adam clarke's commentary on the bible

adam clarke's commentary on the bible

ABRIDGED BY RALPH EARLE

BB

BAKER BOOK HOUSE
Grand Rapids, Michigan

Library of Congress Catalog Card Number 67-13093

ISBN: 0-8010-2321-1

First printing, March 1967
Second printing, October 1967
Third printing, January 1969
Fourth printing, May 1970
Fifth printing, March 1971
Sixth printing, April 1972
Seventh printing, April 1973
Eighth printing, August 1974
Ninth printing, January 1976
Tenth printing, August 1977
Eleventh printing, February 1979
Twelfth printing, April 1980

EDITOR'S PREFACE

Adam Clarke's monumental commentary on the Bible has been a standard reference work for over a century, widely used by men of all evangelical denominations. Its thorough and authoritative scholarship has been recognized by Arminians and Calvinists alike.

The actual work on the commentary was begun on May 1, 1798. As often happens today in writing commentaries, Adam Clarke began with Matthew, writing first on the New Testament. By the end of that year he had finished the first two Gospels, and in November of 1799 the notes on all four Gospels had been written. Actual publication, however, was delayed for ten years.

Finally, in 1809 a Prospectus appeared, and 1,600 subscribers were secured for the new work. The first printing of 11,000 copies (in 1810) sold out very quickly. The title chosen was *The New Testament of Our Lord and Saviour Jesus Christ.*

In March of 1825, Adam Clarke wrote to a friend: "For some time past I have suffered much in my eyes: it is impossible they should last. All winter I have written several hours before day, and several after night. Under this they have failed. But I want to get the Commentary done."

The project was completed on March 28, 1825, "at eight o'clock in the evening." Clarke wrote to an acquaintance: "I wrote upon my knees the last note on the last verse of the last chapter of Malachi. Thus terminated the work on which I have been painfully employed upwards of thirty years." The whole set, in eight large volumes, was published in 1826.

The rest of Clarke's life was spent in going through the *Commentary,* carefully correcting any errors. At the end of Genesis there is appended this note: "Finished the correction of this Part, April 6th, 1827." At the close of Revelation one finds this entry: "Finished correcting for a new edition, Jan. 9, 1832." A few months later, on August 25, he left for his eternal reward.

The *Commentary* has continued to be published in six large volumes right down to the present. But the need has become apparent for a one-volume condensation of this massive work.

The actual words of Adam Clarke have not been changed, except to modernize the language and to abbreviate where appropriate. In a very few instances a word or so has been inserted in brackets to complete the sense in the abridgment. Thus the great scholar is allowed to speak for himself. But much material that is "dated" or is extraneous to the needs of the reader today has been eliminated.

The abridgment was completed in thirteen months of spare time from a busy schedule of teaching and preaching. But it has been a labor of love.

—RALPH EARLE

Kansas City, Mo.
February 17, 1966

SKETCH OF CLARKE'S LIFE

Adam Clarke was born at Moybeg in County Londonderry, Ireland. Unfortunately no record of his birth was made at the time. Shortly before he died Clarke told a friend, Samuel Dunn, that his mother claimed he was born in 1760, while his father said it was in 1763. So the matter is still unsettled, with "about 1762" usually suggested. His father was a man of English extraction, who studied at the great universities of Edinburgh and Glasgow (M.A.). His mother was Scottish. As would be expected, the discipline of the home was strict.

John Clarke, the father, maintained an English and classical school. His two sons, Adam and Tracy, cultivated his farm. They alternated this each day with going to school. Each one, in turn, reported to his working brother what he had just learned.

One phase of Adam Clarke's childhood is described thus by his literary executor:

> Adam was rather a dull boy, and was about eight years of age before he was capable of "putting vowels and consonants together." Having on one occasion failed again and again in his attempts to commit his task to memory, he threw down the book in despair; when the threats of his teacher, who told him he should be a beggar all his days, together with the jeers of the other scholars, roused him as from a lethargy: he felt as if something had broken within him;—his memory in a moment was all light. "What!" said he to himself, "shall I ever be a dunce, and the butt of these fellows' insults!" He resumed his book, conquered his task, speedily went up, and repeated it without missing a word, and proceeded with an ease he had never known before. He soon became passionately fond of reading. Into a wood near the school he oft retired, and there read the Eclogues and the Georgics of Virgil, with living illustrations of them before his eyes. He also amused himself with making hymns, and versifying the Psalms of David, and other portions of the sacred volume. He soon conquered the whole of the heathen mythology and biography. Of Littleton's Classical Dictionary he made himself complete master.[1]

At six years of age young Adam was talking with another little boy about eternal punishment. The conversation ended with their weeping and asking God to forgive them for their sins. Adam reported this to his mother and she encouraged him to live a Christian life. She was a devout Presbyterian, who on Sunday would read, pray, and sing with her children.

Later he was sent to a singing school. Here he received instruction in dancing, which he claimed had a bad moral influence on his life.

In 1777 some Methodist preachers visited the parish where he lived. Coming under great conviction, the teen-age boy sought the open fields. There he wrestled in prayer until he was almost exhausted. Finally in despair he started to leave. Suddenly he thought he heard a voice saying, "Try Jesus." Returning to the place of prayer he called on Jesus. Immediately he felt peace and an overwhelming joy. His darknss had turned to light.

He also experienced an intellectual quickening. He began to study astronomy and philosophy, feeling that these were an aid to religion.

---

[1]Adam Clarke, *Christian Theology:* Selected from his published and unpublished writings and systematically arranged: with a life of the author, by Samuel Dunn (2nd ed.; New York: T. Mason and G. Lane, 1840), p. 8.

Always a serious lad, he induced his parents to have family worship twice a day. The result was that many of his relatives became Methodists. Soon he was going from house to house, and village to village, praying and exhorting in the homes of the people.

In 1782 he preached his first sermon, from I John 5:19. He made such a favorable impression that John Wesley was informed about him. As a result he was sent to the Kingswood school, near Bristol. About a month later Wesley summoned him to Bristol, and soon Adam Clarke, at about twenty years of age, found himself appointed to a Methodist circuit. It was a very busy one, consisting of thirty-one towns and villages. The young preacher made the most of his time by doing solid reading while riding his horse. In the cold of winter he often had to sleep in lofts and outhouses, while bullies disturbed his services. Often he preached in the open air, even when there was heavy snow on the ground.

During a three-year appointment in the Norman Isles he devoted all his spare time to the study of the Hebrew Old Testament, the Samaritan Pentateuch, the Syriac Scriptures, the Latin Vulgate, and the Septuagint, as found in Walton's Polyglot—a copy of which he purchased for ten pounds ($50.00).

In 1788, Adam Clarke was married to Mary Cooke, who outlived him by about a year. They had six sons and six daughters.

After a year as superintendent of the Bristol Circuit, Clarke was sent to Dublin in 1790. The next year John Wesley passed away. In his will Adam Clarke was appointed as one of seven trustees of Wesley's literary property.

Soon he was ministering in Manchester, Liverpool, and London. During this period he began his illustrious career of writing. He was also active in the work of the British and Foreign Bible Society. He was given the degree of LL.D. by the University of Aberdeen and honored by membership in the Royal Irish Academy, in recognition of his scholarly writings. Three times he was chosen as president of the British Conference of Methodism.

His most extensive and most lasting work was his commentary. When he finished it in 1826, he wrote: "I have laboured alone for nearly twenty-five years previously to the work being sent to the press; and fifteen years have been employed to bring it through the press to the public: and thus about forty years of my life have been consumed."[2] He passed away on August 26, 1832. Almost to the very last he was engaged in revising his great commentary.

2Ibid., p. 44.

GENERAL PREFACE
by Adam Clarke

At an early age I took for my motto Prov. xviii. 1: "Through desire a man, having separated himself, seeketh and intermeddleth with all wisdom." Being convinced that the Bible was the Source whence all the principles of true wisdom, wherever found in the world, had been derived, my desire to comprehend adequately its great design, and to penetrate the meaning of all its parts, led me to separate myself from every pursuit that did not lead, at least indirectly, to the accomplishment of this end; and while seeking and intermeddling with different branches of human knowledge, as my limited means would permit, I put each study under contribution to the object of my pursuit, endeavoring to make everything subservient to the information of my own mind, that, as far as Divine Providence might think proper to employ me, I might be the better qualified to instruct others.

At first I read and studied, scarcely committing anything to paper, having my own edification alone in view, as I could not then hope that anything I wrote could be of sufficient importance to engage the attention or promote the welfare of the public. But as I proceeded I thought it best to note down the result of my studies, especially as far as they related to the Septuagint, which about the year 1785 I began to read regularly, in order to acquaint myself more fully with the phraseology of the New Testament, as I found that this truly venerable version was that to which the Evangelists and apostles appear to have had constant recourse, and from which in general they make their quotations. The study of this version served more to illuminate and expand my mind than all the theological works I had ever consulted. I had proceeded but a short way in it before I was convinced that the prejudices against it were utterly unfounded, and that it was of incalculable advantage toward a proper understanding of the literal sense of Scripture, and am astonished that the study of it should be so generally neglected.

About nine years after this, my health having been greatly impaired by the severity of my labors, and fearing that I should soon be obliged to relinquish my public employment, I formed the purpose of writing short notes on the New Testament, collating the common printed text with all the versions and collections from MSS. to which I could have access. Scarcely had I projected this work when I was convinced that another was previously necessary, namely, a careful perusal of the original text. I began this work, and soon found that it was perfectly possible to read and not understand. Under this conviction I sat down determining to translate the whole before I attempted any comment, that I might have the sacred text the more deeply impressed on my memory.

I accordingly began my translation, collating the original text with all the ancient and with several of the modern versions, as well as those which I was able to collect from the most authentic copies of the Greek text. A worse state of health ensuing, I was obliged to remit almost all application to study, and the work was thrown aside for nearly two years. Having returned to it when a state of comparative convalescence took place, I found I had not gone through the whole of my preliminary work. The New Testament I plainly saw was a comment on the Old; and to understand such a comment, I knew it was absolutely necessary to be well acquainted with the original text. I then formed the plan of reading consecutively a portion of the Hebrew Bible daily. Accordingly I began to read the Old Testament, noting down on the different books, chapters, and verses such things as appeared to me of most importance, intending the work as an outline for one on a more extensive scale, should it please God to spare my life and give me health and leisure to complete it. In this preliminary work I spent a little more than one year and two months, in which time I translated every sentence, Hebrew and Chaldee, in the Old Testament.

In such a work it would be absurd to pretend that I had not met with many difficulties. I was attemping to illustrate the most ancient and most learned Book in the universe, replete with allusions to arts that are lost, to nations that are extinct, to customs that are no longer observed, and abounding in modes of speech and turns of phraseology which can be traced out only through the medium of the cognate Asiatic languages. On these accounts I was often much perplexed, but I could not proceed till I had done the utmost in my power to make everything plain. The frequent occurrence of such difficulties led me closely to examine and compare all the original texts, versions, and translations, as they stand in the London Polyglot, with some others not inserted in that work; and from these, especially the Samaritan, Chaldee Targums, Septuagint, and Vulgate, I derived the most assistance, though all the rest contributed their quota in cases of difficulty.

Almost as soon as this work was finished I began my comment on the four Gospels, and notwithstanding the preparations already made, and my indefatigable application early and late to the work, I did not reach the end of the fourth Evangelist till eighteen months after its commencement. Previously to this I had purposed to commit what I had already done to the press; but when I had all my arrangements made, a specimen actually set up and printed, and advertisements circulated, a sudden rise in the price of paper, which I fondly hoped would not be of long continuance, prevented my proceeding. When this hope vanished, another work on the Scriptures by a friend was extensively announced. As I could not bear the thought of even the most distant appearance of opposition to any man, I gave place, being determined not to attempt to divide the attention of the public mind, nor hinder the general spread of a work which for aught I knew might supersede the necessity of mine. That work has been for some time completed, and the numerous subscribers supplied with their copies.

My plan however is untouched; and still finding from the call of many judicious friends, and especially of my brethren in the ministry, who have long been acquainted with my undertaking and its progress, that the religious public would gladly receive a work on the plan which I had previously announced, I have, after much hesitation, made up my mind; and, in the name of God, with a simple desire to add my mite to the treasury, having recommenced the revival and improvement of my papers, I now present them to the public. I am glad that Divine Providence has so ordered it that the publication has been hitherto delayed, as the years which have elapsed since my first intention of printing have afforded me a more ample opportunity to reconsider and correct what I had before done, and to make many improvements.

Should I be questioned as to my specific object in bringing this work before the religious world at a time when works of a similar nature abound, I would simply answer, I wish to do a little good also, and contribute my quota to enable men the better to understand the records of their salvation. That I am in hostility to no work of this kind, the preceding pages will prove;

and I have deferred my own as long as in prudence I can. My tide is turned; life is fast ebbing out; and what I do in this way I must do now, or relinquish the design forever. This I would most gladly do, but I have been too long and too deeply pledged to the public to permit me to indulge my own feelings in this respect. Others are doing much to elucidate the Scriptures; I wish them all God's speed. I also will show my opinion of these divine records, and do a little in the same way. I wish to assist my fellow laborers in the vineyard to lead men to Him who is the Fountain of all excellence, goodness, truth, and happiness; to magnify His law and make it honorable; to show the wonderful provision made in His gospel for the recovery and salvation of a sinful world; to prove that God's great design is to make His creatures happy; and that such a salvation as it becomes God to give, and such as man needs to receive, is within the grasp of every human soul.

CONTENTS

THE BOOKS OF THE OLD TESTAMENT

THE BOOKS OF THE NEW TESTAMENT

THE OLD TESTAMENT

The Book of
GENESIS

Every believer in divine revelation finds himself amply justified in taking for granted that the Pentateuch is the work of Moses. For more than 3,000 years this has been the invariable opinion of those who were best qualified to form a correct judgment on this subject. The Jewish church, from its most remote antiquity, has ascribed the work to no other hand; and the Christian Church, from its foundation, has attributed it to the Jewish lawgiver alone. The most respectable heathens have concurred in this testimony, and Jesus Christ and His apostles have completed the evidence, and have put the question beyond the possibility of being doubted by those who profess to believe the divine authenticity of the New Testament. As to those who, in opposition to all these proofs, obstinately persist in their unbelief, they are worthy of little regard, as argument is lost on their unprincipled prejudices, and demonstration on their minds, because ever wilfully closed against the light. When they have *proved* that Moses is *not* the author of this work, the advocates of divine revelation will reconsider the grounds of their faith.

That there are a few things in the Pentateuch which *seem* to have been added by a later hand there can be little doubt; among these some have reckoned, perhaps without reason, the following passage, Gen. xii. 6: "And the Canaanite was then in the land"; but see the note on this place. Num. xxi. 14, "In the book of the wars of the Lord," was probably a marginal note, which in process of time got into the text; see the note on this passage also. To these may be added the first five verses of Deuteronomy, chap. i; the twelfth of chap. ii; and the eight concluding verses of the last chapter, in which we have an account of the death of Moses. These last words could not have been added by Moses himself, but are very probably the work of Ezra, by whom, according to uninterrupted tradition among the Jews, the various books which constitute the canon of the Old Testament were collected and arranged, and such expository notes added as were essential to connect the different parts; but as he acted under divine inspiration, the additions may be considered of equal authority with the text. A few other places might be added, but they are of little importance, and are mentioned in the notes.

The book of GENESIS has its name from the title it bears in the Septuagint, "The book of the Generation"; but it is called in Hebrew *Bereshith*, "In the beginning," from its initial word. It is the most ancient history in the world; and, from the great variety of its singular details and most interesting accounts, is as far superior in its value and importance to all others as it is in its antiquity. This book contains an account of the creation of the world, and its first inhabitants; the original innocence and fall of man; the rise of religion; the invention of arts; the general corruption and degeneracy of mankind; the universal deluge; the repeopling and division of the earth; the origin of nations and kingdoms; and a particular history of the patriarchs from Adam down to the death of Joseph; including a space, at the lowest computation, of 2,369 years.

CHAPTER 1

First day's work—creation of the heavens and the earth, 1-2. Of the light and its separation from the darkness, 3-5. Second day's work—the creation of the firmament, and the separation of the waters above the firmament from those below it, 6-8. Third day's work—the waters are separated from the earth and formed into seas, etc., 9-10. The earth rendered fruitful, and clothed with trees, herbs, grass, etc., 11-13. Fourth day's work—creation of the celestial luminaries intended for the measurement of time, the distinction of periods, seasons, etc., 14; and to illuminate the earth, 15. Distinct account of the formation of the sun, moon, and stars, 16-19. Fifth day's work—the creation of fish, fowls, and reptiles in general, 20. Of great aquatic animals, 21. They are blessed so as to make them very prolific, 22-23. Sixth day's work—wild and tame cattle created, and all kinds of animals which derive their nourishment from the earth, 24-25. The creation of man in the image and likeness of God, with the dominion given him over the earth and all inferior animals, 26. Man or Adam, a general name for human beings, including both male and female, 27. Their peculiar blessing, 28. Vegetables appointed as the food of man and all other animals, 29-30. The judgment which God passed on His works at the conclusion of His creative acts, 31.

1. Many attempts have been made to define the term GOD. As to the word itself, it is pure Anglo-Saxon, and among our ancestors signified, not only the Divine Being, now commonly designated by the word, but also "good," as in their apprehensions it appeared that "God" and "good" were correlative terms; and when they thought or spoke of Him, they were doubtless led from the word itself to consider Him as the Good Being, a Fountain of infinite benevolence and beneficence towards His creatures.

A general definition of this great First Cause, as far as human words dare attempt one, may be thus given: The eternal, independent, and self-existent Being; the Being whose purposes and actions spring from himself, without foreign motive or influence; He who is absolute in dominion; the most pure, the most simple, and most spiritual of all essences; infinitely benevo-

15

lent, beneficent, true, and holy; the Cause of all being, the Upholder of all things; infinitely happy, because infinitely perfect; and eternally self-sufficient, needing nothing that He has made; illimitable in His immensity, inconceivable in His mode of existence, and indescribable in His essence; known fully only to himself, because an infinite mind can be fully apprehended only by itself. In a word, a Being who, from His infinite wisdom, cannot err or be deceived; and who, from His infinite goodness, can do nothing but what is eternally just, right, and kind.

The original word *Elohim*, God, is certainly the plural form of *El*, or *Eloah*, and has long been supposed, by the most eminiently learned and pious men, to imply a plurality of Persons in the divine nature. As this plurality appears in so many parts of the sacred writings to be confined to three Persons, hence the doctrine of the Trinity, which has formed a part of the creed of all those who have been deemed sound in the faith, from the earliest ages of Christianity. The verb *bara*, "he created," being joined in the singular number with this plural noun, has been considered as pointing out the unity of the divine Persons in this work of creation. In the ever-blessed Trinity, from the infinite and indivisible unity of the Persons, there can be but one will, one purpose, and one infinite and uncontrollable energy.

In the beginning. Before the creative acts mentioned in this chapter all was *eternity*. Time signifies duration measured by the revolutions of the heavenly bodies; but prior to the creation of these bodies there could be no measurement of duration, and consequently no time; therefore *in the beginning* must necessarily mean the commencement of time which followed, or rather was produced by, God's creative acts, as an effect follows or is produced by a cause.

Created. Caused existence where previously to this moment there was no being. The rabbins, who are legitimate judges in a case of verbal criticism on their own language, are unanimous in asserting that the word *bara* expresses the commencement of the existence of a thing. The supposition that God formed all things out of a preexisting, eternal nature is certainly absurd, for if there had been an eternal nature besides an eternal God, there must have been two self-existing, independent, and eternal beings, which is a most palpable contradiction.

Eth hashshamayim. The word *eth*, which is generally considered as a particle, simply denoting that the word following is in the accusative or oblique case, is often understood by the rabbins in a much more extensive sense. "The particle *eth*," says Aben Ezra, "signifies the *substance* of the thing." On this ground these words should be translated, "God in the beginning created the substance of the heavens and the substance of the earth," i.e., the *prima materia*, or first elements, out of which the heavens and the earth were successively formed.

The heaven and the earth. As the word *shamayim* is plural, we may rest assured that it means more than the atmosphere, to which some have endeavored to restrict its meaning. Nor does it appear that the atmosphere is particularly intended here, as this is spoken of in v. 6 under the term "firmament." The word *heaven* must, therefore, comprehend the whole

solar system, as it is very likely the whole of this was created in these six days. In the word *earth* everything relative to the globe is included, that is, all that belongs to the solid and fluid parts of our world with its surrounding atmosphere.

2. *The earth was without form, and void.* The original terms *tohu* and *bohu*, which we translate *without form, and void*, are of uncertain etymology; but in this place, and wherever else they are used, they convey the idea of confusion and disorder. God seems at first to have created the elementary principles of all things; and this formed the grand mass of matter, which in this state must be without arrangement, or any distinction of parts: a vast collection of indescribably confused materials, of nameless entities strangely mixed.

When this congeries of elementary principles was brought together, God was pleased to spend six days in asismilating, assorting, and arranging the materials, out of which He built up, not only the earth, but the whole of the solar system.

The Spirit of God. This has been variously and strangely understood. Some think a violent wind is meant, because *ruach* often signifies "wind," as well as "spirit," as *pneuma* does in Greek; and the term *God* is connected with it merely, as they think, to express the superlative degree. Others understand by it an elementary fire. Others, the sun, penetrating and drying up the earth with his rays. Others, the angels, who were supposed to have been employed as agents in creation. But it is sufficiently evident from the use of the word in other places that the Holy Spirit of God is intended; which our blessed Lord represents under the notion of "wind," John iii. 8; and which, as a "mighty rushing wind" on the Day of Pentecost, filled the house where the disciples were sitting, Acts ii. 2, which was immediately followed by their speaking with other tongues, because they were filled with the Holy Ghost, v. 4. These scriptures sufficiently ascertain the sense in which the word is used by Moses.

Moved. "Was brooding over"; for the word expresses that tremulous motion made by the hen while either hatching her eggs or fostering her young. It here probably signifies the communicating of a vital or prolific principle to the waters.

3. *And God said, Let there be light.* Nothing can be conceived more dignified than this form of expression. It argues at once uncontrollable authority, and omnific power; and in human language it is scarcely possible to conceive that God can speak more like himself.

Many have asked, "How could light be produced on the first day, and the sun, the fountain of it, not created till the fourth day?" I shall observe that the original word signifies not only *light* but "fire," see Isa. xxxi. 9; Ezek. v. 2. I therefore conclude that, as God has diffused the matter of caloric or latent heat through every part of nature, without which there could be neither vegetation nor animal life, it is caloric or latent heat which is principally intended by the original word.

4. *God divided the light from the darkness.* These words simply refer us by anticipation to the rotation of the earth round its own axis once in twenty-three hours, fifty-six minutes,

and four seconds, which is the cause of the distinction between day and night, by bringing the different parts of the surface of the earth successively into and from under the solar rays; and it was probably at this moment that God gave this rotation to the earth, to produce this merciful provision of day and night.

6. *And God said, Let there be a firmament.* Our translators, by following the *firmamentum* of the Vulgate, have deprived this passage of all sense and meaning. The Hebrew word *rakia*, from *raka*, to "spread out as the curtains of a tent or pavilion," simply signifies an "expanse" or "space," and consequently that space or expansion separating the clouds which are in the higher regions of it, from the seas, etc., which are below it. This we call the "atmosphere"; but the word appears to have been used by Moses in a more extensive sense, and to include the whole of the planetary vortex, or the space which is occupied by the whole solar system.

10. *And God called the dry land Earth; and the gathering together of the waters called he Seas.* These two constitute what is called the terraqueous globe, in which the earth and the water exist in a most judicious proportion to each other.

And God saw that it was good. This is the judgment which God pronounced on His own works. They were "beautiful" and "perfect" in their kind, for such is the import of the word *tob.* They were in weight and measure perfect and entire, lacking nothing. But the reader will think it strange that this approbation should be expressed once on the first, fourth, fifth, and sixth days, twice on the third, and not at all on the second! I suppose that the words, *And God saw that it was good,* have been either lost from the conclusion of the eighth verse, or that the clause in the tenth verse originally belonged to the eighth. It appears, from the Septuagint translation, that the words in question existed originally at the close of the eighth verse, in the copies which they used. If the account of the second day stood originally as it does now, no satisfactory reason can be given for the omission of this expression of the divine approbation of the work wrought by His wisdom and power on that day.

11. *Let the earth bring forth grass . . . herb . . . fruit tree.* In these general expressions all kinds of vegetable productions are included. *Fruit tree* is not to be understood here in the restricted sense in which the term is used among us; it signifies all trees, not only those which bear fruit, but also those which had the power of propagating themselves by seeds.

12. *Whose seed was in itself.* Which has the power of multiplying itself by seeds, slips, roots, etc., *ad infinitum;* which contains in itself all the rudiments of the future plant through its endless generations. The astonishing power with which God has endued the vegetable creation to multiply its different species may be instanced in the seed of the elm. This tree produces millions of seeds; and each of these seeds has the power of producing the same number. How astonishing is this produce!

14. *And God said, Let there be lights.* One principal office of these was to divide between day and night. When night is considered a state of comparative darkness, how can lights divide or distinguish it? The answer is easy: The sun is the monarch of the day, which is the state of light; the moon, of the night, the state of darkness.

And let them be for signs. Let them ever be considered as continual tokens of God's tender care for man, and as standing proofs of His continual miraculous interference; for so the word *oth* is often used. And is it not the almighty energy of God that upholds them in being? The sun and moon also serve as *signs* of the different changes which take place in the atmosphere, and which are so essential for all purposes of agriculture, commerce.

For days. Both the hours of the day and night, as well as the different lengths of the days and nights, are distinguished by the longer and shorter spaces of time the sun is above or below the horizon.

And years. That is, those grand divisions of time by which all succession in the vast lapse of duration is distinguished. This refers principally to a complete revolution of the earth round the sun.

16. *And God made two great lights.* Moses speaks of the sun and moon here, not according to their bulk or solid contents, but according to the proportion of light they shed on the earth. The expression has been objected to by some who are as devoid of mental capacity as of candor. "The moon," say they, "is not a *great* body; on the contrary, it is the very smallest in our system." Well, and has Moses said the contrary? He has said it is a *great light;* had he said otherwise he had not spoken the truth. It is, in reference to the earth, next to the sun himself, the greatest light in the solar system; and so true is it that the moon is a great light that it affords more light to the earth than all the planets in the solar system, and all the innumerable stars in the vault of heaven, put together.

He made the stars also. Or rather, "He made the lesser light, with the stars, to rule the night."

20. *Let the waters bring forth abundantly.* There is a meaning in these words which is seldom noticed. Innumerable millions of animalcula are found in water. Eminent naturalists have discovered not less than 30,000 in a single drop! But the fecundity of fishes is another point intended in the text; no creatures are so prolific as these. A tench lays 1,000 eggs, a carp 20,000, and Leuwenhoek counted in a middling-sized cod 9,384,000! Thus, according to the purpose of God, *the waters bring forth abundantly.*

21. *And God created great whales.* Though this is generally understood by the different versions as signifying *whales,* yet the original must be understood rather as a general than a particular term, comprising all the great aquatic animals.

22. *Let fowl multiply in the earth.* It is truly astonishing with what care, wisdom, and minute skill God has formed the different genera and species of birds, whether intended to live chiefly on land or in water. The structure of a single feather affords a world of wonders; and as God made the fowls that they might fly in the firmament of heaven, v. 20, so He has adapted the form of their bodies, and the structure and disposition of their plumage, for that very purpose. The head and neck in flying are drawn principally within the breastbone, so that

the whole underpart exhibits the appearance of a ship's hull. The wings are made use of as sails, or rather oars, and the tail as a helm or rudder. By means of these the creature is not only able to preserve the center of gravity, but also to go with vast speed through the air, either straight forward or downwards. In these also God has shown His skill and His power in the great and in the little—in the vast ostrich and in the beautiful hummingbird, which in plumage excels the splendor of the peacock, and in size is almost on a level with the bee.

24. *Let the earth bring forth the living creature.* A general term to express all creatures endued with animal life, in any of its infinitely varied graduations, from the half-reasoning elephant down to the polyp, which seems equally to share the vegetable and animal life. The word *chaitho*, in the latter part of the verse, seems to signify all wild animals, as lions, tigers, and especially such as are carnivorous, or live on flesh, in contradistinction from domestic animals, such as live on grass and other vegetables, and are capable of being tamed, and applied to domestic purposes. See on v. 29. These latter are probably meant by *behemah* in the text, which we translate *cattle*, such as horses, kine, sheep, dogs. *Creeping thing, remes,* all the different genera of serpents, worms, and such animals as have no feet. In *beasts* also God has shown His wondrous skill and power; in the vast elephant, or still more colossal mammoth or mastodon.

25. *And God made the beast of the earth after his kind.* Everything in both the animal and vegetable world was made so according to its kind, in both genus and species, as to produce its own kind through endless generations. Thus the several races of animals and plants have been kept distinct from the foundation of the world to the present day.

26. *And God said, Let us make man.* It is evident that God intends to impress the mind of man with a sense of something extraordinary in the formation of his body and soul, when He introduces the account of his creation thus: "Let *us* make man." The word *Adam,* which we translate *man,* is intended to designate the species of animal, as *chaitho* marks the wild beasts that live in general a solitary life; *behemah,* domestic or gregarious animals; and *remes,* all kinds of reptiles, from the largest snake to the microscopic eel. Though the same kind of organization may be found in man as appears in the lower animals, yet there is a variety and complication in the parts, a delicacy of structure, a nice arrangement, a judicious adaptation of the different members to their great offices and functions, a dignity of mien, and a perfection of the whole, which are sought for in vain in all other creatures.

In our image, after our likeness. What is said above refers only to the body of man; what is here said refers to his soul. This was made in the *image* and *likeness* of God. Now, as the Divine Being is infinite, He is neither limited by parts, nor definable by passions; therefore He can have no corporeal image after which He made the body of man. The image and likeness must necessarily be intellectual; his mind, his soul, must have been formed after the nature and perfections of his God. The human mind is still endowed with most extraordinary capac-

ities; it was more so when issuing out of the hands of its Creator. God was now producing a spirit, and a spirit, too, formed after the perfections of His own nature. God is the Fountain whence this spirit issued; hence the stream must resemble the spring which produced it. God is holy, just, wise, good, and perfect; so must the soul be that sprang from Him: there could be in it nothing impure, unjust, ignorant, evil, low, base, mean, or vile. It was created after the image of God; and that image, St. Paul tells us, consisted in "righteousness," "true holiness," and "knowledge," Eph. iv. 24; Col. iii. 10. Hence man was wise in his mind, holy in his heart, and righteous in his actions.

Gregory Nyssen has very properly observed that the superiority of man to all other parts of creation is seen in this, that all other creatures are represented as the effect of God's *word,* but man is represented as the *work of God,* according to plan and consideration: "Let us make man in our image, after our likeness."

And let them have dominion. Hence we see that the dominion was not the image. God created man capable of governing the world, and when fitted for the office, He fixed him in it. We see God's tender care and parental solicitude for the comfort and well-being of this masterpiece of His workmanship, in creating the world previously to the creation of man. He prepared everything for his subsistence, convenience, and pleasure, before He brought him into being; so that, comparing little with great things, the house was built, furnished, and amply stored, by the time the destined tenant was ready to occupy it.

28. *And God blessed them.* Marked them as being under His especial protection, and gave them power to propagate and multiply their own kind on the earth. A large volume would be insufficient to contain what we know of the excellence and perfection of man, even in his present degraded, fallen state. Both his body and soul are adapted with astonishing wisdom to their residence and occupations; and also the place of their residence, as well as the surrounding objects, in their diversity, color, and mutual relations, to the mind and body of this lord of the creation. The contrivance, arrangement, action, and reaction of the different parts of the body show the admirable skill of the wondrous Creator; while the various powers and faculties of the mind, acting on and by the different organs of this body, proclaim the soul's divine origin, and demonstrate that he who was made in the image and likeness of God was a transcript of His own excellency, destined to know, love, and dwell with his Maker throughout eternity.

31. *And, behold, it was very good.* "Superlatively, or only good"; as good as they could be. The plan wise, the work well executed, the different parts properly arranged; their nature, limits, mode of existence, manner of propagation, habits, mode of sustenance, properly and permanently established and secured; for everything was formed to the utmost perfection of its nature, so that nothing could be added or diminished.

And the evening and the morning were the sixth day. The word *ereb,* which we translate *evening,* comes from the root *arab,* to "mingle"; and properly signifies that state in which neither absolute darkness nor full light prevails. It has nearly the same grammatical signification as our "twilight." The Hebrews extended the meaning of this term to the whole duration of night, because it was ever a mingled state, the moon, the planets, or the stars, tempering the darkness with some rays of light.

The morning—boker; from *bakar,* he "looked out"; a beautiful figure which represents the morning as looking out at the east, and illuminating the whole of the upper hemisphere.

The evening and the morning were the sixth day. It is somewhat remarkable that through the whole of this chapter, whenever the division of days is made, the evening always precedes the morning. The reason of this may perhaps be that darkness was preexistent to light and, therefore, time is reckoned from the first act of God towards the creation of the world, which took place before light was called forth into existence. It is very likely, for this same reason, that the Jews began their day at six o'clock in the evening in imitation of Moses' division of time in this chapter.

CHAPTER 2

The seventh day is consecrated for a Sabbath, and the reasons assigned, 1-3. A recapitulation of the six days' work of creation, 4-7. The Garden of Eden planted, 8. Its trees, 9. Its rivers, and the countries watered by them, 10-14. Adam placed in the garden, and the command given not to eat of the tree of knowledge on pain of death, 15-17. God purposes to form a companion for the man, 18. The different animals brought to Adam that he might assign them their names, 19-20. The creation of the woman, 21-22. The institution of marriage, 23-24. The purity and innocence of our first parents. 25.

1. *And all the host of them.* The word *host* signifies literally an army, composed of a number of companies of soldiers under their respective leaders; and seems here applied to the various celestial bodies in our system, placed by the divine wisdom under the influence of the sun.

2. *On the seventh day God ended.* It is the general voice of Scripture that God finished the whole of the creation in six days, and rested the seventh, giving us an example that we might labor six days and rest the seventh from all manual exercises. It is worthy of notice that the Septuagint, the Syriac, and the Samaritan read the sixth day instead of the seventh; and this should be considered the general reading, which appears from these versions to have been originally that of the Hebrew text.

3. *And God blessed the seventh day.* The original word *barach,* which is generally rendered "to bless," has a very extensive meaning. It is frequently used in Scripture in the sense of speaking good of or to a person; and hence literally and properly rendered by the Septuagint *eulogesen,* from *eu,* "good" or "well," and *lego,* "I speak." So God has spoken well of the Sabbath, and good to them who conscientiously observe it.

Because that in it he had rested. Shabath, "he rested"; hence "Sabbath," the name of the seventh day, signifying "a day of rest"—rest to the body from labor and toil, and rest to the soul from all worldly care and anxieties. He who labors with his mind by worldly schemes and plans on the Sabbath day is as culpable as he who labors with his hands in his accustomed calling. It is by the authority of God that the Sabbath is set apart for rest and religious purposes, as the six days of the week are appointed for labor. Without this consecrated day religion itself would fail, and the human mind, becoming sensualized, would soon forget its origin and end.

As God formed both the mind and the body of man on principles of activity, so He assigned him proper employment; and it is His decree that the mind shall improve by exercise, and the body find increase of vigor and health in honest labor. He who idles away his time in the six days is equally culpable in the sight of God as he who works on the seventh.

4. *In the day that the Lord God made.* The word *Yehovah* is for the first time mentioned here. What it signifies see on Exod. xxxiv. 5-6. Wherever this word occurs in the sacred writings we translate it LORD, which word is, through respect and reverence, always printed in capitals. Though our English term "Lord" does not give the particular meaning of the original word, yet it conveys a strong and noble sense. The word implies the "giver of bread," i.e., who deals out all the necessaries of life. Our ancient English noblemen were accustomed to keep a continual open house, where all their vassals, and all strangers, had full liberty to enter and eat as much as they would; and hence those noblemen had the honorable name of "lords," i.e., "the dispensers of bread."

5. *Every plant of the field before it was in the earth.* It appears that God created everything, not only perfect as it respects its nature, but also in a state of maturity, so that every vegetable production appeared at once in full growth; and this was necessary that man, when he came into being, might find everything ready for his use.

6. *There went up a mist.* This passage appears to have greatly embarrassed many commentators. The plain meaning seems to be this, that the aqueous vapors, ascending from the earth, and becoming condensed in the colder regions of the atmosphere, fell back upon the earth in the form of dews, and by this means an equal portion of moisture was distributed to the roots of plants. As Moses had said, v. 5, that "the Lord had not caused it to rain upon the earth," He probably designed to teach us, in v. 6, how rain is produced, namely, by the condensation of the aqueous vapors, which are generally through the heat of the sun and other causes raised to a considerable height in the atmosphere, where, meeting with cold air, the watery particles which were before so small and light that they could float in the air, becoming condensed, i.e., many drops being driven into one, become too heavy to be any longer suspended, and then, through their own gravity, fall down in the form which we term rain.

7. *God formed man of the dust.* In the most distinct manner God shows us that man is a compound being, having a body and soul distinctly and separately created; the body out of the dust of the earth, the soul immediately breathed from God himself. Of the soul it is said, *God breathed into his nostrils the breath of life;* "the breath of lives," i.e., animal and intellectual. While this breath of God expanded the lungs and set them in play, His inspiration gave both spirit and understanding.

8. *A garden eastward in Eden.* Though the word *Eden* signifies "pleasure" or "delight," it is certainly the name of a place. See chap. iv. 16; 2 Kings xix. 12; Isa. xxxvii. 12; Ezek. xxvii. 23; Amos i. 5.

9. *Every tree that is pleasant to the sight.* If we take up these expressions literally, they may bear the following interpretation: the tree pleasant to the sight may mean every beautiful tree or plant which for shape, color, or fragrance, delights the senses, such as flowering shrubs.

And good for food. All fruit-bearing trees, whether of the pulpy fruits, as apples, or of the kernel or nut kind, such as dates and nuts.

The tree of life. It is likely that this *tree of life* which was placed *in the midst of the garden* was intended as an emblem of that life which man should ever live, provided he continued in obedience to his Maker. And probably the use of this tree was intended as the means of preserving the body of man in a state of continual vital energy, and an antidote against death. This seems strongly indicated from chap. iii. 22.

And the tree of knowledge of good and evil. Considering this also in a merely literal point of view, it may mean any tree or plant which possessed the property of increasing the knowledge of what was in nature. The prohibition was intended to exercise this faculty in man that should constantly teach him this moral lesson, that there were some things fit and others unfit to be done, and that in reference to this point the tree itself should be both a constant teacher and monitor. The eating of its fruit would not have increased this moral faculty, but the prohibition was intended to exercise the faculty he already possessed.

10. *A river went out of Eden.* The most probable account of its situation is that given by Hadrian Reland. He supposes it to have been in Armenia, near the sources of the great rivers Euphrates, Tigris, Phasis, and Araxes. He thinks *Pison* was the Phasis, a river of Colchis, emptying itself into the Black Sea. This country was famous for *gold*, whence the fable of the golden fleece, attempted to be carried away from that country by the heroes of Greece. The *Gihon* he thinks to be the Araxes, which runs into the Caspian Sea, both the words having the same signification, namely, a "rapid motion." The *Hiddekel* all agree to be the Tigris, and the other river, *Phrat*, or *Perath*, to be the Euphrates. All of these rivers rise in the same tract of mountainous country, though they do not arise from one head.

15. *Put him into the garden . . . to dress it and to keep it.* Horticulture, or gardening, is the first kind of employment on record, and that in which man was engaged while in a state of perfection and innocence. Though the garden may be supposed to produce all things spontaneously, as the whole vegetable surface of the earth certainly did at the creation, yet dressing and tilling were afterwards necessary to maintain the different kinds of plants and vegetables in their perfection, and to repress luxuriance. Even in a state of innocence we cannot conceive it possible that man could have been happy if inactive. God gave him work to do, and his employment contributed to his happiness; for the structure of his body, as well as

of his mind, plainly proves that he was never intended for a merely contemplative life.

17. *Of the tree of the knowledge . . . thou shalt not eat.* This is the first positive precept God gave to man; and it was given as a test of obedience, and a proof of his being in a dependent, probationary state. It was necessary that, while constituted lord of this lower world, he should know that he was only God's vicegerent, and must be accountable to Him for the use of his mental and corporeal powers, and for the use he made of the different creatures put under his care. The man from whose mind the strong impression of this dependence and responsibility is erased necessarily loses sight of his origin and end, and is capable of any species of wickedness. As God is sovereign, He has a right to give to His creatures what commands He thinks proper.

Thou shalt surely die. Literally, "a death thou shalt die"; or, "dying thou shalt die." Thou shalt not only die spiritually, by losing the life of God, but from that moment thou shalt become mortal, and shalt continue in a dying state till thou die. This we find literally accomplished; every moment of man's life may be considered as an act of dying, till soul and body are separated.

18. *It is not good that the man should be alone.* "Only himself." *I will make him an help meet for him;* a help, a counterpart of himself, one formed from him, and a perfect resemblance of his person. If the word be rendered scrupulously literally, it signifies one "like," or "as himself," standing opposite to or before him. And this implies that the woman was to be a perfect resemblance of the man, possessing neither inferiority nor superiority, but being in all things like and equal to himself. As man was made a social creature, it was not proper that he should be alone; for to be alone, i.e., without a matrimonial companion, was not good.

19. *Out of the ground.* Concerning the formation of the different kinds of animals, see the preceding chapter.

20. *And Adam gave names to all cattle.* Two things God appears to have had in view by causing man to name all the cattle: (1) To show him with what comprehensive powers of mind his Maker had endued him; and (2) To show him that no creature yet formed could make him a suitable companion. And that this twofold purpose was answered we shall shortly see; for,

(1) *Adam gave names;* but how? From an intimate knowledge of the nature and properties of each creature. Here we see the perfection of his knowledge; for it is well known that the names affixed to the different animals in Scripture always express some prominent feature and essential characteristic of the creatures to which they are applied.

(2) Adam was convinced that none of these creatures could be a suitable companion for him, and that, therefore, he must continue in the state that was not good, or be a farther debtor to the bounty of his Maker; for among all the animals which he had named *there was not found an help meet for him.* Hence we read,

21. *The Lord God caused a deep sleep to fall upon Adam.* This was neither swoon nor

ecstasy, but what our translation very properly terms a deep sleep.

And he took one of his ribs. It is immaterial whether we render *tsela* a rib or a part of his side, for it may mean either: some part of man was to be used on the occasion, whether bone or flesh it matters not, though it is likely, from v. 23, that a part of both was taken; for Adam, knowing how the woman was formed, said, "This is *flesh* of my *flesh,* and *bone* of my *bones."* As God formed her out of a part of the man himself, he saw she was of the same nature, the same identical flesh and blood, and of the same constitution in all respects, and consequently having equal powers, faculties, and rights. This at once ensured his affection, and excited his esteem.

23. *Adam said, This is now bone of my bones.* There is a very delicate and expressive meaning in the original which does not appear in our version. When the different genera of creatures were brought to Adam, that he might assign them their proper names, it is probable that they passed in pairs before him, and as they passed received their names. To this circumstance the words in this place seem to refer. Instead of *this now is* we should render more literally "this turn," this creature, which now passes or appears before me, is flesh of my flesh. The creatures that had passed already before him were not suitable to him, and therefore it was said, "For Adam there was not a help meet found," v. 20; but when the woman came, formed out of himself, he felt all that attraction which consanguinity could produce, and at the same time saw that she was in her person and in her mind every way suitable to be his companion.

She shall be called Woman. A literal version of the Hebrew would appear strange, and yet a literal version is the only proper one. *Ish* signifies "man," and the word used to express what we term woman is the same with a feminine termination, *ishshah,* and literally means "she-man."

24. *Therefore shall a man leave his father and his mother.* There shall be, by the order of God, a more intimate connection formed between the man and woman than can subsist even between parents and children.

And they shall be one flesh. These words may be understood in a twofold sense. (1) These two shall be one flesh, shall be considered as one body, having no separate or independent rights, privileges, cares, concerns, each being equally interested in all things that concern the marriage state. (2) These two shall be for the production of one flesh; from their union a posterity shall spring, as exactly resembling themselves as they do each other. Our Lord quotes these words, Matt. xix. 5, with some variation from this text: "They twain shall be one flesh." So in Mark x. 8. St. Paul quotes in the same way, 1 Cor. vi. 16, and in Eph. v. 31. The Vulgate Latin, the Septuagint, the Syriac, the Arabic, and the Samaritan, all read the word "two." That this is the genuine reading I have no doubt.

We have here the first institution of marriage, and we see in it several particulars worthy of our most serious regard. (1) God pronounces the state of celibacy to be not a good one. (2) God made the woman *for* the man, and thus He has shown us that every son of Adam should be united to a daughter of Eve to the end of the world. (3) God made the woman *out* of the man, to intimate that the closest union, and the most affectionate attachment, should subsist in the matrimonial connection, so that the man should ever consider and treat the woman as a part of himself.

25. *They were both naked.* The weather was perfectly temperate, and therefore they had no need of clothing, the air being of the same temperature with their bodies. And as sin had not yet entered into the world, and no part of the human body had been put to any improper use, therefore there was no shame, for shame can only arise from a consciousness of sinful or irregular conduct.

CHAPTER 3

Satan, by means of a creature here called the serpent, deceives Eve, 1-5. Both she and Adam transgress the divine command, and fall into sin and misery, 6-7. They are summoned before God, and judged, 8-13. The creature called the serpent is degraded and punished, 14. The promise of redemption by the incarnation of Christ, 15. Eve sentenced, 16. Adam sentenced, 17. The ground cursed, and death threatened, 18-19. Why the woman was called Eve, 20. Adam and Eve clothed with skins, 21. The wretched state of our first parents after their fall, and their expulsion from the garden of paradise, 22-24.

1. *Now the serpent was more subtil.* We have here one of the most difficult as well as the most important narratives in the whole Book of God. The last chapter ended with a short but striking account of the perfection and felicity of the first human beings, and this opens with an account of their transgression, degradation, and ruin. That man is in a fallen state, the history of the world, with that of the life and miseries of every human being, establishes beyond successful contradiction.

3. *Neither shall ye touch it.* Did not the woman add this to what God had before spoken?

4. *Ye shall not surely die.* Here the father of lies at once appears; and appears, too, in flatly contradicting the assertion of God. The tempter insinuates the impossibility of her dying, as if he had said, God has created thee immortal; thy death, therefore, is impossible; and God knows this, for as thou livest by the tree of life, so shalt thou get increase of wisdom by the tree of knowledge.

5. *Your eyes shall be opened.* Your understanding shall be greatly enlightened and improved; *and ye shall be as gods, kelohim,* "like God," so the word should be translated; for what idea could our first parents have of *gods* before idolatry could have had any being, because sin had not yet entered into the world? The Syriac has the word in the singular number, and is the only one of all the versions which has hit on the true meaning. As the original word is the same which is used to point out the Supreme Being, chap. i. 1, so it has here the same signification, and the object of the tempter appears to have been this: to persuade our first parents that they should, by eating of this fruit, become wise and powerful as God (for knowledge is power), and be able to exist forever, independently of Him.

6. *The tree was good for food.* (1) The fruit appeared to be wholesome and nutritive. *And that it was pleasant to the eyes.* (2) The beauty of the fruit tended to whet and increase ap-

petite. *And a tree to be desired to make one wise*, which was (3) an additional motive to please the palate. From these three sources all natural and moral evil sprang: they are exactly what the apostle calls the "desire of the flesh," the tree was good for food; "the desire of the eye," it was pleasant to the sight; and "the pride of life," it was a tree to be desired to make one wise. God had undoubtedly created our first parents not only very wise and intelligent, but also with a great capacity and suitable propensity to increase in knowledge. We see at once how transgression came; it was natural for them to desire to be increasingly wise. God had implanted this desire in their minds; but He showed them that this desire should be gratified in a certain way; that prudence and judgment should always regulate it; that they should carefully examine what God had opened to their view; and should not pry into what He chose to conceal. He alone who knows all things knows how much knowledge the soul needs to its perfection and increasing happiness, in what subjects this may be legitimately sought, and where the mind may make excursions and discoveries to its prejudice and ruin.

7. *The eyes of them both were opened.* They now had a sufficient discovery of their sin and folly in disobeying the command of God; they could discern between good and evil; and what was the consequence? Confusion and shame were engendered, because innocence was lost and guilt contracted.

8. *The voice of the Lord.* The *voice* is properly used here, for as God is an infinite Spirit, and cannot be confined to any form, so He can have no personal appearance. It is very likely that God used to converse with them in the garden, and that the usual time was the decline of the day, in the "evening breeze"; and probably this was the time that our first parents employed in the more solemn acts of their religious worship, at which God was ever present. The time for this solemn worship is again come, and God is in His place; but Adam and Eve have sinned, and therefore, instead of being found in the place of worship, are hidden among the trees!

10. *I was afraid, because I was naked.* See the immediate consequences of sin. (1) Shame, because of the ingratitude marked in the rebellion, and because that in aiming to be like God they were now sunk into a state of the greatest wretchedness. (2) Fear, because they saw they had been deceived by Satan, and were exposed to that death and punishment from which he had promised them an exemption. Shame and fear were the first fruits of sin, and fruits which it has invariably produced, from the first transgression to the present time.

12-13. *And the man said.* We have here some farther proofs of the fallen state of man, and that the consequences of that state extend to his remotest posterity. (1) On the question, "Hast thou eaten of the tree?" Adam is obliged to acknowledge his transgression; but he does this in such a way as to shift off the blame from himself, and lay it upon God and upon the woman! "This woman whom Thou didst give to be with me," to be my companion, (for so the word is repeatedly used,) "she gave me, and I did eat." I have no farther blame in this trans-

gression; I did not pluck the fruit; she took it and gave it to me.

(2) When the woman is questioned, she lays the blame upon God and the serpent, "The serpent beguiled me, and I did eat." Thou didst make him much wiser than Thou didst make me, and therefore my simplicity and ignorance were overcome by his superior wisdom and subtlety. I can have no fault here; the fault is his, and His who made him so wise and me so ignorant. Thus we find that, while the eyes of their body were opened to see their degraded state, the eyes of their understanding were closed, so that they could not see the sinfulness of sin; and at the same time their hearts were hardened through its deceitfulness.

14. *And the Lord God said unto the serpent.* The tempter is not asked why he deceived the woman; he cannot roll the blame on any other; self-tempted, he fell, and it is natural for him, such is his enmity, to deceive and destroy all he can. His fault admits of no excuse, and therefore God begins to pronounce sentence on him first. And here we must consider a twofold sentence, one on Satan and the other on the agent he employed.

15. *I will put enmity between thee and the woman.* This has been generally supposed to apply to a certain enmity subsisting between men and serpents; but this is rather a fancy than a reality. There is a deeper meaning in the text than this, especially in these words, *it shall bruise thy head,* or rather, *He.* Who? The Seed of the woman; the Person is to come by the woman, and by her alone, without the concurrence of man. Therefore the address is not to Adam and Eve, but to Eve alone; and it was in consequence of this purpose of God that Jesus Christ was born of a virgin; this, and this alone, is what is implied in the promise of the Seed of the woman bruising the head of the serpent. Jesus Christ died to put away sin by the sacrifice of himself, and to destroy him who had the power of death, that is, the devil. Thus He bruises his head—destroys his power and lordship over mankind, turning them from the power of Satan unto God; Acts xxvi. 18. And Satan bruises His heel—God so ordered it, that the salvation of man could only be brought about by the death of Christ; and even the spiritual seed of our blessed Lord have the heel often bruised, as they suffer persecution, temptation, which may be all that is intended by this part of the prophecy.

16. *Unto the woman he said.* She being second in the transgression is brought up the second to receive her condemnation, and to hear her punishment: *I will greatly multiply,* or "multiplying I will multiply"; i.e., I will multiply thy sorrows, and multiply those sorrows by other sorrows, and this during conception and pregnancy, and particularly so in parturition or childbearing. And this curse has fallen in a heavier degree on the woman than on any other female. It is added farther, *Thy desire shall be to thy husband*—thou shalt not be able to shun the great pain and peril for childbearing, for thy desire, thy appetite, shall be to thy husband; *and he shall rule over thee,* though at their creation both were formed with equal rights, and the woman had probably as much right to rule as the man; but subjection to the will of her husband is one part of her curse;

and so very capricious is this will, often, that a sorer punishment no human being can well have, to be at all in a state of liberty, and under the protection of wise and equal laws.

17. *Unto Adam he said.* The man being the last in the transgression is brought up last to receive his sentence: *Because thou hast hearkened unto the voice of thy wife*—"Thou wast not deceived, she only gave and counselled thee to eat; this thou shouldst have resisted"; and that he did not is the reason of his condemnation. *Cursed is the ground for thy sake*—from henceforth its fertility shall be greatly impaired; *in sorrow shalt thou eat of it*—be in continual perplexity concerning the seedtime and the harvest, the cold and the heat, the wet and the dry.

18. *Thorns also and thistles.* Instead of producing nourishing grain and useful vegetables, noxious weeds shall be peculiarly prolific, injure the ground, choke the good seed, and mock the hopes of the husbandman; *and thou shalt eat the herb of the field*—thou shalt no longer have the privilege of this garden of delights, but must go to the common country, and feed on such herbs as thou canst find, till by labor and industry thou hast raised others more suitable to thee and more comfortable.

In the curse pronounced on the *ground* there is much more implied than generally appears. The amazing fertility of some of the most common thistles and thorns renders them the most proper instruments for the fulfillment of this sentence against man.

19. *In the sweat of thy face.* Though the whole body may be thrown into a profuse sweat, if hard labor be long continued, yet the *face* or "forehead" is the first part whence this sweat begins to issue; this is occasioned by the blood being strongly propelled to the brain, partly through stooping, but principally by the strong action of the muscles; in consequence of this the blood vessels about the head become turgid through the great flux of blood, the fibres are relaxed, the pores enlarged, and the sweat or serum poured out. Thus then the very commencement of every man's labor may put him in mind of his sin and its consequences. *Dust thou art, and unto dust shalt thou return.* God had said that in the day they ate of the forbidden fruit, "dying they should die" —they should then become mortal, and continue under the influence of a great variety of unfriendly agencies in the atmosphere and in themselves, from heats, colds, drought, and damps in the one, and morbid increased and decreased action in the solids and fluids of the other, till the spirit, finding its earthly house no longer tenable, should return to God, who gave it; and the body, being decomposed, should be reduced to its primitive dust. It is evident from this that man would have been immortal had he never transgressed, and that this state of continual life and health depended on his obedience to his Maker.

20. *And Adam called his wife's name Eve; because she was the mother of all living.* A man who does not understand the original cannot possibly comprehend the reason of what is said here. What has the word *Eve* to do with being *the mother of all living?* Our translators often follow the Septuagint; it is a pity they had not done so here, as the Septuagint translation is literal and correct: "And Adam called

his wife's name *Life,* because she was the mother of all the *living.*" This is a proper and faithful representation of the Hebrew text. It is probable that God designed by this name to teach our first parents these two important truths: (1) That though they had merited immediate death, yet they should be respited, and the accomplishment of the sentence be long delayed; they should be spared to propagate a numerous progeny on the earth. (2) That though much misery would be entailed on his posterity, and death should have a long and universal empire, yet One should in the fulness of time spring from the woman, who should destroy death, and bring life and immortality to light, 2 Tim. i. 10. Therefore Adam called his wife's name "Life," because she was to be the mother of all human beings, and because she was to be the mother of *Him* who was to give life to a world dead in trespasses, and dead in sins, Eph. ii. 1.

21. *God made coats of skins.* It is very likely that the *skins* out of which their clothing was made were taken off animals whose blood had been poured out as a sin offering to God; for as we find Cain and Abel offering sacrifices to God, we may fairly presume that God had given them instructions on this head; nor is it likely that the notion of a sacrifice could have ever occurred to the mind of man without an express revelation from God.

22. *Behold, the man is become as one of us.* On all hands this text is allowed to be difficult, and the difficulty is increased by our translation, which is opposed to the original Hebrew and the most authentic versions. The Hebrew signifies "was," not *is.* The Samaritan text, the Samaritan version, the Syriac, and the Septuagint have the same tense. These lead us to a very different sense, and indicate that there is an ellipsis of some words which must be supplied in order to make the sense complete. A very learned man has ventured the following paraphrase, which should not be lightly regarded: "And the Lord God said, The man who was like one of us in purity and wisdom, is now fallen and robbed of his excellence; he has added to the knowledge of the good, by his transgression, the knowledge of the evil; and now, lest he put forth his hand, and take also of the tree of life, and eat and live forever in this miserable state, I will remove him, and guard the place lest he should reenter. Therefore the Lord God sent him forth from the Garden of Eden." This seems to be the most natural sense of the place.

In chap. i. 26-27, we have seen man in the perfection of his nature, the dignity of his office, and the plenitude of his happiness. Here we find the same creature, but stripped of his glories and happiness, so that the word "man" no longer conveys the same ideas it did before. Man and intellectual excellence were before so intimately connected as to appear inseparable; man and misery are now equally so.

24. *So he drove out the man.* Three things are noted here: (1) God's displeasure against sinful man, evidenced by His expelling him from this place of blessedness; (2) Man's unfitness for the place, of which he had rendered himself unworthy by his ingratitude and transgression; and (3) His reluctance to leave this place of happiness. He was, as we may natural-

ly conclude, unwilling to depart, and God *drove*
him out.

He placed at the east. Or "before" *the garden
of Eden,* before what may be conceived its gate
or entrance; *Cherubims,* "The cherubim." Hebrew plurals in the masculine end in general
in *im;* to add an *s* to this when we introduce
such words into English is very improper;
therefore the word should be written *cherubim,*
not *cherubims.* But what were these? They
are utterly unknown.

The word *kerub* never appears as a verb in
the Hebrew Bible, and therefore is justly supposed to be a word compounded of *ke,* a particle
of resemblance, "like to, like as," and *rab,* he
was "great, powerful." On this ground, I suppose, the cherubim were emblematical representations of the eternal power and Godhead
of the Almighty. These angelic beings were
for a time employed in guarding the entrance
to paradise, and keeping the way of or road to
the tree of life. This, I say, for a time; for it
is very probable that God soon removed the
tree of life, and abolished the garden, so that
its situation could never after be positively
ascertained.

By a flaming sword which turned every way,
or flame folding back upon itself, we may
understand the formidable appearances which
these cherubim assumed, in order to render
the passage to the tree of life inaccessible.

CHAPTER 4

The birth, trade, and religion of Cain and Abel, 1-7.
Cain murders his brother, Abel, 8. God calls him into
judgment for it, 9-10. He is cursed, 11-12. He despairs,
13-14. A promise given him of preservation, and a mark
set on him to prevent his being killed, 15. He departs
from God's presence, 16. Has a son whom he calls Enoch;
and builds a city, which he calls after his name, 17. Cain
has several children, among whom are Lamech, the first
bigamist, 18-19. Jabal, who taught the use of tents and
feeding cattle, 20. Jubal, the inventor of musical instruments, 21. Tubal-cain, the inventor of smithwork, 22.
Strange speech of Lamech to his wives, 23-24. Seth born
to Adam and Eve in the place of Abel, 25. Enoch born,
and the worship of God restored, 26.

1. *I have gotten a man from the Lord.* Cain
signifies "acquisition"; hence Eve says *kanithi,*
I have gotten or "acquired" a man, *eth Yehovah,*
"the Lord." It is extremely difficult to ascertain
the sense in which Eve used these words, which
have been as variously translated as understood. Most expositors think that Eve imagined
Cain to be the promised "seed" that should
bruise the head of the serpent. This exposition
really seems too refined for that period. It is
very likely that she meant no more than to
acknowledge that it was through God's peculiar
blessing that she was enabled to conceive and
bring forth a son, and that she had now a well-
grounded hope that the race of man should be
continued on the earth. Unless she had been
under divine inspiration she could not have
called her son (even supposing him to be the
promised "seed") *Jehovah;* and that she was
not under such an influence her mistake sufficiently proves, for Cain, so far from being the
Messiah, was of the wicked one; 1 John iii. 12.
We may therefore suppose that *eth Yehovah,*
"the Lord," is an elliptical form of expression
for *meeth Yehovah,* "from the Lord," or
"through the divine blessing."

2. *And she again bare his brother Abel.* Literally, "She added to bear his brother." From

the very face of this account it appears evident
that Cain and Abel were twins. In most cases
where a subject of this kind is introduced in
the Holy Scriptures, and the successive births
of children of the same parents are noted, the
acts of conceiving and bringing forth are mentioned in reference to each child; here it is not
said that she conceived and brought forth Abel,
but simply "she added to bring forth Abel his
brother"; that is, as I understand it, Cain was
the firstborn; Abel, his twin brother, came next.

Abel was a keeper of sheep. Adam was
originally a gardener, Abel a shepherd, and
Cain an agriculturist or farmer. These were
the three primitive employments, and I may
add, the most rational, and consequently the
best calculated to prevent strife and an immoderate love of the world.

3. *In process of time.* "At the end of days."
Some think the anniversary of the creation to
be here intended; it is more probable that it
means the Sabbath, on which Adam and his
family undoubtedly offered oblations to God,
as the divine worship was certainly instituted,
and no doubt the Sabbath properly observed
in that family. This worship was, in its original
institution, very simple. It appears to have
consisted of two parts: (1) Thanksgiving to
God as the Author and Dispenser of all the
bounties of nature, and oblations indicative of
that gratitude. (2) Sacrifices to His justice
and holiness, implying a conviction of their
own sinfulness, confession of transgression, and
faith in the promised Deliverer.

*Cain brought of the fruit of the ground an
offering* [*minchah*] *unto the Lord.* The word
minchah is explained, Lev. ii. 1, etc., to be an
offering of fine flour, with oil and fran kin-
cense. It was in general a eucharistic or gratitude offering, and is simply what is implied in
the *fruit of the ground* brought by Cain to
the Lord, by which he testified his belief in
Him as the Lord of the universe, and the Dispenser of secular blessings.

4. *Abel, he also brought of the firstlings of
his flock.* It was by this alone that he acknowledged himself a sinner, and professed faith in
the promised Messiah. To this circumstance the
apostle seems evidently to allude, Heb. xi. 4:
"By faith Abel offered a more or greater sacrifice." Thus his offerings were accepted, while
those of Cain were rejected; for this, as the
apostle says, was done by faith, and therefore
he obtained witness that he was righteous, or
a justified person, God testifying with his gifts,
the thank offering and the sin offering, by
accepting them, that faith in the promised Seed
was the only way in which He could accept the
services and offerings of mankind.

5. *Unto Cain.* As being unconscious of his
sinfulness, and consequently unhumbled, *and
to his offering,* as not being accompanied, as
Abel's was, with faith and a sacrifice for sin,
he had not respect—He could not, consistently
with His holiness and justice, approve of the
one or receive the other. Of the manner in
which God testified His approbation we are not
informed; it was probably, as in the case of
Elijah, by sending down fire from heaven, and
consuming the sacrifice.

Cain was very wroth. That displeasure which
should have been turned against his own unhumbled heart was turned against his innocent

brother, who, though not more highly privileged than he, made a much better use of the advantages which he shared in common with his ungodly and unnatural brother.

6. *Why art thou wroth?* This was designed as a gracious warning, and a preventive of the meditated crime.

7. *If thou doest well,* that which is right in the sight of God, *shalt thou not be accepted?* Does God reject any man who serves Him in simplicity and godly sincerity? *And if thou doest not well,* can wrath and indignation against thy righteous brother save thee from the displeasure under which thou art fallen? On the contrary, have recourse to thy Maker for mercy; "a sin offering lieth at thy door"; an animal proper to be offered as an atonement for sin is now "couching" at the door of thy fold.

The words *chattath* and *chattaah* frequently signify "sin"; but I have observed more than a hundred places in the Old Testament where they are used for "sin offering."

Unto thee shall be his desire. That is, Thou shalt ever have the right of primogeniture, and in all things shall thy brother be subject unto thee. These words are not spoken of sin, as many have understood them, but of Abel's submission to Cain as his superior, and the words are spoken to remove Cain's envy.

8. *Cain talked with Abel his brother.* "And Cain said"; not *talked,* for this construction the word cannot bear without great violence to analogy and grammatical accuracy. But why should it be thus translated? Because our translators could not find that anything was spoken on the occasion; and therefore they ventured to intimate that there was a conversation, indefinitely. In the most correct editions of the Hebrew Bible there is a small space left here in the text, and a circular mark which refers to a note in the margin, intimating that there is a hiatus or deficiency in the verse. Now this deficiency is supplied in the principal ancient versions, and in the Samaritan text. In this the supplied words are, "Let us walk out into the field." The Syriac has, "Let us go to the desert." The Vulgate, "Let us walk out." The Septuagint, "Let us go out into the field." The two Chaldee Targums have the same reading; so has the Coptic version. The words may therefore be safely considered as a part of the sacred text, and with them the whole passage reads clear and consistently: "And Cain said unto Abel his brother, Let us go out into the field: and it came to pass, when they were in the field, that Cain rose up."

10. *The voice of thy brother's blood.* It is probable that Cain, having killed his brother, dug a hole and buried him in the earth, hoping thereby to prevent the murder from being known; and that this is what is designed in the words, "Thy brother's blood crieth unto me from the ground—which hath opened her mouth to receive it from thy hand." Some think that by *the voice of thy brother's blood* the cries of Abel's widow and children are to be understood, as it is very probable that he was father of a family; indeed his occupation and sacrifices seem to render this probable, and probability is all we can expect on such a subject. God represents these as calling aloud for the punishment of the murderer; and it is evident that

Cain expected to fall by the hands of some person who had the right of the avenger of blood; for now that the murder is found out, he expects to suffer death for it. See. v. 14.

12. *A fugitive and a vagabond shalt thou be.* Thou shalt be expelled from the presence of God, and from thy family connections, and shalt have no fixed, secure residence in any place. The Septuagint renders this, "Thou shalt be groaning and trembling" upon the earth—the horror of thy crime shall ever haunt thee, and thou shalt never have any well-grounded hope that God will remit the punishment thou deservest.

13. *My punishment is greater than I can bear.* The margin reads, "Mine iniquity is greater than that it may be forgiven." The original words may be translated, "Is my crime too great to be forgiven?" words which we may presume he uttered on the verge of black despair. It is most probable that *avon* signifies rather the crime than the punishment; in this sense it is used, Lev. xxvi. 41, 43; 1 Sam. xxviii. 10; 2 Kings vii. 9; and *nasa* signifies to remit or forgive. The marginal reading is, therefore, to be preferred to that in the text.

14. *Behold, thou hast driven me out.* In verses 11-12, God states two parts of Cain's punishment: (1) The ground was cursed, so that it was not to yield any adequate recompense for his most careful tillage. (2) He was to be a fugitive and a vagabond, having no place in which he could dwell with comfort or security. To these Cain himself adds others. (1) His being hidden from the face of God; which appears to signify his being expelled from that particular place where God had manifested His presence, in or contiguous to paradise, whither our first parents resorted as to an oracle, and where they offered their daily adorations. So in verse 16, it is said, "Cain went out from the presence of the Lord," and was not permitted anymore to associate with the family in acts of religious worship. (2) The continual apprehension of being slain, as all the inhabitants of the earth were at that time of the same family, the parents themselves still alive, and each having a right to kill this murderer of his relative. Add to all this (3) the terrors of a guilty conscience; his awful apprehension of God's judgments, and of being everlastingly banished from the beatific vision. To this part of the punishment of Cain, St. Paul probably alludes, 2 Thess. i. 9: "Who shall be punished with everlasting destruction from the presence of the Lord, and from the glory of his power." The words are so similar that we can scarcely doubt of the allusion.

15. *The Lord set a mark upon Cain.* Dr. Shuckford observes that the Hebrew word *oth,* which we translate *a mark,* signifies "a sign" or "token." Thus, Gen. ix. 13, the bow was to be "for a sign" or "token" that the world should not be destroyed; therefore the words, *And the Lord set a mark upon Cain,* should be translated, "And the Lord appointed to Cain a token or sign," to convince him that no person should be permitted to slay him. To have *marked* him would have been the most likely way to have brought all the evils he dreaded upon him; therefore the Lord gave him some miraculous sign or token that he should not be slain, to the end that he should not despair, but,

having time to repent, might return to a gracious God and find mercy.

16. *The land of Nod.* As *nod* signifies the same as *nad*, a "vagabond," some think this verse should be rendered, "And Cain went out from the presence of the Lord, from the east of Eden, and dwelt a vagabond on the earth"; thus the curse pronounced on him, verse 12, was accomplished.

17. *She . . . bare Enoch.* As *Chanoch* signifies "instructed, dedicated, or initiated," and especially in sacred things, it may be considered some proof of Cain's repentance, that he appears to have dedicated this son to God, who, in his father's stead, might minister in the sacerdotal office, from which Cain, by his crime, was forever excluded.

19. *Lamech took . . . two wives.* He was the first who dared to reverse the order of God by introducing polygamy; and from him it has been retained, practiced, and defended to the present day.

20. *Jabal . . . was the father.* The "inventor" or "teacher," for so the word is understood, 1 Sam. x. 12. He was the first who invented tent making, and the breeding and managing of cattle; or he was, in these respects, the most eminent in that time. Though Abel was a shepherd, it is not likely he was such on an extensive scale.

21. *Jubal . . . the father.* I.e., the "inventor" of musical instruments, such as the *kinnor*, which we translate *harp*, and the *ugab*, which we render *organ*; it is very likely that both words are generic, the former including under it all stringed instruments, and the latter, all wind instruments.

22. *Tubal-cain.* The first smith on record, who taught how to make warlike instruments and domestic utensils out of brass and iron. Agricultural instruments must have been in use long before, for Cain was a tiller of the ground, and so was Adam, and they could not have cultivated the ground without spades, hooks, etc. Some of these arts were useless to man while innocent and upright, but after his fall they became necessary. Thus is the saying verified: "God hath made man upright; but they have sought out many inventions." As the power to get wealth is from God, so also is the invention of useful arts.

23. *And Lamech said unto his wives.* The speech of Lamech to his wives is in hemistichs in the original, and consequently, as nothing of this kind occurs before this time, it is very probably the oldest piece of poetry in the world.

The following is, as nearly as possible, a literal translation:

"And Lamech said unto his wives,
Adah and Tsillah, hear ye my voice;
Wives of Lamech, hearken to my speech;
For I have slain a man for wounding me,
And a young man for having bruised me.
If Cain shall be avenged sevenfold,
Also Lamech seventy and seven."

It is supposed that Lamech had slain a man in his own defense, and that his wives being alarmed lest the kindred of the deceased should seek his life in return, to quiet their fears he makes this speech, in which he endeavors to prove that there was no room for fear on this account; for if the slayer of the wilful murderer, Cain, should suffer a sevenfold punishment, surely he who should kill Lamech for having slain a man in self-defense might expect a seventy-seven-fold punishment.

25. *God . . . hath appointed me another seed instead of Abel.* Eve must have received on this occasion some divine communication, else how could she have known that this son was appointed in the place of Abel, to continue that holy line by which the Messiah was to come? From this we see that the line of the Messiah was determined from the beginning, and that it was not first fixed in the days of Abraham; for the promise was then only renewed, and that branch of his family designated by which the sacred line was to be continued. And it is worthy of remark that Seth's posterity alone continued after the Flood, when all the other families of the earth were destroyed, Noah being the tenth descendant from Adam through Seth.

26. *Then began men to call upon the name of the Lord.* The marginal reading is, "Then began men to call themselves *by the* name of the Lord"; which words are supposed to signify that in the time of Enos the true followers of God began to distinguish themselves, and to be distinguished by others, by the appellation of "sons of God"; those of the other branch of Adam's family, among whom the divine worship was not observed, being distinguished by the name "children of men."

CHAPTER 5

A recapitulation of the account of the creation of man, 1-2; and of the birth of Seth, 3. Genealogy of the ten antediluvian patriarchs, 3-31. Enoch's extraordinary piety, 22; his translation to heaven without seeing death, 24. The birth of Noah, and the reason of his name, 29; his age at the birth of Japheth, 32.

1. *The book of the generations.* Sepher in Hebrew, which we generally translate *book*, signifies a "register," an "account," any kind of writing, even a "letter," such as the bill of divorce. Here it means the account or register of the generations of Adam or his descendants to the five hundredth year of the life of Noah.

In the likeness of God made he him. This account is again introduced to keep man in remembrance of the heights of glory whence he had fallen; and to prove to him that the miseries and death consequent on his present state were produced by his transgression, and did not flow from his original state. For, as he was created in the image of God, he was created free from natural and moral evil. As the deaths of the patriarchs are now to be mentioned, it was necessary to introduce them by this observation, in order to justify the ways of God to man.

3. *And Adam lived an hundred and thirty years.* The Scripture chronology, especially in the ages of some of the antediluvian and postdiluvian patriarchs, has exceedingly puzzled chronologists, critics, and divines. The printed Hebrew text, the Samaritan, the Septuagint, and Josephus are all different, and have their respective vouchers and defenders.

And begat a son in his own likeness, after his image. Words nearly the same with those of chap. i. 26: "Let us make man in our image, after our likeness." What this *image* and *like-*

ness of God were, we have already seen, and we may rest assured that the same image and likeness are not meant here. The body of Adam was created provisionally immortal, i.e., while he continued obedient he could not die; but his obedience was voluntary, and his state a probationary one. The soul of Adam was created in the moral image of God, in knowledge, righteousness, and true holiness. He had now sinned, and consequently had lost his moral resemblance to his Maker; he had also become mortal through his breach of the law. His image and likeness were therefore widely different at this time from what they were before; and his begetting children in this image and likeness plainly implies that they were imperfect like himself, mortal like himself, sinful and corrupt like himself.

22. *And Enoch walked with God . . . three hundred years.* Enoch, from *chanack,* which signifies to "instruct," to "initiate," to "dedicate." From his subsequent conduct we are authorized to believe he was early instructed in the things of God, initiated into the worship of his Maker, and dedicated to His service. By these means, under the influence of the Divine Spirit, which will ever attend pious parental instructions, his mind got that sacred bias which led him to act a part so distinguished through the course of a long life. He *walked with God;* "he set himself to walk"; he was fixedly purposed and determined to live to God.

27. *The days of Methuselah were nine hundred sixty and nine years.* This is the longest life mentioned in Scripture, and probably the longest ever lived; but we have not authority to say positively that it was the longest. Before the Flood, and before artificial refinements were much known and cultivated, the life of man was greatly protracted, and yet of him who lived within thirty-one years of a thousand it is said he *died;* and the longest life is but as a moment when it is past.

29. *This same shall comfort us.* This is an allusion, as some think, to the name of Noah, which they derive from *nacham,* "to comfort"; but it is much more likely that it comes from *nach* or *nuach,* "to rest, to settle." And what is more comfortable than rest after toil and labor? These words seem to have been spoken prophetically concerning Noah, who built the ark for the preservation of the human race, and who seems to have been a typical person; for when he offered his sacrifice after the drying up of the waters, it is said that God smelled a savor of rest and said He would not curse the ground anymore for man's sake, chap. viii. 21; and from that time the earth seems to have had upon an average the same degree of fertility; and the life of man, in a few generations after, was settled in the mean at threescore years and ten. See chap. ix. 3.

32. *Noah begat Shem, Ham, and Japheth.* From chap. x. 21; 1 Chron. i. 5, etc., we learn that Japheth was the eldest son of Noah, but Shem is mentioned first, because it was from him, in a direct line, that the Messiah came. Ham was certainly the youngest of Noah's sons, and from what we read, chap. ix. 22, the worst of them; and how he comes to be mentioned out of his natural order is not easy to be accounted for. When the Scriptures design to mark precedency, though the subject be a younger son or brother, he is always mentioned first; so Jacob is named before Esau, his elder brother, and Ephraim before Manasseh. See chap. xxviii. 5; xlviii. 20.

CHAPTER 6

The children of God, among whom the true religion was at first preserved, corrupt it by forming matrimonial connections with irreligious women, 1-2. God, displeased with these connections and their consequences, limits the continuance of the old world to 120 years, 3. The issue of those improper connections termed giants, 4. An affecting description of the depravity of the world, 5-6. God threatens the destruction of every living creature, 7. Noah and his family find grace in His sight, 8. The character and family of Noah, 9-10. And a further description of the corruption of man, 11-12. Noah is forewarned of the approaching destruction of the human race, 13; and is ordered to build an ark for the safety of himself and household, the form and dimensions of which are particularly described, 14-16. The deluge threatened, 17. The covenant of God's mercy is to be established between Him and the family of Noah, 18. A male and female of all kinds of animals that could not live in the waters to be brought into the ark, 19-20. Noah is commanded to provide food for their sustenance, 21; and punctually follows all these directions, 22.

1. *When men began to multiply.* It was not at this time that men began to multiply, but the inspired penman speaks now of a fact which had taken place long before. As there is a distinction made here between men and those called the "sons of God," it is generally supposed that the immediate posterity of Cain and that of Seth are intended. The first were mere men, such as fallen nature may produce, degenerate sons of a degenerate father, governed by the desire of the flesh, the desire of the eye, and the pride of life. The others were "sons of God," not angels, as some have dreamed, but such as were, according to our Lord's doctrine, born again, born from above, John iii. 3, 5-6, etc., and made children of God by the influence of the Holy Spirit, Gal. v. 6. The former were apostates from the true religion; the latter were those among whom it was preserved and cultivated.

3. *My spirit shall not always strive.* It is only by the influence of the Spirit of God that the carnal mind can be subdued and destroyed; but those who wilfully resist and grieve that Spirit must be ultimately left to the hardness and blindness of their own hearts, if they do not repent and turn to God. God delights in mercy, and therefore a gracious warning is given. Even at this time the earth was ripe for destruction; but God promised them 120 years' respite: if they repented in that interim, well; if not, they should be destroyed by a flood. See on v. 5.

4. *There were giants in the earth.* Nephilim, from *naphal,* "he fell." Those who had apostatized or fallen from the true religion. The Septuagint translates the original word by *gigantes,* which literally signifies "earth-born," and which we, following them, term *giants,* without having any reference to the meaning of the word, which we generally conceive to signify persons of enormous stature. But the word when properly understood makes a very just distinction between the sons of men and the sons of God; those were the nephilim, the fallen earth-born men, with the animal and devilish mind. These were the sons of God, who were born from above; children of the Kingdom, because children of God.

The same became mighty men . . . men of renown. Gibborim, which we render *mighty men,* signifies properly "conquerors, heroes," from *gabar,* "he prevailed, was victorious," and "men of the name"; the same as we render "men of renown," "twice named," as the word implies, having one name which they derived from their fathers, and another which they acquired by their daring exploits and enterprises.

It may be necessary to remark here that our translators have rendered seven different Hebrew words by the one term "giants," namely, *nephilim, gibborim, enachim, rephaim, emim,* and *zamzummim;* by which appellatives are probably meant in general persons of great knowledge, piety, courage, wickedness, etc., and not men of enormous stature, as is generally conjectured.

5. *The wickedness of man was great.* What an awful character does God give of the inhabitants of the antediluvian world! (1) They were "flesh" (v. 3), wholly sensual, the desires of the mind overwhelmed and lost in the desires of the flesh. (2) They were in a state of "wickedness." All was corrupt within, and all unrighteous without. (3) This wickedness was "great," *rabbah,* "was multiplied"; it was continually increasing and multiplying increase by increase, so that the whole earth was corrupt before God, and was filled with violence (v. 11). (4) "All the imaginations of their thoughts were evil"—the very first embryo of every idea, the figment of every thought, the very materials out of which perception, conception, and ideas were formed, were all *evil;* the fountain which produced them, with every thought, purpose, wish, desire, and motive, was incurably poisoned. (5) All these were evil without any mixture of good—the Spirit of God which strove with them was continually resisted, so that evil had its sovereign sway. (6) They were evil "continually"—there was no interval of good, no moment allowed for serious reflection, no holy purpose, no righteous act. What a finished picture of a fallen soul! (7) To complete the whole, God represents himself as "repenting" because he had made them, and as "grieved at the heart" because of their iniquities! (8) So incensed is the most holy and the most merciful God that He is determined to destroy the work of His hands: "And the Lord said, I will destroy man whom I have created," v. 7. Fools make a mock at sin, but none except fools.

8. *Noah found grace in the eyes of the Lord.* Why? Because he was (1) *A just man,* a man who "gave to all their due"; for this is the ideal meaning of the original word. (2) He was *perfect in his generations*—he was in all things a consistent character, never departing from the truth in principle or practice. (3) He *walked with God*—he was not only righteous in his conduct, but he was pious, and had continual communion with God. The same word is used here as before in the case of Enoch. See chap. v. 22.

13. *I will destroy them with the earth.* Not only the human race was to be destroyed, but all terrestrial animals, i.e., those which could not live in the waters.

14. *Make thee an ark.* Tebath, a word which is used only to express this vessel, and that in which Moses was preserved, Exod. ii. 3, 5. It signifies no more than our word "vessel" in its common acceptation—a hollow place capable of containing persons, goods, etc., without any particular reference to shape or form.

Gopher wood. Some think the cedar is meant; others, the cypress.

15. *Thou shalt make . . . the length of the ark . . . three hundred cubits, the breadth of it fifty cubits, and the height of it thirty cubits.* Allowing the cubit, which is the length from the elbow to the tip of the middle finger, to be 18 inches, the ark must have been 450 feet in length, 75 in breadth, and 45 in height.

16. *A window shalt thou make.* What this was cannot be absolutely ascertained. The original word signifies "clear" or "bright." It is probably a word which should be taken in a collective sense, signifying apertures for air and light.

17. *I . . . do bring a flood.* Mabbul, a word used only to designate the general deluge, being never applied to signify any other kind of inundation; and does not the Holy Spirit intend to show by this that no other flood was ever like this, and that it should continue to be the sole one of the kind? There have been many partial inundations in various countries, but never more than one general deluge; and we have God's promise, chap. ix. 15, that there shall never be another.

18. *With thee will I establish my covenant.* The word *berith,* from *bar,* "to purify or cleanse," signifies properly a purification or purifier (see on chap. xv. 18), because in all covenants made between God and man, sin and sinfulness were ever supposed to be on man's side, and that God could not enter into any covenant or engagement with him without a purifier; hence, in all covenants, a sacrifice was offered for the removal of offenses, and the reconciliation of God to the sinner; and hence the word *berith* signifies not only a *covenant,* but also the sacrifice offered on the occasion, Exod. xxiv. 8; Ps. i. 5; and Jesus Christ, the great Atonement and Purifier, has the same word for His title, Isa. xlii. 6; xlix. 8; and Zech. ix. 11.

Almost all nations, in forming alliances, etc., made their covenants or contracts in the same way. A sacrifice was provided, its throat was cut, and its blood poured out before God; then the whole carcass was divided through the spinal marrow from the head to the rump; so as to make exactly two equal parts; these were placed opposite to each other, and the contracting parties passed between them, or entering at opposite ends met in the center, and there took the covenant oath. This is particularly referred to by Jeremiah, chap. xxxiv. 18-20: "I will give the men [into the hands of their enemies, v. 20] that have transgressed my covenant, which have not performed the words of the covenant which they had made before me, when they cut the calf in twain, and passed between the parts thereof." See also Deut. xxix. 12.

The covenant made with Noah signified, on God's part, that He should save Noah and his family from death by the ark. On Noah's part, that he should in faith and obedience make and enter into the ark—"Thou shalt come into the ark," so committing himself to God's preservation, Heb. xi. 7. And under this the covenant or testament of eternal salvation by Christ was also implied, the apostle testifying, 1 Pet. iii. 21, that the antitype, baptism, doth also now save us; for baptism is a seal of our salvation, Mark xvi. 16. To provide a Saviour, and the means of salvation, is God's part; to accept this is ours. Those who refuse the way and means of salvation must perish; those who accept of the great Covenant Sacrifice cannot perish, but shall have eternal life.

19. *To keep them alive.* God might have destroyed all the animal creation, and created others to occupy the new world, but He chose rather to preserve those already created.

21. *Of all food that is eaten.* That is, of the food proper for every species of animals.

22. *Thus did Noah.* He prepared the ark; and during 120 years preached righteousness to that sinful generation, 2 Pet. ii. 5. And this we are informed, 1 Pet. iii. 18-19, he did by the Spirit of Christ; for it was only through Him that the doctrine of repentance could ever be successfully preached. The people in Noah's time are represented as shut up in prison—arrested and condemned by God's justice, but graciously allowed the space of 120 years to repent in. This respite was an act of great mercy; and no doubt thousands who died in the interim availed themselves of it, and believed to the saving of their souls. But the great majority of the people did not, else the Flood had never come.

CHAPTER 7

God informs Noah that within seven days He shall send a rain upon the earth, that shall continue for forty days and nights; and, therefore, commands him to take his family, with the different clean and unclean animals, and enter the ark, 1-4. This command punctually obeyed, 5-9. In the seventeenth day of the second month, in the six hundredth year of Noah's life, the waters, from the opened windows of heaven, and the broken-up fountains of the great deep, are poured out upon the earth, 10-12. The different quadrupeds, fowls, and reptiles come unto Noah, and the Lord shuts him and them in, 13-16. The waters increase, and the ark floats, 17. The whole earth is covered with water fifteen cubits above the highest mountains, 18-20. All terrestrial animals die, 21-23. And the waters prevail 150 days, 24.

1. *Thee have I seen righteous.* See on chap. vi. 9.

2. *Of every clean beast.* So we find the distinction between clean and unclean animals existed long before the Mosaic law. This distinction seems to have been originally designed to mark those animals which were proper for sacrifice and food, from those that were not. See Leviticus xi.

4. *For yet seven days.* God spoke these words probably on the seventh or Sabbath day, and the days of the ensuing week were employed in entering the ark, in embarking the mighty troop, for whose reception ample provision had been already made.

Forty days. This period afterwards became sacred, and was considered a proper space for humiliation. Moses fasted forty days, Deut. ix. 9, 11; so did Elijah, 1 Kings xix. 8; so did our Lord, Matt. iv. 2.

11. *In the six hundredth year.* This must have been in the beginning of the six hundredth year of his life; for he was a year in the ark, chap. viii. 13; and lived 350 years after the Flood, and died when he was nine hundred and fifty years old, chap. ix. 29.

15. *And they went in.* It was physically impossible for Noah to have collected such a vast number of tame and ferocious animals, nor could they have been retained in their wards by mere natural means. How then were they brought from various distances to the ark and preserved there? Only by the power of God. He who first miraculously brought them to Adam that he might give them their names now brings them to Noah that he may preserve their lives. And now we may reasonably suppose that their natural enmity was so far removed or suspended that the lion might dwell with the lamb, and the wolf lie down with the kid, though each might still require his peculiar aliment. This can be no difficulty to the power of God, without the immediate interposition of which neither the deluge nor the concomitant circumstances could have taken place.

16. *The Lord shut him in.* This seems to imply that God took him under His especial protection, and as He shut him in, so He shut the others out. God had waited 120 years upon that generation; they did not repent; they filled up the measure of their iniquities, and then wrath came upon them to the uttermost.

22. *Of all that was in the dry land.* From this we may conclude that such animals only as could not live in the water were preserved in the ark.

24. *And the waters prevailed upon the earth an hundred and fifty days.* The breaking up of the fountains of the great deep, and the raining 40 days and nights, had raised the waters 15 cubits above the highest mountains; after which 40 days it appears to have continued at this height for 150 days more.

CHAPTER 8

At the end of 150 days the waters begin to subside, 1-3. The art rests on Mount Ararat, 4. On the first of the tenth month the tops of the hills appear, 5. The window opened and the raven sent out, 6-7. The dove sent forth, and returns, 8-9. The dove sent forth a second time, and returns with an olive leaf, 10-11. The dove sent out the third time, and returns no more, 12. On the twentieth day of the second month the earth is completely dried, 13-14. God orders Noah, his family, and all the creatures to come out of the ark, 15-19. Noah builds an altar, and offers sacrifices to the Lord, 20. They are accepted; and God promises that the earth shall not be cursed thus anymore, notwithstanding the iniquity of man, 21-22.

1. *And God made a wind to pass over the earth.* Such a wind as produced a strong and sudden evaporation.

4. *The mountains of Ararat.* That Ararat was a mountain of Armenia is almost universally agreed.

7. *He sent forth a raven, which went forth to and fro.* It is generally supposed that the raven flew off, and was seen no more, but this meaning the Hebrew text will not bear: "and it went forth, going forth and returning." From which it is evident that she did return, but was not taken into the ark. She made frequent excursions, and continued on the wing as long as she could, having picked up such aliment as she found floating on the waters; and then, to rest herself, regained the ark, where she might perch, though she was not admitted. Indeed this must be allowed, as it is impossible she could have continued twenty-one days upon the wing, which she must have done had she not

returned. But the text itself is sufficiently determinate.

8. *He sent forth a dove.* The dove was sent forth thrice; the first time she speedily returned, having, in all probability, gone but a little way from the ark, as she must naturally be terrified at the appearance of the waters. After seven days, being sent out a second time, she returned with an olive leaf plucked off, v. 11, an emblem of the restoration of peace between God and the earth; and from this circumstance the olive has been the emblem of peace among all civilized nations. At the end of the other seven days the dove, being sent out the third time, returned no more, from which Noah conjectured that the earth was now sufficiently drained and, therefore, removed the covering of the ark, which probably gave liberty to many of the fowls to fly off, which circumstance would afford him the greater facility in making arrangements for disembarking the beasts and reptiles, and heavy-bodied domestic fowls, which might yet remain.

14. *And in the second month, on the seven and twentieth day.* From this it appears that Noah was in the ark a complete solar year, or 365 days; for he entered the ark the seventeenth day of the second month, in the six hundredth year of his life, chap. vii. 11, 13, and continued in it till the twenty-seventh day of the second month, in the six hundredth and first year of his life, as we see above. The months of the ancient Hebrews were lunar; the first 6 consisted of 30 days each, the latter 6 of 29; the whole 12 months making 354 days: add to this 11 days (for though he entered the ark the preceding year on the seventeenth day of the second month, he did not come out till the twenty-seventh of the same month in the following year), which make exactly 365 days.

20. *Noah builded an altar.* As we have already seen that Adam, Cain, and Abel offered sacrifices, there can be no doubt that they had altars on which they offered them; but this, builded by Noah, is certainly the first on record. The word which we render *altar* signifies properly a "place for sacrifice," as the root signifies simply to "slay." *Altar* comes from the Latin *altus,* high or elevated, because places for sacrifice were generally either raised very high or built on the tops of hills and mountains; hence they are called high places in the Scriptures; but such were chiefly used for idolatrous purposes.

Burnt offerings. See the meaning of every kind of offering and sacrifice largely explained on Leviticus vii.

21. *The Lord smelled a sweet savour.* That is, He was well pleased with this religious act, performed in obedience to His own appointment, and in faith of the promised Saviour. That this sacrifice prefigured that which was offered by our blessed Redeemer in behalf of the world is sufficiently evident from the words of Paul, Eph. v. 2: "Christ also hath loved us, and given himself for us an offering and a sacrifice to God for a sweetsmelling savour"; where the words of the apostle are the very words used by the Septuagint in this place.

I will not again curse the ground. "I will not add to curse the ground"—there shall not be another deluge to destroy the whole earth: *for the imagination of man's heart,* "although the

imagination of man's heart should be evil," i.e., should they become afterwards as evil as they have been before, I will not destroy the earth by a flood. God has other means of destruction; and the next time He visits by a general judgment, fire is to be the agent, 2 Pet. iii. 7.

22. *While the earth remaineth, seedtime and harvest.* There is something very expressive in the original, "until all the days of the earth"; for God does not reckon its duration by centuries, and the words themselves afford a strong presumption that the earth shall not have an endless duration.

Seedtime and harvest. This is a very merciful promise to the inhabitants of the earth. There may be a variety in the seasons, but no season essentially necessary to vegetation shall utterly fail. The times which are of greatest consequence to the preservation of man are distinctly noted; there shall be both *seedtime* and *harvest*—a proper time to deposit the different grain in the earth, and a proper time to reap the produce of this seed.

CHAPTER 9

God blesses Noah and his sons, 1. The brute creation to be subject to them through fear, 2. The first grant of animal food. 3. Eating of blood forbidden, 4. Cruelty to animals forbidden, 5. A manslayer to forfeit his life, 6. The covenant of God established between Him and Noah and the whole brute creation, 8-11. The rainbow given as the sign and pledge of this covenant, 12-17. The three sons of Noah people the whole earth, 18-19. Noah plants a vineyard, drinks of the wine, is intoxicated, and lies exposed in his tent, 20-21. The reprehensible conduct of Ham, 22. The laudable carriage of Shem and Japheth, 23. Noah prophetically declares the servitude of the posterity of Ham, 24-25; and the dignity and increase of Shem and Japheth, 26-27. The age and death of Noah, 28-29.

1. *God blessed Noah.* Even the increase of families, which appears to depend on merely natural means, and sometimes fortuitous circumstance, is all of God. It is by His power and wisdom that the human being is formed, and it is by His providence alone that man is supported and preserved.

2. *The fear of you and the dread.* Prior to the Fall, man ruled the inferior animals by love and kindness, for then gentleness and docility were their principal characteristics. After the Fall untractableness, with savage ferocity, prevailed among almost all orders of the brute creation; enmity to man seems particularly to prevail; and had not God in His mercy impressed their minds with the *fear* and *terror* of man, so that some *submit* to his will while others *flee* from his residence, the human race would long ere this have been totally destroyed by the beasts of the field.

3. *Every moving thing . . . shall be meat.* There is no positive evidence that animal food was ever used before the Flood. Noah had the first grant of this kind, and it has been continued to all his posterity ever since.

4. *But flesh with the life thereof, which is the blood.* Though animal food was granted, yet the *blood* was most solemnly forbidden, because it was the life of the beast, and this life was to be offered to God as an atonement for sin. Hence the blood was ever held sacred, because it was the grand instrument of expiation, and because it was typical of that Blood by which we enter into the holiest.

5. *Surely your blood . . . will I require; at the hand of every beast.* This is very obscure, but if taken literally it seems to be an awful warning against cruelty to the brute creation.

6. *Whoso sheddeth man's blood, by man shall his blood.* Hence it appears that whoever kills a man, unless "unwittingly," as the Scripture expresses it, shall forfeit his own life.

13. *I do set my bow in the cloud.* From the well-known cause of this phenomenon it cannot be rationally supposed that there was no rainbow in the heavens before the time mentioned in the text, for as the rainbow is the natural effect of the sun's rays falling on drops of water, and of their being refracted and reflected by them, it must have appeared at different times from the creation of the sun and the atmosphere. Nor does the text intimate that the bow was now created for a sign to Noah and his posterity; but that what was formerly created, or rather that which was the necessary effect in certain cases of the creation of the sun and atmosphere, should now be considered by them as an unfailing token of their continual preservation from the waters of a deluge; therefore the text speaks of what had already been done, and not of what was now done, "My bow I *have* given, or put in the cloud."

17. *This is the token.* The divine sign or portent: "The bow shall be in the cloud." For the reasons above specified it must be there, when the circumstances already mentioned occur; if therefore it cannot fail because of the reasons before assigned, no more shall My promise; and the bow shall be the proof of its perpetuity.

20. *Noah began to be an husbandman.* A man of the ground, a farmer; by his beginning to be a husbandman we are to understand his recommencing his agricultural operations, which undoubtedly he had carried on for six hundred years before, but this had been interrupted by the Flood. And the transaction here mentioned might have occurred many years posterior to the deluge, even after Canaan was born and grown up, for the date of it is not fixed in the text.

21. *He drank of the wine.* It is very probable that this was the first time the vine was cultivated; and it is as probable that the strength or intoxicating power of the expressed juice was never before known. Noah, therefore, might have drunk it at this time without the least blame, as he knew not till this trial the effects it would produce.

22-24. *And Ham, the father of Canaan.* There is no occasion to enter into any detail here; the sacred text is circumstantial enough. Ham, and very probably his son Canaan, had treated their father on this occasion with contempt or reprehensible levity. Had Noah not been innocent, as my exposition supposes him, God would not have endued him with the spirit of prophecy on this occasion, and testified such marked disapprobation of their conduct. The conduct of Shem and Japheth was such as became pious and affectionate children, who appear to have been in the habit of treating their father with decency, reverence, and obedient respect. On the one the spirit of prophecy (not the incensed father) pronounces a curse; on the others the same spirit (not parental tenderness) pronounces a blessing. The curse pronounced on Canaan neither fell immediately upon himself nor on his worthless father, but upon the Canaanites; and from the history we have of this people, in Leviticus xviii; xx; and Deut. ix. 4; xii. 31, we may ask, Could the curse of God fall more deservedly on any people than on these? Their profligacy was great, but it was not the effect of the curse; but, being foreseen by the Lord, the curse was the effect of their conduct.

29. *The days of Noah were nine hundred and fifty years.* The oldest patriarch on record, except Methuselah and Jared.

CHAPTER 10

The generations of the sons of Noah, 1. Japheth and his descendants, 2-4. The isles of the Gentiles, or Europe, peopled by the Japhethites, 5. Ham and his posterity, 6-20. Nimrod, one of his descendants, a mighty hunter, 8-9, founds the first kingdom, 10. Nineveh and other cities founded, 11-12. The Canaanites in their nine grand branches or families, 15-18. Their territories, 19. Shem and his posterity, 21-31. The earth divided in the days of Peleg, 25. The territories of the Shemites, 30. The whole earth peopled by the descendants of Noah's three sons, 32.

1. *Now these are the generations.* It is extremely difficult to say what particular nations and people sprang from the three grand divisions of the family of Noah, because the names of many of those ancient people have become changed in the vast lapse of time from the deluge to the Christian era; yet some are so very distinctly marked that they can be easily ascertained, while a few still retain their original names.

Moses does not always give the name of the first settler in a country, but rather that of the people from whom the country afterwards derived its name. Thus *Mizraim* is the dual of *Mezer,* and could never be the name of an individual. The like may be said of *Kittim, Dodanim, Ludim, Anamim, Lehabim, Naphtuhim, Pathrusim, Casluhim, Philistim,* and *Caphtorim,* which are all plurals, and evidently not the names of individuals, but of families or tribes. See vv. 4, 6, 13-14. In the posterity of Canaan we find whole nations reckoned in the geneaology, instead of the individuals from whom they sprang; thus the *Jebusite, Amorite, Girgasite, Hivite, Arkite, Sinite, Arvadite, Zemarite,* and *Hamathite,* vv. 16-18, were evidently whole nations or tribes which inhabited the Promised Land, and were called *Canaanites* from *Canaan,* the son of Ham, who settled there.

Moses also, in this genealogy, seems to have introduced even the name of some places that were remarkable in the sacred history, instead of the original settlers. Such as *Hazarmaveth,* v. 26; and probably *Ophir* and *Havilah,* v. 29. But this is not infrequent in the sacred writings, as may be seen, I Chron. ii. 51, where *Salma* is called "the father of Bethlehem," which certainly never was the name of a man, but of a place sufficiently celebrated in the sacred history; and in chap. iv. 14, where Joab is called "the father of the valley of Charashim," which no person could ever suppose was intended to designate an individual, but the society of craftsmen or artificers who lived there.

2. *The sons of Japheth.* Japheth is supposed to be the same with the "Japetus" of the Greeks, from whom, in an extremely remote antiquity, that people were supposed to have derived their

origin. *Gomer.* Supposed by some to have peopled Galatia; so Josephus, who says that the Galatians were anciently named Gomerites. *Magog.* Supposed by many to be the father of the Scythians and Tartars, or "Tatars," as the word should be written; and in great Tartary many names are still found which bear such a striking resemblance to the Gog and Magog of the Scriptures as to leave little doubt of their identity. *Javan.* It is almost universally agreed that from him sprang the Ionians, of Asia Minor. *Tubal.* Some think he was the father of the Iberians, and that a part at least of Spain was peopled by him and his descendants; and that *Meshech,* who is generally in Scripture joined with him, was the founder of the Cappadocians, from whom proceeded the Muscovites. *Tiras.* From this person, according to general consent, the Thracians derived their origin.

4. *Elishah.* As *Javan* peopled a considerable part of Greece, it is in that region that we must seek for the settlements of his descendants; *Elishah* probably was the first who settled at Elis, in Pelopennesus. *Tarshish.* He first inhabited Cilicia, whose capital anciently was the city of Tarsus, where the Apostle Paul was born. *Kittim.* We have already seen that this name was rather the name of a people than of an individual; some think by *Kittim* Cyprus is meant.

5. *Isles of the Gentiles.* Europe, of which this is allowed to be a general epithet. *Every one after his tongue.* This refers to the time posterior to the confusion of tongues and dispersion from Babel.

6. *Cush.* Who peopled the Arabic nome near the Red Sea in Lower Egypt. Some think the Ethiopians descended from him. *Mizraim.* This family certainly peopled Egypt; and both in the East and in the West, Egypt is called *Mizraim.* *Phut.* Who first peopled an Egyptian nome or district, bordering on Libya. *Canaan.* He who first peopled the land so called, known also by the name of the Promised Land.

7. *Seba.* The founder of the Sabeans. There seem to be three different people of this name mentioned in this chapter, and a fourth in chap. xxv. 3.

8. *Nimrod.* Of this person little is known, as he is not mentioned except here and in 1 Chron. i. 10, which is evidently a copy of the text in Genesis. He is called "a mighty hunter before the Lord"; and from v. 10, we learn that he founded a "kingdom" which included the cities "Babel, and Erech, and Accad, and Calneh, in the land of Shinar." Though the words are not definite, it is very likely he was a very bad man. His name Nimrod comes from *marad,* "he rebelled"; and the Targum, on 1 Chron. i. 10, says: "Nimrod began to be a mighty man in sin, a murderer of innocent men, and a rebel before the Lord." The word which we render *hunter* signifies "prey"; and is applied in the Scriptures to the hunting of men by persecution, oppression, and tyranny. Hence it is likely that Nimrod, having acquired power, used it in tyranny and oppression; and by rapine and violence founded that domination which was the first distinguished by the name of a *kingdom* on the face of the earth.

10. *The beginning of his kingdom was Babel.* *Babel* signifies "confusion"; and it seems to have been a very proper name for the commencement of a kingdom that appears to have been founded in apostasy from God and to have been supported by tyranny, rapine, and oppression. *In the land of Shinar.* The same as mentioned in chap. xi. 2. It appears that, as Babylon was built on the river Euphrates, and the Tower of Babel was in the land of Shinar, consequently Shinar itself must have been in the southern part of Mesopotamia.

11. *Out of that land went forth Asshur.* The marginal reading is to be preferred here. "He—Nimrod—went out into Assyria and built Nineveh"; and hence Assyria is called the "land of Nimrod," Mic. v. 6. Thus did this mighty hunter extend his dominations in every possible way.

14. *Philistim.* The people called Philistines, the frequent oppressors of the Israelites, whose history may be seen at large in the Books of Samuel, Kings.

15. *Sidon.* Who probably built the city of this name, and was the father of the Sidonians. *Heth.* From whom came the Hittites, so remarkable among the Canaanitish nations.

16. *The Jebusite . . . Amorite, etc.* Are well-known as being the ancient inhabitants of Canaan, expelled by the children of Israel.

20. *These are the sons of Ham, after their families.* No doubt all these were well-known in the days of Moses, and for a long time after; but at this distance, when it is considered that the political state of the world has been undergoing almost incessant revolutions through all the intermediate portions of time, the impossibility of fixing their residences or marking their descendants must be evident, as both the names of the people and the places of their residences have been changed beyond the possibility of being recognized.

21. *Shem also, the father of all the children of Eber.* It is generally supposed that the Hebrews derived their name from Eber or Heber, son of Shem; but it appears much more likely that they had it from the circumstance of Abraham "passing over" (for so the word *abar* signifies) the river Euphrates to come into the land of Canaan.

22. *Elam.* From whom came the Elamites, near to the Medes, and whose chief city was Elymais. *Asshur.* Who gave his name to a vast province (afterwards a mighty empire) called Assyria. *Lud.* The founder of the Lydians, in Asia Minor; or of the Ludim, who dwelt at the confluence of the Euphrates and Tigris. *Aram.* The father of the Aramaeans, afterwards called Syrians.

23. *Uz.* Supposed to have been the founder of *Damascus.*

25. *Peleg.* From *palag,* "to divide," because *in his days,* which is supposed to be about one hundred years after the Flood, *the earth was divided* among the sons of Noah. Though some are of opinion that a physical division, and not a political one, is what is intended here, namely, a separation of continents and islands from the main land; the earthy parts having been united into one great continent previously to the days of Peleg. This opinion appears to me the most likely, for what is said, v. 5, is spoken by way of anticipation.

CHAPTER 11

All the inhabitants of the earth, speaking one language and dwelling in one place, 1-2, purpose to build a city and a tower to prevent their dispersion, 3-4. God confounds their language, and scatters them over the whole earth, 5-9. Account of the lives and families of the postdiluvian patriarchs. Shem, 10-11. Arphaxad, 12-13. Salah, 14-15. Eber, 16-17. Peleg, 18-19. Ragau or Reu, 20-21. Serug, 22-23. Nahor, 24-25. Terah and his three sons, Haran, Nahor, and Abram, 26-27. The death of Haran, 28. Abram marries Sarai, and Nahor marries Milcah, 29. Sarai is barren, 30. Terah, Abram, Sarai, and Lot leave Ur of the Chaldees, and go to Haran, 31. Terah dies in Haran, aged two hundred and five years, 32.

1. *The whole earth was of one language. The whole earth*—all mankind—*was of one language,* in all likelihood the Hebrew; *and of one speech* —articulating the same words in the same way. It is generally supposed that, after the confusion mentioned in this chapter, the Hebrew language remained in the family of Heber. The proper names and their significations given in the Scripture seem incontestable evidences that the Hebrew language was the original language of the earth—the language in which God spake to man, and in which He gave the revelation of His will to Moses and the prophets.

2. *As they journeyed from the east.* Assyria, Mesopotamia, and the country on the borders and beyond the Euphrates are called the *east* in the sacred writings. Balaam said that the king of Moab had brought him "from the mountains of the east," Num. xxiii. 7. Now it appears, from chap. xxii. 5, that Balaam dwelt at Pethor, on the river Euphrates. And it is very probable that it was from this country that the wise men came to adore Christ; for it is said they came "from the east" to Jerusalem, Matt. ii. 1. Abraham is said to have come "from the east" to Canaan, Isa. xli. 2; but it is well-known that he came from Mesopotamia and Chaldea. Isa. xlvi. 11 represents Cyrus as coming "from the east" against Babylon.

Noah and his family, landing after the Flood on one of the mountains of Armenia, would doubtless descend and cultivate the valleys; as they increased, they appear to have passed along the banks of the Euphrates, till, at the time specified here, they came to the plains of Shinar, allowed to be the most fertile country in the east. That Babel was built in the land of Shinar we have the authority of the sacred text to prove; and that Babylon was built in the same country we have the testimony of Eusebius and Josephus.

3. *Let us make brick.* It appears they were obliged to make use of *brick*, as there was an utter scarcity of stones in that district; and on the same account they were obliged to use *slime for morter*: so it appears they had neither common stone nor limestone; hence they had *brick* for stone, and *asphaltus* or *bitumen* instead of mortar.

4. *Let us build us a city and a tower.* It is probable that their being "of one language, and of one speech" implies not only a sameness of language but also a unity of sentiment and design, as seems pretty clearly intimated in v. 6. Being therefore strictly united in all things, coming to the fertile plains of Shinar they proposed to settle themselves there, instead of spreading themselves over all the countries of the earth according to the design of God; and in reference to this purpose they encouraged one another to build a *city* and a *tower,*

probably a temple, to prevent their separation, "lest," say they, "we be scattered abroad upon the face of the whole earth": but God, miraculously interposing, confounded or frustrated their rebellious design, which was inconsistent with His will; see Deut. xxxii. 8; Acts xvii. 26; and, partly by confounding their language, and disturbing their counsels, they could no longer keep in a united state.

7. *Go to.* A form of speech which, whatever it might have signified formerly, now means nothing. The Hebrew *habah* signifies "come, make preparation," as it were for a journey, the execution of a purpose, etc. Almost all the versions understand the word in this way; the Septuagint has *deute*, the Vulgate *venite*, both signifying *come*, or *come ye*. This makes a very good sense, "Come, let us go down."

9. *Therefore is the name of it called Babel. Babel,* from *bal,* to "mingle, confound, destroy"; hence *Babel,* from the mingling together and confounding of the projects and language of these descendants of Noah; and this confounding did not so much imply the producing new languages as giving them a different method of pronouncing the same words, and leading them to affix different ideas to them.

10. *These are the generations of Shem.* This may be called the "holy family," as from it sprang Abraham, Isaac, Jacob, the twelve patriarchs, David, Solomon, and all the great progenitors of the Messiah.

26. *And Terah lived seventy years, and begat Abram, Nahor, and Haran.* Haran was certainly the eldest son of Terah, and he appears to have been born when Terah was about seventy years of age, and his birth was followed in successive periods with those of *Nahor* his second, and *Abram* his youngest son. Many have been greatly puzzled with the account here, supposing because Abram is mentioned first, that therefore he was the eldest son of Terah; but he is only put first by way of dignity. An instance of this we have already seen, chap. v. 32, where Noah is represented as having Shem, Ham, and Japheth in this order of succession; whereas it is evident from other scriptures that Shem was the youngest son, who for dignity is named first, as Abram is here; and Japheth, the eldest, named last, as Haran is here. Terah died two hundred and five years old, v. 32; then Abram departed from Haran when seventy-five years old, chap. xii. 4; therefore Abram was born, not when his father, Terah, was seventy, but when he was one hundred and thirty.

29. *Milcah, the daughter of Haran.* Many suppose *Sarai* and *Iscah* are the same person under two different names; but this is improbable, as *Iscah* is expressly said to be the daughter of Haran, and *Sarai* was the daughter of Terah, and half sister of Abram.

CHAPTER 12

God calls Abram to leave Haran and go into Canaan, 1; promises to bless him, and through him all the families of the earth, 2-3. Abram, Sarai, Lot, and all their household depart from Canaan, 4-5; pass through Sichem, 6. God appears to him, and renews the promise, 7. His journey described, 8-9. On account of a famine in the land he is obliged to go into Egypt, 10. Fearing lest, on account of the beauty of his wife, the Egyptians should kill him, he desires her not to acknowledge that she is his wife, but only his sister, 11-13. Sarai, because of her beauty, is taken into the palace of Pharaoh, king of

Egypt, who is very liberal to Abram on her account, 14-16. God afflicts Pharaoh and his household with grievous plagues on account of Sarai, 17. Pharaoh, on finding that Sarai was Abram's wife, restores her honorably, and dismisses the patriarch with his family and their property, 18—20.

1. *Get thee out of thy country.* There is great dissension between commentators concerning the call of Abram; some supposing he had two distinct calls, others that he had but one. At the conclusion of the preceding chapter, v. 31, we find Terah and all his family leaving Ur of the Chaldees, in order to go to Canaan. This was, no doubt, in consequence of some divine admonition. While resting at Haran, on their road to Canaan, Terah died, chap. xi. 32; and then God repeats His call to Abram, and orders him to proceed to Canaan, chap. xii. 1.

Thy kindred. Nahor and the different branches of the family of Terah, Abram and Lot excepted. That Nahor went with Terah and Abram as far as Padan-aram, in Mesopotamia, and settled there, so that it was afterwards called Nahor's city, is sufficiently evident from the ensuing history, see chap. xxv. 20; xxiv. 10, 15; and that the same land was Haran, see chap. xxviii. 2, 10, and there were Abram's kindred and country here spoken of, chap. xxiv. 4.

Thy father's house. Terah being now dead, it is very probable that the family were determined to go no farther, but to settle at Charran; and as Abram might have felt inclined to stop with them in this place, hence the ground and necessity of the second call recorded here, and which is introduced in a very remarkable manner: "Go for thyself." If none of the family will accompany thee, yet go for thyself unto that land *that I will shew thee.* God does not tell him what land it is, that He may still cause him to walk by faith and not by sight. This seems to be particularly alluded to by Isaiah, chap. xli. 2: "Who raised up the righteous man [Abram] from the east, and called him to his foot"; that is, to follow implicitly the divine direction. The apostle assures us that in all this Abram had spiritual views; he looked for a better country, and considered the land of promise only as typical of the heavenly inheritance.

2. *I will make of thee a great nation.* i.e., The Jewish people; *and make thy name great,* alluding to the change of his name from Abram, a high father, to Abraham, the father of a multitude.

3. *In thee.* In thy posterity, in the Messiah, who shall spring from thee, shall all families of the earth be blessed.

4. *And Abram was seventy and five years old.* As Abram was now seventy-five years old, and his father, Terah, had just died, at the age of two hundred and five, consequently Terah must have been one hundred and thirty when Abram was born; and the seventieth year of his age mentioned in Gen. xi. 26 was the period at which Haran, not Abram, was born.

5. *The souls that they had gotten in Haran.* This may apply either to the persons who were employed in the service of Abram or to the persons he had been the instrument of converting to the knowledge of the true God; and in this latter sense the Chaldee paraphrasts understood the passage, translating it, "The souls of those whom they proselyted in Haran." *They went forth to go into the land of Canaan.* A

good land, possessed by a bad people, who for their iniquities were to be expelled, see Lev. xviii. 25.

6. *The plain of Moreh. Elon* should be translated "oak," not *plain;* the Septuagint translates, "the lofty oak"; and it is likely the place was remarkable for a grove of those trees, or for one of a stupendous height and bulk. *The Canaanite was then in the land.* This is thought to be an interpolation, because it is supposed that these words must have been written after the Canaanites were expelled from the land by the Israelites under Joshua; but this by no means follows. All that Moses states is simply that at the time in which Abram passed through Sichem the land was inhabited by the descendants of Canaan.

7. *The Lord appeared.* In what way this appearance was made we know not; it was probably by the great Angel of the covenant, Jesus the Christ. The appearance, whatsoever it was, perfectly satisfied Abram, and proved itself to be supernatural and divine. It is worthy of remark that Abram is the first man to whom God is said to have shown himself or *appeared:* (1) In Ur of the Chaldees, Acts vii. 2; and (2) At the oak of Moreh, as in this verse. As Moreh signifies a "teacher," probably this was called the oak of Moreh because God manifested himself here and instructed Abram concerning the future possession of that land by his posterity, and the dispensation of the mercy of God to all the families of the earth through the promised Messiah.

8. *Beth-el.* The place which was afterwards called *Beth-el* by Jacob, for its first name was Luz. See chap. xxviii. 19. *Beith El* literally signifies "the house of God." *And pitched his tent . . . and . . . builded an altar unto the Lord.* Where Abram has a *tent,* there God must have an *altar,* as he well knows there is no safety but under the divine protection. The house in which the worship of God is not established cannot be considered as under the divine protection.

10. *There was a famine in the land.* Of Canaan. God made it desolate for the wickedness of those who dwelt in it.

11. *Thou art a fair woman to look upon.* Widely differing in her complexion from the swarthy Egyptians, and consequently more likely to be coveted by them. It appears that Abram supposed they would not scruple to take away the life of the husband in order to have the undisturbed possession of the wife.

13. *Say, I pray thee, thou art my sister.* Abram did not wish his wife to tell a falsehood, but he wished her to suppress a part of the truth. From chap. xx. 12, it is evident she was his stepsister, i.e., his sister by his father, but by a different mother.

15. *The woman was taken into Pharaoh's house. Pharaoh* appears to have been the common appellative of the shepherd kings of Egypt, who had conquered this land. The word is supposed to signify "king" in the ancient Egyptian language. When a woman was brought into the harem of the Eastern princes, she underwent for a considerable time certain purifications before she was brought into the king's presence. It was in this interim that God *plagued Pharaoh and his house with plagues,*

so that Sarai was restored before she could have been taken to the bed of the Egyptian king.

16. *He had sheep, and oxen.* As some of these terms are liable to be confounded, and as they frequently occur, especially in the Pentateuch, it may be necessary to consider and fix their meaning in this place. *Sheep; tson,* from *tsaan,* to be "plentiful" or "abundant"; a proper term for the Eastern sheep, which almost constantly bring forth twins, Cant. iv. 2, and sometimes three and even four at a birth. Hence their great fruitfulness is often alluded to in the Scripture. See Ps. lxv. 13; cxliv. 13. But under this same term, which almost invariably means a "flock," both sheep and goats are included. *Oxen; bakar,* from the root, to "examine, look out," because of the full, broad, steady, unmoved look of most animals of the beef kind. *He asses; chamorim,* from *chamar,* to be "disturbed, muddy"; probably from the dull, stupid appearance of this animal, as if it were always affected with melancholy. *She asses; athonoth,* from *ethan,* "strength," probably the strong animal, as being superior in muscular force to every other animal of its size. Under this term both the male and female are sometimes understood. *Camels; gemallim,* from *gamal,* to "recompense, return, repay"; so called from its resentment of injuries, and revengeful temper, for which it is proverbial in the countries of which it is a native. From this enumeration of the riches of Abram we may conclude that this patriarch led a pastoral and itinerant life.

17. *The Lord plagued Pharaoh.* What these plagues were we know not. In the parallel case, chap. xx. 18, all the females in the family of Abimelech, who had taken Sarah in nearly the same way, were made barren; possibly this might have been the case here; yet much more seems to be signified by the expression *great plagues.* Whatever these plagues were, it is evident they were understood by Pharaoh as proofs of the disapprobation of God; and, consequently, even at this time in Egypt there was some knowledge of the primitive and true religion.

20. *Commanded his men concerning him.* Gave particular and strict orders to afford Abram and his family every accommodation for their journey; for having received a great increase of cattle and servants, it was necessary that he should have the favor of the king, and his permission to remove from Egypt with so large a property.

CHAPTER 13

Abram and his family return out of Egypt to Canaan, 1-2. He revisits Beth-el, and there invokes the Lord, 3-4. In consequence of the great increase in the flocks of Abram and Lot, their herdmen disagree; which obliges the patriarch and his nephew to separate, 5-9. Lot being permitted to make his choice of the land, chooses the plains of Jordan, 10-11, and pitches his tent near to Sodom, while Abram abides in Canaan, 12. Bad character of the people of Sodom, 13. The Lord renews His promise to Abram, 14-17. Abram removes to the plains of Mamre, near Hebron, and builds an altar to the Lord, 18.

1. *Abram went up out of Egypt . . . into the south.* Probably the south of Canaan.

2. *Abram was very rich.* The property of these patriarchal times did not consist in flocks only, but also in *silver* and *gold;* and in all these respects Abram was "exceeding rich."

6. *Their substance was great.* As their families increased, it was necessary their flocks should increase also, as from those flocks they derived their clothing, food, and drink. Many also were offered in sacrifice to God. *They could not dwell together.* (1) Because their flocks were great. (2) Because the Canaanites and the Perizzites had already occupied a considerable part of the land. (3) Because there appears to have been envy between the herdmen of Abram and Lot. To prevent disputes among them, that might have ultimately disturbed the peace of the two families, it was necessary that a separation should take place.

9. *Is not the whole land before thee?* As the patriarch or head of the family, Abram, by prescriptive right, might have chosen his own portion first, and appointed Lot his; but intent upon peace, and feeling pure and parental affection for his nephew, he permitted him to make his choice first.

11. *Then Lot chose him all the plain.* A little civility or good breeding is of great importance in the concerns of life. Lot either had none, or did not profit by it. He certainly should have left the choice to the patriarch and should have been guided by his counsel; but he took his own way, trusting to his own judgment, and guided only by the sight of his eyes. *He beheld all the plain of Jordan, that it was well watered;* so he chose the land without considering the character of the inhabitants or what advantages or disadvantages it might afford him in spiritual things. This choice, as we shall see in the sequel, had nearly proved the ruin of his body, soul, and family.

13. *The men of Sodom were wicked. Raim,* from *ra,* "to break in pieces, destroy, and afflict"; meaning persons who broke the established order of things, destroyed and confounded the distinctions between right and wrong, and who afflicted and tormented both themselves and others. *And sinners, chattaim,* from *chata,* "to miss the mark, to step wrong, to miscarry"; so a sinner is one who is ever aiming at happiness and constantly missing his mark; because, being wicked—radically evil within, every affection and passion depraved and out of order, he seeks for happiness where it never can be found, in worldly honors and possessions, and in sensual gratifications, the end of which is disappointment, affliction, vexation, and ruin. The people of Sodom were "exceedingly sinful and wicked before," or against, the Lord—they were sinners of no common character; they excelled in unrighteousness, and soon filled up the measure of their iniquities.

14. *The Lord said unto Abram.* It is very likely that the Angel of the covenant appeared to Abram in open day, when he could take a distinct view of the length and the breadth of this good land. The revelation made in chap. xv. 5 was evidently made in the night; for then he was called to number the stars; here he is called on to number the dust of the earth. v. 16.

15. *To thee will I give it, and to thy seed for ever.* This land was given to Abram, that it might lineally and legally descend to his posterity; and though Abram himself cannot be said to have possessed it, Acts vii. 5, yet it was the gift of God to him in behalf of his seed; and this was always the design of God, not that

Abram himself should possess it, but that his posterity should, till the manifestation of Christ in the flesh. And this is chiefly what is to be understood by the words *for ever,* to the end of the present dispensation and the commencement of the new.

18. *Abram removed his tent.* Continued to travel and pitch in different places, till at last he fixed his tent in the *plain,* or "by the oak," of *Mamre,* see chap. xii. 6, *which is in Hebron;* i.e., the district in which Mamre was situated was called Hebron. Mamre was an Amorite then living, with whom Abram made a league, chap. xiv. 13; and the oak probably went by his name, because he was the possessor of the ground. *Built there an altar unto the Lord.* On which he offered sacrifice, as the word *mizbach,* from *zabach,* "to slay," imports.

CHAPTER 14

The war of four confederate kings against the five kings of Canaan, 1-3. The confederate kings overrun and pillage the whole country, 4-7. Battle between them and the kings of Canaan, 8-9. The latter are defeated, and the principal part of the armies of the kings of Sodom and Gomorrah slain, 10; on which these two cities are plundered, 11. Lot, his goods, and his family are also taken and carried away, 12. Abram, being informed of the disaster of his nephew, 13, arms 318 of his servants, and pursues the enemy, 14; overtakes and routs them, and recovers Lot and his family, and their goods, 15-16; is met on his return by the king of Sodom, and by Melchizedek, king of Salem, with refreshments for himself and men, 17-18. Melchizedek blesses Abram, and receives from him, as priest of the most high God, the tenth of all the spoils, 19-20. The king of Sodom offers to Abram all the goods he has taken from the enemy, 21; which Abram positively refuses, having vowed to God to receive no recompense for a victory of which he knew God to be the sole Author, 22-23; but desires that a proportion of the spoils be given to Aner, Eshcol, and Mamre, who had accompanied him on this expedition, 24.

1. *In the days of Amraphel.* Who this king was is not known; and yet, from the manner in which he is spoken of in the text, it would seem that he was a person well known, even when Moses wrote this account. *Tidal king of nations. Goyim,* different peoples or clans. Probably some adventurous person, whose subjects were composed of refugees from different countries.

2. *These made war with Bera.* It appears, from v. 4, that these five Canaanitish kings had been subdued by Chedorlaomer, and were obliged to pay him tribute; and that, having been enslaved by him twelve years, wishing to recover their liberty, they revolted in the thirteenth; in consequence of which Chedorlaomer, the following year, summoned to his assistance three of his vassals, invaded Canaan, fought with and discomfited the kings of the Pentapolis or five cities—Sodom, Gomorrah, Zeboiim, Zoar, and Admah, which were situated in the fruitful plain of Siddim, having previously overrun the whole land.

5. *Rephaims.* A people of Canaan: chap. xv. 20. *Emims.* A people great and many in the days of Moses, and tall as the Anakim. They dwelt among the Moabites, by whom they were reputed *giants;* Deut. ii. 10-11. *Shaveh Kiriathaim.* Rather, as the margin, the "plain of Kiriathaim," which was a city afterwards belonging to Sihon, king of Heshbon; Josh. xiii. 19.

6. *The Horites.* A people that dwelt in Mount Seir, till Esau and his sons drove them thence; Deut. ii. 22. *El-paran.* The "plain or oak of Paran," which was a city in the wilderness of Paran; chap. xxi. 21.

7. *En-mishpat.* The "well of judgment"; probably so called from the judgment pronounced by God on Moses and Aaron for their rebellion at that place; Num. xx. 1-10. *Amalekites.* So called afterwards, from Amalek, son of Esau; chap. xxxvi. 12. *Hazenon-tamar.* Called, in the Chaldee, Engaddi; a city in the land of Canaan, which fell to the lot of Judah; Josh. xv. 62. See also 2 Chron. xx. 2. It appears, from Cant. i. 13, to have been a very fruitful place.

8. *Bela (the same is Zoar).* That is, it was called Zoar after the destruction of Sodom, mentioned in chap. xix.

10. *Slimepits.* Places where *asphaltus* or *bitumen* sprang out of the ground; this substance abounded in that country. *Fell there.* It either signifies they were defeated on this spot, and many of them slain, or that multitudes of them had perished in the bitumen pits which abounded there; that the place was full of pits we learn from the Hebrew, which reads here *beeroth beeroth,* "pits, pits," i.e., multitudes of pits. A bad place to maintain a fight on or to be obliged to run through in order to escape.

12. *They took Lot.* The people, being exceedingly wicked, had provoked God to afflict them by means of those marauding kings; and Lot also suffered, being found in company with the workers of iniquity.

13. *Abram the Hebrew.* See on chap. x. 21. It is very likely that Abram had this appellation from his coming from beyond the river Euphrates to enter Canaan; for *haibri,* which we render *the Hebrew,* comes from *abar,* to "pass over," or come from beyond. *These were confederate with Abram.* It seems that a kind of convention was made between Abram and the three brothers, Mamre, Eshcol, and Aner, who were probably all chieftains in the vicinity of Abram's dwelling: all petty princes, similar to the nine kings before mentioned.

14. *He armed his trained servants.* These amounted to 318 in number: and how many were in the divisions of Mamre, Eshcol, and Aner, we know not; but they and their men certainly accompanied him in this expedition. See v. 24.

15. *And he divided himself against them.* It required both considerable courage and address in Abram to lead him to attack the victorious armies of these four kings with so small a number of troops, and on this occasion both his skill and his courage are exercised. His affection for Lot appears to have been his chief motive; he cheerfully risks his life for that nephew who had lately chosen the best part of the land and left his uncle to live as he might, on what he did not think worthy his own acceptance. But it is the property of a great and generous mind not only to forgive but to forget offenses, and at all times to repay evil with good.

16. *And he brought back . . . the women also.* This is brought in by the sacred historian with peculiar interest and tenderness. All who read the account must be in pain for the fate of wives and daughters fallen into the hands of a ferocious, licentious, and victorious soldiery. Other spoils the routed confederates might have left behind; and yet on their swift asses, camels, and dromedaries, have carried off the female captives. However, Abram had disposed his attack so judiciously, and so promptly executed

his measures, that not only all the baggage, but all the females also, were recovered.

17. *The king of Sodom went out to meet him.* This could not have been Bera, mentioned in v. 2, for it seems pretty evident, from v. 10, that both he and Birsha, king of Gomorrah, were slain at the bitumen pits in the vale of Siddim; but another person in the meantime might have succeeded to the government.

18. *And Melchizedek king of Salem.* A thousand idle stories have been told about this man, and a thousand idle conjectures spent on the subject of his short history given here and in Hebrews vii. At present it is only necessary to state that he appears to have been as real a personage as Bera, Birsha, or Shinab, though we have no more of his genealogy than we have of theirs. *Brought forth bread and wine.* Certainly to refresh Abram and his men, exhausted with the late battle and fatigues of the journey; not in the way of *sacrifice;* this is an idle conjecture. *He was the priest of the most high God.* He had preserved in his family and among his subjects the worship of the true God, and the primitive patriarchal institutions; by these the father of every family was both king and priest, so Melchizedek, being a worshipper of the true God, was priest among the people, as well as king over them.

Melchizedek is called here *king of Salem,* and the most judicious interpreters allow that by Salem, Jerusalem is meant. That it bore this name anciently is evident from Ps. lxxvi. 1-2: "In Judah is God known: his name is great in Israel. In Salem also is his tabernacle, and his dwelling place in Zion." From the use made of this part of the sacred history by David, Ps. cx. 4, and by St. Paul, Heb. vii. 1-10, we learn that there was something very mysterious, and at the same time typical, in the person, name, office, residence, and government of this Canaanitish prince. (1) In his *person* he was a representative and type of Christ; see the scriptures above referred to. (2) His name signifies "my righteous king," or "king of righteousness." (3) *Office;* he was a *priest of the most high God.* The word *cohen,* which signifies both "prince" and "priest," because the patriarchs sustained this double office, has both its root and proper signification in the Arabic; *kahana* signifies "to approach, draw near, have intimate access to"; and from hence to officiate as priest before God, and thus have intimate access to the divine presence. (4) His *residence;* he was king of *Salem. Shalam* signifies "to make whole, complete, or perfect"; and hence it means "peace." Christ is called "The Prince of Peace" because, by His incarnation, sacrifice, and mediation, He procures and establishes peace between God and man. His residence is peace and quietness and assurance forever in every believing, upright heart.

19. *And he blessed him.* This was a part of the priest's office, to bless in the name of the Lord forever. See the form of this blessing, Num. vi. 23-26; and for the meaning of the word "to bless," see Gen. ii. 3.

20. *And he gave him tithes.* A tenth part of all the spoils he had taken from the confederate kings. These Abram gave as a tribute to the most high God, who, being the "possessor of heaven and earth," dispenses all spiritual and temporal favors, and demands the gratitude, and submissive, loving obedience, of all His subjects. Almost all nations of the earth agreed in giving a tenth part of their property to be employed in religious uses.

22. *I have lift up mine hand.* The primitive mode of appealing to God, and calling Him to witness a particular transaction.

23. *From a thread even to a shoelatchet.* This was certainly a proverbial mode of expression.

24. *Save only that which the young men have eaten.* His own servants had partaken of the victuals which the confederate kings had carried away; see v. 11. This was unavoidable, and this is all he claims; but as he had no right to prescribe the same liberal conduct to his assistants, Aner, Eshcol, and Mamre, he left them to claim the share that by right of conquest belonged to them of the recaptured booty.

CHAPTER 15

God appears to Abram in a vision, and gives him great encouragement, 1. Abram's request and complaint, 2-3. God promises him a son, 4; and an exceedingly numerous posterity, 5. Abram credits the promise, and his faith is counted unto him for righteousness, 6. Jehovah proclaims himself, and renews the promise of Canaan to his posterity, 7. Abram requires a sign of its fulfillment, 8. Jehovah directs him to offer a sacrifice of five different animals, 9; which he accordingly does, 10-11. God reveals to him the affliction of his posterity in Egypt, and the duration of that affliction, 12-13. Promises to bring them back to the land of Canaan with great affluence, 14-16. Renews the covenant with Abram, and mentions the possessions which should be given to his posterity, 18-21.

1. *The word of the Lord came unto Abram.* This is the first place where God is represented as revealing himself by His word. Some learned men suppose that the *debar Yehovah,* translated here *word of the Lord,* means the same with the *logos tou theou* of St. John, chap. i. 1. There have been various conjectures concerning the manner in which God revealed His will, not only to the patriarchs, but also to the prophets, evangelists, and apostles. It seems to have been done in different ways. (1) By a personal appearance of Him who was afterwards incarnated for the salvation of mankind. (2) By an audible voice, sometimes accompanied with emblematical appearances. (3) By visions which took place either in the night in ordinary sleep, or when the persons were cast into a temporary trance by daylight, or when about their ordinary business. (4) By the ministry of angels appearing in human bodies, and performing certain miracles to accredit their mission. (5) By the powerful agency of the Spirit of God upon the mind, giving it a strong conception and supernatural persuasion of the truth of the things perceived by the understanding. We shall see all these exemplified in the course of the work. It was probably in the third sense that the revelation in the text was given; for it is said, God appeared to Abram in a vision.

I am thy shield. Can it be supposed that Abram understood these words as promising him temporal advantages at all corresponding to the magnificence of these promises? If he did he was disappointed through the whole course of his life, for he never enjoyed such a state of worldly prosperity as could justify the strong language in the text.

6. *And he believed in the Lord; and he counted it to him for righteousness.* This I

conceive to be one of the most important passages in the whole Old Testament. It properly contains and specifies that doctrine of justification by faith which engrosses so considerable a share of the Epistles of St. Paul, and at the foundation of which is the atonement made by the Son of God: *And he* (Abram) *believed* (put faith) in Jehovah, *and he counted it* (the faith he put in Jehovah) *to him for righteousness* (or justification), though there was no act in the case but that of the mind and heart, no work of any kind. Hence the doctrine of justification by faith, without any merit of works; for in this case there could be none—no works of Abram which could merit the salvation of the whole human race.

8. *And he said, Lord God. Adonai Yehovah,* "my Lord Jehovah." *Adonai* is the word which the Jews in reading always substitute for Jehovah, as they count it impious to pronounce this name. *Adonai* signifies my "director, basis, supporter, prop, or stay"; and scarcely a more appropriate name can be given to that God who is the Framer and Director of every righteous word and action; the Basis or Foundation on which every rational hope rests; the Supporter of the souls and bodies of men, as well as of the universe in general; the Prop and Stay of the weak and fainting, and the Buttress that shores up the building, which otherwise must necessarily fall. This word often occurs in the Hebrew Bible, and is rendered in our translation *Lord,* the same term by which the word Jehovah is expressed; but to distinguish between the two, and to show the reader when the original is *Yehovah* and when *Adonai,* the first is always put in capitals, LORD, the latter in plain Roman characters, Lord. *Whereby shall I know?* By what sign shall I be assured that I shall inherit this land? It appears that he expected some sign, and that on such occasions one was ordinarily given.

9. *Take me an heifer.* It is worthy of remark that every animal allowed or commanded to be sacrificed under the Mosaic law is to be found in this list. And is it not a proof that God was now giving to Abram an epitome of that law and its sacrifices which He intended more fully to reveal to Moses, the essence of which consisted in its sacrifices, which typified the Lamb of God that takes away the sin of the world?

10. *Divided them in the midst.* The ancient method of making covenants, as well as the original word, have been already alluded to and in a general way explained. See chap. vi. 18. The word "covenant" from *con,* "together," and *venio,* "I come," signifies an agreement, association, or meeting between two or more parties; for it is impossible that a covenant can be made between an individual and himself, whether God or man. Rabbi Solomon Jarchi says, "It was a custom with those who entered into covenant with each other to take a heifer and cut it in two, and then the contracting parties passed between the pieces." *But the birds divided he not.* According to the law, Lev. i. 17, fowls were not to be divided asunder but only cloven for the purpose of taking out the intestines.

11. *And when the fowls,* "birds of prey," *came down upon the carcases to devour them, Abram,* who stood by his sacrifice waiting for the man-

ifestation of God, who had ordered him to prepare for the ratification of the covenant, *drove them away,* that they might neither pollute nor devour what had been thus consecrated to God.

12. *A deep sleep.* The same word which is used to express the sleep into which Adam was cast, previous to the formation of Eve; chap. ii. 21. *An horror of great darkness.* Which God designed to be expressive of the affliction and misery into which his posterity should be brought during the four hundred years of their bondage in Egypt, as the next verse particularly states.

14. *And also that nation.* How remarkably was this promise fulfilled, in the redemption of Israel from its bondage, in the plagues and destruction of the Egyptians, and in the immense wealth which the Israelites brought out of Egypt! Not a more circumstantial or literally fulfilled promise is to be found in the Sacred Writings.

15. *Thou shalt go to thy fathers in peace.* This verse strongly implies the immortality of the soul, and a state of separate existence.

16. *In the fourth generation.* In former times most people counted by generations, to each of which was assigned a term of years amounting to 20, 25, 30, 33, 100, 108, or 110; for the generation was of various lengths among various people, at different times. It is probable that the *fourth generation* here means the same as the "four hundred years" in v. 13.

17. *A smoking furnace, and a burning lamp.* Probably the *smoking furnace* might be designed as an emblem of the sore afflictions of the Israelites in Egypt; but the *burning lamp* was certainly the symbol of the divine presence, which, passing between the pieces, ratified the covenant with Abram, as the following verse immediately states.

18. *The Lord made a covenant. Carath berith* signifies to "cut a covenant," or rather the covenant sacrifice; for as no covenant was made without one, and the creature was cut in two that the contracting parties might pass between the pieces, hence cutting the covenant signified making the covenant. *From the river of Egypt.* Not the Nile, but the river called Sichor, which was on the border of Egypt, near to the isthmus of Suez; see Josh. xiii. 3; though some think that by this a branch of the Nile is meant. This promise was fully accomplished in the days of David and Solomon. See 2 Sam. viii. 3, etc., and 2 Chron. ix. 26.

19. *The Kenites.* Here are ten nations mentioned, though afterwards reckoned but seven; see Deut. vii. 1; Acts xiii. 19. Probably some of them which existed in Abram's time had been blended with others before the time of Moses, so that seven only out of the ten then remained; see part of these noticed in Genesis x.

CHAPTER 16

Sarai, having no child, gives Hagar, her maid, to Abram for wife, 1-3. She conceives and despises her mistress, 4. Sarai is offended and upbraids Abram, 5. Abram vindicates himself; and Hagar, being hardly used by her mistress, runs away, 6. She is met by an angel, and counselled to return to her mistress, 7-9. God promises greatly to multiply her seed, 10. Gives the name of Ishmael to the child that should be born of her, 11. Shows his disposition and character, 12. Hagar calls the name of the Lord who spoke to her, Thou God seest me, 13. She calls the name of the well at which the angel met her, Beer-lahairoi, 14. Ishmael is born in the eighty-sixth year of Abram's age, 15-16.

1. *She had a handmaid, an Egyptian.* As Hagar was an Egyptian, St. Chrysostom's conjecture is very probable, that she was one of those female slaves which Pharaoh gave to Abram when he sojourned in Egypt; see chap. xii. 16. Her name, *Hagar*, signifies a "stranger" or "sojourner," and it is likely she got this name in the family of Abram, as the word is pure Hebrew.

2. *Go in unto my maid.* It must not be forgotten that female slaves constituted a part of the private patrimony or possessions of a wife, and that she had a right, according to the usages of those times, to dispose of them as she pleased, the husband having no authority in the case. *I may obtain children by her.* The slave, being the absolute property of the mistress, not only her person, but the fruits of her labor, with all her children, were her owner's property also. The children, therefore, which were born of the slave, were considered as the children of the mistress. It was on this ground that Sarai gave her slave to Abram; and we find, what must necessarily be the consequence in all cases of polygamy, that strifes and contentions took place.

5. *My wrong be upon thee.* This appears to be intended as a reproof to Abram, containing an insinuation that it was his fault that she herself had not been a mother, and that now he carried himself more affectionately towards Hagar than he did to her, in consequence to which conduct the slave became petulant. To remove all suspicion of this kind, Abram delivers up Hagar into her hand, who was certainly under his protection while his concubine or secondary wife; but this right given to him by Sarai he restores, to prevent her jealousy and uneasiness.

6. *Sarai dealt hardly with her.* "She afflicted her"; the term implying stripes and hard usage, to bring down the body and humble the mind. If the slave was to blame in this business the mistress is not less liable to censure. She alone had brought her into those circumstances in which it was natural for her to value herself beyond her mistress.

7. *The angel of the Lord.* That Jesus Christ, in a body suited to the dignity of His nature, frquently appeared to the patriarchs, has been already intimated. That the person mentioned here was greater than any created being is sufficiently evident from the following particulars: (1) From his promising to perform what God alone could know, and foretelling what God alone could know: "I will multiply thy seed exceedingly," v. 10; "Thou art with child, and shalt bear a son," v. 11; "He will be a wild man," v. 12. (2) Hagar considers the person who spoke to her as God, calls him Eli, and addresses him in the way of worship, which, had he been a created angel, he would have refused. See Rev. xix. 10; xxii. 9. (3) Moses, who relates the transaction, calls this angel expressly Jehovah; for, says he, she called *shem Yehovah*, the name of the Lord that spake to her, v. 13. (4) This person, who is here called *malach Yehovah*, the Angel of the Lord, is the same who is called "the redeeming Angel" or "the Angel the Redeemer," Gen. xlviii. 16; the Angel of God's

presence, Isa. lxiii. 9; and the Angel of the Covenant, Mal. iii. 1. *In the way to Shur.* As this was the road from Hebron to Egypt, it is probable she was now returning to her own country.

8. *Hagar, Sarai's maid.* This mode of address is used to show her that she was known, and to remind her that she was the property of another.

10. *I will multiply thy seed exceedingly.* Who says this? The person who is called the Angel of the Lord; and he certainly speaks with all the authority which is proper to God.

11. *And shalt call his name Ishmael.* Yishmael, from *shama*, "he heard," and *El*, "God"; for, says the Angel, "the Lord hath heard thy affliction." Thus the name of the child must ever keep the mother in remembrance of God's merciful interposition in her behalf, and remind the child and the man that he was an object of God's gracious and providential goodness. Afflictions and distresses have a voice in the ears of God, even when prayer is restrained; but how much more powerfully do they speak when endured in meekness of spirit, with confidence in and supplication to the Lord!

12. *He will be a wild man. Pere adam.* As the root of this word does not appear in the Hebrew Bible, it is probably found in the Arabic *farra*, "to run away, to run wild." What is said of the wild ass, Job xxxix. 5-8, affords the very best description that can be given of the Ishmaelites (the Bedouins and wandering Arabs), the descendants of Ishmael.

13. *And she called the name of the Lord.* She "invoked the name of Jehovah who spake unto her," thus: *Thou God seest me!* She found that the eye of a merciful God had been upon her in all her wanderings and afflictions; and her words seem to intimate that she had been seeking the divine help and protection, for she says, *Have I also* (or *have I not also*) *looked after him that seeth me?*

14. *Wherefore the well was called Beer-lahai-roi.* It appears, from v. 7, that Hagar had sat down by a fountain or well of water in the wilderness of Shur, at which the Angel of the Lord found her; and, to commemorate the wonderful discovery which God had made of himself, she called the name of the well *Beer-lahai-roi*, "A well to the Living One who seeth me." Two things seem implied here: (1) A dedication of the well to Him who had appeared to her; and (2) Faith in the promise; for He who is the Living One, existing in all generations, must have it ever in His power to accomplish promsies which are to be fulfilled through the whole lapse of time.

15. *And Hagar bare Abram a son.* It appears, therefore, that Hagar returned at the command of the angel, believing the promise that God had made to her. *Called his son's name . . . Ishmael.* Finding by the account of Hagar that God had designed that he should be so called.

CHAPTER 17

In the ninety-ninth year of Abram's life God again appears to him, announces His name as God Almighty, and commands him to walk perfectly before Him, 1; proposes to renew the covenant, 2. Abram's prostration, 3. The covenant specified, 4. Abram's name changed to Abraham, and the reason given, 5. The privileges of the covenant enumerated, 6-8. The conditions of the covenant to be observed, not only by Abraham, but all his posterity, 9. Circumcision appointed as a sign or token of the covenant, 10-11. The age at which and the persons on whom this was to be performed, 12-13. The danger of neglecting this rite, 14. Sarai's name changed to Sarah, and a particular promise made to her, 15-16. Abraham's joy at the prospect of the performance of a matter which, in the course of nature, was impossible, 17. His request for the preservation and prosperity of Ishmael, 18. The birth and blessedness of Isaac foretold, 19. Great prosperity promised to Ishmael, 20. But the covenant to be established, not in his, but in Isaac's posterity, 21. Abraham, Ishmael, and all the males in the family circumcised, 23-27.

1. *The Lord appeared to Abram.* See on chap. xv. 1. *I am the Almighty God.* El shaddai, "God all-sufficient"; from *shadah,* to "shed," to "pour out." I am that God who pours out blessings, who gives them richly, abundantly, continually. *Walk before me.* "Set thyself to walk"—be firmly purposed, thoroughly determined to obey, *before me;* for My eye is ever on thee, therefore ever consider that God seeth thee. Who can imagine a stronger incitement to conscientious, persevering obedience? *Be thou perfect.* "And thou shalt be perfections," i.e., altogether perfect. Be just such as the holy God would have thee to be, as the almighty God can make thee, and live as the all-sufficient God shall support thee; for He alone who makes the soul holy can preserve it in holiness. Our blessed Lord appears to have had these words pointedly in view, Matt. v. 48: "Ye shall be perfect, as your Father who is in heaven is perfect." But what does this imply? Why, to be saved from all the power, the guilt, and the contamination of sin. This is only the negative part of salvation, but it has also a positive part; to be made perfect—to be perfect as our Father who is in heaven is perfect, to be filled with the fulness of God, to have Christ dwelling continually in the heart by faith, and to be rooted and grounded in love. This is the state in which man was created, for he was made in the image and likeness of God. This is the state from which man fell, for he broke the command of God. And this is the state into which every human soul must be raised, who would dwell with God in glory; for Christ was incarnated and died to put away sin by the sacrifice of himself. What a glorious privilege! And who can doubt the possibility of its attainment who believes in the omnipotent love of God, the infinite merit of the Blood of atonement, and the all-pervading and all-purifying energy of the Holy Ghost?

3. *And Abram fell on his face.* The Eastern method of prostration was thus: the person first went down on his knees, and then lowered his head to his knees, and touched the earth with his forehead. A very painful posture, but significative of great humiliation and reverence.

5. *Thy name shall be Abraham.* Abram literally signifies a "high or exalted father." Abraham differs from the preceding in only one letter; it has *he* before the last radical. Though this may appear very simple and easy, yet the true etymology and meaning of the word are very difficult to be assigned. The reason given for the change made in the patriarch's name is this: *For a father of many nations have I made thee,* "a father of a multitude of nations." This has led some to suppose that Abraham is a contraction for *ab-rab-hamon,* "the father of a great multitude."

The same difficulty occurs, v. 15, on the word *Sarai,* which signifies "my prince" or "princess," and *Sarah,* where the whole change is made by the substitution of a *he* for a *yod.* This latter might be translated "princess" in general; and while the former seems to point out her government in her own family alone, the latter appears to indicate her government over the nations of which her husband is termed the father or lord; and hence the promise states that *she shall be a mother of nations,* and that *kings of people shall be of her.* See vv. 15-16.

Now as the only change in each name is made by the insertion of a single letter, and that letter the same in both names, I cannot help concluding that some mystery was designed by its insertion; and therefore the opinion of Clarius and some others is not to be disregarded, which supposes that God shows He had conferred a peculiar dignity on both, by adding to their names one of the letters of His own; a name by which His eternal power and Godhead are peculiarly pointed out.

7. *An everlasting covenant. Berith olam.* See on chap. xiii. 15. Here the word *olam* is taken in its own proper meaning, as the words immediately following prove—*to be a God unto thee, and thy seed after thee;* for as the soul is to endure forever, so it shall eternally stand in need of the supporting power and energy of God; and as the reign of the gospel dispensation shall be as long as sun and moon endure, and its consequences eternal, so must the covenant be on which these are founded.

8. *Everlasting possession.* Here *olam* appears to be used in its accommodated meaning, and signifies the completion of the divine counsel in reference to a particular period or dispensation. And it is literally true that the Israelites possessed the land of Canaan till the Mosaic dispensation was terminated in the complete introduction of that of the gospel. But as the spiritual and temporal covenants are both blended together, and the former was pointed out and typified by the latter, hence the word even here may be taken in its own proper meaning, that of ever-during, or eternal; because the spiritual blessings pointed out by the temporal covenant shall have no end. And hence it is immediately added, *I will be their God,* not for a time, certainly, but for ever and ever.

11. *And it shall be a token.* For a sign of spiritual things; for the circumcision made in the flesh was designed to signify the purification of the heart from all unrighteousness, as God particularly showed in the law itself. See Deut. x. 16; see also Rom. ii. 25-29; Col. ii. 11. And it was a seal of that righteousness or justification that comes by faith, Rom. iv. 11. That some of the Jews had a just notion of its spiritual intention is plain from many passages in the Chaldee paraphrases and in the Jewish writers.

12. *He that is eight days old.* Because previously to this they were considered unclean, Lev. xii. 2-3, and circumcision was ever understood as a consecration of the person to God. Neither calf, lamb, nor kid, was offered to God till it was eight days old for the same reason, Lev. xxii. 27.

14. *The uncircumcised . . . shall be cut off from his people.* By being cut off some have imagined that a sudden temporal death was implied; but the simple meaning seems to be that such should have no right to nor share in

the blessings of the covenant, which we have already seen were both of a temporal and spiritual kind; and if so, then eternal death was implied, for it was impossible for a person who had not received the spiritual purification to enter into eternal glory. The spirit of this law extends to all ages, dispensations, and people; he whose heart is not purified from sin cannot enter into the kingdom of God.

15. *Thou shalt not call her name Sarai, but Sarah.* See on v. 5.

16. *I will bless her.* Sarah certainly stands at the head of all the women of the Old Testament, on account of her extraordinary privileges. I am quite of Calmet's opinion that Sarah was a type of the blessed Virgin. St. Paul considers her a type of the New Testament and heavenly Jerusalem; and as all true believers are considered as the children of Abraham, so all faithful, holy women are considered the daughters of Sarah, Gal. iv. 22, 24, 26. See also 1 Pet. iii. 6.

17. *Then Abraham . . . laughed.* I am astonished to find learned and pious men considering this as a token of Abraham's weakness of faith or unbelief, when they have the most positive assurance from the Spirit of God himself that "Abraham was not weak but strong in the faith"; that "he staggered not at the promise through unbelief, but gave glory to God," Rom. iv. 19-20. It is true the same word is used, chap. xviii. 12, concerning Sarah, in whom it was certainly a sign of doubtfulness, though mixed with pleasure at the thought of the possibility of her becoming a mother; but we know how possible it is to express both faith and unbelief in the same way, and even pleasure and disdain have been expressed by a smile or laugh. By laughing Abraham undoubtedly expressed his joy at the prospect of the fulfilment of so glorious a promise; and from this very circumstance Isaac had his name. *Yitschak*, which we change into *Isaac*, signifies "laughter"; and it is the same word which is used in the verse before us.

18. *O that Ishmael might live before thee!* Abraham, finding that the covenant was to be established in another branch of his family, felt solicitous for his son Ishmael, whom he considered as necessarily excluded; on which God delivers that most remarkable prophecy which follows in the twentieth verse, and which contains an answer to the prayer and wish of Abraham: *And as for Ishmael, I have heard thee;* so that the object of Abraham's prayer was that his son Ishmael might be the head of a prosperous and potent people.

20. *Twelve princes shall he beget.* See the names of these twelve princes, chap. xxv. 12-16. From Ishmael proceeded the various tribes of the Arabs. They were anciently, and still continue to be, a very numerous and powerful people.

21. *My covenant will I establish with Isaac.* All temporal good things are promised to Ishmael and his posterity, but the establishment of the Lord's covenant is to be with Isaac. Hence it is fully evident that this covenant referred chiefly to spiritual things—to the Messiah, and the salvation which should be brought to both Jews and Gentiles by His incarnation, death, and glorification.

22. *God went up from Abraham.* Ascended evidently before him, so that he had the fullest proof that it was no human being, no earthly angel or messenger, that talked with him; and the promise of a son in the course of a single year, "at this set time in the next year," v. 21, which had every human probability against it, was to be the sure token of the truth of all that had hitherto taken place, and the proof that all that was farther promised should be fulfilled in its due time.

23. *And Abraham took Ishmael.* Had not Abraham, his son (who was of age to judge for himself), and all the family been fully convinced that this thing was of God, they could not have submitted to it. A rite so painful, so repugnant to every feeling of delicacy, and every way revolting to nature, could never have sprung up in the imagination of man. To this day the Jews practice it as a divine ordinance; and all the Arabians do the same.

CHAPTER 18

The Lord appears unto Abraham in Mamre, 1. Three angels, in human appearance, come towards his tent, 2. He invites them in to wash and refresh themselves, 3-5; prepares a calf, bread, butter, and milk, for their entertainment; and himself serves them, 6-8. They promise that within a year Sarah shall have a son, 9-10. Sarah, knowing herself and husband to be superannuated, smiles at the promise, 11-12. One of the three, who is called the Lord or Jehovah, chides her, and asserts the sufficiency of the divine power to accomplish the promise, 13-14. Sarah, through fear, denies that she had laughed or showed signs of unbelief, 15. Abraham accompanies these divine persons on their way to Sodom, 16; and that One who is called Jehovah informs him of His purpose to destroy Sodom and Gomorrah, because of their great wickedness, 17-21. The two former proceed toward Sodom, while the latter (Jehovah) remains with Abraham, 22. Abraham intercedes for the inhabitants of those cities, entreating the Lord to spare them provided fifty righteous persons should be found in them, 23-25. The Lord grants this request, 26. He pleads for the same mercy should only forty-five be found there, which is also granted, 27-28. He pleads the same for forty, which is also granted, 29; for thirty, with the same success, 30; for twenty, and receives the same gracious answer, 31; for ten, and the Lord assures him that should ten righteous persons be found there, He will not destroy the place, 32. Jehovah then departs, and Abraham returns to his tent, 33.

1. *And the Lord appeared.* See on chap. xv. 1. *Sat in the tent door.* For the purpose of enjoying the refreshing air *in the heat of the day,* when the sun had most power. A custom still frequent among the Asiatics.

2. *Three men stood by him.* Were "standing over against him"; for if they had been standing by him, as our translation says, he needed not to have "run from the tent door to meet them." To Abraham these appeared at first as *men;* but he "entertained angels unawares," see Heb. xiii. 2.

3. *And said, My Lord.* The word is *Adonai*, not *Yehovah*, for as yet Abraham did not know the quality of his guests. For an explanation of this word, see on chap. xv. 8.

4. *Let a little water . . . be fetched, and wash your feet.* In these verses we find a delightful picture of primitive hospitality. In those ancient times shoes such as ours were not in use; and the foot was protected only by sandals or soles, which fastened round the foot with straps. It was, therefore, a great refreshment in so hot a country to get the feet washed at the end of a day's journey; and this is the first thing that Abraham proposes. *Rest yourselves under the tree.* We have already heard of the oak grove of Mamre, chap. xii. 6, and this was the second

requisite for the refreshment of a weary traveller, namely, rest in the shade.

5. *I will fetch a morsel of bread.* This was the third requisite, and is introduced in its proper order, as eating immediately after exertion or fatigue is very unwholesome. *For therefore are ye come.* In those ancient days every traveller conceived he had a right to refreshment, when he needed it, at the first tent he met with on his journey. *So do, as thou hast said.* How exceedingly simple was all this! On neither side is there any compliment but such as a generous heart and sound sense dictate.

6. *Three measures of fine meal.* The *seah*, which is here translated "measure," contained, according to Bishop Cumberland, about two gallons and a half; and Mr. Ainsworth translates the word "peck." *Make cakes upon the hearth.* Or under the ashes. This mode is used in the East to the present day. When the hearth is strongly heated with the fire that has been kindled on it, they remove the coals, sweep off the ashes, lay on the bread, and then cover it with the hot cinders.

10. *I will certainly return.* Abraham was now ninety-nine years of age, and this promise was fulfilled when he was a hundred; so that the phrase *according to the time of life* must mean either a complete year, or nine months from the present time, the ordinary time of pregnancy. Taken in this latter sense, Abraham was now in the ninety-ninth year of his age, and Isaac was born when he was in his hundredth year.

11. *It ceased to be with Sarah after the manner of women.* And consequently, naturally speaking, conception could not take place; therefore, if she is to have a son it must be in a supernatural or miraculous way.

12. *Sarah laughed.* Partly through pleasure at the bare idea of the possibility of the thing, and partly from a conviction that it was extremely improbable. She appears to have been in the same spirit, and to have had the same feelings of those who, unexpectedly hearing of something of great consequence to themselves, smile and say, "The news is too good to be true"; see chap. xxi. 6. There is a case very similar to this mentioned in Ps. cxxvi. 1-2.

13. *And the Lord [Jehovah] said.* So it appears that One of those three persons was Jehovah, and as this name is never given to any created being, consequently the ever-blessed God is intended; and as He was never seen in any bodily shape, consequently the great Angel of the covenant, Jesus Christ, must be meant.

·14. *Is any thing too hard for the Lord?* "Shall a word (or thing) be wonderful from the Lord?" i.e., Can anything be too great a miracle for Him to effect? It was to correct Sarah's unbelief, and to strengthen her faith, that God spoke these most important words; words which state that where human wisdom, prudence, and energy fail, and where nature herself ceases to be an agent, through lack of energy to act, or laws to direct and regulate energy, there also God has full sway, and by His own omnific power works all things after the counsel of His own will. Is there an effect to be produced? God can produce it as well without as with means.

16. *Abraham went with them to bring them on the way.* This was another piece of primitive hospitality—to direct strangers in the way. Public roads did not then exist, and guides were essentially necessary in countries where villages were seldom to be met with and where solitary dwellings did not exist.

17. *Shall I hide from Abraham?* That is, I will not hide. A common mode of speech in Scripture—a question asked when an affirmative is designed.

18. *Shall surely become a great and mighty nation.* The revelation that I make to him shall be preserved among his posterity; and the exact fulfilment of My promises, made so long before, shall lead them to believe in My name and trust in My goodness.

19. *And they shall keep the way of the Lord.* The true religion; God's way; that in which God walks himself, and in which, of course, His followers walk also.

22. *And the men turned their faces.* That is, the two angels who accompanied Jehovah were now sent towards Sodom; while the third, who is called the Lord or *Jehovah,* remained with Abraham for the purpose of teaching him the great usefulness and importance of faith and prayer.

23. *Wilt thou also destroy the righteous with the wicked?* A form of speech similar to that in verse 17, an invariable principle of justice, that the righteous shall not be punished for the crimes of the impious. And this Abraham lays down as the foundation of his supplications. Who can pray with any hope of success who cannot assign a reason to God and his conscience for the petitions he offers? The great sacrifice offered by Christ is an infinite reason why a penitent sinner should expect to find the mercy for which he pleads.

25. *Shall not the Judge of all the earth do right?* God alone is the Judge of all men. Abraham, in thus addressing himself to the person in the text, considers him either as the Supreme Being or His representative.

27. *Which am but dust and ashes. Aphar vaepher,* words very similar in sound, as they refer to matters which so much resemble each other. *Dust*—the lightest particles of earth. *Ashes*—the residuum of consumed substances. By these expressions he shows how deeply his soul was humbled in the presence of God. He who has high thoughts of himself must have low thoughts of the dignity of the divine nature, of the majesty of God, and the sinfulness of sin.

32. *Peradventure ten shall be found there.* Knowing that in the family of his nephew the true religion was professed and practiced, he could not suppose there could be less than ten righteous persons in the city; he did not think it necessary to urge his supplication farther; he therefore left off his entreaties, and the Lord departed from him. It is highly worthy of observation that while he continued to pray the presence of God was continued; and when Abraham ended, "the glory of the Lord was lifted up," as the Targum expresses it.

CHAPTER 19

The two angels mentioned in the preceding chapter come in the evening to Sodom. 1. Lot, who was sitting at the gate, invites them to enter his house, take some refreshment, and tarry all night; which they at first refuse, 2; but on being pressingly solicited, at last comply, 3. The abominable conduct of the men of

Sodom, 4-5. Lot's deep concern for the honor and safety of his guests, which leads him to make a most exceptionable proposal to those wicked men, 6-8. The violent proceedings of the Sodomites, 9. Lot rescued from their barbarity by the angels, who smite them with blindness, 10-11. The angels exhort Lot and his family to flee from that wicked place, as God was about to destroy it, 12-13. Lot's fruitless exhortation to his sons-in-law, 14. The angels hasten Lot and his family to depart, 15-16. Their exhortation, 17. Lot's request, 18-20. He is permitted to escape to Zoar, 21-23. Fire and brimstone are rained down from heaven upon all the cities of the plain, by which they are entirely destroyed, 24-25. Lot's wife, looking behind, becomes a pillar of salt, 26. Abraham, early in the morning, discovers the desolation of those iniquitous cities, 27-29. Lot, fearing to continue in Zoar, went with his two daughters to the mountain, and dwelt in a cave, 30. The strange conduct of his daughters, and his unhappy deception, 31-36. Moab and Ammon born, from whom sprang the Moabites and Ammonites, 37-38.

1. *Two angels.* The two referred to in chap. xviii. 22. *Sat in the gate.* Probably, in order to prevent unwary travellers from being entrapped by his wicked townsmen, he waited at the gate of the city to bring the strangers he might meet with to his own house, as well as to transact his own business. Or, as the gate was the place of judgment, he might have been sitting there as magistrate to hear and determine disputes. *Bowed himself.* Not through religious reverence, for he did not know the quality of his guests; but through the customary form of civility.

2. *Nay; but we will abide in the street.* Instead of "nay" some MSS. have "to him"; "And they said unto him, For we lodge in the street," where, nevertheless, the negation is understood. Knowing the disposition of the inhabitants, and appearing in the mere character of travellers, they preferred the open street to any house; but as Lot pressed them vehemently, and they knew him to be a righteous man, not yet willing to make themselves known, they consented to take shelter under his hospitable roof. Our Lord, willing for the time being to conceal His person from the knowledge of the disciples going to Emmaus, made as though He would go farther, Luke xxiv. 13; but at last, like the angels here, yielded to the importunity of His disciples, and went into their lodgings.

5. *Where are the men which came in to thee?* This account justifies the character given of this depraved people in the preceding chapter, v. 20, and in chap. xiii. 13. As their crime was the deepest disgrace to human nature, so it is too bad to be described; in the sacred text it is sufficiently marked; and the iniquity which, from these most abominable wretches, has been called "Sodomy" is punished in our country with death.

8. *Behold now, I have two daughters.* Nothing but that sacred light in which the rights of hospitality were regarded among the Eastern nations could either justify or palliate this proposal of Lot. A man who had taken a stranger under his care and protection was bound to defend him even at the expense of his own life. In this light the rights of hospitality are still regarded in Asiatic countries; and on these high notions only, the influence of which an Asiatic mind alone can properly appreciate, Lot's conduct on this occasion can be at all excused: but even then, it was not only the language of anxious solicitude, but of unwarrantable haste.

9. *And he will needs be a judge.* So his sitting in the gate is perhaps a farther proof of his being there in a magisterial capacity, as some have supposed.

11. *And they smote the men . . . with blindness.* This has been understood two ways: (1) The angels, by the power which God had given them, deprived these wicked men of a proper and regular use of their sight; or (2) They caused such a deep darkness to take place that they could not find Lot's door. The author of the book of Wisdom was evidently of this latter opinion, for he says they were compassed about with horrible great darkness, chap. xix. 17. See a similar case of Elisha and the Syrians, 2 Kings vi. 18, etc.

12. *Hast thou here any besides? son in law.* Here there appears to be but one meant, as the word is in the singular number; but in v. 14 the word is plural, his sons-in-law. These were only two in number, as we do not hear that Lot had more than two daughters; and these daughters but only betrothed, as is evident from what Lot says, v. 8; for they had not known man, but were the spouses elect of those who are here called his sons-in-law. But though these might be reputed as a part of Lot's family, and entitled on this account to God's protection, yet it is sufficiently plain that they did not escape the perdition of these wicked men; and the reason is given, v. 14, they received the solemn warning as a ridiculous tale, the creature of Lot's invention, or the offspring of his fear. Therefore they made no provision for their escape, and doubtless perished, notwithstanding the sincerely offered grace, in the perdition that fell on this ungodly city.

16. *While he lingered.* Probably in affectionate though useless entreaties to prevail on the remaining parts of his family to escape from the destruction that was now descending; *laid hold upon his hand*—pulled them away by mere force, *the Lord being merciful;* else they had been left to perish in their lingering.

17. *When they had brought them forth.* Every word here is emphatic, *Escape for thy life;* thou art in the most imminent danger of perishing; thy life and thy soul are both at stake. *Look not behind thee*—thou hast but barely time enough to escape from the judgment that is now descending; no lingering, or thou art lost! One look back may prove fatal to thee, and God commands thee to avoid it. *Neither stay thou in all the plain,* because God will destroy that as well as the city. *Escape to the mountain,* on which these judgments shall not light, and which God has appointed thee for a place of refuge, *lest thou be consumed.* It is not an ordinary judgment that is coming; a fire from heaven shall burn up the cities, the plain, and all that remain in the cities and in the plain.

19. *I cannot escape to the mountain.* He saw the destruction so near that he imagined he should not have time sufficient to reach the mountain before it arrived. He did not consider that God could give no command to His creatures that it would be impossible for them to fulfil; but the hurry and perturbation of his mind will at once account for and excuse this gross oversight.

20. *It is a little one.* Probably Lot wished to have it for an inheritance, and therefore pleaded its being a little one, that his request might be the more readily granted. Or he might suppose that, being a little city, it was less depraved than Sodom and Gomorrah, and therefore not so

ripe for punishment; which was probably the case.

22. *I cannot do any thing till thou be come thither.* So these heavenly messengers had the strictest commission to take care of Lot and his family; and even the purposes of divine justice could not be accomplished on the rebellious till this righteous man and his family had escaped from the place. A proof of Abraham's assertion, "The Judge of all the earth will do right."

The name of the city was called Zoar. "Little," its former name being Bela.

24. *Brimstone and fire.* The word which we translate *brimstone* is of very uncertain derivation. It is evidently used metaphorically to point out the utmost degrees of punishment executed on the most flagitious criminals, in Deut. xxix. 23; Job xviii. 15; Ps. xi. 6; Isa. xxxiv. 9; Ezek. xxxviii. 22. And as hell, or an everlasting separation from God and the glory of His power, is the utmost punishment that can be inflicted on sinners, hence brimstone and fire are used in Scripture to signify the torments in that place of punishment. See Isa. xxx. 33; Rev. xiv. 10; xix. 20; xx. 10; xxi. 8. We may safely suppose that it was quite possible that a shower of nitrous particles might have been precipitated from the atmosphere, here, as in many other places, called heaven, which by the action of fire would be immediately ignited, and so consume the cities; and, as we have already seen that the plains about Sodom and Gomorrah abounded with asphaltus or bitumen pits (see chap. xiv. 10), that what is particularly meant here in reference to the plain is the setting fire to this vast store of inflammable matter by the agency of lightning.

26. *She became a pillar of salt.* The vast variety of opinions, both ancient and modern, on the crime of Lot's wife, her change, and the manner in which that change was effected, are in many cases as unsatisfactory as they are ridiculous. On this point the sacred Scripture says little. God had commanded Lot and his family not to look behind them; the wife of Lot disobeyed this command; she *looked back from behind him*—Lot, her husband, *and she became a pillar of salt.* This is all the information the inspired historian has thought proper to give us on this subject.

27. *Abraham gat up early in the morning.* Anxious to know what was the effect of the prayers which he had offered to God the preceding day; what must have been his astonishment when he found that all these cities, with the plain which resembled the garden of the Lord, chap. xiii. 10, burnt up, and the smoke ascending like the smoke of a furnace, and was thereby assured that even God himself could not discover ten righteous persons in four whole cities!

29. *God remembered Abraham.* Though he did not descend lower than ten righteous persons (see chap. xviii. 32), yet the Lord had respect to the spirit of his petitions, and spared all those who could be called righteous, and for Abraham's sake offered salvation to all the family of Lot, though neither his sons-in-law elect nor his own wife ultimately profited by it.

30. *Lot went up out of Zoar.* From seeing the universal desolation that had fallen upon the land, and that the fire was still continuing its depredations, *he feared to dwell in Zoar,* lest that also should be consumed, and then went to those very mountains to which God had ordered him at first to make his escape.

31. *Our father is old,* and consequently not likely to remarry, *and there is not a man in the earth*—none left, according to their opinion, in all the land of Canaan, of their own family and kindred.

32. *Come, let us make our father drink wine.* On their flight from Zoar it is probable they had brought with them certain provisions to serve them for the time being, and the wine here mentioned among the rest.

CHAPTER 20

Abraham leaves Mamre, and, after having sojourned at Kadesh and Shur, settles in Gerar, 1. Abimelech takes Sarah, Abraham having acknowledged her only as his sister, 2. Abimelech is warned by God in a dream to restore Sarah, 3. He asserts his innocence, 4-5. He is farther warned, 6-7. Expostulates with Abraham, 8-10. Abraham vindicates his conduct, 11-13. Abimelech restores Sarah, makes Abraham a present of sheep, oxen, and male and female slaves, 14; offers him a residence in any part of the land, 15; and reproves Sarah, 16. At the intercession of Abraham, the curse of barrenness is removed from Abimelech and his household, 17-18.

1. *And Abraham journeyed.* It is very likely that this holy man was so deeply affected with the melancholy prospect of the ruined cities, and not knowing what was become of his nephew Lot and his family, that he could no longer bear to dwell within sight of the place. Having, therefore, struck his tents, and sojourned for a short time at Kadesh and Shur, he fixed his habitation in Gerar, which was a city of Arabia Petraea, under a king of the Philistines called Abimelech, "my father king," who appears to have been not only the father of his people, but also a righteous man.

2. *She is my sister.* See the parallel account, chap. xxii, and the notes there. Sarah was now about ninety years of age, and probably pregnant with Isaac. Her beauty, therefore, must have been considerably impaired since the time she was taken in a similar manner by Pharaoh, king of Egypt; but she was probably now chosen by Abimelech more on the account of forming an alliance with Abraham, who was very rich, than on account of any personal accomplishments.

3. *But God came to Abimelech.* Thus we find that persons who were not of the family of Abraham had the knowledge of the true God.

5. *In the integrity of my heart.* Had Abimelech any other than honorable views in taking Sarah, he could not have justified himself thus to his Maker; and that these views were of the most honorable kind God himself, to whom the appeal was made, asserts in the most direct manner, "Yea, I know that thou didst this in the integrity of thy heart."

7. *He is a prophet, and he shall pray for thee.* The word prophet, which we have from the Greek *prophetes*, and which is compounded of *pro*, "before," and *phemi*, "I speak," means, in its general acceptation, one who speaks of things before they happen, i.e., one who foretells future events. But that this was not the original notion of the word, its use in this place sufficiently proves. Abraham certainly was not a prophet in the present general acceptation of

the term, and for the Hebrew *nabi* we must seek some other meaning. I have, in a discourse entitled "The Christian Prophet and His Work," proved that the proper ideal meaning of the original word is to "pray, entreat, make supplication," and this meaning of it I have justified at large both from its application in this place and from its pointed use in the case of Saul, mentioned in 1 Samuel x, and from the case of the priests of Baal, 1 Kings xviii, where prophesying most undoubtedly means making prayer and supplication. As those who were in habits of intimacy with God by prayer and faith were found the most proper persons to communicate His mind to man, both with respect to the present and the future, hence *nabi*, the "intercessor," became in process of time the public instructor or preacher, and also the predictor of future events, because to such faithful praying men God revealed the secret of His will.

8. *Abimelech rose early.* God came to Abimelech in a dream by night, and we find as the day broke he arose, assembled his servants, and communicated to them what he had received from God. They were all struck with astonishment, and discerned the hand of God in this business. Abraham is then called, and in a most respectful and pious manner the king expostulates with him for bringing him and his people under the divine displeasure, by withholding from him the information that Sarah was his wife, when by taking her he sought only an honorable alliance with his family.

11. *And Abraham said.* The best excuse he could make for his conduct, which in this instance is far from defensible.

12. *She is my sister.* I have not told a lie; I have suppressed only a part of the truth. In this place it may be proper to ask, What is a lie? It is _any action done or word spoken, whether true or false in itself, which the doer or speaker wishes the observer or hearer to take in a contrary sense to that which he knows to be true. It is, in a word, any action done or speech delivered with the intention to deceive, though both may be absolutely true and right in themselves.

16. *And unto Sarah he said.* But what did he say? Here there is scarcely any agreement among interpreters; the Hebrew is exceedingly obscure, and every interpreter takes it in his own sense. *A thousand pieces of silver.* Shekels are very probably meant here, and so the Targum understands it. *Behold, he is to thee a covering of the eyes.* "It"—the one thousand shekels (not *he*—Abraham)—is to thee for a covering—to procure thee a veil to conceal thy beauty (*unto all that are with thee, and with all other*) from all thy own kindred and acquaintance, and from all strangers, that none, seeing thou art another man's wife, may covet thee on account of thy comeliness.

Thus she was reproved. Paraphrased: "Behold, I have given thy brother (Abraham, gently alluding to the equivocation, vv. 2, 5) a thousand shekels of silver; behold, it is (that is, the silver is, or may be, or let it be) to thee a covering of the eyes (to procure a veil) with regard to all those who are with thee, and to all (or and in all) speak thou the truth." Correctly translated by the Septuagint "and in all things speak the truth"—not only tell a part of the truth, but

tell the whole; say not merely, "He is my brother," but say also, "He is my husband too." Thus in all things speak the truth. I believe the above to be the *sense* of this difficult passage.

17. *So Abraham prayed.* This was the prime office of the *nabi;* see v. 7.

18. *For the Lord had fast closed up all the wombs.* Probably by means of some disease with which He had smitten them, hence it is said they were healed at Abraham's intercession; and this seems necessarily to imply that they had been afflicted by some disease that rendered it impossible for them to have children till it was removed.

CHAPTER 21

Isaac is born according to the promise, 1-3; and is circumcised when eight days old, 4. Abraham's age, and Sarah's exultation at the birth of their son, 5-7. Isaac is weaned, 8. Ishmael mocking on the occasion, Sarah requires that both he and his mother, Hagar, shall be dismissed, 9-10. Abraham, distressed on the account, is ordered by the Lord to comply, 11-12. The promise renewed to Ishmael, 13. Abraham dismisses Hagar and her son, who go to the wilderness of Beer-sheba, 14. They are greatly distressed for want of water, 15-16. An angel of God appears to and relieves them, 17-19. Ishmael prospers and is married, 20-21. Abimelech and Phichol, his chief captain, make a covenant with Abraham, and surrender the well of Beer-sheba for seven ewe lambs, 22-32. Abraham plants a grove, and invokes the name of the everlasting God, 33.

1. *The Lord visited Sarah.* That is, God fulfilled His promise to Sarah by giving her, at the advanced age of ninety, power to conceive and bring forth a son.

3. *Isaac.* See the reason and interpretation of this name in the note on chap. xvii. 7.

6. *God hath made me to laugh.* Sarah alludes here to the circumstance mentioned in chap. xviii. 12; and as she seems to use the word *to laugh* in this place, not in the sense of being incredulous, but to express such pleasure or happiness as almost suspends the reasoning faculty for a time, it justifies the observation on the above-named verse. See a similar case in Luke xxiv. 41, where the disciples were so overcome with the good news of our Lord's resurrection that it is said, "They believed not for joy."

8. *The child grew, and was weaned.* At what time children were weaned among the ancients is a disputed point. St. Jerome says there were two opinions on this subject. Some hold that children were always weaned at five years of age; others, that they were not weaned till they were twelve. From the speech of the mother to her son, 2 Mac. vii. 27, it seems likely that among the Jews they were weaned when three years old: "O my son, have pity upon me that bare thee nine months in my womb, and gave thee suck three years, and nourished thee and brought thee up." And this is farther strengthened by 2 Chron. xxxi. 16, where Hezekiah, in making provision for the Levites and priests, includes the children from three years old and upwards; which is a presumptive proof that previously to this age they were wholly dependent on the mother for their nourishment. The term among the Mohammedans is fixed by the Koran, chap. xxxi. 14, at two years of age.

9. *Mocking.* What was implied in this mocking is not known. St. Paul, Gal. iv. 29, calls it persecuting; but it is likely he meant no more than some species of ridicule used by Ishmael on the occasion, and probably with respect to

the age of Sarah at Isaac's birth, and her previous barrenness.

10. *Cast out this bondwoman and her son.* Both Sarah and Abraham have been accused of cruelty in this transaction, because every word reads harsh to us. *Cast out; garash* signifies not only to "thrust out, drive away, and expel," but also to "divorce" (see Lev. xxi. 7); and it is in this latter sense the word should be understood here. The child of Abraham by Hagar might be considered as having a right at least to a part of the inheritance; and as it was sufficiently known to Sarah that God had designed that the succession should be established in the line of Isaac, she wished Abraham to divorce Hagar, or to perform some sort of legal act by which Ishmael might be excluded from all claim on the inheritance.

12. *In Isaac shall thy seed be called.* Here God shows the propriety of attending to the counsel of Sarah; and lest Abraham, in whose eyes the thing was grievous, should feel distressed on the occasion, God renews His promises to Ishmael and his posterity.

14. *Took bread, and a bottle.* By the word *bread* we are to understand the food or provisions which were necessary for her and Ishmael till they should come to the place of their destination; which, no doubt, Abraham particularly pointed out. The *bottle,* which was made of skin, ordinarily a goat's skin, contained water sufficient to last them till they should come to the next well; which, it is likely, Abraham particularly specified also. This well, it appears, Hagar missed, and therefore wandered about in the wilderness seeking more water, till all she had brought with her was expended. We may therefore safely presume that she and her son were sufficiently provided for their journey had they not missed their way. Travellers in those countries take only provisions sufficient to carry them to the next village or encampment, and water to supply them till they shall meet with the next well. What adds to the appearance of cruelty in this case is that our translation seems to represent Ishmael as being a young child; and that Hagar was obliged to carry him, the bread, and the bottle of water on her back or shoulder at the same time. But that Ishmael could not be carried on his mother's shoulder will be sufficiently evident when his age is considered; Ishmael was born when Abraham was eighty-six years of age, chap. xvi. 16; Isaac was born when he was one hundred years of age, chap. xxi. 5; hence Ishmael was fourteen years old at the birth of Isaac. Add to this the age of Isaac when he was weaned, which, from v. 8 of this chapter (see the note), was probably three, and we shall find that Ishmael was at the time of his leaving Abraham not less than seventeen years old.

15. *And she cast the child.* "And she sent the lad under one of the shrubs," namely, to screen him from the intensity of the heat. Here Ishmael appears to be utterly helpless, and this circumstance seems farther to confirm the opinion that he was now in a state of infancy; but the preceding observations do this supposition entirely away, and his present helplessness will be easily accounted for on this ground: (1) Young persons can bear much less fatigue than those who are arrived at mature age. (2) They require much more fluid from the greater quantum of heat in their bodies. (3) Their digestion is much more rapid, and hence they cannot bear hunger and thirst as well as the others. On these grounds Ishmael must be much more exhausted with fatigue than his mother.

19. *God opened her eyes.* These words appear to me to mean no more than that God directed her to a well, which probably was at no great distance from the place in which she then was; and therefore she is commanded, v. 18, to "support the lad," literally, to "make her hand strong in his behalf"—namely, that he might reach the well and quench his thirst.

20. *Became an archer.* And by his skill in this art, under the continual superintendence of the divine providence (for *God was with the lad*), he was undoubtedly enabled to procure a sufficient supply for his own wants and those of his parent.

21. *He dwelt in the wilderness of Paran.* This is generally allowed to have been a part of the desert belonging to Arabia Petraea, in the vicinity of Mount Sinai; and this seems to be its uniform meaning in the sacred writings.

22. *At that time.* This may either refer to the transactions recorded in the preceding chapter or to the time of Ishmael's marriage, but most probably to the former.

23. *Now therefore swear unto me.* The oath on such occasions probably meant no more than the mutual promise of both the parties, when they slew an animal, poured out the blood as a sacrifice to God, and then passed between the pieces. See this ceremony, chap. v. 18, and on chap. xv. *According to the kindness that I have done.* The simple claims of justice were alone set up among virtuous people in those ancient times.

25. *Abraham reproved Abimelech.* Wells were of great consequence in those hot countries, and especially where the flocks were numerous, because the water was scarce and digging to find it was accompanied with much expense of time and labor.

26. *I wot not who hath done this thing.* The servants of Abimelech had committed these depredations on Abraham without any authority from their master, who appears to have been a very amiable man.

27. *Took sheep and oxen.* Some think that these were the sacrifices which were offered on the occasion, and which Abraham furnished at his own cost, and in order to do Abimelech the greater honor gave them to him to offer before the Lord.

28. *Seven ewe lambs.* These were either given as a present or they were intended as the price of the well; and being accepted by Abimelech, they served as a witness that he had acknowledged Abraham's right to the well in question.

31. *He called that place Beer-sheba.* Literally, the "well of swearing" or "of the oath," because they both sware there—mutually confirmed the covenant.

33. *Abraham planted a grove.* The original word has been variously translated a "grove," a "plantation," an "orchard," a "cultivated field," and an "oak." As Abraham, agreeably, no doubt, to the institutes of the patriarchal religion,

planted an oak in Beer-sheba, and called on the name of Jehovah, the everlasting God (compare Gen. xii. 8; xviii. 1), so we find that oaks were sacred among the idolaters also. "Ye shall be ashamed of the oaks ye have chosen," says Isaiah, chap. i. 29, to the idolatrous Israelites.

And called there on the name of the Lord. On this important passage Dr. Shuckford speaks thus: "Our English translation very erroneously renders this place, *he called upon the name of Jehovah;* but the expression never signifies 'to call upon the name'; *kara beshem* signifies 'to invoke in the name,' and seems to be used where the true worshippers of God offered their prayers in the name of the true Mediator." I believe this to be a just view of the subject, and therefore I admit it without scruple.

The everlasting God. Yehovah el olam, "Jehovah, the strong God, the eternal one." This is the first place in Scripture in which *olam* occurs as an attribute of God, and here it is evidently designed to point out His eternal duration; that it can mean no limited time is self-evident, because nothing of this kind can be attributed to God.

CHAPTER 22

The faith and obedience of Abraham put to a most extraordinary test, 1. He is commanded to offer his beloved son Isaac for a burnt offering, 2. He prepares, with the utmost promptitude, to accomplish the will of God, 3-6. Affecting speech of Isaac, 7; and Abraham's answer, 8. Having arrived at Mount Moriah he prepares to sacrifice his son, 9-10; and is prevented by an angel of the Lord, 11-12. A ram is offered in the stead of Isaac, 13; and the place is named Jehovah-jireh, 14. The angel of the Lord calls to Abraham a second time, 15; and, in the most solemn manner, he is assured of innumerable blessings in the multiplication and prosperity of his seed, 16-18. Abraham returns and dwells at Beer-sheba, 19; hears that his brother Nahor has eight children by his wife Milcah, 20; their names, 21-23; and four by his concubine Reumah, 24.

1. *God did tempt Abraham.* The original here is very emphatic: "And the Elohim He tried this Abraham"; God brought him into such circumstances as exercised and discovered his faith, love, and obedience. Though the word *tempt* signifies no more than to "prove" or "try," yet as it is now generally used to imply a solicitation to evil, in which way God never tempts any man, it would be well to avoid it here.

2. *Take now thy son.* Bishop Warburton's observations on this passage are weighty and important. "The order in which the words are placed in the original gradually increases the sense, and raises the passions higher and higher: *Take now thy son* (rather, take I beseech thee), *thine only son whom thou lovest, even Isaac.* Abraham desired earnestly to be let into the mystery of *redemption;* and God, to instruct him in the infinite extent of the divine goodness to mankind, *who spared not his own Son, but delivered him up for us all,* let Abraham feel by experience what it was to lose a beloved son, the son born miraculously when Sarah was past childbearing, as Jesus was miraculously born of a virgin. The *duration,* too, of the action, v. 4, was the same as that between Christ's death and resurrection, both which are designed to be represented in it; and still farther not only the final archetypical sacrifice of the Son of God was figured in the command to offer Isaac, but the *intermediate typical* sacrifice in the Mosaic economy was represented by the *permitted* sacrifice of the ram offered up, v. 13,

instead of Isaac." *Only son.* All that he had by Sarah, his legal wife. *The land of Moriah.* This is supposed to mean all the mountains of Jerusalem. Beer-sheba, where Abraham dwelt, is about forty-two miles distant from Jerusalem, and it is not to be wondered at that Abraham, Isaac, the two servants, and the ass laden with wood for the burnt offering did not reach this place till the third day; see v. 4.

5. *I and the lad will go . . . and come again.* How could Abraham consistently with truth say this, when he knew he was going to make his son a burnt offering? The apostle answers for him: "By faith Abraham, when he was tried, offered up Isaac . . . accounting that God was able to raise him up, even from the dead, from whence also he received him in a figure," Heb. xi. 17, 19. He knew that previously to the birth of Isaac both he and his wife were dead to all the purposes of procreation; that his birth was a kind of life from the dead; that the promise of God was most positive, "In Isaac shall thy seed be called," chap. xxi. 12; that this promise could not fail; that it was his duty to obey the command of his Maker; and that it was as easy for God to restore him to life after he had been a burnt offering as it was for Him to give him life in the beginning. Therefore he went fully purposed to offer his son, and yet confidently expecting to have him restored to life again.

7. *Behold the fire and the wood: but where is the lamb?* Nothing can be conceived more tender, affectionate, and affecting then the question of the son and the reply of the father on this occasion. A paraphrase would spoil it; nothing can be added without injuring those expressions of affectionate submission on the one hand and dignified tenderness and simplicity on the other.

8. *My son, God will provide himself a lamb.* Here we find the same obedient, unshaken faith for which this pattern of practical piety was ever remarkable. But we must not suppose that this was the language merely of faith and obedience; the patriarch spoke prophetically, and referred to that Lamb of God which He had provided for himself, who in the fulness of time should take away the sin of the world, and of whom **Isaac** was a most expressive type.

9. *And bound Isaac his son.* If the patriarch had not been upheld by the conviction that he was doing the will of God, and had he not felt the most perfect confidence that his son should be restored even from the dead, what agony must his heart have felt at every step of the journey, and through all the circumstances of this extraordinary business? What must his affectionate heart have felt at the questions asked by his innocent and amiable son? What must he have suffered while building the altar, laying on the wood, binding his lovely son, placing him on the wood, taking the knife, and stretching out his hand to slay the child of his hopes? Every view we take of the subject interests the heart and exalts the character of this father of the faithful. But has the character of Isaac been duly considered? Is not the consideration of his excellence lost in the supposition that he was too young to enter particularly into a sense of his danger, and too feeble to have made any resistance, had he been unwilling to submit? Josephus supposes that Isaac was now twenty-five, some rabbins that he was thirty-six; but it

is more probable that he was now about thirty-three. Allowing him to be only twenty-five, he might have easily resisted; for can it be supposed that an old man of at least one hundred and twenty-five years of age could have bound, without his consent, a young man in the very prime and vigor of life? In this case we cannot say that the superior strength of the father prevailed, but the piety, filial affection, and obedience of the son yielded. All this was most illustriously typical of Christ. In both cases the father himself offers up his only begotten son, and the father himself binds him on the wood or to the Cross; in neither case is the son forced to yield, but yields of his own accord; in neither case is the life taken away by the hand of violence; Isaac yields himself to the knife, Jesus lays down His life for the sheep.

11. *The angel of the Lord.* The very Person who was represented by this offering; the Lord Jesus, who calls himself Jehovah, v. 16, and on His own authority renews the promises of the covenant. He was ever the great Mediator between God and man.

12. *Lay not thine hand upon the lad.* As Isaac was to be the representative of Jesus Christ's real sacrifice, it was sufficient for this purpose that in his own will, and the will of his father, the purpose of the immolation was complete. Isaac was now fully offered both by his father and by himself. The father yields up the son, the son gives up his life; on both sides, as far as will and purpose could go, the sacrifice was complete.

14. *Jehovah-jireh.* Literally interpreted in the margin, "The Lord will see"; that is, God will take care that everything shall be done that is necessary for the comfort and support of them who trust in Him. Hence the words are usually translated, "The Lord will provide"; so our translators, v. 8. But all this seems to have been done under a divine impulse, and the words to have been spoken prophetically; hence Houbigant and some others render the words thus: "The Lord shall be seen"; and this translation the following clause seems to require, "As it is said to this day, on this mount the Lord shall be seen." From this it appears that the sacrifice offered by Abraham was understood to be a representative one, and a tradition was kept up that Jehovah should be seen in a sacrificial way on this mount. And this renders the opinion on v. 1 more than probable, namely, that Abraham offered Isaac on that very mountain on which, in the fulness of time, Jesus suffered.

16. *By myself have I sworn.* So we find that the person who was called the "angel of the Lord" is here called "Jehovah"; see on v. 2.

17. *Shall possess the gate of his enemies.* By the gates may be meant all the strength, whether troops, counsels, or fortified cities of their enemies. So Matt. xvi. 18: "On this rock I will build my church, and the gates of hell shall not prevail against it"—the counsels, stratagems, and powers of darkness shall not be able to prevail against or overthrow the true Church of Christ.

18. *And in thy seed.* We have the authority of St. Paul, Gal. iii. 8, 16, 18, to restrain this to our blessed Lord, who was the Seed through whom alone all God's blessings of providence, mercy, grace, and glory should be conveyed to the nations of the earth.

20. *Behold, Milcah, she hath also borne children unto thy brother.* This short history seems introduced solely for the purpose of preparing the reader for the transactions related in chap. xxiv, and to show that the providence of God was preparing, in one of the branches of the family of Abraham, a suitable spouse for his son Isaac.

21. *Huz.* He is supposed to have peopled the land of *Uz* in Arabia Deserta, the country of Job. *Buz his brother.* From this person Elihu the Buzite, one of the friends of Job, is thought to have descended. *Kemuel the father of Aram.* "The father of the Syrians," according to the Septuagint.

23. *Bethuel begat Rebekah.* Who afterward became the wife of Isaac.

24. *His concubine.* We borrow this word from the Latin compound *concubina*, from *con*, "together," and *cubo*, "to lie," and apply it solely to a woman cohabiting with a man without being legally married. The concubine in Scripture is a kind of secondary wife, not unlawful in the patriarchal times, though the progeny of such could not inherit.

CHAPTER 23

The age and death of Sarah, 1-2. Abraham mourns for her, and requests a burial place from the sons of Heth, 2-4. They freely offer him the choice of all their sepulchres, 5-6. Abraham refuses to receive any as a free gift, and requests to buy the cave of Machpelah from Ephron, 7-9. Ephron proffers the cave and the field in which it was situated as a free gift to Abraham, 10-11. Abraham insists on giving its value in money, 12-13. Ephron at last consents, and names the sum of 400 shekels, 14-15. Abraham weighs him the money in the presence of the people; in consequence of which the cave, the whole field, trees, etc., are made sure to him and his family for a possession, 16-18. The transaction being completed, Sarah is buried in the cave, 19. The sons of Heth ratify the bargain, 20.

1. *And Sarah was an hundred and seven and twenty years old.* It is worthy of remark that Sarah is the only woman in the sacred writings whose age, death, and burial are distinctly noted. And she has been deemed worthy of higher honor, for St. Paul, Gal. iv. 22-23, makes her a type of the Church of Christ; and her faith in the accomplishment of God's promise that she should have a son, when all natural probabilities were against it, is particularly celebrated in the Epistle to the Hebrews, chap. xi. Sarah was about ninety-one years old when Isaac was born, and she lived thirty-six years after, and saw him grown up to man's estate. With Sarah the promise of the incarnation of Christ commenced, though a comparatively obscure prophecy of it had been delivered to Eve, chap. iii. 15; and with Mary it terminated, having had its exact completion. Thus God put more honor upon these two women than upon all the daughters of Eve besides.

2. *Sarah died in Kirjath-arba.* Literally "in the city of the four." It seems evidently to have had its name from a Canaanite, one of the Anakim, probably called Arba, who was the chief of the four brothers who dwelt there; the names of the others being Sheshai, Ahiman, and Talmai. See Judg. i. 10. *Abraham came to mourn for Sarah.* From verse 19 of the preceding chapter it appears that Abraham had settled at Beer-sheba; and here we find that Sarah died at Hebron, which was about twenty-four miles distant from Beer-sheba. For the convenience of feeding his numerous flocks, Abraham had

probably several places of temporary residence, and particularly one at Beer-sheba, and another at Hebron; and it is likely that while he sojourned at Beer-sheba, Sarah died at Hebron; and his coming to mourn and weep for her signifies his coming from the former to the latter place on the news of her death.

3. *Abraham stood up from before his dead.* He had probably sat on the ground some days in token of sorrow, as the custom then was (see Isa. xlvii. 1 and Gen. xxxvii. 35), and when this time was finished he arose and began to treat about a burying place.

4. *I am a stranger and a sojourner.* It appears from Heb. xi. 13-16; 1 Pet. ii. 11 that these words refer more to the state of his mind than of his body. He felt that he had no certain dwelling place, and was seeking by faith a city that had foundations. *Give me a possession of a buryingplace.* In different nations it was deemed ignominious to be buried in another's ground; probably this idea prevailed in early times in the East, and it may be in reference to a sentiment of this kind that Abraham refuses to accept the offer of the children of Heth to bury in any of their sepulchres, and earnestly requests them to sell him one, that he might bury his wife in a place that he could claim as his own.

6. *Thou art a mighty prince. Nesi Elohim,* "a prince of God"—a person whom we know to be divinely favored, and whom, in consequence, we deeply respect and reverence.

8. *Entreat for me to Ephron.* Abraham had already seen the cave and field, and finding to whom they belonged, and that they would answer his purpose, came to the gate of Hebron, where the elders of the people sat to administer justice, and where bargains and sales were made and witnessed, and having addressed himself to the elders, among whom was Ephron, though it appears he was not personally known to Abraham, he begged them to use their influence with the owner of the cave and field to sell it to him, that it might serve him and his family for a place of sepulture.

10. *And Ephron dwelt among the children of Heth.* "And Ephron was sitting among the children of Heth," but, as was before conjectured, was personally unknown to Abraham; he therefore answered for himself, making a free tender of the field to Abraham, in the presence of all the people, which amounted to a legal conveyance of the whole property to the patriarch.

13. *If thou wilt give it.* Instead of, *If thou wilt give it,* we should read, "But if thou wilt sell it, I will give thee money for the field"; silver, not coined money, for it is not probable that any such was then in use.

15. *The land is worth four hundred shekels of silver.* Though the words *is worth* are not in the text, yet they are necessarily expressed here to adapt the Hebrew to the idiom of our tongue. A shekel, according to the general opinion, was equal to 2 shillings and sixpence; but according to Dr. Prideaux, whose estimate I shall follow, 3 shillings English, 400 of which are equal to 60 pounds sterling; but it is evident that a certain weight is intended, and not a coin; for in verse 16 it is said, "And Abraham weighed . . . the silver," and hence it appears that this weight itself passed afterwards as a current coin.

16. *Current with the merchant.* "Passing to or with the traveller"—such as was commonly used by those who travelled about with merchandise of any sort.

17. *All the trees that were in the field.* It is possible that all these were specified in the agreement.

20. *And the field, etc., were made sure.* "Were established, caused to stand," the whole transaction having been regulated according to all the forms of law then in use.

CHAPTER 24

Abraham, being solicitous to get his son Isaac properly married, calls his confidential servant, probably Eliezer, and makes him swear that he will not take a wife for Isaac from among the Canaanites, 1-3, but from among his own kindred, 4. The servant proposes certain difficulties, 5, which Abraham removes by giving him the strongest assurances of God's direction in the business, 6-7, and then specifies the conditions of the oath, 8. The form of the oath itself, 9. The servant makes preparations for his journey, and sets out for Mesopotamia, the residence of Abraham's kindred, 10. Arrives at a well near to the place, 11. His prayer to God, 12-14. Rebekah, the daughter of Bethuel, son of Nahor, Abraham's brother, comes to the well to draw water, 15. She is described, 16. Conversation between her and Abraham's servant, in which everything took place according to his prayer to God, 17-21. He makes her presents, and learns whose daughter she is, 22-24. She invites him to her father's house, 25. He returns thanks to God for having thus far given him a prosperous journey, 26-27. Rebekah runs home and informs her family, 28; on which her brother, Laban, comes out, and invites the servant home, 29-31. His reception, 32-33. Tells his errand, 34, and how he had proceeded in executing the trust reposed in him, 35-48. Requests an answer, 49. The family of Rebekah consent that she should become the wife of Isaac, 50-51. The servant worships God, 52, and gives presents to Milcah, Laban, and Rebekah, 53. He requests to be dismissed, 54-56. Rebekah, being consulted, consents to go, 57-58. She is accompanied by her nurse, 59; and having received the blessing of her parents and relatives, 60, she departs with the servant of Abraham, 61. They are met by Isaac, who was on an evening walk for the purpose of meditation, 62-65. The servant relates to Isaac all that he had done, 66. Isaac and Rebekah are married, 67.

1. *And Abraham was old.* He was now about one hundred and forty years of age, and consequently Isaac was forty, being born when his father was one hundred years old. See chap. xxi. 5; xxv. 20.

2. *Eldest servant.* As this eldest servant is stated to have been the ruler over all that he had, it is very likely that Eliezer is meant. See chap. xv. 2-3.

4. *My country.* Mesopotamia, called here Abraham's country because it was the place where the family of Haran, his brother, had settled; and where he himself had remained a considerable time with his father, Terah. In this family, as well as in that of Nahor, the true religion had been in some sort preserved, though afterwards considerably corrupted; see chap. xxxi. 19.

5. *Peradventure the woman will not be willing.* We may see by this and other passages of Scripture, Josh. ix. 18, what the sentiments of the ancients were relative to an oath. They believed they were bound precisely by what was spoken, and had no liberty to interpret the intentions of those to whom the oath was made.

7. *The Lord God.* He expresses the strongest confidence in God, that the great designs for which He had brought him from his own kindred to propagate the true religion in the earth would be accomplished; and that therefore, when earthly instruments failed, heavenly ones should be employed. *He shall send his angel,* probably meaning the Angel of the Covenant, of whom see chap. xv. 7.

9. *Put his hand under the thigh of Abraham.* When we put the circumstances mentioned in this and the third verse together, we shall find that they fully express the ancient method of binding by oath in such transactions as had a religious tendency. (1) The rite or ceremony used on the occasion: the person binding himself put his hand under the thigh of the person to whom he was to be bound; i.e., he put his hand on the part that bore the mark of circumcision, the sign of God's covenant. (2) The form of the oath itself: the person swore by Jehovah, the God of heaven and the God of the earth. Three essential attributes of God are here mentioned: (1) His self-existence and eternity in the name *Jehovah.* (2) His dominion of glory and blessedness in the kingdom of *Heaven.* (3) His providence and bounty in the *earth.* The meaning of the oath seems to be this: "As God is unchangeable in His nature and purposes, so shall I be in this engagement, under the penalty of forfeiting all expectation of temporal prosperity, the benefits of the mystical covenant, and future glory."

10. *Took ten camels.* It appears that Abraham had left the whole management of this business to the discretion of his servant, to take with him what retinue and what dowry he pleased; for it is added, *All the goods of his master were in his hand;* and in those times it was customary to give a dowry for a wife, and not to receive one with her.

11. *He made his camels to kneel down.* To rest themselves, or lie down.

15. *Behold, Rebekah came out.* How admirably had the providence of God adapted every circumstance to the necessity of the case, and so as in the most punctual manner to answer the prayer which His servant had offered up!

19. *I will draw water for thy camels also.* Had Rebekah done no more than Eliezer had prayed for, we might have supposed that she acted not as a free agent, but was impelled to it by the absolutely controlling power of God; but as she exceeds all that was requested, we see that it sprang from her native benevolence, and sets her conduct in the most amiable point of view.

21. *The man wondering at her.* And he was so lost in wonder and astonishment at her simplicity, innocence, and benevolence that he permitted this delicate female to draw water for ten camels, without ever attempting to afford her any kind of assistance! I know not which to admire most, the benevolence and condescension of Rebekah, or the cold and apparently stupid indifference of the servant of Abraham. Surely they are both of an uncommon cast.

22. *The man took a golden earring.* That this could not be an *earring* is very probable from its being in the singular number. The margin calls it a "jewel for the forehead"; but it most likely means a jewel for the nose, or nose ring, which is in universal use through all parts of Arabia and Persia, particularly among young women. They are generally worn in the left nostril. *Half a shekel.* For the weight of a shekel, see chap. xx. 16.

26. *Bowed down his head, and worshipped.* Two acts of adoration are mentioned here: (1) bowing the head; and (2) prostration upon the earth.

27. *The Lord led me.* By desire of his master he went out on this journey; and as he acknowledged God in all his ways, the Lord directed all his steps.

28. *Her mother's house.* Some have conjectured from this that her father, Bethuel, was dead; and the person called Bethuel, verse 50, was a younger brother. This is possible, but the mother's house might be mentioned were even the father alive; for in Asiatic countries the women have apartments entirely separate from those of the men, in which their little children and grown-up daughters reside with them. This was probably the case here, though it is very likely that Bethuel was dead, as the whole business appears to be conducted by Rebekah's brothers.

31. *Thou blessed of the Lord.* Probably a usual mode of wishing prosperity, as he that is blessed of the Lord is worthy of all respect.

32. *Provender for the camels.* These were the first objects of his care; for a good man is merciful to his beast. *Water to wash his feet.* Thus it appears that he had servants with him; and as the fatigues of the journey must have fallen as heavily upon them as upon himself, so we find no distinction made, but water is provided to wash their feet also.

33. *I will not eat, until I have told.* Here is a servant who had his master's interest more at heart than his own. He refuses to take even necessary refreshment till he knows whether he is likely to accomplish the object of his journey. Did not our blessed Lord allude to the conduct of Abraham's servant, John iv. 34: "My meat is to do the will of him that sent me, and to finish his work"?

36. *Unto him hath he given all that he hath.* He has made Isaac his sole heir. These things appear to be spoken to show the relatives of Rebekah that his master's son was a proper match for her; for even in those primitive times there was regard to the suitableness of station and rank in life, as well as of education, in order to render a match comfortable.

42. *O Lord God of my master.* As Abraham was the friend of God, Eliezer makes use of this to give weight and consequence to his petitions.

43. *When the virgin.* Haalmah, from *alam,* to hide, cover, or conceal; a pure virgin, a woman not uncovered, and in this respect still concealed from man. The same as *bethulah,* v. 16, which, from the explanation there given, incontestably means a virgin in the proper sense of the word—a young woman, not that is covered or kept at home, but who was not uncovered in the delicate sense in which the Scripture uses this word.

45. *Before I had done speaking in mine heart.* So we find that the whole of this prayer, so circumstantially related in verses 12-14, and again in 42-44, was mental, and heard only by that God to whom it was directed. It would have been improper to use public prayer on the occasion, as his servants could have felt no particular interest in the accomplishment of his petitions because they were not concerned in them, having none of the responsibility of this mission.

49. *That I may turn to the right hand, or to the left.* That is, That I may go elsewhere and seek a proper match for the son of my master.

50. *Laban and Bethuel*. These seem both to be brothers, of whom Laban was the eldest and chief; for the opinion of Josephus appears to be very correct, namely, that Bethuel, the father, had been some time dead. See v. 28. *Bad or good*. We can neither speak for nor against; it seems to be entirely the work of God, and we cordially submit. Consult Rebekah; if she be willing, take her and go.

53. *Jewels of silver, and jewels of gold*. The word which we here translate *jewels* signifies properly "vessels" or "instruments"; and those presented by Eliezer might have been of various kinds. What he had given before, v. 22, was in token of respect; what he gave now appears to have been in the way of dowry. *Precious things*. This word is used to express exquisite fruits or delicacies, Deut. xxxiii. 13-16; precious plants or flowers, Cant. iv. 16; vii. 13. But it may mean gifts in general.

54. *And they did eat and drink*. When Eliezer had got a favorable answer, then he and his servants sat down to meat; this he had refused to do till he had told his message, v. 33.

55. *Let the damsel abide with us a few days, at the least ten*. The original is very abrupt and obscure, because we are not acquainted with the precise meaning of the form of speech which is here used; *days* or *ten* probably meaning a year or ten months, as the margin reads it, or a week or ten days. This latter is the most likely sense, as there would be no propriety after having given their consent that she should go in detaining her for a year or ten months. In matters of simple phraseology, or in those which concern peculiar customs, the Septuagint translation, especially in the Pentateuch, where it is most accurate and pure, may be considered a legitimate judge; this translation renders the words "about ten days."

58. *Wilt thou go with this man?* So it appears it was left ultimately to the choice of Rebekah whether she would accept the proposals now made to her, unless we suppose that the question meant, "Wilt thou go immediately, or stay with us a month longer?" *She said, I will go*. It fully appears to be the will of God that it should be so, and I consent. This at once determined the whole business.

59. *And her nurse*. Whose name, we learn from chap. xxxv. 8, was Deborah, and who, as a second mother, was deemed proper to accompany Rebekah. This was a measure dictated by good sense and prudence. Rebekah had other female attendants. See v. 61.

60. *Be thou the mother of thousands of millions*. "For thousands ten thousand," or "for myriads of thousands," a large family being ever considered, in ancient times, as a proof of the peculiar blessing and favor of God.

62. *And Isaac came*. Concerning this *well* see chap. xvi. 13, etc. As it appears from chap. xxv. 11 that Isaac dwelt at the well Lahai-roi, it has been conjectured that he had now come on a visit to his aged father at Beer-sheba, where he waited in expectation of his bride. *For he dwelt in the south country*. The southern part of the land of Canaan.

63. *Isaac went out to meditate*. "To bend down" the body, or the mind, or both. He was probably in deep thought, with his eyes fixed upon the ground.

65. *She took a veil*. This is the first time this word occurs, and it is of doubtful signification; but most agree to render it a veil or a cloak. The former is the most likely, as it was generally used by women in the East as a sign of chastity, modesty, and subjection.

67. *Sarah's tent*. Sarah being dead, her tent became now appropriated to the use of Rebekah. *And took Rebekah*. After what form this was done we are not told; or whether there was any form used on the occasion, more than solemnly receiving her as the person whom God had chosen to be his wife; for it appears from v. 66 that the servant told him all the especial providential circumstances which had marked his journey. The primitive form of marriage we have already seen, chap. ii. 23-24, which, it is likely, as far as form was attended to, was that which was commonly used in all the patriarchal times.

CHAPTER 25

Abraham marries Keturah, 1. Their issue, 2-4. Makes Isaac his heir, 5; but gives portions to the sons of his concubines, and sends them eastward from Isaac, to find settlements, 6. Abraham's age, 7, and death. 8. Is buried by his sons, Isaac and Ishmael, in the cave of Machpelah, 9-10. God's blessing upon Isaac, 11. The generations of Ishmael, 12-16. His age, 17, and death, 18. Of the generations of Isaac, 19, who was married in his fortieth year, 20. Rebekah, his wife, being barren, on his prayer to God she conceives, 21. She inquires of the Lord concerning her state, 22. The Lord's answer, 23. She is delivered of twins, 24. Peculiarities in the birth of her sons, Esau and Jacob, from which they had their names, 25-26. Their different manner of life, 27-28. Esau, returning from the field faint, begs pottage from his brother, 29-30. Jacob refuses to grant him any but on condition of his selling him his birthright, 31. Esau, ready to die, parts with his birthright to save his life, 32. Jacob causes him to confirm the sale with an oath, 33. He receives bread and pottage of lentiles, and departs, 34.

2. *Medan, and Midian*. Probably those who peopled that part of Arabia Petraea contiguous to the land of Moab eastward of the Dead Sea. *Shuah*. Or *Shuach*. From this man the Sacceans, near to Batania, at the extremity of Arabia Deserta, towards Syria, are supposed to have sprung. Bildad the Shuhite, one of Job's friends, is supposed to have descended from this son of Abraham.

3. *Sheba*. From whom sprang the Sabeans, who robbed Job of his cattle. *Asshurim, and Letushim, and Leummim*. We know not who these were, but as each name is plural they must have been tribes or families, and not individuals.

5. *Gave all that he had unto Isaac*. His principal flocks, and especially his right to the land of Canaan, including a confirmation to him and his posterity of whatever was contained in the promises of God.

6. *Unto the sons of the concubines*. Namely, Hagar and Keturah, Abraham gave gifts. Cattle for breed, seed to sow the land, and implements for husbandry may be what is here intended. *And sent them away . . . while he yet lived*. Lest after his death they should dispute a settlement in the Land of Promise with Isaac; therefore he very prudently sent them to procure settlements during his lifetime, that they might be under no temptation to dispute the settlement with Isaac in Canaan. From this circumstance arose that law which has prevailed in almost all countries, of giving the estates to the eldest son by a lawful wife; for though concubines, or wives of the second rank, were perfectly legitimate in those ancient times, yet their children

did not inherit, except in case of the failure of legal issue, and with the consent of the lawful wife; and it is very properly observed that it was in consequence of the consent of Leah and Rachel that the children of their slaves by Jacob had a common and equal lot with the rest. *Eastward, unto the east country.* Arabia Deserta, which was eastward of Beer-sheba, where Abraham lived.

7. *The days of the years.* There is a beauty in this expression which is not sufficiently regarded. Good men do not count their lives by *years,* but by *days,* living as if they were the creatures only of a day; having no more time that they can with any propriety call their own, and living that day in reference to eternity.

8. *Then Abraham gave up the ghost.* Highly as I value our translation for general accuracy, fidelity, and elegance, I must beg leave to dissent from this version. The original word signifies "to pant for breath, to expire, to cease from breathing, or to breathe one's last"; and here, and wherever the original word is used, the simple term "expired" would be the proper expression. In our translation this expression occurs in Gen. xxv. 8, 17; xxxv. 29; xliv. 33; Job iii. 11; x. 18; xi. 20; xiii. 19; xiv. 10; Lam. i. 19. Now as our English word *ghost,* from the Anglo-Saxon *gast,* an "inmate, inhabitant, guest" (a casual visitant), also "spirit," is now restricted among us to the latter meaning, always signifying the immortal spirit or soul of man, the guest of the body; and as giving up the spirit, ghost, or soul, is an act not proper to man, though commending it to God, in our last moments, is both an act of faith and piety; and as giving up the ghost, i.e., dismissing His spirit from His body, is attributed to Jesus Christ, to whom alone it is proper, I therefore object against its use in every other case.

An old man. Namely, one hundred and seventy-five, the youngest of all the patriarchs; *and full of years.* The word *years* is not in the text; but as our translators saw that some word was necessary to fill up the text, they added this in italics. It is probable that the true word is "days," as in Gen. xxxv. 29; and this reading is found in the Samaritan text, Septuagint, Vulgate, Syriac, Arabic, Persic, and Chaldee. On these authorities it might be safely admitted into the text.

It was the opinion of Aristotle that a man should depart from life as he should rise from a banquet. Thus Abraham died "full of days," and satisfied with life, but in a widely different spirit from that recommended by the above writers—he left life with a hope full of immortality, which they could never boast; for he saw the day of Christ, and was glad; and his hope was crowned, for here it is expressly said, "He was gathered to his fathers"; surely not to the bodies of his sleeping ancestors, who were buried in Chaldea and not in Canaan, nor with his fathers in any sense, for he was deposited in the cave where his wife alone slept; but he was gathered to the "spirits of just men made perfect, and to the Church of the firstborn, whose names are written in heaven," Heb. xii. 23.

9. *His sons Isaac and Ishmael buried him.* Though Ishmael and his mother had been expelled from Abraham's family on the account of Isaac, yet, as he was under the same obliga-

tion to a most loving, affectionate father as his brother, Isaac, if any personal feuds remained, they agreed to bury them on this occasion, that both might dutifully join in doing the last offices to a parent who was an honor to them and to human nature; and, considering the rejection of Ishmael from the inheritance, this transaction shows his character in an amiable point of view; for though he was "a wild man" (see chap. xvi. 12), yet this appellation appears to be more characteristic of his habits of life than of his disposition.

11. *God blessed his son Isaac.* The peculiar blessings and influences by which Abraham had been distinguished now rested upon Isaac; but how little do we hear in him of the work of faith, the patience of hope, and the labor of love!

12. *These are the generations of Ishmael.* The object of the inspired writer seems to be to show how the promises of God were fulfilled to both the branches of Abraham's family. Isaac has been already referred to; God blessed him according to the promise. He had also promised to multiply Ishmael, and an account of his generation is introduced to show how exactly the promise had also been fulfilled to him.

13. *Nebajoth*—from whom came the Nabatheans, whose capital was Petra.

14. *Mishma,* and *Dumah,* and *Massa*—These three names have passed into a proverb among the Hebrews, because of their signification. *Mishma* signified "hearing"; *Dumah,* "silence"; and *Massa,* "patience." Hence, "Hear much, say little, and bear much."

15. *Hadar*—This name should be read "Hadad" as in 1 Chron. i. 30. This reading is supported by more than three hundred manuscripts, versions, and printed editions. *Tema*—Supposed to be a place in Arabia Deserta, the same of which Job speaks, chap. vi. 19. *Jetur*—From whom came the Itureans, who occupied a small tract of country beyond Jordan, which was afterwards possessed by the half-tribe of Manasseh. *Naphish*—These are evidently the same people mentioned in 1 Chron. v. 19, who, with the Itureans and the people of Nadab, assisted the Hagarenes against the Israelites, but were overcome by the two tribes of Reuben and Gad, and the half-tribe of Manasseh. *Kedemah*—Probably the descendants of this person dwelt at *Kedemoth,* a place mentioned in Deut. ii. 26.

16. *These are their names*—by which their descendants were called. *Their towns*—places of encampment in the wilderness, such as have been used by the Arabs from the remotest times. *Their castles,* "their towers," probably mountaintops, fortified rocks, and fastnesses of various kinds in woods and hilly countries.

18. *They dwelt from Havilah unto Shur.* The descendants of Ishmael possessed all that country which extends from east to west, from *Havilah* on the Euphrates, near its junction with the Tigris, to the desert of *Shur* eastward of Egypt, and which extends along the isthmus of Suez. *He died in the presence of all his brethren.* The original will not well bear this translation. In v. 17 it is said, "He gave up the ghost and died; and was gathered unto his people." Then follows the account of the district occupied by the Ishmaelites, at the conclusion of which it is added, "It [the lot or district] fell [or

was divided] to him in the presence of all his brethren"; and this was exactly agreeable to the promise of God, chap. xvi. 12, "He shall dwell in the presence of all his brethren"; and to show that this promise had been strictly fulfilled, it is here remarked that his lot or inheritance was assigned him by divine providence, contiguous to that of the other branches of the family. The same word, *naphal*, is used, Josh. xxiii. 4, for "to divide by lot."

19. *These are the generations of Isaac.* This is the history of Issac and his family.

21. *Isaac intreated the Lord for his wife.* Isaac and Rebekah had now lived nineteen years together without having a child; for he was forty years old when he married Rebekah, v. 20, and he was threescore years of age when Jacob and Esau were born, v. 26.

22. *The children struggled together.* They dashed against or bruised each other." There was a violent agitation, so that the mother was apprehensive both of her own and her children's safety; and, supposing this was an uncommon case, she went to inquire of the Lord, as the good women in the present day would go to consult a surgeon or physician. It appears she was in considerable perplexity, hence that imperfect speech, "If so, why am I thus?" the simple meaning of which is probably this: If I must suffer such things, why did I ever wish to have a child?

23. *Two nations are in thy womb.* "We have," says Bishop Newton, "in the prophecies delivered respecting the sons of Isaac, ample proof that these prophecies were not meant so much of single persons as of whole nations descended from them; for what was predicted concerning Esau and Jacob was not verified in themselves, but in their posterity. The Edomites were the offspring of Esau, the Israelites were of Jacob; and who but the Author and Giver of life could foresee that two children in the womb would multiply into two nations? The Edomites and Israelites have been from the beginning two such different people in their manners, customs, and religion, as to be at perpetual variance among themselves. The children struggled together in the womb, which was an omen of their future disagreement." *The one people shall be stronger than the other people.* The same author continues to observe that "for some time the family of Esau was the more powerful of the two; but David and his captains made an entire conquest of the Edomites, slew several thousands of them, and compelled the rest to become tributaries.

24. *There were twins.* Thomim, from which comes "Thomas," properly interpreted by the word *Didymus*, which signifies a "twin."

25. *Red, all over like an hairy garment.* This simply means that he was covered all over with red hair or down; and that this must be intended here is sufficiently evident from another part of his history, where Rebekah, in order to make her favorite son, Jacob, pass for his brother, Esau, was obliged to take the skins of kids, and put them upon his hands and on the smooth part of his neck.

26. *His name was called Jacob.* Yaacob, from akab, to "defraud, deceive, to supplant," i.e., to overthrow a person by tripping up his heels. Hence this name was given to Jacob, because it

was found he had laid hold on his brother's heel, which was emblematical of his supplanting Esau and defrauding him of his birthright.

27. *A man of the field.* One who supported himself and family by hunting and by agriculture. *Jacob was a plain man. Ish tam,* "a perfect or upright man"; *dwelling in tents—subsisting* by breeding and tending cattle, which was considered in those early times the most perfect employment; and in this sense the word *tam* should be here understood, as in its moral meaning it certainly could not be applied to Jacob till after his name was changed, after which time only his character stands fair and unblemished. See chap. xxxii. 26-30.

28. *Isaac loved Esau . . . but Rebekah loved Jacob.* This is an early proof of unwarrantable parental attachment to one child in preference to another. And in consequence of this the interests of the family were divided and the house set in opposition to itself. The fruits of this unreasonable and foolish attachment were afterwards seen in a long catalogue of both natural and moral evils among the descendants of both families.

29. *Sod pottage. Yazed nazid,* "he boiled a boiling"; and this we are informed, v. 34, was of "lentiles," a sort of pulse.

30. *I am faint.* He had been either hunting or laboring in the field, and was now returning for the purpose of getting some food, but had been so exhausted that his strength utterly failed before he had time to make the necessary preparations.

31. *Sell me this day thy birthright.* What the *bechorah* or birthright was has greatly divided both ancient and modern commentators. It is generally supposed that the following rights were attached to the primogeniture: (1) Authority and superiority over the rest of the family. (2) A double portion of the paternal inheritance. (3) The peculiar benediction of the father. (4) The priesthood, previous to its establishment in the family of Aaron.

34. *Pottage of lentiles.* See. v. 29. *Thus Esau despised his birthright.* On this account the apostle, Heb. xii. 16, calls Esau a "profane person," because he had by this act alienated from himself and family those spiritual offices connected with the rights of primogeniture. Jacob verified his right to the name of "supplanter," a name which in its first imposition appears to have had no other object in view than the circumstance of his catching his brother by the heel; but all his subsequent conduct proved that it was truly descriptive of the qualities of his mind, as his whole life, till the time his name was changed (and then he had a change of nature), was a tissue of cunning and deception, the principles of which had been very early instilled in him by a mother whose regard for truth and righteousness appears to have been very superficial. See on chap. xxvii.

CHAPTER 26

A famine in the land obliges Isaac to leave Beer-sheba and go to Gerar, 1. God appears to him, and warns him not to go to Egypt, 2. Renews the promises to him which He had made to his father, Abraham, 3-5. Isaac dwells at Gerar, 6. Being questioned concerning Rebekah, and fearing to lose his life on her account, he calls her his sister, 7. Abimelech, the king, discovers, by certain familiarities which he had noticed between Isaac and Rebekah, that she was his wife, 8. Calls Isaac and reproaches him for his insincerity, 9-10. He gives a strict command to all his people not to molest either Isaac or his wife, 11. Isaac applies himself to husbandry and breeding of cattle, and has a great increase, 12-14. Is envied by the Philistines, who stop up the wells he had digged, 15. Is desired by Abimelech to remove, 16. He obeys, and fixes his tent in the valley of Gerar, 17. Opens the wells dug in the days of Abraham, which the Philistines had stopped up, 18. Digs the well Ezek, 19-20; and the well Sitnah, 21; and the well Rehoboth, 22. Returns to Beer-sheba, 23. God appears to him, and renews His promises, 24. He builds an altar there, pitches his tent, and digs a well, 25. Abimelech, Ahuzzath, and Phichol visit him, 26. Isaac accuses them of unkindness, 27. They beg him to make a covenant with them, 28-29. He makes them a feast, and they bind themselves to each other by an oath, 30-31. The well dug by Isaac's servants (v. 25) called Shebah, 32-33. Esau, at forty years of age, marries two wives of the Hittites, 34, at which Isaac and Rebekah are grieved, 35.

1. *There was a famine.* When this happened we cannot tell; it appears to have been after the death of Abraham. Concerning the first famine, see chap. xii. 10. *Abimelech.* As we know not the time when the famine happened, so we cannot tell whether this was the same Abimelech, Phichol, etc., which are mentioned chap. xx. 1, etc., or the sons or other descendants of these persons.

2. *Go not down into Egypt.* As Abraham had taken refuge in that country, it is probable that Isaac was preparing to go thither also; and God, foreseeing that he would there meet with trials which might prove fatal to his peace or to his piety, warns him not to fulfil his intention.

3. *Sojourn in this land.* In Gerar, whither he had gone, v. 1, and where we find he settled, v. 6, though the land of Canaan in general might be here intended.

4. *I will make thy seed . . . as the stars of heaven.* A promise often repeated to Abraham, and which has been most amply fulfilled in both its literal and spiritual sense.

5. *Abraham obeyed my voice.* "My word." *My charge.* Mishmarti, from *shamar*; he kept, observed, the "ordinances" or "appointments" of God. These were always of two kinds: (1) such as tended to promote moral improvement, the increase of piety; and (2) such as were typical of the promised Seed, and the salvation which was to come by Him.

7. *He said, She is my sister.* It is very strange that in the same place, and in similar circumstances, Isaac should have denied his wife, precisely as his father had done before him! Isaac could not say of Rebekah, as Abraham had done of Sarah, "She is my sister." In the case of Abraham this was literally true; it was not so in the case of Isaac, for Rebekah was only his cousin.

8. *Isaac was sporting with Rebekah his wife.* Whatever may be the precise meaning of the word, it evidently implies that there were liberties taken and freedom used on the occasion which were not lawful but between man and wife.

10. *Thou shouldest have brought guiltiness upon us.* It is likely that Abimelech might have had some knowledge of God's intentions concerning the family of Abraham, and that it must be kept free from all impure and alien mixtures; and that consequently, had he or any of his people taken Rebekah, the divine judgment might have fallen upon the land. Abimelech was a good and holy man; and he appears to have considered adultery as a grievous and destructive crime.

11. *He that toucheth.* He who injures Isaac or defiles Rebekah shall certainly die for it. Death was the punishment for adultery among the Canaanites, Philistines, and Hebrews. See chap. xxxviii. 24.

12. *Isaac sowed in that land.* Being now perfectly free from the fear of evil, he betakes himself to agricultural and pastoral pursuits, in which he has the special blessing of God, so that his property becomes greatly increased. *An hundredfold.* Literally, "A hundredfold of barley;" and so the Septuagint. Perhaps such a crop of this grain was a rare occurrence in Gerar. The words, however, may be taken in a general way, as signifying a very great increase; so they are used by our Lord in the parable of the sower.

13. *The man waxed great.* There is a strange and observable recurrence of the same term in the original: "And the man was great; and he went, going on, and was great, until that he was exceeding great." How simple is this language and yet how forcible!

14. *He had possession of flocks.* He who blessed him in the increase of his fields blessed him also in the increase of his flocks; and as he had extensive possessions, so he must have many hands to manage such concerns. Therefore it is added, *he had . . . great store of servants*—he had many domestics, some born in his house, and others purchased by his money.

15. *For all the wells . . . the Philistines had stopped them.* In such countries a good well was a great acquisition; and hence in predatory wars it was usual for either party to fill the wells with earth or sand, in order to distress the enemy. The filling up the wells in this case was a most unprincipled transaction, as they had pledged themselves to Abraham, by a solemn oath, not to injure each other in this or any other respect. See chap. xxi. 25-31.

16. *Go from us; for thou art much mightier than we.* This is the first instance on record of what was termed among the Greeks "ostracism"; i.e., the banishment of a person from the state, of whose power, influence, or riches, the people were jealous. The Philistines appear to have been jealous of Isaac's growing prosperity, and to have considered it, not as a due reward of his industry and holiness, but as their individual loss, as though his gain was at their expense; therefore they resolved to drive him out, and take his well-cultivated ground to themselves, and compelled Abimelech to dismiss him, who gave this reason for it, "Thou hast obtained much wealth among us," and my people are envious of thee.

18. *In the days of Abraham.* Instead of *bimey*, "in the days," Houbigant contends we should read *abdey*, "servants." Isaac digged again the wells which the servants of Abraham, his father, had digged. This reading is supported by the Samaritan, Septuagint, Syriac, and Vulgate; and it is probably the true one.

19. *A well of springing water.* "A well of living waters." This is the oriental phrase for a spring, and this is its meaning in both the Old and New Testaments: Lev. xiv. 5, 50; xv. 30; Num. xix. 17; Cant. iv. 15. See also John iv. 10-14; vii. 38; Rev. xxi. 6; xxii. 1. And by these scriptures we find that an unfailing spring was an emblem of the graces and influences of the Spirit of God.

21. *They digged another well.* Never did any man more implicitly follow the divine command, "Resist not evil," than Isaac; whenever he found that his work was likely to be a subject of strife and contention, he gave place, and rather chose to suffer wrong than to have his own peace of mind disturbed. Thus he overcame evil with good.

24. *The Lord appeared unto him.* He needed special encouragement when insulted and outraged by the Philistines.

25. *Builded an altar there.* That he might have a place for God's worship, as well as a place for himself and family to dwell in. *And called upon the name of the Lord.* And invoked in the name of Jehovah. See on chap. xii. 8; xiii. 15.

26. *Abimelech went to him.* When a man's ways please God, He makes even his enemies to be at peace with him; so Isaac experienced on this occasion. Whether this was the same Abimelech and Phichol mentioned in chap. xxi. 22 we cannot tell; it is possible both might have been now alive, provided we suppose them young in the days of Abraham; but it is more likely that *Abimelech* was a general name of the Gerarite kings, and that *Phichol* was a name of office.

27. *Seeing ye hate me.* He was justified in thinking thus, because if they did not injure him, they had connived at their servants doing it.

28. *Let there be now an oath betwixt us.* Let us make a covenant by which we shall be mutually bound and let it be ratified in the most solemn manner.

30. *He made them a feast.* Probably on the sacrifice that was offered on the occasion of making this covenant. This was a common custom.

31. *They rose up betimes.* Early rising was general among the primitive inhabitants of the world, and this was one cause which contributed greatly to their health and longevity.

33. *He called it Shebah.* This was probably the same well which was called Beer-sheba in the time of Abraham, which the Philistines had filled up, and which the servants of Isaac had reopened. *The name of the city is Beer-sheba.* This name was given to it a hundred years before this time; but as the well from which it had this name originally was closed up by the Philistines, probably the name of the place was abolished with the well; when therefore Isaac reopened the well, he restored the ancient name of the place.

34. *He took to wife . . . the daughter.* It is very likely that the wives taken by Esau were daughters of chiefs among the Hittites, and by this union he sought to increase and strengthen his secular power and influence.

35. *Which were a grief of mind.* Not the marriage, though that was improper, but the persons; they, by their perverse and evil ways, brought bitterness into the hearts of Isaac and Rebekah.

CHAPTER 27

Isaac, grown old and feeble and apprehending the approach of death, desires his son Esau to provide some savory meat for him, that having eaten of it he might convey to him the blessing connected with the right of primogeniture, 1-4. Rebekah, hearing of it, relates the matter to Jacob, and directs him how to personate his brother, and by deceiving his father, obtain the blessing, 5-10. Jacob hesitates, 11-12; but being counselled and encouraged by his mother, he at last consents to use the means she prescribes, 13-14. Rebekah disguises Jacob, and sends him to personate his brother, 15-17. Jacob comes to his father, and professes himself to be Esau, 18-19. Isaac doubts, questions, and examines him closely, but does not discover the deception, 20-24. He eats of the savory meat, and confers the blessing upon Jacob, 25-27. In what the blessing consisted, 28-29. Esau arrives from the field with the meat he had gone to provide, and presents himself before his father, 30-31. Isaac discovers the fraud of Jacob, and is much affected, 32-33. Esau is greatly distressed on hearing that the blessing had been received by another, 34. Isaac accuses Jacob of deceit, 35. Esau expostulates, and prays for a blessing, 36. Isaac describes the blessing which he has already conveyed, 37. Esau weeps and earnestly implores a blessing, 38. Isaac pronounces a blessing on Esau, and prophesies that his posterity should, in process of time, cease to be tributary to the posterity of Jacob, 39-40. Esau purposes to kill his brother, 41. Rebekah hears of it, and counsels Jacob to take refuge with her brother, Laban, in Padan-aram, 42-45. She professes to be greatly alarmed, lest Jacob should take any of the Canaanites to wife, 46.

1. *Isaac was old.* It is conjectured, on good grounds, that Isaac was now about one hundred and seventeen years of age, and Jacob about fifty-seven; though the commonly received opinion makes Isaac one hundred and thirty-seven, and Jacob seventy-seven. *And his eyes were dim.* This was probably the effect of that affliction, of what kind we know not, under which Isaac now labored; and from which, as well as from the affliction, he probably recovered, as it is certain he lived forty if not forty-three years after this time, for he lived till the return of Jacob from Padan-aram; chap. xxxv. 27-29.

2. *I know not the day of my death.* From his present weakness he had reason to suppose that his death could not be at any great distance, and therefore would leave no act undone which he believed it his duty to perform. He who lives not in reference to eternity lives not at all.

3. *Thy weapons.* The original word *keley* signifies "vessels" and "instruments" of any kind; and is probably used here for a hunting spear, javelin, sword, etc. *Quiver. Teli,* from *talah,* to "hang or suspend."

4. *Savoury meat. Matammim,* from *taam,* to "taste or relish." *That I may eat.* The blessing which Isaac was to confer on his son was a species of divine right, and must be communicated with appropriate ceremonies. As eating and drinking were used among the Asiatics on almost all religious occasions, and especially in making and confirming covenants, it is reasonable to suppose that something of this kind was essentially necessary on this occasion and that Isaac could not convey the right till he had eaten of the meat provided for the purpose by him who was to receive the blessing. As Isaac was now old and in a feeble and languishing condition, it was necessary that the flesh used on this occasion should be prepared so as to invite the appetite, that a sufficiency of it might be taken to revive and recruit his drooping strength, that he might be the better able to go through the whole of this ceremony.

5. *And Rebekah heard.* And was determined, if possible, to frustrate the design of Isaac, and procure the blessing for her favorite son. Some pretend that she received a divine inspiration to the purpose; but if she had she needed not to have recourse to deceit to help forward the accomplishment. Isaac, on being informed, would have had too much piety not to prefer the will of his Maker to his own partiality for his eldest son; but Rebekah had nothing of the

kind to plead, and therefore had recourse to the most exceptionable means to accomplish her ends.

12. *I shall bring a curse upon me.* For even in those early times the spirit of that law was understood, Deut. xxvii. 18: "Cursed be he that maketh the blind to wander out of the way"; and Jacob seems to have possessed at this time a more tender conscience than his mother.

13. *Upon me be thy curse, my son.* What a dreadful responsibility did this woman take upon her at this time!

19. *I am Esau thy firstborn.* Here are many palpable falsehoods, and such as should neither be imitated nor excused.

23. *And he discerned him not, because his hands were hairy.* From this circumstance we may learn that Isaac's sense of feeling was much impaired by his present malady. When he could not discern the skin of a kid from the flesh of his son we see that he was, through his infirmity, in a fit state to be imposed on by the deceit of his wife and the cunning of his younger son.

27. *The smell of my son is as the smell of field.* The smell of these garments, the goodly raiment which had been laid up in the house, was probably occasioned by some aromatic herbs, which we may naturally suppose were laid up with the clothes—a custom which prevails in many countries to the present day.

29. *Let people serve thee.* It appears that Jacob was, on the whole, a man of more religion and believed the divine promises more than Esau. The posterity of Jacob likewise preserved the true religion and the worship of one God, while the Edomites were sunk in idolatry; and of the seed of Jacob was born at last the Saviour of the world. This was the peculiar privilege and advantage of Jacob, to be the happy instrument of conveying these blessings to all nations. This was his greatest superiority over Esau; and in this sense St. Paul understood and applied the prophecy: "The elder shall serve the younger," Rom. ix. 12.

33. *And Isaac trembled.* The marginal reading is very literal and proper, "And Isaac trembled with a great trembling greatly." And this shows the deep concern he felt for his own deception, and the iniquity of the means by which it had been brought about. Though Isaac must have heard of that which God had spoken to Rebekah, "The elder shall serve the younger," and could never have wished to reverse this divine purpose; yet he might certainly think that the spiritual blessing might be conveyed to Esau, and by him to all the nations of the earth, notwithstanding the superiority of secular dominion on the other side. *Yea, and he shall be blessed.* From what is said in this verse, collated with Heb. xii. 17, we see how binding the conveyance of the birthright was when communicated with the rites already mentioned. When Isaac found that he had been deceived by Jacob, he certainly would have reversed the blessing if he could; but as it had been conveyed in the sacramental way, this was impossible. "I have blessed him," says he, "yea, and he must, or will, be blessed." Hence it is said by the apostle, Esau "found no place of repentance"—no place for change of mind or purpose in his father—"though he sought it carefully with tears." The father could not reverse it because the grant had already been made and confirmed. But this had nothing to do with the final salvation of poor outwitted Esau, nor indeed with that of his unnatural brother.

35. *Hath taken away thy blessing.* This blessing, which was a different thing from the birthright, seems to consist of two parts: (1) The dominion, generally and finally, over the other part of the family; and (2) Being the progenitor of the Messiah.

36. *Is not he rightly named Jacob?* See on chap. xxv. 26. *He took away my birthright.* So he might say with considerable propriety; for though he sold it to Jacob, yet as Jacob had taken advantage of his perishing situation, he considered the act as a species of robbery.

40. *By thy sword shalt thou live.* This does not absolutely mean that the Edomites should have constant wars; but that they should be of a fierce and warlike disposition, gaining their sustenance by hunting, and by predatory excursions upon the possessions of others. *And when thou shalt have the dominion.* It is here foretold that there was to be a time when the elder was to have dominion and shake off the yoke of the younger. The word *tarid*, which we translate *have dominion*, is of rather doubtful meaning, as it may be deduced from three different roots: *yarad*, to "descend, to be brought down or brought low"; *radah*, to "obtain rule or have dominion"; and *rud*, to "complain"—meaning either that when reduced very low God would magnify His power in their behalf, and deliver them from the yoke of their brethren; or when they should be increased so as to venture to set up a king over them, or when they mourned for their transgressions, God would turn their captivity.

41. *The days of mourning for my father are at hand.* Such was the state of Isaac's health at that time, though he lived more than forty years afterwards, that his death was expected by all; and Esau thought that would be a favorable time for him to avenge himself on his brother, Jacob, as, according to the custom of the times, the sons were always present at the burial of the father. Ishmael came from his own country to assist Isaac to bury Abraham; and both Jacob and Esau assisted in burying their father, Isaac, but the enmity between them had happily subsided long before that time.

42. *Doth comfort himself, purposing to kill thee.* There is no doubt that Esau, in his hatred to his brother, felt himself pleased with the thought that he should soon have the opportunity of avenging his wrongs.

44. *Tarry with him a few days.* It was probably forty years before he returned, and it is likely Rebekah saw him no more; for it is the general opinion of the Jewish rabbins that she died before Jacob's return from Padan-aram, whether the period of his stay be considered twenty or forty years.

45. *Why should I be deprived also of you both?* If Esau should kill Jacob, then the nearest akin to Jacob, who was by the patriarchial law, Gen. ix. 6, the avenger of blood, would kill Esau; and both these deaths might possibly take place in the same day. This appears to be the meaning of Rebekah.

46. *I am weary of my life.* It is very likely that Rebekah kept many of the circumstances related above from the knowledge of Isaac; but as Jacob could not go to Padan-aram without his knowledge, she appears here quite in her own character, framing an excuse for his departure and concealing the true cause. Abraham had been solicitous to get a wife for his son Isaac from a branch of his own family; hence she was brought from Syria. She is now afraid, or pretends to be afraid, that her son Jacob will marry among the Hittites, as Esau had done; and therefore makes this to Isaac the ostensible reason why Jacob should immediately go to Padan-aram, that he might get a wife there. Isaac, not knowing the true cause of sending him away, readily falls in with Rebekah's proposal, and immediately calls Jacob, gives him suitable directions and his blessing, and sends him away. This view of the subject makes all consistent and natural; and we see at once the reason of the abrupt speech contained in this verse, which should be placed at the beginning of the following chapter.

CHAPTER 28

Isaac directs Jacob to take a wife from the family of Laban, 1-2; blesses and sends him away, 3-4. Jacob begins his journey, 5. Esau, perceiving that the daughters of Canaan were not pleasing to his parents, and that Jacob obeyed them in going to get a wife of his own kindred, 6-8, went and took to wife Mahalath, the daughter of Ishmael, his father's brother, 9. Jacob, in his journey towards Haran, came to a certain place (Luz, v. 19), where he lodged all night, 10-11. He sees in a dream a ladder reaching from earth to heaven, on which he beholds the angels of God ascending and descending, 12. God appears above this ladder, and renews those promises which He had made to Abraham and to Isaac, 13-14; promises Jacob personal protection and a safe return to his own country, 15. Jacob awakes, and makes reflections upon his dream, 16-17. Sets up one of the stones he had for his pillow, and pours oil on it, and calls the place Beth-el, 18-19. Makes a vow that if God will preserve him in his journey, and bring him back in safety, the stone shall be God's house, and that he will give Him the tenth of all that he should have, 20-22.

1. *And Isaac called Jacob.* See the note on v. 46 of the preceding chapter. *And blessed him.* Now voluntarily and cheerfully confirmed to him the blessing, which he had before obtained through subtlety.

2. *Go to Padan-aram.* This mission, in its spirit and design, is nearly the same as that in chap. xxiv, which see. There have been several ingenious conjectures concerning the retinue which Jacob had, or might have had, for his journey; and by some he has been supposed to have been well attended. Of this nothing is mentioned here, and the reverse seems to be intimated elsewhere. It appears, from v. 11, that he lodged in the open air, with a stone for his pillow; and from chap. xxxii. 10, that he went on foot with his staff in his hand. He no doubt took provisions with him sufficient to carry him to the nearest encampment or village on the way, where he would naturally recruit his bread and water to carry him to the next stage, and so on. The oil that he poured on the pillar might be a little of that which he had brought for his own use.

3. *That thou mayest be a multitude of people.* There is something very remarkable in the original words: they signify literally "for an assembly, congregation, or church of peoples"; referring no doubt to the Jewish church in the wilderness, but more particularly to the Christian Church, composed of every kindred, and nation, and people, and tongue. This is one essential part of the blessing of Abraham.

4. *Give thee the blessing of Abraham.* May He confirm the inheritance with all its attendant blessings to thee, to the exclusion of Esau; as He did to me, to the exclusion of Ishmael. But, according to St. Paul, much more than this is certainly intended here. For it appears, from Gal. iii. 6-14, that the blessing of Abraham, which is to come upon the Gentiles through Jesus Christ, comprises the whole doctrine of justification by faith, and its attendant privileges, namely, redemption from the curse of the law, remission of sins, and the promise of the Holy Spirit, including the constitution and establishment of the Christian Church.

5. *Bethuel the Syrian.* Literally the "Aramean," so called, not because he was of the race of Aram, the son of Shem, but because he dwelt in that country which had been formerly possessed by the descendants of Aram.

9. *Then went Esau unto Ishmael.* Those who are apt to take everything by the wrong handle, and who think it was utterly impossible for Esau to do any right action, have classed his taking a daughter of Ishmael among his crimes, whereas there is nothing more plain than that he did this with a sincere desire to obey and please his parents. Having heard the pious advice which Isaac gave to Jacob, he therefore went and took a wife from the family of his grandfather Abraham, as Jacob was desired to do out of the family of his maternal uncle, Laban. *Mahalath,* whom he took to wife, stood in the same degree of relationship to Isaac, his father, as Rachel did to his mother, Rebekah. Esau married his father's niece; Jacob married his mother's niece. It was therefore most obviously to please his parents that Esau took this additional wife.

11. *A certain place, and tarried there.* From v. 19 we find this *certain place* was Luz, or some part of its vicinity. Jacob had probably intended to reach Luz; but the sun being set, and night coming on, he either could not reach the city or he might suspect the inhabitants, and rather prefer the open field. Or the gates might be shut by the time he reached it, which would prevent his admission. *He took of the stones.* He took one of the stones that were in that place; from v. 18 we find it was one stone only which he had for his pillow. Luz was about forty-eight miles distant from Beer-sheba, too great a journey for one day through what we may conceive very unready roads.

12. *He dreamed, and behold a ladder.* A multitude of fanciful things have been spoken of Jacob's vision of the ladder, and its signification. It might have several designs, as God chooses to accomplish the greatest number of ends by the fewest and simplest means possible. (1) It is very likely that its primary design was to point out the providence of God. (2) It might be intended also to point out the intercourse between heaven and earth, and the connection of both worlds by the means of angelic ministry. (3) It was probably a type of Christ, in whom both worlds meet, and in whom the divine and human nature are conjoined. The ladder was set up on the earth, and the top of it reached to heaven; for God was manifested in the flesh, and in Him dwelt all the fulness of the Godhead bodily. Nothing could be a more expres-

sive emblem of the Incarnation and its effects; Jesus Christ is the grand connecting Medium between heaven and earth, and between God and man. By Him, God comes down to man; through Him, man ascends to God. It appears that our Lord applies the vision in this way himself: First, in that remarkable speech to Nathanael, "Hereafter ye shall see heaven open, and the angels of God ascending and descending upon the Son of man," John i. 51. Secondly, in His speech to Thomas, John xiv. 6: "I am the way, the truth, and the life: no man cometh unto the Father, but by me."

13. *I am the Lord God of Abraham.* Here God confirms to him the blessing of Abraham, for which Isaac had prayed, vv. 3-4.

14. *Thy seed shall be as the dust.* The people that shall descend from thee shall be extremely numerous; *and in thee and in thy seed*—the Lord Jesus descending from thee, according to the flesh, *shall all the families of the earth*—not only all of thy race, but all the other families or tribes of mankind which have not proceeded from any branch of the Abrahamic family, *be blessed;* for Jesus Christ by the grace of God tasted death for every man, Heb. ii. 9.

16. *The Lord is in this place; and I knew it not.* That is, God has made this place His peculiar residence; it is a place in which He meets with and reveals himself to His followers.

18. *And Jacob . . . took the stone . . . and set it up for a pillar.* He placed the stone in an erect posture, that it might stand as a monument of the extraordinary vision which he had in this place; *and [he] poured oil upon . . . it,* thereby consecrating it to God, so that it might be considered an altar on which libations might be poured, and sacrifices offered unto God.

There is a foolish tradition that the stone set up by Jacob was afterwards brought to Jerusalem, from which, after a long lapse of time, it was brought to Spain, from Spain to Ireland, from Ireland to Scotland, and on it the kings of Scotland sat to be crowned. Edward I had it brought to Westminster; and there this stone, called Jacob's pillar, and Jacob's pillow, is now placed under the chair on which the king sits when crowned!

19. *He called the name of that place Beth-el.* That is, the "house of God"; for in consequence of his having anointed the stone, and thus consecrated it to God, he considered it as becoming henceforth His pecular residence. This word should be always pronounced as two distinct syllables, each strongly accented, Beth-el.

20. *Vowed a vow.* A vow is a solemn, holy promise, by which a man bound himself to do certain things in a particular way, time, etc., and for power to accomplish which he depended on God; hence all vows were made with prayer.

22. *This stone . . . shall be God's house.* That is, should I be preserved to return in safety, I shall worship God in this place. And this purpose he fulfilled, for there he built an altar, anointed it with oil, and poured a drink offering thereon.

CHAPTER 29

Jacob proceeds on his journey, 1. Comes to a well where the flocks of his uncle Laban, as well as those of several others, were usually watered, 2-3. Inquires from the shepherds concerning Laban and his family, 4-6. While they are conversing about watering the sheep, 7-8. Rachel arrives, 9. He assists her to water her flock, 10;

makes himself known unto her, 11-12. She hastens home and communicates the tidings of Jacob's arrival to her father, 12. Laban hastens to the well, embraces Jacob, and brings him home, 13. After a month's stay, Laban proposes to give Jacob wages, 14-15. Leah and Rachel described, 16-17. Jacob proposes to serve seven years for Rachel, 18. Laban consents, 19. When the seven years are fulfilled, Jacob demands his wife, 20-21. Laban makes a marriage feast, 22; and in the evening substitutes Leah for Rachel, to whom he gives Zilpah for handmaid, 23-24. Jacob discovers the fraud and upbraids Laban, 25. He excuses himself, 26; and promises to give him Rachel for another seven years of service, 27. After abiding a week with Leah, he receives Rachel for wife, to whom Laban gives Bilhah for handmaid, 28-29. Jacob loves Rachel more than Leah, and serves seven years for her, 30. Leah being despised, the Lord makes her fruitful, while Rachel continues barren, 31. Leah bears Reuben, 32. and Simeon, 33, and Levi, 34, and Judah; after which she leaves off bearing, 35.

1. *Then Jacob went on his journey.* The original is very remarkable: "And Jacob lifted up his feet, and he travelled unto the land of the children of the east." There is a certain cheerfulness marked in the original which comports well with the state of mind into which he had been brought by the vision of the ladder and the promises of God. He now saw that, having God for his Protector, he had nothing to fear, and therefore he went on his way rejoicing. *People of the east.* The inhabitants of Mesopotamia and the whole country beyond the Euphrates are called "easterns" in the sacred writings.

2. *Three flocks of sheep.* Small cattle, such as sheep, goats, etc. The *three flocks,* if flocks and not shepherds be meant, which were lying now at the well, did not belong to Laban, but to three other chiefs; for Laban's flock was yet to come, under the care of Rachel, v. 6.

3. *All the flocks.* Instead of *hadarim,* flocks, the Samaritan reads *haroim,* "shepherds"; for which reading Houbigant strongly contends, as well in this verse as in v. 8. It is probable that the same reading was originally that of the second verse also. *And put the stone again upon the well's mouth.* It is very likely that the stone was a large one, which was necessary to prevent ill-minded individuals from either disturbing the water or filling up the well; hence a great stone was provided, which required the joint exertions of several shepherds to remove it; and hence those who arrived first waited till all the others were come up, that they might water their respective flocks in concert.

4. *My brethren, whence be ye?* The language of Laban and his family was Chaldee and not Hebrew; but from the names which Leah gave to her children we see that the two languages had many words in common, and therefore Jacob and the shepherds might understand each other with little difficulty. It is possible also that Jacob might have learned the Chaldee language from his mother, as this was his mother's tongue.

5. *Laban the son of Nahor.* Son is here put for grandson, for Laban was the son of Bethuel, the son of Nahor.

6. *Is he well? Hashalom lo?* Is there peace to him? Peace among the Hebrews signified all kinds of prosperity. Is he a prosperous man in his family and in his property? *And they said, He is well*—shalom, He prospers. *Rachel . . . cometh with the sheep.* Rachel (the ch sounded guttural) signifies a "sheep" or "ewe"; and she probably had her name from her fondness for these animals.

7. *It is yet high day.* The day is but about half run; *neither is it time that the cattle should*

be gathered together—it is surely not time yet to put them into the folds; give them, therefore, water and take them again to pasture.

8. *We cannot, until all the flocks be gathered together.* It is a rule that the stone shall not be removed till all the shepherds and the flocks which have a right to this well be gathered together; then we may water the sheep.

9. *Rachel came with her father's sheep.* So we find that young women were not kept concealed in the house till the time they were married. Nor was it beneath the dignity of the daughters of the most opulent chiefs to carry water from the well, as in the case of Rebekah; or tend sheep, as in the case of Rachel. The chief property in those times consisted in flocks: and who so proper to take care of them as those who were interested in their safety and increase? Honest labor, far from being a discredit, is an honor to both high and low.

10. *Jacob went near, and rolled the stone.* Probably the flock of Laban was the last of those which had a right to the well; that flock being now come, Jacob assisted the shepherds to roll off the stone (for it is not likely he did it by himself) and so assisted his cousin, to whom he was as yet unknown, to water her flock.

11. *Jacob kissed Rachel.* A simple and pure method by which the primitive inhabitants of the earth testified their friendship to each other. *And lifted up his voice.* It may be, in thanksgiving to God for the favor He had shown him, in conducting him thus far in peace and safety. *And wept.* From a sense of the goodness of his Heavenly Father, and his own unworthiness of the success with which he had been favored. The same expressions of kindness and pure affection are repeated on the part of Laban, v. 13.

14. *My bone and my flesh.* One of my nearest relatives.

15. *Because thou art my brother.* Though thou art my nearest relative, yet I have no right to thy services without giving thee an adequate recompense. Jacob had passed a whole month in the family of Laban, in which he had undoubtedly rendered himself of considerable service. As Laban, who was of a very saving if not covetous disposition, saw that he was to be of great use to him in his secular concerns, he wished to secure his services, and therefore asked him what wages he wished to have.

17. *Leah was tender eyed.* "Soft, delicate, lovely." I believe the word means just the reverse of the signification generally given to it. The design of the inspired writer is to compare both the sisters together, that the balance may appear to be greatly in favor of Rachel. The chief recommendation of Leah was her soft and beautiful eyes; but Rachel was "beautiful in her shape, person, mien, and gait," and "beautiful in her countenance." The words plainly signify a fine shape and fine features, all that can be considered as essential to personal beauty. Therefore Jacob loved her and was willing to become a bond servant for seven years, that he might get her to wife; for in his destitute state he could produce no dowry, and it was the custom of those times for the father to receive a portion for his daughter, and not to give one with her.

21. *My days are fulfilled.* My seven years are now completed; let me have my wife, for whom I have given this service as a dowry.

22. *Laban . . . made a feast.* Mishteh signifies a feast of "drinking." As marriage was a very solemn contract, there is much reason to believe that sacrifices were offered on the occasion, and libations poured out; and we know that on festival occasions a cup of wine was offered to every guest; and as this was drunk with particular ceremonies, the feast might derive its name from this circumstance, which was the most prominent and observable on such occasions.

23. *In the evening . . . he took Leah his daughter.* As the bride was always veiled, and the bridechamber generally dark, or nearly so, and as Leah was brought to Jacob in the evening, the imposition here practiced might easily pass undetected by Jacob till the ensuing day discovered the fraud.

24. *And Laban gave . . . Zilpah his maid.* Slaves given in this way to a daughter on her marriage were the peculiar property of the daughter; and over them the husband had neither right nor power.

26. *It must not be so done in our country.* It was an early custom to give daughters in marriage according to their seniority; and it is worthy of remark that the Hindoos have this not merely as a custom, but as a positive law; and they deem it criminal to give a younger daughter in marriage while an elder daughter remains unmarried.

27. *Fulfil her week.* The marriage feast, it appears, lasted seven days; it would not, therefore, have been proper to break off the solemnities to which all the men of the place had been invited, v. 22, and probably Laban wished to keep his fraud from the public eye; therefore he informs Jacob that, if he will fulfil the marriage week for Leah, he will give him Rachel at the end of it, on condition of his serving seven years more. To this the necessity of the case caused Jacob to agree; and thus Laban had fourteen years' service instead of seven; for it is not likely that Jacob would have served even seven days for Leah, as his affection was wholly set on Rachel, the wife of his own choice. By this stratagem Laban gained a settlement for both his daughters. What a man soweth, that shall he reap. Jacob had practiced deceit, and is now deceived; and Laban, the instrument of it, was afterwards deceived himself.

28. *And Jacob did so . . . and he gave him Rachel.* It is perfectly plain that Jacob did not serve seven years more before he got Rachel to wife; but having spent a week with Leah, and in keeping the marriage feast, he then got Rachel, and served afterwards seven years for her.

31. *The Lord saw that Leah was hated.* From this and the preceding verse we get the genuine meaning of the word *sane,* "to hate," in certain disputed places in the Scriptures. The word simply signifies "a less degree of love"; so it is said, v. 30: Jacob "loved . . . Rachel more than Leah," i.e., he loved Leah less than Rachel; and this is called hating in v. 31: *When the Lord saw that Leah was hated*—that she had less affection shown to her than was her due, as one of the legitimate wives of Jacob, *he opened her womb* —He blessed her with children. So "Jacob have

I loved, but Esau have I hated," simply means, I have shown a greater degree of affection for Jacob and his posterity than I have done for Esau and his descendants, by giving the former a better earthly portion than I have given to the latter, and by choosing the family of Jacob to be the progenitors of the Messiah. But not one word of all this relates to the eternal state of either of the two nations.

32. *She called his name Reuben.* Literally, "behold a son"; *for Jehovah hath looked upon,* "beheld," *my affliction;* behold then the consequence, I have got a son!

33. *She called his name Simeon.* "Hearing"; i.e., God had blessed her with another son, because He had heard that she was hated—loved less than Rachel was.

34. *Therefore was his name called Levi.* "Joined"; because she supposed that, in consequence of all these children, Jacob would become joined to her in as strong affection, at least, as he was to Rachel. From Levi sprang the tribe of Levites, who, instead of the first-born, were joined unto the priests in the service of the sanctuary. See Num. xviii. 2, 4.

35. *She called his name Judah.* *Yehudah,* a "confessor"; one who acknowledges God, and acknowledges that all good comes from His hands, and gives Him the praise due to His grace and mercy. From this patriarch the Jews have their name, and could it be now rightly applied to them, it would intimate that they were a people that confess God, acknowledge His bounty, and praise Him for His grace. *Left bearing.* That is, for a time; for she had several children afterwards. Literally translated, "she stood still from bearing" certainly does not convey the same meaning as that in our translation; the one appearing to signify that she ceased entirely from having children; the other, that she only desisted for a time, which was probably occasioned by a temporary suspension of Jacob's company, who appears to have deserted the tent of Leah through the jealous management of Rachel.

CHAPTER 30

Rachel envies her sister, and chides Jacob, 1. He reproves her and vindicates himself, 2. She gives him her maid Bilhah, 3-4. She conceives, and bears Dan, 5-6; and afterwards Naphtali, 7-8. Leah gives Zilpah, her maid, to Jacob, 9. She conceives and bears Gad, 10-11, and also Asher, 12-13. Reuben finds mandrakes, of which Rachel requests a part, 14. The bargain made between her and Leah, 15. Jacob in consequence lodges with Leah instead of Rachel, 16. She conceives, and bears Issachar, 17-18, and Zebulun, 19-20, and Dinah, 21. Rachel conceives, and bears Joseph, 22-24. Jacob requests permission from Laban to go to his own country, 25-26. Laban entreats him to tarry, and offers to give him what wages he shall choose to name, 27-28. Jacob details the importance of his services to Laban, 29-30, and offers to continue those services for the speckled and spotted among the goats, and the brown among the sheep, 31-33. Laban consents, 34, and divides all the ring-streaked and spotted among the he-goats, the speckled and spotted among the she-goats, and the brown among the sheep, and puts them under the care of his sons, and sets three days' journey between himself and Jacob, 35-36. Jacob's stratagem of the pilled rods, to cause the cattle to bring forth the ring-streaked, speckled, and spotted, 37-39. In consequence of which he increased his flock greatly, getting all that was strong and healthy in the flock of Laban, 40-43.

1. *Give me children, or else I die.* This is a most reprehensible speech, and argues not only envy and jealousy, but also a total want of dependence on God. She had the greatest share of her husband's affection, and yet was not satisfied unless she could engross all the privileges which her sister enjoyed! How true are those sayings, "Envy [is as] the rottenness of the bones," and, "Jealousy is cruel as the grave"!

2. *Am I in God's stead?* Am I greater than God, to give thee what He has refused?

3. *She shall bear upon my knees.* The handmaid was the sole property of the mistress, as has already been remarked in the case of Hagar; and therefore not only all her labor, but even the children borne by her, were the property of the mistress. These female slaves, therefore, bore children vicariously for their mistresses; and this appears to be the import. *That I may also have children by her.* "And I shall be built up by her." Hence *ben,* "a son," from *banah,* "to build"; because, as a house is formed of the stones that enter into its composition, so is a family by children.

6. *Called she his name Dan.* Because she found God had *judged* for her, and decided she should have a son by her handmaid; hence she called his name *Dan,* "judging."

8. *She called his name Naphtali.* "My wrestling," according to the common mode of interpretation.

11. *She called his name Gad.* This has been variously translated: a "troop," an "army," a "soldier." *A troop cometh. Ba gad,* the marginal reading, has it in two words, "a troop cometh"; whereas the textual reading has it only in one, *bagad,* "with a troop."

13. *And Leah said, Happy am I.* "In my happiness"; therefore *she called his name Asher,* that is, "blessedness" or "happiness."

14. *Reuben . . . found mandrakes. Dudaim.* What these were is utterly unknown, and learned men have wasted much time and pains in endeavoring to guess out a probable meaning.

15. *Thou hast taken my husband.* It appears probable that Rachel had found means to engross the whole of Jacob's affection and company, and that she now agreed to let him visit the tent of Leah, on account of receiving some of the fruits or plants which Reuben had found.

16. *I have hired thee.* We may remark among the Jewish women an intense desire of having children; and it seems to have been produced, not from any peculiar affection for children, but through the hope of having a share in the blessing of Abraham, by bringing forth Him in whom all the nations of the earth were to be blessed.

18. *God hath given me my hire. Sechari.* And she called his name *Issachar.* This word is compounded of *yesh,* "is," and *sachar,* "wages," from *sachar,* to "content, satisfy, saturate"; hence a satisfaction or compensation for work done.

20. *Now will my husband dwell with me. Yizbeleni;* and *she called his name Zebulun,* "a dwelling or cohabitation," as she now expected that Jacob would dwell with her, as he had before dwelt with Rachel.

21. *And called her name Dinah.* "Judgment." As Rachel had called her son by Bilhah Dan, v. 6, so Leah calls her daughter Dinah, God having judged and determined for her, as well as for her sister in the preceding instance.

22. *And God hearkened to her.* After the severe reproof which Rachel had received from her husband, v. 2, it appears that she sought God by prayer, and that He heard her; so that

her prayer and faith obtained what her impatience and unbelief had prevented.

24. *She called his name Joseph. Yoseph,* "adding," or "he who adds"; thereby prophetically declaring that God would add unto her another son, which was accomplished in the birth of Benjamin, chap. xxxv. 18.

25. *Jacob said unto Laban, Send me away.* Having now, as is generally conjectured, fulfilled the fourteen years which he had engaged to serve for Leah and Rachel.

27. *I have learned by experience. Nichashti,* from *nachash,* "to view attentively, to observe, to pry into." I have diligently considered the whole of thy conduct, and marked the increase of my property, and find that the Lord hath blessed me for thy sake.

30. *For it was little which thou hadst before I came.* Jacob takes advantage of the concession made by his father-in-law, and asserts that it was for his sake that the Lord had blessed him. *Since my coming,* "according to my footsteps"—every step I took in thy service, God prospered to the multiplication of thy flocks and property. *When shall I provide for mine own house?* Jacob had already laid his plan; and, from what is afterwards mentioned, we find him using all his skill and experience to provide for his family by a rapid increase of his flocks.

32. *I will pass through all thy flock.* All smaller cattle, such as sheep, goats. *All the speckled and spotted cattle. Seh,* which we translate *cattle,* signifies the young either of sheep or goats, what we call a lamb or a kid. *Speckled* signifies interspersed with variously colored spots. *Spotted.* Spotted with large spots, either of the same or different colors. I have never seen such sheep as are here described but in the islands of Zetland. There I have seen the most beautiful brown or fine chocolate color among the sheep; and several of the ring-streaked, spotted, speckled, and piebald among the same; and some of the latter description I have brought over, and can exhibit a specimen of Jacob's flock brought from the North Seas, feeding in Middlesex.

35. *The he goats that were ringstraked. The he goats* that had rings of black or other colored hair around their feet or legs.

It is extremely difficult to find out, from the thirty-second and thirty-fifth verses, in what the bargain of Jacob with his father-in-law properly consisted. The true meaning appears to be this: Jacob had agreed to take all the partly-colored for his wages. As he was now only beginning to act upon this agreement, consequently none of the cattle as yet belonged to him; therefore Laban separated from the flock, v. 35, all such cattle as Jacob might afterwards claim in consequence of his bargain; therefore Jacob commenced his service to Laban with a flock that did not contain a single animal of the description of those to which he might be entitled; and the others were sent away under the care of Laban's sons, three days' journey from those of which Jacob had the care. The bargain, therefore, seemed to be wholly in favor of Laban; and to turn it to his own advantage, Jacob made use of the stratagems afterwards mentioned. This mode of interpretation removes all the apparent contradiction between the thirty-second and thirty-fifth

verses, with which commentators in general have been grievously perplexed.

37. *Rods of green poplar. Libneh lach.* The *Libneh* is generally understood to mean the white poplar; and the word *lach,* which is here joined to it, does not so much imply greenness of color as being fresh, in opposition to witheredness. Had they not been fresh, just cut off, he could not have pilled the bark from them. *And of the hazel. Luz,* the nut or filbert tree, translated by others the almond tree; which of the two is here intended is not known. *And chestnut tree. Armon,* the plane tree, from *aram,* "he was naked." The plane tree is properly called by this name, because of the outer bark naturally peeling off, and leaving the tree bare in various places, having smooth places where it has fallen off. *Pilled white strakes in them.* Probably cutting the bark through in a spiral line, and taking it off in a certain breadth all round the rods, so that the rods would appear party-colored, the white of the wood showing itself where the bark was stripped off.

38. *And he set the rods which he had pilled before the flocks.* It has long been an opinion that whatever makes a strong impression on the mind of a female in the time of conception and gestation will have a corresponding influence on the mind or body of the fetus. This opinion is not yet rationally accounted for.

40. *Jacob did separate the lambs.* When Jacob undertook the care of Laban's flock, according to the agreement already mentioned, there were no partly-colored sheep or goats among them. Therefore the *ringstraked,* etc., mentioned in this verse, must have been born since the agreement was made; and Jacob makes use of them precisely as he used the pilled rods, that, having these before their eyes during conception, the impression might be made upon their imagination which would lead to the results already mentioned.

41. *Whensoever the stronger cattle did conceive.* The word which we translate *stronger* is understood by several of the ancient interpreters as signifying the "early, first-born, or early spring" cattle; and hence it is opposed to *feeble,* which Symmachus properly renders cattle of the "second birth." Now this more particularly refers to early and late lambs in the same year; as those that are born just at the termination of winter, and in the very commencement of spring, are every way more valuable than those which are born later in the same spring. Jacob therefore took good heed not to try his experiments with those late produced cattle, because he knew these would produce a degenerate breed, but with the early cattle, which were strong and vigorous, by which his breed must be improved.

43. *And the man increased exceedingly.* No wonder, when he used such means as the above. And had *maidservants, and menservants*—he was obliged to increase these as his cattle multiplied. *And camels and asses,* to transport his tents, baggage, and family from place to place, being obliged often to remove for the benefit of pasturage.

CHAPTER 31

father, 4-5; the services he had rendered him, 6; the various attempts made by Laban to defraud him of his hire, 7; how, by God's providence, his evil designs had been counteracted, 8-12; and then informs them that he is now called to return to his own country, 13. To the proposal of an immediate departure, Leah and Rachel agree; and strengthen the propriety of the measure by additional reasons, 14-16; on which Jacob collects all his family, his flocks, and his goods, and prepares for his departure, 17-18. Laban having gone to shear his sheep, Rachel secretes his images, 19. Jacob and his family, unknown to Laban, take their departure, 20-21. On the third day Laban is informed of their flight, 22; and pursues them to Mount Gilead, 23. God appears to Laban in a dream, and warns him not to mole.t Jacob, 24. He comes up with Jacob at Mount Gilead, 25; reproaches him with his clandestine departure, 26-29; and charges him with having stolen his gods, 30. Jacob vindicates himself, and protests his innocence in the matter of the theft, 31-32. Laban makes a general search for his images in Jacob's, Leah's, Bilhah's, and Zilpah's tents; and not finding them, proceeds to examine Rachel's, 33. Rachel, having hidden them among the camel's furniture, sat upon them, 34; and following her delicate excuse for not rising up, Laban desists from farther search, 35. Jacob, ignorant of Rachel's theft, reproaches Laban for his suspicions, 36-37; enumerates his long and faithful services, his fatigues, and Laban's injustice, 38-41; and shows that it was owing to God's goodness alone that he had any property, 42. Laban is moderated, and proposes a covenant, 43-44. Jacob sets up a stone, and the rest bring stones and make a heap, which Laban calls Jegar-sahadutha, and Jacob calls Galeed, 45-47. They make a covenant, and confirm it by an oath, 48-53. Jacob offers a sacrifice; they eat together; and Laban and his companions, having lodged in the mount all night, take a friendly leave of Jacob and his family next morning, and depart, 54-55.

1. *And he heard the words of Laban's sons.* The multiplication of Jacob's cattle, and the decrease and degeneracy of those of Laban, were sufficient to arouse the jealousy of Laban's sons. This, with Laban's unfair treatment and the direction he received from God, determined him to return to his own country. *Hath he gotten all this glory.* All these riches, this wealth, or property. The original word signifies both to be "rich" and to be "heavy"; and perhaps for this simple reason, that riches ever bring with them heavy weight and burden of cares and anxieties.

3. *And the Lord said unto Jacob, Return . . . and I will be with thee.* I will take the same care of thee in thy return, as I took of thee on thy way to this place.

4. *Jacob sent and called Rachel and Leah.* He had probably been at some considerable distance with the flocks; and for the greater secrecy, he rather sends for them to the field, to consult them on this most momentous affair, than visit them in their tents, where probably some of the family of Laban might overhear their conversation, though Laban himself was at the time three days' journey off. It is possible that Jacob sheared his sheep at the same time; and that he sent for his wives and household furniture to erect tents on the spot, that they might partake of the festivities usual on such occasions. Thus they might all depart without being suspected.

7. *Changed my wages ten times.* There is a strange diversity among the ancient versions, and ancient and modern interpreters, on the meaning of these words. It is most natural to suppose that Jacob uses the word *ten times* for an indefinite number, which we might safely translate "frequently"; and that it means an indefinite number in other parts of the sacred writings is evident from Lev. xxvi. 26: "Ten women shall bake your bread in one oven." Eccles. vii. 19: "Wisdom strengtheneth the wise more than ten mighty men in the city." Num, xiv. 22: "Because all those men . . . have tempted me now these ten times." Job xix. 3: "These ten times have ye reproached me." Zech. viii. 23:

"In those days . . . ten men shall take hold . . . of the skirt of him that is a Jew." Rev. ii. 10: "Ye shall have tribulation ten days."

12. *Grisled. Beruddim; barad* signifies "hail," and the meaning must be, they had white spots on them similar to hail. Our word *grisled* comes from the old French, *greslé*, "hail."

15. *Are we not counted of him strangers?* Rachel and Leah, who well knew the disposition of their father, gave him here his true character. He has treated us as *strangers*—as slaves whom he had a right to dispose of as he pleased; in consequence, *he hath sold us*—disposed of us on the mere principle of gaining by the sale. *And hath quite devoured also our money.* Has applied to his own use the profits of the sale, and has allowed us neither portion nor inheritance.

19. *Laban went to shear his sheep.* Laban had gone; and this was a favorable time not only to take his images, but to return to Canaan without being perceived. *Rachel had stolen the images. Teraphim.* In v. 30 they are termed *elohai,* "gods."

21. *Passed over the river.* The Euphrates. But how could he pass such a river with his flocks? There might have been fords well known to both Jacob and Laban, by which they might readily pass. *The mount Gilead.* What the ancient name of this mountain was we know not; but it is likely that it had not the name of *Gilead* till after the transaction mentioned in v. 47. The mountains of Gilead were eastward of the country possessed by the tribes of Reuben and Gad, and extended from Mount Hermon to the mountains of Moab.

24. *And God came to Laban.* God's caution to Laban was of high importance to Jacob— *Take heed that thou speak not to Jacob either good or bad;* or rather, as is the literal meaning of the Hebrew *ra,* "from good to evil," for had he neither spoken good nor evil to Jacob, they could have had no intercourse at all. The original is, therefore, peculiarly appropriate; for when people meet, the language at first is the language of friendship; the command therefore implies, "Do not begin with 'Peace be unto thee,' and then proceed to injurious language and acts of violence."

27. *I might have sent thee away with mirth.* "With rejoicing," making a feast or entertainment on the occasion; *and with songs,* odes either in the praise of God or to commemorate the splendid acts of their ancestors; *with tabret,* the "tympanum" used in the East to the present day, a thin, broad wooden hoop, with parchment extended over one end of it, to which are attached small pieces of brass, tin, etc., which make a jingling noise; it is held in the air with one hand, and beat on with the fingers of the other. It appears to have been precisely the same with that which is called the "tambourine," and which is frequently to be met with in our streets. *And with harp,* a sort of stringed instrument, a lute or harp. These four things seem to include all that was used in those primitive times as expressive of gladness and satisfaction on the most joyous occasions.

29. *It is in the power of my hand to do you hurt.* Literally, "My hand is unto God to do you evil," i.e., I have vowed to God that I will punish thee for thy flight, and the stealing of

my teraphim; but the *God of your father* has prevented me from doing it.

32. *Let him not live.* It appears that anciently theft was punished by death; and we know that the patriarchs had the power of life and death in their hands. But previously to the law the punishment of death was scarcely ever inflicted but for murder. The rabbins consider that this was an imprecation used by Jacob, as if he had said, Let God take away the life of the person who has stolen them! And that this was answered shortly after in the death of Rachel, chap. xxxv.

35. *The custom of women is upon me.* This she knew must be a satisfactory reason to her father; for if the teraphim were used to any religious purpose, and they seem to have been used in this way, as Laban calls them his "gods," he therefore could not suspect that a woman in such a situation, whose touch was considered as defiling, would have sat upon articles that were either the objects of his adoration or used for any sacred purpose. The stratagem succeeded to her wish and Laban departed without suspicion.

36. *And Jacob was wroth, and chode with Laban.* The expostulation of Jacob with Laban and their consequent agreement are told in this place with great spirit and dignity. Jacob was conscious that, though he had made use of cunning to increase his flocks, yet Laban had been on the whole a great gainer by his services. He had served him at least twenty years, fourteen for Rachel and Leah, and six for the cattle. Laban's constitutional sin was covetousness, and it was an easily besetting sin; for it appears to have governed all his conduct, and to have rendered him regardless of the interests of his children, so long as he could secure his own. That he had frequently falsified his agreement with Jacob, though the particulars are not specified, we have already had reason to conjecture from v. 7, and with this Jacob charges his father-in-law, in the most positive manner, v. 41.

39. *That which was torn . . . of my hand didst thou require it.* This more particularly marks the covetous and rigorous disposition of Laban; for the law of God required that what had been torn by beasts the shepherd should not be obliged to make good, Exod. xxii. 10, 13. And it is very likely that this law was in force from the earliest times.

42. *The fear of Isaac.* It is strange that Jacob should say, the *God of Abraham* and the *fear of Isaac,* when both words are meant of the same Being. The reason perhaps was this: Abraham was long since dead, and God was his unalienable Portion forever. Isaac was yet alive in a state of probation, living in the fear of God, not exempt from the danger of falling; therefore God is said to be his *fear*—not only the Object of his religious worship in a general way, but that holy and just God before whom he was still working out his salvation with fear and trembling—fear lest he should fall, and trembling lest he should offend.

46. *Made an heap. Gal,* translated *heap,* signifies properly a round heap; and this heap was probably made for the double purpose of an altar and a table, and Jacob's stone or pillar was set on it for the purpose of a memorial.

47. *Laban called it Jegar-sahadutha.* "The heap or round heap of witness"; but *Jacob called it Galeed,* which signifies the same thing. The first is pure Chaldee, the second pure Hebrew.

48-49. I think these two verses are badly divided, and should be read thus:

48. *And Laban said, This heap is a witness between me and thee this day.*

49. *Therefore was the name of it called Galeed and Mizpah; for he said, The Lord watch between me and thee, when we are absent one from another.*

Mizpah. Mitspah signifies a "watchtower"; and Laban supposes that in consequence of the consecration of the place, and the covenant now solemnly made and ratified, God would take possession of this heap, and stand on it as on a watchtower, to prevent either of them from trenching on the conditions of their covenant.

50. *No man is with us.* Though all were present at the sacrifice offered, yet it appears that in making the contract Jacob and Laban withdrew, and transacted the business in private, calling on God to witness it. Jacob had already four wives; but Laban feared that he might take others, whose children would naturally come in for a share of the inheritance to the prejudice of his daughters and grandchildren.

51. *And Laban said to Jacob . . . behold this pillar, which I have cast betwixt me and thee.* But this pillar, not *cast* but "set up," was certainly set up by Jacob; for in v. 45 we read, "And Jacob took a stone, and set it up for a pillar."

53. *The God of their father.* As Laban certainly speaks of the true God here, with what propriety can he say that this God was the God of Terah, the father of Abraham and Nahor? It is certain that Terah was an idolater; of this we have the most positive proof, Josh. xxiv. 2. Because the clause is not in the Septuagint, and is besides wanting in some MSS., Dr. Kennicott considers it an interpolation. But there is no need of having recourse to this expedient if we adopt the reading "your father," for "their father," which is supported by several of Kennicott's and De Rossi's MSS., and is precisely the same form made use of by Laban, v. 29, when addressing Jacob, and appears to me to be used here in the same way; for he there most manifestly uses the plural pronoun, when speaking only to Jacob himself. It is therefore to be considered as a form of speech peculiar to Laban; at least we have two instances of his use of it in this chapter. *Jacob sware by the fear of his father Isaac.* See on v. 42.

54. *Offered sacrifice upon the mount.* It is very likely that Laban joined in this solemn religious rite, and that, having offered the blood and fat to God, they feasted upon the sacrifice.

55. *Kissed his sons and his daughters.* That is, his grandchildren, Jacob's eleven sons with Dinah, their sister, and their mothers, Leah and Rachel. All these he calls his "children," v. 43. *And blessed them*—prayed heartily for their prosperity, though we find from v. 29 that he came having bound himself by a vow to God to do them some injury. Thus God turned his intended curse into a blessing.

CHAPTER 32

Jacob, proceeding on his journey, is met by the angels
of God, 1-2. Sends messengers before him to his brother
Esau, requesting to be favorably received, 3-5. The messengers return without an answer, but with the intelligence that Esau, with 400 men, was coming to meet
Jacob, 6. He is greatly alarmed, and adopts prudent
means for the safety of himself and family, 7-8. His
affecting prayer to God, 9-12. Prepares a present of five
droves of different cattle for his brother, 13-15. Sends
them forward before him, at a certain distance from each
other, and instructs the drivers what to say when met by
Esau, 15-20. Sends his wives, servants, children, and baggage over the brook Jabbok, by night, 21-23. Himself
stays behind, and wrestles with an angel until the break
of day, 24. He prevails and gets a new name, 25-29. Calls
the name of the place Peniel, 30. Is lame in his thigh
in consequence of his wrestling with the angel, 31-32.

1. *The angels of God met him.* Our word
angel comes from the Greek *aggelos,* which
literally signifies a messenger; or, as translated
in some of our old Bibles, a "tidings-bringer."
The Hebrew word *malach,* from *laach,* "to send,
minister to, employ," is nearly of the same
import; and hence we may see the propriety
of St. Augustine's remark: "It is a name, not of
nature, but of office"; and hence it is applied
indifferently to a human agent or messenger,
2 Sam. ii. 5; to a prophet, Hag. i. 13; to a priest,
Mal. ii. 7; to celestial spirits, Ps. ciii. 19-20, 22;
civ. 4.

2. *Mahanaim.* The "two hosts," if read by
the points, the angels forming one, and Jacob
and his company forming another; or simply
"hosts" or "camps" in the plural. There was a
city built afterwards here, and inhabited by
the priests of God, Josh. xxi. 38. For what
purpose the angels of God met Jacob does not
appear from the text; probably it was intended
to show him that he and his company were
under the care of an especial providence, and
consequently to confirm his trust and confidence
in God.

3. *Jacob sent messengers. Malachim,* the same
word which is before translated "angels." It is
very likely that these messengers had been sent
some time before he had this vision at
Mahanaim, for they appear to have returned
while Jacob encamped at the brook Jabbok,
where he had the vision of angels; see vv. 6 and
23. *The land of Seir, the country of Edom.* This
land which was, according to Dr. Wells, situated
on the south of the Dead Sea, extending from
thence to the Arabian Gulf, 1 Kings ix. 26, was
formerly possessed by the Horites, Gen. xiv. 6;
but Esau with his children drove them out,
destroyed them, and dwelt in their stead, Deut.
ii. 22; and thither Esau went from the face of
his brother, Jacob, chap. xxxvi. 6-7. Thus we
find he verified the prediction, "By thy sword
shalt thou live," chap. xxvii. 40.

4. *Thus shall ye speak unto my lord Esau.*
Jacob acknowledges the superiority of his brother; for the time was not yet come in which it
could be said, "The elder shall serve the
younger."

6. *Esau . . . cometh . . . and four hundred men
with him.* Jacob, conscious that he had injured
his brother, was now apprehensive that he was
coming with hostile intentions, and that he had
every evil to fear from his displeasure. Conscience is a terrible accuser. It does not appear
that Esau in this meeting had any hostile intention, but was really coming with a part of
his servants or tribe to do his brother honor.
If he had had any contrary intention, God had

removed it; and the angelic host which Jacob
met with before might have inspired him with
sufficient confidence in God's protection.

7. *He divided the people.* His prudence and
cunning were now turned into a right channel,
for he took the most effectual method to appease
his brother, had he been irritated, and save at
least a part of his family. This dividing and
arranging of his flocks, family, and domestics,
has something in it highly characteristic. To
such a man as Jacob such expedients would
naturally present themselves.

9. *O God of my father Abraham.* This prayer
is remarkable for its simplicity and energy; and
it is a model too for prayer, of which it contains
the essential constituents: (1) Deep self-abasement. (2) Magnification of God's mercy.
(3) Deprecation of the evil to which he was
exposed. (4) Pleading the promises that God
had made to him. And (5) Taking encouragement from what God had already wrought.

10. *I am not worthy of the least of all the
mercies.* The marginal reading is more consistent with the original: "I am less than all the
compassions, and than all the faithfulness, which
thou hast showed unto thy servant." Probably
St. Paul had his eye on this passage when he
wrote, "Unto me, who am less than the least
of all saints." A man who sees himself in the
light of God will ever feel that he has no good
but what he has received, and that he deserves
nothing of all that he has. *For with my staff.*
i.e., "myself alone," without any attendants, as
the Chaldee has properly rendered it.

11. *And the mother with the children.* He
must have had an awful opinion of his brother
when he used this expression, which implies
the utmost cruelty, proceeding in the work of
slaughter to total extermination.

12. *Make thy seed as the sand.* Having come
to the promise by which the covenant was
ratified both to Abraham and Isaac, he ceased,
his faith having gained strong confirmation in
a promise which he knew could not fail, and
which he found was made over to him, as it had
been to his father and grandfather.

13. *And took of that which came to his hand.*
"Which came under his hand," i.e., what, in the
course of God's providence, came under his
power.

14. *Two hundred she goats.* This was a
princely present, and such as was sufficient to
have compensated Esau for any kind of temporal
loss he might have sustained in being deprived
of his birthright and blessing. The *thirty milch
camels* were particularly valuable.

15. *Ten bulls.* The Syriac and Vulgate have
"twenty"; but *ten* is a sufficient proportion to
the *forty kine.* By all this we see that Jacob
was led to make restitution for the injury he
had done to his brother. Restitution for injuries
done to man is essentially requisite if in our
power. He who can and will not make restitution for the wrongs he has done can have no
claim even on the mercy of God.

22. *Passed over the ford Jabbok.* This brook
or rivulet rises in the mountains of Galaad, and
falls into the Jordan at the south extremity of
the lake of Gennesaret.

24. *And there wrestled a man with him.* This
was doubtless the Lord Jesus Christ, who, among

the patriarchs, assumed that human form which in the fulness of time He really took of a woman, and in which He dwelt thirty-three years among men.

25. *The hollow of Jacob's thigh was out of joint.* What this implies is difficult to find out; it is not likely that it was complete luxation of the thigh bone. It may mean no more than he received a stroke on the groin, not a "touch"; for the Hebrew word *naga* often signifies to "smite with violence," which stroke, even if comparatively slight, would effectually disable him for a time, and cause him to halt for many hours, if not for several days.

26. *Let me go, for the day breaketh.* Probably meaning that, as it was now morning, Jacob must rejoin his wives and children, and proceed on their journey.

28. *Thy name shall be called no more Jacob, but Israel. Yisrael,* from *sar,* "a prince," or *sarah,* "he ruled as a prince," and *el,* "God"; or rather from *ish,* "a man," and *raah,* "he saw," *el,* "God"; and this corresponds with the name which Jacob imposed on the place, calling it *Peniel,* the "faces of God, or of Elohim," which faces being manifested to him caused him to say, v. 30, "I have seen the Elohim faces-to-faces (i.e., fully and completely without any medium), and my soul is redeemed."

We may learn from this that the redemption of the soul will be the blessed consequence of wrestling by prayer and supplication with God: "The kingdom of heaven suffereth violence, and the violent take it by force." From this time Jacob became a new man; but it was not till after a severe struggle that he got his name, his heart, and his character changed. After this he was no more Jacob, the supplanter, but Israel— the man who prevails with God, and sees Him face-to-face.

And hast prevailed. More literally, "Thou hast had power with God, and with man thou shalt also prevail." *In Elohim,* "with the strong God"; *im anashim,* "with weak, feeble man." There is a beautiful opposition here between the two words: Seeing thou hast been powerful with the Almighty, surely thou shalt prevail over perishing mortals; as thou hast prevailed with God, thou shalt also prevail with men.

29. *Tell me, I pray thee, thy name.* It is very likely that Jacob wished to know the name of this angel, that he might invoke him in his necessities: but this might have led him into idolatry, for the doctrine of the Incarnation could be but little understood at this time; hence He refuses to give himself any name, yet shows himself to be the true God, and so Jacob understood Him (see v. 28); but he wished to have heard from His own lips that name by which He desired to be invoked and worshipped. *Wherefore is it that thou dost ask after my name?* Canst thou be ignorant who I am? *And he blessed him there*—gave him the new heart and the new nature which God alone can give to fallen man, and by the change He wrought in him, sufficiently showed who He was.

31. *The sun rose upon him.* Did the Prophet Malachi refer to this, chap. iv. 2: "Unto you that fear my name shall the Sun of righteousness arise with healing in his wings"? Possibly with the rising of the sun, which may here be understood as emblematical of "the Sun of righteous-

ness"—the Lord Jesus—the pain and weakness of his thigh passed away, and he felt in both soul and body that he was healed of his plagues.

32. *Therefore the children of Israel eat not of the sinew.* What this sinew was neither Jew nor Christian can tell; and it can add nothing either to science or to a true understanding of the text to multiply conjectures. I have already supposed that the part which the angel touched or "struck" was the groin; and if this be right, the *sinew,* nerve, or muscle that *shrank,* must be sought for in that place.

CHAPTER 33

Esau, with 400 men, meets Jacob, 1. He places his children under their respective mothers, passes over before them, and bows himself to his brother, 2-3. Esau receives him with great affection, 4. Receives the homage of the handmaids, Leah, Rachel, and their children, 5-7. Jacob offers him the present of cattle, which he at first refuses, but after much entreaty accepts, 8-11. Invites Jacob to accompany him to Mount Seir, 12. Jacob excuses himself because of his flocks and his children, but promises to follow him, 13-14. Esau offers to leave him some of his attendants, which Jacob declines, 15. Esau returns to Seir, 16, and Jacob journeys to Succoth, 17, and to Shalem, in the land of Canaan, 18. Buys a parcel of ground from the children of Hamor, 19, and erects an altar which he calls El-elohe-Israel, 20.

1. *Behold, Esau came, and with him four hundred men.* It has been generally supposed that Esau came with an intention to destroy his brother, and for that purpose brought with him 400 armed men. But (1) There is no kind of evidence of this pretended hostility. (2) There is no proof that the 400 men that Esau brought with him were at all armed. (3) But there is every proof that he acted towards his brother, Jacob, with all openness and candor and with such a forgetfulness of past injuries as none but a great mind could have been capable of. Why then should the character of this man be perpetually vilified? Here is the secret. With some people, on the most ungrounded assumption, Esau is a reprobate and the type and figure of all reprobates, and therefore he must be everything that is bad.

2. *He put the handmaids and their children foremost.* There is something so artificial in this arrangement of Jacob's family that it must have had some peculiar design. Was Jacob still apprehensive of danger, and put those foremost whom he least esteemed, that if the foremost met with any evil, those who were behind might escape on their swift beasts? Or did he intend to keep his choicest treasure to the last, and exhibit his beautiful *Rachel* and favorite *Joseph* after Esau had seen all the rest, in order to make the deeper impression on his mind?

4. *Esau ran to meet him.* How sincere and genuine is this conduct of Esau, and at the same time how magnanimous! He had buried all his resentment, and forgotten all his injuries; and receives his brother with the strongest demonstrations, not only of forgiveness, but of fraternal affection. *And kissed him.* In the Masoretic Bibles each letter of this word is noted with a point over it to make it emphatic. And by this kind of notation the rabbins wished to draw the attention of the reader to the change that had taken place in Esau and the sincerity with which he received his brother, Jacob.

10. *Receive my present at my hand.* Jacob could not be certain that he had found favor with Esau unless the present had been received;

for in accepting it Esau necessarily became his friend, according to the custom of those times and in that country. In the Eastern countries, if your present be received by your superior, you may rely on his friendship; if it be not received, you have everything to fear.

14. *Until I come unto my lord unto Seir.* It is very likely that Jacob was perfectly sincere in his expressed purpose of visiting Esau at Seir, but it is as likely that circumstances afterwards occurred that rendered it either improper or impracticable; and we find that Esau afterwards removed to Canaan, and he and Jacob dwelt there together for several years.

17. *Journeyed to Succoth.* So called from *succoth,* the "booths" or "tents" which Jacob erected there for the resting and convenience of his family, who in all probability continued there for some considerable time.

18. *And Jacob came to Shalem, a city of Shechem.* The word *shalem,* in the Samaritan *shalom,* should be translated here "in peace," or "in safety." After resting some time at Succoth, which was necessary for the safety of his flocks and the comfort of his family, he got safely to a city of Shechem, in health of body, without any loss of his cattle or servants, his wives and children being also in safety. Coverdale and Matthews translate this word as above, and with them agree the Chaldee and the Arabic; it is not likely to have been the name of a city, as it is nowhere else to be found.

20. *And he erected there an altar.* It appears that Jacob had a very correct notion of the providence and mercy of God; hence he says, v. 5: "The children which God hath graciously given thy servant"; and in v. 11 he attributes all his substance to the bounty of his Maker: "Take, I pray thee, my blessing . . . because God hath dealt graciously with me, and because I have enough." Hence he viewed God as the God of all grace, and to Him he erected an altar, dedicating it to "God, the God of Israel," referring to the change of his own name, and the mercies which he then received; and hence perhaps it would be best to translate the words, "The strong God [is] the God of Israel"; as by the power of His grace and goodness He had rescued, defended, blessed, and supported him from his youth up until now. The erecting altars with particular names appears in other places; so, Exod. xvii. 15, Moses calls his altar *Jehovah-nissi,* "the Lord is my banner."

(1) "When a man's ways please the Lord, he maketh even his enemies to be at peace with him." When Jacob had got reconciled to God, God reconciled his brother to him. The hearts of all men are in the hands of God, and He turns them howsoever He will.

(2) Since the time in which Jacob wrestled with the Angel of the covenant, we see in him much dependence on God, accompanied with a spirit of deep humility and gratitude. God's grace alone can change the heart of man, and it is by that grace only that we get a sense of our obligations; this lays us in the dust, and the more we receive the lower we shall lie.

CHAPTER 34

Dinah, the daughter of Jacob and Leah, going out to see the daughters of the land, is ravished by Shechem, the son of Hamor, 1-2. He entreats his father to get her for him to wife, 3-4. Jacob and his sons hear of the in- dignity offered to Dinah, 5-7. Hamor proposes the suit of Shechem to Jacob and his sons, and offers them a variety of advantages, 8-10. Shechem himself comes forward, begs to have Dinah to wife, and offers dowry to any extent, 11-12. The sons of Jacob pretend scruples of conscience to give their sister to one who was uncircumcised; and require, as a condition of this marriage, and of intermarriages in general, that all the Shechemites should be circumcised, 13-17. Hamor and Shechem consent, 18-19. They lay the business before the elders of their city, dwell on the advantages of a connection with Jacob and his family, and propose to them the condition required by the sons of Jacob, 20-23. The elders consent, and all the males are circumcised, 24. While the Shechemites are incapable of defending themselves, on the third day after their circumcision, Simeon and Levi, the brothers of Dinah, come upon the city, slay all the males, sack the city, take the women and children captives, and seize on all the cattle belonging to the Shechemites, 25-29. Jacob is greatly displeased and alarmed at this treachery and cruelty of his sons, and lays before them the probable consequences, 30. They endeavor to vindicate their conduct, 31.

1. *And Dinah . . . went out to see the daughters of the land.* It is supposed that Jacob had been now about seven or eight years in the land, and that Dinah, who was about seven years of age when Jacob came to Canaan, was now about fourteen or fifteen. Why or on what occasion she went out we know not, but the reason given by Josephus is very probable, namely, that it was on one of their festivals.

2. *Prince of the country.* I.e., Hamor was prince; Shechem was the son of the prince or chief.

3. *Spake kindly unto the damsel.* Literally, "he spake to the heart of the damsel"—endeavored to gain her affections, and to reconcile her to her disgrace. It appears sufficiently evident from this and the preceding verse that there had been no consent on the part of Dinah, that the whole was an act of violence, and that she was now detained by force in the house of Shechem. Here she was found when Simeon and Levi sacked the city, v. 26.

7. *He had wrought folly in Israel.* The land, afterwards generally called "Israel," was not as yet so named; and the sons of Jacob were called neither Israel, Israelites, nor Jews, till long after this. How then can it be said that Shechem had *wrought folly in Israel?* The words are capable of a more literal translation: "against Israel." Shechem wrought folly against *Israel,* the prince of God, in lying with the daughter of Jacob. Here both the names are given; *Jacob,* whose daughter was defiled, and *Israel,* the "prince of God," against whom the offense was committed.

12. *Ask me never so much dowry.* See the law relative to this, Exod. xxii. 16-17.

13. *Answered . . . deceitfully.* Which nothing could excuse; yet, to show that they had had much provocation, it is immediately subjoined, "they spoke thus because he had defiled Dinah their sister"; for so this parenthesis should be read.

14. *That were a reproach unto us.* Because the uncircumcised were not in the covenant of God; and to have given an heiress of the promise to one who had no kind of right to its spiritual blessings, from whom might spring children who would naturally walk in the way of their father, would have been absurd, reproachful, and wicked. Thus far they were perfectly right; but to make this holy principle a cloak for their deceitful and murderous purposes was the full sum of all wickedness.

17. *Then will we take our daughter, and we will be gone.* It is natural to suppose that the tribe of Hamor was very inconsiderable, else they would not have sought an alliance with the

family of Jacob, and have come so readily into a painful, disgraceful measure, without having either the sanction of divine authority or reason; for it does not appear that the sons of Jacob urged either. And they are threatened here that, if they do not agree to be circumcised, Dinah shall be taken from them and restored to her family; and this is probably what the Shechemites saw they had not power at present to prevent.

23. *Shall not their cattle and their substance . . . be ours?* This was a bait held out for the poor, unsuspecting people of Hamor by their prince and his son, who were not much less deceived than the people themselves.

24. *Every male was circumcised.* These simple people must have had very great affection for their chief and his son, or have been under the influence of the most passive obedience, to have come so readily into this measure, and to have submitted to this rite. But the petty princes in Asiatic countries have ever been absolute and despotic, their subjects paying them the most prompt and blind obedience.

25. *On the third day, when they were sore.* When the inflammation was at the height, and a fever ensued which rendered the person utterly helpless, and his state critical, *Simeon and Levi,* the brothers of Dinah, *took each man his sword,* probably assisted by that portion of the servants which helped them to take care of the flock, *came upon the city boldly,* "securely"— without being suspected, and being in no danger of meeting with resistance—*and slew all the males.* Great as the provocation was, and it certainly was very great, this was an act of unparalleled treachery and cruelty.

27. *The sons of Jacob.* The rest of Jacob's sons, the remaining brothers of Simeon and Levi, spoiled the city. Though the others could slay the defenseless males, it was not likely that they could have carried away all the booty, with the women, children, and cattle; it is therefore most natural to suppose that the rest of the sons of Jacob assisted at last in the business.

30. *Ye have troubled me.* Brought my mind into great distress, and endangered my personal safety; *to make me to stink*—to render me odious to the surrounding tribes, so that there is every reason to suspect that when this deed is come abroad they will join in a confederacy against me and extirpate my whole family. And had he not been under the peculiar protection of God, this in all human probability would have been the case; but he had prevailed with God, and he was also to prevail with men. That Jacob's resentment was not dissembled we have the fullest proof in his depriving these two sons of the birthright, which otherwise they had doubtless enjoyed. See chap. xlix. 5, 7.

31. *Should he deal with our sister as with an harlot?* On this outrage alone they vindicated their flagitious conduct. The word *harlot* first occurs here. The original is not *pilegesh,* which we render "concubine," but *zonah,* which ordinarily signifies "one who prostitutes herself to any person for hire."

CHAPTER 35

Jacob is commanded of God to go to Beth-el, and to build an altar there, 1. His exhortation to his family to put away all strange gods, etc., 2-3. They deliver them all up, and Jacob hides them in the earth, 4. They com-mence their journey, 5; come to Luz, 6; build there the altar El-beth-el, 7. Burial place of Deborah, Rebekah's nurse, 8. God appears again unto Jacob, 9. Blesses him and renews the promises, 10-13. To commemorate this manifestation of God, Jacob sets up a pillar, and calls the place Beth-el, 14-15. They journey to Ephrath, where Rachel, after hard labor, is delivered of Benjamin, and dies, 16-19. Jacob sets up a pillar on her grave, 20. They journey to Edar, 21. While at this place, Reuben defiles his father's bed, 22. Account of the children of Jacob, according to the mothers, 23-26. Jacob comes to Mamre to his father, Isaac, who was probably then in the one hundred and fifty-eighth year of his age, 27. Isaac dies, and is buried by his sons, Esau and Jacob, 29.

1. *Arise, go up to Beth-el.* The transaction that had lately taken place rendered it unsafe for Jacob to dwell any longer at the city of Shechem; and it seems that while he was reflecting on the horrible act of Simeon and Levi, and not knowing what to do, God graciously appeared to him and commanded him to go up to Beth-el, build an altar there, and thus perform the vow he had made, chap. xxviii. 20, 22.

2. *Put away the strange gods.* "The gods of the foreigners." Jacob's servants were all Syrians, and no doubt were addicted more or less to idolatry and superstition. These gods might belong to them, or, as some have conjectured, they were the *teraphim* which Rachel stole. But it is more natural to suppose that these gods found now in Jacob's family were images of silver, gold, or curious workmanship, which were found among the spoils of the city of Shechem. Lest these should become incitements to idolatry, Jacob orders them to be put away. *Be clean, and change your garments.* Personal or outward purification, as emblematical of the sanctification of the soul, has been in use among all the true worshipers of God from the beginning of the world.

3. *Answered me in the day of my distress.* Not only when he fled from the face of his brother, but more particularly when he was in his greatest strait at the brook of Jabbok.

4. *And . . . earrings which were in their ears.* Earrings were worn as amulets and charms, first consecrated to some god, or formed under some constellation, on which magical characters and images were drawn.

5. *The terror of God.* A supernatural awe sent by the Almighty *was upon the cities that were round about,* so that they were not molested in their departure. This could be owing to nothing less than the especial providence of God.

7. *El-beth-el.* "The strong God, the house of the strong God."

8. *But Deborah Rebekah's nurse died.* She was sent with Rebekah when taken by Abraham's servant to be wife to Isaac, chap. xxiv. 59. How she came to be in Jacob's family, expositors are greatly puzzled to find out; but the text does not state that *she was in Jacob's family.* Her death is mentioned merely because Jacob and his family had now arrived at the place where she was buried, and the name of that place was called *Allon-bachuth,* "the oak of weeping," as it is likely her death had been greatly regretted. and a general and extraordinary mourning had taken place on the occasion. Of Rebekah's death we know nothing. After her counsel to her son, chap. xxvii. we hear no more of her history from the sacred writings, except of her burial in chap. xlix. 31. Her name is written in the dust. And is not this designed as a mark of the disapprobation of God? It seems strange that such an

inconsiderable person as a nurse should be mentioned, when even the person she brought up is passed by unnoticed!

9. *God appeared unto Jacob again.* He appeared to him first at Shechem, when He commanded him to go to Beth-el; and now that he is arrived at the place, God appears to him the second time, and confirms to him the Abrahamic blessing. To Isaac and Jacob these frequent appearances of God were necessary, but they were not so to Abraham; for to him one word was sufficient—"Abraham believed God."

13. *And God went up from him.* This was not a vision, nor a strong mental impression, but a real manifestation of God. Jacob saw and heard Him speak, and before his eyes He *went up*— ascended to heaven. This was no doubt the future Saviour, the Angel of the covenant.

14. *A drink offering.* A "libation." These were afterwards very common in all countries. At first they consisted probably of water only, afterwards wine was used; see on Lev. vii. 1, etc. The *pillar* which Jacob set up was to commemorate the appearance of God to him; the *drink offering* and the *oil* were intended to express his gratitude and devotion to his Preserver. It was probably the same pillar which he had set up before, which had since been thrown down, and which he had consecrated afresh to God.

16. *There was but a little way to come to Ephrath.* *Ephrath*, called also Bethlehem, and Bethlehem Ephrata, was the birthplace of our blessed Redeemer. See its meaning, Matt. ii. 6.

18. *As her soul was in departing.* "In the going away of her soul." *She called his name Ben-oni.* "The son of my sorrow," because of the hard labor she had in bringing him into the world; *but his father called him Benjamin,* "the son of my right hand," i.e., the son peculiarly dear to me.

20. *Jacob set a pillar upon her grave.* Was not this the origin of funeral monuments? In ancient times, and among rude nations, a heap of stones designated the burial place of the chief; many of these still remain in different countries. It is very likely from the circumstances of Jacob that a single stone constituted the *pillar* in this case.

21. *Tower of Edar.* Literally, "the tower of the flock," and so translated in Mic. iv. 8. By the "tower of the flock" we may understand a place built by the shepherds near to some well for the convenience of watering their flocks and keeping watch over them by night.

22. *And Israel heard it.* Not one word is added farther in the Hebrew text; but a break is left in the verse, opposite to which there is a Masoretic note, which simply states that there is a hiatus in the verse. This hiatus the Septuagint has thus supplied: "and it appeared evil in his sight." *Now the sons of Jacob were twelve.* Called afterwards the "twelve patriarchs," because they became heads or chiefs of numerous families or tribes, Acts vii. 8; and the people that descended from them are called the "twelve tribes," Acts xxvi. 7; Jas. i. · 1. Twelve princes came from Ishmael, chap. xxv. 16, who were heads of families and tribes. And in reference to the twelve patriarchs, our Lord chose twelve apostles.

23. *The sons of Leah.* The children are arranged under their respective mothers, and not in order of their birth.

26. *Born to him in Padan-aram.* I.e., all but Benjamin, who was born in Canaan, vv. 16-17. It is well known that Padan-aram is the same as Mesopotamia, and hence the Septuagint translate "Mesopotamia of Syria." The word signifies "between the two rivers." It is situated between the Euphrates and Tigris, having Assyria on the east, Arabia Deserta, with Babylonia, on the south, Syria on the west, and Armenia on the north.

27. *The city of Arbah, which is Hebron.* See chap. xxiii. 2. It has been conjectured that Jacob must have paid a visit to his father before this time, as previously to this he had been some years in Canaan; but now, as he was approaching to his end, Jacob is supposed to have gone to live with and comfort him in his declining days.

29. *Isaac gave up the ghost . . . and was gathered unto his people.* See on chap. xxv. 8. *Esau and Jacob buried him.* See chap. xxv. 9. Esau, as we have seen in chap. xxxiii, was thoroughly reconciled to his brother, Jacob, and now they both join in fraternal and filial affection to do the last kind office to their amiable father. It is generally allowed that the death of Isaac is mentioned here out of its chronological order, as several of the transactions mentioned in the succeeding chapters, especially xxxvii and xxxviii, must have happened during his life; but that the history of Joseph might not be disturbed, his death is anticipated in this place.

CHAPTER 36

The genealogy of Esau, i.e., his sons, by his Canaanitish wives, Adah, Aholibamah, and Bashemath, 1-3. The children of Adah and Bashemath, 4. Of Aholibamah, 5. Esau departs from Canaan and goes to Mount Seir, 6-8. The generations of Esau, i.e., his grandchildren, while in Seir, 9-19. The generations of Seir, the Horite, 20-30. Anah finds mules (*Yemim*) in the wilderness, 24. The kings which reigned in Edom, 31-39. The dukes that succeeded them, 40-43.

1. *These are the generations of Esau.* We have here the genealogy of Esau in his sons and grandsons, and also the genealogy of Seir the Horite. The genealogy of the sons of Esau, born in Canaan, is related in vv. 1-8; those of his grandchildren born in Seir, 9-19; those of Seir the Horite, 20-30. The generations of Esau are particularly marked, to show how exactly God fulfilled the promises He made to him, chaps. xxv and xxvii; and those of Seir the Horite are added, because his family became in some measure blended with that of Esau.

2. *His wives.* It appears that Esau's wives went by very different names. Aholibamah is named Judith, chap. xxvi. 34; Adah is called Bashemath in the same place; and she who is here called Bashemath is called Mahalath, chap. xxviii. 9. These are variations which cannot be easily accounted for; and they are not of sufficient importance to engross much time. It is well known that the same persons in Scripture are often called by different names.

Anah the daughter of Zibeon. But this same Anah is said to be the son of Zibeon, v. 24, though in this and the fourteenth verse he is said to be the daughter of Zibeon. But the

Samaritan, the Septuagint (and the Syriac, in v. 2), read "son" instead of "daughter," which Houbigant and Kennicott contend to be the true reading. Others say that "daughter" should be referred to Aholibamah, who was the daughter of Anah, and granddaughter of Zibeon. I should rather prefer the reading of the Samaritan, Septuagint, and Syriac, and read, both here and in v. 14, "Aholibamah, the daughter of Anah the son of Zibeon," and then the whole will agree with v. 24.

6. *Esau took his wives.* So it appears that Esau and Jacob dwelt together in Canaan, whither the former removed from Seir, probably soon after the return of Jacob. That they were on the most friendly footing this sufficiently proves; and Esau shows the same dignified conduct as on other occasions, in leaving Canaan to Jacob, and returning again to Mount Seir—certainly a much less fruitful region than that which he now in behalf of his brother voluntarily abandoned.

12. *Timna was concubine to Eliphaz.* As Timna was sister to Lotan the Horite, v. 22, we see how the family of Esau and the Horites got intermixed. This might give the sons of Esau a pretext to seize the land, and expel the ancient inhabitants, as we find they did, Deut. ii. 12. *Amalek.* The father of the Amalekites, afterwards bitter enemies to the Jews, and whom God commanded to be entirely exterminated, Deut. xxv. 17, 19.

15. *Dukes of the sons of Esau.* The word *duke* comes from the Latin *dux,* a "captain" or "leader." The Hebrew *alluph* has the same signification; and as it is also the term for a "thousand," which is a grand capital or leading number, probably the *dukes* had this name from being leaders of or captains over a company of one thousand men; just as those among the Greeks called *chiliarchs,* which signifies the same; and as the Romans called those *centurions* who were captains over one hundred men, from the Latin word *centum,* which signifies a hundred. The ducal government was that which prevailed first among the Idumeans, or descendants of Esau. Here fourteen dukes are reckoned to Esau: seven that came of his wife, Adah, four of Bashemath, and three of Aholibamah.

16. *Duke Korah.* This Dr. Kennicott pronounces to be an interpolation. Everything considered, I incline to the opinion that these words were not originally in the text.

20. *These are the sons of Seir the Horite.* These Horites were the original inhabitants of the country of Seir, called the land of the Horites, and afterwards the land of the Idumeans, when the descendants of Esau had driven them out. These people are first mentioned in chap. xiv. 6.

21. *These are the dukes of the Horites.* It appears pretty evident that the Horites and the descendants of Esau were mixed together in the same land, as before observed.

24. *This was that Anah that found the mules in the wilderness.* The word here translated *mules* has given rise to a great variety of conjectures and discordant opinions. St. Jerome, who renders it "warm springs," says there are as many opinions concerning it as there are commentators. My own opinion is that *mules* were not known before the time of Anah; and

that he was probably the first who coupled the mare and ass together to produce this mongrel, or the first who met with creatures of this race in some very secluded part of the wilderness.

31. *Before there reigned any king over* . . . *Israel.* I suppose all the verses, from this to the thirty-ninth inclusive, have been transferred to this place from 1 Chron. i. 43-50, as it is not likely they could have been written by Moses; and it is quite possible they might have been, at a very early period, written in the margin of an authentic copy, to make out the regal succession in Edom, prior to the consecration of Saul; which words being afterwards found in the margin of a valuable copy, from which others were transcribed, were supposed by the copyist to be a part of the text; on this conviction he would not hesitate to transcribe them consecutively in his copy.

I know there is another way of accounting for those words on the ground of their being written originally by Moses; but to me it is not satisfactory. It is simply this: the word *king* should be considered as implying any kind of regular government, whether by chiefs, dukes, judges, and therefore when Moses says these are the *kings* which reigned in Edom, before there was any king in Israel, he may be only understood as saying that these kings reigned among the Edomites before the family of Jacob had acquired any considerable power, or before the time in which his twelve sons had become the fathers of numerous tribes.

Esau, after his dukes, had eight kings, who reigned successively over their people, while Israel was in affliction in Egypt.

40. *These are the names of the dukes that came of Esau.* These dukes did not govern the whole nation of the Idumeans, but they were chiefs in their respective *families,* in *their places* —the districts they governed, and to which they gave *their names.*

43. *He is Esau the father of the Edomites.* That is, the preceding list contains an account of the posterity of Esau, who was the father of Edom. Thus ends Esau's history; for after this there is no further account of his life, actions, or death, in the Pentateuch.

CHAPTER 37

Jacob continues to sojourn in Canaan, 1. Joseph, being seventeen years of age, is employed in feeding the flocks of his father, 2. Is loved by his father more than the rest of his brethren, 3. His brethren envy him, 4. His dream of the sheaves, 5-7. His brethren interpret it, and hate him on the account, 8. His dream of the sun, moon, and eleven stars, 9-11. Jacob sends him to visit his brethren, who were with the flock in Shechem, 12-14. He wanders in the field, and is directed to go to Dothan, whither his brethren had removed the flocks, 15-17. Seeing him coming, they conspire to destroy him, 18-20. Reuben, secretly intending to deliver him, counsels his brethren not to kill, but to put him into a pit, 21-22. They strip Joseph of his coat of many colors, and put him into a pit, 23-24. They afterwards draw him out, and sell him to a company of Ishmaelite merchants for twenty pieces of silver, who carry him into Egypt, 25-28. Reuben returns to the pit, and not finding Joseph, is greatly affected, 29-30. Joseph's brethren dip his coat in a goat's blood to persuade his father that he had been devoured by a wild beast, 31-33. Jacob is greatly distressed, 34-35. Joseph is sold in Egypt to Potiphar, captain of Pharaoh's guard, 36.

1. *Wherein his father was a stranger.* Jacob dwelt in the land "of his father's sojournings," as the margin very properly reads it. The place was probably the vale of Hebron, see v. 14.

2. *These are the generations. Toledoth,* "the history of the lives and actions of Jacob and

his sons"; for in this general sense the original must be taken, as in the whole of the ensuing history there is no particular account of any genealogical succession. Yet the words may be understood as referring to the tables or genealogical lists in the preceding chapter; and if so, the original must be understood in its common acceptation.

3. *A coat of many colours.* A coat made up of stripes of differently colored cloth. Similar to this was the *toga praetexta* of the Roman youth, which was white, striped or fringed with purple; this they wore till they were seventeen years of age, when they changed it for the *toga virilis*, or *toga pura*, which was all white. It is no wonder that his brethren should envy him when his father had thus made him such a distinguished object of his partial love.

4. *And could not speak peaceably unto him.* Does not this imply, in our use of the term, that they were continually quarrelling with him? But this is no meaning of the original: "they could not speak peace to him," i.e., they would not accost him in a friendly manner. They would not even wish him well. The Eastern method of salutation is, "Peace be to thee!" Now as "peace" among those nations comprehends all kinds of blessings spiritual and temporal, so they are careful not to say it to those whom they do not cordially wish well. It is not an unusual thing for an Arab or a Turk to hesitate to return the *salam*, if given by a Christian, or by one of whom he has not a favorable opinion; and this, in their own country, may be ever considered as a mark of hostility; not only as a proof that they do not wish you well, but that if they have an opportunity they will do you an injury. This was precisely the case with respect to Joseph's brethren; they would not give him the *salam*, and therefore felt themselves at liberty to take the first opportunity to injure him.

7. *We were binding sheaves in the field.* Though in these early times we read little of tillage, yet it is evident from this circumstance that it was practiced by Jacob and his sons.

14. *Go . . . see whether it be well with thy brethren.* Literally, "Go, I beseech thee, and see the peace of thy brethren, and the peace of the flock." Go and see whether they are all in prosperity. See on v. 4. As Jacob's sons were now gone to feed the flock on the parcel of ground they had bought from the Shechemites (see chap. xxxiii. 19), and where they had committed such a horrible slaughter, their father might feel more solicitous about their welfare, lest the neighboring tribes should rise against them and revenge the murder of the Shechemites. As Jacob appears to have been at this time in the vale of Hebron, it is supposed that Shechem was about sixty English miles distant from it, and that Dothan was about eight miles farther.

19. *Behold, this dreamer cometh.* This "master of dreams," this "master dreamer." A form of speech which conveys great contempt.

20. *Come now . . . and let us slay him.* What unprincipled savages these must have been to talk thus coolly about imbruing their hands in an innocent brother's blood!

21. *Reuben heard it.* Though Reuben appears to have been a transgressor of no ordinary

magnitude, if we take chap. xxxv. 22 according to the letter, yet his bosom was not the habitation of cruelty. He determined, if possible, to save his brother from death and deliver him safely to his father, with whose fondness for him he was sufficiently acquainted.

23. *They stript Joseph out of his coat.* This probably was done that, if ever found, he might not be discerned to be a person of distinction, and consequently no inquiry made concerning him.

25. *They sat down to eat bread.* Every act is perfectly in character, and describes forcibly the brutish and diabolic nature of their ruthless souls. *A company of Ishmeelites.* We may naturally suppose that this was a caravan, composed of different tribes that, for their greater safety, were travelling together, and of which Ishmaelites and Midianites made the chief.

28. *For twenty pieces of silver.* This, I think, is the first instance on record of selling a man for a slave. But the practice certainly did not commence now; it had doubtless been in use long before.

29. *Reuben returned unto the pit.* It appears he was absent when the caravan passed by, to whom the other brethren had sold Joseph.

32. *Sent the coat of many colours . . . to their father.* What deliberate cruelty to torture the feelings of their aged father, and thus harrow up his soul!

33-34. *Joseph is without doubt rent in pieces.* It is likely he inferred this from the lacerated state of the coat, which, in order the better to cover their wickedness, they had not only besmeared with the blood of the goat, but it is probable reduced to tatters. And what must a father's heart have felt in such a case! As this coat is rent, so is the body of my beloved son rent in pieces! *And Jacob rent his clothes.*

35. *All his sons and all his daughters.* He had only one daughter, Dinah; but his sons' wives may be here included. But what hypocrisy in his sons to attempt to comfort him concerning the death of a son who they knew was alive; and what cruelty to put their aged father to such torture, when, properly speaking, there was no ground for it!

36. *Potiphar, an officer of Pharaoh's.* The word *saris*, translated *officer*, signifies a "eunuch," and lest any person should imagine that, because this Potiphar had a wife, therefore it is absurd to suppose him to have been a eunuch, let such persons know that it is not uncommon in the East for eunuchs to have wives.

Captain of the guard. "Chief of the butchers"; a most appropriate name for the guards of an Eastern despot. If a person offend one of the despotic Eastern princes, the order to one of the life-guards is, "Go and bring me his head"; and this command is instantly obeyed, without judge, jury, or any form of law. Potiphar, we may therefore suppose, was captain of those guards whose business it was to take care of the royal person, and execute his sovereign will on all the objects of his displeasure.

CHAPTER 38

Judah marries the daughter of a Canaanite, 1-2; and begets of her Er, 3, Onan, 4, and Shelah, 5. Er marries Tamar, 6; is slain for his wickedness, 7. Onan, required to raise up seed to his brother, refuses, 8-9. He also is slain, 10. Judah promises his son Shelah to Tamar, when he should be of age; but performs not his promise, 11. Judah's wife dies, 12. Tamar in disguise receives her father-in-law; he leaves his signet, bracelets, and staff in her hand, and she conceives by him, 13-23. Judah is informed that his daughter-in-law is with child; and, not knowing that himself was the father, condemns her to be burnt, 24. She produces the signet, bracelets, and staff, and convicts Judah, 25-26. She is delivered of twins, who are called Pharez and Zarah, 27-30.

1-2. *And it came to pass at that time.* The facts mentioned here could not have happened at the times mentioned in the preceding chapter, as those times are all unquestionably too recent, for the very earliest of the transactions here recorded must have occurred long before the selling of Joseph. *Adullamite.* An inhabitant of Adullam, a city of Canaan, afterwards given for a possession to the sons of Judah, Josh. xv. 1, 35. It appears as if this Adullamite had kept a kind of lodging house, for *Shuah* the Canaanite and his family lodged with him; and there Judah lodged also. As the woman was a Canaanitess, Judah had the example of his fathers to prove at least the impropriety of such a connection.

5. *And he was at Chezib, when she bare him.* This town is supposed to be the same with Achzib, which fell to the tribe of Judah, Josh. xv. 44.

7. *Er . . . was wicked in the sight of the Lord.* What this wickedness consisted in we are not told; but the phrase *sight of the Lord* being added proves that it was some very great evil. It is worthy of remark that the Hebrew word used to express Er's wickedness is his own name, the letters reversed. As if the inspired writer had said, "Er was altogether wicked, a completely abandoned character."

9. *Onan knew that the seed should not be his.* That is, that the child begotten of his brother's widow should be reckoned as the child of his deceased brother, and his name, though the real father of it, should not appear in the genealogical tables. We find from this history that long before the Mosaic law it was an established custom, probably founded on a divine precept, that if a man died childless his brother was to take his wife, and the children produced by this second marriage were considered as the children of the first husband, and in consequence inherited his possessions.

12. *In process of time.* This phrase, which is in general use in the Bible, needs explanation; the original is "and the days were multiplied." Though it implies an indefinite time, yet it generally embraces a pretty long period, and in this place may mean several years.

15. *Thought her to be an harlot.* See the original of this term, chap. xxxiv. 31. The Hebrew is *zonah* and signifies generally a person who prostitutes herself to the public for hire, or one who lives by the public. It appears that in very ancient times there were public persons of this description; and they generally veiled themselves, sat in public places by the highway side, and received certain hire.

17. *Wilt thou give me a pledge, till thou send it?* The word *erabon* signifies an "earnest" of something promised, a part of the price agreed for between a buyer and seller, by giving and receiving of which the bargain was ratified; or a deposit, which was to be restored when the thing promised should be given. St. Paul uses the same word in Greek letters, 2 Cor. i. 22; Eph. i. 14. From the use of the term in this history we may at once see what the apostle means by the Holy Spirit being the "earnest" of the promised inheritance; namely, a security given in hand for the fulfilment of all God's promises relative to grace and eternal life. We may learn from this that eternal life will be given in the great day to all who can produce this *erabon* or "pledge." He who has the earnest of the Spirit then in his heart shall not only be saved from death, but have that eternal life of which it is the pledge and the evidence. What the pledge given by Judah was, see on v. 25.

21. *Where is the harlot, that was openly by the way side?* Our translators often render different Hebrew words by the same term in English, and thus many important shades of meaning, which involve traits of character, are lost. In v. 15 Tamar is called a "harlot," *zonah,* which, as we have already seen, signifies a person who prostitutes herself for money; in this verse she is called a *harlot* in our version; but the original is *kedeshah,* a holy or "consecrated person," from *kadash,* "to make holy," or "to consecrate to religious purposes." And the word here must necessarily signify a person consecrated by prostitution to the worship of some impure goddess.

23. *Lest we be shamed.* Not of the act, for this he does not appear to have thought criminal; but lest he should fall under the raillery of his companions and neighbors for having been tricked out of his signet, bracelets, and staff, by a prostitute.

24. *Bring her forth, and let her be burnt.* As he had ordered Tamar to live as widow in her own father's house till his son Shelah should be marriageable, he considers her therefore as the wife of his son; and as Shelah was not yet given to her, and she is found with child, she is reputed by him as an adulteress, and burning, it seems, was anciently the punishment of this crime. Judah, being a patriarch or head of a family, had, according to the custom of those times, the supreme magisterial authority over all the branches of his own family; therefore he only acts here in his juridical capacity. How strange that in the very place where adultery was punished by the most violent death, prostitution for money and for religious purposes should be considered as no crime!

25. *The signet.* Properly a "seal," or instrument with which impressions were made to ascertain property. *Bracelets. Pethilim,* from *pathal,* "to twist, wreathe, twine," may signify a girdle or a collar by which precedency might be indicated. *Staff.* Either what we would call a common walking stick or the staff which was the ensign of his tribe.

26. *She hath been more righteous than I.* It is probable that Tamar was influenced by no other motive than that which was common to all the Israelitish women, the desire to have children who might be heirs of the promise made to Abraham. And as Judah had obliged her to continue in her widowhood under the promise of giving her his son Shelah when he should be of age, consequently his refusing or delaying to accomplish this promise was a breach of truth, and an injury done to Tamar.

28. *The midwife . . . bound upon his hand a scarlet thread.* The binding of the scarlet thread about the wrist of the child whose arm appeared first in the birth serves to show us how solicitously the privileges of the birthright were preserved. Had not this caution been taken by the midwife, Pharez would have had the right of primogeniture to the prejudice of his elder brother, Zarah. And yet Pharez is usually reckoned in the genealogical tables before Zarah; and from him, not Zarah, does the line of our Lord proceed. See Matt. i. 3. Probably the two brothers, as being twins, were conjoined in the privileges belonging to the birthright.

29. *How hast thou broken forth?* Thou shalt bear the name of the *breach* thou hast made, i.e., in coming first into the world. Therefore his name was called *Parets,* i.e., the person who made the breach.

30. *His name was called Zarah. Zarach,* "risen or sprung up," applied to the sun, rising and diffusing his light.

CHAPTER 39

Joseph, being brought to Potiphar's house, prospers in all his undertakings, 1-3. Potiphar makes him his overseer, 4. Is prospered in all his concerns for Joseph's sake, in whom he puts unlimited confidence, 5-6. The wife of Potiphar solicits him to criminal correspondence, 7. He refuses, and makes a fine apology for his conduct, 8-9. She continues her solicitations, and he his refusals, 10. She uses violence, and he escapes from her hand, 11-13. She accuses him to the domestics, 14-15, and afterward to Potiphar, 16-18. Potiphar is enraged, and Joseph is cast into prison, 19-20. The Lord prospers him, and gives him great favor in the sight of the keeper of the prison, 21, who entrusts him with the care of the house and all the prisoners, 22-23.

4. *He made him overseer. Hiphkid,* from *pakad,* "to visit, take care of, superintend"; the same as *episcopos,* "overseer" or "bishop," among the Greeks. This is the term by which the Septuagint often express the meaning of the original.

6. *Joseph was a goodly person, and well favoured.* "Beautiful in his person," and "beautiful in his countenance." The same expressions are used relative to Rachel; see them explained in chap. xxix. 17. The beauty of Joseph is celebrated over all the East, and the Persian poets vie with each other in descriptions of his comeliness. Mohammed spends the twelfth chapter of the Koran entirely on Joseph, and represents him as a perfect beauty, and the most accomplished of mortals.

8. *My master wotteth not.* Knoweth not, from the old Anglo-Saxon *witan,* "to know"; hence "wit," intellect, understanding, wisdom, prudence.

9. *How then.* "And how?" Joseph gives two most powerful reasons for his noncompliance with the wishes of his mistress: (1) Gratitude to his master, to whom he owed all that he had. (2) His fear of God, in whose sight it would be a heinous offense, and who would not fail to punish him for it.

14. *He hath brought in an Hebrew unto us.* Potiphar's wife affects to throw great blame on her husband, whom we may reasonably suppose she did not greatly love. *He hath brought in—* he hath raised this person to all his dignity and eminence, to give him the greater opportunity to mock us. *Letsachek,* here translated "to mock," is the same word used in chap. xxvi. 8, relative to Isaac and Rebekah; and is certainly used by Potiphar's wife in v. 17 to signify some kind of familiar intercourse not allowable but between man and wife.

20. *Put him into the prison.* Literally the "round house"; in such a form the prison was probably built.

21. *The Lord was with Joseph.* It is but of little consequence where the lot of a servant of God may be cast; like Joseph he is ever employed for his Master, and God honors him and prospers his work.

CHAPTER 40

Pharaoh's chief butler and his chief baker, having offended their lord, are put in prison, 1-3. The captain of the guard gives them into the care of Joseph, 4. Each of them has a dream, 5. Joseph, seeing them sad, questions them on the subject, 6-7. Their answer, 8. The chief butler tells his dream, 9-11. Joseph interprets it, 12-13. Gives a slight sketch of his history to the chief butler, and begs him to think upon him when restored to his office, 14-15. The chief baker tells his dream, 16-17. Joseph interprets this also, 18-19. Both dreams are fulfilled according to the interpretation, the chief butler being restored to his office, and the chief baker hanged, 20-22. The chief butler makes no interest for Joseph, 23.

1. *The butler.* "Cupbearer." *Baker.* Rather "cook, confectioner," or the like. *Had offended.* They had probably been accused of attempting to take away the king's life, one by poisoning his drink, the other by poisoning his bread or confectionaries.

3. *Where Joseph was bound.* The place in which Joseph was now "confined"; this is what is implied in being *bound;* for, without doubt, he had his personal liberty. As the butler and the baker were state criminals they were put in the same prison with Joseph, which we learn from the preceding chapter, v. 20, was the king's prison.

4. *They continued a season.* Literally "days"; how long we cannot tell.

5. *Each man according to the interpretation.* Not like dreams in general, the disordered workings of the mind, the consequence of disease or repletion; these were dreams that had an interpretation, that is, that were prophetic.

6. *They were sad.* They concluded that their dreams portended something of great importance, but they could not tell what.

8. *There is no interpreter.* They either had access to none, or those to whom they applied could give them no consistent, satisfactory meaning. *Do not interpretations belong to God?* God alone, the Supreme Being, knows what is in futurity; and if He have sent a significant dream, He alone can give the solution.

11. *And I took the grapes, and pressed them into Pharaoh's cup.* From this we find that wine anciently was the mere expressed juice of the grape, without fermentation. The cupbearer took the bunch, pressed the juice into the cup, and instantly delivered it into the hands of his master.

12. *The three branches are three days.* That is, the three branches signify three days; a form of speech frequently used in the sacred writings, for the Hebrew has no proper word by which our terms "signifies, represents," etc., are expressed.

14. *Make mention of me unto Pharaoh.* One would have supposed that the very circumstance of his restoration, according to the prediction of Joseph, would have almost necessarily prevented him from forgetting so extraordinary a person. But what have mere courtiers to do with either gratitude or kindness?

15. *For indeed I was stolen.* "Stolen, I have been stolen"—most assuredly I was stolen; *and here also have I done nothing.* These were simple assertions, into the proof of which he was ready to enter if called on.

19. *Lift up thy head from off thee.* Thus we find that beheading, hanging, and gibbeting were modes of punishment among the ancient Egyptians; but the criminal was beheaded before he was hanged, and then either hanged on hooks or by the hands. See Lam. v. 12.

20. *Pharaoh's birthday.* The distinguishing a birthday by a feast appears from this place to have been a very ancient custom. It probably had its origin from a correct notion of the immortality of the soul, as the commencement of life must appear of great consequence to that person who believed he was to live forever. St. Matthew, xiv. 6, mentions Herod's keeping his birthday; and examples of this kind are frequent to the present time in most nations. *Lifted up the head of the chief butler.* By lifting up the head, probably no more is meant than bringing them to trial, tantamount to what was done by Jezebel and the nobles of Israel to Naboth: "Set Naboth on high among the people: and set two men, sons of Belial . . . to bear witness against him," 1 Kings xxi. 9, etc. The issue of the trial was, the baker alone was found guilty and hanged; and the butler, being acquitted, was restored to his office.

23. *Yet did not the chief butler remember Joseph.* Had he mentioned the circumstance to Pharaoh, there is no doubt that Joseph's case would have been examined into, and he would in consequence have been restored to his liberty; but, owing to the ingratitude of the chief butler, he was left two years longer in prison.

CHAPTER 41

Pharaoh's dream of the seven well-favored and seven ill-favored kine, 1-4. His dream of the seven full and seven thin ears of corn, 5-7. The magicians and wise men applied to for the interpretation of them, but can give no solution, 8. The chief butler recollects and recommends Joseph, 9-13. Pharaoh commands him to be brought out of prison, 14. Joseph appears before Pharaoh, 15-16. Pharaoh repeats his dreams, 17-24. Joseph interprets them, 25-32, and gives Pharaoh directions how to provide against the approaching scarcity, 33-36. Pharaoh, pleased with the counsel, appoints Joseph to be superintendent of all his affairs, 37-41. Joseph receives the badges of his new office, 42-43, and has his powers defined, 44; receives a new name, and marries Asenath, daughter of Potipherah, priest of On, 45. Joseph's age when brought before Pharaoh, 46. Great fertility of Egypt in the seven plenteous years, 47. Joseph hoards up the grain, 48-49. Ephraim and Manasseh born, 50-52. The seven years of famine commence with great rigor, 53-55. Joseph opens the storehouses to the Egyptians, 56. People from the neighboring countries come to Egypt to buy corn, the famine being in all those lands, 57.

1. *Two full years.* "Two years of days," two complete solar revolutions, after the events mentioned in the preceding chapter. *The river.* The Nile, the cause of the fertility of Egypt.

2. *There came up out of the river seven well favoured kine.* This must certainly refer to the hippopotamus or river horse, as the circumstances of coming up out of the river and feeding in the field characterize that animal alone. The hippopotamus is the well-known inhabitant of the Nile and frequently by night comes out of the river to feed in the fields, or in the sedge by the riverside.

6. *Blasted with the east wind.* It has been very properly observed that all the mischief

done to corn or fruit, by blasting, smutting, mildews, locusts is attributed to the *east wind.* See Exod. x. 13; xiv. 21; Ps. lxxviii. 26; Ezek. xvii. 10; Jonah iv. 8. In Egypt it is peculiarly destructive, because it comes through the parched deserts of Arabia, often destroying vast numbers of men and women. The action of this destructive wind is referred to by the Prophet Hosea, chap. xiii. 15: "Though he be fruitful among his brethren, an east wind shall come, the wind of the Lord shall come up from the wilderness, and his spring shall become dry, and his fountain shall be dried up: he shall spoil the treasure of all pleasant vessels."

8. *Called for all the magicians.* The word here used may probably mean no more than interpreters of abstruse and difficult subjects. They seem to have been such persons as Josephus (*Ant.,* lib. ii, c. 9, s. 2) calls "sacred scribes, or professors of sacred learning." *Wise men.* The persons who, according to Porphyry, "addicted themselves to the worship of God and the study of wisdom, passing their whole life in the contemplation of Divine things. Contemplation of the stars, self-purification, arithmetic, and geometry, and singing hymns in honour of their gods, was their continual employment."

9. *I do remember my faults.* It is not possible he could have forgotten the circumstance to which he here alludes; it was too intimately connected with all that was dear to him to permit him ever to forget it. But it was not convenient for him to remember this before; and probably he would not have remembered it now, had he not seen that giving this information in such a case was likely to serve his own interest.

14. *They brought him hastily out of the dungeon.* Pharaoh was in perplexity on account of his dreams; and when he heard of Joseph, he sent immediately to get him brought before him. *He shaved himself*—having let his beard grow all the time he was in prison, he now trimmed it, for it is not likely that either the Egyptians or Hebrews shaved themselves in our sense of the word. The change of raiment was, no doubt, furnished out of the king's wardrobe; as Joseph, in his present circumstances, could not be supposed to have any changes of raiment.

16. *It is not in me.* "Without or independently of me"—I am not essential to thy comfort; God himself has thee under His care. And "he will send thee," or answer thee, "peace"; thou shalt have prosperity howsoever ominous thy dreams may appear. By this answer he not only conciliated the mind of the king, but led him to expect his help from that God from whom alone all comfort, protection, and prosperity must proceed.

18. *Seven kine, fatfleshed.* See on v. 2. And observe further that the seven fat and the seven lean kine coming out of the same river plainly show, at once, the cause of both the plenty and the dearth. It is well known that there is scarcely any rain in Egypt; and that the country depends for its fertility on the overflowing of the Nile; and that the fertility is in proportion to the duration and quantity of the overflow. We may therefore safely conclude that the seven years of plenty were owing to an extraordinary overflowing of the Nile; and that the seven years of dearth were occasioned by a very partial or total want of this essentially necessary

inundation. Thus then the two sorts of cattle, signifying years of plenty and want, might be said to "come out of" the same river, as the inundation was either complete, partial, or wholly restrained.

21. *And when they had eaten them up.* Nothing can more powerfully mark the excess and severity of the famine than creatures eating each other, and yet without any effect, remaining as lean and as wretched as they were before.

25. *God hath shewed Pharaoh what he is about to do.* Joseph thus shows the Egyptian king that, though the ordinary cause of plenty or want is the river Nile, yet its inundations are under the direction of God; the dreams are sent by Him, not only to signify beforehand the plenty and want, but to show also that all these circumstances, however fortuitous they may appear to man, are under the direction of an overruling Providence.

31. *The plenty shall not be known in the land by reason of that famine following.* As Egypt depends for its fertility on the flowing of the Nile, and this flowing is not always equal, there must be a point to which it must rise to saturate the land sufficiently in order to produce grain sufficient for the support of its inhabitants. Pliny, *Hist. Nat.*, lib. v, c. 9, has given us a scale by which the plenty and the dearth may be ascertained. "The ordinary height of the inundations is sixteen cubits. When the waters are lower than this standard they do not overflow the whole ground; when above this standard, they are too long in running off. In the first place the ground is not saturated: by the second, the waters are detained so long on the ground that seed-time is lost. The province marks both. If it rise only twelve cubits, a famine is the consequence. Even at thirteen cubits hunger prevails; fourteen cubits produces general rejoicing; fifteen, perfect security; and sixteen, all the luxuries of life."

33. *A man discreet and wise.* As it is impossible that Joseph could have foreseen his own elevation, consequently he gave this advice without any reference to himself. The counsel, therefore, was either immediately inspired by God or was dictated by policy, prudence, and sound sense.

34. *Let him appoint officers.* "Visitors, overseers"; see chap. xxxix. 1.

37. *The thing was good.* Pharaoh and his courtiers saw that the counsel was prudent and should be carefully followed.

38. *In whom the Spirit of God is?* Ruach Elohim, the identical words used in chap. i. 2; and certainly to be understood here as in the preceding place. If the Egyptians were idolaters, they acknowledged Joseph's God.

40. *According unto thy word shall all my people be ruled.* Literally, "At thy mouth shall all my people kiss." In the Eastern countries it is customary to kiss anything that comes from a superior, and this is done by way of testifying respect and submission. In this sense the words in the text are to be understood: All the people shall pay the profoundest respect and obedience to all thy orders and commands. *Only in the throne will I be greater than thou.* This, in one word, is a perfect description of a prime minister. Thou shalt have the sole management, under me, of all state affairs.

42. *And Pharaoh took off his ring . . . and put it upon Joseph's hand.* In this ring was probably set the king's signet, by which the royal instruments were sealed; and thus Joseph was constituted what we would call lord chancellor, or lord keeper of the privy seal. *Vestures of fine linen.* Whether this means linen or cotton is not known. It seems to have been a term by which both were denominated; or it may be some other substance or cloth with which we are unacquainted. If the fine linen of Egypt was such as that which invests the bodies of the mummies, and these in general were persons of the first distinction, and consequently were enveloped in cloth of the finest quality, it was only fine comparatively speaking, Egypt being the only place at that time where such cloth was manufactured. I have often examined the cloth about the bodies of the most splendidly ornamented mummies, and found it sackcloth when compared with the fine Irish linens.

43. *He made him to ride in the second chariot.* That which usually followed the king's chariot in public ceremonies. *Bow the knee. Abrech,* which we translate bow the knee, and which we might as well translate anything else, is probably an Egyptian word, the signification of which is utterly unknown. If we could suppose it to be a Hebrew word, it might be considered as compounded of *ab,* "father," and *rach,* "tender"; for Joseph might be denominated a "father," because of his care over the people, and the provision he was making for their preservation; and tender because of his youth. Or it may be compounded of *ab,* "father," and *barech,* "blessing."

44. *I am Pharaoh.* The same as if he had said, "I am the king"; for "Pharaoh" was the common title of the sovereigns of Egypt.

45. *Zaphnath-paaneah.* The meaning of this title is as little known as that of *abrech* in the preceding verse. Some translate it, "The revealer of secrets"; others, "The treasury of glorious comfort." All the etymologies hitherto given of this word are, to say the least of them, doubtful. I believe it also to be an Egyptian epithet, designating the office to which he was now raised; and similar to our compound terms, prime minister, lord chancellor. *Asenath the daughter of Poti-pherah.* There is no likelihood that the Poti-pherah mentioned here is the same as the Potiphar who had purchased Joseph and on the false accusations of his wife cast him into prison. *Priest of On. On* is rendered Heliopolis (the city of the sun) by the Septuagint. *Joseph went out over all the land.* No doubt for the building of granaries, and appointing proper officers to receive the corn in every place.

46. *Joseph was thirty years old.* As he was seventeen years old when he was sold into Egypt, chap. xxxvii. 2, and was now thirty, he must have been thirteen years in slavery. *Stood before Pharaoh.* This phrase always means admission to the immediate presence of the sovereign, and having the honor of his most unlimited confidence.

47. *The earth brought forth by handfuls.* This probably refers principally to rice, as it grows in tufts, a great number of stalks proceeding from the same seed. In those years the Nile probably rose sixteen cubits; see on v. 31.

50. *Two sons.* Whom he called by names expressive of God's particular and bountiful providence towards him. Manasseh signifies "forgetfulness"; and Ephraim "fruitfulness"; and he called his sons by these names, because God had enabled him to forget all his toil, disgrace, and affliction, and had made him fruitful in the very land in which he had suffered the greatest misfortune and indignities.

54. *The seven years of dearth began to come.* Owing in Egypt to the Nile not rising more than twelve or thirteen cubits (see on v. 31); but there must have been other causes which affected other countries, not immediately dependent on the Nile, though remotely connected with Egypt and Canaan. *The dearth was in all lands.* All the countries dependent on the Nile. And it appears that a general drought had taken place, at least through all Egypt and Canaan; for it is said, v. 57, "that the famine was sore in all lands"—Egypt and Canaan, and their respective dependencies.

55. *When all the land of Egypt was famished.* As Pharaoh, by the advice of Joseph, had exacted a fifth part of all the grain during the seven years of plenty, it is very likely that no more was left than what was merely necessary to supply the ordinary demand both in the way of home consumption and for the purpose of barter or sale to neighboring countries.

56. *Over all the face of the earth.* The original should be translated, "all the face of that land," namely, Egypt, as it is explained at the end of the verse.

57. *All countries came into Egypt . . . to buy.* As there had not been a sufficiency of rains to swell the Nile, to effect a proper inundation in Egypt, the same cause would produce drought, and consequently scarcity, in all the neighboring countries; and this may be all that is intended in the text.

CHAPTER 42

Jacob sends his ten sons to Egypt to buy corn, 1-3; but refuses to permit Benjamin to go, 4. They arrive in Egypt, and bow themselves before Joseph, 5-6. He treats them roughly and calls them spies, 7-10. They defend themselves and give an account of their family, 11-13. He appears unmoved, and puts them all in prison for three days, 14-17. On the third day he releases them on condition of their bringing Benjamin, 18-20. Being convicted by their consciences, they reproach themselves with their cruelty to their brother Joseph, and consider themselves under the displeasure of God, 21-23. Joseph is greatly affected, detains Simeon as a pledge for Benjamin, orders their sacks to be filled with corn, and the purchase money to be put in each man's sack, 24-25. When one of them is going to give his ass provender he discovers his money in the mouth of his sack, at which they are greatly alarmed, 26-28. They come to their father in Canaan, and relate what happened to them in their journey, 29-34. On emptying their sacks, each man's money is found in his sack's mouth, which causes alarm both to them and their father, 35. Jacob deplores the loss of Joseph and Simeon, and refuses to let Benjamin go, though Reuben offers his two sons as pledges for his safety, 36-38.

1. *Jacob saw that there was corn.* That is, Jacob heard from the report of others that there was plenty in Egypt. Before agriculture was properly known and practiced, famines were frequent; Canaan seems to have been peculiarly vexed by them. There was one in this land in the time of Abraham, chap. xii. 10; another in the days of Isaac, chap. xxvi. 1; and now a third in the time of Jacob.

6. *Joseph was the governor.* A "protector." *Bowed down themselves before him.* Thus fulfilling the prophetic dream, chap. xxxvii. 7-8, which they had taken every precaution to render null and void. But there is neither might nor counsel against the Lord.

9. *Ye are spies.* "Ye are footmen, trampers about, foot-pads, vagabonds," lying in wait for the property of others; persons who, under the pretense of wishing to buy corn, desire only to find out whether the land be so defenseless that the tribes to which ye belong (see v. 11) may attack it successfully, drive out the inhabitants, and settle in it themselves; or, having plundered it, retire to their deserts. Thus Joseph spake roughly to them merely to cover that warmth of affection which he felt towards them; and that being thus brought, apparently, into straits and dangerous circumstances, their consciences might be awakened to reflect on and abhor their own wickedness.

11. *We are all one man's sons.* We do not belong to different tribes, and it is not likely that one family would make a hostile attempt upon a whole kingdom. This seems to be the very ground that Joseph took, namely, that they were persons belonging to different tribes. Against this particularly they set up their defense, asserting that they all belonged to one family; and it is on the proof of this that Joseph puts them, v. 15, in obliging them to leave one as a hostage, and insisting on their bringing their remaining brother; so that he took exactly the same precautions to detect them as if he had had no acquaintance with them, and had every reason to be suspicious.

13. *One is not.* An elliptical sentence, "One is not alive."

15. *By the life of Pharaoh.* "Pharaoh liveth." As if he said, As surely as the king of Egypt lives, so surely shall ye not go hence unless your brother come hither. Here, therefore, is no oath; it is just what they themselves make it in their report to their father, chap. xliii. 3: "The man did solemnly protest unto us"; and our translators should not have put it in the form of an oath, especially as the original not only will bear another version, but is absolutely repugnant to this in our sense of the word.

18. *I fear God.* He seems to say to his brethren, I am a worshipper of the true God, and ye have nothing to fear.

21. *We are verily guilty.* How finely are the office and influence of conscience exemplified in these words! It was about twenty-two years since they had sold their brother, and probably their consciences had been lulled asleep to the present hour. God combines and brings about those favorable circumstances which produce attention and reflection and give weight to the expostulations of conscience.

23. *For he spake unto them by an interpreter.* Either there was a very great difference between the two languages as then spoken, or Joseph, to prevent all suspicion, might affect to be ignorant of both. We have many evidences in this book that the Egyptians, Hebrews, Canaanites, and Syrians could understand each other in a general way, though there are also proofs that there was a considerable difference between their dialects.

25. *Commanded to fill their sacks.* "Their vessels"; probably large woolen bags, or baskets lined with leather. These vessels, of whatever

sort, must have been different from those called *sak* in the twenty-seventh and following verses, which was probably only a small "sack" or "bag," in which each had reserved a sufficiency of corn for his ass during the journey; the larger vessels or bags serving to hold the wheat or rice they had brought, and their own packages. The reader will at once see that the English word "sack" is plainly derived from the Hebrew.

26. *They laded their asses.* Amounting, no doubt, to several scores, if not hundreds, else they could not have brought a sufficiency of corn for the support of so large a family as that of Jacob.

27. *One of them opened his sack.* From v. 35 we learn that each of the ten brethren on emptying his sack when he returned found his money in it; can we suppose that this was not discovered by them all before? It seems not; and the reason was probably this: the money was put in the mouth of the sack of one only, in the sacks of the others it was placed at or near to the bottom; hence only one discovered it on the road, the rest found it when they came to empty their sacks at their father's house. *In the inn.* Our word *inn* gives us a false idea here; there were no such places of entertainment at that time in the desert over which they had to pass, nor are there any to the present day. Travellers generally endeavor to reach a well, where they fill their leathern bottles with fresh water, and having clogged their camels, asses, etc., permit them to crop any little verdure there may be in the place, keeping watch over them by turns.

28. *Their heart failed them.* "Their heart went out." This refers to that spasmodic affection which is felt in the breast at any sudden alarm or fright. Among the common people in our own country we find an expression exactly similar, "My heart was ready to leap out at my mouth," used on similar occasions. *What is this that God hath done unto us?* Their guilty consciences, now thoroughly awakened, were in continual alarms; they felt that they deserved God's curse, and every occurrence served to confirm and increase their suspicions.

36. *All these things are against me.* Literally, "All these things are upon me." They lie upon me as heavy loads, hastening my death; they are more than I can bear.

37. *Slay my two sons, if I bring him not to thee.* What a strange proposal made by a son to his father, concerning his grandchildren! But they show the honesty and affection of Reuben's heart; he felt deeply for his father's distress, and was determined to risk and hazard everything in order to relieve and comfort him. There is scarcely a transaction in which Reuben is concerned that does not serve to set his character in an amiable point of view, except the single instance mentioned in chap. xxxv. 22.

38. *He is left alone.* That is, Benjamin is the only remaining son of Rachel; for he supposed Joseph, who was the other son, to be dead. *Shall ye bring down my gray hairs with sorrow.* Here he keeps up the idea of the oppressive burden mentioned in v. 36, to which every occurrence was adding an additional weight, so that he felt it impossible to support it any longer.

CHAPTER 43

The famine continuing, Jacob desires his sons to go again to Egypt and buy some food, 1-2. Judah shows the necessity of Benjamin's accompanying them, without whom it would be useless to return to Egypt, 3-5. Jacob expostulates with him, 6. Judah replies, and offers to become surety for Benjamin, 7-10. Jacob at last consents, and desires them to take a present with them for the governor of Egypt; and double money, that which they had brought back in their sacks' mouth, and the price of the load they were now to bring; and, having prayed for them, sends them away, 11-15. They arrive in Egypt, and are brought to Joseph's house to dine with him, at which they are greatly alarmed, 16-18. They speak to the steward of Joseph's house concerning the money returned in their sacks, 19-22. He gives them encouragement, 23-24. Having made ready the present, they bring it to Joseph when he came home to dine, 25-26. He speaks kindly to them, and inquires concerning their health, and that of their father, 27-28. Joseph is greatly affected at seeing his brother Benjamin, 29-31. They dine with him, and are distinguished according to their seniority; but Benjamin receives marks of peculiar favor, 32-34.

8. *Send the lad with me.* As the original is not *yeled*, from which we have derived our word "lad," but *naar*, it would have been better had our translators rendered it by some other term, such as "the youth," or "the young man," and thus the distinction in the Hebrew would have been better kept up. Benjamin was at this time at least twenty-four years of age, some think thirty, and had a family of his own. See chap. xlvi. 21. *That we may live, and not die.* An argument drawn from self-preservation, what some have termed "the first law of nature." By your keeping Benjamin we are prevented from going to Egypt; if we go not to Egypt we shall get no corn; if we get no corn we shall all perish by famine; and Benjamin himself, who otherwise might live, must, with thee and the whole family, infallibly die.

9. *Let me bear the blame for ever.* "Then shall I sin against thee all my days," and consequently be liable to punishment for violating my faith.

11. *Carry down the man a present.* From the very earliest times presents were used as means of introduction to great men. This is particularly noticed by Solomon: "A man's gift maketh room for him, and bringeth him before great men," Prov. xviii. 16. But what was the present brought to Joseph on this occasion? After all the labor of commentators, we are obliged to be contented with probabilities and conjecture. According to our translation, the gifts were balm, honey, spices, myrrh, nuts, and almonds.

12. *Double money.* What was returned in their sacks, and what was farther necessary to buy another load.

14. This verse may be literally translated thus: "And God, the all-sufficient, shall give you tender mercies before the man, and send to you your other brother, and Benjamin; and I, as I shall be childless, so I shall be childless." That is, I will submit to this privation, till God shall restore my children. It appears that this verse is spoken prophetically; and that God at this time gave Jacob a supernatural evidence that his children should be restored.

16. *Slay, and make ready. Teboach tebach,* "slay a slaying," or make a great slaughter—let preparations be made for a great feast or entertainment. See a similar form of speech, Prov. ix. 2; 1 Sam. xxv. 11; and Gen. xxxi. 54.

18. *And the men were afraid.* A guilty conscience needs no accuser. Everything alarms them; they now feel that God is exacting ret-

ribution, and they know not what the degrees shall be, nor where it shall stop. *Fall upon us.* "Roll himself upon us." A metaphor taken from wrestlers; when a man has overthrown his antagonist, he rolls himself upon him, in order to keep him down. *And our asses.* Which they probably had in great number with them; and which, if captured, would have been a great loss to the family of Jacob, as such cattle must have constituted a principal part of its riches.

20. *O sir, we came indeed . . . to buy food.* There is a frankness now in the conduct of Joseph's brethren that did not exist before; they simply and honestly relate the whole circumstance of the money being found in their sacks on their return from their last journey. Afflictions from the hand of God, and under His direction, have a wonderful tendency to humble the soul. Did men know how gracious His designs are in sending such, no murmur would ever be heard against the dispensations of Divine Providence.

23. *And he said.* The address of the steward in this verse plainly proves that the knowledge of the true God was in Egypt. It is probable that the steward himself was a Hebrew, and that Joseph had given him intimation of the whole affair; and though he was not at liberty to reveal it, yet he gives them assurances that the whole business will issue happily. *I had your money.* "Your money comes to me." As I am the steward, the cash for the corn belongs to me. Ye have no reason to be apprehensive of any evil; the whole transaction is between myself and you; receive, therefore, the money as a present from the God of your father, no matter whose hands He makes use of to convey it. The conduct of the steward, as well as his words, had a great tendency to relieve their burdened minds.

24. *Brought the men into Joseph's house.* This is exactly the way in which a Hindoo receives a guest. As soon as he enters, one of the civilities is the presenting of water to wash his feet.

27. *And he asked them of their welfare.* This verse may be thus translated: "And he asked them concerning their prosperity; and he said, Is your father prosperous, the old man who ye told me was alive? And they said, Thy servant our father prospers; he is yet alive."

29. *He lifted up his eyes, and saw his brother Benjamin.* They were probably introduced to him successively; and as Benjamin was the youngest, he would of course be introduced last. *God be gracious unto thee, my son.* A usual salutation in the East from the aged and superiors to the younger and inferiors.

32. *They set on for him by himself.* From the text it appears evident that there were three tables, one for Joseph, one for the Egyptians, and one for the eleven brethren. *The Egyptians might not eat bread with the Hebrews.* There might have been some *political* reason for this, with which we are unacquainted; but independently of this, two may be assigned. (1) The Hebrews were shepherds; and Egypt had been almost ruined by hordes of lawless wandering banditti, under the name of *Hyksos,* or "king-shepherds." (2) The Hebrews sacrificed those animals which the Egyptians held sacred, and fed on their flesh.

33. *The firstborn according to his birthright.* This must greatly astonish these brethren, to find themselves treated with so much ceremony and at the same time with so much discernment of their respective ages.

34. *Benjamin's mess was five times so much as any of theirs.* The circumstance of Benjamin's having a mess five times as large as any of his brethren shows the peculiar honor which Joseph designed to confer upon him.

CHAPTER 44

Joseph commands his steward to put his cup secretly into Benjamin's sack, 1-2. The sons of Jacob depart with the corn they had purchased, 3. Joseph commands his steward to pursue them, and charge them with having stolen his cup, 4-6. The brethren excuse themselves, protest their innocence, and offer to submit to be slaves should the cup be found with any of them, 7-9. Search is made, and the cup is found in Benjamin's sack, 10-12. They are brought back and submit themselves to Joseph, 13-16. He determines that Benjamin alone, with whom the cup is found, shall remain in captivity, 17. Judah, in a most affecting speech, pleads for Benjamin's enlargement, and offers himself to be a bondman in his stead, 18-34.

2. *Put my cup . . . in the sack's mouth of the youngest.* The stratagem of the cup seems to have been designed to bring Joseph's brethren into the highest state of perplexity and distress, that their deliverance by the discovery that Joseph was their brother might have its highest effect.

5. *Whereby . . . he divineth?* Divination by cups has been from time immemorial prevalent among the Asiatics; and for want of knowing this, commentators have spent a profusion of learned labor upon these words, in order to reduce them to that kind of meaning which would at once be consistent with the scope and design of the history, and save Joseph from the impeachment of sorcery and divination. I take the word *nachash* here in its general acceptation of "to view attentively, to inquire." Now though it is not at all likely that Joseph practiced any kind of divination, yet probably, according to the superstition of those times, supernatural influence might be attributed to his cup; and as the whole transaction related here was merely intended to deceive his brethren for a short time, he might as well affect divination by his cup, as he affected to believe they had stolen it. The steward, therefore, uses the word *nachash* in its proper meaning: "Is not this it out of which my lord drinketh, and in which he inspecteth accurately?" And hence Joseph says, v. 15: *Wot ye not*—did ye not know, *that such a person as I* (having such a cup) *would accurately and attentively look into it?*

16. *What shall we say?* No words can more strongly mark confusion and perturbation of mind. They, no doubt, all thought that Benjamin had actually stolen the cup; and the probability of this guilt might be heightened by the circumstance of his having that very cup to drink out of at dinner; for as he had the most honorable mess, so it is likely he had the most honorable cup to drink out of at the entertainment.

18. *Thou art even as Pharaoh.* As wise, as powerful, and as much to be dreaded as he. In the Asiatic countries, the reigning monarch is always considered to be the pattern of all perfection; and the highest honor that can be

conferred on any person is to resemble him to the monarch, as the monarch himself is likened, in the same complimentary way, to an angel of God. See 2 Sam. xiv. 17-18. Judah is the chief speaker here, because it was in consequence of his becoming surety for Benjamin that Jacob permitted him to accompany them to Egypt. See chap. xliii. 9.

No paraphrase can heighten the effect of Judah's address to Joseph. It is perhaps one of the most tender, affecting pieces of natural oratory ever spoken or penned; and we need not wonder to find that when Joseph heard it he could not refrain himself, but wept aloud. His soul must have been insensible beyond what is common to human nature had he not immediately yielded to a speech so delicately tender and so powerfully impressive. We cannot but deplore the unnatural and unscientific division of the narrative in our common Bibles, which obliges us to have recourse to another chapter in order to witness the effects which this speech produced on the heart of Joseph.

CHAPTER 45

Joseph, deeply affected with the speech of Judah, could no longer conceal himself, but discovers himself to his brethren, 1-4. Excuses their conduct towards him, and attributes the whole to the providence of God, 5-8. Orders them to hasten to Canaan, and bring up their father and their own families, cattle, etc., because there were five years of the famine yet to come, 9-13. He embraces and converses with all his brethren, 14-15. Pharaoh, hearing that Joseph's brethren were come to Egypt, and that Joseph had desired them to return to Canaan and bring back their families, not only confirms the order, but promises them the best part of the land of Egypt to dwell in; and provides them carriages to transport themselves and their households, 16-20. Joseph provides them with wagons according to the commandment of Pharaoh; and having given them various presents, sends them away with suitable advice, 21-24. They depart, arrive in Canaan, and announce the glad tidings to their father, who for a time believes not, but being assured of the truth of their relation, is greatly comforted, and resolves to visit Egypt, 25-28.

1. *Joseph could not refrain himself.* The word *hithappek* is very emphatic; it signifies to "force one's self, to do something against nature, to do violence to one's self." Joseph could no longer constrain himself to act a feigned part—all the brother and the son rose up in him at once, and overpowered all his resolutions; he felt for his father, he realized his disappointment and agony; and he felt for his brethren, "now at his feet submissive in distress"; and, that he might give free and full scope to his feelings, and the most ample play of the workings of his affectionate heart, he ordered all his attendants to go out, while he made himself known to his brethren.

2. *The Egyptians and the house of Pharaoh heard.* Pharaoh's servants, or any of the members of his household, such as those whom Joseph had desired to withdraw, and who might still be within hearing of his voice. The words may only mean that the report was brought to Pharaoh's house.

5. *Be not grieved, nor angry with yourselves.* This discovers a truly noble mind; he not only forgives and forgets, but he wishes even those who had wronged him to forget the injury they had done, that they might not suffer distress on the account; and with deep piety he attributes the whole to the providence of God; for, says he, *God did send me before you to preserve life.* On every word here a strong emphasis may be laid. It is not *you,* but *God;* it is not you that

sold me, but God who *sent* me; Egypt and Canaan must both have perished had not a merciful provision been made; you were to come down hither, and God sent me before you; death must have been the consequence of this famine had not God sent me here to preserve life.

6. *There shall neither be earing nor harvest.* Earing has been supposed to mean collecting the ears of corn, which would confound it with harvest. The word, however, means ploughing or seedtime, and plainly means that there should be no seedtime, and consequently no *harvest;* and why? Because there should be a total want of rain in other countries, and the Nile should not rise above twelve cubits in Egypt; see on chap. xli. 31. But the expressions here must be qualified a little, as we find from chap. xlvii. 19 that the Egyptians came to Joseph to buy seed; and it is probable that even during this famine they sowed some of the ground, particularly on the borders of the river, from which a crop, though not an abundant one, might be produced. The passage, however, in the above chapter may refer to the last year of the famine, when they came to procure seed for the ensuing year.

8. *He hath made me a father to Pharaoh.* It has already been conjectured that father was a name of office in Egypt, and that "father of Pharaoh" might among them signify the same as prime minister or the king's minister does among us. In Judg. xvii. 10, Micah says to the young Levite, "Dwell with me, and be unto me a father and a priest."

10. *Thou shalt dwell in the land of Goshen.* Probably this district had been allotted to Joseph by the king of Egypt, else we can scarcely think he could have promised it so positively without first obtaining Pharaoh's consent. Goshen was the most easterly province of Lower Egypt, not far from the Arabian Gulf, lying next to Canaan, from whence it is supposed to have been about fourscore miles distant, though Hebron was distant from the Egyptian capital about three hundred miles. At Goshen, Jacob stayed till Joseph visited him, chap. xlvi. 28. It is also called the "land of Rameses," chap. xlvii. 11, from a city of that name, which was the metropolis of the country. Josephus, *Antiq.,* 1. ii, c. 4, makes Heliopolis, the city of Joseph's father-in-law, the place of the Israelites' residence. As *geshem* signifies "rain" in Hebrew, St. Jerome and some others have supposed that *Goshen* comes from the same root, and that the land in question was called thus because it had rain, which was not the case with Egypt in general; and as it was on the confines of the Arabian Gulf, it is very probable that it was watered from heaven, and it might be owing to this circumstance that it was peculiarly fertile, for it is stated to be the "best" of the land of Egypt. See chap. xlvii. 6, 11.

12. *That it is my mouth that speaketh unto you.* Undoubtedly Joseph laid considerable stress on his speaking with them in the Hebrew tongue, without the assistance of an interpreter, as in the case mentioned in chap. xlii. 23.

14. *He fell upon his brother Benjamin's neck.* Among the Asiatics kissing the beard, the neck, and the shoulders is in use to the present day; and probably falling on the neck signifies no more than kissing the neck or shoulders, with the arms around.

20. *Regard not your stuff.* Literally, "Let not your eye spare your instruments" or vessels. *Keleychem,* a general term, in which may be included household furniture, agricultural utensils, or implements of any description. They were not to delay nor encumber themselves with articles which could be readily found in Egypt, and were not worth so long a carriage.

21. *Joseph gave them wagons.* Agaloth, from *agal,* which, though not used as a verb in the Hebrew Bible, evidently means to "turn round, roll round," and hence very properly applied to wheel carriages. It appears from this that such vehicles were very early in use, and that the road from Egypt to Canaan must have been very open and much frequented, else such carriages could not have passed by it.

22. *Changes of raiment.* It is a common custom with all the Asiatic sovereigns to give both garments and money to ambassadors and persons of distinction whom they particularly wish to honor. Hence they keep in their wardrobes several hundred changes of raiment, ready made up for presents of this kind. That such were given by way of reward and honor, see Judg. xiv. 12, 19; Rev. vi. 11.

23. *Meat for his father by the way.* Mazon, from *zan,* to "prepare, provide." Hence "prepared meat," some made-up dish. As the word is used, 2 Chron. xvi. 14, for aromatic preparations, it may be restrained in its meaning to something of that kind here.

24. *See that ye fall not out by the way.* This prudent caution was given by Joseph to prevent his brethren from accusing each other for having sold him; and to prevent them from envying Benjamin for the superior favor shown him by his brother. It is strange, but so it is, that children of the same parents are apt to envy each other, fall out, and contend; and therefore the exhortation in this verse must be always seasonable in a large family.

26. *Jacob's heart fainted.* Probably the good news so overpowered him as to cast him into a swoon. *He believed them not*—he thought it was too good news to be true.

27. *When he saw the wagons ... the spirit of Jacob ... revived.* The wagons were additional evidences of the truth of what he had heard from his sons; and the consequence was that he was restored to fresh vigor, he seemed as if he had gained new life, *vattechi,* "and he lived."

28. *It is enough; Joseph my son is yet alive.* It was not the state of dignity to which Joseph had arisen that particularly affected Jacob; it was the consideration that he was still alive. It was this that caused him to exclaim *rab;* "Much! Multiplied! My son is yet alive! I will go and see him before I die." None can realize this scene; the words, the circumstances, all refer to indescribable feelings.

This chapter, which contains the unravelling of the plot, and wonderfully illustrates the mysteries of these particular providences, is one of the most interesting in the whole account; the speech of Joseph to his brethren, vv. 1-13, is inferior only to that of Judah in the preceding chapter. He saw that his brethren were confounded at his presence, that they were struck with his present power, and that they keenly remembered and deeply deplored their own guilt. It was necessary to comfort them, lest their hearts should have been overwhelmed with overmuch sorrow. How delicate and finely wrought is the apology he makes for them! The whole heart of the affectionate brother is at once seen in it—art is confounded and swallowed up by nature—"Be not grieved, nor angry with yourselves ... it was not *you* that sent me hither, but God." What he says also concerning his father shows the warmest feelings of a benevolent and filial heart. Indeed, the whole chapter is a masterpiece of composition, and it is the more impressive because it is evidently a simple relation of facts just as they occurred.

CHAPTER 46

Jacob begins his journey to Egypt, comes to Beer-sheba, and offers sacrifices to God, 1. God appears to him in a vision, gives him gracious promises, and assures him of His protection, 2-4. He proceeds, with his family and their cattle, on his journey towards Egypt, 5-7. A genealogical enumeration of the seventy persons who went down to Egypt, 8, etc. The posterity of Jacob by Leah. Reuben and his sons. 9. Simeon and his sons. 10. Levi and his sons, 11. Judah and his sons, 12. Issachar and his sons. 13. And Zebulun and his sons. 14. All the posterity of Jacob by Leah, thirty and three, 15. The posterity of Jacob by Zilpah. Gad and his sons, 16. Asher and his sons, 17. All the posterity of Jacob by Zilpah, sixteen, 18. The posterity of Jacob by Rachel. Joseph and his sons, 19-20. Benjamin and his sons, 21. All the posterity of Jacob by Rachel, fourteen, 22. The posterity of Jacob by Bilhah. Dan and his sons, 23. Naphtali and his sons, 24. All the posterity of Jacob by Bilhah, seven, 25. All the immediate descendants of Jacob by his four wives, threescore and six, 26; and all the descendants of the house of Jacob, seventy souls, 27. Judah is sent before to inform Joseph of his father's coming, 28. Joseph goes to Goshen to meet Jacob, 29. Their affecting interview, 30. Joseph proposes to return to Pharaoh, and inform him of the arrival of his family, 31, and of their occupation, as keepers of cattle, 32. Instructs them what to say when called before Pharaoh, and questioned by him, that they might be permitted to dwell unmolested in the land of Goshen, 33-34.

1. *And came to Beer-sheba.* This place appears to be mentioned, not only because it was the way from Hebron, where Jacob resided, to Egypt, whither he was going, but because it was a consecrated place, a place where God had appeared to Abraham, chap. xxi. 33, and to Isaac, chap. xxvi. 23, and where Jacob is encouraged to expect a manifestation of the same goodness. He chooses, therefore, to begin his journey with a visit to God's house; and as he is going into a strange land, he feels it right to renew his covenant with God by sacrifice. There is an old proverb which applies strongly to this case: "Prayers and provender never hinder any man's journey." He who would travel safely must take God with him.

3. *Fear not to go down into Egypt.* It appears that there had been some doubts in the patriarch's mind relative to the propriety of this journey; he found, from the confession of his own sons, how little they were to be trusted. But every doubt is dispelled by this divine manifestation. (1) He may go down confidently; no evil shall befall him. (2) Even in Egypt the covenant shall be fulfilled: God will make of him there a great nation. (3) God himself will accompany him on his journey, be with him in the strange land, and even bring back his bones to rest with those of his fathers. (4) He shall see Joseph, and this same beloved son shall be with him in his last hours, and do the last kind office for him. "Joseph shall put his hand upon thine eyes." It is not likely that Jacob would have at all attempted to go down to Egypt had he not received these assurances from God; and it is very likely that he offered his sacrifice merely to obtain this information. It was now a

time of famine in Egypt, and God had forbidden his father, Isaac, to go down to Egypt when there was a famine there, chap. xxvi. 1-3; besides, he may have had some general intimation of the prophecy delivered to his grandfather, Abraham, that his seed should be afflicted in Egypt, chap. xv. 13-14; and he also knew that Canaan, not Egypt, was to be the inheritance of his family, chap. xii. On all these accounts it was necessary to have the most explicit directions from God before he should take such a journey.

7. *All his seed brought he with him into Egypt.* When Jacob went down into Egypt he was in the one hundred and thirtieth year of his age, 215 years after the promise was made to Abraham, chap. xii. 1-4.

8. *These are the names of the children of Israel.* It may be necessary to observe here, *First,* that several of these names are expressed differently elsewhere; compare Num. xxvi. 12; 1 Chron. iv. 24. But it is no uncommon case for the same person to have different names, or the same name to be differently pronounced; see chap. xxv. 15. *Secondly,* that it is probable that some names in this list are brought in by prolepsis or anticipation, as the persons were born (probably) during the seventeen years which Jacob sojourned in Egypt, see v. 12. *Thirdly,* that the families of some are entered more at large than others because of their peculiar respectability, as in the case of Judah, Joseph, and Benjamin.

12. *The sons of Pharez were Hezron and Hamul.* It is not likely that Pharez was more than ten years of age when he came into Egypt, and if so he could not have had children; therefore it is necessary to consider Hezron and Hamul as being born during the seventeen years that Jacob sojourned in Egypt, see on v. 8; and it appears necessary, for several reasons, to take these seventeen years into the account, as it is very probable that what is called the going down into Egypt includes the seventeen years which Jacob spent there.

20. *Unto Joseph . . . were born Manasseh and Ephraim.* There is a remarkable addition here in the Septuagint, which must be noticed: "These were the sons of Manasseh whom his Syrian concubine bore unto him: Machir; and Machir begat Galaad. The sons of Ephraim, Manasseh's brother, were Sutalaam and Taam; and the sons of Sutalaam, Edem." These add five persons to the list, and make out the number given by Stephen, Acts vii. 14, which it seems he had taken from the text of the Septuagint. The addition in the Septuagint is not found in either the Hebrew or the Samaritan at present; and some suppose that it was taken either from Num. xxvi. 29, 35 or 1 Chron. vii. 14-20, but in none of these places does the addition appear as it stands in the Septuagint, though some of the names are found interspersed. Various means have been proposed to find the seventy persons in the text, and to reconcile the Hebrew with the Septuagint and the New Testament.

Dr. Hales's method is, I think, satisfactory: "Moses states that all the souls that came with Jacob into Egypt, which issued from his loins (except his sons' wives), were sixty-six souls, Gen. xlvi. 26. . . . If to these sixty-six children, and grandchildren, and great-grandchildren, we add Jacob himself, Joseph and his two sons,

the amount is seventy, the whole amount of Jacob's family which settled in Egypt.

"In this statement the wives of Jacob's sons, who formed part of the household, are omitted; but they amounted to nine, for of the twelve wives of the twelve sons of Jacob, Judah's wife was dead, chap. xxxviii. 12, and Simeon's also, as we may collect from his youngest son Shaul by a Canaanitess, v. 10, and Joseph's wife was already in Egypt. These nine wives, therefore, added to the sixty-six, give seventy-five souls, the whole amount of Jacob's household that went down with him to Egypt; critically corresponding with the statement in the New Testament, that 'Joseph sent for his father Jacob and all his kindred, amounting to seventy-five souls.' "

28. *He sent Judah before him unto Joseph.* Judah was certainly a man of sense, and also an eloquent man; and of him Joseph must have had a very favorable opinion from the speech he delivered before him, chap. xliv. 18, etc.; he was therefore chosen as the most proper person to go before and announce Jacob's arrival to his son Joseph.

29. *And Joseph made ready his chariot.* In chap. xli. 43 we have the first mention of a chariot, and if the translation be correct, it is a proof that the arts were not in a rude state in Egypt even at this early time. When we find wagons used to transport goods from place to place, we need not wonder that these suggested the idea of forming chariots for carrying persons, and especially those of high rank and authority.

30. *Now let me die, since I have seen thy face.* Perhaps old Simeon had this place in view when, seeing the salvation of Israel, he said, "Lord, now lettest thou thy servant depart in peace," Luke ii. 29.

34. *Thy servants' trade hath been about cattle.* As this land was both fruitful and pleasant, Joseph wished to fix his family in that part of Egypt; hence he advises them to tell Pharaoh that their trade had been in cattle from their youth: and because every shepherd is an abomination to the Egyptians, hence he concluded that there would be less difficulty to get them quiet settlement in Goshen, as they would then be separated from the Egyptians, and consequently have the free use of all their religious customs. This scheme succeeded, and the consequence was the preservation of both their religion and their lives. As it is well known that the Egyptians had cattle and flocks themselves, and that Pharaoh even requested that some of Joseph's brethren should be made rulers over his cattle, how could it be said, *Every shepherd is an abomination unto the Egyptians?* Three reasons may be assigned for this: (1) Shepherds and feeders of cattle were usually a sort of lawless, freebooting banditti. (2) They must have abhorred shepherds if Manetho's account of the Hyksos or king-shepherds can be credited. Hordes of marauders under this name, from Arabia, Syria, and Ethiopia, made a powerful irruption into Egypt, which they subdued and ruled with great tyranny for 259 years. (3) The last and probably the best reason why the Egyptians abhorred such shepherds as were the Israelites was that they sacrificed those very animals, the ox particularly, and the sheep, which the Egyptians held sacred. Hence the

Roman historian Tacitus, speaking of the Jews, says: "They sacrifice the ram in order to insult Jupiter Ammon, and they sacrifice the ox, which the Egyptians worship under the name of Apis."

CHAPTER 47

Joseph informs Pharaoh that his father and brethren are arrived in Goshen, 1. He presents five of his brethren before the king, 2, who questions them concerning their occupation; they inform him that they are shepherds, and request permission to dwell in the land of Goshen, 3-4. Pharaoh consents, and desires that some of the most active of them should be made rulers over his cattle, 5-6. Joseph presents his father to Pharaoh, 7, who questions him concerning his age, 8, to which Jacob returns an affecting answer, and blesses Pharaoh, 9-10. Joseph places his father and family in the land of Rameses (Goshen), and furnishes them with provisions, 11-12. The famine prevailing in the land, the Egyptians deliver up all their money to Joseph to get food, 13-15. The next year they bring their cattle, 16-17. The third, their lands and their persons, 18-21. The land of the priests Joseph does not buy, as it was a royal grant to them from Pharaoh, 22. The people receive seed to sow the land on condition that they shall give a fifth part of the produce to the king, 23-24. The people agree, and Joseph makes it a law all over Egypt, 25-26. The Israelites multiply exceedingly, 27. Jacob, having lived seventeen years in Goshen, and being one hundred and forty-seven years old, 28, makes Joseph promise not to bury him in Egypt, but in Canaan, 29-30. Joseph promises and confirms it with an oath, 31.

2. *He took some of his brethren.* There is something very strange in the original; literally translated it signifies "from the end or extremity of his brethren he took five men." It is certain that in Judg. xviii. 2 the word may be understood as implying dignity, valor, excellence, and preeminence. But the word may be understood simply as signifying *some;* out of the whole of his brethren he took only five men.

6. *In the best of the land make thy father and brethren to dwell; in the land of Goshen let them dwell.* So it appears that the land of Goshen was the best of the land of Egypt. *Men of activity.* "Stout or robust men"—such as were capable of bearing fatigue, and of rendering their authority respectable. *Rulers over my cattle.* *Mikneh* signifies not only *cattle,* but "possessions" or "property" of any kind; though most usually cattle are intended, because in ancient times they constituted the principal part of a man's property. The word may be taken here in a more extensive sense, and the circumstances of the case seem obviously to require it. If every shepherd was an abomination to the Egyptians, however we may understand or qualify the expression, is it to be supposed that Pharaoh should desire that the brethren of his prime minister, of his chief favorite, should be employed in some of the very meanest offices in the land? We may therefore safely understand Pharaoh as expressing his will that the brethren of Joseph should be appointed as overseers or superintendents of his domestic concerns, while Joseph superintended those of the state.

7. *Jacob blessed Pharaoh.* Saluted him on his entrance with "Peace be unto thee," or some such expression of respect and goodwill.

9. *The days of the years of my pilgrimage.* Of my "sojourning" or "wandering." Jacob had always lived a migratory or wandering life, in different parts of Canaan, Mesopotamia, and Egypt, scarcely ever at rest; and in the places where he lived longest, always exposed to the fatigues of the field and the desert.

Have not attained unto the . . . life of my fathers. Jacob lived in the whole one hundred and forty-seven years; Isaac, his father, lived one hundred and eighty; and Abraham, his grandfather, one hundred and seventy-five.

14. *Gathered up all the money.* I.e., by selling corn out of the public stores to the people; and this he did till the money failed, v. 15, till all the money was exchanged for corn, and brought into Pharaoh's treasury. Besides the fifth part of the produce of the seven plentiful years, Joseph had bought additional corn with Pharaoh's money to lay up against the famine that was to prevail in the seven years of dearth; and it is very likely that this was sold out at the price for which it was bought, and the fifth part, which belonged to Pharaoh, sold out at the same price. And as money at that time could not be plentiful, the cash of the whole nation was thus exhausted, as far as that had circulated among the common people.

16. *Give your cattle.* This was the wisest measure that could be adopted, for the preservation both of the people and of the cattle also. As the people had not grain for their own sustenance, consequently they could have none for their cattle; hence the cattle were in the most imminent danger of starving; and the people also were in equal danger, as they must have divided a portion of that bought for themselves with the cattle, which for the sake of tillage they wished of course to preserve till the seven years of famine should end. The cattle being bought by Joseph were supported at the royal expense, and very likely returned to the people at the end of the famine; for how else could they cultivate their ground, transport their merchandise, etc.? For this part of Joseph's conduct he certainly deserves high praise and no censure.

18. *When that year was ended.* The sixth year of the famine, *they came unto him the second year,* which was the last or seventh year of the famine, in which it was necessary to sow the land that there might be a crop the succeeding year; for Joseph, on whose prediction they relied, had foretold that the famine should continue only seven years, and consequently they expected the eighth year to be a fruitful year provided the land was sowed, without which, though the inundation of the land by the Nile might amount to the sixteen requisite cubits, there could be no crop.

21. *And as for the people, he removed them to cities.* It is very likely that Joseph was influenced by no political motive in removing the people to the cities, but merely by a motive of humanity and prudence. As the corn was laid up in the cities, he found it more convenient to bring them to the place where they might be conveniently fed, each being within the reach of an easy distribution. Thus then the country which could afford no sustenance was abandoned for the time being, that the people might be fed in those places where the provision was deposited.

22. *The land of the priests bought he not.* From this verse it is natural to infer that whatever the religion of Egypt was, it was established by law and supported by the state. Hence when Joseph bought all the lands of the Egyptians for Pharaoh, he bought not the land

of the priests, for that was a *portion assigned them of Pharaoh, and they did eat,* did live on, that *portion.* This is the earliest account we have of an established religion supported by the state.

23. *I have bought you this day and your land for Pharaoh.* It fully appears that the kingdom of Egypt was previously to the time of Joseph a very limited monarchy. The king had his estates; the priests had their lands; and the common people their patrimony independently of both. The land of Rameses, or Goshen, appears to have been the king's land, v. 11. The priests had their lands, which they did not sell to Joseph, vv. 22, 26; and that the people had lands independent of the crown is evident from the purchases Joseph made, vv. 19-20; and we may conclude from those purchases that Pharaoh had no power to levy taxes upon his subjects to increase his own revenue until he had bought the original right which each individual had in his possessions. And when Joseph bought this for the king he raised the crown an ample revenue, though he restored the lands, by obliging each to pay one-fifth of the product to the king, v. 24. And it is worthy of remark that the people of Egypt well understood the distinction between subjects and servants; for when they came to sell their land, they offered to sell themselves also, and said: "Buy us and our land . . . and we and our land will be servants unto Pharaoh," v. 19.

26. *And Joseph made it a law.* That the people should hold their land from the king and give him the fifth part of the produce as a yearly tax. Beyond this it appears the king had no further demands. The whole of this conduct of Joseph has been as strongly censured by some as applauded by others. It is natural for men to run into extremes in attacking or defending any position. Sober and judicious men will consider what Joseph did by divine appointment as a prophet of God, and what he did merely as a statesman from the circumstances of the case, the complexion of the times, and the character of the people over whom he presided.

30. *I will lie with my fathers.* As God had promised the land of Canaan to Abraham and his posterity, Jacob considered it as a consecrated place, under the particular superintendence and blessing of God: and as Sarah, Abraham, and Isaac were interred near Hebron, he in all probability wished to lie, not only in the same place, but in the same grace; and it is not likely that he would have been solicitous about this had he not considered that promised land as being a type of the rest that remains for the people of God, and a pledge of the inheritance among the saints in light.

31. *And Israel bowed himself upon the bed's head.* Jacob was now both old and feeble, and we may suppose him reclined on his couch when Joseph came; that he afterwards sat up erect (see chap. xlviii. 2) while conversing with his son, and receiving his oath and promise; and that when this was finished he *bowed himself upon the bed's head*—exhausted with the conversation, he again reclined himself on his bed as before. This seems to be the simple meaning which the text, unconnected with any religious system or prejudice, naturally proposes. But because *shachah* signifies not only to "bow" but to "worship," because acts of religious worship

were performed by bowing or prostration, and because *mittah,* "a bed," by the change of the points, only becomes *matteh,* "a staff," in which sense the Septuagint took it, translating the original words thus: "And Israel worshipped upon the top of his staff," which the writer of the Epistle to the Hebrews, chap. xi. 21, quotes *literatim;* therefore some have supposed that Jacob bowed himself to the staff or scepter of Joseph, thus fulfilling the prophetic import of his son's dreams! The sense of the Hebrew text is given above. If the reader prefers the sense of the Septuagint and the Epistle to the Hebrews, the meaning is that Jacob, through feebleness, supported himself with a staff, and that, when he got the requisite assurance from Joseph that his dead body should be carried to Canaan, leaning on his staff he bowed his head in adoration to God, who had supported him all his lifelong, and hitherto fulfilled all His promises.

CHAPTER 48

Joseph, hearing that his father was near death, took his two sons, Ephraim and Manasseh, and went to Goshen, to visit him, 1. Jacob strengthens himself to receive them, 2. Gives Joseph an account of God's appearing to him at Luz, and repeating the promise, 3-4. Adopts Ephraim and Manasseh as his own sons, 5-6. Mentions the death of Rachel at Ephrath, 7. He blesses Ephraim and Manasseh, preferring the former, who was the younger, to his elder brother, 8-17. Joseph, supposing his father had mistaken in giving the right of primogeniture to the youngest, endeavors to correct him, 18. Jacob shows that he did it designedly, prophesies much good concerning both; but sets Ephraim, the younger, before Manasseh, 19-20. Jacob speaks of his death, and predicts the return of his posterity from Egypt, 21. And gives Joseph a portion above his brethren, which he had taken from the Amorites, 22.

1. *One told Joseph, Behold, thy father is sick.* He was ill before, and Joseph knew it; but it appears that a messenger had now been dispatched to inform Joseph that his father was apparently at the point of death.

2. *Israel strengthened himself, and sat upon the bed.* He had been confined to his bed before (see chap. xlvii. 31), and now, hearing that Joseph was come to see him, he made what efforts his little remaining strength would admit to sit up in bed to receive his son. This verse proves that a bed, not a staff, is intended in the preceding chapter, v. 31.

3. *God Almighty. El Shaddai,* "the all-sufficient God," the Outpourer and Dispenser of mercies (see chap. xvii. 1), *appeared unto me at Luz,* afterwards called Beth-el; see chap. xxviii. 13; xxxv. 6, 9.

5. *And now thy two sons, Ephraim and Manasseh . . . are mine.* I now adopt them into my own family, and they shall have their place among my twelve sons, and be treated in every respect as those, and have an equal interest in all the spiritual and temporal blessings of the covenant.

7. *Rachel died by me.* Rachel was the wife of Jacob's choice, and the object of his unvarying affection; he loved her in life—he loves her in death. "Many waters cannot quench love, neither can the floods drown it."

8. *Who are these?* At verse 10 it is said that Jacob's eyes were dim for age, that he "could not see"—could not discern any object unless it were near him; therefore, though he saw Ephraim and Manasseh, yet he could not distinguish them till they were brought nigh unto him.

11. *I had not thought to see thy face.* There is much delicacy and much tenderness in these expressions. He feels himself now amply recompensed for his long grief and trouble on account of the supposed death of Joseph, in seeing not only himself but his two sons, whom God, by an especial act of favor, is about to add to the number of his own. Thus we find that as Reuben and Simeon were heads of two distinct tribes in Israel, so were Ephraim and Manasseh; because Jacob, in a sort of sacramental way, had adopted them with equal privileges to those of his own sons.

12. *Joseph . . . bowed himself with his face to the earth.* Joseph, in thus reverencing his father, only followed the customs of the Egyptians among whom he lived, who, according to Herodotus, were particularly remarkable for the reverence they paid to old age. "For if a young person meet his senior, he instantly turns aside to make way for him; if an aged person enter an apartment, the youth always rise from their seats."

14. *Israel stretched out his right hand.* Laying hands on the head was always used among the Jews in giving blessings, designating men to any office, and in the consecration of solemn sacrifices. This is the first time we find it mentioned; but we often read of it afterwards. See Num. xxvii. 18, 23; Deut. xxxiv. 9; Matt. xix. 13, 15; Acts vi. 6; 1 Tim. iv. 14. Jacob laid his right hand on the head of the younger, which we are told he did *wittingly*—well knowing what he was about, *for* (or "although") *Manasseh was the firstborn,* knowing by the Spirit of prophecy that Ephraim's posterity would be more powerful than that of Manasseh. It is observable how God from the beginning has preferred the younger to the elder, as Abel before Cain, Shem before Japheth, Isaac before Ishmael, Jacob before Esau, Judah and Joseph before Reuben, Ephraim before Manasseh, Moses before Aaron, and David before his brethren.

15. *He blessed Joseph.* The father first, and then the sons afterwards. And this is an additional proof to what has been adduced under v. 12, of Jacob's superiority; for the less is always blessed of the greater. *The God which fed me all my life long.* Jacob is now standing on the verge of eternity, with his faith strong in God. He sees his life to be a series of mercies; and as he had been affectionately attentive, provident, and kind to his most helpless child, so has God been unto him; He has fed him all his lifelong; he plainly perceives that he owes every morsel of food which he has received to the mere mercy and kindness of God.

16. *The Angel which redeemed me from all evil. Hammalac haggoel.* "The Messenger, the Redeemer or Kinsman"; for so *goel* signifies; for this term, in the law of Moses, is applied to that person whose right it is, from his being nearest akin, to redeem or purchase back a forfeited inheritance. But of whom does Jacob speak? We have often seen, in the preceding chapters, an angel of God appearing to the patriarchs; and we have full proof that this was no created angel, but the Messenger of the Divine Council, the Lord Jesus Christ. Who then was the angel that *redeemed Jacob,* and whom he invoked to bless Ephraim and Manasseh? Is it not *Jesus*? He alone can be called *Goel,* the "redeeming Kinsman"; for He alone took part of our flesh and blood that the right of redemption might be His; and that the forfeited possession of the favor and image of God might be redeemed, brought back, and restored to all those who believe in His name. To have invoked any other angel or messenger in such a business would have been impiety.

Let my name be named on them. "Let them be ever accounted as a part of my own family; let them be true Israelites—persons who shall prevail with God as I have done; and *the name of . . . Abraham*—being partakers of his faith; and *the name of . . . Isaac*—let them be as remarkable for submissive obedience as he was. Let the virtues of Abraham, Isaac, and Jacob be accumulated in them, and invariably displayed by them!" These are the very words of adoption; and by the imposition of hands, the invocation of the Redeemer, and the solemn blessing pronounced, the adoption was completed. From this moment Ephraim and Manasseh had the same rights and privileges as Jacob's sons, which as the sons of Joseph they could never have possessed.

And let them grow into a multitude. "Let them increase like fishes into a multitude." This prophetic blessing was verified in a most remarkable manner; see Num. xxvi. 34, 37; Deut. xxxiii. 17; Josh. xvii. 17. At one time the tribe of Ephraim amounted to 40,500 effective men, and that of Manasseh to 52,700, amounting in the whole to 93,200.

18. *Joseph said . . . Not so, my father.* Joseph supposed that his father had made a mistake in laying his right hand on the head of the younger, because the right hand was considered as the most noble, and the instrument of conveying the highest dignities, and thus it has ever been considered among all nations, though the reason of it is not particularly obvious. Even in the heavens the right hand of God is the place of the most exalted dignity. It has been observed that Joseph spoke here as he was moved by natural affection, and that Jacob acted as he was influenced by the Holy Spirit.

20. *In thee shall Israel bless.* That is, In future generations the Israelites shall take their form of wishing prosperity to any nation or family from the circumstance of the good which it shall be known that God has done to Ephraim and Manasseh: "May God make thee as fruitful as Ephraim, and multiply thee as Manasseh!" So, to their daughters when married, the Jewish women are accustomed to say, "God make thee as Sarah and Rebekah!" The forms are still in use.

21. *Behold, I die.* With what composure is this most awful word expressed! Surely of Jacob it might be now said, "He turns his sight undaunted on the tomb"; for though it is not said that he was full of days, as were Abraham and Isaac, yet he is perfectly willing to bid adieu to earthly things, and lay his body in the grave. Could any person act as the patriarchs did in their last moments who had no hopes of eternal life, no belief in the immortality of the soul? Impossible! With such a conviction of the being of God, with such proofs of His tenderness and regard, with such experience of His providential and miraculous interference in their behalf, could they suppose that they were only creatures of a day, and that God had wasted so much care, attention, providence, grace, and goodness, on

creatures who were to be ultimately like the beasts that perish? The supposition that they could have no correct notion of the immortality of the soul is as dishonorable to God as to themselves.

22. *Moreover I have given to thee one portion. Shechem achad,* one *shechem* or one "shoulder." We have already seen the transactions between Jacob and his family on one part, and Shechem and the sons of Hamor on the other. See chap. xxxiii. 18-19 and chap. xxxiv. As he uses the word *shechem* here, I think it likely that he alludes to the purchase of the field or parcel of ground mentioned in chap. xxxiii. 18-19. It has been supposed that this parcel of ground which Jacob bought from Shechem had been taken from him by the Amorites and that he afterwards had recovered it by his *sword* and by his *bow,* i.e., by force of arms. Shechem appears to have fallen to the lot of Joseph's sons (see Josh. xvii. 1 and xx. 7), and in our Lord's time there was a parcel of ground near to Sychar, or Shechem, which was still considered as that portion which Jacob gave to his son Joseph, John iv. 5; and on the whole it was probably the same that Jacob bought for a hundred pieces of money, chap. xxxiii. 18-19.

CHAPTER 49

Jacob, about to die, calls his sons together that he may bless them, or give prophetic declarations concerning their posterity, 1-2. Prophetic declaration concerning Reuben, 3-4; concerning Simeon and Levi, 5-7; concerning Judah, 8-12; concerning Zebulun, 13; concerning Issachar, 14-15; concerning Dan, 16-18; concerning Gad, 19; concerning Asher, 20; concerning Naphtali, 21; concerning Joseph, 22-26; concerning Benjamin, 27. Summary concerning the twelve tribes, 28. Jacob gives directions concerning his being buried in the cave of Machpelah, 29-32. Jacob dies, 33.

1. *That which shall befall you in the last days.* It is evident from this, and indeed from the whole complexion of these important prophecies, that the twelve sons of Jacob had very little concern in them, personally considered, as they were to be fulfilled in the last days, i.e., in times remote from that period, and consequently to their posterity, and not to themselves, or to their immediate families. The whole of these prophetic declarations, from v. 2 to v. 27 inclusive, is delivered in strongly figurative language, and in the poetic form, which, in every translation, should be preserved as nearly as possible, rendering the version line for line with the original. This order I shall pursue in the succeeding notes, always proposing the verse first, in as literal a translation as possible, line for line with the Hebrew after the hemistich form, from which the sense will more readily appear; but to the Hebrew text and the common version the reader is ultimately referred.

Come together and hear, O sons of Jacob!
And hearken unto Israel your father.
Reuben, my firstborn art thou!
My might, and the prime of my strength,
Excelling in eminence, and excelling in power:
Pouring out like the waters:—thou shalt not
*   excel,*
For thou wentest up to the bed of thy
*   father,—*
Then thou didst defile: to my couch he went
*   up!*

3. Reuben as the *firstborn* had a right to a double portion of all that the father had; see Deut. xxi. 17.

The "eminence" or *dignity* mentioned here may refer to the priesthood; the "power," to the regal government or kingdom. In this sense it has been understood by all the ancient Targumists. The Targum of Onkelos paraphrases it thus: "Thou shouldst have received three portions, the birthright, the priesthood, and the kingdom"; and to this the Targums of Jonathan ben Uzziel and Jerusalem add: "But because thou hast sinned, the birthright is given to Joseph, the kingdom to Judah, and the priesthood to Levi." That the birthright was given to the sons of Joseph we have the fullest proof from 1 Chron. v. 1.

4. *"Pouring out* like *the waters."* This is an obscure sentence because unfinished. It evidently relates to the defilement of his father's couch; and the word *pachaz,* here translated "pouring out," and in our version "unstable," has a bad meaning in other places of the Scripture, being applied to dissolute, debauched, and licentious conduct. See Judg. ix. 4; Zeph. iii. 4; Jer. xxiii. 14, 32; xxix. 23. *Thou shalt not excel.* —This tribe never rose to any eminence in Israel; was not so numerous by one-third as either Judah, Joseph, or Dan, when Moses took the sum of them in the wilderness, Num. i. 21; and was among the first that were carried into captivity, 1 Chron. v. 26.

"Then thou didst defile." Another unfinished sentence, similar to the former, and upon the same subject, passing over a transaction covertly which delicacy forbade Jacob to enlarge upon. For the crime of Reuben, see chap. xxxv. 22.

Simeon and Levi, brethren:
They have accomplished their fraudulent
*   purposes.*
Into their secret council my soul did not come;
In their confederacy my honor was not united:
For in their anger they slew a man,
And in their pleasure they murdered a prince.
Cursed was their anger, for it was fierce!
And their excessive wrath, for it was in-
*   flexible!*
I will divide them out in Jacob,
And I will disperse them in Israel.

5. *Simeon and Levi are brethren.* Not only springing from the same parents, but they have the same kind of disposition, headstrong, deceitful, vindictive, and cruel.

"They have accomplished." Our margin has it, "Their swords are weapons of violence," i.e., Their swords, which they should have used in defense of their persons or the honorable protection of their families, they have employed in the base and dastardly murder of an innocent people.

The Septuagint gives a different turn to this line from our translation, and confirms the translation given above: "They have accomplished the iniquity of their purpose"; with which the Samaritan Version agrees.

6. "Into their secret council." Jacob here exculpates himself from all participation in the guilt of Simeon and Levi in the murder of the Shechemites. He most solemnly declares that he knew nothing of the confederacy by which it was executed, nor of the secret council in which it was plotted. *For in their anger they*

slew a man. Ish, a noble, an honorable man, namely, Shechem. "And in their pleasure." This marks the highest degree of wickedness and settled malice; they were delighted with their deed. As the original word *ratson* signifies, in general, "pleasure, benevolence, delight," it should neither be translated *selfwill* nor "wilfulness," as some have done, but simply as above; and the reasons appear sufficiently obvious. "They murdered a prince"—Hamor, the father of Shechem. Instead of *shor,* which we have translated *a wall,* and others an "ox," I read *sar,* "a prince," which makes a consistent sense.

7. "Cursed was their anger." The first motions of their violence were savage; "and their excessive (or overflowing) wrath, for it was inflexible"—neither the supplications of the males, nor the entreaties, tears, cries, and shrieks of the helpless females, could deter them from their murderous purpose; for this, v. 5, they are said to have accomplished.

"I will divide them out," *achallekem,* "I will make them into lots," giving a portion of them to one tribe, and a portion to another; but they shall never attain to any political consequence. This appears to have been literally fulfilled. Levi had no inheritance except forty-eight cities, scattered through different parts of the land of Canaan; and as to the tribe of Simeon, it is generally believed among the Jews that they became schoolmasters to the other tribes; and when they entered Canaan they had only a small portion, a few towns and villages in the worst part of Judah's lot, Josh. xix. 1, which afterwards finding too little, they formed different colonies in districts which they conquered from the Idumeans and Amalekites, 1 Chron. iv. 39, etc. Thus these two tribes were not only separated from each other, but even divided from themselves, according to this prediction of Jacob.

Judah! thou! Thy brethren shall praise thee.
Thy hand, in the neck of thine enemies:
The sons of thy father shall bow themselves
*   to thee.*
A lion's whelp is Judah:
From the prey, my son, thou hast ascended.
He couched, lying down like a strong lion,
And like a lioness; who shall arouse him?
From Judah the sceptre shall not depart,
Nor a teacher from his offspring,
Until that Shiloh shall come,
And to him shall be assembled the peoples.
Binding his colt to the vine,
And to the choice vine the foals of his ass,
He washed his garments in wine,
His clothes in the blood of the grape.
With wine shall his eyes be red,
And his teeth shall be white with milk.

8. "Thy brethren shall praise thee." As the name Judah signifies "praise," Jacob takes occasion from its meaning to show that this tribe should be so eminent and glorious that the rest of the tribes should praise it; that is, they should acknowledge its superior dignity, as in its privileges it should be distinguished beyond all the others.

10. "From Judah the sceptre shall not depart." Judah shall continue a distinct tribe till the Messiah shall come; and it did so; and after His coming it was confounded with the others, so that all distinction has been ever since lost.

"Nor a teacher from his offspring." I am sufficiently aware that the literal meaning of the original is "from between his feet," and I am as fully satisfied that it should never be so translated; "from between the feet" and "out of the thigh" simply mean progeny, natural offspring, for reasons which surely need not be mentioned.

At the haven of the seas shall Zebulun dwell,
And he shall be a haven for ships.
And his border shall extend unto Sidon.
Issachar is a strong ass
Couching between two burdens.
And he saw the resting place that it was good,
And the land that it was pleasant;
And he inclined his shoulder to the load,
And he became a servant unto tribute.

13. Zebulun's lot or portion in the division of the Promised Land extended from the Mediterranean Sea on the west to the lake of Gennesareth on the east; see his division, Josh. xix. 10, etc. The Targum of Jonathan paraphrases the passage thus: "Zebulun shall be on the coasts of the sea, and he shall rule over the havens; he shall subdue the provinces of the sea with his ships, and his border shall extend unto Sidon."

14. *Issachar is a strong ass. Chamor garem* is properly a "strong-limbed ass"; *couching down between two burdens*—bearing patiently, as most understand it, the fatigues of agriculture, and submitting to exorbitant taxes rather than exert themselves to drive out the old inhabitants. The *two burdens* literally mean the two sacks or panniers, one on each side of the animal's body; and couching down between these refers to the well-known propensity of the ass, whenever wearied or overloaded, to lie down even with its burden on its back.

15. *He saw that rest.* The inland portion that was assigned to him between the other tribes. "He inclined his shoulder to the load"; the Chaldee paraphrase gives this a widely different turn to that given it by most commentators: "He saw his portion that it was good, and the land that it was fruitful; and he shall subdue the provinces of the people, and drive out their inhabitants, and those who are left shall be his servants, and his tributaries." Grotius understands it nearly in the same way. The pusillanimity which is generally attributed to this tribe certainly does not agree with the view in which they are exhibited in Scripture. In the song of Deborah this tribe is praised for the powerful assistance which it then afforded, Judg. v. 15. And in 1 Chron. vii. 1-5, they are expressly said to have been "valiant men of might in all their families, and in all their generations"; i.e., through every period of their history. It appears they were a laborious, hardy, valiant tribe, patient in labor, and invincible in war, bearing both these burdens with great constance whenever it was necessary. When Tola of this tribe judged Israel, the land had rest twenty-three years, Judg. x. 1.

Dan shall judge his people,
As one of the tribes of Israel.
Dan shall be a serpent on the way,
A cerastes upon the track,
Biting the heels of the horse,
And his rider shall fall backwards.

16. *Dan shall judge.* Dan, whose name signifies "judgment," was the eldest of Jacob's sons by Bilhah, Rachel's maid, and he is here promised an equal rule with those tribes that sprang from either Leah or Rachel, the legal wives of Jacob. Some Jewish and some Christian writers understand this prophecy of Samson, who sprang from this tribe, and judged, or as the word might be translated "avenged," the people of Israel twenty years. See Judg. xiii. 2; xv. 20.

17. *Dan shall be a serpent.* The original word is *nachash,* and this has a great variety of significations. It is probable that a serpent is here intended, but of what kind we know not. "A cerastes upon the track." The word *shephiphon,* which is nowhere else to be found in the Bible, is thus translated by the Vulgate. The cerastes has its name from two little horns upon its head, and is remarkable for the property here ascribed to the *shephiphon.* The word *orach,* which we translate *path,* signifies the track or rut made in the ground by the wheel of a cart, wagon, etc. And the description that Nicander gives of this serpent in his *Theriaca* perfectly agrees with what is here said of the *shephiphon:* "It lies under the sand, or in some cart rut by the way."

It is intimated that this tribe should gain the principal part of its conquests more by cunning and stratagem than by valor; and this is seen particularly in their conquest of Laish, Judges xviii, and even in some of the transactions of Samson, such as burning the corn of the Philistines, and at last pulling down their temple, and destroying 3,000 at one time; see Judg. xvi. 26-30.

For thy salvation have I waited, O Lord!

18. This is a remarkable ejaculation, and seems to stand perfectly unconnected with all that went before and all that follows; though it is probable that certain prophetic views which Jacob now had and which he does not explain gave rise to it; and by this he at once expressed both his faith and hope in God. As the tribe of Dan was the first that appears to have been seduced from the true worship of God (see Judg. xviii. 30), some have thought that Jacob refers particularly to this and sees the end of the general apostasy only in the redemption by Jesus Christ, considering the *nachash* above as the seducer and the Messiah the promised Seed.

Gad, an army shall attack him,
And he shall attack in return.

19. This is one of the most obscure prophecies in the whole chapter, and no two interpreters agree in the translation of the original words. The prophecy seems to refer generally to the frequent disturbances to which this tribe should be exposed, and their hostile, warlike disposition, that would always lead them to repel every aggression. It is likely that the prophecy had an especial fulfillment when this tribe, in conjunction with that of Reuben and the half-tribe of Manasseh, had a great victory over the Hagarites, taking captive 100,000 men, 2,000 asses, 50,000 camels, and 250,000 sheep; see 1 Chron. v. 18-22.

From Asher his bread shall be fat,
And he shall produce royal dainties.

20. This refers to the great fertility of the lot that fell to Asher, and which appears to have corresponded with the name, which signifies "happy" or "blessed." His great prosperity is

described by Moses in this figurative way: "Let Asher be blessed with children; let him be acceptable to his brethren, and let him dip his foot in oil," Deut. xxxiii. 24.

Naphtali is a spreading oak,
Producing beautiful branches.

21. This is Bochart's translation; and perhaps no man who understands the genius of the Hebrew language will attempt to dispute its propriety; it is as literal as it is correct. Our own translation scarcely gives any sense. The fruitfulness of this tribe in children may be here intended. But as great increase in this way was not an uncommon case in the descendants of Jacob, this may refer particularly to the fruitfulness of their soil, and the especial providential care and blessing of the Almighty; to which indeed Moses seems particularly to refer, Deut. xxxiii. 23: "O Naphtali, satisfied with favour, and full with the blessing of the Lord." So that he may be represented under the notion of a tree planted in a rich soil, growing to a prodigious size, extending its branches in all directions, becoming a shade for men and cattle and a harbor for the fowls of heaven.

The son of a fruitful [vine] is Joseph;
The son of a fruitful [vine] by the fountain:
The daughters [branches] shoot over the wall.
They sorely afflicted him and contended with him;
The chief archers had him in hatred.
But his bow remained in strength,
And the arms of his hands were made strong
By the hand of the Mighty One of Jacob:
By the name of the Shepherd, the Rock of Israel.
By the God of thy father, for He helped thee;
And God All-sufficient, He blessed thee.
The blessing of the heavens from above,
And the blessings lying in the deep beneath,
The blessings of the breasts and of the womb,
The blessings of thy father have prevailed
Over the blessings of the eternal mountains,
And the desirable things of the everlasting hills.
These shall be on the head of Joseph,
And on his crown who was separated from his brethren.

22. "The son of a fruitful vine." This appears to me to refer to Jacob himself, who was blessed with such a numerous posterity that in 215 years after this his own descendants amounted to upwards of 600,000 effective men; and the figures here are intended to point out the continual growth and increase of his posterity. Jacob was a fruitful tree planted by a fountain, which because it was good would yield good fruit; and because it was planted near a fountain, from being continually watered, would be perpetually fruitful. "The daughters," *banoth,* put here for "branches," shoot over or run upon the wall. Alluding probably to the case of the vine, which requires to be supported by a wall, trees, etc.

23. "The chief archers." "The masters of arrows"—Joseph's brethren, who either used such weapons, while feeding their flocks in the deserts, for the protection of themselves and cattle or for the purpose of hunting, and who probably excelled in archery. It may however refer to the bitter speeches and harsh words that they spoke to and of him, for "they hated him, and could not speak peaceably unto him," chap. xxxvii. 4. Thus they sorely afflicted him, and were incessantly scolding or finding fault.

24. "But his bow remained in strength." The more he was persecuted, either by his brethren or in Egypt, the more resplendent his uprightness and virtues shone. *And the arms*—his extended power and influence—*of his hands* —plans, designs, and particular operations of his prudence, judgment, and discretion—were all rendered successful by the "hand"—the powerful succor and protection, "of the Mighty One of Jacob"—that God who blessed and protected all the counsels and plans of Jacob, and protected and increased him also when he was in a strange land, and often under the power of those who sought opportunities to oppress and defraud him. "By the name of the Shepherd, the Rock of Israel." This appears to me to refer to the subject of the thirty-second chapter, where Jacob wrestled with God, had God's name revealed to him, and his own name changed from Jacob to Israel, in consequence of which he built an altar and dedicated it to God, who had appeared to him under the name of *Elohey-Israel*, the "strong God of Israel"; which circumstance led him to use the term "Rock," which, as an emblem of power, is frequently given to God in the sacred writings, and may here refer to the stone which Jacob set up. It is very probable that the word *shepherd* is intended to apply to our blessed Lord, who is the Shepherd of Israel, the Good Shepherd, John x. 11-17; and who, beyond all controversy, was the Person with whom Jacob wrestled.

25. *The God of thy father.* How frequently God is called the "God of Jacob" none needs to be told who reads the Bible. "God All-sufficient." Instead of *Eth Shaddai*, "The Almighty or All-sufficient," I read *El Shaddai*, "God All-sufficient," which is the reading of the Samaritan, Septuagint, Syriac, and Coptic. "The blessing of the heavens from above." A generally pure, clear, serene sky, frequently dropping down fertilizing showers and dews, so as to make a very fruitful soil and salubrious atmosphere. "Blessings lying in the deep beneath." Whatever riches could be gained from the sea or rivers, from mines and minerals in the bowels of the earth, and from abundant springs in different parts of his inheritance. Our translation of this line is excessively obscure: *Blessings of the deep that lieth under.* What is it that lies under the deep? By connecting "blessings" with "lying," all ambiguity is avoided, and the text speaks a plain and consistent sense. "The blessings of the breasts and of the womb." A numerous offspring, and an abundance of cattle. The progeny of Joseph by Ephraim and Manasseh amounted at the first census or enumeration (Numbers i) to 75,900 men, which exceeded the sum of any one tribe; Judah, the greatest of the others, amounting to no more than 74,600. Indeed, Ephraim and Manasseh had multiplied so greatly in the days of Joshua that a common lot was not sufficient for them. See their complaint, Josh. xvii. 14.

26. *The blessings of thy father.* The blessings which thy father now prays for and pronounces are neither temporal nor transitory; they shall exceed in their duration the eternal mountains, and in their value and spiritual nature all the conveniences, comforts, and delicacies which the everlasting hills can produce. They shall last when the heavens and the earth are no more, and shall extend throughout eternity. They are the blessings which shall be communicated to the world by means of the Messiah.

Benjamin is a ravenous wolf:
In the morning he shall devour the prey,
And in the evening he shall divide the spoil.

27. This tribe is very fitly compared to a ravenous *wolf,* because of the rude courage and ferocity which they have invariably displayed, particularly in their war with the other tribes, in which they killed more men than the whole of their own numbers amounted to.

28. *Every one according to his blessing.* That is, guided by the unerring Spirit of prophecy, Jacob now foretold to each of his sons the important events which should take place during their successive generations and the predominant characteristic of each tribe; and at the same time made some comparatively obscure references to the advent of the Messiah and the redemption of the world by Him.

29. *Bury me with my fathers.* From this it appears that the cave at Machpelah was a common burying place for Hebrews of distinction, and indeed the first public burying place mentioned in history. From v. 31 we find that Abraham, Sarah, Isaac, Rebekah, and Leah had already been deposited there, and among them Jacob wished to have his bones laid; and he left his dying charge with his children to bury him in this place, and this they conscientiously performed.

33. *He gathered up his feet into the bed.* It is very probable that while delivering these prophetic blessings Jacob sat upon the side of his bed, leaning upon his staff; and having finished, he lifted up his feet into the bed, stretched himself upon it, and expired! *And was gathered unto his people.* The testimony that this place bears to the immortality of the soul, and to its existence separate from the body, should not be lightly regarded. In the same moment in which Jacob is said to have *gathered up his feet into the bed,* and to have expired, it is added, *and was gathered unto his people.*

CHAPTER 50

Joseph bewails the death of his father, and commands the physicians to embalm him, 1-2. The Egyptians mourn for him seventy days, 3. Joseph begs permission from Pharaoh to accompany his father's corpse to Canaan, 4-5. Pharaoh consents, 6. Pharaoh's domestics and elders, the elders of Egypt, Joseph and his brethren, with chariots, horsemen, etc., form the funeral procession, 7-9. They come to the threshing floor of Atad, and mourn there seven days, 10. The Canaanites call the place Abelmizraim, 11. They bury Jacob in the cave of Machpelah, 12-13. Joseph returns to Egypt, 14. His brethren, fearing his displeasure, send messengers to him to entreat his forgiveness of past wrongs, 15-17. They follow, and prostrate themselves before him, and offer to be his servants, 18. Joseph receives them affectionately, and assures them and theirs of his care and protection, 19-21. Joseph and his brethren dwell in Egypt, and he sees the third generation of his children, 22-23. Being about to die, he prophesies the return of the children of Israel from Egypt, 24, and causes them to swear that they will carry his bones to Canaan, 25. Joseph dies, aged one hundred and ten years; is embalmed, and put in a coffin in Egypt, 26.

1. *Joseph fell upon his father's face.* Though this act appears to be suspended by the unnatural division of this verse from the preceding chapter, yet we may rest assured it was the immediate consequence of Jacob's death.

2. *The physicians.* The "healers," those whose business it was to heal or restore the body from

sickness by the administration of proper medicines; and when death took place, to heal or preserve it from dissolution by embalming, and thus give it a sort of immortality or everlasting duration. In the art of embalming, the Egyptians excelled all nations in the world; with them it was a common practice. Instances of the perfection to which they carried this art may be seen in the numerous mummies which have been brought from Egypt.

3. *Forty days.* The body it appears required this number of days to complete the process of embalming; afterwards it lay thirty days more, making in the whole seventy days, during which the mourning was continued.

4. *Speak, I pray you, in the ears of Pharaoh.* But why did not Joseph apply himself? Because he was now in his mourning habits, and in such none must appear in the presence of the Eastern monarchs. See Esther iv. 2.

7. *The elders of his house.* Persons who, by reason of their age, had acquired much experience; and who on this account were deemed the best qualified to conduct the affairs of the king's household. The funeral procession of Jacob must have been truly grand. Joseph, his brethren and their descendants, the servants of Pharaoh, the elders of his house, and all the elders—all the principal men—of the land of Egypt, with chariots and horsemen, must have appeared a very great company indeed. He was a national blessing; and the nation mourns in his affliction, and unites to do him honor.

10. *The threshingfloor of Atad.* As *Atad* signifies a "bramble" or "thorn," it has been understood by the Arabic, not as a man's name, but as the name of a *place;* but all the other versions and the Targums consider it as the name of a man.

The mourning of the ancient Hebrews was usually of seven days' continuance, Num. xix. 19; 1 Sam. xxxi. 13; though on certain occasions it was extended to thirty days, Num. xx. 29; Deut. xxi. 13; xxiv. 8, but never longer. The seventy days' mourning mentioned above was that of the Egyptians, and was rendered necessary by the long process of embalming, which obliged them to keep the body out of the grave for seventy days, as we learn both from Herodotus and Diodorus. Seven days by the order of God a man was to mourn for his dead, because during that time he was considered as unclean: but when those were finished he was to purify himself, and consider the mourning as ended, Num. xix. 11, 19.

15. *Saw that their father was dead.* This at once argues both a sense of guilt in their own consciences and a want of confidence in their brother. They might have supposed that hitherto he had forborne to punish them merely on their father's account; but now that he was dead, and Joseph having them completely in his power they imagined that he would take vengeance on them for their former conduct towards him.

16. *Thy father did command.* Whether he did or not we cannot tell. Some think they had feigned this story, but that is not so likely. Jacob might have had suspicions too, and might have thought that the best way to prevent evil was to humble themselves before their brother and get a fresh assurance of his forgiveness.

17. *The servants of the God of thy father.* These words were wonderfully well chosen and spoken in the most forcible manner to Joseph's piety and filial affection. No wonder then that he *wept when they spake unto him.*

22. *Joseph dwelt in Egypt.* Continued in Egypt after his return from Canaan till his death; *he, and his father's house*—all the descendants of Israel, till the exodus or departure under the direction of Moses and Aaron, which was 144 years after.

23. *Were brought up upon Joseph's knees.* They were educated by him, or under his direction; his sons and their children continuing to acknowledge him as patriarch, or head of the family, as long as he lived.

24. *Joseph said ... I die.* That is, I am dying; *and God will surely visit you*—He will yet again give you, in the time when it shall be essentially necessary, the most signal proof of His unbounded love towards the seed of Jacob. *And bring you out of this land.* Though ye have here everything that can render life comfortable, yet this is not the typical land, the land given by covenant, the land which represents the rest that remains for the people of God.

25. *Ye shall carry up my bones.* That I may finally rest with my ancestors in the land which God gave to Abraham, to Isaac, and to Jacob; and which is a pledge as it is a type of the kingdom of Heaven. Thus says the author of the Epistle to the Hebrews, chap. xi. 22: "By faith Joseph, when he died [when dying], made mention of the departing [of the Exodus] of the children of Israel; and gave commandment concerning his bones." From this it is evident that Joseph considered all these things as typical, and by this very commandment expressed his faith in the immortality of the soul and the general resurrection of the dead. This oath, by which Joseph then bound his brethren, their posterity considered as binding on themselves; and Moses took care, when he departed from Egypt, to carry up Joseph's body with him, Exod. xiii. 19; which was afterwards buried in Shechem, Josh. xxiv. 32, the very portion which Jacob had purchased from the Amorites, and which he gave to his son Joseph, Gen. lxviii. 22; Acts vii. 16.

26. *Joseph died, being an hundred and ten years old.* Literally, "the son of a hundred and ten years." *They embalmed him.* The same precautions were taken to preserve his body as to preserve that of his father, Jacob; and this was particularly necessary in his case, because his body was to be carried to Canaan 144 years after.

The Book of

EXODUS

The name by which this book is generally distinguished is borrowed from the Septuagint, in which it is called Exodus, the "going out" or "departure"; and by the Codex Alexandrinus, "the departure from Egypt," because the departure of the Israelites from Egypt is the most remarkable fact mentioned in the whole book. In the Hebrew Bibles it is called *Ve-elleh She-moth*, "these are the names," which are the words with which it commences. It contains a history of the transactions of 145 years, beginning at the death of Joseph, where the Book of Genesis ends, and coming down to the erection of the Tabernacle in the wilderness at the foot of Mount Sinai.

In this book Moses details the causes and motives of the persecution raised up against the Israelites in Egypt, the orders given by Pharaoh to destroy all the Hebrew male children, and the prevention of the execution of those orders through the humanity and piety of the midwives appointed to deliver the Hebrew women. The marriage of Amram and Jochebed is next related; the birth of Moses; the manner in which he was exposed on the river Nile, and in which he was discovered by the daughter of Pharaoh; his being providentially put under the care of his own mother to be nursed, and educated as the son of the Egyptian princess; how, when forty years of age, he left the court, visited and defended his brethren; the danger to which he was in consequence exposed; his flight to Arabia; his contract with Jethro, priest or prince of Midian, whose daughter Zipporah he afterwards espoused. While he was employed in keeping the flocks of his father-in-law, God appeared to him in a burning bush, and commissioned him to go and deliver his countrymen from the oppression under which they groaned. Having given him the most positive assurance of protection and power to work miracles, and having associated with him his brother, Aaron, He sent them first to the Israelites to declare the purpose of Jehovah, and afterwards to Pharaoh to require him, in the name of the Most High, to set the Israelites at liberty. Pharaoh, far from submitting, made their yoke more grievous; and Moses, on a second interview with him, to convince him by whose authority he made the demand, wrought a miracle before him and his courtiers. This being in a certain way imitated by Pharaoh's magicians, he hardened his heart, and refused to let the people go, till God, by ten extraordinary plagues, convinced him of His omnipotence, and obliged him to consent to dismiss a people over whose persons and properties he had claimed and exercised a right founded only on the most tyrannical principles. The plagues by which God afflicted the whole land of Egypt, Goshen excepted, where the Israelites dwelt, were the following:—

(1) He turned all the waters of Egypt into *blood*. (2) He caused innumerable *frogs* to come over the whole land. (3) He afflicted both man and beast with immense *swarms of vermin*. (4) Afterwards with a multitude of different kinds of *insects*. (5) He sent a grievous *pestilence* among their cattle. (6) Smote both man and beast with *boils*. (7) Destroyed their crops with grievous storms of *hail*, accompanied with the most terrible thunder and lightning. (8) Desolated the whole land by innumerable swarms of *locusts*. (9) He spread a palpable *darkness* all over Egypt; and (10) In one night *slew* all the *firstborn*, both of man and beast, through the whole of the Egyptian territories. What proved the miraculous nature of all these plagues most particularly was: *First,* their coming exactly according to the prediction and at the command of Moses and Aaron; *Secondly,* their extending only to the Egyptians, and leaving the land of Goshen, the Israelites, their cattle and substance, entirely untouched.

After relating all these things in detail, with their attendant circumstances, Moses describes the institution, reason, and celebration of the Passover; the preparation of the Israelites for their departure; their leaving Goshen and beginning their journey to the Promised Land, by the way of Rameses, Succoth, and Etham. How Pharaoh, repenting of the permission he had given them to depart, began to pursue them with an immense army of horse and foot, and overtook them at their encampment at Baal-zephon, on the borders of the Red Sea. Their destruction appearing then to be inevitable, Moses further relates that having called earnestly upon God, and stretched his rod over the waters, they became divided, and the Israelites entered into the bed of the sea, and passed over to the opposite shore. Pharaoh and his host madly pursued in the same track, the rear of their army being fairly entered by the time the last of the Israelites had made good their landing on the opposite coast. Moses stretching his rod again over the waters, they returned to their former channel and overwhelmed the Egyptian army, so that every soul perished.

Moses next gives a circumstantial account of the different encampments of the Israelites in the wilderness, during the space of nearly forty years: the miracles wrought in their behalf, the chief of which were the pillar of cloud by day, and the pillar of fire by night, to direct and protect them in the wilderness; the bringing water out of a rock for them and their cattle; feeding them with manna from heaven; bringing innumerable flocks of quails to their camp; giving them a complete victory over the Amalekites at the intercession of Moses; and particularly God's astonishing manifestation of himself on Mount Sinai, when He delivered to Moses an epitome of His whole law, in what was called the Ten Words or Ten Commandments.

Moses proceeds to give a circumstantial detail of the different laws, statutes, and ordinances which he received from God, and particularly the giving of the Ten Commandments on Mount Sinai, and the awful display of the divine majesty on that solemn occasion; the formation of the ark, holy table, and candlestick; the Tabernacle, with its furniture, covering, courts, etc., the brazen altar, golden altar, brazen laver, anointing oil, perfume, sacerdotal garments for Aaron and his sons, and the artificers employed on the work of the Tabernacle. He then gives an account of Israel's idolatry in the matter of the golden calf, made under the direction of Aaron; God's displeasure, and the death of the principal idolaters; the erection and consecration of the Tabernacle, and its being filled and encompassed with the divine glory, with the order and manner of their marches by direction of the miraculous pillar; with which the book concludes.

CHAPTER 1

The names and number of the children of Israel that went down into Egypt, 1-5. Joseph and all his brethren of that generation die, 6. The great increase of their posterity, 7. The cruel policy of the king of Egypt to destroy them, 8-11. They increase greatly, notwithstanding their affliction, 12. Account of their hard bondage, 13-14. Pharaoh's command to the Hebrew midwives to kill all the male children. 15-16. The midwives disobey the king's command, and, on being questioned, vindicate themselves, 17-19. God is pleased with their conduct, blesses them, and increases the people, 20-21. Pharaoh gives a general command to the Egyptians to drown all the male children of the Hebrews, 22.

1. *These are the names.* Though this book is a continuation of the Book of Genesis, with which probably it was in former times conjoined, Moses thought it necessary to introduce it with an account of the names and number of the family of Jacob when they came to Egypt, to show that though they were then very few, yet in a short time, under the especial blessing of God, they had multiplied exceedingly; and thus the promise to Abraham had been literally fulfilled. See the notes on Genesis xlvi.

6. *Joseph died, and all his brethren.* That is, Joseph had now been some time dead, as also all his brethren, and all the Egyptians who had known Jacob and his twelve sons; and this is a sort of reason why the important services performed by Joseph were forgotten.

7. *The children of Israel were fruitful. Paru,* a general term, signifying that they were like healthy trees, bringing forth an abundance of fruit. *And increased.* "They increased like fishes," as the original word implies. *Abundantly. Yirbu,* "they multiplied"; this is a separate term, and should not have been used as an adverb by our translators. *And waxed exceeding mighty.* And they became strong beyond measure—"superlatively, superlatively"—so that *the land* (Goshen) *was filled with them.* This astonishing increase was, under the providence of God, chiefly owing to two causes: (1) The

Hebrew women were exceedingly fruitful, suffered very little in parturition, and probably often brought forth twins. (2) There appear to have been no premature deaths among them. Thus in about two hundred and fifteen years they were multiplied to upwards of 600,000, independently of old men, women, and children.

8. *Which knew not Joseph.* The verb *yada,* which we translate "to know," often signifies to "acknowledge" or "approve." See Judg. ii. 10; Ps. i. 6; xxxi. 7; Hos. ii. 8; Amos iii. 2. We may therefore understand by the new king's not knowing Joseph his disapproving of that system of government which Joseph had established, as well as his haughtily refusing to acknowledge the obligations under which the whole land of Egypt was laid to this eminent prime minister of one of his predecessors.

9. *He said unto his people.* He probably summoned a council of his nobles and elders to consider the subject; and the result was to persecute and destroy them, as is afterwards stated.

10. *They join also unto our enemies.* It has been conjectured that Pharaoh had probably his eye on the oppressions which Egypt had suffered under the shepherd-kings, who for a long series of years had, according to Manetho, governed the land with extreme cruelty. As the Israelites were of the same occupation (namely, shepherds), the jealous, cruel king found it easy to attribute to them the same motives, taking it for granted that they were only waiting for a favorable opportunity to join the enemies of Egypt, and so overrun the whole land.

11. *Set over them taskmasters.* "Chiefs or princes of burdens, works, or tribute"; Septuagint, "overseers of the works." The persons who appointed them their work, and exacted the performance of it. The work itself being oppressive, and the manner in which it was exacted

still more so, there is some room to think that they not only worked them unmercifully, but also obliged them to pay an exorbitant tribute at the same time. *Treasure cities.* "Store cities —public granaries."

12. *But the more they afflicted them.* The margin has pretty nearly preserved the import of the original: "And as they afflicted them, so they multiplied and so they grew." That is, in proportion to their afflictions was their prosperity.

13. *To serve with rigour.* With cruelty, great oppression; being ferocious with them. This kind of cruelty to slaves, and ferociousness, unfeelingness, and hardheartedness, were particularly forbidden to the children of Israel. See Lev. xxv. 43, 46, where the same word is used: "Thou shalt not rule over him with rigour; but shalt fear thy God."

14. *They made their lives bitter.* So that they became weary of life, through the severity of their servitude. *With hard bondage.* "With grievous servitude." This was the general character of their life in Egypt; it was a life of the most painful servitude, oppressive enough in itself, but made much more so by the cruel manner of their treatment while performing their tasks. *In morter, and in brick. First,* in digging the clay, kneading, and preparing it, and *secondly,* forming it into bricks, drying them in the sun. *Service in the field.* Carrying these materials to the places where they were to be formed into buildings, and serving the builders while employed in those public works.

15. *Hebrew midwives. Shiphrah* and *Puah,* who are here mentioned, were probably certain chiefs, under whom all the rest acted and by whom they were instructed in the obstetric art.

17. *The midwives feared God.* Because they knew that God had forbidden murder of every kind; for though the law was not yet given, Exod. xx. 13, being Hebrews they must have known that God had from the beginning declared, "Whosoever sheddeth man's blood, by man shall his blood be shed," Gen. ix. 6. Therefore they saved the male children of all to whose assistance they were called.

19. *The Hebrew women are not as the Egyptian women.* This is a simple statement of what general experience shows to be a fact, namely, that women who during the whole of their pregnancy are accustomed to hard labor, especially in the open air, have comparatively little pain in parturition. With the strictest truth the midwives might say, *The Hebrew women are not as the Egyptian women.* The latter fare delicately, are not inured to labor, and are kept shut up at home; therefore they have hard, difficult, and dangerous labors. But the Hebrew women are *lively, chayoth,* are "strong, hale, and vigorous," and therefore *are delivered ere the midwives come in unto them.* In such cases we may naturally conclude that the midwives were very seldom even sent for.

20. *Therefore God dealt well with the midwives: and the people multiplied, and waxed very mighty.* This shows an especial providence and blessing of God; for though in all cases where females are kept to hard labor they have comparatively easy and safe travail, yet in a state of slavery the increase is generally very small, as the children die for want of proper nursing, the women, through their labor, being obliged to neglect their offspring; so that in the slave countries the stock is obliged to be recruited by foreign imports.

21. *He made them houses.* That the *houses* in question were not made for the midwives, but for the Israelites in general, the Hebrew text seems pretty plainly to indicate, for the pronoun *lahem,* "to them," is the masculine gender; had the midwives been meant, the femine pronoun *lahen* would have been used.

22. *Ye shall cast into the river.* As the Nile, which is here intended, was a sacred river among the Egyptians, it is not unlikely that Pharaoh intended the young Hebrews as an offering to his god, having two objects in view: (1) To increase the fertility of the country by thus procuring, as he might suppose, a proper and sufficient annual inundation; and (2) To prevent an increase of population among the Israelites, and in process of time procure their entire extermination.

It is conjectured, with a great show of probability, that the edict mentioned in this verse was not made till after the birth of Aaron, and that it was revoked soon after the birth of Moses; as, if it had subsisted in its rigor during the eighty-six years which elapsed between this and the deliverance of the Israelites, it is not at all likely that their males would have amounted to six hundred thousand, and those all effective men.

CHAPTER 2

Amram and Jochebed marry, 1. Moses is born, and is hidden by his mother three months, 2. Is exposed in an ark of bulrushes on the river Nile, and watched by his sister, 3-4. He is found by the daughter of Pharaoh, who commits him to the care of his own mother, and has him educated as her own son, 5-9. When grown-up, he is brought to Pharaoh's daughter, who receives him as her own child, and calls him Moses, 10. Finding an Egyptian smiting a Hebrew, he kills the Egyptian, and hides him in the sand, 11-12. Reproves two Hebrews that were contending together, and one of whom charges him with killing the Egyptian, 13-14. Pharaoh, hearing of the death of the Egyptian, seeks to slay Moses, who, being alarmed, escapes to the land of Midian, 15. Meets with the seven daughters of Reuel, priest or prince of Midian, who came to water their flocks, and assists them, 16-17. On their return they inform their father, Reuel, who invites Moses to his house, 18-20. Moses dwells with him, and receives Zipporah, his daughter, to wife, 21. She bears him a son, whom he calls Gershom, 22. The children of Israel, grievously oppressed in Egypt, cry for deliverance, 23. God remembers His covenant with Abraham, Isaac, and Jacob, and hears their prayer, 24-25.

1. *There went a man.* Amram, son of Kohath, son of Levi, chap. vi. 16-20. *A daughter of Levi,* Jochebed, sister to Kohath, and consequently both the wife and aunt of her husband, Amram, chap. vi. 20; Num. xxvi. 59. Such marriages were at this time lawful, though they were afterwards forbidden, Lev. xviii. 12. But it is possible that *daughter of Levi* means no more than a descendant of that family, and that probably Amram and Jochebed were only cousins-german. As a new law was to be given and a new priesthood formed, God chose a religious family out of which the lawgiver and the high priest were both to spring.

2. *Bare a son.* This certainly was not her first child, for Aaron was fourscore and three years old when Moses was but fourscore, see chap. vii. 7: and there was a sister, probably Miriam, who was older than either; see below, v. 4, and see Num. xxvi. 59. Miriam and Aaron had no doubt both been born before the decree was

passed for the destruction of the Hebrew male children, mentioned in the preceding chapter.

Goodly child. The text simply says "that he was good," which signifies that he was not only a perfect, well-formed child, but that he was very beautiful; hence the Septuagint translate the place, "Seeing him to be beautiful," which Stephen interprets, "He was comely to God," or "divinely beautiful." This very circumstance was wisely ordained by the kind providence of God to be one means of his preservation. Scarcely anything interests the heart more than the sight of a lovely babe in distress. His beauty would induce even his parents to double their exertions to save him, and was probably the sole motive which led the Egyptian princess to take such particular care of him, and to educate him as her own, which in all likelihood she would not have done had he been only an ordinary child.

3. *An ark of bulrushes.* A small boat or basket made of the Egyptian reed called papyrus, so famous in all antiquity. This plant grows on the banks of the Nile, and in marshy grounds; the stalk rises to the height of six or seven cubits above the water. This reed was of the greatest use to the inhabitants of Egypt, the pith contained in the stalk serving them for food, and the woody part to build vessels with, which vessels frequently appear on engraved stones and other monuments of Egyptian antiquity. *She laid it in the flags.* Not willing to trust it in the stream for fear of a disaster, and probably choosing the place to which the Egyptian princess was accustomed to come for the purpose specified in the note on the following verse.

5. *To wash herself at the river.* Whether the daughter of Pharaoh went to bathe in the river through motives of pleasure, health, or religion, or whether she bathed at all, the text does not specify. It is merely stated by the sacred writer that she went down to the river to wash; for the word *herself* is not in the original.

6. *She had compassion on him.* The sight of a beautiful babe in distress could not fail to make the impression here mentioned; see on v. 2. It has already been conjectured that the cruel edict of the Egyptian king did not continue long in force; see chap. i. 22. And it will not appear unreasonable to suppose that the circumstance related here might have brought about its abolition. The daughter of Pharaoh, struck with the distressed state of the Hebrew children from what she had seen in the case of Moses, would probably implore her father to abolish this sanguinary edict.

7. *Shall I go and call . . . a nurse?* Had not the different circumstances marked here been placed under the superintendence of an especial providence, there is no human probability that they could have had such a happy issue. The parents had done everything to save their child that piety, affection, and prudence could dictate, and having done so, they left the event to God. "By faith," says the apostle, Heb. xi. 23, "Moses, when he was born, was hid three months of his parents, because they saw he was a proper child; and they were not afraid of the king's commandment." Because of the king's commandment they were obliged to make use of the most prudent caution to save the child's life; and their faith in God enabled them to risk their own

safety, for they were not afraid of the king's commandment—they feared God, and they had no other fear.

10. *And he became her son.* From this time of his being brought home by his nurse his education commenced, and he "was learned in all the wisdom of the Egyptians," Acts vii. 22, who in the knowledge of nature probably exceeded all the nations then on the face of the earth. *And she called his name, Mosheh,* because "out of the waters have I drawn him." *Mashah* signifies "to draw out"; and *mosheh* is the person drawn out; the word is used in the same sense in Ps. xviii. 17 and 2 Sam. xxii. 17. What name he had from his parents we know not; but whatever it might be, it was ever after lost in the name given to him by the princess of Egypt.

11. *When Moses was grown.* Being full forty years of age, as Stephen says, Acts vii. 23, "it came into his heart to visit his brethren," i.e., he was excited to it by a divine inspiration; "and seeing one of them suffer wrong," by an Egyptian smiting him, probably one of the taskmasters, he "avenged him . . . and smote"—slew "the Egyptian," supposing that God, who had given him commission, had given also his brethren to understand that they were to be delivered by his hand; see Acts vii. 23-25. Probably the Egyptian killed the Hebrew, and therefore on the Noahic precept Moses was justified in killing him; and he was authorized so to do by the commission which he had received from God, as all succeeding events amply prove.

13. *Two men of the Hebrews strove together.* How strange that, in the very place where they were suffering a heavy persecution because they were Hebrews, the very persons themselves who suffered it should be found persecuting each other! It has been often seen that, in those times in which the ungodly oppressed the Church of Christ, its own members have been separated from each other by disputes concerning comparatively unessential points of doctrine and discipline, in consequence of which both they and the truth have become an easy prey to those whose desire was to waste the heritage of the Lord.

14. *And Moses feared.* He saw that the Israelites were not as yet prepared to leave their bondage; and that though God had called him to be their leader, yet His providence had not yet sufficiently opened the way; and had he stayed in Egypt he must have endangered his life. Prudence therefore dictated an escape for the present to the land of Midian.

15. *Pharaoh . . . sought to slay Moses. But Moses fled from the face of Pharaoh.* How can this be reconciled with Heb. xi. 27: "By faith he [Moses] forsook Egypt, not fearing the wrath of the king"? Very easily. The apostle speaks not of this forsaking of Egypt, but of his and the Israelites' final departure from it, and of the bold and courageous manner in which Moses treated Pharaoh and the Egyptians, disregarding his threatenings and the multitudes of them that pursued after the people whom, in the name and strength of God, he led in the face of their enemies out of Egypt. *Dwelt in the land of Midian.* A country generally supposed to have been in Arabia Petraea, on the eastern coast of the Red Sea, not far from Mount Sinai.

16. *The priest of Midian.* Or "prince," or both; for the original *cohen* has both meanings.

17. *The shepherds . . . drove them.* The verb being in the masculine gender seems to imply that the shepherds drove away the flocks of Reuel's daughters, and not the daughters themselves. The fact seems to be that, as the daughters of Reuel filled the troughs and brought their flocks to drink, the shepherds drove those away, and, profiting by the young women's labor, watered their own cattle. Moses resisted this insolence, and assisted them to water their flocks, in consequence of which they were enabled to return much sooner than they were wont to do, v. 18.

18. *Reuel their father.* In Num. x. 29 this person is called Raguel, but the Hebrew is the same in both places. The person in question appears to have several names. Here he is Reuel; in Num. x. 29, Raguel; in Exod. iii. 1, *Jethro;* in Judg. iv. 11, *Hobab;* and in Judg. i. 16 he is called *Keyni;* which in chap. iv we translate Kenite. Some suppose that Reuel was father to Hobab, who was also called Jethro. This is the most likely.

20. *That he may eat bread.* That he may be entertained, and receive refreshment to proceed on his journey. *Bread* among the Hebrews was used to signify all kinds of food commonly used for the support of man's life.

21. *Zipporah his daughter.* It appears that Moses obtained Zipporah something in the same way that Jacob obtained Rachel; namely, for the performnce of certain services, probably keeping of sheep; see chap. iii. 1.

22. *Called his name Gershom.* Literally, "a stranger"; the reason of which Moses immediately adds, "for I have been an alien in a strange land."

23. *In process of time . . . the king of Egypt died.* According to Stephen (Acts vii. 30, compared with Exod. vii. 7), the death of the Egyptian king happened about forty years after the escape of Moses to Midian. The words which we translate, *And it came to pass in process of time,* signify, "And it was in many days from these."

24. *God remembered his covenant.* God's covenant is God's engagement; He had promised to Abraham, to Isaac, and to Jacob, to give their posterity a land flowing with milk and honey. They were now under the most oppressive bondage, and this was the most proper time for God to show them His mercy and power in fulfilling His promise. This is all that is meant by God's "remembering" His covenant, for it was now that He began to give it its effect.

25. *And God had respect unto them.* God "knew" them. i.e., He "approved" of them, and therefore it is said that their cry came up before God and He heard their groaning. The word *yada,* "to know," in the Hebrew Bible is frequently used in the sense of approving.

CHAPTER 3

Moses keeping the flock of Jethro at Mount Horeb, the angel of the Lord appears to him in a burning bush, 1-2. Astonished at the sight, he turns aside to examine it, 3, when God speaks to him out of the fire, and declares himself to be the God of Abraham, Isaac, and Jacob, 4-6; announces His purpose of delivering the Israelites from their oppression, and of bringing them into the Promised Land, 7-9; commissions him to go to Pharaoh, and to be leader of the children of Israel from Egypt, 10. Moses excuses himself, 11; and God, to encourage him, promises him His protection, 12. Moses doubts whether the Israelites will credit him, 13, and God reveals to him His name, and informs him what he is to say to the people, 14-17, and instructs him and the elders of Israel to apply unto Pharaoh for permission to go three days' journey into the wilderness, to sacrifice unto the Lord, 18; foretells the obstinacy of the Egyptian king, and the miracles which he himself should work in the sight of the Egyptians, 19-20; and promises that, on the departure of the Israelites, the Egyptians should be induced to furnish them with all necessaries for their journey, 21-22.

1. *Jethro his father in law.* Concerning Jethro, see the note on chap. ii. 18. Learned men are not agreed on the signification of the word *chothen,* which we translate "father in law," and which in Gen. xix. 14 we translate "son in law." It seems to be a general term for a "relative by marriage," and the connection only in which it stands can determine its precise meaning. It is very possible that Reuel was now dead, it being forty years since Moses came to Midian; that Jethro was his son, and had succeeded him in his office of prince and priest of Midian; that Zipporah was the sister of Jethro; and that consequently the word *chothen* should be translated "brother-in-law" in this place: as we learn from Gen. xxxiv. 9; Deut. vii. 3; Josh. xxiii. 12, and other places, that it simply signifies to contract affinity by marriage. If this conjecture be right, we may well suppose that, Reuel being dead, Moses was continued by his brother-in-law, Jethro, in the same employment he had under his father.

Mountain of God. Sometimes named Horeb, at other times Sinai. The mountain itself had two peaks; one was called Horeb, the other Sinai. Horeb was probably the primitive name of the mountain, which was afterwards called the *mountain of God* because God appeared upon it to Moses; and Mount Sinai, from *seneh,* a "bush," because it was in a bush, in a flame of fire, that this appearance was made.

2. *The angel of the Lord.* Not a created angel certainly; for He is called Jehovah, v. 4, and has the most expressive attributes of the Godhead applied to Him, vv. 14, etc. Yet He is an *angel, malach,* a "Messenger," in whom was the name of God, chap. xxiii. 21; and in whom dwelt all the fulness of the Godhead bodily, Col. ii. 9; and who, in all these primitive times, was the Messenger of the covenant, Mal. iii. 1. And who was this but Jesus, the Leader, Redeemer, and Saviour of mankind? *A flame of fire out of the midst of a bush.* Fire was, not only among the Hebrews but also among many other ancient nations, a very significant emblem of the Deity. *And the bush was not consumed.* (1) An emblem of the state of Israel in its various distresses and persecutions: it was in the fire of adversity, but was not consumed. (2) An emblem also of the state of the Church of God in the wilderness, in persecutions often, in the midst of its enemies, in the region of the shadow of death—yet not consumed. (3) An emblem also of the state of every follower of Christ: cast down, but not forsaken; grievously tempted, but not destroyed; walking through the fire, but still unconsumed! Why are all these preserved in the midst of those things which have a natural tendency to destroy them? Because God is in the midst of them; it was this that preserved the bush from destruction; and it was this that preserved the Israelites; and it is this, and this alone, that preserves the Church, and holds the

soul of every genuine believer in the spiritual life.

5. *Put off thy shoes.* It is likely that from this circumstance all the Eastern nations have agreed to perform all the acts of their religious worship barefooted. All the Mohammedans, Brahmins, and Parsees do so still. The Jews were remarked for this in the time of Juvenal; hence he speaks of their performing their sacred rites barefooted. It is probable that *nealim* in the text signifies "sandals," translated by the Chaldee *sandal* (see Gen. xiv. 23), which was the same as the Roman *solea*, a "sole" alone, strapped about the foot. As this sole must let in dust, gravel, and sand about the foot in travelling, hence the custom of frequently washing the feet in those countries where these sandals were worn. Pulling off the shoes was, therefore, an emblem of laying aside the pollutions contracted by walking in the way of sin.

6. *I am the God of thy father.* Though the word *abi*, "father," is here used in the singular, Stephen, quoting this place, Acts vii. 32, uses the plural, "The God of thy fathers"; and that this is the meaning the following words prove: *The God of Abraham, the God of Isaac, and the God of Jacob. And Moses hid his face.* For similar acts, see the passages referred to in the margin. *He was afraid to look*—he was overawed by God's presence, and dazzled with the splendor of the appearance.

7. *I have surely seen.* "Seeing, I have seen"— I have not only seen the afflictions of this people because I am omniscient, but I have considered their sorrows, and My eye affects My heart.

8. *And I am come down to deliver them.* This is the very purpose for which I am now come down upon this mountain, and for which I manifest myself to thee. *Large . . . land.* Canaan, when compared with the small tract of Goshen, in which they were now situated, and where, we learn from chap. i. 7, they were straitened for room, might be well called a large land. See a fine description of this land, Deut. viii. 7. *A land flowing with milk and honey.* Excellent for pasturage, because abounding in the most wholesome herbage and flowers; and from the latter an abundance of wild honey was collected by the bees.

11. *Who am I . . . that I should bring?* He was so satisfied that this was beyond his power, and all the means that he possessed, that he was astonished that even God himself should appoint him to this work! Such indeed was the bondage of the children of Israel, and the power of the people by whom they were enslaved, that had not their deliverance come through supernatural means, their escape had been utterly impossible.

12. *Certainly I will be with thee.* This great event shall not be left to thy wisdom and to thy power; My counsel shall direct thee, and My power shall bring all these mighty things to pass. *And this shall be a token.* Literally, "And this to thee for a sign," i.e., this miraculous manifestation of the burning bush shall be a proof that I have sent thee; or, "My being with thee," to encourage thy heart, strengthen thy hands, and enable thee to work miracles, shall be to thyself and to others the evidence of thy divine mission. *Ye shall serve God upon this mountain.* This was not the sign, but God shows him that in their return from Egypt they should

take this mountain in their way, and should worship Him in this place. There may be a prophetic allusion here to the giving of the law on Mount Sinai. As Moses received his commands here, so likewise should the Israelites receive theirs in the same place.

13. *They shall say . . . What is his name?* Does not this suppose that the Israelites had an idolatrous notion even of the Supreme Being? They had probably drunk deep into the Egyptian superstitions, and had gods many and lords many; and Moses conjectured that, hearing of a supernatural deliverance, they would inquire who that God was by whom it was to be effected.

14. *I AM THAT I AM. Eheyeh asher Eheyeh.* These words have been variously understood. The Vulgate translates, "I am who am." The Septuagint, "I am he who exists." The Syriac, the Persic, and the Chaldee preserve the original words without any gloss. The Arabic paraphrases them, "The Eternal, who passes not away." As the original words literally signify, "I will be what I will be," some have supposed that God simply designed to inform Moses that what He had been to his fathers Abraham, Isaac, and Jacob, He would be to him and the Israelites; and that He would perform the promises He had made to his fathers, by giving their descendants the Promised Land. It is difficult to put a meaning on the words; they seem intended to point out the eternity and self-existence of God.

15. *This is my name for ever.* The name here referred to is that which immediately precedes, *Yehovah Elohim*, which we translate the Lord God, the name by which God had been known from the creation of the world (see Gen. ii. 4) and the name by which He is known among the same people to the present day. Even the heathen knew this name of the true God; and hence out of our *Yehovah* they formed their *Jove.* As to be self-existent and eternal must be attributes of God forever, does it not follow that the *leolam, for ever,* in the text signifies eternity?

16. *Elders of Israel.* Though it is not likely the Hebrews were permitted to have any regular government at this time, yet there can be no doubt of their having such a government in the time of Joseph, and for some considerable time after; the elders of each tribe forming a kind of court of magistrates, by which all actions were tried, and legal decisions made, in the Israelitish community. *I have surely visited you.* An exact fulfillment of the prediction of Joseph, Gen. 1 24, "God will surely visit you," and in the same words too.

18. *They shall hearken to thy voice.* This assurance was necessary to encourage him to an enterprise so dangerous and important. *Three days' journey into the wilderness.* Evidently intending Mount Sinai, which is reputed to be about three days' journey, the shortest way, from the land of Goshen. In ancient times, distances were computed by the time required to pass over them. Thus, instead of miles, furlongs. it was said, the distance from one place to another was so many days', so many hours' journey; and it continues the same in all countries where there are no regular roads or highways.

19. *I am sure that the king of Egypt will not let you go, no, not by a mighty hand.* When the facts detailed in this history have been considered in connection with the assertion as it stands in our Bibles, the most palpable contradiction has appeared. That the king of Egypt did let them go, and that by a mighty hand, the book itself amply declares. We should, therefore, seek for another meaning of the original word. *Velo*, which generally means "and not," has sometimes the meaning of "if not, unless, except"; and in Becke's Bible, 1549, it is thus translated: "I am sure that the kyng of Egypt wyl not let you go, except wyth a mighty hand." The meaning, therefore, is very plain: The king of Egypt, who now profits much by your servitude, will not let you go till he sees My hand stretched out, and he and his nation be smitten with ten plagues. Hence God immediately adds, v. 20: "I will stretch out my hand, and smite Egypt with all my wonders . . . and after that, he will let you go."

22. *Every woman shall borrow.* This is certainly not a correct translation: the original word *shaal* signifies simply to "ask, request, demand, require, inquire"; but it does not signify to *borrow* in the proper sense of that word, though in a very few places of Scripture it is thus used. In this and the parallel place, chap. xii. 35, the word signifies to "ask" or "demand," and not to *borrow*, which is a gross mistake into which scarcely any of the versions, ancient or modern, have fallen, except our own. The Septuagint has "she shall ask"; the Vulgate, "she shall demand." The European versions are generally correct on this point; and our common English version is almost the sole transgressor. God commanded the Israelites to "ask" or "demand" a certain recompense for their past services, and He inclined the hearts of the Egyptians to give liberally; and this, far from a matter of oppression, wrong, or even charity, was no more than a very partial recompense for the long and painful services which we may say six hundred thousand Israelites had rendered to Egypt, during a considerable number of years.

Jewels of silver. The word *keley* we have already seen signifies "vessels, instruments, weapons," and may be very well translated by our English term "articles" or "goods." The Israelites got both gold and silver, and such raiment as was necessary for the journey which they were about to undertake.

Ye shall spoil the Egyptians. The verb *natsal* signifies, not only to "spoil, snatch away," but also to "get away, to escape, to deliver, to regain, or recover." Spoil signifies what is taken by violence; but this cannot be the meaning of the original word here, as the Israelites only asked, and the Egyptians without fear, terror, or constraint, freely gave. It is worthy of remark that the original word is used, 1 Sam. xxx. 22, to signify the recovery of property that had been taken away by violence. In this sense we should understand the word here. The Israelites recovered a part of their property—their wages, of which they had been most unjustly deprived by the Egyptians.

CHAPTER 4

Moses continues to express his fear that the Israelites should not credit his divine mission, 1; God, to strengthen his faith, and to assure him that his countrymen would believe him, changed his rod into a serpent, and the serpent into a rod, 2-5; made his hand leprous, and afterwards restored it, 6-7; intimating that He had now endued him with power to work such miracles, and that the Israelites would believe, 8; and further assures him that he should have power to turn the water into blood, 9. Moses excuses himself on the ground of his not being eloquent, 10, and God reproves him for his unbelief, and promises to give him supernatural assistance, 11-12. Moses expressing his utter unwillingness to go on any account, God is angry, and then promises to give him his brother, Aaron, to be his spokesman, 13-16, and appoints his rod to be the instrument of working miracles, 17. Moses returns to his relative Jethro, and requests liberty to visit his brethren in Egypt, and is permitted, 18. God appears to him in Midian, and assures him that the Egyptians who sought his life were dead, 19. Moses, with his wife and children, sets out on their journey to Egypt, 20. God instructs him what he shall say to Pharaoh, 21-23. He is in danger of losing his life, because he had not circumcised his son, 24. Zipporah immediately circumcising the child, Moses escapes unhurt, 25-26. Aaron is commanded to go and meet his brother, Moses; he goes and meets him at Horeb, 27. Moses informs him of the commission he has received from God, 28. They both go to their brethren, deliver their message, and work miracles, 29-30. The people believe and adore God, 31.

1. *They will not believe me.* As if he had said, Unless I be enabled to work miracles, and give them proofs by extraordinary works as well as by words, they will not believe that Thou hast sent me.

2. *A rod. Matteh*, a "staff," probably his shepherd's crook; see Lev. xxvii. 32. As it was made the instrument of working many miracles, it was afterwards called the "rod of God"; see v. 20.

3. *A serpent.* Of what sort we know not, as the word *nachash* is a general name for serpents.

4. *He put forth his hand, and caught it.* Considering the light in which Moses had viewed this serpent, it required considerable faith to induce him thus implicitly to obey the command of God; but he obeyed, and the noxious serpent became instantly the miraculous rod in his hand! Implicit faith and obedience conquer all difficulties; and he who believes in God and obeys Him in all things has really nothing to fear.

5. *That they may believe.* This is an example of what is called an imperfect or unfinished speech, several of which occur in the sacred writings. It may be thus supplied: "Do this before them, that they may believe that the Lord hath appeared unto thee."

6. *His hand was leprous as snow.* That is, the leprosy spread itself over the whole body in thin white scales. The leprosy, at least among the Jews, was a most inveterate and contagious disorder and deemed by them incurable. Among the heathen it was considered as inflicted by their gods, and it was supposed that they alone could remove it. It is certain that a similar belief prevailed among the Israelites; hence, when the king of Syria sent his general, Naaman, to the king of Israel to cure him of his leprosy, he rent his clothes, saying, "Am I God, to kill and to make alive, that this man doth send unto me to recover a man of his leprosy?" 2 Kings v. 7. This appears, therefore, to be the reason why God chose this sign, as the instantaneous infliction and removal of this disease were demonstrations which all would allow of the sovereign power of God.

8. *If they will not believe . . . the voice of the first sign.* Probably intimating that some would be more difficult to be persuaded than others: some would yield to the evidence of the first miracle; others would hesitate till they had seen the second; and others would not believe till they had seen the water of the Nile turned into blood, when poured upon the dry land, v. 9.

10. *I am not eloquent. Lo ish debarim,* "I am not a man of words"; a periphrasis common in the Scriptures. So Job xi. 2, "a man of lips," signifies one that is talkative. But how could it be said that Moses was *not eloquent,* when Stephen asserts, Acts vii. 22, that he was "mighty in words" as well as in deeds? Though Moses was slow of speech, yet when acting as the messenger of God his word was with power, for at his command the plagues came and the plagues were stayed; thus was he mighty in words as well as in deeds: and this is probably the meaning of Stephen. By the expression *neither heretofore, nor since thou hast spoken unto thy servant,* he might possibly mean that the natural inaptitude to speak readily, which he had felt, he continued to feel, even since God has begun to discover himself; for though He had wrought several miracles for him, yet He had not healed this infirmity.

11. *Who hath made man's mouth?* Cannot He who formed the mouth, the whole organs of speech, and hath given the gift of speech also, cannot He give utterance? God can take away those gifts and restore them again. Do not provoke Him; He who created the eye, the ear, and the mouth, hath also made the blind, the deaf, and the dumb.

13. *Send . . . by the hand of him whom thou wilt send.* The Hebrew literally translated is, "Send now [or, I beseech Thee] by the hand thou wilt send"; which seems to intimate, Send a person more fit for the work than I am. So the Septuagint: "Elect another powerful person, whom thou wilt send."

14. *I know that he can speak well.* "I know that in speaking he will speak." That is, he is apt to talk, and has a ready utterance. *He cometh forth to meet thee.* He shall meet thee at My mount (v. 27), shall rejoice in thy mission, and most heartily cooperate with thee in all things. A necessary assurance to prevent Moses from suspecting that Aaron, who was his elder brother, would envy his superior call and office.

15. *I will be with thy mouth, and with his mouth.* Ye shall be both, in all things which I appoint you to do in this business, under the continual inspiration of the Most High.

16. *He shall be thy spokesman.* Literally, "He shall speak for thee [or in thy stead] to the people." *He shall be to thee instead of a mouth.* He shall convey every message to the people; *and thou shalt be to him instead of God*—thou shalt deliver to him what I communicate to thee.

18. *Let me go, I pray thee, and return unto my brethren.* Moses, having received his commission from God, and directions how to execute it, returned to his father-in-law, and asked permission to visit his family and brethren in Egypt, without giving him any intimation of the great errand on which he was going.

19. *In Midian.* This was a new revelation, and appears to have taken place after Moses returned to his father-in-law previous to his departure for Egypt.

20. *His wife and his sons.* Both Gershom and Eliezer, though the birth of the latter has not yet been mentioned in the Hebrew text. See the note on chap. ii. 22.

Set them upon an ass. The Septuagint reads the word in the plural "upon asses," as it certainly required more than one to carry Zipporah, Gershom, and Eliezer. *The rod of God.* The sign of sovereign power, by which he was to perform all his miracles; once the badge of his shepherd's office, and now that by which he is to feed, rule, and protect his people Israel.

21. *But I will harden his heart.* The case of Pharaoh has given rise to many fierce controversies, and to several strange and conflicting opinions. Would men but look at the whole account without the medium of their respective creeds, they would find little difficulty to apprehend the truth. If we take up the subject in a theological point of view, all sober Christians will allow the truth of this proposition of St. Augustine, when the subject in question is a person who has hardened his own heart by frequently resisting the grace and spirit of God: "God does not harden men by infusing malice into them, but by not imparting mercy to them." And this other will be as readily credited: "God does not work this hardness of heart in man; but he may be said to harden him whom he refuses to soften, to blind him whom he refuses to enlighten, and to repel him whom he refuses to call." It is but just and right that He should withhold those graces which He had repeatedly offered, and which the sinner had despised and rejected. Thus much for the general principle. The verb *chazak,* which we translate *harden,* literally signifies to "strengthen, confirm, make bold or courageous"; and is often used in the sacred writings to excite to duty, perseverance, etc., and is placed by the Jews at the end of most books in the Bible as an exhortation to the reader to take courage, and proceed with his reading and with the obedience it requires. It constitutes an essential part of the exhortation of God to Joshua, chap. i. 7: "Only be thou strong," *rak chazak.* And of Joshua's dying exhortation to the people, chap. xxiii. 6: "Be ye therefore very courageous," *vachazaktem,* "to keep and to do all that is written in the book of the law." Now it would be very strange in these places to translate the word "harden": "Only be thou hard"; "Be ye therefore very hard"; and yet if we use the word "hardy," it would suit the sense and context perfectly well: "Only be thou hardy"; "Be ye therefore very hardy." Now suppose we apply the word in this way to Pharaoh, the sense would be good, and the justice of God equally conspicuous. I will make his heart hardy, bold, daring, presumptuous; for the same principle acting against God's order is presumption which when acting according to it is undaunted courage. It is true that the verb *kashah* is used, chap. vii. 3, which signifies to render stiff, tough, or stubborn, but it amounts to nearly the same meaning with the above.

All those who have read the Scriptures with care and attention know well that God is frequently represented in them as doing what He only *permits* to be done. So because a man has grieved His Spirit and resisted His grace He withdraws that Spirit and grace from him, and thus he becomes bold and presumptuous in sin. Pharaoh made his own heart stubborn against God, chap. ix. 34; and God gave him up to judicial blindness, so that he rushed on stubbornly to his own destruction. From the whole of Pharaoh's conduct we learn that he was bold, haughty, and cruel; and God chose to *permit* these dispositions to have their full sway in his heart without check or restraint from divine influence. The consequence was what God intended: he did not immediately comply with the requisition to let the people go; and this was done that God might have the fuller opportunity of manifesting His power by multiplying signs and miracles, and thus impress the hearts both of the Egyptians and Israelites with a due sense of His omnipotence and justice. The whole procedure was graciously calculated to do endless good to both nations. The Israelites must be satisfied that they had the true God for their Protector, and thus their faith was strengthened. The Egyptians must see that their gods could do nothing against the God of Israel, and thus their dependence on them was necessarily shaken. These great ends could not have been answered had Pharaoh at once consented to let the people go. This consideration alone unravels the mystery, and explains everything. Let it be observed that there is nothing spoken here of the eternal state of the Egyptian king; nor does anything in the whole of the subsequent account authorize us to believe that God hardened his heart against the influences of His own grace, that He might occasion him so to sin that His justice might consign him to hell. This would be such an act of flagrant injustice as we could scarcely attribute to the worst of men. He who leads another into an offense that he may have a fairer pretense to punish him for it, or brings him into such circumstances that he cannot avoid committing a capital crime, and then hangs him for it, is surely the most execrable of mortals. What then should we make of the God of justice and mercy should we attribute to Him a decree, the date of which is lost in eternity, by which He has determined to cut off from the possibility of salvation millions of millions of unborn souls, and leave them under a necessity of sinning, by actually hardening their hearts against the influences of His own grace and Spirit, that He may, on the pretext of justice, consign them to endless perdition? Whatever may be pretended in behalf of such unqualified opinions, it must be evident to all who are not deeply prejudiced that neither the justice nor the sovereignty of God can be magnified by them.

22. *Israel is my son, even my firstborn.* That is, The Hebrew people are unutterably dear to Me.

23. *Let my son go, that he may serve me.* Which they could not do in Goshen, consistently with the policy and religious worship of the Egyptians; because the most essential part of the Israelites' worship consisted in sacrifice, and the animals which they offered to God were sacred among the Egyptians. Moses gives Pharaoh this reason in chap. viii. 26. *I will slay thy son, even thy firstborn.* Which, on Pharaoh's utter refusal to let the people go, was accordingly done; see chap. xii. 29.

24. *By the way in the inn.* See the note on Gen. xlii. 27. The meaning of the whole passage seems to be this: The son of Moses, Gershom or Eliezer, had not been circumcised, though it would seem that God had ordered the father to

do it; but as he had neglected this, therefore Jehovah was about to have slain the child, because not in covenant with Him by circumcision, and thus He intended to have punished the disobedience of the father by the natural death of his son. Zipporah, getting acquainted with the nature of the case and the danger to which her firstborn was exposed, took a sharp stone and cut off the foreskin of her son. By this act the displeasure of the Lord was turned aside, and Zipporah considered herself as now allied to God because of this circumcision. The sharp stone mentioned in v. 25 was probably a knife made of flint, for such were anciently used, even where knives of metal might be had, for every kind of operation about the human body. Ancient authors are full of proofs of these facts. It is probable that Zipporah, being alarmed by this circumstance, and fearing worse evils, took the resolution to return to her father's house with her two sons. See chap. xviii. 1, etc.

27. *The Lord said to Aaron.* See v. 14. By some secret but powerful movement on Aaron's mind, or by some voice or angelic ministry, he was now directed to go and meet his brother, Moses; and so correctly was the information given to both that they arrived at the same time on the sacred mountain.

30. *Aaron spake all the words.* It is likely that Aaron was better acquainted with the Hebrew tongue than his brother, and on this account he became the spokesman. *Did the signs.* Turned the rod into a serpent, made the hand leprous, and changed the water into blood. See on vv. 8 and 9.

31. *The people believed.* They credited the account given of the divine appointment of Moses and Aaron to be their deliverers out of their bondage, the miracles wrought on the occasion confirming the testimony delivered by Aaron. *They bowed their heads and worshipped.* See a similar act mentioned, and in the same words, Gen. xxiv. 26. The bowing the head here may probably refer to the Eastern custom of bowing the head down to the knees, then kneeling down and touching the earth with the forehead.

CHAPTER 5

Moses and Aaron open their commission to Pharaoh, 1. He insultingly asks who Jehovah is, in whose name they require him to dismiss the people, 2. They explain, 3. He charges them with making the people disaffected, 4-5; and commands the taskmasters to increase their work, and lessen their means of performing it, 6-9. The taskmasters do as commanded, and refuse to give the people straw to assist them in making brick, and yet require the fulfillment of their daily tasks as formerly, when furnished with all the necessary means, 10-13. The Israelites failing to produce the ordinary quantity of brick, their own officers, set over them by the taskmasters, are cruelly insulted and beaten, 14. The officers complain to Pharaoh, 15-16; but find no redress, 17-18. The officers, finding their case desperate, bitterly reproach Moses and Aaron for bringing them into their present circumstances, 19-21. Moses retires, and lays the matter before the Lord, and pleads with Him, 22-23.

1. *And afterward Moses and Aaron went.* This chapter is properly a continuation of the preceding, as the succeeding is a continuation of this; and to preserve the connection of the facts they should be read together.

How simply, and yet with what authority, does Moses deliver his message to the Egyptian king! "Thus saith JEHOVAH, God of Israel, Let My people go." It is well in this, as in almost every other case where "Jehovah" occurs, to preserve the original word: our using the word Lord is not sufficiently expressive and often leaves the sense indistinct.

2. *Who is the Lord?* Who is Jehovah, *that I should obey his voice?* What claims has He on me? I am under no obligation to Him. Pharaoh spoke here under the common persuasion that every place and people had a tutelary deity, and he supposed that this Jehovah might be the tutelary deity of the Israelites, to whom he, as an Egyptian, could be under no kind of obligation.

3. *Three days' journey.* The distance from Goshen to Sinai; see chap. iii. 18. *And sacrifice unto the Lord.* Great stress is laid on this circumstance. God required sacrifice; no religious acts which they performed could be acceptable to Him without this. He had now showed them that it was their indispensable duty thus to worship Him, and that if they did not they might expect Him to send the pestilence —some plague or death proceeding immediately —from himself, or the *sword*—extermination by the hands of an enemy. The original word *deber*, from *dabar*, "to drive off, draw under," which we translate *pestilence* from the Latin *pestis*, "the plague," signifies any kind of disease by which an extraordinary mortality is occasioned, and which appears from the circumstances of the case to come immediately from God. The Israelites could not sacrifice in the land of Egypt, because the animals they were to offer to God were held sacred by the Egyptians; and they could not omit this duty, because it was essential to religion even before the giving of the law.

4. *Wherefore do ye, Moses and Aaron?* He hints that the Hebrews are in a state of revolt, and charges Moses and Aaron as being ringleaders of the sedition. This unprincipled charge has been, in nearly similar circumstances, often repeated since. Men who have labored to bring the mass of the common people from ignorance irreligion, and general profligacy of manners, to an acquaintance with themselves and God, and to a proper knowledge of their duty to Him and to each other, have often been branded as being disaffected to the state, and as movers of sedition among the people! *Let the people. Taphriu*, from *para*, to "loose or disengage," which we translate *to let*, from the Anglo-Saxon *lettan*, to "hinder." Ye hinder the people from working. "Get ye to your burdens." "Let religion alone, and mind your work." The language not only of tyranny, but of the basest irreligion also.

5. *The people of the land now are many.* The sanguinary edict had no doubt been repealed long before, or they could not have multiplied so greatly.

6. *The taskmasters of the people, and their officers.* The taskmasters were Egyptians (see on chap. i. 11), the officers were Hebrews; see v. 14. But it is probable that the taskmasters, chap. i. 11, who are called "princes of the burdens or taxes," were different from those termed *taskmasters* here, as the words are different; *nogesim* signifies "exactors" or "oppressors"—persons who exacted from them an unreasonable proportion of either labor or money. *Officers—shoterim;* those seem to have been an inferior sort of officers, who attended on superior officers or magistrates to execute their orders.

7. *Straw to make brick.* There have been many conjectures concerning the use of straw in making bricks. Some suppose it was used merely for burning them, but this is unfounded. The Eastern bricks are often made of clay and straw kneaded together, and then not burned, but thoroughly dried in the sun. This is expressly mentioned by Philo in his life of Moses, who says, describing the oppression of the Israelites in Egypt, that some were obliged to work in clay for the formation of bricks, and others to gather straw for the same purpose, "because straw is the bond by which the brick is held together."

8. *And the tale of the bricks. Tale* signifies the "number." *For they be idle; therefore they cry . . . Let us go and sacrifice.* Thus their desire to worship the true God in a proper manner was attributed to their unwillingness to work.

16. *The fault is in thine own people. Chatath*, the "sin," is in thy own people. *First*, Because they require impossibilities; and *Secondly*, Because they punish us for not doing what cannot be performed.

17. *Ye are idle: therefore ye say, Let us go and do sacrifice.* It is common for those who feel unconcerned about their own souls to attribute the religious earnestness of others, who feel the importance of eternal things, to idleness or a disregard of their secular concerns. Strange that they cannot see there is a medium! He who has commanded them to be "diligent in business" has also commanded them to be "fervent in spirit, serving the Lord."

19. *Did see that they were in evil case.* They saw that they could neither expect justice nor mercy; that their deliverance was very doubtful, and their case almost hopeless.

21. *The Lord look upon you, and judge.* These were hasty and unkind expressions; but the afflicted must be allowed the privilege of complaining. *Put a sword in their hand.* Given them a pretense which they had not before, to oppress us even unto death.

22. *And Moses returned unto the Lord.* This may imply, either that there was a particular place into which Moses ordinarily went to commune with Jehovah; or it may mean that kind of turning of heart and affection to God which every pious mind feels itself disposed to practice in any time or place. The old adage will apply here: "A praying heart never lacks a praying place." *Lord, wherefore hast thou so evil entreated this people?* It is certain that in this address Moses uses great plainness of speech. Whether the offspring of a testy impatience and undue familiarity, or of strong faith which gave him more than ordinary access to the throne of his gracious Sovereign, it would be difficult to say. The latter appears to be the most probable, as we do not find, from the succeeding chapter, that God was displeased with his freedom; we may therefore suppose that it was kept within due bounds and that the principles and motives were all pure and good. However, it should be noted that such freedom of speech with the Most High should never be used but on very special occasions and then only by His extraordinary messengers.

23. *He hath done evil to this people.* Their misery is increased instead of being diminished. *Neither hast thou delivered thy people at all.* The marginal reading is both literal and correct: "And delivering thou hast not delivered." Thou hast begun the work by giving us counsels and a commission, but Thou hast not brought the people from under their bondage.

CHAPTER 6

God encourages Moses, and promises to show wonders upon Pharaoh, and to bring out His people with a strong hand, 1. He confirms this promise by His essential name JEHOVAH, 2-3; by the covenant He had made with their fathers, 4-5. Sends Moses with a fresh message to the Hebrews, full of the most gracious promises, and confirms the whole by appealing to the name in which His unchangeable existence is implied, 6-8. Moses delivers the message to the Israelites, but through anguish of spirit they do not believe, 9. He receives a new commission to go to Pharaoh, 10-11. He excuses himself on account of his unreadiness of speech, 12. The Lord gives him and Aaron a charge both to Pharaoh and to the children of Israel, 13. The genealogy of Reuben, 14; of Simeon, 15; of Levi, from whom descended Gershon, Kohath, and Merari, 16. The sons of Gershon, 17; of Kohath, 18; of Merari, 19. The marriage of Amram and Jochebed, 20. The sons of Izhar and Uzziel, the brothers of Amram, 21-22. Marriage of Aaron and Elisheba, and the birth of their sons, Nadab, Abihu, Eleazar, and Ithamar, 23. The sons of Korah, the nephew of Aaron, 24. The marriage of Eleazar to one of the daughters of Putiel, and the birth of Phinehas, 25. These genealogical accounts introduced for the sake of showing the line of descent of Moses and Aaron, 26-27. A recapitulation of the commission delivered to Moses and Aaron, 28-29, and a repetition of the excuse formerly made by Moses, 30.

1. *With a strong hand. Yad chazakah,* the same verb which we translate "to harden"; see on chap. iv. 21. The *strong hand* here means sovereign power, suddenly and forcibly applied. God purposed to manifest His sovereign power in the sight of Pharaoh and the Egyptians; in consequence of which Pharaoh would manifest his power and authority as sovereign of Egypt, in dismissing and thrusting out the people.

2. *I am the Lord.* It should be, "I am JEHOVAH," and without this the reason of what is said in the third verse is not sufficiently obvious.

3. *By the name of God Almighty. El-Shaddai,* "God All-sufficient"; God the Dispenser or Pourer-out of gifts.
But by my name JEHOVAH was I not known to them. This passage has been a sort of *crux criticorum,* and has been variously explained. It is certain that the name Jehovah was in use long before the days of Ab.aham, see Gen. ii. 4, where the words *Jehovah Elohim* occur, as they do frequently afterwards; and see Gen. xv. 2, where Abraham expressly addresses Him by the name *Adonai Jehovah;* and see the seventh verse, where God reveals himself to Abraham by this very name: "And he said unto him, I am Jehovah, that brought thee out of Ur of the Chaldees." How then can it be said that by His name Jehovah He was not known unto them?
I believe the simple meaning is this, that though from the beginning the name Jehovah was known as one of the names of the Supreme Being, yet what it really implied they did not know. *El-Shaddai,* "God All-sufficient," they knew well by the continual provision He made for them and the constant protection He afforded them; but the name Jehovah is particularly to be referred to the accomplishment of promises already made; to the giving them a being, and thus bringing them into existence, which could not have been done in the order of His provi-

dence sooner than here specified. This name, therefore, in its power and significancy was not known unto them; nor fully known unto their descendants till the deliverance from Egypt and the settlement in the Promised Land.

4. *I have also established my covenant.* I have now fully purposed to give present effect to all My engagements with your fathers in behalf of their posterity.

6. *Say unto the children of Israel, I am the Lord, and I will bring you out.* This confirms the explanation given of v. 3.

7. *I will take you to me for a people.* This was precisely the covenant that He had made with Abraham. See Gen. xvii. 7, and the notes there. *And ye shall know that I am the Lord your God.* By thus fulfilling My promises ye shall know what is implied in My name. See on v. 3.

8. *Which I did swear.* "I have lifted up my hand." The usual mode of making an appeal to God, and hence considered to be a form of swearing. It is thus that Isa. lxii. 8 is to be understood: "The Lord hath sworn by his right hand, and by the arm of his strength."

9. *But they hearkened not.* Their bondage was become so extremely oppressive that they had lost all hope of ever being redeemed from it. *Anguish of spirit. Kotzer ruach,* "shortness of spirit or breath." The words signify that their labor was so continual and their bondage so cruel and oppressive that they had scarcely time to breathe.

12. *Uncircumcised lips?* The word *aral,* which we translate *uncircumcised,* seems to signify anything exuberant or superfluous. The word must refer to some natural impediment in his speech; and probably means a want of distinct and ready utterance, either occasioned by some defect in the organs of speech or impaired knowledge of the Egyptian language after an absence of forty years.

14. *These be the heads.* The "chiefs" or "captains." The following genealogy was simply intended to show that Moses and Aaron came in a direct line from Abraham, and to ascertain the time of Israel's deliverance. The whole account from this verse to v. 26 is a sort of parenthesis, and does not belong to the narration; and what follows from v. 28 is a recapitulation of what was spoken in the preceding chapters.

20. *His father's sister. Dodatho.* The true meaning of this word is uncertain. Parkhurst observes that *dod* signifies "uncle" in 1 Sam. x. 14; Lev. x. 4, and frequently elsewhere. It signifies also an "uncle's son"; compare Jer. xxxii. 8 with v. 12, where the Vulgate renders *dodi* by "my paternal cousin"; and in Amos vi. 10, for *dodo,* the Targum has "his near relation." So the Vulgate, "his relative," and the Septuagint, "those of their household." The best critics suppose that Jochebed was the cousin-german of Amram, and not his aunt. *Bare him Aaron and Moses.* The Samaritan, Septuagint, Syriac, and one Hebrew MS. add, "And Miriam their sister."

21. *Korah.* Though he became a rebel against God and Moses (see Num. xvi. 1, etc.), yet Moses, in his great impartiality, inserts his name among those of his other progenitors.

22. *Uzziel.* He is called Aaron's uncle, Lev. x. 4.

23. *Elisheba.* The oath of the Lord. It is the same name as Elizabeth, so very common among Christians. She was of the royal tribe of Judah, and was sister to Nahshon, one of the princes; see Num. ii. 3. *Eleazar.* He succeeded to the high priesthood on the death of his father, Aaron, Num. xx. 25, etc.

25. *Phinehas.* Of the celebrated act of this person and the most honorable grant made to him and his posterity, see Num. xxv. 7-13.

26. *According to their armies.* Their "battalions"—regularly arranged troops.

28. *And it came to pass.* Here the seventh chapter should commence, as there is a complete ending of the sixth with v. 27, and the thirtieth verse of this chapter is intimately connected with the first verse of the succeeding.

CHAPTER 7

The dignified mission of Moses and Aaron to Pharaoh—the one to be as God, the other as a prophet of the Most High, 1-2. The prediction that Pharaoh's heart should be hardened, that God might multiply His signs and wonders in Egypt, that the inhabitants might know He alone was the true God, 3-6. The age of Moses and Aaron, 7. God gives them directions how they should act before Pharaoh, 8-9. Moses turns his rod into a serpent, 10. The magicians imitate this miracle, and Pharaoh's heart is hardened, 11-13. Moses is commanded to wait upon Pharaoh next morning when he should come to the river, and threaten to turn the waters into blood if he did not let the people go, 14-18. The waters in all the land of Egypt are turned into blood, 19-20. The fish die, 21. The magicians imitate this, and Pharaoh's heart is again hardened, 22-23. The Egyptians sorely distressed because of the bloody waters, 24. This plague endures seven days, 25.

1. *I have made thee a god.* At thy word every plague shall come, and at thy command each shall be removed. Thus Moses must have appeared as a god to Pharaoh. *Shall be thy prophet.* Shall receive the word from thy mouth, and communicate it to the Egyptian king, v. 2.

3. *I will harden Pharaoh's heart.* I will permit his stubbornness and obstinacy still to remain, that I may have the greater opportunity to multiply My wonders in the land, that the Egyptians may know that I only am Jehovah, the self-existent God.

5. *And bring out the children of Israel.* Pharaoh's obstinacy was either caused or permitted in mercy to the Egyptians, that he and his magicians being suffered to oppose Moses and Aaron to the uttermost of their power, the Israelites might be brought out of Egypt in so signal a manner, in spite of all the opposition of the Egyptians, their king, and their gods, that Jehovah might appear to be "All-mighty" and "All-sufficient."

7. *Moses was fourscore years old.* He was forty years old when he went to Midian, and he had tarried forty years in Midian (see chap. ii. 11 and Acts vii. 30); and from this verse it appears that Aaron was three years older than Moses. We have already seen that Miriam, their sister, was older than either, chap. ii. 4.

9. *Shew a miracle for you.* A miracle, *mopheth,* signifies an effect produced in nature which is opposed to its laws, or such as its powers are inadequate to produce. As Moses and Aaron professed to have a divine mission, and to come to Pharaoh on the most extraordinary occasion, making a most singular and

unprecedented demand, it was natural to suppose, if Pharaoh should even give them an audience, that he would require them to give him some proof by an extraordinary sign that their pretensions to such a divine mission were well-founded and incontestable. For it appears to have ever been the sense of mankind that he who has a divine mission to effect some extraordinary purpose can give a supernatural proof that he has got this extraordinary commission. *Take thy rod.* This rod, whether a common staff, an ensign of office, or a shepherd's crook, was now consecrated for the purpose of working miracles; and is indifferently called the rod of God, the rod of Moses, and the rod of Aaron. God gave it the miraculous power, and Moses and Aaron used it.

10. *It became a serpent. Tannin.* What kind of serpent is here intended, learned men are not agreed. From the manner in which the original word is used in Ps. lxxiv. 13; Isa. xxvii. 1; li. 9; Job vii. 12, some very large creature, either aquatic or amphibious, is probably intended; some have thought that the crocodile, a well-known Egyptian animal, is here intended. In chap. iv. 3 it is said that this rod was changed into a "serpent," but the original word there is *nachash,* and here *tannin,* the same word which we translate "whale," Gen. i. 21.

11. *Pharaoh . . . called the wise men. Chacamim,* the men of learning. *Sorcerers, cashshephim,* those who "reveal" hidden things. *Magicians, chartummey,* "decipherers" of abstruse writings. *They also did in like manner with their enchantments.* The word *lahatim,* comes from *lahat,* "to burn, to set on fire"; and probably signifies such incantations as required lustral fires, sacrifices, fumigations, burning of incense, aromatic and odoriferous drugs, as the means of evoking departed spirits or assistant demons, by whose ministry, it is probable, the magicians in question wrought some of their deceptive miracles. There can be no doubt that real serpents were produced by the magicians. On this subject there are two opinions: *First,* That the serpents were such as they, either by juggling or sleight of hand, had brought to the place, and had secreted till the time of exhibition, as our common conjurers do in the public fairs, etc. *Secondly,* That the serpents were brought by the ministry of a familiar spirit, which, by the magic flames already referred to, they had evoked for the purpose. Both these opinions admit the serpents to be real and no illusion of the sight. The first opinion appears to me insufficient to account for the phenomena of the case referred to.

12. *Aaron's rod swallowed up their rods.* As Egypt was remarkably addicted to magic, sorcery, etc., it was necessary that God should permit Pharaoh's wise men to act to the utmost of their skill in order to imitate the work of God, that His superiority might be clearly seen and His powerful working incontestably ascertained; and this was fully done when Aaron's rod swallowed up their rods.

13. *And he hardened Pharaoh's heart.* "And the heart of Pharaoh was hardened," the identical words which in v. 22 are thus translated, and which should have been rendered in the same way here, lest the hardening, which was evidently the effect of his own obstinate shut-

ting of his eyes against the truth, should be attributed to God. See on chap. iv. 21.

14. *Pharaoh's heart is hardened. Cabed,* is become "heavy" or "stupid"; he receives no conviction, notwithstanding the clearness of the light which shines upon him.

15. *Lo, he goeth out unto the water.* Probably for the purpose of bathing, or of performing some religious ablution.

17. *Behold, I will smite.* Here commences the account of the ten plagues which were inflicted on the Egyptians by Moses and Aaron, by the command and through the power of God.

19. *That there may be blood . . . both in vessels of wood, and in vessels of stone.* Not only the Nile itself was to be thus changed into blood in all its branches, and the canals issuing from it, but all the water of lakes, ponds, and reservoirs was to undergo a similar change. And this was to extend even to the water already brought into their houses for culinary and other domestic purposes.

THE FIRST PLAGUE—
THE WATERS TURNED INTO BLOOD

20. *All the waters . . . were turned to blood.* Not merely in appearance, but in reality; for these changed waters became corrupt so that even the fish that were in the river died; and the smell became highly offensive, so that the waters could not be drunk, v. 21.

22. *And the magicians . . . did so.* But if all the water in Egypt was turned into blood by Moses, where did the magicians get the water which they changed into blood? This question is answered in verse 24. The Egyptians digged round about the river for water to drink, and it seems that the water obtained by this means was not bloody like that in the river; on this water, therefore, the magicians might operate. Again, though a general commission was given to Moses, not only to turn the waters of the river (Nile) into blood, but also those of their streams, rivers, ponds, and pools, yet it seems pretty clear from verse 20 that he did not proceed thus far, at least in the first instance; for it is there stated that only the waters of the river were turned into blood. Afterwards the plague doubtless became general.

The plague of the bloody waters may be considered as a display of retributive justice against the Egyptians, for the murderous decree which enacted that all the male children of the Israelites should be drowned in that river, the waters of which, so necessary to their support and life, were now rendered not only insalubrious but deadly, by being turned into blood. As it is well known that the Nile was a chief object of Egyptian idolatry (see on v. 15) and that annually they sacrificed a girl, or as others say, both a boy and a girl, to this river, in gratitude for the benefits received from it, God might have designed this plague as a punishment for such cruelty; and the contempt poured upon this object of their adoration, by turning its waters into blood and rendering them fetid and corrupt, must have had a direct tendency to correct their idolatrous notions and lead them to acknowledge the power and authority of the true God.

25. *And seven days were fulfilled.* So we learn that this plague continued at least a whole week.

CHAPTER 8

The plague of frogs threatened, 1-2. The extent of this plague, 3-4. Aaron commanded to stretch out his hand, with the rod, over the river and waters of Egypt, in consequence of which the frogs came, 5-6. The magicians imitate this miracle, 7. Pharaoh entreats Moses to remove the frogs, and promises to let the people go, 8. Moses promises that they shall be removed from every part of Egypt, the river excepted, 9-11. Moses prays to God, and the frogs die throughout the land of Egypt, 12-14. Pharaoh, finding himself respited, hardens his heart, 15. The plague of lice on man and beast, 16-17. The magicians attempt to imitate this miracle, but in vain, 18. They confess it to be the finger of God, and yet Pharaoh continues obstinate, 19. Moses is sent again to him to command him to let the people go, and in case of disobedience he is threatened with swarms of flies, 20-21. A promise made that the land of Goshen, where the Israelites dwelt, should be exempted from this plague, 22-23. The flies are sent, 24. Pharaoh sends for Moses and Aaron, and offers to permit them to sacrifice in the land, 25. They refuse, and desire to go three days' journey into the wilderness, 26-27. Pharaoh consents to let them go a little way, provided they would entreat the Lord to remove the flies, 28. Moses consents, prays to God, and the flies are removed, 29-31. After which Pharaoh yet hardened his heart, and refused to let the people go, 32.

THE SECOND PLAGUE—FROGS

1. *Let my people go.* God, in great mercy to Pharaoh and the Egyptians, gives them notice of the evils He intends to bring upon them if they continue in their obstinacy. Having had, therefore, such warning, the evil might have been prevented by a timely humiliation and return to God.

2. *If thou refuse.* Nothing can be plainer than that Pharaoh had it still in his power to dismiss the people, and that his refusal was the mere effect of his own wilful obstinacy.

3. *The river shall bring forth frogs abundantly.* The river Nile, which was an object of their adoration, was here one of the instruments of their punishment. The expression *bring forth . . . abundantly* not only shows the vast numbers of those animals which should now infest the land, but it seems also to imply that all the spawn or ova of those animals which were already in the river and marshes should be brought miraculously to a state of perfection. We may suppose that the animals were already in an embryo existence, but multitudes of them would not have come to a state of perfection had it not been for this miraculous interference. This supposition will appear the more natural when it is considered that the Nile was remarkable for breeding frogs.

Into thine ovens. In various parts of the East, instead of what we call *ovens* they dig a hole in the ground, in which they insert a kind of earthen pot, which having sufficiently heated, they stick their cakes to the inside, and when baked remove them and supply their places with others, and so on. To find such places full of frogs when they came to heat them, in order to make their bread, must be both disgusting and distressing in the extreme.

5. *Stretch forth thine hand . . . over the streams, over the rivers.* The streams and rivers here may refer to the grand divisions of the Nile in the Lower Egypt, which were at least seven, and to the canals by which these were connected, as there were no other streams but what proceeded from this great river.

9. *Glory over me. Hithpaer alai.* These words have greatly puzzled commentators in general; and it is not easy to assign their true meaning. The Septuagint render the words thus: "Appoint unto me when I shall pray." The Vulgate is

exactly the same; and in this sense almost all the versions understood this place. This countenances the conjectural emendation of Le Clerc, who, by the change of a single letter, reading *hithbaer* for *hithpaer,* gives the same sense as that in the ancient versions. This appears to be the genuine import of the words, and the sense taken in this way is strong and good. Nothing could be a fuller proof that this plague was supernatural than the circumstance of Pharaoh's being permitted to assign himself the time of its being removed, and its removal at the intercession of Moses according to that appointment. And this is the very use made of it by Moses himself, v. 10, when he says, "Be it according to thy word: that thou mayest know that there is none like unto the Lord our God."

14. *They gathered them together upon heaps.* The killing of the frogs was a mitigation of the punishment; but the leaving them to rot in the land was a continual proof that such a plague had taken place, and that the displeasure of the Lord still continued.

The conjecture of Calmet is at least rational: he supposes that the plague of flies originated from the plague of frogs; that the former deposited their ova in the putrid masses and that from these the innumerable swarms afterwards mentioned were hatched. In vindication of this supposition it may be observed that God never works a miracle when the end can be accomplished by merely natural means; and in the operations of divine providence we always find that the greatest number of effects possible are accomplished by the fewest causes. As, therefore, the natural means for this fourth plague had been miraculously provided by the second, the Divine Being had a right to use the instruments which He had already prepared.

THE THIRD PLAGUE—LICE

16. *Smite the dust of the land, that it may become lice.* If the vermin commonly designated by this name be intended, it must have been a very dreadful and afflicting plague to the Egyptians, and especially to their priests, who were obliged to shave the hair off every part of their bodies, and to wear a single tunic, that no vermin of this kind might be permitted to harbor about them.

The circumstance of their being *in* man and *in* beast agrees so well with the nature of the "tick" that I am ready to conclude this is the insect meant. This animal buries both its sucker and head equally in man or beast; and can with very great difficulty be extracted before it is grown to its proper size, and filled with the blood and juices of the animal on which it preys. When fully grown, it has a glossy black, oval body. Not only horses, cows, and sheep are infested with it in certain countries, but even the common people, especially those who labor in the field, in woods. I know no insect to which the Hebrew term so properly applies. This is the fixed, established insect, which will permit itself to be pulled in pieces rather than let go its hold; and this is literally "in man and in beast," burying its trunk and head in the flesh of both.

18. *The magicians did so.* That is, They tried the utmost of their skill, either to produce these insects or to remove this plague. *But they could not;* no juggling could avail here, because in-

sects must be produced which would stick to and infix themselves in man and beast, which no kind of trick could possibly imitate; and to remove them, as some would translate the passage, was to their power equally impossible. If the magicians even acted by spiritual agents, we find from this case that these agents had assigned limits, beyond which they could not go; for every agent in the universe is acting under the direction or control of the Almighty.

19. *This is the finger of God.* That is, The power and skill of God are here evident. Probably before this the magicians supposed Moses and Aaron to be conjurers, like themselves; but now they are convinced that no man could do these miracles which these holy men did, unless God were with him. God permits evil spirits to manifest themselves in a certain way that men may see that there is a spiritual world and be on their guard against seduction. He at the same time shows that all these agents are under His control, that men may have confidence in His goodness and power.

THE FOURTH PLAGUE—FLIES

21. *Swarms of flies upon thee.* It is not easy to ascertain the precise meaning of the original word *hearob;* as the word comes from *arab,* he "mingled," it may be supposed to express a multitude of various sorts of insects. And if the conjecture be admitted that the putrid frogs became the occasion of this plague (different insects laying their eggs in the bodies of those dead animals, which would soon be hatched, see on verse 14), then the supposition that a multitude of different kinds of insects is meant will seem the more probable. Though the plague of the locusts was miraculous, yet God both brought it and removed it by natural means; see chap. x. 13-19.

22. *I will sever in that day.* Hiphleythi has been translated by some good critics, "I will miraculously separate"; so the Vulgate: "I will do a marvellous thing." And the Septuagint, "I will render illustrious" the land of Goshen in that day; and this He did, by exempting that land and its inhabitants, the Israelites, from the plagues by which He afflicted the land of Egypt.

23. *And I will put a division.* Peduth, "a redemption," *between my people and thy people,* God hereby showing that He had redeemed them from those plagues to which He had abandoned the others.

24. *The land was corrupted.* Everything was spoiled, and many of the inhabitants destroyed, being probably stung to death by these venomous insects. This seems to be intimated by the Psalmist, "He sent divers sorts of flies among them, which devoured them," Ps. lxxviii. 45.

25. *Sacrifice to your God in the land.* That is, Ye shall not leave Egypt, but I shall cause your worship to be tolerated here.

26. *We shall sacrifice the abomination of the Egyptians.* That is, The animals which they hold sacred, and will not permit to be slain, are those which our customs require us to sacrifice to our God; and should we do this in Egypt the people would rise in a mass, and stone us to death. Perhaps few people were more superstitious than the Egyptians. Almost every production of nature was an object of their religious worship: the sun, moon, planets, stars,

the river Nile, animals of all sorts, from the human being to the monkey, dog, cat, and ibis, and even the onions and leeks which grew in their gardens. Jupiter was adored by them under the form of a ram, Apollo under the form of a crow, Bacchus under that of a goat, and Juno under that of a heifer.

27. *And sacrifice to the Lord . . . as he shall command us.* It is very likely that neither Moses nor Aaron knew as yet in what manner God would be worshipped; and they expected to receive a direct revelation from Him relative to this subject when they should come into the wilderness.

28. *I will let you go . . . only ye shall not go very far away.* Pharaoh relented because the hand of God was heavy upon him; but he was not willing to give up his gain. The Israelites were very profitable to him; they were slaves of the state, and their hard labor was very productive: hence he professed a willingness, first to tolerate their religion in the land (v. 25); or to permit them to go into the wilderness, so that they went not far away and would soon return. How ready is foolish man, when the hand of God presses him sore, to compound with his Maker! He will consent to give up some sins, provided God will permit him to keep others. *Intreat for me.* Exactly similar to the case of Simon Magus, who, like Pharaoh, fearing the divine judgments, begged an interest in the prayers of Peter, Acts viii. 24.

31. *The Lord did according to the word of Moses.* How powerful is prayer! God permits His servant to prescribe even the manner and time in which He shall work. *He removed the swarms.* Probably by means of a strong wind which swept them into the sea.

32. *Pharaoh hardened his heart at this time also.* See v. 15. This hardening was the mere effect of his self-determining obstinacy. He preferred his gain to the will and command of Jehovah, and God made his obstinacy the means of showing forth His own power and providence in a supereminent degree.

CHAPTER 9

The Lord sends Moses to Pharaoh to inform him that, if he did not let the Israelites depart, a destructive pestilence should be sent among his cattle, 1-3; while the cattle of the Israelites shou'd be preserved, 4. The next day this pestilence, which was the fifth plague, is sent, and all the cattle of the Egyptians die, 5-6. Though Pharaoh finds that not one of the cattle of the Israelites had died, yet, through hardness of heart, he refuses to let the people go, 7. Moses and Aaron are commanded to sprinkle handfuls of ashes from the furnace, that the sixth plague, that of boils and blains, might come on man and beast, 8-9; which having done, the plague takes place, 10. The magicians cannot stand before this plague, which they can neither imitate nor remove, 11. Pharaoh's heart is again hardened, 12. God's awful message to Pharaoh, with the threat of more severe plagues than before, 13-17. The seventh plague of rain, hail, and fire threatened, 18. The Egyptians commanded to house their cattle that they might not be destroyed, 19. Those who feared the word of the Lord brought home their servants and cattle, and those who did not regard that word left their cattle and servants in the fields, 20-21. The storm of hail, thunder, and lightning takes place, 22-24. It nearly desolates the whole land of Egypt, 25, while the land of Goshen escapes, 26. Pharaoh confesses his sin, and begs an interest in the prayers of Moses and Aaron, 27-28. Moses promises to intercede for him, and while he promises that the storm shall cease, he foretells the continuing obstinacy of both Pharaoh and his servants, 29-30. The flax and barley, being in a state of maturity, are destroyed by the tempest, 31; while the wheat and the rye, not being grown up, are preserved, 32. Moses obtains a cessation of the storm, 33. Pharaoh and his servants, seeing this, harden their hearts, and refuse to let the people go, 34-35.

1. *The Lord God of the Hebrews.* It is very likely that the term Lord, *Yehovah,* is used here to point out particularly His eternal power and Godhead; and that the term God, *Elohey,* is intended to be understood in the sense of Supporter, Defender, Protector. Thus saith the self-existent, omnipotent, and eternal Being, the Supporter and Defender of the Hebrews, "Let My people go, that they may worship Me."

THE FIFTH PLAGUE—THE MURRAIN

3. *The hand of the Lord.* The power of God manifested in judgment. *Upon the horses. Susim.* This is the first place the horse is mentioned, a creature for which Egypt and Arabia were always famous. *Sus* is supposed to have the same meaning with *sas,* which signifies to be "active, brisk, or lively," all which are proper appellatives of the horse, especially in Arabia and Egypt. Because of their activity and swiftness they were sacrificed and dedicated to the sun, and perhaps it was principally on this account that God prohibited the use of them among the Israelites. *A very grievous murrain.* The murrain is a very contagious disease among cattle, the symptoms of which are a hanging down and swelling of the head, abundance of gum in the eyes, rattling in the throat, difficulty of breathing, palpitation of the heart, staggering, a hot breath, and a shining tongue; which symptoms prove that a general inflammation has taken place. The original word *deber* is variously translated. The Septuagint has "death"; the Vulgate has *pestis,* a "plague" or "pestilence." Our English word *murrain* comes either from the French *mourir,* "to die," or from the Greek *maraino,* to "grow lean, waste away." The term "mortality" would be the nearest in sense to the original, as no particular disorder is specified by the Hebrew word.

4. *The Lord shall sever.* See on chap. viii. 22.

5. *To morrow the Lord shall do this.* By thus foretelling the evil, he showed His prescience and power; and from this both the Egyptians and Hebrews must see that the mortality that ensued was no casualty, but the effect of a predetermined purpose in the divine justice.

6. *All the cattle of Egypt died.* That is, all the cattle that did die belonged to the Egyptians, but not one died that belonged to the Israelites, vv. 4 and 6. That the whole stock of cattle belonging to the Egyptians did not die we have the fullest proof, because there were cattle both to be killed and saved alive in the ensuing plague, vv. 19-25. By this judgment the Egyptians must see the vanity of the whole of their national worship, when they found the animals which they not only held sacred, but deified, slain without distinction among the common herd by a pestilence sent from the hand of Jehovah. One might naturally suppose that after this the animal worship of the Egyptians could nevermore maintain its ground.

7. *And Pharaoh sent.* Finding so many of his own cattle and those of his subjects slain, he sent to see whether the mortality had reached to the cattle of the Israelites, that he might know whether this were a judgment inflicted by their God, and probably designing to replace the lost cattle of the Egyptians with those of the Israelites.

THE SIXTH PLAGUE—THE BOILS AND THE BLAINS

8. *Handfuls of ashes of the furnace.* As one part of the oppression of the Israelites consisted in their labor in the brickkilns, some have observed a congruity between the crime and the punishment. The furnaces, in the labor of which they oppressed the Hebrews, now yielded the instruments of their punishment; for every particle of those *ashes,* formed by unjust and oppressive labor, seemed to be a boil or a blain on the tyrannic king and his cruel and hard-hearted people.

9. *Shall be a boil. Shechin.* This word is generally expounded, "an inflammatory swelling, a burning boil"; one of the most poignant afflictions, not immediately mortal, that can well affect the surface of the human body. If a single boil on any part of the body throws the whole system into a fever, what anguish must a multitude of them on the body at the same time occasion! *Breaking forth with blains. Ababuoth,* supposed to come from *baah,* to "swell, bulge out"; any inflammatory swelling in any part of the body, but more especially in the more glandular parts, the neck, armpits, groin. The Septuagint translates it thus: "And it shall be an ulcer with burning pustules." It seems to have been a disorder of an uncommon kind, and hence it is called by way of distinction "the botch of Egypt," Deut. xxviii. 27, perhaps never known before in that or any other country.

11. *The boil was upon the magicians.* They could not produce a similar malady by throwing ashes in the air; and they could neither remove the plague from the people, nor from their own tormented flesh. Whether they perished in this plague we know not, but they are no more mentioned. If they were not destroyed by this awful judgment, they at least left the field and no longer contended with these messengers of God. The triumph of God's power was now complete, and both the Hebrews and the Egyptians must see that there was neither might, nor wisdom, nor counsel against the Lord.

15. *For now I will stretch out my hand.* In the Hebrew the verbs are in the past tense, and not in the future, as our translation improperly expresses them, by which means a contradiction appears in the text; for neither Pharaoh nor his people were smitten by a pestilence, nor was he by any kind of mortality *cut off from the earth.* It is true the firstborn were slain by a destroying angel, and Pharaoh himself was drowned in the Red Sea; but these judgments do not appear to be referred to in this place. If the words be translated, as they ought, in the subjunctive mood, or in the past instead of the future, this seeming contradiction to facts, as well as all ambiguity, will be avoided: "For if now I had stretched out [*shalachti,* had set forth] My hand, and had smitten thee and thy people with the pestilence, thou shouldst have been cut off from the earth. 16. But truly on this very account, have I caused thee to subsist, that I might cause thee to see My power, and that My name might be declared throughout all the earth [or, *becol haarets,* in all this land]."

Thus God gave this impious king to know that it was in consequence of His especial providence that both he and his people had not been already destroyed by means of the past plagues; but God had preserved him for this very purpose, that he might have a further opportunity of manifesting that He, Jehovah, was the only true God for the full conviction of both the Hebrews and the Egyptians, that the former might follow and the latter fear before Him. Judicious critics of almost all creeds have agreed to translate the original as above, a translation which it not only can bear but requires, and which is in strict conformity to both the Septuagint and the Targum. Neither the Hebrew, "I have caused thee to stand"; nor the apostle's translation of it, Rom. ix. 17, "I have raised thee"; nor that of the Septuagint, "On this account art thou preserved," namely, in the past plagues, can countenance that most exceptionable meaning put on the words by certain commentators, namely, "That God ordained or appointed Pharaoh from all eternity, by certain means, to this end; that He made him to exist in time; that He raised him to the throne; promoted him to that high honor and dignity; that He preserved him, and did not cut him off as yet; that He strengthened and hardened his heart; irritated, provoked, and stirred him up against His people Israel, and suffered him to go all the lengths he did go in his obstinacy and rebellion; all which was done to show in him His power in destroying him in the Red Sea. The sum of which is, that this man was raised up by God in every sense for God to show His power in his destruction." So man speaks; thus God hath not spoken.

17. *As yet exaltest thou thyself against my people?* So it appears that at this time he might have submitted, and thus prevented his own destruction.

THE SEVENTH PLAGUE—THE HAIL

18. *To morrow about this time.* The time of this plague is marked thus circumstantially to show Pharaoh that Jehovah was Lord of heaven and earth, and that the water, the fire, the earth, and the air, which were all objects of Egyptian idolatry, were the creatures of His power, and subservient to His will; and that, far from being able to help them, they were now, in the hands of God, instruments of their destruction.

To rain a very grievous hail. "To rain hail" may appear to some superficial observers as an unphilosophical mode of expression, but nothing can be more correct. "Drops of rain falling through a cold region of the atmosphere are frozen and converted into hail"; and thus the *hail* is produced by *rain.* When it begins to fall it is rain; when it is falling it is converted into hail; thus it is literally true that it rains hail. The farther a hailstone falls the larger it generally is, because in its descent it meets with innumerable particles of water, which, becoming attached to it, are also frozen, and thus its bulk is continually increasing till it reaches the earth.

19. *Send . . . now, and gather thy cattle.* So in the midst of judgment, God remembered mercy. The miracle should be wrought that they might know He was the Lord; but all the lives both of men and beasts might have been saved had Pharaoh and his servants taken the warning so mercifully given them. While some regarded not the word of the Lord, others feared it, and their cattle and their servants were saved. See vv. 20-21.

23. *The Lord sent thunder. Koloth,* "voices";

but loud, repeated peals of thunder are meant. *And the fire ran along upon the ground.* "And the fire walked upon the earth." It was not a sudden flash of lightning, but a devouring fire, walking through every part, destroying both animals and vegetables; and its progress was irresistible.

26. *Only in the land of Goshen . . . was there no hail.* What a signal proof of a most particular providence! Surely both the Hebrews and Egyptians profited by this display of the goodness and severity of God.

27. *The Lord is righteous, and I and my people are wicked.* The original is very emphatic: "The Lord is the righteous One [*hatstaddik*], and I and my people are the sinners [*hareshaim*]"; i.e., He is alone righteous, and we alone are transgressors. Who could have imagined that, after such an acknowledgment and confession, Pharaoh should have again hardened his heart?

28. *It is enough.* There is no need of any further plague; I submit to the authority of Jehovah and will rebel no more. *Mighty thunderings. Koloth Elohim*, "voices of God"—that is, superlatively loud thunder. So "mountains of God" (Ps. xxxvi. 6) means exceeding high mountains. So "a prince of God" (Gen. xxiii. 6) means a mighty prince. See a description of thunder, Ps. xxix. 3-8.

29. *I will spread abroad my hands.* That is, I will make supplication to God that He may remove this plague. This may not be an improper place to make some observations on the ancient manner of approaching the Divine Being in prayer. Kneeling down, stretching out the hands, and lifting them up to heaven were in frequent use among the Hebrews in their religious worship. Solomon kneeled down on his knees, and spread forth his hands to heaven, 2 Chron. vi. 13. So David, Ps. cxliii. 6: "I stretch forth my hands unto thee." So Ezra: "I fell upon my knees, and spread out my hands unto the Lord my God"; chap. ix. 5. See also Job xi. 13: "If thou prepare thine heart, and stretch out thine hands towards him." Most nations who pretended to any kind of worship made use of the same means in approaching the objects of their adoration, namely, kneeling down and stretching out their hands, which custom it is very likely they borrowed from the people of God. Kneeling was ever considered to be the proper posture of supplication, as it expresses humility, contrition, and subjection.

31. *The flax and the barley was smitten.* The word *pishtah*, *flax*, Mr. Parkhurst thinks, is derived from the root *pashat*, "to strip," because the substance which we term *flax* is properly the bark or rind of the vegetable, pilled or stripped off the stalks. From time immemorial Egypt was celebrated for the production and manufacture of flax: hence the linen and fine linen of Egypt, so often spoken of in ancient authors. *Barley. Seorah*, from *saar*, "to stand on end, to be rough, bristly"; hence *barley* because of the rough and prickly beard with which the ears are covered and defended. *The flax was bolled.* Meaning, I suppose, was grown up into a stalk: the original is *gibol*, "podded" or was "in the pod." The word well expresses that globous pod on the top of the stalk of flax which succeeds the flower and contains the seed, very properly expressed by the Septuagint, "but the flax was in seed or was seeding."

32. *But the wheat and the rie were not smitten. Wheat, chittah,* which Mr. Parkhurst thinks should be derived from the Chaldee and Samaritan *chati*, which signifies "tender, delicious, delicate," because of the superiority of its flavor to every other kind of grain. *Rie, cussemeth,* from *casam*, "to have long hair"; and hence, though the particular species is not known, the word must mean some bearded grain.

33. *Spread abroad his hands.* Probably with the rod of God in them. See what has been said on the spreading out of the hands in prayer, v. 29.

34. *He sinned yet more, and hardened his heart.* These were merely acts of his own.

35. *And the heart of Pharaoh was hardened.* In consequence of his sinning yet more, and hardening his own heart against both the judgments and mercies of God, we need not be surprised that, after God had given him the means of softening and repentance, and he had in every instance resisted and abused them, he should at last have been left to the hardness and darkness of his own obstinate heart, so as to fill up the measure of his own iniquity and rush headlong to his own destruction.

CHAPTER 10

Moses is again sent to Pharaoh, and expostulates with him on his refusal to let the Hebrews go, 1-3. The eighth plague, namely, of locusts, is threatened, 4. The extent and oppressive nature of this plague, 5-6. Pharaoh's servants counsel him to dismiss the Hebrews, 7. He calls for Moses and Aaron, and inquires who they are of the Hebrews who wish to go, 8. Moses having answered that the whole people, with their flocks and herds, must go and hold a feast to the Lord, 9, Pharaoh is enraged, and having granted permission only to the men, drives Moses and Aaron from his presence, 10-11. Moses is commanded to stretch out his hand and bring the locusts, 12. He does so, and an east wind is sent, which, blowing all that day and night, brings the locusts the next morning, 13. The devastation occasioned by these insects, 14-15. Pharaoh is humbled, acknowledges his sin, and begs Moses to intercede with Jehovah for him, 16-17. Moses does so, and at his request a strong west wind is sent, which carries all the locusts to the Red Sea, 18-19. Pharaoh's heart is again hardened, 20. Moses is commanded to bring the ninth plague—an extraordinary darkness over all the land of Egypt, 21. The nature, duration, and effects of this, 22-23. Pharaoh, again humbled, consents to let the people go, provided they leave their cattle behind, 24. Moses insists on having all their cattle, because of the sacrifices which they must make to the Lord, 25-26. Pharaoh, again hardened, refuses, 27. Orders Moses from his presence, and threatens him with death should he ever return, 28. Moses departs with the promise of returning no more, 29.

1. *Hardened his heart.* God suffered his natural obstinacy to prevail, that He might have further opportunities of showing forth His eternal power and Godhead.

2. *That thou mayest tell in the ears of thy son.* That the miracles wrought at this time might be a record for the instruction of the latest posterity, that Jehovah alone, the God of the Hebrews, was the sole Maker, Governor, and Supporter of the heavens and the earth.

3. *How long wilt thou refuse to humble thyself?* Had it been impossible for Pharaoh, in all the preceding plagues, to have humbled himself and repented, can we suppose that God could have addressed him in such language as the preceding? We may rest assured that there was always a time in which he might have

relented, and that it was because he hardened his heart at such times that God is said to harden him, i.e., to give him up to his own stubborn and obstinate heart.

THE EIGHTH PLAGUE—THE LOCUSTS

4. *To morrow will I bring the locusts.* The word *arbeh*, a *locust*, is probably from the root *rabah*, he "multiplied, became great, mighty"; because of the immense swarms of these animals by which different countries, especially the East, are infested. See this circumstance referred to, Judg. vi. 5; vii. 12; Ps. cv. 34; Jer. xlvi. 23; li. 14; Joel i. 6; Nah. iii. 15; where the most numerous armies are compared to the *arbeh* or "locust." The locust has a large, open mouth; and in its two jaws it has four incisive teeth, which traverse each other like scissors, being calculated, from their mechanism, to gripe or cut.

7. *How long shall this man be a snare unto us?* As there is no noun in the text, the pronoun *zeh* may refer either to the Israelites, to the plague by which they were then afflicted, or to Moses and Aaron, the instruments used by the Most High in their chastisement. *Let the men go, that they may serve the Lord their God.* Much of the energy of several passages is lost in translating *Yehovah* by the term "Lord." The Egyptians had their gods, and they supposed that the Hebrews had a god like unto their own; that this Jehovah required their services, and would continue to afflict Egypt till His people were permitted to worship Him in his own way. *Egypt is destroyed.* This last plague had nearly ruined the whole land.

8. *Who are they that shall go?* Though the Egyptians, about fourscore years before, wished to destroy the Hebrews, yet they found them now so profitable to the state that they were unwilling to part with them.

9. *We will go with our young and with our old.* As a feast was to be celebrated to the honor of Jehovah, all who were partakers of His bounty and providential kindness must go and perform their part in the solemnity. The men and the women must make the feast, the children must witness it, and the cattle must be taken along with them to furnish the sacrifices necessary on this occasion.

10. *Let the Lord be so with you.* This is an obscure sentence. Some suppose that Pharaoh meant it as a curse, as if he had said, "May your God be as surely with you, as I shall let you go!" For as he purposed not to permit them to go, so he wished them as much of the divine help as they should have of his permission. *Look . . . for evil is before you.* "See ye that evil is before your faces"—if you attempt to go, ye shall meet with the punishment ye deserve. Probably Pharaoh intended to insinuate that they had some sinister designs, and that they wished to go in a body that they might the better accomplish their purpose; but if they had no such designs they would be contented for the males to go, and leave their wives and children behind; for he well knew if the men went and left their families they would infallibly return, but that if he permitted them to take their families with them, they would undoubtedly make their escape; therefore he says, v. 11, "Go now ye that are men, and serve the Lord."

13. *The Lord brought an east wind.* As locusts abounded in those countries, and particularly in Ethiopia, and more especially at this time of the year, God had no need to create new swarms for this purpose; all that was requisite was to cause such a wind to blow as would bring those which already existed over the land of Egypt. The miracle in this business was the bringing the locusts at the appointed time and causing the proper wind to blow for that purpose; and then taking them away after a similar manner.

14. *Before them there were no such locusts.* They exceeded all that went before, or were since, in number and in the devastations they produced. Probably both these things are intended in the passage. See v. 15.

17. *Forgive, I pray thee, my sin only this once.* What a strange case! And what a series of softening and hardening, of sinning and repenting! Had he not now another opportunity of returning to God? But the love of gain, and the gratification of his own self-will and obstinacy, finally prevailed.

19. *A mighty strong west wind.* Literally the "wind of the sea"; the wind that blew from the Mediterranean Sea, which lay northwest of Egypt, which had the Red Sea on the east. Here again God works by natural means; He brought the locusts by the east wind, and took them away by the west or northwest wind, which carried them to the Red Sea, where they were drowned. *The Red sea.* The "weedy sea"; so called, as some suppose, from the great quantity of seaweed which grows in it and about its shores. In the Septuagint it is called the "Red Sea," from which version we have borrowed the name. The *Red sea*, called also the Arabic Gulf, separates Arabia from Upper Ethiopia and part of Egypt.

THE NINTH PLAGUE—THICK DARKNESS

21. *Darkness which may be felt.* Probably this was occasioned by a superabundance of aqueous vapors floating in the atmosphere, which were so thick as to prevent the rays of the sun from penetrating through them; an extraordinarily thick mist supernaturally, i.e., miraculously, brought on. An awful emblem of the darkened state of the Egyptians and their king.

23. *They saw not one another.* So deep was the obscurity, and probably such was its nature, that no artificial light could be procured; as the thick, clammy vapors would prevent lamps from burning, or if they even could be ignited, the light through the palpable obscurity could diffuse itself to no distance from the burning body. The author of the Book of Wisdom, chap. xvii. 2-19, gives a fearful description of this plague. *All the children of Israel had light.* By thus distinguishing the Israelites, God showed the Egyptians that the darkness was produced by His power; that He sent it in judgment against them for their cruelty to His people; that because they trusted in Him they were exempted from these plagues; that in the displeasure of such a Being His enemies had everything to fear, and in His approbation His followers had everything to hope.

24. *Only let your flocks and your herds be stayed.* Pharaoh cannot get all he wishes; and

as he sees it impossible to contend with Jehovah, he now consents to give up the Israelites, their wives, and their children, provided he may keep their *flocks* and their *herds*. The cruelty of this demand is not more evident than its avarice. Had six hundred thousand men, besides women and children, gone three days' journey into the wilderness without their cattle, they must have inevitably perished, being without milk for their little ones, and animal food for their own sustenance, in a place where little as a substitute could possibly be found. It is evident from this that Pharaoh intended the total destruction of the whole Israelitish host.

26. *We know not with what we must serve the Lord.* The law was not yet given, the ordinances concerning the different kinds of sacrifices and offerings not known. What kind and what number of animals God should require to be sacrificed, even Moses himself could not as yet tell. He therefore very properly insists on taking the whole of their herds with them, and not leaving even *one hoof behind*.

27. *The Lord hardened Pharaoh's heart.* He had yet another miracle to work for the complete conviction of the Egyptians and triumph of His people; and till that was wrought He permitted the natural obstinacy of Pharaoh's haughty heart to have its full sway, after each resistance of the gracious influence which was intended to soften and bring him to repentance.

28. *See my face no more.* Hitherto Pharaoh had left the way open for negotiation; but now, in wrath against Jehovah, he dismisses His ambassador and threatens him with death if he should attempt anymore to come into his presence.

29. *I will see thy face again no more.* It is very likely that this was the last interview that Moses had with Pharaoh, for what is related, chap. xi. 4-8, might have been spoken on this very occasion, as it is very possible that God gave Moses to understand His purpose to slay the firstborn while before Pharaoh at this time; so, in all probability, the interview mentioned here was the last which Moses had with the Egyptian king. It is true that in v. 31 of chap. xii it is stated that Pharaoh "called for Moses and Aaron by night," and ordered them to leave Egypt, and to take all their substance with them, which seems to imply that there was another interview, but the words may imply no more than that Moses and Aaron received such a message from Pharaoh. If, however, this mode of interpreting these passages should not seem satisfactory to any, he may understand the words of Moses thus: *I will see thy face*—seek thy favor—*no more* in behalf of my people, which was literally true; for if Moses did appear anymore before Pharaoh, it was not as a supplicant, but merely as the ambassador of God, to denounce His judgments by giving him the final determination of Jehovah relative to the destruction of the firstborn.

CHAPTER 11

God purposes to bring another plague upon Pharaoh, after which he should let the Israelites go, 1. They are commanded to ask gold and silver from the Egyptians, 2. The estimation in which Moses was held among the Egyptians, 3. Moses predicts the destruction of the firstborn of the Egyptians, 4-6, and Israel's protection, 7.

On seeing which, Pharaoh and his servants should entreat the Hebrews to depart, 8. The prediction of his previous obstinacy, 9-10.

1. *The Lord said unto Moses.* Calmet contends that this should be read in the pluperfect tense, "For the Lord had said to Moses," as the fourth, fifth, sixth, seventh, and eighth verses appear to have been spoken when Moses had the interview with Pharaoh mentioned in the preceding chapter; see the note there on verse 29. If, therefore, this chapter be connected with the preceding, as it should be, and the first three verses not only read in the past tense but also in a parenthesis, the sense will be much more distinct and clear than it now appears.

2. *Let every man borrow.* For a proper correction of the strange mistranslation of the word *shaal* in this verse, see the note on chap. iii. 22.

3. *The man Moses was very great.* The miracles which Pharaoh and his servants had already seen him work had doubtless impressed them with a high opinion of his wisdom and power. Had he not appeared in their sight as a very extraordinary person, whom it would have been very dangerous to molest, we may naturally conclude that some violence would long ere this have been offered to his person.

4. *About midnight will I go out.* Whether God did this by the ministry of a good or of an evil angel is a matter of little importance, though some commentators have greatly magnified it. Both kinds of angels are under His power and jurisdiction, and He may employ them as He pleases. Such a work of destruction as the slaying of the firstborn is supposed to be more proper for a bad than for a good angel. But the works of God's justice are not less holy and pure than the works of His mercy; and the highest archangel may, with the utmost propriety, be employed in either.

5. *The firstborn of Pharaoh.* From the heir to the Egyptian throne to the son of the most abject slave, or the principal person in each family. *The maidservant that is behind the mill.* The meanest slaves were employed in this work. In many parts of the East they still grind all their corn with a kind of portable millstones, the upper one of which is turned round by a sort of lever fixed in the rim.

6. *There shall be a great cry.* Of the dying and for the dead.

7. *Not a dog move his tongue.* This passage has been generally understood as a proverbial expression, intimating that the Israelites should not only be free from this death, but that they should depart without any kind of molestation. For though there must be much bustle and comparative confusion in the sudden removal of six hundred thousand persons with their wives, children, goods, cattle, yet this should produce so little alarm that even the dogs should not bark at them, which it would be natural to expect, as the principal stir was to be about midnight.

8. *And all these thy servants shall come.* A prediction of what actually took place. See chap. xii. 31-33.

9. *Pharaoh shall not hearken unto you.* Though *shall* and *will* are both reputed signs of the future tense, and by many indiscriminately used, yet they make a most essential difference in composition in a variety of cases. For in-

stance, if we translate *lo yishma,* "Pharaoh shall not hearken," as in our text, the word *shall* strongly intimates that it was impossible for Pharaoh to hearken, and that God had placed him under that impossibility; but if we translate as we should do, "Pharaoh will not hearken," it alters the case most essentially, and agrees with the many passages in the preceding chapters, where he is said to have hardened his own heart; as this proves that he, without any impulsive necessity, obstinately refused to attend to what Moses said or threatened; and that God took the advantage of this obstinacy to work another miracle, and thus multiply His wonders in the land. "Pharaoh will not hearken unto you"; and because he would not, God hardened his heart—left him to his own obstinacy.

CHAPTER 12

The month Abib is to be considered as the commencement of the year, 1-2. The Passover instituted; the lamb or kid to be used on the occasion to be taken from the flock the tenth day of the month, and each family to provide one, 3-4. The lamb or kid to be a male of the first year without blemish, 5. To be killed on the fourteenth day, 6, and the blood to be sprinkled on the side posts and lintels of the doors, 7. The flesh to be prepared by roasting, and not to be eaten either sodden or raw, 8-9; and no part of it to be left till the morning, 10. The people to eat it with their loins girded, etc., as persons prepared for a journey, 11. Why called the Passover, 12. The blood sprinkled on the doorposts, etc., to be a token to them of preservation from the destroying angel, 13. The fourteenth day of the month Abib to be a feast forever, 14. Unleavened bread to be eaten seven days, 15. This also to be observed in all their generations forever, 17-20. Moses instructs the elders of Israel how they are to offer the lamb and sprinkle his blood, and for what purpose, 21-23. He binds them to instruct their children in the nature of this rite, 24-27. The children of Israel act as commanded, 28. All the firstborn of Egypt slain, 29-30. Pharaoh and the Egyptians urge Moses, Aaron, and the Israelites to depart, 31-33. They prepare for their departure, and get gold, silver, and raiment from the Egyptians, 34-36. They journey from Rameses to Succoth, in number six hundred thousand men, besides women and children, and a mixed multitude, 37-38. They bake unleavened cakes of the dough they brought with them out of Egypt, 39. The time in which they sojourned in Egypt, 40-42. Different ordinances concerning the Passover, 43-49; which are all punctually observed by the people, who are brought out of Egypt the same day, 50-51.

2. *This month shall be unto you the beginning of months.* It is supposed that God now changed the commencement of the Jewish year. The month to which this verse refers, the month *Abib,* answers to a part of our March and April; whereas it is supposed that previously to this the year began with *Tisri,* which answers to a part of our September; for in this month the Jews suppose God created the world, when the earth appeared at once with all its fruits in perfection. From this circumstance the Jews have formed a twofold commencement of the year, which has given rise to a twofold denomination of the year itself, to which they afterwards attended in all their reckonings: that which began with *Tisri* or September was called their civil year; that which began with *Abib* or March was called the sacred year.

3. *In the tenth day of this month.* In after times they began their preparation on the thirteenth day or day before the Passover, which was not celebrated till the fourteenth day, see v. 6; but on the present occasion, as this was their first Passover, they probably required more time in which to get ready, as a state of very great confusion must have prevailed at this time. *A lamb.* The original word *seh* signifies the young of sheep and of goats, and may be indifferently translated either "lamb" or "kid." See v. 5. *A lamb for an house.* The whole host

of Israel was divided into twelve tribes, these tribes into families, the families into houses, and the houses into particular persons; Numbers i; Josh. vii. 14.

4. *If the household be too little.* That is, if there be not persons enough in one family to eat a whole lamb, then two families must join together. The rabbins allow that there should be at least ten persons to one paschal lamb, and not more than twenty. *Take it according to the number of the souls.* The persons who were to eat of it were to be first ascertained, and then the lamb was to be slain and dressed for that number.

5. *Without blemish.* Having no natural imperfection, no disease, no deficiency or redundancy of parts. *From the sheep, or from the goats.* The *seh* means either; and either was equally proper if without blemish. The Hebrews however in general preferred the lamb to the kid.

6. *Ye shall keep it up until the fourteenth day.* The lamb or kid was to be taken from the flock on the tenth day, and kept up and fed by itself till the fourteenth day, when it was to be sacrificed. This was never commanded nor practiced afterwards. *The whole assembly . . . shall kill it.* Any person might kill it, the sacrificial act in this case not being confined to the priests. *In the evening.* "Between the two evenings." The Jews divided the day into morning and evening: till the sun passed the meridian all was morning or forenoon; after that, all was afternoon or evening. Their first evening began just after twelve o'clock, and continued till sunset; their second evening began at sunset and continued till night, i.e., during the whole time of twilight; between twelve o'clock, therefore, and the termination of twilight, the passover was to be offered.

7. *Take of the blood, and strike it on the two side posts.* This was to be done by dipping a bunch of hyssop into the blood, and thus sprinkling it upon the posts; see v. 22. That this sprinkling of the blood of the paschal lamb was an emblem of the sacrifice and atonement made by the death of Jesus Christ is most clearly intimated in the sacred writings, 1 Pet. i. 2; Heb. ix. 13-14; viii. 10.

8. *They shall eat the flesh . . . roast with fire.* As it was the ordinary custom of the Jews to boil their flesh, some think that the command given here was in opposition to the custom of the Egyptians, who ate raw flesh in honor of Osiris.

Unleavened bread. Matstsoth, from *matsah,* to "squeeze" or "compress," because the bread prepared without leaven or yeast was generally compressed. *Bitter herbs.* What kind of herbs or salad is intended by the word *merorim,* which literally signifies "bitters," is not well known.

9. *With the purtenance thereof.* All the intestines, for these were abused by the heathen to purposes of divination; and when roasted in the manner here directed they could not be thus used. The command also implies that the lamb was to be roasted whole; neither the head nor the legs were to be separated, nor the intestines removed. I suppose that these last simply included the heart, lungs, liver, kidneys, and not the intestinal canal.

10. *Ye shall let nothing of it remain until*

the morning. Merely to prevent putrefaction; for it was not meet that a thing offered to God should be subjected to corruption, which in such hot countries it must speedily undergo. Thus the body of our blessed Lord "saw no corruption," Ps. xvi. 10; Acts ii. 27, because, like the paschal lamb, it was a sacrifice offered to God.

11. *And thus shall ye eat it; with your loins girded.* As in the Eastern countries they wear long, loose garments, whenever they travel they tuck up the foreparts of their garments in the girdle which they wear round their loins. *Your shoes on your feet.* This seems particularly mentioned because not customary. "The easterns throw off their shoes when they eat, because it would be troublesome," says Sir J. Chardin, "to keep their shoes upon their feet, they sitting cross-legged on the floor, and having no hinder quarters to their shoes, which are made like slippers; and as they do not use tables and chairs as we do in Europe, but have their floors covered with carpets, they throw off their shoes when they enter their apartments, lest they should soil those beautiful pieces of furniture." On the contrary the Israelites were to have their *shoes on,* because now about to commence their journey. *Your staff in your hand.* The same writer observes that the Eastern people universally make use of a *staff* when they travel on foot.

Ye shall eat it in haste. Because they were suddenly to take their departure: the destroying angel was at hand, their enemies were coming against them, and they had not a moment to lose.

It is the Lord's passover. That is, Jehovah is now about to "pass over" the land, and the houses only where the blood is sprinkled shall be safe from the stroke of death. The Hebrew word *pesach,* which we very properly translate *passover,* and which we should always be pronounced as two words, has its name from the angel of God passing by or over the houses of the Israelites, on the posts and lintels of which the blood of the lamb was sprinkled, while he stopped at the houses of the Egyptians to slay their firstborn.

12. *Against all the gods of Egypt.* As different animals were sacred among the Egyptians, the slaying of the *firstborn* of all the beasts might be called executing judgment upon the gods of Egypt. As this however does not appear very clear and satisfactory, some have imagined that the word *elohey* should be translated "princes," which is the rendering in our margin; for as these princes, who were rulers of the kingdom under Pharaoh, were equally hostile to the Hebrews with Pharaoh himself, therefore these judgments fell equally heavy on them also.

13. *The blood shall be to you for a token.* It shall be the sign to the destroying angel that the house on which he sees this blood sprinkled is under the protection of God, and that no person in it is to be injured. See on v. 11.

14. *A memorial.* To keep up a remembrance of the severity and goodness, or justice and mercy, of God. *Ye shall keep it a feast*—it shall be annually observed, and shall be celebrated with solemn religious joy, *throughout your generations*—as long as ye continue to be a distinct people; an *ordinance*—a divine appointment, an institution of God himself, neither to be altered nor set aside by any human authority. *For ever. Chukkath olam,* an everlasting or endless statute, because representative of the Lamb of God, who taketh away the sin of the world; whose mediation, in consequence of His sacrifice, shall endure while time itself lasts; and to whose merits and efficacy the salvation of the soul shall be ascribable throughout eternity. This, therefore, is a statute and ordinance that can have no end, either in this world or in the world to come.

15. *Seven days shall ye eat unleavened bread.* This has been considered as a distinct ordinance, and not essentially connected with the Passover. The Passover was to be observed on the fourteenth day of the first month; the Feast of Unleavened Bread began on the fifteenth and lasted seven days, the first and last of which were holy convocations. *That soul shall be cut off.* There are thirty-six places in which this excision or cutting off is threatened against the Jews for neglect of some particular duty; and what is implied in the thing itself is not well known. Some think it means a violent death, some a premature death, and some an eternal death. It is very likely that it means no more than a separation from the rights and privileges of an Israelite; so that after this excision the person was considered as a mere stranger, who had neither lot nor part in Israel, nor any right to the blessings of the covenant. This is probably what St. Paul means, Rom. ix. 3.

16. *In the first day . . . and in the seventh day there shall be an holy convocation.* This is the first place where we meet with the account of an assembly collected for the mere purpose of religious worship. Such assemblies are called *holy convocations,* which is a very appropriate appellation for a religious assembly; they were called together by the express command of God, and were to be employed in a work of holiness.

17. *Selfsame day. Beetsem,* "in the body of this day," or "in the strength of this day"; probably they began their march about daybreak, called here the body or strength of the day, and in Deut. xvi. 1, by night—sometime before the sun rose.

19. *No leaven found in your houses.* To meet the letter of this precept in the fullest manner possible, the Jews, on the eve of this festival, institute the most rigorous search through every part of their houses, not only removing all leavened bread, but sweeping every part clean, that no crumb of bread shall be left that had any leaven in it. And so strict were they in the observance of the letter of this law that if even a mouse was seen to run across the floor with a crumb of bread in its mouth they considered the whole house as polluted, and began their purification afresh. Leaven was an emblem of sin, because it proceeded from corruption; and the putting away of this implied the turning to God with simplicity and uprightness of heart.

21. *Kill the passover.* That is, the lamb, which was called the paschal or passover lamb. The animal that was to be sacrificed on this occasion got the name of the institution itself. St. Paul copies the expression, 1 Cor. v. 7: "Christ our passover" (that is, our Paschal Lamb) "is sacrificed for us."

22. *A bunch of hyssop.* The original word *ezob* has been variously translated *musk, rosemary, mint, marjoram,* and *hyssop;* the latter seems to be the most proper. It was used in sprinkling the blood of the paschal lamb, in cleansing the leprosy, Lev. xiv. 4, 6, 51-52; in composing the water of purification, Num. xix. 6, and sprinkling it, v. 18. It was a type of the purifying virtue of the bitter sufferings of Christ. And it is plain, from Ps. li. 7, that the Psalmist understood its meaning.

26. *What mean ye by this service?* The establishment of this service annually was a very wise provision to keep up in remembrance this wonderful deliverance. From the remotest antiquity the institution of feasts, games, etc., has been used to keep up the memory of past grand events. Hence God instituted the Sabbath to keep up the remembrance of the creation, and the Passover to keep up the remembrance of the deliverance from Egypt. All the other feasts were instituted on similar reasons. The Jews never took their sons to the Tabernacle or Temple till they were twelve years of age, nor suffered them to eat of the flesh of any victim till they had themselves offered a sacrifice at the Temple, which they were not permitted to do before the twelfth year of their age. It was at this age that Joseph and Mary took our blessed Lord to the Temple, probably for the first time, to offer His sacrifice.

27. *It is the sacrifice of the Lord's passover.* We have already intimated that the paschal lamb was an illustrious type of Christ; and we shall find that everything in this account is typical or representative. The bondage and affliction of the people of Israel may be considered as emblems of the hard slavery and wretchedness consequent on a state of sinfulness.

29. *Smote all the firstborn.* If we take the term *firstborn* in its literal sense only, we shall be led to conclude that in a vast number of the houses of the Egyptians there could have been no death, as it is not at all likely that every firstborn child of every Egyptian family was still alive, and that all the firstborn of their cattle still remained. And yet it is said, v. 30, that there was "not a house where there was not one dead." The word, therefore, must not be taken in its literal sense only. From its use in a great variety of places in the Scriptures it is evident that it means the chief, most excellent, best beloved, most distinguished. In this sense our blessed Lord is called "the firstborn of every creature," Col. i. 15, and "the firstborn among many brethren," Rom. viii. 29; that is, He is more excellent than all creatures, and greater than all the children of men. And the people of Israel are often called by the same name, see Exod. iv. 22: "Israel is my son, my firstborn"; that is, the people in whom I particularly delight, and whom I will especially support and defend.

30. *There was a great cry.* No people in the universe were more remarkable for their mournings than the Egyptians, especially in matters of religion; they whipped, beat, tore themselves, and howled in all the excess of grief. When a relative died, the people left the house, ran into the streets, and howled in the most lamentable and frantic manner.

31. *Called for Moses and Aaron.* That is, he sent the message here mentioned to them; for

it does not appear that he had any further interview with Moses and Aaron, after what is mentioned in chap. x. 28-29 and xi. 8. See the notes there.

33. *The Egyptians were urgent upon the people.* They felt much, they feared more; and therefore wished to get immediately rid of a people on whose account they found they were smitten with so many and such dreadful plagues.

34. *The people took their dough before it was leavened.* There was no time now to make any regular preparation for their departure, such was the universal hurry and confusion. The Israelites could carry but little of their household utensils with them; but some, such as they kneaded their bread and kept their meal in, they were obliged to carry with them. The kneading troughs of the Arabs are comparatively small wooden bowls, which, after kneading their bread in, serve them as dishes out of which they eat their victuals. And as to these being bound up in their clothes, no more may be intended than their wrapping them up in their long, loose garments.

35. *They borrowed of the Egyptians.* See the note on chap. iii. 22, where the very exceptionable term *borrow* is largely explained.

37. *From Rameses to Succoth. Rameses* appears to have been another name for Goshen, though it is probable that there might have been a chief city or village in that land, where the children of Israel rendezvoused previously to their departure, called Rameses. As the term *Succoth* signifies "booths" or "tents," it is probable that this place was so named from its being the place of the first encampment of the Israelites. *Six hundred thousand.* That is, there was this number of effective men, twenty years old and upwards, who were able to go out to war.

40. *Now the sojourning of the children of Israel.* The statement in this verse is allowed on all hands to be extremely difficult and, therefore, the passage stands in especial need of illustration. The Samaritan Pentateuch, in all its manuscripts and printed copies, reads the place thus: "Now the sojourning of the children of Israel, and of their fathers, which they sojourned in the land of Canaan and in the land of Egypt, was 430 years." This same sum is given by St. Paul, Gal. iii. 17, who reckons from the promise made to Abraham, when God commanded him to go to Canaan, to the giving of the law, which soon followed the departure from Egypt; and this chronology of the apostle is concordant with the Samaritan Pentateuch, which, by preserving the two passages, "they and their fathers," and "in the land of Canaan," which are lost out of the present copies of the Hebrew text, has rescued this passage from all obscurity and contradiction. It may be necessary to observe that the Alexandrian copy of the Septuagint has the same reading as that in the Samaritan. That these three witnesses have the truth, the chronology itself proves; for from Abraham's entry into Canaan to the birth of Isaac was 25 years, Gen. xii. 4; xvii. 1-21; Isaac was 60 years old at the birth of Jacob, Gen. xxv. 26; and Jacob was 130 at his going down into Egypt, Gen. xlvii. 9; which three sums make 215 years. And then Jacob and his children having continued in Egypt 215 years

more, the whole sum of 430 years is regularly completed.

42. *A night to be much observed.* A night to be held in everlasting remembrance, because of the peculiar display of the power and goodness of God, the observance of which annually was to be considered a religious precept while the Jewish nation should continue.

43. *This is the ordinance of the passover.* From the last verse of this chapter it appears pretty evident that this, to the fiftieth verse inclusive, constituted a part of the directions given to Moses relative to the proper observance of the first Passover, and should be read conjointly with the preceding account beginning at verse 21. It may be supposed that these latter parts contain such particular directions as God gave to Moses after He had given those general ones mentioned in the preceding verses, but they seem all to belong to this first Passover. *There shall no stranger eat thereof. Ben nechar,* the "son of a stranger or foreigner," i.e., one who was not of the genuine Hebrew stock, or one who had not received circumcision; for any circumcised person might eat the Passover, as the total exclusion extends only to the uncircumcised, see v. 48.

45. *A foreigner. Toshab,* from *yashab,* to "sit down or dwell"; one who is a mere sojourner, for the purpose of traffic, merchandise, etc. *And an hired servant.* None of these shall eat of it, because not circumcised—not brought under the bond of the covenant; and not being under obligation to observe the Mosaic law, had no right to its privileges and blessings.

46. *In one house shall it be eaten.* In one family, if that be large enough; if not, a neighboring family might be invited, v. 4. *Thou shalt not carry forth ought of the flesh.* Every family must abide within doors because of the destroying angel, none being permitted to go out of his house till the next day, v. 22. *Neither shall ye break a bone thereof.* As it was to be eaten in haste (v. 11), there was no time either to separate the bones or to break them in order to extract the marrow; and lest they should be tempted to consume time in this way, therefore this ordinance was given. It is very likely that, when the whole lamb was brought to table, they cut off the flesh without even separating any of the large joints, leaving the skeleton, with whatever flesh they could not eat, to be consumed with fire, v. 10. This precept was also given to point out a most remarkable circumstance which fifteen hundred years after was to take place in the crucifixion of the Saviour of mankind, who was the true Paschal Lamb, that Lamb of God that takes away the sin of the world; who, though He was crucified as a common malefactor, and it was a universal custom to break the legs of such on the cross, yet so did the providence of God order it that a bone of Him was not broken. See the fulfillment of this wondrously expressive type, John xix. 33, 36.

48. *And when a stranger . . . will keep the passover.* Let all who sojourn among you, and who desire to partake of this sacred ordinance, not only be circumcised themselves, but all the males of their families likewise, that they may all have an equal right to the blessings of the covenant.

49. *One law shall be to him that is homeborn.* As this is the first place that the term *torah* or "law" occurs, a term of the greatest importance in divine revelation, and on the proper understanding of which much depends, I judge it best to give its genuine explanation once for all.

The word *torah* comes from the root *yarah,* which signifies to "aim at, teach, point out, direct, lead, guide, make straight or even"; and from these significations of the word (and in all these senses it is used in the Bible) we may see at once the nature, properties, and design of the law of God. It is a system of instruction in righteousness; it teaches the difference between moral good and evil; ascertains what is right and fit to be done, and what should be left undone, because improper to be performed.

The word *lex,* "law," among the Romans, has been derived from *lego,* "I read"; because when a law or statute was made, it was hung up in the most public places, that it might be seen, read, and known by all men, that those who were to obey the laws might not break them through ignorance, and thus incur the penalty. The Greeks call a law *nomos,* from *nemo,* to "divide, distribute, minister to, or serve," because the law divides to all their just rights, appoints or distributes to each his proper duty, and thus serves or ministers to the welfare of the individual and the support of society.

51. *By their armies. Tsibotham,* from *tsaba,* to "assemble, meet together," in an orderly or regulated manner, and hence to "war," to act together as troops in battle; whence *tsebaoth,* "troops, armies, hosts." It is from this that the Divine Being calls himself *Yehovah tsebaoth,* "the Lord of hosts or armies," because the Israelites were brought out of Egypt under His direction, marshalled and ordered by himself, guided by His wisdom, supported by His providence, and protected by His might. This is the true and simple reason why God is so frequently styled in Scripture the "Lord of hosts"; for *the Lord did bring the children of Israel out of the land of Egypt by their armies.*

CHAPTER 13

God establishes the law concerning the firstborn, and commands that all such, both of man and beast, should be sanctified unto Him, 1-2. Orders them to remember the day in which they were brought out of Egypt, when they should be brought to the land of Canaan; and to keep this service in the month Abib, 3-5. Repeats the command concerning the unleavened bread, 6-7, and orders them to teach their children the cause of it, 8, and to keep strictly in remembrance that it was by the might of God alone they had been delivered from Egypt, 9. Shows that the consecration of the firstborn, both of man and beast, should take place when they should be settled in Canaan, 10-12. The firstborn of man and beast to be redeemed, 13. The reason of this also to be shown to their children, 14-15. Frontlets or phylacteries for the hands and forehead commanded, 16. And the people are not led directly to the Promised Land, but about through the wilderness; and the reason assigned, 17-18. Moses takes the bones of Joseph with him, 19. They journey from Succoth and come to Etham, 20. And the Lord goes before them by day in a pillar of cloud, and by night in a pillar of fire, 21, which miracle is regularly continued both by day and night, 22.

1. *The Lord spake unto Moses.* The commands in this chapter appear to have been given at Succoth, on the same day in which they left Egypt.

2. *Sanctify unto me all the firstborn.* To sanctify, *kadash,* signifies to "consecrate, separate, and set apart" a thing or person from all secular purposes to some religious use; and exactly answers to the import of the Greek *hagiazo,* from *a,* privative, and *ge,* "the earth," because everything offered or consecrated to God was separated from all earthly uses. Hence a holy person or saint is termed *hagios,* i.e., a person separated from the earth; one who lives a holy life, entirely devoted to the service of God. Thus the persons and animals sanctified to God were employed in the service of the Tabernacle and Temple; and the animals, such as were proper, were offered in sacrifice. *Whatsoever openeth the womb.* That is, the firstborn, if a male; for females were not offered, nor the first male, if a female had been born previously. Again, if a man had several wives, the firstborn of each, if a male, was to be offered to God. And all this was done to commemorate the preservation of the firstborn of the Israelites, when those of the Egyptians were destroyed.

5. *When the Lord shall bring thee into the land.* Hence it is pretty evident that the Israelites were not obliged to celebrate the Passover, or keep the Feast of Unleavened Bread, till they were brought into the Promised Land.

9. *And it shall be for a sign . . . upon thine hand.* This direction, repeated and enlarged in v. 16, gave rise to "phylacteries," and this is one of the passages which the Jews write upon them to the present day. The manner in which the Jews understood and kept these commands may appear in their practice. They wrote the following four portions of the law upon slips of parchment or vellum: "Sanctify unto me the firstborn," Exod. xiii, from verse 2 to 10 inclusive. "And it shall be, when the Lord shall bring thee into the land," Exod. xiii, from verse 11 to 16 inclusive. "Hear, O Israel: the Lord our God is one Lord," Deut. vi, from verse 4 to 9 inclusive. "And it shall come to pass, if ye shall hearken diligently," Deut. xi, from verse 13 to 21 inclusive. These four portions, making in all thirty verses, written as mentioned above, and covered with leather, they tied to the forehead and to the hand or arm.

These which were for the head (the frontlets) they wrote on four slips of parchment, and rolled up each by itself, and placed them in four compartments, joined together in one piece of skin or leather. Those which were designed for the hand were formed of one piece of parchment, the four portions being written upon it in four columns, and rolled up from one end to the other. These were all correct transcripts from the Mosaic text, without one redundant or deficient letter; otherwise they were not lawful to be worn. Those for the head were tied on so as to rest on the forehead. Those for the hand or arm were usually tied on the left arm, a little above the elbow, on the inside, that they might be near the heart, according to the command, Deut. vi. 6: "And these words which I command thee this day shall be in thine heart." These phylacteries formed no inconsiderable part of a Jew's religion; they wore them as a sign of their obligation to God, and as representing some future blessedness. Hence they did not wear them on feast days nor on the Sabbath, because these things were in themselves signs; but they wore them always when they read the law, or when they prayed, and hence they called them *tephillin,* "prayer ornaments, oratories, or incitements to prayer." In process of time the

spirit of this law was lost in the letter, and when the word was not in their mouth, nor the law in their heart, they had their phylacteries on their heads and on their hands. And the Pharisees, who in our Lord's time affected extraordinary piety, made their phylacteries very broad, that they might have many sentences written upon them, or the ordinary portions in very large and observable letters.

It appears that the Jews wore these for three different purposes: (1) As signs or remembrancers. This was the original design, as the institution itself sufficiently proves. (2) To procure reverence and respect in the sight of the heathen. This reason is given in the *Gemara,* Berachoth, chap. i: "Whence is it proved that the phylacteries or tephillin are the strength of Israel? *Ans.* From what is written, Deut. xxviii. 10: 'All the people of the earth shall see that thou art called by the name of the Lord [Yehovah]; and they shall be afraid of thee.' " (3) They used them as amulets or charms, to drive away evil spirits. This appears from the Targum on Canticles viii. 3: "His left hand is under my head," etc. "The congregation of Israel hath said, I am elect above all people, because I bind my phylacteries on my left hand and on my head, and the scroll is fixed to the right side of my gate, the third part of which looks to my bed-chamber, that demons may not be permitted to injure me."

13. *Every firstling of an ass thou shalt redeem with a lamb.* Or a "kid," as in the margin. In Num. xviii. 15 it is said: "The firstborn of man shalt thou surely redeem; and the firstling of an unclean beast shalt thou redeem." Hence we may infer that *ass* is put here for any unclean beast, or for unclean beasts in general. The *lamb* was to be given to the Lord, that is, to His priest, Num. xviii. 8, 15. And then the owner of the ass might use it for his own service, which without this redemption he could not do; see Deut. xv. 19.

The firstborn of man . . . shalt thou redeem. This was done by giving to the priests five standard shekels, or shekels of the sanctuary, every shekel weighing twenty gerahs.

17. *God led them not through the way of the land of the Philistines.* Had the Israelites been obliged to commence their journey to the Promised Land by a military campaign, there is little room to doubt that they would have been discouraged, have rebelled against Moses and Aaron, and have returned back to Egypt. Their long slavery had so degraded their minds that they were incapable of any great or noble exertions; and it is only on the ground of this mental degradation, the infallible consequence of slavery, that we can account for their many dastardly acts, murmurings, and repinings after their escape from Egypt.

18. *Went up harnessed. Chamushim.* It is truly astonishing what a great variety of opinions are entertained relative to the meaning of this word. After having maturely considered all that I have met with on the subject, I think it probable that the word refers simply to that "orderly" or "well-arranged" manner in which the Israelites commenced their journey from Egypt. For to "arrange, array, or set in order" seems to be the ideal meaning of the word *chamash.*

19. *Moses took the bones of Joseph.* See the

note on Gen. i. 25. It is supposed that the Israelites carried with them the bones or remains of all the twelve sons of Jacob, each tribe taking care of the bones of its own patriarch, while Moses took care of the bones of Joseph. Stephen expressly says, Acts vii. 15-16, that not only Jacob but the "fathers" were carried from Egypt into Sychem; and this was the only opportunity that seems to have presented itself for doing this; and certainly the reason that rendered it proper to remove the bones of Joseph to the Promised Land had equal weight in reference to those of the other patriarchs. See the notes on Gen. xlix. 29.

20. *Encamped in Etham.* As for the reasons assigned on v. 17, God would not lead the Israelites by the way of the Philistines' country, He directed them towards the wilderness of Shur, chap. xv. 22, upon the edge or extremity of which, next to Egypt, at the bottom of the Arabian Gulf, lay *Etham*, which is the second place of encampment mentioned.

21. *The Lord went before them.* That by the Lord here is meant the Lord Jesus, we have the authority of St. Paul to believe, 1 Cor. x. 9; it was He whose Spirit they tempted in the wilderness, for it was He who led them through the desert to the promised rest. *Pillar of a cloud.* This *pillar* or "column," which appeared as a *cloud* by day and a *fire* by night, was the symbol of the Divine Presence. This was the *Shechinah* or divine dwelling place, and was the continual proof of the presence and protection of *God.* It was necessary that they should have a guide to direct them through the wilderness, even had they taken the most direct road; and how much more so when they took a circuitous route not usually travelled, and of which they knew nothing but just as the luminous pillar pointed out the way! Besides, it is very likely that even Moses himself did not know the route which God had determined on, nor the places of encampment, till the pillar that went before them became stationary, and thus pointed out, not only the road, but the different places of rest.

22. *He took not away the pillar of the cloud.* Neither Jews nor Gentiles are agreed how long the cloud continued with the Israelites. It is very probable that it first visited them at Succoth, if it did not accompany them from Rameses; and that it continued with them till they came to the river Jordan, to pass over opposite to Jericho, for after that it appears that the ark alone was their guide, as it always marched at their head. See Josh. iii. 10, etc.

CHAPTER 14

The Israelites are commanded to encamp before Pi-hahiroth, 1-2. God predicts the pursuit of Pharaoh, 3-4. Pharaoh is informed that the Israelites are fled, and regrets that he suffered them to depart, 5. He musters his troops and pursues them, 6-8. Overtakes them in their encampment by the Red Sea, 9. The Israelites are terrified at his approach, 10. They murmur against Moses for leading them out, 11-12. Moses encourages them, and assures them of deliverance, 13-14. God commands the Israelites to advance, and Moses to stretch out his rod over the sea that it might be divided, 15-16; and promises utterly to discomfit the Egyptians, 17-18. The angel of God places himself between the Israelites and the Egyptians, 19. The pillar of the cloud becomes darkness to the Egyptians, while it gives light to the Israelites, 20. Moses stretches out his rod, and a strong east wind blows, and the waters are divided, 21. The Israelites enter and walk on dry ground, 22. The Egyptians enter also in pursuit of the Israelites, 23. The Lord looks out of the pillar of cloud on the Egyptians, terrifies them, and disjoints their chariots, 24-25. Moses is commanded

to stretch forth his rod over the waters, that they may return to their former bed, 26. He does so, and the whole Egyptian army is overwhelmed, 27-28, while every Israelite escapes, 29. Being thus saved from the hand of their adversaries, they acknowledge the power of God, and credit the mission of Moses, 30-31.

2. *Encamp before Pi-hahiroth. Pi hachiroth*, the "mouth, strait, or bay of Chiroth." Between *Migdol*, the "tower," probably a fortress that served to defend the bay. *Over against Baal-zephon*, the "lord or master of the watch," probably an idol temple, where a continual guard, watch, or light was kept up for the defense of one part of the haven or as a guide to ships.

3. *They are entangled in the land.* God himself brought them into straits from which no human power or art could extricate them. Consider their situation when once brought out of the open country, where alone they had room either to fight or fly. Now they had the Red Sea before them, Pharaoh and his host behind them, and on their right and left hand fortresses of the Egyptians to prevent their escape; nor had they one boat or transport prepared for their passage! If they be now saved, the arm of the Lord must be seen, and the vanity and nullity of the Egyptian idols be demonstrated. By bringing them into such a situation He took from them all hope of human help, and gave their adversaries every advantage against them, so that they themselves said, *They are entangled in the land, the wilderness hath shut them in.*

4. *I will harden Pharaoh's heart.* After relenting and giving them permission to depart, he now changes his mind and determines to prevent them; and without any further restraining grace, God permits him to rush on to his final ruin, for the cup of his iniquity was now full.

5. *And it was told the king ... that the people fled.* Of their departure he could not be ignorant, because himself had given them liberty to depart; but the word *fled* here may be understood as implying that they had utterly left Egypt without any intention to return, which is probably what he did not expect, for he had only given them permssion to go three days' journey into the wilderness, in order to sacrifice to Jehovah; but from the circumstances of their departure, and the property they had received from the Egyptians, it was taken for granted that they had no design to return; and this was in all likelihood the consideration that weighed most with this avaricious king, and determined him to pursue, and either recover the spoil or bring them back, or both. Thus *the heart of Pharaoh and of his servants was turned against the people, and they said, Why have we ... let Israel go from serving us?* Here was the grand incentive to pursuit; their service was profitable to the state, and they were determined not to give it up.

7. *Six hundred chosen chariots.* According to the most authentic accounts we have of war-chariots, they were frequently drawn by two or by four horses, and carried three persons; one was charioteer, whose business it was to guide the horses, but he seldom fought; the second chiefly defended the charioteer; and the third alone was properly the combatant. It appears that in this case Pharaoh had collected all the cavalry of Egypt (see v. 17); and though these might not have been very numerous, yet,

humanly speaking, they might easily overcome the unarmed and encumbered Israelites, who could not be supposed to be able to make any resistance against cavalry and war-chariots.

10. *The children of Israel cried out unto the Lord.* Had their prayer been accompanied with faith, we should not have found them in the next verses murmuring against Moses, or rather against the Lord, through whose goodness they were now brought from under that bondage from which they had often cried for deliverance.

13. *Moses said . . . Fear ye not.* This exhortation was not given to excite them to resist, for of that there was no hope; they were unarmed, they had no courage, and their minds were deplorably degraded. *Stand still.* Ye shall not be even workers together with God; only be quiet, and do not render yourselves wretched by your fears and your confusion. *See the salvation of the Lord.* Behold the deliverance which God will work, independently of all human help and means. *Ye shall see them again no more.* Here was strong faith, but this was accompanied by the spirit of prophecy. God showed Moses what He would do; he believed, and therefore he spoke in the encouraging manner related above.

14. *The Lord shall fight for you.* Ye shall have no part in the honor of the day; God alone shall bring you off, and defeat your foes. *Ye shall hold your peace.* Your unbelieving fears and clamors shall be confounded, and ye shall see that by might none shall be able to prevail against the Lord, and that the feeblest shall take the prey when the power of Jehovah is exerted.

15. *Wherefore criest thou unto me?* We hear not one word of Moses' praying, and yet here the Lord asks him why he cries unto Him. From which we may learn that the heart of Moses was deeply engaged with God, though it is probable he did not articulate one word; but the language of sighs, tears, and desires is equally intelligible to God with that of words. This consideration should be a strong encouragement to every feeble, discouraged mind.

16. *Lift thou up thy rod.* Neither Moses nor his rod could be any effective instrument in a work which could be accomplished only by the omnipotence of God; but it was necessary that he should appear in it, in order that he might have credit in the sight of the Israelites, and that they might see that God had chosen him to be the instrument of their deliverance.

18. *Shall know that I am the Lord.* Pharaoh had just recovered from the consternation and confusion with which the late plagues had overwhelmed him, and now he is emboldened to pursue after Israel; and God is determined to make his overthrow so signal by such an exertion of omnipotence that He shall get himself honor by this miraculous act, and that the Egyptians shall know, i.e., "acknowledge," that He is Jehovah, the omnipotent, self-existing, eternal God.

19. *The angel of God.* It has been thought by some that the *angel,* i.e., "messenger," of the Lord and the pillar of cloud mean here the same thing. An angel might assume the appearance of a cloud; and even a material cloud thus particularly appointed might be called an angel or "messenger" of the Lord, for such is the literal import of the word *malach,* "an angel." It is however most probable that the Angel of

the covenant, the Lord Jesus, appeared on this occasion in behalf of the people; for as this deliverance was to be an illustrious type of the deliverance of man from the power and guilt of sin by His incarnation and death, it might have been deemed necessary, in the judgment of divine wisdom, that He should appear Chief Agent in this most important and momentous crisis.

20. *It was a cloud and darkness to them.* That the Israelites might not be dismayed at the appearance of their enemies, and that these might not be able to discern the object of their pursuit, the pillar of cloud moved from the front to the rear of the Israelitish camp, so as perfectly to separate between them and the Egyptians. It appears also that this cloud had two sides, one dark and the other luminous: the luminous side gave light to the whole camp of Israel during the night of passage; and the dark side, turned towards the pursuing Egyptians, prevented them from receiving any benefit from that light. How easily can God make the same thing an instrument of destruction or salvation, as seems best to His godly wisdom!

21. *The Lord caused the sea to go back.* That part of the sea over which the Israelites passed was, according to Mr. Bruce and other travellers, about four leagues across and, therefore, might easily be crossed in one night. In the dividing of the sea two agents appear to be employed, though the effect produced can be attributed to neither. By stretching out the rod the waters were divided; by the blowing of the vehement, ardent, east wind the bed of the sea was dried.

22. *And the waters were a wall unto them on their right hand, and on their left.* This verse demonstrates that the passage was miraculous.

24. *The morning watch.* A *watch* was the fourth part of the time from sunsetting to sunrising. As the Israelites went out of Egypt at the vernal equinox, the morning watch, or, according to the Hebrew, the "watch of daybreak," would answer to our four o'clock in the morning. *The Lord looked unto.* This probably means that the cloud suddenly assumed a fiery appearance where it had been dark before; or they were appalled by violent thunders and lightning, which we are assured by the Psalmist did actually take place, together with great inundations of rain: "The clouds poured out water: the skies sent out a sound: thine arrows also went abroad. The voice of thy thunder was in the heaven: the lightnings lightened the world: the earth trembled and shook. Thy way is in the sea, and thy path in the great waters . . . Thou leddest thy people like a flock by the hand of Moses and Aaron," Ps. lxxvii. 17-20. Such tempests as these would necessarily terrify the Egyptian horses, and produce general confusion. By their dashing hither and thither the wheels must be destroyed, and the chariots broken; and foot and horse must be mingled together in one universal ruin; see v. 25. During the time that this state of horror and confusion was at its summit the Israelites had safely passed over; and then Moses, at the command of God (v. 26), having stretched out his rod over the waters, the "sea returned to his strength" (v. 27); i.e., the waters by their natural gravity resumed their level, and the whole Egyptian host were completely overwhelmed, v. 28. Thus the enemies of the Lord perished; and that people

who decreed that the male children of the Hebrews should be drowned were themselves destroyed in the pit which they had destined for others. God's ways are all equal, and He renders to every man "according to his works."

30. *Israel saw the Egyptians dead upon the sea shore.* By the extraordinary agitation of the waters, no doubt multitudes of the dead Egyptians were cast on the shore, and by their spoils the Israelites were probably furnished with considerable riches, and especially clothing and arms; which latter were essentially necessary to them in their wars with the Amalekites and Amorites on their way to the Promised Land. If they did not get their arms in this way, we know not how they got them, as there is not the slightest reason to believe that they brought any with them out of Egypt.

31. *The people feared the Lord.* They were convinced by the interference of Jehovah that His power was unlimited, and that He could do whatsoever He pleased, both in the way of judgment and in the way of mercy. *And believed the Lord, and his servant Moses.* They now clearly discerned that God had fulfilled all His promises, and that not one thing had failed of all the good which He had spoken concerning Israel. And they *believed . . . his servant Moses* —they had now the fullest proof that he was divinely appointed to work all these miracles, and to bring them out of Egypt into the Promised Land.

CHAPTER 15

Moses and the Israelites sing a song of praise to God for their late deliverance, in which they celebrate the power of God, gloriously manifested in the destruction of Pharaoh and his host, 1; express their confidence in Him as their Strength and Protector, 2-3; detail the chief circumstances in the overthrow of the Egyptians, 4-8; and relate the purposes they had formed for the destruction of God's people, 9, and how He destroyed them in the imaginations of their hearts, 10. Jehovah is celebrated for the perfections of His nature and His wondrous works, 11-13. A prediction of the effect which the account of the destruction of the Egyptians should have on the Edomites, Moabites, and Canaanites, 14-16. A prediction of the establishment of Israel in the Promised Land, 17. The full chorus of praise, 18. Recapitulation of the destruction of the Egyptians, and the deliverance of Israel, 19. Miriam and the women join in and prolong the chorus, 20-21. The people travel three days in the wilderness of Shur, and find no water, 22. Coming to Marah, and finding bitter waters, they murmur against Moses, 23-24. In answer to the prayer of Moses, God shows him a tree by which the waters are sweetened, 25. God gives them statutes and gracious promises, 26. They come to Elim, where they find twelve wells of water and seventy palm trees, and there they encamp, 27.

1. *Then sang Moses and the children of Israel this song.* Poetry has been cultivated in all ages and among all people, from the most refined to the most barbarous; and to it principally, under the kind providence of God, we are indebted for most of the original accounts we have of the ancient nations of the universe. Equally measured lines, with a harmonious collocation of expressive, sonorous, and sometimes highly metaphorical terms, the alternate lines either answering to each other in sense or ending with similar sounds, were easily committed to memory and easily retained. As these were often accompanied with a pleasing air or tune, histories formed thus became the amusement of youth, the softeners of the tedium of labor, and even the solace of age. In such a way the histories of most nations have been preserved. The interesting events celebrated, the rhythm or metre, and the accompanying tune rendered

them easily transmissible to posterity; and by means of tradition they passed safely from father to son through the times of comparative darkness, till they arrived at those ages in which the pen and the press have given them a sort of deathless duration and permanent stability, by multiplying the copies. Though this is not the first specimen of poetry we have met with in the Pentateuch (see Lamech's speech to his wives, Gen. iv. 23-24; Noah's prophecy concerning his sons, chap. ix. 25-27; and Jacob's blessing to the twelve patriarchs, chap. xlix. 2-27), yet it is the first regular ode of any considerable length, having but one subject; and it is all written in hemistichs, or half-lines, the usual form in Hebrew poetry; and though this form frequently occurs, it is not attended to in our common printed Hebrew Bibles, except in this and three other places (Deuteronomy xxxii, Judges v, and 2 Samuel xxii).

I will sing unto the Lord. Moses begins the song, and in the first two hemistichs states the subject of it; and these first two lines became the grand chorus of the piece, as we may learn from v. 21. *Triumphed gloriously.* "He is exceedingly exalted," rendered by the Septuagint, "He is gloriously glorified"; and surely this was one of the most signal displays of the glorious majesty of God ever exhibited since the creation of the world. And when it is considered that the whole of this transaction shadowed out the redemption of the human race from the thraldom and power of sin and iniquity by the Lord Jesus, and the final triumph of the Church of God over all its enemies, we may also join in the song and celebrate Him who triumphed so gloriously, having conquered death and opened the kingdom of Heaven to all believers.

2. *The Lord is my strength and song.* How judiciously are the members of this sentence arranged! He who has God for his Strength will have Him for his Song; and he to whom Jehovah is become Salvation will exalt His name. It is worthy of observation that the word which we translate *Lord* here is not Jehovah in the original, but *Jah. Jah* is several times joined with the name *Jehovah,* so that we may be sure that it is not, as some have supposed, a mere abbreviation of that word. See Isa. xii. 2; xxvi. 4. Our blessed Lord solemnly claims to himself what is intended in this divine name *Jah,* John viii. 58: "Before Abraham was, I AM," not "I was," but "I am," plainly intimating His divine, eternal existence. Compare Isa. xliii. 13. And the Jews appear to have well understood Him, for "then took they up stones to cast at him" as a blasphemer. Compare Col. i. 16-17, where the Apostle Paul, after asserting that all things that are in heaven and that are in earth, visible and invisible, were created by and for Christ, adds, "And He is [not 'was'] before all things, and by Him all things have subsisted, and still subsist."

I will prepare him an habitation. It has been supposed that Moses, by this expression, intended the building of the Tabernacle; but it seems to come in very strangely in this place. Most of the ancient versions understood the original in a very different sense. The Vulgate has *et glorificabo eum;* the Septuagint, "I will glorify him"; with which the Syriac, Coptic, the Targum of Jonathan, and the Jerusalem Targum agree. From the Targum of Onkelos the present translation seems to have been originally derived; he has translated the place, "And I will build him a sanctuary," which not one of the other versions, the Persian excepted, acknowledges. Our own old translations are generally different from the present: Coverdale, "This my God, I will magnify him"; Matthew's, Cranmer's, and the Bishops' Bible render it "glorify," and the sense of the place seems to require it. *My father's God.* I believe Houbigant to be right, who translates the original, *Elohey abi,* "My God is my Father." Every man may call the Divine Being his God; but only those who are His children by adoption through grace can call Him their Father. See Gal. iv. 6.

3. *The Lord is a man of war.* Perhaps it would be better to translate the words, "Jehovah is the Man or Hero of the battle." *The Lord is his name.* That is, *Jehovah.* He has now, as the name implies, given comple *existence* to all His promises. See the notes on Gen. ii. 4 and Exod. vi. 3.

4. *Pharaoh's chariots . . . his host . . . his chosen captains.* On such an expedition it is likely that the principal Egyptian nobility accompanied their king, and that the overthrow they met with here had reduced Egypt to the lowest extremity. Had the Israelites been intent on plunder or had Moses been influenced by a spirit of ambition, how easily might both have gratified themselves, as, had they returned, they might have soon overrun and subjugated the whole land!

6. *Thy right hand.* Thy omnipotence, manifested in a most extraordinary way.

7. *In the greatness of thine excellency.* To this wonderful deliverance the Prophet Isaiah refers, chap. lxiii. 11-14.

8. *The depths were congealed.* The strong east wind (chap. xiv. 21) employed to dry the bottom of the sea is here represented as the blast of God's nostrils that had *congealed* or "frozen" the waters, so that they stood in heaps like a wall on the right hand and on the left.

9. *The enemy said.* As this song was composed by divine inspiration, we may rest assured that these words were spoken by Pharaoh and his captains, and the passions they describe felt, in their utmost sway, in their hearts; but how soon was their boasting confounded? "Thou didst blow with thy wind, the sea covered them: they sank as lead in the mighty waters."

11. *Who is like unto thee, O Lord, among the gods?* We have already seen that all the Egyptian gods, or the objects of the Egyptians' idolatry, were confounded, and rendered completely despicable, by the ten plagues, which appear to have been directed principally against them. *Glorious in holiness.* Infinitely resplendent in this attribute, essential to the perfection of the divine nature. *Fearful in praises.* Such glorious holiness cannot be approached without the deepest reverence and fear, even by angels, who veil their faces before the majesty of God. *Doing wonders.* Every part of the work of God is wonderful; not only miracles, which imply an inversion or suspension of the laws of nature, but every part of nature itself. Who can conceive how a single blade of grass is formed; or how earth, air, and water become consolidated in the body of the oak? And who can comprehend how the different tribes of plants and

animals are preserved, in all the distinctive characteristics of their respective natures? And who can conceive how the human being is formed, nourished, and its different parts developed? These are wonders which God alone works, and to himself only are they fully known.

12. *The earth swallowed them.* It is very likely there was also an earthquake on this occasion, and that chasms were made in the bottom of the sea, by which many of them were swallowed up, though multitudes were overwhelmed by the waters, whose dead bodies were afterward thrown ashore. The Psalmist strongly intimates that there was an earthquake on this occasion: "The voice of thy thunder was in the heaven: the lightnings lightened the world: the earth trembled and shook," Ps. lxxvii. 18.

13. *Thou hast guided them in thy strength unto thy holy habitation.* As this ode was dictated by the Spirit of God, it is most natural to understand this and the following verses, to the end of the eighteenth, as containing a prediction of what God would do for this people which He had so miraculously redeemed. On this mode of interpretation it would be better to read several of the verbs in the future tense.

15. *The dukes of Edom.* Idumea was governed at this time by those called *alluphim,* "heads, chiefs, or captains." See the note on Gen. xxxvi. 15.

16. *Till thy people pass over.* Not over the Red Sea, for that event had been already celebrated; but over the desert and Jordan, in order to be brought into the Promised Land.

17. *Thou shalt bring them in.* By Thy strength and mercy alone shall they get the promised inheritance. *And plant them.* Give them a fixed habitation in Canaan, after their unsettled, wandering life in the wilderness. *In the mountain.* Meaning Canaan, which was a very mountainous country, Deut. xi. 11; or probably Mount Zion, on which the Temple was built. Where the pure worship of God was established, there the people might expect both rest and safety.

18. *The Lord shall reign for ever and ever.* This is properly the grand chorus in which all the people joined. The words are expressive of God's everlasting dominion, not only in the world, but in the Church; not only under the law, but also under the gospel; not only in time, but through eternity. The original *leolam vaed* may be translated, "for ever and onward"; or, by our very expressive compound term, "for evermore," i.e., "for ever and more"—not only through time, but also through all duration. His dominion shall be ever the same, active and infinitely extending. With this verse the song seems to end, as with it the hemistichs, or poetic lines, terminate. The twentieth and beginning of the twenty-first are in plain prose, but the latter part of the twenty-first is in hemistichs, as it contains the response made by Miriam and the Israelitish women at different intervals during the song.

20. *And Miriam the prophetess.* We have already seen that Miriam was older than either Moses or Aaron; for when Moses was exposed on the Nile, she was a young girl capable of managing the stratagem used for the preservation of his life; and then Aaron was only three

years and three months old, for he was fourscore and three years old when Moses was but fourscore (see chap. vii. 7); so that Aaron was older than Moses, and Miriam considerably older than either, not less probably than nine or ten years of age. The name *Miriam* is the same with the Greek *Mariam,* the Latin *Maria,* and the English *Mary.*

The prophetess. Hannebiah. For the meaning of the word prophet, *nabi,* see the note on Gen. xx. 7. It is very likely that Miriam was inspired by the Spirit of God to instruct the Hebrew women, as Moses and Aaron were to instruct the men; and when she and her brother Aaron sought to share in the government of the people with Moses, we find her laying claim to the prophetic influence, Num. xii. 2: "Hath the Lord indeed spoken only by Moses? hath he not spoken also by us?" And that she was constituted joint leader of the people with her two brothers, we have the express word of God by the Prophet Micah, chap. vi. 4: "For I brought thee up out of the land of Egypt . . . and I sent before thee Moses, Aaron, and Miriam." Hence it is very likely that she was the instructress of the women, and regulated the times, places, etc., of their devotional acts; for it appears that from the beginning to the present day the Jewish women all worshipped apart.

A timbrel. Toph, the same word which is translated "tabret," Gen. xxxi. 27. *And with dances. Mecholoth.* Many learned men suppose that this word means some instruments of wind music, because the word comes from the root *chalal,* the ideal meaning of which is to "perforate, penetrate, pierce, stab." Pipes or hollow tubes, such as flutes and the like, may be intended. Both the Arabic and Persian understand it as meaning instruments of music of the pipe, drum, or sistrum kind; and this seems to comport better with the scope and design of the place than the term *dances.* Miriam is the first prophetess on record, and by this we find that God poured out His Spirit not only upon men, but upon women also; and we learn also that Miriam was not only a prophetess, but a poetess also, and must have had considerable skill in music to have been able to conduct her part of these solemnities.

22. *The wilderness of Shur.* This was on the coast of the Red Sea on their road to Mount Sinai.

23. *Marah.* So called from the "bitter waters" found there.

24. *The people murmured.* They were in a state of great mental degradation, owing to their long and oppressive vassalage, and had no firmness of character. See the note on chap. xiii. 17.

25. *He cried unto the Lord.* Moses was not only their leader, but also their mediator. Of prayer and dependence on the Almighty, the great mass of Israelites appear to have had little knowledge at this time. Moses, therefore, had much to bear from their weakness, and the merciful Lord was long-suffering. *There he made for them.* Though it is probable that the Israelites are here intended, yet the word *lo* should not be translated *for them,* but "to him," for these statutes were given to Moses that he might deliver them to the people. *There he proved them. Nissahu,* "he proved him." By this murmuring of the people He proved Moses,

to see, speaking after the manner of men, whether he would be faithful, and, in the midst of the trials to which he was likely to be exposed, whether he would continue to trust in the Lord and seek all his help from Him.

26. *If thou wilt diligently hearken.* What is contained in this verse appears to be what is intended by the *statute* and *ordinance* mentioned in the preceding: "If thou wilt diligently hearken to the voice of the Lord thy God, and wilt do that which is right in his sight, and wilt give ear to his commandments, and keep all his statutes, I will put none of these diseases upon thee." This statute and ordinance implied the three following particulars: (1) That they should acknowledge Jehovah for their God, and thus avoid all idolatry. (2) That they should receive His word and testimony as a divine revelation, binding on their hearts and lives, and thus be saved from profligacy of every kind, and from acknowledging the maxims or adopting the customs of the neighboring nations. (3) That they should continue to do so, and adorn their profession with a holy life. These things being attended to, then the promise of God was that they should have none of the diseases of the Egyptians put on them; that they should be kept in a state of health of body and peace of mind; and if at any time they should be afflicted, on application to God the evil should be removed, because He was their Healer or Physician—*I am the Lord that healeth thee.* That the Israelites had in general a very good state of health, their history warrants us to believe; and when they were afflicted, as in the case of the fiery serpents, on application to God they were all healed.

27. *They came to Elim.* This was in the desert of Sin. *Twelve wells of water.* One for each of the tribes of Israel, say the Targums of Jonathan and Jerusalem. *And threescore and ten palm trees.* One for each of the seventy elders (*ibid.*).

CHAPTER 16

The Israelites journey from Elim and come to the wilderness of Sin, 1. They murmur for lack of bread, 2-3. God promises to rain bread from heaven for them, 4, of which they were to collect a double portion on the sixth day, 5. A miraculous supply of flesh in the evening and bread in the morning promised, 6-9. The glory of the Lord appears in the cloud, 10. Flesh and bread promised as a proof of God's care over them, 11-12. Quails come and cover the whole camp, 13. And a dew falls which leaves a small, round substance on the ground, which Moses tells them is the bread which God has sent, 14-15. Directions for gathering it, 16. The Israelites gather each an omer, 17-18. They are directed to leave none of it till the next day, 19; which some neglecting, it becomes putrid, 20. They gather it every morning, because it melts when the sun waxes hot, 21. Each person gathers two omers on the sixth day, 22. Moses commands them to keep the seventh as a Sabbath to the Lord, 23. What was laid up for the Sabbath did not putrefy, 24. Nothing of it fell on that day; hence the strict observance of the Sabbath was enjoined, 25-30. The Israelites name the substance that fell with the dew manna; its appearance and taste described, 31. An omer of the manna is commanded to be laid up for a memorial of Jehovah's kindness, 32-34. The manna now sent continued daily for the space of forty years, 35. How much an omer contained, 36.

1. *The wilderness of Sin.* This desert lies between Elim and Sinai. *The fifteenth day of the second month.* They had now left Egypt one month, during which it is probable they lived on the provisions they brought with them from Rameses, though it is possible they might have had a supply from the seacoast. Concerning Mount Sinai, see the note on chap. xix. 1.

2. *The whole congregation . . . murmured.* This is an additional proof of the degraded state of the minds of this people; see the note on chap. xiii. 17. And this very circumstance affords a convincing argument that a people so stupidly carnal could not have been induced to leave Egypt had they not been persuaded so to do by the most evident and striking miracles.

3. *The flesh pots.* As the Hebrews were in a state of slavery in Egypt, they were doubtless fed in various companies by their taskmasters in particular places, where large pots or boilers were fixed for the purpose of cooking their victuals.

4. *I will rain bread.* Therefore this substance was not a production of the desert; nor was the dew that was the instrument of producing it common there, else they must have had this bread for a month before.

6. *Ye shall know that the Lord hath brought you out.* After all the miracles they had seen, they appear still to suppose that their being brought out of Egypt was the work of Moses and Aaron; for though the miracles they had already seen were convincing for the time, yet as soon as they had passed by they relapsed into their former infidelity. God therefore saw it necessary to give them a daily miracle in the fall of the manna, that they might have the proof of His divine interposition constantly before their eyes. Thus they knew that *Jehovah* had brought them out, and that it was not the act of Moses and Aaron.

7. *Ye shall see the glory of the Lord.* Does it not appear that the *glory of the Lord* is here spoken of as something distinct from the Lord? for it is said, *He* (the glory) *heareth your murmurings against the Lord;* though *the Lord* may be here put for "himself," the antecedent instead of the relative. This passage may receive some light from Heb. 1. 3: "Who being the brightness of his glory, and the express image of his person." And as St. Paul's words are spoken of the Lord Jesus, is it not likely that the words of Moses refer to Him also? "No man hath seen God at any time"; hence we may infer that Christ was the visible Agent in all the extraordinary and miraculous interferences which took place both in the patriarchal times and under the law.

8. *In the evening flesh to eat.* Namely, the quails; *and in the morning bread to the full,* namely, the manna. *And what are we?* Only His servants, obeying His commands. *Your murmurings are not against us,* for we have not brought you up from Egypt; *but against the Lord,* who, by His own miraculous power and goodness, has brought you out of your slavery.

9. *Come near before the Lord.* This has been supposed to refer to some particular place where the Lord manifested His presence. The great Tabernacle was not yet built, but there appears to have been a small tabernacle, or tent, called the "tabernacle of the congregation," which, after the sin of the golden calf, was always placed without the camp; see chap. xxxiii. 7: "And Moses took the tabernacle, and pitched it without the camp, afar off from the camp, and called it the Tabernacle of the congregation. And it came to pass, that every one which sought the Lord went out unto the tabernacle of the congregation, which was without the camp." May

we not conclude that Moses invited them to come near before the Lord, and so witness His glory, that they might be convinced it was God and not he that led them out of Egypt, and that they ought to submit to Him, and cease from their murmurings? It is said, chap. xix. 17, that Moses brought forth the people out of the camp "to meet with God." And in this instance there might have been a similar though less awful manifestation of the Divine Presence.

10. *As Aaron spake.* So he now became the spokesman or minister of Moses to the Hebrews, as he had been before unto Pharaoh; according to what is written, chap. vii. 1, etc.

13. *At even the quails came. Selav,* from *salah,* to be "quiet, easy, or secure"; and hence the quail, from their remarkably living at ease and plenty among the corn. "An amazing number of these birds," says Hasselquist, *Travels,* p. 209, "come to Egypt at this time (March), for in this month the wheat ripens. They conceal themselves among the corn, but the Egyptians know that they are thieves, and when they imagine the field to be full of them they spread a net over the corn and make a noise, by which the birds, being frightened, and endeavouring to rise, are caught in the net in great numbers, and make a most delicate and agreeable dish."

14. *Behold, upon the face of the wilderness there lay a small round thing.* It appears that this small, round thing fell with the dew, or rather the dew fell first, and this substance fell on it. The dew might have been intended to cool the ground, that the manna on its fall might not be dissolved; for we find, from v. 21, that the heat of the sun melted it. The ground therefore being sufficiently cooled by the dew, the manna lay unmelted long enough for the Israelites to collect a sufficient quantity for their daily use.

15. *They said one to another, It is manna: for they wist not what it was.* This is a most unfortunate translation, because it not only gives no sense, but it contradicts itself. The Hebrew *man hu* literally signifies, "What is this?" *for,* says the text, *they wist not what it was* and therefore they could not give it a name. Moses immediately answers the question, and says, *This is the bread which the Lord hath given you to eat.* From v. 31 we learn that this substance was afterwards called *man,* probably in commemoration of the question they had asked on its first appearance. Almost all our own ancient versions translate the words, "What is this?"

What this substance was we know not. It was nothing that was common to the wilderness. It is evident the Israelites never saw it before, for Moses says, Deut. viii. 3, 16: "He . . . fed thee with manna, which thou knewest not, neither did thy fathers know"; and it is very likely that nothing of the kind had ever been seen before; and by a pot of it being laid up in the ark, it is as likely that nothing of the kind ever appeared again, after the miraculous supply in the wilderness had ceased. It seems to have been created for the present occasion and, like Him whom it typified, to have been the only thing of the kind, the only bread from heaven, which God ever gave to preserve the life of man, as Christ is the True Bread that came down from heaven and was given for the life of the world. See John vi. 31-58.

16. *An omer for every man.* I shall here

once for all give a short account of the measures of capacity among the Hebrews.

"Omer," from the root *amar*, to "press, squeeze, collect, and bind together." It is supposed that the *omer*, which contained about three quarts English, had its name from this circumstance; that it was the most contracted or the smallest measure of things dry known to the ancient Hebrews.

The "ephah," *eiphah*, from *aphah*, "to bake," because this was probably the quantity which was baked at one time. According to Bishop Cumberland the *ephah* contained seven gallons, two quarts, and about half a pint, wine measure; and as the *omer* was the tenth part of the ephah, v. 36, it must have contained about six pints English.

The "kab" is said to have contained about three pints and one-third English.

The "homer," *chomer*, mentioned in Lev. xxvii. 16, was quite a different measure from that above, and is a different word in the Hebrew. The *chomer* was the largest measure of capacity among the Hebrews, being equal to ten baths or ephahs, amounting to about seventy-five gallons, three pints, English. See Ezek. xlv. 11, 13-14. Goodwin supposes that this measure derived its name from *chamor*, an "ass," being the ordinary load of that animal.

The "bath" was the largest measure of capacity next to the homer, of which it was the tenth part. It was the same as the ephah, and consequently contained about seven gallons, two quarts, and half a pint, and is always used in Scripture as a measure of liquids.

The "seah" was a measure of capacity for things dry, equal to about two gallons and a half English. See 2 Kings vii. 1, 16, 18.

The "hin," according to Bishop Cumberland, was the one-sixth part of an ephah, and contained a little more than one gallon and two pints. See Exod. xxix. 40.

The "log" was the smallest measure of capacity for liquids among the Hebrews: it contained about three-quarters of a pint. See Lev. xiv. 10, 12.

Take ye . . . for them which are in his tents. Some might have been confined in their tents through sickness or infirmity, and charity required that those who were in health should gather a portion for them.

17. *Some more, some less.* According to their respective families, an *omer* for a man; and according to the number of infirm persons, whose wants they undertook to supply.

18. *He that gathered much had nothing over.* Because his gathering was in proportion to the number of persons for whom he had to provide. And some having fewer, others more in family, and the gathering being in proportion to the persons who were to eat of it, therefore *he that gathered much had nothing over, and he that gathered little had no lack.* Probably every man gathered as much as he could; and then when brought home and measured by an omer, if he had a surplus, it went to supply the wants of some other family that had not been able to collect a sufficiency, the family being large, and the time in which the manna might be gathered, before the heat of the day, not being sufficient to collect enough for so numerous a household, several of whom might be so confined as not to be able to collect for themselves. Thus there

was an equality, and in this light the words of St. Paul, 2 Cor. viii. 15, lead us to view the passage. Here the thirty-sixth verse should come in: "Now an omer is the tenth part of an ephah."

19. *Let no man leave of it till the morning.* For God would have them to take no thought for the morrow, and constantly to depend on Him for their daily bread. And is not that petition in our Lord's prayer founded on this very circumstance, "Give us day by day our daily bread"?

20. *It bred worms.* Their sinful curiosity and covetousness led them to make the trial; and they had a mass of loathsome putrefaction for their pains. How gracious is God! He is continually rendering disobedience and sin irksome to the transgressor; that finding his evil ways to be unprofitable, he may return to his Maker and trust in God alone.

22. *On the sixth day they gathered twice as much.* This they did that they might have a provision for the Sabbath, for on that day no manna fell, vv. 26-27. What a convincing miracle was this! No manna fell on the Sabbath! Had it been a natural production it would have fallen on the Sabbath as at other times; and had there not been a supernatural influence to keep it sweet and pure, it would have been corrupted on the Sabbath as well as on other days. By this series of miracles God showed His own power, presence, and goodness.

23. *To morrow is the rest of the holy sabbath.* There is nothing in either text or context that seems to intimate that the Sabbath was now first given to the Israelites, as some have supposed; on the contrary, it is here spoken of as being perfectly well known, from its having been generally observed. The commandment, it is true, may be considered as being now renewed; because they might have supposed that in their unsettled state in the wilderness they might have been exempted from the observance of it.

29. *Abide ye every man in his place.* Neither go out to seek manna nor for any other purpose; rest at home and devote your time to religious exercises.

34. *Laid it up before the Testimony.* The *Testimony* belonged properly to the Tabernacle, but that was not yet built. Some are of opinion that the Tabernacle, built under the direction of Moses, was only a renewal of one that had existed in the patriarchal times. The word signifies "reference to something beyond itself"; thus the Tabernacle, the manna, the tables of stone, Aaron's rod, all bore reference and testimony to that spiritual good which was yet to come, namely, Jesus Christ and His salvation.

CHAPTER 17

The Israelites journey from the wilderness of Sin to Rephidim, 1. where they murmur for lack of water, 2-3. Moses asks counsel of God, 4. who commands him to take his rod and smite the rock, 5. and promises that water should proceed from it for the people to drink, 6. The place is called Massah and Meribah, 7. The Amalekites attack Israel in Rephidim, 8. Joshua is commanded to fight with them, 9. Moses, Aaron, and Hur go to the top of a hill, and while Moses holds up his hands, the Israelites prevail; when he lets them down, Amalek prevails, 10-11. Moses, being weary, sits down, and Aaron and Hur hold up his hands, 12. The Amalekites are totally routed, 13. and the event commanded to be recorded, 14. Moses builds an altar, and calls it Jehovah-nissi, 15. Amalek is threatened with continual wars, 16.

1. *Pitched in Rephidim.* In Num. xxxiii. 12-14 it is said that when the Israelites came from Sin they encamped in Dophkah, and next in Alush, after which they came to Rephidim. Here, therefore, two stations are omitted, probably because nothing of moment took place at either.

2. *Why chide ye with me?* God is your Leader, complain to Him. *Wherefore do ye tempt the Lord?* As He is your Leader, all your murmurings against me He considers as directed against himself; why therefore do ye tempt Him? Has He not given you sufficient proofs that He can destroy His enemies and support His friends?

3. *And the people murmured.* The reader must not forget what has so often been noted relating to the degraded state of the minds of the Israelites. A strong argument however may be drawn from this in favor of their supernatural escape from Egypt. Had it been a scheme concerted by the heads of the people, provision would necessarily have been made for such exigencies as these. But as God chose to keep them constantly dependent upon himself for every necessity of life, and as they had Moses alone as their mediator to look to, they murmured against him when brought into straits and difficulties, regretted their having left Egypt, and expressed the strongest desire to return. This shows that they had left Egypt reluctantly; and as Moses and Aaron never appear to have any resources but those which came most evidently in a supernatural way, therefore the whole exodus or departure from Egypt proves itself to have been no human contrivance, but a measure concerted by God himself.

6. *I will stand before thee there upon the rock in Horeb. The rock.* It seems as if God had directed the attention of Moses to a particular rock, with which he was well acquainted; for every part of the mount and its vicinity must have been well known to Moses during the time he kept Jethro's flocks in those quarters.

7. *He called the name of the place Massah, and Meribah. Massah* signifies "temptation" or "trial"; and *Meribah,* "contention." From I Cor. x. 4, we learn that this rock was a type of Christ, and their drinking of it is represented as their being made partakers of the grace and mercy of God through Christ Jesus; and yet many who drank fell and perished in the wilderness in the very act of disobedience! Reader, be not high-minded, but fear!

8. *Then came Amalek, and fought with Israel.* The Amalekites seem to have attacked the Israelites in the same way and through the same motives that the wandering Arabs attack the caravans which annually pass through the same desert. It does not appear that the Israelites gave them any kind of provocation; they seem to have attacked them merely through the hopes of plunder. The Amalekites were the posterity of Amalek, one of the dukes of Eliphaz, the son of Esau, and consequently Israel's brother, Gen. xxxvi. 15-16. *Fought with Israel.* In the most treacherous and dastardly manner; for they came at the rear of the camp, smote the hindmost of the people, even all that were feeble behind, when they were faint and weary; see Deut. xxv. 18. The baggage, no doubt, was the object of their avarice; but finding the women, children, aged, and infirm persons behind with the baggage, they smote them and took away their spoils.

9. *Moses said unto Joshua.* This is the first place in which Joshua the son of Nun is mentioned; the illustrious part which he took in Jewish affairs, till the settlement of his countrymen in the Promised Land, is well known. He was captain-general of the Hebrews under Moses; and on this great man's death he became his successor in the government. Joshua was at first called Hoshea, Num. xiii. 16, and afterwards called Joshua by Moses. Both in the Septuagint and in the Greek Testament he is called Jesus. The name signifies "Saviour"; and he is allowed to have been a very expressive type of our blessed Lord. He fought with and conquered the enemies of his people, brought them into the Promised Land, and divided it to them by lot. *Top of the hill.* Probably some part of Horeb or Sinai, to which they were then near.

10. *Moses, Aaron, and Hur went up.* It is likely that the Hur mentioned here is the same with that Hur mentioned in 1 Chron. ii. 19, who appears from the chronology in that chapter to have been the son of Caleb, the son of Ezron, the son of Pharez, the son of Judah. The rabbins and Josephus say he was the brother-in-law of Moses, having married his sister, Miriam. He was a person in whom Moses put much confidence; for he left him conjoint governor of the people with Aaron, when he went to confer with God on the mount, chap. xxiv. 14. His grandson Bezaleel was the chief director in the work of the Tabernacle; see chap. xxxi. 2-5.

11. *When Moses held up his hand.* We cannot understand this transaction in any literal way; for the lifting up or letting down the hands of Moses could not, humanly speaking, influence the battle. It is likely that he held up the rod of God in his hand, v. 9, as an ensign to the people. We have already seen that in prayer the hands were generally lifted up and spread out (see the note on chap. ix. 29), and therefore it is likely that by this act prayer and supplication are intended.

13. *Joshua discomfited Amalek and his people.* Amalek might have been the name of the ruler of this people continued down from their ancestor (see on v. 8), as Pharaoh was the name of all succeeding kings in Egypt. If this were the case, then *Amalek and his people* mean the prince and the army that fought under him. But if *Amalek* stands here for the Amalekites, then *his people* must mean the confederates he had employed on this occasion.

14. *Write this for a memorial in a book.* This is the first mention of writing on record. *Rehearse it in the ears of Joshua.* Thus showing that Joshua was to succeed Moses, and that this charge should be given to every succeeding governor. *I will utterly put out the remembrance of Amalek.* This threatening was accomplished by Saul, 412 years after. Judgment is God's strange work; but it must take place when the sins which incensed it are neither repented of nor forsaken. This people, by their continued transgressions, proved themselves totally unworthy of a political existence; and therefore said God to Saul, "Go and utterly destroy the sinners the Amalekites," 1 Sam. xv. 18. So their continuance in sin was the cause of their final destruction.

15. *Jehovah-nissi.* "Jehovah is my Ensign or Banner." The hands and rod of Moses were held up as soldiers are wont to hold up their standards in the time of battle; and as these standards bear the arms of the country, the soldiers are said to fight under that banner, i.e., under the direction and in the defense of that government. Thus the Israelites fought under the direction of God, and in the defense of His truth; and therefore the name of Jehovah became the armorial bearing of the whole congregation. By His direction they fought, and in His name and strength they conquered, each one feeling himself, not his own, but the Lord's soldier.

16. *The Lord hath sworn that the Lord will have war with Amalek.* This is no translation of the words *ki yad al kes yah milckamah,* which have been variously rendered by different translators and critics, the most rational version of which is the following: "Because the hand of Amalek is against the throne of God, therefore will I have war with Amalek from generation to generation."

CHAPTER 18

Jethro, called the father-in-law of Moses, hearing of the deliverance which God had granted to Israel, 1, took Zipporah and her two sons, Gershom and Eliezer, and brought them to Moses, when the Israelites were encamped near Horeb, 2-5. He sends to Moses, announcing his arrival, 6. Moses goes out to meet him, 7, and gives him a history of God's dealings with the Israelites, 8. Jethro greatly rejoices, and makes striking observations on the power and goodness of God, 9-11. He offers burnt offerings and sacrifices to Jehovah, and Aaron and all the elders of Israel feast with him, 12. The next day Jethro, observing how much Moses was fatigued by being obliged to sit as judge and hear causes from morning to eevning, 13, inquires why he did so, 14. Moses answers, and shows that he is obliged to determine causes between man and man, and to teach them the statutes and laws of God, 15-16. Jethro finds fault, and counsels him to appoint men who fear God, love truth, and hate covetousness, to be judges over thousands, hundreds, fifties, and tens, to judge and determine in all smaller matters, and refer only the greater and most important to himself, 17-22; and shows that this plan will be advantageous both to himself and to the people, 23. Moses hearkens to the counsel of Jethro, and appoints proper officers over the people, who enter upon their functions, determine all minor causes, and refer only the most difficult to Moses, 24-26. Moses dismisses Jethro, who returns to his own country, 27.

1. *When Jethro, the priest of Midian.* Concerning this person and his several names, see the notes on chap. ii. 15-16, 18; iii. 1; and iv. 20, 24. Jethro was probably the son of Reuel, the father-in-law of Moses, and consequently the brother-in-law of Moses; for the word *chothen,* which we translate *father in law,* in this chapter means simply a "relative by marriage."

2. *After he had sent her back.* Why Zipporah and her two sons returned to Midian is not certainly known. From the transaction recorded in chap. iv. 20, 24, it seems as if she had been alarmed at the danger to which the life of one of her sons had been exposed, and fearing worse evils, left her husband and returned to her father. It is however possible that Moses, foreseeing the troubles to which his wife and children were likely to be exposed had he taken them down to Egypt, sent them back till it should please God to deliver His people. Jethro, now finding that God had delivered them and totally discomfited the Egyptians, their enemies, thought it proper to bring Zipporah and her sons to Moses, while he was in the vicinity of Horeb.

3. *The name of the one was Gershom.* See the note on chap. ii. 22.

5. *Jethro . . . came with his sons.* There are several reasons to induce us to believe that the fact related here is out of its due chronological order, and that Jethro did not come to Moses till the beginning of the second year of the Exodus (see Num. x. 11), some time after the Tabernacle had been erected, and the Hebrew commonwealth established, both in things civil and ecclesiastical. This opinion is founded on the following reasons:

(1) On this verse, where it is said that Jethro came to Moses "while he encamped at the mount of God." Now it appears, from chap. xix. 1-2, that they were not yet come to Horeb, the mount of God, and that they did not arrive there till the third month after their departure from Egypt; and the transactions with which this account is connected certainly took place in the second month; see chap. xvi. 1.

(2) Moses, in Deut. i. 6, 9-10, 12-15, relates that when they were about to depart from Horeb, which was on the twentieth day of the second month of the second year from their leaving Egypt, he then complained that he was not able to bear the burden alone of the government of a people so numerous; and that it was at that time that he established judges and captains over thousands and hundreds and fifties and tens, which appears to be the very transaction recorded in this place; the measure itself being recommended by Jethro, and done in consequence of his advice.

(3) From Num. x. 11, 29, etc., we find that when the cloud was taken up, and the Israelites were about to depart from Horeb, Moses addressed Hobab, who is supposed to have been the same as Jethro, and who then was about to return to Midian, his own country, entreating him to stay with them as a guide while they travelled through the wilderness. It therefore seems necessary that the transaction recorded in this chapter should be inserted in Numbers x, between the tenth and eleventh verses.

(4) It has been remarked that shortly after they had departed from Sinai the dispute took place between Miriam, Aaron, and Moses, concerning the Ethiopian woman Zipporah, whom he had married (see Num. xii. 1, etc.); and this is supposed to have taken place shortly after she had been brought back by Jethro.

(5) In the discourse between Moses and Jethro, mentioned in this chapter, we find that Moses speaks of the statutes and laws of the Lord as things already revealed and acknowledged, which necessarily implies that these laws had already been given (v. 16), which we know did not take place till several months after the transactions mentioned in the preceding chapters.

(6) Jethro offers burnt offerings and sacrifices to God apparently in that way in which they were commanded in the law.

From all these reasons, but particularly from the first two and the last two, it seems most likely that this chapter stands out of its due chronological order. As Moses had in the preceding chapter related the war with Amalek and the curse under which they were laid, he may be supposed to have introduced here the account concerning Jethro the Midianite, to show that he was free from that curse, although the Midianites and the Kenites, the family of Jethro, were as one people, dwelling with the Amalekites. See Judg. i. 16; I Chron. ii. 55; 1 Sam. xv. 6. For although the Kenites were some of those people whose lands God had promised to the descendants of Abraham (see Gen. xv. 18-19), yet, in consideration of Jethro, the relative of Moses, all of them who submitted to the Hebrews were suffered to live in their own country; the rest are supposed to have taken refuge among the Edomites and Amalekites.

6. *And he said unto Moses.* That is, by a messenger; in consequence of which Moses went out to meet him, as is stated in the next verse, for an interview had not yet taken place. This is supported by reading *hinneh*, "behold," for *ani*, "I," which is the reading of the Septuagint and Syriac, and several Samaritan MSS.; instead, therefore, of *I thy father*, we should read, "Behold thy father."

7. *And did obeisance.* "He bowed himself down" (see on Gen. xvii. 3 and Exod. iv. 31); this was the general token of respect. *And kissed him;* the token of friendship. *And they asked each other of their welfare;* literally, "and they inquired, each man of his neighbor, concerning peace" (or prosperity), the proof of affectionate intercourse. *And they came into the tent.* Some think that the Tabernacle is meant, which is likely had been erected before this time; see the note on v. 5. Moses might have thought proper to take his relative first to the house of God, before he brought him to his own tent.

9. *And Jethro rejoiced for all the goodness.* Every part of Jethro's conduct proves him to have been a religious man and a true believer. His thanksgiving to Jehovah (v. 10) is a striking proof of it; he first blesses God for the preservation of Moses, and next for the deliverance of the people from their bondage.

11. *Now I know that the Lord is greater than all gods.* Some think that Jethro was now converted to the true God; but it is very probable that he enjoyed this blessing before he knew anything of Moses, for it is not likely that Moses would have entered into an alliance with this family had they been heathens. Jethro no doubt had the true patriarchal religion. *Wherein they dealt proudly.* Acting as tyrants over the people of God; enslaving them in the most unprincipled manner, and still purposing more tyrannical acts. *He was above them*—He showed himself to be infinitely superior to all their gods, by the miracles which He wrought. Various translations have been given of this clause; the above I believe to be the sense.

12. *Jethro . . . took a burnt offering. Olah.* Though it be true that in the patriarchal times we read of a "burnt offering" (see Gen. xxii. 2, etc.), yet we only read of one in the case of Isaac and, therefore, though this offering made by Jethro is not a decisive proof that the law relative to burnt offerings had already been given, yet, taken with other circumstances in this account, it is a presumptive evidence that the meeting between Moses and Jethro took place after the erection of the Tabernacle. See the note on v. 5.

Sacrifices for God. Zebachim, "slain beasts," as the word generally signifies. We have already seen that sacrifices were instituted by God himself as soon as sin entered into our world; and we see that they were continued and regularly practiced among all the people who had the knowledge of the only true God, from that time until they became a legal establishment. Jethro, who was a priest (chap. ii. 16), had a right to offer these sacrifices.

And Aaron came, and all the elders of Israel, to eat bread. The burnt offering was wholly consumed; every part was considered as the Lord's portion and, therefore, it was entirely burnt up. The other sacrifices mentioned here were such that, after the blood had been poured out before God, the officers and assistants might feed on the flesh. Thus, in ancient times, contracts were made and covenants sealed. It is very likely, therefore, that the sacrifices offered on this occasion were those on the flesh of which Aaron and the elders of Israel feasted with Jethro. *Before God.* Before the Tabernacle, where God dwelt; for it is supposed that the Tabernacle was now erected. See on v. 5; and see Deut. xii. 5-7 and 1 Chron. xxix. 21-22, where the same form of speech, "before the Lord," is used, and plainly refers to His manifested presence in the Tabernacle.

13. *To judge the people.* To hear and determine controversies between man and man, and to give them instruction in things appertaining to God. *From the morning unto the evening.* Moses was obliged to sit all day, and the people were continually coming and going.

15. *The people come unto me to enquire of God.* To know the mind and will of God on the subject of their inquiries. Moses was the mediator between God and the people; and as they believed that all justice and judgment must come from Him, therefore they came to Moses to know what God had spoken.

16. *I do make them know the statutes of God, and his laws.* These words are so very particular that they leave little room for doubt that the law had been given. Such words would scarcely have been used had not the *statutes* and *laws* been then in existence. And this is one of the proofs that the transaction mentioned here stands out of its due chronological order; see on v. 5.

18. *Thou wilt surely wear away. Nabol tibbol,* "in wearing away, thou wilt wear away" —by being thus continually employed, thou wilt soon become finally exhausted. *And this people that is with thee;* as if he had said, "Many of them are obliged to wait so long for the determination of their suit that their patience must be soon necessarily worn out, as there is no one to hear every cause but thyself."

19. *I will give thee counsel, and God shall be with thee.* Jethro seems to have been a man of great understanding and prudence. His advice to Moses was most appropriate and excellent; and it was probably given under the immediate inspiration of God, for after such sacrificial rites, and public acknowledgment of God, the prophetic spirit might be well expected to descend and rest upon him. God could have showed Moses the propriety and necessity of adopting such measures before, but He chose in this case to help man by man.

20. *Thou shalt teach them ordinances. Chukkim,* all such "precepts" as relate to the ceremonies of religion and political economy. *And laws, hattoroth,* the instructions relative to the whole system of morality. *And shalt shew them*

the way. Eth hadderech, "that very way," that *only* way, which God himself has revealed, and in which they should walk in order to please Him and get their souls everlastingly saved. *And the work that they must do.* For it was not sufficient that they should know their duty both to God and man, but they must *do it too; yaasun,* they must do it "diligently, fervently, effectually"; for the paragogic *nun* deepens and extends the meaning of the verb.

21. *Able men.* Persons of wisdom, discernment, judgment, prudence, and fortitude; for who can be a ruler without these qualifications? *Such as fear God.* Who are truly religious, without which they will feel little concerned either for the bodies or souls of the people. *Men of truth.* Honest and true in their own hearts and lives; speaking the truth, and judging according to the truth. *Hating covetousness.* Doing all for God's sake, and love to man; laboring to promote the general good; never perverting judgment. *Rulers of thousands, etc.* "Millenaries, centurions, quinquagenaries, and decurions"; each of these, in all probability, dependent on that officer immediately above himself. So the decurion, or ruler over ten, if he found a matter too hard for him, brought it to the quinquagenary, or ruler of fifty; if, in the course of the exercise of his functions, he found a cause too complicated for him to decide on, he brought it to the centurion, or ruler over a hundred. In like manner the centurion brought his difficult case to the millenary, or ruler over a thousand; the case that was too hard for him to judge, he brought to Moses; and the case that was too hard for Moses, he brought immediately to God. It is likely that each of these classes had a court composed of its own members, in which cases were heard and tried.

23. *If thou shalt do this thing, and God command thee.* Though the measure was obviously of the utmost importance, and plainly recommended itself by its expediency and necessity; yet Jethro very modestly leaves it to the wisdom of Moses to choose or reject it; and, knowing that in all things his relative was now acting under the immediate direction of God, intimates that no measure can be safely adopted without a positive injunction from God himself. As the counsel was doubtless inspired by the Divine Spirit, we find that it was sanctioned by the same, for Moses acted in every respect according to the advice he had received.

27. *And Moses let his father in law depart.* But if this be the same transaction with that mentioned in Num. x. 29, etc., we find that it was with great reluctance that Moses permitted so able a counsellor to leave him; for, having the highest opinion of his judgment, experience, and discretion, he pressed him to stay with them, that he might be instead of eyes to them in the desert. But Jethro chose rather to return to his own country, where probably his family were so settled and circumstanced that they could not be conveniently removed, and it was more his duty to stay with them, to assist them with his counsel and advice, than to travel with the Israelites.

CHAPTER 19

The children of Israel, having departed from Rephidim, come to the wilderness of Sinai in the third month, 1-2. Moses goes up into the mount to God, and receives a message which he is to deliver to the people, 3-6. He returns and delivers it to the people before the elders, 7. The people promise obedience, 8. The Lord proposes to meet Moses in the cloud, 9. He commands him to sanctify the people, and promises to come down visibly on Mount Sinai on the third day, 10-11. He commands him also to set bounds, to prevent the people or any of the cattle from touching the mount, on pain of being stoned or shot through with a dart, 12-13. Moses goes down and delivers this message, 14-15. The third day is ushered in with the appearance of the thick cloud upon the mount, and with thunders, lightning, and the sound of a trumpet; at which the people are greatly terrified, 16. Moses brings forth the people out of the camp to meet with God, 17. Mount Sinai is enveloped with smoke and fire, 18. After the trumpet had sounded long and loud, Moses spoke, and God answered him by a voice, 19. God calls Moses up to the mount, 20, and gives him a charge to the people and to the priests, that they do not attempt to come near to the mount, 21-22. Moses, alleging that it was impossible for them to touch it because of the bounds, 23, is sent down to bring up Aaron, and to warn the people again not to break through the bounds, 24. Moses goes down and delivers this message, 25; after which we may suppose that he and Aaron went up to meet God in the mount.

1. *In the third month.* This was called *Sivan,* and answers to our May. *The wilderness of Sinai.* Mount Sinai is called by the Arabs *Jibel Mousa* or the Mount of Moses, or, by way of eminence, *El Tor, The Mount.* It is one hill, with two peaks or summits; one is called Horeb, the other Sinai. Horeb was probably its most ancient name, and might designate the whole mountain; but as the Lord had appeared to Moses on this mountain in a "bush," *seneh,* chap. iii. 2, from this circumstance it might have received the name of *Sinai.*

3. *Moses went up unto God.* It is likely that the cloud which had conducted the Israelitish camp had now removed to the top of Sinai; and as this was the symbol of the divine presence, Moses went up to the place, there to meet the Lord. *The Lord called unto him.* This, according to Stephen, was the Angel of the Lord, Acts vii. 38. And from several scriptures we have seen that the Lord Jesus was the Person intended; see the notes on Gen. xvi. 7; xviii. 13; Exod. iii. 2.

4. *Brought you unto myself.* In this and the two following verses we see the design of God in selecting a people for himself. (1) They were to obey His voice, v. 5, to receive a revelation from Him, and to act according to that revelation. (2) They were to obey His voice *indeed, shamoa tishmen, in hearing they should hear;* they should consult His testimonies, hear them whenever read or proclaimed, and obey them as soon as heard, affectionately and steadily. (3) They must keep His covenant. (4) They should then be God's peculiar treasure, *segullah,* His own "patrimony," a people in whom He should have all right, and over whom He should have exclusive authority above all the people of the earth. (5) They should be a "kingdom of priests," v. 6. Their state should be a theocracy; and as God should be the sole Governor, so all His subjects should be priests, all worshippers, all sacrificers, every individual offering up the victim for himself. A beautiful representation of the gospel dispensation, to which the apostles Peter and John apply it, 1 Pet. ii. 5, 9; Rev. i. 6; v. 10; and xx. 6; under which dispensation every believing soul offers up for himself that Lamb of God which was slain for and which takes away the sin of the world and through which alone a man can have access to God.

6. *And an holy nation.* They should be a *nation,* one people; firmly united among themselves, living under their own laws; and powerful, because united, and acting under the direction and blessing of God. They should be

an holy nation, saved from their sins, righteous in their conduct, holy in their hearts.

7. *The elders of the people.* The head of each tribe, and the chief of each family, by whose ministry this gracious purpose of God was speedily communicated to the whole camp.

8. *And all the people answered.* The people, having such gracious advantages laid before them, most cheerfully consented to take God for their portion; as He had graciously promised to take them for His people. Thus a covenant was made, the parties being mutually bound to each other. *Moses returned the words.* When the people had on their part consented to the covenant, Moses appears to have gone immediately up to the mountain and related to God the success of his mission; for he was now on the mount, as appears from v. 14.

9. *A thick cloud.* This is interpreted by v. 18: "And mount Sinai was altogether on a smoke . . . and the smoke thereof ascended as the smoke of a furnace"; His usual appearance was in the cloudy pillar, which we may suppose was generally clear and luminous. *That the people may hear.* See the note on chap. xv. 9. The Jews consider this as the fullest evidence their fathers had of the divine mission of Moses; they themselves were permitted to see this awfully glorious sight, and to hear God himself speak out of the thick darkness.

10. *Sanctify them.* See the meaning of this term, chap. xiii. 2. *Let them wash their clothes.* And consequently bathe their bodies; for, according to the testimony of the Jews, these always went together. It was necessary that, as they were about to appear in the presence of God, everything should be clean and pure about them; that they might be admonished by this of the necessity of inward purity, of which the outward washing was the emblem.

12. *Thou shalt set bounds.* Whether this was a line marked out on the ground, beyond which they were not to go, or whether a fence was actually made to keep them off, we cannot tell. This verse strictly forbids the people from coming near and touching Mount Sinai, which was burning with fire. The words, therefore, in v. 15, *al tiggeshu el ishshah,* "come not at your wives," seem rather to mean, "come not near unto the fire." *Whosoever toucheth the mount shall be surely put to death.* The place was awfully sacred, because the dreadful majesty of God was displayed on it. And this taught them that "God is a consuming fire," and that "it is a fearful thing to fall into the hands of the living God."

13. *There shall not an hand touch it. Bo,* "him," not the mountain, but the man who had presumed to touch the mountain. He should be considered altogether as an unclean and accursed thing, not to be touched for fear of conveying defilement; but should be immediately stoned or pierced through with a dart, Heb. xii. 20.

16. *Thunders and lightnings, and a thick cloud . . . and the voice of the trumpet.* The thunders, lightnings, etc., announced the coming, as they proclaimed the majesty, of God. Of the thunders and lightnings, and the deep, dark, dismal, electric cloud, from which the thunders and lightnings proceeded, we can form a tolerable apprehension; but of the loud, long-sounding trumpet we can scarcely form a conjecture.

Such were the appearances and the noise that all the people in the camp trembled, and Moses himself was constrained to say, "I exceedingly fear and quake," Heb. xii. 21.

17. *And Moses brought forth the people . . . to meet with God.* For though they might not touch the mount till they had permission, yet when the trumpet sounded long, it appears they might come up to the *nether part of the mount* (see v. 13 and Deut. iv. 11); and when the trumpet had ceased to sound, they might then go up unto the mountain, as to any other place. The whole scope and design of the chapter prove that no soul can possibly approach this holy and terrible Being but through a mediator; and this is the use made of this whole transaction by the author of the Epistle to the Hebrews, chap. xii. 18-24.

20. *The Lord came down.* This was undoubtedly done in a visible manner, that the people might witness the awful appearance. We may suppose that everything was arranged thus: The glory of the Lord occupied the top of the mountain, and near to this Moses was permitted to approach. Aaron and the seventy elders were permitted to advance some way up the mountain, while the people were permitted to come up only to its base. Moses, as the lawgiver, was to receive the statutes and judgments from God's mouth; Aaron and the elders were to receive them from Moses, and deliver them to the people; and the people were to act according to the direction received. Nothing can be imagined more glorious, terrible, majestic, and impressive than the whole of this transaction; but it was chiefly calculated to impress deep reverence, religious fear, and sacred awe; and he who attempts to worship God uninfluenced by these has a proper sense neither of the divine majesty nor of the sinfulness of sin. It seems in reverence to this that the apostle says, "Let us have grace, whereby we may serve God acceptably with reverence and godly fear: for our God is a consuming fire," Heb. xii. 28-29.

22. *Let the priests also . . . sanctify themselves.* That there were priests among the Hebrews before the consecration of Aaron and his sons cannot be doubted; though their functions might be in a considerable measure suspended while under persecution in Egypt, yet the persons existed whose right and duty it was to offer sacrifices to God. Moses requested liberty from Pharaoh to go into the wilderness to sacrifice; and had there not been among the people both sacrifices and priests, the request itself must have appeared absurd. Sacrifices from the beginning had constituted an essential part of the worship of God, and there certainly were priests whose business it was to offer them to God before the giving of the law; though this, for especial reasons, was restricted to Aaron and his sons after the law had been given.

23. *The people cannot come up.* Either because they had been so solemnly forbidden that they would not dare, with the penalty of instant death before their eyes, to transgress the divine command; or the bounds which were set about the mount were such as rendered their passing them physically impossible. *And sanctify it. Vekiddashto.* Here the word *kadash* is taken in its proper literal sense, signifying the "separating" of a thing, person, or place from all profane

or common uses, and devoting it to sacred purposes.

24. *Let not the priests and the people break through.* God knew that they were heedless, criminally curious, and stupidly obstinate; and therefore His mercy saw it right to give them line upon line, that they might not transgress to their own destruction.

CHAPTER 20

The preface to the Ten Commandments, 1-2. The first commandment, against mental or theoretic idolatry, 3. The second, against making and worshiping images, or practical idolatry, 4-6. The third, against false swearing, blasphemy, and irreverent use of the name of God, 7. The fourth, against profanation of the Sabbath, and idleness on the other days of the week, 8-11. The fifth, against disrespect and disobedience to parents, 12. The sixth, against murder and cruelty, 13. The seventh, against adultery and uncleanness, 14. The eighth, against stealing and dishonesty, 15. The ninth, against false testimony, perjury, etc., 16. The tenth, against covetousness, 17. The people are alarmed at the awful appearance of God on the mount, and stand afar off, 18. They pray that Moses may be mediator between God and them, 19. Moses encourages them, 20. He draws near to the thick darkness, and God communes with him, 21-22. Further directions against idolatry, 23. Directions concerning making an altar of earth, 24; and an altar of hewn stone, 25. None of these to be ascended by steps, and the reason given, 26.

1. *All these words.* Houbigant supposes, and with great plausibility of reason, that the clause *eth col haddebarim haelleh,* "all these words," belongs to the latter part of the concluding verse of chap. xix, which he thinks should be read thus: "And Moses went down unto the people, and spake unto them all these words"; i.e., delivered the solemn charge relative to their not attempting to come up to that part of the mountain on which God manifested himself in His glorious majesty. When Moses, therefore, had gone down and spoken *all these words,* and he and Aaron had reascended the mount, then the Divine Being, as supreme Legislator, is majestically introduced thus: *And God spake . . . saying.* This gives a dignity to the commencement of this chapter of which the clause above mentioned, if not referred to the speech of Moses, deprives it.

THE TEN COMMANDMENTS

The laws delivered on Mount Sinai have been variously named. In Deut. iv. 13, they are called *asereth haddebarim,* "the ten words." In the preceding chapter, v. 5, God calls them *eth berithi,* "my covenant," i.e., the agreement He entered into with the people of Israel to take them for His peculiar people, if they took Him for their God and portion. "If ye will obey my voice indeed, and keep my covenant, then shall ye be a peculiar treasure unto me." And the word "covenant" here evidently refers to the laws given in this chapter, as is evident from Deut. iv. 13: "And he declared unto you his covenant, which he commanded you to perform, even ten commandments." Sometimes they have been termed *the law, hattorah,* by way of eminence, as containing the grand system of spiritual instruction, direction, guidance. See on the word "law," chap. xii. 49. And frequently "the Decalogue," which is a literal translation into Greek of the *asereth haddebarim,* or "ten words," of Moses.

Among divines they are generally divided into what they term the first and second tables: the first table containing the first, second, third, and fourth commandments and comprehending the

whole system of theology, the true notions we should form of the divine nature, the reverence we owe and the religious service we should render to Him; the second containing the last six commandments, and comprehending a complete system of ethics, or moral duties, which man owes to his fellows. By this division the first table contains our duty to God; the second, our duty to our neighbor. This division, which is natural enough, refers us to the grand principle, love to God and love to man, through which both tables are observed. (1) Thou shalt love the Lord thy God with all thy heart, soul, mind, and strength. (2) Thou shalt love thy neighbor as thyself. On these two hang all the law and the prophets. See Matt. xxii. 37-40.

THE FIRST COMMANDMENT:
AGAINST MENTAL OR THEORETIC IDOLATRY

2. *I am the Lord thy God. Yehovah eloheycha.* On the word Jehovah, which we here translate *Lord,* see the notes on Gen. ii. 4 and Exod. vi. 3. And on the word *Elohim,* here translated *God,* see on Gen. i. 1. It is worthy of remark that each individual is addressed here, and not the people collectively, though they are all necessarily included, that each might feel that he was bound for himself to hear and do all these words. Moses labored to impress this personal interest on the people's minds, when he said, Deut. v. 3-4: "The Lord made . . . this covenant . . . with us, even us, who are all of us here alive this day." *Brought thee out of the land of Egypt.* And by this very thing have proved myself to be superior to all gods, unlimited in power, and most gracious as well as fearful in operation. This is the preface or introduction, but should not be separated from the commandment. Therefore—

3. *Thou shalt have no other gods before me. Elohim acherim,* no "strange" gods—none that thou art not acquainted with, none who has not given thee such proofs of his power and godhead as I have done in delivering thee from the Egyptians, dividing the Red Sea, bringing water out of the rock, quails into the desert, manna from heaven to feed thee, and the pillar of cloud to direct, enlighten, and shield thee. By these miracles God had rendered himself familiar to them, they were intimately acquainted with the operation of His hands; and therefore with great propriety He says, Thou shalt have no strange gods *before me; al panai,* "before or in the place of" those manifestations which I have made of myself.

THE SECOND COMMANDMENT:
AGAINST MAKING AND WORSHIPING IMAGES

4. *Thou shalt not make unto thee any graven image.* As the word *pasal* signifies to "hew, carve, grave," *pesel* may here signify any kind of image, either of wood, stone, or metal, on which the axe, the chisel, or the graving tool has been employed. This commandment includes in its prohibitions every species of idolatry known to have been practiced among the Egyptians.

Or any likeness. To know the full spirit and extent of this commandment, this place must be collated with Deut. iv. 15, etc.: "Take ye therefore good heed unto yourselves . . . lest ye corrupt yourselves, and make you a graven image, the similitude of any figure, the likeness of male or female." All who have even the slightest acquaintance with the ancient history of Egypt know that Osiris and his wife, Isis, were supreme divinities among that people. The likeness of any beast, *behemah,* such as the ox and the heifer: Among the Egyptians the ox was not only sacred but adored, because they supposed that in one of these animals Osiris took up his residence; hence they always had a living ox, which they supposed to be the habitation of this deity; and they imagined that on the death of one he entered into the body of another, and so on successively. This famous ox-god they called Apis. The likeness of any winged fowl: The ibis, or stork, or crane, and hawk, may be here intended, for all these were objects of Egyptian idolatry. The likeness of anything that creepeth: The crocodile, serpents, the scarabeus or beetle, were all objects of their adoration. The likeness of any fish: All fish were esteemed sacred animals among the Egyptians.

To countenance its image worship, the Roman Catholic church has left the whole of this second commandment out of the Decalogue, and thus lost one whole commandment out of the ten; but to keep up the number they have divided the tenth into two. This is totally contrary to the faith of God's elect and to the acknowledgment of that truth which is according to godliness. The verse is found in every MS. of the Hebrew Pentateuch that has ever been discovered. It is in all the ancient versions, Samaritan, Chaldee, Syriac, Septuagint, Vulgate, Coptic, and Arabic; also in the Persian, and in all modern versions. This commandment prohibits every species of external idolatry, as the first does all idolatry that may be called internal or mental. All false worship may be considered of this kind, together with all image worship, and all other superstitious rites and ceremonies.

5. *Jealous God.* This shows in a most expressive manner the love of God to this people. He felt for them as the most affectionate husband could do for his spouse; and was *jealous* for their fidelity, because He willed their invariable happiness. *Visiting the iniquity of the fathers upon the children.* This necessarily implies—if the children walk in the steps of their fathers; for no man can be condemned by divine justice for a crime of which he was never guilty; see Ezekiel xviii. Idolatry is however particularly intended, and visiting sins of this kind refers principally to national judgments. By withdrawing the divine protection the idolatrous Israelites were delivered up into the hands of their enemies, from whom the gods in whom they had trusted could not deliver them. This God did to *the third and fourth generation,* i.e., "successively," as may be seen in every part of the Jewish history, and particularly in the Book of Judges. And this, at last, became the grand and the only effectual and lasting means in His hand of their final deliverance from idolatry; for it is well known that after the Babylonish captivity the Israelites were so completely saved from idolatry as nevermore to have disgraced themselves by it as they had formerly done. These national judgments, thus continued from generation to generation, appear to be what are designed by the words in the text, *Visiting the iniquity of the fathers upon the children.*

6. *And shewing mercy unto thousands.* Mark;

even those who love God and keep His commandments merit nothing from Him, and therefore the salvation and blessedness which they enjoy come from the mercy of God: *shewing mercy.* What a disproportion between the works of justice and mercy! Justice works to the third or fourth, mercy to thousands of generations! *That love me, and keep my commandments.* It was this that caused Christ to comprise the fulfilment of the whole law in love to God and man; see the note on v. 1. And as love is the grand principle of obedience, and the only incentive to it, so there can be no obedience without it.

THE THIRD COMMANDMENT:
AGAINST FALSE SWEARING, BLASPHEMY, AND IRREVERENT USE OF THE NAME OF GOD

7. *Thou shalt not take the name of the Lord thy God in vain.* This precept not only forbids all false oaths, but all common swearing where the name of God is used, or where He is appealed to as a Witness of the truth. It also necessarily forbids all light and irreverent mention of God, or any of His attributes, and this the original word *lashshav* particularly imports; and we may safely add to all these that every prayer, ejaculation, etc., that is not accompanied with deep reverence and the genuine spirit of piety is here condemned also. *The Lord will not hold him guiltless.* Whatever the person himself may think or hope, however he may plead in his own behalf, and say he intends no evil, if he in any of the above ways, or in any other way, takes the name of God in vain, God will not hold him guiltless—He will account him guilty and punish him for it.

THE FOURTH COMMANDMENT:
AGAINST PROFANATION OF THE SABBATH, AND IDLENESS ON THE OTHER DAYS OF THE WEEK

8. *Remember the sabbath day, to keep it holy.* See what has been already said on this precept, Gen. ii. 2, and elsewhere. As this was the most ancient institution, God calls them to *remember* it: as if He had said, Do not forget that when I had finished My creation I instituted the Sabbath, and remember why I did so, and for what purposes. The word *shabbath* signifies "rest" or "cessation from labor"; and the sanctification of the seventh day is commanded, as having something representative in it; and so indeed it has, for it typifies the rest which remains for the people of God, and in this light it evidently appears to have been understood by the apostle, Hebrews iv. Because this commandment has not been particularly mentioned in the New Testament as a moral precept binding on all, therefore some have presumptuously inferred that there is no Sabbath under the Christian dispensation. The truth is, the Sabbath is considered as a type. All types are of full force till the thing signified by them takes place. But the thing signified by the Sabbath is that rest in glory which remains for the people of God; therefore the moral obligation of the Sabbath must continue till time be swallowed up in eternity.

9. *Six days shalt thou labour.* Therefore he who idles away time on any of the six days is as guilty before God as he who works on the Sabbath. No work should be done on the Sabbath that can be done on the preceding days,

or can be deferred to the succeeding ones. Works of absolute necessity and mercy are alone excepted.

THE FIFTH COMMANDMENT:
AGAINST DISRESPECT AND DISOBEDIENCE TO PARENTS

12. *Honour thy father and thy mother.* There is a degree of affectionate respect which is owing to parents that no person else can properly claim. For a considerable time parents stand as it were in the place of God to their children, and therefore rebellion against their lawful commands has been considered as rebellion against God. This precept therefore prohibits, not only all injurious acts, irreverent and unkind speeches to parents, but enjoins all necessary acts of kindness, filial respect, and obedience. We can scarcely suppose that a man honors his parents who, when they fall weak, blind, or sick, does not exert himself to the uttermost in their support. In such cases God as truly requires the children to provide for their parents as He required the parents to feed, nourish, support, instruct, and defend the children when they were in the lowest state of helpless infancy. *That thy days may be long.* This, as the apostle observes, Eph. vi. 2, is the first commandment to which God has annexed a promise; and therefore we may learn in some measure how important the duty is in the sight of God. In Deut. v. 16 it is said, "And that it may go well with thee"; we may therefore conclude that it will go ill with the disobedient.

THE SIXTH COMMANDMENT:
AGAINST MURDER AND CRUELTY

13. *Thou shalt not kill.* This commandment, which is general, prohibits murder of every kind. (1) All actions by which the lives of our fellow creatures may be abridged. (2) All wars for extending empire, commerce, etc. (3) All sanguinary laws, by the operation of which the lives of men may be taken away for offenses of comparatively trifling demerit. (4) All bad dispositions which lead men to wish evil to, or meditate mischief against, one another; for, says the Scripture, He that hateth his brother in his heart is a murderer. (5) All want of charity to the helpless and distressed; for he who has it in his power to save the life of another by a timely application of succor, food, raiment, and does not do it, and the life of the person either fails or is abridged on this account, is in the sight of God a murderer. (6) All riot and excess, all drunkenness and gluttony, by which life may be destroyed or shortened; all these are point-blank sins against the sixth commandment.

THE SEVENTH COMMANDMENT:
AGAINST ADULTERY AND UNCLEANNESS

14. *Thou shalt not commit adultery.* Adultery, as defined by our laws, is of two kinds: double, when between two married persons; single, when one of the parties is married, the other single. One principal part of the criminality of adultery consists in its injustice. (1) It robs a man of his right by taking from him the affection of his wife. (2) It does him a wrong by fathering on him and obliging him to maintain as his own a spurious offspring—a child which is not his. The act itself, and everything leading to the act, is prohibited by this commandment; for our Lord says, "He who looks on a woman to lust after her has already committed adultery with her in his heart." And not only adultery (the unlawful commerce between two married persons) is forbidden here, but also fornication and all kinds of mental and sensual uncleanness. All impure books, songs, paintings, etc., which tend to inflame and debauch the mind, are against this law.

THE EIGHTH COMMANDMENT:
AGAINST STEALING AND DISHONESTY

15. *Thou shalt not steal.* All rapine and theft are forbidden by this precept; as well national and commercial wrongs as petty larceny, highway robberies, and private stealing; even the taking advantage of a seller's or buyer's ignorance, to give the one less and make the other pay more for a commodity than its worth, is a breach of this sacred law. All withholding of rights and doing of wrongs are against the spirit of it. But the word is principally applicable to clandestine stealing, though it may undoubtedly include all political injustice and private wrongs.

THE NINTH COMMANDMENT:
AGAINST FALSE TESTIMONY, PERJURY, ETC.

16. *Thou shalt not bear false witness.* Not only false oaths, to deprive a man of his life or of his right, are here prohibited, but all whispering, talebearing, slander, and calumny; in a word, whatever is deposed as a truth, which is false in fact, and tends to injure another in his goods, person, or character, is against the spirit and letter of this law. Suppressing the truth when known, by which a person may be defrauded of his property or his good name, or lie under injuries or disabilities which a discovery of the truth would have prevented, is also a crime against this law. By the term *neighbour* any human being is intended, whether he rank among our enemies or friends.

THE TENTH COMMANDMENT:
AGAINST COVETOUSNESS

17. *Thou shalt not covet thy neighbour's house . . . wife.* Covet signifies to desire or long after in order to enjoy as a property the person or thing coveted. He breaks this commandment who by any means endeavors to deprive a man of his house or farm by taking them "over his head," as it is expressed in some countries; who lusts after his neighbor's wife, and endeavors to ingratiate himself into her affections and to lessen her husband in her esteem; and who endeavors to possess himself of the servants, cattle, etc., of another in any clandestine or unjustifiable manner.

18. *And all the people saw the thunderings.* They had witnessed all these awful things before (see chap. xix. 16) but here they seem to have been repeated; probably at the end of each command, there was a peal of thunder, a blast of the trumpet, and a gleam of lightning, to impress their hearts the more deeply with a due sense of the divine majesty, of the holiness of the law which was now delivered, and of the fearful consequences of disobedience. This had the desired effect; the people were impressed with a deep religious fear and a terror of God's judgments; acknowledged themselves perfectly satisfied with the discoveries God had made of

himself; and requested that Moses might be constituted the mediator between God and them, as they were not able to bear these tremendous discoveries of the divine majesty. "Speak thou with us, and we will hear; but let not God speak with us, lest we die," v. 19. This teaches us the absolute necessity of that great Mediator between God and man, Christ Jesus, as no man can come unto the Father but by Him.

20. *And Moses said . . . Fear not: for God is come to prove you, and that his fear may be before your faces.* The maxim contained in this verse is, "Fear not, that ye may fear"—do not fear with such a fear as brings consternation into the soul, and produces nothing but terror and confusion; but fear with that *fear* which reverence and filial affection inspire, *that ye sin not*—that, through the love and reverence ye feel to your Maker and Sovereign, ye may abstain from every appearance of evil, lest you should forfeit that love which is to you better than life.

22. *I have talked with you from heaven.* Though God manifested himself by the fire, the lightning, the earthquake, the thick darkness, yet the ten words or commandments were probably uttered from the higher regions of the air, which would be an additional proof to the people that there was no imposture in this case; for though strange appearances and voices might be counterfeited on earth—as was often, no doubt, done by the magicians of Egypt—yet it would be utterly impossible to represent a voice, in a long continued series of instruction, as proceeding from heaven itself, or the higher regions of the atmosphere. This, with the earthquake and repeated thunders (see on v. 18) would put the reality of this whole procedure beyond all doubt; and this enabled Moses, Deut. v. 26, to make such an appeal to the people on a fact incontrovertible and of infinite importance, that God had indeed talked with them face-to-face.

23. *Ye shall not make with me gods of silver.* The expressions here are very remarkable. Before it was said, "Thou shalt have no other gods before me," v. 3. Here they are commanded, "Ye shall not make gods of silver or gold with Me," as emblems or representatives of God, in order, as might be pretended, to keep these displays of His magnificence in memory; on the contrary, He would have only an *altar of earth*—of plain turf, on which they should offer those sacrifices by which they should commemorate their own guilt and the necessity of an atonement to reconcile themselves to God.

24. *Thy burnt offerings, and thy peace offerings.* The law concerning which was shortly to be given, though sacrifices of this kind were in use from the days of Abel. *In all places where I record my name.* Wherever I am worshipped, whether in the open wilderness, at the Tabernacle, in the Temple, the synagogues, or elsewhere, *I will come unto thee . . . and bless thee.* These words are precisely the same in signification with those of our Lord, Matt. xviii. 20: "For where two or three are gathered together in my name, there am I in the midst of them." And as it was JESUS who was the "angel" that spoke to them in the wilderness, Acts vii. 38; from the same mouth this promise in the law and that in the gospel proceeded.

25. *Thou shalt not build it of hewn stone.* Because they were now in a wandering state,

and had as yet no fixed residence; and therefore no time should be wasted to rear costly altars, which could not be transported with them, and which they must soon leave. Besides, they must not lavish skill or expense on the construction of an altar; the altar of itself, whether costly or mean, was nothing in the worship; it was only the place on which the victim should be laid, and their mind must be attentively fixed on that God to whom the sacrifice was offered, and on the sacrifice itself, as that appointed by the Lord to make an atonement for their sins.

26. *Neither shalt thou go up by steps unto mine altar.* The word *altar* comes from *altus*, "high" or "elevated," though the Hebrew word *mizbach*, from *zabach*, to "slay, kill," signifies merely a place for sacrifice. But the heathen, who imitated the rites of the true God in their idolatrous worship, made their altars very high; whence they derived their name, *altaria*, "altars."

CHAPTER 21

Laws concerning servants. They shall serve for only seven years, 1-2. If a servant brought a wife to servitude with him, both should go out free on the seventh year, 3. If his master had given him a wife, and she bore him children, he might go out free on the seventh year, but his wife and children must remain, as the property of the master, 4. If, through love to his master, wife, and children, he did not choose to avail himself of the privilege granted by the law, of going out free on the seventh year, his ear was to be bored to the doorpost with an awl, as an emblem of his being attached to the family forever, 5-6. Laws concerning maidservants, betrothed to their masters or to the sons of their masters, 7-11. Laws concerning battery and murder, 12-15. Concerning men-stealing, 16. Concerning him that curses his parents, 17. Of strife between man and man, 18-19; between a master and his servants, 20-21. Of injuries done to women in pregnancy, 22. The *lex talionis*, or law of like, 23-25. Of injuries done to servants, by which they gain the right of freedom, 26-27. Laws concerning the ox which has gored men, 28-32. Of the pit left uncovered, into which a man or a beast has fallen, 33-34. Laws concerning the ox that kills another, 35-36.

1. *Now these are the judgments.* There is so much good sense, feeling, humanity, equity, and justice in the following laws that they cannot but be admired by every intelligent reader; and they are so very plain as to require very little comment. The laws in this chapter are termed political, those in the succeeding chapter judicial laws; and are supposed to have been delivered to Moses alone, in consequence of the request of the people, chap. xx. 19, that God should communicate His will to Moses, and that Moses should, as mediator, convey it to them.

2. *If thou buy an Hebrew servant.* Calmet enumerates six different ways in which a Hebrew might lose his liberty: (1) In extreme poverty he might sell his liberty, Lev. xxv. 39: "If thy brother . . . be waxen poor, and be sold unto thee." (2) A father might sell his children. "If a man sell his daughter to be a maidservant"; see v. 7. (3) Insolvent debtors became the slaves of their creditors. "My husband is dead . . . and the creditor is come to take unto him my two sons to be bondmen," 2 Kings iv. 1. (4) A thief, if he had not money to pay the fine laid on him by the law, was to be sold for his profit whom he had robbed. "If he have nothing, then he shall be sold for his theft," chap. xxii. 3-4. (5) A Hebrew was liable to be taken prisoner of war, and so sold for a slave. (6) A Hebrew slave who had been ransomed from a Gentile by a Hebrew might be sold by him who ransomed him, to one of his own nation.

Six years he shall serve. It was an excellent provision in these laws that no man could finally injure himself by any rash, foolish, or precipitate act. No man could make himself a servant or slave for more than seven years; and if he mortgaged the family inheritance, it must return to the family at the jubilee, which returned every fiftieth year. It is supposed that the term *six years* is to be understood as referring to the sabbatical years; for let a man come into servitude at whatever part of the interim between two sabbatical years, he could not be detained in bondage beyond a sabbatical year; so that if he fell into bondage the third year after a sabbatical year, he had but three years to serve; if the fifth, but one. See on chap. xxiii. 11, etc. Others suppose that this privilege belonged only to the year of jubilee, beyond which no man could be detained in bondage, though he had been sold only one year before.

3. *If he came in by himself.* If he and his wife came in together, they were to go out together; in all respects as he entered, so should he go out.

4. *The wife and her children shall be her master's.* It was a law among the Hebrews that, if a Hebrew had children by a Canaanitish woman, those children must be considered as Canaanitish only, and might be sold and bought, and serve forever. The law here refers to such a case only.

6. *Shall bring him unto the judges.* El haelohim, literally, "to God"; or, "to the judgment of God." *Bore his ear through with an aul.* This was a ceremony sufficiently significant, as it implied, (1) That he was closely attached to that house and family. (2) That he was bound to hear all his master's orders, and to obey them punctually. Boring of the ear was an ancient custom in the East.

7. *If a man sell his daughter.* This the Jews allowed no man to do but in extreme distress—when he had no goods, either movable or immovable, left, even to the clothes on his back; and he had this permission only while she was unmarriageable. It may appear at first view strange that such a law should have been given; but let it be remembered that this servitude could extend, at the utmost, only to six years; and that it was nearly the same as in some cases of apprenticeship among us, where the parents bind the child for seven years and have from the master so much per week during that period.

9. *Betrothed her unto his son, he shall deal with her.* He shall give her the same dowry he would give to one of his own daughters. From these laws we learn that if a man's son married his servant, by his father's consent, the father was obliged to treat her in every respect as a daughter; and if the son married another woman, as it appears he might do, v. 10, he was obliged to make no abatement in the privileges of the first wife, either in her food, raiment, or duty of marriage. The word *onathah* here is the same with the *homilian* of the Septuagint, which signifies the cohabitation of man and wife.

11. *These three.* (1) Her *food*, her "flesh," for she must not, like a common slave, be fed merely on vegetables. (2) Her *raiment*—her private wardrobe, with all occasional necessary additions. And, (3) The "marriage debt"—a due proportion of the husband's time and company.

13. *I will appoint thee a place whither he shall flee.* From the earliest times the nearest akin had a right to revenge the murder of his relation, and as this right was universally acknowledged, no law was ever made on the subject; but as this might be abused, and a person who had killed another accidentally, having had no previous malice against him, might be put to death by the avenger of blood, as the nearest kinsman was termed, therefore God provided the cities of refuge to which the accidental manslayer might flee till the affair was inquired into, and settled by the civil magistrate.

14. *Thou shalt take him from mine altar.* Before the cities of refuge were assigned, the altar of God was the common asylum.

15. *That smiteth his father, or his mother.* As such a case argued peculiar depravity, therefore no mercy was to be shown to the culprit.

16. *He that stealeth a man.* By this law every man-stealer, and every receiver of the stolen person, should lose his life.

19. *Shall pay for the loss of his time, and shall cause him to be thoroughly healed.* This was a wise and excellent institution, and most courts of justice still regulate their decisions on such cases by this Mosaic precept.

21. If the slave who had been beaten by his master died under his hand, the master was punished with death; see Gen. ix. 5-6. But if he survived the beating a day or two, the master was not punished, because it might be presumed that the man died through some other cause. And all penal laws should be construed as favorably as possible to the accused.

22. *And hurt a woman with child.* As a posterity among the Jews was among the peculiar promises of their covenant, and as every man had some reason to think that the Messiah should spring from his family, therefore any injury done to a woman with child, by which the fruit of her womb might be destroyed, was considered a very heavy offense; and as the crime was committed principally against the husband, the degree of punishment was left to his discretion. But if mischief followed, that is, if the child had been fully formed, and was killed by this means, or the woman lost her life in consequence, then the punishment was as in other cases of murder—the person was put to death, v. 23.

24. *Eye for eye.* This is the earliest account we have of the *lex talionis*, or law of like for like, which afterwards prevailed among the Greeks and Romans. Among the latter, it constituted a part of the "twelve tables," so famous in antiquity; but the punishment was afterwards changed to a pecuniary fine, to be levied at the discretion of the praetor. Nothing, however, of this kind was left to private revenge; the magistrate awarded the punishment when the fact was proved; otherwise the *lex talionis* would have utterly destroyed the peace of society and have sown the seeds of hatred, revenge, and all uncharitableness.

27. *If he smite out his . . . tooth.* It was a noble law that obliged unmerciful slaveholders to set the slave at liberty whose eye or tooth they had knocked out. If this did not teach them humanity, it taught them caution, as one rash blow might have deprived them of all right to the future services of the slave; and thus self-interest obliged them to be cautious and circumspect.

28. *If an ox gore a man.* It is more likely that a "bull" is here intended, as the word signifies both, see chap. xxii. 1; and the Septuagint translates the *shor* of the original by *tauros,* "a bull." *His flesh shall not be eaten.* This served to keep up a due detestation of murder, whether committed by man or beast; and at the same time punished the man as far as possible, by the total loss of the beast.

30. *If there be laid on him a sum of money . . . the ransom of his life.* So it appears that, though by the law he forfeited his life, yet this might be commuted for a pecuniary mulct, at which the life of the deceased might be valued by the magistrates.

32. *Thirty shekels.* Each worth about three shillings English; see Gen. xx. 16; xxiii. 15. So, counting the shekel at its utmost value, the life of a slave was valued at four pounds ten shillings. And at this price these same vile people valued the life of our blessed Lord; see Zech. xi. 12-13; Matt. xxvi. 15.

33. *And if a man shall open a pit, or . . . dig a pit.* That is, if a man shall open a well or cistern that had been before closed up, or dig a new one (for these two cases are plainly intimated), and if he did this in some public place where there was danger that men or cattle might fall into it; for a man might do as he pleased in his own grounds, as those were his private right. In the above case, if he had neglected to cover the pit, and his neighbor's ox or ass was killed by falling into it, he was to pay its value in money. The thirty-third and thirty-fourth verses seem to be out of their places. They probably should conclude the chapter, as where they are, they interrupt the statutes concerning the goring ox, which begin at verse 28.

CHAPTER 22

Laws concerning theft, 1-4; concerning trespass, 5; concerning casualties, 6. Laws concerning deposits, or goods left in custody of others, which may have been lost, stolen, or damaged, 7-13. Laws concerning things borrowed or let out on hire, 14-15. Laws concerning seduction, 16-17. Laws concerning witchcraft, 18; bestiality, 19; idolatry, 20. Laws concerning strangers, 21; concerning widows, 22-24; lending money to the poor, 25; concerning pledges, 26-27; concerning respect to magistrates, 28; concerning the first-ripe fruits, and the first-born of man and beast, 29-30. Directions concerning carcasses found torn in the field, 31.

1. *If a man shall steal.* This chapter consists chiefly of judicial laws, as the preceding chapter does of political; and in it the same good sense, and well-marked attention to the welfare of the community and the moral improvement of each individual, are equally evident.

In our translation of this verse, by rendering different Hebrew words by the same term in English, we have greatly obscured the sense. I shall produce the verse with the original words which I think improperly translated, because one English term is used for two Hebrew words, which in this place certainly do not mean the same thing. *If a man shall steal an ox [shor], or a sheep [seh], and kill it, or sell it; he shall restore five oxen [bakar] for an ox [shor], and four sheep [tson] for a sheep [seh].* I think it must appear evident that the sacred writer did not intend that these words should be understood as above. A *shor* certainly is different from a *bakar,* and a *seh* from a *tson.* Where the difference in every case lies, wherever these

words occur, it is difficult to say. The *shor* and the *bakar* are doubtless creatures of the beef kind, and are used in different parts of the sacred writings to signify the bull, the ox, the heifer, the steer, and the calf. The *seh* and the *tson* are used to signify the ram, the ewe, the lamb, the he-goat, the she-goat, and the kid. And the latter word *tson* seems frequently to signify the flock, composed of either of these lesser cattle, or both sorts conjoined.

As *shor* is used, Job xxi. 10, for a "bull," probably it may mean so here. "If a man steal a bull, he shall give five oxen for him," which we may presume was no more than his real value, as very few bulls could be kept in a country destitute of horses, where oxen were so necessary to till the ground. *Tson* is used for a flock either of sheep or goats, and *seh* for an individual of either species. For every *seh,* four, taken indifferently from the *tson* or flock, must be given; i.e., a sheep stolen might be recompensed with four out of the "flock," whether of sheep or goats.

2. *If a thief be found.* If a thief was found breaking into a house in the night season, he might be killed; but not if the sun had risen, for then he might be known and taken, and the restitution made which is mentioned in the succeeding verse.

4. *He shall restore double.* In no case of theft was the life of the offender taken away; the utmost that the law says on this point is that if, when found breaking into a house, he should be smitten so as to die, no blood should be shed for him, v. 2. If he had stolen and sold the property, then he was to restore four- or five-fold, v. 1; but if the animal was found alive in his possession, he was to restore double.

7. *Deliver unto his neighbour.* This is called "pledging"; it is a deposit of goods by a debtor to his creditor, to be kept till the debt be discharged. Whatever goods were thus left in the hands of another person, that person, according to the Mosaic law, became responsible for them; if they were stolen, and the thief was found, he was to pay double; if he could not be found, the oath of the person who had them in keeping, made before the magistrates, that he knew nothing of them, was considered a full acquittance.

8. *Unto the judges.* See the note on chap. xxi. 6.

9. *Challengeth to be his.* It was necessary that such a matter should come before the judges, because the person in whose possession the goods were found might have had them by a fair and honest purchase; and, by sifting the business, the thief might be found out, and if found, be obliged to pay double to his neighbor.

11. *An oath of the Lord be between them.* So solemn and awful were all appeals to God considered in those ancient times that it was taken for granted that the man was innocent who could by an oath appeal to the omniscient God that he had not put his hand to his neighbor's goods.

13. *If it be torn in pieces . . . let him bring it for witness.* Rather, "Let him bring a testimony or evidence of the torn thing," such as the horns, hoofs, etc.

16. *If a man entice a maid.* This was an exceedingly wise and humane law, and must

have operated powerfully against seduction and fornication; because the person who might feel inclined to take the advantage of a young woman knew that he must marry her, and give her a dowry, if her parents consented; and if they did not consent that their daughter should wed her seducer, in this case he was obliged to give her the full dowry which could have been demanded had she been still a virgin.

19. *Lieth with a beast.* If this most abominable crime had not been common, it never would have been mentioned in a sacred code of laws. It is very likely that it was an Egyptian practice.

20. *Utterly destroyed.* The word *cherem* denotes a thing utterly and finally separated from God and devoted to destruction, without the possibility of redemptio..

21. *Thou shalt neither vex a stranger, nor oppress him.* This was not only a very humane law, but it was also the offspring of a sound policy: "Do not vex a stranger; remember ye were strangers. Do not oppress a stranger; remember ye were oppressed. Therefore do unto all men as ye would they should do to you."

22. *Ye shall not afflict any widow, or fatherless child.* It is remarkable that offenses against this law are not left to the discretion of the judges to be punished; God reserves the punishment to himself, and by this He strongly shows His abhorrence of the crime.

25. *Neither shalt thou lay upon him usury. Neshech,* from *nashach,* to "bite, cut, or pierce with the teeth"; "biting usury." So the Latins call it *usura vorax,* "devouring usury."

It is evident that what is here said must be understood of accumulated usury, or what we call "compound interest" only; and accordingly *neshech* is mentioned with and distinguished from *tarbith* and *marbith,* "interest" or "simple interest," Lev. xxv. 36-37; Prov. xxviii. 8; Ezek. xviii. 8, 13, 17; and xxii. 12. Perhaps *usury* may be more properly defined "unlawful interest," receiving more for the loan of money than it is really worth and more than the law allows. It is a wise regulation in the laws of England that if a man be convicted of usury, taking unlawful interest, the bond or security is rendered void and he forfeits treble the sum borrowed.

26. *If thou . . . take thy neighbour's raiment to pledge.* It seems strange that any pledge should be taken which must be so speedily restored; but it is very likely that the pledge was restored by night only; and that he who pledged it brought it back to his creditor next morning. The opinion of the rabbins is that whatever a man needed for the support of life he had the use of it when absolutely necessary, though it was pledged. Thus he had the use of his working tools by day, but he brought them to his creditor in the evening. His *hyke* was probably the *raiment* here referred to; it is a sort of coarse blanket, about six yards long, and five or six feet broad, which an Arab always carries with him, and on which he sleeps at night, it being his only substitute for a bed.

28. *Thou shalt not revile the gods.* Most commentators believe that the word *gods* here means "magistrates." The original is *Elohim,* and should be understood of the true God only: "Thou shalt not blaspheme or make light of God," the Fountain of justice and power, *nor*

curse the ruler of thy people, who derives his authority from God.

29. *The first of thy ripe fruits.* This offering was a public acknowledgment of the bounty and goodness of God.

30. *Seven days it shall be with his dam.* For the mother's health it was necessary that the young one should suck so long; and prior to this time the process of nutrition in a young animal can scarcely be considered as completely formed.

31. *Neither shall ye eat . . . flesh . . . torn of beasts in the field.* The reason of the prohibition against eating the flesh of animals that had been torn appears to have been simply this: That the people might not eat the blood, which in this case must be coagulated in the flesh; and the blood, being the life of the beast, and emblematical of the blood of the covenant, was ever to be held sacred, and was prohibited from the days of Noah. See on Gen. ix. 4.

CHAPTER 23

Laws against evil speaking, 1. Against bad company, 2. Against partiality, 3. Laws commanding acts of kindness and humanity, 4-5. Against oppression, 6. Against unrighteous decisions, 7. Against bribery and corruption, 8. Against unkindness to strangers, 9. The ordinance concerning the sabbatical year, 10-11. The Sabbath a day of rest, 12. General directions concerning circumcision, etc., 13. The three annual festivals, 14. The Feast of Unleavened Bread, 15. The Feast of Harvest and the Feast of Ingathering, 16. All the males to appear before God thrice in a year, 17. Different ordinances—no blood to be offered with leavened bread—no fat to be left till the next day—the firstfruits to be brought to the house of God—and a kid not to be seethed in its mother's milk, 18-19. Description of the Angel of God, who was to lead the people into the Promised Land, and drive out the Amorites, etc., 20-23. Idolatry to be avoided, and the images of idols destroyed, 24. Different promises to obedience, 25-27. Hornets shall be sent to drive out the Canaanites, etc., 28. The ancient inhabitants to be driven out by little and little, and the reason why, 29-30. The boundaries of the Promised Land, 31. No league or covenant to be made with the ancient inhabitants, who are all to be utterly expelled, 32-33.

1. *Thou shalt not raise a false report.* Acting contrary to this precept is a sin against the ninth commandment. And the inventor and receiver of false and slanderous reports are almost equally criminal. The word seems to refer to either, and our translators have very properly retained both senses, putting *raise* in the text, and "receive" in the margin. The original *lo tissa* has been translated, Thou shalt not "publish."

2. *Thou shalt not follow a multitude to do evil.* Be singular. But *rabbim,* which we translate *multitude,* sometimes signifies the "great, chiefs, or mighty ones"; and is so understood by some eminent critics in this place: "Thou shalt not follow the example of the great or rich, who may so far disgrace their own character as to live without God in the world, and trample under foot his laws." It is supposed that these directions refer principally to matters which come under the eye of the civil magistrate; as if He had said, "Do not join with great men in condemning an innocent or righteous person, against whom they have conceived a prejudice on the account of his religion."

3. *Neither shalt thou countenance a poor man in his cause.* The word *dal,* which we translate *poor man,* is probably put here in opposition to *rabbim,* the great, or noblemen, in the preceding verse. If so, the meaning is, Thou shalt neither be influenced by the great to make an unrighteous decision, nor by the poverty or dis-

tress of the poor to give thy voice against the dictates of justice and truth.

4. *If thou meet thine enemy's ox . . . going astray.* From the humane and heavenly maxim in this and the following verse, our blessed Lord has formed the following precept: "Love your enemies, bless them that curse you, do good to them that hate you, and pray for them which despitefully use you, and persecute you," Matt. v. 44.

6. *Thou shalt not wrest the judgment of thy poor.* Thou shalt neither countenance him in his crimes, nor condemn him in his righteousness.

8. *Thou shalt take no gift.* A strong ordinance against selling justice, which has been the disgrace and ruin of every state where it has been practiced.

9. *Ye know the heart of a stranger.* Having been strangers yourselves, under severe, long continued, and cruel oppression, ye know the fears, cares, anxieties, and dismal forebodings which the heart of a stranger feels.

11. *The seventh year thou shalt let it rest.* As every seventh day was a Sabbath day, so every seventh year was to be a Sabbath year. That God intended to teach them the doctrine of providence by this ordinance, there can be no doubt; and this is marked very distinctly, Lev. xxv. 20-21: "And if ye shall say, What shall we eat the seventh year? behold, we shall not sow, nor gather in our increase: then I will command my blessing upon you in the sixth year, and it shall bring forth fruit for three years." That is, There shall be, not three crops in one year, but one crop equal in its abundance to three, because it must supply the wants of three years.

12. *Six days thou shalt do thy work.* Though they were thus bound to keep the sabbatical year, yet they must not neglect the seventh day's rest or weekly Sabbath; for that was of perpetual obligation, and was paramount to all others. That the sanctification of the Sabbath was of great consequence in the sight of God, we may learn from the various repetitions of this law; and we may observe that it has still for its object, not only the benefit of the soul, but the health and comfort of the body also. *The son of thy handmaid, and the stranger . . . be refreshed.* Yinnaphesh, may be "re-spirited" or "new-souled"; have a complete renewal of both bodily and spiritual strength.

14. *Three times thou shalt keep a feast unto me in the year.* The three feasts here referred to were Passover, Pentecost, Tabernacles. The Feast of the Passover was celebrated to keep in remembrance the wonderful deliverance of the Hebrews from Egypt. The Feast of Pentecost, called also the "feast of harvest" and the "feast of weeks," chap. xxxiv. 22, was celebrated fifty days after the Passover to commemorate the giving of the law on Mount Sinai. The Feast of Tabernacles, called also the "feast of the ingathering," was celebrated about the fifteenth of the month Tisri to commemorate the Israelites' dwelling in tents for forty years, during their stay in the wilderness. See on Leviticus xxiii.

17. *All thy males.* Old men, sick men, male idiots, and male children under thirteen years

of age, excepted; for so the Jewish doctors understand this command.

18. *The blood of my sacrifice with leavened bread.* The sacrifice here mentioned is undoubtedly the Passover (see chap. xxxiv. 25); this is called by way of eminence *my sacrifice*, because God had instituted it for that especial purpose, the redemption of Israel from the Egyptian bondage, and because it typified the Lamb of God, who taketh away the sin of the world. We have already seen how strict the prohibition against leaven was during this festival, and what was signified by it. See on chap. xii.

19. *Thou shalt not seethe a kid in his mother's milk.* This passage has greatly perplexed commentators; but Dr. Cudworth is supposed to have given it its true meaning by quoting a MS. comment of a Karaite Jew, which he met with, on this passage. "It was a custom of the ancient heathens, when they had gathered in all their fruits, to take a kid and boil it in the milk of its dam; and then, in a magical way, to go about and besprinkle with it all their trees and fields, gardens and orchards; thinking by these means to make them fruitful, that they might bring forth more abundantly in the following year." After all the learned labor which critics have bestowed on this passage, the simple object of the precept seems to be this: "Thou shalt do nothing that may have any tendency to blunt thy moral feelings, or teach thee hardness of heart." Even human nature shudders at the thought of causing the mother to lend her milk to seethe the flesh of her young one!

20. *Behold, I send an Angel before thee.* Some have thought that this was Moses, others Joshua, because the word *malach* signifies an *angel* or "messenger"; but as it is said, v. 21, "My name is in him" (*bekirbo*, "intimately, essentially in him"), it is more likely that the great Angel of the Covenant, the Lord Jesus Christ, is meant, in whom dwelt "all the fulness of the Godhead bodily." Of Him, Joshua was a very expressive type, the names *Joshua* and *Jesus,* in Hebrew and Greek, being of exactly the same signification, from *yasha*, "he saved, delivered, preserved, or kept safe." Nor does it appear that the description given of the Angel in the text can belong to any other person.

21. *He will not pardon your transgressions.* He is not like a man, with whom ye may think that ye may trifle; were He either man or angel, in the common acceptation of the term, it need not be said, *He will not pardon your transgressions,* for neither man nor angel could do it. *My name is in him.* The Jehovah dwells in Him; in Him dwelt "all the fulness of the Godhead bodily"; and because of this He could either pardon or punish.

23. *Unto the Amorites.* There are only six of the seven nations mentioned here, but the Septuagint, Samaritan, Coptic, and one Hebrew MS., add Girgashite, thus making the seven nations.

24. *Break down their images.* "Pillars, anointed stones."

25. *Shall bless thy bread, and thy water.* That is, all thy provisions, no matter of what sort; the meanest fare shall be sufficiently nutritive when God's blessing is in it.

26. *There shall nothing cast their young, nor*

be barren. Hence there must be a very great increase both of men and cattle. *The number of thy days I will fulfil.* Ye shall all live to a good old age, and none die before his time. This is the blessing of the righteous, for wicked men live not out half their days, Ps. lv. 23.

31. *I will set thy bounds from the Red sea,* on the southeast, *even unto the sea of the Philistines*—the Mediterranean, on the north-west; *and from the desert*—of Arabia, or the wilderness of Shur, on the west, *unto the river* —the Euphrates, on the northeast. Or in general terms, from the Euphrates on the east to the Mediterranean Sea on the west, from Mount Libanus on the north to the Red Sea on the south. This promise was not completely fulfilled till the days of David and Solomon. The general disobedience of the people before this time prevented a more speedy accomplishment; and their disobedience afterwards caused them to lose the possession.

32. *Thou shalt make no covenant with them.* They were incurable idolaters, and the cup of their iniquity was full. And had the Israelites contracted any alliance with them, either sacred or civil, they would have enticed them into their idolatries, to which the Jews were at all times most unhappily prone; and as God intended that they should be the preservers of the true religion till the coming of the Messiah, hence He strictly forbade them to tolerate idolatry.

33. *They shall not dwell in thy land.* They must be utterly expelled. The land was the Lord's, and He had given it to the progenitors of this people, to Abraham, Isaac, and Jacob.

CHAPTER 24

Moses and Aaron, Nadab and Abihu, and the seventy elders, are commanded to go to the mount to meet the Lord, 1. Moses alone to come near to the Divine Presence, 2. He informs the people, and they promise obedience, 3. He writes the words of the Lord, erects an altar at the foot of the hill, and sets up twelve pillars for the twelve tribes, 4. The young priests offer burnt offerings and peace offerings, 5. Moses reads the book of the covenant, sprinkles the people with the blood, and they promise obedience, 6-8. Moses, Aaron, Nadab, Abihu, and the seventy elders of Israel go up to the mount, and get a striking display of the majesty of God, 9-11. Moses alone is called up into the mount, in order to receive the tables of stone, written by the hand of God, 12. Moses and his servant Joshua go up, and Aaron and Hur are left regents of the people during his absence, 13-14. The glory of the Lord rests on the mount, and the cloud covers it for six days, and on the seventh God speaks to Moses out of the cloud, 15-16. The terrible appearance of God's glory on the mount, 17. Moses continues with God on the mount forty days, 18.

1. *Come up unto the Lord.* Moses and Aaron were already on the mount, or at least some way up (chap. xix. 24), where they had heard the voice of the Lord distinctly speaking to them; and the people also saw and heard, but in a less distinct manner, probably like the hoarse grumbling sound of distant thunder; see chap. xx. 18.

2. *Moses alone shall come near.* The people stood at the foot of the mountain. Aaron and his two sons and the seventy elders went up, probably about halfway, and Moses alone went to the summit.

3. *Moses . . . told the people all the words of the Lord.* That is, the Ten Commandments, and the various laws and ordinances mentioned from the beginning of the twentieth to the end of the twenty-third chapter.

4. *Moses wrote all the words of the Lord.* After the people had promised obedience (v. 3) and so entered into the bonds of the covenant, "it was necessary," says Calmet, "to draw up an act by which the memory of these transactions might be preserved, and confirm the covenant by authentic and solemn ceremonies." And this Moses does. (1) As legislator, he reduces to writing all the articles and conditions of the agreement, with the people's act of consent. (2) As their mediator and the deputy of the Lord, he accepts on his part the resolution of the people; and Jehovah on His part engages himself to Israel, to be their God, their King, and Protector, and to fulfil to them all the promises He had made to their fathers. (3) To make this the more solemn and affecting, and to ratify the covenant, which could not be done without sacrifice, shedding and sprinkling of blood, Moses builds an altar and erects twelve pillars, no doubt of unhewn stone, and probably set round about the altar. The altar itself represented the throne of God; the twelve stones, the twelve tribes of Israel. These were the two parties who were to contract, or enter into covenant, on this occasion.

5. *He sent young men.* Stout, able, reputable young men, chosen out of the different tribes, for the purpose of killing, flaying, and offering the oxen mentioned here. *Burnt offerings.* They generally consisted of sheep and goats, Lev. i. 10. These were wholly consumed by fire. *Peace offerings.* Bullocks or goats; see Heb. ix. 19. The blood of these was poured out before the Lord, and then the priests and people might feast on the flesh.

7. *The book of the covenant.* The writing containing the laws mentioned in the three preceding chapters. As this writing contained the agreement made between God and them, it was called *the book of the covenant;* but as no covenant was considered to be ratified and binding till a sacrifice had been offered on the occasion, hence the necessity of the sacrifices mentioned here. Half of the blood being sprinkled on the altar, and half of it sprinkled on the people, showed that both God and they were mutually bound by this covenant. God was bound to the people to support, defend, and save them; the people were bound to God to fear, love, and serve Him.

10. *They saw the God of Israel.* The seventy elders, who were representatives of the whole congregation, were chosen to witness the manifestation of God, that they might be satisfied of the truth of the revelation which He had made of himself and of His will; and on this occasion it was necessary that the people also should be favored with a sight of the glory of God; see chap. xx. 18. Thus the certainty of the revelation was established by many witnesses, and by those especially of the most competent kind. *A paved work of a sapphire stone.* Or "sapphire brickwork." I suppose that something of the mosaic pavement is here intended: floors inlaid with variously colored stones or small square tiles, disposed in a great variety of ornamental forms. *Sapphire* is a precious stone of a fine blue color, next in hardness to the diamond. The ruby is considered by most mineralogists of the same genus; so is also the topaz. Hence we cannot say that the sapphire is only of a blue color; it is blue, red, or yellow, as it

may be called sapphire, ruby, or topaz; and some of them are blue or green, according to the light in which they are held; and some white. The ancient oriental sapphire is supposed to have been the same with the *lapis lazuli*. Supposing that these different kinds of sapphires are here intended, how glorious must a pavement be, constituted of polished stones of this sort, perfectly transparent, with an effulgence of heavenly splendor poured out upon them! There is a similar description of the glory of the Lord in the Book of Revelation, chap. iv. 3: "And he that sat [upon the throne] was to look upon like a jasper and a sardine stone: and there was a rainbow round about the throne, in sight like unto an emerald."

11. *Upon the nobles of . . . Israel he laid not his hand.* This laying on of the hand has been variously explained. (1) He did not conceal himself from the nobles of Israel by covering them with His hand, as He did Moses, chap. xxxiii. 22. (2) He did not endue any of the nobles, i.e., the seventy elders, with the gift of prophecy; for so laying on of the hand has been understood. (3) He did not slay any of. them; none of them received any injury; which is certainly one meaning of the phrase: see Neh. xiii. 21; Ps. lv. 20. *Also they saw God,* i.e., although they had this discovery of His majesty, yet they did eat and drink, i.e., were preserved alive and unhurt. Perhaps the eating and drinking here may refer to the peace offerings on which they feasted, and the libations that were then offered on the ratification of the covenant.

12. *Come up to me into the mount, and be there.* We may suppose Moses to have been, with Aaron, Nadab, Abihu, and the seventy elders, about midway up the mount.

13. *Moses rose up.* In verse 16 it is said that "the glory of the Lord abode upon mount Sinai, and the cloud covered it." The glory was probably above the cloud, and it was to the cloud that Moses and his servant Joshua ascended at this time, leaving Aaron and the elders below. After they had been in this region, namely, where the cloud encompassed the mountain, for six days, God appears to have called Moses up higher; compare the sixteenth and eighteenth verses. Moses then ascended to the glory, leaving Joshua in the cloud, with whom he had, no doubt, frequent conferences during the forty days he continued with God on the mount.

14. *Tarry ye here for us.* Probably Moses did not know that he was to continue so long on the mount, nor is it likely that the elders tarried the whole forty days where they were. They doubtless, after waiting some considerable time, returned to the camp; and their return is supposed to have been the grand cause why the Israelites made the golden calf, as they probably reported that Moses was lost. *Aaron and Hur are with you.* Not knowing how long he might be detained on the mount, and knowing that many cases might occur which would require the interference of the chief magistrate, Moses constituted them regents of the people during the time he should be absent.

16. *And the seventh day he called.* It is very likely that Moses went up into the mount on the first day of the week; and having with Joshua remained in the region of the cloud during six days, on the seventh, which was the Sabbath,

God spake to him, and delivered successively to him, during forty days and forty nights, the different statutes and ordinances which are afterwards mentioned.

17. *The glory of the Lord was like devouring fire.* This appearance was well calculated to inspire the people with the deepest reverence and godly fear; and this is the use the apostle makes of it, Heb. xii. 28-29, where he evidently refers to this place. Seeing the glory of the Lord upon the mount like a devouring fire, Moses having tarried long, the Israelites probably supposed that he had been devoured or consumed by it, and therefore the more easily fell into idolatry. But how could they do this, with this tremendous sight of God's glory before their eyes?

18. *Forty days and forty nights.* During the whole of this time he neither ate bread nor drank water; see chap. xxxiv. 28; Deut. ix. 9. Both his body and soul were so sustained by the invigorating presence of God that he needed no earthly support, and this may be the simple reason why he took none. Elijah fasted forty days and forty nights, sustained by the same influence, 1 Kings xix. 8; as did likewise our blessed Lord, when He was about to commence the public ministry of His own gospel, Matt. iv. 2.

CHAPTER 25

The Lord addresses Moses out of the divine glory, and commands him to speak unto the Israelites that they may give Him freewill offerings, 1-2. The different kinds of offerings, gold, silver, and brass, 3. Purple, scarlet, fine linen, and goats' hair, 4. Rams' skins, badgers' skins (rather violet-colored skins), and shittim wood, 5. Oil and spices, 6. Onyx stones, and stones for the ephod and breastplate, 7. A sanctuary is to be made after the pattern of the Tabernacle, 8-9. The ark and its dimensions, 10. Its crown of gold, 11. Its rings, 12. Its staves and their use, 13-15. The testimony to be laid up in the ark, 16. The mercy seat and its dimensions, 17. The cherubim, how made and placed, 18-20. The mercy seat to be placed on the ark, and the testimony to be put within it, 21. The Lord promises to commune with the people from the mercy seat, 22. The table of shewbread and its dimensions, 23. Its crown and border of gold, 24-25. Its rings, 26-27. Staves, 28. Dishes, spoons, and bowls, 29. Its use, 30. The golden candlestick; its branches, bowls, knops, and flowers, 31-36. Its seven lamps, 37. Tongs and snuffers, 38. The weight of the candlestick and its utensils, one talent of gold, 39. All to be made according to the pattern showed to Moses on the mount, 40.

2. *That they bring me an offering.* The offering here mentioned is the *terumah,* a kind of freewill offering, consisting of anything that was necessary for the occasion. It signifies properly anything that was "lifted up," the heave offering, because in presenting it to God it was lifted up to be laid on His altar; but see on chap. xxix. 26.

3. *This is the offering.* There were three kinds of metals: (1) *Gold, zahab,* which may properly signify "wrought gold"; what was bright and resplendent, as the word implies. (2) *Silver, keseph,* from *casaph,* to be "pale, wan, or white"; so called from its well-known color. (3) *Brass, nechosheth,* "copper"; unless we suppose that the factitious metal commonly called brass is intended; this is formed by a combination of the oxide or ore of zink with copper. Brass seems to have been very anciently in use, as we find it mentioned in Gen. iv. 22. Because brass was capable of so fine a polish as to become exceedingly bright and keep its luster a considerable time, hence it was used for all weapons of war and defensive armor among ancient nations; and copper seems to have been in no repute but for its use in making *brass.*

4. *Blue.* *Techeleth,* generally supposed to mean an "azure or sky color." *Purple.* *Argaman,* a very precious color, extracted from the *murex,* a species of shellfish, from which it is supposed the famous Tyrian purple came, so costly, and so much celebrated in antiquity. *Scarlet.* *Tolaath,* signifies a "worm," of which this coloring matter was made. *Fine linen.* *Shesh;* whether this means linen, cotton, or silk is not agreed on among interpreters. Because *shesh* signifies "six," the rabbins suppose that it always signifies the fine linen of Egypt, in which six folds constituted one thread. *Goats' hair.* *Izzim,* "goats," but used here elliptically for goats' hair. In different parts of Asia Minor, Syria, Cilicia, and Phyrgia, the goats have long, fine, and beautiful hair, in some cases almost as fine as silk, which they shear at proper times, and manufacture into garments.

5. *Rams' skins dyed red.* Literally, "the skins of red rams." It is a fact attested by many respectable travellers that in the Levant sheep are often to be met with that have red or violet-colored fleeces. And almost all ancient writers speak of the same thing. *Badgers' skins.* *Oroth techashim.* Few terms have afforded greater perplexity to critics and commentators than this. Bochart has exhausted the subject, and seems to have proved that no kind of animal is here intended, but a color. None of the ancient versions acknowledge an animal of any kind except the Chaldee, which seems to think the badger is intended, and from it we have borrowed our translation of the word. The Septuagint and Vulgate have skins dyed a violet color; the Syriac, azure; the Arabic, black; the Coptic, violet; the modern Persic, ram-skins. The color contended for by Bochart is a very deep blue. *Shittim wood.* By some supposed to be the finest species of the cedar; by others, the *acacia Nilotica,* a species of thorn, solid, light, and very beautiful. This acacia is known to have been plentiful in Egypt, and it abounds in Arabia Deserta, the very place in which Moses was when he built the Tabernacle; and hence it is reasonable to suppose that he built it of that wood, which was every way proper for his purpose.

6. *Oil for the light.* This they must have brought with them from Egypt, for they could not get any in the wilderness, where there were no olives; but it is likely that this and some other directions refer more to what was to be done when in their fixed and settled residence than while wandering in the wilderness. *Spices,* to make a confection *for sweet incense,* abounded in different parts of these countries.

7. *Onyx stones.* We have already met with the stone called *shoham,* Gen. ii. 12, and acknowledged the difficulty of ascertaining what is meant by it. Some think the onyx, some the sardine, and some the emerald, is meant. *Stones to be set in the ephod.* "Stones of filling up." Stones so cut as to be proper to be set in the gold work of the breastplate. *The ephod.* It is very difficult to tell what this was or in what form it was made. It was a garment of some kind peculiar to the priests, and ever considered essential to all the parts of divine worship for without it no person attempted to inquire of God. As the word itself comes from the root *aphad,* "he tied or bound close," Calmet supposes that it was a kind of girdle, which, brought from

behind the neck and over the shoulders, and so hanging down before, was put cross upon the stomach, and then carried round the waist, and thus made a girdle to the tunic. Where the ephod crossed on the breast there was a square ornament called *choshen,* the *breastplate,* in which twelve precious stones were set, each bearing one of the names of the twelve sons of Jacob engraven on it. There were two sorts of ephods, one of plain linen for the priests, the other very much embroidered for the high priest. As there was nothing singular in this common sort, no particular description is given; but that of the high priest is described very much in detail, chap. xxviii. 6-8. It was distinguished from the common ephod by being composed of gold, blue, purple, scarlet, fine twisted linen, and cunning work, i.e., superbly ornamented and embroidered. This ephod was fastened on the shoulders with two precious stones, on which the names of the twelve tribes of Israel were engraved, six names on each stone.

8. *Let them make me a sanctuary.* Mikdash, a "holy place," such as God might dwell in; this was that part of the Tabernacle that was called the most holy place, into which the high priest entered only once a year, on the great Day of Atonement. *That I may dwell among them.* As the dwelling in this Tabernacle was the highest proof of God's grace and mercy towards the Israelites, so it typified Christ's dwelling by faith in the hearts of believers, and thus giving them the highest and surest proof of their reconciliation to God, and of His love and favor to them; see Eph. i. 22; iii. 17.

9. *After the pattern of the tabernacle.* It has been supposed that there had been a tabernacle before that erected by Moses, though it probably did not now exist; but the Tabernacle which Moses is ordered to make was to be formed exactly on the model of this ancient one, the pattern of which God showed him in the mount, v. 40. The word *mishcan* signifies literally the "dwelling" or "habitation"; and this was so called because it was the dwelling place of God.

10. *They shall make an ark.* Aron signifies an ark, chest, coffer, or coffin. It is used particularly to designate that chest or coffer in which the testimony or two tables of the covenant was laid up, on the top of which was the propitiatory or mercy seat (see on v. 17) and at the end of which were the cherubim of gold (vv. 18-20), between whom the visible sign of the presence of the supreme God appeared as seated upon His throne. The ark was the most excellent of all the holy things which belonged to the Mosaic economy, and for its sake the Tabernacle and the Temple were built, chap. xxvi. 33; xl. 18, 21. It was considered as conferring a sanctity wherever it was fixed, 2 Chron. viii. 11; 2 Sam. vi. 12.

15. *The staves . . . shall not be taken from it.* Because it should ever be considered as in readiness to be removed, God not having told them at what hour He should command them to strike their tents. If the staves were never to be taken out, how can it be said, as in Num. iv. 6, that when the camp should set forward, they should "put in the staves thereof," which intimates that when they encamped they took out the staves, which appears to be contrary to what is here said? To reconcile these two places, it

has been supposed, with great show of probability, that besides the staves which passed through the rings of the ark, and by which it was carried, there were two other staves or poles in the form of a bier or hand-barrow, on which the ark was laid in order to be transported in their journeyings, when it and its own staves, still in their rings, had been wrapped up in the covering of what is called badgers' skins and blue cloth. The staves of the ark itself, which might be considered as its handles simply to lift it by, were never taken out of their rings; but the staves or poles which served as a bier were taken from under it when they encamped.

16. *The testimony.* The two tables of stone which were not yet given; these tables were called *eduth,* from "forward, onward, to bear witness to or of a person or thing." Not only the tables of stone, but all the contents of the ark, Aaron's rod, the pot of manna, the holy anointing oil, bore testimony to the Messiah in His prophetic, sacerdotal, and regal offices.

17. *A mercy seat. Capporeth,* from *caphar,* to "cover or overspread"; because by an act of pardon sins are represented as being covered, so that they no longer appear in the eye of divine justice to displease and call for punishment; and the person of the offender is covered or protected from the stroke of the broken law. In the Greek version of the Septuagint the word *hilasterion* is used, which signifies a "propitiatory," and is the name used by the apostle, Heb. ix. 5. This mercy seat or propitiatory was made of pure gold; it was properly the lid or covering of that vessel so well known by the name of the "ark" and "ark of the covenant." On and before this, the high priest was to sprinkle the blood of the expiatory sacrifices on the great Day of Atonement: and it was in this place that God promised to meet the people (see v. 22), for there He dwelt, and there was the symbol of the Divine Presence. At each end of this propitiatory was a cherub, between whom this glory was manifested; hence in Scripture it is so often said that "he dwelleth between the cherubim," as the word "propitiatory" or "mercy seat," is applied to Christ, Rom. iii. 25, "whom God hath set forth to be a propitiation through faith in his blood . . . for the remission of sins that are past," hence we learn that Christ was the true Mercy Seat, the thing signified by the *capporeth,* to the ancient believers. And we learn further that it was by His blood that an atonement was to be made for the sins of the world. And as God showed himself between the cherubim over this propitiatory or mercy seat, so it is said, "God was in Christ, reconciling the world unto himself," 2 Cor. v. 19; etc. See on Leviticus vii.

18. *Thou shalt make two cherubims.* What these were we cannot distinctly say. It is probable that the term often means a figure of any kind, such as was ordinarily sculptured on stone, engraved on metal, carved on wood, or embroidered on cloth. It may be only necessary to add that "cherub" is the singular number; "cherubim," not *cherubims,* the plural.

22. *And there I will meet with thee.* That is, over the mercy seat, between the cherubim. In this place God chose to give the most especial manifestations of himself; here the divine glory was to be seen; and here Moses was to come in order to consult Jehovah relative to the management of the people.

23. *Thou shalt also make a table of shittim wood.* The same wood, the *acacia,* of which the ark staves were made.

29. *The dishes thereof. Kearothaiv,* probably the deep bowls in which they kneaded the mass out of which they made the shewbread. *And spoons thereof. Cappothaiv,* probably "censers," on which they put up the incense; as seems pretty evident from Num. vii. 14, 20, 26, 32, 38, 44, 50, 56, 62, 68, 74, 80, 86, where the same word is used, and the instrument, whatever it was, is always represented as being filled with incense. *Covers thereof. Kesothaiv,* supposed to be a large cup in which pure wine was kept on the table along with the shewbread for libations, which were poured out before the Lord every Sabbath, when the old bread was removed, and the new bread laid on the table. *Bowls thereof. Menakkiyothaiv,* from *nakah,* to "clear away, remove, empty"; supposed by Calmet to mean either the sieves by which the Levites cleansed the wheat they made into bread or the ovens in which the bread was baked.

30. *Shewbread. Lechem panim,* literally "bread of faces." The Hebrew text seems to intimate that they were called the "bread of faces" because, as the Lord says, they were set *lephanai,* "before My face." These loaves or cakes were twelve, representing, as is generally supposed, the twelve tribes of Israel. They were in two rows of six each. On the top of each row there was a golden dish with frankincense, which was burned before the Lord as a memorial at the end of the week, when the old loaves were removed and replaced by new ones, the priests taking the former for their domestic use.

31. *A candlestick of pure gold.* This *candlestick* or "chandelier" is generally described as having one shaft or stock, with six branches proceeding from it, adorned at equal distances with six flowers like lilies, with as many bowls and knops placed alternately. On each of the branches there was a lamp, and one on the top of the shaft which occupied the center; thus there were seven lamps in all, v. 37. These seven lamps were lighted every evening and extinguished every morning. We are not so certain of the precise form of any instrument or utensil of the Tabernacle or Temple as we are of this, the golden table, and the two silver trumpets.

Titus, after the overthrow of Jerusalem, A.D. 70, had the golden candlestick and the golden table of the shewbread, the silver trumpets, and the book of the law, taken out of the Temple and carried in triumph to Rome; and Vespasian lodged them in the temple which he had consecrated to the goddess of Peace. At the foot of Mount Palatine there are the ruins of an arch on which the triumph of Titus for his conquest of the Jews is represented, and on which the several monuments which were carried in the procession are sculptured, and particularly the golden candlestick, the table of the shewbread, and the two silver trumpets.

39. *Of a talent of pure gold shall he make it, with all these vessels.* That is, a talent of gold in weight was used in making the candlestick, and the different vessels and instruments which belonged to it. According to Bishop Cumber-

land, a talent was 3,000 shekels. A total of 7,013 pounds was expended on the candlestick and its furniture. It is no wonder that Titus should think it of sufficient consequence to be one of the articles, with the golden table and silver trumpets, that should be employed to grace his triumph.

40. *And look that thou make.* This verse should be understood as an order to Moses after the Tabernacle had been described to him; as if he had said: "When thou comest to make all the things that I have already described to thee, with the other matters of which I shall afterwards treat, see that thou make everything according to the pattern which thou didst see in the mount."

CHAPTER 26

The ten curtains of the Tabernacle, and of what composed, 1. Their length, 2-3; their loops, 4-5; their taches, 6. The curtains of goats' hair for a covering, 7; their length and breadth, 8. Coupled with loops, 9-10, and taches, 11. The remnant of the curtains, how to be employed, 12-13. The covering of rams' skins, 14. The boards of the Tabernacle for the south side, 15; their length, 16, tenons, 17, number, 18, sockets, 19. Boards, etc., for the north side, 20-21. Boards, etc., for the west side, 22; for the corners, 23; their rings and sockets, 24-25. The bars of the Tabernacle, 26-30. The veil, its pillars, hooks, and taches, 31-33. How to place the mercy seat, 34. The table and the candlestick, 35. The hanging for the door of the tent, 36; and the hangings for the pillars, 37.

1. *Thou shalt make the tabernacle. Mischan,* from *shachan,* "to dwell," means simply a dwelling place or habitation of any kind, but here it means the dwelling place of Jehovah, who, as a king in his camp, had His dwelling or pavilion among His people, His table always spread, His lamps lighted, and the priests, His attendants, always in waiting. From the minute and accurate description here given, a good workman, had he the same materials, might make a perfect facsimile of the ancient Jewish Tabernacle. It was a movable building, and so constructed that it might be easily taken to pieces, for the greater convenience of carriage, as they were often obliged to transport it from place to place in their various journeyings.

Cunning work. Chosheb probably means a sort of diaper, in which the figures appear equally perfect on both sides; this was probably formed in the loom. Another kind of curious work is mentioned, v. 36, *rokem,* which we term "needlework"; this was probably similar to our embroidery or tapestry. The whole of this account shows that not only necessary but ornamental arts had been carried to a considerable pitch of perfection, among both the Israelites and the Egyptians. The inner curtains of the Tabernacle were ten in number, and each in length twenty-eight cubits, and four in breadth. The curtains were to be coupled together, five and five of a side, by fifty loops, v. 5, and as many golden clasps, v. 6, so that each might look like one curtain, and the whole make one entire covering, which was the *first.*

7. *Curtains of goats' hair.* See the note on chap. xxv. 4. This was the *second* covering.

14. *Rams' skins dyed red.* See on chap. xxv. 5. This was the *third* covering; and what is called the *badgers' skins* was the *fourth.* See the note on chap. xxv. 5. Why there should have been four coverings does not appear. They might have been designed partly for respect; and partly to keep off dust and dirt, and the extremely

fine sand which in that desert rises as it were on every breeze; and partly to keep off the intense heat of the sun.

15. *Thou shalt make boards.* These formed what might be called the walls of the Tabernacle, and were made of shittim wood, the *acacia Nilotica,* which Dr. Shaw says grows here in abundance.

29. *Thou shalt overlay the boards with gold.* It is not said how thick the gold was by which these boards were overlaid; it was no doubt done with gold plates, but these must have been very thin, else the boards must have been insupportably heavy.

31. *Thou shalt make a veil. Parocheth,* from *parach,* "to break or rend"; the inner veil of the Tabernacle or Temple (2 Chron. iii. 14), which broke, interrupted, or divided between the holy place and the most holy; "the holy Ghost this signifying, that the way into the holiest of all was not yet made manifest, while as the first tabernacle was yet standing." Compare Heb. ix. 8. Does not the Hebrew name *parocheth* intimate the typical correspondence of this veil to the body or flesh of Christ? For this veil was His flesh (Heb. x. 20), which, being rent, affords us "a new and living way" into the holiest of all, i.e., "into heaven itself." Compare Heb. x. 19-20; ix. 24. And accordingly when His blessed body was rent upon the Cross, this veil also "was rent in twain from the top to the bottom," Matt. xxvii. 51.

32. *Their hooks shall be of gold. Vaveyhem,* which we translate *their hooks,* is rendered "capitals" by the Septuagint, and *capita* by the Vulgate. On the whole it appears much more reasonable to translate the original by "capitals" than by *hooks.*

After this verse the Samaritan Pentateuch introduces the first ten verses of chap. xxx, and this appears to be their proper place. Those ten verses are not repeated in the thirtieth chapter in the Samaritan, the chapter beginning with the eleventh verse.

36. *A hanging for the door of the tent.* This may be called the "first veil," as it occupied the door or entrance to the Tabernacle; the veil that separated the holy place from the holy of holies is called the "second veil," Heb. ix. 3. These two veils and the inner covering of the Tabernacle were all of the same materials, and of the same workmanship. See chap. xxvii. 16.

CHAPTER 27

The altar of burnt offerings, and its dimensions, 1; its horns, 2; pans, shovels, etc., 3; its grate and network, 4-5; its staves, 6-7. Court of the Tabernacle, with its pillars and hangings, 9-15. Gate of the court, its pillars, hangings, length, breadth, and height, 16-18. All the vessels used in the court of the Tabernacle to be of brass, 19. The Israelites to provide pure olive oil for the light, 20. Everything to be ordered by Aaron and his sons, 21.

2. *Thou shalt make the horns of it.* The horns might have three uses: (1) For ornament. (2) To prevent carcasses from falling off. (3) To tie the victim to, previously to its being sacrificed. So David: "Bind the sacrifice with cords, even unto the horns of the altar," Ps. cxviii. 27.

3. *Thou shalt make his pans. Sirothaiv,* a sort of large brazen dishes, which stood under the altar to receive the ashes that fell through the grating. *His shovels. Yaaiv.* Some kind of fire shovels or scuttles, which were used to

carry off the ashes that fell through the grating into the large pan. *His basons. Mizrekothaiv,* from *zarak,* to "sprinkle" or "disperse"; bowls or basins to receive the blood of the sacrifices, in order that it might be sprinkled on the people before the altar. *His fleshhooks. Mizlegothaiv.* That this word is rightly translated *fleshhooks* is fully evident from 1 Sam. ii. 13-14, where the same word is used in such a connection as demonstrates its meaning: "And the priest's custom with the people was, that, when any man offered sacrifice, the priest's servant came, while the flesh was in seething, with a fleshhook of three teeth [prongs] in his hand; and he struck it into the pan . . . all that the fleshhook brought up the priest took for himself." It was probably a kind of trident, or fork with three prongs, and these bent to a right angle at the middle, as the ideal meaning of the Hebrew seems to imply crookedness or curvature in general. *His firepans. Machtothaiv.* Bishop Patrick and others suppose that "this was a larger sort of vessel, wherein, probably, the sacred fire which came down from heaven (Lev. ix. 24) was kept burning, whilst they cleansed the altar and the grate from the coals and the ashes; and while the altar was carried from one place to another, as it often was in the wilderness."

8. *Hollow with boards.* It seems to have been a kind of framework, and to have had nothing solid in the inside, and only covered with the grating at the top. This rendered it more light and portable.

9. *The court of the tabernacle.* The Tabernacle stood in an enclosure or court, open at the top. This court was made with pillars or posts, and hangings. It was *an hundred cubits* in length; the breadth we learn from verses 12 and 18; and *five cubits* high, v. 18. And as this was but half the height of the Tabernacle, chap. xxvi. 16, that sacred building might easily be seen by the people from without.

16. *And for the gate of the court.* It appears that the hangings of this gate were of the same materials and workmanship with that of the inner covering of the Tabernacle, and the outer and inner veil. See chap. xxvi. 36.

19. *All the vessels . . . shall be of brass.* It would have been improper to use instruments made of the more precious metals about this altar, as they must have been soon worn out by the severity of the service.

20. *Pure oil olive beaten.* That is, such oil as could easily be expressed from the olives after they had been bruised in a mortar. *To cause the lamp to burn always.* It was to be kept burning through the whole of the night, and some think all the day besides. This oil and continual flame were not only emblematical of the unction and influences of the Holy Ghost, but also of that pure spirit of devotion which ever animates the hearts and minds of the genuine worshippers of the true God.

21. *The tabernacle of the congregation.* The place where all the assembly of the people were to worship, where the God of that assembly was pleased to reside, and to which, as the habitation of their King and Protector, they were ever to turn their faces in all their adorations. *Before the testimony.* That is, the ark where the tables of the covenant were deposited. See chap. xxv.

16. *Aaron and his sons.* These and their descendants being the only legitimate priests, God having established the priesthood in this family. *Shall order it from evening to morning.* Josephus says the whole of the seven lamps burned all the night; in the morning four were extinguished, and three kept burning through the whole day. Others assert that the whole seven were kept lighted both day and night continually; but it appears sufficiently evident, from 1 Sam. iii. 3, that these lamps were extinguished in the morning: "And ere the lamp of God went out in the temple of the Lord, where the ark of God was, and Samuel was laid down to sleep." See also chap. xxx. 8: "And when Aaron lighteth the lamps at even."

CHAPTER 28

Aaron and his sons are set apart for the priest's office, 1. Garments to be provided for them, 2-3. What these garments were, 4, and of what made, 5. The ephod, its shoulder pieces, and girdle, 6-8. The two onyx stones, on which the names of the twelve tribes were to be engraven, 9-14. The breastplate of judgment; its twelve precious stones, engraving, rings, chains, and its use, 15-29. The Urim and the Thummim, 30. The robe of the ephod, its border, bells, pomegranates, etc., and their use, 31-35. The plate of pure gold and its motto, 36, to be placed on Aaron's mitre, 37-38. The embroidered coat for Aaron, 39. Coats, girdles, and bonnets, 40. Aaron and his sons are to be anointed for the priest's office, 41. Other articles of clothing and their use, 42-43.

1. *Aaron . . . and his sons.* The priesthood was to be restrained to this family because the public worship was to be confined to one place; and previously to this the eldest in every family officiated as priest, there being no settled place of worship. It has been very properly observed that, if Moses had not acted by the divine appointment, he would not have passed by his own family, which continued in the condition of ordinary Levites, and established the priesthood, the only dignity in the nation, in the family of his brother, Aaron.

2. *For glory and for beauty.* Four articles of dress were prescribed for the priests in orinary, and four more for the high priest. Those for the priests in general were a coat, drawers, a girdle, and a bonnet. Besides these the high priest had a robe, an ephod, a breastplate, and a plate or diadem of gold on his forehead. The garments, says the sacred historian, were for honor and for beauty. They were emblematical of the office in which they ministered.

3. *Whom I have filled with the spirit of wisdom.* So we find that ingenuity in arts and sciences, even those of the ornamental kind, comes from God. It is not intimated here that these persons were filled with the spirit of wisdom for this purpose only; for the direction to Moses is to select those whom he found to be expert artists, and those who were such, God shows by these words, had derived their knowledge from himself.

4. *Robe. Meil,* from *alah,* "to go up, go upon"; hence the *meil* may be considered as an upper coat. It is described by Josephus as a garment that reaches down to the feet, not made of two distinct pieces, but was one entire long garment, woven throughout. This was immediately under the ephod. *Broidered coat. Kethoneth,* what Parkhurst translates "a close, strait coat or garment"; according to Josephus, "a tunic circumscribing or closely encompassing the body, and having tight sleeves for the arms." This

was immediately under the *meil* or robe, and answered the same purpose to the priests that our "shirts" do for us. *Mitre. Mitsnepheth.* As this word comes from the root *tsanaph*, "to roll or wrap round," it evidently means that covering of the head so universal in the Eastern countries which we call "turban." *A girdle. Abnet,* "a belt" or "girdle." This seems to have been the same kind of sash or girdle, so common in the Eastern countries, that confined the loose garments about the waist, and in which their long skirts were tucked up when they were employed in work or on a journey.

8. *The curious girdle of the ephod.* The word *chesheb*, rendered here *curious girdle*, signifies merely a kind of embroidered work (see the note on chap. xxvi. 1); and it is widely different from *abnet*, which is properly translated "girdle" in v. 4.

11. *Like the engravings of a signet.* So signets or seals were in use at this time, and engraving on precious stones was then an art, and this art, which was one of the most elegant and ornamental, was carried in ancient times to a very high pitch of perfection, particularly among the ancient Greeks; such a pitch of perfection as has never been rivalled and cannot now be even well imitated.

12. *Aaron shall bear their names before the Lord.* He was to consider that he was the representative of the children of Israel; and the stones on the ephod and the stones on the breastplate were for a memorial to put Aaron in remembrance that he was the priest and mediator of the twelve tribes.

13. *Ouches of gold. Mishbetsoth,* "straight places," sockets to insert the stones in, from *shabats*, "to close, inclose, straiten." "Socket" in this place would be a more proper translation, as *ouch* cannot be traced up to any legitimate authority.

15. *The breastplate of judgment. Choshen mishpat,* the same as the *choshen*, see chap. xxv. 7, but here called the *breastplate of judgment,* because the high priest wore it upon his breast when he went to ask counsel of the Lord, to give judgment in any particular case; as also when he sat as judge to teach the law, and to determine controversies. See Lev. x. 11; Deut. xvii. 8-9.

16. *Foursquare it shall be.* Here we have the exact dimensions of this breastplate, or more properly "breast piece." It was a *span* in length and breadth when *doubled,* and consequently two spans long one way before it was doubled. Between these doublings, it is supposed, the Urim and the Thummim were placed. See on v. 30.

17. *Four rows of stones.* With a name on each stone, making in all the twelve names of the twelve tribes. (1) A *sardius, odem,* from the root *adam*, he was "ruddy"; the ruby, a beautiful gem of a fine, deep *red* color. The *sardius* is defined to be a precious stone of a blood-red color, the best of which come from Babylon.

(2) A *topaz, pitdah,* a precious stone of a pale dead-green, with a mixture of yellow, sometimes of a fine yellow; and hence it was called "chrysolite" by the ancients, from its gold color. It is now considered by mineralogists as a variety of the sapphire.

(3) *Carbuncle, bareketh,* from *barak,* "to lighten, glitter, or glisten"; a very elegant gem of a deep red color, with an admixture of scarlet. From its bright, lively color it had the name *carbunculus*, which signifies a "little coal"; and among the Greeks *anthrax*, a "coal," because when held before the sun it appears like a piece of bright burning charcoal. It is found only in the East Indies, and there but rarely.

(4) *Emerald, nophech;* it is one of the most beautiful of all the gems, and is of a bright green color, without any other mixture.

(5) *Sapphire, sappir.* See this described, chap. xxiv. 10.

(6) *Diamond, yahalom,* from *halam,* "to beat or smite upon." The diamond is supposed to have this name from its resistance to a blow, for the ancients have assured us that if it be struck with a hammer, upon an anvil, it will not break. This is a complete fable, as it is well known that the diamond can be easily broken. It is, however, the hardest, as it is the most valuable, of all the precious stones hitherto discovered.

(7) *Ligure, leshem,* the same as the jacinth or hyacinth; a precious stone of a dead red or cinnamon color, with a considerable mixture of yellow.

(8) *Agate, shebo.* This is a stone that assumes such a variety of hues and appearances that Mr. Parkhurst thinks it derives its name from the root *shab*, "to turn, to change." Agates have a white, reddish, yellowish, or greenish ground.

(9) *Amethyst, achlamah,* a gem generally of a purple color, composed of a strong blue and deep red.

(10) *The beryl, tarshish.* Mr. Parkhurst derives this name from *tar,* "to go round," and *shash,* "to be vivid or bright in color." If the beryl be intended, it is a pellucid gem of a bluish green color, found in the East Indies, and about the gold mines of Peru. But some of the most learned mineralogists and critics suppose the chrysolite to be meant. This is a gem of a yellowish green. Its name in Greek, *chrysolite*, literally signifies the "golden stone."

(11) *The onyx, shoham.* See the notes on Exod. xxv. 7. There are a great number of different sentiments on the meaning of the original; it has been translated beryl, emerald, prasius, sapphire, sardius, ruby, cornelian, onyx, and sardonyx. It is well known that the onyx is of a darkish horny color, resembling the hoof or nail, from which circumstance it has its name.

(12) *Jasper, yashepheh.* The similarity of the Hebrew name has determined most critics and mineralogists to adopt the *jasper* as intended by the original word. The jasper is usually defined a hard stone, of a beautiful bright green color, sometimes clouded with white, and spotted with red or yellow.

30. *Thou shalt put in the breastplate . . . the Urim and the Thummim.* What these were has, I believe, never yet been discovered. As the word *urim* signifies "lights," and the word *tummim*, "perfections," they were probably designed to point out the "light"—the abundant information, in spiritual things, afforded by the wonderful revelation which God made of himself by and under the law; and the "perfection," entire holiness and strict conformity to himself, which this dispensation required and which are introduced and accomplished by that dispensation of light and truth, the gospel.

31. *The robe of the ephod.* See on v. 4. From this description, and from what Josephus says, who must have been well acquainted with its form, we find that this *meil*, or robe, was one long, straight piece of blue cloth, with a hole or opening in the center for the head to pass through; which hole or opening was bound about, that it might not be rent in putting it on or taking it off, v. 32.

35. *His sound shall be heard.* The bells were doubtless intended to keep up the people's attention to the very solemn and important office which the priest was then performing, that they might all have their hearts engaged in the work; and at the same time to keep Aaron himself in remembrance that he ministered before Jehovah and should not come into His presence without due reverence.

36. *Thou shalt make a plate of pure gold.* The word *tsits*, which we render *plate*, means a "flower," or any appearance of this kind. The Septuagint translate it by "a leaf"; hence we might be led to infer that this plate resembled a wreath of flowers or leaves; it is called, chap. xxix. 6, *nezer*, a "crown."

HOLINESS TO THE LORD. This we may consider as the grand badge of the sacerdotal office. (1) The priest was to minister in holy things. (2) He was the representative of a holy God. (3) He was to offer sacrifices to make an atonement for and to put away sin. (4) He was to teach the people the way of righteousness and true holiness. (5) As mediator, he was to obtain for them those divine influences by which they should be made holy, and be prepared to dwell with holy spirits in the Kingdom of glory. (6) In the sacerdotal office he was the type of that holy and just One who, in the fulness of time, was to come and put away sin by the sacrifice of himself.

38. *May bear the iniquity of the holy things.* "And Aaron shall bear [in a vicarious and typical manner] the sin of the holy or separated things"—offerings or sacrifices. Aaron was, as the high priest of the Jews, the type or representative of our blessed Redeemer; and as he offered the sacrifices prescribed by the law to make an atonement for sin, and was thereby represented as bearing their sins because he was bound to make an atonement for them, so Christ is represented as bearing their sins, i.e., the punishment due to the sins of the world, in His becoming a Sacrifice for the human race. See Isa. liii. 4, 12, where the same verb, *nasa*, is used; and see 1 Pet. ii. 24. By the inscription on the plate on his forehead Aaron was acknowledged as the holy minister of the holy God. *It shall be always upon his forehead.* The plate inscribed with "HOLINESS TO THE LORD" should be always on his forehead, to teach that the law required holiness; that this was its aim, design, and end. And the same is required by the gospel; for under this dispensation it is expressly said, Without holiness "no man shall see the Lord," Heb. xii. 14.

42. *Linen breeches.* This command had in view the necessity of purity and decency in every part of the divine worship, in opposition to the shocking indecency of the pagan worship in general, in which the priests often ministered naked, as in the sacrifices to Bacchus.

CHAPTER 29

Ceremonies to be used in consecrating Aaron and his sons, 1-3. They are to be washed, 4. Aaron is to be clothed with the holy vestments, 5-6; to be anointed, 7. His sons to be clothed and girded, 8-9. They are to offer a bullock for a sin offering, 10-14; and a ram for a burnt offering, 15-18; and a second ram for a consecration offering, 19-22. A loaf, a cake, and a wafer or thin cake for a wave offering, 23-25. The breast of the wave offering and the shoulder of the heave offering to be sanctified, 26-28. Aaron's vestments to descend to his son, who shall succeed him, 29-30. Aaron and his sons to eat the flesh of the ram of consecration, 31-32. No stranger to eat of it, 33. Nothing of it to be left till the morning, but to be burnt with fire, 34. Seven days to be employed in consecrating Aaron and his sons, 35-37. Two lambs, one for the morning and the other for the evening sacrifice, to be offered continually, 38-42. God promises to sanctify Israel with His glory, and to dwell among them, 43-46.

1. *Take one young bullock.* This consecration did not take place till after the erection of the Tabernacle. See Lev. viii. 9-10.

2. *Unleavened bread.* Three kinds of bread as to its form are mentioned here, but all unleavened: (1) *matstsoth*, unleavened bread, no matter in what shape; (2) *challoth*, *cakes*, "pricked or perforated," as the root implies; (3) *rekikey*, an exceeding thin cake, from *rak*, "to be attenuated," properly enough translated *wafer*. The manner in which these were prepared is sufficiently plain from the text, and probably these were the principal forms in which flour was prepared for household use during their stay in the wilderness. These were all waved before the Lord, v. 24, as an acknowledgment that the bread that sustains the body, as well as the mercy which saves the soul, comes from God alone.

4. *Thou . . . shalt wash them.* This was done emblematically, to signify that they were to put away all filthiness of the flesh and spirit, and perfect holiness in the fear of God, 2 Cor. vii. 1.

5. *Thou shalt take the garments.* As most offices of spiritual and secular dignity had appropriate habits and insignia, hence, when a person was appointed to an office and habited for the purpose, he was said to be "invested" with that office, from *in*, used intensively, and *vestio*, "I clothe," because he was then clothed with the vestments peculiar to that office.

7. *Then shalt thou take the anointing oil.* It appears, from Isa. lxi. 1, that anointing with oil, in consecrating a person to any important office, whether civil or religious, was considered as an emblem of the communication of the gifts and graces of the Holy Spirit. This ceremony was used on three occasions, namely, the installation of prophets, priests, and kings, into their respective offices. In the Hebrew language *mashach* signifies to "anoint," and *mashiach*, the "anointed person." But as no man was ever dignified by holding the three offices, so no person ever had the title *mashiach*, the "anointed one," but Jesus the Christ. He alone is King of Kings and Lord of Lords: the King who governs the universe, and rules in the hearts of His followers; the Prophet, to instruct men in the way wherein they should go; and the great High Priest, to make atonement for their sins. Hence He is called the Messias, a corruption of the word *hammashiach*, "the anointed one," in Hebrew; which gave birth to *ho Christos*, which has precisely the same signification in Greek. Of Him, Melchizedek, Abraham, Aaron, David, and others were illustrious types. But none of

these had the title of the Messiah, or the Anointed of God.

10. *Shall put their hands upon the head of the bullock.* By this rite the animal was consecrated to God, and was then proper to be offered in sacrifice. Imposition of hands also signified that they offered the life of this animal as an atonement for their sins, and to redeem their lives from that death which, through their sinfulness, they had deserved. In the case of the sin offering and trespass offering, the person who brought the sacrifice placed his hands on the head of the animal between the horns, and confessed his sin over the sin offering, and his trespass over the trespass offering, saying, "I have sinned, I have done iniquity; I have trespassed, and have done thus and thus; and do return by repentance before Thee, and with *this* I make atonement." Then the animal was considered as vicariously bearing the sins of the person who brought it.

14. *It is a sin offering.* See the note on Lev. vii. 1, etc.

18. *It is a burnt offering.* See the note on Lev. vii. 1, etc.

19. *The other ram.* There were two rams brought on this occasion: one was for a burnt offering, and was to be entirely consumed; the other was the ram of consecration, v. 22, *eil millum,* the "ram of filling up," because when a person was dedicated or consecrated to God his hands were filled with some particular offering proper for the occasion, which he presented to God. Hence the word "consecration" signifies the "filling up or filling the hands."

20. *Take of his blood.* The putting the blood of the sacrifice on the *tip* of the *right ear,* the *thumb* of the *right hand,* and the *great toe* of the *right foot* was doubtless intended to signify that they should dedicate all their faculties and powers to the service of God; their *ears* to the hearing and study of His law, their *hands* to diligence in the sacred ministry and to all acts of obedience, and their *feet* to walking in the way of God's precepts. And this sprinkling appears to have been used to teach them that they could neither hear, work, nor walk profitably, uprightly, and well pleasing in the sight of God without this application of the blood of the sacrifice.

22. *The fat and the rump.* The *rump* or "tail" of some of the Eastern sheep is the best part of the animal, and is counted a great delicacy. They are also very large, some of them weighing from twelve to forty pounds' weight.

23. *And one loaf of bread.* The bread of different kinds (see on v. 2) in this offering seems to have been intended as a *minchah,* or offering of grateful acknowledgment for providential blessings. The essence of worship consisted in acknowledging God, (1) As the Creator, Governor, and Preserver of all things, and the Dispenser of every good and perfect gift. (2) As the Judge of men, the Punisher of sin, and He who alone could pardon it. The *minchahs,* heave offerings, wave offerings, and thank offerings, referred to the *first* point. The burnt offerings, sin offerings, and sacrifices in general referred to the *second.*

24. *For a wave offering.* See the notes on Leviticus vii, where an ample account of all the offerings, sacrifices, etc., under the Mosaic

dispensation, and the reference they bore to the great sacrifice offered by Christ, is given in detail.

25. *Thou shalt receive them of their hands.* Aaron and his sons are here considered merely as any common persons bringing an offering to God, and not having, as yet, any authority to present it themselves, but through the medium of a priest. Moses, therefore, was now to Aaron and his sons what they were afterwards to the children of Israel; and as the minister of God he now consecrates them to the sacred office, and presents their offerings to Jehovah.

27. *The breast of the wave offering, and the shoulder of the heave offering.* As the *wave offering* was agitated to and fro, and the *heave offering* up and down, some have conceived that this twofold action represented the figure of the Cross, on which the great Peace Offering between God and man was offered in the personal sacrifice of our blessed Redeemer. The breast and the shoulder, thus waved and heaved, were by this consecration appointed to be the priests' portion forever. Moses, as priest, received on this occasion the breast and the shoulder, which became afterwards the portion of the priests; see v. 28, and Lev. vii. 34. It is worthy of remark that, although Moses himself had no consecration to the sacerdotal office, yet he acts here as high priest, consecrates a high priest, and receives the breast and the shoulder, which were the priests' portion! But Moses was an extraordinary messenger and derived his authority, without the medium of rites or ceremonies, immediately from God himself.

29. *The holy garments . . . shall be his sons' after him.* These garments were to descend from father to son, and no new garments were to be made.

30. *Seven days.* The priest in his consecration was to abide seven days and nights at the door of the Tabernacle, keeping the Lord's watch. See Lev. viii. 33, etc. The number *seven* is what is called among the Hebrews a number of "perfection"; and it is often used to denote the completion, accomplishment, fulness, or perfection of a thing, as this period contained the whole course of that time in which God created the world and appointed the day of rest. As this act of consecration lasted seven days, it signified a perfect consecration, and intimated to the priest that his whole body and soul, his time and talents, should be devoted to the service of God and His people.

33. *But a stranger shall not eat thereof.* That is, no person who was not of the family of Aaron—no Israelite, and not even a Levite.

34. *Burn the remainder with fire.* Common, voluntary, and peace offerings might be eaten even on the second day; see Lev. vii. 16; xix. 5-6. But this being a peculiar consecration, in order to qualify a person to offer sacrifices for sin, like that great sacrifice, the paschal lamb, that typified the atonement made by Christ, none of it was to be left till the morning lest putrefaction should commence, which would be utterly improper in a sacrifice that was to make expiation for sin and bring the soul into a state of holiness and perfection with God. See the note on Exod. xii. 10.

36. *Thou shalt cleanse the altar.* The altar was to be sanctified for seven days; and it is

likely that on each day, previously to the consecration service, the altar was wiped clean, and the former day's ashes, etc., removed.

37. *Whatsoever toucheth the altar shall be holy.* To this our Lord refers in Matt. xxiii. 19, where He says the altar sanctifies the gift; and this may be understood as implying that whatever was laid on the altar became the Lord's property, and must be wholly devoted to sacred uses, for in no other sense could such things be sanctified by touching the altar.

39. *One lamb thou shalt offer in the morning.* These two lambs, one in the morning, and the other in the evening, were generally termed the morning and evening daily sacrifices, and were offered from the time of their settlement in the Promised Land to the destruction of Jerusalem by the Romans. The use of these sacrifices according to the Jews was this: "The morning sacrifice made atonement for the sins committed in the night, and the evening sacrifice expiated the sins committed during the day."

40. *A tenth deal of flour.* Deal signifies a "part." From Num. xxviii. 5 we learn that this *tenth deal* was the tenth part of an ephah, which constituted what is called an omer. See chap. xvi. 36. *The fourth part of an hin.* The *hin* contained one gallon and two pints. The *fourth* part of this was about one quart and a half of a pint. *Drink offering.* A libation poured out before the Lord. See its meaning, Lev. vii. 1, etc.

44. *I will sanctify . . . both Aaron and his sons.* So we find the sanctification by Moses according to the divine institution was only symbolical; and that Aaron and his sons must be sanctified, i.e., made holy, by God himself before they could officiate in holy things. From this, as well as from many other things mentioned in the sacred writings, we may safely infer that no designation by man only is sufficient to qualify any person to fill the office of a minister of the sanctuary. The approbation and consecration of man have both their propriety and use, but must never be made substitutes for the unction and inspiration of the Almighty. Let holy men ordain, but let God sanctify; then we may expect that His Church shall be built up on its most holy faith.

45. *I will dwell among the children of Israel.* This is the great charter of the people of God, under both the Old and New Testaments; see chap. xxv. 8; Lev. xxvi. 11-12; 2 Cor. vi. 16; Rev. xxi. 3. God dwells among them: He is ever to be found in His Church to enlighten, quicken, comfort, and support it; to dispense the light of life by the preaching of His Word, and the influences of His Spirit for the conviction and conversion of sinners. And He dwells in those who believe; and this is the very tenor of the new covenant which God promised to make with the house of Israel; see Jer. xxxi. 31-34; Ezek. xxxvii. 24-28; Heb. viii. 7-12; and 2 Cor. vi. 16. And because God had promised to dwell in all His genuine followers, hence the frequent reference to this covenant and its privileges in the New Testament. And hence it is so frequently and strongly asserted that every believer is a habitation of God through the Spirit, Eph. ii. 22.

46. *And they shall know that I am the Lord their God.* That is, they shall "acknowledge" God, and their infinite obligations to Him. In a multitude of places in Scripture the word *know*

should be thus understood. *That I may dwell among them.* For without this acknowledgment and consequent dependence on and gratitude and obedience to God, they could not expect Him to dwell among them.

CHAPTER 30

The altar of burnt incense, 1. Dimensions, 2. Golden crown, 3. Rings and staves, 4-5. Where placed, 6-7. Use, 8-10. The ransom price of half a shekel, 11-13. Who were to pay it, 14. The rich and the poor to pay alike, 15. The use to which it was applied, 16. The brazen laver and its uses, 17-21. The holy anointing oil, and its component parts, 22-25. To be applied to the Tabernacle, ark, golden table, candlestick, altar of burnt offerings, and the laver, 26-29. And to Aaron and his sons, 30. Never to be applied to any other uses, and none like it ever to be made, 31-33. The perfume, and how made, 34-35. Its use, 36. Nothing similar to it ever to be made, 37-38.

1. *Altar to burn incense.* The Samaritan omits the ten first verses of this chapter, because it inserts them after the thirty-second verse of chap. xxvi. See the note there. *Shittim wood.* The same of which the preceding articles were made, because it was abundant in those parts, and because it was very durable; hence everywhere the Septuagint translation, which was made in Egypt, renders the original by "incorruptible wood."

2. *Foursquare.* That is, on the upper or under surface, as it showed four equal sides; but it was twice as high as it was broad. It was called, not only the "altar of incense," but also the "golden altar," Num. iv. 11. For the *crown, horns, staves,* etc., see on the altar of burnt offering, chap. xxvi.

6. *Before the mercy seat that is over the testimony.* These words in the original are supposed to be a repetition, by mistake, of the preceding clause; the word *happarocheth,* the "veil," being corrupted by interchanging two letters into *haccapporeth,* the "mercy seat"; and this, as Dr. Kennicott observes, places the altar of incense before the mercy seat, and consequently in the holy of holies! Now this could not be, as the altar of incense was attended every day, and the holy of holies entered only once in the year. The five words which appear to be a repetition are wanting in twenty-six of Kennicott's and De Rossi's MMS., and in the Samaritan. The verse reads better without them and is more consistent with the rest of the account.

7. *When he dresseth the lamps.* Prepares the wicks and puts in fresh oil for the evening. *Shall burn incense upon it.* Where so many sacrifices were offered, it was essentially necessary to have some pleasing perfume to counteract the disagreeable smells that must have arisen from the slaughter of so many animals, the sprinkling of so much blood, and the burning of so much flesh. The perfume that was to be burnt on this altar is described in v. 34. No blood was ever sprinkled on this altar, except on the day of general expiation, which happened only once in the year, v. 10. But the perfume was necessary in every part of the Tabernacle and its environs.

9. *No strange incense.* None made in any other way. *Nor burnt sacrifice.* It should be an altar for incense, and for no other use.

10. *An atonement . . . once in a year.* On the tenth day of the seventh month. See Lev. xvi. 18, etc.

12. *Then shall they give every man a ransom for his soul.* This was a very important ordinance, and should be seriously considered.

13. *Half a shekel.* Each of the Israelites was ordered to give as a ransom for his soul (i.e., for his life) half a shekel, according to the shekel of the sanctuary. St. Peter seems to allude to this, and to intimate that this mode of atonement was ineffectual in itself, and only pointed out the great sacrifice which, in the fulness of time, should be made for the sin of the world. "Ye know," says he, "that ye were not redeemed with corruptible things, as silver and gold, from your vain conversation received by tradition from your fathers; but with the precious blood of Christ, as of a lamb without blemish and without spot: who verily was foreordained before the foundation of the world," 1 Pet. i. 18-20.

18. *A laver of brass.* Kiyor sometimes signifies a "caldron," 1 Sam. ii. 14; but it seems to signify any large, round vessel or basin used for washing the hands and feet. There were doubtless spigots in it to draw off the water, as it is not likely the feet were put into it in order to be washed. The *foot* of the laver must mean the pedestal on which it stood.

20. *They shall wash with water, that they die not.* This was certainly an emblematical washing; and as the hands and the feet are particularly mentioned, it must refer to the purity of their whole conduct. Their *hands* (all of their works), their *feet* (all their goings) must be *washed*—must be holiness unto the Lord. And this washing must be repeated every time they entered into the Tabernacle, or when they came near to the altar to minister. This washing was needful because the priests all ministered barefoot; but it was equally so because of the guilt they might have contracted, for the washing was emblematical of the putting away of sin, or what St. Paul calls the "washing [laver] of regeneration, and renewing of the Holy Ghost" (Titus iii. 5), as the influences of the Spirit must be repeated for the purification of the soul as frequently as any moral defilement has been contracted.

21. *And it shall be a statute for ever.* To continue in its literal meaning as long as the Jewish economy lasted, and in its spiritual meaning to the end of time. What an important lesson does this teach the ministers of the gospel of Christ! Each time they minister in public, whether in dispensing the Word or the sacraments, they should take heed that they have a fresh application of the grace and spirit of Christ to do away past transgressions or unfaithfulness and to enable them to minister with the greater effect, as being in the divine favor, and consequently entitled to expect all the necessary assistances of the divine unction to make their ministrations spirit and life to the people.

24. *Oil olive.* Olive oil is supposed to be the best preservative of odors. As the gifts and graces of the Holy Spirit are termed the anointing of the Holy Ghost, therefore this holy ointment appears to have been designed as emblematical of those gifts and graces. See Acts i. 5; x. 38; 2 Cor. i. 21; 1 John ii. 20, 27.

25. *After the art of the apothecary.* The original, *rokeach,* signifies a "compounder" or "confectioner"; any person who compounds *drugs, aromatics,* etc.

34. *Take unto thee sweet spices.* The holy perfume was compounded of the following ingredients: *Stacte. Nataph,* supposed to be the same with what was afterwards called the balm of Jericho. *Stacte* is the gum which spontaneously flows from the tree which produces myrrh. *Onycha. Shecheleth,* allowed by the best critics to be the external crust of the shellfish *murex,* and is the basis of the principal perfumes made in the East Indies. *Galbanum, Chelbenah,* the African *ferula;* it rises with a ligneous stalk from eight to ten feet, and is garnished with leaves at each joint. When any part of the plant is broken, there issues out a little thin milk of a cream color. The gummy, resinous juice which proceeds from this plant is what is commonly called *galbanum,* from the *chelbenah* of the Hebrew. *Pure frankincense. Labonah Zaccah.* Frankincense is supposed to derive its name from *frank,* "free," because of its liberal or ready distribution of its odors. It is a dry, resinous substance in pieces or drops of a pale yellowish-white color, has a strong smell, and bitter, acrid taste.

CHAPTER 31

Bezaleel appointed for the work of the Tabernacle, 1-5. Aholiab appointed for the same, 6. The particular things on which they were to be employed, the ark and mercy seat, 7. Table, candlestick, and altar of incense, 8. Altar of burnt offering and the laver, 9. Priest's garments, 10. Anointing oil and sweet incense, 11. God renews the command relative to the sanctification of the Sabbath, 12-17. Delivers to Moses the two tables of stone, 18.

2. *I have called by name Bezaleel.* That is, I have particularly appointed this person to be the chief superintendent of the whole work. His name is significant, *betsal-el,* "in or under the shadow of God," meaning under the especial protection of the Most High.

3. *In wisdom. Chochmah,* from *chacham,* to be "wise, skilful, or prudent," denoting the compass of mind and strength of capacity necessary to form a wise man; hence our word "wisdom," the power of judging what is wise or best to be done. *Understanding. Tebunah,* from *ban,* to "separate, distinguish, discern"; capacity to comprehend the different parts of a work, how to connect, arrange, in order to make a complete whole. *Knowledge. Daath,* denoting particular "acquaintance" with a person or thing; practical, experimental knowledge.

4. *Cunning works. Machashaboth,* works of invention or genius, in the goldsmith and silversmith line.

5. *In cutting of stones.* Everything that concerned the lapidary's, jeweler's, and carver's art.

6. *In the hearts of all that are wise hearted I have put wisdom.* So every man that had a natural genius, as we term it, had an increase of wisdom by immediate inspiration from God, so that he knew how to execute the different works which divine wisdom designed for the Tabernacle and its furniture.

8. *The pure candlestick.* Called so either because of the pure gold of which it was made, or the brightness and splendor of its workmanship, or of the light which it imparted in the Tabernacle, as the purest, finest oil was always burnt in it.

9. *The altar of burnt offering.* See on chap. xxvii. 1. *The laver and his foot.* The pedestal on which it stood.

10. *Cloths of service.* Vestments for the ordinary work of their ministry; *the holy garments*—those which were peculiar to the high priest.

13. *My sabbaths ye shall keep.* See the notes on Exod. xx. 8.

14. *Every one that defileth it.* By any kind of idolatrous or profane worship. *Shall surely be put to death.* The magistrates shall examine into the business, and if the accused be found guilty, he shall be stoned to death. *Shall be cut off.* Because that person who could so far contemn the Sabbath, which was a sign to them of the rest which remained for the people of God, was of course an infidel, and should be cut off from all the privileges and expectations of an Israelite.

16. *A perpetual covenant.* Because it is a sign of this future rest and blessedness, therefore the religious observance of it must be perpetually kept up.

17. *Rested, and was refreshed.* God, in condescension to human weakness, applies to himself here what belongs to man. If a man religiously rests on the Sabbath, both his body and soul shall be refreshed; he shall acquire new light and life.

18. *When he had made an end of communing.* When the forty days and forty nights ended. *Two tables of testimony.* See on chap. xxxiv. 1. *Tables of stone.* That the record might be lasting, because it was a testimony that referred to future generations, and therefore the materials should be durable. *Written with the finger of God.* That these tables were written, not by the commandment but by the power of God himself, the following passages seem to prove: "And the Lord said unto Moses, Come up to me into the mount, and be there: and I will give thee tables of stone . . . which I have written; that thou mayest teach them," Exod. xxiv. 12. "And he gave unto Moses . . . upon mount Sinai, two tables of testimony, tables of stone, written with the finger of God," chap. xxxi. 18. "And Moses . . . went down from the mount, and the two tables of testimony were in his hand: the tables were written on both their sides . . . And the tables were the work of God, and the writing was the writing of God, graven upon the tables," chap. xxxii. 15-16. "These words [the Ten Commandments] the Lord spake . . . in the mount out of the midst of the fire, of the cloud, and of the thick darkness, with a great voice: and he added no more. And he wrote them in two tables of stone," Deut. v. 22.

CHAPTER 32

The Israelites, finding that Moses delayed his return, desire Aaron to make them gods to go before them, 1. Aaron consents, and requires their ornaments, 2. They deliver them to him, and he makes a molten calf, 3-4. He builds an altar before it, 5; and the people offer burnt offerings and peace offerings, 6. The Lord commands Moses to go down, telling him that the people had corrupted themselves, 7-8. The Lord is angry, and threatens to destroy them, 9-10. Moses intercedes for them, 11-13; and the Lord promises to spare them, 14. Moses goes down with the tables in his hands, 15-16. Joshua, hearing the noise they made at their festival, makes some remarks on it, 17-18. Moses, coming to the camp, and seeing their idolatrous worship, is greatly distressed, throws down and breaks the two tables, 19. Takes the calf, reduces it to powder, strews it upon the water, and causes them to drink it, 20. Moses expostulates with Aaron, 21. Aaron vindicates himself, 22-24. Moses orders the Levites to slay the transgressors, 25-27. They do so, and 3,000 fall, 28-29. Moses returns to the Lord on the mount, and makes supplication for the people,

30-32. God threatens and yet spares, 33. Commands Moses to lead the people, and promises him the direction of an angel, 34. The people are plagued because of their sin, 35.

1. *When the people saw that Moses delayed.* How long this was before the expiration of the forty days, we cannot tell; but it certainly must have been some considerable time, as the ornaments must be collected, and the calf or ox, after having been founded, must require a considerable time to fashion it with the graving tool; and certainly not more than two or three persons could work on it at once. This work, therefore, must have required several days. *The people gathered themselves together.* They came in a tumultuous and seditious manner, insisting on having an object of religious worship made for them, as they intended under its direction to return to Egypt. See Acts vii. 39-40. *As for this Moses, the man that brought us up.* This seems to be the language of great contempt, and by it we may see the truth of the character given them by Aaron, v. 22, "they are set on mischief." It is likely they might have supposed that Moses had perished in the fire, which they saw had invested the top of the mountain into which he went.

2. *Golden earrings.* Both men and women wore these ornaments, and we may suppose that these were a part of the spoils which they brought out of Egypt.

3. *And all the people brake off the golden earrings.* The human being is naturally fond of dress, though this has been improperly attributed to the female sex alone, and those are most fond of it who have the shallowest capacities; but on this occasion the bent of the people to idolatry was greater than even their love of dress, so that they readily stripped themselves of their ornaments in order to get a molten god.

4. *Fashioned it with a graving tool.* There has been much controversy about the meaning of the word *cheret* in the text: some make it a mold; others a garment, cloth, or apron; some a purse or bag, and others a graver. It is likely that some mold was made on this occasion, that the gold when fused was cast into it, and that afterwards it was brought into form and symmetry by the action of the chisel and graver. *These be thy gods, O Israel.* Was it possible that Aaron could have imagined that he could make any god that could help them? Possibly he only intended to make them some symbolical representation of the divine power and energy. It must, however, be granted that Aaron does not appear to have even designed a worship that should supersede the worship of the Most High; hence we find him making proclamation, "To morrow is a feast to the Lord." It has been supposed that this calf was an exact resemblance of the famous Egyptian god Apis, who was worshipped under the form of an ox, which worship the Israelites no doubt saw often practiced in Egypt.

6. *The people sat down to eat and to drink.* The burnt offerings were wholly consumed; the peace offerings, when the blood had been poured out, became the food of the priests. They *rose up to play, letsachek,* a word of ominous import, which seems to imply here fornicating and adulterous intercourse; and in some countries the verb "to play" is still used precisely in this sense. In this sense the original is evidently used, Gen. xxxix. 14.

7. *Thy people . . . have corrupted themselves.* They had not only got into the spirit of idolatry, but they had become abominable in their conduct, so that God disowns them to be His: *Thy people* have broken the covenant, and are no longer entitled to My protection and love.

9. *A stiffnecked people.* Probably an allusion to the stiff-necked ox, the object of their worship.

10. *Now therefore let me alone.* Moses had already begun to plead with God in the behalf of this rebellious and ungrateful people; and so powerful was his intercession that even the Omnipotent represents himself as incapable of doing anything in the way of judgment unless His creature desists from praying for mercy!

14. *And the Lord repented of the evil.* This is spoken merely after the manner of men who, having formed a purpose, permit themselves to be diverted from it by strong and forcible reasons, and so change their minds relative to their former intentions.

16. *The tables were the work of God.* Because such a law could proceed from none but himself; God alone is the Fountain and Author of law, of what is right, just, holy, and good. *The writing was the writing of God.* For as He is the sole Author of law and justice, so He alone can write them on the heart of man. This is agreeable to the spirit of the new covenant which God had promised to make with men in the latter days: "I will make [a new covenant] with the house of Israel . . . I will put my laws into their mind, and write them in their hearts," Jer. xxxi. 33; Heb. viii. 10; 2 Cor. iii. 3.

17. *Joshua . . . said . . . There is a noise of war in the camp.* How natural was this thought to the mind of a military man! Hearing a confused noise, he supposed that the Israelitish camp had been attacked by some of the neighboring tribes.

18. *And he said.* That is, Moses returned this answer to the observations of Joshua.

19. *He cast the tables out of his hands, and brake them.* He might have done this through distress and anguish of spirit, on beholding their abominable idolatry and dissolute conduct; or he probably did it emblematically, intimating thereby that, as by this act of his the tables were broken in pieces, on which the law of God was written; so they, by their present conduct, had made a breach in the covenant, and broken the laws of their Maker.

20. *He took the calf . . . and burnt . . . and ground it to powder.* How truly contemptible must the object of their idolatry appear when they were obliged to drink their god, reduced to powder and strewed on the water!

21. *What did this people unto thee?* It seems, if Aaron had been firm, this evil might have been prevented.

22. *Thou knowest the people.* He excuses himself by the wicked and seditious spirit of the people, intimating that he was obliged to accede to their desires.

24. *I cast it into the fire, and there came out this calf.* What a silly and ridiculous subterfuge! He seems to insinuate that he only threw the metal into the fire, and that the calf came unexpectedly out by mere accident.

25. *Moses saw that the people were naked.* It is likely that the word *parua* implies that they were reduced to the most helpless and wretched state, being abandoned by God in the midst of their enemies. This is exactly similar to that expression, 2 Chron. xxviii. 19: "For the Lord brought Judah low because of Ahaz king of Israel; for he made Judah naked [*hiphria*], and transgressed sore against the Lord."

26. *Who is on the Lord's side?* That is, Who among you is free from this transgression? *And all the sons of Levi.* It seems they had no part in this idolatrous business.

28. *There fell . . . about three thousand men.* These were, no doubt, the chief transgressors; having broken the covenant by having other gods besides Jehovah, they lost the divine protection, and then the justice of God laid hold on and slew them. Moses, doubtless, had positive orders from God for this act of justice (see v. 27); for though, thorugh his intercession, the people were spared so as not to be exterminated as a nation, yet the principal transgressors, those who were "set on mischief," v. 22, were to be put to death.

29. *For Moses had said, Consecrate yourselves.* "Fill your hands" to the Lord. See the reason of this form of speech in the note on chap. xxiv. 19.

32. *Forgive their sin—; and if not, blot me . . . out of thy book.* "This people have sinned a great sin, and have made them gods of gold"; thus they had broken the covenant (see the first and second commandments), and by this had forfeited their right to Canaan. Yet *now*, he adds, *if thou wilt forgive their sin*, that they may yet attain the promised inheritance—; *and if not, blot me, I pray thee, out of thy book which thou hast written*—if Thou wilt blot out their names from this register, and never suffer them to enter Canaan, blot me out also; for I cannot bear the thought of enjoying that blessedness while my people and their posterity shall be forever excluded. And God, in kindness to Moses, spared him the mortification of going into Canaan without taking the people with him. They had forfeited their lives, and were sentenced to die in the wilderness; and Moses' prayer was answered in mercy to him, while the people suffered under the hand of justice. But the promise of God did not fail; for, although those who sinned were blotted out the book, yet their posterity enjoyed the inheritance.

This seems to be the simple and pure light in which this place should be viewed; and in this sense St. Paul is to be understood, Rom. ix. 3, where he says: "For I could wish that myself were accursed from Christ for my brethren, my kinsmen according to the flesh: who are Israelites; to whom pertaineth the adoption, and the glory, and the covenants." Moses could not survive the destruction of his people by the neighboring nations, nor their exclusion from the Promised Land; and St. Paul, seeing the Jews about to be cut off by the Roman sword for their rejection of the gospel, was willing to be deprived of every earthly blessing, and even to become a sacrifice for them, if this might contribute to the preservation and salvation of the Jewish state. Both those eminent men, engaged in the same work, influenced by a spirit of unparalleled patriotism, were willing to forfeit every blessing of a secular kind, even die for the welfare of the people. But certainly neither of them could wish to go to eternal perdition to save their countrymen from being cut off, the one by the sword of the Philistines, the other by that of the Romans. Even the supposition is monstrous.

33. *Whosoever hath sinned against me, him will I blot out.* As if the Divine Being had said: "All My conduct is regulated by infinite justice and righteousness: in no case shall the innocent ever suffer for the guilty. That no man may transgress through ignorance, I have given you My law, and thus published My covenant; the people themselves have acknowledged its justice and equity, and have voluntarily ratified it. He then that sins against Me (for sin is the transgression of the law, 1 John iii. 4, and the law must be published and known that it may be binding), him will I blot out of My book." And is it not remarkable that to these conditions of the covenant God strictly adhered, so that not one soul of these transgressors ever entered into the promised rest? Here was justice. And yet, though they deserved death, they were spared! Here was mercy. Thus, as far as justice would permit, mercy extended; and as far as mercy would permit, justice proceeded.

34. *Lead the people unto the place.* The word *place* is not in the text, and is with great propriety omitted. For Moses never led this people into that place; they all died in the wilderness except Joshua and Caleb. But Moses led them "towards" the place, and thus the particle *el* here should be understood, unless we suppose that God designed to lead them "to" the borders of the land but not to take them into it. *I will visit their sin.* I will not destroy them, but they shall not enter into the Promised Land. They shall wander in the wilderness till the present generation become extinct.

35. *The Lord plagued the people.* Every time they transgressed afterwards, divine justice seems to have remembered this transgression against them. The Jews have a metaphorical saying, apparently founded on this text: "No affliction has ever happened to Israel in which there was not some particle of the dust of the golden calf."

CHAPTER 33

Moses is commanded to depart from the mount, and lead up the people towards the Promised Land, 1. An angel is promised to be their guide, 2. The land is described, and the Lord refuses to go with them, 3. The people mourn, and strip themselves of their ornaments, 4-6. The Tabernacle or tent is pitched without the camp, 7. Moses goes to it to consult the Lord, and the cloudy pillar descends on it, 8-9. The people, standing at their tent doors, witness this, 10. The Lord speaks familiarly with Moses: he returns to the camp, and leaves Joshua in the Tabernacle, 11. Moses pleads with God, and desires to know whom He will send to be their guide, and to be informed of the way of the Lord, 12-13. The Lord promises that His presence shall go with them, 14. Moses pleads that the people may be taken under the divine protection, 15-16. The Lord promises to do so, 17. Moses requests to see the divine glory, 18. And God promises to make His goodness pass before him, and to proclaim His name, 19. Shows that no man can see His glory and live, 20; but promises to put Moses in the cleft of a rock, and to cover him with His hand while His glory passed by, and then to remove His hand and let him see His back parts, 21-23.

1. *Unto the land.* That is, towards it, or to the borders of it. See chap. xxxii. 34.

2. *I will send an angel.* In chap. xxiii. 20, God promises to send an angel to conduct them into the good land, in whom the name of God should be; that is, in whom God should dwell. Here He promises that an angel shall be their conductor; but as there is nothing particularly specified of him, it has been thought that an ordinary angel is intended, and not that Angel of the Covenant promised before. And this sentiment seems to be confirmed by the following verse.

3. *I will not go up in the midst of thee.* Consequently the angel here promised to be their guide was not that angel in whom Jehovah's name was; and so the people understood it; hence the mourning which is afterwards mentioned.

7. *Moses took the tabernacle. Eth haohel,* "the tent"; not *eth hammishcan,* "the tabernacle," the dwelling place of Jehovah, see chap. xxv. 11, for this was not as yet erected; but probably the tent of Moses, which was before in the midst of the camp, and to which the congregation came for judgment, and where, no doubt, God frequently met with His servant. This is now removed to a considerable distance from the camp, as God refuses to dwell any longer among this rebellious people. And as this was the place to which all the people came for justice and judgment, hence it was probably called the tabernacle, more properly the "tent," *of the congregation.*

9. *The cloudy pillar descended.* This very circumstance precluded the possibility of deception. The cloud descending at these times, and at none others, was a full proof that it was miraculous, and a pledge of the divine presence. It was beyond the power of human art to counterfeit such an appearance; and let it be observed that all the people saw this, v. 10.

11. *The Lord spake unto Moses face to face.* That there was no personal appearance here we may readily conceive; and that the communications made by God to Moses were not by visions, ecstasies, dreams, inward inspirations, or the mediation of angels, is sufficiently evident. We may therefore consider the passage as implying that familiarity and confidence with which the Divine Being treated His servant, and that He spake with him by articulate sounds in his own language, though no shape or similitude was then to be seen. *Joshua, the son of Nun, a young man.* There is a difficulty here. Joshua certainly was not a young man in the literal sense of the word; "but he was called so," says Mr. Ainsworth, "in respect of his service, not of his years; for he was now above fifty years old, as may be gathered from Josh. xxiv. 29." Perhaps the word *naar,* here translated *young man,* means a "single person, one unmarried."

12. *Moses said unto the Lord.* We may suppose that after Moses had quitted the tabernacle he went to the camp and gave the people some general information relative to the conversation he lately had with the Lord; after which he returned to the tabernacle or tent, and began to plead with God, as we find in this and the following verses. *Thou hast not let me know.* As God had said He would not go up with this people, Moses wished to know whom He would send with him, as He had only said in general terms that he would send an angel.

13. *Shew me now thy way.* Let me know the manner in which Thou wouldst have this people led up and governed, because this nation is *thy*

people and should be governed and guided in Thy own way.

14. *My presence shall go with thee. Panai yelechu,* "My faces shall go." I shall give thee manifestations of My grace and goodness through the whole of thy journey. I shall vary My appearances for thee, as thy necessities shall require.

15. *If thy presence go not. Im ein paneycha holechim,* "if Thy faces do not go"—if we have not manifestations of Thy peculiar providence and grace, *carry us not up hence.* Without supernatural assistance, and a most particular providence, he knew that it would be impossible either to govern such a people or support them in the desert; and therefore he wishes to be well assured on this head, that he may lead them up with confidence and be able to give them the most explicit assurances of support and protection. But by what means should these manifestations take place? This question seems to be answered by the Prophet Isaiah, chap. lxiii. 9: "In all their affliction he was afflicted, and the angel of his presence [*panaiv,* of His faces] saved them." So we find that the goodness and mercy of God were to be manifested by the Angel of the Covenant, the Lord Jesus, the Messiah; and this is the interpretation which the Jews themselves give of this place.

16. *So shall we be separated.* By having this divine protection we shall be saved from idolatry and be preserved in Thy truth and in the true worshipping of Thee; and thus "shall we be separated . . . from all the people that are upon the face of the earth," as all the nations of the world, the Jews only excepted, were at this time *idolaters.*

17. *I will do this thing also.* "My presence shall go with thee," and I will keep thee separate from all the people of the earth. Both these promises have been remarkably fulfilled. God continued miraculously with them till He brought them into the Promised Land; and from the day in which He brought them out of Egypt to the present day He has kept them a distinct, unmixed people!

18. *Shew me thy glory.* Moses probably desired to see that which constitutes the peculiar glory or excellence of the divine nature as it stands in reference to man. By many this is thought to signify His eternal mercy in sending Christ Jesus into the world. Moses perceived that what God was now doing had the most important and gracious designs which at present he could not distinctly discover; therefore he desires God to show him His glory. God graciously promises to indulge him in this request as far as possible by proclaiming His name and making all His goodness pass before him, v. 19. But at the same time He assures him that he could not see His face, the fulness of His perfections and the grandeur of His designs, and live, as no human being could bear, in the present state, this full discovery. But He adds, "Thou shalt see my back parts," *eth achorai,* probably meaning that appearance which He should assume in after times when it should be said, God is manifest in the flesh. This appearance did take place, for we find God putting him into a cleft of the rock, covering him with His hand, and passing by in such a way as to exhibit a human similitude.

19. *I will make all my goodness pass before thee.* Thou shalt not have a sight of My justice, for thou couldst not bear the infinite splendor of My purity; but I shall show myself to thee as the Fountain of inexhaustible compassion, the sovereign Dispenser of My own mercy.

20. *No man see me, and live.* The splendor would be insufferable to man; he only, whose mortality is swallowed up of life, can see God as He is. See I John iii. 2.

21. *Behold, there is a place by me.* There seems to be a reference here to a well-known place on the mount where God was accustomed to meet with Moses. This was a *rock;* and it appears there was a cleft or cave in it, in which Moses was to stand while the Divine Majesty was pleased to show him all that human nature was capable of bearing. But this appears to have referred more to the counsels of His mercy and goodness, relative to His purpose of redeeming the human race, than to any visible appearance of the Divine Majesty itself.

CHAPTER 34

Moses is commanded to hew two tables similar to the first, and bring them up to the mount, to get the covenant renewed, 1-3. He prepares the tables and goes up to meet the Lord, 4. The Lord descends, and proclaims His name JEHOVAH, 5. What this name signifies, 6-7. Moses worships and intercedes, 8-9. The Lord promises to renew the covenant, work miracles among the people, drive out the Canaanites, etc., 10-11. No covenant to be made with the idolatrous nations, but their altars and images to be destroyed, 12-15. No matrimonial alliances to be contracted with them, 16. The Israelites must have no molten gods, 17. The commandment of the Feast of Unleavened Bread, and of the sanctification of the firstborn, renewed, 18-20; as also that of the Sabbath, and the three great annual feasts, 21-23. The promise that the surrounding nations shall not invade their territories while all the males were at Jerusalem celebrating the annual feasts, 24. Directions concerning the Passover, 25; and the firstfruits, 26. Moses is commanded to write all these words, as containing the covenant which God had now renewed with the Israelites, 27. Moses, being forty days with God without eating or drinking, writes the words of the covenant; and the Lord writes the Ten Commandments upon the tables of stone, 28. Moses descends with the tables; his face shines, 29. Aaron and the people are afraid to approach him, because of his glorious appearance, 30. Moses delivers to them the covenant and commandments of the Lord; and puts a veil over his face while he is speaking, 31-33, but takes it off when he goes to minister before the Lord, 34-35.

1. *Hew thee two tables of stone like unto the first.* In chap. xxxii. 16 we are told that the first two "tables were the work of God, and the writing was the writing of God"; but here Moses is commanded to provide tables of his own workmanship, and God promises to write on them the words which were on the first. That God wrote the first tables himself seems proved by different passages of Scripture at the end of chap. xxxii. But here, in v. 27, it seems as if Moses was commanded to "write . . . these words," and in v. 28 it is said, "And he wrote upon the tables"; but in Deut. x. 1-4 it is expressly said that God wrote the second tables as well as the first.

In order to reconcile these accounts let us suppose that the "ten words," or Ten Commandments, were written on both tables by the hand of God himself, and that what Moses wrote, v. 27, was a copy of these to be delivered to the people, while the tables themselves were laid up in the ark before the testimony, whither the people could not go to consult them, and therefore a copy was necessary for the use of the congregation; this copy, being taken off under the direction of God, was authenticated equally with the original, and the original itself was laid up as a record to which all succeeding copies might be continually referred, in order to prevent corruption.

6. *And the Lord passed by . . . and proclaimed, The Lord.* It would be much better to read this verse thus: "And the Lord passed by before him, and proclaimed Jehovah," that is, showed Moses fully what was implied in this august name. Moses had requested God to show him His glory (see the preceding chapter, eighteenth verse) and God promised to proclaim or fully declare the name Jehovah (v. 19), by which proclamation or interpretation Moses should see how God "will be gracious to whom I will be gracious," and how He would be merciful to those to whom He would show mercy. Here, therefore, God fulfils that promise by proclaiming this name. It has long been a question what is the meaning of the word Jehovah. Some have maintained that it is utterly inexplicable. How strange is it that none of these learned men have discovered that God himself interprets this name in verses 6 and 7 of this chapter! "And the Lord passed by before him, and proclaimed, The Lord [Jehovah], The Lord God, merciful and gracious, longsuffering, and abundant in goodness and truth, keeping mercy for thousands, forgiving iniquity and transgression and sin, and that will by no means clear the guilty." These words contain the proper interpretation of the venerable and glorious name JEHOVAH.

7. *That will by no means clear the guilty.* This last clause is rather difficult; literally translated it signifies, "in clearing He will not clear." But the Samaritan, reading "to him," instead of the negative "not," renders the clause thus: "With whom the innocent shall be innocent"; i.e., an innocent or holy person shall never be treated as if he were a transgressor, by this just and holy God.

9. *O Lord, let my Lord, I pray thee, go among us.* The original is not *Jehovah*, but *Adonai* in both these places, and seems to refer particularly to the Angel of the Covenant, the Messiah.

10. *I will do marvels.* This seems to refer to what God did in putting them in possession of the land of Canaan, causing the walls of Jericho to fall down, making the sun and moon to stand still, etc. And thus God made His covenant with them; binding himself to put them in possession of the Promised Land, and binding them to observe the precepts laid down in the following verses, from the eleventh to the twenty-sixth inclusive.

13. *Ye shall destroy their . . . images.* See the subjects of this and all the following verses, to the twenty-eighth, treated at large in the notes on chap. xxiii.

21. *In earing time and in harvest thou shalt rest.* This commandment is worthy of especial note. Many break the Sabbath on the pretense of absolute necessity, because, if in harvesttime the weather happens to be what is called bad, and the Sabbath day be fair and fine, they judge it perfectly lawful to employ that day in endeavoring to save the fruits of the field, and think that the goodness of the day beyond the preceding is an indication from Providence that it should be thus employed. But is not the above command pointed directly against this?

24. *Neither shall any man desire thy land.* What a manifest proof was this of the power and particular providence of God! How easy would it have been for the surrounding nations to take possession of the whole Israelitish land with all their fenced cities when there were none left to protect them but women and children!

25. *The blood of my sacrifice.* That is, the paschal lamb. See on chap. xxiii. 18.

26. *Thou shalt not seethe a kid in his mother's milk.* See this amply considered in chap. xxiii. 19.

27. *Write thou these words.* Either a transcript of the whole law now delivered, or the words included from verse 11 to 26. God certainly wrote the "ten words" on both sets of tables. Moses either wrote a transcript of these and the accompanying precepts for the use of the people, or he wrote the precepts themselves in addition to the Ten Commandments, which were written by the finger of God. See on v. 1. Allowing this mode of interpretation, the accompanying precepts were, probably, what was written on the back side of the tables by Moses; the Ten Commandments, what were written on the front by the finger of Jehovah.

29. *The skin of his face shone.* Karan, "was horned": having been long in familiar intercourse with his Maker, his flesh, as well as his soul, was penetrated with the effulgence of the divine glory, and his looks expressed the light and life which dwelt within. Probably Moses appeared now as he did when in our Lord's transfiguration he was seen with Elijah on the mount, Matthew xvii. As the original word *karan* signifies to "shine out, to dart forth," as horns on the head of an animal, or rays of light reflected from a polished surface, we may suppose that the heavenly glory which filled the soul of this holy man darted out from his face in coruscations, in that manner in which light is generally represented. The Vulgate renders the passage, "And he did not know that his face was horned"; which version, misunderstood, has induced painters in general to represent Moses with two very large horns, one proceeding from each temple. But we might naturally ask, while they were indulging themselves in such fancies, why only two horns? for it is very likely that there were hundreds of these radiations, proceeding at once from the face of Moses.

30. *They were afraid to come nigh him.* A sight of his face alarmed them; their consciences were still guilty from their late transgression, and they had not yet received the atonement. The very appearance of superior sanctity often awes the guilty into respect.

33. *And till Moses had done speaking.* The meaning of the verse appears to be this: As often as Moses spoke in public to the people, he put the veil on his face, because they could not bear to look on the brightness of his countenance; but when he entered into the tabernacle to converse with the Lord, he removed this veil, v. 34. St. Paul, 2 Cor. iii. 7, etc., makes a very important use of the transactions recorded in this place. He represents the brightness of the face of Moses as emblematical of the glory or excellence of that dispensation; but he shows that, however glorious or excellent that was, it had no glory when compared with the superior ex-

cellence of the gospel. As Moses was glorious in the eyes of the Israelites, but that glory was absorbed and lost in the splendor of God when he entered into the tabernacle, or went to meet the Lord upon the mount, so the brightness and excellence of the Mosaic dispensation are eclipsed and absorbed in the transcendent brightness or excellence of the gospel of Christ. The apostle further considers the veil on the face of Moses as being emblematical of the metaphorical nature of the different rites and ceremonies of the Mosaic dispensation, each "covering" some spiritual meaning or a spiritual subject; and that the Jews did not lift the veil to penetrate the spiritual sense, and did not look to "the end of the commandment," which was to be "abolished," but rested in the letter or literal meaning, which conferred neither light nor life. He considers the veil also as being emblematical of that state of intellectual darkness into which the Jewish people, by their rejection of the gospel, were plunged, and from which they have never yet been recovered. When a Jew, even at the present day, reads the law in the synagogue, he puts over his head an oblong woolen veil, with four tassels at the four corners, which is called the *taled.* This is a very remarkable circumstance, as it appears to be an emblem of the intellectual veil referred to by the apostle, which is still upon their hearts when Moses is read, and which prevents them from looking to the end of that which God designed should be abrogated, and which has been abolished by the introduction of the gospel. The veil is upon their hearts, and prevents the light of the glory of God from shining into them; "But we all," says the apostle, speaking of believers in Christ, "with open face," without any veil, "beholding as in a glass the glory of God, are changed into the same image from glory to glory, as by the Spirit of the Lord," 2 Cor. iii. 18.

CHAPTER 35

Moses assembles the congregation to deliver to them the commandments of God, 1. Directions concerning the Sabbath, 2-3. Freewill offerings of gold, silver, brass, etc., for the Tabernacle, 4-7. Of oil and spices, 8. Of precious stones, 9. Proper artists to be employed, 10. The Tabernacle and its tent, 11. The ark, 12. Table of the shewbread, 13. Candlestick, 14. Altar of incense, 15. Altar of burnt offering, 16. Hangings, pins, etc., 17-18. Cloths of service, and holy vestments, 19. The people cheerfully bring their ornaments as offerings to the Lord, 20-22; together with blue, purple, scarlet, etc., etc., 23-24. The women spin, and bring the produce of their skill and industry, 25-26. The rulers bring precious stones, etc., 27-28. All the people offer willingly, 29. Bezaleel and Aholiab appointed to conduct and superintend all the work of the Tabernacle, for which they are qualified by the spirit of wisdom, 30-35.

1. *And Moses gathered.* The principal subjects in this chapter have been already largely considered in the notes on chapters xxv, xvi, xxvii, xxviii, xxix, xxx, and xxxi, and to those the reader is particularly desired to refer, together with the parallel texts in the margin.

3. *Ye shall kindle no fire.* The Jews understand this precept as forbidding the kindling of fire only for the purpose of doing work or dressing victuals; but to give them light and heat they judge it lawful to light a fire on the Sabbath day, though themselves rarely kindle it—they get Christians to do this work for them.

5. *An offering.* A *terumah* or heave offering; see Lev. vii. 1, etc.

5 and 6. See on these metals and colors, chap. xxv. 3-4, etc.

7. *Rams' skins, etc.* See on chap. xxv. 5.

8. *Oil for the light.* See chap. xxv. 6.

9. *Onyx stones.* See chap. xxv. 7.

11. *The tabernacle.* See chap. xxv. 8.

12. *The ark.* See chap. xxv. 10-17.

13. *The table.* See chap. xxv. 23-28.

14. *The candlestick.* See chap. xxv. 31-39.

15. *The incense altar.* The golden altar, see chap. xxx. 1-10.

16. *The altar of burnt offering.* The brazen altar, see chap. xxvii. 1-8.

17. *The hangings of the court.* See chap. xxvii. 9.

19. *The cloths of service.* Probably aprons, towels, and suchlike, used in the common service, and different from the vestments for Aaron and his sons. See these latter described, chap. xxviii. 1, etc.

21. *Every one whose heart stirred him up.* Literally, "whose heart was lifted up"—whose affections were set on the work, being cordially engaged in the service of God.

22. *As many as were willing hearted.* For no one was forced to lend his help in this sacred work; all was a freewill offering to the Lord. *Bracelets. Chach,* whatever "hooks together"; ornaments for the wrists, arms, legs, or neck. *Earrings. Nezem,* see this explained, Gen. xxiv. 22. *Rings. Tabbaath,* from *taba,* to "penetrate, enter into"; probably rings for the fingers. *Tablets. Cumaz,* a word only used here and in Num. xxxi. 50, supposed to be a girdle to support the breasts.

25. *All the women that were wise hearted did spin.* They had before learned this art, they were wisehearted; and now they practice it, and God condescends to require and accept their services. In building this house of God, all were ambitious to do something by which they might testify their piety to God, and their love for His worship. The spinning practiced at this time was simple, and required little apparatus. It was the plain distaff or twirling pin, which might be easily made out of any wood they met with in the wilderness.

27. *The rulers brought onyx stones.* These, being persons of consequence, might be naturally expected to furnish the more scarce and costly articles. See how all join in this service! The men worked and brought offerings; the women spun and brought their ornaments; the rulers united with them, and delivered up their jewels; and all the children of Israel "brought a willing offering unto the Lord," v. 29.

CHAPTER 36

Moses appoints Bezaleel, Aholiab, and their associates, to the work, and delivers to them the freewill offerings of the people, 1-3. The people bring offerings more than are needed for the work, and are restrained only by the proclamation of Moses, 4-7. The curtains, their loops, taches, etc., for the Tabernacle, 8-18. The covering for the tent, 19. The boards, 20-30. The bars, 31-34. The veil and its pillars, 35-36. The hangings and their pillars, 37-38.

1. *Then wrought.* The first verse of this chapter should end the preceding chapter, and this should begin with the second verse; as it now stands, it does not make a very consistent sense. By reading the first word *veasah, then wrought,* in the future tense instead of the past, the proper connection will be preserved; for all

grammarians know that the conjunction *vau* is often *conversive,* i.e., it turns the preterite tense of those verbs to which it is prefixed into the future, and the future into the preterite. This power it evidently has here; and joined with the last verse of the preceding chapter the connection will appear thus, chap. xxxv. 30, etc.: "The Lord hath called by name Bezeleel . . . and Aholiab . . . them hath he filled with wisdom of heart, to work all manner of work." Chap. xxxvi. 1: And Bezaleel and Aholiab shall work, "and every wise hearted man, in whom the Lord put wisdom."

5. *The people bring much more than enough.* With what a liberal spirit do these people bring their freewill offerings unto the Lord! Moses is obliged to make a proclamation to prevent them from bringing any more, as there was at present more than enough! Had Moses been intent upon gain, and had he not been perfectly disinterested, he would have encouraged them to continue their contributions, as thereby he might have multiplied to himself gold, silver, and precious stones. But he was doing the Lord's work, under the inspiration of the Divine Spirit, and therefore he sought no secular gain. Everything necessary for the worship of God will be cheerfully provided by a people whose hearts are in that worship.

8. *Cherubims of cunning work.* See on chap. xxvi. 18. Probably the word means no more than figures of any kind wrought in the loom, or by the needle in embroidery, or by the chisel or graving tool in wood, stone, or metal; see on chap. xxv. 18. In some places the word seems to be restricted to express a particular figure then well-known; but in many other places it seems to imply any kind of figure commonly formed by sculpture on stone, by carving on wood, by engraving upon brass, and by weaving in the loom.

9. *The length of one curtain.* Concerning these curtains, see chap. xxvi. 1, etc.

20. *And he made boards.* See the notes on chap. xxvi. 15, etc.

31. *He made bars.* See on chap. xxvi. 26, etc.

35. *He made a veil.* See on chap. xxvi. 31, etc.

37. *Hanging for the . . . door.* See on chap. xxvi. 36.

38. *The five pillars of it with their hooks.* Their capitals. See the note on chap. xxvi. 32.

CHAPTER 37

Bezaleel and Aholiab make the ark, 1-5. The mercy seat, 6. The two cherubim, 7-9. The table of the shewbread, and its vessels, 10-16. The candlestick, 17-24. The golden altar of incense, 25-28. The holy anointing oil and perfume, 29.

1. *And Bezaleel made the ark.* For a description of the ark, see chap. xxv. 10, etc.

6. *He made the mercy seat.* See this described in chap. xxv. 17.

10. *He made the table.* See chap. xxv. 23.

16. *He made the vessels.* See all these particularly described in the notes on chap. xxv. 29.

17. *He made the candlestick.* See this described in the note on chap. xxv. 31.

25. *He made the incense altar.* See this described in chap. xxx. 1.

29. *He made the holy anointing oil.* See this and the *perfume,* and the materials out of which they were made, described at large in the notes on chap. xxx. 23-25 and 34-38.

CHAPTER 38

Bezaleel makes the altar of burnt offering, 1-7. He makes the laver and its foot out of the mirrors given by the women, 8. The court, its pillars, hangings, etc., 9-20. The whole Tabernacle and its work finished by Bezaleel, Aholiab, and their assistants, 21-23. The amount of the gold contributed, 24. The amount of the silver, and how it was expended, 25-28. The amount of the brass, and how this was used, 29-31.

1. *The altar of burnt offering.* See the notes on chap. xxvii. 1; and for its horns, pots, shovels, basins, etc., see the meaning of the Hebrew terms explained, chap. xxvii. 3-5.

8. *He made the laver.* See the notes on chap. xxx. 18, etc. *The lookingglasses.* The word *maroth,* from *raah,* "he saw," signifies reflectors or mirrors of any kind. Here metal, highly polished, must certainly be meant, as glass was not yet in use; and had it even been in use, we are sure that looking glasses could not make a brazen laver. The word, therefore, should be rendered "mirrors," not *lookingglasses,* which in the above verse is perfectly absurd, because from those *maroth* the brazen laver was made. *Of the women . . . which assembled at the door.* What the employment of these women was at the door of the Tabernacle is not easily known. Some think they assembled there for purposes of devotion. Others, that they kept watch there during the night; and this is the most probable opinion, for they appear to have been in the same employment as those who assembled at the door of the Tabernacle of the congregation in the days of Samuel, who were abused by the sons of the high priest Eli, 1 Sam. ii. 22. Among the ancients women were generally employed in the office of porters or doorkeepers.

9. *The court.* See on chap. xxvii. 9.

17. *The hooks . . . and their fillets.* The capitals, and the silver bands that went round them; see the note on chap. xxvi. 32.

21. *This is the sum of the tabernacle.* That is, the foregoing account contains a detail of all the articles which Bezaleel and Aholiab were commanded to make; and which were reckoned up by the Levites, over whom Ithamar, the son of Aaron, presided.

24. *All the gold that was occupied for the work,* etc. The total value of all the *gold, silver,* and *brass* of the Tabernacle will amount to 244,127£ 14s. 6d. And the total weight of all these three metals amounts to 29,124 pounds troy, which, reduced to avoirdupois weight, is nearly ten tons and a half. When all this is considered, besides the quantity of gold which was employed in the golden calf, and which was all destroyed, it is no wonder that the sacred text should say the Hebrews spoiled the Egyptians, particularly as in those early times the precious metals were in probably not very plentiful in Egypt.

26. *A bekah for every man.* The Hebrew word *beka,* from *baka,* to "divide, separate into two," seems to signify, not a particular coin, but a shekel broken or cut in two; so, anciently, our farthing was a penny divided in the midst and then subdivided, so that each division contained the fourth part of the penny; hence its name *fourthing* or *fourthling,* since corrupted into "farthing."

CHAPTER 39

Bezaleel makes the cloths of service for the holy place, and the holy garments, 1. The ephod, 2. Gold is beaten into plates, and cut into wires for embroidery, 3. He makes the shoulder pieces of the ephod, 4. The curious girdle, 5. Cuts the onyx stones for the shoulder pieces, 6. Makes the breastplate, its chains, ouches, rings, etc., 7-21. The robe of the ephod, 22-26. Coats of fine linen, 27. The mitre, 28. The girdle, 29. The plate of the holy crown, 30-31. The completion of the work of the Tabernacle, 32. All the work is brought unto Moses, 33-41. Moses, having examined the whole, finds everything done as the Lord had commanded, in consequence of which he blesses the people, 42-43.

1. *Blue, and purple, and scarlet.* See this subject explained in the notes on chap. xxv. 4.

2. *Ephod.* See this described, chap. xxv. 7.

3. *They did beat the gold into thin plates.* For the purpose, as it is supposed, of cutting it into wires or threads; for to "twist" or "twine" is the common acceptation of the root *pathal.* I cannot suppose that the Israelites had not then the art of making gold thread, as they possessed several ornamental arts much more difficult.

6. *Onyx stones.* See chap. xxv. 7; xxviii. 17; etc.

8. *Breastplate.* See on chap. xxviii. 18.

10. *And they set in it four rows of stones.* See all these precious stones particularly explained in the notes on chap. xxviii. 17, etc.

23. *As the hole of an habergeon.* The *habergeon* was a small coat of mail, something in form of a half shirt, made of small iron rings curiously united together. It covered the neck and breast, was very light, and resisted the stroke of a sword. Sometimes it went over the whole head as well as over the breast. This kind of defensive armor was used among the Asiatics, particularly the ancient Persians, among whom it is still worn.

30. *The holy crown of pure gold.* On Asiatic monuments, particularly those that appear in the ruins of Persepolis and on many Egyptian monuments, the priests are represented as wearing crowns or tiaras, and sometimes their heads are crowned with laurel.

32. *Did according to all that the Lord commanded Moses.* This refers to the command given in chap. xxv. 40; and Moses has taken care to repeat everything in the most circumstantial detail, to show that he had conscientiously observed all the directions he had received.

37. *The pure candlestick.* See the note on chap. xxv. 31. *The lamps to be set in order.* To be trimmed and fresh oiled every day for the purpose of being lighted in the evening. See the note on chap. xxvii. 21.

43. *And Moses did look upon all the work.* As being the general superintendent of the whole, under whom Bezaleel and Aholiab were employed, as the other workmen were under them. *They had done it as the Lord had commanded.* Exactly according to the pattern which Moses received from the Lord, and which he laid before the workmen to work by. *And Moses blessed them.* Gave them that praise which was due to their skill, diligence, and fidelity. See this meaning of the original word in the note on Gen. ii. 3. It is very probable that Moses prayed to God in their behalf that they might be prospered in all their undertakings, saved from every evil, and be brought at last to the inheritance that fadeth not away. This blessing seems to have been given, not only to the workmen, but to all the people. The people contributed liberally, and the workmen wrought faithfully, and the blessing of God was pronounced upon all.

CHAPTER 40

Moses is commanded to set up the Tabernacle, the first day of the first month of the second year of their departure from Egypt, 1-2. The ark to be put into it, 3. The table and candlestick to be brought in also with the golden altar, 4-5. The altar of burnt offering to be set up before the door, and the laver between the tent and the altar, 6-7. The court to be set up, 8. The Tabernacle and its utensils to be anointed, 9-11. Aaron and his sons to be washed, clothed, and anointed, 12-15. All these things are done accordingly, 16. The Tabernacle is erected; and all its utensils, etc., placed in it on the first of the first month of the second year, 17-33. The cloud covers the tent, and the glory of the Lord fills the Tabernacle, so that even Moses is not able to enter, 34-35. When they were to journey, the cloud was taken up; when to encamp, the cloud rested on the Tabernacle, 36-37. A cloud by day and a fire by night was upon the Tabernacle, in the sight of all the Israelites, through the whole course of the journeyings, 38.

2. *The first day of the first month.* It is generally supposed that the Israelites began the work of the Tabernacle about the sixth month after they had left Egypt; and as the work was finished about the end of the first year of their exodus (for it was set up the first day of the second year), that therefore they had spent about six months in making it. Such a building, with such a profusion of curious and costly workmanship, was never put up in so short a time. But it was the work of the Lord, and the people did service as unto the Lord; for the people had a mind to work.

4. *Thou shalt bring in the table, and set in order the things.* That is, Thou shalt place the twelve loaves upon the table in the order before mentioned. See the note on chap. xxv. 30.

15. *For their anointing shall surely be an everlasting priesthood.* By this anointing a right was given to Aaron and his family to be high priests among the Jews forever; so that all who should be born of this family should have a right to the priesthood without the repetition of this unction, as they should enjoy this honor in their father's right, who had it by a particular grant from God. But it appears that the high priest, on his consecration, did receive the holy unction; see Lev. iv. 3; vi. 22; xxi. 10. And this continued till the destruction of the first Temple, and the Babylonish captivity; and according to Eusebius, Cyril of Jerusalem, and others, this custom continued among the Jews to the advent of our Lord, after which there is no evidence it was ever practiced. The Jewish high priest was a type of Him who is called the "high priest over the house of God," Heb. x. 21; and when He came, the functions of the other necessarily ceased.

19. *He spread abroad the tent over the tabernacle.* By the *tent,* in this and several other places, we are to understand the coverings made of rams' skins, goats' hair, etc., which were thrown over the building; for the Tabernacle had no other kind of roof.

20. *And put the testimony into the ark.* That is, the two tables on which the Ten Commandments had been written. See chap. xxv. 16. The ark, the golden table with the shewbread, the golden candlestick, and the golden altar of incense, were all in the Tabernacle, "within the veil" or curtains, which served as a door, vv. 22, 24, 26. And the altar of burnt offering was "by the door," v. 29. And the brazen laver, between the tent of the congregation and the brazen altar, v. 30; still farther outward, that it might be the first thing the priests met with when entering into the court to minister, as their

hands and feet must be washed before they could perform any part of the holy service, vv. 31-32. When all these things were thus placed, then the *court* that surrounded the Tabernacle, which consisted of posts and hangings, was set up, v. 33.

34. *Then a cloud covered the tent.* Thus God gave His approbation of the work; and as this was visible, so it was a sign to all the people that Jehovah was among them. *And the glory of the Lord filled the tabernacle.* How this was manifested we cannot tell; it was probably by some light or brightness which was insufferable to the sight, for Moses himself could not enter in because of the cloud and the glory, v. 35. Precisely the same happened when Solomon had dedicated his Temple; for it is said that "the cloud filled the house of the Lord, so that the priests could not stand to minister because of the cloud: for the glory of the Lord had filled the house of the Lord," 1 Kings viii. 10-11. Previously to this the cloud of the divine glory had rested upon that tent which Moses had pitched without the camp, after the transgression in the matter of the molten calf; but now the cloud removed from that tabernacle and rested upon this one, which was made by the command and under the direction of God himself. And there is reason to believe that this Tabernacle was pitched in the center of the camp, all the twelve tribes pitching their different tents in a certain order around it.

36. *When the cloud was taken up.* The subject of these last three verses has been very largely explained in the notes on chap. xiii. 21, to which, as well as to the general remarks on that chapter, the reader is requested immediately to refer.

38. *For the cloud of the Lord was upon the tabernacle by day.* This daily and nightly appearance was at once both a merciful providence and a demonstrative proof of the divinity of their religion: and these tokens continued with them *throughout all their journeys;* for, notwithstanding their frequently repeated disobedience and rebellion, God never withdrew these tokens of His presence from them, till they were brought into the Promised Land. When, therefore, the Tabernacle became fixed, because the Israelites had obtained their inheritance, this mark of the divine presence was no longer visible in the sight of all Israel, but appears to have been confined to the holy of holies, where it had its fixed residence upon the mercy seat between the cherubim; and in this place continued till the first Temple was destroyed, after which it was no more seen in Israel till God was manifested in the flesh.

The Book of

LEVITICUS

The Greek version of the Septuagint and the Vulgate Latin have given the title of Leviticus to the third book of the Pentateuch, and the name has been retained in almost all the modern versions. The book was thus called because it treats principally of the laws and regulations of the *Levites* and priests in general. In Hebrew it is termed *Vaiyikra,* "And he called," which is the first word in the book, and which, as in preceding cases, became the running title to the whole. It contains an account of the ceremonies to be observed in the offering of burnt sacrifices; meat, peace, and sin offerings; the consecration of priests, together with the institution of the three grand national festivals of the Jews, the Passover, Pentecost, and Tabernacles, with a great variety of other ecclesiastical matters. It seems to contain little more than the history of what passed during the eight days of the consecration of Aaron and his sons, though Archbishop Ussher supposes that it comprises the history of the transactions of a whole month, namely, from April 21 to May 21, which answers to the first month of the second year after the departure from Egypt.

CHAPTER 1

The Lord calls to Moses out of the Tabernacle, and gives him directions concerning burnt offerings of the beef kind, 1-2. The burnt offering to be a male without blemish, 3. The person bringing it to lay his hands upon its head, that it might be accepted for him, 4. He is to kill, flay, and cut it in pieces, and bring the blood to the priests, that they might sprinkle it round about the altar, 5-6 All the pieces to be laid upon the altar and burnt, 7-9. Directions concerning offerings of the smaller cattle, such as sheep and goats, 10-13. Directions concerning offerings of fowls, such as doves and pigeons, 14-17.

1. *And the Lord called unto Moses.* From the manner in which this book commences, it appears plainly to be a continuation of the preceding; and indeed the whole is but one law, though divided into five portions, and why thus divided is not easy to be conjectured.

Previously to the erection of the Tabernacle, God had given no particular directions concerning the manner of offering the different kinds of sacrifices; but as soon as this divine structure was established and consecrated, Jehovah took it as His dwelling place; described the rites and ceremonies which He would have observed in His worship, that His people might know what was best pleasing in His sight; and that, when thus worshipping Him, they might have confidence that they pleased Him, everything being done according to His own directions. A consciousness of acting according to the revealed will of God gives strong confidence to an upright mind.

2. *Bring an offering.* The word *korban,* from *karab,* "to approach or draw near," signifies an *offering* or "gift" by which a person had access unto God; and this receives light from the universal custom that prevails in the East, no man being permitted to approach the presence of a superior without a present or gift; and the offering thus brought was called *korban,* which properly means the "introduction offering," or "offering of access." *Of the cattle. Habbehemah,* animals of the beef kind, such as the bull, heifer, bullock, and calf; and restrained to these alone by the term *herd, bakar,* which, from its general use in the Levitical writings, is known to refer to the ox, heifer, etc. And therefore other animals of the beef kind were excluded. *Of the flock. Tson,* "sheep" and "goats"; for we have already seen that this term implies both kinds; and we know, from its use, that no other animal of the smaller, clean, domestic quadrupeds is intended, as no other animal of this class, besides the sheep and goat, was ever offered in sacrifice to God. The animals mentioned in this chapter as proper for sacrifice are the very same which God commanded Abraham to offer; see Gen. xv. 9. And thus it is evident that God delivered to the patriarchs an epitome of that law which was afterwards given in detail to Moses, the essence of which consisted in its sacrifices; and those sacrifices were of clean animals.

3. *Burnt sacrifice.* The most important of all the sacrifices offered to God; called by the Septuagint *holokautoma,* because it was "wholly consumed," which was not the case in any other offering. *His own voluntary will. Lirtsono,* "to gain himself acceptance" before the Lord. In this way all the versions appear to have understood the original words, and the connection in which they stand obviously requires this meaning.

4. *He shall put his hand upon the head of the burnt offering.* By the imposition of hands the person bringing the victim acknowledged, (1) The sacrifice as his own. (2) That he offered it is an atonement for his sins. (3) That he was worthy of death because he had sinned, having forfeited his life by breaking the law. (4) That he entreated God to accept the life of the innocent animal in place of his own. (5) And all this, to be done profitably, must have respect to Him whose life, in the fulness of time, should be made a sacrifice for sin. (6) The blood was to be sprinkled round about upon the altar, v. 5, as by the sprinkling of blood the atonement was made; for the blood was the life of the beast, and it was always supposed that life went to redeem life.

6. *He shall flay.* Probably meaning the person who brought the sacrifice, who, according to some of the rabbins, killed, flayed, cut up, and washed the sacrifice, and then presented the parts and the blood to the priest, that he might burn the one, and sprinkle the other upon the altar. But it is certain that the priests also, and the Levites, flayed the victims, and the priest had the skin to himself; see chap. vii. 8, and 2 Chron. xxix. 34.

7. *Put fire.* The fire that came out of the Tabernacle from before the Lord, and which was kept perpetually burning; see chap. ix. 24. Nor was it lawful to use any other fire in the service of God. See the case of Nadab and Abihu, chap. x.

8. *The priests . . . shall lay the parts.* The sacrifice was divided according to its larger joints. The sacred fire was then applied, and the whole mass was consumed. This was the *holocaust,* or complete burnt offering.

9. *An offering . . . of a sweet savour.* A "fire offering, an odor of rest," or, as the Septuagint express it, "a sacrifice for a sweet-smelling savor"; which place St. Paul had evidently in view when he wrote Eph. v. 2: "Christ . . . hath loved us, and hath given himself for us an offering and a sacrifice to God for a sweet-smelling savour," where he uses the same terms as the Septuagint. Hence we find that the *holocaust,* or burnt offering, typified the sacrifice and death of Christ for the sins of the world.

16. *Pluck away his crop with his feathers.* In this sacrifice of fowls the head was violently wrung off, then the blood was poured out, then the feathers were plucked off, the breast was cut open, and the crop, stomach, and intestines taken out, and then the body was burnt. Though the bird was split up, yet it was not divided asunder.

CHAPTER 2

The meat offering of flour with oil and incense, 1-3. The oblation of the meat offering baked in the oven and in the pan, 4-6. The meat offering baked in the frying pan, 7-10. No leaven nor honey to be offered with the meat offering, 11. The oblation of the firstfruits, 12. Salt to be offered with the meat offering, 13. Green ears dried by the fire, and corn to be beaten out of full ears, with oil and frankincense, to be offered as a meat offering of firstfruits, 14-16.

1. *Meat offering. Minchah.* There are *five* kinds of the *minchah* mentioned in this chapter. (1) *Soleth,* simple flour or meal, v. 1. (2) Cakes and wafers, or whatever was baked in the oven, v. 4. (3) Cakes baked in the pan, v. 5. (4) Cakes baked on the frying pan, or probably, a gridiron, v. 7. (5) Green ears of corn parched, v. 14. All these were offered without honey or leaven, but accompanied with wine, oil, and frankincense. It is very likely that the *minchah,* in some or all of the above forms, was the earliest oblation offered to the Supreme Being, and probably was in use before sin entered into the world, and consequently before bloody sacrifices had been ordained. The *minchah* of green ears of corn dried by the fire was properly the gratitude offering for a good seedtime, and the prospect of a plentiful harvest. This appears to have been the offering brought by Cain, Gen. iv. 3. The *flour,* whether of wheat, rice, barley, rye, or any other grain, was in all likelihood equally proper; for in Num. v. 15, we find the flour of barley, or barley meal, is called *minchah.* It is plain that in the institution of the *minchah* no animal was here included, though in other places it seems to include both kinds; but in general the *minchah* was not a bloody offering, nor used by way of

atonement or expiation, but merely in a eucharistic way, expressing gratitude to God for the produce of the soil.

2. *His handful of the flour.* This was for a *memorial*, to put God in mind of His covenant with their fathers, and to recall to their minds His gracious conduct towards them and their ancestors. In this case a handful only was burnt, the rest was reserved for the priest's use; but all the frankincense was burnt, because from it the priest could derive no advantage.

4. *Baken in the oven.* Tannur, from *nar*, to "split, divide," says Mr. Parkhurst; and hence the *oven*, because of its burning, dissolving, and melting heat.

5. *Baken in a pan.* Machabath, supposed to be a flat iron plate, placed over the fire; such as is called a griddle in some countries.

7. *The fryingpan.* Marchesheth, supposed to be a shallow earthen vessel like a *fryingpan*, used not only to fry in, but for other purposes.

8. *Thou shalt bring the meat offering.* It is likely that the person himself who offered the sacrifice brought it to the priest, and then the priest presented it before the Lord.

11. *No meat offering . . . shall be made with leaven.* See the reason of this prohibition in the note on Exod. xii. 8. *Nor any honey.* Because it was apt to produce acidity, as some think, when wrought up with flour paste; or rather because it was apt to prove purgative. On this latter account the College of Physicians have totally left it out of all medicinal preparations.

13. *With all thine offerings thou shalt offer salt.* Salt was the opposite to leaven, for it preserved from putrefaction and corruption, and signified the purity and persevering fidelity that were necessary in the worship of God. Everything was seasoned with it, to signify the purity and perfection that should be extended through every part of the divine service and through the hearts and lives of God's worshippers. It was called the *salt of the covenant of thy God*, because as salt is incorruptible, so was the covenant made with Abram, Isaac, Jacob, and the patriarchs, relative to the redemption of the world by the incarnation and death of Jesus Christ.

14. *Green ears of corn dried by the fire.* Green or half-ripe ears of wheat parched with fire is a species of food in use among the poor people of Palestine and Egypt to the present day. As God is represented as keeping a table among His people (for the Tabernacle was His house, where He had the golden table, shewbread, etc.), so He represents himself as partaking with them of all the aliments that were in use, and even sitting down with the poor to a repast on parched corn!

CHAPTER 3

The law of the peace offering in general, 1-5. That of the peace offering taken from the flock, 6-11; and the same when the offering is a goat, 12-17.

1. *Peace offering.* Shelamim, an offering to make peace between God and man.

2. *Lay his hand upon the head of his offering.* See this rite explained on Exod. xxix. 10, and chap. i. 4. "As the *burnt offering* (chap. i)," says Mr. Ainsworth, "figured our reconciliation

to God by the death of Christ, and the *meat offering* (chap. ii), our sanctification in him before God, so this *peace offering* signified both Christ's oblation of himself whereby he became our *peace* and salvation (Eph. ii. 14-16; Acts xiii. 47; Heb. v. 9; ix. 28), and our oblation of praise, thanksgiving, and prayer unto God."

5. *Aaron's sons shall burn it.* As the fat was deemed the most valuable part of the animal, it was offered in preference to all other parts.

9. *The whole rump, it shall he take off hard by the backbone.* The "tails" of the Eastern sheep (note on Exod. xxix. 22).

11. *It is the food of the offering.* We have already remarked that God is frequently represented as feasting with His people on the sacrifices they offered; and because these sacrifices were consumed by that fire which was kindled from heaven, therefore they were considered as the food of that fire, or rather of the Divine Being who was represented by it.

12. *A goat.* Implying the whole species, he-goat, she-goat, and kid, as we have already seen.

17. *That ye eat neither fat nor blood.* It is not likely that the *fat* should be forbidden in the same manner and in the same latitude as the *blood.* The blood was the life of the beast, and that was offered to make an atonement for their souls; consequently, this was never eaten in all their generations. But it was impossible to separate the fat from the flesh, which in many parts is so intimately intermixed with the muscular fibers. By the fat, therefore, mentioned here and in the preceding verse, we may understand any fat that exists in a separate or unmixed state.

CHAPTER 4

The law concerning the sin offering for transgressions committed through ignorance, 1-2. For the priest thus sinning, 3-12. For the sins of ignorance of the whole congregation, 13-21. For the sins of ignorance of a ruler, 22-26. For the sins of ignorance of any of the common people, 27-35.

2. *If a soul shall sin through ignorance.* That is, if any man shall do what God has forbidden, or leave undone what God has commanded, through ignorance of the law relative to these points; as soon as the transgression or omission comes to his knowledge he shall offer the sacrifice here prescribed, and shall not suppose that his *ignorance* is an excuse for his sin.

3. *If the priest that is anointed.* Meaning, most probably the high priest. *According to the sin of the people;* for although he had greater advantages than the people could have, in being more conversant with the law of God, yet it was possible even for him to transgress through ignorance; and his transgression might have the very worst tendency, because the people might be thereby led into sin. Hence several critics understand this passage in this way, and translate it thus: "If the anointed priest shall lead the people to sin"; or, literally, "If the anointed priest shall sin to the sin of the people"; that is, so as to cause the people to transgress, the shepherd going astray, and the sheep following after him.

4. *Lay his hand upon the bullock's head.* See on chap. i. 4.

6. *Seven times.* See the note on Exod. xxix. 30. The blood of this sacrifice was applied in

three different ways: (1) The priest put his finger in it, and sprinkled it seven times before the veil, v. 6. (2) He put some of it on the horns of the altar of incense. (3) He poured the remaining part at the bottom of the altar of burnt offerings, v. 7.

12. *Without the camp.* This was intended figuratively to express the sinfulness of this sin, and the availableness of the atonement. The sacrifice, as having the sin of the priest transferred from himself to it by his confession and imposition of hands, was become unclean and abominable, and was carried, as it were, out of the Lord's sight; from the Tabernacle and congregation it must be carried without the camp, and thus its own offensiveness was removed, and the sin of the person in whose behalf it was offered. The apostle (Heb. xiii. 11-13) applies this in the most pointed manner to Christ: "For the bodies of those beasts, whose blood is brought into the sanctuary by the high priest for sin, are burned without the camp. Wherefore Jesus also, that he might sanctify the people with his own blood, suffered without the gate. Let us go forth therefore unto him without the camp, bearing his reproach."

13. *If the whole congregation of Israel sin.* This probably refers to some oversight in acts of religious worship, or to some transgression of the letter of the law, which arose out of the peculiar circumstances in which they were then found, such as the case mentioned in 1 Sam. xiv. 32, etc., where the people, through their long and excessive fatigue in their combat with the Philistines, being faint, "flew on the spoil, and took sheep, and oxen, and calves, and slew them on the ground: and . . . did eat them with the blood"; and this was partly occasioned by the rash adjuration of Saul mentioned in v. 24: "Cursed be the man that eateth any food until evening." The sacrifices and rites in this case were the same as those prescribed in the preceding, only here the elders of the congregation, i. 3., three of the Sanhedrim, according to Maimonides, laid their hands on the head of the victim in the name of all the congregation.

22. *When a ruler hath sinned.* Under the term *nasi* it is probable that any person is meant who held any kind of political dignity among the people, though the rabbins generally understand it of the king. *A kid of the goats* was the sacrifice in this case, the rites nearly the same as in the preceding cases, only the fat was burnt as that of the peace offering. See v. 26, and chap. iii. 5.

27. *The common people. Am haarets,* "the people of the land," that is, any individual who was not a priest, king, or ruler among the people; any of the poor or ordinary sort. Any of these, having transgressed through ignorance, was obliged to bring a lamb or a kid, the ceremonies being nearly the same as in the preceding cases. The original may denote the very lowest of the people, the laboring or agricultural classes.

CHAPTER 5

Concerning witnesses who, being adjured, refuse to tell the truth, 1. Of those who contract defilement by touching unclean things or persons, 2-3. Of those who bind themselves by vows or oaths, and do not fulfil them, 4-5. The trespass offering prescribed in such cases, a lamb or a kid, 6; a turtledove or two young pigeons, 7-10; or an ephah of fine flour with oil and frankincense, 11-13. Other laws relative to trespasses, through ignorance in holy things, 14-16. Of trespasses in things unknown, 17-19.

1. *If a soul sin.* It is generally supposed that the case referred to here is that of a person who, being demanded by the civil magistrate to answer upon oath, refuses to tell what he knows concerning the subject; such a one *shall bear his iniquity*—shall be considered as guilty in the sight of God of the transgression which he has endeavored to conceal, and must expect to be punished by Him for hiding the iniquity to which he was privy, or suppressing the truth which, being discovered, would have led to the exculpation of the innocent, and the punishment of the guilty.

2. *Any unclean thing.* Either the dead body of a clean animal or the living or dead carcass of any unclean creature. All such persons were to wash their clothes and themselves in clean water, and were considered as unclean till the evening, chap. xi. 24-31. But if this had been neglected, they were obliged to bring a trespass offering. What this meant, see in the notes on chap. vii.

4. *To do evil, or to do good.* It is very likely that rash promises are here intended; for if a man vow to do an act that is evil, though it would be criminal to keep such an oath or vow, yet he is guilty because he made it, and therefore must offer the trespass offering. If he neglect to do the good he has vowed, he is guilty, and must in both cases confess his iniquity, and bring his trespass offering.

5. *He shall confess that he hath sinned.* Even restitution was not sufficient without this confession, because a man might make restitution without being much humbled; but the confession of sin has a direct tendency to humble the soul, and hence it is so frequently required in the Holy Scriptures, as without humiliation there can be no salvation.

7. *If he be not able to bring a lamb.* See the conclusion of chap. i.

10. *He shall offer the second for a burnt offering.* The pigeon for the burnt offering was wholly consumed, it was the Lord's property; that for the sin offering was the priest's property, and was to be eaten by him after its blood had been partly sprinkled on the side of the altar, and the rest poured out at the bottom of the altar. See also chap. vi. 26.

11. *Tenth part of an ephah.* About three quarts. The ephah contained a little more than seven gallons and a half.

15. *In the holy things of the Lord.* This law seems to relate particularly to sacrilege, and defrauds in spiritual matters; such as the neglect to consecrate or redeem the firstborn, the withholding of the firstfruits, tithes, and suchlike; and, according to the rabbins, making any secular gain of divine things, keeping back any part of the price of things dedicated to God, or witholding what man had vowed to pay. *With thy estimation.* The wrong done or the defraud committed should be estimated at the number of shekels it was worth, or for which it would sell. These the defrauder was to pay down, to which he was to add a fifth part more, and bring a ram without blemish for a sin offering besides. There is an obscurity in the text, but this seems to be its meaning.

16. *Shall make amends.* Make restitution for the wrong he had done according to what is laid down in the preceding verse.

19. *He hath certainly trespassed.* And because he hath sinned, therefore he must bring a sacrifice. On no other ground shall he be accepted by the Lord.

CHAPTER 6

Laws relative to detention of property intrusted to the care of another, to robbery, and deceit, 1-2; finding of goods lost, keeping them from their owner, and swearing falsely, 3. Such a person shall not only restore what he has thus unlawfully gotten, but shall add a fifth part of the value of the property besides, 4-5; and bring a ram without blemish, for a trespass offering to the Lord, 6-7. Laws relative to the burnt offering and the perpetual fire, 8-13. Law of the meat offering, and who may lawfully eat of it, 14-18. Laws relative to the offerings of Aaron and his sons and their successors, on the day of their anointing, 19-23. Laws relative to the sin offering, and those who might eat of it, 24-30.

2. *Lie unto his neighbour.* This must refer to a case in which a person delivered his property to his neighbor to be preserved for him, and took no witness to attest the delivery of the goods; such a person therefore might deny that he had ever received such goods, for he who had deposited them with him could bring no proof of the delivery. On the other hand, a man might accuse his neighbor of detaining property which had never been confided to him, or, after having been confided, had been restored again; hence the law here is very cautious on these points. And because in many cases it was impossible to come at the whole truth without a direct revelation from God, which should in no common case be expected, the penalties are very moderate; for in such cases, even when guilt was discovered, the man might not be so criminal as appearances might intimate. See the law concerning this laid down and explained on Exod. xxii. 7, etc.

3. *Have found that which was lost.* The Roman lawyers laid it down as a sound maxim of jurisprudence "that he who found any property and applied it to his own use should be considered as a thief whether he knew the owner or not; for in their view the crime was not lessened, supposing the finder was totally ignorant of the right owner."

5. *All that about which he hath sworn falsely.* That supposes the case of a man who, being convicted by his own conscience, comes forward and confesses his sin. *Restore it in the principal.* The property itself if still remaining, or the full value of it, to which a fifth part more was to be added.

8. *And the Lord spake unto Moses.* At this verse the Jews begin the twenty-fifth section of the law; and here, undoubtedly, the sixth chapter should commence, as the writer enters upon a new subject, and the preceding verses belong to the fifth chapter. The best edited Hebrew Bibles begin the sixth chapter at this verse.

9. *This is the law of the burnt offering.* This law properly refers to that burnt offering which was daily made in what was termed the morning and evening sacrifice; and as he had explained the nature of this burnt offering in general, with its necessary ceremonies, as far as the persons who brought them were concerned, he now takes up the same in relation to the priests who were to receive them from the hands of the offerer, and present them to the Lord on the altar of burnt offerings.

Because of the burning upon the altar all night. If the burnt offering were put all upon the fire at once, it could not be burning all night. We may therefore reasonably conclude that the priests sat up by turns the whole night, and fed the fire with portions of this offering till the whole was consumed, which they would take care to lengthen out till the time of the morning sacrifice. The same we may suppose was done with the morning sacrifice; it was also consumed by piecemeal through the whole day, till the time of offering the evening sacrifice. Thus there was a continual offering by fire unto the Lord; and hence in v. 13 it is said: "The fire shall ever be burning upon the altar; it shall never go out."

11. *And put on other garments.* The priests approached the altar in their holiest garments; when carrying the ashes from the altar, they put on other garments, the holy garments being only used in the holy place. *Clean place.* A place where no dead carcasses, dung, or filth of any kind was laid; for the ashes were holy, as being the remains of the offerings made by fire unto the Lord.

13. *The fire shall ever be burning.* See on v. 9 and v. 20. In imitation of this perpetual fire, the ancient Persian Magi, and their descendants the Parsees, kept up a perpetual fire; the latter continue it to the present day.

15. *His handful, of the flour.* An omer of flour, which was the tenth part of an ephah, and equal to about three quarts of our measure, was the least quantity that could be offered even by the poorest sort, and this was generally accompanied with a log of oil, which was a little more than half a pint. This quantity both of flour and oil might be increased at pleasure, but no less could be offered.

20. *In the day when he is anointed.* Not only in that day, but from that day forward, for this was to them and their successors a statute forever. See v. 22.

23. *For every meat offering for the priest shall be wholly burnt.* Whatever the priest offered was wholly the Lord's and, therefore, must be entirely consumed. The sacrifices of the common people were offered to the Lord, but the priests partook of them; and thus they who ministered at the altar were fed by the altar. Had the priests been permitted to live on their own offerings as they did on those of the people, it would have been as if they had offered nothing, as they would have taken again to themselves what they appeared to give unto the Lord.

25. *In the place where the burnt offering is killed.* The place here referred to was the north side of the altar. See chap. i. 11.

26. *The priest . . . shall eat it.* From the expostulation of Moses with Aaron, chap. x. 17, we learn that the priest, by eating the sin offering of the people, was considered as bearing their sin, and typically removing it from them; and besides, this was a part of their maintenance, or what the Scripture calls their inheritance; see Ezek. xliv. 27-30. This was afterwards greatly abused; for improper persons endeavored to get into the priest's office merely that they might get a secular provision, which is a horri-

ble profanity in the sight of God. See 1 Sam. ii. 36; Jer. xxiii. 1-2; Ezek. xxxiv. 2-4; and Hos. iv. 8.

28. *The earthen vessel . . . shall be broken.* Calmet states that this should be considered as implying the vessels brought by individuals to the court of the Temple or Tabernacle, and not of the vessels that belonged to the priests for the ordinary service. That the people dressed their sacrifices sometimes in the court of the Tabernacle, he gathers from 1 Sam. ii. 13-14, to which the reader is desired to refer.

In addition to what has been already said on the different subjects in this chapter, it may be necessary to notice a few more particulars. The perpetual meat offering, *minchah tamid,* v. 20, the perpetual fire, *esh tamid,* v. 13, and the perpetual burnt offering, *olath tamid,* Exod. xxix. 42, all cast much light on Heb. vii. 25, where it is said, Christ "is able also to save them to the uttermost [perpetually, to all intents and purposes] that come unto God by him, seeing he ever liveth [He is perpetually living] to make intercession for them"; in which words there is a manifest allusion to the perpetual *minchah,* the perpetual fire, and the perpetual burnt offering, mentioned here by Moses. As the *minchah* or gratitude offering should be perpetual, so our gratitude for the innumerable mercies of God should be perpetual. As the burnt offering must be perpetual, so should the sacrifice of our blessed Lord be considered as a perpetual offering, that all men, in all ages, should come unto God through Him who is ever living, in His sacrificial character, to make intercession for men. And as the fire on the altar must be perpetual, so should the influences of the Holy Spirit in every member of the Church, and the flame of pure devotion in the hearts of believers, be ever energetic and permanent.

CHAPTER 7

The law of the trespass offering, and the priest's portion in it, 1-7. As also in the sin offerings and meat offerings, 8-10. The law of the sacrifice of peace offering, 11, whether it was a thanksgiving offering, 12-15; or a vow or voluntary offering, 16-18. Concerning the flesh that touched any unclean thing, 19-20, and the person who touched anything unclean, 21. Laws concerning eating of fat, 22-25, and concerning eating of blood, 26-27. Further ordinances concerning the peace offerings and the priest's portion in them, 28-36. Conclusion of the laws and ordinances relative to burnt offerings, meat offerings, sin offerings, and peace offerings, delivered in this and the preceding chapter, vv. 37-38.

2. *In the place where they kill the burnt offering.* Namely, on the north side of the altar, chap. i. 11.

3. *The rump.* See the notes on chap. iii. 9, where the principal subjects in this chapter are explained, being nearly the same in both.

4. *The fat that is on them.* Chiefly the fat that was found in a detached state, not mixed with the muscles.

9. *Baken in the oven.* See the notes on chap. ii. 5, etc.

15. *He shall not leave any of it until the morning.* Because in such a hot country it was apt to putrefy, and as it was considered to be holy, it would have been very improper to expose that to putrefaction which had been consecrated to the Divine Being.

20. *Having his uncleanness upon him.* Having touched any unclean thing by which he became legally defiled, and had not washed his clothes, and bathed his flesh.

21. *The uncleanness of man.* Any ulcer, sore, or leprosy; or any sort of cutaneous disorder, either loathsome or infectious.

23. *Fat, of ox, or of sheep, or of goat.* Any other fat they might eat, but the fat of these was sacred, because they were the only animals which were offered in sacrifice, though many others ranked among the clean animals as well as these. But it is likely that this prohibition is to be understood of these animals when offered in sacrifice, and then only in reference to the inward fat, as mentioned on v. 4. Of the fat in any other circumstances it cannot be intended, as it was one of the especial blessings which God gave to the people. "Butter of kine, and milk of sheep, with fat of lambs, and rams of the breed of Bashan, and goats" were the provision that He gave to His followers. See Deut. xxxii. 12-14.

27. *Whatsoever soul . . . that eateth any manner of blood.* See the note on Gen. ix. 4. *Shall be cut off*—excommunicated from the people of God, and so deprived of any part in their inheritance, and in their blessings. See the note on Gen. xvii. 14.

29. *Shall bring his oblation.* Meaning those things which were given out of the peace offerings to the Lord and to the priest.

30. *Wave offering.* See on Exod. xxix. 27.

32. *The right shoulder.* See on Exod. xxix. 27.

36. *In the day that he anointed them.* See the note on Exod. xl. 15.

38. *In the wilderness of Sinai.* These laws were probably given to Moses while he was on the mount with God; the time was quite sufficient, as he was there with God not less than fourscore days in all; forty days at the giving, and forty days at the renewing of the law.

As in the course of this book the different kinds of sacrifices commanded to be offered are repeatedly occurring, I think it best, once for all, to give a general account of them, and a definition of the original terms, as well as of all others relative to this subject which are used in the Old Testament, and the reference in which they all stood to the great sacrifice offered by Christ.

(1) *Asham, trespass offering,* from *asham,* to be "guilty, or liable to punishment"; for in this sacrifice the guilt was considered as being transferred to the animal offered up to God, and the offerer redeemed from the penalty of his sin, v. 37. Christ is said to have made His soul an offering for sin, Isa. liii. 10.

(2) *Ishsheh, fire offering,* probably from *ash-ash,* to be "grieved, angered, inflamed"; either pointing out the distressing nature of sin, or its property of incensing divine justice against the offender, who, in consequence, deserving burning for his offense, made use of this sacrifice to be freed from the punishment due to his transgression. It occurs in Exod. xxix. 18, and in many places of this book.

(3) *Habhabim, iterated or repeated offerings,* from *yahab,* to "supply." The word occurs only in Hos. viii. 13, and probably means no more than the continual repetition of the accustomed offerings, or continuation of each part of the sacred service.

(4) *Zebach, a sacrifice,* a creature slain in sacrifice, from *zabach,* to "slay"; hence the altar on which such sacrifices were offered was termed *mizbeach,* the place of sacrifice. *Zebach* is a common name for sacrifices in general.

(5) *Chag,* a "festival," especially such as had a periodical return, from *chagag,* to "celebrate a festival, to dance round and round in circles." See Exod. v. 1; xii. 24.

(6) *Chattath* and *chattaah, sin offering,* from *chata,* to "miss the mark"; it also signifies sin in general, and is a very apt term to express its nature by. A sinner is continually aiming at and seeking happiness; but as he does not seek it in God, hence the Scripture represents him as missing his aim, or missing the mark. This is precisely the meaning of the Greek word *hamartia,* translated "sin" and "sin offering" in our version; and this is the term by which the Hebrew word is translated by both the Septuagint and the inspired writers of the New Testament. The sin offering was an acknowledgment of guilt. This word often occurs.

(7) *Copher,* the expiation or atonement, from *caphar,* to "cover," or annul a contract. Used often to signify the atonement or expiation made for the pardon or cancelling of iniquity.

(8) *Moed,* an appointed *annual festival,* from *yaad,* to "appoint or constitute," signifying such feasts as were instituted in commemoration of some great event or deliverance, such as the deliverance from Egypt. See Exod. xiii. 10, and thus differing from the *chag* mentioned above. See the note on Gen. i. 14.

(9) *Milluim,* consecrations or *consecration offerings,* from *mala,* to "fill"; those offerings made in consecrations, of which the priests partook, or, in the Hebrew phrase, had their "hands filled," or which had filled the hands of them that offered them. See the note on Exod. xxix. 19; and see 2 Chron. xiii. 9.

(10) *Minchah, meat offering,* from *nach,* to "rest, settle" after toil. It generally consisted of things without life, such as green ears of corn, full ears of corn, flour, oil, and frankincense (see on chap. ii. 1, etc.); and may be considered as having its name from that "rest" from labor and toil which a man had when the fruits of the autumn were brought in, or when, in consequence of obtaining any rest, ease, etc., a significant offering or sacrifice was made to God. If sin occurs. See the note on Gen. iv. 3. The jealousy offering (Num. v. 15) was a simple *minchah,* consisting of barley meal only.

(11) *Mesech and mimsach, a mixture offering,* or mixed libation, called a *drink offering,* Isa. lv. 11, from *masach,* to "mingle"; it seems in general to mean old wine mixed with the lees, which made it extremely intoxicating. This offering does not appear to have had any place in the worship of the true God; but from Isa. lxv. 11 and Prov. xxiii. 30, it seems to have been used for idolatrous purposes.

(12) *Masseeth,* an oblation, things "carried" to the Temple to be presented to God, from *nasa,* to "bear or carry," to bear sin; typically, Exod. xxviii. 38; chap. x. 17; xvi. 21; really, Isa. liii. 4, 12. The sufferings and death of Christ were the true *masseeth* or vicarious bearing of the sins of mankind, as the passage in Isaiah above referred to sufficiently proves. This is alluded to by the Evangelist John, chap. i. 29.

(13) *Nedabah, freewill* or *voluntary offering;* from *nadab,* to be "free, liberal, princely." An offering not commanded, but given as a particular proof of extraordinary gratitude to God for especial mercies, or on account of some vow or engagement voluntarily taken, v. 16.

(14) *Nesech, libation,* or *drink offering,* from *nasach,* to "pour out." Water or wine poured out at the conclusion or confirmation of a treaty or covenant. To this kind of offering there is frequent allusion and reference in the New Testament, as it typified the blood of Christ poured out for the sin of the world; and to this our Lord himself alludes in the institution of the Holy Eucharist. The whole gospel economy is represented as a covenant or treaty between God and man, Jesus Christ being not only the Mediator, but the covenant Sacrifice, whose blood was poured out for the ratification and confirmation of this covenant or agreement between God and man.

(15) *Olah, burnt offering,* from *alah,* to "ascend," because this offering, as being wholly consumed, ascended as it were to God in smoke and vapor. It was a very expressive type of the sacrifice of Christ, as nothing less than His complete and full sacrifice could make atonement for the sin of the world. In most other offerings the priest, and often the offerer, had a share, but in the whole burnt offering *all* was given to God.

(16) *Ketoreth,* incense or perfume offering, from *katar,* to "burn," i.e., the frankincense, and other aromatics used as a perfume in different parts of the divine service. To this Paul compares the agreeableness of the sacrifice of Christ to God, Eph. v. 2: "Christ . . . hath given himself for us an offering . . . to God for a sweetsmelling savour." From Rev. v. 8 we learn that it was intended also to represent the prayers of the saints, which, offered up on the Altar, Christ Jesus, that sanctifies every gift, are highly pleasing in the sight of God.

(17) *Korban,* the *gift offering,* from *karab,* to "draw nigh or approach." See this explained on chap. i. 2. *Korban* was a general name for any kind of offering, because through these it was supposed a man had access to his Maker.

(18) *Shelamim, peace offering,* from *shalam,* to "complete, make whole"; for by these offerings that which was lacking was considered as being now made up, and that which was broken, viz., the covenant of God, by His creatures' transgression, was supposed to be made whole; so that after such an offering the sincere and conscientious mind had a right to consider that the breach was made up between God and it, and that it might lay confident hold on this covenant of peace. To this the apostle evidently alludes, Eph. ii. 14-19: "He is our peace [i.e., our *shalam* or Peace Offering], who hath made both one, and broken down the middle wall . . . having abolished in his flesh the enmity."

(19) *Todah, thank offering,* from *yadah,* to "confess"; offerings made to God with public confession of His power, goodness, mercy.

(20) *Tenuphah, wave offering,* from *naph,* to "stretch out"; an offering of the firstfruits stretched out before God, in acknowledgment of His providential goodness. This offering was moved from the right hand to the left.

(21) *Terumah, heave offering,* from *ram,* to "lift up," because the offering was lifted up towards heaven, as the wave offering, in token

of the kindness of God in granting rain and fruitful seasons, and filling the heart with food and gladness. As the wave offering was moved from right to left, so the heave offering was moved up and down; and in both cases this was done several times. These offerings had a blessed tendency to keep alive in the breasts of the people a due sense of their dependence on the divine providence and bounty, and of their obligation to God for His continual and liberal supply of all their wants.

CHAPTER 8

Moses is commanded to consecrate Aaron and his sons, 1-3. Moses convenes the congregation; washes, clothes, and anoints Aaron, 4-12. He also clothes Aaron's sons, 13. Offers a bullock for them as a sin offering, 14-17. And a ram for a burnt offering, 18-21. And another ram for a consecration offering, 22-24. The fat, with cakes of unleavened bread, and the right shoulder of the ram, he offers as a wave offering, and afterwards burns, 25-28. The breast, which was the part of Moses, he also waves, 29. And sprinkles oil and blood upon Aaron and his sons, 30. The flesh of the consecration ram is to be boiled and eaten at the door of the Tabernacle, 31-32. Moses commands Aaron and his sons to abide seven days at the door of the Tabernacle of the congregation, which they do accordingly, 33-36.

2. *Take Aaron and his sons.* The whole subject of this chapter has been anticipated in the notes on Exod. xxviii. 1, etc., and xxix. 1, etc., in which all the sacrifices, rites, and ceremonies have been explained in considerable detail. It is only necessary to observe that Aaron and his sons were not anointed until now. Before, the thing was commanded; now, first performed.

8. *He put in the breastplate the Urim and the Thummim.* The Urim and Thummim are here supposed to be something different from the breastplate itself. See the note on Exod. xxviii. 30.

14. *The bullock for the sin offering.* This was offered each day during the seven days of consecration. See Exod. xxix. 36.

23. *Put it upon the tip of Aaron's right ear.* See this significant ceremony explained in the note on Exod. xxix. 20.

27. *And waved them for a wave offering.* See the nature of this and the *heave offering* in the note on Exod. xxix. 27.

30. *And Moses took . . . the blood . . . and sprinkled it upon Aaron.* Thus we find that the high priest himself must be sprinkled with the blood of the sacrifice.

33. *For seven days shall he consecrate you.* This number was the number of perfection among the Hebrews; and the seven days' consecration implied a perfect and full consecration to the sacerdotal office. See the note on Exod. xxix. 30.

36. *So Aaron and his sons did.* This chapter shows the exact fulfillment of the commands delivered to Moses, Exodus xxix; and consequently the complete preparation of Aaron and his sons to fill the awfully important office of priests and mediators between God and Israel, to offer sacrifices and make atonement for the sins of the people.

CHAPTER 9

Aaron is commanded to offer, on the eighth day, a sin offering and a burnt offering, 1-2. The people are commanded also to offer a sin offering, a burnt offering, peace offerings, and a meat offering, 3-4. They do as they were commanded; and Moses promises that God shall

appear among them, 5-6. Aaron is commanded to make an atonement for the people, 7. He and his sons prepare and offer the different sacrifices, 8-21. Aaron and Moses bless the congregation, 22-23. And the fire of the Lord consumes the sacrifice, 24.

1. *On the eighth day.* This was the first day after their consecration, before which they were deemed unfit to minister in holy things, being considered as in a state of imperfection.

2. *Take thee a young calf.* As these sacrifices were for Aaron himself, they are furnished by himself and not by the people, for they were designed to make atonement for his own sin. See chap. iv. 3. And this is supposed by the Jews to have been intended to make an atonement for his sin in the matter of the golden calf. This is very probable, as no formal atonement for that transgression had yet been made.

3. *Take ye a kid.* In chap. iv. 14 a young bullock is commanded to be offered for the sin of the people; but here the offering is a *kid*, which was the sacrifice appointed for the sin of the ruler, chap. iv. 22-23, and hence some think that the reading of the Samaritan and the Septuagint is to be preferred. "Speak unto the elders of Israel," these being the only princes or rulers of Israel at that time; and for them it is possible this sacrifice was designed. It is however supposed that the sacrifice appointed in chap. iv. 14 was for a particular sin, but this for sin in general; and it is on this account that the sacrifices differ.

6. *And the glory of the Lord shall appear.* God shall give the most sensible signs of His presence among you; this He did in general by the cloud on the Tabernacle, but in this case the particular proof was the fire that came out from before the Lord, and consumed the burnt offering; see vv. 23-24.

7. *Make an atonement for thyself.* This showed the imperfection of the Levitical law; the high priest was obliged to make an expiation for his own sins before he could make one for the sins of the people. See the use made of this by the apostle, Heb. v. 3; vii. 27; ix. 7.

22. *And Aaron lifted up his hand toward the people, and blessed them.* On lifting up the hands in prayer, see Exod. ix. 29. The form of the blessing we have in Num. vi. 23, etc.: "The Lord bless thee, and keep thee: the Lord make his face shine upon thee, and be gracious unto thee: the Lord lift up his countenance upon thee, and give thee peace." *And came down from offering of the sin offering.* A sin offering, a burnt offering, a meat offering, and peace offerings, were made to God that His glory might appear to the whole congregation. This was the end of all sacrifice and religious service; not to confer any obligation on God, but to make an atonement for sin, and to engage Him to dwell among and influence His worshippers.

23. *Moses and Aaron went into the tabernacle.* It is supposed that Moses accompanied Aaron into the Tabernacle to show him how to offer the incense, prepare the lamps and the perfume, adjust the shewbread, etc. *And the glory of the Lord appeared.* To show that everything was done according to the divine mind, (1) The glory of Jehovah appeared unto all the people; (2) A fire came out from before the Lord, and consumed the burnt offering. This was the proof which God gave upon extraordinary occasions of His acceptance of the sacrifice.

24. *When all the people saw, they shouted, and fell on their faces.* (1) The miracle was done in such a way as gave the fullest conviction to the people of its reality. (2) They exulted in the thought that the God of almighty power and energy had taken up His abode among them. (3) They prostrated themselves in His presence, thereby intimating the deep sense they had of His goodness, of their unworthiness, and of the obligation they were under to live in subjection to His authority, and obedience to His will. This celestial fire was carefully preserved among the Israelites till the time of Solomon, when it was renewed, and continued among them till the Babylonish captivity. This divine fire was the emblem of the Holy Spirit. And as no sacrifice could be acceptable to God which was not "salted," i.e., as our Lord says, Mark ix. 49, so no soul can offer acceptable sacrifices to God but through the influences of the Divine Spirit. Hence the promise of the Spirit under the emblem of fire, Matt. iii. 11, and its actual descent in this similitude on the Day of Pentecost, Acts ii. 3-4.

CHAPTER 10

Nadab and Abihu offer strange fire before the Lord, and are destroyed, 1-5. Aaron and his family forbidden to mourn for them, 6-7. He and his family are forbidden the use of wine, 8-11. Directions to Aaron and his sons concerning the eating of the meat offerings, etc., 12-15. Moses chides Aaron for not having eaten the sin offering, 16-18. Aaron excuses himself, and Moses is satisfied, 19-20.

1. *And Nadab and Abihu . . . took either of them his censer.* In the preceding chapter we have seen how God intended that every part of His service should be conducted; and that every sacrifice might be acceptable to Him. He sent His own fire as the emblem of His presence, and the means of consuming the sacrifice. Here we find Aaron's sons neglecting the divine ordinance, and offering incense with strange, that is, common, fire—fire not of a celestial origin; and therefore the fire of God consumed them. So that very fire which, if properly applied, would have sanctified and consumed their gift, becomes now the very instrument of their destruction!

Which he commanded them not. Every part of the religion of God is divine. He alone knew what He designed by its rites and ceremonies, for that which they prefigured—the whole economy of redemption by Christ—was conceived in His own mind, and was out of the reach of human wisdom and conjecture. He therefore who altered any part of this representative system, who omitted or added anything, assumed a prerogative which belonged to God alone, and was certainly guilty of a very high offense against the wisdom, justice, and righteousness of his Maker. This appears to have been the sin of Nadab and Abihu, and this at once shows the reason why they were so severely punished. The most awful judgments are threatened against those who either add to, or take away from, the declarations of God. See Deut. iv. 2; Prov. xxx. 6; and Rev. xxii. 18-19.

3. *And Aaron held his peace.* "And Aaron was dumb." How elegantly expressive is this of his parental affection, his deep sense of the presumption of his sons, and his own submission to the justice of God!

4. *Uzziel the uncle of Aaron.* He was brother to Amram, the father of Aaron; see Exod. vi. 18-22.

6. *Uncover not your heads.* They were to use no sign of grief or mourning: (1) Because those who were employed in the service of the sanctuary should avoid everything that might incapacitate them for that service; and (2) Because the crime of their brethren was so highly provoking to God, and so fully merited the punishment which *He* had inflicted, that their mourning might be considered as accusing the divine justice of undue severity.

7. *The anointing oil of the Lord is upon you.* They were consecrated to the divine service, and this required their constant attendance and most willing and cheerful service.

9. *Strong drink.* The word *shechar*, from *shachar*, to "inebriate," signifies any kind of fermented liquors. This is exactly the same prohibition that was given in the case of *John Baptist*, Luke i. 15: "Wine and sikera he shall not drink." Any inebriating liquor, says Jerome, is called *sicera*, whether made of corn, apples, honey, dates, or other fruit.

10. *That we may put difference between holy and unholy.* This is a strong reason why they should drink no inebriating liquor, that their understanding being clear, and their judgment correct, they might always be able to discern between the clean and the unclean, and ever pronounce righteous judgment.

14. *Wave breast and heave shoulder.* See chap. vii, and on Exod. xxix. 27.

16. *Moses diligently sought the goat.* The goat which was offered the same day for the sins of the priests and the people (see chap. ix. 15-16) and which, through the confusion that happened on account of the death of Nadab and Abihu, was burned instead of being eaten. See v. 18.

19. *And such things have befallen me.* The excuse which Aaron makes for not feasting on the sin offering according to the law is at once appropriate and dignified; as if he had said: "God certainly has commanded me to eat of the sin offering; but when such things as these have happened unto me, could it be good in the sight of the Lord? Does He not expect that I should feel as a father under such afflicting circumstances?" With this spirited answer Moses was satisfied.

20. *When Moses heard that, he was content.* The argument used by Aaron had in it both good sense and strong reason, and Moses, as a reasonable man, felt its force; and as God evidenced no kind of displeasure at this irregularity, which was, in a measure at least, justified by the present necessity, he thought proper to urge the matter no further.

CHAPTER 11

Laws concerning clean and unclean animals, 1-2. Of quadrupeds, those are clean which divide the hoof and chew the cud, 3. Those to be reputed unclean which do not divide the hoof, though they chew the cud, 4-6. Those to be reputed unclean also which, though they divide the hoof, do not chew the cud, 7. Whosoever eats their flesh, or touches their carcasses, shall be reputed unclean, 8. Of fish, those are clean and may be eaten which have fins and scales, 9. Those which have no fins and scales to be reputed unclean, 10-12. Of fowls, those which are unclean, 13-21. Of insects, the following may be eaten: the bald locust, beetle, and grasshopper, 22.

All others are unclean and abominable, their flesh not to be eaten, nor their bodies touched, 23-25. Further directions relative to unclean beasts, 26-28. Of reptiles, and some small quadrupeds, those which are unclean, 29-30. All that touch them shall be unclean, 31; and the things touched by their dead carcasses are unclean also, 32-35. Large fountains, or pits of water, are not defiled by their carcasses, provided a part of the water be drawn out, 36. Nor do they defile seed by accidentally touching it, provided the water which has touched their flesh do not touch or moisten the seed, 37-38. A beast that dieth of itself is unclean, and may not be touched or eaten, 39-40. All creeping things are abominable, 41-44. The reason given for these laws, 45-47.

1. *And the Lord spake unto Moses.* Having delivered the law against drinking wine, Moses proceeds to deliver a series of ordinances, all well calculated to prevent the Israelites from mixing with the surrounding nations, and consequently from being contaminated by their idolatry. In chap. xi he treats of unclean meats. In chaps. xii, xiii, xiv, and xv he treats of unclean persons, garments, and dwellings. In chap. xvi he treats of the uncleanness of the priests and the people, and prescribes the proper expiations and sacrifices for both. In chap. xvii he continues the subject, and gives particular directions concerning the mode of offering. In chap. xviii he treats of unclean matrimonial connections. In chap. xix he repeats sundry laws relative to these subjects, and introduces some new ones. In chap. xx he mentions certain uncleannesses practiced among the idolatrous nations, and prohibits them on pain of death. In chap. xxi he treats of the mourning, marriages, and personal defects of the priests, which rendered them unclean. And in chap. xxii he speaks of unclean sacrifices, or such as should not be offered to the Lord. After this, to the close of the book, many important and excellent political and domestic regulations are enjoined, the whole forming an ecclesiastico-political system superior to anything the world ever saw.

3. *Whatsoever parteth the hoof, and is cloven-footed.* These two words mean the same thing—a divided hoof, such as that of the ox, where the hoof is divided into two toes, and each toe is cased with horn. *Cheweth the cud.* Ruminates; casts up the grass which had been taken into the stomach for the purpose of mastication.

5. *The coney.* Shaphan, not the rabbit, but rather a creature nearly resembling it, which abounds in Judea, Palestine, and Arabia.

6. *The hare.* Arnebeth, as Bochart and others suppose, from arah, to "crop," and nib, the "produce of the ground," these animals being remarkable for destroying the fruits of the earth. That they are notorious for destroying the tender blade of the young corn is well known. It is very likely that different species of these animals are included under the general terms shaphan, and arnebeth, for some travellers have observed that there are four or five sorts of these animals, which are used for food in the present day in those countries.

7. *And the swine.* Chazir, one of the most gluttonous, libidinous, and filthy quadrupeds in the universe; and because of these qualities sacred to the Venus of the Greeks and Romans, and the Friga of our Saxon ancestors; and perhaps on these accounts forbidden, as well as on account of its flesh being strong and difficult to digest, affording a very gross kind of aliment, apt to produce disorders, especially in hot climates.

9. *Whatsoever hath fins and scales.* Because these, of all the fish tribe, are the most nourishing; the others which are without scales, or whose bodies are covered with a thick, glutinous matter, being in general very difficult of digestion.

13. *And these . . . among the fowls . . . the eagle.* Nesher, from nashar, to "lacerate, cut, or tear to pieces"; hence the *eagle*, a most rapacious bird of prey, from its tearing the flesh of the animals it feeds on; and for this purpose birds of prey have, in general, strong, crooked talons and a hooked beak. *The ossifrage.* Or bone-breaker, from os, a "bone," and frango, "I break," because it not only strips off the flesh, but breaks the bone in order to extract the marrow. In Hebrew it is called peres, from paras, to "break or divide in two," and probably signifies that species of the eagle anciently known by the name of ossifraga, and which we render "ossifrage." *Ospray.* Ozniyah, from azan, to be "strong, vigorous"; generally supposed to mean the black eagle, such as that described by Homer, *Iliad*, lib. xxi, v. 252. "Having the rapidity of the black eagle, that bird of prey, at once the swiftest and the strongest of the feathered race." Among the Greeks and Romans the eagle was held sacred, and is represented as carrying the thunderbolts of Jupiter.

14. *The vulture.* Daah, from the root "to fly," and therefore more probably the kite or glede, from its remarkable property of gliding or sailing with expanded wings through the air. The *daah* is a different bird from the *daiyah*, which signifies the vulture. *The kite.* Aiyah, thought by some to be the vulture. That it is a species of the hawk, most learned men allow.

15. *Every raven.* Oreb, a general term comprehending the raven, crow, rook, jackdaw, and magpie.

16. *The owl.* Bath haiyaanah, the "daughter of vociferation," the female ostrich, probably so called from the noise it makes. *The night hawk.* Tachmas, from chamas, to "force away, act violently and unjustly"; supposed by Bochart to signify the male ostrich, from its cruelty towards its young (see Job xxxix. 17-19); but others, with more reason, suppose it to be the bird described by Hasselquist, which he calls the Oriental owl. *The cuckow.* Shachaph, supposed rather to mean the sea mew; called shachaph, from shachepheth, a "wasting distemper," or "atrophy" (mentioned in chap. xxvi. 16; Deut. xxviii. 22), because its body is the leanest, in proportion to its bones and feathers, of most other birds, always appearing as if under the influence of a wasting distemper. *And the hawk.* Nets, from the root natsah, to "shoot forth or spring forward," because of the rapidity and length of its flight, the hawk being remarkable for both. As this is a bird of prey, it is forbidden, and all others of its kind.

17. *The little owl.* Cos, the bittern, night raven or night owl, according to most interpreters. *The cormorant.* Shalach, from the root which signifies to "cast down"; hence the Septuagint, the "cataract," or bird which falls precipitately down upon its prey. It probably signifies the diver, a sea fowl, which I have seen at sea dart down as swift as an arrow into the water and seize the fish which it had discovered while even flying, or rather soaring, at a very great height. *The great owl.* Yanshuph, ac-

cording to the Septuagint and the Vulgate, signifies the ibis, a bird well known and held sacred in Egypt.

18. *The swan. Tinshemeth.* The Septuagint translate the word by *porphyrion,* "purple" or "scarlet" bird. Could we depend on this translation, we might suppose the flamingo or some such bird to be intended. *The pelican. Kaath.* As *kaah* signifies to "vomit up," the name is supposed to be descriptive of the pelican, who receives its food into the pouch under its lower jaw, and, by pressing it on its breast with its bill, throws it up for the nourishment of its young. *The gier eagle. Racham.* As the root of this word signifies "tenderness" and "affection," it is supposed to refer to some bird remarkable for its attachment to its young; hence some have thought that the pelican is to be understood.

19. *The stork. Chasidah,* from *chasad,* which signifies "to be abundant in kindness, or exuberant in acts of beneficence"; hence applied to the stork, because of its affection to its young, and its kindness in tending and feeding its parents when old, facts attested by the best informed and most judicious of the Greek and Latin natural historians. It is remarkable for destroying and eating serpents, and on this account might be reckoned by Moses among *unclean* birds. *The heron. Anaphah.* This word has been variously understood: some have rendered it the kite, others the woodcock, others the curlew, some the peacock, others the parrot, and others the crane. The root, *anaph,* signifies to "breathe short" through the nostrils, to "snuff," as in anger; hence "to be angry"; and it is supposed that the word is sufficiently descriptive of the heron, from its very irritable disposition. It will attack even a man in defense of its nest; and I have known a case where a man was in danger of losing his life by the stroke of a heron's bill, near the eye, who had climbed up into a high tree to take its nest. *The lapwing. Duchiphath,* the hoop, a crested bird, with beautiful plumage, but very unclean. *The bat. Atalleph,* so called, according to Parkhurst, from *at,* to "fly," and *alaph,* "darkness or obscurity," because it flies about in the dusk of the evening, and in the night.

20. *All fowls that creep.* Such as the bat, already mentioned, which has claws attached to its leathern wings, and which serve in place of feet to crawl by, the feet and legs not being distinct; but this may also include all the different kinds of insects, with the exceptions in the following verse. *Going upon all four.* May signify no more than walking regularly or progressively, foot after foot as quadrupeds do; for it cannot be applied to insects literally, as they have in general six feet, many of them more, some reputed to have a hundred, hence called "centipedes."

21. *Which have legs above their feet.* This appears to refer to the different kinds of locusts and grasshoppers, which have very remarkable hind legs, long, and with high joints, projecting above their backs, by which they are enabled to spring up from the ground, and leap high and far.

22. *The locust. Arbeh,* either from *arab,* to "lie in wait or in ambush," because often immense flights of them suddenly alight upon the fields, vineyards, etc., and destroy all the produce of the earth; or from *rabah,* he "multiplied," because of their prodigious swarms. *The bald locust. Solam,* compounded, says Mr. Parkhurst, from *sala,* to "cut, break," and *am,* "contiguity"; a kind of locust, probably so called from its rugged, craggy form. *The beetle. Chargol.* "The Hebrew name seems a derivative from *charag,* to shake, and *regel,* the foot; and so to denote the nimbleness of its motions. Thus in English we call an animal of the locust kind a grasshopper."—Parkhurst. This word occurs only in this place. The *beetle* never can be intended here, as that insect never was eaten by man, perhaps, in any country of the universe. *The grasshopper. Chagab.* Bochart supposes that this species of locust has its name from the Arabic verb *hajaba,* to "veil"; because when they fly, as they often do, in great swarms, they eclipse even the light of the sun.

27. *Whatsoever goeth upon his paws. Cappaiv,* his "palms" or "hands," probably referring to those animals whose feet resemble the hands and feet of the human being, such as apes, monkeys, and all creatures of that genus; together with bears, frogs, etc.

29. *The weasel. Choled,* from *chalad,* to "creep in." Bochart conjectures, with great propriety, that the mole, not the weasel, is intended by the Hebrew word; its property of digging into the earth, and creeping or burrowing under the surface, is well known. *The mouse. Achbar.* Probably the large field rat. *The tortoise. Tsab.* Most critics allow that the tortoise is not intended here, but rather the crocodile, the frog, or the toad. The frog is most probably the animal meant, and all other creatures of its kind.

30. *The ferret. Anakah,* from *anak,* to "groan, to cry out"; a species of lizard which derives its name from its piercing, doleful cry. *The chameleon. Coach. Cach,* to be "strong, firm, vigorous"; it is probably the same with the mongoose, a creature still well known in India, where it is often domesticated in order to keep the houses free from snakes, rats, mice. *The lizard. Letaah.* Bochart contends that this also is a species of lizard, which creeps close to the ground, and is poisonous. *The snail. Chomet,* another species of lizard, according to Bochart, which lives chiefly in the sand. *The mole. Tinshameth,* from *nasham,* to "breathe." Bochart seems to have proved that this is the chameleon, which has its Hebrew name from its wide, gaping mouth, very large lungs, and its deriving its nourishment from small animals which float in the air, so that it has been conjectured by some to feed on the air itself. A bird of the same name is mentioned v. 13, which Bochart supposes to be the night owl.

32. *Any vessel of wood.* Such as the wooden bowls still in use among the Arabs. *Or raiment, or skin*—any baskets covered with skins, another part of the furniture of an Arab tent; the goatskins, in which they churn their milk, also may be intended. *Or sack*—any haircloth used for the purpose of transporting goods from place to place.

33. *And every earthen vessel.* Such pitchers as are commonly used for drinking out of and for holding liquids. M. De la Roque observes that hair sacks, trunks, and baskets, covered with skin, are used among the travelling Arabs

to carry their household utensils in, which are kettles or pots, great wooden bowls, hand mills, and pitchers. It is very likely that these are nearly the same with those used by the Israelites in their journeyings in the wilderness.

35. *Ranges for pots.* To understand this, we must observe that the Arabs dig a hole in their tent, about a foot and a half deep; three-fourths of this they lay about with stones, and the fourth part is left open for the purpose of throwing in their fuel.

36. *A fountain or pit.* This must either refer to running water, the stream of which soon carries off all impurities, or to large reservoirs where the water soon purifies itself; the water in either which touched the unclean thing being considered as impure, the rest of the water being clean.

37. *Any sowing seed.* If any part of an impure carcass fall accidentally on seed about to be sown, it shall not on that account be deemed unclean; but if the water put to the seed to prepare it for being sown shall be touched by such impure carcass, the seed shall be considered as unclean, v. 38. Probably this may be the meaning of these passages.

42. *Whatsoever goeth upon the belly.* This is the middle verse of the Pentateuch. Whatsoever *hath more feet.* Than four; that is, all many-footed reptiles, as well as those which go upon the belly having no feet, such as serpents; besides the four-footed smaller animals mentioned above.

44. *Ye shall . . . sanctify yourselves.* You shall keep yourselves separate from all the people of the earth, that *ye shall be holy; for I am holy.* And this was the grand design of God in all these prohibitions and commands; for these external sanctifications were only the emblems of the internal purity which the holiness of God requires here, and without which none can dwell with Him in glory hereafter.

CHAPTER 12

Ordinances concerning the purification of women after childbirth, 1; after the birth of a son, who is to be circumcised the eighth day, 2-3. The mother to be considered unclean for forty days, 4. After the birth of a daughter, fourscore days, 5. When the days of her purifying were ended, she was to bring a lamb for a burnt offering, and a young pigeon or a turtledove for a sin offering, 6-7. If poor, and not able to bring a lamb, she was to bring either two turtledoves or two young pigeons, 8.

3. *And in the eighth day.* Before this time the child could scarcely be considered as having strength sufficient to bear the operation; after this time it was not necessary to delay it as the child was not considered to be in covenant with God, and consequently not under the especial protection of the divine providence and grace, till this rite had been performed. Circumcision was to every man a constant, evident sign of the covenant into which he had entered with God, and of the moral obligations under which he was thereby laid. It was also a means of purity, and was especially necessary among a people naturally incontinent, and in a climate not peculiarly favorable to chastity.

4. *The blood of her purifying.* The term *purifying* here does not imply that there is anything impure in the blood at this time; on the contrary, the blood is pure, perfectly so, as to its quality, but is excessive in quantity.

6. *When the days of her purifying.* It is not easy to account for the difference in the times of purification, after the birth of a male and female child. After the birth of a boy the mother was considered unclean for forty days; after the birth of a girl, fourscore days. There is probably no physical reason for this difference. *She shall bring . . . a burnt offering, and . . . a sin offering.* It is likely that all these ordinances were intended to show man's natural impurity and original defilement by sin, and the necessity of an atonement to cleanse the soul from unrighteousness.

8. *And if she be not able to bring a lamb, then she shall bring two turtles, or two young pigeons.* As the Virgin Mary brought only the latter, hence it is evident that she was not able, i.e., she was not rich enough to provide the former; for such a holy woman would not have brought the less offering had she been capable of bringing the greater. How astonishing is this! The only Heir to the throne of David was not able to bring a lamb to offer in sacrifice to God!

The priest shall make an atonement for her. Every act of man is sinful, but such as proceed from the influence of the grace and mercy of God. Her sorrow in conception, and her pain in bringing forth children, reminded the woman of her original offense—an offense which deserved death, an offense which she could not expiate, and for which a sacrifice must be offered; and in reference to better things the life of an animal must be offered as a ransom for her life. And being saved in childbed, though she deserved to die, she is required, as soon as the days of her separation were ended, to bring a sacrifice according to her ability to the priest, that he might offer it to God as an atonement for her. Thus, wherever God keeps up the remembrance of *sin,* He keeps up also the memorial of *sacrifice,* to show that the state of a sinner, howsoever deplorable, is not hopeless, for that He himself has found out a ransom.

CHAPTER 13

Laws relative to the leprosy. It is to be known by a rising in the flesh, a scab, or a bright spot, 1-2. When the priest sees these signs he shall pronounce the man unclean, infected with the leprosy, and unfit for society, 3. Dubious or equivocal signs of this disorder, and how the person is to be treated in whom they appear, 4-8. In what state of this disorder the priest may pronounce a man clean or unclean, 9-13. Of the raw flesh, the sign of the unclean leprosy, 14-15. Of the white flesh, the sign of the leprosy called clean, 16-17. Of the leprosy which succeeds a boil, 18-20. Equivocal marks relative to this kind of leprosy, 21-22. Of the burning boil, 23. Of the leprosy arising out of the burning boil, 24-25. Equivocal marks relative to this kind of leprosy, 26-28. Of the plague on the head or in the beard, 29. Of the scall, and how it is to be treated, 30-37. Of the plague of the bright white spots, 38-39. Of the bald head, 40-41. Of the white reddish sore in the bald head, 42-44. The leper shall rend his clothes, put a patch on his upper lip, and cry, "Unclean," 45. He shall be obliged to avoid society, and live by himself without the camp, 46. Of the garments infected by the leprosy, and the signs of this infection, 47-52. Equivocal marks relative to this infection, and how the garment is to be treated, by washing or by burning, 53-58. Conclusion relative to the foregoing particulars, 59.

2. *The plague of leprosy.* This dreadful disorder has its name *leprosy* from the Greek *lepra,* from *lepis,* a "scale," because in this disease the body was often covered with thin, white scales, so as to give it the appearance of snow. Hence it is said of the hand of Moses, Exod. iv. 6, that it was "leprous as snow"; and of Miriam, Num. xii. 10, that she became "leprous, white as snow"; and of Gehazi, 2 Kings

v. 27, that, being judicially struck with the disease of Naaman, he went out from Elisha's presence "a leper as white as snow." In Hebrew this disease is termed *tsaraath,* from *tsara,* to "smite or strike."

There were three signs by which the leprosy was known: (1) A bright spot; (2) A rising (enamelling) of the surface; (3) A scab; the enamelled place producing a variety of layers, or stratum super stratum, of these scales.

3. *The priest shall . . . pronounce him unclean. Vetimme otho;* literally, "shall pollute him," i.e., in the Hebrew idiom, shall "declare or pronounce him polluted"; and in v. 23 it is said, "the priest shall pronounce him clean," *vetiharo haccohen,* the "priest shall cleanse him," i.e., "declare him clean." In this phrase we have the proper meaning of Matt. xvi. 19: "Whatsoever thou shalt bind on earth shall be bound in heaven: and whatsoever thou shalt loose on earth shall be loosed in heaven." By which our Lord intimates that the disciples, from having the "keys," i.e., the true knowledge of the doctrine, of the kingdom of Heaven, should, from particular evidences, be at all times able to distinguish between the clean and the unclean, the sincere and the hypocrite; and pronounce a judgment as infallible as the priest did in the case of the leprosy, from the tokens already specified.

13. *If the leprosy have covered all his flesh, he shall pronounce him clean.* Why is it that the partial leper was pronounced unclean, and the person totally covered with the disease clean? This was probably owing to a different species or stage of the disease; the partial disease was contagious, the total not contagious.

29. *A plague upon the head or the beard.* This refers to a disease in which, according to the Jews, the hair on either the head or the chin dropped out by the roots.

33. *The scall shall he not shave.* Lest the place should be irritated and inflamed, and assume in consequence other appearances besides those of a leprous infection, in which case the priest might not be able to form an accurate judgment.

45. *His clothes shall be rent.* The leprous person was required to be as one that mourned for the dead, or for some great and public calamity. He was to have his clothes rent in token of extreme sorrow; his head was to be made bare, the ordinary bonnet or turban being omitted; and he was to have a *covering upon his upper lip,* his jaws being tied up with a linen cloth, after the same manner in which the Jews bind up the dead. He was also to cry, *Unclean, unclean,* in order to prevent any person from coming near him, lest the contagion might be thus communicated and diffused through society.

47. *The garment also.* The whole account here seems to intimate that the garment was fretted by this contagion; and hence it is likely that it was occasioned by a species of small animals, which we know to be the cause of the itch; these, by breeding in the garments, must necessarily multiply their kind, and fret the garments, i.e., corrode a portion of the finer parts, after the manner of moths, for their nourishment. See v. 52.

52. *He shall therefore burn that garment.*

There being scarcely any means of radically curing the infection. It is well known that the garments infected by the itch animal have been known to communicate the disease even six or seven years after the first infection. This has been also experienced by the sorters of rags at some paper mills.

54. *He shall shut it up seven days more.* To give time for the spreading of the contagion, if it did exist there; that there might be the most unequivocal marks and proofs that the garment was or was not infected.

58. *It shall be washed the second time.* According to the Jews the first washing was to put away the plague, the second to cleanse it.

CHAPTER 14

Introduction to the sacrifices and ceremonies to be used in cleansing the leper, 1-3. Two living birds, cedarwood, scarlet, and hyssop, to be brought for him who was to be cleansed, 4. One of the birds to be killed, 5; and the living bird, with the cedarwood, scarlet, and hyssop, to be dipped in the blood, and to be sprinkled on him who had been infected with the leprosy, 6-7; after which he must wash his clothes, shave his head, eyebrows, beard, etc., bathe himself, tarry abroad seven days, 8-9; on the eighth day he must bring two he-lambs, one ewe-lamb, a tenth deal of flour, and a log of oil, 10; which the priest was to present as a trespass offering, wave offering, and sin offering before the Lord, 11-13. Afterwards he was to sprinkle both the blood and oil on the person to be cleansed, 14-18. The atonement made by these offerings, 19-20. If the person were poor, one lamb, with the flour and oil, two turtledoves, or two young pigeons, were only required, 21-22. These to be presented, and the blood and oil applied as before, 23-32. Laws and ordinances relative to houses infected by the leprosy, 33-48. An atonement to be made in order to cleanse the house, similar to that made for the healed leper, 49-53. A summary of this and the preceding chapter, relative to leprous persons, garments, and houses, 54-56. The end for which these different laws were given, 57.

3. *The priest shall go forth out of the camp.* As the leper was separated from the people, and obliged, because of his uncleanness, to dwell without the camp, and could not be admitted till the priest had declared that he was clean; hence it was necessary that the priest should go out and inspect him, and, if healed, offer for him the sacrifices required, in order to his readmission to the camp. As the priest alone had authority to declare a person clean or unclean, it was necessary that the healed person should show himself to the priest, that he might make a declaration that he was clean and fit for civil and religious society, without which, in no case, could he be admitted; hence, when Christ cleansed the lepers, Matt. viii. 2-4, He commanded them to go and show themselves to the priest.

4. *Two birds alive and clean.* Whether these birds were sparrows, or turtledoves, or pigeons, we know not; probably any kind of clean bird, or bird proper to be eaten, might be used on this occasion, though it is more likely that turtledoves or pigeons were employed, because these appear to have been the only birds offered in sacrifice. Of the cedarwood, hyssop, clean bird, and scarlet wool were made an instrument to *sprinkle* with. The cedarwood served for the handle; the hyssop and living bird were attached to it by means of the scarlet wool. The bird was so bound to this handle as that its tail should be downwards, in order to be dipped into the blood of the bird that had been killed. The whole of this made an instrument for the sprinkling of this blood, and when this business was done, the living bird was let loose, and permitted to go whithersoever it would.

5. *Over running water.* Literally, "living," that is, spring water. The meaning appears to be this: Some water was taken from a spring, and put into a clean earthen vessel, and they killed the bird over this water, that the blood might drop into it; and in this blood and water mixed they dipped the instrument before described, and sprinkled it seven times upon the person who was to be cleansed. The "living" or spring water was chosen because it was purer than what was taken from pits or wells, the latter being often in a putrid or corrupt state; for in a ceremony of purifying or cleansing, everything must be as pure and perfect as possible.

7. *Shall let the living bird loose.* The Jews teach that wild birds were employed on this occasion; no tame or domestic animal was used.

8. *And shave off all his hair.* That the water by which he was to be washed should reach every part of his body, that he might be cleansed from whatever defilement might remain on any part of the surface of his body.

10. *Two he lambs.* One for a trespass offering, v. 12, the other for a burnt offering, vv. 19-20. *One ewe lamb.* This was for a sin offering, v. 19. *Three tenth deals.* Three parts of an ephah, or three omers; see all these measures explained, Exod. xvi. 16. The *three tenth deals* of flour were for a *minchah,* meat or gratitude offering, v. 20. The sin offering was for his *impurity,* the trespass offering for his transgression, and the gratitude offering for his gracious cleansing. These constituted the offering which each was ordered to bring to the priest; see Matt. viii. 4.

12. *Wave offering.* See Exod. xxix. 27, and chap. vii., where the reader will find an ample account of all the various offerings and sacrifices used among the Jews.

21. *And if he be poor . . . he shall take one lamb.* There could be no cleansing without a sacrifice. On this ground the apostle has properly observed that "all things are by the law purged with blood"; and that "without shedding of blood [there] is no remission." Even if the person be poor, he must provide one lamb; this could not be dispensed with. So every soul to whom the word of divine revelation comes must bring that Lamb of God, which takes away the sin of the world. There is no redemption but in His blood.

34. *When ye be come into the land . . . and I put the plague of leprosy.* It was probably from this text that the leprosy has been generally considered to be a disease inflicted immediately by God himself; but it is well known that in Scripture God is frequently represented as doing what, in the course of His providence, He only permits or suffers to be done.

53. *He shall let go the living bird.* This might as well be called the "scape-bird"; as the goat, in chap. xvi., is called the scapegoat. The rites are similar in both cases, and probably had nearly the same meaning.

CHAPTER 15

Laws concerning uncleanness of men, 1-12. Mode of cleansing, 13-15. Of uncleanness, accidental and casual, 16-18. Laws concerning the uncleanness of women, 19-27. Mode of cleansing, 28-30. Recapitulation of the ordinances relative to the preceding cases, 31-33.

2. *When any man hath a running issue.* The cases of natural uncleanness, of both men and women, mentioned in this chapter, taken in a theological point of view, are not of such importance to us as to render a particular description necessary, the letter of the text being, in general, plain enough. The disease mentioned in the former part of this chapter appears to some to have been either the consequence of a very bad infection or of some criminal indulgence; for they find that it might be communicated in a variety of ways, which they imagine are here distinctly specified. On this ground the person was declared unclean, and all commerce and connection with him strictly forbidden. The Septuagint version renders *hazzab,* the man with the *issue,* by the man with a *gonorrhoea,* no less than nine times in this chapter; and that it means what in the present day is commonly understood by that disorder, taken not only in its mild but in its worst sense, they think there is little room to doubt. The disgraceful disorder referred to here is a foul blot which the justice of God in the course of providence has made in general the inseparable consequence of these criminal indulgences, and serves in some measure to correct and restrain the vice itself. In countries where public prostitution was permitted, where it was even a religious ceremony among those who were idolaters, this disease must necessarily have been frequent and prevalent. That the Israelites might have received it from the Egyptians, and that it must, through the Baal-peor and Ashteroth abominations which they learned and practiced, have prevailed among the Moabites, there can be little reason to doubt. Supposing this disease to be at all hinted at here, the laws and ordinances enjoined were at once wisely and graciously calculated to remove and prevent it. By contact, contagion of every kind is readily communicated; and to keep the whole from the diseased must be essential to the check and eradication of a contagious disorder. This was the wise and grand object of this enlightened Legislator in the ordinances which He lays down in this chapter.

11. *And whomsoever he toucheth.* Here we find that the saliva, sitting on the same seat, lying on the same bed, riding on the same saddle, or simple contact, was sufficient to render the person unclean, meaning, possibly, in certain cases, to communicate the disorder; and it is well known that in all these ways the contagion of this disorder may be communicated.

18. *They shall both bathe themselves.* What a wonderful tendency had these ordinances to prevent all excesses! The pains which such persons must take, the separations which they must observe, and the privations which, in consequence, they must be exposed to in the way of commerce, traffic, etc., would prevent them from making an unlawful use of lawful things.

24. In chap. xx. 18, persons guilty of this are condemned to death; here only to a seven days' separation; because, in the former case, Moses speaks of the act when both the man and the woman were acquainted with the situation; in the latter, he speaks of a case where the circumstance was not known till afterwards.

29. *Two turtles, or two young pigeons.* In all these cases moral pollution was ever considered as being less or more present, as even such infirmities sprang from the original defection of man. On these accounts sacrifices must be of-

fered; and in the case of the woman, one of the birds above mentioned must be sacrificed as a sin offering, the other as a burnt offering, v. 30.

31. *Thus shall ye separate the children of Israel from their uncleanness.* By this separation the cause became less frequent, and the contagion, if it did exist, was prevented from spreading. So fever wards are constructed for the purpose of separating the infected from the sound; and thus contagion is lessened, and its diffusion prevented. *That they die not.* That life may be prolonged by these prudential cares; and that he who is morally and legally unclean may not presume to enter into the Tabernacle of God till purified, lest he provoke divine justice to consume him, while attempting to worship with a polluted mind and impure hands.

CHAPTER 16

The solemn yearly expiation for the high priest, who must not come at all times into the holy place, 1-2. He must take a bullock for a sin offering, and a ram for a burnt offering, bathe himself, and be dressed in his sacerdotal robes, 3-4. He shall take two goats, one of which is to be determined by lot to be a sacrifice; the other to be a scapegoat, 5-10. He shall offer a bullock for himself and for his family, 11-14. And shall kill the goat as a sin offering for the people, and sprinkle its blood upon the mercy seat, and hallow the altar of burnt offerings, 15-19. The scapegoat shall be then brought, on the head of which he sh?ll lay his hands, and confess the iniquities of the children of Israel; after which the goat shall be permitted to escape to the wilderness, 20-22. After this Aaron shall bathe himself, and make a burnt offering for himself and for the people, 23-28. This is to be an everlasting statute, and the day on which the atonement is to be made shall be a sabbath, or day of rest, through all their generations, 29-34.

1. *After the death of the two sons of Aaron.* It appears from this verse that the natural place of this chapter is immediately after the tenth, where probably it originally stood; but the transposition, if it did take place, must be very ancient, as all the versions acknowledge this chapter in the place in which it now stands.

2. *That he come not at all times into the holy place.* By the holy place we are to understand here what is ordinarily called the "holy of holies," or "most holy place"; that place within the veil where the ark of the covenant, etc., were laid up; and where God manifested His presence between the cherubim. In ordinary cases the high priest could enter this place only once in the year, that is, on the day of annual atonement; but in extraordinary cases he might enter more frequently, viz., while in the wilderness, in decamping and encamping, he must enter to take down or adjust the things; and on solemn, pressing public occasions he was obliged to enter in order to consult the Lord. But he never entered without the deepest reverence and due preparation.

That it may appear that the grand subject of this chapter, the ordinance of the scapegoat, typified the death and resurrection of Christ, and the atonement thereby made, I beg leave to refer to Heb. ix. 7-12 and 24-26.

3. *With a young bullock for a sin offering.* The *bullock* was presented as a *sin offering* for himself, his family, the whole priesthood, and probably the Levites. The *ram* was for a *burnt offering*, to signify that he and his associates were wholly consecrated, and to be wholly employed in this work of the ministry. The ceremonies with which these two sacrifices were accompanied are detailed in the following verses.

4. *He shall put on the holy linen coat.* He was not to dress in his pontifical garments, but in the simple sacerdotal vestments, or those of the Levites, because it was a day of humiliation; and as he was to offer sacrifices for his own sins, it was necessary that he should appear in habits suited to the occasion. Hence he has neither the robe, the ephod, the breastplate, the mitre, etc.; these constituted his dress of dignity as the high priest of God, ministering for others and the representative of Christ. But now he appears before God as a sinner, offering an atonement for his transgressions, and his garments are those of humiliation.

7. *And he shall take the two goats.* It is allowed on all hands that this ceremony, taken in all its parts, pointed out the Lord Jesus dying for our sins and rising again for our justification; being put to death in the flesh, but quickened by the Spirit. *Two goats* are brought, one to be slain as a sacrifice for sin, the other to have the transgressions of the people confessed over his head, and then to be sent away into the wilderness. The animal by this act was represented as bearing away or carrying off the sins of the people. The two goats made only one sacrifice, yet only one of them was slain. One animal could not point out both the divine and human nature of Christ, nor show both His death and resurrection, for the goat that was killed could not be made alive. The divine and human natures in Christ were essential to the grand expiation; yet the human nature alone suffered, for the divine nature could not suffer; but its presence in the human nature, while agonizing unto death, stamped those agonies, and the consequent death, with infinite merit. The goat therefore that was slain prefigured His human nature and its death; the goat that escaped pointed out His resurrection. The one shows the atonement for sin, as the ground of justification; the other Christ's victory, and the total removal of sin in the sanctification of the soul.

8. *Aaron shall cast lots upon the two goats.* The Jews inform us that there were two *lots* made either of wood, stone, or any kind of metal. On one was written *lashshem*, "for the name," i.e., *Jehovah*, which the Jews will neither write nor pronounce; on the other was written *laazazel*, "for the scapegoat." Then they put the two lots into a vessel which was called *kalpey*, the goats standing with their faces towards the west. Then the priest came, and the goats stood before him, one on the right hand and the other on the left. The *kalpey* was then shaken, and the priest put in both his hands and brought out a lot in each. That which was in his right hand he laid on the goat that was on his right, and that in his left hand he laid on the goat that was on his left; and according to what was written on the lots, the scapegoat and the goat for sacrifice were ascertained. The determining of this solemn business by *lot*, the disposal of which is with the Lord, Prov. xvi. 33, shows that God alone was to select and point out the person by whom this great atonement was to be made; hence He says: "Behold, I lay in Sion a . . . stone elect [that is, chosen by himself], precious"—of infinite value.

10. *To be the scapegoat.* Azazel, from *az*, a "goat," and *azal*, to "dismiss"; the dismissed or sent-away goat, to distinguish it from the goat

that was to be offered in sacrifice. Most ancient nations had vicarious sacrifices, to which they transferred by certain rites and ceremonies the guilt of the community at large, in the same manner in which the scapegoat was used by the Jews.

21. *Aaron shall lay both his hands upon the head.* What this imposition of hands meant see in the notes on Exod. xxix. 10, and on chap. i. 4.

And confess over him all the iniquities . . . transgressions . . . sins. The three terms used here, *iniquities, avonoth,* from *avah,* to "pervert, distort, or turn aside"; *transgressions, peshaim,* from *pasha,* to "transgress, to rebel"; and *sins, chattaoth,* from *chata,* to "miss the mark," are supposed by the Jews to comprise everything that implies a breach of the divine law or an offense against God. Maimonides gives us the confession in the following words: "O Lord, thy people, the house of Israel, have sinned and done iniquity, and trespassed before thee. O Lord, make atonement now for the iniquities and transgressions and sins that thy people, the house of Israel, have sinned and transgressed against thee; as it is written in the law of Moses thy servant, saying: That in this day he shall make atonement for you, to cleanse you from all your sins before the Lord, and ye shall be clean."

When this confession was finished, the goat was sent by a proper hand to the wilderness, and there let loose; and nothing further was ever heard of it. Did not all this signify that Christ has so carried and borne away our sins that against them who receive Him as the only true atoning Sacrifice they should never more be brought to remembrance?

26. *He that let go the goat . . . shall wash.* Not only the person who led him away, but the priest who consecrated him, was reputed unclean, because the goat himself was unclean, being considered as bearing the sins of the whole congregation. On this account both the priest and the person who led him to the wilderness were obliged to wash their clothes and bathe themselves before they could come into the camp.

29. *The seventh month, on the tenth day of the month.* The commandment of fasting, and sanctifying this *tenth* day, is again repeated, chap. xxiii. 27-32; but in the last verse it is called the "ninth day . . . at even," because the Jewish day began with the evening. The sacrifices which the Day of Atonement should have more than other days are mentioned in Num. xxix. 7-11; and the jubilee which was celebrated every fiftieth year was solemnly proclaimed by sound of trumpet on this tenth day, chap. xxv. 8-9. This seventh month was Tisri, and answers to a part of our September and October.

CHAPTER 17

The people are commanded to bring all the cattle they intend to kill to the door of the Tabernacle, where they are to be made an offering to the Lord; and those who disobey are to be cut off, 1-5. The priest is to sprinkle the blood, 6. They are forbidden to offer sacrifices to devils, 7. The injunction to bring their offerings to the door of the Tabernacle is repeated, 8-9. The eating of blood is solemnly forbidden, 10. It is the life of the beast, and is given to make an atonement for their souls, 11-14. If a bird or beast be taken in hunting, its blood must be poured out and covered with dust, for the reasons before assigned, 13-14. None shall eat an animal that dies of itself or is torn by beasts; if any act otherwise he must bathe his clothes and his flesh, or bear his iniquity, 15-16.

4. *And bringeth it not unto the door.* As sacrifice was ever deemed essential to true religion, it was necessary that it should be performed in such a way as to secure the great purpose of its institution. God alone could show how this should be done so as to be pleasing in His sight, and therefore He has given the most plain and particular directions concerning it. The Israelites, from their long residence in Egypt, an idolatrous country, had doubtless adopted many of their usages; and many portions of the Pentateuch seem to have been written merely to correct and bring them back to the purity of the divine worship. *Blood shall be imputed unto that man.* Having poured out the blood improperly, he shall be considered as guilty of murder, because that blood, had it been properly and sacrificially employed, might have made atonement for the life of a man.

7. *They shall no more offer their sacrifices unto devils.* They shall not sacrifice *lasseirim,* to the "hairy ones," to goats. The famous heathen god, Pan, was represented as having the posteriors, horns, and ears of a goat. Herodotus says that all goats were worshipped in Egypt, but the he-goat particularly. *After whom they have gone a whoring.* Though this term is frequently used to express idolatry, yet we are not to suppose that it is not to be taken in a literal sense in many places in Scripture, even where it is used in connection with idolatrous acts of worship. It is well-known that Baalpeor and Ashtaroth were worshipped with unclean rites; and that public prostitution formed a grand part of the worship of many deities among the Egyptians, Moabites, Canaanites, Greeks, and Romans. The great god of the latter nations, Jupiter, was represented as the general corrupter of women.

11. *For the life of the flesh is in the blood.* This sentence, which contains a most important truth, had existed in the Mosaic writings for 3,600 [3,000] years before the attention of any philosopher was drawn to the subject. This is the more surprising, as the nations in which philosophy flourished were those which especially enjoyed the divine oracles in their respective languages. That the blood actually possesses a living principle, and that the life of the whole body is derived from it, is a doctrine of divine revelation, and a doctrine which the observations and experiments of the most accurate anatomists have served strongly to confirm. The proper circulation of this important fluid through the whole human system was first taught by Solomon in figurative language, Eccles. xii. 6; and discovered, as it is called, and demonstrated by Dr. Harvey in 1628, though some Italian philosophers had the same notion a little before. This accurate anatomist was the first who fully revived the Mosaic notion of the vitality of the blood; which notion was afterward adopted by the justly celebrated Dr. John Hunter, professor of anatomy in London, and fully established by him by a great variety of strong reasoning and accurate experiments.

15. *That which died of itself, or that which was torn.* Because, in both cases, the blood was retained in the body; hence the council at Jerusalem forbade "things strangled" as well as "blood," because in such beasts the blood was coagulated in the veins and arteries. See Acts xv. 28.

CHAPTER 18

The people are commanded to avoid the doings of the Egyptians and Canaanites, 1-3. They are to do God's judgments, and to keep His ordinances, that they may live, 4-5. Marriages with those who are near of kin are prohibited, 6. None to marry with his mother or step-mother, 7-8; with his sister or step sister, 9; with his granddaughter, 10; nor with the daughter of his step-mother, 11; nor with his aunt, by father or mother, 12-13; nor with his uncle's wife, 14; nor with his daughter-in-law, 15; nor sister-in-law, 16; nor with a woman and her daughter, son's daughter, or daughter's daughter, 17; nor with two sisters at the same time, 18. Several abominations prohibited, 19-23, of which the Canaanites, etc., were guilty, and for which they were cast out of the land, 24-25. The people are exhorted to avoid these abominations, lest they be treated as the ancient inhabitants of the land were treated, and so cast out, 26-28. Threatenings against the disobedient, 29, and promises to the obedient, 30.

6. *Any that is near of kin. Col shear besaro,* "any remnant of his flesh," i.e., to any particularly allied to his own family, the prohibited degrees in which are specified from the seventh to the seventeenth verse inclusive. Notwithstanding the prohibitions here, it must be evident that in the infancy of the world persons very near of kin must have been joined in matrimonial alliances, and that even brothers must have matched with their own sisters. This must have been the case in the family of Adam. In these first instances necessity required this; when this necessity no longer existed, the thing became inexpedient and improper for two reasons: (1) That the duties owing by nature to relatives might not be confounded with those of a social or political kind; for could a man be a brother and a husband, a son and a husband, at the same time, and fulfil the duties of both? (2) That by intermarrying with other families the bonds of social compact might be strengthened and extended, so that the love of our neighbor might at once be felt to be not only a maxim of sound policy, but also a very practicable and easy duty; and thus feuds, divisions, and wars be prevented.

16. *Thy brother's wife.* This was an illegal marriage, unless the brother died childless. In that case it was not only lawful for her to marry her brother-in-law, but he was obliged by the law, Deut. xxv. 5, to take her to wife.

18. *A wife to her sister.* You shall not marry two sisters at the same time, as Jacob did Rachel and Leah; but there is nothing in this law that rendered it illegal to marry a sister-in-law when her sister was dead; therefore the text says, Thou shalt not take her *in her life time, to vex her,* alluding probably to the case of the jealousies and vexations which subsisted between Leah and Rachel, and by which the family peace was so often disturbed. Some think that the text may be so understood as also to forbid polygamy.

21. *Pass through the fire to Molech.* The name of this idol is mentioned for the first time in this place. As the word *molech* or *melech* signifies "king" or "governor," it is very likely that this idol represented the sun; and more particularly as the fire appears to have been so much employed in his worship. There are several opinions concerning the meaning of passing through the fire to Molech. That some were actually burned alive to this idol several scriptures, according to the opinion of commentators, seem strongly to intimate; see, among others, Ps. cvi. 38; Jer. vii. 31; and Ezek. xxiii. 37-39. That others were only consecrated to his service

by passing between two fires the rabbins strongly assert; and if Ahaz had but one son, Hezekiah (though it is probable he had others, see 2 Chron. xxviii. 3), he is said to have passed through the fire to Molech, 2 Kings xvi. 3, yet he succeeded his father in the kingdom, chap. xviii. 1; therefore this could only be a consecration, his idolatrous father intending thereby to initiate him early into the service of this demon.

22. *With mankind.* This abominable crime [was] frequent among the Greeks and Romans as well as the Canaanites.

23. *Any woman stand before a beast.* That this was often done in Egypt there can be no doubt; and we have the testimony of Herodotus that a fact of this kind actually took place while he was in Egypt.

25. *The land itself vomiteth out her inhabitants.* This is a personification. Here the *land* is represented as an intelligent being, with a deep and refined sense of moral good and evil. Information concerning the abominations of the people is brought to this personified land, with which it is so deeply affected that a nausea is produced, and it vomits out its abominable and accursed inhabitants.

30. *Shall ye keep mine ordinance.* The only way to be preserved from all false worship is seriously to consider and devoutly to observe the ordinances of the true religion. He who in the things of God goes no further than he can say, "Thus it is written, and thus it behooves me to do," is never likely to receive a false creed, nor perform a superstitious act of worship.

CHAPTER 19

Exhortations to holiness, and a repetition of various laws, 1-2. Duty to parents, and observance of the Sabbath, 3. Against idolatry, 4. Concerning peace offerings, 5-8. The gleanings of the harvest and vintage to be left for the poor, 9-10. Against stealing and lying, 11; false swearing, 12; defrauding the hireling, 13. Laws in behalf of the deaf and the blind, 14. Against respect of persons in judgment, 15; talebearing, 16; hatred and uncharitableness, 17; revenge, 18; unlawful mixtures in cattle, seed, and garments, 19. Laws relative to the bond-maid that is betrothed, 20-22. The fruit of the trees of the land not to be eaten for the first three years, 23; but this is lawful in the fourth and fifth years, 24-25. Against eating of blood, and using incantations, 26; superstitious cutting of the hair, 27; and cutting of the flesh in the times of mourning, 28; prostitution, 29. Sabbaths to be reverenced, 30. Against consulting those who are wizards, and have familiar spirits, 31. Respect must be shown to the aged, 32. The stranger shall not be oppressed, 33-34. They shall keep just measures, weights, and balances, 35-36. Conclusion, 37.

3. *Ye shall fear every man his mother.* You shall have the profoundest reverence and respect for them. See the notes on Gen. xlviii. 12 and on Exod. xx. 8, 12.

4. *Turn ye not unto idols. Elilim,* literally "nothings"; and to this Paul seems to allude 1 Cor. viii. 4, where he says, "We know that an idol is nothing in the world."

5. *Peace offerings.* See the notes at the conclusion of chap. vii.

7. *If it be eaten . . . on the third day.* See the note on chap. vii. 15.

9. *When ye reap the harvest.* Liberty for the poor to glean both the cornfields and vineyards was a divine institution among the Jews; for the whole of the Mosaic dispensation, like the Christian, breathed love to God and benevolence to man. The poor in Judea were to live by gleanings from the cornfields and vineyards.

11. *Ye shall not steal.* See the notes on Exodus xx.

13. *The wages . . . shall not abide with thee all night.* For this plain reason, it is the support of the man's life and family, and they need to expend it as fast as it is earned.

14. *Thou shalt not curse the deaf.* Or "speak evil" of him, because he cannot hear, and so cannot vindicate his own character. *Nor put a stumbling block before the blind.* He who is capable of doing this must have a heart cased with cruelty. The spirit and design of these precepts are that no man shall in any case take advantage of the ignorance, simplicity, or inexperience of his neighbor, but in all things do to his neighbor as he would, on a change of circumstances, that his neighbor should do to him.

16. *Thou shalt not go up and down as a talebearer.* Rachil signifies a "trader," a "pedlar," and is here applied to the person who travels about dealing in scandal and calumny, getting the secrets of every person and family, and retailing them wherever he goes. A more despicable character exists not; such a person is a pest to society, and should be exiled from the habitations of men. *Neither shalt thou stand against the blood.* You shall not be as a false witness, because by such testimony the blood— the "life" of an innocent man—may be endangered.

17. *Thou shalt not hate thy brother.* You shall not only not do him any kind of evil, but you shall harbor no hatred in your heart towards him. On the contrary, thou shalt love him as thyself, v. 18. Many persons suppose, from misunderstanding our Lord's words, John xiii. 34, "A new commandment I give unto you, That ye love one another," that loving our neighbor as ourselves was first instituted under the gospel. This verse shows the opinion to be unfounded. But to love another as Christ has loved us, i.e., to lay down our lives for each other, is certainly a "new" commandment; we have it simply on the authority of Jesus Christ alone. *And not suffer sin upon him.* If you see him sin, or know him to be addicted to anything by which the safety of his soul is endangered, you shall mildly and affectionately reprove him, and by no means permit him to go on without counsel and advice in a way that is leading him to perdition. In a multitude of cases timely reproof has been the means of saving the soul. Speak to him privately if possible; if not, write to him in such a way that himself alone shall see it.

19. *Gender with a diverse kind.* These precepts taken literally seem to imply that they should not permit the horse and the she-ass, nor the he-ass and the cow, to couple together; nor sow different kinds of seeds in the same field or garden; nor have garments of silk and woolen, cotton and silk, linen and wool. And if all these were forbidden, there must have been some moral reason for the prohibitions, because domestic economy required several of these mixtures, especially those which relate to seeds and clothing. With respect to heterogeneous mixtures among *cattle,* there is something very unnatural in it, and it was probably forbidden to prevent excitements to such unnatural lusts as those condemned in the preceding chapter, vv. 22-23. As to *seed,* in many cases it would be very improper to sow different kinds in the same plot of ground. As to different kinds of *garments,* the prohibition here might be intended as much against pride and vanity as any thing else. But we really do not know what the original word *shaatnez,* which we translate *linen* and *woollen,* means. It is true that in Deut. xxii. 11, where it is again used, it seems to be explained by the words immediately following, "Thou shalt not wear a garment of divers sorts, as of linen and woollen together"; but this may as well refer to a garment made up of a sort of patchwork differently colored and arranged for pride and for show.

20. *A woman, that is a bondmaid.* Had she been free, the law required that she should be put to death (see Deut. xxii. 24); but as she was a slave, she is supposed to have less self-command, and therefore less guilt. But as it is taken for granted she did not make resistance, or did consent, she is to be scourged, and the man is to bring a ram for a trespass offering.

23. *Three years shall it be as uncircumcised.* I see no reason to seek for mystical meanings in this prohibition. The fruit of a young tree cannot be good; for not having arrived at a state of maturity, the juices cannot be sufficiently elaborated to produce fruit excellent in its kind. The Israelites are commanded not to eat of the fruit of a tree till the fifth year after its planting. In the first three years the fruit is unwholesome; in the fourth year the fruit is holy, it belongs to God, and should be consecrated to Him, v. 24; and in the fifth year and afterward the fruit may be employed for common use, v. 25.

26. *Neither shall ye use enchantment.* Lo *thenachashu.* Conjecture itself can do little towards a proper explanation of the terms used in this verse. *Nachash* in Gen. iii. 1 we translate "serpent." Possibly the superstition here prohibited may be what the Greeks called "divination by serpents." *Nor observe times.* Velo *teonenu,* you shall "not divine by clouds," which was also a superstition much in practice among the heathen, as well as divination by the flight of birds.

27. *Ye shall not round the corners of your heads.* This and the following verse evidently refer to customs which must have existed among the Egyptians when the Israelites sojourned in Egypt; and what they were it is now difficult, even with any probability, to conjecture. Herodotus observes that the Arabs shave or cut their hair round, in honor of Bacchus, who, they say, had his hair cut in this way. *The corners of thy beard.* Probably meaning the hair of the cheek that connects the hair of the head with the beard. This was no doubt cut in some peculiar manner, for the superstitious purposes mentioned above.

28. *Any cuttings in your flesh for the dead.* That the ancients were very violent in their grief, tearing the hair and face, beating the breast, is well-known.

29. *Do not prostitute thy daughter.* This was a very frequent custom, and with examples of it writers of antiquity abound. The Cyprian women, according to Justin, gained that portion which their husbands received with them at marriage by previous public prostitution. And the Phoenicians, according to Augustine, made a gift to Venus of the gain acquired by the public

prostitution of their daughters, previously to their marriage.

31. *Regard not them that have familiar spirits.* The Hebrew word *oboth* probably signifies a kind of ventriloquist, or such as the Pythoness mentioned Acts xvi. 16, 18; persons who, while under the influence of their demon became greatly "inflated," as the Hebrew word implies, and gave answers in a sort of frenzy. *Neither seek after wizards. Yiddeonim,* the "wise or knowing ones," from *yada,* to "know or understand"; called wizard in Scotland, "wise or cunning man" in England. Not only all real dealers with familiar spirits, or necromantic or magical superstitions, are here forbidden, but also all pretenders to the knowledge of futurity, fortune-tellers, astrologers. To attempt to know what God has not thought proper to reveal is a sin against His wisdom, providence, and goodness.

33. *If a stranger sojourn.* This law to protect and comfort the stranger was at once humane and politic. None is so desolate as the stranger, and none needs the offices of benevolence and charity more; and we may add that he who is not affected by the desolate state of the stranger has neither benevolence nor charity. Moses also uses a powerful motive: *Ye were strangers in the land of Egypt.* The spirit of the precept here laid down may be well expressed in our Lord's words: "Do unto all men as ye would they should do unto you."

35. *Ye shall do no unrighteousness.* You shall not act contrary to the strictest justice in any case, and especially in the four following, which, properly understood, comprise all that can occur between a man and his fellow. (1) *Judgment* in all cases that come before the civil magistrate; he is to judge and decide according to the law. (2) *Meteyard, bammiddah,* in measures of length. (3) *Weight, bammishkal,* in anything that is weighed, the weights being all according to the standards kept for the purpose of trying the rest in the sanctuary, as appears from Exod. xxx. 13; 1 Chron. xxiii. 29. (4) *Measure, bammesurah,* from which we derive our term. This refers to all measures of capacity, such as the homer, ephah, seah, hin, omer, kab, and log. See all these explained, Exod. xvi. 16.

36. *Just balances*—"scales." *Weights, abanim*—"stones," as the weights appear to have been originally formed out of stones.

37. *Shall ye observe all my statutes. Chukkothi,* from *chak,* to "describe, mark, or trace out"; the righteousness which I have described, and the path of duty which I have traced out. *Judgments, mishpatai,* from *shaphat,* to "discern, determine, direct"; that which divine wisdom has discerned to be best for man, has determined shall promote his best interest, and has directed him conscientiously to use.

CHAPTER 20

Of giving seed to Molech, and the punishment of this crime, 1-5. Of consulting wizards, etc., 6-8. Of disrespect to parents, 9. Of adultery, 10. Of incestuous mixtures, 11-12. Bestiality, 13-16. Different cases of incest and uncleanness, 17-21. Exhortations and promises, 22-24. The difference between clean and unclean animals to be carefully observed, 25. The Israelites are separated from other nations, that they may be holy, 26. A repetition of the law against wizards and them that have familiar spirits, 27.

2. *That giveth any of his seed unto Molech.* To what has been said in the note on chap. xviii. 21 we may add, that the rabbins describe

this idol, who was probably a representative or emblematical personification of the solar influence, as made of brass, in the form of a man, with the head of an ox; that a fire was kindled in the inside, and the child to be sacrificed to him was put in his arms, and roasted to death. The passing through the fire, so frequently spoken of, might mean no more than a simple rite of consecration to the service of this idol. See the note on chap. xviii. 21.

6. *Familiar spirits.* See the notes on chap. xix. 31; and Exod. xxii. 18.

9. *Curseth his father or his mother.* See the notes on Gen. xlviii. 12 and Exod. xx. 12. He who conscientiously keeps the fifth commandment can be in no danger of this judgment. The term *yekallel* signifies not only to "curse," but to speak of a person contemptuously and disrespectfully, to make light of; so that all speeches which have a tendency to lessen our parents in the eyes of others, or to render their judgment or piety suspected and contemptible, may be here included; though the act of cursing, or of treating the parent with injurious and opprobrious language, is that which is particularly intended.

10. *Committeth adultery.* The word *adultery* comes from the Latin *adulterium,* which is compounded of *ad,* "to or with," and *alter,* "another."

12. *They have wrought confusion.* See chap. xviii, and especially the note on v. 6.

14. *They shall be burnt with fire.* As there are worse crimes mentioned here (see vv. 11 and 17) where the delinquent is ordered simply to be put to death, or to be cut off, it is very likely that the crime mentioned in this verse was not punished by burning alive, but by some kind of branding, by which they were ever after rendered infamous. I need not add that the original, *baesh yishrephu,* may, without violence to its grammatical meaning, be understood as above, though in other places it is certainly used to signify a consuming by fire. But the case in question requires some explanation, It is this: A man marries a wife, and afterward takes his mother-in-law or wife's mother to wife also. Now for this offense the text says all three shall be *burned with fire,* and this is understood as signifying that they shall be burned alive. Now the first wife, we may safely presume, was completely innocent, and was legally married; for a man may take to wife the daughter if single, or the mother if a widow, and in neither of these cases can any blame attach to the man or the party he marries; the crime therefore lies in taking both. Either, therefore, they were all branded as infamous persons, and this certainly was severe enough in the case of the first wife; or the man and the woman taken last were burnt. But the text says, *both he and they;* therefore we should seek for another interpretation of *they shall be burnt with fire* than that which is commonly given. Branding with a hot iron would certainly accomplish every desirable end both for punishment and prevention of the crime; and because the Mosaic laws are so generally distinguished by humanity, it seems to be necessary to limit the meaning of the words as above.

22. *The land, whither I bring you to dwell therein, spue you not out.* See this explained in the note on chap. xviii. 25. From this

we learn that the cup of the iniquities of the Canaanitish nations was full; and that, consistently with divine justice, they could be no longer spared.

24. *A land that floweth with milk and honey.* See this explained in Exod. iii. 8.

25. *Between clean beasts and unclean.* See the notes on chap. xi.

27. *A familiar spirit.* A spirit or demon, which, by magical rites, is supposed to be bound to appear at the call of his employer. See the notes on Gen. xli. 8; Exod. vii. 11, 22, 25; and chap. xix. 31.

CHAPTER 21

The priests shall not mourn for the dead, except for near relatives, such as mother, father, son, daughter, and sister if a virgin, 1-4. They shall not shave their heads nor beards, nor make any cuttings in the flesh, because they are holy unto God, 5-6. A priest shall not marry a woman who is a whore, profane, or divorced from her husband, 7-8. Of the priest's daughter who profanes herself, 9. The high priest shall not uncover his head, or rend his clothes, 10; nor go in unto a dead body, 11; nor go out of the sanctuary, 12. Of his marriage and offspring, 13-15. No person shall be made a priest that has any blemish, nor shall any person with any of the blemishes mentioned here be permitted to officiate in the worship of God, 16-24.

1. *There shall none be defiled for the dead.* No priest shall assist in laying out a dead body, or preparing it for interment. Any contact with the dead was supposed to be of a defiling nature, probably because putrefaction had then taken place; and animal putrefaction was ever held in detestation by all men.

4. *A chief man among his people.* The word *baal* signifies a "master, chief, husband" and is as variously translated here.

5. *They shall not make baldness.* See the note on chap. xix. 27. It is supposed that these things were particularly prohibited, because used superstitiously by the Egyptian priests, who, according to Herodotus, shaved the whole body every third day, that there might be no uncleanness about them when they ministered in their temple. This appears to have been a general custom among the heathen.

7. *That is a whore.* A prostitute, though even reclaimed. *Profane.* A heathen, or one who is not a cordial believer in the true God. *Put away from her husband.* Because this very circumstance might lead to suspicion that the priest and the divorced woman might have been improperly connected before.

9. *She shall be burnt with fire.* Probably not burned alive, but strangled first, and then burned afterward, though it is barely possible that some kind of branding may be intended.

10. *He that is the high priest.* This is the first place where this title is introduced; the title is very emphatic, *haccohen haggadol,* "that priest, the great one." For the meaning of *cohen,* see the note on Gen. xiv. 18. As the chief or high priest was a representative of our blessed Lord, therefore he was required to be especially holy; and he is represented as God's king among the people.

12. *The crown of the anointing oil . . . is upon him.* By his office the priest represented Christ in His sacrificial character; by his anointing, the prophetic influence; and by the crown, the regal dignity of our Lord.

13. *He shall take a wife in her virginity. Bethuleyha.* This is a full proof that *bethulah*

is the proper Hebrew term for a "virgin," from the emphatic root *bathal,* to "separate"; because such a person was in her separate state, and had never been in any way united to man.

17. *Whosoever . . . hath any blemish, let him not approach to offer the bread of his God.* Never was a wiser, a more rational, and a more expedient law enacted relative to sacred matters. The man who ministers in holy things, who professes to be the interpreter of the will of God, should have nothing in his person nor in his manner which cannot contribute to render him respectable in the eyes of those to whom he ministers.

18. *A blind man.* That is, in one eye; for he that was utterly blind could not possibly be employed in such a service. *A flat nose,* like that of an ape; so the best versions. *Any thing superfluous,* such as six fingers, six toes.

19. *Brokenfooted, or brokenhanded.* Clubfooted, bandy-legged; or having the ankle, wrist, or fingers dislocated.

20. *Crookbackt.* Hunchbacked. *A dwarf, dak,* a person too "short" or too "thin," so as to be either particularly observable or ridiculous in his appearance. *A blemish in his eye.* A protuberance on the eye, observable spots or suffusions. *Stones broken.* Is ruptured; an infirmity which would render him incapable of fulfilling the duties of his office, which often might be very fatiguing.

CHAPTER 22

Of the uncleanness of the priests, by which they were prevented from ministering in holy things, 1-5. How they should be cleansed, 6-7. The priest must not eat of any animal that had died of itself or was torn by wild beasts, but must keep God's ordinances, 8-9. No stranger, sojourner, nor hired servant shall eat of the holy things, 10. A servant bought with money may eat of them, 11. Who of the priest's family may not eat of them, 12-13. Of improper persons who partake of the holy things unknowingly, 14-16. Freewill offerings, and sacrifices in general, must be without blemish, 17-25. The age at which different animals were to be offered to God, 26-27. No animal and its young shall be offered on the same day, 28. How the sacrifice of thanksgiving was to be offered, 29-30. All God's testimonies to be observed, and the reason, 31-33.

2. *Speak unto Aaron and to his sons, that they separate themselves.* The same subject is continued in this chapter as in the preceding, with this addition, that besides the perfection of the priests, it was indispensably necessary that the sacrifices also should be perfect. In the service of God, according to the law, neither an imperfect offering nor an imperfect offerer could be admitted. What need then of a mediator between a holy God and sinful men! And can we expect that any of our services, however sincere and well-intentioned, can be accepted, unless offered on that living Altar that sanctifies the gift?

4. *Is a leper, or hath a running issue.* See the case of the leper treated at large in the notes on chapters xiii and xiv; and for other uncleannesses, see the notes on chap. xv.

14. *Then he shall put the fifth part thereof unto it.* The holy thing of which he has unknowingly eaten shall be fairly valued, and to this value he shall add one-fifth more, and give the whole to the priest.

20. *Whatsoever hath a blemish.* The same perfection is required in the sacrifice that was

required in the priest; see on v. 2, and the notes on the preceding chapter.

23. *That hath any thing superfluous or lacking.* The term *sarua* signifies anything "extended" beyond the usual size, and the term *kalut* signifies anything unusually "contracted."

24. *Bruised, or crushed, or broken, or cut.* That is, no bullock or lamb that is injured in any of the above ways shall be offered unto the Lord.

25. *Their corruption is in them.* Viz., they are bruised, crushed, broken.

27. *When a bullock . . . is brought forth.* This is a most unfortunate as well as absurd translation. The creature called an ox is a bull castrated; surely then a *bullock* was never yet *brought forth!* The original word *shor* signifies a bull, a bullock, or indeed anything of the meat kind: here, even common sense required that it should be translated "calf"; and did I not hold myself sacredly bound to print the text of the common version with scrupulous exactness, I should translate the former clause of this verse thus, and so enter it into the text: "When a calf, or a lamb, or a kid is brought forth," instead of, *When a bullock, or a sheep, or a goat is brought forth,* the absurdity of which is glaring.

28. *Ye shall not kill it and her young . . . in one day.* This precept was certainly intended to inculcate mercy and tenderness of heart; and so the Jews understood it.

30. *Leave none of it until the morrow.* See the note on chap. vii. 18.

32. *Neither shall ye profane my holy name.* He profanes God's holy name who does not both implicitly believe and conscientiously obey all His words and all His precepts. *I will be hallowed among the children of Israel.* The words *children of Israel, beney Yishrael,* which so frequently occur, should be translated either "the descendants" or "posterity of Israel," or "the people of Israel." The word *children* has a tendency to beget a false notion, especially in the minds of young people, and lead them to think that children, in the proper sense of the word, i.e., "little ones," are meant.

33. *Brought you out of the land of Egypt.* By such a series of miraculous interferences, *to be your God*—to save you from all idolatry, false and superstitious worship, teach you the right way, lead and support you in it, and preserve you to My eternal kingdom and glory.

CHAPTER 23

The feast of the Lord, 1-2. The Sabbath, 3. The Passover and Unleavened Bread, 4-8. The Feast of Firstfruits, 9-14. The Feast of Pentecost, 15-21. Gleanings to be left for the poor, 22. The Feast of Trumpets, 23-25. The great Day of Atonement, 26-32. The Feast of Tabernacles, 33-44.

2. *These are my feasts.* The original word *moad* is properly applied to any solemn anniversary, by which great and important ecclesiastical, political, or providential facts were recorded; see Gen. i. 14. Anniversaries of this kind were observed in all nations; and some of them, in consequence of scrupulously regular observation, became chronological epochs of the greatest importance in history.

3. *The seventh day is the sabbath.* This, because the first and greatest solemnity, is first mentioned. He who kept not this, in the most

religious manner, was not capable of keeping any of the others. The religious observance of the Sabbath stands at the very threshold of all religion. See Gen. ii. 3.

5. *The Lord's passover.* See this largely explained in the notes on Exod. xii. 21-27.

11. *He shall wave the sheaf.* He shall move it to and fro before the people, and thereby call their attention to the work of divine providence, and excite their gratitude to God for preserving to them the kindly fruits of the earth. See notes on Exod. xxix. 27 and chap. vii at end.

14. *Ye shall eat neither bread, nor parched corn, nor green ears.* It is right that God, the Dispenser of every blessing, should be acknowledged as such, and the firstfruits of the field, etc., dedicated to Him. Concerning the dedication of the firstfruits, see the note on Exod. xxii. 29. Parched ears of corn and green ears, fried, still constitute a part, and not a disagreeable one, of the food of the Arabs now resident in the Holy Land.

15. *Ye shall count unto you . . . seven sabbaths.* That is, from the sixteenth of the first month to the sixth of the third month. These seven weeks, called here *sabbaths,* were to be complete, i.e., the forty-nine days must be finished, and the next day, the fiftieth, is what, from the Septuagint, we call Pentecost.

24. *A memorial of blowing of trumpets.* This is generally called the Feast of Trumpets; and as it took place on the first day of the seventh month, Tisri, which answers to September, which month was the commencement of what was called the civil year, the feast probably had no other design than to celebrate the commencement of that year, if indeed such a distinction obtained among the ancient Jews.

28. *A day of atonement.* See the note on chap. xvi, 3, etc., where this subject is largely explained.

34. *The feast of tabernacles.* In this solemnity the people left their houses, and dwelt in booths or tents made of the branches of "goodly trees" and "thick trees" (of what kind the text does not specify), together with "palm trees" and "willows of the brook," v. 40. And in these they dwelt *seven days,* in commemoration of their forty years' sojourning and dwelling in tents in the wilderness while destitute of any fixed habitations.

40. *Boughs of goodly trees.* The Jews and many critics imagine the citron tree to be intended, and by *boughs of thick trees* the myrtle.

43. *That your generations may know.* By the institution of this feast God had two great objects in view: (1) To perpetuate the wonderful display of His providence and grace in bringing them out of Egypt, and in preserving them in the wilderness; (2) To excite and maintain in them a spirit of gratitude and obedience, by leading them to consider deeply the greatness of the favours which they had received for His most merciful hands.

CHAPTER 24

Pure olive oil must be provided for the lamps, 1-2. Aaron is to take care that the lamps be lighted from evening to morning continually, 3-4. How the shewbread is to be made and ordered, 5-8. Aaron and his sons shall eat this bread in the holy place, 9. Of the son of Shelomith, an Israelitish woman, who blasphemed the name, 10-11. He is imprisoned till the mind of the Lord should be known, 12. He is commanded to be stoned to death, 13-14. The ordinance concerning cursing and blaspheming the Lord, 15-16. The law against murder, 17. The lex talionis, or law of like for like, repeated, 18-21. This law to be equally binding both on themselves and on strangers, 22. The blasphemer is stoned, 23.

5. *Bake twelve cakes.* See the whole account of the shewbread in the notes on Exod. xxv. 30; and relative to the table on which they stood, the golden candlestick and silver trumpets, carried in triumph to Rome, see the note on Exod. xxv. 31.

10. *The son of a Israelitish woman, whose father was an Egyptian.* What the cause of the strife between this mongrel person and the Israelitish man was is not even hinted at. The sacred text does not tell us what name he blasphemed; it is simply said *vaiyikkob eth hashshem,* "He pierced through, distinguished, explained, or expressed the name." As the Jews hold it impious to pronounce the name *Yehovah,* they always put either *Adonai, Lord,* or *hashshem,* "the name," in the place of it; but in this sense *hashshem* was never used prior to the days of rabbinical superstition, and therefore it cannot be put here for the word *Jehovah.* Blaspheming the name of the Lord is mentioned in v. 16, and there the proper Hebrew term is used *shem Yehovah,* and not the rabbinical *hashshem,* as in v. 11. The fifteenth verse seems to countenance the supposition that the god whose name was produced on this occasion was not the true God, for it is there said, "Whosoever curseth his god [*elohaiv*], shall bear his sin"— shall have the punishment due to him as an *idolater;* but "he that blasphemeth the name of the Lord [*shem Yehovah*], . . . shall surely be put to death . . . when he blasphemeth the name [*shem*]" he shall die, v. 16. The verb *nakab,* which we translate "blaspheme," signifies "to pierce, bore, make hollow"; also "to express or distinguish by name"; see Isa. lxii. 2; Num. i. 17; 1 Chron. xii. 31; xvi. 41; xxviii. 15. Hence all that we term blasphemy here may only signify the particularizing some false god, i.e., naming him by his name, or imploring his aid as a helper.

14. *Lay their hands upon his head.* It was by this ceremony that the people who heard him curse bore their public testimony in order to his being fully convicted, for without this his punishment would not have been lawful. By this ceremony also they in effect said to the man, "Thy blood be upon thy own head."

15. *Whosoever curseth his God. Yekallel Elohaiv,* he who "makes light" of Him, who does not treat Him and sacred things with due reverence, *shall bear his sin*—shall have the guilt of this transgression imputed to him, and may expect the punishment.

16. *Blasphemeth the name of the Lord. Venokeb shem Yehovah,* he who "pierces, transfixes," the name of Jehovah; see the note on the tenth verse. This being the name by which especially the Divine Essence was pointed out, it should be held peculiarly sacred. We have already seen that the Jews never pronounce this name, and so long has it been disused among them that the true pronunciation is now totally lost.

17. *He that killeth any man.* Blasphemy against God, i.e., speaking injuriously of His name, His attributes, His government, and His revelation, together with murder, is to be pun-

ished with death. He that blasphemes God is a curse in society, and he who takes away, wilfully and by malicious intent, the life of any man, should certainly be put to death. In this respect God has absolutely required that life shall go for life.

20. *Breach for breach.* This is a repetition of the *lex talionis,* which see explained Exod. xxi. 24.

22. *Ye shall have one manner of law, as well for the stranger, as for one of your own country.* Equal laws, where each individual receives the same protection and the same privileges, are the boast only of a sound political constitution. He who respects and obeys the laws has a right to protection and support, and his person and property are as sacred in the sight of justice as the person and property of the prince. He who does not obey the laws of his country forfeits all right and title to protection and privilege; his own actions condemn him, and justice takes him up on the evidence of his own transgressions.

23. *And stone him with stones.* We are not to suppose that the culprit was exposed to the unbridled fury of the thousands of Israel; this would be brutality, not justice, for the very worst of tempers and passions might be produced and fostered by such a procedure. The Jews themselves tell us that their manner of stoning was this: they brought the condemned person without the camp, because his crime had rendered him unclean, and whatever was unclean must be put without the camp. When they came within four cubits of the place of execution, they stripped the criminal, if a man, leaving him nothing but a cloth about the waist. The place on which he was to be executed was elevated, and the witnesses went up with him to it, and laid their hands upon him, for the purposes mentioned in v. 14. Then one of the witnesses struck him with a stone upon the loins; if he was not killed with that blow, then the witnesses took up a great stone, as much as two men could lift, and threw it upon his breast. This was the *coup de grace,* and finished the tragedy.

CHAPTER 25

The law concerning the sabbatical or seventh year repeated, 1-7. The law relative to the jubilee, or fiftieth year, and the hallowing of the fiftieth, 8-12. In the year of jubilee every one to return unto his possessions, 13. None to oppress another in buying and selling, 14. Purchases to be rated from jubilee to jubilee, according to the number of years unexpired, 15-17. Promises to obedience, 18-19. Promises relative to the sabbatical year, 20-22. No inheritance must be finally alienated, 23-24. No advantage to be taken of a man's poverty in buying his land, 25-28. Ordinances relative to the selling of a house in a walled city, 29-30; in a village, 31. Houses of the Levites may be redeemed at any time, 32-33. The fields of the Levites in the suburbs must not be sold, 34. No usury to be taken from a poor brother, 35-38. If an Israelite be sold to an Israelite, he must not be obliged to serve as a slave, 39, but be as a hired servant or as a sojourner, till the year of jubilee, 40, when he and his family shall have liberty to depart, 41; because God claims all Israelites as His servants, having redeemed them from bondage in Egypt, 42-43. The Israelites are permitted to have bondmen and bondwomen of the heathen, who, being bought with their money, shall be considered as their property, 44-46. If an Israelite, grown poor, be sold to a sojourner who has waxed rich, he may be redeemed by one of his relatives, an uncle or uncle's son, 47-49. In the interim between the jubilees, he may be redeemed; but if not redeemed, he shall go free in the jubilee, 50-54. Obedience enforced by God's right over them as His servants, 55.

2. *The land keep a sabbath.* See this ordinance explained in the note on Exod. xxiii. 11.

It may be asked here: If it required all the annual produce of the field to support the inhabitants, how could the people be nourished the seventh year, when no produce was received from the fields? To this it may be answered that God sent His blessing in an especial manner on the sixth year (see vv. 21-22) and it brought forth fruit for three years.

8. *Thou shalt number seven sabbaths of years.* This seems to state that the jubilee was to be celebrated on the forty-ninth year; but in vv. 10 and 11 it is said, "Ye shall hallow the fiftieth year," and, "A jubile shall this fiftieth year be." Probably in this verse Moses either includes the preceding jubilee, and thus with the forty-ninth makes up the number fifty; or he speaks of proclaiming the jubilee on the forty-ninth, and celebrating it on the fiftieth year current.

11. *A jubile shall that fiftieth year be.* The literal meaning of the word *jubile, yobel* in Hebrew, has not been well ascertained. The most natural derivation is from *hobil,* to "cause to bring back," or "recall," because estates which had been alienated were then brought back to their primitive owners. This was a wise and excellent institution, but appears to have been little regarded by the Jews after the Babylonish captivity. Indeed, it is not mentioned under the second Temple, and the observance must have ceased among the Jews when they were brought under a foreign yoke.

The jubilee seems to have been typical, (1) Of the great time of release, the gospel dispensation, when all who believe in Christ Jesus are redeemed from the bondage of sin—repossess the favor and image of God, the only inheritance of the human soul, having all debts cancelled, and the right of inheritance restored. To this the prophet Isaiah seems to allude, chap. xxvi. 13, and particularly lxi. 1-3. (2) Of the general resurrection. It is worthy of remark that the jubilee was not proclaimed till the tenth day of the seventh month, on the very day when the great annual atonement was made for the sins of the people; and does not this prove that the great liberty or redemption from thraldom, published under the gospel, could not take place till the great atonement, the sacrifice of the Lord Jesus, had been offered up?

14. *Ye shall not oppress one another.* You shall not take advantage of each other's ignorance in either buying or selling; for he that buys an article at less than it is worth, or sells one for more than it is worth, taking advantage in both cases of the ignorance of the vender or buyer, is no better than a thief, as he actually robs his neighbor of as much property as he has bought the article at below or sold it above its current value.

15. *According to the number of years.* The purchases that were to be made of lands were to be regulated by the number of years unelapsed of the current jubilee. This was something like buying the unexpired term of a lease among us; the purchase is always regulated by the number of years between the time of purchase and the expiration of the term.

20. *What shall we eat the seventh year?* A very natural question, which could be laid at rest only by the sovereign promise in the next verse: "I will command my blessing upon you in the sixth year, and it shall bring forth fruit for three years."

23. *The land shall not be sold for ever . . . the land is mine.* As God in a miraculous manner gave them possession of this land, they were therefore to consider themselves merely as tenants to Him; and on this ground He, as the great Landholder or Lord of the soil, prescribes to them all the conditions on which they shall hold it.

25. *Any of his kin come to redeem it.* The land that was sold might be redeemed, in the interim between jubilee and jubilee, by the former owner or by one of his kinsmen or relatives. This kinsman is called in the text *goel* or "redeemer"; and was not this a lively emblem of the redemption of man by Christ Jesus? That *He* might have a right to redeem man, He took upon Him human nature, and thus became a Kinsman of the great family of the human race, and thereby possessed the right of redeeming that fallen nature of which He took part, and of buying back to man that inheritance which had been forfeited by transgression.

29. *Sell a dwelling house in a walled city.* A very proper difference is put between houses in a city and houses in the country. If a man sold his house in the city, he might redeem it any time in the course of a year; but if it were not redeemed within that time, it could no more be redeemed, nor did it go out even in the jubilee. It was not so with a house in the country; such a house might be redeemed during any part of the interim; and if not redeemed, must go out at the jubilee. The reason in both cases is sufficiently evident. The house in the city might be built for purposes of trade or traffic merely; the house in the country was built on or attached to the inheritance which God had divided to the respective families, and it was therefore absolutely necessary that the same law should apply to the house as to the inheritance.

32. *The cities of the Levites.* The law in this and the following verses was also a very wise one. A Levite could not ultimately sell his house. If sold, he could redeem it at any time in the interim between the two jubilees; but if not redeemed, it must go out at the following jubilee. And why? They had no inheritance in Israel, only their cities, to dwell in: and because their houses in these cities were the whole that they could call their own, therefore these houses could not be ultimately alienated. All that they had to live on besides was from that most precarious source of support, the freewill offerings of the people, which depended on the prevalence of pure religion in the land.

36. *Take thou no usury of him.* Usury, at present, signifies unlawful interest for money. Properly, it means the reward or compensation given for the use of a thing, but is principally spoken of money. See the definition of the original term in the note on Exod. xxii. 25.

42. *For they are my servants.* As God redeemed every Israelite out of Egyptian bondage, they were therefore to consider themselves as His property, and that consequently they should not alienate themselves from Him. It was in being His servants, and devoted to His work, that both their religious and political service consisted. And although their political liberty might be lost, they knew that their spiritual liberty never could be forfeited except by an

utter alienation from God. God therefore claims the same right to their persons which He does to their lands; see the note on v. 23.

50. *The price of his sale shall be.* This was a very equitable law, both for the sojourner to whom the man was sold and to the Israelite who had been thus sold. The Israelite might redeem himself, or one of his kindred might redeem him; but this must not be done to the prejudice of his master, the sojourner. They were therefore to reckon the years he must have served from that time till the jubilee; and then, taking the current wages of a servant per year at that time, multiply the remaining years by that sum, and the aggregate was the sum to be given to his master for his redemption. The Jews hold that the kindred of such a person were bound, if in their power, to redeem him, lest he should be swallowed up among the heathen; and we find, from Neh. v. 8, that this was done by the Jews on their return from the Babylonish captivity: "We after our ability have redeemed our brethren the Jews, which were sold unto the heathen."

55. *For unto me the children of Israel are servants.* The reason of this law we have already seen (see on v. 42) but we must look further to see the great end of it. The Israelites were a typical people; they represented those under the gospel dispensation who are children of God by faith in Christ Jesus. But these last have a peculiarity of blessing: they are not merely servants, but they are sons; though they also serve God, yet it is in the newness of the spirit, and not in the oldness of the letter. And to this difference of state the apostle seems evidently to allude, Gal. iv. 6, etc.: "And because ye are sons, God hath sent forth the Spirit of his Son into your hearts, crying, Abba, Father. Wherefore thou art no more a servant, but a son; and if a son, then an heir of God through Christ"—genuine believers in Christ not being heirs of an earthly inheritance, nor merely of a heavenly one, for they are heirs of God. God himself therefore is their Portion, without whom even heaven itself would not be a state of consummate blessedness to an immortal spirit.

CHAPTER 26

Idolatry forbidden, 1. The Sabbath to be sanctified, 2-3. Promises to obedience, of fruitful fields, plentiful harvests, and vintage, 4-5. Of peace and security, 6. Discomfiture of their enemies, 7-9. Of abundance, 10. Of the divine presence, 11-13. Threatenings against the disobedient, 14-15. Of terror and dismay, 16. Their enemies shall prevail against them, 17-18. Of barrenness, 19-20. Of desolation by wild beasts, 21-22. And if not humbled and reformed, worse evils shall be inflicted upon them, 23-24. Their enemies shall prevail, and they shall be wasted by the pestilence, 25-26. If they should still continue refractory, they shall be yet more sorely punished, 27-28. The famine shall so increase that they shall be obliged to eat their own children, 29. Their carcasses shall be cast upon the carcasses of their idols, 30. Their cities shall be wasted, and the sanctuary desolated, 31; the land destroyed, 32. themselves scattered among their enemies, and pursued with utter confusion and distress, 33-39. If under these judgments they confess their sin and return to God, He will remember them in mercy, 40-43; visit them even in the land of their enemies, 44; and remember His covenant with their fathers, 45. The conclusion, stating these to be the judgments and laws which the Lord made between himself and the children of Israel in Mount Sinai. 46.

1. *Ye shall make you no idols.* See the note on Exod. xx. 4, and see the note on Gen. xxviii. 18-19, concerning consecrated stones. Not only idolatry in general is forbidden here, but also the superstitious use of innocent and lawful things. Probably the stones or pillars which were first set up, and anointed by holy men in

commemoration of signal interposition of God in their behalf, were afterward abused to idolatrous and superstitious purposes, and therefore prohibited. This we know was the case with the brazen serpent, 2 Kings xviii. 4.

3. *If ye walk in my statutes.* For the meaning of this and similar words used in the law, see the note on v. 15.

5. *Your threshing shall reach unto the vintage.* According to Pliny, *Hist. Nat.*, 1. xviii., c. 18, the Egyptians reaped their barley six months, and their oats seven months, after seedtime; for they sowed all their grain about the end of summer, when the overflowings of the Nile had ceased. It was nearly the same in Judea: they sowed their corn and barley towards the end of autumn, and about the month of October; and they began their barley harvest after the Passover, about the middle of March; and in one month or six weeks after, about Pentecost, they began that of their wheat. After their wheat heavest their vintage commenced. Moses here leads the Hebrews to hope, if they continued faithful to God, that between their harvest and vintage, and between their vintage and seedtime, there should be no interval, so great should the abundance be. And these promises would appear to them the more impressive, as they had just now come out of a country where the inhabitants were obliged to remain for nearly three months shut up within their cities, because the Nile had then inundated the whole country.

11. *I will set my tabernacle among you.* This and the following verse contain the grand promise of the gospel dispensation, viz., the presence, manifestation, and indwelling of God in human nature, and His constant indwelling in the souls of His followers. So John i. 14: "The Word was made flesh, and dwelt [made His tabernacle] among us." And to this promise of the law Paul evidently refers, 2 Cor. vi. 16-18 and vii. 1.

15. *If ye shall despise my statutes . . . abhor my judgments.* As these words, and others of a similar import, which point out different properties of the revelation of God, are frequently occurring, I judge it best to take a general view of them, once for all, in this place, and show how they differ among themselves, and what property of the divine law each points out.

(1) *Statutes. Chukkoth,* from *chak,* "to mark out, define." This term seems to signify the things which God has defined, marked, and traced out, that men might have a perfect copy of pure conduct always before their eyes, to teach them how they might walk so as to please Him in all things, which they could not do without such instruction as God gives in His Word, and the help which He affords by His Spirit.

(2) *Judgments. Shephatim,* from *shaphat,* to "distinguish, regulate, and determine"; meaning those things which God has determined that men shall pursue, by which their whole conduct shall be regulated, making the proper distinction between virtue and vice, good and evil, right and wrong, justice and injustice; in a word, between what is proper to be done and what is proper to be left undone.

(3) *Commandments. Mitsvoth,* from *tsavah,* to "command, ordain, and appoint, as a legis-

lator." This term is properly applied to those parts of the law which contain the obligation the people are under to act according to the statutes, judgments, etc., already established, and which prohibit them by penal sanctions from acting contrary to the laws.

(4) *Covenant. Berith,* from *bar,* to "clear, cleanse, or purify"; because the covenant, the whole system of revelation given to the Jews, was intended to separate them from all the people of the earth, and to make them holy. *Berith* also signifies the covenant sacrifice, which prefigured the atonement made by Christ for the sin of the world, by which He purifies believers unto himself, and makes them "a peculiar people, zealous of good works." Besides those four, we may add the following, from other places of Scripture.

(5) *Testimonies. Edoth,* from *ad,* "beyond, farther, besides"; because the whole ritual law referred to something farther on or beyond the Jewish dispensation, even to that Sacrifice which in the fulness of time was to be offered for the sins of men. Thus all the sacrifices of the Mosaic law referred to Christ, and bore *testimony* to Him who was to come.

(6) *Ordinances. Mishmaroth,* from *shamar,* to "guard, keep safe, watch over"; those parts of divine revelation which exhorted men to watch their ways, keep their hearts, and promised them, in consequence, the continual protection and blessing of God their Maker.

(7) *Precepts. Pikkudim,* from *pakad,* to "overlook, take care or notice of, to visit"; a very expressive character of the divine testimonies, the overseers of a man's conduct, those who stand by and look on to see whether he acts according to the commands of his Master.

(8) *Truth. Emeth,* from *am,* to "support, sustain, confirm"; because God is immutable, who has promised, threatened, commanded, and therefore all His promises, threatenings.

(9) *Righteousness. Tsedakah,* which, though not having a verb in the Hebrew Bible, seems to convey, from its use as a noun, the idea of giving just weight or good measure; see chap. xix. 36.

(10) *Word of Jehovah. Debar Yehovah,* from *dabar,* "to drive, lead, bring forward," hence to bring forward, or utter one's sentiments; so the word of God is what God has brought forth to man from His own mind and counsel.

(11) *Imrah,* "speech or word," variously modified from *amar,* to "branch out," because of the interesting details into which the word of God enters in order to instruct man and make him wise unto salvation.

(12) All these collectively are termed the *law torah,* or *torath Yehovah,* "the law of the Lord," from *yarah,* to "direct, set straight and true, as stones in a building, to teach and instruct," because this whole system of divine revelation is calculated to direct men to the attainment of present and eternal felicity.

16. *I will even appoint over you terror.* How dreadful is this curse! A whole train of evils are here personified and appointed to be the governors of a disobedient people. *Terror* is to be one of their keepers. *Consumption, sha-chepheth,* generally allowed to be some kind of atrophy by which the flesh was consumed and the whole body dried up by raging fever through lack of sustenance.

22. *I will also send wild beasts among you.* God fulfilled these threatenings at different times. He sent fiery serpents among them, Num. xxi. 6; lions, 2 Kings xvii. 25; bears, 2 Kings ii. 24, and threatened them with total desolation, so that their land should be overrun with *wild beasts,* etc., see Ezek. v. 17.

26. *Ten women shall bake your bread in one oven.* Though in general every family in the East bakes its own bread, yet there are some public bakehouses where the bread of several families is baked at a certain price. Moses here foretells that the desolation should be so great and the want so pressing that there should be many idle hands to be employed, many mouths to be fed, and very little for each.

29. *Ye shall eat the flesh of your sons.* This was literally fulfilled at the siege of Jerusalem. Josephus, *Wars of the Jews,* book vii, chap. ii, gives us a particular instance in dreadful detail of a woman named Mary, who, in the extremity of the famine during the siege, killed her sucking child, roasted, and had eaten part of it when discovered by the soldiers! See this threatened, Jer. xix. 9.

34. *Then shall the land enjoy her sabbaths.* This Houbigant observes to be a historical truth. "From Saul to the Babylonish captivity are numbered about four hundred and ninety years, during which period there were seventy Sabbaths of years; for 7, multiplied by 70, make 490. Now the Babylonish captivity lasted seventy years, and during that time the land of Israel *rested.* Therefore the land rested just as many years in the Babylonish captivity, as it should have rested Sabbaths if the Jews had observed the laws relative to the Sabbaths of the land."

38. *The land of your enemies shall eat you up.* Does this refer to the total loss of the ten tribes? These are so completely swallowed up in some enemies' land that nothing concerning their existence or place of residence remains but mere conjecture.

44. *Neither will I abhor them, to destroy them utterly.* Though God has literally fulfilled all His threatenings upon this people, in dispossessing them of their land, destroying their polity, overturning their city, demolishing their Temple, and scattering themselves over the face of the whole earth; yet He has, in His providence, strangely preserved them as a *distinct* people, and in very considerable numbers also.

46. *These are the statutes and judgments.* See on v. 15. This verse appears to be the proper concluding verse of the whole book; and I rather think that the twenty-seventh chapter originally followed the twenty-fifth. As the law was anciently written upon skins of parchment, sheep or goat skins, pasted or stitched together, and all rolled up in one roll, the matter being written in columns, one of those columns might have been very easily displaced, and thus whole chapters might have been readily interchanged. It is likely that this might have been the case in the present instance. Others endeavor to solve this difficulty by supposing that the twenty-seventh chapter was added after the book had been finished; and therefore there is apparently a double conclusion, one at the end of the twenty-sixth and the other at the end of the twenty-seventh chapter. However the above may have been, all the ancient versions

agree in concluding both the chapters in nearly the same way; yet the twenty-sixth chapter must be allowed to be by far the most natural conclusion of the book.

CHAPTER 27

Laws concerning vows, 1-2. Of males and females from twenty to sixty years of age, and their valuation, 3-4. Of the same from five to twenty years, 5. Of the same from a month to five years of age, 6. Of males and females from sixty years old and upwards, and their valuation, 7. The priest shall value the poor according to his ability, 8. Concerning beasts that are vowed, and their valuation, 9-13. Concerning the sanctification of a house, 14-15. Concerning the field that is sanctified or consecrated to the Lord, to the year of jubilee, 16-24. Every estimation shall be made in shekels, according to the shekel of the sanctuary, 25. The firstlings of clean beasts, being already the Lord's, cannot be vowed, 26. That of an unclean beast may be redeemed, 27. Everything devoted to God shall be unalienable and unredeemable, and continue the Lord's property till death, 28-29. All the tithe of the land is the Lord's, 30; but it may be redeemed by adding a fifth part, 31. The tithe of the herd and the flock is also His, 32. The tenth that passes under the rod shall not be changed, 33. The conclusion of the book, 34.

2. *When a man shall make a singular vow.* The verse is short and obscure, and may be translated thus: "A man who shall have separated a vow, according to thy estimation, of souls unto the Lord"; which may be paraphrased thus: He who shall have vowed or consecrated a soul, i.e., a living creature, whether man or beast, if he wish to redeem what he has thus vowed or consecrated, he shall ransom or redeem it according to the priest's estimation; for the priest shall judge of the properties, qualifications, and age of the person or beast, and the circumstances of the person who has vowed it, and shall regulate the value accordingly; and the money shall be put into his hands for the service of the sanctuary. A vow is a religious promise made unto the Lord, and for the most part with prayer, and paid with thanksgiving, Num. xxi. 2-3; Ps. lxvi. 13-14. Vows were either of abstinence, such as are spoken of in Numbers xxx, and the vow of the Nazarite, Numbers vi; or they were to give something to the Lord, as sacrifices, Lev. vii. 16, or the value of persons, beasts, houses, or lands, concerning which the law is here given. A man might vow or devote himself, his children (vv. 5-6), his domestics, his cattle, his goods. And in this chapter rules are laid down for the redemption of all these things. But if, after consecrating these things, he refused to redeem them, then they became the Lord's property forever. The persons continued all their lives devoted to the service of the sanctuary; the goods were sold for the profit of the Temple or the priests; the animals, if clean, were offered in sacrifice; if not proper for sacrifice, were sold, and the price devoted to sacred uses. This is a general view of the different laws relative to vows, mentioned in this chapter.

3. *From twenty years old even unto sixty . . . fifty shekels.* A man from twenty to sixty years of age, if consecrated to the Lord by a vow, might be redeemed for fifty shekels, which, at 3s. each, amounted to 7l. 10s. sterling.

4. *And if it be a female.* The woman, at the same age, vowed unto the Lord, might be redeemed for thirty shekels, 4l. 10s. sterling, a little more than one-half of the value of the man; for this obvious reason, that a woman, if employed, could not be of so much use in the service of the sanctuary as the man, and was therefore of much less value.

5. *From five years old.* The boy that was vowed might be redeemed for twenty shekels, 3l. sterling; the girl, for ten shekels, just one-half, 1l. 10s.

6. *A month old.* The male child, five shekels, 15s.; the female, three shekels, 9s. Being both in comparative infancy, they were nearly of an equal value. None were vowed under a month old; the firstborn, being always considered as the Lord's property, could not be vowed, see v. 26.

7. *Sixty years old.* The old man and the old woman, being nearly past labor, were nearly of an equal value; hence the one was estimated at fifteen shekels, 2l. 5s., the other at ten shekels, 1l. 10s. This was about the same ratio as that of the children, v. 5, and for the same reason.

10. *He shall not alter it, nor change it, a good for a bad.* Whatever was consecrated to God by a vow, or purpose of heart, was considered from that moment as the Lord's property; to change which was impiety; to withhold it, sacrilege.

13. *Shall add a fifth part.* This was probably intended to prevent rash vows and covetous redemptions. The priest alone was to value the thing; and to whatever his valuation was, a fifth part must be added by him who wished to redeem the consecrated thing.

14. *Shall sanctify his house.* The yearly rent of which, when thus consecrated, went towards the repairs of the Tabernacle, which was the house of the Lord.

16. *Some part of a field.* Though the preceding words are not in the text, yet it is generally allowed they should be supplied here, as it was not lawful for a man to vow his whole estate, and thus make his family beggars, in order to enrich the Lord's sanctuary; this God would not permit.

21. *As a field devoted.* It is *cherem*, a thing so "devoted to God" as never more to be capable of being redeemed. See on v. 29.

25. *Shekel of the sanctuary.* A standard shekel, the standard being kept in the sanctuary by which to try and regulate all the weights in the land.

28. *No devoted thing . . . shall be sold or redeemed.* This is the *cherem*, which always meant an absolute, unredeemable grant to God.

29. *Which shall be devoted of men.* Every man who is devoted shall surely be put to death; or be the Lord's property, or be employed in His service, till death.

30. *All the tithe of the land.* This God claims as His own; and it is spoken of here as being a point perfectly settled, and concerning which there was neither doubt nor difficulty.

32. *Whatsoever passeth under the rod.* It seems to be in reference to this custom that the Prophet Ezekiel, speaking to Israel, says: "I will cause you to pass under the rod, and I will bring you into the bond of the covenant"—you shall be once more claimed as the Lord's property, and be in all things devoted to His service, being marked or ascertained, by especial providences and manifestations of His kindness, to be His peculiar people.

34. *These are the commandments.* This conclusion is very similar to that at the end of the preceding chapter. I have already supposed that this chapter should have followed the twenty-fifth and that the twenty-sixth originally terminated the book.

The Book of

NUMBERS

This, which is the fourth book in order of the Pentateuch, has been called Numbers, from its containing an account of the numbering and marshalling the Israelites in their journey through the wilderness to the Promised Land. Its English name is derived from the title it bears in the Vulgate Latin, *Numeri*, which is a literal translation of the Greek word *Arithmoi*, its title in the Septuagint; and from both, our Saxon ancestors called it *numeration*, "because in this the children of Israel were numbered." This title, however, does not properly apply to more than the three first chapters, and the twenty-sixth. This book, like the preceding, takes its name among the Hebrews from a distinguishing word in the commencement. It is frequently called *Vaidabber*, "and he spoke," from its initial word; but in most Hebrew Bibles its running title is *Bemidbar*, "in the wilderness," which is the fifth word in the first verse.

CHAPTER 1

On the first day of the second month of the second year after Israel came out of Egypt, God commands Moses to number all the males of the people from twenty years and upward, who were effective men and able to go to war, 1-3. A chief of each tribe is associated with Moses and Aaron in this business, 4; the names of whom are given, 5-16. Moses assembles the people, who declare their pedigrees according to their families, 17-19. The descendants of Reuben are numbered, and amount to 46,500, vv. 20-21. Those of Simeon, 59,300, vv. 22-23. Those of Gad, 45,650, vv. 24-25. Those of Judah, 74,600, vv. 26-27. Those of Issachar, 54,400, vv. 28-29. Those of Zebulun, 57,400, vv. 30-31. Those of Ephraim, 40,500, vv. 32-33. Those of Manasseh, 32,200, vv. 34-35. Those of Benjamin, 35,400, vv. 36-37. Those of Dan, 62,700, vv. 38-39. Those of Asher, 41,500, vv. 40-41. Those of Naphtali, 53,400, vv. 42-43. The amount of all the effective men in Israel, from twenty years old and upward, was 603,500, vv. 44-46. The Levites are not numbered with the tribes, because they were dedicated to the service of God. Their particular work is specified, 47-54.

1. *The Lord spake unto Moses . . . on the first day of the second month.* As the Tabernacle was erected upon the first day of the first month, in the second year after their coming out of Egypt, Exod. xl. 17; and this muster of the people was made on the first day of the second month, in the same year; it is evident that the transactions related in the preceding book must all have taken place in the space of one month, and during the time the Israelites were encamped at Mount Sinai, before they had begun their journey to the Promised Land.

2. *Take ye the sum.* God, having established the commonwealth of Israel by just and equitable laws, ordained everything relative to the due performance of His own worship, erected His tabernacle, which was His throne, and the place of His residence among the people, and consecrated His priests who were to minister before Him; He now orders His subjects to be mustered.

3. *From twenty years old and upward.* In this census no women were reckoned, nor children, nor strangers, nor the Levites, nor old men, which, collectively, must have formed an immense multitude; the Levites alone amounted to 22,300. Trueborn Israelites only are reckoned;

such as were able to carry arms, and were expert for war.

14. *Eliasaph, the son of Deuel.* This person is called Reuel, chap. ii. 14. As the *daleth* is very like the *resh*, it was easy to mistake the one for the other. The Septuagint and the Syriac have Reuel in this chapter; and in chap. ii. 14, the Vulgate, the Samaritan, and the Arabic have Deuel instead of Reuel, with which reading a vast number of MSS. concur; and this reading is supported by chap. x. 20. We may safely conclude therefore that *Deuel*, not *Reuel*, was the original reading.

16. *These were the renowned.* Literally, "the called," *of the congregation*—those who were summoned by name to attend.

33. *The tribe Ephraim . . . forty thousand and five hundred.* Ephraim, as he was blessed beyond his elder brother, Manasseh, Gen. xlviii. 20, so here he is increased by thousands more than Manasseh, and more than the whole tribe of Benjamin, and his blessing continued above his brother, Deut. xxxiii. 17. And thus the prophecy, Gen. xlviii. 19, was fulfilled: "His younger brother [Ephraim] shall be greater than he [Manasseh]."

46. *All they that were numbered were six hundred thousand and three thousand and five hundred and fifty.* What an astonishing increase from seventy souls that went down into Egypt, Gen. xlvi. 27, about two hundred fifteen years before, where latterly they had endured the greatest hardships!

In the second census, mentioned chap. xxvi. 34, Judah still has the preeminence; and Simeon, the third in number before, is become the least. Now we see also that the little tribe of Manasseh occupies the seventh place for number. Seven of the tribes had an increase; five, a decrease.

CHAPTER 2

Moses commanded to teach the Israelites how they are to pitch their tents, and erect the ensigns of their fathers houses, 1-2. Judah, Issachar, and Zebulun, on the east, amounting to 186,400 men, 3-9. Reuben, Simeon, and

Gad, on the south, with 151,450 men, 10-16. The Levites to be in the midst of the camp, 17. Ephraim, Manasseh, and Benjamin, on the west, with 108,100 men, 18-24. Dan, Asher, and Naphtali, on the north, with 157,600 men, 25-31. The sum total of the whole, 603,550 men, 32. But the Levites are not included, 33. The people do as the Lord commands them, 34.

CHAPTER 3

The generations of Aaron and Moses, 1-4. The tribe of Levi to minister to the Lord under Aaron and his sons, 5-10. They are taken in the place of the firstborn, 11-13. Moses is commanded to number them, 14-16. Gershon, Kohath, and Merari, the names of the three heads of families of the Levites, 17. Of Gershon and his family, 1821. Their number, 7,500, v. 22. Their place behind the Tabernacle, westward, 23. Their chief, Eliasaph, 24. Their charge, 25-26. Of Kohath and his family, 27. Their number, 8,600, v. 28. Their place, beside the Tabernacle, southward, 29. Their chief, Elizaphan, 30. Their charge, 31. The chief of the Levites, Eleazar, son of Aaron, 32. Of Merari and his family, 33. Their number, 6,200, v. 34. Their chief, Zuriel; they shall pitch beside the Tabernacle, northward, 35. Their charge, 35-37. Moses and Aaron to encamp before the Tabernacle, eastward, 38. The amount of all the males among the Levites from a month old and upwards, 22,000, v. 39. Moses is commanded to number the firstborn, 40; and to take the Levites and their cattle instead of the firstborn of man and beast among the Israelites, 41. Moses numbers the firstborn, who amount to 22,273, v. 43. As the firstborn were 273 more than the Levites, Moses is commanded to take from the people 5 shekels apiece for them, 44-47, which is to be given to Aaron and his sons, 48. Moses does accordingly, and finds the amount of the money to be 1,365 shekels, 49-50, which is given to Aaron and his sons, 51.

1. *The generations of Aaron and Moses.* Though Aaron and Moses are both mentioned here, yet the family of Aaron alone appears in the list; hence some have thought that the word *Moses* was not originally in the text. Others think that the words *veeleh toledoth*, "these are the generations," should be rendered "these are the acts," or transactions, or the history of the lives, as the same phrase may be understood in Gen. ii. 4; vi. 9. However this may be, it is evident that in this genealogy the family of Aaron are alone mentioned, probably because these belonged to the priesthood.

4. *Nadab and Abihu died.* See Lev. chap. x.

6. *Bring the tribe of Levi near.* The original word *hakreb* is properly a sacrificial word, and signifies the presenting of a sacrifice or offering to the Lord. As an offering, the tribe of Levi was given up entirely to the service of the sanctuary, to be no longer their own, but the Lord's property.

7. *The charge of the whole congregation.* They shall work for the whole congregation, and instead of the firstborn.

8. *All the instruments.* The Tabernacle itself and all its contents; see all described, vv. 25-26, 31, 36-37. The Levites were to perform the most common and laborious offices. It was their business to take down, put up, and carry the Tabernacle and its utensils; for it was the object of their peculiar care. In a word, they were the servants of the priests.

10. *Aaron and his sons . . . shall wait on their priest's office.* It was the business of the priests to offer the different sacrifices to God; to consecrate the shewbread, pour out the libations, burn the incense, sprinkle the blood of the victims, and bless the people. In a word, they were the servants of God alone.

12. *I have taken the Levites . . . instead of all the firstborn.* The Levites are taken for the service of the sanctuary in place of the firstborn. The firstborn were dedicated to God in commemoration of His slaying the firstborn of the Egyptians, and preserving those of the Israelites. Even the cattle of the Levites were taken in place of the firstborn of the cattle of the rest of the tribes. See v. 45.

Several reasons have been assigned why God should give this honor to the tribe of Levi in preference to all the others, but they do not seem to me to be conclusive. Their zeal in destroying those who had corrupted the worship of God in the business of the golden calf, Exod. xxxii. 28, has been thought a sufficient reason. A better reason is that this was the smallest tribe, and they were quite enough for the service. To have had a more numerous tribe at this time would have been very inconvenient.

15. *A month old and upward.* The males of all the other tribes were numbered from twenty years and upward; had the Levites been numbered in this way, they would not have been nearly equal in number to the firstborn of the twelve tribes. Add to this that, as there must have been firstborn of all ages in the other tribes, it was necessary that the Levites, who were to be their substitutes, should be also of all ages; and it appears to have been on this ground, at least partly, that the Levites were numbered from four weeks old and upward.

16. *Moses numbered them.* Though Moses and Aaron conjointly numbered the twelve tribes, yet Moses alone numbered the Levites; "for as the money with which the firstborn of Israel, who exceeded the number of Levites, were redeemed was to be paid to Aaron and his sons, v. 48, it was decent that he, whose advantage it was that the number of the firstborn of Israel should exceed, should not be authorized to take that number himself."

22. *Seven thousand and five hundred.* Perhaps originally *resh*, 200, instead of *caph*, 500; see the following note.

39. *Which Moses and Aaron numbered.* The word *veaharon*, "and Aaron," has a point over each of its letters, probably designed as a mark of spuriousness. The word is wanting in the Samaritan, Syriac, and Coptic; it is wanting also in eight of Dr. Kennicott's MSS., and in four of De Rossi's. Moses alone is commanded to take the number of the Levites; see vv. 5, 11, 40, 44, and 51.

All the males . . . were twenty and two thousand. This total does not agree with the particulars; for the Gershonites were 7,500, the Kohathites 8,600, the Merarites 6,200, total 22,300. Several methods of solving this difficulty have been proposed by learned men; Dr. Kennicott's is the most simple. Formerly the numbers in the Hebrew Bible were expressed by letters, and not by words at full length; and if two nearly similar letters were mistaken for each other, many errors in the numbers must be the consequence. Now it is probable that an error has crept into the number of the Gershonites, v. 22, where, instead of 7,500, we should read 7,200, as *caph*, 500, might have been easily mistaken for *resh*, 200, especially if the down stroke of the *caph* had been a little shorter than ordinary, which is often the case in MSS. The extra 300 being taken off, the total is just 22,000, as mentioned in the thirty-ninth verse.

43. *All the firstborn males . . . were twenty and two thousand two hundred and threescore and thirteen.* Thus we find there were 273 firstborn beyond the number of the Levites.

These are ordered, v. 46, to be redeemed; and the redemption price is to be 5 shekels each, v. 47, about 15s. And this money, amounting to 1,365 shekels, equal to £204 15s. English, he took of the firstborn of Israel, v. 50.

CHAPTER 4

Moses is commanded to take the sum of the sons of Kohath from thirty years old and upward, 1-4. The service which they had to perform, 5-15. The office of Eleazar, 16. The family of Kohath to be continued among the Levites, 17-19. They are not to go into the holy of holies, 20. The sum of the sons of Gershon, 21-23. The service they had to perform, 24-27. They are to be under Ithamar, 28. The sum of the sons of Merari, 29-30. The service they had to perform, 31-33. The sum of all the families of Kohath, 2,750, vv. 34-37. The sum of the families of Gershon, 2,630, vv. 38-41. The sum of the families of Merari, 3,200, vv. 42-45. The sum total of the families of Gershon, Kohath, and Merari, 8,580, vv. 46-49.

3. *From thirty years old.* In chap. viii. 24, the Levites are ordered to enter on the service of the Tabernacle at the age of twenty-five years; and in 1 Chron. xxiii. 24, they were ordered to commence that work at twenty years of age. How can these different times be reconciled? (1) At the time of which Moses speaks here, the Levitical service was exceedingly severe, and consequently required men full-grown, strong, and stout, to perform it; the age therefore of thirty years was appointed as the period for commencing this service. (2) In chap. viii. 24, Moses seems to speak of the service in a general way; the severe, which was to be performed by the full-grown Levites, and the less laborious work which younger men might assist in; hence the age of twenty-five is fixed. (3) In David's time and afterwards, in the fixed Tabernacle and Temple, the laboriousness of the service no longer existed, and hence twenty years was the age fixed on for all Levites to enter into the work of the sanctuary. *Until fifty years old.* This was allowing twenty years for public severe service, a very considerate and merciful ordinance.

20. *When the holy things are covered.* Literally, *keballa,* when they are "swallowed down"; which shows the promptitude with which everything belonging to the holy of holies was put out of sight, for these mysteries must ever be treated with the deepest reverence; and indeed without this they could not have been to them the representatives of heavenly realities.

36. *Those that were numbered.* In chap. iii. 27, etc., we have an account of the whole number of the Levites, and here of those only who were able to serve the Lord in the sanctuary. Thus we find that the whole number of the Levites amounted to 22,300, of whom 8,580 were fit for service, and 13,720 unfit, being either too old or too young.

From this and the preceding chapter we see the very severe labor which the Levites were obliged to perform while the journeyings of the Israelites lasted. When we consider that there was almost ten tons and fourteen hundred pounds' weight of metal employed in the Tabernacle, besides the immense weight of the skins, hangings, cords, boards, and posts, we shall find it was no very easy matter to transport this movable Temple from place to place. The Gershonites, who were 7,500 men in the service, had to carry the tent, coverings, veils, hangings of the court, etc., chap. iii. 25-26. The Kohathites, who were 8,600 men, had to carry the ark, table, candlestick, altars, and instruments of the sanctuary, chap. iii. 31. The Merarites, who were 6,200 men, had to carry the boards, bars, pillars, sockets, and all matters connected with these belonging to the Tabernacle, with the pillars of the court, their sockets, pins, and cords, chap. iii. 36-37.

CHAPTER 5

The Israelites are commanded to purify the camp by excluding all lepers, and all diseased and unclean persons, 1-3. They do so, 4. Law concerning him who has defrauded another—he shall confess his sin, restore the principal, and add besides one-fifth of its value, 5-7. If he have no kinsman to whom the recompense can be made, it shall be given unto the Lord, 8. All the holy things offered to the Lord shall be the priest's portion, 9-10. The law concerning jealousy, 11-14. The suspected woman's offering, 15. She is to be brought before the Lord, 16. The priest shall take holy water, and put it in dust from the floor of the Tabernacle, 17. Shall put the offering in her hand, and adjure her, 18-20. The form of the oath, 21-22; which is to be written on a book, blotted out in the bitter waters, and these the suspected person shall be obliged to drink, 23-24. The jealousy offering shall be waved before the Lord, 25-26. The effect which shall be produced if the suspected person be guilty, 27. The effect if not guilty, 28. Recapitulation, with the purpose and design of the law, 29-30.

2. *Put out of the camp every leper.* According to the preceding plan, it is sufficiently evident that each camp had a space behind it, and on one side, whither the infected might be removed, and where probably convenient places were erected for the accommodation of the infected; for we cannot suppose that they were driven out into the naked wilderness. But the expulsion mentioned here was founded (1) On a purely physical reason, viz., the diseases were contagious, and therefore there was a necessity of putting those afflicted by them apart, that the infection might not be communicated. (2) There was also a spiritual reason; the camp was the habitation of God, and nothing impure should be permitted to remain where He dwelt.

4. *And the children of Israel . . . put them out.* This is the earliest account we have of such separations; and probably this ordinance gave the first idea of a hospital, where all those who are afflicted with contagious disorders are put into particular wards, under medical treatment.

7. *Shall confess their sin.* Without confession or acknowledgment of sin, there was no hope of mercy held out. *He shall recompense.* For without restitution, in every possible case, God will not forgive the iniquity of a man's sin. How can any person in a case of defraud, with his neighbor's property in his possession, expect to receive mercy from the hand of a just and holy God?

8. *If the man have no kinsman.* The Jews think that this law respects the stranger and the sojourner only, because every Israelite is in a state of affinity to all the rest; but there might be a stranger in the camp who has no relative in any of the tribes of Israel.

14. *The spirit of jealousy.* *Ruach kinah,* either a supernatural diabolic influence, exciting him to jealousy, or the passion or affection of jealousy, for so the words may be understood.

17. *Holy water.* Water out of the laver, called *holy* because consecrated to sacred uses. This is the most ancient case of the trial by ordeal. *In an earthen vessel.* Supposed by the Jews to be such as had never been previously used. *Dust that is in the floor.* Probably intended to

point out the baseness of the crime of which she was accused.

18. *Uncover the woman's head.* To take off a woman's veil, and expose her to the sight of men, would be considered a very great degradation in the East. To this Paul appears to allude, 1 Cor. xi. 5-6, 10.

21. *The Lord make thee a curse and an oath.* Let thy name and punishment be remembered and mentioned as an example and terror to all others. Like that mentioned Jer. xxix. 22-23: "The Lord make thee like Zedekiah and like Ahab, whom the king of Babylon roasted in the fire; because they have committed villany in Israel, and have committed adultery with their neighbours' wives."

22. *Thy belly to swell, and thy thigh to rot.* What is meant by these expressions cannot be easily ascertained. *Lanpel yarech* signifies literally thy "thigh to fall." As the *thigh,* feet, etc., were used among the Hebrews delicately to express the parts which nature conceals (see Gen. xlvi. 26), the expression here is probably to be understood in this sense; and the falling down of the thigh here must mean something similar to the falling down of the womb, which might be a natural effect of the preternatural distension of the abdomen. *And the woman shall say, Amen, amen.* This is the first place where this word occurs in the common form of a concluding wish in prayer. The root *aman* signifies to be "steady, true, permanent." And in prayer it signifies, "Let it be so—make it steady—let it be ratified."

23. *The priest shall write these curses . . . and he shall blot them out.* It appears that the curses which were written down with a kind of ink prepared for the purpose, as some of the rabbins think, without any calx of iron or other material that could make a permanent dye, were washed off the parchment into the water which the woman was obliged to drink, so that she drank the very words of the execration. The ink used in the East is almost all of this kind— a wet sponge will completely efface the finest of their writings. The rabbins say that the trial by the waters of jealousy was omitted after the Babylonish captivity, because adulteries were so frequent among them that they were afraid of having the name of the Lord profaned by being so frequently appealed to! This is a most humiliating confession.

24. *The bitter water that causeth the curse.* Though the rabbins think that the priest put some bitter substance in the water, yet as nothing of the kind is intimated by Moses, we may consider the word as used here metaphorically for affliction, death, etc. These waters were afflicting and deadly to her who drank them, being guilty. In this sense afflictions are said to be bitter, Isa. xxxviii. 17; so also is death, 1 Sam. xv. 32; Eccles. vii. 26.

29. *This is the law of jealousies.* And this is the most singular law in the whole Pentateuch: a law that seems to have been copied by almost all the nations of the earth, whether civilized or barbarian, as we find that similar modes of trial for suspected offenses were used when complete evidence was wanting to convict; and where it was expected that the object of their worship would interfere for the sake of justice, in order that the guilty should be brought to punishment, and the innocent be cleared.

31. *This woman shall bear her iniquity.* That is, her belly shall swell, and her thigh shall rot; see on v. 22.

CHAPTER 6

The vow of the Nazarite, 1-2. In what it consisted, 3-8. When accidentally defiled, how he is to be purified, 9-12. The sacrifices he is to bring, and the rites he is to perform, when the vow of his separation is fulfilled, 13-21. The manner in which the priests are to bless the people, 22-26. The name of the Lord is to be put on the children of Israel, whom He promises to bless, 27.

2. *When either man or woman shall separate.* The word *nazir,* from *nazar,* to *separate,* signifies merely a separated person, i.e., one peculiarly devoted to the service of God by being separated from all service employments. From the Nazarites sprang the Rechabites, from the Rechabites the Essenes, from the Essenes the Anchorites or Hermits, and in imitation of those, the different monastic orders.

3. *No vinegar of wine.* *Chomets* signifies fermented wine, and is probably used here to signify wine of a strong body, or any highly intoxicating liquor.

5. *There shall no razor come upon his head.* The vow of the Nazarite consisted in the following particulars: (1) He consecrated himself in a very especial and extraordinary manner to God. (2) This was to continue for a certain season, probably never less than a whole year, that he might have a full growth of hair to "burn in the fire which is under the sacrifice of the peace offerings," v. 18. (3) During the time of his separation, or *nazarate,* he drank no wine nor strong drink; nor used any vinegar formed from any inebriating liquor, nor ate the flesh or dried grapes, nor tasted even the kernels or husks of anything that had grown upon the vine. (4) He never shaved his head, but let his hair grow, as the proof of his being in this separated state, and under vows of peculiar austerity. (5) He never touched any dead body, nor did any of the last offices, even to his nearest kin; but was considered as the priests, who were wholly taken up with the service of God, and regarded nothing else. (6) All the days of his separation he was holy, v. 8. During the whole time he was to be incessantly employed in religious acts.

7. *The consecration of his God is upon his head.* Literally, "The separation of his God is upon his head"; meaning his hair, which was the proof and emblem of his separation.

10. *Two turtles, or two young pigeons.* The same kind of offering made by him who had an issue, Lev. xv. 14, etc.

18. *Shall take the hair . . . and put it in the fire.* The hair was permitted to grow for this purpose; and as the Nazarite was a kind of sacrifice, offered to God through the whole term of his *nazarate* or separation, and no human flesh or blood could be offered on the altar of the Lord, he offered his hair at the conclusion of his separation, as a sacrifice—that hair which was the token of his complete subjection to the Lord and which was now considered as the Lord's property.

23. *On this wise ye shall bless the children of Israel.* The prayer which God makes for His followers and puts into their mouth we are sure must be right; and to it, when sincerely, faithfully, and fervently offered, we may confidently

expect an answer. If He condescended to give us a form of blessings or a form of prayer, we may rest assured that He will accept what He himself has made. This consideration may produce great confidence in them who come with either prayer or praise to the throne of grace, both of which should be, as far as circumstances will admit, in the very words of Scripture; for we can readily attach a consequence to the words of God which we shall find difficult to attach to the best ordered words of men.

24. *The Lord bless thee.* There are three forms of blessing here, any or all of which the priests might use on any occasion. The following is a verbal translation:

> *May Jehovah bless thee and preserve thee!*
> *May Jehovah cause His faces to shine upon thee, and be gracious unto thee!*
> *May Jehovah lift up His faces upon thee, and may He put prosperity unto thee!*

CHAPTER 7

When the Tabernacle was fully set up, it appeared that the princes of the twelve tribes had prepared six covered wagons, drawn by two oxen each, one wagon for two tribes, for the service of the Tabernacle, 1-3. Moses is commanded to receive this offering, and distribute the whole to the Levites according to their service, 4-5. Moses does so, and gives two wagons and four oxen to the sons of Gershon, 6-7; and four wagons and eight oxen to the sons of Merari, 8. The sons of Kohath have none, because they are to bear the ark, etc., on their shoulders, 9. Each prince is to take a day for presenting his offerings, 10-11. On the first day, Nahshon, of the tribe of Judah, offers a silver charger, a silver bowl, a golden spoon, a young bullock, a ram, a lamb, and a kid, for a sin offering; two oxen, five rams, five he-goats, and five lambs, for a peace offering, 12-17. On the second day Nethaneel, of the tribe of Issachar, offers the like, 18-23. On the third day Eliab, of the tribe of Zebulun, offers the like, 24-29. On the fourth day Elizur, of the tribe of Reuben, offers the like, 30-35. On the fifth day Shelumiel, of the tribe of Simeon, made a similar offering, 36-41. On the sixth day Eliasaph, of the tribe of Gad, made his offering, 42-47. On the seventh day Elishama, of the tribe of Ephraim, made his offering, 48-53. On the eighth day Gamaliel, of the tribe of Manasseh, made his offering, 54-59. On the ninth day Abidan, of the tribe of Benjamin, made his offering, 60-65. On the tenth day Ahiezer, of the tribe of Dan, made his offering, 66-71. On the eleventh day of Pagiel, of the tribe of Asher, made his offering, 72-77. On the twelfth day Ahira, of the tribe of Naphtali, made the same kind of offering, 78-83. The sum total of all vessels and cattle which were offered was twelve silver chargers and twelve silver bowls; twelve golden spoons; twelve bullocks, twelve rams, and twelve kids; twenty-four bullocks, sixty rams, sixty he-goats, and sixty lambs, 84-88. The offerings being ended, Moses goes into the Tabernacle, and hears the voice of the Lord from the mercy seat, 89.

1. *On the day that Moses had fully set up the tabernacle.* The transactions mentioned in this chapter took place on the second day of the second month of the second year after their departure from Egypt; and the proper place of this account is immediately after the tenth chapter of Leviticus.

5. *According to his service.* That is, distribute them among the Levites as they may need them, giving most to those who have the heaviest burdens to bear.

7. *Two wagons . . . unto the sons of Gershon.* The Gershonites carried only the curtains, coverings, and hangings, chap. iv. 25. And although this was a cumbersome carriage, and they needed the wagons, yet it was not a heavy one.

8. *Four wagons . . . unto the sons of Merari.* Because they had the boards, bars, pillars, and sockets of the Tabernacle to carry, chap. iv. 31-32, therefore they had as many more wagons as the Gershonites.

9. *Unto the sons of Kohath he gave none.* Because they had the charge of the ark, table, candlestick, altars, etc., chap. iv. 5-15, which were to be carried upon their shoulders; for those sacred things must not be drawn by beasts.

10. *And the princes offered.* Every prince or chief offered in the behalf, and doubtless at the expense, of his whole tribe.

13. *One silver charger. Kaarath,* a "dish," or deep bowl, in which they kneaded the paste. *One silver bowl. Mizrak,* a "bason," to receive the blood of the sacrifice in.

14. *One spoon. Caph,* a "censer," on which they put the incense.

48. *On the seventh day.* Both Jewish and Christian writers have been surprised that this work of offering went forward on the seventh day, which they suppose to have been a Sabbath, as well as on the other days. But (1) There is no absolute proof that this seventh day of offering was a Sabbath. (2) Were it even so, could the people be better employed than in thus consecrating themselves and their services to the Lord?

72. *On the eleventh day.* The Hebrew form of expression, here and in the seventy-eighth verse, has something curious in it. *Beyom ashtey asar yom,* "In the day, the first and tenth day"; *beyom sheneym asar yom,* "In the day, two and tenth day." But this is the idiom of the language, and to an original Hebrew our almost anamalous words eleventh and twelfth, by which we translate the original, would appear as strange as his, literally translated, would appear to us. In reckoning after twelve, it is easy to find out the composition of the words thirteen, as three and ten, fourteen, four and ten, and so on; but eleven and twelve bear scarcely any analogy to ten and one, and ten and two, which nevertheless they intend.

84. *This was the dedication of the altar, in the day.* Meaning here the time in which it was dedicated; for as each tribe had a whole day for its representative or prince to present the offerings it had provided, consequently the dedication, in which each had his day, must have lasted twelve days. The words therefore, in this text, refer to the last day or twelfth, in which this dedication was completed.

88. *After that it was anointed.* By the anointing the altar was consecrated to God; by this dedication it was solemnly appointed to that service for which it had been erected.

89. *To speak with him.* To confer with God, and to receive farther discoveries of His will. *He heard the voice of one speaking unto him.* Though Moses saw no similitude, but only heard a voice, yet he had the fullest proof of the presence as well as of the being of the Almighty. In this way God chose to manifest himself during that dispensation. *The mercy seat.* See the note on Exod. xxv. 17. As God gave oracular answers from this place, and spoke to Moses as it were face-to-face, hence the place was called the "oracle," *debir,* or "speaking place," from *dabar,* "he spoke," 1 Kings vi. 23. And as this *mercy seat* represented our blessed Redeemer, so the apostle says that "God, who at sundry times and in divers manners spake in time past unto the fathers by the prophets, hath in these last days spoken unto us by his Son," Heb. i. 1-2.

Hence the *incarnated* Christ is the true *debir* or "oracle," in and by whom God speaks unto man.

CHAPTER 8

Directions how the lamps are to be lighted, 1-3. How the candlestick was formed, 4. The Levites to be consecrated to their service by being cleansed, sprinkled, shaved, purified, and their clothes washed, 5-7. To offer a meat offering and a sin offering, 8. The people to put their hands upon them, 9-10. Aaron is to offer them before the Lord, 11. The Levites to lay their hands on the heads of the bullocks, etc., 12. The Levites are taken to assist Aaron and his sons in the place of all the first-born of Israel, 13-19. Moses and Aaron do as they were commanded; the Levites are presented, purified, and commence their service, 20-22. They are to begin their service at twenty-five years of age, and leave off at fifty, 23-25. After this they shall have the general inspection of the service, 26.

2. *The seven lamps shall give light.* The whole seven shall be lighted at one time, that seven may be ever burning.

4. *This work of the candlestick.* See many curious particulars relative to this candlestick in the notes on Exod. xxv. 31 and 39. The candlestick itself was an emblem of the Church of Christ; the oil, of the graces and gifts of the Spirit of God; and the light, of those gifts and graces in action among men. See Rev. i. 12-20. God builds His Church and sends forth His Spirit to dwell in it, to sanctify and cleanse it, that it may be shown unto the world as His own workmanship. The seven lights in the candlesticks point out "the seven Spirits of God," the Holy Ghost being thus termed, Rev. iii. 1, from the variety and abundance of His gifts and influences; seven being used among the Hebrews to denote anything full, complete, and perfect. A candlestick or lamp without oil is of no use; oil not burning is of no use. So a church or society of religious people without the influence of the Holy Ghost are dead while they have a name to live; and if they have a measure of this light, and do not let it shine by purity of living and holy zeal before men, their religion is neither useful to themselves nor to others.

7. *Sprinkle water of purifying. Mey chattath,* "water of sin," or "water of the sin offering." As this purifying water was made by the ashes of the red heifer, cedarwood, hyssop, and scarlet; and the blood of the heifer itself was sprinkled seven times before the Tabernacle, Num. xix. 3-6; she may be considered as a proper sacrifice for sin, and consequently the water thus prepared be termed the "water of the sin offering." As the ashes were kept ready at hand for purifying from all legal pollutions, the preparation might be considered as a concentration of the essential properties of the sin offering, and might be resorted to at all times with comparatively little expense or trouble and no loss of time. As there were so many things by which legal pollution might be contracted, it was necessary to have always at hand, in all their dwellings, a mode of purifying at once convenient and inexpensive. We see from Heb. ix. 13-14 that these ashes, mingled with water and sprinkled on the unclean, and which sanctified to the purification of the flesh, were intended to typify the blood of Christ, which purges the "conscience from dead works to serve the living God," v. 14. For as without this sprinkling with the water of the sin offering the Levites were not fit to serve God in the wilderness, so without this sprinkling of the blood of Christ no conscience can be purged "from dead

works to serve the living God." See the notes on chap. xix. 1-10.

10. *Shall put their hands upon the Levites.* It has been argued from this that the congregation had a part in the appointment of their own ministers, and that this was done by the imposition of hands. However that may be, it appears that what was done on this occasion meant no more than that the people gave up this whole tribe to God in place of their first-born; and that by this act they bound themselves to provide for them who, because of their sacred service, could follow no secular work.

17. *For all the firstborn . . . are mine.* See the manner of redeeming the firstborn, chap. xviii. 6.

21. *And Aaron made an atonement for them.* Though the Levites had been most solemnly consecrated to the Lord's service, and though all legal washings and purifications were duly performed on the occasion, yet they could not approach God till an atonement had been made for them. How strange is it, after all these significations, of the will and purpose of God relative to man, that any priest or any people will attempt to draw nigh to God without an atonement! As sure as God hath spoken it, there is no entrance into the holiest but through the blood of Jesus, Heb. x. 19-20.

24. *From twenty and five years old.* See the note on chap. iv. 47, where the two terms of twenty-five and thirty years are reconciled.

26. *To keep the charge, and shall do no service.* They shall no longer be obliged to perform any laborious service, but act as general directors and counsellors. Therefore they were to be near the camp, sing praises to God, and see that no stranger or unclean person was permitted to enter. So the Jews and many other persons have understood this place.

CHAPTER 9

The Israelites are reminded of the law that required them to keep the Passover at its proper time, and with all its rites, 1-3. They kept the Passover on the fourteenth day of the first month, 4-5. The case of the men who, being unclean through touching a dead body, could not keep the Passover, 6-7. Moses inquires of the Lord concerning them, 8; and the Lord appoints the fourteenth day of the second month for all those who through any accidental uncleanness, or by being absent on a journey, could not keep it at the usual time, 9-12. He who neglects to keep this solemn feast to be cut off from among his people, 13. The stranger who wishes to keep the Passover is at liberty to do it, 14. The cloud covers the Tabernacle by both day and night, from the time of its dedication, 15-16. This cloud regulates all the encampments and marchings of the Israelites through the wilderness, 17-22. Their journeyings and restings are all directed by the commandment of the Lord, 23.

1. *The Lord spake unto Moses.* The first fourteen verses of this chapter certainly refer to transactions that took place at the time of those mentioned in the commencement of this book, before the numbering of the people, and several learned men are of opinion that these fourteen verses should be referred back to that place. We have already met with instances where transpositions have very probably taken place, and it is not difficult to account for them. As in very early times writing was generally on leaves of the Egyptian flag *papyrus*, facts and transactions thus entered were very liable to be deranged; so that when afterwards a series was made up into a book, many transactions might be inserted in wrong places, and thus the exact chronology of the facts be greatly disturbed.

This one consideration will account for several transpositions, especially in the Pentateuch, where they occur more frequently than in any other part of the sacred writings.

3. *According to all the rites of it.* See all those rites and ceremonies largely explained in the notes on Exodus xii.

7. *We are defiled by the dead body of a man.* It is probable that the defilement mentioned here was occasioned by assisting at the burial of some person—a work of both necessity and mercy. This circumstance however gave rise to the ordinance delivered in verses 10-14, so that on particular occasions the Passover might be twice celebrated: (1) At its regular time, the fourteenth of the first month; (2) An extra time, the fourteenth of the second month. But the man who had no legal hinderance, and did not celebrate it on one or other of these times, was to be cut off from the people of God; and the reason given for this cutting off is that he brought not the offering of God in His appointed season—therefore "that man shall bear his sin," v. 13.

15. *The cloud covered the tabernacle.* See the whole account of this supernatural cloud largely explained, Exod. xiii. 21 and xl. 34-38.

21. *Whether . . . by day or by night.* As the heat of the day is very severe in that same desert, the night season is sometimes chosen for the performance of a journey, though it is very likely that in the case of the Israelites this was seldom resorted to.

23. *Kept the charge of the Lord.* When we consider the strong disposition which this people ever testified to follow their own will in all things, we may be well surprised to find them, in these journeyings, so implicitly following the directions of God. There could be no trick or imposture here. Moses, had he been the most cunning of men, never could have imitated the appearances referred to in this chapter. The cloud, and everything in its motion, was so evidently supernatural that the people had no doubt of its being the symbol of the divine presence.

CHAPTER 10

Moses is commanded to make two silver trumpets for calling the assembly, 1-2. On what occasions these trumpets should be sounded. First, for calling the assembly to the door of the Tabernacle, 3. Secondly, to summon the princes and captains of the thousands of Israel, 4. Thirdly, to make the eastern camps strike their tents, 5. Fourthly, to make those on the south do the like, 6. No alarm to be sounded when the congregation only is to be assembled, 7. The sons of Aaron alone shall sound these trumpets; it shall be a perpetual ordinance, 8. Fifthly, the trumpets are to be sounded in the time of war, 9. Sixthly, on festival occasions, 10. On the twentieth day of the second month, in the second year, the Israelites began their journey from the wilderness of Sinai, and came to the wilderness of Paran, 11-12. By the commandment of God to Moses the first division, at the head of which was the standard of *Judah*, marched first, 13-14. Under him followed the tribe of Issachar, 15, and after them the tribe of Zebulun, 16. Then the Gershonites and Merarites followed with the Tabernacle, 17. At the head of the second division was the standard and camp of Reuben, 18; and under him were that of Simeon, 19; and that of Gad, 20. Next followed the Kohathites, bearing the sanctuary, 21. Then followed the third division, at the head of which was the standard of the camp of *Ephraim*, 22; and under him Manasseh, 23; and Benjamin, 24. At the head of the fourth division was the standard of the camp of *Dan*, 25; and under him Asher, 26; and Naphtali, 27. This was their ordinary method of marching in the wilderness, 28. Moses entreats Hobab the Midianite to accompany them through the wilderness, 29. He refuses, 30. Moses continues and strengthens his entreaties with reasonings and promises, 31-32. They depart from Sinai three days' jour-

ney, 33. The cloud accompanies them by day and night, 34. The words used by Moses when the ark set forward, 35, and when it rested, 36.

2. *Make thee two trumpets of silver.* As the trumpets were to be blown by the priests only, the sons of Aaron, there were only 2, because there were only 2 such persons to use them at this time, Eleazar and Ithamar. In the time of Joshua there were 7 trumpets used by the priests, but these were made, according to our text, of rams' horns, Josh. vi. 4. In the time of Solomon, when the priests had greatly increased, there were 120 priests sounding with trumpets, 2 Chron. v. 12. Josephus intimates that one of these trumpets was always used to call the nobles together, the other to assemble the people; see v. 4. It is possible that these trumpets were made of different lengths and wideness, and consequently they would emit different tones. Thus the sound itself would at once show which was the summons for the congregation, and which for the princes only. These trumpets were allowed to be emblematical of the sound of the gospel, and in this reference they appear to be frequently used.

5. *When ye blow an alarm.* Teruah, probably meaning "short, broken, sharp" tones, terminating with long ones, blown with both the trumpets at once.

6. *When ye blow an alarm the second time.* A single alarm, as above stated, was a signal for the eastward division to march; two such alarms, the signal for the south division; and probably three for the west division, and four for the north. It is more likely that this was the case than that a single alarm served for each, with a small interval between them.

9. *If ye go to war.* These trumpets shall be sounded for the purpose of collecting the people together, to deliberate about the war, and to implore the protection of God against their enemies.
Ye shall be remembered before the Lord. When you decamp, encamp, make war, and hold religious festivals, according to His appointment, which appointment shall be signified to you by the priests, who at the command of God, for such purposes, shall blow the trumpets, then you may expect both the presence and blessing of Jehovah in all that you undertake.

10. *In the day of your gladness.* On every festival the people shall be collected by the same means.

11. *The twentieth day of the second month.* The Israelites had lain encamped in the wilderness of Sinai about eleven months and twenty days; compare Exod. xix. 1 with this verse. They now received the order of God to decamp, and proceeded towards the Promised Land; and therefore the Samaritan introduces at this place the words which we find in Deut. i. 6-8: "The Lord our God spake unto us in Horeb, saying, Ye have dwelt long enough in this mount: turn you, and take your journey," etc.

12. *The cloud rested in the wilderness of Paran.* This was three days' journey from the wilderness of Sinai (see v. 33) and the people had three stations; the first at Kibroth-hattaavah, the second at Hazeroth, chap. xi. 35, and the third in the wilderness of Paran, see chap. xii. 16.

14. *The standard . . . of Judah.* The following

is the order in which this vast company proceeded in their march:

Judah, Issachar, Zebulun, Gershonites and Merarites carrying the Tabernacle

Reuben, Simeon, Gad, and the Kohathites with the sanctuary

Ephraim, Manasseh, Benjamin, Dan, Asher, Naphtali

29. *Moses said unto Hobab.* For a circumstantial account of this person see the notes on Exod. ii. 15-16, 18; iii. 1; iv. 20, 24; and for the transaction recorded here, and which is probably out of its place, see Exod. xviii. 5, where the subject is discussed at large. *We are journeying.* God has brought us out of thraldom, and we are thus far on our way through the wilderness, travelling towards the place of rest which He has appointed us, trusting in His promise, guided by His presence, and supported by His power. *Come thou with us, and we will do thee good.* Those who wish to enjoy the heavenly inheritance must walk in the way towards it, and associate with the people who are going in that way. True religion is ever benevolent. They who know most of the goodness of God are the most forward to invite others to partake of that goodness. *The Lord hath spoken good concerning Israel.* The name Israel is taken in a general sense to signify the followers of God, and to them all the promises in the Bible are made. God has spoken good of them, and He has spoken good to them; and not one word that He hath spoken shall fail.

30. *I will not go; but I will depart to mine own land, and to my kindred.* From the strong expostulations in verses 31 and 32, and from Judg. i. 16; iv. 11; and 1 Sam. xv. 6, it is likely that Hobab changed his mind; or that, if he did go back to Midian, he returned again to Israel, as the above scriptures show that his posterity dwelt among the Israelites in Canaan.

31. *Thou mayest be to us instead of eyes.* But what need had they of Hobab, when they had the pillar and fire continually to point out their way? Answer: The cloud directed their general journeys, but not their particular excursions. Parties took several journeys while the grand army lay still. (See chaps. xiii, xx, xxxi, xxxii, etc.) They therefore needed such a person as Hobab, who was well acquainted with the desert, to direct these particular excursions; to point them out watering places, and places where they might meet with fuel, etc.

33. *The ark . . . went before them.* We find from v. 21 that the ark was carried by the Kohathites in the center of the army; but as the army never moved till the cloud was taken up, it is said to go before them, i.e., to be the first to move, as without this motion the Israelites continued in their encampments.

35. *Rise up, Lord, and let thine enemies be scattered.* If God did not arise in this way and scatter His enemies, there could be no hope that Israel could get safely through the wilderness. God must go first, if Israel would wish to follow in safety.

36. *Return, O Lord, unto the many thousands of Israel.* These were the words spoken by Moses, at the moment the divisions halted in order to pitch their tents. In reference to this subject, and the history with which it is connected, Psalms 68 seems to have been composed,

though applied by David to the bringing of the ark from Kirjath-jearim to Jerusalem. *Many thousands,* literally "the ten thousand thousands."

CHAPTER 11

The people complain, the Lord is displeased, and many of them are consumed by fire, 1. Moses intercedes for them, and the fire is quenched, 2. The place is called Taberah, 3. The mixed multitude long for flesh, and murmur, 4-6. The manna described, 7-9. The people weep in their tents, and the Lord is displeased, 10. Moses deplores his lot in being obliged to hear and bear with all their murmurings, 11-15. He is commanded to bring seventy of the elders to God that He may endue them with the same spirit, and cause them to divide the burden with him, 16-17. He is also commanded to inform the people that they shall have flesh for a whole month, 18-20. Moses expresses his doubt of the possibility of this, 21-22. The Lord confirms His promise, 23. The seventy men are brought to the Tabernacle, 24; and the spirit of prophecy rests upon them, 25. Eldad and Medad stay in the camp and prophesy, 26-27. Joshua beseeches Moses to forbid them, 28. Moses refuses, 29-30. A wind from the Lord brings quails to the camp, 31-32. While feeding on the flesh, a plague from the Lord falls upon them, and many of them die, 33. The place is called Kibroth-hattaavah, or the graves of lust, 34. They journey to Hazeroth, 35.

1. *And when the people complained.* What the cause of this complaining was, we know not. The conjecture of Jerome is probable; they complained because of the length of the way. *It displeased the Lord.* For His extraordinary kindness was lost on such an ungrateful and rebellious people. *And his anger was kindled—*divine justice was necessarily incensed against such inexcusable conduct. *And the fire of the Lord burnt among them.* Either a supernatural fire was sent for this occasion, or the lightning was commissioned against them, or God smote them with one of those hot, suffocating winds which are very common in those countries. *And consumed . . . in the uttermost parts of the camp.* It pervaded the whole camp, from the center to the circumference, carrying death with it to all the murmurers; for we are not to suppose that it was confined to the uttermost parts of the camp, unless we could imagine that there were none culpable anywhere else. If this were the same with the case mentioned in v. 4, then, as it is possible that the mixed multitude occupied the outermost parts of the camp, consequently the burning might have been confined to them.

2. *The fire was quenched.* Was "sunk," or swallowed up, as in the margin. The plague, of whatever sort, ceased to act, and the people had respite.

4. *The mixt multitude. Hasaphsuph,* the "collected or gathered people." Such as came out of Egypt with the Israelites; and are mentioned Exod. xii. 38. This mongrel people, who had comparatively little of the knowledge of God, feeling the difficulties and fatigues of the journey, were the first to complain.

5. *We remember.* The choice aliments which those murmurers complained of having lost by their leaving Egypt were the following: fish, cucumbers, melons, leeks, onions, and garlic. This enumeration takes in almost all the commonly attainable delicacies in those countries.

7. *The manna was as coriander seed.* Probably this short description is added to show the iniquity of the people in murmuring, while they had so adequate a provision. But the baseness of their minds appears in every part of their conduct.

11-15. The complaint and remonstrance of Moses in these verses serve at once to show the deeply distressed state of his mind and the degradation of the minds of the people. We have already seen that the slavery they had so long endured had served to debase their minds, and to render them incapable of every high and dignified sentiment, and of every generous act.

22. *Shall the flocks and the herds be slain?* There is certainly a considerable measure of weakness and unbelief manifested in the complaints and questions of Moses on this occasion; but his conduct appears at the same time so very simple, honest, and affectionate that we cannot but admire it, while we wonder that he had not stronger confidence in that God whose miracles he had so often witnessed in Egypt.

23. *Is the Lord's hand waxed short?* Have you forgotten the miracles which I have already performed? or think you that My power is decreased? The power that is unlimited can never be diminished.

25. *When the spirit rested upon them, they prophesied.* By prophesying here we are to understand their performing those civil and sacred functions for which they were qualified; exhorting the people to quiet and peaceable submission, to trust and confidence in the goodness and providence of God, would make no small part of the duties of their new office. The ideal meaning of the word *naba* is to "pray, entreat." The prophet is called *nabi*, because he prays, supplicates, in reference to God; exhorts, entreats, in reference to man.

27. *Eldad and Medad do prophesy.* These, it seems, made two of the seventy elders; they were written, though they went not out to the Tabernacle; they were enrolled as of the elders, but not to meet God at the Tabernacle, probably at that time prevented by some legal hinderance, but they continued in the camp using their new function in exhorting the people.

28. *My lord Moses, forbid them.* Joshua was afraid that the authority and influence of his master Moses might be lessened by the part Eldad and Medad were taking in the government of the people, which might ultimately excite sedition or insurrection among them.

29. *Enviest thou for my sake?* Are you jealous of their influence only on my account? I am not alarmed; on the contrary, I would to God that all His people were endued with the same influence, and actuated by the same motives.

31. *A wind from the Lord.* An extraordinary one, not the effect of a natural cause. *And brought quails,* a bird which in great companies visits Egypt about the time of the year, March or April, at which the circumstance marked here took place. *Two cubits high upon the face of the earth.* We may consider the quails as flying within two cubits of the ground; so that the Israelites could easily take as many of them as they wished, while flying within the reach of their hands or their clubs. The common notion is that the quails were brought round about the camp, and fell there in such multitudes as to lie two feet thick upon the ground; but the Hebrew will not bear this version. The Vulgate has expressed the sense, "And they flew in the air, two cubits high above the ground."

32. *The people stood up.* While these immense flocks were flying at this short distance from the ground, fatigued with the strong wind and the distance they had come, they were easily taken by the people; and as various flocks continued to succeed each other for two days and a night, enough for a month's provision might be collected in that time. If the quails had fallen about the tents, there was no need to have stood up two days and a night in gathering them; but if they were on the wing, as the text seems to suppose, it was necessary for them to use dispatch, and avail themselves of the passing of these birds while it continued. *And they spread them all abroad.* Maillet observes that birds of all kinds come to Egypt for refuge from the cold of a northern winter; and that the people catch them, pluck, and bury them in the burning sand for a few minutes, and thus prepare them for use. This is probably what is meant by spreading them all abroad round the camp.

33. *The wrath of the Lord was kindled.* In what way, and with what effects, we cannot precisely determine. Some heavy judgment fell upon those murmurers and complainers, but of what kind the sacred writer says nothing.

34. *Kibroth-hattaavah.* "The graves of lust"; and thus their scandalous crime was perpetuated by the name of the place.

CHAPTER 12

Miriam and Aaron raise a sedition against Moses, because of the Ethiopian woman he had married, 1, and through jealousy of his increasing power and authority, 2. The character of Moses, 3. Moses, Aaron, and Miriam are suddenly called to the Tabernacle, 4. The Lord appears in the pillar of the cloud, and converses with them, 5. Declares His purpose to communicate His will to Moses only, 6-8. His anger is kindled against Miriam, and she is smitten with the leprosy, 9-10. Aaron deplores his transgression, and entreats for Miriam, 11-12. Moses intercedes for her, 13. The Lord requires that she be shut out of the camp for seven days, 14. The people rest till she is restored, 15, and afterwards leave Hazeroth, and pitch in the wilderness of Paran, 16.

1. *Miriam and Aaron spake against Moses.* It appears that jealousy of the power and influence of Moses was the real cause of their complaint, though his having married an Ethiopian woman—*haishshah haccushith,* "that woman, the Cushite," probably meaning Zipporah, who was an Arab born in the land of Midian—was the ostensible cause.

2. *Hath the Lord indeed spoken only by Moses?* It is certain that both Aaron and Miriam had received a portion of the prophetic spirit (see Exod. iv. 15 and xv. 20), and therefore they thought they might have a share in the government; for though there was no kind of gain attached to this government and no honor but such as came from God, yet the love of power is natural to the human mind; and in many instances men will sacrifice even honor, pleasure, and profit to the lust of power.

3. *Now the man Moses was very meek.* How could Moses, who certainly was as humble and modest as he was meek, write this encomium upon himself? I think the word is not rightly understood; *anav,* which we translate *meek,* comes from *anah,* to "act upon," to "humble, depress, afflict," and is translated so in many places in the Old Testament; and in this sense it should be understood here: "Now this man Moses was depressed or afflicted more than any man [*haadamah*] of that land." And why was he so? Because of the great burden he had

to bear in the care and government of this people, and because of their ingratitude and rebellion both against God and himself; of this depression and affliction, see the fullest proof in the preceding chapter.

4. *And the Lord spake suddenly.* The sudden interference of God in this business shows at once the importance of the case and His displeasure.

6. *If there be a prophet.* We see here the different ways in which God usually made himself known to the prophets, viz., by *visions*—emblematic appearance, and by *dream,* in which the future was announced by *dark speeches, bechiaoth,* by enigmas or figurative representations, v. 8. But to Moses, God had communicated himself in a different way—He spoke to him face-to-face, *apparently,* showing him His glory, not in *dark* or enigmatical *speeches.* This could not be admitted in the case in which Moses was engaged, for he was to receive laws by divine inspiration, the precepts and expressions of which must all be within the reach of the meanest capacity. As Moses, therefore, was chosen of God to be the lawgiver, so was he chosen to see these laws duly enforced for the benefit of the people among whom he presided.

7. *Moses . . . is faithful. Neeman,* a "prefect" or "superintendent." So Samuel is termed, 1 Sam. ii. 35; iii. 20; David is so called, 1 Sam. xviii. 27, *Neeman,* and son-in-law of the king. Job xii. 20, speaks of the *Neemanim* as a name of dignity. It seems also to have been a title of respect given to ambassadors, Prov. xiii. 17; xxv. 13.

10. *Miriam became leprous.* It is likely Miriam was chief in this mutiny; and it is probable that it was on this ground she is mentioned first (see v. 1) and punished here, while Aaron is spared. Had he been smitten with the leprosy, his sacred character must have greatly suffered, and perhaps the priesthood itself have fallen into contempt.

14. *If her father had but spit in her face.* This appears to have been done only in cases of great provocation on the part of the child, and strong irritation on the side of the parent. Spitting in the face was a sign of the deepest contempt. See Job xxx. 10; Isa. l. 6; Mark xiv. 65. In a case where a parent was obliged by the disobedient conduct of his child to treat him in this way, it appears he was banished from the father's presence for seven days. If then this was an allowed and judged case in matters of high provocation on the part of a child, should not the punishment be equally severe where the creature has rebelled against the Creator? Therefore Miriam was shut out of the camp for seven days, and thus debarred from coming into the presence of God, her Father, who is represented as dwelling among the people.

CHAPTER 13

Twelve men, one out of every tribe, are sent to examine the nature and state of the land of Canaan, 1-3. Their names, 4-16. Moses gives them particular directions, 17-20. They proceed on their journey, 21-22. Come to Eshcol, and cut down a branch with a cluster of grapes, which they bear between two of them upon a staff, 23-24. After forty days they return to Paran, from searching the land, and show to Moses and the people the fruit they had brought with them, 25-26. Their report—they acknowledge that the land is good, but that the inhabitants are such as the Israelites cannot hope to conquer,

27-29. Caleb endeavors to do away the bad impression made by the report of his fellows upon the minds of the people, 30. But the others persist in their former statement, 31; and greatly amplify the difficulties of conquest, 32-33.

2. *Send thou men, that they may search.* It appears from Deut. i. 19-24 that this was done in consequence of the request of the people. *Every one a ruler.* Not any of the princes of the people (see chap. i.), for these names are different from those; but these now sent were men of consideration and importance in their respective tribes.

18. *See the land, what it is.* What sort of country it is; how situated; its natural advantages or disadvantages. *And the people . . . whether they be strong or weak.* Healthy, robust, hardy men; or little, weak, and pusillanimous.

20. *The land . . . whether it be fat or lean.* Whether the soil be rich or poor; which might be known by its being well wooded, and by the fruits it produced; and therefore they were desired to examine it as to the trees, and to bring some of the fruits with them.

21. *From the wilderness of Zin.* The place called *Tsin,* here, is different from that called *Sin,* Exod. xvi. 1; the latter was nigh to Egypt, but the former was near Kadesh-barnea, not far from the borders of the Promised Land.

22. *Hebron was built seven years before Zoan in Egypt.* The Zoan of the Scriptures is allowed to be the Tanis of the heathen historians, which was the capital of Lower Egypt. Some think it was to humble the pride of the Egyptians, who boasted the highest antiquity, that this note concerning the higher antiquity of Hebron was introduced by Moses. Some have supposed that it is more likely to have been originally a marginal note, which in process of time crept into the text; but all the versions and all the MSS. that have as yet been collated acknowledge it.

23. *They bare it between two upon a staff.* It would be very easy to produce a great number of witnesses to prove that grapes in the Promised Land, and indeed in various other hot countries, grow to a prodigious size. From the most authentic accounts the Egyptian grape is very small, and this being the only one with which the Israelites were acquainted, the great size of the grapes of Hebron would appear still more extraordinary. I myself once cut down a bunch of grapes nearly twenty pounds in weight. From what is mentioned v. 20, "Now the time was the time of the firstripe grapes," it is very probable that the spies received their orders about the beginning of August, and returned about the middle of September, as in those countries grapes, pomegranates, and figs are ripe about this time.

27. *We came unto the land.* It is astonishing that men so dastardly as these should have had courage enough to risk their persons in searching the land. But probably though destitute of valor they had a sufficiency of cunning, and this carried them through. The report they brought was exceedingly discouraging, and naturally tended to produce the effect mentioned in the next chapter. The conduct of Joshua and Caleb was alone magnanimous, and worthy of the cause in which they were embarked.

32. *Men of a great stature. Anshey middoth,*

"men of measures"—two men's height; i.e., exceedingly tall men.

33. *There we saw the giants. Nephilim.* It is evident that they had seen a robust, sturdy, warlike race of men, and of great stature; for the asserted fact is not denied by Joshua or Caleb.

CHAPTER 14

The whole congregation weep at the account brought by the spies, 1. They murmur, 2-3; and propose to make themselves a captain, and go back to Egypt, 4. Moses and Aaron are greatly affected, 5. Joshua and Caleb endeavor to appease and encourage the people, 6-9. The congregation are about to stone them, 10. The glory of the Lord appears, and He is about to smite the rebels with the pestilence, 11-12. Moses makes a long and pathetic intercession in their behalf, 13-19. The Lord hears and forbears to punish, 20; but purposes that not one of that generation shall enter into the Promised Land save Joshua and Caleb, 21-24. Moses is commanded to turn and get into the wilderness by way of the Red Sea, 25. The Lord repeats His purpose that none of that generation shall enter into the Promised Land—that their carcasses shall fall in the wilderness, and that their children alone, with Joshua and Caleb, shall possess the land of the Canaanites, etc., 26-32. As many days as they have searched the land shall they wander years in the desert, until they shall be utterly consumed, 33-35. All the spies save Joshua and Caleb die by a plague, 36-38. Moses declares God's purpose to the people, at which they are greatly affected, 39. They acknowledge their sin, and purpose to go up at once and possess the land, 40. Moses cautions them against resisting the purpose of God, 41-43. They, notwithstanding, presume to go, but Moses and the ark abide in the camp, 44. The Amalekites and Canaanites come down from the mountains, and defeat them, 45.

1. *Cried; and . . . wept that night.* In almost every case this people gave deplorable evidence of the degraded state of their minds. With scarcely any mental firmness, and with almost no religion, they could bear no reverses, and were ever at their wit's end. They were headstrong, presumptuous, pusillanimous, indecisive, and fickle. And because they were such, therefore the power and wisdom of God appeared the more conspicuously in the whole of their history.

4. *Let us make a captain.* Here was a formal renunciation of the authority of Moses, and flat rebellion against God. And it seems from Neh. ix. 17 that they had actually appointed another leader, under whose direction they were about to return to Egypt. How astonishing is this! Their lives were made bitter because of the rigor with which they were made to serve in the land of Egypt; and yet they were willing, yes, eager, to get back into the same circumstances again! Great evils, when once some time past, affect the mind less than present ills, though much inferior. They had partly forgotten their Egyptian bondage, and now smart under a little discouragement, having totally lost sight of their high calling, and of the power and goodness of God.

9. *Their defence. Tsillam,* "their shadow," a metaphor highly expressive of protection and support in the sultry Eastern countries. The protection of God is so called; see Ps. xci. 1; cxxi. 5; see also Isa. li. 16; xlix. 2; xxx. 2.

10. *The glory of the Lord appeared.* This timely appearance of the divine glory prevented these faithful servants of God from being stoned to death by this base and treacherous multitude.

14. *That thy cloud standeth over them.* This cloud, the symbol of the divine glory, and proof of the divine presence, appears to have assumed three different forms for three important purposes. (1) It appeared by day in the form of a pillar of sufficient height to be seen by all the camp, and thus went before them to point out their way in the desert, Exod. xl. 38. (2) It appeared by night as a pillar of fire to give them light while travelling by night, which they probably sometimes did (see chap. ix. 21); or to illuminate their tents in their encampment; Exod. xiii. 21-22. (3) It stood at certain times above the whole congregation, overshadowing them from the scorching rays of the sun; and probably at other times condensed the vapors and precipitated rain or dew for the refreshment of the people. "He spread a cloud for a covering; and fire to give light in the night," Ps. cv. 39. It was probably from this circumstance that the shadow of the Lord was used to signify the divine protection.

19. *Pardon, I beseech thee, the iniquity of this people.* From v. 13 to v. 19 inclusive we have the words of Moses' intercession. They need no explanation; they are full of simplicity and energy. His arguments with God (for he did reason and argue with his Maker) are pointed, cogent, and respectful; and while they show a heart full of humanity, they evidence the deepest concern for the glory of God.

20. *I have pardoned.* That is, They shall not be cut off as they deserve, because you have interceded for their lives.

21. *All the earth shall be filled. Kol haarets,* "all this land," i.e., the land of Canaan, which was fulfilled to the letter only when the preaching of Christ and His apostles was heard through all the cities and villages of Judea. It does not appear that the whole of the terraqueous globe is meant by this expression in any of the places where it occurs connected with this promise of the diffusion of the divine light. See Ps. lxxii. 19; Isa. xl. 5; Hab. ii. 14.

24. *But my servant Caleb.* Caleb had *another spirit*—not only a bold, generous, courageous, noble, and heroic spirit; but the Spirit and influence of the God of heaven thus raised him above human inquietudes and earthly fears. Therefore he *followed* God, *fully; vaimalle acharai,* literally, "he filled after Me." God showed him the way he was to take, and the line of conduct he was to pursue, and he filled up this line, and in all things followed the will of his Maker. He therefore shall see the Promised Land, and his seed shall possess it.

34. *After the number of the days.* The spies were forty days in searching the land, and the people who rebelled on their evil report are condemned to wander forty years in the wilderness! Now let them make them a captain and go back to Egypt if they can. God had so hedged them about with His power and providence that they could neither go back to Egypt nor get forward to the Promised Land! *And ye shall know my breach of promise.* This is certainly a most harsh expression; and most learned men agree that the words *eth tenuathi* should be translated "my vengeance," which is the rendering of the Septuagint, Vulgate, Coptic, and Anglo-Saxon, and which is followed by almost all our ancient English translations. The meaning however appears to be this: As God had promised to bring them into the good land, provided they kept His statutes, ordinances, etc., and they had now broken their engagements, He was no longer held by His covenant; and

therefore, by excluding them from the Promised Land, He showed them at once His annulling of the covenant which they had broken and His vengeance because they had broken it.

37. *Those men that did bring up the evil report . . . died.* Thus ten of the twelve that searched out the land were struck dead, by the justice of God, on the spot! Caleb, of the tribe of Judah, and Joshua, of the tribe of Ephraim, alone escaped, because they had followed God fully.

40. *We . . . will go up unto the place.* They found themselves on the very borders of the land, and they heard God say they should not enter it, but should be consumed by a forty years' wandering in the wilderness; notwithstanding, they are determined to render vain this purpose of God, probably supposing that the temporary sorrow they felt for their late rebellion would be accepted as a sufficient atonement for their crimes. They accordingly went up, and were cut down by their enemies; and why? God went not with them.

CHAPTER 15

Directions concerning the different offerings they should bring unto the Lord when they should come to the land of Canaan, 1-3. Directions relative to the meat offering, 4; to the drink offering, 5. Of the burnt offering, vow offering, peace offering, drink offering, etc., 6-12. All born in the country must perform these rites, 13, and the strangers also, 14-16. They shall offer unto the Lord a heave offering of the firstfruits of the land, 17-21. Concerning omissions through ignorance, and the sacrifices to be offered on such occasions, 22-29. He who sins presumptuously shall be cut off, 30-31. History of the person who gathered sticks on the Sabbath, 32. He is brought to Moses and Aaron, 33. They put him in confinement till the mind of the Lord should be known on the case, 34. The Lord commands him to be stoned, 35. He is stoned to death, 36. The Israelites are commanded to make fringes to the borders of their garments, 37-38. The end for which these fringes were to be made, that they might remember the commandments of the Lord, that they might be holy, 39-41.

2. *When ye be come into the land.* Some learned men are of opinion that several offerings prescribed by the law were not intended to be made in the wilderness, but in the Promised Land, the former not affording those conveniences which were necessary to the complete observance of the divine worship in this and several other respects.

3. *And will make an offering.* For the different kinds of offerings, sacrifices, etc., see Lev. i. 2 and vii.

5. *The fourth part of an hin.* The quantity of meal and flour was augmented in proportion to the size of the sacrifice with which it was offered. With a lamb or a kid were offered one-tenth deal of flour (the tenth part of an ephah, see on Exod. xxix. 40), the fourth part of a hin of oil, and *the fourth part of an hin of wine.* With a ram, two tenth deals of flour, a third part of a hin of oil, a third part of a hin of wine. With a bullock, three tenth deals of flour, half a hin of oil, and half a hin of wine. See vv. 4-11.

14. *If a stranger sojourn.* See the notes on Lev. xix. 33; xxii. 9. When the case of the Jewish people is fairly considered, and their situation with respect to the surrounding idolatrous nations, we shall see the absolute necessity of having but one form of worship in the land. That alone was genuine which was prescribed by the Almighty, and no others could be tolerated, because they were idolatrous. All

strangers, all that came to sojourn in the land, were required to conform to it; and it was right that those who did conform to it should have equal rights and privileges with the Hebrews themselves, which we find was the case.

20. *Ye shall offer . . . the first of your dough.* Concerning the offerings of firstfruits, see the notes on Exod. xxii. 29.

24. *If ought be committed by ignorance.* See the notes on Lev. iv. 2 and v. 17. The case here probably refers to the whole congregation; the cases above, to the sin of an individual.

25. *The priest shall make an atonement.* Even sins committed through ignorance required an atonement; and God in His mercy has provided one for them.

30. *But the soul that doeth ought presumptuously.* Bold, daring acts of transgression against the fullest evidence, and in despite of the divine authority, admitted of no atonement; the person was to be cut off—to be excluded from God's people, and from all their privileges and blessings.

32. *They found a man that gathered sticks upon the sabbath.* This was in all likelihood a case of that kind supposed above: the man despised the word of the Lord, and therefore broke His commandment; see v. 31. On this ground he was punished with the utmost rigor of the law.

36. *Stoned him.* See the note on Lev. xxiv. 23.

38. *Bid them . . . make them fringes.* We learn from v. 39 that these fringes were emblematical of the various commands of God.

CHAPTER 16

The rebellion of Korah and his company against Moses, 1-3. He directs them how to try, in the course of the next day, whom God had called to the priesthood, 4-11. Dathan and Abiram use the most seditious speeches, 12-14. Moses is wroth, 15; and orders Korah and his company to be ready on the morrow with their censers and incense, 16-8. Korah gathers his company together, 19. The glory of the Lord appears, and he threatens to consume them, 20-21. Moses and Aaron intercede for them, 22. The people are commanded to leave the tents of the rebels, 23-26. They obey, and Korah and his company come out and stand before the door of their tents, 27. Moses in a solemn address puts the contention to issue, 28-30. As soon as he had done speaking, the earth clave and swallowed them, and all that appertained to them, 31-34; and the 250 men who offered incense are consumed by fire, 35. The Lord commands Eleazar to preserve the censers, because they were hallowed, 36-38. Eleazar makes of them a covering for the altar, 39-40. The next day the people murmur anew, the glory of the Lord appears, and Moses and Aaron go to the Tabernacle, 41-43. They are commanded to separate themselves from the congregation, 44-45. Moses, perceiving that God had sent a plague among them, directs Aaron to hasten and make an atonement, 46. Aaron does so, and the plague is stayed, 47-48. The number of those who died by the plague, 14,700 men, 49-50.

1. *Now Korah . . . took men.* Had not these been the most brutish of men, could they have possibly so soon forgotten the signal displeasure of God manifested against them so lately for their rebellion? The word *men* is not in the original; and the verb *vaiyikkach,* "and he took," is not in the plural but the singular; hence it cannot be applied to the act of all these chiefs. In every part of the Scripture where this rebellion is referred to it is attributed to Korah (see chap. xxvi. 3 and Jude, v. 11). Therefore the verb here belongs to him, and the whole verse should be translated thus: "Now Korah, son of Yitsar, son of Kohath, son of Levi, he took even Dathan and Abiram, the sons of Eliab, and On,

son of Peleth, son of Reuben; and they rose up . . ."

3. *Ye take too much upon you.* The original is simply *rab lachem,* "too much for you." The spirit of this saying appears to me to be the following: "Holy offices are not equally distributed: you arrogate to yourselves the most important ones, as if your superior holiness entitled you alone to them; whereas all the congregation are holy, and have an equal right with you to be employed in the most holy services." Moses retorts this saying, v. 7: "Ye take too much upon you," *rab lachem;* You have too much already, "ye sons of Levi"; i.e., by your present spirit and disposition you prove yourselves to be wholly unworthy of any spiritual employment.

15. *Respect not thou their offering.* There was no danger of this; they wished to set up a priesthood and a sacrificial system of their own; and God never has blessed, and never can bless, any scheme of salvation which is not of His own appointment.

30. *If the Lord make a new thing.* Veim beriah yibra Yehovah, "And if Jehovah should create a creation," i.e., do such a thing as was never done before. *And they go down quick into the pit. Sheolah,* a proof, among many others, that *sheol* signifies here a "chasm" or "pit" of the earth, and not the place called hell; for it would be absurd to suppose that their houses had gone to hell; and it would be wicked to imagine that their little innocent children had gone thither, though God was pleased to destroy their lives with those of their iniquitous fathers.

33. *They, and all that appertained to them.* Korah, Dathan, and Abiram, and all that appertained to their respective families, went down into the pit caused by this supernatural earthquake; while the fire from the Lord consumed the 250 men that bare censers. Thus there were two distinct punishments, the pit and the fire, for the two divisions of these rebels.

37. *The censers . . . are hallowed. Kadeshu,* are "consecrated," i.e., to the service of God, though in this instance improperly employed.

41. *On the morrow all the congregation . . . murmured.* It is very likely that the people persuaded themselves that Moses and Aaron had used some cunning in this business, and that the earthquake and fire were artificial; else, had they discerned the hand of God in this punishment, could they have dared the anger of the Lord in the very face of justice?

46. *The plague is begun.* God now punished them by a secret blast, so as to put the matter beyond all dispute; His hand, and His alone, was seen, not only in the plague, but in the manner in which the mortality was arrested. It was necessary that this should be done in this way that the whole congregation might see that those men who had perished were not the people of the Lord; and that God, not Moses and Aaron, had destroyed them.

48. *He stood between the dead and the living; and the plague.* What the plague was we know not, but it seems to have begun at one part of the camp and to have proceeded regularly onward; and Aaron went to the quarter where it was then prevailing, and stood with his atonement where it was now making its ravages. *And the plague was stayed;* but not before 14,700 had fallen victims to it, v. 49.

CHAPTER 17

The twelve chiefs of the tribes are commanded to take their rods, and to write the name of each tribe upon the rod that belonged to its representative; but the name of Aaron is to be written on the rod of the tribe of Levi, 1-3. The rods are to be laid up before the Lord, who promises that the man's rod whom He shall choose for priest shall blossom, 4-5. The rods are produced and laid up before the Tabernacle, 6-7. Aaron's rod alone buds, blossoms, and bears fruit, 8-9. It is laid up before the testimony as a token of the manner in which God had disposed of the priesthood, 10-11. The people are greatly terrified, and are apprehensive of being destroyed, 12-13.

2. *And take of every one of them a rod. Matteh,* the "staff" or "scepter," which the prince or chief of each tribe bore, and which was the sign of office or royalty among almost all the people of the earth.

5. *The man's rod, whom I shall choose, shall blossom.* It was necessary that something further should be done to quiet the minds of the people, and forever to settle the dispute in what tribe the priesthood should be fixed. God therefore took the method described in the text, and it had the desired effect; the Aaronical priesthood was never after disputed.

8. *The rod of Aaron . . . was budded.* That is, on the same rod or staff were found buds, blossoms, and ripe fruit. This fact was so unquestionably miraculous as to decide the business forever; and probably this was intended to show that in the priesthood, represented by that of Aaron, the beginning, middle, and end of every good work must be found. The buds of good desires, the blossoms of holy resolutions and promising professions, and the ripe fruit of faith, love, and obedience, all spring from the priesthood of the Lord Jesus.

12. *Behold, we die, we perish, we all perish. Gavaenu* signifies not so much to *die* simply, as to feel an extreme difficulty of breathing, which, producing suffocation, ends at last in death. See the folly and extravagance of this sinful people. At first every person might come near to God, for all, they thought, were sufficiently holy, and every way qualified to minister in holy things. Now no one, in their apprehension, can come near to the Tabernacle without being consumed, v. 13. In both cases they were wrong; some there were who might approach, others there were who might not. God had put the difference. His decision should have been final with them.

CHAPTER 18

The priests are to bear the iniquity of the sanctuary, 1. The Levites to minister to the priests, and have charge of the Tabernacle, 2-4. The priests alone to have the charge of the sanctuary, etc.; no stranger to come nigh on pain of death, 5-7. The portion allowed for their maintenance, 8. They shall have every meat offering; and they shall eat them in the holy place, 9-10. The wave offerings, 11. The firstfruits of the oil, wine, and wheat, and whatever is first ripe, and every devoted thing, 12-14; also all the firstborn of men and beasts, 15-18; and heave offerings, 19. The priests shall have no inheritance, 20. The Levites shall have no inheritance, but shall have the tenth of the produce in Israel, 21-24, of which they are to give a tenth to the priests, taken from the best parts, 25-30.

1. *Thou and thy sons . . . shall bear the iniquity of the sanctuary.* That is, They must be answerable for its legal pollutions, and must make the necessary atonements and expiations. By this they must feel that, though they had a high and important office confirmed to them by a miraculous interference, yet it was a place of

the highest responsibility; and that they must not be high-minded, but fear.

2. *Thy brethren also of the tribe of Levi . . . may be joined unto thee.* There is a fine paronomasia, or play upon words, in the original. *Levi* comes from the root *lavah,* to "join to, couple, associate"; hence Moses says, The Levites, *yillavu,* shall be *joined,* or associated, with the priests; they shall conjointly perform the whole of the sacred office, but the priests shall be principal, the Levites only their associates or assistants.

15. *The firstborn of man . . . and the firstling of unclean beasts.* Thus vain man is ranked with the beasts that perish; and with the worst kinds of them too, those deemed unclean.

16. *Shalt thou redeem . . . for the money of five shekels.* Redemption of the firstborn is one of the rites which is still practiced among the Jews.

19. *It is a covenant of salt.* That is, an incorruptible, everlasting covenant. As *salt* was added to different kinds of viands, not only to give them a relish, but to preserve them from putrefaction and decay, it became the emblem of incorruptibility and permanence. Hence, *a covenant of salt* signified an everlasting covenant.

20. *I am thy part and thine inheritance.* The principal part of what was offered to God was the portion of the priests; therefore they had no inheritance of land in Israel—independently of that they had a very ample provision for their support.

21. *Behold, I have given the children of Levi all the tenth.* (1) The Levites had the tenth of all the productions of the land. (2) They had 48 cities, each forming a square of 4,000 cubits. (3) They had 2,000 cubits of ground round each city. (4) They had the firstfruits and certain parts of all the animals killed in the land.

28. *Thus ye also shall offer an heave offering.* As the Levites had the tithe of the whole land, they themselves were obliged to give the tithe of this tithe to the priests, so that this considerably lessened their revenue. And this tithe or tenth they were obliged to select from the best part of the substance they had received, vv. 29, etc. A portion of all must be given to God, as an evidence of His goodness, and their dependence on Him. See the end of chap. xx.

CHAPTER 19

The ordinance of the red heifer, 1-2. She shall be slain by Eleazar without the camp, and her blood sprinkled before the Tabernacle, 3-4. Her whole body and appurtenance shall be reduced to ashes, and while burning, cedarwood, scarlet, and hyssop, shall be thrown into the fire, 5-6. The priest, and he that burns her, to bathe themselves, and be reputed unclean till the evening, 7-8. Her ashes to be laid up for a water of purification, 9. How and in what cases it is to be applied, 10-13. The law concerning him who dies in a tent, or who is killed in the open field, 14-16. How the persons, tent, and vessels are to be purified by the application of these ashes, 17-19. The unclean person who does not apply them, to be cut off from the congregation, 20. This is to be a perpetual statute, 21-22.

2. *Speak unto the children of Israel, that they bring thee.* The ordinance of the *red heifer* was a sacrifice of general application. All the people were to have an interest in it, and therefore the people at large were to provide the sacrifice. This Jewish rite certainly had a ref-

erence to things done under the gospel, as the author of the Epistle to the Hebrews has remarked: "For if," says he, "the blood of bulls and of goats," alluding probably to the sin offerings and the scapegoat, "and the ashes of an heifer sprinkling the unclean, sanctifieth to the purifying of the flesh: how much more shall the blood of Christ, who through the eternal Spirit offered himself without spot to God, purge your conscience from dead works to serve the living God?" Heb. ix. 13-14.

9. *For a water of separation.* That is, the ashes were to be kept, in order to be mixed with water, v. 17, and sprinkled on those who had contracted any legal defilement.

11. *He that toucheth the dead body of any man shall be unclean seven days.* How low does this lay man! He who touched a dead beast was unclean for only one day, Lev. xi. 24, 27, 39; but he who touches a dead man is unclean for seven days. This was certainly designed to mark the peculiar impurity of man, and to show his sinfulness—seven times worse than the vilest animal!

12. *He shall purify himself with it.* Yithchatta bo, literally, "He shall sin himself with it." This Hebrew form of speech is common enough among us in other matters. Thus to fleece, to bark, and to skin do not signify to add a fleece, another bark, or a skin, but to take one away; therefore to "sin himself," in the Hebrew idiom, is not to add sin, but to take it away, to purify. The verb *chata* signifies to "miss the mark, to sin, to purify from sin, and to make a sin offering."

CHAPTER 20

The Israelites come to Zin, and Miriam dies, 1. They murmur for want of water, 2-5. Moses and Aaron make supplication at the Tabernacle, and the glory of the Lord appears, 6. He commands Moses to take his rod, gather the congregation together, and bring water out of the rock, 7-8. Moses takes the rod, gathers the Israelites together, chides with them, and smites the rock twice, and the waters flow out plenteously, 9-11. The Lord is offended with Moses and Aaron because they did not sanctify Him in the sight of the children of Israel, 12. The place is called Meribah, 13. Moses sends a friendly message to the king of Edom, begging liberty to pass through his territories, 14-17. The Edomites refuse, 18. The Israelites expostulate, 19. The Edomites still refuse, and prepare to attack them, 20-21. The Israelites go to Mount Hor, 22. Aaron is commanded to prepare for his death, 23-24. Aaron is stripped on Mount Hor, and his vestments put on Eleazar, his son; Aaron dies, 25-28. The people mourn for him thirty days, 29.

1. *Then came the children of Israel.* This was the first month of the fortieth year after their departure from Egypt. See chap. xxxiii. 38, compared with v. 28 of this chapter, and Deut. i. 3. The transactions of thirty-seven years Moses passes by, because he writes not as a historian but as a legislator; and gives us particularly an account of the laws, ordinances, and other occurrences of the first and last years of their peregrinations. The year now spoken of was the last of their journeyings; for from the going out of the spies, chap. xiii, unto this time, was about thirty-eight years, Deut. i. 22-23; ii. 14.

And Miriam died there. Miriam was certainly older than Moses. When he was an infant, exposed on the river Nile, she was entrusted by her parents to watch the conduct of Pharaoh's daughter, and to manage a most delicate business, that required much address and prudence.

See Exodus ii. It is supposed that she was at the time of her death one hundred and thirty years of age, having been at least ten years old at her birth.

2. *And there was no water for the congregation.* The same occurrence took place to the children of Israel at Kadesh as did formerly to their fathers at Rephidim, see Exod. xvii. 1; and as the fathers murmured, so also did the children

12. *Because ye believed me not.* What was the offense for which Moses was excluded from the Promised Land? It appears to have consisted in some or all of the following particulars: (1) God had commanded him (v. 8) to take the rod in his hand, and go and speak to the rock, and it should give forth water. It seems Moses did not think speaking would be sufficient; therefore he smote the rock without any command so to do. (2) He did this twice, which certainly in this case indicated a great perturbation of spirit and want of attention to the presence of God. (3) He permitted his spirit to be carried away by a sense of the people's disobedience, and thus, being provoked, he was led to speak unadvisedly with his lips: "Hear now, ye rebels," v. 10. (4) He did not acknowledge God in the miracle which was about to be wrought, but took the honor to himself and Aaron: "Must we fetch you water out of this rock?" Thus it plainly appears that they did not properly believe in God, and did not honor Him in the sight of the people; for in their presence they seem to express a doubt whether the thing could possibly be done. As Aaron appears to have been consenting in the above particulars, therefore he is also excluded from the Promised Land.

14. *Thus saith thy brother Israel.* The Edomites were the descendants of Edom or Esau, the brother of Jacob or Israel, from whom the Israelites were descended.

17. *We will go by the king's high way.* This is the first time this phrase occurs; it appears to have been a public road made by the king's authority at the expense of the state.

21. *Thus Edom refused to give Israel passage through his border.* Though every king has a right to refuse passage through his territories to any strangers, yet in a case like this, and in a time also in which emigrations were frequent and universally allowed, it was both cruelty and oppression in Edom to refuse a passage to a comparatively unarmed and inoffensive multitude, who were all their own near kinsmen. It appears however that it was only the Edomites of Kadesh that were thus unfriendly and cruel; for from Deut. ii. 29 we learn that the Edomites who dwelt in Mount Seir treated them in a hospitable manner. This cruelty in the Edomites of Kadesh is strongly reprehended, and threatened by the Prophet Obadiah, vv. 10, etc.

26. *Strip Aaron of his garments.* This was, in effect, depriving him of his office; and putting the clothes on his son Eleazar implied a transfer of that office to him. A transfer of office, from this circumstance of putting the clothes of the late possessor on the person intended to succeed him, was called "investing" or "investment" (clothing), as removing a person from an office was termed divesting or unclothing.

CHAPTER 21

Arad, a king of the Canaanites, attacks Israel, and makes some prisoners, 1. They devote him and his people to destruction, 2; which they afterwards accomplished, 3. They journey from Hor, and are greatly discouraged, 4. They murmur against God and Moses, and loathe the manna, 5. The Lord sends fiery serpents among them, 6. They repent, and beg Moses to intercede for them, 7. The Lord directs him to make a brazen serpent, and set it on a pole, that the people might look on it and be healed, 8. Moses does so, and the people who behold the brazen serpent live, 9. They journey to Oboth, Ije-abarim, Zared, and Arnon, 10-13. A quotation from "the book of the wars of the Lord," 14-15. From Arnon they come to Beer, 16. Their song of triumph, 17-20. Moses sends messengers to the Amorites for permission to pass through their land, 21-22. Sihon, their king, refuses, attacks Israel, is defeated, and all his cities destroyed, 23-26. The poetic proverbs made on the occasion, 27-30. Israel possesses the land of the Amorites, 31-32. They are attacked by Og, king of Bashan, 33. They defeat him, destroy his troops and family, and possess his land, 34-35.

1. *The way of the spies. Atharim.* Some think that this signifies the way that the spies took when they went to search the land. But this is impossible, as Dr. Kennicott justly remarks, because Israel had now marched from Meribath-kadesh to Mount Hor, beyond Ezion-gaber, and were turning round Edom to the southeast; and therefore the word is to be understood here as the name of a place.

3. *The Lord hearkened to the voice of Israel.* The whole of this verse appears to me to have been added after the days of Joshua. It is certain the Canaanites were not utterly destroyed at the time here spoken of, for this did not take place till after the death of Moses. If, instead of *utterly destroyed them, vaiyacharem,* we translate, "They devoted them to utter destruction," it will make a good sense, and not repugnant to the Hebrew; though some think it more probable that the verse was added afterwards by Joshua or Ezra, in testimony of the fulfillment of God's promise; for Arad, who is mentioned as being destroyed here, is mentioned among those destroyed by Joshua long after (see Josh. xii. 14). But this is quite consistent with their being "devoted to destruction," as this might be fulfilled any time after.

5. *This light bread. Hakkelokel,* a word of excessive scorn; as if they had said, This innutritive, unsubstantial, cheat-stomach stuff.

6. *Fiery s e r p e n t s. Hannechashim hasseraphim. Seraphim* is one of the orders of angelic beings, Isa. vi. 2, 6; but as it comes from the root *saraph,* which signifies to "burn," it has been translated *fiery* in the text.

8. *Make thee a fiery serpent.* Literally, make thee a seraph. *And set it upon a pole. Al nes,* upon a standard or ensign.

9. *And Moses made a serpent of brass. Nechash nechosheth.* Hence we find that the word for brass or copper comes from the same root with *nachash,* which here signifies a serpent, probably on account of the color; as most serpents, especially those of the bright spotted kind, have a very glistening appearance, and those who have brown or yellow spots appear something like burnished brass. But the true meaning of the root cannot be easily ascertained. On the subject of the cure of the serpent-bitten Israelites, by looking at the brazen serpent, there is a good comment in the book of Wisdom, chap. xvi. 4-12, in which are these remarkable words: "They were admonished, having a sign of salvation (i.e., the brazen serpent), to put them in remembrance of the commandments of

thy law. For he that turned himself towards it was not saved by the thing that he saw, but by thee, that art the Saviour of all." To the circumstance of looking at the brazen serpent in order to be healed, our Lord refers, John iii. 14-15: "As Moses lifted up the serpent in the wilderness, even so must the Son of man be lifted up: that whosoever believeth in him should not perish, but have eternal life."

12. *They . . . pitched in the valley of Zared. Nachal zared.* This should be translated "the brook Zared," as it is in Deut. ii. 13-14. This stream has its origin in the mountains eastward of Moab, and runs from east to west, and discharges itself into the Dead Sea.

13. *Arnon.* Another river which takes its rise in the mountains of Moab, and, after having separated the ancient territories of the Moabites and Ammonites, falls into the Dead Sea, near the mouth of Jordan.

14. *The book of the wars of the Lord.* There are endless conjectures about this book, among both ancients and moderns. Dr. Lightfoot's opinion is the most simple, and to me bears the greatest appearance of being the true one. "This book seems to have been some book of remembrances and directions, written by Moses for Joshua's private instruction for the management of the wars after him. See Exod. xvii. 14-16. It may be that this was the same book which is called the *book of Jasher,* i.e., the *book of the upright,* or a directory for Joshua, from Moses, what to do and what to expect in his wars; and in this book it seems as if Moses directed the setting up of *archery,* see 2 Sam. i. 18, and warrants Joshua to command the sun, and expect its obedience, Josh. x. 13."

What he did in the Red sea, and in the brooks of Arnon. This clause is impenetrably obscure. All the versions, all the translators, all the commentators have been puzzled with it. Scarcely any two agree. The original is *eth vaheb besuphah,* which our translators render, *What he did in the Red sea,* following here the Chaldee Targum. As I judge the whole clause to have been a common proverb in those days, and *Vaheb* to be a proper name, I therefore propose the following translation, which I believe to be the best: "From Vaheb unto Suph, and unto the streams of Arnon." If we allow it to have been a proverbial expression, used to point out extensive distance, then it was similar to that well-known phrase, "From Dan even unto Beer-sheba."

17. *Spring up, O well.* This is one of the most ancient war songs in the world, but is not easily understood, which is commonly the case with all very ancient compositions, especially the poetic.

18. *The princes digged the well . . . with their staves.* This is not easily understood. Who can suppose that the princes dug this well with their *staves?* And is there any other idea conveyed by our translation? The word *chapharu,* which is translated *they digged,* should be rendered "they searched out," which is a frequent meaning of the root; and *bemishanotham,* which we render *with their staves,* should be translated "on their borders or confines," from the root *shaan,* to "lie along."

26. *For Heshbon was the city of Sihon.* It appears therefore that the territory now taken from Sihon by the Israelites was taken from a former king of Moab, in commemoration of which an *epikedion* or war song was made, several verses of which, in their ancient poetic form, are here quoted by Moses.

27. *They that speak in proverbs. Hammoshelim,* from *mashal,* to "rule, to exercise authority"; hence a weighty proverbial saying, because admitted as an axiom for the government of life.

The ode from verses 27 to 30 is composed of three parts. The first takes in verses 27 and 28; the second, verse 29; and the third, verse 30. The first records with bitter irony the late insults of Sihon and his subjects over the conquered Moabites. The second expresses the compassion of the Israelites over the desolations of Moab, with a bitter sarcasm against their god Chemosh, who had abandoned his votaries in their distress, or was not able to rescue them out of the hands of their enemies. The third sets forth the revenge taken by Israel upon the whole country of Sihon, from Heshbon to Dibon, and from Nophah even to Medeba. See Isa. xv. 1-2.

CHAPTER 22

The Israelites pitch in the plains of Moab, 1. Balak, king of Moab, is greatly terrified, 2-4; and sends to Balaam, a diviner, to come and curse them, 5-6. The elders of Moab take a reward and carry it to Balaam, 7. He inquires of the Lord, and is positively ordered not to go with them, 8-12. He communicates this to the elders of Moab, 13. They return to Balak with this information, 14. He sends some of his princes to Balaam with promises of great honor, 15-17. He consults God, and is permitted to go, on certain conditions, 18-20. Balaam sets off, is opposed by an angel of the Lord, and the Lord miraculously opens the mouth of his ass to reprove him, 21-30. Balaam sees the angel, and is reproved by him, 31-33. He humbles himself, and offers to go back, 34; but is ordered to proceed, on the same conditions as before, 35. The king of Moab goes out to meet him, 36. His address to him, 37. Balaam's firm answer, 38. Balak sacrifices, and takes Balaam to the high places of Baal, that he may see the whole of the Israelitish camp, 39-41.

1. *And pitched in the plains of Moab.* They had taken no part of the country that at present appertained to the Moabites; they had taken only that part which had formerly belonged to this people, but had been taken from them by Sihon, king of the Amorites. *On this side Jordan.* On the east side. By Jericho, that is, over against it.

5. *To Pethor, which is by the river of the land of the children of his people.* "Twelve Hebrew MSS. confirm the Samaritan text here in reading, instead of *ammo,* 'his people,' *Ammon,* with the Syriac and Vulgate versions." It should therefore stand thus: "by the river of the land of the children of Ammon"; and thus it agrees with Deut. xxiii. 4.

6. *Come now therefore, I pray thee, curse me this people.* Balaam, once a prophet of the true God, appears to have been one of the *Moshelim* who had added to his poetic gift that of sorcery or divination. It was supposed that prophets and sorcerers had a power to curse persons and places so as to confound all their designs, frustrate their counsels, enervate their strength, and fill them with fear, terror, and dismay. See Gen. ix. 25; Ps. cix. 6, 20; Josh. vi. 26; Jer. xvii. 5-6.

7. *The rewards of divination.* Whoever went to consult a prophet took with him a present, as it was on such gratuitous offerings the prophets lived; but here more than a mere present

is intended, perhaps everything necessary to provide materials for the incantation. The drugs, etc., used on such occasions were often very expensive. It appears that Balaam was very covetous, and that he "loved the wages of unrighteousness," and probably lived by them; see 2 Pet. ii. 15.

8. *I will bring you word again, as the Lord shall speak.* So it appears he knew the true God and had been in the habit of consulting Him, and receiving oracles from His mouth.

12. *Thou shalt not go with them; thou shalt not curse the people.* That is, You shalt not go with them to curse the people. With them he might go, as we find he afterwards did by God's own command, but not to curse the people; this was wholly forbidden. Probably the command, *Thou shalt not go,* refers here to that time, viz., the first invitation; and in this sense it was most punctually obeyed by Balaam; see v. 13.

18. *I cannot go beyond the word of the Lord my God.* Balaam knew God too well to suppose he could reverse any of His purposes; and he respected Him too much to attempt to do anything without His permission. Though he was covetous, yet he dared not, even when strongly tempted by both riches and honors, to go contrary to the command of his God.

19. *What the Lord will say unto me more.* He did not know but God might make a further discovery of His will to him, and therefore he might very innocently seek further information.

20. *If the man come . . . go with them.* This is a confirmation of what was observed on the twelfth verse, though we find his going was marked with the divine displeasure because he wished, for the sake of the honors and rewards, to fulfil as far as possible the will of the king of Moab. Mr. Shuckford observes that the pronoun *hu* is sometimes used to denote a person's doing a thing out of his own head, without regard to the directions of another. Thus in the case of Balaam, when God had allowed him to go with the messengers of Balak, if they came in the morning to call him; because he was more hasty than he ought to have been, and went to them instead of staying till they should come to him, it was said of him, not *ki halach,* "He went," but *ki holech hu,* i.e., "He went of his own head"—without being called; and in this, Mr. Shuckford supposes, his iniquity chiefly lay.

23. *And the ass saw the angel.* When God granted visions, those alone who were particularly interested saw them while others in the same company saw nothing; see Dan. x. 7; Acts ix. 7.

26. *And the angel . . . stood in a narrow place.* In this carriage of the angel, says Mr. Ainsworth, the Lord shows us the proceedings of His judgments against sinners. First, He mildly shakes His rod at them but lets them go untouched. Secondly, He comes nearer and touches them with an easy correction as it were wringing their foot against the wall. Thirdly when all this is ineffectual, He brings them into such straits that they can neither turn to the right hand nor to the left, but must fall before His judgments if they do not fully turn to Him.

28. *The Lord opened the mouth of the ass.* And where is the wonder of all this? If the ass had opened her own mouth, and reproved the rash prophet, we might well be astonished; but when God opens the mouth, an ass can speak as well as a man. It is worthy of remark here that Balaam testifies no surprise at this miracle, because he saw it was the Lord's doing.

33. *Surely now also I had slain thee.* How often are the meanest animals, and the most trivial occurrences, instruments of the preservation of our lives and of the salvation of our souls! The messenger of justice would have killed Balaam had not the mercy of God prevented the ass from proceeding.

34. *If it displease thee, I will get me back again.* Here is a proof that, though he "loved the wages of unrighteousness," yet he still feared God; and he is now willing to drop the enterprise if God be displeased with his proceeding.

38. *The word that God putteth in my mouth, that shall I speak.* Here was a noble resolution, and he was certainly faithful to it. Though he wished to please the king, and get wealth and honor, yet he would not displease God to realize even these bright prospects. Many who slander this poor prophet have not half his piety.

40. *And Balak offered oxen.* This was to gain the favor of his gods, and perhaps to propitiate Jehovah, that the end for which he had sent for Balaam might be accomplished.

41. *That . . . he might see the utmost part of the people.* As he thought Balaam must have them all in his eye when he pronounced his curse, lest it might not extend to those who were not in sight. On this account he took him up into the high places of Baal.

CHAPTER 23

Being arrived at the high places of Baal (chap. xxii. 41), Balaam orders Balak to build seven altars, and prepare oxen and rams for sacrifice, 1-2. Balaam inquires of the Lord, receives an answer, with which he returns to Balak, 3-10. Balak, finding that this was a prediction of the prosperity of the Israelites, is greatly troubled, 11. Balaam excuses himself, 12. He brings him to another place, where he might see only a part of Israel, and repeats his sacrifices, 13-14. Balaam again consults the Lord. 15-17. Returns with his answer, and again predicts the glory of Israel, 18-24. Balak is angry, 25; and Balaam again excuses himself. Balak proposes another trial, takes him to another place, and repeats the same sacrifices, 26-30.

1. *Build me here seven altars.* The *oxen* and the *rams* were such as the Mosaic law had ordered to be offered to God in sacrifice; the building of seven altars was not commanded. As *seven* was a number of perfection, Balaam chose it on this occasion because he intended to offer a grand sacrifice, and to offer a bullock and a ram upon each of the altars, the whole to be made a burnt offering at the same time. And as he intended to offer seven bullocks and seven rams at the same time, it could not be conveniently done on one altar; therefore he ordered seven to be built.

3. *Stand by thy burnt offering.* We have already seen that blessing and cursing in this way were considered as religious rites, and therefore must always be preceded by sacrifice. See this exemplified in the case of Isaac, before he blessed Jacob and Esau, Genesis xxvii, and the notes there. The venison that was brought to Isaac, of which he did eat, was properly the preparatory sacrifice.

7. *And he took up his parable. Meshalo,* see on chap. xxi. 27. All these oracular speeches of Balaam are in hemistich meter in the original.

They are highly dignified, and may be considered as immediate poetic productions of the Spirit of God; for it is expressly said, v. 5, that God put the word in Balaam's mouth, and that "the spirit of God came upon him," chap. xxiv. 2.

8. *How shall I curse, whom God hath not cursed?* It was granted on all hands that no incantations nor imprecations could avail unless God concurred and ratified them. From God's communication to Balaam he saw that God was determined to bless and defend Israel, and therefore all endeavors to injure them must be in vain.

9. *From the top of the rocks I see him.* That is, from the high places of Baal where he went, chap. xxii. 41, that he might the more advantageously see the *whole* camp of Israel. *The people shall dwell alone.* They shall ever be preserved as a distinct nation. This prophecy has been literally fulfilled through a period of 3,300 years to the present day. This is truly astonishing.

10. *Let me die the death of the righteous.* Probably Balaam had some presentiment that he should be taken off by a premature death, and therefore he lodges this petition against it. The death of the righteous in those times implied being gathered to one's fathers in a good old age, having seen his children and children's children; and to this, probably, the latter part of this petition applies: *And let my last end be like his!* ("And let my posterity be like his!")

13. *Thou shalt see but the utmost part of them.* Balak thought that the sight of such an immense camp had intimidated Balaam, and this he might gather from what he said in the tenth verse: "Who can count the dust of Jacob?" He thought therefore that he might get Balaam to curse them in detached parties, till the whole camp should be devoted to destruction by successive execrations.

17. *What hath the Lord spoken?* Balak himself now understood that Balaam was wholly under the influence of Jehovah, and would say nothing but what God commanded him; but not knowing Jehovah as Balaam did, he hoped that he might be induced to change his mind, and curse a people whom he had hitherto determined to bless.

19. *God is not a man, that he should lie.* This seems to be spoken to correct the foregoing supposition of Balak that God could change his mind.

21. *He hath not beheld iniquity in Jacob, neither hath he seen perverseness in Israel.* This is a difficult passage; for if we take the words as spoken of the people Israel, as their *iniquity* and their *perverseness* were almost unparalleled, such words cannot be spoken of them with strict truth. If we consider them as spoken of the patiarch Jacob and Israel, or of Jacob after he became Israel, they are most strictly true, as after that time a more unblemished and noble character (Abraham excepted) is not to be found in the page of history, whether sacred or profane; and for his sake, and for the sake of his father, Isaac, and his grandfather, Abraham, God is ever represented as favoring, blessing, and sparing a rebellious and undeserving people. In this way, I think, this difficult text may be safely understood.

There is another way in which the words may be interpreted, which will give a good sense.

Aven not only signifies *iniquity,* but most frequently "trouble, labor, distress, and affliction"; and these indeed are its ideal meanings, and *iniquity* is only an accommodated or metaphorical one, because of the pain, distress, etc., produced by sin. *Amal,* translated here *perverseness,* occurs often in Scripture, but is never translated "perverseness" except in this place. It signifies simply "labor," especially that which is of an afflictive or oppressive kind. The words may therefore be considered as implying that God will not suffer the people either to be exterminated by the sword or to be brought under a yoke of slavery. Either of these methods of interpretation gives a good sense, but our common version gives none.

22. *The strength of an unicorn.* Reem and reim. It is generally allowed that there is no such beast in nature as the *unicorn;* i.e., a creature of the horse kind, with one long, rich, curled horn in the forehead. The creature painted from fancy is represented as one of the supporters of the royal arms of **Great Britain.** It is difficult to say what kind of beast is intended by the original word. But I believe the rhinoceros is that intended by the sacred writers.

23. *There is no enchantment.* Because God has determined to save them, therefore no enchantment can prevail against them. *According to this time.* I think this clause should be read thus: "As at this time it shall be told to Jacob and to Israel what God worketh"; i.e., this people shall always have prophetic information of what God is about to work. And indeed they are the only people under heaven who ever had this privilege. When God himself designed to punish them because of their sins, He always forewarned them by the prophets, and also took care to apprise them of all the plots of their enemies against them.

24. *Behold, the people shall rise up as a great lion.* Labi, the "great, mighty, or old lion," the king of the forest, who is feared and respected by all the other beasts of the field; so shall Israel be the subduer and possessor of the whole land of Canaan. And *as a young lion, ari* from *arah,* "to tear off," the predatory lion, or the lion in the act of seizing and tearing his prey; the nations against whom the Israelites are now going shall be no more able to defend themselves against their attacks than the feeblest beasts of the forest are against the attacks of the strong lion.

28. *Unto the top of Peor.* Probably the place where the famous Baal-peor had his chief temple. He appears to have been the Priapus of the Moabites, and to have been worshipped with the same obscene and abominable rites.

CHAPTER 24

Balaam, finding that God was determined to bless Israel, seeks no longer for enchantments, 1. The Spirit of God coming upon him, he delivers a most important prophetic parable, 2-9. Balak's anger is kindled against him, and he commands him to depart to his own country, 10-11. Balaam vindicates his conduct, 12-13; and delivers a prophecy relative to the future destruction of Moab by the Israelites, 14-17; also of Edom, 18-19; of the Amalekites, 20; and of the Kenites, 21-22. Predicts also the destruction of Asshur and Eber, by the naval power of Chittim, which should afterwards be itself destroyed, 23-24. Balaam and Balak separate, 25.

1. *He went not, as at other times, to seek for enchantments.* We have already had occasion to observe that the proper meaning of the word

nachash is not easily ascertained. Here the plural *nechashim* is rendered *enchantments*, but it probably means no more than the knowledge of future events. When Balaam saw that it pleased God to bless Israel, he therefore thought it unnecessary to apply for any further propetic declarations of God's will as he had done before, for he could safely infer every good to this people from the evident disposition of God towards them.

2. *The spirit of God came upon him.* This divine afflatus he had not expected on the present occasion, but God had not yet declared the whole of His will.

3. *He took up his parable.* His prophetic declaration couched in highly poetic terms, and in regular meter, as the preceding were. *The man whose eyes are open.* I believe the original *shethum* should be translated "shut," not *open;* for in the next verse, where the opening of his eyes is mentioned, a widely different word is used, *galah*, which signifies to "open" or "reveal." At first the eyes of Balaam were shut, and so closely too that he could not *see* the angel who withstood him, till God opened his eyes; nor could he see the gracious intentions of God towards Israel, till the eyes of his understanding were opened by the powers of the Divine Spirit.

4. *Falling into a trance.* There is no indication in the Hebrew that he fell into a *trance;* these words are added by our translators, but they are not in the original. *Nophel* is the only word used, and simply signifies "falling, or falling down," perhaps in this instance by way of religious prostration.

6. *Lign aloes which the Lord hath planted.* Or, "as the tents which the Lord hath pitched"; for it is the same word, *ohalim*, which is used in the fifth verse. But from other parts of Scripture we find that the word also signifies a species of tree called by some the sandal tree, and by others the lignum or wood aloes. This tree is described as being eight or ten feet high, with very large leaves growing at the top; and it is supposed that a forest of those at some distance must bear some resemblance to a numerous encampment. As the word comes from the root *ahal*, which signifies to "spread or branch out," and therefore is applied to tents, because of their being extended or spread out on the ground, so when it is applied to trees it must necessarily mean such as were remarkable for their widely extended branches; but what the particular species is cannot be satisfactorily ascertained. By the Lord's planting are probably meant such trees as grow independently of the cultivation of man.

7. *He shall pour the water out of his buckets.* Here is a very plain allusion to their method of raising water in different parts of the East. By the well a tall pole is erected, which serves as a fulcrum to a very long lever, to the smaller end of which a bucket is appended. On the opposite end, which is much larger, are many notches cut in the wood, which serve as steps for a man, whose business it is to climb into the well. When the bucket is filled, he raises it by walking back on the opposite arm, till his weight brings the bucket above the well's mouth. A person standing by the well empties the bucket into a trench, which communicates with the ground intended to be watered. *His seed shall*

be in many waters. Another simple allusion to the sowing of rice. The ground must not only be well-watered, but flooded, in order to serve for the proper growth of this grain. The rice that was sown in *many waters* must be the most fruitful. By an elegant and chaste metaphor all this is applied to the procreation of a numerous posterity.

His king shall be higher than Agag. This name is supposed to have been as common to all the Amalekitish kings as Pharaoh was to those in Egypt. But several critics, with the Septuagint, suppose that a small change has taken place here in the original word, and that instead of *meagag*, "than Agag," we should read *miggog*, "than Gog." As Gog in Scripture seems to mean the enemies of God's people, then the promise here may imply that the true worshippers of the Most High shall ultimately have dominion over all their enemies.

8. *God brought him forth out of Egypt.* They were neither expelled thence nor came voluntarily away. God alone, with a high hand and uplifted arm, brought them forth. Concerning the *unicorn*, see on chap. xxiii. 22.

9. *He couched, he lay down as a lion.* See the original terms explained, chap. xxiii. 24.

These oracles, delivered by Balaam, are evident prophecies of the victories which the Israelites should gain over their enemies, and of their firm possession of the Promised Land. They may also refer to the great victories to be obtained by the Lord Jesus Christ, that Lion of the tribe of Judah, over sin, death, and Satan, the grand enemies of the human race; and to that most numerous posterity of spiritual children which should be begotten by the preaching of the gospel.

11. *Lo, the Lord hath kept thee back from honor.* A bitter and impious sarcasm. "Hadst thou cursed this people, I would have promoted thee to great honor; but thou hast chosen to follow the directions of Jehovah rather than mine, and what will He do for thee?"

15. *The man whose eyes are open.* See on v. 3. It seems strange that our version should have fallen into such a mistake as to render *shethum* "open," which it does not signify, when the very sound of the word expresses the sense. The Vulgate has very properly preserved the true meaning, by rendering the clause "he whose eyes are shut." The Targum first paraphrased the passage falsely, and most of the versions followed it.

17. *I shall see him, but not now.* Or, "I shall see him, but he is not now." *I shall behold him, but not nigh*—I shall have a full view of him, but the time is yet distant. That is, The person of whom I am now prophesying does not at present exist among these Israelites, nor shall he appear in this generation. *There shall come a Star out of Jacob, and a Sceptre shall rise out of Israel*—a person eminent for wisdom, and formidable for strength and power, shall arise as king among this people. *He shall smite the corners of Moab*—he shall bring the Moabites perfectly under subjection (see 2 Sam. viii. 2), *and destroy all the children of Sheth.*

19. *Out of Jacob shall come.* This is supposed to refer to Christ, because of what is said in Gen. xlix. 10.

20. *Amalek was the first of the nations.* The

most ancient and most powerful of all the nations or states then within the view of Balaam; *but his latter end shall be that he perish for ever,* or "his posterity [*acharitho*] shall be destroyed, or shall utterly fail." This oracle began to be fulfilled by Saul, 1 Sam. xv. 7-8, who overthrew the Amalekites and took their king, Agag, prisoner. Afterwards they were nearly destroyed by David, 1 Sam. xxvii. 8, and they were finally exterminated by the sons of Simeon in the days of Hezekiah, 1 Chron. iv. 41-43; since that time they have ceased to exist as a people, and now no vestige of them remains on the face of the earth.

21. *He looked on the Kenites.* Commentators are not well agreed who the Kenites were. Dr. Dodd's opinion is, I think, nearest to the truth. Jethro, the father-in-law of Moses, is called a priest or prince of Midian, Exod. iii. 1, and in Judg. i. 16 he is called a Kenite; we may infer, therefore, says he, that the Kenites and the Midianites were the same, or at least that the Kenites and the Midianites were confederate tribes. Some of these, we learn from Judges i, followed the Israelites; others abode still among the Midianites and Amalekites.

22. *Until Asshur shall carry thee away captive.* The Assyrians and Babylonians who carried away captive the ten tribes, 2 Kings xvii. 6, and the Jews into Babylon, 2 Kings xxv, probably carried away the Kenites also. Indeed this seems pretty evident, as we find some Kenites mentioned among the Jews after their return from the Babylonish captivity, 1 Chron. ii. 55.

24. *Ships shall come from the coast of Chittim.* Some think by Chittim the Romans, others the Macedonians under Alexander the Great, are meant. *And shall afflict Eber.* Probably not the Hebrews, as some think, but the people on the other side the Euphrates, from *abar*, "to pass over, go beyond"; all which people were discomfited and their empire destroyed by Alexander the Great.

25. *And Balaam . . . returned to his place.* Intended to have gone to Mesopotamia, his native country (see Deut. xxiii. 4), but seems to have settled among the Midianites, where he was slain by the Israelites; see chap. xxxi. 8.

CHAPTER 25

While Israel abides in Shittim the people commit whoredom with the daughters of Moab, 1. They become idolaters, 2. The anger of the Lord is kindled against them, and He commands the ringleaders to be hanged, 3-4. Moses causes the judges to slay the transgressors, 5. Zimri, one of the Israelitish princes of the tribe of Simeon, brings a Midianitish princess, named Cozbi, into his tent, while the people are deploring their iniquity before the Tabernacle, 6. Phinehas, the son of Eleazar, incensed by this insult to the laws and worship of God, runs after them and pierces them both with a javelin, 7-8. Twenty-four thousand die of the plague, sent as a punishment for their iniquity, 9. The Lord grants to Phinehas a covenant of peace and an everlasting priesthood, 10-13. The name and quality of the Israelitish man and Midianitish woman, 14-15. God commands the Israelites to vex and smite the Midianites, who had seduced them to the worship of Baal-peor, 16-18.

3. *Israel joined himself unto Baal-peor.* The same as the Priapus of the Romans, and worshipped with the same obscene rites as we have frequently had occasion to remark. The joining to Baal-peor, mentioned here, was probably what Paul had in view when he said, 2 Cor. vi. 14: "Be ye not unequally yoked together with unbelievers." And this joining, though done even in a matrimonial way, was nevertheless fornication (see Rev. ii. 14), as no marriage between an Israelite and a Midianite could be legitimate, according to the law of God.

4. *Take all the heads of the people.* Meaning the chiefs of those who had transgressed; as if he had said, "Assemble the chiefs and judges, institute an inquiry concerning the transgressors, and hang them who shall be found guilty before the Lord, as a matter required by his justice." *Against the sun*—in the most public manner, and in daylight.

5. *Slay ye every one his men.* In the different departments where you preside over thousands, hundreds, fifties, and tens, slay all the culprits that shall be found.

6. *One of the children of Israel.* Zimri, the son of Salu, a prince of a chief family in the tribe of Simeon, v. 14, *brought . . . a Midianitish woman,* Cozbi, daughter of Zur, head over a people of one of the chief families in Midian, v. 15. The condition of these two persons plainly proves it to have been a matrimonial alliance; the one was a prince, the other a princess. Therefore I must conclude that fornication or whoredom, in the common sense of the word, was not practiced on this occasion. Josephus positively says that Zimri had married Cozbi, *Antiq.,* l. iv, chap. 6; and if he had not said so, still the thing is nearly self-evident.

The children of Israel, who were weeping. This aggravated the crime, because the people were then in a state of great humiliation because of the late impure and illegal transactions.

8. *Thrust both of them through.* Inspired undoubtedly by the Spirit of the God of justice to do this act, which can never be a precedent on any common occasion.

9. *Those that died . . . were twenty and four thousand.* Paul, 1 Cor. x. 8, reckons only twenty-three thousand; though some MSS. and versions, particularly the latter Syriac and the Armenian, have twenty-four thousand, with the Hebrew text. Allowing the 24,000 to be the genuine reading, and none of the Hebrew MSS. exhibit any various reading here, the two places may be reconciled thus: 1,000 men were slain in consequence of the examination instituted, v. 4, and 23,000 in consequence of the orders given, v. 5, making 24,000 in the whole. Paul probably refers only to the latter number.

12-13. *My covenant of peace . . . of an everlasting priesthood.* As the word *peace* implied all kinds of blessings, both spiritual and temporal, it may mean no more here than the promise of God to grant him and his family the utmost prosperity in reference to both worlds. The *everlasting priesthood* refers properly to the priesthood of Christ, which was shadowed out by the priesthood under the law, no matter in what family it was continued. Therefore the *kehunnath olam,* or "eternal priesthood," does not merely refer to any sacerdotal ministrations which should be continued in the family of Phinehas during the Mosaic dispensation, but to that priesthood of Christ typified by that of Aaron and his successors.

17. *Vex the Midianites.* See this order fulfilled, chap. xxxi. 1-20. Twelve thousand Israelites attacked the Midianites, destroyed all their cities, slew their five kings, every male, and every grown-up woman, and took all their spoils.

CHAPTER 26

Moses and Eleazar are commanded to take the sum of the Israelites, in the plains of Moab, 1-4. Reuben and his posterity, 43,730, vv. 5-11. Simeon and his posterity, 22,200, vv. 12-14. Gad and his posterity, 40,500, vv. 15-18. Judah and his posterity, 76,500, vv. 19-22. Issachar and his posterity, 64,300, vv. 23-25. Zebulun and his posterity, 60,500, vv. 26-27. Manasseh and his posterity, 52,700, vv. 28-34. Ephraim and his posterity, 32,500, vv. 35-37. Benjamin and his posterity, 45,600, vv. 38-41. Dan and his posterity, 64,400, vv. 42-43. Asher and his posterity, 53,400, vv. 44-47. Naphtali and his posterity, 45,400, vv. 48-50. Total amount of the twelve tribes, 601,730, v. 51. The land is to be divided by lot, and how, 52-56. The Levites and their families, 57-58. Their genealogy, 59-61. Their number, 23,000, v. 62. In this census or enumeration not one man was found save Joshua and Caleb, of all who had been reckoned thirty-eight years before, the rest having died in the wilderness, 63-65.

2. *Take the sum of all the congregation.* After thirty-eight years God commands a second census of the Israelites to be made, to preserve the distinction in families and to regulate the tribes previously to their entry into the Promised Land, and to ascertain the proportion of land which should be allowed to each tribe. For though the whole was divided by lot, yet the portions were so disposed that a numerous tribe did not draw where the lots assigned small inheritances. See verses 53-56, and also the note on chap. i. 1.

10. *Together with Korah.* The Samaritan text does not intimate that Korah was *swallowed . . . up*, but that he was burned, as appears, in fact, to have been the case. "And the earth swallowed them up, what time that company died; and the fire devoured Korah with the two hundred and fifty men, who became a sign."

11. *The children of Korah died not.* It is difficult to reconcile this place with chap. xvi. 27, 31-33, where it seems to be intimated that not only the men, but the wives, and the sons, and the little ones of Korah, Dathan, and Abiram, were swallowed up by the earthquake; see especially v. 27, collated with v. 33, of chap. xvi. But the text here expressly says, *The children of Korah died not;* and on a close inspection of v. 27 of the above-mentioned chapter, we shall find that the sons and the little ones of Dathan and Abiram alone are mentioned. "So they gat up from the tabernacle of Korah, Dathan, and Abiram, on every side: and Dathan and Abiram came out . . . and their wives, and their sons, and their little ones." Here is no mention of the children of Korah; they therefore escaped, while it appears those of Dathan and Abiram perished with their fathers.

51. *These were the numbered of the children of Israel, six hundred thousand and a thousand seven hundred and thirty.* Let it be observed, (1) That among these there was not a man of the former census, save Joshua and Caleb, see vv. 64-65. (2) That though there was an increase in seven tribes of not less than 74,800 men, yet so great was the decrease in the other five tribes that the balance against the present census is 1,820.

55. *The land shall be divided by lot.* The word *goral*, translated *lot*, is supposed by some to signify the stone or pebble formerly used for the purpose of what we term casting lots. A *lot* in the promised land was evidently typical of a place in eternal glory. "That they may receive forgiveness of sins, and an inheritance [a *lot*] among them which are sanctified," Acts xxvi. 18. Who "hath made us meet to be partakers of the inheritance [of the *lot*] of the saints in light," Col. i. 12. "Which is the earnest

of our inheritance" (of our *allotted portion*)," Eph. i. 14. "What [is] the riches of the glory of his inheritance" (*allotted portion*), Eph. i. 18.

CHAPTER 27

The daughters of Zelophehad claim their inheritance, 1-4. Moses brings their case before the Lord. 5. He allows their claim, 6-7; and a law is made to regulate the inheritance of daughters, 8-11. Moses is commanded to go up to Mount Abarim, and view the Promised Land, 12; is apprised of his death, 13; and because he did not sanctify God at the waters of Meribah, he shall not enter into it, 14. Moses requests the Lord to appoint a person to supply his place as leader of the Israelites, 15-17. God appoints Joshua, commands Moses to lay his hands upon him, to set him before Eleazar, the priest, and give him a charge in the sight of the people, 18-20. Eleazar shall ask counsel for him by Urim and at his command shall the Israelites go out and come in, 21. Moses does as the Lord commanded him, and consecrates Joshua, 22-23.

1. *The daughters of Zelophehad.* The singular case of these women caused an additional law to be made to the civil code of Israel, which satisfactorily ascertained and amply secured the right of succession in cases of inheritance. The law, which is as reasonable as it is just, stands thus: (1) On the demise of the father the estate goes to the sons; (2) If there be no son, the daughters succeed; (3) If there be no daughter, the brothers of the deceased inherit; (4) If there be no brethren or paternal uncles, the estate goes to the brothers of his father; (5) If there be no granduncles or brothers of the father of the deceased, then the nearest akin succeeds to the inheritance.

12. *Get thee up into this mount Abarim.* The mountain which Moses was commanded to ascend was certainly Mount Nebo, see Deut. xxxii. 49, etc., which was the same as Pisgah, see Deut. xxxiv. 1. The mountains of Abarim, according to Dr. Shaw, are a long ridge of frightful, rocky, precipitous hills, which are continued all along the eastern coast of the Dead Sea, as far as the eye can reach. As in Hebrew *abar* signifies to "pass over," *Abarim* here probably signifies "passages"; and the ridge in this place had its name in all likelihood from the passage of the Israelites, as it was opposite to these that they passed the Jordan into the Promised Land.

17. *That the congregation of the Lord be not as sheep which have no shepherd.* This is a beautiful expression, and shows us in what light Moses viewed himself among his people. He was their shepherd; he sought no higher place; he fed and guided the flock of God under the direction of the Divine Spirit, and was faithful in all his Master's house. To this saying of Moses our Lord alludes, Matt. ix. 36.

18. *In whom is the spirit.* This must certainly mean the Spirit of God; and because he was endued with this Spirit, therefore he was capable of leading the people.

20. *And thou shalt put.* Mechodecha, of "thine honor or authority" upon him. You shall show to the whole congregation that you have associated him with yourself in the government of the people.

21. *Eleazar the priest . . . shall ask counsel for him.* Here was a remarkable difference between him and Moses. God talked with Moses face-to-face, but to Joshua only through the medium of the high priest.

23. *He laid his hands upon him.* As a proof of his being appointed to and qualified for the

work. So at the word of Joshua they were to go out, and at his word to come in, v. 21. And thus he was a type of our blessed Lord as to his mediatorial office and divine appointment as man to the work of our salvation.

CHAPTER 28

All the offerings of God to be offered in their due season, 1-2. The continual burnt offering for the morning, 3-6; and its drink offering, 7. The continual burnt offering for the evening, 8. The offerings for the Sabbath, 9-10. The offerings for the beginning of each month, 11-15. Repetition of the ordinances concerning the Passover, 16-25. Ordinances concerning the day of first-fruits or Pentecost, 26-31.

2. Command the children of Israel. It is not easy to account for the reason of the introduction of these precepts here, which had been so circumstantially delivered before in different parts of the Books of Exodus and Leviticus. It is possible that the daily, weekly, monthly, and yearly services had been considerably interrupted for several years, owing to the unsettled state of the people in the wilderness, and that it was necessary to repeat these laws for two reasons: (1) Because they were now about to enter into the Promised Land, where these services must be established and constant. (2) Because the former generations being all dead, multitudes of the present might be ignorant of these ordinances.

In their due season. Moses divides these offerings into (1) *Daily.* The morning and evening sacrifices: a lamb each time, vv. 3-4. (2) *Weekly.* The Sabbath offerings, two lambs of a year old, vv. 9, etc. (3) *Monthly.* At the beginning of each month two young bullocks, one ram, and seven lambs of a year old, and a kid for a sin offering, vv. 11, etc. (4) *Annually.* (*a*) The Passover to last seven days; the offerings, two young bullocks, one ram, seven lambs of a year old, and a he-goat for a sin offering, vv. 16, etc. (*b*) The day of firstfruits. The sacrifices, the same as on the beginning of the month, vv. 26, etc. With these sacrifices were offered libations, or drink offerings, of strong wine, vv. 7, 14, and *minchahs*, or meat offerings, composed of fine flour mingled with oil, vv. 8, 12, etc. For an ample account of all these offerings, see the notes on Leviticus vii and Exodus xii.

7. Strong wine. *Sikera:* see the note on chap. x. 9, where this is largely explained.

26. Day of the firstfruits. Called also the Feast of Weeks, and the Feast of Pentecost. See it explained, Exod. xxiii. 14 and Lev. xxiii. 15.

31. Without blemish. This is to be understood as applying, not only to the animals, but also to the flour, wine, and oil; everything must be perfect in its kind.

CHAPTER 29

The Feast of Trumpets on the first day of the seventh month, and its sacrifices, 1-6. The feast of expiation, or annual atonement, on the tenth day of the same month, with its sacrifices, 7-11. The Feast of Tabernacles, held on the fifteenth day of the same month, with its eight days' offerings, 12. The offerings of the first day, thirteen bullocks, two rams, fourteen lambs, and one kid, 13-16. The offerings of the second day, twelve bullocks, two rams, fourteen lambs, and one kid, 17-19. The offerings of the third day, eleven bullocks; the rest as before, 20-22. The offerings of the fourth day, ten bullocks; the rest as before, 23-25. The offerings of the fifth day, nine bullocks, etc., 26-28. The offerings of the sixth day, eight bullocks, etc., 29-31. The offerings of the seventh day, seven bullocks, etc., 32-34. The offerings of the eighth day, one bullock, one ram, seven lambs, and one

goat, 35-38. These sacrifices to be offered, and feasts to be kept, besides vows, freewill offerings, etc., 39. Moses announces all these things to the people, 40.

1. And in the seventh month. This was the beginning of their civil year, and was a time of great festivity, and was ushered in by the blowing of trumpets. It answers to a part of our September.

7. On the tenth day. See the notes on Lev. xvi. 29; xxiii. 24.

12. On the fifteenth day of the seventh month. On this day there was to be a solemn assembly, and for seven days sacrifices were to be offered; on the first day 13 young bullocks, 2 rams, and 14 lambs. On each succeeding day one bullock less, till on the seventh day there were only 7, making in all 70. What an expensive service! How should we magnify God for being delivered from it! Yet these were all the taxes they had to pay. At the public charge there were annually offered to God, independently of trespass offerings and voluntary vows, 15 goats, 21 kids, 72 rams, 132 bullocks, and 1,101 lambs! But how little is all this when compared with the lambs slain every year at the Passover, which amounted in one year to the immense number of 255,600 slain in the Temple itself, which was the answer that Cestius, the Roman general, received when he asked the priests how many persons had come to Jerusalem at their annual festivals; the priests, numbering the people by the lambs that had been slain, said, "twenty-five myriads, five thousand and six hundred." For an account of the Feast of Tabernacles, see on Lev. xxiii. 34.

35. On the eighth day ye shall have a solemn assembly. This among the Jews was esteemed the chief or high day of the feast, though fewer sacrifices were offered on it than on the others. The people seem to have finished the solemnity with a greater measure of spiritual devotion, and it was on this day of the feast that our blessed Lord called the Jews from the letter to the spirit of the law, proposing himself as the sole Fountain whence they could derive the streams of salvation, John vii. 37. On the subject of this chapter see the notes on Leviticus xii; xvi; and xxiii.

CHAPTER 30

The law concerning vows of men, 1-2. Of women under age, and in what cases the father may annul them, 3-5. The vows of a wife, and in what cases the husband may annul them, 6-8. The vows of a widow, or divorced woman, in what cases they may be considered either as confirmed or annulled, 9-15. Recapitulation of these ordinances, 16.

2. If a man vow a vow. A vow is a religious promise made to God. Vows were of several kinds: (1) Of abstinence or humiliation, see v. 13; (2) Of the Nazarite, see chap. vi; (3) Of giving certain things or sacrifices to the Lord, Lev. vii. 16; (4) Of alms given to the poor, see Deut. xxiii. 21. The law in this chapter must have been very useful, as it both prevented and annulled rash vows, and provided a proper sanction for the support and performance of those that were rationally and piously made. Besides, this law must have acted as a great preventive of lying and hypocrisy. If a vow was properly made, a man or woman was bound, under penalty of the displeasure of God, to fulfil it.

3. In her youth. That is, say the rabbins, under twelve years of age; and under thirteen in case of a young man. Young persons of this age were considered to be under the authority of their parents, and had consequently no power to vow away the property of another. A married woman was in the same circumstances, because she was under the authority of her husband. If however the parents or the husband heard of the vow, and objected to it in the same day in which they heard of it (v. 5), the vow was annulled; or if, having heard of it, they held their peace, this was considered a ratification of the vow.

12. *Concerning the bond of her soul.* Her life is at stake if she fulfil not the obligation under which she has laid herself.

16. *These are the statutes.* It is very probable that this law, like that concerning the succession of daughters (chap. xxvii), rose from the exigency of some particular case that had just then occurred.

CHAPTER 31

The command of the Lord to make war on the Midianites, 1-2. One thousand men are chosen out of each of the twelve tribes, and sent with Phinehas against the Midianites, 3-6. They slay all the males, 7; their five kings and Balaam, 8. They take all the women captives, with the flocks and goods, 9; burn their cities and bring away the spoil, 10-11. They bring the captives, etc., to Moses, who is wroth with the officers for sparing the women, who had formerly been the cause of their transgression and punishment, 12-16. He commands all the male children and all the grown-up females to be slain, 17-18. How the soldiers were to purify themselves, 19-20; and the different articles taken in war, 21-24. They are commanded to take the sum of the prey, to divide it into two parts: one for the 12,000 warriors, and the other for the rest of the congregation, 25-27. One of 500, both of persons and cattle, of the share of the warriors, to be given to the Lord, 28-29; and one part of 50, of the people's share, to be given to the Levites, 30. The sum of the prey remaining after the above division: sheep 675,000, beeves 72,000, asses 61,000, young women 32,000, vv. 31-35. How the soldiers' part was divided, 36-40. How the part belonging to the congregation was divided, 41-47. The officers report that they had not lost a man in this war, 48-49. They bring a voluntary oblation to God, of gold and ornaments, 50-51; the amount of which was 16,750 shekels, 52-53. Moses and Eleazar bring the gold into the Tabernacle for a memorial, 54.

2. *Gathered unto thy people.* Where? Not in the grave surely. Moses was gathered with none of them; his burial place no man ever knew. "But being gathered unto one's people means dying." It does imply dying, but it does not mean this only. The truth is, God considers all those who are "dead" to men in a state of conscious existence in another world. Therefore He calls himself the "God of Abraham, and the God of Isaac, and the God of Jacob. [Now] God is not the God of the dead, but of the living," because all live to Him, whether dead to men or not. Moses therefore was to be gathered to his people—to enter into that republic of Israel which, having died in the faith, fear, and love of God, were now living in a state of conscious blessedness beyond the confines of the grave.

3. *Avenge the Lord of Midian.* It was God's quarrel, not their own, that they were now to take up. These people were idolaters; idolatry is an offense against God. The civil power has no authority to meddle with what belongs to Him, without especial directions, certified in the most unequivocal way. Private revenge, extension of territory, love of plunder were to have no place in this business; the Lord is to be avenged, and through Him the children of Israel (v. 2), because their souls as well as their bodies had been well-nigh ruined by their idolatry.

6. *A thousand of every tribe.* Twelve thousand men in the whole. *And Phinehas the son of Eleazar;* some think he was made general in this expedition, but this is not likely. The ark and its contents must proceed to this battle, because the battle was the Lord's and He dwelt between the cherubim over the ark; and Phinehas, who had before got a grant in the eternal priesthood, was chosen to accompany the ark in place of his father, Eleazar, who was probably now too far advanced in years to undergo the fatigue. Who then was general? Joshua, without doubt, though not here mentioned, because the battle being the Lord's, He alone is to have the supreme direction, and all the glory. Besides, it was an extraordinary war, and not conducted on the common principle, for we do not find that peace was offered to the Midianites, and that they refused it; see Deut. xx. 10, etc. In such a case only hostilities could lawfully commence; but they were sinners against God; the cup of their iniquity was full, and God thought proper to destroy them.

8. *Balaam . . . they slew with the sword.* This man had probably committed what John calls the "sin unto death"—a sin which God punishes with temporal death, while at the same time He extends mercy to the soul.

17. *Kill every male among the little ones.* For this action I account simply on the principle that God, who is the Author and Supporter of life, has a right to dispose of it when and how He thinks proper; and the Judge of all the earth can do nothing but what is right. Of the women killed on this occasion it may be safely said their lives were forfeited by their personal transgressions; and yet even in this case there can be little doubt that God showed mercy to their souls. The little ones were safely lodged; they were taken to heaven and saved from the evil to come.

23. *The water of separation.* The water in which the ashes of the red heifer were mingled; see on chap. viii. 7; xix. 2, etc. Garments, whether of cloth or skins, were to be washed. Gold, silver, brass, iron, tin, and lead, to pass through the fire, probably to be melted down.

28. *And levy a tribute unto the Lord . . . one soul of five hundred.* The person to be employed in the Lord's service, under the Levites—the cattle either for sacrifice or for the use of the Levites, v. 30.

32. *The booty.* It appears from the enumeration here that the Israelites, in this war against the Midianites, took 32,000 female prisoners, 61,000 asses, 72,000 beeves, 675,000 sheep and small cattle; besides the immense number of males who fell in battle, and the women and children who were slain by the divine command, v. 17. And it does not appear that in this expedition a single man of Israel fell! This was naturally to be expected, because the battle was the Lord's, v. 49.

50. *We have . . . brought an oblation for the Lord.* So it appears there was a great deal of booty taken which did not come into the general account; and of this the soldiers, of their own will, made a very extensive offering to God because He had preserved them from falling in battle. *To make an atonement for our souls.* That is, to make an acknowledgment to God for the preservation of their lives.

CHAPTER 32

The Reubenites and Gadites request Moses to give them their inheritance on this side of Jordan, 1-5. Moses expostulates with and reproves them, 6-15. They explain themselves, and propose conditions, with which Moses is satisfied—they are to build cities for their wives and children, and folds for their cattle, and go over Jordan armed with the other tribes, and fight against their enemies till the land is subdued; after which they are to return, 16-27. Moses proposes the business to Eleazar, Joshua, and the elders, 28-30. The Gadites and Reubenites promise a faithful observance of the conditions, 31-32; on which Moses assigns to them, and the half-tribe of Manasseh, the kingdom of Sihon, king of the Amorites, and the kingdom of Og, king of Bashon, 33. The cities built by the Gadites, 34-36. The cities built by the Reubenites, 37-38. The children of Machir, the son of Manasseh, expel the Amorites from Gilead, 39, which Moses grants to them, 40. Jair, the son of Manasseh, takes the small towns of Gilead, 41. And Nobah takes Kenath and its villages, 42.

3. *Ataroth, and Dibon.* The places mentioned here belonged to Sihon, king of the Amorites, and Og, king of Bashan, which, being conquered by the Israelites, constituted ever after a part of their territories, v. 33.

5. *Let this land be given unto thy servants.* Because it was good for pasturage, and they had many flocks, v. 1.

12. *Caleb the son of Jephunneh the Kenezite.* It was Jephunneh that was the Kenezite, and not Caleb. Kenaz was probably the father of Jephunneh.

16. *We will build . . . cities for our little ones.* It was impossible for these, numerous as they might be, to build cities and fortify them for the defense of their families in their absence.

17. *Because of the inhabitants of the land.* These were the Ammonites, Moabites, Idumeans, and the remains of the Midianites and Amorites. But could the women and children even keep the defensed cities when placed in them? This certainly cannot be supposed possible. Many of the man of war must, of course, stay behind. In the last census, chap. xxvi., the tribe of Reuben consisted of 43,730 men; the tribe of Gad, 40,500; the tribe of Manasseh, 52,700, the half of which is 26,350. Add this to the sum of the other two tribes, and the amount is 110,580. Now from Joshua iv. 13 we learn that of the tribes of Reuben and Gad, and the half of the tribe of Manasseh, only 40,000 armed men passed over Jordan to assist their brethren in the reduction of the land; consequently the number of 70,580 men were left behind for the defense of the women, the children, and the flocks. This was more than sufficient to defend them against a people already panic-stuck by their late discomfitures and reverses.

34. *The children of Gad built . . . Aroer.* This was situated on the river Arnon, Deut. ii. 36; 2 Kings x. 33. It was formerly inhabited by the *Emim,* a warlike and perhaps gigantic people. They were expelled by the Moabites; the Moabites, by the Amorites; and the Amorites, by the Israelites. The Gadites then possessed it till the captivity of their tribe, with that of Reuben and the half of the tribe of Manasseh, by the Assyrians, 2 Kings xv. 29, after which the Moabites appear to have repossessed it, as they seem to have occupied it in the days of Jeremiah, chap. xlviii. 15-20.

38. *And Nebo . . . (their names being changed).* That is, Those who conquered the cities called them after their own names. Thus the city Kenath, being conquered by Nobah, was called after his name, v. 42.

41. *Havoth-jair.* That is, the "villages" or "habitations of Jair"; and thus they should have been translated. As these two tribes and a half were the first, says Ainsworth, who had their inheritance assigned to them in the Promised Land, so they were the first of all Israel that were carried captive out of their own land, because of their sins. "For they transgressed against the God of their fathers, and went a whoring after other gods. And God delivered them into the hands of Pul and Tiglath-Pilneser, kings of Assyria, and they brought them to Halah, Habor, Hara, and Gozan, unto this day." See 1 Chron. v. 25-26.

CHAPTER 33

The journeyings of the Israelites written out by Moses, according to the commandment of the Lord, 1-2. They depart from Rameses on the fifteenth day of the first month, on the day after the Passover, the firstborn of the Egyptians having been slain, 3-4. Their forty-two stations enumerated, 5-49. They are authorized to expel all the former inhabitants, and destroy all remnants of idolatry, 50-53. The land is to be divided by lot, 54. Should they not drive out the former inhabitants, they shall be to them as pricks in their eyes and thorns in their sides, 55. And if not obedient, God will deal with them as He has purposed to do with the Canaanites, 56.

2. *And Moses wrote their goings out according to their journeys.* We may consider the whole Book of Numbers as a diary, and indeed the first book of travels ever published.

3. *From Rameses.* This appears to have been the metropolis of the land of Goshen, and the place of rendezvous whence the whole Israelitish nation set out on their journey to the Promised Land; and is supposed to be the same as Cairo.

[There follows in verses 5-49 an outline of the journey in which the forty-two stations or stopping places are listed.]

52. *Ye shall . . . destroy all their pictures.* *Maskiyotham,* from *sachah,* "to be like, or resemble," either pictures, carved work, or embroidery, as far as these things were employed to exhibit the abominations of idolatry. *Molten images, tsalmey massechotham,* metallic talismanical figures, made under certain constellations, and supposed in consequence to be possessed of some extraordinary influences and virtues.

55. *Shall be pricks in your eyes.* Under these metaphors the continual mischief that should be done to them, in both soul and body, by these idolaters is set forth in a very expressive manner. What can be more vexatious than a continual goading of each side, so that the attempt to avoid the one throws the body more forcibly on the other? And what can be more distressing than a continual pricking in the eye?

CHAPTER 34

The land of Canaan is described, 1-2. The south quarter, 3-5. The western border, 6. The north border, 7-9. The east border, 10-12. This land to be divided by lot among the nine tribes and half, 13; two tribes and half, Reuben and Gad, and the half of Manasseh, having already got their inheritance on the east side of Jordan, 14-15. Eleazar, the priest, and Joshua, to assist in dividing the land, 16-17; and with them a chief out of every tribe, 18. The names of the twelve chiefs, 19-29.

2. *The land of Canaan with the coasts thereof.* All description here is useless. The situation and boundaries of the land of Canaan can be known only by actual survey, or by consulting a good map.

3. *The salt sea.* The Dead Sea, or Lake Asphaltites.

5. *The river of Egypt.* The eastern branch of the river Nile; or, according to others, a river which is south of the land of the Philistines.

6. *Ye shall even have the great sea for a border.* The Mediterranean Sea, called here the Great Sea, to distinguish it from the Dead Sea, the Sea of Tiberias, etc., which were only a sort of lakes. In Hebrew there is properly but one term, *yam*, which is applied to all collections of water apparently stagnant, and which is generally translated "sea."

11. *The sea of Chinnereth.* The same as the sea of Galilee, Sea of Tiberias, and Sea of Gennesareth.

12. *The border shall go down to Jordan.* This river is famous in both the Old and New Testaments. It takes its rise at the foot of Mount Libanus, passes through the Sea of Chinnereth or Tiberias, and empties itself into the Lake Asphaltites or Dead Sea, from which it has no outlet. In and by it God wrought many miracles. God cut off the waters of this river as He did those of the Red Sea, so that they stood on a heap on each side, and the people passed over on dry ground. Both Elijah and Elisha separated its waters in a miraculous way, 2 Kings ii. 8-14. Naaman, the Syrian general, by washing in it at the command of the prophet, was miraculously cured of his leprosy, 2 Kings v. 10-14. In this river John baptized great multitudes of Jews; and in it was Christ himself baptized, and the Spirit of God descended upon Him, and the voice from heaven proclaimed Him the great and only Teacher and Saviour of men, Matt. iii. 16-17; Mark i. 5-11.

13. *This is the land which ye shall inherit by lot.* Much of what is said concerning this land is peculiarly emphatic. It is a land that contains a multitude of advantages in its climate, its soil, situation, etc. It is bounded on the south by a ridge of mountains, which separate it from Arabia, and screen it from the burning and often pestiferous winds which blow over the desert from that quarter. On the west it is bounded by the Mediterranean Sea; on the north, by Mount Libanus, which defends it from the cold northern blasts; and on the east by the river Jordan, and its fertile, well-watered plains. It is described by God himself as "a good land, a land of brooks of water, of fountains and depths that spring out of valleys and hills; a land of wheat, and barley, and vines, and fig trees, and pomegranates; a land of olive oil and honey"; a land wherein there was no scarcity of bread, and where both iron and copper mines abounded, Deut. viii. 7-9; a land finely diversified with hills and valleys, and well watered by the rain of heaven, in this respect widely different from Egypt; a land which God cared for, on which His eyes were continually placed from the beginning to the end of the year; watched over by a most merciful Providence; in a word, a land which flowed with milk and honey, and was the most pleasant of all lands, Deut. xi. 11-12; Ezek. xx. 6.

19, etc. *And the names of the men are these.* It is worthy of remark that Moses does not follow any order hitherto used of placing the tribes, neither that in chap. i, nor that in chap. vii, nor that in chap. xxvi, nor any other; but

places them here exactly in that order in which they possessed the land: Judah, Simeon, Benjamin, Dan, Manasseh, Ephraim, Zebulun, Issachar, Asher, Naphtali. Judah is first, having the first lot; and he dwelt in the south part of the land, Josh. xv. 1, etc.; and next to him Simeon, because his inheritance was "within the inheritance of the children of Judah," Josh. xix. 1. Benjamin was third; he had his inheritance by Judah, "between the children of Judah and the children of Joseph," Josh. xviii. 11. Dan was the fourth; his lot fell westward of that of Benjamin, in the country of the Philistines, as may be seen in Josh. xix. 40-41, etc. Fifth, Manasseh; and sixth, by him, his brother, Ephraim, whose inheritances were behind that of Benjamin, Josh. xvi. 7. Next to these dwelt, seventh, Zebulun; and eighth, Issachar; concerning whose lots see Josh. xix. 10-17. Ninth, Asher; and tenth, Naphtali; see Josh. xix. 24, 32, etc. And as in encamping about the Tabernacle they were arranged according to their fraternal relationship, so they were in the division and inheriting of the Promised Land. Judah and Simeon, both sons of Leah, dwelt abreast of each other. Benjamin, son of Rachel, and Dan, son of Rachel's maid, dwelt next abreast. Manasseh and Ephraim, both sons of Joseph, son of Rachel, had the next place abreast. Zebulun and Issachar, who dwelt next together, were both sons of Leah; and the last pair were Asher, of Leah's maid, and Naphtali, of Rachel's maid. Thus God, in nominating princes that should divide the land, signified beforehand the manner of their possession, and that they should be so situated as to dwell together as brethren in unity, for the mutual help and comfort of each other.

CHAPTER 35

The Israelites are commanded to give the Levites, out of their inheritances, cities and their suburbs for themselves and for their cattle, goods, etc., 1-3. The suburbs to be 3,000 cubits round about from the wall of the city, 4-5. The cities to be forty-two, to which six cities of refuge should be added, in all forty-eight cities, 6-7. Each tribe shall give of these cities in proportion to its possessions, 8. These cities to be appointed for the person who might slay his neighbor unawares, 9-12. Of these six cities there shall be three on each side Jordan, 13-14. The cities to be places of refuge for all who kill a person unawares, whether they be Israelites, strangers, or sojourners, 15. Cases of murder to which the benefit of the cities of refuge shall not extend, 16-21. Cases of manslaughter to which the benefits of the cities of refuge shall extend, 22-23. How the congregation shall act between the manslayer and the avenger of blood, 24-25. The manslayer shall abide in the city of refuge till the death of the high priest; he shall then return to the land of his possession, 26-28. Two witnesses must attest a murder before a murderer can be put to death, 29-30. Every murderer to be put to death, 31. The manslayer is not to be permitted to come to the land of his inheritance till the death of the high priest, 32. The land must not be polluted with blood, for the Lord dwells in it, 33-34.

4. *And the suburbs of the cities . . . shall reach from the wall of the city and outward a thousand cubits round about.*

5. *And ye shall measure from without the city . . . two thousand cubits.* Commentators have been much puzzled with the accounts in these two verses. In v. 4 the measure is said to be 1,000 cubits from the wall; in v. 5 the measure is said to be 2,000 from without the city. It is likely these two measures mean the same thing; at least so it was understood by the Septuagint and Coptic, who have 2,000 cubits in the fourth as well as in the fifth verse; but this reading of the Septuagint and Coptic is not acknowledged

by any other of the ancient versions, nor by any of the MSS. collated by Kennicott and De Rossi. We must seek therefore for some other method of reconciling this apparently contradictory account. Sundry modes have been proposed by commentators, which appear to me, in general, to require fully as much explanation as the text itself. Maimonides is the only one intelligible on the subject. "The suburbs," says he, "of the cities are expressed in the law to be 3,000 cubits on every side from the wall of the city and outwards. The first thousand cubits are the suburbs, and the 2,000, which they measured without the suburbs, were for fields and vineyards."

11. *Ye shall appoint . . . cities of refuge.* The cities of refuge among the Israelites were widely different from the *asyla* among the Greeks and Romans, as also from the privileged altars among the Roman Catholics. Those among the Hebrews were for the protection of such only as had slain a person involuntarily. The temples and altars among the latter often served for the protection of the most profligate characters. Cities of refuge among the Hebrews were necessary because the old patriarchal law still remained in force, viz., that the nearest akin had a right to avenge the death of his relation by slaying the murderer; for the original law enacted that "whoso sheddeth man's blood, by man shall his blood be shed," Gen. ix. 6, and none was judged so proper to execute this law as the man who was nearest akin to the deceased.

12. *Until he stand before the congregation in judgment.* So one of these cities was not a perpetual asylum; it was only a *pro tempore* refuge, till the case could be fairly examined by the magistrates in the presence of the people, or the elders—their representatives; and this was done in the city or place where he had done the murder, Josh. xx. 4, 6. If he was found worthy of death, they delivered him to the avenger that he might be slain, Deut. xix. 12; if not, they sent him back to the city of refuge, where he remained till the death of the high priest, v. 25. Before the cities of refuge were appointed, the altar appears to have been a sanctuary for those who had killed a person unwittingly.

19. *The revenger of blood.* Goel haddam, the "redeemer of blood," the next in blood to him who was slain.

30. *But one witness shall not testify against any.* This was a just and necessary provision. One may be mistaken, or so violently prejudiced as to impose even on his own judgment, or so

wicked as to endeavor through malice to compass the life of his neighbor, but it is not likely that two or more should be of this kind; and even were they, their separate examination would lead to a discovery of the truth, and to their conviction.

31. *Ye shall take no satisfaction for the life of a murderer.* No atonement could be made for him, nor any commutation, so as to save him from death.

32. *Until the death of the priest.* Probably intended to typify that no sinner can be delivered from his banishment from God, or recover his forfeited inheritance, till Jesus Christ, the great High Priest, had died for his offenses and risen again for his justification.

33. *For blood it defileth the land.* The very land was considered as guilty till the blood of the murderer was shed in it.

CHAPTER 36

The inconveniences which might be produced by daughters, inheritrixes, marrying out of their own tribe, remedied on the recommendation of certain chiefs of the tribe of Joseph, who stated the case of the daughters of Zelophehad, 1-4. The daughters of Zelophehad are commanded to marry in their own tribe, 5-6; which is to be an ordinance in all similar circumstances, 7-9. The daughters of Zelophehad marry their father's brothers' sons, and thus their inheritance is preserved in their own tribe, 10-12. The conclusion of the commandments given by the Lord to the Israelites in the plains of Moab, 13.

2. *To give the inheritance of Zelophehad . . . unto his daughters.* See this case spoken of at large on chap. xxvii. Either the first eleven verses of chap. xxvii should come in before this chapter or this chapter should come in immediately after those eleven verses; they certainly both make parts of the same subject. Here Moses determines that heiresses should marry in their own tribe, that no part of the ancient inheritance might be alienated from the original family.

6. *Let them marry to whom they think best.* Here was latitude sufficient, and yet a salutary and reasonable restraint, which prevented a vexatious mixture of property and possession.

8. *Every daughter, that possesseth an inheritance.* This law affected none but heiresses; all others were at liberty to marry into any of the other tribes. The priests and Levites, who could have no inheritance, were exempt from the operation of this law. Jehoiada had the king of Judah's daughter to wife, 2 Chron. xxii. 11. And another priest had for wife one of the daughters of Barzillai the Gileadite, Ezra ii. 61.

The Book of

DEUTERONOMY

We have borrowed the name of this book, as in former cases, from the Vulgate Latin, *Deuteronomium,* as the Vulgate has done from the Greek version of the Septuagint, *Deuter-ronomion,* which is a compound term literally signifying the "second law," because it seems to contain a repetition of the preceding laws, from which circumstance it has been termed by the rabbins *mishneh,* the "iteration" or "doubling."

It appears that both these names are borrowed from chap. xvii. 18, where the king is commanded to write him a copy of this law; the original is *mishneh hattorah,* a "repetition or doubling of the Law," which the Septuagint have translated *to deuteronomion,* "this second law," which we properly enough translate a "copy of the law." But in Hebrew, like the preceding books, it takes its name from its commencement, *elleh haddebarim,* "these are the words"; and in the best rabbinical Bibles its running title is *Sepher Debarim,* or "the book of the words."

The Book of Deuteronomy contains an account of what passed in the wilderness from the first day of the eleventh month of the fortieth year after the departure of the Israelites from Egypt to the seventh day of the twelfth month of the same, making in the whole a history of the transactions of exactly five weeks. The history is continued about seven days after the death of Moses; for he began to deliver his first discourse to the people in the plains of Moab the first day of the eleventh month of the fortieth year, chap. i. 3, and died on the first day of the twelfth month of the same year, aged one hundred twenty years.

As the Israelites were now about to enter into the Promised Land, and many of them had not witnessed the different transactions in the wilderness, the former generations having been all destroyed except Joshua and Caleb, to impress their hearts with a deep sense of their obligation to God, and to prepare them for the inheritance which God had prepared for them, Moses here repeats the principal occurrences of the forty years, now almost elapsed; shows them the absolute necessity of fearing, loving, and obeying God; repeats the Ten Commandments, and particularly explains each, and the ordinances belonging to them, adding others which he had not delivered before; confirms the whole law in a most solemn manner, with exceeding great and precious promises to them that keep it, and a denunciation of the most awful judgments against those who should break it; renews the covenant between God and the people; prophesies of things which should come to pass in the latter days; blesses each of the tribes, prophetically, with the choicest spiritual and temporal blessings; and then, having viewed the whole extent of the land, from the top of Mount Nebo or Pisgah, he yielded up the ghost, and was privately buried by God, leaving Joshua the son of Nun for his successor.

The Book of Deuteronomy and the Epistle to the Hebrews contain the best comment on the nature, design, and use of the law; the former may be considered as an evangelical commentary on the four preceding books, in which the spiritual reference and signification of the different parts of the law are given, and given in such a manner as none could give who had not a clear discovery of the glory which was to be revealed. It may be safely asserted that very few parts of the Old Testament Scriptures can be read with greater profit by the genuine Christian than the Book of Deteronomy.

CHAPTER 1

Introduction to the book, 1-2. Moses addresses the people in the fortieth year after the exodus from Egypt, 3-5; and shows how God had spoken to them in Horeb, and the directions He gave them, 6-8. How, at the commandment of the Lord, he had appointed officers, judges, etc., to share the government with him, 9-18. Of their travels in the terrible wilderness, 19-21. The people's request to have spies sent to search out the land, 22-25. Of their murmuring and rebellion when they heard the report of the spies, 26-28. How Moses encouraged them, 29-33. The displeasure of the Lord against them because of their murmurings, and His purpose to exclude them from the good land, and give it to their children only, 34-40. How they repented, and yet, without the authority of God, went against the Amorites, by whom they were defeated, 41-44. Their return to Kadesh, where they abode many days, 45-46.

1. *These be the words which Moses spake.* The first five verses of this chapter contain the introduction to the rest of the book; they do not appear to be the work of Moses, but were added probably by either Joshua or Ezra.

On this side Jordan. Beeber, "at the passage" of Jordan, i.e., near or opposite to the place where the Israelites passed over after the death of Moses. Though *eber* is used to signify both on "this side" and on "the other side," and the connection in which it stands can only determine the meaning, yet here it signifies neither, but simply the place or ford where the Israelites passed over Jordan. *In the plain.* That is, of Moab; *over against the Red sea*—not the Red Sea, for they were now farther from it than they had been: the word *sea* is not in the text, and the word *suph*, which we render *red*, does not signify the Red Sea, unless joined with *yam*, "sea"; here it must necessarily signify a place in or adjoining to the plains of Moab. *Paran.* This could not have been the Paran which was contiguous to the Red Sea, and not far from Mount Horeb; for the place here mentioned lay on the very borders of the Promised Land, at a vast distance from the former. *Dizahab.* The word should be separated, as it is in the Hebrew, *Di Zahab.* As *Zahab* signifies "gold," the Septuagint have translated it "the gold mines"; and the Vulgate, "where there is much gold." It is more likely to be the name of a place.

2. *There are eleven days' journey.* The Israelites were eleven days in going from Horeb to Kadesh-barnea, where they were near the verge of the Promised Land; after which they were thirty-eight years wandering up and down in the vicinity of this place, not being permitted, because of their rebellions, to enter into the promised rest, though they were the whole of that time within a few miles of the land of Canaan!

3. *The fortieth year.* This was a melancholy year to the Hebrews in different respects; in the first month of this year Miriam died, Numbers xx.; on the first day of the fifth month Aaron died, Num. xxxiii. 38; and about the conclusion of it, Moses himself died.

5. *Began Moses to declare this law. Began,* hoil, "willingly undertook"; *to declare, beer,* "to make bare, clear," "fully to explain," *this law.*

6. *Ye have dwelt long enough.* They came to Sinai in the third month after their departure from Egypt, Exod. xix. 1-2, and left it the twentieth of the second month of the second year; so it appears they had continued there nearly a whole year.

7. *Go to the mount of the Amorites.* On the south of the land of Canaan, towards the Dead Sea. *The river Euphrates.* Thus Moses fixes the bounds of the land, to which on all quarters the territories of the Israelites might be extended should the land of Canaan, properly so called, be found insufficient for them. Their south border might extend to the mount of the Amorites, their west to the borders of the Mediterranean Sea, their north to Lebanon, and their east border to the river Euphrates; and to this extent Solomon reigned; see 1 Kings iv. 21. So that in his time, at least, the promise to Abraham was literally fulfilled.

10. *Ye are this day as the stars of heaven for multitude.* This was the promise God made to Abraham, Gen. xv. 5-6; and Moses considers it now as amply fulfilled. But was it really so? Many suppose the expression to be hyperbolical; and others, no friends to revelation, think it a vain, empty boast, because the stars amount to innumerable millions. Let us consider this subject. How many in number are the stars which appear to the naked eye? For it is by what appears to the naked eye we are to be governed in this business, for God brought Abraham forth abroad, i.e., out of doors, and

bade him look towards heaven, not with a telescope, but with his naked eyes, Gen. xv. 5. Now I shall beg the objector to come forth abroad, and look up in the brightest and most favorable night, and count the stars; and I shall pledge myself to find a male Israelite in the very last census taken of this people, Numbers xxvi., for every star he finds in the whole upper hemisphere of heaven. The truth is, only about 3,010 stars can be seen by the naked eye in both the northern and southern hemispheres; and the Israelites, independently of women and children, were at the above time more than 600,000.

13. *Take you wise men. Chachamim,* such as had gained knowledge by great labor and study. *Understanding, nebonim,* persons of discernment, judicious men. *Known, yeduim,* persons practiced in the operations of nature, capable of performing important works.

15. *Captains over thousands.* What a well-regulated economy was that of the Israelites! See its order and arrangement: (1) God, the King and Supreme Judge; (2) Moses, God's prime minister; (3) The priests, consulting Him by *Urim* and *Thummim;* (4) The chiefs or princes of the twelve tribes; (5) Chiliarchs, or captains over thousands; (6) Centurions, or captains over hundreds; (7) Tribunes, or captains over fifty men; (8) Decurions, or captains over ten men; and (9) Officers, persons who might be employed by the different chiefs in executing particular commands. All these held their authority from God, and yet were subject and accountable to each other.

17. *Ye shall not respect persons.* Hebrew, "faces." Let not the bold, daring countenance of the rich or mighty induce you to give an unrighteous decision; and let not the abject look of the poor man induce you either to favor him in an unrighteous cause or to give judgment against him at the demand of the oppressor. Be uncorrupt and incorruptible, for *the judgment is God's.* You minister in the place of God; act like Him.

22. *We will send men before us.* See on Numbers xiii.

28. *Cities . . . walled up to heaven.* That is, with very high walls which could not be easily scaled.

34. *The Lord . . . was wroth.* That is, His justice was incensed, and He evidenced His displeasure against you; and He could not have been a just God if He had not done so.

36. *Caleb . . . wholly followed the Lord.* See on Num. xiv. 24.

37. *The Lord was angry with me.* See on Num. xx. 10, etc., where a particular account is given of the sin of Moses.

44. *The Amorites . . . chased you.* See the note on Num. xiv. 40; *as bees do*—by irresistible numbers.

46. *According unto the days that ye abode there.* They had been a long time at this place; see Num. xiii. 27; xx. 1, 14, 21. And some think that the words mean, "Ye abode as long at Kadesh, when you came to it the second time, as ye did at the first." Or, according to others, "While ye were in that part of the desert, ye encamped at Kadesh."

CHAPTER 2

Moses continues to relate how they compassed Mount Seir, 1. And the commands they received not to meddle with the descendants of Esau, 2-8; nor to distress the Moabites, 9. Of the Emims, 10-11; the Horims, 12. Their passage of the brook Zered, 13. The time they spent between Kadesh-barnea and Zered, 14; during which all the men of war that came out of Egypt were consumed, 15-16. The command not to distress the Ammonites, 17-19. Of the Zamzummims, 20. the Anakims, 21. the Horims, 22. the Avims and Caphtorims, all destroyed by the Ammonites, 23. They are commanded to cross the river Arnon, and are promised the land of Sihon, king of the Amorites, 24-25. Of the message sent to Sihon, to request a passage through his territories, 26-29. His refusal, 30. The consequent war, 31-32. His total overthrow, 33; and extermination of his people, 34. The spoils that were taken, 35. And his land possessed from Aroer to Arnon by the Israelites, 36; who took care, according to the command of God, not to invade any part of the territories of the Ammonites, 37.

3. *Turn you northward.* From Mount Seir, in order to get to Canaan. This was not the way they went before, viz., by Kadesh-barnea, but they were to proceed between Edom on the one hand, and Moab and Ammon on the other, so as to enter into Canaan through the land of the Amorites.

5. *Meddle not with them.* That is, the Edomites. See on Num. xx. 14-21.

7. *The Lord . . . hath blessed thee.* God had given them much property, and therefore they had no need of plunder; they had gold and silver to buy the provender they needed, and therefore God would not permit them to take anything by violence.

10. *The Emims dwelt therein.* They are generally esteemed as giants; probably they were a hardy, fierce, and terrible people, who lived, like the wandering Arabs, on the plunder of others.

11. *Which also were accounted giants.* This is not a fortunate version. The word is not *giants*, but *Rephaim*, the name of a people. It appears that the *Emim*, the *Anakim*, and the *Rephaim* were probably the same people, called by different names in the different countries where they dwelt; for they appear originally to have been a kind of wandering freebooters, who lived by plunder. It must be granted, however, that there were several men of this race of extraordinary stature. And hence all gigantic men have been called *Rephaim*.

12. *The Horims also dwelt in Seir.* The whole of this verse was probably added by Joshua or Ezra.

20. *That also was accounted a land of giants.* That was accounted the land or territory of the *Rephaim*. *Zamzummims.* Supposed to be the same as the *Zuzim*, Gen. xiv. 5. From the tenth to the twelfth, and from the twentieth to the twenty-third verse inclusive, we have certain historical remarks introduced which do not seem to have been made by Moses, but rather by Joshua or Ezra. By the introduction of these verses the thread of the narrative suffers considerable interruption. That they could not have made a part of the speech of Moses originally needs little proof.

29. *As the children of Esau which dwell in Seir.* See the note on Num. xx. 21.

30. *The Lord . . . hardened his spirit.* See the notes on Exod. iv. 21; ix. 15; etc.

36. *From Aroer . . . by the brink of the river of Arnon.* See on Num. xxi. 13, etc.

37. *Only unto the land of the children of Ammon thou camest not.* God gave them their

commission; and those only were to be cut off, the cup of whose iniquity was full. Though the Moabites and Ammonites were thus spared, they requited good with evil, for they fought against the Israelites, and cast them out of their possessions, Judg. xi. 4-5; 2 Chron. xx. 1; etc., and committed the most shocking cruelties; see Amos i. 13. Hence God enacted a law that none of these people should enter into the congregation of the Lord even to their tenth generation; see chap. xxiii. 3-6.

CHAPTER 3

The war with Og, king of Bashan, 1-2. He is defeated, 3. Sixty fortified cities with many unwalled towns taken, 4-5. The utter destruction of the people, 6. The spoils, 7; and extent of the land taken, 8-10. Account of Og's iron bedstead, 11. The land given to the Reubenites, Gadites, and half tribe of Manasseh, 12-13. Jair takes the country of Argob, 14. Gilead is given unto Machir, 15. And the rest of the land possessed by the Reubenites and Gadites, 16-17. The directions given to those tribes, 18-20. The counsel given to Joshua, 21-22. Moses' prayer to God for permission to go into the Promised Land, 23-25; and God's refusal, 26. He is commanded to go up to Mount Pisgah to see it, 27; and to encourage Joshua, 28. They continue in the valley opposite to Beth-peor, 29.

4. *All the region of Argob.* Col chebel Argob, all the "cable" or "cord of Argob." This expression, which is used in various other parts of Scripture (see, in the original, Amos vii. 17; Mic. ii. 5; Deut. xxii. 9; Ps. xv. 6), shows that anciently land was measured by lines or cords of a certain length.

9. *Hermon the Sidonians call . . . Shenir.* I suppose this verse to have been a marginal remark, which afterwards got incorporated with the text, or an addition by Joshua or Ezra.

11. *Og king of Bashan remained.* Og was the last king of the Amorites; his kingdom appears to have taken its name from the hill of Bashan; the country has been since called Batanaea. *Remnant of giants.* Of the *Rephaim.* See on chap. ii. 10-11. *His bedstead was . . . of iron.* Iron was probably used partly for its strength and durability, and partly to prevent noxious vermin from harboring in it. *Is it not in Rabbath, of the children of Ammon?* The bedstead was probably taken in some battle between the Ammonites and Amorites, in which the former had gained the victory. The bedstead was carried a trophy and placed in Rabbath, which appears, from 2 Sam. xii. 26, to have been the royal city of the children of Ammon. *Nine cubits was the length . . . four cubits the breadth.* Allowing the bedstead to have been one cubit longer than Og, which is certainly sufficient, and allowing the cubit to be about *eighteen* inches long, for this is perhaps the average of the cubit of a man, then Og was twelve feet high.

14. *Bashan-havoth-jair.* Bashan of the cities of Jair; see Num. xxxii. 41.

17. *From Chinnereth.* See on Num. xxxiv. 11.

24-25. The prayer of Moses recorded in these two verses, and his own reflections on it, v. 26, are very affecting. He had suffered much in both body and mind in bringing the people to the borders of the Promised Land; and it was natural enough for him to wish to see them established in it, and to enjoy a portion of that inheritance himself, which he knew was a type of the heavenly country. But notwithstanding his very earnest prayer, and God's especial favor towards him, he was not permitted to go over

Jordan! He had grieved the Spirit of God, and He passed a sentence against him of exclusion from the Promised Land. Yet He permitted him to see it, and gave him the fullest assurances that the people whom he had brought out of Egypt should possess it. Thus God may choose to deprive those of earthly possessions to whom He is nevertheless determined to give a heavenly inheritance.

26. *Let it suffice thee. Rab lach,* "there is an abundance to thee"—you have had honor enough already, and may well dispense with going over Jordan. He surely has no reason to complain who is taken from earthly felicity to heavenly glory. In this act God showed to Moses both His goodness and severity.

28. *But charge Joshua.* Give him authority in the sight of the people; let them see that he has the same commission which I gave to you. *Encourage him,* for he will meet with many difficulties in the work to which he is called. *And strengthen him*—show him My unfailing promises, and exhort him to put his trust in Me alone; *for he shall go over before this people, and shall cause them to inherit the land*—of this let him rest perfectly assured.

29. *Beth-peor.* This was a city in the kingdom of Sihon, king of the Amorites; and as *beth* signifies a "house," the place probably had its name from a temple of the god Peor, who was worshipped there. Peor was nearly the same among the Moabites that Priapus was among the Romans—the obscene god of an obscene people.

CHAPTER 4

Exhortations to obedience, 1. Nothing to be added to or taken from the testimonies of God, 2. The people are exhorted to recollect how God had destroyed the ungodly among them, 3; and preserved those who were faithful, 4. The excellence of the divine law, 5-6. No nation in the world could boast of any such statutes, judgments, etc., 7-8. They are exhorted to obedience by the wonderful manifestations of God in their behalf, 9-13. Moses exhorts them to beware of idolatry, and to make no likeness of anything in heaven or earth as an object of adoration, 14-20. He informs them that he must die in that land, as God had refused to let him go into the Promised Land, being angry with him on their account, 21-22. Repeats his exhortation to obedience, 23-24. Predicts the judgments of God against them should they turn to idolatry, 25-28. Promises of God's mercy to the penitent, 29-31. The grand and unparalleled privileges of the Israelites, 32-40. Moses severs three cities on the east side of Jordan for cities of refuge, 41-42. Their names, 43. When and where Moses gave these statutes and judgments to Israel, 44-49.

1. *Harken . . . unto the statutes.* Everything that concerned the rites and ceremonies of religion; *judgments*—all that concerned matters of civil right and wrong.

2. *Ye shall not add.* Any book, chapter, verse, or word which I have not spoken; nor give any comment that has any tendency to corrupt, weaken, or destroy any part of this revelation. *Neither shall ye diminish.* You shall not only not take away any larger portion of this word, but you shall not take one jot or tittle from the law; it is that word of God that abideth forever.

6. *Keep . . . and do them; for this is your wisdom.* There was no mode of worship at this time on the face of the earth that was not wicked, obscene, puerile, foolish, or ridiculous, except that established by God himself among the Israelites. And every part of this, taken in its connection and reference, may be truly called a wise and reasonable service. *The nations . . . and say, Surely this great nation is a*

wise and understanding people. Almost all the nations in the earth showed that they had formed this opinion of the Jews, by borrowing from them the principal part of their civil code.

9. *Only take heed to thyself.* Be circumspect and watchful. *Keep thy soul diligently.* Be mindful of your eternal interests. Whatever becomes of the body, take care of the soul. *Lest thou forget.* God does His work that they may be had in everlasting remembrance; and he that forgets them forgets his own mercies. *Lest they depart from thy heart.* It is not sufficient to lay up divine things in the memory; they must be laid up in the *heart.* "Thy word have I hid in mine heart," says David, "that I might not sin against thee." The life of God in the soul of man can alone preserve the soul to life everlasting; and this grace must be retained all the days of our life. *But teach them thy sons.* If a man know the worth of his own soul, he will feel the importance of the salvation of the souls of his family. Those who neglect family religion neglect personal religion; if more attention were paid to the former, even among those called religious people, we should soon have a better state of civil society. On family religion God lays much stress; and no head of a family can neglect it without endangering the final salvation of his own soul.

15. *Ye saw no manner of similitude.* Howsoever God chose to appear or manifest himself, he took care never to assume any describable form. He would have no image worship, because He is a Spirit, and they who worship Him "must worship him in spirit and in truth."

16. *The likeness of male or female.* Such as Baal-peor and the Roman Priapus, Ashtaroth or Astarte, and the Greek and Roman Venus, after whom most nations of the world literally went a whoring.

17. *The likeness of any beast.* Such as the Egyptian god Apis, who was worshipped under the form of a white bull; the ibis and hawk, among the fowls, had also divine honors paid to them; serpents and the crocodile, among reptiles.

19. *When thou seest the sun and the moon, and the stars.* The worship of the heavenly bodies was the oldest species of idolatry. Those who had not the knowledge of the true God were led to consider the sun, moon, planets, and stars as not only self-existing, but the authors of all the blessings possessed by mankind.

21. *The Lord was angry with me.* And if with me, so as to debar me from entering into the Promised Land, can you think to escape if guilty of greater provocations?

24. *Thy God is a consuming fire.* They had seen Him on the mount as an unconsuming fire, while appearing to Moses, and giving the law; and they had seen Him as a consuming fire in the case of Korah, Dathan, Abiram, and their company. They had, therefore, every good to expect from His approbation, and every evil to dread from His displeasure.

26. *I call heaven and earth to witness against you.* A most solemn method of adjuration, in use among all nations in the world.

27. *The Lord shall scatter you among the nations.* This was amply verified in their different captivities and dispersions.

28. *There ye shall serve gods . . . wood and stone.* This was also true of the Israelites, not

only in their captivities, but also in their own land.

29. *But if from thence thou shalt seek the Lord.* God is long-suffering, and of tender mercy; and waits, ever ready, to receive a backsliding soul when it returns to Him.

30. *When thou art in tribulation . . . in the latter days.* Are not these the times spoken of? And is there not still hope for Israel?

33. *Did ever people hear the voice of God?* It seems to have been a general belief that if God appeared to men it was for the purpose of destroying them; and indeed most of the extraordinary manifestations of God were in the way of judgment. But here it was different; God did appear in a sovereign and extraordinary manner, but it was for the deliverance and support of the people. They heard His voice speaking with them in a distinct, articulate manner. They saw the fire, the symbol of His presence, the appearances of which demonstrated it to be supernatural. Notwithstanding God appeared so terrible, yet no person was destroyed, for He came, not to destroy, but to save.

34. *From the midst of another nation.* This was a most extraordinary thing, that a whole people, consisting of upwards of 600,000 effective men, besides women and children, should, without striking a blow, be brought out of the midst of a very powerful nation, to the political welfare of which their services were so essential: that they should be brought out in so open and public a manner; that the sea itself should be supernaturally divided to afford this mighty host a passage; and that, in a desert utterly unfriendly to human life, they should be sustained for forty years. These were such instances of the almighty power and goodness of God as never could be forgotten.

In this verse Moses enumerates seven different means used by the Almighty in effecting Israel's deliverance. (1) *Temptations, massoth,* from *nasah,* "to try or prove"; the miracles which God wrought to try the faith and prove the obedience of the children of Israel. (2) *Signs, othoth,* from *athah,* "to come near"; such signs as God gave them of His continual presence and especial providence, particularly the pillar of cloud and pillar of fire, keeping near to them night and day, and always directing their journeys. (3) *Wonders, mophethim,* from *yaphath,* "to persuade." It probably means "typical" representations; in this signification the word is used, Zech. iii. 8. Joshua, the high priest, and his companions were *anshey mopheth,* "typical men," raised up by God as types of Christ, and proofs that God would bring His Servant, the Branch. (4) *War, milchamah,* "hostile engagements"; such as those with the Amalekites, the Amorites, and the Bashanites, in which the hand of God was seen rather than the hand of man. (5) *A mighty hand, yad chazakah;* one that is strong to deal its blows, irresistible in its operations, and grasps its enemies hard, so that they cannot escape, and protects its friends so powerfully that they cannot be injured. (6) *A stretched out arm, zeroa netuyah;* a series of almighty operations, following each other in quick, astonishing succession. Let it be noted that in the Scriptures: The *finger* of God denote any manifestation of the divine power where effects are produced beyond the power of art or nature. The *hand* of God signifies the same

power, but put forth in a more signal manner. The *arm* of God, the divine omnipotence manifested in the most stupendous miracles. The *arm* of God *stretched out,* this same omnipotence exerted in a continuation of stupendous miracles, in the way of both judgment and mercy. In this latter sense it appears to be taken in the text: the judgments were poured out on the Egyptians; the mercies wrought in favor of the Israelites. (7) *Great terrors, moraim gedolim;* such terror, dismay, and consternation as were produced by the ten plagues, to which probably the inspired penman here alludes; or, as the Septuagint has it, "with great or portentous sights"; such as that when God looked out of the cloud upon the Egyptians, and their chariot wheels were taken off, Exod. xiv. 24-25 More awful displays of God's judgments, power, and might, were never witnessed by man.

41. *Then Moses severed three cities.* See the law relative to the cities of refuge explained, Num. xxxv. 9, etc.

43. *Bezer in the wilderness.* As the cities of refuge are generally understood to be types of the salvation provided by Christ for sinners, so their names have been thought to express some attribute of the Redeemer of mankind.

I suppose the last nine verses of this chapter to have been added by either Joshua or Ezra.

CHAPTER 5

God's covenant with the people in Horeb, 1-4. Moses the mediator of it, 5. A repetition of the Ten Commandments, 6-21; which God wrote on two tables of stone, 22. The people are filled with dread at the terrible majesty of God, 23-26; and beseech Moses to be their mediator, 27. The Lord admits of their request, 28; and deplores their ungodliness, 29. They are exhorted to obedience, that they may be preserved in the possession of the Promised Land, 30-33.

1. *And Moses called all Israel, and said . . . Hear.* (1) God speaks to the people. (2) The people are called to *hear* what God speaks. (3) To *learn* what they heard, that they may be thoroughly instructed in the will of God. (4) To *keep* God's testimonies ever in mind, and to treasure them up in a believing and upright heart. (5) That they might *do them*—obey the whole will of God, taking His word for the invariable rule of their conduct. Should not all these points be kept in view by every Christian assembly?

3. *The Lord made not this covenant with our fathers* (only), *but with us* (also).

6. *I am the Lord thy God.* See these commandments explained in the notes on Exodus xx.

15. *And remember that thou wast a servant.* In this and the latter clause of the preceding verse Moses adds another reason why one day in seven should be sanctified, viz., that the servants might rest, and this is urged upon them on the consideration of their having been servants in the land of Egypt. We see therefore that God had three grand ends in view by appointing a Sabbath: (1) To commemorate the creation. (2) To give a due proportion of rest to man and beast. When in Egypt they had no rest; their cruel taskmasters caused them to labor without intermission; now God had given rest, and as He had showed them mercy, He teaches them to show mercy to their servants: *Remember that thou wast a servant.* (3) To afford peculiar spiritual advantages to the soul,

that it might be kept in remembrance of the rest which remains at the right hand of God.

Therefore the Lord thy God commanded thee to keep the sabbath day. Here is a variation in the manner of expression, *sabbath day* for "seventh," owing, it is supposed, to a change of the day at the Exodus from Sunday to Saturday, effected upon the gathering of the manna, Exod. xvi. 23. The Sabbath now became a twofold memorial of the deliverance, as well as of the creation; and this accounts for the new reason assigned for its observance: "Therefore the Lord thy God commanded thee to keep the sabbath day."

21. *His field.* This clause is not in the tenth commandment as it stands in Exod. xx. 17.

29. *O that there were such an heart in them*— or rather, *mi yitten vehayah lebabam zeh,* "Who will give such a heart to them"—*that they may fear,* etc.! They refuse to receive such a heart from Me; who then can supply it?

32. *Ye shall observe to do.* He who marks not the word of God is never likely to fulfil the will of God. *Ye shall not turn aside to the right hand or to the left.* The way of truth and righteousness is a right line; a man must walk straight forward who wishes to go to glory; no crooked or devious path ever led to God or happiness.

33. *Ye shall walk in all the ways.* God never gave a commandment to man which He did not design that he should obey. He who selects from the divine testimonies such precepts as he feels but little inclination to transgress, and lives in the breach of others, sins against the grand legislative authority of God, and shall be treated as a rebel. *That ye may live. Ticheyun,* that ye "may enjoy life" (for the paragogic *nun,* at the end of the word, deepens the sense), *that it may be well with you, vetob lachem,* "and good shall be to you"—God will prosper you in all things essential to the welfare of your bodies, and the salvation of your souls. *That ye may prolong your days in the land.* That you may arrive at a good old age, and grow more and more meet for the inheritance among the saints in light.

CHAPTER 6

The great design of God in giving His laws is that the people may fear and obey Him, that they may continue in peace and prosperity, and be mightily increased, 1-3. The great commandment of the law, 4-5, which shall be laid up in their hearts, 6; taught to their children, 7; and affixed as a sign to their hands, heads, doors, and gates, 8-9. How they are to act when they shall come into the Promised Land, 10-19. How they shall instruct their children, and relate the history to them of God's wonderful acts, 20-25.

1. *Now these are the commandments.* See the difference between commandments, statutes, judgments, etc., pointed out in Lev. xxvi. 15. *Do them.* That is, live in the continual practice of them; for by this they were to be distinguished from all the nations of the world, and all these were to be in force till the Son of God should come. *Whither ye go, oberim,* whither "ye pass over," referring to the river Jordan, across which they must pass to get into Canaan.

2. *That thou mightest fear the Lord.* Respect His sovereign authority as a Lawgiver, and ever feel thyself bound to obey Him. No man can walk either conscientiously or safely who has not the fear of God continually before his eyes. *Thou, and thy son, and thy son's son.* Through all thy successive generations. Whoever fears God will endeavor to bring up his children in the way of righteousness.

3. *Hear therefore, O Israel, and observe to do it.* Literally, "Ye shall hear, O Israel, and thou shalt keep to do them."

4. *Hear, O Israel. Shema Yisrael, Yehovah Eloheinu, Yehovah achad.* These words may be variously rendered into English; but almost all possible verbal varieties in the translation amount to the same sense: "Israel, hear! Jehovah, our God, is one Jehovah"; or, "Jehovah is our God, Jehovah is one"; or, "Jehovah is our God, Jehovah alone"; or, "Jehovah is our God, Jehovah who is one"; or, "Jehovah, who is our God, is the one Being." On this verse the Jews lay great stress; it is one of the four passages which they write on their phylacteries, and they write the last letter in the first and last words very large, for the purpose of exciting attention to the weighty truth it contains.

5. *Thou shalt love the Lord.* Here we see the truth of that word of the apostle, 1 Tim. i. 5: "Now the end of the commandment is . . . [love] out of a pure heart." See the whole of the doctrine contained in this verse explained on Matt. xxii. 36-40.

6. *Shall be in thine heart.* For where else can love be? If it be not in the heart, it exists not. And if *these words* be not *in thine heart*— if they are not esteemed, prized, and received as a high and most glorious privilege—what hope is there that this love shall ever reign there?

7. *Thou shalt teach them diligently. Shinnantam,* from *shanan,* "to repeat, iterate, or do a thing again and again"; hence to whet or sharpen any instrument, which is done by reiterated friction or grinding. We see here the spirit of this divine injunction. God's testimonies must be taught to our children, and the utmost diligence must be used to make them understand them. This is a most difficult task; and it requires much patience, much prudence, much judgment, and much piety in the parents, to enable them to do this good, this most important work, in the best and most effectual manner. *And shalt talk of them when thou sittest in thine house.* You shall have religion at home, as well as in the Temple and Tabernacle. *And when thou walkest by the way.* You shall be religious abroad as well as at home, and not be ashamed to own God wherever you are. *When thou liest down, and when thou risest up.* You shall begin and end the day with God, and thus religion will be the great business of your life.

8. *Thou shalt bind them for a sign upon thine hand.* Is not this an allusion to an ancient and general custom observed in almost every part of the world? When a person wishes to remember a thing of importance, and is afraid to trust to the common operations of memory, he ties a knot on some part of his clothes, or a cord on his hand or finger, that his memory may be whetted to recollection, and his eye affect his heart. God, who knows how slow of heart we are to understand, graciously orders us to make use of every help, and through the means of things sensible, to rise to things spiritual. *And they shall be as frontlets. Totaphoth* seems to have the same meaning as

"phylacteries" has in the New Testament; and for the meaning and description of these appendages to a Jew's dress and to his religion, see the notes on Exod. xiii. 9 and on Matt. xxiii. 5.

9. *Write them upon the posts of thy house, and on thy gates.* The Jews, forgetting the spirit and design of this precept, used these things as superstitious people do amulets and charms, and supposed, if they had these passages of Scripture written upon slips of pure parchment, wrapped round their foreheads, tied to their arm, or nailed to their doorposts, that they should then be delivered from every evil!

12. *Beware lest thou forget the Lord.* In earthly prosperity men are apt to forget heavenly things. While the animal senses have everything they can wish, it is difficult for the soul to urge its way to heaven; the animal man is happy, and the desires of the soul are absorbed in those of the flesh. God knows this well; and therefore, in His love to man, makes comparative poverty and frequent affliction his general lot. Should not every soul therefore magnify God for this lot in life? "Before I was afflicted," says David, "I went astray"; and had it not been for poverty and affliction, as instruments in the hands of God's grace, multitudes of souls now happy in heaven would have been wretched in hell. It is not too much to speak thus far, because we ever see that the rich and the affluent are generally negligent of God and the interests of their souls. It must however be granted that extreme poverty is as injurious to religion as excessive affluence. Hence the wisdom as well as piety of Agur's prayer, Prov. xxx. 7-9: "Give me neither poverty nor riches . . . lest I be full, and deny thee . . . or lest I be poor, and steal."

13. *Thou shalt fear the Lord thy God.* You shall respect and reverence Him as your Lawgiver and Judge; as your Creator, Preserver, and the sole Object of your religious adoration. *And serve him.* Our blessed Lord, in Matt. iv. 10; Luke iv. 8, quotes these words thus: "And him *only* shalt thou serve." It appears, therefore, that *lebaddo* was anciently in the Hebrew text, as it was and is in the Septuagint, from which our Lord quoted it. The Coptic preserves the same reading; so do also the Vulgate (*illi soli*) and the Anglo-Saxon. Dr. Kennicott argues that without the word "only" the text would not have been conclusive for the purpose for which our Lord advanced it; for as we learn from Scripture that some men worshipped false gods in conjunction with the true, the quotation here would not have been full to the point without this exclusive word. It may be proper to observe that the omitted word *lebaddo*, retained in the above versions, does not exist in the Hebrew printed text, nor in any MS. hitherto discovered. *Shalt swear by his name. Tishshabea*, from *shaba*, "he was full, satisfied, or gave that which was full or satisfactory." Hence an oath and swearing, because appealing to God, and taking Him for Witness in any case of promise, etc., gave full and sufficient security for the performance; and if done in evidence, or to the truth of any particular fact, it gave full security for the truth of that evidence. An oath, therefore, is an appeal to God, who knows all things, of the truth of the matter in question; and when a religious man takes such an oath, he gives

full and reasonable satisfaction that the thing is so, as stated.

14. *Ye shall not go after other gods.* The object of religious worship among every people, whether that object be true or false, is ever considered as the pattern or exemplar to his worshippers. Christians are termed the "followers" of God; they take God for their Pattern, and "walk"—act—as He does. Hence we see the meaning of the terms in this verse: *Ye shall not go after*—you shall not take false gods for your patterns. The Canaanites, Greeks, Romans, etc., were a most impure people, because the objects of their worship were impure, and they went after them, i.e., were like their gods. This serves to show us that such as our Redeemer is, such should we be; and indeed this is the uniform language of God to man: "Be ye holy, for I am holy," see Lev. xxi. 8; "Be ye therefore perfect, even as your Father which is in heaven is perfect," Matt. v. 48.

15. *A jealous God.* Jehovah has betrothed you to himself as a bride is to her husband. Do not be unfaithful, else that love wherewith He has now distinguished you shall assume the form of jealousy, and so divorce and consume you.

16. *Ye shall not tempt the Lord.* You shall not provoke Him by entertaining doubts of His mercy, goodness, providence, and truth. *As ye tempted him in Massah.* How did they tempt Him in Massah? They said, "Is the Lord among us, or not?" Exod. xvii. 1-7. After such proofs as they had of His presence and His kindness, this was exceedingly provoking. Doubting God's kindness where there are so many evidences of it is highly insulting to God Almighty.

17. *Ye shall diligently keep.* On this and the following verse see the note on v. 3.

20. *And when thy son asketh thee.* "Here," as Mr. Ainsworth justly remarks, "followeth a brief *catechism*, containing the grounds of religion." *What mean the testimonies?* The Hebrew language has no word to express to "mean" or "signify," and therefore uses simply the substantive verb "what is?" i.e., "what mean or signify?" The seven thin ears are, i.e., "signify," seven years of famine. This form of speech frequently occurs.

25. *It shall be our righteousness.* The evidence that we are under the influence of the fear and love of God. Moses does not say that this righteousness could be wrought without the influence of God's mercy, nor does he say that they should purchase heaven by it; but God required them to be conformed to His will in all things, that they might be holy in heart, and righteous in every part of their moral conduct.

CHAPTER 7

With the seven nations that God shall cast out, 1, they shall make no covenant, 2, nor form any matrimonial alliances, 3; lest they should be enticed into idolatry, 4. All monuments of idolatry to be destroyed, 5. The Israelites are to consider themselves a holy people, 6; and that the Lord had made them such, not for their merits, but for his own mercies, 7-8. They shall therefore love Him, and keep His commandments, 9-11. The great privileges of the obedient, 12-24. All idolatry to be avoided, 25-26.

1. *Seven nations greater and mightier than thou.* In several places of the Hebrew text, each of these seven nations is not enumerated, some

one or other being left out, which the Septuagint in general supplies.

2. *Thou shalt smite them.* These idolatrous nations were to be utterly destroyed, and all the others also which were contigious to the boundaries of the promised land, provided they did not renounce their idolatry and receive the true faith. For if they did not, then no covenant was to be made with them on any secular or political consideration whatever; no mercy was to be shown to them, because the cup of their iniquity also was now full; and they must either embrace, heartily embrace, the true religion, or be cut off.

3. *Neither shalt thou make marriages.* The heart being naturally inclined to evil, there is more likelihood that the idolatrous wife should draw aside the believing husband than that the believing husband should be able to bring over his idolatrous wife to the true faith.

6. *Thou art an holy people.* And therefore should have no connection with the workers of iniquity.

8. *But because the Lord loved you.* It was no good in them that induced God to choose them at this time to be His peculiar people; He had His reasons, but these sprang from His infinite goodness. He intended to make a full discovery of His goodness to the world, and this must have a commencement in some particular place, and among some people. He chose that time, and He chose the Jewish people, but not because of their goodness or holiness.

12. *The Lord . . . shall keep unto thee the covenant.* So we find their continuance in the state of favor was to depend on their faithfulness to the grace of God. If they should rebel, though God had chosen them through His love, yet He would cast them off in His justice. The elect, we see, may become unfaithful, and so become reprobates. So it happened to 24,000 of them, whose carcasses fell in the wilderness because they had sinned; yet these were of the elect that came out of Egypt. Let him that standeth take heed lest he fall.

22. *Put out those nations . . . by little and little.* The Israelites were not as yet sufficiently numerous to fill the whole land occupied by the seven nations mentioned in v. 1. And as wild and ferocious animals might be expected to multiply where either there are no inhabitants or the place is but thinly peopled, therefore God tells them that, though at present by force of arms they might be able to expel them, it would be impolitic so to do, lest the beasts of the field should multiply upon them.

25. *Thou shalt not desire the silver or gold that is on them.* Some of the ancient idols were plated over with gold, and God saw that the value of the metal and the excellence of the workmanship might be an inducement for the Israelites to preserve them; and this might lead, remotely at least, to idolatry. As the idols were accursed, all those who had them, or anything appertaining to them, were accursed also, v. 26.

CHAPTER 8

An exhortation to obedience from a consideration of God's past mercies, 1-2. Man is not to live by bread only, but by every word of God, 3. How God provided for them in the wilderness, 4. The Lord chastened them that they might be obedient, 5-6. A description of the land into which they were going, 7-9. Cautions lest they should

forget God in their prosperity, 10-16, and lest they should attribute that prosperity to themselves, and not to God, 17-18. The terrible judgments that shall fall upon them, should they prove unfaithful, 19-20.

2. *Thou shalt remember all the way.* The various dealings of God with you; the dangers and difficulties to which you were exposed, and from which God delivered you; together with the various miracles which He wrought for you, and His long-suffering towards you.

3. *He . . . suffered thee to hunger, and fed thee.* God never permits any tribulation to befall His followers which He does not design to turn to their advantage. When He permits us to hunger, it is that His mercy may be the more observable in providing us with the necessaries of life. Privations, in the way of providence, are the forerunners of mercy and goodness abundant.

4. *Thy raiment waxed not old.* The plain meaning of this much-tortured text appears to me to be this: "God so amply provided for them all the necessaries of life that they never were obliged to wear tattered garments, nor were their feet injured for lack of shoes or sandals." If they had carvers, engravers, silversmiths, and jewellers among them, as plainly appears from the account we have of the Tabernacle and its utensils, is it to be wondered at if they also had habit and sandal makers, as we are certain they had weavers, embroiderers, and suchlike? And the traffic which we may suppose they carried on with the Moabites, or with travelling hordes of Arabians, doubtless supplied them with the materials; though, as they had abundance of sheep and meat cattle, they must have had much of the materials within themselves. It is generally supposed that God, by a miracle, preserved their clothes from wearing out; but if this sense be admitted, it will require, not one miracle, but a chain of the most successive and astonishing miracles ever wrought, to account for the thing.

9. *A land whose stones are iron.* Not only meaning that there were iron mines throughout the land, but that the loose stones were strongly impregnated with iron, ores of this metal. *Out of whose hills thou mayest dig brass.* As there is no such thing in nature as a *brass* mine, the word *nechosheth* should be translated "copper"; of which, by the addition of the *lapis calaminaris*, brass is made. See on Exod. xxv. 3.

15. *Who led thee through that . . . terrible wilderness.* See the account of their journeying in the notes on Exod. xvi. 1, etc.; Numbers xxi, etc. *Fiery serpents.* Serpents whose bite occasioned a most violent inflammation, accompanied with an unquenchable thirst, and which terminated in death. See on Num. xxi. 6.

16. *Who fed thee . . . with manna.* See this miracle described in Exod. xvi. 13, etc.

18. *God . . . giveth thee power to get wealth.* Who among the rich and wealthy believes this saying? Who gives wisdom, understanding, skill, bodily strength, and health? Is it not God? And without these, how can wealth be acquired?

CHAPTER 9

The people are informed that they shall shortly pass over Jordan, and that God shall go over before them, to expel the ancient inhabitants, 1-3. They are cautioned not to suppose that it is on account of their righteousness that God is to give them that land, 4-6. They are exhorted to remember their various provocations of the Divine Majesty, especially at Horeb, 7-14; and how Moses interceded for them, and destroyed the golden calf, 15-21. How they murmured at Taberah, 22; and rebelled at Kadesh-barnea, 23; and had been perverse from the beginning, 24. An account of the intercession of Moses in their behalf, 25-29.

1. *Thou art to pass over Jordan this day.* Haiyom, "this time"; they had come thirty-eight years before this nearly to the verge of the Promised Land, but were not permitted at that day or time to pass over, because of their rebellions; but "this time" they shall certainly pass over. This was spoken about the eleventh month of the fortieth year of their journeying, and it was on the first month of the following year they passed over; and during this interim Moses died.

5. *For the wickedness of these nations.* So then it was not by any sovereign act of God that these people were cast out, but for their wickedness; they had transgressed the law of their Creator; they had resisted His Spirit, and could no longer be tolerated. The Israelites were to possess their land, not because they deserved it, but first, because they were less wicked than the others; and secondly, because God thus chose to begin the great work of His salvation among men. Thus then the Canaanites were cut off, and the Israelites were grafted in; and the Israelites, because of their wickedness, were afterwards cut off, and the Gentiles grafted in. Let the latter not be high-minded, but fear. "If God spared not the natural branches, take heed lest he also spare not thee."

10. *Tables of stone.* See the notes on Exod. xxxi. 18 and xxxii. 15-16.

12. *Thy people . . . have corrupted themselves.* Debased themselves by making and worshipping an Egyptian idol. See on Exodus xxxii.

21. *I took your sin, the calf which ye had made.* See this fully explained, Exod. xxxii. 20.

22. *At Kibroth-hattaavah.* See the note on Num. xi. 18.

27. *Remember thy servants, Abraham, Isaac, and Jacob.* As if he had said: "These are their descendants, and the covenant was made with those patriarchs in behalf of these."

CHAPTER 10

Moses is commanded to make a second set of tables, 1-2. He makes an ark, prepares the two tables, God writes on them the Ten Commandments, and Moses lays them up in the ark, 3-5. The Israelites journey from Beeroth to Mosera, where Aaron dies, 6; and from thence to Gudgodah and Jotbath, 7. At that time God separated the tribe of Levi for the service of the sanctuary, 8-9. How long Moses stayed the second time in the mount, 10-11. What God requires of the Israelites, 12-15. Their hearts must be circumcised, 16. God's character and conduct, 17-18. They are commanded to love the stranger, 19; to fear, love, and serve God, 20, because He has done such great things for them and their fathers, 21-22.

1. *Hew thee two tables of stone.* See the notes on Exod. xxxiv. 1.

3. *Shittim wood.* See the note on Exod. xxv. 5, and succeeding verses.

4. *Ten commandments.* See the note on Exod. xx. 1, etc.

12. *Now, Israel, what doth the Lord . . . require of thee?* An answer is immediately given. God requires: (1) That ye *fear* Him as Jehovah your God; Him who made, preserves, and governs you. (2) That ye *walk in all his ways*—

that, having received His precepts, ye obey the whole; walking in God's ways, not your own, nor in the ways of the people of the land. (3) That ye *love him*—have confidence in Him as your Father and Friend, have recourse to Him in all your necessities, and love Him in return for His love. (4) That you *serve* Him—give Him that worship which He requires, performing it with all your *heart*—the whole of your affections, and with all your *soul*—your will, understanding, and judgment. In a word, putting forth your whole strength and energy of body and soul in the sacred work.

14. *Behold, the heaven and the heaven of heavens.* All these words in the original are in the plural number: *hen hashshamayim, ushemey hashshamayim;* "behold, the heavens and the heavens of heavens." But what do they mean? To say that the first means the atmosphere, the second the planetary system, and the third the region of the blessed, is saying but very little in the way of explanation. The words were probably intended to point out the immensity of God's creation, in which we may readily conceive one system of heavenly bodies, and others beyond them, and others still in endless progression through the whole vortex of space, every star in the vast abyss of nature being a sun, with its peculiar and numerous attendant worlds! Thus there may be systems of systems in endless gradation up to the throne of God!

16. *Circumcise . . . the foreskin of your heart.* A plain proof from God himself that this precept pointed out spiritual things, and that it was not the cutting away a part of the flesh that was the object of the divine commandment, but the purification of the soul, without which all forms and ceremonies are of no avail. Loving God with all the heart, soul, mind, and strength, the heart being circumcised to enable them to do it, was, from the beginning, the end, design, and fulfillment of the whole law.

17. *God of gods, and Lord of lords.* That is, He is the Source whence all being and power proceed; every agent is finite but himself; and He can counteract, suspend, or destroy all the actions of all creatures whensoever He pleases. If He determine to save, none can destroy; if He purpose to destroy, none can save. How absolutely necessary to have such a God for our Friend! *A great God . . . mighty.* Hael haggibbor, "the mighty God"; this is the very title that is given to our blessed Lord and Saviour, Isa. ix. 6.

21. *He is thy praise.* It is an eternal honor to any soul to be in the friendship of God. Why are people ashamed of being thought religious? Because they know nothing of religion. He who knows his Maker may glory in his God, for without Him what has any soul but disgrace, pain, shame, and perdition?

22. *With threescore and ten persons.* And now, from so small a beginning, they were multiplied to more than 600,000 souls; and this indeed in the space of forty years, for the 603,000 which came out of Egypt were at this time all dead but Moses, Joshua, and Caleb. How easily can God increase and multiply, and how easily diminish and bring low! In all things, because of His unlimited power, He can do whatsoever He will; and He will do whatsoever is right.

CHAPTER 11

The people are exhorted to obedience from a consideration of God's goodness to their fathers in Egypt, 1-4, and what He did in the wilderness, 5, and the judgment on Dathan and Abiram, 6, and from the mercies of God in general, 7-9. A comparative description of Egypt and Canaan, 10-12. Promises to obedience, 13-15. Dissuasives from idolatry, 16-17. The words of God to be laid up in their hearts, to be for a sign on their hands, foreheads, gates, etc., 18, taught to their children, made the subject of frequent conversation, to the end that their days may be multiplied, 19-21. If obedient, God shall give them possession of the whole land, and not one of their enemies shall be able to withstand them, 22-25. Life and death, a blessing and a curse, are set before them, 26-28. The blessings to be put on Mount Gerizim and the curses on Mount Ebal, 29-30. The promise that they should pass over Jordan, and observe these statutes in the Promised Land, 31-32.

1. *Thou shalt love the Lord.* Because without this there could be no obedience to the divine testimonies, and no happiness in the soul; for the heart that is destitute of the love of God is empty of all good, and consequently miserable.

6. *What he did unto Dathan.* See the notes on Numbers xvi.

8. *Therefore shall ye keep all the commandments.* Because God can execute such terrible judgments, and because He has given such proofs of His power and justice; and because in similar provocations, He may be expected to act in a similar way; therefore keep His charge, that He may keep you unto everlasting life.

10. *Wateredst it with thy foot.* Rain scarcely ever falls in Egypt, and God supplies the lack of it by the inundations of the Nile. In order to water the grounds where the inundations do not extend, water is collected in ponds, and directed in streamlets to different parts of the field where irrigation is necessary. It is no unusual thing in the East to see a man, with a small mattock, making a little trench for the water to run by, and as he opens the passage, the water following, he uses his *foot* to raise up the mold against the side of this little channel, to prevent the water from being shed unnecessarily before it reaches the place of its destination. Thus he may be said to water the ground with his foot. But after all, the expression *wateredst it with thy foot* may mean no more than doing it by labor; for, as in the land of Egypt there is scarcely any rain, the watering of gardens, etc., must have been all artificial. But in Judea it was different, as there they had their proper seasons of rain. The compound word *beregel,* "with, under, or by the foot," is used to signify anything under the power, authority, etc., of a person; and this very meaning it has in the sixth verse, "all the substance that was in their possession" is, literally, all the substance that was "under their feet," *beragleyhem,* that is, in their power, possession, or what they had acquired by their labor.

14. *The rain . . . in his due season, the first rain and the latter rain.* By the *first* or "former" rain we are to understand that which fell in Judea about November, when they sowed their seed, and this served to moisten and prepare the ground for the vegetation of the seed. The *latter rain* fell about April, when the corn was well grown up, and served to fill the ears, and render them plump and perfect. Rain rarely fell in Judea at any other seasons than these. If the former rain were withheld, or not sent in due season, there could be no vegetation; if the latter rain were withheld, or not sent in its due season, there could be no full corn in the ear,

and consequently no harvest. Of what consequence then was it that they should have their rain in *due season!* God, by promising this provided they were obedient, and threatening to withhold it should they be disobedient, shows that it is not a general providence that directs these things, but that the very rain of heaven falls by particular direction, and the showers are often regulated by an especial providence.

18. *Therefore shall ye lay up these my words.* See chap. vi. 4-8, and see on Exod. xiii. 9.

24. *From the river*—Euphrates, which was on the east—*unto the uttermost sea*—the Mediterranean, which lay westward of the Promised Land. This promise, notwithstanding the many provocations of the Israelites, was fulfilled in the time of Solomon, for "he reigned over all the kings from the river [Euphrates] even unto the land of the Philistines, and to the border of Egypt," 2 Chron. ix. 26.

26. *Behold, I set before you . . . a blessing and a curse.* If God had not put it in the power of this people either to obey or disobey; if they had not had a free will, over which they had complete authority, to use it either in the way of willing or nilling; could God, with any propriety, have given such precepts as these, sanctioned with such promises and threatenings? If they were not free *agents,* they could not be punished for disobedience, nor could they, in any sense of the word, have been rewardable for obedience.

29. *Thou shalt put the blessing upon mount Gerizim, and the curse upon mount Ebal.* The etymology of these names may be supposed to cast some light on this institution. *Gerizim,* from *garaz,* "to cut, cut off, cut down"; hence *gerizim,* the "cutters down, fellers, and reapers or harvestmen," this mountain being supposed to have its name from its great fertility, or the abundance of the crops it yielded. Of *ebal* or *eybal* the root is not found in Hebrew; but in Arabic *abala* signifies "rough, rugged, curled"; and *abalo,* from the same root, signifies "white stones," and a mountain in which such stones are found; *alabalo,* "the mount of white stones." And as it is supposed that the mountain had this name because of its barrenness, on this metaphorical interpretation the sense of the passage would appear to be the following: God will so superintend the land, and have it continually under the eye of His watchful providence, that no change can happen in it but according to His divine counsel, so that its fertility shall ever be the consequence of the faithful obedience of its inhabitants, and a proof of the blessing of God upon it; on the contrary, its barrenness shall be a proof that the people have departed from their God, and that His curse has in consequence fallen upon the land. See the manner of placing these blessings and curses, chap. xxvii. 12, etc. That Gerizim is very fruitful, and that Ebal is very barren, is the united testimony of all who have travelled in those parts.

CHAPTER 12

All monuments of idolatry in the Promised Land to be destroyed, 1-3; and God's service to be duly performed, 4-7. The difference between the performance of that service in the wilderness and in the Promised Land, 8-11. The people are to be happy in all their religious observances, 12. The offerings must be brought to the place which God appoints, and no blood is to be eaten, 13-16.

The tithe of corn, wine, oil, etc., to be eaten in the place that God shall choose, 17-18. The Levite must not be forsaken, 19. All clean beasts may be eaten, but the blood must be poured out before the Lord, and be eaten on no pretence whatever, 20-25. Of vows, burnt offerings, etc., 26-27. These precepts are to be carefully obeyed, 28. Cautions against the abominations of the heathen, 29-31. Nothing to be added to or diminished from the word of God, 32.

3. *Ye shall overthrow their altars,* where unholy sacrifices have been offered; *and break their pillars,* probably meaning statues and representations of their gods cut out of stone; and burn their groves, such as those about the temple of Ashtaroth, the Canaanitish Venus, whose impure rites were practiced in different parts of the enclosures or groves round her temples; *and ye shall hew down the graven images,* probably implying all images carved out of wood; *and destroy the names of them,* which, no doubt were at first graven on the stones, and carved on the trees, and then applied to the surrounding districts. In various instances the names of whole mountains, valleys, and districts were borrowed from the gods worshipped there.

14. *The place which the Lord shall choose.* To prevent idolatry and bring about a perfect uniformity in the divine worship, which at that time was essentially necessary. Because every rite and ceremony had a determinate meaning, and pointed out the good things which were to come, therefore one place must be established where those rites and ceremonies should be carefully and punctually observed. Had it not been so, every man would have formed his worship according to his own mind, and the whole beauty and importance of the grand representative system would have been destroyed, and the Messiah and the glories of His kingdom could not have been seen through the medium of the Jewish ritual.

15. *Thou mayest kill and eat flesh in all thy gates.* With the proviso that the blood be poured out on the ground. (1) The blood should not be eaten. (2) It should be poured out by way of sacrifice. *The roebuck, and . . . the hart.* It is very likely that by *tsebi* the antelope is meant; and by *aiyal,* the hart or deer.

19. *Forsake not the Levite.* These had no inheritance, and were to live by the sanctuary; if therefore the offerings were withheld by which the Levites were supported, they of course must perish. Those who have devoted themselves to the service of God in ministering to the salvation of the souls of men certainly should be furnished at least with all the necessaries of life.

23. *For the blood is the life.* And the life being offered as an atonement, consequently the blood should not be eaten. See the notes on Lev. xvii. 11.

31. *Their sons and their daughters they have burnt in the fire.* Almost all the nations in the world agreed in offering human victims to their gods on extraordinary occasions, by which it is evident that none of those nations had any right notion of the divine nature. How necessary, then, was the volume of revelation, to teach men what that religion is with which God can be well pleased!

CHAPTER 13

Of false prophets and their lying signs, 1-6. Of those who endeavor to entice and seduce people to idolatry, 7-8. The punishment of such, 9-11. Of cities perverted

from the pure worship of God, 12-14. How that city is to be treated, 15. All the spoil of it to be destroyed, 16. Promises to them who obey these directions, 17-18.

1. *If there arise among you a prophet.* Any pretending to have a divine influence, so as to be able perfectly to direct others in the way of salvation; *or a dreamer of dreams*—one who pretends that some deity has spoken to him in the night season; *and giveth thee a sign, oth,* what appears to be a miraculous proof of his mission; *or a wonder, mopheth,* some type or representation of what he wishes to bring you over to, as some have pretended to have received a consecrated image from heaven. But here the word seems to mean some portentous sign, such as an eclipse, which he who knew when it would take place might predict to the people who knew nothing of the matter, and thereby accredit his pretensions.

3. *The Lord your God proveth you.* God permits such imposters to arise to try the faith of His followers, and to put their religious experience to the test; for he who experimentally knows God cannot be drawn away after idols. He who has no experimental knowledge of God may believe anything. Experience of the truths contained in the Word of God can alone preserve any man from false religion. They who have not this are a prey to the pretended prophet, and to the dreamer of dreams.

6. *If thy brother . . . or thy son.* The teacher of idolatry was to be put to death; and so strict was this order that a man must neither spare nor conceal his *brother, son, daughter, wife,* or *friend,* because this was the highest offense that could be committed against God, and the most destructive to society; hence the severest laws were enacted against it.

13. *Children of Belial.* From *bal,* "not," and *yaal,* "profit"; Septuagint, "lawless men"; persons good for nothing to themselves or others, and capable of nothing but mischief.

15. *Thou shalt surely smite the inhabitants.* If one city were permitted to practice idolatry, the evil would soon spread; therefore the contagion must be destroyed in its birth.

17. *And there shall cleave nought of the cursed thing.* As God did not permit them to take the spoils of these idolatrous cities, they could be under no temptation to make war upon them. It could be done only through a merely religious motive, in obedience to the command of God, as they could have no profit by the subversion of such places. How few religious wars would there ever have been in the world had they been regulated by this principle: "Thou shalt neither extend thy territory, nor take any spoils"!

CHAPTER 14

The Israelites are not to adopt superstitious customs in mourning, 1-2. The different kinds of clean and unclean animals, 3-20. Nothing to be eaten that dieth of itself, 21. Concerning offerings which, from distance, cannot be carried to the altar of God, and which may be turned into money, 22-26. The Levite is not to be forsaken, 27. The third year's tithe for the Levite, stranger, widow, etc., 28-29.

1. *Ye are the children of the Lord.* The very highest character that can be conferred on any created beings; *ye shall not cut yourselves,* i.e., their hair, for it was a custom among idolatrous nations to consecrate their hair to their deities, though they sometimes also made incisions in their flesh.

4. *These are the beasts which ye shall eat.* On Leviticus xi I have entered into considerable detail relative to the clean and unclean animals there mentioned. For the general subject, the reader is referred to the notes on that chapter; but as there are particulars mentioned here which Moses does not introduce in Leviticus, it will be necessary to consider them in this place. *The ox.* Shor. This term includes all clean animals of the beef kind; not only the *ox* properly so called, but also the bull, the cow, heifer, and calf. *The sheep.* Seh: including the ram, the wether, the ewe, and the lamb. *The goat.* Az: including the he-goat, she-goat, and kid. The words in the text, *seh chesabim,* signify the lamb or young of sheep; and *seh izzim,* the young or kid of goats: but this is a Hebrew idiom which signifies every creature of the genus. The flesh of these animals is universally allowed to be the most wholesome and nutritive. They live on the very best vegetables; and having several stomachs, their food is well concocted, and the chyle formed from it the most pure because the best elaborated, as it is well refined before it enters into the blood. On ruminating or chewing the cud, see the note on Lev. xi. 3.

5. *The hart.* Aiyal, the deer, according to Dr. Shaw. *The roebuck.* Tsebi, generally supposed to be the antelope. It has round, twisted, spiral horns, hairy tufts on the knees, browses on tender shoots, lives in hilly countries, is fond of climbing rocks, and is remarkable for its beautiful black eyes. The flesh is good and well-flavored. *The fallow deer.* Yachmur, from *chamar,* to be "troubled, disturbed, disordered"; this is supposed to mean, not the *fallow deer,* but the "buffalo." According to 1 Kings iv. 23, this was one of the animals which was daily served up at the table of Solomon. Though the flesh of the buffalo is not considered very delicious, yet in the countries where it abounds it is eaten as frequently by all classes of persons as the ox is in England. The *yachmur* is not mentioned in the parallel place, Leviticus xi. *The wild goat.* Akko. It is not easy to tell what creature is intended by the *akko.* Dr. Shaw supposed it to be a kind of very timorous goat, bearing a resemblance to both the goat and the stag, whence the propriety of the name given it by the Septuagint and Vulgate, the "goat-stag"; probably the rock goat. The word is found nowhere else in the Hebrew Bible.

The pygarg. Dishon. As this word is nowhere else used, we cannot tell what animal is meant by it. The word *pygarg* literally signifies "white buttocks," and is applied to a kind of eagle with a white tail; but here it evidently means a quadruped. It was probably some kind of goat, common and well-known in Judea. *The wild ox.* Teo. This is supposed to be the *oryx* of the Greeks, which is a species of large "stag." *The chamois.* Zemer. This was probably a species of goat or deer, but of what kind we know not; that it cannot mean the *chamois* is evident from this circumstance, "that the chamois inhabits only the regions of snow and ice, and cannot bear the heat." The Septuagint and Vulgate translate it the *Camelopard,* but this creature is only found in the torrid zone and probably was never seen in Judea; consequently could never be prescribed as a clean animal, to be used as ordinary food. Once more I must be permitted to say that to ascertain the natural history of the

Bible is a hopeless case. Of a few of its animals and vegetables we are comparatively certain, but of the great majority we know almost nothing.

13. *The vulture after his kind.* The word *daiyah* in this verse is not only different from that in Leviticus, but means also a different animal, properly enough translated *vulture.* See the note on Lev. xi. 14.

21. *Thou shalt not seethe a kid in his mother's milk.* Mr. Calmet thinks that this precept refers to the paschal lamb only, which was not to be offered to God till it was weaned from its mother; but see the note on Exod. xxiii. 19.

22. *Thou shalt truly tithe.* Meaning the second tithe, which themselves were to eat, v. 23, for there was a first tithe that was given to the Levites, out of which they paid a tenth part to the priests, Num. xviii. 24-28; Neh. x. 37-38. Then of that which remained, the owners separated a second tithe, which they ate before the Lord the first and second year; and in the third year it was given to the Levites and to the poor, Deut. xiv. 28-29. In the fourth and fifth years it was eaten again by the owners, and in the sixth year was given to the poor. The seventh year was a Sabbath to the land, and then all things were common, Exod. xxiii. 10-11.

26. *Or for strong drink.* What the *sikera* or strong drink of the Hebrews was, see in the note on Lev. x. 9.

29. *And the Levite (because he hath no part nor inheritance).* And hence much of his support depended on the mere freewill offerings of the people. God chose to make His ministers thus dependent on the people, that they might be induced (among other motives) to labor for their spiritual profiting, that the people, thus blessed under their ministry, might feel it their duty and privilege to support and render them comfortable.

CHAPTER 15

The sabbatical year of release, 1. **The manner in which** this release shall take place, 2-5. Of lending to the poor, and the disposition in which it should be done, 6-11. Of the Hebrew servant who has served six years, and who shall be dismissed well-furnished, 12-15. The ceremny of boring the ear, when the servant wishes to continue with his master, 16-18. Of the firstlings of the flock and herd, 19-20. Nothing shall be offered that has any blemish, 21. The sacrifice to be eaten by both the clean and unclean, except the blood, which is never to be eaten, but poured out upon the ground, 22-23.

1. *At the end of every seven years thou shalt make a release.* For an explanation of many things in this chapter, see the notes on Exodus xxi and xxiii and Leviticus xxv.

4. *There shall be no poor.* That is, comparatively; see v. 11.

8. *Thou shalt open thine hand wide.* Your benevolence shall be in proportion to his distress and poverty, and your ability. You shall have no other rule to regulate your charity by.

9. *Beware that there be not a thought in thy wicked heart.* Lebabecha beliyaal, "thy belial heart," that is, thy good-for-nothing or unprofitable heart; see on chap. xiv. 13. *And thine eye be evil.* An evil eye signifies a covetous disposition. See the same form of expression used by our Lord in the same sense, Matt. vi. 23. "If thine eye be evil"—if you are a covetous person. "Evil eye" is by our Lord opposed to "single eye," i.e., a person of a liberal, benev-

olent mind. Covetousness darkens the soul; liberality and benevolence enlighten it. *And he cry unto the Lord against thee.* What a consolation to the poor and the oppressed, that they have a sure Friend in God, who will hear their cry and redress their grievances!

11. *For the poor shall never cease out of the land.* To this passage our Lord appears to allude in Mark xiv. 7: "For ye have the poor with you always." God leaves these in mercy among men to exercise the feelings of compassion, tenderness, mercy. And without occasions afforded to exercise these, man would soon become a Stoic or a brute.

13. *Thou shalt not let him go away empty.* Because during the time he served you he made no property for himself, having been always honest towards you; and now when he leaves you, he has nothing to begin the world with.

14. *Thou shalt furnish him . . . out of thy flock.* You shall give him some cattle to breed with; *out of thy floor*—some corn for seed and for bread; *and out of thy winepress*—an adequate provision of wine for present necessity.

17. *Thou shalt take an aul.* See the note on Exod. xxi. 6.

20. *Thou shalt eat it . . . in the place which the Lord shall choose.* Thus God in His mercy made their duty and interest go hand in hand. And in every case God acts thus with His creatures.

21. *If there be any blemish.* See the notes on Lev. xxii. 20. God will have both a perfect priest and a perfect offering.

CHAPTER 16

The month of Abib to be observed, 1. The Feast of the Passover and of Unleavened Bread, 2-8. The Feast of Weeks, 9-12. The Feast of Tabernacles, 13-15. All the males to appear before the Lord thrice in the year, none to come empty, each to give according to his ability, 16-17. Judges and officers to be made in all their cities, 18. Strict justice shall be executed, 19-20. No grove to be planted near the altar of God nor any image to be set up, 21-22.

1. *Keep the passover.* A feast so called because the angel that destroyed the firstborn of the Egyptians, seeing the blood of the appointed sacrifice sprinkled on the lintels and doorposts of the Israelites' houses, "passed over them," and did not destroy any of their firstborn. See the notes on Exod. xii. 2, etc.

3. *Bread of affliction.* Because, being baked without leaven, it was unsavory, and put them in mind of their afflictive bondage in Egypt.

11. *Thou shalt rejoice.* The offerings of the Israelites were to be eaten with festivity, communicated to their friends with liberality, and bestowed on the poor with great generosity, that they might partake with them in these repasts with joy before the Lord. To answer these views it was necessary to eat the flesh while it was fresh, as in that climate putrefaction soon took place; therefore they were commanded to let nothing remain until the morning, v. 4.

16. *Three times in a year.* See Exod. xxiii. 14, where all the Jewish feasts are explained. See also Lev. xxiii. 34.

18. *Judges and officers shalt thou make.* Judges, *shophetim,* among the Hebrews, were probably the same as our magistrates or "justices of the peace." *Officers, shoterim,* seem to have been the same as our sergeants, whose office it was to go into the houses, shops, etc., and examine weights, measures, and the civil conduct of the people. When they found anything amiss, they brought the person offending before the magistrate, and he was punished by the officer on the spot.

21. *Thou shalt not plant thee a grove.* We have already seen that groves were planted about idol temples for the purpose of the obscene worship performed in them. On this account God would have no groves or thickets about His altar, that there might be no room for suspicion that anything contrary to the strictest purity was transacted there. Every part of the divine worship was publicly performed, for the purpose of general edification.

CHAPTER 17

All sacrifices to be without blemish, 1. Of persons convicted of idolatry and their punishment, 2-7. Difficult matters in judgment to be laid before the priests and judges, and to be determined by them; and all to submit to their decision, 8-13. The king that may be chosen to be one of their brethren; no stranger to be appointed to that office, 14-15. He shall not multiply horses to himself, nor cause the people to return unto Egypt, 16. Nor multiply wives, money, etc., 17. He shall write a copy of the law for his own use, and read and study it all his days, that his heart be not lifted up above his brethren, 18-20.

1. *Wherein is blemish.* God must not have that offered to Him which you would not use yourself. This not only refers to the perfect sacrifice offered by Christ Jesus, but to that sincerity and uprightness of heart which God requires in all those who approach Him in the way of worship.

4. *If it be told thee*—in a private way by any confidential person. *And thou hast heard of it*—so that it appears to be notorious, very likely to be true, and publicly scandalous. *And enquired diligently*—sought to find out the truth of the report by the most careful examination of persons reporting, circumstances of the case, etc. *And, behold, it be true*—the report is not founded on vague rumor, hearsay, or malice. *And the thing certain*—substantiated by the fullest evidence. *Then shalt thou bring forth that man,* v. 5. As the charge of idolatry was the most solemn and awful that could be brought against an Israelite, because it affected his life, therefore God required that the charge should be substantiated by the most unequivocal facts, and the most competent witnesses. Hence all the precautions mentioned in the fourth verse must be carefully used, in order to arrive at so affecting and so awful a truth.

6. *Two witnesses.* One might be deceived, or be prejudiced or malicious; therefore God required two substantial witnesses for the support of the charge.

8. *If there arise a matter too hard for thee.* These directions are given to the common magistrates, who might not be able to judge of or apply the law in all cases that might be brought before them. The priests and Levites, who were lawyers by birth and continual practice, were reasonably considered as the best qualified to decide on difficult points.

12. *The man that will do presumptuously!* The man who refused to abide by this final

determination forfeited his life, as being then in a state of rebellion against the highest authority, and consequently the public could have no pledge for his conduct.

15. *One from among thy brethren shalt thou set king over thee.* It was on the ground of His command that the Jews proposed that insidious question to our Lord, "Is it lawful to give tribute unto Caesar, or not?" Matt. xxii. 17; for they were then under the authority of a foreign power. Had Christ said, "Yes," then they would have condemned Him by this law; had He said, "No," then they would have accused Him to Caesar.

16. *He shall not multiply horses.* As *horses* appear to have been generally furnished by Egypt, God prohibits these: (1) Lest there should be such commerce with Egypt as might lead to idolatry; (2) Lest the people might depend on a well-appointed cavalry as a means of security, and so cease from trusting in the strength and protection of God; and (3) That they might not be tempted to extend their dominion by means of cavalry, and so get scattered among the surrounding idolatrous nations, and thus cease, in process of time, to be that distinct and separate people which God intended they should be, and without which the prophecies relative to the Messiah could not be known to have their due and full accomplishment.

17. *Neither shall he multiply wives.* For this would necessarily lead to foreign alliances, and be the means of introducing the manners and customs of other nations, and their idolatry also. Solomon sinned against this precept, and brought ruin on himself and on the land by it; see 1 Kings xi. 4.

18. *He shall write him a copy of this law.* *Mishneh hattorah hazzoth*, and "iteration or duplicate of this law"; translated by the Septuagint, "this deuteronomy." From this version both the Vulgate Latin and all the modern versions have taken the name of this book; and from the original word the Jews call it *Mishneh*. See the preface to this book.

Out of that which is before the priests the Levites. It is likely this means that the copy which the king was to write out was to be taken from the autograph kept in the Tabernacle before the Lord, from which, as a standard, every copy was taken, and with which doubtless every copy was compared; and it is probable that the priests and Levites had the revising of every copy that was taken off, in order to prevent errors from creeping into the sacred text.

19. *And it shall be with him.* It was the surest way to bring the king to an acquaintance with the divine law to oblige him to write out a fair copy of it with his own hand, in which he was to read daily. This was essentially necessary, as these laws of God were all permanent, and no Israelitish king could make any new law, the kings of this people being ever considered as only the vicegerents of Jehovah.

20. *He, and his children, in the midst of Israel.* From this verse it has been inferred that the crown of Israel was designed to be hereditary, and this is very probable; for long experience has proved to almost all the nations of the world that hereditary succession in the regal government is, on the whole, the safest, and best calculated to secure the public tranquillity.

CHAPTER 18

The priests and Levites to have no inheritance, 1-2. What is the priest's due, 3-5. Of the Levites that come from any of the other cities, 6-8. The Israelites must not copy the abominations of the former inhabitants, 9. None to cause his son or daughter to pass through the fire, or use any kind of divination or enchantment, as the former inhabitants did, 10-14. The great prophet which God promised to raise up, 15-19. Of false prophets, 20; and how to discern them, 21-22.

2. *The Lord is their inheritance.* He is the portion of their souls; and as to their bodies, they shall live by the offerings of the Lord made by fire, i.e., the meat offering, the sin offering, and the trespass offering; and whatever was the Lord's right, in these or other offerings, He gave to the priests.

3. *Offer a sacrifice. Zobechey hazzebach.* The word *zebach* is used to signify, not only an animal sacrificed to the Lord, but also one killed for common use. See Gen. xliii. 15; Prov. xvii. 1; Ezek. xxv. 6. And in this latter sense it probably should be understood here; and, consequently, the command in this verse relates to what the people were to allow the priests and Levites from the animals slain for common use. The parts to be given to the priests were: (1) The *shoulder;* (2) The *two cheeks,* which may include the whole head; (3) The *maw*—the whole of those intestines which are commonly used for food.

4. *The firstfruit also of thy corn, of thy wine, and of thine oil.* All these firstfruits and firstlings were the Lord's portion, and these He gave to the priests.

8. *The sale of his patrimony.* So we find that, though the Levites might have no part of the land by lot, yet they were permitted to make purchases of houses, goods, and cattle, yea, of fields also. See the case of Abiathar, 1 Kings ii. 26, and of Jeremiah, Jer. xxxii. 7-8.

10. *To pass through the fire.* Probably in the way of consecration to Molech, or some other deity. *Divination. Kosem kesamim,* one who endeavors to find out futurity by auguries, using lots, etc. *Observer of times. Meonen,* one who pretends to foretell future events by present occurrences, and who predicts great political or physical changes from the aspects of the planets, eclipses, motion of the clouds, etc. *Enchanter. Menachesh,* from *nichesh,* to "view attentively"; one who inspected the entrails of beasts, observed the flight of birds, etc., and drew auguries thence. Some think divination by serpents is meant, which was common among the heathen. *A witch. Mechashsheph,* probably those who by means of drugs, herbs, perfumes, etc., pretended to bring certain celestial influences to their aid. See the note on Lev. xix. 26.

11. *A charmer. Chober chaber,* one who uses spells; a peculiar conjunction, as the term implies, of words, or things, tying knots, etc., for the purposes of divination. This was a custom among the heathen. *A consulter with familiar spirits. Shoel ob,* a Pythoness, one who inquires by the means of one spirit to get oracular answers from another of a superior order. See on Lev. xix. 31. *A wizard. Yiddeoni,* "a wise one," a knowing one. *Wizard* was formerly considered as the masculine of "witch," both practicing divination by similar means. See on Exod. xxii. 18 and Lev. xix. 31. *Or a necromancer. Doresh el hammethim,* one who seeks from or inquires of the dead, such as the witch at Endor, who

professed to evoke the dead, in order to get them to disclose the secrets of the spiritual world.

15. *The Lord thy God will raise up unto thee a Prophet.* Instead of diviners, observers of times, etc., God here promises to give them an infallible Guide, who should tell them all things that make for their peace, so that His declarations should completely answer the end of all the knowledge that was pretended to be gained by the persons already specified. *Like unto me.* Viz., a Prophet, a Legislator, a King, a Mediator, and the Head or Chief of the people of God. This was the very Person of whom Moses was the type, and who should accomplish all the great purposes of the Divine Being. Such a Prophet as had never before appeared, and who should have no equal till the consummation of the world. This Prophet is the Lord Jesus, who was in the bosom of the Father, and who came to declare Him to mankind. Every word spoken by Him is a living, infallible oracle from God himself; and must be received and obeyed as such, on pain of the eternal displeasure of the Almighty. See v. 19, and Acts iii. 22-23.

22. *If the thing follow not.* It is worthy of remark that the prophets in general predicted those things which were shortly to come to pass, that the people might have the fullest proof of their divine mission, and of the existence of God's providence in the administration of the affairs of men.

CHAPTER 19

Three cities of refuge to be appointed in the midst of the Promised Land; the land being divided into three parts, a city is to be placed in each, a proper way to which is to be prepared, 1-3. In what cases of manslaughter the benefit of those cities may be claimed, 4-6. Three cities more to be added should the Lord enlarge their coasts, and the reasons why, 7-10. The intentional murderer shall have no benefit from these cities, 11-13. The landmark is not to be shifted, 14. One witness shall not be deemed sufficient to convict a man, 15. How a false witness shall be dealt with—he shall bear the punishment which he designed should have been inflicted on his neighbor, 16-20. Another command to establish the *lex talionis*, 21.

2. *Thou shalt separate three cities.* See on Num. xxxv. 10, etc.

3. *Thou shalt prepare thee a way.* The Jews inform us that the roads to the cities of refuge were made very broad, thirty-two cubits; and even, so that there should be no impediments in the way; and were constantly kept in good repair.

9. *Shalt thou add three cities more.* This was afterwards found necessary, and accordingly six cities were appointed, three on either side Jordan. See Josh. xxi. 1, etc. In imitation of these cities of refuge the heathens had their *asyla,* and the Catholics their privileged altars.

11. *If any man hate his neighbour.* See on Exod. xxi. 13.

14. *Thou shalt not remove thy neighbour's landmark.* Before the extensive use of fences, landed property was marked out by stones or posts, set up so as to ascertain the divisions of family estates. It was easy to remove one of these landmarks, and set it in a different place; and thus the dishonest man enlarged his own estate by contracting that of his neighbor. The *termini* or landmarks among the Romans were held very sacred, and were at last deified.

15. *One witness shall not rise up, etc.* See Num. xxxv. 30.

19. *Then shall ye do unto him as he had thought to have done unto his brother.* Nothing can be more equitable or proper than this, that if a man endeavor to do any injury to or take away the life of another, on detection he shall be caused to undergo the same evil which he intended for his innocent neighbor.

21. *Life . . . for life, eye for eye.* The operation of such a law as this must have been very salutary; if a man prized his own members, he would naturally avoid injuring those of others.

CHAPTER 20

Directions concerning campaigns, 1. The priest shall encourage the people with the assurance that God will accompany and fight for them, 2-4. The officers shall dismiss from the army all who had just built a new house, but had not dedicated it, 5. All who had planted a vineyard, but had not yet eaten of its fruits, 6. All who had betrothed a wife, but had not brought her home, 7. And all who were timid and fainthearted, 8. The commanders to be chosen after the timid, etc., had retired, 9. No city to be attacked till they had proclaimed conditions of peace to it, provided it be a city beyond the bounds of the seven Canaanitish nations; if it submitted, it was to become tributary; if not, it was to be besieged, sacked, and all the males put to the sword; the women, children, and cattle to be taken as booty, 10-15. No such offers to be made to the cities of the Canaanites; of them nothing shall be preserved, and the reason, 16-18. In besieging a city no trees to be cut down but those which do not bear fruit, 19-20.

1. *When thou goest out to battle.* This refers chiefly to the battles they were to have with the Canaanites, in order to get possession of the Promised Land; for it cannot be considered to apply to any wars which they might have with the surrounding nations for political reasons, as the divine assistance could not be expected in wars which were not undertaken by the divine command.

2. *The priest shall approach and speak unto the people.* The priest on these occasions was the representative of that God whose servant he was, and whose worship he conducted. It is remarkable that almost all ancient nations took their priests with them to battle, as they did not expect success without having the object of their adoration with them, and they supposed they secured his presence by having that of his representative.

5. *That hath built a new house, and hath not dedicated it?* From the title of Psalms xxx—"A Psalm and Song at the Dedication of the House of David," it is evident that it was a custom in Israel to dedicate a new house to God with prayer, praise, and thanksgiving; and this was done in order to secure the divine presence and blessing, for no pious or sensible man could imagine he could dwell safely in a house that was not under the immediate protection of God.

7. *Betrothed a wife, and hath not taken her?* It was customary among the Jews to contract matrimony, espouse, or betroth, and for some considerable time to leave the parties in the houses of their respective parents; when the bridegroom had made proper preparations, then the bride was brought home to his house, and thus the marriage was consummated. The provisions in this verse refer to a case of this kind; for it was deemed an excessive hardship for a person to be obliged to go to battle, where there was a probability of his being slain, who had left a new house unfinished, a newly purchased

heritage half-tilled, or a wife with whom he had just contracted marriage.

8. *What man is there that is fearful and fainthearted?* The original *rach* signifies "tender" or "softhearted." And a soft heart the man must have who, in such a contest, after such a permission, could turn his back upon his enemies and his brethren. However, such were the troops commanded by Gideon in his war against the Midianites; for after he gave this permission, out of 32,000 men only 10,000 remained to fight! Judges vii. 3. There could be no deception in a business of this kind; for the departure of the 22,000 was the fullest proof of their dastardliness which they could possibly give.

10. *Proclaim peace unto it.* The text, taken in connection with the context (see vv. 15-18), appears to state that this proclamation or offer of peace to a city is to be understood only of those cities which were situated beyond the limits of the seven anathematized nations, because these latter are commanded to be totally destroyed. Nothing can be clearer than this from the bare letter of the text.

19. (*For the tree of the field is man's life*) *to employ them in the siege.* The original is exceedingly obscure, and has been variously translated. The following are the chief versions: "For, O man, the trees of the field are for thee to employ them in the siege"; or, "For it is man, and the tree of the field, that must go before thee for a bulwark"; or, "For it is a tree, and not men, to increase the number of those who come against thee to the siege"; or, lastly, "The tree of the field (is as) a man, to go before thy face for a bulwark." The sense is sufficiently clear, though the strict grammatical meaning of the words cannot be easily ascertained: it was a merciful provision to spare all fruit-bearing trees, because they yielded the fruit which supported man's life; and it was sound policy also, for even the conquerors must perish if the means of life were cut off.

CHAPTER 21

If a man be found slain in a field, and the cause of his death be unknown, the murder shall be expiated by the sacrifice of a heifer in an uncultivated valley, 1-4. The rites to be u~ed on the occasion, 5-9. The ordinance concerning marriage with a captive, 10-14. The law relative to the children of the hated and beloved wives: if the son of the hated wife should be the firstborn he shall not be disinherited by the son of the beloved wife, but shall have a double portion of all his father's goods, 15-18. The law concerning the stubborn and rebellious son, who when convicted, is to be stoned to death, 19-21. Of the person who is to be hanged, 22. His body shall not be left on the tree all night; everyone that is hanged on a tree is accursed of God, 23.

4. *Shall bring down the heifer unto a rough valley. Nachal eythan* might be translated a "rapid stream," probably passing through a piece of uncultivated ground where the elders of the city were to strike off the head of the heifer, and to wash their hands over her in token of their innocence. The spot of ground on which this sacrifice was made must be uncultivated, because it was considered to be a sacrifice to make atonement for the murder, and consequently would pollute the land. This regulation was calculated to keep murder in abhorrence, and to make the magistrates alert in their office, that delinquents might be discovered and punished, and thus public expense saved.

6. *Shall wash their hands over the heifer.* Washing the hands, in reference to such a subject as this, was a rite anciently used to signify that the persons thus washing were innocent of the crime in question. It was probably from the Jews that Pilate learned this symbolical method of expressing his innocence.

11. *And seest . . . a beautiful woman.* No forcible possession was allowed even in this case, when the woman was taken in war, and was, by the general consent of ancient nations adjudged as a part of the spoils. The person to whose lot or share such a woman as is here described fell might, if he chose, have her for a wife on certain conditions; but he was not permitted to use her under any inferior character.

12. *She shall shave her head.* This was in token of her renouncing her religion, and becoming a proselyte to that of the Jews. This is still a custom in the East; when a Christian turns Mohammedan his head is shaven, and he is carried through the city crying, *La alahila allah we Mohammed resooli Allah,* "There is no God but God, and Mohammed is the prophet of God." *Pare her nails.* "She shall make her nails." Now whether this signifies paring or letting them grow is greatly doubted among learned men. Possibly it means neither, but coloring the nails, staining them red with the hennah, which is much practiced in India to the present day, and which was undoubtedly practiced among the ancient Egyptians, as is evident from the nails of mummies which are found thus stained.

15. *One beloved, and another hated.* That is one loved less than the other. This is the true notion of the word *hate* in Scripture. So "Jacob hated Leah," that is, he loved her less than he did Rachel; and "Jacob have I loved, but Esau have I hated"—that is, I have shown a more particular affection to the posterity of Jacob than I have to the posterity of Esau. See the note on Gen. xxix. 31. From this verse we see that polygamy did exist under the Mosaic laws, and that it was put under certain regulations. But it was not enjoined; Moses merely suffered it, because of the hardness of their hearts, as our Lord justly remarks in Matt. xix. 8.

23. *His body shall not remain all night upon the tree.* Its exposure for the space of one day was judged sufficient. The law which required this answered all the ends of public justice, exposed the shame and infamy of the conduct, but did not put to torture the feelings of humanity by requiring a perpetual exhibition of a human being, a slow prey to the most loathsome process of putrefaction. *For he that is hanged is accursed of God.* That is, he has forfeited his life to the law; for it is written, "Cursed is every one that continueth not in all things which are written in the book of the law to do them"; and on his body, in the execution of the sentence of the law, the curse was considered as alighting; hence the necessity of removing the accursed thing out of sight.

CHAPTER 22

Ordinances relative to strayed cattle and lost goods, 1-3. Humanity to oppressed cattle, 4. Men and women shall not wear each other's apparel, 5. No bird shall be taken with her nest of eggs or young ones, 6-7. Battlements must be made on the roofs of houses, 8. Improper mixtures to be avoided, 9-11. Fringes on the garments, 12.

Case of the hated wife, and the tokens of virginity, and the proceedings thereon, 13-21. The adulterer and adulteress to be put to death, 22. Case of the betrothed damsel corrupted in the city, 23-24. Cases of rape and the punishment, 25-27; of fornication, 28-29. No man shall take his father's wife, 30.

1. *Thou shalt not see thy brother's ox or his sheep go astray.* The same humane, merciful, and wise regulations which we met with before, Exod. xxiii. 4-5, well calculated to keep in remembrance the second grand branch of the law of God, "Thou shalt love thy neighbour as thyself." A humane man cannot bear to see even an ass fall under his burden, and not endeavor to relieve him; and a man who loves his neighbor as himself cannot see his property in danger without endeavoring to preserve it. These comparatively small matters were tests and proofs of matters great in themselves, and in their consequences.

3. *Thou mayest not hide thyself.* You shall not keep out of the way of affording help, nor pretend you did not see occasion to render your neighbor any service. The priest and the Levite, when they saw the wounded man, passed by on the other side of the way, Luke x. 31-32. This was a notorious breach of the merciful law mentioned above.

5. *The woman shall not wear that which pertaineth unto a man. Keli geber,* "the instruments or arms of a man." As the word *geber* is here used, which properly signifies a "strong man" or "man of war," it is very probable that armor is here intended; especially as we know that in the worship of Venus, to which that of Astarte or Ashtaroth among the Canaanites bore a striking resemblance, the women were accustomed to appear in armor before her. It certainly cannot mean a simple change in dress, whereby the men might pass for women, and vice versa. This would have been impossible in those countries where the dress of the sexes had but little to distinguish it, and where every man wore a long beard.

7. *Thou shalt . . . let the dam go, and take the young to thee; that it may be well with thee.* This passage may be understood literally. If they destroyed both young and old, must not the breed soon fail, and would it not in the end be ill with them; and by thus cutting off the means of their continual support, must not their days be shortened on the land? But we may look for a humane precept in this law. The young never knew the sweets of liberty; the dam did. They might be taken and used for any lawful purpose, but the dam must not be brought into a state of captivity.

8. *A battlement for thy roof.* Houses in the East are in general built with flat roofs, and on them men walk to enjoy the fresh air, converse together, sleep, etc.; it was therefore necessary to have a sort of battlement or balustrade to prevent persons from falling off. If a man neglected to make a sufficient defense against such accidents, and the death of another was occasioned by it, the owner of the house must be considered in the light of a murderer.

9. *Divers seeds.* See the note on Lev. xix. 19.

10. *Thou shalt not plow with an ox and an ass.* It is generally supposed that mixtures of different sorts in seed, breed, etc., were employed for superstitious purposes, and therefore prohibited in this law. It is more likely, however, that there was a physical reason for this;

two beasts of a different species cannot associate comfortably together, and on this ground never pull pleasantly either in cart or plough; and every farmer knows that it is of considerable consequence to the comfort of the cattle to put those together that have an affection for each other. This may be very frequently remarked in certain cattle, which, on this account, are termed true yokefellows. After all, it is very probable that the general design was to prevent improper alliances in civil and religious life. And to this Paul seems evidently to refer, 2 Cor. vi. 14: "Be ye not unequally yoked together with unbelievers," which is simply to be understood as prohibiting all intercourse between Christians and idolaters in social, matrimonial, and religious life. And to teach the Jews the propriety of this, a variety of precepts relative to improper and heterogeneous mixtures were interspersed through their law, so that in civil and domestic life they might have them ever before their eyes.

12. *Fringes.* See on Num. xv. 38.

15. *Tokens of the damsel's virginity.* This was a perfectly possible case in all places where girls were married at ten, twelve, and fourteen years of age, which is frequent in the East. I have known several instances of persons having had two or three children at separate births before they were fourteen years of age. Such tokens, therefore, as the text speaks of must be infallibly exhibited by females so very young on the consummation of their marriage.

17. *They shall spread the cloth.* A usage of this kind argues a roughness of manners which would ill comport with the refinement of European ideas on so delicate a subject. Attempts have been made to show that the law here is to be understood metaphorically; but they so perfectly fail to establish anything like probability that it would be wasting my own and my reader's time to detail them. A custom similar to that above is observed among the Mohammedans to the present day.

22. *Shall both of them die.* Thus we find that in the most ancient of all laws adultery was punished with death in both the parties.

25. *And the man force her.* A rape also, by these ancient institutions, was punished with death, because a woman's honor was considered equally as precious as her life; therefore the same punishment was inflicted on the ravisher as upon the murderer.

30. *A man shall not take his father's wife.* This is to be understood as referring to the case of a stepmother. A man in his old age may have married a young wife, and on his dying, his son by a former wife may desire to espouse her; this the law prohibits. It was probably on pretense of having broken this law that Solomon put his brother Adonijah to death, because he had desired to have his father's concubine to wife, 1 Kings ii. 13-25.

CHAPTER 23

Neither eunuchs, bastards, Ammonites, nor Moabites shall be incorporated with the genuine Israelites, 1-3. The reason why the Ammonites and Moabites were excluded, 4-6. Edomites and Egyptians to be respected, 7. Their descendants in the third generation may be incorporated with the Israelites, 8. Cautions against wickedness when they go forth against their enemies, 9. To keep the camp free from every defilement, and the reason why, 10-14. The slave who had taken refuge among them is not to be delivered up to his former master, 15-16. There shall be no prostitutes nor sodomites in the land, 17. The hire of a prostitute or the price of a dog is not to be brought into the house of God, 18. The Israelites shall not lend on usury to each other, 19; but they may take usury from strangers, 20. Vows must be diligently paid, 21-23. In passing through a vineyard or field a man may eat of the grapes or corn, but must carry none away with him, 24-25.

1. *Shall not enter into the congregation.* If by entering the congregation be meant the bearing a civil office among the people, such as magistrate, judge, etc., then the reason of the law is very plain; no man with any such personal defect as might render him contemptible in the sight of others should bear rule among the people, lest the contempt felt for his personal defects might be transferred to his important office, and thus his authority be disregarded. The general meaning of these words is simply that the persons here designated should not be so incorporated with the Jews as to partake of their civil privileges.

2. *A bastard shall not enter.* Mamzer, which is here rendered *bastard*, should be understood as implying the offspring of an illegitimate or incestuous mixture.

3. *An Ammonite or Moabite.* These nations were subjected for their impiety and wickedness (see vv. 4 and 5) to peculiar disgrace, and on this account were not permitted to hold any office among the Israelites. But this did not disqualify them from being proselytes; Ruth, who was a Moabitess, was married to Boaz, and she became one of the progenitors of our Lord. *Even to their tenth generation.* That is, "for ever," as the next clause explains; see Neh. xiii. 1.

12-14. These directions may appear trifling to some, but they were essentially necessary to this people in their present circumstances. Decency and cleanliness promote health, and prevent many diseases.

15. *Thou shalt not deliver . . . the servant which is escaped . . . unto thee.* That is, a servant who left an idolatrous master that he might join himself to God and to His people. In any other case, it would have been injustice to harbor the runaway.

17. *There shall be no whore.* See on Gen. xxxviii. 15-21.

18. *The hire of a whore, or the price of a dog.* Many public prostitutes dedicated to their gods a part of their impure earnings; and some of these prostitutes were publicly kept in the temple of Venus Melytta, whose gains were applied to the support of her abominable worship.

19. *Usury.* See on Lev. xxv. 36.

21. *When thou shalt vow.* See on Num. xxx. 1, etc.

24. *Thou shalt not put any in thy vessel.* You shall carry none away with you. The old English proverb, "Eat thy fill but pocket none," seems to have been founded on this law.

25. *Thou mayest pluck the ears with thine hand.* It was on the permission granted by this law that the disciples plucked the ears of corn, as related Matt. xii. 1. This was both a considerate and humane law, and is no dishonor to the Jewish code.

CHAPTER 24

The case of a divorced wife, 1-4. No man shall be obliged to undertake any public service for the first year of his marriage, 5. The mill-stones shall not be taken as a pledge, 6. The manstealer shall be put to death, 7. Concerning cases of leprosy, 8-9. Of receiving pledges, and returning those of the poor before bedtime, 10-13. Of servants and their hire, 14, 15. Parents and children shall not be put to death for each other, 16. Of humanity to the stranger, fatherless, widow, and bondman, 17-18. Gleanings of the harvest, etc., to be left for the poor, stranger, widow, fatherless, etc., 19-22.

1. *Some uncleanness.* Any cause of dislike, for this great latitude of meaning the fact itself authorizes us to adopt, for it is certain that a Jew might put away his wife for any cause that seemed good to himself; and so hard were their hearts that Moses suffered this; and we find they continued this practice even to the time of our Lord, who strongly reprehended them on the account, and showed that such license was wholly inconsistent with the original design of marriage; see Matt. v. 31, etc.; xix. 3, etc., and the notes there.

3. *And write her a bill of divorcement.* These bills, though varying in expression, are the same in substance among the Jews in all places.

4. *She is defiled.* Does not this refer to her having been divorced, and married in consequence to another? Though God, for the hardness of their hearts, suffered them to put away their wives, yet He considered all after-marriages in that case to be pollution and defilement; and it is on this ground that our Lord argues in the places referred to above that whoever marries the woman that is put away is an adulterer. Now this could not have been the case if God had allowed the divorce to be a legal and proper separation of the man from his wife; but in the sight of God nothing can be a legal cause of separation but adultery on either side. In such a case, according to the law of God, a man may put away his wife, and a wife may put away her husband; see Mark x. 12.

5. *When a man hath taken a new wife.* Other people made a similar provision for such circumstances. Alexander ordered those of his soldiers who had married that year to spend the winter with their wives, while the army was in winter quarters.

6. *The nether or the upper millstone.* Small hand-mills which can be worked by a single person were formerly in use among the Jews, and are still used in many parts of the East. As therefore the day's meal was generally ground for each day, they keeping no stock beforehand, hence they were forbidden to take either of the stones to pledge, because in such a case the family must be without bread. On this account the text terms the millstone the *man's life.*

8-9. *The plague of leprosy.* See on Leviticus xiii and xiv.

12. *And if the man be poor.* Did not this law preclude pledging entirely, especially in case of the abjectly poor? For who would take a pledge in the morning which he knew, if not redeemed, he must restore at night? However, he might resume his claim in the morning, and have the pledge daily returned, and thus keep up his property in it till the debt was discharged; see the note on Exod. xii. 26. The Jews in several cases did act contrary to this rule, and we find them cuttingly reproved for it by the Prophet Amos, chap. ii. 8.

15. *He is poor, and setteth his heart upon it.* How exceedingly natural is this! The poor servant who seldom sees money, yet finds from his master's affluence that it procures all the conveniences and comforts of life, longs for the time when he shall receive his wages. Should his pay be delayed after the time is expired, he may naturally be expected to cry unto God against him who withholds it. See most of these subjects treated at large on Exod. xxii. 21-27.

16. *The fathers shall not be put to death for the children.* This law is explained and illustrated in sufficient detail, Ezekiel xviii.

18. *Thou shalt remember that thou wast a bondman.* Most people who have affluence rose from comparative penury; such therefore should remember what their feelings, their fears, and anxieties were when *they* were poor and abject. A want of attention to this most wholesome precept is the reason why pride and arrogance are the general characteristics of those who have risen in the world from poverty to affluence; and it is the conduct of those men which gave rise to the rugged proverb, "Set a beggar on horseback, and he will ride to the devil."

19. *When thou cuttest down thine harvest* This is an addition to the law, Lev. xix. 9; xxiii. 22. The corners of the field, the gleanings, and the forgotten sheaf were all the property of the poor. This the Hebrews extended to any part of the fruit or produce of a field which had been forgotten in the time of general ingathering, as appears from the concluding verses of this chapter.

CHAPTER 25

Punishment by whipping not to exceed forty stripes, 1-3. The ox that treads out the corn is not to be muzzled, 4. The ordinance concerning marrying the wife of that brother who has died childless, 5-10. Of the woman who acts indecently in succoring her husband, 11-12. Of false weights and measures, 13-16. Amalek is to be destroyed, 17-19.

1. *They shall justify the righteous.* This is a very important passage, and is a key to several others. The word *tsadak* is used here precisely in the same sense in which Paul sometimes uses the corresponding word, not to "justify" or "make just," but to "acquit, declare innocent, to remit punishment, or give reasons why such a one should not be punished"; so here the magistrates, *hitsdiku*, "shall acquit" *the righteous*—declare him innocent, because he is found to be righteous and not wicked. So the Septuagint: "they shall make righteous the righteous"—declare him free from blame, not liable to punishment, acquitted; using the same word with Paul when he speaks of a sinner's justification, i.e., his acquittance from blame and punishment, because of the death of Christ in his stead.

3. *Forty stripes he may give him, and not exceed.* According to God's institution a criminal may receive forty stripes; not one more! But is the institution from above or not that for any offense sentences a man to receive 300, yes, 1,000 stripes? *Thy brother should seem vile,* or be contemptible. By this God teaches us to hate and despise the sin, not the sinner, who is by this chastisement to be amended; as the power which the Lord hath given is "to edification, and not to destruction," 2 Cor. xiii. 10.

4. *Thou shalt not muzzle the ox.* While the oxen were at work, some muzzled their mouths

to hinder them from eating the corn, which Moses here forbids, instructing the people by this symbolical precept to be kind to their servants and laborers, but especially to those who ministered to them in holy things; so Paul applies it in 1 Cor. ix. 9, etc.; 1 Tim. v. 18.

9. *And loose his shoe.* It is difficult to find the reason of these ceremonies of degradation. Perhaps the *shoe* was the emblem of power; and by stripping it off, deprivation of that power and authority was represented. Spitting in the face was a mark of the utmost ignominy; but the Jews, who are legitimate judges in this case, say that the spitting was not in his face, but before his face on the ground. And this is the way in which the Asiatics express their detestation of a person to the present day, intelligent travellers assure us. It has been remarked that the prefix *beth* is seldom applied to *peney;* but when it is it signifies as well "before" as *in* the face. See Josh. xxi. 44; xxiii. 9; Esther ix. 2; and Ezek. xliii. 12, which texts are supposed to be proofs in point. The act of spitting, whether *in* or *before* the face, marked the strong contempt the woman felt for the man who had slighted her. And it appears that the man was ever after disgraced in Israel; for so much is certainly implied in the saying, v. 10: "And his name shall be called in Israel, The house of him that hath his shoe loosed."

13. *Divers weights. Eben vaaben,* "a stone and a stone," because the weights were anciently made of stone, and some had two sets of stones, a light and a heavy. With the latter they bought their wares; by the former they sold them. In our own country this was once a common case; smooth, round, or oval stones were generally chosen by the simple country people for selling their wares, especially such as were sold in pounds and half pounds. And hence the term a "stone weight," which is still in use, though lead or iron be the matter that is used as a counterpoise; but the name itself shows us that a stone of a certain weight was the material formerly used as a weight. See the notes on Lev. xix. 35-36.

14. *Divers measures.* Literally, "an ephah and an ephah"; one large, to buy your neighbor's wares, another small, to sell your own by. See the notes on Exod. xvi. 16 and Lev. xix. 35.

18. *Smote the hindmost of thee.* See the note on Exod. xvii. 8. It is supposed that this command had its final accomplishment in the death of Haman and his ten sons, Esther iii, vii, ix, and from this time the memory and name of Amalek were blotted out from under heaven, for through every period of their history it might be truly said, They "feared not God."

CHAPTER 26

Firstfruits must be offered to God, 1-2. The form of confession to be used on the occasion, 3-11. The third year's tithe is to be given to the Levites and the poor, 12, and the form of confession to be used on this occasion, 13-15. The Israelites are to take Jehovah for their God, and to keep His testimonies, 16-17. And Jehovah is to take them for His people, and make them high above all the nations of the earth, 18-19.

2. *Thou shalt take of the first of all the fruit.* This was intended to keep them in continual remembrance of the kindness of God, in preserving them through so many difficulties and literally fulfilling the promises He had made to them. God being the Author of all their bless-

ings, the firstfruits of the land were consecrated to Him, as the Author of every good and perfect gift.

5. *A Syrian ready to perish was my father.* This passage has been variously understood, both by the ancient versions and by modern commentators. The Vulgate renders it thus: "A Syrian persecuted my father." The Septuagint thus: "My father abandoned Syria." The Targum thus: "Laban the Syrian endeavoured to destroy my father." The Syriac: "My father was led out of Syria into Egypt." The Arabic: "Surely, Laban the Syrian had almost destroyed my father." The Targum of Jonathan ben Uzziel: "Our father Jacob went at first into Syria of Mesopotamia, and Laban sought to destroy him." It is pretty evident from the text that by a *Syrian* we are to understand Jacob, so called from his long residence in Syria with his father-in-law, Laban. And his being ready to perish may signify the hard usage and severe labor he had in Laban's service, by which, as his health was much impaired, so his life might have often been in imminent danger.

8. *With a mighty hand.* See on Deut. iv. 34.

11. *Thou shalt rejoice.* God intends that His followers shall be happy; that they shall eat their bread with gladness and singleness of heart, praising Him. Those who eat their meat grudgingly, under the pretense of their unworthiness, profane God's bounties and shall have no thanks for their voluntary humility. *Thou, and the Levite, and the stranger.* They were to take care to share God's bounties among all those who were dependent on them. The *Levite* has no inheritance; let him rejoice with you. The *stranger* has no home; let him feel you to be his friend and his father.

12. *The third year, which is the year of tithing.* This is supposed to mean the third year after the seventh or sabbatical year, in which the tenths were to be given to the poor. See the law, chap. xiv. 28. But from the letter in both these places it would appear that the tithe was for the Levites, and that this tithe was drawn only once in three years.

14. *I have not . . . given ought thereof for the dead.* That is, I have not consecrated any of it to an idol, which was generally a dead man whom superstition and ignorance had deified. From 1 Cor. x. 27-28 we learn that it was customary to offer that flesh to idols which was afterwards sold publicly in the shambles; probably the blood was poured out before the idol in imitation of the sacrifices offered to the true God. Perhaps the text here alludes to a similar custom.

17. *Thou hast avouched the Lord.* The people *avouch*, publicly declare, that they have taken Jehovah to be their God.

18. *And the Lord hath avouched.* Publicly declared, by the blessings He pours down upon them, that He has taken them to be His peculiar people. Thus the covenant is made and ratified between God and His followers.

19. *Make thee high above all nations.* It is written, "Righteousness exalteth a nation, but sin is a reproach to any people," Prov. xiv. 34. While Israel regarded God's word and kept His testimonies, they were the greatest and most respectable of all nations; but when they forsook God and His law, they became the most contemptible.

CHAPTER 27

Moses commands the people to write the law upon stones, when they shall come to the Promised Land, 1-3. And to set up these stones on Mount Ebal, 4; and to build an altar of unhewn stones, and to offer on it burnt offerings and peace offerings, 5-7. The words to be written plainly, and the people to be exhorted to obedience, 8-10. The six tribes which should stand on Mount Gerizim to bless the people, 11-12. Those who are to stand upon Mount Ebal to curse the transgressors, 13. The different transgressors against whom the curses are to be denounced, 14-26.

2. *Thou shalt set thee up great stones.* How many is not specified, possibly twelve, and possibly only a sufficient number to make a surface large enough to write the blessings and the curses on. *Plaister them with plaister.* Perhaps the original should be translated, "Thou shalt cement them with cement," because this was intended to be a durable monument. In similar cases it was customary to set up a single stone, or a heap, rudely put together, where no cement or mortar appears to have been used; and because this was common, it was necessary to give particular directions when the usual method was not to be followed.

3. *All the words of this law.* After all that has been said by ingenious critics concerning the *law* ordered to be written on these stones, some supposing the whole Mosaic law to be intended, others, only the Decalogue, I am fully of opinion that the (*torah*) law or ordinance in question simply means the blessings and curses mentioned in this and in the following chapter; and indeed these contained a very good epitome of the whole law in all its promises and threatenings, in reference to the whole of its grand moral design.

4. *Set up these stones . . . in mount Ebal.* So the present Hebrew text, but the Samaritan has "Mount Gerizim." On all hands it is allowed that Gerizim abounds with springs, gardens, and orchards, and that it is covered with a beautiful verdure, while Ebal is as naked as and as barren as a rock. On this very account the former was highly proper for the ceremony of blessing, and the latter for the ceremony of cursing.

12. *These shall stand upon mount Gerizim to bless the people.* Instead of *upon* we may translate "by," as the particle *al* is sometimes used; for we do not find that the tribes did stand on either mount, for in Josh. viii. 88, when this direction was reduced to practice, we find the people did not stand on the mountains, but "over against" them on the plain.

15. *Cursed be the man.* Other laws, previously made, had prohibited all these things; and penal sanctions were necessarily understood; but here God more openly declares that he who breaks them is cursed—falls under the wrath and indignation of his Maker and Judge.

16. *Setteth light by his father or his mother.* See the note on Exod. xx. 12.

17. *Removeth his neighbour's landmark.* See before on Deut. xix. 14 and on Exod. xx. 17. And for all the rest of these curses, see the notes on Exodus xx.

18. *The blind to wander out of the way.* A sin against the sixth commandment. See on Exod. xx. 13.

26. *That confirmeth not all the words of this law.* The word *col, all,* is not found in any printed copy of the Hebrew text; but the Samaritan preserves it, and so do six MSS. in the

collections of Kennicott and De Rossi, besides several copies of the Chaldee Targum. The Septuagint also, and Paul in his quotations of this place, Gal. iii. 10. Jerome says that the Jews suppressed the word, that it might not appear that they were bound to fulfill all the precepts in the law of Moses.

CHAPTER 28

The blessings which God pronounces on the obedient, 1-6. Particular privileges which the faithful shall receive, 7-13. The curses pronounced against the ungodly and idolatrous, 14-19. A detailed account of the miseries which should be inflicted on them should they neglect the commandments of the Lord, 20. They shall be smitten with the pestilence, 21; with consumption, fever, etc., 22; drought and barrenness, 23-24; they shall be defeated by their enemies, 25-26; they shall be afflicted with the botch of Egypt, 27; with madness and blindness, 28-29; they shall be disappointed in all their projects, 30; deprived of all their possessions, and afflicted in all their members, 31-35; they and their king shall go into captivity, 36, and become a byword among the nations, 37. Their land shall be unfruitful, and they shall be the lowest of all people, 38-44. All these curses shall come on them should they be disobedient, 45-48. Character of the people by whom they should be subdued, 49-50. Particulars of their dreadful sufferings, 51-57. A recapitulation of their wretchedness, 58-63. The prediction that they shall be scattered among all the nations of the earth, 64-68.

2. *All these blessings shall come on thee.* God shall pour out His blessing from heaven upon thee. *And overtake thee.* Upright men are represented as going to the kingdom of God, and God's blessings as following and overtaking them in their heavenly journey.

3. *In the city*—in all civil employments. *In the field*—in all agricultural pursuits.

4. *Fruit of thy body*—all your children. *Increase of thy kine*, etc.—every animal employed in domestic and agricultural purposes shall be under the especial protection of divine providence.

5. *Thy basket.* Your olive gathering and vintage, as the *basket* was employed to collect those fruits. *Store. Mishereth,* kneading trough, or "remainder"; all that is laid up for future use, as well as what is prepared for present consumption. Some think that by *basket* all their property abroad may be meant, and by *store* all that they have at home, i.e., all that is in the fields, and all that is in the houses.

6. *When thou comest in,* from your employment, you shall find that no evil has happened to the family or dwelling in your absence. *When thou goest out.* Your way shall be made prosperous before you, and you shall have the divine blessing in all your labors. 7. *The Lord shall cause thine enemies.* This is a promise of security from foreign invasion, or total discomfiture of the invaders should they enter the land. *They shall come out against thee one way* —in the firmest and most united manner. *And flee . . . seven ways*—shall be utterly broken, confounded, and finally routed.

8. *The Lord shall command the blessing upon thee.* Everything that you have shall come by divine appointment; you shall have nothing casually, but everything, both spiritual and temporal, shall come by the immediate *command* of God.

9. *The Lord shall establish thee an holy people unto himself.* This is the sum of all blessings, to be made *holy*, and be preserved in holiness. *If thou shalt keep.* Here is the solemn condition; if they did not keep God's testimonies,

taking them for the regulators of their lives, and according to their direction walking in His ways, under the influence and aids of His grace, then the curses, and not the blessings, must be their portion. See vv. 15, etc.

12. *The Lord shall open unto thee his good treasure.* The clouds, so that a sufficiency of showers should descend at all requisite times, and the vegetative principle in the earth should unfold and exert itself, so that their crops should be abundant.

14. *Thou shalt not go aside . . . to the right hand, or to the left.* The way of obedience is a straight way; it goes right forward; he who declines either to right or left from this path goes astray and misses heaven.

20. *Cursing*—this shall be your state; *vexation* —grief, trouble, and anguish of heart; *rebuke*— continual judgments, and marks of God's displeasure.

21. *The pestilence cleave unto thee.* "The Lord shall cement the pestilence or plague to thee." Septuagint, "The Lord will glue the death unto thee." How dreadful a plague it must be that ravages without intermission, any person may conceive who has ever heard the name.

22. *Consumption. Shachepheth,* a t r o p h y through lack of food; from *shacaph,* "to be in want." *Fever. Kaddachath,* from *kadach,* "to be kindled, burn, sparkle"; a burning, inflammatory fever. *Inflammation. Dalleketh,* from *dalak,* "to pursue eagerly, to burn after"; probably a rapidly consuming cancer. *Extreme burning. Charchur,* "burning upon burning," scald upon scald; from *char,* to be "heated, enraged." This probably refers not only to excruciating inflammations on the body but also to the irritation and agony of a mind utterly abandoned by God, and lost to hope. What an accumulation of misery! how formidable! and especially in a land where great heat was prevalent and dreadful. *Sword.* War in general, enemies without, and civil broils within. This was remarkably the case in the last siege of Jerusalem. *Blasting.* Probably either the blighting east wind that ruined vegetation or those awful pestilential winds which suffocate both man and beast wherever they come. These often prevail in different parts of the East. *Mildew. Yerakon,* an exudation of the vegetative juice from different parts of the stalk, by which the maturity and perfection of the plant are utterly prevented. It comes from *yarak,* "to throw out moisture."

Of these seven plagues, the five former were to fall on their bodies, the two latter upon their substance. What a fearful thing it is to fall into the hands of the living God!

23. *Thy heaven . . . shall be brass, and the earth . . . iron.* The atmosphere should not be replenished with aqueous vapors, in consequence of which they should have neither the early nor the latter rain; hence the *earth*—the ground— must be wholly intractable, and through its hardness, incapable of cultivation. God shows them by this that He is Lord of nature; and that drought and sterility are not casualties, but proceed from the immediate appointment of the Lord.

24. *The rain of thy land powder and dust.* As their heavens—atmosphere, clouds, etc.—were to be as brass—yielding no rain—so the surface of the earth must be reduced to powder; and

this, being frequently taken up by the strong winds, would fall down in showers instead of rain.

27. *The Lord will smite thee with the botch.* Shechin, a violent, inflammatory swelling. *Emerods.* Ophalim, from *aphal*, "to be elevated, raised up"; swellings, protuberances; probably the bleeding piles. *Scab.* Garab does not occur as a verb in the Hebrew Bible, but *gharb*, in Arabic, signifies a distemper in the corner of the eye, and may amount to the Egyptian ophthalmia, which is so epidemic and distressing in that country; some suppose the scurvy to be intended. *Itch.* Cheres, a burning itch, probably what is commonly called "St. Anthony's fire." *Whereof thou canst not be healed.* For as they were inflicted by God's justice, they could not, of course, be cured by human art.

28. *The Lord shall smite thee with madness.* Shiggaon, "distraction," so that you shall not know what to do. *And blindness.* Ivvaron, blindness, both physical and mental; the *garab* (v. 27) destroying their eyes, and the judgments of God confounding their understandings. *Astonishment.* Timmahon, stupidity and amazement. By the just judgments of God they were so completely confounded as not to discern the means by which they might prevent or remove their calamities, and to adopt those which led directly to their ruin.

29. *Thou shalt be only oppressed.* Perhaps no people under the sun have been more oppressed and spoiled than the rebellious Jews. And still they *grope at noonday, as the blind gropeth in darkness*—they do not yet discover, notwithstanding the effulgence of the light by which they are encompassed, that the rejection of their own Messiah is the cause of all their calamities.

30. *Thou shalt betroth a wife.* Can any heart imagine anything more grievous than the evils threatened in this and the following verses? To be on the brink of all social and domestic happiness, and then to be suddenly deprived of all, and see an enemy possess and enjoy everything that was dear to them, must excite them to the utmost pitch of distraction and madness.

32. *Thy sons and thy daughters shall be given unto another people.* In several countries, particularly in Spain and Portugal, the children of the Jews have been taken from them by order of government, and educated in the popish faith. There have been some instances of Jewish children being taken from their parents even in Protestant countries.

35. *With a sore botch.* Shechin, an inflammatory swelling, a burning boil. See v. 27.

36-45. Can anything be conceived more dreadful than the calamities threatened in these verses?

48. *Therefore shalt thou serve thine enemies.* Because they would not serve God, therefore they became slaves to men.

49. *A nation . . . from far.* Probably the Romans. *As the eagle flieth.* The very animal on all the Roman standards. The Roman eagle is proverbial. *Whose tongue thou shalt not understand.* The Latin language, than which none was more foreign to the structure and idiom of the Hebrew.

52. *He*—Nebuchadnezzar first (2 Kings xxv. 1-2, etc.), and Titus next; *shall besiege thee*—beset you round on every side, and cast a trench

around you, viz., lines of circumvallation, as our Lord predicted (see Matt. xxiv. 1, etc., and Luke xxi. 5, etc.); *in all thy gates throughout all thy land*—all your fenced cities, which points out that their subjugation should be complete, as both Jerusalem and all their fortified places should be taken. This was done literally by Nebuchadnezzar and the Romans.

56. *The tender and delicate woman.* This was literally fulfilled when Jerusalem was besieged by the Romans; a woman named Mary, of a noble family, driven to distraction by famine, boiled and ate her own child! See a similar case 2 Kings vi. 29; and see on Lev. xxvi. 29.

64. *The Lord shall scatter thee among all people.* How literally has this been fulfilled! The people of the Jews are scattered over every nation under heaven.

65. *No ease . . . a trembling heart, and failing of eyes.* The trembling of heart may refer to their state of continual insecurity, being, under every kind of government, proscribed, and, even under the most mild, uncertain of toleration and protection; and the failing of eyes, to their vain and ever-disappointed expectation of the Messiah.

68. *And the Lord shall bring thee into Egypt again.* That is, into another state of slavery and bondage similar to that of Egypt, out of which they had been lately brought. *And there ye shall be sold,* that is, be exposed to sale, or "expose yourself to sale," as the word *hithmaccartem* may be rendered. They were vagrants, and wished to become slaves that they might be provided with the necessaries of life. *And no man shall buy you;* even the Romans thought it a reproach to have a Jew for a slave, they had become so despicable to all mankind. When Jerusalem was taken by Titus, many of the captives which were above seventeen years of age were sent into the works in Egypt. See Josephus, *antiq.*, b. xii., c. 1, 2, *War* b. vi., c. 9, s. 2.

CHAPTER 29

A recapitulation of God's gracious dealings with Israel, 1-8. An exhortation to obedience, and to enter into covenant with their God, that they and their posterity may be established in the good land, 9-15. They are to remember the abominations of Egypt, and to avoid them, 16-17. He who hardens his heart, when he hears these curses, shall be utterly consumed, 18-21. Their posterity shall be astonished at the desolations that shall fall upon them, 22-23; shall inquire the reason, and shall be informed that the Lord has done thus to them because of their disobedience and idolatry, 24-28. A caution against prying too curiously into the secrets of the divine providence, and to be contented with what God has revealed, 29.

1. *These are the words of the covenant.* This verse seems properly to belong to the preceding chapter, as a widely different subject is taken up at v. 2 of this; and it is distinguished as the sixty-ninth verse in some of the most correct copies of the Hebrew Bible. *Commanded Moses to make.* Lichroth, "to cut," alluding to the covenant sacrifice which was offered on the occasion and divided, as is explained, Gen. xv. 18. *Beside the covenant which he made . . . in Horeb.* What is mentioned here is an additional institution to the ten words given on Horeb; and the curses denounced here are different from those denounced against the transgressors of the Decalogue.

4. *The Lord hath not given you an heart.* Some critics read this verse interrogatively:

"And hath not God given you a heart?" because they suppose that God could not reprehend them for the nonperformance of a duty, when He had neither given them a mind to perceive the obligation of it nor strength to perform it had that obligation been known. Though this is strictly just, yet there is no need for the interrogation, as the words only imply that they had not such a heart, not because God had not given them all the means of knowledge, and helps of His grace and Spirit, which were necessary; but they had not made a faithful use of their advantages, and therefore they had not that wise, loving, and obedient heart which they otherwise might have had. Hence God himself is represented as grieved because they were unchanged and disobedient: "O that there were such an heart in them, that they would fear me, and keep all my commandments always, that it might be well with them, and with their children for ever!" See chap. v. 29.

5. *Your clothes are not waxen old.* See on chap. viii. 4.

6. *Ye have not eaten bread.* That is, you have not been supported in an ordinary providential way; I have been continually working miracles for you, *that ye might know that I am the Lord.* Thus we find that God had furnished them with all the means of this knowledge, and that the means were ineffectual, not because they were not properly calculated to answer God's gracious purpose, but because the people were not workers with God; consequently they received the grace of God in vain. See 2 Cor. vi. 1.

10. *Ye stand . . . all of you before the Lord.* They were about to enter into a covenant with God; and as a covenant implies two parties contracting, God is represented as being present, and they and all their families, old and young, come before Him.

12. *That thou shouldest enter.* Leaber, "to pass through," that is, between the separated parts of the covenant sacrifice. See Gen. xv. 18.

15. *Him that standeth here.* The present generation. *Him that is not here*—all future generations of this people.

18. *A root that beareth gall and wormwood.* That is, as the apostle expresses it, Heb. iii. 12, "an evil heart of unbelief, in departing from the living God," for to this place he evidently refers.

19. *To add drunkenness to thirst.* A proverbial expression denoting the utmost indulgence in all sensual gratifications.

26. *Gods . . . whom he had not given unto them.* This is an unhappy translation. *Chalak* signifies a "portion, lot, inheritance," and God is frequently represented in Scripture as the Portion or Inheritance of His people. Here, therefore, I think the original should be rendered, "And there was no portion to them," that is, the gods they served could neither supply their wants nor save their souls.

29. *The secret things belong unto the Lord.* This verse has been variously translated. The simple general meaning seems to be this: "What God has thought proper to reveal He has revealed; what He has revealed is essential to the well-being of man, and this revelation is intended not for the present time merely, nor for one people, but for all succeeding generations. The things which He has not revealed concern

not man but God alone, and are therefore not to be inquired after." Thus, then, the things that are hidden belong unto the Lord, those that are revealed belong unto us and our children.

CHAPTER 30

Gracious promises are given to the penitent, 1-6. The Lord will circumcise their hearts, and put all these curses on their enemies, if they hearken to His voice and keep His testimonies, 7-10. The word is near to them, and easy to be understood, 11-14. Life and death, a blessing and a curse, are set before them; and they are exhorted to love the Lord, obey His voice, and cleave unto Him, that they may inherit the land promised to Abraham, 15-20.

1. *When all these things are come upon thee, the blessing and the curse.* So fully did God foresee the bad use these people would make of their free agency in resisting the Holy Ghost that He speaks of their sin and punishment as certain; yet at the same time shows how they might turn to himself and live, even while He was pouring out His indignation upon them because of their transgressions.

3. *Gather thee from all the nations.* This must refer to a more extensive captivity than that which they suffered in Babylon.

5. *Will bring thee into the land.* As this promise refers to a return from a captivity in which they had been scattered among all nations, consequently it is not the Babylonish captivity which is intended; and the repossession of their land must be different from that which was consequent on their return from Chaldea.

6. *God will circumcise thine heart.* This promise remains yet to be fulfilled. Their heart, as a people, has never yet been circumcised; nor have the various promises in this chapter ever yet been fulfilled. There remaineth, therefore, a rest for this people of God. Now, as the law, properly speaking, made no provision for the circumcision of the heart, which implies the remission of sins, and purification of the soul from all unrighteousness; and as circumcision itself was only a sign of spiritual good, consequently the promise here refers to the days of the Messiah, and to this all the prophets and all the apostles give witness: for "circumcision is that of the heart, in the spirit, and not in the letter," Rom. ii. 29; and the genuine followers of God "are circumcised with the circumcision made without hands . . . by the circumcision of Christ," Col. ii. 11-12. Hence we see these promises cannot be fulfilled to the Jews but in their embracing the gospel of Christ.

11. *This commandment . . . is not hidden.* Not too "wonderful" or difficult for thee to comprehend or perform, as the word *niphleth* implies. *Neither is it far off*—the word or doctrine of salvation shall be proclaimed in your own land; for He is to be born in Bethlehem of Judah, who is to feed and save Israel; and the Prophet who is to teach them is to be raised up from among their brethren.

12. *It is not in heaven.* Shall not be communicated in that way in which the prophets received the living oracles; but the Word shall be made flesh, and dwell among you.

13. *Neither is it beyond the sea.* You shall not be obliged to travel for it to distant nations, because "salvation is of the Jews."

14. *But the word is very nigh unto thee.* The doctrine of salvation preached by the apostles;

n thy mouth—the promises of redemption made by the prophets forming a part of every Jew's creed; *in thy heart*—the power to believe with the heart unto righteousness, that the tongue may make confession unto salvation. In this way, it is evident, Paul understood these passages; see Rom. x. 6, etc.

15. *Life and good.* Present and future blessings. *Death and evil.* Present and future miseries: termed, v. 19, "Life and death, blessing and cursing." Were there no such thing as *free will* in man, who could reconcile these sayings with either sincerity or common sense? God has made the human will free, and there is no power or influence either in heaven, earth, or hell, except the power of God, that can deprive it of its free volitions; of its power to will and nill, to choose and refuse, to act or not act or force it to sin against God. Hence man is accountable for his actions, because they are his; were he necessitated by fate, or sovereign constraint, they could not be his.

20. *That thou mayest love the Lord.* Without love there can be no obedience. *Obey his voice.* Without obedience love is fruitless and dead. *And . . . cleave unto him.* Without close attachment and perseverance, temporary love, however sincere and fervent—temporary obedience, however disinterested, energetic, and pure while it lasts—will be ultimately ineffectual. He alone who "endureth to the end shall be saved."

CHAPTER 31

Moses, being one hundred and twenty years old and about to die, calls the people together, and exhorts them to courage and obedience. 1-6. Delivers a charge to Joshua, 7-8. Delivers the law which he had written to the priests, with a solemn charge that they should read it every seventh year, publicly to all the people, 9-13. The Lord calls Moses and Joshua to the Tabernacle, 14. He appears to them, informs Moses of his approaching death, and delivers to him a prophetical and historical song, or poem, which he is to leave with Israel, for their instruction and reproof, 15-21. Moses writes the song the same day, and teaches it to the Israelites, 22; gives Joshua a charge, 23; finishes writing the book of the law, 24. Commands the Levites to lay it up in the side of the ark, 25-26. Predicts their rebellions, 27. Orders the elders to be gathered together, and shows them what evils would befall the people in the latter days, 28-29, and repeats the song to them, 30.

2. *I am an hundred and twenty years old.* The life of Moses, the great prophet of God and lawgiver of the Jews, was exactly the same in length as the time Noah employed in preaching righteousness to the antediluvian world. These 120 years were divided into three remarkable periods: 40 years he lived in Egypt, in Pharaoh's court, acquiring all the learning and wisdom of the Egyptians (see Acts vii. 20, 23); 40 years he sojourned in the land of Midian in a state of preparation for his great and important mission (Acts vii. 29-30); and 40 years he guided, led, and governed the Israelites under the express direction and authority of God.

3. *Joshua, he shall go over before thee.* See on Num. xxvii. 17, etc.

6. *Be strong. Chizku,* the same word that is used Exod. iv. 21; ix. 15, for hardening Pharaoh's heart. The Septuagint, in this and the following verse, have, "Play the man, and be strong"; and from this Paul seems to have borrowed his ideas, 1 Cor. xvi. 13: "Stand firm in the faith; play the man"—act like heroes; be vigorous.

8. *The Lord . . . doth go before thee.* To prepare your way, and to direct you. *He will be with thee.* Accompany you in all your journeys, and assist you in all your enterprises. *He will not fail thee.* Your expectation, however strong and extensive, shall never be disappointed; you cannot expect too much from Him. *Neither forsake thee.* He knows that without Him you can do nothing, and therefore He will continue with you, and in such a manner too that the excellence of the power shall appear to be of Him, and not of man.

9. *Moses wrote this law.* Not the whole Pentateuch, but either the discourses and precepts mentioned in the preceding chapters or the Book of Deuteronomy, which is most likely.

10-11. *At the end of every seven years . . . thou shalt read this law.* Every seventh year was a year of release, chap. xv. 1, at which time the people's minds, being under a peculiar degree of solemnity, were better disposed to hear and profit by the words of God. I suppose on this ground also that the whole Book of Deuteronomy is meant, as it alone contains an epitome of the whole Pentateuch. And in this way some of the chief Jewish rabbins understand this place.

It is strange that this commandment, relative to a public reading of the law every seven years, should have been rarely attended to. It does not appear that from the time mentioned in Josh. viii. 30, at which time this public reading first took place, till the reign of Jehoshaphat, 2 Chron. xvii. 7, there was any public seventh-year reading—a period of 530 years. The next seventh-year reading was not till the eighteenth year of the reign of Josiah, 2 Chron. xxxiv. 30, a space of 282 years. Nor do we find any other publicly mentioned from this time till the return from the Babylonish captivity, Neh. viii. 2. Nor is there any other on record from that time to the destruction of Jerusalem.

16. *Behold, thou shalt sleep with thy fathers. Shocheb,* thou "shalt lie down"; it signifies to rest, take rest in sleep, and, metaphorically, "to die."

18. *I will surely hide my face.* Withdraw My approbation and My protection. This is a general meaning of the word in Scripture.

19. *Write ye this song.* The song which follows in the next chapter. Things which were of great importance and of common concern were, among the ancients, put into verse, as this was found the best method of keeping them in remembrance, especially in those times when writing was little practiced.

21. *This song shall testify against them.* Because in it their general defection is predicted, but in such a way as to show them how to avoid the evil; and if they did not avoid the evil, and the threatened punishment should come upon them, then the song should testify against them, by showing that they had been sufficiently warned, and might have lived to God, and so escaped those disasters.

26. *Take this book of the law.* The standard copy to which all transcripts must ultimately refer; another copy was put into the hands of the priests. See the note on v. 9.

27. *While I am yet alive . . . ye have been rebellious.* Such was the disposition of this people to act contrary to moral goodness that Moses felt himself justified in inferring what would take place from what had already happened.

CHAPTER 32

The prophetical and historical song of Moses, showing forth the nature of God's doctrine, 1-3. The character of God, 4. The corruption of the people, 5-6. They are called to remember God's kindness, 7, and His dealings with them during their travels in the wilderness, 8-14. Their ingratitude and iniquity, 15-18. They are threatened with His judgments, 19-28. A pathetic lamentation over them because of their sins, 29-35. Gracious purposes in their behalf, mixed with reproaches for their manifold idolatries, and threatenings against His enemies, 36-42. A promise of salvation to the Gentiles, 43. Moses, having finished the song, warmly exhorts the people to obedience, 44-47. God calls him up to the mount, that he may see the good land and then die, 48-52.

1. On the inimitable excellence of this ode much has been written by commentators, critics, and poets; and it is allowed by the best judges to contain a specimen of almost every species of excellence in composition. It is so thoroughly poetic that even the dull Jews themselves found they could not write it in the prose form; and hence it is distinguished as poetry in every Hebrew Bible by being written in its own hemistichs or short half-lines, which is the general form of the Hebrew poetry; and were it translated in the same way it would be more easily understood. The song itself has suffered by both transcribers and translators, the former having mistaken some letters in different places, and made wrong combinations of them in others. *Give ear, O ye heavens.* Let angels and men hear, and let this testimony of God be registered in both heaven and earth. Heaven and earth are appealed to as *permanent* witnesses.

2. *My doctrine. Likchi,* from *lakach,* to "take, carry away"; to "attract or gain over the heart" by eloquence or persuasive speech. *Shall drop as the rain.* It shall come drop by drop as the shower, beginning slowly and distinctly, but increasing more and more till the plenitude of righteousness is poured down, and the whole canon of divine revelation completed. *My speech shall distil as the dew. Imrathi;* My familiar, friendly, and affectionate speeches shall descend gently and softly, on the ear and the heart, as the dew, moistening and refreshing all around. In hot regions *dew* is often a substitute for rain; without it there could be no fertility, especially in those places where rain seldom falls. And in such places only can the metaphor here used be felt in its perfection. *As the small rain. Seirim,* from *saar,* to be "rough" or "tempestuous"; sweeping showers, accompanied with a strong gale of wind. *And as the showers. Rebibim,* from *rabah,* "to multiply, to increase greatly"; shower after shower, or rather a continual rain, whose drops are multiplied beyond calculation, upon the earth; alluding perhaps to the rainy seasons in the East, or to those early and latter rains so essentially necessary for the vegetation and perfection of the grain.

No doubt these various expressions point out that great variety in the word or revelation of God whereby it is suited to every place, occasion, person, and state; being profitable for doctrine, reproof, and edification in righteousness. Hence the apostle says that God "at sundry times and in divers manners spake in time past unto the fathers by the prophets," and "in these last times [has] spoken unto us by his Son, Heb. i. 1-2. By every prophet, evangelist, and apostle, God speaks a particular language; all is His *doctrine,* His great system of instruction, for the information and salvation of the souls of men. But some portions are like the "sweeping showers," in which the tempest of God's wrath appears against sinners. Others are like the "incessant showers of gentle rain," preparing the soil for the germination of the grain, and causing it to take root. And others still are like the "dew," mildly and gently insinuating convictions, persuasions, reproofs, and consolations.

4. *He is the Rock.* The word *tsur* is rendered "Creator" by some eminent critics. Rab. Moses ben Maimon observes that the word *tsur,* which is ordinarily translated "rock," signifies "origin, fountain, first cause," and in this way it should be translated here: "He is the First Principle; His work is perfect."

5. *Their spot is not the spot of his children.* This verse is variously translated and variously understood. "They are corrupted, not his, children of pollution."—Kennicott. "They are corrupt, they are not his children, they are blotted."—Houbigant. This is according to the Samaritan. The interpretation commonly given to these words is as unfounded as it is exceptionable: "God's children have their spots, i.e., their sins, but sin in them is not like sin in others; in others sin is exceedingly sinful, but God does not see the sins of His children as He sees the sins of His enemies." Unfortunately for this bad doctrine, there is no foundation for it in the sacred text, which, though very obscure, may be thus translated: "He [Israel] hath corrupted himself. They [the Israelites] are not His children: they are spotted." Coverdale renders the whole passage thus: "The froward and overthwart generation have marred themselves to himward, and are not his children because of their deformity." This is the sense of the verse. Let it be observed that the word *spot,* which is repeated in our translation, occurs but once in the original, and the marginal reading is greatly to be preferred: "He hath corrupted to himself, that they are not his children, that is their blot."

8. *When the most High divided to the nations.* Verses 8 and 9, says Dr. Kennicott, give us express authority for believing that the earth was very early divided in consequence of a divine command, and probably by *lot* (see Acts xvii. 26); and as Africa is called the land of Ham (Ps. lxxviii. 51; cv. 23, 27; cvi. 22), probably that country fell to him and to his descendants, at the same time that Europe fell to Japheth, and Asia to Shem, with a particular reserve of Palestine to be the Lord's portion, for some one peculiar people. *He set the bounds of the people according to the number of the children of Israel.* The Septuagint is very curious, "He established the bounds of the nations according to the number of the angels of God." The meaning of the passage seems to be that, when God divided the earth among mankind, He reserved twelve lots, according to the number of the sons of Jacob, which He was now about to give to their descendants, according to His promise.

9. *The Lord's portion is his people.* What an astonishing saying! As holy souls take God for their portion, so God takes them for His portion. He represents himself as happy in His followers; and they are infinitely happy in, and satisfied with, God as their portion. This is what is implied in being a saint. He who is seeking for an earthly portion has little commerce with the Most High.

10. *He*—the Lord, *found him*—Jacob, in his descendants, *in a desert land*—the wilderness. *He led him about* forty years in this wilderness, Deut. viii. 2, or *yesobebenhu;* "he compassed him about," i.e., God defended them on all hands, and in all places. *He instructed him*—taught them that astonishing law through which we have now almost passed, giving them statutes and judgments which, for depth of wisdom, and correct political adaptation to times, places, and circumstances, are so wondrously constructed as essentially to secure the comfort, peace, and happiness of the individual, and the prosperity and permanency of the moral system. *He kept him as the apple of his eye.* Nothing can exceed the force and delicacy of this expression. As deeply concerned and as carefully attentive as man can be for the safety of his eyesight, so was God for the protection and welfare of this people. How amazing this condescension!

11. *As an eagle stirreth up her nest,* flutters over her brood to excite them to fly; or, as some think, disturbs her nest to oblige the young ones to leave it; so God by His plagues in Egypt obliged the Israelites, otherwise very reluctant, to leave a place which He appeared by His judgments to have devoted to destruction. *Fluttereth over her young. Yeracheph,* broodeth over them, communicating to them a portion of her own vital warmth. So did God, by the influences of His Spirit, enlighten, encourage, and strengthen their minds. It is the same word which is used in Gen. i. 2. *Spreadeth abroad her wings.* In order, not only to teach them how to fly, but to bear them when weary. For to this fact there seems an allusion, it having been generally believed that the eagle, through extraordinary affection for her young, takes them upon her back when they are weary of flying. The same figure is used in Exod. xix. 4.

12. *So the Lord alone did lead him.* By His power, and by His only, were they brought out of Egypt, and supported in the wilderness. *And there was no strange god.* They had help from no other quarter. The Egyptian idols were not able to save their own votaries; but God not only saved His people, but destroyed the Egyptians.

13. *He made him ride. Yarkibehu,* "he will cause him to ride." All the verbs here are in the future tense, because this is a prophecy of the prosperity they should possess in the Promised Land. The Israelites were to *ride*—exult, *on the high places,* the mountains and hills of their land, in which they are promised the highest degrees of prosperity, as even the rocky part of the country should be rendered fertile by the peculiar benediction of God. *Suck honey out of the rock, and oil out of the flinty rock.* This promise states that even the most barren places in the country should yield an abundance of aromatic flowers, from which the bees should collect *honey* in abundance; and even the tops of the rocks afford sufficient support for olive trees, from the fruit of which they should extract oil in abundance; and all this should be occasioned by the peculiar blessing of God upon the land.

14. *Fat of kidneys of wheat.* Almost every person knows that the kidney is enveloped in a coat of the purest fat in the body of the animal, for which several anatomical reasons might be given. As the kidney itself is to the abundantly surrounding fat, so is the germ of the grain to the lobes. The expression here may be considered as a very strong and peculiarly happy figure to point out the finest wheat, containing the healthiest and most vigorous germ, growing in a very large and nutritive grain; and consequently the whole figure points out to us a species of wheat, equally excellent for both seed and bread. *Pure blood of the grape.* Red wine, or the pure juice of whatever color, expressed from the grapes, without any adulteration or mixture with water; *blood* here is synonymous with juice. This intimates that their vines should be of the best kind, and their wine in abundance, and of the most delicious flavor.

15. *Jeshurun.* The "upright." This appellative is here put for Israel, and as it comes from *yashar,* "he was right, straight," may be intended to show that the people who once not only promised fair, but were really upright, walking in the paths of righteousness, should, in the time signified by the prophet, not only revolt from God, but actually fight against Him; like a full-fed horse, who not only will not bear the harness, but breaks away from his master, and endeavors to kick him as he struggles to get loose. All this is spoken prophetically, and is intended as a warning, that the evil might not take place. For were the transgression unavoidable, it must be the effect of some necessitating cause, which would destroy the turpitude of the action, as it referred to Israel; for if evil were absolutely unavoidable, no blame could attach to the unfortunate agent, who could only consider himself the miserable instrument of a dire necessity. See a case in point, 1 Sam. xxiii. 11-12, where the prediction appears in the most absolute form, and yet the evil was prevented by the person receiving the prediction as a warning.

The Rock of his salvation. He ceased to depend on the fountain whence his salvation issued; and thinking highly of himself, he lightly esteemed his God; and having ceased to depend on Him, his fall became inevitable. The figure is admirably well supported through the whole verse. We see, first, a miserable, lean steed, taken under the care and into the keeping of a master who provides him with an abundance of provender. We see, secondly, this horse waxing fat under this keeping. We see him, thirdly, breaking away from his master, leaving his rich pasturage, and running to the wilderness, unwilling to bear the yoke or harness, or to make any returns for his master's care and attention. We see, fourthly, whence this conduct proceeds —from a want of consciousness that his strength depends upon his master's care and keeping; and a lack of consideration that leanness and wretchedness must be the consequence of his leaving his master's service, and running off from his master's pasturage. How easy to apply all these points to the case of the Israelites! and how illustrative of their former and latter state! And how powerfully do they apply to the case of many called Christians who, having increased in riches, forget that God from whose hand alone those mercies flowed!

17. *They sacrificed unto devils.* The original word *shedim* has been variously understood. The Syriac, Chaldee, Targums of Jerusalem and Jonathan, and the Samaritans retain the original word: the Vulgate, Septuagint, Arabic, Persic,

Coptic, and Anglo-Saxon have devils or demons. The Septuagint has, "They sacrificed to demons"; the Vulgate copies the Septuagint. *New gods that came newly up. Mikkarob bau,* "which came up from their neighbours"; viz., the Moabites and Amorites, whose gods they received and worshipped on their way through the wilderness, and often afterwards.

18. *Of the Rock that begat thee. Tsur,* the "first cause," the Fountain of your being. See the note on v. 4.

19. *When the Lord saw it.* More literally, "And the Lord saw it, and through indignation He reprobated His sons and His daughters." That is, When the Lord shall see such conduct, He shall be justly incensed, and so reject and deliver up to captivity His sons and daughters.

20. *Children in whom is no faith. Lo emon bam,* "There is no steadfastness in them"; they can never be depended on. They are fickle, because they are faithless.

21. *They have moved me to jealousy.* This verse contains a very pointed promise of the calling of the Gentiles, in consequence of the rejection of the Jews, threatened in v. 19; and to this great event it is applied by Paul, Rom. x. 19.

22. *The lowest hell. Sheol tachtith,* the very deepest destruction; a total extermination, so that *the earth,* their land, and its *increase,* and all their property, should be seized; and the *foundations of the mountains,* their strongest fortresses, should be razed to the ground. All this was fulfilled in a most remarkable manner in the last destruction of Jerusalem by the Romans, so that of the fortifications of that city not one stone was left on another. See the notes on Matthew xxiv.

23. *I will spend mine arrows upon them.* The judgments of God in general are termed the "arrows of God," Job vi. 4; Ps. xxxviii. 2-3; xci. 5; see also Ezek. v. 16; Jer. i. 14; 2 Sam. xxii. 14-15. In this and the following verses, to the twenty-eighth inclusive, God threatens this people with every species of calamity that could possibly fall upon man. How strange it is that, having this law continually in their hands, they should not discern those threatened judgments, and cleave to the Lord that they might be averted!

24. *They shall be burnt with hunger.* Their land shall be cursed, and famine shall prevail. This is one of the arrows. *Burning heat.* No showers to cool the atmosphere; or rather boils, blains, and pestilential fevers; this was a second. *Bitter destruction.* The plague; this was a third. *Teeth of beasts . . . with the poison of serpents.* The beasts of the field should multiply upon and destroy them—this was a fourth; and poisonous serpents, infesting all their steps, and whose mortal bite should produce the utmost anguish, were to be a fifth arrow. Added to all these, the *sword* of their enemies—*terror* among themselves, v. 25, and captivity were to complete their ruin, and thus the arrows of God were to be spent upon them.

27. *Were it not that I feared the wrath of the enemy.* Houbigant and others contend that *wrath* here refers not to the *enemy,* but to God, and that the passage should be thus translated: "Indignation for the adversary deters me, lest their enemies should be alienated, and say, The strength of our hands, and not of the Lord's,

hath done this." Had not God punished them in such a way as proved that His hand and not the hand of man had done it, the heathens would have boasted of their prowess, and Jehovah would have been blasphemed, as not being able to protect His worshippers or to punish their infidelities. Titus, when he took Jerusalem, was so struck with the strength of the place that he acknowledged that, if God had not delivered it into his hands, the Roman armies never could have taken it.

29. *That they would consider their latter end! Archaritham,* properly, "their latter times"—the glorious days of the Messiah, who, according to the flesh, should spring up among them. Should they carefully consider this subject, and receive the promised Saviour, they would consequently act as persons under infinite obligations to God; His strength would be their shield, and then—

30. *How should one chase a thousand?* If therefore they had not forgotten their Rock, God, their Author and Defense, it could not possibly have come to pass that a thousand of them should flee before *one* of their enemies.

31. *For their rock.* The gods and pretended protectors of the Romans. *Is not as our Rock.* Have neither power nor influence like our God. *Our enemies themselves being judges.* For they often acknowledged the irresistible power of that God who fought for Israel. See Exod. xiv. 25; Num. xxiii. 8-12, 19-21; 1 Sam. iv. 8.

32. *For their vine is of the vine of Sodom.* The Jews are as wicked and rebellious as the Sodomites; for by the *vine* the inhabitants of the land are signified; see Isa. v. 2, 7. *Their grapes.* Their actions, are *gall* and wormwood—producing nothing but mischief and misery to themselves and others. *Their clusters are bitter.* Their united exertions, as well as their individual acts, are sin, and only sin, continually. That by *vine* is meant the people, and by *grapes* their moral conduct, is evident from Isa. v. 1-7. It is very likely that the grapes produced about the Lake Asphaltitis, where Sodom and Gomorrah formerly stood, were not only of an acrid, disagreeable taste, but of a deleterious quality; and to this, it is probable, Moses here alludes.

33. *Their wine.* Their system of doctrines and teaching, *is the poison of dragons,* fatal and destructive to all them who follow it.

34. *Sealed up among my treasures?* Deeds or engagements by which persons were bound at a specified time to fulfil certain conditions were *sealed* and *laid up* in places of safety; so here God's justice is pledged to avenge the quarrel of His broken covenant on the disobedient Jews, but the time and manner were sealed in His treasures, and known only to himself. Hence it is said,

35. *Their foot shall slide in due time.* But Calmet thinks that this verse is spoken against the Canaanites, the enemies of the Jewish people.

36. *The Lord shall judge his people.* He has an absolute right over them as their Creator, and authority to punish them for their rebellions as their Sovereign; yet He will *repent himself*—He will change His manner of conduct towards them, *when he seeth that their power is gone*—when they are entirely subjugated by their adversaries, so that their political power is en-

tirely destroyed; *and there is none shut up, or left*—not one strong place untaken, and not one family left, all being carried into captivity, or scattered into strange lands. Or, He will do justice to His people, and avenge them of their adversaries; see v. 35.

37. *He shall say.* He shall begin to expostulate with them, to awaken them to a due sense of their ingratitude and rebellion. This may refer to the preaching of the gospel to them in the latter days.

39. *See now that I . . . am he.* Be convinced that God alone can save, and God alone can destroy, and that your idols can neither hurt nor help you. *I kill, and I make alive.* My mercy is as great as my justice, for I am as ready to save the penitent as I was to punish the rebellious.

40. *For I lift up my hand to heaven.* See concerning oaths and appeals to God in the note on chap. vi. 13.

42. *From the beginning of revenges.* The word *paroth*, rendered *revenges*, a sense in which it never appears to be taken, has rendered this place very perplexed and obscure. Probably *merosh paroth* may be properly translated, "from the naked head"—The enemy shall have nothing to shield him from My vengeance; the crown of dignity shall fall off, and even the helmet be no protection against the sword and arrows of the Lord.

43. *Rejoice, O ye nations.* You Gentiles, for the casting off of the Jews shall be the means of your ingathering with *his people,* for they shall not be utterly cast off. (See Rom. xv. 9, for in this way the apostle applied it.) But how shall the Gentiles be called, and the Jews have their iniquity purged? *He will be merciful unto his land, and, to his people; vechipper,* "He shall cause an atonement" to be made for His land and people; i.e., Jesus Christ, the long-promised Messiah, shall be crucified for Jews and Gentiles, and the way to the holiest be made plain by His blood. The people have long been making atonements for themselves, but to none effect, for their atonements were but signs, and not the thing signified, for the body is Christ; now the Lord himself makes an atonement, for the Lamb of God alone taketh away the sin of the world. This is a very proper and encouraging conclusion to the awfully important matter of this poem. Israel shall be long scattered, peeled, and punished, but they shall have mercy in the latter times; they also shall rejoice with the Gentiles, in the common salvation purchased by the blood of the Saviour of all mankind.

44. *And Moses came.* Probably from the Tabernacle, where God had given him this prophetic ode, and he rehearsed it in the ears of the people.

46. *Set your hearts unto all the words.* Another proof that all these awful denunciations of divine wrath, though delivered in an absolute form, were only declaratory of what God would do if they rebelled against Him.

47. *Through this thing ye shall prolong your days.* Instead of being cut off, as God here threatens, you shall be preserved and rendered prosperous in the land which, when they passed over Jordan, they should possess.

49. *Get thee up into this mountain Abarim.* The mount of the "passages," i.e., of the Israel-

ites when they entered into the Promised Land. See the notes on Num. xxvii. 12.

50. *And die in the mount . . . as Aaron.* Some have supposed that Moses was translated; but if so, then Aaron was translated, for what is said of the death of the one is said of the death of the other.

51. *Ye trespassed against me . . . at the waters of Meribah.* See the note on Num. xx. 8.

52. *Thou shalt see the land before thee.* See Num. xxvii. 12, etc. How glorious to depart out of this life with God in his heart and heaven in his eye! his work, his great, unparalleled usefulness, ending only with his life. The serious reader will surely join in the following pious ejaculation of Charles Wesley, one of the best Christian poets:

> *O that without a lingering groan*
> *I may the welcome word receive;*
> *My body with my charge lay down,*
> *And cease at once to work and live!*

CHAPTER 33

Moses delivers a prophetical blessing to the children of Israel, 1. The introduction, 2-5. Prophetic declarations concerning Reuben, 6; concerning Judah. 7; concerning Levi, 8-11; concerning Benjamin, 12; concerning Joseph, 13-17; concerning Zebulun. 18-19; concerning Gad. 20-21; concerning Dan, 22; concerning Naphtali, 23; concerning Asher, 24-25. The glory of the God of Jeshurun, and the glorious privileges of His true followers, 26-29.

1. *And this is the blessing, wherewith Moses . . . blessed.* The general nature of this solemn introduction, says Kennicott, is to show the foundation which Moses had for blessing his brethren, viz., because God had frequently manifested His glory in their behalf; and the several parts of this introduction are disposed in the following order: (1) The manifestation of the divine glory on Sinai, as it was prior in time and more magnificent in splendor, is mentioned first. (2) That God manifested His glory at Seir is evident from Judg. v. 4: "Lord. when thou wentest out of Seir, when thou marchedst out of the fields of Edom. the earth trembled. and the heavens dropped." (3) The next place is Paran, where the "glory of the Lord appeared . . . before all the children of Israel," Num. xiv. 10.

2. Instead of *he came with ten thousands of saints,* by which our translators have rendered *meribeboth kodesh,* Kennicott reads Meribah-Kadesh, the name of a place; for we find that, towards the end of forty years, the Israelites came to Kadesh, Num. xx. 1, which was also called Meribah, on account of their contentious opposition to the determinations of God in their favor, v. 13; and there the glory of the Lord again appeared, as we are informed in v. 6. These four places, *Sinai, Seir, Paran,* and *Meribah-Kadesh,* mentioned by Moses in the text, are the identical places where God manifested His glory in a fiery appearance, the more illustriously to proclaim His special providence over and care of Israel.

3. *Yea, he loved the people.* This is the inference which Moses makes from those glorious appearances, that God truly loved the people; and that all His saints, *kedoshaiv,* the people whom He had "consecrated" to himself, were under His especial benediction; and that in order to make them a holy nation, God had

displayed His glory on Mount Sinai, where they had fallen prostrate at His feet with the humblest adoration, sincerely promising the most affectionate obedience; and that God had there commanded them a *law* which was to be the possession and inheritance of the children of Jacob, v. 4. And to crown the whole, He had not only blessed them as their Lawgiver, but had also vouchsafed to be their King, v. 5.

6. *Let Reuben live, and not die.* Though his life and his blessings have been forfeited by his transgression with his father's concubine, Gen. xlix. 3-4, and in his rebellion with Korah, Num. xvi. 1, etc., let him not become extinct as a tribe in Israel. "It is very usual," says Mr. Ainsworth, "in the Scripture, to set down things of importance and earnestness, by affirmation of the one part, and denial of the other; Isa. xxxviii. 1: 'Thou shalt die, and not live'; Num. iv. 19: 'That they may live, and not die'; Ps. cxviii. 17: 'I shall not die, but live'; Gen. xliii. 8: 'That we may live, and not die.' "

And let not his men be few. It is possible that this clause belongs to Simeon. In the Alexandrian copy of the Septuagint the clause stands thus: "Let Simeon be very numerous," but none of the other versions insert the word. As the negative particle is not in the Hebrew, but is supplied in our translation, and the word Simeon is found in one of the most ancient and most authentic copies of the Septuagint version; and as Simeon is nowhere else mentioned here, if not implied in this place, probably the clause anciently stood: "Let Reuben live, and not die; but let the men of Simeon be few." That this tribe was small when compared with the rest, and with what it once was, is evident enough from the first census, taken after they came out of Egypt, and that in the plains of Moab nearly forty years after. In the first, Simeon was 59,300; in the last, 22,200, a decrease of 37,100 men!

7. *And this is the blessing of Judah.* Though the word *blessing* is not in the text, yet it may be implied from v. 1; but probably the words, "he spake," are those which should be supplied: "And this he spake of Judah, Lord, hear the voice of Judah." *Let his hands be sufficient for him*—let him have a sufficiency of warriors always to support the tribe, and vindicate its rights; and let his enemies never be able to prevail against him! Three things are expressed here: (1) That the tribe of Judah, conscious of its weakness, shall depend on the Most High, and make prayer and supplication to Him; (2) That God will hear such prayer; and, (3) That his hands shall be increased, and that he shall prevail over his enemies. This blessing has a striking affinity with that which this tribe received from Jacob, Gen. xlix. 9; and both may refer to our blessed Lord, who sprang from this tribe, as is noticed on the above passage, who has conquered our deadly foes by His death, and whose praying posterity ever prevail through His might.

8. *Of Levi he said.* Concerning the *Urim* and *Thummim* see Exod. xxviii. 30. *Thy holy one.* Aaron primarily, who was anointed the high priest of God, and whose office was the most holy that man could be invested with. Therefore Aaron was called God's *holy one,* and the more especially so as he was the type of the most holy and blessed Jesus, from whom the *Urim*—all

light and wisdom, and *Thummim*—all excellence, completion, and perfection, are derived. *Whom thou didst prove.* God contended with Aaron as well as with Moses at the waters of Meribah, and excluded him from the Promised Land because he did not sanctify the Lord before the people. From the words of Paul, 1 Cor. x. 8-12, it is evident that these words, at least in a secondary sense, belong to Christ. He is the Holy One who was tempted by them at Massah, who suffered their manners in the wilderness, who slew 23,000 of the most incorrigible transgressors, and who brought them into the Promised Land by His deputy, Joshua, whose name and that of Jesus have the same signification.

9. *Who said unto his father.* There are several difficulties in this and the following verses. Some think they are spoken of the tribe of Levi; others, of all the tribes; others, of the Messiah; but several of the interpretations founded on these suppositions are too recondite, and should not be resorted to till a plain literal sense is made out. I suppose the whole to be primarily spoken of Aaron and the tribe of Levi. Let us examine the words in this way, *Who said unto his father.* The law had strictly enjoined that if the father, mother, brother, or child of the high priest should die, he must not mourn for them, but act as if they were not his kindred; see Lev. xxi. 11-12. Neither must Aaron mourn for his sons Nadab and Abihu, though not only their death, but the circumstances of it, were the most afflicting that could possibly affect a parent's heart. Besides, the high priest was forbidden, on pain of death, to go out from the door of the Tabernacle, Lev. x. 2-7, for God would have them more to regard their function and duty in His service than any natural affection whatever. And herein Christ was figured, who, when He was told that His mother and brethren stood without, and wished to speak with Him, said: "Who is my mother? and who are my brethren? . . . whosoever shall do the will of my Father which is in heaven, the same is my brother, and sister, and mother," Matt. xii. 46-50. It is likely also that Moses may refer here to the fact of the Levites, according to the command of Moses, killing every man his brother, friend, neighbor, and even son, who had sinned in worshipping the golden calf, Exod. xxxii. 26; and in this way the Chaldee paraphrast understands the words.

10. *They shall teach Jacob.* This was the office of the Levites, to teach, by their significant service and typical ceremonies, the way of righteousness and truth to the children of Israel. And of their faithfulness in this respect God bears testimony by the prophet, "My covenant was with him of life and peace," Mal. ii. 5; and, "The law of truth was in his mouth, and iniquity was not found in his lips: he walked with me in peace and equity, and did turn many away from iniquity," v. 6. These words are a sufficient comment on the words of the text.

11. *Bless, Lord, his substance.* The blessing of God to the tribe of Levi was peculiarly necessary, because they had no inheritance among the children of Israel, and lived more immediately than others upon the providence of God. Yet, as they lived by the offerings of the people and the tithes, the increase of their substance necessarily implied the increase of the people at large: the more fruitful the land was, the more abundant would the tithes of the Levites be; and thus

in the increased fertility of the land the substance of Levi would be blessed.

12. *Of Benjamin . . . The beloved of the Lord.* Alluding to his being particularly beloved of his father, Jacob, Gen. xlix. 27. *Shall dwell in safety by him.* That is, by the Lord, whose Temple, which is considered as His dwelling place, was in the tribe of Benjamin, for a part of Jerusalem belonged to this tribe. *Shall cover him all the day.* Be his continual Protector; *and he shall dwell between his shoulders—* within his coasts, or in his chief city, viz., Jerusalem, where the temple of God was built, on his mountains Zion and Moriah, here poetically termed his shoulders.

13. *Blessed . . . be his land.* The whole of this passage certainly relates to the peculiar fertility of the soil in the portion that fell to this tribe, which, the Jews say, yielded a greater abundance of all good things than any other part of the Promised Land. *The precious things of heaven.* The peculiar mildness and salubrity of its atmosphere. *For the dew.* A plentiful supply of which was a great blessing in the dry soil of a hot climate. *The deep that coucheth beneath.* Probably referring to the plentiful supply of water which should be found in digging wells; hence the Septuagint has "fountains of the deeps." Some suppose there has been a slight change made in the word *mittal, for the dew,* which was probably at first *meal,* "from above," and then the passage would read thus: "For the precious things of heaven from above, and for the deep that coucheth beneath." This reading is confirmed by several of Kennicott's and De Rossi's MSS. The Syriac and Chaldee have both readings: "The dew of heaven from above."

14. *The precious fruits brought forth by the sun.* All excellent and important productions of the earth, which come to perfection once in the year. So *the precious things put forth by the moon* may imply those vegetables which require but about a month to bring them to perfection, or vegetables of which several crops may be had in the course of a year.

15. *The chief things of the ancient mountains. Umerosh harerey kedem,* "and from the head or top of the ancient or eastern mountains," the precious things or productions being still understood. And this probably refers to the large trees growing on the mountaintops, and the springs of water issuing from them. The mountains of Gilead may be here intended, as they fell to the half-tribe of Manasseh. And *the precious things of the lasting hills* may signify the metals and minerals which might be digged out of them.

16. *The good will of him that dwelt in the bush.* The favour of Him who appeared in the burning bush on Mount Sinai, who there, in His *good will,* mere love and compassion, took Israel to be His people; and who has preserved and will preserve, in tribulation and distress, all those who trust in Him, so that they shall as surely escape unhurt as the bush, though enveloped with fire, was unburnt. *The top of the head.* The same words are used by Jacob in blessing this tribe, Gen. xlix. 26. The meaning appears to be that God should distinguish this tribe in a particular way, as Joseph himself was separated, *nazir,* a Nazarite, a consecrated

prince to God, from among and in preference to all his brethren. See the notes on Gen. xlix. 25, etc.

17. *His glory is like the firstling of his bullock.* This similitude is very obscure. A bullock was the most excellent of animals among the Jews, not only because of its acceptableness in sacrifice to God, but because of its great usefulness in agriculture. There is something peculiarly noble and dignified in the appearance of the ox, and his greatest ornaments are his fine horns; these the inspired penman has particularly in view, as the following clause proves; and it is well known that in scriptural language horns are the emblem of strength, glory, and sovereignty; Ps. lxxv. 5, 10; lxxxix. 17, 24; cxii. 9; Dan. viii. 3, etc.; Luke i. 69; Rev. xvii. 3, etc. *His horns are like the horns of unicorns. Reem,* which we interpret *unicorn,* signifies, according to Bochart, the "mountain goat"; and according to others, the "rhinoceros," a very large quadruped with one great horn on his nose, from which circumstance his name is derived. See the notes on Num. xxiii. 22; xxiv. 8. *Reem* is in the singular number, and because the horns of a unicorn, a one-horned animal, would have appeared absurd, our translators, with an unfaithfulness not common to them, put the word in the plural number. *To the ends of the earth.* Of the land of Canaan, for Joshua with his armies conquered all this land, and drove the ancient inhabitants out before him. *They are the ten thousands of Ephraim.* That is, The horns signify the ten thousands of Ephraim, and the thousands of Manasseh. Jacob prophesied, Gen. xlviii. 19, that the younger should be greater than the elder; so here *tens of thousands* are given to Ephraim, and only *thousands* to Manasseh. See the census, Num. i. 33-35.

18. *Rejoice, Zebulun, in thy going out.* That is, You shall be very prosperous in your coasting voyages; for this tribe's situation was favorable for traffic, having many seaports. *And, Issachar, in thy tents.* That is, as Zebulon should be prosperous in his shipping and traffic, so should Issachar be in his *tents*—his agriculture and pasturage.

19. *They shall call the people unto the mountain.* By their traffic with the "Gentiles" (for so I think *ammim* should be understood here) they shall be the instruments in God's hands of converting many to the true faith; so that instead of sacrificing to idols, they should offer *sacrifices of righteousness. They shall suck of the abundance of the seas.* That is, grow wealthy by merchandise. *And of treasures hid in the sand.* Jonathan ben Uzziel has probably hit upon the true meaning of this difficult passage: "From the sand," says he, "are produced looking-glasses and glass in general; the *treasures*—the method of finding and working this, was revealed to these tribes." Several ancient writers inform us that there were havens in the coasts of the Zebulunites in which the vitreous sand, or sand proper for making glass, was found. See Strabo, lib. xvi.; see also Pliny, *Hist. Nat.* 1. xxxvi., c. 26; Tacitus, *Hist.* 1. v., c. 7. The words of Tacitus are remarkable: "The river Belus falls into the Jewish sea, about whose mouth those sands, mixed with nitre, are collected, out of which glass is formed," or which is melted into glass. Some think that the celebrated shellfish called *murex,* out of which the

precious purple dye was extracted, is here intended by the *treasures hid in the sand;* this also Jonathan introduces in this verse.

20. *Blessed be he that enlargeth Gad.* As deliverance out of distress is termed "enlarging" (see Ps. iv. 1), this may refer to God's deliverance of the tribe of Gad out of that distress mentioned Gen. xlix. 19, and to the enlargement obtained through means of Jephthah, Judg. xi. 33, and probably also the victories obtained by Gad and Reuben over the Hagarites, 1 Chron. v. 18-20. *He dwelleth as a lion.* Probably the epithet of *lion* or lionlike was applied to this tribe from their fierce and warlike disposition. And on this supposition, 1 Chron. xii. 8, will appear to be a sufficient comment: "And of the Gadites there [were] . . . men of might, and men of war for the battle, that could handle shield and buckler, whose faces were like the faces of lions, and were as swift as the roes upon the mountains." Tearing the *arm* or "shoulder" *with the crown of the head* seems simply to mean that no force should be able to prevail over them, or stand against them; as the arm or shoulder signifies dominion, and the crown of the head, sovereign princes.

21. *He provided the first part.* That is, he chose for himself a very excellent portion, viz., the land of Sihon and Og, in which this tribe had requested to be settled by the lawgiver, viz., Moses, from whom they requested this portion, Num. xxxii. 1-5. *He came with the heads of the people.* Notwithstanding this portion fell unto them on the east side of Jordan, yet they proceeded with the *heads of the people,* the chiefs of the other tribes. To execute *the justice of the Lord.* To extirpate the old inhabitants of the country, according to the decree and purpose of the Lord. See on Num. xxxii.

22. *Dan is a lion's whelp: he shall leap from Bashan.* The Jewish interpreters observe that Bashan was a place much frequented by lions, who issued thence into all parts to look for prey. By this probably Moses intended to point out the strength and prowess of this tribe, that it should extend its territories, and live a sort of predatory life. It appears from Josh. xix. 47 that the portion originally assigned to this tribe was not sufficient for them; hence we find them going out to war against Leshem and taking it, adding it to their territories, and calling it by the name of the tribe. Jacob, in his prophetic blessing of this tribe, represents it under the notion of a "serpent in the path," Gen. xlix. 17. The character there, and that given here, constitute the complete warrior—stratagem and courage.

23. *O Naphtali, satisfied with favour.* Though this may refer to the very great fertility of the country that fell to this tribe, yet certainly something more is intended. Scarcely any of the tribes was more particularly favored by the wondrous mercy and kindness of god than this and the tribe of Zebulun. The light of the glorious gospel of Christ shone brightly here, Matt. iv. 13, 15-16. Christ's chief residence was at Capernaum in this tribe, Matt. ix. 1; Mark ii. 1, and this city, through Christ's constant residence, and the mighty miracles He wrought in it, is represented as being "exalted unto heaven," Matt. xi. 23. And it is generally allowed that the apostles were principally of the tribe of Naph-

tali, who were to *possess . . . the west and the south*—to dispense the gospel through all the other tribes. The word *yam,* which we here translate *west,* literally signifies the "sea," and probably refers to the Sea of Gennesareth, which was in this tribe.

24. *Let Asher be blessed with children.* Let him have a numerous posterity, continually increasing. *Let him be acceptable to his brethren.* May he be in perfect union and harmony with the other tribes. *Let him dip his foot in oil.* Let him have a fertile soil, and an abundance of all the conveniences and comforts of life.

25. *Thy shoes shall be iron and brass.* Some suppose this may refer to the iron and copper mines in their territory; but it is more likely that it relates to their warlike disposition, as we know that greaves, boots, shoes, etc., of iron, brass, and tin, were used by ancient warriors. Goliath had greaves of brass on his legs, 1 Sam. xvii. 6; and "the brazen-booted Greeks" is one of the epithets given by Homer to his heroes.

And as thy days, so shall thy strength be. If we take this clause as it appears here, we have at once an easy sense; and the saying, I have no doubt, has comforted the souls of multitudes. The meaning is obvious: "Whatever thy trials or difficulties may be, I shall always give thee grace to support thee under and bring thee through them." The original is only two words, the latter of which has been translated in a great variety of ways, *ucheyameycha dobecha.* Of the first term there can be no doubt; it literally means, *and as thy days;* the second word, *dobe,* occurs nowhere else in the Hebrew Bible. The Septuagint have rendered it by *strength,* and most of the versions have followed them; but others have rendered it "affliction, old age, fame, weakness," etc. It would be almost endless to follow interpreters through their conjectures concerning its meaning. It is allowed among learned men that where a word occurs not as a verb in the Hebrew Bible its root may be legitimately sought in the Arabic. He who controverts this position knows little of the ground on which he stands. In this language the root is found; *daba* signifies "he rested, was quiet." This gives a very good sense, and a very appropriate one; for as the borders of this tribe lay on the vicinity of the Phoenicians, it was naturally to be expected that they should be constantly exposed to pillage; but God, to give them confidence in His protection, says, "According to thy days [all circumstances and vicissitudes], so shall thy rest be"—While faithful to your God, no evil shall touch you; your days shall increase, and your quiet be lengthened out. This is an unfailing promise of God: "I will keep him in perfect peace, whose mind is stayed upon Me, because he trusteth in Me"; therefore "trust ye in the Lord for ever: for in the Lord Jehovah is everlasting strength," Isa. xxvi. 4.

26. *There is none like unto the God of Jeshurun.* We have already seen the literal meaning of Jeshurun, chap. xxxii. 15; but besides its literal meaning, it seems to be used as an expression of particular affection. Hence the Septuagint seem to have apprehended the full force of the word by translating it "the beloved one," the object of God's especial delight. *Rideth upon the heaven.* Unites heaven and earth in

your defense and support, and comes with irresistible velocity to succor and defend you, and to discomfit your adversaries.

27. *The eternal God. Elohey kedem,* the "former God," He who was of old. Not like the gods which were lately come up. He who ever was and ever will be; and He who was, is, and will be unchangeably holy, wise, just, and merciful. *Everlasting arms.* As the arm is the emblem of power, and of power in a state of exertion, the words here state that an unlimited and unconquerable power shall be eternally exerted in the defense of God's Church, and in the behalf of all those who trust in Him. *Thrust out the enemy.* He will expel all the ancient inhabitants, and put you in possession of their land.

28. *Israel then shall dwell . . . alone.* This people shall not be incorporated with any other people under heaven. A prophecy which continues to be fulfilled to the very letter. Every attempt to unite them with any other people has proved absolutely ineffectual. *The fountain of Jacob.* His "offspring" shall possess a most fertile land; such was Palestine.

29. *Happy art thou.* Oh, the happiness of Israel! it is ineffable, inconceivable, because they are a *people saved by the Lord*—have such a salvation as it becomes the infinite perfections of God to bestow; He is their *help,* their never-failing Strength, and the *shield* of that help— He defends their defense, saves them and preserves them in the state of salvation. *Sword of thy excellency.* Or "whose sword"—His all-conquering Word, "is thine excellency," in its promises, threatenings, precepts. Paul, in his exhortation to the Christians at Ephesus, uses the same metaphor, "Take unto you . . . the sword of the Spirit, which is the word of God." *Thine enemies shall be found liars.* Who said you should never be able to gain the possession of this good land; for you *shall tread on,* subdue, their *high places*—even their best fortified cities.

CHAPTER 34

Moses goes up Mount Nebo to the top of Pisgah, and God shows him the whole extent of the land which He promised to give to the descendants of Abraham, 1-4. There Moses died, and was so privately buried by the Lord that his sepulchre was never discovered, 5-6. His age and strength of constitution, 7. The people weep for him thirty days, 8. Joshua being filled with the spirit of wisdom, the Israelites hearken to him, as the Lord commanded them, 9. The character of Moses as a prophet, and as a worker of the most extraordinary miracles, both in the sight of the Egyptians and the people of Israel: conclusion of the Pentateuch, 10-12.

1. *And Moses went up.* This chapter could not have been written by Moses. A man certainly cannot give an account of his own death and burial. We may therefore consider Moses' words as ending with the conclusion of the preceding chapter, as what follows could not possibly have been written by himself. To suppose that he anticipated these circumstances, or that they were shown to him by an especial revelation, is departing far from propriety and necessity, and involving the subject in absurdity;

for God gives no prophetic intimations but such as are absolutely necessary to be made. But there is no necessity here, for the Spirit which inspired the writer of the following book would naturally communicate the matter that concludes this. I believe, therefore, that Deuteronomy xxxiv should constitute the first chapter of the Book of Joshua.

On this subject the following note from an intelligent Jew cannot be unacceptable to the reader: "Most commentators are of opinion that Ezra was the author of the last chapter of Deuteronomy; some think it was Joshua, and others the seventy elders, immediately after the death of Moses; adding, that the book of Deuteronomy originally ended with the prophetic blessing upon the twelve tribes: 'Happy art thou, O Israel: who is like unto thee, O people saved by the Lord!' and that what now makes the last chapter of Deuteronomy was formerly the first of Joshua, but was removed from thence and joined to the former by way of supplement."

5. *So Moses . . . died . . . according to the word of the Lord. Al pi Yehovah,* "at the mouth of Jehovah," i.e., by the especial command and authority of the Lord; but it is possible that what is here said refers only to the sentence of his exclusion from the Promised Land, when he offended at the waters of Meribah.

6. *He buried him.* It is probable that the reason why Moses was buried thus privately was lest the Israelites, prone to idolatry, should pay him divine honors; and God would not have the body of His faithful servant abused in this way.

7. *His eye was not dim.* Even at the advanced age of a hundred and twenty; *nor his natural force abated*—he was a young man even in old age, notwithstanding the unparalleled hardships he had gone through.

9. *Laid his hands upon him.* See on Num. xxvii. 18-23.

10. *There arose not a prophet.* Among all the succeeding prophets none was found so eminent in all respects nor so highly privileged as Moses; with him God spoke *face to face*— admitted him to the closest familiarity and greatest friendship with himself. Now all this continued true till the advent of Jesus Christ, of whom Moses said, "A prophet shall the Lord your God raise up unto you of your brethren, like unto me"; but how great was this Person when compared with Moses! Moses desired to see God's glory; this sight he could not bear; he saw his "back parts," probably meaning God's design relative to the latter days. But Jesus, the almighty Saviour, in whom dwells all the fulness of the Godhead bodily, who lay in the bosom of the Father, He hath "declared" God to man.

Now to the ever blessed and glorious Trinity, Father, Word, and Spirit, the infinite and eternal One, from whom alone wisdom, truth, and goodness can proceed, be glory and dominion for ever and ever. Amen.

The Book of
JOSHUA

Joshua, the son of Nun, of the tribe of Ephraim, was first called *Oshea* or *Hoshea*, Num. xiii. 16, which signifies "saved," a "saviour," or "salvation"; but afterwards Moses, guided no doubt by a prophetic spirit, changed his name into *Yehoshua* or Joshua, which signifies "he shall save," or "the salvation of Jehovah"; referring, no doubt, to his being God's instrument in saving the people from the hands of their enemies, and leading them from victory to victory over the different Canaanitish nations, till he put them in possession of the Promised Land. By the Septuagint he is called *Jesus Naue,* or "Jesus son of Nave"; and in the New Testament he is expressly called Jesus; see Acts vii. 45; Heb. iv. 8. Joshua was denominated the "servant of Moses," as he seems to have acted sometimes as his secretary, sometimes as his aid-de-camp, and sometimes as the general of the army. He was early appointed to be the successor of Moses, see Exod. xvii. 14; and under the instruction of this great master he was fully qualified for the important office. He was a great and pious man, and God honored him in a most extraordinary manner, as the sequel of the history amply proves. From the preceding books it appears that he became attached to Moses shortly after the exodus from Egypt; that he was held by him in the highest esteem; had the command of the army confided to him in the way with the Amalekites; and accompanied his master to the mount, when he went up to receive the law from God. These were the highest honors he could possibly receive during the lifetime of Moses.

Commentators and critics are divided in opinion whether the book that goes under his name was actually compiled by him.

It is argued by those who deny Joshua to be the author that there are both names and transactions in it which did not exist till considerably after Joshua's time. The account we have, chap. iv. 9, of the twelve stones set up by Joshua in the midst of Jordan remaining to the present day seems to prove that the book, at least this verse, was not written till after Joshua's time; the same may be said of the account of Ai, that Joshua made it a heap forever, even a desolation to the present day, chap. viii. 28, which is a proof, however, that the book was not written after the time of the kings, as Ai subsisted after the return from the Captivity; see Ezra ii. 28: "The men of Beth-el and Ai, two hundred twenty and three." It is supposed also that the relation of the marriage of Achsah, daughter of Caleb, with Othniel, the son of Kenaz, necessarily belongs to the time of the Judges; Josh. xv. 16-19; as also the account of the capture of Leshem by the Danites, chap. xix. 47, compared with Judges xviii. 7, 29.

What is related, chap. xv. 63, concerning the Jebusites dwelling with the children of Judah at Jerusalem unto this day must certainly have been written before the time of David; for he took the stronghold of Zion, and expelled the Jebusites; see 2 Sam. v. 7-9. Also, what is said, chap. xvi. 10, "They drave not out the Canaanites that dwelt in Gezer: but the Canaanites dwell among the Ephraimites unto this day," must have been written before the time of Solomon; for in his time Pharaoh, king of Egypt, had taken Gezer, burned it with fire, slain the Canaanites that dwelt in it, and given it a present to his daughter, the wife of Solomon, 1 Kings ix. 16. The country of Cabul, mentioned chap. xix. 27, had not this name till the time of Solomon, as appears from 1 Kings ix. 13; and the city called Joktheel, chap. xv. 38, had not this name till the reign of Joash, as appears from 2 kings xiv. 7, it having been previously called Selah. The like may be said of Tyre, chap. xix. 29; and of Galilee chap. xx. 7 and xxi. 32.

These are the principal objections which are made against the book as being the work of Joshua. Some of these difficulties might be so removed as to render it still probable that Joshua was the author of the whole book, as some think to be intimated chap. xxiv. 26: "And Joshua wrote these words in the book of the law of God" (but this probably refers to nothing more than the words of the covenant which was then made, and which is included in vv. 2-24). But there are other difficulties that cannot be removed on the above supposition, and therefore it has been generally supposed that the book was written by some inspired person after the time of Joshua, and postively before many kings had reigned in Israel. The book has been attributed to Samuel, though some give this honor to Ezra.

After all, I cannot help considering the book in the main as the composition of Joshua himself. It is certain that Moses kept an accurate register of all the events that took place during *his* administration in the wilderness, at least from the giving of the law to the time of his death. And in that wilderness he wrote the Book of Genesis, as well as the others that bear his name.

Now it is not likely that Joshua, the constant servant and companion of Moses, could see all this and not adopt the same practice, especially as at the death of Moses he came into the same office. I therefore take it for granted that the Book of Joshua is as truly his work as the Commentaries of Caesar are his; and all the real difficulties mentioned above may be rationally and satisfactorily accounted for on the ground that in transcribing this book in after ages, especially between the times of Joshua and the Kings, some few changes were made, and a very few slight additions which referred chiefly to the insertion of names by which cities were than known instead of those by which they had been anciently denominated. This book therefore I conceive to be not the work of Ezra, nor of Samuel, nor of any other person of those times; nor can I allow that "it is called the Book of Joshua, because he is the chief subject of it, as the heroic poem of Virgil is called the Aeneis, because of the prince whose travels and actions it relates." But I conceive it to be called the Book of Joshua; (1) Because Joshua wrote it; (2) Because it is the relation of his own conduct in the conquest, division, and settlement of the Promised Land; (3) Because it contains a multitude of particulars that only himself, or a constant eyewitness, could possibly relate; (4) Because it was evidently designed to be a continuation of the Book of Deuteronomy, and is so connected with it, in narrative, as to prove that it must have been immediately commenced on the termination of the other; and (5) I might add to this that, with the exception of a few individuals, the whole of the ancient Jewish and Christian churches have uniformly acknowledged Joshua to be its author.

The Book of Joshua is one of the most important writings in the old covenant, and should never be separated from the Pentateuch, of which it is at once both the continuation and completion. Between this book and the five Books of Moses there is the same analogy as between the four Gospels and the Acts of the Apostles. The Pentateuch contains a history of the Acts of the great Jewish legislator, and the laws on which the Jewish church should be established. The Book of Joshua gives an account of the establishment of that church in the land of Canaan, according to the oft-repeated promises and declarations of God. The Gospels give an account of the transactions of Jesus Christ, the great Christian Legislator, and of those laws on which His Church should be established, and by which it should be governed. The Acts of the Apostles gives an account of the actual establishment of that Church, according to the predictions and promises of its great Founder. Thus, then, the Pentateuch bears as pointed a relation to the Gospels as the Book of Joshua does to the Acts of the Apostles. And we might, with great appearance of probability, carry this analogy yet further, and show that the writings of several of the prophets bear as strict a relation to the apostolical Epistles as the Books of Ezekiel and Daniel do to the Apocalypse. On this very ground of analogy Christ obviously founded the Christian Church; hence He had His twelve disciples, from whom the Christian Church was to spring, as the Jewish church or twelve tribes sprang from the twelve sons of Jacob. He had His seventy or seventy-two disciples, in reference to the seventy-two elders, six chosen out of each of the twelve tribes, who were united with Moses and Aaron in the administration of justice, etc., among the people. Christ united in His person the characters of both Moses and Aaron, or Legislator and High Priest; hence He ever considers himself, and is considered by His apostles and followers, the same in the Christian Church that Moses and Aaron were in the Jewish. As a rite of initiation into His Church, He instituted baptism in the place of circumcision, both being types of the purification of the heart and holiness of life; and as a rite of establishment and confirmation, the holy Eucharist in place of the paschal lamb, both being intended to commemorate the atonement made to God for the sins of the people. The analogies are so abundant, and indeed universal, that time would fail to enumerate them. On this very principle it would be a matter of high utility to read these Old Testament and the New Testament books together, as they reflect a strong and mutual light on each other, bear the most decided testimony to the words and truth of prophecy, and show the ample fulfilment of all the ancient and gracious designs of God. This appears particularly evident in the five Books of Moses and the Book of Joshua compared and collated with the four Gospels and the Acts of the Apostles.

CHAPTER 1

Moses being dead, God commissions Joshua to bring the people into the Promised Land, 1-2. The extent of the land to be possessed, 3-4. Joshua is assured of victory over all his enemies, and is exhorted to courage and activity, 5-6; and to be careful to act, in all things, according to the law of Moses, in which he is to meditate day and night, 7-8. He is again exhorted to courage. with the promise of continual support, 9. Joshua commands the officers to prepare the people for their passage over Jordan, 10-11. The Reubenites, Gadites, and half tribe of Manasseh, are put in mind of their engagement to pass over with their brethren, 12-15. They promise the strictest obedience, and pray for the prosperity of their leader, 16-18.

1. *Now after the death of Moses.* Vayehi, "and it was or happened" after the death of

Moses. Even the first words in this book show it to be a continuation of the preceding, and intimately connected with the narrative in the last chapter in Deuteronomy, of which I suppose Joshua to have been the author, and that chapter to have originally made the commencement of this book. The time referred to here must have been at the conclusion of the thirty days in which they mourned for Moses.

2. *Moses my servant.* The word *servant*, as applied both to Moses and Joshua, is to be understood in a very peculiar sense. It signifies God's prime minister, the person by whom He issued His orders, and by whom He ac-

complished all his purposes and designs. No person ever bore this title in the like sense but the Redeemer of mankind, of whom Moses and Joshua were types.

3. *The sole of your foot shall tread upon.* That is, the whole land occupied by the seven Canaanitish nations, and as far as the Euphrates on the east; for this was certainly the utmost of the grant now made to them; and all that was included in what is termed the Promised Land, the boundaries of which have already been defined. See Deut. xxxiv. 1-4, and see v. 4 below. It has been supposed that the words *Every place that the sole of your foot shall tread upon* were intended to express the ease with which they were to conquer the whole land, an instance of which occurs in the taking of Jericho. It was only their unfaithfulness to God that rendered the conquest in any case difficult.

4. *From the wilderness and this Lebanon.* The utmost of their limits should be from the desert of Arabia Petraea on the south to Lebanon on the north, and from the Euphrates on the east to the Mediterranean Sea on the west. The Israelites did not possess the full extent of this grant till the days of David. See 2 Sam. viii. 3, etc., and 2 Chron. ix. 26.

Land of the Hittites. These are generally reputed to have been the most hardy and warlike of all the Canaanitish nations; and as they occupied the mountainous countries on the south of the land of Canaan, it is natural to suppose that they would be the most difficult to subdue, and on this account, it is supposed, God particularly specifies these. But it is probable that under this one term all the other nations are included, as it is certain they are in other places under the term *Amorites.*

Great sea—the Mediterranean, called *great* in respect of the lakes in the land of Judea, such as the Sea of Galilee and the Dead Sea, which were comparatively small lakes; but the Hebrews gave the name of *sea, yam,* to every large collection of waters.

5. *Be able to stand before thee.* Because God shall be with you, therefore you shall be irresistible. This promise was most punctually and literally fulfilled.

7. *Only be thou strong, and very courageous.* "Be strong therefore, and play the man to the uttermost." Though God had promised him that no man should be able to stand before him, yet it was on condition that he should use all his military skill, and avail himself to the uttermost of all the means, natural and providential, which God should place within his reach. God will not help them who refuse to help themselves.

8. *This book of the law shall not depart out of thy mouth.* Though there was a copy of the law laid up in the sanctuary, yet this was not sufficient. Joshua must have a copy for himself, and he was to consult it incessantly, that his way might be made prosperous. If he kept God's word, God would keep him in body and soul; if he should observe to do according to that word, then God would cause all his way to be prosperous.

10. *Commanded the officers. Shoterim.* These were different from the *shophetim,* who were judges among the people, and whose business it was to determine in all civil cases. The *shoterim*

have been supposed to be subordinate officers, whose business it was to see the decisions of the *shophetim* carried into effect.

11. *Prepare you victuals. Tsedah,* such prey or provisions as they had taken from the conquered countries, such as corn, oxen, sheep, etc.; for the word signifies "prey," or what is taken by hunting. This was necessary, as they were about to undergo considerable fatigue in marching, and in making preparations for the passage of the Jordan; for although the manna had not ceased to fall, yet such other provisions as are mentioned above were necessary on this occasion. *For within three days he shall pass.* The text is supposed to mean, "Prepare victuals for three days' march," for "on the third day after your decampment from Shittim ye shall pass over this Jordan."

13. *Remember the word.* He puts the Reubenites, etc., in remembrance of the agreement they had made with Moses (see Num. xxxii. 20) when he granted them their portion on the east side of Jordan.

14. *Your wives, your little ones.* And with these it appears, from Num. xxxii. 17, were left behind 70,580 effective men to guard them and their property, only 40,000 having passed over Jordan to assist the nine tribes and a half to conquer the land. See chap. iv. 13, *Armed, chamushim,* "by fives"; in several lines, five in front, probably the usual method of marching; but it seems to signify "arrayed, equipped, accoutred, well-armed," and ready for battle. See the note on Exod. xiii. 18.

16. *All that thou commandest us we will do.* Here they acknowledge the divine mission of Joshua, as they had done that of Moses, and consequently promise to follow his directions in all things.

17. *Only the Lord thy God be with thee.* Provided God be with thee, as He was with Moses, we will implicitly obey thee. The words however may mean no more than an earnest prayer for Joshua's prosperity: May God be with thee, as He was with Moses!

18. *He shall be put to death.* This was martial law; he who disobeyed the command of his general should be put to death. To this the people agreed, and it was essentially necessary in order that proper discipline should be kept up in this great army. By insubordination their fathers had suffered much in the wilderness; they rejected the authority of Moses, mutinied, and made themselves a leader to conduct them back to Egypt (see Num. xiv. 4). And Joshua himself, for attempting to encourage them against their fears, was near being stoned to death. It was necessary, therefore, that they should give him the most positive assurance that they would not act as their fathers had done.

CHAPTER 2

Joshua sends out two spies to examine the state of the inhabitants of the land, particularly those of Jericho, who are entertained at the house of Rahab, 1. The king of Jericho is informed of their being in the town, and sends to Rahab, commanding her to deliver them up, 2-3. She hides the spies, and tells the messengers that the men were departed and gone towards the mountain, 4-5. When the officers of the king of Jericho were departed, she took the spies to the housetop, and covered them with flax, 6-7. She relates to them that the fear of the Israelites had fallen on all the inhabitants of the country on hearing of their victories over the Amorites; that she knew none could resist the God of Israel, and therefore desired them to give her an oath that, when they took Jericho, they would preserve the lives of her and her family, 8-13. The spies swear to her. 14. She lets them down by a cord from the housetop, and gives them directions how to proceed, in order to avoid the pursuers, 15-16. She is to tie a scarlet line to the window, through which she had let them down, which should be the sign to the Israelites to spare that house and its inhabitants, 17-19. Having bound her to secrecy, they depart, 20-21. After three days' stay in the mountain, they return to Joshua, and make a favourable report, 22-24.

1. *Joshua . . . sent . . . two men to spy secretly.* It is very likely that these spies had been sent out soon after the death of Moses, and therefore our marginal reading, "had sent," is to be preferred. *Secretly*—It is very probable also that these were confidential persons, and that the transaction was between them and him alone. As they were to pass over the Jordan opposite to Jericho, it was necessary that they should have possession of this city, that in case of any reverses they might have no enemies in their rear.

An harlot's house. Harlots and innkeepers seem to have been called by the same name, as no doubt many who followed this mode of life, from their exposed situation, were not the most correct in their morals. I am fully satisfied that the term *zonah* in the text, which we translate *harlot*, should be rendered "tavern or innkeeper," or "hostess." The spies who were sent out on this occasion were undoubtedly the most confidential persons that Joshua had in his host; they went on an errand of the most weighty importance, and which involved the greatest consequences. The risk they ran of losing their lives in this enterprise was extreme. Is it therefore likely that persons who could not escape apprehension and death, without the miraculous interference of God, should in despite of that law go into a place where they might expect, not the blessing, but the curse, of God? Is it not therefore more likely that they went rather to an inn to lodge than to a brothel? But what completes in my judgment the evidence on this point is that this very Rahab, whom we call a harlot, was actually married to Salmon, a Jewish prince, see Matt. i. 5. And is it probable that a prince of Judah would have taken to wife such a person as our text represents Rahab to be?

3. *The king of Jericho sent unto Rahab.* This appears to be a proof of the preceding opinion. Had she been a prostitute or a person of ill fame he could at once have sent officers to seize the persons lodged with her as vagabonds; but if she kept a house of entertainment, the persons under her roof were sacred, according to the universal custom of the Asiatics, and could not be molested on any trifling grounds.

4. *And hid them.* Probably she secreted them for the time being in some private corner, till she had the opportunity of concealing them on the housetop in the manner mentioned v. 6

5. *When it was dark.* So it appears that it was after night that the king of Jericho sent to Rahab, ordering her to produce the persons who lodged with her. The season itself was friendly to the whole plot; had these transactions taken place in daylight, it is scarcely possible that the spies could have escaped. But this is no excuse for the woman's prevarication; for God could have saved His messengers independently of her falsity. God never says to any, Do evil that good may come of it.

6. *Hid them with the stalks of flax.* As this was about the season, viz., the end of March or the beginning of April, in which the flax is ripe in that country, consequently Rahab's flax might have been recently pulled, and was now drying on the roof of her house. *Upon the roof.* We have already seen that all the houses in the east were made flat-roofed; for which a law is given Deut. xxii. 8. On these flat roofs the Asiatics to this day walk, converse, and oftentimes even sleep and pass the night.

9. *I know that the Lord hath given you the land.* It is likely she had this only from conjecture, having heard of their successes against the Amorites, their prodigious numbers, and seeing the state of terror and dismay to which the inhabitants of her own land were reduced.

11. *He is God in heaven above, and in earth beneath.* This confession of the true God is amazingly full, and argues considerable light and information, as if she had said, "I know your God to be omnipotent and omnipresent"; and in consequence of this faith she hid the spies, and risked her own life in doing it. But how had she this clear knowledge of the divine nature? Possibly she received this instruction from the spies, with whom she appears to have had a good deal of conversation; or she had it from a supernatural influence of God upon her own soul.

12. *Swear unto me by the Lord.* This is a further proof that this woman had received considerable instruction in the Jewish faith; she acknowledged the true God by His essential character Jehovah, and knew that an oath in His name was the deepest and most solemn obligation under which a Jew could possibly come. Does not this also refer to the command of God, "Thou shalt fear the Lord, and shalt swear by his name"? See the note on Deut. vi. 13.

13. *Deliver our lives from death.* She had learned, either from the spies or otherwise, that all the inhabitants of the land were doomed to destruction, and therefore she obliges them to enter into a covenant with her for the preservation of herself and her household.

14. *Our life for yours.* "May our life be destroyed if we suffer yours to be injured!"

15. *Then she let them down by a cord.* The natural place of this verse is after the first clause of v. 21; for it is certain that she did not let them down in the basket till all those circumstances marked from vv. 16-20 inclusive had taken place. *She dwelt upon the wall.* That is, either the wall of the city made a part of her house or her house was built close to the wall, so that the top or battlements of it were above the wall, with a window that looked out to the country. As the city gates were now shut, there was no way for the spies to escape but through this window; and in order for them to do this she let them down through the window in a basket suspended by a cord, till they reached the ground on the outside of the wall.

16. *Hide yourselves there three days.* They were to travel by night, and hide themselves in the daytime; otherwise they might have been discovered by the pursuers who were in search of them.

18. *This line of scarlet thread.* Probably this may mean "this piece of scarlet cloth," or "this

cloth [made] of scarlet thread." When the Israelites took the city, this piece of red cloth seems to have been hung out of the window by way of flag; and this was the sign on which she and the spies had agreed.

20. *If thou utter this our business.* It was prudent to make her life depend on her secrecy; had it been otherwise she might have been tempted to give information, not only concerning the spies, but concerning the designs of the Israelites.

23. *So the two men returned.* Having concealed themselves in the mountains that night, all the next day, and the night ensuing, on the third day they returned to Joshua.

24. *Truly the Lord hath delivered into our hands all the land.* How different was this report from that brought by the spies on a former occasion! They found that all the inhabitants of the land were panic-struck. The people had heard of the great exploits of the Israelites on the other side of Jordan; and as they had destroyed the potent kings of the Amorites, they took it for granted that nothing could stand before them. This information was necessary to Joshua to guide him in forming the plan of his campaign.

CHAPTER 3

The Israelitish camp removes from Shittim to Jordan, 1. The officers inform them how they are to pass the river, and the distance they are to keep from the ark, 2-4. Joshua directs the people, 5-6; and the Lord gives directions to Joshua, 7-8. He delivers the Lord's message to the people, and foretells the miraculous passage and division of Jordan, 9-13. The priests, bearing the ark, enter the river, and immediately the waters are cut off, and the priests stand on dry ground, in the bed of the river, till all the camp passes over, 14-17.

1. *Joshua rose early.* From Shittim, where they had lately been encamped, to Jordan, was about sixty stadia, according to Josephus; that is, about eight English miles.

2. *After three days.* These three days are probably to be thus understood: As soon as Joshua took the command of the army, he sent the spies to ascertain the state of Jericho; as we have seen chap. i. 12. They returned at the end of three days, or rather on the third day, and made their report. It was at this time, immediately on the return of the spies, that he made the proclamation mentioned here; in consequence of which the people immediately struck their tents, and marched forward to Jordan.

4. *About two thousand cubits.* This distance they were to keep, (1) for the greater respect, because the presence of the ark was the symbol and pledge of the divine presence; (2) that the ark, which was to be their pilot over these waters, might be the more conspicuous, which it could not have been had the people crowded upon it.

5. *Sanctify yourselves.* What was implied in this command we are not informed; but it is likely that it was the same as that given by Moses, Exod. xix. 10-14. They were to wash themselves and their garments, and abstain from everything that might indispose their minds from a profitable attention to the miracle about to be wrought in their behalf.

6. *Spake unto the priests, saying, Take up the ark.* It is remarkable that the priests, not the Levites, whose ordinary business it was, were employed to carry the ark on this occasion.

7. *This day will I begin to magnify thee.* By making him the instrument in this miraculous passage, He did him honor and gave him high credit in the sight of the people; hence his authority was established, and obedience to him as their leader fully secured. What must have confirmed this authority was his circumstantially foretelling how the waters should be cut off as soon as the feet of the priests had touched them, v. 13. This demonstrated that the secret of the Lord was with him.

8. *Ye shall stand still in Jordan.* The priests proceeded first with the ark, and entered into the bed of the river, the course of which was immediately arrested, the waters collecting above the place where the priests stood, while the stream fell off towards the Dead Sea, so that the whole channel below where the priests were standing became dry. The whole camp, therefore, passed over below where the priests were standing, keeping at the distance of two thousand cubits from the ark; this they would readily do, as the whole bed of the river was dry for many miles below the place where the priests entered.

10. *Hereby ye shall know that the living God is among you.* The Israelites were apt to be discouraged, and to faint at even the appearance of danger; it was necessary, therefore, that they should have the fullest assurance of the presence and assistance of God in the important enterprise on which they were now entering. They were to combat idolaters, who had nothing to trust in and help them but gods of wood, stone, and metal; whereas they were to have the living God in the midst of them—He who is the Author of life and of being—who can give, or take it away, at His pleasure; and who by this miracle proved that He had undertaken to guide and defend them; and Joshua makes this manifestation of God the proof that He will drive out the Hittites, Hivites, etc., before them.

15. *And the feet of the priests . . . were dipped in the brim of the water.* Thus we find that everything occurred exactly in the way in which Joshua had foretold it. This must have greatly increased his credit among the people. *For Jordan overfloweth all his banks.* It has often been remarked that there was no need of a miracle in crossing Jordan, as it is but an inconsiderable stream, easily fordable, being but about twenty yards in breadth. But the circumstance marked here by the sacred historian proves that there was a time in the year, viz., in the harvest, that this river overflowed its banks; and this is confirmed by another place in Scripture, 1 Chron. xii. 15. As the miracle reported here took place about the beginning of April, a time in which rivers in general are less than in winter, it may be asked how there could be such an increase of waters at this time. The simple fact is that the Jordan, as we have already seen, has its origin at the foot of Mount Lebanon, which mountain is always covered with snow during the winter months; in those months therefore the river is low. But when the summer's sun has melted these snows, there is consequently a prodigious increase of waters, so that the old channel is not capable of containing them.

16. *Rose up upon an heap.* That is, they continued to accumulate, filling up the whole of the channel toward the source, and the adjacent ground over which they were now spread, to a much greater depth, the power of God giving a contrary direction to the current. We need not suppose them to be gathered up "like a mountain," as the Vulgate expresses it, but that they continued to flow back in the course of the channel; and ere they could have reached the lake of Gennesareth, where they might have been easily accumulated, the whole Israelitish army would have all got safely to the opposite side. *Very far from the city Adam . . . beside Zaretan.* Where these places were it is difficult to say. The city *Adam* is wholly unknown.

17. *The priests . . . stood firm on dry ground.* They stood in the mid channel and shifted not their position till the camp, consisting of nearly six hundred thousand effective men, besides women, children, etc., had passed over.

CHAPTER 4

When the people are passed over, Joshua commands twelve men, one taken out of each tribe, to take up a stone on his shoulder out of the midst of the river, and carry it to the other side, to be set up as a memorial of this miraculous passage, 1-7. They do so, and set up the stones in the place where they encamp the first night, 8-9. The priests stand in the river, till all the people are passed over, 10-11. Of the tribes of Reuben and Gad, and the half-tribe of Manasseh, 40,000 fighting men pass over with the other tribes, 12-13. Joshua is magnified in the sight of the people, and they fear him as they did Moses, 14. The priests are commanded to come up out of the river, which, on their leaving it, immediately returns, and overflows its banks as before, 15-18. This miraculous passage takes place the tenth day of the first month, 19. The stones are set up in Gilgal, and Joshua teaches the people what use they are to make of them, 20-24.

2. *Take you twelve men.* From chap. iii. 12, it appears that the twelve men had been before appointed, one taken out of each of the twelve tribes; and now they are employed for that purpose for which they had been before selected.

3. *Where ye shall lodge this night.* This was in the place that was afterwards called Gilgal. See v. 19.

4. *Twelve men, whom he had prepared.* This must refer to their appointment, chap. iii. 12.

6. *This may be a sign.* Stand as a continual memorial of this miraculous passage, and consequently a proof of their lasting obligation to God.

9. *And Joshua set up twelve stones in the midst of Jordan.* It seems from this chapter that there were two sets of stones erected as a memorial of this great event: twelve at Gilgal, v. 20; and twelve in the bed of Jordan, v. 9. The twelve stones in the bed of Jordan might have been so placed on a base of strong stonework so high as always to be visible, and serve to mark the very spot where the priests stood with the ark. The twelve stones set up at Gilgal would stand as a monument of the place of the first encampment after this miraculous passage.

10. *And the people hasted and passed over.* How very natural is this circumstance! The people seeing the waters divided, and Jordan running back, might be apprehensive that it would soon resume its wonted course; and this would naturally lead them to hasten to get over, with as much speed as possible. The circumstance itself thus marked is a proof that the

relater was an eyewitness of this miraculous passage.

14. *The Lord magnified Joshua.* See the note on chap. iii. 7.

18. *The waters of Jordan returned unto their place.* It is particularly remarked by the sacred historian that as soon as the soles of the priests' feet touched the water the stream of the Jordan was cut off, chap. iii. 15, and the course of the river continued to be inverted all the time they continued in its channel; and that as soon as the soles of their feet had touched the dry land, on their return from the bed of the river, the waters immediately resumed their natural course.

19. *On the tenth day of the first month.* As the Israelites left Egypt on the fifteenth day of the first month (see Exodus xiv) and they entered into Canaan the tenth of the first month, it is evident that forty years, wanting five days, had elapsed from the time of their exodus from Egypt to their entrance into the promised inheritance. *Encamped in Gilgal.* That is, in the place that was afterwards called Gilgal, see chap. v. 9; for here the name is given it by anticipation. In Hebrew, *gal* signifies to "roll"; and the doubling of the root, *galgal* or *gilgal*, signifies "rolling round and round," or "rolling off or away," because, in circumcising the children that had been born in the wilderness, Joshua rolled away, rolled off completely, the reproach of the people. Gilgal was about ten furlongs from Jericho, and fifty from Jordan—Jericho being on the west, and Jordan on the east, Gilgal being between both.

20. *Those twelve stones.* It is very likely that a base of masonwork was erected of some considerable height, and then the twelve stones placed on the top of it, and that this was the case both in Jordan and Gilgal. For twelve such stones as a man could carry a considerable way on his shoulder, see v. 5, could scarcely have made any observable altar, or pillar of memorial; but erected on a high base of masonwork they would be very conspicuous, and thus properly answer the end for which God ordered them to be set up.

22. *Then ye shall let your children know.* The necessity of an early religious education is inculcated through the whole oracles of God. The parents who neglect it have an awful account to give to the Judge of quick and dead.

24. *That all the people of the earth might know.* It is very likely that *col ammey haarets* means simply, "all the people of this land"—all the Canaanitish nations.

CHAPTER 5

The effect produced on the minds of the Canaanites by the late miracle, 1. Joshua is commanded to circumcise the Israelites, 2. He obeys, 3. Who they were that were circumcised, and why it was now done, 4-7. They abide in the camp till they are whole, 8. The place is called Gilgal, and why, 9. They keep the Passover in the same place, 10. They eat unleavened cakes and parched corn on the morrow after the Passover, 11. The manna ceases, 12. The captain of the Lord's host appears to Joshua, 13-15.

1. *The Amorites, which were on the side of Jordan westward.* It has already been remarked that the term *Amorites* is applied sometimes to signify all the nations or tribes of Canaan. It appears from this verse that there were people thus denominated that dwelt on both sides of the

Jordan. Those on the east side had already been destroyed in the war which the Israelites had with Sihon and Og; with those on the west side Joshua had not yet waged war. It is possible however that the *Amorites,* of whom we read in this verse, were the remains of those who dwelt on the east side of the Jordan, and who had taken refuge here on the defeat of Og and Sihon.

2. *Make thee sharp knives.* "Knives of rock, stone, or flint." *Circumcise again the children of Israel the second time.* This certainly does not mean that they should repeat circumcision on those who had already received it. This would have been as absurd as impracticable. But the command implies that they were to renew the observance of a rite which had been neglected in their travels in the desert.

4. *This is the cause why Joshua did circumcise.* The text here explains itself. Before the Israelites left Egypt all the males were circumcised; and some learned men think that all those who were born during their encampment at Sinai were circumcised also, because there they celebrated the Passover; but after that time, during the whole of their stay in the wilderness, there were none circumcised till they entered into the Promised Land. Owing to their unsettled state, God appears to have dispensed, for the time being, with this rite. But as they were about to celebrate another Passover, it was necessary that all the males should be circumcised; for without this they could not be considered within the covenant, and could not keep the Passover, which was the seal of that covenant.

8. *They abode . . . in the camp, till they were whole.* This required several days; see the notes on Genesis xxxiv.

9. *The reproach of Egypt.* Their being uncircumcised made them like the uncircumcised Egyptians, and the Hebrews ever considered all those who were uncircumcised as being in a state of the grossest impurity. Being now circumcised, the reproach of uncircumcision was rolled away. *The place is called Gilgal.* "A rolling away" or "rolling off." See the note on chap. iv. 19, where the word is largely explained.

11. *They did eat of the old corn of the land.* The Hebrew word *abur,* which we translate "old corn," occurs only in this place in such a sense, if that sense be legitimate. The noun, though of doubtful signification, is evidently derived from *abar,* "to pass over, to go beyond"; and here it may be translated simply "the produce," that which passes from the land into the hands of the cultivator; or according to Cocceius, what passes from person to person in the way of traffic; hence bought corn, what they purchased from the inhabitants of the land. *On the morrow after the passover.* That is, on the fifteenth day, for then the Feast of Unleavened Bread began. But they could eat neither bread. nor parched corn, nor green ears, till the firstfruits of the harvest had been waved at the Tabernacle (see Lev. xxiii. 9, etc.); and therefore in this case we may suppose that the Israelites had offered a sheaf of the barley harvest, the only grain that was then ripe, before they ate of the unleavened cakes and parched corn.

12. *And the manna ceased . . . after they had eaten of the old corn.* This miraculous supply continued with them as long as they needed it. While they were in the wilderness they required such a provision; nor could such a multitude, in such a place, be supported without a miracle. Now as they entered into the Promised Land, and there was an ample provision made in the ordinary way of Providence, there was no longer any need of a miraculous supply; therefore the manna ceased which they had enjoyed for forty years.

13. *When Joshua was by Jericho.* The sixth chapter should have commenced here, as this is an entirely new relation; or these two chapters should have made but one, as the present division has most unnaturally divided the communication which Joshua had from the angel of the Lord, and which is continued to v. 5 of chap. vi. It is very likely that Joshua had gone out privately to reconnoiter the city of Jericho when he had this vision; and while he was contemplating the strength of the place, and probably reflecting on the extreme difficulty of reducing it, God, to encourage him, granted him this vision, and instructed him in the means by which the city should be taken.

There stood a man over against him. It has been a very general opinion, both among the ancients and moderns, that the person mentioned here was no other than the Lord Jesus in that form which, in the fulness of time, He was actually to assume for the redemption of man. *And Joshua went unto him.* The whole history of Joshua shows him to have been a man of the most undaunted mind and intrepid courage—a genuine hero. An ordinary person, seeing this man armed, with a drawn sword in his hand, would have endeavored to regain the camp, and sought safety in flight; but Joshua, undismayed, though probably slightly armed, walked up to this terrible person and immediately questioned him, *Art thou for us, or for our adversaries?* probably at first supposing that he might be the Canaanitish general, coming to reconnoitre the Israelitish camp, as himself was come out to examine the city of Jericho.

14. *But as captain of the host of the Lord am I now come.* By this saying Joshua was both encouraged and instructed. As if he had said, "Fear not; Jehovah hath sent from heaven to save thee and thy people from the reproach of them that would swallow thee up. Israel is the Lord's host; and the Lord of hosts is Israel's Captain. Thou thyself shalt only be captain under me, and I am now about to instruct thee relative to thy conduct in this war." *And Joshua . . . did worship.* Nor was he reprehended for offering divine worship to this person, which he would not have received had he been a created angel. See Rev. xxii. 8-9.

15. *Loose thy shoe from off thy foot.* These were the same words which the angel, on Mount Sinai spoke to Moses (see Exod. iii. 5-8); and from this it seems likely that it was the same person that appeared in both places: in the first, to encourage Moses to deliver the oppressed Israelites, and bring them to the Promised Land; in the second, to encourage Joshua in his arduous labor in expelling the ancient inhabitants, and establishing the people in the inheritance promised to their fathers.

There is scarcely a more unfortunate division of chapters in the whole Bible than that here. Through this very circumstance many persons have been puzzled to know what was intended by this extraordinary appearance, because they supposed that the whole business ends with the chapter, whereas it is continued in the succeeding one, the first verse of which is a mere parenthesis, simply relating the state of Jericho at the time that Joshua was favored by this encouraging vision.

CHAPTER 6

The inhabitants of Jericho close their gates, 1. Continuation of the discourse between the captain of the Lord's host and Joshua. He commands the people to march round the city six days, the seven priests blowing with their trumpets; and to give a general shout, then marching round it on the seventh, and promises that then the walls of the city shall fall down, 2-5. Joshua delivers these directions to the priests and to the people, 6-7. The priests and people obey; the order of their procession, 8-16. He commands them to spare the house of Rahab, 17, and not to touch any part of the property of the city, the whole of which God had devoted to destruction, 18-19. On the seventh day the walls fall down, and the Israelites take the city, 20-21. The spies are ordered to take care of Rahab and her family—the city is burned, but the silver, gold, brass, and iron are put into the treasury of the house of the Lord, 22-24. Rahab dwells among the Israelites, 25; and the city is laid under a curse, 26.

1. *Now Jericho was straitly shut up.* The king of Jericho, finding that the spies had escaped, though the city was always kept shut by night, took the most proper precaution to prevent everything of the kind in future by keeping the city shut both day and night, having no doubt laid in a sufficiency of provisions to stand a siege, being determined to defend himself to the uttermost.

2. *And the Lord said unto Joshua.* This is the same person who in the preceding chapter is called the captain or prince of the Lord's host, the discourse being here continued that was begun at the conclusion of the preceding chapter, from which the first verses of this are unnaturally divided. *I have given into thine hand Jericho.* From v. 11 of chap. xxiv. it seems as if there had been persons of all the seven Canaanitish nations then in Jericho, who might have come together at this time to help the king of Jericho against the invading Israelites.

3. *Ye shall compass the city.* In what order the people marched round the city does not exactly appear from the text. Some think they observed the same order as in their ordinary marches in the desert; others think that the soldiers marched first, then the priests who blew the trumpets, then those who carried the ark, and lastly the people.

4. *Seven trumpets of rams' horns.* The Hebrew word *yobelim* does not signify *rams' horns;* nor do any of the ancient versions, the Chaldee excepted, give it this meaning. The instruments used on this occasion were evidently of the same kind with those used on the jubilee, and were probably made of horn or of silver; and the text in this place may be translated, "And seven priests shall bear before the ark the seven jubilee trumpets." *Seven times.* The time was thus lengthened out that the besiegers and the besieged might be the more deeply impressed with that supernatural power by which *alone* the walls fell.

5. *The wall of the city shall fall down flat.* Several commentators, both Jews and Christians, have supposed that the ground under the foundation of the walls opened, and the wall sunk into the chasm, so that there remained nothing

but plain ground for the Israelites to walk over. Of this the text says nothing; literally, "The wall of the city shall fall down under itself," which appears to mean no more than, "The wall shall fall down from its very foundations." And this probably was the case in every part, though large breaches in different places might be amply sufficient to admit the armed men first, after whom the whole host might enter, in order to destroy the city.

9. *The rereward came after the ark.* The word *measseph,* from *asaph,* to "collect" or "gather up," may signify either the *rearward,* as our translation understands it, or the people who carried the baggage of the army; for on the seventh day this was necessary, as much fighting might be naturally expected in the assault, and they would need a supply of arms, darts, etc., as well as conveniences for those who might happen to be wounded. Or the persons here intended might be such as carried the sacred articles belonging to the ark, or merely such people as might follow in the procession, without observing any particular order. The Jews think the division of Dan is meant, which always brought up the rear. See Numbers x.

14. *So they did six days.* It is not likely that the whole Israelitish host went each day round the city. This would have been utterly impossible; the fighting men alone amounted to nearly six hundred thousand, independently of the people, who must have amounted at least to two or three millions. We may therefore safely assert that only a select number, such as was deemed necessary for the occasion, were employed.

15. *The seventh day . . . they rose early.* Because on this day they had to encompass the city seven times; a proof that the city could not have been very extensive, else this going round it seven times, and having time sufficient left to sack and destroy it, would have been impossible.

17. *The city shall be accursed.* That is, it shall be devoted to destruction; you shall take no spoils, and put all that resist to the sword. Though this may be the meaning of the word *cherem* in some places (see the note on Lev. xxvii. 29), yet here it seems to imply the total destruction of all the inhabitants, (see v. 21); but it is likely that peace was offered to this city, and that the extermination of the inhabitants was in consequence of the rejection of this offer.

20. *The people shouted with a great shout, that the wall fell down.* There has been much learned labor spent to prove that the shouting of the people might be the natural cause that the wall fell down! The whole relation evidently supposes it to have been a supernatural interference.

21. *They utterly destroyed . . . both man and woman.* As this act was ordered by God himself, who is the Maker and Judge of all men, it must be right; for the Judge of all the earth cannot do wrong. Nothing that breathed was permitted to live; hence the oxen, sheep, and asses were destroyed, as well as the inhabitants.

23. *Brought out Rahab, and her father.* Rahab having been faithful to her vow of secrecy, the Israelites were bound by the oath of the spies,

who acted as their representatives in this business, to preserve her and her family alive. *And left them without the camp.* They were considered as persons unclean, and consequently left without the camp (see Lev. xiii. 46; Num. xii. 14). When they had abjured heathenism, were purified, and the males had received circumcision, they were doubtless admitted into the camp and became incorporated with Israel.

24. *Only the silver, and the gold . . . they put into the treasury.* The people were to have no share of the spoils, because they had no hand in the conquest. God alone overthrew the city; and only into His treasury the spoils were brought.

25. *And she dwelleth in Israel even unto this day.* This is one proof that the book was written in the time to which it is commonly referred; and certainly might have been done by the hand of Joshua himself, though doubtless many marginal notes may have since crept into the text, which, to superficial observers, give it the appearance of having been written after the days of Joshua. See the Preface to this book.

26. *And Joshua adjured them at that time.* It appears that he had received intimations from God that this idolatrous city should continue a monument of the divine displeasure; and having convened the princes and elders of the people, he bound them by an oath that they should never rebuild it; and then, in their presence, pronounced a curse upon the person who should attempt it. The ruins of this city continuing would be a permanent proof, not only of God's displeasure against idolatry, but of the miracle which He had wrought in behalf of the Israelites.

He shall lay the foundation thereof. This is a strange execration, but it may rather be considered in the light of a prediction. It seems to intimate that he who should attempt to rebuild this city should lose all his children in the interim from laying the foundation to the completion of the walls; which the author of 1 Kings xvi. 34 says was accomplished in Hiel the Beth-elite, who rebuilt Jericho under the reign of Ahab, and "laid the foundation thereof in Abiram his firstborn, and set up the gates thereof in his youngest son Segub."

CHAPTER 7

The trespass of the Israelites, 1. Joshua sends men to view the state of Ai, 2. They return with a favorable report, 3. Three thousand men are sent against it, who are defeated, and thirty-six killed, 4-5. Joshua is greatly distressed, prostrates himself, and inquires of the Lord the reason why He has abandoned Israel to their enemies, 6-9. The Lord raises him, and informs him that, contrary to the command, some of the people had secreted some of the spoils of Jericho, 10-12. He is directed how to discover the delinquent, 13-15. Joshua inquires in what tribe the guilt is found, and finds it to be in the tribe of Judah; in what family, and finds it to be among the Zarhites; in what household, and finds it to be in that of Zabdi; in what individual, and finds it to be Achan, son of Carmi, son of Zabdi, 16-18. Joshua exhorts him to confess his sin, 19. He does so, and gives a circumstantial account, 20-21. Joshua sends for the stolen articles, 22-23. Achan and all that belonged to him are brought to the valley of Achor, stoned, and burned, 24-26.

1. *The children of Israel committed a trespass.* It is certain that one only was guilty, and yet the trespass is imputed here to the whole congregation; and the whole congregation soon suffered shame and disgrace on the account, as their armies were defeated, thirty-six persons slain, and general terror spread through the whole camp. Being one body, God attributed the crime of the individual to the whole till the trespass was discovered, and by a public act of justice inflicted on the culprit the congregation had purged itself of the iniquity. *The accursed thing.* A portion of the spoils of the city of Jericho, the whole of which God had commanded to be destroyed. *For Achan, the son of Carmi.* Judah had two sons by Tamar: Pharez and Zarah. Zarah was father of Zabdi, and Zabdi of Carmi, the father of Achan.

2. *Sent men from Jericho to Ai.* This is the place called Hai, Gen. xii. 8. It was in the east of Bethel, north of Jericho, from which it was distant about ten or twelve miles. From verses 4 and 5 it appears to have been situated upon a hill, and belonged to the Amorites, as we learn from v. 7. It is very likely that it was a strong place, as it chose to risk a siege, notwithstanding the extraordinary destruction of Jericho, which it had lately witnessed.

4. *About three thousand men.* The spies sent to reconnoitre the place (v. 3) reported that the town was meanly garrisoned, and that two or three thousand men would be sufficient to take it. These were accordingly sent up, and were repulsed by the Amorites.

5. *They chased them from before the gate even unto Shebarim.* They seem to have presumed that the men of Ai would have immediately opened their gates to them, and therefore they marched up with confidence; but the enemy appearing, they were put to flight, their ranks utterly broken, and thirty-six of them killed. *Shebarim* signifies "breaches" or "broken places," and may here apply to the ranks of the Israelites, which were broken by the men of Ai; for the people were totally routed, though there were but few slain. *The hearts of the people melted.* They were utterly discouraged, and by this gave an ample proof that without the supernatural assistance of God they could never have conquered the land.

6. *Joshua rent his clothes.* It was not in consequence of this slight discomfiture, simply considered in itself, that Joshua laid this business so much to heart; but (1) because the people melted, and became as water, and there was little hope that they would make any stand against the enemy; and (2) because this defeat evidently showed that God had turned His hand against them. *Put dust upon their heads.* Rending the clothes, beating the breast, tearing the hair, putting dust upon the head, and falling down prostrate were the usual marks of deep affliction and distress. Most nations have expressed their sorrow in a similar way.

7. *Alas, O Lord God.* Particles of exclamations and distress, or what are called interjections, are nearly the same in all languages; and the reason is because they are the simple voice of nature. The Hebrew word which we translate *alas* is *ahah*. The complaint of Joshua in this and the following verses seems principally to have arisen from his deep concern for the glory of God, and the affecting interest he took in behalf of the people. He felt for the thousands of Israel, whom he considered as abandoned to destruction; and he felt for the glory of God, for he knew should Israel be destroyed God's name would be blasphemed among the heathen. His expostulations with his Maker,

which have been too hastily blamed by some as savoring of too great freedom and impatience, are founded on God's own words, Deut. xxxii. 26-27, and on the practice of Moses himself, who had used similar expressions on a similar occasion; see Exod. v. 22-23; Num. xiv. 13-18.

10. *Wherefore liest thou thus upon thy face?* It is plain there was nothing in Joshua's prayer or complaint that was offensive to God, for here there is no reprehension.

11. *Israel hath sinned.* It is impossible that God should turn against His people, if they had not turned away from Him. *They have taken of the accursed thing,* notwithstanding My severe prohibition. They *have also stolen,* supposing, if not seen by their brethren, I should either not see or not regard it. They have *dissembled—* pretended to have kept strictly the command I gave them; *and they have put it even among their own stuff*—considered it now as a part of their own property.

12. *Because they were accursed.* From this verse it appears that the nature of the execration or anathema was such that those who took of the thing doomed to destruction fell immediately under the same condemnation.

13. *Up, sanctify the people.* Joshua, all the time that God spake, lay prostrate before the ark; he is now commanded to get up, and sanctify the people, i.e., cause them to wash themselves, and get into a proper disposition to hear the judgment of the Lord relative to the late transactions.

14. *Ye shall be brought according to your tribes.* It has been a subject of serious inquiry in what manner and by what means the culpable tribe, family, household, and individual were discovered. It is probable that the whole was determined by the lot; and that God chose this method to detect the guilty *tribe,* next the *family,* thirdly the *household,* and lastly the individual. This was nearly the plan pursued in the election of Saul by Samuel, 1 Sam. x. 19-20. The same mode was used to find out who it was that transgressed the king's command, when it was found that Jonathan had eaten a little honey, 1 Sam. xiv. 40-43.

19. *My son, give . . . glory to the Lord God.* The person being now detected, Joshua wishes him to acknowledge the omniscience of God, and confess his crime. And doubtless this was designed, not only for the edification of the people, and a vindication of the righteous judgment of God, but in reference to his own salvation; for as his life was now become forfeited to the law, there was the utmost necessity of humiliation before God, that his soul might be saved. *Give . . . glory to God* signifies the same as, Make a thorough confession as in the presence of God, and disguise no part of the truth. In this way and in these very words the Jews adjured the man who had been born blind that he would truly tell who had healed him, John ix. 24.

20. *I have sinned against the Lord God.* This seems a very honest and hearty confession, and there is hope that this poor culprit escaped perdition.

21. *A goodly Babylonish garment.* Addereth *shinar,* a "splendid or costly robe of Shinar"; but as Babylon or Babel was built in the plain of Shinar, the word has in general been trans-

lated Babylon in this place. It is very probable that this was the robe of the king of Jericho, for the same word is used, Jon. iii. 6, to express the royal robe of the king of Nineveh, which he laid aside in order to humble himself before God. *A wedge of gold.* A tongue of gold, *leshon zahab* what we commonly call an "ingot of gold," a corruption of the word *lingot,* signifying a "little tongue." This verse gives us a notable instance of the progress of sin. It (1) enters by the eye; (2) sinks into the heart; (3) actuates the hand, and (4) leads to secrecy and dissimulation.

24. *Joshua . . . took Achan . . . and all that he had.* He and his cattle and substance were brought to the valley to be consumed; his sons and his daughters, probably, to witness the judgments of God inflicted on their disobedient parent. See v. 25.

25. *Why hast thou troubled us?* Here is a reference to the meaning of Achan's or Achar's name, *meh achar-tanu;* and as *achar* is used here, and not *achan,* and the valley is called the "valley of Achor," and not the "valley of Achan," hence some have supposed that Achar was his proper name, as it is read in 1 Chron. ii. 7.

And all Israel stoned him with stones, and burned them with fire, after they had stoned them with stones. With great deference to the judgment of others, I ask, Can it be fairly proved from the text that the sons and daughters of Achan were stoned to death and burned as well as their father? The text certainly leaves it doubtful, but seems rather to intimate that Achan alone was stoned, and that his substance was burned with fire. The reading of the present Hebrew text is, "They stoned him with stones, and burned them with fire, after they had stoned them with stones." The singular number being used in the first clause of the verse, and the plural in the last, makes the matter doubtful. The Vulgate is very clear: "All Israel stoned him: and all that he had was consumed with fire." The Septuagint add this and the first clause of the next verse together: "And all Israel stoned him with stones, and raised over him a great heap of stones." The Syriac says simply, "They stoned him with stones, and burned what pertained to him with fire."

CHAPTER 8

The Lord encourages Joshua, and promises to deliver Ai into his hands, and instructs him how he is to proceed against it, 1-2. Joshua takes 30,000 of his best troops, and gives them instructions concerning his intention of taking Ai by stratagem, 3-8. The men dispose themselves according to these directions, 9-13. The king of Ai attacks the Israelites, who, feigning to be beaten, fly before him, in consequence of which all the troops of Ai issue out, and pursue the Israelites, 14-17. Joshua, at the command of God, stretches out his spear towards Ai, and then 5,000 men that he had placed in ambush in the valley rise up, enter the city, and set it on fire, 18-19. Then Joshua and his men turned against the men of Ai, and, at the same time, those who had taken the city sallied forth and attacked them in the rear; thus the men of Ai were defeated, their king taken prisoner, the city sacked, and 12,000 persons slain, 20-26. The Israelites take the spoils, and hang the king of Ai, 27-29. Joshua builds an altar to God on Mount Ebal, and writes on it a copy of the law of Moses, 30-32. The elders, officers, and judges stand on each side of the ark, one half over against Mount Gerizim, and the other against Mount Ebal, and read the blessings and curses of the law, according to the command of Moses, 33-35.

1. *Fear not.* The iniquity being now purged away, because of which God had turned His hand against Israel, there was now no cause to

dread any other disaster, and therefore Joshua is ordered to take courage.

Take all the people of war with thee. From the letter of this verse it appears that all that were capable of carrying arms were to march out of the camp on this occasion: 30,000 chosen men formed an ambuscade in one place; 5,000 Joshua placed in another, who had all gained their positions in the night season; with the rest of the army he appeared the next morning before Ai, which the men of that city would naturally suppose were the whole of the Israelitish forces, and consequently be the more emboldened to come out and attack them. But some think that 30,000 men were the whole that were employed on this occasion; 5,000 of whom were placed as an ambuscade on the west side of the city between Bethel and Ai, v. 12, and with the rest Joshua appeared before the city in the morning. The king of Ai seeing but about 25,000 coming against him, and being determined to defend his city and crown to the last extremity, though he had but 12,000 persons in the whole city, v. 25, scarcely one-half of whom we can suppose to be effective men, he was determined to risk a battle; and accordingly issued out, and was defeated by the stratagem mentioned in the preceding part of this chapter.

Several eminent commentators are of opinion that the whole Israelitish force was employed on this occasion, because of what is said in the first verse; but this is not at all likely. (1) It appears that but 30,000 were chosen out of the whole camp for this expedition, the rest being drawn up in readiness should their cooperation be necessary. See vv. 3 and 10. (2) That all the people were mustered in order to make this selection, v. 1. (3) That these 30.000 were sent off by night, v. 3, Joshua himself continuing in the camp a part of that night, v. 9, with the design of putting himself at the head of the army next morning. (4) That of the 30,000 men 5,000 were directed to lie in ambush between Bethel and Ai, on the west side of the city, v. 12, the 25,000 having taken a position on the north side of the city, v. 11.

8. *Ye shall set the city on fire.* Probably this means no more than that they should kindle a fire in the city, the smoke of which should be an indication that they had taken it. For as the spoils of the city were to be divided among the people, had they at this time set fire to the city itself, all the property must have been consumed, for the 5,000 men did not wait to save anything, as they immediately issued out to attack the men of Ai in the rear.

10. *Numbered the people.* "He visited the people"—inspected their ranks to see whether everything was in perfect readiness, that in case they should be needed they might be led on to the attack. There is no doubt that Joshua had left the rest of the army so disposed and ready, part of it having probably advanced towards Ai, that he might easily receive reinforcements in case of any disaster to the 30,000 which had advanced against the city; and this consideration will serve to remove a part of the difficulty which arises from vv. 1, 3, and 10, collated with other parts of this chapter. Had he brought all his troops in sight, the people of Ai would not have attempted to risk a battle, and would consequently have kept within their walls, from which it was the object of Joshua to decoy them.

17. *There was not a man left in Ai or Beth-el.* It is very likely that the principal strength of Bethel had been previously brought into Ai, as the strongest place to make a stand in, Bethel being but about three miles distant from Ai, and probably not greatly fortified. Therefore Ai contained on this occasion all the men of Bethel —all the warriors of that city, as well as its own troops and inhabitants. Others think that the Bethelites, seeing the Israelites flee, sallied out of their city as against a common enemy; but that, finding the men of Ai discomfited and the city taken, they returned to Bethel, which Joshua did not think proper to attack at this time. From Judg. i. 24 we find that Bethel was then a walled city, in the hands of the Canaanites, and was taken by the house of Joseph.

18. *Stretch out the spear.* It is very probable that Joshua had a flag or ensign at the end of his spear, which might be easily seen at a considerable distance; and that the unfurling or waving of this was the sign agreed on between him and the ambush.

19. *Set the city on fire.* See on v. 8.

20. *They had no power to flee this way or that way.* They were in utter consternation. They saw that the city was taken; they found themselves in the midst of their foes; that their wives, children, and property, had fallen a prey to their enemies, in consequence of which they were so utterly panic-struck as to be incapable of making any resistance.

24. *Returned unto Ai, and smote it with the edge of the sword.* This must refer to the women, children, and old persons, left behind; for it is likely that all the effective men had sallied out when they imagined the Israelites had fled.

26. *Joshua drew not his hand back.* He was not only the general, but the standard-bearer or ensign of his own army, and continued in this employment during the whole of the battle. Some commentators understand this and v. 18 figuratively, as if they implied that Joshua continued in prayer to God for the success of his troops; nor did he cease till the armies of Ai were annihilated and the city taken and destroyed. The Hebrew word *kidon*, which we render *spear*, is rendered by the Vulgate "buckler"; and it must be owned that it seems to have this signification in several passages of Scripture (see 1 Sam. xvii. 6, 45; Job xxxix. 23). But it is clear enough also that it means a spear, or some kind of offensive armor, in other places (see Job xli. 29; Jer. vi. 23). I cannot therefore think that it has any metaphorical meaning, such as that attributed to the holding up of Moses' hands, Exod. xvii. 10-12.

27. *Only the cattle and the spoil.* In the case of Jericho these were all consigned to destruction, and therefore it was criminal to take anything pertaining to the city, as we have already seen; but in the case before us the cattle and spoils were expressly given to the conquerors by the order of God.

28. *Unto this day.* This last clause was probably added by a later hand.

29. *The king of Ai he hanged on a tree.* He had gone out at the head of his men, and had been taken prisoner, v. 23; and the battle being over, he was ordered to be hanged, probably after having been strangled, or in some way deprived of life, as in the case mentioned chap.

x. 26, for in those times it was not customary to hang people alive. *As soon as the sun was down.* It was not lawful to let the bodies remain all night upon the tree. See the note on Deut. xxi. 23. *Raise thereon a great heap of stones.* This was a common custom through all antiquity in every country, as we have already seen in the case of Achan, chap. vii. 20.

30. *Then Joshua built an altar.* This was done in obedience to the express command of God, Deut. xxvii. 4-8.

32. *A copy of the law of Moses. Mishneh torath,* the "repetition of the law"; that is, a copy of the blessings and curses, as commanded by Moses; not a copy of the Decalogue, as some imagine, nor of the Book of Deuteronomy, as others think; much less of the whole Pentateuch; but merely of that part which contained the blessings and curses, and which was to be read on this solemn occasion.

35. *With the women, and the little ones.* It was necessary that all should know that they were under the same obligations to obey; even the *women* are brought forward, not only because of their personal responsibility, but because to them was principally intrusted the education of the children. The *children* also witness this solemn transaction, that a salutary fear of offending God might be early, diligently, and deeply impressed upon their hearts.

CHAPTER 9

All the kings of the Hittites, Amorites, Canaanites, Perizzites, Hivites, and Jebusites unite their forces against Joshua, 1-2. The inhabitants of Gibeon, hearing what Joshua had done to Ai, sent ambassadors to him, feigning themselves to come from a very distant tribe, requesting a friendly alliance with him, 3-5. Their address to Joshua, and the means they used to deceive the Israelites, 6-13. The Israelitish elders are deceived, and make a league with them, which they confirm with an oath, 14-15. After three days they are informed that the Gibeonites belong to the seven Canaanitish nations, yet they spare their cities, 16-17. The congregation murmuring because of this, the elders excuse themselves because of their oath, 18-19. They purpose to make the Gibeonites slaves to the congregation, 20-21. Joshua calls them, and pronounces this sentence against them, 22-23. They vindicate themselves, and submit to their lot, 24-25. They are spared, and made hewers of wood and drawers of water to the congregation and to the altar, 26-27.

1. *And it came to pass, when all the kings . . . heard thereof.* From this account it appears that the capture and destruction of Jericho and Ai had been heard of to the remotest parts of the land, that a general fear of the Israelitish arms prevailed, and that the different dynasties or petty governments into which the land was divided, felt all their interests at stake and determined to make the defense of their country a common cause.

3. *The inhabitants of Gibeon heard.* These alone did not join the confederation. Gibeon is supposed to have been the capital of the Hivites. In the division of the land it fell to the lot of Benjamin, chap. xviii. 25, and was afterwards given to the priests, chap. xxi. 17.

4. *Old sacks . . . and wine bottles, old.* They pretended to have come from a very distant country, and that their sacks and the goatskins that served them for carrying their wine and water were worn out by the length of the journey.

5. *Old shoes and clouted.* Their sandals they pretended had been worn out by long and difficult travelling, and they had been obliged to

have them frequently patched during the way; their garments also were worn thin; and what remained of their bread was moldy—spotted with age, or, as our old version has it, "bored" —pierced with many holes by the vermin which had bred in it, through the length of the time it had been in their sacks; and this is the most literal meaning of the original *nikkudim,* which means "spotted or pierced with many holes."

7. *Peradventure ye dwell among us.* It is strange they should have had such a suspicion, as the Gibeonites had acted so artfully; and it is as strange that, having such a suspicion, they acted with so little caution.

8. *We are thy servants.* This appears to have been the only answer they gave to the question of the Israelitish elders, and this they gave to Joshua, not to them, as they saw that Joshua was commander in chief of the host. *Who are ye? and from whence come ye?* To these questions, from such an authority, they felt themselves obliged to give an explicit answer; and they do it very artfully by a mixture of truth, falsehood, and hypocrisy.

9. *Because of the name of the Lord thy God.* They pretend that they had undertaken this journey on a religious account, and seem to intimate that they had the highest respect for Jehovah, the object of the Israelites' worship; this was hypocrisy. *We have heard the fame of him.* This was true: the wonders which God did in Egypt, and the discomfiture of Sihon and Og, had reached the whole land of Canaan; and it was on this account that the inhabitants of it were panic-struck. The Gibeonites, knowing that they could not stand where such mighty forces had fallen, wished to make the Israelites their friends. This part of their relation was strictly true.

11. *Wherefore our elders.* All this, and what follows to the end of verse 13, was false, contrived merely for the purpose of deceiving the Israelites, and this they did to save their own lives, as they expected all the inhabitants of Canaan to be put to the sword.

14. *The men took of their victuals.* This was done in all probability in the way of friendship; for, from time immemorial to the present day, eating together, in the Asiatic countries, is considered a token of unalterable friendship; and those who eat even salt together feel themselves bound thereby in a perpetual covenant. But the marginal reading of this clause should not be hastily rejected. *And asked not counsel at the mouth of the Lord.* They made the covenant with the Gibeonites without consulting God by Urim and Thummim, which was highly reprehensible in them, as it was a state transaction in which the interests and honor of God, their King, were intimately concerned.

15. *Joshua made peace with them.* Joshua agreed to receive them into a friendly connection with the Israelites, and to respect their lives and properties; and the elders of Israel bound themselves to the observance of it, and confirmed it with an oath. As the same words are used here as in verse 6, we may suppose that the covenant was made in the ordinary way, a sacrifice being offered on the occasion, and its blood poured out before the Lord.

16. *At the end of three days.* Gibeon is reputed to be only about eight leagues distant

from Gilgal, and on this account the fraud might be easily discovered in the time mentioned above.

17. *The children of Israel . . . came unto their cities.* Probably when the fraud was discovered, Joshua sent out a detachment to examine their country, and to see what use could be made of it in the prosecution of their war with the Canaanites. Some of the cities mentioned here were afterwards in great repute among the Israelites; and God chose to make one of them, Kirjath-jearim, the residence of the ark of the covenant for twenty years, in the reigns of Saul and David. There is no evidence that the preservation of the Gibeonites was displeasing to Jehovah.

18. *All the congregation murmured.* Merely because they were deprived of the spoils of the Gibeonites. They were now under the full influence of a predatory spirit; God saw their proneness to this and therefore, at particular times, totally interdicted the spoils of conquered cities, as in the case of Jericho.

19. *We have sworn unto them.* Although the Israelites were deceived in this business, and the covenant was made on a certain supposition which was afterwards proved to have had no foundation in truth, and consequently the whole engagement on the part of the deceived was hereby vitiated and rendered null and void, yet because the elders had eaten with them, offered a covenant sacrifice, and sworn by Jehovah, they did not consider themselves at liberty to break the terms of the agreement, as far as the lives of the Gibeonites were concerned. That their conduct in this respect was highly pleasing to God is evident from this, that Joshua is nowhere reprehended for making this covenant and sparing the Gibeonites; and that Saul, who four hundred years after this thought himself and the Israelites loosed from this obligation, and in consequence oppressed and destroyed the Gibeonites, was punished for the breach of this treaty, being considered as the violator of a most solemn oath and covenant engagement (see 2 Sam. xxi. 2-9 and Ezek. xvii. 18-19). All these circumstances laid together prove that the command to destroy the Canaanites was not so absolute as is generally supposed, and should be understood as rather referring to the destruction of the political existence of the Canaanitish nations than to the destruction of their lives.

21. *Hewers of wood and drawers of water.* Perhaps this is a sort of proverbial expression, signifying the lowest state of servitude, though it may also be understood literally.

23. *Now therefore ye are cursed.* Does not this refer to what was pronounced by Noah, Gen. ix. 25, against Ham and his posterity? Did not the curse of Ham imply slavery, and nothing else? "Cursed be Canaan; a servant of servants shall he be"; and does it not sufficiently appear that nothing else than perpetual slavery is implied in the curse of the Gibeonites? *Hewers of wood and drawers of water.* The disgrace of this state lay not in the laboriousness of it, but in its being the common employment of the females, if the ancient customs among the same, people were such as prevail now.

24. *We were sore afraid of our lives.* Self-preservation, which is the most powerful law of nature, dictated to them those measures which they adopted; and they plead this as the motive of their conduct.

25. *We are in thine hand.* Entirely in thy power. *As it seemeth good and right unto thee . . . do.* Whatever justice and mercy dictate to thee to do to us, that perform. They expect justice, because they deceived the Israelites; but they expect mercy also, because they were driven to use this expedient for fear of losing their lives.

26. *And so did he unto them.* That is, he acted according to justice and mercy. He delivered them out of the hands of the people, so that they slew them not—here was mercy; and he made them hewers of wood and drawers of water for the congregation, and to the altar of God—here was justice. Thus Joshua did nothing but what was good and right, not only in his own eyes, but also in the eyes of the Lord.

CHAPTER 10

Adoni-zedec, king of Jerusalem, hearing of the capture of Ai, and that the Gibeonites had made peace with Israel, calls to his assistance four other kings to fight against Gibeon, 1-4. They join forces, and encamp against Gibeon, 5. The Gibeonites send to Joshua for succor, 6, who immediately marches to their relief receives encouragement from God, and falls suddenly on the confederate forces, 7-9, and defeats them; they fly, and multitudes of them are slain by a miraculous shower of hailstones, 10-11. Joshua, finding that the day began to fail, prayed that the sun and moon might stand still, that they might have time to pursue and utterly destroy these confederate forces, 12. The sun and moon stand still, and make that day as long as two, 13-14. Joshua and the people return to their camp at Gilgal, 15. The five kings having taken shelter in a cave at Makkedah, Joshua commands the people to roll great stones against the mouth of the cave, and set a watch to keep it, while Israel are pursuing their enemies, 16-19. The Israelites return to Makkedah, bring forth the five kings, then slay and hang them on five trees, 20-27. The Israelites take and destroy Makkedah, 28, and Libnah, 29-30, and Lachish 31-32, and defeat Horam, king of Gezer, 33, and take Eglon, 34-35, and Hebron, 36-37, and Debir, 38-39, and all the country of the hills, south, vale, and springs, and the whole country from Kadesh-barnea to Gibeon, 40-42. They return to Gilgal, 43.

1. *Adoni-zedec.* This name signifies the "Lord of justice or righteousness"; and it has been conjectured that the Canaanitish kings assume this name in imitation of that of the ancient patriarchal king of this city, Melchizedek, whose name signifies "king of righteousness," or "my righteous king." *Jerusalem. Yerushalam.* This word has been variously explained; if it be compounded of *shalam,* "peace, perfection," and *raah,* "he saw," it may signify "the vision of peace"—or "he shall see peace or perfection."

2. *As one of the royal cities.* Not a regal city, but great, well-inhabited and well-fortified, as those cities which served for the royal residence generally were.

3. *Hoham king of Hebron.* This city was situated in the mountains, southward of Jerusalem, from which it was about thirty miles distant. It fell to the tribe of Judah. *Piram king of Jarmuth.* There were two cities of this name; one belonged to the tribe of Issachar, see chap. xxi. 29; that mentioned here fell to the tribe of Judah, see chap. xv. 35; it is supposed to have been about eighteen miles distant from Jerusalem. *Japhia king of Lachish.* This city is celebrated in Scripture. In that city Amaziah was slain by conspirators, 2 Kings xiv. 19. It was besieged by Sennacherib, 2 Kings xviii. 14, 17; and without effect by the king of Assyria, as we learn from Isa. xxxvii. 8; it was also

besieged by the army of Nebuchadnezzar, see Jer. xxxiv. 7. It also fell to the lot of Judah, chap. xv. 39.

5. *The five kings of the Amorites.* This is a general name for the inhabitants of Canaan, otherwise called Canaanites; and it is very likely that they had this appellation because the Amorites were the most powerful tribe or nation in that country.

9. *Joshua . . . came unto them suddenly.* This he did by a forced march during the night, for he *went up from Gilgal all night;* from Gilgal to Gibeon was about eighteen or twenty miles; and, having fallen so unexpectedly on these confederate kings, they were immediately thrown into confusion.

10. *Slew them with a great slaughter at Gibeon.* Multitudes of them fell in the onset; after which they fled, and the Israelites pursued them by the way of *Beth-horon.* There were two cities of this name, the upper and lower, both in the tribe of Ephraim, and built by Sherah, the daughter of Ephraim, 1 Chron. vii. 24. *To Azekah, and unto Makkedah.* These two cities were in the tribe of Judah, chap. xv. 35-41.

11. *The Lord cast down great stones from heaven upon them.* Some have contended that stones, in the common acceptation of the word, are intended here; and that the term *hailstones* is used only to point out the celerity of their fall, and their quantity. But it is more likely that hailstones, in the proper sense of the word, are meant as well as expressed in the text. That God on other occasions has made use of hailstones to destroy both men and cattle we have ample proof in the plague of hail that fell on the Egyptians. See the note on Exod. ix. 18.

12. *Then spake Joshua to the Lord.* Though Joshua saw that the enemies of his people were put to flight, yet he well knew that all which escaped would rally again, and that he should be obliged to meet them once more in the field of battle if permitted now to escape. Finding that the day was drawing towards a close, he feared that he should not have time sufficient to complete the destruction of the confederate armies. In this moment, being suddenly inspired with divine confidence, he requested the Lord to perform the most stupendous miracle that had ever been wrought, which was no less than to arrest the sun in his course, and prolong the day till the destruction of his enemies had been completed!

Sun, stand thou still upon Gibeon; and thou, Moon, in the valley of Ajalon. The terms in this command are worthy of particular note. Joshua does not say to the sun, "Stand still," as if he had conceived him to be running his race round the earth; but, "Be silent," or "inactive"; that is, as I understand it, "Restrain thy influence"—no longer act upon the earth, to cause it to revolve round its axis, a mode of speech which is certainly consistent with the strictest astronomical knowledge. And the writer of the account, whether Joshua himself or the author of the book of Jasher, in relating the consequence of this command is equally accurate, using a word widely different when he speaks of the effect the retention of the solar influence had on the moon. In the first case the sun was "silent" or "inactive," *dom;* in the latter, the moon "stood still," *amad.* The standing still of the moon, or its continuance above the horizon, would be the natural effect of the cessation of the solar influence, which obliged the earth to discontinue her diurnal rotation, which of course would arrest the moon; and thus both it and the sun were kept above the horizon, probably for the space of a whole day. As to the address to the moon, it is not conceived in the same terms as that to the sun, and for the most obvious philosophical reasons; all that is said is simply, ". . . and the moon on the vale of Ajalon," which may be thus understood: "Let the sun restrain his influence or be inactive, as he appears now upon Gibeon, that the moon may continue as she appears now over the vale of Ajalon." It is worthy of remark that every word in this poetic address is apparently selected with the greatest caution and precision.

13. *Book of Jasher.* The book of the upright. See the note on Num. xxi. 14. Probably this was a book which, in reference to Joshua and his transactions, was similar to the commentaries of Caesar on his wars with the Gauls.

14. *And there was no day like that.* There was no period of time in which the sun was kept so long above the horizon as on that occasion.

15. *And Joshua returned . . . unto the camp to Gilgal.* That the Israelitish army did not return to the camp at Gilgal till after the hanging of the five kings and the destruction of their cities is sufficiently evident from the subsequent parts of this chapter. When all this business was done, and not before, they returned unto the camp to Gilgal; see v. 43. This verse is omitted by the Septuagint and by the Anglo-Saxon, and it does not appear to have existed in the ancient hexaplar versions; it stands in its proper place in v. 43, and is not only useless where it is, but appears to be an encumbrance to the narrative.

16. *Hid themselves in a cave.* It is very likely that this cave was a fortified place among some rocks, for there were many such places in different parts of Palestine.

21. *None moved his tongue.* The whole transaction of this important day had been carried on so evidently under the direction of God that there was not the least murmuring, nor cause for it, among them, for their enemies were all discomfited. There is an expression similar to this in Exod. xi. 7.

24. *Put your feet upon the necks of these kings.* This act was done symbolically, as a token, not only of the present complete victory, but of their approaching triumph over all their adversaries, which is the interpretation given of it by Joshua in the succeeding verse.

28. *That day Joshua took Makkedah.* It is very possible that Makkedah was taken on the evening of the same day in which the miraculous solstice took place; but as to the other cities mentioned in this chapter, they certainly were subdued some days after, as it is not possible that an army, exhausted as this must have been with a whole night's march and two days' hard fighting, could have proceeded farther than Makkedah that night; the other cities were successively taken in the following days.

29. *Fought against Libnah.* This city was near Makkedah, see chap. xv. 42, and fell to the tribe of Judah, vv. 20, 42, and was given to the priests, chap. xxi. 13. Sennacherib besieged it, after he had been obliged to raise the siege of Lachish (see 2 Kings xix. 8; Isa. xxxvii. 8).

32. *Lachish.* It appears that this was anciently a very strong place; notwithstanding the people were panic-struck, and the Israelites flushed with success, yet Joshua could not reduce it till the second day, and the king of Assyria afterwards was obliged to raise the siege.

33. *Horam king of Gezer.* It is likely that Horam was in a state of alliance with the king of Lachish, and therefore came to his assistance as soon as it appeared that he was likely to be attacked. Joshua probably sent a detachment against him before he was able to form a junction with the forces of Lachish, and utterly destroyed him and his army.

36-38. *Hebron . . . and the king thereof.* See the note on v. 3. From v. 23 we learn that the king of Hebron was one of those five whom Joshua slew and hanged on five trees at Makkedah. How then can it be said that he slew the king of Hebron when he took the city, which was some days after the transactions at Makkedah? Either this slaying of the king of Hebron must refer to what had already been done, or the Hebronites, finding that their king fell in battle, had set up another in his place.

It appears that the city of *Hebron* had fallen back into the hands of the Canaanites, for it was again taken from them by the tribe of Judah, Judg. i. 10. *Debir* had also fallen into their hands, for it was reconquered by Othniel, the son-in-law of Caleb, Judg. i. 11-13. The manner in which Calmet accounts for this is very natural; Joshua, in his rapid conquests, contented himself with taking, demolishing, and burning those cities; but did not garrison any of them, for fear of weakening his army. In several instances no doubt the scattered Canaanites returned, repeopled, and put those cities in a state of defense. Hence the Israelites were obliged to conquer them a second time.

39. *Destroyed all the souls.* They brought every person under an anathema; they either slew them or reduced them to a state of slavery. Is it reasonable to say those were slain who were found in arms, of the others they made slaves?

40. *All the country of the hills.* See the note on Deut. i. 7. Destroyed all that breathed. Every person found in arms who continued to resist; these were all destroyed. Those who submitted were spared; but many no doubt made their escape, and afterwards reoccupied certain parts of the land. See vv. 36-37.

41. *And all the country of Goshen.* It appears plain that there was a city named *Goshen* in the tribe of Judah (see chap. xv. 51); and this probably gave name to the adjacent country, which may be that referred to above.

42. *Did Joshua take at one time.* That is, he defeated all those kings, and took all their cities, in one campaign; this appears to be the rational construction of the Hebrew. But these conquests were so rapid and stupendous that they cannot be attributed either to the generalship of Joshua or to the valor of the Israelites; and hence the author himself, disclaiming the merit of them, modestly and piously adds, *because the Lord God of Israel fought for Israel.*

CHAPTER 11

The kings of Hazor, Madon, Shimron, and Achshaph, with those of the mountains, plains, etc., and various chiefs of the Canaanites and Amorites, confederate against Israel, 1-3. They pitch their tents at the waters of Merom, 4-5. The Lord encourages Joshua, 6. He attacks and discomfits them, 7-8. Houghs all their horses, and burns all their chariots, 9. Takes and burns several of their cities, 10-13. The Israelites take the spoils, 14-15. An account of the country taken by Joshua, 16-18. Only the Gibeonites make peace with Israel, 19. All the rest resist and are overcome, 20. Joshua cuts off the Anakim, 21-22. The conquered lands are given to Israel, and the war is concluded, 23.

1. *Jabin king of Hazor.* It is probable that Jabin was the common name of all the kings of Hazor. That king, by whom the Israelites were kept in a state of slavery for twenty years, and who was defeated by Deborah and Barak, was called by this name; see Judg. iv. 2-3, 23. The name signifies "wise" or "intelligent." The city of Hazor was situated above the Lake Semechon, in upper Galilee, according to Josephus, *Antiq.* lib. v., c. 6. It was given to the tribe of Naphtali, Josh. xix. 36, who it appears did not possess it long; for though it was burned by Joshua, v. 11, it is likely that the Canaanites rebuilt it, and restored the ancient government, as we find a powerful king there about one hundred and thirty years after the death of Joshua, Judg. iv. 1. It is the same that was taken by Tiglath-pileser, together with Kadesh, to which it is contiguous; see 2 Kings xv. 29. *Jobab king of Madon.* This royal city is nowhere else mentioned in Scripture except in chap. xii. 19. *King of Shimron.* This city is supposed to be the same with Symira, joined to Maron or Marath, by Pliny. It cannot be Samaria, as that had its name long after by Omri, king of Israel. See 1 Kings xvi. 24.

2. *On the north of the mountains.* Or "the mountain," probably Hermon, or some mountain not far from the Lake of Gennesareth. *And of the plains.* That is, the valleys of the above mountains, which had the Sea of Chinneroth or Gennesareth on the south. *Chinneroth.* This city is supposed by Jerome and several others since his time to be the same as was afterwards called Tiberias. From this city or village the Sea of Chinneroth or Gennesareth probably had its name.

3. *The Canaanite on the east.* Those who dwelt on the borders of Jordan, south of the Sea of Tiberias. *The Hivite under Hermon.* Mount Hermon was to the east of Libanus and the fountains of Jordan; it is the same with Syrion and Baal-hermon in Scripture. *The land of Mizpeh.* There were several cities of this name: one in the tribe of Judah (chap. xv. 38); a second in the tribe of Benjamin (chap. xviii. 26); a third beyond Jordan, in the tribe of Gad; and a fourth beyond Jordan, in the tribe of Manasseh, which is that mentioned in the text.

4. *Much people, even as the sand.* This form of speech, by some called a hyperbole, conveys simply the idea of a vast or unusual number—a number of which no regular estimate could be easily formed. That *chariots* were frequently used in war all the records of antiquity prove; but it is generally supposed that among the Canaanites they were armed with iron scythes fastened to their poles and to the naves of their wheels. Terrible things are spoken of these, and the havoc made by them when furiously driven among the ranks of infantry. Of what sort the cavalry was, we know not; but from the account here given we may see what great advantages these allies possessed over the Israelites, whose armies consisted of infantry only.

5. *The waters of Merom.* Where these waters

were, interpreters are not agreed. Whether they were the waters of the Lake Semechon, or the waters of Megiddo, mentioned Judg. v. 19, cannot be easily determined. The latter is the more probable opinion.

6. *Be not afraid . . . of them.* To meet such a formidable host so well-equipped, in their own country, furnished with all that was necessary to supply a numerous army, required more than ordinary encouragement in Joshua's circumstances. This communication from God was highly necessary, in order to prevent the people from desponding on the eve of a conflict in which their all was at stake.

7. *By the waters of Merom suddenly.* Joshua, being apprised of this grand confederation, lost no time, but marched to meet them; and before they could have supposed him at hand, fell suddenly upon them, and put them to the rout.

9. *He houghed their horses.* The Hebrew word *akar*, which we render to "hough" or "hamstring," signifies to "wound, cut, or lop off." It is very likely that it means here an act by which they were not only rendered useless, but destroyed.

13. *The cities that stood still in their strength.* The word *tillam*, which we translate *their strength*, and the margin, "their heap," has been understood two ways: (1) As signifying those cities which had made peace with the Israelites, when conditions of peace were offered according to the command of the law; and consequently were not destroyed, such as the cities of the Hivites; see v. 19; (2) The cities which were situated upon hills and mountains, which, when taken, might be retained with little difficulty. In this sense the place is understood by the Vulgate, as pointing out the cities "which were situated on hills and eminences."

14. *All the spoil of these cities . . . Israel took.* With the exception of those things which had been employed for idolatrous purposes; see Deut. vii. 25.

16. *The mountain of Israel, and the valley of the same.* This place has given considerable trouble to commentators; and it is not easy to assign such a meaning to the place as may appear in all respects satisfactory. (1) If we consider this verse and the twenty-first to have been added after the times in which the kingdoms of Israel and Judah were divided, the difficulty is at once removed. (2) The difficulty will be removed if we consider that *mountain* and *valley* are put here for "mountains" and "valleys," and that these include all mountains and valleys which were not in the lot that fell to the tribe of Judah. Or, (3) If by *mountain of Israel* we understand Bethel, where God appeared to Jacob, afterwards called Israel, and promised him the land of Canaan, a part of the difficulty will be removed. But the first opinion seems best founded; for there is incontestable evidence that several notes have been added to this book since the days of Joshua. See the Preface.

17. *From the mount Halak.* All the mountainous country that extends from the south of the land of Canaan towards *Seir* unto *Baal-gad*, which lies at the foot of Mount Libanus or Hermon, called by some the mountains of "Separation," which serve as a limit between the land of Canaan and that of Seir; see chap.

xii. 7. *The valley of Lebanon.* The whole extent of the plain which is on the south, and probably north, of Mount Libanus.

18. *Joshua made war a long time.* The whole of these conquests were not effected in one campaign; they probably required six or seven years. Calmet allows the term of seven years for the conquest of the whole land. "Caleb was forty years old when sent from Kadesh-barnea to spy out the land. At the conclusion of the war he was eighty-five years old, as himself says, chap. xiv. 10. From this sum of eighty-five subtract forty, his age when he went from Kadesh-barnea, and the thirty-eight years which he spent in the wilderness after his return, and there will remain the sum of seven years, which was the time spent in the conquest of the land."

20. *It was of the Lord to harden their hearts.* They had sinned against all the light they had received, and God left them justly to the hardness, obstinacy, and pride of their own hearts; for as they chose to retain their idolatry, God was determined that they should be cut off. For as no city made peace with the Israelites but Gibeon and some others of the Hivites, v. 19, it became therefore necessary to destroy them; for their refusal to make peace was the proof that they willfully persisted in their idolatry.

21. *Cut off the Anakims . . . from Hebron . . . from Debir.* This is evidently a recapitulation of the military operations detailed in chap. x. 36-41. *Destroyed . . . their cities.* That is, those of the Anakims; for from v. 13 we learn that Joshua preserved certain other cities.

22. *In Gaza, in Gath, and in Ashdod.* The whole race of the Anakims was extirpated in this war, except those who had taken refuge in the above cities, which belonged to the Philistines, and in which some of the descendants of Anak were found even in the days of David.

23. *So Joshua took the whole land.* All the country described here and in the preceding chapter. *And Joshua gave it for an inheritance unto Israel.* He claimed no peculiar jurisdiction over it; his own family had no peculiar share of it, and himself only the ruined city of Timnath-serah, in the tribe of Ephraim, which he was obliged to rebuild. See chap. xix. 49-50. *And the land rested from war.* The whole territory being now conquered, which God designed the Israelites should possess at this time.

CHAPTER 12

A list of the kings on the east of Jordan which were conquered by Moses, with their territories, 1-6. A list of those on the west side of Jordan conquered by Joshua, in number thirty-one, 7-24.

1. *From the river Arnon unto Mount Hermon.* Arnon was the boundary of all the southern coast of the land occupied by the Israelites beyond Jordan, and the mountains of Hermon were the boundaries on the north. Arnon takes its rise in the mountains of Gilead, and having run a long way from north to south falls into the Dead Sea, near the same place into which Jordan discharges itself. *And all the plain on the east.* All the land from the plains of Moab to Mount Hermon.

2. *From Aroer.* Aroer was situated on the western side of the river Arnon, in the middle

of the valley through which this river takes its course. The kingdom of Sihon extended from the river Arnon and the city of Aroer on the south to the river Jabbok on the north. *And from half Gilead.* The mountains of Gilead extended from north to south from Mount Hermon towards the source of the river Arnon, which was about the midst of the extent of the kingdom of Sihon; thus Sihon is said to have possessed the half of Gilead, that is, the half of the mountains and of the country which bore the name of Gilead on the east of his territories. *River Jabbok.* This river has its source in the mountains of Gilead, and running from east to west, falls into Jordan. It bounds the territories of Sihon on the north and those of the Ammonites on the south.

3. *The sea of Chinneroth.* Or Gennesareth, the same as the Lake or Sea of Tiberias. *The salt sea on the east.* Some think that the Dead Sea is here intended. *Beth-jeshimoth.* A city near the Dead Sea in the plains of Moab. *Ashdoth-pisgah.* Supposed to be a city at the foot of Mount Pisgah.

4. *Coast of Og king of Bashan.* Concerning this person see the notes on Deut. iii. 11 and on Num. xxi. 35, etc. *The remnant of the giants.* Or Rephaim. See the notes on Gen. vi. 4; xiv. 5; and Deut. ii. 7, 11.

5. *The border of the Geshurites.* The country of Bashan, in the days of Moses and Joshua, extended from the river Jabbok on the south to the frontiers of the Geshurites and Maachathites on the north, to the foot of the mountains of Hermon.

7. *From Baal-gad.* A repetition of what is mentioned chap. xi. 17.

9. *The king of Jericho.* On this and the following verses see the notes on chap. x. 1-3.

14. *The king of Hormah.* Supposed to be the place where the Israelites were defeated by the Canaanites, see Num. xiv. 45; and which probably was called Hormah, or "destruction," from this circumstance.

15. *Adullam.* A city belonging to the tribe of Judah, chap. xv. 35. In a cave at this place David often secreted himself during his persecution by Saul, 1 Sam. xxii. 1.

18. *Aphek.* There were several cities of this name: one in the tribe of Asher, chap. xix. 30; another in the tribe of Judah, 1 Sam. iv. 1 and xxix. 1; and a third in Syria, 1 Kings xx. 26 and 2 Kings xiii. 17. Which of the two former is here intended cannot be ascertained.

21. *Taanach.* A city in the half-tribe of Manasseh, to the west of Jordan, not far from the frontiers or Zebulun, chap. xvii. 11. This city was assigned to the Levites, chap. xxi. 25.

22. *Kedesh.* There was a city of this name in the tribe of Naphtali, chap. xix. 37. It was given to the Levites, and was one of the cities of refuge, chap. xx. 7.

23. *The king of Dor.* The city of this name fell to the lot of the children of Manasseh, chap. xvii. 11. Bochart observes that it was one of the oldest royal cities in Phoenicia. The Canaanites held it, Judg. i. 27. *The king of the nations of Gilgal.* This is supposed to mean the higher Galilee, surnamed "Galilee of the Gentiles" or "nations," as the Hebrew word *goyim* means. On this ground it should be read "king of Galilee of the nations." Others suppose it is the same country with that of which Tidal was king; see Gen. xiv. 1. The place is very uncertain, and commentators have rendered it more so by their conjectures.

24. *King of Tirzah.* This city appears to have been for a long time the capital of the kingdom of Israel, and the residence of its kings. See 1 Kings xiv. 17; xv. 21, 33. Its situation cannot be exactly ascertained; but it is supposed to have been situated on a mountain about three leagues south of Samaria. *All the kings thirty and one.* So many kings in so small a territory shows that their kingdoms must have been very small indeed. The kings of Bethel and Ai had but about twelve thousand subjects in the whole; but in ancient times all kings had very small territories.

CHAPTER 13

Joshua being old, the Lord informs him of the land yet remaining to be possessed, 1. Of the unconquered land among the Philistines, 2-3. Among the Canaanites, Sidonians, and Amorites, 4-5. The inhabitants of the hill country and the Sidonians to be driven out, 6. The land on the east side of Jordan, that was to be divided among the tribes of Reuben and Gad and the half-tribe of Manasseh, 7-12. The Geshurites and the Maachathites not expelled, 13. The tribe of Levi receive no inheritance, 14. The possessions of Reuben described, 15-23. The possessions of Gad, 24-28. The possessions of the half-tribe of Manasseh, 29-31. Recapitulation of the subjects contained in this chapter, 32-33.

1. *Joshua was old.* He is generally reputed to have been at this time about a hundred years of age. He had spent about seven years in the conquest of the land, and is supposed to have employed about one year in dividing it; and he died about ten years after, aged one hundred and ten years. It is very likely that he intended to subdue the whole land before he made the division of it among the tribes, but God did not think proper to have this done. So unfaithful were the Israelites that He appears to have purposed that some of the ancient inhabitants should still remain to keep them in check, and that the respective tribes should have some labor to drive out from their allotted borders the remains of the Canaanitish nations. *There remaineth yet very much land to be possessed.* That is, very much when compared with that on the other side Jordan, which was all that could as yet be said to be in the hands of the Israelites.

2. *The borders of the Philistines, and all Geshuri.* The borders of the Philistines may mean the land which they possessed on the sea-coast, southwest of the land of Canaan.

3. *From Sihor, which is before Egypt.* Supposed by some to be the Pelusiac branch of the Nile, near to the Arabian Desert. *Ekron northward.* Ekron was one of the five lordships of the Philistines, and the most northern of all the districts they possessed. Baal-zebub, its idol, is famous in Scripture; see 2 Kings i. 2, etc. The five lordships of the Philistines were Gaza, Ashdod, Askelon, Gath, and Ekron. There is no proof that the Israelites ever possessed Ekron.

Counted to the Canaanite. It is generally allowed that the original possessors of this country were the descendants of Canaan, the youngest son of Ham. The Philistines sprang from Mizraim, the second son of Ham, and, having dispossessed the Avim from the places they held in this land, dwelt in their stead. See Gen. x. 13-14. *Five lords of the Philistines.* These dynasties are famous in the Scriptures for their successful wars against the Israelites, of whom they were almost the perpetual scourge. *Also the Avites.* These must not be confounded with the Hivites. The Avites seem to have been a very inconsiderable tribe, who dwelt in some of the outskirts of Palestine. They had been originally deprived of their country by the Caphtorim; and though they lived as a distinct people, they had never afterwards arrived to any authority.

5. *The land of the Giblites.* This people dwelt beyond the precincts of the land of Canaan, on the east of Tyre and Sidon. See Ezek. xxvii. 9; Ps. lxxxiii. 7; their capital was named Gebal.

6. *Them will I drive out.* That is, if the Israelites continued to be obedient; but they did not, and therefore they never fully possessed the whole of that land which, on this condition alone, God had promised them. The Sidonians were never expelled by the Israelites, and were only brought into a state of comparative subjection in the days of David and Solomon.

7. *The nine tribes, and the half tribe of Manasseh.* The other half-tribe of Manasseh, and the two tribes of Reuben and Gad, received their inheritance on the other side of Jordan, in the land formerly belonging to Og, king of Bashan, and Sihon, king of the Amorites.

9. *From Aroer.* See on chap. xii. 2.

11. *Border of the Geshurites.* See on chap. xii. 5.

17. *Bamoth-baal.* The high places of Baal, probably so called from altars erected on hills for the impure worship of this Canaanitish Priapus.

18. *Jahaza.* A city near Medeba and Dibon. It was given to the Levites, 1 Chron. vi. 78. *Kedemoth.* Mentioned in Deut. ii. 26; supposed to have been situated beyond the river Arnon. *Mephaath.* Situated on the frontiers of Moab, on the eastern part of the desert. It was given to the Levites, chap. xxi. 37.

19. *Sibmah.* A place remarkable for its vines. See Isa. xvi. 8-9; Jer. xlviii. 32. *Zareth-shahar, in the mount of the valley.* This probably means a town situated on or near to a hill in some flat country.

20. *Beth-peor.* The "house" or temple of Peor, situated at the foot of the mountain of the same name. See Num. xxv. 3.

21. *The princes of Midian.* See the history of this war, Num. xxxi. 1, etc.; and from that place this and the following verse seem to be borrowed, for the introduction of the death of Baalam here seems quite irrelevant.

23. *The cities and the villages.* By *villages* it is likely that movable villages or tents are meant, such as are in use among the Bedouin Arabs, places where they were accustomed to feed and pen their cattle.

25. *Half the land of the children of Ammon.* This probably was land which had been taken from the Ammonites by Sihon, king of the Amorites, and which the Israelites possessed by right of conquest. For although the Israelites were forbidden to take the land of the Ammonites, Deut. ii. 37, yet this part, as having been united to the territories of Sihon, they might possess when they defeated that king and subdued his kingdom.

26. *Ramath-mizpeh.* The same as Ramothgilead. It was one of the cities of refuge, chap. xx. 8; Deut. iv. 47. *Mahanaim.* Or the "two camps." Situated on the northern side of the brook Jabbok, celebrated for the vision of the two camps of angels which Jacob had there; see Gen. xxxii. 2.

27. *Succoth.* A place between Jabbok and Jordan where Jacob pitched his "tents," from which circumstance it obtained its name; see Genesis xxxiii. 17.

29. *The half tribe of Manasseh.* When the tribes of Reuben and Gad requested to have their settlement on the east side of Jordan, it does not appear that any part of the tribe of Manasseh requested to be settled in the same place. But as this tribe was numerous, and had much cattle, Moses thought proper to appoint one half of it to remain on the east of Jordan, and the other to go over and settle on the west side of that river.

30. *The towns of Jair.* These were sixty cities; they are mentioned afterwards, and in 1 Chron. ii. 21, etc. They are the same with the Havoth-jair mentioned Num. xxxii. 41. Jair was son of Segub, grandson of Esron or Hezron, and great-grandson of Machir on his grandmother's side, who married Hezron of the tribe of Judah. See his genealogy, 1 Chron. ii. 21-24.

32. *Which Moses did distribute.* Moses had settled everything relative to these tribes before his death, having appointed them to possess the territories of Og, king of Bashan, and Sihon, king of the Amorites.

CHAPTER 14

Eleazar, Joshua, and the heads of the fathers distribute the land by lot to the people, 1-3. The Levites receive no land, but cities to dwell in, and suburbs for their cattle, 4-5. Caleb requests to have Mount Hebron for an inheritance, because of his former services, 6-12. Joshua grants his request, 13-15.

1. *Eleazar the priest.* Eleazar, as being the minister of God in sacred things, is mentioned first. Joshua, as having the supreme command in all things civil, is mentioned next. And the heads or princes of the twelve tribes, who in all things acted under Joshua, are mentioned last. These *heads* or "princes" were twelve, Joshua and Eleazar included; and the reader may find their names in Num. xxxiv. 19-28. It is worthy of remark that no prince was taken from the tribes of Reuben and Gad, because these had already received their inheritance on the other side of Jordan, and therefore could not be interested in this division.

2. *By lot was their inheritance.* Concerning the meaning and use of the lot, see the note on Num. xxxvi. 55.

4. *The children of Joseph were two tribes.* This was ascertained by the prophetic declaration of their grandfather Jacob, Gen. xlviii. 5-6; and as Levi was taken out of the tribes for the service of the sanctuary, one of these sons of Joseph came in his place, and Joseph was treated as the firstborn of Jacob, in the place of Reuben, who forfeited his right of primogeniture.

5. *They divided the land.* This work was begun some time before at Gilgal, and was

finished some time after at Shiloh. It must have required a very considerable time to make all the geographical arrangements that were necessary for this purpose.

6. *Caleb the son of Jephunneh the Kenezite.* In the note on the parallel place, Num. xxxii. 12, it is said Kenaz was probably the father of Jephunneh, and that Jephunneh, not Caleb, was the Kenezite; but still, allowing this to be perfectly correct, Caleb might also be called the Kenezite, as it appears to have been a family name, for Othniel, his nephew and son-in-law, is called the son of Kenaz, chap. xv. 17; Judg. i. 13; and 1 Chron. iv. 13; and a grandson of Caleb is also called the son of Kenaz, 1 Chron. iv. 15. In 1 Chron. ii. 18, Caleb is called the son of Hezron, but this is only to be understood of his having Hezron for one of his ancestors; and *son* here may be considered the same as descendant.

Thou knowest the thing that the Lord said. In the place to which Caleb seems to refer, viz., Num. xiv. 24, there is not a word concerning a promise of Hebron to him and his posterity, nor in the place (Deut. i. 36) where Moses repeats what had been done at Kadesh-barnea; but it may be included in what is there spoken. God promised, because he had another spirit within him, and had followed God fully, therefore he should enter into the land whereinto he came, and his seed should possess it. Probably this relates to Hebron, and was so understood by all parties at that time. This seems tolerably evident from the pointed reference made by Caleb to this transaction.

7. *As it was in mine heart.* Neither fear nor favor influenced him on the occasion; he told what he believed to be the truth, the whole truth, and nothing but the truth.

9. *The land whereon thy feet have trodden.* This probably refers to Hebron, which was no doubt mentioned on this occasion.

11. *Even so is my strength now.* I do not ask this place because I wish to sit down now, and take my ease; on the contrary, I know I must fight to drive out the Anakim, and I am as able and willing to do it as I was forty-five years ago, when Moses sent me to spy out the land.

12. *I shall be able to drive them out.* He cannot mean Hebron merely, for that had been taken before by Joshua; but in the request of Caleb doubtless all the circumjacent country was comprised, in many parts of which the Anakim were still in considerable force.

13. *Joshua blessed him.* As the word bless often signifies to "speak good or well of or to" any person, here it may mean the praise bestowed on Caleb's intrepidity and faithfulness by Joshua, as well as a prayer to God that he might have prosperity in all things; and especially that the Lord might be with him, as himself had expressed in the preceding verse.

14. *Hebron therefore became the inheritance of Caleb.* Joshua admitted his claim, recognized his right, and made a full conveyance of Hebron and its dependencies to Caleb and his posterity; and this being done in the sight of all the elders of Israel, the right was publicly acknowledged, and consequently this portion was excepted from the general determination by lot, God having

long before made the cession of this place to him and to his descendants.

15. *And the name of Hebron before was Kirjath-arba.* That is, "the city of Arba," or rather, "the city of the four," for thus *kiryath arba* may be literally translated. It is very likely that this city had its name from four Anakim, gigantic or powerful men, probably brothers, who built or conquered it. This conjecture receives considerable strength from chap. xv. 14, where it is said that Caleb drove from Hebron the three sons of Anak, Sheshai, Ahiman, and Talmai. Now it is quite possible that Hebron had its former name, Kirjath-arba, "the city of the four," from these three sons and their father, who, being men of uncommon stature or abilities, had rendered themselves famous by acts proportioned to their strength and influence in the country. It appears however from chap. xv. 13 that Arba was a proper name, as there he is called the father of Anak.

The land had rest from war. There were no more general wars; the inhabitants of Canaan collectively could make no longer any head, and when their confederacy was broken by the conquests of Joshua, he thought proper to divide the land and let each tribe expel the ancient inhabitants that might still remain in its own territories.

CHAPTER 15

The lot of the tribe of Judah described, 1. Their south border, 2-4. Their east border, 5-11. Their west border, 12. Caleb's conquest, 13-15. Promises his daughter to the person who should take Kirjath-sepher, 16. Othniel, his kinsman, renders himself master of it, and gets Achsah to wife, 17. Her request to her father to get a well-watered land, which is granted, 18-19. The cities of the tribe of Judah are enumerated, 20-63.

1. *By their families.* It is supposed that the family divisions were not determined by lot. These were left to the prudence and judgment of Joshua, Eleazar, and the ten princes, who appointed to each family a district in proportion to its number, etc., the general division being that alone which was determined by the lot. *To the border of Edom.* The tribe of Judah occupied the most southerly part of the land of Canaan. Its limits extended from the extremity of the Dead Sea southward, along Idumea, possibly by the desert of Sin, and proceeding from east to west to the Mediterranean Sea.

2. *From the bay that looketh southward.* These were the southern limits of the tribe of Judah, which commenced at the extremity of the Dead Sea and terminated at Sihor or the river of Egypt and Mediterranean Sea.

3. *Maaleh-acrabbim.* The ascent of the Mount of Scorpions, probably so called from the multitude of those animals found in that place. *Kadesh-barnea.* This place was on the edge of the Wilderness of Paran, and about twenty-four miles from Hebron. Here Miriam, the sister of Moses and Aaron, died; and here Moses and Aaron rebelled against the Lord.

4. *Toward Azmon.* This was the last city they possessed toward Egypt.

5. *The east border was the salt sea.* The Salt Sea is the same as the Dead Sea. And here it is intimated that the eastern border of the tribe of Judah extended along the Dead Sea, from its lowest extremity to the *end of Jordan,* i.e., to the place where Jordan falls into this sea.

6. *Beth-hogla.* A place between Jericho and the Dead Sea, belonging to the tribe of Benjamin, chap. xviii. 21, though here serving as a frontier to the tribe of Judah.

7. *The valley of Achor.* The *valley of Achor* had its name from the punishment of Achan. See the account, chap. vii. 24, etc. *En-shemesh.* The "fountain of the sun"; it was eastward of Jerusalem, on the confines of Judah and Benjamin.

8. *The valley of the son of Hinnom.* It was situated on the east of Jerusalem, and is often mentioned in Scripture. The image of the idol Molech appears to have been set up there; and here the idolatrous Israelites caused their sons and daughters to pass through the fire in honor of that demon, 2 Kings xxiii. 10. It was also called Tophet; see Jer. vii. 32. When King Josiah removed the image of this idol from this valley, it appears to have been held in such universal execration that it became the general receptacle of all the filth and impurities which were carried out of Jerusalem; and it is supposed that continual fires were there kept up, to consume those impurities and prevent infection. From the Hebrew words *gei ben Hinnom,* "the valley of the son of Hinnom," and by contraction, *gei Hinnom,* the "valley of Hinnom," came the *Gehenna* of the New Testament, called also the *Gehenna of fire,* which is the emblem of hell, or the place of the damned. See Matt. v. 22, 29-30; x. 28; xviii. 9.

The same is Jerusalem. This city was formerly called Jebus; a part of it was in the tribe of Benjamin. Zion, called its citadel, was in the tribe of Judah. *The valley of the giants.* Of the *Rephaim.* See the notes on Gen. vi. 4; xiv. 5; Deut. ii. 7, 11.

9. *Baalah, which is Kirjath-jearim.* This place was rendered famous in Scripture, in consequence of its being the residence of the ark for twenty years after it was sent back by the Philistines; see 1 Sam. v; vi; and vii. 1-2.

10. *Beth-shemesh.* The "house or temple of the sun." It is evident that the sun was an object of adoration among the Canaanites; and hence fountains, hills, etc., were dedicated to him. Beth-shemesh is remarkable for the slaughter of its inhabitants, in consequence of their prying curiously into the ark of the Lord, when sent back by the Philistines. See 1 Samuel vii.

12. *The great sea.* The Mediterranean.

15. *Kirjath-sepher.* The "city of the book." Why so named is uncertain.

16. *Will I give Achsah my daughter.* In ancient times fathers assumed an absolute right over their children, especially in disposing of them in marriage; and it was customary for a king or great man to promise his daughter in marriage to him who should take a city, kill an enemy, etc. So Saul promised his daughter in marriage to him who should kill Goliath, 1 Sam. xvii. 25; and Caleb offers his on this occasion to him who should take Kirjath-sepher.

18. *As she came.* As she was now departing from the house of her father to go to that of her husband. *She moved him.* Othniel, *to ask of her father a field,* one on which she had set her heart, as contiguous to the patrimony already granted. *She lighted off her ass.* She

"hastily, suddenly" alighted, as if she had forgotten something, or was about to return to her father's house. Which being perceived by her father, he said, *What wouldest thou?* What is the matter? What do you want?

19. *Give me a blessing.* Do me an act of kindness. Grant me a particular request. *Thou hast given me a south land.* Which was probably dry, or very ill-watered. *Give me also springs of water.* Let me have some fields in which there are brooks or wells already digged. *The upper springs, and the nether springs.* He gave her even more than she requested; he gave her a district among the mountains and another in the plains well-situated and well-watered.

24. *Ziph.* There were two cities of this name in the tribe of Judah: that mentioned here, and another in v. 55. One of these two is noted for the refuge of David when persecuted by Saul, and the attempts made by its inhabitants to deliver him into the hands of his persecutor. See 1 Sam. xxiii. 14-24.

28. *Beer-sheba.* A city famous in the Book of Genesis as the residence of the patriarchs Abraham and Jacob, chap. xxii. 19; xxviii. 10; xlvi. 1, (see the note on Gen. xxi. 31). It lay on the way between Canaan and Egypt, about forty miles from Jerusalem.

30. *Hormah.* A place rendered famous by the defeat of the Hebrews by the Canaanites. See Num. xiv. 45; Deut. i. 44.

31. *Ziklag.* The Philistines seem to have kept possession of this city till the time of David, who received it from Achish, king of Gath, 1 Sam. xxvii. 6; after which time it remained in the possession of the kings of Judah.

32. *All the cities are twenty and nine, with their villages.* But on a careful examination we shall find thirty-eight; but it is supposed that nine of these are excepted, viz., Beer-sheba, Moladah, Hazar-shual, Baalah, Azem, Hormah, Ziklag, Ain, and Rimmon, which were afterwards given to the tribe of Simeon. This may appear satisfactory, but perhaps the truth will be found to be this: Several cities in the Promised Land are expressed by compound terms; not knowing the places, different translations combine what should be separated, and in many cases separate what should be combined. On this ground we have thirty-eight cities as the sum here, instead of twenty-nine.

33. *Eshtaol, and Zoreah.* Here Samson was buried, it being the burial place of his fathers; see Judg. xvi. 31. These places, though first given to Judah, afterwards fell to the lot of Dan, chap. xix. 41.

35. *Jarmuth.* See the note on chap. x. 3. *Adullam.* See the note on chap. xii. 15. *Socoh.* It was near this place that David fought with and slew Goliath, the champion of the Philistines, 1 Sam. xvii. 1.

36. *Gederah.* See the note on chap. xii. 13. *Fourteen cities.* Well-reckoned, we shall find fifteen cities here; but probably Gederah and Gederothaim (v. 36) are the same. See the note on v. 32.

39. *Lachish . . . and Eglon.* See on chap. x. 3.

41. *Beth-dagon.* The "house" or temple of Dagon. This is a well-known idol of the Philistines, and probably the place mentioned here

was in some part of their territories; but the situation at present is unknown.

42. *Libnah.* See the note on chap. x. 29. *Ether.* From chap. xix. 7 we learn that this city was afterwards given to the tribe of Simeon.

44. *Keilah.* This town was near Hebron, and is said to have been the burying place of the prophet Habakkuk. David obliged the Philistines to raise the siege of it (see 1 Sam. xxiii. 1-13); but finding that its inhabitants had purposed to deliver him into the hands of Saul, who was coming in pursuit of him, he made his escape. *Mareshah.* Called also Maresheth and Marasthi; it was the birthplace of the prophet Micah. Near this place was the famous battle between Asa, king of Judah, and Zera, king of Cush or Ethiopia, who was at the head of "a thousand thousand [men], and three hundred chariots." Asa defeated this immense host and took much spoil, 2 Chron. xiv. 9-15.

46. *Ekron.* One of the five Philistine lordships (see the note on chap. xiii. 3).

37. *Ashdod.* Called also Azotus, Acts viii. 40. *The great sea.* The Mediterranean.

51. *Giloh.* The country of the traitor Ahithophel, 2 Sam. xv. 12.

53. *Beth-tappuah.* The "house of the apple" or citron tree. Probably a place where these grew in great abundance and perfection.

55. *Maon.* In a desert to which this town gave name David took refuge for a considerable time from the persecution of Saul; and in this place Nabal the Carmelite had great possessions. See 1 Sam. xxiii. 24-25; xxv. 2. *Carmel.* Not the celebrated mount of that name, but a village, the residence of Nabal. See 1 Sam. xxv. 2. It was near Maon, mentioned above, and was about ten miles eastward of Hebron. It is the place where Saul erected a trophy to himself after the defeat of the Amalekites; see 1 Sam. xv. 12.

57. *Timnah.* A frontier town of the Philistines. It was in this place that Samson got his wife; see Judges xiv and xv.

62. *The city of Salt.* Or of Melach. This city was somewhere in the vicinity of the Lake Asphaltites, the waters of which are the saltiest perhaps in the world. The whole country abounds with salt; see the note on Gen. xix. 25. *En-gedi.* The "well of the kid." It was situated between Jericho and the Lake of Sodom or Dead Sea.

63. *The Jebusites dwell . . . at Jerusalem unto this day.* The whole history of Jerusalem, previously to the time of David, is encumbered with many difficulties. Sometimes it is attributed to Judah, sometimes to Benjamin; and it is probable that, being on the frontiers of both those tribes, each possessed a part of it. If the Jebusites were ever driven out before the time of David, it is certain they recovered it again, or at least a part of it—what is called the citadel or stronghold of Zion (see 2 Sam. v. 7), which he took from them, after which the city fell wholly into the hands of the Israelites. This verse is an additional proof that the Book of Joshua was not written after the times of the Jewish kings, as some have endeavored to prove; for when this verse was written, the Jebusites dwelt with the children of Judah, which they did not after the days of David. Therefore the

book was written before there were any kings in Judea.

CHAPTER 16

Borders of the children of Joseph, 1-4. The borders of the Ephraimites, 5-9. The Canaanites dwell tributary among them, 10.

1. *The children of Joseph.* Ephraim and Manasseh, and their descendants. The limits of the tribe of Ephraim extended along the borders of Benjamin and Dan, from Jordan on the east to the Mediterranean on the west.

2. *From Beth-el to Luz.* From Gen. xxviii 19 it appears that the place which Jacob called Bethel was formerly called Luz (see the note there), but here they seem to be two distinct places. It is very likely that the place where Jacob had the vision was not in Luz, but in some place within a small distance of that city or village (see the note on Gen. xxviii. 12) and that sometimes the whole place was called Bethel, at other times Luz, and sometimes, as in the case above, the two places were distinguished. *Archi to Ataroth.* Archi was the country of Hushai, the friend of David, 2 Sam xv. 32, who is called Hushai the Archite Ataroth, called Ataroth-addar, "Ataroth the illustrious," v. 5, and simply Ataroth, v. 7, is supposed to have been about fifteen miles from Jerusalem.

3. *Beth-horon the nether.* This city was about twelve miles from Jerusalem, on the side of Nicopolis, formerly Emmaus.

8. *Tappuah.* This was a city in the tribe of Manasseh, and gave name to a certain district called the "land of Tappuah." *The sea.* The Mediterranean, as before.

9. *And the separate cities.* That is, the cities that were separated from the tribe of Manasseh to be given to Ephraim; see chap. xvii. 9.

10. *The Canaanites that dwelt in Gezer.* It appears that the Canaanites were not expelled from this city till the days of Solomon, when it was taken by the king of Egypt, his father-in-law, who made it a present to his daughter, Solomon's queen (see 1 Kings ix. 16). The Ephraimites, however, had so far succeeded in subjecting these people as to oblige them to pay tribute, though they could not, or at least did not, totally expel them.

CHAPTER 17

The lot of the half-tribe of Manasseh, 1-2. Case of the daughters of Zelophehad, 3-6. The borders of Manasseh described, 7-11. The Canaanites dwell among them, but are laid under tribute, 12-13. The children of Joseph complain of the scantiness of their lot, 14-16. Joshua authorizes them to possess the mountainous wood country of the Perizzites, and gives them encouragement to expel them, though they were strong and had chariots of iron, 17-18.

1. *There was also a lot for the tribe of Manasseh.* It was necessary to mark this because Jacob, in his blessing (Gen. xlviii. 19-20) did in a certain sense set Ephraim before Manasseh, though the latter was the firstborn; but the place here shows that this preference did not affect the rights of primogeniture. *For Machir . . . because he was a man of war.* It is not likely that Machir himself was now alive; if he were, he must have been nearly two hundred years old. It is therefore probable that

what is spoken here is spoken of his children, who now possessed the lot that was originally designed for their father, who it appears had signalized himself as a man of skill and valor in some of the former wars, though the circumstances are not marked. His descendants, being of a warlike, intrepid spirit, were well-qualified to defend a frontier country, which would be naturally exposed to invasion.

2. *The rest of the children of Manasseh.* That is, his grandchildren; for it is contended that Manasseh had no other son than Machir; and these were very probably the children of Gilead, the son of Machir.

3. *Zelophehad . . . had no sons, but daughters.* See this case considered at large in the notes on Num. xxvii. 1-7, and xxxvi. 1, etc.

5. *There fell ten portions to Manasseh.* The Hebrew word *chabley,* which we translate *portions,* signifies literally "cords" or "cables," and intimates that by means of a cord, cable, or what we call a chain, the land was divided. As there were six sons and five daughters, among whom this division was to be made, there should be eleven portions; but Zelophehad, son of Hepher, having left five daughters in his place, neither he nor Hepher is reckoned. The lot of Manasseh therefore was divided into ten parts: five for the five sons of Gilead, who were Abiezer, Helek, Asriel, Shechem, and Shemida; and five for the five daughters of Zelophehad, viz., Mahlah, Noah, Hoglah, Milcah, and Tirzah.

9. *Unto the river Kanah.* Literally, the "river or valley of the reeds." The tribe of Manasseh appears to have been bounded on the north by this torrent or valley, and on the south by the Mediterranean Sea.

11. *Beth-shean.* Called afterwards Scythopolis; the city of the Scythians or Cuthites, those who were sent into the different Samaritan cities by the kings of Assyria. *Dor.* On the Mediterranean Sea, about eight miles from Caesarea, on the road to Tyre. *En-dor.* The "well or fountain of Dor," the place where Saul went to consult the witch; 1 Sam. xxviii. 7, etc.

12. *Could not drive out.* They had neither grace nor courage to go against their enemies, and chose rather to share their territories with those whom the justice of God had proscribed than exert themselves to expel them. But some commentators give a different turn to this expression, and translate the passage thus: "But the children of Manasseh could not (resolve) to destroy those cities, but the Canaanites consented to dwell in the land."

15. *If thou be a great people.* Joshua takes them at their own word; they said, v. 14, that they were a great people; then said he, "If thou be a great people [or seeing thou art a great people, go to the wood country, and clear away for thyself." Joshua would not reverse the decision of the lot; but as there was much woodland country, he gave them permission to clear away as much of it as they found necessary to extend themselves as far as they pleased.

16. *The hill is not enough for us.* The mountain of Gilboa being that which had fallen to them by lot. *Chariots of iron.* We cannot possess the plain country, because that is occupied by the Canaanites; and we cannot conquer them, because they have *chariots of iron,*

that is, very strong chariots, and armed with scythes, as is generally supposed.

CHAPTER 18

The Tabernacle is set up at Shiloh, 1. Seven of the tribes having not yet received their inheritance, 2, Joshua orders three men from each tribe to be chosen, and sent to examine the land and divide it into seven parts, which should be distributed among them by lot, 3-7. The men go and do as commanded, and return to Joshua, 8-9. Joshua casts lots for them, 10. The lot of Benjamin, how situated, 11. Its northern boundaries, 12-14. Its southern boundaries, 15-19. Its eastern boundary, 20. Its cities, 21-28.

1. *Israel assembled together at Shiloh.* This appears to have been a considerable town about fifteen miles from Jerusalem, in the tribe of Ephraim, and nearly in the center of the whole land. To this place both the camp of Israel and the ark of the Lord were removed from Gilgal, after a residence there of 7 years. Here the Tabernacle remained 120 years, as is generally supposed, being the most conveniently situated for access to the different tribes, and for safety, the Israelites having possession of the land on all sides; for it is here added, *The land was subdued before them*—the Canaanites were so completely subdued that there was no longer any general resistance to the Israelitish arms.

3. *How long are ye slack to go to possess the land?* We find an unaccountable backwardness in this people to enter on the inheritance which God had given them! They had so long been supported by miracle, without any exertions of their own, that they found it difficult to shake themselves from their inactivity.

4. *Three men for each tribe.* Probably meaning only three from each of the seven tribes who had not yet received their inheritance. It is likely that these twenty-one men were accompanied by a military guard, for without this they might have been easily cut off by straggling parties of the Canaanites. *They shall . . . describe it.* It is likely they were persons well-acquainted with geography, without which it would have been impossible for them to divide the land in the way necessary on this occasion.

5. *Judah shall abide . . . on the south, and the house of Joseph . . . on the north.* Joshua does not mean that the tribe of Judah occupied the south and the tribe of Ephraim and Manasseh the north of the Promised Land; this was not the fact. But being now at Shiloh, a considerable way in the territory of Ephraim, and not far from that of Judah, he speaks of them in relation to the place in which he then was.

7. *The priesthood of the Lord is their inheritance.* We have already seen that the priests and Levites had the sacrifices, oblations, tithes, firstfruits, redemption money of the firstborn, etc., for their inheritance; they had no landed possessions in Israel; the Lord was their Portion.

9. *And described it . . . in a book.* This, as far as I can recollect, is the first act of surveying on record. These men and their work differed widely from those who had searched the land in the time of Moses; they went only to discover the nature of the country and the state of its inhabitants, but these went to take an actual geographical survey of it, in order to divide it among the tribes which had not yet received their portions. We may suppose that

the country was exactly described *in a book*, that is, a map, pointing out the face of the country, accompanied with descriptions of each part.

11. *And the lot . . . of Benjamin came up.* There were probably two urns, one of which contained the names of the seven tribes, and the other that of the seven portions. They therefore took out one name out of the first urn, and one portion out of the second, and thus the portion was adjudged to that tribe.

12. *The wilderness of Beth-aven.* This was the same as Bethel, but this name was not given to it till Jeroboam had fixed one of his golden calves there. It first name signifies the "house of God"; its second, "the house of iniquity."

16. *To the side of Jebusi.* The mountain of Zion, that was near Jerusalem; for Jebusi, or Jebus, was the ancient name of this city.

17. *En-shemesh.* The fountain of the sun; a proof of the idolatrous nature of the ancient inhabitants of this land. *Geliloth.* As the word signifies "borders" or "limits," it is probably not the proper name of a place: "And went forth towards the borders which are over against the ascent to Adummim."

19. *The north bay of the salt sea. Leshon* signifies the "tongue."

21. *Now the cities.* Some of these cities have been mentioned before, and described; of others we know nothing but the name.

24. *And Gaba.* Supposed to be the same as Gibeah of Saul, a place famous for having given birth to the first king of Israel; and infamous for the shocking act towards the Levite's wife, mentioned in Judges xix, which was the cause of a war in which the tribe of Benjamin was nearly exterminated, Judges xx.

25. *Gibeon.* See before, chap. x. This place is famous for the confederacy of the five kings against Israel, and their miraculous defeat. *Ramah,* a place about six or eight miles north of Jerusalem. *Beeroth,* i.e., "wells"; one of the four cities which belonged to the Gibeonites, who made peace with the Israelites by stratagem.

26. *And Mizpeh.* This place is celebrated in the sacred writings. Here the people were accustomed to assemble often in the presence of the Lord, as in the deliberation concerning the punishment to be inflicted on the men of Gibeah, for the abuse of the Levite's wife, Judg. xx. 1-3. Samuel assembled the people here to exhort them to renounce their idolatry, 1 Sam. vii. 5-6. In this same place Saul was chosen to be king, 1 Sam. x. 17. It was deemed a sacred place among the Israelites; for we find, from 1 Mac. iii. 46, that the Jews assembled here to seek God, when their enemies were in possession of the Temple.

28. *And Zelah.* This was the burying place of Saul, Jonathan, and the family of Kish. See 2 Sam. xxi. 14. *Jebusi, which is Jerusalem.* We often meet with this name, and it is evident that it was the ancient name of Jerusalem, which was also called Salem, and was probably the place in which Melchizedek reigned in the days of Abraham. That this was a name of Jerusalem is evident from Ps. lxxvi. 1-2: "In Judah is God known: his name is great in Israel. In Salem also is his tabernacle, and his dwelling place in Zion." This must refer to Jerusalem, where the Temple was situated. Whether Jebus or Jebusi had its name from the Jebusites, or the Jebusites from it, cannot be ascertained.

CHAPTER 19

The lot of Simeon, 1-9. Of Zebulun, 10-16. Of Issachar, 17-23. Of Asher, 24-31. Of Naphtali, 32-39. Of Dan, 40-48. Joshua's portion, 49-50. The conclusion of the division of the land, 51.

1. *The second lot came forth to Simeon.* In this appointment the providence of God may be especially remarked. For the iniquitous conduct of Simeon and Levi, in the massacre of the innocent Shechemites, Genesis xxxiv, Jacob, in the spirit of prophecy, foretold that they should be "divided in Jacob," and "scattered in Israel," Gen. xlix. 7. And this is most literally fulfilled in the manner in which God disposed of both these tribes afterwards. Levi was scattered through all Palestine, not having received any inheritance, only cities to dwell in, in different parts of the land; and Simeon was dispersed in Judah, with what could scarcely be said to be their own or a peculiar lot. See the note on Gen. xlix. 7.

2. *Beer-sheba.* The "well of the oath." See the note on Gen. xxi. 31.

3. *Hazar-shual.* For this and several of the following places, see the notes on chap. xv.

5. *Beth-marcaboth.* The "house or city of chariots."

6. *Beth-lebaoth.* The "house or city of lionesses."

8. *Baalath-beer.* The "well of the mistresses." Probably so called from some superstitious or impure worship set up there.

13. *Gittah-hepher.* The same as Gath-hepher, the birthplace of the prophet Jonah.

15. *Shimron.* See on chap. xii. *Beth-lehem.* The "house of bread"; a different place from that in which our Lord was born.

17. *The fourth lot came out to Issachar.* It is remarkable that, though Issachar was the eldest brother, yet the lot of Zebulun was drawn before his lot; and this is the order in which Jacob himself mentions them, Gen. xlix. 13-14.

18. *Shunem.* This city was rendered famous by being the occasional abode of the prophet Elisha, and the place where he restored the son of a pious woman to life, 2 Kings iv. 8. It was the place where the Philistines were encamped on that ruinous day in which the Israelites were totally routed at Gilboa, and Saul and his sons killed, 1 Sam. xxviii. 4; xxxi. 1, etc.

22. *Beth-shemesh.* "The house or temple of the sun"; there were several cities or towns of this name in Palestine, an ample proof that the worship of this celestial luminary had generally prevailed in that idolatrous country.

26. *Carmel.* "The vineyard of God"; a place greatly celebrated in Scripture, and especially for the miracles of Elijah; see 1 Kings xviii. The mountain of Carmel was so very fruitful as to pass into a proverb. There was another Carmel in the tribe of Judah (see chap. xv. 55), but this, in the tribe of Asher, was situated about one hundred and twenty furlongs south from Prolemais, on the edge of the Mediterranean Sea.

27. *Cabul on the left hand.* That is, to the

north of Cabul, for so the *left hand,* when referring to place, is understood among the Hebrews.

28. *Unto great Zidon.* The city of Sidon and the Sidonians are celebrated from the remotest antiquity. They are frequently mentioned by Homer.

29. *The strong city Tyre.* I suspect this to be an improper translation. Perhaps the words of the original should be retained: "And the coast turneth to Ramah and to the city." Our translators have here left the Hebrew, and followed the Septuagint and Vulgate, a fault of which they are sometimes guilty. The word *Tsor,* which we translate or change into *Tyre,* signifies a "rock" or "strong place"; and as there were many rocks in the land of Judea that with a little art were formed into strong places of defense, hence several places might have the name of Tyre. *Achzib.* Called now Zib; it is about nine miles' distance from Ptolemais, towards Tyre.

30. *Twenty and two cities.* There are nearly thirty cities in the above enumeration instead of twenty-two, but probably several are mentioned that were but frontier towns, and that did not belong to this tribe, their border only passing by such cities; and on this account, though they are named, yet they do not enter into the enumeration in this place. Perhaps some of the villages are named as well as the cities.

34. *And to Judah upon Jordan.* It is certain that the tribe of Naphtali did not border on the east upon Judah, for there were several tribes betwixt them. Some think that, as these two tribes were bounded by Jordan on the east, they might be considered as in some sort conjoined, because of the easy passage to each other by means of the river; but this might be said of several other tribes as well as of these. There is considerable difficulty in the text as it now stands. But if, with the Septuagint, we omit *Judah,* the difficulty vanishes, and the passage is plain; but this omission is supported by no MS. hitherto discovered.

38. *Nineteen cities.* But if these cities be separately enumerated they amount to twenty-three; this is probably occasioned by reckoning frontier cities belonging to other tribes, which are mentioned here only as the boundaries of the tribe. See on v. 30.

41. *Ir-shemesh.* "The city of sun"; another proof of the idolatry of the Canaanites. Some think this was the same as Beth-shemesh.

42. *Shaalabbin.* "The foxes." Of this city the Amorites kept constant possession. See Judg. i. 35. *Ajalon.* There was a place of this name about two miles from Nicopolis or Emmaus, on the road to Jerusalem.

43. *Thimnathah.* Probably the same as Timnah. See on chap. xv. 57. *Ekron.* A well-known city of the Philistines, and the metropolis of one of their five dynasties.

45. *Jehud, and Bene-berak.* Or Jehud of the children of Berak.

46. *Japho.* The place since called Joppa, lying on the Mediterranean, and the chief seaport, in the possession of the twelve tribes.

47. *Went out too little for them.* This is certainly the meaning of the passage, but our translators have been obliged to add the words *too little* to make this sense apparent. *And called Leshem, Dan.* This city was situated near the origin of Jordan, at the utmost northern extremity of the Promised Land, as Beersheba was at that of the south; and as after its capture by the Danites it was called Dan, hence arose the expression "from Dan even to Beer-sheba," which always signified the whole extent of the Promised Land.

50. *Timnath-serah.* Called Timnath-heres in Judg. ii. 9, where we find that the mountain on which it was built was called Gaash. It is generally allowed to have been a barren spot in a barren country.

51. *At the door of the tabernacle.* All the inheritances were determined by lot, and this was cast *before the Lord*—everything was done in his immediate presence, as under his eye; hence there was no murmuring, each having received his inheritance as from the hand of God himself, though some of them thought they must have additional territory because of the great increase of their families.

CHAPTER 20

Joshua is commanded to appoint cities of refuge, 1-2 The purpose of their institution, 3-6. Three cities are appointed in the Promised Land, 7; and three on the east side of Jordan, 8-9.

2. *Cities of refuge.* An institution of this kind was essentially necessary wherever the patriarchal law relative to the right of redemption and the avenging of blood was in force. We have already seen that the nearest of kin to a deceased person had not only the right of redeeming an inheritance that had been forfeited or alienated, but had also authority to slay on the spot the person who had slain his relative. Now, as a man might casually kill another against whom he had no ill will, and with whom he had no quarrel, and might have his life taken away by him who was called the avenger of blood, though he had not forfeited his life to the law; therefore these privileged cities were appointed, where the person might have protection till the cause had been fully heard by the magistrates, who certainly had authority to deliver him up to the avenger if they found, on examination, that he was not entitled to this protection. On this subject see the notes on Num. xxxv. 11 to the end.

7. *They appointed Kedesh in Galilee.* The cities of refuge were distributed through the land at proper distances from each other, that they might be convenient to every part of the land; and it is said they were situated on eminences, that they might be easily seen at a distance, the roads leading to them being broad, even, and always kept in good repair. In the concluding note on Numbers xxxv it has been stated that these cities were a type of our blessed Lord, and that the apostle refers to them as such, Heb. vi. 17-18. Hence their names have been considered as descriptive of some character or office of Christ. I shall give each and its signification, and leave the application to others. (1) *Kedesh,* from *kadash,* to "separate" or "set apart," because it implies the consecration of a person or thing to the worship or service of God alone; hence to "make or be holy," and hence *Kedesh,* "holiness," the full consecration of a person to God. (2) *Shechem,* from *shacham,*

"to be ready, forward, and diligent"; hence Shechem, the "shoulder," because of its readiness to bear burdens, prop up, sustain, and from this ideal meaning it has the metaphorical one of government. (3) *Hebron,* from *chabar,* "to associate, join, conjoin, unite as friends"; and hence *chebron,* "fellowship, friendly association." (4) *Bezer,* from *batsar,* "to restrain, enclose, shut up, or encompass with a wall"; and hence the goods or treasure thus secured, and hence a fortified place, a fortress. (5) *Ramoth,* from *raam,* "to be raised, made high or exalted," and hence *Ramoth,* high places, eminences. (6) *Golan,* from *galah,* "to remove, transmigrate, or pass away"; hence Golan, a transmigration or passage.

Kedesh and *Hebron* were at the two extremities of the Promised Land; one was in Galilee, the other in the tribe of Judah, both in mountainous countries; and *Shechem* was in the tribe of Ephraim, nearly in the middle, between both. *Bezer* was on the east side of Jordan, in the plain, opposite to Jericho. *Ramoth* was about the midst of the country occupied by the two tribes and a half, about the middle of the mountains of Gilead. *Golan* was the capital of a district called Gaulonitis, in the land of Bashan, towards the southern extremity of the lot of Manasseh.

9. *For all the children of Israel, and for the stranger.* As these typified the great provision which God was making for the salvation of both Jews and Gentiles, hence the stranger as well as the Israelite had the same right to the benefits of these cities of refuge. *Until he stood before the congregation.* The judges and elders of the people, in trying civil and criminal causes, always sat; the persons who came for judgment, or who were tried, always stood; hence the expressions so frequent in Scripture, "standing before the Lord, the judges, the elders."

CHAPTER 21

The Levites apply to Eleazar, Joshua, and the elders for the cities to dwell in which Moses had promised, 1-2. Their request is granted, 3. The priests receive thirteen cities out of the tribes of Judah, Simeon, and Benjamin, 4. The Levites receive ten cities out of the tribes of Ephraim, Dan, and the half-tribe of Manasseh, 5; and thirteen out of the other half-tribe of Manasseh, and the tribes of Issachar, Asher, and Naphtali, 6. The children of Merari had twelve cities out of the tribes of Reuben, Gad, and Zebulun, 7. The names of the cities given out of the tribes of Judah and Simeon, 8-16. Those granted out of the tribe of Benjamin, 17-19. Out of Ephraim, 20-22. Those out of Dan, 23-24. Those out of both the halves of the tribe of Manasseh, 25-27. Those out of the tribe of Issachar, 28-29. Those out of Asher, 30-31. Those out of Naphtali, 32. These were the cities of the Gershonites, 33. The cities of the Merarites, 34-40. The sum of the cities given to the Levites, forty-eight, 41-42. The exact fulfilment of all God's promises, 43-45.

1. *The heads of the fathers of the Levites.* The Levites were composed of three grand families, the Gershonites, Koathites, and Merarites, independently of the family of Aaron, who might be said to form a fourth. To none of these had God assigned any portion in the division of the land. But in this general division it must have been evidently intended that the different tribes were to furnish them with habitations; and this was according to a positive command of God, Num. xxxv. 2, etc. Finding now that each tribe had its inheritance appointed to it, the heads of the Levites came before Eleazar, Joshua, and the chiefs of the tribes who had been employed in dividing the land, and

requested that cities and suburbs should be granted them according to the divine command.

3. *And the children of Israel gave unto the Levites.* They cheerfully obeyed the divine command, and cities for habitations were appointed to them out of the different tribes by lot, that it might as fully appear that God designed them their habitations as He designed the others their inheritances.

4. *Out of the tribe of Judah . . . Simeon, and . . . Benjamin, thirteen cities.* These tribes furnished more habitations to the Levites in proportion than any of the other tribes, because they possessed a more extensive inheritance; and Moses had commanded, Num. xxxv. 8, "From them that have many ye shall give many; but from them that have few ye shall give few: every one shall give of his cities unto the Levites according to his inheritance." It is worthy of remark that the principal part of this tribe, whose business was to minister at the sanctuary, which sanctuary was afterwards to be established in Jerusalem, had their appointment nearest to that city, so that they were always within reach of the sacred work which God had appointed them.

5. *And the rest of the children of Kohath.* That is, the remaining part of that family that were not priests, for those who were priests had their lot in the preceding tribes. Those, therefore, of the family of Kohath who were simply Levites, and not of the priests or Aaron's family (see v. 10), had their habitations in Ephraim, Dan, and the half-tribe of Manasseh.

12. *The fields of the city . . . gave they to Caleb.* This was an exclusive privilege to him and his family, with which the grant to the Levites did not interfere.

18. *Anathoth.* Celebrated as the birthplace of Jeremiah, about three miles northward of Jerusalem, according to Jerome.

19. *Thirteen cities with their suburbs.* At the time mentioned here certainly thirteen cities were too large a proportion for the *priests,* as they and their families amounted to a very small number; but this ample provision was made in reference to their great increase in after times, when they formed twenty-four courses, as in the days of David.

27. *Golan in Bashan.* On this and the other cities of refuge mentioned here, see the note on chap. xx. 7.

35. *Dimnah with her suburbs.* It is well known to every Hebrew scholar that the two following verses are wholly omitted by the Masora, and are left out in some of the most correct and authentic Hebrew Bibles.

43. *And the Lord gave . . . all the land which he sware.* All was now divided by lot unto them, and their enemies were so completely discomfited that there was not a single army of the Canaanites remaining to make head against them; and those which were left in the land served under tribute, and the tribute that they paid was the amplest proof of their complete subjugation.

CHAPTER 22

Joshua assembles, commends, blesses, and then dismisses the two tribes of Reuben and Gad, and the half-tribe of Manasseh, 1-8. They return and build an altar by the side of Jordan, 9-10. The rest of the Israelites hearing of this, and suspecting that they had built the altar for idolatrous purposes, or to make a schism in the national worship, prepare to go to war with them, 11-12; but first send a deputation to know the truth, 13-14. They arrive and expostulate with their brethren, 15-20. The Reubenites, Gadites, and half-tribe of Manasseh make a noble defense, and show that their altar was built as a monument only to prevent idolatry, 21-29. The deputation are satisfied, and return to the ten tribes and make their report, 30-32. The people rejoice and praise God, 33; and the Reubenites and Gadites call the altar they had raised Ed, that it might be considered a witness between them and their brethren on the other side Jordan, 34.

1. *Then Joshua called the Reubenites.* We have already seen that 40,000 men of the tribes of Reuben and Gad and the half-tribe of Manasseh had passed over Jordan armed, with their brethren, according to their stipulation with Moses. The war being now concluded, Joshua assembles these warriors, and with commendations for their services and fidelity he dismisses them, having first given them the most pious and suitable advices. They had now been about seven years absent from their respective families; and though there was only the river Jordan between the camp at Gilgal and their own inheritance, yet it does not appear that they had during that time ever revisited their own home, which they might have done anytime in the year, the harvest excepted, as at all other times that river was easily fordable.

5. *But take diligent heed.* Let us examine the force of this excellent advice; they must ever consider that their prosperity and continued possession of the land depended on their fidelity and obedience to God; to this they must take diligent heed. *Do the commandment.* They must pay the strictest regard to every moral precept. *And the law.* They must observe all the rites and ceremonies of their holy religion. *Love the Lord your God.* Without an affectionate filial attachment to their Maker, duty would be irksome, grievous, and impossible. *Walk in all his ways.* They must not only believe and love, but obey: Walk not in your own ways, but walk in those which God has pointed out. *Keep his commandments.* They must love Him with all their heart, soul, mind, and strength, and their neighbor as themselves. *Cleave unto him.* They must be cemented to Him in a union that should never be dissolved. *Serve him.* They must consider Him as their Master, having an absolute right to appoint them when, where, how, and in what measure they should do His work. *With all your heart.* Having all their affections and passions sanctified and united to Him. *And with all your soul.* Giving up their whole life to Him, and employing their understanding, judgment, and will in the contemplation and adoration of His perfections, that their love and obedience might increase in proportion to the cultivation and improvement of their understanding.

7. *Then he blessed them.* Spoke respectfully of their fidelity and exertions, wished them every spiritual and temporal good, prayed to God to protect and save them, and probably gave some gifts to those leaders among them that had most distinguished themselves in this seven years' war. In all the above senses the word *bless* is frequently taken in Scripture.

8. *Return with much riches.* It appears they had their full proportion of the spoils that were taken from the Canaanites, and that these spoils consisted in cattle, silver, gold, brass, iron, and raiment. *Divide the spoil . . . with your brethren.* It was right that those who stayed at home to defend the families of those who had been in the wars, and to cultivate the ground, should have a proper proportion of the spoils taken from the enemy; for had they not acted as they did, the others could not have safely left their families.

17. *Is the iniquity of Peor too little?* See this history, Num. xxv. 3, etc. Phinehas takes it for granted that this altar was built in opposition to the altar of God erected by Moses, and that they intended to have a separate service, priesthood, etc., which would be rebellion against God, and bring down His curse on them and their posterity.

19. *If the land of your possessions be unclean.* The generous mind of Phinehas led him to form this excuse for them. If you suppose that this land is impure, as not having been originally included in the covenant, and you think that you cannot expect the blessing of God unless you have an altar, sacrifices, etc., then *pass ye over unto the land of the possession of the Lord, wherein the Lord's tabernacle dwelleth,* the only legitimate place where sacrifices and offerings can be made. We will divide this land with you, and rather straiten ourselves than that you should conceive yourselves to be under any necessity of erecting a new altar *beside the altar of the Lord our God.*

20. *Did not Achan the son of Zerah?* Your sin will not be merely against yourselves; your transgressions will bring down the wrath of God upon all the people. This was the case in the transgression of Achan; he alone sinned, and yet God on that account turned His face against the whole congregation, so that they fell before their enemies.

21. *Then the children of Reuben . . . answered.* Though conscious of their own innocency they permitted Phinehas to finish his discourse, though composed of little else than accusations.

22. *The Lord God of gods.* The original words are exceedingly emphatic, and cannot be easily translated. *El Elohim Yehovah* are the three principal names by which the supreme God was known among the Hebrews, and may be thus translated, "the strong God, Elohim, Jehovah." And the Reubenites, by using these in their very solemn appeal, expressed at once their strong, unshaken faith in the God of Israel; and by this they fully showed the deputation from the ten tribes that their religious creed had not been changed; and in the succeeding part of their defense they show that their practice corresponded with their creed. The repetition of these solemn names by the Reubenites shows their deep concern for the honor of God, and their anxiety to wipe off the reproach which they consider cast on them by the supposition that they had been capable of defection from the pure worship of God, or of disaffection to their brethren.

Save us not this day. This was putting the affair to the most solemn issue; and nothing but the utmost consciousness of their own integrity could have induced them to make such an appeal, and call for such a decision. "Let God, the Judge, cause us to perish this day if in principle or practice we have knowingly departed from Him."

24. *For fear of this thing.* The motive that actuated us was directly the reverse of that of which we have been suspected.

26. *An altar, not for burnt offering, nor for sacrifice.* Because this would have been in flat opposition to the law, Lev. xvii. 8-9; Deut. xii. 4-6, 10-11, 13-14, which most positively forbade any sacrifice or offering to be made in any other place than that one which the Lord should choose. Therefore the altar built by the Reubenites, etc., was for no religious purpose, but merely to serve as a testimony that they were one people with those on the west of Jordan, having the same religious and civil constitution, and bound by the same interests to keep that constitution inviolate.

33. *And did not intend to go up against them in battle.* That is, they now relinquished the intention of going against them in battle, as this explanation proved there was no cause for the measure.

34. *Called the altar Ed.* The word *Ed,* which signifies "witness" or "testimony," is not found in the common editions of the Hebrew Bible, and is supplied in italics by our translators, at least in our modern copies; for in the first edition of this translation it stands in the text without any note of this kind.

CHAPTER 23

Joshua, being old, calls for the rulers and different heads of the Israelites, 1-2, to whom he relates how God had put them in possession of the Promised Land, 3-4; from which all their remaining enemies should be expelled, 5. Exhorts them to be faithful to God, and to avoid all connections with the idolatrous nations. 6-8. Encourages them with the strongest promises, that no enemy should ever be able to prevail against them, if they continued to love the Lord their God. 9-11. Lays also before them the consequences of disobedience, 12-13. Shows them that, as all God's promises had been fulfilled to them while they were obedient, so His threatenings should be fulfilled on them if they revolted from His service; and that if they did so, they should be utterly destroyed from off the good land. 14-16.

1. *A long time after that the Lord had given rest.* This is supposed to have been in the last or one hundred and tenth year of the life of Joshua, about thirteen or fourteen years after the conquest of Canaan, and seven after the division of the land among the tribes.

2. *Joshua called for all Israel.* There are four degrees of civil distinction mentioned here: (1) *zekenim,* the *elders* or senate, the princes of the tribes; (2) *rashim,* the chiefs or *heads* of families; (3) *shophetim,* the *judges* who interpreted and decided according to the law; (4) *shoterim,* the *officers,* sergeants, etc., who executed the decisions of the judges. Whether this assembly was held at Timnath-serah, where Joshua lived, or at Shiloh, where the ark was, or at Shechem, as in chap. xxiv. 1, we cannot tell.

3. *For the Lord your God is he that hath fought for you.* There is much of both piety and modesty in this address. It was natural for the Israelites to look on their veteran, worn-out general, who had led them on from conquest to conquest, with profound respect; and to be ready to say, "Had we not had such a commander, we had never got possession of this good land." Joshua corrects this opinion, and shows them that all their enemies had been defeated because the Lord their God had fought for them; that the battle was the Lord's, and not his; and that God alone should have the glory.

4. *I have divided . . . these nations that remain.* The whole of the Promised Land had been portioned out, as well as those parts which had not yet been conquered as those from which the ancient inhabitants had been expelled. The Canaanitish armies had long ago been broken in pieces, so that they could make no head against the Israelites, but in many districts the old inhabitants remained, more through the supineness of the Israelites than through their own bravery.

5. *And drive them . . . out . . . and ye shall possess.* The same Hebrew word *yarash* is used here to signify to "expel from an inheritance," and to "succeed" those thus expelled. "Ye shall disinherit them from your sight, and ye shall inherit their land."

6. *Be ye therefore very courageous to keep and to do.* It requires no small courage to keep a sound creed in the midst of scoffers, and not less to maintain a godly practice among the profane and profligate. *That is written in the book.* By the Word of God alone His followers are bound. Nothing is to be received as an article of faith which God has not spoken.

7. *Come not among these nations.* Have no civil or social contracts with them (see v. 12), as these will infallibly lead to spiritual affinities, in consequence of which you will make honorable *mention of the name of their gods . . . swear by them* as the judges of your motives and actions, *serve them* in their abominable rites, and *bow yourselves* unto them as your creators and preservers, thus giving the whole worship of God to idols—and all this will follow from simply coming among them.

10. *One man of you shall chase a thousand.* Do not remain inactive on the supposition that you must be much more numerous before you can drive out your enemies, for it is the Lord that shall drive out nations great and strong; and under His direction and influence *one . . . of you shall chase a thousand.*

11. *Take good heed . . . unto yourselves, that ye love the Lord.* "Take heed to your souls," literally; but *nephesh* and *nefs,* both in Hebrew and Arabic, signify the whole self, as well as soul and life. Both soul and body must be joined in this work, for it is written, "Thou shalt love the Lord thy God with all thy heart . . . soul . . . mind, and . . . strength."

12. *Else if ye do . . . go back.* The soldier who draws back when going to meet the enemy forfeits his life. These were the Lord's soldiers, and if they drew back they drew back unto perdition, their lives being forfeited by their infidelity.

13. *They shall be snares.* Lephach, a net set by the artful fowler to catch heedless birds. *And traps.* Mokesh, any snare, toil, or trap placed on the ground to catch the unwary traveller or wild beast by the foot. *Scourges in your sides, and thorns in your eyes.* Nothing can be conceived more vexatious and distressing than a continual goad in the side or thorn in the eye.

14. *The way of all the earth.* I am about to die; I am going into the grave. Not one thing

hath failed. God had so remarkably and literally fulfilled His promises that not one of His enemies could state that even the smallest of them had not had its most literal accomplishment; this all Israel could testify.

15. *So shall the Lord bring upon you all evil things.* His faithfulness in fulfilling His promises is a proof that He will as faithfully accomplish His threatenings, for the veracity of God is equally pledged for both.

CHAPTER 24

Joshua gathers all the tribes together at Shechem, 1; and gives them a history of God's gracious dealings with Abraham, 2-3; Isaac, Jacob, and Esau, 4; Moses and Aaron and their fathers in Egypt, 5-6. His judgments on the Egyptians, 7. On the Amorites, 8. Their deliverance from Balak and Balaam, 9-10. Their conquests in the Promised Land, and their establishment in the possession of it, 11-13. Exhorts them to abolish idolatry, and informs them of his and his family's resolution to serve Jehovah, 14-15. The people solemnly promise to serve the Lord alone, and mention His merciful dealings towards them, 16-18. Joshua shows them the holiness of God, and the danger of apostasy, 19-20. The people again promise obedience, 21. Joshua calls them to witness against themselves, that they had promised to worship God alone, and exhorts them to put away the strange gods. 22-23. They promise obedience, 24. Joshua makes a covenant with the people, writes it in a book, sets up a stone as a memorial of it, and dismisses the people. 25-28. Joshua's death, 29, and burial, 30. The people continue faithful during that generation, 31. They bury the bones of Joseph in Shechem, 32. Eleazar, the high priest, dies also, 33.

1. *Joshua gathered all the tribes.* This must have been a different assembly from that mentioned in the preceding chapter, though probably held not long after the former. *To Shechem.* As it is immediately added that they *presented themselves before God,* this must mean the Tabernacle; but at this time the Tabernacle was not at Shechem but at Shiloh. The Septuagint appear to have been struck with this difficulty, and therefore read "Shiloh," both here and in v. 25.

2. *On the other side of the flood.* The river Euphrates. *They served other gods.* Probably Abraham as well as Terah, his father, was an idolater, till he received the call of God to leave that land. See on Gen. xi. 31; xii. 1.

9. *Then Balak . . . arose and warred against Israel.* This circumstance is not related in Numbers xxii, nor does it appear in that history that the Moabites attacked the Israelites; and probably the warring here mentioned means no more than his attempts to destroy them by the curses of Balaam and the wiles of the Midianitish women.

11. *The men of Jericho fought against you.* See the notes on chap. iii and chap. vi. 1, etc. The people of Jericho are said to have fought against the Israelites because they opposed them by shutting their gates.

14. *Fear the Lord.* Reverence Him as the sole Object of your religious worship. *Serve him.* Perform His will by obeying His commands. *In sincerity.* Having your whole heart engaged in His worship. *And in truth.* According to the directions He has given you in His infallible word. *Put away the gods.* From this exhortation of Joshua we learn of what sort the gods were, to the worship of whom these Israelites were still attached: (1) those which their fathers worshipped on the other side of the flood: i.e., the gods of the Chaldeans, fire, light, the sun; (2) those of the Egyptians, Apis, Anubis, the ape, serpents, vegetables; (3) those of the Canaanites, Moabites, Baal-peor or Priapus, Astarte or Venus.

15. *Choose you this day whom ye will serve.* Joshua well knew that all service that was not free and voluntary could be only deceit and hypocrisy. He therefore calls upon the people to make their choice, for God himself would not force them—they must serve Him with all their hearts if they served Him at all.

16. *God forbid that we should forsake the Lord.* That they were now sincere cannot be reasonably doubted, for they served the Lord all the days of Joshua, and the elders that outlived him, v. 31; but afterwards they turned aside, and did serve other gods.

19. *Ye cannot serve the Lord: for he is an holy God.* If we are to take this literally, we cannot blame the Israelites for their defection from the worship of the true God; for if it was impossible for them to serve God, they could not but come short of His kingdom. But surely this was not the case. Instead of *lo thuchelu,* "ye cannot serve," some eminent critics read *lo thechallu,* "ye shall not cease to serve." This is a very ingenious emendation, but there is not one MS. in all the collections of Kennicott and De Rossi to support it. If the common reading be preferred, the meaning of the place must be, "Ye cannot serve the Lord, for He is holy and jealous, *unless* ye put away the gods which your fathers served beyond the flood. For He is a jealous God, and will not give to nor divide His glory with any other. He is a holy God, and will not have His people defiled with the impure worship of the Gentiles."

21. *And the people said . . . Nay; but we will serve.* So they understood the words of Joshua to imply no moral impossibility on their side; and had they earnestly sought the gracious assistance of God, they would have continued steady in His covenant.

22. *Ye are witnesses against yourselves.* You have been sufficiently apprised of the difficulties in your way—of God's holiness—your own weakness and inconstancy—the need you have of divine help, and the awful consequences of apostasy; and now you deliberately make your choice. Remember, then, that you are witnesses against yourselves.

23. *Now therefore put away.* As you have promised to reform, begin instantly the work of reformation. A man's promise to serve God soon loses its moral hold of his conscience if he do not instantaneously begin to put it in practice. The grace that enables him to promise is that by the strength of which he is to begin the performance.

25. *Joshua made a covenant.* Literally, "Joshua cut the covenant," alluding to the sacrifice offered on the occasion. *And set them a statute and an ordinance.* He made a solemn and public act of the whole, which was signed and witnessed by himself and the people, in the presence of Jehovah; and having done so, he wrote the words of the covenant in the book of the law of God, probably in some part of the skin constituting the great roll, on which the laws of God were written, and of which there were some blank columns to spare. Having done this, he took a great stone and set it up under an oak—that this might be *ed* or "witness"

that, at such a time and place, this covenant was made, the terms of which might be found written in the book of the law, which was laid up beside the ark. See Deut. xxxi. 26.

27. *This stone . . . hath heard all the words.* That is, the stone itself, from its permanency, shall be in all succeeding ages as competent and as substantial a witness as one who had been present at the transaction, and heard all the words which on both sides were spoken on the occasion.

28. *So Joshua.* After this verse the Septuagint insert v. 31.

29. *Joshua the son of Nun . . . died.* This event probably took place shortly after this public assembly; for he was old and stricken in years when he held the assembly mentioned in chap. xxiii. 2; and as his work was now all done, and his soul ripened for a state of blessedness, God took him to himself, being one hundred and ten years of age, exactly the same age as that of the patriarch Joseph. See Gen. i. 26.

30. *And they buried him . . . in Timnath-serah.* This was his own inheritance, as we have seen chap. xix. 50. It is very strange that there is no account of any public mourning for the death of this eminent general; probably, as he was buried in his own inheritance, he had forbidden all funeral pomp, and it is likely was privately interred.

31. *And Israel served the Lord.* Though there was private idolatry among them, for they had strange gods, yet there was no public idolatry all the days of Joshua and of the elders that overlived Joshua, most of whom must have been advanced in years at the death of this great man.

32. *And the bones of Joseph.* See the note on Gen. i. 25 and on Exod. xiii. 19. This burying of the bones of Joseph probably took place when the conquest of the land was completed, and each tribe had received its inheritance; for it is not likely that this was deferred till after the death of Joshua.

33. *And Eleazar . . . died.* Probably about the same time as Joshua, or soon after, though some think he outlived him six years. Thus, nearly all the persons who had witnessed the miracles of God in the wilderness were gathered to their fathers; and their descendants left in possession of the great inheritance, with the law of God in their hands, and the bright example of their illustrious ancestors before their eyes. *A hill that pertained to Phinehas his son.* This grant was probably made to Phinehas as a token of the respect of the whole nation, for his zeal, courage, and usefulness; for the priests had properly no inheritance.

The last six verses in this chapter were, doubtless, not written by Joshua; for no man can give an account of his own death and burial. Eleazar, Phinehas, or Samuel might have added them, to bring down the narration so as to connect it with their own times and thus preserve the thread of the history unbroken.

The Book of
JUDGES

The persons called judges, *Shophetim,* from *shaphat,* "to judge, discern, regulate, and direct," were the heads or chiefs of the Israelites who governed the Hebrew republic from the days of Moses and Joshua till the time of Saul. The word *judge* is not to be taken here in its usual signification, i.e., one who determines controversies, and denounces the judgment of the law in criminal cases, but one who directs and rules a state or nation with sovereign power, administers justice, makes peace or war, and leads the armies of the people over whom he presides. Officers with the same power, and with nearly the same name, were established by the Tyrians in new Tyre, after the destruction of old Tyre, and the termination of its regal state. The Carthaginian *Suffetes* appear to have been the same as the Hebrew *Shophetim,* as were also the *Archons* among the Athenians, and the *Dictators* among the ancient Romans. But they were neither hereditary governors nor were they chosen by the people; they were properly vicegerents or lieutenants of the Supreme God; and were always, among the Israelites, chosen by Him in a supernatural way. They had no power to make or change the laws; they were only to execute them under the direction of the Most High. God, therefore, was King in Israel: the government was a theocracy; and the judges were His deputies. The office, however, was not continual, as there appear intervals in which there was no judge in Israel. And, as they were extraordinary persons, they were raised up only on extraordinary occasions to be instruments in the hands of God of delivering their nation from the oppression and tyranny of the neighboring powers. They had neither pomp nor state nor, probably, any kind of emoluments.

The chronology of the Book of Judges is extremely embarrassed and difficult; and there is no agreement among learned men concerning it. When the deliverances and consequent periods of rest, so frequently mentioned in this book, took place cannot be satisfactorily ascertained.

Who the author of the Book of Judges was is not known; some suppose that each judge wrote his own history, and that the book has been compiled from those separate accounts, which is very unlikely. Others ascribe it to Phinehas, to Samuel, to Hezekiah, and some to Ezra. But it is evident that it was the work of an individual and of a person who lived posterior to the time of the judges (see chap. ii. 10, etc.), and most probably of Samuel.

CHAPTER 1

After the death of Joshua the Israelites purpose to attack the remaining Canaanites; and the tribe of Judah is directed to go up first, 1-2. Judah and Simeon unite, attack the Canaanites and Perizites, kill ten thousand of them, take Adoni-bezek prisoner, cut off his thumbs and great toes, and bring him to Jerusalem, where he dies, 3-7. Jerusalem conquered, 8. A new war with the Canaanites under the direction of Caleb, 9-11. Kirjath-sepher taken by Othniel, on which he receives, as a reward, Achsah, the daughter of Caleb, and with her a "south land" with springs of water, 12-15. The Kenites dwell among the people, 16. Judah and Simeon destroy the Canaanites in Zephath, Gaza, etc., 17-19. Hebron is given to Caleb, 20. Of the Benjamites, house of Joseph, tribe of Manasseh, etc., 21-27. The Israelites put the Canaanites to tribute, 28. Of the tribes of Ephraim, Zebulun, Asher, and Naphtali, 29-33. The Amorites force the children of Dan into the mountains, 34-36.

1. *Now after the death of Joshua.* How long after the death of Joshua this happened we cannot tell; it is probable that it was not long. The enemies of the Israelites, finding their champion dead, would naturally avail themselves of their unsettled state and make incursions on the country. *Who shall go up?* Joshua had left no successor, and everything relative to the movements of this people must be determined either by caprice or an especial direction of the Lord.

2. *The Lord said, Judah shall go up.* They had inquired of the Lord by Phinehas, the high priest; and he had communicated to them the divine counsel.

3. *Come up with me into my lot.* It appears that the portions of Judah and Simeon had not been cleared of the Canaanites, or that these were the parts which were now particularly invaded.

5. *And they found Adoni-bezek.* The word *matsa*, "he found," is used to express a hostile encounter between two parties; to "attack, surprise." This is probably its meaning here. *Adoni-bezek* is literally the "lord of Bezek." It is very probable that the different Canaanitish tribes were governed by a sort of chieftains.

6. *Cut off his thumbs.* That he might never be able to draw his bow or handle his sword; and *great toes*, that he might never be able to pursue or escape from an adversary.

7. *Threescore and ten kings.* Chieftains, heads of tribes, or military officers. For the word *king* cannot be taken here in its proper and usual sense. *Having their thumbs and their great toes cut off.* That this was an ancient mode of treating enemies we learn from Aelian, who tells us that "the Athenians, at the instigation of Cleon, son of Cleaenetus, made a decree that all the inhabitants of the island of Aegina should have the thumb cut off from the right hand, so that they might ever after be disabled from holding a spear, yet might handle an oar." *Gathered their meat under my table.* I think this was a proverbial mode of expression, to signify reduction to the meanest servitude. *So God hath requited me.* The king of Bezek seems to have had the knowledge of the true God, and a proper notion of a divine providence. He now feels himself reduced to that state to which he had cruelly reduced others. Those acts in him were acts of tyrannous cruelty; the act towards him was an act of retributive justice. *And there he died.* He continued at Jerusalem in a servile and degraded condition till the day of his death. How long he lived after his disgrace we know not.

8. *Had fought against Jerusalem.* We read this verse in a parenthesis, because we suppose that it refers to the taking of this city by Joshua; for as he had conquered its armies and slew its king, Josh. x. 26, it is probable that he took the city. Yet we find that the Jebusites still dwelt in it, Josh. xv. 63; and that the men of Judah could not drive them out, which probably refers to the stronghold or fortress on Mount Zion, which the Jebusites held till the days of David, who took it, and totally destroyed the Jebusites. See 2 Sam. v. 6-9, and 1 Chron. xi. 4-8. It is possible that the Jebusites, who had been discomfited by Joshua, had again become sufficiently strong to possess themselves of Jerusalem; and that they were now defeated, and the city itself set on fire, but that they still were able to keep possession of their strong fort on Mount Zion, which appears to have been the citadel of Jerusalem.

9. *The Canaanites, that dwelt in the mountain.* The territories of the tribe of Judah lay in the most southern part of the Promised Land, which was very mountainous, though towards the west it had many fine plains. In some of these the Canaanites had dwelt, and the expedition marked here was for the purpose of finally expelling them. But probably this is a recapitulation of what is related Josh. x. 36; xi. 21; xv. 13.

12-15. *And Caleb.* See this whole account, which is placed here by way of recapitulation, in Josh. xv. 13-19.

16. *The children of the Kenite, Moses' father in law.* For an account of Jethro, the father-in-law of Moses, see Exod. xviii. 1-27; Num. x. 29, etc. *The city of palm trees.* This seems to have been some place near Jericho, which city is expressly called "the city of palm trees," Deut. xxxiv. 3; and though destroyed by Joshua, it might have some suburbs remaining where these harmless people had taken up their residence.

The Kenites, the descendants of Jethro, the father-in-law of Moses, were always attached to the Israelites. They received there a lot with the tribe of Judah, and remained in the city of palm trees during the life of Joshua; but after his death, not contented with their portion, or molested by the original inhabitants, they united with the tribe of Judah, and went with them to attack Arad. After the conquest of that country, the Kenites established themselves there, and remained in it till the days of Saul, mingled with the Amalekites. When this king received a commandment from God to destroy the Amalekites, he sent a message to the Kenites to depart from among them, as God would not destroy them with the Amalekites. From them came Hemath, who was the father of the house of Rechab, 1 Chron. ii. 55, and the Rechabites, of whom we have a remarkable account Jer. xxxv. 1, etc.

17. *The city was called Hormah.* This appears to be the same transaction mentioned in Num. xxi. 1, etc.

18. *Judah took Gaza . . . and Askelon . . . and Ekron.* There is a most remarkable variation here in the Septuagint: "But Judah did not possess Gaza, nor the coast thereof; neither Askelon, nor the coasts thereof; neither Ekron, nor the coasts thereof; neither Azotus, nor its adjacent places: and the Lord was with Judah." This is the reading of the Vatican and other copies of the Septuagint; but the Alexandrian MS. and the text of the Complutensian and Antwerp Polyglots agree more nearly with the Hebrew text. St. Augustine and Procopius read the same as the Vatican MS.; and Josephus expressly says that the Israelites took only Askelon and Azotus, but did not take Gaza nor Ekron. And the whole history shows that these cities were not in the possession of the Israelites, but of the Philistines; and if the Israelites did take them at this time, as the Hebrew text states, they certainly lost them in a very short time after.

19. *And the Lord was with Judah; and he drave out the inhabitants of the mountain; but could not drive out the inhabitants of the valley, because they had chariots of iron.* Strange! were the iron chariots too strong for Omnipotence? The whole of this verse is improperly rendered. The first clause, *The Lord was with Judah,* should terminate the eighteenth verse, and this gives the reason for the success of this tribe. Here then is a complete period; the remaining part of the verse refers either to a different time or to the rebellion of Judah against the Lord, which caused Him to withdraw His support. This is the turn given to the verse by Jonathan ben Uzziel, the Chaldee paraphrast: "And the word of Jehovah was in the support of the house of Judah, and they extirpated the inhabitants of the mountains; but afterwards, when they sinned, they were not able to extirpate the inhabitants of the plain country, because they had chariots of iron."

20. *They gave Hebron unto Caleb.* See this whole transaction explained Josh. xiv. 12, etc.

21. *The Jebusites dwell with the children of Benjamin.* Jerusalem was situated partly in the tribe of Judah and partly in the tribe of Benjamin the northern part belonging to the latter tribe, the sourthern to the former. The Jebusites had their strongest position in the part that belonged to Benjamin, and from this place they were not wholly expelled till the days of David. See the notes on v. 8. What is said here of Benjamin is said of Judah, Josh. xv. 63. There must be an interchange of the names in one or other of these places. *Unto this day.* As the Jebusites dwelt in Jerusalem till the days of David, by whom they were driven out, and the author of the Book of Judges states them to have been in possession of Jerusalem when he wrote, therefore this book was written before the reign of David.

22. *The house of Joseph, they also went up against Beth-el.* That is, the tribe of Ephraim and the half-tribe of Manasseh, who dwelt beyond Jordan. Bethel was not taken by Joshua, though he took Ai, which was nigh to it.

23. *Beth-el . . . the name of the city before was Luz.* Concerning this city and its names, see the notes on Gen. xxviii. 19.

24. *Shew us . . . the entrance into the city.* Taken in whatever light we choose, the conduct of this man was execrable. He was a traitor to his country, and he was accessory to the destruction of the lives and property of his fellow citizens, which he most sinfully betrayed, in order to save his own. According to the rules and laws of war, the children of Judah might avail themselves of such men and their information, but this does not lessen, on the side of this traitor, the turpitude of the action.

26. *The land of the Hittites.* Probably some place beyond the land of Canaan, in Arabia, whither this people emigrated when expelled by Joshua. The man himself appears to have been a Hittite, and to perpetuate the name of his city he called the new one which he now founded Luz, this being the ancient name of Bethel.

27. *Beth-shean.* Called by the Septuagint Scythopolis, or "the city of the Scythians." On these towns see the notes, Josh. xvii. 12-13.

29. *Neither did Ephraim.* See the notes on the parallel passages, Josh. xvi. 5-10.

30. *Neither did Zebulun drive out.* See on Josh. xix. 10-15.

31. *Neither did Asher.* See on Josh. xix. 24-31.

Accho. Supposed to be the city of Ptolemais, near to Mount Carmel.

33. *Neither did Naphtali.* See the notes on Josh. xix. 32-39.

35. *The Amorites would dwell in mount Heres.* They perhaps agreed to dwell in the mountainous country, being unable to maintain themselves on the plain, and yet were so powerful that the Danites could not totally expel them; they were, however, laid under tribute, and thus the house of Joseph had the sovereignty.

36. *Akrabbim.* Of "scorpions"; probably so called from the number of those animals in that place. *From the rock, and upward.* The Vulgate understand by *sela,* "a rock," the city Petra, which was the capital of Arabia Petraea.

CHAPTER 2

An angel comes to the Israelites at Bochim, and gives them various reproofs, at which they are greatly affected, 1-5. They served the Lord during the days of Joshua, and the elders who succeeded him, 6-7. Joshua having died, and all that generation, the people revolted from the true God and served idols, 8-13. The Lord, being angry, delivered them into the hands of spoilers, and they were greatly distressed, 14-15. A general account of the method which God used to reclaim them, by sending them judges whom they frequently disobeyed, 16-19. Therefore God left the various nations of the land to plague and punish them, 20-23.

1. *An angel of the Lord.* In the preceding chapter we have a summary of several things which took place shortly after the death of Joshua, especially during the time in which the elders lived (that is, the men who were contemporary with Joshua, but survived him) and while the people continued faithful to the Lord. In this chapter, and some parts of the following,

we have an account of the same people abandoned by their God and reduced to the heaviest calamities because they had broken their covenant with their Maker. This chapter, and the first eight verses of the next, may be considered as an epitome of the whole book, in which we see on one hand the crimes of the Israelites, and on the other the punishments inflicted on them by the Lord; their repentance, and return to their allegiance; and the long-suffering and mercy of God, shown in pardoning their backslidings and delivering them out of the hands of their enemies.

The *angel of the Lord,* mentioned here, is variously interpreted. Some think it was Phinehas, the high priest, which is possible; others, that it was a prophet, sent to the place where they were now assembled, with an extraordinary commission from God, to reprove them for their sins, and to show them the reason why God had not rooted out their enemies from the land; this is the opinion of the Chaldee paraphrast, consequently of the ancient Jews. Others think that an angel, properly such, is intended; and several are of opinion that it was the Angel of the Covenant, the Captain of the Lord's host, which had appeared unto Joshua, chap. v. 14, and no less than the Lord Jesus Christ himself. I think it more probable that some extraordinary human messenger is meant, as such messengers, and indeed prophets, apostles, etc., are frequently termed *angels,* that is, "messengers" of the Lord. The person here mentioned appears to have been a resident at Gilgal, and to have come to Bochim on this express errand.

I will never break my covenant. Nor did God ever break it. A covenant is never broken but by him who violates any of the conditions, the covenant is then broken, and by that party alone; and the conditions on the other side are null and void.

3. *I will not drive them out from before you.* Their transgressions, and breach of the covenant, were the reasons why they were not put in entire possession of the Promised Land. See note at the end of this chapter.

5. *They called the name of that place Bochim.* The word *bochim* signifies "weepings" or "lamentations"; and is translated by the Septuagint "bewailings"; and it is supposed that the place derived its name from these lamentations of the people. Some think the place itself, where the people were now assembled, was Shiloh, now named *Bochim* because of the above circumstance. It should be observed that the angel speaks here in the person of God, by whom he was sent, as the prophets frequently do.

11. *Served Baalim.* The word *baalim* signifies "lords." Their false gods they considered supernatural rulers or governors, each having his peculiar district and office; but when they wished to express a particular *baal,* they generally added some particular epithet, a Baalzephon, Baal-peor, Baal-zebub, Baal-shamayim. The two former were adored by the Moabites; Baal-zebub, by the Ekronites. Baal-berith was honored at Shechem; and Baal-shamayim, the "lord or ruler of the heavens," was adored among the Phoenicians, Syrians, Chaldeans.

12. *Which brought them out of the land of Egypt.* This was one of the highest aggravations of their offense; they forsook the God who brought them out of Egypt, a place in which

they endured the most grievous oppression, and were subjected to the most degrading servitude, from which they never could have rescued themselves; and they were delivered by such a signal display of the power, justice, and mercy of God as should never have been forgotten, because the most stupendous that had ever been exhibited.

14. *The hands of spoilers.* Probably marauding parties of the Canaanites, making frequent incursions in their lands, carrying away cattle, spoiling their crops.

15. *The hand of the Lord was against them.* The "power" which before protected them when obedient was now turned against them because of their disobedience. They not only had not God with them, but they had God against them.

16. *The Lord raised up judges.* That is, leaders, generals, and governors, raised up by an especial appointment of the Lord, to deliver them from, and avenge them on, their adversaries.

17. *Went a whoring after other gods.* Idolatry, or the worship of strange gods, is frequently termed adultery, fornication, and whoredom in the sacred writings. As many of their idolatrous practices were accompanied with impure rites, the term was not only metaphorically but literally proper.

18. *The Lord was with the judge.* God himself was King, and the judge was His representative. *It repented the Lord.* He changed His purpose towards them; He purposed to destroy them because of their sin; they repented and turned to Him, and He changed this purpose.

19. *When the judge was dead.* It appears that in general the office of the judge was for life. *Their stubborn way.* Their "hard or difficult way." Most sinners go through great tribulation in order to get to eternal perdition; they would have had less pain in their way to heaven.

20. *The anger of the Lord was hot.* They were as fuel by their transgressions; and the displeasure of the Lord was as a fire about to kindle and consume that fuel.

22. *That through them I may prove Israel.* There appeared to be no other way to induce this people to acknowledge the true God but by permitting them to fall into straits from which they could not be delivered but by His especial providence.

23. *Without driving them out hastily.* Had God expelled all the ancient inhabitants at once, we plainly see from the subsequent conduct of the people that they would soon have abandoned His worship, and in their prosperity forgotten their Deliverer. At first He drove out as many as were necessary in order to afford the people, as they were then, a sufficiency of room to settle in; as the tribes increased in population, they were to extend themselves to the uttermost of their assigned borders, and expel all the remaining inhabitants.

CHAPTER 3

An account of the nations that were left to prove Israel, 1-4. How the people provoked the Lord, 5-7. They are delivered into the power of the king of Mesopotamia, by whom they are enslaved eight years, 8. Othniel is raised up as their deliverer; he discomfits the king of Mesopotamia, delivers Israel, and the land enjoys peace for forty years, 9-11. They again rebel, and are delivered into the hand of the king of Moab, by whom they are enslaved eighteen years, 12-14. They are delivered by Ehud, who kills Eglon, king of Moab, and slays 10,000 Moabites, and the land rests fourscore years, 15-30.

1. *Now these are the nations.* The nations left to prove the Israelites were the five lordships or satrapies of the Philistines, viz., Gath, Askelon, Ashdod, Ekron, and Gaza; the Sidonians, the Hivites of Lebanon, Baal-hermon, etc.; with the remains of the Canaanites, viz., the Hittites, Amorites, Perizzites, and Jebusites.

2. *That . . . Israel might know, to teach them war.* This was another reason why the Canaanites were left in the land, that the Israelites might not forget military discipline, but habituate themselves to the use of arms, that they might always be able to defend themselves against their foes. Had they been faithful to God, they would have had no need of learning the art of war; but now arms became a sort of necessary substitute for that spiritual strength which had departed from them.

4. *To know whether they would hearken.* This would be the consequence of the Canaanites being left among them: if they should be faithful to God, their enemies would not be able to enslave them; should they be rebellious, the Lord would abandon them to their foes.

6. *And they took their daughters.* They formed matrimonial alliances with those proscribed nations, served their idols, and thus became *one* with them in politics and religion.

7. *Served Baalim and the groves.* No *groves* were ever worshipped, but the deities who were supposed to be resident in them; and in many cases temples and altars were built in groves, and the superstition of consecrating groves and woods to the honor of the deities was a practice very usual with the ancients. But it is very probable that the word *asheroth,* which we translate *groves,* is a corruption of the word *ashtaroth,* the moon or Venus. *Ashtaroth* is read in this place by the Chaldee Targum, the Syriac, the Arabic, and the Vulgate.

8. *Chushan-rishathaim. Kushan,* the "wicked" or "impious"; and so the word is rendered by the Chaldee Targum, the Syriac, and the Arabic, wherever it occurs in this chapter. *King of Mesopotamia.* King of *Aram naharayim,* "Syria of the two rivers," translated *Mesopotamia* by the Septuagint and Vulgate. It was the district situated between the Tigris and Euphrates. *Served Chushan . . . eight years.* He overran their country, and forced them to pay a very heavy tribute.

9. *Raised up . . . Othniel the son of Kenaz.* This noble Hebrew was of the tribe of Judah, and nephew and son-in-law to Caleb, whose praise stands without abatement in the sacred records. Othniel had already signalized his valor in taking Kirjath-sepher, which appears to have been a very hazardous exploit. By his natural valor, experience in war, and the peculiar influence of the Divine Spirit, he was well qualified to inspire his countrymen with courage, and to lead them successfully against their oppressors.

10. *His hand prevailed.* We are not told of what nature this war was, but it was most decisive; and the consequence was an undisturbed peace of forty years, during the whole life of Othniel. By *the spirit of the Lord* coming upon him the Chaldee understands the spirit of

prophecy; others understand the spirit of fortitude and extraordinary courage, as opposed to the spirit of fear or faintness of heart; but as Othniel was judge, and had many offices to fulfil besides that of a general, he had need of the Spirit of God, in the proper sense of the word, to enable him to guide and govern this most refractory and fickle people; and his receiving it for these purposes shows that the political state of the Jews was still a theocracy.

12. *The children of Israel did evil.* They forgot the Lord and became idolaters, and God made those very people, whom they had imitated in their idolatrous worship, the means of their chastisement. *The Lord strengthened Eglon the king of Moab.* The success he had against the Israelites was by the especial appointment and energy of God. *Eglon* is supposed to have been the immediate successor of Balak. Some great men have borne names which, when reduced to their grammatical meaning, appear very ridiculous; the word *Eglon* signifies a "little calf"!

13. *The city of palm trees.* This the Targum renders "the city of Jericho"; but Jericho had been destroyed by Joshua, and certainly was not rebuilt till the reign of Ahab, long after this, 1 Kings xvi. 34. However, as Jericho is expressly called "the city of palm trees," Deut. xxxiv. 3, the city in question must have been in the vicinity or plain of Jericho, and the king of Moab had seized it as a frontier town contiguous to his own estates.

15. *Ehud the son of Gera . . . a man left-handed.* "A man lame in his right hand," and therefore obliged to use his left. The Septuagint render it "an ambidexter," a man who could use both hands alike. It is well known that to be an ambidexter was in high repute among the ancients. In chap. xx. 16 of this book we have an account of 700 men of Benjamin, each of whom was "lame of his right hand," and yet slinging stones to a hair's breadth without missing; these are generally thought to be ambidexters. *Sent a present unto Eglon.* This is generally understood to be the tribute money which the king of Moab had imposed on the Israelites.

17. *Eglon was a very fat man.* The *ish bari* of the text is translated by the Septuagint "a very beautiful or polite man," and in the Syriac, "a very rude man." It probably means what we call lusty or corpulent.

18. *Made an end to offer the present.* Presents, tribute, etc., in the Eastern countries were offered with very great ceremony; and to make the more parade several persons, ordinarily slaves, sumptuously dressed, and in considerable number, were employed to carry what would not be a burden even to one. This appears to have been the case in the present instance.

19. *He . . . turned . . . from the quarries. Pesilim.* Some of the versions understand this word as meaning idols or graven images, or some spot where the Moabites had a place of idolatrous worship. As *pasal* signifies to "cut, hew, or engrave," it may be applied to the images thus cut, or the place or quarry whence they were digged; but it is most likely that idols are meant.

20. *I have a message from God unto thee. Debar elohim li aleycha,* "a word of the gods to me, unto thee." It is very likely that the word *elohim* is used here to signify idols, or the

pesilim mentioned above, v. 19. Ehud, having gone so far as this place of idolatry, might feign he had there been worshipping, and that the *pesilim* had inspired him with a message for the king; and this was the reason why the king commanded silence, why every man went out, and why he rose from his seat or throne, that he might receive it with the greater respect. This, being an idolater, he would not have done to any message coming from the God of Israel.

22. *The haft also went in after the blade.* As the instrument was very short, and Eglon very corpulent, this might readily take place.

24. *He covereth his feet.* He has lain down on his sofa in order to sleep; when this was done they dropped their slippers, lifted up their feet, and covered them with their long, loose garments.

26. *Passed beyond the quarries.* Beyond the *pesilim*, which appear to have been the Moabitish borders, where they had set up those hewn stones as landmarks, or sacred boundary stones.

28. *Took the fords of Jordan.* It is very likely that the Moabites, who were on the western side of Jordan, hearing of the death of Eglon, were panic-struck, and endeavored to escape over Jordan at the fords near Jericho, when Ehud blew his trumpet in the mountains of Ephraim, and thus to get into the land of the Moabites, which lay on the east of Jordan; but Ehud and his men, seizing the only pass by which they could make their escape, slew 10,000 of them in their attempt to cross at those fords. What is called here *the fords* was doubtless the place where the Israelites had passed over Jordan when they (under Joshua) took possession of the Promised Land.

29. *All lusty, and all men of valour.* Picked, chosen troops, which Eglon kept among the Israelites to reduce and overawe them.

31. *And after him was Shamgar the son of Anath.* Dr. Hales supposes that "Shamgar's administration in the West, included Ehud's administration of eighty years in the East; and that, as this administration might have been of some continuance, so this Philistine servitude, which is not noticed elsewhere, might have been of some duration; as may be incidentally collected from Deborah's thanksgiving, chap. v. 6."

CHAPTER 4

The Israelites again rebel against God, and they are delivered into the hands of Jabin, king of Canaan, 1-2. They cry unto God, and He raises up Deborah and Barak to deliver them, 3-10. Some account of Heber the Kenite, 11. Barak attacks Sisera, captain of Jabin's army, at the river Kishon, and gives him a total overthrow, 12-16. Siser leaves his chariot, and flies away on foot; enters the tent of Jael, the wife of Heber, by whom he is slain, while secreting himself in her apartment, 17-24.

1. *When Ehud was dead.* Why not "when Shamgar was dead"? Does this not intimate that Shamgar was not reckoned in the number of the judges?

2. *Jabin king of Canaan.* Probably a descendant of the Jabin mentioned Josh. xi. 1, etc., who had gathered together the wrecks of the army of that Jabin defeated by Joshua.

3. *Nine hundred chariots of iron.* Chariots armed with iron scythes, as is generally supposed; they could not have been made all of iron, but they might have been shod with iron, or had iron scythes projecting from the axle on each side, by which infantry might be easily cut down or thrown into confusion.

4. *Deborah, a prophetess.* One on whom the Spirit of God descended, and who was the instrument of conveying to the Israelites the knowledge of the divine will, in things sacred and civil. *She judged Israel.* This is, I believe, the first instance of female government on record. Deborah seems to have been supreme in both civil and religious affairs; and *Lapidoth,* her husband, appears to have had no hand in the government. But the original may as well be translated "a woman of Lapidoth" as *the wife of Lapidoth.*

6. *She sent and called Barak.* She appointed him to be general of the armies on this occasion, which shows that she possessed the supreme power in the state.

9. *The Lord shall sell Sisera into the hand of a woman.* Does not this mean, If I go with thee, the conquest shall be attributed to me, and thou wilt have no honor? Or is it a prediction of the exploit of Jael? In both these senses the words have been understood. It seems, however, more likely that Jael is intended.

The Septuagint made a remarkable addition to the speech of Barak: "If thou wilt go with me I will go; but if thou wilt not go with me, I will not go; because I know not the day in which the Lord will send his angel to give me success." By which he appears to mean that, although he was certain of a divine call to this work, yet, as he knew not the time in which it would be proper for him to make the attack, he wished that Deborah, on whom the Divine Spirit constantly rested, would accompany him to let him know when to strike that blow, which he knew would be decisive.

10. *Ten thousand men at his feet.* Ten thousand footmen. He had no chariots; his army was all composed of infantry.

11. *Hobab the father in law of Moses.* For a circumstantial account of this person, and the meaning of the original word *chothen,* which is translated "son in law" in Gen. xix. 14, see the notes on Exod. ii. 15-16, 18; iii. 1; iv. 20, 24; and xviii. 5.

14. *Up; for this is the day.* This is exactly the purpose for which the Septuagint states, v. 8, that Barak wished Deborah to accompany him. *Went down from mount Tabor.* He had probably encamped his men on and near the summit of this mount.

15. *The Lord discomfited Sisera.* "The Lord confounded, threw them all into confusion, drove them pell-mell"—caused chariots to break and overthrow chariots, and threw universal disorder into all their ranks. In this case Barak and his men had little to do but kill and pursue, and Sisera, in order to escape, was obliged to abandon his chariot. There is no doubt all this was done by supernatural agency; God sent His angel and confounded them.

18. *Jael went out to meet Sisera.* He preferred the woman's tent because of secrecy; for, according to the etiquette of the Eastern countries, no person ever intrudes into the apartments of the women.

19. *She opened a bottle of milk.* She gave

more than he requested, and her friendship increased his confidence and security.

20. *Stand in the door of the tent.* As no man would intrude into the women's apartment without permission, her simply saying, "There is no man in my tent," would preclude all search.

21. *A nail of the tent.* One of the spikes by which they fasten to the ground the cords which are attached to the cloth or covering. *He was fast asleep and weary.* As he lay on one side, and was overwhelmed with sleep through the heat and fatigues of the day, the piercing of his temples must have in a moment put him past resistence.

24. *The hand of the children of Israel prospered.* "It went, going"—they followed up this victory, and the consequence was, they utterly destroyed Jabin and his kingdom.

CHAPTER 5

The triumphant song of Deborah and Barak, after the defeat of Sisera, captain of the armies of Jabin, king of Canaan.

1. *Then sang Deborah and Barak.* There are many difficulties in this very sublime song, and learned men have toiled much to remove them. That there are several gross mistakes in our version will be instantly acknowledged by all who can critically examine the original.

4. *When thou wentest out of Seir.* Here is an illusion to the giving of the law, and the manifestation of God's power and glory at that time; and as this was the most signal display of His majesty and mercy in behalf of their forefathers, Deborah very properly begins her song with a commemoration of this transaction.

6. *The highways are unoccupied.* The land was full of anarchy and confusion, being everywhere infested with banditti. No public road was safe.

7. *The villages ceased.* The people were obliged to live together in fortified places; or in great numbers, to protect each other against the incursions of bands of spoilers.

8. *They chose new gods.* This was the cause of all their calamites; they forsook Jehovah, and served other gods; and *then was war in their gates*—they were hemmed up in every place, and besieged in all their fortified cities. And they were defenseless, they had no means of resisting their adversaries; for even *among forty thousand* men, there was neither spear nor shield to be seen.

10. *Ye that ride on white asses.* Perhaps *athonoth tsechoroth* should be rendered "sleek or well-fed asses." *Ye that sit in judgment. Yoshebey al middin;* some have rendered this, "ye who dwell in Middin." This was a place in the tribe of Judah, and is mentioned in Josh. xv. 61. *And walk by the way.* Persons who go from place to place for the purposes of traffic.

11. *In the places of drawing water.* As wells were very scarce in every part of the East, and travellers in such hot countries must have water, robbers and banditti generally took their stations near tanks, pools, and springs, in order that they might suddenly fall upon those who came to drink; and when the country was badly governed, annoyances of this kind were very frequent. The victory gained now by the Israel-

ites put the whole country under their own government, and the land was cleansed from such marauders. *Go down to the gates.* They may go down to the gates to receive judgment and justice as usual. It is well known that the gate was the place of judgment in the East.

12. *Lead thy captivity captive.* Make those captives who have formerly captivated us.

13. *Made him that remaineth.* This appears to be spoken of Barak, who is represented as being only a remnant of the people.

14. *Out of Ephraim . . . a root of them.* Deborah probably means that out of Ephraim and Benjamin came eminent warriors. Joshua, who was of the tribe of *Ephraim*, routed the Amalekites a short time after the Israelites came out of Egypt, Exod. xvii. 10. Ehud, who was of the tribe of *Benjamin*, slew Eglon, and defeated the Moabites, the friends and allies of the Ammonites and Amalekites. *Machir*, in the land of Gilead, produced eminent warriors; and *Zebulun* produced eminent statesmen, and men of literature. Probably Deborah speaks here of the past wars, and not of anything that was done on this occasion; for we know that no person from Gilead were present in the war between Jabin and Israel. See v. 17: "Gilead abode beyond Jordan."

15. *The princes of Issachar.* They were at hand and came willingly forth, at the call of Deborah, to this important war. *Barak . . . was sent on foot.* Should be translated "with his footmen or infantry." Thus the Alexandrian Septuagint understood it, rendering the clause thus: "Barak also sent forth his footmen into the valley." Luther has perfectly hit the meaning, "Barak with his footmen."

For the divisions of Reuben. Either the Reubenites were divided among themselves into factions, which prevented their cooperation with their brethren, or they were divided in their judgment concerning the measures now to be pursued, which prevented them from joining with the other tribes till the business was entirely settled. The *thoughts of heart* and *searchings of heart* might refer to the doubts and uneasiness felt by the other tribes when they found the Reubenites did not join them; for they might have conjectured that they were either unconcerned about their liberty or were meditating a coalition with the Canaanites.

17. *Gilead abode beyond Jordan.* That is, the Gadites, who had their lot in those parts, and could not well come to the aid of their brethren at a short summons. But the words of Deborah imply a criminal neglect on the part of the Danites; they were intent upon their traffic, and trusted in their ships. Joppa was one of their seaports. *Asher continued on the sea shore.* The lot of Asher extended along the Mediterranean Sea; and being contiguous to Zebulun and Naphtali, they might have easily succored their brethren; but they had the pretense that their posts were unguarded, and they abode in their *breaches*, in order to defend them.

18. *Zebulun and Naphtali . . . jeoparded their lives.* The original is very emphatic, "They desolated their lives to death"—they were determined to conquer or die, and therefore plunged into the thickest of the battle.

19. *The kings came and fought.* It is conjectured that Jabin and his confederates had

invaded Manasseh, as both Taanach and Megiddo were in that tribe, and that they were discomfited by the tribes of Zebulun and Naphtali at Taanach and Megiddo, while Barak defeated Sisera at Mount Tabor. *They took no gain of money.* They expected much booty in the total rout of the Israelites; but they were defeated, and got no prey; or, if applied to the Israelites. They fought for liberty, not for plunder.

20. *They fought from heaven.* The angels of God came to the assistance of Israel, and "the stars in their orbits fought against Sisera"; probably some thunderstorm, or great inundation from the river Kishon, took place at that time, which in poetic language was attributed to the stars.

21. *The river of Kishon swept them away.* This gives plausibility to the above conjecture, that there was a storm at this time which produced an inundation in the river Kishon, which the routed Canaanites attempting to ford were swept away.

22. *Then were the horsehoofs broken.* In very ancient times horses were not shod, nor are they to the present day in several parts of the East. Sisera had iron chariots when his hosts were routed; the horses that drew these, being strongly urged on by those who drove them, had their hoofs broken by the roughness of the roads; in consequence of which they became lame, and could not carry off their riders. This is marked as one cause of their disaster.

23. *Curse ye Meroz.* Where Meroz was is not known. *Curse ye bitterly.* "Curse with cursing" —use the most awful execrations. *Said the angel of the Lord.* That is, Barak, who was Jehovah's *angel* or "messenger" in this war; the person sent by God to deliver His people. *To the help of the Lord.* That is, to the help of the people of the Lord. *Against the mighty.* Baggibborim, "with the heroes"; that is, Barak and his men, together with Zebulun and Naphtali. These were the mighty men, or heroes, with whom the inhabitants of Meroz would not join.

24. *Blessed above women shall Jael . . . be.* She shall be highly celebrated as a most heroic woman; all the Israelitish women shall glory in her. I do not understand these words as expressive of the divine approbation towards Jael. The word *bless,* in both Hebrew and Greek, often signifies "to praise, to speak well of, to celebrate." This is most probably its sense here.

25. *She brought forth butter.* As the word *chemah,* here translated *butter,* signifies "disturbed, agitated," it is probable that buttermilk is intended.

26. *She smote off his head.* The original does not warrant this translation, nor is it supported by fact. "She smote his head," and transfixed him through the temples. It was his head that received the death wound, and the place where this wound was inflicted was the temples. The manner in which Jael dispatched Sisera seems to have been this: (1) Observing him to be in a profound sleep, she took a *workmen's hammer* and with one blow on the head deprived him of all sense. (2) She then took a tent nail and drove it through his temples, and thus pinned him to the earth, which she could not have done had she not previously stunned him with the blow on the head.

27. *At her feet he bowed. Bein ragleyha,* "between her feet." After having stunned him she probably sat down, for the greater convenience of driving the nail through his temples. *He bowed . . . he fell.* He probably made some struggles after he received the blow on the head, but could not recover his feet.

28. *Cried through the lattice.* This is very natural; in the women's apartments in the East the windows are latticed, to prevent them from sending or receiving letters, etc. The latticing is the effect of the jealousy which universally prevails in those countries. *Why is his chariot so long in coming?* Literally, Why is his chariot ashamed to come?

CHAPTER 6

The Israelites again do evil, and are delivered into the hands of the Midianites, by whom they are oppressed seven years, 1-2. Different tribes spoil their harvests, and take away their cattle, 3-5. They cry unto the Lord, and He sends them a prophet to reprehend and instruct them, 6-10. An angel appears unto Gideon, and gives him commission to deliver Israel, and works several miracles, to prove that he is divinely appointed to this work, 11-23. Gideon builds an altar to the Lord, under the name of Jehovah-shalom; and throws down the altar of Baal, 24-27. His townsmen conspire against him; he expostulates with them, and they are pacified, 28-32. The Midianites and Amalekites gather together against Israel; Gideon summons Manasseh, Asher, Zebulun, and Naphtali, who join his standard, 33-35. The miracle of the fleece of wool, 36-40.

1. *Delivered them into the hand of Midian.* The Midianites were among the most ancient and inveterate of the enemies of Israel. They joined with the Moabites to seduce them to idolatry, and were nearly extirpated by them, Numbers xxxi. The Midianites dwelt on the eastern borders of the Dead Sea, and their capital was Arnon.

2. *Made them the dens which are in the mountains.* Nothing can give a more distressing description of the state of the Israelites than what is here related. They durst not reside in the plain country, but were obliged to betake themselves to dens and caves of the mountains, and live like wild beasts, and were hunted like them by their adversaries.

3. *Children of the east.* Probably those who inhabited Arabia Deserta, Ishmaelites.

4. *Encamped against them.* Wandering hordes of Midianites, Amalekites, and Ishmaelites came, in the times of harvest and autumn, and carried away their crops, their fruit, and their cattle. And they appear to have come early, encamped in the plains, and watched the crops till they were ready to be carried off. This is frequently the case even to the present day. *Till thou come unto Gaza.* That is, the whole breadth of the land, from Jordan to the coast of the Mediterranean Sea.

5. *They came up with their cattle and their tents.* All this proves that they were different tribes of wanderers who had no fixed residence; but, like their descendants the Bedouins or wandering Arabs, removed from place to place to get prey for themselves and forage for their cattle.

8. *The Lord sent a prophet.* The Jews say that this was Phinehas; but it is more likely that it was some prophet or teacher raised up by the Lord to warn and instruct them.

11. *There came an angel of the Lord.* The prophet came to teach and exhort; the angel

comes to confirm the word of the prophet, to call and commission him who was intended to be their deliverer, and to work miracles, in order to inspire him with supernatural courage and a confidence of success. *Ophrah.* Or Ephra, was a city, or village rather, in the half-tribe of Manasseh, beyond Jordan.

His son Gideon threshed wheat. This is not the only instance in which a man taken from agricultural employments was made general of an army, and the deliverer of his country. Shamgar was evidently a ploughman, and with his oxgoad he slew many Philistines, and became one of the deliverers of Israel. *Threshed wheat by the winepress.* This was a place of privacy; he could not make a threshing floor in open day as the custom was, for fear of the Midianites, who were accustomed to come and take it away as soon as threshed. He got a few sheaves from the field and brought them home to have them privately threshed for the support of the family. As there could be no vintage among the Israelites in their present distressed circumstances, the winepress would never be suspected by the Midianites to be the place of threshing corn.

13. *And Gideon said unto him.* This speech is remarkable for its energy and simplicity; it shows indeed a measure of despondency, but not more than the circumstances of the case justified.

14. *Go in this thy might.* What does the angel mean? He had just stated that Jehovah was with Gideon; and he now says, *Go in this thy might,* i.e., in the might of Jehovah, who is with thee.

15. *Wherewith shall I save Israel?* I have neither men nor money. *Behold, my family is poor in Manasseh.* "Behold, my thousand is impoverished." Tribes were anciently divided into tens, and fifties, and hundreds, and thousands; the thousands therefore marked grand divisions, and consequently numerous families; Gideon here intimates that the families of which he made a part were very much diminished.

16. *Thou shalt smite the Midianites as one man.* You shall as surely conquer all their host as if you had but one man to contend with; or, You shall destroy them to a man.

17. *Shew me a sign.* Work a miracle, that I may know that you have wisdom and power sufficient to authorize and qualify me for the work.

18. *And bring forth my present.* My *minchah;* generally an offering of bread, wine, oil, flour, and suchlike. It seems from this that Gideon supposed the person to whom he spoke to be a divine person. Nevertheless, what he prepared and brought out appears to be intended simply as an entertainment to refresh a respectable stranger.

20. *Take the flesh.* The angel intended to make the flesh and bread an offering to God, and the broth a libation.

21. *The angel . . . put forth the end of the staff.* He appeared like a traveller with a staff in his hand; this he put forth, and having touched the flesh, fire rose out of the rock and consumed it. Here was the most evident proof of supernatural agency. *Then the angel . . . departed out of his sight.* Though the angel vanished out of his sight, yet God continued to converse with him either by secret inspiration in his own heart or by an audible voice.

22. *Alas, O Lord God! for because I have seen.* This is an elliptical sentence, a natural expression of the distressed state of Gideon's mind; as if he had said, Have mercy on me, O Lord God! else I shall die; because I have seen an angel of Jehovah face-to-face. We have frequently seen that it was a prevalent sentiment, as well before as under the law, that if any man saw God, or His representative angel, he must surely die.

23. *Fear not: thou shalt not die.* Here the discovery is made by God himself; Gideon is not curiously prying into forbidden mysteries, therefore he shall not die.

24. *Gideon built an altar . . . and called it Jehovah-shalom.* The words *Yehovah shalom* signify, "The Lord is my peace," or, "The peace of Jehovah"; and this name he gave the altar in reference to what God had said, v. 23, "Peace be unto thee."

25. *Take thy father's young bullock, even the second bullock.* There is some difficulty in this verse, for, according to the Hebrew text, two bullocks are mentioned here; but there is only one mentioned in verses 26 and 28. But what was this second bullock? Some think that it was a bullock that was fattened in order to be offered in sacrifice to Baal. This is very probable, as the *second bullock* is so particularly distinguished from another which belonged to Gideon's father. As the altar was built upon the ground of Joash, yet appears to have been public property (see vv. 29-30), so this second ox was probably reared and fattened at the expense of the men of that village; else why should they so particularly resent its being offered to Jehovah?

26. *With the wood of the grove.* It is probable that *Asherah* here signifies *Astarte;* and that there was a wooden image of this goddess on the altar of Baal.

27. *He feared his father's household.* So it appears that his father was an idolater; but as Gideon had ten men of his own servants whom he could trust in this matter, it is probable that he had preserved the true faith, and had not bowed his knee to the image of Baal.

28. *The second bullock was offered.* It appears that the second bullock was offered because it was just seven years old, v. 25, being calved about the time that the Midianitish oppression began; and it was now to be slain to indicate that their slavery should end with its life. The young bullock, v. 25, is supposed to have been offered for a peace offering; the bullock of seven years old, for a burnt offering.

29. *Gideon the son of Joash hath done this thing.* They fixed on him the more readily because they knew he had not joined with them in their idolatrous worship.

30. *The men of the city said.* They all felt an interest in the continuance of rites in which they had often many sensual gratifications. Baal and Ashtaroth would have more worshippers than the true God, because their rites were more adapted to the fallen nature of man.

31. *Will ye plead for Baal?* The words are very emphatic: "Will ye plead in earnest for Baal? Will ye really save *him?* If *he* be God, *Elohim,* let him contend for himself, seeing his altar is thrown down."

32. *He called him Jerubbaal.* That is, "Let Baal contend"; changed, 2 Sam. xi. 21, into

Jerubbesheth, "He shall contend against confusion or shame"; thus changing *baal,* "lord," into *bosheth,* "confusion or ignominy."

33. *Then all the Midianites.* Hearing of what Gideon had done, and apprehending that this might be a forerunner of attempts to regain their liberty, they formed a general association against Israel.

34. *The Spirit of the Lord came upon Gideon.* He was endued with preternatural courage and wisdom.

36. *If thou wilt save Israel.* Gideon was very bold, and God was very condescending. But probably the request itself was suggested by the Divine Spirit.

CHAPTER 7

The Lord commands Gideon to make a selection of a small number of his men to go against the Midianites. Three hundred only are selected; and into the hands of these God promises to deliver the whole Midianitish host, 1-8. Gideon is directed to go down unto the host in the night, that he may be encouraged on hearing what they say, 9-12. He obeys, and hears a Midianite tell a remarkable dream unto his fellow, which predicted the success of his attack, 13-15. He takes encouragement, divides his men into three companies, and gives each a trumpet with a lighted lamp concealed in a pitcher, with directions how to use them, 16-18. They come to the Midianitish camp at night, when all suddenly blowing their trumpets and exposing their lamps, the Midianites are thrown into confusion, fly, and are stopped by the Ephraimites at the passage of Jordan and slain, 19-24. Oreb and Zeeb, two Midianitish princes, are slain, 25.

1. *Then Jerubbaal, who is Gideon.* It appears that Jerubbaal was now a surname of Gideon, from the circumstance mentioned chap. vi. 32. See chap. viii. 35. *The well of Harod.* If this was a town or village, it is nowhere else mentioned. Probably, as *charad* signifies to "shake or tremble through fear," the fountain in question may have had its name from the terror and panic with which the Midianitish host was seized at this place.

2. *The people that are with thee are too many.* Had he led up a numerous host against his enemies, the excellence of the power by which they were discomfited might have appeared to be of man and not of God. By the manner in which this whole transaction was conducted, both the Israelites and Midianites must see that the thing was of God. This would inspire the Israelites with confidence, and the Midianites with fear.

3. *Whosoever is fearful and afraid, let him return . . . from mount Gilead.* Gideon is certainly not at Mount Gilead at this time, but rather near Mount Gilboa. Gilead was on the other side of Jordan. Calmet thinks there must either have been two Gileads, which does not from the Scripture appear to be the case, or that the Hebrew text is here corrupted, and that for Gilead we should read Gilboa. This reading, though adopted by Houbigant, is not countenanced by any MS., nor by any of the versions.

Dr. Hales endeavors to reconcile the whole by the supposition that there were in Gideon's army many of the eastern Manasses, who came from Mount Gilead; and that these probably were more afraid of their neighbors, the Midianites, than were the western tribes; and therefore proposes to read the text thus: "Whosoever from Mount Gilead is fearful and afraid, let him return (home) and depart early. So there returned (home) twenty-two thousand of the people." Perhaps this is on the whole the best method of solving this difficulty.

5. *Every one that lappeth of the water . . . as a dog.* The original word *yalok* is precisely the sound which a dog makes when he is drinking.

6. *The number of them that lapped.* From this account it appears that some of the people went down on their knees, and putting their mouths to the water, sucked up what they needed; the others stooped down, and taking up water in the hollow of their hands, applied it to their mouth.

8. *So the people took victuals.* The 300 men that he reserved took the victuals necessary for the day's expenditure, while the others were dismissed to their tent and their houses as they thought proper.

9. *I have delivered it into thine hand.* I have determined to do it, and it is as sure as if it were done.

13. *Told a dream.* Both the dream and the interpretation were inspired by God for the purpose of increasing the confidence of Gideon, and appalling his enemies.

14. *Into his hand hath God delivered Midian.* This is a full proof that God had inspired both the dream and its interpretation.

16. *He divided the three hundred men.* Though the victory was to be from the Lord, yet he knew that he ought to use prudential means; and those which he employed on this occasion were the best calculated to answer the end.

18. *The sword of the Lord, and of Gideon.* The word *chereb,* sword, is not found in this verse, though it is necessarily implied, and is found in v. 20.

20. *Blew the trumpets, and brake the pitchers.* How astonishing must the effect be, in a dark night, of the sudden glare of 300 torches, darting their splendor, in the same instant, on the half-awakened eyes of the terrified Midianites, accompanied with the clangor of 300 trumpets, alternately mingled with the thundering shout of "A sword for the Lord and for Gideon!"

21. *They stood every man in his place.* Each of the three companies kept their station, and continued to sound their trumpets. The Midianites seeing this, and believing that they were the trumpets of a numerous army which had then penetrated their camp, were thrown instantly into confusion; and supposing that their enemies were in the midst of them, they turned their swords against every man they met, while at the same time they endeavored to escape for their lives. No stratagem was ever better imagined, better executed, or more completely successful.

22. *Fled to Beth-shittah.* This is nowhere else mentioned in Scripture. *Zererath.* This and *Tabbath* are nowhere else to be found. *Abel-meholah.* This was the birthplace of the prophet Elisha, 1 Kings xix. 16. It was beyond Jordan, in the tribe of Manasseh, 1 Kings iv. 12.

23. *The men of Israel gathered.* It is very likely that these were some persons whom Gideon had sent home the day before, who, now hearing that the Midianites were routed, went immediately in pursuit.

24. *Take before them the waters unto Beth-barah.* This is probably the same place as that mentioned John i. 28, where the Hebrews forded Jordan under the direction of Joshua. To this place the Midianites directed their flight, that they might escape into their own country; and here, being met by the Ephraimites, they appear to have been totally overthrown, and their two generals taken.

25. *They slew Oreb upon the rock Oreb.* These two generals had taken shelter, one in the cavern of the rock, the other in the vat of a winepress; both of which places were, from this circumstance, afterwards called by their names. *Brought the heads of Oreb and Zeeb to Gideon.* *Oreb* signifies a "raven," and *Zeeb* a "wolf." In all ancient nations we find generals and princes taking their names from both birds and beasts.

CHAPTER 8

The Ephraimites are angry with Gideon because he did not call them particularly to his assistance; he pacifies them, 1-3. Gideon and his 300 men pass over Jordan, pursuing the Midianites: and, being faint, ask victuals from the princes of Succoth, but are refused, 4-7. They make the like application to the people of Penuel, and are also refused, 8-9. Gideon defeats Zebah and Zalmunna, the two kings of Midian, and takes them prisoners, 10-12. He chastises the men of Succoth and Penuel, 13-17. He slays Zebah and Zalmunna, who had killed his brethren, 18-21. The Israelites offer him the kingdom, which he refuses, 22-23. He requires from them the gold rings which they had taken from the Ishmaelites, and makes an ephod, which he sets up at Ophrah; and it became an instrument of idolatry, 24-27. The land enjoys peace forty years; Gideon dies, having 71 sons, 28-32. The Israelites fall into idolatry, and forget their obligations to Gideon's family, 33-35.

1. *The men of Ephraim said.* This account is no doubt displaced; for what is mentioned here could not have taken place till the return of Gideon from the pursuit of the Midianites, for he had not yet passed Jordan, v. 4. And it was when he was beyond that river that the Ephraimites brought the heads of Oreb and Zeeb to him, chap. vii. 25.

2. *Is not the gleaning?* That is, The Ephraimites have performed more important services than Gideon and his men; and he supports the assertion by observing that it was they who took the two Midianitish generals, having discomfited their hosts at the passes of Jordan.

3. *Then their anger was abated.* "A soft answer turneth away wrath." He might have said that he could place but little dependence on his brethren when, through faintheartedness, 22,000 left him at one time; but he passed this by, and took a more excellent way.

5. *Give, I pray you, loaves of bread.* As Gideon was engaged in the common cause of Israel, he had a right to expect succor from the people at large. His request to the men of Succoth and Penuel was both just and reasonable.

6. *Are the hands of Zebah and Zalmunna now in thine hand?* They feared to help Gideon, lest, if he should be overpowered, the Midianites would revenge it upon them; and they dared not trust God.

7. *I will tear your flesh.* What this punishment consisted in I cannot say. It must mean a severe punishment; as if he had said, I will thresh your flesh with briers and thorns, as corn is threshed out with threshing instruments; or, You shall be trodden down under the feet of my victorious army, as the corn is trodden out with the feet of the ox.

8. *Succoth* was beyond Jordan, in the tribe of Gad. *Penuel* was also in the same tribe, and not far distant from Succoth.

9. *I will break down this tower.* Probably they had not only denied him, but insultingly pointed to a tower in which their chief defense lay; and intimated to him that he might do his worst, for they could amply defend themselves.

10. *Zebah and Zalmunna were in Karkor.* If this were a place, it is nowhere else mentioned in Scripture. Some contend that *karkor* signifies "rest"; and thus the Vulgate understood it: Zebah and Zalmunna "rested," with all their army. And this seems the most likely, for it is said, v. 11, that Gideon smote the host, for the host was "secure."

13. *Returned from battle before the sun was up.* This does not appear to be a proper translation. It should be rendered "from the ascent of Chares"; this is the reading of the Septuagint, the Syriac, and the Arabic.

14. *He described unto him the princes of Succoth.* The young man probably gave him the names of seventy persons, the chief men of Succoth, who were those who were most concerned in refusing him and his men the refreshment he requested.

16. *He taught the men of Succoth.* Instead of *he taught,* Houbigant reads "he tore"; and this is not only agreeable to what Gideon had threatened, v. 7, but is supported by the Vulgate, Septuagint, Chaldee, Syriac, and Arabic. The Hebrew text might have been easily corrupted in this place by the change of *shin* into *ain,* letters very similar to each other.

18. *What manner of men were they whom ye slew at Tabor?* We have no antecedent to this question, and are obliged to conjecture one. It seems as if Zebah and Zalmunna had massacred the family of Gideon while he was absent on this expedition. Gideon had heard some confused account of it, and now questions them concerning the fact. They boldly acknowledge it, and describe the persons whom they slew, by which he found they were his own brethren. This determines him to avenge their death by slaying the Midianitish kings, whom he otherwise was inclined to save.

20. *He said unto Jether his firstborn.* By the ancient laws of war, prisoners taken in war might be either slain, sold, or kept for slaves. To put a captive enemy to death no executioner was required. Gideon slays Zebah and Zalmunna with his own hand. So Samuel is said to have hewn Agag in pieces, 1 Sam. xv. 33.

21. *The ornaments that were on their camels' necks.* The heads, necks, bodies, and legs of camels, horses, and elephants are highly ornamented in the Eastern countries; and indeed this was common, from the remotest antiquity, in all countries. Instead of *ornaments,* the Septuagint translate "the crescents" or "half-moons"; and this is followed by the Syriac and Arabic. We learn from v. 24 that the Ishmaelites, or Arabs, as they are termed by the Targum, Syriac, and Arabic, had golden earrings, and probably a crescent in each; for it is well known that the Ishmaelites, and the Arabs who descended from them, were addicted very early to the worship of the moon; and so attached were they to this superstition that, although Mohammed destroyed the idolatrous use of the

crescent, yet it was universally borne in their ensigns, and on the tops of their mosques.

22. *Rule thou over us, both thou, and thy son, and thy son's son.* That is, Become our king, and let the crown be hereditary in your family. What a weak, foolish, and inconstant people were these! As yet their government was a theocracy; and now, dazzled with the success of a man who was only an instrument in the hands of God to deliver them from their enemies, they wish to throw off the divine yoke, and shackle themselves with an unlimited hereditary monarchy!

23. *The Lord shall rule over you.* Few with such power at their command would have acted as Gideon. His speech calls them back to their first principles, and should have excited in them both shame and contrition.

24. *Give me every man the earrings of his prey.* The spoils taken from their enemies in this warfare. This is a transaction very like to that of the Israelites and Aaron when they brought him their golden earrings, out of which he made the molten calf, Exod. xxxii. 2, etc. Whether Gideon designed this ephod for an instrument of worship or merely as a trophy is not very clear. It is most likely that he had intended to establish a place of worship at Ophrah, and he took this occasion to provide the proper sacerdotal vestments.

27. *Gideon made an ephod thereof.* That is, he made an ephod out of this mass of gold; but he could not employ it all in making this one garment, for it is not likely that any man could wear a coat of nearly one hundred pounds' weight. It is likely that he made a whole Tabernacle service in miniature out of this gold. *All Israel went thither a whoring after it.* This form of speech often occurs, and has been often explained. The whole Jewish nation is represented as being united to God as a wife is to her husband. Any act of idolatry is considered as a breach of their covenant with God, as an act of whoredom is the breach of the marriage agreement between man and wife.

28. *Forty years in the days of Gideon.* The Midianites were so completely humbled that they could make head no more against Israel during the forty years in which the government of Gideon lasted.

31. *His concubine.* A lawful but secondary wife, whose children could not inherit. *Whose name he called Abimelech.* That is, "my father is king" or "my father hath reigned." This name was doubtless given by the mother, and so it should be understood here; she wished to raise her son to the supreme government, and therefore gave him a name which might serve to stimulate him to seek that which she hoped he should enjoy in his father's right.

33. *A whoring after Baalim.* This term has probably a different meaning here from what it has v. 7; for it is very likely that in most parts of the pagan worship there were many impure rites, so that going *a whoring after Baalim* may be taken in a literal sense. *Baal-berith.* Literally, "the lord of the covenant."

34. *Remembered not the Lord their God.* They attributed their deliverance to some other cause, and did not give Him the glory of their salvation.

35. *Neither shewed they kindness to the house of . . . Gideon.* They were both unthankful and unholy. Though they had the clearest proofs of God's power and goodness before their eyes, yet they forgot Him. And although they were under greatest obligations to Gideon, and were once so sensible of them that they offered to settle the kingdom on him and his family, yet they forgot him also.

Jerubbaal, namely, Gideon. This is improper; it should be "Jerubbaal Gideon," as we say "Simon Peter," or call any man by his Christian name and surname.

CHAPTER 9

Abimelech is made king and, to secure himself in the kingdom, slays his brethren; only Jotham, the youngest, escapes, 1-6. Jotham reproves him and the Shechemites by a curious and instructive parable, 7-21. Abimelech having reigned three years, the Shechemites, headed by Gaal, the son of Ebed, conspire against him, 22-29. Zebul, governor of the city, apprises Abimelech of the insurrection, who comes with his forces and discomfits Gaal, 30-40. Abimelech assaults the city, takes it, beats it down, and sows it with salt, 41-45. Several of the Shechemites take refuge in the temple of Baal-berith; Abimelech sets fire to it, and destroys in it about one thousand men and women, 46-50. He afterwards besieges and takes Thebez; but while he is assaulting the citadel, a woman throws a piece of millstone upon his head, and kills him. Thus God requites him and the men of Shechem for their wickedness, and their ingratitude to the family of Gideon, 51-57.

1. *Abimelech . . . went to Shechem.* We have already seen that Abimelech was the son of Gideon by his concubine at Shechem. His going thither immediately after his father's death was to induce his townsmen to proclaim him governor in the place of his father. Shechem was the residence of his mother, and of all her relatives.

2. *Whether is better for you, either that all the sons?* This was a powerful argument: Whether will you have seventy tyrants or only one? For, as he had no right to the government, and God alone was King at that time in Israel, so he must support his usurped rule by whatever means were most likely to effect it: a usurped government is generally supported by oppression and the sword.

3. *He is our brother.* We shall be raised to places of trust under him, and our city will be the capital of the kingdom.

4. *Threescore and ten pieces of silver.* Probably shekels; and this was the whole of his exchequer. As he was now usurping the government of God, he began with a contribution from the idol temple. A work begun under the name and influence of the devil is not likely to end to the glory of God or to the welfare of man. *Hired vain and light persons.* "Worthless and dissolute men"; persons who were living on the public, and had nothing to lose. Such was the foundation of his Babel government. By a cunning management of such rascals most revolutions have been brought about.

5. *Slew his brethren.* His brothers by the father's side, chap. viii. 30. This was a usual way of securing an ill-gotten throne, the person who had no right destroying all those that had right, that he might have no competitors. *Yet Jotham . . . was left.* That is, all the seventy were killed except Jotham, if there were not seventy besides Jotham.

6. *And all the house of Millo.* If *Millo* be the name of a place, it is nowhere else mentioned in the sacred writings. But it is probably the

name of a person of note and influence in the city of Shechem—"the men of Shechem and the family of Millo."

7. *Stood in the top of mount Gerizim.* Gerizim and Ebal were mounts very near to each other; the former lying to the north, the latter to the south, and at the foot of them Shechem. *That God may hearken unto you.* It appears that Jotham received this message from God, and that he spoke on this occasion by divine inspiration.

8. *The trees went forth on a time.* This is the oldest, and without exception the best, fable in the world. It is not to be supposed that a fable, if well-formed, requires much illustration; every part of this, a few expressions excepted, illustrates itself, and tells its own meaning. *To anoint a king.* Hence it appears that anointing was usual in the installation of kings long before there was any king in Israel; for there is much evidence that the Book of Judges was written before the days of Saul and David. *The olive tree.* The olive was the most useful of all the trees in the field or forest, as the bramble was the meanest and the most worthless.

9. *Wherewith . . . they honor God and man.* I believe the word *elohim* here should be translated "gods," for the parable seems to be accommodated to the idolatrous state of the Shechemites. Thus it was understood by the Vulgate, Arabic, and others.

11. *But the fig tree said . . . Should I forsake my sweetness?* The fruit of the fig tree is the sweetest or most luscious of all fruits.

13. *Which cheereth God and man.* I believe *elohim* here is to be taken in the same sense proposed on v. 9. Vast libations of wine, as well as much oil, were used in heathenish sacrifices and offerings; and it was their opinion that the gods actually partook of, and were delighted with, both the wine and oil.

14. *Then said all the trees unto the bramble.* The word *atad,* which we translate *bramble,* is supposed to mean the *rhamnus,* which is the largest of thorns, producing dreadful spikes, similar to darts.

15. *Come and put your trust in my shadow.* The vain boast of the would-be sovereign, and of the man who is seeking to be put into power by the suffrages of the people. All promise, no performance. *Let fire come out of the bramble.* The bramble was too low to give shelter to any tree, and so far from being able to consume others that the smallest fire will reduce it to ashes, and that in the shortest time. Hence the very transitory mirth of fools is said to be like the cracking of thorns under a pot. Abimelech was the *bramble;* and the *cedars of Lebanon,* all the nobles and people of Israel. Could they therefore suppose that such a lowborn, uneducated, cruel, and murderous man could be a proper protector or a humane governor? He who could imbrue his hands in the blood of his brethren in order to get into power was not likely to stop at any means to retain that power when possessed. If therefore they took him for their king, they might rest assured that desolation and blood would mark the whole of his reign. The condensed moral of the whole fable is this: Weak, worthless, and wicked men will ever be foremost to thrust themselves into power; and, in the end, to bring ruin upon them-

selves, and on the unhappy people over whom they preside.

20. *Let fire come out from Abimelech.* As the thorn or bramble may be the means of kindling other wood, because it may be easily ignited, so shall Abimelech be the cause of kindling a fire of civil discord among you that shall consume the rulers and great men of your country. A prophetic declaration of what would take place.

23. *God sent an evil spirit.* He permitted jealousies to take place which produced factions; and these factions produced insurrections, civil contentions, and slaughter.

25. *The men of Shechem set liers in wait.* It pleased God to punish this bad man by the very persons who had contributed to his iniquitous elevation. So God often makes the instruments of men's sins the means of their punishment. It is likely that although Abimelech had his chief residence at Shechem, yet he frequently went to Ophrah, the city of his father, his claim to which there was none to oppose, as he had slain all his brethren. It was probably in his passage between those two places that the Shechemites had posted cutthroats, in order to assassinate him; as such men had no moral principle, they robbed and plundered all who came that way.

26. *Gaal the son of Ebed.* Of this person we know no more than is here told. He was probably one of the descendants of the Canaanites, who hoped from the state of the public mind, and their disaffection to Abimelech, to cause a revolution, and thus to restore the ancient government as it was under Hamor, the father of Shechem.

28. *Zebal his officer. Pekido,* "his overseer"; probably governor of Shechem in his absence.

29. *Would to God this people were under my hand!* The very words and conduct of a sly, hypocritical demagogue. *Increase thine army, and come out.* When he found his party strong, and the public feeling warped to his side, then he appears to have sent a challenge to Abimelech to come out and fight him.

31. *They fortify the city against thee.* Under pretense of repairing the walls and towers, they were actually putting the place in a state of defense, intending to seize on the government as soon as they should find Abimelech coming against them.

35. *Stood in the entering of the gate.* Having probably got some intimation of the designs of Zebul and Abimelech.

37. *By the plain of Meonenim.* Some translate, "by the way of the oaks," or oaken groves; others, "by the way of the magicians," or "regarders of the times," as in our margin. Probably it was a place in which augurs and soothsayers dwelt.

45. *And sowed it with salt.* Intending that the destruction of this city should be a perpetual memorial of his achievements. The salt was not designed to render it barren, as some have imagined; for who would think of cultivating a city? But as salt is an emblem of incorruption and perpetuity, it was no doubt designed to perpetuate the memorial of this transaction, and as a token that he wished this desolation to be eternal. This sowing a place with salt was a custom in different nations to express permanent desolation and abhorrence.

46. *An hold of the house of the god Berith.* This must mean the precincts of the temple, as we find there were a thousand men and women together in that place.

53. *A piece of a millstone.* "A piece of a chariot wheel"; but the word is used in other places for upper millstones, and is so understood here by the Vulgate, Septuagint, Syriac, and Arabic. *And all to break his skull.* A most nonsensical version of *vattarits eth gulgolto,* which is literally, "And she brake (or fractured) his skull." Plutarch, in his life of Pyrrhus, observes that this king was killed at the siege of Thebes by a piece of a tile, which a woman threw upon his head.

54. *Draw thy sword, and slay me.* It was a disgrace to be killed by a woman. Abimelech was also afraid that, if he fell thus mortally wounded into the hands of his enemies, they might treat him with cruelty and insult.

56. *Thus God rendered.* Both fratricide Abimelech and the unprincipled men of Shechem had the iniquity visited upon them of which they had been guilty. Man's judgment may be avoided, but there is no escape from the judgments of God.

CHAPTER 10

Tola judges Israel twenty-three years, 1-2. Jair is judge twenty-two years, 3-5. After him the Israelites rebel against God, and are delivered into the hands of the Philistines and Ammonites eighteen years, 6-9. They humble themselves, and God reproves them, 10-14. They put away their strange gods, and gather together against the Ammonites, 15-17. The chiefs of Gilead inquire concerning a captain to head them against the Ammonites, 18.

1. *Tola the son of Puah.* As this Tola continued twenty-three years a judge of Israel after the troubles of Abimelech's reign, it is likely that the land had rest, and that the enemies of the Israelites had made no hostile incursions into the land during his presidency and that of Jair, which together continued forty-five years.

4. *He had thirty sons.* It appears that there were both peace and prosperity during the time that Jair governed Israel. He had, it seems, provided for his family, and given a village to each of his thirty sons; which were, in consequence, called *Havoth Jair* or the "villages of Jair." Their riding *on thirty ass colts* seems to intimate that they were persons of consideration, and kept up a certain dignity in their different departments.

6. *And served Baalim.* They became universal idolaters, adopting every god of the surrounding nations. *Baalim and Ashtaroth* may signify "gods" and "goddesses" in general.

7. *The anger of the Lord was hot.* This divine displeasure was manifested in delivering them into the hands of the Philistines and the Ammonites. The former dwelt on the western side of Jordan, the latter on the eastern; and it appears that they joined their forces on this occasion to distress and ruin the Israelites, though the Ammonites were the most active.

11. *And the Lord said.* By what means these reproofs were conveyed to the Israelites, we know not; it must have been by an angel, a prophet, or some holy man inspired for the occasion.

15. *We have sinned.* The reprehension of this people was kind, pointed, and solemn; and their repentance, deep. And they gave proofs that their repentance was genuine by putting away all their idols, but they were ever fickle and uncertain.

17. *The children of Ammon were gathered together.* Literally, "They cried against Israel"—they sent out criers in different directions to stir up all the enemies of Israel; and when they had made a mighty collection, they encamped in Gilead.

18. *What man is he that will begin to fight?* It appears that, although the spirit of patriotism had excited the people at large to come forward against their enemies, yet they had no general, none to lead them forth to battle. God, however, who had accepted their sincere repentance, raised them up an able captain in the person of Jephthah; and in him the suffrages of the people were concentrated, as we shall see in the following chapter. In those ancient times much depended on the onset; a war was generally terminated in one battle. The first impression was therefore of great consequence, and it required a person skillful, valorous, and strong, to head the attack. Jephthah was a person in whom all these qualifications appear to have met. When God purposes to deliver, He, in the course of His providence, will find out, employ, and direct the proper means.

CHAPTER 11

The history of Jephthah, and his covenant with the Gileadites, 1-10. He is elected by the people, 11. Sends an embassy to the king of the Ammonites, to inquire why they invaded Israel; and receives an answer, to which he sends back a spirited reply, 12-27. This is disregarded by the Ammonites, and Jephthah prepares for battle, 28-29. His vow, 30-31. He attacks and defeats them, 32-33. On his return to Mizpeh he is met by his daughter, whom, according to his vow, he dedicates to the Lord, 34-40.

1. *Now Jephthah ... was the son of an harlot.* I think the word *zonah,* which we here render *harlot,* should be translated, as is contended for on Josh. ii. 1, viz., a "hostess," keeper of an inn or tavern for the accommodation of travellers; and thus it is understood by the Targum of Jonathan on this place: "and he was the son of a woman, a tavern keeper." See the note referred to above. She was very probably a Canaanite, as she is called, v. 2, a *strange woman,* a "woman of another race"; and on this account his brethren drove him from the family, as he could not have a full right to the inheritance, his mother not being an Israelite.

3. *There were gathered vain men to Jephthah. Reykim,* "empty men"—persons destitute of good sense, and profligate in their manners. The word may, however, mean in this place "poor persons," without property, and without employment. The versions in general consider them as plunderers.

4. *The children of Ammon made war.* They had invaded the land of Israel, and were now encamped in Gilead. See chap. x. 17.

6. *Come, and be our captain.* The Israelites were assembled in Mizpeh, but were without a captain to lead them against the Ammonites. And we find, from the conclusion of the preceding chapter, that they offered the command to any that would accept it.

8. *Therefore we turn again to thee now.* We

are convinced that we have dealt unjustly by thee, and we wish now to repair our fault, and give thee this sincere proof of our regret for having acted unjustly, and of our confidence in thee.

11. *Jephthah went with the elders.* The elders had chosen him for their head; but, to be valid, this choice must be confirmed by the people; therefore it is said, *The people made him head.* But even this did not complete the business; God must be brought in as a Party to this transaction; and therefore *Jephthah uttered all his words before the Lord*—the terms made with the elders and the people on which he had accepted the command of the army; and, being sure of the divine approbation, he entered on the work with confidence.

12. *Jephthah sent messengers.* He wished the Ammonites to explain their own motives for undertaking a war against Israel, as then the justice of his cause would appear more forcibly to the people.

13. *From Arnon even unto Jabbok, and unto Jordan.* That is, all the land that had formerly belonged to the Amorites, and to the Moabites, who it seems were confederates on this occasion.

22. *From the wilderness even unto Jordan.* From Arabia Deserta on the east to Jordan on the west.

23. *The Lord God of Israel hath dispossessed the Amorites.* Jephthah shows that the Israelites did not take the land of the Moabites or Ammonites, but that of the Amorites, which they had conquered from Sihon, their king, who had without cause or provocation attacked them; and although the Amorites had taken the lands in question from the Ammonites, yet the title by which Israel held them was good, because they took them not from the Ammonites, but conquered them from the Amorites.

So now the Lord . . . hath dispossessed the Amorites. The circumstances in which the Israelites were when they were attacked by the Amorites plainly proved that, unless Jehovah had helped them, they must have been overcome. God defeated the Amorites and made a grant of their lands to the Israelites; and they had, in consequence, possessed them for three hundred years, v. 26.

24. *Wilt not thou possess that which Chemosh thy god giveth thee?* As if he had said: "It is a maxim with you, as it is among all nations, that the lands which they conceive to be given them by their gods, they have an absolute right to, and should not relinquish them to any kind of claimant. You suppose that the land which you possess was given you by your god Chemosh; and therefore you will not relinquish what you believe you hold by a divine right. Now we know that Jehovah, our God, who is the Lord of heaven and earth, has given the Israelites the land of the Amorites; and therefore we will not give it up."

27. *The Lord the Judge be judge . . . between the children of Israel.* If you be right, and we be wrong, then Jehovah, who is the sovereign and incorruptible Judge, shall determine in your favor; and to Him I submit the righteousness of my cause.

29. *Then the Spirit of the Lord came upon Jephthah.* The Lord qualified him for the work He had called him to do, and thus gave him the most convincing testimony that his cause was good.

31. *Shall surely be the Lord's, and I will offer it up for a burnt offering.* The translation, according to the most accurate Hebrew scholars, is this: "I will consecrate it to the Lord, or I will offer it for a burnt offering"; that is, "If it be a thing fit for a burnt offering, it shall be made one; if fit for the service of God, it shall be consecrated to Him." That conditions of this kind must have been implied in the vow is evident enough. If a dog had met him, this could not have been made a burnt offering; and if his neighbor or friend's wife, son, or daughter had been returning from a visit to his family, his vow gave him no right over them. Besides, human sacrifices were ever an abomination to the Lord, and this was one of the grand reasons why God drove out the Canaanites.

From v. 39 it appears evident that Jephthah's daughter was not sacrificed to God, but consecrated to Him in a state of perpetual virginity; for the text says, "She knew no man, for this was a statute in Israel"; viz., that persons thus dedicated or consecrated to God should live in a state of unchangeable celibacy. Thus this celebrated place is, without violence to any part of the text, or to any proper rule of construction, cleared of all difficulty, and caused to speak a language consistent with itself, and with the nature of God.

The Targumist refers here to the law, Lev. xxvii. 1-5, where the Lord prescribes the price at which either males or females, who had been vowed to the Lord, might be redeemed. "When a man shall make a singular vow, the persons shall be for the Lord by thy estimation . . . the male from twenty years old even unto sixty . . . shall be fifty shekels of silver . . . And if it be a female, then thy estimation shall be thirty shekels. And if it be from five years old even unto twenty years . . . the male twenty shekels, and for the female ten." This also is an argument that the daughter of Jephthah was not sacrificed, as the father had it in his power, at a very moderate price, to have redeemed her; and surely the blood of his daughter must have been of more value in his sight than thirty shekels of silver!

33. *Twenty cities.* That is, he either took or destroyed twenty cities of the Ammonites, and completely routed their whole army.

34. *With timbrels and with dances.* From this instance we find it was an ancient custom for women to go out to meet returning conquerors with musical instruments, songs, and dances; and that it was continued afterwards is evident from the instance given 1 Sam. xviii. 6.

35. *Thou hast brought me very low.* He was greatly distressed to think that his daughter, who was his only child, should be, in consequence of his vow, prevented from continuing his family in Israel; for it is evident that he had not any other child, for *beside her*, says the text, *he had neither son nor daughter*, v. 34. He might, therefore, well be grieved that thus his family was to become extinct in Israel.

36. *And she said unto him.* What a pattern of filial piety and obedience! She was at once obedient, pious, and patriotic. A woman to have

no offspring was considered to be in a state of the utmost degradation among the Hebrews; but she is regardless of all this, seeing her father is in safety, and her country delivered.

37. *I and my fellows.* Whether she meant the young women of her own acquaintance or those who had been consecrated to God in the same way, though on different accounts, is not quite clear; but it is likely she means her own companions. And her going up and down upon the mountains may signify no more than her paying each of them a visit at their own houses, previously to her being shut up at the Tabernacle; and this visiting of each at their own homes might require the space of two months. This I am inclined to think is the meaning of this difficult clause.

39. *And she knew no man.* She continued a virgin all the days of her life.

40. *To lament the daughter of Jephthah.* I am satisfied that this is not a correct translation of the original. Houbigant translates the whole verse thus: "But this custom prevailed in Israel, that the virgins of Israel went at different times, four days in the year, to the daughter of Jephthah that they might comfort her." This verse also gives evidence that the daughter of Jephthah was not sacrificed; nor does it appear that the custom or statute referred to here lasted after the death of Jephthah's daugher.

CHAPTER 12

The Ephraimites are incensed against Jephthah, because he did not call them to war against the Ammonites; and threaten his destruction, 1. He vindicates himself, 2-3; and arms the Gileadites against the men of Ephraim; they fight against them, and kill forty-two thousand Ephraimites at the passages of Jordan, 4-6. Jephthah dies, having judged Israel six years, 7. Ibzan judges seven years, 8. His posterity and death, 9-10. Elon judges ten years, and dies, 11-12. Abdon judges eight years, 13. His posterity and death, 14-15.

1. *The men of Ephraim gathered themselves together.* "They called each other to arms," summoning all their tribe and friends to arm themselves to destroy Jephthah and the Gileadites, being jealous lest they should acquire too much power.

3. *I put my life in my hands.* I exposed myself to the greatest difficulties and dangers. But whence did this form of speech arise? Probably from a man's laying hold of his sword, spear, or bow. "This is the defender of my life; on this, and my proper use of it, my life depends."

4. *And fought with Ephraim.* Some commentators suppose that there were two battles in which the Ephraimites were defeated: the first mentioned in the above clause, and the second occasioned by the taunting language mentioned in the conclusion of the verse, "Ye Gileadites are fugitives of Ephraim." Where the point of this reproach lies, or what is the reason of it, cannot be easily ascertained.

6. *Say now Shibboleth: and he said Sibboleth.* The original differs only in the first letter *samech*, instead of *sheen*. But there must have been a very remarkable difference in the pronunciation of the Ephraimites, when instead of *shibboleth*, an "ear of corn" (see Job xxiv. 24), they said *sibboleth*, which signifies "a burden," Exod. vi. 6; and a heavy burden were they obliged to bear who could not pronounce this test letter. The sound of *th* cannot be pro-

nounced by the Persians in general; and yet it is a common sound among the Arabians. *For he could not frame to pronounce it right.* This is not a bad rendering of the original; "and they did not direct to speak it thus."

8. *And after him Ibzan.* It appears that during the administration of *Jephthah*, six years—*Ibzan*, seven years—*Elon*, ten years—and *Abdon*, eight years (in the whole thirty-one years), the Israelites had peace in all their borders; and we shall find by the following chapter that in this time of rest they corrupted themselves, and were afterwards delivered into the power of the Philistines.

CHAPTER 13

The Israelites corrupt themselves, and are delivered into the hands of the Philistines forty years, 1. An angel appears to the wife of Manoah, foretells the birth of her son, and gives her directions how to treat both herself and her child, who is to be a deliverer of Israel, 2-5. She informs her husband of this transaction, 6-7. Manoah prays that the angel may reappear; he is heard, and the angel appears to him and his wife, and repeats his former directions concerning the mother and the child, 8-14. Manoah presents an offering to the Lord, and the angel ascends in the flame, 15-20. Manoah is alarmed, but is comforted by the judicious reflections of his wife, 21-23. Samson is born, and begins to feel the influence of the Divine Spirit, 24-25.

1. *Delivered them into the hand of the Philistines.* It does not appear that after Shamgar, to the present time, the Philistines were in a condition to oppress Israel, or God had not permitted them to do it; but now they have a commission, the Israelites having departed from the Lord. Nor is it evident that the Philistines had entirely subjected the Israelites, as there still appears to have been a sort of commerce between the two people. They had often vexed and made inroads upon them, but they had them not in entire subjection; see chap. xv. 11.

2. *A certain man of Zorah.* A town in the tribe of Judah, but afterwards given to Dan.

3. *The angel of the Lord.* Generally supposed to have been the same that appeared to Moses, Joshua, Gideon, etc., and no other than the Second Person of the ever-blessed Trinity.

4. *Beware . . . drink not wine.* As Samson was designed to be a Nazarite from the womb, it was necessary that, while his mother carried and nursed him, she should live the life of a Nazarite, neither drinking wine nor any inebriating liquor, nor eating any kind of forbidden meat. See the account of the Nazarite and his vow in the notes on Num. vi. 2, etc.

5. *He shall begin to deliver Israel.* Samson only began this deliverance, for it was not till the days of David that the Israelites were completely redeemed from the power of the Philistines.

6. *But I asked him not whence he was, neither told he me his name.* This clause is rendered very differently by the Vulgate, the negative not being omitted: "Who, when I asked who he was and whence he came, and by what name he was called, would not tell me; but this he said."

The negative is also wanting in the Septuagint, as it stands in the Complutensian Polyglot: "And I asked him whence he was, and his name, but he did not tell me." This is also the reading of the Codex Alexandrinus; but the Septuagint, in the London Polyglot, together with the Chaldee, Syriac, and Arabic, read the negative particle with the Hebrew text, "I asked not his name."

9. *The angel of God came again.* This second appearance of the angel was probably essential to the peace of Manoah, who might have been jealous of his wife had he not had this proof that the thing was of the Lord.

15. *Until we shall have made ready a kid.* Not knowing his quality, Manoah wished to do this as an act of hospitality.

16. *I will not eat of thy bread.* As I am a spiritual being, I subsist not by earthly food. *And if thou wilt offer a burnt offering.* Neither shall I receive that homage which belongs to God; you must therefore offer your burnt offering to Jehovah.

18. *Seeing it is secret.* It was because it was *secret* that they wished to know it. The angel does not say that it was *secret,* but *hy peli,* "It is wonderful"; the very character that is given to Jesus Christ, Isa. ix. 6: "His name shall be called Wonderful"; and it is supposed by some that the angel gives this as his name, and consequently that he was our blessed Lord.

19. *The angel did wonderously.* He acted according to his name; he, being "wonderful," performed wonderful things, probably causing fire to arise out of the rock and consume the sacrifice, and then ascending in the flame.

22. *We shall surely die, because we have seen God.* See the note on chap. vi. 22.

23. *If the lord were pleased to kill us.* This is excellent reasoning, and may be of great use to every truly religious mind, in cloudy and dark dispensations of divine providence. It is not likely that God, who has preserved you so long, borne with you so long, and fed and supported you all your life long, girding you when you knew Him not, is less willing to save and provide for you and yours now than He was when, probably, you trusted less in Him. He who freely gave His Son to redeem you can never be indifferent to your welfare; and if He gave you power to pray to and trust in Him, is it at all likely that He is now seeking an occasion against you, in order to destroy you? Nor would He have told you such things of His love, mercy, and kindness, and unwillingness to destroy sinners, as He has told you in His sacred Word if He had been determined not to extend His mercy to you.

24. *And called his name Samson.* The original, *shimshon,* which is from the root *shamash,* "to serve" (whence *shemesh,* "the sun"), probably means either a "little sun" or a "little servant"; and this latter is so likely a name to be imposed on an only son, by maternal fondness, that it leaves but little doubt of the propriety of the etymology. *And the Lord blessed him.* Gave evident proofs that the child was under the peculiar protection of the Most High, causing him to increase daily in stature and extraordinary strength.

25. *The Spirit of the Lord began to move him.* He felt the degrading bondage of his countrymen, and a strong desire to accomplish something for their deliverance. These feelings and motions he had from the Divine Spirit. *Camp of Dan.* Probably the place where his parents dwelt; for they were Danites, and the place is

supposed to have its name from its being the spot where the Danites stopped when they sent some men of their company to rob Micah of his teraphim (see chap. xviii). As he had these influences *between Zorah and Eshtaol,* it is evident that this was while he dwelt at home with his parents, for Zorah was the place where his father dwelt; see v. 2. Thus God began, from Samson's infancy, to qualify him for the work to which He had called him.

CHAPTER 14

Samson marries a wife of the Philistines, 1-4. Slays a young lion at Timnath, in the carcass of which he afterwards finds a swarm of bees, 5-9. He makes a feast; they appoint him thirty companions, to whom he puts forth a riddle, which they cannot expound, 10-14. They entice his wife to get the interpretation from him; she succeeds, informs them, and they tell the explanation, 15-18. He is incensed, and slays thirty of the Philistines, 19-20.

1. *Went down to Timnath.* A frontier town of the Philistines, at the beginning of the lands belonging to the tribe of Judah, Josh. xv. 57; but afterwards given up to Dan, Josh. xix. 43. David took this place from the Philistines, but they again got possession of it in the reign of Ahaz, 2 Chron. xxviii. 18.

3. *Is there never a woman?* To marry with any that did not belong to the Israelitish stock was contrary to the law, Exod. xxxiv. 16; Deut. vii. 3. But this marriage of Samson was said to be "of the Lord," v. 4; that is, God permitted it (for in no other sense can we understand the phrase) that it might be a means of bringing about the deliverance of Israel. *For she pleaseth me well.* "For she is right in my eyes."

5. *A young lion roared against him.* Came fiercely out upon him, ready to tear him to pieces.

6. *He rent him as he would have rent a kid.* Now it is not intimated that he did this by his own natural strength, but by the Spirit of the Lord coming mightily upon him; so that his strength does not appear to be his own, nor to be at his command. His might was, by the will of God, attached to his hair and to his being a Nazarite.

7. *And talked with the woman.* That is, concerning marriage; thus forming the espousals.

8. *After a time.* Probably about one year, as this was the time that generally elapsed between espousing and wedding. *A swarm of bees and honey in the carcase.* By length of time the flesh had been entirely consumed off the bones, and a swarm of bees had formed their combs within the region of the thorax, nor was it an improper place; nor was the thing unfrequent, if we may credit ancient writers, the carcasses of slain beasts becoming a receptacle for wild bees.

10. *Samson made there a feast.* The marriage feast, when he went to marry his espoused wife.

11. *They brought thirty companions.* These are called in Scripture "children of the bride-chamber," and friends of the bridegroom.

12. *I will now put forth a riddle.* Probably this was one part of the amusements at a marriage feast, each in his turn proposing a riddle, to be solved by any of the rest on a particular forfeit; the proposer forfeiting, if solved, the same which the company must

forfeit if they could not solve it. *Thirty sheets.* I have no doubt that the Arab *hyke* is here meant, a dress in which the natives of the East wrap themselves, as a Scottish Highlander does in his plaid.

17. *And she wept before him.* Not through any love to him, for it appears she had none, but to oblige her paramours; and of this he soon had ample proof.

18. *If ye had not plowed with my heifer.* If my wife had not been unfaithful to my bed, she would not have been unfaithful to my secret; and, you being her paramours, your interest was more precious to her than that of her husband. She has betrayed me through her attachment to you.

19. *The Spirit of the Lord came upon him.* "The spirit of fortitude from before the Lord." —Targum. He was inspired with unusual courage, and he felt strength proportioned to his wishes. *He . . . slew thirty men . . . and took their spoil.* He took their *hayks*, their *kumjas*, and *caftans*, and gave them to the thirty persons who, by unfair means, had solved his riddle; thus they had what our version calls "thirty sheets, and thirty changes of raiment."

20. *But Samson's wife was given to his companion.* This was the same kind of person who is called "the friend of the bridegroom," John iii. 29. And it is very likely that she loved this person better than she loved her husband, and went to him as soon as Samson had gone to his father's house at Zorah. She might, however, have thought herself abandoned by him, and therefore took another; this appears to have been the persuasion of her father, chap. xv. 2. But her betraying his secret and his interests to his enemies was a full proof he was not very dear to her; though, to persuade him to the contrary, she shed many crocodile tears; see v. 16.

CHAPTER 15

Samson, going to visit his wife, finds her bestowed on another, 1-2. He is incensed, vows revenge, and burns the corn of the Philistines, 3-5. They burn Samson's wife and her father, 6. He is still incensed, makes a great slaughter among them, 7-8. The Philistines gather together against Israel, and to appease them the men of Judah bind Samson, and deliver him into their hands, 9-13. The Spirit of the Lord comes upon him; he breaks his bonds, finds the jawbone of an ass, and therewith kills a thousand men, 14-16. He is sorely fatigued; and, being thirsty, God miraculously produces water from an opening of the ground in Lehi, and he is refreshed, 17-19. He judges Israel in the time of the Philistines twenty years, 20.

1. *Visited his wife with a kid.* On her betraying him, he had, no doubt, left her in great disgust. After some time his affection appears to have returned; and, taking a kid, or perhaps a fawn, as a present, he goes to make reconciliation, and finds her given to his brideman, probably the person to whom she betrayed his riddle.

2. *Thou hadst utterly hated her.* As he was conscious she had given him great cause so to do. *Her younger sister.* The father appears to have been perfectly sincere in this offer.

4. *Went and caught three hundred foxes.* There has been much controversy concerning the meaning of the term *shualim*, some supposing it to mean "foxes" or "jackals," and others "handfuls or sheaves of corn." Much of the force

of the objections against the common version will be diminished by the following considerations: (1) Foxes, or jackals, are common and gregarious in that country. (2) It is not hinted that Samson collected them alone; he might have employed several hands in this work. (3) It is not said he collected them all in one day; he might have employed several days, as well as many persons, to furnish him with these means of vengeance.

8. *He smote them hip and thigh.* This also is variously understood, but the general meaning seems plain. He appears to have had no kind of defensive weapon; therefore he was obliged to grapple with them, and, according to the custom of wrestlers, trip up their feet, and then bruise them to death. *The top of the rock Etam.* It is very likely that this is the same place as that mentioned in 1 Chron. iv. 32; it was in the tribe of Simeon, and on the borders of Dan, and probably a fortified place.

10. *To bind Samson are we come up.* It seems they did not wish to come to an open rupture with the Israelites, provided they would deliver up him who was the cause of their disasters.

11. *Three thousand men of Judah went.* It appears evidently from this that Samson was strongly posted, and they thought that no less than three thousand men were necessary to reduce him.

12. *That ye will not fall upon me yourselves.* He could not bear the thought of contending with and slaying his own countrymen, for there is no doubt that he could have as easily rescued himself from their hands as from those of the Philistines.

13. *They bound him with two new cords.* Probably his hands with one and his legs with the other.

14. *When he came unto Lehi.* This was the name of the place to which they brought him, either to put him to death, or keep him in perpetual confinement. *Shouted against him.* His capture was a matter of public rejoicing.

15. *He found a new jawbone of an ass.* I rather think that the word *teriyah*, which we translate *new*, and the margin "moist," should be understood as signifying the *tabia* or putrid state of the ass from which this jawbone was taken.

16. *With the jawbone of an ass, heaps upon heaps.* I cannot see the propriety of this rendering of the Hebrew words *bilchi hachamor, chamor chamorathayim;* I believe they should be translated thus:

"With the jawbone of this ass, an ass [the foal] of two asses;
With the jawbone of this ass I have slain a thousand men."

This appears to have been a triumphal song on the occasion; and the words are variously rendered both by the versions and by expositors.

17. *Ramath-lehi.* The "lifing up (or casting away) of the jawbone." Lehi was the name of the place before, Ramath was now added to it here; he lifted up the jawbone against his enemies, and slew them.

18. *I die for thirst.* The natural consequence of the excessive fatigue he had gone through in this encounter.

19. *God clave an hollow place that was in the jaw.* "That was in Lehi"; that is, there was a hollow place in this Lehi, and God caused a fountain to spring up in it. *En-hakkore.* "The well of the implorer"; this name he gave to the spot where the water rose, in order to perpetuate the bounty of God in affording him this miraculous supply. *Which is in Lehi unto this day.* Consequently not "in the jawbone of the ass," a most unfortunate rendering.

20. *He judged Israel . . . twenty years.* In the margin it is said, "He seems to have judged southwest Israel during twenty years of their servitude of the Philistines," chap. xiii. 1. Instead of *twenty years,* the Jerusalem Talmud has "forty years"; but this reading is not acknowledged by any MS. or version.

CHAPTER 16

Samson comes to Gaza; they lay wait for him; he rises by night, and carries away the city gates, 1-3. Falls in love with Delilah, 4. The lords of the Philistines promise her money if she will obtain from Samson the secret in which his strength lies, 5. By various artifices she at last obtains this; and communicates it to the Philistines, who seize and bind him, put out his eyes, and cause him to grind in the prison house. 6-21. At a public festival to Dagon he is brought out to make sport; when, being weary, he requests to be placed between the two pillars which supported the roof of the house, on which 3,000 men and women are stationed to see him make sport, 22-27. He prays to God to strengthen him, and pulls down the pillars; by which (the house falling) both himself, the lords of the Philistines, and a vast multitude of the people are slain, 28-39. His relatives come and take away his body, and bury it, 31.

1. *Then went Samson to Gaza, and saw there an harlot.* The Chaldee, as in the former case, renders the clause thus: "Samson saw there a woman, an inn-keeper." Perhaps the word *zonah* is to be taken here in its double sense: one who keeps a house for the entertainment of travellers, and who also prostitutes her person. Gaza was situated near the Mediterranean Sea, and was one of the most southern cities of Palestine. It has been supposed by some to have derived its name from the treasures deposited there by Cambyses, king of the Persians, because they say *Gaza,* in Persian, signifies "treasure"; so Pomponius Mela, and others. But it is more likely to be a Hebrew word, and that this city derived its name, *azzah,* from *azaz,* "to be strong," it being a strong or well-fortified place.

2. *They compassed him in.* They shut up all the avenues, secured the gates, and set persons in ambush near them, that they might attack him on his leaving the city early the next morning.

3. *An hill . . . before Hebron.* Possibly there were two Hebrons; it could not be the city generally understood by the word Hebron, as that was about twenty miles distant from Gaza; unless we suppose that *al peney Chebron* is to be understood of the road "leading to Hebron": he carried all to the top of that hill which was on the road leading to Hebron.

4. *He loved a woman in the valley of Sorek.* Some think Samson took this woman for his wife; others, that he had her as a concubine. It appears she was a Philistine; and however strong his love was for her, she seems to have had none for him. He always matched improperly, and he was cursed in all his matches. Where the *valley* or "brook" *of Sorek* was is not easy to be ascertained.

5. *See wherein his great strength lieth.* They saw that his stature was not remarkable and that, nevertheless, he had most extraordinary strength; therefore they supposed that it was the effect of some charm or amulet.

7. *Seven green withs.* That is, any kind of pliant, tough wood, twisted in the form of a cord or rope.

9. *Men lying in wait.* They probably did not appear, as Samson immediately broke his bonds when this bad woman said, *The Philistines be upon thee.*

11. *If they bind me fast with new ropes.* Samson wishes to keep up the opinion which the Philistines held, viz., that his mighty strength was the effect of some charm; and therefore he says, "Seven green withs which had not been dried; new ropes that were never occupied; weave the seven locks of my hair with the web." The *green* withs, the *new* ropes, and the number *seven* are such matters as would naturally be expected in a charm or spell.

13. *The seven locks of my head.* Probably Samson had his long hair plaited into seven divisions. Every person must see that this verse ends abruptly, and does not contain a full sense. Houbigant has particularly noticed this, and corrected the text from the Septuagint, the reading of which I shall here subjoin: "If thou shalt weave the seven locks of my head with the web, and shalt fasten them with the pin in the wall, I shall become weak like other men. And so it was that, when he slept, Dalida took the seven locks of his head, and wove them with the web, and fastened it with the pin to the wall and said unto him."

16. *His soul was vexed unto death.* What a consummate fool was this strong man! Might he not have seen, from what already took place, that Delilah intended his ruin? After trifling with her, and lying thrice, he at last commits to her his fatal secret, and thus becomes a traitor to himself and to his God.

17. *If I be shaven, then my strength will go from me.* The miraculous strength of Samson must not be supposed to reside either in his hair or in his muscles, but in that relation in which he stood to God as a Nazarite, such a person being bound by a solemn vow to walk in a strict conformity to the laws of his Maker. It was a part of the Nazarite's vow to permit no razor to pass on his head; and his long hair was the mark of his being a Nazarite, and of his vow to God. When Samson permitted his hair to be shorn off, he renounced and broke his Nazarite vow, in consequence of which God abandoned him; and therefore we are told, in v. 20, that "the Lord was departed from him."

19. *She began to afflict him.* She had probably tied his hands slyly, while he was asleep, and after having cut off his hair, she began to insult him before she called the Philistines, to try whether he were really reduced to a state of weakness. Finding he could not disengage himself, she called the Philistines, and he, being alarmed, rose up, thinking he could exert himself as before, and shake himself, i.e., disengage himself from his bonds and his enemies. But *he wist not that the Lord was departed from him;* for as Delilah had cut off his locks while he was asleep, he had not yet perceived that they were gone.

21. *Put out his eyes.* Thus was the lust of the eye, in looking after and gazing on strange women, punished. As the Philistines did not know that his strength might not return, they put out his eyes, that he might never be able to plan any enterprise against them. *He did grind in the prison house.* Before the invention of wind and water mills, the grain was at first bruised between two stones, afterwards ground in hand mills.

22. *The hair of his head began to grow again.* And may we not suppose that, sensible of his sin and folly, he renewed his Nazarite vow to the Lord, in consequence of which his supernatural strength was again restored?

23. *Unto Dagon their god.* Diodorus Siculus describes their god thus: "It had the head of a woman, but all the rest of the body resembled a fish."

25. *Call for Samson, that he may make us sport.* What the sport was we cannot tell; probably it was an exhibition of his prodigious strength.

27. *Now the house was full of men.* It was either the prison house, house of assembly, or a temple of Dagon, raised on pillars, open on all sides, and flat-roofed, so that it could accommodate a multitude of people on the top.

28. *Samson called unto the Lord.* It was in consequence of his faith in God that he should be strengthened to overthrow his enemies and the enemies of his country that he is mentioned, Hebrews xi., among those who were remarkable for their faith.

29. *The two middle pillars upon which the house stood.* Much learned labor has been lost on the attempt to prove that a building like this might stand on two pillars. But what need of this? There might have been as many pillars here as were in the temple of Diana at Ephesus, and yet the two center pillars be the key of the building; these being once pulled down, the whole house would necessarily fall.

30. *So the dead which he slew.* We are informed that the house was full of men and women, with about three thousand of both sexes on the top; now as the whole house was pulled down, consequently the principal part of all these were slain; and among them we find there were the lords of the Philistines. The death of these, with so many of the inferior chiefs of the people, was such a crush to the Philistine ascendancy that they troubled Israel no more for several years, and did not even attempt to hinder Samson's relatives from taking away and burying his dead body.

31. *He judged Israel twenty years.* It is difficult to ascertain the time of Samson's magistracy, and the extent of country over which he presided. His jurisdiction seems to have been very limited, and to have extended no farther than over those parts of the tribe of Dan contiguous to the land of the Philistines. This is what our margin intimates on v. 20 of chap. xv. Many suppose that he and Eli were contemporaries, Samson being rather an executor of the divine justice upon the enemies of his people than an administrator of the civil and religious laws of the Hebrews. Allowing Eli and Samson to have been contemporaries, this latter part might have been entirely committed to the care of Eli.

CHAPTER 17

Micah, an Ephraimite, restores to his mother eleven hundred shekels of silver, which he had taken from her, 1-2. She dedicates this to God; and out of a part of it makes a graven image and a molten image, and sets them up in the house of Micah, 3-4; who consecrates one of his sons to be his priest, 5. He afterwards finds a Levite, whom he consecrates for a priest, and gives him annually ten shekels of silver, with his food and clothing, 6-13.

1. *And there was a man of mount Ephraim.* It is extremely difficult to fix the chronology of this and the following transactions. Some think them to be here in their natural order; others, that they happened in the time of Joshua, or immediately after the ancients who outlived Joshua. All that can be said with certainty is this, that they happened when there was no king in Israel; i.e., about the time of the judges, or in some time of the anarchy, v. 6.

2. *About which thou cursedst.* Houbigant and others understand this of putting the young man to his oath. It is likely that when the mother of Micah missed the money, she poured imprecations on the thief; and that Micah, who had secreted it, hearing this, was alarmed, and restored the money lest the curses should fall on him.

3. *I had wholly dedicated.* From this it appears that Micah's mother, though she made a superstitious use of the money, had no idolatrous design, for she expressly says she had dedicated it "to Jehovah"; and this appears to have been the reason why she poured imprecations on him who had taken it.

4. *A graven image and a molten image.* What these images were we cannot positively say; they were most probably some resemblance of matters belonging to the Tabernacle.

5. *The man Micah had an house of gods.* Beith Elohim should, I think, be translated "house (or temple) of God"; for it is very likely that both the mother and the son intended no more than a private or domestic chapel, in which they proposed to set up the worship of the true God.

Made an ephod. Perhaps the whole of this case may be stated thus: Micah built a house of God—a chapel in imitation of the sanctuary; he made a graven image representing the ark, a molten image to represent the mercy seat, teraphim to represent the cherubim above the mercy seat, and an ephod in imitation of the sacerdotal garments; and he consecrated one of his sons to be priest. Thus gross idolatry was not the crime of Micah; he only set up in his own house an epitome of the divine worship as performed at Shiloh. What the *teraphim* were, see the note on Gen. xxxi. 19; for the *ephod,* see the note on Exod. xxv. 7; and for the sacerdotal vestments in general, see the note on Exod. xxviii. 5, etc.

6. *There was no king in Israel.* The word *melech,* which generally means *king,* is sometimes taken for a supreme governor, judge, magistrate, or ruler of any kind (see Gen. xxxvi. 31 and Deut. xxxiii. 5), and it is likely it should be so understood here. *Every man did that which was right in his own eyes.* He was his own governor, and what he did he said was

right; and, by his cunning and strength, defended his conduct. When a man's own will, passions, and caprice are to be made the rule of law, society is in a most perilous and ruinous state.

7. *Of the family of Judah.* The word *family* may be taken here for "tribe"; or the young man might have been of the tribe of Judah by his mother, and of the tribe of Levi by his father, for he is called here a Levite; and it is probable that he might have officiated at Shiloh, in the Levitical office. A Levite might marry into any other tribe, providing the woman was not an heiress.

8. *To sojourn where he could find.* He went about the country seeking for some employment, for the Levites had no inheritance.

10. *Be unto me a father and a priest.* You shall be master of my house, as if you were my father; and, as priest, you shall appear in the presence of God for me. The term *father* is often used to express honor and reverence. *Ten shekels of silver.* About thirty shillings per annum, with board, lodging, and clothes. Very good wages in those early times.

11. *The Levite was content.* He thought the place a good one, and the wages respectable.

12. *Micah consecrated the Levite.* "He filled his hands"; i.e., he gave him an offering to present before the Lord, that he might be accepted by Him.

13. *Now know I that the Lord will do me good.* As he had already provided an epitome of the Tabernacle, a model of the ark, mercy seat, and cherubim, and had got proper sacerdotal vestments, and a Levite to officiate, he took for granted that all was right, and that he should now have the benediction of God.

CHAPTER 18

Some Danites, seeking an inheritance, send five men to search the land, who arrive at the house of Micah, 1-2. They employ the Levite, who served in his house as priest, to ask counsel for them of God, 3-5. He inquires, and promises them success, 6. They depart, and go to Laish, and find the inhabitants secure, 7. They return to their brethren, and encourage them to attempt the conquest of the place, 8-10. They send 600 men, who, coming to the place where Micah dwelt, enter the house, and carry off the priest and his consecrated things, 11-21. Micah and his friends pursue them; but, being threatened, are obliged to return, 22-26. The Danites come to Laish, and smite it, and build a city here, which they call Dan, 27-29. They make the Levite their priest, and set up the images at this new city, 30-31.

1. *There was no king in Israel.* See chap. xvii. 6. The circumstances related here show that this must have happened about the time of the preceding transactions. *The tribe of the Danites.* That is, a part of this tribe; some families of it. *All their inheritance.* That is, they had not received an extent of country sufficient for them. Some families were still unprovided for, or had not sufficient territory; for we find from Josh. chap. xix. 40, etc., that, although the tribe of Dan did receive their inheritance with the rest of the tribes of Israel, yet their coasts "went out too little for them," and they went and fought "against Leshem [called here Laish], and took it." This circumstance is marked here more particularly than in the Book of Joshua. See on Josh. xix. 47.

2. *Five men . . . men of valour.* The Hebrew word *chayil* has been applied to personal prowess, to mental energy, and to earthly possessions. They sent those in whose courage, judgment, and prudence they could safely confide.

3. *They knew the voice of the young man.* They knew by his dialect or mode of pronunciation that he was not an Ephraimite. We have already seen (chap. xii. 6) that the Ephraimites could not pronounce certain letters.

5. *Ask counsel . . . of God.* As the Danites use the word *Elohim* here for *God,* we are necessarily led to believe that they meant the true God; especially as the Levite answers, v. 6, "Before the Lord [*Yehovah*] is your way." Though the former word sometimes may be applied to idols, whom their votaries clothed with the attributes of God, yet the latter is never applied but to the true *God* alone. As the Danites succeeded according to the oracle delivered by the Levite, it is a strong presumption that the worship established by Micah was not of an idolatrous kind.

7. *After the manner of the Zidonians.* Probably the people of *Laish* or Leshem were originally a colony of the *Sidonians,* who, it appears, were an opulent people; and, being in possession of a strong city, lived in a state of security, not being afraid of their neighbors. In this the Leshemites imitated them, though the sequel proves they had not the same reason for their confidence.

They were far from the Zidonians. Being, as above supposed, a Sidonian colony, they might naturally expect help from their countrymen; but, as they dwelt a considerable distance from Sidon, the Danites saw that they could strike the blow before the news of invasion could reach Sidon.

And had no business with any man. In the most correct copies of the Septuagint, this clause is thus translated: "And they had no transactions with Syria." Now it is most evident that, instead of *adam,* "man," they read *aram,* "Syria"; words which are so nearly similar that the difference which exists is only between the *resh* and *daleth,* and this, both in MSS. and in printed books, is often indiscernible. It may be proper to observe that *Laish* was on the frontiers of Syria; but as they had no intercourse with the Syrians, from whom they might have received the promptest assistance, this was an additional reason why the Danites might expect success.

9. *Arise.* This is a very plain address, full of good sense, and well adapted to the purpose. It seems to have produced an instantaneous effect.

11. *Six hundred men.* These were not the whole, for we find they had children, v. 21; but these appear to have been 600 armed men.

12. *Mahaneh-dan.* "The camp of Dan"; so called from the circumstance of this armament encamping there. See chap. xiii. 25, which affords some proof that this transaction was previous to the days of Samson.

14. *Consider what ye have to do.* They probably had formed the design to carry off the priest and his sacred utensils.

18. *These went into Micah's house.* The 5 men went in, while the 600 armed men stood at the gate.

19. *Lay thine hand upon thy mouth.* This was the token of silence. The god of silence,

Harpocrates, is represented on ancient statues with his finger pressed on his lips.

20. *Went in the midst of the people.* He was glad to be employed by the Danites; and went into the crowd, that he might not be discovered by Micah or his family.

21. *The little ones and the cattle.* These men were so confident of success that they removed their whole families, household goods, cattle, and all. *And the carriage.* Their "substance, precious things, or valuables"; or rather the "luggage" or "baggage."

24. *Ye have taken away my gods.* As Micah was a worshipper of the true God, as we have seen, he cannot mean any kind of idols by the word *elohai* here used. He undoubtedly means those representations of divine things and symbols of the divine presence such as the teraphim, ephod, etc.; for they are all evidently included under the word *elohai,* which we translate *my gods.*

27. *Unto a people . . . at quiet and secure.* They found the report given by the spies to be correct. The people were apprehensive of no danger, and were unprepared for resistance; hence they were all put to the sword, and their city burned up.

28. *There was no deliverer.* They had no succor; because the Sidonians, from whom they might have expected it, were at too great a distance.

29. *Called the name of the city Dan.* This city was afterwards very remarkable as one of the extremities of the Promised Land. The extent of the Jewish territories was generally expressed by the phrase, "From Dan to Beersheba"; that is, "From the most northern to the southern extremity."

30. *The children of Dan set up the graven image.* They erected a chapel, or temple, among themselves, as Micah had done before, having the same implements and the same priest. *And Jonathan the son of Gershom.* Either this was the name of the young Levite or they had turned him off and got this Jonathan in his place. *The son of Manasseh.* Who this Manasseh was, none can tell; nor does the reading appear to be genuine. Instead of *Manasseh,* the word should be read *Mosheh,* "Moses," as it is found in some MSS., in the Vulgate, and in the concessions of the most intelligent Jews. The Jews, as R. D. Kimchi acknowledges, have suspended the letter *nun* over the word *Mosheh,* which, by the addition of the points, they have changed into *Manasseh,* because they think it would be a great reproach to their legislator to have had a grandson who was an idolater. That Gershom the son of Moses is here intended is very probable.

Until the day of the captivity of the land. Calmet observes, "The posterity of this Jonathan executed the office of priest in the city of Dan, all the time that the idol of Micah (the teraphim, ephod, etc.) was there. But this was only while the house of the Lord was at Shiloh; and, consequently, the sons of Jonathan were priests at Dan only till the time in which the ark was taken by the Philistines, which was the last year of Eli, the high priest; for after that the ark no more returned to Shiloh." This is evident; and on this very ground Houbigant contends that, instead of *haarets,* "the land," we

should read *haaron,* "the ark"; for nothing is easier than the *vau* and *final nun* to be mistaken for the *final tsade,* which is the only difference between "the captivity of the land" and "the captivity of the ark." And this conjecture is the more likely, because the next verse tells us that Micah's graven image continued at Dan "all the time that the house of God was in Shiloh," which was till the ark was taken by the Philistines.

CHAPTER 19

A Levite and his concubine disagree, and she leaves him and goes to her father's house, 1-2. He follows to bring her back, and is kindly entertained by her father five days, 3-8. He returns; and lodges the first night at Gibeah, in the tribe of Benjamin, 9-21. The men of Gibeah attack the house, and insist on abusing the body of the Levite; who, to save himself, delivers to them his concubine, whose life falls a victim to their brutality, 22-27. The Levite divides her dead body into twelve pieces, and sends one to each of the twelve tribes; they are struck with horror, and call a council on the subject, 28-30.

1. *There was no king in Israel.* All sorts of disorders are attributed to the want of civil government; justice, right, truth, and humanity had fallen in the streets. *Took to him a concubine.* We have already seen that the *concubine* was a sort of secondary wife; and that such connections were not disreputable, being according to the general custom of those times.

2. *Played the whore.* Neither the Vulgate, Septuagint, Targum, nor Josephus understand this word as implying any act of conjugal infidelity on the woman's part. They merely state that the parties disagreed, and the woman returned to her father's house. Indeed all the circumstances of the case vindicate this view of the subject. If she had been a *whore,* or adulteress, it is not very likely that her husband would have gone after her to *speak friendly,* literally, "to speak to her heart," and entreat her to return. The Vulgate simply states that she "left him"; the Septuagint, that she "was angry with" him; the Targum, that she "despised him"; Josephus, that she "was alienated," or separated herself, from him. Houbigant translates the clause: "Who when she was alienated from him or angry with him, left him." I think the true meaning to be among the above interpretations.

3. *He rejoiced to meet him.* He hoped to be able completely to reconcile his daughter and her husband.

8. *And they tarried until afternoon.* Merely that they might avoid the heat of the day, which would have been very inconvenient in travelling.

9. *The day groweth to an end.* "The day is about to pitch its tent"; that is, it was near the time in which travellers ordinarily pitched their tents, to take up their lodging for the night.

11. *When they were by Jebus.* This was Jerusalem, in which, though after the death of Joshua it appears to have been partly conquered by the tribe of Judah, yet the Jebusites kept the stronghold of Zion till the days of David, by whom they were finally expelled.

15. *No man . . . took them into his house to lodging.* There was probably no inn in this place, and therefore they could not have a lodging unless furnished by mere hospitality.

20. *All thy wants lie upon me.* Here was

genuine hospitality: "Keep your bread and wine for yourselves, and your straw and provender for your asses; you may need them before you finish your journey; I will supply all your wants for this night, therefore do not lodge in the street."

22. *Sons of Belial.* Profligate fellows. *That we may know him.* See Genesis xix. These were genuine sodomites as to their practice; sons of Belial, rascals and miscreants of the deepest dye; worse than brutes, being a compound of beast and devil inseparably blended.

24. *Here is my daughter a maiden.* Such a proposal was made by Lot to the men of Sodom, Genesis xix, but nothing can excuse either. That the rights of hospitality were sacred in the East, the most highly regarded, we know; and that a man would defend, at the expense of his life, the stranger whom he had admitted under his roof, is true; but how a father could make such a proposal relative to his virgin daughter must remain among those things which are incomprehensible.

25. *So the man took his concubine.* The word *yachazek,* which we here translate simply *took,* signifies rather to "take or seize by violence." The woman would not go out to them; but her graceless husband forced her to go, in order that he might save his own body. He could have had but little love for her, and this was the cause of their separation before. The men of Gibeah who wished to abuse the body of the Levite; the Levite who wished to save his body at the expense of the modesty, reputation, and life of his wife; and the old man who wished to save his guest at the expense of the violation of his daughter are all characters that humanity and modesty wish to be buried in everlasting oblivion. *When the day began to spring.* Their turpitude could not bear the full light of the day, and they dismissed the poor woman when the day began to break.

26. *Fell down at the door.* She had strength to reach the door, but not to knock for admittance; when she reached the door she fell down dead!

29. *Divided her . . . into twelve pieces.* There is no doubt that with the pieces he sent to each tribe a circumstantial account of the barbarity of the men of Gibeah; and it is very likely that they considered each of the pieces as expressing an execration, "If ye will not come and avenge my wrongs, may ye be hewn in pieces like this abused and murdered woman!"

30. *There was no such deed done nor seen.* They were all struck with the enormity of the crime, and considered it a sovereign disgrace to all the tribes of Israel. *Consider of it.* Literally, "Put it to yourselves; take counsel upon it; and speak." This was the prelude to the council held, and the subsequent operations, which are mentioned in the following chapter.

CHAPTER 20

The heads of the eleven tribes come before the Lord in Mizpeh, and examine the Levite relative to the murder of his wife, who gives a simple narrative of the whole affair, 1-7. They unanimously resolve to avenge the wrong, and make provision for a campaign against the Benjamites, 8-11. They desire the Benjamites to deliver up the murderers; they refuse, and prepare for battle, having assembled an army of 26,700 men, 12-16. The rest of the Israelites amount to 400,000, who, taking counsel of God, agree to send the tribe of Judah against the

Benjamites, 17-18. They attack the Benjamites, and are routed with the loss of 22,000 men, 19-21. They renew the battle next day, and are discomfited with the loss of 18,000 men, 22-25. They weep, fast, and pray, and offer sacrifices; and again inquire of the Lord, who promises to deliver Benjamin into their hands, 26-28. They concert plans, attack the Benjamites, and rout them, killing 25,100 men, and destroy the city of Gibeah, 29-37. A recapitulation of the different actions in which they were killed, 38-46. Six hundred men escape to the rock Rimmon, 47. The Israelites destroy all the cities of the Benjamites, 48.

1. *Unto the Lord in Mizpeh.* This city was situated on the confines of Judah and Benjamin, and is sometimes attributed to the one, sometimes to the other. It seems that there was a place here in which the Lord was consulted, as well as at Shiloh; in 1 Mac. iii. 46 we read, "In Maspha was the place where they prayed aforetime in Israel." These two passages cast light on each other.

2. *The chief of all the people.* The "corners," *pinnoth;* for as the cornerstones are the strength of the walls, so are the chiefs the strength of the people. Hence Christ is called the "chief cornerstone." *In the assembly of the people of God.* The Septuagint translate, "And all the tribes of Israel stood up before the face of the Lord, in the Church of the people of God."

3. *Tell us, how was this wickedness?* They had heard before, by the messengers he sent with the fragments of his wife's body; but they wish to hear it, in full council, from himself.

10. *Ten men of an hundred.* Expecting that they might have a long contest, they provide sutlers for the camp; and it is probable that they chose these tenths by lot.

13. *Deliver us the men.* Nothing could be fairer than this. They wish only to make the murderers answerable for their guilt. *Benjamin would not hearken.* Thus making their whole tribe partakers of the guilt of the men of Gibeah. By not delivering up those bad men, they in effect said: "We will stand by them in what they have done, and would have acted the same part had we been present." This proves that the whole tribe was excessively depraved.

15. *Twenty and six thousand.* Some copies of the Septuagint have 23,000, others 25,000. The Vulgate has this latter number; the Complutensian Polyglot and Josephus have the same.

16. *Left-handed.* They were ambidexters—could use the right hand and the left with equal ease and effect. See the note on chap. iii. 15. *Could sling stones at a hair . . . and not miss.* *Velo yachati,* "and not sin." Here we have the true import of the term "sin"; it signifies simply to "miss the mark." Men miss the mark of true happiness in aiming at sensual gratifications; which happiness is to be found only in the possession and enjoyment of the favor of God, from whom their passions continually lead them. He alone hits the mark, and ceases from sin, who attains to God through Christ Jesus.

18. *Went up to the house of God.* Some think that a deputation was sent from Shiloh, where Phinehas, the high priest, was, to inquire, not concerning the expediency of the war, nor of its success, but which of the tribes should begin the attack. Having so much right on their side, they had no doubt of the justice of their cause. Having such a superiority of numbers, they had no doubt of success. *And the Lord said, Judah.* But He did not say that they should conquer.

21. *Destroyed down to the ground . . . twenty*

and two thousand men. That is, so many were left dead on the field of battle.

23. *Go up against him.* It appears most evident that the Israelites did not seek the protection of God. They trusted in the goodness of their cause and in the multitude of their army. God humbled them, and delivered them into the hands of their enemies, and showed them that the race was not to the swift, nor the battle to the strong.

26. *And wept.* Had they humbled themselves, fasted and prayed, and offered sacrifices at first, they had not been discomfited. *And fasted that day until even.* This is the first place where fasting is mentioned as a religious ceremony, or as a means of obtaining help from God. And in this case, and many since, it has been powerfully effectual. At present it is but little used— a strong proof that self-denial is wearing out of fashion.

28. *Phinehas, the son of Eleazar.* This was the same Phinehas who is mentioned Numbers xxv, and consequently these transactions must have taken place shortly after the death of Joshua.

29. *Israel set liers in wait.* Though God had promised them success, they knew they could expect it only in the use of the proper means. They used all prudent precaution, and employed all their military skill.

32. *Let us . . . draw them from the city.* They had two reasons for this: (1) They had placed an ambuscade behind Gibeah, which was to enter and burn the city as soon as the Benjamites had left it. (2) It would seem that the slingers, by being within the city and its fortifications, had great advantage against the Israelites by their slings, whom they could not annoy with their swords, unless they got them to the plain country.

33. *Put themselves in array at Baal-tamar.* The Israelites seem to have divided their army into three divisions: one was at Baal-tamar, a second behind the city in ambush, and the third skirmished with the Benjamites before Gibeah.

35. *Twenty and five thousand and an hundred.* As the Benjamites consisted only of 26,700 slingers; or, as the Vulgate, Septuagint, and others read, 25,000, which is most probably the true reading, then the whole of the Benjamites were cut to pieces, except 600 men, who we are informed fled to the rock Rimmon, where they fortified themselves.

38. *Now there was an appointed sign.* From this verse to the end of the chapter we have the details of the same operations which are mentioned, in a general way, in the preceding part of the chapter.

45. *Unto the rock of Rimmon.* This was some strong place, but where situated is not known. Here they maintained themselves four months, and it was by these alone that the tribe of Benjamin was preserved from utter extermination. See the following chapter.

CHAPTER 21

The Israelites mourn because of the desolation of Benjamin, and consult the Lord, 1-4. They inquire who of Israel had not come to this war, as they had vowed that those who would not make this a common cause should be put to death, 5-6. They consult how they shall procure wives for the 600 men who had fled to the rock

Rimmon, 7. Finding that the men of Jabesh-gilead had not come to the war, they send 12,000 men against them, smite them, and bring off 400 virgins, which they give for wives to those who had taken refuge in Rimmon, 8-14. To provide for the 200 which remained, they propose to carry off 200 virgins of the daughters of Shiloh, who might come to the annual feast of the Lord, held at that place, 15-22. They take this counsel, and each carries away a virgin from the feast, 23-25.

1. *Now the men of Israel had sworn.* Of this oath we had not heard before; but it appears they had commenced this war with a determination to destroy the Benjamites utterly, and that if any of them escaped the sword, no man should be permitted to give him his daughter to wife. By these means the remnant of the tribe must soon have been annihilated.

2. *The people came to the house of God.* Literally, "the people came to Bethel"; this is considered as the name of a place by the Chaldee, Syriac, Arabic, and Septuagint. *And wept sore.* Their revenge was satisfied, and now reflection brought them to contrition for what they had done.

3. *Why is this come to pass?* This was a very impertinent question. They knew well enough how it came to pass. It was right that the men of Gibeah should be punished, and it was right that they who vindicated them should share in that punishment; but they carried their revenge too far. They endeavored to exterminate both man and beast, chap. xx. 48.

4. *Built there an altar.* This affords some evidence that this was not a regular place of worship, else an altar would have been found in the place; and their act was not according to the law, as may be seen in several places of the Pentateuch. But there was neither king nor law among them, and they did whatever appeared right in their own eyes.

7. *How shall we do for wives for them?* From this it appears that they had destroyed all the Benjamitish women and children! They had set out with the purpose of exterminating the whole tribe, and therefore they massacred the women, that if any of the men escaped, they might find neither wife nor daughter; and they bound themselves under an oath not to give any of their females to any of the remnant of this tribe, that thus the whole tribe might utterly perish.

8. *There came none to the camp from Jabesh-gilead.* As they had sworn to destroy those who would not assist in this war, v. 5, they determined to destroy the men of Jabesh, and to leave none alive except the virgins, and to give these to the 600 Benjamites that had escaped to the rock Rimmon. So 12,000 men went, smote the city, and killed all the males and all the married women. The whole account is dreadful; and none could have been guilty of all these enormities but those who were abandoned of God. The crime of the men of Gibeah was of the deepest dye; the punishment, involving both the guilty and the innocent, was extended to the most criminal excess; and their mode of redressing the evil which they had occasioned was equally abominable.

13. *And to call peaceably unto them.* To proclaim peace to them; to assure them that the enmity was all over, and that they might with safety leave their stronghold.

14. *Yet so they sufficed them not.* There were 600 men at Rimmon, and all the young women

they saved from Jabesh were only 400; therefore there were 200 still wanting.

19. *There is a feast of the Lord.* What this feast was is not known; it might be either the Passover, Pentecost, or the Feast of Tabernacles, or indeed some other peculiar to this place. All the above feasts were celebrated at that time of the year when the vines were in full leaf; therefore the Benjamites might easily conceal themselves in the vineyards; and the circumstances will answer to any of those feasts.

On the east side of the highway. I can see no reason for this minute description, unless it intimates that this feast was to be held this year in rather a different place to that which was usual; and, as the Benjamites had been shut up in their stronghold in Rimmon, they might not have heard of this alteration; and it was necessary, in such a case, to give them the most circumstantial information, that they might succeed in their enterprise without being discovered.

21. *And catch you every man his wife.* That is, Let each man of the 200 Benjamites seize and carry off a woman, whom he is, from that hour, to consider as his *wife.*

22. *Be favourable unto them.* They promise to use their influence with the men of Shiloh to induce them to consent to a connection thus fraudulently obtained, and which the necessity of the case appeared to them to justify.

We reserved not to each man his wife in the war. The reading of the Vulgate is very remarkable: "Pardon them, for they have not taken them as victors take captives in war; but when

they requested you to give them you did not therefore the fault is your own." Here it is intimated that application had been made to the people of Shiloh to furnish these 200 Benjamites with wives, and that they had refused; and it was this refusal that induced the Benjamites to seize and carry them off. Houbigant translates the Hebrew thus: "Pardon them, I beseech you, for they have not each taken his wife to the war; and unless you now give these to them, you will sin."

23. *They went and returned unto their inheritance.* It appears that the Benjamites acted in the most honorable way by the women whom they had thus violently carried off; and we may rest assured they took them to an inheritance at least equal to their own, for it does not appear that any part of the lands of the Benjamites was alienated from them, and the 600 men in question shared, for the present, the inheritance of many thousands.

24. *Every man to his tribe.* Though this must have been four months after the war with Benjamin, chap. xx. 47, yet it appears the armies did not disband till they had got the remnant of Benjamin settled, as is here related.

25. *In those days there was no king in Israel.* Let no one suppose that the sacred writer, by relating the atrocities in this and the preceding chapters, justifies the actions themselves; by no means. Indeed, they cannot be justified; and the writer by relating them gives the strongest proof of the authenticity of the whole, by such an impartial relation of facts that were highly to the discredit of his country.

The Book of
RUTH

When and by whom the Book of Ruth was written are points not agreed on among critics and commentators.

As to the transactions recorded in it, they are variously placed. In the book itself there is no other notation of time than merely this, that the things came to pass in the days when the judges ruled; therefore some have placed these transactions under Ehud; others, under Gideon; others, under Barak; others, under Abimelech; and others, under Shamgar. This last is the opinion of Archbishop Ussher; and most chronologers adopt it. The book is evidently an appendix to the Book of Judges, and contains a perfect history in itself; and therefore should not be inserted in any part of that book. It also seems to be an introduction to the Books of Samuel, in which the history of David is contained, as it gives the genealogy of this prince. It is also not without its use in matters which respect the Gospels, as it ascertains the line by which Jesus Christ came.

As to the author, he is as uncertain as the time. It has been attributed to Hezekiah, to Ezra, and to Samuel; and it is most likely that the author of the two Books of Samuel was also the writer of this little book, as it seems necessary to complete his plan of the history of David.

The sum of the history contained in this book is the following: A man of Bethlehem, named Elimelech, with his wife, Naomi, and his two sons, Mahlon and Chilion, left his own country in the time of a famine, and went to sojourn in the land of Moab. There he died; and Naomi married her two sons to two Moabitish women. Mahlon married Ruth, who is the chief subject of this book; and Chilion married one named Orpah. In about ten years both these brethren died; and Naomi, accompanied by her two daughters-in-law, set out to return to the land of Judah, she having heard that plenty was again restored to her country. On the way she besought her daughters to return to their own country and kindred. Orpah took her advice and, after an affectionate parting, returned; but Ruth insisted on accompanying her mother-in-law. They arrived in Bethlehem about the time of harvest, and Ruth went into the fields to glean for their support. The ground on which she was accidentally employed belonged to Boaz, one of the relatives of Elimelech, her father-in-law; who, finding who she was, ordered her to be kindly treated, and appointed her both meat and drink with his own servants. Finding that she was by marriage his kinswoman, he purposed to take her to wife, if a nearer kinsman who was then living should refuse. He was accordingly applied to, refused to take Ruth, and surrendered his right to her, according to the custom of those times, at the gate of Bethlehem, before the elders of the city. Boaz then took her to wife, by whom she had Obed, who was father to Jesse, the father of David.

CHAPTER 1

Elimelech, his wife, Naomi, and their two sons, Mahlon and Chilion, flee from a famine in the land of Israel, and go to sojourn in Moab, 1-2. Here his two sons marry; and, in the space of ten years, both their father and they die, 3-6. Naomi sets out on her return to her own country, accompanied by her daughters-in-law, Orpah and Ruth, whom she endeavors to persuade to return to their own people, 7-13. Orpah returns, but Ruth accompanies her mother-in-law, 14-18. They arrive at Bethlehem in the time of the barley harvest, 19-22.

1. *When the judges ruled.* We know not under what judge this happened. *There was a famine.* Probably occasioned by the depredations of the Philistines, Ammonites, etc., carrying off the corn as soon as it was ripe, or destroying it on the field.

2. *Elimelech.* That is, "God is my king." *Naomi.* "Beautiful" or "amiable." *Mahlon.* "Infirmity." *Chilion.* "Finished, completed."

3. *Elimelech . . . died.* Probably a short time after his arrival in Moab.

4. *And they took them wives.* The Targum very properly observes that "they transgressed the decree of the word of the Lord, and took to themselves strange women."

5. *And Mahlon and Chilion died.* The Targum adds, "And because they transgressed the decree of the word of the Lord, and joined affinity with strange people, therefore their days were cut off."

11. *Are there yet any more sons.* This was spoken in allusion to the custom that, when a married brother died without leaving posterity, his brother should take his widow; and the children of such a marriage were accounted the children of the deceased brother.

14. *And Orpah kissed her mother in law.* The Septuagint adds, "And returned to her own people." The Vulgate, Syriac, and Arabic are to the same purpose.

15. *Gone back . . . unto her gods.* They were probably both idolaters; their having been proselytes is an unfounded conjecture. Chemosh was the grand idol of the Moabites. The conversion of Ruth probably commenced at this time.

16. *And Ruth said.* A more perfect surrender was never made of friendly feelings to a friend: "I will not leave you—I will follow you; I will lodge where you lodge—take the same fare with which you meet. *Thy people shall be my people*—I most cheerfully abandon my own country, and determine to end my days in yours. I will also henceforth have no god but thy God —and be joined with you in worship, as I am in affection and consanguinity. I will cleave unto you even unto death; die where you die; and be buried, if possible, in the same grave. This was a most extraordinary attachment, and evidently without any secular motive.

17. *The Lord do so to me, and more.* May He inflict any of those punishments on me, and any worse punishment, if I part from you till death. And it appears that she was true to her engagement; for Naomi was nourished in the house of Boaz in her old age, and became the fosterer and nurse of their son Obed, chap. iv. 15-16.

19. *All the city was moved about them.* It appears that Naomi was not only well-known, but highly respected also, at Bethlehem—a proof that Elimelech was of high consideration in that place.

20. *Call me not Naomi.* That is, "beautiful" or "pleasant." *Call me Mara.* That is, "bitter"; one whose life is grievous to her. *The Almighty. Shaddai,* He who is self-sufficient, has taken the props and supports of my life.

21. *I went out full.* Having a husband and two sons. *The Lord hath brought me home again empty.* Having lost all three by death. It is also likely that Elimelech took considerable property with him into the land of Moab; for as he fled from the face of the famine, he would naturally take his property with him; and on this Naomi subsisted till her return to Bethlehem, which she might not have thought of till all was spent.

22. *In the beginning of barley harvest.* This was in the beginning of spring, for the barley harvest began immediately after the Passover, and that feast was held on the fifteenth of the month Nisan, which corresponds nearly with our March.

CHAPTER 2

Ruth goes to glean in the field of Boaz, 1-3. Boaz finds her, and inquires who she is, 4-7. He speaks kindly to her, gives her permission to follow his reapers, and orders them to use her well, 8-16. She returns in the evening to Naomi, and tells her of her fare; from whom she receives encouragement and advice, 17-23.

1. *A mighty man of wealth.* Some suppose Boaz to have been one of the judges of Israel; he was no doubt a man of considerable property.

2. *Glean ears of corn.* The word *glean* comes from the French *glaner*, to gather ears or grains of corn. This was formerly a general custom in England and Ireland; the poor went into the fields and collected the straggling ears of corn after the reapers. *After him in whose sight I shall find grace.* She did not mean Boaz; but she purposed to go out where they were now reaping, and glean after any person who might permit her, or use her in a friendly manner. The words seem to intimate that, notwithstanding the law of Moses, the gleaners might be prevented by the owner of the field.

3. *And her hap was.* So she was accidentally

or providentially led to that part of the cultivated country which belonged to Boaz.

4. *Boaz came from Beth-lehem.* This salutation between Boaz and his reapers is worthy of particular regard; he said, "Jehovah be with you!" They said, "May Jehovah bless thee!" Can a pious mind read these godly salutations without wishing for a return of those simple primitive times?

7. *That she tarried a little in the house.* It seems as if the reapers were now resting in their tent, and that Ruth had just gone in with them to take her rest also.

8. *Abide here fast by my maidens.* These were probably employed in making bands, and laying on them enough to form a sheaf, which the binders would tie and form into shocks. When the maidens had gathered up the scattered handfuls thrown down by the reapers, Ruth picked up any straggling heads or ears which they had left.

9. *The young men that they shall not touch thee.* This was peculiarly necessary, as she was a stranger and unprotected.

10. *Then she fell on her face.* Prostrated herself, as was the custom in the East when inferiors approached those of superior rank.

12. *The Lord recompense thy work.* The dutiful respect which you have paid to your husband, and your tender and affectionate attachment to your aged mother-in-law. *And a full reward be given thee.* This is spoken with great modesty and piety: The kindness I show you is little in comparison of your desert; God alone can give you a *full reward* for your kindness to your husband and mother-in-law; and He will do it, because you are come to trust under His wings—to become a proselyte to His religion. It is evident from this that Ruth had already attached herself to the Jewish religion.

13. *Not like unto one of thine handmaidens.* I am as unworthy of your regards as any of your own maidservants, and yet you show me distinguished kindness.

14. *Dip thy morsel in the vinegar.* The *chomets,* which we here translate *vinegar,* seems to have been some refreshing kind of acid sauce used by the reapers to dip their bread in, which both cooled and refreshed them. *Parched corn.* This was a frequent repast among the ancients in almost countries.

15. *Let her glean even among the sheaves.* This was a privilege; for no person should glean till the sheaves were all bound, and the shocks set up.

17. *An ephah of barley.* Not less than seven gallons and a half; a good day's work.

18. *And gave to her that she had reserved.* As Ruth had received a distinct portion at dinnertime, of which she had more than she could eat, v. 14; it appears she brought the rest home to her mother-in-law, as is here related.

20. *To the living and to the dead.* Naomi and Ruth were the living; and they were also the representatives of Elimelech and Mahlon, who were dead. *One of our next kinsmen. Miggoaleynu,* or our "redeemers"; one who has the right to redeem the forfeited inheritance of the family. The word *goel* signifies a "near kinsman"—one who by the Mosiac law had a right to redeem an inheritance.

21. *Keep fast by my young men.* The word *hannearim* should be translated "servants," both the male and female being included in it; the latter especially, as we see in vv. 22-23.

23. *And of wheat harvest.* That is, she was to continue gleaning in the farm of Boaz to the end of the barley harvest; and then, when the wheat harvest began, to continue to its conclusion in the same way. In the interim, as well as each night, she lodged with her mother-in-law.

CHAPTER 3

Naomi's advice to Ruth, how to procure herself a marriage with Boaz, 1-5. She acts according to her mother-in-law's direction, and is kindly received by Boaz, who promises to marry her, should her nearer kinsman refuse, 6-13. He gives her six measures of barley, and sends her away privately to her mother-in-law, who augurs favorably of the issue of the plan she had laid, 14-18.

1. *Shall I not seek rest for thee?* That is, Shall I not endeavor to procure you a proper husband?

2. *He winnoweth barley to night.* It is very likely that the winnowing of grain was effected by taking up, in a broad, thin vessel or sieve, a portion of the corn, and letting it down slowly in the wind. It is said here that this was done at night; probably what was threshed out in the day was winnowed in the evening, when the sea breeze set in, which was common in Palestine.

3. *Wash thyself therefore.* She made Ruth put on her best dress, that Boaz might, in the course of the day, be the more attracted by her person, and be the better disposed to receive her as Naomi wished.

4. *Uncover his feet, and lay thee down.* It is said that women in the East, when going to the bed of their lawful husbands, through modesty, and in token of subjection, go to the bed's foot, and gently raising the clothes, creep under them up to their place.

7. *Went to lie down.* As the threshing floors of the Eastern nations are in general in the open air, it is very likely that the owner continued in the fields till the grain was secured, having a tent in the place where the corn was threshed and winnowed. Boaz seems to have acted thus.

9. *Spread therefore thy skirt over thine handmaid.* Hebrew, "Spread thy wing." The wing is the emblem of protection, and is a metaphor taken from the young of fowls, which run under the wings of their mothers, that they may be saved from birds of prey. The meaning here is, "Take me to thee for wife."

10. *In the latter end than at the beginning.* It is not easy to find out what Boaz means. Perhaps *chesed,* which we translate *kindness,* means "piety"; as if he had said: You have given great proof of your piety in this latter instance, when you have avoided the young, and those of your own age, to associate yourself with an elderly man, merely for the purpose of having the divine injunction fulfilled, viz., that the brother, or next akin, might take the wife of the deceased, and raise a family to him who had died childless, that his name might not become extinct in Israel. *Whether poor or rich.* So it appears from this that it was not to mend her condition in life that Ruth endeavored to get Boaz for her husband, for she might have had a rich young man, but she preferred the building up the house of her deceased husband.

12. *There is a kinsman nearer than I.* It is very likely that Naomi was not acquainted with this circumstance.

13. *As the Lord liveth.* Thus he bound himself by an oath to take her to wife if the other should refuse.

15. *Bring the veil.* This seems to have been a cloak. *Six measures of barley.* We supply the word *measures,* for the Hebrew mentions no quantity. If the omer be meant, which is about six pints, this would amount to but about four gallons and a half.

CHAPTER 4

Boaz gathers a council of the elders at the city gates, states the case, and proposes to the nearest kinsman to redeem the inheritance of Elimelech, and take Ruth to wife, 1-5. The kinsman refuses, and relinquishes his right to Boaz, 6. The manner of redemption in such cases, 7-8. Boaz redeems the inheritance in the presence of the elders, and of the people, who witness the contract, and pray for God's blessing upon the marriage, 9-12. Boaz takes Ruth for wife, and she bears a son, 13. The people's observations on the birth of the child, 14-15. It is given to Naomi to nurse, 16. The neighboring women name the child, and the book concludes with the genealogy of David, 17-22.

1. *Then went Boaz up to the gate.* We have often had occasion to remark that the *gate* or entrance to any city or town was the place where the court of justice was ordinarily kept. *Ho, such a one! . . . sit down here.* This familiar mode of compellation is first used here. The original is *shebah poh, peloni almoni!* "Hark ye, Mr. Such-a-one of such a place! come and sit down here." This is used when the person of the individual is known, and his name and residence unknown. *Almoni* comes from *alam,* "to be silent or hidden"; hence the Septuagint render it by "thou unknown person": *peloni* comes from *palah,* "to sever or distinguish"; you of such a particular place.

2. *He took ten men.* Probably it required this number to constitute a court. How simple and how rational was this proceeding!

4. *I thought to advertise thee.* Both Kennicott and Houbigant have noticed several corruptions in the pronouns of this and the following verses; and their criticisms have been confirmed by a great number of MSS. since collated. The text corrected reads thus: "And I said I will reveal this to thy ear, saying, Buy it before the inhabitants, and before the elders of my people. If thou wilt redeem it, redeem it; but if thou wilt not redeem it, tell me, that I may know; for there is none to redeem it but thou, and I who am next to thee. And he said, I will redeem it. And Boaz said, In the day that thou redeemest the land from the hand of Naomi, thou wilt also acquire Ruth, the wife of the dead, that thou mayest raise up the name of the dead upon his inheritance," vv. 4-5.
I will redeem it. I will pay down the money which it is worth. He knew not of the following condition.

5. *Thou must buy it also of Ruth.* More properly, "Thou wilt also acquire Ruth." You cannot get the land without taking the wife of the deceased; and then the children which you may have shall be reputed the children of Mahlon, your deceased kinsman.

6. *I cannot redeem it for myself.* The Targum

gives the proper sense of this passage: "And the kinsman said, On this ground I cannot redeem it because I have a wife already; and I have no desire to take another, lest there should be contention in my house, and I should become a corrupter of my inheritance. Do thou redeem it, for thou hast no wife; for I cannot redeem it."

7. *A man plucked off his shoe.* The law of such a case is given at large in Deut. xxv. 5-9. It was simply this: If a brother, who had married a wife, died without children, the eldest brother was to take the widow, and raise up a family to the brother deceased; and he had a right to redeem the inheritance, if it had been alienated. But if the person who had the right of redemption would not take the woman, she was to pull off his shoe and spit in his face; and he was ever after considered as a disgraced man. In the present case the shoe only is taken off, probably because the circumstances of the man were such as to render it improper for him to redeem the ground and take Ruth to his wife; and because of this reasonable excuse, the contemptuous part of the ceremony is omitted.

11. *We are witnesses.* It is not very likely that any writing was drawn up. There was an appeal made to the people then present, whether they had seen and understood the transaction; who answered, "We have witnessed it." *The Lord make the woman . . . like Rachel and like Leah.* May your family be increased by her means, as the tribes were formed by means of Rachel and Leah, wives of the patriarch Jacob! *Which two did build the house of Israel.* We have already seen that *ben,* a "son," comes from the root *banah,* "he built"; and hence *eben,* a "stone," because as a house is built of stones, so is a family of children.

12. *Like the house of Pharez.* This was very appropriate; for from Pharez, the son of Judah, by Tamar, came the family of the Bethlehemites and that of Elimelech.

13. *So Boaz took Ruth.* The law of Moses had prohibited the Moabites, even to the tenth generation, from entering into the congregation of the Lord; but this law, the Jews think, did not extend to women; and even if it had, Ruth's might be considered an exempt case, as she already had been incorporated into the family by marriage; and left her own country, people, and gods, to become a proselyte to the true God in the land of Israel.

15. *Better to thee than seven sons.* If Naomi had had even a numerous family of sons, it is most likely that they would have been scattered to different quarters from her, and settled in life; whereas Ruth cleaved to her, and it was by her affectionate services that Naomi was preserved alive.

17. *Her neighbours gave it a name.* That is, they recommended a name suitable to the circumstances of the case; and the parents and grandmother adopted it. *They called his name Obed.* "Serving," from *abad,* "he served." Why was this name given? Because he was to be the "nourisher of her old age," v. 15. *He is the father of Jesse, the father of David.* And for the sake of this conclusion, to ascertain the line of David, and in the counsel of God to fix and ascertain the line of the Messiah, was this instructive little book written.

19. *Hezron begat Ram.* He is called Aram here by the Septuagint, and also by Matthew, chap. i. 3.

20. *Amminadab begat Nahshon.* The Targum adds, "And Nahshon was chief of the house of his father in the tribe of Judah."

The ten persons whose genealogy is recorded in the last five verses may be found, with a trifling change of name, in the genealogical list in Matt. i. 3-6, as forming important links in the line of the Messiah. To introduce this appears to have been the principal object of the writer, as introductory to the following books, where the history of David, the regal progenitor and type of the Messiah, is so particularly detailed.

The First Book of
SAMUEL

This and the three following books were formerly termed the First, Second, Third, and Fourth Books of Kings; and the two Books of Samuel made, in ancient times, but one. These books are, properly speaking, a continuation of the Book of Judges, as they give us an account of the remaining judges of Israel, down to the election of Saul; and of all the kings of Israel and Judah to the Babylonish captivity.

Of this book, called the First Book of Samuel, the following are the contents: The birth and education of Samuel; the high priesthood of Eli; the Philistines attack the Israelites, overthrow them with a terrible slaughter, take the ark of the Lord, and set it up in the temple of their god Dagon; they are visited with divine judgments, and are obliged to send back the ark with offerings and presents; Samuel, long acknowledged as a prophet of the Lord, takes the government of the people. Under his wise and pious administration, the affairs of Israel become reestablished, and the Philistines are subdued. The sons of Samuel, who principally administered the secular concerns of the kingdom, acting unworthily, the people desire to have a king, who should be supreme in both civil and military affairs. Samuel, after expostulations, yields to their entreaties; and, under the direction of God, Saul, the son of Kish, while seeking the lost asses of his father, is met by the prophet, and anointed king over Israel. This man, not conducting himself in the government according to the direction of God, is rejected, and David, the son of Jesse, anointed king in his place, though Saul continues still in the government. This person soon becomes advantageously known to Israel by his single combat with a gigantic Philistine chief, called Goliath, whom he slays; on which the Israelites attack the Philistines, and give them a total overthrow. Saul, envious of David's popularity, seeks his destruction; he is in consequence obliged to escape for his life, and take refuge sometimes among the Moabites, sometimes among the Philistines, and sometimes in the caves of the mountains of Judah, everywhere pursued by Saul, and everywhere visibly protected by the Lord. At last Saul, being pressed by the Philistines, and finding that the Lord has forsaken him, has recourse to a witch that dwelt at Endor, whom he consults relative to the issue of the present war with the Philistines; he loses the battle, and being sorely wounded, and his three sons slain, he falls on his own sword, and expires on Mount Gilboa.

The Philistines find his body, and the bodies of his three sons, among the slain; they cut off Saul's head, and affix the bodies to the walls of Beth-shan. The men of Jabesh-gilead, hearing this, go by night, and takes the bodies from the walls of Beth-shan, bring them to Jabesh, burn them there, bury the bones, and mourn over their fallen king, fasting seven days. Thus concludes the First Book of Samuel.

Concerning the author of these books there have been various conjectures. Because in most of the Hebrew copies they bear the name of Samuel as a running title, it has been generally supposed that he was the author. But his name does not appear to have been anciently prefixed to these books, at least in those copies used by the Greek interpreters, commonly called the Septuagint, as they simply term each "The History (or Book) of Kingdoms." The Jews, in general, believe that Samuel is the author of the first twenty-seven chapters of this book, which contain the history of his own life and government, and what respects Saul and David during that time. The remaining four chapters they suppose were added by the prophets Gad and Nathan. This opinion is founded on what is said in 1 Chron. xxix. 29: "Now the acts of David the king, first and last, behold, they are written in the book of Samuel the seer, and in the book of Nathan the prophet, and in the book of Gad the seer." Others suppose the books to be more recent than the persons already named, but that they were compiled out of their memoirs.

But who was the compiler? Some of the most learned among the Jews supposed it to have been Jeremiah, the prophet, and that the style bears a near resemblance to his prophecies. That they were the work of a more recent author than Samuel, Grotius thinks evident from this circumstance, that the names of the months are comparatively modern, and were not known among the ancient Jews. Others have atributed them to David; others, to Hezekiah; and others, to Ezra the scribe on his return from the Babylonish captivity.

Calmet's opinion is as probable as any, viz., "That these books were written by the same hand, though composed out of the memoirs left by persons of that time; and that the compiler has generally used the same terms he found in those memoirs, adding here and there something of his own by way of illustration."

CHAPTER 1

Some account of Elkanah and his two wives, Peninnah and Hannah, 1-2. His annual worship at Shiloh and the portions he gave at such times to his wives, 3-5. Hannah, being barren, is reproached by Peninnah, especially in their going up to Shiloh; at which she is sorely grieved, 6-7. Elkanah comforts her, 8. Her prayer and vow in the temple, that if God would give her a son, she would consecrate him to His service, 9-11. Eli, the high priest, indistinctly hearing her pray, charges her with being drunk, 12-14. Her defense of her conduct, 15-16. Eli, undeceived, blesses her; on which she takes courage, 17-18. Hannah and Elkanah return home; she conceives. bears a son, and calls him Samuel, 19-20. Elkanah and his family go again to Shiloh to worship; but Hannah stays at home to nurse her child, purposing, as soon as he is weaned, to go and offer him to the Lord, according to her vow, 21-23. When weaned, she takes him to Shiloh, presents her child to Eli to be consecrated to the Lord, and offers three bullocks, an ephah of flour, and a bottle of wine, for his consecration, 24-28.

1. *Ramathaim-zophim.* Literally, "the two high places of the watchman"; these were, no doubt, two contiguous hills, on which watch-towers were built, and in which watchmen kept continual guard for the safety of the country, and which afterwards gave name to the place.

2. *He had two wives.* The custom of those times permitted polygamy; but wherever there was more than one wife, we find the peace of the family greatly disturbed by it. *The name of the one was Hannah.* Channah, which signifies "fixed" or "settled"; and *the other Peninnah,* which signifies a "jewel" or "pearl."

3. *Went up out of his city yearly to worship.* As the ark was at Shiloh, there was the temple of God, and thither all the males were bound by the law to go once a year, on each of the great national festivals: viz., the Passover, Pentecost, and Feast of Tabernacles.

The Lord of hosts. Yehovah tsebaoth, "Jehovah of armies." As all the heavenly bodies were called the "hosts of heaven," tseba hash-shamayim, Jehovah being called Lord of this host showed that He was their Maker and Governor; and consequently He, not they, was the proper object of religious worship. The sun, moon, planets, and stars were the highest objects of religious worship to the heathen in general. The Jewish religion, teaching the knowlegde of a Being who was the Lord of all these, showed at once its superiority to all that heathenism could boast. This is the first place where *Lord of hosts* is mentioned in the Bible; and this is so much in the style of the prophets Isaiah, Jeremiah, that it gives some weight to the supposition that this book was written by a person who lived in or after the times of these prophets.

4. *He gave . . . portions.* The sacrifices which were made were probably peace offerings, of which the blood was poured out at the foot of the altar; the fat was burnt on the fire; the breast and right shoulder were the portion of the priest; and the rest belonged to him who made the offering; on it he and his family feasted, each receiving his portion; and to these feasts God commands them to invite the Levite, the poor, the widow, and the orphan, Deut. xvi. 11.

5. *Unto Hannah he gave a worthy portion.* The Hebrew here is very obscure; "He gave her one portion of two faces." As the showbread that was presented to the Lord was called the "bread of faces," because it was placed before the face or appearances of the Lord; probably this was called *manah appayim,* because it was the portion that belonged to, or was placed before, the person who had offered the sacrifice. On this ground it might be said that Elkanah gave Hannah his own portion, or a part of that which was placed before himself. Whatever it was, it was intended as a proof of his especial love to her.

6. *And her adversary.* That is, Peninnah. *Provoked her sore.* Was constantly striving to irritate and vex her, *to make her fret*—to make her discontented with her lot, because the Lord had denied her children.

7. *And as he did so year by year.* As the whole family went up to Shiloh to the annual festivals, Peninnah had both sons and daughters to accompany her, v. 4, but Hannah had none; and Peninnah took this opportunity particularly to twit Hannah with her barrenness, by making an ostentatious exhibition of her children. *Therefore she wept.* She was greatly distressed, because it was a great reproach to a woman among the Jews to be barren; because, say some, everyone hoped that the Messiah should spring from her line.

8. *Am not I better to thee than ten sons?* Ten, a certain for an uncertain number. Is not my especial affection for you better than all the comfort you could gain, even from a numerous family?

9. *Eli . . . sat upon a seat.* Al hakkisse, upon the throne, i.e., of judgment; for he was then judge of Israel. *By a post of the temple of the Lord.* I think this is the first place where heychal Yehovah, "temple of Jehovah," is mentioned. This gives room for a strong suspicion that the Books of Samuel were not compiled till the first Temple was built, or after the days of Solomon. After this the word *temple* is frequent in the books of Kings, Chronicles, and in the prophets.

11. *I will give him unto the Lord.* Samuel, as a descendant of the house of Levi, was the

Lord's property from twenty-five years of age till fifty; but the vow here implies that he should be consecrated to the Lord from his infancy to his death, and that he should act not only as a Levite, but as a Nazarite, on whose head no razor should pass.

13. *Spake in her heart; only her lips moved.* She prayed; her whole heart was engaged. And though she spake not with an audible voice, yet her lips formed themselves according to the pronunciation of the words which her *heart* uttered.

15. *I have drunk neither wine nor strong drink.* "Neither wine nor inebriating drink has been *poured out unto me;* but I have poured out my soul unto the Lord." There is a great deal of delicacy and point in this vindication.

16. *Count not thine handmaid for a daughter of Belial.* "Put not thy handmaiden before the faces of a daughter of Belial." "If I am a drunkard, and strive by the most execrable hypocrisy (praying in the house of God) to cover my iniquity, then I am the chief of the daughters of Belial." Or, "Give not thy handmaid (to reproach) before the faces of the daughters of Belial."

17. *Grant thee thy petition.* He was satisfied he had formed a wrong judgment, and by it had added to the distress of one already sufficiently distressed. The fact that Eli supposed her to be *drunken,* and the other of the conduct of Eli's sons, prove that religion was at this time at a very low ebb in Shiloh; for it seems drunken women did come to the place, and lewd women were to be found there.

18. *Let thine handmaid find grace.* Continue to think favorably of me, and to pray for me.

20. *Called his name Samuel.* As she gave this name to her son because she had *asked him of the Lord,* the word *Shemuel* must be here considerably contracted; if it express this sentiment, the component parts of it are the following: *shaul meEl,* "asked of God." This name would put both the mother and the son in continual remembrance of the divine interposition at his birth (see on v. 28).

21. *The man Elkanah, and all his house.* He and the whole of his family, Hannah and her child excepted, who purposed not to go up to Shiloh till her son was old enough to be employed in the divine service. *And his vow.* Probably he had also made some vow to the Lord on the occasion of his wife's prayer and vow; in which, from his love to her, he could not be less interested than herself.

24. *With three bullocks.* The Septuagint, the Syriac, and the Arabic read, "a bullock of three years old"; and this is probably correct, because we read, v. 25, that they slew "the bullock." We hear of no more, and we know that a bullock or heifer of three years old was ordinarily used; see Gen. xv. 9. *One ephah of flour.* Seven gallons and a half. *A bottle of wine.* "A skin full of wine." Their bottles for wine and fluids in general were made out of skins of goats, stripped off without being cut up; the places whence the legs were extracted sewed up, as also the lower part; and the top tied. These three things, the ox, the flour, and the wine, probably constituted the consecration offering.

26. *As thy soul liveth.* As sure as you are a living soul, so surely am I the person who stood by you here praying.

28. *Therefore also I have lent him to the Lord.* There is here a continual reference to her vow, and to the words which she used in making that vow. The word "Samuel," as we have already seen, is a contraction of the words *Shaul meEl,* that is, "asked or lent of God"; for his mother said, v. 27, "The Lord hath given me my petition, which [*shaalti*] I asked of him." In v. 28 she says: *hu shaul layhovah,* "He shall be lent unto the Lord." Here we find the verb is the same; and it is remarked by grammarians that *shaal,* "he asked," making in the participle *pahul shaul,* "asked," in the conjugation *hiphil* signifies to "lend"; therefore, says his mother, v. 28, *hishiltihu layhovah,* "I have lent him to the Lord." This twofold meaning of the Hebrew root is not only followed by our translators, but also by the Vulgate, Septuagint, and Syriac.

And he worshipped the Lord there. Instead of *he worshipped,* "they worshipped" is the reading of six of Kennicott's and De Rossi's MSS., of some copies of the Septuagint, and of the Vulgate, Syriac, and Arabic.

CHAPTER 2

Hannah's prophetic hymn, 1-10. Samuel ministers to the Lord, 11. The abominable conduct of Eli's sons, 12-17. Further account of Samuel, and of the divine blessing on Elkanah and Hannah, 18-21. Eli's reprehensible remissness towards his sons in not retraining them in their great profligacy, 22-26. The message of God to Eli, and the prophecy of the downfall of his family, and slaughter of his wicked sons, Hophni and Phinehas, 27-36.

1. *And Hannah prayed, and said.* The Chaldee very properly says, "And Hannah prayed in the spirit of prophecy"; for indeed the whole of this prayer, or as it may be properly called "oracular declaration," is a piece of regular prophecy, every part of it having respect to the future, and perhaps not a little of it declaratory of the Messiah's kingdom. In the best MSS. the whole of this hymn is written in hemistich or poetic lines. I shall here produce it in this order, following the plan as exhibited in Kennicott's Bible, with some trifling alterations of our present version:

1. *My heart exulteth in Jehovah;*
   My horn is exalted in Jehovah.
   My mouth is incited over mine enemies,
   For I have rejoiced in thy salvation.
2. *There is none holy like Jehovah,*
   For there is none besides thee;
   There is no rock like our God.
3. *Do not magnify yourselves, speak not proudly, proudly.*
   Let not prevarication come out of your mouth;
   For the God of knowledge is Jehovah,
   And by him actions are directed.
4. *The bows of the heroes are broken,*
   And the tottering are girded with strength.
5. *The full have hired out themselves for bread,*
   And the famished cease for ever.
   The barren hath borne seven,
   And she who had many children is greatly enfeebled.
6. *Jehovah killeth, and maketh alive;*
   He bringeth down to the grave, and bringeth up.

7. *Jehovah maketh poor, and maketh rich;*
   He bringeth down, and he even exalteth.
8. *He lifteth up the poor from the dust;*
   From the dunghill he exalteth the beggar,
   To make him sit with the nobles,
   And inherit the throne of glory.
   For to Jehovah belong the pillars of the
   earth,
   And upon them he hath placed the globe.
9. *The foot of his saints he shall keep*
   And the wicked shall be silent in dark-
   ness;
   For by strength shall no man prevail.
10. *Jehovah shall bruise them who contend*
    with him;
    Upon them shall be thunder in the earth;
    And he shall give strength to his King,
    And shall exalt the horn of his Messiah.

It is not particularly stated here when Hannah composed or delivered this hymn; it appears from the connection to have been at the very time in which she dedicated her son to God at the Tabernacle, though some think that she composed it immediately on the birth of Samuel. The former sentiment is probably the most correct.

Mine horn is exalted in the Lord. We have often seen that *horn* signifies power, might, and dominion. It is thus constantly used in the Bible, and was so used among the heathens. *My mouth is enlarged.* My faculty of speech is "incited, stirred up," to express God's disapprobation against my adversaries.

2. *None holy.* Holiness is peculiar to the God of Israel; no false god ever pretended to holiness. It was no attribute of heathenism, nor of any religion ever professed in the world before or since the true revelation of the true God. *There is none beside thee.* There can be but one unoriginated, infinite, and eternal Being; that Being is Jehovah. *Any rock like our God.* Rabbi Maimon has observed that the word *tsur*, which we translate *rock*, signifies, when applied to Jehovah, "fountain, source, spring." There is no source whence continual help and salvation can arise but our God.

3. *A God of knowledge.* He is the most wise, teaching all good, and knowing all things. *Actions are weighed.* Nithkenu, they are "directed"; it is by His counsel alone that we can successfully begin, continue, or end, any work.

5. *They that were full.* All the things mentioned in these verses frequently happen in the course of the divine providence; and indeed it is the particular providence of God that Hannah seems more especially to celebrate through the whole of this simple yet sublime ode.

6. *The Lord killeth.* God is the Arbiter of life and death; He only can give life, and He only has a right to take it away. *He bringeth down to the grave.* The Hebrew word *sheol*, which we translate *grave*, seems to have the same meaning in the Old Testament with *hades* in the New, which is the word generally used by the Septuagint for the other. It means the grave, the state of the dead, and the invisible place, or place of separate spirits. Sometimes we translate it "hell," which now means the state of perdition, or place of eternal torments. The Targum seems to understand it of death and the resurrection. "He kills and commands to give life; he causes to descend into Sheol, that in the time to come he may bring them into the lives of eternity," i.e., the life of shame and everlasting contempt, and the life of glory.

7. *The Lord maketh poor.* For many cannot bear affluence, and if God should continue to trust them with riches, they would be their ruin. *Maketh rich.* Some He can trust, and therefore makes them stewards of His secular bounty.

8. *To set them among princes.* There have been many cases where, in the course of God's providence, a person has been raised from the lowest and most abject estate to the highest; from the plough to the imperial dignity; from the dungeon to the throne; from the dunghill to nobility. The story is well-known of the patriarch Joseph. *For the pillars of the earth are the Lord's.* He is almighty, and upholds all things by the word of His power.

9. *He will keep the feet of his saints.* He will order and direct all their goings, and keep them from every evil way. The wicked shall be silent in darkness. The Targum understands this of their being sent to the darkness of hell; they shall be slain. *By strength shall no man prevail.* Because God is omnipotent, and no power can be successfully exerted against Him.

10. *The adversaries of the Lord shall be broken.* Those who "contend with him" by sinning against His laws, opposing the progress of His word, or persecuting His people. *Shall judge the ends of the earth.* His empire shall be extended over all mankind by the preaching of the everlasting gospel, for to this the afterpart of the verse seems to apply: "He shall give strength unto his king, and shall exalt the horn of his anointed [Christ]," or, as the Targum says, "He shall multiply the kingdom of the Messiah." Here *the horn* means spiritual as well as secular dominion.

12. *The sons of Eli were sons of Belial.* They were perverse, wicked, profligate men.

13. *When any man offered sacrifice.* That is, when a peace offering was brought, the right shoulder and the breast belonged to the priest, the fat was burnt upon the altar, and the blood was poured at the bottom of the altar; the rest of the flesh belonged to the offerer. Under pretense of taking only their own part, they took the best of all they chose, and as much as they chose.

15. *Before they burnt the fat.* They would serve themselves before God was served! This was iniquity and arrogance of the first magnitude. *He will not have sodden flesh.* He chooses roast meat, not boiled; and if they had it in the pot before the servant came, he took it out that it might be roasted.

17. *Wherefore the sin of the young men was very great.* That is, Hophni and Phinehas, the sons of Eli. *Men abhorred the offering.* As the people saw that the priests had no piety, and that they acted as if there was no God, they despised God's service, and became infidels.

19. *Made him a little coat.* "A little cloak," an upper garment; probably intended to keep him from the cold, and to save his other clothes from being abused in his meaner services. It is probable that she furnished him with a new

one each year, when she came up to one of the annual sacrifices.

20. *Eli blessed Elkanah.* The natural place of this verse seems to be before the eleventh; after which the twenty-first should come in; after the twenty-first, perhaps the twenty-sixth should come in. The subjects in this chapter seem very much entangled and confused by the wrong position of the verses.

22. *They lay with the women that assembled.* It is probable that these were persons who had some employment about the Tabernacle. See the note on Exod. xxxviii. 8, where the Hebrew text is similar to that in this place.

23. *Why do ye such things?* Eli appears to have been a fondly affectionate, easy father, who wished his sons to do well, but did not bring them under proper discipline, and did not use his authority to restrain them. As judge, he had power to cast them immediately out of the vineyard, as wicked and unprofitable servants; this he did not, and his and their ruin was the consequence.

25. *If one man sin against another.* All differences between man and man may be settled by the proper judge; but if a man sin against the Supreme Judge, God himself, who shall reconcile him to his Maker? Your sin is immediately against God himself, and is the highest insult that can be offered, because it is in the matter of His own worship; therefore you may expect His heaviest judgments. *Because the Lord would slay them.* The particle *ki*, which we translate *because*, and thus make their continuance in sin the effect of God's determination to destroy them, should be translated "therefore," as it means in many parts of the sacred writings.

27. *There came a man of God.* Who this was we know not, but the Chaldee terms him *nebiya daya*, "a prophet of Jehovah." Unto the *house of thy father.* That is, to Aaron; he was the first high priest; the priesthood descended from him to his eldest son, Eleazar, then to Phinehas. Afterwards it became established in the younger branch of the family of Aaron; for Eli was a descendant of Ithamar, Aaron's youngest son. From Eli it was transferred back again to the family of Eleazar, because of the profligacy of Eli's sons.

28. *And did I choose him?* The high priesthood was a place of the greatest honor that could be conferred on man, and a place of considerable emolument; for from their part of the sacrifices they derived a most comfortable livelihood.

29. *Wherefore kick ye at my sacrifice?* They disdained to take the part allowed by law, and would take for themselves what part they pleased, and as much as they pleased, vv. 13-16; thus they kicked at the sacrifices. *Honourest thy sons above me.* Permitting them to deal, as above, with the offerings and sacrifices, and take their part before the fat, etc., was burned unto the Lord; thus they were first served. At this Eli connived, and thus honored his sons above God.

30. *Should walk before me for ever.* See Exod. xxix. 9; xl. 15; Num. xxv. 10-13, where it is positively promised that the priesthood should be continued in the family of Aaron forever. But although this promise appears to be absolute, yet we plainly see that, like all other apparently absolute promises of God, it is conditional, i.e., a condition is implied though not expressed. *But now . . . be it far from me.* You have walked unworthily; I shall annul My promise, and reverse My ordinance (see Jer. xviii. 8, 10). *For them that honour me.* This is a plan from which God will never depart; this can have no alteration; every promise is made in reference to it: They who honor God shall be honored; they who despise Him "shall be lightly esteemed."

31. *I will cut off thine arm.* I will destroy the strength, power, and influence of your family.

32. *Thou shalt see an enemy in my habitation.* Every version and almost every commentator understands this clause differently. The word *tsar*, which we translate an *enemy*, and the Vulgate a "rival," signifies "calamity"; and this is the best sense to understand it in here. The calamity which he saw was the defeat of the Israelites, the capture of the ark, the death of his wicked sons, and the triumph of the Philistines. All this he saw, that is, knew to have taken place, before he met with his own tragical death. *In all the wealth which God shall give Israel.* This also is dark. The meaning may be this: God has spoken good concerning Israel; He will, in the end, make the triumph of the Philistines their own confusion; and the capture of the ark shall be the desolation of their gods; but the Israelites shall first be sorely pressed with calamity. *There shall not be an old man.* This is repeated from the preceding verse; all the family shall die in the flower of their years, as is said in the following verse.

34. *They shall die both of them.* Hophni and Phinehas were both killed very shortly after in the great battle with the Philistines in which the Israelites were completely routed, and the ark taken (see chap. iv).

35. *A faithful priest.* This seems to have been spoken of Zadok, who was anointed high priest in the room of Abiathar, the last descendant of the house of Eli (see 1 Kings ii. 26-27). Abiathar was removed because he had joined with Adonijah, who had got himself proclaimed king (see 1 Kings i. 7). *I will build him a sure house.* I will continue the priesthood in his family. *He shall walk before mine anointed.* He shall minister before Solomon, and the kings which shall reign in the land. The Targum says, "He shall walk before my Messiah," and the Septuagint expresses it, "before my Christ."

36. *Shall come and crouch to him.* Shall prostrate himself before him in the most abject manner, begging to be employed even in the meanest offices about the Tabernacle, in order to get even the most scanty means of support. *A morsel of bread.* A mouthful; what might be sufficient to keep body and soul together. See the sin and its punishment. They formerly pampered themselves, and fed to the full on the Lord's sacrifices; and now they are reduced to a *morsel of bread.*

CHAPTER 3

Samuel ministers to the Lord before Eli, 1. He is thrice called by the Lord, who informs him of the evils which shall be brought on the house of Eli, 2-15. Eli inquires of Samuel what the Lord had said, 16-17. He gives a faithful relation of the whole, which Eli receives with great submission, 18. Samuel prospers; is established as a prophet in Israel; and the Lord reveals himself to him in Shiloh, 19-21.

1. *Samuel ministered unto the Lord.* He performed minor services in the Tabernacle, under the direction of Eli, such as opening the doors, etc. (see v. 15). *The word of the Lord was precious.* There were but few revelations from God; and because the word was scarce, therefore it was valuable. The author of this book probably lived at a time when prophecy was frequent. *There was no open vision.* There was no public accredited prophet; one with whom the secret of the Lord was known to dwell, and to whom all might have recourse in cases of doubt or public emergency.

2. *Eli was laid down in his place.* It is very likely that, as the ark was a long time at Shiloh, they had built near to it certain apartments for the high priest and others more immediately employed about the Tabernacle. In one of these, near to that of Eli, perhaps under the same roof, Samuel lay when he was called by the Lord.

3. *Ere the lamp of God went out.* Before sunrise; for it is likely that the lamps were extinguished before the rising of the sun (see Exod. xxvii. 21; Lev. xxiv. 3).

4. *The Lord called Samuel.* The voice probably came from the holy place, near to which Eli and Samuel were both lying.

7. *Samuel did not yet know the Lord.* He had not been accustomed to receive any revelation from Him. He knew and worshipped the God of Israel; but he did not know Him as communicating especial revelation of His will.

9. *Speak, Lord; for thy servant heareth.* This was the usual way in which the prophets spoke when they had intimations that the Lord was about to make some especial revelation.

10. *The Lord came, and stood.* He heard the voice as if it was approaching nearer and nearer, till at last, from the sameness of the tone, he could imagine that it ceased to approach; and this is what appears to be represented under the notion of God standing and calling.

11. *The Lord said to Samuel.* He probably saw nothing, and only heard the voice; for it was not likely that any extraordinary representation could have been made to the eyes of a person so young. *The ears . . . shall tingle.* It shall be a piercing word to all Israel; it shall astound them all; and, after having heard it, it will still continue to resound in their ears.

12. *I will perform . . . all things which I have spoken.* That is, what He had declared by the prophet, whose message is related in chap. ii. 27, etc. *When I begin, I will also make an end.* I will not delay the execution of My purpose: when I begin, nothing shall deter Me from bringing all My judgments to a conclusion.

13. *I will judge his house for ever.* I will continue to execute judgments upon it till it is destroyed. *His sons made themselves vile* (see chap. ii. 12-17, 22-25). *He restrained them not.* He did not use his parental and juridical authority to curb them, and prevent the disorders which they committed.

14. *Shall not be purged with sacrifice nor offering.* That is, God was determined that they

should be removed by a violent death. They had committed the sin unto death; and no offering or sacrifice could prevent this. What is spoken here relates to their temporal death only.

15. *Samuel feared to show Eli.* He reverenced him as a father, and he feared to distress him by showing what the Lord had purposed to do.

17. *God do so to thee, and more also.* This was a very solemn adjuration; he suspected that God had threatened severe judgments, for he knew that his house was very criminal; and he wished to know what God had spoken. The words imply thus much: If thou do not tell me fully what God has threatened, may the same and greater curses fall on thyself.

18. *Samuel told him every whit.* "Everything." The Hebrew, "all these words." *It is the Lord.* He is sovereign, and will do what He pleases; He is righteous, and will do nothing but what is just. *Let him do what seemeth him good.* There is much of a godly submission, as well as a deep sense of his own unworthiness, found in these words. He also had sinned, so as to be punished with temporal death; but surely there is no evidence that the displeasure of the Lord against him was extended to a future state.

20. *All Israel from Dan even to Beer-sheba.* Through the whole extent of Palestine; Dan being at the northern, Beer-sheba at the southern extremity. *Was established to be a prophet.* The word *neeman,* which we translate established, signifies "faithful": "The faithful Samuel was a prophet of the Lord."

21. *The Lord appeared again.* "And Jehovah added to appear"; that is, He continued to reveal himself to Samuel at Shiloh. *By the word of the Lord.* By the spirit and word of prophecy.

CHAPTER 4

A battle between Israel and the Philistines, in which the former are defeated, with the loss of 4,000 men, 1-2. They resolve to give the Philistines battle once more, and bring the ark of the Lord, with Hophni and Phinehas, the priests, into the camp, 3-4. They do so, and become vainly confident, 5. At this the Philistines are dismayed, 6-9. The battle commences; the Israelites are again defeated, with the loss of 30,000 men; Hophni and Phinehas are among the slain; and the ark of the Lord is taken, 10-11. A Benjamite runs with the news to Eli; who, hearing of the capture of the ark, falls from his seat, and breaks his neck, 12-18. The wife of Phinehas, hearing of the death of her husband, and father-in-law, and of the capture of the ark, is taken in untimely travail, brings forth a son, calls him Ichabod, and expires, 19-22.

1. *The word of Samuel came to all Israel.* This clause certainly belongs to the preceding chapter, and is so placed by the Vulgate, Septuagint, Syriac, and Arabic. *Pitched beside Eben-ezer.* This name was not given to this place till more than twenty years after this battle (see chap. vii. 12; for the monument called the "Stone of Help" was erected by Samuel in the place which was afterwards, from this circumstance, called Ebenezer when the Lord had given the Israelites a signal victory over the Philistines. It was situated in the tribe of Judah, between Mizpeh and Shen, and not far from the Aphek here mentioned. This is another proof that this book was compiled after the times and transactions which it records, and probably from memoranda which had been made by a contemporary writer.

3. *Let us fetch the ark.* They vainly supposed that the ark could save them when the God of it had departed from them because of their wickedness. They knew that in former times their fathers had been beaten by their enemies when they took not the ark with them to battle, as in the case of their wars with the Canaanites, Num. xiv. 44-45; and that they had conquered when they took this with them, as in the case of the destruction of Jericho, Josh. vi. 4. It was customary with all the nations of the earth to take their gods and sacred ensigns with them to war.

4. *The Lord of hosts.* See on chap. i. 3. *Dwelleth between the cherubims.* Of what shape the cherubim were, we know not; but there was one of these representative figures placed at each end of the ark of the covenant; and between them, on the lid or cover of that ark, which was called the "propitiatory" or "mercy seat," the *shechinah*, or symbol of the Divine Presence, was said to dwell. They thought, therefore, if they had the ark, they must necessarily have the presence and influence of Jehovah.

5. *All Israel shouted.* Had they humbled themselves, and prayed devoutly and fervently for success, they would have been heard and saved.

7. *God is come into the camp.* They took for granted, as did the Israelites, that His presence was inseparable from His ark or shrine.

8. *These mighty Gods.* "From the hand of these illustrious Gods." Probably this should be translated in the singular, and not in the plural: "Who shall deliver us from the hand of this illustrious God?"

9. *Be strong.* This was the address to the whole army, and very forcible it was. "If ye do not fight, and acquit yourselves like men, ye will be servants to the Hebrews, as they have been to you; and you may expect that they will avenge themselves of you for all the cruelty you have exercised towards them."

11. *Hophni and Phinehas were slain.* They probably attempted to defend the ark, and lost their lives in the attempt.

12. *Came to Shiloh the same day.* The field of battle could not have been at any great distance, for this young man reached Shiloh the same evening after the defeat. *With his clothes rent, and with earth upon his head.* These were signs of sorrow and distress among all nations. The *clothes rent* signified the rending, dividing, and scattering of the people; the *earth*, or "ashes," on the head signified their humiliation: "We are brought down to the dust of the earth; we are near to our graves."

13. *His heart trembled for the ark of God.* He was a most mild and affectionate father, and yet the safety of the ark lay nearer to his heart than the safety of his two sons. Who can help feeling for this aged, venerable man?

17. *And the messenger answered.* Never was a more afflictive message, containing such a variety of woes, each rising above the preceding, delivered in so few words. (1) *Israel is fled before the Philistines.* (2) *There hath also been a great slaughter among the people.* (3) *Thy two sons also, Hophni and Phinehas, are dead.* (4) *The ark of God is taken.*

This was the most dreadful of the whole; now Israel is dishonored in the sight of the heathen, and the name of the Lord will be blasphemed by them. Besides, the capture of the ark shows that God is departed from Israel; and now there is no further hope of restoration for the people, but every prospect of the destruction of the nation, and the final ruin of all religion!

18. *When he made mention of the ark of God.* Eli bore all the relation till the messenger came to this solemn word; he had trembled before for the ark, and now, hearing that it was captured, he was transfixed with grief, fell down from his seat, and dislocated his neck! Behold the judgments of God! But shall we say that this man, however remiss in the education of his children, and criminal in his indulgence towards his profligate sons, which arose more from the easiness of his disposition than from a desire to encourage vice, is gone to perdition? God forbid! *He had judged Israel forty years.* Instead of *forty years*, the Septuagint was here "twenty years." All the other versions, as well as the Hebrew text, have forty years.

19. *And his daughter in law.* This is another very affecting story; the defeat of Israel, the capture of the ark, the death of her father-in-law, and the slaughter of her husband were more than a woman in her circumstances, near the time of her delivery, could bear. *She bowed, travailed, was delivered of a son, gave the child a name indicative of the ruined state of Israel, and expired!*

21. *She named the child I-chabod.* The versions are various on the original words. It is pretty evident they did not know well what signification to give the name; and we are left to collect its meaning from what she says afterwards, *The glory is departed from Israel;* the words literally mean, "Where is the glory?" And indeed where was it, when the armies of Israel were defeated by the Philistines, the priests slain, the supreme magistrate dead, and the ark of the Lord taken?

CHAPTER 5

The Philistines set up the ark in the temple of Dagon at Ashdod, whose image is found next morning prostrate before it, broken in pieces, 1-5. The Philistines are also smitten with a sore disease, 6. The people of Ashdod refuse to let the ark stay with them; and the lords of the Philistines, with whom they consulted, order it to be carried to Gath, 7-8. They do so; and God smites the inhabitants of that city, young and old, with the same disease, 9. They send the ark to Ekron, and a heavy destruction falls upon that city, and they resolve to send it back to Shiloh, 10-12.

1. *Brought it from Eben-ezer unto Ashdod.* Ashdod or Azotus was one of the five satrapies or lordships of the Philistines.

2. *The house of Dagon.* On this idol, which was supposed to be partly in a human form and partly in that of a fish, see the note on Judg. xvi. 23.

The motive which induced the Philistines to set up the ark in the temple of Dagon may be easily ascertained. It was customary in all nations to dedicate the spoils taken from an enemy to their gods: (1) as a gratitude offering for the help which they supposed them to have furnished; and (2) as a proof that their gods, i.e., the gods of the conquerors, were more powerful than those of the conquered. It was, no doubt, to insult the God of Israel, and to insult and terrify His people, that they placed His ark in the temple of Dagon.

3. *They of Ashdod arose early on the morrow.* Probably to perform some act of their superstition in the temple of their idol. *Dagon was fallen upon his face.* This was one proof, which they little expected, of the superiority of the God of Israel. *Set him in his place again.* Supposing his fall might have been merely accidental.

4. *Only the stump of Dagon was left.* Literally, Only *dagon* (i.e., the "little fish") was left. Dagon had the head, arms, and hands of a man or woman, and the rest of the idol was in the form of a fish, to which Horace is supposed to make allusion in the following words: "The upper part resembling a beautiful woman; the lower, a fish." All that was human in his form was broken off from what resembled a fish. Here was a proof that the affair was not accidental; and these proofs of God's power and authority prepared the way for His judgments.

5. *Tread on the threshold.* Because the arms of Dagon were broken off by his fall on the threshold, the threshold became sacred, and neither his priests nor worshippers ever tread on the threshold. Thus it was ordered in the divine providence that, by a religious custom of their own, they should perpetuate their disgrace, the insufficiency of their worship, and the superiority of the God of Israel.

It is supposed that the idolatrous Israelites, in the time of Zephaniah, had adopted the worship of Dagon: and that in this sense chap. i. 9 is to be understood: "In the same day also will I punish all those that leap on the threshold." In order to go into such temples, and not tread on the threshold, the people must step or leap over them; and in this way the above passage may be understood.

6. *Smote them with emerods.* The word *apholim,* from *aphal,* to be "elevated," probably means the disease called the bleeding piles, which appears to have been accompanied with dysentery, bloody flux, and ulcerated anus.

7. *His hand is sore upon us, and upon Dagon our god.* Here the end was completely answered: they now saw that they had not prevailed against Israel on account of their god being more powerful than Jehovah; and they now felt how easily this God can confound and destroy their whole nation.

8. *The lords of the Philistines.* The word *sarney,* which we translate *lords,* is rendered by the Chaldee "tyrants." The Syriac is the same. By the Vulgate and Septuagint, "satraps." Palestine was divided into five satrapies: Ashdod, Ekron, Askelon, Gath, and Gaza (see Josh. xiii. 8). But these were all federates, and acted under one general government, for which they assembled in council. *Let the ark . . . be carried about.* They probably thought that their affliction rose from some natural cause; and therefore they wished the ark to be carried about from place to place, to see what the effects might be. If they found the same evil produced wherever it came, then they must conclude that it was a judgment from the God of Israel.

9. *The hand of the Lord was against the city.* As it was at Ashdod, so it was at Gath.

12. *The men that died not.* Some it seems were smitten with instant death; others, with the hemorrhoids; and there was a universal consternation; *and the cry of the city went up to heaven*—it was an exceeding great cry.

CHAPTER 6

After the ark had been seven months in the land of the Philistines, they consult their priests and diviners about sending it to Shiloh, 1-2. They advise that it be sent back with a trespass offering of five golden emerods and five golden mice, 3-6. They advise also that it be sent back on a new cart, drawn by two milch kine, from whom their calves shall be tied up; and then conclude that if these cows shall take the way of Beth-shemesh, as going to the Israelitish border, then the Lord had afflicted them; if not, then their evils were accidental, 7-9. They do as directed; and the kine take the way of Beth-shemesh, 10-13. They stop in the field of Joshua; and the men of Beth-shemesh take them, and offer them to the Lord for a burnt offering, and cleave the wood of the cart to burn them, and make sundry other offerings, 14-15. The offerings of the five lords of the Philistines, 16-18. For too curiously looking into the ark, the men of Beth-shemesh are smitten of the Lord, 19-20. They send to the inhabitants of Kirjath-jearim, that they may take away the ark, 21.

2. *The diviners. Kosemim,* from *kasam,* "to presage or prognosticate" (see Deut. xviii. 10). In what their pretended art consisted, we know not.

3. *Send it not empty.* As it appears you have trespassed against Him, send Him an offering for this trespass. *Why his hand is not removed.* The sense is, If you send Him a trespass offering, and you be cured, then you shall know why His judgments have not been taken away from you previously to this offering.

4. *Five golden emerods, and five golden mice.* One for each satrapy. The emerods had afflicted their bodies; the mice had marred their land. Both they considered as sent by God; and, making an image of each, and sending them as a trespass offering, they acknowledged this.

6. *Wherefore then do ye harden your hearts?* They had heard how God punished the Egyptians, and they are afraid of similar plagues. *Did they not let the people go?* And has He not wrought wonderfully among us? And should we not send back His ark?

7. *Make a new cart.* It was indecent and improper to employ in any part of the worship of God anything that had before served for a common purpose. When David removed the ark from the house of Abinadab, he put it on a new cart, 2 Sam. vi. 3. *Bring their calves home from them.* So it appears that their calves had been with them in the fields. This was a complete trial: unless they were supernaturally influenced, they would not leave their calves: unless supernaturally directed, they would not leave their home, and take a way unguided, which they had never gone before.

8. *The jewels of gold.* The word *keley,* which our translators so often render *jewels,* signifies "vessels, implements, ornaments."

9. *A chance that happened to us.* The word *mikreh,* from *karah,* to "meet or coalesce," signifies an event that naturally arises from such concurring causes as, in the order and nature of things, must produce it.

12. *Lowing as they went.* Calling for their calves. *To the right hand or to the left.* Some think they were placed where two roads met: one going to Ekron, the other to Beth-shemesh. It is possible that they were put in such cir-

cumstances as these for the greater certainty of the affair: to have turned from their own homes, from their calves and known pasture, and to have taken the road to a strange country, must argue supernatural influence. *The lords of the Philistines went after.* They were so jealous in this business that they would trust no eyes but their own. All this was wisely ordered, that there might be the fullest conviction of the being and interposition of God.

14. *They clave the wood of the cart.* Both the cart and the cattle, having been thus employed, could no longer be devoted to any secular services; therefore the cattle were sacrificed, and the cart was broken up for fuel to consume the sacrifice.

15. *The Levites took down.* It appears there were some of the tribe of Levi among the people of Beth-shemesh; to them appertained the service of the Tabernacle.

17. *These are the golden emerods.* Each of these cities, in what may be called its corporate capacity, sent a golden emerod.

19. *He smote of the people fifty thousand and threescore and ten men.* The present Hebrew text of this most extraordinary reading stands thus: "And he smote among the men of Beth-shemesh, (because they looked into the ark of Jehovah,) and he smote among the people seventy men, fifty thousand men."

From the manner in which the text stands, and from the great improbability of the thing, it is most likely that there is a corruption in this text, or that some explanatory word is lost, or that the number *fifty thousand* has been added by ignorance or design; it being very improbable that such a small village as Beth-shemesh should contain or be capable of employing fifty thousand and seventy men in the fields at wheat harvest, much less that they could all peep into the ark on the stone of Abel, in the cornfield of Joshua.

That the words are not naturally connected in the Hebrew text is evident; and they do not stand better in the versions. (1) The Vulgate renders it thus: "And he smote of the [chief] people seventy men, and fifty thousand of the [common] people." (2) The Targum of Jonathan is something similar to the Vulgate: "And he smote of the elders of the people seventy men; and of the congregation fifty thousand men." (3) The Septuagint follow the Hebrew text: "And he smote of them seventy men; and fifty thousand men." (4) The Syriac is as follows: "And the Lord smote among the people five thousand and seventy men." (5) The Arabic is nearly similar: "And the Lord smote among the people; and there died of them five thousand and seventy men." (6) Josephus is different from all the rest, for he renders the place thus, *Antiq. Jud.,* lib. vi, cap. i, sect. 4: "But the displeasure and wrath of God pursued them so, that seventy men of the village of Beth-shemesh, approaching the ark, which they were not worthy to touch (not being priests), were struck with lightning." Here we find the whole *fifty thousand* is omitted.

The common reading may be defended if we only suppose the omission of a single letter, the particle of comparison *ke,* "like, as, or equal to." The passage would then read: "And he smote of the people seventy men, equal to fifty thousand men"; that is, they were the elders or governors of the people. Some solve the difficulty by translating, "He slew seventy men out of fifty thousand men." There are various other methods invented by learned men to remove this difficulty, which I shall not stop to examine; all, however, issue in this point, that only seventy men were slain; and this is without doubt the most probable.

With a great slaughter. Seventy men slain, out of an inconsiderable village in a harvest day, was certainly a great slaughter.

20. *Who is able to stand?* Why this exclamation? They knew that God had forbidden any to touch His ark but the priests and Levites; but they endeavored to throw that blame on God, as a Being hard to be pleased, which belonged solely to themselves.

21. *To the inhabitants of Kirjath-jearim.* They wished the ark away out of their village, but why they sent to this city instead of sending to Shiloh does not appear. Probably Shiloh had been destroyed by the Philistines, after the late defeat of Israel. This is most likely, as the ark was never more taken back to that place.

CHAPTER 7

The men of Kirjath-jearim bring the ark from Beth-shemesh, and consecrate Eleazar, the son of Abinadab, to keep it; and there it continued twenty years, 1-2. Samuel reproves and exhorts the people, and gathers them together at Mizpeh, where they fast and pray, and confess their sins, 3-6. The Philistines go up against them; the Israelites cry unto the Lord for help; Samuel offers sacrifices; and the Lord confounds the Philistines with thunder; Israel discomfits and pursues them to Beth-car, 7-11. Samuel erects a stone for a memorial, and calls it Eben-ezer, 12. The Philistines are totally subdued, and Israel recovers all its lost cities, 13-14. Samuel acts as an itinerant judge in Israel, 15-17.

1. *Fetched up the ark.* When these people received the message of the Beth-shemites, they probably consulted Samuel, with whom was the counsel of the Lord, and he encouraged them to go and bring it up, else they might have expected such destruction as happened to the Beth-shemites. *Sanctified Eleazar.* Perhaps this sanctifying signifies no more than setting this man apart, simply to take care of the ark.

2. *It was twenty years.* This chapter contains the transactions of at least twenty years, but we know not the date of each event.

3. *And Samuel spake.* We have heard nothing of this judge since he served in the Tabernacle. He was now grown up, and established for a prophet in the land of Israel. *If ye do return.* From your backsliding and idolatry. *With all your hearts.* For outward services and professions will avail nothing.

4. *Put away Baalim and Ashtaroth.* These were not two particular deities, but two *genera* of idols: the one masculine, Baalim; the other feminine, Ashtaroth; both the words are in the plural number, and signify all their "gods" and "goddesses."

5. *Gather all Israel to Mizpeh.* This appears to have been an armed assembly, though probably collected principally for religious and political purposes; but Samuel knew that an unarmed multitude could not safely be convened in the vicinity of the Philistines.

6. *Drew water, and poured it out.* It is not easy to know what is meant by this; it is true

that pouring out water, in the way of libation, was a religious ordinance among the Hebrews (Isa. xii. 3), and among most other nations, particularly the Greeks and Romans, who used, not only water, but wine, milk, honey, and blood. The Chaldee paraphrast understands the place differently, for he translates: "And they poured out their hearts in penitence, as waters, before the Lord." That deep penitential sorrow was represented under the notion of pouring out water. We have a direct proof in the case of David, who says, Ps. xxii. 14, "I am poured out like water . . . my heart is like wax; it is melted in the midst of my bowels." And to repentance, under this very similitude, the prophet exhorts fallen Jerusalem: "Arise, cry out in the night: in the beginning of the watches pour out thine heart like water before the face of the Lord," Lam. ii. 19.

And Samuel judged. He gave them ordinances, heard and redressed grievances, and taught them how to get reconciled to God. The assembly, therefore, was held for religio-politico-military purposes.

7. *The Philistines went up against Israel.* They went to give them battle before that, by continual accessions of numbers, they should become too powerful.

8. *Cease not to cry unto the Lord.* They had strong confidence in the intercession of Samuel, because they knew he was a holy man of God.

9. *Samuel took a sucking lamb.* This sucking lamb must have been eight days under its mother before it could be offered, as the law says, Lev. xxii. 27.

10. *The Lord thundered with a great thunder.* Literally, "The Lord thundered with a great voice"—He confounded them with a mighty tempest of thunder and lightning, and no doubt slew many by the lightning.

11. *Under Beth-car.* We know not where this place was; the Septuagint have Beth-chor; the Targum, Beth-saron; and the Syriac and Arabic, Beth-jasan.

12. *Called the name of it Eben-ezer. Eben haezer,* "The Stone of Help"; perhaps a pillar is meant by the word *stone.*

13. *They came no more into the coast of Israel.* Perhaps a more signal victory was never gained by Israel; the Lord had brought them low, almost to extermination; and now, by His miraculous interference, He lifts them completely up, and humbles to the dust their proud oppressors. God often suffers nations and individuals to be brought to the lowest extremity, that He may show His mercy and goodness by suddenly rescuing them from destruction, when all human help has most evidently failed.

14. *The cities which the Philistines had taken.* We are not informed of the particulars of these reprisals, but we may rest assured all this was not done in one day; perhaps the retaking of the cities was by slow degrees, through the space of several years. *There was peace between Israel and the Amorites.* That is, all the remaining Canaanites kept quiet, and did not attempt to molest the Israelites, when they found the Philistines, the most powerful of the ancient inhabitants of the land, broken and subdued before them.

16-17. *He went from year to year in circuit.* When he was at Bethel, the tribe of Ephraim,

and all the northern parts of the country, could attend him; when at Gilgal, the tribe of Benjamin, and those beyond Jordan, might have easy access to him; and when at Mizpeh, he was within reach of Judah, Simeon, and Gad. But *Ramah* was the place of his ordinary abode; and there he held his court, for *there he judged Israel;* and, as it is probable that Shiloh was destroyed, it is said that *there* (viz., at Ramah) *he built an altar unto the Lord.* This altar, being duly consecrated, the worship performed at it was strictly legal. *Ramah,* which is said to be about six miles from Jerusalem, was the seat of prophecy during the life of Samuel; and there it is probable all Israel came to consult him on matters of a spiritual nature, as there was the only altar of God in the land of Israel.

CHAPTER 8

Samuel, grown old, makes his sons judges in Beersheba, 1-2. They pervert judgment; and the people complain, and desire a king, 3-5. Samuel is displeased, and inquires of the Lord, 6. The Lord is also displeased; but directs Samuel to appoint them a king, and to show them solemnly the consequences of their choice, 7-9. Samuel does so; and shows them what they may expect from an absolute monarch, and how afflicted they should be under his administration, 10-18. The people refuse to recede from their demand; and Samuel lays the matter before the Lord, and dismisses them, 19-22.

1. *When Samuel was old.* Supposed to be about sixty. *He made his sons judges.* He appointed them as his lieutenants to superintend certain affairs in Beersheba, which he could not conveniently attend to himself. But they were never *judges* in the proper sense of the word; Samuel was the last judge in Israel, and he judged it to the day of his death. See chap. vii. 15.

3. *His sons walked not in his ways.* Their iniquity is pointed out in three words: (1) they *turned aside after lucre;* the original (*batsa*) signifies to "cut, clip, break off." It expresses here the idea of avarice, of getting money by hook or by crook. (2) They *took bribes;* "gifts or presents" blind their eyes. (3) They *perverted judgment*—they turned judgment aside; they put it out of its regular path; they sold it to the highest bidder. Thus the wicked rich man had his cause, and the poor man was oppressed and deprived of his right.

5. *Make us a king.* Hitherto, from the time in which they were a people, the Israelites were under a theocracy; they had no other king but God. Now they desire to have a king like the other nations around them, who may be their general in battle; for this is the point at which they principally aim.

6. *The thing displeased Samuel.* Because he saw that this amounted to a formal renunciation of the divine government. *Samuel prayed unto the Lord.* He begged to know His mind in this important business.

7. *They have rejected me.* They wish to put that government in the hands of a mortal which was always in the hands of their God. But *hearken unto the voice of the people*—grant them what they request. So we find God grants that in His displeasure which He withholds in His mercy.

9. *Shew them the manner of the king.* The word *mishpat,* which we here render *manner,* signifies simply what the king would and might require, according to the *manner* in which kings

in general ruled; all of whom, in those times, were absolute and despotic.

19. *The people refused to obey.* They would have the king, his manner and all, notwithstanding the solemn warning which they here receive.

20. *May judge us.* This appears to be a rejection of Samuel. *Go out before us.* Be in every respect our head and governor. And *fight our battles.* Be the general of our armies.

21. *Rehearsed them in the ears of the Lord.* He went to the altar, and in his secret devotion laid the whole business before God.

22. *Hearken unto their voice.* Let them have what they desire, and let them abide the consequences. *Go ye every man unto his city.* It seems the elders of the people had tarried all this time with Samuel, and when he had received his ultimate answer from God, he told them of it and dismissed them.

CHAPTER 9

Saul's lineage and description; he is sent by his father to seek some lost asses, 1-5. Not finding them, he purposes to go and consult Samuel concerning the proper method of proceeding, 6-14. The Lord informs Samuel that he should anoint Saul king, 15-16. Samuel invites Saul to dine with him, and informs him that the asses are found; and gives him an intimation that he is to be king, 17-21. Saul dines with Samuel, and afterwards he is taken to the housetop, where both commune together, 22-27.

1. *A mighty man of power.* Literally, a "strong man"; this appears to be the only power he possessed; and the physical strength of the father may account for the extraordinary size of the son. See v. 2.

2. *From his shoulders and upward.* It was probably from this very circumstance that he was chosen for king; for, where kings were elective, in all ancient times great respect was paid to personal appearance.

3. *The asses of Kish . . . were lost.* What a wonderful train of occurrences were connected in order to bring Saul to the throne of Israel! Everything seemed to go on according to the common course of events, and yet all conspired to favor the election of a man to the kingdom who certainly did not come there by the approbation of God.

7. *There is not a present to bring to the man of God.* We are not to suppose from this that the prophets took money to predict future events; Saul only refers to an invariable custom, that no man approached a superior without a present of some kind or other. We have often seen this before; even God, who needs nothing, would not that His people should approach Him with empty hands.

9. *Beforetime in Israel.* This passage could not have been a part of this book originally; but we have already conjectured that Samuel, or some contemporary author, wrote the memoranda out of which a later author compiled this book. This hypothesis, sufficiently reasonable in itself, solves all difficulties of this kind. *Was beforetime called a Seer.* The word *seer*, *roeh*, occurs for the first time in this place; it literally signifies a "person who sees." A "seer" and a "prophet" were the same in most cases; only with this difference, the seer was always a prophet, but the prophet was not always a seer.

I think the ninth verse comes more naturally in after the eleventh.

11. *Young maidens going out to draw water.* So far is it from being true that young women were always kept closely shut up at home, that we find them often in the field, drawing and carrying water, as here.

12. *He came to day to the city.* Though Samuel lived chiefly in Ramah, yet he had a dwelling in the country, at a place called Naioth, where it is probable there was a school of the prophets (see chap. xix. 18-24). *A sacrifice of the people.* A great feast. The animals used were first sacrificed to the Lord; that is, their blood was poured out before Him; and then all the people fed on the flesh. By *high place* probably Samuel's altar is alone meant, which no doubt was raised on an eminence.

13. *He doth bless the sacrifice.* He alone can perform the religious rites which are used on this occasion.

14. *Came out against them.* Met them.

15. *Now the Lord had told Samuel.* How this communication was made we cannot tell.

16. *Thou shalt anoint him to be captain.* Not to be "king," but to be *nagid* or captain of the Lord's host. But in ancient times no king was esteemed who was not an able warrior.

17. *Behold the man whom I spake to thee of!* What an intimate communion must Samuel have held with his God! A constant familiarity seems to have existed between them.

19. *I am the seer.* This declaration would prepare Saul for the communications afterwards made.

20. *As for thine asses.* Thus he shows him that he knows what is in his heart, God having previously revealed these things to Samuel. *And on whom is all the desire of Israel?* Saul understood this as implying that he was chosen to be king.

21. *Am not I a Benjamite?* This speech of Saul is exceedingly modest; he was now becomingly humble; but who can bear elevation and prosperity? The tribe of Benjamin had not yet recovered its strength after the ruinous war it had with the other tribes, Judges xx.

22. *Brought them into the parlour.* It might as well be called "kitchen"; it was the place where they sat down to feast.

23. *Said unto the cook.* *Tabbach*, here rendered *cook*, the singular of *tabbachoth*, "female cooks," chap. viii. 13, from the root *tabach*, "to slay or butcher." Probably the butcher is here meant.

24. *The shoulder, and that which was upon it.* Probably the shoulder was covered with a part of the caul, that it might be the better roasted. Why was the shoulder set before Saul? Not because it was the best part, but because it was an emblem of the government to which he was now called. See Isa. ix. 6: "And the government shall be upon his shoulder."

25. *Upon the top of the house.* All the houses in the East were flat-roofed; on these people walked, talked, and frequently slept, for the sake of fresh and cooling air.

26. *Called Saul to the top of the house.* Saul had no doubt slept there all night; and now, it being the "break of day," "Samuel called to

Saul on the top of the house, saying, Up, that I may send thee away." There was no calling him to the housetop a second time; he was sleeping there, and Samuel called him up.

27. *As they were going down.* So it appears that Saul arose immediately, and Samuel accompanied him out of the town, and sent the servant on, that he might show Saul the *word*— the "counsel" or "design," of the Lord. What this was we shall see in the following chapter.

CHAPTER 10

Samuel anoints Saul captain of the Lord's inheritance, 1. Instructs him concerning his return home, whom he should meet, and what he should do, 2-8. Saul meets a company of prophets, the Spirit of the Lord comes on him, and he prophesies among them, 9-13. He meets his uncle, and converses with him, 14-16. Samuel calls the people together to Mizpeh, and upbraids them for having rejected the Lord as their King, 17-19. Lots are cast to find out the person proper to be appointed king; Saul is chosen, 20-24. Samuel shows the manner of the king, and writes it in a book, 25. Saul goes to Gibeah; and certain persons refuse to acknowledge him as king, 26-27.

1. *Took a vial of oil.* The reasons of this rite the reader will find largely stated in the note on Exod. xxix. 7. The anointing mentioned here took place in the open field. See the preceding chapter, vv. 26-27. How simple was the ancient ceremony of consecrating a king! A prophet or priest poured oil upon his head, and kissed him; and said, "Thus the Lord hath anointed thee to be captain over his inheritance." This was the whole of the ceremony. Even in this anointing, Saul is not acknowledged as king, but simply *nagid*, "a captain"—one who goes before and leads the people.

2. *Rachel's sepulchre.* This was nigh to Bethlehem (see Gen. xxxv. 19). *At Zelzah.* If this be the name of a place, nothing is known of it. The Hebrew *betseltsach* is translated by the Septuagint "dancing greatly"; now this may refer to the joy they felt and expressed on finding the asses, or it may refer to those religious exultations, or playing on instruments of music, mentioned in the succeeding verses.

3. *Three men going up to God to Beth-el.* Jacob's altar was probably still there, Gen. xxviii. 19. However this might be, it was still considered, as its name implies, "the house of God"; and to it they were now going, to offer sacrifice. The *three kids* were for sacrifice; the *three loaves of bread*, to be offered probably as a thank offering; and the *bottle* or skin full of *wine*, for a libation. When the blood was poured out before the Lord, they feasted on the flesh and on the bread; and probably had a sufficiency of the wine left for their own drinking.

4. *And they will salute thee.* "And they will inquire of thee concerning peace," i.e., welfare. In the East, if this salutation be given, then the person or persons giving it may be reckoned friends; if the others return it, then there is friendship on both sides.

5. *The hill of God.* The Targum says, "The hill on which the ark of the Lord was." Calmet supposes it to be a height near Gibeah. *The garrison of the Philistines.* Probably they kept a watch on the top of this hill, with a company of soldiers to keep the country in check. *A company of prophets.* A company of scribes, says the Targum. Probably the scholars of the prophets; for the prophets seem to have been

the only accredited teachers, at particular times, in Israel; and at this time there does not appear to have been any other prophet besides Samuel in this quarter.

A psaltery. Nebel. As the word signifies in other places a "bottle or flagon," it was probably something like the bagpipe. *A tabret. Toph;* a sort of drum or cymbal. *A pipe. Chalile,* from *chal,* "to make a hole or opening"; a sort of pipe, flute, clarinet, or the like. *A harp. Kinnor;* a stringed instrument similar to our harp, or that on the model of which a harp was formed.

7. *Thou do as occasion serve thee.* After God has shown you all these signs that you are under His especial guidance, fear not to undertake anything that belongs to your office, for God is with you.

8. *Seven days shalt thou tarry.* I will come to you within seven days, offer sacrifices, receive directions from the Lord, and deliver them to you. It is likely that these seven days referred to the time in which Samuel came to Saul to Gilgal, offered sacrifices, and confirmed the kingdom to him, after he had defeated the Ammonites (see chap. xi. 14-15).

10. *Behold, a company of prophets.* See on v. 5.

12. *But who is their father?* The Septuagint, in its principal editions, adds, "Is it not Kish?" This makes the sense more complete.

13. *He came to the high place.* I suppose this to mean the place where Saul's father lived, as it is evident the next verse shows him to be at *home.*

14. *Saul's uncle.* The word *dod* signifies a "beloved one, love, a lover, friend," and is the same as "David." It is supposed to mean *uncle* here, but I think it means some familiar friend.

18. *I brought up Israel out of Egypt.* These are similar to the upbraidings in chap. vii. 7, etc.

19. *Present yourselves . . . by your tribes.* It appears that, in order to find out the proper person who should be made their king, they must determine by lot: (1) the tribe, (2) the thousands or grand divisions by families, (3) the smaller divisions by families, and (4) the individual.

21. *When they sought him, he could not be found.* Through modesty or fear he had secreted himself.

22. *The Lord answered.* What a continual access to God! and what condescension in His attention to all their requests! The *stuff* among which he had secreted himself may mean the carts, baggage, etc., brought by the people to Mizpeh.

24. *God save the king.* There is no such word here; no, nor in the whole Bible; nor is it countenanced by any of the versions. The words which we thus translate here and elsewhere are simply *yechi hammelech,* "May the king live"; and so all the versions, the Targum excepted, which says, "May the king prosper!"

25. *The manner of the kingdom.* It is the same word as in chap. viii. 9; and doubtless the same thing is implied as is there related. But possibly there was some kind of compact or covenant between them and Saul; and this was the thing that was written in a book, and laid up before the Lord, probably near the ark.

26. *A band of men.* Not a military band, as I imagine, but some secret friends, or companions, who were personally attached to him.

27. *Brought him no presents.* They gave him no proofs that they acknowledged either the divine appointment or his authority. Saul was now a public character, and had a right to support from the public. These sons of Belial refused to bear their part; they brought him no presents. He marked it, but at present held his peace; "he was as if he were deaf."

CHAPTER 11

Nahash, king of the Ammonites, besieges Jabesh-gilead; and proposes to its inhabitants the most degrading conditions of peace, 1-2. They apply to their brethren for help, 3-4. Saul hears of their distress; takes a yoke of oxen, hews them in pieces, and sends them throughout the coasts of Israel, with the threat that all who did not come to his standard should have his cattle served in like manner; in consequence of which he is soon at the head of an army of 330,000 men, 5-8. He sends to Jabesh-gilead, and promises help, 9-10. Saul attacks the Ammonites next morning, and gives them a total overthrow, 11. The people are greatly encouraged, and propose to put to death those who are opposed to Saul's government; but this he prevents, 12-13. Samuel leads the people to Gilgal: they offer sacrifices, and renew the kingdom to Saul, 14-15.

2. *I may thrust out all your right eyes.* This cruel condition would serve at once as a badge of their slavery, and a means of incapacitating them from being effective warriors.

3. *Give us seven days' respite.* Such promises are frequently made by besieged places: "We will surrender if not relieved in so many days"; and such conditions are generally received by the besiegers.

5. *Saul came after the herd.* He had been bred up to an agricultural life, and after his consecration he returned to it, waiting for a call of divine providence, which he considered he had now received in the message from Jabesh-gilead.

6. *The Spirit of God came upon Saul.* He felt himself strongly excited to attempt the relief of his brethren. *And his anger was kindled greatly.* I believe this means no more than that "his courage was greatly excited"—he felt himself strong for fight, and confident of success.

7. *He took a yoke of oxen.* The sending the pieces of the oxen was an act similar to that of the Levite, Judg. xix. 29.

10. *To morrow we will come out unto you.* They concealed the information they had received of Saul's promised assistance. They did come out unto them; but it was in a different manner to what the Ammonites expected.

11. *Put the people in three companies.* Intending to attack the Ammonites in three different points, and to give his own men more room to act. *In the morning watch.* He probably began his march in the evening, passed Jordan in the night, and reached the camp of the Ammonites by daybreak. *That two of them were not left together.* This proves that the rout was complete.

12. *Who is he that said, Shall Saul reign?* Now, flushed with victory and proud of their leader, they wished to give him a proof of their attachment by slaying, even in cold blood, the

persons who were at first averse from his being entrusted with the supreme power!

13. *There shall not a man be put to death.* This was as much to Saul's credit as the lately proposed measure was to the discredit of his soldiers.

14. *Renew the kingdom.* The unction of Saul, in the first instance, was a very private act; and his being appointed to be king was not known to the people in general. He had now shown himself worthy to command the people; and Samuel takes advantage of this circumstance to gain the general consent in his favor.

15. *There they made Saul king.* It is likely, from these words, that Saul was anointed a second time; he was now publicly acknowledged, and there was no gainsayer. Thus far Saul acted well, and the kingdom seemed to be confirmed in his hand; but soon through imprudence he lost it.

CHAPTER 12

Samuel, grown old, testifies his integrity before the people, which they confirm, 1-5. He reproves them for their ingratitude and disobedience; and gives a summary of the history of their fathers, 6-12. He exhorts them to future obedience, and calls for a sign from heaven to confirm his authority, and to show them their disobedience: God sends an extraordinary thunder and rain, 13-19. He warns them against idolatry, and exhorts to obedience, and promises to intercede for them, 20-23. Sums up their duty, and concludes with a solemn warning, 24-25.

1. *And Samuel said.* It is very likely that it was at this public meeting Samuel delivered the following address; no other time seems to be given for it, and this is the most proper that could be chosen.

2. *My sons are with you.* It is generally agreed that these words intimate that Samuel had deprived them of their public employ, and reduced them to a level with the common people. *Have walked before you from my childhood.* He had been a long, steady, and immaculate servant of the public.

3. *Witness against me.* Did ever a minister of state, in any part of the world, resign his office with so much self-consciousness of integrity, backed with the universal approbation of the public?

7. *Now therefore stand still.* I have arraigned myself before God and you; I now arraign you before God.

8. *The Lord sent Moses and Aaron.* He shows them that through all their history God had ever raised them up deliverers, when their necessities required such interference.

11. *Jerubbaal.* That is, Gideon. *And Bedan:* instead of *Bedan,* whose name occurs nowhere else as a judge or deliverer of Israel, the Septuagint have "Barak"; the same reading is found in the Syriac and Arabic. The Targum has Samson. Instead of *Samuel,* the Syriac and Arabic have "Samson"; and it is most natural to suppose that Samuel does not mention himself in this place.

12. *When ye saw that Nahash.* This was not the first time they had demanded a king; see before, chap. viii. 5. But at the crisis mentioned here they became more importunate; and it was in consequence of this that the kingdom was a second time confirmed to Saul. Saul was elected at Mizpeh, he was confirmed at Gilgal.

14. *If ye will fear the Lord.* On condition that you rebel no more, God will take you and your king under His merciful protection, and He and His kingdom shall be confirmed and continued.

17. *Is it not wheat harvest to day?* That is, This is the time of wheat harvest. According to Jerome, who spent several years in the Promised Land, this harvest commenced about the end of June or beginning of July, in which he says he never saw rain in Judea.

18. *The Lord sent thunder and rain that day.* This was totally unusual; and, as it came at the call of Samuel, was a most evident miracle. *Greatly feared the Lord.* They dreaded His terrible majesty; and they feared Samuel, perceiving that he had so much power with God.

19. *Pray for thy servants . . . that we die not.* As they knew they had rebelled against God, they saw that they had everything to fear from His justice and power.

20. *Ye have done all this wickedness.* That is, although you have done all this wickedness: what was past God would pass by, provided they would be obedient in the future.

21. *After vain things.* That is, idols; which he calls here *hattohu,* the same expression found in Gen. i. 2. The earth was *tohu;* it was waste, empty, and formless; so idols—they are confusion, and things of naught.

24. *Only fear the Lord.* Know, respect, and reverence Him. *Serve him.* Consider Him your Lord and Master; consider yourselves His servants. *In truth.* Be ever honest, ever sincere; *with all your heart*—have every affection engaged in the work of obedience; act not merely from a principle of duty, but also from a pious, affectionate sense of obligation. Act towards your God as an affectionate child should act towards a tender and loving parent.

25. *Ye shall be consumed.* If you do wickedly you shall be destroyed, your kingdom destroyed, and your king destroyed.

CHAPTER 13

Saul chooses a body of troops, 1-2. Jonathan smites a garrison of the Philistines, 3-4. The Philistines gather together an immense host against Israel, 5. The Israelites are afraid; and some hide themselves in caves, and others flee over Jordan, 6-7. Samuel delaying his coming, Saul offers sacrifice, 8-9. Samuel comes and reproves him, and Saul excuses himself, 10-12. Samuel shows him that God has rejected him from being captain over His people, 13-14. Samuel departs; and Saul and Jonathan, with 600 men, abide in Gibeah, 15-16. The Philistines send out foraging companies, and waste the land, 17-18. Desolate state of the Israelitish army, having no weapons of defense against their enemies, 19-23.

1. *Saul reigned one year.* A great deal of learned labor has been employed and lost on this verse, to reconcile it with propriety and common sense. I shall not recount the meanings put on it. I think this clause belongs to the preceding chapter, either as a part of the whole or a chronological note added afterwards; as if the writer had said, "These things [related in chap. xii] took place in the first year of Saul's reign"; and then he proceeds in the next place to tell us what took place in the second year, the two most remarkable years of Saul's reign. In the first he is appointed, anointed, and twice confirmed, viz., at Mizpeh and at Gilgal; in the second, Israel is brought into the lowest state of degradation by the Philistines,

Saul acts unconstitutionally, and is rejected from being king. These things were worthy of an especial chronological note.

And when he had reigned. This should begin the chapter, and be read thus: "And when Saul had reigned two years over Israel, he chose him three thousand." The Septuagint has left the clause out of the text entirely, and begins the chapter thus: "And Saul chose to himself three thousand men out of the men of Israel."

2. *Two thousand were with Saul.* Saul, no doubt, meditated the redemption of his country from the Philistines; and having chosen 3,000 men, he thought best to divide them into companies, and send one against the Philistine garrison at *Michmash,* another against that at *Beth-el,* and the third against that at *Gibeah.* He perhaps hoped, by surprising these garrisons, to get swords and spears for his men, of which we find (v. 22) they were entirely destitute.

3. *Jonathan smote.* He appears to have taken this garrison by surprise, for his men had no arms for a regular battle, or taking the place by storm. This is the first place in which this brave and excellent man appears, a man who bears one of the most amiable characters in the Bible. *Let the Hebrews hear.* Probably this means the people who dwelt beyond Jordan, who might very naturally be termed here *haibrim,* from *abar,* "he passed over"; those who are beyond the river Jordan, as Abraham was called *Ibri* because he dwelt beyond the river Euphrates.

4. *The people were called together.* The smiting of this garrison was the commencement of a war, and in effect the shaking off of the Philistine yoke; and now the people found that they must stand together, and fight for their lives.

5. *Thirty thousand chariots, and six thousand horsemen.* There is no proportion here between the chariots and the cavalry. The largest armies ever brought into the field, even by mighty emperors, never were furnished with *thirty thousand* chariots. I think *sheloshim,* "thirty," is a false reading for *shalosh,* "three." The Syriac and the Arabic both signify "three thousand"; and this was a fair proportion to the horsemen. This is most likely to be the true reading.

6. *The people did hide themselves.* They, being few in number, and totally unarmed as to swords and spears, were terrified at the very numerous and well-appointed army of the Philistines. Judea was full of rocks, caves, thickets, where people might shelter themselves from their enemies.

7. *While some hid themselves others fled beyond Jordan;* and those who did cleave to Saul *followed him trembling.*

8. *He tarried seven days, according to the set time.* Samuel in the beginning had told Saul to wait seven days, and he would come to him, and show him what to do, chap. x. 8. What is here said cannot be understood of that appointment, but of a different one. Samuel had at this time promised to come to him within seven days, and he kept his word, for we find him there before the day was ended; but as Saul found he did not come at the beginning of the seventh day, he became impatient, took the whole business into his own hand, and acted

the parts of prophet, priest, and king; and thus he attempted a most essential change in the Israelitish constitution. In it the king, the prophet, and the priest are in their nature perfectly distinct. What such a rash person might have done, if he had not been deprived of his authority, who can tell? But his conduct on this occasion sufficiently justifies that deprivation. That he was a rash and headstrong man is also proved by his senseless adjuration of the people about "food," chap. xiv. 24, and his unfeeling resolution to put the brave Jonathan, his own son, to death, because he had unwittingly acted contrary to this adjuration, v. 44. Saul appears to have been a brave and honest man, but he had few of those qualities which are proper for a king.

9. *And he offered the burnt offering.* This was most perfectly unconstitutional; he had no authority to offer, or cause to be offered, any of the Lord's sacrifices.

10. *Behold, Samuel came.* Samuel was punctual to his appointment; one hour longer of delay would have prevented every evil, and by it no good would have been lost.

11. *And Saul said.* Here he offers three excuses for his conduct: (1) the people were fast leaving his standard; (2) Samuel did not come "at the time"; at the very commencement of the time he did not come, but within that time he did come; (3) the Philistines were coming fast upon him. Saul should have waited out the time; and at all events he should not have gone contrary to the counsel of the Lord.

12. *I forced myself.* It was with great reluctance that I did what I did. In all this Saul was sincere, but he was rash, and regardless of the precept of the Lord, which precept or command he most evidently had received, v. 13. And one part of this precept was, that the Lord should tell him what he should do. Without this information, in an affair under the immediate cognizance of God, he should have taken no step.

14. *The Lord hath sought him a man after his own heart.* That this man was David is sufficiently clear from the sequel. But in what sense he was a man after God's own heart? Answer: (1) in his strict attention to the law and worship of God; (2) in his admitting, in the whole of his conduct, that God was King in Israel, and that he himself was but His vicegerent; (3) in never attempting to alter any of those laws, or in the least change the Israelitish constitution; (4) in all his public official conduct he acted according to the divine mind, and fulfilled the will of his Maker; thus was he a man after God's own heart. In reference to his private or personal moral conduct, the word is never used.

15. *And Samuel arose.* Though David, in the divine purpose, is appointed to be captain over the people, yet Saul is not to be removed from the government during his life; Samuel therefore accompanies him to Gibeah, to give him the requisite help in this conjuncture. *About six hundred men.* The whole of the Israelitish army at this time, and not one sword or spear among them!

17. *The spoilers came out.* The Philistines, finding that the Israelites durst not hazard a battle, divided their army into three bands, and sent them in three different directions to pillage and destroy the country. Jonathan profited by this circumstance, and attacked the remains of the army at Michmash, as we shall see in the succeeding chapter.

19. *Now there was no smith found.* It is very likely that in the former wars the Philistines carried away all the smiths from Israel.

21. *Yet they had a file.* The Hebrew *petsirah,* from *patsar,* "to rub hard," is translated very differently by the versions and by critics. Our translation may be as likely as any: they permitted them the use of *a file* (I believe the word means grindstone) to restore the blunted edges of their *axes* and *goads.*

22. *In the day of battle . . . there was neither sword nor spear.* But if the Israelites enjoyed such profound peace and undisturbed dominion under Samuel, how is it that they were totally destitute of arms, a state which argues the lowest circumstances of oppression and vassalage? In answer to this we may observe, that the bow and the sling were the principal arms of the Israelites; for these they needed no smith. The most barbarous nations, who have never seen iron, have nevertheless bows and arrows; the arrowheads generally made of flint.

CHAPTER 14

Jonathan and his armor-bearer purpose to attack a garrison of the Philistines, 1. Saul and his army, with Ahiah, the priest, tarry in Gibeah, 2-3. Jonathan plans his attack of the Philistine garrison, 4-10. He and his armor-bearer climb over a rock: attack and rout the garrison, 11-15. Saul and his company, seeing confusion in the Philistine host, come out against them, as did the men who had hidden themselves; and the Philistines are defeated, 16-23. Saul lays every man under a curse who shall eat food until the evening, in consequence of which the people are sorely distressed, 24-26. Jonathan, not hearing the adjuration, eats a little honey, which he found on the ground, 27-30. The Philistines being defeated, the people seize on the spoil, and begin to eat flesh without previously bleeding the animals, which Saul endeavors to prevent, 31-34. He builds an altar there, 35. Inquires of the Lord if he may pursue the Philistines by night, but receives no answer, 36-37. Attributes this to some sin committed by some unknown person; makes inquiry by lot, and finds that Jonathan had tasted the honey, on which he purposes to put him to death, 38-44. The people interpose, and rescue Jonathan, 45. Saul fights against the Moabites, Ammonites, and Amalekites, 46-48. An account of the family of Saul, 49-52.

1. *Come, and let us go over.* This action of Jonathan was totally contrary to the laws of war; no military operation should be undertaken without the knowledge and command of the general. But it is likely that he was led to this by a divine influence.

2. *Under a pomegranate tree.* Under *Rimmon,* which not only signifies a *pomegranate tree,* but also a strong rock, in which 600 Benjamites took shelter, Judg. xx. 45. Probably it was in this very rock that Saul and his 600 men now lay hidden.

3. *Ahiah, the son of Ahitub.* Phinehas, son of Eli, the high priest, had two sons, Ahitub and Ichabod; the latter was born when the ark was taken, and his mother died immediately after. Ahiah is also called Ahimelech, chap. xxii. 9. *Wearing an ephod.* That is, performing the functions of the high priest. This man does not appear to have been with Saul when he offered the sacrifices, chap. xiii. 9, etc.

4. *The name of the one was Bozez.* "Slippery"; *and the name of the other Seneh,* "treading down."—Targum.

6. *Let us go over.* Moved, doubtless, by a divine impulse. *There is no restraint to the Lord.* This is a fine sentiment; and where there is a promise of defense and support, the weakest, in the face of the strongest enemy, may rely on it with the utmost confidence.

9. *If they say thus unto us.* Jonathan had no doubt asked this as a sign from God; exactly as Eliezer, the servant of Abraham, did, Gen. xxiv. 12.

12. *Come up to us, and we will shew you a thing.* This was the favorable sign which Jonathan had requested. The Philistines seem to have meant, Come, and we will show you how well fortified we are, and how able to quell all the attacks of your countrymen.

13. *Jonathan climbed up.* It seems he had a part of the rock still to get over. When he got over, he began to slay the guards, which were about twenty in number; these were a sort of outpost or advanced guard to the garrison. *Slew after him.* Jonathan knocked them down, and the armor-bearer dispatched them. This seems to be the meaning.

14. *An half acre of land.* The ancients measured land by the quantum which a yoke of oxen could plough in a day. The original is obscure, and is variously understood. It is probably a proverbial expression for a "very small space."

16. *The watchmen of Saul.* Those who were sent out as scouts to observe the motions of the army. *Melted away.* There was no order in the Philistine camp, and the people were dispersing in all directions. The Vulgate has, "And behold the multitude were prostrate"; many lay dead upon the field, partly by the sword of Jonathan and his armor-bearer, and partly by the swords of each other, v. 20.

17. *Number now.* Saul perceived that the Philistines were routed, but could not tell by what means; supposing that it must be by some of his own troops, he called a muster to see who and how many were absent.

18. *Bring hither the ark of God.* He wished to inquire what use he should make of the present favorable circumstances, and to proceed in the business as God should direct.

19. *While Saul talked unto the priest.* Before he had made an end of consulting him, the increasing noise of the panic-struck Philistines called his attention; and finding there was no time to lose, he immediately collected his men and fell on them.

21. *The Hebrews that were with the Philistines.* We may understand such as they held in bondage, or who were their servants. Instead of *Hebrews* the Septuagint read, "the slaves"; from which it is evident that, instead of *Ibrim,* "Hebrews," they found in their text *abadim,* "servants."

24. *Saul had adjured the people.* He was afraid if they waited to refresh themselves the Philistines would escape out of their hands, and therefore he made the taking any food till sunset a capital crime. This was the very means of defeating his own intention; for as the people were exhausted for want of food, they could not continue the pursuit of their enemies. Had it not been for this foolish adjuration, there had been a greater slaughter of the Philistines, v. 30.

25. *There was honey upon the ground.* There were many wild bees in that country, and Judea is expressly said to be a land flowing with milk and honey.

26. *The honey dropped.* It seems to have dropped from the trees on the ground. Honey dews, as they are called, are not uncommon in most countries; and this appears to have been something of this kind.

27. *His eyes were enlightened.* Hunger and fatigue affect and dim the sight; on taking food, this affection is immediately removed.

33. *Roll a great stone unto me.* Probably this means that they should set up an altar to the Lord, on which the animals might be properly slain, and the blood poured out upon the earth; and a large stone was erected for an altar.

35. *Saul built an altar.* And this we are informed was *the first* he had built; Samuel, as prophet, had hitherto erected the altars, and Saul thought he had sufficient authority to erect one himself without the prophet, as he once offered sacrifice without him.

36. *Then said the priest.* It is evident that Ahiah doubted the propriety of pursuing the Philistines that night; and as a reverse of fortune might be ruinous after such a victory, he wished to have specific directions from the Lord.

37. *He answered him not that day.* Why was this answer delayed? Surely Jonathan's eating the honey was no sin. This could not have excited God's displeasure. And yet the lot found out Jonathan! But did this argue that he had incurred guilt in the sight of God? I answer: It did not; for Jonathan was delivered, by the authority of the people, from his father's rash curse; no propitiation is offered for his supposed transgression to induce God to pardon it; nor do we find any displeasure of God manifested on the occasion.

41. *Lord God of Israel, Give a perfect lot.* Both the Vulgate and Septuagint add much to this verse: "And Saul said to the Lord God of Israel, Lord God of Israel, give judgment. Why is it that thou hast not answered thy servant to-day? If the iniquity be in me, or Jonathan my son, make it manifest. Or if this iniquity be in thy people, give sanctification."

42. *And Jonathan was taken.* The object of the inquiry most evidently was, Who has gone contrary to the king's adjuration today? The answer to that must be Jonathan.

45. *And the people said . . . Shall Jonathan die, who hath wrought this great salvation in Israel? God forbid: as the Lord liveth, there shall not one hair of his head fall to the ground.* Here was a righteous and impartial jury, who brought in a verdict according to the evidence: No man should die but for a breach of the law of God; but Jonathan hath not broken any law of God; therefore Jonathan should not die. *He hath wrought with God this day.* God has been Commander in chief; Jonathan has acted under His directions. *So the people rescued Jonathan.* And God testified no displeasure; and perhaps He permitted all this that He might correct Saul's propensity to rashness.

47. *So Saul took the kingdom.* The Targum appears to give the meaning of this expression: "Saul prospered in his government over Israel."

And the proofs of his prosperity are immediately subjoined. *Fought against all his enemies.* Of the wars which are mentioned here we have no particulars; they must have endured a long time, and have been, at least in general, successful.

48. *Smote the Amalekites.* This war is mentioned in the following chapter.

49. *Now the sons of Saul.* We do not find Ishbosheth here.

52. *When Saul saw any strong man.* This was very politic. He thus continued to recruit his army with strong and effective men.

CHAPTER 15

Samuel sends Saul to destroy the Amalekites, and all their substance, 1-3. Saul collects an immense army and comes against their city, 4-5. He desires the Kenites to remove from among the Amalekites, 6. He smites the Amalekites, and takes their king Agag, prisoner, and saves the best of the spoil, 7-9. The Lord is displeased, and sends Samuel to reprove him, 10-11. The conversation between Samuel and Saul, in which the latter endeavors to justify his conduct, 12-23. He is convinced that he has done wrong, and asks pardon, 24-31. Samuel causes Agag to be slain, for which he assigns the reasons, 32-35.

1. *The Lord sent me to anoint thee.* This gave him a right to say what immediately follows.

2. *I remember that which Amalek did.* The Amalekites were a people of Arabia Petraea, who had occupied a tract of country on the frontiers of Egypt and Palestine. They had acted with great cruelty towards the Israelites on their coming out of Egypt (Exod. xvii. 8). They came upon them when they were "faint and weary," and "smote the hindmost of the people"—those who were too weak to keep up with the rest (see Deut. xxv. 18). And God then purposed that Amalek, as a nation, should be blotted out from under heaven, which purpose was now fulfilled by Saul upwards of four hundred years afterwards!

3. *Slay both man and woman.* Nothing could justify such an exterminating decree but the absolute authority of God. This was given. All the reasons of it we do not know; but this we know well, the Judge of all the earth doth right. This war was not for plunder, for God commanded that all the property as well as all the people should be destroyed.

5. *Saul came to a city of Amalek.* I believe the original should be translated, "And Saul came to the city Amalek," their capital being called by the name of their tribe.

6. *Said unto the Kenites.* The Kenites were an ancient people. Jethro, the father-in-law of Moses, was a Kenite. Hobab, his son (if the same person be not meant), was guide to the Hebrews through the wilderness. They had a portion of the Promised Land, near to the city Arad (see Judg. i. 16); and for more particulars concerning them and the Amalekites see the notes on Num. xxvi. 20-21.

11. *It repenteth me that I have set up Saul.* That is, I placed him on the throne; I intended, if he had been obedient, to establish his kingdom. He has been disobedient; I change My purpose, and the kingdom shall not be established in his family. This is what is meant by God's repenting—"changing a purpose" according to conditions already laid down or mentally determined.

12. *He set him up a place.* Literally, a "hand," *yad.* Some say it was a monument; others, a triumphal arch. Probably it was no more than a hand, pointing out the place where Saul had gained the victory. Absalom's pillar is called "the hand of Absalom," 2 Sam. xviii. 18.

15. *The people spared the best of the sheep.* It is very likely that the people did spare the best of the prey; and it is as likely that Saul might have restrained them if he would. That they might not love war, God had interdicted spoil and plunder; so the war was undertaken merely from a sense of duty, without any hope of enriching themselves by it.

21. *To sacrifice unto the Lord.* Thus he endeavors to excuse the people. They did not take the spoil in order to enrich themselves by it, but to *sacrifice unto the Lord;* and did not this motive justify their conduct?

22. *Hath the Lord as great delight?* This was a very proper answer to and refutation of Saul's excuse. Is not obedience to the will of God the end of all religion, of its rites, ceremonies, and sacrifices?

23. *For rebellion is as the sin of witchcraft, and stubbornness is as iniquity and idolatry.* This is no translation of those difficult words. It appears to me that the three nouns which occur first in the text refer each to the three last in order. Thus, *chattah,* "transgression," refers to *aven,* "iniquity," which is the principle whence transgression springs. *Kesem,* "divination," refers to *teraphim,* consecrated images used in incantations. And *meri,* "rebellion," refers evidently to *haphstar,* "stubbornness," whence rebellion springs. The meaning therefore of this difficult place may be the following: As transgression comes from iniquity, divination from teraphim, and rebellion from stubbornness, so, because you have rejected the word of the Lord, He has also rejected you from being king.

24. *I have sinned . . . because I feared the people.* This was the best excuse he could make for himself; but had he feared God more, he need have feared the people less.

25. *Pardon my sin.* Literally, "bear my sin"; take it away; forgive what I have done against thee, and be my intercessor with God, that He may forgive my offense against Him.

26. *I will not return with thee.* I cannot acknowledge you as king, seeing the Lord has rejected you.

29. *The Strength of Israel will not lie.* What God has purposed He will bring to pass, for He has all power in the heavens and in the earth; and He will not *repent*—change His purpose—concerning you.

32. *Agag came unto him delicately.* The Septuagint have "trembling"; the original, "delicacies"; probably *ish,* "man," understood; "a man of delights, a pleasure-taker"; the Vulgate, "very fat and trembling." *Surely the bitterness of death is past.* Almost all the versions render this differently from ours. "Surely death is bitter," is their general sense; and this seems to be the true meaning.

33. *As thy sword hath made women childless.* It appears that Agag had forfeited his life by his own personal transgressions, and that his death now was the retribution of his cruelties.

35. *And Samuel came no more to see Saul.* But we read, chap. xix. 22-24, that Saul went to see Samuel at Naioth, but this does not affect what is said here. From this time Samuel had no connection with Saul; he never more acknowledged him as king; he mourned and prayed for him, and continued to perform his prophetic functions at Ramah, and at Naioth, superintending the school of the prophets in that place.

CHAPTER 16

Samuel is sent from Ramah to Bethlehem, to anoint David, 1-13. The Spirit of the Lord departs from Saul, and an evil spirit comes upon him, 14. His servants exhort him to get a skilful harper to play before him, 15-16. He is pleased with the counsel, and desires them to find such a person, 17. They recommend David, 18. He is sent for, comes, plays before Saul, and finds favor in his sight, 19-23.

1. *Fill thine horn with oil.* Horns appear to have been the ancient drinking vessels of all nations; and we may suppose that most persons who had to travel much always carried one with them, for the purpose of taking up water from the fountains to quench their thirst.

2. *Take an heifer with thee, and say, I am come to sacrifice.* This was strictly true; Samuel did offer a sacrifice; and it does not appear that he could have done the work which God designed unless he had offered this sacrifice, and called the elders of the people together, and thus collected Jesse's sons. But he did not tell the principal design of his coming. Had he done so, it would have produced evil and no good; and though no man, in any circumstances, should ever tell a lie, yet in all circumstances he is not obliged to tell the whole truth, though in every circumstance he must tell nothing but the truth, and in every case so tell the truth that the hearer shall not believe a lie by it.

3. *Call Jesse to the sacrifice.* The common custom was, after the blood of the victim had been poured out to God, and the fat burned, to feast on the flesh of the sacrifice. This appears to have been the case in all except in the whole burnt offering; this was entirely consumed.

4. *The elders of the town trembled at his coming.* They knew he was a prophet of the Lord, and they were afraid that he was now come to denounce some judgments of the Most High against their city.

5. *Sanctify yourselves.* Change your clothes, and wash your bodies in pure water, and prepare your minds by meditation, reflection, and prayer; that, being in the spirit of sacrifice, you may offer acceptably to the Lord.

7. *Man looketh on the outward appearance.* And it is well he should, and confine his looks to that; for when he pretends to sound the heart, he usurps the prerogative of God.

10. *Seven of his sons.* This certainly was not done publicly; Samuel, Jesse, and his children must have been in a private apartment, previously to the public feast on the sacrifice; for Samuel says, v. 11, "We will not sit down till he [David] come."

12. *He was ruddy.* I believe the word here means "red-haired."

13. *The Spirit of the Lord came upon David.* God qualified him to be governor of his people, by infusing such graces as wisdom, prudence, counsel, courage, liberality, and magnanimity.

14. *The Spirit of the Lord departed from Saul.* He was thrown into such a state of mind by the judgments of God as to be deprived of any regal qualities which he before possessed. God seems to have taken what gifts he had and given them to David; and then the evil spirit came upon Saul; for what God fills not, the devil will. *An evil spirit from the Lord.* The evil spirit was either immediately sent from the Lord or permitted to come. Whether this was a diabolic possession or a mere mental malady, the learned are not agreed; it seems to have partaken of both. That Saul had fallen into a deep melancholy, there is little doubt.

23. *The evil spirit from God.* The word *evil* is not in the common Hebrew text, but it is in the Vulgate, Septuagint, Targum, Syriac, and Arabic. The Septuagint leave out "of God," and have "the evil spirit." The Targum says, "The evil spirit from before the Lord"; and the Arabic has it, "The evil spirit by the permission of God"; this is at least the sense.

CHAPTER 17

The Philistines gather together against Israel at Ephes-dammim, and Saul and his men pitch their camp near the valley of Elah, 1-3. Goliath of Gath, a gigantic man, whose height was six cubits and a span, defies the armies of Israel, and proposes to end all contests by single combat; his armor is described, 4-11. Saul and his host are greatly dismayed, 12. David, having been sent by his father with provisions to his brethren in the army, hears the challenge, inquires into the circumstances, thinks it a reproach to Israel that no man can be found to accept the challenge, is brought before Saul, and proposes to undertake the combat, 13-32. Saul objects to his youth and inexperience, 33. David shows the grounds on which he undertakes it, 34-37. Saul arms him with his own armor; but David, finding them an encumbrance, puts them off, and takes his staff, his sling, and five stones out of the brook, and goes to meet Goliath, 38-40. The Philistine draws near, despises, defies, and curses him, 41-44. David retorts his defiance, 45-47. They draw near to each other, and David slings a stone, hits Goliath in the forehead, slays him, and cuts off his head with his own sword, 48-51. The Philistines flee, and are pursued by the Israelites, 52-53. David brings the head of the Philistine to Jerusalem, 54. Conversation between Saul and Abner concerning David, who is in consequence brought before Saul, 55-58.

1. *Now the Philistines gathered together.* We have already seen that there was war between Saul and the Philistines all his days (see chap. xiv. 52). *Shochoh and Azekah.* Places which lay to the south of Jerusalem and to the west of Bethlehem.

2. *The valley of Elah.* Some translate this the "turpentine valley" or "the valley of the terebinth trees"; and others, "the valley of oaks."

3. *The Philistines stood on a mountain.* These were two eminences or hills from which they could see and talk with each other.

4. *There went out a champion.* Our word *champion* comes from *campus*, "the field." "Champion is he, properly, who fights in the field; i.e., in camps." But is this the meaning of the original *ish habbenayim*, a "middle man," the "man between two"; that is, as here, the man who undertakes to settle the disputes between two armies or nations? So our ancient champions settled disputes between contending parties by what was termed camp fight; hence the *campio* or "champion."

Whose height was six cubits and a span. The word *cubit* signifies the length from *cubitus*, the elbow, to the top of the middle finger, which is generally rated at eighteen inches. The *span* is the distance from the top of the middle finger to the end of the thumb, when extended as far as they can stretch on a plain; this is ordinarily nine inches. The height of this Philistine would then be nine feet nine inches, which is a tremendous height for a man. But the versions are not all agreed in his height. The Septuagint read "four cubits and a span"; and Josephus reads the same. It is necessary however to observe that the Septuagint, in the Codex Alexandrinus, read with the Hebrew text.

5. *He was armed with a coat of mail.* The words in the original mean "a coat of mail" formed of plates of brass overlapping each other, like the scales of a fish, or tiles of a house. *The weight . . . five thousand shekels.* Goliath's coat of mail, weighing *five thousand shekels*, was exactly 156 pounds 4 ounces avoirdupois. A vast weight for a coat of mail, but not all out of proportion to the man!

6. *Greaves of brass upon his legs.* This species of armor may be seen on many ancient monuments. It was a plate of brass which covered the shin or forepart of the leg, from the knee down to the instep, and was buckled with straps behind the leg.

A target of brass between his shoulders. There are different opinions concerning this piece of armor, called here *kidon.* Some think it was a covering for the shoulders; others, that it was a javelin or dart; others, that it was a lance; some, a club; and others, a sword. It is certainly distinguished from the shield, v. 41, and is translated a "spear," Josh. viii. 18.

7. *His spear's head weighed six hundred shekels of iron.* That is, his spear's head was of iron, and it weighed *six hundred shekels;* this, according to the former computation, would amount to eighteen pounds twelve ounces. *And one bearing a shield. Hatstsinnah,* from *tsan,* "pointed or penetrating," if it does not mean some kind of lance, must mean a *shield* with what is called the *umbo,* a sharp protuberance in the middle, with which they could as effectually annoy their enemies as defend themselves.

10. *I defy.* "I strip and make bare" the armies of Israel, for none dared to fight him.

11. *Saul and all Israel . . . were dismayed.* They saw no man able to accept the challenge.

12. Verses 12 to 31 inclusive are wanting in the Septuagint; as also v. 41; and from v. 54 to the end; with the first five verses of chap. xviii, and verses 9-11, 17-19 of the same.

18. *Carry these ten cheeses.* "Cheeses of milk," says the margin. In the East they do not make what we call cheese; they press the milk but slightly, and carry it in rush baskets. It is highly salted, and little different from curds.

29. *Is there not a cause? Halo dabar hu.* I believe the meaning is what several of the versions express: "I have spoken but a word."

32. *And David said.* This properly connects with the eleventh verse.

33. *Thou art but a youth.* Supposed to be about twenty-two or twenty-three years of age.

34. *Thy servant kept his father's sheep.* He found it necessary to give Saul the reasons why he undertook this combat, and why he expected to be victorious.

35. *The slaying of the lion and the bear* mentioned here must have taken place at two different times; perhaps the verse should be read thus: "I went out after him [the lion] and smote him, etc. And when he [the bear] rose up against me, I caught him by the beard and slew him."

37. *Go, and the Lord be with thee.* Saul saw that these were reasonable grounds of confidence, and therefore wished him success.

39. *I cannot go with these.* In ancient times it required considerable exercise and training to make a man expert in the use of such heavy armor. *I have not proved them,* says David; I am wholly unaccustomed to such armor and it would be an encumbrance to me.

40. *He took his staff.* What we would call his crook. *A shepherd's bag.* That in which he generally carried his provisions while keeping the sheep in the open country. *And his sling.* The sling, among both the Greeks and Hebrews, has been a powerful offensive weapon. See what has been said on Judg. xx. 16. It is composed of two strings and a leathern strap; the strap is in the middle, and is the place where the stone lies. The string on the right end of the strap is firmly fastened to the hand; that on the left is held between the thumb and middle joint of the forefinger. It is then whirled two or three times round the head; and when discharged, the finger and thumb let go their hold of the left-end string. The velocity and force of the sling are in proportion to the distance of the strap from the shoulder joint.

42. *He disdained him.* He held him in contempt; he saw that he was young, and from his ruddy complexion supposed him to be effeminate.

43. *Am I a dog, that thou comest to me with staves?* It is very likely that Goliath did not perceive the sling, which David might have kept coiled up within his hand. *Cursed David by his gods.* Prayed his gods to curse him. This long parley between David and Goliath is quite in the style of those times.

44. *Come to me, and I will give thy flesh.* He intended, as soon as he could lay hold on him, to pull him to pieces.

45. *Thou comest to me with a sword.* "I come to thee with the name [*beshem*] of Jehovah of hosts, the God of the armies of Israel." What Goliath expected from his arms, David expected from the ineffable name.

46. *This day will the Lord deliver thee into mine hand.* This was a direct and circumstantial prophecy of what did take place.

47. *For the battle is the Lord's.* It is the Lord's war. You are fighting against Him and His religion, as the champion of your party; I am fighting for God, as the champion of His cause.

49. *Smote the Philistine in his forehead.* Except his face, Goliath was everywhere covered over with strong armor. Either he had no beaver to his helmet, or it was lifted up so as to expose his forehead; but it does not appear that the ancient helmets had any covering for the face.

CHAPTER 18

Jonathan and David commence a lasting friendship; and David acts prudently with respect to Saul, 1-5. Saul becomes jealous of David, on account of the esteem in which he is held in Israel; and, in his fury, endeavors to destroy him, 6-12. David is made captain over a thousand; and the people love and respect him, 13-16. Saul, in order to ensnare him, offers him his daughter in marriage, 17-24; and requires a hundred foreskins of the Philistines for dowry; hoping that, in endeavoring to procure them, David might fall by the hands of the Philistines, 25. David agrees to the conditions, fulfils them, and has Michal to wife, 26-30.

6. *The women came out.* It was the principal business of certain women to celebrate victories, sing at funerals, etc. *With instruments of music.* The original word (*shalishim*) signifies instruments with three strings.

7. *Saul hath slain his thousands.* As it cannot literally be true that Saul had slain thousands, and David ten thousands, it would be well to translate the passage thus: "Saul hath smitten or fought against thousands; David, against tens of thousands."

10. *The evil spirit from God.* See on chap. xvi. 14, etc. *He prophesied in the midst of the house.* He was beside himself; made prayers, supplications, and incoherent imprecations. But let us examine the original more closely: it is said that Saul prophesied in the midst of his house, that is, he prayed in his family, while David was playing on the harp; and then suddenly threw his javelin, intending to have killed David. Let it be observed that the word *vaiyithnabbe* is the third person singular of the future *hithpael*, the sign of which is not only to do an action on or for oneself, but also to feign or pretend to do it. The meaning seems to be, Saul pretended to be praying in his family, the better to conceal his murderous intentions, and render David unsuspicious; who was, probably, at this time performing the musical part of the family worship. This view of the subject makes the whole case natural and plain.

11. *Saul cast the javelin.* The *javelin* or "spear" was the emblem of regal authority; kings always had it at hand, and in ancient monuments they are always represented with it.

13. *Made him his captain.* This was under pretense of doing him honor, when it was in effect only to rid himself of the object of his envy.

15. *He was afraid of him.* He saw that, by his prudent conduct, he was every day gaining increasing influence.

21. *That she may be a snare to him.* Saul had already determined the condition on which he would give his daughter to David; viz., that he should slay 100 Philistines. This he supposed David would undertake for the love of Michal, and that he must necessarily perish in the attempt; and thus Michal would become a snare to him.

25. *But an hundred foreskins.* That is, You shall slay 100 Philistines, and you shall produce their foreskins as a proof not only that you have killed 100 men but that these are of the uncircumcised.

27. *Slew . . . two hundred men.* The Septuagint has only "one hundred men." Saul covenanted with David for a hundred; and David himself says, 2 Sam. iii. 14, that he

espoused Michal for a hundred; hence it is likely that "one hundred" is the true reading.

30. *Then the princes of the Philistines went forth.* Probably to avenge themselves on David and the Israelites; but of this war we know no more than that David was more skillful and successful in it than any of the other officers of Saul. His military skill was greater, and his success was proportionate to his skill and courage; hence it is said he *behaved himself more wisely than all the servants of Saul.*

CHAPTER 19

Jonathan pleads for David before Saul, who is for the present reconciled, 1-7. David defeats the Philistines; and Saul becomes again envious, and endeavors to slay him, but he escapes, 8-10. Saul sends men to David's house, to lie in wait for him; but Michal saves him by a stratagem, 11-17. David flees to Samuel, at Ramah, 18. Saul, hearing of it, sends messengers there several times to take him; but the Spirit of God coming upon them, they prophesy, 19-21. Saul, hearing of this, goes after David himself, and falls under the same influence, 22-24.

1. *That they should kill David.* Nothing less than the especial interposition of God could have saved David's life, when every officer about the king's person, and every soldier, had got positive orders to dispatch him.

2. *Take heed to thyself until the morning.* Perhaps the order was given to slay him the next day; and therefore Jonathan charges him to be particularly on his guard at that time, and to hide himself.

5. *For he did put his life in his hand.* The pleadings in this verse, though short, are exceedingly cogent; and the argument is such as could not be resisted.

6. *He shall not be slain.* In consequence of this oath, we may suppose he issued orders contrary to those which he had given the preceding day.

7. *He was in his presence, as in times past.* By Jonathan's advice he had secreted himself on that day on which he was to have been assassinated; the king having sworn that he should not be slain, David resumes his place in the palace of Saul.

9. *And the evil spirit from the Lord.* His envy and jealousy again returned, producing distraction of mind, which was exacerbated by diabolic influence (see on chap. xvi. 14).

10. *But he slipped away.* He found he could not trust Saul, and therefore was continually on his watch. His agility of body was the means of his preservation at this time.

11. *To slay him in the morning.* When they might be able to distinguish between him and Michal, his wife; for had they attempted his life in the night season, there would have been some danger to Michal's life. Besides, Saul wished to represent him as a traitor; and consequently an attack upon him was justifiable at any time, even in the fullest daylight.

12. *Let David down through a window.* As Saul's messengers were sent to David's house to watch him, they would naturally guard the gate, or lie in wait in that place by which David would come out. Michal, seeing this, let him down to the ground through a window, probably at the back part of the house.

13. *Michal took an image. Eth hatteraphim,* "the teraphim." The Hebrew word appears to mean any kind of image, in any kind of form,

as a representative of some reality. Here it must have been something in the human form, because it was intended to represent a man lying in bed, indisposed. *A pillow of goats' hair.* Perhaps she formed the appearance of a sick man's head muffled up by this pillow or bag of goats' hair. So I think the original might be understood. The goats' hair was merely accidental, unless we could suppose that it was designed to represent the hair of David's head, which is not improbable.

17. *Let me go; why should I kill thee?* That is, If you do not let me go, I will kill you. This she said to excuse herself to her father; as a wife she could do not less than favor the escape of her husband, being perfectly satisfied that there was no guilt in him. It is supposed that it was on this occasion that David wrote the fifty-ninth psalm, "Deliver me from mine enemies."

18. *David fled, and escaped . . . to Samuel.* He, no doubt, came to this holy man to ask advice; and Samuel thought it best to retain him for the present, with himself at Naioth, where it is supposed he had a school of prophets.

20. *The company of the prophets prophesying.* Employed in religious exercises. *Samuel . . . appointed over them.* Being head or president of the school at this place. *The Spirit of God was upon the messengers.* They partook of the same influence, and joined in the same exercise, and thus were prevented from seizing David.

23. *He went on, and prophesied.* The Divine Spirit seemed to have seized him at the well of Sechu; and he went on from that prophesying—praying, singing praises—till he came to Naioth.

24. *He stripped off his clothes.* Threw off his royal robes or military dress, retaining only his tunic; and continued so all that day and all that night, uniting with the sons of the prophets in prayers, singing praises, and other religious exercises, which were unusual to kings and warriors; and this gave rise to the saying, *Is Saul also among the prophets?* By bringing both him and his men thus under a divine influence, God prevented them from injuring the person of David.

CHAPTER 20

David complains to Jonathan of Saul's enmity against him; Jonathan comforts him, 1-10. They walk out into the field, and renew their covenant, 11-17. David asks Jonathan's leave to absent himself from Saul's court; and Jonathan informs him how he shall ascertain the disposition of his father towards him, 18-23. David hides himself; is missed by Saul; Jonathan is questioned concerning his absence; makes an excuse for David; Saul is enraged, and endeavors to kill Jonathan, 24-33. Jonathan goes out to the field; gives David the sign which they had agreed on, and by which he was to know that the king had determined to take away his life, 34-39. He sends his servant back into the city; and then he and David meet, renew their covenant, and have a very affectionate parting, 40-42.

1. *David fled from Naioth.* On hearing that Saul had come to that place, knowing that he was no longer in safety, he fled for his life.

2. *My father will do nothing.* Jonathan thought that his father could have no evil design against David, because of the oath which he had sworn to himself, chap. xix. 6; and at any rate, that he would do nothing against David without informing him.

3. *There is but a step between me and death.* My life is in the most imminent danger. Your father has, most assuredly, determined to destroy me.

5. *To morrow is the new moon.* The months of the Hebrews were lunar months, and they reckoned from new moon to new moon. And as their other feasts, particularly the Passover, were reckoned according to this, they were very scrupulous in observing the first appearance of each new moon. On these new moons they offered sacrifices, and had a feast; as we learn from Num. x. 10; xxviii. 11. And we may suppose that the families, on such occasions, sacrificed and feasted together.

12. *Jonathan said . . . O Lord God of Israel.* There is, most evidently, something wanting in this verse. The Septuagint has, "The Lord God of Israel doth know." The Syriac and Arabic, "The Lord God of Israel is witness." Either of these makes a good sense. But two of Dr. Kennicott's MSS. supply the word *chai,* "liveth"; and the text reads thus, "As the Lord God of Israel liveth, when I have sounded my father—if there be good, and I then send not unto thee, and show it thee, the Lord do so and much more to Jonathan." This makes a still better sense.

13. *The Lord be with thee, as he hath been with my father.* From this and other passages here it is evident that Jonathan knew that the Lord had appointed David to the kingdom.

14. *Shew me the kindness of the Lord.* When you come to the kingdom, if I am alive, you shall show kindness to me, and you shall continue that kindness to my family after me.

25. *The king sat upon his seat.* It seems that there was one table for Saul, Jonathan, David, and Abner—Saul having the chief seat, that next to the wall. As only four sat at this table, the absence of any one would soon be noticed.

29. *Our family hath a sacrifice.* Such sacrifices were undoubtedly festal ones; the beasts slain for the occasion were first offered to God, and their blood poured out before Him; afterwards all that were bidden to the feast ate of the flesh. This was a family entertainment, at the commencement of which God was peculiarly honored.

30. *Thou son of the perverse rebellious woman.* The Hebrew might be translated, "Son of an unjust rebellion"; that is, "Thou art a rebel against thy own father."

34. *Jonathan arose . . . in fierce anger.* We should probably understand this rather of Jonathan's grief than of his *anger,* the latter clause explaining the former: *for he was grieved for David.*

38. *Make speed, haste, stay not.* Though these words appear to be addressed to the lad, yet they were spoken to David, indicating that his life was at stake, and only a prompt flight could save him.

40. *Jonathan gave his artillery.* I believe this to be the only place in our language where the word *artillery* is not applied to cannon or ordnance. The original (*keley*) signifies simply "instruments," and here means the bow, quiver, and arrows.

41. *Until David exceeded.* David's distress must, in the nature of things, be the greatest.

Besides his friend Jonathan, whom he was now about to lose forever, he lost his wife, relatives, country; and, what was most afflictive, the altars of his God, and the ordinances of religion.

CHAPTER 21

David comes to Ahimelech at Nob, receives provisions from him, and the sword of Goliath; and is noticed by Doeg, one of the servants of Saul, 1-9. He leaves Nob, and goes to Achish, king of Gath, 10. But on being recognized as the vanquisher of Goliath by the servants of Achish, he feigns himself deranged, and Achish sends him away, 11-15.

1. *Then came David to Nob.* There were two places of this name, one on this side, the second on the other side of Jordan. But it is generally supposed that Nob, near Gibeah of Benjamin, is the place here intended; it was about twelve miles from Jerusalem. *Why art thou alone?* Ahimelech probably knew nothing of the difference between Saul and David; and as he knew him to be the king's son-in-law, he wondered to see him come without any attendants.

2. *The king hath commanded me a business.* All said here is an untruth, and could not be dictated by the Spirit of the Lord; but there is no reason to believe that David was under the influence of divine inspiration at this time.

6. *So the priest gave him hallowed bread.* To this history our Lord alludes, Mark ii. 25, in order to show that in cases of absolute necessity a breach of the ritual law was no sin. It was lawful for the priests only to eat the shewbread; but David and his companions were starving, no other bread could be had at the time, and therefore he and his companions ate of it without sin.

7. *Detained before the Lord.* Probably fulfilling some vow to the Lord, and therefore for a time resident at the Tabernacle. *And his name was Doeg.* From chap. xxii. 9 we learn that this man betrayed David's secret to Saul, which caused him to destroy the city, and slay eighty-five priests. We learn from its title that the fifty-second psalm was made on this occasion; but titles are not to be implicitly trusted.

9. *The sword of Goliath.* It has already been conjectured (see chap. xvii) that the sword of Goliath was laid up as a trophy in the Tabernacle.

10. *Went to Achish the king of Gath.* This was the worst place to which he could have gone; it was the very city of Goliath, whom he had slain, and whose sword he now wore; and he soon found, from the conversation of the servants of Achish, that his life was in the most imminent danger in this place.

13. *And he changed his behaviour.* Some imagine David was so terrified at the danger to which he was now exposed that he was thrown into a kind of frenzy, accompanied with epileptic fits. This opinion is countenanced by the Septuagint, who render the passage thus: "Behold, ye see an epileptic man. Why have ye introduced him to me? Have I any need of epileptics, that ye have brought him to have his fits before me?" It is worthy of remark that the spittle falling upon the beard, i.e., frothing at the mouth, is a genuine concomitant of an epileptic fit.

If this translation be allowed, it will set the conduct of David in a clearer point of view than the present translation does. But others think the whole was a feigned conduct, and that he acted the part of a lunatic or madman in order to get out of the hands of Achish and his courtiers.

CHAPTER 22

David flees to the cave of Adullam, where he is joined by 400 men of various descriptions, 1-2. He goes afterwards to Moab; and by the advice of the prophet Gad, to the forest of Hareth, 3-5. Saul, suspecting his servants of infidelity, upbraids them, 6-8. Doeg informs him of David's coming to Nob; of his being entertained by Ahimelech; on which Saul slays Ahimelech and all the priests, to the number of 85, and destroys the city of Nob, 9-19. Abiathar, the son of Ahimelech, alone escapes; he joins with David, by whom he is assured of protection, 20-23.

1. *The cave Adullam.* This was in the tribe of Judah, and, according to Eusebius and Jerome, ten miles eastward of what they call Eleutheropolis.

2. *And every one that was in distress . . . debt . . . discontented.* It is very possible that these several disaffected and exceptionable characters might at first have supposed that David, unjustly persecuted, would be glad to avail himself of their assistance that he might revenge himself upon Saul, and so they in the meantime might profit by plunder. But if this were their design they were greatly disappointed, for David never made any improper use of them. Whatever they were before they came to David, we find that he succeeded in civilizing them, and making profitable to the state those who were before unprofitable.

3. *He said unto the king of Moab.* David could not trust his parents within the reach of Saul, and he found it very inconvenient to them to be obliged to go through all the fatigues of a military life, and therefore begs the king of Moab to give them shelter.

5. *Get thee into the land of Judah.* Gad saw that in this place alone he could find safety.

6. *Saul abode in Gibeah.* Saul and his men were in pursuit of David, and had here, as in the general custom in the East, encamped on a "height," for so *Ramah* should be translated, as in the margin. His *spear,* the ensign of power (see on chap. xviii. 11) was at hand, that is, stuck in the ground where he rested, which was the mark to the soldiers that there was their general's tent. *And all his servants were standing about him.* That is, they were encamped around him, or perhaps here there is a reference to a sort of council of war called by Saul for the purpose of delivering the speech recorded in the following verses.

9. *Doeg the Edomite, which was set over the servants of Saul.* In chap. xxi. 7 he is said to be "the chiefest of the herdmen that belonged to Saul," and the Septuagint intimate that he was over the mules of Saul.

14. *And who is so faithful?* The word *neeman,* which we here translate *faithful,* is probably the name of an officer.

15. *Did I then begin to enquire of God?* He probably means that his inquiring now for David was no new thing, having often done so before, and without ever being informed it was either wrong in itself or displeasing to the king. Nor is it likely that Ahimelech knew of any disagreement between Saul and David. He knew

him to be the king's son-in-law, and he treated him as such.

17. *But the servants of the king would not.* They dared to disobey the commands of the king in a case of such injustice, inhumanity, and irreligion.

18. *And Doeg . . . fell upon the priests.* A ruthless Edomite, capable of any species of iniquity.

19. *And Nob . . . smote he with the edge of the sword.* This is one of the worst acts in the life of Saul; his malice was implacable, and his wrath was cruel, and there is no motive of justice or policy by which such a barbarous act can be justified.

20. *Abiathar, escaped.* This man carried with him his sacerdotal garments, as we find from chap. xxiii. 6, 9.

CHAPTER 23

David succors Keilah, besieged by the Philistines; defeats them, and delivers the city, 1-6. Saul, hearing that David was at Keilah, determines to come and seize him, 7-8. David inquires of the Lord concerning the fidelity of the men of Keilah towards him; is informed that, if he stays in the city, the men of Keilah will betray him to Saul, 9-12. David and his men escape from the city, and come to the wilderness of Ziph, 13-15. Jonathan meets David in the wood of Ziph, strengthens his hand in God, and they renew their covenant, 16-18. The Ziphites endeavor to betray David to Saul, but he and his men escape to Maon, 19-24. Saul comes to Maon; and having surrounded the mountain on which David and his men were, they must inevitably have fallen into his hands, had not a messenger come to call Saul to the succor of Judah, then invaded by the Philistines, 25-27. Saul leaves the pursuit of David, and goes to succor the land; and David escapes to En-gedi, 28-29.

1. *The Philistines fight against Keilah.* Keilah was a fortified town in the tribe of Judah near to Eleutheropolis, on the road to Hebron. *Rob the threshingfloors.* This was an ancient custom of the Philistines, Midianites, and others (see Judg. vi. 4). When the corn was ripe and fit to be threshed, and they had collected it at the threshing floors, which were always in the open field, their enemies came upon them and spoiled them of the fruits of their harvest.

2. *Therefore David enquired of the Lord.* In what way David made this inquiry we are not told, but it was proably by means of Abiathar; and therefore I think, with Houbigant, that the sixth verse should be read immediately after the first. *The Lord said . . . Go, and smite.* He might now go with confidence, being assured of success.

4. *David enquired of the Lord yet again.* This was to satisfy his men, who made the strong objections mentioned in the preceding verse.

5. *Brought away their cattle.* The forage and spoil which the Philistines had taken, driving the country before them round about Keilah.

8. *Saul called all the people together.* That is, all the people of that region or district, that they might scour the country, and hunt out David from all his haunts.

9. *Bring hither the ephod.* It seems as if David himself, clothed with the ephod, had consulted the Lord; vv. 10-12 contain the words of the consultation and the Lord's answer.

14. *Wilderness of Ziph.* Ziph was a city in the southern part of Judea, not far from Carmel.

25. *The wilderness of Maon.* Maon was a mountainous district in the most southern parts of Judah.

28. *They called that place Sela-hammah-lekoth.* That is, "the rock of divisions"; because, says the Targum, "the heart of the king was divided to go hither and thither." Here Saul was obliged to separate himself from David, in order to go and oppose the invading Philistines.

29. *Strong holds at En-gedi.* En-gedi was situated near to the western coast of the Dead Sea, not far from Jeshimon. It literally signifies the "kid's well," and was celebrated for its vineyards, Cant. i. 14. It was also celebrated for its balm. It is reported to be a mountainous territory, filled with caverns; and consequently proper for David in his present circumstances.

CHAPTER 24

Saul is informed that David is at En-gedi, and goes to seek him with 3,000 men, 1-2. He goes into a cave to repose, where David and his men lie hid; who, observing this, exhort David to take away his life; David refuses, and contents himself with privily cutting off Saul's skirt, 3-7. When Saul departs, not knowing what was done, David calls after him; shows him that his life had been in his power; expostulates strongly with him; and appeals to God, the Judge of his innocence, 8-15. Saul confesses David's uprightness; acknowledges his obligation to him for sparing his life; and causes him to swear that, when he should come to the kingdom, he would not destroy his seed, 16-21. Saul returns home, and David and his men stay in the hold, 22.

1. *Saul was returned.* It is very probable that it was only a small marauding party that had made an excursion in the Israelitish borders, and this invasion was soon suppressed.

2. *Rocks of the wild goats.* The original is variously understood. The Vulgate makes a paraphrase: "On the most precipitous rocks over which the ibexes alone can travel." The Targum: "the caverns of the rocks." The Septuagint make the original a proper name.

3. *The sheepcotes.* Caves in the rocks, in which it is common, even to the present time, for shepherds and their flocks to lodge. According to Strabo there are caverns in Syria one of which is capable of containing 4,000 men.

13. *Wickedness proceedeth from the wicked.* This proverb may be thus understood: He that does a wicked act gives proof thereby that he is a wicked man.

14. *After a dead dog.* A term used among the Hebrews to signify the most sovereign contempt (see 2 Sam. xvi. 9). One utterly incapable of making the least resistance against Saul, and the troops of Israel. The same idea is expressed in the term *flea.* The Targum properly expresses both thus: "one who is weak, one who is contemptible."

19. *If a man find his enemy, will he let him go well away?* Or rather, "Will he send him in a good way?" But Houbigant translates the whole clause thus: "If a man, finding his enemy, send him by a good way, *the Lord will give him his reward.*" The words which are here put in italic are not in the Hebrew text, but they are found, at least in the sense, in the Septuagint, Syriac, and Arabic, and seem necessary to complete the sense. "Therefore," adds Saul, "the Lord will reward thee good for what thou hast done unto me."

20. *I know well that thou shalt surely be king.* Hebrew, "Reigning, thou shalt reign."

He knew this before, and yet he continued to pursue David with the most deadly hatred.

21. *Swear now.* Saul knew that an oath would bind David, though it was insufficient to bind himself (see chap. xix. 6). He had sworn to his son Jonathan that David should not be slain, and yet sought by all means in his power to destroy him!

22. *David and his men gat them up unto the hold.* "Went up to Mizpeh," according to the Syriac and Arabic. David could not trust Saul with his life.

CHAPTER 25

The death of Samuel, 1. The history of Nabal, and his churlishness towards David and his men, 2-12. David, determining to punish him, is appeased by Abigail, Nabal's wife, 13-35. Abigail returns, and tells Nabal of the danger that he has escaped, who on hearing it is thunderstruck, and dies in ten days, 36-38. David, hearing of this, sends and takes Abigail to wife. 39-42. He marries also Ahinoam of Jezreel, Saul having given Michal, David's wife, to Phalti, the son of Laish, 43-44.

1. *And Samuel died.* Samuel lived, as is supposed, about ninety-eight years. *Buried him in his house.* Probably this means, not his dwelling house, but the house or tomb he had made for his sepulchure; and thus the Syriac and Arabic seem to have understood it. *David . . . went down to the wilderness of Paran.* This was either on the confines of Judea or in the Arabia Petraea, between the mountains of Judah and Mount Sinai; it is evident from the history that it was not far from Carmel, on the south confines of Judah.

3. *The name of the man was Nabal.* The word *nabal* signifies to be "foolish, base, or villainous." *The name of his wife Abigail.* The "joy or exultation of my father." *Of the house of Caleb. Vehu Chalibi,* "He was a Calebite." But as the word *caleb* signifies "a dog," the Septuagint have understood it as implying a man of a canine disposition, and translate it thus, "He was a doggish man." It is understood in the same way by the Syriac and Arabic.

6. *Peace be both to thee.* This is the ancient form of sending greetings to a friend: "Peace to thee, peace to thy household, and peace to all that thou hast." That is, "May both thyself, thy family, and all that pertain unto thee, be in continual prosperity!"

7. *Thy shepherds which were with us, we hurt them not.* It is most evident that David had a claim upon Nabal, for very essential services performed to his herdmen at Carmel. He not only did them no hurt, and took none of their flocks for the supply of his necessities, but he protected them from the rapacity of others. "They were a wall unto us," said Nabal's servants, "both by night and day."

8. *Whatsoever cometh to thine hand.* As you are making a great feast for your servants, and I and my men, as having essentially served you, would naturally come in for a share were we present, send a portion by my ten young men for me and my men, that we also may rejoice with you. Certainly this was a very reasonable and a very modest request.

10. *Who is David?* Nabal's answer shows the surliness of his disposition. It was unjust to refuse so reasonable a request, and the manner of the refusal was highly insulting. It is true what his own servants said of him, "He is such a son of Belial, that a man cannot speak to him," v. 17.

18. *Took two hundred loaves.* The Eastern bread is ordinarily both thin and small, and answers to our cakes. *Two bottles of wine.* That is, two goatskins full. The hide is pulled off the animal without ripping up; the places where the legs, etc., were are sewed up, and then the skin appears one large bag. This is properly the Scripture and Eastern "bottle." *Five sheep.* Not one sheep to one hundred men. *Clusters of raisins.* Raisins dried in the sun. *Cakes of figs.* Figs cured, and then pressed together.

Now all this provision was a matter of little worth, and, had it been granted in the first instance, it would have perfectly satisfied David, and secured the good offices of him and his men. Abigail showed both her wisdom and prudence in making this provision. Out of 3,000 sheep Nabal could not have missed 5; and as this claim was made only in the time of sheep-shearing, it could not have been made more than once in the year; and it certainly was a small price for such important services.

20. *She came down . . . and . . . David . . . came down.* David was coming down Mount Paran; Abigail was coming down from Carmel.

22. *So and more also do God.* Nothing can justify this part of David's conduct. Whatever his provocation might have been, he had suffered, properly speaking, no wrongs; and his resolution to cut off a whole innocent family, because Nabal had acted ungenerously towards him, was abominable and cruel, not to say diabolic. *Any that pisseth against the wall.* This expression certainly means either men or dogs, and should be thus translated, "if I leave any male."

29. *Shall be bound in the bundle of life.* Thy life shall be precious in the sight of the Lord. *Them shall he sling out.* Far from being bound and kept together in union with the Fountain of life, He will cast them off from himself as a stone is cast out from a sling. This betokens both force and violence.

37. *His heart died within him, and he became as a stone.* He was thunderstruck, and was so terrified at the apprehension of what he had escaped that the fear overcame his mind, he became insensible to all things around him, probably refused all kinds of nourishment, and died in ten days.

39. *To take her to him to wife.* It is likely that he had heard before this that Saul, to cut off all his pretensions to the throne, had married Michal to Phalti; and this justified David in taking Abigail or any other woman; and, according to the then custom, it was not unlawful for David to take several wives. By his marriage with Abigail it is probable he became possessed of all Nabal's property in Carmel and Maon.

43. *David also took Ahinoam.* Many think that this was his wife before he took Abigail; she is always mentioned first in the list of his wives and she was the mother of his eldest son, Ammon.

44. *Phalti.* Called also Phaltiel, 2 Sam. iii. 15. *Of Gallim.* Probably a city or town in the tribe of Benjamin; see Isa. x. 30. It is likely

therefore that Saul chose this man because he was of his own tribe.

CHAPTER 26

The Ziphites inform Saul of David's hiding place, 1. Saul, with 3,000 men, goes in pursuit of him, 2-3. David sends out spies and finds where Saul had pitched his camp; he and Abishai come to the camp by night, find all asleep, and bring away Saul's spear, and the cruse of water that was at his head, 4-12. David goes to the opposite hill; awakes Abner, captain of Saul's host; chides him for being so careless of his master's life; calls on Saul to send one of his servants for the spear; and severely chides him for his continued hostility to him, 13-24. Saul humbles himself to David, promises to persecute him no more, and returns to his own place, 25.

1. *The Ziphites came.* This is the second time that these enemies of David endeavored to throw him into the hands of Saul (see chap. xxiii. 19).

2. *Three thousand chosen men.* Though they knew that David was but 600 strong, yet Saul thought it was not safe to pursue such an able general with a less force than that mentioned in the text; and, that he might the better depend on them, they were all elect or picked men out of the whole of his army.

5. *David arose.* As David and his men knew the country, they had many advantages over Saul and his men, and no doubt could often watch them without being discovered. *Saul lay in the trench.* The word *bammaegal,* which we translate *in the trench,* and in the margin "in the midst of his carriages," is rendered by some "in a ring of carriages," and by others "in the circle," i.e., which was formed by his troops. As *agal* signifies anything "round," it may here refer to a round pavilion or tent made for Saul, or else to the form of his camp.

6. *Abishai the son of Zeruiah.* She was David's sister, and therefore Abishai and Joab were nephews to David.

8. *God hath delivered thine enemy into thine hand.* Here Abishai uses the same language as did David's men when Saul came into the cave at En-gedi (see chap. xxiv. 4, etc.), and David uses the same language in reply.

10. *The Lord shall smite him*—he shall die by a stroke of the divine judgment; *or his day shall come to die*—he shall die a natural death, which in the course of things must be before mine, and thus I shall get rid of mine enemy; *or he shall descend into the battle, and perish*—he shall fall by the enemies of his country. These are the three ordinary ways by which man accomplishes his day. Murder David could not consider to be lawful; this would have been taking the matter out of God's hand, and this David would not do.

12. *David took the spear and the cruse.* The *spear,* we have already seen, was the emblem of power and regal dignity. But it is usual, in Arab camps, for every man to have his lance stuck in the ground beside him, that he may be ready for action in a moment. The cruse of water resembled, in some measure, the canteens of our soldiers. In such a climate, where water was always scarce, it was necessary for each man to carry a little with him, to refresh him on his march.

15. *Art not thou a valiant man?* This is a strong irony. "Ye are worthy to die; ye are sons of death"—You deserve death for this neglect of your king.

19. *Let him accept an offering.* If God have stirred you up against me, why, then, let Him deliver my life into your hand, and accept it as a sacrifice. But as the word is *minchah,* a gratitude offering, perhaps the sense may be this: Let God accept a gratitude offering from you, for having purged the land of a worker of iniquity.

Saying, Go, serve other gods. His being obliged to leave the Tabernacle, and the place where the true worship of God was performed, and take refuge among idolaters, said in effect, *Go, serve other gods.*

20. *As when one doth hunt a partridge.* It is worthy of remark that the Arabs, observing that partridges, being put up several times, soon become so weary as not to be able to fly; they in this manner hunt them upon the mountains, till at last they can knock them down with their clubs. It was in this manner that Saul hunted David, coming hastily upon him, and putting him up from time to time, in hopes that he should at length, by frequent repetitions of it, be able to destroy him.

21. *I have sinned.* Perhaps the word *chatathi,* "I have sinned," should be read, "I have erred, or, have been mistaken."

25. *Thou shalt both do great things, and also shalt still prevail.* The Hebrew is, "Also in doing thou shalt do, and being able thou shalt be able"; which the Targum translates, "Also in reigning thou shalt reign, and in prospering thou shalt prosper"—which in all probability is the meaning.

CHAPTER 27

David flees to Achish, king of Gath, who receives him kindly, and gives him Ziklag to dwell in, where he continues a year and four months, 1-7. David invades the Geshurites and Amalekites, and leaves neither man nor woman alive, 8-9. He returns to Achish, and pretends that he has been making inroads on the Israelites, and Achish believes it, 10-12.

1. *I shall now perish one day by the hand of Saul.* This was a very hasty conclusion; God had so often interposed in behalf of his life that he was authorized to believe the reverse.

2. *David arose, and he passed over . . . unto Achish.* There is not one circumstance in this transaction that is not blameable. David joins the enemies of his God and of his country, acts a most inhuman part against the Geshurites and Amalekites, without even the pretense of a divine authority; tells a most deliberate falsehood to Achish, his protector, relative to the people against whom he had perpetrated this cruel act, giving him to understand that he had been destroying the Israelites, his enemies. I undertake no defense of this conduct of David; it is all bad, all defenseless; God vindicates him not.

3. *Every man with his household.* So it appears that the men who consorted with David had wives and families. David and his company resembled a tribe of the wandering Arabs.

5. *Why should thy servant dwell in the royal city?* He seemed to intimate that two princely establishments in the same city were too many. Achish appears to have felt the propriety of his proposal, and therefore appoints him Ziklag.

6. *Achish gave him Ziklag.* Ziklag was at first given to the tribe of Judah, but afterwards

it was ceded to that of Simeon, Josh. xv. 31; xix. 5. The Philistines had, however, made themselves masters of it, and held it to the time here mentioned; it then fell into the tribe of Judah again, and continued to be the property of the kings of Judah. This verse is a proof that this book was written long after the days of Samuel, and that it was formed by a later hand, out of materials which had been collected by a contemporary author.

9. *David smote the land.* Here was a complete extirpation of all these people, not one being left alive, lest he should carry tidings of the disasters of his country! The spoil which David took consisted of sheep, oxen, asses, camels, and apparel.

10. *Whither have ye made a road to day?* He had probably been in the habit of making predatory excursions. This seems to be implied in the question of Achish.

CHAPTER 28

The Philistines prepare to attack the Israelites, and Achish informs David that he shall accompany him to battle, 1-2. Saul, unable to obtain any answer from God, applies to a witch at En-dor to bring up Samuel, that he may converse with him on the issue of the war, 3-11. Samuel appears, 12-14. He reproaches Saul with his misconduct, and informs him of his approaching ruin, 15-19. He is greatly distressed; but at the solicitation of the woman and his own servants he takes some food, and departs the same night, 20-25.

2. *Surely thou shalt know what thy servant can do.* This was another equivocal answer, and could be understood only by his succeeding conduct. It might imply what he could do in favor of the Philistines against Israel, or in favor of Israel against the Philistines. Achish understood it in the former sense, and therefore he said to David, *I will make thee keeper of mine head for ever;* i.e., You shall be captain of my lifeguards.

3. *Samuel was dead.* And there was no longer a public accredited prophet to consult. *Those that had familiar spirits, and the wizards.* See the note on Lev. xix. 31, and Exod. xxii. 18.

5. *When Saul saw.* He saw from the superiority of his enemies, from the state of his army, and especially from his own state towards God, that he had everything to fear.

6. *The Lord answered him not.* He used the three methods by which supernatural intelligence was ordinarily given: (1) *Dreams.* The person prayed for instruction, and begged that God would answer by a significant dream. (2) *Urim.* This was a kind of oracular answer given to the high priest when clothed with the ephod, on which were the Urim and Thummim. How these communicated the answer is not well-known. (3) *Prophets.* Who were requested by the party concerned to consult the Lord on the subject in question, and to report his answer. The prophets at that time could only be those in the schools of the prophets, which Samuel had established at Naioth and Gibeah.

7. *At En-dor.* This was a city in the valley of Jezreel, at the foot of Mount Gilboa, where the army of Saul had now encamped.

8. *Saul disguised himself.* That he might not be known by the woman, lest she, being terrified, should refuse to use her art.

13. *I saw gods ascending out of the earth.* The word *elohim,* which we translate *gods,* is the word which is used for the Supreme Being throughout the Bible; but all the versions, the Chaldee excepted, translate it in the plural number, as we do. The Chaldee has, "I see an angel of the Lord ascending from the earth."

17. *The Lord hath done to him.* I believe these words are spoken of Saul; and as they are spoken to him, it seems evident that *him* should be "thee." The Septuagint, "to thee."

20. *Then Saul fell straightway all along the earth.* Literally, "He fell with his own length," or "with the fulness of his stature." He was so overwhelmed with this most dreadful message that he swooned away, and thus fell at his own length upon the ground.

23. *I will not eat.* It is no wonder that not only his strength, but also his appetite, had departed from him. *And sat upon the bed.* Beds or couches were the common places on which the ancients sat to take their repasts.

24. *The woman had a fat calf.* In hot countries they could not keep flesh meat by them any length of time; hence they generally kept young animals, such as calves, lambs, and kids, ready for slaughter; and when there was occasion, one of them was killed, and dressed immediately. *Unleavened bread.* There was not time to bake leavened bread; that would have taken considerable time, in order that the leaven might leaven the whole lump.

CHAPTER 29

The Philistines gather their armies together against Israel, and encamp at Aphek, while the Israelites encamp at Jezreel, 1. The lords of the Philistines refuse to let David go to battle with them, lest he should betray them, 2-5. Achish expresses his confidence in David, but begs him to return, 6-10. David and his men return, 11.

1. *To Aphek.* This was a place in the valley of Jezreel between Mounts Tabor and Gilboa. *Pitched by a fountain.* To be near a *fountain,* or "copious spring of water," was a point of great importance to an army in countries such as these, where water was so very scarce.

3. *These days, or these years.* I suppose these words to mark no definite time, and may be understood thus: "Is not this David, who has been with me for a considerable time?"

4. *The princes of the Philistines were wroth.* It is strange that they had not yet heard of David's destruction of a village of the Geshurites, Gezrites, and Amalekites, chap. xxvii. Had they heard of this, they would have seen much more cause for suspicion.

6. *Thou hast been upright.* So he thought, for as yet he had not heard of the above transaction, David having given him to understand that he had been fighting against Israel.

8. *David said . . . what have I done?* It was in the order of God's gracious providence that the Philistine lords refused to let David go with them to this battle. Had he gone, he had his choice of two sins: (1) If he had fought for the Philistines, he would have fought against God and his country. (2) If he had in the battle gone over to the Israelites, he would have deceived and become a traitor to the hospitable Achish.

CHAPTER 30

While David is absent with the army of Achish, the Amalekites invade Ziklag, and burn it with fire, and carry away captive David's wives, and those of his men, 1-2. David and his men return, and finding the desolate state of their city, are greatly affected, 3-5. The men mutiny, and threaten to stone David, who encourages himself in the Lord, 6. David inquires of the Lord, and is directed to pursue the Amalekites, with the promise that he shall recover all, 7-8. He and his men begin the pursuit, but 200, through fatigue, are obliged to stay behind at the brook Besor, 9-10. They find a sick Egyptian, who directs them in their pursuit, 11-15. David finds the Amalekites secure, feasting on the spoils they had taken; he attacks and destroys the whole host, except 400, who escape on camels, 16-17. The Israelites recover their wives, their families, and all their goods, 18-20. They come to the 200 who were so faint as not to be able to pursue the enemy, with whom they divide the spoil; and this becomes a statute in Israel, 21-25. David sends part of the spoil which he had taken to different Jewish cities, which had suffered by the incursion of the Amalekites, and where David and his men had been accustomed to resort, 26-31.

7. *Bring me hither the ephod.* It seems as if David had put on the ephod, and inquired of the Lord for himself; but it is more likely that he caused Abiathar to do it.

9. *The brook Besor.* This had its source in the mountain of Idumea, and fell into the Mediterranean Sea beyond Gaza.

14. *Upon the south of the Cherethites.* In 2 Sam. xv. 18 we find that the Cherethites formed a part of David's guards. *South of Caleb.* Somewhere about Kirjath-arba, or Hebron, and Kirjath-sepher, these being in the possession of Caleb and his descendants.

15. *Swear unto me.* At the conclusion of this verse the Vulgate, Syriac, and Arabic add that "David swore to him." This is not expressed in the Hebrew, but is necessarily implied.

16. *Out of the land of the Philistines.* That these Amalekites were enemies to the Philistines is evident, but it certainly does not follow from this that those whom David destroyed were enemies also.

17. *There escaped not a man of them.* It is well-known to every careful reader of the Bible that the Amalekites were a proscribed people, even by God himself.

20. *And David took all the flocks.* He and his men not only recovered all their own property, but they recovered all the spoil which these Amalekites had taken from the south of Judah, the Cherethites, and the south of Caleb. When this was separated from the rest, it was given to David, and called "David's spoil."

22. *Men of Belial.* This is a common expression to denote the sour, the rugged, the severe, the idle, and the profane.

23. *That which the Lord hath given us.* He very properly attributes this victory to God, the numbers of the Amalekites being so much greater than his own. Indeed, as many fled away on camels as were in the whole host of David.

25. *He made it a statute and an ordinance for Israel.* Nothing could be more just and proper than this law; he who stays at home to defend house and property has an equal right to the booty taken by those who go out to the war. There was a practice of this kind among the Israelites long before this time; see Num. xxxi. 27; Josh. xxii. 8; and the note on this

latter verse. *Unto this day.* This is another indication that this book was composed long after the facts it commemorates.

26. *Unto the elders of Judah.* These were the persons among whom he sojourned during his exile, and who had given him shelter and protection. Gratitude required these presents.

27. *To them which were in Beth-el.* This was in the tribe of Ephraim. *South Ramoth.* So called to distinguish it from Ramoth-gilead, beyond Jordan. This Ramoth belonged to the tribe of Simeon, Josh. xix. 8. *In Jattir.* It was situated in the mountains, and belonged to Judah.

28. *In Aroer.* Situated beyond Jordan, on the banks of the river Arnon, in the tribe of Gad.

29. *And . . . the cities of the Kenites.* A very small tract on the southern coast of the Dead Sea.

30. *Hormah.* The general name of those cities which belonged to Arad, king of Canaan, and were devoted to destruction by the Hebrews, and thence called Hormah (see Num. xxi. 1-3). *In Chor-ashan.* Probably the same as Ashan in the tribe of Judah (see Josh. xv. 42). It was afterwards ceded to Simeon, Josh. xix. 7.

31. *To them which were in Hebron.* This was a place strongly attached to David, and David to it, and the place where he was proclaimed king, and where he reigned more than seven years previously to the death of Ish-bosheth, Saul's son, who was, for that time, his competitor in the kingdom.

CHAPTER 31

A battle in Mount Gilboa between Israel and the Philistines, in which the former are defeated, and Saul's three sons slain, 1-2. Saul, being mortally wounded, and afraid to fall alive into the hands of the Philistines, desires his armor-bearer to dispatch him; which he refusing, Saul falls on his sword, and his armor-bearer does the same, 3-6. The Israelites on the other side of the valley forsake their cities, and the Philistines come and dwell in them, 7. The Philistines, finding Saul and his three sons among the slain, strip them of their armor, which they put in the house of Ashtaroth, cut off their heads, send the news to all the houses of their idols, and fasten the bodies of Saul and his three sons to the walls of Beth-shan, 8-10. Valiant men of Jabesh-gilead go by night and take away the bodies, burn them at Jabesh, bury their bones under a tree, and fast seven days, 11-13.

1. *Now the Philistines fought.* This is the continuation of the account given in chap. xxix. *The men of Israel fled.* It seems as if they were thrown into confusion at the first onset, and turned their backs upon their enemies.

2. *Followed hard upon Saul and upon his sons.* They, seeing the discomfiture of their troops, were determined to sell their lives as dear as possible, and therefore maintained the battle till the three brothers were slain.

3. *He was sore wounded of the archers.* It is likely that Saul's sons were slain by the archers, and that Saul was now mortally wounded by the same. Houbigant translates, "The archers rushed upon him, from whom he received a grievous wound."

6. *And all his men.* Probably meaning those of his troops which were his life or body guards: as to the bulk of the army, it fled at the commencement of the battle, v. 1.

7. *The men of Israel that were on the other side of the valley.* They appear to have been panic-struck, and therefore fled as far as they could out of the reach of the Philistines. As the Philistines possessed Beth-shan, situated near to Jordan, the people on the other side of that river, fearing for their safety, fled also.

8. *On the morrow.* It is very likely that the battle and pursuit continued till the night, so that there was no time till the next day to strip and plunder the slain.

9. *And they cut off his head.* It is possible that they cut off the heads of his three sons likewise; for although only his head is said to be cut off, and his body only to be fastened to the walls of Beth-shan, yet we find that the men of Jabesh-gilead found both his body and the bodies of his three sons fastened to the walls, v. 12.

10. *They put his armour in the house of Ashtaroth.* As David had done in placing the sword of Goliath in the Tabernacle. We have already seen that it was common for the conquerors to consecrate armor and spoils taken in war to those who were the objects of religious worship. *They fastened his body to the wall.* Probably by means of iron hooks; but it is said, 2 Sam. xxi. 12, that these bodies were fastened "in the street of Beth-shan." This may mean that the place where they were fastened

to the wall was the main street or entrance into the city.

11. *When the inhabitants of Jabesh-gilead heard.* This act of the men of Jabesh-gilead was an act of gratitude due to Saul, who, at the very commencement of his reign, rescued them from Nahash, king of the Ammonites (see chap. xi. 1, etc.) and by his timely succors saved them from the deepest degradation and the most oppressive tyranny.

12. *And burnt them there.* It has been denied that the Hebrews burned the bodies of the dead, but that they buried them in the earth, or embalmed them, and often burned spices around them. These, no doubt, were the common forms of sepulture, but neither of these could be conveniently practiced in the present case. They could not have buried them about Beth-shan without being discovered; and as to embalming, that was most likely out of all question, as doubtless the bodies were now too putrid to bear it. They therefore burned them, because there was no other way of disposing of them at that time so as to do them honor; and the bones and ashes they collected, and buried under a tree or in a grove at Jabesh.

13. *And fasted seven days.* To testify their sincere regret for his unfortunate death, and the public calamity that had fallen upon the land.

The Second Book of SAMUEL

As this is a continuation of the preceding history, without any interruption, it can scarcely be called another book. Originally this and the preceding made but one book, and they have been separated. For a general account of both, see the preface to the First Book of Samuel. It is generally allowed that this book comprehends a period of forty years.

It has been divided into three parts: in the first we have an account of the happy commencement of David's reign, cc. i—x. In the second, David's unhappy fall, and its miserable consequences, cc. xi—xviii. In the third, his restoration to the divine favor, the reestablishment of his kingdom, and the events which signalized the latter part of his reign, cc. xix—xxiv.

CHAPTER 1

An Amalekite comes to David, and informs him that the Philistines had routed the Israelites, and that Saul and his sons were slain, 1-4. Pretends that he himself had dispatched Saul, finding him ready to fall alive into the hands of the Philistines, and had brought his crown and bracelets to David, 5-10. David and his men mourn for Saul and his sons, 11-12. He orders the Amalekite, who professed that he had killed Saul, to be slain, 13-16. David's funeral song for Saul and Jonathan, 17-27.

2. *A man came out of the camp.* The whole account which this young man gives is a fabrication; in many of the particulars it is grossly self-contradictory. There is no fact in the case but the bringing of the crown, or diadem, and bracelets of Saul, which, as he appears to have been a plunderer of the slain, he found on the field of battle; and he brought them to David,

and told the lie of having dispatched Saul, merely to ingratiate himself with David.

16. *Thy blood be upon thy head.* If he killed Saul, as he said he did, then he deserved death; at that time it was not known to the contrary, and this man was executed on his own confession.

18. *The use of the bow.* The use of is not in the Hebrew; it is simply *the bow*, that is, a song thus entitled. This lamentation is justly admired as a picture of distress the most tender and most striking; unequally divided by gr¹ into longer and shorter breaks, as nature could pour them forth from a mind interrupted by the alternate recurrence of the most lively images of love and greatness. His reverence

for Saul and his love for Jonathan have their strongest colorings; but their greatness and bravery come full upon him, and are expressed with peculiar energy. Being himself a warrior, it is in that character he sees their greatest excellence; and though his imagination hurries from one point of recollection to another, yet we hear him—at first, at last, everywhere—lamenting, "How are the mighty fallen!" It is almost impossible to read the noble original without finding every word swollen with a sign or broken with a sob. A heart pregnant with distress, and striving to utter expressions descriptive of its feelings, which are repeatedly interrupted by an excess of grief, is most sensibly painted throughout the whole.

CHAPTER 2

David, by the direction of God, goes up to Hebron, and is there anointed king over the house of Judah, 1-4. He congratulates the inhabitants of Jabesh-gilead on their kindness in rescuing the bodies of Saul and his sons from the Philistines, 5-7. Abner anoints Ish-bosheth, Saul's son, king over Gilead, the Ashurites, Jezreel, Ephraim, Benjamin, and all Israel; over whom he reigned two years, 8-10. David reigns over Judah, in Hebron, seven years and six months, 11. Account of a battle between Abner, captain of the Israelites, and Joab, captain of the men of Judah; in which the former are routed with the loss of 360 men: but Asahel, the brother of Joab, is killed by Abner, 12-32.

1. *David enquired of the Lord.* By means of Abiathar, the priest; for he did not know whether the different tribes were willing to receive him, though he was fully persuaded that God had appointed him king over Israel. *Unto Hebron.* The metropolis of the tribe of Judah, one of the richest regions in Judea.

4. *Anointed David king.* He was anointed before by Samuel, by which he acquired a right to the kingdom; by the present anointing he had authority over the kingdom. The other parts of the kingdom were, as yet, attached to the family of Saul.

5. *David sent messengers unto . . . Jabesh-gilead.* This was a generous and noble act, highly indicative of the grandeur of David's mind. He respected Saul as his once legitimate sovereign; he loved Jonathan as his most intimate friend.

8. *Abner the son of Ner.* This man had long been one of the chief captains of Saul's army, and commander in chief on several occasions; he was probably envious of David's power, by whom he had often been outgeneralled in the field.

9. *Made him king over Gilead.* These were places beyond Jordan; for as the Philistines had lately routed the Israelites, they were no doubt in possession of some of the principal towns. Abner was therefore afraid to bring the new king to any place where he was likely to meet with much resistance, till he had got his army well-recruited.

10. *Ish-bosheth . . . reigned two years.* It is well observed that Ish-bosheth reigned all the time that David reigned in Hebron, which was seven years and six months. Some think that Abner in effect reigned the last five years of Ish-bosheth, who had only the name of king after the first two years. Or the text may be understood thus: "When Ish-bosheth had reigned two years over Israel, he was forty years of age."

14. *Let the young men . . . play before us.* This was diabolical play, where each man thrust his sword into the body of the other, so that the twenty-four (twelve on each side) fell down dead together!

16. *Caught every one his fellow by the head.* Probably by the beard, if these persons were not too young to have one, or by the hair of the head. Alexander ordered all the Macedonians to shave their beards; and being asked by Parmenion why they should do so, answered, "Dost thou not know that in battle there is no better hold than the beard?"

18. *Asahel was as light of foot as a wild roe.* To be swift of foot was deemed a great accomplishment in the heroes of antiquity; "the swift-footed Achilles" is an epithet which Homer gives to that hero no less than thirty times in the course of the *Iliad.*

27. *And Joab said.* The meaning of this verse appears to be this: If Abner had not provoked the battle (see v. 14) Joab would not have attacked the Israelites that day, as his orders were probably to act on the defensive. Therefore the blame fell upon Israel.

29. *They came to Mahanaim.* So they returned to the place whence they set out (see v. 12). This was the commencement of the civil wars between Israel and Judah, and properly the commencement of the division of the two kingdoms, through which both nations were deluged with blood.

CHAPTER 3

Account of the children born to David in Hebron, 1-5. Abner being accused by Ish-bosheth of familiarities with Rizpah, Saul's concubine, he is enraged; offers his services to David; goes to Hebron, and makes a league with him, 6-22. Joab, through enmity to Abner, pretends to David that he came as a spy, and should not be permitted to return, 23-25. He follows Abner, and treacherously slays him, 26-27. David hearing of it is greatly incensed against Joab, and pronounces a curse upon him and upon his family, 28-29. He commands a general mourning for Abner, and himself follows the bier weeping, 30-32. David's lamentation over Abner, 33-34. The people solicit David to take meat; but he fasts the whole day, and complains to them of the insolence and intrigues of Joab and his brothers; the people are pleased with his conduct, 35-39.

1. *There was long war.* Frequent battles and skirmishes took place between the followers of David and the followers of Ish-bosheth, after the two years mentioned above, to the end of the fifth year, in which Ish-bosheth was slain by Rechab and Baanah.

6. *Abner made himself strong.* This strengthening of himself, and going in to the late king's concubine, were most evident proofs that he wished to seize upon the government (see 1 Kings ii. 21-22; xii. 8; xvi. 21).

8. *Am I a dog's head?* Do you treat a man with indignity who has been the only prop of your tottering kingdom, and the only person who could make head against the house of David?

9. *Except, as the Lord hath sworn to David.* And why did he not do this before, when he knew that God had given the kingdom to David? Was he not now, according to his own concession, fighting against God?

13. *Except thou first bring Michal.* David had already six wives at Hebron; and none of them could have such pretensions to legitimacy as Michal, who had been taken away from him

and married to Phaltiel. However distressing it was to take her from a husband who loved her most tenderly (see v. 16), yet prudence and policy required that he should strengthen his own interest in the kingdom as much as possible; and that he should not leave a princess in the possession of a man who might, in her right, have made pretensions to the throne. Besides, she was his own lawful wife, and he had a right to demand her when he pleased.

16. *Weeping behind her.* If genuine affection did not still subsist between David and Michal, it was a pity to have taken her from Phaltiel, who had her to wife from the conjoint authority of her father and her king. Nevertheless David had a legal right to her, as she had never been divorced, for she was taken from him by the hand of violence.

18. *The Lord hath spoken of David.* Where is this spoken? Such a promise is not extant. Perhaps it means no more than, "Thus, it may be presumed, God hath determined."

21. *He went in peace.* David dismissed him in good faith, having no sinister design in reference to him.

27. *And smote him there.* Joab feared that, after having rendered such essential services to David, Abner would be made captain of the host. He therefore determined to prevent it by murdering the man, under pretense of avenging the death of his brother Asahel. The murder, however, was one of the most unprovoked and wicked; and such was the power and influence of this nefarious general that the king dared not bring him to justice for his crime. In the same way he murdered Amasa a little time afterwards (see chap. xx. 10).

29. *Let it rest on the head.* All these verbs may be rendered in the future tense: it will rest on the head of Joab, etc. This was a prophetic declaration which sufficiently showed the displeasure of God against this execrable man.

31. *David said to Joab.* He commanded him to take on him the part of a principal mourner.

33. *The king lamented over Abner.* This lamentation, though short, is very pathetic. It is a high strain of poetry; but the measure cannot be easily ascertained. Our own translation may be measured thus:

Died Abner as a fool dieth?
Thy hands were not bound,
Nor thy feet put into fetters.
As a man falleth before the wicked,
So hast thou fallen!

Or thus:

Shall Abner die
A death like to a villain's?
Thy hands not bound,
Nor were the fetters to thy feet applied.
Like as one falls before the sons of guilt,
So hast thou fallen!

36. *The people took notice.* They saw that the king's grief was sincere, and that he had no part nor device in the murder of Abner; see v. 37.

39. *I am this day weak.* Had Abner lived, all the tribes of Israel would have been brought under my government. *Though anointed king.* I have little else than the title: first, having only one tribe under my government; and secondly, the sons of Zeruiah, Joab and his

brethren, having usurped all the power, and reduced me to the shadow of royalty. *The Lord shall reward the doer of evil.* That is, Joab, whom he appears afraid to name.

CHAPTER 4

Some account of Rechab and Baanah, two of Ish-bosheth's captains, and of Mephibosheth, the son of Jonathan, 1-4. Rechab and Baanah murder Ish-bosheth, and escape; and bring his head to David, 5-8. David is greatly irritated, and commands them to be slain, 9-12.

1. *All the Israelites were troubled.* Abner was their great support, and on him they depended; for it appears that Ish-bosheth was a feeble prince, and had few of those qualities requisite for a sovereign.

2. *Captains of bands.* Whether Ish-bosheth kept bands of marauders, whose business it was to make sudden incursions into the country places, and carry off grain, provisions, cattle, etc., we know not; but such persons would be well-qualified for the bloody work in which these two men were afterwards employed.

3. *The Beerothites fled to Gittaim.* Probably the same as Gath, as Ramathaim is the same as Ramah.

4. *He fell, and became lame.* Dislocated his ankle, knee, or thigh, which was never after reduced, and thus he became lame.

5. *Lay on a bed at noon.* It is a custom in all hot countries to travel or work very early and very late, and rest at noonday, in which the heat chiefly prevails.

6. *As though they would have fetched wheat.* As these men were accustomed to bring wheat from these stores, from which it appears there was an easy passage to the king's chamber, no man would suspect their present errand, as they were in the habit of going frequently to that place.

8. *They brought the head . . . unto David.* They thought, as did the poor lying Amalekite, to ingratiate themselves with David by this abominable act.

9. *Who hath redeemed my soul out of all adversity.* This was, in David's case, a very proper view of the goodness and watchful providence of God towards him.

10. *A reward for his tidings. Euangelia,* Septuagint. Here is a proof that *evangelium,* or "gospel," signifies the *reward* which the bringer of good tidings is entitled to receive.

11. *How much more?* Here are several things which aggravated the guilt of those wicked men. (1) Ish-bosheth was an innocent man, and therefore none could have any ground of quarrel against him. (2) He was in his own house, which was his sanctuary, and none but the worst of men would disturb him there. (3) He was upon his bed, resting in the heat of the day, and so free from suspicion that he was not even attended by his guards, nor had he his doors secured. To take away the life of such a man in such circumstances, whom also they professed to hold as their sovereign, was the most abandoned treachery.

12. *And they slew them.* None ever more richly deserved death; and by this act of justice David showed to all Israel that he was a decided enemy to the destruction of Saul's family, and that none could lift up their hands against any

of them without meeting with condign punishment. In all these cases I know not that it was possible for David to show more sincerity or a stricter regard for justice.

CHAPTER 5

The elders of all the tribes of Israel come and anoint David king over all Israel, 1-5. He goes against the Jebusites, and takes the stronghold of Zion, and afterwards the city itself, which is called the city of David, 6-9. David's prosperity, and friendship with Hiram, king of Tyre, 10-12. He takes more concubines, and begets several sons and daughters, 13-16. The Philistines gather together against him in the valley of Rephaim; he defeats them; they abandon their idols, and David and his men burn them, 17-21. They assemble once more in the valley of Rephaim, and David smites them from Geba to Gazer, 22-25.

1. *Then came all the tribes of Israel.* Ish-bosheth, the king, and Abner, the general, being dead, they had no hope of maintaining a separate kingdom, and therefore thought it better to submit to David's authority. And they founded their resolution on three good arguments: (1) David was their own countryman; *We are thy bone and thy flesh.* (2) Even in Saul's time David had been their general, and had always led them to victory; *Thou wast he that leddest out and broughtest in Israel.* (3) God had appointed him to the kingdom, to govern and protect the people; *The Lord said to thee, Thou shalt feed my people Israel, and . . . be a captain over Israel.*

3. *They anointed David king.* This was the third time that David was anointed, having now taken possession of the whole kingdom.

6. *The king and his men went to Jerusalem.* This city was now in the hands of the Jebusites, but how they got possession of it is not known; probably they took it during the wars between Ish-bosheth and David. After Joshua's death, what is called the lower city was taken by the Israelites; and it is evident that the whole city was in their possession in the time of Saul, for David brought the head of Goliath thither, 1 Sam. xvii. 54. It appears to have been a very strong fortress and, from what follows, deemed impregnable by the Jebusites. It was right that the Israelites should repossess it, and David very properly began his reign over the whole country by the siege of this city. *Except thou take away the blind and the lame.* It appears that the Jebusites, vainly confiding in the strength of their fortress, placed lame and blind men upon the walls, and thus endeavored to turn into ridicule David's attempt to take the place.

11. *Hiram king of Tyre.* He was a very friendly man, and no doubt a believer in the true God. He was not only a friend to David, but also of his son Solomon, to whom, in building the Temple, he afforded the most important assistance.

13. *David took him more concubines.* He had, in all conscience, enough before; he had, in the whole, eight wives and ten concubines.

14. *These be the names.* Eleven children are here enumerated in the Hebrew text, but the Septuagint has no less than twenty-four.

17. *The Philistines came up to seek David.* Ever since the defeat of the Israelites and the fall of Saul and his sons, the Philistines seem to have been in undisturbed possession of the principal places in the land of Israel; now, finding that David was chosen king by the whole nation, they thought best to attack him before his army got too numerous, and the affairs of the kingdom were properly settled.

19. *David enquired of the Lord.* He considered himself only the captain of the Lord's host, and therefore would not strike a stroke without the command of his Superior.

20. *The Lord hath broken forth.* He very properly attributes the victory of Jehovah, without whose strength and counsel he could have done nothing. *Baal-perazim.* The "plain or chief of breaches," because of the breach which God made in the Philistine army.

21. *They left their images.* It was the custom of most nations to carry their gods with them to battle.

23. *Fetch a compass behind them.* When they may be had, God will not work without using human means. By this He taught David caution, prudence, and dependence on the divine strength.

24. *When thou hearest the sound of a going.* If there had not been an evident supernatural interference, David might have thought that the sleight which he had used was the cause of his victory. By the going in the tops of the mulberry trees, probably only a rustling among the leaves is intended.

25. *And David did so.* He punctually obeyed the directions of the Lord, and then everything succeeded to his wish.

CHAPTER 6

David goes with 30,000 men to bring the ark from Kirjath-jearim to Jerusalem, 1-5. The oxen stumbling, Uzzah, who drove the cart on which the ark was placed, put forth his hand to save it from falling; the Lord was displeased, and smote him so that he died, 6-7. David, being alarmed, carries the ark to the house of Obed-edom, 8-10. Here it remains three months; and God prospers Obed-edom, in whose house it was deposited, 11. David, hearing of this, brings the ark, with sacrifices and solemn rejoicings, to Jerusalem, 12-15. Michal, seeing David dance before the ark, despises him, 16. He offers burnt offerings and peace offerings, and deals among all the people, men and women, a cake of bread, a good piece of flesh, and a flagon of wine each, 17-19. Michal coming to meet him, and seeing him dance extravagantly before the ark, reproaches him for his conduct; he vindicates himself, reproves her, and she dies childless, 20-23.

1. *Thirty thousand.* This is supposed to have been a new levy; and thus he augmented his army by 30,000 fresh troops. The Septuagint has 70,000.

2. *From Baale of Judah.* This is supposed to be the same city which, in Josh. xv. 60, is called Kirjath-baal or Kirjath-jearim (see 1 Chron. xiii. 6); or Baalah, Josh. xv. 9. *Whose name is called by the name of the Lord.* That is, "The ark is called the ark of the Lord of hosts." But this is not a literal version. The word *shem*, "name," occurs twice together; probably one of them should be read *sham*, "there." There the name of the Lord of hosts was invoked.

3. *A new cart.* Everything used in the worship of God was hallowed or set apart for that purpose; a new cart was used through respect, as that had never been applied to any profane or common purpose. But this is not sufficient, for the ark should have been carried on the shoulders of the priests; and the neglect of this ceremony was the cause of the death of Uzzah.

5. *On all manner of instruments made of fir wood.* This place should be corrected from the parallel place, 1 Chron. xiii. 8: "All Israel

played before God, with all their might, and with singing, and with harps, and with psalteries." Instead of *bechol atsey*, "with all woods" or "trees," the parallel place is *bechol oz*, "with all their strength." This makes a good sense; the first makes none. The Septuagint, in this place, has the same reading: "with might."

6. *Uzzah put forth his hand.* In Num. iv. 15-20, the Levites are forbidden to touch the ark on pain of death; this penalty was inflicted upon Uzzah, and he was the first that suffered for a breach of this law.

7. *Smote him there for his error.* Uzzah sinned through ignorance and precipitancy; he had not time to reflect. The oxen suddenly stumbled; and, fearing lest the ark should fall, he suddenly stretched out his hand to prevent it. Had he touched the ark with impunity, the populace might have lost their respect for it and its sacred service; the example of Uzzah must have filled them with fear and sacred reverence; and, as to Uzzah, no man can doubt of his eternal safety.

10. *But David carried it aside.* The house of Obed-edom appears to have been very near the city which they were about to enter.

11. *The Lord blessed Obed-edom.* And why? Because he had the ark of the Lord in his house. Whoever entertains God's messengers or consecrates his house to the service of God will infallibly receive God's blessing.

19. *A cake of bread.* Such as those which are baked without leaven, and are made very thin. *A good piece of flesh, and a flagon of wine.* The words *of flesh* and *of wine* we add; they are not in the Hebrew.

20. *To bless his household.* This was according to the custom of the patriarchs, who were priests in their own families. It is worthy of remark that David is called "patriarch" by Stephen, Acts ii. 29, though living upwards of four hundred years after the termination of the patriarchal age. *How glorious was the king of Israel!* This is a strong irony. From what Michal says, it is probable that David used some violent gesticulations, by means of which some parts of his body became uncovered.

21. *It was before the Lord, which chose me.* David felt the reproach, and was strongly irritated, and seems to have spoken to Michal with sufficient asperity.

22. *I will yet be more vile.* The plain meaning of these words appears to be this: "I am not ashamed of humbling myself before that God who rejected thy father because of his obstinacy and pride, and chose me in his stead to rule his people; and even those maidservants, when they come to know the motive of my conduct, shall acknowledge its propriety, and treat me with additional respect; and as for thee, thou shalt find that thy conduct is as little pleasing to God as it is to me."

CHAPTER 7

1. *When the king sat in his house.* That is, when he became resident in the palace which

Hiram, king of Tyre, had built for him. *And the Lord had given him rest.* This was after he had defeated the Philistines, and cast them out of all the strong places in Israel which they had possessed after the overthrow of Saul.

3. *Nathan said to the king.* In this case he gave his judgment as a pious and prudent man, not as a prophet; for the prophets were not always under a divine afflatus; it was only at select times they were thus honored.

5. *Shalt thou build me an house?* That is, You shall not; this is the force of the interrogative in such a case.

7. *With any of the tribes.* "Spake I a word to any of the judges?" is the reading in the parallel place, 1 Chron. xvii. 6; and this is probably the true reading. Indeed, there is but one letter of difference between them, and letters which might be easily mistaken for each other.

10. *I will appoint a place.* I "have" appointed a place, and "have" planted them.

11. *The Lord . . . will make thee an house.* You have in your heart to make Me a house; I have it in My heart to make you a house.

13. *He shall build.* That is, Solomon shall build My temple, not you, because you have shed blood abundantly, and have made great wars (see 1 Chron. xxii. 8). *The throne of his kingdom for ever.* This is a reference to the government of the spiritual Kingdom, the kingdom of the Messiah, agreeably to the predictions of the prophet long after, and by which this passage is illustrated: "Of the increase of his government and peace there shall be no end, upon the throne of David, and upon his kingdom, to order it, and to establish it with judgment and with justice from henceforth even for ever," Isa. ix. 7.

14. *If he commit iniquity*—depart from the holy commandment delivered to him, *I will chasten him with the road of men*—he shall have affliction, but his government shall not be utterly subverted.

19. *And is this the manner of man?* Literally: "And this, O Lord God, is the law of Adam." Does he refer to the promise made to Adam, "The seed of the woman shall bruise the head of the serpent"? From my line shall the Messiah spring and be the spiritual and triumphant King for ever and ever.

20. *What can David say more?* How can I express my endless obligation to Thee?

25. *And do as thou hast said.* David well knew that all the promises made to himself and family were conditional, and therefore he prayed that they might be fulfilled. His posterity did not walk with God, and therefore they were driven from the throne. All the promises have failed to David and his natural posterity, and to Christ and His spiritual seed alone are they fulfilled.

CHAPTER 8

1. *David took Metheg-ammah.* This is variously translated. The Vulgate has, "David removed the bondage of the tribute," which the Israelites paid to the Philistines. Some think it means a fortress, city, or strong town; but no such place as Metheg-ammah is known. Probably the Vulgate is nearest the truth.

2. *And measured them with a line . . . even with two lines.* It has been generally conjectured that David, after he had conquered Moab, consigned two-thirds of the inhabitants to the sword; but I think the text will bear a meaning much more reputable to that king. The first clause of the verse seems to determine the sense: *he measured them with a line, casting them down to the ground*—to put to death, and with one line to keep alive. Death seems here to be referred to the cities by way of metaphor; and from this view of the subject we may conclude that two-thirds of the cities, that is, the strong places of Moab, were erased; and not having strong places to trust to, the text adds, *So the Moabites became David's servants, and brought gifts,* i.e., were obliged to pay tribute. The word *line* may mean the same here as our rod, i.e., the instrument by which land is measured.

3. *David smote . . . Hadadezer.* He is supposed to have been king of all Syria, except Phoenicia, and, wishing to extend his dominions to the Euphrates, invaded a part of David's dominions which lay contiguous to it; but being attacked by David, he was totally routed.

4. *A thousand chariots.* It is strange that there were 1,000 chariots, and only 700 horsemen taken, and 20,000 footmen. But as the discomfiture appears complete, we may suppose that the chariots, being less manageable, might be more easily taken, while the horsemen might, in general, make their escape. The infantry also seem to have been surrounded, when 20,000 of them were taken prisoners. *David houghed all the chariot horses.* "And David disjointed all the chariots," except a hundred chariots which he reserved for himself.

6. *Brought gifts.* Paid tribute.

7. *David took the shields of gold.* We know not what these were. Some translate "arms," others "quivers," others "bracelets," others "collars," and others "shields." They were probably costly ornaments by which the Syrian soldiers were decked and distinguished. And those who are called *servants* here were probably the choice troops or bodyguard of Hadadezer.

13. *David gat him a name.* Became a very celebrated and eminent man. The Targum has it, "David collected troops"; namely, to recruit his army when he returned from smiting the Syrians. His many battles had no doubt greatly thinned his army.

14. *He put garrisons in Edom.* He repaired the strong cities which he had taken, and put garrisons in them to keep the country in awe.

16. *Joab . . . was over the host.* General and commander in chief over all the army. *Ahilud . . . recorder. Mazkir,* "remembrancer"; one who kept a strict journal of all the proceedings of the king and operations of his army; a chronicler.

17. *Seraiah . . . the scribe.* Most likely the king's private secretary.

18. *Benaiah.* The chief of the second class of David's worthies. We shall meet with him again. *The Cherethites and the Pelethites.* The former supposed to be those who accompanied David when he fled from Saul; the latter, those who came to him at Ziklag. But the Targum translates these two names thus, "the archers and the slingers"; and this is by far the most likely.

CHAPTER 9

David inquires after the family of Jonathan, and is informed of Mephibosheth, his son, 1-4. He sends for him and gives him all the land of Saul, 5-8; and appoints Ziba, the servant of Saul, and his family to till the ground for Mephibosheth, 9-13.

1. *Is there yet any that is left?* David, recollecting the covenant made with his friend Jonathan, now inquires after his family. It is supposed that political considerations prevented him from doing this sooner.

3. *That I may shew the kindness of God unto him?* That is, the utmost, the highest degrees of kindness.

7. *Will restore thee all the land.* I believe this means the mere family estate of the house of Kish, which David as king might have retained, but which most certainly belonged, according to the Israelitish law, to the descendants of the family. *And thou shalt eat bread at my table.* This was kindness (the giving up the land was justice), and it was the highest honor that any subject could enjoy, as we may see from the reference made to it by our Lord, Luke xxii. 30: "That ye may eat and drink at my table in my kingdom." For such a person David could do no more. His lameness rendered him unfit for any public employment.

10. *Thou therefore, and thy sons . . . shall till the land.* It seems that Ziba and his family had the care of the whole estate, and cultivated it at their own expense, yielding the half of the produce to the family of Mephibosheth.

11. *So shall thy servant do.* The promises of Ziba were fair and specious, but he was a traitor in his heart, as we shall see in the rebellion of Absalom.

CHAPTER 10

The king of Ammon being dead, David sends ambassadors to comfort his son Hanun, 1-2. Hanun, misled by his courtiers, treats the messengers of David with great indignity, 3-5. The Ammonites, justly dreading David's resentment, send and hire the Syrians to make war upon him, 6. Joab and Abishai meet them at the city of Medeba, and defeat them, 7-14. The Syrians collect another army, but are defeated by David with great slaughter, and make with him a separate peace, 15-19.

2. *I will shew kindness unto Hanun the son of Nahash.* We do not know exactly the nature or extent of the obligation which David was under to the king of the Ammonites.

4. *Shaved off the one half of their beards.* The beard is held in high respect in the East; the possessor considers it his greatest ornament, often swears by it, and in matters of great importance *pledges* it. Nothing can be more secure than a pledge of this kind; its owner will redeem it at the hazard of his life. The beard was never cut off but in mourning, or as a sign of slavery. Cutting off half of the beard and the clothes rendered the men ridiculous,

and made them look like slaves; what was done to these men was an accumulation of insult.

6. *The children of Ammon saw that they stank.* That is, that their conduct rendered them abominable. This is the Hebrew mode of expressing such a feeling. *The Syrians of Beth-rehob.* This place was situated at the extremity of the valley between Libanus and Anti-libanus. The Syrians of Zoba were subject to Hadadezer. *Maacah* was in the vicinity of Mount Hermon, beyond Jordan, in the Trachonitis. *Ish-tob.* This was probably the same with Tob, to which Jephthah fled from the cruelty of his brethren. It was situated in the land of Gilead.

7. *All the host of the mighty.* All his worthies, and the flower of his army.

8. *At the entering in of the gate.* This was the city of Medeba, as we learn from 1 Chron. xix. 7.

9. *Before and behind.* It is probable that one of the armies was in the field, and the other in the city, when Joab arrived. When he fronted this army, the other appears to have issued from the city, and to have taken him in the rear. He was therefore obliged to divide his army as here mentioned, one part to face the Syrians commanded by himself, and the other to face the Ammonites commanded by his brother Abishai.

12. *Be of good courage.* This is a very fine military address, and is equal to anything in ancient or modern times.

14. *The Syrians were fled.* They betook themselves to their own confines, while the Ammonites escaped into their own city.

16. *The Syrians that were beyond the river.* That is, the Euphrates. *Hadarezer.* This is the same that was overthrown by David, chap. viii, and there called Hadadezer, which is the reading here of about thirty of Kennicott's and De Rossi's MSS. But the *resh* and *daleth* are easily interchanged.

17. *David . . . gathered all Israel together.* He thought that such a war required his own presence.

18. *Seven hundred chariots . . . and forty thousand horsemen.* In the parallel place, 1 Chron. xix. 18, it is said, "David slew of the Syrians seven thousand men which fought in chariots." It is difficult to ascertain the right number in this and similar places. The Jews expressed their numbers, not by words at full length, but by numeral letters; and, as many of the letters bear a great similarity to each other, mistakes might easily creep in when the numeral letters came to be expressed by words at full length. This alone will account for the many mistakes which we find in the numbers in these books, and renders a mistake here very probable. The letter *zain,* with a dot above, stands for 7,000; *nun,* for 700. The great similarity of these letters might easily cause the one to be mistaken for the other, and so produce an error in this place.

19. *Made peace with Israel.* They made this peace separately, and were obliged to pay tribute to the Israelites.

We have now done with the first part of this book, in which we find David great, glorious, and pious. We come to the second part, in which we shall have the pain to observe him fallen from God, and his horn defiled in the dust by crimes of the most flagitious nature. Let him that most assuredly standeth take heed lest he fall.

CHAPTER 11

David sends Joab against the Ammonites, who besieges the city of Rabbah, 1. He sees Bath-sheba, the wife of Uriah, bathing; is enamored of her; sends for and takes her to his bed, 2-4. She conceives, and informs David, 5. David sends to Joab, and orders him to send to him Uriah, 6. He arrives; and David having inquired the state of the army, dismisses him, desiring him to go to his own house, 7-8. Uriah sleeps at the door of the king's house, 9. The next day the king urges him to go to his house; but he refuses to go, and gives the most pious and loyal reasons for his refusal, 10-11. David after two days sends him back to the army, with a letter to Joab, desiring him to place Uriah in the front of the battle, that he may be slain, 12-15. He does so; and Uriah falls, 16-17. Joab communicates this news in an artful message to David, 18-25. David sends for Bath-sheba and takes her to wife, and she bears him a son, 26-27.

1. *When kings go forth.* This was about a year after the war with the Syrians spoken of before, and about the spring of the year, as the most proper season for military operations.

2. *In an eveningtide . . . David arose.* He had been reposing on the roof of his house, to enjoy the breeze, as the noonday was too hot for the performance of business. This is still a constant custom on the flat-roofed houses in the East. *He saw a woman washing herself.* How could any woman of delicacy expose herself where she could be so fully and openly viewed? Did she not know that she was at least in view of the king's terrace? Was there no design in all this?

3. *The daughter of Eliam.* Called, 1 Chron. iii. 5, Ammiel; a word of the same meaning; "The people of my God, The God of my people." This name expressed the covenant—"I will be your God; we will be Thy people."

4. *And she came in unto him.* We hear nothing of her reluctance, and there is no evidence that she was taken by force.

8. *Go down to thy house, and wash thy feet.* Uriah had come off a journey, and needed this refreshment; but David's design was that he should go and lie with his wife, that the child now conceived should pass for his, the honor of Bath-sheba be screened, and his own crime concealed. *A mess of meat from the king.* All this was artfully contrived.

9. *Slept at the door.* That is, in one of the apartments or niches in the court of the king's house.

10. *Camest thou not from thy journey?* It is not your duty to keep watch or guard; you are come from a journey, and need rest and refreshment.

11. *The ark, and Israel . . . abide in tents.* It appears therefore that they had taken the ark with them to battle. This was the answer of a brave, generous, and disinterested man. I will not indulge myself while all my fellow soldiers are exposed to hardships, and even the ark of the Lord in danger.

13. *He made him drunk.* Supposing that in this state he would have been off his guard, and hasten down to his house.

14. *David wrote a letter.* This was the sum of treachery and villainy. He made this most noble man the carrier of letters which prescribed the mode in which he was to be murdered.

27. *When the mourning was past.* Probably it lasted only seven days. *She became his wife.* This hurried marriage was no doubt intended on both sides to cover the pregnancy. *But the thing that David had done displeased the Lord.* It was necessary to add this, lest the splendor of David's former virtues should induce any to suppose his crimes were passed over, or looked on with an indulgent eye, by the God of purity and justice. Sorely he sinned, and sorely did he suffer for it; he sowed one grain of sweet, and reaped a long harvest of calamity and woe.

CHAPTER 12

The Lord sends Nathan the prophet to reprove David, which he does by means of a curious parable, 1-4. David is led, unknowingly, to pronounce his own condemnation, 5-6. Nathan charges the guilt home on his conscience, and predicts a long train of calamities which should fall on him and his family, 7-12. David confesses his sin; Nathan gives him hope of God's mercy, and foretells the death of the child born in adultery, 13-14. The child is taken ill; David fasts and prays for its restoration, 15-17. On the seventh day the child dies, and David is comforted, 18-24. Solomon is born of Bath-sheba, 25-26. Joab besieges Rabbah of the Ammonites, takes the city of waters, and sends for David to take Rabbah, 27-28. He comes, takes it, gets much spoil, and puts the inhabitants to hard labor, 29-31.

1. *There were two men in one city.* There is nothing in this parable that requires illustration; its bent is evident; and it was constructed to make David, unwittingly, pass sentence on himself. It was in David's hand what his own letters were in the hands of the brave but unfortunate Uriah.

5. *The man . . . shall surely die.* Literally, "He is a son of death," a very bad man, and one who deserves to die. But the law did not sentence a sheep-stealer to death. Let us hear it: "If a man steal an ox, or a sheep . . . he shall restore five oxen for an ox, and four sheep for a sheep," Exod. xxii. 1; and hence David immediately says, "He shall restore the lamb fourfold."

7. *Thou art the man.* What a terrible word! And by it David appears to have been transfixed, and brought into the dust before the messenger of God.

8. *Thy master's wives into thy bosom.* Perhaps this means no more than that he had given him absolute power over everything possessed by Saul; and as it was the custom for the new king to succeed even to the wives and concubines, the whole harem of the deceased king, so it was in this case; and the possession of the wives was a sure proof that he had got all regal rights.

9. *Thou hast killed Uriah.* You are the murderer, as having planned his death; the sword of the Ammonites was your instrument only.

11. *I will take thy wives.* That is, In the course of My providence I will permit all this to be done. Had David been faithful, God, by His providence, would have turned all this aside; but now, by his sin, he has made that providence his enemy which before was his friend.

13. *The Lord . . . hath put away thy sin.* Many have supposed that David's sin was now actually pardoned, but this is perfectly erroneous. David, as an adulterer, was condemned to death by the law of God, and he had according to that law passed sentence of death

upon himself. God alone, whose law that was, could revoke that sentence, or dispense with its execution. Therefore Nathan, who had charged the guilt home upon his conscience, is authorized to give him the assurance that he should not die a temporal death for it: *The Lord also hath put away thy sin; thou shalt not die.* There is something very remarkable in the words of Nathan: *The Lord also hath put away thy sin; thou shalt not die.* "Also Jehovah hath caused thy sin to pass over, or transferred thy sin; thou shalt not die." God has transferred the legal punishment of this sin to the child; he shall die, you shall not die. And this is the very point on which the prophet gives him the most direct information: The child that is born unto you shall surely die—"dying he shall die."

16. *David . . . besought God for the child.* How could he do so after the solemn assurance that he had from God that the child should die? The justice of God absolutely required that the penalty of the law should be exacted; either the father or the son shall die. This could not be reversed.

22. *Who can tell?* David, and indeed all others under the Mosaic dispensation, were so satisfied that all God's threatenings and promises were conditional that even in the most positive assertions relative to judgments, etc., they sought for a change of purpose. And notwithstanding the positive declaration of Nathan relative to the death of the child, David sought for its life, not knowing but that might depend on some unexpressed condition, such as earnest prayer, fasting, humiliation, and in these he continued while there was hope.

23. *I shall go to him, but he shall not return to me.* It is not clear whether David by this expressed his faith in the immortality of the soul; going to him may only mean, "I also shall die, and be gathered to my fathers, as he is."

24. *David comforted Bath-sheba.* His extraordinary attachment to this beautiful woman was the cause of all his misfortunes. *He called his name Solomon.* This name seems to have been given prophetically, for *sholomah* signifies "peaceable," and there was almost uninterrupted peace during his reign.

25. *Called . . . Jedidiah.* Literally, "the beloved of the Lord."

26. *And took the royal city.* How can this be, when Joab sent to David to come to take the city, in consequence of which David did come and take that city? The explanation seems to be this: Rabbah was composed of a city and citadel; the former, in which was the king's residence, Joab had taken, and supposed he could soon render himself master of the latter, and therefore sends to David to come and take it, lest, he taking the whole, the city should be called after his name.

27. *And have taken the city of waters.* The city where the tank or reservoir was that supplied the city and suburbs with water. Some think that the original should be translated, "I have intercepted, or cut off, the waters of the city"; and Houbigant translates the place, "And I have already drawn off the waters from the city." This perfectly agrees with the account in Josephus, who says, "Having cut off their waters," *Antiq.,* lib. vii, cap. 7. This was the reason why David should come speedily, as

the citadel, deprived of water, could not long hold out.

30. *The weight whereof was a talent of gold.* If this talent was only seven pounds, as Whiston says, David might have carried it on his head with little difficulty; but this weight, according to common computation, would amount to more than one hundred pounds! If, however, *mish-kalah* be taken for the value, not the weight, then all is plain. Now this seems to be the true sense, because of the added words *with the precious stones;* i.e., the gold of the crown, and the jewels with which it was adorned, were equal in value to a talent of gold.

31. *He brought forth the people . . . and put them under saws.* From this representation a great cry has been raised against "David's unparalleled, if not diabolic, cruelty." I believe this interpretation was chiefly taken from the parallel place, 1 Chron. xx. 3, where it is said he "cut them with saws . . . and with axes." Instead of *vaiyasar,* "he sawed," we have here (in Samuel) *vaiyasem,* "he put them"; and these two words differ from each other only in a part of a single letter, *resh* for *mem.* And it is worthy of remark that, instead of *vaiyasar,* "he sawed," in 1 Chron. xx. 3, six or seven MSS. collated by Dr. Kennicott have *vaiyasem,* "he put them"; nor is there found any various reading in all the MSS. yet collated for the text in this chapter that favors the common reading in Chronicles. The meaning therefore is, He made the people slaves, and employed them in sawing, making iron harrows, or mining (for the word means both), and in hewing of wood, and making of brick.

CHAPTER 13

Amnon falls in love with his half sister Tamar, and feigns himself sick, and requests her to attend him, 1-6. David sends her to him, and he violates her, 7-14. He then hates her, and expels her from his house, 15-17. She rends her garments, puts ashes on her head, and goes forth weeping, 18-19. She is met by Absalom, her brother, who, understanding her case, determines the death of Amnon, 20-22. Two years after, he invites all his brothers to a sheep-shearing, when he orders his servants to murder Amnon, 23-29. Tidings come to David that Absalom has slain all the king's sons, which fill him with the bitterest distress, 30-31. The rest soon arrive, and he finds that Amnon only is killed, 32-36. Absalom flees to Talmai, king of Geshur, where he remains three years, 37-38. David longs after Absalom, having become reconciled to the death of Amnon, 39.

1. *Whose name was Tamar.* Tamar was the daughter of David and Maacah, daughter of the king of Geshur, and the sister of Absalom. Amnon was David's eldest son by Ahinoam. She was therefore sister to Amnon only by the father's side, i.e., half sister; but whole sister to Absalom.

2. *Amnon was so vexed . . . for she was a virgin.* It has been well remarked that "the passion of love is nowhere so wasting and vexatious as where it is unlawful."

12. *Nay, my brother.* There is something exceedingly tender and persuasive in this speech of Tamar; but Amnon was a mere brute, and it was all lost on him.

21. *But when King David heard.* To this verse the Septuagint add the following words: "But he would not grieve the soul of Amnon his son, for he loved him, because he was his firstborn." The same addition is found in the Vulgate and in Josephus, and it is possible that this once made a part of the Hebrew text.

23. *Absalom had sheepshearers.* These were times in which feasts were made, to which the neighbors and relatives of the family were invited.

26. *Let my brother Amnon go.* He urged this with the more plausibility because Amnon was the firstborn, and presumptive heir to the kingdom; and he had disguised his resentment so well before that he was not suspected.

30. *Absalom hath slain all the king's sons.* Fame never lessens but always magnifies a fact. Report, contrary to the nature of all other things, gains strength by going.

32. *And Jonadab . . . said . . . Amnon only is dead.* This was a very bad man, and here speaks coolly of a most bloody tragedy, which himself had contrived.

37. *Absalom fled.* As he had committed willful murder, he could not avail himself of a city of refuge, and was therefore obliged to leave the land of Israel and take refuge with Talmai, king of Geshur, his grandfather by his mother's side.

39. *David longed to go forth unto Absalom.* We find that he had a very strong paternal affection for this young man, who appears to have had little to commend him but the beauty of his person. David wished either to go to him or to bring him back, for the hand of time had now wiped off his tears for the death of his son Amnon. Joab had marked this disposition, and took care to work on it, in order to procure the return of Absalom. It would have been well for all parties had Absalom ended his days at Geshur. His return brought increasing wretchedness to his unfortunate father. And it may be generally observed that those undue, unreasonable paternal attachments are thus rewarded.

CHAPTER 14

A woman of Tekoah, by the advice of Joab, comes to the king, and by a fictitious story persuades him to recall Absalom, 1-20. Joab is permitted to go to Geshur, and bring Absalom from thence, 21-23. Absalom comes to Jerusalem to his own house, but is forbidden to see the king's face, 24. An account of Absalom's beauty, and the extraordinary weight of his hair, 25-26. His children, 27. He strives to regain the king's favor, and employs Joab as an intercessor, 28-32. David is reconciled to him, 33.

2. *Joab sent to Tekoah.* Tekoah, according to Jerome, was a little city in the tribe of Judah, about twelve miles from Jerusalem.

5. *I am indeed a widow woman.* It is very possible that the principal facts mentioned here were real, and that Joab found out a person whose circumstances bore a near resemblance to that which he wished to represent.

7. *The whole family is risen.* They took on them the part of the avenger of blood, the nearest akin to the murdered person having a right to slay the murderer. *They shall quench my coal which is left.* A man and his descendants or successors are often termed in Scripture a lamp or light. Thus, *quench my coal that is left* means destroying all hope of posterity, and extinguishing the family from among the people.

9. *The iniquity be on me.* She intimates that, if the king should suppose that the not bringing the offender to the assigned punishment might reflect on the administration of

justice in the land, she was willing that all blame should attach to her and her family, *and the king and his throne be guiltless.*

10. *Whosoever saith ought unto thee.* Neither did this bring the matter to such a bearing that she could come to her conclusion, which was to get the king pledged by a solemn promise that all proceedings relative to the case should be stopped.

11. *Let the king remember the Lord thy God.* Consider that when God is earnestly requested to show mercy He does it in the promptest manner; He does not wait till the case is hopeless. The danger to which my son is exposed is imminent; if the king do not decide the business instantly, it may be too late. *And he said, As the Lord liveth.* Thus he binds himself by a most solemn promise and oath, and this is what the woman wanted to extort.

13. *Wherefore then hast thou thought such a thing?* The woman, having now received the king's promise confirmed by an oath, that her son should not suffer for the murder of his brother, comes immediately to her conclusion: Is not the king to blame? Does he now act a consistent part? He is willing to pardon the meanest of his subjects the murder of a brother at the instance of a poor widow, and he is not willing to pardon his son Absalom, whose restoration to favor is the desire of the whole nation.

14. *For we must needs die.* Whatever is done must be done quickly; all must die; God has not exempted any person from this common lot. Though Amnon be dead, yet the death of Absalom cannot bring him to life nor repair this loss. The argument contained in v. 14 is very elegant, and powerfully persuasive; but one clause of it has been variously understood, *Neither doth God respect any person.* The Hebrew is, "And God doth not take away the soul." The Septuagint has it, "And God will receive the soul." This intimates that, after human life is ended, the soul has a state of separate existence with God. This was certainly the opinion of these translators, and was the opinion of the ancient Jews.

20. *According to the wisdom of an angel of God.* This is quite in the style of Asiatic flattery.

21. *And the king said unto Joab.* It appears that Joab was present at the time when the woman was in conference with the king, and no doubt others of David's courtiers or officers were there also.

24. *Let him not see my face.* He would not at once restore him to favor, though he had now remitted his crime, so that he should not die for it.

25. *None to be so much praised as Absalom.* It was probably his personal beauty that caused the people to interest themselves so much in his behalf.

27. *Unto Absalom there were born.* These children did not survive him (see chap. xviii. 18). *Tamar.* The Septuagint adds, "And she became the wife of Roboam, the son of Solomon, and bare to him Abia" (see Matt. i. 7). Josephus says the same. This addition is not found in the other versions.

30. *Go and set it on fire.* This was strange conduct, but it had the desired effect. He had not used his influence to get Absalom to court; now he uses it, and succeeds.

CHAPTER 15

Absalom conspires against his father, and uses various methods to seduce the people from their allegiance to their king, 1-6. Under pretense of paying a vow at Hebron, he obtains leave from David to go thither; and, by emissaries sent through the land, prepares the people for revolt, 7-11. He gains over Ahithophel, David's counsellor, 12. David is informed of the general defection of the people; on which he, and his lifeguards and friends, leave the city and go towards the wilderness, 13-18. The steadfast friendship of Ittai, the Gittite, 19-22. David's affecting departure from the city, 23. He sends Zadok and Abiathar with the ark back to Jerusalem, 24-29. He goes up Mount Olivet; prays that the counsel of Ahithophel may be turned into foolishness, 30-31. He desires Hushai to return to Jerusalem, and to send him word of all that occurs, 32-37.

1. *Absalom prepared him chariots and horses.* After all that has been said to prove that *horses* here mean "horsemen," I think it most likely that the writer would have us to understand *chariots* drawn by *horses*. *Fifty men to run before him.* Affecting in every respect the regal state by this establishment.

6. *So Absalom stole the hearts.* His manner of doing this is circumstantially related above. He was thoroughly versed in the arts of the demagogue, and the common people heard him gladly. He used the patriot's arguments, and was everything of the kind, as far as promise could go. He found fault with men in power; and he only wanted their place, like all other pretended patriots, that he might act as they did, or worse.

7. *After forty years.* There is no doubt that this reading is corrupt, though supported by the commonly printed Vulgate, the Septuagint, and the Chaldee. But the Syriac has "four years," the Arabic the same, and Josephus has the same; so also the Sistine edition of the Vulgate and several MSS. of the same version. Theodoret also reads "four," not "forty"; and most learned men are of opinion that *arbaim,* "forty," is an error for *arba,* "four"; yet this reading is not supported by any Hebrew MS. yet discovered.

8. *While I abode at Geshur in Syria.* Geshur, the country of Talmai, was certainly not in Syria, but lay on the south of Canaan, in or near Edom, as is evident from Judg. i. 10; 1 Sam. xxvii. 8; chap. xiii. 37. Hence it is probable that *Aram,* "Syria," is a mistake for "Edom," *daleth* and *resh* being easily interchangeable. "Edom" is the reading of both the Syriac and Arabic.

10. *Absalom sent spies.* These persons were to go into every tribe; and the trumpet was to be blown as a signal for all to arise, and proclaim Absalom in every place. The trumpet was probably used as a kind of telegraph by the spies, trumpet exciting trumpet from place to place, so that in a few minutes all Israel would hear the proclamation.

11. *Went two hundred men.* These were probably soldiers, whom he supposed would be of considerable consequence to him. They had been seduced by his specious conduct, but knew nothing of his present design.

12. *Sent for Ahithophel.* When Absalom got him, he in effect got the prime minister of the kingdom to join him.

14. *David said . . . Arise . . . let us flee.* This, I believe, was the first time that David turned his back to his enemies. And why did he now flee? Jerusalem, far from not being in a state to sustain a siege, was so strong that even the blind and the lame were supposed to be a sufficient defense for the walls (see chap. v. 6). And he had still with him his faithful Cherethites and Pelethites, besides 600 faithful Gittites, who were perfectly willing to follow his fortunes. There does not appear any reason why such a person, in such circumstances, should not act on the defensive, at least till he should be fully satisfied of the real complexion of affairs. But he appears to take all as coming from the hand of God; therefore he humbles himself, weeps, goes barefoot, and covers his head!

17. *And tarried in a place.* He probably waited till he saw all his friends safely out of the city.

19. *Thou art a stranger, and also an exile.* Some suppose that Ittai was the son of Achish, king of Gath, who was very much attached to David, and banished from his father's court on that account. He and his 600 men are generally supposed to have been proselytes to the Jewish religion.

23. *The brook Kidron.* This was an inconsiderable brook, and furnished with water only in winter, and in the rains (see John xviii. 1).

24. *Bearing the ark.* The priests knew that God had given the kingdom to David; they had no evidence that He had deposed him. They therefore chose to accompany him, and take the ark, the object of their charge, with them.

25. *Carry back the ark.* David shows here great confidence in God, and great humility. The ark was too precious to be exposed to the dangers of his migrations; he knew that God would restore him if He delighted in him, and he was not willing to carry off from the city of God that without which the public worship could not be carried on. He felt, therefore, more for this public worship and the honor of God than he did for his own personal safety.

31. *Turn the counsel of Ahithophel into foolishness.* Ahithophel was a wise man, and well versed in state affairs, and God alone could confound his devices.

32. *Where he worshipped God.* Though in danger of his life, he stops on the top of Mount Olivet for prayer! *Hushai the Archite.* He was the particular friend of David, and was now greatly affected by his calamity.

33. *Then thou shalt be a burden unto me.* It appears that Hushai was not a warrior, but was a wise, prudent, and discreet man, who could well serve David by gaining him intelligence of Absalom's conspiracy; and he directs him to form a strict confederacy with the priests Zadok and Abiathar, and to make use of their sons as couriers between Jerusalem and David's place of retreat.

37. *Absalom came into Jerusalem.* It is very probable that he and his partisans were not far from the city when David left it, and this was one reason which caused him to hurry his departure.

CHAPTER 16

Ziba, servant of Mephibosheth, meets David with provisions, and by false insinuations obtains the grant of his master's property, 1-4. Shimei abuses and curses David, who restrains Abishai from slaying him, 5-14. Hushai makes a feigned tender of his services to Absalom, 15-19. Absalom calls a council and Ahithophel advises him to go in to his father's concubines, 20-22. Character of Ahithophel as a counsellor, 23.

1. *Two hundred loaves of bread.* The word *loaf* gives us a false idea of the ancient Jewish bread; it was thin cakes, not yeasted and raised like ours. *A bottle of wine.* A goat's skin full of wine.

2. *The asses be for the king's household.* This is the Eastern method of speaking when anything is presented to a great man: "This and this is for the slaves of the servants of Your Majesty," when at the same time the presents are intended for the sovereign himself, and are so understood. It is a high Eastern compliment: These presents are not worthy of your acceptance; they are fit only for the slaves of your slaves.

3. *To day shall the house of Israel.* What a base wretch was Ziba! and how unfounded was this accusation against the peaceable, loyal, and innocent Mephibosheth!

4. *Thine are all.* This conduct of David was very rash; he spoiled an honorable man to reward a villain, not giving himself time to look into the circumstances of the case. But David was in heavy afflictions, and these sometimes make even a wise man mad.

5. *David came to Bahurim.* This place lay northward of Jerusalem, in the tribe of Benjamin. It is called Almon, Josh. xxi. 18; and Alemeth, 1 Chron. vi. 60. Bahurim signifies "youths," and Almuth "youth"; so the names are of the same import. *Cursed still as he came.* Used imprecations and execrations.

10. *Because the Lord hath said.* The particle *vechi* should be translated "for if," not *because.* "For if the Lord hath said unto him, Curse David, who shall then say, Wherefore hast thou done so?"

11. *Let him curse; for the Lord hath bidden him.* No soul of man can suppose that God ever bade one man to curse another, much less that He commanded such a wretch as Shimei to curse such a man as David; but this is a peculiarity of the Hebrew language, which does not always distinguish between permission and commandment.

15. *The men of Israel.* These words are wanting in the Chaldee, Septuagint, Syriac, Vulgate, and Arabic.

18. *Whom the Lord, and this people . . . choose.* Here is an equivocation; Hushai meant in his heart that God and all the people of Israel had chosen David; but he spake so as to make Absalom believe that he spoke of him. For whatever of insincerity may appear in this, Hushai is alone answerable. What he says afterwards may be understood in the same way.

21. *Go in unto thy father's concubines.* It may be remembered that David left ten of them behind to take care of the house; see chap. xv. 16. Ahithophel advised this infernal measure in order to prevent the possibility of a reconciliation between David and his son; thus was the prophecy to Nathan fulfilled, chap. xii. 11. And this was probably transacted in

the very same place where David's eye took the adulterous view of Bath-sheba (see chap. xi. 2). The wives of the conquered king were always the property of the conqueror; and in possessing these, he appeared to possess the right to the kingdom.

CHAPTER 17

Ahithophel counsels Absalom to pursue his father with 12,000 men, 1-4. Hushai gives a different coun.el, and is followed, 5-14. Hushai informs Zadok and Abiathar, and they send word to David, 15-21. David and his men go beyond Jordan, 22. Ahithophel, finding his counsel slighted, goes home, sets his house in order, and hangs himself, 23. David moves to Mahanaim, and Absalom follows him over Jordan, 24-26. Several friends meet David at Mahanaim with refreshments and provisions, 27-29.

1. *Let me now choose out twelve thousand men.* Had this counsel been followed, David and his little troop would soon have been destroyed; nothing but the miraculous interposition of God could have saved them.

3. *The man whom thou seekest is as if all returned.* Only secure David, and all Israel will be on your side. He is the soul of the whole; destroy him, and all the rest will submit.

13. *Shall all Israel bring ropes to that city.* The original word *chabalim,* which signifies *ropes,* and from which we have our word "cable," may have some peculiarity of meaning here; for it is not likely that any city could be pulled down with ropes. The Chaldee, which should be best judge in this case, translates the original word by "towers"; this gives an easy sense.

17. *En-rogel.* The "fullers' well," the place where they were accustomed to tread the clothes with their feet; hence the name *ein,* a "well," and *regel,* the "foot." *And a wench went and told them.* The word *wench* occurs nowhere else in the Holy Scriptures: and, indeed, has no business here, as the Hebrew word should have been translated "girl, maid, maidservant."

23. *Put his household in order.* This self-murder could not be called lunacy, as every step to it was deliberate. He foresaw Absalom's ruin; he did not choose to witness it, and share in the disgrace, and he could expect no mercy at the hands of David.

25. *Amasa captain of the host.* From the account in this verse it appears that Joab and Amasa were sisters' children, and both nephews to David.

28. *Brought beds.* These no doubt consisted in skins of beasts, mats, carpets, and suchlike things. *Basons.* Probably wooden bowls, such as the Arabs still use to eat out of, and to knead their bread in. *Earthen vessels.* Probably clay vessels, baked in the sun. These were perhaps used for lifting water, and boiling those articles which required to be cooked. *Wheat, and barley.* There is no direct mention of flesh-meat here; little was eaten in that country, and it would not keep. Whether the *sheep* mentioned were brought for their flesh or their milk, I cannot tell.

CHAPTER 18

David reviews and arranges the people, and gives the command to Joab, Abishai, and Ittai, 1-2. On his expressing a desire to accompany them to the battle, they will not permit him, 3. He reviews them as they go out of the city, and gives commandment to the captains to save Absalom, 4-5. They join battle with Absalom and his army, who are discomfited with the loss of 20,000 men, 6-8. Absalom, fleeing away, is caught by his head in an oak; Joab finds him, and transfixes him with three darts, 9-15. The servants of David are recalled, and Absalom buried, 16-18. Ahimaaz and Cushi bring the tidings to David, who is greatly distressed at hearing of the death of Absalom, and makes bitter lamentation for him, 19-33.

1. *And set captains of thousands.* By this time David's small company was greatly recruited, but what its number was we cannot tell. Josephus says it amounted to 4,000 men. Others have supposed that they amounted to 10,000, for thus they understand a clause in v. 3, which they think should be read, "We are now ten thousand strong."

5. *Deal gently . . . with the young man.* David was the father of this worthless young man; and is it to be wondered at that he feels as a father? Who in his circumstances, that had such feelings as every man should have, would have felt or acted otherwise?

7. *Twenty thousand men.* Whether these were slain on the field of battle or whether they were reckoned with those slain in the wood of Ephraim, we know not.

8. *The wood devoured more people.* It is generally supposed that, when the army was broken, they betook themselves to the wood, fell into pits, swamps, etc., and, being entangled, were hewn down by David's men.

9. *And his head caught hold of the oak.* It has been supposed that Absalom was caught by the hair, but no such thing is intimated in the text. Probably his neck was caught in the fork of a strong bough, and he was nearly dead when Joab found him; for it is said, v. 14, "He was yet alive," an expression which intimates he was nearly dead.

11. *And a girdle.* The military belt was the chief ornament of a soldier, and was highly prized in all ancient nations; it was also a rich present from one chieftain to another. Jonathan gave his to David, as the highest pledge of his esteem and perpetual friendship, 1 Sam. xvii. 4.

13. *Thou thyself wouldest have set thyself against me.* This is a strong appeal to Joab's loyalty, and respect for the orders of David; but he was proof against every fine feeling, and against every generous sentiment.

14. *I may not tarry thus with thee.* He had nothing to say in vindication of the purpose he had formed. *Thrust them through the heart of Absalom.* He was determined to make sure work, and therefore he pierced his heart.

15. *Ten young men . . . smote Absalom, and slew him.* That is, they all pierced the body; but there could be no life in it after three darts had been thrust through the heart.

16. *Joab blew the trumpet.* He knew that the rebellion was now extinguished by the death of Absalom, and was not willing that any further slaughter should be made of the deluded people.

17. *And laid a very great heap of stones.* This was the method of burying heroes, and even traitors, the heap of stones being designed to perpetuate the memory of the event, whether good or bad.

18. *Absalom's place.* Literally "Absalom's hand." See the note on 1 Sam. xv. 12.

21. *Tell the king what thou hast seen.* At

this time the death of Absalom was not publicly known, but Joab had given Cushi private information of it. This Ahimaaz had not, for he could not tell the king whether Absalom was dead. To this Joab seems to refer, v. 22: "Thou hast no tidings ready."

24. *David sat between the two gates.* He was probably in the seat of justice.

25. *If he be alone, there is tidings.* That is, "good tidings." For if the battle had been lost, men would have been running in different directions through the country.

29. *I saw a great tumult.* It was very probable that Ahimaaz did not know of the death of Absalom; he had seen the rout of his army, but did not know of his death.

30. *Stand here.* He intended to confront two messengers, and compare their accounts.

32. *Is the young man Absalom safe?* This was the utmost of his solicitude, and it well merited the reproof which Joab gave him, chap. xix. 5.

CHAPTER 19

David continues his lamentation for his son, and the people are greatly discouraged, 1-4. Joab reproves and threatens him with the general defection of the people, 5-7. David lays aside his mourning, and shows himself to the people, who are thereby encouraged, 8. The tribes take counsel to bring the king back to Jerusalem, 9-12. He makes Amasa captain of the host in place of Joab, 13. The king, returning, is met by Judah at Gilgal, 14-15. Shimei comes to meet David, and entreats for his life, which David grants, 16-23. Mephibosheth also meets him, and shows how he had been slandered by Ziba, 24-30. David is met by Barzillai, and between them there is an affecting interview, 31-40. Contention between the men of Judah and the men of Israel about bringing back the king, 41-43.

2. *The victory . . . was turned into mourning.* Instead of rejoicing that a most unnatural and ruinous rebellion had been quashed, the people mourned over their own success, because they saw their king so immoderately afflicted for the loss of his worthless son.

4. *The king covered his face.* This was the custom of mourners.

5. *Thou hast shamed this day.* Joab's speech to David on his immoderate grief for the death of his rebellious son is not only remarkable for the insolence of office but also for good sense and firmness. Every man who candidly considers the state of the case must allow that David acted imprudently at least, and that Joab's firm reproof was necessary to arouse him to a sense of his duty to his people. But still, in his manner, Joab had far exceeded the bonds of that reverence which a servant owes to his master, or a subject to his prince. Joab was a good soldier, but in every respect a bad man, and a dangerous subject.

8. *The king . . . sat in the gate.* The place where justice was administered to the people.

11. *Speak unto the elders of Judah.* David was afraid to fall out with this tribe; they were in possession of Jerusalem, and this was a city of great importance to him. They had joined Absalom in his rebellion, and doubtless were now ashamed of their conduct. David appears to take no notice of their infidelity, but rather to place confidence in them, that their confidence in him might be naturally excited: and, to oblige them yet farther, purposes to make Amasa captain of the host in the place of Joab.

14. *And he bowed the heart of all the men of Judah.* The measures that he pursued were the best calculated that could be to accomplish this salutary end.

16. *Shimei the son of Gera.* It appears that Shimei was a powerful chieftain in the land; for he had here, in his retinue, no less than a thousand men.

18. *There went over a ferry boat.* This is the first mention of anything of the kind. Some think a bridge or raft is what is here intended.

20. *For thy servant doth know that I have sinned.* This was all he could do; his subsequent conduct alone could prove his sincerity. On such an avowal as this David could not but grant him his life.

24. *Neither dressed his feet.* He had given the fullest proof of his sincere attachment to David and his cause, and by what he had done, amply refuted the calumnies of his servant Ziba.

27. *The king is as an angel of God.* As if he had said, I state my case plainly and without guile; you are too wise not to penetrate the motives from which both myself and servant have acted. I shall make no appeal; with whatsoever you determine I shall rest contented.

29. *I have said, Thou and Ziba divide the land.* At first David gave the land of Saul to Mephibosheth; Ziba, his sons, and his servants were to work that land; and to Mephibosheth, as the lord, he was to give the half of the produce. Ziba met David in his distress with provisions, and calumniated Mephibosheth; David made him on the spot a grant of his master's land. Now he finds that he has acted too rashly, and therefore confirms the former grant; i.e., that Ziba should cultivate the ground, and still continue to give to Mephibosheth, as the lord, the half of the produce.

37. *Thy servant Chimham.* It is generally understood that this was Barzillai's son; and this is probable from 1 Kings ii. 7, where, when David was dying, he said, "Shew kindness unto the sons of Barzillai": and it is very probable that this Chimham was one of them. In Jer. xli. 17 mention is made of the "habitation of Chimham," which was near to Bethlehem; and it is reasonably conjectured that David had left that portion, which was probably a part of his paternal estate, to this son of Barzillai.

39. *The king kissed Barzillai, and blessed him.* The kiss was the token of friendship and farewell; the blessing was a prayer to God for his prosperity, probably a prophetical benediction.

42. *Wherefore then be ye angry for this matter?* We have not done this for our own advantage; we have gained nothing by it; we did it through loyal attachment to our king.

43. *We have ten parts in the king, and . . . more right.* We are ten tribes to one, or we are ten times as many as you, and consequently should have been consulted in this business. *The words of the men of Judah were fiercer than the words of the men of Israel.* They had more weight, for they had more reason on their side.

CHAPTER 20

Sheba raises an insurrection, and gains a party in Israel, 1-2. David shuts up the ten concubines who were defiled by Absalom, 3. Amasa is sent to assemble the men of Judah, 4-5. And in the meantime Abishai is sent to pursue Sheba, 6-7. Joab treacherously murders Amasa, 8-12. Joab and the army continue the pursuit of Sheba, 13-14. He is besieged in Abel; and, by the counsels of a wise woman, the people of Abel cut off his head, and throw it over the wall to Joab; who blows the trumpet of peace, and he and his men return to Jerusalem, 15-22. Account of David's civil and military officers, 23-26.

1. *Sheba, the son of Bichri.* As this man was a Benjamite, he probably belonged to the family of Saul, and he seems to have had considerable influence in Israel to raise such an insurrection: but we know nothng further of him than what is related in this place. *We have no part in David.* We of Israel, we of the ten tribes, are under no obligation to the house of David. Leave him, and let every man fall into the ranks under his own leader.

3. *The ten women.* He could not well divorce them; he could not punish them, as they were not in the transgression; he could no more be familiar with them, because they had been defiled by his son; and to have married them to other men might have been dangerous to the state. Therefore he shut them up and *fed them*—made them quite comfortable, and they continued as widows to their death.

4. *Then said the king to Amasa.* Thus he invests him with the command of the army, and sends him to collect the men of Judah, and to come back to receive his orders in relation to Sheba, in three days. It appears that Amasa found more difficulty in collecting his countrymen than was at first supposed; and this detaining him beyond the three days, David, fearing that Sheba's rebellion would get head, sent Abishai, who it appears was accompanied by Joab, to pursue after Sheba. Amasa, it seems, caught up with them at Gibeon, v. 8, where he was treacherously murdered by the execrable Joab. 8. *Joab's garment.* It appears that this was not a military garment, and that Joab had no arms but a short sword, which he had concealed in his girdle; and this sword, or knife, was so loose in its sheath that it could be easily drawn out.

10. *In the fifth rib.* I believe *chomesh*, which we render here and elsewhere the *fifth rib*, means any part of the abdominal region. The Septuagint translate it "the groin"; the Targum, "the right side of the thigh." That it means some part of the abdominal region is evident from what follows, *and shed out his bowels to the ground.*

11. *He that favoreth Joab.* As if he had said, There is now no other commander besides Joab, and Joab is steadily attached to David; let those therefore who are loyal follow Joab.

14. *Unto Abel.* This is supposed to have been the capital of the district called Abilene in Luke's Gospel, chap. iii. 1. *Beth-maachah.* Is supposed to have been in the northern part of the Holy Land, on the confines of Syria, and probably in the tribe of Naphtali.

15. *They cast up a bank against the city.* The word which we render *bank* means most probably a "battering engine" of some kind, or a "tower" overlooking the walls, on which archers and slingers could stand and annoy the inhabitants, while others of the besiegers could proceed to sap the walls.

16. *A wise woman.* She was probably governess.

18. *They shall surely ask counsel at Abel.*

Abel was probably famed for the wisdom of its inhabitants; and parties who had disputes appealed to their judgment, which appears to have been in such high reputation as to be final by consent of all parties.

19. *I . . . peaceable and faithful in Israel.* I am for peace, not contention of any kind; I am *faithful*—I adhere to David, and neither seek nor shall sanction any rebellion or anarchy in the land. Why then do you proceed in such a violent manner? Perhaps the woman speaks here in the name and on behalf of the city: "I am a peaceable city, and am faithful to the king." *A mother in Israel.* That is, a chief city of a district; for it is very likely that the woman speaks of the city, not of herself.

21. *His head shall be thrown to thee.* Thus it appears she had great sway in the counsels of the city; and that the punishment of a state rebel was then, what it is now in this kingdom, beheading.

23. *Joab was over all the host.* He had murdered Amasa and seized on the supreme command; and such was his power at present, and the service which he had rendered to the state by quelling the rebellion of Sheba, that David was obliged to continue him, and dared not to call him to account for his murders without endangering the safety of the state by a civil war. *Benaiah . . . over the Cherethites.* Benaiah was over the "archers and slingers." See the notes on chap. viii. 18.

24. *Adoram was over the tribute.* Probably the chief receiver of the taxes; or chancellor of the exchequer, as we term it. *Jehoshaphat . . . recorder.* The registrar of public events.

25. *Shevah was scribe.* The king's secretary.

26. *Ira . . . was a chief ruler about David.* The Hebrew is *cohen ledavid,* "a priest to David"; and so the Vulgate, Septuagint, Syriac, and Arabic. The Chaldee has *rab,* a "prince, or chief." He was probably a sort of domestic chaplain to the king. We know that the kings of Judah had their seers, which is nearly the same: Gad was David's seer, chap. xxiv. 11; and Jeduthun was the seer of King Josiah, 2 Chron. xxxv. 15.

CHAPTER 21

A famine taking place three successive years in Israel, David inquired of the Lord the cause, and was informed that it was on account of Saul and his bloody house, who had slain the Gibeonites, 1. David inquires of the Gibeonites what atonement they require, and they answer, seven sons of Saul, that they may hang them up in Gibeah, 2-6. Names of the seven sons thus given up, 7-9. Affecting account of Rizpah, who watched the bodies through the whole of the time of harvest, to prevent them from being devoured by birds and beasts of prey, 10. David is informed of Rizpah's conduct, and collects the bones of Saul, Jonathan, and the seven men that were hanged at Gibeah, and buries them; and God is entreated for the land, 11-14. War between the Israelites and Philistines, in which David is in danger of being slain by Ishbi-benob, but is succored by Abishai, 15-17. He and several gigantic Philistines are slain by David and his servants, 18-22.

1. *Then there was a famine.* Of this famine we know nothing; it is not mentioned in any part of the history of David. *Because he slew the Gibeonites.* No such fact is mentioned in the life and transactions of Saul, nor is there any reference to it in any other part of Scripture.

2. *The remnant of the Amorites.* The Gibeon-

ites were Hivites, not Amorites, as appears from Josh. xi. 19: but *Amorites* is a name often given to the Canaanites in general, Gen. xv. 16; Amos ii. 8; and elsewhere.

3. *Wherewith shall I make the atonement?* It is very strange that a choice of this kind should be left to such a people. Why not ask this of God himself?

6. *Seven men of his sons.* Meaning sons, grandsons, or other near branches of his family.

8. *Five sons of Michal . . . whom she brought up.* Michal, Saul's daughter, was never married to Adriel, but to David, and afterwards to Phaltiel; though it is here said "she bore," *yaledah,* not *brought up,* as we falsely translate it. But we learn from 1 Sam. xviii. 19 that Merab, one of Saul's daughters, was married to Adriel.

9. *In the beginning of barley harvest.* This happened in Judea about the vernal equinox, or the twenty-first of March.

10. *Rizpah . . . took sackcloth.* Who can read the account of Rizpah's maternal affection for her sons that were now hanged without feeling his mind deeply impressed with sorrow? *Until water dropped upon them.* Until the time of the autumnal rains, which in that country commence about October.

12. *Took the bones of Saul.* The reader will recollect that the men of Jabesh-gilead burned the bodies of Saul and his sons, and buried the remaining bones under a tree at Jabesh (see 1 Sam. xxxi. 12-13). These David might have digged up again, in order to bury them in the family sepulchre.

15. *Moreover the Philistines had yet war.* There is no mention of this war in the parallel place, 1 Chron. xx. 4, etc. *David waxed faint.* This circumstance is nowhere else mentioned.

16. *Being girded with a new sword.* As the word *sword* is not in the original, we may apply the term *new* to his armor in general. He had got new arms, a new coat of mail, or something that defended him well, and rendered him very formidable; or it may mean a strong or sharp sword.

17. *That thou quench not the light of Israel.* David is here considered as the lamp by which all Israel was guided, and without whom all the nation must be involved in darkness. The lamp is the emblem of direction and support.

18. *A battle . . . at Gob.* Instead of *Gob,* several editions, and about forty of Kennicott's and De Rossi's MSS., have *nob;* but "Gezer" is the name in the parallel place, 1 Chron. xx. 4.

19. *Elhanan the son of Jaare-oregim . . . slew . . . Goliath the Gittite.* Here is a most manifest corruption of the text, or gross mistake of the transcriber; David, not *Elhanan,* slew *Goliath.* In 1 Chron. xx. 5, the parallel place, it stands thus: "Elhanan the son of Jair slew Lahmi the brother of Goliath the Gittite, whose spear staff was like a weaver's beam." This is plain, and our translators have borrowed some words from Chronicles to make both texts agree. The corruption may be easily accounted for by considering that *oregim,* which signifies "weavers," has slipped out of one line into the other; and that *beith hallachmi,* the Bethlehemite, is corrupted from *eth Lachmi;* then the reading will be the same as in Chronicles.

CHAPTER 22

David's psalm of thanksgiving for God's powerful deliverance and manifold blessings, including prophetic declarations relative to the humiliation and exaltation of the Messiah, 1-51.

1. *David spake unto the Lord the words of this song.* This is the same in substance, and almost in words, with Psalms xviii; and therefore the exposition of it must be reserved till it occurs in its course in that book, with the exception of a very few observations.

5. *When the waves of death compassed me.* Though in a primary sense many of these things belong to David, yet generally and fully they belong to the Messiah alone.

11. *He rode upon a cherub, and did fly . . . he was seen upon the wings of the wind.* In the original of this sublime passage, sense and sound are astonishingly well connected. The clap of the wing, the agitation and rush through the air are expressed here in a very extraordinary manner.

CHAPTER 23

The last words of David, 1-7. The names and exploits of his thirty-seven worthies, 8-39.

1. *These be the last words of David.* I suppose the "last poetical composition" is here intended. He might have spoken many words after these in prose, but none in verse. The words of this song contain a glorious prediction of the Messiah's kingdom and conquests, in highly poetic language. *The sweet psalmist of Israel.* This character not only belonged to him as the finest poet in Israel, but as the finest and most divine poet of the whole Christian world. The *sweet psalmist of Israel* has been the sweet Psalmist of every part of the habitable world where religion and piety have been held in reverence.

2. *The Spirit of the Lord spake by me.* Hence the matter of his writing came by direct and immediate inspiration. *His word was in my tongue.* Hence the words of this writing were as directly inspired as the matter.

3. *The Rock of Israel.* The Fountain whence Israel was derived. *He that ruleth over men must be just.* More literally, "He that ruleth in man is the just one"; or, "The just one is the ruler among men." *Ruling in the fear of God.* It is by God's fear that Jesus Christ rules the hearts of all His followers; and he who has not the fear of God before his eyes can never be a Christian.

4. *He shall be as the light of the morning.* This verse is very obscure, for it does not appear from it who the person is of whom the prophet speaks. As the Messiah seems to be the whole subject of these last words of David, He is probably the Person intended. *As the tender grass.* The effects of this shining, and of the rays of His grace, shall be like the shining of the sun upon the young grass or corn, after a plentiful shower of rain.

5. *Although my house be not so with God.* Instead of *ken,* "so," read *kun,* "established"; and let the whole verse be considered as an interrogation, including a positive assertion, and the sense will be at once clear and consistent: "For is not my house (family) established with

God; because He hath made with me an ever-lasting covenant, ordered in all, and preserved? For this (He) is all my salvation, and all my desire, although He make it (or him) not to spring up." All is sure relative to my spiritual successor, though he do not as yet appear; the covenant is firm, and it will spring forth in due time.

6. *But the sons of Belial shall be all of them as thorns.* There is no word in the text for *sons*; it is simply *Belial*, the "good-for-nothing man," and may here refer—first to Saul, and secondly to the enemies of our Lord.

8. *These be the names of the mighty men.* This chapter should be collated with the parallel place, 1 Chronicles xi. *The Tachmonite that sat in the seat.* Literally and properly, "Jasho-beam the Hachmonite." See 1 Chron. xi. 11. *The same was Adino the Eznite.* This is a corruption for *he lift up his spear* (see 1 Chron. xi. 11). *Eight hundred, whom he slew at one time.* "Three hundred" is the reading in Chron-icles, and seems to be the true one. The word *chalal*, which we translate "slain," should prob-ably be translated "soldiers," as in the Sep-tuagint; he withstood "three hundred soldiers" at one time.

9. *When they defied the Philistines that were there gathered.* This is supposed to refer to the war in which David slew Goliath.

11. *A piece of ground full of lentiles.* In 1 Chron. xi. 13 it is "a parcel of ground full of barley." There is probably a mistake of *ada-shim*, "lentiles," for *seorim*, "barley," or vice versa. Some think there were both *lentiles* and *barley* in the field, and that a marauding party of the Philistines came to destroy or carry them off, and these worthies defeated the whole, and saved the produce of the field. This is not unlikely.

13. *And three of the thirty.* The word *shalishim*, which we translate *thirty*, probably signifies an office or particular description of men. Of these *shalishim* we have here thirty-seven, and it can scarcely be said with propriety that we have thirty-seven out of thirty; and besides, in the parallel place, 1 Chronicles xi, there are sixteen added. The captains over Pharaoh's chariots are termed *shalishim*, Exod. xiv. 7. *The Philistines pitched in the valley of Rephaim.* This is the same war which is spoken of in chap. v. 17, etc.

16. *Poured it out unto the Lord.* To make libations, both of water and of wine, was a frequent custom among the heathen.

20. *Two lionlike men of Moab.* Some think that two real lions are meant; some that they were two savage, gigantic men; others, that two fortresses are meant. The words may signify, as the Targum has rendered it, "The two princes of Moab."

21. *He slew an Egyptian.* This man in 1 Chron. xi. 23 is stated to have been five cubits high, about seven feet six inches. *He went down to him with a staff.* I have known men who, with a staff only for their defense, could render the sword of the best-practiced soldier of no use to him.

23. *David set him over his guard.* The Vul-gate renders this, "David made him his privy counsellor"; or according to the Hebrew, "He

put him to his ears," i.e., confided his secrets to him.

24. *Asahel . . . was one of the thirty.* Asahel was one of those officers, or troops, called the *shalishim*. This Asahel, brother of Joab, was the same that was killed by Abner, chap. ii. 23.

25. *Shammah the Harodite.* There are several varieties in the names of the following *shali-shim;* which may be seen by comparing these verses with 1 Chron. xi. 27.

39. *Uriah the Hittite: thirty and seven in all.* To these the author of 1 Chron. xi. 41 adds Zabad son of Ahlai.

CHAPTER 24

David is tempted by Satan to number Israel and Judah, 1. Joab remonstrates against it, but the king deter-mines that it shall be done; and Joab and the captains accomplish the work, and bring the sum total to the king: viz., 800,000 warriors in Israel, and 500,000 in Judah, 2-9. David is convinced that he has done wrong; and the prophet Gad is sent to him to give him his choice of three judgments, one of which God is determined to inflict upon the nation, 10-13. David humbles himself before God, and a pestilence is sent, which destroys 70,000 men, 14-15. The angel of the Lord being about to destroy Jerusalem, David makes intercession, and the plague is stayed, 16-17. Gad directs him to build an altar to the Lord on the threshing floor of Araunah, where the plague was stayed, 18. He purchases this place for the purpose, and offers burnt offerings and peace offer-ings, 19-25.

1. *He moved David against them.* God could not be angry with David for numbering the people if He moved him to do it; but in the parallel place (1 Chron. xxi. 1) it is expressly said, "Satan stood up against Israel, and pro-voked David to number Israel." David, in all probability, slackening in his piety and con-fidence toward God, and meditating some ex-tension of his dominions without the divine counsel or command, was naturally curious to know whether the number of fighting men in his empire was sufficient for the work which he had projected. He therefore orders Joab and the captains to take an exact account of all the effective men in Israel and Judah. God is justly displeased with this conduct, and deter-mines that the props of his vain ambition shall be taken away, by either famine, war, or pes-tilence.

3. *Joab said unto the king.* This very bad man saw that the measure now recommended by the king was a wrong one, and might be ruinous to the people, and therefore he remon-strated against it in a very sensible speech; but the king was infatuated, and would hear no reason.

5. *And pitched in Aroer.* This was beyond Jordan, on the river Arnon, in the tribe of Gad; hence it appears that they began their census with the most eastern parts of the country beyond Jordan.

6. *To Dan-jaan.* Or to "Dan of the woods." This is the place so frequently mentioned, sit-uated at the foot of Mount Libanus, near to the source of the Jordan, the most northern city of all the possessions of the Israelites in what was called the Promised Land, as Beer-sheba was the most southern.

7. *The strong hold of Tyre.* This must have been the old city of Tyre, which was built on the mainland; the new city was built on a rock in the sea.

8. *Nine months and twenty days.* This was

a considerable time; but they had much work to do, nor did they complete the work, as appears from 1 Chron. xxi. 6; xxvii. 24.

9. *In Israel eight hundred thousand . . . the men of Judah were five hundred thousand.* In the parallel place, 1 Chron. xxi. 5, the sums are widely different: in Israel 1,100,000, in Judah 470,000. Neither of these sums is too great, but they cannot both be correct, and which is the true number is difficult to say. The former seems the most likely; but more corruptions have taken place in the numbers of the historical books of the Old Testament than in any other part of the sacred records. To attempt to reconcile them in every part is lost labor; better at once acknowledge what cannot be successfully denied, that although the original writers of the Old Testament wrote under the influence of the Divine Spirit, yet we are not told that the same influence descended on all copiers of their words, so as absolutely to prevent them from making mistakes. They might mistake, and they did mistake; but a careful collation of the different historical books serves to correct all essential errors of the scribes.

10. *David said . . . I have sinned greatly.* We know not exactly in what this sin consisted. I have already hinted, v. 1, that probably David now began to covet an extension of empire, and purposed to unite some of the neighboring states with his own; and having, through the suggestions of Satan or some other "adversary" (for so the word implies), given way to this covetous disposition, he could not well look to God for help, and therefore wished to know whether the thousands of Israel and Judah might be deemed equal to the conquests which he meditated. When God is offended and refuses assistance, vain is the help of man.

11. *For when David was up.* It is supposed that David's contrition arose from the reproof given by Gad, and that in the order of time the reproof came before the confession stated in the tenth verse. *David's seer.* A holy man of God, under the divine influence, whom David had as a domestic chaplain.

13. *Shall seven years of famine?* In 1 Chron. xxi. 12, the number is "three," not *seven;* and here the Septuagint has "three," the same as in Chronicles. This is no doubt the true reading, the letter *zain,* "seven," being mistaken for *gimel,* "three." A mistake of this kind might be easily made from the similarity of the letters.

14. *I am in a great strait: let us fall now into the hand of the Lord.* David acted nobly in this business. Had he chosen war, his own personal safety was in no danger, because there was already an ordinance preventing him from going to battle. Had he chosen famine, his own wealth would have secured his and his own family's support. But he showed the greatness of his mind in choosing the pestilence, to the ravages of which himself and household were exposed equally with the meanest of his subjects.

15. *From the morning . . . to the time appointed.* That is, from the morning of the day after David had made his election till the third day, according to the condition which God had proposed, and he had accepted. But it seems that the plague was terminated before the conclusion of the third day, for Jerusalem might have been destroyed, and it was not. Throughout the land, independently of the city, 70,000 persons were slain! This was a terrible mortality in the space of less than three days.

16. *The angel stretched out his hand upon Jerusalem.* By what means this destruction took place, we know not. It appears that an angel was employed in it, and that this minister of divine justice actually appeared as an object of sight; for it is said, v. 17, "When he [David] saw the angel that smote the people"; and both Ornan and his four sons saw him and were affrighted, 1 Chron. xxi. 20.
The threshingplace of Araunah. These threshing places, we have already seen, were made in the open air. In the parallel place, 1 Chron. xxi. 15, 20, etc., this person is called Ornan. The word that we render *Araunah* is written in this very chapter "Avarnah," v. 16; "Araniah," v. 18; "Araunah" or "Aravnah," v. 20 and the following; but in every place in 1 Chronicles xxi where it occurs it is written "Ornan." It is likely he had both names, "Araunah" and "Ornan"; but the varieties of spelling in 2 Samuel must arise from the blunders of transcribers.

17. *But these sheep, what have they done?* It seems that in the order of Providence there is no way of punishing kings in their regal capacity but by afflictions on their land, in which the people must necessarily suffer. If the king, therefore, by his own personal offenses, in which the people can have no part, bring down God's judgments upon his people (though they suffer innocently), grievous will be the account that he must give to God. *Against my father's house.* That is, against his own family; even to cut it off from the face of the earth.

18. *Go up, rear an altar unto the Lord.* This place is supposed to be Mount Moriah, where Abraham attempted to sacrifice Isaac, and where the temple of Solomon was afterwards built.

22. *Here be oxen for burnt sacrifice.* He felt for the king, and showed his loyalty to him by this offer. He felt for the people, and was willing to make any sacrifice to get the plague stayed. He felt for his own personal safety, and therefore was willing to give up all to save his life. He felt for the honor of God, and therefore was glad that he had a sacrifice to offer, so that God might magnify both His justice and mercy.

23. *As a king, give unto the king.* Literally, "All these did King Araunah give unto the king." That there could not be a king of the Jebusites on Mount Moriah is sufficiently evident; and that there was no other king than David in the land is equally so. The word *hammelech,* "the king," given here to Araunah, is wanting in the Septuagint, Syriac, and Arabic; and, it is very probable, never made a part of the text. Perhaps it should be read, "All these did Araunah give unto the king."

The First Book of

KINGS

In the most correct and ancient editions of the Hebrew Bible, the two Books of Kings make but one, with sometimes a little break, the first book beginning with 1 Sam. xxii. 40. Some of the ancient fathers seem to have begun the First Book of Kings at the death of David, chap. ii. 12. The more modern copies of the Hebrew Bible have the same division as ours; but in the time of the Masoretes they certainly made but one book; as both, like the Books of Samuel, are included under one enumeration of sections, verses, etc., in the Masora.

The titles to these books have been various, though it appears from Origen that they had their name from their first words, *vehammelech David,* "and King David," as Genesis had its name from *bereshith,* "in the beginning." The Septuagint simply term it "of reigns," or kingdoms; of which it calls Samuel the first and second, and these two the third and fourth.

The author of these books is unknown. That they are a compilation out of public and private records, as the Books of Samuel are, there is little doubt; but by whom this compilation was made nowhere appears. Some have attributed it to Isaiah and to Jeremiah, because there are several chapters in both these prophets which are similar to some found in the First and Second Books of Kings; cf. 2 Kings xviii—xx with Isaiah xxxvi—xxxix; and 2 Kings xxiv. 18 and xxv. 1, etc., with Jer. lii. 1, etc. But rather than allow those prophets to be the authors or compilers of these books, some very learned men have judged that the chapters in question have been taken from the Books of Kings in after times and inserted in those prophets. It is worthy of remark that the fifty-second chapter found in Jeremiah is marked so as to intimate that it is not the composition of that prophet; for at the end of chap. li we find these words, "Thus far are the words of Jeremiah," intimating that the following chapter is not his.

But the most common opinion is that Ezra was the author, or rather the compiler of the history found in these books. Allowing only the existence of ancient documents from which it was compiled, it appears: (1) That it is the work of one person, as is sufficiently evident from the uniformity of the style and the connection of events; (2) That this person had ancient documents from which he compiled, and which he often only abridged, is evident from his own words, "The rest of the acts" of such and such a prince, "are they not written in the chronicles of the kings of Judah?" or "of Israel?" which occur frequently; (3) These books were written during or after the Babylonish captivity, as at the end of the second book that event is particularly described; (4) That the writer was not contemporary with the facts which he relates is evident from the reflections he makes on the facts that he found in the memoirs which he consulted (see 2 Kings xvii from v. 6 to v. 24); (5) There is every reason to believe that the author was a priest or a prophet; he studies less to describe acts of heroism, successful battles, conquests, political address, etc., than what regards the Temple, religion, religious ceremonies, festivals, the worship of God, the piety of princes, the fidelity of the prophets, the punishment of crimes, the manifestation of God's anger against the wicked, and His kindness to the righteous. He appears everywhere strongly attached to the house of David; he treats of the kings of Israel only accidentally; his principal object seems to be the kingdom of Judah, and the matters which concern it.

Now all this agrees well with the supposition that Ezra was the compiler of these books. He was not only a priest, a zealous servant of God, and a reformer of the corruptions which had crept into the divine worship, but is universally allowed by the Jews to have been the collector and compiler of the whole sacred code, and author of the arrangement of the different books which constitute the Old Testament. If some things be found in these Books of Kings which do not agree to his time, they may be easily accounted for on his often taking the facts as he found them in the documents which he consults, without any kind of alteration; and this is so far a proof of his great sincerity and scrupulous exactness.

The First Book of Kings contains the history of 119 years. It contains a great variety of interesting particulars, the chief of which are the following: The death of David; the reign of Solomon; the building and dedication of the Temple; the building of Solomon's palace; an account of his great wisdom; his magnificence, and his fall; the division of Israel and Judah under Rehoboam; the idolatry of the ten tribes over whom Jeroboam became king. It states how Judah, Benjamin, and Levi attached themselves to the house of David; how Rehoboam was attacked by Shishak, king of Egypt, who pillaged the Temple; how Baasha destroyed the house of Jeroboam, and seized on the government of Israel; how Jehu predicted the ruin of Baasha; how Ahab married the impious Jezebel, and persecuted the prophets of the Lord. It relates the acts of Elijah; the destruction of the prophets of Baal; the cruel death of Naboth; the death of Ahab; the good reign of Jehoshaphat, king of Judah; and the wicked reign of Ahaziah, king of Israel, etc.

CHAPTER 1

David, grown old, is, by the advice of his physicians, cherished by Abishag the Shunammite, 1-4. Adonijah conspires with Joab and Abiathar to seize on the government, 5-10. Nathan and Bath-sheba communicate these tidings to the aged king, 11-27. David immediately pronounces Solomon his successor, and causes Zadok and Nathan to proclaim and anoint him king, 28-40. Adonijah and his friends hear of it, are afraid, and flee away, Adonijah laying hold on the horns of the altar, from which he refused to go till Solomon shall promise him his life; this he does, and banishes him to his own house, 41-53.

1. *Now King David was old.* He was probably now about sixty-nine years of age. He was thirty years old when he began to reign, reigned forty, and died in the seventieth year of his age, 2 Sam. v. 4, and chap. ii. 11; and the transactions mentioned here are supposed to have taken place about a year before his death. *But he gat no heat.* Sixty-nine was not an advanced age; but David had been exhausted with various fatigues, and especially by family afflictions, so that he was much older in constitution than he was in years. Besides he seems to have labored under some wasting maladies, to which there is frequent reference in the Psalms.

2. *Let there be sought . . . a young virgin.* This was the best remedy which in his state c o u l d be prescribed. His nearly exhausted frame would infallibly absorb from her young and healthy body an additional portion of animal heat, and consequently trim and revive the flame of animal life.

5. *Adonijah the son of Haggith.* Who this woman was we know not; Adonijah was evidently David's eldest son now living, and one of whom his father was particularly fond; see v. 6. *Prepared him chariots and horsemen.* He copied the conduct of his brother Absalom in every respect. See 2 Sam. xv. 1.

7. *And he conferred with Joab.* Joab well knew if he made the new king he would necessarily be continued in the command of the army, and so govern him.

8. *And Nathan.* Some suppose that he was the preceptor of Solomon.

9. *Slew sheep and oxen.* Making a royal feast, in reference to his inauguration. As he had Abiathar the priest with him, no doubt these animals were offered sacrificially, and then the guests fed on the flesh of the victims.

11. *Hast thou not heard that Adonijah the son of Haggith doth reign?* He was now considered as being legally appointed to the regal office, and no doubt was about to begin to perform its functions.

12. *Save thine own life, and the life of thy son.* Nathan took for granted that Adonijah would put both Bath-sheba and Solomon to death as state criminals if he got established on the throne.

13. *Go and get thee in unto King David.* He knew that this woman had a sovereign influence over the king. *Didst not thou . . . swear?* It is very likely that David made such an oath, and that was known only to Bath-sheba and Nathan. It is nowhere else mentioned.

20. *That thou shouldest tell . . . who shall sit on the throne.* This was a monarchy neither hereditary nor elective; the king simply named his successor. This obtained less or more, anciently, in most countries.

21. *Shall be counted offenders.* When Adonijah and his party shall find that I and my son have had this promise from thee by oath, he will slay us both.

28. *Call me Bath-sheba.* She had gone out when Nathan came in, and he retired when she was readmitted. Each had a separate audience, but to Nathan the king did not express any will.

33. *Take with you the servants of your lord.* By these we may understand the king's guards, the guards of the city, the Cherethites and Pelethites, who were under the command of Benaiah; and in short, all the disposable force that was at hand. *Solomon . . . to ride upon mine own mule.* No subject could use anything that belonged to the prince without forfeiting his life. As David offered Solomon to ride on his own mule, this was full evidence that he had appointed him his successor.

34. *Blow ye with the trumpet.* After he has been anointed, make proclamation that he is king.

40. *The people piped with pipes.* They danced, sang, and played on what instruments of music they possessed. *The earth rent.* We use a similar expression in precisely the same sense: They rent the air with their cries.

43. *Jonathan answered.* He was properly a messenger about the court; we have met with him and Ahimaaz before, 2 Sam. xv. 36. He had now been an observer, if not a spy, on all that was doing, and relates the transactions to Adonijah, in the very order in which they took place.

50. *Adonijah feared.* He knew he had usurped the kingdom, and had not his father's consent; and, as he finds now that Solomon is appointed by David, he knows well that the people will immediately respect that appointment, and that his case is hopeless. He therefore took sanctuary, and, fleeing to the Tabernacle, laid hold on one of the horns of the altar, as if appealing to the protection of God against the violence of men. The altar was a privileged place, and it was deemed sacrilege to molest a man who had taken refuge there.

52. *If he will shew himself a worthy man.* If from henceforth he behave well, show himself to be contented, and not endeavor to make partisans, or stir up insurrections among the people, he shall be safe; *but if wickedness shall be found in him*—if he act at all contrary to this—*he shall die;* his blood shall be upon him.

53. *Go to thine house.* Intimating that he should have no place about the king's person

nor under the government. Adonijah must have seen that he stood continually on his good behavior.

CHAPTER 2

David leaves his dying charge with Solomon, relative to his own personal conduct, 1-4; to Joab, 5-6; to Barzillai, 7; to Shimei, 8-9. He dies, and Solomon is established in the kingdom, 10-12. Adonijah requests to have Abishag to wife, and is put to death by Solomon, 13-25. Abiathar, the priest, is banished to his estate at Anathoth, 26-27. Joab, fearing for his life, flees to the horns of the altar, and is slain there by Benaiah, 28-34. Benaiah is made captain of the host in his stead, 35. Shimei is ordered to confine himself to Jerusalem, and never leave it on pain of death, 36-38. After three years he follows some of his runaway servants to Gath, and thereby forfeits his life, 39-40. Solomon sends for him, upbraids him, and commands him to be slain by Benaiah, 41-46.

2. *I go the way of all the earth.* I am dying. All the inhabitants of the earth must come to the dust. In life, some follow one occupation, some another; but all must, sooner or later, come to the grave. *Shew thyself a man.* Act like a rational being, and not like a brute; and remember that he acts most like a man who is most devoted to his God.

3. *Keep the charge of the Lord.* Keep what God has given you to keep. (1) *Walk in his ways.* Not in your own, nor in the ways of a wicked, perishing world. (2) *Keep his statutes.* Consider all His appointments to be holy, just, and good; receive them as such and conscientiously observe them. (3) *Keep . . . his commandments.* Whatever He has bidden you to do, perform; what He has forbidden you to do, omit. (4) *Keep . . . his judgments.* What He has determined to be right is essentially and inherently right; what He has determined to be wrong or evil is inherently and essentially so. (5) *Keep . . . his testimonies.* Bear witness to all to which He has borne witness. His testimonies are true; there is no deceit or falsity in them.

4. *That the Lord may continue his word.* The prosperity which God has promised to grant to my family will depend on their faithfulness to the good they receive; if they live to God, they shall sit forever on the throne of Israel.

5. *Thou knowest . . . what Joab . . . did to me.* He did everything bad and dishonorable in itself, in the murder of Abner and Amasa, and indeed in the death of the profligate Absalom. *Shed the blood of war . . . upon his girdle . . . and in his shoes.* He stabbed them while he pretended to embrace them, so that their blood gushed out on his girdle, and fell into his shoes!

6. *Let not his hoar head go down to the grave in peace.* It would have been an insult to justice not to take the life of Joab. David was culpable in delaying it so long, but probably the circumstances of his government would not admit of his doing it sooner. According to the law of God, Joab, having murdered Abner and Amasa, should die.

7. *But shew kindness unto the sons of Barzillai.* See the notes on 2 Sam. xix. 31, etc.

8. *Thou hast with thee Shimei.* See on 2 Sam. xvi. 5, etc., and the notes on 2 Sam. xix. 18-23.

9. *Hold him not guiltless.* Do not consider him as an innocent man, though I have sworn to him that I would not put him to death by the sword. Yet as you are a wise man, and know how to treat such persons, treat him as he deserves. Only as I have sworn to him, and he is an aged man, let him not die a violent death; bring not down his hoary head to the grave with blood. So Solomon understood David, and so I think David should be understood; for the negative particle *lo* in the former clause, "hold him not guiltless," should be repeated in this latter clause, though not expressed, "his hoary head bring thou not down"—instances of which frequently occur in the Hebrew Bible.

27. *So Solomon thrust out Abiathar.* This was for having taken part before with Adonijah, but by it a remarkable prophecy was fulfilled; see 1 Sam. ii. 13-35, and the notes there. God had told Eli that the priesthood should depart from his house; Abiathar was the last of the descendants of Ithamar, of which family was Eli, the high priest. Zadok, who was made priest in the stead of Abiathar, was of the family of Eliezer; and by this change the priesthood reverted to its ancient channel. Abiathar deserved this degradation; he supported Adonijah in his unnatural assumption of the royal dignity, even during the life of his father.

28. *Tidings came to Joab.* He heard that Adonijah had been slain and Abiathar banished, and probably he had heard of David's dying charge to Solomon. Fearing therefore for his personal safety, he takes refuge at the Tabernacle, as claiming divine protection, and desiring to have his case decided by God alone.

30. *Nay; but I will die here.* The altars were so sacred among all the people that, in general, even the vilest wretch found safety if he once reached the altar. This led to many abuses and the perversion of public justice; and at last it became a maxim that the guilty should be punished, should they even have taken refuge at the altars. God decreed that the presumptuous murderer who had taken refuge at the altar should be dragged thence and put to death; see Exod. xxi. 14.

36. *Build thee an house.* Thus he gave him the whole city for a prison, and this certainly could have reduced him to no hardships.

37. *Thy blood shall be upon thine own head.* You know what to expect; if you disobey my orders you shall certainly be slain, and then you shall be considered as a self-murderer; you alone shall be answerable for your own death. Solomon knew that Shimei was a seditious man, and he chose to keep him under his own eye; for such a man at large, in favorable circumstances, might do much evil. His bitter revilings of David were a sufficient proof.

40. *And Shimei . . . went to Gath.* It is astonishing that with his eyes wide open he would thus run into the jaws of death.

45. *King Solomon shall be blessed.* He seems to think that, while such bad men remained unpunished, the nation could not prosper; that it was an act of justice which God required him to perform, in order to the establishment and perpetuity of his throne.

CHAPTER 3

Solomon marries Pharaoh's daughter, 1-2. He serves God, and offers a thousand burnt offerings upon one altar, at Gibeon, 3-4. God appears to him in a dream at Gibeon; and asks what He shall give him, 5. He asks wisdom; with which God is well pleased, and promises to give him not only that, but also riches and honor; and, if obedient, long life, 6-14. He comes back to Jerusalem; offers burnt offerings and peace offerings, and makes a feast for his servants, 15. His judgment between the two harlots, 16-27. He rises in the esteem of the people, 28.

1. *Solomon made affinity with Pharaoh.* This was no doubt a political measure in order to strengthen his kingdom, and on the same ground he continued his alliance with the king of Tyre; and these were among the most powerful of his neighbors. But should political considerations prevail over express laws of God? God had strictly forbidden His people to form alliances with heathenish women, lest they should lead their hearts away from Him into idolatry. Let us hear the law: "Neither shalt thou make marriages with them; thy daughter thou shalt not give unto his son, nor his daughter shalt thou take unto thy son. For they will turn away thy son from following me," Exod. xxxiv. 16; Deut. vii. 3-4. Now Solomon acted in direct opposition to these laws, and perhaps in this alliance were sown those seeds of apostasy from God and goodness in which he so long lived, and in which he so awfully died.

5. *The Lord appeared to Solomon in a dream.* This was the night after he had offered the sacrifices (see 2 Chron. i. 7), and probably after he had earnestly prayed for wisdom; see *Wisdom,* chap. vii. 7: "Wherefore I prayed, and understanding was given me: I called upon God, and the spirit of wisdom came to me." If this were the case, the dream might have been the consequence of his earnest prayer for wisdom. The images of those things which occupy the mind during the day are most likely to recur during the night; and this, indeed, is the origin of the greater part of our dreams. But this appears to have been supernatural.

7. *I know not how to go out or come in.* I am just like an infant learning to walk alone, and can neither go out nor come in without help.

9. *Give . . . an understanding heart to judge thy people.* He did not ask wisdom in general, but the true science of government. This wisdom he sought, and this wisdom he obtained.

12. *I have given thee a wise and an understanding heart.* I have given you a capacious mind, one capable of knowing much. Make a proper use of your powers, under the direction of My Spirit, and you shall excel in wisdom all that have gone before thee; neither after thee shall any arise like unto thee. But was not all this conditional? If he should walk in His ways, and keep His statutes and commandments, v. 14. Did not his unfaithfulness prevent the fulfillment of the divine purpose? No character in the sacred writings disappoints us more than the character of Solomon.

16. *Then came there two women . . . harlots.* The word *zonoth,* which we here, and in some other places, improperly translated *harlots,* is by the Chaldee (the best judge in this case) rendered "tavern keepers" (see on Josh. ii. 1). If these had been harlots, it is not likely they would have dared to appear before Solomon; and if they had been common women, it is not likely they would have had children; nor is it likely that such persons would have been permitted under the reign of David.

28. *They feared the king.* This decision proved that they could not impose upon him, and they were afraid to do those things which might bring them before his judgment seat. *They saw that the wisdom of God was in him.* They perceived that he was taught of God, judged impartially, and could not be deceived.

CHAPTER 4

An account of Solomon's chief officers, 1-6. Names of the twelve officers that were over twelve districts, to provide victuals for the king's household monthly, 7-19. Judah and Israel are very populous, and Solomon reigns over many provinces, 20-21. The daily provision for his family, 22-23. The extent and peace of his dominions, 24-25. His horses, chariots, and dromedaries, with the provision made for them, 26-28. His wisdom and understanding, 29-31. The number of his proverbs and songs; and his knowledge in natural history, 32-33. People from all nations come to hear his wisdom, 34.

2. *These were the princes which he had; Azariah the son of Zadok the priest.* These were his great, chief, or principal men. None of them were princes in the common acceptation of the word.

3. *Elihoreph and Ahiah . . . scribes.* "Secretaries" to the king. *Jehoshaphat . . . recorder.* Historiographer to the king, who chronicled the affairs of the kingdom. He was in this office under David (see 2 Sam. xx. 24).

5. *Azariah . . . was over the officers.* He had the superintendence of the twelve officers mentioned below (see v. 7). *Zabud . . . was principal officer.* Perhaps what we call "premier," or "prime minister." *The king's friend.* His chief favorite—his confidant.

6. *Ahishar was over the household.* The king's chamberlain. *Adoniram . . . was over the tribute.* What we call "chancellor of the exchequer." He received and brought into the treasury all the proceeds of taxes and tributes. He was in this office under David (see 2 Sam. xx. 24).

7. *Twelve officers.* The business of these twelve officers was to provide daily, each for a month, those provisions which were consumed in the king's household (see vv. 22-23). And the task for such a daily provision was not an easy one.

13. *Threescore great cities with walls and brazen bars.* These were fortified cities, their gates and bars covered with plates of brass.

20. *Eating and drinking, and making merry.* They were very comfortable, very rich, very merry, and very corrupt. And this full feeding and dissipation led to a total corruption of manners.

21. *Solomon reigned over all kingdoms.* The meaning of this verse appears to be that Solomon reigned over all the provinces from the river Euphrates to the land of the Philistines, even to the frontiers of Egypt. The Euphrates was on the east of Solomon's dominions; the Philistines were westward on the Mediterranean Sea; and Egypt was on the south. Solomon had, therefore, as tributaries the kingdoms of Syria, Damascus, Moab, and Ammon, which lay between the Euphrates and the Mediterranean. Thus he appears to have possessed all the land that God covenanted with Abraham to give to his posterity.

22. *Solomon's provision for one day:* Of fine flour—*thirty measures,* or "cors." The cor was the same as the homer, and contained nearly seventy-six gallons.

25. *Every man under his vine.* They were no longer obliged to dwell in fortified cities for fear of their enemies; they spread themselves over all the country, which they everywhere cultivated; and had always the privilege of eating the fruits of their own labors.

26. *Solomon had forty thousand stalls of horses . . . and twelve thousand horsemen.* In 2 Chron. ix. 25, instead of *forty thousand stalls,* we read "four thousand"; and even this number might be quite sufficient to hold horses for 12,000 horsemen; for stalls and stables may be here synonymous. In chap. x. 26 it is said he had "a thousand and four hundred chariots, and twelve thousand horsemen"; and this is the reading in 2 Chron. i. 14. In 2 Chron. ix. 25, already quoted, instead of *forty thousand stalls of horses,* the Septuagint has "four thousand mares." From this collation of parallel places we may rest satisfied that there is a corruption in the numbers somewhere; and as a sort of medium, we may take for the whole 4,000 stalls, 1,400 chariots, and 12,000 horsemen.

28. *And dromedaries.* The word *rechesh,* which we translate thus, is rendered "beasts," or "beasts of burden," by the Vulgate; "mares" by the Syriac and Arabic; "chariots" by the Septuagint; and "racehorses" by the Chaldee. The original word seems to signify a very swift kind of horse, and racehorse or post-horse is probably its true meaning. To communicate with so many distant provinces, Solomon had need of many animals of this kind.

29. *God gave Solomon wisdom.* He gave him a capacious mind, and furnished him with extraordinary assistance to cultivate it.

30. *The children of the east country.* That is the Chaldeans, Persians, and Arabians, who, with the Egyptians, were famed for wisdom and knowledge through all the world.

31. *He was wiser than all men.* He was wiser than any of those who were most celebrated in his time, among whom were the four after mentioned, viz., *Ethan, Heman, Chalcol,* and *Darda.* Ethan was probably the same as is mentioned in some of the psalms, particularly Psalms lxxxix, title; and among the singers in 1 Chron. vi. 42. There is a Heman mentioned in the title to Psalms lxxxviii. In 1 Chron. ii. 6 we have all the four names, but they are probably not the same persons, for they are there said to be the sons of Zerah, and he flourished long before Solomon's time.

32. *He spake three thousand proverbs.* The Book of Proverbs, attributed to Solomon, contains only about nine hundred or nine hundred and twenty-three distinct proverbs; and if we grant with some that the first nine chapters are not the work of Solomon, then all that can be attributed to him is only about six hundred and fifty. Of all his *thousand and five* songs or poems we have only one, the Book of Canticles, remaining, unless we include Psalms cxxvii, "Except the Lord build the house," etc., which in the title is said to be by or for him, though it appears more properly to be a psalm of direction, left him by his father, David, relative to the building of the Temple.

33. *He spake of trees . . . beasts . . . fowl . . . creeping things, and of fishes.* This is a complete system of natural history, as far as relates to the animal and vegetable kingdoms, and the first intimation we have of anything of the kind. Solomon was probably the first natural historian in the world.

CHAPTER 5

Hiram, king of Tyre, sends to congratulate Solomon on his accession to the kingdom, 1. Solomon consults him on building a temple for the Lord, and requests his assistance, 2-6. Hiram is pleased, and specifies the assistance which he will afford, 7-9. He sends cedars and fir trees, 10. The return made by Solomon, 11. They form a league, 12. Solomon makes a levy of men in Israel to prepare wood and stones, 13-18.

6. *Any that can skill to hew timber.* An obsolete and barbarous expression for "any that know how to cut timber." They had neither carpenters nor builders among them, equal to the Sidonians. Sidon was a part of the territories of Hiram, and its inhabitants appear to have been the most expert workmen.

9. *Shall bring them down from Lebanon unto the sea.* As the river Adonis was in the vicinity of the forest of Lebanon, and emptied itself into the Mediterranean Sea, near Biblos, Hiram could transport the timber all squared, and cut so as to occupy the place it was intended for in the building, without any further need of axe or saw. It might be readily sent down the coast on rafts and landed at Joppa, or Jamnia, just opposite to Jerusalem, at the distance of about twenty-five miles. See 2 Chron. ii. 16.

11. *And Solomon gave Hiram.* The information in this verse of the annual stipend paid to Hiram is deficient, and must be supplied out of 2 Chron. ii. 10. Here *twenty thousand measures of wheat . . . and twenty measures of pure oil* is all that is promised. There, "twenty thousand measures of beaten wheat, and twenty thousand measures of barley, and twenty thousand baths of wine, and twenty thousand baths of oil" is the stipulation; unless we suppose the first to be for Hiram's own family, the latter for his workmen. Instead of *twenty* measures of oil, the Syriac, Arabic, and Septuagint, have "twenty thousand" measures, as in Chronicles. In 2 Chronicles, instead of *cors* of oil, it is *baths.* The *bath* was a measure much less than the *cor.*

13. *The levy was thirty thousand men.* We find from the following verse that only 10,000 were employed at once, and those only for one month at a time; and having rested two months, they again resumed their labor. These were the persons over whom Adoniram was superintendent, and were all Israelites.

15. *Threescore and ten thousand that bare burdens.* These were all strangers, or proselytes, dwelling among the Israelites, as we learn from the parallel place, 2 Chron. ii. 17-18.

16. *Besides . . . three thousand and three hundred which ruled over the people.* In the parallel place, 2 Chron. ii. 18, it is "three thousand and six hundred." The Septuagint has here the same number.

17. *Great stones.* Stones of very large dimensions. *Costly stones.* Stones that cost much labor and time to cut them out of the rock. *Hewed stones.* Everywhere squared and polished.

18. *And the stonesquarers.* Instead of *stonesquarers* the margin very properly reads "Giblites," *haggiblim,* and refers to Ezek. xxvii.

9, where we find the inhabitants of Gebal celebrated for their knowledge in shipbuilding. Some suppose that these Giblites were the inhabitants of Biblos, at the foot of Mount Libanus, northward of Sidon, on the coast of the Mediterranean Sea.

but the ornamenting, gilding, or overlaying with gold, making the carved work, cherubim, trees, flowers, etc., must have consumed a considerable time. The month *Bul* answers to a part of our October and November, as Zif, in which it was begun, answers to a part of April and May.

CHAPTER 6

In the four hundred and eightieth year from the Exodus, in the fourth year of Solomon's reign, and in the second month, he laid the foundations of the Temple; the length sixty cubits, the breadth twenty, and the height thirty cubits; besides the porch, which was twenty cubits in length, and ten cubits in height, 1-3. A description of its different external parts, 4-10. God's promise to Solomon, 11-13. Description of its internal parts and contents, 14-36. Temple finished in the eighth month of the eleventh year of Solomon's reign, being seven years in building, 37-38.

1. *The month Zif.* This answers to a part of our April and May; and was the second month of the sacred year, but the eighth month of the civil year. Before the time of Solomon, the Jews do not appear to have had any names for their months, but mentioned them in the order of their consecutive occurrence, first month, second month, third month, etc. In this chapter we find *Zif* and *Bul;* and in chap. viii. v. 2, we find another, *Ethanim;* and these are supposed to be borrowed from the Chaldeans; and consequently this book was written after the Babylonish captivity. Before this time we find only the word *Abib* mentioned as the name of a month, Exod. xiii. 4.

4. *Windows of narrow lights.* The Hebrew is "windows to look through, which shut." Probably latticed windows: windows through which a person within could see well; but a person without, nothing. "Windows," says the Targum, "which were open within and shut without."

7. *The house . . . was built of stone.* It appears that every stone was hewn and squared, and its place in the building ascertained, before it came to Jerusalem; the timbers were fitted in like manner. This greatly lessened the trouble and expense of carriage. On this account, that all was prepared at Mount Lebanon, *there was neither hammer nor ax nor any tool of iron heard in the building.* Nothing except mallets to drive the tenons into the mortices, and drive in the pins to fasten them, was necessary; therefore there was no noise.

9. *Covered the house with beams and boards of cedar.* The Eastern custom is very different from ours. We ceil with plaster, and make our floors of wood; they make their floors of plaster or painted tiles, and make their ceilings of wood.

11. *The word of the Lord came to Solomon.* Some think that this is the same revelation as that mentioned in chap. ix. 2, etc., which took place after the dedication of the Temple; but to me it appears different. It was a word to encourage him while building, to warn him against apostasy, and to assure him of God's continued protection of him and his family, if they continued faithful to the grace which God had given.

38. *In the eleventh year . . . was the house finished.* It is rather strange that this house required seven years and about six months to put all the stones and the timbers in their places, for we have already seen that they were all prepared before they came to Jerusalem;

CHAPTER 7

Solomon builds his own house, and completes it in thirteen years, 1. He builds another called the house of the forest of Lebanon, and a house for Pharaoh's daughter, 2-12. He brings Hiram, a coppersmith, out of Tyre, who makes much curious work for the Temple, 13-20. He makes the two pillars Jachin and Boaz, 21-22. The molten sea, and the twelve oxen that bare it, 23-26. And ten brazen bases, and the ten lavers, with pots, shovels, and basins, all of which he cast in the plain of Jordan, 27-46. The quantity of brass too great to be weighed; and the vessels of the Temple were all of pure gold, 47-50. Solomon brings into the house the silver and gold which his father had dedicated, 51.

1. *Building his own house.* This house is said to have been situated in Jerusalem, and probably was, what some call it, his winter's residence.

2. *The house of the forest of Lebanon.* It was not built in Lebanon, but is thought to have been on Mount Sion. It was probably called *the house of the forest of Lebanon* because it was built almost entirely of materials brought from that place.

7. *A porch for the throne.* One porch appears to have been devoted to the purposes of administering judgment, which Solomon did in person.

8. *An house for Pharaoh's daughter.* This appears to have been a third house. Probably the whole three made but one building, and were in the same place, but distinguished from each other: the first as Solomon's palace; the second as a house of judgment, a courthouse; the third, the harem, or apartments for the women.

13. *Solomon sent and fetched Hiram out of Tyre.* This was not the Tyrian king, mentioned before, but a very intelligent coppersmith, of Jewish extraction by his mother's side, who was probably married to a Tyrian. In 2 Chron. ii. 14, this woman is said to be "of the daughters of Dan," but here "of the tribe of Naphtali." The king of Tyre, who gives the account as we have it in Chronicles, might have made the mistake, and confounded the two tribes; or she might have been of Naphtali by her father, and of Dan by her mother, and so be indifferently called of the tribe of Naphtali or of the daughters of Dan. This appears to be the best solution of the difficulty.

15. *A line of twelve cubits.* In circumference.

21. *The right pillar . . . Jachin.* That is, "He shall establish." *The left pillar . . . Boaz,* that is, "in strength." These were no doubt emblematical; for notwithstanding their names, they seem to have supported no part of the building.

27. *He made ten bases.* That is, "pedestals," for the ten lavers to rest on.

38. *Then made he ten lavers.* These were set on the ten bases or pedestals, and were to hold water for the use of the priests in their sacred office, particularly to wash the victims that were to be offered as a burnt offering, as we learn from 2 Chron. iv. 6; but the brazen sea was for the priests to wash in. The whole was a building of vast art, labor, and expense.

CHAPTER 8

Solomon assembles the elders of Israel, and brings up the ark, and the holy vessels, and the tabernacle, out of the city of David, and places them in the Temple; on which account a vast number of sheep and oxen are sacrificed, 1-8. There was nothing in the ark save the two tables of stone, which Moses put there at Horeb, 9. The cloud of God's glory fills the house, 10-11. Solomon blesses the people, 12-21. His dedicatory prayer, 22-53. Afterwards he blesses and exhorts the people, 54-61. They offer a sacrifice of 22,000 oxen, and 120,000 sheep, 62-63. He hallows the middle of the court for offerings, as the brazen altar which was before the Lord was too small, 64. He holds the Feast of the Dedication for seven days; and for other seven days, the Feast of Tabernacles; and on the eighth day blesses the people, and sends them away joyful, 65-66.

1. *Then Solomon assembled.* Solomon deferred the dedication of the Temple to the following year after it was finished, because that year, according to Archbishop Ussher, was a jubilee.

2. *At the feast in the month Ethanim.* The Feast of Tabernacles, which was celebrated in the seventh month of what is called the ecclesiastical year.

8. *And there they are unto this day.* This proves that the book was written before the destruction of the first Temple, but how long before we cannot tell.

10. *When the priests were come out.* That is, after having carried the ark into the holy of holies, before any sacred service had yet commenced.

11. *The glory of the Lord had filled the house.* The cloud, the symbol of the divine glory and presence, appears to have filled not only the holy of holies, but the whole Temple, court and all, and to have become evident to the people; and by this Solomon knew that God had honored the place with His presence, and taken it for His habitation in reference to the people of Israel.

12. *The Lord said . . . he would dwell.* It was under the appearance of a cloud that God showed himself present with Israel in the wilderness (see Exod. xiv. 19-20). And at the dedication of the Tabernacle in the wilderness, God manifested himself in the same way that He did here at the dedication of the Temple; see Exod. xl. 34-35.

14. *Blessed all the congregation.* Though this blessing is not particularly stated, yet we may suppose that it was such as the high priest pronounced upon the people: "The Lord bless thee, and keep thee: the Lord make his face shine upon thee, and be gracious unto thee: the Lord lift up his countenance upon thee, and give thee peace" (see Num. vi. 24-26), for Solomon seems now to be acting the part of the high priest. But he may have in view more particularly the conduct of Moses, who, when he had seen that the people had done all the work of the Tabernacle, as the Lord had commanded them, blessed them, Exod. xxxix. 43; and the conduct of his father, David, who, when the ark had been brought into the city of David, and the burnt offerings and peace offerings completed, blessed the people in the name of the Lord, 2 Sam. vi. 18.

21. *Wherein is the covenant of the Lord.* As it is said, v. 9, that there was nothing in the ark but the two tables of stone, consequently these are called the covenant, i.e., a sign of the covenant, as our Lord calls the cup the new covenant in His blood, that is, the sign of the new covenant; for "This is my body" implies, "This is the *sign* or *emblem* of My body."

22. *Stood.* He ascended the brazen scaffold, five cubits long, and five cubits broad, and three cubits high, and then kneeled down upon his knees, with his hands spread up to heaven, and offered up the following prayer (see v. 54, and 2 Chron. v. 12-13).

And spread forth his hands toward heaven. This was a usual custom in all nations. In prayer the hands were stretched out to heaven, as if to invite and receive assistance from thence; while, humbly kneeling on their knees, they seemed to acknowledge at once their dependence and unworthiness.

24. *Who hast kept with thy servant David.* This is in reference to 2 Sam. vii. 13, where God promises to David that Solomon shall build a house for the name of the Lord. The Temple being now completed, this promise was literally fulfilled.

27. *But will God indeed dwell on the earth?* This expression is full of astonishment, veneration, and delight. He is struck with the immensity, dignity, and grandeur of the Divine Being, but especially at His condescension to dwell with men; and though he sees, by His filling the place, that He has come now to make His abode with them, yet he cannot help asking the question, How can such a God dwell in such a place, and with such creatures?

Behold, the heaven. The words are all in the plural number in the Hebrew: *hashshamayim, ushemey hashshamayim;* "the heavens, and the heavens of heavens."

29. *My name shall be there.* I will there show forth My power and My glory by enlightening, quickening, pardoning, sanctifying, and saving all My sincere worshippers.

30. *Toward this place.* Both Tabernacle and Temple were types of our Lord Jesus, or of God manifested in the flesh; and He was and is the Mediator between God and man. All prayer, to be acceptable, and to be entitled to a hearing, must go to God through Him.

31. *If any man trespass against his neighbour.* Solomon puts here seven cases, in all of which the mercy and intervention of God would be indispensably requisite; and he earnestly bespeaks that mercy and intervention on condition that the people pray towards that holy place, and with a feeling heart make earnest supplication. The first case is one of doubtfulness; where a man has sustained an injury, and charges it on a suspected person, though not able to bring direct evidence of the fact, the accused is permitted to come before the altar of God and purge himself by his personal oath.

33. *When thy people Israel be smitten down.* The second case—when their enemies make inroads upon them, and defeat them in battle, and lead them into captivity.

35. *When heaven is shut up, and there is no rain.* The third case—when, because of their sin, and their ceasing to walk in the good way in which they should have walked, God refuses to send the early and latter rain, so that the appointed weeks of harvest come in vain, as there is no crop.

37. *If there be in the land famine . . . pestilence.* The fourth case includes several kinds of evils: (1) *Famine,* necessarily springing from the preceding clause, drought. (2) *Pestilence.* (3) *Blasting.* (4) *Mildew.* (5) *Locust.* (6) *Caterpillar.* The former refers to locusts brought by winds from other countries and settling on the land; the latter, to the young locusts bred in the land. (7) An *enemy,* having attacked their defensed cities. (8) Any other kind of *plague.* (9) *Sickness.*

41. *Moreoevr, concerning a stranger.* The fifth case relates to heathens coming from other countries with the design to become proselytes to the true religion; that they might be received, blessed, and protected as the true Israelites, that the name of Jehovah might be known over the face of the earth.

44. *If thy people go out to battle.* The sixth case refers to wars undertaken by divine appointment: *whithersoever thou shalt send them.*

46. *If they sin against thee.* This seventh case must refer to some general defection from truth, to some species of false worship, idolatry, or corruption of the truth and ordinances of the Most High.

In v. 46 we read, *If they sin against thee, (for there is no man that sinneth not).* On this verse we may observe that the second clause, as it is here translated, renders the supposition in the first clause entirely nugatory; for if there be "no man that sinneth not," it is useless to say, "if they sin." But this contradiction is taken away by reference to the original, which should be translated, "If they shall sin against Thee, or should they sin against Thee; for there is no man that may not sin"; i.e., there is no man impeccable, none infallible, none that is not liable to transgress.

50. *And give them compassion before them who carried them captive.* He does not pray that they may be delivered out of that captivity, but that their enemies may use them well; and that they may, as formerly, be kept a separate and distinct people.

55. *He stood, and blessed all the congregation.* This blessing is contained in vv. 57 and 58.

59. *And let these my words.* This and the following verse is a sort of supplement to the prayer which ended in v. 53; but there is an important addition to this prayer in the parallel place, 2 Chron. vi. 41-42: "Now therefore arise, O Lord God, into thy resting place, thou, and the ark of thy strength: let thy priests, O Lord God, be clothed with salvation, and let thy saints rejoice in goodness. O Lord God, turn not away the face of thine anointed: remember the mercies of David thy servant."

61. *Let your heart therefore be perfect.* Be sincere in your faith; be irreproachable in your conduct.

63. *Two and twenty thousand oxen.* This was the whole amount of the victims that had been offered during the fourteen days; i.e., the seven days of the dedication, and the seven days of the Feast of Tabernacles.

64. *Did the king hallow the middle of the court.* The great altar of burnt offerings was not sufficient for the number of sacrifices which were then made; therefore the middle of the court was set apart, and an altar erected there for the same purpose.

65. *From . . . Hamath.* Supposed to be Antioch of Syria; *unto the river of Egypt:* i.e., from one extremity of the land to the other.

CHAPTER 9

The Lord appears a second time to Solomon, and assures him that He had heard his prayer; and that He would establish His worship forever in that Temple, and him and his successors on the throne of I rael, provided he and they would keep His statutes and judgments, 1-5. But if they should transgress and forsake the Lord, then they should be cast off, the Temple itself abandoned, and their enemies permitted to prevail over them, 6-9. Solomon having finished the Temple and the king's house, about which he was employed twenty years, and having received assistance from Hiram, king of Tyre, he gave him in return twenty cities in Galilee, with which he was not pleased, 10-14. Solomon's levies, buildings, and the persons employed, 15-23. Pharaoh's daughter comes to the city of David, 24. He sacrifices thrice a year at the Temple, 25. Solomon's navy, and the gold they brought from Ophir, 26-28.

2. *The Lord appeared to Solomon.* The design of this appearance, which was in a dream, as that was at Gibeon, was to assure Solomon that God had accepted his service, and had taken that house for His dwelling place, and would continue it, and establish him and his descendants upon the throne of Israel forever, provided they served Him with an upright heart; but, on the contrary, if they forsook Him, He would abandon both them and His temple.

10. *At the end of twenty years.* He employed seven years and a half in building the Temple, and twelve years and a half in building the king's house (see chap. vii. 1; 2 Chron. viii. 1).

11. *Solomon gave Hiram twenty cities.* It is very likely that Solomon did not give those cities to Hiram so that they should be annexed to his Tyrian dominions, but rather gave him the produce of them till the money was paid which he had advanced to Solomon for his buildings. It appears however that either Hiram did not accept them or that, having received the produce till he was paid, he then restored them to Solomon; for in the parallel place, 2 Chron. viii. 2, it is said, "The cities which Huram had restored to Solomon, Solomon built them, and caused the children of Israel to dwell there." Some think that they were heathen *cities* which Solomon had conquered, and therefore had a right to give them if he pleased, as they were not any part of the land given by promise to the Israelites.

14. *Sixscore talents of gold.* This was the sum which Hiram had lent, and in order to pay this Solomon had laid a tax upon his people, as we afterward learn.

15. *This is the reason of the levy.* That is, in order to pay Hiram the sixscore talents of gold which he had borrowed from him (Hiram not being willing to take the Galilean cities mentioned above; or, having taken them, soon restored them again), he was obliged to lay a tax upon the people; and that this was a grievous and oppressive tax we learn from chap. xii. 1-4, where the elders of Israel came to Rehoboam, complaining of their heavy state of taxation, and entreating that their yoke might be made lighter. *And Millo.* This is supposed to have been a deep valley between Mount Sion and what was called the city of Jebus, which Solomon filled up, and it was built on and became a sort of fortified place, and a place for public assemblies.

16. *Pharaoh . . . had gone up, and taken Gezer.* This city Joshua had taken from the Canaanites, Josh. x. 33 and xii. 12, and it was divided by lot to the tribe of Ephraim, and was intended to be one of the Levitical cities. But it appears that the Canaanites had retaken it, and kept possession till the days of Solomon, when his father-in-law, Pharaoh, king of Egypt, retook it, and gave it to Solomon in dowry with his daughter.

18. *And Tadmor in the wilderness.* This is almost universally allowed to be the same with the celebrated Palmyra, the ruins of which remain to the present day, and give us the highest idea of Solomon's splendor and magnificence. Palmyra stood upon a fertile plain surrounded by a barren desert, having the river Euphrates on the east.

19. *And all the cities of store.* Though by the multitude and splendor of his buildings Solomon must have added greatly to the magnificence of his reign; yet, however plenteous silver and gold were in his times, his subjects must have been greatly oppressed with the taxation necessary to defray such a vast public expenditure.

21. *A tribute of bondservice.* He made them do the most laborious part of the public works, the Israelites being generally exempt.

25. *Three times in a year did Solomon offer.* These three times were: (1) the *Passover,* (2) the Feast of *Pentecost,* (3) the Feast of *Tabernacles.*

26. *A navy of ships.* Literally, *oni,* "a ship." In the parallel place, 2 Chron. viii. 18, it is said that Hiram sent him *oniyoth,* "ships"; but it does not appear that Solomon in this case built more than one ship, and this was manned principally by the Tyrians.

CHAPTER 10

The queen of Sheba visits Solomon, and brings rich presents; and tries him by hard questions, which he readily solves, 1-3. She expresses great surprise at his wisdom, his buildings, his court, etc., and praises God for placing him on the Jewish throne, 4-9. She gives him rich presents, 10. What the navy of Hiram brought from Ophir, 11-12. The queen of Sheba returns, 13. Solomon's annual revenue, 14-15. He makes 200 targets and 300 shields of gold, 16-17. His magnificent ivory throne, 18-20. His drinking vessels all of gold, 21. What the navy of Tharshish brought every three years to Solomon, 22. His great riches, numerous chariots, and horsemen, 23-27. He brings chariots and horses out of Egypt, 28-29.

1. *When the queen of Sheba heard.* As our Lord calls her "queen of the south" (Matt. xii. 42), it is likely the name should be written *Saba,* the "south." *With hard questions.* Septuagint, "riddles." With "parables and riddles," says the Arabic.

2. *She came to Jerusalem with . . . spices.* Those who contend that she was queen of the Sabaeans, a people of Arabia Felix, towards the southern extremity of the Red Sea, find several proofs of their opinion: (1) That the Sabaeans abounded in riches and spices. (2) All ancient authors speak, not only of their odoriferous woods, but of their rich gold and silver mines, and of their precious stones. (3) It is also well known that the Sabaeans had queens for their sovereigns, and not kings.

3. *Solomon told her all her questions.* Riddles, problems, fables, apologues formed the principal part of the wisdom of the East.

4. *Had seen all Solomon's wisdom.* By the answers which he gave to her subtle questions. *And the house that he had built.* Most probably his own house.

5. *The meat of his table.* The immense supply of all kinds of food daily necessary for the many thousands which were fed at and from his table. See chap. iv. 22-23. *And the sitting of his servants.* The various orders and distinctions of his officers. *The attendance of his ministers.* See the account of these and their attendance, chap. iv. 1, etc. *And their apparel.* The peculiarity of their robes, and their splendor and costliness. *And his cupbearers.* The original may as well be applied to his beverage, or to his drinking utensils, as to his cupbearers. *And his ascent by which he went up.* It seems very strange that the steps to the Temple should be such a separate matter of astonishment. All the versions have translated the original, "And the holocausts which he offered in the house of the Lord." The Vulgate, Septuagint, Chaldee, Syriac, and Arabic, all express this sense; so does the German translation of Luther, from which, in this place, we have most pitifully departed: "And his burnt offering which he offered in the house of the Lord." *There was no more spirit in her.* She was overpowered with astonishment; she fainted.

8. *Happy are thy men.* All these are very natural expressions from a person in her state of mind.

10. *An hundred and twenty talents of gold.* After this verse the thirteenth should be read, which is here most evidently misplaced; and then the account of the queen of Sheba will be concluded, and that of Solomon's revenue will stand without interruption.

11. *Great plenty of almug trees.* In the parallel place, 2 Chron. ix. 10-11, these are called *algum trees.*

13. *All her desire, whatsoever she asked.* Some imagine she desired progeny from the wise king of Israel; and all the traditions concerning her state that she had a son by Solomon called Menilek, who was brought up at an Israelitish court, succeeded his mother in the kingdom of Saba, and introduced among his subjects the Jewish religion.

17. *He made three hundred shields.* The *magen* was a large shield by which the whole body was protected.

19. *The throne was round behind: and there were stays on either side.* This description seems to indicate that the throne was in the form of one of our ancient round-topped, two-armed chairs. This throne or chair of state was raised on a platform, the ascent to which consisted of six steps. What we call *stays* is in the Hebrew *yadoth,* "hands," which serves to confirm the conjecture above.

25. *They brought every man his present.* This means tribute; and it shows us of what sort that tribute was, viz., vessels of gold and silver, probably ingots; garments of very rich stuffs; armor, for little of this kind was ever made in Judea; spices, which doubtless sold well in that country; horses, which were very rare; and mules, the most necessary animal for all the purposes of life.

26. *He had a thousand and four hundred chariots.* See the note on chap. iv. 26.

27. *Made silver . . . as stones.* He destroyed its value by making it so exceedingly plenty. *As the sycomore trees.* He planted many cedars, and doubtless had much cedarwood imported; so that it became as common as the sycomore trees, which appear to have grown there in great abundance.

28. *Horses brought out of Egypt.* It is thought that the first people who used horses in war were the Egyptians; and it is well known that the nations who knew the use of this creature in battle had greatly the advantage of those who did not. God had absolutely prohibited horses to be imported or used, but in many things Solomon paid little attention to the divine command. *And linen yarn.* The original word, *mikveh,* is hard to be understood. The versions are all puzzled with it: the Vulgate and Septuagint make it a proper name: "And Solomon had horses brought out of Egypt, and from Coa, or Tekoa."

29. *A chariot came up . . . for six hundred shekels.* This was the ordinary price of a chariot, as 150 shekels were for a horse. *Kings of the Hittites.* These must have been the remains of the original inhabitants of Canaan, who had gone to some other country, probably Syria, and formed themselves into a principality there. It seems that neither horses nor chariots came out of Egypt but by means of Solomon's servants.

CHAPTER 11

Solomon's attachment to strange women, and consequent idolatry, 1-2. Number of his wives and concubines, 3. In his old age they turn away his heart from God, 4. He builds temples to idols, burns incense and sacrifices to them, 5-8. The Lord is angry with him, and threatens to deprive him of the kingdom, but will leave one tribe for David's sake, 9-13. The Lord stirs up Hadad, the Edomite, to be his enemy; the history of this man, 14-22. He stirs another adversary against him, Rezon the son of Eliadah. He and Hadad plague Israel, 23-25. Jeroboam also becomes his enemy, and the reason why, 26-28. Ahijah, the prophet, meets Jeroboam and promises, in the name of the Lord, that God will rend Israel from the family of Solomon and give him ten tribes, 29-39. Solomon, hearing of this, seeks to put Jeroboam to death, who escapes to Egypt, where he continues till the death of Solomon, 40. Solomon dies, after having reigned over Israel forty years, and his son Rehoboam reigns in his stead, 41-43.

1. *Many strange women.* That is, idolaters; *together with the daughter of Pharaoh*—she was also one of those strange women and an idolater. But many think she became a proselyte to the Jewish religion; of this there is no evidence.

3. *He had seven hundred wives, princesses.* How he could get so many of the blood royal from the different surrounding nations is astonishing; but probably the daughters of noblemen, generals, etc., may be included. *And three hundred concubines.* These were wives of the second rank, who were taken according to the usages of those times; but their offspring could not inherit.

7. *The hill that is before Jerusalem.* This was the Mount of Olives.

9. *The Lord was angry with Solomon.* Had not this man's delinquency been strongly marked by the divine disapprobation, it would have had a fatal effect on the morals of mankind. Vice is vice, no matter who commits it. Solomon was wise; he knew better; his understanding showed him the vanity as well as the wickedness of idolatry. God *had appeared unto him twice,* and thus given him the most direct proof of His being and of His providence. The promises of God had been fulfilled to him in the most remarkable manner, and in such a way as to prove that they came by a divine counsel. All these were aggravations of Solomon's crimes, as to their demerit.

11. *Forasmuch as this is done of thee.* Was not this another warning from the Lord? And might not Solomon have yet recovered himself? Was there not mercy in this message which he might have sought and found?

13. *Will give one tribe . . . for David my servant's sake.* The line of the Messiah must be preserved.

14. *The Lord stirred up an adversary.* "A satan." When he sent to Hiram to assist him in building the temple of the Lord, he could say, "There was no satan," see chap. v. 4; and all his kingdom was in peace and security; "every man [dwelt] under his vine and under his fig tree," chap. iv. 25. But now that he had turned away from God, three satans rise up against him at once, Hadad, Rezon, and Jeroboam.

15. *Was gone up to bury the slain.* The slain Edomites; for Joab had in the course of six months exterminated all the males, except Hadad and his servants, who escaped to Egypt. Instead of *bury the slain,* the Targum has to "take the spoils of the slain."

17. *Hadad being yet a little child.* "A little boy"; one who was apprehensive of his danger, and could, with his father's servants, make his escape—not an infant.

18. *They arose out of Midian.* They at first retired to Midian, which lay to the southwest of the Dead Sea. Not supposing themselves in safety there, they went afterwards to Paran in the south of Idumea, and getting a number of persons to join them in Paran, they went straight to Egypt, where we find Hadad became a favorite with Pharaoh, who gave him his sister-in-law to wife, and incorporated him and his family with his own.

22. *Let me go in any wise.* It does not appear that he avowed his real intention to Pharaoh; for at this time there must have been peace between Israel and Egypt, Solomon having married the daughter of Pharaoh.

23. *Rezon the son of Eliadah.* Thus God fulfilled His threatening by the prophet Nathan: "If he commit iniquity, I will chasten him with the rod of men, and with the stripes of the children of men," 2 Sam. vii. 14.

24. *And reigned in Damascus.* Rezon was one of the captains of Hadadezer, whom David defeated. It seems that at this time Rezon escaped with his men; and having lived, as is supposed, some time by plunder, he seized on Damascus, and reigned there till David took Damascus, when he subdued Syria, and drove out Rezon. But after Solomon's defection from God, Rezon, finding that God had departed from Israel, recovered Damascus; and joining with Hadad, harassed Solomon during the remaining part of his reign. But some think that Hadad and Rezon were the same person.

26. *Jeroboam the son of Nebat.* From the context we learn that Jeroboam while a young

man was employed by Solomon to superintend the improvements and buildings at Millo, and had so distinguished himself there by his industry and good conduct as to attract general notice, and to induce Solomon to set him over all the laborers employed in that work, belonging to the tribes of Ephraim and Manasseh, called here the "house of Joseph." At first it appears that Solomon employed none of the Israelites in any drudgery; but it is likely that as he grew profane, he grew tyrannical and oppressive; and at the works of Millo he changed his conduct; and there, in all probability, were the seeds of disaffection sown. And Jeroboam, being a clever and enterprising man, knew well how to avail himself of the general discontent.

29. *When Jeroboam went out of Jerusalem.* On what errand he was going out of Jerusalem, we know not. *Ahijah the Shilonite.* He was one of those who wrote the history of the reign of Solomon, as we find from 2 Chron. ix. 29, and it is supposed that it was by him God spake twice to Solomon; and particularly delivered the message which we find in this chapter, vv. 11-13.

31. *Take thee ten pieces.* The *garment* was the symbol of the kingdom of Israel; the *twelve pieces,* the symbol of the twelve tribes; the *ten pieces* given to Jeroboam, of the ten tribes which would be given to him, and afterwards form the kingdom of Israel, ruling in Samaria, to distinguish it from the kingdom of Judah, ruling in Jerusalem.

36. *That David my servant may have a light alway.* That his posterity may never fail, and the regal line never become extinct. This, as we have already seen, was in reference to the Messiah. He was not only David's Light, but he was a Light to enlighten the Gentiles.

37. *According to all that thy soul desireth.* It appears from this that Jeroboam had affected the kingdom, and was seeking for an opportunity to seize on the government. God now tells him, by His prophet, what he shall have, and what he shall not have, in order to prevent him from attempting to seize on the whole kingdom, to the prejudice of the spiritual seed of David.

38. *And build thee a sure house.* He would have continued his posterity on the throne of Israel had he not by his wickedness forfeited the promises of God, and thrown himself out of the protection of the Most High.

39. *But not for ever.* They shall be in affliction and distress till the Messiah come, who shall sit on the throne of David to order it and establish it in judgment and justice forever. Jarchi says, on this verse, "When the Messiah comes, the kingdom shall be restored to the house of David."

40. *Sought . . . to kill Jeroboam.* He thought by this means to prevent the punishment due to his crimes.
Unto Shishak king of Egypt. This is the first time we meet with the proper name of an Egyptian king, *Pharaoh* being the common name for all the sovereigns of that country.

41. *The book of the acts of Solomon.* These acts were written by "Nathan the prophet . . . Ahijah the Shilonite, and . . . Iddo the seer," as we learn from 2 Chron. ix. 29. Probably from these were the Books of Kings and Chronicles

composed, but the original documents are long since lost.

42. *Solomon reigned . . . forty years.* Josephus says "fourscore years," which is sufficiently absurd.

43. *Solomon slept with his fathers.* He died in almost the flower of his age and, it appears, unregretted. His government was no blessing to Israel; and laid, by its exactions and oppressions, the foundation of that schism which was so fatal to the unhappy people of Israel and Judah.

CHAPTER 12

The people go to Shechem to make Rehoboam king, and send for Jeroboam out of Egypt, who, with the heads of the tribes, requests relief from the heavy burdens laid on them by Solomon, 1-4. He requires three days to consider their petition, 5. He rejects the counsel of the elders, who served his father, and follows that of young men, and returns the people a provoking answer, 6-15. The people therefore renounce the family of David, stone to death Adoram, who came to receive their tribute, and make Jeroboam king, none cleaving to Rehoboam but the tribes of Judah and Benjamin, 16-20. Rehoboam comes to Jerusalem, assembles all the fighting men of Judah and Benjamin, and finds the number to be 180,000; and with these he purposes to reduce the men of Israel to his allegiance, but is forbidden by the prophet Shemaiah, 21-24. Jeroboam builds Shechem in Mount Ephraim and Penuel, 25. And lest the people should be drawn away from their allegiance to him by going up to Jerusalem to worship, he makes two golden calves, and sets them up, one in Dan, the other in Bethel, and the people worship them, 26-30. He makes priests of the lowest of the people, and establishes the fifteenth day of the eighth month as a feast to his new gods; makes offerings, and burns incense, 31-33.

1. *Rehoboam went to Shechem.* Rehoboam was probably the only son of Solomon; for although he had a thousand wives, he had not the blessing of a numerous offspring; and although he was the wisest of men himself, his son was a poor, unprincipled fool. Had Solomon kept himself within reasonable bounds in matrimonial affairs, he would probably have had more children; and such as would have had common sense enough to discern the delicacy of their situation, and rule according to reason and religion.

4. *The grievous service . . . and . . . heavy yoke.* They seem here to complain of two things —excessively laborious service and a heavy taxation.

7. *If thou wilt be a servant unto this people.* This is a constitutional idea of a king. He is the *servant,* but not the slave, of his people; every regal act of a just king is an act of service to the state. *They will be thy servants for ever.* The way to insure the obedience of the people is to hold the reins of empire with a steady and impartial hand; let the people see that the king lives for them and not for himself, and they will obey, love, and defend him.

10. *And the young men that were grown up with him.* It was a custom in different countries to educate with the heir to the throne young noblemen of nearly the same age.

11. *Chastise you with scorpions.* Should you rebel, or become disaffected, my father's *whip* shall be a *scorpion* in my hand. His was chastisement; mine shall be punishment. Isidore and after him Calmet and others, assert that the scorpion was a sort of severe whip, the lashes of which were armed with iron points that sunk into and tore the flesh.

15. *The cause was from the Lord. Sibbah* "the revolution, was from the Lord." God

stirred up the people to revolt from a man who had neither skill nor humanity to govern them.

16. *So Israel departed unto their tents.* That is, the ten tribes withdrew their allegiance from Rehoboam; only Judah and Benjamin, frequently reckoned one tribe, remaining with him.

18. *King Rehoboam sent Adoram.* As this was the person who was superintendent over the tribute, he was probably sent to collect the ordinary taxes; but the people, indignant at the master who had given them such a brutish answer, stoned the servant to death. The sending of Adoram to collect the taxes when the public mind was in such a state of fermentation was another proof of Rehoboam's folly and incapacity to govern.

20. *Made him king over all Israel.* What is called Israel here was ten-twelfths of the whole nation.

24. *For this thing is from me.* That is, the separation of the ten tribes from the house of David. *They . . . returned to depart.* This was great deference, in both Rehoboam and his officers, to relinquish, at the demand of the prophet, a war which they thought they had good grounds to undertake. The remnant of the people heard the divine command gratefully, for the mass of mankind are averse from war.

27. *And they shall kill me.* He found he had little cause to trust this fickle people; though they had declared for him it was more from caprice, desire of change, and novelty than from any regular and praiseworthy principle.

28. *Made two calves of gold.* It is strange that in pointing out his calves to the people he should use the same words that Aaron used when he made the golden calf in the wilderness, when they must have heard what terrible judgments fell upon their forefathers for this idolatry.

29. *One in Beth-el, and the other . . . in Dan.* One at the southern and the other at the northern extremity of the land. Solomon's idolatry had prepared the people for Jeroboam's abominations!

31. *An house of high places.* A temple of temples; he had many *high places* in the land, and to imitate the Temple at Jerusalem, he made one chief over all the rest, where he established a priesthood of his own ordination.

32. *Ordained a feast.* The Jews held their Feast of Tabernacles on the fifteenth day of the seventh month; Jeroboam, who would meet the prejudices of the people as far as he could, appointed a similar feast on the fifteenth of the eighth month, thus appearing to hold the thing while he subverted the ordinance.

CHAPTER 13

A man of God prophesies against Jeroboam's altar, and foretells the destruction of that altar, and of its idolatrous priests by Josiah; and gives Jeroboam a sign that the prophecy should be accomplished, 1-3. Jeroboam is enraged, and orders the man of God to be seized; and stretching out his hand for this purpose, his arm dries up, 4. The altar is rent, and the ashes poured out, according to the sign given by the man of God; and at his intercession Jeroboam's arm is restored, 5-6. Jeroboam wishes to engage him in his service, but he refuses, and tells him that he was ordered by God not even to eat or drink in that place; and he accordingly departs, 7-10. An old prophet that dwelt at Bethel, hearing of this, rides after the man of God, deceives him, brings him back to

his house, and persuades him to eat and drink, 11-19. While he is eating, the word of the Lord comes to the old prophet, and he foretells the death of the man of God; who departing is met by a lion, and slain, 20-25. On hearing this, the old prophet goes to the place, finds the carcass, brings it home, buries it, and mourns over it, charging his sons to bury him, when dead, in the same grave, 26-32. Notwithstanding these warnings, Jeroboam continues in his idolatry, 33-34.

1. *There came a man of God.* Who this was we know not. The Chaldee, Syriac, and Arabic call him a "prophet." The Vulgate and Septuagint follow the Hebrew.

2. *He cried against the altar.* He denounced the destruction of this idolatrous system. *A child shall be born . . . Josiah by name.* This is one of the most remarkable and most singular prophecies of the Old Testament. It here most circumstantially foretells a fact which took place 340 years after the prediction, a fact which was attested by the two nations. The Jews, in whose behalf this prophecy was delivered, would guard it most sacredly; and it was the interest of the Israelites, against whom it was levelled, to impugn its authenticity and expose its falsehood, had this been possible. This prediction not only showed the knowledge of God, but His power. He gave, as it were, this warning to idolatry, that it might be on its guard, and defend itself against this Josiah whenever a person of that name should be found sitting on the throne of David. And no doubt it was on the alert, and took all prudent measures for its own defense; but all in vain, for Josiah, in the eighteenth year of his reign, literally accomplished this prophecy, as we may read in 2 Kings xxiii. 15-20.

3. *And he gave a sign.* A miracle to prove that the prophecy should be fulfilled in its season.

4. *Lay hold on him.* No doubt stretching out his own hand at the same time, through rage, pride, and haste, to execute his own orders. *And his hand . . . dried up.* The whole arm suddenly became rigid.

5. *The altar was also rent.* It split or clave of its own accord; and, as the split parts would decline at the top from the line of their perpendicular, so the ashes and coals would fall off, or be poured out.

6. *Intreat . . . the face of the Lord thy God.* The *face* of God is His favor, as we see in many parts of the sacred writings. He says, *thy God;* for Jeroboam knew that He was not his God, for he was now in the very act of acknowledging other gods, and had no portion in the God of Jacob. *And the king's hand was restored.* Both miracles were wrought to show the truth of the Jewish religion, and to convince this bold innovator of his wickedness, and to reclaim him from the folly and ruinous tendency of his idolatry.

7. *Come home with me . . . and I will give thee a reward.* Come and be one of my priests, and I will give you a proper salary.

9. *For so it was charged me . . . Eat no bread.* That is, Have no kind of communication with those idolaters. He was charged also not to return by the way that he came; probably lest the account of what was done should have reached the ears of any of the people through whom he had passed, and he suffer inconveniences on the account, either by persecution from the idolaters or from curious people delaying

him in order to cause him to give an account of the transactions which took place at Bethel.

11. *An old prophet.* Probably once a prophet of the Lord, who had fallen from his steadfastness, and yet not so deeply as to lose the knowledge of the true God and join with Jeroboam in his idolatries.

14. *And went after the man of God.* I can hardly think that this was with any evil design. His sons had given him such an account of the prediction, the power, and influence of this prophet that he wished to have a particular acquaintance with him, in order that he might get further information relative to the solemn import of the prophecy which he had denounced against the idolatry at Bethel.

18. *An angel spake unto me.* That he lied unto him is here expressly asserted and is amply proved by the event. But why should he deceive him? The simple principle of curiosity to know all about this prediction and the strange facts which had taken place, of which he had heard at second hand by means of his sons, was sufficient to induce such a person to get the intelligence he wished by any means.

19. *So he went back with him.* He permitted himself to be imposed on; he might have thought, as he had accomplished every purpose for which God sent him, and had actually begun to return by another way, God, who had given him the charge, had authority to say, "As thy purpose was to obey every injunction, even to the letter, I now permit thee to go with this old prophet, and take some refreshment."

20. *The word of the Lord came unto the prophet that brought him back.* "A great clamour," says Kennicott, "has been raised against this part of the history, on account of God's denouncing sentence on the true prophet by the mouth of the false prophet: but if we examine with attention the original words here, they will be found to signify either *he who brought him back;* or, *whom he had brought back;* for the very same words, *asher heshibo,* occur again in ver. 23, where they are now translated, *whom he had brought back;* and where they cannot be translated otherwise. This being the case, we are at liberty to consider the word of the Lord as delivered to the true prophet thus brought back; and then the sentence is pronounced by God himself, calling to him out of heaven, as in Gen. xxii. 11."

21. *And he.* That is, according to the above interpretation, the voice of God from heaven addressing the man of God, the old prophet having nothing to do in this business.

22. *Thy carcase shall not come.* This intimated to him that he was to die an untimely death, but probably did not specify by what means.

28. *The lion had not eaten the carcase, nor torn the ass.* All here was preternatural. The lion, though he had killed the man, does not devour him; the ass stands quietly by, not fearing the lion; and the lion does not attempt to tear the ass. Both stand as guardians of the fallen prophet. How evident is the hand of God in all!

30. *Alas, my brother!* This lamentation is very simple, very short, and very pathetic. Perhaps the old prophet said it as much in reference to himself, who had been the cause of his untimely death, as in reference to the man of God, whose corpse he now committed to the tomb.

31. *Lay my bones beside his bones.* This argues a strong conviction in the mind of the old prophet that the deceased was a good and holy man of God, and he is willing to have place with him in the general resurrection.

33. *Jeroboam returned not from his evil way.* There is something exceedingly obstinate and perverse, as well as blinding and infatuating, in idolatry. The prediction lately delivered at Bethel and the miracles wrought in confirmation of it were surely sufficient to have affected and alarmed any heart not wholly and incorrigibly hardened; and yet they had no effect on Jeroboam!

Made . . . the lowest of the people priests. So hardy was this bad man in his idolatry that he did not even attempt to form anything according to the model of God's true worship. *Whosoever would, he consecrated him.* He made no discrimination; any vagabond that offered was accepted even of those who had no character, who were too idle to work, and too stupid to learn.

34. *And this thing became sin.* These abominations were too glaring, and too insulting to the divine majesty, to be permitted to last; therefore his house was cut off, and destroyed from the face of the earth.

CHAPTER 14

Abijah, son of Jeroboam, falls sick, 1. Jeroboam sends his wife disguised to Ahijah, the prophet, and with her a present, to inquire concerning his son, 2-4. Ahijah discovers her by a divine intimation and delivers to her a heavy message concerning the destruction of Jeroboam's house and the death of her son, 5-16. The child dies, according to the prediction of Ahijah, 17. Jeroboam's reign and death, 18-20. Rehoboam's bad reign, and the apostasy of Judah, 21-24. Shishak, king of Egypt, invades Judea, spoils the Temple, and takes away the golden shields made by Solomon; instead of which Rehoboam makes others of brass, 25-28. Rehoboam's reign and death, 29-31.

1. *Abijah . . . fell sick.* This was but a prelude to the miseries which fell on the house of Jeroboam; but it was another merciful warning, intended to turn him from his idolatry and wickedness.

3. *Ten loaves.* Probably common or household bread. *Cracknels.* "Spotted or perforated bread."

5. *Feign herself to be another woman.* It would have been discreditable to Jeroboam's calves if it had been known that he had consulted a prophet of Jehovah.

8. *And rent the kingdom away from the house of David.* That is, permitted it to be rent, because of the folly and insolence of Rehoboam.

10. *Him that pisseth against the wall.* "Every male." The phrase should be thus rendered wherever it occurs.

11. *Shall the dogs eat.* They shall not have an honorable burial, and shall not come into the sepulchres of their fathers.

13. *In him there is found some good thing.* Far be it from God to destroy the righteous with the wicked; God respects even a little good, because it is a seed from himself.

15. *For the Lord shall smite Israel.* See this prophecy fulfilled, chap. xv. 28-30, when Baasha destroyed all the house and posterity of Jeroboam.

19. *The rest of the acts of Jeroboam . . . are written in the . . . chronicles.* For some important particulars relative to this reign, see 2 Chron. xiii. 1-20.

24. *There were also sodomites in the land.* Kedeshim, "consecrated persons"; persons who had devoted themselves in practices of the greatest impurity, to the service of the most impure idols.

26. *He took away the treasures.* All the treasures which Solomon had amassed, both in the Temple and in his own houses; a booty the most immense ever acquired in one place. *All the shields of gold which Solomon had made.* These were 300 in number, and were all made of beaten gold.

28. *The guard bare them.* The guard probably were just 300, answering to the number of the shields.

31. *Naamah an Ammonitess.* He was born of a heathen mother, and begotten of an apostate father. From such an impure fountain could sweet water possibly spring?

CHAPTER 15

Abijam's wicked reign, and death, 1-8. Asa succeeds him in the kingdom of Judah, and rules well, 9-15. He makes a league with the king of Syria against Baasha, king of Israel, who is obliged to desist in his attempts against Judah, 16-22. He is diseased in his feet and dies, and is succeeded by his son Jehoshaphat, 23-25. Nadab, son of Jeroboam, reigns over Israel; but is slain by Baasha, who reigns in his stead, 26-28. Baasha destroys all the house of Jeroboam, according to the prediction of Ahijah, 29-30. Baasha continues the idolatry of Jeroboam, 31-34.

1. *Reigned Abijam over Judah.* Of this son of Rehoboam, of his brethren, and of Rehoboam's family in general, see 2 Chronicles xii, where many particulars are added.

3. *His heart was not perfect.* He was an idolater, or did not support the worship of the true God. This appears to be the general meaning of the heart not being perfect with God.

4. *The Lord . . . give him a lamp.* That is, a son to succeed him (see chap. xi. 36).

5. *Save only in the matter of Uriah.* Properly speaking, this is the only flagrant fault or crime in the life of David. It was a horrible offense, or rather a whole system of offenses. See the notes on 2 Samuel xi and xii.

6. *There was war between Rehoboam and Jeroboam.* This was mentioned in the preceding chapter, v. 30, and it can mean no more than this: There was a continual spirit of hostility kept up between the two kingdoms, and no doubt frequent skirmishing between bordering parties; but it never broke out into open war, for this was particularly forbidden (see chap. xii. 24).

But why is this circumstance repeated, and the history of Abijam interrupted by the repetition? There is some reason to believe that *Rehoboam* is not the true reading, and that it should be "Abijam": "Now there was war between Abijam and Jeroboam all the days of his life." And this is the reading of *fourteen* of Kennicott's and De Rossi's MSS. The Syriac has "Abia the son of Rehoboam"; the Arabic has "Abijam." Some copies of the Targum have

"Abijam" also. This is doubtless the true reading, as we know there was a very memorable war between Abijam and Jeroboam; see it particularly described in 2 Chron. xiii. 3, etc.

10. *His mother's name.* Our translators thought that "grandmother" was likely to be the meaning, and therefore have put it in the margin. *The daughter of Abishalom.* She is called, says Calmet, the "daughter of Absalom," according to the custom of the Scriptures, which give the name of "daughter" indifferently to the niece, the granddaughter, and great-granddaughter.

12. *The sodomites. Hakkedeshim;* literally, "the holy or consecrated ones" (see chap. xiv. 24).

14. *The high places were not removed.* He was not able to make a thorough reformation; this was reserved for his son Jehoshaphat. *Asa's heart was perfect.* He worshipped the true God, and zealously promoted His service (see on v. 3). And even the high places which he did not remove were probably those where the true God alone was worshipped.

15. *Which his father had dedicated.* On what account he and his father dedicated the things mentioned below, we know not; but it appears that Asa thought himself bound by the vow of his father.

16. *There was war.* That is, there was continual enmity (see on v. 6). But there was no open war till the thirty-sixth year of Asa, when Baasha, king of Israel, began to build Ramah, that he might prevent all communication between Israel and Judah (see 2 Chron. xv. 19 and xvi. 1). But this does not agree with what is said here, chap. xvi. 8-9, that Elah, the son and successor of Baasha, was killed by Zimri in the twenty-sixth year of the reign of Asa. Chronologers endeavor to reconcile this by saying that the years should be reckoned, not from the beginning of the reign of Asa, but from the separation of the kingdoms of Israel and Judah. It is most certain that Baasha could not make war upon Asa in the thirty-sixth year of his reign, when it is evident from this chapter that he was dead in the twenty-sixth year of that king. We must either adopt the mode of solution given by chronologists or grant that there is a mistake in some of the numbers; most likely in the parallel places in Chronicles, but which we have no direct means of correcting. But the reader may compare 2 Chron. xiv. 1 with xv. 10, 19 and xvi. 1.

17. *And Baasha . . . built Ramah.* As the word signifies a "high place," what is here termed *Ramah* was probably a hill (commanding a defile through which lay the principal road to Jerusalem) which Baasha fortified in order to prevent all intercourse with the kingdom of Judah, lest his subjects should cleave to the house of David.

18. *Asa took all the silver.* Shishak, king of Egypt, had not taken the whole; or there had been some treasures brought in since that time. *Ben-hadad.* This was the son of Rezon, called here Hezion, who founded the kingdom of Damascus (see chap. xi. 23-24).

19. *There is a league between me and thee.* Or, Let there be a league between me and thee, as there was *between my father and thy*

father. There was no reason why Asa should have emptied his treasures at this time to procure the aid of the Syrian king, as it does not appear that there was any danger which himself could not have turned aside. He probably wished to destroy the kingdom of Israel; and to effect this purpose, even robbed the house of the Lord.

20. *Ijon, and Dan.* He appears to have attacked and taken those towns which constituted the principal strength of the kingdom of Israel.

21. *Dwelt in Tirzah.* This seems to have been the royal city (see v. 33 and chap. xiv. 17); and in this Baasha was probably obliged to shut himself up.

22. *None was exempted.* Every man was obliged to go and help to dismantle the fortress at Ramah which Baasha had built.

23. *And the cities which he built.* Such as Geba and Mizpah, which he built out of the spoils of Ramah. *He was diseased in his feet.* Probably he had a strong rheumatic affection. This took place in the thirty-ninth year of his reign, three years before his death; and it is said that he sought to physicians rather than to the Lord, 2 Chron. xvi. 12-13.

24. *Asa slept with his fathers.* Of his splendid and costly funeral we read in 1 Chron. xvi. 14.

27. *Smote him at Gibbethon.* This was a city in the tribe of Dan, and generally in the possession of the Philistines.

29. *He smote all the house of Jeroboam.* This was according to Ahijah's prophetic declaration (see chap. xiv. 10, 14). Thus God made use of one wicked man to destroy another.

CHAPTER 16

Jehu, the prophet, denounces the destruction of Baasha, 1-7. Zimri conspires against him, and slays him and his family, and reigns seven days, 8-15. The people make Omri king, and besiege Zimri in Tirzah; who, finding no way to escape, sets fire to his palace, and consumes himself in it, 16-20. The people are divided, half following Tibni, and half Omri; the latter faction overcomes the former. Tibni is slain, and Omri reigns alone, 21-23. He founds Samaria, 24. His bad character and death, 25-28. Ahab reigns in his stead; marries Jezebel, restores idolatry, and exceeds his predecessors in wickedness, 29-33. Hiel the Bethelite rebuilds Jericho, 34.

1. *Then the word of the Lord came to Jehu.* Of this prophet we know nothing but from this circumstance. It appears from 2 Chron. xvi. 7-10 that his father, Hanani, was also a prophet, and suffered imprisonment in consequence of the faithful discharge of his ministry to Asa.

2. *Made thee prince over my people.* That is, in the course of My providence, I suffered thee to become king; for it is impossible that God should make a rebel, a traitor, and a murderer, king over His people, or over any people. God is ever represented in Scripture as doing those things which, in the course of His providence, He permits to be done.

7. *And because he killed him.* This the Vulgate understands of Jehu, the prophet, put to death by Baasha: "On this account he killed him, that is, Jehu the prophet, the son of Hanani." Some think Baasha is intended, others Jeroboam, and others Nadab, the son of Jeroboam. The order is here confused, and the seventh verse should probably be placed between the fourth and fifth.

9. *Captain of half his chariots.* It is probable

that Zimri, and some other who is not here named, were commanders of the cavalry.

11. *He slew all the house of Baasha.* He endeavored to exterminate his race, and blot out his memory.

13. *For all the sins of Baasha.* We see why it was that God permitted such judgments to fall on this family. Baasha was a grievous offender, and so also was his son Elah; they caused the people to sin, and they provoked God to anger by their idolatries.

15. *The people were encamped against Gibbethon.* It appears that, at this time, the Israelites had war with the Philistines, and were now besieging Gibbethon, one of their cities. This army, hearing that Zimri had rebelled and killed Elah, made Omri, their general, king, who immediately raised the siege of Gibbethon, and went to attack Zimri in the royal city of Tirzah; who, finding his affairs desperate, chose rather to consume himself in his palace than to fall into the hands of his enemies.

23. *In the thirty and first year of Asa.* There must be a mistake here in the number thirty-one; for, in vv. 10 and 15, it is said that Zimri slew his master, and began to reign in the twenty-seventh year of Asa; and as Zimri reigned only seven days, and Omri immediately succeeded him, this could not be in the thirty-first, but in the twenty-seventh, year of Asa. Jarchi reconciles the two places thus: "The division of the kingdom between Tibni and Omri began in the twenty-seventh year of Asa; this division lasted five years, during which Omri had but a share of the kingdom. Tibni dying, Omri came into the possession of the whole kingdom, which he held seven years; this was in the thirty-first year of Asa."

24. *He bought the hill Samaria of Shemer.* This should be read, "He bought the hill of Shomeron from Shomer, and called it Shomeron [i.e., Little Shomer], after the name of Shomer, owner of the hill." At first the kings of Israel dwelt at Shechem, and then at Tirzah; but this place having suffered much in the civil broils, and the place having been burned down by Zimri, Omri purposed to found a new city, to which he might transfer the seat of government. He fixed on a hill that belonged to a person of the name of *Shomer;* and bought it from him for *two talents of silver.* Shomeron, or, as it is corruptly written, *Samaria,* is situated in the midst of the tribe of Ephraim, not very far from the coast of the Mediterranean Sea, and about midway between Dan and Beersheba; thus Samaria became the capital of the ten tribes, the metropolis of the kingdom of Israel, and the residence of its kings. The kings of Israel adorned and fortified it; Ahab built a "house of ivory" in it, chap. xxii. 39; the kings of Syria had magazines or storehouses in it, for the purpose of commerce (see chap. xx. 34). And it appears to have been a place of considerable importance and great strength.

31. *He took to wife Jezebel.* This was the head and chief of his offending; he took to wife, not only a heathen, but one whose hostility to the true religion was well-known, and carried to the utmost extent.

33. *Ahab made a grove.* Asherah, Astarte, or Venus; what the Syriac calls an "idol."

34. *Did Hiel the Beth-elite build Jericho.* Joshua's curse is well-known: "Cursed be the man before the Lord, that riseth up and buildeth this city Jericho: he shall lay the foundation thereof in his firstborn, and in his youngest son shall he set up the gates of it," Josh. vi. 26. There are three opinions on the words, "lay the foundation . . . in his firstborn," and "set up the gates" in his youngest son. (1) It is thought that when he laid the foundation of the city his eldest son, the hope of his family, died by the hand and judgment of God, and that all his children died in succession; so that when the doors were ready to be hung, his youngest and last child died, and thus, instead of securing himself a name, his whole family became extinct. (2) These expressions signify only great delay in the building; that he who should undertake it should spend nearly his whole life in it. (3) That he who rebuilt this city should, in laying the foundation, slay or sacrifice his firstborn, in order to consecrate it, and secure the assistance of the objects of his idolatrous worship; and should slay his youngest at the completion of the work, as a gratitude offering for the assistance received. None of the versions, the Chaldee excepted, intimates that the children were either slain or died, which circumstance seems to strengthen the opinion that the passage is to be understood of delays and hindrances.

CHAPTER 17

Elijah's message to Ahab concerning the three years' drought, 1. He is commanded to go to the brook Cherith, where he is fed by ravens, 2-7. He afterwards goes to a widow's house at Zarephath, and miraculously multiplies her meal and oil, 8-16. Her son dies, and Elijah restores him to life, 17-24.

1. *Elijah the Tishbite.* The history of this great man is introduced very abruptly; his origin is enveloped in perfect obscurity. He is here said to be a *Tishbite.* Tishbeh, says Calmet, is a city beyond Jordan, in the tribe of Gad, and in the land of Gilead. Who was his father, or from what tribe he sprang, is not intimated; he seems to have been the prophet of Israel peculiarly, as we never find him prophesying in Judah. His Hebrew name, which we have corrupted into *Elijah* and "Elias," is *Alihu,* or, according to the vowel points, *Eliyahu;* and signifies "he is my God."

3. *Hide thyself by the brook Cherith.* This brook, and the valley through which it ran, are supposed to have been on the western side of Jordan, and not far from Samaria. Others suppose it to have been on the eastern side, because the prophet is commanded to go eastward, v. 3.

4. *I have commanded the ravens to feed thee.* You shall not lack the necessaries of life; you shall be supplied by an especial providence.

6. *And the ravens brought him bread and flesh.* This is the first account we have of flesh-meat breakfasts and flesh-meat suppers; and as this was the food appointed by the Lord for the sustenance of the prophet, we may naturally conjecture that it was the food of the people at large.

7. *The brook dried up.* Because there had been no rain in the land for some time, God having sent this drought as a testimony against the idolatry of the people (see Deut. xi. 16-17).

9. *Get thee to Zarephath.* This was a town between Tyre and Sidon, but nearer to the latter, and is therefore called in the text *Zarephath, which belongeth to Sidon;* or, as the Vulgate and other versions express it, "Sarepta of the Sidonians." Sarepta is the name by which it goes in the New Testament.

12. *An handful of meal in a barrel.* The word *cad* is to be understood as implying an earthen jar; not a wooden vessel, or barrel of any kind. In the East they preserve their corn and meal in such vessels, without which precaution the insects would destroy them.

13. *But make me thereof a little cake first.* This was certainly putting the widow's faith to an extraordinary trial; to take and give to a stranger, of whom she knew nothing, the small pittance requisite to keep her child from perishing was too much to be expected.

16. *The barrel of meal wasted not.* She continued to take out of her jar and out of her bottle the quantity of meal and oil requisite for the consumption of her household.

17. *There was no breath left in him.* He ceased to breathe and died.

18. *To call my sin to remembrance.* She now seems to be conscious of some secret sin which she had either forgotten or too carelessly passed over, and to punish this she supposes the life of her son was taken away.

21. *Stretched himself upon the child three times.* It is supposed that he did this in order to communicate some natural warmth to the body of the child, in order to dispose it to receive the departed spirit. Elisha, his disciple, did the same in order to restore the dead child of the Shunammite, 2 Kings iv. 34. And Paul appears to have stretched himself on Eutychus in order to restore him to life, Acts xx. 10. *Let this child's soul come into him again.* Surely this means no more than the "breath." Though the word *nephesh* may sometimes signify the "life," yet does not this imply that the spirit must take possession of the body in order to produce and maintain the flame of animal life?

22. *And the soul [Nephesh] of the child came into him again; al kirbo,* into the midst of him; *and he revived,* "and he became alive."

24. *The word of the Lord in thy mouth is truth.* Three grand effects were produced by this temporary affliction: (1) The woman was led to examine her heart, and try her ways; (2) The power of God became highly manifest in the resurrection of the child; (3) She was convinced that the word of the Lord was truth, and that not one syllable of it could fall to the ground.

The subject in the fourth verse of this chapter deserves a more particular consideration. *I have commanded the ravens to feed thee.* It is contended that if we consider *orebim* to signify *ravens,* we shall find any interpretation on this ground to be clogged with difficulties. I need mention but a few. The raven is an unclean bird, "And these . . . ye shall have in abomination among the fowls . . . every raven after his kind," Lev. xi. 13-15. Is it therefore likely that God would employ this most unclean bird to feed His prophet? Besides, where could the ravens get any flesh that was not unclean? The original word *orebim* has been considered by some as meaning "merchants," persons occasionally trading through that country, whom God directed, by inspiration, to supply the prophet with food. To get a constant supply from such hands in an extraordinary way was miracle enough; it showed the superintendence of God, and that the hearts of all men are in His hands.

CHAPTER 18

Elijah is commanded by the Lord to show himself to Ahab, 1-2. Ahab, and Obadiah, his steward, search the land to find provender for the cattle, 3-6. Obadiah meets Elijah, who commands him to inform Ahab that he is ready to present himself before him, 7-15. Elijah and Ahab meet, 16-18. Elijah proposes that the 450 priests of Baal should be gathered together at Mount Carmel; that they should offer a sacrifice to their god, and he to Jehovah; and the God who should send down fire to consume the sacrifice should be acknowledged as the true God, 19-24. The proposal is accepted, and the priests of Baal call in vain upon their god through the whole day, 25-29. Elijah offers his sacrifice, prays to God, and fire comes down from heaven and consumes it; whereupon the people acknowledge Jehovah to be the true God, and slay all the prophets of Baal, 30-40. Elijah promises Ahab that there shall be immediate rain; it comes accordingly, and Ahab and Elijah come to Jezreel, 41-46.

1. *After many days . . . in the third year.* We learn from our Lord, Luke iv. 25, that the drought which brought on the famine in Israel lasted three years and six months. Jas. v. 17 gives it the same duration. Probably Elijah spent six months at the brook Cherith, and three years with the widow at Sarepta. *I will send rain upon the earth.* The word *haadamah* should be translated "the ground" or "the land," as it is probable that this drought did not extend beyond the land of Judea.

3. *Obadiah feared the Lord greatly.* He was a sincere and zealous worshipper of the true God, and his conduct towards the persecuted prophets was the full proof of both his piety and his humanity.

4. *Fed them with bread and water.* By these are signified the necessaries of life, of whatsoever kind.

5. *Unto all fountains of water.* All marshy or well-watered districts, where grass was most likely to be preserved.

10. *There is no nation or kingdom.* He had sent through all his own states and to the neighboring governments to find out the prophet, as he knew, from his own declaration, that both rain and drought were to be the effect of his prayers. *He took an oath.* Ahab must have had considerable power and authority among the neighboring nations to require and exact this, and Elijah must have kept himself very secret to have shunned such an extensive and minute search.

13. *When Jezebel slew the prophets.* This persecution was probably during the dearth, for as this bad woman would attribute the public calamity to Elijah, not being able to find him, she would naturally wreak her vengeance on the prophets of Jehovah who were within her reach.

18. *I have not troubled Israel.* Here the cause of the dearth is placed on its true ground: the king and the people had forsaken the true God, and God shut up the heavens that there was no rain. Elijah was only the minister whom God used to dispense this judgment.

19. *Gather to me all Israel.* The heads of tribes and families, the rulers of the people.

The prophets of Baal four hundred and fifty . . . the prophets of the groves four hundred. The king and queen had different religious establishments. The king and his servants worshipped Baal, the supreme lord and master of the world, the sun. For this establishment 450 priests were maintained. The queen and her women worshipped *Asherah,* Astarte or Venus; and for this establishment 400 priests were maintained. These latter were in high honor; they ate at Jezebel's table; they made a part of her household.

21. *How long halt ye between two opinions?* Literally, "How long hop ye about upon two boughs?" This is a metaphor taken from birds hopping about from bough to bough, not knowing on which to settle. Perhaps the idea of "limping" through lameness should not be overlooked. They were halt; they could not walk uprightly. They dreaded Jehovah, and therefore could not totally abandon Him; they feared the king and queen, and therefore thought they must embrace the religion of the state.

22. *I only, remain a prophet of the Lord.* That is, I am the only prophet of God present, and can have but the influence of an individual, while the prophets of Baal are 450 men! It appears that the queen's prophets, amounting to 400, were not at this great assembly; and these are they whom we meet in chap. xxii. 6, and whom the king consulted relative to the battle at Ramoth-gilead.

24. *The God that answereth by fire.* Elijah gave them every advantage when he granted that the God who answered by fire should be acknowledged as the true God; for as the Baal who was worshipped here was incontestably Apollo, or the sun, he was therefore the god of fire, and had only to work in his own element.

25. *For ye are many.* And therefore shall have the preference, and the advantage of being first in your application to the deity.

26. *From morning even until noon.* It seems that the priests of Baal employed the whole day in their desperate rites. The time is divided into two periods: (1) *From morning until noon;* this was employed in preparing and offering the sacrifice, and in earnest supplication for the celestial fire. Still there was no answer, and at noon Elijah began to mock and ridicule them, and this excited them to commence anew. And (2) They continued *from noon till the time of offering the evening sacrifice,* dancing up and down, cutting themselves with knives, mingling their own blood with their sacrifice, praying, supplicating, and acting in the most frantic manner. *And they leaped upon the altar.* Perhaps it will be more correct to read with the margin, "they leaped up and down at the altar"; they danced round it with strange and hideous cries and gesticulations, tossing their heads to and fro, with a great variety of bodily contortions.

27. *At noon . . . Elijah mocked them.* Had not Elijah been conscious of the divine protection, he certainly would not have used such freedom of speech while encompassed by his enemies. *For he is a god.* Ki Elohim hu, "he is the supreme God," you worship him as such he must needs be such, and no doubt jealous of his own honor and the credit of his votaries! A strong irony. *He is talking.* He may be

giving audience to some others; let him know that he has other worshippers, and must not give too much of his attention to one. Perhaps the word *siach* should be interpreted as in the margin, "he meditateth." *He is pursuing.* He may be taking his pleasure in hunting.

28. *They cried aloud.* The poor fools acted as they were bidden. *And cut themselves after their manner.* This was done according to the rites of that barbarous religion; if the blood of the bullock would not move him, they thought their own blood might; and with it they smeared themselves and their sacrifice.

29. *They prophesied.* They made incessant prayer and supplication; a further proof that to pray or supplicate is the proper ideal meaning of the word *naba,* which we constantly translate "to prophesy," when even all the circumstances of the time and place are against such a meaning.

31. *Took twelve stones.* He did this to show that all the twelve tribes of Israel should be joined in the worship of Jehovah.

32. *He made a trench.* This was to detain the water that might fall down from the altar when the barrels should be poured upon it, v. 35.

33. *Fill four barrels.* This was done to prevent any kind of suspicion that there was fire concealed under the altar.

36. *Lord God of Abraham.* He thus addressed the Supreme Being, that they might know when the answer was given that it was the same God whom the patriarchs and their fathers worshipped, and thus have their hearts turned back again to the true religion of their ancestors.

38. *Then the fire of the Lord fell.* It did not burst out from the altar; this might still, notwithstanding the water, have afforded some ground for suspicion that fire had been concealed, after the manner of the heathens, under the altar. *Consumed the burnt sacrifice.* The process of this consumption is very remarkable, and all calculated to remove the possibility of a suspicion that there was any concealed fire.

39. *Fell on their faces.* Struck with awe and reverence at the sight of this incontestable miracle. *And they said.* We should translate the words thus: "Jehovah, He is the God! Jehovah, He is the God!" Baal is not the God; Jehovah alone is the God of Israel.

40. *Let not one of them escape.* They had committed the highest crime against the state and the people by introducing idolatry, and bringing down God's judgments upon the land; therefore their lives were forfeited to that law which had ordered every idolater to be slain. It seems also that Ahab, who was present, consented to this act of impartial justice.

41. *Get thee up, eat and drink.* It appears most evidently that Ahab and the prophet were now on good terms, and this is a further evidence that the slaying of the false prophets was by the king's consent.

42. *Put his face between his knees.* He kneeled down, and then bowed his head to the earth, so that, while his face was between his knees, his forehead touched the ground.

43. *Look toward the sea.* From the top of Mount Carmel the Mediterranean Sea was in full view.

44. *There ariseth a little cloud out of the sea, like a man's hand.* "Like the hollow of a man's hand." In the form of the hand bent, the concave side downmost.

46. *Ran before Ahab.* Many think that Elijah ran before the king in order to do him honor. I believe all these entirely mistake the writer's meaning. Ahab yoked his chariot, and made all speed to Jezreel. The hand of the Lord, or, as the Targum says, the "spirit of strength," came upon Elijah, and he girded up his loins, that is, tucked up his long garments in his girdle, and ran; and notwithstanding the advantage the king had by means of his chariot, the prophet reached Jezreel before him. All this was intended to show that he was under the peculiar influence and inspiration of the Almighty, that the king might respect and fear him, and not do or permit to be done to him any kind of outrage.

CHAPTER 19

Ahab tells Jezebel what Elijah had done; she is enraged, and threatens to take away his life, 1-2. He leaves Jezreel, and comes to Beersheba, and thence to the wilderness, where he is fed and encouraged by an angel, 3-9. His complaint, and the vision by which God instructs him, 10-14. He is sent to Damascus, in order to anoint Hazael king over Syria, and Jehu king over Israel, 15-18. He meets with Elisha, who becomes his servant, 19-21.

1. *Ahab told Jezebel.* Probably with no evil design against Elijah.

2. *So let the gods do.* If I do not slay you, let the gods slay me with the most ignominious death.

3. *He arose, and went for his life.* He saw it was best to give place to this storm, and go to a place of safety. He probably thought that the miracle at Carmel would have been the means of effecting the conversion of the whole court and of the country, but, finding himself mistaken, he is greatly discouraged. *To Beer-sheba.* This being at the most southern extremity of the Promised Land, and under the jurisdiction of the king of Judah, he might suppose himself in a place of safety. *Left his servant there.* Being alone, he would be the more unlikely to be discovered; besides, he did not wish to risk the life of his servant.

4. *A day's journey into the wilderness.* Probably on his way to Mount Horeb (see v. 8). *Juniper tree.* A tree that afforded him a shade from the scorching sun. *It is enough.* I have lived long enough! I can do no more good among this people; let me now end my days.

5. *As he lay and slept.* Excessive anguish of mind frequently induces sleep, as well as great fatigue of body. *An angel touched him.* He needed refreshment, and God sent an angel to bring him what was necessary.

6. *A cake baken on the coals.* All this seems to have been supernaturally provided.

7. *The journey is too great for thee.* From Beersheba to Horeb was about one hundred fifty miles.

8. *Forty days and forty nights.* So he fasted just the same time as Moses did at Horeb, and as Christ did in the wilderness.

9. *He came thither unto a cave.* Conjectured by some to be the same cave in which God put Moses that He might give him a glimpse of His glory (see Exod. xxxiii. 22). *What doest thou here, Elijah?* Is this a reproach for having fled from the face of Jezebel, through what some call unbelieving fears that God would abandon him to her rage?

10. *I have been very jealous for the Lord.* The picture which he draws here of apostate Israel is very affecting: (1) They *have forsaken thy covenant.* They have now cleaved to and worshipped other gods. (2) *Thrown down thine altars.* Endeavored, as much as they possibly could, to abolish Thy worship, and destroy its remembrance from the land. (3) *And slain thy prophets.* That there might be none to reprove their iniquity or teach the truth. (4) *I only, am left.* They have succeeded in destroying all the rest of the prophets, and they are determined not to rest till they slay me.

11. *Stand upon the mount before the Lord.* God was now treating Elijah nearly in the same way that He treated Moses; and it is not unlikely that Elijah was now standing on the same place where Moses stood when God revealed himself to him in the giving of the law (see Exod. xix. 9, 16). *The Lord passed by.* It appears that the passing by of the Lord occasioned the strong wind, the earthquake, and the fire; but in none of these was God to make a discovery of himself unto the prophet. Yet these, in some sort, prepared His way, and prepared Elijah to hear the "still small voice."

13. *Wrapped his face in his mantle.* This he did to signify his respect; so Moses hid his face, for he dared not to look upon God, Exod. iii. 6. Covering the face was a token of respect among the Asiatics, as uncovering the head is among the Europeans.

15. *To the wilderness of Damascus.* He does not desire him to take a road by which he might be likely to meet Jezebel, or any other of his enemies. *Anoint Hazael.* For what reason the Lord was about to make all these revolutions, we are told in v. 17. God was about to bring His judgments upon the land, and especially on the house of Ahab. This He exterminated by means of Jehu, and Jehu himself was a scourge of the Lord to the people. Hazael also grievously afflicted Israel; see the accomplishment of these purposes, 2 Kings viii and ix.

17. *Shall Elisha slay.* The meaning of the prophecy may be this: Hazael, Jehu, and Elisha shall be the ministers of My vengeance against this disobedient and rebellious people. The order of time, here, is not to be regarded.

18. *Seven thousand in Israel.* That is, "many thousands"; for seven is a number of perfection, as we have often seen: so, "The barren has born seven"—has had a numerous offspring; "Gold seven times purified"—purified till all the dross is perfectly separated from it. The court and multitudes of the people had gone after Baal, but perhaps the majority of the common people still worshipped in secret the God of their fathers. *Every mouth which hath not kissed him.* Idolaters often kissed their hands in honor of their idols; and hence the origin of "adoration"—bringing the hand to the mouth after touching the idol, if it were within reach; and if not, kissing the right hand in token of respect and subjection. The word is compounded of *ad*, "to," and *os, oris*, "the mouth."

19. *Twelve yoke of oxen.* Elisha must have had a considerable estate, when he kept twelve yoke of oxen to till the ground. If, therefore, he obeyed the prophetic call, he did it at considerable secular loss. *He with the twelfth.* Every owner of an inheritance among the Hebrews, and indeed among the ancients in general, was a principal agent in its cultivation. *Cast his mantle upon him.* Either this was a ceremony used in a call to the prophetic office or it indicated that he was called to be the servant of the prophet. The *mantle* was the peculiar garb of the prophet, as we may learn from Zech. xiii. 4; and this was probably made of skin dressed with the hair on (see also 2 Kings i. 8). It is likely, therefore, that Elijah threw his mantle on Elisha to signify to him that he was called to the prophetic office.

20. *Let me . . . kiss my father and my mother.* Elisha fully understood that he was called by this ceremony to the prophetic office; and it is evident that he conferred not with flesh and blood, but resolved, immediately resolved, to obey; only he wished to bid farewell to his relatives. *What have I done to thee?* Your call is not from me, but from God; to Him, not to me, are you accountable for your use or abuse of it.

21. *He returned back.* He went home to his house; probably he yet lived with his parents, for it appears he was a single man. He slew a yoke of the oxen—he made a feast for his household, having boiled the flesh of the oxen with his agricultural implements, probably in token that he had abandoned secular life. Then, having bidden them an affectionate farewell, he arose, went after Elijah, who probably still awaited his coming in the field or its vicinity, and ministered unto him.

CHAPTER 20

Ben-hadad, king of Syria, and thirty-two kings, besiege Samaria, 1. He sends an insulting message to Ahab, and insists on pillaging the whole city, 2-7. The elders of Israel counsel the king not to submit to such shameful conditions, 8. He sends a refusal to Ben-hadad; who, being enraged, vows revenge, 9-13. A prophet comes to Ahab, promises him victory, and gives him directions how he should order the battle, 13-19. The Syrians are discomfited, and Ben-hadad scarcely escapes, 20-21. The prophet warns Ahab to be on his guard, for the Syrians would return next year, 22. The counsellors of the king of Syria instruct him how he may successfully invade Israel, 23-25. He leads an immense army to Aphek, to fight with Ahab, 26-27. A man of God encourages Ahab, who attacks the Syrians and kills 100,000 of them, 28-29. They retreat to Aphek, where 27,000 of them are slain by a casualty, 30. Ben-hadad and his courtiers, being closely besieged in Aphek, and unable to escape, surrender themselves with sackcloth on their loins, and halters on their heads; the king of Israel receives them in a friendly manner, and makes a covenant with Ben-hadad, 31-34. A prophet, by a symbolical action, shows him the impolicy of his conduct in permitting Ben-hadad to escape, and predicts his death and the slaughter of Israel, 35-43.

1. *Ben-hadad.* Several MSS., and some early printed editions, have *Ben-hadar,* or "the son of Hadar," as the Septuagint. He is supposed to be the same whom Asa stirred up against the king of Israel, xv. 18; or, as others, his son or grandson. *Thirty and two kings.* Tributary chieftains of Syria and the adjacent countries. In former times every town and city had its independent chieftain. Both the Septuagint and Josephus place this war after the history of Naboth.

4. *I am thine, and all that I have.* He probably hoped by this humiliation to soften this barbarous king, and perhaps to get better conditions.

6. *Whatsoever is pleasant in thine eyes.* It is not easy to discern in what this second requisition differed from the first; for surely his silver, gold, wives, and children were among his most pleasant or desirable things. It is evident that Ben-hadad meant to sack the whole city, and after having taken the royal treasures, and the wives and children of the king, to deliver up the whole to be pillaged by his soldiers.

8. *Hearken not unto him.* The elders had everything at stake, and they chose rather to make a desperate defense than tamely to yield to such degrading and ruinous conditions.

10. *If the dust of Samaria shall suffice.* This is variously understood. Jonathan translates thus: "If the dust of Shomeron shall be sufficient for the soles of the feet of the people that shall accompany me"; i.e., I shall bring such an army that there will scarcely be room for them to stand in Samaria and its vicinity.

11. *Let not him that girdeth on.* This was no doubt a proverbial mode of expression. Jonathan translates, "Tell him, Let not him who girds himself and goes down to the battle, boast as he who has conquered and returned from it."

13. *There came a prophet.* Who this was we cannot tell.

14. *By the young men of the princes of the provinces.* These were probably some chosen persons out of the militia of different districts, raised by *the princes of the provinces.*

15. *Two hundred and thirty two.* These were probably the king's life or body guards; not all the militia, but 230 of them who constituted the royal guard in Samaria. They were therefore the king's own regiment, and he is commanded by the prophet to put himself at their head. *Seven thousand.* How low must the state of Israel have been at this time!

18. *Take them alive.* He was confident of victory. Do not slay them; bring them to me, they may give us some useful information.

20. *The Syrians fled.* They were doubtless panic-struck.

23. *Their gods are gods of the hills.* It is very likely that the small Israelitish army availed itself of the heights and uneven ground, that they might fight with greater advantage against the Syrian cavalry, for Ben-hadad came up against Samaria with horses and chariots, v. 1. These therefore must be soon thrown into confusion when charging in such circumstances; indeed, the chariots must be nearly useless. *Let us fight against them in the plain.* There our horses and chariots will all be able to bear on the enemy, and there their gods, whose influence is confined to the hills, will not be able to help them. It was a general belief in the heathen world that each district had its tutelary and protecting deity, who could do nothing out of his own sphere.

24. *Take the kings away.* These were not acquainted with military affairs, or they had not competent skill. Put experienced *captains* in their place, and fight not but on the plains, and you will be sure of victory.

26. *Ben-hadad numbered the Syrians, and went up to Aphek.* There were several towns of this name (see the notes on Josh. xii. 18). It is supposed that the town mentioned here was situated in Libanus, upon the river Adonis, between Heliopolis and Biblos.

28. *Because the Syrians have said.* God resents their blasphemy, and is determined to punish it. They shall now be discomfited in such a way as to show that God's power is everywhere, and that the multitude of a host is nothing against Him.

29. *Slew . . . an hundred thousand footmen in one day.* This number is enormous; but the MSS. and versions give no various reading.

30. *A wall fell upon twenty and seven thousand.* From the first view of this text it would appear that when the Syrians fled to Aphek, and shut themselves within the walls, the Israelites immediately brought all hands and sapped the walls, in consequence of which a large portion fell, and buried 27,000 men. But perhaps the hand of God was more immediately in this disaster; probably a burning wind is meant. *Came into the city, into an inner chamber.* However the passage above may be understood, the city was now, in effect, taken; and Ben-hadad either betook himself with his few followers to the citadel or to some secret hiding place, where he held the council with his servants immediately mentioned.

31. *Put sackcloth on our loins, and ropes upon our heads.* Let us show ourselves humbled in the deepest manner, and let us put ropes about our necks, and go submitting to his mercy, and deprecating his wrath.

32. *Thy servant Ben-hadad.* See the vicissitude of human affairs! A little before he was the haughtiest of all tyrants, and Ahab calls him his lord; now, so much is he humbled that he will be glad to be reputed Ahab's slave!

33. *Did hastily catch it.* They were watching to see if any kind word should be spoken by him, from which they might draw a favorable omen; and when they heard him use the word "brother," it gave them much encouragement.

34. *Thou shalt make streets for thee in Damascus.* It appears that it was customary for foreigners to have a place assigned to them, particularly in maritime towns, where they might deposit and vend their merchandise.

35. *In the word of the Lord.* By the word or command of the Lord; that is, God has commanded thee to smite me. Refusing to do it, this man forfeited his life, as we are informed in the next verse. By this emblematical action he intended to inform Ahab that, as the man forfeited his life who refused to smite him when he had the Lord's command to do it, so he (Ahab) had forfeited his life, because he did not smite Ben-hadad when he had him in his power.

36. *A lion found him, and slew him.* This seems a hard measure, but there was ample reason for it. This person was also one of the sons of the prophets, and he knew that God frequently delivered His counsels in this way, and should have immediately obeyed. For the smiting could have had no evil in it when God commanded it, and it could be no outrage or injury to his fellow when he himself required him to do it.

38. *Disguised himself with ashes upon his face.* It does not immediately appear how putting *ashes* upon his face could disguise him. Instead of *apher*, "dust," Houbigant conjectures that it should be *aphad*, a "fillet" or "bandage." It is only the corner of the last letter which makes the difference, for the *daleth* and *resh* are nearly the same; only the shoulder of the former is square, the latter round. That "bandage," not "dust," was the original reading seems pretty evident from its remains in two of the oldest versions, the Septuagint and the Chaldee. The former has, "And he bound his eyes with a fillet." The latter has, "And he covered his eyes with a cloth."

39. *Keep this man.* The drift of this is at once seen; but Ahab, not knowing it, was led to pass sentence on himself.

41. *Took the ashes away.* He took the bandage from off his eyes (see on v. 38). It was no doubt of thin cloth, through which he could see, while it served for a sufficient disguise.

42. *Thy life shall go for his life.* This was fulfilled at the battle of Ramoth-gilead, where he was slain by the Syrians (see chap. xxii 34-35).

43. *Heavy and displeased.* Heavy or afflicted because of these dreadful tidings, and displeased with the prophet for having announced them. Had he been displeased with himself, and humbled his soul before God, even those judgments, so circumstantially foretold, might have been averted.

CHAPTER 21

Ahab covets the vineyard of Naboth, and wishes to have it by either purchase or exchange, 1-2. Naboth refuses to alienate it on any account, because it was his inheritance from his fathers, 3. Ahab becomes disconsolate, takes to his bed, and refuses to eat, 4. Jezebel, finding out the cause, promises to give him the vineyard, 5-7. She writes to the nobles of Jezreel to proclaim a fast, to accuse Naboth of blasphemy, carry him out, and stone him to death; which is accordingly done, 8-14. She then tells Ahab to go and take possession of the vineyard; he goes, and is met by Elijah, who denounces on him the heaviest judgments, 15-24. Ahab's abominable character, 25-26. He humbles himself; and God promises not to bring the threatened public calamities in his days, but in the days of his son, 27-29.

1. *After these things.* This and the twentieth chapter are transposed in the Septuagint, this preceding the account of the Syrian war with Ben-hadad. Josephus gives the history in the same order.

2-3. *Give me thy vineyard.* The request of Ahab seems at first view fair and honorable. Naboth's vineyard was nigh to the palace of Ahab, and he wished to add it to his own for a "kitchen garden," or perhaps a "grass-plat"; and he offers to give him either a better vineyard for it or to give him its worth in money. Naboth rejects the proposal with horror: *The Lord forbid it me, that I should give the inheritance of my fathers unto thee.* No man could finally alienate any part of the parental inheritance; it might be sold or mortgaged till the jubilee, but at that time it must revert to its original owner, if not redeemed before; for this God had particularly enjoined, Lev. xxv. 14-17, 25-28. Ahab most evidently wished him to alienate it finally, and this is what God's law had expressly forbidden. Therefore he could not, consistently with his duty to God, indulge Ahab; and it was high iniquity in Ahab to tempt him to do it, and to covet it showed the depravity of Ahab's soul.

4. *He laid him down upon his bed.* Poor soul! He was lord over ten-twelfths of the land, and became miserable because he could not get a poor man's vineyard added to all that he possessed!

7. *Dost thou now govern the kingdom of Israel?* Naboth, not Ahab, is king. If he has authority to refuse, and you have no power to take, he is the greater man of the two. This is the vital language of despotism and tyranny.

8. *She wrote letters in Ahab's name.* She counterfeited his authority by his own consent, and he lent his signet to stamp that authority.

9. *Proclaim a fast.* Intimate that there is some great calamity coming upon the nation, because of some evil tolerated in it. *Set Naboth on high.* Bring him to a public trial.

10. *Set two men.* For life could not be attainted but on evidence of two witnesses at least. *Sons of Belial.* Men who will not scruple to tell lies and take a false oath. *Thou didst blaspheme God and the king.* The words literally are, "Naboth hath blessed God and the king"; or, as Parkhurst contends, "Thou hast blessed the false gods and Molech." And though Jezebel was herself an abominable idolatress, yet, as the law of Moses still continued in force, she seems to have been wicked enough to destroy Naboth, upon the false accusation of blessing the heathen Molech, which subjected him to death by Deut. xii. 6; xvii. 2-7. The first meaning appears the most simple.

13. *And stoned him with stones.* As they pretended to find him guilty of treason against God and the king, it is likely they destroyed the whole of his family; and then the king seized on his grounds as confiscated, without any heir at law. That his family was destroyed appears strongly intimated, 2 Kings ix. 26; "Surely I have seen yesterday the blood of Naboth, and the blood of his sons, saith the Lord."

18. *Go down to meet Ahab.* This was the next day after the murder, as we learn from the above quotation, 2 Kings ix. 26.

19. *In the place where dogs licked.* Thus it would have been fulfilled, but the humiliation of Ahab induced the merciful God to say, "I will not bring the evil in his days, but in the days of his son" (see v. 29). Now dogs did lick the blood of Ahab; but it was at the pool of Samaria, where his chariot and his armor were washed, after he had received his death wound at Ramoth-gilead; but some think this was the place where Naboth was stoned (see chap. xxii. 38). And how literally the prediction concerning his son was fulfilled (see 2 Kings ix. 25), where we find that the body of Jehoram, his son, just then slain by an arrow that had passed through his heart, was thrown "into the portion of the field of Naboth the Jezreelite"; and there, doubtless, the dogs licked his blood, if they did not even devour his body!

20. *Thou hast sold thyself to work evil.* See a similar form of speech, Rom. vii. 14. You have totally abandoned yourself to the service of sin.

23. *The dogs shall eat Jezebel.* This was most literally fulfilled (see 2 Kings ix. 36).

25. *Did sell himself to work wickedness.* He hired himself to the devil for this very purpose, that he might work wickedness. *In the sight of the Lord, whom Jezebel his wife stirred up.* A good wife is from the Lord; a bad wife is from the devil. Jezebel was of this kind, and she has had many successors.

27. *He rent his clothes.* He was penetrated with sorrow, and that evidently unfeigned. *Put sackcloth upon his flesh.* He humbled himself before God and man. *And fasted.* He afflicted his body for his soul's benefit. *Lay in sackcloth.* Gave the fullest proof that his repentance was real. *And went softly.* "Walked barefooted"; so the Chaldee, Syriac, and Arabic. The Vulgate has: "with his head hanging down." Houbigant translates "went groaning." Jarchi says that the word *at*, used here, signifies "to be unshod." This is its most likely sense. All these things prove that Ahab's repentance was genuine, and God's approbation of it puts it out of doubt.

29. *Seest thou how Ahab humbleth himself?* He did abase himself; he did truly repent him of his sins, and it was such a repentance as was genuine in the sight of God. *He humbleth himself before me.*

CHAPTER 22

Jehoshaphat, king of Judah, and Ahab, king of Israel, unite against the Syrians, in order to recover Ramoth-gilead, 1-4. They inquire of false prophets, who promise them success. Micaiah, a true prophet, foretells the disasters of the war, 5-17. A lying spirit in the mouths of Ahab's prophets persuades Ahab to go up against Ramoth, 18-29. The confederate armies are routed, and the king of Israel is slain, 30-36. Death and burial of Ahab, 37-40. Character of Jehoshaphat, 41-47. He makes a fleet in order to go to Ophir for gold, which is wrecked at Ezion-geber, 48. His death, 49. He is succeeded by his son Jehoram, 50. Ahaziah succeeds his father, Ahab, and reigns wickedly, 51-52.

1. *Three years without war.* That is, from the time that Ahab made the covenant with Ben-hadad, mentioned in chap. xx. 34. And probably in that treaty it was stipulated that Ramoth-gilead should be restored to Israel; which not being done, Ahab formed a confederacy with Judah, and determined to take it by force.

4. *Wilt thou go with me?* We find that there was a good understanding between Jehoshaphat and Ahab, which no doubt was the consequence of a matrimonial alliance between the son of the former, Jehoram, and the daughter of the latter, Athaliah (see 2 Chron. xviii. 1; 2 Kings viii. 18). This coalition did not please God, and Jehoshaphat is severely reproved for it by Jehu, the seer, 2 Chron. xix. 1-3.

6. *About four hundred men.* These were probably the prophets of Asherah maintained by Jezebel, who were not present at the contention on Mount Carmel (see chap. xviii. 19, etc.).

8. *Micaiah the son of Imlah.* The Jews suppose that it was this prophet who reproved Ahab for dismissing Ben-hadad, chap. xx. 35, etc. And that it was because of the judgments with which he had threatened him that Ahab hated him: *I hate him; for he doth not prophesy good concerning me, but evil.*

9. *The king of Israel called an officer.* Saris, literally "a eunuch"; probably a foreigner, for it was not lawful to disgrace an Israelite by reducing him to such a state.

11. *Zedekiah . . . made him horns of iron.* This was in imitation of that sort of prophecy which instructed by significative actions. This was frequent among the prophets of the Lord.

13. *The words of the prophets declare good.* What notion could these men have of prophecy,

when they supposed it was in the power of the prophet to model the prediction as he pleased, and have the result accordingly?

15. *Go, and prosper.* This was a strong irony; as if he had said, All your prophets have predicted success; you wish me to speak as they speak. *Go, and prosper; for the Lord shall deliver it into the hand of the king.* These were the precise words of the false prophets (see vv. 6 and 12) and were spoken by Micaiah in such a tone and manner as at once showed to Ahab that he did not believe them. Hence the king adjures him, v. 16, that he would speak to him nothing but truth; and on this the prophet immediately relates to him the prophetic vision which pointed out the disasters which ensued.

17. *These have no master.* Here the prophet foretells the defeat of Israel, and the death of the king; they were as sheep that had not a shepherd, people that had no master. The political shepherd and master (Ahab) shall fall in battle.

22. *Go forth, and do so.* This is no more than, "God has permitted the spirit of lying to influence the whole of your prophets; and He now, by my mouth, apprizes you of this, that you may not go and fall at Ramoth-gilead." Never was a man more circumstantially and fairly warned; he had counsels from the God of truth, and counsels from the spirit of falsity. He obstinately forsook the former and followed the latter.

23. *The Lord hath put a lying spirit.* He has permitted or suffered a lying spirit to influence your prophets.

24. *Which way went the Spirit of the Lord from me?* This is an expression of as great insolence as the act was of brutal aggression. "Did the Spirit of the Lord, who rests solely upon me, condescend to inspire you? Was it at this ear [where he smote him] that it entered, in order to hold communion with you?"

25. *When thou shalt go into an inner chamber.* It is probable that this refers to some divine judgment which fell upon this deceiver. Hearing of the tragical result of the battle, he no doubt went into a secret place to hide himself from the resentment of Jezebel and the Israelitish courtiers, and there it is probable he perished; but how, when, or where is not mentioned.

27. *Feed him with bread of affliction.* Deprive him of all the conveniences and comforts of life; treat him severely; just keep him alive, that he may see my triumph.

30. *I will disguise myself.* Probably he had heard of the orders given by Ben-hadad to his thirty-two captains, to fight with the king of Israel only. *But put thou on thy robes.* What is meant by this? He could not mean, "Appear as the king of Judah, for they will not molest you, as the matter of contention lies between them and me." For if Jehoshaphat aided Ahab, is it to be supposed that the Syrians would spare him in battle? The Septuagint gives the clause a different and more intelligible turn: "I will cover (conceal) myself, and enter into the battle; but put thou on my robes." And does it not appear that he did put on Ahab's robes? And was it not this that caused the Syrians to mistake him for the king of Israel (v. 32)?

34. *Drew a bow at a venture.* It is supposed that he shot, as the archers in general did, not aiming at any person in particular. The word *lethummo,* which we translate "in his simplicity," has been variously understood: "in his integrity, his uprightness; in his perfection"; i.e., to the utmost of his skill and strength. This is most probably the meaning.

35. *The king was stayed up.* He did not wish his misfortune should be known, lest his troops should be discouraged.

36. *Every man to his city.* It appears that the Israelites and Jews maintained the fight the whole of the day; but when at evening the king died, and this was known, there was a proclamation made, probably with the consent of both Syrians and Israelites, that the war was over. Ahab being dead, his subjects did not choose to contend for Ramoth-gilead; so the Israelites went to their own cities, and the Syrians to their own country.

38. *The dogs licked up his blood.* Some of the rabbins think that this was in the very place where Naboth was stoned (see on chap. xxi. 19).

39. *Ivory house.* A royal palace which he built in Samaria, decorated with ivory, and hence called the *ivory house.* Amos, the prophet, speaks against this luxury, chap. iii. 15.

43. *The high places were not taken away.* In 2 Chron. xvii. 6, it is expressly said that he did take away the high places. Allowing that the text is right in 2 Chronicles, the two places may be easily reconciled. There were two kinds of high places in the land: (1) those used for idolatrous purposes, (2) those that were consecrated *to God,* and were used before the Temple was built. The former he did take away; the latter he did not. But some think the parallel place in 2 Chron. xvii. 6 is corrupted, and that, instead of *veod,* "and moreover he took away," we should read, *velo hesir,* "and he did not take away."

46. *The remnant of the sodomites.* "Of the consecrated persons"; or it may rather apply here to the system of pollution, effeminacy, and debauch. He destroyed the thing itself— the abominations of Priapus, and the rites of Venus, Baal, and Ashtaroth. No more of that impure worship was to be found in Judea.

47. *There was then no king in Edom.* It is plain that the compiler of this book lived after the days of Jehoshaphat, in whose time the Edomites revolted (see 2 Kings viii. 22). David had conquered the Edomites, and they continued to be governed by deputies, appointed by the kings of Judah, till they recovered their liberty, as above. This note is introduced by the writer to account for Jehoshaphat's building ships at Ezion-geber, which was in the territory of the Edomites, and which showed them to be at that time under the Jewish yoke.

48. *Ships of Tharshish to go to Ophir for gold.* In the parallel place, 2 Chron. xx. 36, it is said that Jehoshaphat joined himself to Ahaziah "to make ships to go to Tharshish: and they made the ships in Ezion-gaber." Some translate, instead of ships of *Tharshish,* ships of "burden."

49. *But Jehoshaphat would not.* It appears from the above cited place in Chronicles that Jehoshaphat did join in making and sending ships to Tharshish, and it is possible that what is here said is spoken of a second expedition, in which Jehoshaphat *would not* join Ahaziah. But instead of *velo abah,* "he would not," perhaps we should read *velo abah,* "he consented to him"; two words pronounced exactly in the same way, and differing but in one letter, viz., an *aleph* for a *vau.* This reading, however, is not supported by any MS. or version. But the emendation seems just, for there are several places in these historical books in which there are mistakes of transcribers which nothing but criticism can restore, and to this it is dangerous to resort but in cases of the last necessity. Critics have recommended the forty-eighth and forty-ninth verses to be read thus: "Jehoshaphat had built ships of burden at Ezion-geber, to go to Ophir for gold. And Ahaziah, the son of Ahab, had said to Jehoshaphat, Let my servants, I pray thee, go with thy servants in the ships: to which Jehoshaphat consented. But the ships went not thither; for the ships were broken at Ezion-geber." This is Houbigant's translation, who contends that "the words of the forty-eighth verse, *but they went not,* should be placed at the end of the forty-ninth verse, for who can believe that the sacred writer should first relate that *the ships were broken,* and then that Ahaziah requested of Jehoshaphat that his servants might embark with the servants of Jehoshaphat?" This bold critic, who understood the Hebrew language better than any man in Europe, has, by happy conjectures, since verified by the testimony of MSS., removed the blots of many careless transcribers from the sacred volume.

The Second Book of
KINGS

The Second Book of Kings contains the history of 308 years, from the rebellion of Moab to the ruin of the kingdom of Judah. The history, on the whole, exhibits little less than a series of crimes, disasters, divine benefits, and divine judgments. In the kingdom of Judah we meet with a few kings who feared God, and promoted the interests of pure religion in the land; but the major part were idolaters and profligates of the highest order.

The kingdom of Israel was still more corrupt. All its kings were determined idolaters; profligate, vicious, and cruel tyrants. Elijah and Elisha stood up in the behalf of God and truth in this fallen, idolatrous kingdom, and bore a strong testimony against the corruptions of the princes and the profligacy of the people. Their powerful ministry was confined to the ten tribes; Judah had its own prophets, and those in considerable number.

At length the avenging hand of God fell first upon Israel, and afterwards upon Judah. Israel, after many convulsions, torn by domestic and foreign wars, was at length wholly subjugated by the king of Assyria, the people led away into captivity, and the land repeopled by strangers.

The kingdom of Judah continued some time longer, but was at last overthrown by Nebuchadnezzar. Zedekiah, its last king, was taken prisoner; his eyes put out; and the principal part of the people were carried into captivity, which lasted about seventy years. There was after this a partial restoration of the Jews, but they never more rose to any consequence among the nations; and at last their civil polity was finally dissolved by the Romans, and their Temple burned, A.D. 70; and from that time until now they became fugitives and vagabonds over the face of the earth.

CHAPTER 1

Ahaziah, being hurt by a fall, sends messengers to Baal-zebub to inquire whether he shall recover, 1-2. They are met by Elijah, who sends them back with the information that he shall surely die, 3-8. The king sends a captain and fifty men, to bring Elijah to Samaria, on which fire comes down from heaven and destroys both him and his men, 9-10. Another captain and fifty men are sent, who are likewise destroyed, 11-12. A third is sent, who behaves himself humbly, and Elijah is commanded to accompany him; he obeys, comes to the king, reproves his idolatry, and announces his death, 13-16. Ahaziah dies and Jehoram reigns in his stead, 17-18.

1. *Moab rebelled.* The Moabites had been subdued by David, and laid under tribute, chap. iii. 4 and 2 Sam. viii. 2. After the division of the two kingdoms, the Moabites fell partly under the dominion of Israel, and partly under that of Judah, until the death of Ahab, when they arose and shook off this yoke. Jehoram confederated with the king of Judah and the king of Edom, in order to reduce them. See this war, chap. iii. 5.

2. *Fell down through a lattice.* Perhaps either through the flat roof of his house or over or through the balustrades with which the roof was surrounded. *Go, enquire of Baal-zebub.* Literally, the "fly-god," or "master of flies." The Septuagint has "Baal the fly." He was the tutelary god of Ekron, and probably was used at first to drive away flies. Afterwards he became a very respectable devil, and was supposed to have great power and influence. In the New Testament, Beelzebub is a common name for Satan himself, or the prince of devils.

4. *But shalt surely die.* The true God tells you this, He in whose hands are both life and death, who can kill and make alive. Baal-zebub

can do nothing; God has determined that your master shall die.

8. *He was an hairy man.* That is, he wore a rough garment, either made of camels' hair, as his successor John Baptist's was; or he wore a skin dressed with the hair on. Some think that the meaning is, he had very long hair and a long beard. The ancient prophets all wore rough garments, or upper coats made of the skins of beasts: "They wandered about in sheepskins and goatskins," says the apostle, Heb. xi. 37.

9. *A captain of fifty with his fifty.* It is impossible that such a man as Ahaziah, in such circumstances, could have had any friendly designs in sending a captain and fifty soldiers for the prophet; and the manner in which they are treated shows plainly that they went with a hostile intent. *And he spake unto him, Thou man of God.* You prophet of the Most High.

10. *And there came down fire.* Some have blamed the prophet for destroying these men, by bringing down fire from heaven upon them. But they do not consider that it was no more possible for Elijah to bring down fire from heaven than for them to do it. God alone could send the fire; and as He is just and good, He would not have destroyed these men had there not been a sufficient cause to justify the act. It was not to please Elijah, or to gratify any vindictive humor in him, that God thus acted; but to show His own power and justice. No entreaty of Elijah could have induced God to perform an act that was wrong in itself. God led him simply to announce on these occasions what He himself had determined to do. *If I*

359

be a man of God, fire [shall] come down from heaven, and [shall] consume thee and thy fifty. This is the literal meaning of the original; and by it we see that Elijah's words were only declarative, and not imprecatory.

15. *And the angel of the Lord said . . . Go down with him.* This is an additional proof that Elijah was then acting under particular inspirations; he had neither will nor design of his own. *And he arose, and went down.* He did not even regard his personal safety or his life; he went to the king without the least hesitation, though he had reason to suppose he would be doubly irritated by his prediction and the death of 100 of his men.

17. *And Jehoram reigned in his stead.* The Vulgate, Septuagint, and Syriac say, "Jehoram his brother reigned in his stead, in the second year of Jehoram." There were two Jehorams who were contemporary: the first, the son of Ahab, brother to Ahaziah, and his successor in the kingdom of Israel; the second, the son of Jehoshaphat, king of Judah, who succeeded his father in Judah. But there is a difficulty here: "How is it that Jehoram the brother of Ahaziah began to reign in the second year of Jehoram son of Jehoshaphat, seeing that, according to chap. iii. 1, he began his reign in the eighteenth year of the reign of Jehoshaphat; and, according to chap. viii. 16, Jehoram son of Jehoshaphat began to reign in the fifth year of Jehoram king of Israel?" Calmet and others answer thus: "Jehoram king of Israel began to reign in the eighteenth year of Jehoshaphat king of Judah, which was the second year after this same Jehoshaphat had given the vice-royalty to his son Jehoram; and afterwards Jehoshaphat communicated the royalty to Jehoram his successor, two years before his death, and the fifth year of Jehoram, king of Israel."

CHAPTER 2

Elijah, about to be taken up to heaven, goes in company with Elisha from Gilgal to Bethel, 1-2. Thence to Jericho, 3-5. And thence to Jordan, 6-7. Elijah smites the waters with his mantle; they divide, and he and Elisha pass over on dry ground, 8. Elijah desires Elisha to ask what he should do for him; who requests a double portion of his spirit, which is promised on a certain condition, 9-10. A chariot and horses of fire descend; and Elijah mounts, and ascends by a whirlwind to heaven, 11. Elisha gets his mantle, comes back to Jordan, smites the waters with it, and they divide, and he goes over, 12-14. The sons of the prophets see that the spirit of Elijah rests on Elisha, 15. They propose to send fifty men to seek Elijah, supposing the Spirit of the Lord might have cast him on some mountain or valley; after three days' search, they return, not having found him, 16-18. The people of Jericho apply to Elisha to heal their unwholesome water, 19. He casts salt into the spring in the name of Jehovah, and the water becomes wholesome, 20-22. Forty-two young persons of Bethel, mocking him, are slain by two she-bears, 23-24. He goes to Carmel, and returns to Samaria, 25.

1. *When the Lord would take up Elijah.* It appears that God had revealed this intended translation, not only to Elijah himself, but also to Elisha, and to the schools of the prophets, at both Bethel and Jericho, so that they were all expecting this solemn event.

2. *Tarry here, I pray thee.* He either made these requests through humility, not wishing any person to be witness of the honor conferred on him by God, or with the desire to prove the fidelity of Elisha, whether he would continue to follow and serve him.

3. *Knowest thou that the Lord?* Thus we see that it was a matter well-known to all the sons of the prophets.

7. *Fifty men of the sons of the prophets.* They fully expected this extraordinary event, and they could have known it only from Elijah himself, or by a direct revelation from God.

8. *Took his mantle.* "His sheep-skin," says the Septuagint. *They were divided hither and thither.* This was a most astonishing miracle, and could be performed only by the almighty power of God.

9. *A double portion of thy spirit be upon me.* This in reference to the law, Deut. xxi. 17: "He shall acknowledge . . . the firstborn, by giving him a double portion of all that he hath . . . the right of the firstborn is his." Elisha considered himself the only child or firstborn of Elijah, as the disciples of eminent teachers were called their children; so here he claims a double portion of his spiritual influence, any other disciples coming in for a single share only. "Sons of the prophets" means no more than the disciples or scholars of the prophets. The original words *pi shenayim* mean rather "two parts" than double the quantity.

10. *A hard thing.* This is what is not in my power; God alone can give this. Yet *if thou see me . . . taken from thee, it shall be so.* Perhaps this means no more than, "If thou continue with me till I am translated, God will grant this to thee."

11. *A chariot of fire, and horses of fire.* That is, a chariot and horses of the most resplendent glory.

12. *The chariot of Israel and the horsemen thereof.* The Chaldee translates these words thus: "My master, my master! who, by thy intercession, wast of more use to Israel than horses and chariots." This is probably the sense. *And rent them in two pieces.* As a sign of sorrow for having lost so good and glorious a master.

13. *He took . . . the mantle.* The same with which he had been called by Elijah to the prophetic office, and the same by which Elijah divided Jordan. His having the mantle was a proof that he was invested with the authority and influence of his master.

15. *The spirit of Elijah doth rest on Elisha.* This was a natural conclusion, from seeing him with the mantle, and working the same miracle. This disposed them to yield the same obedience to him they had done to his master: and in token of this, they went out "to meet him, and bowed themselves to the ground before him."

16. *Fifty strong men.* Probably the same fifty who are mentioned in v. 7, and who saw Elijah taken up in the whirlwind. *Cast him upon some mountain.* Though they saw him taken up towards heaven, yet they thought it possible that the Spirit of the Lord might have descended with him, and left him on some remote mountain valley. *Ye shall not send.* He knew that he was translated to heaven, and that therefore it would be useless.

17. *Till he was ashamed.* He saw they would not be satisfied unless they made the proposed search; he felt therefore that he could not, with any good grace, resist their importunity any longer.

19. *The water is naught, and the ground*

barren. The barrenness of the ground was the effect of the badness of the water.

21. *And cast the salt in there.* He cast in the salt at the place where the waters sprang out of the earth. Jarchi well observes here, "Salt is a thing which corrupts water; therefore, it is evident that this was a true miracle."

23-24. *There came forth little children out of the city.* These were probably the school of some celebrated teacher; but under his instruction they had learned neither piety nor good manners. *Go up, thou bald head; go up, thou bald head.* Does not this imply the grossest insult? "Ascend, you empty skull, to heaven," as it is pretended your master did! This was blasphemy against God; and their punishment (for they were Bethelite idolaters) was only proportioned to their guilt. Elisha *cursed them,* i.e., pronounced a curse upon them, *in the name of the Lord, beshem Yehovah,* "by the name (or authority) of Jehovah." The spirit of their offense lies in their ridiculing a miracle of the Lord; the offense was against the Lord, and He punished it. It was no petulant humor of the prophet that caused him to pronounce this curse; it was God alone. Had it proceeded from a wrong disposition of the prophet, no miracle would have been wrought in order to gratify it.

"But was it not a cruel thing to destroy forty-two little children, who, in mere childishness, had simply called the prophet bare skull, or bald head?" I answer, Elisha did not destroy them; he had no power by which he could bring two she-bears out of the wood to destroy them. It was evidently either accidental or a divine judgment; and if a judgment, God must be the sole Author of it. Elisha's "curse" must be only declaratory of what God was about to do. "But then, as they were little children, they could scarcely be accountable for their conduct; and consequently, it was cruelty to destroy them." But were they *little children?* for here the strength of the objection lies. Now I suppose the objection means children from four to seven or eight years old, for so we use the word; but the original, *nearim ketannim,* may mean "young men," for *katon* signifies to be "young," in opposition to "old," and is so translated in various places in our Bible; and *naar* signifies not only a "child" but a "young man," a "servant," or even a "soldier," or one fit to go out to battle; and is so translated in a multitude of places in our common English version. Isaac was called *naar* when twenty-eight years old, Gen. xxi. 5-12; and Joseph was so called when he was thirty-nine, Gen. xli. 12. Add to these 1 Kings xx. 14: "And Ahab said, By whom [shall the Assyrians be delivered into my hand]? And he said, Thus saith the Lord, Even by the young men of the princes of the provinces." That these were soldiers, probably militia, or a selection from the militia, which served as a bodyguard to Ahab, the event sufficiently declares; and the persons that mocked Elisha were perfectly accountable for their conduct.

But is it not possible that these forty-two were a set of unlucky young men, who had been employed in the wood, destroying the whelps of these same *she-bears,* who now pursued them, and tore them to pieces, for the injury they had done? We have already heard of the ferocity of "a bear robbed of her whelps"; see at the end of 2 Samuel, chap. xvii. The mention of *she-bears* gives some color to the above conjecture; and, probably, at the time when these young fellows insulted the prophet, the bears might be tracing the footsteps of the murderers of their young, and thus came upon them in the midst of their insults, God's providence ordering these occurrences so as to make this natural effect appear as a divine cause.

CHAPTER 3

The reign and idolatry of Jehoram, king of Israel, 1-3. Mesha, king of Moab, rebels against Israel, 4-5. Jehoram, Jehoshaphat, and the king of Edom join against the Moabites, and are brought into great distress for want of water, 6-10. The three kings go to Elisha to inquire of the Lord; who promises them water, and a complete victory, 11-19. Water comes the next morning, and fills the trenches which these kings had made in the valley, 20. The Moabites arm against them; and suppose, when they see the sun shining upon the waters, which look like blood, that the confederate kings have fallen out, and slain each other; and that they have nothing to do but take the spoil, 21-23. The Israelites attack and completely rout them, beat down their cities, and mar their land, 24-25. The king of Moab, having made an unsuccessful attack on the king of Edom, takes his eldest son, and offers him for a burnt offering upon the wall; and there is great indignation against Israel, 26-27.

2. *He put away the image of Baal.* He abolished his worship; but he continued that of the calves at Dan and Bethel.

4. *Was a sheepmaster.* The original is *naked,* of which the Septuagint could make nothing, and therefore retained the Hebrew word; but the Chaldee has "a sheepmaster." The original signifies one who "marks" or "brands," probably from the marking of sheep. He fed many sheep and had them all marked in a particular way, in order to ascertain his property. *An hundred thousand lambs.* The Chaldee and Arabic have "a hundred thousand fat oxen."

7. *My people as thy people.* We find that Jehoshaphat maintained the same friendly intercourse with the son as he did with the father. See 1 Kings xxii. 4.

8. *Through the wilderness of Edom.* Because he expected the king of Edom to join them, as we find he did; for, being tributary to Judah, he was obliged to do it.

9. *A compass of seven days' journey.* By taking a circuitous route, to go round the southern part of the Dead Sea, they probably intended to surprise the Moabites; but it appears their journey was ill-planned, as they at last got into a country in which it was impossible to obtain water, and they were brought in consequence to the utmost extremity.

10. *The Lord hath called these three kings together.* That is, This is a divine judgment; God has judicially blinded us, and permitted us to take this journey to our destruction.

11. *Is there not here a prophet of the Lord.* The kings of Judah still acknowledged the true God, and Him only. *Poured water on the hands of Elijah.* That is, was his constant and confidential servant.

12. *The word of the Lord is with him.* He has the gift of prophecy.

13. *Get thee to the prophets of thy father.* This was a just but cutting reproof.

14. *Were it not that I regard the presence of Jehoshaphat.* He worshipped the true God; Jehoram was an idolater.

15. *Bring me a minstrel.* A person who played on the harp. To be able to discern the voice of God, and the operation of His hand, it is necessary that the mind be calm, and the passions all in harmony, under the direction of reason, that reason may be under the influence of the Divine Spirit. *The hand of the Lord came upon him.* The playing of the harper had the desired effect; his mind was calmed, and the power of God descended upon him.

16. *Make this valley full of ditches.* The word *nachal* may be translated "brook," as it is by the Vulgate and Septuagint. There probably was a river here, but it was now dry; and the prophet desires that they would enlarge the channel, and cut out various canals from it, and reservoirs, where water might be collected for the refreshment of the army and of the cattle; and these were to be made so wide that the reflection of the sun's rays from this water might be the means of confounding and destroying the Moabites.

17. *Ye shall not see wind.* There shall be no wind to collect vapors, and there shall be no showers, and yet the whole bed of this river, and all the new-made canals, shall be filled with water.

19. *Shall fell every good tree.* Every tree by which your enemies may serve themselves for fortifications. But surely fruit trees are not intended here; for this was positively against the law of God, Deut. xx. 19-20. *Stop all wells of water.* In those hot countries this would lead sooner than anything else to reduce an enemy. *Mar every good piece of land with stones.* Such a multitude of men, each throwing a stone on a good field as they passed, would completely destroy it.

20. *When the meat offering was offered.* This was the first of all offerings, and was generally made at sunrising. *There came water.* This supply was altogether miraculous, for there was neither wind nor rain, nor any other natural means by which it could be supplied.

22. *Saw the water on the other side as red as blood.* This might have been an optical deception.

23. *Therefore, Moab, to the spoil.* Thus they came on in a disorderly manner, and fell an easy prey to their enemies.

25. *On every good piece of land.* On all cultivated ground, and especially fields that were sown. *Only in Kir-haraseth.* This was the royal city of the Moabites, and, as we learn from Scripture, exceedingly strong (see Isa. xvi. 7, 11), so that it is probable the confederate armies could not easily reduce it. The *slingers*, we are informed, went about the wall, and smote all the men that appeared on it, while no doubt the besieging army was employed in sapping the foundations.

26. *Seven hundred men.* These were no doubt the choice of all his troops, and being afraid of being hemmed up and perhaps taken by his enemies, whom he found on the eve of gaining possession of the city, he made a desperate sortie in order to regain the open country; and supposing that the quarter of the Edomites was weakest, or less carefully guarded, he endeavored to make his impression

there; but they were so warmly received by the king of Edom that they failed in the attempt, and were driven back into the city. Hence he was led to that desperate act mentioned in the following verse.

CHAPTER 4

A widow of one of the prophets, oppressed by a merciless creditor, applies to Elisha, who multiplies her oil; by a part of which she pays her debt, and subsists on the rest, 1-7. His entertainment at the house of a respectable woman in Shunem, 8-10. He foretells to his hostess the birth of a son, 11-17. After some years the child dies, and the mother goes to Elisha at Carmel; he comes to Shunem, and raises the child to life, 18-37. He comes to Gilgal, and prevents the sons of the prophets from being poisoned by wild gourds, 38-41. He multiplies a scanty provision, so as to make it sufficient to feed 100 men, 42-44.

1. *Sons of the prophets.* "Disciples of the prophets"; so the Targum here, and in all other places where the words occur, and properly too. *To take unto him my two sons to be bondmen.* Children, according to the laws of the Hebrews, were considered the property of their parents, who had a right to dispose of them for the payment of their debts. And in cases of poverty, the law permitted them, expressly, to sell both themselves and their children; Exod. xxi. 7 and Lev. xxv. 39.

2. *Save a pot of oil.* Oil was used as aliment, for anointing the body after bathing, and to anoint the dead. Some think that this pot of oil was what this widow had kept for her burial (see Matt. xxvi. 12).

6. *And the oil stayed.* While there was a vessel to fill, there was oil sufficient; and it ceased to flow only when there was no vessel to receive it. This is a good emblem of the grace of God. While there is an empty, longing heart, there is a continual overflowing fountain of salvation. If we find in any place or at any time that the oil ceases to flow, it is because there are no empty vessels there, no souls hungering and thirsting for righteousness. We find fault with the dispensations of God's mercy, and ask, Why were the former days better than these? Were we as much in earnest for our salvation as our forefathers were for theirs, we should have equal supplies, and as much reason to sing aloud of divine mercy.

8. *Elisha passed to Shunem.* This city was in the tribe of Issachar, to the south of the brook Kishon, and at the foot of Mount Tabor. *Where was a great woman.* Instead of *great woman*, the Chaldee has "a woman fearing sin"; the Arabic, "a woman eminent for piety before God." This made her truly great.

9. *This is an holy man of God.* That is, "a prophet," as the Chaldee interprets it. *Which passeth by us continually.* It probably lay in his way to some school of the prophets that he usually attended.

10. *Let us make a little chamber.* As the woman was convinced that Elisha was a prophet, she knew that he must have need of more privacy than the general state of her house could afford; and therefore she proposed what she knew would be a great acquisition to him, as he could live in this little chamber in as much privacy as if he were in his own house. The *bed*, the *table*, the *stool*, and the *candlestick* were really everything he could need by way of accommodation in such circumstances.

12. *Gehazi his servant.* This is the first time we hear of this very indifferent character.

13. *Wouldest thou be spoken for to the king?* Elisha must have had considerable influence with the king, from the part he took in the late war with the Moabites. *Or to the captain of the host?* As if he had said, Will you that I should procure you and your husband a place at court? *I dwell among mine own people.* I am perfectly satisfied and contented with my lot in life; I live on the best terms with my neighbors, and am here encompassed with my kindred, and feel no disposition to change my connections or place of abode. How few are there like this woman on the earth! How few are there that will not sacrifice everything—peace, domestic comfort, their friends, their conscience, and their God—for money, honors, grandeur, and parade?

14. *What then is to be done for her?* It seems that the woman retired as soon as she had delivered the answer mentioned in the preceding verse.

16. *Thou shalt embrace a son.* This promise, and the circumstances of the parties, are not very dissimilar to that relative to the birth of Isaac, and those of Abraham and Sarah.

18. *When the child was grown.* We know not of what age he was, very likely four or six, if not more years.

19. *My head, my head.* Probably affected by sunstroke, which might, in so young a subject, soon occasion death, especially in that hot country.

21. *Laid him on the bed of the man of God.* She had no doubt heard that Elijah had raised the widow's son of Zarephath to life, and she believed that he who had obtained this gift from God for her could obtain his restoration to life.

23. *Wherefore wilt thou go?* She was a very prudent woman; she would not harass the feelings of her husband by informing him of the death of his son till she had tried the power of the prophet.

24. *Drive, and go forward.* It is customary in the East for a servant to walk alongside or drive the ass his master rides.

26. *It is well.* How strong was her faith in God and submission to His authority! Though the heaviest family affliction that could befall her and her husband had now taken place, yet, believing that it was a dispensation of Providence which was in itself neither unwise nor unkind, she said, "It is well with me, with my husband, and with my child."

27. *The Lord hath hid it from me, and hath not told me.* In reference to this point he had not now the discernment of spirits. This, and the gift of prophecy, were influences which God gave and suspended as His infinite wisdom saw good.

28. *Did I desire a son of my lord?* I expressed no such wish to you; I was contented and happy; and when you did promise me a son, *did I not say, Do not deceive me?*

29. *Salute him not.* Make all the haste you possibly can, and lay my staff on the face of the child. He probably thought that it might be a case of mere suspended animation or a

swoon, and that laying the staff on the face of the child might act as a stimulus to excite the animal motions.

30. *I will not leave thee.* The prophet it seems had no design to accompany her; he intended to wait for Gehazi's return. But as the woman was well assured the child was dead, she was determined not to return till she brought the prophet with her.

33. *Prayed unto the Lord.* He had no power of his own by which he could restore the child.

34. *Lay upon the child.* Endeavored to convey a portion of his own natural warmth to the body of the child; and probably endeavored, by blowing into the child's mouth, to inflate the lungs and restore respiration. He uses every natural means in his power to restore life, while praying to the Author of it to exert a miraculous influence. Natural means are in our power; those that are supernatural belong to God. We should always do our own work, and beg of God to do His.

35. *Walked in the house to and fro.* In order, no doubt, that he might recover that natural warmth which was absorbed by the cold body of the child, that he might, by again taking it in his arms, communicate more warmth. *The child sneezed seven times.* That is, it sneezed "abundantly." When the nervous influence began to act on the muscular system, before the circulation could be in every part restored, particular muscles, if not the whole body, would be thrown into strong contractions and shiverings, and sneezing would be a natural consequence.

37. *She went in, and fell at his feet.* Few can enter into the feelings of this noble woman. What suspense must she have felt during the time that the prophet was employed in the slow process referred to above! for slow in its own nature it must have been, and exceedingly exhausting to the prophet himself.

38. *Came again to Gilgal.* He had been there before with his master, a short time prior to his translation. *Set on the great pot, and seethe pottage for the sons of the prophets.* It was in a time of dearth, and all might now stand in need of refreshment; and it appears that the prophet was led to put forth the power he had from God to make a plentiful provision for those who were present.

40. *There is death in the pot.* As if they had said, "We have here a deadly mixture; if we eat of it, we shall all die."

41. *Bring meal.* Though this might, in some measure, correct the strong acrid and purgative quality, yet it was only a miracle which could make a lapful of this fruit shred into pottage salutary.

42. *Bread of the firstfruits.* This was an offering to the prophet, as the firstfruits themselves were an offering to God. *Corn in the husk.* Probably parched corn or corn to be parched, a very frequent food in the East.

43. *Thus saith the Lord, They shall eat, and shall leave thereof.* It was God, not the prophet, who fed 100 men with these 20 loaves, etc. This is something like our Lord's feeding the multitude miraculously. Indeed, there are many things in this chapter similar to facts in our Lord's history.

CHAPTER 5

The history of Naaman, captain of the host of the king of Syria, a leper; who was informed by a little Israelitish captive maid that a prophet of the Lord, in Samaria, could cure him, 1-4. The king of Syria sends him, with a letter and rich presents, to the king of Israel, that he should recover him of his leprosy, 5-6. On receiving the letter, the king of Israel is greatly distressed, supposing that the Syrian king designed to seek a quarrel with him; in desiring him to cleanse a leper, when it was well-known that none could cure that disorder but God, 7. Elisha, hearing this, orders Naaman to be sent to him, 8. He comes to Elisha's house in great state, 9. And the prophet sends a messenger to him, ordering him to wash in Jordan seven times, and he should be made clean, 10. Naaman is displeased that he is received with so little ceremony, and departs in a rage, 11-12. His servants reason with him; he is persuaded, goes to Jordan, washes, and is made clean, 13-14. He returns to Elisha; acknowledges the true God; and offers him a present, which the prophet refuses, 15-16. He asks directions, promises never to sacrifice to any other god, and is dismissed, 17-19. Gehazi runs after him, pretends he is sent by his master for a talent of silver and two changes of raiment; which he receives, brings home, and hides, 20-24. Elisha questions him; convicts him of his wickedness; pronounces a curse of leprosy upon him, with which he is immediately afflicted; and departs from his master a leper, as white as snow, 25-27.

1. *Naaman, captain of the host.* Of Naaman we know nothing more than is related here. *King of Syria.* The Hebrew is *melech Aram,* "king of Aram," which is followed by the Chaldee and Arabic. The Septuagint and Vulgate have "Syria," and this is a common meaning of the term in Scripture. If the king of Syria be meant, it must be Ben-hadad; and the contemporary king of Israel was Jehoram. *A mighty man in valour.* "He was a giant, and very strong," according to the Arabic. He had, in a word, all the qualifications of an able general. *But he was a leper.* Here was a heavy tax upon his grandeur; he was afflicted with a disorder the most loathsome and the most humiliating that could possibly disgrace a human being.

2. *The Syrians had gone out by companies.* "Troops." *A little maid.* Who, it appears, had pious parents, who brought her up in the knowledge of the true God. Behold the goodness and the severity of the divine providence! Affectionate parents are deprived of their promising daughter by a set of lawless freebooters, without the smallest prospect that she should have any lot in life but that of misery, infamy, and woe. *Waited on Naaman's wife.* Her decent, orderly behavior, the consequence of her sober and pious education, entitled her to this place of distinction; in which her servitude was at least easy, and her person safe. If God permitted the parents to be deprived of their pious child by the hands of ruffians, He did not permit the child to be without a guardian.

3. *Would God my lord.* "I wish"; or, as the Chaldee, Syriac, or Arabic have, "Happy would it be for my master if he were with the prophet." Here the mystery of the divine providence begins to develop itself. By the captivity of this little maid one Syrian family at least, and that one of the most considerable in the Syrian empire, is brought to the knowledge of the true God.

5. *The king of Syria said.* He judged it the best mode of proceeding to send immediately to the king, under whose control he supposed the prophet must be, that he would order the prophet to cure his general.

7. *Am I God, to kill and to make alive?* He spoke thus under the conviction that God alone could cure the leprosy; which, indeed, was universally acknowledged.

8. *Let him come now to me.* Do not be afflicted; the matter belongs to me, as the prophet of the Most High. Send him to me, and he shall know that I am such.

9. *Came with his horses and with his chariot.* In very great pomp and state. Closely inspected, this was preposterous enough; a leper sitting in state, and affecting it!

10. *Sent a messenger.* Did not come out to speak with him; he had got his orders from God, and he transmitted them to Naaman by his servant. *Wash in Jordan seven times.* The waters of Jordan had no tendency to remove this disorder, but God chose to make them the means by which He would convey His healing power.

11. *Naaman was wroth.* And why? Because the prophet treated him without ceremony, and because he appointed him an expenseless and simple mode of cure. *Behold, I thought.* God's ways are not as our ways; He appoints that mode of cure which He knows to be best. Naaman expected to be treated with great ceremony; and instead of humbling himself before the Lord's prophet, he expected the prophet of the Lord to humble himself before him! *Behold, I thought*—and what did he think? Hear his words, for they are all very emphatic: (1) *I thought, He will surely come out to me.* He will never make his servant the medium of communication between me and himself. (2) *And stand*—present himself before me, and stand as a servant to hear the orders of his God. (3) *And call on the name of the Lord his God,* so that both his God and himself shall appear to do me service and honor. (4) *And strike his hand over the place;* for can it be supposed that any healing virtue can be conveyed without contact?

13. *My father.* A title of the highest respect and affection. *Had bid thee do some great thing.* If the prophet had appointed you to do something very difficult in itself, and very expensive to you, would you not have done it? With much greater reason should you do what will occupy little time, be no expense, and is easy to be performed.

14. *Then went he down.* He felt the force of this reasoning, and made a trial, probably expecting little success.

15. *He returned to the man of God.* He saw that the hand of the Lord was upon him; he felt gratitude for his cleansing; and came back to acknowledge, in the most public way, his obligation to God and His servant. *Stood before him.* He was now truly humbled, and left all his state behind him. *Take a blessing.* Accept a present.

16. *I will receive none.* It was very common to give presents to all great and official men; and among these, prophets were always included. But as it might have appeared to the Syrians that he had taken the offered presents as a remuneration for the cure performed, he refused; for as God alone did the work, He alone should have all the glory.

17. *Shall there not then, I pray thee?* This verse is understood two different ways. I will give them both in a paraphrase: (1) "Shall there not then be given unto thy servant [viz., Naaman] two mules' burden of this Israelitish earth, that I may build an altar with it, on

which I may offer sacrifices to the God of Israel?" (2) "Shall there not be given to thy [Elisha's] servant [Gehazi] two mules' burden of this earth?" i.e., the gold and silver which he brought with him; and which he esteemed as earth, or dust, in comparison of the cure he received.

18. *In this thing the Lord pardon thy servant.* It is useless to enter into the controversy concerning this verse. By no rule of right reasoning, nor by any legitimate mode of interpretation, can it be stated that Naaman is asking pardon for offenses which he may commit, or that he could ask or the prophet grant indulgence to bow himself in the temple of Rimmon, thus performing a decided act of homage, the very essence of that worship which immediately before he solemnly assured the prophet he would never practice. The original may legitimately be read, and ought to be read, in the past, and not in the future tense. "For this thing the Lord pardon thy servant, for that when my master hath gone into the house of Rimmon to worship there, and he hath leaned upon mine hand, that I also have bowed myself in the house of Rimmon; for my worshipping in the house of Rimmon, the Lord pardon thy servant in this thing." This is the translation of Lightfoot, the most able Hebraist of his time in Christendom.

20. *My master hath spared . . . this Syrian.* He has neither taken anything from him for himself, nor permitted him to give anything to me.

21. *He lighted down from the chariot.* He treats even the prophet's servant with the profoundest respect, alights from his chariot, and goes to meet him. *Is all well? Hashalom;* "Is it peace (or prosperity)?"

22. *And he said. Shalom.* "It is peace"; all is right. This was a common mode of address and answer. *There be come to me from mount Ephraim.* There was probably a school of the prophets at this mount.

23. *He . . . bound two talents of silver.* It required two servants to carry these two talents, for, according to the computation above, each talent was about 120 pounds in weight.

24. *When he came to the tower.* The Chaldee, Septuagint, Syriac, and Arabic understand the word *ophel,* which we translate *tower,* as signifying a secret, dark, or hiding place.

26. *Went not mine heart with thee?* The Chaldee gives this a good turn: "By the prophetic spirit it was shown unto me, when the man returned from his chariot to meet thee." *Is it a time to receive money?* He gave him further proof of this all-discerning prophetic spirit in telling him what he designed to do with the money; he intended to set up a splendid establishment, to have *menservants* and *maidservants,* to have *oliveyards* and *vineyards,* and *sheep* and *oxen.*

27. *The leprosy . . . of Naaman shall cleave unto thee.* You have received much money, and you shall have much to do with it. You have received Naaman's silver, and you shall have Naaman's leprosy. Gehazi is not the last who has received money in an unlawful way, and has received God's curse with it. *A leper as white as snow.* The moment the curse was pronounced, that moment the signs of the leprosy began to appear. The white shining spot was the sign that the infection had taken place (see Lev. xiii. 2).

CHAPTER 6

The sons of the prophets wish to enlarge their dwelling place, and go to the banks of Jordan to cut down wood, when one of them drops his axe into the water, which Elisha causes to swim, 1-7. Elisha, understanding all the secret designs of the king of Syria against Israel, informs the king of Israel of them, 8-10. The king of Syria, finding that Elisha had thus penetrated his secrets and frustrated his attempts, sends a great host to Dothan, to take the prophet; the Lord strikes them with blindness; and Elisha leads the whole host to Samaria, and delivers them up to the king of Israel, 11-19. The Lord opens their eyes, and they see their danger, 20. But the king of Israel is prevented from destroying them; and, at the order of the prophet, gives them meat and drink, and dismisses them to their master, 21-23. Ben-hadad besieges Samaria, and reduces the city to great distress, of which several instances are given, 24-30. The king of Israel vows the destruction of Elisha, and sends to have him beheaded, 31-33.

1. *The place . . . is too strait for us.* Notwithstanding the general profligacy of Israel, the schools of the prophets increased. This was no doubt owing to the influence of Elisha.

2. *Every man a beam.* They made a sort of log houses with their own hands.

5. *Alas, master! for it was borrowed.* "Ah! ah, my master; and it has been sought." It has fallen in, and I have sought it in vain. Or, "it was borrowed," and therefore I am the more afflicted for its loss.

6. *He cut down a stick.* This had no natural tendency to raise the iron; it was only a sign or ceremony which the prophet chose to use on the occasion. *The iron did swim.* This was a real miracle.

8. *The king of Syria warred against Israel.* This was probably the same Ben-hadad who is mentioned in v. 24. *In such and such a place.* The Syrian king had observed, from the disposition of the Israelitish army, in what direction it was about to make its movements; and therefore laid ambuscades where he might surprise it to the greatest advantage.

9. *Beware that thou pass not such a place.* Elisha must have had this information by immediate revelation from heaven.

10. *Sent to the place.* To see if it were so. But the Vulgate gives it quite a different turn: "The king of Israel sent previously to the place, and took possession of it"; and thus the Syrians were disappointed. This is very likely, though it is not expressed in the Hebrew text.

13. *Behold, he is in Dothan.* This is supposed to be the same place as that mentioned in Gen. xxxvii. 17. It lay about twelve miles from Samaria.

14. *He sent thither horses.* It is strange he did not think that he who could penetrate his secrets with respect to the Israelitish army could inform himself of all his machinations against his own life.

16. *For they that be with us are more.* What astonishing intercourse had this man with heaven! It seems the whole heavenly host had it in commission to help him.

18. *Smite this people . . . with blindness.* Confound their sight so that they may not know what they see, and so mistake one place for another.

19. *I will bring you to the man whom ye seek.* And he did so; he was their guide to

Samaria, and showed himself to them fully in that city.

20. *Open the eyes of these men.* Take away their confusion of vision, that they may discern things as they are, and distinguish where they are.

21. *My father, shall I smite?* This was dastardly; the utmost he could have done with these men, when thus brought into his hand, was to make them prisoners of war.

22. *Whom thou hast taken captive.* Those who in open battle either lay down their arms, or are surrounded, and have their retreat cut off, are entitled to their lives, much more those who are thus providentially put into your hand, without having been in actual hostility against you. Give them meat and drink, and send them home to their master, and let them thus know that you fear him not, and are incapable of doing an ungenerous or unmanly action.

23. *He prepared great provision for them.* These, on the return to their master, could tell him strange things about the power of the God of Israel, and the magnanimity of its king. *So the bands of Syria came no more.* Marauding parties were no more permitted by the Syrian king to make inroads upon Israel. And it is very likely that for some considerable time after this there was no war between these two nations. What is mentioned in the next verse was more than a year afterwards.

25. *And, behold, they besieged it.* They had closed it in on every side, and reduced it to the greatest necessity. *And the fourth part of a cab of dove's dung.* The *cab* was about a quart or three pints. *Dove's dung.* Whether this means pigeon's dung literally or a kind of pulse has been variously disputed by learned men. It is probable a sort of peas are meant, which the Arabs to this day call by this name.

27. *If the Lord do not help thee.* Some read this as an imprecation, "May God save thee not! how can I save thee?"

29. *So we boiled my son.* This very evil Moses had foretold should come upon them if they forsook God (see Deut. xxviii. 53, 57). The same evil came upon this wretched people when besieged by Nebuchadnezzar (see Ezek. v. 10). And also when Titus besieged Jerusalem (see Josephus, De Bell. Judaic., lib. vi, cap. 3).

30. *He had sackcloth within upon his flesh.* The king was in deep mourning for the distresses of the people.

31. *If the head of Elisha . . . shall stand on him.* Either he attributed these calamities to the prophet, or else he thought he could remove them and yet would not.

32. *This son of a murderer.* Jehoram, the son of Ahab and Jezebel. Ahab is called a *murderer* because of the murder of Naboth. *Shut the door.* He was obliged to make use of this method for his personal safety, as the king was highly incensed. *The sound of his master's feet behind him.* That is, King Jehoram is following his messenger, that he may see him take off my head.

33. *Behold, this evil is of the Lord.* It is difficult to know whether it be the prophet, the messenger, or the king that says these words. It might be the answer of the prophet from within to the messenger who was without,

and who sought for admission, and gave his reason; to whom Elisha might have replied: "I am not the cause of these calamities; they are from the Lord; I have been praying for their removal; but why should I pray to the Lord any longer, for the time of your deliverance is at hand?" And *then* Elisha said—see the following chapter, where the removal of the calamity is foretold in the most explicit manner; and indeed the chapter is unhappily divided from this. The seventh chapter should have begun with v. 24 of this chapter, as by the present division the story is unnaturally interrupted.

CHAPTER 7

Elisha foretells abundant relief to the besieged inhabitants of Samaria, 1. One of the lords questions the possibility of it; and is assured that he shall see it on the morrow, but not taste of it, 2. Four lepers, perishing with hunger, go to the camp of the Syrians to seek relief, and find it totally deserted, 3-5. How the Syrians were alarmed, and fled, 6-7. The lepers begin to take the spoil, but at last resolve to carry the good news to the city, 8-11. The king, suspecting some treachery, sends some horsemen to scour the country, and see whether the Syrians are not somewhere concealed; they return, and confirm the report that the Syrians are totally fled, 12-15. The people go out and spoil the camp, in consequence of which provisions become as plentiful as Elisha had foretold, 16. The unbelieving lord, having the charge of the gate committed to him, is trodden to death by the crowd, 17-20.

1. *To morrow about this time.* This was in reply to the desponding language of the king, and to vindicate himself from the charge of being author of this calamity. See the end of the preceding chapter. *A measure of fine flour . . . for a shekel.* A *seah* of fine flour. The *seah* was about two gallons and a half; the *shekel,* two shillings and fourpence at the lowest computation. A wide difference between this and the price of the ass's head mentioned above!

2. *Then a lord.* Shalish. This word as a name of office occurs often, and seems to point out one of the highest offices in the state. So unlikely was this prediction to be fulfilled that he thought God must pour out wheat and barley from heaven before it could have a literal accomplishment. *But shalt not eat thereof.* This was a mere prediction of his death, but not as a judgment for his unbelief; any person in his circumstances might have spoken as he did.

5. *The uttermost part of the camp.* Where the Syrian advanced guards should have been.

6. *The Lord had made the . . . Syrians to hear a noise.* This threw them into confusion; they imagined that they were about to be attacked by powerful auxiliaries, which the king of Israel had hired against them.

13. *And one of his servants answered.* This is a very difficult verse, and the great variety of explanations given of it cast but little light on the subject. I am inclined to believe, with Kennicott, that there is an interpolation here which puzzles, if not destroys, the sense. "Several instances," says he, "have been given of words improperly repeated by Jewish transcribers, who have been careless enough to make such mistakes, and yet cautious not to alter or erase, for fear of discovery. This verse furnishes another instance in a careless repetition of seven Hebrew words. The exact English of this verse is this: And the servant said, Let

them take now five of the remaining horses, which remain in it; behold they are as all the multitude of Israel which remain in it; behold, they are as all the multitude of Israel which are consumed; and let us send and see. Whoever considers that the second set of these seven words is neither in the Septuagint nor Syriac versions, and that those translators who suppose these words to be genuine alter them to make them look like sense, will probably allow them to have been at first an improper repetition; consequently to be now an interpolation strangely continued in the Hebrew text."

That are consumed. The words should be translated, "which are perfect"; i.e., fit for service. The rest of the horses were either dead of the famine, killed for the subsistence of the besieged, or so weak as not to be able to perform such a journey.

14. *They took . . . two chariot horses.* They had at first intended to send five; probably they found on examination that only two were effective.

15. *All the way was full of garments and vessels.* A manifest proof of the hurry and precipitancy with which they fled.

17. *And the people trode upon him.* This officer being appointed by the king to have the command of the *gate*, the people rushing out to get spoil, and to carry it to their houses, he was borne down by the multitude, and trodden to death.

CHAPTER 8

Account of the sojourning of the Shunammite in the land of the Philistines, during the seven years' famine, 1-2. She returns, and solicits the king to let her have back her land; which, with its fruits, he orders to be restored to her, 3-6. Elisha comes to Damascus, and finds Ben-hadad sick; who sends his servant Hazael to the prophet to inquire whether he shall recover, 7-9. Elisha predicts his death, tells Hazael he shall be king, and shows him the atrocities he will commit, 10-14. Hazael returns, stifles his master with a wet cloth, and reigns in his stead, 15. Jehoram, son of Jehoshaphat, becomes king over Judah; his bad reign, 16-19. Edom and Libnah revolt, 20-22. Jehoram dies, and his son Ahaziah reigns in his stead, 23-24. His bad reign, 25-27. He joins with Joram, son of Ahab, against Hazael; Joram is wounded by the Syrians, and goes to Jezreel to be healed, 28-29.

1. *Then spake Elisha.* As this is the relation of an event far past, the words should be translated, "But Elisha *had* spoken unto the woman whose son he *had* restored unto life; and the woman *had* arisen, and acted according to the saying of the man of God, and *had* gone with her family, and *had* sojourned in the land of the Philistines seven years." What is mentioned in these two verses happened several years before the time specified in the third verse.

5. *This is the woman, and this is her son, whom Elisha restored to life.* This was a very providential occurrence in behalf of the Shunammite. The relation given by Gehazi was now corroborated by the woman herself; the king was duly affected, and gave immediate orders for the restoration of her land.

8. *Take a present in thine hand.* But what an immense present was this—forty camels' burden of every good thing of Damascus.

10. *Thou mayest certainly recover: howbeit the Lord hath shewed me that he shall surely die.* That is, God has not determined your death, nor will it be a necessary consequence of the disease by which you are now afflicted;

but this wicked man will abuse the power and trust you have reposed in him, and take away your life.

11. *He settled his countenance stedfastly.* Of whom does the author speak? Of Hazael, or of Elisha? Several apply this action to the prophet. He had a murderer before him, and he saw the bloody acts he was about to commit, and was greatly distressed; but he endeavored to conceal his feelings. At last his face reddened with anguish, his feelings overcame him, and he burst out and wept. The Septuagint, as it stands in the Complutensian and Antwerp Polyglots, makes the text very plain: "And Hazael stood before his face, and he presented before him gifts till he was ashamed; and the man of God wept." The Codex Vaticanus and the Codex Alexandrinus are nearly as the Hebrew. All the versions follow the Hebrew.

12. *I know the evil that thou wilt do.* We may see something of the accomplishment of this prediction, chap. x. 32-33 and xiii. 3, 7.

13. *But what, is thy servant a dog, that he should do this great thing?* I believe this verse to be wrongly interpreted by the general run of commentators. It is generally understood that Hazael was struck with horror at the prediction; that these cruelties were most alien from his mind; that he then felt distressed and offended at the imputation of such evils to him; and yet so little did he know his own heart that when he got power, and had opportunity, he did the whole with a willing heart and a ready hand. On the contrary, I think he was delighted at the prospect; and his question rather implies a doubt whether a person so inconsiderable as he is shall ever have it in his power to do such great, not such evil things. The Hebrew text stands thus: "But, what! thy servant, this dog! that he should do this great work!" Or, "Can such a poor, worthless fellow, such a dead dog, perform such mighty actions? thou fillest me with surprise." And that this is the true sense, his immediate murder of his master on his return fully proves.

15. *A thick cloth.* The versions, in general, understand this of a hairy or woolen cloth. *So that he died.* He was smothered, or suffocated.

16. *In the fifth year of Joram.* The three Hebrew words, "and of Jehoshaphat king of Judah," greatly disturb the chronology in this place. It is certain that Jehoshaphat reigned twenty-five years, and that Jehoram, his son, reigned but eight; 1 Kings xxii. 42; 2 Kings viii. 17; 2 Chron. xx. 31 and xxi. 5. So that he could not have reigned during his father's life without being king twenty years, and eight years! These words are wanting in three of Kennicott's and De Rossi's MSS., in the Complutensian and Aldine editions of the Septuagint, in the Peshito Syriac, in the Arabic, and in many copies of the Vulgate.

17. *He reigned eight years in Jerusalem.* Beginning with the fifth year of Joram, king of Israel. He reigned three years with Jehoshaphat, his father, and five years alone.

18. *The daughter of Ahab was his wife.* This was the infamous Athaliah, and through this marriage Jehoshaphat and Ahab were confederates; and this friendship was continued after Ahab's death.

19. *To give him alway a light.* To give him a successor in his own family.

21. *Joram went over to Zair.* This is the same as Seir, a chief city of Idumea. So Isa. xxi. 11: "The burden of Dumah [Idumea]. He calleth to me out of Seir." *Smote the Edomites.* It appears that the Israelites were surrounded by the Idumeans; and that in the night Joram and his men cut their way through them, and so got every man to his tent, for they were not able to make any further head against these enemies; and therefore it is said, that "Edom revolted from under the hand of Judah unto this day."

23. *Are they not written in the book of the chronicles.* Several remarkable particulars relative to Joram may be found in 2 Chronicles xxi.

26. *Two and twenty years old was Ahaziah when he began to reign.* In 2 Chron. xxii. 2, it is said, "Forty and two years old was Ahaziah when he began to reign"; this is a heavy difficulty, to remove which several expedients have been used. It is most evident that, if we follow the reading in Chronicles, it makes the son two years older than his own father! for his father began to reign when he was thirty-two years old, and reigned eight years, and so died, being forty years old (see v. 17).

After all, here is a most manifest contradiction that cannot be removed but by having recourse to violent modes of solution. I am satisfied the reading in 2 Chron. xxii. 2 is a mistake; and that we should read there, as here, "twenty-two" instead of "forty-two" years. And may we not say with Calmet, Which is most dangerous, to acknowledge that transcribers have made some mistakes in copying the sacred books, or to acknowledge that there are contradictions in them, and then to have recourse to solutions that can yield no satisfaction to any unprejudiced mind?

28. *The Syrians wounded Joram.* Ahaziah went with Joram to endeavor to wrest Ramoth-gilead out of the hands of the Syrians, which belonged to Israel and Judah. Ahab had endeavored to do this before, and was slain there (see 1 Kings xxii. 3, etc.).

29. *Went back to be healed in Jezreel.* And there he continued till Jehu conspired against and slew him there. And thus the blood of the innocents, which had been shed by Ahab and his wife, Jezebel, was visited on them in the total extinction of their family. See the following chapters, where the bloody tale of Jehu's conspiracy is told at large.

CHAPTER 9

Elisha sends one of the disciples of the prophets to Ramoth-gilead, to anoint Jehu king of Israel, 1-3. He acts according to his orders, and informs Jehu that he is to cut off the whole house of Ahab, 4-10. Jehu's captains proclaim him king, 11-15. He goes against Jezreel; where he finds Joram and Ahaziah, king of Judah, who had come to visit him; he slays them both. The former is thrown into the portion of Naboth; the latter, having received a mortal wound, flees to Megiddo, and dies there, and is carried to Jerusalem, and buried in the city of David, 15-29. He commands Jezebel to be thrown out of her window; and she is trodden under the feet of his horses; and the dogs eat her, according to the word of the Lord, 30-37.

1. *One of the children of the prophets.* The Jews say that this was Jonah, the prophet, the son of Amittai. *Gird up thy loins.* What you have to do requires the utmost dispatch.

4. *The young man the prophet.* This should be translated, "The servant of the prophet"; that is, the servant which Elisha now had in place of Gehazi.

6. *King over the people of the Lord.* This pointed out to Jehu that he was to rule that people according to God's law; and consequently, that he was to restore the pure worship of the Most High in Israel.

7. *Thou shalt smite the house of Ahab.* For their most cruel murders they have forfeited their own lives, according to that immutable law, "He that sheddeth man's blood, by man shall his blood be shed." This and the following two verses contain the commission which Jehu received from the Lord against the bloody house of Ahab.

10. *The dogs shall eat Jezebel.* How most minutely was this prophecy fulfilled (see v. 33, etc.)!

11. *Wherefore came this mad fellow to thee?* Was it because he was a holy man of God that he was reputed by a club of irreligious officers to be a madman? *Ye know the man, and his communication.* You know that he is a madman, and that his message must be a message of folly. Jehu did not appear willing to tell them what had been done, lest it should promote jealousy and envy.

12. *They said, It is false.* Or, as the Chaldee has it, "Thou liest."

13. *Took every man his garment.* This was a ceremony by which they acknowledged him as king; and it was by such a ceremony that the multitudes acknowledged Jesus Christ for the Messiah and King of Israel, a little before His passion (see Matt. xxi. 7). The ceremony was expressive: "As we put our garments under his feet, so we place everything under his authority, and acknowledge ourselves his servants."

On the top of the stairs. The Chaldee, the rabbins, and several interpreters understand this of the public sundial; which, in those ancient times, was formed of steps like stairs, each step serving to indicate, by its shadow, one hour, or such division of time as was commonly used in that country. This dial was, no doubt, in the most public place; and upon the top of it, or on the platform on the top, would be a very proper place to set Jehu, while they blew their trumpets, and proclaimed him king. The Hebrew *maaloth* is the same word which is used in chap. xx. 9-11 to signify the "dial" of Ahaz, and this was probably the very same dial on which that miracle was afterwards wrought.

14. *Joram had kept Ramoth-gilead.* The confederate armies appear to have taken this city; but they were obliged to watch their conquests, as they perceived that Hazael was determined to retake it if possible.

16. *Jehu . . . went to Jezreel; for Joram lay there.* From the preceding verse we learn that Joram had been wounded in his attack on Ramoth-gilead, and had gone to Jezreel to be cured; and neither he nor Ahaziah knew anything of the conspiracy in Ramoth-gilead, because Jehu and his captains took care to prevent any person from leaving the city.

17. *A watchman on the tower.* These watchmen, fixed on elevated places, and generally

within hearing of each other, served as a kind of telegraphs, to communicate intelligence through the whole country. But, in some cases, it appears that the intelligence was conveyed by a horseman to the next stage, as in the case before us. At this time, when the armies were at Ramoth-gilead, they were, no doubt, doubly watchful to observe the state of the country and to notice every movement.

18. *What hast thou to do with peace?* "What is it to thee whether there be peace or war? Join my company, and fall into the rear."

20. *He driveth furiously.* Jehu was a bold, daring, prompt, and precipitate general. In his various military operations he had established his character, and now it was almost proverbial.

21. *Joram . . . and Ahaziah . . . went out.* They had no suspicion of what was done at Ramoth-gilead; else they would not have ventured their persons as they now did.

22. *What peace, so long as the whoredoms?* Though the words whoredom, adultery, and fornication are frequently used to express idolatry and false religion in general, yet here they may be safely taken in their common and most obvious sense, as there is much reason to believe that Jezebel was the patroness and supporter of a very impure system of religion.

23. *There is treachery, O Ahaziah.* This was the first intimation he had of it; he feels for the safety of his friend Ahaziah, and now they fly for their lives.

24. *Drew a bow with his full strength.* The marginal reading is correct: "He filled his hand with a bow." That is, "He immediately took up his bow, set his arrow, and let fly." *Between his arms.* That is, between his shoulders; for he was now turned, and was flying from Jehu.

25. *Cast him in the portion of the field.* This was predicted, 1 Kings xxi; and what now happened to the son of Ahab is foretold in v. 29 of that chapter.

26. *The blood of Naboth, and the blood of his sons.* We are not informed in 1 Kings xxi that any of Naboth's family was slain but himself. But as the object of both Ahab and Jezebel was to have Naboth's vineyard entirely, and forever, it is not likely that they would leave any of his posterity, who might at a future time reclaim it as their inheritance.

27. *Fled by the way of the garden.* The account of the death of Ahaziah, as given in 2 Chron. xxii. 8-9, is: "When Jehu was executing judgment upon the house of Ahab . . . he sought Ahaziah: and they caught him, (for he was hid in Samaria,) and brought him to Jehu: and when they had slain him, they buried him."

29. *In the eleventh year of Joram.* The note in our margin contains as good an account of this chronological difficulty as can be reasonably required: Then he began to reign "as viceroy to his father in his sickness, 2 Chron. xxi 18-19. But in Joram's twelfth year he began to reign alone, chap. viii. 25."

30. *She painted her face, and tired her head.* She endeavored to improve the appearance of her complexion by paint, and the general effect of her countenance by a tiara or turban headdress. Jonathan, the Chaldee Targumist, translates this, "She stained her eyes with *stibium* or *antimony.*"

33. *So they threw her down.* What a terrible death! She was already, by the fall, almost dashed to pieces; and the brutal Jehu trampled her already mangled body under his horses' feet!

34. *She is a king's daughter.* She was daughter of the king of Tyre; wife of Ahab, king of Israel; mother of Joram, king of Israel; mother-in-law of Joram, king of Judah; and grandmother of Ahaziah, king of Judah.

37. *And the carcase of Jezebel shall be as dung.* As it was not buried under the earth, but was eaten by the dogs, this saying was also literally fulfilled. *They shall not say, This is Jezebel.* There was not even a solitary stone to say, "Here lies Jezebel!"

CHAPTER 10

Jehu sends an ironical letter to the elders of Samaria, telling them to choose one of the best of their master's sons, and put him on the throne; to which they return a submissive answer, 1-6. He writes a second letter, and orders them to send him the heads of Ahab's seventy sons; they do so, and they are laid in two heaps at the gate of Jezreel, 7-8. Jehu shows them to the people, and excuses himself, and states that all is done according to the word of the Lord, 9-10. He destroys all the kindred of Ahab that remained in Jezreel, 11. He also destroys forty-two men, the brethren of Ahaziah, king of Judah. 12-14. He meets with Jehonadab, and takes him with him in his chariot, 15-16. He comes to Samaria, and destroys all that were of the kindred of Ahab there, 17. He pretends a great zeal for the worship of Baal, and gathers all his priests together, under the pretense of a grand sacrifice, and slays them all, 18-25. He burns Baal's images, and makes his temple a draughthouse, 26-28. But he does not depart from the sins of Jeroboam, and does not prosper, 29-31. Hazael vexes Israel, 32-33. Jehu dies, having reigned over Israel, in Samaria, twenty-eight years, 34-36.

1. *Ahab had seventy sons.* As he had several wives, he might have many children. *Unto the rulers of Jezreel.* It certainly should be, "unto the rulers of Samaria"; for to them and to that city the whole context shows us the letters were sent (see v. 6). *To them that brought up Ahab's children.* It appears that the royal children of Israel and Judah were entrusted to the care of the nobles, and were brought up by them (see v. 6); and to these, therefore, Jehu's letters are directed. It is supposed Isaiah (xlix. 23) alludes to this custom: "Kings shall be thy nursing fathers, and queens thy nursing mothers."

2. *A fenced city also.* All here seems to refer to Samaria alone; in it were the magazines and implements of war. No reader need be told that these letters were all ironical. It was the same as if he had said, "Ye have no means of defense; Israel is with me. If you yield not up yourselves and the city, I will put you all to the sword."

4. *Two kings stood not before him.* That is, Joram and Ahaziah.

5. *He that was over the house.* Thus all the constituted authorities agreed to submit. *Will do all that thou shalt bid us.* They made no conditions, and stood pledged to commit the horrid murders which this most execrable man afterwards commanded.

6. *Come to me to Jezreel.* Therefore the letters were not written to Jezreel, but from Jezreel to Samaria.

7. *Put their heads in baskets.* What cold-blooded wretches were the whole of these people!

8. *Lay ye them in two heaps.* It appears that the heads of these princes had arrived at Jezreel

in the nighttime. Jehu ordered them to be left at the gate of the city, a place of public resort, that all the people might see them, and be struck with terror, and conclude that all resistance to such authority and power would be vain.

9. *Ye be righteous.* Another irony, intended partly to excuse himself, and to involve them in the odium of this massacre, and at the same time to justify the conduct of both, by showing that all was done according to the commandment of the Lord.

11. *Jehu slew all.* So it appears that the *great men* who had so obsequiously taken off the heads of Ahab's seventy sons fell also a sacrifice to the ambition of this incomparably bad man.

12. *The shearing house.* Probably the place where the shepherds met for the annual sheep shearing.

13. *The brethren of Ahaziah.* The relatives of his family; for it does not appear that he had any brethren, properly so called. But we know that the term brethren among the Jews signified the relatives of the same family, and especially brothers' and sisters' children; and that these were such (see 2 Chron. xxii. 8). *We go down to salute.* So promptly had Jehu executed all his measures that even the nearest relatives of the murdered kings had not heard of their death, and consequently had no time to escape. They were all taken as in a net.

14. *The pit of the shearing house.* Probably the place where they washed the sheep previously to shearing, or the fleeces after they were shorn off.

15. *Jehonadab the son of Rechab.* For particulars concerning this man, his ancestry, and posterity see the notes on Jeremiah xxxv. *Is thine heart right* with me, in the prosecution of a reform in Israel, *as my heart is with thy heart* in the true religion of Jehovah, and the destruction of Baal? *It is.* I wish a reform in the religion of the country; I am his friend who shall endeavor to promote it. *Give me thine hand.* Jehonadab was doubtless a very honorable man in Israel; and by carrying him about with him in his chariot, Jehu endeavored to acquire the public esteem.

18. *Ahab served Baal a little.* Jehu had determined to have no worship in Israel but that of the golden calves at Dan and Bethel; therefore he purposes to destroy all the worshippers of Baal. And that he may do it without suspicion, he proclaims a great sacrifice; and that he may do it the more easily, he gathers them all together into one place.

19. *Whosoever shall be wanting, he shall not live.* Because, as he will thereby show himself without zeal for the service of his God, he will justly forfeit his life. All this was done in the very spirit of deceit.

22. *He said unto him that was over the vestry.* The word *vestry* comes from *vestiarium,* and that from *vestes,* "garments," from *vestio,* "I clothe"; and signifies properly the place where the sacerdotal robes are kept. The priests of Baal had their robes as well as the priests of the Lord, but the garments were such that one could be easily distinguished from the other.

25. *To the guard and to the captains.* To the couriers or runners, and the *shalashim,* the men of the third rank; those officers who were next to the nobles, the king and these being only their superiors. The runners were probably a sort of light infantry. *The city of the house of Baal.* Does not this mean a sort of holy of holies, where the most sacred images of Baal were kept?

27. *Made it a draught house.* A place for human excrement; so all the versions understand it. Nothing could be more degrading than this.

30. *Thy children of the fourth generation.* These four descendants of Jehu were Jehoahaz, Jehoash, Jeroboam II, and Zechariah (see chaps. xiv and xv). This was all the compensation Jehu had in either world, as a recompense of his zeal for the Lord.

31. *Jehu took no heed.* He never made it his study; indeed, he never intended to walk in this way; it suited neither his disposition nor his politics.

32. *The Lord began to cut Israel short.* The marginal reading is best: "The Lord cut off the ends"; and this He did by permitting Hazael to seize on the *coasts,* to conquer and occupy the frontier towns. This was the commencement of those miserable ravages which Elisha predicted (see chap. viii. 12). And we find from the next verse that he seized on *all the land of Gilead,* and that of Reuben and Gad, and the half-tribe of Manasseh; in a word, whatever Israel possessed on the east side of Jordan.

34. *Are they not written in the book of the chronicles?* We have no chronicles in which there is anything further spoken of this bad man. His reign was long, twenty-eight years; and yet we know nothing of it but the commencement.

CHAPTER 11

Athaliah destroys all that remain of the seed royal of Judah, 1. Jehosheba hides Joash, the son of Ahaziah, and he remains hidden in the house of the Lord six years; and Athaliah reigns over the land, 2-3. Jehoiada, the high priest, calls the nobles privately together into the Temple, shows them the king's son, takes an oath of them, arms them, places guards around the Temple, and around the young king's person; they anoint and proclaim him, 4-12. Athaliah is alarmed, comes into the Temple, is seized, carried forth, and slain, 13-16. Jehoiada causes the people to enter into a covenant with the Lord; they destroy Baal's house, priest, and images, 17-18. Joash is brought to the king's house, reigns, and all the land rejoices, 19-21.

1. *Athaliah.* This woman was the daughter of Ahab, and granddaughter of Omri, and wife of Joram, king of Judah, and mother of Ahaziah. *Destroyed all the seed royal.* All that she could lay her hands on whom Jehu had left, in order that she might get undisturbed possession of the kingdom.

2. *Daughter of . . . Joram, sister of Ahaziah.* It is not likely that Jehosheba was the daughter of Athaliah; she was sister, we find, to Ahaziah, the son of Athaliah, but probably by a different mother. The mother of Jehoash was Zibiah of Beersheba (see chap. xxii. 1).

3. *He was . . . hid in the house of the Lord.* This might be readily done, because none had access to the Temple but the priests; and the high priest himself was the chief manager of this business.

4. *And the seventh year Jehoiada sent.* He had certainly sounded them all, and brought them into the interests of the young king, before

this time. The plot having been laid, and now ripe for execution, he brings the chief officers of the army and those of the bodyguard into the Temple, and there binds them by an oath of secrecy, and shows them the king's son, in whose behalf they are to rise.

5. *That enter in on the sabbath.* It appears that Jehoiada chose the Sabbath day to proclaim the young king because, as that was a day of public concourse, the gathering together of the people who were in this secret would not be noticed; and it is likely that they all came unarmed, and were supplied by Jehoiada with the spears and shields which David had laid up in the Temple, v. 10.

12. *Put the crown upon him.* This was a diadem or golden band that went round the head. *And . . . the testimony.* Probably the book of the law, written on a roll of vellum. This was his sceptre. *They clapped their hands.* This I believe is the first instance on record of clapping the hands as a testimony of joy. *God save the king.* "May the king live!" So the words should be translated wherever they occur.

14. *The king stood by a pillar.* "Stood on a pillar or tribunal," the place or throne on which they were accustomed to put the kings when they proclaimed them. *Treason, Treason.* "A conspiracy, a conspiracy!" from *kashar,* "to bind, unite together."

15. *Have her forth.* She had pressed in among the guards into the Temple. *And him that followeth.* The person who takes her part, let him instantly be slain.

16. *By the way . . . which the horses came.* They probably brought her out near the king's stables.

17. *Jehoiada made a covenant.* A general covenant was first made between the *Lord,* the Supreme King, the *king,* His viceroy, and the *people,* that they should all be *the Lord's people,* each being equally bound to live according to the divine law. Then, secondly, a particular covenant was made between the *king* and the *people,* by which the king was bound to rule according to the laws and constitution of the kingdom, and to watch and live for the safety of the public. And the people were bound, on their part, to love, honor, succor, and obey the king.

18. *His altars and images brake they in pieces.* It is probable that Athaliah had set up the worship of Baal in Judah, as Jezebel had done in Israel; or probably it had never been removed since the days of Solomon. It was no wonder that Jehoiada began his reform with this act, when we learn from 2 Chron. xxiv. 7 that "the sons of Athaliah, that wicked woman, had broken up the house of God; and also all the dedicated things of the house of the Lord did they bestow upon Baalim."

20. *The people . . . rejoiced.* They were glad to get rid of the tyranny of Athaliah. *And the city was in quiet.* She had no partisans to rise up and disturb the king's reign.

21. *Seven years old was Jehoash.* The first instance on record of making a child seven years old the king of any nation, and especially of such a nation as the Jews, who were at all times very difficult to be governed.

CHAPTER 12

Jehoash reigns well under the instructions of Jehoiada the priest. 1-3. He directs the repairing of the Temple; the account of what was done, 4-16. Hazael takes Gath; and, proceeding to besiege Jerusalem, is prevented by Jehoash, who gives him all the treasures and hallowed things of the house of the Lord. 17-18. The servants of Jehoash conspire against and slay him, 19-21.

2. *Jehoash did . . . right in the sight of the Lord.* While Jehoiada, the priest, who was a pious, holy man, lived, Jehoash walked uprightly; but it appears from 2 Chron. xxiv. 17-18 that he departed from the worship of the true God after the death of this eminent high priest, lapsed into idolatry, and seems to have had a share in the murder of Zechariah, who testified against his transgressions and those of the princes of Judah.

3. *The high places were not taken away.* Without the total destruction of these there could be no radical reform. Jehoiada did not use his influence as he might have done; for as he had the king's heart and hand with him, he might have done what he pleased.

4. *All the money of the dedicated things.* From all this account we find that the Temple was in a very ruinous state; the walls were falling down, some had perhaps actually fallen, and there was no person so zealous for the pure worship of God as to exert himself to shore up the falling Temple! The king himself seems to have been the first who noticed these dilapidations, and took measures for the necessary repairs. The repairs were made from the following sources: (1) The *things* which pious persons had *dedicated* to the service of God. (2) The freewill offerings of strangers who had visited Jerusalem: *the money of every one that passeth.* (3) The half-shekel which the males were obliged to pay from the age of twenty years (Exod. xxx. 12) for the redemption of their souls, that is, their lives, which is here called *the money that every man is set at.*

6. *In the three and twentieth year.* In what year Jehoash gave the orders for these repairs, we cannot tell; but the account here plainly intimates that they had been long given, and that nothing was done, merely through the inactivity and negligence of the priests (see 2 Chron. xxiv. 5). It seems that the people had brought money in abundance, and the pious Jehoiada was over the priests, and yet nothing was done! Though Jehoiada was a good man, he does not appear to have had much of the spirit of an active zeal; and simple piety, without zeal and activity, is of little use when a reformation in religion and manners is necessary to be brought about.

9. *Jehoiada . . . took a chest.* This chest was at first set *beside the altar,* as is here mentioned; but afterwards, for the convenience of the people, it was set without the gate (see 2 Chron. xxiv. 8).

10. *The king's scribe and the high priest.* It was necessary to associate with the high priest some civil authority and activity, in order to get the neglected work performed.

13. *Howbeit there were not made . . . bowls.* That is, there were no vessels made for the service of the Temple till all the outward repairs were completed; but after this was done, "they brought the rest of the money before the king and Jehoiada, whereof were made . . . vessels of gold and silver," 2 Chron. xxiv. 14.

15. *They reckoned not with the men.* They placed great confidence in them, and were not disappointed, *for they dealt faithfully.*

17. *Hazael . . . fought against Gath, and took it.* This city, with its satrapy or lordship, had been taken from the Philistines by David (see 2 Sam. viii. 1 and 1 Chron. xviii. 1) and it had continued in the possession of the kings of Judah till this time.

18. *Took all the hallowed things.* He dearly bought a peace which was of short duration, for the next year Hazael returned, and Jehoash, having no more treasures, was obliged to hazard a battle, which he lost, with the principal part of his nobility, so that Judah was totally ruined, and Jehoash shortly after slain in his bed by his own servants, 2 Chron. xxiv. 23.

19. *The rest of the acts of Joash.* We have already seen that this man, so promising in the beginning of his reign, apostatized, became an idolater, encouraged idolatry among his subjects, and put the high priest Zechariah, the son of Jehoiada, his benefactor, to death; and now God visited that blood upon him by the hands of the tyrannous king of Syria, and by his own servants.

20. *The house of Millo.* Was a royal palace, built by David (see 2 Sam. v. 9), and *Silla* is supposed to be the name of the road or causeway that led to it. Millo was situated between the old city of Jerusalem and the city of David.

21. *For Jozachar.* This person is called Zabad in 2 Chron. xxiv. 26; and Shimeath, his mother, is said to be an Ammonitess, as Jehozabad is said to be the son, not of *Shomer,* but of Shimrith, a Moabitess. *They buried him with his fathers in the city of David.* But they did not bury him in the sepulchres of the kings; this is supposed to express the popular disapprobation of his conduct.

CHAPTER 13

Jehoahaz reigns in Israel seventeen years; his various acts, and wars with the Syrians, 1-8. He dies, and Joash reigns in his stead, and does evil in the sight of the Lord, 9-13. Elisha's last sickness; he foretells a threefold defeat of the Syrians, and dies, 14-20. A dead man raised to life by touching the bones of Elisha, 21. Hazael dies, having long oppressed Israel; but Jehoash recovers many cities out of the hands of Ben-hadad, his successor, and defeats him three times, 22-25

1. *In the three and twentieth year of Joash.* The chronology here is thus accounted for; Jehoahaz began his reign at the commencement of the twenty-third year of Joash, and reigned seventeen years—fourteen alone, and three years with his son Joash. The fourteenth year was but just begun.

5. *And the Lord gave Israel a saviour.* This was undoubtedly Joash, whose successful wars against the Syrians are mentioned at the conclusion of the chapter.

6. *The grove also in Samaria.* Asherah, or Astarte, remained in Samaria, and there she was worshipped, with all her abominable rites.

10. *In the thirty and seventh year.* Joash, the son of Jehoahaz, was associated with his father in the government two years before his death. It is this association that is spoken of here. He succeeded him two years after, a little before the death of Elisha. Joash reigned *sixteen years,* which include the years he governed conjointly with his father.

12. *Wherewith he fought against Amaziah.* This war with Amaziah may be seen in ample detail, 2 Chronicles xxv; it ended in the total defeat of Amaziah, who was taken prisoner by Joash, and afterwards slain in a conspiracy at Lachish. Joash took Jerusalem, broke down 400 cubits of the wall, and took all the royal treasures, and the treasures of the house of God (see 2 Chron. xxv. 20-27).

14. *Now Elisha was fallen sick.* This is supposed to have taken place in the tenth year of Joash; and if so, Elisha must have prophesied about sixty-five years. *O my father, my father.* "What shall I do now thou art dying? thou art the only defense of Israel." He accosts him with the same words which himself spoke to Elijah when he was translated (see chap. ii. 12).

15. *Take bow and arrows.* The bow, the arrows, and the smiting on the ground were all emblematical things, indicative of the deliverance of Israel from Syria.

17. *Open the window eastward.* This was towards the country beyond Jordan, which Hazael had taken from the Israelites. *The arrow of . . . deliverance from Syria.* That is, As surely as that arrow is shot towards the lands conquered from Israel by the Syrians, so surely shall those lands be reconquered and restored to Israel. It was an ancient custom to shoot an arrow or cast a spear into the country which an army intended to invade. *Thou shalt smite the Syrians in Aphek.* This was a city of Syria, and probably the place of the first battle; and there, it appears, they had a total overthrow. They were, in the language of the text, consumed or "exterminated."

23. *And the Lord was gracious unto them.* He had tender affection for them, as a husband has for his wife, or a father for his own children. *And had compassion on them.* "His bowels yearned over them"; He felt for them; He sympathized with them in all their distress. "Therefore my bowels are troubled for him; I will surely have mercy upon him, saith the Lord," Jer. xxxi. 20. *And had respect unto them.* "He turned face towards them"; He received them again into favor, and this because of His *covenant* with their fathers. They must not be totally destroyed; the Messiah must come from them.

25. *Three times did Joash beat him.* The particulars of these battles we have not, but these three victories were according to the prediction of Elisha, v. 19. That these victories were very decisive we learn from their fruits, for Joash took from the Syrians the cities which Hazael had taken from Israel: viz., Gilead, the possessions of Reuben, Gad, and the half-tribe of Manasseh, and the country of Bashan (see chap. x. 33).

CHAPTER 14

Amaziah begins to reign well; his victory over the Edomites, 1-7. He challenges Jehoash, king of Israel, 8. Jehoash' parable of the thistle and the cedar, 9-10. The two armies meet at Beth-shemesh; and the men of Judah are defeated, 11-12. Jehoash takes Jerusalem, breaks down 400 cubits of the wall; takes the treasures of the king's house, and of the Temple; and takes hostages, and returns to Samaria, 13-14. The death and burial of both these kings, 15-20. Azariah, the son of Amaziah, made king; he builds Elath, 21-22. Jeroboam II is made king over Israel; his wicked reign and death, 23-29.

1. *In the second year of Joash.* This second year should be understood as referring to the

time when his father, Jehoahaz, associated him with himself in the kingdom, for he reigned two years with his father; so this *second* year of Joash is the first of his absolute and independent government.

5. *As soon as the kingdom was confirmed in his hand.* No doubt those wicked men, Jozachar and Jehozabad, who murdered his father, had considerable power and influence; and therefore he found it dangerous to bring them to justice till he was assured of the loyalty of his other officers. When this was clear, he called them to account, and put them to death.

6. *But the children of the murderers he slew not.* Here he showed his conscientious regard for the law of Moses; for God had positively said, "The fathers shall not be put to death for the children, neither shall the children be put to death for the fathers: every man shall be put to death for his own sin," Deut. xxiv. 16.

7. *He slew of Edom in the valley of salt.* This war is more circumstantially related in 2 Chron. xxv. 5, etc. The Idumeans had arisen in the reign of Joram, king of Judah, and shaken off the yoke of the house of David. Amaziah determined to reduce them to obedience; he therefore levied an army of 300,000 men to his own kingdom, and hired 100,000 Israelites, at the price of 100 talents. When he was about to depart at the head of this numerous army, a prophet came to him and ordered him to dismiss the Israelitish army, for God was not with them; and on the king of Judah expressing regret for the loss of his 100 talents, he was answered that the Lord could give him much more than that. He obeyed, sent back the Israelites, and at the head of his own men attacked the Edomites in the valley of salt, slew 10,000 on the spot, and took 10,000 prisoners, all of whom he precipitated from the "rock," or *Selah,* a place or city supposed to be the same with Petra, where there must have been a great precipice, from which the place took its name of *Selah* or Petra.

8. *Come, let us look one another in the face.* This was a real declaration of war; and the ground of it is most evident from this circumstance: that the 100,000 men of Israel that had been dismissed, though they had the stipulated money, taking the advantage of Amaziah's absence, "fell upon the cities of Judah, from Samaria even unto Beth-horon, and smote three thousand of them, and took much spoil," 2 Chron. xxv. 10-13. Amaziah no doubt remonstrated with Jehoash, but to no purpose; and therefore he declared war against him.

9. *Jehoash . . . sent to Amaziah . . . saying.* The meaning of this parable is plain. *The thistle that was in Lebanon*—Amaziah, king of Judah, *sent to the cedar that was in Lebanon*—Jehoash, king of Israel, *saying, Give thy daughter*—a part of your kingdom, *to my son to wife* —to be united to, and possessed by the kings of Judah. *And there passed by a wild beast*— his troops, pillaged the Temple, and broke down *the thistle*—utterly discomfited Amaziah and his troops, pillaged the Temple, and broke down the walls of Jerusalem (see vv. 12-14). Probably Amaziah had required certain cities of Israel to be given up to Judah; if so, this accounts for that part of the parable, "Give thy daughter to my son to wife."

10. *Glory of this, and tarry at home.* There is a vast deal of insolent dignity in this remonstrance of Jehoash; but it has nothing conciliatory, no proposal of making amends for the injury his army had done to the unoffending inhabitants of Judah. The ravages committed by the army of Jehoash were totally unprovoked, and they were base and cowardly; they fell upon women, old men, and children, and butchered them in cold blood, for all the effective men were gone off with their king against the Edomites. The quarrel of Amaziah was certainly just, yet he was put to rout; he did meddle to his hurt; he fell, and Judah fell with him, as Jehoash had said. But why was this? Why, it came of God; for he had brought the gods "of Seir, and set them up to be his gods, and bowed down himself before them, and burned incense unto them." Therefore God delivered "them into the hand of their enemies, because they sought after the gods of Edom," 2 Chron. xxv. 14, 20. This was the reason why the Israelites triumphed.

13. *Took Amaziah king of Judah.* It is plain that afterwards Amaziah had his liberty; but how or on what terms he got it is not known. See on the following verse.

14. *And he took . . . hostages.* "Pledges"; from *arab,* "to pledge, give security," for the performance of some promise. It is likely that Amaziah gave some of the nobles or some of his own family as hostages, that he might regain his liberty; and they were to get their liberty when he had fulfilled his engagements; but of what kind these were we cannot tell, nor, indeed, how he got his liberty.

15. *How he fought with Amaziah.* The only fighting between them was the battle already mentioned, and this is minutely related in 2 Chronicles xxv.

19. *They made a conspiracy against him.* His defeat by Jehoash, and the consequent pillaging of the Temple, and emptying the royal exchequer, and the dismantling of Jerusalem, had made him exceedingly unpopular; so that probably the whole of the last fifteen years of his life were a series of troubles and distresses.

21. *Took Azariah.* He is also called Uzziah, 2 Chron. xxvi. 1. The former signifies, "The help of the Lord"; the latter, "The strength of the Lord."

22. *He built Elath.* This city belonged to the Edomites, and was situated on the eastern branch of the Red Sea. It had probably suffered much in the late war, and was now rebuilt by Uzziah, and brought entirely under the dominion of Judah.

25. *He restored the coast of Israel.* From the description that is here given it appears that Jeroboam reconquered all the territory that had been taken from the kings of Israel; so that Jeroboam II left the kingdom as ample as it was when the ten tribes separated under Jeroboam I.

26. *The Lord saw the affliction of Israel.* It appears that about this time Israel had been greatly reduced, and great calamities had fallen upon all indiscriminately; even the diseased and captives in the dungeon had the hand of God heavy upon them, and there was no helper. And then God sent Jonah to encourage them, and to assure them of better days. He

was the first of the prophets, after Samuel, whose writings are preserved; yet the prophecy delivered on this occasion is not extant, for what is now in the prophecies of Jonah relates wholly to Nineveh.

28. *How he warred, and . . . recovered Damascus.* We learn from 1 Chron. xviii. 3-11 that David had conquered all Syria, and put garrisons in Damascus and other places, and laid all the Syrians under tribute; but this yoke they had not only shaken off, but they had conquered a considerable portion of the Israelitish territory and added it to Syria. These latter Jeroboam now recovered; and thus the places which anciently belonged to Judah by David's conquests, and were repossessed by Syria, he now conquered and added to Israel.

29. *Jeroboam slept with his fathers.* He died a natural death; and was regularly succeeded by his son Zachariah, who, reigning badly, was, after six months, slain by Shallum, who succeeded him, and reigned but one month, being slain by Menahem, who succeeded him, and reigned ten years over Israel. Amos, the prophet, lived in the reign of Jeroboam; and was accused by Amaziah, one of the idolatrous priests of Bethel, of having predicted the death of Jeroboam by the sword, but this was a slander. What he did predict, and which came afterwards to pass, may be seen in Amos vii. 10-17.

CHAPTER 15

Azariah begins to reign over Judah, and acts well, but does not remove the high places. 1-4. He becomes leprous, and dies, after having reigned fifty-two years; and Jotham, his son, reigns in his stead. 5-7. Zachariah reigns over Israel, and acts wickedly; Shallum conspires against him and slays him, after he had reigned six months, 8-12. Shallum reigns one month, and is slain by Menahem, 13-15. Menahem's wicked and oppressive reign; he subsidizes the king of Assyria, and dies, after having reigned ten years, 16-22. Pekahiah, his son, reigns in his stead; does wickedly; Pekah, one of his captains, conspires against and kills him, after he had reigned ten years, 23-26. Pekah reigns in his stead, and acts wickedly, 27-28. Tiglath-pileser, king of Assyria, carries into captivity the inhabitants of many cities, 29. Hoshea conspires against and slays Pekah, after he had reigned twenty years; and reigns in his stead, 30-31. Jotham begins to reign over Judah; he reigns well; dies after a reign of sixteen years, and is succeeded by his son Ahaz, 32-38.

1. *In the twenty and seventh year of Jeroboam.* There are insuperable difficulties in the chronology of this place. The marginal note says, "This is the twenty-seventh year of Jeroboam's partnership in the kingdom with his father, who made him consort at his going to the Syrian wars. It is the sixteenth year of Jeroboam's monarchy." Lightfoot endeavors to reconcile this place with chap. xiv. 16-17 thus: "At the death of Amaziah, his son and heir Uzziah was but four years old, for he was about sixteen in Jeroboam's twenty-seventh year; therefore, the throne must have been empty eleven years, and the government administered by protectors while Uzziah was in his minority."

3. *He did that which was right.* It is said, 2 Chron. xxvi. 5, that he sought the Lord in the days of Zechariah the prophet, and "God made him to prosper."

10. *Smote him before the people.* In some public assembly: he probably became very unpopular.

12. *This was the word of the Lord . . . unto Jehu.* God had promised to Jehu that his sons should sit on the throne of Israel to the fourth

generation; and so it came to pass, for Jehoahaz, Joash, Jeroboam, and Zachariah succeeded Jehu, to whom this promise was made. But because he executed the divine purpose with an uncommanded cruelty, therefore God cut his family short, according to his word by Hosea, "I will avenge the blood of Jezreel upon the house of Jehu, and will cause to cease the kingdom of the house of Israel," i. 4.

13. *He reigned a full month.* Menahem is supposed to have been one of Zachariah's generals. Hearing of the death of his master, when he was with the troops at Tirzah, he hastened to Samaria, and slew the murderer, and had himself proclaimed in his stead. But, as the people of Tiphsah did not open their gates to him, he took the place by assault; and as the text tells us, practiced the most cruel barbarities, even ripping up the women that were with child!

19. *Pul the king of Assyria.* This is the first time we hear of *Assyria* since the days of Nimrod, its founder, Gen. x. 11. *That his hand.* That is, "his power and influence," might be with him. In this sense is the word *hand* frequently used in Scripture.

20. *Each man fifty shekels of silver.* Upwards of five pounds sterling a man.

21. *Are they not written in . . . the chronicles?* There are no chronicles extant in which there is anything further relative to this king.

25. *Smote him in Samaria, in the palace of the king's house, with Argob and Arieh.* Who Argob and Arieh were we know not. Some make them men; some make them statues. Pekah had *fifty . . . Gileadites* in the conspiracy with him.

29. *Took Ijon.* These places belonged to Israel; and were taken by Ben-hadad, king of Syria, when he was in league with Asa, king of Judah (see 1 Kings xv. 20). They were regained by Jeroboam II, and now they are taken from Israel once more by Tiglath-pileser. From 1 Chron. v. 26 we learn that Pul and Tiglath-pileser, kings of Assyria, carried away into captivity the two tribes of Reuben, and Gad, and the half-tribe of Manasseh—all that belonged to Israel, on the other side of Jordan. These were never restored to Israel.

30. *Hoshea the son of Elah . . . in the twentieth year of Jotham.* There are many difficulties in the chronology of this place. To reconcile the whole Calmet says: "Hoshea conspired against Pekah, the twentieth year of the reign of this prince, which was the eighteenth after the beginning of the reign of Jotham, king of Judah. Two years after this, that is, the fourth year of Ahaz, and the twentieth of Jotham, Hoshea made himself master of a part of the kingdom, according to v. 30. Finally, the twelfth year of Ahaz, Hoshea had peaceable possession of the whole kingdom, according to chap. xvii. v. 1."

36. *Now the rest of the acts of Jotham.* These acts are distinctly stated in 2 Chronicles xxvii. He built the high gate of the house of the Lord, and he built much on the wall of Ophel. He built cities in the mountains of Judah, and in the forests he built castles and towers. He overthrew the Ammonites, and obliged them to give him 100 talents of silver, 10,000 measures of wheat, and 10,000 of barley, for three con-

secutive years. He was twenty-five years old when he began to reign, and he reigned sixteen years. These are the particulars which we learn from the place in Chronicles quoted above, few of which are mentioned in this place. As to the *higher gate* of the house of the Lord, commentators are not well agreed. Some think it was a gate which he then made, and which did not exist before, and is the same that is called the "new gate," Jer. xxvi. 10—which is very likely.

37. *In those days the Lord began to send.* It was about this time that the Assyrian wars so ruinous to the Jews began; but it was in the following reigns that they arrived at their highest pitch of disaster to those unfaithful and unfortunate people.

CHAPTER 16

Ahaz begins to reign, acts wickedly, and restores idolatry in Judea, 1-4. Rezin, king of Syria, besieges Jerusalem, but cannot take it; he takes Elath, and drives the Jews thence, 5-6. Ahaz hires Tiglath-pileser against the king of Syria and the king of Israel, and gives him the silver and gold that were found in the treasures of the house of the Lord, 7-8. Tiglath-pileser takes Damascus and slays Rezin, 9. Ahaz goes to meet him at Damascus; sees an altar there, a pattern of which he sends to Urijah, the priest, and orders him to make one like it, which he does, 10-15. He makes several alterations in the Temple; dies; and Hezekiah, his son, reigns in his stead, 16-20.

2. *Twenty years old was Ahaz.* Here is another considerable difficulty in the chronology. Ahaz was but twenty years old when he began to reign, and he died after he had reigned sixteen years; consequently his whole age amounted only to thirty-six years. But Hezekiah, his son, was twenty-five years old when he began to reign; and if this were so, then Ahaz must have been the father of Hezekiah when he was but eleven years of age! Some think that the twenty years mentioned here respect the beginning of the reign of Jotham, father of Ahaz; so that the passage should be thus translated: "Ahaz was twenty years of age when his father began to reign"; and consequently he was fifty-two years old when he died, seeing Jotham reigned sixteen years; and therefore Hezekiah was born when his father was twenty-seven years of age. This however is a violent solution, and worthy of little credit. It is better to return to the text as it stands, and allow that Ahaz might be only eleven or twelve years old when he had Hezekiah. This is not at all impossible, as we know that the youth of both sexes in the Eastern countries are marriageable at ten or twelve years of age.

3. *Made his son to pass through the fire.* On this passage I beg leave to refer the reader to my notes on Lev. xviii. 21; xx. 2, 14, where the subject is considered at large.

5. *But could not overcome him.* It is likely that this was the time when Isaiah was sent to console Ahaz (see Isa. vii. 1); and predicted the death of both Rezin and Pekah, his enemies.

6. *Recovered Elath to Syria.* See the note on chap. xiv. 22.

7. *I am thy servant and thy son.* I will obey you in all, and become tributary to you; only help me against Syria and Israel.

9. *The king of Assyria hearkened unto him.* It is said, 2 Chron. xxviii. 20, that "Tilgath-pilneser . . . distressed him, but strengthened

him not." Though he came against the Syrians, and took Damascus, and slew Rezin, yet he did not help Ahaz against the Philistines, nor did he lend him any forces to assist against Israel; and he distressed him by taking the royal treasures, and the treasures of the Temple, and did him little service for so great a sacrifice. He helped him a little, but distressed him on the whole. It appears that, about this time, Pekah, king of Israel, nearly ruined Judea: it is said, 2 Chron. xxviii. 6, that he slew 120,000 valiant men in one day; and that he carried away captive to Samaria 200,000 women and children, and much spoil; but, at the instance of the prophet Oded, these were all sent back, fed, and clothed, ib. 8-15.

10. *Ahaz went to Damascus.* He had received so much help on the defeat of Rezin that he went to Damascus to meet the king of Assyria and render him thanks. *Ahaz sent to Urijah the priest the fashion of the altar.* This was some idolatrous altar, the shape and workmanship of which pleased Ahaz so well that he determined to have one like it at Jerusalem. For this he had no divine authority, and the compliance of Urijah was both mean and sinful. That Ahaz did this for an idolatrous purpose is evident from 2 Chron. xxviii. 21-25.

14. *Put it on the north side.* He seems to have intended to conform everything in the Lord's house as much as possible to the idolatrous temples which he saw at Damascus, and to model the divine worship in the same way; in a word, to honor and worship the gods of Syria, and not the God of heaven. All the alterations specified here were in contempt of the true God. Thus "he provoked to anger the Lord God of his fathers," 2 Chron. xxviii. 25.

18. *And the covert for the sabbath.* There are a great number of conjectures concerning this *covert*, or, as it is in the Hebrew, the *musach*, of the Sabbath. As the word, and others derived from the same root, signify "covering" or "booths," it is very likely that this means either a sort of canopy which was erected on the Sabbath days for the accommodation of the people who came to worship, and which Ahaz took away to discourage them from that worship, or a canopy under which the king and his family reposed themselves, and which he transported to some other place to accommodate the king of Assyria when he visited him.

20. *Was buried with his fathers in the city of David.* But it is expressly declared, 2 Chron. xxviii. 27, that he was not buried in the sepulchres of the kings of Israel; and this was undoubtedly intended as a mark of degradation.

CHAPTER 17

Hoshea's wicked reign, 1-2. Shalmaneser comes up against him, makes him tributary, and then casts him into prison, 3-4. He besieges Samaria three years; and at last takes it, and carries Israel captive into Assyria, and places them in different cities of the Assyrians and Medes, 5-6. The reason why Israel was thus afflicted; their idolatry, obstinacy, divination, etc., 7-18. Judah copies the misconduct of Israel, 19. The Lord rejects all the seed of Israel, 20-23. The king of Assyria brings different nations and places them in Samaria, and the cities from which the Israelites had been led away into captivity, 24. Many of these strange people are destroyed by lions, 25. The king of Assyria sends back some of the Israelitish priests to teach these nations the worship of Jehovah, which worship they incorporate with their own idolatry, 26-33. The state of the Israelites, and strange nations in the land of Israel, 34-41.

3. *Shalmaneser.* This was the son and successor of Tiglath-pileser. He is called Shalman by Hosea, x. 14. *Gave him presents.* Became tributary to him.

4. *Found conspiracy in Hoshea.* He had endeavored to shake off the Assyrian yoke, by entering into a treaty with So, king of Egypt; and having done so, he ceased to send the annual tribute to Assyria.

5. *Besieged it three years.* It must have been well-fortified, well-provisioned, and well-defended to have held out so long.

6. *Took Samaria.* According to the prophets Hosea (xiii. 16) and Micah (i. 6), he exercised great cruelties on this miserable city, ripping up the women with child, dashing young children against the stones.

Thus ended the kingdom of Israel, after it had lasted 254 years, from the death of Solomon and the schism of Jeroboam till the taking of Samaria by Shalmaneser, in the ninth year of Hoshea, after which the remains of the ten tribes were carried away beyond the river Euphrates.

The rest of this chapter is spent in vindicating the divine providence and justice, showing the reason why God permitted such a desolation to fall on a people who had been so long His peculiar children.

9. *From the tower of the watchmen to the fenced city.* That is, the idolatry was universal; every place was made a place for some idolatrous rite or act of worship; from the largest city to the smallest village, and from the public watchtower to the shepherd's cot.

10. *Images and groves.* Images of different idols, and places for the abominable rites of Ashtaroth.

13. *Yet the Lord testified against Israel.* What rendered their conduct the more inexcusable was that the Lord had preserved among them a succession of prophets, who testified against their conduct and preached repentance to them, and the readiness of God to forgive, provided they would return unto Him and give up their idolatries.

18. *None left but the tribe of Judah only.* Under this name all those of Benjamin and Levi and the Israelites who abandoned their idolatries and joined with Judah are comprised. It was the ten tribes that were carried away by the Assyrians.

24. *The king of Assyria brought men from Babylon.* He removed one people entirely, and substituted others in their place; and this he did to cut off all occasion for mutiny or insurrection. *From Cuthah.* This is supposed to be the same as *Cush,* the Chaldeans and Syrians changing *shin* into *tau. From Ava.* The Avim were an ancient people, expelled by the Caphtorim from Hazerim, Deut. ii. 23. *From Hamath.* This was Hemath or Emath of Syria, frequently mentioned in the sacred writings.

25. *The Lord sent lions among them.* The land being deprived of its inhabitants, wild beasts would necessarily increase, even without any supernatural intervention; and this the superstitious newcomers supposed to be a plague sent upon them, because they did not know how to worship Him who was the God of the land; for they thought, like other heathens, that every district had its own tutelary deity. Yet it is likely that God did send lions as a scourge on this bad people.

26. *The manner of the God of the land.* Mishpat, the "judgment," the way in which the God of the land is to be worshipped.

27. *Carry thither one of the priests.* Imperfect as this teaching was, it in the end overthrew the idolatry of these people, so that soon after the Babylonish captivity they were found to be as free from idolatry as the Jews themselves, and continue so to the present day. But they are now nearly annihilated; the small remains of them is found at Naplouse and Jaffa. They are about thirty families; and men, women, and children amount to about two hundred persons! They have a synagogue, which they regularly attend every Sabbath; and they go thither clothed in white robes.

29. *Every nation made gods of their own.* That is, they made gods after the fashion of those which they had worshipped in their own country.

30. *The men of Babylon made Succoth-benoth.* This, literally, signifies "the tabernacles of the daughters" or young women, and most evidently refers to those public prostitutions of young virgins at the temple of Venus among the Babylonians. *The men of Cuth made Nergal.* This is supposed to have been the solar orb or light. *The men of Hamath made Ashima.* Perhaps "the fire"; from *asham,* "to make atonement or to purify."

31. *The Avites made Nibhaz.* This was supposed to be the same as the Anubis of the Egyptians; and was in form partly of a dog, and partly of a man. *And Tartak.* This is supposed by some to be another name of the same idol. *Adrammelech.* From *adar,* "glorious," and *melech,* "king." Probably the sun. *Anammelech.* From *anah,* "to return," and *melech,* "king." Probably, the Moloch of the Ammonites.

32. *Of the lowest of them priests.* One priest was not enough for this motley population; and, as the priesthood was probably neither respectable nor lucrative, it was only the lowest of the people who would enter into the employment.

33. *They feared the Lord, and served their own gods.* They did not relinquish their own idolatry but incorporated the worship of the true God with that of their idols. They were afraid of Jehovah, who had sent lions among them, and therefore they offered Him a sort of worship that He might not thus afflict them; but they *served* other gods, devoted themselves affectionately to them, because their worship was such as gratified their grossest passions and most sinful propensities.

36. *But the Lord.* Jehovah, the supreme, self-existent, and eternal Being; Author of all being and life. This was to be the whole Object of their adoration. *Who brought you up.* This was a strong reason why they should adore Him only. He had saved them from the hands of their enemies, and He did it in such a way as to show His power to be irresistible; in such a Being they might safely confide. *Him shall ye fear.* Here is the manner in which He is to be worshipped. Him you shall "reverence" as your Lawgiver and Judge. *Him shall ye worship.* Before Him you shall bow the knee, living in the spirit of obedience, and performing

every religious act in the deepest humility. *And to him shall ye do sacrifice.* You shall consider that, as you have sinned, so you deserve death; you shall therefore bring your living victims to the altar of the Lord, and let their life's blood be poured out there, as an atonement for your souls.

41. *So do they unto this day.* This must have been written before the Babylonish captivity, because after that time none of the Israelites ever lapsed into idolatry. But this may chiefly refer to the heathenish people who were sent to dwell among the remains of the ten tribes.

CHAPTER 18

Hezekiah begins to reign; he removes the high places, breaks to pieces the brazen serpent, and walks uprightly before God, 1-6. He endeavors to shake off the Assyrian yoke, and defeats the Philistines, 7-8. Shalmaneser comes up against Samaria, takes it, and carries the people away into captivity, 9-12. And then comes against Judah, and takes all the fenced cities, 13. Hezekiah sends a message to him at Lachish to desist, with the promise that he will pay him any tribute he chooses to impose; in consequence of which Shalmaneser exacts 300 talents of silver, and 30 talents of gold; to pay which Hezekiah is obliged to take all his own treasures and those belonging to the Temple, 14-16. The king of Assyria sends, notwithstanding, a great host against Jerusalem; and his general, Rab-shakeh, delivers an insulting and blasphemous message to Hezekiah, 17-35. Hezekiah and his people are greatly afflicted at the words of Rab-shakeh, 36-37.

4. *Brake in pieces the brasen serpent.* The history of this may be seen in Num. xxi. 8-9. We find that this brazen serpent had become an object of idolatry, and no doubt was supposed to possess extraordinary virtues, and that incense was burned before it which should have been burned before the true God. *And he called it Nehushtan.* Not one of the versions has attempted to translate this word. Jarchi says, "He called it Nechustan, through contempt, which is as much as to say, *a brazen serpent.*"

5-7. *He trusted in the Lord.* See the character of this good king: (1) *He trusted in the Lord God of Israel;* (2) *He clave to the Lord;* (3) He was steady in his religion; he *departed not from following the Lord;* (4) He *kept* God's *commandments.* And what were the consequences? (1) The *Lord was with him;* (2) *He prospered whithersoever he went.*

8. *From the tower of the watchmen.* See the same words, chap. xvii. 9. It seems a proverbial mode of expression. He reduced every kind of fortification; nothing was able to stand before him.

17. *The king of Assyria sent Tartan.* Calmet has very justly remarked that these are not the names of persons but of offices. *Tartan* signifies him who presides over the gifts or tribute, chancellor of the exchequer. *Rabsaris.* "The chief of the eunuchs." *Rab-shakeh,* "Master or chief over the wine cellar," or he who had the care of the king's drink.

From Lachish. It seems as if the Assyrian troops had been worsted before Lachish, and were obliged to raise the siege, from which they went and sat down before Libnah. While Sennacherib was there with the Assyrian army, he heard that Tirhakah, king of Ethiopia, had invaded the Assyrian territories. Being obliged therefore to hasten, in order to succor his own dominions, he sent a considerable force under the aforementioned officers against Jerusalem, with a most fearful and bloody manifesto, commanding Hezekiah to pay him tribute, to deliver up his kingdom to him, and to submit, he and his people, to be carried away captives into Assyria! This manifesto was accompanied with the vilest insults and the highest blasphemies. God interposed and the evils threatened against others fell upon himself.

Conduit of the upper pool. The aqueduct that brought the water from the upper or eastern reservoir, near to the valley of Kidron, into the city. Probably they had seized on this in order to distress the city. *The fuller's field.* The place where the washermen stretched out their clothes to dry.

18. *Called to the king.* They wished him to come out that they might get possession of his person. *Eliakim . . . over the household.* What we would call lord chamberlain. *Shebna the scribe.* The king's secretary. *Joah . . . the recorder.* The writer of the public annals.

19. *What confidence is this?* The words are excessively insulting: "What little, foolish, or unavailing cause of confidence is it, in which thou trustest?"

21. *The staff of this bruised reed.* Egypt had already been greatly bruised and broken, through the wars carried on against it by the Assyrians.

22. *Whose high places and whose altars Hezekiah hath taken away.* This was artfully malicious. Many of the people sacrificed to Jehovah on the high places; Hezekiah had removed them (v. 4) because they were incentives to idolatry. Rab-shakeh insinuates that by so doing he had offended Jehovah, deprived the people of their religious rights, and he could neither expect the blessing of God nor the cooperation of the people.

23. *I will deliver thee two thousand horses.* Another insult: Were I to give you 2,000 Assyrian horses, you could not find riders for them. How then can you think that you shall be able to stand against even the smallest division of my troops?

25. *Am I now come up without the Lord?* As Rab-shakeh saw that the Jews placed the utmost confidence in God, he wished to persuade them that by Hezekiah's conduct Jehovah had departed from them and was become Ally to the king of Assyria, and therefore they could not expect any help from that quarter.

26. *Talk not with us in the Jews' language.* The object of this blasphemous caitiff was to stir up the people to sedition, that the city and the king might be delivered into his hand.

34. *Where are the gods of Hamath?* Sennacherib is greater than any of the gods of the nations. The Assyrians have already overthrown the gods of *Hamath, Arpad, Hena,* and *Ivah;* therefore Jehovah shall be like one of them, and shall not be able to deliver Jerusalem out of the hand of my master. The impudent blasphemy of this speech is without parallel. Hezekiah treated it as he ought. It was not properly against him, but against the Lord; therefore he refers the matter to Jehovah himself, who punishes this blasphemy in the most signal manner.

36. *Answer him not.* The blasphemy is too barefaced. Jehovah is insulted, not you; let Him avenge His own quarrel. See the succeeding chapter.

37. *Then came Eliakim . . . and Shebna . . . and Joah . . . to Hezekiah with their clothes rent.* It was the custom of the Hebrews, when they heard any blasphemy, to rend their clothes, because this was the greatest of crimes, as it immediately affected the majesty of God; and it was right that a religious people should have in the utmost abhorrence every insult offered to the Object of their religious worship. These three ambassadors lay the matter before the king, as God's representative; he lays it before the prophet, as God's minister; and the prophet lays it before God, as the people's Mediator.

CHAPTER 19

Hezekiah is greatly distressed, and sends to Isaiah to pray for him, 1-4. Isaiah returns a comfortable answer, and predicts the destruction of the king of Assyria and his army, 5-8. Sennacherib, hearing that his kingdom was invaded by the Ethiopians, sends a terrible letter to Hezekiah, to induce him to surrender, 9-13. Hezekiah goes to the Temple, spreads the letter before the Lord, and makes a most affecting prayer, 14-19. Isaiah is sent to him to assure him that his prayer is heard, that Jerusalem shall be delivered, and that the Assyrians shall be destroyed, 20-34. That very night a messenger of God slays 185,000 Assyrians, 35. Sennacherib returns to Nineveh, and is slain by his own sons, 36-37.

2. *To Isaiah the prophet.* His fame and influence were at this time great in Israel; and it was well-known that the word of the Lord was with him.

3. *The children are come to the birth.* The Jewish state is here represented under the emblem of a woman in travail, who has been so long in pangs that her strength is now entirely exhausted and her deliverance is hopeless, without a miracle. The image is very fine and highly appropriate.

4. *The remnant that are left.* That is, the Jews, the ten tribes having been already carried away captive by the kings of Assyria.

7. *Behold, I will send a blast . . . and he shall hear a rumour.* The *rumour* was that Tirhakah had invaded Assyria. The blast was that which slew 185,000 of them in one night (see v. 35). *Cause him to fall by the sword.* Alluding to his death by the hands of his two sons, at Nineveh (see vv. 35-37).

8. *Libnah . . . Lachish.* These two places were not very distant from each other; they were in the mountains of Judah, southward of Jerusalem.

10. *Let not thy God in whom thou trustest.* This letter is nearly the same with the speech delivered by Rab-shakeh (see chap. xviii. 29).

14. *Spread it before the Lord.* The Temple was considered to be God's dwelling place, and that whatever was there was peculiarly under His eye. Hezekiah spread the letter before the Lord, as he wished Him to read the blasphemies spoken against himself.

15. *Thou art the God.* Thou art not only God of Israel, but God also of Assyria, and of all the nations of the world.

23. *The tall cedar trees . . . the choice fir trees.* Probably meaning the princes and nobles of the country. *The forest of his Carmel.* Better in the margin: "the forest and his fruitful field."

24. *I have digged and drunk strange waters.* I have conquered strange countries, in which I have digged wells for my army; or, I have gained the wealth of strange countries. *With the sole of my feet.* My infantry have been so numerous that they alone have been sufficient to drink up the rivers of the places I have besieged.

25. *Hast thou not heard?* Here Jehovah speaks, and shows this boasting king that what he had done was done by the divine appointment, and that of his own counsel and might he could have done nothing. It was because God had appointed them to this civil destruction that he had overcome them, and it was not through his might; for God had made their inhabitants of small power, so that he got the victory only over men whom God had confounded, dismayed, and enervated, v. 26.

28. *I will put my hook in thy nose.* This seems to be an allusion to the method of guiding a buffalo. He has a sort of ring put into his nose, to which a cord or bridle is attached, by which he can be turned to the right, or to the left, or round about, according to the pleasure of his driver.

29. *This shall be a sign unto thee.* To Hezekiah; for to him this part of the address is made. *Ye shall eat this year.* Sennacherib had ravaged the country, and seedtime was now over, yet God shows them that He would so bless the land that what should grow of itself that year would be quite sufficient to supply the inhabitants and prevent all famine; and though the second year was the sabbatical rest or jubilee for the land, in which it was unlawful to plough or sow, yet even then the land, by an especial blessing of God, should bring forth a sufficiency for its inhabitants; and in the third year they should sow and plant and have abundance. Now this was to be a *sign* to Hezekiah that his deliverance had not been effected by natural or casual means; for as without a miracle the ravaged and uncultivated land could not yield food for its inhabitants, so not without miraculous interference could the Assyrian army be cut off and Israel saved.

30. *The remnant . . . shall yet again take root.* As your corn shall take root in the soil, and bring forth and abundantly multiply itself, so shall the Jewish people; the population shall be greatly increased, and the desolations occasioned by the sword soon be forgotten.

31. *Out of Jerusalem shall go forth a remnant.* The Jews shall be so multiplied as to fill not only Jerusalem, but all the adjacent country.

32. *He shall not.* Here follow the fullest proofs that Jerusalem shall not be taken by the Assyrians. (1) *He shall not come into this city;* (2) He shall not be able to get so near as to *shoot an arrow* into it; (3) He shall not be able to bring an army before it; (4) Nor shall he be able to raise any redoubt or mound against it.

33. *By the way that he came.* Though his army shall not return, yet he shall return to Assyria; for because of his blasphemy he is reserved for a more ignominious death.

35. *That night.* The very night after the blasphemous message had been sent, and this prophecy delivered. *The angel of the Lord went out.* I believe this *angel* or "messenger of the Lord" was simply a suffocating or pestilential wind by which the Assyrian army was destroyed, as in a moment, without noise, confusion, or any warning. Thus was the threatening, v. 7, fulfilled, "I will send a blast upon

him." For he had heard the rumor that his territories were invaded; and on his way to save his empire, in one night the whole of his army was destroyed, without anyone even seeing who had hurt them. *When they arose early.* That is, Sennacherib, and probably a few associates, who were preserved as witnesses and relaters of this most dire disaster. Rab-shakeh, no doubt, perished with the rest of the army.

36. *Dwelt at Nineveh.* This was the capital of the Assyrian empire.

37. *Nisroch his god.* We know nothing of this deity; he is nowhere else mentioned.

CHAPTER 20

Hezekiah's sickness, and the message of the prophet to him, to prepare for death, 1. His distress and prayer to God, 2-3. The Lord hears, and promises to add fifteen years to his life, and Isaiah prescribes a means of cure, 4-7. Hezekiah seeks a sign; and to assure him of the truth of God's promise, the shadow on the dial of Ahaz goes back ten degrees, 8-11. The king of Babylon sends a friendly message to Hezekiah, to congratulate him on his recovery; and to these messengers he ostentatiously shows all his treasures, 12-13. Isaiah reproved him, and foretells that the Babylonians will come and take away all those treasures, and take the people into captivity; and degrade the royal family of Judah, 14-18. Hezekiah bows to the divine judgment, 19. His acts and death, 20-21.

1. *Set thine house in order.* It appears from the text that he was smitten with such a disorder as must terminate in death, without the miraculous interposition of God; and he is now commanded to set his house in order, or to give charge concerning his house. Hezekiah reigned only twenty-nine years, chap. xviii. 2. He had reigned fourteen years when the war with Sennacherib began, chap. xviii. 13, and he reigned fifteen years after this sickness, chap. xx. 6. That Hezekiah's sickness happened before the destruction of Sannacherib's army is asserted by the text itself (see v. 6).

3. *I beseech thee, O Lord.* Hezekiah knew that, although the words of Isaiah were delivered to him in an absolute form, yet they were to be conditionally understood; else he could not have prayed to God to reverse a purpose which he knew to be irrevocable. Even this passage is a key to many prophecies and divine declarations (see chap. xviii of Jeremiah).

7. *Take a lump of figs . . . and laid it on the boil.* We cannot exactly say in what Hezekiah's malady consisted. *Shechin* signifies any inflammatory tumor, boil, abscess.

8. *What shall be the sign?* He wishes to be fully convinced that his cure was to be entirely supernatural; and, in order to this, he seeks one miracle to prove the truth of the other, that nothing might remain equivocal.

11. *He brought the shadow ten degrees backward.* We cannot suppose that these *ten degrees* meant ten hours. There were ten divisions of time on this dial; and perhaps it would not be right to suppose that the sun went ten degrees back in the heavens, or that the earth turned back upon its axis from east to west, in a contrary direction to its natural course. But the miracle might be effected by means of refraction, for a ray of light we know can be refracted from a right line by passing through a dense medium. And we know also, by means of the refracting power of the atmosphere, the sun, when near rising and setting, seems to be higher above the horizon than he really is; and,

by horizontal refraction, we find that the sun appears above the horizon when he is actually below it, and literally out of sight. Therefore, by using dense clouds or vapors, the rays of light in that place might be refracted from their direct course ten, or any other number, of degrees; so that the miracle might have been wrought by occasioning this extraordinary refraction, rather than by disturbing the course of the earth, or any other of the celestial bodies.

12. *At that time Berodach-baladan.* He is called Merodach-Baladan, Isa. xxix. 1, and by the Septuagint, Syriac, and Arabic versions; and also by the Babylonian and Jerusalem Talmuds. The true reading seems to be Merodach. *Sent letters and a present.* It appears that there was friendship between the king of Babylon and Hezekiah, when the latter and the Assyrians were engaged in a destructive war. The king of Babylon had not only heard of his sickness, but he had heard of the miracle, as we learn from 2 Chron. xxxii. 31.

13. *Hezekiah hearkened unto them.* Instead of *vaiyishma,* "he hearkened," *vaiyismach,* "he rejoiced" or "was glad," is the reading of twelve of Kennicott's and De Rossi's MSS., the parallel place, Isa. xxxix. 2, the Septuagint, Syriac, Vulgate, Arabic, some copies of the Targum, and the Babylonian Talmud. *All the house of his precious things.* Interpreters are not well-agreed about the meaning of the original *nechothoh,* which we here translate *precious things,* and in the margin "spicery" or "jewels." I suppose the last to be meant. *There was nothing in his house.* He showed them, through a spirit of folly and exultation, all his treasures, and no doubt those in the house of the Lord. And it is said, 2 Chron. xxxii. 31, that in this business "God left him, to try him, that he might know all that was in his heart"; and this trial proved that in his heart there was little else than pride and folly.

17. *Behold, the days come.* This was fulfilled in the days of the latter Jewish kings, when the Babylonians had led the people away into captivity, and stripped the land, the Temple, etc., of all their riches (see Dan. i. 1-3).

18. *They shall be eunuchs.* Perhaps this means no more than that they should become household servants to the kings of Babylon. See the fulfillment, chap. xxiv. 13-15 and Dan i. 1-3.

CHAPTER 21

Manasseh succeeds his father, Hezekiah, reigns fifty-five years, and fills Jerusalem and the whole land with abominable idolatry and murder, 1-9. God denounces the heaviest judgments against him and the land. 10-15. Manasseh's acts and death, 16-18. Amon. his son, succeeds him, and reigns two years; is equally profligate with his father; is slain by his servants, and buried in the garden of Uzza; and Josiah, his son, reigns in his stead. 19-26.

1. *Manasseh was twelve years old.* He was born about three years after his father's miraculous cure; he was carried captive to Babylon, repented, was restored to his kingdom, put down idolatry, and died at the age of sixty-seven years (see 2 Chron. xxxiii. 1-20).

2. *After the abominations of the heathen.* He exactly copied the conduct of those nations which God had cast out of that land.

3. *Made a grove.* "He made Asherah," the Babylonian Melitta or Roman Venus. Wor-

shipped all the host of heaven. All the stars and planets, but particularly the sun and the moon.

4. *Built altars.* He placed idolatrous altars even in the Temple.

6. *Made his son pass through the fire.* Consecrated him to Moloch. *Observed times.* He practiced divination by the clouds; by observing their course at particular times, their different kinds, contrary directions. *Used enchantments.* He used incantations, spells, and charms. *Dealt with familiar spirits.* He was a necromancer; was a raiser of spirits, whom he endeavored to press into his service. *And wizards.* The "knowing ones."

7. *He set a graven image of the grove that he had made in the house.* Everyone may see that *Asherah* here must signify an idol, and not a grove.

8. *Neither will I make the feet of Israel.* Had they been faithful to God's testimonies, they never would have gone into captivity, and should even at this day have been in possession of the Promised Land.

9. *Seduced them to do more evil.* He did all he could to pervert the national character, and totally destroy the worship of the true God; and he succeeded.

10. *The Lord spake by . . . the prophets.* The prophets were Hosea, Joel, Nahum, Habakkuk, and Isaiah. These following five verses contain the sum of what these prophets spoke. It is said that Isaiah not only prophesied in those days, but also that he was put to death by Manasseh, being sawn asunder by a wooden saw.

12. *Both his ears shall tingle. Titstsalnah;* something expressive of the sound in what we call, from the same sensation, the "tingling" of the ears. This is the consequence of having the ears suddenly pierced with a loud and shrill noise; the ears seem to ring for some time after. The prophets spoke to them vehemently, so that the sound seemed to be continued even when they had left off speaking. This was a faithful and solemn testimony.

13. *The line of Samaria.* I will treat Jerusalem as I have treated Samaria. Samaria was taken, pillaged, ruined, and its inhabitants led into captivity; Jerusalem shall have the same measure. *I will wipe Jerusalem as a man wipeth a dish.* The Vulgate translates this clause as follows: "I will blot out Jerusalem as tablets are wont to be blotted out." This is a metaphor taken from the ancient method of writing. They traced their letters with a style on boards thinly spread over with wax; for this purpose one end of the style was sharp, the other end blunt and smooth, with which they could rub out what they had written, and so smooth the place and spread back the wax as to render it capable of receiving any other word. Thus the Lord had written down Jerusalem, never intending that its name or its memorial should be blotted out. But the idea of emptying out and wiping a dish expresses the same meaning equally well. Jerusalem shall be emptied of all its wealth, and of all its inhabitants, as truly as a dish turned up is emptied of all its contents; and it shall be turned upside down, never to be filled again.

14. *I will forsake the remnant of mine in-* *heritance.* One part (the ten tribes) was already forsaken and carried into captivity; the *remnant* (the tribe of Judah) was now about to be forsaken.

16. *Shed innocent blood very much.* Like the deities he worshipped, he was fierce and cruel; an unprincipled, merciless tyrant. He slew innocent people and God's prophets.

17. *Now the rest of the acts.* In 2 Chron. xxxiii. 11, etc., we read that the Assyrians took Manasseh, bound him with fetters, and took him to Babylon; that there he repented, sought God, and was, we are not told how, restored to his kingdom; that he fortified the city of David, destroyed idolatry, restored the worship of the true God, and died in peace. *Are they not written?* There are several particulars referred to here, and in 2 Chronicles xxxiii, which are not found in any chronicles or books which now remain, and what the "books of the seers" were, mentioned in Chronicles, we cannot tell.

18. *In the garden of his own house.* It was probably a burying place made for his own family, for Amon, his son, is said to be buried in the same place, v. 26.

19. *He reigned two years in Jerusalem.* The remark of the rabbins is not wholly without foundation, that the sons of those kings who were idolaters and who succeeded their fathers seldom reigned more than two years. So Nadab, the son of Jeroboam, 1 Kings xv. 25; Elah, the son of Baasha, 1 Kings xvi. 8; Ahaziah, the son of Ahab, 1 Kings xxii. 51; and Amon, the son of Manasseh, as mentioned here, v. 19.

23. *The servants of Amon conspired.* What their reason was for slaying their king we cannot tell. It does not seem to have been a popular act, for the people of the land rose up and slew the regicides. We hear enough of this man when we hear that he was as bad as his father was in the beginning of his reign, but did not copy his father's repentance.

26. *The garden of Uzza.* The family sepulchre or burying place.

CHAPTER 22

Josiah succeeds Amon, his father, and reigns thirty-one years, 1-2. He repairs the breaches of the Temple, 3-7. Hilkiah finds the book of the law in the Temple, 8. It is read by Shaphan, the scribe, before the king and his servants, 9-10. The king, greatly affected, sends to inquire of Huldah, the prophetess, 11-13. She delivers an afflictive prophecy concerning the evils that were coming upon the land, 14-17. But promises Josiah that these evils shall not come in his time, 18-20.

1. *Josiah was eight years old.* He was one of the best, if not the best, of all the Jewish kings since the time of David. He began well, continued well, and ended well.

4. *That he may sum the silver.* As Josiah began to seek the Lord as soon as he began to reign, we may naturally conclude that the worship of God that was neglected and suppressed by his father was immediately restored, and the people began their accustomed offerings to the Temple. Ten years therefore had elapsed since these offerings began; no one had as yet taken account of them, nor were they applied to the use for which they were given, viz., the repairing the breaches of the Temple.

8. *I have found the book of the law.* Was this the autograph of Moses? It is very probable

that it was, for in the parallel place, 2 Chron. xxxiv. 14, it is said to be the book of "the law of the Lord by Moses." It is supposed to be that part of Deuteronomy (xxviii; xxix; xxx; and xxxi) which contains the renewing of the covenant in the plains of Moab, and which contains the most terrible invectives against the corrupters of God's word and worship.

14. *Went unto Huldah, the prophetess.* This is a most singular circumstance. At this time Jeremiah was certainly a prophet in Israel, but it is likely he now dwelt at Anathoth, and could not be readily consulted. Zephaniah also prophesied under this reign, but probably he had not yet begun. Hilkiah was high priest, and the priest's lips should retain knowledge. Shaphan was scribe, and must have been conversant in sacred affairs to have been at all fit for his office. And yet *Huldah,* a prophetess, of whom we know nothing but by this circumstance, is consulted on the meaning of the book of the law.

17. *My wrath shall be kindled.* The decree is gone forth. Jerusalem shall be delivered into the hands of its enemies; the people will revolt more and more; towards them long-suffering is useless. The wrath of God is kindled, *and shall not be quenched.* This was a dreadful message.

20. *Thou shalt be gathered into thy grave in peace.* During your life none of these calamities shall fall upon the people, and no adversary shall be permitted to disturb the peace of Judea, and you shall die in peace with God. But was Josiah gathered to the grave in peace? Is it not said, chap. xxiii. 29, that Pharaohnechoh slew him at Megiddo? On this we may remark that the Assyrians and the Jews were at peace; that Josiah might feel it his duty to oppose the Egyptian king going against his friend and ally, and endeavor to prevent him from passing through his territories; and that in his endeavors to oppose him he was mortally wounded at Megiddo, but certainly was not killed there. For his servants put him in his second chariot and brought him to Jerusalem, where he died in peace (see 2 Chron. xxxv. 24).

CHAPTER 23

Josiah reads in the Temple to the elders of Judah, the priests, the prophets, and the people, the book of the covenant which had been found, 1-2. He makes a covenant, and the people stand to it, 3. He destroys the vessels of Baal and Asherah, and puts down the idolatrous priests; breaks down the houses of the sodomites, and the high places; defiles Topheth; takes away the horses of the sun; destroys the altars of Ahaz; breaks in pieces the images; and breaks down and burns Jeroboam's altar at Bethel, 4-15. Fulfils the word of the prophet who cried against the altar at Bethel, 16-18. Destroys the high places in Samaria, slays the idolatrous priests, and celebrates a great Passover, 19-23; and puts away all the dealers with familiar spirits, 24. His eminent character; he is mortally wounded at Megiddo, and buried at Jerusalem, 25-30. Jehoahaz reigns in his stead, and does evil in the sight of the Lord, 31-32. Is dethroned by Pharaoh-nechoh; and Eliakim, his brother, called also Jehoiakim, made king in his stead; the land is laid under tribute by the king of Egypt, and Jehoiakim reigns wickedly, 33-37.

2. *The king went up into the house of the Lord.* Here is another very singular circumstance. The high priest, scribes, priest, and prophets are gathered together, with all the elders of the people, and the king himself reads the book of the covenant which lately had been found! It is strange that either the high priest, Jeremiah, Zephaniah, or some other of the

prophets, who were certainly present there, did not read the sacred book! It is likely that the king considered himself a mediator between God and them, and therefore read and made the covenant.

3. *Stood by a pillar.* He stood, *al haammud,* "upon the stairs or pulpit." This is what is called the brazen scaffold or pulpit which Solomon made, and on which the kings were accustomed to stand when they addressed the people (see 2 Chron. vi. 13 and the parallel places).

4. *The priests of the second order.* These were probably such as supplied the place of the high priest when he was prevented from fulfilling the functions of his office. But the words may refer to those of the second course or order established by David; though it does not appear that those orders were now in use, yet the distinction was continued even to the time of our Lord. We find the course of Abia, which was the eighth, mentioned in Luke i. 5. *All the vessels.* These had been used for idolatrous purposes; the king is now to destroy them; for although no longer used in this way, they might, if permitted to remain, be an incentive to idolatry at a future time.

6. *He brought out the grove.* He brought out the idol Asherah. *Upon the graves of the children of the people.* I believe this means the burial place of the common people.

7. *The houses of the sodomites.* We have already often met with these *kedeshim* or "consecrated persons." The word implies all kinds of prostitutes, as well as abusers of themselves with mankind. *Wove hangings for the grove.* For *Asherah;* curtains or tent coverings for the places where the rites of the impure goddess were performed.

8. *The gate of Joshua.* The place where he, as governor of the city, heard and decided causes. Near this we find there were public altars, where sometimes the true God, at other times false gods, were honored.

9. *The priests of the high places came not up.* As these priests had offered sacrifices on the high places, though it was to the true God, yet they were not thought proper to be employed immediately about the Temple; but as they were acknowledged to belong to the priesthood, they had a right to their support. Therefore a portion of the tithes, offerings, and unleavened bread, shewbread, was appointed to them for their support. Thus they were treated as priests who had some infirmity which rendered it improper for them to minister at the altar (see Lev. xxi. 17, etc., and particularly vv. 22 and 23).

10. *He defiled Topheth.* Jerome says that Topheth was a fine and pleasant place, wellwatered with fountains, and adorned with gardens. The valley of the son of Hinnom, or *Gehenna,* was in one part; here it appears the sacred rites of Molech were performed, and to this all the filth of the city was carried, and perpetual fires were kept up in order to consume it. Hence it has been considered a type of hell, and in this sense it is used in the New Testament.

11. *The horses that the kings of Judah had given to the sun.* Throughout the East the horse, because of his swiftness and utility, was ded-

icated to the sun; and the Greeks and Romans feigned that the chariot of the sun was drawn by four horses. Whether these were living or sculptured horses, we cannot tell; the latter is the more reasonable supposition.

12. *On the top of the upper chamber.* Altars built on the flat roof of the house. Such altars were erected to the sun, moon, and stars, etc.

13. *Mount of corruption.* This, says Jarchi, following the Chaldee, was the mount of Olives, for this is the mount *hammishchah*, "of unction"; but because of the idolatrous purposes for which it was used, the Scripture changed the appellation to the mount *hammashchith*, "of corruption." *Ashtoreth the abomination* (see on 1 Kings xi. 7).

14. *Filled their places with the bones of men.* This was allowed to be the utmost defilement to which anything could be exposed.

16. *And as Josiah turned himself.* See 1 Kings xiii. 2, where these things were predicted.

17. *What title is that?* There was either a stone, an image, or an inscription here; no doubt the old prophet took care to have the place made sufficiently remarkable.

18. *The prophet that came out of Samaria.* See the note on 1 Kings xiii. 32.

19. *That were in the cities of Samaria.* Israel had now no king; and Josiah, of the blood royal of Judah, certainly had a direct right to the kingdom. He had, at this time, an especial commission from God to reform every abuse through the whole land—all that ground that was given by the Lord as an inheritance to the twelve sons of Jacob. Therefore he had every right to carry his plans of reformation into the Samaritan states.

20. *Slew all the priests.* The lives of these, as corrupters of the people, were forfeited to the law.

22. *Surely there was not holden such a passover.* Not one on purer principles, more heartily joined in by the people present, more literally consecrated, or more religiously observed. The words do not apply to the number present, but to the manner and spirit. See the particulars and mode of celebrating this Passover in 2 Chron. xxxv. 1-18.

24. *And the images.* The *teraphim.* See the note on Gen. xxxi. 19.

25. *Like unto him was there no king.* Perhaps not one from the time of David; and, morally considered, including David himself, none ever sat on the Jewish throne so truly exemplary in his own conduct, and so thoroughly zealous in the work of God. David was a greater but not a better man than Josiah.

26. *The Lord turned not.* It was of no use to try this fickle and radically depraved people any longer. They were respited merely during the life of Josiah.

30. *Dead from Megiddo.* The word *meth* should here be considered as a participle, "dying," for it is certain he was not *dead.* He was mortally wounded at Megiddo, was carried in a dying state to Jerusalem, and there he died and was buried (see 2 Chron. xxxv. 24).

31. *Jehoahaz was twenty and three years old.* This was not the eldest son of Josiah, which is

evident from this, that he was twenty-three years old when he began to reign; that he reigned but three months; that, being dethroned, his brother Eliakim was put in his place, who was then twenty-five years of age. Eliakim, therefore, was the eldest brother; but Jehoahaz was probably raised to the throne by the people, as being of a more active and martial spirit.

33. *Nechoh put him in bands.* But what was the cause of his putting him in bands? It is conjectured, and not without reason, that Jehoahaz, otherwise called Shallum, raised an army, met Nechoh in his return from Carchemish, fought, was beaten, taken prisoner, put in chains, and taken into Egypt, where he died (v. 34 and Jer. xxii. 11-12). *Riblah* or Diblath, the place of this battle, was probably a town in Syria, *in the land* or district *of Hamath.*

34. *Turned his name to Jehoiakim.* These names are precisely the same in signification. Eliakim is "God shall arise"; Jehoiakim, "Jehovah shall arise." That is, God's rising again to show His power, justice. The change of the name was to show Nechoh's supremacy, and that Jehoiakim was only his vassal or viceroy. Proofs of this mode of changing the name, when a person of greater power put another in office under himself, may be seen in the case of Mattaniah, changed into Zedekiah; Daniel, Mishael, Hananiah, and Azariah into Belteshazzar, Shadrach, Meshach, and Abed-nego; and Joseph into Zaphnath-paaneah (see Dan. i. 6-7; Gen. xli. 45).

35. *Jehoiakim gave the silver and the gold.* Nechoh had placed him there as viceroy, simply to raise and collect his taxes. *Every one according to his taxation.* That is, each was assessed in proportion to his property. That was the principle avowed: but there is reason to fear that this bad king was not governed by it.

37. *He did that which was evil in the sight of the Lord.* He was a most unprincipled and oppressive tyrant. Jeremiah gives us his character at large, chap. xxii. 13-19, to which the reader will do well to refer. Jeremiah was at that time in the land, and was an eyewitness of the abominations of this cruel king.

CHAPTER 24

Nebuchadnezzar brings Jehoiakim under subjection, who, after three years, rebels, 1. Bands of Chaldeans, Syrians, Moabites, and Ammonites invade the land, 2-4. Jehoiakim dies, and Jehoiachin, his son, reigns in his stead, 5-6. The Babylonians overcome the Egyptians, 7. Nebuchadnezzar takes Jehoiachin and his family, and all his treasures, and those of the Temple, and all the chief people and artificers, and carries them to Babylon, 8-16; and makes Mattaniah, brother of Jehoiakim, king, who reigns wickedly, and rebels against the king of Babylon, 17-20.

1. *Nebuchadnezzar.* This man, so famous in the writings of the prophets, was son of Nabopolassar. He was sent by his father against the rulers of several provinces that had revolted; and he took Carchemish, and all that belonged to the Egyptians, from the Euphrates to the Nile. Jehoiakim, who was tributary to Nechoh, king of Egypt, he attacked and reduced, and obliged to become tributary to Babylon. At the end of three years he revolted; and then a mixed army, of Chaldeans, Syrians, Moabites, and Ammonites, was sent against him, who

ravaged the country and took 3,023 prisoners, whom they brought to Babylon, Jer. lii. 28.

2. *According to the word of the Lord.* See what Huldah predicted, chap. xxii. 16; and see chaps. xiv; xv; and xvi of Jeremiah.

6. *Jehoiachin his son.* As this man reigned only three months, and was a mere vassal to the Babylonians, his reign is scarcely to be reckoned; and therefore Jeremiah says of Jehoiakim, "He shall have none to sit upon the throne of David," chap. xxxvi. 30, for at that time it belonged to the king of Babylon, and Jehoiachin was a mere viceroy or governor. Jehoiachin is called Jechonias in Matt. i. 11.

7. *The king of Egypt came not again.* He was so crushed by the Babylonians that he was obliged to confine himself within the limits of his own states, and could no more attempt any conquests. The text tells us how much he had lost by the Babylonians.

8. *Jehoiachin was eighteen years old.* He is called Jeconiah, 1 Chron. iii. 16; and Coniah, Jer. xxii. 24. In 2 Chron. xxxvi. 9, he is said to be only eight years of age, but this must be a mistake. For we find that, having reigned only three months, he was carried captive to Babylon, and there he had wives; and it is very improbable that a child between eight and nine years of age could have wives; and of such a tender age, it can scarcely be said that, as a king, "he did that which was evil in the sight of the Lord." The place in Chronicles must be corrupted.

12. *Jehoiachin . . . went out.* He saw that it was useless to attempt to defend himself any longer; and he therefore surrendered himself, hoping to obtain better terms.

13. *He carried out thence all the treasures.* It has been remarked that Nebuchadnezzar spoiled the Temple three times: (1) He took away the greater part of those treasures when he took Jerusalem under Jehoiakim, and the vessels that he took then he placed in the temple of his god, Dan. i. 2. And these were the vessels which Belshazzar profaned, Dan. v. 2; and which Cyrus restored to Ezra when he went up to Jerusalem, Ezra i. 2. It was at this time that he took Daniel and his companions. (2) He took the remaining part of those vessels, and broke them or cut them in pieces, when he came the second time against Jerusalem under Jeconiah; as is mentioned here, v. 13. (3) He pillaged the Temple, took away all the brass, the brazen pillars, brazen vessels, and vessels of gold and silver, which he found there when he besieged Jerusalem under Zedekiah, chap. xxv. 13-17.

14. *He carried away all Jerusalem.* That is, all the chief men, the nobles, and artificers. Among these there were of mighty men 7,000; of craftsmen and smiths, 1,000.

17. *Made Mattaniah his father's brother king in his stead.* He was the son of Josiah, and brother to Jehoiakim. *Changed his name to Zedekiah.* See the note on chap. xxiii. 34.

19. *He did . . . evil.* How astonishing is this! not one of them takes warning by the judgments of God, which fell on their sinful predecessors.

20. *Zedekiah rebelled.* This was in the eighth year of his reign; and he is strongly reproved for having violated the oath he took to the king of Babylon (see 2 Chron. xxxvi. 13).

CHAPTER 25

Nebuchadnezzar besieges Jerusalem; it is taken, after having been sorely reduced by famine, etc.; and Zedekiah, endeavoring to make his escape, is made prisoner, and his sons are slain before his eyes; then, his eyes being put out, he is put in chains and carried to Babylon, 1-7. Nebuzar-adan burns the Temple, breaks down the walls of Jerusalem, and carries away the people captives, leaving only a few to till the ground, 8-12. He takes away all the brass, and all the vessels of the Temple, 13-17. Several of the chief men and nobles found in the city, he brings to Nebuchadnezzar at Riblah, who puts them all to death, 18-21. Nebuchadnezzar makes Gedaliah governor over the poor people that were left, against whom Ishmael rises, and slays him, and others with him; on which the people in general, fearing the resentment of the Chaldeans, flee to Egypt, 22-26. Evil-merodach, king of Babylon, releases Jehoiachin out of prison, treats him kindly, and makes him his friend, 27-30.

1. *In the ninth year of his reign.* Zedekiah having revolted against the Chaldeans, Nebuchadnezzar, wearied with his treachery, and the bad faith of the Jews, determined the total subversion of the Jewish state. Having assembled a numerous army, he entered Judea on the tenth day of the tenth month of the ninth year of the reign of Zedekiah, which was a sabbatical year; whereon the men of Jerusalem, hearing that the Chaldean army was approaching, proclaimed liberty to their servants (see Jer. xxxiv. 8-10), according to the law, Exod. xxi. 2; Deut. xv. 1-2, 12. For Nebuchadnezzar, marching with his army against Zedekiah, having wasted all the country, and taken their strongholds, except Lachish, Azekah, and Jerusalem, came against the latter with all his forces (see Jer. xxxiv. 1-7). On the very day the siege and utter destruction of Jerusalem were revealed to Ezekiel, the prophet, then in Chaldea, under the type of a seething pot; and his wife died in the evening, and he was charged not to mourn for her, because of the extraordinary calamity that had fallen upon the land (see Ezek. xxiv. 1-2, etc.).

Jeremiah, having predicted the same calamities, Jer. xxxiv. 1-7, was by the command of Zedekiah shut up in prison, xxxii. 1-16. Pharaoh-hophra, hearing how Zedekiah was pressed, and fearing for the safety of his own dominions should the Chaldeans succeed against Jerusalem, determined to succor Zedekiah. Finding this, the Chaldeans raised the siege of Jerusalem, and went to meet the Egyptian army, which they defeated and put to flight, Joseph., *Antiq.,* lib. 10, cap. 10. In the interim the Jews, thinking their danger was passed, reclaimed their servants, and put them again under the yoke; Jer. xxxiv. 8, etc.

2-4. *And the city was besieged.* Nebuchadnezzar, having routed the Egyptian army, returned to Jerusalem, and besieged it so closely that, being reduced by famine, and a breach made in the wall, the Chaldeans entered it on the ninth day of the fourth month, Zedekiah and many others endeavoring to make their escape by night.

5. *The army of the Chaldeans pursued.* Zedekiah was taken, and brought captive to Riblah in Syria, where Nebuchadnezzar then lay, who ordered his sons to be slain before his face, and then put out his eyes; and having loaded him with chains, sent him to Babylon (see Jer. xxxix. 4, 7; lii. 7, 11), thus fulfilling the prophetic declarations that his eyes should see the eyes of the king of Babylon, Jer. xxxii. 4 and xxxiv. 3; but Babylon he should not see, though he was to die there, Ezek. xii. 13.

8. *In the fifth month.* On the seventh day of the fifth month Nebuzar-adan made his entry into the city; and having spent two days in making provision, on the tenth day of the same month he set fire to the Temple and the king's palace, and the houses of the nobility, and burned them to the ground (Jer. lii. 13, compared with xxxix. 8). Thus the Temple was destroyed in the eleventh year of Zedekiah, the nineteenth of Nebuchadnezzar.

10. *Brake down the walls.* In the same fifth month, Jer. i. 3, the walls of Jerusalem being razed to the ground, all that were left in the city, and all that had fled over formerly to Nebuchadnezzar, and all the common people of the city, with all the king's treasures, those of the nobles, and the whole furniture of the Temple, did Nebuzar-adan carry off to Babylon (see Jer. xxxix. 8-9; lii. 14, 23).

18. *Seraiah the chief priest . . . Zephaniah.* The person who is here called the *second priest* was what the Jews call *sagan,* a sort of deputy, who performed the functions of the high priest when he was prevented by any infirmity from attending the Temple service (see on chap. xxiii. 4).

19. *And five men of them that were in the king's presence.* These were principal counsellors and confidential officers. In Jer. lii. 25 it is said he took seven men who were near the king's person, and the same number is found in the Arabic in this place; and the Chaldee has no less than fifty men; but in Jeremiah this, as well as all the rest of the versions, reads "seven." Probably they were no more than five at first, or perhaps Jeremiah reckoned with the five the officer that was set over the men of war and the principal scribe of the host mentioned here, as two with the five; and thus made seven in the whole.

21. *The king of Babylon smote them.* He had, no doubt, found that these had counselled Zedekiah to revolt.

22. *Made Gedaliah . . . ruler.* This was no regal dignity; he was only a sort of overseer, appointed to regulate the husbandmen.

23. *To Mizpah.* This is said to have been situated on the east side of the river Jordan, and most contiguous to Babylon, and therefore the most proper for the residence of Gedaliah, because nearest to the place from which he was to receive his instructions.

24. *Gedaliah sware to them.* He pledged himself in the most solemn manner to encourage and protect them.

25. *Smote Gedaliah.* This was at an entertainment which Gedaliah had made for them (see Jer. xli. 1, etc.). He was not content with this murder, but slew fourscore more, who were coming with offerings to the Temple, and took several as prisoners, among whom were some of the king's daughters; and set off to go to the Ammonites. But Johanan, the son of Kareah, hearing of these outrages, raised a number of men, and pursued Ishmael; upon which Ishmael's prisoners immediately turned and joined Johanan; so that he, and eight of his accomplices, with difficulty escaped to the Ammonites (see Jer. xli. 1, etc.). Baalis, king of the Ammonites, had sent Ishmael to murder Gedaliah; and of this he was informed by Johanan, who offered to prevent it by taking away the life of this murderer. But Gedaliah could not believe that he harbored such foul designs, and therefore took no precaution to save his life (see Jer. xl. 13-16).

27. *And it came to pass.* Nebuchadnezzar was just now dead; and Evil-merodach, his son, succeeded to the kingdom in the thirty-seventh year of the captivity of Jehoiachin. And on the seven and twentieth day [Jeremiah says five and twentieth] of the twelfth month of that year, he brought the long captivated Jewish king out of prison, treated him kindly, and ever after, during his life, reckoned him among the king's friends. This is particularly related in the last four verses of the Book of Jeremiah.

30. *A continual allowance given him of the king.* He lived in a regal style, and had his court even in the city of Babylon, being supplied with every requisite by the munificence and friendship of the king. In about two years after this, Evil-merodach was slain in a conspiracy; and it is supposed that Jehoiachin, then about fifty-eight years of age, fell with his friend and protector. Thus terminates the catastrophe of the Jewish kings, people, and state; the consequence of unheard-of rebellions and provocations against the Majesty of heaven.

The First Book of

CHRONICLES

THE TWO BOOKS OF CHRONICLES

Anciently these two books were considered but as one. For this we have not only the testimony of Jerome, but also that of the Masoretes, who gave the sum of all the sections, chapters, and verses, under one notation at the end of the second book, without mentioning any division; and although the modern Jews divide them, yet they give the Masoretic enumeration of sections as it was given of old; and all editors of the Masoretic Bibles, whether Jewish or Christian, follow the same plan.

These books have had several *names*. In Hebrew they are denominated *dibrey haiyamim;* literally, "The Words of the Days," i.e., "The Journals," particularly of the kings of Israel and kings of Judah. But this name does not appear to have been given by the inspired writer.

The Septuagint has "of the things that were left"; supposing that these books were a supplement either to Samuel and to the Books of Kings, or to the whole Bible. To this the Greek translators might have been led by finding that these books in their time closed the Sacred Canon, as they still do in the most correct editions of the Hebrew Bible.

In our English Bibles these books are termed Chronicles, from the Greek *chronos*, "time," i.e., "A History of Times."

Concerning the author of these books, nothing certain is known. Some think they are the works of different authors; but the uniformity of the style, the connection of the facts, together with the recapitulations and reflections which are often made, prove that they are the work of one and the same person.

The Jews, and Christian interpreters in general, believe they were the work of Ezra, assisted by the prophets Haggai, Zechariah, and Malachi. That Ezra was the author is, on the whole, the most probable opinion. That he lived at the conclusion of the Babylonish captivity is well-known; and the Second Book of Chronicles terminates at that period, barely reciting the decree of Cyrus to permit the return of the captivated Israelites to their own land; which subject is immediately taken up in the book of Ezra, in which the operation of that decree is distinctly marked.

We are not to suppose that these books are the "chronicles of the kings of Judah and Israel" so often referred to in the historical books of the Old Testament; these have been long lost, and the books before us can only be abridgments, either of such chronicles or of works of a similar kind.

That the ancient Jews took great care to register their civil, military, and ecclesiastical transactions is sufficiently evident from frequent reference to such works in the sacred writings; and that these registers were carefully and correctly formed, we learn from the character of the persons by whom they were compiled. They were in general prophets, and seem to have been employed by the kings under whom they lived to compile the annals of their reigns; or most likely this was considered a part of the prophet's regular office.

Though the writer gives many important particulars in the life of David, yet he passes by his adultery with Bath-sheba and all its consequences. He says nothing of the incest of Amnon with his sister Tamar, nor a word of the rebellion and abominations of Absalom. He says very little of the kings of Israel, and takes no notice of what concerned that state, from the capture of Amaziah, king of Judah, by Joash, king of Israel—2 Chron. xxv. 17, etc. And of the last wars of these kings, which terminated in the captivity of the ten tribes, he says not one word!

The principal design of the writer appears to have been this: to point out, from the public registers, which were still preserved, what had been the state of the different families previously to the Captivity, that at their return they might enter on and repossess their respective inheritances. He enters particularly into the functions, genealogies, families, and orders of the priests and Levites; and this was peculiarly necessary after the return from the Captivity, to the end that the worship of God might be conducted in the same way as before, and by the proper, legitimate persons.

He is also very particular relative to what concerns religion, the worship of God, the Temple and its utensils, the kings who authorized or tolerated idolatry, and those who maintained the worship of the true God. In his distribution of praise and blame, these are the qualities which principally occupy his attention and influence his pen.

CHAPTER 1

The genealogy of Adam to Noah, 1-3. Of Noah to Abraham, 4-27. The sons of Abraham, Ishmael, and Isaac, 28. The sons of Ishmael, 29-33. The sons of Esau, 34-42. A list of the kings of Edom, 43-50. A list of the dukes of Edom, 51-54.

1. *Adam, Sheth, Enosh.* That is, Adam was the father of Sheth or Seth, Seth was the father of Enosh, Enosh the father of Kenan, and so on. No notice is taken of Cain and Abel, or of any of the other sons of Adam. One line of patriarchs, from Adam to Noah, is what the historian intended to give.

43. *Before any king reigned over . . . Israel.* See Gen. xxxvi. 31, etc., where the same verses occur, as I have supposed borrowed from this place; and see the notes there.

For various particulars in this chapter see Genesis x and xxxvi and the parallel places.

CHAPTER 2

The twelve sons of Jacob, 1-2. The posterity of Judah down to David, 3-15. The posterity of the children of Jesse and Caleb, 16-55.

42. *Now the sons of Caleb.* This was not Caleb the son of Jephunneh, but Caleb the son of Hezron, vv. 18, 50.

CHAPTER 3

The children of David which were born to him in Hebron, 1-4. Those born to him in Jerusalem, 5-9. The regal line from Solomon, 10-24.

1. *The second, Daniel.* In 2 Sam. iii. 3, this person is called Chileab; he probably had two names. The Targum says, "The second, Daniel, who was also called Chileab, because he was in every respect like to his father." The Targumist refers here to the import of the word *ke-le-ab*, "like to the father."

5. *Shimea, and Shobab.* Solomon is mentioned last, though he was the eldest of these four sons, because the genealogy was to be continued from him. *Bath-shua* is the same as Bath-sheba.

6. *Elishama, and Eliphelet.* In this and the eighth verse these two names occur twice; some think this is a mistake, but others suppose that two persons of these names died young, and that the next born received the name of the deceased.

8. *Nine.* There are thirteen if we count the four sons of Bath-sheba, and nine without them; and in the Second Book of Samuel there are eleven, reckoning the above four, and without them only seven. In the Book of Samuel probably only those who were alive were reckoned, while the author of the Chronicles comprises those also who were dead in this enumeration. Jarchi supposes that the duplicate Elishama and Eliphelet are those which increase the regular number seven to nine.

9. *And Tamar their sister.* This is the only daughter of David whose name is on record; and yet he is said to have had both sons and daughters, 2 Sam. v. 13.

16. *Zedekiah his son.* If this be the same who was the last king of Judah, before the Captivity, the word *son* must be taken here to signify "successor"; for it is certain that Zedekiah was the successor of Jeconiah, and that Zedekiah was the son of Josiah, and not of Jehoiakim.

17. *The sons of Jeconiah.* Jeremiah has said, chap. xxii. 30, that Jeconiah, or as he calls him, Coniah, should be childless. But this must refer to his posterity being deprived of the throne, and indeed thus the prophet interprets it himself: "For no man of his seed shall prosper, sitting upon the throne of David, and ruling any more in Judah." *Assir.* Salathiel was not the son of Assir, but of Jeconiah, Matt. i. 12. Who then was Assir? Possibly nobody; for as the Hebrew *assir* signifies a "prisoner," it may be considered as an epithet of Jeconiah, who we know was a very long time prisoner in Babylon (see 2 Kings xxiv. 15).

19. *The sons of Pedaiah.* Houbigant thinks these words should be omitted. *Pedaiah* is wanting in the Arabic and Syriac. If this be omitted, Zerubbabel will appear to be the son of Salathiel, according to Matt. i. 12, and not the son of Pedaiah, as here stated.

22. *The sons of Shemaiah . . . six.* Five only are found in the text, and the versions give us no assistance; neither do the MSS. correct the place. If the father be not here included with his sons, some name must be lost out of the text.

CHAPTER 4

A second genealogy of Judah, 1-23. The account of Jabez, 9-10. The genealogy of Simeon, 24-27. Their cities, 28-31. Their villages, and where situated, 32-33. The heads of families, 34-38. Where they settled, and what was their occupation, 39-43.

1. *The sons of Judah.* A genealogy of this tribe has already been given in the second chapter. It is here introduced again, with some variations. Probably there were different copies in the public registers; and the writer of this book, finding that this second one contained some remarkable particulars, thought proper to insert it in this place.

7. *And Ethnan.* After this word we should, with the Targum, read Coz, whose posterity is mentioned in the next verse. Coz was probably the same as Kenaz.

8. *The son of Harum.* Jabez should be mentioned at the end of this verse, else he is as a consequent without an antecedent.

15. *Caleb the son of Jephunneh.* We have already met with this eminent person in Num. xiii. 6, 30; xiv. 24; and elsewhere, and seen his courageous piety and inflexible integrity.

23. *These were the potters.* They were probably brickmakers; perhaps potters also, who had their dwelling in low grounds, and fabricated the clay into pots and bricks that was digged up in forming fences in the king's domains.

24. *The sons of Simeon.* This genealogy is very different from that given in Gen. xlvi. 10, and Num. xxvi. 12. This may be occasioned by the same person having several names, one list taking one name, another list some other, and so on. To reconcile is impossible; to attempt it, useless.

27. *Neither did all their family multiply.* In Num. i. 23 the number of all the families of Simeon was 59,300; and that of Judah was, v. 27, not less than 74,600. When the next census was made, Numbers xxvi, the tribe of Judah amounted to 76,500, an increase of 1,900; while the tribe of Simeon amounted only to 22,200, a decrease of 37,100. It was at that time the smallest tribe in Israel.

31. *These were their cities unto the reign of David.* It appears that David took some of the cities of the Simeonites, and added them to Judah; Ziklag, for instance, 1 Sam. xxvii. 6. As the tribe of Simeon had withdrawn their allegiance from the house of David, the kings of Judah extended their domination as far as possible into the territories of that tribe, so that they were obliged to seek pasture for their flocks at Gedor and in the mountains of Seir, as we find in vv. 39-42.

40. *They of Ham had dwelt there of old.* These were probably either Philistines or Egyptians, who dwelt at Gedor, which was situated in the environs of Joppa and Samnia. Those whom the 500 Simeonites expelled from Seir were Amalekites, v. 43.

43. *They smote the rest of the Amalekites.* Those who had escaped in the war which Saul made against them (see 1 Sam. xiv. 48) and from David, who had attacked them afterwards, 2 Sam. viii. 12.

CHAPTER 5

The genealogies of Reuben, 1-10. Of Gad, 11-17. The exploits of Reuben, Gad, and the half-tribe of Manasseh, 18-22. The genealogy of the half-tribe of Manasseh, 23-24. The idolatry of these tribes and their captivity by the Assyrians, 25-26.

1. *The sons of Reuben the firstborn.* As Reuben was the eldest son of Jacob, why was not his genealogy reviewed first? This verse answers the question; he lost the birthright because of the transgression mentioned in Gen. xxxv. 22 and xlix. 4, and the precedency was given to Judah; from him therefore came the chief ruler. This appears to be the meaning of the place.

2. *And of him came the chief ruler.* This is, by both the Syriac and Arabic, understood of Christ: "From Judah the King Messiah shall proceed."

6. *Beerah his son.* After their separation from the house of David the ten tribes continued to have princes of the tribes; and this continued till the time that Tiglath-pileser carried them captives into Assyria. At that time *Beerah* was their *prince* or "chief"; and with him this species of dominion or precedency terminated.

8. *Who dwelt in Aroer.* This town was situated on the river Arnon; and *Nebo* was both a city and a mountain in the same country. They both lay on the other side of Jordan.

10. *And they dwelt in their tents.* The *Hagarites* were tribes of nomad Arabs; people who lived in tents, without any fixed dwellings, and whose property consisted in cattle. The descendants of Reuben extirpated these Hagarites, seized on their property and their tents, and dwelt in their place.

16. *The suburbs of Sharon.* There were three places of this name: that mentioned here was a district in the country of Bashan beyond Jordan (see Josh. xii. 18); there was another that lay between Caesarea of Palestine and Joppa; and there was a third between Mount Tabor and the Sea of Tiberias.

19. *They made war with the Hagarites.* This is probably the same war that is mentioned in v. 10.

21. *They took away their cattle.* This was a war of extermination as to the political state of the people, which nothing could justify but an especial direction of God; and this He could never give against any, unless the cup of their iniquity had been full. The Hagarites were full of idolatry (see v. 25).

22. *For there fell down many slain.* The hundred thousand men mentioned above were probably made slaves, and were not slain.

25. *The gods of the people of the land.* We see the reason why God delivered the Hagarites into the hands of these tribes; they were abominable idolaters, and therefore God destroyed them.

26. *Tilgath-pilneser.* Many MSS. have *Tiglath* instead of *Tilgath*. The Syriac, the Septuagint, and the Chaldee have the same reading as in 2 Kings xv. 29, etc.

CHAPTER 6

The genealogy of Levi and Aaron, 1-30. The offices of the priests and Levites, 31-53. The cities assigned them, 54-81.

1. *The sons of Levi.* It has been well remarked that the genealogy of *Levi* is given here more amply and correctly than that of any of the others. And this is perhaps an additional proof that the author was a priest, felt much for the priesthood, and took care to give the genealogy of the Levitical and sacerdotal families from the most correct tables; for with such tables we may presume he was intimately acquainted.

4. *Eleazar begat Phinehas.* As the high priesthood continued in this family for a long time, the sacred historian confines himself to this chiefly, omitting Nadab and Abihu, and even the family of Ithamar.

8. *Ahitub begat Zadok.* Through this person the high priesthood came again into the family of Eleazar.

10. *Johanan.* Supposed to be the same as Jehoiada. *Executed the priest's office.* Probably this refers to the dignified manner in which Azariah opposed King Uzziah, who wished to invade the priest's office, and offer incense in the Temple (see 2 Chron. xxvi. 17-18).

14. *Seraiah.* He was put to death by Nebuchadnezzar, 2 Kings xxv. 18, 21.

22. *Korah.* See the history of this man, and his rebellion, Numbers xvi.

28. *The firstborn Vashni, and Abiah.* There is a great mistake in this verse: in 1 Sam. viii. 2 we read, "Now the name of his [Samuel's] firstborn was Joel; and the name of his second, Abiah." The word *Joel* is lost out of the text, in this place, and *vesheni*, which signifies "the second," and which refers to *Abiah*, is made here into a proper name. These, Joel and Abiah, were the two sons of Samuel, who administered justice so badly that the people, being oppressed, began to murmur, and demanded a king (see 1 Sam. viii. 1, etc).

31. *After that the ark had rest.* That is, when it was brought from the house of Obed-edom.

32. *According to their order.* This order is specified below.

39. *Asaph.* This person, with Heman, the sons of Korah, Ethan, Jeduthun, etc., are celebrated in these books, and in the Psalms, for their skill in singing, and the part they performed in the public worship of God.

50. *These are the sons of Aaron.* We have

already had a list of these (see vv. 3-16); this is a second, but less extensive, and is a proof that the writer of this book had several lists before him, from which he borrowed as he judged proper.

54. *Theirs was the lot.* All the tribes and families obtained their respective inheritances by lot, but to the sons of Aaron was the "first lot"; and so the Syriac and Arabic have understood this place. See an account of the possessions of the priests and Levites, Joshua xx; xxi.

60. *All their cities . . . were thirteen.* But there are only eleven reckoned here, Gibeon and Juttah being omitted, and the names of some of the others changed. None of the versions give the full number of names, although they all give the whole sum "thirteen."

65. *Which are called by their names.* Probably each family gave its own name to the city that fell to its lot.

69. *Aijalon with her suburbs.* There are two cities wanting here, Eltekeh and Gibethon (see Josh. xxi. 23).

71-77. We shall see from Josh. xxi. 28, etc., that several of these cities have different names.

CHAPTER 7

The genealogy of Issachar, 1-5. Of Benjamin, 6-12. Of Naphtali, 13. Of Manasseh, 14-19. Of Ephraim, 20-29. And of Asher, 30-40.

2. *Whose number was in the days of David.* Whether this was the number returned by Joab and his assistants, when they made that census of the people with which God was so much displeased, we know not. It is worthy of remark that we read here the sum of three tribes, Benjamin, Issachar, and Asher, under the reign of David, which is mentioned nowhere else; and yet we have no account here of the other tribes, probably because the author found no public registers in which such enumeration was recorded.

3. *The sons of Izrahiah . . . five.* There are, however, only four names in the text. Instead of *five,* the Syriac and Arabic read "four." If *five* be the true reading, then Izrahiah must be reckoned with his four sons.

6. *The sons of Benjamin; Bela, and Becher, and Jediael.* In Gen. xlvi. 21, ten sons of Benjamin are reckoned. In Num. xxvi. 38, etc., five sons only of Benjamin are mentioned. In the beginning of the following chapter, five sons of Benjamin are mentioned, viz., Bela, Ashbel, Aharah, Nohah, and Rapha; where also Addar, Gera, Abihud, Abishua, Naaman, Ahoah, a second Gera, Shephuphan, and Huram are all represented as grandsons, not sons of Bejamin. Hence we see that in many cases grandsons are called sons, and both are often confounded in the genealogical tables. To attempt to reconcile such discrepancies would be a task as endless as it would be useless. The rabbins say that Ezra, who wrote this book, did not know whether some of these were sons or grandsons; and they intimate also that the tables from which he copied were often defective, and here we must leave all such matters.

21. *Whom the men of Gath . . . slew.* We know nothing of this circumstance but what is related here.

24. *His daughter was Sherah.* That is, "remnant"; "called so," says the Targum, "because she was the remnant that escaped from the slaughter mentioned above."

32. *And Shua their sister.* It is very rarely that women are found in the Jewish genealogies, and they are never inserted but for especial reasons.

CHAPTER 8

The genealogy of Benjamin down to Saul, 1-32. The children and descendants of Saul, 33-40.

1. *Now Benjamin begat.* See what has been said on the preceding chapter, v. 6.

9. *He begat of Hodesh his wife.* In the preceding verse it is said that Hushim and Baara were his wives; and here it is said, *He begat of Hodesh his wife.* And then his children by Hushim are mentioned, but not a word of Baara! It is likely therefore that Hodesh was another name for Baara, and this is asserted by the Targum: "And he begot of Baara, that is Chodesh, his wife; so called because he espoused her anew." It is supposed that he had put her away before, and now remarried her.

29. *And at Gibeon.* This passage to the end of the thirty-eighth verse is found, with a little variety in the names, in chap. ix. 35-44. The rabbins say that Ezra, having found two books that had these passages with a variety in the names, as they agreed in general, he thought best to insert them both, not being able to discern which was the best.

34. *Merib-baal.* The same as Mephibosheth; for, as the Israelites detested *Baal,* which signifies "lord," they changed it into *bosheth,* which signifies "shame" or "reproach."

CHAPTER 9

All Israel reckoned by genealogies, 1. The first inhabitants of Jerusalem, after their return from their captivity, who were chiefs of the fathers, 2-9. Of the priests, 10-13; Levites, 14-16; porters, their work, lodgings, etc., 17-29; other officers, 30-32; the singers, 33-34. A repetition of the genealogy of Saul and his sons, 35-44.

1. *Were reckoned by genealogies.* Jarchi considers these as the words of Ezra, the compiler of the book; as if he had said: I have given the genealogies of the Israelites as I have found them in a book which was carried into Babylon, when the people were carried thither for their transgressions; and this book which I found is that which I have transcribed in the preceding chapters.

2. *Now the first inhabitants.* This is spoken of those who returned from the Babylonish captivity, and of the time in which they returned; for it is insinuated here that other persons afterwards settled at Jerusalem, though these mentioned here were the *first* on the return from the Captivity. Properly speaking, the divisions mentioned in this verse constituted the whole of the Israelitish people, who were, ever since the days of Joshua, divided into the four following classes: (1) the *priests;* (2) the *Levites;* (3) the common people, or simple *Israelites;* (4) the *Nethinims,* or slaves of the Temple, the remains of the Gibeonites, who, having deceived Joshua, were condemned to this service, Josh. ix. 21, etc. In David's time it is probable that other conquered people were added, as the

successors of the Gibeonites were not sufficient to perform all the drudgery of the Temple service.

3. *And in Jerusalem dwelt.* Several of the tribes of Judah, Benjamin, Ephraim, and Manasseh took advantage of the proclamation of Cyrus to return to Jerusalem, and so mingled with the Israelites, and those to whom Jerusalem had previously appertained; and this was necessary in order to provide a sufficient population for so large a city.

4. *Uthai the son of Ammihud.* The list here is nearly the same with those found in Ezra and Nehemiah, and contains those who returned to Jerusalem with Zerubbabel; but the list in Nehemiah is more ample, probably because it contains those who came afterwards. The object of the sacred writer here was to give the list of those who came *first.* "Now the first inhabitants."

11. *The ruler of the house of God.* The high priest at this time was Jeshua, the son of Jozadak (Ezra iii. 8); and Seraiah (Neh. xi. 11), called here *Azariah,* was the *ruler of the house;* the person next in authority to the high priest, and who probably had the guard of the Temple and command of the priests, Levites, etc. It is likely that the person here was the same as is called the "second priest," 2 Kings xxv. 18, who was the *sagan* or high priest's deputy.

13. *And their brethren.* What a prodigious number of ecclesiastics to perform the divine service of one temple! No less than 1,780 able-bodied men! And this number is reckoned independently of the 212 porters who served at the gates of the house of the Lord, v. 22.

18. *The king's gate.* That by which the kings of Judah went to the Temple (see 2 Kings xvi. 18).

19. *Keepers of the entry.* Whose business it was to suffer no person to come to the tabernacle but the priests, during the performance of the sacred service.

30. *The sons of the priests made the ointment.* Only the priests were permitted to make this ointment; all others were forbidden to do it on pain of death (see Exod. xxx. 34-38, and the notes there).

35. *Whose wife's name was Maachah.* Here our translators have departed from the original, for the word is *achotho,* "his sister"; but the Vulgate, Septuagint, Syriac, Arabic, and Chaldee have "wife"; to which may be added chap. viii. 29, the parallel place. Almost all the early editions, as well as the MS. editions, have the same reading. There is most certainly a fault somewhere, for Maachah could not be both the sister and the wife of Jehiel. Whether, therefore, chap. viii. 29 has been altered from this, or this altered from that, who can tell? A single letter makes the whole difference. If the word be written with *cheth,* it is "sister"; if with *shin,* it is "wife." The latter is most probably the true reading.

41. *And Ahaz.* This is added by our translators from chap. viii. 35, but such liberties should be taken only in a note; for although the words are now sufficiently distinguished from the text by being printed in italics, yet it is too much to expect that every editor of a Bible will attend to such distinctions, and in process of

time the words will be found incorporated with the text.

35, and the following verses, are a repetition of what we find in chap. viii. 29-38.

CHAPTER 10

A fatal battle between the Israelites and Philistines in Gilboa, in which Saul is mortally wounded, and his three sons slain, 1-6. The Israelites being totally routed, the Philistines, coming to strip the dead, find Saul and his three sons among the slain; they cut off Saul's head, and send it and his armor about the country to the idol temples; and then fix them up in the house of Dagon, 7-10. The men of Jabesh-gilead come by night and take away the bodies of Saul and his three sons, and bury them in Jabesh, 11-12. The reason of Saul's tragic death; the kingdom is transferred to David, 13-14.

1. *Now the Philistines fought against Israel.* The reader will find the same history in almost the same words, in 1 Sam. xxxi. 1-13.

6. *So Saul died . . . and all his house.* Every branch of his family that had followed him to the war was cut off; his three sons are mentioned as being the chief. No doubt all his officers were slain.

11. *When all Jabesh-gilead heard.* For a general account of the principles of heroism and gratitude from which this action of the men of Jabesh-gilead proceeded, see 1 Sam. xxxi. 11-12.

CHAPTER 11

David is anointed king in Hebron, 1-3. He wars against the Jebusites and takes their city, 4-9. An account of David's three mightiest heroes; and particularly of their hazardous exploit in bringing water from the well of Bethlehem, 10-19. A list of the rest, and an account of their acts, 20-47.

1. *Then all Israel gathered themselves to David.* See 2 Sam. v. 1-10 for the history contained in the first nine verses of this chapter.

11. *The number of the mighty men.* See 2 Sam. xxiii. 8, etc.

CHAPTER 12

The different persons, captains, etc., who joined themselves to David at Ziklag, 1-22. Those who joined him at Hebron, out of the different tribes: Judah, Simeon, Levi, the house of Aaron, Benjamin, Ephraim, Manasseh, Issachar, Zebulun, Naphtali, Dan, Asher, Reuben, etc., to the amount of 120,000, 23-37. Their unanimity, and the provisions they brought for his support, 38-40.

1. *Came to David to Ziklag.* Achish, king of Gath, had given Ziklag to David as a safe retreat from the wrath of Saul.

8. *And were as swift as the roes.* That swiftness was considered to be a grand accomplishment in a warrior appears from all ancient writings which treat of military affairs.

15. *In the first month.* Perhaps this was the month Nisan, which answers to a part of our March and April. This was probably before the snows on the mountains were melted, just as Jordan began to overflow its banks; or if we allow that it had already overflowed its banks, it made their attempt more hazardous, and afforded additional proof of their heroism.

23. *And came to David to Hebron.* That is, after the death of Ish-bosheth, Saul's son. See 2 Sam. iv. 5.

27. *Jehoiada was the leader of the Aaronites.* Abiathar was then high priest, and Jehoiada captain over the warriors of the house of Aaron.

32. *Children of Issachar.* According to the Targum they were all astronomers and astrologers.

It appears that in their wisdom, experience, and skill their brethren had the fullest confidence; and nothing was done but by their direction and advice.

CHAPTER 13

David consults with his officers, and resolves to bring back the ark from the house of Abinadab, 1-4. They place it on a new cart, and Uzza and Ahio drive the cart; the oxen stumbling, Uzza puts forth his hand to save the ark from falling, and he is smitten by the Lord, 5-10. David is displeased, and orders the ark to be carried to the house of Obed-edom the Gittite, 11-13. The ark abides there three months, and the Lord blesses Obed-edom, 14.

1. *David consulted.* Having taken the stronghold of Zion from the Jebusites, organized his army, got assurances of the friendly disposition of the Israelites towards him, he judged it right to do what he could for the establishment of religion in the land; and as a first step, consulted on the propriety of bringing the ark from an obscure village, where it had remained during the reign of Saul, to the royal city or seat of government.

6. *Whose name is called on it.* "Where his name is invoked."—T. And so the Hebrew should be understood; his name was not *called on it,* but "invoked at it."

7. *In a new cart.* Lest it should be profaned by being placed on any carriage that had been employed about common uses. *Uzza and Ahio.* All the versions understand *achyo* as signifying "brother" or "brothers"; so does Jarchi, who observes, from 2 Sam. vi. 3, that these were the sons of Abinadab.

9. *Uzza put forth his hand.* See this transaction explained, 2 Sam. vi. 6, etc.

14. *The Lord blessed the house of Obed-edom.* That this man was only a sojourner at Gath, whence he was termed Gittite, and that he was originally a Levite, is evident from chap. xv. 17-18.

CHAPTER 14

Hiram sends artificers and materials to David, to build him a house, 1-2. David's wives and children, 3-7. He defeats the Philistines in two battles: one in the valley of Rephaim, 8-12; and the other at Gibeon and Gazer, 13-16. His fame goes out into all the surrounding nations, 17.

1. *Now Hiram king of Tyre.* See the transactions of this chapter related, 2 Sam. v. 11-25.

4. *These are the names of his children.* In 2 Sam. v. 14-16, eleven persons only are mentioned in the Hebrew text, but the Septuagint has twenty-four; here there are thirteen, and all the versions have the same number, with certain varieties in the names.

8. *The Philistines went up to seek David.* See 2 Sam. v. 17.

17. *Into all lands.* That is, all the surrounding or neighboring lands and nations, for no others can possibly be intended.

CHAPTER 15

David prepares to bring home the ark, and musters the Levites, 1-11. They sanctify themselves, and bear the ark upon their shoulders, 12-15. The solemnities observed on the occasion, 16-26. David dances before the ark, and is despised by his wife Michal, 27-29.

1. *Made him houses.* One for himself, and one for the ark; in the latter was a tent, under which the ark was placed.

2. *None ought to carry the ark . . . but the Levites.* It was their business; and he should have thought of this sooner, and then the unfortunate breach on Uzza would have been prevented; see v. 13.

15. *Upon their shoulders.* That is, the staves which went through the rings rested on their shoulders, but the ark itself rested on the staves like a sedan on its poles. *As Moses commanded.* See Num. iv. 5, 15.

17. *Heman . . . Asaph . . . Ethan.* These were the three chief musicians in the time of David; see chap. vi. 31.

20. *With psalteries on Alamoth.* Some suppose that the word signifies "virgins," or "women singers," the persons mentioned here being appointed to accompany them with psalteries, and preside over them.

21. *On the Sheminith.* According to the Targum, this signifies an instrument that sounded an octave, or, according to others, an instrument with eight strings.

22. *Chenaniah . . . instructed about the song.* This appears to have been the master singer; he gave the key and the time, for he presided *bemassa,* "in the elevation," probably meaning what is called pitching the tune, for *he was skilful* in music, and powerful in his voice, and well qualified to lead the band.

26. *God helped the Levites.* When they saw that God had made no breach among them, as he had in the case of Uzza, in gratitude for their preservation, and His acceptance of their labor, they sacrificed seven bullocks and seven rams.

27. *A robe of fine linen.* A robe made of *buts,* probably the tuft or beard of the Pinna Magna, a species of mussel found everywhere on the shores of the Mediterranean.

29. *Michal . . . saw . . . David dancing . . . and she despised him.* See this whole business explained, 2 Sam. vi. 20, etc.

CHAPTER 16

David brings the ark into its tent; and offers sacrifices, peace offerings, and burnt offerings, 1-2; and gives portions to the people of Israel, 3. He appoints proper ministers and officers for the ark, 4-6. He delivers a solemn thanksgiving on the occasion, 7-36. How the different officers served at the ark, 37-42. The people return home, 43.

5. *Asaph.* See the preceding chapter, v. 17. etc.

7. *David delivered first this psalm.* I believe the meaning of this place to be this: David made the psalm on the occasion above specified; and delivered it to Asaph, who was the musician, and to his brethren, to be sung by them in honor of what God had done in behalf of His people.

12. *Remember his marvellous works.* The whole of the psalm refers to God's wondrous actions among the nations in behalf of Israel.

22. *Touch not mine anointed.* By this title the patriarchs are generally understood; they had a regal and sacerdotal power in the order of God. In the behalf of the patriarchs God had often especially interfered: in behalf of Abraham, Gen. xii. 17 and xx. 3; and of Jacob, Gen. xxxi. 24; xxxiv. 26; and xxxv. 5. But the title may be applied to all the Jewish people, who were the anointed, as they were the elect and peculiar people of God. See Heb. xi. 26.

35. *Save us, O God of our salvation.* As He is the saving God, so we may pray to Him to save us.

39. *Zadok the priest.* Both Zadok and Abiathar were high priests at this time. The former David established at Gibeah, or Gibeon, where the ark had been all the days of Saul; and the latter he established at Jerusalem, where the ark now was. So there were two high priests, and two distinct services; but there was only one ark. How long the service at Gibeon was continued we cannot tell; the principal functions were no doubt performed at Jerusalem.

CHAPTER 17

David consults Nathan about building a temple for God, 1-2. God sends him an answer by Nathan, informing him that Solomon shall build the house, 3-14. David receives the divine purpose with humility and joy, and gives God praise, 15-27.

1. *Now it came to pass.* See everything recorded in this chapter amply detailed in the notes on 2 Sam. vii. 1, etc.

9. *Neither shall the children of wickedness.* They shall no more be brought into servitude as they were in the time they sojourned in Egypt. This is what is here referred to.

12. *I will stablish his throne for ever.* David was a type of Christ, and concerning him the prophecy is literally true. See Isa. ix. 7, where there is evidently the same reference.

13. *I will not take my mercy away from him.* I will not cut off his family from the throne, as I did that of his predecessor, Saul.

16. *And what is mine house, that thou hast brought me hitherto?* I am not of any regal family, and have no natural right to the throne.

CHAPTER 18

David smites the Philistines, and takes Gath, 1. Reduces the Moabites, 2. Vanquishes Hadarezer, king of Zobah, 3-4. Overcomes the Syrians of Damascus, and takes several of their cities, 5-8. Tou, king of Hamath, congratulates him on his victory, and sends him vessels of silver, gold, and brass, 9-10. Those and the different spoils he had taken from the conquered nations, he dedicates to God, 11. Abishai defeats the Edomites, 12-13. David reigns over all Israel, 14. His officers, 15-17.

1. *David . . . took Gath and her towns.* See 2 Sam. viii. 1, etc.

2. *Brought gifts.* Were laid under tribute.

9. *Tou king of Hamath.* Called Toi in 2 Sam. viii. 9.

12. *Abishai . . . slew of the Edomites.* This victory is attributed to David, 2 Sam. viii. 13. He sent Abishai against them, and he defeated them; this is with great propriety attributed to David as commander in chief.

15. *Joab . . . was over the host.* General in chief. *Jehoshaphat . . . recorder.* The king's remembrancer, or historiographer royal.

16. *Zadok . . . and Abimelech . . . priests.* Both high priests; one at Gibeon, and the other at Jerusalem, as we have seen, chap. xvi. 39. *Shavsha was scribe.* Called Seraiah, 2 Sam. viii. 17.

CHAPTER 19

David sends a congratulatory message to Hanun, king of Ammon, 1-2. He treats the messengers with great incivility, 3-4. David is exasperated, but condoles with the degraded messengers, 5. The Ammonites prepare for

war, and hire 32,000 chariots, and besiege Medeba, 6-7. David sends Joab to attack them; he defeats the Syrians and Ammonites, 8-15. The discomfited Syrians recruit their army, and invade David's territories beyond Jordan; he attacks them, kills Shophach, their general, 7,000 charioteers, and 40,000 of their infantry, 16-18. The Syrians abandon the Ammonites and make a separate peace with David, 19.

1. *Now it came to pass.* See the same history, 2 Sam. x. 1, etc.

6. *Chariots and horsemen out of Mesopotamia.* These are not mentioned in the parallel place in Samuel; probably they did not arrive till the Ammonites and their other allies were defeated by the Israelites in the first battle.

7. *Thirty and two thousand.* The whole number mentioned in Samuel is: Syrians, of Bethrehob, and of Zoba, 20,000; of King Maacah, 1,000; of Ishtob, 12,000; in all, 33,000. Of chariots or cavalry there is no mention. These could not have been the whole army.

13. *Be of good courage.* See the note on 2 Sam. x. 12.

18. *Forty thousand footmen.* See this number accounted for in the note on 2 Sam. x. 18.

19. *They made peace with David, and became his servants.* See on 2 Sam. x. 19.

CHAPTER 20

Joab smites the city of Rabbah; and David puts the crown of its king upon his own head, and treats the people of the city with great rigor, 1-3. First battle with the Philistines, 4. Second battle with the Philistines, 5. Third battle with the Philistines, 6-7. In these battles three giants are slain, 8.

1. *After the year was expired, at the time that kings go out to battle.* About the spring of the year; see the note on 2 Sam. xi. 1. After this verse the parallel place in Samuel relates the whole story of David and Bath-sheba, and the murder of Uriah, which the compiler of these books passes over as he designedly does almost everything prejudicial to the character of David. All he states is, *But David tarried at Jerusalem;* and while he thus tarried, and Joab conducted the war against the Ammonites, the awful transactions above referred to took place.

2. *David took the crown of their king . . . off his head.* See 2 Sam. xii. 30.

3. *He brought out the people.* See this transaction particularly explained in the notes on the parallel places, 2 Sam. xii. 30-31.

5. *Elhanan the son of Jair.* See 2 Sam. xxi. 19.

CHAPTER 21

David is tempted by Satan to take the numbers of the people of Israel and Judah, 1-2. Joab remonstrates, but the king is determined, and Joab pleads in vain, 3-4. He returns, and delivers in the number to the king, but reckons not Levi and Benjamin, 5. The Lord is displeased, and sends Gad to offer David his choice of three great national calamities; famine, war, or pestilence, 6-12. David submits himself to God, and a pestilence is sent, which destroys 70,000, 13-14. At David's intercession the destroying angel is restrained at the threshing floor of Ornan, 15-17. He buys the piece of ground, builds an altar to the Lord, and offers sacrifices, and the plague is stayed, 18-20.

1. *And Satan stood up against Israel.* See the notes on the parallel place, 2 Sam. xxiv. 1, etc.

5. *All they of Israel were a thousand thousand . . . Judah was four hundred threescore and ten thousand.* In the parallel place, 2 Sam. xxiv. 9, the men of Israel are reckoned 800,000 and the men of Judah 500,000.

6. *Levi and Benjamin counted he not.* The rabbins give the following reason for this: Joab, seeing that this would bring down destruction upon the people, purposed to save two tribes. Should David ask, Why have you not numbered the Levites? Joab purposed to say, Because the Levites are not reckoned among the children of Israel. Should he ask, Why have you not numbered Benjamin? he would answer, Benjamin has been already sufficiently punished, on account of the treatment of the woman at Gibeah; if therefore this tribe were to be again punished, who would remain?

12. *Three days . . . the pestilence, in the land.* In 2 Sam. xxiv. 13, seven years of famine are mentioned.

20. *Ornan turned back, and saw the angel.* The Septuagint say, "And Orna turned and saw the king." The Syriac and Arabic say, "David saw the angel," and do not mention Ornan in this place.

24. *For the full price.* That is, 600 shekels full weight of pure gold.

26. *He answered him . . . by fire.* In answer to David's prayers, God, to show that He had accepted him, and was now pacified towards him and the people, sent fire from heaven and consumed the offerings.

30. *Because of the sword of the angel.* This is given as a reason why David built an altar in the threshing floor of Ornan. He was afraid to go to Gibeon, because of the sword of the destroying angel, or he was afraid of delaying the offerings so long as his going thither would require, lest the destroying angel should in the meanwhile exterminate the people. Therefore he hastily built an altar in that place, and on it made the requisite offerings; and by the fire from heaven God showed that He had accepted his act and his devotion. Such interventions as these must necessarily maintain in the minds of the people a full persuasion of the truth and divine origin of their religion.

CHAPTER 22

David makes great preparations for building a temple to the Lord, 1-5; gives the necessary directions to Solomon concerning it, 6-16; and exhorts the princes of Israel to assist in the undertaking, 17-19.

1. *David said, This is the house of the Lord.* Till a temple is built for His name, this place shall be considered the temple of God; and on this altar, and not on that at Gibeon, shall the burnt offerings of Israel be made. David probably thought that this was the place on which God designed that His house should be built.

2. *The strangers that were in the land.* Those who had become proselytes to the Jewish religion, at least so far as to renounce idolatry, and keep what were called the seven Noahic precepts. These were to be employed in the more servile and difficult parts of the work; see on 1 Kings ix. 21. For the account of building the Temple, see 1 Kings v—ix.

3. *Iron . . . for the nails.* Iron for bolts, bars, hinges, etc.

9. *His name shall be Solomon. Shelomoh,* from *shalam,* "he was peaceable"; and therefore, says the Lord, alluding to the name, *I will give peace [shalom] . . . in his days.*

14. *In my trouble I have prepared.* Notwithstanding all the wars in which I have been engaged, all the treacheries with which I have been surrounded, all the domestic troubles with which I have been overwhelmed, I never lost sight of this great object, the building of a house for God, that His worship might be established in the land. *An hundred thousand talents of gold.* One hundred thousand talents would amount to 507,578,125 pounds sterling. *A thousand thousand talents of silver.* A thousand thousand, or a million, talents would amount to the immense sum of 353,591,666 pounds, 13 shillings, and 4 pence, sterling. *Thou mayest add thereto.* Save as I have saved, out of the revenues of the state, and thou mayest also add something for the erection and splendor of this house. This was a gentle though pointed hint, which was not lost on Solomon.

18. *Hath he not given you rest on every side?* David at this time was not only king of Judea, but had also subdued most of the surrounding nations.

CHAPTER 23

David makes Solomon king, 1. Numbers the Levites, and appoints them their work, 2-5. The sons of Levi, Gershom, Kohath, Merari, and their descendants, 6-12. The sons of Amram, and their descendants, 13. The sons of Moses, and their descendants, 14-24. David appoints the Levites to wait on the priests for the service of the sanctuary, 25-32.

1. *David was old and full of days.* On the phrase *full of days,* see Gen. xxv. 8.

3. *Thirty years and upward.* The enumeration of the Levites made in the desert, Num. iv. 3, was from thirty years upwards to fifty years. In this place, the latter limit is not mentioned, probably because the service was not so laborious now; for the ark being fixed, they had no longer any heavy burdens to carry, and therefore even an old man might continue to serve the Tabernacle. David made another ordinance afterwards; see on vv. 24 and 27.

5. *Four thousand praised the Lord.* David made this distribution according to his own judgment, and from the dictates of his piety; but it does not appear that he had any positive divine authority for such arrangements. As to the instruments of music which he made, they are condemned elsewhere; see Amos vi. 5, to which this verse is allowed to be the parallel.

11. *Therefore they were in one reckoning.* The family of Shimei, being small, was united with that of Laadan, that the two families might do that work which otherwise belonged to one, but which would have been too much for either of these separately.

13. *To bless in his name.* To bless the people by invoking the name of the Lord.

22. *Their brethren the sons of Kish took them.* This was according to the law made, Num. xxvii. 1, etc; and xxxvi. 5-9, in favor of the daughters of Zelophehad, that women who were heiresses should marry in the family of the tribe of their father, and that their estates should not be alienated from them.

24. *Twenty years and upward.* It appears that this was a different ordinance from that mentioned in v. 3. At first he appointed the Levites to serve from thirty years and upward; now from twenty years. These were David's last orders; see v. 27. They should begin at an earlier age, and continue later. This was not a very painful task; the ark being now fixed, and the Levites very numerous, there could be no drudgery.

28. *Purifying of all holy things.* Keeping all the vessels and utensils belonging to the sacred service clean and neat.

29. *Both for the shewbread.* It was the priests' office to place this bread before the Lord, and it was their privilege to feed on the old loaves when they were replaced by the new. *For all manner of measure and size.* The standards of all weights and measures were kept at the sanctuary, and by those there deposited all the weights and measures of the land were to be tried. See Exod. xxx. 13.

30. *To stand every morning.* At the offering of the morning and evening sacrifice they sounded their musical instruments and sang praises to God.

32. *The charge of the sons of Aaron.* It was the priests' business to kill, flay, and dress, as well as to offer, the victims; but being few, they were obliged to employ the Levites to flay those animals. The Levites were, properly speaking, servants to the priests, and were employed about the more servile part of divine worship.

CHAPTER 24

David divides the families of Eleazar and Ithamar, by lot, into twenty-four courses, 1-19. How the rest of the sons of Levi were disposed of, 20-31.

2. *Nadab and Abihu died before their father.* That is, during his lifetime. *Eleazar and Ithamar executed the priest's office.* These two served the office during the life of their father, Aaron; after his death Eleazar succeeded in the high priesthood. And under Eli, the high priest, the family of Ithamar reentered into that office.

3. *And Ahimelech.* Ahimelech is put here for Abiathar, who was high priest in the days of David. Abiathar had also the name of Ahimelech as well as his father.

5. *They divided by lot.* This prevented jealousies; for, as all the families were equally noble, they had equal right to all ecclesiastical and civil distinctions.

6. *One principal household . . . for Eleazar.* The family of Eleazar was the most illustrious of the sacerdotal families, because Eleazar was the firstborn of Aaron; Ithamar's family was the second in order and dignity. Therefore one of the principal families of Eleazar was first taken, and then one of Ithamar's, and thus alternately till the whole was finished.

19. *Under Aaron their father.* That is, they followed the order and plans laid down by Aaron during his lifetime.

26. *The sons of Merari.* It is remarkable that not a word is here spoken of the family of Gershom.

31. *These likewise cast lots.* The Levites were divided into twenty-four orders; and these were appointed by lot to serve under the twenty-four orders of the priests: the first order of Levites under the first order of priests, and so on.

CHAPTER 25

The number and offices of the singers and players on musical instruments, and their division by lot into twenty-four courses, 1-31.

1. *David and the captains of the host.* The chiefs of those who formed the several orders, not military captains. *Should prophesy.* Should accompany their musical instruments with prayer and singing.

2. *Which prophesied.* Sung hymns and prayed.

3. *The sons of Jeduthun . . . six.* That is, six with their father; otherwise there are but five.

5. *Three daughters.* These also were employed among the singers.

9. *For Asaph to Joseph.* His firstborn. *The second to Gedaliah.* The firstborn of Jeduthun.

10. *The third to Saccur.* The firstborn of Asaph.

11. *The fourth to Izri.* The second son of Jeduthun.

12. *The fifth to Nethaniah.* The third son of Asaph. Thus we find the lot did not run in any particular kind of order.

14. *Jesharelah.* Supposed to be the same with Uzziel, son of Heman.

31. *Romamti-ezer.* Both these names belong to the same person. He is mentioned also in v. 4.

CHAPTER 26

The divisions of the porters, 1-12. The gates assigned to them, 13-19. Those who were over the treasures, 20-28. Different officers, 29-32.

1. *The divisions of the porters.* There were four classes of these, each of which belonged to one of the four gates of the Temple, which opened to the four cardinal points of heaven. The eastern gate fell to Shelemiah; the northern, to Zechariah, v. 14; the southern, to Obed-edom, v. 15; the western, to Shuppim and Hosah, v. 16. These several persons were captains of these porter bands or doorkeepers at the different gates. There were probably a thousand men under each of these captains; as we find, from chap. xxiii. 5, that there were 4,000 in all.

6. *They were mighty men of valour.* They were not only porters or doorkeepers in the ordinary sense of the word, but they were a military guard for the gates; and perhaps in this sense alone we are to understand their office.

12. The rest of this chapter, with the whole of the twenty-eighth, is wanting in both the Syriac and Arabic.

13. *They cast lots . . . for every gate.* None of these captains or their companies were permitted to choose which gate they would guard, but each took his appointment by lot.

15. *The house of Asuppim.* The house of the "collections"; the place where either the supplies of the porters or the offerings made for the use of the priests and Levites were laid up.

16. *The gate Shallecheth.* The gate of the projections, probably that through which all the offal of the Temple was carried out.

17. *Eastward were six Levites.* It is supposed that there were more guards set at this eastern gate because it was more frequented than the

others. At each of the other gates were only four; at this, six.

20. *The treasures of the house of God.* Where the money was kept, which was to be expended in oblations for the Temple.

29. *Outward business.* Work done without the city: cutting the timber, hewing stones, ploughing the fields belonging to the sanctuary.

30. *In all the business of the Lord.* Everything that concerned ecclesiastical matters. *In the service of the king.* Everything that concerned civil affairs: see also v. 32.

CHAPTER 27

An account of the 12 captains who were over the monthly course of 24,000 men, each captain serving one month in turn, 1. The names of the 12, and the months in which they served, 2-15. The names of the rulers of the 12 tribes, 16-22. The reasons why the whole number of Israel and Judah had not been taken, 23-24. The persons who were over the king's property, treasures, fields, flocks, etc., 25-31. His officers of state, 32-34.

1. *The chief fathers and captains of thousands.* The patriarchs, chief generals, or generals of brigade. This enumeration is widely different from the preceding. In that, we have the orders and courses of the priests and the Levites in their ecclesiastical ministrations; in this, we have the account of the order of the civil service, that which related simply to the political state of the king and the kingdom. Twenty-four persons, chosen out of David's worthies, each of whom had a second, were placed over 24,000 men, who all served a month in turn at a time; and this was the whole of their service during the year, after which they attended to their own affairs. Thus the king had always on foot a regular force of 24,000, who served without expense to him or the state, and were not oppressed by the service, which took up only a twelfth part of their time. And by this plan he could at any time, when the exigency of the state require it, bring into the field 12 times 24,000, or 288,000 fighting men, independently of the 12,000 officers, which made in the whole an effective force of 300,000 soldiers—and all these men were prepared, disciplined, and ready at a call, without the smallest expense to the state or the king. These were, properly speaking, the militia of the Israelitish kingdom.

5. *Benaiah the son of Jehoiada, a chief priest.* Why should not this clause be read as it is in the Hebrew? "Benaiah, the son of Jehoiada the priest, a captain; and in his course"? Or, as the Targum has it, "The third captain of the host for the month Sivan was Benaiah, the son of Jehoiada the priest, who was constituted a chief"?

7. *Asahel the brother of Joab.* This verse proves that the division and arrangement mentioned above were made before David was acknowledged king in Hebron; for Asahel, the brother of Joab, who was fourth captain, was slain by Abner, while Ish-bosheth reigned over Israel at Mahanaim, 2 Sam. ii. 19-23.

16. *Over the tribes of Israel.* In this enumeration there is no mention of the tribes of Asher and Gad. Probably the account of these has been lost from this register. These rulers appear to have been all honorary men, without pay, like the lords lieutenants of our counties.

24. *Neither was the number put in the ac-*

count. Joab did not return the whole number. Probably the plague began before he had finished; or he did not choose to give it in, as he had entered on this work with extreme reluctance, and he did not choose to tell the king how numerous they were.

25-31. *Over the king's treasures.* We see from these verses in what the personal property of David consisted: (1) *Treasures,* gold, silver. (2) *Goods* and grain in castles, *cities, villages,* and in the *fields.* (3) *Vineyards* and their produce. (4) *Olive trees* and their produce. (5) Meat cattle, in different districts. (6) *Camels* and *asses;* they had no horses. (7) *Flocks,* sheep, goats.

CHAPTER 28

David assembles the princes of Israel, and informs them that the Temple is to be built by Solomon, to whom God had given the most gracious promises, 1-7. He exhorts them and him to be obedient to God, that they might continue to prosper, 8-10. He gives Solomon a pattern of the work, 11-12; directs him concerning the courses of the priests and Levites, 13; gives also gold, by weight, for the different utensils of the Temple, as God had directed him, 14-19; encourages Solomon to undertake the work, 20-21.

1. *David assembled.* This refers to the persons whose names and offices we have seen in the preceding chapter.

2. *David . . . stood up upon his feet.* He was now very old, and chiefly confined to his bed (see 1 Kings i. 47); and while he was addressing his son Solomon he continued on the bed; but when all the principal nobles of his kingdom came before him, he received strength to arise and address them, standing on his feet.

3. *Thou shalt not build an house.* See 2 Sam. vii. 5, 13.

4. *Over Israel for ever.* The government should have no end, provided they continued to walk according to the commandments of God; see v. 7. The government, as referring to Christ, is, and will be, without end.

11. *David gave to Solomon . . . the pattern.* He gave him an ichnography of the building, with elevations, sections, and specifications of every part; and all this he received by inspiration from God himself (see vv. 12 and 19), just as Moses had received the plan of the Tabernacle.

14. *Of gold by weight.* The quantity of gold which was to be put in each article.

15. *For the candlesticks.* There was but one chandelier in the Tabernacle; there were ten in the Temple. See 1 Kings vii. 49.

19. *Understand in writing.* In some vision of ecstasy he had seen a regularly sketched out plan, which had made so deep an impression on his mind that he could readily describe it to his son.

CHAPTER 29

David enumerates the gifts which he designed for the building of the Temple, and exhorts the princes and people to make their offerings, 1-5. They offer willingly, and to a great amount, 6-9. David's thanksgiving and prayer to God on the occasion, 10-19. The princes and people praise God, offer sacrifices and feasts before Him, make Solomon king, and do him homage, 20-24. The Lord magnifies Solomon, 25. Concluding account of David's reign, character, and death, 26-30.

2. *And marble stones. Abney shayish,* which the Vulgate translates, "Parian marble." Paros

was one of the Cyclades islands, and produced the whitest and finest marble, that of which most of the finest works of antiquity have been made.

5. *To consecrate his service.* "To fill his hand"; to bring an offering to the Lord.

7. *Of gold five thousand talents.* These amount to 25,378,906 pounds, 5 shillings, sterling. *Ten thousand drams.* Probably golden *darics,* amounting to 10,000 pounds. *Of silver ten thousand talents.* These amount to 3,535,937 pounds. *Brass eighteen thousand talents.* Amount to 1,026 tons, 11 hundredweight, and one quarter. *One hundred thousand talents of iron.* Amount to 5,703 tons, 2 hundredweight, and a half.

15. *Our days on the earth are as a shadow.* They are continually declining, fading, and passing away. *There is none abiding.* However we may wish to settle and remain in this state of things, it is impossible, because every earthly form is passing swiftly away. All is in a state of revolution and decay, and there is no abiding, *mikveh,* no "expectation," that we shall be exempt from those changes and chances to which our fathers were subjected.

18. *Keep this for ever.* All the good dispositions which myself and my people have came from Thee; continue to support and strengthen them by the same grace by which they have been inspired!

19. *Give unto Solomon . . . a perfect heart.* This He did, but Solomon abused His mercies.

20. *Worshipped the Lord, and the king.* They did reverence to God as the supreme Ruler, and to the king as His deputy.

21. *With their drink offerings.* The Targum says a thousand drink offerings, making these libations equal in number to the other offerings. *And sacrifices.* These were peace offerings offered for the people, and on the flesh of which they feasted.

22. *They made Solomon . . . king the second time.* The first time of his being anointed and proclaimed king was when his brother Adonijah affected the throne; and Zadok, Nathan, and Benaiah anointed and proclaimed him in a hurry, and without pomp. See 1 Kings i. 39. Now that all is quiet, and David, his father, dead (for he was probably so at the time of the second anointing), they anointed and proclaimed him afresh, with due ceremonies, sacrifices, etc. *To be the chief governor.* To be the vicegerent or deputy of Jehovah; for God never gave up His right of king in Israel. Those called kings were only His lieutenants; hence it is said, v. 23, that "Solomon sat on the throne of the Lord as king instead of David his father."

24. *Submitted themselves.* "They gave the hand under Solomon"; they swore fealty to him.

28. *And he died.* David, at his death, had everything that his heart could wish. (1) *A good old age;* having lived as long as living could be desirable, and having in the main enjoyed good health. (2) *Full of days;* having lived till he saw everything that he lived for either accomplished or in a state of forwardness. (3) *Full of . . . riches;* witness the immense sums left for the Temple. (4) *Full of . . . honour;* having gained more renown than any crowned head ever did, either before his time or since.

29. *The acts of David . . . first and last.* Those which concerned him in private life, as well as those which grew out of his regal government. All these were written by three eminent men, personally acquainted with him through the principal part of his life. These were *Samuel* and *Gad,* the seers; and *Nathan,* the prophet. These writings are all lost, except the particulars interspersed in the books of Samuel, Kings, and Chronicles, none of which are the records mentioned here.

30. *The times that went over him.* The transactions of his reign, and the occurrences and vicissitudes in his own kingdom, as well as those which were over all the kingdoms of the countries, i.e., in the surrounding nations, in most of which David had a share during his forty years' reign.

The Second Book of
CHRONICLES

(See page 385 for preface to the Books of Chronicles.)

CHAPTER 1

Solomon, and the chiefs of the congregation, go to Gibeon, where was the Tabernacle of the Lord, and the brazen altar; and there he offers a thousand sacrifices, 1-6. The Lord appears to him in a dream, and gives him permission to ask any gift, 7. He asks wisdom, 8-10, which is granted; and riches, wealth, and honor besides, 11-12. His kingdom is established, 13. His chariots, horsemen, and horses, 14. His abundant riches, 15. He brings horses, linen yarn, and chariots, at a fixed price, out of Egypt, 16-17.

1. *And Solomon the son of David.* The very beginning of this book shows that it is a continuation of the preceding, and should not be thus formally separated from it. See the preface to the first book.

2. *Then Solomon spake.* This is supposed to have taken place in the second year of his reign.

4. *But the ark.* The Tabernacle and the bra-

zen altar remained still at Gibeon; but David had brought away the ark out of the Tabernacle, and placed it in a tent at Jerusalem; 2 Sam. vi. 2, 17.

5. *Sought unto it.* Went to seek the Lord there.

7. *In that night.* The night following the sacrifice. On Solomon's choice, see 1 Kings iii. 5-15.

9. *Let thy promise. Debarcha,* "thy word"; *pithgamach,* Targum. It is very remarkable that when either God or man is represented as having spoken a word then the noun *pithgam* is used by the Targumist; but when "word" is used personally, then he employs the noun *meymera,* which appears to answer to the *Logos* of St. John, ch. i. 1.

14. *He had a thousand and four hundred chariots.* For these numbers, see the notes on 1 Kings iv. 26.

17. *An horse for an hundred and fifty.* Suppose we take the shekel at the utmost value at which it has been rated, three shillings; then the price of a horse was about twenty-two pounds ten shillings.

CHAPTER 2

Solomon determines to build a temple, 1. The number of his workmen, 2. Sends to Huram for artificers and materials, 3-10. Huram sends him a favorable answer, and makes an agreement with him concerning the labor to be done, and the wages to be paid to his men, 11-16. The number of strangers in the land, and how employed, 17-18.

1. *An house for the name of the Lord.* A temple for the worship of Jehovah. *An house for his kingdom.* A royal palace for his own use as king of Israel.

3. *Solomon sent to Huram.* This man's name is written *Chiram* in Kings; and in Chronicles, *Churam.* There is properly no difference, only a *yod* and a *vau* interchanged.

6. *Save only to burn sacrifice.* It is not under the hope that the house shall be able to contain Him, but merely for the purpose of burning incense to Him, and offering Him sacrifice, that I have erected it.

7. *Send me . . . a man cunning to work.* A person of great ingenuity, who is capable of planning and directing, and who may be over the other artists.

11. *Answered in writing.* Though correspondence among persons of distinction was in these early times carried on by confidential messengers, yet we find that epistolary correspondence did exist.

13. *I have sent a cunning man.* His name appears to have been *Hiram,* or *Hiram Abi;* see the notes on 1 Kings vii. 13-14.

16. *In floats by sea to Joppa.* See the note on 1 Kings v. 9, and on the parallel places, for other matters contained in this chapter.

CHAPTER 3

Solomon begins to build the Temple on Mount Moriah, in the fourth year of his reign, 1-2. Its dimensions, ornaments, and pillars, 3-17.

4. *The height was an hundred and twenty.* Some think this should be twenty only; but if the same building is spoken of as in 1 Kings vi. 2, the height was only thirty cubits. "Twenty" is the reading of the Syriac, the Arabic, and the

Septuagint in the Codex Alexandrinus. There is probably a mistake here, which, from the similarity of the letters, might easily occur.

6. The Vulgate translates the passage thus: "And he made the pavement of the temple of the most precious marble; and moreover the gold was of the best quality."

9. *The weight of the nails was fifty shekels.* "Bolts" must be here intended, as it would be preposterous to suppose nails of nearly two pounds' weight. *The upper chambers.* Probably the "ceiling" is meant.

CHAPTER 4

The brazen altar, 1. Molten sea, and its supporters, 2-5. The ten lavers, 6. Ten golden candlesticks, 7. Ten tables, the hundred golden basons, and the priests' court, 8-10. The works which Huram performed, 11-17. Solomon finishes the Temple and its utensils, 18-22.

3. *Under it was the similitude of oxen.* In 1 Kings vii. 24, instead of "oxen," *bekarim,* we have "knops," *pekaim;* and this last is supposed by able critics to be the reading which ought to be received here. What we call *knops* may signify grapes, mushrooms, apples, or some such ornaments placed round about under the turned-over lip or brim of this caldron. The reader will at once see that what are called the "oxen," v. 3, said to be round about the brim, are widely different from those in v. 4, by which this molten sea was supported.

5. *It . . . held three thousand baths.* In 1 Kings vii. 26, it is said to hold only 2,000 baths. As this book was written after the Babylonish captivity, it is very possible that reference is here made to the Babylonish bath, which might have been less than the Jewish.

6. *He made also ten lavers.* The lavers served to wash the different parts of the victims in, and the molten sea was for the use of the priests. In this they bathed, or drew water from it for their personal purification.

8. *An hundred basons of gold.* These were doubtless a sort of sacrificial spoons with which they made libations.

9. *He made the court of the priests.* This was the inner court. *And the great court.* This was the outer court, or place for the assembling of the people.

16. *Huram his father. Ab,* "father," is often used in Hebrew to signify a "master, inventor, chief operator," and is very probably used here in the former sense by the Chaldee: "All these Chiram his master made for King Solomon."

17. *In the clay ground.* See on 1 Kings vii. 46. Some suppose that he did not actually cast those instruments at those places, but that he brought the clay from that quarter, as being the most proper for making moulds to cast in.

21. *And the flowers, and the lamps.* Probably each branch of the chandelier was made like a plant in flower, and the opening of the flower was either the lamp or served to support it.

22. *The doors . . . were of gold.* That is, were overlaid with golden plates, the thickness of which we do not know.

CHAPTER 5

Solomon, having finished the Temple, brings in the things which his father had consecrated, 1. He assembles the elders and chiefs of Israel and the Levites.

in order to bring up the ark from the city of David,
2-3. They bring it and its vessels, and having offered
innumerable sacrifices, place it in the Temple, under the
wings of the cherubim, 4-10. The Levites, singers, and
trumpeters praise God; and His glory descends and fills
the house, so that the priests cannot stand to minister,
11-14.

1. *Brought in all the things.* See the note on
1 Kings vii. 51.

3. *The feast.* "That is, the feast of tabernacles, which was held in the seventh month."
—Targum. See 1 Kings viii. 2.

9. *They drew out the staves.* As the ark was
no longer to be carried about, these were unnecessary.

10. *There was nothing in the ark save.* The
Chaldee paraphrases thus: "There was nothing
put in the ark but the two tables which Moses
placed there, after the first had been broken on
account of the calf which they made in Horeb,
and the two other tables had been confirmed
which were written with writing expressed in
the ten words."

11. *When the priests were come out.* After
having carried the ark into the holy of holies,
before the sacred service had commenced.

CHAPTER 6

Solomon's prayer at the dedication of the Temple, 1-42.

1. *The Lord hath said that he would dwell.*
Solomon, seeing the cloud descend and fill the
house, immediately took for granted that the
Lord had accepted the place, and was now present. What occurred now was precisely the same
with what took place when Moses reared the
Tabernacle in the wilderness; see Exod. xl. 34-
35.

22. *If a man sin against his neighbour.* For
the seven cases put here by Solomon in his
prayer, see the notes on 1 Kings viii. 31-46.

36. *For there is no man which sinneth not.*
See this case considered in the note on 1 Kings
viii. 46.

CHAPTER 7

Solomon having ended his prayer, the fire of the Lord
comes down from heaven and consumes the offerings, 1.
The people and the priests see this, and glorify God, and
offer sacrifices, 2-4. Solomon offers 22,000 oxen, and
120,000 sheep; and the priests and Levites attend in their
offices, 5-6. He keeps the feast seven days, and the
dedication of the altar seven days, and dismisses the
people, 7-11. The Lord appears unto him by night, and
assures him that He has heard his prayer, 12-16; promises
him and his posterity a perpetual government, if they be
obedient, 17-18; but utter destruction should they disobey,
and become idolaters, 19-22.

1. *The fire came down.* The cloud had come
down before; now the fire consumes the sacrifice, showing that both the house and the sacrifices were accepted by the Lord.

4. *The king and all the people offered sacrifices.* They presented the victims to the priests,
and they and the Levites slew them, and sprinkled the blood. Or perhaps the people themselves slew them and, having caught the blood,
collected the fat, etc., presented them to the
priests to be offered as the law required.

5. *Twenty and two thousand oxen.* The
amount of all the victims that had been offered
during the seven days of the Feast of Tabernacles, and the seven days of the Feast of the
Dedication.

10. *On the three and twentieth day.* This was
the ninth day of the dedication of the Temple;
but in 1 Kings viii. 66 it is called the eighth
day. "The meaning is this," says Jarchi: "he
gave them liberty to return on the eighth day,
and many of them did then return: and he dismissed the remainder on the ninth, what is called
here the twenty-third, reckoning the fourteen
days for the duration of the two feasts; in all,
twenty-three."

12. *The Lord appeared to Solomon.* This was
a second manifestation; see 1 Kings ix. 2-9, and
the notes there.

18. *There shall not fail thee a man.* This
promise was not fulfilled, because the condition
was not fulfilled; they forsook God, and He cut
them off, and the throne also.

20. *Then will I pluck them up by the roots.*
How completely has this been fulfilled! Not
only all the branches of the Jewish political
tree have been cut off, but the very *roots* have
been plucked up; so that the day of the Lord's
anger has left them neither root nor branch.

CHAPTER 8

Solomon's buildings, conquests, and officers, 1-10. He
brings Pharaoh's daughter to his new-built palace, 11.
His various sacrifices, and arrangement of the priests,
Levites, and porters, 12-16. He sends a fleet to Ophir,
17-18.

1. *At the end of twenty years.* He employed
seven years and a half in building the Temple,
and twelve and a half, or thirteen, in building
his own house. Compare this with 1 Kings
vii. 1.

2. *The cities which Huram had restored.* See
the note on 1 Kings ix. 11.

4. *Tadmor. Palmyra.* See the note on 1 Kings
ix. 18 for an account of this superb city.

6. *All the store cities.* See 1 Kings ix. 19.

9. *But of the children of Israel.* See 1 Kings
ix. 21.

11. *Because the places are holy.* Is not this
a proof that he considered his wife to be a
heathen, and not proper to dwell in a place
which had been sanctified? Solomon had not
yet departed from the true God.

13. *Three times in the year.* These were the
three great annual feasts.

15. *The commandment of the king.* The institutions of David.

18. *Knowledge of the sea.* Skillful sailors.
Solomon probably bore the expenses and his
friend, the Tyrian king, furnished him with
expert sailors; for the Jews, at no period of
their history, had any skill in maritime affairs, their navigation being confined to the
lakes of their own country, from which they
could never acquire any nautical skill. The Tyrians, on the contrary, lived on and in the sea.

CHAPTER 9

The queen of Sheba visits Solomon, and is sumptuously
entertained by him, 1-12. His great riches, 13-14. He
makes targets and shields of beaten gold, and a magnificent ivory throne, and various utensils of gold, 15-20. His
navigation to Tarshish, and the commodities brought
thence, 21. His magnificence and political connections,
22-28. The writers of his life, 29. He reigns forty years,
and is succeeded by his son Rehoboam, 30-31.

1. *The queen of Sheba.* See all the particulars of this royal visit distinctly marked and explained in the notes on 1 Kings x. 1-10.

12. *Beside that which she had brought unto the king.* In 1 Kings x. 13 it is stated that Solomon gave her all she asked, beside that which he "gave her of his royal bounty." It is not at all likely that he gave her back the presents which she brought to him, and which he had accepted. She had, no doubt, asked for several things which were peculiar to the land of Judea, and would be curiosities in her own kingdom; and besides these, he gave her other valuable presents.

25. *Four thousand stalls for horses.* See the note on 1 Kings iv. 26, where the different numbers in these two books are considered. The Targum, instead of *four thousand,* has *arba meah,* "four hundred."

29. *Nathan the prophet.* These books are all lost.

CHAPTER 10

The people apply to Rehoboam to ease them of their burdens, 1-4. Rejecting the advice of the aged counsellors, and following that of the young men, he gives them an ungracious answer, 5-14. The people are discouraged, and ten tribes revolt, 15-17. They stone Hadoram, who went to collect the tribute; and Rehoboam but barely escapes, 18-19.

1. *Rehoboam went to Shechem.* This chapter is almost word for word the same as 1 Kings xii, to the notes on which the reader is referred.

10. *My little finger shall be thicker.* "My weakness shall be stronger than the might of my father."—Targum.

CHAPTER 11

Rehoboam raises an army, purposing to reduce the ten tribes; but is prevented by Shemaiah the prophet, 1-4. He builds several cities of defense, and fortifies others, 5-12. The priests and Levites, being turned out by Jeroboam, come to Rehoboam, 13-14. Jeroboam's gross idolatry, 15. The pious of the land join with Judah, and strengthen the kingdom of Rehoboam, 16-17. His wives, concubines, and numerous issue, 18-21. He places his own sons for governors in the different provinces, 22-23.

1. *Gathered of the house of Judah.* See this account, 1 Kings xii. 21-24.

5. *And built cities for defence in Judah.* He was obliged to strengthen his frontiers against the encroachments of the men of Israel; and Jeroboam did the same thing on this part, to prevent the inroads of Judah. See 1 Kings xii. 25.

11. *Store of victual.* In these places he laid up stores of provisions, not only to enable them to endure a siege, but also that they might be able, from their situation, to supply desolate places.

14. *The Levites left their suburbs.* They and the priests were expelled from their offices by Jeroboam, lest they should turn the hearts of the people to the true God, and then they would revolt to Judah, 1 Kings xii. 26; and therefore he established a new worship, and made new gods.

15. *And he ordained him priests . . . for the devils. Seirim,* "the hairy ones"; probably goats. For as the golden calves, or oxen, were in imitation of the Egyptian ox-god, Apis, so they no doubt paid divine honors to the goat, which we know was an object of religious veneration in Egypt.

16. *Such as set their hearts to seek the Lord.* All the truly pious joined him out of every tribe; and the whole tribe of Levi, being deprived of their functions, joined him also. Thus he had Judah, Benjamin, and Levi, and probably a part of Simeon; for he had Etam, which was in that tribe, and the truly religious out of all the other tribes, for they could not bear Jeroboam's idolatry.

17. *For three years they walked in the way of David.* During this time he prospered; but for fourteen years after this he and the people were unfaithful to the Lord, except at such intervals as the hand of God's judgments was upon them.

18. *Took him Mahalath.* By marrying thus in the family of David, he strengthened his right to the Jewish throne.

20. *Maachah the daughter of Absalom.* See the note on 1 Kings xv. 10. She is called Michaiah, the daughter of Uriel, chap. xiii. 2. For this the Targum gives the following reason: "Abijah reigned three years in Jerusalem; and his mother's name was Michaiah, daughter of Uriel of Gibeatha. She is the same as Michah, the daughter of Absalom; but because she was an upright woman, her name was changed into the more excellent name Michaiah, and her father's name into that of Uriel of Gibeatha, that the name of Absalom might not be remembered."

21. *Eighteen wives, and threescore concubines.* Bad enough, but not so abandoned as his father. Of these marriages and concubinage the issue was twenty-eight sons and sixty daughters; eighty-eight children in the whole, to the education of the whole of whom he could pay but little attention.

22. *Made Abijah . . . the chief.* Abijah certainly was not the firstborn of Rehoboam; but as he loved Maachah more than any of his wives, so he preferred her son, probably through his mother's influence.

23. *He dealt wisely.* It was true policy to disperse his own sons through the different provinces who were not likely to form any league with Jeroboam against their father.

CHAPTER 12

Rehoboam and his subjects, forsaking the Lord, are delivered into the hands of Shishak, king of Egypt, 1-4. Shemaiah, the prophet, remonstrates with them, and they humble themselves, and Jerusalem is not destroyed; but Shishak takes away all the treasures, and the golden shields, instead of which Rehoboam makes shields of brass, 5-12. He reigns badly seventeen years, dies, and is succeeded by his son Abijah, 13-16.

1. *He forsook the law of the Lord.* This was after the three years mentioned in chap. xi. 17.

2. *Shishak king of Egypt.* Concerning this man, and the motive which led him to attack the Jews, see the note on 1 Kings xiv. 31.

3. *The Lubims.* Supposed to be a people of Libya, adjoining to Egypt; sometimes called Phut in Scripture, as the people are called Lehabim and Ludim. *The Sukkiims.* The Troglodytes, a people of Egypt on the coast of the Red Sea. They were called *Troglodytes,* "because they dwelt in caves." *The Ethiopians. Cushim.* Various people were called by this name, particularly a people bordering on the northern coast of the Red Sea; but these are

supposed to have come from a country of that name on the south of Egypt.

6. *Whereupon the princes of Israel and the king humbled themselves.* This is not mentioned in the parallel place, 1 Kings xiv. This was the sole reason why Jerusalem was not at this time totally destroyed, and the house of David entirely cut off; for they were totally incapable of defending themselves against this innumerable host.

8. *They shall be his servants.* They shall be preserved, and serve their enemies, that they may see the difference between the service of God and that of man. While they were pious, they found the service of the Lord to be perfect freedom; when they forsook the Lord, they found the fruit to be perfect bondage. A sinful life is both expensive and painful.

9. *Took away the treasures.* Such a booty as never had before, nor has since, come into the hand of man. *The shields of gold.* These shields were the mark of the king's bodyguard.

13. *Was one and forty years old.* Houbigant things he was but sixteen years old when he began to reign, and brings many and forcible arguments to prove that the number forty-one must be a mistake. That he was young when he came to the throne is evident from his consulting "the young men that were brought up with him," chap. x. 8, 10. Besides, Abijah, in his speech to Jeroboam, chap. xiii. 7, says that at the time Rehoboam came to the throne he was tenderhearted, and therefore could not withstand the children of Belial raised up against him by Jeroboam. But surely at that time no man could be reputed young and tenderhearted, quite devoid of experience, who was above forty years of age.

16. *Abijah his son.* Concerning the many varieties in this king's name, see the note on 1 Kings xiv. 31.

CHAPTER 13

Abijah begins to reign over Judah, and has war with Jeroboam, 1-3. His speech from Mount Zemaraim to Jeroboam, before the commencement of hostilities, 4-12. While thus engaged, Jeroboam dispatches some troops, which come on the rear of Abijah's army, 13. Perceiving this, they cry unto the Lord, and the Israelites are defeated with the loss of 500,000 men, 14-18. Abijah retakes several cities from Jeroboam, who is smitten by the Lord, and dies, 19-20. Abijah's marriages and issue, 21-22.

2. *His mother's name . . . was Michaiah.* See on chap. xi. 20.

3. *Abijah set the battle in array.* The numbers in this verse and in the seventeenth seem almost incredible. Abijah's army consisted of 400,000 effective men; that of Jeroboam consisted of 800,000; and the slain of Jeroboam's army were 500,000. Now it is very possible that there is a cipher too much in all these numbers, and that they should stand thus: Abijah's army, 40,000; Jeroboam's, 80,000; the slain, 50,000.

9. *A young bullock and seven rams.* He who could provide these for his own consecration was received into the order of this spurious and wicked priesthood. Some think he who could give to Jeroboam a young bullock and seven rams was thereby received into the priesthood, this being the price for which the priesthood was conferred. The former is most likely.

10. *The Lord is our God.* We have not abandoned the Lord, and we still serve Him according to His own law.

12. *God himself is with us.* You have golden calves; we have the living and omnipotent Jehovah. *With . . . trumpets to cry alarm against you.* This was appalling. When the priests sound their trumpets, it will be a proof that the vengeance of the Lord shall speedily descend upon you.

13. *But Jeroboam caused an ambushment.* While Abijah was thus employed in reproving them, Jeroboam divided his army privately, and sent a part to take Abijah in the rear; and this must have proved fatal to the Jews had not the Lord interposed.

20. *The Lord struck him, and he died.* Who died? Abijah or Jeroboam? Some think it was Jeroboam; some, that it was Abijah. Both rabbins and Christians are divided on this point, nor is it yet settled. The prevailing opinion is that Jeroboam is meant, who was struck then with that disease of which he died about two years after, for he did not die till two years after Abijah; see 1 Kings xiv. 20; xv. 9.

21. *Married fourteen wives.* Probably he made alliances with the neighboring powers, by taking their daughters to him for wives.

22. *Written in the story.* Bemidrash, "in the commentary"; this, as far as I recollect, is the first place where a *midrash* or "commentary" is mentioned. *His ways, and his sayings.* The commentary *of the prophet Iddo* is lost. What his *sayings* were we cannot tell; but from the specimen in this chapter he appears to have been a very able speaker, and one who knew well how to make the best use of his argument.

CHAPTER 14

Asa succeeds his father Abijah, reigns piously, and has peace for ten years, 1. He makes a great reformation in Judah, and builds cities of defense, 2-7. His military strength, 8. He is attacked by Zerah the Ethiopian, with an immense army; Asa cries to the Lord, attacks the Ethiopians, and gives them a total overthrow, 9-12. He takes several of their cities, their cattle, etc., and returns to Jerusalem, laden with spoils, 13-15.

1. *The land was quiet ten years.* Calmet thinks these years should be counted from the fifth to the fifteenth of Asa's reign.

2. *Did that which was good.* He attended to what the law required relative to the worship of God. He was no idolater, though, morally speaking, he was not exempt from faults, 1 Kings xv. 14. He suppressed idolatry universally, and encouraged the people to worship the true God; see vv. 3-5.

6. *Fenced cities.* To preserve his territories from invasion, and strengthen the frontiers of his kingdom, see v. 7.

8. *Targets and spears.* Probably targets with the dagger in the center, and javelins for distant fight. *Bare shields and drew bows.* They were not only archers, but had shield and sword for close fight.

9. *Zerah the Ethiopian.* Probably of that Ethiopia which lay on the south of Egypt, near to Libya, and therefore the Libyans are joined with them, chap. xvi. 8. *A thousand thousand.* If this people had come from any great distance, they could not have had forage for such an immense army.

11. *Whether with many.* The same sentiment

as that uttered by Jonathan, 1 Sam. xiv. 6, when he attacked the garrison of the Philistines.

14. *There was . . . much spoil in them.* These cities being on the rear of this vast army, they had laid up much forage in them, and to get this the Jews overthrew the whole.

CHAPTER 15

Azariah's prophecy concerning Israel, and his exhortation to Asa, 1-7. Asa completes the reformation which he had begun, his kingdom is greatly strengthened, and all the people make a solemn covenant with the Lord, 8-15. His treatment of his mother, Maachah, 16. He brings into the house of God the things that his father had dedicated, 17-18. And he has no war till the thirty-fifth year of his reign, 19.

1. *Azariah the son of Obed.* We know nothing of this prophet but what is related of him here.

2. *The Lord is with you, while ye be with him.* This the settled and eternal purpose of God; to them who seek Him, He will ever be found propitious, and them alone will He abandon who forsake Him.

5. *But great vexations.* Does not our Lord allude to this and the following verse in Matt. xxiv. 6-7, 9, 13?

8. *Renewed the altar.* Dedicated it afresh, or perhaps enlarged it, that more sacrifices might be offered on it than ever before; for it cannot be supposed that this altar had no victims offered on it till the fifteenth year of the reign of Asa, who had previously been so zealous in restoring the divine worship.

9. *And the strangers.* Many out of the different tribes, particularly out of Simeon, Ephraim, and Manasseh, having reflected that the divine blessing was promised to the house of David, and finding the government of Jeroboam founded in idolatry, would naturally, through a spirit of piety, leave their own country and go where they might enjoy the worship of the true God.

10. *The third month.* At the Feast of Pentecost, which was held on the third month.

11. *The spoil which they had brought.* The spoil which they had taken from Zerah and his auxiliaries, chap. xiv. 14-15.

12. *They entered into a covenant.* The covenant consisted of two parts: (1) We will seek the God of our fathers with all our hearts, and with all our souls. (2) Whosoever, great or small, man or woman, will not worship the true God, and serve Him alone, shall be put to death. Thus no toleration was given to idolatry, so that it must be rooted out; and that this covenant might be properly binding, they confirmed it with an oath; and God accepted them and their services.

16. *Concerning Maachah.* See the matter fully explained in the note on 1 Kings xv. 13.

17. *The high places were not taken away.* He had totally suppressed or destroyed the idolatry; but some of the places, buildings, or altars, he permitted to remain.

18. *The things that his father had dedicated.* As it was a custom to dedicate a part of the spoils taken from an enemy to the service and honor of God, it is natural to suppose that Abijah, having so signally overthrown Jeroboam (chap. xiii. 15-19), had dedicated a part of the spoils to the Lord; but they had not been brought into the Temple till this time. *Silver, and gold, and vessels.* The word *kelim,* which we translate *vessels,* signifies "instruments, utensils, ornaments."

19. *The five and thirtieth year of the reign of Asa.* Archbishop Ussher thinks that this should be counted from the separation of the kingdom, and that this fell on the fifteenth year of Asa's reign. Probably we should read here "the five and twentieth year." See the margin, and the note on 1 Kings xv. 16.

CHAPTER 16

Baasha, king of Israel, begins to build Ramah, to prevent his subjects from having any intercourse with the Jews, 1. Asa hires Ben-hadad, king of Syria, against him; and obliges him to leave off building Ramah, 2-5. Asa and his men carry the stones and timbers of Ramah away, and build therewith Geba and Mizpah, 6. Asa is reproved by Hanani, the seer, for his union with the king of Syria: he is offended with the seer, and puts him in prison, 7-10. Of his acts, 11. He is diseased in his feet, and seeks to physicians and not to God, and dies, 12-13. His sumptuous funeral, 14.

1. *The six and thirtieth year.* After the division of the kingdoms of Israel and Judah, according to Ussher. This opinion is followed in our margin; see the note on 1 Kings xv. 16, where this subject is further considered. Concerning Baasha's building of Ramah, see the note on 1 Kings xv. 17.

3. *There is a league.* Let there be a treaty, offensive and defensive, between me and thee: see on 1 Kings xv. 22.

6. *Took all Judah.* See on 1 Kings xv. 22.

7. *Escaped out of thine hand.* It is difficult to know what is here intended. Perhaps the divine providence had intended to give Asa a grand victory over the Syrians, who had always been the inveterate enemies of the Jews; but by this unnecessary and very improper alliance between Asa and Ben-hadad, this purpose of the divine providence was prevented, and thus the Syrians escaped out of his hands.

9. *Therefore . . . thou shalt have wars.* And so he had with Israel during the rest of his reign, 1 Kings xv. 32.

10. *Asa was wroth with the seer.* Instead of humbling himself, and deprecating the displeasure of the Lord, he persecuted His messenger; and having thus laid his impious hands upon the prophet, he appears to have got his heart hardened through the deceitfulness of sin. Then he began to oppress the people, either by unjust imprisonments or by excessive taxations.

12. *Diseased in his feet.* He had a strong and long fit of the gout; this is most likely.

14. *And laid him in the bed.* It is very likely that the body of Asa was burnt; that the *bed* spoken of here was a funeral pyre, on which much spices and odoriferous woods had been placed; and then they set fire to the whole and consumed the body with the aromatics. Some think the body was not burned, but the aromatics only, in honor of the king.

CHAPTER 17

Jehoshaphat succeeds his father, Asa, and reigns piously, and is particularly blessed, 1-6. He establishes an itinerant ministry, for the instruction of the people, through all the cities of Judah, which produces the most beneficial effects, 7-10. The Philistines and Arabians bring him gifts, 11. His greatness, 12-13. The commanders of his troops, 14-19.

1. *Jehoshaphat . . . and strengthened himself against Israel.* The kingdoms of Israel and Judah were rivals from the beginning; sometimes one, sometimes the other, prevailed. Asa and Baasha were nearly matched; but after Baasha's death Israel was greatly weakened by civil contentions, and Jehoshaphat got the ascendancy. See 1 Kings xvi. 16-23.

2. *The cities of Ephraim.* This conquest from the kingdom of Israel is referred to in chap. xv. 8, but when it was made we do not know.

7-9. *To teach in the cities of Judah.* "To teach the fear of the Lord in the cities of Judah."—Targum.

In these verses we find a remarkable account of an itinerant ministry established by Jehoshaphat; and in this work he employed three classes of men: (1) the *princes,* (2) the *Levites,* (3) the *priests.* We may presume that the princes instructed the people in the nature of the civil law and constitution of the kingdom; the Levites instructed them in everything that appertained to the Temple service and ritual law; and the priests instructed them in the nature and design of the religion they professed. Thus the nation became thoroughly instructed in their duty to God, to the king, and to each other.

9. *Had the book of the law of the Lord with them.* This was their textbook; it was the book of God; they taught it as such, and as such the people received it. By these means the nation enjoyed peace and prosperity; and all insurrections, seditions, and popular commotions were prevented. The surrounding nations, perceiving this, saw that there was no hope of subduing such a people, so "they made no war against Jehoshaphat," v. 10. And they took care not to provoke such a people to fall on them; therefore it is said, "The fear of the Lord fell upon all the kingdoms of the lands that were round about Judah."

11. *The Philistines brought . . . presents.* They and the *Arabians* purchased peace with the king of Judah by paying an annual *tribute.* The Philistines brought *silver,* and no doubt different kinds of merchandise. The Arabs, whose riches consisted in cattle, *brought him flocks* in great abundance, principally *rams* and *he goats.*

13. *He had much business in the cities.* He kept the people constantly employed; they had wages for their work, and by their labors the empire was both enriched and strengthened.

14. *Adnah the chief.* He was generalissimo of all his host.

19. *These waited on the king.* They were disposable forces, always at the king's command, and were independent of those by which the cities of Judah were garrisoned.

CHAPTER 18

Jehoshaphat joins affinity with Ahab, king of Israel, 1-2; who invites him to assist him in the war against the Syrians, to which Jehoshaphat agrees, 3. They consult the prophets concerning the success of the war; and all except Micaiah promise Ahab victory, 4-17. Micaiah relates his vision concerning the lying spirit in the mouth of Ahab's prophets, 18-22. Zedekiah, a false prophet, opposes Micaiah, and Micaiah is put in prison, 23-27. Both the kings go against the Syrians; the confederate armies are defeated, and the king of Israel is slain, 28-31.

1. *Jehoshaphat had riches and honour.* The preceding chapter gives ample proof of this.

Joined affinity with Ahab. Took his daughter Athaliah to be wife to his son Joram.

3. *To Ramoth-gilead.* This place belonged to the Israelites, and was now held by the king of Syria. The whole of this chapter is circumstantially explained in the note on 1 Kings xxii.

29. *I will disguise myself.* See the note on 1 Kings xxii. 30.

34. *Stayed himself up . . . against the Syrians.* There was a great deal of true personal courage and patriotism in this last act of the king of Israel. He well knew that if his troops found that he was mortally wounded they would immediately give way, and the battle would not only be lost, but the slaughter would be great in the pursuit. Therefore he stayed himself up till the evening, when the termination of the day must necessarily bring the battle to a close, and when this was done, the Israelites found that their king was slain, and so they left the field of battle to their foes. Thus Israel had a great loss, and the Syrians had got a great deliverance. Had it not been for this accident, the Syrians had probably been defeated. See on 1 Kings xxii. 36.

CHAPTER 19

Jehoshaphat, on his return from Ramoth-gilead, is met by the prophet Jehu, and reproved, 1-3. He makes a further reformation in the land, establishing courts of justice, and giving solemn and pertinent directions to the judges, Levites, etc., to do judgment and justice among the people, in the fear of God, 4-11.

1. *Returned to his house in peace.* That is, in safety, notwithstanding he had been exposed to a danger so imminent, from which only the especial mercy of God could have saved him.

2. *Jehu the son of Hanani.* We have met with this prophet before; see the note on 1 Kings xvi. 7. *Therefore is wrath upon thee.* That is, Thou deservest to be punished. And who can doubt this, who knows that he did help the ungodly, and did love them that hated Jehovah?

4. *From Beer-sheba to Mount Ephraim.* Before the separation of the ten tribes, in speaking of the extent of the land it was said, "From Dan to Beer-sheba"; but since that event, the kingdom of Judah was bounded on the south by Beer-sheba, and on the north by the mountains of Ephraim. This shows that Jehoshaphat had gone through all his territories to examine everything himself, to see that judgment and justice were properly administered among the people.

6. *Take heed what ye do.* A very solemn and very necessary caution; judges should feel themselves in the place of God, and judge as those who know they shall be judged for their judgments.

8. *And for controversies, when they returned to Jerusalem.* Who were they that returned to Jerusalem? Some suppose that it means Jehoshaphat and his courtiers, who returned to Jerusalem after the expedition mentioned in v. 4. But if this were so, or if the text spoke of any person returning to Jerusalem, would not "to Jerusalem," and not the simple word *Yerushalem,* without the preposition, be used? Learned men have supposed, with great plausibility, that the word *vaiyashubu,* "and they returned," should be written *yoshebey,* "the inhabitants," and that the words should be read, "And for the

controversies of the inhabitants of Jerusalem." That this was the original reading is very probable from its vestiges in the Vulgate, "its inhabitants"; and in the Septuagint it is, "And to judge the inhabitants of Jerusalem."

10. *Between blood and blood.* Cases of manslaughter or accidental murder, or cases of consanguinity, the settlement of inheritance, family claims, etc. *Between law and commandment.* Whatsoever concerns the moral precepts, rites, and ceremonies of the law, or whatsoever belongs to civil affairs.

11. *Behold, Amariah.* Here was a twofold jurisdiction, ecclesiastical and civil. In the ecclesiastical court, Amariah, the high priest, was supreme judge; in the civil court, Zebadiah was supreme. To assist both, the Levites were a sort of counsellors.

CHAPTER 20

The Moabites, Ammonites, and Edomites invade Judah, 1-2. Jehoshaphat proclaims a fast, and gathers the people together to seek the Lord, 3-4. His prayer to God, 5-12. Great and small, male and female, seek the Lord, 13. Jahaziel predicts the downfall of their enemies, 14-17. The king, the Levites, and the people take courage; praise and magnify God; and go forth to meet their enemies, 18-21. The enemies are confounded, and destroy each other, 22-24. The men of Judah take the spoil, praise the Lord, and return with joy to Jerusalem, 25-28. The fear of the Lord falls upon all their enemies round about, and the land has rest, 29-30. Transactions and character of Jehoshaphat, 31-34. He joins with Ahaziah, king of Israel, in building a fleet of ships to go to Tarshish, but they are wrecked at Ezion-geber, 35-37.

1. *Children of Ammon, and with them other beside the Ammonites.* Here there must be a mistake; surely the *Ammonites* are the same as the *children of Ammon.* Our translators have falsified the text by inserting the words "other beside," which have nothing properly to represent them in the Hebrew. Literally translated, the words are: "And it happened after this, the children of Moab, and the children of Ammon, and with them of the Ammonites"; and thus the Vulgate. "And with them some of the Edomites." This is very likely to be the true reading, as we find from vv. 10, 22-23 that they procured men from Mount Seir; and these were the Idumeans or Edomites. We should, in my opinion, read the text thus: "The children of Moab, and the children of Ammon, and with them some of the Edomites."

2. *On this side Syria.* Instead of *mearam,* "from Syria," I would read with one of Kennicott's MSS. *meedom,* "from Edom," which alteration brings it to truth, and does not require the change of half a letter, as it consists in the almost imperceptible difference between *resh* and *daleth.* We do not read of any Syrians in the invasion, but we know there were Edomites, or inhabitants of Mount Seir. *Hazazon-tamar.* "In the wood of palm trees, that is, in Engedi."—Targum. This is the meaning of the word, and it is probable that they lay hid there.

3. *Jehoshaphat feared.* He found that he could not possibly stand against such a numerous army, and therefore could not expect to be delivered except by the strong arm of God. To get this assistance, it was necessary to seek it; and to get such extraordinary help, they should seek it in an extraordinary way; hence he proclaimed a universal fast, and all the people came up to Jerusalem to seek the Lord.

5. *Jehoshaphat stood.* What an instructive

sight was this! The king who proclaimed the fast was foremost to observe it, and was on this occasion the priest of the people; offering in the congregation, without form or any premeditation, one of the most sensible, pious, correct, and as to its composition one of the most elegant prayers ever offered under the Old Testament dispensation.

12. *Wilt thou not judge them?* That is, Thou wilt inflict deserved punishment upon them.

15. *For the battle is not yours, but God's.* God will not employ you in the discomfiture of this great host; He himself will take the matter in hand, deliver you, and destroy them.

22. *The Lord set ambushments.* Houbigant translates the place thus: "The Lord set against the children of Ammon and Moab ambushments of those who came from Mount Seir against Judah; and the children of Ammon and Moab were smitten: but they afterwards rose up against the inhabitants of Mount Seir, and utterly destroyed each other." This is probably the meaning of these verses.

25. *Both riches with the dead bodies.* For *pegarim,* "dead bodies," *begadim,* "garments," is the reading of eight MSS. in the collections of Kennicott and De Rossi, and in several ancient editions. None of the versions have *dead bodies* except the Chaldee. The words might be easily mistaken for each other, as the *pe,* if a little faint in the under dot, might easily pass for a *beth;* and we know that the *resh* and *daleth* are frequently interchanged and mistaken for each other, in both Hebrew and Syriac. I believe "garments" to be the true reading.

26. *Assembled themselves in the valley of Berachah.* "The valley of Benediction"; and so in the latter clause.—Targum.

27. *Jehoshaphat in the forefront of them.* He was their leader in all these spiritual, holy, fatiguing, and self-denying exercises. What a noble and persuasive pattern!

33. *The high places were not taken away.* The idolatry, as we have seen, was universally suppressed; but some of the places where that worship had been performed were not destroyed. Some of them still remained; and these, to such a fickle people, became the means of idolatry in reigns less propitious to truth and religion.

34. *In the book of Jehu.* This is totally lost, though it is evident that it was in being when the Books of Chronicles were written.

36. *To go to Tarshish.* "In the great sea."—Targum. By which expression they always meant the Mediterranean Sea.

CHAPTER 21

Jehoram succeeds his father, Jehoshaphat; and commences his reign with the murder of his brethren, and of several of the princes of Israel, 1-5. He walks in the way of Ahab, whose bad daughter, Athaliah, he had married, 6. God remembers His covenant with David, and does not destroy the nation, 7. The Edomites revolt, 8-10. Jehoram restores the high places in the mountains of Judah, and greatly corrupts the morals of the people, 11. A letter comes to him from Elijah, 12-15. The Philistines and Arabians come up against him, pillage his house, and take away his wives, with all his sons except Jehoahaz, 16-17. He is smitten with an incurable disease in his bowels, of which, in two years, he dies miserably, after a profligate reign of eight years, 18-20.

2. *And he had brethren . . . the sons of Jehoshaphat king of Israel.* Jehoshaphat certainly was not king of Israel, but king of Judah.

Yisrael must be a corruption in the text, for *Yehudah*, which is the reading of the Syriac, Arabic, Septuagint, and Vulgate; the Chaldee only agrees with the Hebrew text. And the reading of the versions is supported by thirty-eight of Kennicott's and De Rossi's MSS. The word "Judah" should therefore be restored to the text.

3. *The kingdom gave he to Jehoram.* He made him copartner with himself in the kingdom about three years before his death, so that he reigned only five years after the death of his father, Jehoshaphat. See the notes on 2 Kings viii. 16, etc.; and on the same, chap. i. 17, where an attempt is made to settle this disturbed chronology.

6. *He had the daughter of Ahab to wife.* This was Athaliah, daughter of Ahab and Jezebel, who was famous for her impieties and cruelty, as was her most profligate mother. It is likely that she was the principal cause of Jehoram's cruelty and profaneness.

7. *To give a light to him.* To give him a descendant.

8. *In his days the Edomites revolted.* See on 2 Kings viii. 21.

11. *To commit fornication.* That is, to serve idols. The Israelites were considered as joined to Jehovah as a woman is joined to her husband. When she associates with other men, this is adultery; when they served other gods, this was called by the same name—it was adultery against Jehovah. This is frequently the only meaning of the terms adultery and fornication in the Scriptures.

12. *There came a writing to him from Elijah the prophet.* From 2 Kings ii. 11, it is evident that Elijah had been translated in the reign of Jehoshaphat, the father of Jehoram. How then could he send a letter to the son? It is certainly a possible case that this writing might have been a prediction of Jehoram's impiety and miserable death, delivered in the time of the prophet, and which was now laid before this wicked king for the first time; and by it the prophet, though not among mortals, still continued to speak. I can see no solid reason against this opinion.

16. *The Philistines, and . . . the Arabians.* We have no other account of this war. Though it was a predatory war, yet it appears to have been completely ruinous and destructive.

17. *Save Jehoahaz the youngest.* This person had at least three names, Jehoahaz, Ahaziah (chap. xxii. 1), and Azariah (v. 6.)

20. *Departed without being desired.* He was hated while he lived, and neglected when he died; visibly cursed of God, and necessarily execrated by the people whom he had lived only to corrupt and oppress. No annalist is mentioned as having taken the pains to write any account of his vile life.

CHAPTER 22

Ahaziah begins to reign, and reigns wickedly under the counsels of his bad mother, 1-4. He is slain by Jehu, who destroys all the house of Ahab, 5-9. Athaliah destroys all the seed royal of Judah, except Joash, who is hidden by his nurse in the Temple six years, 10-12.

1. *Made Ahaziah his youngest son king.* All the others had been slain by the Arabians, etc.; see the preceding chapter, v. 17.

2. *Forty and two years old was Ahaziah.* See the note on 2 Kings viii. 26. Ahaziah might have been twenty-two years old, according to 2 Kings viii. 26, but he could not have been forty-two, as stated here, without being two years older than his own father! The Syriac and Arabic have "twenty-two," and the Septuagint, in some copies, "twenty." And it is very probable that the Hebrew text read so originally; for when numbers were expressed by single letters it was easy to mistake *mem,* "forty," for *caph,* "twenty." And if this book was written by a scribe who used the ancient Hebrew letters, now called the Samaritan, the mistake was still more easy and probable, as the difference between *caph* and *mem* is very small, and can in many instances be discerned only by an accustomed eye. The reading in 2 Kings is right, and any attempt to reconcile this in Chronicles with that is equally futile and absurd. Both readings cannot be true; is that therefore likely to be genuine that makes the son two years older than the *father* who begat him?

3. *His mother was his counsellor.* Athaliah, the wicked daughter of a wicked parent, and the wicked spouse of an unprincipled king.

5. *Went with Jehoram.* See on 2 Kings viii. 28.

9. *He sought Ahaziah.* See a different account, 2 Kings ix. 27, and the note there, where the accounts are reconciled.

10. *All the seed royal of the house of Judah.* Nothing but the miraculous intervention of the divine providence could have saved the line of David at this time, and preserved the prophecy relative to the Messiah. The whole truth of that prophecy, and the salvation of the world, appeared to be now suspended on the brittle thread of the life of an infant of a year old (see chap. xxiv. 1), to destroy whom was the interest of the reigning power! But God can save by few as well as by many.

CHAPTER 23

Jehoiada the priest, after having taken counsel with the captains, Levites, etc., proclaims Joash, and anoints him king, 1-11. Athaliah, endeavoring to prevent it, is slain, 12-15. He makes the people enter into a covenant that they would serve the Lord, 16. The people break down the temple of Baal and slay Mattan, his priest, 17. Jehoiada makes several alterations, and remodels the kingdom, 18-21.

1. *And in the seventh year.* See on 2 Kings xi. 4, etc.

9. *Spears, and bucklers.* See on 2 Kings xi. 10.

11. *God save the king.* "May the king live!" See on 2 Kings xi. 12.

14. *And whoso followeth her, let him be slain with the sword.* He who takes her part, or endeavors to prevent the present revolution, let him be immediately slain.

15. *Of the horse gate.* See on 2 Kings xi. 16.

16. *Made a covenant between him.* The high priest was, on this occasion, the representative of God, whom both the people and the king must have had in view, through the medium of His priest.

21. *The city was quiet.* There was no attempt at a counterrevolution.

CHAPTER 24

Joash begins to reign when seven years old, and reigns well all the days of Jehoiada, the priest, 1-3. He purposes to repair the temple of God, and makes a proclamation that the people should bring in the money prescribed by Moses, 4-9. They all contribute liberally; and the different artificers soon perfect the work, 10-13. The rest of the money is employed to form utensils for the Temple, 14. Jehoiada dies, 15-16. And the people after his death become idolaters, 17-18. Prophets are sent unto them, 19. And among the rest Zechariah, the son of Jehoiada, who testifies against them; and they stone him to death, 20-22. The Syrians come against Jerusalem and spoil it, 23-24. Joash is murdered by his own servants, 25-26. His acts, 27.

1. *Joash was seven years old.* As he was hidden six years in the Temple, and was but seven when he came to the throne, he could have been but one year old when he was secreted by his aunt; see on chap. xxii. 10.

4. *To repair the house of the Lord.* During the reigns of Joram and Athaliah, the temple of God had been pillaged to enrich that of Baal, and the whole structure permitted to fall into decay; see v. 7.

5. *Gather of all Israel money.* As the Temple was the property of the whole nation, and the services performed in it were for the salvation of the people at large, it was right that each should come forward on an occasion of this kind and lend a helping hand. This is the first instance of such a general collection for building or repairing a house of God. *From year to year.* It must have been in a state of great dilapidation when it required such annual exertions to bring it into a thorough state of repair.

6. *The collection . . . of Moses.* This was the poll tax, fixed by Moses, of half a shekel, which was levied on every man from twenty years old and upward, and which was considered as a ransom for their souls, that there might be no plague among them. See Exod. xxx. 12-14.

8. *They made a chest.* See the notes on the parallel places, 2 Kings xii. 4, etc.

16. *They buried him . . . among the kings.* He had, in fact, been king in Judah; for Joash, who appears to have been a weak man, was always under his tutelage. Jehoiada governed the state in the name of the king, and his being buried among the kings is a proof of the high estimation in which he was held among the people.

17. *The princes of Judah . . . made obeisance to the king.* I believe the Targum has given the true sense of this verse: "After the death of Jehoiada, the great men of Judah came and adored King Joash, and seduced him; and then the king received from them their idols."

20. *And the Spirit of God came upon Zechariah.* "When he saw the transgression of the king and of the people, burning incense to an idol in the house of the sanctuary of the Lord, on the day of expiation; and preventing the priests of the Lord from offering the burnt-offerings, sacrifices, daily oblations, and services, as written in the book of the law of Moses; he stood above the people, and said."—Targum.

21. *Stoned him . . . at the commandment of the king.* What a most wretched and contemptible man was this, who could imbrue his hands in the blood of a prophet of God, and the son of the man who had saved him from being murdered, and raised him to the throne!

22. *The Lord look upon it, and require it.*

And so he did; for at the end of that year the Syrians came against Judah, destroyed all the princes of the people, sent their spoils to Damascus; and Joash, the murderer of the prophet, the son of his benefactor, was himself murdered by his own servants. Here was a most signal display of the divine retribution.

26. *These are they that conspired against him.* The two persons here mentioned were certainly not Jews; the mother of one was an Ammonitess, and the mother of the other was a Moabitess. Who their fathers were we know not; they were probably foreigners and aliens. Some suppose that these persons were of the king's chamber, and therefore could have the easiest access to him.

27. *The greatness of the burdens laid upon him.* Meaning, probably, the heavy tribute laid upon him by the Syrians, though some think the vast sums amassed for the repairs of the Temple are here intended. *Written in the story, Midrash,* the "commentary," *of the book of the kings.* We have met with this before; but these works are all lost, except the extracts found in Kings, Chronicles, and Ezra. These abridgments were the cause of the neglect, and finally of the destruction, of the originals.

CHAPTER 25

Amaziah succeeds his father, Joash, and begins his reign well, 1-2. He slays his father's murderers, but spares their children, 3-4. He reviews and remodels the army, 5; and hires 100,000 soldiers out of Israel, whom, on the expostulation of a prophet, he sends home again, without bringing them into active service; at which they are greatly offended, 6-10. He attacks the Syrians, kills 10,000, and takes 10,000 prisoners, whom he precipitates from the top of a rock, so that they are dashed to pieces, 11-12. The Israelitish soldiers, sent back, ravage several of the cities of Judah, 13. Amaziah becomes an idolater, 14. Is reproved by a prophet, whom he threatens, and obliges to desist, 15-16. He challenges Joash, king of Israel, 17; who reproves him by a parable, 18-19. Not desisting, the armies meet, the Jews are overthrown, and Amaziah taken prisoner by Joash, who ravages the Temple and takes away all the treasures of the king, 20-24. The reign of Amaziah: a conspiracy is formed against him; he flees to Lachish, whither he is pursued and slain; is brought to Jerusalem, and buried with his fathers, 25-28.

2. *He did that which was right.* He began his reign well, but soon became an idolater, vv. 14-15.

5. *Gathered Judah together.* He purposed to avenge himself of the Syrians, but wished to know his military strength before he came to a rupture.

9. *The Lord is able to give thee much more than this.* Better lose the money than keep the men, for they will be a curse unto thee.

10. *They returned home in great anger.* They thought they were insulted, and began to meditate revenge. See the notes on 2 Kings xiv. 1-20, where almost every circumstance in this chapter is examined and explained.

16. *Art thou made of the king's counsel?* How darest *thou* give advice to, or reprove, a king?

18. *The thistle that was in Lebanon.* See the explanation of this 2 Kings xiv. 9.

24. *In the house of God with Obed-edom.* From 1 Chron. xxvi. 15 we learn that to Obed-edom and his descendants was allotted the keeping of the house of *Asuppim* or "collections" for the divine treasury. *And . . . the hostages.* See on 2 Kings xiv. 14.

CHAPTER 26

Uzziah, the son of Amaziah, succeeds; and begins his reign piously and prosperously, which continued during the life of Zechariah, the prophet, 1-5. He fights successfully against the Philistines, and takes and dismantles some of their chief cities, 6; prevails over the Arabians and Mehunims, 7; and brings the Ammonites under tribute, 8. He fortifies Jerusalem, and builds towers in different parts of the country, and delights in husbandry, 9-10. An account of his military strength, warlike instruments, and machines, 11-15. He is elated with his prosperity, invades the priest's office, and is smitten with the leprosy, 16-20. He is obliged to abdicate the regal office and dwell apart from the people, his son Jotham acting as regent, 21. His death and burial, 22-23.

1. *The people of Judah took Uzziah.* They all agreed to place this son on his father's throne.

2. *He built Eloth.* See the notes on 2 Kings xiv. 21. This king is called by several different names; see the note on 2 Kings xv. 1.

5. *In the days of Zechariah.* Who this was we know not, but by the character that is given of him here. He was wise in the visions of God—in giving the true interpretation of divine prophecies. He was probably the tutor of Uzziah.

8. *The Ammonites gave gifts.* Paid an annual tribute.

10. *Built towers in the desert.* For the defense of his flocks, and his shepherds and husbandmen.

14. *Shields, and spears.* He prepared a vast number of military weapons, that he might have them in readiness to put into the hands of his subjects on any exigency.

15. *Engines . . . to shoot arrows and great stones.* This is the very first intimation on record of any warlike engines for the attack or defense of besieged places, and this account is long prior to anything of the kind among either the Greeks or Romans. Previously to such inventions the besieged could only be starved out, and hence sieges were very long and tedious. Shalmaneser consumed three years before such an inconsiderable place as Samaria, 2 Kings xvii. 5-6. The Jews alone were the inventors of such engines; and the invention took place in the reign of Uzziah, about eight hundred years before the Christian era. It is no wonder that, in consequence of this, *his name spread far abroad* and struck terror into his enemies.

16. *Went into the temple . . . to burn incense.* Thus assuming to himself the priest's office. See this whole transaction explained in the notes on 2 Kings xv. 5.

21. *And dwelt in a several house.* He was separated, because of the infectious nature of his disorder, from all society, domestic, civil, and religious.
Jotham . . . was over the king's house. He became regent of the land, his father being no longer able to perform the functions of the regal office.

22. *The rest of the acts of Uzziah, first and last, did Isaiah the prophet . . . write.* This work, however, is totally lost; for we have not any history of this king in the writings of Isaiah. He is barely mentioned, Isa. i. 1 and vi. 1.

23. *They buried him . . . in the field of the burial.* As he was a leper, he was not permitted to be buried in the common burial place of the kings, as it was supposed that even a place of sepulture must be defiled by the body of one who had died of this most afflictive and dangerous malady.

CHAPTER 27

Jotham succeeds his father, Uzziah, and reigns well, 1-2. His buildings, 3-4. His successful wars, 5-6. General account of his acts, reign, and death, 7-9.

2. *He entered not into the temple.* He copied his father's conduct as far as it was constitutional, and avoided his transgression. See the preceding chapter.

3. *On the wall of Ophel.* The wall, says the Targum, of the interior palace. Ophel was some part of the wall of Jerusalem that was most pregnable, and therefore Jotham fortified it in a particular manner.

4. *Castles and towers.* These he built for the protection of the country people against marauders.

5. *He fought also with . . . the Ammonites.* We find here that he brought them under a heavy tribute for three years, but whether this was the effect of his prevailing against them is not so evident. Some think that they paid this tribute for three years and then revolted; that, in consequence, he attacked them, and their utter subjection was the result.

7. *The rest of the acts of Jotham, and all his wars, and his ways.* It was in his days, according to 2 Kings xv. 37, that Rezin, king of Syria, and Pekah, king of Israel, began to cut Judah short. See the notes on 2 Kings xv. 36-37. *Written in the book of the kings.* There is not so much found in the Books of Kings which we have now as in this place of the Chronicles. In both places we have abridged accounts only; the larger histories have long been lost. The reign of Jotham was properly the last politically prosperous reign among the Jews. Hezekiah and Josiah did much to preserve the divine worship, but Judah continued to be cut short, till at last it was wholly ruined.

CHAPTER 28

Ahaz succeeds his father, Jotham, and reigns wickedly for sixteen years, 1. He restores idolatry in its grossest forms, 2-4; and is delivered into the hands of the kings of Israel and Syria, 5. Pekah slays 120,000 Jews in one day, and carries away captive 200,000 of the people, whom, at the instance of Oded the prophet, they restore to liberty, and send home, clothed and fed, 6-15. Ahaz sends to the king of Assyria for help against the Edomites, Philistines, etc., from whom he receives no effectual succor, 16-21. He sins yet more, spoils and shuts up the temple of God, and propagates idolatry throughout the land, 22-25. A reference to his acts, his death, and burial, 26-27.

1. *Ahaz was twenty years old.* For the difficulties in this chronology, see the notes on 2 Kings xvi. 1.

5. *Delivered him into the hand of the king of Syria.* For the better understanding of these passages the reader is requested to refer to what has been advanced in the notes on the sixteenth chapter of 2 Kings, vv. 5, etc.

6. *An hundred and twenty thousand.* It is very probable that there is a mistake in this number. It is hardly possible that 120,000 men could have been slain in one day, yet all the versions and MSS. agree in this number. The whole people seem to have been given up into the hands of their enemies.

9. *But a prophet of the Lord . . . whose name was Oded.* To this beautiful speech nothing can be added by the best comment; it is simple, humane, pious, and overwhelmingly convincing

—no wonder it produced the effect mentioned here.

16. *The kings of Assyria to help him.* Instead of *malchey*, "kings," the Vulgate, Syriac, Arabic, and Chaldee, and the parallel place, 2 Kings xvi. 7, have *melek*, "king," in the singular number. This king was Tiglath-pileser, as we learn from the Second Book of Kings.

21. *But he helped him not.* He did him no ultimate service. See the note on 2 Kings xvi. 9.

23. *He sacrificed unto the gods of Damascus, which smote him.* "This passage," says Mr. Hallet, "greatly surprised me; for the sacred historian himself is here represented as saying, *The gods of Damascus had smitten Ahaz.* But it is impossible to suppose that an inspired author could say this; for the Scripture everywhere represents the heathen idols as nothing and vanity, and as incapable of doing either good or hurt. All difficulty is avoided if we follow the old Hebrew copies, from which the Greek translation was made, *And King Ahaz said, I will seek to the gods of Damascus which have smitten me;* and then it follows, both in Hebrew and Greek, *He said moreover, Because the gods of the king of Syria help them; therefore will I sacrifice to them, that they may help me.* Both the Syriac and Arabic give it a similar turn; and say that *Ahaz sacrificed to the gods of Damascus, and said, Ye are my gods and my lords; you will I worship, and to you will I sacrifice.*"

24. *Shut up the doors.* He caused the divine worship to be totally suspended; and they continued shut till the beginning of the reign of Hezekiah, one of whose first acts was to reopen them, and thus to restore the divine worship, chap. xxix. 3.

27. *The kings of Israel.* It is a common thing for the writer of this book to put *Israel* for "Judah." He still considers them as one people, because proceeding from one stock. The versions and MSS. have the same reading with the Hebrew; the matter is of little importance, and with this interpretation none can mistake.

CHAPTER 29

Hezekiah's good reign, 1-2. He opens and repairs the doors of the Temple, 3. He assembles and exhorts the priests and Levites, and proposes to renew the covenant with the Lord, 4-11. They all sanctify themselves and cleanse the Temple, 12-17. They inform the king of their progress, 18-19. He collects the rulers of the people, and they offer abundance of sin offerings, and burnt offerings, and worship the Lord, 20-30. Every part of the divine service is arranged, and Hezekiah and all the people rejoice, 31-36.

2. *He did that which was right.* See the note on 2 Kings xviii. 3.

10. *To make a covenant.* To renew the covenant under which the whole people were constantly considered, and of which circumcision was the sign; and the spirit of which was, "I will be your God; ye shall be My people."

16. *And the priests went.* The priests and Levites cleansed first the courts both of the priests and of the people. On this labor they spent eight days. Then they cleansed the interior of the Temple; but as the Levites had no right to enter the Temple, the priests carried all the dirt and rubbish to the porch, whence they were collected by the Levites, carried away, and cast into the brook Kidron. In this work eight days

more were occupied, and thus the Temple was purified in sixteen days.

21. *They brought seven bullocks.* This was more than the law required; see Lev. iv. 13, etc. It ordered one calf or ox for the sins of the people, and one he-goat for the sins of the prince; but Hezekiah here offers many more. And the reason appears sufficiently evident: the law speaks only of sins of ignorance; but here were sins of every kind and every die—idolatry, apostasy from the divine worship, profanation of the Temple, etc., etc. The sin offerings, we are informed, were offered, first for the kingdom—for the transgressions of the king and his family; secondly, for the sanctuary, which had been defiled and polluted, and for the priests who had been profane, negligent, and unholy; and, finally, for Judah—for the whole mass of the people, who had been led away into every kind of abomination by the above examples.

23. *They laid their hands upon them.* That is, they confessed their sin; and as they had by their transgression forfeited their lives, they now offer these animals to die as vicarious offerings, their life being taken for the life of their owners.

34. *They could not flay all the burnt offerings.* Peace offerings, and suchlike, the Levites might flay and dress; but the whole burnt offerings, that is, those which were entirely consumed on the altar, could be touched only by the priests, unless in a case of necessity, such as is mentioned here. *The Levites were more upright in heart.* The priests seem to have been very backward in this good work; the Levites were more ready to help forward this glorious reformation. Why the former should have been so backward is not easy to tell, but it appears to have been the fact. Indeed it often happens that the higher orders of the priesthood are less concerned for the prosperity of true religion than the lower.

36. *And Hezekiah rejoiced.* Both he and the people rejoiced that God had prepared their hearts to bring about so great a reformation in so short a time; *for,* it is added, *the thing was done suddenly.*

CHAPTER 30

Hezekiah invites all Israel and Judah, and writes letters to Ephraim and Manasseh to come up to Jerusalem, and hold a Passover to the Lord, 1-4. The posts go out with the king's proclamation from Dan to Beersheba, and pass from city to city through the coasts of Ephraim, Manasseh, and Zebulun, but are generally mocked in Israel, 5-10. Yet several of Asher, Manasseh, and Zebulun humble themselves and come to Jerusalem, 11. But in Judah they are all of one heart, 12-13. They take away the idolatrous altars, kill the Passover, sprinkle the blood, and, as circumstances will permit, sanctify the people, 14-15. Many having eaten of the Passover who were not purified according to the law, Hezekiah prays for them; and the Lord accepts his prayer, and heals them, 16-20. Hezekiah exhorts them; and they hold the feast seven additional days, fourteen in all, and the people greatly rejoice, 21-26. The priests and the Levites bless the people, and God accepts their prayers and thanksgivings, 27.

1. *Hezekiah sent to all Israel.* It is not easy to find out how this was permitted by the king of Israel; but it is generally allowed that Hoshea, who then reigned over Israel, was one of their best kings. And as the Jews allow that at this time both the golden calves had been carried away by the Assyrians—that at Dan by Tiglath-pileser, and that at Bethel by Shalmaneser—the people who chose to worship Jehovah at Jerusalem were freely permitted to do it, and

Hezekiah had encouragement to make the proclamation in question.

2. *In the second month.* In Ijar, as they could not celebrate it in Nisan, the fourteenth of which month was the proper time. But as they could not complete the purgation of the Temple till the sixteenth of that month, therefore they were obliged to hold it now, or else adjourn it till the next year, which would have been fatal to that spirit of reformation which had now taken place. The law itself had given permission to those who were at a distance and could not attend to the fourteenth of the first month, and to those who were accidentally defiled and ought not to attend, to celebrate the Passover on the fourteenth of the second month; see Num. ix. 10-11.

6. *So the posts went.* "The runners or couriers"; persons who were usually employed to carry messages; men who were light of foot, and confidential.

18. *A multitude of the people . . . had not cleansed themselves.* As there were men from Ephraim, Manasseh, Issachar, and Zebulun, they were excusable, because they came from countries that had been wholly devoted to idolatry.

22. *Spake comfortably unto all the Levites.* On such occasions the priests and Levites had great fatigue and suffered many privations, and therefore had need of that encouragement which this prudent and pious king gave. It is a fine and expressive character given of these men, "They taught the good knowledge of God to the people."

25. *The strangers that came out of the land of Israel.* That is, the proselytes of the covenant who had embraced Judaism and had submitted to the rite of circumcision, for none others could be permitted to eat of the Passover.

26. *Since the time of Solomon . . . there was not the like in Jerusalem.* For from that time the ten tribes had been separated from the true worship of God, and now many of them for the first time, especially from Asher, Issachar, Ephraim, Manasseh, and Zebulun, joined to celebrate the Passover.

27. *And their voice was heard.* God accepted the fruits of that pious disposition which himself had infused. *And their prayer came up.* As the smoke of their sacrifices ascended to the clouds, so did their prayers, supplications, and thanksgivings ascend to the heavens.

CHAPTER 31

The people destroy all traces of idolatry throughout Judah, Benjamin, Ephraim, and Manasseh, 1. Hezekiah reforms the state of religion in general; and the tithes are brought in from all quarters, and proper officers set over them, 2-13. They bring in also the freewill offerings, and regulate the priests and Levites, and their families, according to their genealogies, 14-19. Hezekiah does everything in sincerity and truth, and is prosperous, 20-21.

1. *Brake the images in pieces.* This species of reformation was not only carried on through Judah, but they carried it into Israel; whether through a transport of religious zeal or whether with the consent of Hoshea the Israelitish king, we cannot tell.

2. *In the gates of the tents of the Lord.* That is in the Temple; for this was the house, tabernacle, tent, and camp of the Most High.

3. *The king's portion of his substance for the*

burnt offerings. It is conjectured that the Jewish kings, at least from the time of David, furnished the morning and evening sacrifice daily at their own expense, and several others also.

5. *Brought . . . the firstfruits.* These were principally for the maintenance of the priests and Levites. They brought tithes of all the produce of the field, whether commanded or not, as we see in the instance of *honey,* which was not to be offered to the Lord, Lev. ii. 11, yet it appears it might be offered to the priests as firstfruits, or in the way of tithes.

7. *In the third month.* "The month *Sivan;* the seventh, *Tisri.*"—Targum. *The heaps.* The vast collections of grain which they had from the tithes over and above their own consumption; see v. 10.

11. *To prepare chambers.* To make granaries to lay up this superabundance.

12. *Shimei . . . was the next.* He was assistant to Cononiah.

15. *And Miniamin.* Instead of *Miniamin, Benjamin* is the reading of three of Kennicott's and De Rossi's MSS.; and this is the reading of the Vulgate, Syriac, Septuagint, and Arabic.

17. *From twenty years old.* Moses had ordered that the Levites should not begin their labor till they were thirty years of age; but David changed this order, and obliged them to begin at twenty.

CHAPTER 32

Sennacherib invades Judea, 1. Hezekiah takes proper measures for the defense of his kingdom, 2-6. His exhortation, 7-8. Sennacherib sends a blasphemous message to Hezekiah and to the people, 9-15. His servants rail against God, and he and they blaspheme most grievously, 16-19. Hezekiah and the prophet Isaiah cry to God; He answers, and the Assyrians are destroyed, and Sennacherib is slain by his own sons, 20-21. The Lord is magnified, 22-23. Hezekiah's sickness and recovery, 24. His ingratitude, 25. His humiliation, 26. His riches, 27-30. His error relative to the Babylonish ambassadors, 31. His acts and death, 32-33.

1. *After these things.* God did not permit this pious prince to be disturbed till he had completed the reformation which he had begun.

2. *When Hezekiah saw.* This was in the fourteenth year of the reign of Hezekiah; and at first the Jewish king bought him off at the great price of 300 talents of silver and 30 talents of gold; and even emptied his own treasures, and spoiled the house of the Lord, to gratify the oppressive avarice of the Assyrian king. See the whole account, 2 Kings xviii. 13, etc.

4. *Stopped all the fountains.* This was prudently done, for without water how could an immense army subsist in an arid country?

5. *Raised it up to the towers.* He built the wall up to the height of the towers, or, having built the wall, he raised towers on it.

6. *Set captains of war over the people . . . in the street of the gate of the city.* That is, the open places at the gate of the city, whither the people came for judgment.

7. *There be more with us than with him.* We have more power than they have. (These words he quotes from the prophet Elisha, 2 Kings vi. 16). This was soon proved to be true by the slaughter made by the angel of the Lord in the Assyrian camp.

9. *After this did Sennacherib.* Having received the silver and gold mentioned above, he withdrew his army, but shortly after he sent Rab-

shakeh with a blasphemous message. This is the fact mentioned here.

10. *Thus saith Sennacherib.* See all these circumstances largely explained, 2 Kings xviii. 17-36.

17. *Wrote also letters.* See 2 Kings xix. 9, 14.

21. *The Lord sent an angel.* See 2 Kings xix. 35 and the note there. *House of his god.* Nisroch. *They that came forth of his own bowels.* His sons Adrammelech and Sharezer.

23. *Many brought gifts unto the Lord.* They plainly saw that Jehovah was the Protector of the land. *And presents to Hezekiah.* They saw that God was his Friend and would undertake for him, and they did not wish to have such a man for their enemy.

24. *Hezekiah was sick.* See 2 Kings xx. 1, etc., and the notes there.

25. *Hezekiah rendered not again.* He got into a vain confidence, took pleasure in his riches, and vainly showed them to the messengers of the king of Babylon. See on 2 Kings xx. 12, etc.

26. *Humbled himself.* Awoke from his sleep, was sorry for his sin, deprecated the wrath of God, and the divine displeasure was turned away from him.

27. *Pleasant jewels.* Desirable "vessels" or "utensils."

30. *The upper watercourse.* He made canals to bring the waters of Gihon from the west side of Jerusalem to the west side of the city of David.

31. *Of the ambassadors.* See 2 Kings xx. 13.

32. *The vision of Isaiah.* See this prophet, cc. xxxvi—xxxix.

33. *Chiefest of the sepulchres.* This respect they paid to him who, since David, had been the best of all their kings.

CHAPTER 33

Manasseh reigns fifty-five years, and restores idolatry, pollutes the Temple, and practices all kinds of abominations, 1-9. He and the people are warned in vain, 10. He is delivered into the hands of the Assyrians, bound with fetters, and carried to Babylon, 11. He humbles himself and is restored, 12-13. He destroys idolatry and restores the worship of God, 14-16. The people keep the high places but sacrifice to the Lord on them, 17. His acts, prayer, and death, 18-20. His son Amon succeeds him, and after a wicked, idolatrous reign of two years is slain by his own servants in his own house, 21-24. The people rise up and slay his murderers, and make Josiah, his son, king in his stead, 25.

1. *Manasseh was twelve years old.* We do not find that he had any godly director; his youth was therefore the more easily seduced. But surely he had a pious education; how then could the principles of it be so soon eradicated?

3. *Altars for Baalim.* The sun and moon. *And made groves, Asheroth,* "Astarte"; *the host of heaven,* all the planets and stars. These were the general objects of his devotion.

5. *He built altars.* See the principal facts in this chapter explained in the notes on 2 Kings xxi. 1-17.

14. *He built a wall.* This was probably a weak place that he fortified; or a part of the wall which the Assyrians had broken down, which he now rebuilt.

15. *He took away the strange gods.* He appears to have done everything in his power to destroy the idolatry which he had set up and to restore

the pure worship of the true God. His repentance brought forth fruits meet for repentance. How long he was in captivity, and when or by whom he was delivered, we know not. The fact of his restoration is asserted, and we believe it on divine testimony.

21. *Amon . . . reigned two years.* See on 2 Kings xxi. 19.

22. *Sacrificed unto all the carved images.* How astonishing is this! with his father's example before his eyes, he copies his father's vices, but not his repentance.

23. *Trespassed more and more.* He appears to have exceeded his father, and would take no warning.

25. *The people of the land slew all them.* His murder was not a popular act, for the people slew the regicides. They were as prone to idolatry as their king was. We may rest satisfied that idolatry was accompanied with great licentiousness and sensual gratifications, else it never, as a mere religious system, could have had any sway in the world.

CHAPTER 34

Josiah reigns thirty-one years; destroys idolatry in Judah, as also in Manasseh, Ephraim, Simeon, and even to Naphtali, 1-7. He begins to repair the Temple, and collects money for the purpose, and employs workmen, 8-13. Hilkiah, the priest, finds the book of the law in the Temple, which is read by Shaphan before the king, 14-19. He is greatly troubled and consults Huldah, the prophetess, 20-22. Her exhortation and message to the king, 23-28. He causes it to be read to the elders of Judah, and they make a covenant with God, 29-32. Josiah removes every abomination, and the people serve God all his days, 33.

2. *He . . . declined neither to the right hand, nor to the left.* He never swerved from God and truth; he never omitted what he knew to be his duty to God and his kingdom; he carried on his reformation with a steady hand; timidity did not prevent him from going far enough; and zeal did not lead him beyond due bounds.

4. *The altars of Baalim.* How often have these been broken down, and how soon set up again! We see that the religion of a land is as the religion of its king. If the king were idolatrous, up went the altars; on the other hand, when the king was truly religious, down went the idolatrous altars.

6. *The cities of Manasseh.* Even those who were under the government of the Israelitish king permitted their idols and places of idolatry to be hewn down and destroyed; after the truth was declared and acknowledged, the spade and the axe were employed to complete the reformation.

9. *And they returned to Jerusalem.* Instead of *vaiyashubu,* "they returned," we should read *yoshebey,* "the inhabitants"—a reading which is supported by many MSS., printed editions, and all the versions, as well as by necessity and common sense. See the note on chap. xix. 8, where a similar mistake is rectified.

14. *Found a book of the law.* See on 2 Kings xxii. 8.

22. *Huldah the prophetess.* See on 2 Kings xxii. 14.

28. *Gathered to thy grave in peace.* See particularly the note on 2 Kings xxii. 20.

30. *The king went.* See on 2 Kings xxiii. 1.

31. *Made a covenant.* See on 2 Kings xxiii. 3.

32. *To stand to it.* It is likely that he caused them all to arise when he read the terms of the covenant, and thus testify their approbation of the covenant itself, and their resolution to observe it faithfully and perseveringly.

CHAPTER 35

Josiah celebrates a Passover, 1; regulates the courses of the priests; assigns them, the Levites, and the people their portions; and completes the greatest Passover ever celebrated since the days of Solomon, 2-19. Pharaoh-necho passes with his army through Judea, 20. Josiah meets and fights with him at Megiddo, and is mortally wounded, 21-23. He is carried to Jerusalem, where he dies, 24. Jeremiah laments for him, 25. Of his acts and deeds, and where recorded, 26-27.

3. *Put the holy ark in the house.* It is likely that the priests had secured this when they found that the idolatrous kings were determined to destroy everything that might lead the people to the worship of the true God. And now, as all appears to be well-established, the ark is ordered to be put into its own place. For an ample account of this Passover and the reformation that was then made, see on 2 Kings xxiiii. 1, etc.

11. *They killed the passover.* The people themselves might slay their own paschal lambs, and then present the blood to the priests, that they might sprinkle it before the altar; and the Levites flayed them, and made them ready for dressing.

18. *There was no passover like to that.* "That which distinguished this passover from all the former was," says Calmet, "the great liberality of Josiah, who distributed to his people a greater number of victims than either David or Solomon had done."

20. *Necho king of Egypt.* "Pharaoh the lame," says the Targum.

24. *The second chariot.* Perhaps this means no more than that they took Josiah out of his own chariot and put him into another, either for secrecy or because his own had been disabled. The chariot into which he was put might have been that of the officer who attended his master to the war. See the note on 2 Kings xxii. 20.

27. *And his deeds, first and last.* These general histories are lost, but in the Books of Kings and Chronicles we have the leading facts.

CHAPTER 36

Jehoahaz made king on the death of his father, Josiah, and reigns only three months, 1-2. He is dethroned by the king of Egypt, and Jehoiakim, his brother, is made king in his stead, who reigns wickedly eleven years, and is dethroned and led captive to Babylon by Nebuchadnezzar, 3-8. Jehoiachin is made king in his stead, and reigns wickedly three months and ten days, and is also led captive to Babylon, 9-10. Zedekiah begins to reign, and reigns wickedly eleven years, 11-12. He rebels against Nebuchadnezzar, and he and his people cast all the fear of God behind their backs; the wrath of God comes upon them to the uttermost; the Temple is destroyed; and the whole nation is subjugated, and led into captivity, 13-21. Cyrus, king of Persia, makes a proclamation to rebuild the temple of the Lord, 22-23.

1. *Took Jehoahaz.* It seems that after Necho had discomfited Josiah he proceeded immediately against Charchemish, and in the interim, Josiah dying of his wounds, the people made his son king.

3. *The king of Egypt put him down.* He now considered Judah to be conquered and tributary to him, and because the people had set up Jehoahaz without his consent, he dethroned him, and put his brother in his place, perhaps for no other reason but to show his supremacy. For other particulars see the notes on 2 Kings xxiii. 31-35.

6. *Came up Nebuchadnezzar.* See the notes on 2 Kings xxiv. 1.

9. *Jechoiachin was eight.* See on 2 Kings xxiv.

10. *Made Zedekiah . . . king.* His name was at first Mattaniah, but the king of Babylon changed it to Zedekiah. See 2 Kings xxiv. 17, and the notes there.

12. *Did that which was evil.* Was there ever such a set of weak, infatuated men as the Jewish kings in general? They had the fullest evidence that they were only deputies to God Almighty, and that they could not expect to retain the throne any longer than they were faithful to their Lord; and yet with all this conviction they lived wickedly, and endeavored to establish idolatry in the place of the worship of their Maker! After bearing with them long, the divine mercy gave them up, as their case was utterly hopeless.

19. *They burnt the house of God.* Here was an end to the Temple, the most superb and costly edifice ever erected by man. *Brake down the wall of Jerusalem.* So it ceased to be a fortified city. *Burnt all the palaces.* So it was no longer a dwelling place for kings or great men. *Destroyed all the goodly vessels.* Beat up all the silver and gold into masses, keeping only a few of the finest in their own shape. See v. 18.

21. *To fulfil the word of the Lord.* See Jer. xxv. 9, 12; xxvi. 6-7; xxix. 12. For the miserable death of Zedekiah, see 2 Kings xxv. 4, etc.

22. *Now in the first year of Cyrus.* This and the following verse are supposed to have been written by mistake from the Book of Ezra, which begins in the same way. The Book of the Chronicles, properly speaking, does close with the twenty-first verse, as then the Babylonish captivity commences; and these two verses speak of the transactions of a period seventy years after.

The Book of

EZRA

At the conclusion of 2 Kings, and also of the preceding book, 2 Chronicles, we have seen the state of misery and desolation to which the kingdoms of Israel and Judah were reduced through their unparalleled ingratitude to God and their innumerable backslidings and rebellions. These at last issued in their captivity, the inhabitants of the former country being carried away by the Assyrians, and those of the latter by the Chaldeans. The former never recovered their ancient territories, and were so disposed of by their enemies that they either became amalgamated with the heathen nations, so as to be utterly undistinguishable, or they were transported to some foreign and recluse place of settlement, that the place of their existence, though repeatedly guessed at, has for more than two thousand years been totally unknown.

In mercy to the less polluted inhabitants of the kingdom of Judah, though delivered up into the hands of their enemies, God had promised by His prophet that at the expiration of *seventy years* they should be enlarged, and restored to their own country. This prediction was most literally fulfilled; and the Books of Ezra, Esther, and Nehemiah inform us how the divine goodness accomplished this most gracious design, and the movers and agents He employed on the occasion. The writer of the following book was undoubtedly the chief agent under God.

CHAPTER 1

The proclamation of Cyrus for the rebuilding of the Temple, 1-4. The people provide for their return, 5-6. Cyrus restores to Sheshbazzar the vessels taken by Nebuchadnezzar out of the temple of Solomon, 7-11.

1. *Now in the first year.* This is word for word with the two last verses of the preceding book, which stand here in their proper place and connection, but there are entirely destitute of chronological connection and reference. *Cyrus.* This prince, so eminent in antiquity, is said to have been the son of Cambyses, king of Persia, and Mandane, daughter of Astyages, king of the Medes, and was born about six hundred years before Christ. Josephus accounts for his partiality to the Jews from this circumstance, that he was shown the places in Isaiah the prophet where he is mentioned by name, and his exploits and conquests foretold: see Isa. xliv. 28 and xlv. 1. Finding himself thus distinguished by the God of the Jews, he was anxious to give Him proofs of his gratitude in return; and so made the decree in favor of the Jews, restored their sacred vessels, gave them liberty to return to their own land, and encouraged them to rebuild the temple of Jehovah. It is very probable that when Cyrus took Babylon he found Daniel there, who had been long famed as one of the wisest ministers of state in all the East; and it is most likely that it was this person who pointed out to him the prophecy of Isaiah, and gave him those further intimations relative to the divine will which were revealed to himself.

By ... Jeremiah. This prophet, chap. xxv. 12 and xxix. 11, had foretold that the Babylonish captivity should last only seventy years; these were now ended. Cyrus had given the Jews permission and encouragement to return to Judea

and rebuild the temple of the Lord, and thus the prediction of Jeremiah was fulfilled.

2. *The Lord God of heaven.* It is not unworthy of remark that, in all the books written prior to the Captivity, Jehovah is called "The Lord of Hosts"; but in all the books written after the Captivity, as 2 Chronicles, Ezra, Nehemiah, and Daniel, He is styled "The God of Heaven." The words however have the same meaning. *All the kingdoms of the earth.* At this time the empire of the Medo-Persians was very extensive; according to ancient writers, Cyrus at this time, reigned over the Medes, Persians, Hyrcanians, Armenians, Syrians, Assyrians, Arabians, Cappadocians, Phrygians, Lydians, Phoenicians, Babylonians, Bactrians, Indians, Saci, Cilicians, Paphlagonians, Moriandrians, and many others. His empire extended on the east to the Red Sea; on the north, to the Euxine Sea; on the west, to the island of Cyprus and Egypt; and on the south, to Ethiopia.

4. *Whosoever remaineth in any place.* Everyone was at liberty to go, but none was obliged to go. Thus their attachment to God was tried. He whose heart was right with God went; he who was comfortably settled in Babylon might go if he chose. Those who did not go were commanded to assist their brethren who went.

6. *Vessels of silver.* Articles of silver, gold etc.

7. *The king brought forth the vessels.* See on vv. 9-11.

8. *Sheshbazzar, the prince of Judah.* This was probably the Chaldean name of him who was originally called Zerubbabel. The former signifies "joy in affliction"; the latter, "a stranger in Babylon." The latter may be designed to refer to his captive state; the former, to the prospect

of release. Some think this was quite a different person; a Persian or Chaldean, sent by Cyrus to superintend whatever officers or men Cyrus might have sent to assist the Jews on their return and to procure them help in the Chaldean provinces, through which they might be obliged to travel.

11. *All the vessels . . . were five thousand and four hundred.* This place is without doubt corrupted; here it is said the sum of all the vessels, of every quality and kind, was 5,400; but the enumeration of the articles, as given in vv. 9 and 10, gives the sum of 2,499 only. But we can correct this account from 1 Esdras ii. 13-14.

CHAPTER 2

An account of those who returned from Babylon, 1-35. The children of the priests who returned, 36-39. Of the Levites, 40. Of the singers, 41. Of the porters, 42. Of the Nethinim, and the children of Solomon's servants. 43-58. Others who could not find out their registers, 59-62. The number of the whole congregation, 63-64. Of their servants, maids, and singers, 65. Their horses and mules, 66. Their camels and asses, 67. The offerings of the chief men when they came to Jerusalem, 68-69. The priests, Levites, singers, porters, and Nethinim betake themselves to their respective cities, 70.

1. *These are the children of the province.* That is, of Judea—once a kingdom and a flourishing nation; now a province, subdued, tributary, and ruined! Some think Babylon is meant by *the province;* and that *the children of the province* means those Jews who were born in Babylon. But the first is most likely to be the meaning, for thus we find Judea styled, chap. v. Besides, the *province* is contradistinguished from Babylon even in this first verse. *The children of the province*—"that had been carried away unto Babylon."

2. *Which came with Zerubbabel.* There are many difficulties in this table of names; but as we have no less than three copies of it, that contained here from vv. 1-67, a second in Neh. vii. 6-69, and a third in 1 Esdras v. 7-43, on a careful examination they will be found to correct each other. Though the sum total at the end of each of these enumerations is equal, namely, 42,360, yet the particulars reckoned up make in Ezra only 29,818. and in Nehemiah 31,089. We find that Nehemiah mentions 1,765 persons which are not in Ezra, and Ezra has 494 not mentioned by Nehemiah. Mr. Alting thinks that this circumstance, which appears to render all hope of reconciling them impossible, is precisely the very point by which they can be reconciled; for if we add Ezra's surplus to the sum in Nehemiah, and the surplus of Nehemiah to the number in Ezra, the numbers will be equal.

3. *The children of Parosh.* Where the word *children* is found in this table, prefixed to the name of a man, it signifies the descendants of that person, as from this verse to v. 21. Where it is found prefixed to a place, it signifies the inhabitants of that place, as from v. 21 to v. 35.

33. *The children of Lod, Hadid, and Ono.* There were cities in the tribe of Benjamin; see on 1 Chron. viii. 12.

36. *The priests.* The preceding list takes in the census of Judah and Benjamin.

55. *The children of Solomon's servants.* The Nethinim, and others appointed to do the meaner services of the holy house.

63. *The Tirshatha.* This is generally supposed to be Nehemiah, or the person who was the

commandant; see Neh. viii. 9 and x. 1, for the word appears to be the name of an office. *Should not eat of the most holy things.* There was a high priest then, but no Urim and Thummim, these having been lost in the Captivity.

66. *Their horses . . . seven hundred.* They went into captivity, stripped of everything; they now return from it, abounding in the most substantial riches, viz., horses 736, or, according to Esdras, 7,036; mules, 245; camels, 435; asses, 6,720; besides gold, and silver, and rich stuffs.

69. *Threescore and one thousand drams of gold.* Drakmons or darics; a Persian coin. always of gold, and worth about 1£. 5s.; not less than £76,250 sterling in gold. *Five thousand pound of silver.* Manehs or minas. As a weight, the maneh was 100 shekels; as a coin, 60 shekels in value, or about 9£; 5,000 of these manehs therefore will amount to £45,000, making in the whole a sum of about £120,000; and in this are not included the 100 garments for priests.

70. *Dwelt in their cities.* They all went to those cities which belonged originally to their respective families.

CHAPTER 3

The altar of burnt offerings is set up, 1-3. They keep the Feast of Tabernacles, 4-6. They make provision for rebuilding the Temple, and lay its foundation in the second month of the second year, 7-8. Ceremonies observed in laying the foundation, 9-11. Some weep aloud, and others shout for joy, 12-18.

1. *When the seventh month was come.* The month Tisri, which answers to the latter part of our September and beginning of October. It seems that the Israelites had left Babylon about the spring of the year; that on their arrival at Jerusalem they constructed themselves huts and sheds to lodge in among the ruins, in which they must have spent some months. After this they rebuilt the altar of burnt offerings and kept the Feast of Tabernacles, which happened about this time, and continued to offer sacrifices regularly, as if the Temple were standing.

2. *Jeshua the son of Jozadak.* He was grandson of Seraiah, the high priest, who was put to death by Nebuchadnezzar, 2 Kings xxv. 18, 21. This Jeshua or Joshua was the first high priest after the Captivity.

3. *They set the altar upon his bases.* Rebuilt it on the same spot on which it had formerly stood. As it was necessary to keep up the divine worship during the time they should be employed in reedifying the Temple, they first reared this altar of burnt offerings; and all this they did, though *fear was upon them*, because of the unfriendly disposition of their surrounding neighbors.

4. *They kept also the feast of tabernacles, as it is written.* This began on the fifteenth day of the seventh month; but they had begun the regular offerings from the first day of this month, v. 6. And these were religiously continued all the time they were building the Temple.

7. *They gave money also.* They copied the conduct of Solomon while he was building his temple; see 1 Kings v. 11. He employed the Tyrians, gave them meat and drink; and this permission they now had from Cyrus.

8. *In the second year.* The previous time had been employed in clearing the ground, felling timber, hewing stones, and transporting them to

the place, and making other necessary preparations for the commencement of the building.

10. *After the ordinance of David.* With psalms which he composed, acting in the manner which he directed.

12. *Wept with a loud voice.* They saw that the glory had departed from Israel; in their circumstances it was impossible to build such a house as the first Temple was; and had this been even possible, still it would have been greatly inferior, because it wanted the ark of the covenant, the heavenly fire, the mercy seat, the heavenly manna, Aaron's rod that budded, the divine Shekinah, the spirit of prophecy, and most probably the Urim and Thummim. *Many shouted . . . for joy.* Finding they were now restored to their own land, and to the worship of their God in His own peculiar city. These, in general, had not seen the original Temple, and therefore could not feel affected in that way which the elderly people did.

CHAPTER 4

The Samaritans endeavor to prevent the rebuilding of the Temple, 1-5. They send letters to Artaxerxes, against the Jews, 6-9. A copy of the letter, 10-16. He commands the Jews to cease from building the Temple, which they do; nor was anything further done in the work till the second year of Darius, 17-24.

1. *Now when the adversaries.* These were the Samaritans, and the different nations with which the kings of Assyria had peopled Israel, when they had carried the original inhabitants away into captivity, see v. 9.

2. *Let us build with you.* We acknowledge the same God, are solicitous for His glory, and will gladly assist you in this work. But that they came with no friendly intention, the context proves.

3. *Ye have nothing to do with us.* We cannot acknowledge you as worshippers of the true God, and cannot participate with you in anything that relates to His worship.

4. *Weakened the hands.* Discouraged and opposed them by every possible means.

5. *Hired counsellors.* They found means to corrupt some of the principal officers of the Persian court, so that the orders of Cyrus were not executed—or at least so slowly as to make them nearly ineffectual. *Until the reign of Darius.* This was probably Darius the son of Hystaspes.

6. *In the reign of Ahasuerus.* This is the person who is called Cambyses by the Greeks. He reigned seven years and five months, and during the whole of that time the building of the Temple was interrupted.

7. *In the days of Artaxerxes.* It is generally believed that, from the time of Cyrus the great, Xerxes and Artaxerxes were names assumed by the Persian sovereigns, whatever their names had been before. *Written in the Syrian tongue.* That is, the Syrian or Chaldean character was used— not the Hebrew. *Interpreted in the Syrian tongue.* That is, the language, as well as the character, was the Syriac or Chaldaic.

8. *Rehum the chancellor.* With this verse the Chaldee part of the chapter begins, and the same language continues to the end of v. 18 of chap. vi. These men wrote to Darius in their own language; and the king in the same dialect returns an answer, chap. v. This circumstance adds authenticity to what is written; so scrupulous was the inspired penman that he not only gave the words which each spoke and wrote, but he gave them also in the very language in which they were conceived, and in the character peculiar to that language.

10. *The great and noble Asnapper.* Whether this was Shalmaneser, or Esar-haddon, or some other person, learned men and chronologists are not agreed.

11. *And at such a time.* The word *ucheeneth* has greatly perplexed all commentators and critics. The versions give us no light; and the Vulgate translates it "and they wish prosperity." Some translate it "and so forth"; and our translators supposed that it referred to the date, which however is not specified, and might have been as easily entered as the words *and at such a time.*

13. *Toll, tribute, and custom.* The first term is supposed to imply the capitation tax; the second, an excise on commodities and merchandise; the third, a sort of land tax. Others suppose the first means a property tax; the second, a poll tax; and the third, what was paid on imports and exports. In a word, if you permit these people to rebuild and fortify their city, they will soon set you at naught, and pay you no kind of tribute.

14. *Now because we have maintenance from the king's palace.* More literally: "Now because at all times we are salted with the salt of the palace"; i.e., We live on the king's bounty, and must be faithful to our benefactor. Salt was used as the emblem of an incorruptible covenant, and those who ate bread and salt together were considered as having entered into a very solemn covenant. These hypocrites intimated that they felt their conscience bound by the league between them and the king, and therefore could not conscientiously see the thing going on that was likely to turn to the king's damage. They were probably also persons in the pay of the Persian king.

15. *The book of the records of thy fathers.* That is, the records of the Chaldeans, to whom the Persians succeeded.

17. *Peace, and at such a time.* The word *ucheeth* is like that which we have already considered on v. 10, and probably has the same meaning.

19. *Hath made insurrection against kings.* The struggles of the Israelites to preserve or regain their independency, which they had from God, are termed insurrection, rebellion, and sedition, because at last they fell under the power of their oppressors.

20. *Beyond the river.* That is, the Euphrates. Both David and Solomon carried their conquests beyond this river. See 2 Sam. viii. 3, etc., and 1 Kings iv. 21, where it is said, "Solomon reigned over all kingdoms from the river [Euphrates] unto the land of the Philistines, and unto the border of Egypt."

21. *Until another commandment shall be given from me.* The rebuilding was only provisionally suspended. The decree was, Let it cease for the present; nor let it proceed at any time without an order express from me.

CHAPTER 5

Haggai and Zechariah, the prophets, encourage Zerubbabel and Jeshua to proceed with the building of the Temple, 1-2. Tatnai, the governor of the provinces on this side the Euphrates, and his companions, inquire by what authority they do this, 3-5. They write to Darius; a copy of the letter, 6-16. They request to know how they are to proceed, 17.

1. *Haggai . . . and Zechariah.* These are the same whose writings we have among the twelve minor prophets. *The son of Iddo.* That is, the grandson of Iddo; for Zechariah was the son of Berechiah, the son of Iddo. See his prophecy, chap. i. 1.

2. *Then rose up Zerubbabel.* Here we find three classes of men joining in the sacred work: Zerubbabel, the civil governor; Jeshua, the high priest or ecclesiastical governor; and Haggai and Zechariah, the prophets.

3. *Tatnai, governor.* He was governor of the provinces which belonged to the Persian Empire on their side of the Euphrates, comprehending Syria, Arabia Deserta, Phoenicia, and Samaria. He seems to have been a mild and judicious man, and to have acted with great prudence and caution, and without any kind of prejudice. The manner in which he represented this to the king is a full proof of this disposition.

4. *What are the names?* It is most evident that this is the answer of the Jews to the inquiry of Tatnai, v. 3, and the verse should be read thus: "Then said we unto them after this manner: These are the names of the men who make this building."

8. *With great stones.* They are making a very strong and a very costly building.

16. *Sheshbazzar.* Probably the military officer that conducted the people from Babylon, and had the oversight of the work; but some think that Ezra is meant.

17. *The . . . treasure house.* This is a Persian word, "a treasury."

CHAPTER 6

Darius orders search to be made for the edict of Cyrus, 1. It is found at Achmetha, 2. A transcript of this edict, 3-5. Darius confirms it, 6-12. Tatnai encourages the Jews to proceed, and they finish the Temple in the sixth year of Darius, 13-15. They dedicate the Temple, 16-18; keep the Passover, 19-21, and the Feast of Unleavened Bread, 22.

1. *In the house of the rolls.* The "house of the books," the king's library. This is the first time we hear of a library.

2. *At Achmetha.* Ecbatana in India, whither it is probable all the records of Cyrus had been carried. This was a sort of summer residence for the kings of Persia.

3. *The height thereof threescore cubits.* This was much larger than the temple of Solomon. This was sixty cubits high and sixty cubits broad, whereas Solomon's was only twenty cubits broad and thirty cubits high.

4. *Three rows of great stones, and a row of new timber.* We have noticed this kind of building before, three courses of stones, and then a course of strong balk; and this continued to the square of the building. *And let the expenses be given.* Cyrus had ordered wood to be cut at Libanus, and conveyed to Joppa at his expense; but it does not appear that he furnished the other expenses of the building, for we have

already seen that the Jews contributed for the defraying of all others. But it appears that he provided at his own expense the sacrifices and offerings for the Temple. See v. 9.

6. *Be ye far from thence.* Do not interrupt the Jews in their building but, on the contrary, further them all in your power.

10. *And pray for the life of the king, and of his sons.* Even heathens believed that offerings made in their behalf to the God of the Jews would be available.

11. *Let timber be pulled down.* Whether this refers to the punishment of hanging and gibbeting, or whipping at a post, or of impaling, is not quite clear. *Let his house be made a dunghill.* Let it be reduced to ruins, and never more used, except for the most sordid and unclean purposes.

14. *According to the commandment of the God of Israel.* He first gave the order, and stirred up the hearts of the following Persian kings to second that order.

17. *Twelve he goats.* This was a sin offering for every tribe.

18. *And they set the priests.* With this verse the Chaldee or Aramitic part of this chapter ends.

20. *The Levites were purified together.* They were all ready at one time to observe the proper rites and ceremonies, and had no need of having a second Passover, which was appointed by the law for those who had been accidentally defiled or were at a distance from the Tabernacle. See 2 Chron. xxx. 3.

21. *And all such as had separated themselves.* These were the proselytes who had embraced the Jewish religion by having mingled with the Jews in their captivity. This proves that there the poor captives had so acted according to the principles of their religion that the heathen saw it and walked in the light of the Lord with them.

22. *Turned the heart of the king of Assyria.* I am of Calmet's mind, that *king of Assyria* is here put for "king of Persia." Cyrus and his successors possessed all the rights and estates of the ancient kings of Assyria and therefore the same monarch may be styled king of Assyria as well as king of Persia.

CHAPTER 7

In the seventh year of Artaxerxes, king of Persia, Ezra goes up to Jerusalem, and with him certain of the priests, Levites, porters, and Nethinim; his character, 1-10. The letter and decree of Artaxerxes in behalf of the Jews, 11-26. Ezra's thanksgiving to God for these mercies, 27-28.

1. *In the reign of Artaxerxes.* This was Artaxerxes Longimanus. *Son of Seraiah.* Either this could not have been Seraiah, the high priest, who had been put to death by Nebuchadnezzar 121 years before this time, or the term *son* here must signify only one of his descendants. In this place there are only 16 generations reckoned between Ezra and Aaron, but in 1 Chron. vi. 3-4, etc., there are not less than 22. We must therefore supply the deficient generations from the above place, between Amariah son of Meraioth, 1 Chron. vi. 7, and Azariah son of Johanan, v. 10.

6. *A ready scribe. Sopher machir* does not merely signify a speedy writer or an excellent

penman, but one who was eminently skillful in expounding the law. In this sense the word *scribe* is repeatedly used in the New Testament, and we find that in both the Old and New Testament it had the same signification.

8. *He came to Jerusalem in the fifth month.* From the following verse we learn that Ezra and his company set off from Babylon on the first day of the first month, and thus we find they were upwards of four months on their journey. They could not travel fast, as they were a great company, composed in part of the aged and infirm, besides multitudes of women and children. They appear also to have taken a circuitous route. See on chap. viii.

10. *Ezra had prepared his heart.* Here is a fine character of a minister of God: He prepares, he fixes, purposes, and determines; with his heart, with all his powers and affections; *to seek the law of the Lord, and to do it* himself, that he may be properly qualified to *teach* its *statutes* and *judgments* to Israel.

12. *Artaxerxes, king of kings.* This letter, from the beginning of this verse to the end of v. 26, is in the Aramitic or Chaldee language.

13. *Their own freewill.* None shall be forced either to go or to stay. He who loves his God will avail himself of this favorable opportunity.

14. *His seven counsellors.* It is very likely that the privy counsel of the king consisted of seven persons simply. The names of these seven counsellors or chamberlains may be found in the Book of Esther, chap. i. 10.

16. *And all the silver and gold.* The king and his counsellors had already made a present to the house of the God of Israel, and Ezra is now empowered to receive any contribution which any of the inhabitants of the province of Babylon may think proper to give.

18. *After the will of your God.* He gave them the fullest liberty to order everything according to their own institutions, binding them to no form or mode of worsnip.

22. *An hundred talents of silver.* The talent of silver was 450 *l. An hundred measures of wheat.* A hundred cors; each cor was a little more than seventy-five gallons, one quart, and a pint, wine measure. *An hundred baths of wine.* Each bath was seven gallons and five pints.

23. *Why should there be wrath?* As he believed he was appointed by the Almighty to do this work, he therefore wished to do it heartily, knowing that if he did not, God would be displeased, and that the kingdom would be cut off from him or his posterity.

24. *It shall not be lawful to impose toll.* As these persons had no private revenues, it would have been unreasonable to have laid them under taxation.

26. *Whether it be unto death.* These include almost every species of punishment which should be inflicted on culprits in any civilized state. With this verse the Chaldee part of this chapter ends.

CHAPTER 8

The genealogy of the chief persons who went with Ezra from Babylon. 1-14. He gathers them together at Ahava; and finding among them no Levites, he sends confidential persons to the river of Ahava, who return with many Levites and Nethinim, 15-20. He proclaims a fast at Ahava for divine protection on their journey, 21-23. He delivers to the care of the priests, etc., the silver, gold,

and sacred vessels, that they might carry them to Jerusalem, and deliver them to the high priest, 24-30. They depart from Ahava, and come to Jerusalem, 31-32. The vessels are weighed and the weight registered, 33-34. They offer burnt offerings to God, 35; deliver the king's commissions to his lieutenants, by whom they are furthered in their work, 36.

2. *Gershom.* One of the descendants of Phinehas, son of Eleazar.

3. *Of the sons of Shechaniah.* There were three of this name; the second is mentioned in v. 5, and the third in chap. x. 2. They were all different persons, as may be seen from their fathers' houses.

15. *The river that runneth to Ahava.* Ahava was a river itself. *None of the sons of Levi.* None that were simply Levites.

22. *I was ashamed to require . . . a band.* He had represented God, the object of his worship, as supremely powerful, and as having the strongest affection for His true followers. He could not therefore, consistently with his declarations, ask a band of soldiers from the king to protect them on the way, when they were going expressly to rebuild the temple of Jehovah and restore His worship. He therefore found it necessary to seek the Lord by fasting and prayer, that they might have from Him those succors without which they might become a prey to their enemies; and then the religion which they professed would be considered by the heathen as false and vain. Thus we see that this good man had more anxiety for the glory of God than for his own personal safety.

26. *Silver vessels an hundred talents.* That is, The weight of all the silver vessels amounted to 100 talents; not that there were 100 vessels of silver, each a talent in weight.

35. *Twelve bullocks for all Israel.* Though of tribes there were only Judah and Benjamin, yet they offered a bullock for every tribe, as if present. There can be little doubt that there were individuals there from all the twelve tribes, possibly some families of each, but no complete tribe but those mentioned above.

CHAPTER 9

The princes inform Ezra that many of the people now settled in the land had married heathen wives; and several of the rulers were principal offenders in this thing, 1-2. He is greatly afflicted, 3-4. His prayer to God on this account, 5-15.

1. *The people of Israel.* These were they who had returned at first with Zerubbabel, and were settled in the land of Judea, and whom Ezra found on his arrival to be little better than the Canaanitish nations from whom God had commanded them ever to keep separate.

3. *I rent my garment and my mantle.* The outer and inner garment, in sign of great grief. This significant act is frequently mentioned in the sacred writings, and was common among all ancient nations. *Plucked off the hair.* Shaving the head and beard were signs of excessive grief; much more so the plucking off the hair, which must produce exquisite pain. All this testified his abhorrence, not merely of the act of having taken strange wives, but their having also joined them in their idolatrous abominations.

4. *Those that had been carried away.* Those that had returned long before with Zerubbabel; see v. 1. *Until the evening sacrifice.* The morning sacrifice was the first of all the offerings of the day, the evening sacrifice the last. As the

latter was offered between the two evenings, i.e., between sunset and the end of twilight, so the former was offered between break of day and sunrise. Ezra *sat astonied*—confounded in his mind, distressed in his soul, and scarcely knowing what to do. He probably had withdrawn himself into some sequestered place, or into some secret part of the Temple, spending the time in meditation and reflection.

5. *Fell upon my knees.* In token of the deepest humility. *Spread out my hands,* as if to lay hold on the mercy of God.

6. *I am ashamed and blush.* God had been so often provoked, and had so often pardoned them, and they had continued to transgress, that he was ashamed to go back again to the throne of grace to ask for mercy in their behalf.

8. *And now for a little space.* This interval in which they were returning from servitude to their own land. *Grace hath been shewed.* God has disposed the hearts of the Persian kings to publish edicts in our favor. *To leave us a remnant to escape.* The ten tribes are gone irrecoverably into captivity; a great part even of Judah and Benjamin had continued beyond the Euphrates; so that Ezra might well say there was but a *remnant* which had escaped. *A nail in his holy place.* Even so much ground as to fix our tent poles in. *May lighten our eyes.* To give us a thorough knowledge of ourselves and of our highest interest, and to enable us to re-establish His worship, is the reason why God has brought us back to this place. *A little reviving.* We were perishing, and our hopes were almost dead; and, because of our sins, we were sentenced to death. But God in His great mercy has given us a new trial; and He begins with little, to see if we will make a wise and faithful use of it.

10. *What shall we say after this?* Even in the midst of these beginnings of respite and mercy we have begun to provoke Thee anew!

11. *Have filled it from one end to another.* The abominations have been like a sweeping, mighty torrent that has increased till it filled the whole land and carried everything before it.

13. *Hast punished us less than our iniquities.* Great, numerous, and oppressive as our calamities have been, yet merely as temporal punishments, they have been much less than our provocations have deserved.

15. *Thou art righteous.* Thou art "merciful." This is one of the many meanings of the word *tsedek;* and to this meaning St. Paul refers when he says, God declares "his righteousness for the remission of sins that are past," Rom. iii. 25. *We remain yet escaped.* Because of this righteousness or mercy. *In our trespasses.* We have no righteousness; we are clothed and covered with our trespasses. *We cannot stand before thee because of this.* The parallel place is Ps. cxxx. 3: "If thou, Lord, shouldest mark iniquities, O Lord, who shall stand?" Every man must stand before the judgment seat of Christ; but who shall stand there with joy? No man against whom the Lord marks iniquities.

CHAPTER 10

The people are greatly afflicted by Ezra's prayer, 1. Shechaniah proposes that all who have taken strange wives should put them away, and the children they had by them; and make a covenant to serve God, 2-4. Ezra is encouraged, and makes a proclamation to collect the people, to find who has transgressed, 5-8. They come together on the twentieth day of the ninth month, 9. Ezra exhorts them to put away their strange wives, 10. The people agree to it, and require time, 11-14. This being granted, the business is completed by the first of the first month, 15-17. Some of the priests had taken strange wives; their names, and the names of all who were in the same trespass, 18-44.

1. *The people wept very sore.* They were deeply affected at the thought of God's displeasure, which they justly feared was about to light upon them because of their transgressions.

2. *Shechaniah the son of Jehiel.* He speaks here in the name of the people, not acknowledging himself culpable, for he is not in the following list. *Yet now there is hope in Israel.* Mikveh, "expectation," of pardon; for the people were convinced of the evil, and were deeply penitent. Hence it is said, v. 1, that they wept sore.

3. *Let us make a covenant. Nichrath berith,* "Let us cut or divide the covenant sacrifice." See the notes on Gen. xv. 10.

4. *Arise; for this matter belongeth unto thee.* By the decree of Artaxerxes, he was authorized to do everything that the law of God required; see chap. vii. 23-28. And all officers were commanded to be aiding and assisting; hence Shechaniah says, "We are with you."

5. *And they sware.* The thing was evidently contrary to the law of God, and now he bound them by an oath to rectify the abuse.

6. *Johanan the son of Eliashib.* Eliashib was high priest, and was succeeded in that office by his son Joiada, Neh. xii. 10. Probably Johanan here is the same as Jonathan in Nehemiah, who was the son of Joiada, and grandson of Eliashib. Some suppose that Johanan and Joiada were two names for the same person.

8. *All his substance should be forfeited.* To the use of the Temple. So the Septuagint understood the place: "All his substance shall be devoted to a holy use." *Himself separated.* Excommunicated from the church of God, and exiled from Israel.

9. *Ninth month.* Answering to a part of our December. *Trembling because of . . . the great rain.* "Because of the winter," Septuagint; it was now December, the coldest and most rainy part of the year in Palestine.

11. *Make confession.* Acknowledge your sins before God, with deep compunction of heart, and the fullest resolution to forsake them.

12. *As thou hast said, so must we do.* They all resolved to do what Ezra then commanded. They did put away their wives, even those by whom they had children, v. 44; this was a great hardship on the women and children. Though by the Jewish laws such marriages were null and void, yet as the women they had taken did not know these laws, their case was deplorable. However, we may take it for granted that each of them received a portion according to the circumstances of their husbands, and that they and their children were not turned away desolate, but had such a provision as their necessities required.

17. *The first day of the first month.* So they were three whole months in examining into this affair, and making those separations which the law required.

19. *They gave their hands.* They bound themselves in the most solemn manner to do as the rest of the delinquents had done, and they made an acknowledgment of their iniquity to God by offering each a ram for a trespass offering.

25. *Moreover of Israel.* That is, as Calmet observes, "simple Israelites," to distinguish them from the priests, Levites, and singers, mentioned in vv. 18, 23-24.

44. *Some of them had wives by whom they had children.* This observation was probably intended to show that only a few of them had children; but it shows also how rigorously the law was put in execution.

The Book of

NEHEMIAH

In the introduction to the Book of Ezra, we have already seen those wonderful interferences of divine providence in which Nehemiah bore so large a share. Dr. Prideaux, with his usual perspicuity, has interwoven the whole of the transaction of the mission of Nehemiah with that part of the Persian history with which they are connected; which I shall give in his own words. He connects this book, as it ought to be, with the Book of Ezra. See before.

"He who succeeded Ezra in the government of Judah and Jerusalem was Nehemiah, a very religious and most excellent man; one that was nothing behind his predecessor, saving his learning and great knowledge in the law of God. He came to Jerusalem in the twentieth year of Artaxerxes Longimanus, about four hundred and forty-five years before Christ; and by a commission from him, superseded that of Ezra, and succeeded him in the government of Judah and Jerusalem. He had in that commission, by an express clause therein inserted, full authority to repair the walls, and set up the gates of Jerusalem; and to fortify it again in that manner as it was before it was dismantled and destroyed by the Babylonians.

"He was a Jew, whose ancestors had formerly been citizens of Jerusalem; for there, he says, was the place of his fathers' sepulchres; but as to the tribe or family which he was of, no more is said but only that his father's name was Hachaliah, who seems to have been of those Jews who, having gotten good settlements in the land of their captivity, chose rather to abide in them than return into their own country, when leave was granted for it. It is most likely that Hachaliah was an inhabitant of the city of Sushan, and that it was his dwelling there that gave his son an opportunity of gaining an advancement in the king's palace; for he was one of the cup-bearers of King Artaxerxes, which was a place of great honour and advantage in the Persian court, because of the privilege it gave him of being daily in the king's presence, and the opportunity which he had thereby of gaining his favour for the obtaining of any petition which he should make to him . . . No doubt it was by the favour of Queen Esther, as being of the same nation and people with her, that he obtained so honourable and advantageous a preferment in that court.

"However, neither the honour nor advantage of this place, nor the long settlement of his family out of his country, could make him forget his love for it, or lay aside that zeal which he had for the religion of his forefathers, who had formerly dwelt in it. For though he had been born and bred in a strange land, yet he had a great love for Sion, and a heart thoroughly set for the advancing the prosperity of it, and was in all things a very religious observer of the law of his God; and therefore, when some came from Jerusalem, and told him of the ill state of that city, how the walls of it were still in many places broken down, and the gates of it in the same demolished state as when burnt with fire by the Babylonians, and that, by reason thereof, the remnant of the captivity that dwelt there lay open, not only to the incursions and insults of their enemies, but also to the reproach and contempt of their neighbours, as a mean and despicable people, and that they were in both these respects in great grief and affliction of heart; the good man, being suitably moved with this representation, applied himself in fasting and prayer unto the Lord his God, and earnestly supplicated him for his people Israel, and the place which he had chosen for his worship among them. And having thus implored the Divine mercy against this evil, he resolves next to make his application to the king for the redressing of it, trusting in God for the inclining of his heart thereto; and therefore, when his turn came next to wait in his office, the king, observing his countenance to be sad, which at other times used not to be so, and asking the cause thereof, he took this opportunity to lay before him the distressed state of his country; and, owning this to be the cause of great grief to him, prayed the king to send him there to remedy it. . . .

"Accordingly a royal decree was issued out for the rebuilding of the walls and gates of Jerusalem; and Nehemiah was sent thither with it, as governor of the province of Judea, to put it into execution; and to do him the more honour, the king sent a guard of horsemen with him, under the command of some of the captains of his army, to conduct him safely to his government. And he wrote letters to all the governors on this side the river Euphrates, to further him in the work on which he was sent; and also gave his orders to Asaph, the keeper of the forests in those parts, to allow him as much timber out of them as should be needed for the finishing of it. However, the Ammonites, the Moabites, and the Samaritans, and other neighbouring nations round, did all they could to hinder him from proceeding therein . . .

"Having, on his arrival at Jerusalem, made known to the people the commission with which he was sent, he took a view of the ruins of the old walls, and immediately set about the repairing of them, dividing the people into several companies, and assigning to each of them the quarter where they were to work, but reserving to himself the superintendence and direction of the whole, in which he laboured so effectually that all was finished by the end of the month Elul, within the compass of thirty-two days, notwithstanding all manner of opposition that was made against him, both from within and without. . . . When they had thus far finished the walls and set up the gates, a public dedication of them was celebrated with great solemnity by the priests and Levites, and all the people. . . .

"And thus Nehemiah, having executed the main of the end for which he obtained the favour of the king to be sent to Jerusalem, appointed Hanani and Hananiah to be governors of the city, and returned again unto him into Persia; for a time had been set him for his return again to court, when he first obtained to be sent from thence on this commission . . . On his return to the king, and having given him an account how all things stood in that province, and what farther was needful to be done for the well regulating of it, he soon obtained to be sent back again to take care thereof . . .

"Nehemiah, being returned from the Persian court with a new commission, in the twenty-first year of Artaxerxes, (B.C. 444,) forthwith set himself to carry on the reformation of the Church, and the state of the Jews, which Ezra had begun; and took along with him the advice and direction of that learned and holy scribe in all that he attempted in this work.

"The first thing that he did was to provide for the security of the city, which he had now fortified, by settling rules for the opening and shutting of the gates, and keeping watch and ward on the towers and walls: but finding Jerusalem to be but thinly inhabited, and that to make this burden more easy there needed more inhabitants to bear their share with them in it, he projected the thorough repeopling of the place: in order to which he prevailed first with the rulers and great men of the nation to agree to build them houses there, and dwell in them; and then others following their example, offered themselves voluntarily to do the same; and of the rest of the people every tenth man was taken by lot, and obliged to come to Jerusalem, and there build them houses, and settle themselves and their families in them. And when the city was fortified, and all that had their dwellings in it there well secured by walls and gates against the insults of their enemies, and the incursions of thieves and robbers, who before molested them, all willingly complied; by which means the houses, as well as the walls and gates, being again rebuilt, and fully replenished with inhabitants, it soon after this received its ancient lustre, and became again a city of great note in those parts.

"Nehemiah, finding it necessary to have the genealogies of the people well investigated and clearly stated, next examined into that matter; and this he did, not only for the sake of their civil rights, that all knowing of what tribe and family they were, they might be directed where to take their possessions; but more especially for the sake of the sanctuary, that none might be admitted to officiate, even as Levites, who were not of the tribe of Levi; or as priests, that were not of the family of Aaron. . . .

"Ezra, having completed his edition of the law of God, and written it out fairly and clearly in the Chaldean character, this year, on the feast of trumpets, publicly read it to the people of Jerusalem. . . . Nehemiah and Ezra, finding them so well disposed, applied themselves to make the best improvement they could of it for the honour of God, and the interests of religion; and, therefore, proclaimed a fast to be held the day but one after the festival was ended, to which having called all the people while the sense of these things was fresh in their minds, excited them to make a solemn confession of their sins before God, and also to enter into a solemn vow and covenant with God to avoid them for the future. . . . It being their ignorance which led them into these transgressions, and this ignorance having been occasioned by their not having heard the law of God read to them; to prevent this for the future, they had from this time the most learned of the Levites and scribes that were skilled in the law, to read it to them in every city; which no doubt was at first done by gathering the people together in the most wide street, where all might the better hear it; but the inconvenience of this being soon felt, especially in the winter and stormy seasons of the year, they erected houses or tabernacles to meet in, and these were the original synagogues among them. That they had no synagogues before the Babylonish captivity is plain . . .

"Nehemiah, after having held the government of Judah *twelve* years, returned to the Persian court, either recalled thither by the king, or else going thither to solicit a new commission after the expiration of the former, (32 Artax., B.C. 433.) During all the time that he had been in the government he managed it with great justice. . . . In the *thirty-seventh* year of Artaxerxes, (B.C. 428,) having tarried there about *five* years in the execution, as it may be supposed, of his former office, at length obtained permission from the king to be sent back to Jerusalem with a new commission. . . .

"Many things having gone wrong among the Jews during the absence of Nehemiah, as soon as he was again settled in the government, he applied himself with his accustomed zeal to correct them. That which he first took notice of was a great profanation which had been introduced into the temple for the sake of Tobiah the Ammonite. This man . . . did the utmost he could to obstruct Nehemiah in all that he did for the good of that people, and confederated with Sanballat, their greatest enemy, to carry on this purpose. . . .

"It appears most likely that it was Eliashib the high priest who was the author of this great profanation of the house of God. What was done, however, the text tells us, Nehemiah immediately withstood, as soon as he returned to Jerusalem; for, overruling what the high priest had ordered to be done by the authority which he had as governor, he commanded all the household stuff of Tobiah to be cast out, and the chambers to be cleansed and restored to their former use. . . .

"Among other corruptions that grew up during the absence of Nehemiah, one especially to be noticed was, the neglect of not carrying on the daily service of the house of God in the manner it ought; for the tithes, which were to maintain the ministers of the temple in their offices and stations, either being embezzled by the high priest or other rulers under him, or else subtracted by the laity, and not paid at all; for want of them the Levites and singers were driven from the temple, every one to his own house, there to seek for a subsistence some other way. This abuse the governor, whose piety led him always to attend to the public worship, could not be long without taking notice of and when he had thoroughly informed himself of the cause, he soon provided very effectually for its remedy . . . He also took care that the Sabbath should be duly observed, and made many good orders for the preventing of the profanation of it, and caused them all to be put into effectual execution. . . .

"With this book the general historical books of the Old Testament end; and the succeeding accounts of the Jewish people must be sought partly in the Apocryphal books, and in Josephus."

CHAPTER 1

Account of Nehemiah, 1. His inquiry about the Jews that had returned from their captivity, and concerning the state of Jerusalem, of which he receives the most discouraging information, 2-3. He is greatly affected; fasts and prays, 4. His prayer and confession to God, 5-11.

1. *The words of Nehemiah.* That this book was compiled out of the journal or memoranda made by Nehemiah himself, there can be no doubt; but that he was not the compiler is evident from several passages in the work itself. As it is written consecutively as one book with Ezra, many have supposed that this latter was the author. But whoever compares the style of each, in the Hebrew, will soon be convinced that this is not correct; the style is so very different that they could not possibly be the work of the same person. *The month Chisleu.* Answering to a part of our November and December. *Twentieth year.* That is, of Artaxerxes. *Shushan the palace.* The ancient city of Susa, the winter residence of the Persian kings.

3. *The wall of Jerusalem also is broken down.* This must refer to the walls which had been rebuilt after the people returned from their captivity, for it could not refer to the walls which were broken down and levelled with the dust by Nebuchadnezzar; to hear of this could be no news to Nehemiah.

4. *And mourned certain days.* From the month Chisleu to the month Nisan—about four months from the time he received the above information till the time that Artaxerxes noticed his grief, chap. ii. 1. All this time he probably spent in supplication to God, waiting for a favorable opening in the divine providence.

5. *Lord God of heaven.* What was, before the Captivity, "Jehovah, God of hosts." *Great*—able

to do mighty things. *Terrible*—able to inflict the heaviest judgments.

6. *Let thine ear.* Hear what we say and confess. *Thine eyes open*—see what we suffer.

7. *Have not kept thy commandments.* The moral precepts by which our lives should be regulated. *Statutes.* What refers to the rites and ceremonies of Thy religion. *Judgments.* The precepts of justice relative to our conduct to each other.

8. *Thy servant Moses.* Though in an enemy's country, and far from the ordinances of God, Nehemiah did not forget the law; he read his Bible well, and quotes correctly.

11. *Mercy in the sight of this man.* Favor before the king, Ahasuerus. He seems then to have been giving him the cup. *For I was the king's cupbearer.* The king's "butler," which gave him the opportunity of being frequently with the king; and to be in such a place of trust, he must be in the king's confidence.

CHAPTER 2

Artaxerxes, observing the sorrow of Nehemiah, inquires into the cause, 1-2. Nehemiah shows him the cause, and requests permission to go and rebuild the walls of Jerusalem, 3-6. The king grants it, and gives him letters to the governors beyond the river, 7-8. He sets out on his journey, 9. Sanballat and Tobiah are grieved to find he had got such a commission, 10. He comes to Jerusalem and, without informing any person of his business, examines by night the state of the city, 11-16. He informs the priests, nobles, and rulers of his design and commission, 17-18. The design is turned into contempt by Sanballat, Tobiah, and Geshem, 19. Nehemiah gives them a suitable answer, 20.

1. *Month Nisan.* Answering to a part of our March and April.

4. *So I prayed to the God of heaven.* Before he dared to prefer his request to the king, he

made his prayer to God, that his suit might be acceptable; and this he does by mental prayer. To the spirit of prayer every place is a praying place.

5. *The city of my fathers' sepulchres.* The tombs of the dead were sacred among the ancients, and nothing could appear to them more detestable than disturbing the ashes or remains of the dead. Nehemiah knew that in mentioning this circumstance he should strongly interest the feelings of the Persian king.

6. *The queen also sitting by him.* Who probably forwarded his suit. This was not Esther, as Dean Prideaux supposes, nor perhaps the same Artaxerxes who had taken her to be queen; nor does *shegal* signify "queen," but rather harlot or concubine, she who was chief favorite. The Septuagint translate it "harlot"; and properly too. *I set him a time.* How long this time was we are not told; it is by no means likely that it was long, probably no more than six months or a year; after which he either returned, or had his leave of absence lengthened. For in the same year we find he was made governor of the Jews, in which office he continued twelve years, viz., from the twentieth to the thirty-second year of Artaxerxes, chap. v. 14. He then returned to Susa; and after staying a short time, had leave to return to rectify some abuses that Tobiah the Ammonite had introduced into the Temple, chap. xiii. 6-7, and several others of which the people themselves were guilty. After having performed this service, it is likely he returned to the Persian king, and died in his office of cupbearer; but of this latter circumstance we have no mention in the text.

8. *Asaph the keeper of the king's forest.* The "paradise" of the king. This I believe is originally a Persian word; it frequently occurs in Arabic and in Greek, and in both signifies a "pleasant garden, vineyard, pleasure garden," and what we call a "paradise." *And the king granted me.* This noble-spirited man attributes everything to God. He might have said, I had been long a faithful servant to the king; and he was disposed, in reward of my fidelity, to grant my request; but he would not say so. "He granted my request, because the good hand of my God was upon me."

10. *Sanballat the Horonite.* Probably a native of Horonaim, a Moabite by birth, and at this time governor of the Samaritans under the king of Persia. *Tobiah the servant.* He was an Ammonite; and here, under the Persian king, joint governor with Sanballat. Some suppose that the Sanballat here mentioned was the same who persuaded Alexander to build a temple on Mount Gerizim in favor of the Samaritans. Pelagius thinks there were two governors of this name.

13. *The dragon well.* Perhaps so called because of the representation of a dragon, out of whose mouth the stream issued that proceeded from the well. *Dung port.* This was the gate on the eastern side of the city, through which the filth of the city was carried into the valley of Hinnom.

14. *The gate of the fountain.* Of Siloah. *The king's pool.* Probably the aqueduct made by Hezekiah, to bring the waters of Gihon to the city of David. See 2 Chron. xxxii. 30.

15. *By the brook.* Kidron. *By the gate of the valley.* The valley through which the brook Kidron flowed. It was by this gate he went out; so he went all round the city, and entered by the same gate from which he had gone out.

16. *The rulers knew not whither I went.* He made no person privy to his design, that he might hide everything as much as possible from their enemies till he had all things in readiness, lest they should take measures to defeat the work.

18. *Then I told them.* He opened to them his design and his commission.

19. *Geshem the Arabian.* Some chief of the Arabs contiguous to Samaria, who had joined with Sanballat and Tobiah to distress the Jews and hinder their work. *Will ye rebel against the king?* This they said in order to raise jealousies in the king's mind, and induce him to recall his ordinance.

20. *Ye have no portion, nor right.* To be a citizen of Jerusalem was a high honor, and they would not permit those who did not belong to the tribes of Israel to dwell there. Zerubbabel gave the same answer to the Samaritans, Ezra iv. 3.

CHAPTER 3

The names of those who rebuilt the walls of Jerusalem, and the part assigned to each person, 1-32.

1. *Eliashib the high priest.* It was right that the priests should be first in this holy work, and perhaps *the sheep gate* which is mentioned here is that by which the offerings or sacrifices were brought into the Temple. *They sanctified it.* As they began with the sacred offering as soon as they got an altar built, it was proper that the gate by which these sacrifices entered should be consecrated for this purpose, i.e., set apart, so that it should be for this use only.

3. *The fish gate.* We really know scarcely anything about these gates—what they were, why called by these names, or in what part of the wall situated.

7. *The throne of the governor.* His house, and the place where he dispensed justice and judgment. Previously to the days of Nehemiah, Jerusalem was governed by a deputy from the Persian king (see chap. v. 15); but after this time they were governed by governors and judges chosen from among themselves.

8. *Goldsmiths.* From the remotest period of the history of the Jews they had artists in all elegant and ornamental trades; and it is also evident that goldsmiths, apothecaries, and merchants were formed into companies in the time of Nehemiah. *Apothecaries.* Rather such as dealt in drugs, aromatics, spices, for embalming or for furnishing the Temple with the incense consumed there.

9. *Ruler of the half part of Jerusalem.* Probably the city was divided into two parts: one for Judah, and the other for Benjamin, each having its proper governor. *Rephaiah* mentioned here was one of these governors, and Shallum, mentioned in v. 12, was the other.

11. *Repaired the other piece.* That which was left by Jedaiah after he had repaired the wall opposite to his own house. Probably some of the principal people were obliged to repair those

parts of the wall opposite to their own dwellings. Perhaps this was the case generally.

12. *The son of Halohesh.* Or the son of the "Enchanter," conjectured to be thus named from having the art to charm serpents. *The ruler of the half part.* See on v. 9.

13. *The inhabitants of Zanoah.* This was a town in the tribe of Judah, Josh. xv. 34.

14. *Beth-haccerem.* A village or town in the tribe of Benjamin. See Jer. vi. 1.

15. *The pool of Siloah.* This is probably the same as that mentioned by the Evangelists. *The stairs that go down from the city of David.* Jerusalem being built on very uneven ground, and some hills being taken within the walls, there was a necessity that there should be in different places steps by which they could ascend and descend.

16. *The pool that was made.* Calmet supposes that this was the reservoir made by Hezekiah, when besieged by Sennacherib, 2 Chron. xxxii. 4. *The house of the mighty.* Probably a place where a band of soldiers was kept, or the city guard.

19. *The going up to the armoury.* This was either a tower that defended the angle where the two walls met or the city arsenal, where shields, spears, etc., were kept to arm the people in time of danger.

20. *Earnestly repaired.* He distinguished himself by his zeal and activity.

22. *The priests, the men of the plain.* Some of the officers of the Temple, particularly the singers, dwelt in the plain country round about Jerusalem, chap. xii. 28; and it is likely that several of the *priests* dwelt in the same place.

28. *The horse gate.* The place through which the horses passed in order to be watered; it was near the Temple.

CHAPTER 4

Sanballat and Tobiah mock the Jews, and endeavor to prevent the completing of the wall, 1-3. Nehemiah prays against them, and the people complete one half of the wall, 4-6. The Arabians, Ammonites, and Ashdodites conspire together, and come to fight against the Jews, 7-8. The Jews commend themselves to God, and determine to fight for their lives and liberties, on hearing of which their enemies are disheartened, 9-16. The Jews divide themselves into two bands, one half working, and the other standing ready armed to meet their enemies. Even the workmen are obliged to arm themselves while employed in building, for fear of their enemies, 17-18. Nehemiah uses all precautions to prevent a surprise, and all labor with great fervor in the work, 19-22.

2. *The army of Samaria.* As he was governor, he had the command of the army, and he wished to excite the soldiers to second his views against Nehemiah and his men. *What do these feeble Jews?* We may remark here, in general, that the enemies of God's work endeavor by all means to discredit and destroy it, and those who are employed in it.

4. *Turn their reproach upon their own head.* A prayer of this kind, understood literally, is not lawful for any Christian. Jesus, our great Master, has said, "Love your enemies . . . do good to them that hate you, and pray for them which despitefully use you." Such sayings as the above are excusable in the mouth of a Jew, under severe irritation. See the next verse.

5. *Let not their sin be blotted out.* These are the most terrible imprecations; but probably we should understand them as declaratory, for the same form of the verb, in the Hebrew, is used as precative and imperative. *Turn their reproach*—Their reproach "shall be turned." *Give them for a prey*—"They shall be given for a prey." *Cover not their iniquity*—"Their iniquity shall not be covered." *Let not their sin be blotted out*—"Their sin shall not be blotted out." All who know the genius of the Hebrew language know that the future tense is used to express all these senses. Besides, we may rest assured that Neheimah's curses, or declaration of God's judgments, had respect only to their bodies, and to their life—not to their souls and the world to come. And then they amount to no more than this: What a man soweth, that shall he reap.

6. *For the people had a mind to work.* The original is very emphatic: *vayehi leb leam laasoth,* "For the people had a *heart* to work." Their hearts were engaged in it; and where the heart is engaged, the work of God goes on well. The whole of this sixth verse is omitted by the Septuagint.

7. *The walls of Jerusalem were made up.* That is, they were made up to the half height of the wall; for the preceding verse seems to intimate that the whole wall was thus far built—not half of the wall completed, but the whole wall built to half its height.

9. *We made our prayer unto our God, and set a watch.* The strongest confidence in the protection and favor of God does not preclude the use of all or any of the means of self-preservation and defense which His providence has put in our power.

10. *The strength of the bearers of burdens is decayed.* They worked both day and night, scarcely ever putting off their clothes, except for the purpose of being washed, vv. 21, 23. *Much rubbish.* The ruins they were obliged to clear away before they could dig the foundation for a new wall; and in this labor they were nearly exhausted; see chap. v. 15.

12. *From all places whence ye shall return unto us.* This verse is extremely difficult. Our translators have supplied the words, "they will be upon you," which have nothing correspondent in the Hebrew. The Septuagint have given a good sense. "They come up from all places against us." The sense appears to be this: The Jews which dwelt among the Samaritans came often to Nehemiah from all quarters where they sojourned, and told him the designs of his enemies against him. Therefore he set people with their swords, spears, and bows, to defend the walls. It is probable that instead of *tashubu,* "ye shall return," we should read *chashebu,* "they designed or meditated." This word is very similar to the other, and makes the sense very clear. "The Jews who dwelt among them told us frequently, from all places, what they designed against us."

14. *Be not ye afraid of them.* Are they more terrible or stronger than God? *Fight for your brethren.* Your own countrymen, who worship the same God, and are come from the same stock; *your sons,* whom they wish to slay or lead into captivity; *your daughters* and *wives,* whom they wish to deflower and defile; and *your houses,* which they wish to seize and occupy as their own. They had everything at stake; and therefore they must fight for their religion, their lives, and their property.

15. *Their counsel to nought.* The word *counsel* used here countenances the emendation in the twelfth verse.

16. *Half ... wrought in the work.* This is no unusual thing, even in the present day, in Palestine. People sowing their seed are often attended by an armed man, to prevent the Arabs from robbing them of their seed, which they will not fail to do if not protected. *Habergeons.* Breastplates, or armor for the breast.

17. *With one of his hands wrought in the work, and with the other hand held a weapon.* That is, he had his arms at hand, and was as fully prepared to fight as to work.

20. *Ye hear the sound of the trumpet.* As the walls were very extensive, and the workmen consequently much scattered, their enemies might easily attack and destroy them successively. He therefore ordered them all to work as near to each other as they could; and himself, who was everywhere surveying the work, kept a trumpeter always with him, who was to sound when the enemy approached; and all were instantly to run to the place where they heard the sound.

22. *Let every one with his servant lodge within Jerusalem.* The country people were accustomed, after their day's labor, to return to their families; now being so formidably threatened, he obliged them all to sleep in Jerusalem, that they might be ready, in case of attack, to help their brethren. All this man's arrangements were wise and judicious.

CHAPTER 5

The people complain that they are oppressed and enthralled by their richer brethren, 1-3. Nehemiah calls them to account; upbraids them for their cruelty; and obliges them to swear that they will forgive the debts, restore the mortgaged estates, and free their servants, 4-13. Nehemiah's generosity and liberality, 14-17. The daily provision for his table, 18-19.

2. *We, our sons, and our daughters, are many.* Our families are larger than we can provide for; we are obliged to go in debt; and our richer brethren take advantage of our necessitous situation, and oppress us. The details which are given in the next verse are sufficiently plain.

3. *Because of the dearth.* About the time of Zerubbabel, God had sent a judicial dearth upon the land, as we learn from Haggai, chap. i. 9, etc.; for the people, it seems, were more intent on building houses for themselves than on rebuilding the house of the Lord. This dearth might have been continued, or its effects still felt; but it is more likely that there was a new dearth owing to the great number of people, for whose support the land that had been brought into cultivation was not sufficient.

4. *We have borrowed money.* This should be read, "We have borrowed money for the king's tribute on our lands and vineyards." They had a tax to pay to the Persian king in token of their subjection to him, and though it is not likely it was heavy, yet they were not able to pay it.

5. *We bring into bondage our sons.* The law permitted parents to sell their children in times of extreme necessity, Exod. xxi. 7.

7. *Ye exact usury.* This was expressly contrary to the law of God; and was doubly cruel at this time, when they were just returning out of the land of their captivity, and were suffering from the effects of a dearth. *I set a great assembly against them.* Brought all these delinquents before the rulers of the people.

9. *Ought ye not to walk in the fear of our God?* If ye wish to accredit that religion ye profess which comes from the God of justice and mercy, should you not, in the sight of the heathen, abstain from injustice and cruelty?

11. *Also the hundredth part of the money.* Houbigant contends, (1) That the word *meath*, which we and the Vulgate translate one *hundredth* part, never means so anywhere; and (2) That it would have answered no end to remit to people so distressed merely the one-hundredth part of the money which had been taken from them by usury. He understands *meath* as signifying the same as *min eth*, contracted into *meeth*, a preposition and demonstrative particle joined together, "also a part from the money." Neither the Syriac, Septuagint, nor Arabic acknowledges this *hundredth part*.

13. *Also I shook my lap.* This was a significant action frequent among the Hebrews, and something of the same nature was practiced among other nations.

14. *I and my brethren have not eaten the bread of the governor.* From what is related here, and in the following verse, we find that the table of the governor was always supplied by the people with bread and wine; and, besides, they had forty shekels per diem for their other expenses. The people were also greatly oppressed by the servants and officers of the governor; but during the twelve years that Nehemiah had been with them, he took not this salary, and ate none of their bread. Nor were his servants permitted to take or exact anything from them. Having such an example, it was scandalous for their chiefs, priests, and nobles thus to oppress an afflicted and distressed people.

16. *Neither bought we any land.* Neither he nor his officers took any advantage of the necessities of the people to buy their lands. He even made his own servants to work at the wall.

17. *An hundred and fifty of the Jews.* He kept open house, entertained all comers, besides having 150 Jews who had their food constantly at his table and at his expense. To be able to bear all these expenses, no doubt Nehemiah had saved money while he was cupbearer to the Persian king in Susa.

18. *One ox and six choice sheep.* This was food sufficient for more than two hundred men. *Once in ten days store of all sorts of wine.* It is supposed that every tenth day they drank wine; at all other times they drank water—unless we suppose the meaning of the phrase to be that his servants laid in a stock of wine every ten days.

19. *Think upon me, my God, for good.* Nehemiah wishes for no reward from man; and he only asks mercy at the hand of his God for what His providence enabled him to do; and which, according to the good hand of his God upon him, he had done faithfully.

CHAPTER 6

Sanballat, Tobiah, and Geshem insidiously desire a conference with Nehemiah, which he refuses, 1-4. They then charge him with the design of rebelling and causing himself to be made king. 5-7; which he denies, and prays to God for support, 8-9. A false prophet is hired by Tobiah and Sanballat to put him in fear; he discovers the imposture and defeats their design, 10-13. He prays to God against them, 14. The wall is finished in fifty-two days, 15. He discovers a secret and treasonable correspondence between Tobiah and some of the Jewish nobles, 16-19.

2. *Come, let us meet together in . . . the plain of Ono.* They wished to get him out of Jerusalem from among his friends, that they might either carry him off or murder him. Ono is supposed to have been in the tribe of Benjamin, near Jordan.

3. *I am doing a great work.* Though he knew their design, he did not think it prudent to mention it. Had he done so, they would probably have gone to extremities, finding that they were discovered; and perhaps in a formidable body attacked Jerusalem, when ill provided to sustain such a shock. They wished to effect their purpose rather by treachery than by open violence.

5. *With an open letter in his hand.* This was an insult to a person of Nehemiah's quality, as letters sent to chiefs and governors in the East are always carefully folded up, and put in costly silken bags, and these carefully sealed. The circumstance is thus marked to show the contempt he (Sanballat) had for him.

6. *And Gashmu saith it.* You are accused of crimes against the state, and Geshem, the Arabian, is your accuser.

7. *Thou hast also appointed prophets.* Persons who pretend to be commissioned to preach to the people, and say, "Nehemiah reigneth!" *Come now therefore, and let us take counsel.* Come and justify yourself before me. This was a trick to get Nehemiah into his power.

8. *There are no such things done.* You well know that what you say is false. I shall not, therefore, trouble myself about a false charge.

10. *Who was shut up.* Lived in a sequestered, solitary state, pretending to sanctity and to close intercourse with God.

14. *And on the prophetess Noadiah.* Whether this was a prophet or prophetess, we cannot tell. Only the Hebrew text makes her a *prophetess;* all the versions have "Noadiah the prophet," except the Arabic, which has "Younadaa the prophet." I think we should read, "Noadiah the prophet."

15. *The twenty and fifth . . . of . . . Elul.* This Jewish month answers to a part of our August and September. *Fifty and two days.* I see no difficulty in supposing that several thousand workmen, each of whom was working as for God, should be able to complete this wall in fifty-two days. There is little doubt that several parts of the old wall were entire; in many places the foundations still remained; there were all the materials of the old wall still at hand; and though they had to clear and carry away much rubbish, yet they do not appear to have had any stones to quarry.

16. *This work was wrought of our God.* This is an additional reason why we should not wonder at the shortness of the time in which so great a work was done, for God helped them by an especial providence; and this was so very observable that their *carnal* enemies could discover it.

17. *The nobles of Judah sent many letters.* The circumstances marked in this and the following verses show still more clearly the difficulties which Nehemiah had to encounter; he had enemies without and false friends within. A treacherous correspondence was carried on between the nobles of Judah and the Ammonites; and had almost any other man been at the head of the Jewish affairs, Jerusalem had never been reestablished.

18. *He was the son in law of Shechaniah.* Previously to the coming of Nehemiah, the Jews seemed to be fast intermixing with the heathen, by intermarriages with Ashdodites, Ammonites, and Moabites; see chap. xiii. 23. Ezra had many evils of this kind to redress (Ezra ix. 3, etc.), chiefly among the common people, though there were both chiefs and priests in that trespass. But here we find the heathen and Jewish nobles interlinked; and the latter were so far imbued with the spirit of idolatry that they forgot God, His service, their brethren, and their own souls.

CHAPTER 7

Nehemiah makes use of proper precautions in guarding the city gates, 1-4. He proposes to reckon the people according to their genealogies; and finds a register of those who came out of Babylon, with Zerubbabel, 5-7. A transcript of the register, 8-60. Account of those who came from other provinces; and of priests who, because they could not show their register, were put away from the priesthood as polluted, 61-65. The sum total of the congregation: of their menservants and maidservants; singing men and women; horses, mules, camels, and asses, 66-69. The sums given by different persons for the work, 70-72. All betake themselves to their several cities, 73.

2. *My brother Hanani.* This was the person who gave Nehemiah the account of the desolate state of the Jews, chap. i. 2. He is now made ruler of Jerusalem, probably because Nehemiah was about to return to the Persian court.

3. *Until the sun be hot.* The meaning of this is, the gates were not to be opened before sunrise, and always shut at sunset. *Every one . . . over against his house.* Each was obliged to guard that part of the wall that was opposite to his own dwelling.

4. *The houses were not builded.* The city was not yet rebuilt, only a row of houses in the inside of the wall all round.

5. *God put into mine heart.* With this good man every good thing was of God. If he purposed any good, it was because God put in into his heart; if he did any good, it was because the good hand of his God was upon him; if he expected any good, it was because he earnestly prayed God to remember him for good.

7. *Who came with Zerubbabel.* The register which he found was that of the persons only who came long before Zerubbabel, Ezra, and Joshua, the son of Josedek, which *register* could not answer in every respect to the state of the people then. Several persons and families were no doubt dead, and others had arrived since. Nehemiah probably altered it only in such parts, leaving the body of it as it was before; and this will account for the difference between it and the register that is found in Ezra, chap. ii.

8. *The children of Parosh.* As this chapter is almost entirely the same with the second chapter of the Book of Ezra, it is not necessary to add anything to what is said there.

19. *The children of Bigvai, two thousand threescore and seven.* Some MSS. read 2,066, as in Ezra ii.

33. *The men of the other Nebo.* The word *other* is not in the parallel place, Ezra ii. 29, and is wanting in many of Kennicott's and De Rossi's MSS. This *Nebo* is supposed to be the same as Nob or Nobah, in the tribe of Benjamin.

34. *The other Elam.* To distinguish him from the Elam mentioned in v. 12.

73. *All Israel, dwelt in their cities.* It was in reference to this particularly that the public registers were examined; for by them they found the different families, and consequently the cities, villages, etc., which belonged to them, according to the ancient division of the lands. It seems that the examination of the registers occupied about a month; for as soon as the walls were finished, which was in the sixth month, chap. vi. 15, Nehemiah instituted the examination mentioned in this chapter, v. 5; and by the concluding verse we find that the different families had got into their paternal cities in the seventh month, answering to a part of our September and October. Thus the register determined everything; there was not room for complaint, and none to accuse the governor of partiality.

CHAPTER 8

Ezra, Nehemiah, and the Levites read and interpret the laws to the people, 1-7. The manner in which they do this important work, 8. The effect produced on the people's minds by hearing it, 9. The people are exhorted to be glad, and are told that the joy of the Lord is their strength, 10-12. On the second day they assemble, and find that they should keep the Feast of Tabernacles, which they accordingly religiously solemnize for seven days; and Ezra reads to them from the book of the law, 13-18.

1. *The street that was before the water gate.* The gate which led from the Temple to the brook Kidron.

2. *Upon the first day of the seventh month.* This was the first day of what was called the civil year; and on it was the Feast of Trumpets, the year being ushered in by the sound of these instruments.

4. *Stood upon a pulpit of wood.* Migdal, a "tower," a "platform," raised up for the purpose, to elevate him sufficiently for the people both to see and hear him; for it is said, v. 5, that "he was above all the people."

5. *All the people stood up.* This was out of respect to the sacred word; in imitation of this, when the Gospel for the day is read in our churches, all the people stand up.

8. *So they read in the book.* For an explanation of this verse, see the observations at the end of the chapter.

9. *Nehemiah, which is the Tirshatha.* This puts it out of doubt that, when the Tirshatha is mentioned, Nehemiah himself is intended, Tirshatha being the name of his office. *Mourn not, nor weep.* This is a holy day to God; a day appointed for general rejoicing in Him who has turned our captivity, restored to us His law, and again established among us His ordinances.

10. *Eat the fat, and drink the sweet.* Eat and drink the best that you have; and while ye are feeding yourselves in the fear of the Lord, remember those who cannot feast, and send portions to them, that the joy and the thanksgiving may be general. Let the poor have reason to rejoice as well as you. *For the joy of the Lord is your strength.* This is no gluttonous and drunken festival that enervates the body and enfeebles the mind. From your religious feast your bodies will acquire strength and your minds power and fervor, so that you shall be able to do His will, and to do it cheerfully.

14. *In the feast of the seventh month.* That is, the Feast of Tabernacles, which was held in commemoration of the sojourning of their fathers in the wilderness after they had been delivered from the Egyptian bondage. Now, having been delivered from the Babylonish captivity, and the proper time of the year occurring, it was their especial duty to keep the same feast.

15. *Fetch olive branches.* For everything concerning this Feast of Tabernacles, see the notes on Leviticus xxiii.

16. *Upon the roof of his house.* It need scarcely be repeated that the houses in the East are generally built with flat roofs. On these they reposed; on these they took the air in the heats of summer; and on these they oftentimes slept.

17. *Since the days of Jeshua.* No Feast of Tabernacles since Joshua's time had been so heartily and so piously celebrated.

On the subject in v. 8, I beg leave to make observation: "So they read in the book in the law of God distinctly, and gave the sense, and caused them to undertsand the reading." The Israelites, having been lately brought out of the Babylonish captivity, in which they had continued seventy years, according to the prediction of Jeremiah, chap. xxv. 11, were not only extremely corrupt, but it appears that they had in general lost the knowledge of the ancient Hebrew to such a degree that, when the book of the law was read, they did not understand it; but certain Levites stood by and "gave the sense," i.e., translated into the Chaldee dialect.

CHAPTER 9

On the twenty-fourth day of the seventh month, the people hold a solemn fast unto the Lord, and confess their sins, 1-3. The Levites give a general account of God's kindness and forbearance to them and to their fathers, and acknowledge God's mercies and judgments, 4-37. They make a covenant with the Lord, 38.

1. *Now in the twenty and fourth day.* The Feast of Trumpets was on the first day of this month; on the fourteenth began the Feast of Tabernacles, which, lasting seven days, finished on the twenty-second; on the twenty-third they separated themselves from their illegitimate wives and children; and on the twenty-fourth they held a solemn day of fasting and confession of sin, and reading the law, which they closed by renewing their covenants.

2. *The seed of Israel separated themselves.* A reformation of this kind was begun by Ezra, x. 3; but it appears that either more were found out who had taken strange wives, or else those who had separated from them had taken them again. *And stood and confessed their sins, and the iniquities of their fathers.* They acknowledged that they had been sinners against God throughout all their generations; that their fathers had sinned and were punished; and that they, with this example before their eyes, had copied their fathers' offenses.

3. *One fourth part of the day.* As they did no manner of work on this day of fasting and humiliation, so they spent the whole of it in religious duties.

5. *Stand up and bless the Lord your God.* It is the shameless custom of many congregations of people to sit still while they profess to bless and praise God by singing the psalms of David or hymns made on the plan of the gospel! I ask such persons, Did they ever feel the spirit of devotion while thus employed?

6. *Thou preservest them all.* "And Thou givest life to them all; and the host of the heavens prostrate themselves unto Thee."

14. *Madest known unto them thy holy sabbath.* They appear to have forgotten this first of all the commandments of God, during their sojourning in Egypt.

17. *And in their rebellion appointed a captain.* This clause, read according to its order in the Hebrew text, is thus: "And appointed a captain to return to their bondage in their rebellion." But it is probable that *bemiryam,* "in their rebellion," is a mistake for *bemitsrayim,* "in Egypt." This is the reading in Num. xiv. 4. The clause should undoubtedly be read, "They appointed a captain to return to their bondage in Egypt."

19. *The pillar of the cloud departed not from them.* "From over them."

21. *Their clothes waxed not old.* See Deut. viii. 4.

22. *The land of Og king of Bashan.* It is most evident that Sihon was king of Heshbon. How then can it be said that they possessed *the land of Sihon, and the land of the king of Heshbon?* The words *the land of the king of Heshbon* are wanting in two of De Rossi's MSS. In another MS. the words *and the land of* are wanting; so that the clause is read, "They possessed the land of Sihon, king of Heshbon." The Septuagint has the same reading; the Arabic nearly the same, viz., "the land of Sihon, the land of the king of Heshbon." The Syriac has, "They possessed the land of Sihon, the land of the kings of Heshbon." The reading of the text is undoubtedly wrong; that supported by the MSS. and by the Septuagint is most likely to be the true one. Those of the Arabic and Syriac contain at least no contradictory sense. The *and* in the Hebrew and our version distinguishes two lands and two kings, when it is most certain that only one land and one king can be meant; but the *vau* may be translated here as it often is, *even*: "even the land of the king of Heshbon."

25. *Became fat, and delighted themselves.* They became effeminate, fell under the power of luxury, got totally corrupted in their manners, sinned against all the mercies of God, and then were destroyed by His judgments.

27. *Thou gavest them saviours.* The whole Book of Judges is a history of God's mercies and their rebellions.

30. *Many years didst thou forbear.* It is supposed that Nehemiah refers principally to the ten tribes. And many years did God bear with them, not less than 254 years from their separation from the house of David, till their captivity and utter dispersion under Shalmaneser, during the whole of which time God invariably warned them by His prophets; or, as it is here said, *by thy spirit in thy prophets,* which gives us the true notion of divine inspiration. God's Spirit was given to the prophets; and

they testified to the people, according as they were taught and influenced by this Spirit.

32. *On our kings, on our princes.* I believe Nehemiah in this place mentions the whole of civil society in its officers as they stand related to each other in dignity: (1) *kings,* as supreme; (2) *princes;* (3) *priests;* (4) *prophets;* (5) the *fathers,* heads or chiefs of tribes and families; (6) the common *people.*

35. *For they have not served thee in their kingdom.* Instead of *in their kingdom,* "in thy kingdom" is the reading of two of Kennicott's MSS., as also of the Septuagint, Syriac, and Arabic. This is most likely to be the true reading.

36. *Behold, we are servants.* They had no king of their own, and were under the government of the kings of Persia, to whom they paid a regular tribute.

37. *It yieldeth much increase unto the kings.* Good and fruitful as the land is, yet it profits us little, as the chief profits on all things go to the kings of Persia.

CHAPTER 10

The names of those who sealed the covenant, 1-27. All solemnly promise not to have affinity with the people of the land, 28-30; to observe the Sabbaths, 31; to provide for the sanctuary according to the law, 32-36; and to pay the regular tithes for the support of the priests, Levites, and other officers of the Temple, 37-39.

1. *Now those that sealed.* Four classes here seal. Nehemiah first, as their governor. And after him, secondly, the priests, vv. 2-8. Thirdly, the Levites, vv. 9-13. Fourthly, the chiefs of the people, vv. 14-27.

28. *And the rest of the people.* All had, in one or other of the classes which sealed, their representatives; and by their sealing they considered themselves bound.

29. *They clave to their brethren.* Though they did not sign this instrument, yet they found themselves under a solemn oath that they would fulfil the conditions of the covenant, and walk according to the law of Moses.

30. *Not give our daughters.* Make no affinity with the people of the land.

31. *Bring ware.* We will most solemnly keep the Sabbath. *Leave the seventh year.* We will let the land have its Sabbath, and rest every seventh year. See on Exod. xxiii. 10-11.

32. *Charge ourselves yearly with the third part of a shekel.* According to the law, everyone above twenty years of age was to give half a shekel to the sanctuary, which was called a ransom for their souls. See Exod. xxx. 11-16. But why is one *third* of a shekel now promised instead of the half-shekel, which the law required? To this question no better answer can be given than this: The general poverty of the people occasioned by their wars, overthrows, heavy tributes, etc., in the land of their captivity; and now on their return, having little property, it was impossible for them to give more. Though only a third part of a shekel was given at this time, and probably for the reason above assigned, yet when the people got into a state of greater prosperity the half-shekel was resumed, for it is clear that this sum was paid in the time of our Lord.

34. *Cast the lots . . . for the wood offering.* There does not appear to have been any wood offering under the law. It was the business of

the Nethinim to procure this; and hence they were called "hewers of wood and drawers of water" to the congregation. But it is very likely that after the Captivity few Nethinim were found; for as such, who were the descendants of the Gibeonites, were considered only as slaves among the Israelites, they would doubtless find it as much, if not more, to their interest to abide in the land of their captivity than to return with their former masters.

36. *Also the firstborn.* See this law, and the reasons of it, Exod. xiii. 1-13. As by this law the Lord had a right to all the firstborn, instead of these He was pleased to take the tribe of Levi for the whole; and thus the Levites served at the Tabernacle and Temple, instead of the first-born of all the tribes.

38. *Tithe of the tithes.* The tithes of all the produce of the fields were brought to the Levites; out of these a tenth part was given to the priests. This is what is called the "tithe of the tithes." The law for this is found in Num. xviii. 26.

39. *We will not forsake the house of our God.* Here was a glorious resolution; and had they been faithful to it, they had been a great and good people to the present day.

CHAPTER 11

Lots are cast that a tenth of the people may constantly dwell at Jerusalem, and the other nine parts in the other cities and villages, 1. Some willingly offer themselves to dwell in Jerusalem, and the people bless them, 2. An enumeration of the families that dwell in Jerusalem, of Judah, and Benjamin, 3-9; of those of the priests, 10-12; of the chiefs of the fathers, 13; of the mighty men, 14; of the Levites, 15-18; of the porters, 19; of the residue of Israel and the officers, 20-24. The villages at which they dwelt, 25-35. Certain divisions of the Levites were in Judah and Benjamin, 36.

1. *To bring one of ten.* Jerusalem certainly had many inhabitants at this time; but not sufficient to preserve the city, which was now encompassed with a wall, and the rebuilding of which was going on fast. Nehemiah therefore obliged one-tenth of the country people to come and dwell in it, that the population might be sufficient for the preservation and defense of the city. Ten were set apart, and the lot cast among them to see which one of the ten should take up his residence in the city.

2. *All the men, that willingly offered.* Some volunteered their services, which was considered a sacrifice to patriotism at that time, as Jerusalem afforded very few advantages and was a place of considerable danger; hence the people "spoke well of them," and no doubt prayed for God's blessing upon them.

3. *Now these are the chief.* A good deal of difference will be found between the enumeration here and that in 1 Chron. ix. 2, etc. There, those only who came with Zerubbabel appear to be numbered; here, those, and the persons who came with Ezra and Nehemiah, enter into the account.

9. *And Joel . . . was their overseer.* Joel was chief or magistrate over those, and Judah was his *second* or "deputy." Perhaps each had a different office, but that of Joel was the chief.

11. *Ruler of the house of God.* He had the command over all secular matters, as the high priest had over those which were spiritual.

14. *Mighty men of valour.* Noted for strength of body and military courage.

16. *And Shabbethai.* This verse, with vv. 20-21, 28-29, 32-35, are all wanting in the Septua-

gint and the whole chapter is wanting in the Arabic, the translator not being concerned in Jewish genealogies. *The outward business.* Calmet supposes that he provided the victuals for the priests, victims for the sacrifices, the sacerdotal vestments, the sacred vessels, and other necessaries for the service of the Temple.

17. *The principal to begin the thanksgiving.* The pitcher of the tune.

22. *The overseer also of the Levites.* The "visitant," the "inspector."

23. *It was the king's commandment.* By the *king* some understand David, and others Artaxerxes. It is most probable that it was the latter, who wished that a provision should be made for these, a part of whose office was to offer up prayers also, as well as praises. For we know that Darius made an ample provision for the priests, "that they may offer sacrifices of sweet savours unto the God of heaven, and pray for the life of the king, and of his sons," Ezra vi. 10. Some have thought that they had been Jewish singers employed in the service of the Persian king, to whom he had given a salary, and to whom he wished still to continue the same.

24. *Pethahiah . . . was at the king's hand.* He was the governor appointed by the Persian king over the Jewish nation in those matters in which the civil government interfered with Jewish concerns. He no doubt fixed, levied, and received the tribute.

36. *And of the Levites were divisions.* The Levites had their dwellings in the divisions of Judah and Benjamin. This is probably the meaning.

CHAPTER 12

Account of the priests and Levites that came up with Zerubbabel, 1-7. Of the Levites, 8-21. The Levites in the days of Eliashib, 22-26. Of the dedication of the wall, and its ceremonies, 27-43. Different officers appointed, 44-47.

1. *Now these are the priests.* Not the whole, but the chief of them, as we are informed, vv. 7, 22-24.

7. *The chief of the priests.* They were twenty-four orders or courses in number, all subordinate to each other; as established by David, 1 Chron. xxiv. 18. And these orders or courses were continued till the destruction of Jerusalem by the Romans.

8. *Over the thanksgiving.* The principal singers: see on chap. xi. 17.

23. *The book of the chronicles.* This is not the Book of Chronicles which we have now, no such list being found in it; but some other book or register, which is lost.

27. *At the dedication of the wall.* They sent for the Levites from all quarters, that this dedication might be as solemn and majestic as possible; and it is likely that this was done as soon as convenient after the walls were finished. The dedication seems to have consisted in processions of the most eminent persons around the walls, and thanksgivings to God, who had enabled them to bring the work to so happy a conclusion.

29. *From the house of Gilgal, and out of the fields of Geba and Azmaveth.* Or from Beth-Gilgal; a village erected in the place where the Israelites encamped after they had, under the direction of Joshua, passed over Jordan.

30. *The priests and the Levites purified themselves.* This consisted in washings, abstinence from wine, and other matters, which, on all other occasions, were lawful. And as to the purifying of the gates and the walls, nothing was requisite but to remove all filth from the former, and all rubbish that might have been laid against the latter.

31. *Then I brought up the princes.* Perhaps this verse should be read thus: "Then I caused the princes of Judah to go up on the wall, and appointed two great choirs [to sing praises], and two processions, one on the right hand," etc.

CHAPTER 13

The law is read, which commands that the Ammonite and Moabite should be separated from the congregation, on which they separate all the mixed multitude, 1-3. Eliashib, the high priest, having not only joined opinion with Sanballat, but being also allied to Tobiah the Ammonite, and having given him some of the chambers in the court of the house of God, 4-5. Nehemiah casts out the goods of Tobiah and purifies the chambers, 6-9. He rectifies several evils; and the people bring the tithes of all things to the treasuries, 10-12. He appoints treasurers, 13-14: finds that the Sabbaths had been greatly profaned by buying and selling, and rectifies this abuse, 15-22; finds Jews that had married strange wives, against whom he testifies, and expels one of the priests who had married the daughter of Sanballat the Horonite, 23-29. He cleanses them from all strangers, makes a final regulation, and prays for God's mercy to himself, 30-31.

1. *Should not come into the congregation.* That is, You shall not form any kind of matrimonial alliance with them. This, and this alone, is the meaning of the law.

3. *They separated from Israel all the mixed multitude.* They excluded all strange women, and all persons, young and old, who had been born of these illegal connections.

4. *Eliashib the priest.* Perhaps this was a different person from Eliashib, the high priest; but there is no indubitable evidence that he was not the same. If he was high priest, he was very unfaithful to the high charge which he had received, and a reproach to the priesthood. He had married his grandson to Sanballat's daughter; this produced a connection with Tobiah, the fast friend of Sanballat, in whose favor he polluted the house of God, giving him one of the chambers for his ordinary residence, which were appointed for the reception of the tithes, oblations, etc., that came to the house of God.

6. *Was not I at Jerusalem.* Nehemiah came to Jerusalem in the twentieth year of Artaxerxes, and remained there till the thirty-second year, twelve years; then returned to Babylon, and staid one year; got leave to revisit his brethren; and found matters as stated in this chapter.

8. *I cast forth all the household stuff of Tobiah.* He acted as Jesus Christ did when He found the courts of the Lord's house profaned: "He overthrew the tables of the money-changers, and the seats of them that sold doves."

10. *The portions of the Levites had not been given.* Hence we find they were obliged to abandon the sacred service and betake themselves to cultivate the land for their support. This was the fault of the rulers, who permitted all these abuses.

11. *Why is the house of God forsaken?* They had all solemnly promised, chap. x. 39, that they would never forsake the house of their God; but, alas, how soon is this forgotten! Nehemiah used their own words here by way of reproof.

13. *They were counted faithful.* They were reported to me as persons in whom I could confide; they had been steady in God's ways and work, while others had been careless and relaxed.

15. *Treading wine presses.* The Sabbath appears to have been totally disregarded.

17. *I contended with the nobles.* These evils took place through their negligence, and this I proved before them.

19. *When the gates . . . began to be dark.* After sunset on Friday evening he caused the gates to be shut, and kept them shut all the Sabbath; and, as he could not trust the ordinary officers, he set some of his own servants to watch the gates, that no person might enter for the purpose of traffic.

20. *So the merchants . . . lodged without Jerusalem.* They exposed their wares for sale on the outside of the walls.

21. *I will lay hands on you.* I will imprison every man of you. This had the desired effect; they *came . . . no more.*

24. *Half in the speech of Ashdod.* There were children in the same family by Jewish and Philistine mothers. As the Jewish mother would always speak to her children in Hebrew or Chaldee, so they learned to speak these languages; and as the Ashdod mother would always speak to her children in the Ashdod language, so they learned that tongue.

25. *I contended with them.* Proved the fact against these iniquitous fathers, in a legal assembly. *And cursed them.* Denounced the judgments of God and the sentence of the law upon them. *Smote certain of them.* Had them punished by whipping. *And plucked off their hair.* Had them shaven, as a mark of the greatest ignominy. *And made them swear by God, saying, Ye shall not give.* Caused them to bind themselves by an oath that they would make no intermarriages with those who were not of the seed of Israel.

26. *Did not Solomon?* Have you not had an awful example before you? What a heavy curse did Solomon's conduct bring upon himself and upon the people, for a conduct such as yours?

27. *Shall we then hearken unto you?* If God spared not Solomon, who was so much beloved of Him, shall we spare you, who by your conduct are bringing down God's judgments upon Israel?

28. *One of the sons of Joiada.* This was Manasseh, brother of Jaddua, son of Joiada, and grandson of Eliashib, the high priest. *I chased him from me.* Struck him off the list of the priests, and deemed him utterly unworthy of all connection and intercourse with truly religious people.

29. *Because they have defiled the priesthood.* God, therefore, will remember their iniquities against them, and punish them for their transgressions. These words of Nehemiah are to be understood declaratively.

31. *For the word offering.* This was a most necessary regulation; without it the Temple service could not have gone forward; and therefore Nehemiah mentions this as one of the most important services he had rendered to his nation. See chap. x. 34, *Remember me, O my God, for good.* This has precisely the same meaning with, "O my God, have mercy upon me!" and thus alone it should be understood.

The Book of
ESTHER

The son and successor of the famous Persian king Xerxes was Artaxerxes, surnamed Longimanus. This prince, on coming to the throne, had powerful opponents and competitors in the children of Artabanus, uncle to Xerxes, and in his own brother Hystaspes. The former, and their adherents, he overthrew in a bloody battle; and in the following year obtained a complete victory over his brother, and totally subdued the Bactrians, who had espoused his cause; and thus rendered himself the undisputed possessor of the Persian Empire. About his third year, which was 462 before Christ, the history of Esther begins.

CHAPTER 1

Ahasuerus makes royal feasts for his nobles and people, 1-9. Vashti is sent for by the king, but refuses to come, 10-12. Vashti is disgraced, and a law made for the subjection of women, 13-22.

1. *Now it came to pass.* The Ahasuerus of the Romans, the Artaxerxes of the Greeks, and Ardsheer of the Persians are the same. *Reigned, from India even unto Ethopia.* This is nearly the same account that is given by Xenophon.

2. *Sat on the throne of his kingdom.* Having subdued all his enemies, and brought universal peace to his empire. *Shushan the palace.* The ancient city of Susa. This, with Ecbatana and Babylon, was a residence of the Persian kings. The word which we render *the palace* should be rendered "the city," as in the Septuagint.

4. *The riches of his glorious kingdom.* Luxury was the characteristic of the Eastern monarchs, and particularly of the Persians. In their feasts, which were superb and of long continuance, they made a general exhibition of their wealth, grandeur, etc., and received the highest encomiums from their poets and flatterers.

5. *A feast unto all the people.* The first was a feast for the nobles in general; this, for the people of the city at large. *In the court of the garden.* As the company was very numerous that was to be received, no apartments in the palace could be capable of containing them; therefore the *court of the garden* was chosen.

6. *White, green, and blue hangings.* It was customary, on such occasions, not only to hang the place about with elegant curtains of the above colors, but also to have a canopy of rich stuffs suspended on cords from side to side of the place in which they feasted. The *beds . . . of gold and silver* mentioned here were the couches covered with gold and silver cloth, on which the guests reclined.

7. *Vessels being diverse.* They had different services of plate.

8. *None did compel: for so the king had appointed.* Every person drank what he pleased; he was not obliged to take more than he had reason to think would do him good.

9. *Also Vashti the queen.* Vashti is a mere Persian word, and signifies a "beautiful or excellent woman." *Made a feast for the women.* The king, having subdued all his enemies, left no competitor for the kingdom; and being thus quietly and firmly seated on the throne, made this a time of general festivity. As the women of the East never mingle with the men in public, Vashti made a feast for the Persian ladies by themselves; and while the men were in the court of the garden, the women were in the royal house.

10. *He commanded Mehuman.* All these are doubtless Persian names, but so disguised by passing through a Hebrew medium that some of them can scarcely be known. *Mehuman* signifies a "stranger or guest."

12. *Vashti refused to come.* And much should she be commended for it. What woman, possessing even a common share of prudence and modesty, could consent to expose herself to the view of such a group of drunken Bacchanalians? Her courage was equal to her modesty: she would resist the royal mandate rather than violate the rules of chaste decorum.

14. *And the next unto him . . . the seven princes.* Probably the privy counsellors of the king. *Which saw the king's face*—were at all times admitted to the royal presence.

18. *The ladies of Persia.* The "princesses."

19. *That it be not altered.* Let it be inserted among the permanent laws.

CHAPTER 2

The counsellors advise that a selection of virgins should be made throughout the empire, out of whom the king should choose one to be queen in place of Vashti, 1-4. Account of Mordecai and his cousin Esther, 5-7. She is chosen among the young women, and is placed under the care of Hegai, the king's chamberlain, to go through a year's purification, 8-11. The manner in which these young women were introduced to the king, and how these were disposed of who were not called again to the king's bed, 12-14. Esther pleases the king, and is set above all the women; and he makes her queen in the place of Vashti, and does her great honor, 15-20. Mordecai, sitting at the king's gate, discovers a conspiracy formed against the king's life by two of his chamberlains; he informs the king, the matter is investigated, they are found guilty and hanged, and the transaction is recorded, 21-23.

2. *Let there be fair young virgins sought for the king.* This was the usual way in which the harem was furnished; the finest women in the

land, whether of high or low birth, were sought out, and brought to the harem. They all became the king's concubines; but one was raised, as chief wife, to the throne, and her issue was specially entitled to inherit.

3. *Hege the king's chamberlain.* "Hege, the king's *eunuch*"; so the Septuagint, Vulgate, Targum, and Syriac. In the Eastern countries the women are intrusted to the care of the eunuchs only. *Let their things for purification be given them.* "Their cosmetics." What these were we are told in v. 12; "oil of myrrh" and "sweet odours." The myrrh was employed for six months, and the "odours" for six months more, after which the person was brought to the king. This space was sufficient to show whether the young woman had been chaste, whether she were with child or not, that the king might not be imposed on, and be obliged to father a spurious offspring, which might have been the case had not this precaution been used.

7. *He brought up Hadassah.* Hadassah signifies a "myrtle" in Chaldee; this was probably her first or Babylonish name. When she came to the Persian court, she was called Esther, which signifies a "star" in Persian. Esther was the daughter of Abihail, the uncle of Mordecai, and therefore must have been Mordecai's cousin.

9. *The maiden pleased him.* He conceived a partiality for her above the rest, probably because of the propriety of her deportment, and her engaging though unassuming manners. *Seven maidens.* These were to attend her to the bath, to anoint and adorn her, and be her servants in general.

10. *Esther had not shewed her people.* This might have prejudiced her with the king, for it was certainly no credit at the Persian court to be a Jew; and we shall find from the sequel that those who were in the Persian dominions were far from being reputable, or in a safe state. Besides, had her lineage been known, envy might have prevented her from ever having access to the king.

13. *Whatsoever she desired.* When any of the young women were called to go to the king, it appears that it was an ordinance that whatever kind of dress stuff, color, jewels, etc., they thought best to set off their persons, and render them more engaging, should be given them.

14. *She returned into the second house.* This was the place where the king's concubines were kept. They went out no more, and were never given in marriage to any man, and saw the king's face no more unless specially called. *Custody of Shaashgaz.* This is probably another Persian name; "beardless," a proper epithet of a eunuch.

15. *She required nothing.* She left this entirely to her friend Hege, who seems to have been intent on her success. She therefore left her decorations to his judgment alone, and went in that dress and in those ornaments which he deemed most suitable.

16. *The tenth month . . . Tebeth.* Answering to part of our December and January.

18. *Made a release to the provinces.* Remitted some kind of tribute or impost in honor of Esther at her coronation.

21. *Mordecai sat in the king's gate.* Mordecai might have been one of the officers of the king, as the gate was the place where such usually

attended to await the king's call. It has been observed that the name of God does not once occur in this book. This is true of the Hebrew text, and all translations from it; but in the Septuagint we find the following words, in v. 20, after, "Esther had not yet shewed her kindred": "For so Mordecai had charged her to fear God, and to keep his commandments, as she did when with him."

CHAPTER 3

Ahasuerus exalts Haman, the Agagite, and commands all his officers to do him reverence, which Mordecai refuses, 1-3. Haman, informed of Mordecai's refusal, plots his destruction, and that of the Jews, 4-6. Lots are cast to find out the proper time, 7. Haman accuses the Jews to Ahasuerus, counsels him to destroy them, and offers 10,000 talents of silver for the damage which the revenue might sustain by their destruction, 8-9. The king refuses the money, but gives Haman full authority to destroy them, 10-11. Letters are written to this effect, and sent to the king's lieutenants throughout the empire, and the thirteenth day of the month Adar is appointed for the massacre, 12-15.

1. *Haman . . . the Agagite.* Perhaps he was some descendant of that Agag, king of the Amalekites, spared by Saul, but destroyed by Samuel; and on this ground might have had an antipathy to the Jews. *Set his seat above all the princes.* Made him his prime minister, and put all the officers of state under his direction.

2. *The king's servants, that were in the king's gate.* By *servants* here, certainly a higher class of officers are intended than porters; and Mordecai was one of those officers, and came to the gate with the others who were usually there in attendance to receive the commands of the king. *Mordecai bowed not.* "He did not bow down"; *nor did him reverence, velo yishtachaveh,* "nor did he prostrate himself." I think it most evident, from these two words, that it was not civil reverence merely that Haman expected and Mordecai refused; this sort of respect is found in the word *cara,* to "bow." This sort of reverence Mordecai could not refuse without being guilty of the most inexcusable obstinacy, nor did any part of the Jewish law forbid it. But Haman expected, what the Persian kings frequently received, a species of divine adoration; and this is implied in the word *shachah,* which signifies that kind of prostration which implies the highest degree of reverence that can be paid to God or man, lying down flat on the earth, with the hands and feet extended, and the mouth in the dust.

7. *The first month.* That is, of the civil year of the Jews. *The month Nisan.* Answering to a part of our March and April. *The twelfth year of King Ahasuerus.* According to the chronology in our Bibles, about five hundred and ten years before Christ. *They cast Pur, that is, the lot.* This appears to be the Hebrew corruption of the pure Persian word *pari,* which signifies anything that "happens fortuitously." We see plainly intimated by the Hebrew text that they cast lots, or used a species of divination, to find which of the twelve months would be the most favorable for the execution of Haman's design; and, having found the desired month, then they cast lots, or used divination, to find out which day of the said month would be the lucky day for the accomplishment of the enterprise. The Hebrew text does not tell us the result of this divination; we are left to guess it out. But the Greek supplies this deficiency, and makes all clear. From it we find that, when they cast for the month, the

month Adar was taken; and when they cast for the day, the fourteenth (Heb., thirteenth) of that month was taken.

8. *Their laws are diverse from all people.* Such they certainly were, for they worshipped the true God according to His own laws; and this was not done by any other people then on the face of the earth.

9. *Let it be written that they may be destroyed.* Let it be enacted that they may all be put to death. By this he would throw all the odium off himself, and put it on the king and his counsellors; for he wished the thing to pass into a law, in which he could have but a small share of the blame. *I will pay ten thousand talents of silver.* He had said before that it was not for the king's profit to suffer them; but here he is obliged to acknowledge that there will be a loss to the revenue, but that loss he is willing to make up out of his own property. Ten thousand talents of silver is an immense sum indeed, which, counted by the Babylonish talent, amounts to 2,119,000 pounds sterling; but, reckoned by the Jewish talent, it makes more than double that sum.

10. *The king took his ring.* In this ring was no doubt included his privy seal, and he gave this to Haman, that when he had formed such a decree as he thought fit, he might seal it with this ring, which would give it its due force and influence among the rulers of the provinces.

12. *Unto the king's lieutenants. Achashdarpeney.* This is in all probability another Persian word, for there is nothing like it in the Hebrew language, nor can it be fairly deduced from any roots in that tongue. The Vulgate translates "to all the *satraps* of the king." It is very likely that this is the true sense of the word.

13. *To destroy, to kill, and to cause to perish.* To put the whole of them to death in any manner, or by every way and means. *Take the spoil of them for a prey.* Thus, whoever killed a Jew had his property for his trouble! And thus the hand of every man was armed against this miserable people.

15. *The posts.* Literally, the "couriers," those who carried the public dispatches. *The decree was given in Shushan.* It was dated from the royal Susa, where the king then was. *The city Shushan was perplexed.* They saw that in a short time, by this wicked measure, the whole city would be thrown into confusion; for, although the Jews were the only objects of this decree, yet, as it armed the populace against them, even the Persians could not hope to escape without being spoiled, when a desperate mob had begun to taste of human blood, and enrich themselves with the property of the murdered.

orders Mordecai to gather all the Jews of Shushan, and fast for her success three days, night and day; and resolves to make the attempt, though at the risk of her life, 15-17.

1. *Mordecai rent his clothes.* He gave every demonstration of the most poignant and oppressive grief. Nor did he hide this from the city; and the Greek says that he uttered these words aloud: "A people are going to be destroyed, who have done no evil!"

2. *Before the king's gate.* He could not enter into the gate of the place where the officers waited, because he was in the habit of a mourner, for this would have been contrary to law.

3. *Fasting, and weeping, and wailing.* How astonishing that in all this there is not the slightest intimation given of praying to God!

4. *Sent raiment.* She supposed that he must have been spoiled of his raiment by some means, and therefore sent him clothing.

5. *Then called Esther for Hatach.* This eunuch the king had appointed to wait upon her, partly, as is still the case in the East, to serve her, and partly to observe her conduct; for no despot is ever exempt from a twofold torture, jealousy and suspicion.

11. *Into the inner court.* The Persian sovereigns affected the highest degree of majesty, even to the assuming of divine honors. No man nor woman dared to appear unveiled before them without hazarding their lives; into the inner chamber of the harem no person ever entered but the king, and the woman he had chosen to call thither.

13. *Think not . . . that thou shalt escape.* This confirms the suspicion that Haman knew something of the relationship between Mordecai and Esther; and therefore he gives her to understand that, although in the king's palace, she should no more escape than the Jews.

14. *Then shall there enlargment and deliverance arise.* He had a confidence that deliverance would come by some means, and he thought that Esther would be the most likely; and that, if she did not use the influence which her providential station gave her, she would be highly culpable.

16. *Fast ye for me, and neither eat nor drink three days.* What a strange thing that still we hear nothing of prayer, nor of God! What is the ground on which we can account for this total silence? I know it not. She could not suppose there was any charm in fasting, sackcloth garments, and lying on the ground. If these were not done to turn away the displeasure of God, which seemed now to have unchained their enemies against them, what were they done for?

CHAPTER 4

On hearing the king's decree to exterminate the Jews, Mordecai mourns, and clothes himself in sackcloth, 1-2. The Jews are filled with consternation, 3. Esther, perceiving Mordecai in distress at the palace gate, sends her servant Hatach to inquire the reason, 4-6. Hatach returns with the information, and also the express desire of Mordecai that she should go instantly to the king, and make supplication in behalf of her people, 7-9. Esther excuses herself on the ground that she has not been called by the king for thirty days past; and that the law was such that anyone approaching his presence, without express invitation, should be put to death, unless the king should, in peculiar clemency, stretch out to such persons the golden sceptre, 10-12. Mordecai returns an answer, insisting on her compliance, 13-14. She then

CHAPTER 5

Esther presents herself before the king, and finds favor in his sight, 1-2. He asks what her request is, and promises to grant it, 3. She invites him and Haman to a banquet, which they accept, 4-5. He then desires to know her request; she promises to make it known on the morrow, if they will again come to her banquet, 6-8. Haman, though overjoyed at the manner in which he was received by the queen, is indignant at the indifference with which he is treated by Mordecai, 9. He goes home and complains of this conduct to his friends, and his wife, Zeresh, 10-13. They counsel him to make a gallows of fifty cubits high, and to request the king that Mordecai may be hanged on it, which they take for granted the king will not refuse; and the gallows is made accordingly, 14.

1. *On the third day.* Most probably the third day of the fast which she has prescribed to Mordecai and the Jews.

4. *Let the king and Haman come this day unto the banquet.* It was necessary to invite Haman to prevent his suspicion, and that he might not take any hasty step which might have prevented the execution of the great design.

6. *The banquet of wine.* At that part of the banquet when *wine* was introduced.

8. *I will do tomorrow.* She saw she was gaining on the king's affections; but she was not yet sufficiently confident, and therefore wished another interview, that she might ingratiate herself more fully in the king's favor, and thus secure the success of her design. But Providence disposed of things thus, to give time for the important event mentioned in the succeeding chapter.

9. *That he stood not up, nor moved for him.* This was certainly carrying his integrity or inflexibility to the highest pitch. But still we are left to conjecture that some reverence was required which Mordecai could not conscientiously pay.

11. *The multitude of his children.* The Asiatic sovereigns delight in the number of their children, and this is one cause why they take so many wives and concubines.

13. *Yet all this availeth me nothing.* Pride will ever render its possessor unhappy. He has such a high opinion of his own worth that he conceives himself defrauded by everyone who does not pay him all the respect and homage which he conceives to be his due.

14. *Let a gallows be made of fifty cubits high.* The word *ets*, which we translate *gallows*, signifies simply "wood, a tree, or pole"; and this was to be seventy-five feet high, that he might suffer the greater ignominy, and be a more public spectacle.

CHAPTER 6

That night the king, not being able to sleep, orders the chronicles of the kingdom to be read to him, and finds there the record concerning the discovery of the treason of the two eunuchs, made by Mordecai, 1-2. He inquires whether Mordecai had been rewarded, and was answered in the negative, 3. At this time Haman arrives, in order to request the king's permission to hang Mordecai; and being suddenly asked what should be done to the man whom the king delighted to honor, supposing that himself must be meant, presented the ceremonial, 4-9. The king orders him to give Mordecai those honors; which he performs, to his extreme moritification, 10-11. He informs his wife, Zeresh, of these transactions, who predicts his downfall, 12-13. He is hurried by the eunuchs to the queen's banquet, 14.

3. *What honour and dignity hath been done to Mordecai?* It is certain he found nothing in the record; and had anything been done, that was the most likely place to find it.

6. *The king said unto him.* He did not give him time to make his request; and put a question to him which, at the first view, promised him all that his heart could wish.

8. *Let the royal apparel be brought.* Pride and folly ever go hand in hand. What he asked would have been in any ordinary case against his own life; but he wished to reach the pinnacle of honor, never reflecting that the higher he rose, the more terrible would be his fall. The *royal apparel* was never worn but by the king; even when the king had lain them aside, it was

death to put them on. *And the horse . . . and the crown royal.* Interpreters are greatly divided whether what is called here the *crown royal* be not rather an ornament worn on the head of the horse than what may be called the royal crown. The original may be understood both ways, and our version seems to favor the former opinion; but I think it more likely that the royal crown is meant, for why mention the ordinary trappings of the royal steed?

9. *One of the king's most noble princes.* Alas, poor Haman! Never was the fable of the dog and shadow more literally fulfilled. Thou didst gape at the shadow, and didst lose the substance.

12. *Mordecai came again to the king's gate.* He resumed his former humble state; while Haman, ashamed to look up, covered his face, and ran home to hide himself in his own house. Covering the head and face was a sign of shame and confusion, as well as of grief, among most people of the earth.

14. *Hasted to bring Haman.* There was a dreadful banquet before him, of which he knew nothing, and he could have little appetite to enjoy that which he knew was prepared at the palace of Esther.

CHAPTER 7

The king at the banquet urges Esther to prefer her petition, with the positive assurance that it shall be granted, 1-2. She petitions for her own life, and the life of her people, who were sold to be destroyed, 3-4. The king inquires the author of this project and Haman is accused by the queen, 5-6. The king is enraged; Haman supplicates for his life, but the king orders him to be hanged on the gallows he had prepared for Mordecai, 7-10.

3. *Let my life be given me.* This was very artfully, as well as very honestly, managed, and was highly calculated to work on the feelings of the king. What! is the life of the queen, whom I most tenderly love, in any kind of danger?

4. *To be destroyed, to be slain.* She here repeats the words which Haman put into the decree. See chap. iii. 13. *Could not countervail the king's damage.* Even the 10,000 talents of silver could not be considered as a compensation to the state for the loss of a whole nation of people throughout all their generations.

5. *Who is he, and where is he?* There is a wonderful abruptness and confusion in the original words, highly expressive of the state of mind in which the king then was: *mi hu zeh veey zeh hu asher melao libbo laasoth ken.* "Who? He? This one? And where? This one? He? Who hath filled his heart to do thus?" He was at once struck with the horrible nature of a conspiracy so cruel and diabolic.

7. *Haman stood up.* He rose from the table to make request for his life, as soon as the king had gone out; and then he fell on his knees before the queen, she still sitting upon her couch.

8. *Will he force the queen?* On the king's return he found him at the queen's knees; and, professing to think that he intended to do violence to her honor, used the above expressions; though he must have known that, in such circumstances, the thought of perpetrating an act of this kind could not possibly exist. *They covered Haman's face.* This was a sign of his being devoted to death, for the attendants saw that the king was determined on his destruction.

9. *Behold also, the gallows.* As if he had said, Besides all he has determined to do to the Jews, he has erected a very high gallows, on which he had determined, this very day, to hang Mordecai, who has saved the king's life. *Hang him thereon.* Let him be instantly impaled on the same post.

CHAPTER 8

Ahasuerus invests Mordecai with the offices and dignities possessed by Haman, 1-2. Esther begs that the decree of destruction gone out against the Jews may be reversed, 3-6. He informs her that the acts that had once passed the king's seal cannot be reversed; but he instructs her and Mordecai to write other letters in his name, and seal them with his seal, and send them to all the provinces in the empire, giving the Jews full liberty to defend themselves, which is accordingly done, and the letters are sent off with the utmost speed to all the provinces; in consequence, the Jews prepare for their own defense, 8-14. Mordecai appears publicly in the dress of his high office, 15. The Jews rejoice in every place; and many of the people become Jews, because the fear of the Jews has fallen upon them, 16-17.

1. *The king . . . give the house of Haman.* As Haman was found guilty of treasonable practices against the peace and prosperity of the king and his empire, his life was forfeited, and his goods confiscated. And as Mordecai had been the means of preserving the king's life, and was the principal object of Haman's malice, it was but just to confer his property upon him, as well as his dignity and office, as Mordecai was found deserving of the former, and fit to discharge the duties of the latter.

2. *The king took off his ring.* In the ring was the seal of the king. Giving the ring to Mordecai was tantamount to giving him the seal of the kingdom, and constituting him the same as lord chancellor among us.

6. *To see the destruction of my kindred?* She had now informed the king that she was cousin to Mordecai, and consequently a Jewess; and though her own life and that of Mordecai were no longer in danger, Haman being dead, yet the decree that had gone forth was in full force against the Jews; and if not repealed, their destruction would be inevitable.

8. *May no man reverse.* Whatever had passed the royal signet could never be revoked; no succeeding edict could destroy or repeal a preceding one. But one of a similar nature to the Jews against the Persians, as that to the Persians was against the Jews, might be enacted, and thus the Jews be enabled legitimately to defend themselves and, consequently, placed on an equal footing with their enemies.

9. *The month Sivan.* This answers to a part of our May and June.

10. *On mules, camels, and young dromedaries.* What these beasts were is difficult to say. The word which we translate *mules* signifies a "swift chariot horse."

11. *To destroy, to slay, and to cause to perish.* The same words as in Haman's decree; therefore the Jews had as much authority to slay their enemies as their enemies had to slay them. *Little ones and women.* This was the ordinary custom, to destroy the whole family of those convicted of great crimes; and whether this was right or wrong, it was the custom of the people, and according to the laws. Besides, as this edict was to give the Jews the same power against their enemies as they had by the former decree against them, and the women and children were

there included, consequently they must be included here.

14. *The decree was given at Shushan.* The contrary effect which it was to produce considered, this decree was in every respect like the former. See chap. iii.

15. *Blue and white.* Probably stripe interchanged with stripe, or blue faced and bordered with white fur. *A great crown of gold.* A large turban, ornamented with gold, jewels, etc. *Shushan . . . was glad.* Haman was too proud to be popular; few lamented his fall.

CHAPTER 9

On the thirteenth of the month Adar the Jews destroy their enemies, and the governors of the provinces assist them, 1-5. They slay 500 in Shushan, and kill the 10 sons of Haman, but take no spoil, 6-10. The king is informed of the slaughter in Shushan, 11. He desires to know what Esther requests further, who begs that the Jews may be permitted to act on the following day as they had done on the preceding, and that Haman's sons may be hanged upon the gallows, which is granted; and they slay 300 more in Shushan, and in the other provinces 75,000, 12-16. A recapitulation of what was done, and of the appointment of the feast of Purim to be observed through all their generations every year, 17-28. Esther writes to confirm this appointment, 29-32.

1. *Now in the twelfth month.* What a number of providences, and none of them apparently of an extraordinary nature, concurred to preserve a people so signally, and to all human appearance so inevitably, doomed to destruction!

3. *And all the rulers of the provinces.* Mordecai being raised to the highest confidence of the king, and to have authority over the whole realm, these officers assisted the Jews, no doubt, with the troops under their command, to overthrow those who availed themselves of the former decree to molest the Jews. For it does not appear that the Jews slew any person who did not rise up to destroy them. See v. 5.

6. *And in Shushan.* It is strange that in this city, where the king's mind must have been so well known, there should be found 500 persons to rise up in hostility against those whom they knew the king befriended!

10. *The ten sons of Haman.* Their names are given above. And it is remarked here, and in v. 16, where the account is given of the number slain in the provinces, that the Jews laid no hands on the spoil. They stood for their lives, and gave full proof that they sought their own personal safety, and not the property of their enemies, though the decree in their favor gave them authority to take the property of all those who were their adversaries, chap. viii. 11.

13. *Let Haman's ten sons be hanged.* They had been slain the preceding day, and now she requests that they may be exposed on posts or gibbets, as a terror to those who sought the destruction of the Jews.

15. *And slew three hundred men.* Esther had probably been informed by Mordecai that there were still many enemies of the Jews who sought their destruction, who had escaped the preceding day, and therefore begs that this second day be added to the former permission. This being accordingly granted, they found 300 more, in all 800. And thus Susa was purged of all their enemies.

18. *The Jews . . . assembled . . . on the thirteenth . . . and on the fourteenth.* These two

days they were employed in slaying their enemies, and they rested on the fifteenth.

19. *The Jews of the villages.* They joined that to the preceding day, and made it a day of festivity, and of sending portions to each other; that is, the rich sent portions of the sacrifices slain on this occasion to the poor, that they also might be enabled to make the day a day of festivity; that as the sorrow was general, so also might the joy be.

20. *Mordecai wrote these things.* It has been supposed that thus far that part of the Book of Esther which was written by Mordecai extends. What follows, to the end, was probably added either by Ezra or the men of the Great Synagogue—though what is said here may refer only to the letters sent by Mordecai to the Jews of the provinces. From this to the end of the chapter is nothing else than a recapitulation of the chief heads of the preceding history, and an account of the appointment of an annual feast, called the Feast of Purim, in commemoration of their providential deliverance from the malice of Haman.

23. *The Jews undertook to do as they had begun.* They had already kept the fifteenth day, and some of them in the country the fourteenth also, as a day of rejoicing. Mordecai wrote to them to bind themselves and their successors, and all their proselytes, to celebrate this as an annual feast throughout all their generations; and this they undertook to do. And it has been observed among them, in all places of their dispersion, from that day to the present time, without any interruption.

26. *They called these days Purim.* That is from *pari*, "the lot"; because, as we have seen, Haman cast lots to find what month, and what

day of the month, would be the most favorable for the accomplishment of his bloody designs against the Jews. See on chap. iii. 7. *And of that which they had seen.* The first letter to which this second refers must be that sent by Mordecai himself. See v. 20.

29. *Esther . . . wrote with all authority.* Esther and Mordecai had the king's license so to do, and their own authority was great and extensive.

31. *As they had decreed for themselves and for their seed.* There is no mention of their receiving the approbation of any high priest, nor of any authority beyond that of Mordecai and Esther. The king could not join in such a business, as he had nothing to do with the Jewish religion, that not being the religion of the country.

32. *The decree of Esther confirmed these matters.* It was received by the Jews universally with all respect, and they bound themselves to abide by it.

CHAPTER 10

Ahasuerus lays a tribute on his dominions, 1. Mordecai's advancement under him, 2. His character, 3.

1. *Laid a tribute upon the land.* On the 127 provinces of which we have already heard. *The isles of the sea.* Probably the isles of the Aegean Sea, which were conquered by Darius Hystaspes.

2. *The book of the chronicles . . . of Media and Persia?* The Persians have ever been remarkable for keeping exact chronicles of all public events.

3. *Was next unto king Ahasuerus.* He was his prime minister; and, under him, was the governor of the whole empire.

The Book of

JOB

This is the most singular book in the whole of the Sacred Code. Though written by the same inspiration, and in reference to the same end, the salvation of men, it is so different from every other book of the Bible that it seems to possess nothing in common with them, for even the language, in its construction, is dissimilar from that in the law, the prophets, and the historical books. Except the first two chapters and the last ten verses, which are merely prose, all the rest of the book is poetic; and is everywhere reducible to the hemistich form, in which all the other poetic books of the Bible are written. It is therefore properly called a poem; but whether it belongs to the dramatic or epic species has not been decided by learned men. Genuine poetry is like a mountain flood; it pours down, resistless, bursts all bounds, scoops out its own channel, carries woods and rocks before it, and spreads itself abroad, both deep and wide, over all the plain. Such, indeed, is the poetry which the reader will meet with in this singular and astonishing book.

As to the Book of Job, it is most evidently a poem, and a poem of the highest order; dealing in subjects the most grand and sublime; using imagery the most chaste and appropriate; described by language the most happy and energetic; conveying instruction, in both divine and human things, the most ennobling and useful; abounding in precepts the most pure and exalted, which are enforced by arguments the most strong and conclusive, and illustrated by examples the most natural and striking.

All these points will appear in the strongest light to every attentive reader of the book, and to such its great end will be answered. They will learn from it: that God has sway everywhere; that the wicked, though bearing rule for a time, can never be ultimately prosperous and happy; and that the righteous, though oppressed with sufferings and calamities, can never be forgotten by Him in whose hands are His saints, and with whom their lives are precious; that in this world neither are the wicked ultimately punished nor the righteous ultimately rewarded; that God's judgments are a great deep, and His ways past finding out; but the issues of all are to the glory of His wisdom and grace, and to the eternal happiness of those who trust in Him. This is the grand design of the book.

CHAPTER 1

Character of Job, 1. His family, 2. His substance, 3. Care of his family, 4-5. Satan accuses him to God as a selfish person, who served God only for the hope of secular rewards, 6-11. Satan is permitted to strip him of all his children and property, 12-19. Job's remarkable resignation and patience, 20-22.

1. *In the land of Uz.* This country was situated in Idumea, or the land of Edom, in Arabia Petraea, of which it comprised a very large district. *Whose name was Job.* The original is *Aiyob.* From the Vulgate we borrow *Job,* not very dissimilar from the *Iob* of the Septuagint. The name signifies "sorrowful," or "he that weeps." *Perfect and upright.* "Complete" as to his mind and heart, and "straight" or "correct" as to his moral deportment. *Feared God.* Had Him in continual reverence. *Eschewed evil.* Departing from or avoiding evil. We have the word "eschew" from the old French *eschever,* which signifies "to avoid."

3. *His substance also was seven thousand sheep.* A thousand, says the Chaldee, for each of his sons. *Three thousand camels,* a thousand for each of his daughters. *Five hundred yoke of oxen* for himself. And *five hundred she asses* for his wife. Thus the Targum divides the substance of this eminent man. *A very great household.* "A very great estate." The word *abuddah* refers chiefly to husbandry, including all manner of labor in the field, with cattle, and every description of servants. *The greatest of all the men of the east.* He was more eminent than any other person in that region in wisdom, wealth, and piety.

4. *Feasted in their houses, every one his day.* It is likely that a birthday festival is here intended. When the birthday of one arrived, he invited his brothers and sisters to feast with him; and each observed the same custom.

5. *When the days of their feasting were gone about.* At the conclusion of the year, when the birthday of each had been celebrated, the pious father appears to have gathered them all together, that the whole family might hold a feast to the Lord, offering burnt offerings in order to make an atonement for sins of all kinds, whether presumptuous or committed through ignorance. This we may consider as a general custom among the godly in those ancient times. *And cursed God in their hearts.* In this book, according to most interpreters, the verb *barach* signifies both to "bless" and to "curse"; and the noun *Elohim* signifies the true God, false gods, and great or mighty. The reason why Job offered the burnt offerings appears to have been this: In a country where idolatry flourished, he thought it possible that his children might, in their festivity, have given way to idolatrous thoughts, or done something prescribed by idolatrous rites; and therefore the words may be rendered thus: "It may be that my children have blessed the gods in their hearts."

6. *There was a day when the sons of God.* All the versions, and indeed all the critics, are puzzled with the phrase *sons of God; beney haelohim,* literally, "sons of the God," or "sons of the gods." The Vulgate has simply "sons of God." The Septuagint, "the angels of God." But what are we to make of this whole account? Expositions are endless. That of Mr. Peters appears to me to be at once the most simple and the most judicious: The Scripture speaks of God after the manner of men. As kings, therefore, transact their most important affairs in a solemn council or assembly, so God is pleased to represent himself as having His council likewise, and as passing the decrees of His providence in an assembly of His holy angels. We have here, in the case of Job, the same grand assembly held as was before in that of Ahab, I Kings xxii. *And Satan came also.* This word *also* is emphatic in the original, *hassatan,* "the Satan," or "the adversary." St. Peter, 1st Epist., chap. v, v. 8, plainly refers to this place; and fully proves that *hassatan,* which he literally translates "the adversary," is no other than "the devil," or chief of bad demons, which he adds to others by way of explanation. There are many demons mentioned in Scripture; but the word "Satan" or "devil" is never found in the originals of the Old and New Testaments in the plural number. Hence we reasonably infer that all evil spirits are under the government of one chief, the devil, who is more powerful and more wicked than the rest.

7. *From going to and fro in the earth.* The translation of the Septuagint is curious: "Having gone round the earth, and walked over all that is under heaven, I am come hither." St. Peter, as has been already stated, v. 8, refers to this: "Be sober, be vigilant; for your adversary the devil, as a roaring lion, walketh about, seeking whom he may devour."

8. *Hast thou considered my servant Job?* Literally, "Hast thou placed thy heart on My servant Job?" Hast thou viewed his conduct with attention, whilst thou wert roaming about, seeking whom thou mightest devour?

9. *Doth Job fear God for nought?* Thou hast made it his interest to be exemplary in his conduct. For this assertion Satan gives his reasons in what immediately follows.

10. *Hast not thou made an hedge about him?* Thou hast fortified him with spikes and spears. Thou hast defended him as by an unapproachable hedge. He is an object of Thy peculiar care, and is not exposed to the common trials of life,

11. *But put forth thine hand.* Shoot the dart of poverty and affliction against him. *And he will curse thee to thy face.* "If he will not bless Thee to Thy appearances." He will bless Thee only in proportion to the temporal good Thou bestowest upon him, to the providential and gracious appearances or displays of Thy power in his behalf. The exact maxim of a great statesman Sir Robert Walpole: "Every man has his price."

13. *There was a day.* It no doubt refers to one of those birthday festivals mentioned before.

14. *The asses feeding beside them.* The she-asses, which appear to have been more domesticated, as of more worth and use than the others, for both their milk and their work.

15. *And the Sabeans fell.* The Vulgate alone understands this of a people. The Septuagint, Syriac, and Arabic understand it as implying a marauding party.

16. *The fire of God is fallen.* Though *the fire of God* may mean a great, a tremendous fire, yet it is most natural to suppose lightning is meant; for as thunder was considered to be the voice of God, so lightning was the fire of God.

17. *The Chaldeans made out three bands.* The *Chaldeans* inhabited each side of the Euphrates near to Babylon, which was their capital. They were also mixed with the wandering Arabs, and lived like them on rapine. They divided themselves into *three bands,* in order the more speedily and effectually to encompass, collect, and drive off the 3,000 camels; probably they mounted the camels and rode off.

19. *A great wind from the wilderness.* Here was another proof of the influence of "the prince of the power of the air." What mischief might he not do with this tremendous agent, were he not constantly under the control of the Almighty! He seems to have directed four different currents, which, blowing against the four corners or sides of the house, crushed it together, and involved all within in one common ruin.

20. *Rent his mantle.* Tearing the garments, shaving or pulling off the hair of the head, throwing dust or ashes on the head, and sitting on the ground were acts by which immoderate grief was expressed. Job must have felt the bitterness of anguish when he was told that, in addition to the loss of all his property, he was deprived of his ten children by a violent death. *Worshipped.* Prostrated himself; lay all along upon the ground, with his face in the dust.

21. *Naked came I out of my mother's womb.* I had no earthly possessions when I came into the world; I cannot have less going out of it. *Naked shall I return thither.* As I came out of my mother's womb destitute of the earthly possessions, so shall I return there; i.e., to the earth on which he was now falling.

22. *In all this Job sinned not.* He did not give way to any action, passion, or expression offensive to his Maker. That Job lived after the giving of the law seems to me clear from many references to the rites and ceremonies instituted by Moses. In chap. i. 5, we are informed that he sanctified his children, and offered burnt offerings daily in the morning for each of them. This was a general ordinance of the law, as we may see, Lev. ix. 7.

Job appears to have thought that his children might have sinned through ignorance, or sinned privately; and it was consequently necessary to make the due sacrifices to God in order to prevent His wrath and their punishment; he therefore offered the burnt offering, which was prescribed by the law in cases of sins committed through ignorance. See the ordinances, Lev. iv. 1-35; v. 15-19, and particularly Num. xv. 24-29.

CHAPTER 2

The sons of God once more present themselves before Him; and Satan comes also, accusing Job as a person whose steadfastness would be soon shaken provided his body were to be subjected to sore afflictions, 1-5. He receives permission to afflict Job, and smites him with sore boils, 6-8. His wife reviles him, 9. His pious reproof, 10. His three friends come to visit and mourn with him.

3. *To destroy him without cause.* Thou wishedst Me to permit thee to destroy a man whose sins have not called for so heavy a judgment. The original word signifies to "swallow down" or "devour"; and this word Peter had no doubt in view in the place quoted on v. 7 of the preceding chapter: "Your adversary the devil, as a roaring lion, walketh about, seeking whom he may devour"—seeking whom he may swallow or gulp down.

4. *Skin for skin.* That is, A man will part with all he has in the world to save his life.

5. *He will curse thee to thy face.* Literally, "If he will not bless Thee to Thy face." See the note on chap. i. 11.

6. *But save his life.* His body thou shalt have permission to afflict, but against his life thou shalt have no power.

7. *Sore boils.* "With an evil inflammation." What this diabolical disorder was interpreters are not agreed. Some think it was the leprosy; and this is the reason why he dwelt by himself, and had his habitation in an unclean place, without the city, or in the open air; and the reason why his friends beheld him "afar off," v. 12, was because they knew that the disorder was infectious. His scraping himself with a potsherd indicates a disease accompanied with intolerable itching, one of the characteristics of smallpox.

9. *Then said his wife.* We translate *barech Elohim vamuth,* "Curse God, and die." The verb *barach* is supposed to include in it the ideas of cursing and blessing; but it is not clear that it has the former meaning in any part of the sacred writings, though we sometimes translate it so. Here it seems to be a strong irony. Job was exceedingly afflicted, and apparently dying through sore disease, yet his soul was filled with gratitude to God. His wife, destitute of the salvation which her husband possessed, gave him this ironical reproof. "Bless God, and die"— What! bless Him for His goodness while He is destroying all that thou hast! bless Him for His support while He is casting thee down and destroying thee! Bless on, and die.

10. *Thou speakest as one of the foolish.* Thou speakest like an infidel; like one who has no knowledge of God, of religion, or of a future state.

11. *Job's three friends.* The first was *Eliphaz the Temanite.* Eliphaz was one of the sons of Esau; and Teman, of Eliphaz, Gen. xxxvi. 10-11. Teman was a city of Edom, Jer. xlix. 7-20; Ezek. xxv. 13; Amos i. 11-12. *Bildad the Shuhite.*

Shuah was the son of Abraham by Keturah, and his posterity is reckoned among the Easterns. *Zophar the Naamathite.* He most probably came from the Naamah which was bordering upon the Edomites to the south and fell by lot to the tribe of Judah, Josh. xv. 21-41. These circumstances prove that Job must have dwelt in the land of Edom, and that all his friends dwelt in Arabia Petraea, or in the countries immediately adjacent. That some of those Eastern people were highly cultivated, we have at least indirect proof in the case of the Temanites, Jer. xlix. 7: "Concerning Edom, thus saith the Lord of hosts; Is wisdom no more in Teman? is counsel perished from the prudent? is their wisdom vanished?" It is evident that the inhabitants of those districts were celebrated for their knowledge, and the sayings of Job's three friends are proofs that their reputation for wisdom stood on a very solid foundation.

12. *They rent every one his mantle.* I have already had frequent occasions to point out and illustrate, by quotations from the ancients, the actions that were used in order to express profound grief; such as wrapping themselves in sackcloth, covering the face, strewing dust or ashes upon the head, sitting upon the bare ground, etc., etc.—significant actions which were in use among all nations.

13. *They sat down with him upon the ground seven days.* They were astonished at the unprecedented change which had taken place in the circumstances of this most eminent man; they could not reconcile his present situation with anything they had met with in the history of divine providence. The *seven days* mentioned here were the period appointed for mourning. The Israelites mourned for Jacob seven days, Gen. l. 10. The men of Jabesh mourned so long for the death of Saul, 1 Sam. xxxi. 13; 1 Chron. x. 12. And Ezekiel sat on the ground with the captives at Chebar, and mourned with and for them seven days, Ezek. iii. 15. The wise son of Sirach says, "Seven days do men mourn for him that is dead," Ecclus. xxii. 12. So calamitous was the state of Job that they considered him as a dead man, and went through the prescribed period of mourning for him. *They saw that his grief was very great.* This is the reason why they did not speak to him. They believed him to be suffering for heavy crimes and, seeing him suffer so much, they were not willing to add to his distresses by invectives or reproach. Job himself first broke silence.

CHAPTER 3

Job curses the day of his birth, and regrets that he ever saw the light, 1-12. Describes the empire of death and its inhabitants, 13-19. Regrets that he is appointed to live in the midst of sorrows, for the calamities which he feared had overtaken him, 20-26.

1. *After this opened Job his mouth.* After the seven days' mourning was over, there being no prospect of relief, Job is represented as thus cursing the day of his birth. Here the poetic part of the book begins. *Cursed his day.* That is, the day of his birth. We find a similar execration to this in Jeremiah, chap. xx. 14-18, and in other places; which, by the way, are no proofs that the one borrowed from the other, but that this was the common mode of Asiatic thinking, speaking, and feeling on such occasions.

3. *There is a man child conceived.* The word

harah signifies to "conceive"; yet here, it seems, it should be taken in the sense of being born, as it is perfectly unlikely that the night of conception should be either distinctly known or published.

4. *Let that day be darkness.* The meaning is exactly the same with our expression, "Let it be blotted out of the calendar." *Let not God regard it from above.* "Let Him not require it"—let Him not consider it essential to the completion of the days of the year; and therefore he adds, *neither let the light shine upon it.* If it must be a part of duration, let it not be distinguished by the light of the sun.

5. *Let darkness and the shadow of death stain it.* "Pollute or avenge it," from *gaal,* to "vindicate, avenge"; hence *goel,* the nearest of kin, whose right it was to redeem an inheritance, and avenge the death of his relative by slaying the murderer. Let this day be pursued, overtaken, and destroyed. *Let a cloud dwell upon it.* "Let the thickest clouds have there their dwelling-place." *Let the blackness of the day terrify it.* Leaving out the semicolon, we had better translate the whole clause thus: "Let the thickest cloud have its dwelling-place upon it, and let the bitterness of a day fill it with terror."

6. *As for that night, let darkness seize upon it.* I think the Targum has hit the sense of this whole berse: "Let darkness seize upon that night; let it not be reckoned among the annual festivals; in the number of the months of the calendar let it not be computed."

7. *Lo, let that night be solitary.* "Let that night be grievous, oppressive, as destitute of good as a bare rock is of verdure." *Let no joyful voice come therein.* The word *renanah* signifies any brisk movement, such as the vibration of the rays of light, or the brisk modulation of the voice in a cheerful ditty.

8. *Let them curse it that curse the day.* "Let them curse it who detest the day; them who are ready to raise up the leviathan." That is, Let them curse my birthday who hate daylight, such as adulterers, murderers, thieves, and banditti, for whose practices the night is more convenient; and let them curse it who, being like me weary of life, are desperate enough to provoke the leviathan, the crocodile, to tear them to pieces.

9. *Let the stars of the twilight thereof.* The stars of the twilight may here refer to the planets Venus, Jupiter, Mars, and Mercury, as well as to the brighter fixed stars. *Let it look for light.* The darkness is represented as waiting for the lustre of the evening star, but is disappointed; and then for the dawn, but equally in vain.

12. *Why did the knees prevent me?* Why was I dandled on the knees? Why was I nourished by *the breasts?*

13. *For now should I have lain still.* In that case I had been insensible; *quiet*—without these overwhelming agitations; *slept*—unconscious of evil; *been at rest*—been out of the reach of calamity and sorrow.

14. *With kings and counsellors of the earth.* These mighty agitators of the world are at rest in their graves, after the lives of commotion which they have led among men, most of whom indeed have been the troublers of the peace of the globe. *Which built desolate places.* Who erect mausoleums, funeral monuments, sepul-

chral pyramids to keep their names from perishing, while their bodies are turned to corruption.

15. *Or with princes that had gold.* Chief or mighty men who got gold in abundance, filled their houses with silver, left all behind, and had nothing reserved for themselves but the empty places which they had made for their last dwelling, and where their dust now sleeps, devoid of care, painful journeys, and anxious expectations.

16. *Or as a hidden untimely birth.* An early miscarriage, which was scarcely perceptible by the parent herself; and in this case he *had not been*—he had never had the distinguishable form of a human being.

17. *There the wicked cease.* In the grave the oppressors of men cease from irritating, harassing, and distressing their fellow creatures and dependents. *And there the weary be at rest.* Those who were worn out with the cruelties and tyrannies of the above.

18. *The prisoners rest together.* Those who were slaves, feeling all the troubles, and scarcely tasting any of the pleasures of life, are quiet in the grave together; and the voice of the oppressor, the hard, unrelenting taskmaster, which was more terrible than death, is heard no more.

19. *The small and great are there.* All sorts and conditions of men are equally blended in the grave, and ultimately reduced to one common dust; and between the bond and free there is no difference.

20. *Wherefore is light given?* Why is life granted to him who is incapable of enjoying it, or of performing its functions?

21. *Which long for death.* They look to it as the end of all their miseries, and long more for a separation from life than those who love gold do for a rich mine.

22. *Which rejoice exceedingly.* L i t e r a l l y, "They rejoice with joy, and exult when they find the grave."

23. *To a man whose way is hid.* Who knows not what is before him in either world, but is full of fears and trembling concerning both. *God hath hedged in.* Leaving him no way to escape, and not permitting him to see one step before him. There is an exact parallel to this passage in Lam. iii. 7, 9: "He hath hedged me about, that I cannot get out . . . He hath inclosed my ways with hewn stone."

24. *For my sighing cometh.* Some think that this refers to the ulcerated state of Job's body, mouth, hands, etc. He longed for food, but was not able to lift it to his mouth with his hands, nor masticate it when brought thither. But perhaps it is most natural to suppose that he means his sighing took away all appetite, and served him in place of meat. There is the same thought in Ps. xlii. 3: "My tears have been my meat day and night." *My roarings are poured out.* My lamentations are like the noise of the murmuring stream, or the dashings of the overswollen torrent.

25. *For the thing which I greatly feared.* Literally, "the fear that I feared"; or, "I feared a fear," as in the margin. While I was in prosperity I thought adversity might come, and I had a dread of it. I feared the loss of my family and my property, and both have occurred.

26. *I was not in safety.* If this verse be read interrogatively, it will give a good and easy sense: "Was I not in safety? Had I not rest? Was I not in comfort? Yet trouble came."

CHAPTER 4

Eliphaz answers, and accuses Job of impatience, and of despondence in the time of adversity, 1-6; asserts that no innocent man ever perished, and that the wicked are afflicted for their sins, 7-11; relates a vision that he had, 12-16, and what was said to him on the occasion, 17-21.

1. *Then Eliphaz the Temanite answered.* For seven days this person and his two friends had observed a profound silence, being awed and confounded at the sight of Job's unprecedented affliction. Having now sufficiently contemplated his afflicted state, and heard his bitter complaint, forgetting that he came as a comforter, and not as a reprover, he loses the feeling of the friend in the haughtiness of the censor, endeavoring to strip him of his only consolation by insinuating that, if his ways had been upright, he would not have been abandoned to such distress and affliction, and if his heart possessed that righteousness of which he boasted, he would not have been so suddenly cast down by adversity.

2. *If we assay to commune with thee.* As if he had said, Should I and my friends endeavor to reason with you ever so mildly, because we shall have many things to say by way of reprehension, you will be grieved and faint; and this we may reasonably infer from the manner in which you bear your present afflictions. Yet as you have uttered words which are injurious to your Maker, who can forbear speaking? It is our duty to rise up on the part of God, though thereby we shall grieve him who is our friend. This was a plausible beginning, and certainly was far from being insincere.

5. *But now it is come upon thee.* Now it is your turn to suffer, and give an example of the efficacy of your own principles; but instead of this, behold, you faint. Either, therefore, you pretended to what you had not or you are not making a proper use of the principles which you recommended to others.

6. *Is not this thy fear?* I think Coverdale hits the true meaning: "Where is now thy feare of God, thy stedfastnesse, thy pacience, and the perfectnesse of thy life?" If these be genuine, surely there is no cause for all this complaint, vexation, and despair.

7. *Remember, I pray thee.* Recollect, if you can, a single instance where God abandoned an innocent man, or suffered him to perish. Did you ever hear of a case in which God abandoned a righteous man to destruction? Were you a righteous man, and innocent of all hidden crimes, would God abandon you thus to the malice of Satan? or let loose the plagues of affliction and adversity against you?

8. *They that plow iniquity.* A proverbial form of speech drawn from nature. Whatever seed a man sows in the ground, he reaps the same kind, for every seed produces its like. Thus Prov. xxii. 8: "He that soweth iniquity shall reap vanity." And Gal. vi. 7-8: "Be not deceived, God is not mocked: for whatsoever a man soweth, that shall he also reap. For he that soweth to his flesh shall of the flesh reap corruption; but he that soweth to the Spirit shall of the Spirit reap life everlasting." The same figure

is employed by the prophet Hosea, viii. 7: "They have sown the wind, and they shall reap the whirlwind"; and chap. x. 12-13: "Sow to yourselves in righteousness, reap in mercy . . . Ye have plowed wickedness, ye have reaped iniquity." The last sentence contains not only the same image but almost the same words as those used by Eliphaz.

9. *By the blast of God they perish.* As the noxious and parching east wind blasts and destroys vegetation, so the wicked perish under the indignation of the Almighty.

10. *The roaring of the lion.* By the roaring lion, fierce lion, old lion, stout lion, and lion's whelps, tyrannous rulers of all kinds are intended. The design of Eliphaz in using these figures is to show that even those who are possessed of the greatest authority and power—the kings, rulers, and princes of the earth—when they become wicked and oppressive to their subjects are cast down, broken to pieces, and destroyed by the incensed justice of the Lord; and their *whelps,* their children and intended successors, scattered without possessions over the face of the earth.

11. *The old lion perisheth.* In this and the preceding verse the word *lion* occurs five times; and in the original the words are all different.

12. *Now a thing was secretly brought to me.* To give himself the more authority, he professes to have received a vision from God, by which he was taught the secret of the divine dispensations in providence, and a confirmation of the doctrine which he was now stating to Job, and which he applied in a different way to what was designed in the divine communication. *Mine ear received a little thereof.* Mr. Good translates, "And mine ear received a whisper along with it."

18. *Behold, he put no trust in his servants.* This verse is generally understood to refer to the fall of angels; for there were some of those heavenly beings who "kept not their first estate" and are "reserved in . . . chains under darkness unto the judgment of the great day," Jude 6. *And his angels he charged with folly.* Not "chargeth," as many quote the passage. He *charged* those with folly who kept not their first estate. It does not appear that He is charging the others in the same way, who continue steadfast.

19. *How much less?* Rather, with the Vulgate, "How much more?" If angels may be unstable, how can man arrogate stability to himself, who dwells in an earthly tabernacle, and who must shortly return to dust? *Crushed before the moth.* The slightest accident oftentimes destroys. "A fly, a grapestone, or a hair can kill."

20. *They are destroyed from morning to evening.* In almost every moment of time some human being comes into the world, and someone departs from it. Thus are they *destroyed from morning to evening. They perish for ever.* They "pass by"; they "go out of sight"; they moulder with the dust, and are soon forgotten.

21. *Doth not their excellency . . . go away?* Personal beauty, corporeal strength, powerful eloquence, and various mental endowments pass away, or are "plucked up by the roots"; they are no more seen or heard among men, and their memory soon perisheth. *They die, even without wisdom.* If wisdom means "the pursuit of the best end, by the most legitimate and appropriate means," the great mass of mankind

appear to perish without it. But, if we consider the subject more closely, we shall find that all men die in a state of comparative ignorance. With all our boasted science and arts, how little do we know!

CHAPTER 5

Eliphaz proceeds to show that the wicked are always punished by the justice of God, though they may appear to flourish for a time, 1-8; extols the providence of God, by which the counsels of the wicked are brought to naught, and the poor fed and supported, 9-16; shows the blessedness of being corrected by God, in the excellent fruits that result from it; and exhorts Job to patience and submission, with the promise of all secular prosperity, and a happy death in a mature and comfortable old age, 17-27.

1. *Call now, if there be any.* This appears to be a strong irony. From whom among those whose foundations are in the dust, and who are crushed before the moth, canst thou expect succor? *To which of the saints wilt thou turn?* To whom among the *holy ones (kedoshim)* or among those who are equally dependent on divine support with thyself, and can do no good but as influenced and directed by God, canst thou turn for help?

2. *For wrath killeth the foolish man.* "Foolish," "silly," and "simple," are epithets given by Solomon to sinners and transgressors of all kinds. Such parallelisms have afforded a presumptive argument that Solomon was the author of this book. The words of Eliphaz may be considered as a sort of maxim, which the wisdom and experience of ages had served to establish; viz., The wrath of God is manifested only against the wicked and impious; and if you were not such, God would not thus contend with you.

3. *I have seen the foolish taking root.* I have seen wicked men for a time in prosperity, and becoming established in the earth; but I well knew, from God's manner of dealing with men, that they must soon be blasted. I even ventured to pronounce their doom; for I knew that, in the order of God's providence, that was inevitable.

4. *His children are far from safety.* His posterity shall not continue in prosperity. "Ill gotten, ill spent"; whatever is got by wrong must have God's curse on it. *They are crushed in the gate.* There is reference here to a custom which I have often had occasion to notice: viz., that in the Eastern countries the courthouse, or tribunal of justice, was at the gate of the city; here the magistrates attended, and hither the plaintiff and defendant came for justice.

5. *Whose harvest.* Their possessions, because acquired by unjust means, shall not be under the protection of God's providence; He shall abandon them to be pillaged and destroyed by the wandering, half-starved hordes of the desert banditti. *The robber swalloweth up.* Or, more properly, the *thirsty,* as is plain from their "swallowing up" or "gulping down"; opposed to the "hungry" or half-starved, mentioned in the preceding clause. The hungry shall eat up their grain, and the thirsty shall drink down their wine and oil, here termed their "strength" or "power," for the most obvious reasons.

6. *Affliction cometh not forth of the dust.* If there were not an adequate cause, you could not be so grievously afflicted. *Spring out of the ground.* It is not from mere natural causes that affliction and trouble come; God's justice inflicts them upon offending man.

7. *Yet man is born unto trouble.* "To labour." He must toil and be careful; and if in the course of his labor he meet with trials and difficulties, he should rise superior to them, and not sink as you do. *As the sparks fly upward.* "And the sons of the coal lift up their flight," or "dart upwards." And who are the sons of the coal? Are they not bold, intrepid, ardent, fearless men, who rise superior to all their trials; combat what are termed chance and occurrence; succumb under no difficulties; and rise superior to time, tide, fate, and fortune?

8. *I would seek unto God.* Were I in your place, instead of wasting my time, and irritating my soul with useless complaints, I would apply to my Maker, and, if conscious of my innocence, would confidently commit my cause to Him.

9. *Which doeth great things.* No work, however complicated, is too deep for His counsel to plan; none, however stupendous, is too great for His power to execute. He who is upright is always safe in referring his cause to God, and trusting in Him.

11. *To set up on high those that be low.* He so distributes His providential blessings without partiality that the land of the poor man is as well sunned and watered as that of the rich, so that he is thus set upon a level with the lords of the soil.

13. *He taketh the wise in their own craftiness.* So counterworks them as to cause their feet to be taken in their own snares, and their evil dealings to fall on their own pate.

14. *They meet with darkness in the daytime.* They act in noonday as if the sun were extinct, and their eyes put out.

16. *So the poor.* He who is made "thin," who is wasted, extenuated; *hath hope*—he sees what God is accustomed to do, and he expects a repetition of gracious dealings in his own behalf; and because God deals thus with those who trust in Him, therefore the mouth of impiety is stopped.

17. *Behold, happy is the man.* See Heb. xii. 5; Jas. i. 12; and Prov. iii. 12.

18. *For he maketh sore, and bindeth up.* Thus nervously rendered by Coverdale, "For though he make a wounde, he giveth a medicyne agayne; though he smyte, his hande maketh whole agayne."

19. *He shall deliver thee in six troubles.* The numbers *six* and *seven* are put here for "many."

21. *Thou shalt be hid from the scourge of the tongue.* Perhaps no evil is more dreadful than the *scourge of the tongue*: evil speaking, detraction, backbiting, calumny, slander, talebearing, whispering, and scandalizing are some of the terms which we use when endeavoring to express the baleful influence and effects of that member, which is a "world of fire," kindled from the nethermost hell. The Scripture abounds with invectives and execrations against it. See Ps. xxxi. 20; lii. 2-4; Prov. xii. 18; xiv. 3; Jas. iii. 5-8.

23. *Thou shalt be in league with the stones of the field.* Coverdale translates the verse thus: "But the castels in the londe shall be confederate with the, And the beastes of the felde shall give the peace."

24. *Thou shalt know.* You shall be so fully satisfied of the friendly disposition of all your neighbors that you shall rest secure in your bed, and not be afraid of any danger, though sleeping in your "tent" in the field; and when you return from your country excursions, you shall find that your habitation has been preserved in peace and prosperity, and that you have "made no mistake" in your trust, in your confidence, or in your confederates.

The word *thy tabernacle* means simply a tent, or movable dwelling, composed of poles, pins, and cloth, or skin, to be pitched anywhere in a few moments, and struck again with the same ease. The word which we properly translate *thy habitation* signifies solid, permanent dwelling place. As to *techeta*, which we translate *thou . . . shalt not sin*, it comes from *chata*, to "err," to "mistake," to "miss the mark," hence to sin. And it is very likely, from the connection above, that to "mistake" or "err" is its meaning in this place. I need not add that the Arab chiefs, who had their castles or strongholds, frequently in their country excursions lodged in tents in the open fields; and that on such occasions a hostile neighbor sometimes took advantage of their absence, attacked and pillaged their houses, and carried off their families and household.

26. *Thou shalt come to thy grave.* You shall not die before your time; you shall depart from life like a full-fed guest, happy in what you have known, and in what you have enjoyed. *Like as a shock of corn.* You shall completely run through the round of the spring, summer, autumn, and winter of life; and you shall be buried like a wholesome seed in the earth; from which you shall again rise up into an eternal spring!

27. *Lo this, we have searched it.* What I have told you is the sum of our wisdom and experience on these important points. These are established maxims, which universal experience supports. *Know*—understand, and reduce them to practice *for thy good.* Thus ends Eliphaz, the Temanite, "full of wise saws and ancient instances"; but he miserably perverted them in his application of them to Job's case and character. They contain, however, many wholesome truths, of which the wise in heart may make a very advantageous, practical use.

CHAPTER 6

Job answers, and vindicates himself; and shows that the great affliction which he suffered was the cause of his complaining, by which life was rendered burdensome to him, 1-13. He complains that, whereas he expected consolation from his friends, he had received nothing but the bitterest reproaches, on the assumed ground that he must be a wicked man, else God would not so grievously afflict him, 14-20. He shows them that they knew nothing of his case, and that they had no compassion, 21-23. And then entreats them, if they can, to show him in what he has offended, as he is ready to acknowledge and correct every trespass, 24-30.

2. *Oh that my grief were thoroughly weighed!* Job wished to be dealt with according to justice, as he was willing that his sins, if they could be proved, should be weighed against his sufferings; and if this could not be done, he wished that his sufferings and his complainings might be weighed together; and it would then be seen that, bitter as his complaint had been, it was little when compared with the distress which occasioned it.

3. *Heavier than the sand of the sea.* This includes two ideas: their number was too great to be counted; their weight was too great to be estimated.

4. *The arrows of the Almighty.* There is an evident reference here to wounds inflicted by poisoned arrows; and to the burning fever occasioned by such wounds, producing such an intense, parching thirst as to dry up all the moisture in the system, stop all the salivary ducts, thicken and inflame the blood, induce putrescency, and terminate in raging mania, producing the most terrifying images, from which the patient is relieved only by death.

5. *Doth the wild ass?* This meaning of Job appears to be this: You condemn me for complaining; do I complain without a cause? The wild ass will not bray, and the ox will not low, unless in want.

8. *Oh that I might have!* As Job had no hope that he should ever be redeemed from his present helpless state, he earnestly begs God to shorten it by taking away his life.

9. *Let loose his hand.* A metaphor taken from an archer drawing his arrow to the head, and then loosing his hold, that the arrow may fly to the mark.

10. *Then should I yet have comfort.* The expectation that He will speedily make an end of me would cause me to rejoice with great joy. *I would harden myself in sorrow.* To know that I should shortly have an end put to my miseries would cause me to endure the present with determinate resolution. *Let him not spare*—let Him use whatever means he chooses, for I will not resist His decree; He is *holy,* and His decrees must be just.

11. *What is my strength?* I can never suppose that my strength will be restored; and, were that possible, have I any comfortable prospect of a happy termination of my life? Had I any prospect of future happiness, I might well bear my present ills; but the state of my body and the state of my circumstances preclude all hope.

12. *Is my strength the strength of stones?* I am neither a rock, nor is my flesh brass, that I can endure all these calamities. This is a proverbial saying, and exists in all countries.

13. *Is not my help in me?* My help is all in myself; and, alas! that is perfect weakness: "and my subsistence," all that is real, stable, and permanent, is *driven quite from me.* My friends have forsaken me, and I am abandoned to myself; my property is all taken away, and I have no resources left. I believe Job neither said, nor intended to say, as some interpreters have it, "Reason is utterly driven from me." Surely there is no mark in this chapter of his being deranged, or at all impaired in his intellect.

14. *To him that is afflicted pity should be shewed from his friend; but he forsaketh the fear of the Almighty.* The Vulgate gives a better sense, "He who takes away mercy from his friend, hath cast off the fear of the Lord."

15. *Have dealt deceitfully as a brook.* There is probably an allusion here to those land torrents which make a sudden appearance, and as suddenly vanish, being produced by the rains that fall upon the mountains during the rainy season, and are soon absorbed by the thirsty sands over which they run. At first they seem to promise a permanent stream, and are noticed with delight by the people, who fill their tanks or reservoirs from their waters; but sometimes they are so large and rapid as to carry everything before them—and then suddenly fail, so that there is no time to fill the tanks. The approach of Job's friends promised much of sympathy and compassion; his expectations were raised, but their conduct soon convinced him that they were physicians of no value.

16. *Blackish by reason of the ice.* He represents the waters as being sometimes suddenly frozen, their foam being turned into the semblance of snow. When the heat comes, they are speedily liquefied; and the evaporation is so strong from the heat, and the absorption so powerful from the sand, that they soon disappear.

18. *The paths of their way.* They sometimes forsake their ancient channels; and, growing smaller and smaller from being divided into numerous streams, *they go to nothing, and perish*—are at last utterly lost in the sands.

19-20. *The troops of Tema looked.* The caravans coming from Tema are represented as arriving at those places where it was well known torrents did descend from the mountains, and they were full of expectation that here they could not only slake their thirst, but fill their waterskins; but when they arrive, they find the waters totally dissipated and lost. In vain did the caravans of Sheba wait for them; they did not reappear; and they *were confounded because they had hoped* to find here refreshment and rest.

21. *For now ye are nothing.* Ye are just to me as those deceitful torrents to the caravans of Tema and Sheba. *Ye see my casting down.* Ye see that I have been hurried from my eminence into want and misery, as the flood from the top of the mountains, which is divided, evaporated, and lost in the desert. *And are afraid.* Ye are terrified at the calamity that has come upon me; and instead of drawing near to comfort me, ye start back at my appearance.

22. *Did I say, Bring unto me?* Why do you stand aloof? Have I asked you to bring me any presents? or to supply my wants out of your stores?

23. *Or, Deliver me?* Did I send to you to come and avenge me of the destroyers of my property, or to rescue my substance out of the hands of my enemies?

24. *Teach me.* Show me where I am mistaken. Bring proper arguments to convince me of my errors, and you will soon find that I shall gladly receive your counsels, and abandon the errors of which I may be convicted.

25. *How forcible are right words!* A well-constructed argument, that has truth for its basis, is irresistible. *But what doth your arguing reprove?* Your reasoning is defective, because your premises are false; and your conclusions prove nothing, because of the falsity of the premises whence they are drawn. The last clause, literally rendered, is, "What reproof, in a reproof from you?"

26. *Do ye imagine to reprove words?* Is it some expressions which in my hurry, and under the pressure of unprecedented affliction, I have uttered, that ye catch at? You can find no flaw in my conduct; would ye make me an offender for a word? Why endeavor to take such advantage of a man who complains in the bitterness of his heart, through despair of life and happiness?

27. *Ye overwhelm the fatherless.* Ye see that I am as destitute as the most miserable orphan;

would ye overwhelm such a one? And would you *dig a pit for your friend*—do ye lay wait for me, and endeavor to entangle me in my talk?

28. *Look upon me.* View me; consider my circumstances; compare my words; and you must be convinced that I have spoken nothing but truth.

29. *Return, I pray you.* Reconsider the whole subject. Do not be offended. *My righteousness is in it*—my argumentation is a sufficient proof of my innocence.

30. *Is there iniquity in my tongue?* Am I not an honest man? And if in my haste my tongue had uttered falsity, would not my conscience discern it? And do you think that such a man as your friend is would defend what he knew to be wrong?

CHAPTER 7

Job continues to deplore his helpless and afflicted state, 1-6. He expostulates with God concerning his afflictions, 7-12; describes the disturbed state of his mind by visions in the night season; abhors life, 13-16; and, showing that he is unworthy of the notice of God, begs pardon and respite, 17-21.

1. *Is there not an appointed time to man?* The Hebrew literal rendering is as follows: "Is there not a warfare to miserable man upon the earth?" Coverdale: "Is not the life off man upon earth a very batayle?"

2. *Earnestly desireth the shadow.* As a man who labors hard in the heat of the day earnestly desires to get under a shade, or wishes for the long evening shadows, that he may rest from his labor, get his day's wages, retire to his food, and then go to rest.

3. *So am I made to possess.* But night is no relief to me; it is only a continuance of my anxiety and labor. I am like the hireling; I have my appointed labor for the day. I am like the soldier harassed by the enemy; I am obliged to be continually on the watch, always on the look-out, with scarcely any rest.

4. *When I lie down.* I have so little rest that when I do lie down I long for the return of the light, that I may rise. Nothing can better depict the state of a man under continual afflictions, which afford him no respite, his days and his nights being spent in constant anguish, utterly unable to be in any one posture, so that he is continually changing his position in his bed, finding ease nowhere; thus, as himself expresses it, he is *full of tossings.*

5. *My flesh is clothed with worms.* This is perhaps no figure, but is literally true. *Clods of dust.* I suppose Job to allude to those incrustations of dried pus which are formed on the tops of pustules in a state of decay, such as the scales which fall from the pustules of the smallpox, when the patient becomes convalescent.

9. *As the cloud is consumed.* As the cloud is dissipated, so is the breath of those that go down to the grave. As that cloud shall never return, so shall it be with the dead; they return no more to sojourn with the living.

10. *He shall return no more to his house, neither shall his place know him any more.* He does not mean that he shall be annihilated, but that he shall nevermore become an inhabitant of the earth.

11. *Therefore I will not refrain.* All is hope-less; I will therefore indulge myself in complaining.

12. *Am I a sea, or a whale?* Job was hedged about and shut in with insuperable difficulties of various kinds. He was entangled as a wild beast in a net; the more he struggled, the more he lost his strength, and the less probability there was of his being extricated from his present situation. The *sea* is shut in with barriers, over which it cannot pass; Jer. v. 22; Ps. civ. 9; chap. xxxviii. 8.

14. *Thou scarest me with dreams.* There is no doubt that Satan was permitted to haunt his imagination with dreadful dreams and terrific appearances, so that, as soon as he fell asleep, he was suddenly roused and alarmed by those appalling images. He needed rest by sleep, but was afraid to close his eyes because of the horrid images which were presented to his imagination. Could there be a state more deplorable than this?

16. *I loathe it: I would not live alway.* Life, in such instances, is hateful to me; and though I wished for long life, yet if length of days were offered to me with the sufferings which I now undergo, I would despise the offer and spurn the boon.

17. *What is man, that thou shouldest magnify him? and that thou shouldest set thine heart upon him?* Two different ideas have been drawn from these words:

(a) Man is not worth Thy notice; why therefore dost Thou contend with him?

(b) How astonishing is Thy kindness that Thou shouldest fix Thy heart—Thy strongest affections—on such a poor, base, vile, impotent creature as man (*enosh*), that Thou shouldest so highly exalt him beyond all other creatures, and mark him with the most particular notice of Thy providence and grace!

The paraphrase of Calmet is as follows: "Does man, such as he at present is, merit thy attention! What is man that God should make it his business to examine, try, prove, and afflict him? Is it not doing him too much honour to think thus seriously about him? O Lord! I am not worthy that thou shouldest concern thyself about me!"

19. *Till I swallow down my spittle?* This is a proverbial expression, and exists among the Arabs to the present day, the very language being nearly the same. It signifies the same as, *Let me draw my breath; give me a moment's space; let me have even the twinkling of an eye.* I am urged by my sufferings to continue my complaint; but my strength is exhausted, my *mouth dry* with speaking. Suspend my sufferings even for so short a space as is necessary to swallow my spittle, that my parched tongue may be moistened, so that I may renew my complaint.

20. *I have sinned; what shall I do?* Dr. Kennicott contends that these words are spoken to Eliphaz, and not to God, and would paraphrase them thus: "You say I must have been a sinner. What then? I have not sinned against thee, O thou spy upon mankind! Why hast thou set up me as a butt or mark to shoot at? Why am I become a burden unto thee? Why not rather overlook my transgression, and pass by mine iniquity? I am now sinking to the dust! Tomorrow, perhaps, I shall be sought in vain!" Others consider the address as made to God. Taken in this light, the sense is plain enough.

Those who suppose that the address is made to God translate the twentieth verse thus: "Be it that I have sinned, what injury can I do unto thee, O thou Observer of man? Why hast thou set me up as a mark for thee, and why am I made a burden to thee?"

21. *And why dost thou not pardon?* These words are spoken after the manner of men. If Thou have any design to save me, if I have sinned, why dost Thou not pardon my transgression, as Thou seest that I am a dying man; and tomorrow morning Thou mayest seek me to do me good, but in all probability I shall then be no more, and all Thy kind thoughts towards me shall be unavailing? If I have sinned, then why should not I have a part in that mercy that flows so freely to all mankind?

CHAPTER 8

Bildad answers, and reproves Job for his justifying himself, 1-2. Shows that God is just, and never punishes but for iniquity; and intimates that it was on account of their sins that his children were cut off, 3-4. States that, if Job would humble himself to the Almighty, provided he were innocent, his captivity would soon be turned, and his latter end be abundantly prosperous, 5-7. Appeals to the ancients for the truth of what he says; and draws examples from the vegetable world, to show how soon the wicked may be cut off, and the hope of the hypocrite perish, 8-19. Asserts that God never did cast off a perfect man nor help the wicked; and that, if Job be innocent, his end shall be crowned with prosperity, 20-22.

1. *Bildad the Shuhite.* Supposed to be a descendant of Shuah, one of the sons of Abraham, by Keturah, who dwelt in Arabia Deserta, called in Scripture the "east country." See Gen. xxv. 1-2, 6.

2. *How long wilt thou speak these things?* Will you still go on to charge God foolishly? Your heavy affliction proves that you are under His wrath; and His wrath, thus manifested, proves that it is for your sins that He punishes you. *Be like a strong wind?* Will you continue to "breathe forth a tempest of words?"

3. *Doth God pervert judgment?* God afflicts you; can He afflict you for naught? As He is just, His judgment is just; and He could not inflict punishment unless there be a cause.

4. *If thy children have sinned.* I know your children have been cut off by a terrible judgment; but was it not because by transgression they had filled up the measure of their iniquity?

5. *If thou wouldest seek unto God.* Though God has so severely afflicted you, and removed your children by a terrible judgment, yet if you will now humble yourself before Him, and implore His mercy, you shall be saved. He cut them off in their sins, but He spares you; and this is a proof that He waits to be gracious to you.

6. *If thou wert pure and upright.* Concerning your guilt there can be no doubt; for if you had been a holy man, and these calamities had occurred through accident, or merely by the malice of your enemies, would not God, long ere this, have manifested His power and justice in your behalf, punished your enemies, and restored you to affluence? *The habitation of thy righteousness.* Strongly ironical. If your house had been as a temple of God, in which His worship had been performed, and His commandments obeyed, would it now be in a state of ruin and desolation?

8. *Enquire . . . of the former age.* "Of the first age"; of the patriarchs.

9. *For we are but of yesterday, and know nothing.* The writer of this book probably had before his eyes these words of David, in his last prayer, 1 Chron. xxix. 15: "For we are strangers before thee, and sojourners, as were all our fathers: our days on the earth are as a shadow, and there is no expectation" (marg.)

10. *Shall not they teach thee?* Will you not treat their maxims with the utmost deference and respect? They *utter words out of their heart* —what they say is the fruit of long and careful experience.

11. *Can the rush grow?* The word *gome,* which we translate *rush,* is, without doubt, the Egyptian papyrus, on which the ancients wrote, and from which our paper derives its name. The Septuagint render *gome* by "papyrus," thus: "Can the papyrus flourish without water?" Their translation leaves no doubt concerning the meaning of the original. They were probably writing on the very substance in question, while making their translation. *Can the flag grow without water?* Parkhurst supposes that the word *achu,* which we render *flag,* is the same with that species of reed which Mr. Hasselquist found growing near the river Nile.

12. *Whilst it is yet in his greenness.* We do not know enough of the natural history of this plant to be able to discern the strength of this allusion; but we learn from it that, although this plant be very succulent, and grow to a great size, yet it is short-lived, and speedily withers; and this we may suppose to be in the dry season, or on the retreat of the waters of the Nile. However, "Soon ripe, soon rotten," is a maxim in horticulture.

13. *So are the paths.* The papyrus and the rush flourish while they have a plentiful supply of ooze and water; but take these away, and their prosperity is speedily at an end. So it is with the wicked and profane; their prosperity is of short duration, however great it may appear to be in the beginning. *The hypocrite's hope shall perish.* A *hypocrite,* or rather "profligate," has no inward religion, for his heart is not right with God; he has only hope, and that perishes when he gives up the ghost. This is the first place in which the word *hypocrite* occurs, or the noun *chaneph,* which rather conveys the idea of pollution and defilement than of hypocrisy. A hypocrite is one who only carries the mask of godliness, to serve secular purposes; who wishes to be taken for a religionist, though he is conscious he has no religion. Such a person cannot have hope of any good, because he knows he is insincere. But the person in the text has hope; therefore *hypocrite* cannot be the meaning of the original word. But all the vile, the polluted, and the profligate have hope; they hope to end their iniquities before they end life, and they hope to get at last to the kingdom of Heaven. *Hypocrite* is a very improper translation of the Hebrew.

14. *Whose hope shall be cut off.* Such persons, subdued by the strong habits of sin, hope on fruitlessly, till the last thread of the web of life is cut off from the beam; and then they find no more strength in their hope than is in the threads of the spider's web.

15. *He shall lean upon his house.* This is an allusion to the spider. When he suspects his web, here called his *house,* to be frail or unsure, he leans upon it in different parts, propping himself

on his hinder legs, and pulling with his fore claws, to see if all be safe. If he find any part of it injured, he immediately adds new cordage to that part, and attaches it strongly to the wall. When he finds all safe and strong, he retires into his hole at one corner, supposing himself to be in a state of complete security, when in a moment the *brush* sweeps away both himself, his house, and his confidence. The wicked, whose hope is in his temporal possessions, strengthens and keeps his house in repair, and thus leans on his earthly supports. In a moment, as in the case of the spider, his house is overwhelmed by the blast of God's judgments, and himself probably buried in its ruins.

16. *He is green before the sun.* This is another metaphor. The wicked is represented as a luxuriant plant, in a good soil, with all the advantages of a good situation; well exposed to the sun; the roots intervolving themselves with stones, so as to render the tree more stable. But suddenly a blast comes, and the tree begins to die.

18. *If he destroy him from his place.* Is not this a plain reference to the alienation of his inheritance? God destroys him from it; it becomes the property of another; and on his revisiting it, the place says, "I know thee not; I have never seen thee."

19. *Behold, this is the joy of his way.* A strong irony. Here is the issue of all his mirth, of his sports, games, and pastimes! *Out of the earth shall others grow.* As in the preceding case, when one plant or tree is blasted or cut down, another may be planted in the same place; so, when a spendthrift has run through his property, another possesses his inheritance.

20. *Behold, God will not cast away a perfect man.* This is another of the maxims of the ancients, which Bildad produces: "As sure as he will punish and root out the wicked, so surely will he defend and save the righteous."

21. *Till he fill thy mouth with laughing.* Perhaps it may be well to translate after Mr. Good, "Even yet may he fill thy mouth with laughter!" The two verses may be read as a prayer; and probably they were thus expressed by Bildad, who speaks with less virulence than his predecessor, though with equal positiveness in respect to the grand charge, viz., If you were not a sinner of no mean magnitude, God would not have inflicted such unprecedented calamities upon you.

CHAPTER 9

Job acknowledges God's justice and man's sinfulness, 1-3. Celebrates His almighty power as manifested in the earth and in the heavens, 4-10. Maintains that God afflicts the innocent as well as the wicked, without any respect to their works: and hath delivered the earth into the hands of the wicked, 11-24. Complains of his lot, and maintains his innocence, 25-35.

2. *I know it is so of a truth.* I acknowledge the general truth of the maxims you have advanced. God will not ultimately punish a righteous person, nor shall the wicked finally triumph; and though righteous before man, and truly sincere in my piety, yet I know, when compared with the immaculate holiness of God, all my righteousness is nothing.

3. *If he will contend with him.* God is so holy, and his law so strict, that if He will enter into judgment with His creatures, the most up-

right of them cannot be justified in His sight. *One of a thousand.* Of a thousand offenses of which he may be accused, he cannot vindicate himself in even one. How little that any man does, even in the way of righteousness, truth, and mercy, can stand the penetrating eye of a just and holy God, when all motives, feelings, and objects come to be scrutinized! In His sight, on this ground, no man living can be justified. Oh, how necessary to fallen, weak, miserable, imperfect, and sinful man is the doctrine of justification by faith, and sanctification through the Divine Spirit, by the sacrificial death and mediation of the Lord Jesus Christ!

4. *He is wise in heart, and mighty in strength.* By His infinite knowledge He searches out and sees all things, and by His almighty power He can punish all delinquencies. He that rebels against Him must be destroyed.

5. *Removeth the mountains, and they know not.* This seems to refer to earthquakes. By those strong convulsions, mountains, valleys, hills, even whole islands, are removed in an instant; and to this latter circumstance the words *they know not* most probably refer.

6. *The pillars thereof tremble.* This also refers to an earthquake, and to that tremulous motion which sometimes gives warning of the approaching catastrophe, and from which this violent convulsion of nature has received its name.

7. *Which commandeth the sun.* Obscures it either with clouds, with thick darkness, or with an eclipse. *Sealeth up the stars.* Like the contents of a letter, wrapped up and sealed, so that it cannot be read. Sometimes the heavens become as black as ebony, and no star, figure, or character in this great book of God can be read.

8. *And treadeth upon the waves.* This is a very majestic image. God not only walks upon the waters, but, when the sea runs mountains high, He steps from billow to billow in His almighty and essential majesty. There is a similar sentiment in David, Ps. xxix. 10: "The Lord sitteth upon the flood; yea, the Lord sitteth King for ever." But both are far outdone by the Psalmist, Ps. xviii. 9-15, and especially in these words, v. 10, "He did fly upon the wings of the wind."

9. *Which maketh Arcturus, Orion, and Pleiades, and the chambers of the south.* The original words are thus rendered by the Septuagint: "Who makes the Pleiades, and Hesperus, and Arcturus, and Orion, and the chambers of the south."

11. *Lo, he goeth by me, and I see him not.* He is incomprehensible in all His ways, and in all His works; and He must be so if He be God, and work as God; for His own nature and His operations are past finding out.

12. *He taketh away.* He never gives, but He is ever lending, and while the gift is useful or is improved, He permits it to remain; but when it becomes useless or is misused, He recalls it. *Who can hinder him?* Literally, "Who can cause Him to restore it?"

13. *If God will not withdraw his anger.* It is of no use to contend with God; He cannot be successfully resisted; all His opposers must perish.

14. *How much less shall I answer?* I cannot contend with my Maker. He is the Lawgiver and

the Judge. How shall I stand in judgment before Him?

15. *Though I were righteous.* Though clear of all the crimes, public and secret, of which you accuse me, yet I would not dare to stand before His immaculate holiness.

16. *If I had called, and he had answered.* These sentiments sufficiently confuted that slander of his friends, who said he was presumptuous, had not becoming notions of the majesty of God, and used blasphemous expressions against His sovereign authority.

17. *He breaketh me with a tempest.* The Targum, Syriac, and Arabic have this sense: "He powerfully smites even every hair of my head, and multiplies my wounds without cause." That is, There is no reason known to myself, or to any other man, why I should be thus most oppressively afflicted. It is, therefore, cruel and inconsequent to assert that I suffer for my crimes.

18. *He will not suffer me to take my breath.* I have no respite in my afflictions; I suffer continually in my body, and my mind is incessantly harassed.

19. *If I speak of strength, lo, he is strong.* Human wisdom, power, and influence avail nothing before Him. *Who shall set me a time?* "Who would be a witness for me?" or, Who would dare to appear in my behalf? Almost all the terms in this part of the speech of Job, from v. 11 to v. 24, are forensic or juridical, and are taken from legal processes and pleadings in their gates or courts of justice.

20. *If I justify myself.* God must have some reason for His conduct towards me. I therefore do not pretend to justify myself; the attempt to do it would be an insult to His majesty and justice. Though I am conscious of none of the crimes of which you accuse me, and know not why He contends with me, yet He must have some reason, and that reason He does not choose to explain.

24. *The earth is given into the hand of the wicked.* Is it not most evident that the worst men possess most of this world's goods, and that the righteous are scarcely ever in power or affluence? This was the case in Job's time; it is the case still. Therefore prosperity and adversity in this life are no marks of either God's approbation or His disapprobation. *He covereth the faces of the judges thereof.* Or, "The faces of its decisions he shall cover." God is often stated in Scripture as doing a thing which He only permits to be done. So He permits the eyes of judgment to be blinded, and hence false decisions. *Where, and who is he?* If God does not permit these things, who is it that orders them?

25. *Swifter than a post.* "Than a runner." The light-footed messenger or courier who carries messages from place to place. *They flee away.* The Chaldee says, "My days are swifter than the shadow of a flying bird."

26. *As the swift ships.* "Ships of desire," or "ships of Ebeh," says our margin; perhaps more correctly, "inflated ships," the sails bellying out with a fair brisk wind, tide favorable, and the vessels themselves lightly freighted.

27. *I will forget my complaint.* I will "forsake" or "forego" my complaining. *I will leave off my heaviness.* Vulgate, "I will change my coun-

tenance"—force myself to smile, and endeavor to assume the appearance of comfort.

29. *If I be wicked.* If I am the sinner you suppose me to be, in vain should I labor to counterfeit joy, and cease to complain of my sufferings.

30. *If I wash myself with snow water.* Supposed to have a more detergent quality than common water, and it was certainly preferred to common water by the ancients.

32. *For he is not a man, as I am.* I cannot contend with Him as with one of my fellows in a court of justice.

33. *Neither is there any daysman.* A "reprover," "arguer," or "umpire" between us. Daysman, in our law, means an arbitrator or umpire between party and party; instead of *lo yesh,* "there is not," fifteen of Kennicott's and De Rossi's MSS., with the Septuagint, Syriac, and Arabic, read *lu yesh,* "I wish there were"; or, "Oh, that there were!"

34. *Let him take his rod away.* As *shebet* signifies, not only *rod,* but also "sceptre" or the ensign of royalty, Job might here refer to God sitting in His majesty upon the judgment seat; and this sight so appalled Him that, filled with terror, he was unable to speak.

35. *But it is not so with me.* I am not in such circumstances as to plead with my Judge.

CHAPTER 10

Job is weary of life, and expostulates with God, 1-6. He appeals to God for his innocence; and pleads on the weakness of his frame, and the manner of his formation, 7-13. Complains of his sufferings, and prays for respite, 14-20. Describes the state of the dead, 21-22.

2. *Do not condemn me.* Let me not be afflicted in Thy wrath. *Shew me wherefore thou contendest.* If I am afflicted because of my sins, show me what that sin is. God never afflicts but for past sin, or to try His followers, or for the greater manifestation of His grace in their support and deliverance.

3. *Is it good unto thee?* Surely it can be no gratification to Thee to distress the children of men, as if Thou didst despise the work of Thy own hands. *And shine upon the counsel.* For by my afflictions the harsh judgments of the wicked will appear to be confirmed, viz., that God regards not His most fervent worshippers, and it is no benefit to lead a religious life.

4. *Hast thou eyes of flesh?* Dost Thou judge as *man* judges? Illustrated by the next clause, *Seest thou as man seeth?*

5. *Are thy days as the days of man? Enosh,* "wretched, miserable man." *Thy years as man's days? Gaber,* "the strong man." Thou art not short-lived, like man in his present imperfect state; nor can the years of the long-lived patriarchs be compared with Thine.

6. *That thou enquirest.* Is it becoming Thy infinite dignity to concern thyself so much with the affairs or transgressions of a despicable mortal? A word spoken in the heart of most sinners.

8. *Thine hands have made me.* Thou art well acquainted with human nature, for Thou art its Author. *And fashioned me together round about.* It is Thou who hast refined the materials out of which I have been formed, and modified them into that excellent symmetry and order in which they are now found, so that the union and har-

mony of the different parts (*yachad*) and their arrangement and completion (*sabib*) proclaim equally Thy wisdom, skill, power, and goodness. *Yet thou dost destroy me.* "And thou wilt swallow me up." Men generally care for and prize those works on which they have spent most time, skill, and pains: but, although Thou hast formed me with such incredible skill and labor, yet Thou art about to destroy me!

17. *Thou renewest thy witnesses.* In this speech of Job he is ever referring to trials in courts of judicature, and almost all his terms are forensic. Thou bringest witnesses in continual succession to confound and convict me. *Changes and war.* I am as if attacked by successive troops; one company being wearied, another succeeds to the attack, so that I am harassed by continual warfare.

CHAPTER 11

Zophar answers Job, and reproves him severely for his attempts to justify himself; charges him with secret iniquity, and contends that God inflicts less punishment on him than his iniquities deserve, 1-6. Shows the knowledge and perfections of God to be unsearchable, and that none can resist His power, 7-11. Warns him against vanity of mind, and exhorts him to repentance on the ground that his acceptance with God is still a possible case, and that his latter days may yet become happy and prosperous, 12-20.

1. *Zophar the Naamathite.* Of this man and his friends, see chap. ii. 11. He is the most inveterate of Job's accusers, and generally speaks without feeling or pity. In sour godliness he excelled all the rest. This chapter and the twentieth comprehend all that he said. He was too crooked to speak much in measured verse.

2. *Should not the multitude of words be answered?* Some translate, "To multiply words profiteth nothing." *And should a man full of talk be justified?* "A man of lips," a proper appellation for a great talker.

4. *My doctrine is pure.* "My assumptions."

10. *If he cut off.* Perhaps Zophar may refer to Job's former state, his losses and afflictions. *If he cut off,* as He has done, your children; *if he . . . shut up,* as He has done, yourself by this sore disease; or *gather together* hostile bands to invade your territories and carry away your property; *who can hinder him?*

11. *He knoweth vain men.* "Men of falsehood."

12. *For vain man would be wise.* The original is difficult and uncertain. *Though man be born like a wild ass's colt.* Man is full of self-conceit; and imagines himself born to act as he pleases, to roam at large, to be under no control, and to be accountable to none for his actions.

17. *Thine age shall be clearer than the noonday.* The rest of your life shall be unclouded prosperity.

18. *Yea, thou shalt dig.* I believe this neither refers to digging his grave nor to curiously investigating surrounding circumstances, but to the custom of digging for water in the places where they pitched their tents.

CHAPTER 12

Job reproves the boasting of his friends, and shows their uncharitableness towards himself, 1-5. Asserts that even the tabernacles of robbers prosper; and that, notwithstanding, God is the Governor of the world—a truth which is proclaimed by all parts of the creation whether animate or inanimate, and by the revolutions which take place in states, 6-25.

2. *No doubt but ye are the people.* Doubtless ye are the wisest men in the world; all wisdom is concentrated in you; and when ye die, there will no more be found on the face of the earth! This is a strong irony.

3. *I am not inferior to you.* I do not fall short of any of you in understanding, wisdom, learning, and experiece. *Who knoweth not such things as these?* All your boasted wisdom consists only in strings of proverbs which are in every person's mouth, and are no proof of wisdom and experience in them that use them.

16. *With him is strength and wisdom.* "Strength and sufficiency." Strength or power, springing from an exhaustless and infinite source of potency.

25. *They grope in the dark.* The writer seems to have had his eye on those words of Moses, Deut. xxviii. 28-29: "The Lord shall smite thee with madness, and blindness, and astonishment of heart: and thou shalt grope at noonday, as the blind gropeth in darkness."

CHAPTER 13

Job defends himself against the accusations of his friends, and accuses them of endeavoring to pervert truth, 1-8. Threatens them with God's judgments, 9-12. Begs some respite, and expresses strong confidence in God, 13-19. He pleads with God, and deplores his severe trials and sufferings, 20-28.

3. *Surely I would speak to the Almighty.* "Oh, that—I wish I could speak to the Almighty!" *I desire to reason with God.* He speaks here in reference to the proceedings in a court of justice. Ye pretend to be advocates for God, but ye are forgers of lies. Oh, that God himself would appear! Before Him I could soon prove my innocence of the evils with which ye charge me.

4. *Ye are forgers of lies.* Ye frame deceitful arguments; ye reason sophistically, and pervert truth and justice, in order to support your cause.

6. *Hear now my reasoning.* The speeches in this book are conceived as if delivered in a court of justice, different counsellors pleading against each other. Hence most of the terms are forensic.

12. *Your remembrances are like unto ashes.* Your memorable sayings are proverbs of dust.

14. *Wherefore do I take my flesh in my teeth?* A proverbial expression. I risk everything on the justice of my cause. "I put my life in my hand," 1 Sam. xxviii. 21.

15. *Though he slay me.* I have no dependence but God; I trust in Him alone. Should He even destroy my life by this affliction, yet will I hope that when He has tried me, I shall come forth as gold. In the common printed Hebrew text we have *lo ayachel,* "I will not hope"; but the Vulgate, Syriac, Arabic, and Chaldee have read "him," instead of "not." Our translators have followed the best reading.

22. *Then call thou.* Begin thou first to plead, and I will answer for myself; or I will first state and defend my own case, and then answer *thou* me.

23. *How many are mine iniquities?* What are the specific charges in this indictment? To say I must be a sinner to be thus afflicted is saying nothing; tell me what are the sins, and show me the proofs.

24. *Wherefore hidest thou thy face?* Why is it

that I no longer enjoy thy approbation? *Holdest me for thine enemy?* treatest me as if I were the vilest of sinners?

27. *Thou puttest my feet also in the stocks.* 'In a clog," such as was tied to the feet of slaves, to prevent them from running away.

CHAPTER 14

The shortness, misery, and sinfulness of man's life, 1-4. The unavoidable necessity of death, and the hope of a general resurrection, 5-15. Job deplores his own state, and the general wretchedness of man, 16-22.

1. *Man . . . born of a woman.* There is a delicacy in the original not often observed: *Adam yelud ishah.* "Adam born of a woman, few of days, and full of tremor."

3. *Dost thou open thine eyes upon such an one?* The whole of this chapter is directed to God alone; in no part of it does he take any notice of his friends.

4. *Who can bring a clean thing?* The text refers to man's original and corrupt nature.

5. *Seeing his days are determined.* The general term of human life is fixed by God himself; in vain are all attempts to prolong it beyond this term. Several attempts have been made in all nations to find an elixir that would expel all the seeds of disease and keep men in continual health, but all these attempts have failed.

13. *O that thou wouldest hide me in the grave!* Dreadful as death is to others, I shall esteem it a high privilege; it will be to me a covert from the wind and from the tempest of this affliction and distress. *Keep me secret.* Hide my soul with thyself, where my enemies cannot invade my repose.

14. *If a man die, shall he live again?* The Septuagint: "If a man die, shall he live, having accomplished the days of his life? I will endure till I live again." Here is no doubt, but a strong persuasion, of the certainty of the general resurrection. *All the days of my appointed time.* 'Of my warfare." *Will I wait,* till "my renovation come." This word is used to denote the springing again of grass, Ps. xc. 5-6, after it had once withered, which is in itself a very expressive emblem of the resurrection.

15. *Thou wilt have a desire.* "Thou wilt pant with desire"; or, "Thou wilt yearn over the work of thy hands."

16. *For now thou numberest my steps.* "Although thou."

17. *My transgression is sealed up in a bag.* An allusion to the custom of collecting evidence of state transgressions, sealing them up in a bag, and presenting them to the judges.

20. *Thou changest his countenance.* Probably an allusion to the custom of covering the face when the person was condemned, and sending him away to execution. See the case of Haman, Esther vii. 8.

CHAPTER 15

Eliphaz charges Job with impiety in attempting to justify himself, 1-13; asserts the utter corruption and abominable state of man, 14-16; and, from his own knowledge and the observations of the ancients, shows the desolation to which the wicked are exposed, and insinuates that Job has such calamities to dread, 17-35.

2. *Should a wise man utter vain knowledge?* Or rather, "Should a wise man utter the science

of wind?" A science without solidity or certainty. *And fill his belly with the east wind? Beten,* which we translate *belly,* is used to signify any part of the body; here it evidently refers to the lungs, and may include the cheeks. The *east wind* is a very stormy wind in the Levant, or the eastern part of the Mediterranean Sea. Eliphaz, by these words, seems to intimate that Job's speech was a perfect storm or tempest of words.

4. *Thou castest off fear.* Thou hast no reverence for God. *And restrainest prayer.* Instead of humbling yourself, and making supplication to your Judge, you spend your time in arraigning His providence and justifying yourself.

7. *Art thou the first man that was born?* Literally, "Wert thou born before Adam?" Art thou in the pristine state of purity and innocence?

8. *Hast thou heard the secret of God?* "Hast thou hearkened in God's council?"

16. *How much more abominable and filthy is man?* As in the preceding verse it is said, "He putteth no trust in his saints," it has appeared both to translators and commentators that the original words should be rendered "how much less," not "how much more": How much less would He put confidence in man, who is filthy and abominable in his nature, and profligate in his practice, as he drinks down *iniquity like water?* A man who is under the power of sinful propensities commits sin as greedily as the thirsty man or camel drinks down water. He thinks he can never have enough.

17. *I will shew thee, hear me; and that which I have seen I will declare.* Eliphaz is now about to quote a whole collection of wise sayings from the ancients; all good enough in themselves, but sinfully misapplied to the case of Job.

19. *Unto whom alone the earth was given.* He very likely refers to the Israelites, who got possession of the Promised Land from God himself, *no stranger* being permitted to dwell in it, as the old inhabitants were to be exterminated.

20. *The wicked man travaileth with pain.* This is a most forcible truth: a life of sin is a life of misery, and he that will sin must suffer. The sense of the original is, "He torments himself." He is a true self-tormentor, and he alone is author of his own sufferings and his own ruin.

22. *That he shall return out of darkness.* If he take but a few steps in the dark, he expects the dagger of the assassin.

26. *He runneth upon him.* Calmet has properly observed that this refers to God, who, like a mighty conquering hero, marches against the ungodly, rushes upon him, seizes him.

27. *Maketh collops of fat on his flanks.* A proverbial expression for "His ambition is boundless."

29. *He shall not be rich.* The whole of what follows, to the end of the chapter, seems to be directed against Job himself, whom Eliphaz indirectly accuses of having been a tyrant and oppressor.

32. *It shall be accomplished before his time.* I believe the Vulgate gives the true sense: "He shall perish before his time; before his days are completed."

34. *The congregation of hypocrites.* Job is here classed with *hypocrites,* or rather the impious of all kinds. The *congregation,* or "society," of

such shall be *desolate*, or a "barren rock." See the Arabic word explained in the note on chap. iii. 7. *Fire shall consume the tabernacles of bribery.* Another insinuation against Job, that he had perverted justice and judgment, and had taken bribes.

CHAPTER 16

Job replies to Eliphaz, and through him to all his friends, who, instead of comforting him, had added to his misfortunes; and shows that, had they been in his circumstances, he would have treated them in a different manner, 1-5. Enters into an affecting detail of his suffering, 6-16. Consoles himself with the consciousness of his own innocence, of which he takes God to witness, and patiently expects a termination of all his sufferings by death, 17-22.

3. *Vain words.* Literally, "words of air."

7. *But now he hath made me weary.* The Vulgate translates thus: "But now my grief oppresses me, and all my joints are reduced to nothing."

9. *He teareth me in his wrath.* He (Satan) *gnasheth upon me with his teeth; mine enemy sharpeneth his eyes upon me.*

10. *They* (demons) *have gaped on me with their mouth; they have gathered themselves together against me.*

11. *God hath delivered me to the ungodly* (to the evil one), *and turned me over into the hands of the wicked.*

15. *Defiled my horn in the dust.* The *horn* was an emblem of power.

18. *O earth, cover not thou my blood.* This is evidently an allusion to the murder of Abel. Job here calls for justice against his destroyers.

CHAPTER 17

Job complains of the injustice of his friends, and compares his present state of want and woe with his former honor and affluence, 1-6. God's dealings with him will astonish even upright men; yet the righteous shall not be discouraged, but hold on his way, 7-9. Asserts that there is not a wise man among his friends, and that he has no expectation but of a speedy death, 10-16.

1. *My breath is corrupt.* Rather, "My spirit is oppressed."

3. *Lay down now.* Deposit a pledge; stake your conduct against mine, and your life and soul on the issue. Let the cause come before God; let Him try it, and see whether any of you shall be justified by Him, while I am condemned.

4. *For thou hast hid their heart.* This address is to God; and here He is represented as doing that which in the course of His providence He only permits to be done. *Shalt thou not exalt them.* This was exactly fulfilled; not one of Job's friends was exalted. On the contrary, God condemned the whole, and they were not received into the divine favor till Job sacrificed and made intercession for them.

5. *He that speaketh flattery.* The man who expects much from his friends will be disappointed; while depending on them, his children's eyes may fail in looking for bread.

6. *He hath made me also a byword.* My afflictions and calamities have become a subject of general conversation, so that my poverty and affliction are proverbial. "As poor as Job," "As afflicted as Job," are proverbs that have reached even our times and are still in use. *Aforetime I was as a tabret.* "I shall be as a furnace, or consuming fire (Tophet) before them." They

shall have little reason to mock when they see the end of the Lord's dealings with me; my example will be a consuming fire to them, and my false friends will be confounded.

7. *Mine eye also is dim.* Continual weeping impairs the sight; and indeed any affliction that debilitates the frame generally, weakens the sight in the same proportion. *All my members are as a shadow.* Nothing is left but skin and bone. I am but the shadow of my former self.

9. *The righteous also shall hold on his way.* There shall be no doubt concerning the dispensations of the divine providence. My case shall illustrate all seemingly intricate displays of God's government. *Shall be stronger and stronger.* He shall take encouragement from my case, stay himself on the Lord, and thus gain strength by every blast of adversity. This is one grand use of the Book of Job. It casts much light on seemingly partial displays of divine providence, and has ever been the great textbook of godly men in a state of persecution and affliction.

12. *They change the night into day.* These purposes and thoughts are so very gloomy that they change day into night. *The light is short because of darkness.* "The light is near from the face of darkness."

CHAPTER 18

Bildad, in a speech of passionate invective, accuses Job of impatience and impiety, 1-4; shows the fearful end of the wicked and their posterity; and apparently applies the whole to Job, whom he threatens with the most ruinous end, 5-21.

2. *How long will it be ere ye make an end?* It is difficult to say to whom this address is made; being in the plural number, it can hardly be supposed to mean Job only. It probably means all present; as if he had said, It is vain to talk with this man, and follow him through all his quibbles; take notice of this, and then let us all deliver our sentiments fully to him, without paying any regard to his self-vindications. It must be owned that this is the plan which Bildad followed, and he amply unburdens a mind that was laboring under the spirit of rancor and abuse.

3. *Counted as beasts.* You treat us as if we had neither reason nor understanding.

5. *The light of the wicked shall be put out.* Some think it would be better to translate the original, "Let the light of the wicked be extinguished!" You are a bad man, and you have perverted the understanding which God has given you. Let that understanding, that abused gift, be taken away. From this verse to the end of the chapter is a continual invective against Job.

6. *The light shall be dark in his tabernacle.* His property shall be destroyed, his house pillaged, and himself and his family come to an untimely end. *His candle shall be put out.* He shall have no posterity.

18. *He shall be driven from light.* He shall be taken off by a violent death. *And chased out of the world.* The wicked is driven away in his iniquity. This shows his reluctance to depart from life.

CHAPTER 19

Job complains of the cruelty of his friends, 1-5. Pathetically laments his sufferings, 6-12. Complains of his being forsaken by all his domestics, friends, relatives, and even his wife, 13-19. Details his sufferings in an affecting manner, calls upon his friends to pity him, and earnestly wishes that his speeches may be recorded, 20-24. Expresses his hope in a future resurrection, 25-27. And warns his persecutors to desist, lest they fall under God's judgments, 28-29.

3. *These ten times.* The exact arithmetical number is not to be regarded, *ten times* being put for many times, as we have already seen. See particularly Gen. xxxi. 7. *Ye make yourselves strange to me.* When I was in affluence and prosperity, ye were my intimates, and appeared to rejoice in my happiness; but now ye scarcely know me, or ye profess to consider me a wicked man because I am in adversity.

11. *And he counteth me unto him as one of his enemies.* From the seventh to the thirteenth verse there seems to be an allusion to a hostile invasion, battles, sieges, etc.

14. *My kinsfolk have failed.* Literally, "departed"; they have all left my house, now that there is no more hope of gain.

19. *My inward friends.* Those who were my greatest intimates.

20. *My bone cleaveth to my skin.* My flesh is entirely wasted away, and nothing but skin and bone left. *I am escaped with the skin of my teeth.* To *escape with the skin of the teeth* seems to have been a proverbial expression, signifying great difficulty. I had as narrow an escape from death as the thickness of the enamel on the teeth. I was within a hair's breadth of destruction.

21. *Have pity upon me.* The iteration here strongly indicates the depth of his distress, and that his spirit was worn down with the length and severity of his suffering.

23. *Oh that my words were now written!* Our translators have made a strange mistake by rendering the verb *yuchaku, printed,* when they should have used "described, traced out." Oh, that my words were fairly traced out in a book! Three kinds of writing Job alludes to, as being practiced in his time: (1) writing in a book, (2) cutting with an iron style on plates of lead, (3) engraving on large stones or rocks, many of which are still found in different parts of Arabia.

25. *For I know that my redeemer liveth.* I shall therefore lay down one principle, without which no mode of interpretation hitherto offered can have any weight. The principle is this: Job was now under the especial inspiration of the Holy Spirit, and spoke prophetically. I arrive at the conclusion that the prophecy in question was not designed to point out the future prosperity of Job, but rather the future redemption of mankind by Jesus Christ, and the general resurrection of the human race.
I know, yadati, I have a firm and full persuasion, *that my redeemer, goali,* my "kinsman," he whose right it was among the ancient Hebrews to redeem the forfeited heritages belonging to the family (Lev. xxv. 25; Num. xxv. 12; Ruth iii. 13); but here it must refer to Christ, who has truly the right of redemption, being of the same kindred, who was born of woman, flesh of our flesh and bone of our bone. *Liveth, chai,* is the living One, who has the keys of hell and death; the Creator and Lord of the spirits of all flesh, and the principle and support of all life.
And that he shall stand at the latter day upon the earth. The latter day, or time, when God

comes to judgment. *He shall stand,* "he shall arise, or stand up," i.e., to give sentence in judgment; or He himself shall arise from the dust, as the passage has been understood by some to refer to the resurrection of Christ from the dead. *Upon the earth, al aphar,* "over the dead," or from the dead. *Upon the earth, al aphar,* "over the dead," or those who are reduced to dust. This is the meaning of *aphar* in Ps. xxx. 9: "What profit is there in my blood, when I go down to the pit? Shall the dust [i.e., the dead] praise thee?"

26. *And though after my skin worms destroy this body. My skin,* which is now almost all that remains of my former self, except the bones; see v. 20. *They destroy this*—not body. *They*—diseases and affliction, destroy this wretched composition of misery and corruption. *Yet in my flesh shall I see God.* Either, I shall arise from the dead, have a renewed body, and see Him with eyes of flesh and blood, though what I have now shall shortly molder into dust; or, I shall see Him in the flesh, my Kinsman, who shall partake of my flesh and blood, in order that He may ransom the lost inheritance.

27. *Whom I shall see for myself.* Have a personal interest in the resurrection, as I shall have in the Redeemer. *And mine eyes shall behold.* That very Person who shall be the Resurrection, as He is the Life. *And not another.* And not a "stranger," one who has no relation to human nature; but *goali,* my redeeming Kinsman. *Though my reins be consumed within me.* Though I am now apparently on the brink of death, the thread of life being spun out to extreme tenuity.

28. *But ye should say.* Or, "Then ye shall say." *Why persecute we him?* Or, as Mr. Good, How did we persecute him! Alas! we are not convinced that we did wrong. *Seeing the root of the matter.* Instead of *bi,* "in me," *bo,* "in him," is the reading of more than one hundred of Kennicott's and De Rossi's MSS., and in several of the versions: "Seeing the root of the matter is found in him."

CHAPTER 20

Zophar answers Job, and largely details the wretchedness of the wicked and the hypocrite; shows that the rejoicing of such is short and transitory, 1-9. That he is punished in his family and in his person, 10-14. That he shall be stripped of his ill-gotten wealth, and shall be in misery, though in the midst of affluence, 15-23. He shall at last die a violent death, and his family and property be finally destroyed, 24-29.

2. *Therefore do my thoughts.* It has already been observed that Zophar was the most inveterate of all Job's *enemies,* for we really must cease to call them *friends.* He sets no bounds to his invective, and outrages every rule of charity. A man of such a bitter spirit must have been, in general, very unhappy. With him Job is, by insinuation, everything that is base, vile, and hypocritical. *For this I make haste.* "There is sensibility in me, and my feelings provoke me to reply."

3. *I have heard the check of my reproach.* Zophar assumes his old ground, and retracts nothing of what he had said. Like many of his own complexion in the present day, he was determined to believe that his judgment was infallible and that he could not err.

4. *Knowest thou not this of old?* This is a maxim as ancient as the world; it began with the

first man: A wicked man shall triumph but a short time; God will destroy the proud doer.

6. *Though his excellency mount up to the heavens.* Probably referring to the original state of Adam, of whose fall he appears to have spoken, v. 4. He was created in the image of God; but by his sin against his Maker he fell into wretchedness, misery, death, and destruction.

10. *His children shall seek to please the poor.* They shall be reduced to the lowest degree of poverty and want, so as to be obliged to become servants to the poor.

15. *He shall vomit them up again.* This is also an allusion to an effect of most ordinary poisons; they occasion a nausea, and often excruciating vomiting—nature striving to eject what it knows, if retained, will be its bane.

16. *He shall suck the poison of asps.* That delicious morsel, that secret, easily besetting sin, of his soul as the poison of asps would do on the life of his body.

19. *He hath oppressed and hath forsaken the poor.* Literally, *He hath broken in pieces the forsaken of the poor.*

20. *Surely he shall not feel quietness in his belly.* The meaning seems to be, "He shall never be satisfied; he shall have an endless desire after secular good, and shall never be able to obtain what he covets."

22. *In the fulness of his sufficiency he shall be in straits.* This is a fine saying. It is literally true of every great, rich, wicked man.

23. *When he is about to fill his belly.* Here seems a plain allusion to the lustings of the children of Israel in the desert. God showered down quails upon them, and showered down His wrath while the flesh was in their mouths.

24. *He shall flee from the iron weapon.* Or, "Though he should flee from the iron armour, the brazen bow should strike him through."

26. *A fire not blown shall consume him.* As Zophar is here showing that the wicked cannot escape from the divine judgments, so he points out the different instruments which God employs for their destruction. The "wrath" of God—any secret or supernatural curse. The "iron weapon"—the spear or suchlike. The "bow," and its swift-flying arrow. "Darkness"—deep horror and perplexity. "A fire not blown"—a supernatural fire, lightning—such as fell on Korah and his company, to whose destruction there is probably here an allusion; hence the words, *It shall go ill with him that is left in his tabernacle.*

27. *The heaven shall reveal his iniquity; and the earth shall rise up against him.* Another allusion, if I mistake not, to the destruction of Korah and his company. "And the glory of the Lord appeared unto all the congregation," Num. xvi. 19, etc. And then "the earth rose up against them." "The ground clave asunder that was under them: and the earth opened her mouth, and swallowed them up, and . . . they . . . went down alive into the pit, and the earth closed upon them," Num. xvi. 31-33.

28. *The increase of his house shall depart, and his goods shall flow aawy in the day of his wrath.* A further allusion to the punishment of the rebellious company of Korah, who not only perished themselves, but their houses also, and their goods, Num. xvi. 32.

CHAPTER 21

Job expresses himself as puzzled by the dispensations of divine providence, because of the unequal distribution of temporal goods; he shows that wicked men often live long, prosper in their families, in their flocks, and in all their substance, and yet live in defiance of God and sacred things, 1-16. At other times their prosperity is suddenly blasted, and they and their families come to ruin, 17-21. God, however, is too wise to err, and He deals out various lots to all according to His wisdom. Some come sooner, others later, to the grave; the strong and the weak, the prince and the peasant, come to a similar end in this life; but the wicked are reserved for a day of wrath, 22-33. He charges his friends with falsehood in their pretended attempts to comfort him, 34.

2. *Let this be your consolations.* "And let this be your retractations." Let what I am about to say induce you to retract what you have said, and to recall your false judgments. *Nacham* signifies, not only to "comfort," but to "change one's mind, to repent."

4. *As for me.* "Alas for me!"

7. *Wherefore do the wicked live?* You have frequently asserted that the wicked are invariably punished in this life, and that the righteous are ever distinguished by the strongest marks of God's providential kindness. How then does it come that many wicked men live long and prosperously, and at last die in peace, without any evidence whatever of God's displeasure? This is a fact that is occurring daily; how then will you reconcile it with your maxims?

12. *They take the timbrel and harp.* They "rise up" or "lift themselves up," probably alluding to the rural exercise of dancing. *Toph*, which we translate *timbrel,* means a sort of "drum," such as the tom-tom of the Asiatics. *Kinnor* may mean something of the *harp* kind. *Ugab,* organ, means nothing like the instrument now called the organ. It probably means the syrinx, composed of several unequal pipes, closed at the bottom, which, when blown into at the top, gives a very shrill and lively sound.

13. *They spend their days in wealth.* "They grow old," or wear out as with old age.

18. *They are as stubble before the wind.* The original signifies that they shall be "carried away by a furious storm."

19. *God layeth up his iniquity for his children.* This is according to the declaration of God, Exod. xx. 5: "Visiting the iniquity of the fathers upon the children unto the third and fourth generation of them that hate me." This always supposes that the children, who are thus visited, have copied their parents' example.

23. *One dieth in his full strength.* In this and the three following verses Job shows that the inequality of fortune, goods, health, strength, etc., decides nothing either for or against persons in reference to the approbation or disapprobation of God, as these various lots are no indications of their wickedness or innocence.

29. *Have ye not asked them that go by the way?* This appears to be Job's answer. Consult travellers who have gone through different countries, and they will tell you that they have seen both examples—the wicked in great prosperity in some instances, while suddenly destroyed in others.

33. *The clods of the valley shall be sweet unto him.* Perhaps there is an allusion here to the Asiatic mode of interment for princes, saints, and nobles; a well-watered valley was chosen for the tomb, where a perpetual spring might be secured. This was intended to be the emblem of a resurrection, or of a future life; and to conceal as much as possible the disgrace of the rotting carcass.

CHAPTER 22

Eliphaz reproves Job for his attempts to clear his character and establish his innocence, 1-4. Charges him with innumerable transgressions; with oppressions towards his brethren, cruelty to the poor, hardheartedness to the needy, and uncharitableness towards the widow and the orphan; and says it is on these accounts that snares and desolations are come upon him, 5-11. Speaks of the majesty and justice of God: how He cut off the antediluvians, the inhabitants of Sodom, and the cities of the plain, 12-20. Exhorts him to repent and acknowledge his sins, and promises him great riches and prosperity, 21-30.

2. *Can a man be profitable unto God?* God does not afflict you because you have deprived Him of any excellency.

6. *Thou hast taken a pledge.* You have exacted where nothing was due, so that through you the poor have been unable to procure their necessary clothing.

7. *Thou hast not given water.* It was esteemed a great virtue in the East to furnish thirsty travellers with water; especially in the deserts, where scarcely a *stream* was to be found, and where *wells* were very rare. Some of the Indian devotees are accustomed to stand with a *girbah* or skin full of water, on the public roads, to give drink to weary travellers who are parched with thirst.

8. *But as for the mighty man, he had the earth.* "The man of arm." Finger, hand, and arm are all emblems of strength and power. *The honourable man.* Literally, the man whose "face is accepted," the respectable man, the man of wealth. You were an enemy to the poor and needy, but you favored and flattered the rich and great.

12. *Is not God in the height of heaven?* It appears, from this and the following verses, that Eliphaz was attributing infidel and blasphemous speeches or sentiments to Job.

16. *Whose foundation was overflown with a flood.* The unrighteous in the days of Noah, who appear to have had an abundance of all temporal good (v. 18) and who surpassed the deeds of all the former wicked, said in effect to God, "Depart from us."

18. *But the counsel of the wicked is far from me.* Sarcastically quoting Job's words, chap. xxi. 14, 16.

19. *The righteous see it, and are glad.* They see God's judgments on the incorrigibly wicked, and know that the Judge of all the earth does right; hence they rejoice in all the dispensations of His providence.

29. *When men are cast down.* The following is nearly a literal version: "When they shall humble themselves, thou say, Be exalted [or, There is exaltation]: for the downcast of eye he will save." The same sentiment as that of our Lord, "Every one that exalteth himself shall be abased; and he that humbleth himself shall be exalted."

30. *He shall deliver the island of the innocent.* The text may be translated, "He shall deliver every innocent person: He [the innocent person] shall be delivered by the pureness of thy hands"; i.e., as you love justice, so you will do justice.

CHAPTER 23

Job answers, apologizes for his complaining, wishes to plead his cause in the presence of his Maker, from whom he knows he should receive justice, but regrets that he cannot find Him, 1-9. He however gives himself and his cause up to God, with the conviction of his own innocence, and God's justice and goodness, 10-14. He is nevertheless afraid when he considers the majesty of his Maker, 15-17.

3. *Oh that I knew where I might find him!* This and the following verse may be read thus: "Who will give me the knowledge of God, that I may find Him out? I would come to His establishment (the place or way in which He has promised to communicate himself); I would exhibit, in detail, my judgment (the cause I wish to be tried) before His face; and my mouth would I fill with convincing or decisive arguments."

7. *There the righteous might dispute with him.* Might "argue" or "plead." To dispute with God sounds very harsh.

8. *Behold, I go forward.* These two verses paint in vivid colors the distress and anxiety of a soul in search of the favor of God.

14. *For he performeth the thing that is appointed for me.* "For he hath appointed me my lot; and like these there are multitudes with him." He diversifies human affairs; scarcely any two men have the same lot, nor has the same person the same portion at all times. He has multitudes of resources, expedients, means, etc., which he employs in governing human affairs.

16. *For God maketh my heart soft.* Prostrates my strength, deprives me of courage.

17. *Because I was not cut off.* This verse should be read in connection with the preceding, and then we shall have the following sense. Verse 16: "The Lord hath beaten down my strength, and my soul has been terrified by His fear." Verse 17: "For it is not this deep night in which I am enveloped, nor the evils which I suffer, that have overwhelmed me; I sink only through the fear which the presence of His majesty inspires."

CHAPTER 24

Job asserts that there are various transgressors whose wickedness is not visited on them in this life, and particularizes: the unjust and oppressive, 1-6; those who are cruel to the poor, 7-13; the murderer, 14; the adulterer, 15; thieves and plunderers, 16-17. Nevertheless they have an accursed portion, and shall die, and their memory perish, 18-20. He speaks of the abuse of power, and of the punishment of oppressors, 21-24; and asserts that what he has said on these subjects cannot be contradicted, 25.

1. *Why, seeing times are not hidden from the Almighty?* The wish is that God would appoint such times that the falsely accused might look forward to them with comfort; knowing that, on their arrival, they should have a fair hearing, and their innocence be publicly declared.

2. *Some remove the landmarks.* Stones or posts were originally set up to ascertain the bounds of particular estates, and this was necessary in open countries, before hedges and fences were formed. Wicked and covetous men often removed the landmarks and set them in on their neighbors' ground, that, by contracting their boundaries, they might enlarge their own. The law of Moses denounces curses on those who remove their neighbors' landmarks.

4. *They turn the needy out of the way.* They

will not permit them to go by the accustomed paths; they oblige them to take circuitous routes.

9. *They pluck the fatherless from the breast.* They forcibly take young children in order that they may bring them up in a state of slavery. *Take a pledge of the poor.* Oppressive landlords who let out their grounds at an exorbitant rent, which the poor laborers, though using the utmost diligence, are unable at all times to pay; and then the unfeeling wretch "sells them up," as the phrase here is, or takes their cow or their bed in pledge that the money shall be paid in such a time.

10. *They cause him to go naked.* These cruel, hardhearted oppressors seize the cloth made for the family wear, or the wool and flax out of which such clothes should be made. *And they take away the sheaf.* Seize the grain as soon as it is reaped, that they may pay themselves the exorbitant rent at which they have leased out their land.

11. *Make oil within their walls.* Thus stripped of all that on which they depended for clothing and food, they are obliged to become vassals to their lord, labor in the fields on scanty fare, or tread their winepresses, from the produce of which they are not permitted to quench their thirst.

12. *Men groan from out of the city.* After having shown the oppressions carried on in the country, he takes a view of those carried on in the town. Here the miseries are too numerous to be detailed. *Yet God layeth not folly to them.* He does not impute their calamities to their own folly. But the Hebrew may be translated, "And God doth not attend to their prayers." Job's object was to show, in opposition to the mistaken doctrine of his friends, that God did not hastily punish every evil work, nor reward every good one.

13. *They ... rebel against the light.* Speaking of wicked men. They rebel against the light of God in their consciences, and His light in His Word.

CHAPTER 25

Bildad, the Shuhite, in an irregular speech, shows that God's dominion is supreme, His armies innumerable, and His providence extends over all. 1-3; that man cannot be justified before God; that even the heavenly bodies cannot be reputed pure in His sight; much less man, who is naturally weak and sinful, 4-6.

1. *Bildad the Shuhite.* This is the last attack on Job; the others felt themselves foiled, though they had not humility enough to acknowledge it, but would not again return to the attack. Bildad has little to say, and that little is very little to the point. He makes a few assertions, particularly in reference to what Job had said in the commencement of the preceding chapter, of his desire to appear before God, and have his case tried by Him, as he had the utmost confidence that his innocence should be fully proved. For this Bildad reprehends Job with arguments which had been brought forth often in this controversy, and as repeatedly confuted, chap. iv. 18 and xv. 14-16.

This speech of Bildad is both confused and inconclusive. His reasoning is absurd, and he draws false conclusions from his premises. In the third verse, he says, "Is there any number of his armies? and upon whom doth not his light arise?" But how absurd is the conclusion which

he draws from his questions! "How then can a man be justified with God? or how can he be clean that is born of a woman?" This has no relation to the premises; still, to us the question is not difficult. A man can be "justified with God," through the blood of Christ; and he can "be clean that is born of a woman," through the sanctification of the Spirit.

6. *How much less man, that is a worm?* Or as the Targum: "How much more man, who in his life is a reptile; and the son of man, who in his death is a worm?"

Thus endeth Bildad the Shuhite, who endeavored to speak on a subject which he did not understand; and, having got on bad ground, was soon confounded in his own mind, spoke incoherently, argued inconclusively, and came abruptly and suddenly to an end. Thus, his three friends being confounded, Job was left to pursue his own way. They trouble him no more, and he proceeds in triumph to the end of the thirty-first chapter.

CHAPTER 26

Job, perceiving that his friends could no longer support their arguments on the ground they had assumed, sharply reproves them for their want of both wisdom and feeling, 1-4; shows that the power and wisdom of God are manifest in the works of creation and providence; gives several proofs; and then adds that these are a small specimen of His infinite skill and unlimited power, 5-14.

2. *How hast thou helped him?* This seems a species of irony.

4. *Whose spirit came from thee?* Mr. Good renders the verse thus: "From whom hast thou pillaged speeches? And whose spirit hath issued forth from thee?" The retort is peculiarly severe, and refers immediately to the proverbial sayings which in several of the preceding answers have been adduced against the irritated sufferer, for which see chap. viii. 11-19; xv. 20-35. I concur most fully therefore with Dr. Stock in regarding the remainder of this chapter as a sample, ironically exhibited by Job, of the harangues on the power and greatness of God which he supposes his friends to have taken out of the mouths of other men, to deck their speeches with borrowed lustre. Only, in descanting on the same subject, he shows how much he himself can go beyond them in eloquence and sublimity.

5. *Dead things are formed from under the waters.* This verse, as it stands in our version, seems to convey no meaning, and the Hebrew is obscure; *harephaim,* "the Rephaim," certainly does not mean *dead things.* There is probably here an allusion to the destruction of the earth by the general deluge. Moses, speaking concerning the state of the earth before the Flood, says, Gen. vi. 4, "There were giants [*nephilim*] in the earth in those days." Now it is likely that Job means the same by *rephaim* as Moses does by the *nephilim;* and that both refer to the antediluvians, who were all, for their exceeding great iniquities, overwhelmed by the waters of the Deluge. Can those mighty men and their neighbors, all the sinners who have been gathered to them since, be rejected from under the waters, by which they were judicially overwhelmed?

6. *Hell is naked before him.* Sheol, the place of the dead, or of separate spirits, is always in his view. "And there is no covering to Abaddon"

—the place of the "destroyer," where destruction reigns, and where those dwell who are eternally separated from God. The ancients thought that hell or Tartarus was a vast space in the center or at the very bottom of the earth.

7. *He stretcheth out the north over the empty place.* Al tohu, "to the hollow waste." The same word is as is used, Gen. i. 2, "The earth was without form," *tohu.*

8. *He bindeth up the waters.* Drives the aqueous particles together, which were raised by evaporation, so that, being condensed, they form clouds which float in the atmosphere, till, meeting with strong currents of wind, or by the agency of the electric fluid, they are further condensed; and then, becoming too heavy to be sustained in the air, fall down in the form of rain, when, in this poetic language, *the cloud is . . . rent under them.*

9. *He holdeth back the face of his throne.* The great Agent is not personally discoverable. The words, however, may refer to those obscurations of the face of heaven, and the hiding of the body of the sun, when the atmosphere is laden with dense vapors, and the rain begins to be poured down on the earth.

10. *He hath compassed the waters with bounds.* Perhaps this refers merely to the circle of the horizon, the line that terminates light and commences darkness, called here "until the completion of light with darkness."

11. *The pillars of heaven tremble.* This is probably a poetical description either of thunder or of an earthquake.

12. *He divideth the sea with his power.* Here is a manifest allusion to the passage of the Red Sea by the Israelites, and the overthrow of Pharaoh and his host. *He smiteth through the proud. Rahab,* the very name by which Egypt is called Isa. li. 9 and elsewhere. Let Job live when he might, I am satisfied the Book of Job was written long after the death of Moses, and not earlier than the days of Solomon, if not later. The farther I go in the work, the more this conviction is deepened.

14. *Lo, these are parts of his ways. Ketsoth,* "the ends" or "extremities," the outlines, an indistinct sketch, of his eternal power and Godhead. *How little a portion is heard? Shemets,* "a mere whisper"; admirably opposed to *raam, the thunder,* mentioned in the next clause.

CHAPTER 27

Job strongly asserts his innocence; determines to maintain it, and to avoid every evil way, 1-7. Shows his abhorrence of the hypocrite by describing his infamous character, accumulated miseries, and wretched end, 8-23.

1. *Continued his parable.* After having delivered the preceding discourse, Job appears to have paused to see if any of his friends chose to make any reply; but finding them all silent, he resumed his discourse, which is here called *meshalo, his parable,* his "authoritative weighty discourse"; from *mashal,* "to exercise rule, authority, dominion, or power." And it must be granted that in this speech he assumes great boldness, exhibits his own unsullied character, and treats his friends with little ceremony.

2. *Who hath taken away my judgment.* Who has turned aside my cause, and has not permitted it to come to a hearing, where I might

have justice done to me, but has abandoned me to the harsh and uncharitable judgment of my enemies. There appears to be a great want of reverence in these words of Job; he speaks with a degree of irritation, if not bitterness, which cannot be justified. No man should speak thus of his Maker.

3. *All the while my breath is in me.* "As long as I live and have my understanding."

5. *God forbid.* Far be it from me, *that I should justify you.*

8. *What is the hope of the hypocrite?* The word *chaneph,* which we translate, most improperly, *hypocrite,* means a "wicked fellow, a defiled, polluted wretch, a rascal, a knave."

11. *I will teach you by the hand of God.* Job felt that the good hand of his God was upon him, and that therefore he should make no mistake in his doctrines.

12. *Ye yourselves have seen it.* Your own experience and observation have shown you that the righteous are frequently in affliction, and the wicked in affluence. *Why then are ye thus altogether vain?* "Why then should ye thus babble babblings?" If our language would allow it, we might say "vanitize vanity."

13. *This is the portion of a wicked man.* Job now commences his promised teaching; and what follows is a description of the lot or portion of the wicked man and of tyrants, in general, though the hand of man be not laid upon them. Though God does not at all times show His displeasure against the wicked, by reducing them to a state of poverty and affliction, yet He often does it so that men may see it; and at other times He seems to pass them by; reserving their judgment for *another world,* that men may not forget that there is a day of judgment and perdition for ungodly men, and a future recompense for the righteous.

14. *If his children be multiplied.* As numerous families were supposed to be a proof of the benediction of the Almighty, Job shows that this is not always the case; for the offspring of the wicked shall be partly cut off by *violent deaths,* and partly reduced to great *poverty.*

15. *Those that remain of him.* "His remains," whether meaning himself personally, or his family.

16. *Though he heap up silver.* Though he amass riches in the greatest abundance, he shall not enjoy them. Unsanctified wealth is a curse to its possessor.

17. *The just shall put it on.* Money is God's property. "The silver is mine, and the gold is mine, saith the Lord"; and though it may be abused for a time by unrighteous hands, God, in the course of His providence, brings it back to its proper use; and often the righteous possess the inheritance of the wicked.

18. *He buildeth his house as a moth.* With great skill, great pains, and great industry; but the structure, however skilful, shall be dissolved. To its owner it shall be only a temporary habitation, like that which the moth makes in its caterpillar state. *As a booth that the keeper maketh.* A shed which the watchman or keeper of a vineyard erects to cover him from the scorching sun, while watching the ripening grapes, that they may be preserved from depredation. Travellers in the East have observed

that such booths or sheds are made of the lightest and most worthless materials; and after the harvest or vintage is in, they are quite neglected, and by the winter rains are soon dissolved and destroyed.

19. *The rich man shall lie down.* In the grave. *But he shall not be gathered.* Neither have a respectable burial among men nor be gathered with the righteous in the kingdom of God. *He openeth his eyes.* In the morning of the resurrection. *And he is not.* He is utterly lost and undone forever.

22. *God shall cast upon him.* Or, rather, the storm mentioned above shall incessantly pelt him, and give him no respite; nor can he by any means escape from its fury.

23. *Men shall clap their hands at him.* These two verses refer to the storm which is to sweep away the ungodly; therefore the word *God,* in v. 22, and *men* in this verse, should be omitted. Verse 22: "For it shall fall upon him, and not spare: flying from its power, he shall continue to fly. Verse 23: "It shall clap its hands against him, and *hiss,* 'shriek,' him out of his place." Here the storm is personified, and the wicked actor is hissed and driven by it from off the stage. It seems it was an ancient method to clap the hands against and hiss a man from any public office who had acted improperly in it.

CHAPTER 28

Job, in showing the vanity of human pursuits in reference to genuine wisdom, mentions mining for and refining gold and silver, 1; iron and other minerals, 2; the difficulties of mining, 3-4; produce of grain for bread from the earth, and stones of fire from under it, 5. He speaks of precious stones and gold dust, 6; of the instinct of fowls and wild beasts in finding their way, 7-8; and of the industry and successful attempts of men in mining and other operations, 9-11: but shows that with all their industry, skill, and perseverance they cannot find out true wisdom, 12; of which he gives the most exalted character, 13-22; and shows that God alone, the Fountain of wisdom, knows and can teach it, 23-27; and in what this true wisdom consists, 28.

1. *Surely there is a vein for the silver.* This chapter is the oldest and finest piece of natural history in the world, and gives us very important information on several curious subjects; and could we ascertain the precise meaning of all the original words we might, most probably, find out allusions to several useful arts which we are apt to think are of modern, or comparatively modern, invention. *A place for gold where they fine it.* This should rather be translated, "A place for gold which they refine."

2. *Iron is taken out of the earth.* This most useful metal is hidden under the earth, and men have found out the method of separating it from its ore.

3. *He setteth an end to darkness.* As it is likely Job still refers to mining, the words above may be understood as pointing out the persevering industry of man in penetrating into the bowels of the earth, in order to seek for metals and precious stones.

4. *The flood breaketh out from the inhabitant.* This passage is very difficult. Some think it refers to mining; others, to navigation. *Forgotten of the foot.* No man treads there anymore.

5. *The earth, out of it cometh bread.* Or the earth, *mimmennah,* "from itself," by its own vegetative power, "it sends out bread," or the corn of which bread is made.

9. *He putteth forth his hand upon the rock.* Still there appears to be a reference to mining. Man puts his hand upon the rock, he breaks that to pieces, in order to extract the metals which it contains. *He overturneth the mountains.* He excavates, undermines, or digs them away, when in search of the metals contained in them.

10. *He cutteth out rivers among the rocks.* He cuts canals in the rocks, and drives levels under ground, in order to discover *veins* of ore. *His eye seeth every precious thing.* He sinks those shafts, and drives those levels, in order to discover where the precious minerals lie.

11. *He bindeth the floods.* Prevents the risings of springs from drowning the mines; and conducts rivers and streams from their wonted course, in order to bring forth to light what was hidden under their beds.

12. *But where shall wisdom be found?* Now as these terms *chochmah,* "wisdom," and *binah,* "understanding" or "discernment," are often applied in the sacred writings in their common acceptations, we must have recourse to what Job says of them, to know their meaning in this place. In v. 28, he says, "The fear of the Lord . . . is wisdom; and to depart from evil is understanding." We know that the "fear of the Lord" is often taken for the whole of that religious reverence and holy obedience which God prescribes to man in His Word, and which man owes to his Maker. Hence the Septuagint render *chochmah,* "wisdom," by "Divine worship"; wisdom—all true religion—must come by divine revelation.

14. *The depth saith, It is not in me.* Men may dig into the bowels of the earth, and there find gold, silver, and precious stones; but these will not give them true happiness. *The sea saith, It is not with me.* Men may explore foreign countries, and by navigation connect as it were the most distant parts of the earth; but every voyage and every enjoyment proclaim, True happiness is not here.

15. *It cannot be gotten for gold.* Genuine religion and true happiness are not to be acquired by earthly property.

16. *The gold of Ophir.* Gold is five times mentioned in this and vv. 17 and 19, and four of the times in different words. I shall consider them all at once. (1) *Segor,* from *sagar,* to "shut up": gold in the mine, or shut up in the ore. (2) *Kethem,* from *catham,* to "sign" or "stamp": gold made current by being coined, or stamped with its weight or value.

17. (3) *Zahab,* from *zahab,* to be "clear, bright, or resplendent": the untarnishing metal; the only metal that always keeps its lustre. But probably here it means burnished gold. (4) *Paz,* from *paz,* to *consolidate,* joined here with *keley,* "vessels, ornaments, instruments": hammered or wrought gold; gold in the finest forms, and most elegant utensils. In these verses there are also seven kinds of precious stones mentioned: onyx, sapphire, crystal, coral, pearls, rubies, and topaz.

22. *Destruction and death say, We have heard the fame thereof.* Abaddon, the destroyer, and his offspring, death. This is the very name that is given to the devil in Greek letters, Rev. ix. 11, and is rendered by the Greek word *Apollyon,* a word exactly of the same meaning.

23. *God understandeth the way thereof.* It can be taught only by a revelation from himself.

25. *And he weigheth the waters by measure.* He has exactly proportioned the aqueous surface of the earth to the terrene parts, so that there shall be an adequate surface to produce, by evaporation, moisture sufficient to be treasured up in the atmosphere for the irrigation of the earth.

26. *When he made a decree for the rain.* When he determined how that should be generated. *A way for the lightning of the thunder.* Kol signifies "voice" of any kind; and *koloth* is the plural, and is taken for the frequent claps or rattlings of thunder. *Chaz* signifies to "notch, indentate," as in the edges of the leaves of trees; *chaziz* must refer to the zigzag form which lightning assumes in passing from one cloud into another.

27. *Then did he see it, and declare it.* When He had finished all His creative operations, and tried and proved His work, investigated and found it to be very good, then He gave the needful revelation to man.

28. *Unto man he said. Laadam,* "unto man," He said. This probably refers to the revelation of His will which God gave to Adam after his fall.

CHAPTER 29

Job laments his present condition, and gives an affecting account of his former prosperity, having property in abundance, being surrounded by a numerous family, and enjoying every mark of the approbation of God, 1-6. Speaks of the respect he had from the young, 7-8; and from the nobles, 9-10. Details his conduct as a magistrate and judge in supporting the poor, and repressing the wicked, 11-17; his confidence, general prosperity, and respect, 18-25.

2. *Oh that I were as in months past.* Job seems here to make an apology for his complaints, by taking a view of his former prosperity, which was very great, but was now entirely at an end. He shows that it was not removed because of any bad use he had made of it; and describes how he behaved himself before God and man, and how much, for justice, benevolence, and mercy, he was esteemed and honored by the wise and good.

7. *When I went out to the gate.* Courts of justice were held at the gates or entrances of the cities of the East, and Job was "supreme magistrate."

8. *The young men saw me, and hid themselves.* From all classes of persons I had the most marked respect.

11. *When the ear heard me.* This and the six following verses present us with a fine exhibition of a man full of benevolence and charity, acting up to the highest dictates of those principles, and rendering the miserable of all descriptions happy, by the constant exercise of his unconfined philanthropy.

12. *Because I delivered the poor that cried.* This appears to be intended as a refutation of the charges produced by Eliphaz, chap. xxii. 5-10, to confute which Job appeals to facts, and to public testimony.

19. *My root was spread out by the waters.* A metaphor taken from a healthy tree growing beside a rivulet where there is plenty of water, which in consequence flourishes in all seasons; its leaf does not wither, nor its fruit fall off. See Ps. i. 3; Jer. xvii. 8.

24. *I laughed on them, they believed it not.* We have a similar phrase: "The news was too good to be true."

CHAPTER 30

Job proceeds to lament the change of his former condition, and the contempt into which his adversity had brought him, 1-15. Pathetically describes the afflictions of his body and mind, 16-31.

1. *But now they that are younger than I have me in derision.* Compare this with chap. xxix. 8, where he speaks of the respect he had from the youth while in the days of his prosperity. Now he is no longer affluent, and they are no longer respectful.

2. *The strength of their hands profit me.* He is speaking here of the fathers of these young men. What was the strength of their hands to me? Their old age also has perished.

7. *Among the bushes they brayed.* They cried out among the bushes, seeking for food, as the wild ass when he is in want of provender. *Under the nettles.* The "briers" or "brambles," under the brushwood in the thickest parts of the underwood; they huddled together like wild beasts.

8. *Children of fools.* Children of *nabal. Viler than the earth.* Rather, "driven out of the land"; persons not fit for civil society.

11. *Because he hath loosed my cord.* Instead of *yithri,* "my cord," which is the marginal reading, *yithro,* "his cord," is the reading of the text in many copies; and this reading directs us to a metaphor taken from an archer, who, observing his butt, sets his arrow on the string, draws it to a proper degree of tension, levels, and then loosing his hold, the arrow flies at the mark. He hath let loose his arrow against me; it has hit me, and I am wounded. *They have also let loose the bridle.* When they perceived that God had afflicted me, they then threw off all restraints, like headstrong horses.

12. *Upon my right hand rise the youth.* "Younglings." *They push away my feet.* They trip up my heels, or they in effect trample me under their feet.

13. *They mar my path.* They destroy the waymarks, so that there is no safety in travelling through the deserts, the guideposts and waymarks being gone.

24. *He will not stretch out his hand to the grave.* As if he said, Though I suffer here, I shall not suffer hereafter. Though He add stroke to stroke, so as to destroy my life, yet His displeasure shall not proceed beyond the grave.

25. *Did not I weep for him that was in trouble?* "Should I not then weep for the ruthless day?"

28. *I went mourning without the sun. Chammah,* which we here translate *the sun,* comes from a root of the same letters, which signifies to hide, protect, and may be translated, "I went mourning without a protector or guardian."

29. *I am a brother to dragons.* By my mournful and continual cry I resemble *tannim,* the jackals or hyenas. *And a companion to owls.* "To the daughters of howling," generally understood to be the ostrich; for both the jackal and the female ostrich are remarkable for their mournful cry, and for their attachment to desolate places.

CHAPTER 31

Job makes a solemn protestation of his chastity and integrity, 1-12; of his humanity, 13-16; of his charity and mercy, 17-23; of his abhorrence of covetousness and idolatry, 24-32; and of his readiness to acknowledge his errors, 33-34; and wishes for a full investigation of his case, being confident that this would issue in the full manifestation of his innocence, 36-40.

1. *I made a covenant with mine eyes.* "I have cut" or divided "the covenant sacrifice with my eyes." My conscience and my eyes are the contracting parties; God is the Judge; and I am therefore bound not to look upon anything with a delighted or covetous eye by which my conscience may be defiled or my God dishonored. *Why then should I think upon a maid?* "And why should I set myself to contemplate, or think upon, Bethulah?" That Bethulah may here signify an idol is very likely.

5. *If I have walked with vanity.* If I have been guilty of idolatry, or the worshipping of a false god; for thus *shav,* which we here translate "vanity," is used Jer. xviii. 15 (compare with Ps. xxxi. 6; Hos. xii. 11; and Jonah ii. 9) and it seems evident that the whole of Job's discourse here is a vindication of himself from all idolatrous dispositions and practices.

6. *Mine integrity. Tummathi,* my perfection; the totality of my unblamable life.

7. *If my step hath turned out of the way.* I am willing to be sifted to the uttermost—for every step of my foot, for every thought of my heart, for every look of mine eye, and for every act of my hands.

9. *If mine heart have been deceived by a woman.* The Septuagint add, "another man's wife."

10. *Let my wife grind unto another.* Let her work at the handmill, grinding corn, which was the severe work of the meanest slave.

17. *Or have eaten my morsel myself alone.* Hospitality was a very prominent virtue among the ancients in almost all nations.

24. *Gold my hope, Zahab,* polished gold, and *kethem,* stamped gold (see on chap. xxviii. 15-17).

26. *If I beheld the sun when it shined.* In this verse Job clears himself of that idolatrous worship which was the most ancient and most consistent with reason of any species of idolatry: the worship of the heavenly bodies.

"Adoration," or the religious act of "kissing the hand," comes to us from the Latin; *ad,* to, and *oris,* the mouth.

31. *If the men of my tabernacle said.* I believe the Targum gives the best sense here: "If the men of my tabernacle have not said, Who hath commanded that we should not be satisfied with his flesh?" My domestics have had all kindness shown them; they have lived like my own children, and have been served with the same viands as my family.

33. *If I covered my transgressions as Adam.* Here is a most evident allusion to the Fall. Adam transgressed the commandment of his Maker, and he endeavored to conceal it.

34. *Did I fear a great multitude?* Was I ever prevented by the voice of the many from decreeing and executing what was right?

35. *Oh that one would hear me!* I wish to have a fair and full hearing. *Behold, my desire is.* "There is my pledge." I bind myself, on a great penalty, to come into court, and abide the issue. *That the Almighty would answer me.* That He would call this case immediately before himself, and oblige my adversary to come into court, to put His accusations into a legal form, that I might have the opportunity of vindicating myself in the presence of a Judge who would hear dispassionately my pleadings, and bring the cause to a righteous issue. *And that mine adversary had written a book.* That he would not indulge himself in vague accusations, but would draw up a proper "bill of indictment," that I might know to what I had to plead, and find the accusation in a tangible form.

36. *Surely I would take it upon my shoulder.* I would be contented to stand before the bar as a criminal, bearing upon my shoulder the board to which the accusation is affixed.

37. *I would declare unto him the number of my steps.* I would show this adversary the different stations I had been in, and the offices which I had filled in life, that he might trace me through the whole of my civil, military, and domestic life, in order to get evidence against me. *As a prince would I go near.* Though carrying my own accusation, I would go into the presence of my Judge as the *nagid,* "chief," or sovereign commander and judge, of the people and country, and would not shrink from having my conduct investigated by even the meanest of my subjects.

38. *If my land cry.* Job seems here to refer to that law, Lev. xxv. 1-7, by which the Israelites were obliged to give the land rest every seventh year. He, conscious that he had acted according to this law, states that his land could not cry out against him, nor its *furrows . . . complain.*

39. *If I have eaten the fruits thereof without money.* If I have eaten the fruits of it, I have cultivated it well to produce those fruits; and this has not been without money, for I have gone to expenses on the soil, and remunerated the laborers.

40. *The words of Job are ended.* That is, his defense of himself against the accusations of his friends, as they are called. He spoke afterwards, but never to them; he addresses only God, who came to determine the whole controversy.

CHAPTER 32

Elihu comes forward, and expresses his disapprobation of both Job and his three friends—with the one for justifying himself, and with the others for taking up the subject in a wrong point of view, and not answering satisfactorily—and makes a becoming apology for himself, 1-22.

1. *These three men ceased to answer Job.* They supposed that it was of no use to attempt to reason any longer with a man who justified himself before God. The truth is, they failed to convince Job of any point because they argued from false principles; and, as we have seen, Job had the continual advantage of them. There were points on which he might have been successfully assailed, but they did not know them. Elihu, better acquainted with both human nature and the nature of the divine law, and of God's moral government of the world, steps in, and makes the proper discriminations; acquits Job on the ground of their accusations, but condemns him for his too great self-confidence, and his trusting too much in his external righteousness; and, without duly considering his frailty and imperfections,

his incautiously arraigning the providence of God of unkindness in its dealings with him. This was the point on which Job was particularly vulnerable, and which Elihu very properly clears up. *Because he was righteous in his own eyes.* The Septuagint, Syriac, Arabic, and Chaldee, all read, "Because he was righteous in their eyes," intimating that they were now convinced that he was a holy man, and that they had charged him foolishly.

2. *Then was kindled the wrath.* This means no more than that Elihu was greatly excited, and felt a strong and zealous desire to vindicate the justice and providence of God against the aspersions of Job and his friends. *Elihu the son of Barachel the Buzite.* Buz was the second son of Nahor, the brother of Abram, Gen. xxii. 21. *Of the kindred of Ram.* Kemuel was the third son of Nahor; and is called in Genesis (see above) "the father of Aram," which is the same as Ram. A city of the name of *Buz* is found in Jer. xxv. 23, which probably had its name from this family; and, as it is mentioned with Dedan and Tema, we know it must have been a city in Idumea, as the others were in that district. *Because he justified himself rather than God.* Literally, "he justified his soul," *naphhso,* "before God." He defended, not only the whole of his conduct, but also his motives, thoughts.

6. *I am young.* Among the Asiatics the youth never spoke in the presence of the elders, especially on any subject of controversy.

7. *Days should speak.* That is, men are to be reputed wise and experienced in proportion to the time they have lived. The Easterners were remarkable for treasuring up wise sayings; indeed, the principal part of their boasted wisdom consisted in proverbs and maxims on different subjects.

8. *But there is a spirit in man.* "The spirit itself is in miserable man, and the breath of the Almighty causeth them to understand." The spirit itself is in man as the spring or fountain of his animal existence; and by the afflatus of this spirit he becomes capable of understanding and reason, and consequently of discerning divine truth. The animal and intellectual lives are here stated to be from God, and this appears to be an allusion to man's creation, Gen. ii. 7. In this one saying Elihu spoke more sense and sound doctrine than all Job's friends did in the whole of the controversy.

11. *Whilst ye searched out what to say.* "Whilst ye were searching up and down for words." A fine irony, which they must have felt.

12. *Behold, there was none of you that convinced Job.* "Confuted Job." They spoke multitudes of words, but were unable to overthrow his arguments.

14. *He hath not directed.* He has not spoken a word against me; therefore I have no cause of irritation. I shall speak for truth, not for conquest or revenge. *Neither will I answer him with your speeches;* your passions have been inflamed by contradiction, and you have spoken foolishly with your lips.

16. *When I had waited.* I waited to hear if they had anything to reply to Job; and when I found them in effect speechless, then I ventured to come forward.

17. *I will answer also my part.* "I will recite

my portion." We have already seen that the Book of Job is a sort of drama, in which several persons have their different parts to recite. Probably the book was used in this way, in ancient times, for the sake of public instruction. Eliphaz, Zophar, and Bildad had recited their parts, and Job had responded to each; nothing was brought to issue. Elihu, a bystander, perceiving this, comes forward and takes a part, when all the rest had expended their materials. Yet Elihu, though he spoke well, was incapable of closing the controversy; and God himself appears, and decides the case.

18. *I am full of matter.* "I am full of words," or sayings; i.e., wise sentences, and ancient opinions.

19. *My belly is as wine which hath no vent.* New wine in a state of effervescence. *Like new bottles.* Rather "bags," made of goatskins. When the wine is in a state of fermentation, and the skin has no vent, these bags are ready to *burst;* and if they be old, the new wine destroys them, breaks the old stitching, or rends the old skin. Our Lord makes use of the same figure, Matt. ix. 17.

21. *Let me not . . . accept any man's person.* I will speak the truth without fear or favor. *Neither let me give flattering titles.* I will not give epithets to any man that are not descriptive of his true state.

CHAPTER 33

Elihu offers himself in God's stead to reason with Job in meekness and sincerity, 1-7. Charges Job with irreverent expressions, 8-12. Vindicates the providence of God, and shows the various methods which He uses to bring sinners to himself: by dreams and visions, 13-15; by secret inspirations, 16-18; by afflictions, 19-22; by messengers of righteousness, 23; and by the great atonement, 24. How and from what God redeems men, and the blessings which He communicates, 25-30. Job is exhorted to listen attentively to Elihu's teaching, 31-33.

6. *I am according to thy wish in God's stead: I also am formed out of the clay.* Mr. Good, and before him none other that I have seen, has most probably hit the true meaning: "Behold, I am thy fellow. I too was formed by God out of the clay."

7. *My terror shall not make thee afraid.* This is an allusion to what Job had said, chap. ix. 34: "Let him take his rod away from me, and let not his fear terrify me." Being thy equal, no fear can impose upon thee so far as to overawe thee, so that thou shouldst not be able to conduct thy own defense.

8. *Surely thou hast spoken.* What Elihu speaks here, and in the three following verses, contains, in general, simple quotations from Job's own words, or the obvious sense of them.

12. *In this thou art not just.* Thou hast laid charges against God's dealings, but thou hast not been able to justify those charges; and were there nothing else against thee, these irreverent speeches are so many proofs that thou art not clear in the sight of God.

13. *Why dost thou strive against him?* Is it not useless to contend with God? Can He do anything that is not right? As to His giving thee any account of the reasons why He deals thus and thus with thee, or anyone else, thou needest not expect it; He is sovereign, and is not to be called to the bar of His creatures.

14. *For God speaketh once.* Elihu, having made the general statement that God would not come to the bar of His creatures to give account of His conduct, shows the general means which He uses to bring men to an acquaintance with themselves and with Him. He states these in the six following particulars, which may be collected from vv. 15-24.

15. (1) *In a dream . . . when deep sleep falleth upon men.* Many, by such means, have had the most salutary warnings. (2) *In a vision of the night . . . in slumberings upon the bed.* Visions or images presented in the imagination during slumber, when men are betwixt sleeping and waking, or when, awake and in bed, they are wrapt up in deep contemplation, the darkness of the night having shut out all objects from their sight, so that the mind is not diverted by images of earthly things impressed on the senses.

16. *Then he openeth the ears of men.* (3) By secret inspirations. A dream or a vision simply considered is likely to do no good; it is the opening of the understanding, and the pouring in of the light, that make men wise to salvation.

19. *He is chastened also with pain upon his bed.* (4) Afflictions are a fourth means which God makes use of to awaken and convert sinners. In the hand of God these were the cause of the salvation of David, as himself testifies: "Before I was afflicted I went astray," Ps. cxix. 67, 71, 75.

23. *If there be a messenger with him, an interpreter.* (5) The messengers of righteousness this is a fifth method, "If there be over him an interpreting or mediatorial angel or messenger." *One among a thousand,* "One from the chief, head, or teacher."

24. *Then he is gracious unto him.* He exercises mercy towards fallen man, and gives command for His respite and pardon. (6) *I have found a ransom.* Copher, "an atonement." It is this that gives efficacy to all the preceding means, without which they would be useless, and the salvation of man impossible. I must think that the redemption of a lost world, by Jesus Christ, is not obscurely signified in vv. 23-24.

25. *His flesh shall be fresher than a child's.* He shall be born a new creature. *He shall return to the days of his youth.* He shall be born again, and become a child of God, through faith in Christ Jesus.

27. *He looketh upon men. Anashim,* wretched, fallen men. He "shines into them," to convince them of sin; and if any, under this convincing light of God, say, "*I have sinned, and perverted the right*"—abused the powers, faculties, mercies, and advantages, which Thou didst give me, by seeking rest and happiness in the creature— *and it profited me not,* "and it was not equal to me," did not come up to my expectation, nor supply my wants;

28. *He will deliver his soul.* He will do that to every individual penitent sinner which He has promised in His Word to do for a lost world—He will deliver his soul from going down to the pit of hell.

29. *Lo, all these things worketh God.* God frequently uses one, or another, or all of these means to bring men, *gaber,* stouthearted men, who are far from righteousness, to holiness and heaven.

CHAPTER 34

Elihu begins with an exhortation to Job's friends, 1-4; charges Job with accusing God of acting unrighteously, which he shows is impossible, 5-12; points out the power and judgments of the Almighty, 13-30; shows how men should address God, and how irreverently Job has acted, 31-37.

5. *Job hath said, I am righteous.* Job had certainly said the words attributed to him by Elihu, particularly in chap. xxvii. 2, etc.; but it was in vindication of his aspersed character that he had asserted is own righteousness, and in a different sense to that in which Elihu appears to take it up. He asserted that he was righteous as to the charges his friends had brought against him. And he never intimated that he had at all times a pure heart, and had never transgressed the laws of his Maker. It is true also that he said, *God hath taken away my judgment;* but he most obviously does not mean to charge God with injustice, but to show that He had dealt with him in a way wholly mysterious; and that He did not interpose in his behalf, while his friends were overwhelming him with obloquy and reproach.

8. *Which goeth in company with the workers of iniquity.* Job makes a "track to join fellowship" with the workers of iniquity; i.e., Job's present mode of reasoning, when he says, "I am righteous, yet God hath taken away my judgment," is according to the assertion of sinners, who say, "There is no profit in serving God."

10. *Far be it from God.* Rather, "Wickedness, far be that from God; and from iniquity, the Almighty." The sense is sufficiently evident without the paraphrase in our version.

13. *Who hath given him a charge?* Who is it that governs the world? Is it not God? Who disposes of all things in it? Is it not the Almighty, by His just and merciful providence? The government of the world shows the care, the justice, and the mercy of God.

14. *If he set his heart upon man.* I think this and the following verse should be read thus: "If He set His heart upon man, He will gather his soul and breath to himself; for all flesh shall perish together, and man shall turn again unto dust."

17. *Shall . . . he that hateth right govern?* Or, "Shall he who hateth judgment lie under obligation?" It is preposterous to suppose that he who lives by no rule should impose rules upon others.

18. *Is it fit to say to a king, Thou art wicked?* Literally, "Who calls a king Belial? Who calls princes wicked?" Civil governors should be treated with respect; no man should speak evil of the ruler of the people.

19. *That accepteth not.* If it be utterly improper to speak against a king or civil governor, how much more so to speak disrespectfully of God, who is not influenced by human caprices or considerations, and who regards the rich and the poor alike!

23. *For he will not lay upon man.* The meaning appears to be this: He will not call man a second time into judgment.

25. *He knoweth their works.* He knows what they have done, and what they are plotting to do. *He overturneth them in the night.* In the revolution of a single night the plenitude of power on which the day closed is annihilated. See the cases of Belshazzar and Babylon.

26. *He striketh them as wicked men.* At other times He executes His judgments more openly, and they are suddenly destroyed in the sight of the people.

31. *Surely it is meet to be said unto God.* This is Elihu's exhortation to Job: Humble thyself before God, and say, "I have suffered—I will not offend."

37. *He addeth rebellion unto his sin.* An ill-natured, cruel, and unfounded assertion, borne out by nothing which Job had ever said or intended; and indeed, more severe than the most inveterate of his friends (so called) had ever spoken.

CHAPTER 35

Elihu accuses Job of impious speeches, 1-4. No man can affect God by his iniquity, nor profit Him by his righteousness, 5-8. Many are afflicted and oppressed, but few cry to God for help; and, for want of faith, they continue in affliction, 9-16.

2. *My righteousness is more than God's.* This would indeed be a blasphemous saying; but Job never said so, neither directly nor constructively. It would be much better to translate the words, "I am righteous before God." And Job's meaning most certainly was, "Whatever I am in your sight, I know that in the sight of God I am a righteous man"; and he had a right to assume this character, because God himself had given it to him.

3. *What advantage will it be unto thee?* As if he had said to God, "My righteousness cannot profit Thee, nor do I find that it is of any benefit to myself. Or perhaps Elihu makes here a general assertion, which he afterwards endeavors to exemplify: Thou hast been reasoning how it may profit thee, and thou hast said, "What profit shall I have in righteousness more than in sin?"

9. *By reason of the multitude.* Or rather, "From among the multitude" the oppressed clamor, "They shout because of the mighty." The wicked rich oppress the wicked poor; these cry aloud because of their oppressors; but they have no relief, because they call not upon God.

15. *But . . . because it is not so.* Rather, "But now, because He visiteth not in His anger." The sense of the place appears to be this: Because vengeance is not speedily executed on an evil work, therefore are the hearts of the children of men set in them to do iniquity. This is, in effect, the charge which Elihu brings against Job.

16. *Therefore doth Job open his mouth in vain.* God will execute vengeance when it may best serve the ends of His justice, providence, and mercy. *He multiplieth words without knowledge.* However this may apply to Job, it most certainly applies very strongly and generally to the words, not only of Job's three friends, but to those also of Elihu himself. The contest is frequently a strife of words.

CHAPTER 36

Elihu vindicates God's justice, and His providential and gracious dealings with men, 1-9. Promises of God to the obedient, and threatenings to the disobedient; also promises to the poor and afflicted, 10-16. Sundry proofs of God's mercy, with suitable exhortations and cautions, 17-33.

3. *I will fetch my knowledge from afar.* "From the distant place," meaning probably both remote antiquity and heaven. I will show thee that all antiquity and experience are on my side.

4. *He that is perfect in knowledge is with thee.* "The perfection of knowledge is with thee."

5. *God is mighty, and despiseth not any.* He reproaches no man for his want of knowledge. *He is mighty.* Literally, "He is mighty in strength of heart"; He can never be terrified nor alarmed.

6. *He preserveth not the life.* He will not give life to the wicked; all such forfeit life by their transgressions. *But giveth right.* Justice will He give to the afflicted or "humble."

13. *But the hypocrites in heart.* "The profligates, the impious." *They cry not.* "Though he binds them, yet they cry not." They are too obstinate to humble themselves even under the mighty hand of God.

14. *They die in youth.* Exactly what the Psalmist says, "Bloody and deceitful men shall not live out half their days," Ps. lv. 23. Literally, the words of Elihu are, "They shall die in the youth of their soul."

20. *Desire not the night.* Thou hast wished for death (here called *night*).

21. *Regard not iniquity.* It is sinful to entertain such wishes; it is an insult to the providence of God. He sends affliction; He knows this to be best for thee. But thou hast preferred death to affliction, thereby setting thy wisdom against the wisdom of God.

26. *God is great.* He is omnipotent. *We know him not.* He is unsearchable. *Neither can the number of his years be searched out.* He is eternal.

27. *He maketh small the drops of water.* This appears simply to refer to evaporation.

29. *The noise of his tabernacle?* By the *tabernacle* we may understand the whole firmament, whence He sends forth the rain of His strength, and the thunder of His power.

32. *With clouds he covereth the light.* "By the hollow of his hands he concealeth the light," the fountain of light, i.e., the sun. *And commandeth it not to shine by the cloud that cometh betwixt.* I am afraid this is no translation of the original. Old Coverdale is better: "And at his commandement it cometh agayne."

33. *The noise thereof sheweth concerning it, the cattle also concerning the vapour.* I think this may be translated without any violence to any word in the text: Its loud noise (or His thunder) shall proclaim concerning Him; a magazine of wrath against iniquity.

CHAPTER 37

Elihu continues to set forth the wisdom and omnipotence of God, as manifested in the thunder and lightning, 1-5; in the snows and frosts, 6-8; in various meteors; and shows the end for which they are sent, 9-13. Job is exhorted to consider the wondrous works of God in the light, in the clouds, in the winds, in heat and cold, in the formation of the heavens, and in the changes of the atmosphere, 14-22. The perfections of God, and how He should be reverenced by His creatures, 23-24.

1. *My heart trembleth.* A proper consideration of God's majesty in the thunder and lightning is enough to appall the stoutest heart.

2. *Hear attentively.* "Hear with hearing." The words seem to intimate that there was actually at that time a violent storm of thunder and

lightning, and that the successive peals were now breaking over the house, and the lightning flashing before their eyes. The storm continued till Elihu had finished, and out of that storm the Almighty spoke. See the beginning of the succeeding chapter. *The noise of his voice.* The sudden clap. *And the sound that goeth out.* The peal or continued rattling, pounding, and thumping, to the end of the peal.

3. *He directeth it under the whole heaven.* He directs it (the lightning) under the whole heaven, in the twinkling of an eye from east to west; and its light—the reflection of the flash, not the lightning—*unto the ends of the earth,* so that a whole hemisphere seems to see it at the same instant.

4. *After it a voice roareth.* After the flash has been seen, the peal is heard. *He thundereth with the voice of his excellency.* "Of his majesty"; nor is there a sound in nature more descriptive of, or more becoming, the majesty of God than that of thunder. *And he will not stay them.* "And he hath not limited or circumscribed them."

5. *God thundereth marvellously with his voice.* This is the conclusion of Elihu's description of the lightning and thunder; and here only should chap. xxxvi. have ended. He began, chap. xxxvi. 29, with the noise of God's tabernacle; and he ends here with the marvellous thundering of Jehovah. *Great things doeth he.* This is the beginning of a new paragraph, and relates particularly to the phenomena which are afterwards mentioned.

7. *He sealeth up the hand of every man.* I think that the act of freezing is probably intended; that when the earth is bound up by intense frost, *the hand,* "labour," of *every man* is sealed up; he can do no more labor in the field till the south wind blow, by which a thaw takes place. While the earth is in this state of rigidity, *the beasts go into their* [*dens,*] *and remain in their places,* v. 8, some of them sleeping out the winter in a state of torpor, and others of them feeding on the stores which they had collected in autumn.

11. *By watering he wearieth the thick cloud.* Perhaps it would be better to say, "The brightness dissipates the cloud"; or, if we follow our version, *By watering the earth he wearieth,* weareth out or emptieth, *the thick cloud*—causes it to pour down all its contents upon the earth, that they may cause it to bring forth and bud.

15. *And caused the light of his cloud to shine?* Almost every critic of note understands this of the rainbow.

21. *And now men see not the bright light.* Elihu seems to refer to the insufferable brightness of the sun. Can any man look at the sun shining in his strength, when a clear and strong wind has purged the sky from clouds and vapors? Much less can any gaze on the majesty of God.

22. *Fair weather cometh out of the north.* Is this any version of the original, which is rendered by almost every version, ancient and modern, thus, or to this effect: "From the north cometh gold"?

23. *Touching the Almighty, we cannot find him out.* This is a very abrupt exclamation, and highly descriptive of the state of mind in which Elihu was at this time; full of solemnity, wonder, and astonishment at his own contemplation

of this "great First Cause, least understood." The Almighty! we cannot find Him out. *He will not afflict.* "He will not answer." He will give account of none of His matters to us. We cannot comprehend His motives, nor the ends He has in view.

CHAPTER 38

The Lord answers Job out of a whirlwind, and challenges him to answer, 1-3. He convinces him of ignorance and weakness, by an enumeration of some of His mighty works, particularly of the creation of the earth, 4-7. The sea and the deeps, 8-18. The light, 19-21. Snow, hail, thunder, lightning, rain, dew, ice, and hoarfrost, 22-30. Different constellations and the ordinances of heaven influencing the earth, 31-33. Shows His own power and wisdom in the atmosphere, particularly in the thunder, lightnings, and rain, 34-38. His providence in reference to the brute creation, 39-41.

1. *The Lord answered Job out of the whirlwind.* It is not *suphah,* as in the preceding chapter, v. 9; but *searah,* which signifies something turbulent, tumultuous, or violently agitated; and here may signify what we call a "tempest," and was intended to fill Job's mind with solemnity, and an awful sense of the majesty of God.

5. *Who hath laid the measures thereof?* Who hath adjusted its polar and equatorial distances from the center? *Who hath stretched the line?* Who hath formed its zones and its great circles, and adjusted the whole of its magnitude and gravity to the orbit in which it was to move, as well as its distance from that great center about which it was to revolve?

7. *When the morning stars sang together.* This must refer to some intelligent beings who existed before the creation of the visible heavens and earth, and it is supposed that this and the following clause refer to the same beings; that by the *sons of God* and the *morning stars,* the angelic host is meant, as they are supposed to be first, though perhaps not chief, in the order of creation.

10. *And brake up for it my decreed place.* This refers to the decree, Gen. i. 9: "Let the waters under the heaven be gathered together unto one place."

13. *That the wicked might be shaken out of it.* The meaning appears to be this: As soon as the light begins to dawn upon the earth, thieves, assassins, murderers, and adulterers, who all hate and shun the light, fly like ferocious beasts to their several dens and hiding places.

14. *And they stand as a garment.* The earth receiving these impressions from the solar light and heat, plants and flowers spring up, and decorate its surface as the most beautiful stamped garment does the person of the most sumptuously dressed female.

23. *Reserved against the time of trouble.* "To the season of strictness," i.e., the season when the earth is bound by the frost. *Against the day of battle and war.* Hailstones being often employed as instruments of God's displeasure against His enemies, and the enemies of His people. There is probably an allusion here to the plague of hail sent on the Egyptians. See Exod. ix. 23.

25. *Divided a watercourse.* The original may signify rather a "cloud," or clouds in general, where the waters are stored up.

26. *To cause it to rain on the earth.* It is well-known that rain falls copiously in thunder-

storms. The flash is first seen, the clap is next heard, and last the rain descends.

31. *Canst thou bind the sweet influences of Pleiades?* The Pleiades are a constellation in the sign Taurus. They consist of six stars visible to the naked eye; to a good eye, in a clear night, seven are discernible; but with a telescope ten times the number may be readily counted.

32. *Mazzaroth in his season?* This is generally understood to mean the signs of the zodiac.

37. *Who can number the clouds?* Perhaps the word *saphar*, which is commonly rendered to *number*, may here mean, as in Arabic, to "irridiate," and may refer to those celestial and inimitable tinges which we sometimes behold in the sky. *Bottles of heaven.* The clouds; it is an allusion to the *girbahs*, or bottles made of skin, in which they are accustomed to carry their water from swells.

39. *Wilt thou hunt the prey for the lion?* Rather the lioness, or strong lion. In the best Hebrew Bibles, the thirty-ninth chapter begins with this verse, and begins properly, as a new subject now commences, relating to the natural history of the earth, or the animal kingdom, as the preceding chapter does to astronomy and meteorology.

40. *When they couch in their dens.* Before they are capable of trusting themselves abroad. *Abide in the covert.* Before they are able to hunt down the prey by running. It is a fact that the young lions, before they have acquired sufficient strength and swiftness, lie under cover, in order to surprise those animals which they have not fleetness enough to overtake in the forest; and from this circumstance the *kephirim*, "young lions, or lions' whelps," have their name. The root is *caphar*, to "cover" or "hide."

41. *Who provideth for the raven?* This bird is chosen, perhaps, for his voracious appetite, and general hunger for prey, beyond most other fowls.

CHAPTER 39

Several animals described: the wild goats and hinds, 1-4. The wild ass, 5-8. The unicorn, 9-12. The peacock and ostrich, 13-18. The war-horse, 19-25. The hawk, 26. And the eagle and her brood, 27-30.

9. *Will the unicorn be willing to serve thee?* The animal in question, called *reim*, is undoubtedly the rhinoceros, which has the latter name from the horn that grows on his nose.

12. *That he will bring home thy seed.* Thou canst make no domestic nor agricultural use of him.

13. *The goodly wings unto the peacocks?* I believe *peacocks* are not intended here; and the Hebrew word should be translated "ostriches"; and the term which we translate *ostrich* should be, as it is elsewhere translated, "stork"; and perhaps the word rendered here *feathers* should be translated "hawk," or "pelican." Mr. Good has come nearest both to the original and to the meaning by translating thus: "The wing of the ostrich tribe is for flapping; but of the stork and falcon for flight."

17. *God hath deprived her of wisdom.* Of this foolishness we have an account from the ancients: "It covers its head in the reeds, and thinks itself all out of sight because itself cannot see."

18. *She lifteth up herself.* "When she raiseth up herself to run away." It neither flies nor runs distinctly, but has a motion composed of both; and, using its wings as sails, makes great speed.

21. *He paweth in the valley.* "They dig in the valley," i.e., in his violent galloping, in every pitch of his body, he scoops up sods out of the earth.

25. *He saith among the trumpets, Ha, ha.* The original is peculiarly emphatical: *Heach!* a strong, partly nasal, partly guttural sound, exactly resembling the first note which the horse emits in neighing.

26. *Doth the hawk fly by thy wisdom?* It may very probably mean the falcon. It was owing to its swiftness that the Egyptians in their hieroglyphics made it the emblem of the wind. *Stretch her wings toward the south?* Most of the falcon tribe pass their way toward warmer regions on the approach of winter.

29. *Her eyes behold afar off.* The eagle was proverbial for her strong and clear sight.

30. *Her young ones also suck up blood.* The eagle does not feed her young with carrion, but with prey newly slain, so that they may *suck up blood.* Where the slain are, there is she. These words are quoted by our Lord. "Wheresoever the carcase is, there will the eagles be gathered together," Matt. xxiv. 28. It is likely, however, that this was a proverbial mode of expression; and our Lord adapts it to the circumstances of the Jewish people, who were about to fall a prey to the Romans.

CHAPTER 40

Job humbles himself before the Lord, 1-5. And God again challenges him by a display of His power and judgments, 6-14. A description of behemoth, 15-24.

1. *Moreover the Lord answered.* That is, the Lord continued His discourse with Job. *Answered* does not refer to any thing said by Job, or any question asked.

2. *He that reproveth God, let him answer it.* Let the man who has made so free with God and His government answer to what he has now heard.

9. *Hast thou an arm like God?* Every word from this to the end of v. 14, has a wonderful tendency to humble the soul; and it is no wonder that at the conclusion of these sayings Job fell in the dust confounded, and ascribed righteousness to his Maker.

13. *Hide them in the dust together.* Blend the high and the low, the rich and the poor, in one common ruin. *Bind their faces in secret.* This seems to refer to the custom of preserving mummies.

15. *Behold now behemoth.* I am of the opinion that the animal here described is now extinct. The mammoth, for size, will answer the description in this place, especially v. 19: "He is the chief of the ways of God."

CHAPTER 41

God's great power in the leviathan, of which creature He gives a very circumstantial description, 1-34.

1. *Canst thou draw out leviathan?* A species of whale has been supposed to be the creature in question, but the description suits no animal

but the crocodile or alligator. The crocodile is a natural inhabitant of the Nile, and other Asiatic and African rivers. It is a creature of enormous voracity and strength, as well as fleetness in swimming. He will attack the largest animals, and even men, with the most daring impetuosity. In proportion to his size he has the largest mouth of all monsters. The upper jaw is armed with forty sharp, strong teeth, and the under jaw with thirty-eight. *With an hook.* That crocodiles were caught with a baited hook, at least one species of crocodile, we have the testimony of Herodotus, lib. ii., c. 70.

8. *Lay thine hand upon him.* Mr. Heath translates, "Be sure thou strike home. Mind thy blow: rely not upon a second stroke."

25. *By reason of breakings they purify themselves.* No version, either ancient or modern, appears to have understood this verse; nor is its true sense known.

29. *Darts are counted as stubble.* All these verses state that he cannot be wounded by any kind of weapon, and that he cannot be resisted by any human strength.

CHAPTER 42

Job humbles himself before God, 1-6. God accepts him; censures his three friends; and commands Job to offer sacrifices for them, that He might pardon and accept them, as they had not spoken what was right concerning their Maker, 7-9. The Lord turns Job's captivity; and his friends visit him, and bring him presents, 10-11. Job's affluence becomes double to what it was before, 12. His family is also increased, 13-15. Having lived 140 years after his calamities, he dies, 16-17.

2. *I know that thou canst do every thing.* Thy power is unlimited, Thy wisdom infinite.

3. *Who is he that hideth counsel?* These are the words of Job, and they are a repetition of what Jehovah said, chap. xxxviii. 2: "Who is this that darkeneth counsel by words without knowledge?" Job now, having heard the Almighty's speech, and having received His reproof, echoes back His words: "Who is he that hideth counsel without knowledge?" Alas, I am the man.

8. *Take . . . seven bullocks and seven rams.* From this it appears that Job was considered a priest, not only in his own family, but also for others. For his children he offered burnt offerings, chap. i. 5; and now he is to make the same kind of offerings, accompanied with intercession, in behalf of his three friends. This is a full proof of the innocence and integrity of Job.

A more decided one could not be given that the accusations of his friends, and their bitter speeches, were as untrue as they were malevolent.

10. *The Lord turned the captivity of Job.* It is said that *the Lord turned the captivity of Job, when he prayed for his friends.* He had suffered much through the unkindness of these friends. They had criticized his conduct without feeling or mercy, and he had just cause to be irritated against them; and that he had such a feeling toward them several parts of his discourses sufficiently prove. God was now about to show Job His mercy; but mercy can be shown only to the merciful. Job must forgive his unfeeling friends if he would be forgiven by the Lord.

11. *A piece of money.* Kesitah signifies a "lamb"; and it is supposed that this piece of money had a lamb stamped on it, as that quantity of gold was generally the current value for a lamb. The Vulgate, Chaldee, Septuagint, Arabic, and Syriac have "one lamb or sheep"; so it appears that they did not understand the *kesitah* as implying a piece of money of any kind, but a sheep or a lamb. *Earring of gold.* Literally, a "nose-jewel."

12. *The Lord blessed the latter end of Job.* Was it not in consequence of his friends bringing him a lamb, sheep, or other kind of cattle, and the quantity of gold mentioned, that his stock of sheep was increased so speedily to 14,000, his camels to 6,000, his oxen to 2,000, and his she-asses to 1,000? *He had fourteen thousand sheep.* The reader, by referring to chap. i. 3, will perceive that the whole of Job's property was exactly *doubled.*

13. *Seven sons and three daughters.* This was the same number as before.

14. *The name of the first, Jemima.* "Days upon days." *Kezia.* "Cassia," a well-known aromatic plant. *Keren-happuch.* The "horn of plenty."

15. *Gave them inheritance among their brethren.* This seems to refer to the history of the daughters of Zelophehad, given in Num. xxviii. 1-8, who appear to have been the first who were allowed an inheritance among their brethren.

16. *After this lived Job an hundred and forty years.* How long he had lived before his afflictions we cannot tell.

17. *Job died, being old and full of days.* He died when he was "satisfied with this life"; this the word *seba* implies.

The Book of
PSALMS

This book is termed in Hebrew *Sepher Tehillim*, "The Book of Praises," as the major part of the psalms have for their subject the praises of the Lord.

That the psalms were sung in the Jewish service, and frequently accompanied by musical instruments, there is no doubt, for the fact is repeatedly mentioned; and hence the most ancient translation we have of the Psalms, viz., the Septuagint, as it stands in what is called the Codex Alexandrinus, is called "The Psaltery," which is a species of musical instrument resembling the harp, according to the accounts given of it by some of the ancients. From this term came the *Psalterium* of the Vulgate, and our word "Psalter."

A psalm is called in Hebrew *mizmor*, from *zamar*, "to cut off," because in singing each word was separated into its component syllables, each syllable answering to a note in the music.

The Hebrews divide the Psalms into five books, and this division is noticed by several of the primitive fathers. The origin of this division is not easily ascertained; but as it was considered a book of great excellence, and compared for its importance to the Pentateuch itself, it was probably divided into five books, as the law was contained in so many volumes.

Book I. From Psalm i to Psalm xli inclusive.
Book II. From Psalm xlii to Psalm lxxii inclusive.
Book III. From Psalm lxxiii to Psalm lxxxix inclusive.
Book IV. From Psalm xc to Psalm cvi inclusive.
Book V. From Psalm cvii to Psalm cl inclusive.

That the collection, as it now stands, was made long after David's death is a general opinion among learned men; and Ezra was the collector and compiler is commonly believed. As to the inscriptions, they are of slender authority; several of them do not agree with the subject of the psalm to which they are prefixed, and not a few of them appear to be out of their places. Supposing that the persons mentioned are the authors of those psalms to which their names are prefixed, there are still fifty-three which, as bearing no proper name, must be attributed to uncertain authors, though it is very probable that several of them were made by David.

That there were several authors, and that the psalms were composed at different times, is sufficiently evident from the compositions themselves. The occasions also on which they were written are frequently pointed out by their contents.

PSALM 1

The blessedness of the righteous shown, in his avoiding every appearance of evil, 1. In his godly use of the law of the Lord, 2. This further pointed out under the metaphor of a good tree planted in good, well-watered soil, 3. The opposite state of the ungodly pointed out, under the metaphor of chaff driven away by the wind, 4. The miserable end of sinners, and the final happiness of the godly, 5-6.

1. *Blessed is the man.* This psalm has no title, and has been generally considered, but without especial reason, as a preface or introduction to the whole book.

The Word which we translate *blessed* is properly in the plural form, "blessednesses"; or may be considered as an exclamation produced by contemplating the state of the man who has taken God for his Portion; "Oh, the blessedness of the man!" And the word *haish* is emphatic: "that man"; that one among a thousand who lives for the accomplishment of the end for which God created him. *That walketh not in the counsel of the ungodly.* There is a double climax in this verse: First, there are here three characters, each exceeding the other in sinfulness. (1) The ungodly, *reshaim,* from *rasha,*

to be "unjust"; rendering to none his due. (2) Sinners, *chattaim,* from *chata,* "to miss the mark," "to pass over the prohibited limits," "to transgress." This man not only does no good, but he does evil. (3) Scornful, *letsim,* from *latsah,* "to mock, deride." The second climax is found in the words, (1) Walk; (2) Stand; (3) Sit, which mark three different degrees of evil in the conduct of those persons. The ungodly man walks, the sinner stands, and the scornful man sits down in the way of iniquity.

2. *But his delight is in the law of the Lord.* His will, desire, affection, every motive in his heart, and every moving principle in his soul are on the side of God and His truth.

3. *Like a tree planted.* Not like one growing wild, but one that has been carefully cultivated. *His leaf also shall not wither.* His profession of true religion shall always be regular and unsullied, and his faith be ever shown by his works.

6. *The Lord knoweth.* "Approveth" the way, of the righteous, *tsaddikim,* from *tsadak,* to "give even weight"—the men who give to all their due; opposed to *reshaim,* v. 1, they who withhold right from all.

PSALM 2

This psalm treats of the opposition raised, by both Jew and Gentile, against the kingdom of Christ, 1-3. Christ's victory, and the confusion of His enemies, 4-6. The promulgation of the gospel after His resurrection, 7-9. A call to all the potentates and judges of the earth to accept it, because of the destruction that shall fall on those who reject it, 10-12.

1. *Why do the heathen rage?* It has been supposed that David composed this psalm after he had taken Jerusalem from the Jebusites, and made it the head of the kingdom; 2 Sam. vv. 7-9. The Philistines, hearing this, encamped in the valley of Rephaim, nigh to Jerusalem, and Josephus, *Antiq.* lib. vii. c. 4, says that all Syria, Phoenicia, and the other circumjacent warlike people, united their armies to those of the Philistines, in order to destroy David before he had strengthened himself in the kingdom. David, having consulted the Lord, 2 Sam. vv. 17-19, gave them battle, and totally overthrew the whole of his enemies. In the first place, therefore, we may suppose that this psalm was written to celebrate the taking of Jerusalem, and the overthrow of all the kings and chiefs of the neighboring nations. In the second place we find, from the use made of this psalm by the apostles, Acts iv. 27, that David typified Jesus Christ, and that the psalm celebrates the victories of the gospel. *The heathen, goyim,* the nations; those who are commonly called "the Gentiles." *Rage, rageshu;* the gnashing of teeth, and tumultuously rushing together, of those indignant and cruel people are well expressed by the sound as well as the meaning of the original word.

2. *Against his anointed.* "Against his Messiah." But as this signifies "the anointed" person, it may refer first to David, as it does secondly to Christ.

4. *He that sitteth in the heavens shall laugh.* Words spoken after the manner of men; shall utterly contemn their puny efforts.

7. *This day have I begotten thee.* We have St. Paul's authority for applying to the resurrection of our Lord these words, "Thou art my Son; this day have I begotten thee"—see Acts xiii. 3; see also Heb. v. 5. "I have begotten" is here taken in the sense of "manifesting, exhibiting, or declaring"; and to this sense of it St. Paul (Rom. i. 3-4) evidently alludes when speaking of "Jesus Christ . . . which was made of the seed of David according to the flesh; and declare [exhibited or determined] to be the Son of God with power, according to the spirit of holiness."

8. *Ask of me, and I shall give thee.* Here a second branch of Christ's office as Saviour of the world is referred to; viz., His mediatorial office. Having died as an atoning Sacrifice, and risen again from the dead, He was now to make intercession for mankind.

9. *Thou shalt break them with a rod of iron.* This may refer to the Jewish nation, whose final rejection of the gospel was foreseen, and in whose place the Gentiles or heathen were brought into the Church of Christ.

10. *Be instructed, ye judges.* Rather, "Be ye reformed"; and receive the gospel as the law, or the basis of the law, of the land.

11. *Serve the Lord with fear.* A general direction to all men. Fear God with that reverence which is due to His supreme majesty, and as servants should their Master. *Rejoice with trembling.* If ye serve God aright, ye cannot but be happy; but let a continual filial fear moderate all your joys. Ye must all stand at last before the judgment seat of God; watch, pray, believe, work, and keep humble.

12. *Kiss the Son, lest he be angry.* It is remarkable that the word *son (bar,* a Chaldee word) is not found in any of the versions except the Syriac, nor indeed anything equivalent to it. The Chaldee, Vulgate, Septuagint, Arabic, and Aethiopic, have a term which signifies "doctrine" or "discipline": "Embrace discipline, lest the Lord be angry with you."

This psalm is remarkable, not only for its subject, the future kingdom of the Messiah, but also for the change of person. In the first verse the prophet speaks; in the third, the adversaries; in the fourth and fifth, the prophet answers; in the sixth, Jehovah speaks; in the seventh, the Messiah; in the eighth and ninth, Jehovah answers; and in the tenth to the twelfth, the prophet exhorts the opponents to submission and obedience.

PSALM 3

David complains, in great distress, of the number of his enemies, and the reproaches they cast on him, as one forsaken of God, 1-2; is confident, notwithstanding, that God will be his Protector, 3; mentions his prayers and supplications, and how God heard him, 4-5; derides the impotent malice of his adversaries, and foretells their destruction, 6-7; and ascribes salvation to God, 8.

This is said to be *A Psalm of David, when he fled from Absalom his son.* See the account, 2 Sam. xv. 1, etc. And David is supposed to have composed it when obliged to leave Jerusalem, passing by the mount of Olives, weeping, with his clothes rent, and with dust upon his head. This psalm is suitable enough to these circumstances, and they mutually cast light on each other. If the inscription be correct, this psalm is a proof that the psalms are not placed in any chronological order.

1. *Lord, how are they increased that trouble me!* We are told that the hearts of all Israel went after Absalom, 2 Sam. xv. 13.

2. *No help for him in God.* These were some of the reproaches of his enemies, Shimei and others. These reproaches deeply affected his heart; and he mentions them with that note which so frequently occurs in the Psalms, and which occurs here for the first time, *Selah.* Much has been said on the meaning of this word, and we have nothing but conjecture to guide us. The Septuagint always translate it by *diapsalma,* "a pause in the Psalm." The Chaldee sometimes translates it by *lealmin,* "for ever." The rest of the versions leave it unnoticed. It either comes from *sal,* to "raise or elevate," and may denote a particular elevation in the voices of the performers, which is very observable in the Jewish singing to the present day; or it may come from *salah,* to "strew or spread out," intimating that the subject to which the word is attached should be spread out, meditated on, and attentively considered by the reader.

3. *Thou, O Lord, art a shield.* As a shield covers and defends the body from the strokes of an adversary, so wilt Thou cover and defend me from them that rise up against me. *The lifter up of mine head.* Thou wilt restore me to the state from which my enemies have cast me down. This is the meaning of the phrase, and this he speaks prophetically.

5. *I laid me down and slept.* He who knows that he has God for his Protector may go quietly and confidently to his bed.

7. *Thou hast smitten.* "Thou wilt smite. Breaking the jaws and *the teeth* are expressions which imply confounding and destroying an adversary.

PSALM 4

David prays to be heard, 1; expostulates with the ungodly, 2; exhorts them to turn to God, and make their peace with Him, 3-5; shows the vain pursuits of men in search of happiness, which he asserts exists only in the approbation of God, 6-7; commends himself to the Lord, and then quietly takes his repose, 8.

This psalm seems to have been composed on the same occasion with the preceding, viz., Absalom's rebellion. It appears to have been an evening hymn, sung by David and his company previously to their going to rest. It is inscribed "to the chief Musician on Neginoth." *Neginoth* seems to come from *nagan*, "to strike"; and probably may signify some such instruments as the cymbal, drum, and stringed instruments in general.

1. *Thou hast enlarged me.* I was in prison, and Thou hast brought me forth abroad. *Have mercy upon me*—continue to act in the same way.

2. *Love vanity.* The poor, empty, shallow-brained, pretty-faced Absalom, whose prospects are all vain, and whose promises are all empty! *Seek after leasing?* "Falsehood."

3. *The Lord hath set apart him that is godly. Chasid*, the pious, benevolent man. He has marked such, and put them aside as His own property.

4. *Stand in awe, and sin not.* The Septuagint, which is copied by St. Paul, Eph. iv. 26, translate this clause, "Be ye angry, and sin not." The Vulgate, Syriac, Aethiopic, and Arabic, give the same reading; and thus the original *rigzu* might be translated: If ye be angry, and if ye think ye have cause to be angry, do not let your disaffection carry you to acts of rebellion against both God and your king. *And be still.* "And be dumb." Hold your peace; fear lest ye be found fighting against God.

6. *Who will shew us any good?* This is not a fair translation. The word *any* is not in the text, nor anything equivalent to it. The place is sufficiently emphatic without this. There are multitudes who say, Who will show us good? *Lift thou up the light of thy countenance.* This alone, *the light of thy countenance*—Thy peace and approbation—constitute the supreme good.

7. *Thou hast put gladness in my heart.* Thou hast given my soul what it wanted and wished for. I find now a happiness which earthly things could not produce. I have peace of conscience, and joy in the Holy Ghost; such inward happiness as they cannot boast who have got the highest increase of *corn* and *wine*, those two things in the abundance of which many suppose happiness to be found.

8. *I will both lay me down in peace, and sleep.* Most men lie down, and most sleep, daily, for without rest and sleep life could not be preserved; but alas! how few lie down in peace! peace with their own consciences, and peace with God!

PSALM 5

David continues instant in prayer, 1-2; makes early application to God, 3; and shows the hatred which God bears to the workers of iniquity, 4-6. His determination to worship God, and to implore direction and support, 7-8. He points out the wickedness of his enemies, 9, and the destruction they may expect, 10; and then shows the happiness of those who trust in the Lord, 11-12.

This psalm is inscribed "to the chief Musician upon Nehiloth, A Psalm of David." As *neginoth* may signify all kinds of instruments struck with a plectrum, stringed instruments, those like the drum, cymbals, etc.; so *nechiloth*, from *chal*, to be "hollow," to "bore through," may signify any kind of wind instruments, such as the horn, trumpet, flute.

1. *Give ear to my words.* This is properly a morning hymn, as the preceding was an evening hymn. We have seen from the conclusion of the last psalm that David was very happy, and lay down and slept in the peace and love of his God. When he opens his eyes on the following morning, he not only remembers but feels the happiness of which he spoke; and with his first recollections he meditates on the goodness and mercy of God, and the glorious state of salvation into which he has been brought.

3. *My voice shalt thou hear in the morning.* He finds it good to begin the day with God, to let divine things occupy the first place in his waking thoughts, as that which first occupies the mind on awaking is most likely to keep possession of the heart all the day through.

4. *Neither shall evil dwell with thee.* As Thou art holy, so Thou hast pleasure only in holiness; and as to *evil men*, they shall never enter into Thy glory; lo *yegurecha ra*, "the evil man shall not even *sojourn* with thee."

5. *The foolish shall not stand.* He is a fool and a madman who is running himself out of breath for no prize, who is fighting against the Almighty. This every wicked man does; therefore is every *wicked* man a *fool* and a *madman. Thou hatest all workers of iniquity.* Some sin *now* and *then*, others *generally;* some *constantly,* and some *labor* in it with all their might. These are the *workers of iniquity.* Such even the God of infinite love and mercy *hates.* Alas! what a portion have *the workers of iniquity!* the hatred of God Almighty!

6. *That speak leasing.* See on Ps. iv. 2. *The Lord will abhor the bloody and deceitful man.* "The man of bloods"; for he who has the spirit of a murderer will rarely end with one bloodshedding.

7. *In the multitude of thy mercy.* David considered it an inexpressible privilege to be permitted to attend public worship; and he knew that it was only through the multitude of God's mercy that he, or any man else, could enjoy such a privilege. He who takes David's views of this subject will never, willingly, be absent from the means of grace. *In thy fear.* Duly considering the infinite holiness of Thy majesty *will I worship*, "will I bow and prostrate myself" in the deepest self-abasement and humility. *Toward thy holy temple.* If David was the author of this psalm, as is generally agreed, the Temple was not built at this time; only the Tabernacle then existed; and in the preceding clause he speaks of coming into the house, by which he must mean the Tabernacle. But *temple* here may signify the holy of holies, before which David might prostrate himself while in the house, i.e., the court of the Tabernacle.

10. *Destroy thou them, O God.* All these apparently imprecatory declarations should be translated in the future tense, to which they belong, and which shows them to be prophetic. "Thou wilt *destroy* them; Thou wilt *cast them out*."

11. *Let all those that put their trust in thee rejoice.* Such expressions as these should be translated in the same way, declaratively and prophetically: "All those who put their trust in Thee shall *rejoice*—shall *ever shout for joy*."

12. *With favour.* Literally, "Like a shield Thy favor will crown him."

PSALM 6

This psalm contains a deprecation of eternal vengeance, 1; a petition to God for mercy, 2. This is enforced from a consideration of the Psalmist's sufferings, 3; from that of the divine mercy, 4; from that of the praise and glory which God would fail to receive if man were destroyed, 5; from that of his humiliation and contrition, 6-7. Being successful in his supplication, he exults in God, 8-9; and predicts the downfall of all his enemies, 10.

This psalm has the following inscription: "To the chief Musician on Neginoth, upon Sheminith, A Psalm of David," which the Chaldee translates, "To be sung on neginoth, a harp of eight strings." We have already seen that *neginoth* probably signifies all instruments which emitted sounds by strokes, or stringed instruments in general. This psalm was to be accompanied with such instruments; but one of a particular kind is specified, viz., *sheminith,* so called from its having eight strings. The "chief musician" is directed to accompany the recital of this psalm with the above instrument.

1. *O Lord, rebuke me not.* This psalm, which is one of the seven "Penitential Psalms," is supposed to have been written during some grievous disease with which David was afflicted after his transgression with Bath-sheba. It argues a deep consciousness of sin, and apprehension of the just displeasure of God.

2. *Have mercy.* I have no merit. I deserve all I feel and all I fear. *O Lord, heal me.* No earthly physician can cure my malady. Body and soul are both diseased, and only God can help me. *I am weak. Umlal.* "I am exceedingly weak"; I cannot take nourishment, and my strength is exhausted.

7. *Mine eye is consumed.* Is blasted, withered, sunk in my head.

10. *Ashamed and sore vexed.* May they as deeply deplore their transgressions as I have done mine! May they return; may they be suddenly converted! The original will bear this meaning, and it is the most congenial to Christian principles.

PSALM 7

The Psalmist prays against the malice of his enemies, 1-2; protests his own innocence, 3-5; prays to God that He would vindicate him, for the edification of His people, 6-8; prays against the wickedness of his enemies, 9; expresses strong confidence in God, 10; threatens transgressors with God's judgments, 11-13; shows the conduct and end of the ungodly, 14-16; and exults in the mercy and loving-kindness of his Maker, 17.

This psalm is entitled, "Shiggaion of David, which he sang unto the Lord, concerning the words of Cush the Benjamite." The word *shig-*

gayon comes from *shagah,* "to wander," a wandering song; i.e., a psalm composed by David in his wanderings, when he was obliged to hide himself from the fury of Saul.

As to "Cush the Benjamite," he is a person unknown in the Jewish history. The name is probably a name of disguise, and by it he may covertly mean Saul himself, the son of Kish, who was of the tribe of Benjamin. The subject of the psalm will better answer to Saul's unjust persecution and David's innocence than to any other subject in the history of David.

1. *O Lord my God. Yehovah Elohai,* words expressive of the strongest confidence the soul can have in the Supreme Being.

2. *Lest he tear my soul like a lion.* These words seem to answer well to Saul. As the lion is king in the forest, so was Saul king over the land. As the lion in his fierceness seizes at once, and tears his prey in pieces, so David expected to be seized and suddenly destroyed by Saul.

3. *If I have done this.* David was accused by Saul of affecting the kingdom and of waiting for an opportunity to take away the life of his king, his patron, and his friend. In his application to God he refers to these charges, meets them with indignation, and clears himself of them by a strong appeal to his Judge.

4. *Yea, I have delivered him.* When, in the course of Thy providence, Thou didst put his life in my hand in the cave, I contented myself with cutting off his skirt, merely to show him the danger he had been in, and the spirit of the man whom he accused of designs against his life; and yet even for this my heart smote me, because it appeared to be an indignity offered to him who was the Lord's anointed.

7. *For their sakes therefore return thou on high.* Ascend the judgment seat; and let them see, by the dispensations of Thy providence, who is innocent and who is guilty.

11. *God is angry with the wicked every day.* The Hebrew for this sentence according to the *points* is, "And God is angry every day." Our translation seems to have been borrowed from the Chaldee, where the whole verse is as follows: "God is a righteous Judge; and in strength he is angry against the wicked every day." The Vulgate: "God is a Judge righteous, strong, and patient;—will he be angry every day?" The Septuagint: "God is a righteous Judge, strong and long-suffering; not bringing forth his anger every day." Syriac: "God is the Judge of righteousness; he is not angry every day." The Arabic is the same as the Septuagint. The Aethiopic: "God is a just Judge, and strong and long-suffering; he will not bring forth tribulation daily." I have judged it of consequence to trace this verse through all the ancient versions in order to be able to ascertain what is the true reading, where the evidence on one side amounts to a positive affirmation, "God is angry every day"; and, on the other side, to as positive a negation, "He is not angry every day." The mass of evidence supports the latter reading. The Chaldee first corrupted the text by making the addition, "with the wicked," which our translators have followed, though they have put the words into italics, as not being in the Hebrew text. The true sense may be restored thus: *el,* with the vowel point *tsere,* signifies "God"; *al,* the same letters, with the point *pathach,* signifies "not." Several of the versions have read

it in this way: "God judgeth the righteous, and is not angry every day."

12. *If he turn not.* Most of the versions read, "If ye return not."

13. *He hath also prepared for him the instruments of death.* This appears to be all a prophecy of the tragic death of Saul. He was wounded by the arrows of the Philistines; and his own keen sword, on which he fell, terminated his woeful days!

14. *He travaileth with iniquity.* All these terms show the pitch of envy, wrath, and malevolence to which Saul had carried his opposition against David.

15. *He made a pit.* The metaphor is taken from pits dug in the earth, and slightly covered over with reeds, so as not to be discerned from the solid ground; but the animal steps on them, the surface breaks, and he falls into the pit and is taken. "All the world agrees to acknowledge the equity of that sentence, which inflicts upon the *guilty* the punishment intended by them for the *innocent*."—Horne.

16. *Shall come down upon his own pate.* Upon his *scalp*, the top of the head.

PSALM 8

The glory and excellence of God manifested by His works, 1-2; particularly in the starry heavens, 3; in man, 4; in his formation, 5; and in the dominion which God has given him over the earth, the air, the sea, and their inhabitants, 6-8: in consequence of which God's name is celebrated over all the earth, 9.

The inscription of this psalm is the following: "To the chief Musician upon Gittith, A Psalm of David." This has been metaphrased, "To the conqueror, concerning the winepresses," and has been supposed to be a psalm intended for the time of vintage. That the psalm has respect to our Lord and the time of the gospel is evident from the reference made to v. 2, in Matt. xi. 25, the express quotation of it in Matt. xxi. 16, and another reference to it in 1 Cor. i. 27. The *fourth* and *sixth* verses are quoted Heb. ii. 6-9. See also 1 Cor. xv. 27 and Eph. i. 22. The first and second Adam are both referred to, and the first and second creation also; and the glory which God has received, and is to receive, through both. It relates to Christ and redemption.

1. *O Lord our Lord. Yehovah Adoneynu;* "O Jehovah our Prop, our Stay, or Support."

2. *Out of the mouth of babes and sucklings.* We have seen how our Lord applied this passage to the Jewish children, who, seeing His miracles, cried out in the Temple, "Hosanna to the Son of David" Matt. xxi. 16. And we have seen how the *enemy* and the *avenger*—the *chief priests* and the *scribes*—were offended because of these things; and as the psalm wholly concerns Jesus Christ, it is most probable that in this act of the Jewish children the prophecy had its primary fulfilment, and was left to the Jews as a witness and a sign of the Messiah, which they should have acknowledged when our Lord directed their attention to it.

4. *What is man? Mah enosh,* what is wretched, miserable man; man in his fallen state, full of infirmity, ignorance, and sin? *That thou art mindful of him?* That thou settest Thy heart upon him, keepest him continually in Thy merciful view. *And the son of man. Uben Adam,*

and the son of Adam, the first great rebel, the fallen child of a fallen parent.

5. *Thou hast made him a little lower than the angels.* The original is certainly very emphatic: "Thou hast made him less than God for a little time." See these passages explained at large in the notes on Heb. ii. 6.

6. *Thou madest him to have dominion.* See the notes referred to above, and those on Phil. ii. 6-9. *Thou hast put all things under his feet.* Though the whole of the brute creation was made subject to Adam in his state of innocence, yet it could never be literally said of him that God had put all things under his feet, or that he had dominion over the work of God's hands; but all this is most literally true of our Lord Jesus, and to Him the apostle, Heb. ii. 6, etc., applies all these passages.

7. *All sheep and oxen.* All domestic animals. *Beasts of the field.* All wild beasts.

8. *The fowl of the air.* All these were given to man in the beginning, and he has still a general dominion over them; for thus saith the Lord: "The fear of you and the dread of you shall be upon every beast of the earth, and upon every fowl of the air, upon all that moveth upon the earth, and upon all the fishes of the sea; into your hand are they delivered," Gen. ix. 2.

9. *O Lord our Lord.* The Psalmist concludes as he began. Jehovah, our Prop and Support! His name is excellent in all the earth. The name of Jesus is celebrated in almost every part of the habitable globe; for His gospel has been preached, or is in the progress of being preached, through the whole world.

PSALM 9

David praises God for the benefits which He has granted to Israel in general, and to himself in particular, 1-6. He encourages himself in the Lord, knowing that He will ever judge righteously, and be a Refuge for the distressed, 7-10. He exhorts the people to praise God for His judgments, 11-12; prays for mercy and support; and thanks God for His judgments executed upon the heathen, 13-16. He foretells the destruction of the ungodly, 17; prays for the poor and needy, and against their oppressors, 18-20.

The inscription to this psalm in the Hebrew text is, "To the chief Musician upon Muth-labben, A Psalm of David." The title and the psalm have been so variously understood that it would be as painful as it would be useless to follow the different commentators, both ancient and modern, through all their conjectures.

1. *I will praise thee, O Lord, with my whole heart.* And it is only when the *whole heart* is employed in the work that God can look upon it with acceptance. *I will shew forth.* "I will number out, or reckon up," a very difficult task, "thy miracles," supernatural interventions of Thy power and goodness.

5. *Thou hast rebuked the heathen.* We know not what this particularly refers to, but it is most probably to the Canaanitish nations, which God destroyed from off the face of the earth; hence it is said, *Thou hast put out their name for ever and ever.*

6. *Destructions are come to a perpetual end.* Rather, "The enemy is desolated for ever; for thou hast destroyed their cities, and their memory is perished with them." Multitudes of the cities of the Canaanites have perished so utterly that neither name nor vestige remains of them.

9. *A refuge.* "A high place," where their enemies can neither reach nor see them.

15. *The heathen are sunk down in the pit.* See on Ps. vii. 15.

17. *The wicked shall be turned into hell.* "Headlong into hell, down into hell." The original is very emphatic.

20. *Put them in fear.* "O Lord, place a teacher among them," that they may know they also are accountable creatures, grow wise unto salvation, and be prepared for a state of blessedness. *That the nations may know themselves to be but men. Enosh;* Let the Gentiles be taught by the preaching of Thy gospel that they are weak and helpless and stand in need of the salvation which Christ has provided for them.

PSALM 10

The Psalmist complains to God of the oppressions which the poor suffer from the wicked man, whom he describes as the hater of the poor, 1-2; proud, 3; one who will not seek God, 4; and is regardless of His judgments, 5; self-confident, 6; blasphemous and deceitful, 7; strives by subtlety and treachery to destroy the poor, 8-10; and supposes that God is regardless of his conduct, 11. The Psalmist calls earnestly on God to preserve the poor and humble, and cast down the oppressor, 12-15. He foresees that his prayer is heard, that judgment will be executed, and the poor delivered, 16-18.

1. *Why standest thou afar off, O Lord?* This psalm makes a part of the preceding in the Vulgate and Septuagint, and in four of Kennicott's and De Rossi's MSS. It seems to belong to the time of the Captivity, or the return of the captives. It was probably made in reference to Sanballat, and the other enemies of the Jews. There is a great similarity between this and Psalms xiii; xiv; xxxv; and liii. In these we find the same complaints, the same sentiments, and almost the same expressions. God is represented here as standing at some distance, beholding the oppression of His people, and yet apparently disregarding it.

3. *Blesseth the covetous, whom the Lord abhorreth.* Or, "He blesseth the covetous, he abhorreth the Lord."

8-9. *He sitteth in the lurking places.* In this and the following verse there appears to be an allusion to espionage, or setting of spies on a man's conduct; or to the conduct of an assassin or private murderer. *He sitteth in the lurking places . . . in the secret places . . . his eyes—spies—are privily set. He lieth in wait secretly . . . he doth catch the poor, when he draweth him into his net.* He is like a hunter that lays his traps and gins, digs his pits, sets his nets; and when the prey falls into them, he destroys its life.

10. *He croucheth.* The lion squats down and gathers himself together, that he may make the greater spring.

16. *The Lord is King for ever.* He has, and ever will have, the supreme power.

18. *That the man of the earth may no more oppress.* I believe the Hebrew will be better translated thus: "That he may not add any more to drive away the wretched man from the land." Destroy the influence of the tyrant, and let him not have it again in his power to add even one additional act of oppression to those which he has already committed.

PSALM 11

David's friends advise him to flee to the wilderness from Saul's fury, 1-3. He answers that, having put his trust in God, knowing that He forsakes not those who confide in Him, and that He will punish the ungodly, he is perfectly satisfied that he shall be in safety, 4-7.

The inscription is, "To the chief Musician, A Psalm of David." By the "chief musician" we may understand the master singer, the leader of the band, the person who directed the choir; but we know that the word has been translated, "To the Conqueror."

1. *In the Lord put I my trust: how say ye?* Some of David's friends seem to have given him this advice when they saw Saul bent on his destruction: *Flee as a bird to your mountain.*

3. *If the foundations be destroyed.* If Saul, who is the vicegerent of God, has cast aside his fear, and now regards neither truth nor justice, a righteous man has no security for his life. Kimchi supposes this refers to the priests who were murdered by Doeg, at the command of Saul.

4. *The Lord is in his holy temple.* He is still to be sought and found in the place where He has registered His name. Though the priests be destroyed, the God in whose worship they were employed still lives, and is to be found in His temple by His upright worshippers.

5. *The Lord trieth the righteous.* He does not abandon them; He tries them to show their faithfulness, and He afflicts them for their good. *His soul hateth.* The wicked man must ever be abhorred of the Lord; and the violent man—the destroyer and murderer—*his soul hateth.* An expression of uncommon strength and energy—all the perfections of the divine nature have such in abomination.

6. *Upon the wicked he shall rain.* This is a manifest allusion to the destruction of Sodom and Gomorrah. *An horrible tempest.* "The spirit of terrors."

PSALM 12

The Psalmist, destitute of human comfort, craves help from God, 1; gives the character of those who surrounded him, and denounces God's judgments against them, 2-5; confides in the promises of God, and in His protection of him and all good men, 6-8.

The inscription to this psalm is: "To the chief Musician upon Sheminith, A Psalm of David." See on the title of Psalm vi. Some think that this psalm was made when Doeg and the Ziphites betrayed David to Saul, see 1 Samuel xxii and xxiii; but it is most likely that was written during the Babylonish captivity.

2. *They speak vanity every one with his neighbour.* They are false and hollow; they say one thing while they mean another; there is no trusting to what they say. *With flattering lips and with a double heart do they speak.* "With a heart and a heart." They seem to have two hearts: one to speak fair words, and the other to invent mischief.

3. *Proud things. Gedoloth,* "Great things."

5. *For the oppression of the poor.* This seems to refer best to the tribulations which the poor Israelites suffered while captives in Babylon. The Lord represents himself as looking on and seeing their affliction; and, hearing their cry, He determines to come forward to their help.

8. *The wicked walk on every side.* The land is full of them. *When the vilest men are exalted;* rather, "As villainy gains ground among the sons of Adam."

PSALM 13

This psalm contains the sentiments of an afflicted soul that earnestly desires succor from the Lord. The Psalmist complains of delay, 1-3; prays for light and comfort, because he finds himself on the brink of death, 3; dreads the revilings of his enemies, 4; anticipates a favorable answer, and promises thanksgiving, 5-6.

There is nothing particular in the inscription. The psalm is supposed to have been written during the Captivity, and to contain the prayers and supplications of the distressed Israelites, worn out with their long and oppressive bondage.

1. *How long wilt thou forget me?* The words *ad anah,* "to what length, to what time," translated here *how long?* are four times repeated in the two first verses, and point out at once great dejection and extreme earnestness of soul. *Hide thy face from me?* How long shall I be destitute of a clear sense of Thy approbation?

3. *Consider and hear me.* Rather, "Answer me."

4. *Lest mine enemy say.* Satan's ordinary method in temptation is to excite strongly to sin, to blind the understanding, inflame the passions; and when he succeeds, he triumphs by insults and reproaches.

6. *I will sing unto the Lord.* That heart is turned to God's praise which has a clear sense of God's favor. *Because he hath dealt bountifully with me.* "Because he hath recompensed me."

PSALM 14

The sentiments of atheists and deists, who deny the doctrine of a divine providence. Their character: they are corrupt, foolish, abominable, and cruel, 1-4. God fills them with terror, 5; reproaches them for their oppression of the poor, 6. The Psalmist prays for the restoration of Israel, 7.

There is nothing particular in the title; only it is probable that the word *ledavid,* "of David," is improperly prefixed, as it is sufficiently evident, from the construction of the psalm, that it speaks of the Babylonish captivity.

1. *The fool hath said in his heart, There is no God.* Nabal, which we render *fool,* signifies "an empty fellow, a contemptible person, a villain." One who has a muddy head and an unclean heart; and, in his darkness and folly, says in his heart, "There is no God." "And none," says one, "but a *fool* would say so." The word is not to be taken in the strict sense in which we use the term "atheist," that is, one who denies the being of a God, or confounds Him with matter. (1) There have been some, not many, who have denied the existence of God. (2) There are others who, without absolutely denying the divine existence, deny His providence. (3) There are others, and they are very numerous, who, while they profess to acknowledge both, deny them in their heart, and live as if they were persuaded there was no God to either punish or reward.

3. *They are all gone aside.* They will not walk in the straight path. *They are all together become filthy.* They are become "sour" and

"rancid"; a metaphor taken from milk that has fermented, and turned sour, rancid, and worthless. *There is none that doeth good, no, not one.* This is not only the state of heathen Babylon, but the state of the whole inhabitants of the earth, till the grace of God changes their heart. By nature, and from nature, by practice, every man is sinful and corrupt.

5. *There were they in great fear.* This is a manifest allusion to the history of the Canaanitish nations; they were struck with terror at the sight of the Israelites, and by this allusion the Psalmist shows that a destruction similar to that which fell upon them should fall on the Babylonians.

7. *Oh that the salvation!* Or, more literally, "Who will give from Zion salvation to Israel?" From Zion the deliverance must come, for God alone can deliver them; but whom will He make His instruments?

PSALM 15

The important question answered, Who is a proper member of the Church militant? and who shall finally join the Church triumphant? Verse 1 contains the question; vv. 2-5, the answer.

1. *Lord, who shall abide in thy tabernacle?* The literal translation of this verse is, "Lord, who shall sojourn in Thy tabernacle? who shall dwell in the mountain of Thy holiness?"

2. *He that walketh uprightly.* (1) He walks perfectly. *And worketh righteousness.* (2) He is not satisfied with a contemplative life; he has duties to perform. *And speaketh the truth in his heart.* (3) He is a true man; in him there is no false way.

3. *He that backbiteth not with his tongue.* "He foots not upon his tongue." (4) He is one who treats his neighbor with respect. He says nothing that might injure him in his character, person, or property. *Nor doeth evil to his neighbour.* (5) He not only avoids evil speaking, but he avoids also evil acting towards his neighbor. *Nor taketh up a reproach against his neighbour.* (6) The word *cherpah,* which we here translate *a reproach,* comes from *charaph,* "to strip, or make bare, to deprive one of his garments." The application is easy: A man, for instance, of a good character is reported to have done something wrong; the tale is spread, and the slanderers and backbiters carry it about; and thus the man is stripped of his fair character, of his clothing of righteousness, truth, and honesty. The good man *taketh* it not *up.* He cannot prevent the detractor from laying it down; but it is in his power not to take it up, and thus the progress of the slander may be arrested.

4. *In whose eyes a vile person is contemned.* (7) This man judges of others by their conduct; he tries no man's heart. *A vile person,* the "reprobate," one abandoned to sin; is despised, is "loathsome," as if he were covered with leprosy, for so the word implies. *He honoureth them that fear the Lord.* (8) The truly pious man, while he has in contempt the "honourable" profligate, yet *honoureth them that fear the Lord,* though found in the most abject poverty. *Sweareth to his own hurt, and changeth not.* (9) If at any time he have bound himself by a solemn engagement to do so and so, and he finds afterwards that to keep his oath will be greatly to his damage, yet such reverence has he for God

and for truth that he will not change, be the consequences what they may. The Hebrew might be thus translated: "He sweareth to afflict himself, and does not change"; and thus the Chaldee has rendered this clause. He has promised to the Lord to keep his body under, and bring it into subjection; to deny himself that he may not pamper the flesh, and have the more to give to the poor.

5. *Putteth not out his money to usury.* (10) As *usury* signifies unlawful interest, or that which is got by taking advantage of the necessity of a distressed neighbor, no man that fears God can be guilty of it. The word *neshech*, which we translate *usury*, comes from *nashach*, "to bite as a serpent"; and here must signify that biting or devouring usury which ruins the man who has it to pay. *Nor taketh reward against the innocent.* (11) He neither gives nor receives a bribe in order to pervert justice or injure an innocent man in his cause.

PSALM 16

The contents of this psalm are usually given in the following manner: David, sojourning among idolaters, and being obliged to leave his own country through Saul's persecution, cries to God for help; expresses his abhorrence of idolatry, and his desire to be again united to God's people, 1-4; and declares his strong confidence in God, who had dealt bountifully with him, 5-7. Then follows a remarkable prophecy of the resurrection of Christ, 8-11.

The title of this psalm in the Hebrew is *michtam ledavid,* which the Chaldee translates, "A straight sculpture of David." That David was the author there can be no doubt. It is most pointedly attributed to him by St. Peter, Acts ii. 25-31. That its principal parts might have some relation to his circumstances is also probable; but that Jesus Christ is its main scope not only appears from quotations made by the apostle as above, but from the circumstance that some parts of it never did and never could apply to David. From the most serious and attentive consideration of the whole psalm, I am convinced that every verse of it belongs to Jesus Christ, and none other.

1. *Preserve me, O God: for in thee do I put my trust.* I consider this a prayer of the *man* Christ Jesus on His entering on His great atoning work, particularly His passion in the Garden of Gethsemane. In that passion, Jesus Christ most evidently speaks as man; and with the strictest propriety, as it was the manhood, not the Godhead, that was engaged in the suffering. *Shomreni,* "keep me"—preserve, sustain this feeble humanity, now about to bear the load of that punishment due to the whole of the human race. "For in thee have I hoped." No human fortitude, or animal courage, can avail in My circumstances. It is worthy of remark that our Lord here uses the term, *El,* which signifies the "strong God," an expression remarkably suited to the frailty of that human nature which was now entering upon its vicarious sufferings. It will be seen with what admirable propriety the Messiah varies the appellations of the Divine Being in this address, a circumstance which no translation without paraphrase can express.

2-3. *Thou hast said unto the Lord, Thou art my Lord.* Thou hast said to Jehovah, the supreme, self-existing, and eternal Being; *Thou art my Lord, adonai attah,* "Thou art my *Prop, Stay, or Support.*" As the Messiah, or Son of God,

Jesus derived His being and support from Jehovah; and the man Christ was supported by the eternal divinity that dwelt within Him, without which He could not have sustained the sufferings which He passed through, nor have made an atonement for the sin of the world. It is the suffering Messiah, or the Messiah in prospect of His sufferings, who here speaks. *My goodness extendeth not to thee.* There are almost endless explanations of this clause. I think the words should be understood of what the Messiah was doing for men. My goodness, "my bounty," is not to Thee. What I am doing can add nothing to Thy divinity. Thou art not providing this astonishing sacrifice because Thou canst derive any excellence from it; but this bounty extends *to the saints*—to all the spirits of just men made perfect, whose bodies are still in the earth; *and to the excellent,* "the noble or supereminent ones," those who through faith and patience inherit the promises.

4. *Their sorrows shall be multiplied that hasten after another god.* In the Hebrew text there is no word for *God,* and therefore *Messiah* or *Saviour* might be as well substituted, and then the whole will refer to the unbelieving Jews. They would not have the true Christ; they have sought, and are seeking, another Messiah; and how amply fulfilled has the prophetic declaration been in them! *Their drink offerings of blood will I not offer. Nesech* is a "libation," whether of wine or of water, poured out on the sacrifice. A drink offering of blood is not a correct form of expression; it is rather the libation on the blood of the sacrifice already made.

5. *The Lord is the portion of mine inheritance.* The Messiah speaks. Jehovah is the Portion of mine inheritance. I seek no earthly good; I desire to do the will of God, and that only.

6. *The lines are fallen unto me in pleasant places.* Here is an allusion to the ancient division of the land by lot among the Israelites, the breadth and length being ascertained by lines which were used in measuring. I have got a rich inheritance of immortal spirits. *I have a goodly heritage.* A Church, an innumerable multitude of saints, partakers of the divine nature, and filled with all the fullness of God.

7. *Who hath given me counsel.* Jesus, as man, received all His knowledge and wisdom from God, Luke ii. 40-52. And in Him were hidden all the treasures of wisdom and knowledge. *My reins also instruct me. Reins* or "kidneys," which from their retired situation in the body, says Parkhurst, and being hidden in fat, are often used in Scripture for the most secret workings and affections of the heart. The kidneys and their fat were always to be burnt in sacrifice, to indicate that the most secret purposes and affections of the soul are to be devoted to God. *In the night seasons.* That is, in the time of My passion, My secret purposes and determinations concerning the redemption of man support Me. "For the joy that was set before him [he] endured the cross, despising the shame," Heb. xii. 2.

8. *I have set the Lord always before me.* This verse and all to the end of v. 11 are applied by St. Peter to the death and resurrection of Christ, Acts ii. 25, etc. *He is at my right hand.* That is, I have His constant presence, approbation, and support. All this is spoken by Christ as *man.*

I shall not be moved. Nothing can swerve Me from My purpose; nothing can prevent Me from fulfilling the divine counsel, in reference to the salvation of men.

9. *Therefore my heart is glad.* Unutterably happy in God, always full of the divine presence, because whatsoever I do pleaseth Him. *My glory rejoiceth.* My "tongue," so called by the Hebrews (see Ps. lvii. 8; xxx. 12) because it was bestowed on us to glorify God, and because it is our *glory*, being the instrument of expressing our thoughts by words. *My flesh also shall rest in hope.* There is no sense in which these and the following words can be spoken of David. Jesus, even on the Cross, and breathing out His soul with His life, saw that His rest in the grave would be very short—just a sufficiency of time to prove the reality of His death, but not long enough to produce corruption; and this is well argued by St. Peter, Acts ii. 31.

11. *Thou wilt shew me the path of life.* I first shall find the way out of the regions of death, to die no more. Thus Christ was the Firstfruits of them that slept. Several had before risen from the dead, but they died again. Jesus Christ's resurrection from the dead was the first entrance out of the grave to eternal life or lives, *chaiyim*, for the word is in the plural, and with great propriety too, as this resurrection implies the life of the body, and the life of the rational soul also. *In thy presence.* "Thy faces." Every holy soul has, throughout eternity, the beatific vision, i.e., it sees God as He is, because it is like Him, 1 John iii. 2. *Thy right hand.* The place of honor and dignity; repeatedly used in this sense in the Scriptures. *Pleasures for evermore.* "Onwardly; perpetually, continually," well expressed by our translation, *ever* and *more*—an eternal progression.

PSALM 17

David implores the succor of God against his enemies; and professes his integrity and determination to live in God's glory, 1. He prays for support, and expresses strong confidence in God, 5-9; describes the malice and cruelty of his enemies, and prays against them, 10-14; receives a strong persuasion of support and final victory, 15.

David was most probably the author of this psalm; and it appears to have been written about the time in which Saul had carried his persecution against him to the highest pitch. See 1 Samuel xxvii.

1. *Hear the right.* Attend to the justice of my cause. "O righteous Jehovah, attend unto my cry."

3. *Thou hast tried me.* "Thou hast put me to the test," as they do metals, in order to detect their alloy, and to purify them; well expressed by the Vulgate, "Thou hast tried me by fire."

4. *The paths of the destroyer.* Some render, "hard or difficult paths."

8. *Keep me as the apple of the eye.* Or, "as the black of the daughter of eye." *Hide me under the shadow of thy wings.* This is a metaphor taken from the hen and her chickens. See Matt. xxiii. 37. The Lord says of His followers, Zech. ii. 8: "He that toucheth you toucheth the apple of mine eye." How dear are our eyes to us! how dear must His followers be to God!

9. *From my deadly enemies, who compass me about.* This is a metaphor taken from huntsmen who spread themselves around a large track of forest, driving in the deer from every part of the circumference, till they are forced into the nets or traps which they have set for them in some particular narrow passage. The metaphor is carried on in the following verses.

10. *They are inclosed in their own fat.* Dr. Kennicott, Bishop Horsley, Houbigant, and others read the passage thus: "They have closed their net upon me." This continues the metaphor which was introduced in the preceeding verse, and which is continued in the two following.

11. *They have set their eyes bowing down to the earth.* It is the attitude of the huntsmen looking for the track of the hart's, hind's, or antelope's foot on the ground.

12. *Like as a lion that is greedy of his prey.* I believe the word *lion* is here used to express Saul in his strength, kingly power, and fierce rapacity.

13. *Arise, O Lord, disappoint him.* When he arises to spring upon and tear me to pieces, arise Thou, O Lord; disappoint him of his prey; seize him, and cast him down. *Deliver my soul.* Save my life. *From the wicked, which is thy sword.* Saul is still meant.

14. *From men of the world, which have.* "From mortal men of time"; temporizers; men who shift with the times; who have no fixed principle but one, that of securing their own secular interest. And this agrees with what follows—*which have their portion in this life;* who never seek after anything spiritual; who have bartered heaven for earth, and have got the portion they desired. For Thou *fillest their belly . . . with thy hid treasure.* Their *belly*—their sensual appetites—is their god; and, when their animal desires are satisfied, they take their rest without consideration, like the beasts that perish.

PSALM 18

David's address of thanks to Jehovah, 1-3. A relation of sufferings undergone, and prayers made for assistance, 4-6. A magnificent description of divine interposition in behalf of the sufferer, 7-15; and of the deliverance wrought for him, 16-19. That this deliverance was in consideration of his righteousness, 20-24; and according to the tenor of God's equitable proceedings, 25-28. To Jehovah is ascribed the glory of the victory, 29-36; which is represented as complete by the destruction of all his opponents, 37-42. On these events the heathen submit, 43-45. And for all these things God is glorified, 46-50.

The title: "To the chief Musician, A Psalm of David, the servant of the Lord, who spake unto the Lord the words of this song in the day that the Lord delivered him from the hand of all his enemies, and from the hand of Saul." Except the first clause, this title is taken from 2 Sam. xxii. 1.

1. *I will love thee.* Love always subsists on motive and reason. The verb *racham* signifies to "love with all the tender feelings of nature." Why should he love Jehovah? Not merely because He was infinitely great and good, possessed of all possible perfections, but because He was good to him; and he here enumerates some of the many blessings he received from Him. *My strength.* (1) Thou who hast given me power over my adversaries, and hast enabled me to avoid evil and do good.

2. *The Lord is my rock.* (2) I stand on Him as my Foundation, and derive every good from Him who is the Source of good. The word *sela* signifies those craggy precipices which afford

shelter to men and wild animals. (3) He was his *fortress*; a place of strength and safety, where he could be safe from his enemies. He refers to those inaccessible heights in the rocky, mountainous country of Judea where he had often found refuge from the pursuit of Saul. What these have been to my body, such has the Lord been to my soul. *Deliverer.* (4) He who causes me to escape. He was often almost surrounded and taken, but still the Lord made a way for his escape—made a way out as his enemies got in. These escapes were so narrow and so unlikely that he plainly saw the hand of the Lord was in them. (5) *My God, Eli,* "my strong God," not only the Object of my adoration, but He who puts strength in my soul. (6) *My strength, tsuri.* This is a different word from that in the first verse. Rabbi Maimon has observed that *tsur,* when applied to God, signifies "fountain, source, origin." God is not only the Source whence my being was derived, but He is the Fountain whence I derive all my good; *in whom,* says David, *I will trust.* And why? Because he knew Him to be an eternal and inexhaustible Fountain of goodness. This fine idea is lost in our translation; for we render two Hebrew words of widely different meaning by the same term in English, "strength." (7) *My buckler,* my Shield, my Defender, He who covers my head and my heart, so that I am neither slain nor wounded by the darts of my adversaries. (8) *Horn of my salvation. Horn* was the emblem of power, and power in exercise. This has been already explained; see on 1 Sam. ii. 1. The *horn of salvation* means a powerful, an efficient salvation. (9) *My high tower;* not only a place of defense, but one from which I can discern the country round about, and always be able to discover danger before it approaches me.

3. *I will call upon the Lord.* When he was conscious that the Object of his worship was such as he has pointed out in the above nine particulars, it is no wonder that he resolves to call upon Him; and no wonder that he expects, in consequence, to be saved from his enemies. For who can destroy him whom such a God undertakes to save?

4. *The sorrows of death compassed me.* "The cables or cords of death." He was almost taken in those nets or stratagems, by which, if he had been entangled, he would have lost his life. *The floods of ungodly men.* Troops of wicked men were rushing upon him like an irresistible torrent; or like the waves of the sea, one impelling another forward in successive ranks; so that, thinking he must be overwhelmed by them, he was for the moment affrighted. But God turned the torrent aside, and he escaped.

5. *The sorrows of hell.* "The cables or cords of the grave." Is not this a reference to the cords or ropes with which they lowered the corpse into the grave? or the bandages by which the dead were swathed? He was as good as dead. *The snares of death prevented me.* I was just on the point of dropping into the pit which they had digged for me. In short, I was all but a dead man; and nothing less than the immediate interference of God could have saved my life.

10. *He rode upon a cherub, and did fly.* I.e., the cherub supported and led on the tempest, in which the Almighty rode as in His chariot. This is agreeable to the office elsewhere ascribed to the cherubim. Thus they supported the mercy seat, which was peculiarly the throne of God under the Jewish economy. God is expressly said to make "the clouds his chariot," Ps. civ. 3; and to ride "upon a swift cloud," Isa. xix. 1: so that riding upon a cherub, and riding upon a swift cloud, are riding in the cloud as His chariot, supported and guided by the ministry of the cherubim.

11. *He made darkness his secret place.* God is represented as dwelling in the thick darkness, Deut. iv. 11; Ps. xcvii. 2. This representation in the place before us is peculiarly proper; as thick, heavy clouds deeply charged, and with lowering aspects, are always the forerunners and attendants of a tempest, and greatly heighten the horrors of the appearance; and the representation of them, spread about the Almighty as a tent, is truly grand and poetic. *Dark waters.* The vapors strongly condensed into clouds, which, by the stroke of the lightning, are about to be precipitated in torrents of rain.

12. *At the brightness that was before him his thick clouds passed.* The word *nogah* signifies the "lightning." This goes before Him; the flash is seen before the thunder is heard, and before the rain descends; and then the thick cloud passes. Its contents are precipitated on the earth, and the cloud is entirely dissipated. *Hail stones and coals of fire.* This was the storm that followed the flash and the peal, for it is immediately added—

13. *The Lord also thundered in the heavens, and the Highest gave his voice.* And then followed the hail and coals of fire. The former verse mentioned the lightning, with its effects; this gives us the report of the thunder, and the increasing storm of hail and fire that attended it.

14. *He sent out his arrows . . . he shot out lightnings.* I believe the latter clause to be an illustration of the former. *He sent out his arrows*—that is, He shot out *lightnings.*

15. *The channels of water were seen.* This must refer to an earthquake; for in such cases, the ground being rent, water frequently gushes out at the fissures, and often rises to a tremendous height.

16. *He drew me out of many waters.* Here the allusion is still carried on. The waters thus poured out were sweeping the people away; but God, by a miraculous interference, sent and drew David out. Sometimes *waters* are used to denote multitudes of people, and here the word may have that reference; multitudes were gathered together against David, but God delivered him from them all. This seems to be countenanced by the following verse.

17. *He delivered me from my strong enemy.* Does not this refer to his conflict with Ishbi-benob? "And Ishbi-benob, which was of the sons of the giant . . . thought to have slain David. But Abishai the son of Zeruiah succoured him, and smote the Philistine, and killed him. Then the men of David sware unto him, saying, Thou shalt go no more out with us to battle, that thou quench not the light of Israel," 2 Sam. xxi. 16-17. It appears that at this time he was in the most imminent danger of his life, and that he must have fallen by the hands of the giant if God had not sent Abishai to his assistance. *They were too strong for me.* He was nearly overpowered by the Philistines, and his escape was such as evidently to show it to be supernatural.

18. *They prevented me in the day of my calamity.* They took advantage of the time in which I was least able to make head against them, and their attack was sudden and powerful. I should have been overthrown, *but the Lord was my stay.* He had been nearly exhausted by the fatigue of the day, when the giant availed himself of this advantage.

19. *He brought me forth also into a large place.* He enabled me to clear the country of my foes, who had before cooped me up in holes and corners.

20. *The Lord rewarded me.* David proceeds to give the reasons why God had so marvellously interposed in his behalf. *According to my righteousness.* Instead of being an enemy to Saul, I was his friend. I dealt righteously with him while he dealt unrighteously with me.

26. *With the froward.* "The perverse man"; he that is crooked in his tempers and ways. *Thou wilt shew thyself froward.* "Thou wilt set thyself to twist, twine, and wrestle." If he contend, Thou wilt contend with him.

28. *For thou wilt light my candle.* Thou wilt restore me to prosperity, and give me a happy issue out of all my afflictions. By the lamp of David the Messiah may be meant; Thou wilt not suffer my family to become extinct, nor the kingdom which Thou hast promised me utterly to fail.

29. *I have run through a troop.* This may relate to some remarkable victory, and the taking of some fortified place, possibly Zion, from the Jebusites. See the account 2 Sam. v. 6-8.

30. *God, his way is perfect.* His conduct is like His nature, absolutely pure. *The word of the Lord is tried.* Literally "tried in the fire."

31. *For who is God save the Lord?* "For who is Eloah, except Jehovah?" None is worthy of adoration but the self-existent, eternal, infinitely perfect, and all-merciful Being.

32. *God . . . girdeth me with strength.* The girdle was a necessary part of the Eastern dress; it strengthened and supported the loins, served to confine the garments close to the body; and in it they tucked them up when journeying. The strength of God was to his soul what the girdle was to the body.

33. *My feet like hinds' feet.* Swiftness, or speed of foot, was a necessary qualification of an ancient hero.

34. *He teacheth my hands to war.* The success which I have had in my military exercises I owe to the divine help. *A bow of steel is broken by mine arms.* All the versions render this: "Thou hast made my arm like a brazen bow." A bow of steel is out of the question.

35. *The shield of thy salvation.* In all battles and dangers God defended him. *Thy gentleness,* thy "meekness" or "humility."

40. *The necks of mine enemies.* Thou hast made me a complete conqueror. Treading on the neck of an enemy was the triumph of the conqueror, and the utmost disgrace of the vanquished.

41. *They cried.* The Philistines called upon their gods, but there was none to save them. *Even unto the Lord.* Such as Saul, Ish-bosheth, Absalom, who, professing to worship the true God, called on Him while in their opposition to David.

42. *Then did I beat them.* God was with him, and they had only an arm of flesh.

43. *The strivings of the people.* Disaffections and insurrections among my own subjects, as in the revolt of Absalom, the civil war of Abner in favor of Ish-bosheth. *The head of the heathen. Rosh goyim,* "the chief," or "governor, of the nations," all the circumjacent heathen people; all these were subdued by David, and brought under tribute. *A people whom I have not known.* The people whom he knew were those of the twelve tribes; those whom he did not know were the Syrians, Philistines, Idumeans, etc. All these served him, that is, paid him tribute.

44. *As soon as they hear of me.* His victories were so rapid and splendid over powerful enemies that they struck a general terror among the people, and several submitted without a contest.

45. *The strangers shall fade away.* "They shall fall as the leaves fall off the trees in winter." *And be afraid out of their close places.* Those who have formed themselves into banditti, and have taken possession of rocks and fortified places, shall be so afraid when they hear of my successes that they shall surrender at discretion, without standing a siege. Perhaps all these verbs should be understood in the perfect tense, for David is here evidently speaking of a kingdom at rest, all enemies having been subdued; or, as the title is, when the Lord had "delivered him from the hand of all his enemies."

48. *He delivereth me.* That is, He hath delivered me, and continues to deliver me, from all that rise up against me. *The violent man.* Saul; this applies particularly to him.

49. *Will I give thanks unto thee . . . among the heathen.* Quoted by Paul, Rom. xv. 9, to prove that the calling of the Gentiles was predicted, and that what then took place was the fulfillment of that prediction.

50. *Great deliverance giveth he to his king.* David was a king of God's appointment, and was peculiarly favored by Him. Literally, "He is magnifying the salvations of His king." *To his seed.* His "posterity." So the words in the Old and New Testament should be universally translated. The common translation is totally improper. *For evermore. Ad olam,* "forever"; through all duration of created worlds. *And more*—the eternity that is beyond time. This shows that another David is meant, with another kind of posterity, and another sort of kingdom. From the family of David came the man Christ Jesus; His posterity are the genuine Christians; His kingdom, in which they are subjects, is spiritual. This government shall last through all time.

PSALM 19

The heavens and their host proclaim the majesty of God, 2-6; the excellence and perfection of the divine law, 7-10; its usefulness, 11. The Psalmist prays for pardon and preservation from sin, 12-13; and that his words and thoughts may be holy, 14.

1. *The heavens declare the glory of God.* Literally, "The heavens number out the glory of the strong God." *The firmament.* The whole visible expanse; not only containing the celestial bodies above referred to, but also the air, light, rains, dews.

3. *There is no speech nor language, where their voice is not heard.* Leave out the expletives here, which pervert the sense; and what remains is a tolerable translation of the original: "No speech, and no words; their voice without hearing. Into all the earth hath gone out their sound; and to the extremity of the habitable world, their eloquence." St. Paul applies this as a prophecy relative to the universal spread of the gospel of Christ, Rom. x. 18; for God designed that the light of the gospel should be diffused wheresoever the light of the celestial luminaries shone.

5. *Which is as a bridegroom.* The sun is compared to a bridegrrom in his ornaments, because of the glory and splendor of his rays; and to a giant or strong man running a race, because of the power of his light and heat.

7. *The law of the Lord.* And here are two books of divine revelation: (1) the visible heavens, and the works of creation in general; (2) the Bible, or divinely inspired writings contained in the Old and New Testaments. These may all be called *the law of the Lord; torah,* from *yarah,* to "instruct, direct, put straight, guide." *Is perfect. Temimah,* it is perfection; it is perfect in itself as a law, and requires perfection in the hearts and lives of men. *Converting the soul.* Turning it back to God. *The testimony of the Lord. Eduth,* from *ad,* "beyond, forward." The various types and appointments of the law, which refer to something beyond themselves, and point forward to the Lamb of God, who takes away the sin of the world. *Is sure. Neemanah,* are "faithful"; they point out the things beyond them fairly, truly, and fully. They all bear testimony to the great atonement. *Making wise the simple.* The simple is he who has but one end in view, who is concerned about his soul.

8. *The statutes of the Lord. Pikkudim,* from *pakad,* "He visited, cared, took notice of, appointed to a charge." The appointments or charge delivered by God to man for his regard and observance. *Are right. Yesharim,* from *yashar,* "to make straight, smooth, right, upright." *Rejoicing the heart.* As they show a man what he is to observe and keep in charge, and how he is to please God, and the divine help he is to receive from the visitations of God, they contribute greatly to the happiness of the upright—they rejoice the heart. *The commandment. Mitsvah,* from *tsavah,* "to command, give orders, ordain." *Is pure.* From *barah,* "to clear, cleanse, purify." *Enlightening the eyes.* Showing men what they should *do,* and what they should avoid. It is by God's commandments that we see the exceeding sinfulness of sin, and the necessity of redemption.

9. *The fear of the Lord. Yirah,* from *yara,* "to fear, to venerate"; often put for the whole of divine worship. The reverence we owe to the Supreme Being. *Is clean. Tehorah,* from *tahar,* "to be pure, clean"; not differing much from *barah* (see above), to be clean and bright as the heavens. Its object is to purge away all defilement, to make a spotless character. *The judgments of the Lord. Mishpatim,* from *shaphat,* "He judged, regulated, disposed." All God's regulations, all His decisions; what He has pronounced to be right and proper. *Are true. Emeth, truth,* from *am,* "to support, confirm, make stable, and certain." *And righteous altogether.* They are not only according to truth,

but they are righteous, *tsadeku;* they give to "all their due." They show what belongs to *God,* to *man,* and to *ourselves.* And hence the word *altogether, yachdav, equally,* is added; or *truth and righteousness united.*

10. *Honeycomb.* Honey is sweet; but honey just out of the comb has a sweetness, richness, and flavor far beyond what it has after it becomes exposed to the air.

11. *By them is thy servant warned. Nizhar,* from *zahar,* "to be clear." By these laws, testimonies, etc., Thy servant is fully instructed; he sees all clearly, and he discerns that in keeping of them there is great reward.

14. *Let the words of my mouth.* He has prayed against practical sin, the sins of the body; now, against the sins of the mouth and of the heart. *My redeemer. Goali,* my "kinsman," he whose right it is to redeem the forfeited inheritance.

PSALM 20

A prayer for the king in his enterprises, that his prayers may be heard, his offerings accepted, and his wishes fulfilled, 1-4. Confidence of victory expressed, 5-6. Vain hopes exposed, and supplication made for the king.

It is most likely that this psalm was penned on the occasion of David's going to war; and most probably with the Ammonites and Syrians, who came with great numbers of horses and chariots to fight with him. See 2 Sam. x. 6-8; 1 Chron. xix. 7. It is one of the Dialogue Psalms, and appears to be thus divided: Previously to his undertaking the war, David comes to the Tabernacle to offer sacrifice. This being done, the people, in the king's behalf, offer up their prayers; these are included in the three first verses. The fourth was probably spoken by the high priest; the fifth, by David and his attendants; the last clause, by the high priest; the sixth, by the high priest, after the victim was consumed; the seventh and eighth, by David and his men; and the ninth, as a chorus by all the congregation.

1. *The Lord hear thee.* David had already offered the sacrifice and prayed. The people implore God to succor him in the day of trouble. *The name of the God of Jacob.* This refers to Jacob's wrestling with the Angel, Gen. xxxii. 24, etc. And who was this Angel? Evidently none other than the *Angel of the Covenant,* the Lord Jesus.

2. *Send thee help from the sanctuary.* This was the place where God recorded His name, the place where He was to be sought, and the place where He manifested himself. He is now in Christ, reconciling the world to himself. This is the true sanctuary where God must be sought.

3. *Remember all thy offerings.* The *minchah,* which is here mentioned, was a gratitude offering. *Burnt sacrifice.* The *olah* here mentioned was a bloody sacrifice.

4. *Grant thee according to thine own heart.* This was probably the prayer of the high priest.

5. *We will rejoice in thy salvation.* The words of this verse were spoken by David and his officers; immediately after which I suppose the high priest to have added, *The Lord fulfil all thy petitions.*

6. *Now know I that the Lord saveth his anointed.* These are probably the words of the priest after the victim had been consumed.

7. *Some trust in chariots.* The words of the original are short and emphatic: "These in chariots; and these in horses; but we will record in the name of Jehovah our God." This and the following verse I suppose to be the words of David and his officers.

9. *Save, Lord.* This verse was spoken by all the congregation, and was the chorus and conclusion of the piece.

PSALM 21

The Psalmist returns thanks to God for giving him the victory over his enemies, which victory he had earnestly requested, 1-2. He enters into a detail of the blessings that in consequence of the victory he had obtained, 3-7. He predicts the destruction of all those who may hereafter rise up against him, 8-12; and concludes with praising the power of Jehovah, 13.

1. *The king shall joy. Melech Meshicha,* "the King Messiah."

3. *Thou preventest him.* To "prevent," from *praevenio,* literally signifies "to go before." "For thou shalt go before him with the blessings of goodness."

6. *Thou hast made him most blessed for ever.* Literally, "Thou hast set him for blessings for ever." Thou hast made the Messiah the Source whence all blessings for time and for eternity shall be derived.

13. *Be thou exalted.* "Exalt thyself, O Lord" —Thy creatures cannot exalt Thee.

PSALM 22

Under great affliction and distress, the Psalmist prays unto God, 1-3; appeals to God's wonted kindness in behalf of His people, 4-5; relates the insults that he received, 6-8; mentions the goodness of God to him in his youth, as a reason why he should expect help now, 9-11; details his sufferings, and the indignities offered to him, 12-18; prays with the confidence of being heard and delivered, 19-24; praises God, and foretells the conversion of the nations to the true religion, 25-31.

1. *My God, my God, why hast thou forsaken me?* I beg the reader to refer to my note on Matt. xxvii. 46. *The words of my roaring. Shaagathi,* The Vulgate, Septuagint, Syriac, Aethiopic, and Arabic, with the Anglo-Saxon, make use of terms which may be thus translated: "My sins (or foolishness) are the cause why deliverance is so far from me." It appears that these versions have read *shegagathi,* "my sin of ignorance," instead of *shaagathi,* "my roaring"; but no MS. extant supports this reading.

6. *But I am a worm, and no man.* I can see no sense in which our Lord could use these terms. David might well use them to express his vileness and worthlessness.

7. *Laugh me to scorn.* They utterly despised me, set me at naught, treated me with the utmost contempt. *They shoot out the lip, they shake the head.* This is applied by Matthew, chap. xxvii. 39, to the conduct of the Jews toward our Lord when He hung upon the Cross; as is also the following verse.

12. *Many bulls have compassed me.* The bull is the emblem of brutal strength, that gores and tramples down all before it. Such were Absalom, Ahithophel, and others who rose up in rebellion against David; and such were the Jewish rulers who conspired against Christ. *Strong bulls of Bashan.* Bashan was a district beyond Jordan, very fertile, where they were accustomed to fatten cattle, which became, in consequence of

the excellent pasture, the largest, as well as the fattest, in the country.

16. *For dogs have compassed me.* This may refer to the Gentiles, the Roman soldiers, and others by whom our Lord was surrounded in His trial, and at His cross. *They pierced my hands and my feet.* The other sufferings David, as a type of our Lord, might pass through, but the piercing of the hands and feet was peculiar to our Lord; therefore this verse may pass for a direct revelation.

17. *I may tell all my bones.* This may refer to the violent extension of His body when the whole of its weight hung upon the nails which attached His hands to the transverse beam of the Cross. The body being thus extended, the principal bones became prominent, and easily discernible.

18. *They part my garments.* This could be true in no sense of David. The fact took place at the crucifixion of our Lord. The soldiers divided His upper garment into four parts, each soldier taking a part; but His tunic or inward vestment being without seam, woven in one entire piece, they agreed not to divide, but to cast lost whose the whole should be.

20. *Deliver my soul from the sword.* Deliver *naphshi,* "my life"; save Me alive, or raise Me again. *My darling.* "My only one." The only human being that was ever produced since the creation, even by the power of God himself, without the agency of man.

21. *Save me from the lion's mouth.* Probably our Lord here includes His Church with himself. The *lion* may then mean the Jews; the *unicorns,* the Gentiles. For the *unicorn,* see the note on Num. xxiii. 22.

24. *For he hath not despised.* Perhaps it may mean, Though ye have despised Me in My humiliation, yet God has graciously received Me in the character of a sufferer on account of sin, as by that humiliation unto death the great atonement was made for the sin of the world.

26. *The meek shall eat.* "The poor shall eat." In the true only Sacrifice there shall be such a provision for all believers that they shall have a fullness of joy. Those who offfered the sacrifice fed on what they offered. Jesus, the true Sacrifice, is the Bread that came down from heaven; they who eat of this Bread shall never die.

27. *All the ends of the world.* The gospel shall be preached to every nation under heaven; and *all the kindreds of the nations, mishpechoth,* the "families" of the nations.

28. *The kingdom is the Lord's.* That universal sway of the gospel which in the New Testament is called the kingdom of God.

29. *All they that be fat upon earth.* The rich, the great, the mighty, even princes, governors, and kings, shall embrace the gospel. *That go down to the dust.* Every dying man shall put his trust in Christ, and shall expect glory only through the great Saviour of mankind. *None can keep alive his own soul.* The Vulgate has: "And my soul shall live to him, and my seed shall serve him." And with this agree the Syriac, Septuagint, Aethiopic, Arabic, and Anglo-Saxon.

30. *Shall be accounted to the Lord for a generation.* They shall be called Christians after the name of Christ.

PSALM 23

The Lord is the Pastor of His people; therefore it may be inferred that they shall not want, 1. How He guides, feeds, and protects them, 2-3. Even in the greatest dangers they may be confident of His support, 4. His abundant provision for them, 5. The confidence they may have of His continual mercy, and their eternal happiness.

1. *The Lord is my shepherd.* There are two allegories in this psalm which are admirably well adapted to the purpose for which they are produced. The first is that of a shepherd; the second, that of a great feast, set out by a host the most kind and the most liberal.

2. *He maketh me to lie down in green pastures.* Not *green pastures,* but "cottages of turf or sods," such as the shepherds had in open champaign countries; places in which themselves could repose safely; and pens thus constructed where the flock might be safe all the night. *Beside the still waters.* "Deep waters," that the strongest heat could not exhale; not by a rippling current, which argues a shallow stream.

4. *Yea, though I walk through the valley of the shadow of death.* The reference is still to the shepherd. Though I, as one of the flock, should walk through the most dismal valley, in the dead of the night, exposed to pitfalls, precipices, devouring beasts, I should fear no evil under the guidance and protection of such a Shepherd. He knows all the passes, dangerous defiles, hidden pits, and abrupt precipices in the way; and He will guide me around, about, and through them. *Thy rod and thy staff.* "Thy sceptre, rod, ensign" of a tribe, staff of office; for so *shebet* signifies in Scripture. *And thy staff,* "Thy prop or support." The former may signify the shepherd's crook; the latter, some sort of rest or support.

5. *Thou preparest a table before me.* Here the second allegory begins. A magnificent banquet is provided by a most liberal and benevolent host, who has not only the bounty to feed me, but power to protect me; and, though surrounded by enemies, I sit down to this table with confidence, knowing that I shall feast in perfect security. *Thou anointest my head with oil.* Perfumed oil was poured on the heads of distinguished guests when at the feasts of great personages. The woman in the Gospel who poured the box of ointment of spikenard on the head of our Lord (see Matt. xxvi. 6-7; Mark xiv. 8; Luke vii. 46) only acted according to the custom of her own country, which the host, who invited our Lord, had shamefully neglected.

6. *Goodness and mercy shall follow me.* As I pass on through the vale of life, Thy goodness and mercy shall follow my every step; as I proceed, so shall they. *I will dwell in the house,* "and I shall return to the house of the Lord," *for ever,* "for length of days."

PSALM 24

The Lord is sovereign Ruler of the universe, 1-2. The great question, Who is fit to minister to the Lord in His own temple? 3-6. The glory of God in His entrance into His temple, 7-10.

It is probable that this psalm was composed on occasion of bringing the ark from the house of Obed-edom to Mount Zion, and the questions may respect the fitness of the persons who were to minister before this ark. The last verses may refer to the opening of the city gates

in order to admit it. Many of the expressions here are nearly the same with those in Psalm xv.

1. *The earth is the Lord's.* He is the Creator and Governor of it; it is His own property. *The fulness thereof.* "All its creatures."—*Targum.* *They that dwell therein.* All human beings.

3. *Who shall ascend?* Who is sufficiently holy to wait in His temple? Who is fit to minister in the holy place?

4. *He that hath clean hands.* He whose conscience is irreproachable.

5. *He shall receive the blessing.* Perhaps alluding to Obed-edom, at whose house the ark had been lodged, and on whom God had poured out especial blessings. *And righteousness.* Mercy; every kind of necessary good.

6. *This is the generation.* This is the description of people who are such as God can approve of, and delight in. *That seek thy face, O Jacob.* It is most certain that *Elohey,* "O God," has been lost out of the Hebrew text in most MSS., but it is preserved in two of Kennicott's MSS., and also in the Syriac, Vulgate, Septuagint, Aethiopic, Arabic, and Anglo-Saxon. "Who seek thy face, O God of Jacob."

7. *Lift up your heads, O ye gates.* The address of those who preceded the ark, the gates being addressed instead of the keepers of the gates.

8. *Who is this King of glory?* This is the answer of those who are within. Who is this glorious King, for whom ye demand entrance? To which they reply: *The Lord strong and mighty, the Lord mighty in battle.* It is Jehovah, who is come to set up His abode in His imperial city—He who has conquered His enemies and brought salvation to Israel. To make the matter still more solemn, and give those without an opportunity of describing more particularly this glorious Personage, those within hesitate to obey the first summons; and then it is repeated, v. 9—*Lift up your heads, O ye gates; even lift them up, ye everlasting doors; and the King of glory shall come in.* To which a more particular question is proposed: *Who is [He], this King of glory?* To which an answer is given that admits of no reply. *The Lord of hosts*—He who is coming with innumerable armies.

Several, both among ancients and moderns, have thought this psalm speaks of the resurrection of our Lord, and is thus to be understood. It is easy to apply it in this way: Jesus has conquered sin, Satan, and death, by dying. He now rises from the dead; and, as a mighty Conqueror, claims an entrance into the realms of glory.

PSALM 25

The Psalmist, in great distress, calls upon God frequently, 1-5; prays for pardon with the strong confidence of being heard, 6-11; shows the blessedness of the righteous, 12-14; again earnestly implores the divine mercy, and prays for the restoration of Israel, 15-22.

This psalm seems to refer to the case of the captives in Babylon, who complain of oppression from their enemies, and earnestly beg the help and mercy of God. It is the first of those called acrostic psalms, i.e., psalms each line of which begins with a several letter of the Hebrew alphabet in their common order. Of acrostic psalms there are seven, viz., xxv, xxxiv, xxxvii, cxi, cxii, cxix, and cxlv. The letter *vau* is wanting in the fifth verse, and *koph* in the eighteenth; the letter *resh* being twice inserted, once instead of *koph;* and a whole line added at the end, entirely out of the alphabetical series.

1. *Do I lift up my soul.* His soul was cast down, and by prayer and faith he endeavors to lift it up to God.

2. *I trust in thee.* I depend upon Thy infinite goodness and mercy for my support and salvation, *Let me not be ashamed.* Hide my iniquity, and forgive my guilt.

3. *Let none that wait on thee be ashamed.* Though he had burden enough of his own, he felt for others in similar circumstances, and became an intercessor in their behalf.

4. *Shew me thy ways.* That he may get this *showing, teaching,* and *leading,* he comes to God, as the God of his salvation; and that he may not lose his labor, he waits on Him all the day. Many lose the benefit of their earnest prayers because they do not persevere in them.

9. *The meek will he guide. Anavim,* the "poor," the "distressed."

10. *All the paths of the Lord. Orchoth* signifies the "tracks" or "ruts" made by the wheels of wagons by often passing over the same ground. Mercy and truth are the paths in which God constantly walks in reference to the children of men.

13. *His soul shall dwell at ease.* "Shall lodge in goodness"; this is the marginal reading in our version, and is preferable to that in the text. *His seed shall inherit.* His posterity shall be sent up to God by their pious fathers, and God has registered these prayers in their behalf.

16. *Turn thee unto me.* Probably the prayer of the poor captives in Babylon, which is continued through this and the remaining verses.

17. *The troubles of my heart are enlarged.* The evils of our captive state, instead of lessening, seem to multiply, and each to be extended.

21. *Let integrity and uprightness.* I wish to have a perfect heart and an upright life.

PSALM 26

The Psalmist appeals to God for his integrity, and desires to be brought to the divine test in order to have his innocence proved, 1-3; shows that he had avoided all fellowship with the wicked, and associated with the upright, 4-8; prays that he may not have his final lot with the workers of iniquity, 9-10; purposes to walk uprightly before God, 11-12.

This psalm, and the two following, are supposed by Calmet to be all parts of one ode, and to relate to the time of the Captivity, containing the prayers, supplications, complaints, and resolutions of the Israelites in Babylon.

1. *Judge me, O Lord.* There are so many strong assertions in this psalm concerning the innocence and uprightness of its author that many suppose he wrote it to vindicate himself from some severe reflections on his conduct or accusations relative to plots, conspiracies, etc. This seems to render the opinion probable that attributes it to David during his exile, when all manner of false accusations were brought against him at the court of Saul.

4. *I have not sat with vain persons.* "Men of lies," dissemblers, backbiters. *Neither will I go in with dissemblers.* The "hidden ones," the

dark designers, the secret plotters and conspirators in the state.

9. *Gather not my soul with sinners.* Let not my eternal lot be cast with them!

10. *Their right hand is full of bribes.* He speaks of persons in office who took bribes to pervert judgment and justice.

PSALM 27

The righteous man's confidence in God, 1-3; his ardent desire to have the spiritual privilege of worshipping God in His temple, because of the spiritual blessings which he expects to enjoy there, 4-6; his prayer to God for continual light and salvation, 7-9; his confidence that, though even his own parents might forsake him, yet God would not, 10. Therefore he begs to be taught the right way to be delivered from all his enemies, and to see the goodness of the Lord in the land of the living, 11-13; he exhorts others to trust in God, to be of good courage, and to expect strength for their hearts, 14.

In the Hebrew and Chaldee this psalm has no other title than simply *ledavid.* "To or for David."

5. *He shall hide me in his pavilion.* "In his tabernacle." I would make His temple my residence. *He shall set me up upon a rock.* He shall so *strengthen* and *establish* me that my enemies shall not be able to prevail against me.

6. *Now shall mine head be lifted up.* We shall most assuredly be redeemed from this captivity, and restored to our own land, and to the worship of our God in His own temple. There shall we offer *sacrifices of joy;* we *will sing praises unto the Lord,* and acknowledge that it is by His might and mercy alone that we have been delivered.

7. *Hear, O Lord, when I cry.* This is the utmost that any man of common sense can expect—to be heard when he cries. But there are multitudes who suppose God will bless them whether they cry or not; and there are others, and not a few, who, although they listlessly pray and *cry* not, yet imagine God must and will hear them! God will answer them that pray and cry; those who do not are most likely to be without the blessings which they so much need.

8. *When thou saidst, Seek ye my face.* I believe the true rendering to be as follows: "Unto thee, my heart, He hath said, Seek ye My face. Thy face, O Jehovah, I will seek. O my heart, God hath commanded thee to seek His face." Then, "His face I will seek."

10. *When my father and my mother forsake me.* Or, more literally, "For my father and my mother have forsaken me; but the Lord hath gathered me up."

13. *"I had fainted, unless I had believed."* The words in italics are supplied by our translators; but, far from being necessary, they injure the sense. Throw out the words "I had fainted," and leave a break after the verse, and the elegant figure of the Psalmist will be preserved: "Unless I had believed to see the goodness of the Lord in the land of the living" —what! what, alas! should have become of me!

PSALM 28

A righteous man in affliction makes supplication to God, and complains of the malice of his enemies, 1-4; whom he describes as impious, and whose destruction he predicts, 5. He blesses God for hearing his prayers, and for filling him with consolation, 6-7; then prays for God's people, 8-9.

This psalm is of the same complexion with the two preceding, and belongs most probably to the times of the Captivity, though some have preferred it to David in his persecutions. In the first five verses the author prays for support against his enemies, who appear to have acted treacherously against him. In the sixth and seventh he is supposed to have gained the victory, and returns with songs of triumph. The eighth is a chorus of the people sung to their conquering king. The ninth is the prayer of the king for his people.

1. *O Lord my rock.* Tsuri not only means *my rock,* but "my fountain," and the origin of all the good I possess.

4. *Give them.* Is the same as "Thou wilt give them," a prophetic declaration of what their lot will be.

8. *The Lord is their strength.* Instead of *lamo,* "to them," eight MSS. of Kennicott and De Rossi have *leammo,* "to His people"; and this reading is confirmed by the Septuagint, Syriac, Vulgate, Aethiopic, Arabic, and Anglo-Saxon. This makes the passage more precise and intelligible; and of the truth of the reading there can be no reasonable doubt. *The Lord is the strength of His people, and the saving strength of his anointed.* Both king and people are protected, upheld, and saved by Him.

9. *Save thy people.* Continue to preserve them from all their enemies, from idolatry, and from sin of every kind. *Feed them. Raah* signifies both to "feed" and to "govern." Feed them, as a shepherd does his flock; rule them, as a father does his children.

PSALM 29

The Psalmist calls upon the great and mighty to give thanks unto God, and to worship Him in the beauty of holiness, on account of a tempest that had taken place, 1-2. He shows the wonders produced by a thunderstorm, which he calls the voice of God, 3-9. Speaks of the majesty of God, 10; and points out the good He will do to His people, 11.

In the Hebrew, this is called "A Psalms for David." The psalm was probably written to commemorate the abundant rain which fell in the days of David, after the heavens had been shut up for three years, 2 Sam. xxi. 1-10. The whole psalm is employed in describing the effects produced by a thunderstorm which had lately taken place.

2. *In the beauty of holiness.* "The beautiful garments of holiness."

3. *The voice of the Lord.* Thunder, so called, Exod. ix. 23, 28-29; Job xxxvii. 4; Ps. xviii. 13; Isa. xxx. 30. *Upon many waters.* The clouds, which Moses calls the waters which are above the firmament.

4. *Is powerful.* There is no agent in universal nature so powerful as the electric fluid. *Full of majesty.* No sound in nature is so tremendous and majestic as that of thunder; it is the most fit to represent the voice of God.

5. *Breaketh the cedars.* Very tall trees attract the lightning from the clouds, by which they are often torn to pieces.

7. *Divideth the flames of fire.* The forked, zigzag lightning is the cause of thunder; and in a thunderstorm these lightnings are variously dispersed.

8. *The wilderness of Kadesh.* This was on the frontiers of Idumea and Paran. There may be a reference to some terrible thunderstorm and earthquake which had occurred in that place.

9. *Maketh the hinds to calve.* Strikes terror through all the tribes of animals, which sometimes occasions those which are pregnant to cast their young. *Discovereth the forests.* Makes them sometimes evident in the darkest night, by the sudden flash, and often by setting them on fire.

10. *The Lord sitteth upon the flood.* "Jehovah sat upon the deluge." *Sitteth King for ever.* He governs universal nature.

PSALM 30

The Psalmist returns thanks to God for deliverance from great danger, 1-3. He calls upon the saints to give thanks to God at the remembrance of His holiness, because of His readiness to save, 4-5. He relates how his mind stood affected before this great trial, and how soon an unexpected change took place, 6-7; mentions how, and in what terms, he prayed for mercy, 8-10; shows how God heard and delivered him, and the effect it had upon his mind, 11-12.

This psalm or song is said to have been made or used at the dedication of the house of David, or rather the dedication of a house or temple; for the word *David* refers not to the house, but to *mizmor,* a psalm. But what temple or house could this be? Calmet supposes it to have been made by David on the dedication of the place which he built on the threshing floor of Araunah, after the grievous plague which had so nearly desolated the kingdom, 2 Sam. xxiv. 25; 1 Chron. xxi. 26. All the parts of the psalm agree to this; and they agree to this so well, and to no other hypothesis, that I feel myself justified in modelling the comment on this principle alone.

2. *Thou hast healed me.* Thou hast removed the plague from my people by which they were perishing in thousands before my eyes.

3. *Thou hast brought up my soul from the grave.* I and my people were both about to be cut off, and Thou hast spared us in mercy, and given us a most glorious respite.

4. *Sing unto the Lord, O ye saints of his.* Ye priests, who wait upon Him in His sanctuary, and whose business it is to offer prayers and sacrifices for the people, magnify Him for the mercy He has now showed in staying this most destructive plague. *Give thanks at the remembrance of his holiness.* "Be ye holy," saith the Lord, "for I am holy." He who can give thanks at the remembrance of His holiness is one who loves holiness.

5. *For his anger endureth but a moment.* There is an elegant abruptness in these words in the Hebrew text. This is the literal translation: "For a moment in His anger. Lives in His favor. In the evening weeping may lodge: but in the morning exultation."

6. *In my prosperity I said, I shall never be moved.* Peace and prosperity had seduced the heart of David, and led him to suppose that his "mountain"—his dominion—stood so strong that adversity could never affect him. He wished to know the physical and political strength of his kingdom; and, forgetting to depend upon God, he desired Joab to make a census of the people, which God punished in the manner related in 2 Samuel xxiv.

8. *I cried to thee, O Lord.* See his confession and prayer, 2 Sam. xxiv. 17.

11. *Thou hast turned . . . my mourning into dancing.* Rather "into piping." I have not prayed in vain. Though I deserved to be cut off from the land of the living, yet Thou hast spared me, and the remnant of my people. Thou hast taken away *my sackcloth,* the emblem of my distress and misery, *and girded me with gladness,* when Thou didst say to the destroying angel, when he stood over Jerusalem ready to destroy it: "It is enough: stay now thy hand," 2 Sam. xxiv. 16.

PSALM 31

The Psalmist, with strong confidence in God, in a time of distress prays earnestly for deliverance, 1-5. He expresses his abhorrence of evil, 6; gratefully mentions former interpositions of God, 7-8; continues to detail the miseries of his case, 9-18; points out the privileges of them that fear God, 19-20; shows that God had heard his prayers, notwithstanding he had given himself over for lost, 21-22; calls on the saints to love God, and to have confidence in Him, because He preserves the faithful, and plentifully rewards the proud doer, 23-24.

2. *Strong rock.* Rocks, rocky places, or caves in the rocks were often strong places in the land of Judea.

4. *Pull me out of the net.* They have hemmed me in on every side, and I cannot escape but by miracle.

5. *Into thine hand I commit my spirit.* "And when Jesus had cried with a loud voice, he said, Father, into thy hands I commend my spirit," Luke xxiii. 46. The rest of the verse was not suitable to the Saviour of the world, and therefore he omits it; but it is suitable to us who have been redeemed by that sacrificial death. Stephen uses nearly the same words, and they were the last that he uttered, Acts vii. 59.

6. *I have hated them.* That is, I have abominated their ways. *I trust in the Lord.* While they trust in vanities, vain things (for an idol is nothing in the world) and in *lying vanities* (for much is promised and nothing given), I trust in Jehovah, who is God all-sufficient, and is my Shepherd, and therefore I shall lack no good thing.

10. *My life is spent with grief.* My life is a life of suffering and distress, and by grief my days are shortened. *My years with sighing. Anachah.* This is a mere natural expression of grief, the very sounds which proceed from a distressed mind; *an-ach-ah!* common, with little variation, to all nations, and nearly the same in all languages.

13. *I have heard the slander of many.* To this and the two foregoing verses the reader may find several parallels: Jer. xviii. 18 to the end of chap. xix, and first ten verses of chap. xx. This has caused several to suppose that Jeremiah was the author of this psalm.

16. *Make thy face to shine upon thy servant.* Only let me know that Thou art reconciled to and pleased with me, and then, come what will, all must be well. *Save me for thy mercies' sake.* Literally, "Save me in Thy mercy."

20. *Thou shalt hide them in the secret of thy presence.* "With the covering of thy countenance."

21. *In a strong city.* If this psalm was written by David, this must refer to his taking refuge with Achish, king of Gath, who gave him Ziklag, a fortified city, to secure himself and followers in. See 1 Sam. xxvii. 6. Perhaps the passage may mean that, under the protection of God, he was as safe as if he had been in a fortified city.

PSALM 32

True blessedness consists in remission of sin and purification of the heart, 1-2. What the Psalmist felt in seeking these blessings, 3-5. How they should be sought, 6-7. The necessity of humility and teachableness, 8-9. The misery of the wicked, 10. The blessedness of the righteous, 11.

The title of this psalm is significant, *ledavid maskil,* "A Psalm of David, giving instruction," an instructive psalm; so called by way of eminence, because it is calculated to give the highest instruction relative to the guilt of sin, and the blessedness of pardon and holiness, or justification and sanctification. It is supposed to have been composed after David's transgression with Bath-sheba, and subsequently to his obtaining pardon.

1. *Blessed is he whose transgression is forgiven.* In this and the following verse four evils are mentioned: *Transgression, sin, iniquity, guile.* The first signifies the passing over a boundary, doing what is prohibited. The second signifies the missing of a mark, not doing what was commanded; but is often taken to express sinfulness, or sin in the future, producing transgression in the life. The third signifies what is turned out of its proper course or situation, anything morally distorted or perverted. The fourth signifies fraud, deceit, guile. To remove these evils, three acts are mentioned: forgiving, covering, and not imputing. St. Paul quotes this passage, Rom. iv. 6-7, to illustrate the doctrine of justification by faith.

3. *When I kept silence.* Before I humbled myself, and confessed my sin, my soul was under the deepest horror.

5. *I acknowledged my sin.* When this confession was made thoroughly and sincerely, and I ceased to cover my offense, then Thou didst forgive *the iniquity of my sin.*

6. *Surely in the floods.* In violent trials, afflictions, and temptations.

7. *Thou art my hiding place.* An allusion, probably, to the city of refuge. *Thou shalt preserve me from trouble.* The avenger of blood shall not be able to overtake me.

8. *I will instruct thee.* These are probably the Lord's words to David.

PSALM 33

The Lord is praised for His works of creation, 1-9; and for the stability of His own counsels, 10-11. The blessedness of the people who have the knowledge of the true God, His grace, and providence, 12-15. The vanity of all earthly dependence, 16-17. The happiness of them that fear God and trust in His mercy, 18-22.

This psalm has no title in the Hebrew and it was probably written on no particular occasion, but was intended as a hymn of praise in order to celebrate the power, wisdom, and mercy of God. Creation and providence are its principal subjects, and these lead the Psalmist to glance at different parts of the ancient Jewish history.

1. *Rejoice in the Lord.* It is very likely that the last verse of the preceding psalm was formerly the first verse of this. As this psalm has

no title, the verse was the more easily separated. In the preceding psalm we have an account of the happiness of the justified man; in this such are taught how to glorify God, and to praise Him for the great things He had done for them.

2. *The psaltery.* Our translation seems to make a third instrument in this place, by rendering *an instrument of ten strings,* whereas they should both be joined together.

10. *The counsel of the heathen to nought.* This appears to be similar to what is mentioned in the second psalm, the useless attempts of the Gentiles to prevent the extension of the kingdom of Christ in the earth, and it may refer to similar attempts of ungodly nations or men to prevent the promulgation of the gospel and the universal dissemination of truth in the world.

11. *The counsel of the Lord.* What He has determined shall be done. He determined to make a world, and He made it; to create man, and He created him. He determined that at a certain period God should be manifested in the flesh, and it was so; that He should taste death for every man, and He did so; that His gospel should be preached in all the world, and, behold, it has already nearly overrun the whole earth.

13. *The Lord looketh from heaven.* This and the following verse seem to refer to God's providence. He sees all that is done in the earth, and His eye is on all the children of men.

20. *Our soul waiteth.* Our whole life is employed in this blessed work; we trust in nothing but Him—neither in multitudes of armed men, nor in natural strength, nor in the fleetest animals, nor in anything human. We trust in Him alone who is *our help and our shield.*

PSALM 34

David praises God, and exhorts others to do the same, 1-3; shows how he sought the Lord, and how He was found of him, 4-6. All are exhorted to taste and see the goodness of God, with the assurance of support and comfort, 7-10. He shows the way to attain happiness and long life, 11-16; the privileges of the righteous, and of all who sincerely seek God, 17-22.

The title states that this is "A Psalm of David, when he changed his behaviour before Abimelech, who drove him away, and he departed." The history of this transaction may be found in 1 Samuel xxi. But Abimelech is not the person there mentioned; it was Achish, king of Gath, called here Abimelech, because that was a common name of the Philistine kings. This is the second of the acrostic or alphabetical psalms, each verse beginning with a consecutive letter of the Hebrew alphabet. But in this psalm some derangement has taken place. The verse which begins with *vau,* and which should come in between the fifth and sixth, is totally wanting; and the twenty-second verse is entirely out of the series. It is, however, my opinion that this verse (the twenty-second), which now begins with *phe, podeh,* "redeemeth," was originally written *vepodeh* or with *padah,* as more than a hundred of Dr. Kennicott's MSS. read it, thus making *vepodah,* "and will redeem," and this reads admirably in the above connection.

2. *My soul shall make her boast.* Shall "set itself to praise" the Lord—shall consider this its chief work. *The humble.* The afflicted, such as David had been.

6. *This poor man cried.* "This afflicted man," David.

7. *The angel of the Lord encampeth round.* I should rather consider this angel in the light of a watchman going round his circuit, and having for the objects of his especial care such as fear the Lord.

11. *Come, ye children.* All ye that are of a humble, teachable spirit.

18. *A broken heart.* The heart "broken to shivers." *A contrite spirit.* "The beaten-out spirit." In both words the hammer is necessarily implied. This will call to the reader's remembrance Jer. xxiii. 29: "Is not my word like as a fire? saith the Lord; and like a hammer that breaketh the rock in pieces?" The *broken heart* and the *contrite spirit* are two essential characteristics of true repentance.

22. *The Lord redeemeth.* Both the life and soul of God's followers are ever in danger, but God is continually redeeming both. *Shall be desolate.* Literally, "shall be guilty." They shall be preserved from sin, and forfeit neither life nor soul.

PSALM 35

The Psalmist, in great straits, prays for his personal safety, 1-3; and for the confusion of his enemies, 4-8; expresses his confidence in God, 9-10; mentions his kindness to those who had rewarded him evil for his good, 11-16; appeals to God against them, 17-26; prays for those who befriended him; and praises God for His goodness, 27-28.

1. *Plead my cause, O Lord.* Literally, "Contend, Lord, with them that contend with me." The word is often used in a forensic or law sense. The imprecations in these verses against enemies are all legitimate. They are not against the souls or eternal welfare of those sinners, but against their schemes and plans for destroying the life of an innocent man; and the holiest Christian may offer up such prayers against his adversaries.

7. *For without cause have they hid for me their net in a pit.* The word *pit* belongs to the second member of this verse, and the whole should be read thus: For without a cause they have hidden for me their net; without a cause they have digged a pit for my life.

14. *Mourneth for his mother.* As a mourning mother. How expressive is this word!

15. *But in mine adversity they rejoiced.* How David was mocked and insulted in the case of Absalom's rebellion by Shimei and others is well-know. *The abjects.* "The smiters," probably hired assassins. They were everywhere lying in wait, to take away my life.

16. *With hypocritical mockers in feasts.* These verses seem to be prophetic of the treatment of Christ.

17. *My darling.* "My only one," Ps. xxii. 20.

21. *They opened their mouth wide.* Gaped upon me to express their contempt. *And said, Aha, aha, our eye hath seen it.* They said, *Heach, heach,* the last syllable in each word being a protracted, strongly guttural sound, marking insult and triumph at the same time. It is the word which we translate, "Ah," v. 25.

25. *Swallowed him up.* "We have gulped him down."

PSALM 36

The miserable state of the wicked, 1-4. The excellence of God's mercy in itself, and to His followers, 5-9. He prays for the upright, 10; for himself that he may be saved from pride and violence, 11; and shows the end of the workers of iniquity, 12.

The title in the Hebrew is, "To the conqueror, to the servant of Jehovah, to David." It is one of the finest psalms in the whole collection.

1. *The transgression of the wicked saith within my heart.* It is difficult to make any sense of this line as it now stands. How can the transgression of the wicked speak within my heart? But instead of *libbi,* "my heart," four of Kennicott's and De Rossi's MSS. have *libbo,* "his heart." "The speech of transgression to the wicked is in the midst of his heart. There is no fear of God before his eyes." The principle of transgression, sin in the heart, says, or suggests to every sinner, There is no cause for fear; go on, do not fear, for there is no danger. He obeys this suggestion, goes on, and acts wickedly, as God is not *before his eyes.*

5. *Thy mercy, O Lord, is in the heavens.* That is, Thou art abundant, infinite in Thy mercy, else such transgressors must be immediately cut off; but Thy long-suffering is intended to lead them to repentance. *Thy faithfulness reacheth unto the clouds.* To the eternal regions, above all visible space.

6. *Thy righteousness is like the great mountains.* "Like the mountains of God"; exceeding high mountains. *Thy judgments are a great deep.* "The great abyss"; as incomprehensible as the great chaos.

8. *They shall be abundantly satisfied.* "They shall be saturated," as a thirsty field is by showers from heaven.

10. *O continue thy lovingkindness.* Literally, "Draw out Thy mercy." *To the upright in heart.* "To the straight of heart"; to those who have but one end in view, and one aim to that end.

11. *Let not the foot of pride come against me.* Let me not be trampled underfoot by proud and haughty men. *Let not the hand of the wicked remove me.* "Shake me" or "cause me to wander."

PSALM 37

Godly directions for those who are in adversity not to envy the prosperity of the wicked, because it is superficial, and of short duration, 1-22; to put their confidence in God, and live to His glory, as this is the sure way to be happy in this life, and in that which is to come, 23-40.

This psalm is one of the acrostic or alphabetical kind; but it differs from those we have already seen in having two verses under each letter, the first only exhibiting the alphabetical letter consecutively.

4. *Delight thyself also in the Lord.* Expect all thy happiness from Him, and seek it in Him. *The desires of thine heart.* The "petitions." The godly man never indulges a desire which he cannot form into a prayer to God.

5. *Commit thy way unto the Lord.* "Roll thy way upon the Lord." *He shall bring it to pass.* "He will work." Trust God, and He will work for thee.

7. *Rest in the Lord.* "Be silent, be dumb." Do not find fault with thy Maker. He does all

things well for others; He will do all things well for thee. *And wait patiently for him.* And "set thyself" to expect Him; and be determined to expect or wait for Him.

9. *They shall inherit the earth.* The word *arets* throughout this psalm should be translated "land," not *earth;* for it is most probable that it refers to the land of Judea, and in this verse there is a promise of their return thither.

10. *For yet a little while, and the wicked shall not be.* A prediction of the destruction of Babylon. This empire was now in its splendor; and the captives lived to see it totally overturned by Cyrus, so that even the shadow of its power did not remain. *Thou shalt diligently consider his place.* "And he is not." The ruler is killed, the city is taken, and the whole empire is overthrown, in one night!

11. *But the meek. Anavim,* the "afflicted," the poor Jewish captives. *Shall inherit the earth. Arets,* the "land" of Judea, given by God himself as an inheritance to their fathers, and to their posterity forever. See v. 9.

20. *The enemies of the Lord shall be as the fat of lambs.* This verse has given the critics some trouble. Several of the versions read thus: "But the enemies of the Lord, as soon as they are exalted to honour, shall vanish; like smoke they vanish." If we follow the Hebrew, it intimates that "they shall consume as the fat of lambs." That is, as the fat is wholly consumed in sacrifices by the fire on the altar, so shall they consume away in the fire of God's wrath.

21. *The wicked borroweth.* Is often reduced to penury, and is obliged to become debtor to those whom he before despised. *And payeth not again.* May refuse to do it, and because he is a wicked man; or be unable to do it, because he is reduced to beggary. *But the righteous sheweth mercy.* Because he has received mercy from God, therefore he shows mercy to men.

22. *Shall inherit the earth. Arets,* the "land," as before. See v. 11.

23. *The steps of a good man are ordered by the Lord.* There is nothing for *good* in the text. *Geber* is the original word, and it properly signifies a "strong man," a "conqueror" or "hero"; and it appears to be used here to show that even the most powerful must be supported by the Lord, otherwise their strength and courage will be of little avail.

24. *Though he fall, he shall not be utterly cast down.* The original is short and emphatic *ki yippol, lo yutal,* which the Chaldee translates, "Though he should fall into sickness, he shall not die." Neither the text nor any of the versions intimate that a falling into sin is meant; but a falling into trouble, difficulty.

25. *I have been young, and now am old.* I believe this to be literally true in all cases. I am now grey-headed myself; I have travelled in different countries, and have had many opportunities of seeing and conversing with religious people in all situations in life; and I have not, to my knowledge, seen one instance to the contrary.

26. *He is ever merciful, and lendeth.* "All the day he is compassionate."

28. *Forsaketh not his saints.* "His merciful or compassionate ones"; those who, through love to Him and all mankind, are ever ready to give of their substance to the poor.

29. The righteous shall inherit the land. If this be not another promise of return to their own land, from that of their captivity, it must be spiritually understood and refer to their eternal dwelling with God in glory.

31. None of his steps shall slide. His holy heart always dictates to his *eyes*, his *mouth*, his *hands*, and his *feet*. The precepts which direct his conduct are not only *written in his Bible*, but also *in his heart.*

32. The wicked watcheth the righteous, and seeketh to slay him. Similar to what is said in v. 12: "The wicked plotteth against the just [righteous]." But it is added, v. 33: "The Lord will not leave him in his hands"; He will confound his devices, and save His own servants.

34. Wait on the Lord, and keep his way. This is the true mode of waiting on God which the Scripture recommends: keeping God's way—using all His ordinances, and living in the spirit of obedience. *When the wicked are cut off, thou shalt see it.* They did see the destruction of the Babylonish king, Belshazzar, and his empire; and it was in consequence of that destruction that they were enlarged.

35. I have seen the wicked in great power, and spreading himself like a green bay tree. Does not this refer to Nebuchadnezzar, king of Babylon, and to the vision he had of the great tree which was in the midst of the earth, the head of which reached up to heaven? See Dan. iv. 10, etc.

36. Yet he passed away. Both Nebuchadnezzar and his wicked successor, Belshazzar.

37. Mark the perfect man. Him who is described above. Take notice of him. He is perfect in his soul, God having saved him from all sin, and filled him with His own love and image. And he is upright in his conduct; and his end, die when he may or where he may, is peace, quietness, and assurance forever.

PSALM 38

David prays God to have mercy upon him, and gives a most affecting account of his miserable state, 1-10; complains of his being forsaken by his friends, and cruelly persecuted by his enemies, 11-16; confesses his sin, and earnestly implores help, 17-22.

6. I am troubled. In mind. *I am bowed down*—in body. I am altogether afflicted, and full of distress.

7. For my loins are filled with a loathsome disease. Or rather, a "burning," strongly feverish disease.

10. My heart panteth. "Flutters, palpitates," through fear and alarm. *My strength faileth.* Not being able to take nourishment. *The light of mine eyes . . . is gone.* I can scarcely discern anything through the general decay of my health and vigor, particularly affecting my sight.

11. My lovers. Those who professed much affection for me; *my friends*, my "companions," who never before left my company, *stand aloof.* *My kinsmen.* My "neighbors," stand afar off. I am deserted by all, and they stand off because of my "plague."

13. But I, as a deaf man. I was conscious of my guilt; I could not vindicate myself; and I was obliged in silence to bear their insults.

14. No reproofs. "Arguments" or "vindications"; a forensic term. I was as a man accused in open court, and I could make no defense.

17. For I am ready to halt. Literally, "I am prepared to halt." So completely infirm is my soul that it is impossible for me to take one right step in the way of righteousness, unless strengthened by Thee.

18. I will declare mine iniquity. I will confess it with the deepest humiliation and self-abasement.

19. But mine enemies are lively. Instead of *chaiyim*, "lively," I would read *chinam*, "without cause."

20. Because I follow the thing that good is. The translation is as bad as the sentence is awkward. "Because I follow goodness."

PSALM 39

The Psalmist's care and watchfulness over his thoughts, tongue, and actions, 1-3. He considers the brevity and uncertainty of human life, 4-7; prays for deliverance from sin, 8-11; and that he may be protected and spared till he is fitted for another world, 12-13.

The title says, "To the chief Musician, Jeduthun himself, A Psalm of David." It is supposed that this Jeduthun is the same with *Ethan*, 1 Chron. vi. 44, compared with 1 Chron. xvi. 41; and is there numbered among the sons of Merari. And he is supposed to have been one of the four masters of music, or leaders of bands, belonging to the Temple. And it is thought that David, having composed this psalm, gave it to Jeduthun and his company to sing. But several have supposed that Jeduthun himself was the author. It is very likely that this psalm was written on the same occasion with the preceding. It relates to a grievous malady by which David was afflicted after his transgression with Bath-sheba.

1. I said, I will take heed to my ways. I must be cautious because of my enemies; I must be patient because of my afflictions; I must be watchful over my tongue, lest I offend my God, or give my adversaries any cause to speak evil of me.

5. My days as a handbreadth. My life is but a "span." *And mine age is as nothing.* "As if it were not before thee." All time is swallowed up in Thy eternity. *Verily every man at his best state.* "Every man that exists is vanity."

6. Walketh in a vain shew. In a "shadow." He is but the semblance of being; he appears for a while, and then vanisheth away. *He heapeth up riches, and knoweth not who shall gather them.* He "raketh together." This is a metaphor taken from agriculture. The husbandman rakes the corn, etc., together in the field, and yet, so uncertain is life, that he knows not who shall gather them into the granary!

11. When thou with rebukes dost correct man. Tochachoth signifies a "vindication of proceedings in a court of law," a "legal defense." When God comes to maintain the credit and authority of His law against a sinner, He causes *his beauty to consume away*—a metaphor taken from the case of a culprit who, by the arguments of counsel and the unimpeachable evidence of witnesses, has the facts all proved against him, grows pale, looks terrified; his fortitude forsakes him, and he faints in court.

13. O spare me. Take me not from this state of probation till I have a thorough preparation for a state of blessedness. This he terms recovering his strength—being restored to the favor and image of God, from which he had fallen. This should be the daily cry of every human spirit: Restore me to Thine image, guide me by Thy counsel, and then receive me to Thy glory!

PSALM 40

The benefit of confidence in God, 1-3. The blessedness of those who trust in God, 4-5. The termination of the Jewish sacrifices in that of Christ, 6-8. The Psalmist's resolution to publish God's goodness, 9-10; he prays to be delivered from evils, 11-13; against his enemies, 14-15; and in behalf of those who are destitute, 16-17.

I am satisfied the psalm was composed by David, and about the same time and on the same occasion as the two preceding; with this difference, that here he magnifies God for having bestowed the mercy which he sought there. It is, therefore, a thanksgiving for his recovery from the sore disease by which he was afflicted in his body, and for his restoration to the divine favor. The sixth, seventh, and eighth verses contain a remarkable prophecy of the incarnation and sacrificial offering of Jessu Christ. From the eleventh to the end contains a new subject, and appears to have belonged to another psalm. It is the same as the seventieth psalm; only it wants the first two verses.

1. *I waited patiently for the Lord.* The two preceding psalms are proofs of the patience and resignation with which David waited for the mercy of God. *And heard my cry.* The two preceding psalms show how he prayed and waited; this shows how he succeeded.

2. *An horrible pit.* Literally, the "sounding pit," where nothing was heard except the howlings of wild beasts, or the hollow sounds of winds reverberated and broken from the craggy sides and roof. *The miry clay.* Where the longer I stayed, the deeper I sank, and was utterly unable to save myself.

5. *Many . . . are thy wonderful works.* The Psalmist seems here astonished and confounded at the counsels, loving-kindnesses, and marvellous works of the Lord, not in nature, but in grace; for it was the mercy of God towards himself that he had now particularly in view.

6. *Sacrifice and offering.* The apostle, Heb. x. 5, etc., quoting this and the two following verses, says, "When he [the Messiah] cometh into the world"—was about to be incarnated, "he saith"— to God the Father, "Sacrifice and offering thou wouldest not"—it was never Thy will and design that the sacrifices under Thy own law should be considered as making atonement for sin; they were designed only to point out My incarnation and consequent sacrificial death; and therefore "a body hast thou prepared me," by a miraculous conception in the womb of a virgin.

A body hast thou prepared me. The quotation of this and the two following verses by the apostle, Heb. x. 5, etc., is taken from the Septuagint, with scarcely any variety of reading: but, although the general meaning is the same, they are widely different in verbal expression in the Hebrew. David's words we translate, *Mine ears hast thou opened;* but they might be more properly rendered, "My ears hast Thou bored;" that is, Thou hast made me Thy servant forever, to dwell in Thine own house. For the allusion is evidently to the custom mentioned Exod. xxi. 2, etc.: "If thou buy an Hebrew servant, six years he shall serve: and in the seventh he shall go out free . . . and if the servant shall plainly say,

I love my master, etc., I will not go out free: then his master shall bring him to . . . the door post; and . . . shall bore his ear through with an aul; and he shall serve him for ever."

But how is it possible that the Septuagint and the apostle should take a meaning so totally different from the sense of the Hebrew? Dr. Kennicott has a very ingenious conjecture here. He supposes that the Septuagint and the apostle express the meaning of the words as they stood in the copy from which the Greek translation was made; and that the present Hebrew text is corrupted in the word *oznayim,* "ears," which has been written through carelessness for *az gevah,* "then, a body."

It is remarkable that all the offerings and sacrifices which were considered to be of an atoning or cleansing nature, offered under the law, are here enumerated by the Psalmist and the apostle, to show that none of them, nor all of them, could take away sin; and that the grand sacrifice of Christ was that alone which could do it.

Four kinds are here specified, by both the Psalmist and the apostle; viz., sacrifice, offering, burnt offering, sin offering. Of all these we may say, with the apostle, it was impossible that the blood of bulls and goats should take away sin.

7. *In the volume of the book.* "In the roll of the book." Anciently, books were written on skins and rolled up. Among the Romans these were called *volumina,* from *volvo,* "I roll"; and the Pentateuch in the Jewish synagogues is still written in this way. There are two wooden rollers; on one they roll on, on the other they roll off, as they proceed in reading. One now lying before me, written on vellum, is 2 feet 2 inches in breadth, and 102 feet long. To roll and unroll such a MS. was no easy task; and to be managed, must lie flat on a table. This contains the Pentateuch only, and is without points, or any other Masoretic distinction. The *book* mentioned here must be the Pentateuch, or five books of Moses; for in David's time no other part of divine revelation had been committed to writing. This whole book speaks about Christ, and His accomplishing the will of God, not only in "The Seed of the woman shall bruise the head of the serpent" and "In thy seed shall all the nations of the earth be blessed," but in all the sacrifices and sacrificial rites mentioned in the law.

9. *I have preached righteousness.* I think it best to refer these words to Christ and His apostles. In consequence of His having become a Sacrifice for sin, the Jewish sacrificial system being ended, the middle wall of partition was broken down, and the door of faith, the doctrine of justification by faith, opened to the Gentiles. Hence the gospel was preached in all the world, and the mercy of God made known to the Gentiles; and thus *righteousness,* justification by faith, was preached *in the great congregation*— to Jews and Gentiles, throughout the Roman Empire. *The great congregation,* in both this and the following verse, I think, means the Gentiles, contradistinguished from the Jews.

10. *Thy faithfulness.* This means the exact fulfilment of the promises made by the prophets relative to the incarnation of Christ, and the opening of the door of faith to the Gentiles. *Lovingkindness.* Shows the gift itself of Jesus Christ, the highest proof that God could give to a lost world of His loving-kindness.

12. *Innumerable evils have compassed me about.* This part does not comport with the preceding, and either argues a former experience or must be considered a part of another psalm, written at a different time and on another occasion; and were we to prefix the first two verses of the seventieth psalm to it we should find it to be a psalm as complete in itself as that is.

15. *That say unto me, Aha, aha. Heach, heach.* See on Ps. xxxv. 21.

17. *But I am poor.* "Afflicted," greatly depressed. *And needy.* "A beggar." One utterly destitute, and seeking help. *The Lord thinketh upon me.* The words are very emphatic; *Adonai*, my Prop, my Support, *thinketh*, "meditateth," *upon me.*

PSALM 41

The blessedness of the man who is merciful to the poor, 1-3. The Psalmist complains of his enemies, and prays for support, 4-10; and blesses God for having heard his prayer, and preserved him from his adversaries, 11-12. A fine doxology closes the psalm, 13.

3. *Thou wilt make all his bed.* Thou hast "turned up, tossed, and shaken" it; and Thou wilt do so to all his bed—Thou wilt not leave one uneasy place in it—not one lump, or any unevenness, to prevent him from sleeping.

8. *An evil disease, say they, cleaveth fast unto him.* A "thing, word, or pestilence of Belial, is poured out upon him." His disease is of no common sort; it is a diabolical malady.

9. *Mine own familiar friend.* This is either a direct prophecy of the treachery of Judas or it is a fact in David's distresses which our Lord found so similar to the falsity of His treacherous disciple that He applies it to him, John xiii. 18. What we translate *mine own familiar friend* is "the man of my peace." The man who, with the "Peace be to thee!" kissed me, and thus gave the agreed-on signal to my murderers that I was the person whom they should seize, hold fast, and carry away. *Did eat of my bread.* Applied by our Lord to Judas, when eating with Him out of the same dish. See John xiii. 18, 26. Possibly it may refer to Ahithophel, his counsellor, the man of his peace, his prime minister, who, we know, was the strength of Absalom's conspiracy.

10. *Raise me up.* Restore me from this sickness, *that I may requite them.* This has also been applied to our Lord, who, knowing that He must die, prays that He may rise again, and thus disappoint the malice of His enemies.

13. *Blessed be the Lord God of Israel.* By all these circumstances and events glory shall redound to the name of God forever; for the record of these things shall never perish, but be published from one generation to another; and it has been so. *From everlasting, and to everlasting.* "From the hidden time to the hidden time"; from that which had no beginning to that which has no end.

Thus ends what the Hebrews call the First Book of Psalms; for the reader will recollect that this book is divided by the Jews into five books, the first of which ends with this psalm.

PSALM 42

The Psalmist earnestly longs for the ordinances of the Lord's house, 1-4; describes his deep distress, 5-7; endeavors to take comfort from the consideration that the Lord would appear in his behalf, 8-9; speaks of the insults of his enemies, 10; and again takes encouragement, 11.

The title, "to the chief Musician, giving instruction to the sons of Korah." This is the first of the psalms that has this title prefixed, and it is probable that such psalms were composed by the descendants of Korah during the Babylonish captivity, or by some eminent person among those descendants, and that they were used by the Israelites during their long captivity, as a means of consolation. Indeed, most of the psalms which bear this inscription are of the consoling kind and the sentiments appear to belong to that period of the Jewish history, and to none other. The word *maskil*, from *sakal*, signifies to "make wise," to "direct wisely," to "give instruction."

1. *As the hart panteth after the water brooks.* The hart feels himself almost entirely spent; he is nearly hunted down; the dogs are in full pursuit; he is parched with thirst; and in a burning heat pants after the water, and when he comes to the river, plunges in as his last refuge.

3. *My tears have been my meat day and night.* My longing has been so intense after spiritual blessings that I have forgotten to take my necessary food, and my sorrow has been so great that I have had no appetite for any.

4. *When I remember these things.* Or "these things I shall remember." My soul is dissolved, becomes weak as water, when I reflect on what I have had, and on what I have lost. Or, "I pour out my soul to myself" in deep regrets and complaints, when reflecting on these things. There was a *multitude* to worship God in public; with these I often went. But, alas, this is no more; now there are found only a few solitary individuals who sigh for the desolations of Zion. There we had our holy days, our appointed feasts, to commemorate the wonderful works of the Lord; now there are no processions, no festivals, no joyous assemblies. All is desolation in Zion, and all is mourning in our captivity.

5. *Why art thou cast down, O my soul?* Bad as the times are, desolate as Jerusalem is, insulting as are our enemies, hopeless as in the sight of man our condition may be, yet there is no room for despair. All things are possible to God. We have a promise of restoration. He is as good as He is powerful; hope therefore in Him. *I shall yet praise him.* For my restoration from this captivity.

6. *Therefore will I remember thee from the land of Jordan.* That is, from Judea, this being the chief river of that country. *And of the Hermonites.* The "Hermons," used in the plural because Hermon has a double ridge joining in an angle, and rising in many summits. The river Jordan, and the mountains of Hermon, were the most striking features of the Holy Land. *From the hill Mizar.* "From the little hill." The little hill probably means Sion, which was little in comparison of the Hermons.

7. *Deep calleth unto deep.* One wave of sorrow rolls on me, impelled by another. There is something dismal in the sound of the original, *tehom el tehom kore;* something like, "And hollow howlings hung in air."

9. *I will say unto God my rock.* God, my Fortress and Support. *Why hast thou forgotten me?* This and the following verse are badly pointed in our Bibles: "Why go I mourning as with a sword in my bones because of the oppression of the enemy? Mine enemies reproach me daily, while they say unto me, Where is thy God?" Their reproaches are to my soul as cutting and severe as a sword thrust into my body.

11. *Why art thou cast down?* There is no reason why you should despair. God will appear and release you and your brother captives, and soon your sighing and sorrowing shall flee away. *Who is the health of my countenance.* As a healthy state of the constitution shows itself in the appearance of the face, God will so rejoice your heart, heal all your spiritual maladies, that your face shall testify the happiness that is within you.

PSALM 43

The Psalmist begs God to take his part against his enemies, 1-2; to send His light and truth to guide him to the Tabernacle, 3; promises, if brought thither, to be faithful in the divine service, 4; chides himself for despondency, and takes courage, 5.

There is no title to this psalm in the Hebrew. It is most evidently on the same subject with the forty-second psalm, had the same author or authors, and contains the remaining part of the complaint of the captive Jews in Babylon. It is written as a part of the forty-second psalm in forty-six of Kennicott's and De Rossi's MSS.

1. *Judge me, O God, and plead my cause. Ribah ribi,* a forensic term, properly enough translated, "plead my cause," be my Counsellor and Advocate. *Ungodly nation.* The Babylonians. *The deceitful and unjust man.* Nebuchadnezzar.

2. *For thou art the God of my strength.* The Psalmist speaks here, as in other places, in the person of the whole Israelitish people then captive in Babylon. We still acknowledge Thee for our God.

3. *O send out thy light and thy truth.* We are in darkness and distress; oh, send light and prosperity. We look for the fulfillment of Thy promises; oh, send forth Thy truth. Let Thy light guide me to Thy holy hill, to the country of my fathers; let Thy truth lead me to Thy tabernacles, there to worship Thee in spirit and in truth.

4. *Then will I go unto the altar.* When Thy light, a favorable turn in our affairs, leads us to the land of our fathers, and Thy truth, the fulfillment of Thy gracious promises, has placed us again at the door of Thy tabernacles, then will we go to Thy altar, and joyfully offer those sacrifices and offerings which Thy law requires, and rejoice in Thee with exceeding great joy.

PSALM 44

The Psalmist recounts the mercies of God; shows to his people how God in ancient times gave them the victory over all their enemies, 1-8; points out their present miserable state, 9-10; asserts that they have not apostatized, and appeals to God for the truth of his assertion, 17-22; and calls upon the Lord for deliverance from their enemies, 23-26.

The title here is the same as that in Psalms xlii, which see. Like the preceding, it appears to belong to the time of the Captivity.

1. *We have heard with our ears.* The Psalmist begins with recounting the marvellous interpositions of God in behalf of the Jewish people, that he might the better strengthen his confidence, and form a ground on which to build his expectation of additional help.

2. *Thou didst drive out the heathen.* The Canaanites were as a bad tree planted in a good soil, and bringing forth bad fruit with great luxuriance. God plucked up this bad tree from the roots, and in its place planted the Hebrews as a good tree, a good vine, and caused them to take root, and fill the land.

4. *Thou art my King.* What Thou wert to them, be to us. We believe in Thee as they did; we have sinned and are in captivity, but we repent and turn unto Thee; *command,* therefore, *deliverances for Jacob,* for we are the descendants of him in whose behalf Thou hast wrought such wonders.

5. *Through thee will we push down.* "Through Thy words." Literally, "We will toss them in the air with our horn," a metaphor taken from an ox or bull tossing into the air the dogs which attack him. *Through thy name.* Jehovah; the infinite, the omnipotent, the eternal Being, whose power none is able to resist.

6. *I will not trust in my bow.* As he is speaking of what God had already done for his forefathers, these words should be read in the past tense: "We have not trusted."

8. *In God we boast.* We have told the heathen how great and powerful our God is. If Thou do not deliver us by Thy mighty power, they will not believe our report, but consider that we are held in bondage by the superior strength of their gods.

11. *And hast scattered us among the heathen.* This most evidently alludes to the Captivity. From the successful wars of the kings of Assyria and Chaldea against the kings of Israel and Judah, and the dispersion of the tribes under Tiglath-pileser, Shalmaneser, and Nebuchadnezzar, Jews have been found in every province of the East; there they settled, and there their successors may be found to the present day.

12. *Thou sellest thy people for nought.* An allusion to the mode of disposing of slaves by their proprietors or sovereigns. Instead of seeking profit, Thou hast made us a present to our enemies.

14. *Thou makest us a byword.* We are evidently abandoned by Thee, and are become so very miserable in consequence that we are a proverb among the people.

17. *Yet have we not forgotten thee.* These are bold words, but they must be understood in a qualified sense. We have not apostatized from Thee; we have not fallen into idolatry. And this was strictly true; the charge of idolatry could never be brought against the Jewish nation from the time of the Captivity.

19. *Thou hast sore broken us in the place of dragons.* Thou hast delivered us into the hands of a fierce, cruel, and murderous people. We, as a people, are in a similar state to one who has strayed into a wilderness where there are no human inhabitants.

20. *If we have forgotten the name of our God.* That name, Yehovah, by which the true God was particularly distinguished, and which implied the exclusion of all other objects of adoration.

22. *For thy sake are we killed all the day long.* Because of our attachment to Thee and to Thy religion we are exposed to continual death; and some of us fall a daily sacrifice to the persecuting spirit of our enemies, and we all carry our lives

continually in our hands. In the same state were the primitive Christians, and St. Paul applies these words to their case, Rom. viii. 36.

23. *Awake, why sleepest thou, O Lord?* That is, Why dost Thou appear as one asleep, who is regardless of the safety of his friends?

PSALM 45

The contents of this psalm are generally summed up thus: The majesty and grace of Christ's kingdom; or an epithalamium of Jesus Christ and the Christian Church; the duty of this Church, and its privileges. The psalm contains a magnificent description of the beauty, ornaments, valor, justice, and truth of the Divine Bridegroom; the beauty, magnificence, and riches of the bride, who was to become mother of a numerous and powerful posterity. The preamble is found in the title and v. 1. The description and character of the Bridegroom, 2-9. The address to the bride by her companions, 10-15. A prediction of her numerous and glorious descendants, 16-17.

The title is nearly the same with that of Psalms lxix and lxxx. "To the chief musician, or master of the band of those who played on the six-stringed instruments, giving instruction, for the sons of Korah; a song of loves, or a song of the beloved maids." I believe it to be a nuptial song, which primarily respected Solomon's marriage with the daughter of Pharaoh, and that it probably has a prophetic reference to the conversion of the Gentiles.

1. *My heart is inditing a good matter.* Boileth or bubbleth up. It is a metaphor taken from a fountain that sends up its waters from the earth in this way. *I speak of the things which I have made touching the king.* Literally, "I dedicate my work unto the king." *My tongue is the pen of a ready writer.* I shall compose and speak as fluently the divine matter which is now in my heart as the most expert scribe can write from my recitation.

2. *Thou art fairer than the children of men.* By whom are these words spoken? It seems that the whole psalm, except the first verse, was spoken by those who are called in the title the "beloved maids," or female companions, who begin with his perfections and then describe hers. And afterwards there is a prophetical declaration concerning his issue. We may, therefore, consider that what is spoken here is spoken by companions of the bride. *Grace is poured into thy lips.* This probably refers to his speech, or the gracious words which he spoke. Solomon was renowned for wisdom, and especially the wisdom of his conversation. *God hath blessed thee for ever.* This, I am afraid, could in no sense be ever spoken of Solomon; but of the man Christ Jesus it is strictly true.

3. *Gird thy sword upon thy thigh, O most mighty.* This clause should be translated, "O hero, gird thy sword upon thy thigh!" This, I think, cannot be spoken of Solomon. The words more properly apply to Christ, who is King of Kings, and Lord of Lords. *With thy glory and thy majesty.* Be as warlike as thou art glorious and majestic. Solomon's court was splendid, and his person was majestic. But the majesty and glory of Christ are above all.

4. *In thy majesty ride prosperously.* These words cannot be spoken of Solomon; they are true only of Christ. His riding is the prosperous progress of His gospel over the earth. He uses no sword but the Sword of the Spirit. *And thy right hand shall teach thee terrible things.* The Chaldee is different: "And the Lord will teach

thee to perform terrible things by thy right hand." The meaning is, Nothing shall be able to resist thee, and the judgments which thou shalt inflict on thine enemies shall be terrible.

5. *Thine arrows are sharp.* The arrows here may mean the convictions produced in the hearts of man by the preaching of the gospel.

6. *Thy throne, O God, is for ever.* "O God, thy throne is for ever, and eternal!" The word *Elohim* here is the very *first* term or *name* by which the Supreme God has made himself known to the children of men. See Gen. i. 1; and this very verse the apostle, Heb. i. 8, has applied to Jesus Christ.

7. *Oil of gladness.* As an evidence that all causes of *mourning, sorrow,* and *death* were at an end, as in the state of mourning the ancients did not anoint themselves.

8. *All thy garments smell of myrrh.* The Asiatics are very partial to perfumes; everything with them is perfumed, and especially their garments. *Myrrh* and *aloes* are well-known; *cassia* is probably the bark or wood of the cinnamon tree. *Whereby they have made thee glad.* Referring to the effect of strong perfumes refreshing and exhilarating the spirits.

9. *Kings' daughters were among.* Applied to Solomon, these words have no difficulty. We know he had 700 wives, princesses.

10-11. *Hearken, O daughter, and consider.* This is the beginning of the address by the companions of the bride to their mistress; after having, in the preceding verses, addressed the bridegroom; or, rather, given a description of his person, qualities, and magnificence. Supposing the daughter of Pharaoh to be intended, the words import: Thou art now become the spouse of the most magnificent monarch in the universe. To thee he must be all in all. *Forget therefore thine own people*—the Egyptians—and take the Israelites in their place. *Forget* also *thy father's house;* thou art now united to a new family. *So shall the king,* Solomon, *greatly desire thy beauty*—thou wilt be, in all respects, pleasing to him. And it is right thou shouldst act so, for he is now become *thy Lord*—thy supreme governor. *And worship thou him*—submit thyself reverently and affectionately to all his commands.

Taken in reference to Christ and the gospel, this is an address to the Gentiles to forsake their idolatrous customs and connections, to embrace Christ and His gospel in the spirit of reverence and obedience, with the promise that, if beautified with the graces of His Spirit, Christ will delight in them, and take them for His peculiar people—which has been done.

12. *The daughter of Tyre shall be there with a gift.* The Tyrians shall pay tribute to thy spouse, and assist him in all his grand and magnificent operations.

13. *The king's daughter is all glorious within.* This, in some sense, may be spoken of Solomon's bride, the daughter of the king of Egypt; and then the expression may refer either to the cultivation of her mind or the ornaments and splendor of her palace. Spiritually, the *king's daughter* may mean the Christian Church filled with the mind that was in Christ, and adorned with the graces of the Holy Spirit.

16. *Instead of thy fathers shall be thy children.* This is the third part, or prophetic declaration relative to the numerous and powerful issue of

this marriage. This cannot refer either to Solomon or to the daughter of Pharaoh, for there is no evidence that he ever had a child by Pharaoh's daughter. The *children* mentioned here are generally supposed to mean the apostles and their successors in the Christian ministry, founding churches all over the world, by whom the Christian name becomes a memorial through all the earth.

17. *Therefore shall the people praise thee.* They shall magnify the heavenly Bridegroom, and sing the wonderful displays of His love to the Church, His spouse. And the constant use of this psalm in the Christian Church is a literal fulfillment of the prophecy.

PSALM 46

The confidence of believers in God, 1-3. The privileges of the Church, 4-5; her enemies, and her Helper, 6-7. God's judgments in the earth, 8-9. He will be exalted among the heathen, and throughout the earth, 10-11.

The title in the Hebrew is, "To the chief musician for the sons of Korah; an ode upon *Alamoth*, or concerning the virgins," possibly meaning a choir of singing girls.

1. *God is our refuge.* It begins abruptly, but nobly; you may trust in whom and in what you please, but *God* (Elohim) *is our refuge and strength. A very present help.* The words are very emphatic: "He is found an exceeding, or superlative, Help in difficulties."

3. *Though the waters thereof roar. Waters,* in prophetic language, signify people; and, generally, people in a state of political commotion, here signified by the term *roar.* And by these strong agitations of the people, the *mountains*—the secular rulers—*shake with the swelling thereof*—tremble, for fear that these popular tumults should terminate in the subversion of the state.

4. *There is a river, the streams whereof.* The Chaldee understands the *river,* and its *streams* or divisions, as pointing out various peoples who should be converted to the faith, and thus *make glad the city of God,* Jerusalem, by their flowing together to the worship of the true God.

7. *The Lord of hosts is with us.* We, feeble Jews, were but a handful of men; but the *Lord of hosts*—the God of armies—was on our side. *The God of Jacob.* The God who appeared to Jacob in his distress, and saved him out of all his troubles, appeared also for us His descendants, and has amply proved to us that He has not forgotten His covenant.

8. *Come, behold the works of the Lord.* See empires destroyed and regenerated, and in such a way as to show that a supernatural agency has been at work. By the hand of God alone could these great changes be effected.

9. *He maketh wars to cease.* By the death of Cambyses, and setting Darius, son of Hystaspes, upon the Persian throne, he has tranquillized the whole empire. That same God who for our unfaithfulness has delivered us into the hand of our enemies, and subjected us to a long and grievous captivity and affliction, has now turned our captivity, and raised us up the most powerful friends and protectors in the very place in which we have been enduring so great a fight of afflictions.

10. *Be still, and know that I am God.* "Cease" from your provocations of the divine justice; cease from murmuring against the dispensations of His providence.

11. *The Lord of hosts is with us.* Having heard these declarations of God, the people cry out with joy and exultation, *The Lord of hosts,* the God of armies, *is with us;* we will not fear what man can do unto us. *The God of Jacob is our refuge.* He who saved our fathers will save us, and will never abandon His people in distress.

PSALM 47

The Gentiles are invited to celebrate the praises of God as the Sovereign of the world, 1-2. The Jews exult in His kindness to them, 3-4. All then join to celebrate His majesty, as reigning over the heathen, and gathering the dispersed Jews and Gentiles together into one Church, 5-9.

The title, "A Psalm for the sons of Korah," has nothing remarkable in it. The psalm was probably written about the same time with the preceding, and relates to the happy state of the Jews when returned to their own land. They renew their praises and promises of obedience, and celebrate Him for the deliverance they had received. In a spiritual sense, it appears to relate to the calling of the Gentiles to be made partakers of the blessings of the gospel with the converted Jews.

1. *O clap your hands, all ye people.* Let both Jews and Gentiles magnify the Lord: the Jews, for being delivered from the Babylonish captivity; the Gentiles, for being called to enter into the glorious liberty of the children of God.

6. *Sing praises. Zammeru.* This word is four times repeated in this short verse, and shows at once the earnestness and happiness of the people. They are the words of exultation and triumph.

7. *For God is the King of all the earth.* He is not your King only, but the King of the universe. *Sing ye praises with understanding. Zammeru maskil,* "sing an instructive song." Let sense and sound go together. Let your hearts and heads go with your voices. Understand what you sing, and feel what you understand; and let the song be what will give instruction in righteousness to them that hear it.

8. *God reigneth over the heathen.* Though this is literally true in God's universal dominion, yet more is here meant. God reigns over the heathen, when, by the preaching of the gospel, they are brought into the Church of Christ.

9. *The princes of the people are gathered together.* The princely, noble, or free-willed people; those who gladly receive the word of life; those who, like the Bereans, were of a noble or liberal disposition, and when they heard the gospel, searched the Scriptures to see whether these things were so. It is a similar word which is used Ps. cx. 3; and I believe both texts speak of the same people—the Gentiles who gladly come unto His light, and present themselves a freewill offering to the Lord. *The people of the God of Abraham.* The people of the God of Abraham are the Gentiles, who, receiving the gospel, are made partakers of the faith of Abraham, and are his spiritual children. *The shields of the earth belong unto God.* The Septuagint translates this "the strong ones of the earth."

PSALM 48

The ornaments and the privileges of the Church, 1-8.
The duty of God's people, 9-14.

The title: "A Song and Psalm for the sons of
Korah." It is evidently of the same complexion
with the two preceding, and refers to the Jews
returned from captivity; and perhaps was sung
at the dedication of the second Temple, in order
to return thanks to the Lord for the restoration
of their political state and the reestablishment
of their worship.

1. *Great is the Lord.* This verse should be
joined to the last verse of the preceding psalm,
as it is a continuation of the same subject.
The mountain of his holiness. Mount Moriah,
on which the Temple was built. The ancient
city of Jerusalem, which David took from the
Jebusites, was on the south of Mount Zion, on
which the Temple was built, though it might
be said to be more properly on Mount Moriah,
which is one of the hills of which Mount Zion
is composed. The Temple therefore was to the
north of the city, as the Psalmist here states,
v. 2: "Beautiful for situation, the joy of the
whole earth, is Mount Zion, on the sides of the
north, the city of the great King."

2. *The joy of the whole earth.* Commentators
have been greatly puzzled to show in what sense
Zion, or the Temple, could be said to be the
joy of the whole earth. If we take the earth
here for the habitable globe, there is no sense
in which it ever was the joy of the whole earth;
but if we take *col haarets* as signifying the
"whole of this land" (and it has no other meaning), the assertion is plain and easy to be understood, for the Temple was considered the
ornament and glory of the whole land of Judea.

3. *God is known in her palaces for a refuge.*
All those who worship there in spirit and truth
find God for their Refuge. But the words may
be understood: God is known for the defense
of her palaces; and with this view of the subject
agree the three following verses.

4-6. *For, lo, the kings were assembled.* Many
of the neighboring potentates, at different times,
envied the prosperity of the Jewish nation and
coveted the riches of the Temple, but they had no
power against it till the cup of Jewish transgression was full. In vain did they assemble
—confederate, and invade the land. *Saw it*—
reconnoitered the place; *marvelled* at its excellence and strength, for *they were troubled*
—struck with fear; *hasted away* for fear of destruction, for *fear took hold upon them* as pains
seize on *a woman in travail.* Those who came
to destroy were glad to make their own escape.

10. *According to thy name.* As far as Thou
art known, so far art Thou praised; and where
Thou art known, Thou wilt have praise to the
end of the earth. And why? *Thy right hand is
full of righteousness.* Thou art continually dispensing Thy blessings to the children of men.

11. *Let Mount Zion rejoice.* The Temple is
restored in majesty, which was threatened with
total destruction; it is again repaired. *Let the
daughters of Judah be glad.* That Thou hast
turned her captivity, and poured out Thy judgments upon her oppressors.

12. *Walk about Zion.* Consider the beauty and
magnificence of the Temple, count *the towers*
by which it is fortified.

13. *Mark ye well her bulwarks.* See the redoubts by which she is defended. *Consider her
palaces.* See her courts, chambers, altars; make
an exact register of the whole, that you may
have to tell to your children how Jerusalem was
built in troublesome times; how God restored
you; and how He put it into the hearts of the
heathen to assist to build, beautify, and adorn
the temple of our God.

PSALM 49

All men are invited to attend to lessons of wisdom
relative to the insufficiency of earthly good to save or
prolong life; to secure the resurrection from the dead,
1-9. Death is inevitable, 10. The vain expectations of
rich men, 11-13. Death renders all alike, 14. The Psalmist
encourages and fortifies himself against envying the apparently prosperous state of the wicked, who are brutish,
and die like beasts, 15-20.

The title, "To the chief Musician, A Psalm for
the sons of Korah," has nothing particular in it.

1. *Hear this, all ye people.* The first four
verses contain the author's exordium or introduction, delivered in a very pompous style, and
promising the deepest lessons of wisdom and
instruction.

4. *I will incline mine ear to a parable.* This
was the general method of conveying instruction
among the Asiatics. They used much figure and
metaphor to induce the reader to study deeply
in order to find out the meaning. Reflect deeply;
and thus in some measure taught them the use,
government, and managment of their minds.

5. *The iniquity of my heels.* Perhaps *akebai*,
which we translate *my heels*, should be considered the contracted plural of *akebim*, "supplanters." The verse would then read thus:
"Wherefore should I fear in the days of evil,
though the iniquity of my supplanters should
compass me about?"

8. *For the redemption of their soul is precious.*
It is of too high a price to be redeemed with
corruptible things, such as silver or gold, and
has required the sacrificial death of Christ. *And
it ceaseth for ever.* This is very obscure, and
may apply to the ransom which riches could
produce. That ransom must be forever unavailable, because of the value of the soul. Or this
clause should be added to the following verse,
and read thus: "And though he cease to be
during the hidden time, yet he shall live on
through eternity, and not see corruption." This
is probably the "dark saying" which it was the
design of the author to utter in a parable, and
leave it to the ingenuity of posterity to find it
out.

11. *Their inward thought is, that their houses
shall continue for ever.* Thus, by interpolation,
we have endeavored to patch up a sense to this
clause. Instead of *kirbam*, their "inward part,"
the Septuagint appear to have used a copy in
which the second and third letters have been
transposed, *kibram*, "their sepulchres"; for they
translate: "For their graves are their dwellings
for ever." So six or seven feet long, and two or
three wide, is sufficient to hold the greatest conqueror in the universe!

12. *Man being in honour abideth not.* However rich, wise, or honorable, they must die; and
if they die not with a sure hope of eternal life,
they die like beasts.

13. *Their posterity approve their sayings.* Go
the same way; adopt their maxims.

14. *Like sheep they are laid in the grave.* "Into sheol," the place of separate spirits. *Death shall feed on them.* "Death shall feed them!" What an astonishing change! All the good things of life were once their portion, and they lived only to eat and drink; and now **they live in** sheol, and Death himself feeds them! and with what? Damnation.

15. *But God will redeem my soul from the power of the grave.* "From the hand of sheol." That is, by the plainest construction, I shall have a resurrection from the dead, and an entrance into His glory; and death shall have no dominion over me."

19. *They shall never see light.* Rise again they shall; but they shall never see the light of glory, for there is prepared for them the "blackness of darkness" forever.

PSALM 50

God, the sovereign Judge, cites before His throne all his people, and the priests and the judges, 1-6; and reproaches them for their vain confidence in the sacrifices they had offered, 7-13; and shows them the worship He requires, 14-15; and then enters into a particular detail of their hypocrisy, injustice, and union with scandalous transgressors; all of whom He threatens with heavy judgments, 16-22. The blessedness of him who worships God aright, and walks unblamably, 23.

In the title this is said to be "A Psalm of Asaph." There are twelve that go under his name; and most probably he was author of each, for he was of high repute in the days of David, and is mentioned second to him as a composer of psalms: "Moreover Hezekiah the king and the princes commanded the Levites to sing praise unto the Lord with the words of David, and of Asaph the seer." His band, sons or companions, were also eminent in the days of David, as we learn from 1 Chronicles xxv, etc. Asaph himself was one of the musicians who sounded with cymbals of brass, 1 Chron. xv. 19. And he is mentioned with great respect, Neh. xii. 46: "For in the days of David and Asaph of old there were chief of the singers, and songs of praise and thanksgiving unto God." He was certainly a prophetic man; he is called a seer—one on whom the Spirit of God rested; and seems from this, his education, and natural talent, to be well qualified to compose hymns or psalms in the honor of God. Persons capable of judging, on a comparison of those psalms attributed to Asaph with those known to be of David, have found a remarkable difference in the style. The style of David is more polished, flowing, correct, and majestic than that of Asaph, which is more stiff and obscure.

1-6. *The mighty God, even the Lord, hath spoken.* Here the essential names of God are used: El, Elohim, Yehovah, hath spoken. The first six verses of this psalm seem to contain a description of the great judgment. In this light I shall consider this part of the psalm, and show—*First,* The preparatives to the coming of the great Judge. "El Elohim Jehovah *hath spoken, and called the earth,"* all the children of men. *Out of Zion, the perfection of beauty* (the beauty where all perfection is comprised), *God hath shined,* vv. 1-2. (1) He has sent His Spirit to convince men of sin, righteousness, and judgment. (2) He has sent His Word. *Secondly,* The accompaniments. (1) His approach is proclaimed, v. 3: *Our God shall come.* (2) The trumpet proclaims his approach: "He *shall not*

keep silence." (3) Universal nature shall be shaken, and the earth and its works be burnt up: *A fire shall devour before him, and it shall be very tempestuous round about him, v.* 3. *Thirdly,* The witnesses are summoned and collected from all quarters; some from heaven, and some from earth. (1) Guardian angels. (2) Human associates. *He shall call to the heavens from above, and to the earth, that he may judge his people, v.* 4. *Fourthly,* The procedure. As far as it respects the righteous, orders are issued: *Gather my saints,* those who are saved from their sins and made holy, *together unto me.* And that the word *saints* might not be misunderstood, it is explained by *those that have made a covenant with me by sacrifice;* those who have entered into union with God, through the sacrificial offering of the Lord Jesus Christ. *Fifthly,* The final issue: all the angelic host and all the redeemed of the Lord join in applauding acclamation at the decision of the Supreme Judge.

7. *Hear, O my people.* As they were now amply informed concerning the nature and certainty of the general judgment, and were still in a state of probation, Asaph proceeds to show them the danger to which they were exposed, and the necessity of repentance and amendment, that when that great day should arrive, they might be found among those who had made a covenant with God by sacrifice. And he shows them that the sacrifice with which God would be well pleased was quite different from the bullocks, he-goats, etc., which they were in the habit of offering. In short, he shows here that God has intended to abrogate those sacrifices, as being no longer of any service. For when the people began to trust in them, without looking to the thing signified, it was time to put them away.

8. *I will not reprove thee.* I do not mean to find fault with you for not offering sacrifices. You have offered them; they *have been continually before me.* But you have not offered them in the proper way.

From the sixteenth to the twenty-second verse Asaph appears to refer to the final rejection of the Jews from having any part in the true covenant sacrifice.

16. *But unto the wicked.* The bloodthirsty priests, proud Pharisees, and ignorant scribes of the Jewish people.

17. *Seeing thou hatest instruction.* All these rejected the counsel of God against themselves, and refused to receive the instructions of Christ.

23. *Whoso offereth praise.* These are the very same words as those in v. 14, and should be read the same way, "Sacrifice the thank offering." Jesus is the great eucharistic Sacrifice; offer Him up to God in your faith and prayers. *Ordereth his conversation.* "Disposeth his way." *Will I shew the salvation of God.* I will cause him to see into the salvation of God, into God's method of saving sinners by Christ.

PSALM 51

The Psalmist, with a deeply penitent heart, prays for remission of sins, 1-4; which he confesses, and deeply deplores, 5-14; states his willingness to offer sacrifice, but is convinced that God prefers a broken heart to all kinds of oblations, 15-17; prays for the restoration of the walls of Jerusalem, and promises that then the Lord's sacrifice shall be properly performed, 18-19.

The title is long: "To the chief Musician, A Psalm of David, when Nathan the prophet came unto him, after he had gone in to Bath-sheba."

1. *Have mercy upon me, O God.* Without mercy I am totally, finally ruined and undone. *According to thy lovingkindness.* Mark the gradation in the sense of these three words, *Have mercy on me; thy lovingkindness; thy tender mercies,* here used to express the divine compassion. *Blot out my transgressions.* "Wipe out." There is a reference here to an indictment. The Psalmist knows what it contains; he pleads guilty, but begs that the writing may be defaced.

2. *Wash me throughly.* "Wash me again and again—cause my washings to be multiplied."

4. *Against thee, thee only, have I sinned.* This verse is supposed to show the impropriety of affixing the above title to this psalm. It could not have been composed on account of the matter with Bath-sheba and the murder of Uriah, for surely these sins could not be said to have been committed against God only. *That thou mightest be justified when thou speakest.* Perhaps, to save the propriety of the title, we might understand the verse thus: David, being king, was not liable to be called to account by any of his subjects; nor was there any authority in the land by which he could be judged and punished. In this respect, God alone was greater than the king; and to Him alone, as king, he was responsible.

5. *Behold, I was shapen in iniquity.* A genuine penitent will hide nothing of his state; he sees and bewails, not only the acts of sin which he has committed, but the disposition that led to those acts. He deplores, not only the transgression, but the carnal mind, which is enmity against God.

6. *Behold, thou desirest truth.* I am the very reverse of what I should be. Thou desirest truth in the heart, but in me there is nothing but sin and falsity. *Thou shalt make me to know wisdom.* Thou wilt teach me to restrain every inordinate propensity, and to act according to the dictates of sound wisdom, the rest of my life.

7. *Purge me with hyssop.* "Thou shalt make a sin offering for me," probably alluding to the cleansing of the leper, Lev. xiv. 1, etc.

9. *Hide thy face from my sins.* The sentiment here is nearly the same as that in v. 3. His sin was ever before his own face; and he knew that the eye of God was constantly upon him, and that His purity and justice must be highly incensed on the account. He therefore, with a just horror of his transgressions, begs God to turn away His face from them, and to blot them out, so that they may nevermore be seen.

10. *Create in me a clean heart.* Mending will not avail; my heart is altogether corrupted. It must be new made, made as it was in the beginning. This is exactly the sentiment of St. Paul: "Neither circumcision availeth any thing, nor uncircumcision, but a new creature [creation]"; and the salvation given under the gospel dispensation is called a being "created anew in Christ Jesus." *A right spirit within me.* A constant, steady, determined spirit; called in v. 12 a noble spirit; a free, generous, princely spirit; cheerfully giving up itself to thee; no longer bound and degraded by the sinfulness of sin.

14. *Deliver me from bloodguiltiness.* This is one of the expressions that gives most color to

the propriety of the title affixed to this psalm. Here he may have in view the death of Uriah, and consider that his blood cries for vengeance against him, and that nothing but the mere mercy of God can wipe this blood from his conscience. The prayer here is earnest and energetic: *O God! thou God of my salvation,* deliver me!

16. *For thou desirest not sacrifice.* This is the same sentiment which he delivers in Ps. xl. 6, etc.

17. *The sacrifices of God are a broken spirit.* I have the *broken spirit, ruach nishbarah,* and the *broken and contrite heart, leb nishbar venidkeh.* These words are very expressive. *Shabar* signifies exactly the same as our word "shiver," to break into pieces, to reduce into splinters; and *dakah* signifies to "beat out thin," to beat out masses of metal into thin plates. The spirit broken all to pieces, and the heart broken all to pieces, stamped and beaten out, are the sacrifices which, in such cases, Thou requirest; and these *thou wilt not despise.* We may now suppose that God had shone upon his soul, healed his broken spirit, and renewed and removed his broken and distracted heart; and that he had now received the answer to the preceding prayers. And here the psalm properly ends, as in the following two verses there is nothing similar to what we find in the rest of this most important composition.

18. *Do good in thy good pleasure unto Zion.* This and the following verse most evidently refer to the time of the Captivity, when the walls of Jerusalem were broken down and the Temple service entirely discontinued; and, consequently, are long posterior to the times of David. Hence it has been concluded that the psalm was not composed by David, nor in his time, and that the title must be that of some other psalm inadvertently affixed to this. The fourth verse has also been considered as decisive against this title; but the note on that verse has considerably weakened, if not destroyed, that objection. I have been long of opinion that, whether the title be properly or improperly affixed to this psalm, these two verses make no part of it. The subject is totally dissimilar; and there is no rule of analogy by which it can be interpreted as belonging to the psalm, to the subject, or to the person. I think they oiginally made a psalm of themselves, a kind of ejaculatory prayer for the redemption of the captives from Babylon, the rebuilding of Jerusalem, and the restoration of the Temple worship. And, taken in this light, they are very proper and very expressive.

PSALM 52

The Psalmist points out the malevolence of a powerful enemy, and predicts his destruction, 1-5. At which destruction the righteous should rejoice, 6-7. The Psalmist's confidence in God, 8-9.

The title is, "To the chief Musician, and instructive Psalm of David, when Doeg the Edomite came and informed Saul, and said to him, David is come to the house of Ahimelech." The history to which this alludes is the following: David, having learned that Saul was determined to destroy him, went to take refuge with Achish, king of Gath. In his journey he passed by Nob, where the Tabernacle then was, and took thence the sword of Goliath; and, being spent with hunger, took some of the shewbread. Doeg, an

Edomite, one of the domestics of Saul, being there, went to Saul and informed him of these transactions. Saul immediately ordered Ahimelech into his presence, upbraided him for being a partisan of David, and ordered Doeg to slay him and all the priests. Doeg did so, and there fell by his hand eighty-five persons. And Saul sent and destroyed Nob and all its inhabitants, old and young, with all their property; none escaping but Abiathar, the son of Ahimelech, who immediately joined himself to David. The account may be found 1 Sam. xxi. 1-7; xxii. 9-23.

5. *God shall likewise destroy thee.* God shall set himself to destroy you; "He will pull down thy building"; He shall unroof it, dilapidate, and dig up your foundation.

7. *In the abundance of his riches.* Literally, in the "multiplication of his riches." He had got much, he hoped to get more, and expected that his happiness would multiply as his riches multiplied. And this is the case with most rich men. *Strengthened himself in his wickedness.* Loved money instead of God; and thus his depravity, being increased, was *strengthened.*

PSALM 53

The sentiments of atheists and deists, who deny divine providence; their character: they are corrupt, foolish, abominable, and cruel, 1-4; God fills them with terror, 5; reproaches them for their oppression of the poor, 5. The Psalmist prays for the restoration of Israel, 6.

The title, "To the chief Musician upon Mahalath, an instructive Psalm of David." The word *mahalath,* some translate the "president"; others, "hollow instruments." A flute pipe, or wind instrument with holes, appears to be what is intended. "To the chief player on the flute"; or, "To the master of the band of pipers."

1. *The fool hath said in his heart.* The whole of this psalm, except a few inconsiderable differences, is the same as the fourteenth. By referring to the fourteenth, the reader will find the subject of it explained. *Have done abominable iniquity.* Instead of *avel,* "evil" or "iniquity," eight of Kennicott's and De Rossi's MSS. have *alilah,* "work," which is nearly the same as in Psalm xiv.

4. *Have the workers of iniquity.* For *workers* seventy-two of Kennicott's and De Rossi's MSS., with several ancient editions, add the word "all" —"all the workers of iniquity," which is the reading in the parallel place in Psalm xiv.

5. *For God hath scattered the bones of him that encampeth against thee: thou hast put them to shame, because God hath despised them.* The reader will see, on comparing this with the fifth and sixth verses of Psalm xiv., that the words above are mostly added here to what is said there; and appear to be levelled against the Babylonians, who sacked and ruined Jerusalem, and who were now sacked and ruined in their turn . . . *Oh that the salvation of Israel were come out of Zion!* I have already shown that the proper translation is, "Who shall give from Zion salvation to Israel?" The word *salvation* is in the plural here, "deliverances."

PSALM 54

The Psalmist complains that strangers were risen up against him to take away his life, 1-3; expresses his confidence in God that He will uphold him, and punish his enemies, 4-5; on which he promises to sacrifice to God, 6; he speaks of His deliverance, 7.

The title is, "To the chief Musician upon Neginoth, an instructive Psalm of David, when the Ziphites came to Saul, and said, Doth not David conceal himself among us?"

Ziph was a village in the southern part of Palestine. David having taken refuge in the mountains of that country, the Ziphites went to Saul, and informed him of the fact. Saul, with his army, immediately went thither, and was on one side of a mountain while David was on the other. Just when he was about to fall into the hands of his merciless pursuer, an express came to Saul that the Philistines had invaded Israel, on which he gave up the pursuit and returned to save his country, and David escaped to En-gedi. See the account in 1 Sam. xxiii. 19-29. *Neginoth,* from *nagan,* to "strike" or "play" on some kind of instrument, probably signifies stringed instruments, such as were played on with a plectrum.

1. *Save me, O God, by thy name.* Save me by thyself alone; so *name* here may be understood. The name of God is often God himself. David was now in such imminent danger of being taken and destroyed that no human means were left for his escape; if God therefore had not interfered, he must have been destroyed.

2. *Hear my prayer.* In his straits he had recourse to God; for from Him alone, for the reasons alleged above, his deliverance must proceed.

3. *Strangers are risen up against me.* The Ziphites. *And oppressors.* Saul, his courtiers, and his army.

6. *I will freely sacrifice unto thee.* Or, "I will sacrifice nobly unto Thee." Not only with a 'willing mind, but with a liberal hand will I bring sacrifice unto Thee.

7. *For he hath delivered me.* Saul had now decamped, and was returned to save his territories; and David in the meanwhile escaped to En-gedi. God was most evidently the Author of this deliverance. *Mine eye hath seen his desire upon mine enemies.* It is not likely that this psalm was written after the death of Saul, and therefore David could not say that he had seen his desire. The words might be translated, "My eye hath seen my enemies"—they have been so near that I could plainly discover them. Thus almost all the versions have understood the text. I have seen them, and yet they were not permitted to approach me. God has been my Deliverer.

PSALM 55

David, in great danger and distress from the implacable malice of his enemies, calls on God for mercy, 1-5; wishes he had the wings of a dove, that he might flee away, and be at rest, 6-8; prays against his enemies, and describes their wickedness, 9-11; speaks of a false friend, who had been the principal cause of all his distresses, 12-14; again prays against his enemies, 15; expresses his confidence in God, 16-18; gives a further description of the deceitful friend, 19-21; encourages himself in the Lord, and foretells the destruction of his foes, 22-23.

The title, "To the chief Musician upon Neginoth, A Psalm of David, giving instruction." This is the same as the preceding.

1. *Give ear to my prayer.* The frequency of such petitions shows the great earnestness of David's soul.

2. *I mourn in my complaint.* "In my sighing"; a strong guttural sound, expressive of the natural

accents of sorrow. *And make a noise.* I am in a "tumult"—I am strongly agitated.

3. *They cast iniquity upon me.* They charge me with horrible crimes.

4. *The terrors of death are fallen upon me.* I am in hourly expectation of being massacred.

5. *Fearfulness.* How natural is this description! He is in distress—he mourns—makes a noise; sobs and sighs; his heart is wounded; he expects nothing but death; this produces fear; this produces tremor, which terminates in that deep apprehension of approaching and inevitable ruin that overwhelms him with horror. No man ever described a wounded heart like David.

7. *Would I wander far off.* He did escape, and yet his enemies were so near as to throw stones at him; but he escaped beyond Jordan, 2 Sam. xvii. 22-23.

8. *The windy storm.* From the sweeping wind and tempest—Absalom and his party, and the mutinous people in general.

9. *Destroy, O Lord.* "Swallow them up"—confound them. *Divide their tongues.* Let his counsellors give opposite advice. And the prayer was heard. Hushai and Ahithophel gave opposite counsel. Absalom followed that of Hushai; and Ahithophel, knowing that the steps advised by Hushai would bring Absalom's affairs to ruin, went and hanged himself. See 2 Samuel xv; xvi; and xvii.

12. *It was not an enemy.* It is likely that in all these three verses Ahithophel is meant, who, it appears, had been at the bottom of the conspiracy from the beginning.

14. *Walked unto the house of God in company.* Or with haste; for the rabbins teach that we should walk hastily to the Temple, but slowly from it.

15. *Let death seize upon them.* This is a prediction of the sudden destruction which should fall on the ringleaders in this rebellion. And it was so. Ahithophel, seeing his counsel rejected, hanged himself. Absalom was defeated; and, fleeing away, he was suspended by the hair in a tree, under which his mule had passed; and being found thus by Joab, he was dispatched with three darts; and the people who espoused his interests were almost all cut off. *Let them go down quick into hell.* Let them go down alive into the pit. Let the earth swallow them up! And something of this kind actually took place. Absalom and his army were defeated; 20,000 of the rebels were slain on the field; and "the wood devoured more people that day than the sword devoured," 2 Sam. xviii. 7-8.

17. *Evening, and morning, and at noon, will I pray.* This was the custom of the pious Hebrews. See Dan. vi. 10. The Hebrews began their day in the evening, and hence David mentions the evening first.

19. *Because they have no changes.* At first Absalom, Ahithophel, and their party carried all before them. There seemed to be a very general defection of the people; and as in their first attempts they suffered no "reverses," therefore they feared not God. Most of those who have few or no afflictions and trials in life have but little religion. They become sufficient to themselves, and call not upon God.

20. *He hath put forth his hands.* A further description of Ahithophel. He betrayed his friends, and he broke his covenant with his king.

21. *Were smoother than butter.* He was a complete courtier, and a deep, designing hypocrite besides. His words "were as soft as butter, and as smooth as oil," while he meditated war; and the fair words which were intended to deceive were intended also to destroy—they were *drawn swords.* This is a literal description of the words and conduct of Absalom, as we learn from the inspired historian, 2 Sam. xv. 2, etc. He was accustomed to wait at the gate, question the persons who came for justice and judgment, throw out broad hints that the king was negligent of the affairs of his kingdom and had not provided an effective magistracy to administer justice among the people; and added that if he were appointed judge in the land justice should be done to all. He bowed also to the people, and kissed them; and thus "he stole the hearts of the men of Israel." See the passages referred to above.

PSALM 56

David prays for support against his enemies, whose wickedness he describes, 1-6; and foretells their destruction, 7; expresses his confidence in God's mercy, expects deliverance, and promises thanksgiving and obedience, 8-13.

The title of this psalm is very long: "To the conqueror, concerning the dumb dove in foreign places: golden Psalm of David." If the title be at all authentic, David may mean himself and his companions by it, when he escaped from the hands of the Philistines; particularly from the hands of Achish, king of Gath. *Elem* signifies to "compress" or "bind together"; also, a "small band or body of men." And *yonath*, from *yanah*, to "oppress" or "afflict," is properly applied to the dove because of its being so defenseless, and often becoming the prey of ravenous birds. It is possible, therefore, that the title may imply no more than—"A prayer to God in behalf of himself and the oppressed band that followed him, and shared his misfortunes in distant places."

2. *O thou most High. Marom.* I do not think that this word expresses any attribute of God, or indeed is at all addressed to Him. It signifies, literally, "from on high," or "from a high or elevated place": "For the multitudes fight against me from the high or elevated place"; the place of authority—the court and cabinet of Saul.

4. *In God I will praise his word. Belohim* may mean here "through God," or "by the help of God," *I will praise his word.* And that he should have cause to do it, he says, *In God I have put my trust,* and therefore he says, *I will not fear what flesh can do unto me.* He repeats this sentiment in the tenth and eleventh verses.

8. *Thou tellest my wanderings.* Thou seest how often I am obliged to shift the place of my retreat. I am hunted everywhere; but Thou "numberest all my hiding-places," and seest how often I am in danger of losing my life. *Put thou my tears into thy bottle.* Here is an allusion to a very ancient custom, which we know long obtained among the Greeks and Romans, of putting the tears which were shed for the death of any person into small phials, and offering them on the tomb of the deceased. *Are they not in thy book?* Thou hast taken an exact account of

all the tears I have shed in relation to this business, and Thou wilt call my enemies to account for every tear.

10-11. See on v. 4, where the same words occur.

PSALM 57

David cries to God for mercy, with the strongest confidence of being heard, 1-3; he describes his enemies as lions, 4; thanks God for his deliverance, 5; and purposes to publish the praises of the Lord among his people, 6-11.

The title is, "To the chief Musician, Altaschith [destroy not], a golden Psalm of David (or one to be engraven), when he fled from Saul in the cave." It is very likely that this psalm was made to commemorate his escape from Saul in the cave of En-gedi, where Saul had entered without knowing that David was there, and David cut off the skirt of his garment. And it is not improbable that, when he found that Saul was providentially delivered into his hand, he might have formed the hasty resolution to take away his life, as his companions counselled him to do; and in that moment the divine monition came, *al tascheth!* "Destroy not! lift not up thy hand against the Lord's anointed!" Instead, therefore, of taking away his life, he contented himself with taking away his skirt, to show him that he had been in his power. When, afterwards, he composed the psalm, he gave it for title the words which he received as a divine warning. See the history, 1 Samuel xxiv.

1. *Be merciful unto me.* To show David's deep earnestness, he repeats this twice; he was in great danger, surrounded by implacable enemies, and he knew that God alone could deliver him. *In the shadow of thy wings.* A metaphor taken from the brood of a hen taking shelter under her wings when they see a bird of prey, and there they continue to hide themselves till their enemy disappears. In a storm, or tempest of rain, the mother covers them with her wings to afford them shelter and defense.

2. *I will cry unto God most high.* He is the Most High, and therefore far above all my enemies, though the prince of the power of the air be at their head. *Unto God, lael,* unto the "strong God," One against whom no human or diabolic might can prevail. David felt his own weakness, and he knew the strength of his adversaries; and therefore he views God under those attributes and characters which were suited to his state. *That performeth all things for me.* Who *works* for me; *gomer,* He who "completes" for me, and will bring all to a happy issue.

3. *God shall send forth his mercy and his truth.* Here *mercy* and *truth* are personified. They are the messengers that God will send from heaven to save me. His *mercy* ever inclines Him to help and save the distressed. This He has promised to do; and His *truth* binds Him to fulfill the promises or engagements His mercy has made, to both saints and sinners.

4. *My soul is among lions.* I agree with Dr. Kennicott that this should be translated, "My soul dwells in parched places."

6. *They have prepared a net for my steps.* A gin such as huntsmen put in the places which they know the prey they seek frequents. *They have digged a pit.* Another method of catching game and wild beasts. They dig a pit, cover it

over with weak sticks and turf. The beasts, not suspecting danger where none appears, in attempting to walk over it, fall through and are taken. Saul digged a pit, laid snares for the life of David, and fell into one of them himself, particularly at the cave of En-gedi; for he entered into the very pit or cave where David and his men were hidden, and his life lay at the generosity of the very man whose life he was seeking!

7. *My heart is fixed.* My heart is prepared to do and suffer Thy will. It is *fixed*—it has made the firmest purpose through His strength, by which I can do all things.

8. *Awake up, my glory.* I think the Syriac likely to be the true reading: "Awake up, my harp; awake, psaltery and harp: I will awake early." The last five verses of this psalm are nearly the same with the first five verses of Psalm cviii. Rabbi Solomon Jarchi tells us that David had a harp at his bed's head, which played of itself when the north wind blew on it; and then David arose to give praise to God.

9. *Among the people.* The Israelites. *Among the nations.* The Gentiles at large.

10. *Thy mercy is great unto the heavens.* It is as far above all human description and comprehension as the heavens are above the earth. See Ps. xxxvi. 5-6, where nearly the same words occur.

11. *Be thou exalted, O God, above the heavens.* The same sentiments and words which occur in v. 5.

PSALM 58

David reproves wicked counsellors and judges, who pervert justice, and stir up the strong against the weak and innocent, 1-5. He foretells their destruction, and describes the nature of it, 6-9. The righteous, seeing this, will magnify God's justice and providence, 10-11.

The title seems to have no reference to the subject of the psalm. See the introduction to the preceding.

2. *Yea, in heart ye work wickedness.* With their tongues they had spoken maliciously, and given evil counsel. In their hearts they meditated nothing but wickedness. And though in their *hands* they held the scales of justice, yet in their use of them they were balances of injustice and violence. This is the fact to which the Psalmist alludes, and the figure which he uses is that of Justice with her scales or balances, which, though it might be the emblem of the court, yet it did not prevail in the practice of these magistrates and counsellors.

3. *The wicked are estranged from the womb.* "This," says Dr. Kennicott, "and the next two verses, I take to be the answer of Jehovah to the question in the two first verses, as the 6th, 7th, and 8th, are the answer of the psalmist, and the remainder contains the decree of Jehovah."

4. *Their poison is like the poison of a serpent.* When they bite, they convey poison into the wound, as the serpent does. They not only injure you by outward acts, but by their malevolence they poison your reputation. Such is the slanderer, and such his influence in society.

8. *As a snail which melteth.* The Chaldee reads the verse thus: "They shall melt away in their sins as water flows off; as the creeping

snail that smears its track; as the untimely birth and the blind mole, which do not see the sun."

9. *Before your pots can feel the thorns.* Ye shall be destroyed with a sudden destruction. So very short will be the time that it may be likened to the heat of the first blaze of dry thorns under a pot, that has not as yet been able to penetrate the metal, and warm what is contained in it.

10. *The righteous shall rejoice when he seeth the vengeance.* He shall have a strong proof of the divine providence. *He shall wash his feet in the blood of the wicked.* This can only mean that the slaughter would be so great, and at the same time so very nigh to the dwelling of the righteous, that he could not go out without dipping his feet in the blood of the wicked. The Syriac, Vulgate, Septuagint, Aethiopic, Arabic, and Anglo-Saxon read "hands" instead of *feet.* Everything that is vindictive in the psalms must be considered as totally alien from the spirit of the gospel, and not at all, under our dispensation, to be imitated.

11. *So that a man shall say.* That is, people, seeing these just judgments of God, shall say, *There is a reward* ("fruit") to the *righteous* man. He has not sown his seed in vain; he has not planted and watered in vain. He has the fruit of his labours; he eats the fruit of his doings.

PSALM 59

The Psalmist prays for deliverance from his enemies, whose desperate wickedness he describes, 1-7; professes strong confidence in God, 8-10; speaks of the destruction of his enemies, 11-15; praises God for benefits already received, and determines to trust in Him, 16-17.

The title, "To the chief Musician, Al-taschith, Michtam of David," has already occurred, and perhaps means no more than that the present psalm is to be sung as Psalm lvii, the first which bears this title. But there is here added the supposed occasion on which David made this psalm; it was "when Saul sent, and they watched the house to kill him." When the reader considers the whole of this psalm carefully, he will be convinced that the title does not correspond to the contents. The psalm most evidently agrees to the time of Nehemiah, when he was endeavoring to rebuild the walls of Jerusalem, when the enterprise was first mocked; then opposed by Sanballat the Horonite, Tobiah the Ammonite, and Geshem the Arabian, who watched day and night that they might cause the work to cease, and laid ambuscades for the life of Nehemiah himself. Every part of the psalm agrees to this, and I am therefore of Calmet's opinion, that the psalm was composed in that time, and probably by Nehemiah, or by Esdras.

1. *Deliver me from mine enemies, O my God.* A very proper prayer in the mouth of Nehemiah, when resisted in his attempts to rebuild the walls of Jerusalem by Sanballat, Tobiah, and Geshem, who opposed the work, and endeavored to take away the life of the person whom God had raised up to restore and rebuild Jerusalem. I conceive the psalm to have been made on this occasion, and on this hypothesis alone I think it capable of consistent explanation.

2. *The workers of iniquity.* Principally Sanballat the Horonite, Tobiah the Ammonite, and Geshem the Arabian, who were the chief enemies of the poor returned captives. *Bloody men.* The above, who sought the destruction of the Israelites; and particularly that of Nehemiah, whom four times they endeavored to bring into an ambush, that they might take away his life. See Neh. vi. 1-4.

3. *For, lo, they lie in wait for my soul.* For my "life."

4. *They run and prepare themselves.* They leave no stone unturned that they may effect my destruction and prevent the building.

5. *O Lord God of hosts.* This was a proper view to take of God, when Israel, a handful of poor, distressed captives, were surrounded and oppressed by the heathen chiefs above mentioned, and their several tribes. But Jehovah, *God of hosts,* was the *God of Israel;* and hence Israel had little to fear. *Be not merciful to any wicked transgressors.* Do not favor the cause of these wicked men. They are "changers of iniquity"; they go through the whole round of evil, find out and exercise themselves in all the varieties of transgression. How exactly does this apply to Nehemiah's foes! They sought, by open attack, wiles, flattery, foul speeches, fair speeches, threats, and ambuscades to take away his life. Do not show them favor, that they may not succeed in their wicked designs. The prayer here is exactly the same in sentiment with that of Nehemiah, chap. iv. 4-5. "Hear, O our God; for we are despised: and turn their reproach upon their own head ... cover not their iniquity, and let not their sin be blotted out."

6. *They return at evening.* When the beasts of prey leave their dens and go prowling about the cities and villages, these come about the city to see if they may get an entrance, destroy the work, and those engaged in it.

7. *They belch out with their mouth.* They use the lowest insult, the basest abuse. They deal in sarcasm, ridicule, slander, and lies.

8. *Thou, O Lord, shalt laugh at them.* They have mocked us; God will turn them and their schemes into ridicule and contempt. "Thou shalt have all these heathenish nations in derision."

9. *Because of his strength will I wait upon thee.* With this reading, I can make no sense of the passage. But instead of *uzzo,* "his strength," *uzzi,* "my strength," is the reading of fourteen of Kennicott's and De Rossi's MSS., of the Vulgate, Septuagint, Chaldee. "To thee I commit all my strength."

10. *The God of my mercy shall prevent me.* The mercy of God shall "go before me." *God shall let me see my desire.* The sentence is short, "God will let me see concerning my enemies," i.e., how He will treat them.

11. *Slay them not, lest my people forget.* I believe the Chaldee gives the true sense of this verse: "Do not slay them suddenly, lest my people should forget. Drive them from their habitations by thy power, and reduce them to poverty by the loss of their property."

14. *At evening let them return.* He had mentioned before, v. 6, that these persons came like beasts of prey round the city striving to get in, that they might take possession. Now, being fully assured of God's protection, and that they shall soon be made a public example, he says, "Let them return and make a noise like a dog,"

like dogs, jackals, and other famished creatures, who come howling about the city walls for something to eat, and wander up and down for meat, grumbling because they are not satisfied, v. 15. Nehemiah had made up all the breaches, and had the city guarded so well day and night that there was no longer any fear of being taken by surprise.

17. *Unto thee, O my strength.* A similar sentiment to that expressed in v. 9. But the words are very emphatic: "God is my strength; God is my elevation. My God is my mercy."

PSALM 60

The Psalmist complains of the desolations which had fallen on the land; prays for deliverance, 1-5; and promises himself victory over Shechem, Succoth, Gilead, Ephraim, Moab, Idumea, and the Philistines, by the special help and assistance of God, 6-12.

The title, "To the chief Musician upon the hexachord, or lily of the testimony, a golden Psalm of David, for instruction; when he strove with Aram Naharaim, Syria of the two rivers (Mesopotamia) and Aram-Zobah, Syria of the watchmen (Coelosyria), when Joab returned, and smote twelve thousand Edomites in the Valley of Salt." I have only to remark here that there is nothing in the contents of this psalm that bears any relation to this title. According to the title it should be a song of victory and triumph, instead of which the first part of it is a tissue of complaints of disaster and defeat, caused by the divine desertion. Besides, it was not Joab that slew 12,000 men in the Valley of Salt; it was Abishai, the brother of Joab; and the number 12,000 here is not correct; for there were 18,000 slain in that battle, as we learn from 1 Chron. xviii. 12. The Valley of Salt or salt pits is in Idumea. To reconcile the difference between the numbers, various expedients have been hit on; but still the insuperable objection remains: the contents of this psalm and this title are in opposition to each other. That the psalm deplores a defeat is evident from the first three and last two verses. This is the last of the six psalms to which *michtam* is prefixed; the others are Psalms xvi; lvi; lvii; lviii; and lix. I have said something relative to this word in the introduction to Psalm xvi.

1. *O God, thou hast cast us off.* Instead of being our General in the battle, Thou hast left us to ourselves.

3. *Thou hast made us to drink the wine of astonishment.* We reel as drunken men; we are giddy, like those who have drunk too much wine; but our giddiness has been occasioned by the astonishment and dismay that have taken place in consequence of the prevalence of our enemies, and the unsettled state of the land.

4. *Thou hast given a banner.* "A sign," something that was capable of being fixed on a pole. *That it may be displayed.* "That it may be unfurled." *Because of the truth.* "From the face of truth"; which has been thus paraphrased: If we have displayed the ensign of Israel, and gone forth against these our enemies, who have now made such a terrible breach among us (vv. 1-3), it was because of Thy truth—the promises of victory which we supposed would attend us at all times.

6. *God hath spoken.* Judah shall not only be reestablished in Jerusalem, but shall possess

Samaria, where *Shechem* is, and the country beyond Jordan, in which is situated the *valley of Succoth.* Dividing and meting out signify possession.

7. *Gilead is mine.* This country was also beyond Jordan, and *Manasseh* and *Ephraim* are put for the tribes that formed the kingdom of Israel. All these, after the return from the Captivity, formed but one people, the Jews and Israelites being united. *The strength of mine head.* It shall be the principal support of the newfound kingdom, when all distinctions shall be buried. *Judah is my lawgiver.* This tribe was chief of all those who returned from the Captivity; and Zerubbabel, who was their leader, was chief of that tribe, and of the family of David. As this part of the psalm appears to relate to the return of the captives from Babylon, and their repossession of their own land, the Psalmist may refer, not only to the promises of their restoration, but also to the principal person under whose superintendence they returned.

8. *Moab is my washpot.* The Moabites shall be reduced to the meanest slavery. *Over Edom will I cast out my shoe.* I will make a complete conquest of Idumea, and subject the Edomites to the meanest offices, as well as the Moabites. *Philistia, triumph thou because of men.* John Hyrcanus subdued the Idumeans, and caused them to receive circumcision, and profess the Jewish religion. The words here seem to predict their entire subjugation.

In an essay for a new translation of the Bible, there is what appears to me a correct paraphrase of the seventh and eighth verses: "Gilead and Manasseh have submitted unto me; Ephraim furnishes me with valiant men, and Judah with men of prudence and wisdom. I will reduce the Moabites to servitude; I will triumph over the Edomites, and make them my slaves; and the Philistines shall add to my triumph."

PSALM 61

The Psalmist's prayer for those who were banished from their own land, and from the ordinances of God, 1-2. He praises God for His past mercies, 3; purposes to devote himself entirely to His service, 4-5. He prays for the king, 6-7; and promises to perform his vow to the Lord daily, 8.

The title, "To the chief Musician upon Neginah." The verb *nagan* signifies to "strike or play on a musical instrument," especially one of the stringed kind. The psalm appears to have been written about the close of the Captivity, and the most judicious interpreters refer it to that period.

1. *Hear my cry, O God.* In the midst of a long and painful captivity, oppressed with suffering, encompassed with cruel enemies and isolent masters, I address my humble prayer to Thee, O my God.

2. *From the end of the earth. Arets* should be here translated "land," not *earth,* and so it should be in numerous places besides. But here it seems to mean the country beyond the Euphrates, as it is thought to do in Ps. lxv. 5, 8, called there also "the ends of the earth" or land.

4. *I will abide in thy tabernacle.* The greater portion of those psalms which were composed during and after the Captivity, says Calmet, had Levites and priests for their authors. Hence we find the ardent desire so frequently expressed of seeing the Temple; of praising God there; of spending their lives in that place, performing the functions of their sacred office.

6. *Thou wilt prolong the king's life.* The words are very emphatic, and can refer to no ordinary person. Literally, "Days upon days Thou wilt add to the king; and his years shall be like the generations of this world, and the generations of the world to come." I am persuaded no earthly king is intended; and it is Christ, as Mediator, that "shall abide before God for ever," v. 7.

7. *He shall abide before God for ever.* Literally, "He shall sit forever before the faces of God." He shall ever appear in the presence of God for us. *Prepare mercy and truth, which may preserve him.* As Mediator, His attendants will ever be *mercy* and *truth.* He will dispense the *mercy* of God, and thus fulfill the *truth* of the various promises and predictions which had preceded His incarnation.

PSALM 62

David, in imminent danger, flees to God for help and safety, 1-2; points out the designs of his adversaries, 3-4; encourages his soul to wait on God, 5-8; shows the vanity of tru-ting in man, and of trusting in riches, 9-10; and concludes with asserting that power and mercy belong to God, and that He will give to every man according to his works, 11-12.

The title, "To the chief Musician, to Jeduthun," may mean that the psalm was sent to him who was the chief or leader of the band of the family of Jeduthun. It appears that Asaph, Jeduthun, and Heman were chief singers in the time of David; that they, with their families, presided over different departments of the vocal and instrumental worship in the Tabernacle, 1 Chron. xxv. 1, etc.

1. *Truly my soul waiteth upon God.* I do not think that the original will warrant this translation, "Surely to God only is my soul dumb." I am subject to God Almighty. He has a right to lay on me what He pleases; and what He lays on me is much less than I deserve; therefore am I "dumb" before God.

3. *How long will ye imagine mischief?* The original word has been translated variously; "rush upon, rage against, stir yourselves up, thrust against." The root is *hathath* or *hathah,* "to rush violently upon, to assault." It points out the disorderly, riotous manner in which this rebellion was conducted. *As a bowing wall . . . a tottering fence.* Ye are just ready to fall upon others and destroy them; and in that fall yourselves shall be destroyed: "Ye shall be slain the whole of you."

4. *To cast him down from his excellency.* They are consulting to dethrone me, and use treachery and falsehood in order to bring it about: *They delight in lies.*

7. *In God is my salvation. Al Elohim,* "Upon God is my salvation"; He has taken it upon himself.

9. *Men of low degree are vanity. Beney Adam,* which we here translate *men of low degree,* literally, "sons of Adam," are put in opposition to *beney ish, men of high degree,* literally, the "sons of substance," or children of substantial men. *Adam* was the name of the first man when formed out of the earth; *Ish* was his name when united to his wife, and they became one flesh. Before, he was the incomplete man; after, he was the complete man. *Enosh* is another name given to man; but this concerns him in his low, fallen, wretched estate; it properly signifies "weak, poor, afflicted, wretched man." *To be laid in the balance.* "In the balances they ascend." *They are altogether lighter than vanity.* Literally, "Both of them united are vanity."

10. *Trust not in oppression.* Do not suppose that my unnatural son and his partisans can succeed. *Become not vain in robbery.* If you have laid your hands on the spoils of my house, do not imagine that these ill-gotten riches will prosper. God will soon scatter them to all the winds of heaven. All oppressors come to an untimely end, and all property acquired by injustice has God's curse on it.

11. *God hath spoken once.* God has *once* addressed His people in giving the law on Mount Sinai. *Twice have I heard this.* Except some of the ancient versions, almost every version, translation, and commentary has missed the sense and meaning of this verse. The true version is this: "Once hath God spoken; these two things have I heard." Now what are the two things he had heard? (1) "That strength is the Lord's"; that is, He is the Origin of power. (2) "And to thee, Lord, is mercy"; that is, He is the Fountain of mercy. These, then, are the two grand truths that the law, yea, the whole revelation of God, declares through every page. He is the Almighty; He is the most merciful; and hence the inference: The powerful, just, and holy God, the most merciful and compassionate Lord, will by and by judge the world, and will render to man according to his works. How this beautiful meaning should have been unseen by almost every interpreter is hard to say; these verses contain one of the most instructive truths in the Bible.

PSALM 63

David's soul thirsts after God, while absent from the sanctuary, and longs to be restored to the divine ordinances, 1-2. He expresses strong confidence in the Most High, and praises Him for His goodness, 3-8; shows the misery of those who do not seek God, 9-10; and his own safety as king of the people, 11.

The title of this psalm is, "A Psalm of David, when he was in the wilderness of Judah." It is most probable that the psalm was written when David took refuge in the forest of Hareth, in the wilderness of Ziph, when he fled from the court of Achish.

1. *O God, thou art my God.* He who can say so, and feels what he says, need not fear the face of any adversary. He has God, and all sufficiency in Him. *Early will I seek thee.* From the dawn of day. What first lays hold of the heart in the morning is likely to occupy the place all the day.

2. *To see thy power and thy glory . . . in the sanctuary.* In His public ordinances God had often showed His *power* in the judgments He executed, in the terror He impressed, and in awakening the sinful; and His glory in delivering the tempted, succoring the distressed, and diffusing peace and pardon through the hearts of His followers. God shows His *power* and *glory* in His *ordinances;* therefore *public worship* should never be neglected. *We must see God,* says the old Psalter, *that he may see us.* In His temple He dispenses His choicest blessings.

3. *Thy lovingkindness is better than life.* Thy lovingkindness, *chasdecha*, "thy effusive mercy," *is better, mechaiyim,* "than lives; it is better than," or "good beyond," countless ages of human existence.

7. *Therefore in the shadow of thy wings.* I will get into the very secret of Thy presence, into the holy of holies, to the mercy seat, over which the cherubs extend their wings. If the Psalmist does not allude to the overshadowing of the mercy seat by the extended wings of the cherubim, he may have in view, as a metaphor, the young of fowls, seeking shelter, protection, and warmth under the wings of their mothers. See the same metaphor, Ps. lxi. 4.

8. *My soul followeth hard after thee.* "My soul cleaves (or) is glued after thee."

10. *They shall fall by the sword.* "They shall be poured out by the hand of the sword." That is, their life's blood shall be shed either in war or by the hand of justice. *They shall be a portion for foxes.* They shall be left unburied, and the "jackals" shall feed upon their dead bodies.

11. *But the king shall rejoice.* David shall come to the kingdom according to the promise of God. *That sweareth by him.* It was customary to swear by the life of the king. The Egyptians swore by the life of Pharaoh; and Joseph conformed to this custom, as may be seen in the Book of Genesis, chap. xlii. 15-16. But here it may refer to God. He is the King, and swearing by His name signifies binding themselves by His authority.

PSALM 64

The Psalmist prays for preservation from the wicked, 1-2; whom he describes, 3-6; shows their punishment, 7-8; and the effect that this should have on the godly, 9-10.

The title, "To the chief Musician, or conqueror, A Psalm of David."

4. *That they may shoot in secret.* They lurk, that they may take their aim the more surely, and not miss their mark. *Suddenly.* When there is no fear apprehended, because none is seen.

5. *They commune of laying snares.* They lay snares to entrap those whom they cannot slay by open attack or private ambush.

6. *They search out iniquities; they accomplish a diligent search.* The word *chaphash*, which is used three times, as a noun and a verb, in this sentence, signifies "to strip off the clothes." They investigate iniquities; they perfectly investigate an investigation."

7. *But God shall shoot at them with an arrow.* They endeavor to trace me out, that they may shoot me; but God will shoot at them. This, if the psalm refer to the times of David, seems to be prophetic of Saul's death. The archers pressed upon him, and sorely wounded him with their arrows (1 Sam. xxxi. 3).

8. *Their own tongue to fall upon themselves.* All the plottings, counsels, and curses they have formed against me shall come upon themselves.

9. *And all men shall fear.* They endeavored to hide their mischief; but God shall so punish them that all shall see it, and shall acknowledge in their chastisement the just judgment of God. The wicked, in consequence, shall fear, and

10. *The righteous shall be glad.* They shall see that God does not abandon His followers to the malice of bad men.

PSALM 65

God is praised for the fulfillment of His promises, and for His mercy in forgiving sins, 1-3. He is praised for the wonders that He works in nature, which all mankind must acknowledge, 4-8; for the fertilizing showers which He sends upon the earth, and the abundance thereby produced for both men and cattle, 9-13.

1. *Praise waiteth for thee.* Praise is "silent" or "dumb" for Thee. Thou alone art worthy of praise.

3. *Iniquities prevail against me.* This is no just rendering of the original, "Iniquitous words have prevailed against me," or, "The words of iniquity are strong against me." All kinds of calumnies, lies, and slanders have been propagated, to shake my confidence and ruin my credit. *Our transgressions, thou shalt purge them away.* Whatsoever offenses we have committed against Thee, Thou wilt pardon; *tecapperem,* Thou wilt "make atonement" for them, when with hearty repentance and true faith we turn unto Thee.

4. *Blessed is the man whom thou choosest.* This is spoken in reference to the priests, who were chosen of God to minister at the Tabernacle; and who were permitted to *approach,* "draw nigh," to the Divine Majesty by the various offerings and sacrifices which they presented.

8. *Are afraid at thy tokens.* Thunder and lightning, storms and tempests, eclipses and meteors, tornadoes and earthquakes, are proofs to all who dwell even in the remotest parts of the earth that there is a Supreme Being who is wonderful and terrible in His acts. From this verse to the end of the psalm there is a series of the finest poetic imagery in the world. *The outgoings of the morning.* The rising and setting sun, the morning and evening twilight, the invariable succession of day and night, are all ordained by Thee, and contribute to the happiness and continuance of man and beast. Or, All that fear Thee praise Thee in the morning, when they go to their work, and in the evening, when they return home, for Thy great goodness manifested in the continuance of their strength, and the success of their labor.

9. *Thou visitest the earth.* God is represented as going through the whole globe, and examining the wants of every part, and directing the clouds how and where to deposit their fertilizing showers, and the rivers where to direct their beneficial courses. *The river of God.* Some think the Jordan is meant, and the visiting and watering refer to rain after a long drought. But the clouds may be thus denominated which properly are the origin of rivers.

10. *Thou waterest the ridges.* In seedtime Thou sendest that measure of rain that is necessary, in order to prepare the earth for the plough; and then, when the *ridges* are thrown into furrows, thou makest them *soft with showers,* so as to prepare them for the seed. *Thou blessest the springing thereof.* Literally, "Thou wilt bless its germinations"—its springing buds.

11. *Thou crownest the year.* A full and plentiful harvest is the crown of the year, and this

Psalms 65—68

496

springs from the unmerited goodness of God. "Thou encirclest," as with a diadem.

12. *The pastures of the wilderness.* Even the places which are not cultivated have their sufficiency of moisture, so as to render them proper places of pasturage for cattle. The terms "wilderness" and "desert," in the Sacred Writings, mean, in general, places not inhabited and uncultivated, though abounding with timber, bushes, and herbage. *The little hills rejoice.* Literally, "The hills gird themselves with exultation." The metaphor appears to be taken from the frisking of lambs, bounding of kids, and dancing of shepherds and shepherdesses, in the joy-inspiring summer season.

PSALM 66

The Psalmist exhorts all to praise God for the wonders He has wrought, 1-4; calls on Israel to consider His mighty acts in behalf of their fathers, 5-7; His goodness in their own behalf, 8-12. He resolves to pay his vows to God, and offer his promised sacrifices, 13-15; calls on all to hear what God had done for his soul, 15-20.

3. *How terrible art thou!* Consider the plagues with which He afflicted Egypt before He brought your fathers from their captivity, which obliged all His enemies to submit. *Thine enemies submit themselves.* Literally, "lie unto Thee." This was remarkably the case with Pharaoh and the Egyptians. They promised again and again to let the people go, when the hand of the Lord was upon them; and they as frequently falsified their word.

9. *Which holdeth our soul in life.* Literally, "he who placeth our soul in lives." We are preserved alive, have health of body, and feel the life of God in our hearts. *And suffereth not our feet to be moved.* Keeps us steadfast in His testimonies.

10. *For thou, O God, hast proved us.* This is a metaphor taken from melting and refining metals; afflictions and trials of various kinds are represented as a furnace where ore is melted, and a crucible where it is refined.

11. *Thou broughtest us into the net.* This refers well to the case of the Israelites when, in their departure from Egypt, pursued by the Egyptians, having the Red Sea before them and no method of escape, Pharaoh said, "The wilderness hath shut them in . . . they are entangled," comparing their state to that of a wild beast in a net.

14. *When I was in trouble.* This is generally the time when good resolutions are formed, and vows made; but how often are these forgotten when affliction and calamity are removed!

18. *If I regard iniquity in my heart.* "If I have seen iniquity in my heart," if I have known it was there, and encouraged it.

PSALM 67

The Psalmist prays for the enlargement of God's kingdom, 1-2; calls upon all nations to serve Him, because He judges and governs righteously, 3-5; promises prosperity to the faithful and obedient, 6-7.

The title here is the same with that of Psalm iv, where see the notes. It is supposed to have been written at the return from the Babylonish captivity, and to foretell the conversion of the Gentiles to the Christian religion. The prayer for their salvation is very energetic.

1. *God be merciful unto us.* This is nearly the same form of blessing as that used Num. vi. 25.

2. *That thy way may be known.* That Thy will, Thy gracious designs towards the children of men, Thy way of reconciling them to thyself, of justifying the ungodly, and sanctifying the unholy, may be known to all the nations upon the earth! *Thy saving health.* "Thy salvation."

When or by whom this psalm was written cannot be ascertained. It seems to be simply a prophecy concerning the calling of the Gentiles, the preaching of the apostles, and the diffusion and influence of Christianity in the world. It is a fine piece of devotion, and it would be nearly impossible to read or repeat it with a cold and unaffected heart.

PSALM 68

The Psalmist calls upon God to arise, bless His people, and scatter His enemies, 1-3; exhorts them to praise Him for His greatness, tenderness, compassion, and judgments, 4-6; describes the grandeur of His march when He went forth in the redemption of His people, 7-8; how He dispensed His blessings, 9-10; what He will still continue to do in their behalf, 11-13; the effects produced by the manifestation of God's majesty, 14-18. He is praised for His goodness, 19-20; for His judgments, 21-23. He tells in what manner the divine worship was conducted, 24-27; how God is to be honored, 28-31. All are invited to sing His praises and extol His greatness, 32-35.

It is probable that this psalm, or a part of it at least, might have been composed by Moses, to be recited when the Israelites journeyed (see Num. x. 35); and that David, on the same model, constructed this psalm. It might have been sung also in the ceremony of transporting the ark from Kirjath-jearim to Jerusalem, or from the house of Obed-edom to the Tabernacle erected at Sion.

I know not how to undertake a comment on this psalm; it is the most difficult in the whole Psalter. There are customs here referred to which I do not fully understand; there are words whose meaning I cannot, to my own satisfaction, ascertain; and allusions which are to me inexplicable. Yet of the composition itself I have the highest opinion. It is sublime beyond all comparison; it is constructed with an art truly admirable; it possesses all the dignity of the sacred language. None but David could have composed it.

1. *Let God arise.* This was sung when the Levites took up the ark upon their shoulders; see Num. x. 35-36.

4. *Extol him that rideth upon the heavens by his name JAH.* Baaraboth, which we render "in the high heavens," is here of doubtful signification. Probably it may mean the gloomy desert, through which God, in the chariot of His glory, led the Israelites. *By his name JAH.* Yah, probably a contraction of the word *Yehovah*. It might be translated "the Self-existent."

7. *O God, when thou wentest forth.* This and the following verse most manifestly refer to the passage of the Israelites through the wilderness.

9. *Didst send a plentiful rain.* "A shower of liberality." I believe this to refer to the manna by which God refreshed and preserved alive the weary and hungry Israelites.

10. *Thy congregation hath dwelt therein.* "Thy living creature." Does not this refer to the quails that were brought to the camp of the Israelites, and *dwelt*, as it were, round about it?

11. *Great was the company of those that published it. Hammebasseroth tsaba rab;* "Of the

female preachers there was a great host." Such is the literal translation of this passage; the reader may make of it what he pleases. But the publication of good news, or of any joyful event, belonged to the women. It was they who announced it to the people at large; and to this universal custom, which prevails to the present day, the Psalmist alludes.

15. *The hill of God is as the hill of Bashan.* This and the following verse should be read thus: "Is Mount Bashan the craggy mount, Mount Bashan, the mount of God? Why envy ye, ye craggy mounts? This is the mount of God in which He has desired to dwell."

17. *The chariots of God are twenty thousand.* "Two myriads of thousands doubled." Does not this mean simply 40,000? A myriad is 10,000; two myriads, 20,000; these doubled, 40,000.

18. *Thou hast ascended on high.* When the ark had reached the top of Sion, and was deposited in the place assigned for it, the singers joined in the following chorus. This seems to be an allusion to a military triumph. The conqueror was placed on a very elevated chariot. *Led captivity captive.* The conquered kings and generals were usually tied behind the chariot of the conqueror—bound to it, bound together, and walked after it, to grace the triumph of the victor. *Thou hast received gifts for men.* "And gave gifts unto men," Eph. iv. 8. At such times the conqueror threw money among the crowd. *Yea, for the rebellious also.* Even to the rebellious, those who were his enemies. *That the Lord God might dwell among them.* Yah Elohim, "the self-existing God"; see v. 4. The conqueror now coming to fix his abode among the conquered people to organize them under his laws, to govern and dispense justice among them. The whole of this is very properly applied by St. Paul, Eph. iv. 5, to the resurrection and glory of Christ.

19. *Blessed be the Lord, who daily loadeth us.* "With benefits" is not in the text. Perhaps it would be better to translate the clause thus: "Blessed be Adonai, our Prop day by day, who supports us." Or, "Blessed be the Lord, who supports us day by day." Or as the Vulgate, Septuagint, and Arabic: "Blessed be the Lord daily, our God who makes our journey prosperous; even the God of our salvation." The word *amas,* which we translate "to load," signifies "to lift, bear up, support," or "to bear a burden for another." Hence it would not be going far from the ideal meaning to translate: "Blessed is the Lord day by day, who bears our burdens for us."

20. *The issues from death.* The "going out" or "exodus" from death—from the land of Egypt and house of bondage. Or the expression may mean, Life and death are in the hand of God. "He can create, and he destroys."

22. *From the depths of the sea.* All this seems to speak of the defeat of the Egyptians and the miraculous passage of the Red Sea.

27. *There is little Benjamin.* This is a description of another part of the procession.

28. *Thy God hath commanded.* This and the following verses are what they sang.

30. *Rebuke the company of spearmen.* "The wild beast of the reed"—the crocodile or hippopotamus, the emblem of Pharaoh and the Egyptians; thus all the versions. Our translators have mistaken the meaning, but they have put the true sense in the margin.

31. *Ethiopia shall soon stretch out her hands unto God.* There were Egyptians at Jerusalem on the Day of Pentecost, who, St. Hilary tells us, on their return to their own country proclaimed what they had seen, and became in that country the ambassadors of Christ. The Ethiopian eunuch was one of the first among the Gentiles who received the gospel. Thus *princes* or chief men came out of Egypt, and Ethiopia stretched out her hands to God. The Hebrew is very emphatic: "Cush will cause her hands to run out to God."

34. *His strength is in the clouds.* This refers to the bursting, rattling, and pounding of thunder and lightning.

35. *O God, thou art terrible out of thy holy places.* The sanctuary and heaven. Out of the former He had often shone forth with consuming splendor; see the case of Korah and his company. Out of the latter He had often appeared in terrible majesty in storms, thunder, lightning. *He that giveth strength and power unto his people.* Therefore that people must be invincible who have this strong and irresistible God for their Support.

PSALM 69

The Psalmist describes his afflicted state, and the wickedness of his adversaries, 1-21; he declares the miseries that should come upon his enemies, 22-28; enlarges on his afflicted state, and expresses his confidence in God, 29-34; prophesies the restoration of the Jews to their own land and Temple, 35-36.

The title is: "To the chief Musician upon Shoshannim, A Psalm of David." See this title explained on Psalm xlv.

The psalm is supposed to have been written during the Captivity, and to have been the work of some Levite divinely inspired. It is a very fine composition, equal to most in the Psalter. Several portions of it seem to have a reference to our Lord; to His advent, passion, resurrection, the vocation of the Gentiles, the establishment of the Christian Church, and the reprobation of the Jews. The ninth verse is quoted by St. John, chap. ii. 17. The twenty-first verse is quoted by St. Matthew, chap. xxvii. 34, 48; by St. Mark, chap. xv. 23; by St. John, chap. xix. 29; and applied to the sufferings of our Lord, in the treatment He received from the Jews. St. Paul quotes the twenty-second as a prophecy of the wickedness of the Jews, and the punishment they were to receive. He quotes the twenty-third verse in the same way. Those portions which the writers of the New Testament apply to our Lord, we may apply also; of others we should be careful.

1. *The waters are come in unto my soul.* I am in the deepest distress. The waters have broken their dikes, and are just ready to sweep me away! In the first, second, third, fourteenth, and fifteenth verses the Psalmist, speaking in the person of the captives in Babylon, compares their captivity to an abyss of waters, breaking all bounds, and ready to swallow them up; to a deep mire, in which there was no solid bottom, and no standing; and to a pit, in which they were about to be enclosed forever. This is strongly figurative, and very expressive.

3. *I am weary of my crying.* A pathetic de-

scription of the state of the poor captives for about seventy years.

4. *Then I restored that which I took not away.* I think. with Calmet, that this is a sort of proverbial expression, like such as these, "Those who suffered the wrong, pay the costs."

9. *The zeal of thine house hath eaten me up.* The strong desire to promote Thy glory has absorbed all others. This verse is very properly applied to our Lord, John ii. 17.

12. *They that sit in the gate.* At the gates were the courts for public justice.

13. *My prayer is unto thee, O Lord, in an acceptable time.* This seems to refer to the end of the Captivity, which Jeremiah had said should last seventy years, Jer. xxv. 11-12.

16. *Thy lovingkindness is good.* The word *chesed* signifies "exuberance of kindness"; and the word *rachamim*, which we translate *tender mercies*, signifies such affection as mothers bear to their young.

21. *They gave me also gall for my meat.* This is applied to our Lord, Matt. xxvii. 34.

22. *Let their table become a snare.* The execrations here and in the following verses should be read in the future tense, because they are predictive; and not in the imperative mood, as if they were the offspring of the Psalmist's resentment.

27. *Add iniquity unto their iniquity.* "Give iniquity," that is, the reward of it, "upon" or "for their iniquity." Or, as the original signifies "perverseness," treat their perverseness with perverseness.

28. *Let them be blotted out.* They *shall* be blotted out from the land of the living. They shall be cut off from life, which they have forfeited by their cruelty and oppression. The Psalmist is speaking of retributive justice, and in this sense all these passages are to be understood.

29. *I am poor and sorrowful.* Literally, "I am laid low, and full of pain or grief." Hence the prayer, *Let thy salvation, O God, set me up on high.* My oppression has laid me low; Thy salvation shall make me high!

33. *For the Lord heareth the poor.* "The beggars." He perhaps refers here to the case of the captives, many of whom were reduced to the most abject state. *His prisoners.* The captives, shut up by His judgments in Chaldea, without any civil liberty, like culprits in a prison.

35. *God will save Zion.* This fixes the psalm to the time of the Captivity. There was no Zion belonging to the Jews in the time of Saul, when those suppose the psalm to be written who make David the author; for David, after he came to the throne, won the stronghold of Zion from the Jebusites (2 Sam. v. 7; 1 Chron. xi. 5). *Will build the cities of Judah.* This refers to the return from the Captivity, when all the destroyed cities should be rebuilt, and the Jews repossess their forfeited heritages.

PSALM 70

The Psalmist prays for speedy deliverance, 1; prays against those who sought his life, 2-3; and for the blessedness of those who sought God, 3; urges his speedy deliverance, 5.

The title in the Hebrew is, "To the chief Musician, A Psalm of David, to bring to re-

membrance." It is almost word for word the same with the last five verses of Psalm xl, to the notes on which the reader is referred.

3. *That say, Aha, aha. Heach! heach!* a note of supreme contempt. See on Ps. xl. 15.

5. *But I am poor and needy.* I am a poor man, and a beggar—an afflicted beggar.

PSALM 71

The prophet, in confidence, prays for God's favor, 1-5; recounts God's kindness to him from youth to old age, 6-9 shows what his adversaries plot against him, and prays for their confusion, 10-13; promises fidelity, and determines to be a diligent preacher of righteousness even in old age, 14-19; takes encouragement in God's mercy, and foresees the confusion of all his adversaries, 20-24.

There is no title to this psalm in either the Hebrew or Chaldee; and the reason is, it was written as a part of the preceding psalm, as appears by about twenty-seven of Kennicott's and De Rossi's MSS. For the first, second, and third verses, see their parallels, Ps. xxxi. 1-3.

4. *Out of the hand of the wicked.* Probably his unnatural son *Absalom*, called here *rasha*, *the wicked*, because he had violated all laws, human and divine. *The unrighteous and cruel man.* Probably Ahithophel, who was the iniquitous counsellor of a wicked and rebellious son.

7. *I am as a wonder unto many.* I am "as a portent," or "type."

9. *Cast me not off in the time of old age.* The original might be translated and paraphrased thus: "Thou wilt not cast me off till the time of old age; and according to the failure of my flesh, Thou wilt not forsake me."

13. *Let them be confounded.* They *shall* be confounded: these are prophetic denunciations.

16. *I will go.* Abo, I will enter, i.e., into the Tabernacle, *in the strength* or "mightinesses" of *Adonai Jehovah*, the supreme God, who is my Prop, Stay, and Support.

19. *Thy righteousness . . . is very high.* Ad *marom*—is up to the exalted place, reaches up to heaven.

22. *I will also praise thee with the psaltery.* Bichli nebel, "with the instrument nebel." *Unto thee will I sing with the harp; bechinnor,* "with the kinnor." Both were stringed instruments.

24. *Talk of thy righteousness.* The righteousness of God is frequently used in this psalm, and in other places, to signify His justice, judgments, faithfulness, truth, mercy. There are few words of more general import in the Bible.

PSALM 72

David prays to God for Solomon, 1; prescribes Solomon's work, 2; the effects of his administration, 3-7; the extent of his dominion, 8-11; his mercy and kindness to the poor, and the perpetuity of his praise, 12-17. God is blessed for His power and goodness; and the Psalmist prays that the whole earth may be filled with His glory, 18-20.

The title *lishelomoh*, we translate, "A Psalm for Solomon." The Chaldee says, "By the hand of Solomon, spoken prophetically." The Syriac, "A Psalm of David, when he had constituted Solomon king." All the other versions attribute it to Solomon himself. But in the conclusion of the psalm it appears to be attributed to David. "The prayers of David the son of Jesse are ended." It is most probably a psalm of David, composed in his last days, when he had set this beloved son on the throne of the kingdom.

1. *Give the king thy judgments.* Let Solomon receive Thy law, as the civil and ecclesiastical code by which he is to govern the kingdom. *And thy righteousness unto the king's son.* Solomon is called here *the king,* because now set upon the Jewish throne; and he is called *the king's son,* to signify his right to that throne on which he now sat.

3. *The mountains shall bring peace.* Perhaps *mountains* and *hills* are here taken in their figurative sense, to signify princes and petty governors. But what is the meaning of *the little hills, by righteousness?* Why, it has no meaning; and it has none because it is a false division of the verse. The word *bitsedakah,* "in righteousness," at the end of v. 3, should begin v. 4, and then the sense will be plain. V. 3: "The mountains and the hills shall bring prosperity to the people." V. 4: "In righteousness *he shall judge the poor of the people, he shall save the children of the needy, and shall break in pieces the oppressor.*"

5. *They shall fear thee.* There is no sense in which this can be spoken of Solomon, nor indeed of any other man; it belongs to Jesus Christ, and to Him alone.

6. *He shall come down like rain upon the mown grass.* The word which we translate *mown grass* more properly means "pastured grass" or "pastured land," for the dew of the night is intended to restore the grass which has been eaten in the course of the day.

7. *In his days shall the righteous flourish.* There was nothing but peace and prosperity all the days of Solomon. For in his days "Judah and Israel dwelt safely, every man under his vine and under his fig tree, from Dan even to Beer-sheba," 1 Kings iv. 25. *So long as the moon endureth.* "Till there be no more moon."

8. *He shall have dominion also from sea to sea.* The best comment on this, as it refers to Solomon, may be found in 1 Kings iv. 21, 24. *Unto the ends of the earth,* or "land," must mean the tract of country along the Mediterranean Sea, which was the boundary of the land on that side. But, as the words may refer to Christ, everything may be taken in its utmost latitude and extent.

9. *They that dwell in the wilderness.* It is likely that those who dwell by the seacoasts, and support themselves by navigation and fishing, are here intended.

10. *The kings of Tarshish and of the isles shall bring presents.* Minchah signifies a gratitude or friendly offering. *The kings of Sheba and Seba.* Both countries of Arabia. From the former came the queen of Sheba, to hear the wisdom of Solomon. And she brought exceeding great gifts. *Eshcar* signifies "a compensative present, made on account of benefits received."

11. *All kings shall fall down before.* They shall reverence him on account of his great wisdom, riches, etc. *All nations shall serve him.* All the surrounding nations. This and the preceding verses are fully explained by 1 Kings x. 23-25. If we take these expressions to mean literally all the habitable globe, then they cannot be applied to Solomon; but if we take them as they are most evidently used by the sacred writer, then they are literally true.

16. *There shall be a handful of corn.* The earth shall be exceedingly fruitful. Even a handful of corn sown on the top of a mountain shall grow up strong and vigorous; and it shall be, in reference to crops in other times, as the cedars of Lebanon are to common trees or shrubs; and as the earth will bring forth in handfuls, so the people shall be multiplied who are to consume this great produce.

17. *His name shall endure for ever.* Hitherto this has been literally fulfilled. Solomon is celebrated in the east and in the west, in the north and in the south. *All nations shall call him blessed.* Because of the extraordinary manner in which he was favored by the Most High. I well know that all these things are thought to belong properly to Jesus Christ; and, in reference to Him, they are all true, and ten thousand times more than these. But I believe they are all properly applicable to Solomon.

20. *The prayers of David the son of Jesse are ended.* This was most probably the last psalm he ever wrote.

PSALM 73

The Psalmist speaks of God's goodness to His people, 1; shows how much he was stumbled at the prosperity of the wicked, and describes their state, 2-12; details the process of the temptation, and the pain he suffered in consequence, 13-16; shows how he was delivered, and the dismal reverse of the state of the once prosperous ungodly man, by which his own false views were corrected, 17-22; his great confidence in God, and the good consequences of it, 23-28.

This is the commencement of the Third Book of the Psalter; and the psalm before us has for title, "A Psalm of Asaph"; or, as the margin has it, "A Psalm for Asaph." The title in the Hebrew is *mizmor leasaph;* "A Psalm of Asaph," and it is likely that this *Asaph* was the composer of it; that he lived under the Babylonish captivity; and that he published this psalm to console the Israelites under bondage, who were greatly tried to find themselves in such outward distress and misery, while a people much more wicked and corrupt than they were in great prosperity, and held them in bondage.

2. *My feet were almost gone.* I had nearly given up my confidence. I was ready to find fault with the dispensations of providence, and thought the Judge of all the earth did not do right.

3. *I was envious at the foolish.* I saw persons who worshipped not the true God, and others who were abandoned to all vices, in possession of every temporal comfort, while the godly were in straits, difficulties, and affliction.

4. *No bands in their death.* Many of the godly have sore conflicts at their death. Their enemy then thrusts sore at them that they may fall, or that their confidence in their God may be shaken. But of this the ungodly know nothing. Satan will not molest *them;* he is sure of his prey. They are entangled, and cannot now break their nets. Their consciences are seared; they have no sense of guilt. If they think at all of another world, they presume on that mercy which they never sought, and of which they have no distinct notion. Perhaps, "they die without a sigh or a groan; and thus go off as quiet as a lamb" —to the slaughter.

6. *Pride compasseth them about as a chain.* Perhaps there is an allusion here to the office

which some of them bore. Chains of gold were ensigns of magistracy and civil power.

7. *Their eyes stand out with fatness.* "Their countenance is changed because of fatness."—Chaldee. *They have more than heart could wish.* It would be more literal to say, "They surpass the thoughts of their heart." They have more than they expected, though not more than they wish.

8. *They are corrupt.* "They mock, act dissolutely."

9. *Set their mouth against the heavens.* They blaspheme God, ridicule religion, mock at Providence, and laugh at a future state. *Their tongue walketh through the earth.* They find fault with everything; they traduce the memory of the just in heaven, and ridicule the saints that are upon earth. They criticize every dispensation of God.

10. *Therefore his people return h i t h e r.* "Therefore shall my people be converted, where they shall find abundance of waters." That is. The people, seeing the iniquity of the Babylonians, and feeling their oppressive hand, shall be converted to Me; and I shall bring them to their own land, where they shall find an abundance of all the necessaries of life.

15. *If I say, I will speak thus.* I have at last discovered that I have reasoned incorrectly, and that I have the uniform testimony of all Thy children against me. From generation to generation they have testified that the Judge of all the earth does right.

17. *Until I went into the sanctuary.* That this psalm was written during the Captivity there is little room to doubt. How then can the Psalmist speak of *the sanctuary?* There was none at Babylon, and at Jerusalem it had been long since destroyed. There is no way to solve this difficulty but by considering that *mikdeshey* may be taken in the sense of "holy places"—places set apart for prayer and meditation.

18. *Thou didst set them in slippery places.* Affluence is a slippery path; few have ever walked in it without falling.

21. *Thus my heart was grieved.* The different views which I got of this subject quite confounded me; I was equally astonished at their sudden overthrow and my own ignorance. I felt as if I were a beast in stupidity.

25. *Whom have I in heaven but thee?* The original is more emphatic: "Who is there to me in the heavens? And with thee I have desired nothing in the earth."

26. *My flesh . . . faileth.* I shall soon die: *and my heart*—even my natural courage, will fail; and no support but what is supernatural will then be available. Therefore, he adds, *God is the strength of my heart.* Literally, "the Rock of my heart."

PSALM 74

The Psalmist complains of the desolations of the sanctuary, and pleads with God, 1-3; shows the insolence and wickedness of their enemies, 4-8; prays to God to act for them as He had done for their fathers, whom, by His miraculous power, He had saved, 9-17; begs God to arise, and vindicate His own honor against his enemies, and the enemies of His people, 18-23.

The title is, Maschil of Asaph, or, "A Psalm of Asaph, to give instruction." That this psalm was written at a time when the Temple was

ruined, Jerusalem burnt, and the prophets scattered or destroyed, is evident.

4. *Thine enemies roar.* Thy people, who were formerly a distinct and separate people, and who would not even touch a Gentile, are now obliged to mingle with the most profane. Their boisterous mirth, their cruel mockings, their insulting commands are heard everywhere in all our assemblies. *They set up their ensigns for signs.* They set up their standards in the place of ours. The fifth, sixth, and seventh verses give a correct historical account of the ravages committed by the Babylonians, as we may see from 2 Kings xxv. 4, 7-9 and Jer. lii. 7, 18-19.

8. *Let us destroy them.* Their object was totally to annihilate the political existence of the Jewish people. *They have burned up all the synagogues of God in the land.* It is supposed that there were no *synagogues* in the land till after the Babylonish captivity. How then could the Chaldeans burn up any in Judea? The word *moadey,* which we translate *synagogues,* may be taken in a more general sense, and mean any places where religious assemblies were held. This is the only place in the Old Testament where we have the word synagogue. Indeed, wherever there was a place in which God met with patriarch or prophet, and any memorial of it was preserved, there was a *moed,* or place of religious meeting; and all such places the Chaldeans would destroy, pursuant to their design to extinguish the Jewish religion, and blot out all its memorials from the earth.

13. *Thou didst divide the sea.* When our fathers came from Egypt. *Thou brakest the heads of the dragons in the waters.* Pharaoh, his captains, and all his hosts were drowned in the Red Sea, when attempting to pursue them.

15. *Thou didst cleave the fountain.* Thou didst cleave the rock in the wilderness, of which all the congregation drank. *Thou driedst up mighty rivers.* Does not this refer to the cutting off the waters of the Jordan, so that the people passed over dry-shod?

PSALM 75

The Psalmist praises God for present mercies, 1; the Lord answers, and promises to judge the people righteously, 2-3; rebukes the proud and haughty, 4-5; shows that all authority comes from himself, 4-7; that He will punish the wicked, 8. The Psalmist resolves to praise God, 9; and the Most High promises to cast down the wicked and raise up the righteous, 9-10.

The title is, "To the chief Musician, or conqueror, Al-taschith, destroy not, A Psalm or Song of Asaph." See this title Al-taschith explained Psalm lvii. The psalm seems to have been composed during the Captivity, and appears to be a continuation of the subject in the preceding.

1. *Unto thee, O God, do we give thanks.* The numerous manifestations of Thy providence and mercy show that Thou art not far off, but near; this *thy wondrous works declare.* These words would make a proper conclusion to the preceding psalm, which seems to end very abruptly. The second verse is the commencement of the divine answer to the prayer of Asaph.

6. *For promotion cometh neither from the east,* etc. As if the Lord had said, speaking to the Babylonians, None of all the surrounding powers shall be able to help you; none shall pluck you

out of My hand. I am the Judge; I will pull you down, and set My afflicted people up, v. 7.

8. *It is full of mixture.* Alluding to that mingled potion of stupefying drugs given to criminals to drink previously to their execution. See a parallel passage to this, Jer. xxv. 15-26.

10. *All the horns of the wicked.* All their power and influence will I cut off, and will exalt and extend the power of the *righteous.* All was punctually fulfilled: the *wicked*—the Babylonians—were all cut off; the *righteous*—the Jews—were delivered and *exalted.*

PSALM 76

The true God known in Judah, Israel, Salem, and Zion, 1-2. A description of His defeat of the enemies of His people, 3-6. How God is to be worshipped, 7-9. He should be considered as the chief Ruler; all the potentates of the earth are subject to Him, 10-12.

The title, "To the chief Musician on Neginoth, a Psalm or Song of Asaph." See the titles to Psalms iv and vi. If Asaph was its author, it could not be the Asaph that flourished in the days of David but some other gifted and divinely inspired man of the same name, by whom several others of the psalms appear to have been composed during the Captivity.

2. *In Salem also is his tabernacle.* Salem was the ancient name of Jebus, afterward called Jerusalem. Here was the *tabernacle* set up; but afterwards, when the Temple was built on Mount Zion, there was His habitation. The psalm was evidently composed after the building of Solomon's Temple.

3. *There brake he the arrows of the bow.* "The fiery arrows."

5. *The stouthearted are spoiled.* The boasting blasphemers, such as Rab-shakeh, and his master, Sennacherib, the king of Assyria. *They have slept their sleep.* They were asleep in their tent when the destroying angel, the suffocating wind, destroyed the whole; they over whom it passed never more awoke.

7. *Thou, even thou, art to be feared.* The Hebrew is simple, but very emphatic: *attah nora attah,* "Thou art terrible; Thou art." The repetition of the pronoun deepens the sense. *When once thou art angry.* Literally, "From the time thou art angry." In the moment Thy wrath is kindled, in that moment judgment is executed.

9. *The meek of the earth.* The humbled or oppressed people of the land. The poor Jews, now utterly helpless, and calling upon the Lord for succor.

10. *Surely the wrath of man shall praise thee.* The rage of Sennacherib shall only serve to manifest Thy glory. The stronger he is, and the more he threatens, and the weaker Thy people, the more shall Thy majesty and mercy appear in his destruction and their support. *The remainder of wrath shalt thou restrain.* The Hebrew gives rather a different sense: "Thou shalt gird thyself with the remainder of wrath." Even after Thou hast sent this signal destruction upon Sennacherib and his army, Thou wilt continue to pursue the remnant of the persecutors of Thy people; their wrath shall be the cause of the excitement of Thy justice to destroy them. As a man girds himself with his girdle, that he may the better perform his work, so Thou wilt gird thyself with wrath, that Thou mayest destroy Thy enemies.

11. *Vow, and pay unto the Lord.* Bind yourselves to Him, and forget not your obligations. *That ought to be feared.* "To the terrible One."

PSALM 77

The Psalmist's ardent prayer to God in the time of distress, 1-4. The means he used to excite his confidence, 5-12. God's wonderful works in behalf of His people, 13-20.

The title, "To the chief Musician (or conqueror), to Jeduthun, A Psalm of Asaph." On this title we may observe that both Asaph and Jeduthun were celebrated singers in the time of David, and no doubt were masters or leaders of bands which long after their times were called by their names. Hence psalms composed during and after the Captivity have these names prefixed to them. But there is reason to believe also that there was a person of the name of Asaph in the captivity at Babylon. The author must be considered as speaking in the persons of the captive Israelites. It may however be adapted to the case of any individual in spiritual distress through strong temptation, or from a sense of the divine displeasure in consequence of backsliding.

2. *My sore ran in the night, and ceased not.* This is a most unaccountable translation; the literal meaning of *yadi niggerah,* which we translate *my sore ran,* is, "my hand was stretched out," i.e., in prayer. He continued during the whole night with his voice and hands lifted up to God, and ceased not.

3. *My spirit was overwhelmed.* As the verb is in the *hithpael* conjugation, the word must mean, "My spirit was overpowered in itself." It purposed to involve itself in this calamity.

4. *Thou holdest mine eyes waking.* Literally, "Thou keepest the watches of mine eyes"—my grief is so great that I cannot sleep. *I am so troubled that I cannot speak.* This shows an increase of sorrow and anguish. At first he felt his misery, and called aloud. "Small troubles are loquacious; the great are dumb."

5. *I have considered the days of old.* "I have counted up"; I have reckoned up the various dispensations of Thy mercy in behalf of the distressed, marked down in the history of our fathers.

6. *I call to remembrance my song in the night.* I do not think that *neginathi* means *my song.* We know that *neginath* signifies some stringed musical instrument that was struck with a plectrum, but here it possibly might be applied to the psalm that was played on it. But it appears to me rather that the Psalmist here speaks of the circumstances of composing the short ode contained in the seventh, eighth, and ninth verses, which it is probable he sung to his harp as a kind of dirge, if indeed he had a harp in that distressful captivity. *My spirit made diligent search.* The verb *chaphas* signifies such an investigation as a man makes who is obliged to strip himself in order to do it; or, to lift up coverings, to search fold by fold, or in our phrase, to leave no stone unturned.

7. *Will the Lord cast off for ever?* Will there be no end to this captivity?

8. *For evermore?* "To generation and generation."

10. *And I said, This is my infirmity.* The Hebrew is very obscure, and has been differ-

ently translated: "And I said, Is this my weakness? Years the right hand of the Most High."

13. *Thy way . . . is in the sanctuary.* See Ps. lxxiii. 17.

16. *The waters saw thee.* What a fine image! He represents God approaching the Red Sea; and the waters, seeing Him, took fright, and ran off before Him, dividing to the right and left to let Him pass. I have not found anything more majestic than this.

17. *The clouds poured out water.* It appears from this that there was a violent tempest at the time of the passage of the Red Sea. There was a violent storm of thunder, lightning, and rain.

PSALM 78

An enumeration of the principal effects of the goodness of God to His people, 1-16; of their rebellions and punishment, 17-33; their feigned repentance, 34-37; God's compassion towards them, 38-39; their backsliding and forgetfulness of His mercy, 40-42; the plagues which He brought upon the Egyptians, 43-51; the deliverance of His own people, and their repeated ingratitude and disobedience, 52-58; their punishment. 59-64; God's wrath against their adversaries, 65-66; His rejection of the tribes of Israel and His choice of the tribe of Judah, and of David to be king over His people, 67-72.

2. *In a parable.* Or, I will give you instruction by numerous examples; see Ps. xlix. 1-4, which bears a great similarity to this. The term *parable*, in its various acceptations, has already been sufficiently explained; but *mashal* may here mean "example," as opposed to *torah*, "law" or "precept," v. 1.

4. *We will not hide them.* In those ancient times there was very little reading, because books were exceedingly scarce; tradition was therefore the only, or nearly the only, means of preserving the memory of past events. They were handed down from father to son by parables or pithy sayings, and by chronological poems. This very psalm is of this kind, and must have been very useful to the Israelites, as giving instructions concerning their ancient history, and recounting the wonderful deeds of the Almighty in their behalf.

9. *The children of Ephraim . . . turned back.* This refers to some defeat of the Ephraimites; and some think to that by the men of Gath. mentioned in 1 Chron. vii. 21.

12. *The field of Zoan.* "Tanis" was the capital of Pharaoh, where Moses wrought so many miracles. It was situated in the Delta, on one of the most easterly branches of the Nile.

18. *By asking meat for their lust.* "For their souls," i.e., "for their lives"; for they said in their hearts that the light bread, the manna, was not sufficient to sustain their natural force, and preserve their lives.

25. *Man did eat angels' food.* "Man did eat the bread of the mighty ones." They ate such bread as could be expected only at the tables of the rich and great; the best, the most delicate food.

26. *He caused an east wind to blow.* See Num. xi. 31.

32. *For all this they sinned still.* How astonishing is this! They were neither drawn by mercies nor awed by judgments!

33. *Their days did he consume in vanity.* By causing them to wander forty years in the **wilderness**, vainly expecting an end to their labor, and the enjoyment of the promised rest, which, by their rebellions, they had forfeited.

35. *That God was their rock.* They recollected in their affliction that Jehovah was their *Rock*, the Source, not only of their being, but of all their blessings; or that He was their sole Protector. *And the high God their redeemer. Veel elyon goalam,* "And the strong God, the Most High, their kinsman." That one who possessed the right of redemption. The Hebrew word *goel* answers to the Greek *Soter,* a "savior"; and is given to the Lord Jesus Christ, the strong God, the Most High, the Redeemer of a lost world. After this verse there is the following Masoretic note: "The middle of the book." And thus the reader has arrived at the middle of the Psalter.

36. *Nevertheless they did flatter him with their mouth.* I think the Vulgate gives the true sense of the Hebrew: "They loved him with their mouth; and they lied unto him with their tongue."

38. *But he, being full of compassion.* Feeling for them as a father for his children. *Forgave their iniquity. Yechapper,* "made an atonement" for their iniquity. *And did not stir up all his wrath.* The punishment was much less than the iniquity deserved.

39. *He remembered that they were but flesh.* Weak mortals. *A wind that passeth away, and cometh not again.* I believe this to be a bad translation, and may be productive of error; as if when a man dies his being were ended, and death were an eternal sleep. The translation should be, "The spirit goeth away, and it doth not return." The Arabic takes away all ambiguity: "He remembered that they were flesh; and a spirit which, when it departs, does not again return." The human being is composed of flesh and spirit, or body and soul; these are easily separated, and, when separated, the body turns to dust, and the spirit returns no more to animate it in a state of probation.

41. *Limited the Holy One of Israel.* The Chaldee translates, "And the Holy One of Israel they signed with a sign." Here it most obviously means an insult offered to God.

44. *Turned their rivers into blood.* See Exod. vii. 20.

45. *He sent . . . flies . . . and frogs.* See Exod. viii. 6, 24.

46. *The caterpiller, and . . . the locust.* See Exod. x. 13.

48. *He gave up their cattle.* See Exod. ix. 23.

49. *By sending evil angels.* This is the first mention we have of *evil angels.* There is no mention of them in the account we have of the plagues of Egypt in the Book of Exodus, and what they were we cannot tell. An angel or "messenger" may be either animate or inanimate, a disembodied spirit or human being, any thing or being that is an instrument sent of God for the punishment or support of mankind.

54. *The border of his sanctuary.* "Of his holy place," that is, the land of Canaan, called afterwards *the mountain, which his right hand had purchased,* because it was a mountainous country, widely differing from Egypt, which was a long, continued, and almost perfect level.

60. *He forsook the tabernacle of Shiloh.* The Lord, offended with the people, and principally

with the priests, who had profaned His holy worship, gave up His ark into the hands of the Philistines. And so true it is that he *forsook the tabernacle of Shiloh* that He never returned to it again. See 1 Sam. vi. 1; 2 Samuel vi; 1 Kings viii. 1; where the several removals of the ark are spoken of, and which exp'ain the remaining part of this psalm. Because God suffered the Philistines to take the ark, it is said, v. 61: He "delivered his strength into captivity, and his glory into the enemy's hand"; and v. 67, that "he refused the tabernacle of Joseph, and chose not the tribe of Ephraim." For Shiloh was in the tribe of Ephraim, the son of Joseph; and God did not suffer His ark to return thither, but to go to Kirjath-jearim, which was in the tribe of Benjamin; from thence to the house of Obed-edom; and so to Zion in the tribe of Judah, as it follows, v. 68.

63. *Their maidens were not given to marriage. Hullalu,* were not celebrated with marriage songs.

64. *Their priests fell by the sword.* Hophni and Phinehas, who were slain in that unfortunate battle against the Philistines in which the ark of the Lord was taken, 1 Sam. iv. 11.

65. *Then the Lord awaked.* He seemed as if He had totally disregarded what was done to His people, and the reproach that seemed to fall on himself and His worship by the capture of the ark. *Like a mighty man. Kegibbor,* "like a hero" *that shouteth by reason of wine.* One who, going forth to meet his enemy, having taken a sufficiency of wine to refresh himself, and become a proper stimulus to his animal spirits, shouts—gives the war signal for the onset; impatient to meet the foe, and sure of victory. The idea is not taken from the case of a drunken man. A person in such a state would be very unfit to meet his enemy, and could have little prospect of conquest.

66. *He smote his enemies in the hinder parts.* This refers to the hemorrhoids with which he afflicted the Philistines. See 1 Sam. v. 6-10.

67. *He refused the tabernacle of Joseph.* See the note on v. 60.

69. *He built his sanctuary like high palaces.* The temple of God at Jerusalem was the only one in the land. And there He *established* His ark, to go no more out as long as the Temple should last. Before this time it was frequently in a migratory state, not only in the wilderness, but afterwards in the Promised Land. See the notes on v. 60.

70. *He chose David.* See the account, 1 Sam. xvi. 11, etc.

PSALM 79

The Psalmist complains of the cruelty of his enemies and the desolations of Jerusalem, and prays against them, 1-7. He prays for the pardon and restoration of his people, and promises gratitude and obedience, 8-13.

The title, "A Psalm of Asaph," must be understood as either applying to a person of the name of Asaph who lived under the Captivity, or else to the family of Asaph, or to a band of singers still bearing the name of that Asaph who flourished in the days of David; for most undoubtedly the psalm was composed during the Babylonish captivity, when the city of Jerusalem lay in heaps, the Temple was defiled, and the people were in a state of captivity. Some think it was composed by Jeremiah; and it is certain that the sixth and seventh verses are the same with Jer. x. 25: "Pour out thy fury upon the heathen that know thee not, and upon the families that call not on thy name: for they have eaten up Jacob, and devoured him, and consumed him, and have made his habitation desolate."

1. *The heathen are come into thine inheritance.* Thou didst cast them out, and take Thy people in; they have cast us out, and now taken possession of the land that belongs to Thee. They have defiled the Temple, and reduced Jerusalem to a heap of ruins, and made a general slaughter of Thy people.

2. *The dead bodies of thy servants.* It appears that in the destruction of Jerusalem the Chaldeans did not bury the bodies of the slain, but left them to be devoured by birds and beasts of prey. This was the grossest inhumanity.

4. *We are become a reproach to our neighbours.* The Idumeans, Philistines, Phoenicians, Ammonites, and Moabites, all gloried in the subjugation of this people; and their insults to them were mixed with blasphemies against God.

8. *Remember not against us former iniquities.* Visit us not for the sins of our forefathers. *We are brought very low.* Literally, "We are greatly thinned." Few of us remain.

9. *Purge away our sins. Capper,* "be propitiated," or "receive an atonement" on account of our sins.

10. *Where is their God?* Show where Thou art by rising up for our redemption, and the infliction of deserved punishment upon our enemies.

11. *The sighing of the prisoner.* The poor captive Israelites in Babylon, who sigh and cry because of their bondage. *Those that are appointed to die.* "Sons of death." Either those who were condemned to death because of their crimes or condemned to be destroyed by their oppressors. Both these senses apply to the Israelites. They were sons of death, i.e., worthy of death because of their sins against God; they were condemned to death or utter destruction by their Babylonish enemies.

12. *Sevenfold into their bosom.* That is, Let them get in this world what they deserve for the cruelties they have inflicted on us. Let them suffer in captivity who now have us in bondage. Probably this is a prediction.

PSALM 80

A prayer for the captives, 1-3. A description of their miseries, 4-7. Israel compared to a vineyard, 8-14. Its desolate state, and a prayer for its restoration, 15-19.

The title: see Psalms xlv; lx; and lxix, where everything material is explained. This psalm seems to have been written on the same occasion with the former. One ancient MS. in the public library in Cambridge writes the eightieth and the seventy-ninth all as one psalm; the subject matter is precisely the same—was made on the same occasion, and probably by the same author.

1. *O Shepherd of Israel.* The subject continued from the last verse of the preceding psalm. *That dwellest between the cherubims.* It was between the cherubim, over the cover of the ark, called the mercy seat, that the glory of the Lord, or symbol of the Divine Presence, appeared.

Shine forth. Restore Thy worship; and give us such evidences of Thy presence now as our fathers had under the first Tabernacle, and afterwards in the Temple built by Solomon.

2. *Before Ephraim and Benjamin and Manasseh.* It is supposed that these three tribes represent the whole, Benjamin being incorporated with Judah, Manasseh comprehending the country beyond Jordan, and Ephraim all the rest.

3. *Turn us again.* "Convert" or "restore" us. There are four parts in this psalm, three of which end with the above words; see the third, seventh, and nineteenth verses; and one with words similar, v. 14.

5. *Thou feedest them with the bread of tears.* They have no peace, no comfort, nothing but continual sorrow. *In great measure.* "Threefold." Some think it was a certain measure used by the Chaldeans, the real capacity of which is not known. Others think it signifies "abundance" or "abundantly."

8. *Thou hast brought a vine out of Egypt.* This is a most elegant metaphor, and everywhere well-supported. The same similitude is used by Isaiah, chap. v. 1, etc.; by Jeremiah, chap. ii. 21; by Ezekiel, chap. xvii. 5-6; by Hosea, chap. x. 1; by Joel, chap. i. 7; by Moses, Deut. xxxii. 32-33; and often by our Lord himself, Matt. xx. 1, etc; xxi. 33, etc.; Mark xii. 1, etc. And this was the ordinary figure to represent the Jewish church. We may remark several analogies here: (1) This vine was brought out of Egypt that it might be planted in a better and more favorable soil. (2) When the husbandman has marked out a proper place for his vineyard, he hews down and roots up all other trees; gathers out the stones, brambles, etc. So God cast out the heathen nations from the land of Canaan, that His pure worship might be established, and that there might not remain any incitements to idolatry.

9. *Thou preparedst . . . before it.* (3) When the ground is properly cleared, the vines are placed in the ground at proper distances. So when God had cast out the heathen, He caused the land to be divided by lot to the different tribes, and then to the several families of which these tribes were composed. *And didst cause it to take deep root.* (4) By sheltering, propping up, and loosening the ground about the tender plants, they are caused to take a deep and firm rooting in the ground. Thus did God, by especial manifestations of His kind providence, support and protect the Israelites in Canaan. *It filled the land.* (5) To multiply vines, the gardener cuts off a shoot from the old tree, then plants it in proper soil. Thus God so carefully, tenderly, and abundantly blessed the Israelites that they increased and multiplied and, in process of time, filled the whole land of Canaan.

10. *The hills were covered.* (6) The vine, carefully cultivated in a suitable soil, may be spread to any extent. In the land of Judea it formed shades under which the people not only sheltered and refreshed themselves in times of sultry heats; but it is said they even ate, drank, and dwelt under the shelter of their vines. See 1 Kings iv. 25; Mic. iv. 4; 1 Mac. xiv. 12.

11. *She sent out her boughs unto the sea, and her branches unto the river.* The Israelitish empire extended from the river Euphrates on the east to the Mediterranean Sea on the west.

12. *Why hast thou . . . broken down?* (7) When a vineyard is planted, it is properly fenced to preserve it from being trodden down. So God protected Jerusalem and His temple by His own almighty arm, and none of their enemies could molest them as long as they had that protection. As it was now spoiled, it was a proof that that protection had been withdrawn.

13. *The boar out of the wood.* Nebuchadnezzar, king of Babylon, who was a fierce and cruel sovereign.

14. *Return . . . O God of hosts.* Thou hast abandoned us, and therefore our enemies have us in captivity. Come back to us, and we shall again be restored.

15. *The vineyard which thy right hand hath planted.* Thy holy and pure worship, which Thy almighty power had established in this city. *And the branch . . . thou madest strong for thyself.* The original is *veal ben,* "and upon the Son whom thou hast strengthened for thyself." Many have thought that the Lord Jesus is meant.

17. *The man of thy right hand.* The only person who can be said to be at the right hand of God as intercessor is Jesus, the Messiah. Let Him become our Deliverer.

18. *So will not we go back from thee.* We shall no more become idolaters; and it is allowed on all hands that the Jews were never guilty of idolatry after their return from the Babylonish captivity. *Quicken us.* "Make us alive," for we are nearly as good as dead.

19. *Turn us again.* Redeem us from this captivity. *O Lord God of hosts.* Thou who hast all power in heaven and earth, the innumerable hosts of both worlds being at Thy command. *Cause thy face to shine.* Let us know that thou art reconciled to us. Smile upon Thy poor rebels, weary of their sins, and prostrate at Thy feet, imploring mercy. *And we shall be saved.* From the power and oppression of the Chaldeans, from the guilt and condemnation of our sins, and from Thy wrath and everlasting displeasure.

PSALM 81

An exhortation to the people to praise God for His benefits, 1-7; and to attend to what He had prescribed, 8-10; their disobedience lamented, 11; the miseries brought on themselves by their transgressions, 12-16.

The title is the same as to Psalm xiii, which see. There are various opinions concerning the occasion and time of this psalm, but it is pretty generally agreed that it was either written for or used at the celebration of the Feast of Trumpets (see on Lev. xxiii. 24), which was held on the first day of the month Tisri, which was the beginning of the Jewish year; and on that day it is still used in the Jewish worship. The psalm may have been used in celebrating the Feast of Trumpets on the first day of Tisri, the Feast of Tabernacles on the fifteenth of the same month, the creation of the world, the Feasts of the New Moons, and the deliverance of the Israelites from Egypt—to all which circumstances it appears to refer.

1. *Sing aloud unto God our strength.* Their is much meaning here. As God is our Strength, let that strength be devoted to His service; therefore, sing aloud! This is principally addressed to the priests and Levites.

2. *Take a psalm.* Zimrah. I rather think that this was the name of a musical instrument.

Bring hither the timbrel. Toph; some kind of drum or tom-tom. *The pleasant harp. Kinnor.* A stringed instrument. *With the psaltery. Nebel.* The cithara.

3. *Blow up the trumpet. Shophar,* a species of horn. Certainly a wind instrument, as the last two were stringed instruments. The feast of the *new moon* was always proclaimed by sound of trumpet. For want of astronomical knowledge, the Jews were put to sad shifts to know the real time of the new moon. They generally sent persons to the top of some hill or mountain about the time which the new moon should appear. The first who saw it was to give immediate notice to the Sanhedrin; they closely examined the reporter as to his credibility, and whether his information agreed with their calculations. If all was found satisfactory, the president proclaimed the new moon by shouting out, "*Mik-kodesh!*" "It is consecrated!" This word was repeated twice aloud by the people, and was then proclaimed everywhere by blowing of horns, or what is called the sound of trumpets.

4. *This was a statute for Israel.* See the statute, Num. x. 10 and Lev. xxiii. 24.

5. *I heard a language that I understood not.* All the versions, except the Chaldee, read the pronoun in the third person, instead of the first. "He heard a language that he understood not."

7. *Thou calledst in trouble.* They had cried by reason of their burdens, and the cruelty of their taskmasters; and God heard that cry, and delivered them. See Exod. iii. 7, etc. *In the secret place of thunder.* On Mount Sinai, where God was heard but not seen. *At the waters of Meribah.* See this transaction, Exod. xvii. 1, etc.

8. *Hear, O my people.* These are nearly the same words with those spoken at the giving of the law, Exod. xx. 2.

11. *Israel would none of me.* "They willed Me not"; they would not have Me for their God.

12. *Unto their own hearts' lust.* To the obstinate wickedness of their heart.

13. *Oh that my people had hearkened unto me . . . Israel had walked in my ways!* Nothing can be more plaintive than the original; sense and sound are surprisingly united.

15. *Their time should have endured for ever.* That is, Their prosperity should have known no end.

16. *With the finest of the wheat.* Literally, "with the fat of wheat."

PSALM 82

A warning to corrupt judges, 1-2; an exhortation to them to dispense justice without respect of persons, 3-5; they are threatened with the judgments of the Lord, 6-8.

This psalm, which, in the title, is attributed to Asaph, was probably composed in the time when Jehoshaphat reformed the courts of justice throughout his states; see 2 Chron. xix. 6-7, where he uses nearly the same words as in the beginning of this psalm.

1. *God standeth in the congregation of the mighty.* The Hebrew should be translated, "God standeth in the assembly of God."

2. *Accept the persons of the wicked.* "Lift up their faces," encourage them in their oppressions.

3. *Defend the poor.* You are their natural protectors under God.

5. *They know not.* The judges are not acquainted with the law of God, on which all their decisions should be founded. *Neither will they understand.* They are ignorant, and do not wish to be instructed. *All the foundations of the earth.* "All the civil institutions of the land totter."

6. *Ye are gods.* Or, with the prefix of *ke,* the particle of similitude, *keelohim,* "like God."

7. *But ye shall die like men. Keadam,* "ye shall die like Adam," who fell from his high perfection and dignity as ye have done.

8. *Arise, O God, judge the earth.* Justice is perverted in the land; take the sceptre, and rule thyself. *For thou shalt inherit all nations.* Does not this last verse contain a prophecy of our Lord, the calling of the Gentiles, and the prevalence of Christianity over the earth? Thus several of the fathers have understood the passage.

PSALM 83

The Psalmist calls upon God for immediate help against a multitude of confederate enemies who had risen up against Judah, 1-5. He mentions them by name, 6-8; shows how they were to be punished, 9-17; and that this was to be done for the glory of God, 18.

The title, "A Song or Psalm of Asaph," contains nothing particular. Among a multitude of conjectures relative to the time and occasion of this psalm, that which refers it to the confederacy against Jehoshaphat, king of Judah, mentioned in 2 Chronicles xx, is the most likely.

1. *Keep not thou silence.* A strong appeal to God just as the confederacy was discovered.

2. *Thine enemies make a tumult.* They are not merely the enemies of Thy people, but they are the enemies of thyself, Thy worship, ordinances, and laws. They *make a tumult;* they throng together. *They . . . have lifted up the head.* They have made an irruption into the land of Judea, and encamped at En-gedi, by the Dead Sea, 2 Chron. xx. 1-2.

4. *Let us cut them off.* Let us exterminate the whole race, that there may not be a record of them on the face of the earth. And their scheme was well laid. Eight or ten different nations united themselves in a firm bond to do this; and they had kept their purpose so secret that the king of Judah does not appear to have heard of it till his territories were actually invaded, and the different bodies of this coalition had assembled at En-gedi. Never was Judah before in greater danger.

5. *They have consulted together with one consent.* With a united heart, *leb yachdav. They are confederate against thee.* "They have made a covenant," *berith yachrithu,* "they have cut the covenant sacrifice." They have slain an animal, divided him in twain, and passed between the pieces of the victim; and have thus bound themselves to accomplish their purpose.

6. *The tabernacles of Edom.* The "tents" of these different people are seen in the grand encampment. *Hagarenes.* These people dwelt on the east of Gilead; and were nearly destroyed in the days of Saul, being totally expelled from their country, 1 Chron. v. 10, but afterwards recovered some strength and consequence; but where they dwelt after their expulsion by the Israelites is not known.

7. *Gebal.* The Giblites, who were probably the persons here designed, were a tribe of the

ancient inhabitants of the land of Canaan, and are mentioned as unconquered at the death of Joshua, chap. xiii. 5. They are called stone-squarers or Giblites, 1 Kings v. 18, and were of considerable assistance to Hiram, king of Tyre, in preparing timber and stones for the building of the Temple. They appear to have been eminent in the days of Ezekiel, who terms them "the ancients of Gebal and the wise men thereof," who were shipbuilders, chap. xxvii. 9. *Ammon* and *Moab* were the descendants of the children of Lot. Their bad origin is sufficiently known. See Gen. xix. 30, etc. *Amalek.* The Amalekites are well-known as the ancient and inveterate enemies of the Israelites. They were neighbors to the Idumeans. *The Philistines.* These were tributaries to Jehoshaphat, 2 Chron. xvii. 11; but it seems they took advantage of the present times to join in the great confederacy against him. *The inhabitants of Tyre.* These probably joined the confederacy in hopes of making conquests and extending their territory on the mainland.

8. *Assur also is joined.* The Ammonites might have got those auxiliaries from beyond the Euphrates, against Jehoshaphat, as formerly they were brought against David. See 2 Sam. x. 16. *They have holpen the children of Lot.* The Ammonites, who appear to have been the chief instigators in this war.

9. *Do unto them as unto the Midianites.* Who were utterly defeated by Gideon, Judg. vii. 21-22. *As to Sisera.* Captain of the army of Jabin, king of Canaan, who was totally defeated by Deborah and Barak, near Mount Tabor, by the river Kishon; and himself, after having fled from the battle, slain by Jael, the wife of Heber, the Kenite. See Judg. iv. 15, etc.

10. *Perished at En-dor.* This refers to the defeat of the Midianites by Gideon, who were encamped in the Valley of Jezreel, at the foot of Mount Gilboa, and near to Tabor, Judg. vi. 33; vii. 1, and consequently in the environs of En-dor.

11. *Make their nobles like Oreb, and like Zeeb.* They were two of the chiefs, or generals, of the Midianites; and were slain in the pursuit of the Midianites, by the men of Ephraim; and their heads brought to Gideon on the other side of Jordan. Judg. vii. 24-25. *Yea, all their princes as Zebah, and as Zalmunna.* These were kings of Midian who were encamped at Karkor with 15,000 men, whom Gideon attacked there, and defeated, and took the kings prisoners; and finding that they had killed his own brothers, slew them both. See Judg. viii. 10-21.

12. *Let us take to ourselves the houses of God in possession.* Nearly the words spoken by the confederates when they came to attack Jehoshaphat. See 2 Chron. xx. 11.

13. *O my God, make them like a wheel.* Alluding to the manner of threshing corn in the East. A large, broad wheel was rolled over the grain on a threshing floor, which was generally in the open air; and the grain being thrown up by a shovel against the wind, the chaff was thus separated from it, in the place where it was threshed.

14. *The flame setteth the mountains on fire.* This may refer to the burning of the straw and chaff, after the grain was threshed and winnowed.

15. *So persecute them.* In this and the two following verses we find several awful execrations; and all this seems to be done in reference to that ancient custom, "pouring execrations on an enemy previously to battle." The reader is particularly requested to refer to the case of Balaam being hired by the king of Moab to curse Israel previously to his intended attack; see Numbers xxii.

16. *That they may seek thy name.* Let them be confounded in all their attempts on Israel, and see so manifestly that Thou hast done it that they may invoke Thy name and be converted to Thee.

17. *Let them . . . perish.* That is, in their present attempts. Some have objected to the execrations in this psalm, without due consideration. None of these execrations refer either to their souls or to their eternal state, but merely to their discomfiture in their present attempts.

18. *That men may know.* That they may acknowledge, and be converted to Thee. Here is no malice; all is self-defense.

PSALM 84

The Psalmist longs for communion with God in the sanctuary, 1-3. The blessedness of those who enjoy God's ordinances, 4-7. With confidence in God, he prays for restoration to His house and worship, 8-12.

The title here is the same as that of Psalm lxxxi, only that was for Asaph, this for the sons of Korah. This person was one of the chief rebels against Moses and Aaron; there were three, Korah, Dathan, and Abiram, who made an insurrection; and the earth opened, and swallowed up them and their partisans, Numbers xvi. The children of Dathan and Abiram perished with their fathers; but by a particular dispensation of providence the children of Korah were spared. See Num. xxvi. 11. The family of Korah was continued in Israel; and it appears from 1 Chron. xxvi. 1-19 that they were still employed about the Temple, and were porters or keepers of the doors. They were also singers in the Temple; see 2 Chron. xx. 19. This psalm might have been sent to them to be sung, or one of themselves might have been its author.

1. *How amiable are thy tabernacles!* In this plural noun he appears to include all the places in or near the Temple where acts of divine worship were performed.

2. *My soul longeth.* It is a Levite that speaks, who ardently longs to regain his place in the Temple, and his part in the sacred services.

3. *Yea, the sparrow hath found an house.* It is very unlikely that sparrows and swallows, or birds of any kind, should be permitted to build their nests, and hatch their young, in or about altars which were kept in a state of the greatest purity, and where perpetual fires were kept up for the purpose of sacrifice, burning incense, etc. Without altering the text, if the clause be read in a parenthesis, the absurdity will be avoided, and the sense be good. "My heart crieth out for the living God (even the sparrow hath found a house, and the ring-dove, a nest for herself, where she may lay her young), for thine altars, O Lord of hosts!" Or read the parenthesis last: "My heart crieth out for the living God; for thine altars, O Lord of hosts, my King and my God. Even the sparrow hath found out a house, and the swallow (ring-dove) a nest for herself, where she may lay her young"; but I have no place, of either rest or worship, understood.

4. *Blessed are they that dwell in thy house.* They who have such a constant habitation in Thy temple as the sparrow or the swallow has in the house wherein it has built its nest.

5. *In whose heart are the ways of them.* This is no sense. The original, however, is obscure: "The high ways are in their hearts"; that is, the roads winding to Thy temple.

6. *Passing through the valley of Baca make it a well.* I believe *Baca* to be the same here as Bochim, Judg. ii. 1-5, called "The Valley of Weeping." *The rain also filleth the pools.* The Hebrew may be translated differently, and has been differently understood by all the versions. "Yea, the instructor is covered or clothed with blessings."

7. *They go from strength to strength.* They proceed from one degree of grace to another, gaining divine virtue through all the steps of their probation. *Every one of them in Zion appeareth before God.* This is a paraphrase, and a bad one, but no translation. They shall proceed *from strength to strength.* "The God of gods shall be seen in Zion." God shall appear in their behalf, as often as they shall seek Him, in consequence of which they shall increase in spiritual strength.

11. *For the Lord God is a sun and shield.* To illuminate, invigorate, and warm; to protect and defend all such as prefer Him and His worship to everything the earth can produce. It is remarkable that not one of the versions understands the *shemesh*, as signifying *sun*, as we do. They generally concur in the following translation: "For the Lord loveth mercy and truth, and he will give grace and glory." The Chaldee says, "The Lord is as a high wall and a strong shield; grace and glory will the Lord give, and will not deprive those of blessedness who walk in perfection."

PSALM 85

Thanksgiving to God for restoration to the divine favor, 1-3; prayer for further mercies, 4-7; the Psalmist waits for a gracious answer in full confidence of receiving it, 8. He receives the assurance of the greatest blessings, and exults in the prospect, 9-13.

The title of this psalm we have seen before, Psalm xlii. As to the time, it seems to have been written during, or even after, the return from the Babylonish captivity. In the first three verses the Psalmist acknowledges the goodness of God in bringing the people back to their own land; he next prays to God to restore them to their ancient prosperity. In the spirit of prophecy, he waits on God, and hears Him promise to do it; and then exults in the prospect of so great a good. The whole psalm seems also to have a reference to the redemption of the world by Jesus Christ.

1. *Lord, thou hast been favourable.* Literally, "Thou hast been well pleased with Thy land." *Thou hast brought back the captivity.* This seems to fix the time of the psalm to be after the return of the Jews from Babylon.

2. *Thou hast forgiven the iniquity.* "Thou hast borne, or carried away, the iniquity." An allusion to the ceremony of the scapegoat.

3. *Thou hast taken away.* "Thou hast gathered up all Thy wrath." This carries on the

metaphor in the second verse: "Thou hast collected all Thy wrath, and carried it away with all our iniquities."

8. *I will hear what God the Lord will speak.* The Psalmist goes as a prophet to consult the Lord; and, having made his request, waits an answer from the spirit of prophecy. He is satisfied that the answer will be gracious; and having received it, he relates it to the people. *He will speak peace.* He will give prosperity to the people in general; and to *his saints,* His followers, in particular. *But let them not turn again to folly.* Let them not abuse the mercy of their God, by sinning any more against Him.

10. *Mercy and truth are met together.* Where did these meet? In Christ Jesus. When were they reconciled? When He poured out His life on Calvary.

11. *Truth shall spring out of the earth.* In consequence of this wonderful reconciliation, the truth of God shall prevail among men. The seeds of it shall be so plentifully sown by the preaching of Christ and His apostles that true religion shall be diffused over the world.

13. *Righteousness shall go before him.* Perhaps this verse may receive its best solution from Rom. iii. 25: "Whom God hath set forth to be a propitiation through faith in his blood, to declare his righteousness for the remission of sins that are past." This term the apostle uses to point out God's method of justifying or saving mankind. And this, in the preaching of the pure gospel, is ever going before to point out the Lord Jesus, and the redemption that is in His blood.

PSALM 86

The Psalmist prays to God for support, from a conviction that He is merciful, good, ready to forgive, and that there is none like Him, 1-8; all nations shall bow before Him because of His wondrous works, 9-10. He prays to be instructed, and promises to praise God for His great mercy, 11-13; describes his enemies, and appeals to God, 14-16; begs a token for good, that his enemies may be confounded, 17.

The title attributes this psalm to David, and in this all the versions agree; but in its structure it is the same with those attributed to the sons of Korah, and was probably made during the Captivity. It is a very suitable prayer for a person laboring under affliction from persecution or calumny.

1. *Bow down thine ear.* Spoken after the manner of men: I am so low, and so weak, that, unless Thou stoop to me, my voice cannot reach Thee.

2. *For I am holy. Ki chasid ani,* "for I am merciful."

5. *For thou, Lord, art good.* I found my expectations of help on Thy own goodness, through which Thou art always ready to forgive. And I found it also on Thy well-known character, to which all Thy followers bear testimony, viz., that Thou art *plenteous in mercy unto all them that call upon thee.*

10. *For thou art great.* Almighty, infinite, eternal. *And doest wondrous things.* Thou art the "Worker of miracles." This appears to be a prophecy of the calling of the Gentiles to the faith of Christ, and the evidence to be given to His divine mission by the miracles which He should work. *Thou art God alone.* Septuagint, "Thou art the only, the great God."

11. *Teach me thy way.* Instruct me in the steps I should take, for without Thy teaching I must go astray. *Unite my heart. Yached lebabi,* "join" all the purposes, resolutions, and affections of my heart "together," *to fear* and to glorify *thy name.* This is a most important prayer.

12. *I will praise thee . . . with all my heart.* When my heart is united to fear Thy name, then shall I praise Thee with my whole heart.

14. *The assemblies of violent men.* "The congregation of the terrible ones."

PSALM 87

The nature and glorious privileges of Zion and Jerusalem, 1-3. No other city to be compared to this, 4. The privilege of being born in it, 5-6. Its praises celebrated, 7.

The title, "A Psalm or Song for the sons of Korah," gives us no light into the author or meaning of this psalm. It begins and ends so abruptly that many have thought it to be only a fragment of a larger psalm. This opinion is very likely. Those who suppose it to have been made when Jerusalem was rebuilt and fortified imagine it to have been an exclamation of the author on beholding its beauty and contemplating its privileges. If this opinion be allowed, it will account for the apparent abruptness in the beginning and end.

1. *His foundation is in the holy mountains.* Jerusalem was founded on the mountains or hills of Zion and Moriah.

4. *I will make mention of Rahab.* The meaning seems to be, *Rahab;* i.e., "Egypt, Babylon, Tyre, Philistia, and Ethiopia" are not so honorable as Jerusalem.

5. *This and that man was born in her.* It will be an honor to any person to have been born in Zion. But how great is the honor to be born from above, and be a citizen of the Jerusalem that is from above!

6. *The Lord shall count, when he writeth up the people.* "In the register of the people." When He takes account of those who dwell in Jerusalem, He will particularly note those who were born in Zion. This has an easy spiritual meaning. When God takes an account of all professing Christians, He will set apart those for inhabitants of the New Jerusalem who were born in Zion, who were born again, received a new nature, and were fitted for heaven.

7. *As well the singers.* Perhaps this may mean no more than, The burden of the songs of all the singers and choristers shall be, "All my fountains (ancestors and posterity) are in Thee," and consequently entitled to all Thy privileges and immunities.

PSALM 88

The earnest prayer of a person in deep distress, abandoned by his friends and neighbours, and apparently forsaken of God, 1-18.

Perhaps the title of this psalm, which is difficult enough, might be thus translated: "A poem to be sung to the conqueror, by the sons of Korah, responsively, in behalf of a distressed person; to give instruction to Heman the Ezrahite." Heman and Ethan, whose names are separately prefixed to this and the following psalm, are mentioned as the grandsons of Judah by his

daughter-in-law Tamar, 1 Chron. ii. 6. If these were the same persons mentioned in 1 Kings iv. 31, they were eminent in wisdom; for it is there said that Solomon's wisdom "excelled the wisdom of all the children of the east country, and all the wisdom of Egypt. For he was wiser than all men; than Ethan the Ezrahite, and Heman, and Chalcol, and Darda, the sons of Mahol," vv. 30-31.

5. *Free among the dead,* I rather think, means "stripped among the dead." Both the fourth and fifth verses seem to allude to a field of battle. The slain and the wounded are found scattered over the plain; the spoilers come among them and strip, not only the dead, but those also who appear to be mortally wounded, and cannot recover, and are so feeble as not to be able to resist. *They are cut off from thy hand.* An allusion to the roll in which the general has the names of all that compose his army under their respective officers. And when one is killed, he is erased from this register, and remembered no more, as belonging to the army.

8. *Thou hast made me an abomination.* This verse has been supposed to express the state of a leper, who, because of the infectious nature of his disease, is separated from his family, is abominable to all, and at last shut up in a separate house, whence he does not come out to mingle with society.

10. *Wilt thou shew wonders to the dead? Methim,* "dead men." *Shall the dead? Rephaim,* "departed spirits." *Arise and praise thee?* Anymore in this life? The interrogations in this and the following two verses imply the strongest negations.

11. *Or thy faithfulness in destruction?* Faithfulness in God refers as well to His fulfilling His threatenings as to His keeping His promises.

12. *The land of forgetfulness.* The place of separate spirits, or the invisible world.

13. *Shall my prayer prevent thee?* It shall "get before" Thee. I will not wait till the accustomed time to offer my morning sacrifice; I shall call on Thee long before others come to offer their devotions.

18. *Lover and friend.* I have no comfort, and neither friend nor neighbor to sympathize with me. *Mine acquaintance into darkness.* "Darkness is my companion."

PSALM 89

The Psalmist shows God's great mercy to the house o, David, and the promises which He had given to it of support and perpetuity, 1-37; complains that, notwithstanding these promises, the kingdom of Judah is overthrown, and the royal family nearly ruined, 38-45; and earnestly prays for their restoration, 46-52.

It is most probable that this psalm was composed during the Captivity. Of Ethan and Heman we have already seen something in the introduction to the preceding psalm. The title should probably be translated, "To give instruction to Ethan the Ezrahite."

The psalm divides itself into two grand parts. The first extends from v. 1 to 37, in which the Psalmist shows God's mercy to the house of David, and the promises which He has given to it of support and perpetuity. The second part begins with v. 38, and ends with the psalm; and in it the author complains that, notwithstanding these promises, the kingdom of Judah is overthrown and the royal family ruined; and he entreats the Lord to remember His covenant made with that family, and restore them from their captivity.

4. *Thy seed will I establish for ever, and build up thy throne to all generations.* And this covenant had most incontestably Jesus Christ in view. This is the *seed,* or posterity, that should sit on the throne, and reign for ever and ever. David and his family are long since become extinct; none of his race has sat on the Jewish throne for more than two thousand years. But the Christ has reigned invariably since that time, and will reign till all His enemies are put under His feet.

6. *For who in the heaven? Shachak* signifies the ethereal regions, all visible or unbounded space; the universe. Who is like Jesus? Even in His human nature none of *the sons of the mighty* can be compared with Him. He atones for the sin of the world, and saves to the uttermost all who come unto God through Him.

7. *God is greatly to be feared.* In all religious assemblies the deepest reverence for God should rest upon the people. Where this does not prevail, there is no true worship.

8. *Thy faithfulness round about thee?* Or, more properly, "Thy faithfulness is round about thee." Thou still keepest Thy promises in view.

10. *Thou hast broken Rahab.* Thou hast destroyed the power of Egypt, having overthrown the king and its people when they endeavored to prevent Thy people from regaining their liberty. *As one that is slain.* The whole clause in the original is, "Thou, like a hero, hast broken down Egypt."

12. *The north and the south.* It is generally supposed that by these four terms all the four quarters of the globe are intended. *Tabor,* a mountain of Galilee, was on the west of Mount *Hermon,* which was beyond Jordan, to the east of the source of that river.

14. *Justice and judgment are the habitation of thy throne.* The throne—the government—of God is founded in righteousness and judgment. *Mercy and truth shall go before thy face.* These shall be the heralds that shall announce the coming of the Judge. His *truth* binds Him to fulfill all His declarations, and His *mercy* shall be shown to all those who have fled for refuge to the hope that is set before them in the gospel.

15. *Blessed is the people.* "Oh, the blessednesses of that people that know the joyful sound; they shall walk vigorously in the light of Thy countenance."

16. *In thy name shall they rejoice.* Or "greatly exult."

20. *I have found David my servant.* This is the sum of what God had said in prophetic visions to His saints or holy persons, Samuel, Nathan, and Gad. Here the Psalmist begins to reason with God relative to David, his posterity, and the perpetuity of his kingdom; which promises appear now to have utterly failed, as the throne had been overturned and all the people carried into captivity. But all these things may have reference to Christ and His kingdom, for we are assured that David was a type of the Messiah.

22. *The enemy shall not exact upon him.* None of his enemies shall be able to prevail against him. It is worthy of remark that David was never overthrown; he finally conquered every foe that rose up against him.

25. *I will set his hand also in the sea.* This was literally fulfilled in David. *Hand* signifies power or authority; he set his hand on the sea in conquering the Philistines, and extending his empire along the coast of the Mediterranean Sea. All the coasts of the Red Sea, the Persian Gulf, and the Arabic Ocean might be said to have been under his government, for they all paid tribute to him or his son Solomon.

27. *I will make him my firstborn.* I will deal with him as a father by his firstborn son, to whom a double portion of possessions and honors belong. *Firstborn* is not always to be understood literally in Scripture. It often signifies simply a well-beloved or best beloved son; one preferred to all the rest, and distinguished by some eminent prerogative. Thus God calls Israel His son, His firstborn, Exod. iv. 22.

29. *His seed also will I make to endure for ever.* This can apply only to the spiritual David.

34. *My covenant will I not break.* My determination to establish a spiritual Kingdom, the Head of which shall be Jesus, the Son of David, shall never fail.

36. *His throne as the sun.* Splendid and glorious! dispensing light, heat, life, and salvation to all mankind.

38. *But thou hast cast off.* Hitherto the Psalmist has spoken of the covenant of God with David and his family, which led them to expect all manner of prosperity, and a perpetuity of the Jewish throne. Now he shows what appears to him a failure of the promise, and what he calls in the next verse the making void the covenant of His servant. God cannot lie to David; how is it then that His crown is profaned, that it is cast down to the ground; the land being possessed by strangers, and the twelve tribes in the most disgraceful and oppressive captivity?

40. *Thou hast broken down all his hedges.* Thou hast permitted the land to be stripped of all defense; there is not even one strong place in the hands of Thy people.

41. *All that pass by the way spoil him.* The land is in the condition of a vineyard, the hedge of which is broken down, so that they who pass by may pull the grapes, and dismantle or tear down the vines. The Chaldeans and the Assyrians began the ravage; the Samaritans on the one hand, and the Idumeans on the other, have completed it.

52. *Blessed be the Lord for evermore.* Let Him treat us as He will, His name deserves eternal praises; our affliction, though great, is less than we have deserved.

This verse concludes the Third Book of the Psalter; and, I think, has been added by a later hand, in order to make this distinction, as every Masoretic Bible has something of this kind at the end of each book.

PSALM 90

The eternity of God, 1-2; the frailty of the state of man, 3-9; the general limits of human life, 10; the danger of displeasing God, 11; the necessity of considering the shortness of life, and of regaining the favor of the Almighty, 12; earnest prayer for the restoration of Israel, 13-17.

The title of this psalm is, "A Prayer of Moses the man of God." The Chaldee has, "A prayer which Moses the prophet of the Lord prayed when the people of Israel had sinned in the wilderness." All the versions ascribe it to Moses; but that it could not be of Moses the lawgiver is evident from this consideration, that the age of man was not then seventy or eighty years, which is here stated to be its almost universal limit, for Joshua lived one hundred and ten years, and Moses himself one hundred and twenty. Therefore the psalm cannot at all refer to such ancient times.

3. *Thou turnest man to destruction.* Literally, "Thou shalt turn dying man, *enosh,* to the small dust, but Thou wilt say, Return, ye children of Adam." This appears to be a clear and strong promise of the resurrection of the human body, after it has long slept, mingled with the dust of the earth.

4. *For a thousand years in thy sight.* As if he had said, Though the resurrection of the body may be a thousand (or any indefinite number of) years distant, yet, when these are past, they are *but as yesterday,* or a single *watch in the night.*

5. *Thou carriest them away as with a flood.* On the whole, life is represented as a stream; youth, as morning; old age, as evening; death, as sleep; and the resurrection as the return of the flowers in spring. All these images appear in these curious and striking verses, 3-6.

8. *Thou hast set our iniquities before thee.* Every one of our transgressions is set before Thee, noted down in Thy awful register!

9. *We spend our years as a tale.* "We consume our years like a groan."

10. *Threescore years and ten.* This psalm could not have been written by Moses, because the term of human life was much more extended when he flourished than eighty years at the most.

12. *So teach us to number our days.* Let us deeply consider our own frailty, and the shortness and uncertainty of life, that we may live for eternity, acquaint ourselves with Thee, and be at peace; that we may die in Thy favor, and live and reign with Thee eternally.

13. *Return, O Lord, how long?* Wilt Thou continue angry with us forever? *Let it repent thee.* "Be comforted," rejoice over them to do them good. Be glorified rather in our salvation than in our destruction.

14. *O satisfy us early.* Let us have Thy mercy soon (literally, "in the morning").

15. *Make us glad according to the days.* Let Thy people have as many years of prosperity as they have had of adversity. We have now suffered seventy years of a most distressful captivity.

17. *And let the beauty of the Lord.* Let us have Thy presence, blessing, and approbation, as our fathers had. *Establish thou the work of our hands.* This is supposed, we have already seen, to relate to their rebuilding the Temple, which the surrounding heathens and Samaritans wished to hinder.

PSALM 91

The safety of the godly man, and his confidence, 1-2. How he is defended and preserved, 3-10. The angels of God are his servants, 11-12; and he shall tread on the necks of his adversaries, 13. What God says of, and promises to, such a person, 14-16.

4. *He shall cover thee with his feathers.* He shall act towards thee as the hen does to her brood—take thee under His wings when birds of prey appear, and also shelter thee from chilling blasts. *His truth shall be thy shield and buckler.* His revelation; His Bible. That truth contains promises for all times and circumstances, and these will be invariably fulfilled to him that trusts in the Lord. The fulfillment of a promise relative to defense and support is to the soul what the best shield is to the body.

5. *The terror by night.* The Chaldee translates this verse, "Thou shalt not fear the demons that walk by night; nor the arrow of the angel of death which is shot in the daytime." Thou needest not to fear a sudden and unprovided-for death.

7. *A thousand shall fall at thy side.* It is a promise of perfect protection, and the utmost safety.

11. *He shall give his angels charge over thee.* The angels of God shall have an especial charge to accompany, defend, and preserve thee; and against their power, the influence of evil spirits cannot prevail. *To keep thee in all thy ways.* The path of duty is the way of safety.

12. *They shall bear thee up in their hands.* Take the same care of thee as a nurse does of a weak and tender child; lead thee, teach thee to walk, lift thee up out of the way of danger, *lest thou dash thy foot against a stone,* receive any kind of injury, or be prevented from pursuing thy path with safety and comfort.

13. *Thou shalt tread upon the lion and adder.* Even the king of the forest shall not be able to injure thee. And even the "asp," one of the most venomous of serpents, shall not be able to injure thee.

14. *Because he hath set his love upon me.* Here the Most High is introduced as confirming the word of His servant. He has fixed his love, his heart and soul, on Me. *I will set him on high.* I will place him out of the reach of all his enemies.

15. *He shall call upon me.* He must continue to pray; all his blessings must come in this way. When he calls, I will answer him. *I will be with him in trouble.* Literally, "I am with him." *And honour him.* "I will glorify him."

16. *With long life.* Literally, "With length of days will I fill him up." *And shew him my salvation.* "I will make him see (or contemplate) My salvation."

PSALM 92

The Psalmist shows the duty and advantage of praising God, 1-3; speaks of the grandeur of God's works, 4-6; the fall of the wicked, 7-9; the happiness of the righteous, 10-14; and all this founded on the perfections of God.

The title, "A Psalm or Song for the Sabbath," gives no information concerning the time, occasion, or author.

2. *To shew forth thy lovingkindness. Chasdecha,* Thy abundant mercy, *in the morning*—that has preserved me throughout the night, and brought me to the beginning of a new day; *and thy faithfulness every night,* that has so amply fulfilled the promise of preservation during the course of the day. This verse contains a general plan for morning and evening prayer.

12. *The righteous shall flourish like the palm*

tree. Very different from the wicked, v. 7, who are likened to grass. These shall have a short duration, but those shall have a long and useful life. They are compared also to the cedar of Lebanon, an incorruptible wood, and extremely long-lived.

13. *Those that be planted in the house of the Lord.* I believe the Chaldee has the true meaning here: "His children shall be planted in the house of the sanctuary of the Lord, and shall flourish in the courts of our God."

14. *They shall still bring forth fruit in old age.* They shall continue to grow in grace, and be fruitful to the end of their lives. It is a rare case to find a man in old age full of faith, love, and spiritual activity.

PSALM 93

The universal government of God, 1-2; the opposition to that government, 3-4; the truth of God's testimonies, 5.

1. *The Lord reigneth.* He continues to govern everything He has created; and He is every way qualified to govern all things, for *he is clothed with majesty,* and, *with strength*—dominion is His, and He has supreme power to exercise it; and He has so established the world that nothing can be driven out of order; all is ruled by Him. Nature is His agent, or rather, nature is the sum of the laws of His government; the operations carried on by the divine energy, and the effects resulting from those operations.

3. *The floods have lifted up.* Multitudes of people have confederated against Thy people, and troop succeeds troop as the waves of the sea succeed each other.

4. *The Lord . . . is mightier than the noise of many waters.* Greater in strength than all the peoples and nations that can rise up against Him. *Mighty waves of the sea.* Even the most powerful empires can prevail nothing against Him; therefore those who trust in Him have nothing to fear.

5. *Thy testimonies are very sure.* Thou wilt as surely fulfil Thy word as Thou wilt keep possession of Thy throne. *Holiness becometh thine house.* Thy nature is holy, all Thy works are holy, and Thy word is holy; therefore Thy house—Thy Church—should be holy.

PSALM 94

An appeal to God against oppressors, 1-7. Expostulations with the workers of iniquity, 8-11. God's merciful dealings with His followers, 12-15; and their confidence in Him, 16-19. The punishment of the wicked foretold, 20-23.

1. *O Lord God, to whom vengeance belongeth.* God is the Author of retributive justice, as well as of mercy. What is here referred to is that simple act of justice which gives to all their due.

2. *Lift up thyself.* Exert Thy power. *Render a reward to the proud.* To the Babylonians, who oppress and insult us.

3. *How long shall the wicked triumph?* The wicked are often in prosperity; and this only shows us of how little worth riches are in the sight of God, when He bestows them on the most contemptible of mortals.

5. *They break in pieces thy people.* This was true of the Babylonians. Nebuchadnezzar slew many; carried the rest into captivity; ruined

Jerusalem; overturned the Temple; sacked, pillaged, and destroyed all the country.

6. *They slay the widow.* Nebuchadnezzar carried on his wars with great cruelty.

8. *Understand, ye brutish.* These are the same expressions as in Ps. xcii. 6.

9. *He that planted the ear, shall he not hear?* This is allowed to be an unanswerable mode of argumentation. Whatever is found of excellence in the creature must be derived from the Creator, and exist in Him in the plenitude of infinite excellence.

10. *He that chastiseth the heathen, shall not he correct?* You, who are heathens, and heathens of the most abandoned kind. *He that teacheth man knowledge.* We here supply *shall not he know?* But this is not acknowledged by the original, nor by any of the versions. Indeed it is not necessary; for either the words contain a simple proposition, "It is He who teacheth man knowledge," or this clause should be read in connection with v. 11: "Jehovah, who teacheth man knowledge, knoweth the devices of man, that they are vanity."

12. *Blessed is the man whom thou chastenest.* "Whom thou instructest," *and teachest him out of thy law.* Two points here are worthy of our most serious regard: (1) God gives knowledge to man, gives him understanding and reason. (2) He gives him a revelation of himself; He places before that reason and understanding His divine law.

13. *That thou mayest give him rest.* He whom God instructs is made wise unto salvation; and he who is thus taught has rest in his soul, and peace and confidence in adversity.

15. *But judgment shall return unto righteousness.* If we read *yosheb,* "shall sit," for *yashub,* "shall return," we have the following sense: "Until the just one shall sit in judgment, and after him all the upright in heart." Cyrus has the epithet "the just one" in different places in the Prophet Isaiah. See Isa. xli. 2, 10; xlv. 8; li. 5.

16. *Who will rise up for me?* Who is he that shall be the deliverer of Thy people? Who will come to our assistance against these wicked Babylonians?

17. *Unless the Lord had been my help.* Had not God in a strange manner supported us while under His chastising hand, we had been utterly cut off. *My soul had almost dwelt in silence.* The Vulgate has *in inferno;* the Septuagint, "in the invisible world."

18. *When I said, My foot slippeth.* When I found myself weak and my enemy strong. *Thy mercy, O Lord, held me up.* "Propped me." It is a metaphor taken from anything falling, that is propped, shored up, or buttressed. How often does the mercy of God thus prevent the ruin of weak believers!

PSALM 95

An invitation to praise God, 1-2. The reason on which this is founded, the majesty and dominion of God, 3-5. An invitation to pray to God, 6. And the reasons on which that is founded, 7. Exhortation not to act as their fathers had done, who rebelled against God, and were cast out of His favor, 8-11.

This psalm is also without a title, in both the Hebrew and Chaldee; but is attributed to David by the Vulgate, Septuagint, Aethiopic, Arabic, and Syriac, and by the author of the Epistle to the Hebrews, chap. iv. 3-7. Houbigant, and other learned divines, consider this psalm as composed of three parts: (1) The part of the people, v. 1 to the middle of v. 7. (2) The part of the priest or prophet, from the middle of v. 7 to the end of v. 8. (3) The part of Jehovah, vv. 9-11.

2. *Let us come before his presence.* "His faces," with thanksgiving, "with confession," or "with the confession offering."

3. *For the Lord is a great God.* The Supreme Being has three names here: El, Jehovah, Elohim. The first implies His strength; the second, His being and essence; the third, His covenant relation to mankind. In public worship these are the views we should entertain of the Divine Being.

6. *O come, let us worship.* Three distinct words are used here to express three different acts of adoration: (1) *Let us worship,* let us "prostrate" ourselves, the highest act of adoration by which the supremacy of God is acknowledged. (2) *Let us . . . bow down, nichraah,* let us "crouch down, bending the legs under," as a dog in the presence of his master, which solicitously waits to receive his commands. (3) *Let us kneel,* "let us put our knees to the ground," and thus put ourselves in the posture of those who supplicate.

7. *For he is our God.* Here is the reason for this service. He has condescended to enter into a covenant with us, and He has taken us for His own; therefore *we are the people of his pasture.* Or rather, as the Chaldee, Syriac, Vulgate, and Aethiopic read, "We are his people, and the sheep of the pasture of his hand." We are His own; He feeds and governs us, and His powerful hand protects us.

To day if ye will hear his voice. This should commence the eighth verse, as it begins what is supposed to be the part of the priest or prophet who now exhorts the people; as if he had said: Seeing you are in so good a spirit, do not forget your own resolutions, and harden not your hearts, as your fathers did in Meribah and Massah, in the wilderness. The same fact and the same names as are mentioned in Exod. xvii. 7, when the people murmured at Rephidim, because they had no water; hence it was called *Meribah,* contention or provocation, and *Massah,* temptation.

9. *When your fathers tempted me.* "Tried me," by their insolence, unbelief, and blasphemy. They *proved me*—they had full proof of My power to save and to destroy. There they *saw my work*—they saw that nothing was too hard for God.

10. *Forty years long.* They did nothing but murmur, disbelieve, and rebel, from the time they began their journey at the Red Sea till they passed over Jordan, a period of *forty* years. *They have not known my ways.* The verb *yada,* "to know," is used here, as in many other parts of Scripture, to express approbation. They knew God's ways well enough, but they did not like them, and would not walk in them.

PSALM 96

All the inhabitants of the earth are invited to praise the Lord, 1-3. His supreme majesty, 3-6. The tribes of Israel are invited to glorify Him, 7-9; and to proclaim Him among the heathen, 10. The heavens and the earth are commanded to rejoice in Him, 11-13.

This psalm has no title, in either the Hebrew or Chaldee. We have seen in 1 Chron. xvi. 23-33 a psalm nearly like this, composed by David, on bringing the ark to Sion, from the house of Obed-edom. But the psalm, as it stands in the Chronicles, has thirty verses; and this is only a section of it, from the twenty-third to the thirty-third. It is very likely that this part was taken from the psalm above mentioned, to be used at the dedication of the second Temple. The one hundred and fifth psalm is almost the same as that in Chronicles, but much more extensive.

1. *Sing unto the Lord a new song.* A song of peculiar excellence, for in this sense the term *new* is repeatedly taken in the Scriptures.

2. *Shew forth his salvation from day to day.* The original is very emphatic, "Preach the gospel of His salvation from day to day."

3. *Declare his glory among the heathen.* The heathen do not know the true God; as His being and attributes are at the foundation of all religion, these are the first subjects of instruction for the Gentile world. *Declare,* "detail, number out" *his glory,* His "splendour and excellence." *His wonders among all people.* Declare also to the Jews His wonders, "his miracles."

4. *He is to be feared above all gods.* I think the two clauses of this verse should be read thus: Jehovah is great, and greatly to be praised. Elohim is to be feared above all. I doubt whether the word *Elohim* is ever, by fair construction, applied to false gods or idols. The contracted form in the following verse appears to have this meaning.

5. *All the gods of the nations are idols. Elohey.* All those reputed or worshipped as gods among the heathens are *elilim,* "vanities, emptinesses, things of nought." Instead of being *Elohim,* they are *elilim;* they are not only not God, but they are nothing.

8. *Come into his courts.* Probably referring to the second Temple.

9. *Worship the Lord in the beauty of holiness.* I think *behadrath kodesh* signifies "holy ornaments," such as the high priest wore in his ministrations. These were given him for glory and beauty; and the Psalmist calls on him to put on his sacerdotal garments, to bring his offering, *minchah,* and come into the courts of the Lord, and perform his functions, and make intercession for the people.

11-13. The Psalmist here in the true spirit of poetry gives life and intelligence to universal nature, producing them all as exulting in the reign of the Messiah, and the happiness which should take place in the earth when the gospel should be universally preached.

PSALM 97

The reign of Jehovah, its nature and blessedness, 1-2. He is fearful to the wicked, 3-6. Idolaters shall be destroyed, 7. The blessedness of the righteous, 8-12.

The psalm has no title in either the Hebrew or Chaldee. The author of the Epistle to the Hebrews, chap. i. 6, quotes a part of the seventh verse of this psalm, and applies it to Christ. Who the author was is uncertain; it is much in the spirit of David's finest compositions, and yet many learned men suppose it was written to celebrate the Lord's power and goodness in the restoration of the Jews from the Babylonish captivity.

1. *The Lord reigneth.* Here is a simple proposition, which is a self-evident axiom, and requires no proof. Jehovah is infinite and eternal; is possessed of unlimited power and unerring wisdom, as He is the Maker, so He must be the Governor, of all things. His authority is absolute, and His government therefore universal. In all places, on all occasions, and in all times, Jehovah reigns.

2. *Clouds and darkness are round about him.* There must be *clouds and darkness*—an impenetrable obscurity—round about Him; and we can no more comprehend Him in the eternity that passed before time commenced than we can in the eternity that is to come, when time shall be no more.

Righteousness and judgment are the habitation of his throne. Righteousness, tsedek, the principle that acts according to justice and equity; that gives to all their due, and ever holds in all things an even balance. *And judgment, mishpat,* the principle that discerns, orders, directs, and determines everything according to truth and justice. These form *the habitation of his throne;* that is, His government and management of the world are according to these.

3. *A fire goeth before him. Fire* is generally represented as an accompaniment of the appearances of the Supreme Being. He appeared on Mount Sinai in the midst of fire, thunder, and lightnings, Exod. xix. 16-18. St. Paul tells us (2 Thess. i. 7-8) that "the Lord Jesus shall be revealed from heaven with His mighty angels, in flaming fire"; and St. Peter (2 Epist. iii. 7, 10-11), that when the Lord shall come to judgment the heavens and the earth shall be destroyed by fire.

5. *The Lord of the whole earth. Adon col haarets,* the Director, Stay, and Support of the whole earth.

7. *Confounded be all they.* Rather, "They shall be confounded that boast themselves in idols." *Worship him.* Who? Jesus; so says the apostle, Heb. i. 6. *All ye gods.* "His angels"; so the Septuagint and the apostle: "Let all the angels of God worship him." And the words are most certainly applied to the Saviour of the world by the author of the Epistle to the Hebrews.

8. *Zion heard, and was glad.* All the land of Israel, long desolated, heard of the judgments which God had shown among the enemies of His people. *And the daughters of Judah.* All the villages of the land—Zion as the mother, and all the villages in the country as her *daughters*—rejoice in the deliverance of God's people.

10. *Ye that love the Lord, hate evil.* Because it is inconsistent with His love to you, as well as your love to Him. *He preserveth the souls of his saints.* The *saints, chasidaiv,* "His merciful people"; their *souls,* lives, are precious in his sight. He preserves them; keeps them from every evil, and every enemy.

12. *Rejoice in the Lord, ye righteous.* It is your privilege to be happy. Exult in Him through whom ye have received the atonement. *Rejoice;* but let it be *in the Lord. At the remembrance of his holiness.* But why should you give thanks at the remembrance that God is holy? Because He has said, "Be ye holy; for I am holy"; and in holiness alone true happiness is to be found.

PSALM 98

God is celebrated for His wondrous works, 1-2; for the exact fulfilment of His gracious promises, 3. The manner in which He is to be praised, 4-6. Inanimate creation called to bear a part in this concert, 7-8. The justice of His judgments, 9.

In the Hebrew this is simply termed *mizmor,* "a psalm." The psalm in its subject is very like the ninety-sixth. It was probably written to celebrate the deliverance from the Babylonish captivity, but is to be understood prophetically of the redemption of the world by Jesus Christ.

1. *A new song.* "A song of excellence." Give Him the highest praise. See on Ps. xcvi. 1. *Hath done marvellous things.* "Miracles"; the same word as in Ps. xcvi. 3, where we translate it "wonders." *His holy arm.* His almighty power. *Hath gotten him the victory.* "Hath made salvation to himself."

2. *Made known his salvation.* He has delivered His people in such a way as to show that it was supernatural, and that their confidence in the unseen God was not in vain.

3. *He hath remembered his mercy.* His gracious promises to their forefathers. *And his truth.* Faithfully accomplishing what He had promised. All this was fulfilled under the gospel.

5. *With . . . the voice of a psalm.* I think *zimrah,* which we translate "psalm," means either a musical instrument or a species of ode modulated by different voices.

6. *With trumpets.* Some kind of tubular instruments, of the form and management of which we know nothing. *And sound of cornet. Shophar,* the word commonly used for what we call "trumpet."

7. *Let the sea roar.* These are either fine poetic images or, if we take them as referring to the promulgation of the gospel, by *the sea* all maritime countries and commercial nations may be intended.

8. *Let the floods clap their hands.* Properly "the rivers"—possibly meaning immense continents, where only large rivers are found.

9. *For he cometh to judge the earth.* He comes to make known His salvation, and show His merciful designs to all the children of men. *With righteousness shall he judge the world.* See the notes on Psalm xcvi. There is a very great similarity between this psalm and the Magnificat of the Blessed Virgin.

PSALM 99

The empire of God in the world and the Church, 1-2. He ought to be praised, 3. Justice and judgment are His chief glory, 4. He should be worshipped as among the saints of old, whom He graciously answered and saved, 5-8. Exalt Him because He is holy, 9.

The Hebrew and Chaldee have no title; all the versions but the Chaldee attribute it to David.

1. *The Lord reigneth.* See the note on Ps. xcvii. 1. *Let the people tremble.* He will establish His kingdom in spite of His enemies; let those who oppose Him tremble for the consequences. *He sitteth between the cherubims.*

This is in reference to the ark, at each end of which was a cherub of glory; and the Shechinah, or symbol of the Divine Presence, appeared on the lid of the ark, called also the "mercy seat," between the cherubim. Sitting between the cherubim implies God's graciousness and mercy.

2. *The Lord is great in Zion.* It is among His own worshippers that He has manifested His power and glory in an especial manner. There He is known, and there He is worthily magnified.

3. *Let them praise thy great and terrible name.* Let them confess Thee to be great and terrible; let them tremble before Thee. *For it is holy. Kadosh hu.* As this not only ends this verse but the fifth also, and in effect the ninth, it seems to be a species of chorus which was sung in a very solemn manner at the conclusion of each of these parts. His holiness—reason why He should be exalted, praised, and worshipped.

4. *The king's strength.* If this psalm were written by David, he must mean by it that he was God's vicegerent or deputy, and that, even as king, God was his Strength, and the Pattern according to which equity, judgment, and righteousness should be executed in Jacob.

5. *Worship at his footstool.* Probably meaning the ark on which the divine glory was manifested. Sometimes the earth is called God's footstool, Matt. v. 35; Isa. lxvi. 1; sometimes Jerusalem; sometimes the Temple, Lam. ii. 1; sometimes the Tabernacle, Ps. xxxii. 7; and sometimes the ark, 1 Chron. xxviii. 2.

7. *He spake unto them in the cloudy pillar.* That is, He directed all their operations, marchings, and encampments by this cloudy pillar. See Exod. xxxiii. 9.

8. *Thou . . . forgavest them.* When the people had sinned, and wrath was about to descend on them, and Moses and Aaron interceded for them, and they were not destroyed. *Tookest vengeance of their inventions.* God spared them, but showed his displeasure at their misdoings. He chastised, but did not consume them. This is amply proved in the history of this people.

9. *Worship at his holy hill.* Worship Him publicly in the Temple.

PSALM 100

All nations are exhorted to praise the Lord, 1-2; to acknowledge Him to be the sovereign God and the Creator, and that they are His people and the flock of His pasture, 3; to worship Him publicly, and be grateful for His mercies, 4. The reasons on which this is founded: His own goodness, His everlasting mercy, and His ever-during truth, 5.

This psalm is entitled in the Hebrew *mizmor lethodah*, not "A Psalm of praise," as we have it, but "A Psalm for the confession, or for the confession offering," very properly translated by the Chaldee: "Praise for the sacrifice (or offering) of confession." The Vulgate, Septuagint, and Aethiopic have followed this sense.

1. *Make a joyful noise. Hariu,* "exult, triumph, leap for joy." *All ye lands.* Not only Jews, but Gentiles, for the Lord bestows His benefits on all with a liberal hand.

2. *Serve the Lord with gladness.* It is your privilege and duty to be happy in your religious worship. The religion of the true God is intended to remove human misery, and to make mankind happy. He whom the religion of Christ

has not made happy does not understand that religion, or does not make a proper use of it.

3. *Know ye that the Lord he is God.* Acknowledge in every possible way, in both public and private, that Jehovah, the uncreated, self-existent, and eternal Being, is *Elohim,* the God who is in covenant with man, to instruct, redeem, love, and make him finally happy. *It is he that hath made us.* He is our Creator and has consequently the only right in and over us. *And not we ourselves.* I can never think that this is the true reading, though found in the present Hebrew text, in the Vulgate, Septuagint, Aethiopic, and Syriac. In twenty-six of Kennicott's and De Rossi's MSS. we have "and his we are." This is the reading of the Targum, or Chaldee paraphrase, "and his we are," and is the reading of the text in the Complutensian Polyglot, of both the Psalters which were printed in 1477, and is the *keri,* or marginal reading in most Masoretic Bibles. Every person must see, from the nature of the subject, that it is the genuine reading.

4. *Enter into his gates with thanksgiving.* Publicly worship God; and when ye come to the house of prayer, be thankful that you have such a privilege; and when you *enter his courts,* praise Him for the permission. The word which we render *with thanksgiving* is properly "with the confession offering or sacrifice."

5. *For the Lord is good.* Goodness, the perfect, eternal opposition to all badness and evil, is essential to God. Mercy and compassion are modifications of His goodness; and as His nature is eternal, so His mercy, springing from His goodness, must be everlasting. And as truth is an essential characteristic of an infinitely intelligent and perfect nature, therefore God's truth must endure from generation to generation. Whatsoever He has promised must be fulfilled, through all the successive generations of men, as long as sun and moon shall last.

PSALM 101

The subject proposed, mercy and judgment, 1. The Psalmist's resolution in respect to his private conduct, 2. He will put away evil, inward and outward, 3. No evil person shall stand in his presence, 4; nor any slanderer of his neighbor, 4-5. He will encourage the faithful and upright, 6; but the deceitful, the liars, and the profligate, he will cast out of the city of God, 7-8.

The Hebrew and all the versions attribute this psalm to David. It shows us the resolutions he formed when he came to the throne, and it is a perfect model according to which a wise prince should regulate his conduct and his government.

1. *I will sing of mercy and judgment.* David might say, Adverse and prosperous providences have been of the utmost use to my soul; therefore I will thank God for both. Or, as he was probably now called to the government of all the tribes, he might make a resolution that he would show *chesed,* incessant benevolence, to the upright; and *mishpat,* the execution of judgment, to the wicked; and would make the conduct of God the model of his own.

2. *I will behave myself wisely.* God's law prescribes a perfect way of life; in this perfect way I have professed to walk, and I must act wisely in order to walk in it. *When wilt thou come unto me?* I can neither walk in this way nor grow wise unto salvation unless Thou come

unto me by Thy grace and Spirit. *I will walk within my house.* It is easier for most men to walk with a perfect heart in the church, or even in the world, than in their own families. How many are as meek as lambs among others, when at home they are wasps or tigers! The man who, in the midst of family provocations, maintains a Christian character, being meek, gentle, and long-suffering to his wife, his children, and his servants, has got a perfect heart, and adorns the doctrine of God his Saviour in all things. The original is very emphatic: "I will set myself to walk"; I will make it a determined point thus to walk.

4. *A froward heart.* Rash and headstrong men shall not be employed by me. *I will not know a wicked person.* I will give no countenance to sinners of any kind, and whatever is *evil* shall be an object of my abhorrence.

5. *Whoso privily slandereth his neighbour.* The Chaldee gives a remarkable meaning to the Hebrew, "He who speaks with the triple tongue against his neighbour." That is, the tongue by which he slays three persons, viz., (1) The man whom he slanders; (2) Him to whom he communicates the slander; and, (3) Himself, the slanderer. Every slanderer has his triple tongue, and by every slander inflicts those three deadly wounds. Such a person deserves to be *cut off.*

6. *Mine eyes.* My approbation. *Upon the faithful.* The humble, upright followers of God. *That they may dwell with me.* Be my confidants and privy counsellors.

PSALM 102

The complaint and miserable state of the poor captives, 1-11; the expectation of deliverance, 12-14; the conversion of the heathen, 15-18; the termination of the Captivity, 19-22; the great frailty of man, 23-24; the unchangeableness of God, 25-27; the permanence of the Church, 28.

The Hebrew, and nearly all the versions, give the following title to this psalm: "A prayer of the afflicted, when he is overwhelmed, and pours out his sighing before the Lord." There seems to be little doubt that this is the prayer of the captives in Babylon when, towards the end of the Captivity, they were almost worn out with oppression, cruelty, and distress. The author of the Epistle to the Hebrews has applied the twenty-fifth, twenty-sixth, and twenty-seventh verses to our Lord, and the perpetuity of His kingdom.

1. *Hear my prayer.* The chief parts of the psalm answer well to the title; it is the language of the deepest distress, and well directed to Him from whom alone help can come.

3. *My days are consumed like smoke.* He represents himself (for the Psalmist speaks in the name of the people) under the notion of a pile of combustible matter, placed upon a fire, which soon consumes it, part flying away in smoke, and the residue lying on the hearth in the form of charred coal and ashes. The Chaldeans were the fire, and the captive Jews the fuel, thus converted into smoke and ashes.

4. *My heart is smitten, and withered like grass.* The metaphor here is taken from grass cut down in the meadow. It is first *smitten* with the scythe, and then *withered* by the sun.

6. *I am like a pelican of the wilderness.* It may be the pelican or the bittern. The original, *kaath,*

is mentioned in Lev. xi. 18, and is there described.

8. *They that are mad against me are sworn against me.* The Chaldeans are determined to destroy us, and they have bound themselves by oath to do it.

11. *My days are like a shadow that declineth.* Or rather, "My days decline like the shadow."

13. *Thou shalt arise, and have mercy upon Zion.* While he is humbled at the footstool of mercy, and earnestly praying for mercy, an answer of peace is given. He is assured, not only that they shall be delivered, but that the time of deliverance is at hand. The *set time*—the seventy years predicted by Jeremiah—was ended, and God gave him to see that He was ever mindful of His promises.

14. *Thy servants take pleasure in her stones.* Though Jerusalem was at this time in a heap of ruins, yet even her rubbish was sacred in the eyes of the pious, for this had been the city of the great King.

17. *The prayer of the destitute.* Haarar of him who is laid in utter ruin, who is entirely wasted.

18. *The people which shall be created.* "The Gentiles, who shall be brought to the knowledge of salvation by Christ," as the Syriac states in its inscription of this psalm.

19. *For he hath looked down.* This, with the three following verses, seems to me to contain a glorious prophecy of the incarnation of Christ, and the gathering in of the Jews and the Gentiles to Him.

24. *I said, O my God.* This and the following verses seem to be the form of prayer which the captives used previously to their deliverance. *Thy years are throughout all generations.* This was a frequent argument used to induce God to hear prayer. We are frail and perishing; Thou art everlasting; deliver us, and we will glorify Thee.

27. *But thou art the same.* "But thou art He," that is, the Eternal. *Thy years shall have no end.* "They shall not be completed."

28. *The children of thy servants shall continue.* Thy Church shall be permanent, because founded on Thee; it shall live throughout all the revolutions of time.

PSALM 103

God is praised for His benefits to His people, 1-2; He forgives their iniquities, and heals their diseases, 3; redeems their lives, crowns them with loving-kindness, 4; satisfies them with good things, renews their youth, 5. He helps the oppressed, makes His ways known, is merciful and gracious, and keeps not His anger forever, 6-9; His forbearance, and pardoning mercy, 10-12. He is a tender and considerate Father, 13-14. The frail state of man, 15-16; God's everlasting mercy, and universal dominion, 17-19. All His angels, His hosts, and His works are invited to praise Him, 20-22.

The inscription in the Hebrew, and in all the versions, gives this psalm to David; and yet many of the ancients believed it to refer to the times of the Captivity, or rather to its conclusion, in which the redeemed Jews give thanks to God for their restoration.

3. *Who forgiveth.* The benefits are the following, (1) Forgiveness of sin. (2) Restoration of health: *Who healeth all thy diseases.*

4. *Who redeemeth.* (3) Preservation from destruction. *Haggoel,* properly, redemption of life

by the kinsman; possibly looking forward, in the spirit of prophecy, to Him who became Partaker of our flesh and blood, that He might have the right to redeem our souls from death by dying in our stead. (4) Changing and ennobling his state; weaving a crown for him out of *loving-kindness and tender mercies.*

5. *Who satisfieth thy mouth.* (5) For continual communications of spiritual and temporal good, so that the vigor of his mind was constantly supported and increased. *Thy youth is renewed like the eagle's.* He refers to the molting of birds, which, in most, takes place annually, in which they cast their old feathers and get a new plumage.

12. *As far as the east is from the west.* As the east and the west can never meet in one point, but be forever at the same distance from each other, so our sins and their decreed punishment are removed to an eternal distance by His mercy.

13. *Like as a father pitieth his children.* This is a very emphatic verse, and may be thus translated: "As the tender compassions of a father towards his children, so the tender compassions of Jehovah towards them that fear Him."

14. *For he knoweth our frame.* "Our formation"; the manner in which we are constructed, and the materials of which we are made.

15. *His days are as grass.* See the note on Ps. xc. 5.

17. *The mercy of the Lord is from everlasting to everlasting.* Chesed signifies more particularly the "exuberant goodness of God." This is an attribute of His nature, and must be from everlasting to everlasting; and hence His righteousness (*tsidketh*), His merciful mode of justifying the ungodly, is extended from one generation to another.

PSALM 104

The majesty and power of God manifested in the creation of the heavens and the atmosphere, 1-3; of the earth and sea, 4-9; of the springs, fountains, and rivers, 10-13; of vegetables and trees, 14-18; of the sun and moon, 19; of day and night, and their uses, 20-23; of the riches of the earth, 24; of the sea, its inhabitants, and its uses, 25-26; of God's general providence in providing food for all kinds of animals, 27-31; of earthquakes and volcanoes, 32. God is praised for His majesty, and the instruction which His works afford, 33-34. Sinners shall be destroyed, 35.

This psalm has no title in either the Hebrew or Chaldee. It is properly a poem on the works of God in the creation and government of the world; and some have considered it a sort of epitome of the history of the creation, as given in the Book of Genesis.

2. *Who coverest thyself with light.* Light, insufferable splendor, is the robe of the Divine Majesty. Light and fire are generally the accompaniments of the Supreme Being, when He manifests His presence to His creatures.

7. *At thy rebuke they fled.* When God separated the waters which were above the firmament from those below, and caused the dry land to appear. He commanded the separation to take place; and the waters, as if instinct with life, hastened to obey.

13. *From his chambers.* The clouds, as in v. 3.

17. *Where the birds make their nests.* Tsipporim signifies swallows, sparrows, and small birds in general; here opposed to the *chasidah* or *stork.* Perhaps the heron may be understood,

which is said to be the first of all birds to build her nest, and she builds it on the very highest trees. The general meaning is that God has provided shelter and support for the greatest and smallest birds; they are all objects of His providential regard.

25. *This great and wide sea.* The original is very emphatic: "This very sea, great and extensive of hands." Its waters, like arms, encompassing all the terrene parts of the globe. I suppose the Psalmist was within sight of the Mediterranean when he wrote these words.

26. *There go the ships.* He appears at this time to have seen the ships under sail. *That leviathan.* This may mean the whale, or any of the large marine animals.

30. *Thou sendest forth thy spirit, they are created.* "They are created again."

33. *I will sing unto the Lord.* I will sing unto the Lord "with my lives," the life that I now have and the life that I shall have hereafter. *I will sing praise to my God.* "In my eternity"; my going on, my endless progression.

PSALM 105

An exhortation to praise God for His wondrous works, 1-5; His goodness to Abraham, Isaac, and Jacob, 6-16; to Joseph in Egypt, 17-22; to Israel in Egypt, 23-25; to Moses in the same land, 26; the plagues sent on the Egyptians, 27-36; the deliverance of the Israelites out of Egypt, 37-38; how He supported them in the wilderness, 39-43; and brought them into Canaan, 44-45.

We find several verses of this psalm in 1 Chronicles xvi, from which it is evident that David was the author of the principal part of it; but it was probably enlarged and sung at the restoration of the people from the Babylonish captivity.

2. *Talk ye of all his wondrous works.* "Of his miracles." Who have so many of these to boast of as Christians! Christianity is a tissue of miracles, and every part of the work of grace on the soul is a miracle.

7. *He is the Lord our God.* He is *Jehovah,* the self-existent and eternal God. He is *our God,* He is our Portion; has taken us for His people, and makes us happy in His love.

The following abstract of the history of the Israelites presents but few difficulties. See the notes on Psalm lxxviii.

19. *Until the time that his word came.* This appears to refer to the completion of Joseph's interpretation of the dreams of the chief butler and baker. *The word of the Lord tried him.* This seems to refer to the interpretation of Pharaoh's dreams, called *imrath Yehovah,* "the oracle of the Lord," because sent by Him to Pharaoh.

25. *He turned their heart.* "Their heart was turned." So the Syriac and Arabic.

27. *They shewed his signs.* Here is a reference to the plagues with which God afflicted the Egyptians.

28. *They rebelled not against his word.* Instead of *velo maru,* "They rebelled," some think that it should be read *velo shamru,* "They did not observe or keep His word." Or the words may be spoken of Moses and Aaron; they received the commandment of God, and they did not rebel against it. It could not be spoken of the Egyptians, for they rebelled against His words through the whole course of the transactions.

33. He smote their vines also and their fig trees. This is not mentioned in Exodus; but we have had it before, Ps. lxxviii. 47.

41. He opened the rock, and the waters gushed out. See Exod. xvii. 6.

PSALM 106

God is praised for His manifold mercies, 1-3. The prophet prays for himself, 4-5. A recapitulation of the history of the Hebrew people: of God's mercies toward them, and their rebellions, 6-39. The judgments and afflictions which their transgressions brought upon them, 40-42. God's mercy to them notwithstanding their transgressions, 43-46. He prays for their restoration, 47-48.

As a part of the preceding psalm is found in 1 Chronicles xvi, so the first and last two verses of this are found in the same place (vv. 34-36); and yet it is supposed by eminent commentators to be a prayer of the captives in Babylon, who acknowledge the mercies of God, confess their own sins and those of their forefathers, and implore the Lord to gather them from among the heathen, and restore them to their own country.

6. We have sinned. Here the confession begins; what preceded was only the introduction to what follows: Our forefathers sinned, and suffered; we, like them, have sinned, and do suffer.

7. Our fathers understood not. They did not regard the operation of God's hands, and therefore they understood neither His designs nor their own interest. *At the sea, even at the Red sea.* They provoked, (al yam) at the sea; beyam suph, "in the sea Suph," or Red Sea. They provoked Him at it and in it.

8. He saved them for his name's sake. "On account of His name"; to manifest His own power, goodness, and perfections.

10. The hand of him that hated them. Pharaoh.

12. Then believed they. Just while the miracle was before their eyes.

13. They soon forgat his works. Three days afterwards, at the waters of Marah, Exod. xv. 24. *They waited not for his counsel.* They were impatient, and would not wait till God should in His own way fulfill His own designs.

16. They envied Moses. A reference to the case of Korah and his company. *Aaron the saint.* The anointed, the high priest of the Lord.

20. Thus they changed their glory. That is, their God, who was their Glory; and they worshipped an ox in His stead. See the use St. Paul makes of this, Rom. i. 23.

22. Wondrous works in the land of Ham. Egypt is called *the land of Ham* or Cham, because it was peopled by Misraim, the son of Cham.

28. Ate the sacrifices of the dead. Methim, of "dead men." Most of the heathen idols were men who had been deified after their death.

33. They provoked his spirit. Himru, from *marah,* "to rebel." They brought it into a rebellious state; he was soured and irritated, and was off his guard. *So that he spake unadvisedly with his lips.* For this sentence we have only these two words in the Hebrew, *vayebatte bisephathaiv,* "He stuttered or stammered with his lips," indicating that he was transported with anger. See Num. xx. 10-12.

36. They served their idols. Atsabbeyhem,

their "labors" or "griefs"—idols, so called because of the pains taken in forming them, the labor in worshipping them, and the grief occasioned by the divine judgments against the people for their idolatry.

37. They sacrificed their sons and their daughters unto devils. "To demons." Devil is never in Scripture used in the plural; there is but one devil, though there are many demons.

43. Many times did he deliver them. See the Book of Judges; it is a history of the rebellions and deliverances of the Israelites.

46. He made them also to be pitied. This was particularly true as to the Babylonish captivity. For Cyrus gave them their liberty; Darius favored them, and granted them several privileges; and Artaxerxes sent back Nehemiah, and helped him to rebuild Jerusalem and the Temple. See the Books of Ezra and Nehemiah.

48. Blessed be the Lord God of Israel. Here both gratitude and confidence are expressed; gratitude for what God had already wrought, and confidence that He would finish the great work of their restoration. *From everlasting to everlasting.* "From the hidden term to the hidden term," from the beginning of time to the end of time, from eternity and on to eternity.

This is the end of the fourth book of the Psalms.

PSALM 107

A thanksgiving of the people for deliverance from difficulties and dangers; their state compared to a journey through a frightful wilderness, 1-9; to confinement in a dreary dungeon, 10-16; to a dangerous malady, 17-22; to a tempest at sea, 23-32. The Psalmist calls on men to praise God for the merciful dispensations of His providence, in giving rain and fruitful seasons, after affliction by drought and famine, 33-38; for supporting the poor in affliction, and bringing down the oppressors, 39-41. The use which the righteous should make of these providences, 42; and the advantage to be derived from a due consideration of God's merciful providence, 43.

This psalm has no title, either in the Hebrew or in any of the versions. The author is unknown; but it was probably like Psalms cv and cvi, made and sung at the dedication of the second Temple. The three psalms seem to be on the same subject. In them the author has comprised the marvellous acts of the Lord towards his people; the transgressions of this people against God; the captivities and miseries they endured in consequence; and finally God's merciful kindness to them in their restoration from captivity, and reestablishment in their own land. This psalm seems to have been sung in parts: the 8th, 15th, 21st, and 31st verses, with the 6th, 13th, 19th, and 28th, forming what may be called the burden of the song, in singing of which the whole chorus joined.

4. They wandered in the wilderness. Here begins the first comparison: the Israelites in captivity are compared to a traveller in a dreary, uninhabited, and barren desert, spent with hunger and thirst, as well as by the fatigues of the journey, v. 5.

8. Oh that men would praise the Lord! This is the burden of each part of this responsive song; see the introduction.

9. For he satisfieth the longing soul. "The soul that pushes forward in eager desire" after salvation.

10. Such as sit in darkness. Here begins the second similitude, which he uses to illustrate the state of the captives in Babylon, viz., that of a prisoner in a dreary dungeon.

13. *Then they cried unto the Lord in their trouble.* This was the salutary effect which their afflictions produced; they began to cry to God for mercy and help.

15. *Oh that men!* This is the burden of the second part, as it was of the first. See v. 8.

16. *For he hath broken.* This is the reason given for thanks to God for His deliverance of the captives. It was not a simple deliverance; it was done so as to manifest the irresistible power of God. He tore the prison in pieces, and *cut the bars of iron* asunder.

17. *Fools because of their transgression.* This is the third comparison, the Captivity being compared to a person in a dangerous malady. Our version does not express this clause well: "Fools, because of the way of their transgressions, are afflicted."

18. *Their soul abhorreth all manner of meat.* A natural description of a sick man; appetite is gone, and all desire for food fails. See a similar image, Job xxxiii. 20.

19. *Then they cry.* The effect produced by affliction as before.

21. *Oh that men!* The intercalary verse, or burden, as before.

22. *And let them sacrifice.* For their healing they should bring a sacrifice; and they should offer the life of the innocent animal unto God, as He has spared their lives; and let them thus confess that God has spared them when they deserved to die; and let them declare also *his works with rejoicing;* for who will not rejoice when he is delivered from death?

23. *They that go down to the sea in ships.* This is the fourth comparison. Their captivity was as dangerous and alarming as a dreadful tempest at sea to a weather-beaten mariner.

26. *They mount up to the heaven.* This is a most natural and striking description of the state of a ship at sea in a storm: when the sea appears to run mountains high, and the vessel seems for a moment to stand on the sharp ridge of one most stupendous, with a valley of a frightful depth between it and a similar mountain, which appears to be flying in the midst of heaven, that it may submerge the hapless bark, when she descends into the valley of death below. *Their soul is melted because of trouble.* This is not less expressive than it is descriptive. The action of raising the vessel to the clouds, and precipitating her into the abyss, seems to dissolve the very soul. The whole mind seems to melt away, so that neither feeling, reflection, nor impression remains, nothing but the apprehension of inevitable destruction! When the ship is buffeted between conflicting waves, which threaten either to tear her asunder or crush her together; when she reels to and fro, and staggers like a drunken man, not being able to hold any certain course, then indeed are they *at their wit's end;* or, as the inimitable original expresses it, "and all their skill is swallowed up"—seems to be gulped down by the frightful abyss into which the ship is about to be precipitated.

31. *Oh that men!* The intercalary verse, or burden, as before. See v. 8.

PSALM 108

The Psalmist encourages himself to praise the Lord for mercies he had received, 1-5. He prays for the divine succor, 6; and encourages the people to expect their restoration, and the enjoyment of all their former privileges and possessions, 7-13.

This psalm is compounded of two psalms which we have had already under review. Verses 1-5 are the same with the vv. 7-11 of Psalm lvii. And vv. 6-13 are the same with vv. 5-12 of Psalm lx. That the psalms referred to were made by David, and were applicable to the then state of his affairs, has been the opinion of many; and it is probable that the captives in Babylon composed this out of two above, and applied it to the state of their affairs. Their captivity being now ended, or nearly at an end, they look and pray for their restoration to their own land, as amply as it was possessed in the most prosperous days of David.

3. *Among the people.* The Jews. *Among the nations.* The Gentiles. Wherever this psalm is sung or read, among either Jews or Gentiles, David may be said to sing praise to God.

PSALM 109

The Psalmist speaks against his inveterate enemies, 1-5. He prays against them, and denounces God's judgments, 6-15. The reason on which this is grounded, 16-20. He prays for his own safety and salvation, using many arguments to induce God to have mercy upon him, 21-31.

The title of this psalm, "To the chief Musician, A Psalm of David," has already often occurred, and on it the versions offer nothing new. The Syriac says it is "a Psalm of David, when the people, without his knowledge, made *Absalom* king; on which account he was slain: but to us (Christians) he details the passion of Christ." That it contains a prophecy against *Judas* and the enemies of our Lord is evident from Acts i. 20. Probably, in its primary meaning (for such a meaning it certainly has), it may refer to *Ahithophel.* The execrations in it should be rendered in the *future* tense, as they are mere prophetic denunciations of God's displeasure against sinners. Taken in this light, it cannot be a stumbling block to any person. God has a right to denounce those judgments which He will inflict on the workers of iniquity. But perhaps the whole may be the execrations of *David's* enemies against himself. See on v. 20. *Ahithophel,* who gave evil counsel against *David,* and being frustrated hanged himself, was no mean prototype of *Judas,* the traitor; it was probably on this account that St. *Peter,* Acts i. 20, applied it to the case of *Judas,* as a prophetic declaration concerning him, or at least a subject that might be accommodated to his case.

1. *Hold not thy peace.* Be not silent; arise and defend my cause.

4. *But I give myself unto prayer.* "And I prayer." The Chaldee: "but I pray."

6. *Let Satan stand at his right hand.* As the word *satan* means an "adversary" simply, though sometimes it is used to express the evil spirit *Satan,* I think it best to preserve here its grammatical meaning: "Let an adversary stand at his right hand"; i.e., Let him be opposed and thwarted in all his purposes.

7. *Let him be condemned.* "Let him come out a wicked man"; that is, let his wickedness be made manifest. *Let his prayer become sin.* I

once more apprise the reader that if these are not the words of David's enemies against himself (see on v. 20) they are prophetic denunciations against a rebellious and apostate person or people, hardened in crime, and refusing to return to God.

8. *Let another take his office.* The original literally means "superintendence, oversight, inspection from actual visitations."

20. *Let this be the reward of mine adversaries from the Lord, and of them that speak evil against my soul.* Is not this verse a key to all that preceded it? The original, fairly interpreted, will lead us to a somewhat different meaning: "This is the work of my adversaries before the Lord, and of those who speak evil against my soul," or "life." That is, all that is said from the sixth to the twentieth verse consists of the evil words and imprecations of my enemies against my soul, laboring to set the Lord, by imprecations, against me, that their curses may take effect. This, which is a reasonable interpretation, frees the whole psalm from every difficulty. Surely the curses contained in it are more like those which proceed from the mouth of the wicked than from one inspired by the Spirit of the living God. Taking the words in this sense, which I am persuaded is the best, and which the original will well bear and several of the versions countenance, then our translation may stand just as it is; only let the reader remember that at the sixth verse David begins to tell how his enemies cursed him, while he prayed for them.

21. *But do thou for me.* While they use horrible imprecations against me, and load me with their curses, act Thou for me, and deliver me from their maledictions. While they curse, do Thou bless. This verse is a further proof of the correctness of the interpretation given above.

22. *I am poor and needy.* I am afflicted and impoverished; and my heart is wounded—my very life is sinking through distress.

23. *I am gone like the shadow.* "I have walked like the declining shadow"—I have passed my meridian of health and life; and as the sun is going below the horizon, so am I about to go under the earth. *I am tossed up and down as the locust.* When swarms of locusts take wing, and infest the countries in the East, if the wind happen to blow briskly, the swarms are agitated and driven upon each other, so as to appear to be heaved to and fro, or tossed up and down.

25. *When they looked upon me they shaked their heads.* Thus was David treated by Shimei, 2 Sam. xvi. 5-6, and our blessed Lord by the Jews, Matt. xxvii. 39.

28. *Let them curse, but bless thou.* See on v. 20. Of the mode of interpretation recommended there, this verse gives additional proof.

PSALM 110

The Messiah sits in His kingdom at the right hand of God. His enemies being subdued under Him, 1-2. The nature and extent of His government, 3. His everlasting priesthood, 4. His execution of justice and judgment, 5-6. The reason on which all this is founded, His passion and exaltation, 7.

The Hebrew, and all the versions except the Arabic, attribute this psalm to David; nor can this be doubted, as it is thus attributed in the New Testament. We have in it the celebration of some great potentate's accession to the crown; but the subject is so grand, the expressions so noble, and the object raised so far above what can be called human, that no history has ev mentioned a prince to whom a literal application of this psalm can be made. To Jesus Christ alone, to His everlasting priesthood and government, as King of Kings and Lord of Lords, can it be applied.

1. *The Lord said unto my Lord.* Jehovah said unto my *Adoni.* That David's Lord is the Messiah is confirmed by our Lord himself and by the apostles Peter and Paul. *Sit thou at my right hand.* This implies the possession of the utmost confidence, power, and preeminence. *Until I make thine enemies.* Jesus shall reign till all His enemies are subdued under Him.

2. *The rod of thy strength.* The gospel—the doctrine of Christ crucified.

3. *Thy people shall be willing in the day of thy power.* This verse has been woefully perverted. It has been supposed to point out the irresistible operation of the grace of God on the souls of the elect, thereby making them willing to receive Christ as their Saviour. Now whether this doctrine be true or false, it is not in this text, nor can it receive the smallest countenance from it. There has been much spoken against the doctrine of what is called "free will" by persons who seem not to have understood the term. "Will" is a free principle. "Free will" is as absurd as "bound will"; it is not "will" if it be not free. Volition is essential to the being of the soul, and to all rational and intellectual beings. This is the most essential discrimination between matter and spirit. Let us examine the text. The Hebrew words literally translated are, "Thy princely people, or free people, in the day of thy power." It merely expresses the character of the people who shall constitute the kingdom of Christ. *Am nedaboth* is the people of liberality—the princely, noble, and generous people.

In the beauties of holiness. "In the splendid garments of holiness." An allusion to the beautiful garments of the high priest. *From the womb of the morning.* As the dew flows from the womb of the morning, so shall all the godly from Thee. They are *the dew of thy youth;* they are the offspring of Thy own nativity. As the human nature of our Lord was begotten by the creative energy of God in the womb of the Virgin, so the followers of God are "born, not of blood, nor of the will of the flesh," but by the Divine Spirit.

4. *The Lord hath sworn.* Has most firmly purposed, and will most certainly perform it. *And will not repent.* Will never change this purpose. *After the order of Melchizedek.* For the elucidation of this point the reader is requested to refer to Gen. xiv. 18-19.

6. *He shall judge among the heathen.* David shall greatly extend his dominion, and rule over the Idumeans, Moabites, Philistines, etc. *He shall fill . . . with the dead bodies.* He shall fill pits—make heaps of slain; there shall be an immense slaughter among his enemies.

PSALM 111

The Psalmist praises the Lord, and extols His works as great, honorable, glorious, and magnificent, 1-4; His providence and kindness to His followers, 5-8; the redemption He has granted to His people, 9. "The fear of the Lord is the beginning of wisdom," 10.

This is one of the alphabetical or acrostic psalms; but it is rather different from those we have already seen, as the first eight verses each contain two members, and each member commences with a consecutive letter of the Hebrew alphabet. But the last two verses are composed of three members each, characterized the same way, making twenty-two members or hemistichs in the whole, to each of which a consecutive letter of the alphabet is prefixed.

1. *I will praise the Lord with my whole heart.* If we profess to "sing to the praise and glory of God," the heart, and the *whole heart,* without division and distraction, must be employed in the work. *In the assembly. Besod,* in the "secret assembly"—the private religious meetings for the communion of saints. *And in the congregation, edah,* the "general assembly"—the public congregation.

2. *The works of the Lord are great. Gedolim,* "vast in magnitude."

5. *He hath given meat. Tereph,* "prey." This may allude to the quails in the wilderness.

6. *The power of his works.* They have seen that these things did not arrive in the common course of nature; it was "not by might, nor by power," but by the Spirit of the Lord of hosts they were done. And it required a display of the power of God to give them the heritage of the heathen.

8. *They stand fast for ever.* "They are propped up, buttressed, for ever." They can never fail; for God's power supports His works, and His providence preserves the record of what He has done.

9. *He sent redemption.* He sent Moses to redeem them out of Egypt; various judges to deliver them out of the hands of their oppressors; Ezra, Nehemiah, and Zerubbabel to deliver them from Babylon; and the Lord Jesus to redeem a whole lost world from sin, misery, and death. *Holy and reverend is his name.* The word *reverend* comes to us from the Latin *reverendus* and is compounded of *re,* intensive, and *vereor,* "to be feared." But *reverend* is not applied to God in this way; nor does the word *nora* bear this signification. It rather means "terrible": "Holy and terrible," or, "Holy and tremendous is his name." This title belongs not to man; nor does any minister, in assuming the title reverend, assume this.

10. *The fear of the Lord is the beginning of wisdom.* The original stands thus: "The beginning of wisdom is the fear of Jehovah." Wisdom itself begins with this fear. A *good understanding have all they that do his commandments.* These last words we add as necessary to make up the sense; but there is no need of this expedient, as the words of the original literally read thus: "The beginning of wisdom is the fear of Jehovah; good discernment to the doers."

PSALM 112

The blessedness of the man that fears the Lord, as it regards both himself and his family, 1-3; his conduct to his family, his neighbors, and the poor, 4-9; the envy of the wicked at his prosperity, 10.

This is another of the acrostic or alphabetical psalms, under the title *Hallelujah.* It is formed exactly as the preceding in the division of its verses. It has ten verses in the whole. The first

eight each contain two hemistichs, beginning with a consecutive letter of the alphabet; the ninth and tenth verses, three each, making twenty-two in the whole. It is understood to have been written after the Captivity, and probably by Zechariah and Haggai; to them it is ascribed by the Vulgate.

1. *Blessed is the man that feareth the Lord.* This seems to be the continuation of the preceding psalm. There it was asserted that the beginning of wisdom was the fear of the Lord, and here the blessedness of the man who thus fears is stated. *That delighteth greatly.* It is not enough to fear God; we must also love Him. Fear will deter us from evil; love will lead us to obedience. And the more a man fears and loves God, the more obedient will he be, till at last he will delight greatly in the commandments of his Maker.

2. *His seed shall be mighty.* His "posterity." So the word should always be understood in this connection.

3. *Wealth and riches shall be in his house.* This is often the case; a godly man must save both time and money. Before he was converted he lost much time, and squandered his money.

8. *His heart is established.* "His heart is propped up"; he is buttressed up by the strength of his Maker.

9. *He hath dispersed.* He has scattered abroad his munificence; he has given particularly *to the poor; his righteousness*—his almsgiving, his charity—*remaineth for ever.* See v. 3. *His horn* —his power and authority—*shall be exalted with honour.* He shall rise to influence only through his own worth, and not by extortion or flattery.

10. *The wicked shall see it. Rasha,* "the wicked one." Some think Satan is meant. It is distinguished from *reshaim,* "wicked men," in the conclusion of the verse. *Shall gnash with his teeth.* Through spite and ill will. *And melt away.* Through envy and hopeless expectation of similar good; for his *desire* in reference to himself, and in reference to him who is the object of his envy, *shall perish*—shall come to nothing.

PSALM 113

An exhortation to bless God for His own excellencies, 1-6; and for His great mercy to the poor and necessitous, 7-9.

Psalms cxiii; cxiv; cxv; cxvi; cxvii; and cxviii form the great *Hallel,* and were sung by the Jews on their most solemn festivals, and particularly at the Passover. To these reference is made by the Evangelists, Matt. xxvi. 30 and Mark xiv. 26, there called the "hymn" which Jesus and His disciples sung at the Passover, for the whole of the psalms were considered as one grand hymn of thanksgiving. It was probably composed after the return from the Captivity. It has no title but *Hallelujah* in the Hebrew and ancient versions.

1. *Praise, O ye servants.* Probably an address to the Levites.

3. *From the rising of the sun.* From morning to evening be always employed in the work. Or it may be a call on all mankind to praise God for His innumerable mercies to the human

race. Praise Him from one end of the world unto the other. And therefore the Psalmist adds,

4. *The Lord is high above all nations.* He governs all, He provides for all; therefore let all give Him praise.

5. *Who is like unto the Lord?* Those who are highly exalted are generally unapproachable; they are proud and overbearing; or so surrounded with magnificence that to them the poor have no access, but God, though infinitely exalted, humbleth himself to behold even heaven itself, and much more does He humble himself when He condescends to behold earth and her inhabitants (v. 6).

9. *He maketh the barren woman to keep house.* This is a figure to point out the desolate, decreasing state of the captives in Babylon, and the happy change which took place on their return to their own land. These are nearly the words of Hannah, 1 Sam. ii. 5.

PSALM 114

Miracles wrought at the exodus of the Israelites from Egypt, at the Red Sea, and at Jordan, 1-6; and at the rock of Horeb. 7-8.

This psalm has no title. The word *Hallelujah* is prefixed in all the versions except the Chaldee and Syriac. It seems like a fragment, or a part of another psalm. In many MSS. it is only the beginning of the following, both making but one psalm in all the versions except the Chaldee.

1. *A people of strange language.* The language of the Egyptians in the time of Joseph was so different from that of the Hebrews that they could not understand each other. See Gen. xlii. 23.

2. *Judah was his sanctuary.* He set up His true worship among the Jews, and took them for His peculiar people.

5. *What ailed thee, O thou sea?* The original is very abrupt; and the personification very fine and expressive:

> *What to thee, O sea, that thou fleddest away!*
> *O Jordan, that thou didst roll back!*
> *Ye mountains, that ye leaped like rams!*
> *And ye hills, like the young of the fold!*

After these very sublime interrogations God appears, and the Psalmist proceeds as if answering his own questions:

> *At the appearance of the Lord, O earth, thou didst tremble;*
> *At the appearance of the strong God of Jacob.*
> *Converting the rock into a pool of waters;*
> *The granite into water springs.*

I know the present Hebrew text reads *chuli,* "tremble thou," in the imperative; but almost all the versions understood the word in past tense, and read as if the Psalmist was answering his own questions, as stated in the translation above.

PSALM 115

God alone is to be glorified, 1-3. The vanity of idols, 4-8. Israel, the house of Aaron, and all that fear God are exhorted to trust in the Lord, 9-11. The Lord's goodness to His people, and His gracious promises, 12-16. As the dead cannot praise Him, the living should, 17-18.

2. *Wherefore should the heathen say?* This appears to refer to a time in which the Israelites had suffered some sad reverses, so as to be brought very low, and to be marked by the heathen.

12. *The Lord hath been mindful.* He has never yet wholly abandoned us to our enemies. There is a great deal of emphasis in this verse; several words are redoubled to make the subject the more affecting. I give a literal translation: "V. 12. The Lord has been mindful of us; He will bless the house of Israel; He will bless the house of Aaron. V. 13: He will bless them that fear Jehovah, the small with the great. V. 14: Jehovah will add upon you, upon you and upon all your children. V. 15: Blessed are ye of the Lord, the Maker of heaven and earth. V. 16: The heavens of heavens are the Lord's: but the earth He hath given to the sons of Adam."

PSALM 116

The Psalmist praises God for his deliverance from thraldom, which he compares to death and the grave, 1-9. The exercises through which he had passed, 10-11. His gratitude for these mercies, and resolution to live to God's glory, 12-19.

This psalm is also without a title, and its author is unknown. It appears to have been written after the Captivity, and to be a thanksgiving to God for that glorious event. The Psalmist compares this captivity to "death" and the "grave"; and shows the happy return to the Promised Land, called here "the land of the living." The people recollect the vows of God which were upon them, and purpose to fulfill them. They exult at being enabled to worship God in the Temple at Jerusalem.

3. *The sorrows of death.* The "cables" or "cords of death," alluding to their bonds and fetters during their captivity; or to the cords by which a criminal is bound, who is about to be led out to execution. *The pains of hell.* "The straitnesses of the grave."

6. *The Lord preserveth the simple. Pethaim,* which all the versions render "little ones." Those who are meek and lowly of heart, who feel the spirit of little children, these He preserves, as He does little children.

8. *Thou hast delivered my soul from death.* Thou hast rescued my "life" from the destruction to which it was exposed. *Mine eyes from tears.* Thou hast turned my sorrow into joy.

9. *I will walk before the Lord.* "I will set myself to walk." I am determined to walk.

11. *All men are liars.* "The whole of man is a lie."

12. *What shall I render?* "What shall I return?" *For all his benefits.* "His retributions," the returns He had made to my prayers and faith.

13. *I will take the cup of salvation.* Literally, "The cup of salvation, or deliverance, will I lift up." Alluding to the action in taking the cup of blessing among the Jews, which, when the person or master of the family lifted up, he said these words, "Blessed be the Lord, the Maker of the world, who has created the fruit of the vine!"

14. *I will pay my vows unto the Lord now in the presence of all his people.* He was probably now bringing his offering to the Temple. These words are repeated, v. 18.

15. *Precious in the sight of the Lord.* Many have understood this verse as meaning, "The saints are too precious in the Lord's sight lightly to give them over to death."

17. *I will offer to thee.* As it is most probable that this psalm celebrates the deliverance from Babylon, it is not wonder that we find the Psalmist so intent on performing the rites of his religion in the Temple at Jerusalem, which had been burnt with fire, and was now reviving out of its ruins, the Temple service having been wholly interrupted for nearly fourscore years.

19. *In the midst of thee, O Jerusalem.* He speaks as if present in the city, offering his vowed sacrifices in the Temple to the Lord.

PSALM 117

The Psalmist calls upon the nations of the world to praise the Lord for His mercy and kindness, and for the fulfillment of His promises, 1-2.

This is the shortest psalm in the whole collection; it is written as a part of the preceding in thirty-two of Kennicott's and De Rossi's MSS., and is found thus printed in some ancient editions.

2. *For his merciful kindness is great. Gabar,* is "strong." *And the truth of the Lord endureth for ever.* Whatsoever He has promised, that He will most infallibly fulfill.

PSALM 118

A general exhortation to praise God for His mercy, 1-4. The Psalmist, by his own experience, encourages the people to trust in God, and shows them the advantage of it, 5-9; then describes his enemies, and shows how God enabled him to destroy them, 10-13. The people rejoice on the account, 15-16. He speaks again of the help he received from the Lord; and desires admission into the Temple, that he may enter and praise the Lord, 17-19. The gate is opened, 20. He offers praise, 21. The priests, etc., acknowledge the hand of the Lord in the deliverance wrought, 22-24. The Psalmist prays for prosperity, 25. The priest performs his office, blesses the people, and all join in praise, 26-27. The Psalmist expresses his confidence, 28. The general doxology, or chorus, 29.

Most probably David was the author of this psalm, though many think it was written after the Captivity. It partakes of David's spirit, and everywhere shows the hand of a master. The style is grand and noble; the subject, majestic.

7. *The Lord taketh my part with them that help me.* Literally, "The Lord is to me among my helpers." *Therefore shall I see my desire upon them that hate me.* Literally, "And I shall look among them that hate me." As God is on my side, I fear not to look the whole of them in the face. I shall see them defeated.

10. *All nations compassed me about.* This is by some supposed to relate to David, at the commencement of his reign, when all the neighboring Philistine nations endeavored to prevent him from establishing himself in the kingdom. Others suppose it may refer to the Samaritans, Idumeans, Ammonites, and others who endeavored to prevent the Jews from rebuilding their city and their Temple after their return from captivity in Babylon.

19. *Open to me the gates.* Throw open the doors of the Temple, that I may enter and perform my vows unto the Lord.

20. *This gate of the Lord.* Supposed to be the answer of the Levites to the request of the king.

21. *I will praise thee.* He is now got within the gates, and breaks out into thanksgivings for

the mercies he had received. He is *become my salvation*—He himself hath saved me from all mine enemies.

22-23. *The stone which the builders refused.* See a full elucidation of these two verses in the notes on Matt. xxi. 42.

24. *This is the day which the Lord hath made.* As the Lord hath called me to triumph, this is the day which He hath appointed for that purpose. This is a gracious opportunity; I will improve it to His glory.

25. *Save now, I beseech thee.* These words were sung by the Jews on the Feast of Tabernacles, when carrying green branches in their hands; and from the *hoshiah nna,* we have the word *hosanna.* This was sung by the Jewish children when Christ made His public entry into Jerusalem. See Matt. xxi. 9.

26. *We have blessed you.* The answer of the Levites to the king.

27. *God is the Lord.* El Yehovah, "the strong God Jehovah." *Which hath shewed us light.* "And He will illuminate us." Perhaps at this time a divine splendor shone upon the whole procession, a proof of God's approbation.

29. *O give thanks unto the Lord.* This is the general doxology or chorus. All join in thanksgiving, and they end as they began: *His mercy endureth for ever.*

PSALM 119

The various excellencies and important uses of the law or revelation of God.

This is another of the alphabetical or acrostic psalms. It is divided into twenty-two parts, answering to the number of letters in the Hebrew alphabet. Every part is divided into eight verses; and each verse begins with that letter of the alphabet which forms the title of the part, e.g.: The first eight verses have *aleph* prefixed, the second eight *beth,* each of the eight verses beginning with that letter; and so of the rest. It is not easy to give any general analysis of this psalm; it is enough to say that it treats in general on the privileges and happiness of those who observe the law of the Lord. That law is exhibited by various names and epithets tending to show its various excellences. Earnest prayers are offered to God for wisdom to understand it, and for grace to observe it faithfully. The words which express that revelation which God had then given to men, or some particular characteristic of it, are generally reckoned to be the ten following: (1) testimonies; (2) commandments; (3) precepts; (4) word; (5) law; (6) ways; (7) truth; (8) judgments; (9) righteousness; (10) statutes. I believe it is almost universally asserted that in every verse of this psalm one or other of those ten words is used, except in v. 122; but on a closer inspection we shall find that none of them is used in the above sense in the 84th, 90th, 121st, 122nd, and 132nd.

To save myself unnecessary repetition, and the reader time and trouble, I shall here, once for all, explain the above words, which the reader will do well to keep in remembrance.

I. The Law, *torah,* from *yarah,* to "direct, guide, teach, make straight, or even, point forward"; because it guides, directs, and instructs in the way of righteousness; makes our path straight, shows what is even and right, and points us onward to peace, truth, and happiness.

II. Statutes, *chukkim,* from *chak,* "to mark, trace out, describe, and ordain"; because they mark out our way, describe the line of conduct we are to pursue, and order or ordain what we are to observe.

III. Precepts, *pikkudim,* from *pakad,* "to take notice or care of a thing, to attend, have respect to, to appoint, to visit"; because they take notice of our way, have respect to the whole of our life and conversation, superintend, overlook, and visit us in all the concerns and duties of life.

IV. Commandments, *mitsvoth,* from *tasvah,* "to command, order, ordain"; because they show us what we should do, and what we should leave undone, and exact our obedience.

V. Testimonies, *edoth,* from *ad,* denoting "beyond, farther, all along, to bear witness, or testimony." The rites and ceremonies of the law; because they point out matters beyond themselves, being types and representations of the good things that were to come.

VI. Judgments, *mishpatim,* from *shaphat,* "to judge, determine, regulate, order, and discern," because they judge concerning our words and works; show the rules by which they should be regulated; and cause us to discern what is right and wrong, and decide accordingly.

VII. Truth, *emunah,* from *aman,* "to make steady, constant, to settle, trust, believe." The law that is established, steady, confirmed, and ordered in all things, and sure; which should be believed on the authority of God, and trusted to as an infallible testimony from Him who cannot lie nor deceive.

VIII. Word, *dabar,* "to discourse, utter one's sentiments, speak consecutively and intelligibly." Any prophecy or immediate communication from heaven, as well as the whole body of divine revelation.

IX. Way, *derech,* "to proceed, go on, walk, tread." The way in which God goes in order to instruct and save man; the way in which man must tread in order to be safe, holy, and happy.

X. Righteousness, *tsedakah,* from *tsadak,* "to do justice, to give full weight." That which teaches a man to give to all their due. This word is applied to God's judgments, testimonies, and commandments; they are all righteous, give to all their due, and require what is due from everyone.

The three words which some add here are, first, faithfulness, *emunah.* But see this under No. VII; nor does it appear in v. 90, where it occurs, to be used as a characteristic of God's law, but rather His exact fulfillment of His promises to man. The second is judgment, *mishpat.* See this under No. VI. It occurs in vv. 84 and 121: "When wilt thou execute judgment?" etc., but is not used in those places as one of the ten words. The third is name, *shem;* see v. 132. But this is no characteristic of God's law; it refers here simply to himself. *Name* is the same as *those that love Thee.* Bishop Nicholson inserts *promises* among the ten words, but this occurs no where in the psalm.

We might, and with much more propriety, add a fourth, *imrah,* from *amar,* "to branch out, spread, or diffuse itself," as the branches of a tree; and which is often used for a word spoken, a speech. This often occurs in the psalm, and we regularly translate it "word," and put no difference or distinction between it and *dabar,* No. VIII; but it is not exactly the same. *Dabar* may apply more properly to history, relation, description, and suchlike; while *imrathecha,* "thy word," may mean an immediate oracle, delivered solemnly from God to His prophet for the instruction of men. But the two words appear often indifferently used, and it would not be easy to ascertain the different shades of meaning between these two roots.

Letter *Aleph*—First Division

1. *Blessed are the undefiled in the way.* "Oh, the blessedness of the perfect ones in the way! This psalm begins something like the first, By the *perfect,* which is the proper meaning of the original word, we are to understand those who sincerely believe what God has spoken, religiously observe all the rules and ceremonies of His religion, and have their lives and hearts regulated by the spirit of love, fear, and obedience. This is further stated in the second verse.

4. *Thy precepts diligently. Meod,* "superlatively, to the uttermost." God has never given a commandment the observance of which He knew to be impossible.

5. *O that my ways were directed!* "I wish that my way may be confirmed to keep Thy statutes."

8. *O forsake me not utterly. Ad meod,* "to utter dereliction."

Letter *Beth*—Second Division

9. *A young man cleanse his way. Orach,* which we translate *way* here, signifies a "track," a "rut," such as is made by the wheel of a cart or chariot. A young sinner has no broad, beaten path; he has his private ways of offense, his secret pollutions.

16. *I will delight myself.* The word is very emphatic: *eshtaasha,* "I will skip about and jump for joy." He must exult in God's word as his treasure, live in the spirit of obedience as his work, and ever glory in God, who has called him to such a state of salvation.

Letter *Gimel*—Third Division

17. *Deal bountifully. Gemol,* "reward" Thy servant. Let him have the return of his faith and prayers, that the divine *life* may be preserved in his soul! Then he will keep Thy word. From *gamal,* "to reward," comes the name of *gimel,* the third letter in the Hebrew alphabet, which is prefixed to every verse in this part, and commences it with its own name. This is a stroke of the Psalmist's art and ingenuity.

18. *Open thou mine eyes. Gal,* "reveal my eyes," illuminate my understanding, take away the veil that is on my heart, and then shall I see wonders in Thy law. The Holy Scriptures are plain enough; but the heart of man is darkened by sin. The Bible does not so much need a comment as the soul does the light of the Holy Spirit.

20. *My soul breaketh.* We have a similar expression: "It broke my heart." It expresses excessive longing, grievous disappointment, hopeless love, accumulated sorrow.

23. *Princes also did sit.* It is very likely that the nobles of Babylon did often, by wicked misrepresentations, render the minds of the kings of the empire evil affected towards the Jews.

24. *Thy testimonies also are . . . my counsellors.* "The men of my counsel." I sit with them; and I consider every testimony Thou hast given as a particular counsellor, one whose advice I especially need.

Letter *Daleth*—Fourth Division

25. *My soul cleaveth unto the dust.* It would be best to translate *naphshi*, "my life," and then cleaving to the dust may imply an apprehension of approaching death; and this agrees best with the petition, *Quicken thou me.* "Make me alive." Keep me from going down into the dust.

26. *I have declared my ways.* "I have numbered my ways"; I have searched them out; I have investigated them. And that he had earnestly prayed for pardon of what was wrong in them is evident, for he adds, *Thou heardest me.*

28. *My soul melteth. Dalaph* signifies "to distill, to drop as tears from the eye." As my distresses cause the tears to distil from my eyes, so the overwhelming load of my afflictions causes my life to ebb and leak out.

31. *I have stuck.* "I have cleaved to, been glued to," them—the same word as in v. 25.

32. *I will run.* The particle which we translate *when* should be translated "because."

Letter *He*—Fifth Division

33. *Teach me, O Lord, the way of thy statutes.* To understand the spiritual reference of all the statutes under the law required a teaching which could come only from God.

34. *With my whole heart.* I will not trifle with my God, I will not divide my affections with the world; God shall have all.

38. *Stablish thy word.* Fulfill the promises Thou hast made to me.

Letter *Vau*—Sixth Division

41. *Let thy mercies come.* Let me speedily see the accomplishment of all my prayers! Let me have *thy salvation*—such a deliverance as it becomes Thy greatness and goodness to impart. Let it be *according to thy word*—Thy exceeding great and precious promises.

Letter *Zain*—Seventh Division

49. *Remember the word.* Thou hast *promised* to redeem us from our captivity; on that *word* we have built our *hope*. Remember that Thou hast thus promised, and see that we thus *hope.*

50. *This is my comfort.* While enduring our harsh captivity, we anticipated our enlargement; and thy *word of promise* was the *means* of keeping our souls *alive.*

51. *The proud have had me.* We have been treated, not only with oppressive cruelty, but also with contempt, because we still professed to trust in Thee, the living God, who because of our transgressions hadst been greatly displeased with us; yet we have *not declined from thy law.*

52. *I remembered thy judgments of old.* The word *judgments* is here taken for providential dealing, and indeed kind treatment, that which God showed to the Hebrews in bearing with and blessing them. And it was the recollection of these judgments that caused him to comfort himself.

54. *Thy statutes have been my songs.* During our captivity all our consolation was derived from singing Thy praises, and chanting among our fellow captives portions of Thy law, and the precepts it contains.

Letter *Cheth*—Eighth Division

57. *Thou art my portion, O Lord.* From the fifty-seventh to the sixtieth verse may be seen the progress of the work of grace on the human heart, from the first dawn of heavenly light till the soul is filled with the fullness of God. The author has been obliged, for the support of his acrostic plan, to interchange circumstances, putting that sometimes behind which in the order of grace comes before; I shall therefore follow what I conceive to be its order in the connection of grace.

59. First—*I thought on my ways.* I deeply pondered them; I turned them upside down; I viewed my conduct on all sides. The word, as used here, is a metaphor taken from embroidering, where the figure must appear the same on the one side as it does on the other; therefore, the cloth must be turned on each side every time the needle is set in, to see that the stitch be fairly set. Thus narrowly and scrupulously did the Psalmist examine his conduct; and the result was a deep conviction that he had departed from the way of God and truth. Secondly—*And turned my feet unto thy testimonies.* Having made the above discovery, and finding himself under the displeasure of God, he abandoned every evil way, took God's word for his directory, and set out fairly in the way of life and salvation.

60. Thirdly—*I made haste, and delayed not.* He did this with the utmost speed, and did not trifle with his convictions, nor seek to drown the voice of conscience. The original word, which we translate *delayed not*, is amazingly emphatic, *velo hithmahmahti*, "I did not stand what-what-what-ing"; or, as we used to express the same sentiment, "shilly-shallying" with myself. I was determined, and so set out.

58. Fourthly—Being determined in his heart, he tells us *I intreated favour with my whole heart.* He found he had sinned, that he needed mercy, that he had no time to lose, that he must be importunate; and therefore he sought that mercy with all his soul. Fifthly—Feeling that he deserved nothing but wrath, that he had no right to any good, he cries for mercy in the way that God had promised to convey it: *Be merciful unto me.* And to this he is encouraged only by the promise of God; and therefore prays, *Be merciful unto me according to thy word.*

57. Sixthly—To keep himself firm in his present resolutions, he binds himself unto the Lord. *I have said that I would keep thy words.* Seventhly—He did not seek in vain; God reveals himself in the fullness of blessedness to him, so that he is enabled to exclaim, *Thou art my portion, O Lord.*

61. *The bands of the wicked have robbed me. Chebley*, the "cables," "cords," or "snares" of the wicked.

Letter *Teth*—Ninth Division

66. *Teach me good judgment and knowledge.* "Teach me [to have] a good taste and discernment." Let me see and know the importance of divine things, and give me a relish for them.

67. *Before I was afflicted I went astray.* Many have been humbled under affliction, and taught

to know themselves and humble themselves before God, that probably without this could never have been saved; after this, they have been serious and faithful.

As the letter *teth* begins but few words, not forty, in the Hebrew language, there is less variety under this division than under any of the preceding.

Letter *Yod*—Tenth Division

76. *Thy merciful kindness.* Let me derive my comfort and happiness from a diffusion of Thy love and mercy, *chasdecha,* "thy exuberant goodness," through my soul.

77. *Let thy tender mercies.* "Thy fatherly and affectionate feelings."

Letter *Caph*—Eleventh Division

82. *Mine eyes fail.* With looking up for the fulfillment of Thy promise, as my heart fails in longing after Thy presence.

83. *Like a bottle in the smoke.* In the Eastern countries their *bottles* are made of skins; one of these hung in the smoke must soon be parched and shrivelled up. This represents the exhausted state of his body and mind by long bodily affliction and mental distress.

85. *The proud have digged pits.* The Vulgate, Septuagint, Aethiopic, and Arabic translate this verse thus: "They have recited to me unholy fables, which are not according to thy law."

Letter *Lamed*—Twelfth Division

89. *For ever, O Lord, thy word is settled in heaven.* Thy purposes are all settled above, and they shall all be fulfilled below.

90. *Thy faithfulness.* That which binds Thee to accomplish the promise made.

91. *They continue this day.* This verse should be thus read: "All are Thy servants; therefore they continue this day according to Thy ordinances."

96. *I have seen an end of all perfection.* Literally, "Of all consummations I have seen the end"; as if one should say, Everything of human origin has its limits and end, howsoever extensive, noble, and excellent.

Letter *Mem*—Thirteenth Division

97. *O how love I thy law!* This is one of the strongest marks of a gracious and pious heart, cast in the mold of obedience.

100. *I understand more than the ancients.* God had revealed to him more of that hidden wisdom which was in His law than He had done to any of his predecessors. And this was most literally true of David, who spoke more fully about Christ than any who had gone before him; or, indeed, followed after him.

Letter *Nun*—Fourteenth Division

105. *Thy word is a lamp.* This is illustrated thus by Solomon, Prov. vi. 23: "The commandment is a lamp; and the law is light; and reproofs of instruction are the way of life."

107. *I am afflicted very much. Ad meod,* "to extremity, excessively." *Quicken me.* Deliver us from our bondage.

108. *The freewill offerings of my mouth.* "The voluntary offerings which I have promised." Or, As we are in captivity, and cannot sacrifice to Thee, but would if we could, accept the praises of our mouth, and the purposes of our hearts, instead of the sacrifices and offerings which we would bring to Thy altar, but cannot.

109. *My soul is continually in my hand. Naphshi,* "my life." The expression signifies to be in continual danger.

Letter *Samech*—Fifteenth Division

113. *I hate vain thoughts.* I have hated *seaphim,* "tumultuous, violent men."

Letter *Ain*—Sixteenth Division

122. *Be surety for thy servant.* Give a pledge or token that Thou wilt help me in times of necessity. Or, "Be bail for Thy servant." What a word is this! Pledge thyself for me, that Thou wilt produce me safely at the judgment of the great day. Then sustain and keep me blameless till the coming of Christ. Neither of these two verses has any of the ten words in reference to God's law or attributes. The *judgment* and the *justice* refer to the Psalmist's own conduct in v. 121. Verse 122 has no word of the kind.

126. *It is time for thee, Lord, to work.* The *time* is fulfilled in which Thou hast promised deliverance to Thy people.

127. *Above gold. Mizzahab,* more than "resplendent gold"; gold without any strain or rust. *Yea, above fine gold. Umippaz,* "above solid gold"; gold separated from the dross, perfectly refined.

Letter *Pe*—Seventeenth Division

130. *The entrance of thy words giveth light. Pethach,* the "opening" of it. When I open my Bible to read, light springs up in my mind.

131. *I opened my mouth, and panted.* A metaphor taken from an animal exhausted in the chase. He runs, open-mouthed, to take in the cooling air, the heart beating high, and the muscular force nearly expended through fatigue.

133. *Order my steps.* Make them "firm"; let me not walk with a halting or unsteady step. *Have dominion over me. Bi,* "in me." Let me have no governor but God; let the throne of my heart be filled by Him, and none other.

135. *Make thy face to shine.* Give me a sense of Thy approbation. Let me know, by the testimony of Thy Spirit in my conscience, that Thou art reconciled to me.

Letter *Tsaddi*—Eighteenth Division

140. *Thy word is very pure.* It is "purification." It is not a purified thing, but a thing that purifies. "Now ye are clean," said Christ, by "the word which I have spoken unto you." God's Word is a Fire to purify as well as a Hammer to break.

142. *Thy righteousness is an everlasting righteousness.* The word *tsedek* is a word of very extensive meaning in the Bible. It signifies, not only God's inherent righteousness and perfection of nature, but also His method of treating others, His plan of redemption, His method of saving others.

Letter *Koph*—Nineteenth Division

147. *I prevented the dawning.* "I went before the dawn or twilight."

148. *Mine eyes prevent.* "Go before the watches." Before the watchman proclaims the hour, I am awake, meditating on Thy words. The Jews divided the night into three watches, which began at what we call six o'clock in the

evening, and consisted each of four hours. The Romans taught them afterwards to divide it into four watches of three hours each.

152. *Concerning thy testimonies, I h a v e known of old.* "Long ago I have known concerning thy testimonies."

Letter *Resh*—Twentieth Division

154. *Plead my cause. Ribah ribi.* "Be my Advocate in my suit."

156. *Great are thy tender mercies.* They are *rabbim,* "multitudes." They extend to all the wretchednesses of all men.

158. *I beheld the transgressors, and was grieved.* Literally, "I was affected with anguish."

160. *Thy word is true from the beginning. Rosh,* "the head or beginning of Thy word, is true." Does he refer to the first word in the Book of Genesis, *bereshith,* "in the beginning"? The learned reader knows that *rash,* or *raash,* is the root in that word. Every word Thou hast spoken from the first in *Bereshith* (Genesis) to the end of the law and prophets, and all Thou wilt yet speak, must be true; and all shall have, in due time, their fulfillment.

Letter *Schin*—Twenty-first Division

161. *Princes have persecuted me.* This may refer to what was done by prime ministers, and the rulers of provinces, to sour the king against the unfortunate Jews, in order still to detain them in bondage. In reference to David, the plotting against him in Saul's court, and the dangers he ran in consequence of the jealousies of the Philistine lords while he sojourned among them, are well-known.

163. *I . . . abhor lying.* Perhaps they might have made the confessions which the Chaldeans required, and by mental reservation have kept an inward firm adherence to their creed; but this, in the sight of the God of truth, must have been *lying;* and at such a sacrifice they would not purchase their enlargement, even from their captivity.

164. *Seven times a day do I praise thee.* We have often seen that seven was a number expressing perfection, completion, among the Hebrews; and that it is often used to signify many, or an indefinite number, see Prov. xxiv. 16; Lev. xxvi. 28. And here it may mean no more than that his soul was filled with the spirit of gratitude and praise, and that he very frequently expressed his joyous and grateful feelings in this way.

Letter *Tau*—Twenty-second Division

169. *Let my cry come near before thee.* Here the Psalmist's cry for deliverance is personified; made an intelligent being, and sent up to the throne of grace to negotiate in his behalf.

171. *My lips shall utter praise. Tehillah,* a song of praise.

175. *Let my soul live.* Let my "life" be preserved, and my soul quickened!

There is one extraordinary perfection in this psalm: Begin where you will, you seem to be at the commencement of the piece; end where you will, you seem to close with a complete sense. And yet it is not like the Book of Proverbs, a tissue of detached sentences. It is a whole composed of many parts, and all appar-

ently as necessary to the perfection of the psalm as the different alphabetical letters under which it is arranged are to the formation of a complete alphabet.

PSALM 120

The Psalmist, in great distress, calls on the Lord for deliverance from calumny and defamation, 1-2; shows the punishment that awaits his persecutor, 3-4; deplores the necessity of his residence with the ungodly, 5-7.

This psalm, and all the rest that follow it, to the end of Psalm cxxxiv, fifteen in number, are called Psalms of Degrees; for thus the Hebrew title *hammaaloth* is generally translated, as coming from the root *alah,* "to ascend or mount upwards." Hence *maaloth,* "steps or stairs for ascending," 1 Kings x. 19-20; 2 Kings ix. 13. But as the word may be applied to elevation in general, hence some have thought that it may here signify the elevation of voice, "these psalms being sung with the highest elevations of voice and music." Others have thought the word expresses rather the matter of these psalms, as being of peculiar excellence.

1. *In my distress.* Through the causes afterwards mentioned. *I cried unto the Lord.* Made strong supplication for help. *And he heard me.* Answered my prayer by comforting my soul. It appears to be a prayer of the captives in Babylon for complete liberty, or perhaps he recites the prayer the Israelites had made previously to their restoration.

4. *Sharp arrows.* The Chaldee has, "The strong, sharp arrows are like lightning from above, with coals of juniper kindled in hell beneath."

5. *That I sojourn in Mesech.* The Chaldee has it, "Woe is me that I am a stranger with the Asiatics and that I dwell in the tents of the Arabs."

PSALM 121

The resolution of a godly man, 1-2. The safety and prosperity of such, as they and theirs shall be under the continual protection of God, 3-8.

This appears to be a prayer of the Jews in their captivity, who are solicitous for their restoration. It is in the form of a dialogue. Vv. 1-2. The person who worships God speaks the two first verses, "I will lift up mine eyes . . . my help cometh." V. 3. The ministering priest answers him, "He will not suffer thy foot to be moved: He that keepeth thee will not slumber." To which the worshipper answers that he knows that "he that keepeth Israel shall neither slumber nor sleep," v. 4; but he seems to express a doubt whether he shall be an object of the divine attention. Vv. 5, etc. The priest resumes; and, to the conclusion of the psalm, gives him the most positive assurances of God's favor and protection.

1. *Unto the hills.* Jerusalem was built upon a mountain; and Judea was a mountainous country.

4. *He that keepeth Israel.* The Divine Being represents himself as a Watchman, who takes care of the city and its inhabitants during the night watches, and who is never overtaken with slumbering or sleepiness.

8. *Thy going out and thy coming in.* Night

and day—in all your business and undertakings; and this through the whole course of your life: *for evermore.*

PSALM 122

The satisfaction of a gracious soul in the use of God's ordinances, 1-2. Description of the internal government of Jerusalem, 3-5. Prayers for its peace and prosperity, 6-9.

In the preceding psalms we find the poor captives crying to God for deliverance; here they are returning thanks that they find they are permitted to return to their own land and to the ordinances of their God.

1. *I was glad when they said.* When Cyrus published an edict for their return, the very first object of their thanksgiving was the kindness of God in permitting them to return to His ordinances.

2. *Our feet shall stand.* For seventy years we have been exiled from our own land; our heart was in Jerusalem, but our feet were in Chaldea. Now God has turned our captivity, and our feet shall shortly stand within the gates of Jerusalem.

5. *There are set thrones of judgment.* There were the public courts, and thither the people went to obtain justice.

6. *Pray for the peace of Jerusalem. Shalom* signifies both peace and "prosperity."

7. *Peace be within thy walls.* This is the form of prayer that they are to use: "May prosperity ever reside within they walls, on all the people that dwell there; and tranquility within thy palaces or high places, among the rulers and governors of the people."

PSALM 123

The prayer and faith of the godly, 1-2. They desire to be delivered from contempt, 3-4.

This psalm is probably a complaint of the captives in Babylon relative to the contempt and cruel usage they received. The author is uncertain.

2. *As the eyes of servants.* We now wait for Thy commands, feeling the utmost readiness to obey them when made known to us.

4. *Those that are at ease.* The Babylonians, who, having subdued all the people of the neighboring nations, lived *at ease,* had none to contend with them, and now became luxurious, indolent, and insolent; they were contemptuous and proud.

PSALM 124

A thanksgiving of the godly for extraordinary deliverances, 1-6. The great danger they were in, 7. Their confidence in God, 8.

In our present Hebrew copies this psalm is attributed to David; but this inscription is wanting in three of Kennicott's and De Rossi's MSS., as also in the Septuagint, Syriac, Vulgate, Aethiopic, and Arabic; and in most of the ancient fathers, Greek and Latin, who found no other inscription in their copies of the text than "A Psalm of degrees." It was composed long after David's days, and appears to be a thanksgiving either for their deliverance from the Babylonish captivity or for a remarkable deliverance from some potent and insidious enemy after their return to Judea. Or, what appears to be more likely, it is a thanksgiving of the Jews for their escape from the general massacre intended by Haman, prime minister of Ahasuerus, king of Persia.

1. *If it had not been the Lord.* This might refer to the plot against the whole nation of the Jews by Haman, in the days of Mordecai and Esther, when by his treacherous schemes the Jews, wheresoever dispersed in the provinces of Babylon, were all to have been put to death in one day.

5. *Then the proud waters.* The proud Haman had nearly brought the flood of desolation over our lives.

7. *Our soul is escaped as a bird out of the snare.* This is a fine image, and at once shows the weakness of the Jews and the cunning of their adversaries. Haman had laid the snare completely for them; humanly speaking there was no prospect of their escape. But the Lord was on their side; and the providence that induced Ahasuerus to call for the book of the records of the kingdom to be read to him, as well indeed as the once very improbable advancement of Esther to the throne of Persia, was the means used by the Lord for the preservation of the whole Jewish people from extermination. God thus broke the snare, and the bird escaped, while the poacher was caught in his own trap, and executed. See the Book of Esther, which is probably the best comment on this psalm.

PSALM 125

The safety of those who trust in God, 1-2. God's protecting providence in behalf of His followers, 3. A prayer for the godly, 4. The evil lot of the wicked, 5.

This psalm is without a title; it belongs most probably to the times after the Captivity and has been applied, with apparent propriety, to the opposition which Sanballat the Horonite, Geshem the Arabian, and Tobiah the Ammonite gave to the Jews while employed in rebuilding the walls of Jerusalem and restoring the Temple.

3. *For the rod of the wicked shall not rest upon the lot of the righteous.* Rod, here, may be taken for persecution, or for rule; and then it may be thus interpreted: "The wicked shall not be permitted to persecute always, nor to have a permanent rule."

PSALM 126

The joy of the Israelites on their return from captivity, and the effect their deliverance had upon the heathen, 1-3. The prayer which they had offered up, 4. The inference they draw from the whole, 5-6.

This psalm is not of David, has no title in the Hebrew or any of the versions, and certainly belongs to the close of the Captivity.

1. *When the Lord turned again the captivity.* When Cyrus published his decree in favor of the Jews, giving them liberty to return to their own land, and rebuild their city and Temple. *We were like them that dream.* The news was so unexpected that we doubted for a time the truth of it. We believed it was too good news to be true, and thought ourselves in a dream or illusion.

4. *Turn again our captivity.* This is either a recital of the prayer they had used before their

deliverance, or it is a prayer for those who still remained in the provinces beyond the Euphrates. The Jewish captives did not all return at once; they came back at different times, and under different leaders, Ezra, Nehemiah, Zerubbabel, etc.

6. *He that goeth forth and weepeth, bearing precious seed.* The metaphor seems to be this: A poor farmer has had a very bad harvest; a very scanty portion of grain and food has been gathered from the earth. The seedtime is now come, and is very unpromising. Out of the famine a little seed has been saved to be sown, in hopes of another crop; but the badness of the present season almost precludes the entertainment of hope. He carries his all, his *precious seed,* with him in his seed basket; and with a sorrowful heart commits it to the furrow, watering it in effect with his tears, and earnestly imploring the blessing of God upon it. The appointed weeks of harvest come, and the grain is very productive. He fills his arms, his carriages with the sheaves and shocks; and returns to his large, expecting family in triumph, praising God for the wonders He has wrought. So shall it be with this handful of returning Israelites. They also are to be sown—scattered all over the land; the blessing of God shall be upon them, and their faith and numbers shall be abundantly increased.

PSALM 127

The necessity of God's blessing on every undertaking, without which no prosperity can be expected, 1-2. Children are a heritage from the Lord, 3-4. A fruitful wife is a blessing to her husband, 5.

The Hebrew, Chaldee, and Vulgate attribute this psalm to Solomon. The Septuagint, Aethiopic, Arabic, and Anglo-Saxon have no title, but simply "A Psalm of Degrees." It was most likely composed for the building of the second Temple, under Nehemiah, and by some prophet of that time.

1. *Except the Lord build the house.* To build a house is taken in three different senses in the sacred writings. (1) To build the temple of the Lord, which was called *the house,* by way of eminence. (2) To build any ordinary house, or place of dwelling. (3) To have a numerous offspring. *Ben,* "a son," and *bath,* "a daughter," and *beith,* "a house," come from the same root *banah,* "to build"; because sons and daughters build up a household. Now it is true that unless the good hand of God be upon us we cannot prosperously build a place of worship for His name. Unless we have His blessing, a dwelling house cannot be comfortably erected. And if His blessing be not on our children, the house (the family) may be built up, but instead of its being the house of God, it will be the synagogue of Satan.

Except the Lord keep the city. When the returned Jews began to restore the walls of Jerusalem, and rebuild the city, Sanballat, Tobiah, and others formed plots to prevent it. Nehemiah, being informed of this, set up proper watches and guards. To this the Psalmist alludes; and in effect says, Though you should watch constantly, guard every place, and keep on your armor ready to repel every attack, yet remember the success of all depends upon the presence and blessing of God. While, therefore, you are not slothful in business, be fervent in spirit,

serving the Lord; for there is no success in either spiritual or secular undertakings but in consequence of the benediction of the Almighty.

PSALM 128

The blessedness of the man that fears the Lord, 1. He is blessed in his labor, 2; in his wife and children, 3-4; in the ordinances of God, 5; and in a long life and numerous posterity, 6.

This psalm has no title, either in the Hebrew or in any of the versions. It seems to be a continuation of the preceding psalm, or rather the second part of it. The man who is stated to have a numerous offspring, in the preceding psalm, is here represented as sitting at table with his large family. A person in the meanwhile coming in sees his happy state, speaks of his comforts, and predicts to him and his all possible future good. And why? Because the man and his family fear God, and walk in His ways.

2. *Thou shalt eat the labour of thine hands.* You shall not be exempted from *labour.* You shall work; but God will bless and prosper that work, and you and your family shall eat of it.

5. *The Lord shall bless thee out of Zion.* In all your approaches to Him in His house by prayer, by sacrifice, and by offering, you shall have His especial blessing. You shall thrive everywhere, and in all things.

6. *And peace upon Israel.* This is the same conclusion as in Psalm cxxv, and should be translated, "Peace be upon Israel!"

PSALM 129

The Jews give an account of the afflictions which they have passed through, 1-3. And thank God for their deliverance, 4. The judgments that shall fall on the workers of iniquity, 5-8.

This psalm was written after the Captivity. It has no title in any of the versions, nor in the Hebrew text, except the general one of "A Psalm of Degrees."

1. *Many a time have they afflicted me.* The Israelites had been generally in affliction or captivity from the earliest part of their history, here called their *youth.* So Hos. ii. 15: "She shall sing . . . as in the days of her youth . . . when she came up out of the land of Egypt." See Jer. ii. 2 and Ezek. xvi. 4.

2. *Yet they have not prevailed.* They endeavored to annihilate us as a people, but God still preserves us as His own nation.

5. *Let them all be confounded.* They shall be confounded.

6. *As the grass upon the house tops.* As in the East the roofs of the houses were flat, seeds of various kinds falling upon them would naturally vegetate; and, because of the want of proper nourishment, would necessarily dry and wither away.

8. *Neither do they which go by say.* There is a reference here to the salutations which were given and returned by the reapers in the time of the harvest. We find that it was customary, when the master came to them into the field, to say unto the reapers, "The Lord be with you"; and for them to answer, "The Lord bless thee" (Ruth ii. 4).

PSALM 130

The prayer of a penitent to God, with confession of sin, 1-3. Confidence in God's mercy, and waiting upon Him, 4-6. Israel is encouraged to hope in the Lord, because of His willingness to save, 7-8.

This psalm has no author's name, either in the Hebrew or in any of the versions. It was most probably composed during the Captivity; and contains the complaint of the afflicted Jews, with their hopes of the remission of those sins which were the cause of their sufferings, and their restoration from captivity to their own land. This is one of those called "penitential psalms."

3. *If thou . . . shouldest mark iniquities.* If Thou shouldst set down every deviation in thought, word, and deed from Thy holy law; and if Thou shouldst call us into judgment for all our infidelities, of both heart and life, O Lord, who could stand? Who could stand such a trial, and who could stand acquitted in the judgment? This is a most solemn saying; and if we had not the doctrine that is in the next verse, who could be saved?

4. *But there is forgiveness with thee.* Thou canst forgive; mercy belongs to Thee, as well as judgment.

5. *I wait for the Lord.* The word *kavah*, which we translate "to wait," properly signifies the "extension of a cord from one point to another." This is a fine metaphor: God is one point, the human heart is the other; and the extended cord between both is the earnest, believing desire of the soul. This desire, strongly extended from the heart to God, is the active, energetic waiting which God requires, and which will be successful.

6. *More than they that watch for the morning.* I believe the original should be read differently from what it is here. The Chaldee has, "More than they who observe the morning watches, that they may offer the morning oblation." This gives a good sense and is, perhaps, the true meaning.

7. *Let Israel hope in the Lord.* What *reason* is there for this *hope?* A twofold reason: (1) *With the Lord there is mercy. Hachesed*, "that mercy," the fund, the essence of mercy. (2) *And with him is plenteous redemption.* "That abundant redemption."

8. *He shall redeem Israel.* "He will make a ransom for Israel."

PSALM 131

The Psalmist professes his humility, and the peaceableness of his disposition and conduct, 1-2. Exhorts Israel to hope in God, 3.

Some think that David composed this psalm as a vindication of himself, when accused by Saul's courtiers that he affected the crown, and was laying schemes and plots to possess himself of it. Others think the psalm was made during the Captivity, and that it contains a fair account of the manner in which the captives behaved themselves under the domination of their oppressors.

1. *Lord, my heart is not haughty.* The principle of pride has no place in my heart; and consequently the high, lofty, and supercilious look does not appear in my eyes. I neither look up, with desire to obtain, to the state of others, nor look down with contempt to the meanness or poverty of those below me. And the whole of my conduct proves this; for "I have not exercised myself," walked, "in high matters," nor associated myself with the higher ranks of the community, nor *in great matters,* "wonderful" or sublime things; *too high for me,* "alien from me," and that do not belong to a person in my sphere and situation in life.

PSALM 132

The Psalmist prays that God would remember His promises to David, 1. His purpose to bring the ark of the Lord into a place of rest, 2-5. Where it was found, and the prayer in removing it, 6-9. The promises made to David and his posterity, 10-12. God's choice of Zion for a habitation, and His promises to the people, 13-17. All their enemies shall be confounded, 18.

Some attribute this psalm to David, but without sufficient ground; others, to Solomon, with more likelihood; and others, to some inspired author at the conclusion of the Captivity, which is, perhaps, the most probable. It refers to the building of the second Temple, and placing the ark of the covenant in it.

2. *How he sware unto the Lord.* It is only in this place that we are informed of David's vow to the Lord relative to the building of the Temple but we find he had fully purposed the thing.

3. *Surely I will not come.* This must refer to the situation of the Temple; or, as we would express it, he would not pass another day till he had found out the ground on which to build the Temple, and projected the plan, and devised ways and means to execute it.

5. *The mighty God of Jacob.* "The Mighty One of Jacob." We have this epithet of God for the first time in Gen. xlix. 24.

6. *Lo, we have heard of it at Ephratah.* This may be considered as a continuation of David's vow; as if he had said: As I had determined to build a temple for the ark, and heard that it was at Ephratah, I went and found it in the "fields of Jaar"—not the wood, but Kirjath Jaar or Jearim, where the ark was then lodged—and having found it, he entered the Tabernacle, v. 7; and then, adoring that God whose presence was in it, he invited Him to arise and come to the place which he had prepared for Him.

8. *Arise, O Lord, into thy rest; thou, and the ark of thy strength.* Using the same expressions which Solomon used when he dedicated the Temple, 2 Chron. vi. 41-42. If we take vv. 6-8, not as the continuation of David's vow, but as the words of the captives in Babylon, the explanation will be plain and easy: "We have heard, O Lord, from our fathers, that Thy tabernacle was formerly a long time at Shiloh, in the tribe of Ephraim. And our history informs us that it has been also at Kirjath-jearim, *the fields of the wood;* and afterwards it was brought to Jerusalem, and there established; but Jerusalem is now ruined, the Temple destroyed, and Thy people in captivity. Arise, O Lord, and re-establish Thy dwelling place in Thy holy city!"

11. *The Lord hath sworn.* As David sware to the Lord, so the Lord swears to David, that He will establish his throne, and place his posterity on it; and that He had respect to David's Antitype, we learn from St. Peter, Acts ii. 30.

13. *The Lord hath chosen Zion.* Therefore neither Shiloh nor Kirjath-jearim is the place of his rest.

14. *This is my rest for ever.* Here the Christian Church is most indubitably meant. This is God's place forever.

18. *His enemies will I clothe with shame.* Every opponent of the Christian cause shall be confounded. *But upon himself shall his crown flourish.* There shall be no end of the government of Christ's kingdom. From v. 11 to the end, the spiritual David and his posterity are the subjects of which the psalm treats.

PSALM 133

The comfort and benefit of the communion of saints, 1-3.

There are different opinions concerning this psalm; the most probable is that it represents the priests and Levites returned from captivity, and united in the service of God in the sanctuary. This, the preceding, and the following appear to make one subject. In the one hundred and thirty-second, the Lord is entreated to enter His temple, and pour out His benediction; in the one hundred and thirty-third, the beautiful order and harmony of the Temple service is pointed out; and in the one hundred and thirty-fourth, all are exhorted to diligence and watchfulness in the performance of their duty.

1. *Behold, how good and how pleasant!* Unity is, according to this scripture, a *good* thing and a *pleasant;* and especially among *brethren*—members of the same family, of the same Christian community, and of the same nation.

2. *Like the precious ointment.* The composition of this holy anointing oil may be seen, Exod. xxx. 23; sweet cinnamon, sweet calamus, *cassia lignea,* and olive oil. The odor of this must have been very agreeable, and serves here as a metaphor to point out the exquisite excellence of brotherly love. *Ran down upon the beard.* The oil was poured upon the head of Aaron so profusely as to run down upon his garments. It is customary in the East to pour out the oil on the head so profusely as to reach every limb.

3. *As the dew of Hermon, and as the dew that descended upon the mountains of Zion.* This was not Mount Zion in Jerusalem, but "Sion," which is a part of Hermon. See Deut. iv. 48: "Mount Sion, which is Hermon." On this mountain the dew is very copious.

PSALM 134

An exhortation to praise God in His sanctuary, 1-3.

This is the last of the fifteen psalms called "psalms of degrees." It is intimately connected with the preceding two psalms, and is an exhortation to the priests and Levites who kept nightly watch in the Temple to be assiduous in praising the Lord. It seems to consist of two parts: First, An exhortation, probably from the high priest, to those priests and Levites who kept watch in the Temple by night, to spend their time profitably, and duly celebrate the praises of God, vv. 1-2. The second part, which is contained in the third verse, is the prayer of the priests and Levites for the high priest, who seems now to be going to his rest.

1. *Behold, bless ye the Lord.* I believe *hinneh* should be taken here in the sense of "take heed."

Which by night stand. Who minister during the night.

2. *Lift up your hands in the sanctuary.* *Kodesh,* "in holiness." The expression seems very similar to that of St. Paul, 1 Tim. ii. 8: "Lifting up holy hands, without wrath and doubting."

3. *Bless thee out of Zion.* As if they had said, "We will attend to your orders; go in peace, and may God shower down His blessings upon you!" The blessing pronounced by the priests was the following: "The Lord bless thee, and keep thee: the Lord make his face shine upon thee, and be gracious unto thee: the Lord lift up his countenance upon thee, and give thee peace" (Num. vi. 24-26).

PSALM 135

An exhortation to praise God for His goodness and greatness, 1-5; for His wonders in nature, 6-7; His wonders done in Egypt, 8-9; in the wilderness, 10-12; for His goodness to His people, 13-14. The vanity of idols, 15-18. Israel, with its priests and Levites, exhorted to praise the Lord, 19-21.

This psalm is intimately connected with the preceding. It is an exhortation addressed to the priests and Levites, and to all Israel, to publish the praises of the Lord. The conclusion of this psalm is nearly the same with Psalm cxv; and what is said about idols, and the effects of the power of God, seems to be taken from it and the tenth chapter of Jeremiah; and from these and other circumstances it appears the psalm was written after the Captivity; and might, as Calmet conjectures, have been used at the dedication of the second Temple.

1. *Praise ye the Lord.* This may be considered as the title, for it has none other. *Praise ye the name of the Lord.* Perhaps the original, *halelu eth shem Yehovah,* should be translated, "Praise ye the name Jehovah"; that is, Praise God in His infinite essence of being, holiness, goodness, and truth.

2. *Ye that stand.* Priests and Levites. For which he gives several reasons.

3. *The Lord is good.* Here is the first reason why He should be praised; and a second is subjoined—*for it is pleasant.* It is becoming to acknowledge this infinite Being, and our dependence on Him.

4. *For the Lord hath chosen Jacob.* This is a third reason. He has taken the Israelites for His peculiar people, "his peculiar treasure."

5. *The Lord is great.* Unlimited in His power —another reason. *Is above all gods.* Every class of being, whether idolized or not; because he is the Fountain of existence. This is a fifth reason.

15. *The idols of the heathen.* This verse and the following, to the end of the eighteenth, are almost word for word the same as vv. 4-8 of Psalm cxv.

19. *Bless the Lord, O house.* See similar verses, Ps. cxv. 9-13.

PSALM 136

An exhortation to give thanks to God for various mercies granted to all men, 1-9; particularly to the Israelites in Egypt, 10-12; at the Red Sea, 13-15; in the wilderness, 16-20; and in the Promised Land, 21-22; for the redemption of the captives from Babylon, 23-24; and for His providential mercies to all, 25-26.

This psalm is little else than a repetition of the preceding, with the burden, "because his mercy endureth for ever," at the end of every verse. It seems to have been a responsive song; the first part of the verse sung by the Levites, the burden by the people. It has no title in the Hebrew, nor in any of the versions. It was doubtless written after the Captivity. The author is unknown.

1. *O give thanks unto the Lord; for he is good.* This sentiment often occurs: the goodness of the divine nature, as a ground both of confidence and of thanksgiving. *For his mercy endureth for ever.* These words, which are the burden of every verse, *ki leolam chasdo,* might be translated: "For His tender mercy is to the coming age"; meaning, probably, if the psalm be prophetic, that peculiar display of His compassion, the redemption of the world by the Lord Jesus. These very words were prescribed by David as an acknowledgment, to be used continually in the divine worship, see 1 Chron. xvi. 41: also by Solomon, 2 Chron. vii. 3, 6; and observed by Jehoshaphat, 2 Chron. xx. 21; all acknowledging that, however rich in mercy God was to them, the most extensive displays of His goodness were reserved for the age to come; see 1 Pet. i. 10-12.

2. *The God of gods. Ladonai haadonim.* As *adonai* signifies "director," it may apply here, not to idols, for God is not their God, but to the priests and spiritual rulers; as Lord of lords may apply to kings and magistrates, etc. He is God and Ruler over all the rulers of the earth, whether in things sacred or civil.

4. *Who alone doeth great wonders.* "Miracles."

6. *Stretched out the earth above the waters.* Or "upon the waters."

25. *Giveth food to all flesh.* By whose universal providence every intellectual and animal being is supported and preserved. The appointing every living thing food, and that sort of food which is suited to its nature, is an overwhelming proof of the wondrous providence, wisdom, and goodness of God.

PSALM 137

The desolate and afflicted state of the captives in Babylon, 1-2. How they were insulted by their enemies, 3-4. Their attachment to their country, 5-6. Judgments denounced against their enemies, 7-9.

Neither the Hebrew nor Chaldee has any title. Some think it was sung when they returned from Babylon; others, while they were there. It was evidently composed during or at the close of the Captivity.

1. *By the rivers of Babylon.* In their captivity and dispersion, it was customary for the Jews to hold their religious meetings on the banks of rivers. Mention is made of this Acts xvi. 13, where we find the Jews of Philippi resorting to "a river side, where prayer was wont to be made."

2. *We hanged our harps upon the willows.* The *willows* were very plentiful in Babylon. The great quantity of them that were on the banks of the Euphrates caused Isaiah, chap. xv. 7, to call it "the brook [or river] of the willows." This is a most affecting picture. Perhaps resting themselves after toil, and wishing to spend their time religiously, they took their harps, and were about to sing one of the songs of Zion; but, reflecting on their own country, they became so filled with distress that they unstrung their harps with one consent, and hung them on the willow bushes, and gave a general loose to their grief. Some of the Babylonians, who probably attended such meetings for the sake of the music, desired them to sing one of Zion's songs. This is affectingly told.

3. *They that carried us away captive required of us a song.* This was as unreasonable as it was insulting.

4. *How shall we sing the Lord's song? Eich! nashir;* "Oh, we sing!" Who does not hear the deep sigh in the strongly guttural sound of the original *eich!* wrung, as it were, from the bottom of the heart? Can we, in this state of slavery—we, exiles, from our country—we sing, or be mirthful in these circumstances?

7. *Remember . . . the children of Edom.* It appears from Jer. xii. 6; xxv. 14; Lam. iv. 21-22; Ezek. xxv. 12; Obad. 11-14, that the Idumeans joined the army of Nebuchadnezzar against their brethren the Jews; and that they were main instruments in razing the walls of Jerusalem even to the ground.

8. *O daughter of Babylon, who art to be destroyed.* Or, "O thou daughter of Babylon, the destroyer." *Rewardeth thee as thou hast served us.* This was Cyrus, who was chosen of God to do this work, and is therefore called *happy,* as being God's agent in its destruction.

9. *Happy . . . that taketh and dasheth thy little ones.* That is, So oppressive have you been to all under your domination as to become universally hated and detested; so that those who may have the last hand in your destruction, and the total extermination of your inhabitants, shall be reputed *happy*—shall be celebrated and extolled as those who had rid the world of a curse so grievous. These prophetic declarations contain no excitement to any person or persons to commit acts of cruelty and barbarity, but are simply declarative of what would take place in the order of the retributive providence and justice of God, and the general opinion that should in consequence be expressed on the subject.

PSALM 138

The Psalmist praises the Lord for His mercies to himself, 1-3. He foretells that the kings of the earth shall worship Him, 4-5. God's condescension to the humble, 6. The Psalmist's confidence, 7-8.

The Hebrew and all the versions attribute this psalm to David, and it is supposed to have been made by him when, delivered from all his enemies, he was firmly seated on the throne of Israel.

1. *Before the gods will I sing. Neged Elohim,* "in the presence of Elohim"; most probably meaning before the ark, where were the sacred symbols of the Supreme Being.

2. *For thy lovingkindness.* Thy "tender mercy" shown to me; and for the fulfillment of *thy truth*—the promises Thou hast made. *Thou hast magnified thy word above all thy name.* All the versions read this sentence thus: "For thou hast magnified above all the name of thy holiness." Thou hast proved that Thou hast all power in heaven and in earth, and that Thou art true in all Thy words. The original I think might be thus translated: "For Thou hast magnified Thy name and Thy word over all," or, "on every occasion."

8. *The Lord will perfect.* Whatever is further necessary to be done, He will do it.

PSALM 139

A fine account of the omniscience of God, 1-6; of His omnipresence, 7-12; of His power and providence, 13-16. The excellence of His purposes, 17-18. His opposition to the wicked, 19-20; with whom the godly can have no fellowship, 21-22.

The title of this psalm in the Hebrew is, "To the chief Musician [or, To the Conqueror], A Psalm of David." The versions in general follow the Hebrew. And yet, notwithstanding these testimonies, there appears internal evidence that the psalm was not written by David, but during or after the time of the Captivity, as there are several Chaldaisms in it. See vv. 2-3, 7, 9, 19-20, collated with Dan. ii. 29-30; iv. 16; vii. 28; some of these will be noticed in their proper places.

1. *O Lord, thou hast searched me.* "Thou hast investigated me"; Thou hast thoroughly acquainted thyself with my whole soul and conduct.

2. *My downsitting and mine uprising.* Even these inconsiderable and casual things are under Thy continual notice. I cannot so much as take a seat, or leave it, without being marked by Thee. *Thou understandest my thought.* "My Cogitation." This word is Chaldee, see Dan. ii. 29-30. *Afar off.* While the figment is forming that shall produce them.

3. *Thou compassest my path.* Zeritha—thou dost winnow, ventilate, or "sift" my path; *and my lying down, ribi,* my "bed." *And art acquainted.* Thou treasurest up—this is the import of *sachan.* Thou hast the whole number of *my ways,* and the steps I took in them.

4. *There is not a word in my tongue.* "Although [ki] there be not a word in my tongue, behold, O Jehovah, Thou knowest the whole of it"; that is, Thou knowest all my words before they are uttered, as Thou knowest all my thoughts while as yet they are unformed.

5. *Thou hast beset me behind and before.* "The hereafter and the past, Thou hast formed me."

7. *Whither shall I go from thy spirit?* Surely *ruach* in this sense must be taken personally; it certainly cannot mean either breath or wind. To render it so would make the passage ridiculous. *From thy presence?* "From thy faces." Why do we meet with this word so frequently in the plural number when applied to God? And why have we His *spirit,* and His "appearances" or "faces," both here? A Trinitarian would at once say, "The plurality of persons in the Godhead is intended"; and who can prove that he is mistaken?

15. *My substance was not hid from thee.* My "bones" or "skeleton." *Curiously wrought.* Embroidered, made of needlework. These two words, says Bishop Horsley, describe the two principal parts of which the human body is composed: the bony skeleton, the foundation of the whole; and the external covering of muscular flesh, tendons, veins, arteries, nerves, and skin —a curious web of fibers.

16. *Thine eyes did see my substance.* My "embryo state."

17. *How precious also are thy thoughts!* "Thy cogitations"; a Chaldaism, as before. *How great* is the sum of them! "How strongly rational are the heads or principal subjects of them!"

18. *If I should count them.* I should be glad to enumerate so many interesting particulars, but they are beyond calculation. *When I awake.* Thou art my Governor and Protector night and day.

19. *Surely thou wilt slay the wicked.* The remaining part of this psalm has no visible connection with the preceding. I rather think it a fragment or a part of some other psalm. *Ye bloody men.* "Men of blood," men guilty of death.

21. *Do not I hate them?* I hold their conduct in abomination.

22. *With perfect hatred.* Their conduct, their motives, their opposition to Thee, their perfidy and idolatrous purposes, I perfectly abhor.

23. *Search me, O God.* Investigate my conduct, examine my heart, put me to the test, and examine my thoughts.

24. *If there be any wicked way.* "A way of idolatry, or of error." *Lead me in the way everlasting.* "In the old way"—the way in which our fathers walked, who worshipped Thee.

PSALM 140

The Psalmist prays against his enemies, 1-6; returns thanks for help, 7; describes his enemies, and prays further against them, 8-11. His confidence in God, 12-13.

The Hebrew and all the versions attribute this psalm to David; and it is supposed to contain his complaint when persecuted by Saul.

1. *From the evil man.* Saul, who was full of envy, jealousy, and cruelty against David, to whom both himself and his kingdom were under the highest obligations, endeavored by every means to destroy him.

2. *They gathered together.* He and his courtiers form plots and cabals against my life.

3. *They have sharpened their tongues.* They employ their time in forging lies and calumnies against me, and those of the most virulent nature.

4. *Preserve me from the violent man.* Saul again, who was as headstrong and violent in all his measures as he was cruel, and inflexibly bent on the destruction of David.

5. *Have hid a snare for me.* They hunted David as they would a dangerous wild beast.

11. *Let not an evil speaker be established.* "A man of tongue."

PSALM 141

The Psalmist prays that his devotions may be accepted, 1-2. That he may be enabled so to watch that he do not offend with his tongue, and that he may be preserved from wickedness, 3-4. His willingness to receive reproof, 5. He complains of disasters, 6-7. His trust in God, and prayer against his enemies, 8-10.

This psalm is generally attributed to David, and considered to have been composed during his persecution by Saul. Some suppose that he made it at the time that he formed the resolution to go to Achish, king of Gath; see 1 Sam. xxvi. It is generally thought to be an evening prayer, and has long been used as such in the service of the Greek church.

1. *Lord, I cry unto thee.* Many of David's psalms begin with complaints, but they are not those of habitual plaint and peevishness. He

was in frequent troubles and difficulties, and he always sought help in God.

2. *As incense.* Incense was offered every morning and evening before the Lord, on the golden altar, before the veil of the sanctuary (Exod. xxix. 39 and Num. xxviii. 4). *As the evening sacrifice. Minchah,* which is generally taken for a gratitude offering or unbloody sacrifice. The literal translation of the passage is, "Let my prayer be established for incense before Thy faces; and the lifting up of my hands for the evening oblation."

4. *Let me eat not of their dainties.* This may refer to eating things forbidden by the law, or to the partaking in banquets or feasts in honor of idols.

5. *Let the righteous smite me.* This verse is extremely difficult in the original. The following translation, in which the Syriac, Vulgate, Septuagint, Aethiopic, and Arabic nearly agree, appears to me to be the best: "Let the righteous chastise me in mercy, and instruct me; but let not the oil of the wicked anoint my head. It shall not adorn my head; for still my prayer shall be against their wicked works." The oil of the wicked may here mean his smooth, flattering speeches; and the Psalmist intimates that he would rather suffer the cutting reproof of the righteous than the oily talk of the flatterer.

6. *When their judges are overthrown in stony places.* "In the hands of the rock." *They shall hear my words; for they are sweet.* Some think there is here an allusion to David's generous treatment of Saul in the cave of En-gedi, and afterwards at the hill of Hachilah, in this verse, which might be translated: "Their judges have been dismissed in the rocky places; and have heard my words, that they were sweet."

PSALM 142

The Psalmist, in great distress and difficulty, calls upon God, 1-7.

The title says, "An Instruction of David," or a Psalm of David giving instruction; "A Prayer when he was in the cave." David was twice in great peril in caves: (1) At the cave of Adullam, when he fled from Achish, king of Gath, 1 Samuel xxii; (2) When he was in the cave of En-gedi, where he had taken refuge from the pursuit of Saul; and the latter, without knowing that David was in it, had gone into it on some necessary occasion, 1 Samuel xxiv. If the inscription can be depended on, the cave of En-gedi is the most likely of the two, for the scene laid here.

3. *Then thou knewest my path.* When Saul and his army were about the cave in which I was hidden, *thou knewest my path*—that I had then no way of escape but by miracle; but Thou didst not permit them to know that I was wholly in their power.

7. *Bring my soul out of prison.* Bring *naphshi,* "my life," out of this cave in which it is now imprisoned, Saul and his men being in possession of the entrance. *The righteous shall compass me about.* They "shall crown me"; perhaps meaning that the pious Jews, on the death of Saul, would cheerfully join together to make him king, being convinced that God, by His bountiful dealings with him, intended that it should be so.

PSALM 143

The Psalmist prays for mercy, and deprecates judgment, 1-2. His persecutions, 3. His earnest prayer for deliverance, 4-9. Prays for God's quickening Spirit, 10-11. And for the total discomfiture of his adversaries, 12.

The Hebrew and all the versions attribute this psalm to David; and the Vulgate, Septuagint, Aethiopic, and Arabic state that it was composed on the rebellion of his son Absalom. Nor is there anything in the psalm that positively disagrees with this inscription. This is the last of the seven psalms styled "penitential."

3. *He hath made me to dwell in darkness.* Literally, "in dark places." This may be understood of David's taking refuge in caves and dens of the earth, to escape from his persecuting son.

6. *I stretch forth my hands.* This is a natural action. All in distress, or under the influence of eager desire, naturally extend their hands and arms, as if to catch at help and obtain succor. *As a thirsty land,* parched and burned by the sun, longs for rain, so does my thirsty soul for the living God.

7. *Hear me speedily.* "Make haste" to answer me. A few hours, and my state may be irretrievable. In a short time my unnatural son may put an end to my life.

8. *Cause me to hear thy lovingkindness in the morning.* This petition was probably offered in the night season. David had dispatched his messengers in all directions, and prays to God that he might by the morning get some good news. *Cause me to know the way wherein I should walk.* Absalom and his partisans are in possession of all the country. I know not in what direction to go, that I may not fall in with them; point out by Thy especial providence the path I should take.

10. *Teach me to do thy will.* "Thy pleasure." To be found doing the will of God is the only safe state for man.

PSALM 144

The Psalmist praises God for His goodness, 1-2. Exclamations relative to the vanity of human life, 3-4. He prays against his enemies, 5-8; and extols God's mercy for the temporal blessings enjoyed by His people, 9-15.

The Hebrew, and all the versions, attribute this psalm to David. Calmet thinks, and with much probability, that it was composed by David after the death of Absalom, and the restoration of the kingdom to peace and tranquility. From a collation of this with Psalm xviii, of which it appears to be an abridgment, preserving the same ideas and the same forms of expression, there can be no doubt of both having proceeded from the same pen, and that David was the author.

2. *Who subdueth my people.* Who has once more reduced the nation to a state of loyal obedience. This may refer to the peace after the rebellion of Absalom.

4. *Man is like to vanity.* Literally, "Adam is like to Abel," exposed to the same miseries, accidents, and murderers; for in millions of cases the hands of brothers are lifted up to shed the blood of brothers.

9. *I will sing a new song.* A song of peculiar excellence. I will pour forth all my gratitude, and all my skill, on its composition. See Ps. xxxiii. 2-3.

13. *That our garners,* etc. "Our garners are full." These are not prayers put up by David for such blessings, but assertions that such blessings were actually in possession. All these expressions should be understood in the present tense. *Ten thousands in our streets.* "In our pens or sheep-walks."

14. *Our oxen may be strong to labour.* We have not only an abundance of cattle, but they are of the most strong and vigorous breed. *No breaking in.* So well-ordered is the police of the kingdom that there are no depredations, no robbers, housebreakers, or marauding parties in the land.

15. *Happy is that people.* "Oh, how happy are the people!"

PSALM 145

God is praised for His unsearchable greatness, 1-2; for His majesty and terrible acts, 3-6; for His goodness and tender mercies to all, 7-9; for His power and kingdom, 10-13; for His kindness to the distressed, 14; for His providence, 15-17. He hears and answers prayer, 18-20. All should praise Him, 21.

This psalm is attributed to David by the Hebrew and all the versions. It is the last of the acrostic psalms, and should contain twenty-two verses, as answering to the twenty-two letters of the Hebrew alphabet. But the verse between the thirteenth and fourteenth, beginning with the letter *nun,* is lost out of the present Hebrew copies; but a translation of it is found in the Syriac, Septuagint, Vulgate, Aethiopic, Arabic, and Anglo-Saxon. It is an incomparable psalm of praise.

3. *His greatness is unsearchable.* Literally, "To His mightinesses there is no investigation." All in God is unlimited and eternal.

4. *One generation.* Thy creating and redeeming acts are recorded in Thy word; but Thy wondrous providential dealings with mankind must be handed down by tradition, from generation to generation, for they are in continual occurrence, and consequently innumerable.

10. *All thy works shall praise thee.* The God who is good to all. *Thy saints. Chasideycha,* "Thy compassionate ones"; those who are partakers of Thy great mercy, v. 8.

13. *Thy dominion endureth.* There is neither age nor people in and over which God does not manifest His benignly ruling power. As the above verse begins with the letter *mem,* the next in the order of the alphabet should begin with *nun;* but that verse is totally wanting. To say it never was in is false, because the alphabet is not complete without it; and it is an unanswerable argument to prove the careless manner in which the Jews have preserved the divine records. One MS., now in Trinity College, Dublin, has it thus, I suppose by correction, in the bottom of the page: "The Lord is faithful in all his words; and merciful in all his works." The Septuagint and Vulgate are the same with the Hebrew given above.

14. *The Lord upholdeth all that fall.* "The falling," or those who are not able to keep their feet; the weak. He shores them up; he is their Prop.

15. *The eyes of all wait upon thee.* What a fine figure! God is here represented as the universal Father, providing food for every living creature. *In due season.* The kind of food that is suited to every animal, and to all the stages of life in each animal.

16. *Thou openest thine hand.* What a hand is this that holds in it all the food that meets the desires and necessities of the universe of creatures!

17. *The Lord is righteous.* It was the similarity of this to the omitted verse, which should have been the fourteenth, that caused it to be omitted.

20. *The Lord preserveth.* He is the Keeper of all them that love Him. *But all the wicked will he destroy.* There is something curious in the *shomer,* the Keeper or Guardian of the pious; He is *shamid,* the Destroyer of the wicked. The first word implies, He is continually keeping them; the second, that He *causes* the others to be destroyed.

PSALM 146

The Psalmist, full of gratitude, purposes to praise God forever, 1-2; and exhorts not to trust in man, not even the most powerful; for which he gives his reasons, 3-4. The great advantage of trusting in God, 5. The mercies which they who trust in God may expect, 6-9. The divine government is everlasting, 10.

This is the first of the psalms called *Hallelujah* Psalms, of which there are five, and which conclude the book. No author's name is prefixed to this, in either the Hebrew or Chaldee. It was probably written after the Captivity, and may refer to the time when Cyrus, prejudiced by the enemies of the Jews, withdrew his order for the rebuilding of the walls of Jerusalem, to which revocation of the royal edict the third verse may refer: *Put not your trust in princes.*

7. *Which executeth judgment for the oppressed.* For those who suffer by violence or calumny. This may refer to the Israelites, who suffered much by oppression from the Babylonians, and by calumny from the Samaritans, who had prejudiced the king of Persia against them. *Giveth food to the hungry.* No doubt He fed the poor captives by many displays of His peculiar providence. *The Lord looseth the prisoners.* And as He has sustained you so long under your captivity, so will He bring you out of it.

9. *Preserveth the strangers.* He has preserved you strangers in a strange land, where you have been in captivity for seventy years; and though in an enemy's country, He has provided for the widows and orphans as amply as if He had been in the Promised Land. *The way of the wicked he turneth upside down.* He "subverts, turns aside."

PSALM 147

The Psalmist praises God for His goodness to Jerusalem, 1-3; shows His great mercy to them that trust in Him, 4-6; he extols Him for His mercies and providential kindness, 7-11; for His defense of Jerusalem, 12-15; for His wonders in the seasons, 16-18; and His word unto Jacob, 19-20.

This psalm, which is without title in the Hebrew, Chaldee, and Vulgate, is attributed by the other versions to Haggai and Zechariah. It was probably penned after the Captivity, when the Jews were busily employed in rebuilding Jerusalem, as may be gathered from the second and thirteenth verses. It may be necessary to remark that all the versions, except the Chaldee, divide this psalm at the end of the eleventh verse, and begin a new psalm at the twelfth. By this division the numbers of the psalms agree in the versions with the Hebrew; the former having been, till now, one behind.

1. *Praise is comely.* It is decent, befitting, and proper that every intelligent creature should acknowledge the Supreme Being; and as He does nothing but good to the children of men, so they should speak good of His name.

2. *The Lord doth build up.* The Psalmist appears to see the walls rising under his eye, because the outcasts of Israel, those who had been in captivity, are now gathered together to do the work.

3. *He healeth the broken in heart.* "The shivered in heart." From the root *shabar,* "to break in pieces," we have our word "shiver," to break into splinters, into shivers.

4. *He telleth the number of the stars.* He whose knowledge is so exact as to tell every star in heaven can be under no difficulty to find out and collect all the scattered exiles of Israel.

5. *His understanding is infinite.* "To his intelligence there is no number"; though He numbers the stars, His understanding is without number. It is infinite; therefore He can know, as He can do, all things.

6. *The Lord lifteth up the meek.* The humbled, the afflicted.

7. *Sing unto the Lord. Enu,* sing a responsive song, sing in parts, answer one another.

8. *Who covereth the heaven with clouds.* Collects the vapors together, in order to cause it to rain upon the earth. Even the direction of the winds, the collection of the clouds, and the descent of the rain are under the especial management of God. These things form a part of His providential management of the world. *Maketh grass to grow upon the mountains.* After this clause the Vulgate, the Septuagint, Aethiopic, Arabic, and Anglo-Saxon add, "and herb for the service of man." It appears that a hemistich, or half-line, has been lost from the Hebrew text; which, according to the above versions, must have stood thus: as in Ps. civ. 14: "And herbage for the service of mankind."

11. *The Lord taketh pleasure in them that fear him.* That are truly religious. *In those that hope is his mercy.* Even the cry of the penitent is pleasing in the ear of the Lord. With this verse the hundred and forty-sixth psalm ends in all the versions, except the Chaldee. And the hundred and forty-seventh commences with the twelfth verse. I believe these to be two distinct psalms. The subjects of them are not exactly the same, though something similar; and they plainly refer to different periods.

13. *He hath strengthened the bars of thy gates.* He has enabled you to complete the walls of Jerusalem. From the former part of the psalm it appears the walls were then in progress; from this part, they appear to be completed, and provisions to be brought into the city to support its inhabitants.

17. *He casteth forth his ice* (probably hailstones) *like crumbs.*

18. *He sendeth out his word.* He gives a command; the south wind blows; the thaw takes place; and the ice and snow being liquefied, *the waters flow,* where before they were bound up by the ice.

PSALM 148

The Psalmist calls on all the creation to praise the Lord. The angels and visible heavens, 1-6; the earth and the sea, 7; the meteors, 8; mountains, hills, and trees, 9; beasts, reptiles, and fowls, 10; kings, princes, and mighty men, 11; men, women, and children, 12-13; and especially all the people of Israel, 14.

This psalm has no title, but by the Syriac it is attributed to Haggai and Zechariah; and the Septuagint and the Aethiopic follow it. As a hymn of praise, this is the most sublime in the whole book.

1. *Praise ye the Lord from the heavens. Min hashshamayim* signifies whatever belongs to the heavens, all their inhabitants; as *min haarets,* v. 7, signifies all that belongs to the earth, all its inhabitants and productions.

3. *Praise ye him, sun and moon.* The meaning of this address and all others to inanimate nature is this: Every work of God's hand partakes so much of His perfections that it requires only to be studied and known in order to show forth the manifold wisdom, power, and goodness of the Creator.

7. *Praise the Lord from the earth.* As, in the first address, he calls upon the heavens and all that belong to them, so here, in this second part, he calls upon the earth and all that belong to it. *Ye dragons. Tanninim,* whales, porpoises, sharks, and sea monsters of all kinds. *And all deeps.* Whatsoever is contained in the sea, the astonishing flux and reflux of the ocean.

9. *Fruitful trees.* Fruit trees of all kinds. *And all cedars.* Every kind of forest tree.

10. *Beasts.* "Wild beasts" of every kind. *All cattle.* All domestic animals.

13. *Let them,* all already specified, *praise the name of Jehovah,* because He excels all beings; and *his glory,* as seen in creating, preserving, and governing all things, is *al,* "upon" or "over" *the earth and heaven.* All space and place as well as the beings found in them, show forth the manifold wisdom and goodness of God.

14. *He also exalteth the horn.* Raises to power and authority *his people. The praise.* Jehovah is the Subject of the praise of all His *saints.*

PSALM 149

All the congregation are invited to praise God for His mercies, 1-3. Their great privileges, 4-5. Their victories, 6-9.

This seems to be a song of triumph after some glorious victory, probably in the time of the Maccabees. It has been also understood as predicting the success of the gospel in the nations of the earth. It has no title in the Hebrew, nor in any of the versions, and no author's name.

1. *Sing unto the Lord a new song.* That is, as we have often had occasion to remark, an "excellent song," the best we can possibly pronounce. So the word *chadash* is often understood; and so the word *novus,* "new," was often used among the Latin writers.

3. *Let them praise his name in the dance. Bemachol,* "with the pipe," or some kind of wind music, classed here with *toph,* the drum, and *kinnor,* the harp. I know no place in the Bible where *machol* and *machalath* mean *dance* of any kind; they constantly signify some kind of pipe.

4. *The Lord taketh pleasure in his people.* The pleasure or goodwill of God is in His people;

He loves them ardently, and will load them with His benefits while they are humble and thankful; for *he will beautify,* "He will make fair," *the meek,* "the lowly," the humble, *with salvation.*

6. *Let the high praises of God.* Let them sing songs the most sublime, with the loudest noise consistent with harmony. *And a twoedged sword in their hand.* Perhaps there is an allusion here to the manner in which the Jews were obliged to labor in rebuilding the walls of Jerusalem: "Every one with one of his hands wrought in the work, and with the other hand held a weapon," Neh. iv. 17.

7. *To execute vengeance upon the heathen.* This may refer simply to their purpose of defending themselves to the uttermost, should their enemies attack them while building their wall. *Punishments upon the people.* The unfaithful and treacherous Jews; for we find that some, even of their nobles, had joined with Sanballat and Tobiah (see Neh. vi. 17-19); and it appears also that many of them had formed alliances with those heathens, which were contrary to the law; see Neh. xiii. 15-29.

9. *To execute upon them the judgment written.* In Deut. vii. 1, God promises His people complete victory over all their enemies, and over the heathen. God repeatedly promises such victories to His faithful people; and this is, properly speaking, the *judgment written,* i.e., foretold.

PSALM 150

A general exhortation to praise God, 1-2. With the trumpet, psaltery, and harp, 3. With the timbrel and dance, stringed instruments and organs, 4. With the cymbals, 5. All living creatures are called upon to join in the exercise.

This psalm is without title and author in the Hebrew, and in all the ancient versions. It is properly the full chorus of all voices and instruments in the Temple, at the conclusion of the grand *Hallelujah,* to which the five concluding psalms belong.

1. *Praise God in his sanctuary.* In many places we have the compound word *halelu-yah,* "praise ye Jehovah"; but this is the first place in which we find *halelu-el,* "praise God," or "the strong God." Praise Him who is Jehovah, the infinite and self-existent Being; and praise Him who is God, *El* or *Elohim,* the great God in covenant with mankind, to bless and save them unto eternal life. *In his sanctuary*—in the Temple; in whatever place is dedicated to His service. Or, "in his holiness"—through His own holy influence in your hearts. *The firmament of his power.* Through the whole expanse, to the utmost limits of His power. As *rakia* is the

firmament of vast expanse that surrounds the globe, and probably that in which all the celestial bodies of the solar system are included, it may have that meaning here. Praise Him whose power and goodness extend through all worlds; and let the inhabitants of all those worlds share in the grand chorus, that it may be universal.

2. *For his mighty acts.* Whether manifested in creation, government, mercy, or justice. *His excellent greatness.* According to the multitude of His magnitude, or of His majesty.

3. *The sound of the trumpet. Sophar,* from its noble, cheering, and majestic sound; for the original has this ideal meaning. *With the psaltery. Nebel;* the nabla, a hollow stringed instrument; perhaps like the guitar. *And harp. Kinnor,* another stringed instrument, played on with the hands or fingers.

4. *Praise him with the timbrel. Toph,* drum, tabret, or tympanum, or tom-tom of the ancients; a skin stretched over a broad hoop; perhaps something like the tambourine. *And dance. Machol,* the "pipe." It never means *dance;* see the note on Ps. cxlix. 3. *Stringed instruments. Minnim.* This literally signifies "strings put in order"; perhaps a triangular kind of hollow instrument on which the strings were regularly placed, growing shorter and shorter till they came to a point. This would give a variety of sounds, from a deep bass to a high treble. *Organs. Ugab.* Very likely the mouth organ.

5. *Loud cymbals. Tseltselim.* Two hollow plates of brass, which, being struck together, produced a sharp clanging sound. This instrument is still in use. What the *high sounding cymbals* meant I know not, unless those of a larger make, struck above the head, and consequently emitting a louder sound.

6. *Let every thing that hath breath.* Either to make a vocal noise, or a sound by blowing into pipes, fifes, flutes, trumpets, etc. Let all join together, and put forth all your strength and all your skill in sounding the praises of Jehovah; and then let a universal burst with HALLELUJAH! close the grand ceremony. It is evident that this psalm has no other meaning than merely the summoning up all the voices, and all the instruments, to complete the service in full chorus.

Of such peculiar importance did the Book of Psalms appear to our blessed Lord and His apostles that they have quoted nearly fifty of them several times in the New Testament. There is scarcely a state in human life that is not distinctly marked in them; together with all the variety of experience which is found, not merely among pious Jews, but among Christians, the most deeply acquainted with the things of Christ.

The Book of
PROVERBS

There has scarcely been any dispute concerning either the author or divine authority of this book, in either the Jewish or Christian Church. All allow that it was written by Solomon, and the general belief is that he wrote the book of divine inspiration.

It has, indeed, been supposed that Solomon *collected* the major part of these proverbs from those who had preceded him, whether Hebrews or heathens; but the latter opinion has been controverted, as derogating from the authority of the book. But this supposition has very little weight; for, whatever of truth is found in or among men, came originally from God. And if He employed an inspired man to collect those rays of light, and embody them for the use of His Church, He had a right to do so, and to claim His own wheresoever found, and, by giving it a new authentication, to render it more useful in reference to the end for which it was originally communicated. God is "the Father of lights," and from Him came all true wisdom, not only in its discursive teachings, but in all its detached maxims for the government and regulation of life. I think it very likely that Solomon did not compose them all; but he collected everything of this kind within his reach, and what was according to the Spirit of truth, by which he was inspired, he condensed in this book; and as the Divine Spirit gave it, so the providence of God has preserved it, for the use of His Church.

The term *proverb, proverbium,* compounded of *pro,* "for," and *verbum,* "a word, speech, or saying," leads us to an original meaning of the thing itself. It was an allegorical saying, where "more was meant than met the eye"—a short saying that stood for a whole discourse.

But the Hebrew *meshalim,* from *mashal,* "to rule or govern," signifies a set or collection of weighty, wise, and therefore authoritative, sayings, whereby a man's whole conduct, civil and religious, is to be governed; sayings containing rules for the government of life. Or, as the divine Author himself expresses it in the beginning of the first chapter, the design is to lead men "to know wisdom and instruction; to perceive the words of understanding; to receive the instruction of wisdom, justice, and judgment, and equity; to give subtilty to the simple, and to the young man knowledge and discretion," vv. 2-3. This was the design of proverbs; and perhaps it would be impossible to find out a better definition of the design and object of those of Solomon than is contained in the two preceding verses.

The Book of Proverbs has been divided into five parts:

I. A master is represented as instructing his scholar, giving him admonitions, directions, cautions, and excitements to the study of wisdom, chaps. i to ix.

II. This part is supposed to contain the proverbs of Solomon, properly so called; delivered in distinct, independent, general sentences. From chap. ix to xxii. 17:

III. In this part the tutor again addresses himself to his pupil, and gives him fresh admonitions to the study of wisdom; which is followed by a set of instructions, delivered imperatively to the pupil, who is supposed all the while to be standing before him. From chap. xxii. 17 to chap. xxv.

IV. This part is distinguished by being a selection of Solomon's proverbs, made by the men of Hezekiah. This part, like the second, is composed of distinct, unconnected sentences, and extends from chap. xxv to xxx.

V. The fifth part contains a set of wise expostulations and instructions, which Agur, the son of Jakeh, delivered to his pupils, Ithiel and Ucal, chap. xxx. And the thirty-first chapter contains the instructions which a mother, who is not named, gave to Lemuel, her son, being earnestly desirous to guard him against vice, to establish him in the principles of justice, and to have him married to a wife of the best qualities. These last two chapters may be considered a kind of appendix to the Book of Proverbs.

CHAPTER 1

The design of the proverbs, 1-6. An exhortation to fear God, and believe His word, because of the benefit to be derived from it, 7-9; to avoid the company of wicked men, who involve themselves in wretchedness and ruin, 10-19. Wisdom, personified, cries in the streets, and complains of the contempt with which she is treated, 20-23. The dreadful punishment that awaits all those who refuse her counsels, 24-33.

2. *To know wisdom.* That is, this is the design of parabolical writing in general; and the particular aim of the present work. This and the two following verses contain the interpretation of the term "parable," and the author's design in the whole book. The first verse is the title, and the next three verses are an explanation of the nature and design of this very important tract. *Wisdom. Chochmah* may mean here, and in every other part of this book, not only that divine science by which we are enabled to discover the best end and pursue it by the most proper means, but also the whole of that heavenly teaching that shows us both ourselves and God, directs us into all truth, and forms the whole of true religion. *And instruction. Musar,* the "teaching" that discovers all its parts.

3. *To receive the instruction. Haskel,* the deliberate "weighing" of the points contained in the teaching, so as to find out their importance. *Equity. Mesharim,* "rectitude."

4. *To give subtilty to the simple.* The word *simple,* from *simplex,* compounded of *sine,* "without," and *plica,* "a fold," properly signifies "plain and honest."

5. *A wise man will hear.* I shall not only give such instructions as may be suitable to the youthful and inexperienced, but also to those who have much knowledge and understanding.

6. *Dark sayings. Chidoth,* enigmas or riddles, in which the Asiatics abounded.

7. *The fear of the Lord.* In the preceding verses Solomon shows the advantage of acting according to the dictates of wisdom; in the following verses he shows the danger of acting contrary to them. *The fear of the Lord* signifies that religious reverence which every intelligent being owes to his Creator. This fear or religious reverence is said to be *the beginning of knowledge; reshith,* the principle, the first moving influence, begotten in a tender conscience by the Spirit of God. No man can ever become truly wise who does not begin with God, the Fountain of knowledge; and he whose mind is influenced by the fear and love of God will learn more in a month than others will in a year. *Fools despise. Evilim,* evil men. Men of bad hearts, bad heads, and bad ways.

8. *My son, hear.* "Father" was the title of preceptor, and "son" that of disciple, among the Jews. But here the reference appears to be to the children of a family; the *father* and the *mother* have the principal charge, in the first instance, of their children's instruction.

16. *For their feet run to evil.* The whole of this verse is wanting in the Septuagint, and in the Arabic.

17. *Surely in vain the net is spread in the sight of any bird.* The wicked are represented as lurking privily for the innocent.

18. *They lay wait for their own blood.* I believe it is the innocent who are spoken of here, for whose *blood* and *lives* these *lay wait* and *lurk privily;* certainly not their own, by any mode of construction.

20. *Wisdom crieth.* Here wisdom is again personified, as it is frequently, throughout this book; where nothing is meant but the teachings given to man, either by divine revelation or the voice of the Holy Spirit in the heart. And this voice of *wisdom* is opposed to the seducing language of the wicked mentioned above.

22. *Ye simple ones. Pethayim,* ye who have been seduced and deceived.

23. *Turn you at my reproof.* At my "convincing mode of arguing."

24. *Because I have called.* These and the following words appear to be spoken of the persons who are described, vv. 11-19, who have refused to return from their evil ways till arrested by the hand of justice; and here the wise man points out their deplorable state.

32. *For the turning away of the simple.* This difficult place seems to refer to such a case as we term "turning king's evidence," where an accomplice saves his own life by impeaching the rest of his gang. This is called his "turning" or "repentance," *meshubah;* and he was the most likely to turn, because he was of the *pethayim,* seduced or deceived persons. And this evidence was given against them when they were in their prosperity, *shalvah,* their "security," enjoying the fruits of their depredations; and being thus in a state of fancied security, they were the more easily taken and brought to justice.

CHAPTER 2

The teacher promises his pupil the highest advantages if he will follow the dictates of wisdom, 1-9. He shall be happy in its enjoyment, 10-11; shall be saved from wicked men, 12-15; and from the snares of bad women, 16-19; be a companion of the good and upright; and be in safety in the land, when the wicked shall be rooted out of it, 20-22.

7. *He layeth up sound wisdom. Tushiyah.* We have met with this word in Job; see chap. v. 12; vi. 13; xi. 6; xii. 16; especially Job xi. 6.

12. *The man that speaketh froward things. Tahpuchoth,* things of "subversion"; from *taphach,* "to turn or change the course of a thing."

16. *The stranger which flattereth with her words.* She that "smooths" with her words. The original intimates the glib, oily speeches of a prostitute.

22. *Transgressors. Bogedim.* The "garment men," the hypocrites; those who act borrowed characters, who go under a cloak.

CHAPTER 3

An exhortation to obedience, 1-4; trust in God's providence, 4-6; to humility, 7-8; to charity, 9-10; to submission to God's chastenings, 11-12. The profitableness of wisdom in all the concerns of life, 13-26. No act of duty should be deferred beyond the time in which it should be done, 27-28. Brotherly love and forbearance should be exercised, 29-30. We should not envy the wicked, 31-32. The curse of God is in the house of the wicked, but the humble and wise shall prosper, 33-35.

2. *For length of days.* Three eminent blessings are promised here: (1) long days; (2) years of lives; (3) *shalom,* prosperity; i.e., health, long life, and abundance.

3. *Let not mercy and truth forsake thee.* Let these be your constant companions through life.

6. *In all thy ways acknowledge him.* Begin, continue, and end every work, purpose, and device with God. Earnestly pray for His direction at the commencement; look for His continual support in the progress; and so begin and continue that all may terminate in His glory. And then it will certainly be to your good, for we never honor God without serving ourselves.

11. *Despise not the chastening of the Lord.* The word *musar* signifies "correction, discipline, and instruction."

12. *Whom the Lord loveth.* To encourage thee to bear correction, know that it is a proof of God's love to thee; and thereby He shows that He treats thee as a father does his son, even

that one to whom he bears the fondest affection. The last clause the Septuagint translate, "And chasteneth every son whom he receiveth"; and Heb. xii. 6 quotes this *literatim.*

18. *She is a tree of life.* "The tree of lives," alluding most manifestly to the tree so called which God in the beginning planted in the garden of paradise.

19. *The Lord by wisdom hath founded the earth.* Here wisdom is taken in its proper acceptation, for that infinite knowledge and skill which God has manifested in the creation and composition of the earth, and in the structure and economy of the heavens.

21. *Keep sound wisdom and d i s c r e t i o n. Tushiyah umezimmah.* We have met with both these words before. *Tushiyah* is the "essence" or "substance" of a thing; *mezimmah* is the "resolution" or "purpose" formed in reference to something good or excellent. To acknowledge God as the Author of all good is the *tushiyah,* the "essence," of a godly man's creed. To resolve to act according to the directions of His wisdom is the *mezimmah,* the "religious purpose," that will bring good to ourselves and glory to God.

24. *When thou liest down.* In these verses (23-26) the wise man describes the confidence, security, and safety which proceed from a consciousness of innocence.

27. *Withhold not good from them to whom it is due.* "From the lords of it." But who are they? The poor.

31. *Envy thou not the oppressor.* Oh, how bewitching is *power!* Every man desires it; and yet all hate *tyrants.* But query, if all had *power,* would not the major part be *tyrants?*

32. *But his secret. Sodo, his secret assembly;* godly people meet there, and God dwells there.

33. *The curse of the Lord.* No godly people meet in such a house, nor is God ever an inmate there. *But he blesseth the habitation of the just.* He considers it as His own temple. There He is worshipped in spirit and in truth; and hence God makes it His dwelling place.

34. *Surely he scorneth the scorners: but he giveth grace unto the lowly.* The Septuagint has, "The Lord resisteth the proud; but giveth grace to the humble." These words are quoted by St. Peter, 1st Epist. v. 5, and by St. James, chap. iv. 6, just as they stand in the Septuagint, with the change of "God," for "the Lord."

CHAPTER 4

The preceptor calls his pupils and tells them how himself was educated, 1-4; specifies the teachings he received, 5-19; and exhorts his pupil to persevere in well-doing, and to avoid evil, 20-27.

7. *Wisdom is the principal thing. Reshith chochmah,* "Wisdom is the principle." *Wisdom* prescribes the best end, and the means best calculated for its attainment. *Understanding* directs to the ways, times, places, and opportunities of practicing the lessons of wisdom.

13. *Take fast hold. Hachazek,* "Seize it strongly," and keep the hold; and do this as for life.

17. *For they eat the bread of wickedness.* By privately stealing. *And drink the wine of violence.* By highway robbery.

18. *But the path of the just.* The path of the wicked is gloomy, dark, and dangerous; that of the righteous is open, luminous, and instructive.

This verse contains a fine metaphor; it refers to the sun rising above the horizon, and the increasing twilight, till his beams shine full upon the earth. The original may be translated, "going and illuminating unto the prepared day."

23. *Keep thy heart with all diligence.* "Above all keeping," guard your heart. He who knows anything of himself knows how apt his affections are to go astray. *For out of it are the issues of life.* "The goings out of lives."

24. *A froward mouth.* Beware of hastiness, anger, and rash speeches. *And perverse lips.* Do not delight in nor acquire the habit of contradicting and gainsaying; and beware of calumniating and backbiting your neighbor.

CHAPTER 5

Further exhortations to acquire wisdom, 1-2. The character of a loose woman, and the ruinous consequences of attachment to such, 3-14. Exhortations to chastity and moderation, 15-21. The miserable end of the wicked, 22-23.

4. *Bitter as wormwood.* Something as excessive in its bitterness as honey is in its sweetness.

7. *Hear me . . . O ye children. Banim,* "sons," young men in general, for these are the most likely to be deceived and led astray.

11. *When thy flesh and thy body are consumed.* The word *shear,* which we render "body," signifies properly the remains, residue, or remnant of a thing; and is applied here to denote the breathing carcass, putrid with the concomitant disease of debauchery. The mourning here spoken of is of the most excessive kind; the word *naham* is often applied to the growling of a lion, and the hoarse, incessant murmuring of the sea.

15. *Drink waters out of thine own cistern.* Be satisfied with thy own wife; and let the wife see that she reverence her husband, and not tempt him by inattention or unkindness to seek elsewhere what he has a right to expect, but cannot find at home.

CHAPTER 6

Exhortations against becoming surety for others, 1-5; against idleness, from the example of the ant, 6-11; description of a worthless person, 12-15; seven things hateful to God, 16-19; the benefits of instruction, 20-23; further exhortations against bad women, and especially against adultery, 24-33; what may be expected from jealousy, 34-35.

1. *If thou be surety for thy friend.* "For thy neighbor"; i.e., any person. If you pledge yourself in behalf of another, you take the burden off him, and place it on your own shoulders; and when he knows he has got one to stand between him and the demands of law and justice, he will feel little responsibility. Striking or shaking hands when the mouth had once made the promise was considered as the ratification of the engagement, and thus the man became ensnared with the words of his mouth.

3. *Do this . . . deliver thyself.* Continue to press him for whom you are become surety, to pay his creditor; give him no rest till he do it, else you may fully expect to be left to pay the debt.

5. *Deliver thyself as a roe.* The antelope. If you are got into the snare, get out if you possibly canst; make every struggle and exertion, as the antelope taken in the net, and the bird

taken in the snare would, in order to get free from your captivity.

6. *Go to the ant, thou sluggard.* The *ant* is a remarkable creature for foresight, industry, and economy.

11. *So shall thy poverty come as one that travelleth.* That is, with slow but surely approaching steps. *Thy want as an armed man.* That is, with irresistible fury; and you are not prepared to oppose it.

14. *He deviseth mischief.* He plots schemes and plans to bring it to pass. *He soweth discord.* Between men and their wives, by seducing the latter from their fidelity.

15. *Suddenly shall he be broken.* Probably alluding to some punishment of the adulterer, such as being stoned to death.

22. *When thou goest, it shall lead thee.* Here the law is personified; and is represented as a nurse, teacher, and guardian, by night and day.

CHAPTER 7

A further exhortation to acquire wisdom, in order to be preserved from impure connections, 1-5. The character of a harlot, and her conduct towards a youth who fell into her snare, 6-23. Solemn exhortations to avoid this evil, 24-27.

2. *As the apple of thine eye.* As the pupil of the eye, which is of such essential necessity to sight, and so easily injured.

7. *Among the simple ones.* The inexperienced, inconsiderate young men. *A young man void of understanding.* "Destitute of a heart." He had not wisdom to discern the evil intended, nor courage to resist the flatteries of the seducer.

11. *She is loud and stubborn.* She is never at rest, always agitated.

13. *And with an impudent face.* "She strengthened her countenance," assumed the most confident look she could.

14. *I have peace offerings with me.* More literally, "The sacrifices of the peace offerings are with me." *Peace offerings* were offerings the spiritual design of which was to make peace between God and man, to make up the breach between them which sin had occasioned. *Have I payed my vows.* She seems to insinuate that she had made a vow for the health and safety of this young man; and having done so, and prepared the sacrificial banquet, came actually out to seek him, that he might partake of it with her, v. 15.

16. *I have decked my bed.* Arsi, "my couch or sofa"; distinguished from *mishcabi,* "my bed," v. 17, the place to sleep on, as the other was the place to recline on at meals.

18. *Come, let us take our fill of love.* "Let us revel in the breasts"; and then it is added, *Let us solace ourselves with loves;* "Let us gratify each other with loves, with the utmost delights."

19. *For the good man.* Literally, "For the man is not in his house."

20. *He hath taken.* Literally, "The money bag he hath taken in his hand." He is gone a journey of itinerant merchandising. This seems to be what is intended. *And will come home at the day appointed.* The time fixed for a return from such a journey.

CHAPTER 8

The fame and excellence of wisdom, and its manner of teaching, 1-4; the matter of its exhortations, 5-12; its influence among men, 13-21; its antiquity, 22-31; the blessedness of attending to its counsels, 32-35; the misery of those who do not, 36.

1. *Doth not wisdom cry?* Here wisdom is again personified. It is represented in this chapter in a twofold point of view: (1) Wisdom, the power of judging rightly, implying the knowledge of divine and human things. (2) As an attribute of God, particularly displayed in the various and astonishing works of creation.

2. *In the places of the paths.* "The constituted house of the paths." Does not this mean the house of public worship?

4. *Unto you, O men.* Ishim, men of wealth and power, "will I call"; and not to you alone, for my voice is *al beney Adam,* "to all the descendants of Adam," to the whole human race.

5. *O ye simple.* Pethaim, you that are deceived, and with flattering words and fair speeches deluded and drawn away. *Ye fools.* Kesilim, ye stupid, stiff-necked, senseless people.

8. *All the words . . . are in righteousness.* Betsedek, in justice and equity, testifying what man "owes" to his God, to his neighbor, and to himself; giving to each his "due." This is the true import of *tsadak. There is nothing froward.* Niphtal, tortuous, involved, or difficult. *Or perverse.* Ikkesh, distorted, leading to obstinacy. On the contrary,

9. *They are all plain.* Nechochim, straightforward, over against every man, level to every capacity.

10. *Receive my instruction, and not silver.* A Hebrew idiom: "Receive my instruction in preference to silver."

12. *I wisdom dwell with prudence.* Prudence is defined, "wisdom applied to practice"; so wherever true wisdom is, it will lead to action, and its activity will be always in reference to the accomplishment of the best ends by the use of the most appropriate means. Hence comes what is here called *knowledge of witty inventions,* "I have found out knowledge and contrivance."

14. *Counsel is mine.* Tushiyah, "substance, reality, essence," all belong to me.

15. *By me kings reign.* In this and the following verse five degrees of civil power and authority are mentioned: (1) *melachim,* kings; (2) *rozenim,* consuls; (3) *sarim,* princes, chiefs of the people; (4) *nedibim,* nobles; and (5) *shophetim,* judges or civil magistrats. Instead of *shophetey arets, judges of the earth, shophetey tsedek,* "righteous judges," or "judges of righteousness," is the reading of 162 of Kennicott's and De Rossi's MSS., both in the text and in the margin, and of several ancient editions. And this is the reading of the Vulgate, the Chaldee, and the Syriac; and should undoubtedly supersede the other.

17. *And those that seek me early shall find me.* Not merely betimes in the morning, though he who does so shall find it greatly to his advantage (see on Psalm iv.), but early in life.

23. *I was set up from everlasting.* I was diffused or "poured out," Isa. xxix. 10.

24. *When there were no depths.* Tehomoth, before the original chaotic mass was formed.

See Gen. i. 2. *I was brought forth.* "I was produced as by laboring throes."

26. *The highest part of the dust of the world.* "The first particle of matter."

28. *The clouds above.* "The ethereal regions."

30. *Then I was by him, as one brought up.* A "nursling," a darling child.

34. *Watching daily at my gates.* Wisdom is represented as having a school for the instruction of men; and seems to point out some of the most forward of her scholars coming, through their intense desire to learn, even before the gates were opened, and waiting there for admission, that they might hear every word that was uttered, and not lose one accent of the heavenly teaching. Blessed are such.

36. *Wrongeth his own soul.* It is not Satan, it is not sin, properly speaking, that hurts him; it is himself.

CHAPTER 9

Wisdom builds her house, makes her provision for a great feast, calls her guests, and exhorts them to partake of her entertainment, 1-6. Different admonitions relative to the acquisition of wisdom, 7-12. The character and conduct of a bad woman, 13-18.

The same Wisdom speaks here who spoke in the preceding chapter. There she represented herself as manifest in all the works of God in the natural world, all being constructed according to counsels proceeding from an infinite understanding. Here she represents herself as the great potentate who was to rule all that she had constructed; and having an immense family to provide for, had made an abundant provision, and calls all to partake of it.

4. *Whoso is simple.* Let the young, heedless, and giddy attend to my teaching. *Him that wanteth understanding.* Literally, "he that wanteth understanding." Literally, "he that wanteth a heart"; who is without courage, is feeble and fickle, and easily drawn aside from the holy commandment.

5. *Come, eat of my bread.* Not only receive my instructions, but act according to my directions. *Drink of the wine . . . I have mingled.* Enter into my counsels; be not contented with superficial knowledge on any subject, where anything deeper may be attained.

7. *He that reproveth a scorner.* The person who "mocks" at sacred things.

9. *Give instruction to a wise man.* Literally, "Give to the wise, and he will be wise."

16. *Whoso is simple, let him turn in hither.* Folly or Pleasure, here personified, uses the very same expressions as employed by Wisdom, v. 4. Wisdom says, "Let the simple turn in to me." No, says Folly, "Let the simple turn in to me." If he turn in to Wisdom, his folly shall be taken away, and he shall become wise; if he turn in to Folly, his darkness will be thickened, and his folly will remain. Wisdom sets up her school to instruct the ignorant: Folly sets her school up next door, to defeat the designs of Wisdom.

17. *Stolen waters are sweet.* I suppose this to be a proverbial mode of expression, importing that "illicit pleasures are sweeter than those which are legal." The meaning is easy to be discerned; and the conduct of multitudes shows

that they are ruled by this adage. On it are built all the *adulterous intercourses* in the land.

CHAPTER 10

It is impossible to give summaries of such chapters as these, where almost every verse contains a separate subject. Our common version, not being able to exhibit the contents as usual, simply says, "From this chapter to the five and twentieth are sundry observations upon moral virtues, and their opposite vices." In general the wise man states in this chapter the difference between the wise and the foolish, the righteous and the wicked, the diligent and the idle. He speaks also of love and hatred, of the good and the evil tongue, or of the slanderer and the peacemaker.

1. *The proverbs of Solomon.* Some ancient MSS. of the Vulgate have, "The second book of the Proverbs." *A wise son maketh a glad father.* The parallels in this and several of the succeeding chapters are those which Bishop Lowth calls the antithetic: when two lines correspond with eath other by an opposition of terms and sentiments; when the second is contrasted with the first—sometimes in expression, sometimes in sense only.

7. *The memory of the just is blessed.* Or "is a blessing." *But the name of the wicked shall rot.* This is another antithesis.

8. *A prating fool shall fall.* This clause is repeated in the tenth verse.

13. *A rod is for the back of him.* The rod is a most powerful instrument of knowledge.

14. *Wise men lay up knowledge.* They keep secret everything that has a tendency to disturb domestic or public peace; but the foolish man blabs all out, and produces much mischief. Think much, speak little, and always think before you speak. This will promote your own peace and that of your neighbor.

19. *In the multitude of words.* It is impossible to speak much and yet speak nothing but truth, and injure no man's character in the meanwhile.

20. *The heart of the wicked is little worth.* Kimat, is like little or nothing.

22. *The blessing of the Lord, it maketh rich.* Whatever we receive in the way of providence has God's blessing in it, and will do us good.

CHAPTER 11

A parallel of the advantages of the righteous and wise, opposed to the miseries of the wicked and the foolish. True and false riches.

1. *A false balance is abomination.* This refers to the balance itself deceitfully constructed, so that it is sooner turned at one end than at the other. This is occasioned by one end of the beam being longer than the other. *But a just weight.* The "perfect stone," probably because weights were first made of stone; see the law, Deut. xxv. 13-35.

2. *When pride cometh.* The proud man thinks much more of himself than any other can do; and, expecting to be treated according to his own supposed worth, which treatment he seldom meets with, he is repeatedly mortified, ashamed, confounded, and rendered indignant. *With the lowly.* The "humble," the "modest," as opposed to the *proud*, referred to in the first clause. The humble man looks for nothing but justice, expects nothing in the way of commendation or praise, and can never be disappointed but in receiving praise.

9. *An hypocrite with his mouth. Chaneph* might be better translated "infidel" than *hypocrite.* The latter is one that pretends to religion. The former is one who disbelieves divine revelation, and accordingly is polluted, and lives in pollution.

13. *A talebearer.* The walking busybody, the trader in scandal.

15. *He that is surety for a stranger shall smart for it.* He shall find evil upon evil in it. See chap. vi. 1.

16. *A gracious woman retaineth honour.* Instead of this the Septuagint have, "A gracious woman raiseth up honour to the man; but she that hateth righteous things is a throne of dishonour." A good wife is an honor to her husband, and a bad wife is her husband's reproach. If this be so, how careful should a man be whom he marries!

22. *A jewel of gold in a swine's snout.* That is, beauty in a woman destitute of good breeding and modest carriage is as becoming as a gold ring on the snout of a swine.

24. *There is that scattereth, and yet increaseth.* The bountiful man who gives to the poor, never turning away his face from anyone in distress, the Lord blesses his property, and the bread is multiplied in his hand.

25. *The liberal soul shall be made fat.* He who gives to the distressed, in the true spirit of charity, shall get a hundredfold from God's mercy. How wonderful is the Lord! He gives the property, gives the heart to use it aright, and recompenses the man for the deed, though all the fruit was found from himself! *He that watereth.* A man who distributes in the right spirit gets more good himself than the poor man does who receives the bounty. Thus "it is more blessed to give than to receive."

26. *He that withholdeth corn.* Who refuses to sell because he hopes for a dearth, and then he can make his own price.

30. *The fruit of the righteous is a tree of life.* "The tree of lives."

31. *Behold, the righteous shall be recompensed in the earth,* etc. The Septuagint, Syriac, and Arabic read this verse as follows: "And if the righteous scarcely be saved, where shall the ungodly and the sinner appear?" And this St. Peter quotes *literatim,* 1st Epist. iv. 18.

CHAPTER 12

Of the benefit of instruction, and the cultivation of piety. The virtuous woman. The different lot of the just and unjust. The humane man. The industrious man. The fool and the wise man. The uncharitable. The excellence of the righteous. The slothful is in want. Righteousness leads to life, etc.

1. *Whoso loveth instruction. Musar,* discipline or correction, *loveth knowledge;* for correction is the way to knowledge. *But he that hateth reproof is brutish. Baar,* he is a bear.

4. *A virtuous woman is a crown to her husband.* "A strong woman." Our word "virtue" (*virtus*) is derived from *vir,* a "man"; and as man is the noblest of God's creatures, virtue expresses what is becoming to man; that is noble, courageous, and dignified; and as *vir,* a "man," comes from *vis,* "power" or "strength," so it implies what is strong and vigorous in principle.

9. *He that is despised, and hath a servant.* I believe the Vulgate gives the true *sense* of this verse: "Better is the poor man who provides for himself, than the proud who is destitute of bread." The versions in general agree in this sense.

10. *A righteous man regardeth the life of his beast.* One principal characteristic of a holy man is mercy. I once in my travels met with the Hebrew of this clause on the signboard of a public inn, which, being very appropriate, reminded me that I should feed my horse. *The tender mercies of the wicked are cruel.* Are "violent, without mercy, ruthless."

16. *A fool's wrath is presently known.* We have a proverb very like this, and it will serve for illustration: A fool's bolt is soon shot.

18. *There is that speaketh. Boteh,* "blabbing out, blustering."

21. *There shall no evil happen to the just.* No, for all things work together for good to them that love God.

CHAPTER 13

Various moral sentences; the wise child; continence of speech; of the poor rich man and the rich poor man; ill-gotten wealth; delay of what is hoped for; the bad consequences of refusing instruction; providing for one's children; the necessity of correcting them, etc.

1. *A wise son heareth his father's instruction.* The child that has had a proper nurturing will profit by his father's counsels, but the child that is permitted to fulfill its own will and have its own way will jest at the reproofs of its parents.

3. *He that keepeth his mouth keepeth his life.* It has often been remarked that God has given us two eyes, that we may see much; two ears, that we may hear much; but has given us but one tongue, and that fenced in with teeth, to indicate that we should speak but little.

8. *The ransom of a man's life.* In despotic countries, a rich man is often accused of some capital crime, and to save his life though he may be quite innocent, is obliged to give up his riches; but the poor, in such countries, are put to no trouble.

9. *The light of the righteous rejoiceth.* They shall have that measure of prosperity which shall be best for them. *Light* and *lamp* in both cases may signify posterity.

10. *By pride cometh contention.* Perhaps there is not a quarrel among individuals in private life, nor a war among nations, that does not proceed from pride and ambition.

14. *The law of the wise is a fountain of life.* Perhaps it would be better to translate, "The law is to the wise man a fountain of life."

15. *The way of transgressors is hard.* Never was a truer saying; most sinners have more pain and difficulty to get their souls damned than the righteous have, with all their cross-bearings, to get to the kingdom of Heaven.

24. *He that spareth his rod hateth his son.* That is, if he *hated* him, he could not do him a greater disservice than not to correct him when his obstinacy or disobedience requires it. We have met with this subject already, and it is a favorite with Solomon.

CHAPTER 14

Various moral sentiments. The antithesis between wisdom and folly, and the different effects of each.

1. *Every wise woman buildeth her house.* By her prudent and industrious management she increases property in the family, furniture in the house, and food and raiment for her household.

3. *The mouth of the foolish is a rod of pride.* The reproofs of such a person are ill-judged and ill-timed, and generally are conveyed in such language as renders them not only ineffectual, but displeasing, and even irritating.

6. *A scorner seeketh wisdom. I believe the scorner* means, in this book, the man that despises the counsel of God.

9. *Fools make a mock at sin.* And only fools would do so. But he that makes a sport of sinning will find it no sport to suffer the vengeance of an eternal fire.

10. *The heart knoweth his own bitterness. Morrath naphsho,* "The bitterness of its soul."

17. *He that is soon angry.* "Short of nostrils"; because, when a man is angry, his nose is contracted.

29. *That is hasty of spirit. Ketsar ruach,* "the short of spirit"; one that is easily irritated; and, being in a passion, he is agitated so as to be literally short of breath.

34. *But sin is a reproach to any people.* I am satisfied this is not the sense of the original, *vechesed leummim chattath;* which would be better rendered, "And mercy is a sin offering for the people."

CHAPTER 15

The soft answer. Useful correction. Stability of the righteous. The contented mind. The slothful man. The fool. The covetous. The impious. The wicked opposed to the righteous; to the diligent; and to the man who fears the Lord.

1. *A soft answer.* Gentleness will often disarm the most furious, where positive derangement has not taken place. One angry word will always beget another, for the disposition of one spirit always begets its own likeness in another. Thus kindness produces kindness, and rage produces rage. Universal experience confirms this proverb.

2. *Useth knowledge aright.* This is very difficult to know: when to speak, and when to be silent; what to speak, and what to leave unspoken; the manner that is best and most suitable to the occasion, the subject, the circumstances, and the persons. All these are difficulties, often even to the wisest men.

11. *Hell and destruction. Sheol vaabaddon. Hades,* the invisible world, the place of separate spirits till the resurrection, and *Abaddon,* the place of torment, are ever under the eye and control of the Lord.

19. *The way of the slothful man is as an hedge of thorns.* Because he is slothful, he imagines ten thousand difficulties in the way which cannot be surmounted; but they are all the creatures of his own imagination, and that imagination is formed by his sloth.

24. *The way of life is above to the wise.* There is a treble antithesis here: (1) the way of the wise, and that of the fool. (2) The one is above,

the other below. (3) The one is of life, the other is of death.

27. *He that is greedy of gain*—he who *will* be rich. *Troubleth his own house*—he is a torment to himself and his family by his avariciousness and penury, and a curse to those with whom he deals. *But he that hateth gifts*—whatever is given to pervert judgment.

28. *The heart of the righeous studieth to answer.* His tongue never runs before his wit; he never speaks rashly, and never unadvisedly; because he *studieth,* ponders, his thoughts and his words.

31. *The ear that heareth the reproof.* That receives it gratefully and obeys it. "Advice is for them that will take it"; so says one of our own old proverbs.

CHAPTER 16

Man prepares, but God governs. God has made all things for himself; He hates pride. The judgments of God. The administration of kings; their justice, anger, and clemency. God has made all in weight, measure, and due proportion. Necessity produces industry. The patient man. The lot is under the direction of the Lord.

1. *The preparations of the heart in man.* The Hebrew is literally, "To man are the dispositions of the heart; but from the Lord is the answer of the tongue." Man proposes his wishes, but God answers as He thinks proper. The former is the free offspring of the heart of man; the latter, the free volition of God.

3. *Commit thy works unto the Lord.* See that what you do is commanded; and then begin, continue, and end all in His name. *And thy thoughts shall be established*—these schemes or arrangements, though formed in the heart, are agreeable to the divine will, and therefore shall be established.

4. *Even the wicked for the day of evil.* The whole verse is translated by the Chaldee thus: "All the works of the Lord are for those who obey him; and the wicked is reserved for the evil day."

6. *By mercy and truth iniquity is purged.* This may be misunderstood, as if a man, by showing mercy and acting according to truth, could atone for his own iniquity. The Hebrew text is not ambiguous: "By mercy and truth he shall atone for iniquity." He, God, by His *mercy,* in sending His Son, Jesus, into the world, "shall make an atonement for iniquity" according to His *truth*—the word which He declared by His holy prophets since the world began.

11. *All the weights of the bag are his.* Alluding, probably, to the *standard weights* laid up in a bag in the *sanctuary,* and to which all weights in common use in the land were to be referred, in order to ascertain whether they were just.

32. *He that ruleth his spirit than he that taketh a city.* It is much easier to subdue an enemy without than one within. There have been many kings who had conquered nations and yet were slaves to their own passions.

33. *The lot is cast into the lap.* On the *lot,* see Num. xxvi. 55. How far it may be proper now to put difficult matters to the lot, after earnest prayer and supplication, I cannot say. *Formerly,* it was both lawful and efficient; for after it was solemnly cast, the decision was taken as coming immediately from the Lord. But those

who need most to have recourse to the lot are those who have not piety to pray nor faith to trust to God for a positive decision.

CHAPTER 17

Contentment. The wise servant. The Lord tries the heart. Children a crown to their parents. We should hide our neighbor's faults. The poor should not be despised. Litigations and quarrels to be avoided. Wealth is useless to a fool. The good friend. A fool may pass for a wise man when he holds his peace.

1. *Better is a dry morsel.* Peace and contentment, and especially domestic peace, are beyond all other blessings.

7. *Excellent speech becometh not a fool.* This proverb is suitable to those who affect, in public speaking, fine language which comports neither with their ordinary conversation nor with their education.

8. *A gift is as a precious stone.* It both enriches and ornaments. In the latter clause there is an evident allusion to cut stones. Whithersoever you turn them, they reflect the light, are brilliant and beautiful.

12. *Let a bear robbed of her whelps.* At which times such animals are peculiarly fierce.

13. *Whoso rewardeth evil for good.* Here is a most awful warning. As many persons are guilty of the sin of ingratitude, and of paying kindness with unkindness, and good with evil, it is no wonder we find so much wretchedness among men; for God's word cannot fail. Evil shall not depart from the houses and families of such persons.

14. *The beginning of strife is as when one letteth out water.* As soon as the smallest breach is made in the dike or dam, the water begins to press from all parts towards the breach. The resistance becomes too great to be successfully opposed, so that dikes and all are speedily swept away. Such is the beginning of contentions, quarrels, lawsuits. *Leave off contention, before it be meddled with.* As you see what an altercation must lead to, therefore do not begin it. Before it be "mingled together," before the spirits of the contending parties come into conflict, are joined together in battle, and begin to deal out mutual reflections and reproaches. When you see that the dispute is likely to take this turn, leave it off immediately.

17. *A friend loveth at all times.* Equally in adversity as in prosperity. And a *brother,* according to the ties and interests of consanguinity, is *born* to support and comfort a brother in distress.

18. *Striketh hands.* Striking each other's hands, or shaking hands, was anciently the form in concluding a contract. See chap. vi. 1.

19. *He that exalteth his gate.* The exalting of the gate may mean proud boasting and arrogant speaking, such as has a tendency to kindle and maintain strife.

22. *A merry heart doeth good like a medicine.* Instead of *gehah, a medicine,* it appears that the Chaldee and Syriac had read in their copies *gevah,* the "body," as they translate in this way. This makes the apposition here more complete: "A merry heart doeth good to the body; but a broken spirit drieth the bones."

23. *A gift out of the bosom.* Out of his purse; as in their bosoms, above their girdles, the Asiatics carry their purses.

CHAPTER 18

The man who separates himself and seeks wisdom. The fool and the wicked man. Deep wisdom. Contention of fools. The talebearer and the slothful. The name of the Lord. Pride and presumption because of riches. Hastiness of spirit. The wounded spirit. The influence of gifts. The lot. The offended brother. The influence of the tongue. A wife a good from God. The true friend.

1. *Through desire a man, having separated himself.* The original is difficult and obscure. The Vulgate, Septuagint, and Arabic read as follows: "He who wishes to break with his friend, and seeks occasions or pretenses, shall at all times be worthy of blame." The nearest translation to the Hebrew is perhaps the following: "He who is separated shall seek the desired thing [i.e., the object of his desire] and shall intermeddle [mingle himself] with all realities or all essential knowledge." He finds that he can make little progress in the investigation of divine and natural things, if he have much to do with secular or trifling matters. He therefore separates himself as well from unprofitable pursuits as from frivolous company, and then enters into the spirit of his pursuit; is not satisfied with superficial observances, but examines the substance and essence, as far as possible, of those things which have been the objects of his desire. This appears to me the best meaning.

2. *But that his heart may discover itself.* It is a fact that most vain and foolish people are never satisfied in company but in showing their own nonsense and emptiness. But this verse may be understood as confirming the view already given of the preceding, and may be translated thus: "But a fool doth not delight in understanding, though it should even manifest itself."

3. *When the wicked cometh.* Would it not be better to read this verse thus? "When the wicked cometh contempt cometh; and with ignominy cometh reproach."

4. *The words of a man's mouth.* That is, the wise sayings of a wise man are like *deep waters;* howsoever much you pump or draw off, you do not appear to lessen them. *The wellspring of wisdom.* Where there is a sound understanding, and a deep, well-informed mind, its wisdom and its counsels are an incessant stream, *mekor chochmah,* "the vein of wisdom," ever throwing out its healthy streams.

8. *The words of a talebearer.* "The words of the whisperer," the busybody, the busy, meddling croaker.

9. *He also that is slothful.* A slothful man neglects his work, and the materials go to ruin; the waster, he destroys the materials. They are both destroyers.

10. *The name of the Lord is a strong tower. The name of the Lord* may be taken for the Lord himself; He is *a strong tower,* a refuge, and place of complete safety, to all that trust in Him.

11. *The rich man's wealth.* See chap. x. 15.

12. *Before destruction.* See chap. xi. 2 and xvi. 18.

16. *A man's gift maketh room for him.* It is, and ever has been, a base and degrading practice in Asiatic countries to bring a gift or present to the great man into whose presence you come. Without this there is no audience, no favor, no justice.

18. *The lot causeth contentions to cease.* See chap. xvi. 33.

19. *A brother offended is harder to be won than a strong city.* Almost all the versions agree in the following reading: "A brother assisted by a brother, is like a fortified city; and their decisions are like the bars of a city." Coverdale is both plain and terse: "The unitie of brethren is stronger then a castell, and they that holde together are like the barre of a palace."

21. *Death and life are in the power of the tongue.* This may apply to all men. Many have lost their lives by their tongue, and some have saved their lives by it. But it applies most forcibly to *public pleaders;* on many of their tongues hangs *life* or *death.*

22. *Whoso findeth a wife findeth a good thing.* Marriage, with all its troubles and embarrassments, is a blessing from God; and there are few cases where a wife of any sort is not better than none, because celibacy is an evil; for God himself hath said, "It is not good for man to be alone."

24. *There is a friend that sticketh closer than a brother.* In many cases the genuine friend has shown more attachment, and rendered greater benefits, than the natural brother. Some apply this to God; others, to Christ; but the text has no such meaning.

CHAPTER 19

The worth of a poor, upright man. Riches preserve friends. False witnesses. False friends. A king's wrath. The foolish son. The prudent wife. Slothfulness. Pity for the poor. The fear of the Lord. The spendthrift son. Obedience to parents.

1. *Better is the poor.* The upright, poor man is always to be preferred to the rich or self-sufficient fool.

2. *Also, that the soul be without knowledge, it is not good.* Would it not be plainer, as it is more literal, to say, "Also, to be without knowledge, is not good for the soul"?

10. *Delight is not seemly for a fool. Taanug,* splendid or luxurious living, rank, equipage. These sit ill on a *fool,* though he be by birth a lord.

13. *The contentions of a wife are a continual dropping.* The man who has got such a wife is like a tenant who has got a cottage with a bad roof, through every part of which the rain either drops or pours. He can neither sit, stand, work, nor sleep, without being exposed to these droppings.

14. *A prudent wife is from the Lord.* One who has a good understanding; who avoids complaining, though she may often have cause for it.

17. *Lendeth unto the Lord.* Oh, what a word is this! God makes himself debtor for everything that is given to the *poor!* Who would not advance much upon such credit?

18. *Let not thy soul spare for his crying.* This is a hard precept for a parent. Nothing affects the heart of a parent so much as a child's cries and tears. But it is better that the child may be caused to cry, when the correction may be healthful to his soul, than that the parent should cry afterwards, when the child is grown to man's estate and his evil habits are sealed for life.

21. *There are many devices.* The same sentiment as in chap. xvi. 1.

CHAPTER 20

Against wine and strong drink. We should avoid contentions. The sluggard. The righteous man. Weights and measures. Talebearers. The wicked son. The wise king. The glory of young men. The beauty of old men. The benefit of correction.

1. *Wine is a mocker.* It deceives by its fragrance, intoxicates by its strength, and renders the intoxicated ridiculous. *Strong drink. Shechar,* any strong, fermented liquor, whether of the vine, date, or palm species.

2. *The fear of a king.* Almost the same with chap. xix. 12.

3. *It is an honour for a man.* The same sentiment as chap. xix. 11.

9. *Who can say, I have made my heart clean?* No man. But thousands can testify that the blood of Jesus Christ has cleansed them from all unrighteousness. And he is *pure from his sin* who is justified freely through the redemption that is in Jesus.

10. *Divers weights, and divers measures.* Hebrew: "A stone and a stone; an ephah and an ephah." One the standard, the other below it; one to buy with, the other to sell by.

12. *The hearing ear, and the seeing eye.* Every *good* we possess comes from God; and we should neither use our eyes, nor our ears, nor anything we possess, but in strict subserviency to His will.

13. *Love not sleep, lest thou come to poverty.* Sleep is an indescribable blessing; but how often is it turned into a curse! It is like food; a certain measure of it restores and invigorates exhausted nature; more than that oppresses and destroys life. A lover of sleep is a paltry, insignificant character.

14. *It is naught, it is naught, saith the buyer.* How apt are men to decry the goods they wish to purchase, in order that they may get them at a cheaper rate; and, when they have made their bargain and carried it off, boast to others at how much less than its value they have obtained it!

16. *Take his garment that is surety for a stranger.* I suppose the meaning to be, If a stranger or unknown person become surety in a case, greater caution should be used, and such security taken from this stranger as would prevent him from running away from his engagements.

17. *Bread of deceit is sweet.* Property acquired by falsehood, speculation, etc., without labor, is pleasant to the unprincipled, slothful man; but there is a curse in it, and the issue will prove it.

20. *Whoso curseth his father.* Such persons were put to death under the law; see Exod. xxi. 17; Lev. xx. 9; and here it is said, *Their lamp shall be put out*—they shall have no posterity; God shall cut them off both root and branch.

21. *An inheritance . . . gotten hastily.* Gotten by speculation; by lucky hits; not in the fair, progressive way of traffic, in which money has its natural increase. All such inheritances are short-lived; God's blessing is not in them, because they are not the produce of industry; and they lead to idleness, pride, fraud, and knavery.

25. *Who devoureth that which is holy.* It is a sin to take that which belongs to God, His worship, or His work, and devote it to one's own use. *And after vows to make enquiry.* That is, if a man be inwardly making a rash vow, the fitness or unfitness, the necessity, expediency, and propriety of the thing should be first carefully considered. But how foolish to make the vow first, and afterwards to inquire whether it was right in the sight of God to do it!

26. *Bringeth the wheel over them.* He threshes them in his anger, as the wheel does the grain on the threshing floor.

27. *The spirit of man is the candle of the Lord.* God has given to every man a mind, which He so enlightens by His own Spirit that the man knows how to distinguish good from evil; and conscience, which springs from this, searches the inmost recesses of the soul.

28. *Mercy and truth preserve the king.* These are the brightest jewels in the royal crown, and those kings who are most governed by them have the stablest government.

29. *The glory of young men is their strength.* Scarcely any young man affects to be wise, learned, etc.; but all delight to show their strength and to be reputed strong. *And the beauty of old men is the gray head.* They no longer affect strength and agility, but they affect wisdom, experience, prudent counsels, and are fond of being reputed wise, and of having respect paid to their understanding and experience.

30. *The blueness of a wound.* *Chabburoth,* from *chabar,* "to unite, to join together." Does it not refer to the cicatrix of a wound when, in its healing, the two lips are brought together? By this union the wound is healed.

CHAPTER 21

The king's heart is in the hand of God. We should practice mercy and justice. The lying tongue. The quarrelsome woman. The punishment of the wicked. The uncharitable. The private gift. The happiness of the righteous. The wicked a ransom for the righteous. The treasures of the wise. He who guards his tongue. Desire of the sluggard. The false witness. Salvation is of the Lord.

1. *The king's heart is in the hand of the Lord.* The Lord is the only Ruler of princes. He alone can govern and direct their counsels. But there is an allusion here to the Eastern method of watering their lands. Several canals are dug from one stream; and by opening a particular sluice, the husbandman can direct a stream to whatever part he pleases. So the king's heart; i.e., to whomsoever he is disposed to show favor.

3. *To do justice and judgment.* The words of Samuel to Saul. See 1 Sam. xv. 23.

4. *An high look.* The evidence of pride, self-conceit, and vanity. *A proud heart,* from which the high look, etc., come. *And the plowing.* "The lamp," the prosperity and posterity of the wicked; *is sin*—it is evil in the seed, and evil in the root, evil in the branch, and evil in the fruit.

9. *In a corner of the house top.* A shed raised on the flat roof; *a wide house; beith chaber,* "a house of fellowship"; what we should call a lodging house, or a house occupied by several families.

12. *The righteous man wisely considereth.*

This verse is understood as implying the pious concern of a righteous man for a wicked family, whom he endeavors by his instructions to bring into the way of knowledge and peace.

CHAPTER 22

A good reputation. The rich and the poor. The idle. Good habits formed in infancy. Injustice and its effects. The providence of God. The lewd woman. The necessity of timely correction. Exhortation to wisdom. Rob not the poor. Be not the companion of the froward. Avoid suretyship. Be honest. The industrious shall be favored.

1. *A good name.* *Shem,* a "name," put for reputation, credit, fame. Used nearly in the same way that we use it: "He has got a name."

2. *The rich and poor meet together.* *Ashir,* the "opulent," whether in money, land, or property; *rash,* the man that is destitute of these, and lives by his labor, whether a handicraftsman, or one that tills the ground. In the order of God, the rich and the poor live together, and are mutually helpful to each other. Without the poor, the rich could not be supplied with the articles which they consume; for the poor include all the laboring classes of society: and without the rich, the poor could get no vent for the produce of their labor, nor, in many cases, labor itself.

5. *Thorns and snares.* Various difficulties, trials, and sufferings.

6. *Train up a child in the way he should go.* The Hebrew of this clause is curious: "Initiate the child at the opening (the mouth) of his path." *Chanac,* which we translate *train up* or "initiate," signifies also "dedicate"; and is often used for the consecrating anything, house, or person, to the service of God. Dedicate, therefore in the first instance, your child to God; and nurse, teach, and discipline him as God's child, whom He has entrusted to your care.

14. *The mouth of strange women is a deep pit.* In chap. xxiii. 27, he says, "A whore is a deep ditch; and a strange woman is a narrow pit."

17. *Bow down thine ear.* From this to the end of v. 21 are contained, not proverbs, but directions how to profit by that which wisdom has already delivered; the nature of the instruction, and the end for which it was given.

24. *Make no friendship with an angry man.* Spirit has a wonderful and unaccountable influence upon spirit. From those with whom we associate we acquire habits, and learn their ways, imbibe their spirit, show their tempers, and walk in their steps. We cannot be too choice of our company, for we may soon learn ways that will be a snare to our souls.

27. *If thou hast nothing to pay.* Should any man give security for more than he is worth? If he does, is it not a fraud on the very face of the transaction?

28. *Remove not the ancient landmark.* Do not take the advantage, in ploughing or breaking up a field contiguous to that of your neighbor, to set the dividing stones farther into his field that you may enlarge your own. Let all ancient divisions, and the usages connected with them, be held sacred. Bring in no new dogmas, nor rites, nor ceremonies, into religion, or the worship of God, that are not clearly laid down in the sacred writings.

CHAPTER 23

Sobriety in eating and drinking, especially at the tables of the great. Have no fellowship with the covetous. Remove not the ancient landmark. Children should receive due correction. Avoid the company of wine-bibbers. Obedience to parents. Avoid lewd connections. The effect of an unfeeling conscience.

1. *When thou sittest to eat with a ruler.* When invited to the table of your betters, eat moderately. Do not appear as if half starved at home. Eat not of delicacies to which you are not accustomed; they are deceitful meat; they please, but they do not profit. They are pleasant to the sight, the taste, and the smell; but they are injurious to health.

4. *Labour not to be rich.* Let not this be your object. *Cease from thine own wisdom.* Your own "understanding" or "prudence."

6. *Of him that hath an evil eye.* Never eat with a covetous or stingy man; if he entertains you at his own expense, he grudges every morsel you put in your mouth. This is well-marked by the wise man in the next verse: "Eat and drink, saith he . . . but his heart is not with thee."

8. *The morsel which thou hast eaten.* On reflection you will even blame yourself for having accepted his invitation.

10. *Remove not the old landmark.* See the preceding chapter, v. 28. *Enter not into the fields of the fatherless.* Take nothing that belongs to an orphan. The heaviest curse of God will fall upon them that do so.

11. *For their redeemer is mighty. Goalam,* their "kinsman." The word means the person who has a right, being next in blood, to redeem a field or estate, alienated from the family.

14. *Thou shalt beat him with the rod.* A proper correction of children was a favorite point of discipline with Solomon. We have already seen how forcibly he speaks on this subject.

18. *Surely there is an end.* There is another life; and *thine expectation* of the enjoyment of a blessed immortality *shall not be cut off.*

20. *Be not among winebibbers.* There is much of this chapter spent in giving directions concerning eating, drinking, and entertainments in general. (1) The pupil is directed relative to the manner in which he is to conduct himself in his visits to the tables of the rich and great. (2) Relative to the covetous, and his intercourse with them. And (3) To public entertainments, where there were generally riot and debauch.

22. *Despise not thy mother when she is old.* A very necessary caution, as very old women are generally helpless, useless, and burdensome; yet these circumstances do not at all lessen the child's duty. And this duty is strengthened by the divine command here given.

23. *Buy the truth.* Acquire the knowledge of God at all events; and in order to do this, too much pains, industry, and labor cannot be expended. *And sell it not.* When once acquired, let no consideration deprive you of it.

26. *My son, give me thine heart.* This is the speech of God to every human soul. Give your affections to God, so as to love Him with all your heart, soul, mind, and strength.

28. *Increaseth the transgressors among men.* More iniquity springs from this one source of evil than from any other cause in the whole system of sin. Women and strong drink cause many millions to transgress.

29-30. *Who hath woe?* I believe Solomon refers here to the natural effects of drunkenness. And perhaps *oi,* which we translate *woe,* and *aboi,* which we translate *sorrow,* are mere natural sounds or vociferations that take place among drunken men, either from illness or the nauseating effects of too much liquor. As to *contentions* among such; *babbling* on a variety of subjects, which they neither understand nor are fit to discuss; *wounds,* got by falling out about nothing; and *redness of eyes,* bloodshot with excess of drink, or black and blue eyes with fighting—these are such common and general effects of these compotations as naturally to follow from them. So that they who *tarry long at wine,* and use *mixed wine* to make it more inebriating, are the very persons who are most distinguished by the circumstances enumerated above.

31. *Look not thou upon the wine.* Let neither the color, the odor, the sparkling of the wine, when poured out, induce you to drink of it. However good and pure it may be, it will to you be a snare, because you are addicted to it, and have no self-command.

33. *Thine eyes shall behold strange women.* Evil concupiscence is inseparable from drunkenness.

CHAPTER 24

Do not be envious. Of the house wisely built. Counsel necessary in war. Save life when you can. Of honey and the honeycomb. Of the just that falleth seven times. We should not rejoice at the misfortune of others. Ruin of the wicked. Fear God and the king. Prepare your work. The field of the sluggard, and the vineyard of the foolish, described.

3. *Through wisdom is an house builded.* That is, a family; household affairs. See chap. ix. 1.

9. *The thought of foolishness is sin.* "The device of folly is transgression"; or, "An evil purpose is sinful"; or, perhaps more literally, "The device of the foolish is sin."

13. *And the honeycomb.* I have often had occasion to remark how much finer the flavor of honey is in the honeycomb than it is after it has been expressed from it, and exposed to the action of the air. See 1 Sam. xiv. 27; Ps. xix. 10; Prov. v. 3; xvi. 24; xxvii. 7; Cant. iv. 11; v. 1

14 *So shall the knowledge of wisdom be unto thy soul.* True religion shall be to your soul as the honeycomb is to your mouth. *Then there shall be a reward, and thy expectation shall not be cut off.* This is precisely the same with that in the preceding chapter, v. 18. The word *acharith* we translate in the former place "an end," and here we translate it "a reward"; but there is no place I believe in the sacred writings in which it has any such acceptation; nor can such a meaning be deduced from the root *achar,* which always refers to "behind, after, extremity, latter part, time," but never carries the idea of "recompense, compensation," or suchlike. There is another state or life, and your expectation of happiness in a future world shall not be cut off. In this sense the versions all understood it.

15. *The dwelling of the righteous. Tsaddik,* the man who is walking unblamably in all the testimonies of God, who is rendering to every man his due.

16. *For a just man.* Tsaddik, the "righteous," the same person mentioned above. *Falleth seven times.* Gets very often into distresses through his resting place being spoiled by the wicked man, the robber, the spoiler of the desert, lying in wait for this purpose, v. 15. *And riseth up again.* Though God permit the hand of violence sometimes to spoil his tent, temptations to assail his mind, and afflictions to press down his body, he constantly emerges; and every time he passes through the furnace, he comes out brighter and more refined. *But the wicked shall fall into mischief.* And there they shall lie, having no strong arm to uphold them.

18. *And he turn away his wrath from him.* Wrath is here taken for the effect of wrath, punishment; and the meaning must be—lest he take the punishment from him, and inflict it upon you.

20. *For there shall be no reward to the evil man.* Acharith. There shall not be the future state of blessedness to the wicked. See the note on v. 14. His *candle . . . shall be put out;* his prosperity shall finally cease, or he shall have no posterity.

23. *These things also belong to the wise.* "These also to wise." This appears to be a new section; and perhaps what follows belongs to another collection. Probably fragments of sayings collected by wise men from the Proverbs of Solomon.

26. *Kiss his lips.* Shall treat him with affection and respect.

CHAPTER 25

A new series of Solomon's proverbs. God's glory in mysteries. Observations concerning kings. Avoid contentions. Opportune speech. The faithful ambassador. Delicacies to be sparingly used. Avoid familiarity. Amusements not grateful to a distressed mind. Do good to your enemies. The misery of dwelling with a scold. The necessity of moderation and self-government.

1. *These are also proverbs of Solomon.* It seems that the remaining part of this book contains proverbs which had been collected by the order of King Hezekiah, and were added to the preceding book as a sort of supplement, having been collected from traditionary sayings of Solomon.

2. *It is the glory of God to conceal a thing.* This has been understood as referring to the revelation of God's will in His Word, where there are many things concealed in parables, allegories, metaphors, similitudes. And it is becoming the majesty of God so to publish His will that it must be seriously studied to be understood, in order that the truth may be more prized when it is discovered. And if it be God's glory thus partially to conceal his purposes, it is the glory of a king to search and examine this Word, that he may understand how by Him kings reign and princes decree judgment.

3. *The heaven for height.* The simple meaning of this is, the reasons of state, in reference to many acts of the executive government, can no more be fathomed by the common people than the height of the heavens and the depth of the earth.

7. *Come up hither.* Our Lord refers to this; see Luke xiv. 8.

8. *Go not forth hastily to strive.* To enter into a lawsuit.

11. *A word fitly spoken.* "Upon its wheels." An observation, caution, reproof, or advice that comes in naturally, runs smoothly along, is not forced nor dragged in, that appears to be without design, to rise out of the conversation, and though particularly relative to one point, will appear to the company to suit all. *Is like apples of gold in pictures of silver.* Is like the refreshing orange or beautiful citron, served up in open-work or filigree baskets, made of silver. The Asiatics excel in filigree silver work.

12. *As an earring of gold.* I believe *nezem* to mean the nose ring with its pendants; the left nostril is pierced, and a ring put through it, as in the ear.

14. *A false gift.* "A lying gift," one promised but never bestowed.

17. *Withdraw thy foot.* Another proverb will illustrate this: "Too much familiarity breeds contempt."

20. *As vinegar upon nitre.* The original word *nather* is what is known among chemists as the *natron* of the ancients and of the Scriptures, and carbonate of soda. It is used in the East for the purposes of washing. If vinegar be poured on it, Dr. Shaw says a strong fermentation immediately takes place, which illustrates what Solomon says here: "The singing of songs to a heavy heart is like vinegar upon natron"; that is, "there is no affinity between them."

22. *Thou shalt heap coals of fire upon his head.* Not to consume, but to melt him into kindness.

23. *The north wind driveth away rain.* The margin has, "The north wind bringeth forth rain." It is said that the "north wind brings forth rain at Jerusalem, because it brings with it the vapours arising from the sea that lies north of it." *A backbiting tongue.* "A hidden tongue."

24. *It is better to dwell in the corner.* See chap. xxi. 9.

27. *It is not good to eat much honey.* He that searches too much into mysteries is likely to be confounded by them. I really think this is the meaning of the place.

CHAPTER 26

Honor is not seemly in a fool. The correction and treatment suitable to such. Of the slothful man. Of him who interferes with matters which do not concern him. Contentions to be avoided. Of the dissembler and the lying tongue.

2. *As the bird.* As the "sparrow" flies about the house, and the "swallow" emigrates to strange countries, so an undeserved malediction may flutter about the neighborhood for a season; but in a short time it will disappear as the bird of passage.

6. *Cutteth off the feet.* Sending by such a person is utterly useless.

8. *As he that bindeth a stone in a sling, so is he that giveth honour to a fool.* It is entirely thrown away. This, however, is a difficult proverb; and the versions give but little light on the subject. The Hebrew may be translated, "As a piece of precious stone among a heap of stones, so is he that giveth honor to a fool." On this interpretation the meaning would rather be, "It is as useless to throw a jewel among a heap of stones to increase its bulk as to give honor to a fool."

11. *As a dog returneth to his vomit.* See 2 Pet. ii. 22.

13. *The slothful man saith.* See chap. xxii. 13.

16. *Than seven men that can render a reason.* Seven here only means perfection, abundance, or multitude. He is wiser in his own eyes than a multitude of the wisest men.

17. *He that passeth by.* This proverb stands true ninety-nine times out of a hundred, where people meddle with domestic broils, or differences between men and their wives.

20. *Where no wood is, there the fire goeth out.* The tale-receiver and the talebearer are the agents of discord. If none received the slander in the first instance, it could not be propagated. Hence our proverb, "The receiver is as bad as the thief."

22. *The words of a talebearer.* The same with chap. xviii. 8.

23. *Burning lips and a wicked heart.* Splendid, shining, smooth lips; that is, lips which make great professions of friendship are like a vessel plated over with base metal to make it resemble silver; but it is only a vile pot, and even the outside is not pure.

25. *For there are seven abominations in his heart.* That is, he is full of abominations.

27. *Whoso diggeth a pit.* See Ps. vii. 15.

28. *A lying tongue hateth those that are afflicted by it.* He that injures another hates him in proportion to the injury he has done him.

CHAPTER 27

Tomorrow is uncertain. Self-praise forbidden. Anger and envy. Reproof from a friend. Want makes us feel the value of a supply. A good neighbor. Beware of suretyship. Suspicious praise. The quarrelsome woman. One friend helps another. Man insatiable. The incorrigible fool. Domestic cares. The profit of flocks for food and raiment.

1. *Boast not thyself of to morrow.* See Jas. iv. 13, etc.

2. *Let another man praise thee, and not thine own mouth.* We have a similar proverb, which illustrates this: "Self-praise is no commendation."

10. *Thine own friend.* A well and long tried friend is invaluable. Him that has been a friend to your family never forget, and never neglect. And, in the time of adversity, rather apply to such a one than go to your nearest relative who keeps himself at a distance.

12. *A prudent man foreseeth the evil.* The very same as chap. xxii. 3.

13. *Take his garment.* The same as chap. xx. 16.

14. *He that blesseth his friend.* He who makes loud and public protestations of acknowledgments to his friend for favors received subjects his sincerity to suspicion.

15. *A continual dropping.* See chap. xix. 13.

16. *Whosoever hideth her hideth the wind.* You may as well attempt to repress the blowing of the wind as the tongue of a scold; and to conceal this unfortunate propensity of a wife is as impossible as to hush the storm, and prevent its sound from being heard. *The ointment of his right hand.* You can no more conceal such a woman's conduct than you can the smell of the aromatic oil with which your hand has been anointed.

17. *Iron sharpeneth iron.* As hard iron, viz., steel, will bring a knife to a better edge when it is properly whetted against it, so one friend may be the means of exciting another to reflect, dive deeply into, and illustrate a subject, without which whetting or excitement this had never taken place.

19. *As in water face answereth to face.* As a man sees his face perfectly reflected by the water, when looking into it, so the wise and penetrating man sees generally what is in the heart of another by considering the general tenor of his words and actions.

23. *The state of thy flocks.* The directions to the end of the chapter refer chiefly to pastoral and agricultural affairs. Do not trust your flocks to the shepherd merely; number them yourself; look into their condition; see how they are tended; and when, and with what, and in what proportion, they are fed.

24. *For riches are not for ever.* All other kinds of property are very transitory. Money and the highest civil honors are but for a short season. Flocks and herds, properly attended to, may be multiplied and continued from generation to generation. The *crown* itself is not naturally so permanent.

CHAPTER 28

The timidity of the wicked. Quick succession in the government of a country is a punishment to the land. Of the poor who oppress the poor. The upright poor man is preferable to the wicked rich man. The unprofitable conduct of the usurer. The prosperity of the righteous a cause of rejoicing. He is blessed who fears always. A wicked ruler a curse. The murderer generally execrated. The faithful man. The corrupt judge. The foolishness of trusting in one's own heart. The charitable man. When the wicked are elevated, it is a public evil.

3. *A poor man that oppresseth the poor.* Our Lord illustrates this proverb most beautifully by the parable of the two debtors, Matt. xviii. 23.

8. *He that by usury . . . increaseth his substance.* By taking unlawful interest for his money; lending to a man in great distress money, for the use of which he requires an exorbitant sum.

19. *He that tilleth his land.* See chap. xii. 11.

20. *He that maketh haste to be rich.* See chap. xiii. 11; xx. 21.

24. *Whoso robbeth his father.* The father's property is as much his own, in reference to the child, as that of the merest stranger. He who robs his parents is worse than a common robber; to the act of dishonesty and rapine he adds ingratitude, cruelty, and disobedience. Such a person is *the companion of a destroyer;* he may be considered as a murderer.

25. *Shall be made fat.* Shall be prosperous.

26. *He that trusteth in his own heart is a fool.* For his heart, which is deceitful and desperately wicked, will infallibly deceive him.

CHAPTER 29

We must not despise correction. The prudent king. The flatterer. The just judge. Contend not with a fool. The prince who opens his ears to reports. The poor and the deceitful. The pious king. The insolent servant. The humiliation of the proud. Of the partner of a thief. The fear of man. The Lord the righteous Judge.

1. *Hardeneth his neck.* Becomes stubborn and obstinate.

13. *The poor and the deceitful man.* It is difficult to fix the meaning of *techachim,* which we here render *the deceitful man.* I suppose the meaning may be the same as in chap. xxii. 2: "The rich and poor meet together: the Lord is the maker of them all."

18. *Where there is no vision.* Where divine revelation and the faithful preaching of the sacred testimonies are neither reverenced nor attended, the ruin of that land is at no great distance. *But he that keepeth the law, happy is he.* So our Lord: "Blessed are they that hear the word of God, and keep it."

22. *An angry man stirreth up strife.* His spirit begets its like wherever he goes. *And a furious man aboundeth in transgression.* His furious spirit is always carrying him into extremes, and each of these is a transgression.

23. *A man's pride shall bring him low.* A proud man is universally despised, and such are often exposed to great mortifications.

24. *Hateth his own soul. Naphsho,* his "life," as the outraged law may at any time seize on and put him to death. *He heareth cursing.* "The execration," or adjuration, "but he will not tell it." He has no fear of God, nor reverence for an oath, because his heart is hardened through the deceitfulness of sin.

25. *The fear of man bringeth a snare.* How often has this led weak men, though sincere in their general character, to deny their God, and abjure His people! See the case of Peter.

CHAPTER 30

Agur's confession of faith, 1-6. His prayer, 7-9. Of wicked generations, 10-14. Things that are never satisfied, 15-16. Of him who despises his parents, 17. Three wonderful things, 18-20. Three things that disquiet the land, 21-23. Four little but very intelligent animals, 24-28. Four things that go well, 29-31. A man should cease from doing foolishly, and from strife, 32-33.

1. *The words of Agur the son of Jakeh.* The words *Agur, Jakeh, Ithiel,* and *Ucal* have been considered by some as proper names; by others, as descriptive characters. With some, *Agur* is Solomon; and *Jakeh,* David; and *Ithiel* and *Ucal* are epithets of Christ. From this introduction, from the names here used, and from the style of the book, it appears evident that Solomon was not the author of this chapter; and that it was designed to be distinguished from his work by this very preface, which specifically distinguishes it from the preceding work. Nor can the words in verses 2, 3, 8, and 9 be at all applied to Solomon, they suit no part of Solomon's life nor of his circumstances. We must, therefore, consider it an appendix or supplement to the preceding collection.

3. *I neither learned wisdom.* I have never been a scholar in any of those schools of the wise men, nor *have the knowledge of the holy, kedoshim,* of the saints or holy persons.

4. *What is his name?* Show me the nature of this Supreme Being. Point out His eternity, omniscience, omnipresence, omnipotence; comprehend and describe Him, if you can. *What is his son's name?* Many are of opinion that Agur refers here to the first and second persons of the ever-blessed Trinity. It may be so; but who would venture to rest the proof of that most glorious doctrine upon such a text, to say nothing of the obscure author? The doctrine is

true, sublimely true; but many doctrines have suffered in controversy by improper texts being urged in their favor. Every lover of God and truth should be very choice in his selections when he comes forward in behalf of the more mysterious doctrines of the Bible. Quote nothing that is not clear; advance nothing that does not tell. When we are obliged to spend a world of critical labor in order to establish the sense of a text which we intend to allege in favor of the doctrine we wish to support, we may rest assured that we are going the wrong way to work. Those who indiscriminately amass every text of Scripture they think bears upon the subject they defend give their adversaries great advantage against them. I see many a sacred doctrine suffering through the bad judgment of its friends every day.

5. *Every word of God is pure.* "Every oracle of God is purified." A metaphor taken from the purifying of metals. Everything that God has pronounced, every inspiration which the prophets have received, is pure, without mixture of error, without dross. *He is a shield unto them.* And this oracle among the rest. He is the Defense of all *them that put their trust in him.*

6. *Add not thou unto his words.* You can no more increase their value by any addition than you can that of gold by adding any other metal to it.

7. *Two things have I required of thee.* These two petitions are mentioned in the next verse.

8. *Remove far from me vanity and lies* (1) All false shows, all false appearances of happiness, every vain expectation. Let me not set my heart on anything that is not solid, true, durable, and eternal. (2) Lies, all words of deception, empty pretensions, false promises, uncertain dependences, and words that fail; promises which, when they become due, are like bad bills. From the import of the original, I am satisfied that Agur prays against idolatry, false religion, and false worship of every kind. *Give me neither poverty nor riches.* Here are three requests: (1) Give me not poverty. The reason is added: Lest, being poor, I shall get into a covetous spirit, and, impelled by want, distrust my Maker, and take my neighbor's property; and, in order to excuse, hide, or vindicate my conduct, *I take the name of my God in vain; taphasti,* "I catch at the name of God." Or, by swearing falsely, endeavor to make myself pass for innocent.

(2) *Give me* not *riches.* For which petition he gives a reason also: *Lest I be full,* and addict myself to luxurious living, pamper the flesh and starve the soul, and so *deny thee,* the Fountain of goodness; and, if called on to resort to first principles, I say, *Who is the Lord* [Jehovah]?

(3) The third request is, *Feed me with food convenient for me;* the meaning of which is, "Give me as prey my statute allowance of bread," i.e., my daily bread, a sufficient portion for each day.

11. *There is a generation.* There are such persons in the world. In this and the following three verses the wise man points out four grand evils that prevailed in his time.

The *first,* Those who not only did not honor, but who evil-treated, their parents.

12. The *second,* Those who were self-righteous, supposing themselves *pure,* and were not so.

13. The *third,* Those who were full of vanity, pride, and insolence.

14. The *fourth,* The greedy, cruel, and oppressive, and especially oppressive to the poor.

15. *The horseleech hath two daughters, crying, Give, give.* The word *alukah,* which we here translate *horseleech,* is read in no other part of the Bible. May it not, like Agur, Jakeh, Ithiel, and Ucal, be a proper name, belonging to some well-known woman of his acquaintance, and well-known to the public, who had two daughters notorious for their covetousness and lechery?

CHAPTER 31

The words and prophecy of King Lemuel, and what his mother taught him, 1-2. Debauchery and much wine to be avoided, 3-7. How kings should administer justice, 8-9. The praise of a virtuous woman and good housewife, in her economy, prudence, watchfulness, and assiduity in labor, 10-29. Frailty of beauty, 30-31.

1. *The words of king Lemuel. Dibrey lemuel melech,* "The words to Muel the king." So the Syriac; and so I think it should be read, the *lamed* being the article or preposition. There is no evidence whatever that *Muel* or *Lemuel* means Solomon; the chapter seems to be much later than his time, and the several Chaldaisms which occur in the very opening of it are no mean proof of this. If Agur was not the author of it, it may be considered as another supplement to the Book of Proverbs. Most certainly Solomon did not write it. *The prophecy that his mother taught him. Massa* may here signify the "oracle," the subject that came by divine inspiration. From this and some other circumstances it is probable that both these chapters were written by the same author.

2. *What, my son?* The Chaldee *bar* is used twice in this verse, instead of the Hebrew *ben,* "son." This verse is very elliptical; and commentators, according to their different tastes, have inserted words, indeed some of them a whole sentence, to make up the sense. Perhaps Coverdale has hit the sense as nearly as any other: "These are the wordes of Kynge Lemuel; and the lesson that his mother taughte him. My sonne, thou son of my body, O my deare beloved sonne!" *The son of my vows?* A child born after vows made for offspring is called the child of a person's vows.

6. *Give strong drink unto him that is ready to perish.* We have already seen that inebriating drinks were mercifully given to condemned criminals, to render them less sensible of the torture they endured in dying. This is what was offered to our Lord; but He refused it.

8. *Open thy mouth for the dumb.* For such accused persons as have no counsellors, and cannot plead for themselves. *Are appointed to destruction. Beney chaloph,* variously translated, "children of passage"—indigent travellers; "children of desolation"—those who have no possessions, or orphans. I believe it either signifies those who are strangers, and are travelling from place to place, or those who are ready to perish in consequence of want or oppression.

10. *Who can find a virtuous woman?* This and the following verses are acrostic, each beginning with a consecutive letter of the Hebrew alphabet: v. 10, *aleph;* v. 11, *beth;* v. 12, *gimel;* and so on to the end of the chapter, the last

verse of which has the letter *tau.* From this to the end of the chapter we have the character of a woman of genuine worth laid down; first, in general, vv. 10-12; secondly, in its particular or component parts, vv. 13-29; and, thirdly, the summing up of the character, vv. 30-31.

I. Her general character. (1) She is a *virtuous woman*—a woman of power and strength. (2) She is invaluable; her *price is far above rubies*—no quantity of precious stones can be equal to *her* worth.

11. *The heart of her husband.* (3) She is an unspotted wife. *The heart of her husband doth safely trust in her*—he knows she will take care that a proper provision is made for his household, and will not waste anything. He *has no need for spoil*—he is not obliged to go out on predatory excursions, to provide for his family, at the expense of the neighboring tribes.

12. *She will do him good.* (4) She has her husband's happiness in view constantly.

13. *She seeketh wool, and flax, and worketh willingly.*

II. This is the second part of her character, giving the particulars of which it is composed. (1) She did not buy ready woven cloth. She procured the raw material, if wool, most probably from her own flocks; if flax, most probably from her own fields. (2) Here she manufactured; for she *worketh willingly with her hands.* And all her labor is a cheerful service; her will, her heart, is in it.

14. *She is like the merchants' ships.* (3) She acts like merchants. If she buys anything for her household, she sells sufficient of her own manufactures to pay for it.

15. *She riseth also while it is yet night.* (4) She is an economist of time.

16. *She considereth a field, and buyeth it.* (5) She provides for the growing wants of her family. (6) She does not restrict herself to the bare necessaries of life; she is able to procure some of its comforts.

17. *She girdeth her loins with strength.* (7) She takes care of her own health and strength, not only by means of useful labor, but by healthy exercise.

18. *She perceiveth that her merchandise is good.* (8) She takes care to manufacture the best articles of the kind, and to lay on a reasonable price that she may secure a ready sale. (9) She is *watchful* and careful. Her candle—her "lamp"—burns all night, which is of great advantage in case of sudden alarms.

19. *She layeth her hands to the spindle.* (10) She gives an example of skill and industry to her household. She takes the *distaff,* that on which the wool or flax was rolled; and the *spindle,* that by twisting of which she twisted the thread with the right hand, while she held the distaff in the guard of the left arm, and drew down the thread with the fingers of the left hand.

20. *She stretcheth out her hand to the poor.* (11) She is truly charitable.

21. *She is not afraid of the snow.* (12) She is not anxious relative to the health and comfort of her family in the winter season, having provided clothes sufficient for each in the cold weather, in addition to those which they wore in the warm season. *For all her household are*

clothed with scarlet. Not *scarlet,* for the color can avail nothing in keeping off the cold. But *shanim,* from *shanah,* "to double," signifies not only *scarlet,* so called from being twice or doubly dyed, but also "double garments."

22. *She maketh herself coverings of tapestry.* (13) She has tapestry, *marbaddim,* either tapestry, carpeting, or quilted work for her beds; and her own *clothing* is *shesh,* fine flax, or linen cloth, and *purple;* probably for a cloak or mantle.

23. *Her husband is known in the gates.* (14) She is a loving wife, and feels for the respectability and honor of her husband. He is an elder among his people, and he sits as a magistrate in the gate.

24. *She maketh fine linen, and selleth it.* (15) She is here remarkable for carrying on a traffic of splendid and ornamental dresses.

25. *Strength and honour are her clothing.* (16) All the articles manufactured by herself or under her care have a double perfection: (1) They are strong. (2) They are elegant. *Strength and honour are her clothing.*

26. *She openeth her mouth with wisdom.* (17) He comes now to the moral management of her family. *In her tongue is the law of kindness.* This is the most distinguishing excellence of this woman. There are very few of those who are called managing women who are not lords over their husbands, tyrants over their servants, and insolent among their neighbors.

27. *She looketh well to the ways of her household.* (18) She is a moral manager; she takes care that all shall behave themselves well, that none of them shall keep bad company or contract vicious habits. *And eateth not the bread of idleness.* (19) She knows that idleness leads to vice; and therefore everyone has his work, and everyone has his proper food.

28. *Her children arise up, and call her blessed.* (20) She considers a good education next to divine influence; and she knows also that if she train up a child in the way he should go, when he is old he will not depart from it.

29. *Many daughters have done virtuously.* This is undoubtedly the speech of the husband, giving testimony to the excellence of his wife. But high as the character of this Jewish matron stands in the preceding description, I can say that I have met at least her equal in a daughter of the Rev. Dr. Samuel Annesly, the wife of Samuel Wesley, Sr., rector of Epworth in Lincolnshire, and mother of the late extraordinary brothers, John and Charles Wesley.

30. *Favour is deceitful, and beauty is vain.*

III. Here is the *summing up* of the character. (1) *Favour, chen,* "grace" of manner, may be *deceitful;* many a fair appearance of this kind is put on, assumed for certain secular or more unworthy purposes. (2) *Beauty, haiyophi,* elegance of shape, symmetry of features, dignity of mien, and beauty of countenance, are all *hebel,* "vanity"; (3) *But a woman that feareth the Lord,* that possesses true religion, has that grace that harmonizes the soul, that purifies and refines all the tempers and passions, and that ornament of beauty, a meek and quiet mind, which in the sight of God is of great price. *She shall be praised.* This is the lasting grace, the unfading beauty.

The Book of
ECCLESIASTES

The book entitled *Koheleth,* or Ecclesiastes, has ever been received, by both the Jewish and the Christian Church, as written under the inspiration of the Almighty, and was held to be properly a part of the sacred canon. But while this has been almost universally granted, there has been but little unanimity among learned men and critics as to its author. To Solomon it has been most generally attributed, in both ancient and modern times.

Grotius, however, conjectured that it was written a long time after Solomon, showing that there are many words in it which do not savor of the purity of the Hebrew tongue, and are found in the times of the Captivity and afterwards, and such as appear principally in the Books of Ezra and Daniel.

The Jews in general, and St. Jerome, hold the book to be the composition of Solomon, and the fruit of his repentance when restored from his idolatry, into which he had fallen through means of the strange or heathenish women whom he had taken for wives and concubines. Others, of no mean note, who consider Solomon as the author, believe that he wrote it before his fall. Of the restoration of Solomon to the favor of God there is no proof in the sacred history.

That Solomon, son of David, might have been the author of the whole matter of this, and a subsequent writer put it in his own language, is a possible case; and were this to be allowed, it would solve all difficulties. Let us place the supposition thus: Solomon said all these things, and they are highly worthy of his wisdom; and a divine writer, after his time, who does not mention his name, gives us a faithful version of the whole in his own language.

CHAPTER 1

The prophet shows that all human courses are vain, 1-4. The creatures are continually changing, 5-8. There is nothing new under the sun, 9-11. Who the prophet was, his estate and his studies, 12-18.

1. *The words of the Preacher.* Literally, "The words of Choheleth, son of David, king of Jerusalem." The word *Koheleth* is a feminine noun, from the root *kahal*, to collect, gather together, assemble; and means, "she who assembles or collects a congregation"; translated by the Septuagint, "a public speaker, a speaker in an assembly"; and hence translated by us "a preacher."

2. *Vanity of vanities.* As the words are an exclamation, it would be better to translate, "O vanity of vanities!" Emptiness of emptinesses!

5 and 6. These verses are confused by being falsely divided. The first clause of the sixth should be joined to the fifth verse. "The sun also ariseth, and the sun goeth down, and hasteth to his place where he ariseth; going to the south, and circulating to the north."

6. "The wind is continually whirling about, and the wind returneth upon its whirlings." It is plain, from the clause which I have restored to the fifth verse, that the author refers to the approximations of the sun to the northern and southern tropics. All the versions agree in applying the first clause of the sixth verse to the sun, and not to the wind. Our version alone has mistaken the meaning. The author points out two things here: (1) Day and night, marked by the appearance of the sun above the horizon; proceeding apparently from east to west; where he sinks under the horizon, and appears to be lost during the night. (2) His annual course through the twelve signs of the zodiac, when, from the equinoctial, he proceeds southward to the Tropic of Capricorn; and thence turneth about towards the north, till he reaches the Tropic of Cancer.

7. *All the rivers run into the sea; yet the sea is not full.* The reason is, nothing goes into it either by the rivers or by rain that does not come from it; and to the place whence the rivers come, whether from the sea originally by evaporation or immediately by rain, thither they return again. For the water exhaled from the sea by evaporation is collected in the clouds, and in rain falls upon the tops of the mountains; and produces streams, several of which, uniting, make rivers, which flow into the sea.

10. *Is there any thing?* The original is beautiful. "Is there anything which will say, See this! it is new?"

11. *There is no remembrance.* I believe the general meaning to be this: Multitudes of ancient transactions have been lost, because they were not recorded; and of many that have been recorded, the records are lost. And this will be the case with many others which are yet to occur.

12. *I the Preacher was king.* This is a strange verse, and does not admit of an easy solution. It is literally, "I, Choheleth, have been king over Israel, in Jerusalem."

13. *And I gave my heart to seek and search.* While Solomon was faithful to his God, he diligently cultivated his mind. His giving himself to the study of natural history, philosophy, poetry, etc., are sufficient proofs of it. He had not intuitive knowledge from God, but he had a capacity to obtain every kind of knowledge useful to man. *This sore travail.* This is the way in which knowledge is to be acquired; and in order to investigate the operations of nature, the most laborious discussions and perplexing experiments must be instituted, and conducted to their proper results. It is God's determination that knowledge shall be acquired in no other way.

14. *Behold, all is vanity.* After all these discussions and experiments, when even the results have been the most successful, I have found only rational satisfaction, but not that supreme good by which alone the soul can be made happy.

15. *That which is crooked cannot be made straight.* There are many apparent irregularities and anomalies in nature for which we cannot account, and there are many defects that cannot be supplied. This is the impression from a general view of nature; but the more we study and investigate its operations, the more we shall be convinced that all is a consecutive and well-ordered whole; and that in the chain of nature not one link is broken, deficient, or lost.

16. *I communed with mine own heart.* Literally, "I spoke, I, with my heart, saying."

17. *To know madness and folly.* Holloth vesichluth. "Parables and science."—Septuagint. So the Syriac; nearly so the Arabic. "What were error and foolishness."—Coverdale. Perhaps "gaiety" and "sobriety" may be the better meaning for these two difficult words. I can scarcely think they are taken in that bad sense in which our translation exhibits them.

18. *For in much wisdom is much grief.* The more we know of ourselves, the less satisfied shall we be with our own hearts; and the more we know of mankind, the less willing shall we be to trust them, and the less shall we admire them. *He that increaseth knowledge increaseth sorrow.* And why so? Because, independently of God, the principal objects of knowledge are natural and moral evils.

CHAPTER 2

The vanity of human courses in the works of pleasure, planting, building, equipage, amassing wealth, etc., 1-11. Wisdom preferable to folly, 12-14; yet little difference between the wise and the foolish in the events of life, 15-17. The vanity of amassing wealth for heirs, when whether they will be foolish or wise cannot be ascertained, 18-21. There is much sorrow in the labor of man, 22-23. We should enjoy what the providence of God gives, 25-26.

2. *I said of laughter, It is mad.* Literally, "To laughter I said, O mad one! and to mirth, What is this one doing?"

3. *To give myself unto wine, yet acquainting* (*noheg,* "guiding") *mine heart with wisdom.* I did not run into extremes.

4. *I builded me houses.* Palace after palace; the house of the forest of Lebanon, 1 Kings vii. 1, etc.; a house for the queen; the Temple, etc., 2 Chron. viii. 1, etc; 1 Kings ix. 10, etc.; besides many other buildings of various kinds.

5. *I made me gardens and orchards.* Pardesim, "paradises." How well Solomon was qualified to form gardens, orchards, vineyards, conservatories, etc., may be at once conceived when we recollect his knowledge of natural his-

tory; and that he wrote treatises on vegetables and their properties, from the cedar to the hyssop.

7. *Great and small cattle.* And multitudes of most of these he needed, when we are told that his household consumed daily ten stall-fed oxen, with twenty from the pasture, with a hundred sheep; besides harts, roebucks, fallow deer, fatted fowls, and other kinds of provision.

8. *The peculiar treasure of kings and of the provinces.* (1) The *taxes* levied off his subjects. (2) The *tribute* given by the neighboring potentates. *Men singers and women singers.* This includes all instrumental and vocal performers. These may be called the delights of the sons of men. *Musical instruments, and that of all sorts.* For these seven words, there are only two in the original, *shiddah veshiddoth.* These words are acknowledged on all hands to be utterly unknown, if not utterly inexplicable. *Sadeh,* in Hebrew, is a "field," and occurs in various parts of the Bible. *Sadoth* is "fields," 1 Sam. xxii. 7. May not Solomon be speaking here of "farms upon farms" or "estates upon estates," which he had added by purchase to the common regal portion?

11. *And, behold, all was vanity.* Emptiness. *And vexation of spirit.* Because it promised the good I wished for, but did not, could not, perform the promise; and left my soul discontented and chagrined.

15. *As it happeneth to the fool.* Literally, "According as the event is to the fool, it happens to me, even me." There is a peculiar beauty and emphasis in the repetition of *me.*

16. *There is no remembrance.* The wise and the fool are equally subject to death; and, in most instances, they are equally forgotten.

17. *Therefore I hated life.* "The lives," of both the wise, the madman, and the fool. Also all the stages of life, the child, the man, and the sage.

18. *I hated all my labour.* Because (1) It has not answered the end for which it was instituted; (2) I can enjoy the fruits of it but a short time; (3) I must leave it to others, and know not whether a wise man, a knave, or a fool will possess it.

19. *A wise man or a fool?* Alas! Solomon, the wisest of all men, made the worst use of his wisdom, had 300 wives and 700 concubines, and yet left but one son behind him to possess his estates and his throne, and that one was the silliest of fools!

21. *For there is a man.* Does he not allude to himself? As if he had said, "I have labored to cultivate my mind in wisdom and in science, in knowledge of men and things, and have endeavored to establish equity and dispense justice. And now I find I shall leave all the fruits of my labor to a man that hath not labored therein, and consequently cannot prize what I have wrought." Does he not refer to his son Rehoboam?

23. *His days are sorrows.* What a picture of human life where the heart is not filled with the peace and love of God! All his days are sorrows, all his labors griefs, all his nights restless.

25. *For who can eat . . . more than I?* But instead of *chuts mimmenni,* "more than I," *chuts mimmennu,* "without him," is the reading of eight of Kennicott's and De Rossi's MSS., as

also of the Septuagint, Syriac, and Arabic. "For who maye eat, drynke, or bring enythinge to pass without him?"—Coverdale. I believe this to be the true reading. No one can have a true relish of the comforts of life without the divine blessing. This reading connects all the sentences: "This also I saw, that it was from the hand of God—for who can eat, and who can relish without him? For God giveth to man that is good." It is through His liberality that we have anything to eat or drink; and it is only through His blessing that we can derive good from the use of what we possess.

26. *Giveth . . . wisdom, and knowledge, and joy.* (1) God gives *wisdom*—the knowledge of himself, light to direct in the way of salvation. (2) *Knowledge*—understanding to discern the operation of His hand. (3) *Joy.*

CHAPTER 3

Everything has its time and season, 1-8. Men are exercised with labor, 9-10. Everything is beautiful in its season, 11. Men should enjoy thankfully the gifts of God, 12-13. What God does is forever, 14. There is nothing new, 15. The corruption of judgment: but the judgments of God are right, 16-17. Man is brutish; and men and brutes die in like manner, 18-21. Man may enjoy the fruit of his own labors, 22.

1. *To every thing there is a season, and a time to every purpose.* Two general remarks may be made on the first eight verses of this chapter. (1) God by His providence governs the world, and has determined particular things and operations to particular times. In those times such things may be done with propriety and success; but if we neglect the appointed seasons, we sin against this providence, and become the authors of our own distresses. (2) God has given to man that portion of duration called time—the space in which all the operations of nature, of animals, and intellectual beings are carried on. But while nature is steady in its course, and animals faithful to their instincts, man devotes it to a great variety of purposes; but very frequently to that for which God never made time, space, or opportunity.

11. *Beautiful in his time.* God's works are well done; there are order, harmony, and beauty in them all. Even the caterpillar is a finished beauty in all the changes through which it passes, when its structure is properly examined, and the end kept in view in which each change is to issue. Nothing of this kind can be said of the works of man. The most finished works of art are bungling jobs, when compared with the meanest operation of nature. *He hath set the world in their heart.* Haolam, that "hidden time"—the "period beyond" the present—eternity. The proper translation of this clause is the following: "Also that eternity hath he placed in their heart, without which man could not find out the work which God hath made from the commencement to the end." God has deeply rooted the idea of eternity in every human heart, and every considerate man sees that all the operations of God refer to that endless duration. See v. 14. And it is only in eternity that man will be able to discover what God has designed by the various works He has formed.

14. *I know that, whatsoever God doeth, it shall be for ever.* Leolam, "for eternity"; in reference to that grand consummation of men and things intimated in v. 11. *Nothing can be put to it.* No new order of beings, whether animate

or inanimate, can be produced. God will not create more; man cannot add. *Nor any thing taken from it.* Nothing can be annihilated; no power but that which can create can destroy.

15. *And God requireth that which is past,* i.e., that it may return again in its proper order.

21. The word *ruach,* which is used in this and the nineteenth verse, has two significations, "breath" and "spirit." It signifies *spirit,* or an incorporeal substance, as distinguished from flesh, or a corporeal one, 1 Kings xxii. 21-22 and Isa. xxxi. 3. And it signifies the spirit or soul of man, Ps. xxxi. 6; Isa. lvii. 16; in this book, chap. xii. 7, and in many other places. In this book it is used also to signify the breath, spirit, or soul of a beast. While it was said in v. 19, "They have all one breath," i.e., the man and the beast live the same kind of animal life, in this verse a proper distinction is made between the *ruach,* or "soul" of man, and the *ruach,* or "soul" of the beast: the one *goeth upward,* the other *goeth downward.* The literal translation of these important words is this: "Who considereth the [*ruach*] immortal spirit of the sons of Adam, which ascendeth? it is from above; [*hi lemalah*] and the spirit or breath of the cattle which descendeth? it is downwards unto the earth," i.e., it tends to the earth only.

22. *A man should rejoice in his own works.* Do not turn God's blessings into sin by perverseness and complaining; make the best of life. God will sweeten its bitters to you, if you be faithful. Remember this is the state to prepare for glory, and the evils of life may be so sanctified to you as to work for your good.

CHAPTER 4

The vanity of life is increased by oppression, 1-3; by envy, 4; by idleness, 5. The misery of a solitary life and the advantages of society, 6-12. A poor and wise child better than an old and foolish king, 13. The uncertainty of popular favor, 14-16.

1. *Considered all the oppressions. Ashukim* signifies any kind of "injury" which a man can receive in his person, his property, or his good fame.

2. *Wherefore I praised the dead.* I considered those happy who had escaped from the pilgrimage of life to the place where the wicked cease from troubling, and where the weary are at rest.

3. *Which hath not yet been.* Better never to have been born into the world than to have seen and suffered so many miseries.

4. *For this a man is envied.* If a man act uprightly and properly in the world, he soon becomes the object of his neighbor's envy and calumny too. Therefore the encouragement to do good, to act an upright part, is very little. This constitutes a part of the vain and empty system of human life.

6. *Better is an handful with quietness.* These may be the words of the slothful man, and spoken in vindication of his idleness. Or the words may contain Solomon's reflection on the subject.

8. *There is one alone, and there is not a second.* Here covetousness and avarice are characterized. The man who is the center of his own existence— has neither wife, child, nor legal heir—and yet is as intent on getting money as if he had the

largest family to provide for. This is not only *vanity,* the excess of foolishness, but it is also *sore travail.*

9. *Two are better than one.* Married life is infinitely to be preferred to this kind of life, for the very reasons alleged below, and which require no explanation.

CHAPTER 5

The reverence to be observed in attending divine worship, 1-3. We should be faithful to our engagements, 4-7. The oppression of the innocent, 8. The king dependent on the produce of the soil, 9. Against covetousness, 10-11. The peace of the honest laborer, 12. The evil effect of riches, 13-14. Man cannot carry his property to the grave, 15-17. We should thankfully enjoy the blessings of God, 18-20.

1. *Keep thy foot.* This verse the Hebrew and all the versions join to the preceding chapter. Solomon, having before intimated, though very briefly, that the only cure against human vanity is a due sense of religion, now enters more largely on this important subject, and gives some excellent directions with regard to the right performance of divine service, the nature of vocal and mental prayer, the danger of rash vows. The whole verse might be more literally translated thus: "Guard your steps as you are going to the house of God; and approach to hearken, and not to give the sacrifice of fools, for none of them have knowledge about doing evil."

3. *For a dream cometh.* That is, as dreams are generally the effect of the business in which we have been engaged during the day, so a multitude of words evidence the feeble workings of the foolish heart.

4. *When thou vowest a vow.* When in distress and difficulty, men are apt to promise much to God if He will relieve them, but generally forget the vow when the distress or trouble is gone by.

6. *Neither say thou before the angel, that it was an error.* I believe by the *angel* nothing else is intended than the priest, whose business it was to take cognizance of vows and offerings. See Lev. v. 4-5. In Mal. ii. 7 the priest is called the angel of the Lord of hosts.

7. *In . . . dreams . . . are . . . divers vanities; but fear thou God.* If, by the disturbed state of your mind during the day, or by Satanic influence, you dream of evil, do not give way to any unreasonable fears or gloomy forebodings of any coming mischief; fear God. Fear neither the dream nor its interpretation; God will take care of and protect you.

8. *Marvel not at the matter. Hachephets,* the "will," i.e., of God, which permits such evils to take place; for all things shall work together for good to them that love Him.

9. *The profit of the earth is for all.* The earth, if properly cultivated, is capable of producing food for every living creature; and without cultivation none has a right to expect bread. *The king himself is served by the field.* Without the field he cannot have supplies for his own house; and, unless agriculture flourish, the necessary expenses of the state cannot be defrayed.

11. *When goods increase.* An increase of property always brings an increase of expense, by a multitude of servants; and the owner really possesses no more, and probably enjoys much less, than he did when every day provided

its own bread, and could lay up no store for the next.

12. *The sleep of a labouring man is sweet.* His labor is healthy exercise. He is without possessions, and without cares; his sleep, being undisturbed, is sound and refreshing.

13. *Riches kept for the owners thereof to their hurt.* This may be the case through various causes: (1) He may make an improper use of them, and lose his health by them. (2) He may join in an unfortunate partnership and lose all. (3) His riches may excite the desire of the robber; and he may spoil him of his goods, and even take away his life. (4) Or he may leave them to his son, who turns profligate, spends the *whole,* and ruins both his body and soul. I have seen this again and again.

14. *And he begetteth a son, and there is nothing in his hand.* He has been stripped of his property by unfortunate trade or by plunderers, and he has nothing to leave to his children.

15. *As he came forth.* However it may be, he himself shall carry nothing with him into the eternal world. If he die worth millions, those millions are dead to him forever; so he has had no real profit from all his labors, cares, anxieties, and vast property!

17. *All his days also he eateth in darkness.* Even his enjoyments are embittered by uncertainty. He fears for his goods; the possibility of being deprived of them fills his heart with anguish. But instead of *yochel,* "he shall eat," *yelech,* "he shall walk," is the reading of several MSS. He "walks" *in darkness*—he has no evidence of salvation. *And wrath with his sickness.* His last hours are awful.

CHAPTER 6

The vanity of riches without use, 1-2. Of children and of old age without riches and enjoyment, 3-7. Man does not know what is good for himself, 8-12.

2. *A man to whom God hath given riches.* A man may possess much earthly goods and yet enjoy nothing of them.

9. *Better is the sight of the eyes than the wandering of the desire.* This is translated by the Vulgate as a sort of adage: "It is better to see what one desires than to covet what one knows not." It is better to enjoy the present than to feed oneself with vain desires of the future. What we translate *the wandering of the desire, mehaloch nephesh,* is "the travelling of the soul." It shows the soul to be in a restless state, and consequently to be unhappy.

10. *That which hath been is named already.* The Hebrew of this verse might be translated, "Who is he who is? His name has been already called. And it is known that he is Adam; and that he cannot contend in judgment with him who is stronger than he."

12. *For who knoweth what is good for man in this life?* Those things which we deem good are often evil. And those which we think evil are often good.

CHAPTER 7

The value of a good name, 1. Advantages of sorrow and correction, 2-5. The emptiness of a fool's joy, 6. Of oppression, 7. The end better than the beginning, 8. Against hastiness of spirit, 9. Comparison of former and present times, 10. Excellence of wisdom, 11-12. Of the dispensations of Providence, 13-15. Against extremes, 16-18. The strength of wisdom, 19. Man is ever liable to sin and mistake, 20. We should guard our words, 21-22. Difficulty of obtaining wisdom, 23-25. A bad woman dangerous, 26. There are few who are really upright, 27-29.

1. *A good name.* Unsatisfactory as all sublunary things are, yet still there are some which are of great consequence, and among them a good name. The place is well paraphrased in the following verses:

> "A spotless name,
> By virtuous deeds acquired, is sweeter far
> Than fragrant balms, whose odours round diffused
> Regale the invited guests. Well may such men
> Rejoice at death's approach, and bless the hours
> That end their toilsome pilgrimage; assured
> That till the race of life is finish'd none
> Can be completely blest."

2. *It is better to go to the house of mourning.* It is much more profitable to visit the house of mourning for the dead than the house of festivity. In the former we find occasion for serious and deeply edifying thoughts and reflections; from the latter we seldom return with one profitable thought or one solid impression.

3. *Sorrow is better than laughter.* The reason is immediately given; for by the sorrow *of the countenance*—the grief of heart that shows itself in the countenance—*the heart is made better.* In such cases, most men try themselves at the tribunal of their own consciences, and resolve on amendment of life.

4. *The heart of the wise is in the house of mourning.* A wise man loves those occasions from which he can derive spiritual advantage; and therefore prefers visiting the sick, and sympathizing with those who have suffered privations by death. But the fool—the gay, thoughtless, and giddy—prefers places and times of diversion and amusement.

6. *For as the crackling of thorns.* They make a great noise, a great blaze, and are extinguished in a few moments. Such, indeed, comparatively, are the joys of life: they are noisy, flashy, and transitory.

7. *Oppression maketh a wise man mad.* This has been translated with good show of reason, "Surely oppression shall give lustre to a wise man: but a gift corrupteth the heart." The chief difference here is in the word *yeholel,* which, from the root *halal,* signifies "to glister, irradiate," as well as "to move briskly, to be mad, furious, in a rage"; and certainly the former meaning suits this place best.

8. *Better is the end.* We can then judge of the whole, and especially if the matter relate to the conduct of Divine Providence. At the beginning we are often apt to make very rash conjectures, and often suppose that such and such things are against us, and that everything is going wrong.

9. *Anger resteth in the bosom of fools.* A wise man, off his guard, may feel it for a moment, but in him it cannot rest; it is a fire which he immediately casts out of his breast. But the fool—the man who is under the dominion of his own tempers—harbors and fosters it, till it takes the form of malice, and then excites him to seek full revenge on those whom he deems enemies.

10. *The former days were better than these.* This is a common saying, and it is as foolish as it is common. There is no weight nor truth in it. "In former times men might be more religious, use more self-denial, be more exemplary." This is all false. In former days men were wicked as they are now, and religion was unfashionable. God also is the same now as He was then.

11. *Wisdom is good with an inheritance.* In this chapter Solomon introduces many observations which appear to be made by objectors against his doctrine; and as he was satisfied of their futility, he proposes them in their own full strength, and then combats and destroys them. It is quite necessary to attend to this; else we shall take the objector's words for those of Solomon and think, as some have done, that the wise man contradicts and refutes himself. Here an objector, who had listened to the wise man declaiming in favor of wisdom, suddenly interrupts him, and says in effect, "I grant the truth of what you have said. Wisdom is very good in its place; but what is it without property? A man who has a good inheritance may be profited by wisdom, because it will show him how to manage it to the best advantage."

12. *Wisdom is a defence.* To whom Solomon answers: All true wisdom is most undoubtedly a great advantage to men in all circumstances; and money is also of great use, but it cannot be compared to wisdom. *Knowledge* of divine and human things is a great blessing. Money is the means of supporting our animal life; but *wisdom*—the religion of the true God—gives *life to them that have it.*

13. *Consider the work of God.* Such is the nature of His providence that it puts money into the hands of few, but wisdom is within the reach of all. The former can rarely be acquired, for God puts it out of the reach of most men, and you cannot *make that straight, which he has made crooked;* the latter may be easily attained by every person who carefully and seriously seeks it from God.

15. *There is a just man that perisheth.* This is another objection; as if he had said, "I also have had considerable experience; and I have not discovered any marked approbation of the conduct of the righteous, or disapprobation of that of the wicked. On the contrary, I have seen a righteous man perish, while employed in the work of righteousness; and a wicked man prosperous, and even exalted, while living wickedly."

16. *Why shouldest thou destroy t h y s e l f ?* "Make thyself desolate," so that thou shalt be obliged to stand alone. *Neither make thyself over wise;* "Do not pretend to abundance of wisdom." In other words, and in modern language, "There is no need of all this watching, fasting, praying, self-denial; you carry things to extremes." To this the man of God answers:

17. *Be not over much wicked, neither be thou foolish: why shouldest thou die before thy time?* Do not multiply wickedness; do not add direct opposition to godliness to the rest of your crimes. Why should you provoke God to destroy you before your time?

19. *Wisdom strengtheneth the wise.* One wise, thoroughly learned, and scientific man may be of more use in fortifying and defending a city than ten "princes."

20. *There is not a just man upon earth, that* *doeth good, and sinneth not. Lo yechta,* that "may not sin." There is not a man upon earth, however just he may be, and habituated to do good, but is liable to commit sin; and therefore should continually watch and pray, and depend upon the Lord. But the text does not say, "The just man does commit sin," but simply that he "may sin"; and so our translators have rendered it in 1 Sam. ii. 25, twice in 1 Kings viii. 31, 46; and 2 Chron. vi. 36.

21. *Thy servant curse thee.* Make light of you, speak evil of you.

22. *Thou thyself . . . hast cursed others. Kalalta;* you have spoken evil; have vilified others.

25. *I applied mine heart.* I cast about, *sabbothi,* I made a circuit; I circumscribed the ground I was to traverse; and all within my circle I was determined to *know,* and to "investigate," *and to seek out wisdom, and the reason of things.* Has man reason and understanding? If so, then this is his work. God as much calls him to use these powers in this way as to believe on the Lord Jesus that he may be saved. Every doctrine of God is a subject for both reason and faith to work on.

26. *And I find more bitter than death the woman.* After all his investigation of the "wickedness of folly" and the "foolishness of madness," he found nothing equally dangerous and ruinous with the blandishments of cunning women.

27. *Counting one by one.* I have compared one thing with another; man with woman, his wisdom with her wiles; his strength with her blandishments; his influence with her ascendancy; his powers of reason with her arts and cunning; and in a thousand men, I have found one thoroughly upright man; but among a thousand women I have not found one such. This is a lamentable account of the state of morals in Judea, in the days of the wise King Solomon.

29. *Lo, this only have I found, that God hath made man upright.* Whatever evil may be now found among men and women, it is not of God, for God made them all upright. This is a singular verse, and has been most variously translated. I doubt much whether the word *chishbonoth* should be taken in a bad sense. It may signify the whole of human devices, imaginations, inventions, artifice, with all their products; arts, sciences, schemes, plans, and all that they have found out for the destruction or melioration of life. God has given man wondrous faculties; and of them he has made strange uses, and they have been at one time his help, and at another his bane.

CHAPTER 8

A man's wisdom makes his face shine, 1. Kings are to be greatly respected, 2-4. Of him who keeps the commandment; of the misery of man; of the certainty of death, 5-8. Of him that rules another to his own hurt, 9. The end of the wicked, 10. God's long-suffering, 11-12. It shall be ill with wicked men, 13. Strange events in the course of providence, 14-15. God's works cannot be found out, 16-17.

1. *Who knoweth the interpretation? Pesher,* a pure Chaldee word, found nowhere else in the Bible but in the Chaldee parts of Daniel. *A man's wisdom maketh his face to shine.* Every state of the heart shines through the countenance. *The boldness of his face shall be changed.* The verse might be read, "The wisdom of a man

shall illuminate his face; and the strength of his countenance shall be doubled."

2. *To keep the king's commandment.* This sentence would be better translated, "I keep the mouth of the king"; I take good heed not to meddle with state secrets; and if I know, to hide them. Or, I am obedient to the commands of the laws; I feel myself bound by whatever the king has decreed. *In regard of the oath of God.* You have sworn obedience to him; keep your oath, for the engagement was made in the presence of God. It appears that the Jewish princes and chiefs took an oath of fidelity to their kings. This appears to have been done to David, 2 Sam. v. 1-3; to Joash, 2 Kings xi. 17; and to Solomon, 1 Chron. xxix. 24.

3. *Be not hasty.* I consider the first five verses here as directions to courtiers, and the more immediate servants of kings.

11. *Because sentence. Pithgam,* a "divine decree or declaration." This is no Hebrew, but a mere Chaldee word, and occurs only in the later books of the Bible, Esther, Ezra, and Daniel, and nowhere else but in this place.

14. *There be just men.* See chap. vii. 16.

16. *When I applied mine heart to know wisdom.* This is the reply of the wise man: "I have also considered these seeming contradictions. God governs the world; but we cannot see the reasons of His conduct, nor know why He does this, omits that, or permits a third thing. We may study night and day, and deprive ourselves of rest and sleep, but we shall never fathom the depths that are in the divine government; but all is right and just."

CHAPTER 9

No man knows, by any present sign, what is before him, 1. All things happen alike to all, 2-3. Comparison of the state of the dead and the living, 4-6. Enjoy God's mercies, and live to His glory, 7-10. The race is not to the swift, nor the battle to the strong, 11. Man is ignorant of futurity, 12-13. The account of the little city and the poor wise man, 14-18.

1. *The righteous, and the wise, and their works, are in the hand of God.* This is a continuation of the preceding subject; and here the wise man draws a conclusion from what he had seen, and from the well-known character of God, that the righteous, the wise, and their conduct were all in the hand of God, protected by His power, and safe in His approbation. But we cannot judge from the occurrences which take place in life who are the objects of God's love or displeasure.

2. *All things come alike to all.* This is very generally true; but God often makes a difference, and His faithful followers witness many interventions of divine providence in their behalf. But there are general blessings, and general natural evils, that equally affect the just and the unjust. But in this all is right; the evils that are in nature are the effects of the fall of man, and God will not suspend general laws, or alter them, to favor individual cases.

4. *For to him that is joined to all the living there is hope.* While a man lives he hopes to amend, and he hopes to have a better lot; and thus life is spent, hoping to grow better, and hoping to get more. *A living dog is better than a dead lion.* I suppose this was a proverb.

6. *Also their love, and their hatred.* It is evi-

ent that he speaks here of the ignorance, want of power, etc., of the dead, in reference only to this life. And though they have no more a *portion . . . under the sun,* yet he does not intimate that they have none anywhere else.

7. *Go thy way, eat thy bread with joy.* Do not vex and perplex yourselves with the dispensations and mysteries of providence; enjoy the blessings which God has given you, and live to His glory, and then God will accept your works.

8. *Let thy garments be always white.* The Jews wore white garments on festal occasions, as emblems of joy and innocence. Be always pure, and always happy.

9. *Live joyfully with the wife whom thou lovest.* Marry prudently, keep faithfully attached to the wife you have chosen, and rejoice in the labor of your hands.

11. *But time and chance. Eth,* time or opportunity, and *pega,* incident or occurrence—*happeneth to them all.* Every man has what may be called time and space to act in, and opportunity to work.

CHAPTER 10

Observations on wisdom and folly, 1-3. Concerning right conduct towards rulers, 4. Merit depressed, and worthlessness exalted, 5-7. Of him who digs a pit and removes a landmark, 8-9. The use of wisdom and experience, 10. Of the babbler and the fool, 11-15. The infant king, 16. The well-regulated court, 17. Of slothfulness, 18. Of feasting, 19. Speak not evil of the king, 20.

4. *If the spirit of the ruler rise up against thee.* If the king gets incensed against you. *Leave not thy place.* Humble yourself before him; that is *thy place* and duty.

5. *An error which proceedeth from the ruler.* What this error in the ruler is, the two following verses point out: it is simply this—an injudicious distribution of offices, and raising people to places of trust and confidence who are destitute of merit.

8. *Whoso breaketh an hedge, a serpent shall bite him.* While spoiling his neighbor's property, he himself may come to greater mischief; while pulling out the sticks, he may be bit by a serpent, who has his nest there.

9. *Whoso removeth stones.* This verse teaches care and caution. Whoever pulls down an old building is likely to be hurt by the stones; and in cleaving wood, many accidents occur for want of sufficient caution.

10. *If the iron be blunt.* If the axe have lost its edge, and the owner do not sharpen it, he must apply the more strength to make it cut. But the *wisdom* that is *profitable to direct* will teach him that he should *whet* his axe, and spare his *strength.*

11. *The serpent will bite without enchantment. Belo lachash,* "without hissing," as a snake may bite before it hisses, so also will the babbler, talkative person, or calumniator. Without directly speaking evil, he insinuates things injurious to the reputation of his neighbor.

14. *A man cannot tell what shall be.* A foolish babbling man will talk on every subject, though he can say as little on the past as he can on the future.

15. *He knoweth not how to go to the city.* I suppose this to be a proverb: "He knows nothing; he does not know his way to the next village."

16. *Thy princes eat in the morning!* They do nothing in order; turn night into day, and day into night; sleep when they should wake, and wake when they should sleep; attending more to chamberings and banquetings than to the concerns of the state.

CHAPTER 11

Give alms to all, 1-4. The works of God unknown to man, 5. Diligence necessary, 6. Prosperity frequently succeeded by adversity, 7-8. There will be a day of judgment, 9-10.

1. *Cast thy bread upon the waters.* An allusion to the sowing of rice, which was sown upon muddy ground, or ground covered with water, and trodden in by the feet of cattle. It thus took root and grew, and was found after many days in a plentiful harvest. Give alms to the poor, and it will be as seed sown in good ground.

2. *Give a portion to seven.* Never cease giving while you see a person in distress, and have werewithal to relieve him. *Thou knowest not what evil.* Such may be the change of times that you may yet stand in need of similar help yourself. Do as you would be done by.

3. *If the clouds be full of rain.* Act as the clouds; when they are full they pour out their water on the field and on the desert. *Where the tree falleth, there it shall be.* Death is at no great distance; you have but a short time to do good. Acquire a heavenly disposition while here, for there will be no change after this life.

4. *He that observeth the wind shall not sow.* The man that is too scrupulous is never likely to succeed in anything. If a man neither plough nor sow till the weather is entirely to his mind, the season will in all probability pass before he will have done anything. So if you are too nice in endeavoring to find out who are the impostors among those who profess to be in want, the real object may perish whom otherwise you might have relieved, and whose life might have been thereby saved.

5. *As thou knowest not . . . the way of the spirit.* Why God should have permitted such and such persons to fall into want, and how they came into all their distresses, you cannot tell, no more than you can how the soul is united to the body.

6. *In the morning sow thy seed.* Be ready at all times to show mercy; begin in the *morning,* continue till the *evening.* You do not know the most worthy object. It is enough that God knows; and if your motive be good, He will applaud and reward you.

10. *Therefore remove sorrow.* "Anger"; every kind of violent passion.

CHAPTER 12

Youth should remember their Creator, 1. A description of old age and its infirmities, with the causes of death and dissolution, 2-9. How the Preacher taught the people knowledge, 9-11. General directions, and conclusion of the work, 12-14.

2. *While the sun, or the light, or the moon, or the stars, be not darkened.* I.e., in the spring, prime, and prosperity of life. *Nor the clouds return.* The infirmities of old age, of which winter is a proper emblem, as spring is of youth in the former clause of this verse.

3. *In the day when the keepers of the house.* The body of man is here compared to a house; mark the metaphors and their propriety. (1) *The keepers shall tremble*—the hands become paralytic. (2) *The strong men shall bow.* The legs become feeble, and unable to support the weight of the body. (3) *The grinders cease because they are few.* The teeth decayed and mostly lost, and *few* that remain being incapable of properly masticating hard substances or animal food. And so they cease. (4) *Those that look out of the windows.* The optic nerves, which receive impressions, through the medium of the different humors of the eye, from surrounding objects—they *are darkened.*

4. *And the doors shall be shut in the streets.* (5) The *doors*—the lips, which are the doors by which the mouth is closed. (6) *Be shut in the streets.* The *doors* or lips are *shut* to hinder the food in chewing from dropping out; as the teeth, which prevented that before, are now lost. (7) *The sound of the grinding is low.* Little noise is now made in eating, because the teeth are either lost or become so infirm as not to suffer their being pressed close together; and the mouth being kept shut to hinder the food from dropping out, the sound in eating is scarcely heard. (8) *He shall rise up at the voice of the bird.* His sleep is not sound, as it used to be, and the crowing of the cock awakes him. And so much difficulty does he find to respire while in bed that he is glad of the dawn to rise up and get some relief. The chirping of the sparrow is sufficient to awake him. (9) *All the daughters of musick shall be brought low.* The voice becomes feeble and squeaking, and merriment and pleasure are no more.

5. *When they shall be afraid of that which is high.* (10) Being so feeble, they are afraid to trust themselves to ascend steps, stairs, etc., without help. (11) *Fears shall be in the way.* They dare not walk out, lest they should meet some danger which they have not strength to repel nor agility to escape. (12) *The almond tree shall flourish.* Not *flourish,* but "fall off." The hair falls off. The almond tree, having white flowers, is a fit emblem of a hoary head. (13) *The grasshopper shall be a burden.* Even such an inconsiderable thing as a locust, or a very small insect, shall be deemed burdensome, their strength is so exceedingly diminished. (14) *Desire shall fail.* Both relish and appetite for food, even the most delicate, that to which they were formerly so much attached, now fails. (15) *Because man goeth to his long home.* El beith olamo, "to the house of his age"; the place destined to receive him when the whole race or course of life shall be finished, for *olam* takes in the whole course or duration of a thing. (16) He is just departing into the invisible world, and this is known by *the mourners* going *about the streets.*

6. *Or ever the silver cord be loosed.* We have already had all the external evidences of old age, with all its attendant infirmities; next follow what takes place in the body, in order to produce what is called death, or the separation of body and soul. (1) *The silver cord.*—The spinal marrow, from which all the nerves proceed, as itself does from the brain. This is said to be *loosed;* as the nervous system became a little before, and at the article of death, wholly debilitated. (2) *The golden bowl be broken.* The

brain contained in the cranium, or skull. *Broken*—be rendered unfit to perform its functions. (3) *Or the pitcher be broken at the fountain.* The *vena cava*, which brings back the blood to the right ventricle of the heart, here called the *fountain*, the "spring" whence the water gushes up; properly applied here to the heart. (4) *The wheel broken at the cistern.* The great aorta, which receives the blood from the *cistern*, the left ventricle of the heart, and distributes it to the different parts of the system. These may be said, as in the case of the brain above, to be *broken*, i.e., rendered useless.

7. *Then shall the dust return to the earth as it was: and the spirit shall return unto God.* (5) Putrefaction and solution take place; the whole mass becomes decomposed, and in process of time is reduced to dust, from which it was originally made; while *the spirit, haruach*, "that spirit," which God at first breathed into the nostrils of man, returns *to God who gave it.*

8. This affecting and minute description of old age and death is concluded by the author with the same exclamation by which he began this book: *Vanity of vanities*, saith Koheleth; *all is vanity.* Now that man, the masterpiece of God's creation, the delegated sovereign of this lower world, is turned to dust, what is there stable or worthy of contemplation besides?

9. *Because the preacher was wise, he still taught the people knowledge.* And in order to do this he took *good heed*—considered what would be most useful. *He set in order*—collected and arranged, many parables, probably alluding to the book over which we have already passed.

10. *He sought to find out acceptable words.* Dibrey chephets, "words of desire," words of will; the best, the most suitable words; those which the people could best understand. But these words were not such as might merely please the people; they were *words of truth,* such as came from God and might lead them to Him.

11. *The words of the wise.* Doctrines of faith, illustrated by suitable language, are *as nails fastened by the masters of assemblies,* the "masters of collections," those who had made the best collections of this kind, the matter of which was of the most excellent nature.

12. *And further, by these, my son, be admonished.* Hear such teachers, and receive their admonitions, and do not receive the grace of God in vain. *Of making many books there is no end.* Two thousand years have elapsed since this was written; and since that time some millions of treatises have been added, on all kinds of subjects, to those which have gone before.

The Song of

SOLOMON

The book before us is called in the Hebrew "The Song of Songs"; or "An Ode of the Odes," which might be understood, "An Ode the most excellent of all others," this being an idiom common to the Hebrew language.

There have been some doubts concerning the author of this book. Some of the rabbins supposed it to be the work of the prophet Isaiah, but this sentiment never gained much credit. Most have, without hesitation, attributed it to Solomon, whose name it bears; and if the book of Ecclesiastes be his, this will follow in course, as the style is exactly the same, allowing for the difference of the subject. Both books seem to have been written about the same time and to have had the same author.

As to the persons chiefly concerned, it is generally believed that Solomon and Pharaoh's daughter are the bridegroom and bride, with their proper attendants, viz., companions of the bridegroom and companions of the bride.

I had for a long time hesitated whether I should say anything on this book, not because I did not think I understood its chief design and general meaning, for of this I really have no doubt, but because I did not understand it as a spiritual allegory, representing the loves of Christ and His Church. I must own I see no indubitable ground for this opinion. It is much better, therefore, if explained or illustrated at all, to take it in its literal meaning, and explain it in its general sense. The conviction on my mind and the conclusion to which I have conscientiously arrived are the result of frequent examination, careful reading, and close thinking, at intervals, for nearly fifty years. And however I may be blamed by some, and pitied by others, I must say, and I say it as fearlessly as I do conscientiously, that in this inimitably fine, elegant Hebrew ode I see nothing of Christ and His Church, and nothing that appears to have been intended to be thus understood; and nothing, if applied in this way, that, per se, can promote the interests of vital godliness.

CHAPTER 1

The bride's love to her spouse, 1-5. She confesses her unworthiness; desires to be directed to the flock, 6-7; and she is directed to the shepherds' tents, 8. The bridegroom describes his bride, and shows how he will provide for her, and how comfortably they are accommodated, 9-17.

1. *The song of songs.* A song of peculiar excellence. See the Introduction.

2. *Let him kiss me.* She speaks of the bridegroom in the third person, to testify her own modesty, and to show him the greater respect.

3. *Thy name is as ointment poured forth.* Your name is as refreshing to my heart, as the best perfumes diffused through a chamber are to the senses of the guests.

4. *Draw me.* Let me have the full assurance of your affection. *We will run after thee.* Speaking in the plural through modesty, while still herself is meant. *The king hath brought me.* My spouse is a mighty *king,* no ordinary person. *Into his chambers.* He has favored me with his utmost confidence. *The upright love thee.* The most perfect and accomplished find you worthy of their highest esteem.

5. *I am black, but comely.* This is literally true of many of the Asiatic women; though black or brown, they are exquisitely beautiful. *As the tents of Kedar.* I am tawny, like the tents of the Arabians.

6. *Because the sun hath looked upon me.* The bride gives here certain reasons why she was dark-complexioned. *The sun hath looked upon me.* I am sunburnt, tanned by the sun; being obliged, perhaps, through some domestic jealousy or uneasiness, to keep much without: *My mother's children were angry with me; they made me keeper of the vineyards.*

8. *If thou know not.* This appears to be the reply of the virgins. They know not exactly; and therefore direct the bride to the shepherds, who would give information.

9. *I have compared thee . . . to a company of horses.* This may be translated, more literally, "I have compared you to my mare, in the chariots or courses of Pharaoh"; and so the versions understood it. Mares, in preference to horses, were used both for riding and for chariots in the East.

12. *While the king sitteth at his table.* "In his circle," probably meaning the circle of his friends at the marriage festivals, or a round table.

15. *Thou hast doves' eyes.* The large and beautiful dove of Syria is supposed to be here referred to, the eyes of which are remarkably fine.

CHAPTER 2

A description of the bridegroom, and his love to the bride, 1-9. A fine description of spring, 10-13. The mutual love of both, 14-17.

1. *I am the rose of Sharon.* Sharon was a very fruitful place, where David's cattle were fed, 1 Chron. xxvii. 29. It is mentioned as a place of excellence, Isa. xxxv. 2, and as a place of flocks, Isa. lxv. 10. Perhaps it would be better, with almost all the versions, to translate, "I am the rose of the field." The bridegroom had just before called her fair; she, with a becoming modesty, represents her beauty as nothing extraordinary, and compares herself to a common flower of the field. This, in the warmth of his affection, he denies, insisting that she as much surpasses all other maidens as the flower of the lily does the bramble, v. 2.

3. *As the apple tree.* The bride returns the compliment, and says, As the apple or citron tree is *among the trees of the wood,* so is the bridegroom among all other men. *I sat down under his shadow.* I am become his spouse, and my union with him makes me indescribably happy.

8. *Behold, he cometh leaping.* This appears to be highly characteristic of the gambols of the shepherds, and points out the ecstasy with which those who were enamored ran to their mates.

16. *My beloved is mine.* The words of the bride on his entering: "I am your own; you are wholly mine." *He feedeth among the lilies.* The odor with which he is surrounded is as fine as if he passed the night among the sweetest-scented flowers.

17. *Until the day break.* Literally, "until the day breathe"; until the first dawn, which is usually accompanied with the most refreshing breezes. *The shadows flee away.* Referring to the evening or setting of the sun, at which all shadows vanish. *The mountains of Bether.* Translated also "mountains of division," supposed to mean the mountains of Beth-horon.

CHAPTER 3

The bride mentions the absence of her spouse, her search after him, and her ultimate success, 1-5. A description of the bridegroom, his bed, chariot, etc., 6-11.

1. *By night on my bed I sought him.* It appears that the bridegroom saw the bride only by night, that on the night referred to here he did not come as usual. The bride, troubled on the account, rose and sought him, inquired of the city guards, and continued to seek till at last she found him, and brought him to her apartment, vv. 2-4.

4. *Into my mother's house.* The women in the East have all separate apartments, into which no person ever attempts to enter except the husband. We find Isaac bringing Rebecca into his mother's tent, when he made her his wife, Gen. xxiv. 67.

5. *I charge you.* The same adjuration as before, chap. ii. 7.

7. *Threescore valiant men.* These were the guards about the pavilion of the bridegroom, who were placed there because of fear in the night. The security and state of the prince required such a guard as this, and the passage is to be literally understood.

9. *Of the wood of Lebanon.* Of the cedar that grew on that mount. It is very likely that a "nuptial bed," not a *chariot,* is intended by the original word.

10. *The pillars . . . of silver.* The bedposts were made of silver. *The bottom thereof of gold.* This may refer to cords made of gold thread, or to the mattress, which was made of cloth ornamented with gold. *The covering . . . of purple.* Most probably the canopy. *The midst . . . paved with love.* The counterpane, superb piece of embroidery, wrought by some of the noble maids of Jerusalem, and, as a proof of their

affection, respect, and love, presented to the bride and bridegroom on their nuptial day.

CHAPTER 4

The bridegroom's description of his bride, her person, her accomplishments, her chastity, and her general excellence, 1-16.

1. *As a flock of goats.* Because it was black and sleek, as the hair of the goats of Arabia and Palestine is known to be. The mountains of Gilead were beyond Jordan.

2. *Thy teeth are like a flock.* This comparison appears to be founded on the evenness, neatness, and whiteness of the newly shorn and newly washed sheep.

3. *Thy lips are like a thread of scarlet.* Both lips and cheeks were ruddy. "Like the section of a pomegranate," that side cut off on which is the finest blush. She had beautiful hair, beautiful eyes, beautiful cheeks and lips, and a most pleasing and dulcet voice.

9. *Thou hast ravished my heart.* Libbabtini, "Thou hast hearted me," i.e., taken away my heart. *With one of thine eyes.* Beachad meeynayich. "Even one of your eyes, or one glance of your eyes, has been sufficient to deprive me of all power; it has completely overcome me."

12. *A garden inclosed . . . a spring shut up, a fountain sealed.* Different expressions to point out the fidelity of the bride, or of the Jewish queen.

CHAPTER 5

The bridegroom calls on his spouse to admit him, 1-3. She hesitates; but arising finds him gone, seeks him, and is treated unworthily by the city watch, 4-7. Inquires of the daughters of Jerusalem, who question her concerning her beloved, 8-9. This gives her occasion to enter into a fine description of his person and accomplishments, 10-16.

1. *I am come into my garden.* Bathi, "I came, or have come"; this should be translated in the past tense, as the other preterite verbs in this clause.

7. *Took away my veil.* They tore it off rudely, to discover who she was. To tear the veil signifies, in Eastern phrase, to dishonor a woman.

8. *I am sick of love.* "I am exceedingly concerned for his absence, and am distressed on account of my thoughtless carriage towards him."

9. *What is thy beloved more than another beloved?* This question gives the bride an opportunity to break out into a highly wrought description of the beauty and perfections of her spouse.

10. *My beloved is white and ruddy.* Red and white, properly mixed, are essential to a fine complexion, and this is what is intimated. He has the finest complexion *among ten thousand* persons; not one in that number is equal to him. Literally, "He bears the standard among ten thousand men."

11. *His head is as the most fine gold.* He has the most beautiful head, fine and majestic. Gold is here used to express excellence. *His locks are bushy.* Crisped or curled. *Black as a raven.* His hair is black and glossy.

12. *His eyes are as the eyes of doves.* See chap. iv. 1. *Washed with milk.* The white of the eye, exceedingly white.

CHAPTER 6

The companions of the bride inquire after the bridegroom, 1-3. A description of the bride, 4-13.

1. *Whither is thy beloved gone?* These words are supposed to be addressed to the bride by her own companions, and are joined to the preceding chapter by the Hebrew and all the versions.

2. *My beloved is gone down into his garden.* The answer of the bride to her companions.

4. *Beautiful . . . as Tirzah.* This is supposed to be the address of Solomon to the bride. Tirzah was a city in the tribe of Ephraim (Josh. xii. 24) and the capital of that district. It appears to have been beautiful in itself, and beautifully situated, for Jeroboam made it his residence before Samaia was built; and it seems to have been the ordinary residence of the kings of Israel, 1 Kings xiv. 17; xv. 53. Its name signifies "beautiful" or "delightful." *Comely as Jerusalem.* This was called "the perfection of beauty" Ps. xlviii. 2-3; l. 2. And thus the poet compares the bride's beauty to the two finest places in the land of Palestine, and the capitals of the two kingdoms of Israel and Judah.

5. *Thy hair is as a flock of goats.* See chap. iv. 1.

6. *Thy teeth.* See chap. iv. 2.

7. *As a piece of a pomegranate.* See chap. iv. 3.

8. *There are threescore queens.* Though there be sixty queens, and eighty concubines, or secondary wives, and virgins innumerable, in my harem, yet you, my dove, my undefiled, are achath, one, the only one, she in whom I delight beyond all.

10. *Looketh forth as the morning.* The bride is as lovely as the dawn of day.

12. *The chariots of Ammi-nadib.* Probably for their great speed these chariots became proverbial.

13. *Return, O Shulamite.* This appears to be addressed to the bride, as now the confirmed, acknowledged wife of Solomon. *The company of two armies.* Or the "musicians of the camps."

CHAPTER 7

A further description of the bride, 1-9. Her invitation to the bridegroom, 10-13.

1. *How beautiful are thy feet with shoes!* "How graceful is your walking!" In the sixth chapter the bridegroom praises the Shulamite, as we might express it, from head to foot. Here he begins a new description, taking her from foot to head.

7. *Like to a palm tree.* Which is remarkably straight, taper, and elegant.

11. *Let us go forth into the field.* It has been conjectured that the bridegroom arose early every morning, left the bride's apartment, and withdrew to the country; often leaving her asleep, and commanding her companions not to disturb her till she should awake of herself. Here the bride wishes to accompany her spouse to the country, and spend a night at his country house.

12. *Let us get up early to the vineyards.* When in the country, we shall have the better opportunity to contemplate the progress of the spring vegetation; and there she promises to be peculiarly affectionate to him.

CHAPTER 8

The love of the bride to her spouse, and the nature of that love, 1-7. The younger sister, 8-10. Solomon's vineyard, 11-12. The confidence of the bride and bridegroom in each other, 13-14.

1. *O that thou wert as my brother!* The bride, fearing that her fondness for her spouse might be construed into too great a familiarity, wishes that he were her little brother; and then she might treat him in the most affectionate manner, and kiss him even in the streets without suspicion, and without giving offense to anyone.

5. *That cometh up from the wilderness.* Perhaps the words of the daughters of Jerusalem, who, seeing the bride returning from the country, leaning on the arm of her beloved, are filled with admiration at her excellent carriage and beauty.

6. *A most vehement flame.* "The flame of God."

8. *We have a little sister.* This young girl belonged most probably to the bride. *She hath no breasts.* She is not yet marriageable. *What shall we do for our sister?* How shall we secure her comfort and welfare? *In the day when she shall be spoken for?* When any person shall demand her in marriage.

9. *If she be a wall.* All these expressions, says Calmet, show that it was necessary to provide a husband for this young sister. For a woman without a husband is like a wall without towers, and without defense; is like a gate or door without bar or lock; and like a city without walls.

The Book of

ISAIAH

Naba signifies not only to "foretell future events," but also to "pray" and "supplicate"; and *nabi*, the "prophet," was by office not only a "declarer of events still future," but the general "preacher" of the day; and as he frequently foresaw the approach of disastrous times, such was the wickedness of the people, he employed his time in counselling sinners to turn from the error of their ways, and in making strong prayer and supplication to God to avert the threatened judgments; for such predictions, however apparently positive in their terms, were generally conditional.

In ancient times those who were afterwards called "prophets" were termed "seers" (1 Sam. ix. 9). *Haroeh* signifies the "seeing person," he who perceives mentally what the design of God is. Sometimes he is called also *chozeh*, the man who has "visions," or supernatural revelations (1 Kings xxii. 17; 2 Kings xvii. 13). Both these terms are translated "seer" in our common version. They were sometimes called men of God, and messengers or angels of God. In their case it was ever understood that all God's prophets had an extraordinary commission and had their message given them by immediate inspiration.

Of Isaiah, the writer of this book, very little is known. He is supposed to have been of the tribe of Judah, and of the royal family of David. Himself says that he was son of Amoz; and others tell us that this Amoz was the son of Joash, and brother of Amaziah, king of Judah.

Isaiah appears to have had two sons, who were typical in their names; one, Shear-jashub, "a remnant shall return," chap. vii. 3; and the other, Maher-shalal-hash-baz, "haste to the spoil; quick to the prey"; chap. viii. 3; and it is remarkable, that his wife is called a "prophetess."

CHAPTER 1

The prophet, with a boldness and majesty becoming the herald of the Most High, begins with calling on the whole creation to attend while Jehovah speaks, 2. A charge of gross insensibility and ingratitude is then brought against the Jews, by contrasting their conduct with that of the ox and ass, the most stupid of animals, 3. This leads to an amplification of their guilt, 4: highly aggravated by their slighting the chastisements and judgments of God, though repeated till they had been left almost like Sodom and Gomorrah, 5-9. The incidental mention of those places leads to an address to the rulers and people of the Jews, under the character of princes of Sodom, and people of Gomorrah, which is no less spirited and severe than elegant and unexpected, 10. The vanity of trusting to the performance of the outward rites and ceremonies of religion is then exposed, 11-15; and the necessity of repentance and reformation is strongly enjoined, 16-17, and urged by the most encouraging promises as well as by the most awful threatenings, 18-20. But neither of these producing the proper effect on that people who were the prophet's charge, he bitterly laments their degeneracy, 21-23; and concludes with introducing God, declaring His purpose of inflicting such heavy judgments as would entirely cut off the wicked, and excite in the righteous, who should also pass through the furnace, an everlasting shame and abhorrence of everything connected with idolatry, the source of their misery, 24-31.

The kingdom of Judah seems to have been in a more flourishing condition during the reigns of Uzziah and Jotham than at any other time after the revolt of the ten tribes. The former recovered the port of Elath on the Red Sea, which the Edomites had taken in the reign of Joram. He was successful in his wars with the Philistines, and took from them several cities; as likewise against some people of Arabia Deserta, and against the Ammonites, whom he compelled to pay him tribute. He repaired and improved the fortifications of Jerusalem; and had a great army, well appointed and disciplined. He was no less attentive to the arts of peace; and very much encouraged agriculture and the breeding of cattle. Jotham maintained the establishments and improvements made by his father; added to what Uzziah had done in strengthening the frontier places; conquered the Ammonites, who had revolted; and exacted from them a more stated and probably a larger tribute. However, at the latter end of his time, the league between Pekah, king of Israel, and Rezin, king of Syria, was formed against Judah; and they began to carry their designs into execution.

But in the reign of Ahaz, his son, not only all these advantages were lost, but the kingdom of Judah was brought to the brink of destruction. Pekah, king of Israel, overthrew the army of Ahaz, who lost in battle 120,000 men; and the Israelites carried away captives 200,000 women and children, who however were released and sent home again upon the remonstrance of the prophet Oded. After this, as it should seem, the two kings of Israel and Syria, joining their forces, laid siege to Jerusalem; but in this attempt they failed of success. In this distress Ahaz called in the assistance of Tiglath-pileser, king of Assyria, who invaded the kingdoms of Israel and Syria, and slew Rezin. But he was more in danger than ever from his too powerful ally; to purchase whose forbearance, as he had before bought his assistance, he was forced to strip himself and his people of all the wealth he could possibly raise from his own treasury, from the Temple, and from the country. About the time of the siege of Jerusalem the Syrians took Elath, which was never after recovered. The Edomites likewise, taking advantage of the distress of Ahaz, ravaged Judea, and carried away many captives. The Philistines recovered what they had before lost; and took many places in Judea, and maintained themselves there. Idolatry was established by the command of the king in Jerusalem, and throughout Judea; and the service of the Temple was either intermitted or converted into an idolatrous worship.

Hezekiah, his son, on his accession to the throne, immediately set about the restoration of the legal worship of God, both in Jerusalem and through Judea. He cleansed and repaired the Temple, and held a solemn Passover. He improved the city, repaired the fortification, erected magazines of all sorts, and built a new aqueduct. In the fourth year of his reign Shalmaneser, king of Assyria, invaded the kingdom of Israel, took Samaria, and carried away the Israelites into captivity, and replaced them by different people sent from his own country; and this was the final destruction of that kingdom, in the sixth year of the reign of Hezekiah.

Hezekiah was not deterred by this alarming example from refusing to pay the tribute to the king of Assyria, which had been imposed on Ahaz. This brought on the invasion of Sennacherib in the fourteenth year of his reign, an account of which is inserted among the prophecies of Isaiah. After a great and miraculous deliverance from so powerful an enemy, Hezekiah continued his reign in peace. He prospered in all his works, and left his kingdom in a flourishing state to his son Manasseh—a son in every respect unworthy of such a father.

2. *Hear, O heavens*—"Hear, O ye heavens." God is introduced as entering into a public action, or pleading, before the whole world, against His disobedient people. The prophet, as herald or officer to proclaim the summons to the court, calls upon all created beings, celestial and terrestrial, to attend and bear witness to the truth of His plea and the justice of His cause. By the same bold figure, Micah calls upon the mountains, that is, the whole country of Judea, to attend to him, chap. vi. 1-2. With the like invocation, Moses introduces his sublime song: "Give ear, O ye heavens, and I will speak; and hear, O earth, the words of my mouth" (Deut. xxxii. 1). *I have nourished.* The Septuagint have, "I have begotten."

3. *The ox knoweth.* An amplification of the gross insensibility of the disobedient Jews, by comparing them with the most heavy and stupid of all animals, yet not so insensible as they.

4. *Ah sinful nation*—"Degenerate." *Are corrupters*—"Are estranged." *They are gone away backward*—"They have turned their backs upon Him."

5. *Why should ye be stricken any more?*—"On what part?"

6. *They have not been closed*—"It hath not been pressed." The pharmaceutical art in the East consists chiefly in external applications; accordingly the prophet's images in this place are all taken from surgery.

7-9. *Your country is desolate.* The description of the ruined and desolate state of the country in these verses does not suit any part of the prosperous times of Uzziah and Jotham. It very well agrees with the time of Ahaz, when Judea was ravaged by the joint invasion of the Israelites and Syrians, and by the incursions of the Philistines and Edomites. The day of this prophecy is therefore generally fixed to the time of Ahaz. But on the other hand it is said, 2 Kings xv. 37, that in Jotham's time "the Lord began to send against Judah Rezin . . . and Pekah." If we may suppose any invasion from that quarter to have been actually made at the latter end of Jotham's reign, I should choose to refer this prophecy to that time.

8. *As a cottage in a vineyard*—"As a shed in a vineyard." A little, temporary hut covered with boughs, straw, turf, or the like materials, for a shelter from the heat by day and the cold and dews by night, for the watchman that kept the garden or vineyard during the short season the fruit was ripening (see Job xxvii. 18), and presently removed when it had served that purpose. *As a lodge.* That is, after the fruit was gathered, the lodge being then permitted to fall into decay. Such was the desolate, ruined state of the city.

9. *The Lord of hosts.* As this title of God, *Yehovah tsebaoth,* "Jehovah of hosts," occurs here for the first time, I think it proper to note that I translate it always, "Jehovah God of hosts," taking it as an elliptical expression for *Yehovah Elohey tsebaoth.* This title imports that Jehovah is the God or Lord of hosts or armies. *We should have been as Sodom.* As completely and finally ruined as *that* and the cities of the plain were, no vestige of which remains at this day.

10. *Ye rulers of Sodom*—"Ye princes of Sodom." The incidental mention of Sodom and

Gomorrah in the preceding verse suggested to the prophet this spirited address to the rulers and inhabitants of Jerusalem, under the character of princes *of Sodom* and *people of Gomorrah*. Two examples of a sort of elegant turn of the like kind may be observed in St. Paul's Epistle to the Romans, chap. xv. 4-5, 12-13.

11. *To what purpose?*—"What have I to do?" The prophet Amos has expressed the same sentiments with great elegance—Amos v. 21-24. *The fat of fed beasts.* The fat and the blood are particularly mentioned because these were in all sacrifices set apart to God. The fat was always burnt upon the altar, and the blood was partly sprinkled, differently on different occasions, and partly poured out at the bottom of the altar. See Leviticus iv.

12. *When ye come to appear.* The appearing before God here refers chiefly to the three solemn annual festivals. See Exod. xxiii. 14. *Tread my courts* (no more). So the Septuagint divide the sentence, joining the end of this verse to the beginning of the next: "To tread my court ye shall not add . . . ye shall not be again accepted in worship."

13. *The new moons and sabbaths*—"The fast and the day of restraint." The prophet Joel (chap. i. 14 and ii. 15) twice joins together the fast and the day of restraint. *Atsarah,* "the restraint," is rendered, both here and in other places of our English translation, "the solemn assembly." Certain holy days ordained by the law were distinguished by a particular charge that "no servile work" should be done therein (Lev. xxiii. 36; Num. xxix. 35; Deut. xvi. 8). This circumstance clearly explains the reason of the name "the restraint," or "the day of restraint," given to those days.

16. *Wash you.* Referring to the preceding verse, "Your hands are full of blood," and alluding to the legal washing commanded on several occasions. See Lev. xiv. 8-9, 47.

19. *Ye shall eat the good of the land.* Referring to v. 7: it shall not be "devoured by strangers."

20. *Ye shall be devoured with the sword*— "Ye shall be food for the sword."

24. *Ah, I will ease me*—"Aha! I will be eased." Anger, arising from a sense of injury and affront, especially from those who, from every consideration of duty and gratitude, ought to have behaved far otherwise, is an uneasy and painful sensation; and revenge, executed to the full on the offenders, removes that uneasiness, and consequently is pleasing and quieting, at least for the present. Ezekiel v. 13 introduces God expressing himself in the same manner: "And mine anger [shall] be [fully] accomplished, and I will cause my fury to rest upon them, and I will" give myself ease. This is a strong instance of the metaphor called anthropopathism, by which throughout the Scriptures the sentiments, sensations, and affections, the bodily faculties, qualities, and members, of men are attributed to God. The foundation of this is obvious; it arises from necessity. We have no idea of the natural attributes of God, of His pure essence, of His manner of existence, of His manner of acting. When therefore we would treat on these subjects, we find ourselves forced to express them by sensible images.

25. *I will turn my hand upon thee.* This seems to be a metaphor taken from the custom of those who, when the metal is melted, strike off the scoriae with their hands previously to its being poured out into the mould.

27. *With judgment*—"In judgment."

29. *For they shall be ashamed of the oaks.* Sacred groves were a very ancient and favorite appendage of idolatry. They made a principal part of the religion of the old inhabitants of Canaan; and the Israelites were commanded to destroy their groves, among other monuments of their false worship. The Israelites themselves became afterwards very much addicted to this species of idolatry.

29. *For they shall be ashamed*—"For ye shall be ashamed."

CHAPTER 2

Prophecy concerning the kingdom of the Messiah, and the conversion of the Gentile world, 1-5. Great wickedness and idolatry of the unbelieving Jews, 6-9. Terrible consternation that will seize the wicked, who shall in vain seek for rocks and mountains to hide them from the face of God in the day of His judgments, 10-17. Total destruction of idolatry in consequence of the establishment of Messiah's kingdom, 18-21. An exhortation to put no confidence in man, 22.

The prophecy contained in the second, third, and fourth chapters makes one continued discourse. The first five verses of chap. ii foretell the kingdom of Messiah, the conversion of the Gentiles, and their admission into it. From the sixth verse to the end of the second chapter is foretold the punishment of the unbelieving Jews for their idolatrous practices, their confidence in their own strength, and distrust of God's protection; and moreover the destruction of idolatry, in consequence of the establishment of Messiah's kingdom. The whole of the third chapter, with the first verse of the fourth, is a prophecy of the calamities of the Babylonian invasion and captivity; with a particular amplification of the distress of the proud and luxurious daughters of Sion; chap. iv. 2-6 promises to the remnant, which shall have escaped this severe purgation, a future restoration to the favor and protection of God.

This prophecy was probably delivered in the time of Jotham, or perhaps in that of Uzziah, as Isaiah is said to have prophesied in his reign; to which time not any of his prophecies is so applicable as that of these chapters. The seventh verse of the second and the latter part of the third chapter plainly point out times in which riches abounded, and luxury and delicacy prevailed. Plenty of silver and gold could arise only from their commerce, particularly from that part of it which was carried on by the Red Sea. This circumstance seems to confine the prophecy within the limits above mentioned, while the port of Elath was in their hands. It was lost under Ahaz, and never recovered.

2. *In the last days.* "Wherever the latter times are mentioned in Scripture," the days of the Messiah are always meant," says Kimchi on this place. And *the mountain of the Lord's house,* says the same author, is Mount Moriah, on which the Temple was built. The prophet Micah, chap. iv. 1-4, has repeated this prophecy of the establishment of the kingdom of Christ, and of its progress to universality and perfection, in the same words; for as he did not begin to prophesy till Jotham's time, and this seems

to be one of the first of Isaiah's prophecies, I suppose Micah to have taken it from hence.

6. *They be replenished*—"And they multiply." *And are soothsayers*—"They are filled with diviners."

7. *Their land is also full of horses*—"And his land is filled with horses." This was in direct contradiction to God's command in the law: "But he [the king] shall not multiply horses to himself, nor cause the people to return to Egypt, to the end that he should multiply horses . . . neither shall he greatly multiply to himself silver and gold," Deut. xvii. 16-17. Uzziah seems to have followed the example of Solomon (see 1 Kings x. 26-29), who first transgressed in these particulars. He recovered the port of Elath on the Red Sea, and with it that commerce which in Solomon's days had "made silver and gold at Jerusalem as plenteous as stones," 2 Chron. i. 15. He had an army of 307,500 men, in which, as we may infer from the testimony of Isaiah, the chariots and horses made a considerable part.

8. *Their land also is full of idols*—"And his land is filled with idols." Uzziah and Jotham are both said, 2 Kings xv. 3-4, 34-35, to have done "that which was right in the sight of the Lord"; that is, to have adhered to and maintained the legal worship of God, in opposition to idolatry and all irregular worship; "save that the high places were not removed: [where] the people sacrificed and burned incense still." There was hardly any time when they were quite free from this irregular and unlawful practice, which they seem to have looked upon as very consistent with the true worship of God. Even after the conversion of Manasseh, when he had removed the strange gods, and commanded Judah to serve Jehovah the God of Israel, it is added, "Nevertheless the people did sacrifice still in the high places, yet unto the Lord [Jehovah] their God only," 2 Chron. xxxiii. 17. The worshipping on the high places therefore does not necessarily imply idolatry; and from what is said of these two kings, Uzziah and Jotham, we may presume that the public exercise of idolatrous worship was not permitted in their time. The idols therefore here spoken of must have been such as were designed for a private and secret use.

9. *Boweth down*—"Shall be bowed down." This has reference to the preceding verse. They bowed themselves down to their idols; therefore shall they be bowed down and brought low under the avenging hand of God. *Therefore forgive them not.* "And thou wilt not forgive them."

13-16. *And upon all the cedars*—"Even against all the cedars." Princes, potentates, rulers, captains, rich men. These verses afford us a striking example of that peculiar way of writing which makes a principal characteristic of the parabolical or poetical style of the Hebrews, and in which the prophets deal so largely, namely, their manner of exhibiting things divine, spiritual, moral, and political by a set of images taken from things natural, artificial, religious, historical, in the way of metaphor or allegory. Of these nature furnishes much the largest and the most pleasing share; and all poetry has chiefly recourse to natural images, as the richest and most powerful source of illustration. *Ships of Tarshish.* This term is in Scripture frequently used by a metonymy for ships in general, especially such as are employed in carrying on traffic between distant countries, as Tarshish was the most celebrated mart of those times, frequented of old by the Phoenicians, and the principal source of wealth to Judea and the neighboring countries. The learned seem now to be perfectly well agreed that Tarshish is Tartessus, a city of Spain, whence the Phoenicians, who first opened this trade, brought silver and gold (Jer. x. 9; Ezek. xxvii. 12), in which that country then abounded. Tarshish is celebrated in Scripture (2 Chron. viii. 17-18; ix. 21) for the trade which Solomon carried on thither, in conjunction with the Tyrians. Jehoshaphat (1 Kings xxii. 48; 2 Chron. xx. 36) attempted afterwards to renew their trade.

19-21. *Into the holes of the rocks*—"Into caverns of rocks." The country of Judea, being mountainous and rocky, is full of caverns, as appears from the history of David's persecution under Saul. At En-gedi, in particular, there was a cave so large that David with 600 men hid themselves in the sides of it; and Saul entered the mouth of the cave without perceiving that anyone was there, (1 Samuel xxiv). Josephus, *Antiq.* xiv. 15, and Bell. *Jud.* 1. 16, tell us of a numerous gang of banditti, who, having infested the country, and being pursued by Herod with his army, retired into certain caverns almost inaccessible, near Arbela in Galilee, where they were with great difficulty subdued.

20. *Which they made each one for himself to worship*—"Which they have made to worship." *To the moles.* They shall carry their idols with them into the dark caverns, old ruins, or desolate places, to which they shall flee for refuge; and so shall give them up, and relinquish them to the filthy animals that frequent such places, and have taken possession of them as their proper habitation.

22. *Cease ye from man.* Trust neither in him, nor in the gods that he has invented. Neither he, nor they, can either save or destroy.

CHAPTER 3

The whole of this chapter, with the first verse of the next, is a prophecy of those calamities that should be occasioned by the Babylonish invasion and captivity. These calamities are represented as so great and so general that even royal honors, in such a state, are so far from being desirable that hardly any can be got to accept them, 1-7. This visitation is declared to be the consequence of their profanity and guilt; for which the prophet further reproves and threatens them, 8-15. Particular amplification of the distress of the delicate and luxurious daughters of Zion, whose deplorable situation is finely contrasted with their former prosperity and ease, 16-26.

1. *The stay and the staff*—"Every stay and support." Hebrew, "the support masculine, and the support feminine"; that is, every kind of support, whether great or small, strong or weak.

The following two verses, 2-3, are very clearly explained by the sacred historian's account of the event, the captivity of Jehoiachin by Nebuchadnezzar, king of Babylon: "And he carried away all Jerusalem, and all the princes, and all the mighty men of valour, even ten thousand captives, and all the craftsmen and smiths: none remained, save the poorest sort of the people of the land," 2 Kings xxiv. 14.

4. *I will give children to be their princes*—

"I will make boys their princes." This also was fully accomplished in the succession of weak and wicked princes, from the death of Josiah to the destruction of the city and Temple, and the taking of Zedekiah, the last of them, by Nebuchadnezzar.

6. *Of the house of his father*—"Of his father's house." *Thou hast clothing*—"Take by the garment." That is, shall entreat him in an humble and supplicating manner. "Ten men . . . shall take hold of the skirt of him that is a Jew, saying, We will go with you: for we have heard that God is with you," Zech. viii. 23. And so in Isa. iv. 1, the same gesture is used to express earnest and humble entreaty. *And let this ruin be under thy hand*—"And let thy hand support."

7. *In that day shall he swear*—"Then shall he openly declare." *For in my house is neither bread nor clothing*. "It is customary through all the East," says Sir J. Chardin, "to gather together an immense quantity of furniture and clothes; for their fashions never alter." Princes and great men are obliged to have a great stock of such things in readiness for presents upon all occasions. A great quantity of provision for the table was equally necessary. This explains the meaning of the excuse made by him that is desired to undertake the government. He alleges that he has not wherewithal to support the dignity of the station, by such acts of liberality and hospitality as the law of custom required of persons of superior rank.

9. *The shew of their countenance*. Bishop Lowth has it "the steadfastness of their countenance"—they appear to be bent on iniquity; their eyes tell the wickedness of their hearts. *They declare their sin as Sodom*. Impure propensities are particularly legible in the eyes. *They have rewarded evil unto themselves*. Every man's sin is against his own soul.

13. *The people*—"His people."

14. *The vineyard*—"My vineyard."

15. *And grind the faces*. The expression and the image is strong, to denote grievous oppression, but is exceeded by the prophet Micah, chap. iii. 1-3.

16. *And wanton eyes*—"And falsely setting off their eyes with paint." Hebrew, "falsifying" their eyes.

17. *The Lord will smite*—"Will the Lord humble." *Will discover their secret parts*—"Expose their nakedness." It was the barbarous custom of the conquerors of those times to strip their captives naked, and to make them travel in that condition. This is always mentioned as the hardest part of the lot of captives. Nahum, chap. iii. 5-6, denouncing the fate of Nineveh, paints it in very strong colors.

18. *Ornaments about their feet*—"The ornaments of the feet rings." *And their cauls*—"the net-works."

20. *The tablets*. The words which we translate *tablets*, and Bishop Lowth, "perfume boxes," literally signify "houses of the soul"; and may refer to strong-scented bottles used for pleasure and against fainting.

23. *And the veils*.—"The transparent garments."

24. *Instead of sweet smell*—"perfume." *Burning instead of beauty*—"A sunburnt skin."

26. *Sit upon the ground*. Sitting on the ground was a posture that denoted mourning and deep distress. The prophet Jeremiah (Lam. ii. 8) has given it the first place among many indications of sorrow.

CHAPTER 4

The havoc occasioned by war, and those other calamities which the prophet had been describing in the preceding chapter, are represented as 'o terribly great that seven women should be left to one man, 1. Great blessedness of the remnant that shall be accounted worthy to escape these judgments, 2-4. The privileges of the gospel set forth by allusions to the glory and pomp of the Mosaic dispensation, 5-6.

1. *And . . . seven women*. The division of the chapters has interrupted the prophet's discourse, and broken it off almost in the midst of the sentence. "The numbers slain in battle shall be so great that seven women shall be left to one man."

2. *The branch of the Lord*—"The branch of Jehovah." The Branch is an appropriate title of the Messiah; and *the fruit* of the land means the great Person to spring from the house of Judah, and is only a parallel expression signifying the same, or perhaps the blessings consequent upon the redemption procured by Him.

3. *Written among the living*. That is, whose name stands in the enrollment or register of the people; or every man living, who is a citizen of Jerusalem.

4. *The spirit of burning* means the fire of God's wrath, by which He will prove and purify His people; gathering them into His furnace, in order to separate the dross from the silver, the bad from the good. The severity of God's judgments, the fiery trial of His servants, Ezekiel (chap. xxii. 18-22) has set forth at large, after his manner, with great boldness of imagery and force of expression. God threatens to gather them into the midst of Jerusalem, as into the furnace; to blow the fire upon them, and to melt them. Malachi, chap. iii. 2-3, treats the same subject, and represents the same event, under the like images.

5. *A cloud and smoke by day*. This is a manifest allusion to the pillar of a cloud and of fire which attended the Israelites in their passage out of Egypt, and to the glory that rested on the Tabernacle, Exod. xiii. 21; xl. 38. The prophet Zechariah, chap. ii. 5, applies the same image to the same purpose: And I "will be unto her a wall of fire round about, and I will be the glory in the midst of her." That is, the visible presence of God shall protect her.

CHAPTER 5

This chapter begins with representing, in a beautiful parable, the tender care of God for His people, and their unworthy returns for His goodness, 1-7. The parable or allegory is then dropped; and the prophet, in plain terms, reproves and threatens them for their wickedness; particularly for their covetousness, 8-10; intemperance 11; and inattention to the warnings of Providence, 12 Then follows an enumeration of judgments as the necessary consequence. Captivity and famine appear with al their horrors, 13. Hades, or the grave, like a ravenous monster, opens wide its jaws, and swallows down it myriads, 14. Distress lays hold on all ranks. 15 and God is glorified in the execution of His judgments, 16 till the whole place is left desolate, a place for the flocks to range in, 17. The prophet than pauses: and again resumes his subject, reproving them for several other sins, and threatening them with woes and vengeance, 18-24; after which he sums up the whole of hi awful denunciation in a very lofty and spirited epi phonema or conclusion. The God of armies, havin hitherto corrected to no purpose, is represented wit inimitable majesty, as only giving a hist, and a swarm of nations hasten to His standard, 25-27. Upon a guilty race, unpitied by heaven or by earth, they execute their commission; and leave the land desolate and dark, without one ray of comfort to cheer the horrid gloom, 28-30.

1. *Now will I sing to my wellbeloved a song of my beloved*—"Let me sing now a song." *A song of my beloved*—"A song of loves." *In a very fruitful hill*—"On a high and fruitful hill." Hebrews, "on a horn the son of oil."

2. *Wild grapes*—"Poisonous berries."

7. *And he looked for judgment.* The play on the words in this place is very remarkable: *mishpat, mishpach, tsedakah, tseakah.* There are many examples of it in the other prophets, but Isaiah seems peculiarly fond of it.

9. *Many houses.* This has reference to what was said in the preceding verse: "In vain are ye so intent upon joining house to house, and field to field; your houses shall be left uninhabited, and your fields shall become desolate and barren; so that a vineyard of ten acres shall produce but one bath (not eight gallons) of wine, and the husbandman shall reap but a tenth part of the seed which he has sown." This means such an extent of vineyard as would require ten yoke of oxen to plough in one day.

11. *Woe unto them that rise up early!* There is a likeness between this and the following passage of the prophet Amos, chap. vi. 3-6.

13. *And their honourable men*—"And the nobles."

17. *The lambs.* The meaning is, Their luxurious habitations shall be so entirely destroyed as to become a pasture for flocks. *After their manner*—"Without restraint."

18. *With a cart rope*—"As a long cable." "An evil inclination," says Kimchi on this place, from the ancient rabbins, "is at the beginning like a fine hair-string, but at the finishing like a thick cart-rope."

25. *The hills did tremble*—"And the mountains trembled." Probably referring to the great earthquakes in the days of Uzziah, king of Judah, in or not long before the time of the prophet himself, recorded as a remarkable era in the title of the prophecies of Amos, chap. i. 1, and by Zechariah, chap. xiv. 5.

27. *None . . . among them.* Kimchi has well illustrated this continued exaggeration or hyperbole, as he rightly calls it, to the following effect: "Through the greatness of their courage, they shall not be fatigued with their march; nor shall they stumble though they march with the utmost speed: they shall not slumber by day, nor sleep by night; neither shall they ungird their armour, or put off their sandals to take their rest. Their arms shall be always in readiness, their arrows sharpened, and their bows bent. The hoofs of their horses are hard as a rock. They shall not fail, or need to be shod with iron: the wheels of their carriages shall move as rapidly as a whirlwind."

CHAPTER 6

This chapter, by a particular designation of Isaiah to the prophetic office, 1-8, introduces, with great solemnity, a declaration of the whole tenor of the divine conduct in reference to His people, who, on account of their unbelief and impenitence, should for a very long period be given up to a judicial blindness and hardness of heart, 9-10; and visited with such calamities as would issue in the total desolation of their country, and their general dispersion, 11-12. The prophet adds, however, that

under their repeated dispersions (by the Chaldeans, Romans, etc.) a small remnant would be preserved as a seed from which will be raised a people in whom will be fulfilled all the divine promises, 13.

As this vision seems to contain a solemn designation of Isaiah to the prophetic office, it is by most interpreters thought to be the first in order of his prophecies. But this perhaps may not be so; for Isaiah is said, in the general title of his prophecies, to have prophesied in the time of Uzziah, whose acts, first and last, he wrote, 2 Chron. xxvi. 22, which is usually done by a contemporary prophet; and the phrase *in the year that Uzziah died* probably means after the death of Uzziah, as the same phrase (chap. xiv. 28) means after the death of Ahaz.

In this vision the ideas are taken in general from royal majesty, as displayed by the monarchs of the East; for the prophet could not represent the ineffable presence of God by any other than sensible and earthly images. The particular scenery of it is taken from the Temple. God is represented as seated on His throne above the ark, in the most holy place, where the glory appeared above the cherubim, surrounded by His attendant ministers. The veil, separating the most holy place from the holy or outermost part of the Temple, is here supposed to be taken away; for the prophet, to whom the whole is exhibited, is manifestly placed by the altar of burnt offering, at the entrance of the Temple (compare Ezek. xliii. 5-6,) which was filled with the train of the robe, the spreading and overflowing of the divine glory.

2. *Above it stood the seraphims.* From *seraph,* "to burn." He saw, says Kimchi, the angels as flames of fire, that the depravity of that generation might be exhibited, which was worthy of being totally burnt up. *He covered his feet.* "It is a great mark of respect in the East to cover the feet, and to bow down the head in the presence of the king."

3. *Holy, holy, holy.* This hymn, performed by the seraphim, divided into two choirs, the one singing responsively to the other, is formed upon the practice of alternate singing, which prevailed in the Jewish church from the time of Moses, whose ode at the Red Sea was thus performed (see Exod. xv. 20, 32), to that of Ezra, under whom the priests and Levites sung alternately, "O praise Jehovah, for he is gracious; for his mercy endureth for ever," Ezra iii. 11.

5. *Woe is me! for I am undone.* "I am become dumb." There is something exceedingly affecting in this complaint. I am a man of unclean lips; I cannot say, Holy, holy, holy! which the seraphs exclaim. They are holy; I am not so: they see God, and live; I have seen Him, and must die, because I am unholy. Only the pure in heart shall see God, and they only can live in His presence forever.

6. *A live coal.* The word of prophecy which was put into the mouth of the prophet. *From off the altar.* That is, from the altar of burnt offerings, before the door of the Temple, on which the fire that came down at first from heaven (Lev. ix. 24; 2 Chron. vii. 1) was perpetually burning. It was never to be extinguished, Lev. vi. 12-13.

10. *Make the heart of this people fat*—"Gross." The prophet speaks of the event, the fact as it would actually happen, not of God's purpose

and act by his ministry. Or the words may be understood thus, according to the Hebrew idiom: "Ye certainly hear, but do not understand; ye certainly see, but do not acknowledge." Seeing this is the case, make the heart of this people fat—declare it to be stupid and senseless; and remove from them the means of salvation, which they have so long abused.

13. *A tenth.* This passage, though somewhat obscure, and variously explained by various interpreters, has, I think, been made so clear by the accomplishment of the prophecy that there remains little room to doubt of the sense of it. When Nebuchadnezzar had carried away the greater and better part of the people into captivity, there was yet *a tenth* remaining in the land, the poorer sort left to be vinedressers and husbandmen, under Gedaliah, 2 Kings xxv. 12, 22, and the dispersed Jews gathered themselves together, and returned to him, Jer. xl. 12; yet even these, fleeing into Egypt after the death of Gedaliah, contrary to the warning of God given by the prophet Jeremiah, miserably perished there.

CHAPTER 7

The king of Judah and the royal family being in the utmost consternation on receiving accounts of the invasion of the kings of Syria and Israel, the prophet is sent to assure them that God would make good his promises to David and his house; that, although they might be corrected, they could not be destroyed, while these prophecies remained to be accomplished, 1-9. The Lord gives Ahaz a sign that the confederacy against Judah shall be broken, which sign strikingly points out the miraculous conception of the Messiah, who was to spring from the tribe of Judah, 10-16. Prediction of very heavy calamities which the Assyrians would inflict upon the land of Judea, 17-25.

The confederacy of Rezin, king of Syria, and Pekah, king of Israel, against the kingdom of Judah, was formed in the time of Jotham; and perhaps the effects of it were felt in the latter part of his reign; see 2 Kings xv. 37. However, in the very beginning of the reign of Ahaz they jointly invaded Judah with a powerful army, and threatened to destroy or to dethrone the house of David. The king and royal family being in the utmost consternation on receiving advices of their designs, Isaiah is sent to them to support and comfort them in their present distress, by assuring them that God would make good His promises to David and his house. This makes the subject of this, and the following, and the beginning of the ninth chapters. Chapter vii begins with a historical account of the occasion of this prophecy; and then follows, vv. 4-16, a prediction of the ill success of the designs of the Israelites and Syrians against Judah; and from thence to the end of the chapter, a denunciation of the calamities to be brought upon the king and people of Judah by the Assyrians, whom they had now hired to assist them. Chapter viii has a pretty close connection with the foregoing; it contains a confirmation of the prophecy before given of the approaching destruction of the kingdoms of Israel and Syria by the Assyrians, of the denunciation of the invasion of Judah by the same Assyrians. Verses 9-10 give a repeated general assurance that all the designs of the enemies of God's people shall be in the end disappointed, and brought to naught; vv. 11, etc., admonitions and threatenings, concluding with an illustrious prophecy, chap. ix. 1-6, of the manifestation of Messiah, the transcendent dignity of His char-

acter, and the universality and eternal duration of His kingdom.

8. *Threescore and five years.* It was sixty-five years from the beginning of the reign of Ahaz, when this prophecy was delivered, to the total depopulation of the kingdom of Israel by Esarhaddon, who carried away the remains of the ten tribes which had been left by Tiglath-pileser, and Shalmaneser, and who planted the country with new inhabitants.

9. *If ye will not believe.* That is, unless ye believe this prophecy of the destruction of Israel, ye Jews also, as well as the people of Israel, shall not remain established as a kingdom and people; ye also shall be visited with punishment at the same time.

14-15. At the time referred to, the kingdom of Judah, under the government of Ahaz, was reduced very low. Pekah, king of Israel, had slain in Judea 120,000 persons in one day; and carried away captives 200,000, including women and children, together with much spoil. To add to their distress, Rezin, king of Syria, being confederate with Pekah, had taken Elath, a fortified city of Judah, and carried the inhabitants away captive to Damascus. In this critical conjuncture, need we wonder that Ahaz was afraid that the enemies who were now united against him must prevail, destroy Jerusalem, end the kingdom of Judah, and annihilate the family of David? To meet and remove this fear, apparently well-grounded, Isaiah is sent from the Lord to Ahaz, swallowed up now both by sorrow and by unbelief, in order to assure him that the counsels of his enemies should not stand; and that they should be utterly discomfited. To encourage Ahaz, he commands him to ask a sign or miracle, which should be a pledge in hand that God should, in due time, fulfill the predictions of His servant, as related in the context. On Ahaz humbly refusing to ask any sign, it is immediately added, "Therefore the Lord himself shall give you a sign; Behold, a virgin shall conceive, and bear a son, and shall call his name Immanuel. Butter and honey shall he eat." Both the divine and human nature of our Lord, as well as the miraculous conception, appear to be pointed out in the prophecy quoted here by the evangelist: He shall be called *Immanuel;* literally, "The strong God with us": similar to those words in the New Testament: "The word [which] was God . . . was made flesh, and dwelt among us . . . full of grace and truth," John i. 1, 14. And "God was manifest in the flesh," 1 Tim. iii. 16. So that we are to understand *God with us* to imply God incarnated—God in human nature. This seems further evident from the words of the prophet, v. 15: *Butter and honey shall he eat*—He shall be truly man—grow up and be nourished in a human natural way, which refers to His being with us, i.e., incarnated. To which the prophet adds, *That he may know to refuse the evil, and choose the good;* or rather, "According to His knowledge, reprobating the evil, and choosing the good." This refers to Him as God, and is the same idea given by this prophet, chap. liii. 11: "By his knowledge [the knowledge of Christ crucified] shall my righteous servant justify many; for he shall bear their iniquities [offences]." Now this union of the divine and human nature is termed a *sign* or "miracle," i.e., something which exceeds the power of nature to produce. And this miraculous union was to be brought about in a miraculous way: *Behold, a virgin shall conceive.* The word is very emphatic, *haalmah, the virgin;* the only one that ever was, or ever shall be, a mother in this way.

But how could that be a sign to Ahaz, which was to take place so many hundreds of years after? I answer, the meaning of the prophet is plain: not only Rezin and Pekah should be unsuccessful against Jerusalem at that time, which was the fact; but Jerusalem, Judea, and the house of David should be both preserved, notwithstanding their depressed state, and the multitude of their adversaries, till the time should come when a virgin should bear a son. This is a most remarkable circumstance—the house of David could never fail, till a virgin should conceive and bear a son—nor did it. But when that incredible and miraculous fact did take place, the kingdom and house of David became extinct!

18. *Egypt, and . . . Assyria.* Sennacherib, Esarhaddon, Pharaoh-necho, and Nebuchadnezzar, who one after another desolated Judea.

20. *The river.* That is, the Euphrates. *Shall the Lord shave with a razor that is hired.* To shave with the hired razor the head, the feet, and the beard is an expression highly parabolical, to denote the utter devastation of the country from one end to the other; and the plundering of the people, from the highest to the lowest, by the Assyrians, whom God employed as His instrument to punish the Jews. Ahaz himself, in the first place, hired the king of Assyria to come to help him against the Syrians, by a present made to him of all the treasures of the Temple, as well as his own. And God himself considered the great nations whom He thus employed as His mercenaries, and paid them their wages. Thus He paid Nebuchadnezzar for his services against Tyre, by the conquest of Egypt, Ezek. xxix. 18-20. The hairs of the head are those of the highest order in the state; those of the feet, or the lower parts, are the common people; the beard is the king, the high priest, the very supreme in dignity and majesty.

The remaining verses of this chapter, 21-25, contain an elegant and very expressive description of a country depopulated, and left to run wild, from its adjuncts and circumstances: the vineyards and cornfields, before well-cultivated, now overrun with briers and thorns; much grass, so that the few cattle that are left, *a young cow, and two sheep,* have their full range, and abundant pasture, so as to yield milk in plenty to the scanty family of the owner; the thinly scattered people living, not on corn, wine, and oil, the produce of cultivation, but on milk and honey, the gifts of nature; and the whole land given up to the wild beasts, so that the miserable inhabitants are forced to go out armed with bows and arrows, either to defend themselves against the wild beasts or to supply themselves with necessary food by hunting.

CHAPTER 8

Prediction respecting the conquest of Syria and Israel by the Assyrians, 1-4. Israel, for rejecting the gentle stream of Shiloah, near Jerusalem, is threatened to be overflowed by the great river of Assyria, manifestly alluding by this strong figure to the conquests of Tiglath-pileser and Shalmaneser over that kingdom, 5-7. The invasion of the kingdom of Judah by the Assyrians under Sennacherib foretold, 8. The prophet assures the Israelites and Syrians that their hostile attempts against Judah shall be frustrated, 9-10. Exhortation not to be afraid of the wrath of man, but to fear the displeasure of God, 11-13. Judgments which shall overtake those who put no confidence in Jehovah, 14-15. The prophet proceeds to warn his countrymen against idolatry, divination, and the like sinful practices, exhorting them to seek direction from the word of God, professing that this was his own pious resolution. And to enforce this counsel, and strengthen their faith, he points to his children, whose symbolic names were signs or pledges of the divine promises, 16-20. Judgments of God against the finally impenitent, 21-22.

The prophecy of the foregoing chapter relates directly to the kingdom of Judah only. The first part of it promises them deliverance from the united invasion of the Israelites and Syrians; the latter part, from v. 17, denounces the desolation to be brought upon the kingdom of Judah by the Assyrians. The sixth, seventh, and eighth verses of this chapter seem to take in both the kingdoms of Israel and Judah. "This people refuseth the waters of Shiloah" may be meant of both: the Israelites despised the kingdom of Judah, which they had deserted, and now attempted to destroy; the people of Judah, from a consideration of their own weakness and a distrust of God's promises, being reduced to despair, applied to the Assyrians for assistance against the two confederate kings. But how could it be said of Judah that they rejoiced in Rezin and the son of Remaliah, the enemies confederated against them? This, therefore, must be understood of Israel. The prophet denounces the Assyrian invasion, which should overwhelm the whole kingdom of Israel under Tiglath-pileser and Shalmaneser; and the subsequent invasion of Judah by the same power under Sennacherib, which would bring them into the most imminent danger, like a flood reaching to the neck, in which a man can but just keep his head above water. The two next verses, 9 and 10, are addressed by the prophet, as a subject of the kingdom of Judah, to the Israelites and Syrians, and perhaps to all the enemies of God's people, assuring them that their attempts against that kingdom shall be fruitless, for that the promised Immanuel, to whom he alludes by using His name to express the signification of it, "for God is with us" shall be the Defense of the house of David, and deliver the kingdom of Judah out of their hands. He then proceeds to warn the people of Judah against idolatry, divination, and the like forbidden practices; to which they were much inclined, and which would soon bring down God's judgments upon Israel. The prophecy concludes at the sixth verse of chap. ix with promises of blessings in future times by the coming of the great Deliverer already pointed out by the name of Immanuel, whose person and character are set forth in terms the most ample and magnificent.

And here it may be observed that it is almost the constant practice of the prophet to connect in like manner deliverances temporal with spiritual. Thus the eleventh chapter, setting forth the kingdom of Messiah, is closely connected with the tenth, which foretells the destruction of Sennacherib. So likewise the destruction of nations, enemies to God, in the thirty-fourth chapter, introduces the flourishing state of the kingdom of Christ in the thirty-fifth. And thus the chapters from xl to xlix inclusive, plainly relating to the deliverance from the captivity of Babylon, do in some parts plainly relate to the greater deliverance by Christ.

1. *Take thee a great roll.* In this manner he was to record the prophecy of the destruction of Damascus and Samaria by the Assyrians, the subject and sum of which prophecy is here expressed with great brevity in four words, *maher shalal hash baz;* i.e., "to hasten the spoil, to take quickly the prey"; which are afterwards applied as the name of the prophet's son, who was made a sign of the speedy completion of it—Maher-shalal-hash-baz: *Haste-to-the-spoil, Quick-to-the-prey.* And that it might be done with the greater solemnity, and to preclude all doubt of the real delivery of the prophecy before the event, he calls witnesses to attest the recording of it.

4. *Before the child.* The prophecy was accordingly accomplished within three years; when Tiglath-pileser, king of Assyria, went up against Damascus and took it, and carried the people of it captive to Kir, and slew Rezin, and also took the Reubenites and the Gadites, and the half-tribe of Manasseh, and carried them captive to Assyria, 2 Kings xv. 29; xvi. 9; 1 Chron. v. 26.

6. *Forasmuch as this people refuseth.* The gentle *waters of Shiloah,* a small fountain and brook just without Jerusalem, which supplied a pool within the city for the use of the inhabitants, is an apt emblem of the state of the kingdom and house of David, much reduced in its apparent strength, yet supported by the blessing of God; and is finely contrasted with the waters of the Euphrates, great, rapid, and impetuous— the image of the Babylonian empire, which God threatens to bring down like a mighty flood upon all these apostates of both kingdoms, as punishment for their manifold iniquities, and their contemptuous disregard of His promises.

8. *He shall reach even to the neck.* He compares Jerusalem, says Kimchi, to the head of the human body. As when the waters come up to a man's neck, he is very near drowning, so the king of Assyria coming up to Jerusalem was like a flood reaching to the neck—the whole country was overflowed, and the capital was in imminent danger.

9. *Associate yourselves*—"Know ye this." God by His prophet plainly declares to the confederate adversaries of Judah, and bids them regard and attend to His declaration, that all their efforts shall be in vain.

11. *With a strong hand.* That is, with a strong and powerful influence of the prophetic Spirit.

20. *To the law and to the testimony*—"Unto the command, and unto the testimony." *Because there is no light in them*—"In which there is no obscurity." Kimchi says this was the form of an oath: "By the law and by the testimony such and such things are so." Now if they had sworn this falsely, it is because there is *no light,* no "illumination," no scruple of conscience, *in them.*

21. *Hardly bestead*—"Distressed." Instead of *niksheh,* "distressed," the Vulgate, Chaldee, and Symmachus manifestly read *nichshal,* "stumbling, tottering through weakness, ready to fall," a sense which suits very well with the place. *And look upward*—"And he shall cast his eyes upward."

CHAPTER 9

This chapter contains an illustrious prophecy of the Messiah. He is represented under the glorious figure of the sun, or light, rising on a benighted world, and diffusing joy and gladness wherever He sheds His beams, 1-3. His conquests are astonishing and miraculous, as in the day of Midian; and the peace which they procure is to be permanent, as denoted by the burning of all the implements of war, 4-5. The person and character of this great Deliverer are then set forth in the most magnificent terms which the language of mankind could furnish, 6. The extent of His kingdom is declared to be universal, and the duration of it eternal, 7. The prophet foretells most awful calamities which were ready to fall upon the Israelites on account of their manifold impieties, 8-21.

1. *Dimness*—"Accumulated darkness." *The land of Zebulun.* Zebulun, Naphtali, Manasseh, that is, the country of Galilee all round the Sea of Gennesareth, were the parts that principally suffered in the first Assyrian invasion under Tiglath-pileser; see 2 Kings xv. 29; 1 Chron. v. 26. And they were the first that enjoyed the blessings of Christ's preaching the gospel, and exhibiting His miraculous works among them.

3. *And not increased the joy*—"Thou hast increased their joy."

5. *Every battle of the warrior*—"The greaves of the armed warrior." I take it to mean that part of the armor which covered the legs and feet. The burning of heaps of armor, gathered from the field of battle, as an offering made to the god supposed to be the giver of victory, was a custom that prevailed among some heathen nations; and the Romans used it as an emblem of peace, which perfectly well suits with the design of the prophet in this place. A medal struck by Vespasian on finishing his wars both at home and abroad represents the goddess Peace holding an olive branch in one hand, and, with a lighted torch in the other, setting fire to a heap of armor. Ezekiel, chap. xxxix. 8-10, in his bold manner, describes the burning of the arms of the enemy, in consequence of the complete victory to be obtained by the Israelites over God and Magog.

6. *The government shall be upon his shoulder.* That is, the ensign of government; the sceptre, the sword, the key, or the like, which was borne upon or hung from the shoulder. *The everlasting Father*—"The Father of the everlasting age," or "the Father of eternity." *Prince of Peace.* The Prince of prosperity, the Giver of all blessings.

7. This is an illustrious prophecy of the incarnation of Christ, with an enumeration of those characters in which He stands most nearly related to mankind as their Saviour, and of others by which His infinite majesty and Godhead are shown. He shall appear as a child, born of a woman, born as a Jew, under the law, but not in the way of ordinary generation. He is *a Son . . . given*—the human nature, in which the fullness of the Godhead was to dwell, being produced by the creative energy of the Holy Ghost in the womb of the Virgin. See Matt. i. 20-21, 23, 25, and Luke i. 35, and Isa. vii. 14, and the notes on those passages. As being God manifested in the flesh, He was wonderful in His conception, birth, preaching, miracles, sufferings, death, resurrection, and ascension; wonderful in His person, and wonderful in His working. He is the *Counsellor* that expounds the law; shows its origin, nature, and claims; instructs, pleads for the guilty; and ever appears in the presence of God for men. He is the

mighty God; God essentially and efficiently prevailing against His enemies, and destroying ours. He is the *Father* of eternity; the Origin of all being, and the Cause of the existence, and particularly the Father of the spirits of all flesh. The *Prince of Peace*—not only the Author of peace, and the Dispenser of peace, but also He that rules by peace, whose rule tends always to perfection, and produces prosperity.

10. *The bricks.* "The eastern bricks," says Sir John Chardin, "are only clay well moistened with water, and mixed with straw, and dried in the sun." These bricks are properly opposed to hewn stone, so greatly superior in beauty and durableness. *The sycomores,* which, as Jerome on the place says, are timber of little worth, with equal propriety are opposed to the *cedars.* By this *mashal,* or figurative and sententious speech, they boast that they shall easily be able to repair their present losses, suffered perhaps by the first Assyrian invasion under Tiglath-pileser, and to bring their affairs to a more flourishing condition than ever.

11. *The adversaries of Rezin against him*—"The princes of Retsin against him." The princes of Retsin, the late ally of Israel, that is, the Syrians, expressly named in the next verse, shall now be excited against Israel.

12. *With open mouth*—"On every side."

18. *For wickedness.* Wickedness rageth like a fire, destroying and laying waste the nation; but it shall be its own destruction, by bringing down the fire of God's wrath, which shall burn up *the briers and the thorns;* that is, the wicked themselves. Briers and thorns are an image frequently applied in Scripture, when set on fire, to the rage of the wicked; violent, yet impotent, and of no long continuance.

20. *The flesh of his own arm*—"The flesh of his neighbor." Jeremiah has the very same expression: "And every one shall eat the flesh of his neighbour" (see chap. xix. 9); that is, they shall harass and destroy one another. "Manasseh [shall destroy] E p h r a i m; and Ephraim, Manasseh," which two tribes were most closely connected in both blood and situation as brothers and neighbors; "and both of them in the midst of their own dissensions shall agree in preying upon Judah."

CHAPTER 10

God's judgments against oppressive rulers, 1-4. The prophet foretells the invasion of Sennacherib, and the destruction of his army. That mighty monarch is represented as a rod in the hand of God to correct His people for their sins; and his ambitious purposes, contrary to his own intentions, are made subservient to the great designs of Providence, 5-11. Having accomplished this work, the Almighty takes account of his impious vauntings, 12-14; and threatens utter destruction to the small and great of his army, represented by the thorns, and the glory of the forest, 15-19. This leads the prophet to comfort his countrymen with the promise of this signal interposition of God in their favor, 20-27. Brief description of the march of Sennacherib towards Jerusalem, and of the alarm and terror which he spread everywhere as he hastened forward, 28-32. The spirit and rapidity of the description are admirably suited to the subject. The affrighted people are seen fleeing, and the eager invader pursuing; the cries of one city are heard by those of another; and groan swiftly succeeds to groan, till at length the rod is lifted over the last citadel. In this critical situation, however, the promise of a divine inter-position is seasonably renewed. This scene instantly changes; the uplifted arm of this signal conqueror is at once arrested and laid low by the hand of heaven; the forest of Lebanon (a figure by which the immense Assyrian host is elegantly pointed out) is hewn down by the axe of the divine vengeance; and the mind is equally pleased with the equity of the judgment, and the beauty and majesty of the description, 33-34.

4. *Without me.* That is, without my aid; they shall be taken captive even by the captives, and shall be subdued even by the vanquished.

5. *O Assyrian*—"Ho to the Assyrian." Here begins a new and distinct prophecy, continued to the end of the twelfth chapter; and it appears from vv. 9-11 of this chapter that this prophecy was delivered after the taking of Samaria by Shalmaneser, which was in the sixth year of the reign of Hezekiah. And as the former part of it foretells the invasion of Sennacherib, and the destruction of his army, which makes the whole subject of this chapter, it must have been delivered before the fourteenth of the same reign. *The staff in their hand*—"The staff in whose hand."

15. *No wood*—"Its master."

16. *And under his glory.* That is, all that he could boast of as great and strong in his army, expressed afterwards, v. 18, by "the glory of his forest, and of his fruitful field."

17. *And it shall burn and devour his thorns*—"And he shall burn and consume his thorn." The *briers* and *thorns* are the common people; "the glory of his forest" is the nobles and those of highest rank and importance. See note on chap. ix. 17, and compare Ezek. xx. 47. The fire of God's wrath shall destroy them, both great and small; it shall consume them "from the soul to the flesh," a proverbial expression—*soul and body,* as we say. It shall consume them entirely and altogether; and the few that escape shall be looked upon as having escaped from the most imminent danger; "as a firebrand plucked out of the fire," Amos iv. 11.

21. *The remnant shall return . . . unto the mighty God. El gibbor,* the mighty or conquering God; the Messiah, the same Person mentioned in v. 6 of the preceding chapter.

24. *After the manner of Egypt*—"In the way of Egypt." Sennacherib, soon after his return from his Egyptian expedition, which, I imagine, took him up three years, invested Jerusalem. He is represented by the prophet as lifting up his rod in his march from Egypt, and threatening the people of God, as Pharaoh and the Egyptians had done when they pursued them to the Red Sea. But God in His turn will lift up His rod over the sea, as He did at that time, in the way, or after the manner, of Egypt. And as Sennacherib has imitated the Egyptians in his threats, and came full of rage against them from the same quarter, so God will act over again the same part that He had taken formerly in Egypt, and overthrow their enemies in as signal a manner.

25. *The indignation*—"Mine indignation."

26. *And as his rod was upon the sea*—"And like His rod which He lifted up over the sea."

28. *He is come to Aiath.* A description of the march of Sennacherib's army approaching Jerusalem in order to invest it, and of the terror and confusion spreading and increasing through the several places as he advanced; expressed with great brevity, but finely diversified. The places here mentioned are all in the neighborhood of Jerusalem, from *Ai* northward, to *Nob* westward of it; from which last place he might probably have a prospect of Mount *Zion. Anathoth* was within three Roman miles of Jerusalem, according to Eusebius, Jerome, and Josephus. *Nob* was probably still

nearer. And it should seem from this passage of Isaiah that Sennacherib's army was destroyed near the latter of these places.

29. *They are gone over the passage*—"They have passed the strait." The strait here mentioned is that of Michmas, a very narrow passage between two sharp hills or rocks (see 1 Sam. xiv. 4-5), where a great army might have been opposed with advantage by a very inferior force.

CHAPTER 11

The Messiah represented as a slender twig shooting up from the root of an old, withered stem, which tender plant, so extremely weak in its first appearance, should nevertheless become fruitful and mighty, 1-4. Great equity of the Messiah's government, 5. Beautiful assemblages of images by which the great peace and happiness of His kingdom are set forth, 6-8. The extent of His dominion shall be ultimately that of the whole habitable globe, 9. The prophet, borrowing his imagery from the exodus from Egypt, predicts, with great majesty of language, the future restoration of the outcasts of Israel and the dispersed of Judah (viz., the whole of the twelve tribes of Israel) from their several dispersions, and also that blessed period when both Jews and Gentiles shall assemble under the banner of Jesus, and zealously unite in extending the limits of His kingdom, 10-16.

The prophet had described the destruction of the Assyrian army under the image of a mighty forest, consisting of flourishing trees growing thick together, and of a great height; of Lebanon itself crowned with lofty cedars, but cut down and laid level with the ground by the axe wielded by the hand of some powerful and illustrious agent. In opposition to this image he represents the great Person who makes the subject of this chapter as a slender twig shooting out from the trunk of an old tree, cut down, lopped to the very root, and decayed; which tender plant, so weak in appearance, should nevertheless become fruitful and prosper. This contrast shows plainly the connection between this and the preceding chapter, which is moreover expressed by the connecting particle; and we have here a remarkable instance of that method so common with the prophets, and particularly with Isaiah, of taking occasion, from the mention of some great temporal deliverance, to launch out into the display of the spiritual deliverance of God's people by the Messiah. For that this prophecy relates to the Messiah we have the express authority of St. Paul, Rom. xv. 12. Thus in the latter part of Isaiah's prophecies the subject of the great redemption, and of the glories of the Messiah's kingdom, arises out of the restoration of Judah by the deliverance from the captivity of Babylon, and is all along connected and intermixed with it.

4. *With the rod of his mouth*—"By the blast of his mouth."

10. *A root of Jesse, which shall stand*—"The root of Jesse, which standeth." St. John hath taken this expression from Isaiah, Rev. v. 5 and xxii. 16, where Christ hath twice applied it to himself. The one hundred and tenth psalm is a good comment on this verse.

11. *And it shall come to pass in that day.* This part of the chapter contains a prophecy which certainly remains yet to be accomplished.

15. *The Lord . . . shall smite it in the seven streams*—"Smite with a drought." Here is a plain allusion to the passage of the Red Sea. And the Lord's shaking His hand over the river with His vehement wind refers to a particular circumstance of the same miracle;

for He "caused the sea to go back by a strong east wind all that night, and made the sea dry land," Exod. xiv. 21. The *tongue;* a very apposite and descriptive expression for a bay such as that of the Red Sea. It is used in the same sense, Josh. xv. 2, 5; xviii. 19.

CHAPTER 12

Prophetic hymn of praise for the great mercies vouchsafed to the children of Israel in their deliverance from the great Babylonish captivity, and for redemption by the Messiah, 1-6.

This hymn seems, by its whole tenor, and by many expressions in it, much better calculated for the use of the Christian Church than for the Jewish, in any circumstances, or at any time that can be assigned. The Jews themselves seem to have applied it to the times of Messiah. On the last day of the Feast of Tabernacles they fetched water in a golden pitcher from the fountain of Shiloah, springing at the foot of Mount Sion without the city. They brought it through the water gate into the Temple, and poured it, mixed with wine, on the sacrifice as it lay upon the altar, with great rejoicing. They seem to have taken up this custom, for it is not ordained in the law of Moses, as an emblem of future blessings, in allusion to this passage of Isaiah, "Ye shall draw waters with joy from the fountains of salvation," expressions that can hardly be understood of any benefits afforded by the Mosaic dispensation. Our Saviour applied the ceremony, and the intention of it, to himself, and the effusion of the Holy Spirit, promised, and to be given, by Him. The sense of the Jews in this matter is plainly shown by the following passage of the Jerusalem Talmud: "Why is it called the place or house of drawing?" (for that was the term for this ceremony, or for the place where the water was taken up) "Because from thence they draw the Holy Spirit; as it is written, And ye shall draw water with joy from the fountains of salvation."

1. *Though thou wast angry*—"For though thou hast been angry." The Hebrew phrase is exactly the same with that of St. Paul, Rom. vi. 17: "But thanks be to God, that ye were the slaves of sin; but have obeyed from the heart"; that is, "that whereas, or though, ye were the slaves of sin, yet ye have now obeyed from the heart the doctrine on the model of which ye were formed."

6. *Thou inhabitant of Zion.* Not only the Jewish people, to whom His word of salvation was to be sent first, but also all members of the Church of Christ; as in them, and in His Church, the Holy One of Israel dwells.

CHAPTER 13

God mustereth the armies of His wrath against the inhabitants of Babylon, 1-6. The dreadful consequences of this visitation, and the terror and dismay of those who are the objects of it, 7-16. The horrid cruelties that shall be inflicted upon the Babylonians by the Medes, 17-18. Total and irrecoverable desolation of Babylon, 19-22.

This and the following chapter—striking off the last five verses of the latter, which belong to a quite different subject—contain one entire prophecy, foretelling the destruction of Babylon by the Medes and Persians; delivered probably in the reign of Ahaz, about two hundred years before its accomplishment. The captivity itself

of the Jews at Babylon, which the prophet does
not expressly foretell, did not fully take place
till about one hundred and thirty years after
the delivery of this prophecy; and the Medes,
who are expressly mentioned in chap. xiii. 17
as the principal agents in the overthrow of the
Babylonian monarchy, by which the Jews were
released from that captivity, were at this time
an inconsiderable people.

The former part of this prophecy is one of
the most beautiful examples that can be given
of elegance of composition, variety of imagery,
and sublimity of sentiment and diction, in the
prophetic style; and the latter part consists of
an ode of supreme and singular excellence.

The prophecy opens with the command of
God to gather together the forces which He
had destined to this service, vv. 2-3. Upon
which the prophet immediately hears the tumultuous noise of the different nations crowd-
ing together to His standard; he sees them
advancing, prepared to execute the divine
wrath, vv. 4-5. He proceeds to describe the
dreadful consequences of this visitation, the
consternation which will seize those who are
the objects of it; and, transferring unawares
the speech from himself to God, v. 11, sets forth,
under a variety of the most striking images, the
dreadful destruction of the inhabitants of Babylon which will follow, vv. 11-16, and the everlasting desolation to which that great city is
doomed, vv. 17-22.

The deliverance of Judah from captivity, the
immediate consequence of this great revolution,
is then set forth, without being much enlarged
upon, or greatly amplified, chap. xiv. 1-2. This
introduces, with the greatest ease and the utmost propriety, the triumphant song on that
subject, vv. 4-28.

A chorus of Jews is introduced, expressing
their surprise and astonishment at the sudden
downfall of Babylon; and the great reverse of
fortune that had befallen the tyrant, who, like
his predecessors, had oppressed his own, and
harassed the neighboring kingdoms. These oppressed kingdoms, or their rulers, are represented under the image of the fir trees and the
cedars of Libanus, frequently used to express
anything in the political or religious world
that is supereminently great and majestic: the
whole earth shouteth for joy; the cedars of
Libanus utter a severe taunt over the fallen
tyrant, and boast their security, now he is no
more.

The scene is immediately changed, and a new
set of persons is introduced. The regions of the
dead are laid open, and Hades is represented as
rousing up the shades of the departed monarchs. They rise from their thrones to meet
the king of Babylon at his coming, and insult
him on his being reduced to the same low
estate of impotence and dissolution with themselves.

The Jews now resume the speech; they address
the king of Babylon as the morning star fallen
from heaven, as the first in splendor and dignity
in the political world, fallen from his high state.
They introduce him as uttering the most extravagant vaunts of his power and ambitious
designs in his former glory. These are strongly
contrasted in the close with his present low
and abject condition.

Immediately follows a different scene, and a
most happy image, to diversify the same sub-

ject, to give it a new turn, and an additional
force. Certain persons are introduced who light
upon the corpse of the king of Babylon, cast
out and lying naked on the bare ground, among
the common slain, just after the taking of the
city; covered with wounds, and so disfigured
that it is some time before they know him.
They accost him with the severest taunts; and
bitterly reproach him with his destructive ambition, and his cruel usage of the conquered;
which have deservedly brought him this ignominious treatment, so different from that
which those of his rank usually meet with, and
which shall cover his posterity with disgrace.

To complete the whole, God is introduced,
declaring the fate of Babylon, the utter extirpation of the royal family, and the total
desolation of the city; the deliverance of His
people, and the destruction of their enemies;
confirming the irreversible decree by the awful
sanction of His oath.

1. *The burden of Babylon.* The prophecy
that foretells its destruction by the Medes and
Persians.

3. *I have commanded my sanctified ones.*
The persons "consecrated" to this very purpose.
Nothing can be plainer than that the verb
kadash, "to make holy," signifies also to "consecrate" or "appoint" to a particular purpose.
Bishop Lowth translates, "my enrolled warriors." This is the sense.

4. *Of the battle*—"For the battle." Cyrus'
army was made up of many different nations.
Jeremiah calls it "an assembly of different nations
from the north country," chap. l. 9.

5. *From the end of heaven.* Kimchi says,
Media, "the end of heaven," in Scripture phrase,
means the east.

10. *For the stars of heaven*—"Yea, the stars
of heaven." The Hebrew poets, to express
happiness, prosperity, the advancement of states,
kingdoms, and potentates, make use of images
taken from the most striking parts of nature,
from the heavenly bodies, from the sun, moon,
and stars—which they describe as shining with
increased splendor, and never setting. On the
contrary, the destruction of kingdoms is represented by opposite images. The stars are
obscured, the moon withdraws her light, and
the sun shines no more! The earth quakes,
and the heavens tremble; and all things seem
tending to their original chaos. See Joel ii.
10; iii. 15-16; Amos viii. 9; Matt. xxiv. 29.

*And the moon shall not cause her light to
shine.* This in its further reference may belong
to the Jewish polity, in both church and state,
which should be totally eclipsed, and perhaps
shine no more in its distinct state forever.

11. *I will punish the world*—"I will visit the
world." That is, the Babylonish empire.

12. *I will make a man more precious than
fine gold . . . wedge of Ophir.* The Medes and
Persians will not be satisfied with the spoils of
the Babylonians. They seek either to destroy
or enslave them; and they will accept no ransom
for any man—either for *enosh,* the poor man, or
for *adam,* the more honorable person. All must
fall by the sword, or go into captivity together;
for the Medes (v. 17) regard not silver, and
delight not in gold.

14. "And the remnant." Here is plainly a
defect in this sentence, as it stands in the

Hebrew text; the subject of the proposition is lost. What is it that shall be like a roe chased? The Septuagint happily supply it, "the remnant." *They shall . . . turn*—"They shall look." That is, the forces of the king of Babylon, destitute of their leader, and all his auxiliaries, collected from Asia Minor, and other distant countries, shall disperse and flee to their respective homes.

15. *Every one that is found*—"Everyone that is overtaken." That is, none shall escape from the slaughter; neither they who flee singly, dispersed and in confusion, nor they who endeavor to make their retreat in a more regular manner, by forming compact bodies; they shall all be equally cut off by the sword of the enemy.

17. *Which shall not regard silver*—"Who shall hold silver of no account." That is, who shall not be induced, by large offers of gold and silver for ransom, to spare the lives of those whom they have subdued in battle; their rage and cruelty will get the better of all such motives.

18. *Their bows also shall dash.* Both Herodotus, i. 61, and Xenophon, *Anab.* iii., mention that the Persians used large bows, and the latter says particularly that their bows were three cubits long, *Anab.* iv. They were celebrated for their archers, see chap. xxii. 6; Jer. xlix. 35. Probably their neighbors and allies, the Medes, dealt much in the same sort of arms.

19. *And Babylon.* The great city of Babylon was at this time rising to its height of glory, while the prophet Isaiah was repeatedly denouncing its utter destruction. From the first of Hezekiah to the first of Nebuchadnezzar, under whom it was brought to the highest degree of strength and splendor, are about one hundred and twenty years. It was, according to the lowest account given of it by ancient historians, a regular square, 45 miles in compass, enclosed by a wall 200 feet high and fifty broad, in which there were 100 gates of brass. Its principal ornaments were the temple of Belus, in the middle of which was a tower of eight stories of building, upon a base of a quarter of a mile square, a most magnificent palace, and the famous hanging gardens, which were an artificial mountain, raised upon arches, and planted with trees of the largest as well as the most beautiful sorts. Cyrus took the city by diverting the waters of the Euphrates, which ran through the midst of it, and entering the place at night by the dry channel. The river, being never restored afterward to its proper course, overflowed the whole country, and made it little better than a great morass. This and the great slaughter of the inhabitants, with other bad consequences of the taking of the city, was the first step to the ruin of the place. The Persian monarchs ever regarded it with a jealous eye; they kept it under, and took care to prevent its recovering its former greatness. Darius Hystaspes not long afterward most severely punished it for a revolt, greatly depopulated the place, lowered the walls, and demolished the gates. Xerxes destroyed the temples.

CHAPTER 14

Deliverance of Israel from captivity, which shall follow the downfall of the great Babylonish empire, 1-2. Triumphant ode or song of the children of Jacob, for the signal manifestation of divine vengeance against their oppressors, 3-23. Prophecy against the Assyrians, 24-25. Certainty of the prophecy, and immutability of the divine counsels, 26-27. Palestine severely threatened, 28-31. God shall establish Zion in these troublous times, 32.

1. *And will yet choose Israel.* That is, will still regard Israel as His chosen people, however He may seem to desert them, by giving them up to their enemies and scattering them among the nations. Judah is sometimes called Israel; see Ezek. xiii. 16; Mal. i. 1; ii. 11. But the name of Jacob and of Israel, used apparently with design in this place, each of which names includes the twelve tribes, and the other circumstances mentioned in this and the next verse, which did not in any complete sense accompany the return from the captivity of Babylon, seem to intimate that this whole prophecy extends its views beyond that even.

4. *This proverb*—"This parable." *Mashal.* I take this to be the general name for poetic style among the Hebrews, including every sort of it, as ranging under one or other, or all of the characters, of sententious, figurative, and sublime; which are all contained in the original notion, or in the use and application of the word *mashal.* Parables or proverbs, such as those of Solomon, are always expressed in short, pointed sentences; frequently figurative, being formed on some comparison; generally forcible and authoritative, in both the matter and the form. And such in general is the style of the Hebrew poetry. The verb *mashal* signifies to rule; to exercise authority; to make equal; to compare one thing with another; to utter parables or acute, weighty, and powerful speeches, in the form and manner of parables, though not properly such. *The golden city ceased. Madhebah,* which is here translated *golden city,* is a Chaldee word. Probably it means that golden coin which was given to the Babylonians by way of tribute. So the word is understood by the Vulgate, where it is rendered *tributum.*

9. *Hell from beneath is moved for thee to meet thee.* That is, Nebuchadnezzar. Tyrannical kings who have oppressed and spoiled mankind are here represented as enthroned in hell, and as taking a Satanic pleasure in seeing others of the same description enter those abodes of misery!

12. *O Lucifer, son of the morning!* The versions in general agree in this translation, and render *heilel* as signifying *Lucifer,* the morning star, whether Jupiter or Venus; as these are both bringers of the morning light, or morning stars, annually in their turn. And although the context speaks explicitly concerning Nebuchadnezzar, yet this has been, I know not why, applied to the chief of the fallen angels, who is most incongruously denominated Lucifer (the bringer of light!), an epithet as common to him as those of Satan and Devil. But the truth is, the text speaks nothing at all concerning Satan nor his fall, nor the occasion of that fall. Besides, I doubt much whether our translation be correct. *Heilel,* which we translate *Lucifer,* comes from *yalal,* "yell, howl, or shriek," and should be translated, "Howl, son of the morning"; and so the Syriac has understood it.

13. *I will ascend into heaven.* I will get the empire of the whole world. *I will exalt my throne above the stars of God*—above the Israel-

ites, who are here termed the stars of God. This chapter speaks not of the ambition and fall of Satan, but of the pride, arrogance, and fall of Nebuchadnezzar. *The mount of the congregation*—"The mount of the Divine Presence." It appears plainly from Exod. xxv. 22 and xxix. 42-43 (where God appoints the place of meeting with Moses, and promises to meet with him before the ark to commune with him, and to speak unto him, and to meet the children of Israel at the door of the Tabernacle) that the Tabernacle, and afterwards the door of the Tabernacle, and Mount Zion whereon it stood, were called the Tabernacle, and the mount of convention or of appointment, not from the people's assembling there to perform the services of their religion (which is what our translation expresses by calling it "the tabernacle of the congregation"), but because God appointed that for the place where He himself would meet with Moses and commune with him, and would meet with the people.

19. *Like an abominable branch*—"Like the tree abominated." That is, as an object of abomination and detestation, such as the tree is on which a malefactor has been hanged.

28. *In the year that king Ahaz died was this burden.* Uzziah had subdued the Philistines, 2 Chron. xxvi. 6-7; but, taking advantage of the weak reign of Ahaz, they invaded Judea, and took, and held in possession, some cities in the southern part of the kingdom. On the death of Ahaz, Isaiah delivers this prophecy, threatening them with the destruction that Hezekiah, his son, and great-grandson of Uzziah, should bring upon them; which he effected, for "he smote the Philistines, even unto Gaza, and the borders thereof," 2 Kings xviii. 8. Uzziah, therefore, must be meant by the rod that smote them, and by the serpent from whom should spring the *fiery flying serpent*, v. 29, that is, Hezekiah, a much more terrible enemy than even Uzziah had been.

31. *There shall come from the north a smoke* —"From the north cometh a smoke." That is, a cloud of dust raised by the march of Hezekiah's army against Philistia, which lay to the southwest from Jerusalem.

32. *The messengers of the nation*—"The ambassadors of the nations." The ambassadors of the neighbouring nations, that send to congratulate Hezekiah on his success; which in his answer he will ascribe to the protection of God. See 2 Chron. xxxii. 23. Or if the reading of the text be preferred, the ambassadors sent by the Philistines to demand peace.

CHAPTER 15

Prediction of very heavy calamities about to fall upon the Moabites, 1-9.

This and the following chapter, taken together, make one entire prophecy, very improperly divided into two parts. The time of its delivery, and consequently of its accomplishment, which was to be in three years from that time, is uncertain; the former not being marked in the prophecy itself, nor the latter recorded in history. But the most probable account is that it was delivered soon after the foregoing, in the first year of Hezekiah; and that it was accomplished in his fourth year, when Shalman-

eser invaded the kingdom of Israel. He might probably march through Moab; and to secure everything behind him, possess himself of the whole country, by taking their principal strong places, Ar and Kirhares.

Jeremiah has happily introduced much of this prophecy of Isaiah into his own larger prophecy against the same people in his forty-eighth chapter, denouncing God's judgment on Moab, subsequent to the calamity here foretold, and to be executed by Nebuchadnezzar, by which means several mistakes of transcribers in the present text of both prophets may be rectified.

2. *He is gone up to Bajith, and to Dibon. Alah habbayith* should be rendered, "He is gone to the house," i.e., to their chief temple, where they practiced idolatry. Dibon was the name of a tower where also was an idolatrous temple; thither they went to weep and pray before their idols, that they might interpose and save them from their calamities. *On all their heads shall be baldness.* Herodotus, ii. 36, speaks of it as a general practice among all men, except the Egyptians, to cut off their hair as a token of mourning. "Cut off thy hair . . . and cast it away," says Jeremiah, vii. 29, "and take up a lamentation."

4. *The armed soldiers*—"The very loins." So the Septuagint and the Syriac. They cry out violently, with their utmost force.

5. *My heart shall cry out for Moab*—"The heart of Moab crieth within her." *An heifer of three years old*—"A young heifer." In full strength.

7. *To the brook of the willows*—"To the valley of willows." That is, to Babylon.

CHAPTER 16

The distress of Moab pathetically described by the son of the prince, or ruler of the land, being forced to flee for his life through the desert, that he may escape to Judea; and the young women, like young birds scared from their nest, wade helpless through the fords of Arnon, the boundary of their country, to seek protection in some foreign land, 1-2. The prophet addresses Sion, exhorting her to show mercy to her enemies in their distress, that her throne may be established in righteousness, 3-5. Exceeding great pride of Moab, 6. The terrible calamities about to fall upon Moab further described by the languishing of the vine, the ceasing of the vintage, the sound of the prophet's bowels quivering like a harp, etc., 7-13. Awful nearness of the full accomplishment of the prophecy, 14.

1. *Send ye the lamb.*—"I will send forth the son." Both the reading and the meaning of this verse are still more doubtful than those of the preceding. The Septuagint and Syriac read, "I will send"; the Vulgate and Talmud Babylon. read "send," singular imperative. The Syriac, for *car*, "a lamb," reads *bar*, "a son," which is confirmed by five MSS. of Kennicott and De Rossi. The first two verses describe the distress of Moab on the Assyrian invasion, in which even the son of the prince of the country is represented as forced to flee for his life through the desert, that he may escape to Judea; and the young women are driven forth like young birds cast out of the nest, and endeavoring to wade through the fords of the river Arnon. Perhaps there is not so much difficulty in this verse as appears at first view. "Send ye the lamb to the ruler of the land" may receive light from 2 Kings iii. 4-5: "And Mesha king of Moab was a sheepmaster, and rendered unto the king of Israel an hundred thousand lambs

[with their wool], and an hundred thousand rams . . . But . . . when Ahab was dead . . . the king of Moab rebelled against . . . Israel." Now the prophet exhorts them to begin paying the tribute as formerly, that their punishment might be averted or mitigated.

3. *Take counsel*—"Impart counsel."

4. *Let mine outcasts dwell with thee, Moab*—"Let the outcasts of Moab sojourn with thee, O Zion." *The oppressors*—"The oppressor." Perhaps the Israelites, who in the time of Ahaz invaded Judah, defeated his army, slaying 120,000 men, and brought the kingdom to the brink of destruction. Judah, being now in a more prosperous condition, is represented as able to receive and to protect the fugitive Moabites. And with those former times of distress the security and flourishing state of the kingdom under the government of Hezekiah is contrasted.

5. *In mercy shall the throne be established.* May not this refer to the throne of Hezekiah? Here we have the character of such a king as cannot fail to be a blessing to the people.

6. *We have heard of the pride of Moab*—"We have heard the pride of Moab." Zephaniah, chap. ii. 8-10, in his prophecy against Moab, the subject of which is the same with that of Jeremiah in his forty-eighth chapter, enlarges much on the pride of Moab, and their insolent behavior towards the Jews.

7. *For the foundations of Kir-hareseth*—"For the men of Kirhares." A palpable mistake in this place is happily corrected by the parallel text of Jer. xlviii. 31. In the same place of Jeremiah, and in v. 36, and here in v. 11, the name of the city is Kirheres, not Kir-hareseth.

8. *Languish*—"Are put to shame." The meaning of this verse is that the wines of Sibmah and Heshbon were greatly celebrated, and in high repute with all the great men and princes of that and the neighboring countries, who indulged themselves even to intemperance in the use of them; so that their vines were so much in request as not only to be propagated all over the country of Moab to the sea of Sodom, but to have scions of them sent even beyond the sea into foreign countries.

9. *With the weeping*—"As with the weeping." *For thy summer fruits and for thy harvest is fallen*—"And upon thy vintage the destroyer hath fallen."

10. *Neither shall there be shouting*—"An end is put to the shouting."

12. *When it is seen that Moab*—"When Moab shall see."

CHAPTER 17

Judgments of God upon Damascus, 1-3; and upon Israel, 4-6. Good effects of these judgments on the small remnant or gleaning that should escape them, 7-8. The same judgments represented in other but stronger terms, and imputed to irreligion and neglect of God, 9-11. The remaining verses are a distinct prophecy, a beautiful detached piece, worked up with the greatest elegance, sublimity, and propriety; and forming a noble description of the formidable invasion and sudden overthrow of Sennacherib, exactly suitable to the event, 12-14.

This prophecy by its title should relate only to Damascus; but it fully as much concerns, and more largely treats of, the kingdom of Samaria and the Israelites, confederated with Damascus and the Syrians against the kingdom of Judah. It was delivered probably soon after the prophecies of the seventh and eighth chapters, in the beginning of the reign of Ahaz; and was fulfilled by Tiglath-pileser's taking Damascus, and carrying the people captives to Kir (2 Kings xvi. 9) and overrunning a great part of the kingdom of Israel, and carrying a great number of the Israelites also captives to Assyria; and still more fully in regard to Israel, by the conquest of the kingdom, and the captivity of the people, effected a few years after by Shalmaneser.

1. *The burden of Damascus.* If we credit *Midrash*, the Damascenes were the most extensive and flagrant of all idolaters. "There were in Damascus three hundred and sixty-five streets, in each of these was an idol, and each idol had his peculiar day of worship; so that the whole were worshipped in the course of the year." This, or anything like this, was a sufficient reason for this city's destruction.

2. *The cities of Aroer are forsaken*—"The cities are deserted forever."

4. *In that day.* That is, says Kimchi, the time when the ten tribes of Israel, which were *the glory of Jacob*, should be carried into captivity.

5. *As when the harvestman gathereth.* That is, the king of Assyria shall sweep away the whole body of the people, as the reaper strippeth off the whole crop of corn; and the remnant shall be no more in proportion than the scattered ears left to the gleaner. *The valley of Rephaim* near Jerusalem was celebrated for its plentiful harvest; it is here used poetically for any fruitful country.

10. *Strange slips*—"Shoots from a foreign soil." The pleasant plants and shoots from a foreign soil are allegorical expressions for strange and idolatrous worship; vicious and abominable practices connected with it; reliance on human aid, and on alliances entered into with the neighboring nations, especially Egypt; to all which the Israelites were greatly addicted, and in their expectations from which they should be grievously disappointed.

12. *Woe to the multitude!* The last three verses of this chapter seem to have no relation to the foregoing prophecy, to which they are joined. It is a beautiful piece, standing singly and by itself, for neither has it any connection with what follows. Whether it stands in its right place or not, I cannot say. It is a noble description of the formidable invasion and the sudden overthrow of Sennacherib, which is intimated in the strongest terms and the most expressive images, exactly suitable to the event.

14. *He is not*—"He is no more." Though God may permit the wicked to prevail for a time against His people, yet in the end those shall be overthrown, and the glory of the Lord shall shine brightly on them that fear Him; for the earth shall be subdued, and the universe filled with His glory.

CHAPTER 18

This chapter contains a very obscure prophecy, possibly designed to give the Jews, and perhaps the Egyptians, whose country is supposed to be meant, 1-2, and with whom many Jews resided, an intimation of God's interposition in favor of Sion, 3-4; and of His counsels in regard to the destruction of their common enemy, Sennacherib, whose vast army, just as he thought his projects ripe and ready to be crowned with success, 5, should become a prey to the beasts of the field and to the fowls of heaven, 6; and that Egypt should be grateful to God for the deliverance vouchsafed her, 7.

This is one of the most obscure prophecies in the whole Book of Isaiah. The subject of it, the end and design of it, the people to whom it is addressed, the history to which it belongs, the person who sends the messengers, and the nation to whom the messengers are sent, are all obscure and doubtful.

1. *Woe to the land! Hoi arets!* This interjection should be translated "Ho!" for it is properly a particle of calling: Ho, land! Attend! Give ear! *Shadowing with wings*—"The winged cymbal." The Egyptian sistrum is expressed by a periphrasis. *Which is beyond the rivers of Ethiopia*—"Which borders on the rivers of Cush."

2. *In vessels of bulrushes*—"In vessels of papyrus." This circumstance agrees perfectly well with Egypt. It is well-known that the Egyptians commonly used on the Nile a light sort of boats made of the reed papyrus. *Go, ye swift messengers.* To this nation before mentioned, who, by the Nile and by their numerous canals, have the means of spreading the report in the most expeditious manner through the whole country. *Go, ye swift messengers,* and carry this notice of God's designs in regard to them. *Scattered*—"Stretched out in length." Egypt, that is, the fruitful part, exclusive of the deserts on each side, is one long vale, through the middle of which runs the Nile, bounded on each side to the east and west by a chain of mountains 750 miles in length. *Peeled*—"Smoothed." Made smooth, perfectly plain and level, by the overflowing of the Nile. *Meted out*—"Meted out by line." It is generally referred to the frequent necessity of having recourse to mensuration in Egypt, in order to determine the boundaries after the inundations of the Nile, to which even the origin of the science of geometry is by some ascribed. *Trodden down.* Supposed to allude to a peculiar method of tillage in use among the Egyptians. Both Herodotus (lib. ii) and Diodorus (lib. i) say that when the Nile had retired within its banks, and the ground became somewhat dry, they sowed their land, and then sent in their cattle to tread in the seed; and without any further care expected the harvest. *The rivers have spoiled*—"The rivers have nourished."

3. *When he lifteth up an ensign*—"When the standard is lifted up." I take God to be the Agent in this verse; and that by the standard and the trumpet are meant the meteors, the thunder, the lightning, the storm, earthquake, and tempest, by which Sennacherib's army shall be destroyed, or by which at least the destruction of it shall be accompanied; as it is described in chap. x. 16-17; xxix. 6; and xx. 30-31.

4. *For so the Lord said unto me.* The subject of the remaining part of this chapter is that God would comfort and support His own people, though threatened with immediate destruction by the Assyrians; that Sennacherib's great designs and mighty efforts against them should be frustrated; and that his vast expectations should be rendered abortive, when he thought them mature, and just ready to be crowned with success; that the chief part of his army should be made a prey for the beasts of the field and the fowls of the air; and that Egypt, being delivered from his oppression, and avenged by the hand of God of the wrongs which she had suffered, should return thanks for the wonderful deliverance, both of herself and of the Jews, from this most powerful adversary.

5. *The flower*—"The blossom."

7. *The present*—"A gift." The Egyptians were in alliance with the kingdom of Judah, and were fellow sufferers with the Jews under the invasion of their common enemy Sennacherib, and so were very nearly interested in the great and miraculous deliverance of that kingdom by the destruction of the Assyrian army. Upon which wonderful event it is said, 2 Chron. xxxii. 23, that "many brought gifts unto the Lord to Jerusalem, and presents to Hezekiah king of Judah: so that he was magnified in the sight of all nations from thenceforth." It is not to be doubted that among these the Egyptians distinguished themselves in their acknowledgments on this occasion. *Of a people*—"From a people."

CHAPTER 19

Prophecy concerning Egypt, in which her lamentable condition under the Babylonians, Persians, etc., is forcibly pointed out, 1-17. The true religion shall be propagated in Egypt; referring primarily to the great spread of Judaism in that country in the reign of the Ptolemies, and ultimately to its reception of the gospel in the latter days, 18-22. Profound peace between Egypt, Assyria, and Israel, and their blessed condition under the gospel, 23-25.

Not many years after the destruction of Sennacherib's army before Jerusalem, by which the Egyptians were freed from the yoke with which they were threatened by so powerful an enemy, who had carried on a successful war of three years' continuance against them, the affairs of Egypt were again thrown into confusion by broils among themselves, which ended in a perfect anarchy, that lasted some few years. This was followed by an aristocracy, or rather tyranny, of twelve princes, who divided the country between them, and at last by the sole dominion of Psammitichus, which he held for fifty-four years. Not long after that followed the invasion and conquest of Egypt by Nebuchadnezzar, and then by the Persians under Cambyses, the son of Cyrus. The yoke of the Persians was so grievous that the conquest of the Persians by Alexander may well be considered as a deliverance to Egypt, especially as he and his successors greatly favored the people and improved the country. To all these events the prophet seems to have had a view in this chapter; and in particular, from v. 18, the prophecy of the propagation of the true religion in Egypt seems to point to the flourishing state of Judaism in that country, in consequence of the great favor shown to the Jews by the Ptolemies. Alexander himself settled a great many Jews in his new city Alexandria, granting them privileges equal to those of the Macedonians. The first Ptolemy, called Soter, carried great numbers of them thither, and gave them such encouragement that still more of them were collected there from different parts, so that Philo reckons that in his time there were a million of Jews in that country. These worshipped the God of their fathers, and their example and influence must have had a great effect in spreading the knowledge and worship of the true God through the whole country.

1. *The burden of Egypt.* That is, the prophet's declaration concerning Egypt.

4. *A cruel lord*—"Cruel lords." Nebuchadnezzar in the first place, and afterwards the whole succession of Persian kings, who in general where hard masters, and grievously oppressed the country.

5. *The river shall be wasted and dried up.* The Nile shall not overflow its banks; and if no inundation, the land must become barren. For, as there is little or no rain in Egypt, its fertility depends on the overflowing of the Nile.

6. *Shall turn the rivers far away*—"Shall become putrid."

8. *The fishers also.* There was great plenty of fish in Egypt; see Num. xi. 5.

9. *They that work in fine flax.* I.e., flax dressed on the comb used for that purpose.

16. *Shall Egypt be*—"The Egyptians shall be."

17. *And the land of Judah.* The threatening hand of God will be held out and shaken over Egypt, from the side of Judea, through which the Assyrians will march to invade it. It signifies that kind of terror that drives one to his wit's end, that causes him to reel like a drunken man, to be giddy through astonishment.

18. *The city of destruction*—"The city of the sun." This passage is attended with much difficulty and obscurity. First, in regard to the true reading. It is well-known that Onias applied it to his own views, either to procure from the king of Egypt permission to build his temple in the Hieropolitan Nome or to gain credit and authority to it when built; from the notion which he industriously propagated that Isaiah had in this place prophesied of the building of such a temple. He pretended that the very place where it should be built was expressly named by the prophet, *ir hacheres,* "the city of the sun." This possibly may have been the original reading. The present text has *ir haheres,* "the city of destruction"; which some suppose to have been introduced into the text by the Jews of Palestine afterwards, to express their detestation of the place, being much offended with this schismatical temple in Egypt. Some think the latter to have been the true reading; and that the prophet himself gave this turn to the name out of contempt, and to intimate the demolition of this Hieropolitan temple; which in effect was destroyed by Vespasian's orders, after that of Jerusalem. I take the whole passage from the eighteenth verse to the end of the chapter to contain a general intimation of the future propagation of the knowledge of the true God in Egypt and Syria, under the successors of Alexander; and, in consequence of this propagation, of the early reception of the gospel in the same countries, when it should be published to the world.

23. *Shall there be a highway.* Under the latter kings of Persia, and under Alexander, Egypt, Judea, and Assyria lived peaceably under the same government, and were on such friendly terms that there was a regular, uninterrupted intercourse between them, so that the Assyrian came into Egypt and the Egyptian into Assyria, and *Israel* became *the third, i.e.,* was in strict union with the other two; and was a *blessing* to both, as affording them some knowledge of the true God, v. 24.

25. *Blessed be Egypt . . . Assyria . . . and Israel.* All these countries shall be converted to the Lord. Concerning Egypt, it was said, chap. xviii. 7, that it should bring gifts to the Lord at Jerusalem. Here it is predicted, v. 19, that there shall be an altar to the Lord in Egypt itself; and that they, with the Assyrians, shall become the people of God with the Israelites. This remains partly to be fulfilled. These countries shall be all, and perhaps at no very distant time from this, converted to the faith of our Lord Jesus Christ.

CHAPTER 20

The prophet Isaiah a sign to Egypt and Cush or Ethiopia that the captives and exiles of these countries shall be indignantly treated by the king of Assyria, 1-6.

Tartan besieged Ashdod or Azotus, which probably belonged at this time to Hezekiah's dominions; see 2 Kings xviii. 8. The people expected to be relieved by the Cushites of Arabia and by the Egyptians. Isaiah was ordered to go uncovered, that is, without his upper garment, the rough mantle commonly worn by the prophets (see Zech. xiii. 4), probably three days, to show that within three years the town should be taken, after the defeat of the Cushites and Egyptians by the king of Assyria, which event should make their case desperate and induce them to surrender. Azotus was a strong place; it afterwards held out twenty-nine years against Psammitichus, king of Egypt, Herod. ii. 157. Tartan was one of Sennacherib's generals, 2 Kings xviii. 17, and Tirhakah, king of the Cushites, was in alliance with the king of Egypt against Sennacherib. These circumstances make it probable that by Sargon is meant Sennacherib. It might be one of the seven names by which Jerome, on this place, says he was called. The taking of Azotus must have happened before Sennacherib's attempt on Jerusalem, when he boasted of his late conquests, chap. xxxvii. 25. And the warning of the prophet had a principal respect to the Jews also, who were too much inclined to depend upon the assistance of Egypt.

2. *Walking naked and barefoot.* It is not probable that the prophet walked uncovered and barefoot for three years; his appearing in that manner was a sign that within three years the Egyptians and Cushites should be in the same condition, being conquered and made captives by the king of Assyria. The time was denoted as well as the event; but his appearing in that manner for three whole years could give no premonition of the time at all. It is probable, therefore, that the prophet was ordered to walk so for three days to denote the accomplishment of the event in three years; a day for a year, according to the prophetical rule, Num. xiv. 34; Ezek. iv. 6.

CHAPTER 21

Prediction of the taking of Babylon by the Medes and Persians at the time of a great festival, 1-9. Short application of the prophecy to the Jews, partly in the person of God, and partly in his own, 10. Obscure prophecy respecting Dumah, 11-12. Prophecy concerning the Arabians to be fulfilled in a very short time after its delivery, 13-17.

The first ten verses of this chapter contain a prediction of the taking of Babylon by the Medes and Persians. It is a passage singular in its kind for its brevity and force, for the variety and rapidity of the movements, and for the strength and energy of coloring with which the action and event are painted. It opens with the prophet's seeing at a distance the dreadful storm that is gathering and ready to burst upon Babylon. The event is intimated in general terms, and God's orders are issued to the Persians and Medes to set forth upon the expedition which He has given them in charge. Upon this the prophet enters into the midst of the action; and in the person of Babylon expresses, in the strongest terms, the astonishment and horror that seize her on the sudden surprise of the city at the very season dedicated to pleasure and festivity, vv. 3-4. Then, in his own person, describes the situation of things there, the security of the Babylonians, and in the midst of their feasting the sudden alarm of war, v. 5. The event is then declared in a very singular manner. God orders the prophet to set a watchman to look out, and to report what he sees; he sees two companies marching onward, representing by their appearance the two nations that were to execute God's orders, who declare that Babylon is fallen, vv. 6-9.

1. *The desert of the sea.* This plainly means Babylon, which is the subject of the prophecy. The country about Babylon, and especially below it towards the sea, was a great flat morass, overflowed by the Euphrates and Tigris. It became habitable by being drained by the many canals that were made in it. *As whirlwinds in the south*—"Like the southern tempests." The most vehement storms to which Judea was subject came from the desert country to the south of it. "Out of the south cometh the whirlwind," Job xxxvii. 9. For the situation of Idumea, the country (as I suppose) of Job (see Lam. iv. 21 compared with Job i. 1), was the same in this respect with that of Judea.

2. *The treacherous dealer dealeth treacherously, and the spoiler spoileth*—"The plunderer is plundered, and the destroyer is destroyed." *All the sighing thereof have I made to cease*—"I have put an end to all her vexations." Hebrew, "Her sighing; that is, the sighing caused by her."

5. *Prepare the table*—"The table is prepared." In Hebrew the verbs are in the infinitive mood absolute, as in Ezek. i. 14: "And the living creatures ran and returned, as the appearance of a flash of lightning." *Arise, ye princes, and anoint the shield.* Kimchi observes that several of the rabbins understood this of Belshazzar's impious feast and death.

7. *And he saw a chariot*, etc.—"And he saw a chariot with two riders: a rider on an ass, a rider on a camel." This passage is extremely obscure from the ambiguity of the term *recheb*, which is used three times, and which signifies a chariot, or any other vehicle, or the rider in it; or a rider on a horse, or any other animal; or a company of chariots, or riders. The prophet may possibly mean a cavalry in two parts, with two sorts of riders: riders on asses or mules, and riders on camels; or led on by two riders: one on an ass, and one on a camel. However, so far it is pretty clear that Darius and Cyrus, the Medes and the Persians, are intended to be distinguished by the two riders on the two sorts of cattle.

8. *And he cried, A lion*—"He that looked out on the watch." The present reading, *aryeh, a lion*, is so unintelligible, and the mistake so obvious, that I make no doubt that the true reading is *haroeh, the seer;* as the Syriac translator manifestly found it in his copy, who renders it by "a watchman."

9. *Here cometh a chariot of men*—"A man, one of the two riders." So the Syriac understands it.

10. *O my threshing.* The image of threshing is frequently used by the Hebrew poets, with great elegance and force, to express the punishment of the wicked and the trial of the good, or the utter dispersion and destruction of God's enemies.

11. *The burden of Dumah*—"The oracle concerning Dumah." This prophecy, from the uncertainty of the occasion on which it was uttered, and from the brevity of the expression, is extremely obscure. The Edomites as well as the Jews were subdued by the Babylonians. They inquire of the prophet how long their subjection is to last. He intimates that the Jews should be delivered from their captivity; not so the Edomites. Thus far the interpretation seems to carry with it some degree of probability. What the meaning of the last line may be, I cannot pretend to divine.

13. *The burden upon Arabia*—"The oracle concerning Arabia." This prophecy was to have been fulfilled within a year of the time of its delivery, see v. 16; and it was probably delivered about the same time with the rest in this part of the book, that is, soon before or after the fourteenth of Hezekiah, the year of Sennacherib's invasion. In his first march into Judea, or in his return from the Egyptian expedition, he might perhaps overrun these several clans of Arabians; their distress on some such occasion is the subject of this prophecy.

14. *The land of Tema*—"The southern country." To bring forth bread and water is an instance of common humanity in such cases of distress; especially in those desert countries in which the common necessaries of life, more particularly water, are not easily to be met with or procured.

17. *The archers, the mighty men of the children of Kedar*—"The mighty bowmen of the sons of Kedar."

CHAPTER 22

Prophecy concerning Jerusalem, 1-14. Sentence against Shebna, who was over the household, 15-19. Prophecy concerning Eliakim, the son of Hilkiah, 20-21. From Eliakim, Isaiah (agreeably to the mode universally adopted in the prophetical writings, of making the things then present, or which were shortly to be accomplished, types or representations of things to be fulfilled upon a larger scale in distant futurity) makes a transition to the Messiah, of whom Eliakim was a type, to whom the words will best apply, and to whom some passages in the prophecy must be solely restrained, 20-24. The sentence against Shebna again confirmed, 25.

This prophecy, ending with the fourteenth verse of this chapter, is entitled, "The oracle concerning the valley of vision," by which is meant Jerusalem. The prophecy foretells the invasion of Jerusalem by the Assyrians under Sennacherib, or by the Chaldeans under Nebuchadnezzar.

1. *Art . . . gone up to the house tops.* The houses in the East were in ancient times, as they are still, generally built in one and the same uniform manner. The roof or top of the house is always flat, covered with broad

stones, or a strong plaster of terrace, and guarded on every side with a low parapet wall; see Deut. xxii. 8. The terrace is frequented as much as any part of the house. On this, as the season favors, they walk, they eat, they sleep, they transact business (1 Sam. ix. 25), they perform their devotions, Acts x. 9. The house is built with a court within, into which chiefly the windows open. Those that open to the street are so obstructed with latticework that no one either without or within can see through them. Whenever, therefore, anything is to be seen or heard in the streets, any public spectacle, any alarm of a public nature, everyone immediately goes up to the housetop to satisfy his curiosity. In the same manner, when anyone has occasion to make anything public, the readiest and most effectual way of doing it is to proclaim it from the housetops to the people in the streets. "What ye hear in the ear, that publish ye upon the house tops," saith our Saviour, Matt. x. 27. The people running all to the tops of their houses gives a lively image of a sudden general alarm.

8. *The armour*—"The arsenal." Built by Solomon within the city, and called the house of the forest of Lebanon, probably from the great quantity of cedar from Lebanon which was employed in the building. See 1 Kings vii. 2-3.

9. *Ye gathered together the waters*—"And ye shall collect the waters." There were two pools in or near Jerusalem, supplied by springs: the upper pool, or the old pool, supplied by the spring called Gihon, 2 Chron. xxxii. 30, towards the higher part of the city, near Sion, or the city of David; and the lower pool, probably supplied by Siloam, towards the lower part. When Hezekiah was threatened with a siege by Sennacherib, he stopped up all the waters of the fountains without the city, and brought them into the city by a conduit, or subterranean passage cut through the rock; those of the old pool to the place where he had a double wall, so that the pool was between the two walls. This he did in order to distress the enemy, and to supply the city during the siege (2 Kings xx. 20; 2 Chron. xxxii. 2-3, 5, 30).

11. *Unto the maker thereof*—"To him that hath disposed this." That is, to God, the Author and Disposer of this visitation, the invasion with which He now threatens you.

13. *Let us eat and drink; for to morrow we shall die.* This has been the language of all those who have sought their portion in this life, since the foundation of the world. St. Paul quotes the same heathen sentiment, 1 Cor. xv. 32: "Let us eat and drink; for to morrow we die."

14. *It was revealed in mine ears*—"The voice of Jehovah."

15. *Go . . . unto Shebna.* The following prophecy concerning Shebna seems to have very little relation to the foregoing, except that it might have been delivered about the same time; and Shebna might be a principal person among those whose luxury and profaneness are severely reprehended by the prophet in the conclusion of that prophecy, vv. 11-14. Shebna, the scribe, mentioned in the history of Hezekiah, chap. xxxvi, seems to have been a different person from this Shebna, the treasurer or

steward of the household, to whom this prophecy relates. The Eliakim here mentioned was probably the person who, at the time of Sennacherib's invasion, was actually treasurer, the son of Hilkiah. If so, this prophecy was delivered, as the preceding plainly was, some time before the invasion of Sennacherib.

16. *A sepulchre on high . . . in a rock.* Persons of high rank in Judea, and in most parts of the East, were generally buried in large sepulchral vaults, hewn out in the rock for the use of themselves and their families. The vanity of Shebna is set forth by his being so studious and careful to have his sepulchre on high—in a lofty vault; and that probably in a high situation, that it might be more conspicuous. Hezekiah was buried "in the chiefest," says our translation—rather, in the highest part—"of the sepulchres of the sons of David," to do him the more honor, 2 Chron. xxxii. 33.

17. *Cover thee.* That is, thy face. This was the condition of mourners in general, and particularly of condemned persons. See Esther vi. 12; vii. 8.

22. *And the key of the house of David will I lay upon his shoulder.* As the robe and the baldric, mentioned in the preceding verse, were the ensigns of power and authority, so likewise was the key the mark of office, either sacred or civil. This mark of office was likewise among the Greeks, as here in Isaiah, borne on the shoulder. In allusion to the image of the key as the ensign of power, the unlimited extent of that power is expressed with great clearness as well as force by the sole and exclusive authority to open and shut. Our Saviour, therefore, has upon a similar occasion made use of a like manner of expression, Matt. xvi. 19; and in Rev. iii. 7 has applied to himself the very words of the prophet.

23. *A nail.* In ancient times and in the Eastern countries the houses were much more simple than ours at present. They had not that quantity and variety of furniture, nor those accommodations of all sorts, with which we abound. It was convenient and even necessary for them, and it made an essential part in the building of a house, to furnish the inside of the several apartments with sets of spikes, nails, or large pegs, upon which to dispose of and hang up the several movables and utensils in common use. These spikes they worked into the walls at the first erection of them, the walls being of such materials that they could not bear their being driven in afterwards; and they were contrived so as to strengthen the walls by binding the parts together, as well as to serve for convenience.

24. *All the glory.* One considerable part of the magnificence of the Eastern princes consisted in the great quantity of gold and silver vessels which they had for various uses. "Solomon's drinking vessels were of gold, and all the vessels of the house of the forest of Lebanon were of pure gold; none were of silver: it was nothing accounted of in the days of Solomon," 1 Kings x. 21. The vessels "in the house of the forest of Lebanon," the armory of Jerusalem so called, were "two hundred targets," and "three hundred shields of beaten gold," *ibid.* vv. 16-17. These were ranged in order upon the walls of the armory (see Cant. iv. 4), upon pins worked

into the walls on purpose, as above mentioned. Eliakim is considered as a principal stake of this sort, immovably fastened in the wall for the support of all vessels destined for common or sacred uses; that is, as the principal support of the whole civil and ecclesiastical polity. And the consequence of his continued power will be the promotion and flourishing condition of his family and dependents, from the highest to the lowest.

CHAPTER 23

Prophecy denouncing the destruction of Tyre by Nebuchadnezzar, delivered upwards of one hundred and twenty years before its accomplishment, at a period when the Tyrians were in great prosperity, and the Babylonians in abject subjection to the Assyrian empire; and, consequently, when an event of so great magnitude was improbable in the highest degree, 1-14. Tyre shall recover its splendor at the termination of seventy years, the days of one king, or kingdom, by which must be meant the time allotted for the duration of the Babylonish empire, as otherwise the prophecy cannot be accommodated to the event, 15-17. Supposed reference to the early conversion of Tyre to Christianity, 18.

1. *The burden of Tyre.* There were two cities of this name: one on the continent, and the other on an island, about half a mile from the shore. The city on the island was about four miles in circumference. Old Tyre resisted Nebuchadnezzar for thirteen years; then the inhabitants carried, so to speak, the city to the forementioned island, v. 4. This new city held out against Alexander the Great for seven months; who, in order to take it, was obliged to fill up the channel which separated it from the mainland. In A.D 1289 it was totally destroyed by the sultan of Egypt, and now contains only a few huts. *Howl, ye ships of Tarshish.* This prophecy denounces the destruction of Tyre by Nebuchadnezzar. It opens with an address to the Tyrian negotiators and sailors at Tarshish (Tartessus, in Spain), a place which, in the course of their trade, they greatly frequented. The news of the destruction of Tyre by Nebuchadnezzar is said to be brought to them from Chittim, the islands and coasts of the Mediterranean. "For the Tyrians," says Jerome on v. 6, "when they saw they had no other means of escaping, fled in their ships, and took refuge in Carthage and in the islands of the Ionian and Aegean sea." From whence the news would spread and reach Tarshish.

2. *Be still*—"Be silent." Silence is a mark of grief and consternation. See chap. xlvii. 5.

3. *The seed of Sihor*—"The seed of the Nile." The Nile is called here Shichor, as it is in Jer. ii. 18 and 1 Chron. xiii. 5. It had this name from the blackness of its waters, charged with the mud which it brings down from Ethiopia when it overflows. Egypt by its extraordinary fertility, caused by the overflowing of the Nile, supplied the neighboring nations with corn, by which branch of trade the Tyrians gained great wealth.

4. *Be thou ashamed, O Zidon.* Tyre is called, v. 12, the daughter of Sidon. Sidon, as the mother city, is supposed to be deeply affected with the calamity of her daughter.

7. *Whose antiquity is of ancient days*—"Whose antiquity is of the earliest date." Tyre, though not so old as Sidon, was yet of very high antiquity; it was a strong city even in the time of Joshua. It is called "the city of the fortress of Sor," Josh. xix. 29. *Her own feet shall carry her afar off to sojourn.* This may

belong to the new or insular Tyre; *her own feet, that is, her own inhabitants, shall carry her*—shall transport the city from the continent to the island. *Merachok* does not always signify a great distance, but distance or interval in general; for in Josh. iii. 4, *rachok* is used to express the space between the camp and the ark, which we know to have been only 2,000 cubits. Some refer the sojourning afar off to the extent of the commercial voyages undertaken by the Tyrians and their foreign connections.

10. *O daughter of Tarshish.* Tyre is called the daughter of Tarshish; perhaps because, Tyre being ruined, Tarshish was become the superior city, and might be considered as the metropolis of the Tyrian people; or rather because of the close connection and perpetual intercourse between them, according to that latitude of signification in which the Hebrews use the words son and daughter to express any sort of conjunction and dependence whatever.

13. *Behold the land of the Chaldeans.* The Chaldeans, *Chasdim,* are supposed to have had their origin, and to have taken their name, from *Chesed,* the son of Nachor, the brother of Abraham. They were known by that name in the time of Moses, who calls Ur in Mesopotamia, from whence Abraham came, to distinguish it from other places of the same name, "Ur of the Chaldeans." And Jeremiah calls them an ancient nation. This is not inconsistent with what Isaiah here says of them: *This people was not,* that is, they were of no account (see Deut. xxxii. 21); they were not reckoned among the great and potent nations of the world till of later times; they were a rude, uncivilized, barbarous people, without laws, without settled habitations. Such they are represented to have been in the time of Job, chap. i. 17, and such they continued to be till Assur, some powerful king of Assyria, gathered them together, and settled them in Babylon in the neighboring country.

15. *According to the days of one king.* That is, of one "kingdom"; see Dan. vii. 17; viii. 20. Nebuchadnezzar began his conquests in the first year of his reign; from thence to the taking of Babylon by Cyrus are seventy years, at which time the nations subdued by Nebuchadnezzar were to be restored to liberty. These seventy years limit the duration of the Babylonish monarchy. Tyre was taken by him towards the middle of that period, so did not serve the king of Babylon during the whole period, but only for the remaining part of it. This seems to be the meaning of Isaiah. The days allotted to the one king or kingdom are seventy years; Tyre, with the rest of the conquered nations, shall continue in a state of subjection and desolation to the end of that period. Not from the beginning and through the whole of the period; for, by being one of the latest conquests, the duration of that state of subjection in regard to her was not much more than half of it. All "these nations," saith Jeremiah, xxv. 11, "shall serve the king of Babylon seventy years." Some of them were conquered sooner, some later; but the end of this period was the common term for the deliverance of them all.

17. *After the end of seventy years.* Tyre, after its destruction by Nebuchadnezzar, recovered, as it is here foretold, its ancient trade,

wealth, and grandeur, as it did likewise after a second destruction by Alexander. It became Christian early with the rest of the neighboring countries. St. Paul himself found many Christians there, Acts xxi. 4. It suffered much in the Diocletian persecution. It was an archbishopric under the patriarchate of Jerusalem, with fourteen bishoprics under its jurisdiction. It continued Christian till it was taken by the Saracens in 639; was recovered by the Christians in 1124; but in 1280 was conquered by the Mamelukes, and afterwards taken from them by the Turks in 1517. Since that time it has sunk into decay; is now a mere ruin.

CHAPTER 24

Dreadful judgments impending over the people of God, 1-4. Particular enumeration of the horrid impieties which provoked the divine vengeance, 5-6. Great political wretchedness of the transgressors, 7-12. The calamities shall be so great that only a small remnant shall be left in the land, as it were the gleanings of the vintage, 13. The rest, scattered over the different countries, spread there the knowledge of God, 14-16. Strong figures by which the great distress and long captivity of the transgressors are set forth, 17-22. Gracious promise of a redemption from captivity; and of an extension of the kingdom of God in the latter days, attended with such glorious circumstances as totally to eclipse the light and splendor of the previous dispensation, 23.

From the thirteenth chapter to the twenty-third inclusive, the fate of several cities and nations is denounced: of Babylon, of the Philistines, Moab, Damascus, Egypt, Tyre. After having foretold the destruction of the foreign nations, enemies of Judah, the prophet declares the judgments impending on the people of God themselves for their wickedness and apostasy, and the desolation that shall be brought on their whole country.

The twenty-fourth and the following three chapters seem to have been delivered about the same time: before the destruction of Moab by Shalmaneser; see chap. xxv. 10, consequently, before the destruction of Samaria; probably in the beginning of Hezekiah's reign. But concerning the particular subject of the twenty-fourth chapter interpreters are not at all agreed: some refer it to the desolation caused by the invasion of Shalmaneser; others, to the invasion of Nebuchadnezzar; and others, to the destruction of the city and nation by the Romans. Perhaps it may have a view to all of the three great desolations of the country, by Shalmaneser, by Nebuchadnezzar, and by the Romans; especially the last, to which some parts of it may seem more peculiarly applicable.

4. *The world languisheth.* The world is the same with the land; that is, the kingdoms of Judah and Israel.

5. *The laws*—"The law." *Torah*, singular: so read the Septuagint, Syriac, and Chaldee.

6. *Are burned*—"Are destroyed."

8. *The mirth.* "The noise."

9. *Strong drink*—"Palm wine." All enjoyment shall cease; the sweetest wine shall become bitter to their taste.

11. *All joy is darkened*—"All gladness is passed away."

14. *They shall lift up their voice*—"But these shall lift up their voice." That is, they that escaped out of these calamities. The great distresses brought upon Israel and Judah drove the people away, and dispersed them all over the neighboring countries; they fled to Egypt,

to Asia Minor, to the islands, and the coasts of Greece. They were to be found in great numbers in most of the principal cities of these countries. Alexandria was in a great measure peopled by them. They had synagogues for their worship in many places, and were greatly instrumental in propagating the knowledge of the true God among these heathen nations, and preparing them for the reception of Christianity. This is what the prophet seems to mean by the celebration of the name of Jehovah in the waters, in the distant coasts, and in the uttermost parts of the land.

16. *But I said.* The prophet speaks in the person of the inhabitants of the land still remaining there, who should be pursued by divine vengeance, and suffer repeated distresses from the inroads and depredations of their powerful enemies.

17. *Fear, and the pit*—"The terror, the pit." If they escape one calamity, another shall overtake them. The images are taken from the different methods of hunting and taking wild beasts, which were anciently in use. The *terror* was a line strung with feathers of all colors, which fluttering in the air scared and frightened the beasts into the toils, or into the pit which was prepared for them. The *pit* or pitfall, digged deep in the ground, and covered over with green boughs, turf, etc., in order to deceive them, that they might fall into it unawares. The *snare*, or toils; a series of nets, enclosing at first a great space of ground, in which the wild beasts were known to be, and then drawn in by degrees into a narrower compass, till they were at last closely shut up, and entangled in them.

19. *The earth*—"The land."

20. *Like a cottage*—"Like a lodge for a night."

21. *On high . . . upon the earth.* That is, the ecclesiastical and civil polity of the Jews, which shall be destroyed. The nation shall continue in a state of depression and dereliction for a long time. God shall at length revisit and restore His people in the last age.

CHAPTER 25

The short glance which the prophet gave at the promised restoration of the people of God and the Messiah's kingdom, in the close of the preceding chapter, makes him break out into a rapturous song of praise in this, where although he alludes to temporal mercies, such as the destruction of the cities which had been at war with Zion, the ruin of Moab, and other signal interpositions of divine providence in behalf of the Jews, yet he is evidently impressed with a more lively sense of future and much higher blessings under the gospel dispensation, in the plenitude of its revelation, of which the temporal deliverances vouchsafed at various times to the primitive kingdoms of Israel and Judah were the prototypes, 1-5. These blessings are described under the figure of a feast made for all nations, 6; the removing of a veil from their faces, 7; the total extinction of the empire of death by the resurrection from the dead, the exclusion of all sorrow, and the final overthrow of all the enemies of the people of God, 8-12.

1. *Thy counsels of old are faithfulness and truth.* That is, All thy past declarations by the prophets shall be fulfilled in their proper time.

2. *A city*—"The city." Nineveh, Babylon, Ar, Moab, or any other strong fortress possessed by the enemies of the people of God. *A palace of strangers*—"The palace of the proud ones."

4. *As a storm against the wall*—"Like a winter storm."

5. *Of strangers*—"Of the proud." *The heat with the shadow of a cloud*—"As the heat by a thick cloud."

6. *In this mountain.* Zion, at Jerusalem. In His Church. *Shall the Lord of hosts make unto all people a feast.* Salvation by Jesus Christ. A feast is a proper and usual expression of joy in consequence of victory, or any other great success. The feast here spoken of is to be celebrated on Mount Sion; and all people, without distinction, are to be invited to it. This can be no other than the celebration of the establishment of Christ's kingdom, which is frequently represented in the gospel under the image of a feast; where "many shall come from the east and west, and shall sit down [at table] with Abraham, Isaac, and Jacob, in the kingdom of heaven," Matt. viii. 11. See also Luke xiv. 16; xxiv. 29-30. *Of wines on the lees*—"Of old wines"; that is, of wines kept long on the lees.

7. *The face of the covering cast over all people*—"The covering that covered the face of all the peoples." "The face of the covering"; He will unveil all the Mosaic ritual, and show by his apostles that it referred to, and was accomplished in, the sacrificial offering of Jesus Christ.

8. *He will swallow up death.* As in the Arabic countries a *covering* was put over the face of him who was condemned to suffer death, it is probable that the words in v. 7 may refer to this. The whole world was condemned to death, and about to be led out to execution, when the gracious Lord interposed, and, by a glorious sacrifice, procured a general pardon.

10. *Shall the hand of the Lord rest*—"The hand of Jehovah shall give rest." That is, "shall give peace and quiet to Sion, by destroying the enemy," as it follows. *As straw is trodden down*—"As the straw is threshed." *For the dunghill*—"Under the wheels of the car."

11. *As he that swimmeth spreadeth forth his hands to swim*—"As he that sinketh stretcheth out his hands to swim." There is great obscurity in this place. Some understand God as the Agent; others, Moab. I have chosen the latter sense, as I cannot conceive that the stretching out of the hands of a swimmer in swimming can be any illustration of the action of God stretching out His hands over Moab to destroy it.

CHAPTER 26

This chapter, like the foregoing, is a song of praise, in which thanksgivings for temporal and spiritual mercies are beautifully mingled, though the latter still predominate. Even the sublime and evangelical doctrine of the resurrection seems here to be hinted at, and made to typify the deliverance of the people of God from a state of the lowest misery; the captivity, the general dispersion, or both. This hymn too, like the preceding, is beautifully diversified by the frequent change of speakers. It opens with a chorus of the Church, celebrating the protection vouchsafed by God to His people; and the happiness of the righteous, whom He guards, contrasted with the misery of the wicked, whom He punishes, 1-7. To this succeeds their own pious resolution of obeying, trusting, and delighting in God, 8. Here the prophet breaks in, in his own person, eagerly catching the last words of the chorus, which were perfectly in unison with the feelings of his own soul, and which he beautifully repeats, as one musical instrument reverberates the sound of another on the same key with it. He makes likewise a suitable response to what had been said on the judgments of God, and observes their different effects on the good and the bad; improving the one, and hardening the other, 9-11. After this, a chorus of Jews express their gratitude to God for past deliverances, make confession of their sins, and supplicate His power, which they had been long expecting, 12-18. To this God makes

a gracious reply, promising deliverance that should be a life from the dead, 19. And the prophet (apparently alluding to the command of Moses to the Israelites, when the destroying angel was to go through the land of Egypt) concludes with exhorting his people to patience and resignation, till God sends the deliverance He has promised, 20-21.

1. *We have a strong city.* In opposition to the city of the enemy, which God hath destroyed, chap. xxv. See the note there. *Salvation . . . for walls and bulwarks.* Or "the walls and the ditch." *Chel* properly signifies the *ditch* or *trench* without the wall; see Kimchi. The same rabbin says, This song refers to the time of salvation, i.e., the days of the Messiah.

2. *The righteous nation.* The converted Gentiles shall have the gates opened—a full entrance into all the glories and privileges of the gospel, being fellow heirs with the converted Jews. *The truth.* The gospel itself—as the fulfillment of all the ancient types, shadows, and ceremonies; and therefore termed *the truth,* in opposition to all those shadowy rites and ceremonies. "The law was given by Moses, but grace and truth came by Jesus Christ," John i. 17.

3. *In perfect peace.* Shalom, shalom, "peace, peace," i.e., peace upon peace—all kinds of prosperity—happiness in this world and in the world to come.

4. *Everlasting strength.* "The rock of ages"; or, according to Rab. Maimon, the "eternal Fountain, Source, or Spring." Does not this refer to the lasting streams from the rock in the desert? And that Rock was Christ.

8. *Have we waited for thee*—"We have placed our confidence in Thy name."

9. *When thy judgments.* It would be better to read, When Thy judgments were in the earth, the inhabitants of the world have learned righteousness. Men seldom seek God in prosperity; they are apt to rest in an earthly portion. But God in mercy embitters this by adversity; then there is a general cry after himself as our chief, solid, and only permanent Good.

19. *My dead body*—"My deceased." All the ancient versions render it in the plural. *The dew of herbs*—"The dew of the dawn." The deliverance of the people of God from a state of the lowest depression is explained by images plainly taken from the resurrection of the dead. In the same manner the Prophet Ezekiel represents the restoration of the Jewish nation from a state of utter dissolution by the restoring of the dry bones to life, exhibited to him in a vision, chap. xxxvii, which is directly thus applied and explained, vv. 11-13. And this deliverance is expressed with a manifest opposition to what is here said above, v. 14, of the great lords and tyrants, under whom they had groaned: "They are dead, they shall not live; they are deceased [tyrants], they shall not rise": that they should be destroyed utterly, and should never be restored to their former power and glory. It appears from hence that the doctrine of the resurrection of the dead was at that time a popular and common doctrine; for an image which is assumed in order to express or represent anything in the way of allegory or metaphor, whether poetical or prophetical, must be an image commonly known and understood; otherwise it will not answer the purpose for which it is assumed. Kimchi refers these words to the days of the Messiah, and says,

"Then many of the saints shall rise from the dead," and quotes Dan. xii. 2. Do not these words speak of the resurrection of our blessed Lord; and of that resurrection of the bodies of men, which shall be the consequence of His body being raised from the dead? *Thy dead men shall live . . . with my dead body shall they arise.* This seems very express.

20. *Come, my people, enter thou into thy chambers.* An exhortation to patience and resignation under oppression, with a confident expectation of deliverance by the power of God manifestly to be exerted in the destruction of the oppressor. It seems to be an allusion to the command of Moses to the Israelites, when the destroying angel was to go through the land of Egypt, not to "go out at the door of his house until the morning," Exod. xii. 22.

21. *The earth also shall disclose her blood.* Crimes of cruelty and oppression, which have passed away from the eyes of men, God will bring into judgment, and exact punishment for them.

CHAPTER 27

Destruction of the enemies of the Church. 1. God's care of His vineyard, 2-11. Prosperity of the descendants of Abraham in the latter days, 12-13.

2. *A vineyard of red wine.* The redder the wine, the more it was valued, says Kimchi.

3. *Lest any hurt it, I will keep it night and day*—"I will take care of her by night; and by day I will keep guard over her."

4. *Fury is not in me*—"I have no wall." The vineyard wishes for a wall and a fence of thorns—human strength and protection (as the Jews were too apt to apply to their powerful neighbors for assistance, and to trust to the shadow of Egypt). Jehovah replies that this would not avail her, nor defend her against His wrath. He counsels her, therefore, to betake herself to His protection. On which she entreats Him to make peace with her. This song receives much light from being collated with that in chap. v. In v. 5 of that chapter, God threatens to take away the wall of His vineyard. This was done, and here the vineyard complains, "I have no wall," and wishes for any kind of defense rather than be thus naked. *Who would set the briers and thorns against me?*— "Oh, that I had a fence of the thorn and brier."

11. *The boughs thereof*—"Her boughs." That is, the boughs of the vineyard.

13. *The great trumpet shall be blown.* Does not this refer to the time spoken of by our Lord in Matt. xxiv. 31? "He shall send [forth] his angels"—the preachers of His gospel—"with a great sound of a trumpet"—the earnest invitation to be saved by Jesus Christ; "and they shall gather together his elect"—the Jews, His ancient chosen people—"from the four winds"— from all parts of the habitable globe in which they have been dispersed.

CHAPTER 28

This chapter begins with a denunciation of the approaching ruin of the Israelites by Shalmaneser, whose power is compared to a tempest or flood, and his keenness to the avidity with which one plucks and swallows the grape that is soonest ripe, 1-4. It then turns to the two tribes of Judah and Benjamin, who were to continue a kingdom after the final captivity of their brethren; and

gives first a favorable prognostication of their affairs under Hezekiah, 5-6; but soon changes to reproofs and threatenings for their intemperance and their profaneness, 7-8. They are introduced as not only scornfully rejecting, but also mocking and ridiculing, the instructions of the prophet, 9-10. To this God immediately retorts in terms alluding to their own mocking, but differently applied, 11-13. The prophet then addresses these scoffers, 14; who considered themselves as perfectly secure from every evil, 15; and assures them that there was no method under heaven but one, by which they could be saved, 16; that every other vain resource should fail in the day of visitation, 17-18. He then further adds that the judgments of God were particularly levelled against them, and that all the means to which they trusted for warding them off should be to no purpose, 19-20; as the Almighty, who, on account of His patience and long-suffering, is amiably described as unacquainted with punishing, had nevertheless determined to punish them, 21-22. The prophet then concludes with a beautiful parable in explanation and defense of God's dealing with His people, 23-29.

1. *Woe to the crown of pride.* By the crown of pride, etc., Samaria is primarily understood.

3. *The crown of pride, the drunkards of Ephraim*—"The proud crown of the drunkards of Ephraim."

4. *The hasty fruit before the summer*—"The early fruit before the summer." "No sooner doth the *boccore* (the early fig) draw near to perfection in the middle or latter end of June, than the *kermez* or summer fig begins to be formed, though it rarely ripens before August; about which time the same tree frequently throws out a third crop, or the winter fig, as we may call it. This is usually of a much longer shape and darker complexion than the kermez, hanging and ripening upon the tree even after the leaves are shed; and, provided the winter proves mild and temperate, is gathered as a delicious morsel in the spring" (Shaw, *Travels,* p. 370, fol.).

Which when he that looketh upon it seeth— "Which whoso seeth, he plucketh it immediately." The image expresses in the strongest manner the great ease with which the Assyrians shall take the city and the whole kingdom, and the avidity with which they shall seize the rich prey without resistance.

5. *In that day.* Thus far the prophecy relates to the Israelites, and manifestly denounces their approaching destruction by Shalmaneser. Here it turns to the two tribes of Judah and Benjamin, the remnant of God's people who were to continue a kingdom after the final captivity of the Israelites. It begins with a favorable prognostication of their affairs and threatenings for their intemperance, disobedience, and profaneness.

Jonathan's Targum on this verse is worthy of notice: "In that time Messiah, the Lord of hosts, shall be a crown of joy and a diadem of praise to the residue of his people." Kimchi says the rabbins in general are of this opinion. Here then the rabbins, and their most celebrated Targum, give the incommunicable name, *Yehovah tsebaoth,* "the Lord of hosts," to our ever blessed Redeemer, Jesus Christ.

6. *The battle to the gate*—"The war to the gate of the enemy." That is, who pursue the fleeing enemy even to the very gates of their own city. "We were upon them even unto the entering of the gate," 2 Sam. xi. 23; that is, we drove the enemy back to their own gates. The Targum says, The Messiah shall give the victory to those who go out to battle, that He may bring them back to their own houses in peace.

9. *Whom shall he teach knowledge?*—"Whom, say they, would He teach knowledge?" The

scoffers mentioned below, v. 14, are here introduced as uttering their sententious speeches; they treat God's method of dealing with them, and warning them by His prophets, with contempt and derision. What, say they, doth He treat us as mere infants just weaned? Doth He teach us like little children, perpetually inculcating the same elementary lessons, the mere rudiments of knowledge; precept after precept, line after line, here and there, by little and little? imitating at the same time, and ridiculing, in v. 10, the concise prophetical manner. God, by His prophet, retorts upon them with great severity their own contemptuous mockery, turning it to a sense quite different from what they intended. Yes, saith He, it shall be in fact as you say. You shall be taught by a strange tongue and a stammering lip, in a strange country; you shall be carried into captivity by a people whose language shall be unintelligible to you, and which you shall be forced to learn like children. And My dealing with you shall be according to your own words. It shall be command upon command for your punishment; it shall be line upon line, stretched over you to mark your destruction (compare 2 Kings xxi. 13). It shall come upon you at different times, and by different degrees, till the judgments, with which from time to time I have threatened you, shall have their full accomplishment.

10. *For precept must be upon precept.* The original is remarkably abrupt: *latsav tsav latsav tsav ki; lakav kav lakav kav; sham zeeir sham zeeir.* "Command to command, command to command. Line to line, line to line. A little there, a little there." *Tsav* signifies a "little precept," such as is suited to the capacity of a child; see v. 9. *Kav* signifies the "line" that a mason stretches out to build a layer of stones by. After one layer or course is placed, he raises the line and builds another; thus the building is by degrees regularly completed. This is the method of teaching children, giving them such information as their narrow capacities can receive; and thus the prophet dealt with the Israelites.

12. *This is the rest*—"This is the true rest." The sense of this verse is: God had warned them by His prophets that their safety and security, their deliverance from their present calamities and from the apprehensions of still greater approaching, depended wholly on their trust in God, their faith and obedience; but they rejected this gracious warning with contempt and mockery.

15. *A covenant with death.* To be in covenant with is a kind of proverbial expression to denote perfect security from evil and mischief of any sort: "For thou shalt be in league with the stones of the field: and the beasts of the field shall be at peace with thee," Job v. 23. *We have made a covenant with death, and with hell are we at agreement.* We have made a "vision"; we have had an "interview," struck a bargain, and settled all preliminaries. So they had made a covenant with hell by diabolic sacrifice. "We have cut the covenant sacrifice"; they divided it for the contracting parties to pass between the separated victim. For the victim was split exactly down the middle; and being set opposite to each other, the contracting parties entered, one at the head part, the other

at the feet; and, meeting in the center, took the covenant oath. Thus, it is intimated, these bad people made an agreement with *sheol*, with demons, with whom they had an interview; i.e., meeting them in the covenant sacrifice! To such a pitch had the Israelitish idolatry reached at that time!

18. *Your covenant with death shall be disannulled*—"Your covenant with death shall be broken."

20. *For the bed is shorter.* A *mashal* or proverbial saying, the meaning of which is that they will find all means of defense and protection insufficient to secure them, and cover them from the evils coming upon them.

23. *Give ye ear, and hear my voice*—"Listen ye, and hear my voice." The foregoing discourse, consisting of severe reproofs, and threatenings of dreadful judgments impending on the Jews for their vices, and their profane contempt of God's warnings by His messengers, the prophet concludes with an explanation and defense of God's method of dealing with His people in an elegant parable or allegory; in which He employs a variety of images, all taken from the science of agriculture. As the *husbandman* uses various methods in preparing his land, and adapting it to the several kinds of seeds to be sown, with a due observation of times and seasons; and when he hath gathered in his harvest, employs methods as various in separating the corn from the straw and the chaff by different instruments, according to the nature of the different sorts of grain; so God, with unerring wisdom, and with strict justice, instructs, admonishes, and corrects His people; chastises and punishes them in various ways, as the exigence of the case requires, now more moderately, now more severely; always tempering justice with mercy, in order to reclaim the wicked, to improve the good, and, finally, to separate the one from the other.

27-28. Four methods of threshing are here mentioned, by different instruments: the "flail," the "drag," the "wain," and the "treading of the cattle." The staff or flail was used for, says Jerome, the grain that was too tender to be treated in the other methods. The drag consisted of a sort of strong planks, made rough at the bottom, with hard stones or iron; it was drawn by horses or oxen over the corn sheaves spread on the floor, the driver sitting upon it. The wain was much like the former; but had wheels with iron teeth, or edges like a saw.

28. *Bruise it with his horsemen*—"Bruise it with the hoofs of his cattle."

CHAPTER 29

Distress of Ariel, or Jerusalem, on Sennacherib's invasion, with manifest allusion, however, to the still greater distress which it suffered from the Romans, 1-4. Disappointment and fall of Sennacherib described in terms, like the event, the most awful and terrible, 5-8. Stupidity and hypocrisy of the Jews, 9-16. Rejection of the Jews, and calling of the Gentiles, 17. The chapter concludes by a recurrence to the favorite topics of the prophet, viz., the great extension of the Messiah's kingdom in the latter days, and the future restoration of Israel, 18-24.

The subject of this and the following four chapters is the invasion of Sennacherib; the great distress of the Jews while it continued; their sudden and unexpected deliverance by God's immediate interposition in their favor;

the subsequent prosperous state of the kingdom under Hezekiah; interspersed with severe reproofs, and threats of punishment, for their hypocrisy, stupidity, infidelity, their want of trust in God, and their vain reliance on the assistance of Egypt; and with promises of better times, both immediately to succeed, and to be expected in the future age.

1. *Ariel.* That Jerusalem is here called by this name is very certain; but the reason of this name, and the meaning of it as applied to Jerusalem, are very obscure and doubtful. From Ezek. xliii. 15, we learn that Ariel was the name of the altar of burnt offerings, put here for the city itself in which that altar was. In the second verse it is said, "I will distress Ariel . . . and it shall be unto me as Ariel." The first Ariel here seems to mean Jerusalem, which should be distressed by the Assyrians; the second Ariel seems to mean the altar of burnt offerings. But why is it said, "Ariel shall be unto me as Ariel"? As the altar of burnt offerings was surrounded daily by the victims which were offered, so the walls of Jerusalem shall be surrounded by the dead bodies of those who had rebelled against the Lord, and who should be victims to His justice. The translation of Bishop Lowth appears to embrace both meanings: "I will bring distress upon Ariel; and it shall be to me as the hearth of the great altar." *Add ye year to year.* Ironically. Go on year after year, keep your solemn feasts; yet know that God will punish you for your hypocritical worship, consisting of mere form destitute of true piety. Probably delivered at the time of some great feast, when they were thus employed.

2. *There shall be heaviness and sorrow*— "There shall be continual mourning and sorrow," instead of your present joy and festivity. *And it shall be unto me as Ariel*—"And it shall be unto me as the hearth of the great altar." That is, it shall be the seat of the fire of God, which shall issue from thence to consume His enemies. See note on v. 1. Or, perhaps, all on flame, as it was when taken by the Chaldeans; or covered with carcasses and blood, as when taken by the Romans—an intimation of which more distant events, though not immediate subjects of the prophecy, may perhaps be given in this obscure passage.

4. *And thy speech shall be low out of the dust*—"And from out of the dust thou shalt utter a feeble speech."

5. *The multitude of thy strangers*—"The multitude of the proud." The fifth, sixth, and seventh verses contain an admirable description of the destruction of Sennacherib's army, with a beautiful variety of the most expressive and sublime images; perhaps more adapted to show the greatness, the suddenness, and horror of the event than the means and manner by which it was effected. Compare chap. xxx. 30-33.

7. *As a dream.* This is the beginning of the comparison which is pursued and applied in the next verse. Sennacherib and his mighty army are not compared to a dream because of their sudden disappearance; but the disappointment of their eager hopes is compared to what happens to a hungry and thirsty man when he awakes from a dream in which fancy had presented to him meat and drink in abundance, and finds it nothing but a vain illusion.

8. Bishop Stock's translation of the prophet's text is both elegant and just: "As when a hungry man dreameth; and, lo! he is eating: and he awaketh; and his appetite is unsatisfied. And as a thirsty man dreameth; and, lo! he is drinking: and he awaketh; and, lo! he is faint, and his appetite craveth."

9. *Stay yourselves, and wonder.* "Go on what-what-whatting," in a state of mental indetermination, till the overflowing scourge take you away.

13. *And their fear toward me is taught by the precept of men*—"And vain is their fear of Me, teaching the commandments of men."

17. *And Lebanon shall be turned into a fruitful field*—"Ere Lebanon become like Carmel." A *mashal*, or proverbial saying, expressing any great revolution of things; and, when respecting two subjects, an entire reciprocal change—explained here by some interpreters, I think with great probability, as having its principal view beyond the revolutions then near at hand, to the rejection of the Jews, and the calling of the Gentiles. Carmel stands here opposed to Lebanon, and therefore is to be taken as a proper name.

21. *Him that reproveth in the gate*—"Him that pleaded in the gate."

22. *Who redeemed Abraham.* As God redeemed Abraham from among idolaters and workers of iniquity, so will He redeem those who hear the words of the Book, and are humbled before Him, vv. 18-19. *Concerning the house of Jacob.*—"The God of the house of Jacob." I read *El* as a noun, not a preposition. The parallel line favors this sense, and there is no address to the house of Jacob to justify the other. *Neither shall his face now wax pale*— "His face shall no more be covered with confusion."

23. *But when he seeth his children, the work of mine hands*—"For when his children shall see the work of My hands."

CHAPTER 30

The Jews reproved for their reliance on Egypt, 1-7. Threatened for their obstinate adherence to this alliance, 8-17. Images the most elegant and lofty, by which the intense gloriousness of Messiah's reign at the period when all Israel shall be added to the Church is beautifully set forth, 18-26. Dreadful fall of Sennacherib's army, an event most manifestly typical of the terrible and sudden overthrow of Antichrist; as, unless this typical reference be admitted, no possible connection can be imagined between the stupendous events which took place in Hezekiah's reign and the very remote and inconceivably more glorious displays of divine vengeance and mercy in the days of the Messiah, 27-33.

1. *And that cover with a covering*—"Who ratify covenants." Hebrew, "Who pour out a libation." Sacrifice and libation were ceremonies constantly used in ancient times by most nations in the ratifying of covenants; a libation therefore is used for a covenant.

5. *But a shame*—"But proved even a shame."

6. *The burden. Massa* seems here to be taken in its proper sense; the "load," not the "oracle." The same subject is continued, and there seems to be no place here for a new title to a distinct prophecy. Does not *burden of the beasts of the south* in this place relate to the presents sent by Hoshea, king of Israel, to the south, to Egypt, to engage the Egyptians to succor him against the king of Assyria. *Into the land of*

trouble and anguish—"Through a land of distress and difficulty." The same deserts are here spoken of which the Israelites passed through when they came out of Egypt, which Moses describes, Deut. viii. 15, as "that great and terrible wilderness, wherein were fiery serpents, and scorpions, and drought, where there was no water"; and which was designed to be a kind of barrier between them and Egypt, of which the Lord has said, "Ye shall henceforth return no more that way," Deut. xvii. 16.

7. *Their strength is to sit still*—"Rahab the Inactive."

8. *For ever and ever*—"For a testimony forever."

13. *Swelling out in a high wall*—"A swelling in a high wall." It has been observed before that the buildings of Asia generally consist of little better than what we call mud walls.

14. *He shall not spare*—"And spareth it not."

17. *At the rebuke of five shall ye flee*—"At the rebuke of five, ten thousand of you shall flee." In the second line of this verse a word is manifestly omitted, which should answer to *one thousand* in the first. "How should one chase a thousand, and two put ten thousand to flight?" Deut. xxxii. 30 "And five of you shall chase an hundred, and an hundred of you shall put ten thousand to flight," Lev. xxvi. 8.

18. *And therefore will he be exalted*—"Even for this shall he expect in silence."

19. *For the people shall dwell in Zion*—"When a holy people shall dwell in Sion." The word *kadosh*, lost out of the text, but happily supplied by the Septuagint, clears up the sense, otherwise extremely obscure. When the rest of the cities of the land were taken by the king of Assyria, Zion was preserved, and all that were in it. *Thou shalt weep no more*—"Thou shalt implore him with weeping."

21. *When ye turn to the right hand, and when ye turn to the left*—"Turn not aside, to the right or to the left."

22. *Ye shall defile*—"Ye shall treat as defiled." The very prohibition of Moses, Deut. vii. 25, only thrown out of the prose into the poetical form.

25. *When the towers fall*—"When the mighty fall."

26. *Shall be sevenfold.* The text adds *as the light of seven days,* a manifest gloss, taken in from the margin; it is not in most of the copies of the Septuagint. It interrupts the rhythmical construction, and obscures the sense by a false, or at least an unnecessary, interpretation. By *moon, sun, light,* are to be understood the abundance of spiritual and temporal felicity, with which God should bless them in the days of the Messiah, which should be sevenfold, i.e., vastly exceed all that they had ever before possessed.

27. *And the burden thereof is heavy*—"And the flame raged violently."

28. *To sift the nations with a sieve of vanity*—"To toss the nations with the van of perdition." Kimchi's explanation is to the following effect: "*Naphah* is a van with which they winnow corn; and its use is to cleanse the corn from the chaff and straw: but the van with which God will winnow the nations will be the van of emptiness or perdition; for nothing useful shall

remain behind, but all shall come to nothing, and perish. In like manner, a bridle is designed to guide the horse in the right way; but the bridle which God will put in the jaws of the people shall not direct them aright, but shall make them err, and lead them into destruction."

30. *The Lord shall cause his glorious voice to be heard.* Kimchi understands this of the great destruction of the Assyrian host by the angel of the Lord.

31. *Which smote with a rod*—"He that was ready to smite with his staff."

32. *The grounded staff*—"The rod of his correction." *With tabrets and harps.* With every demonstration of joy and thanksgiving for the destruction of the enemy in so wonderful a manner; with hymns of praise, accompanied with musical instruments. See v. 29.

33. *For Tophet is ordained.* Tophet is a valley very near to Jerusalem, to the southeast, called also the valley of Hinnom or Gehenna; where the Canaanites, and afterwards the Israelites, sacrificed their children, by making them pass through the fire, that is, by burning them in the fire, to Molech, as some suppose. It is therefore used for a place of punishment by fire; and by our blessed Saviour in the gospel for hellfire, as the Jews themselves had applied it. Here the place where the Assyrian army was destroyed is called Tophet by a metonymy.

CHAPTER 31

The Jews again reproved for their confidence in Egypt, finely contrasted with their neglect of the power and protection of God, 1-3. Deliverance and protection are, notwithstanding, promised, expressed by two similes—the first remarkably lofty and poetical, the latter singularly beautiful and tender, 4-5. Exhortation to repentance, joined with the prediction of a more reformed period, 6-7. This chapter concludes like the preceding, with a prophecy of the fall of Sennacherib, 8-9.

1. *Woe to them that go down to Egypt.* This is a reproof to the Israelites for forming an alliance with the Egyptians, and not trusting in the Lord. *And stay on horses*—"Who trust in horses."

3. *He that helpeth* (the Egyptians) *shall fall, and he that is holpen* (the Israelites) *shall fall down . . . together.*

5. *Passing over*—"Leaping forward." The generality of interpreters observe in this place an allusion to the deliverance which God vouchsafed to His people when He destroyed the firstborn of the Egyptians, and exempted those of the Israelites sojourning among them by a peculiar interposition. The same word is made use of here which is used upon that occasion, and which gave the name to the feast which was instituted in commemoration of that deliverance, *pesach.* But the difficulty is to reconcile the commonly received meaning of that word with the circumstances of the similitude here used to illustrate the deliverance represented as parallel to the deliverance in Egypt. The common meaning of the word *pasach* upon other occasions is "to halt, to be lame, to leap," as in a rude manner of dancing (as the prophets of Baal did, 1 Kings xviii. 26), all which agrees very well together; for the motion of a lame person is a perpetual springing forward, by throwing himself from the weaker upon the stronger leg. The common notion of God's passage over the houses

of the Israelites is that in going through the land of Egypt to smite the firstborn, seeing the blood on the door of the houses of the Israelites, He passed over, or skipped, those houses, and forbore to smite them. But that this is not the true notion of the thing will be plain from considering the words of the sacred historian, where he describes very explicitly the action: "For Jehovah will pass through to smite the Egyptians; and when He seeth the blood on the lintels and on the two side posts, Jehovah will spring forward over (or before) the door, and will not suffer the destroyer to come into your houses to smite you" (see Exod. xii. 23). Here are manifestly two distinct agents, with which the notion of passing over is not consistent, for that supposes but one agent. The two agents are the destroying angel passing through to smite every house and Jehovah, the Protector, keeping pace with him; and who, seeing the door of the Israelite marked with the blood, *leaps forward*, throws himself with a sudden motion in the way, opposes the destroying angel, and covers and protects that house against the destroying angel, nor suffers him to smite it. In this way of considering the action, the beautiful similitude of the bird protecting her young answers exactly to the application by the allusion to the deliverance in Egypt. As the mother bird spreads her wings to cover her young, throws herself before them, and opposes the rapacious bird that assaults them, so shall Jehovah protect, as with a shield, Jerusalem from the enemy, protecting and delivering, springing forward and rescuing her.

6. *Have deeply revolted*—"Have so deeply engaged in revolt."

7. *Which your own hands have made unto you for a sin*—"The sin, which their own hands have made."

8. *Then shall the Assyrian fall.* Because he was to be discomfited by the angel of the Lord, destroying in his camp, in one night, upwards of one hundred and eighty thousand men; and Sennacherib himself fell by the hands of the princes, his own sons. Not mighty men, for they were not soldiers; not mean men, for they were princes.

CHAPTER 32

Prophecy of great prosperity under Hezekiah; but, in its highest sense, applicable to Christ, 1-8. Description of impending calamities, 9-14. Rejection of the Jews, and calling of the Gentiles, 15. The future prosperity of the Church, 16-20.

1. *Behold, a king shall reign in righteousness.* If King Hezekiah were a type of Christ, then this prophecy may refer to His time; but otherwise it seems to have Hezekiah primarily in view. It is evident, however, that in the fullest sense these words cannot be applied to any man; God alone can do all that is promised here.

2. *As the shadow of a great rock.* The shadow of a great projecting rock is the most refreshing that is possible in a hot country, not only as most perfectly excluding the rays of the sun, but also as having in itself a natural coolness, which it reflects and communicates to everything about it.

3. *And the eyes of them that see shall not be dim*—"And him the eyes of those that see shall regard."

5. *The vile person—nabal,* the pampered, fattened, brainless fellow, who eats to live, and lives to eat; who will scarcely part with anything, and that which he does give he gives with an evil eye and a grudging heart. *Liberal—nadib;* the generous, openhearted, princely man. *The churl—kilai,* the avaricious man; he who starves himself amidst his plenty, and will not take the necessaries of life for fear of lessening his stock. Thus he differs from *nabal,* who feeds himself to the full, and regards no one else; like the rich man in the Gospel. The avaricious man is called *kilai,* from *ki,* "for," and *li,* "myself"; or contracted from *col,* "all," and *li,* "to myself." All is mine; all I have is my own; and all I can get is for myself. *Bountiful—shoa,* he who is abundantly rich; who rejoices in his plenty, and deals out to the distressed with a liberal hand.

6. *The vile person will speak villany*—"The fool will still utter folly."

7. *The instruments also of the churl are evil*—"As for the niggard, his instruments are evil." His machinations, his designs. *To destroy the poor with lying words*—"To defeat the assertions of the poor in judgment."

8. *Liberal things*—"Generous purposes."

9. From this verse to the end of the fourteenth, the desolation of Judea by the Chaldeans appears to be foretold.

12. *They shall lament . . . for the pleasant fields*—"Mourn ye for the pleasant field."

13. *Shall come up thorns and briers*—"The thorn and the brier shall come up." The description of impending distress which begins at v. 13 belongs to other times than that of Sennacherib's invasion, from which they were so soon delivered. It must at least extend to the ruin of the country and city by the Chaldeans. And the promise of blessings which follows was not fulfilled under the Mosiac dispensation; they belong to the kingdom of Messiah. Compare v. 15 with chap. xxix. 17.

14. *The forts*—"Ophel." It was a part of Mount Zion, rising higher than the rest, at the eastern extremity, near to the Temple, a little to the south of it; called by Micah, chap. iv. 8, "Ophel of the daughter of Zion." It was naturally strong by its situation; and had a wall of its own, by which it was separated from the rest of Zion.

17. *The work of righteousness.* Righteousness works and produces peace.

19. *The city shall be low in a low place.*—"The city shall be laid level with the plain." *The city*—probably Nineveh or Babylon; but this verse is very obscure.

20. *That sow beside all waters*—"Who sow your seed in every well-watered place."

CHAPTER 33

This chapter contains the sequel of the prophecy respecting Sennacherib. The prophet addresses himself to the Assyrian monarch, 1-4. The mercy and power of God acknowledged by the Jews, 5-6. Distress and despair of the Jews at the approach of Sennacherib, 7-9. Gracious promise of deliverance, 10-13. Dreadful apprehensions of the wicked, and security of the righteous, 14-17. The security of the Jews under the reign of Hezekiah, and the wretched condition of Sennacherib and his army, 18-24.

The plan of the prophecy continued in this chapter, and which is manifestly distinct from the foregoing, is peculiarly elegant. To set it in a proper light, it will be necessary to mark the transitions from one part of it to another.

In v. 1 the prophet addresses himself to Sennacherib, expressing the injustice of his ambitious designs, and the sudden disappointments of them. In v. 2 the Jews are introduced offering up their earnest supplications to God in their present distressful condition.

In vv. 3 and 4 the prophet in the name of God, or rather God himself, is introduced addressing himself to Sennacherib, and threatening him that, notwithstanding the terror which he had occasioned in the invaded countries, yet he should fall. In vv. 5-6 a chorus of Jews is introduced, acknowledging the mercy and power of God, who had undertaken to protect them; extolling it with direct opposition to the boasted power of their enemies, and celebrating the wisdom and piety of their king, Hezekiah, who had placed his confidence in the favor of God.

Then follows, in vv. 7-9, a description of the distress and despair of the Jews, upon the king of Assyria's marching against Jerusalem, and sending his summons to them to surrender, after the treaty he had made with Hezekiah on the conditions of his paying, as he actually did pay to him, 300 talents of silver and 30 talents of gold, 2 Kings xviii. 14-16. In v. 10, God himself is again introduced, declaring that He will interpose in this critical situation of affairs, and disappoint the vain designs of the enemies of His people, by discomfiting and utterly consuming them.

Then follows, vv. 11-22, still in the person of God, which however falls at last into that of the prophet, a description of the dreadful apprehensions of the wicked in those times of distress and imminent danger; finely contrasted with the confidence and security of the righteous, and their trust in the promises of God that He will be their never-failing Strength and Protector. The whole concludes, in the person of the prophet, with a description of the security of the Jews under the protection of God, and of the wretched state of Sennacherib and his army, wholly discomfited, and exposed to be plundered even by the weakest of the enemy.

1. *And dealest treacherously*—"Thou plunderer." *When thou shalt make an end to deal treacherously*—"When thou art weary of plundering."

2. *Be thou their arm every morning*—"Be Thou our Strength every morning."

3. *At the noise of the tumult*—"From Thy terrible voice."

6. *His treasure*—"Thy treasure."

7. *Their valiant ones shall cry without*—"The mighty men raise a grievous cry."

9. *Bashan and Carmel shake off their fruits*—"Bashan and Carmel are stripped of their beauty."

11. *Your breath*—"And my spirit."

14. *The sinners in Zion are afraid.* Zion has been generally considered as a type of the Church of God. Now all the members of God's Church should be holy, and given to good works; sinners in Zion, therefore, are portentous beings! but, alas! where are they not?

15. *That stoppeth his ears from hearing of blood*—"Who stoppeth his ears to the proposal of bloodshed."

18. *Where is the scribe?* The person appointed by the king of Assyria to estimate their number and property in reference to their being heavily taxed. *Where is the receiver?* Or he who was to have collected this tribute. *Where is he that counted the towers?* That is, the commander of the enemy's forces, who surveyed the fortifications of the city, and took an account of the height, strength, and situation of the walls and towers, that he might know where to make the assault with the greatest advantage.

20. *Look upon Zion*—"Thou shalt see Zion."

21. *The glorious Lord*—"The glorious name of Jehovah."

23. *Thy tacklings are loosed.* Here the Assyrians are represented under the figure of a ship wrecked by a violent storm; and the people on the beach, young, old, feeble, and diseased, gathering the spoil without any to hinder them. *Their mast*—"Thy mast."

24. *And the inhabitant shall not say.* This verse is somewhat obscure. The meaning of it seems to be that the army of Sennacherib shall by the stroke of God be reduced to so shattered and so weak a condition that the Jews shall fall upon the remains of them, and plunder them without resistance; that the most infirm and disabled of the people of Jerusalem shall come in for their share of the spoil; the lame shall seize the prey; even the sick and the diseased shall throw aside their infirmities, and recover strength enough to hasten to the general plunder. The last line of the verse is parallel to the first, and expresses the same sense in other words. Sickness being considered as a visitation from God, a punishment of sin, the forgiveness of sin is equivalent to the removal of a disease. Thus the Psalmist: "Who forgiveth all thy sin; and healeth all thine infirmities" (see Ps. ciii. 3). That this prophecy was exactly fulfilled, I think we may gather from the history of this great event given by the prophet himself. It is plain that Hezekiah, by his treaty with Sennacherib, by which he agreed to pay him 300 talents of silver and 30 talents of gold, had stripped himself of his whole treasure. He not only gave him all the silver and gold that was in his own treasury and in that of the Temple, but was even forced to cut off the gold from the doors of the Temple and from the pillars, with which he had himself overlaid them, to satisfy the demands of the king of Assyria. But after the destruction of the Assyrian army, we find that he "had exceeding much riches," and that "he made himself treasuries for silver, and for gold, and for precious stones," 2 Chron. xxxii. 27. He was so rich that out of pride and vanity he displayed his wealth to the ambassadors from Babylon. This cannot be otherwise accounted for than by the prodigious spoil that was taken on the destruction of the Assyrian army. And thus, in the providence of God, he had the wealth which was exacted from him restored.

CHAPTER 34

The prophet earnestly exhorts all nations to attend to the communication which he has received from Jehovah, as the matter is of the highest importance, and of universal concern, 1. The wrath of God is denounced against all the nations that had provoked to anger the Defender of the cause of Zion, 2-3. Great crowd of images, by which the final overthrow and utter extermination of everything that opposes the spread of true religion in the earth are forcibly and majestically set forth; images so very bold and expressive as to render it impossible, without doing great violence to symbolical language, to restrain their import to the calamities which befell the Edomites in the reign of Nebuchadnezzar, or in that of any other potentate, or even to the calamities which the enemies of the Church have yet suffered since the delivery of the prophecy. Edom must therefore be a type of Antichrist, the last grand adversary of the people of God; and consequently this most awful prophecy, in its ultimate signification, remains to be accomplished, 4-15. The churches of Zion, at the period of the consummation, commanded to consult the book of Jehovah, and note the exact fulfillment of these terrible predictions in their minutest details. Not one jot or tittle relative even to the circumstances shadowed forth by the impure animals shall be found to fail; for what the mouth of the Lord has declared necessary to satisfy the divine justice, His Spirit will accomplish, 16-17.

This and the following chapter make one distinct prophecy; an entire, regular, and beautiful poem, consisting of two parts: the first containing a denunciation of divine vengeance against the enemies of the people or Church of God, the second describing the flourishing state of the Church of God consequent upon the execution of those judgments. The event foretold is represented as of the highest importance, and of universal concern. All nations are called upon to attend to the declaration of it; and the wrath of God is denounced against all the nations, that is, all those that had provoked to anger the Defender of the cause of Zion. Among those, Edom is particularly specified. The principal provocation of Edom was their insulting the Jews in their distress, and joining against them with their enemies, the Chaldeans; see Amos i. 11; Ezek. xxv. 12; xxxv. 15; Ps. cxxxvii. 7. Accordingly the Edomites were, together with the rest of the neighboring nations, ravaged and laid waste by Nebuchadnezzar; see Jer. xxv. 15-26; Mal. i. 3-4. The general devastation spread through all these countries by Nebuchadnezzar may be the event which the prophet has primarily in view in the thirty-fourth chapter. But this event, as far as we have any account of it in history, seems by no means to come up to the terms of the prophecy, or to justify so highly wrought and terrible a description; and it is not easy to discover what connection the extremely flourishing state of the people of God described in the next chapter could have with those events, and how the former could be the consequence of the latter, as it is there represented to be. By a figure, very common in the prophetical writings, any city or people, remarkably distinguished as enemies of the people and kingdom of God, is put for those enemies in general. This seems here to be the case with Edom and Botsra. It seems, therefore, reasonable to suppose, with many learned expositors, that this prophecy has a further view to events still future; to some great revolutions to be effected in later times, antecedent to that more perfect state of the kingdom of God upon earth, and serving to introduce it, which the Holy Scriptures warrant us to expect.

That the thirty-fifth chapter has a view beyond anything that could be the immediate consequence of those events is plain from every part, especially from the middle of it, vv. 5-6, where the miraculous works wrought by our blessed Saviour are so clearly specified that we cannot avoid making the application; and our Saviour himself has moreover plainly referred to this very passage, as speaking of Him and His works, Matt. xi. 4-5. He bids the disciples of John to go and report to their master the

things which they heard and saw, that the blind received their sight, the lame walked, and the deaf heard; and leaves it to him to draw the conclusion in answer to his inquiry, whether He who performed the very works which the prophets foretold should be performed by the Messiah was not indeed the Messiah himself. And where are these works so distinctly marked by any of the prophets as in this place? and how could they be marked more distinctly? To these the strictly literal interpretation of the prophet's words directs us. According to the allegorical interpretation, they may have a further view. This part of the prophecy may run parallel with the former, and relate to the future advent of Christ; to the conversion of the Jews, and their restitution to their land; to the extension and purification of the Christian faith; events predicted in the Holy Scriptures as preparatory to it.

1. *Hearken*—"Attend unto me."

5. *For my sword shall be bathed in heaven*—"For my sword is made bare in the heavens."

6. *The Lord hath a sacrifice*—"For Jehovah celebrateth a sacrifice." Ezekiel, chap. xxxix. 16-17, has manifestly imitated this place of Isaiah. He has set forth the great leaders and princes of the adverse powers under the same emblems of goats, bulls, rams, fatlings, and has added to the boldness of the imagery, by introducing God as summoning all the fowls of the air, and all the beasts of the field, and bidding them to the feast which He has prepared for them by the slaughter of the enemies of His people.

The sublime author of the Revelation, chap. xix. 17-18, has taken this image from Ezekiel, rather than from Isaiah.

7. *The unicorns shall come down. Reemim,* translated "wild goats" by Bishop Lowth.

8. *The year of recompences for the controversy of Zion*—"The year of recompense to the Defender of the cause of Zion."

11. *The cormorant.* "The pelican." *The bittern.* The "hedgehog," or "porcupine." *The line of confusion, and the stones of emptiness*—"The plummet of emptiness over her scorched plains."

13. *A court for owls. Yaanah,* the "ostrich," from *anah,* "to cry," because of the noise it makes.

14. *The wild beasts of the desert.* The "mountain cats."—Bochart. *Wild beasts of the island.* The "jackals." *The satyr. Seir,* the "hairy one," probably the he-goat. *The screech owl. Lilith,* the "night-bird."

15. *The great owl. Kippoz,* the "darter," a serpent so called because of its suddenly leaping up or darting on its prey.

CHAPTER 35

Flourishing state of the Church of God consequent to the awful judgments predicted in the preceding chapter. The images employed in the description are so very consolatory and sublime as to oblige us to extend their fulfillment to that period of the gospel dispensation when Messiah shall take unto himself His great power and reign. The fifth and sixth verses were literally accomplished by our Saviour and His apostles; but that the miracles wrought in the first century were not the only import of the language used by the prophet is sufficiently plain from the context. They therefore have a further application; and are contemporary with, or rather a consequence of, the judgments of God upon the enemies of the Church in the latter days; and so relate to the greater influence and extension of the Christian faith, the conversion of the Jews, their restoration to their own land, and the second advent of Christ. Much of the imagery of this chapter seems to have been borrowed from the exodus from Egypt; but it is greatly enlivened by the life, sentiments, and passions ascribed to inanimate objects; all nature being represented as rejoicing with the people of God in consequence of their deliverance; and administering in such an unusual manner to their relief and comfort as to induce some commentators to extend the meaning of the prophecy to the blessedness of the saints in heaven, 1-10.

The various miracles our Lord wrought are the best comment on this chapter, which predicts those wondrous works and the glorious state of the Christian Church.

1. *Shall be glad.* Probably the true reading is, "The wilderness and the dry place shall be glad." Not *for them.*

2. *Rejoice even with joy and singing*—"The well-watered plain of Jordan shall also rejoice."

7. *The parched ground*—"The glowing sand." The glowing sandy plain, which in the hot countries at a distance has the appearance of water.

8. *But it shall be for those*—"But He himself shall be with them, walking in the way." That is, God; see v. 4. "Who shall dwell among them, and set them an example that they should follow His steps."

9. *It shall not be found there*—"Neither shall he be found there." *The redeemed shall walk there. Geulim.* Those whose forfeited inheritances are brought back by the "kinsman," goel. This has been considered by all orthodox divines as referring to the incarnation of our Lord, and His sacrificial offering.

10. *The ransomed. Peduyey,* from *padah,* "to redeem by paying a price." Those for whom a price was paid down to redeem them from bondage and death.

CHAPTER 36

Sennacherib, king of Assyria, comes against Judah, and takes all the fenced cities, 1. He afterwards sends a great host against Jerusalem; and his general, Rabshakeh, delivers an insulting and blasphemous message to Hezekiah, 2-20. Hezekiah and his people are greatly afflicted at the words of Rabshakeh, 21-22.

The history of the invasion of Sennacherib, and of the miraculous destruction of his army, which makes the subject of so many of Isaiah's prophecies, is very properly inserted here as affording the best light to many parts of those prophecies, and as almost necessary to introduce the prophecy in the thirty-seventh chapter, being the answer of God to Hezekiah's prayer, which could not be properly understood without it. We find the same narrative in the Second Book of Kings, chaps. xviii; xix; xx; and these chapters of Isaiah, xxxvi; xxxvii; xxxviii; xxix, for much the greater part (the account of the sickness of Hezekiah only excepted) are but a different copy of that narration.

3. *Then came forth unto him.* Before these words the other copy, 2 Kings xviii. 18, adds, "And they demanded audience of the king."

5. *I say*—"Thou hast said." *But they are but vain words.* "A word of the lips." You talk about counsels, but you have none; about strength, but there is none with you.

6. *The staff of this broken reed.* A weakened, faithless ally. *It will go into his hand, and pierce it.* Will take subsidy after subsidy, and do nothing for it.

7. *But if thou say*—"But if ye say." *Ye shall worship before this altar*—"To worship only before this altar." See 2 Chron. xxxii. 12.

10. *Am I now come up without the Lord?* Probably some apostate Israelitish priest might have encouraged the king of Assyria by telling him that Jehovah had given him a commission against Jerusalem.

17. *And vineyards.* The other copy, 2 Kings xviii. 32, adds here: "A land of oil olive and of honey, that ye may live, and not die: and hearken not unto Hezekiah, when he persuadeth [seduceth] you."

CHAPTER 37

Hezekiah is greatly distressed, and sends to Isaiah, the prophet, to pray for him, 1-4. Isaiah returns a comfortable answer, and predicts the destruction of the king of Assyria and his army, 5-7. Sennacherib, hearing that his kingdom was invaded by the Ethiopians, sends a terrible letter to Hezekiah, to induce him to surrender, 9-13. Hezekiah goes to the Temple, spreads the letter before the Lord, and makes a most affecting prayer, 14-20. Isaiah is sent to him to assure him that his prayer is heard, that Jerusalem shall be delivered, and that the Assyrians shall be destroyed, 21-35. That very night a messenger of God slays 185,000 Assyrians, 36. Sennacherib returns to Nineveh, and is slain by his own sons, 37-38.

6. *Thus shall ye say.* "Thus shall ye (explicitly, earnestly, and positively) say." The paragogic *nun* deepens and increases the sense.

7. *I will send a blast*—"I will infuse a spirit into him."

8. *Rabshakeh returned.* From chap. xxxvi. 2, we learn that the king of Assyria had sent Rabshakeh from Lachish to Jerusalem; now it is likely that Rabshakeh had besieged that place, and that the king of Assyria had taken his station before this city, and dispatched Rabshakeh against Jerusalem. But, as it is said he had "departed from Lachish," probably he had been obliged to raise the siege, and sat down before *Libnah,* which promised an easier conquest.

9. *He heard say concerning Tirhakah king of Ethiopia.* When he heard that Tirhak, king of Ethiopia, had come out against him, then he sent that blasphemous manifesto which is contained in vv. 10-13, to terrify Hezekiah into submission.

20. *That thou art the Lord, even thou only*—"That Thou Jehovah art the only God." The word *Elohim,* "God," is lost here in the Hebrew text, but preserved in the other copy, 2 Kings xix. 19.

25. *Water*—"Strange waters." The word *zarim,* "strange," lost out of the Hebrew text in this place, is supplied from the other copy. *With the sole of my feet.* With my *infantry. All the rivers of the besieged places*—"All the canals of fenced places." The principal cities of Egypt, the scene of his late exploits, were chiefly defended by deep moats, canals, or large lakes, made by labor and art, with which they were surrounded.

26. *Lay waste defenced cities into ruinous heaps*—"Lay waste warlike nations, strong fenced cities."

CHAPTER 38

Account of Hezekiah's dangerous sickness and miraculous recovery, 1-9. Tender and beautiful song of thanksgiving, in which this pious king breathed out the sentiments of a grateful heart, when his life was, as it were, restored. This ode may be adapted to other cases; and will always afford profit and pleasure to those who are not void of feeling and piety, 10-22.

The narration of this chapter seems to be in some parts an abridgment of that of 2 Kings xx. The abridger, having finished his extract here with the eleventh verse, seems to have observed that the seventh and eighth verses of 2 Kings xx were wanted to complete the narration; he therefore added them at the end of the chapter, after he had inserted the song of Hezekiah.

6. *I will defend this city.* The other copy, 2 Kings xx. 6, adds: "for mine own sake, and for my servant David's sake"; and the sentence seems somewhat abrupt without it.

8. *Which is gone down*—"By which the sun is gone down."

9. *The writing of Hezekiah.* Here the Book of Kings deserts us, the song of Hezekiah not being inserted in it.

12. *Mine age . . . is removed from me as a shepherd's tent.* I shall be removed from this state to another, as a shepherd removes his tent from one place to another for the sake of his flock. *I have cut off like a weaver my life*—"My life is cut off as by the weaver."

13. *I reckoned till morning,* etc.—"I roared until the morning like the lion."

14. *Undertake for me*—"Contend for me."

15. *I shall go softly all my years in the bitterness of my soul.*—"Through the rest of my years will I reflect on this bitterness of my soul."

16. *By these things men live*—"For this cause shall it be declared."

17. *For peace I had great bitterness*—"My anguish is changed into ease."

21. *Let them take a lump of figs.* God, in effecting this miraculous cure, was pleased to order the use of means not improper for that end.

CHAPTER 39

The Babylonish monarch sends letters of congratulation and a present to Hezekiah, on account of his recovery from his late dangerous illness, 1. The king of Judah shows the messengers of Merodach-baladan all the treasures of his house and kingdom, 2. The prophet takes occasion from this ostentatious display of the king to predict the captivity of the royal family, and of the people, by the Babylonians, 3-8.

8. *Then said Hezekiah.* The nature of Hezekiah's crime, and his humiliation on the message of God to him by the prophet, is more expressly declared by the author of the Book of the Chronicles: "But Hezekiah rendered not again according to the benefit done unto him; for his heart was lifted up: therefore there was wrath upon him, and upon Judah and Jerusalem. Notwithstanding Hezekiah humbled himself for the pride of his heart, both he and the inhabitants of Jerusalem, so that the wrath of the Lord came not upon them in the days of Hezekiah. . . . And Hezekiah prospered in all his works. Howbeit in the business of the ambassadors of the princes of Babylon, who sent unto him to enquire of the wonder that was done in the land, God left him, to try him, that he might know all that was in his heart" (2 Chron. xxxii. 25-26, 30-31).

There shall be peace and truth in my days. I rather think these words should be understood as a humble inquiry of the king, addressed to the prophet. "Shall there be prosperity, *shalom,* and truth in my days?—Shall I escape the evil which you predict?" Understood otherwise, they manifest a pitiful unconcern both for his own family and for the nation. This is the view I have taken of the passage in 2 Kings xxi. 19.

CHAPTER 40

In this chapter the prophet opens the subject respecting the restoration of the Church with great force and elegance; declaring God's command to His messengers the prophets to comfort His people in their captivity, and to impart to them the glad tidings that the time of favor and deliverance was at hand, 1-2. Immediately a harbinger is introduced giving orders, as usual in the march of Eastern monarchs, to remove every obstacle, and to prepare the way for their return to their own land, 3-5. The same words, however, the New Testament scriptures authorize us to refer to the opening of the gospel dispensation. Accordingly, this subject, coming once in view, is principally attended to in the sequel. Of this the prophet gives us sufficient notice by introducing a voice commanding another proclamation, which calls off our attention from all temporary, fading things to the spiritual and eternal things of the gospel, 6-11. And to remove every obstacle in the way of the prophecy in either sense, or perhaps to give a further display of the character of the Redeemer, he enlarges on the power and wisdom of God, as the Creator and Disposer of all things. It is impossible to read this description of God, the most sublime that ever was penned, without being struck with inexpressible reverence and self-abasement. The contrast between the great Jehovah and everything reputed great in this world, how admirably imagined, how exquisitely finished! What atoms and inanities are they all before HIM who sitteth on the circle of the immense heavens, and views the potentates of the earth in the light of grasshoppers—those poor insects that wander over the barren heath for sustenance, spend the day in continual chirpings, and take up their humble lodging at night on a blade of grass, 12-26! The prophet concludes with a most comfortable application of the whole, by showing that all this infinite power and unsearchable wisdom is unweariedly and everlastingly engaged in strengthening, comforting, and saving His people, 27-31.

The course of prophecies which follow, from hence to the end of the book, and which taken together constitute the most elegant part of the sacred writings of the Old Testament, interspersed also with many passages of the highest sublimity, was probably delivered in the latter part of the reign of Hezekiah. The prophet in the foregoing chapter had delivered a very explicit declaration of the impending dissolution of the kingdom, and of the captivity of the royal house of David, and of the people, under the kings of Babylon. As the subject of his subsequent prophecies was to be chiefly of the consolatory kind, he opens them with giving a promise of the restoration of the kingdom, and the return of the people from that captivity, by the merciful interposition of God in their favor. But the views of the prophet are not confined to this event. As the restoration of the royal family and of the tribe of Judah, which would otherwise have soon become undistinguished and have been irrecoverably lost, was necessary, in the design and order of Providence, for the fulfilling of God's promises of establishing a more glorious and an everlasting Kingdom, under the Messiah to be born of the tribe of Judah, and of the family of David, the prophet connects these two events together, and hardly ever treats of the former without throwing in some intimations of the latter; and sometimes is so fully possessed with the glories of the future and more remote Kingdom that he seems to leave the more immediate subject of his commission almost out of the question.

I have not the least doubt that the return of the Jews from the captivity of Babylon is the first, though not the principal, thing in the prophet's view. The redemption from Babylon is clearly foretold, and at the same time is employed as an image to shadow out a redemption of an infinitely higher and more important nature.

Yet obvious and plain as I think this literal sense is, we have nevertheless the irrefragable authority of John the Baptist, and of our blessed Saviour himself, as recorded by all the Evangelists, for explaining this exordium of the prophecy of the opening of the gospel by the preaching of John, and of the introduction of the kingdom of Messiah; who was to effect a much greater deliverance of the people of God, Gentiles as well as Jews, from the captivity of sin and the dominion of death. And this we shall find to be the case in many subsequent parts also of this prophecy, where passages manifestly relating to the deliverance of the Jewish nation, effected by Cyrus, are, with good reason, and upon undoubted authority, to be understood of the redemption wrought for mankind by Christ.

2. *Double for all her sins*—"Blessings double to the punishment." It does not seem reconcilable to our notions of the divine justice, which always punishes less than our iniquities deserve, to suppose that God had punished the sins of the Jews in double proportion; and it is more agreeable to the tenor of this consolatory message to understand it as a promise of ample recompense for the effects of past displeasure, on the reconciliation of God to His returning people.

3. *The voice of him that crieth in the wilderness.* The idea is taken from the practice of Eastern monarchs, who, whenever they entered upon an expedition or took a journey, especially through desert and unpracticed countries, sent harbingers before them to prepare all things for their passage, and pioneers to open the passes, to level the ways, and to remove all impediments. The Jewish church, to which John was sent to announce the coming of Messiah, was at that time in a barren and desert condition, unfit, without reformation, for the reception of her King. It was in this desert country, destitute at that time of all religious cultivation, in true piety and good works unfruitful, that John was sent to prepare the way of the Lord by preaching repentance.

6. *The voice said, Cry*—"A voice saith, Proclaim." To understand rightly this passage is a matter of importance; for it seems designed to give us the true key to the remaining part of Isaiah's prophecies, the general subject of which is the restoration of the people and Church of God. The prophet opens the subject with great clearness and elegance; he declares at once God's command to His messengers to comfort His people in captivity, to impart to them the joyful tidings, that their punishment has now satisfied the divine justice, and the time of reconciliation and favor is at hand. He then introduces a harbinger giving orders to prepare the way for God, leading His people from Babylon, as He did formerly from Egypt, through the wilderness; to remove all obstacles, and to clear the way for their passage. Thus far nothing more appears to be intended than a return from the Babylonish captivity; but the next words seem to intimate something much greater: "And the glory of Jehovah shall be revealed; And all flesh shall see together the salvation of our God." He then introduces a voice commanding him to make a solemn proclamation. And what is the import of it? that the people—the *flesh*—is of a vain, temporary nature; that all its glory fadeth, and is soon gone; but that the word of God endureth forever.

7. *Because the spirit of the Lord*—"When the wind of Jehovah." *Ruach Yehovah*, a wind of Jehovah, is a Hebraism, meaning no more than a strong wind. It is well-known that a hot wind in the East destroys every green thing.

9. *O Zion, that bringest good tidings*—"O Daughter, that bringest glad tidings to Zion." The office of announcing and celebrating such glad tidings as are here spoken of belongs peculiarly to the women. On occasion of any great public success, a signal victory, or any other joyful event, it was usual for the women to gather together, and with music, dances, and songs to publish and celebrate the happy news. So in this place, Jehovah having given the word by His prophet, the joyful tidings of the restoration of Zion, and of God's returning to Jerusalem (see chap. lii. 8), the women are exhorted by the prophet to publish the joyful news with a loud voice from eminences, whence they might best be heard all over the country; and the matter and burden of their song was to be, *Behold your God!*

10. *His reward is with him, and his work before him.*—"His reward is with Him, and the recompense of His work before him." That is, the reward and the recompense which He bestows, and which He will pay to His faithful servants; this He has ready at hand with Him, and holds it out before Him, to encourage those who trust in Him and wait for Him.

11. *Shall gently lead those that are with young*—"The nursing ewes shall he gently lead." A beautiful image, expressing, with the utmost propriety as well as elegance, the tender attention of the shepherd to his flock. That the greatest care in driving the cattle in regard to the dams and their young was necessary appears clearly from Jacob's apology to his brother, Esau, Gen. xxxiii. 13.

16. *And Lebanon is not sufficient.* Does not the prophet mean here that all the burnt offerings and sacrifices that could be offered were insufficient to atone for sin? That the nations were as nothing before Him, not merely because of His immensity, but because of their insufficiency to make any atonement by their oblations for the iniquities which they had committed?

19. *And casteth silver chains*—"And forgeth for it chains of silver."

20. *Chooseth a tree that will not rot.* For what? To make a god out of it! The rich, we find, made theirs of gold and silver; the poor man was obliged to put up with a wooden god!

28. *There is no searching of his understanding*—"And that His understanding is unsearchable."

31. *They shall mount up with wings as eagles*—"They shall put forth fresh feathers like the moulting eagle." It has been a common and popular opinion that the eagle lives and retains his vigor to a great age; and that, beyond the common lot of other birds, he molts in his old

age, and renews his feathers, and with them his youth. "Thou shalt renew thy youth like the eagle," says the Psalmist, ciii. 5.

CHAPTER 41

The prophet, having intimated the deliverance from Babylon, and the still greater redemption couched under it, resumes the subject. He begins with the divine vocation of Abraham, the root of the Israelitish family, and his successful exploits against the idolaters, 1-7. He then recurs to the Babylonish captivity, and encourages the seed of Abraham, the friend of God, not to fear, as all their enemies would be ultimately subdued under them, 8-16; and everything furnished necessary to refresh and comfort them in their passage homewards through the desert, 17-20. The prophet then takes occasion to celebrate the prescience of God, from His knowledge of events so very distant, as instanced in the prediction concerning the messenger of glad tidings which should be given to Jerusalem to deliver her from all her enemies; and challenges the idols of the heathen to produce the like proof of their pretended divinity, 21-27. But they are all vanity, and accursed are they that choose them, 28-29.

1. *Keep silence before me, O islands*—"Let the distant nations repair to me with new force of mind."

2. *The righteous man.* Some explain it of Abraham, others of Cyrus. I rather think that the former is meant; because the character of the righteous man, or righteousness, agrees better with Abraham than with Cyrus. Besides, immediately after the description of the success given by God to Abraham and his posterity (who, I presume, are to be taken into the account), the idolaters are introduced as greatly alarmed at this event. Abraham was called out of the east; and his posterity were introduced into the land of Canaan, in order to destroy the idolaters of that country, and they were established there on purpose to stand as a barrier against the idolatry then prevailing, and threatening to overrun the whole face of the earth. *He gave them as the dust to his sword*—"Hath made them like the dust before his sword."

4. *Who hath wrought and done it?*—"Who hath performed and made these things?"

5. *Were afraid*—"And they were terrified."

7. *That it should not be moved*—"That it shall not move."

9. *And called thee from the chief men thereof*—"And called from the extremities thereof."

15. *Thou shalt thresh the mountains.* Mountains and hills are here used metaphorically for the kings and princes of the Gentiles.—Kimchi.

19. *I will plant in the wilderness the cedar.* The preceding two verses express God's mercy to them in their passage through the dry deserts, in supplying them with abundant water, when distressed with thirst, in allusion to the Exodus. This verse expresses the relief afforded to them, fainting with heat in their journey through that hot country, destitute of shelter, by causing shady trees, and those of the tallest and most beautiful kinds, to spring up for their defense. *The oil tree.* This, Kimchi says, is not to be understood of the olive tree, for the olive is distinguished, Neh. viii. 15; but it means the pine or fir, from which pitch is extracted.

21. *Bring forth your strong reasons*—"Produce these your mighty powers." "Let your idols come forward which you consider to be so very strong" (*Hieron, in loc.*).

23. *That we may be dismayed, and behold it together*—"Then shall we be struck at once with admiration and terror."

24. *Your work of nought*—"Your operation is less than naught."

25. *I have raised up one from the north.* "That is," says Kimchi, "the Messiah." *He shall come upon princes*—"He shall trample on princes."

27. *The first shall say to Zion, Behold, behold them*—"I first to Zion gave the word, Behold, they are here." This verse is somewhat obscure by the transposition of the parts of the sentence, and the peculiar manner in which it is divided into two parallel lines. The following paraphrase will explain the form and the sense of it. "I first, by My prophets, give notice of these events, saying, Behold, they are at hand! and I give to Jerusalem a messenger of glad tidings."

28. *Among them*—"Among the idols."

CHAPTER 42

The prophet sets forth the meekness of Messiah's character, and the extent and blessings of His kingdom, particularly among the Gentiles, 1-9. In consequence of this he calls on the whole creation to join him in one song of praise to God, 10-12. After which he seems again to glance at the deliverance from the Captivity, although the words may full as well apply to the deliverance vouchsafed to the Church, to the overthrow of her most powerful enemies, and to the prevalency of true religion over idolatry and error, 13-17. The prophet then reproves the Jews for their blindness and infidelity in rejecting the Messiah, and gives intimations of those judgments which their guilt would draw on them, 18-25.

The prophet, having opened his subject with the preparation for the return from captivity at Babylon, and intimated that a much greater deliverance was covered under the veil of that event, proceeded to vindicate the power of God, as Creator and Disposer of all things; and His infinite knowledge, from His prediction of future events, and in particular of that deliverance. He went still further, and pointed out the instrument by which He should effect the redemption of His people, the Jews, from slavery; namely, a great conqueror, whom He would call forth from the north and the east to execute His orders. In this chapter he proceeds to the greater deliverance; and at once brings forth into full view, without throwing any veil of allegory over the subject, the Messiah. "Behold my servant, Messiah," says the Chaldee. Matthew has applied it directly to Christ; nor can it with any justice or propriety be applied to any other person or character whatever.

1. *Behold my servant, whom I uphold.* "On whom I lean." Alluding to the custom of kings leaning on the arm of their most beloved and faithful servant. All, both Jews and Christians, agree, that the first seven verses of this chapter belong to Christ. Now, as they are evidently a continuation of the prophecy in the preceding chapter, that prophecy cannot belong to Cyrus, but to Christ. *He shall bring forth judgment to the Gentiles*—"He shall publish judgment to the nations." The word *mishpat,* "judgment," like *tsedakah,* "righteousness," is taken in a great latitude of signification. It means "rule, form, order, model, plan; rule of right, or of religion; an ordinance, institution; judicial process, cause, trial, sentence, condemnation, acquittal, deliverance, mercy." It certainly means in this place the law to be published by Messiah, the institution of the gospel.

4. *He shall not fail nor be discouraged*—"His force shall not be abated nor broken."

6. *A covenant of the people*—"A covenant to the people." But I think the word *berith,* here, should not be translated *covenant,* but "covenant sacrifice," which meaning it often has; and undoubtedly in this place. This gives a still stronger and clearer sense.

7. *To open the blind eyes.* In this verse the prophet seems to set forth the spiritual redemption, under images borrowed from the temporal deliverance.

8. *I am the Lord. Ani Yehovah.* This is the famous tetragrammation, or name of four letters, which we write *Jehovah, Yehovah,* etc. The letters are *Y H U H.* The Jews never pronounce it, and the true pronunciation is utterly unknown. *That is my name.* A name peculiar to myself.

11. *Let the wilderness.* The most uncultivated countries, and the most rude and uncivilized people, shall confess and celebrate with thanksgiving the blessing of the knowledge of God graciously imparted to them. *The villages that Kedar doth inhabit.* The Arabs, according to the Targum. *The inhabitants of the rock.* They who dwell in fortified places. The Vulgate has "the inhabitants of Arabia Petraea."

14. *I have been still*—"Shall I keep silence forever?"

19. *As my messenger that I sent*—"As he to whom I have sent My messengers." *As he that is perfect*—"As he who is perfectly instructed."

20. *Seeing many things*—"Thou hast seen indeed." *But he heareth not*—"Yet you will not hear."

21. *He will magnify the law*—"He hath exalted His own praise."

22. *They are all of them snared in holes*—"All their chosen youths are taken in the toils."

24. *We have sinned*—"They have sinned."

25. *The fury of his anger*—"The heat of His wrath."

CHAPTER 43

Prediction of that blessed period when God should gather the posterity of Abraham, with tender care, from their several dispersions in every quarter under heaven, and bring them safely to their own land, 1-7. Struck with astonishment at so clear a display of an event so very remote, the prophet again challenges all the blinded nations and their idols to produce an instance of such foreknowledge, 8-9; and intimates that the Jews should remain (as at this day) a singular monument to witness the truth of the prediction, till it should at length be fulfilled by the irresistible power of God, 10-13. He then returns to the nearer deliverance—that from the captivity of Babylon, 14-15; with which, however, he immediately connects another deliverance described by allusions to that from Egypt, but represented as much more wonderful than that; a character which will not at all apply to the deliverance from Babylon, and must therefore be understood of the restoration from the mystical Babylon, 16-18. On this occasion the prophet, with peculiar elegance, and by a very strong poetic figure, represents the tender care of God in comforting and refreshing His people on their way through the desert, to be so great as to make even the wild beasts haunting those parched places so sensible of the blessing of those copious streams then provided by Him as to join their hissing and howling notes with one consent to praise God, 19-21. This leads to a beautiful contrast of the ingratitude of the Jews and a vindication of God's dealings with regard to them, 22-28.

3. *I gave Egypt for thy ransom.* This is commonly supposed to refer to the time of Sennacherib's invasion; who, when he was just ready to fall upon Jerusalem, soon after his entering Judea, was providentially diverted from that design, and turned his arms against the Egyptians, and their allies the Cushean Arabians, with their neighbors the Sabeans, probably joined with them under Tirhakah. See chap. xx and chap xxxvii. 9. Or as there are some reasonable objections to this opinion, perhaps it may mean more generally that God has often saved His people at the expense of other nations whom He had, as it were in their stead, given up to destruction. Kimchi refers all this to the deliverance of Jerusalem from the invasion of Sennacherib. Tirhakah, king of Ethiopia, had come out to war against the king of Assyria, who was thereupon obliged to raise the siege of Jerusalem. Thus the Ethiopians, Egyptians, and Sabeans were delivered into the hands of the Assyrians as a ransom for Israel. I cannot help thinking this to be a very rational solution of the text.

7. *Every one that is called by my name.* All who worship the true God, and are obedient to His laws. *I have created him.* I have produced him out of nothing. *I have formed him. Yetsartiv.* I have given him that particular form and shape which are best suited to his station in life. *I have made him. Asithiv.* I have adapted him to the accomplishment of My counsels and designs.

8. *Bring forth the blind people that have eyes*—"Bring forth the people, blind, although they have eyes." I understand this of the Gentiles, as the verse following, not of the Jews. Their natural faculties, if they had made a proper use of them, must have led them to the knowledge of the being and attributes of the one true God; for "his eternal power and Godhead," if well attended to, are clearly seen in His works (Rom. i. 20), and would have preserved them from running into the folly and absurdity of worshipping idols. They are here challenged to produce the evidence of the power and foreknowledge of their idol gods; and the Jews are just afterwards, v. 10, appealed to as witnesses for God in this cause. Therefore these latter cannot here be meant by the people blind with eyes and deaf with ears.

10. *Ye* (the Israelites) *are my witnesses . . . and my servant* (the Prophet) *whom I have chosen,* that whatever has been said before concerning Sennacherib has been literally fulfilled. The prophet had predicted it; the Israelites saw it accomplished.

12. *I have declared, and have saved.* My prophets have always predicted your deliverances before they took place; and I have fulfilled their words to the uttermost.

14. *The Chaldeans, whose cry is in the ships*—"The Chaldeaans exulting in their ships." Babylon was very advantageously situated both in respect to commerce and as a naval power. It was open to the Persian Gulf by the Euphrates, which was navigable by large vessels; and being joined to the Tigris above Babylon by the canal called the Royal River, supplied the city with the produce of the whole country to the north of it, as far as the Euxine and Caspian seas (*Herod.* i. 194). Semiramis was the foundress of this part also of the Babylonian greatness. She improved the navigation of the Euphrates (*Herod.* i. 184; *Strabo,* lib. xvi), and is said to have had a fleet of 3,000 galleys. We are not to wonder that in later times we hear little of the commerce and naval power of Babylon; for, after the taking of the city by

Cyrus, the Euphrates was not only rendered less fit for navigation by being on that occasion diverted from its course and left to spread over the whole country; but the Persian monarchs, residing in their own country, to prevent any invasion by sea on that part of their empire, purposely obstructed the navigation of both the rivers by making cataracts in them (*Strabo,* ib.), that is, by raising dams across the channel, and making artificial falls in them, that no vessel of any size or force could possibly come up. Alexander began to restore the navigation of the rivers by demolishing the cataracts upon the Tigris as far up as Seleucia (*Arrian,* lib. vii), but he did not live to finish his great designs; those upon the Euphrates still continued. The prophet therefore might very justly speak of the Chaldeans as glorying in their naval power in his time, though afterwards they had no foundation for making any such boast.

19. *Behold, I will do a new thing.* At v. 16 the prophet had referred to the deliverance from Egypt and the passage through the Red Sea; here he promises that the same power shall be employed in their redemption and return from the Babylonish captivity. This was to be a new prodigy.

20. *The beast of the field shall honour me*—"The wild beast of the field shall glorify Me." The image is elegant and highly poetical. God will give such an abundant miraculous supply of water to His people traversing the dry desert in their return to their country that even the wild beasts, the serpents, the ostriches, and other animals that haunt those arid regions, shall be sensible of the blessing, and shall break forth into thanksgiving and praises to Him for the unusual refreshment which they receive from His so plentifully watering the sandy wastes of Arabia Deserta, for the benefit of His people passing through them.

22. *But thou hast not called upon me.* The connection is: But you, Israel, whom I have chosen, whom I have formed for myself to be My witness against the false gods of the nations; even you have revolted from Me, have neglected My worship, and have been perpetually running after strange gods. The emphasis of this and the following parts of the sentence, on which the sense depends, is laid on the words *me, on my account.* The Jews were diligent in performing the external services of religion; in offering prayers, incense, sacrifices, oblations; but their prayers were not offered with faith, and their oblations were made more frequently to their idols than to the God of their fathers. *But thou hast been weary of me, O Israel*—"Neither on My account have you labored, O Israel."

25. *I, even I, am he.* The original is extremely abrupt: "I, I, he." *For mine own sake.* In the pardon of sin God can draw no reason but from His own infinite goodness.

28. *I have profaned the princes of the sanctuary*— "Your princes have profaned My sanctuary."

CHAPTER 44

This chapter, besides promises of redemption, of the effusion of the Spirit, and success of the gospel, 1-5, sets forth, in a very sublime manner, the supreme power and foreknowledge, and absolute eternity, of the one true God; and exposes the folly and absurdity of idolatry with admirable force and elegance, 6-20. And to show that the knowledge of future events belongs only to Jehovah, whom all creation is again called to adore for the deliverance and reconciliation granted to His people, 21-23, the prophet concludes with setting in a very strong point of view the absolute impotence of everything considered great and insurmountable in the sight of men, when standing in the way of the divine counsel; and mentions the future deliverer of the Jewish nation expressly by name, nearly two hundred years before his birth, 24-28.

2. *Jesurun.* Jeshurun means Israel. This name was given to that people by Moses, Deut. xxxii. 15; xxxiii. 5, 26. The most probable account of it seems to be that in which the Jewish commentators agree; namely, that it is derived from *yashar,* and signifies "upright."

4. *They shall spring up as among the grass*— "They shall spring up as the grass among the waters."

5. *Shall call himself*—"Shall be called." *Another shall subscribe with his hand unto the Lord*—"This shall inscribe his hand to Jehovah."

7. *Let them shew unto them*—"Let them declare unto us."

9-10. *That they may be ashamed. Who hath formed a god?*—"That everyone may be ashamed that he hath formed a god."

11. *And the workmen, they are of men*—"Even the workmen themselves shall blush."

12. *The smith with the tongs*—"The smith cutteth off a portion of iron." The sacred writers are generally large and eloquent upon the subject of idolatry; they treat it with great severity, and set forth the absurdity of it in the strongest light. But this passage of Isaiah, vv. 12-20, far exceeds anything that ever was written upon the subject, in force of argument, energy of expression, and elegence of composition. A heathen author, in the ludicrous way, has, in a line or two, given idolatry one of the severest strokes it ever received: "Formerly I was the stump of a fig tree, a useless log; when the carpenter, after hesitating whether to make me a *god* or a *stool,* at last determined to make me a *god.* Thus I became a god!" (Horat., *Satyr,* lib. 1. sat, viii.) From the tenth to the seventeenth verse, a most beautiful strain of irony is carried on against idolatry. And we may naturally think that every idolater who either read or heard it must have been forever ashamed of his own devices.

17. *He falleth down unto it.* There were four forms of adoration used among the Hebrews: (1) The prostration of the whole body, (2) The bowing of the head, (3) The bending of the upper part of the body down to the knees, (4) Bowing the knee, or kneeling.

18. *He hath shut their eyes*—"Their eyes are closed up."

20. *He feedeth on ashes.* He feedeth on that which affordeth no nourishment; a proverbial expression for using ineffectual means, and bestowing labor to no purpose. In the same sense Hosea says, "Ephraim feedeth on wind," chap. xii. 1.

22. *I have blotted out, as a thick cloud, thy transgressions, and, as a cloud, thy sins*—"I have made your transgressions vanish away like a cloud, and your sins like a vapor."

27. *That saith to the deep, Be dry*—"Who saith to the deep, Be thou wasted." Cyrus took Babylon by laying the bed of the Euphrates

dry, and leading his army into the city by night through the empty channel of the river. The Euphrates, in the middle of the summer, from the melting of the snows on the mountains of Armenia, like the Nile, overflows the country. In order to diminish the inundation, and to carry off the waters, two canals were made by Nebuchadnezzar a hundred miles above the city; the first on the eastern side called Naharmalca, or the Royal River, by which the Euphrates was let into the Tigris; the other on the western side, called Pallacopas, or Naharaga, by which the redundant waters were carried into a vast lake, forty miles square, contrived, not only to lessen the inundation, but for a reservoir, with sluices, to water the barren country on the Arabian side. Cyrus, by turning the whole river into the lake by the Pallacopas, laid the channel, where it ran through the city, almost dry; so that his army entered it, both above and below, by the bed of the river, the water not reaching above the middle of the thigh (Herod. i, 185, 190; Xenophon, *Cyrop.* vii).

28. *That saith of Cyrus, He is my shepherd*— "Who saith to Cyrus, Thou art my shepherd." (1) Cyrus is called God's shepherd. Shepherd was an epithet which Cyrus took to himself; and what He gave to all good kings. (2) This Cyrus should say to the Temple: "Thy foundation shall be laid." Not—*Thou shalt be built.* The fact is, only the foundation was laid in the days of Cyrus; nor was it resumed till the second year of Darius, one of his successors. There is often a precision in the expressions of the prophets which is as honorable to truth as it is unnoticed by careless readers.

CHAPTER 45

Prophecy concerning Cyrus, the first king of the Persians. Every obstruction shall be removed out of his way, and the treasures taken from his enemies shall be immense 1-3. To whom, and on what account, Cyrus was indebted for his wonderful success, 4-6. The prophet refutes the absurd opinion of the Persians that there were two supreme beings, an evil and a good one, represented by light and darkness, here declared to be only the operation of the one true God, 7; and makes a transition to the still greater work of God displayed in the dispensation of the gospel, 8. Great impiety of those who call in question the mysterious providence of God towards His children, 9-12. The remaining part of this chapter, interspersed with strictures on the absurdity of idolatry and some allusions to the dark lying oracles of the heathens, may partly refer to the deliverance begun by Cyrus but chiefly to the salvation by the Messiah, which, it is declared, shall be of universal extent and everlasting duration, 13-25.

1. *Loose the loins of kings*—"Ungird the loins of kings." *To open before him the two leaved gates,* etc.—"That I may open before him the valves; and the gates shall not be shut." The gates of Babylon within the city leading from the streets to the river were providentially left open, when Cyrus' forces entered the city in the night through the channel of the river, in the general disorder occasioned by the great feast which was then celebrated. Otherwise, says Herodotus, i. 191, the Persians would have been shut up in the bed of the river, and taken as in a net, and all destroyed. And the gates of the palace were opened imprudently by the king's orders, to inquire what was the cause of the tumult without; when the two parties under Gobrias and Gadatas rushed in, got possession of the palace, and slew the king (Xenoph., *Cyrop.* vii. p. 528).

2. *The crooked places*—"The mountains." *The gates of brass*—"The valves of brass." Herod-

otus, i. 179: "In the wall all round there are a hundred gates, all of brass; and so in like manner are the sides and the lintels." The gates likewise within the city, opening to the river from the several streets, were of brass; as were those also of the temple of Belus.—Herod. i., 180-81.

3. *I will give thee the treasures of darkness.* Sardes and Babylon, when taken by Cyrus, were the wealthiest cities in the world. Croesus, celebrated beyond all the kings of that age for his riches, gave up his treasures to Cyrus, with an exact account in writing of the whole, containing the particulars with which each wagon was loaded when they were carried away; and they were delivered to Cyrus at the palace of Babylon.—Xenoph. *Cyrop.* lib. vii, pp. 503, 515, 540. *Treasures of darkness* may refer to the custom of burying their jewels and money under the ground in their house floors, fearing robbers.

7. *I form the light, and create darkness.* It was the great principle of the Magian religion, which prevailed in Persia in the time of Cyrus, and in which probably he was educated, that there are two supreme, coeternal, and independent causes always acting in opposition one to the other; one the author of all good, the other of all evil. The good being they called light; the evil being, darkness. That when light had the ascendant, then good and happiness prevailed among men; when darkness had the superiority, then evil and misery abounded. With reference to this absurd opinion, held by the person to whom this prophecy is addressed, God, by His prophet, asserts His omnipotence and absolute supremacy:

I am Jehovah, and none else;
Forming light, and creating darkness,
Making peace, and creating evil;
I, Jehovah, am the Author of all these things.

Declaring that those powers whom the Persians held to be the original authors of good and evil to mankind, representing them by light and darkness, are no other than creatures of God, the instruments which He employs in His government of the world. *I make peace, and create evil.* Evil is here evidently put for war and its attendant miseries. I will procure *peace* for the Israelites, and destroy Babylon by war.

8. *Drop down, ye heavens.* The eighty-fifth psalm is a very elegant ode on the same subject with this part of Isaiah's prophecies, the restoration of Judah from captivity; and is in the most beautiful part of it (10-14) a manifest imitation of this passage of the prophet. *Let them bring forth salvation*—"Let salvation produce her fruit."

9. *Woe unto him that striveth with his Maker!* —"Woe unto him that contendeth with the Power that formed him." The prophet answers or prevents the objections and cavils of the unbelieving Jews, disposed to murmur against God, and to arraign the wisdom and justice of His dispensations in regard to them. *Or thy work, He hath no hands*—"And to the workman, Thou hast no hands."

11. *Ask me of things to come.* The learned bishop therefore reads the passage thus:

Thus saith Jehovah, the Holy One of Israel;
And he that formeth the things which are to come;

Do ye question me concerning my children? And do ye give me directions concerning the work of my hands?

13. *I have raised him up.* This evidently refers to Cyrus, and to what he did for the Jews, and informs us by whom he was excited to do it.

14. *The labour of Egypt*—"The wealth of Egypt." This seems to relate to the future admission of the Gentiles into the Church of God. *The Sabeans, men of stature*—"The Sabeans, tall of stature." That the Sabeans were of a more majestic appearance than common is particularly remarked by Agatharchides, an ancient Greek historian quoted by Bochart. *They shall make supplication unto thee*—"They shall in suppliant guise address thee."

15. *Verily thou art a God that hidest thyself.* At present, from the nations of the world. *O God of Israel, the Saviour.* While Thou revealest thyself to the Israelites and savest them.

16. *They shall be ashamed*—"They are ashamed." The reader cannot but observe the sudden transition from the solemn adoration of the secret and mysterious nature of God's counsels in regard to His people to the spirited denunciation of the confusion of idolaters, and the final destruction of idolatry; contrasted with the salvation of Israel, not from temporal captivity, but the eternal salvation by the Messiah, strongly marked by the repetition and augmentation of the phrase, "to the ages of eternity."

19. *I the Lord speak righteousness, I declare things that are right*—"I am Jehovah, who speak truth, who give direct answers." This also is said in opposition to the false and ambiguous answers given by the heathen oracles, of which there are many noted examples; none more so than that of the answer given to Croesus when he marched against Cyrus. "If Croesus march against Cyrus, he shall overthrow a great empire." He, supposing that this promised him success, fought, and lost his own, while he expected to destroy that of his enemy.

22. *Look unto me, and be ye saved.* This verse and the following contain a plain prediction of the universal spread of the knowledge of God through Christ; see Rom. xiv. 11; Phil. ii. 10.

24. *Surely, shall one say, In the Lord have I righteousness and strength*—"Saying, Only to Jehovah belongeth salvation and power."

CHAPTER 46

The idols of Babylon represented as so far from being able to bear the burden of their votaries that they themselves are borne by beasts of burden into captivity, 1-2. This beautifully contrasted with the tender care of God, in bearing His people from first to last in His arms, and delivering them from their distress, 3-4. The prophet, then, with his usual force and elegance, goes on to show the folly of idolatry, and the utter inability of idols, 5-7. From which he passes with great ease to the contemplation of the attributes and perfections of the true God, 8-10. Particularly that prescience which foretold the deliverance of the Jews from the Babylonish captivity, with all its leading circumstances; and also that very remote event of which it is the type in the days of the Messiah, 11-13.

1. *Their carriages were heavy loaden*—"Their burdens are heavy."

2. *They could not deliver the burden*—"They could not deliver their own charge." That is, their worshippers, who ought to have been borne by them. See the next two verses.

3. *Which are borne by me from the belly*—"Ye that have been borne by me from the birth." The prophet very ingeniously, and with great force, contrasts the power of God, and His tender goodness effectually exerted towards His people, with the inability of the false gods of the heathen. He like an indulgent father had carried His people in His arms, "as a man carrieth his son" (see Deut. i. 31). He had protected them, and delivered them from their distresses; whereas the idols of the heathen are forced to be carried about themselves, and removed from place to place, with great labor and fatigue, by their worshippers.

8. *Shew yourselves men. Hithoshashu.* This word is rather of doubtful derivation and signification. It occurs only in this place, and some of the ancient interpreters seem to have had something different in their copies. The Vulgate read *hithbosheshu*, "take shame to yourselves"; the Syriac, *hithbonenu*, "Consider with yourselves"; the Septuagint, perhaps *hithabbelu*, "Groan or mourn, within yourselves."

11. *Calling a ravenous bird from the east*—"Calling from the east the eagle." A very proper emblem for Cyrus, as in other respects, so particularly because the ensign of Cyrus was a golden eagle.

12. *Hearken unto me, ye stouthearted*—This is an address to the Babylonians, stubbornly bent on the practice of injustice towards the Israelites.

CHAPTER 47

The destruction of Babylon is denounced by a beautiful selection of circumstances, in which her prosperous is contrasted with her adverse condition. She is represented as a tender and delicate female reduced to the work and abject condition of a slave, and bereaved of every consolation, 1-4. And that on account of her cruelty, particularly to God's people, her pride, voluptuousness, sorceries, and incantations, 5-11. The folly of these last practices elegantly exposed by the prophet, 12-15. It is worthy of observation that almost all the imagery of this chapter is applied in the Book of the Revelation (in nearly the same words) to the antitype of the illustrious capital of the Chaldean empire, viz., Babylon the Great.

2. *Take the millstones, and grind meal.* It was the work of slaves to grind the corn. They used hand mills. Water mills were not invented till a little before the time of Augustus; windmills, not until long after. It was not only the work of slaves, but the hardest work, and often inflicted upon them as a severe punishment. The words denote that state of captivity to which the Babylonians should be reduced. *Make bare the leg, uncover the thigh.* This is repeatedly seen in Bengal, where there are few bridges, and both sexes, having neither shoes nor stockings, truss up their loose garments, and walk across, where the waters are not deep. In the deeper water they are obliged to truss very high, to which there seems a reference in the third verse: "Thy nakedness shall be uncovered."

3. *I will not meet thee as a man*—"Neither will I suffer man to intercede with me."

4. *Our redeemer*—"Our Avenger." Here a chorus breaks in upon the midst of the subject, with a change of construction, as well as sentiment.

6. *I was wroth with my people.* God, in the course of His providence, makes use of great conquerors and tyrants as His instruments to

execute His judgments in the earth; He employs one wicked nation to scourge another. The inflicter of the punishment may perhaps be as culpable as the sufferer, and may add to his guilt by indulging his cruelty in executing God's justice. When he has fulfilled the work to which the divine vengeance has ordained him, he will become himself the object of it; see chap. x. 5-12. God charges the Babylonians, though employed by himself to chastise His people, with cruelty in regard to them. They exceeded the bounds of justice and humanity in oppressing and destroying them; and though they were really executing the righteous decree of God, yet, as far as it regarded themselves, they were only indulging their own ambition and violence. The Prophet Zechariah sets this matter in the same light: "I was but a little displeased, and they helped forward the affliction," chap. i. 15.

9. *These two things shall come to thee in a moment.* That is, suddenly. Belshazzar was slain; thus the city became metaphorically a widow, the husband—the governor of it—being slain. In the time in which the king was slain, the Medes and Persians took the city, and slew many of its inhabitants; see Dan. v. 30-31. When Darius took the city, he is said to have crucified 3,000 of its principal inhabitants. *In their perfection*—"On a sudden." Instead of "in their perfection," as our translation renders it, the Septuagint and Syriac read, "suddenly"; parallel to *in a moment,* in the preceding alternate member of the sentence. *For the multitude*—"Notwithstanding the multitude."

15. *To his quarter.* "Everyone shall turn aside to his own business; none shall deliver thee."

CHAPTER 48

The Jews reproved for their obstinate attachment to idols, notwithstanding their experience of the divine providence over them; and of the divine prescience that revealed by the prophets the most remarkable events which concerned them, that they should not have the least pretext for ascribing any portion of their success to their idols, 1-8. The Almighty, after bringing them to the furnace for their perverseness, asserts His glorious sovereignty, and repeats His gracious promises of deliverance and consolation, 9-11. Prophecy concerning that individual (Cyrus) who shall be an instrument in the hand of God of executing His will on Babylon, and His power on the Chaldeans; and the idols of the people are again challenged to give a like proof of their foreknowledge, 12-16. Tender and passionate exclamation of Jehovah respecting the hardened condition of the Jewish nations, to which the very pathetic exclamation of the Divine Saviour when He wept over Jerusalem may be considered a striking parallel, 17-19. Notwithstanding the repeated provocations of the house of Israel, Jehovah will again be merciful to them. They are commanded to escape from Babylon; and God's gracious favor towards them is beautifully represented by images borrowed from the exodus from Egypt, 20-21. Certain perdition of the finally impenitent, 22. It will be proper here to remark that many passages in this chapter, and indeed the general strain of these prophecies, have a plain aspect to a restoration of the Church in the latter days upon a scale much greater than the world has yet witnessed, when the very violent fall of Babylon the Great, mentioned in the Revelation, of which the Chaldean capital was an expressive type, shall introduce by a most tremendous political convulsion (Rev. xvi. 17-21) that glorious epoch of the gospel which forms so conspicuous a part of the prophecies of the Old Testament, and has been a subject of the prayers of all saints in all ages.

1. *Are come forth out of the waters of Judah* —"Ye that flow from the fountain of Judah."

6. *Thou hast heard, see all this*—"Thou didst hear it beforehand; behold, the whole is accomplished."

9. *And for my praise*—"And for the sake of My praise."

10. *I have chosen thee*—"I have tried thee." I cannot think *becheseph,* "with silver," is the true reading. *Kecheseph,* "like silver," as the Vulgate evidently read it, I suppose to have been the original reading, though no MS. yet found supports this word. The similarity of the two letters, *beth* and *caph,* might have easily led to the mistake in the first instance; and it has been but too faithfully copied ever since. *Cur,* which we translate *furnace,* should be rendered "crucible," the vessel in which the silver is melted. The meaning of the verse seems to be this: I have purified you, but not as silver is purified; for when it is purified, no dross of any kind is left behind. Had I done this with you, I should have consumed you altogether; but I have put you in the crucible of affliction, in captivity, that you may acknowledge your sins, and turn unto Me.

11. *For how should my name be polluted?* —"For how would My name be blasphemed?"

14. *Which among them hath declared these things?*—"Who among you hath predicted these things?" *The Lord hath loved him: he will do his pleasure on Babylon*—"He whom Jehovah hath loved will execute His will on Babylon." That is, Cyrus.

16. *From the time that it was*—"Before the time when it began to exist." From the time that the expedition of Cyrus was planned, there was God managing the whole by the economy of His providence. *There am I*—"I had decreed it." I take *sham* for a verb, not an adverb. *And now the Lord God, and his Spirit, hath sent me* —"And now the Lord Jehovah hath sent me, and His Spirit." "Who is it that saith in Isaiah, And now the Lord hath sent me and his Spirit? in which, as the expression is ambiguous, is it the Father and the Holy Spirit who have sent Jesus; or the Father, who hath sent both Christ and the Holy Spirit? The latter is the true interpretation."—Origen *cont. Cels.* lib. i. I have kept to the order of the words of the original on purpose that the ambiguity, which Origen remarks in the version of the Septuagint, and which is the same in the Hebrew, might still remain; and the sense which he gives to it be offered to the reader's judgment, which is wholly excluded in our translation.

18. *As a river*—"Like the river." That is, the Euphrates.

CHAPTER 49

In this chapter the Messiah is introduced, declaring the full extent of His commission, which is to be Saviour not only to the Jews, but also to the Gentiles. The power and efficacy of His word is represented by apt images; the ill success of His ministry among the Jews is intimated, and the great success of the gospel among the Gentiles, 1-12. But the prophet, then casting his eye on the happy, though distant, period of Israel's restoration, makes a beautiful apostrophe to the whole creation to shout forth the praises of God on the prospect of this remarkable favor, 13. The tender mercies of God to His people, with the prosperity of the Church in general, and the final overthrow of all its enemies, make the subject of the remaining verses, 14-26.

1. *Listen, O isles, unto me*—"Hearken unto me, O ye distant lands." Hitherto the subject of the prophecy has been chiefly confined to the redemption from the captivity of Babylon; with strong intimations of a more important deliverance sometimes thrown in, to the refutation of idolatry, and the demonstration of the infinite power, wisdom, and foreknowledge of God. The character and office of the Messiah

were exhibited in general terms at the beginning of chap. xlii; but here He is introduced in person, declaring the full extent of His commission, which is not only to restore the Israelites, and reconcile them to their Lord and Father, from whom they had so often revolted, but to be a Light to lighten the Gentiles, to call them to the knowledge and obedience of the true God, and to bring them to be one Church together with the Israelites, and to partake with them of the same common salvation procured for all by the great Redeemer and Reconciler of man to God.

2. *And he hath made my mouth like a sharp sword*—"And he hath made my mouth a sharp sword." The servant of God, who speaks in the former part of this chapter, must be the Messiah. If any part of this character can in any sense belong to the prophet, yet in some parts it must belong exclusively to Christ, who is represented as having "a sharp twoedged sword" going "out of his mouth," Rev. i. 16; who is himself the Word of God; which word is "quick, and powerful, and sharper than any twoedged sword, piercing even to the dividing asunder of soul and spirit, and of the joints and marrow, and is a discerner of the thoughts and intents of the heart," Heb. iv. 12.

This person, who is (v. 3) called *Israel*, cannot in any sense be Isaiah. That name, in its original design and full import, can only belong to him who contended powerfully with God in behalf of mankind, and prevailed, Gen. xxxii. 28. After all that Vitringa, Bp. Lowth, and others have said in proof of this chapter speaking of the Messiah, and of Him alone, I have my doubts whether sometimes Isaiah, sometimes Cyrus, and sometimes the Messiah be not intended; the former shadowing out the latter, of whom, in certain respects, they may be considered the types. The literal sense should be sought out first; this is of the utmost importance both in reading and interpreting the oracles of God.

5. *And now, saith the Lord*—"And now, thus saith Jehovah." *Though Israel be not gathered*—"And that Israel unto Him might be gathered."

6. *And to restore the preserved of Israel*—"And to restore the branches of Israel."

7. *The Redeemer of Israel, and his Holy One*—"The Redeemer of Israel, His Holy One." *To him whom man despiseth*—"To Him whose person is despised."

17. *Thy children shall make haste*—"They that destroyed you shall soon become your builders." *Shall go forth of thee*—"Shall become your offspring." Shall "proceed, spring, issue, from thee," as your children. The phrase is frequently used in this sense: see chap. xi. 1; Mic. v. 2; Nah. i. 11. The accession of the Gentiles to the Church of God is considered as an addition made to the number of the family and children of Sion: see vv. 21-22 and chap. lx. 4.

18. *Bind them on thee, as a bride doeth*—"Bind them about you, as a bride her jewels." The end of the sentence is manifestly imperfect. Does a bride bind her children, or her new subjects, about her?

23. *With their face toward the earth*—"With their faces to the earth." It is well-known that expressions of submission, homage, and reverence always have been and are still carried to

a great degree of extravagance in the Eastern countries. When Joseph's brethren were introduced to him, they "bowed down themselves before him with their faces to the earth," Gen. xlii. 6.

24. *Shall the prey be taken from the mighty?*—"Shall the prey seized by the terrible be rescued?" These last two verses contain a glorious promise of deliverance to the persecuted Church of Christ from the terrible one—Satan, and all his representatives and vicegerents, persecuting anichristian rulers.

CHAPTER 50

In this chapter God vindicates His dealings with His people, whose alienation is owing to themselves, 1. And, by allusion to the temporal deliverances connected with the drying up of the Red Sea and the Euphrates, asserts His power to save, 2-3; namely, by the obedience and sufferings of the Messiah, 4-6; who was at length to prove victorious over all His enemies, 7-9. The last two verses exhort to faith and trust in God in the most disconsolate circumstances, with a denunciation of vengeance on those who should trust to their own devices, 10-11.

1. *Thus saith the Lord.* This chapter has been understood of the prophet himself; but it certainly speaks more clearly about Jesus of Nazareth than of Isaiah, the son of Amoz. *Where is the bill?*—"Where is this bill?" Husbands, through moroseness or levity of temper, often sent bills of divorcement to their wives on slight occasions, as they were permitted to do by the law of Moses, Deut. xxiv. 1. And fathers, being oppressed with debt, often sold their children, which they might do for a time, till the year of release, Exod. xxi. 7. That this was frequently practiced appears from many passages of Scripture, and that the persons and the liberty of the children were answerable for the debts of the father. The widow, 2 Kings iv. 1, complains that "the creditor is come to take unto him my two sons to be bondmen." And in the parable, Matt. xviii. 25: The lord, forasmuch as his servant "had not to pay, . . . commanded him to be sold, and his wife, and children, and all that he had, and payment to be made." But this, saith God, cannot be My case; I am not governed by any such motives, neither am I urged by any such necessity. Your captivity therefore and your afflictions are to be imputed to yourselves, and to your own folly and wickedness.

2. *Their fish stinketh*—"Their fish is dried up."

5. *Neither turned away back*—"Neither did I withdraw myself backward."

6. *And my cheeks to them that plucked off the hair.* The greatest indignity that could possibly be offered. *I hid not my face from shame and spitting.* Another instance of the utmost contempt and detestation. It was ordered by the law of Moses as a severe punishment, carrying with it a lasting disgrace, Deut. xxv. 9. Among the Medes it was highly offensive to spit in anyone's presence, Herod. i. 99; and so likewise among the Persians, Xenophon, *Cyrop.* lib. i., p. 18. But in this place it certainly means spitting in the face. So it is understood in St. Luke, where our Lord plainly refers to this prophecy: "All things that are written by the prophets concerning the Son of man shall be accomplished. For he shall be delivered unto the Gentiles, and shall be mocked, and spitefully entreated, and spitted

on," xviii. 31-32, which was in fact fulfilled: "And some began to spit on him," Mark xiv. 65; xv. 19. If spitting in a person's presence was such an indignity, how much more spitting in His face?

7. *Therefore have I set my face like a flint.* The Prophet Ezekiel, chap. ii. 8-9, has expressed this with great force in his bold and vehement manner.

10. *Who is among you that feareth the Lord?* I believe this passage has been generally, if not dangerously, misunderstood. It has been quoted, and preached upon, to prove that "a man might conscientiously fear God, and be obedient to the words of the law and the prophets; obey the voice of His Servant—of Jesus Christ himself—that is, be sincerely and regularly obedient to the moral law and the commands of our blessed Lord, and yet walk in darkness and have no light, no sense of God's approbation, and no evidence of the safety of his state." This is utterly impossible; for Jesus hath said. "He that followeth me shall not walk in darkness, but shall have the light of life." Bishop Lowth's translation has set the whole in the clearest light. The text contains two questions, to each of which a particular answer is given: "Q. 1. Who is there among you that feareth Jehovah? Ans. Let him hearken unto the voice of his servant. Q. 2. Who that walketh in darkness and hath no light? Ans. Let him trust in the name of Jehovah; And lean himself (prop himself) upon his God."

That obeyeth the voice of his servant—"Let him hearken unto the voice of His servant."

11. *Ye that kindle a fire.* The fire of their own kindling, by the light of which they walk with security and satisfaction, is an image designed to express, in general, human devices and mere worldly policy, exclusive of faith, and trust in God. *That compass yourselves about with sparks*—"Who heap the fuel round about." Without faith, repentance, or a holy life, they are bold in their professed confidence in God—presumptuous in their trust in the mercy of God; and, while destitute of all preparation for and right to the kingdom of Heaven, would think it criminal to doubt their final salvation! Living in this way, what can they have at the hand of God but an endless bed of sorrow! *Ye shall lie down in sorrow.*

CHAPTER 51

The prophet exhorts the children of Abraham to trust in the Lord; and briefly, but beautifully, describes the great blessedness which should be the consequence, 1-3. Then, turning to the Gentiles, encourages them to look for a portion in the same salvation, 4-5; the everlasting duration of which is majestically described, 6. And as it is everlasting, so is it sure to the righteous, notwithstanding all the machinations of their enemies, 7-8. The faithful, then, with exultation and joy, lift their voices, reminding God of His wondrous works of old, which encourage them to look now for the like glorious accomplishment of these promises, 9-11. In answer to this the Divinity is introduced comforting them under their trials, and telling them that the deliverer was already on his way to save and to establish them. 12-16. On this the prophet turns to Jerusalem to comfort and congratulate her on so joyful a prospect. She is represented, by a bold image, as a person lying in the streets, under the intoxicating effects of the cup of the divine wrath, without a single person from among her own people appointed to give her consolation, and trodden under the feet of her enemies; but, in the time allotted by the divine providence, the cup of trembling shall be taken out of her hand, and put into that of her oppressors; and she shall drink it no more again forever, 17-22.

1. *Ye that follow after righteousness.* The people who, feeling the want of salvation, seek the Lord in order to be justified. *The rock.* Abraham. *The hole of the pit.* Sarah; as explained in v. 2.

2. *I called him alone.* As I have made out of one a great nation, so, although you are brought low, yet I can restore you to happiness, and greatly multiply your number.

4. *My people ... O my nation*—"O ye peoples . . . O ye nations." The difference is very material; for in this case the address is made, not to the Jews, but to the Gentiles, as in all reason it ought to be; for this and the two following verses express the call of the Gentiles, the islands, or the distant lands on the coasts of the Mediterranean and other seas. *A law shall proceed from me.* The new law, the gospel of our Lord Jesus.

5. *My righteousness is near.* The word *tsedek,* "righteousness," is used in such a great latitude of signification, for justice, truth, faithfulness, goodness, mercy, deliverance, salvation, that it is not easy sometimes to give the precise meaning of it without much circumlocution. It means here the faithful completion of God's promises to deliver His people.

14. *The captive exile hasteneth that he may be loosed*—"He marcheth on with speed, who cometh to set free the captive." Cyrus, if understood of the temporal redemption from the captivity of Babylon; in the spiritual sense, the Messiah, who comes to open the prison to them that are bound.

16. *That I may plant the heavens*—"To stretch out the heavens."

17. *The cup of trembling.* "The cup of mortal poison." This may also allude to the ancient custom of taking off criminals by a cup of poison. Socrates is well known to have been sentenced by the Areopagus to drink a cup of the juice of hemlock, which occasioned his death.

19. *These two things . . . desolation, and destruction, and the famine, and the sword.* That is, desolation by famine, and destruction by the sword, taking the terms alternately. *By whom shall I comfort thee?*—"Who shall comfort thee?"

CHAPTER 52

Jerusalem, in manifest allusion to the strong figure employed in the close of the preceding chapter, is represented as fallen asleep in the dust, and in that helpless state bound by her enemies. The prophet, with all the ardor natural to one who had such joyful news to communicate, bids her awake, arise, put on her best attire (holiness to the Lord), and ascend her lofty seat; and then he delivers the message he had in charge, a very consolatory part of which was that no more should enter into her the uncircumcised and the polluted, 1-6. Awaking from her stupefaction, Jerusalem sees the messenger of such joyful tidings on the eminence from which he spied the coming deliverance. She expresses, in beautiful terms, her joy at the news, repeating with peculiar elegance the words of the crier, 7. The rapturous intelligence that Jehovah was returning to resume His residence on His holy mountain immediately spreads to others on the watch, who all join in the glad acclamation, 8; and in the ardor of their joy, they call to the very ruins of Jerusalem to sing along with them, because Jehovah maketh bare His holy arm in the sight of all the nations, and all the ends of the earth are about to see the salvation of Israel's God. 9-10. To complete the deliverance, they are commanded to march in triumph out of Babylon, earnestly exhorted to have nothing to do with any of her abominations, and assured that Jehovah will guide them in all their way, 11-12. The prophet then passes to the procuring cause of this great blessedness to the house of Israel in particular, and to the world in general, viz., the humiliation, sufferings, death, burial, resurrection, and ascension of Jesus Christ; a very celebrated and clear prophecy, which takes up the remainder of this and the whole of the following chapter.

2. *Sit down, O Jerusalem*—"Ascend thy lofty seat, O Jerusalem."

5. *They that rule over them*—"They that are lords over them." *Make them to howl*—"Make their boast of it."

6. *I am he that doth speak*—"I am he, Jehovah, that promised."

7. *How beautiful!* The watchmen discover afar off, on the mountains, the messenger bringing the expected and much-wished-for news of the deliverance from the Babylonish captivity. They immediately spread the joyful tidings, v. 8, and with a loud voice proclaim that Jehovah is returning to Zion, to resume His residence on His holy mountain, which for some time He seemed to have deserted. This is the literal sense of the place. "How beautiful on the mountains are the feet of the joyful messenger!" is an expression highly poetical. For how welcome is his arrival! how agreeable are the tidings which he brings! Nahum, chap. i. 15, who is generally supposed to have lived after Isaiah, has manifestly taken from him this very pleasing image. St. Paul has applied this passage to the preaching of the gospel, Rom. x. 15.

8. *Thy watchmen shall lift up the voice*—"All your watchmen lift up their voices." *They shall see eye to eye.* May not this be applied to the prophets and apostles; the one predicting, and the other discovering in the prediction the truth of the prophecy? The meaning of both Testaments is best understood by bringing them face-to-face. *When the Lord shall bring again Zion*—"When Jehovah returneth to Zion." God is considered as having deserted His people during the Captivity; and at the restoration, as returning himself with them to Zion, His former habitation.

9. *He hath redeemed Jerusalem*—"He hath redeemed Israel."

13. *My servant shall deal prudently. Yaskil,* "shall prosper" or "act prosperously." The subject of Isaiah's prophecy from the fortieth chapter inclusive, has hitherto been, in general, the deliverance of the people of God. This includes in it three distinct parts which, however, have a close connection with one another: (1) The deliverance of the Jews from the captivity of Babylon; (2) The deliverance of the Gentiles from their miserable state of ignorance and idolatry; and (3) The deliverance of mankind from the captivity of sin and death. Cyrus is expressly named as the immediate agent of God in effecting the first deliverance. A greater Person is spoken of as the Agent who is to effect the latter two deliverances, called the *servant,* the elect, of God, in whom His soul delighteth; Israel, in whom God will be glorified. Babylon has hitherto been kept pretty much in sight, at the same time that strong intimations of something much greater have frequently been thrown in. But here Babylon is at once dropped, and I think hardly ever comes in sight again, unless perhaps in chap. lv. 12 and lvii. 14. The prophet's views are almost wholly engrossed by the superior part of his subject. He introduces the Messiah as appearing at first in the lowest state of humiliation, which he had just touched upon before (chap. i. 5-6), and obviates the offense which would be occasioned by it by declaring the important and necessary cause of it, and foreshowing the glory which should follow it.

14. *As many were astonied at thee*—"As many were astonished at Him."

15. *For that which had not been told them.* The mystery of the gospel so long concealed. See Rom. xv. 21; xvi. 25. *Shall they see.* With the eyes of their faith. *And that which they had not heard.* The redemption of the world by Jesus Christ; the conversion of the Gentiles, and making them one flock with the converted Jews.

CHAPTER 53

This chapter foretells the sufferings of the Messiah, the end for which He was to die, and the advantages resulting to mankind from that illustrious event. It begins with a complaint of the infidelity of the Jews, 1; the offense they took at His mean and humble appearance, 2; and the contempt with which they treated Him, 3. The prophet then shows that the Messiah was to suffer for sins not His own; but that our iniquities were laid on Him, and the punishment of them exacted of Him, which is the meritorious cause of our obtaining pardon and salvation, 4-6. He shows the meekness and placid submission with which He suffered a violent and unjust death, with the circumstances of His dying with the wicked, and being buried with the great, 7-9; and that, in consequence of His atonement, death, resurrection, and intercession, He should procure pardon and salvation to the multitudes, insure increasing prosperity to His Church, and ultimately triumph over all His foes, 10-11. This chapter contains a beautiful summary of the most peculiar and distinguishing doctrines of Christianity.

That this chapter speaks of none but Jesus must be evident to every unprejudiced reader who has ever heard the history of His sufferings and death. The Jews have endeavored to apply it to their sufferings in captivity; but, alas for their cause! they can make nothing out in this way. Allowing that it belongs to our blessed Lord, then who can read verses 4, 5, 6, 8, 10, without being convinced that His death was a vicarious sacrifice for the sins of mankind?

2. *He hath no form nor comeliness.* "He hath no form, nor any beauty, that we should regard Him; nor is His countenance such that we should desire Him."—Symmachus; the only one of the ancients that has translated it rightly.

3. *We hid as it were our faces from him*—"As one that hideth his face from us." Mourners covered up the lower part of their faces, and their heads, 2 Sam. xv. 30; Ezek. xxix. 17; and lepers were commanded by the law, Lev. xii. 45, to cover the upper lip.

4. *Surely he hath borne our griefs*—"Surely our infirmities He hath borne." *And carried our sorrows*—"And our sorrows, He hath carried them."

5. *The chastisement of our peace*—"The chastisement by which our peace is effected," that by which we are brought into a state of peace and favor with God.

8. *And who shall declare his generation?*—"And His manner of life who would declare?" A learned friend has communicated to me the following passages from the Mishna, and the Gemara of Babylon, as leading to a satisfactory explication of this difficult place. It is said in the former that before anyone was punished for a capital crime proclamation was made before the prisoner by the public crier, in these words: "Whosoever knows anything of this man's innocence, let him come and declare it." Now it is plain from the history of the four Evangelists that in the trial and condemnation

of Jesus no such rule was observed. And our Saviour seems to refer to such a custom, and to claim the benefit of it, by His answer to the high priest when he asked Him of His disciples and of His doctrine: "I spake openly to the world; I ever taught in the synagogue, and in the temple, whither the Jews always resort; and in secret have I said nothing. Why askest thou me? ask them which heard me, what I have said unto them: behold, they know what I said," John xviii. 20-21. This, therefore, was one remarkable instance of hardship and injustice, among others predicted by the prophet, which our Saviour underwent in His trial and sufferings. St. Paul likewise, in similar circumstances, standing before the judgment seat of Festus, seems to complain of the same unjust treatment: that no one was called, or would appear, to vindicate his character. "My manner of life [my generation] from my youth, which was at the first among mine own nation at Jerusalem, know all the Jews; which knew me from the beginning, if they would testify, that after the most straitest sect of our religion I lived a Pharisee," Acts xxvi. 4-5. *Dor* signifies age, duration, the time which one man or many together pass in this world, in this place; the course, tenor, or manner of life. *Was he stricken*—"He was smitten to death."

9. *With the rich in his death*—"With the rich man was His tomb." It may be necessary to introduce Bishop Lowth's translation: "And his grave was appointed with the wicked; but with the rich man was his tomb."

10. *To grief*—"With affliction." *When thou shalt make his soul*—"If His soul shall make." *When thou shalt make his soul an offering.* The word *nephesh*, "soul," is frequently used in Hebrew to signify "life." Throughout the New Testament the salvation of men is uniformly attributed to the death of Christ. *He shall see his seed.* True converts, genuine Christians. *He shall prolong his days.* Or this spiritual progeny shall prolong their days, i.e., Christianity shall endure to the end of time. *And the pleasure of the Lord.* To have all men saved and brought to the knowledge of the truth. *Shall prosper in his hand.* Shall go on in a state of progressive prosperity; and so completely has this been thus far accomplished that every succeeding century has witnessed more Christianity in the world than the preceding, or any former one.

11. *Shall be satisfied*—"And be satisfied." *Shall my righteous servant justify*—"Shall My Servant justify." Three MSS. (two of them ancient) omit the word *tsaddik;* it seems to be only an imperfect repetition, by mistake, of the preceding word. It makes a solecism in this place; for according to the constant usage of the Hebrew language the adjective, in a phrase of this kind, ought to follow the substantive; and *tsaddik abdi*, in Hebrew, would be as absurd as "shall my servant righteous justify" in English. Add to this that it makes the hemistich too long.

12. *He bare the sin of many.* The "multitudes," the many that were made sinners by the offenses of one; i.e., the whole human race; for all have sinned—all have fallen; and for all that have sinned, and for all that have fallen, Jesus Christ died. *He made intercession for the transgressors.*—This was literally fulfilled

at His death, "Father, forgive them; for they know not what they do," Luke xxiii. 34. And to make intercession for transgressors is one part of His mediatorial office (Heb. vii. 25 and ix. 24).

CHAPTER 54

Some suppose this chapter to have been addressed to the Gentiles; some, to the Jewish Church; and some, to the Christian, in its first stage. On comparing the different parts of it, particularly the seventh and eighth verses, with the remainder, the most obvious import of the prophecy will be that which refers it to the future conversion of the Jews, and to the increase and prosperity of that nation, when reconciled to God after their long rejection, when their glory and security will far surpass what they were formerly in their most favored state, 1-17.

1. *Sing, O barren, thou that didst not bear*— "Shout for joy, O thou barren, that didst not bear." The Church of God under the Old Testament, confined within the narrow bounds of the Jewish nation, and still more so in respect of the very small number of true believers, and which sometimes seemed to be deserted of God, her Husband, is the barren woman, that did not bear, and was *desolate.* She is exhorted to rejoice, and to express her joy in the strongest manner, on the reconciliation of her Husband (see v. 6) and on the accession of the Gentiles to her family. The converted Gentiles are all along considered by the prophet as a new accession of adopted children, admitted into the original Church of God, and united with it. See chap. xlix. 20-21.

4. *For thou shalt forget the shame of thy youth.* That is, "The bondage of Egypt: widowhood, the captivity of Babylon."—Secker.

7. *For a small moment*—"In a little anger."

9. *For this is as the waters of Noah unto me* —"The same will I do now, as in the days of Noah."

11. *Behold, I will lay thy stones*—"Behold, I lay your stones." These seem to be general images to express beauty, magnificence, purity, strength, and solidity, agreeably to the ideas of the Eastern nations.

15. *Shall fall for thy sake*—"Shall come over to your side."

CHAPTER 55

This chapter first displays the fullness, freeness, excellence, and everlasting nature of the blessings of the gospel, and foretells again the enlargement of Messiah's kingdom, 1-5. This view leads the prophet to exhort all to seize the precious opportunity of sharing in such blessings, which were not, however, to be expected without repentance and reformation, 6-7. And as the things now and formerly predicted were so great as to appear incredible, the prophet points to the omnipotence of God, who would infallibly accomplish His word, and bring about those glorious deliverances which He had promised; the happy effects of which are again set forth by images beautiful and poetical in the highest degree, 8-13.

3. *I will make an everlasting covenant.* Heb., "I will cut the old or everlasting covenant sacrifice with you." That covenant sacrifice which was pointed out of old from the very beginning, and which is to last to the consummation of ages; viz., the Lamb of God that was slain from the foundation of the world. *The sure mercies of David.* That is, says Kimchi, "The Messiah," called here *David.*

6. *Seek ye the Lord while he may be found.* Rab. David. Kimchi gives the true sense of this passage: "Seek ye the Lord, because He

may be found: call upon Him, because he is near. Repent before ye die, for after death there is no conversion of the soul."

12. *The mountains and the hills.* These are highly poetical images to express a happy state attended with joy and exultation.

13. *Instead of the thorn*—"Instead of the thorny bushes." These likewise are general poetical images, expressing a great and happy change for the better. The wilderness turned into a paradise, Lebanon into Carmel; the desert of the Gentiles watered with the heavenly snow and rain, which fail not to have their due effect and becoming fruitful in piety and righteousness; or, as the Chaldee gives the moral sense of the emblem, "Instead of the wicked shall arise the just; and instead of sinners, such as fear to sin." Compare chap. xxxv. 1-2; xli. 19.

CHAPTER 56

Whoever would partake of the blessings of the gospel is required to be holy in all manner of life and conversation. And he that will be so is declared to be accepted according to this gracious dispensation, the blessings of which are large as the human race, without any respect to persons or to nations, 1-8. At the ninth verse begins a different subject, or new section of prophecy. It opens with calling on the enemies of the Jews (the Chaldeans, or perhaps the Romans), as beasts of prey against them, for the sins of their rulers, teachers, and other profane people among them, whose guilt drew down judgments on the nation, 9-12.

2. *That keepeth the sabbath from polluting it.* Kimchi has an excellent note here. "The Sabbath is sanctified when it is distinguished in dignity; and separated from other days."

6. *The sons of the stranger.* The Gentiles. *That join themselves to the Lord.* Who shall enter into the Christian covenant by baptism and faith in Christ, as the Jews and proselytes did by circumcision. *To serve him.* To live according to the gospel, and ever do that which is right in the sight of the Lord. *To love the name of the Lord.* The name of Jesus, the Christ, the Saviour of sinners, the Anointed of God, and the Giver of the Holy Spirit to His followers. *To be his servants.* To worship no other God but Jehovah, and to trust in none for salvation but His Christ. *That keepeth the sabbath.* That observes it as a type of the rest that remains for the people of God. *And taketh hold of my covenant.* "Of My covenant sacrifice," as without this he can do nothing good; and without it nothing can be acceptable to the infinite majesty of the Most High.

9. *All ye beasts of the field.* Here manifestly begins a new section. The prophet in the foregoing chapters, having comforted the faithful Jews with many great promises of God's favor to be extended to them, in the restoration of their ruined state, and in the enlargement of His Church by the admission of the Gentiles, here on a sudden makes a transition to the more disagreeable part of the prospect, and to a sharp reproof of the wicked and unbelievers; and especially of the negligent and faithless governors and teachers, of the idolaters and hypocrites, who would still draw down His judgments upon the nation, probably having in view the destruction of their city and polity by the Chaldeans, and perhaps by the Romans. The same subject is continued in the next chapter, in which the charge of corruption and apostasy becomes more general against the whole Jewish church.

11. *Greedy dogs.* Insatiably feeding themselves with the fat, and clothing themselves with the wool, while the flock is scattered, ravaged, and starved!

12. *I will fetch wine*—"Let us provide wine." The spirit of this epicurean sentiment is this: Let us indulge ourselves in the present time to the utmost, and instead of any gloomy forebodings of the future, let us expect nothing but increasing hilarity for every day we shall live.

CHAPTER 57

After mentioning the removal of righteous persons as an awful symptom of the approach of divine judgments, 1-2, the prophet goes on to charge the nation in general with idolatry, and with courting the unprofitable alliance of idolatrous kings, 3-12. In opposition to such vain confidence, the prophet enjoins trust in God, with whom the penitent and humble are sure to find acceptance, and from whom they should obtain temporal and spiritual deliverances, 13-19. Awful condition of the wicked and finally impenitent, 20-21.

I shall give Bishop Lowth's translation of the first two verses, and give the substance of his criticisms with additional evidence.

> "Ver. 1. The righteous man perisheth, and no one considereth;
> And pious men are taken away, and no one understandeth,
> That the righteous man is taken away because of the evil.
>
> "2. He shall go in peace: he shall rest in his bed;
> Even the perfect man: he that walketh in the straight path."

1. *The righteous perisheth.* There is an emphasis here which seems intended to point out a particular person. *Perisheth*—As the root *abad* signifies the straying of cattle, their passing away from one pasture to another, I feel inclined to follow the grammatical meaning of the word "perish," *pereo.* So the Vulgate, *justus periit,* from *per,* "by" or "through," and *eo,* to "go." In his death the righteous man may be said to have passed "through" life, and to have passed by men, i.e., gone or passed before them into the eternal world. There are very few places in Isaiah where Jesus Christ is not intended; and I am inclined to think that He is intended here, that Just One; and perhaps Stephen had this place in view when he thus charged the Jews, "Ye denied the Holy One and the Just," Acts iii. 14. *Merciful men.* If the first refers to Christ, this may well refer to the apostles, and to others of the primitive Christians, who were *taken away,* some by death and martyrdom, and others by a providential escape from the city that they knew was devoted to destruction. *The evil to come.* That destruction which was to come upon this disobedient people by the Romans.

2. *He shall enter into peace*—"He shall go in peace." *Yabo shalom;* the expression is elliptical, such as the prophet frequently uses. The same sense is expressed at large and in full terms, Gen. xv. 15: "And thou shalt go to thy fathers in peace." *They shall rest in their beds, each one walking in his uprightness*—"He shall rest in his bed; even the perfect man." To follow on my application of this to our Lord: He, the Just One, *shall enter into peace*—the peaceable, prosperous possession of the glorious mediatorial Kingdom. *They shall rest in their*

beds—the hand of wrong and oppression can reach these persecuted followers of Christ no more. The perfect man *walking in his uprightness*. This may be considered as a general declaration. The separated spirit, though disunited from its body, walking in conscious existence in the paradise of God, reaping the fruit of righteousness.

6. *Among the smooth stones of the stream*—"Among the smooth stones of the valley." The Jews were extremly addicted to the practice of many superstitious and idolatrous rites, which the prophet here inveighs against with great vehemence. Of the worship of rude stones consecrated, there are many testimonials of the ancients. Kimchi says: "When they found a beautiful polished stone in a brook or river, they paid divine adoration to it."

8. *Behind the doors also and the posts hast thou set up thy remembrance*—"Behind the door, and the doorposts, have you set up your memorial." That is, the image of their tutelary gods, or something dedicated to them; in direct opposition to the law of God, which commanded them to write upon the doorposts of their house, and upon their gates, the words of God's law (Deut. vi. 9; xi. 20). If they chose for them such a situation as more private, it was in defiance of a particular curse denounced in the law against the man who should make a graven or a molten image, and put it in a secret place (Deut. xxvii. 15).

9. *And thou wentest to the king with ointment*—"And you have visited the king with a present of oil." That is, the king of Assyria, or Egypt. Hosea, chap. xii. 1, reproaches the Israelites for the same practice: "They do make a covenant with the Assyrians, and oil is carried into Egypt."

10. *Yet saidst thou not, There is no hope*—"You have said, There is hope." Now if we compare Jer. ii. 25 and xviii. 12, we shall find that the subject is in both places quite the same with this of Isaiah; and the sentiment expressed, that of a desperate resolution to continue at all hazards in their idolatrous practices—the very thing that in all reason we might expect here.

11. *Nor laid it to thy heart*—"Nor revolved it in your hand." *Even of old*—"And winked." "As if not seeing," Vulgate. See Ps. x. 1. In one of my own MSS., "Is it not because I was silent, and winked?"

12. *Thy righteousness*—"My righteousness."

13. *Let thy companies deliver thee*—"Let your associates deliver you."

14. *And shall say*—"Then will I say." They are the words of God, as it is plain from the conclusion of the verse: *my people*.

16. *For I will not contend for ever.* The learned have taken a great deal of pains to little purpose on the latter part of this verse, which they suppose to be very obscure. I think the best and easiest explication of it is given in the two following passages of the Psalms, which I presume are exactly parallel to it, and very clearly express the same sentiment: Ps. lxxviii. 38-39; ciii. 9, 13-14. *For the spirit. Ruach*, "the animal life." *And the souls. Neshamoth*, "the immortal spirits." The Targum understands this of the resurrection. "I will restore the souls of the dead," i.e., to their bodies.

17. *For the iniquity of his covetousness was I wroth*—"Because of his iniquity for a short time was I wroth."

18. *I have seen his ways.* Probably these verses refer to the restoration of the Jews from captivity.

19. *I create the fruit of the lips.* "The sacrifice of praise," saith St. Paul, Heb. xiii. 15, is "the fruit of our lips." God creates this fruit of the lips by giving new subject and cause of thanksgiving by His mercies conferred on those among His people who acknowledge and bewail their transgressions and return to Him. The great subject of thanksgiving is peace—reconciliation and pardon, offered to them that are nigh and to them that are afar off; not only to the Jew, but also to the Gentile, as St. Paul more than once applies those terms (Eph. ii. 13, 17). See also Acts ii. 39. *Peace to him that is far off*—"That is, to the penitent; *and to him that is near*, i.e., the righteous."—Kimchi.

21. *There is no peace, saith my God.* This verse has reference to the nineteenth. The perseveringly wicked and impenitent are excluded from all share in that peace above mentioned, that reconcilement and pardon which is promised to the penitent only. The forty-eighth chapter ends with the same declaration, to express the exclusion of the unbelievers and impenitent from the benefit of the foregoing promises.

CHAPTER 58

This elegant chapter contains a severe reproof of the Jews on account of their vices, particularly their hypocrisy in practicing and relying on outward ceremonies, such as fasting and bodily humiliation, without true repentance, 1-5. It then lays down a clear and comprehensive summary of the duties they owed to their fellow creatures, 6-7. Large promises of happiness and prosperity are likewise annexed to the performance of these duties in a variety of the most beautiful and striking images, 8-12. Great temporal and spiritual blessedness of those who keep holy the Sabbath day, 13-14.

1. *Cry aloud, spare not.* Never was a louder cry against the hypocrisy, nor a more cutting reproof of the wickedness, of a people professing a national established religion, having all the forms of godliness without a particle of its power.

3. *Have we afflicted our soul*—"Have we afflicted our souls." *In the day of your fast ye find pleasure.* Fast days are generally called holidays, and holidays are days of idleness and pleasure. In numberless cases the fast is turned into a feast. *And exact all your labours.* Some disregard the most sacred fast, and will oblige their servant to work all day long; others use fast days for the purpose of settling their accounts, posting up their books, and drawing out their bills to be ready to collect their debts. These are sneaking hypocrites; the others are daringly irreligious.

4. *To smite with the fist of wickedness: ye shall not fast as ye do this day*—"To smite with the fist the poor. Wherefore fast ye unto Me in this manner?"

8. *And thine health shall spring forth speedily*—"And your wounds shall speedily be healed over."

11. *And make fat thy bones*—"And he shall renew your strength."

12. *The restorer of paths to dwell in*—"The

restorer of paths to be frequented by inhabitants."

13. *If thou turn away thy foot from the sabbath.* The meaning of this seems to be that they should be careful not to take their pleasure on the Sabbath day, by paying visits, and taking country jaunts; not going, as Kimchi interprets it, more than a Sabbath day's journey, which was only 2,000 cubits beyond the city's suburbs. How vilely is this rule transgressed by the inhabitants of this land! They seem to think that the Sabbath was made only for their recreation! *Nor speaking thine own words* —"From speaking vain words."

CHAPTER 59

This chapter contains a more general reproof of the wickedness of the Jews, 1-8. After this they are represented confessing their sins, and deploring the unhappy consequences of them, 9-15. On this act of humiliation God, ever ready to pardon the penitent, promises that He will have mercy on them; that the Redeemer will come, mighty to save; and that He will deliver His people, subdue His enemies, and establish a new and everlasting covenant, 16-21.

The foregoing elegant chapter contained a severe reproof of the Jews, in particular for their hypocrisy in pretending to make themselves accepted with God by fasting and outward humiliation without true repentance; while they still continued to oppress the poor, and indulge their own passions and vices; with great promises however of God's favor on condition of their reformation. This chapter contains a more general reproof of their wickedness, bloodshed, violence, falsehood, injustice. At v. 9 they are introduced as making an ample confession of their sins, and deploring their wretched state in consequence of them. On this act of humiliation a promise is given that God, in His mercy and zeal for His people, will rescue them from this miserable condition; that the Redeemer will come like a mighty Hero to deliver them; He will destroy His enemies, convert both Jews and Gentiles to himself, and give them a new covenant, and a law which shall never be abolished.

4. *They conceive mischief, and bring forth iniquity.* There is a curious propriety in this mode of expression. A thought or purpose is compared to conception; a word or act, which is the consequence of it, to the birth of a child. From the third to the fifteenth verse inclusive may be considered a true statement of the then moral state of the Jewish people; and that they were, in the most proper sense of the word, guilty of the iniquities with which they are charged.

10. *We stumble at noon day as in the night*— "We stumble at midday, as in the twilight."

16. *And wondered that there was no intercessor.* This and the following verses some of the most eminent rabbins understand as spoken of the Messiah.

18. *According to their deeds, accordingly he will repay*—"He is mighty to recompense; He that is mighty to recompense will requite."

19. *When the enemy shall come in like a flood.* This all the rabbins refer to the coming of the Messiah. If you see a generation which endures much tribulation, then (say they) expect Him, according to what is written: *When the enemy shall come in like a flood, the spirit of the Lord shall lift up a standard against him.*

20. *Unto them that turn from transgression in Jacob*—"And shall turn away iniquity from Jacob." So the Septuagint and St. Paul, Rom. xi. 26.

21. *My spirit that is upon thee.* This seems to be an address to the Messiah. *And my words which I have put in thy mouth.* Whatsoever Jesus spoke was the word and mind of God himself; and must, as such, be implicitly received. *Nor out of the mouth of thy seed.* The same doctrines which Jesus preached, all His faithful ministers preach; and His seed, genuine Christians who are all born of God, believe; and they shall continue, and the doctrines remain in the seed's seed through all generations, for ever and ever. This is God's covenant, ordered in all things and sure.

CHAPTER 60

The glorious prospect displayed in this chapter seems to have elevated the prophet even above his usual majesty. The subject is the very flourishing condition of the Church of Jesus Christ at that period of the gospel dispensation when both Jews and Gentiles shall become one fold under one Shepherd. The imagery employed is of the most consolatory and magnificent description. This blessed state of the world shall follow a time of gross darkness, 1-2. The universal diffusion of vital godliness beautifully set forth by a great variety of images, 3-14. The everlasting duration and spotless purity of this kingdom of Christ, 15-21. A time appointed in the counsels of Jehovah for the commencement of this happy period; and when this time arrives, the particulars of the prophecy shall have a speedy accomplishment, 22.

The subject of this chapter is the great increase and flourishing state of the Church of God by the conversion and accession of the heathen nations to it, which is set forth in such ample and exalted terms as plainly show that the full completion of this prophecy is reserved for future times. This subject is displayed in the most splendid colors under a great variety of images highly poetical, designed to give a general idea of the glories of that perfect state of the Church of God which we are taught to expect in the latter times; when the fullness of the Gentiles shall come in, and the Jews shall be converted and gathered from their dispersions, and the kingdoms of this world shall become the kingdoms of our Lord and of His Christ.

1. *Arise.* Call upon God through Christ, for His salvation; and *shine. Ori,* "be illuminated"; for till you arise and call upon God you will never receive true light. *For thy light is come.* "For your light cometh." The Messiah is at the door; who, while He is a Light to lighten the Gentiles, will be *the glory*—the effulgence—of His people Israel.

2. *Darkness shall cover the earth.* This is the state of the Gentile people.

3. *And the Gentiles shall come.* This has been in some sort already fulfilled. The Gentiles have received the light of the gospel from the land of Judea, and the Gentile kings have embraced that gospel, so that many nations of the earth are full of the doctrine of Christ.

4. *Shall be nursed at thy side*—"Shall be carried at the side."

5. *Then thou shalt see*—"Then shall you fear."

8. *And as the doves to their windows?*—"And like doves upon the wing?"

9. *The ships of Tarshish first*—"The ships of Tarshish among the first."

13. *And I will make the place of my feet glorious*—"And that I may glorify the place whereon I rest my feet." The temple of Jerusalem was called the house of God, and the place of His rest or residence. The visible symbolical appearance of God, called by the Jews the Shekinah, was in the most holy place, between the wings of the cherubim, above the ark. This is considered as the throne of God, presiding as King over the Jewish state; and as a footstool is a necessary appendage to a throne, the ark is considered as the footstool of God, and is so called, Ps. xcix. 5; 1 Chron. xxviii. 2. *The glory of Lebanon.* That is, the cedar.

19. *Neither for brightness shall the moon give light unto thee*—"Nor by night shall the brightness of the moon enlighten you."

22. *I the Lord will hasten it in his time.* There is a time set for the fulfillment of this prophecy. That time must come before it begins to take place; but when it does begin, the whole will be performed in a short space.

CHAPTER 61

The subject of the preceding chapter is continued in this; and to give it the greater solemnity, the Messiah is introduced, describing His character and office, and confirming the large promises made before, 1-9. In consequence of this the Jewish church is introduced, praising God for the honor done her by her restoration to favor, and by the accession of the Gentiles, which is beautifully described by allusions to the rich, pontifical dress of the high priest—a happy similitude to express the ornaments of a restored nation and of a renewed mind, 10. Certainty of the prophecy illustrated by a figure drawn from the vegetable kingdom, 11.

1. *The Spirit of the Lord God is upon me*—"The Spirit of Jehovah is upon Me." The Septuagint, Vulgate, and St. Luke (chap. iv. 18) omit the word *Adonai*, "the Lord," which was probably added to the text through the superstition of the Jews, to prevent the pronunciation of the word *Yehovah* following. In most of Isaiah's prophecies there is a primary and secondary sense, or a remote subject illustrated by one that is near. The deliverance of the Jews from their captivity in Babylon is constantly used to shadow forth the salvation of men by Jesus Christ. Even the prophet himself is a typical person, and is sometimes intended to represent the great Saviour. It is evident from Luke iv. 18 that this is a prophecy of our blessed Lord and His preaching; and yet it is as evident that it primarily refers to Isaiah preaching the glad tidings of deliverance to the Jews. *The opening of the prison*—"Perfect liberty." Not merely opening of prisons, but every kind of liberty—complete redemption. The proclaiming of perfect liberty to the bound, and the year of acceptance with Jehovah, is a manifest allusion to the proclaiming of the year of jubilee by sound of trumpet. See Lev. xxv. 9, etc. This was a year of general release of debts and obligations, of bondmen and bondwomen, of lands and possessions which had been sold from the families and tribes to which they belonged. Our Saviour, by applying this text to himself (Luke iv. 18-19), a text so manifestly relating to the institution above mentioned, plainly declares the typical design of that institution.

3. *To appoint unto them that mourn in Zion*—"To impart gladness to the mourners of Zion." *Beauty for ashes*—"A beautiful crown instead of ashes." In times of mourning the Jews put on sackcloth, and spread dust and ashes on their heads; on the contrary, splendid clothing and ointment poured on the head were the signs of joy. *Trees of righteousness*—"Trees approved." Hebrew, "oaks of righteousness or truth"; that is, such as by their flourishing condition should show that they were indeed of God's planting.

4. *The desolations of many generations.* It seems that these words cannot refer to the Jews in the Babylonish captivity, for they were not there many generations. But it may refer to their dispersions and state of ruin since the advent of our Lord, and consequently this may be a promise of the restoration of the Jewish people.

5. *Strangers shall . . . feed your flocks.* Gentiles shall first preach to you the salvation of Christ, and feed with divine knowledge the Jewish congregations.

7. *For your shame*—"Instead of your shame."

8. *I hate robbery for burnt offering*—"Who hate rapine and iniquity." The difference lies in the punctuation; *beolah*, "in a burnt offering"; *beavelah*, "in iniquity." The letters are the same in both words.

9. *Their seed shall be known among the Gentiles.* Both Jews and Gentiles are to make but one fold under one Shepherd, Christ Jesus. But still, notwithstanding this, they may retain their peculiarity and national distinction; so that though they are known to be Christians, yet they shall appear to be converted Jews.

10. *I will greatly rejoice in the Lord.* These may be the words of the Jews now converted, and brought into the Church of Christ, and with the Gentiles made fellow heirs of the blessings of the new covenant. *As a bridegroom decketh himself with ornaments*—"As the bridegroom decketh himself with a priestly crown." An allusion to the magnificent dress of the high priest, when performing his functions; and particularly to the mitre, and crown or plate of gold on the front of it, Exod. xxix. 6. The bonnet or mitre of the priests also was made, as Moses expresses it, "for glory and for beauty," Exod. xxviii. 40.

CHAPTER 62

The prophet opens this chapter with ardent prayers that the happy period of reconciliation just now promised, and here again foretold, may be hastened, 1-5. He then calls upon the faithful, particularly the priests and Levites, to join him, urging the promises, and even the oath, of Jehovah, as the foundation of their request, 6-9. And, relying on this oath, he goes on to speak of the general restoration promised, as already performing; and calls to the people to march forth, and to the various nations among whom they are dispersed to prepare the way for them, as God had caused the order for their return to be universally proclaimed, 10-12.

1. *For Zion's sake will I not hold my peace.* These are the words of Jehovah declaring His purpose relative to the events predicted in the preceding chapter.

4. *Thy land Beulah. Beulah*, "married." In the prophets, a desolate land is represented under the notion of a widow; an inhabited land, under that of a married woman, who has both a husband and children.

6. *Ye that make mention of the Lord, keep not silence.* The faithful, and in particular the

priests and Levites, are exhorted by the prophet to beseech God with unremitted importunity to hasten the redemption of Sion. The image in this place is taken from the Temple service, in which there was appointed a constant watch, day and night, by the Levites; and among them this seems to have belonged particularly to the singers, see 1 Chron. ix. 33. Now the watches in the East, even to this day, are performed by a loud cry from time to time of the watchmen, to mark the time, and that very frequently, and in order to show that they themselves are constantly attentive to their duty. Hence the watchmen are said by the prophet, chap. lii. 8, to lift up their voice; and here they are commanded not to keep silence; and the greatest reproach to them is that they are "dumb dogs, they cannot bark"; dreamers; sluggards, "loving to slumber," chap. lvi. 10.

9. *But they that have gathered it shall eat it, and praise the Lord.* This and the following line have reference to the law of Moses: "Thou mayest not eat within thy gates the tithe of thy corn, or of thy wine, or of thy oil . . . but thou must eat them before the Lord thy God, in the place which the Lord thy God shall choose," Deut. xii. 17-18. "And when ye shall come into the land, and shall have planted all manner of trees for food, then ye shall count the fruit thereof as uncircumcised: three years it shall be as uncircumcised unto you; it shall not be eaten of. But . . . in the fifth year shall ye eat of the fruit thereof," Lev. xix. 23-25.

11. *Behold, thy salvation cometh*—"Lo, thy Saviour cometh." *Behold, his reward.* See note on chap. xl. 10-11. This reward He carries as it were in His hand. *His work* [is] *before him*— He perfectly knows what is to be done, and is perfectly able to do it.

CHAPTER 63

The prophet (or rather the Church he represents) sees the great Deliverer, long promised and expected, making His appearance, after having crushed His enemies, like grapes in the wine vat. The comparison suggests a lively idea of the wrath of Omnipotence, which its unhappy objects can no more resist than the grapes can resist the treader. Indeed, there is so much pathos, energy, and sublimity in this remarkable passage as hardly anything can be conceived to exceed. The period to which it refers must be the same with that predicted in the nineteenth chapter of the Revelation, some parts of which are expressed in the same terms with this, and plainly enough refer to the very sudden and total overthrow of Antichrist, and of all his adherents and auxiliaries, of which the destruction of Babylon, the capital of Chaldea, and of Bozrah, the chief city of the Edomites, was the prototype, 1-6. At the seventh verse commences a penitential confession and supplication of the Jews, as uttered in their present dispersion, 7-19.

1. *Who is this that cometh from Edom?* Probably both *Edom* and *Bozrah* are only figurative expressions, to point out the place in which God should discomfit His enemies. Edom signifies "red," and Bozrah, "a vintage." *I that speak in righteousness*—"I who publish righteousness."

3. *And of the people there was none with me.* I was wholly abandoned by them. But a good meaning is, No man has had any part in making the atonement; it is entirely the work of the Messiah alone. No created being could have any part in a sacrifice that was to be of infinite merit. *And I will stain*—"And I have stained."

5. *And my fury*—"And mine indignation."

6. *And make them drunk in my fury*—"And I crushed them in Mine indignation."

7. *I will mention the lovingkindnesses of the Lord.* The prophet connects the preceding mercies of God to the Jews with the present prospect he has of their redemption by the Messiah, thus making a circle in which eternal goodness revolves. The remaining part of this chapter, with the whole chapter following, contains a penitential confession and supplication of the Israelites in their present state of dispersion, in which they have so long marvellously subsisted, and still continue to subsist, as a people; cast out of their country; without any proper form of civil polity or religious worship; their Temple destroyed, their city desolated and lost to them, and their whole nation scattered over the face of the earth, apparently deserted and cast off by the God of their fathers, as no longer His peculiar people. They begin with acknowledging God's great mercies and favors to their nation, and the ungrateful returns made to them on their part, that by their disobedience they had forfeited the protection of God, and had caused Him to become their Adversary. And now the prophet represents them, enduced by the memory of the great things that God had done for them, as addressing their humble supplication for the renewal of His mercies. They beseech Him to regard them in consideration of his former loving-kindness; they acknowledge Him for their Father and Creator; they confess their wickedness and hardness of heart; they entreat His forgiveness, and deplore their present miserable condition under which they have so long suffered. It seems designed as a formulary of humiliation for the Israelites, in order to their conversion.

8-9. *So he was their Saviour. In all their affliction*—"And He became their Saviour in all their distress." An *angel of his presence* means an angel of superior order, in immediate attendance upon God. So the angel of the Lord says to Zacharias, "I am Gabriel, that stand in the presence of God," Luke i. 19.

11. *Moses, and his people*—"Moses his servant." *Where is he that brought them up out of the sea with the shepherd of his flock? where,* etc.?—"How he brought them up from the sea, with the shepherd of His flock; how," etc. *The shepherd of his flock.* That is, Moses.

13-14. *That led them through the deep . . . As a beast goeth down into the valley.* In these verses there is an allusion to the Israelites going through the Red Sea, in the bottom of which they found no more inconvenience than a horse would in running in the desert, where there was neither stone nor mud; nor a beast in the valley, where all was plain and smooth. *The Spirit of the Lord caused him to rest*—"The Spirit of Jehovah conducted them."

15. *And thy strength*—"And Thy mighty power."

16. *Our redeemer; thy name is from everlasting*—"Oh, deliver us for the sake of Thy name."

17. *Why hast thou made us to err?* A mere Hebraism for Why hast Thou permitted us to err?

18. *The people of thy holiness have possessed it but a little while*—"It is little that they have taken possession of Thy holy mountain."

CHAPTER 64

The whole of this chapter, which is very pathetic and tender, may be considered as a formulary of prayer and humiliation intended for the Jews in order to their conversion, 1-12.

1. *Oh, that thou wouldest rend the heavens—* This seems to allude to the wonderful manifestation of God upon Mount Sinai.

2. *As when the melting fire burneth—*"As the fire kindleth the dry fuel."

4. *For since the beginning of the world men have not heard.* I would read the whole verse thus: "Yea, from the time of old they have not heard, they have not hearkened to, an eye hath not seen a God besides Thee. He shall work for that one that waiteth for Him." This I really think on the whole to be the best translation of the original.

5. *Thou meetest him that rejoiceth and worketh righteousness—*"Thou meetest with joy those who work righteousness." *In those is continuance, and we shall be saved.* "Thou art wroth, for we have sinned in them [Thy ways] of old; and can we be saved?"

7. *And hast consumed us, because of our iniquities—*"And hast delivered us up into the hands of our iniquities."

CHAPTER 65

We have here a vindication of God's dealings with the Jews, 1-2. To this end the prophet points out their great hypocrisy, and gives a particular enumeration of their dreadful abominations, many of which were committed under the specious guise of sanctity, 3-5. For their horrid impieties (recorded in writing before Jehovah) the wrath of God shall certainly come upon them to the uttermost; a prediction which was exactly fulfilled in the first and second centuries in the reigns of the Roman emperors Vespasian, Titus, and Hadrian, when the whole Jewish polity was dissolved, and the people dispersed all over the world, 6-7. Though God had rejected the Jews, and called the Gentiles, who sought Him not (Rom. ix. 24-26), yet a remnant from among the former shall be preserved, to whom He will in due time make good all His promises, 8-10. Denunciation of divine vengeance against those idolaters who set in order a table for Gad, and fill out a libation to Meni, ancient idolatries, which, from the context, and from the chronological order of the events predicted, have a plain reference to the idolatries practiced by Antichrist under the guise of Christianity, 11-12. Dreadful fate which awaits these gross idolaters beautifully contrasted with the great blessedness reserved for the righteous, 13-16. Future restoration of the posterity of Jacob, and the happy state of the world in general from that most glorious epoch, represented by the strong figure of the creation of new heavens and a new earth, wherein dwelleth righteousness, and into which no distress shall be permitted to enter, 17-19. In this new state of things the term of human life shall be greatly protracted, and shall possess none of that uncertainty which attaches to it in "the heavens and the earth which are now." This is elegantly illustrated by the longevity of a tree; manifestly alluding to the oak or cedar of Lebanon, some individuals of which are known to have lived from seven to ten centuries, 20-23. Beautiful figures shadowing forth the profound peace and harmony of the Church of Jesus Christ, which shall immediately follow the total overthrow of Antichrist; with a most gracious promise that the great chain of Omnipotence shall be put upon every adversary, so that none will be able any longer to hurt and destroy in all God's holy mountain, 24-25.

This chapter contains a defense of God's proceedings in regard to the Jews, with reference to their complaint in the chapter preceding. God is introduced, declaring that He had called the Gentiles, though they had not sought Him; and had rejected His own people for their refusal to attend to His repeated call; for their obstinate disobedience, their idolatrous practices, and detestable hypocrisy. That nevertheless He would not destroy them all, but would preserve a remnant, to whom He would make good His ancient promises. Severe punishments are threatened to the apostates, and great rewards are promised to the obedient in a future flourishing state of the Church.

1. *I am sought of them that asked not for me—*"I am made known to those that asked not for Me."

3. *That sacrificeth in gardens, and burneth incense upon altars of brick—*"Sacrificing in the gardens, and burning incense on the tiles." These are instances of heathenish superstition, and idolatrous practices, to which the Jews were immoderately addicted before the Babylonish captivity. The heathen worshipped their idols in groves; whereas God, in opposition to this species of idolatry, commanded His people, when they should come into the Promised Land, to destroy all the places wherein the Canaanites had served their gods, and in particular to burn their groves with fire, Deut. xii. 2-3. These apostate Jews sacrificed upon altars built of bricks, in opposition to the command of God in regard to His altar, which was to be of unhewn stone, Exod. xx. 25.

4. *In the monuments—*"In the caverns." *Which eat swine's flesh.* This was expressly forbidden by the law, Lev. xi. 7, but among the heathen was in principal request in their sacrifices and feasts. Antiochus Epiphanes compelled the Jews to eat swine's flesh, as a full proof of their renouncing their religion, 2 Mac. vi. 18 and vii. 1.

6. *Behold, it is written before me.* Their sin is registered in heaven, calling aloud for the punishment due to it.

7. *Your iniquities, and the iniquities of your fathers—*"Their iniquities, and the iniquities of their fathers."

8. *A blessing is in it.* The Hebrews call all things which serve for food *berachah*, "a blessing."

9. *An inheritor of my mountains—*"An inheritor of My mountain."

10. *Sharon . . . and the valley of Achor.* Two of the most fertile parts of Judea, famous for their rich pastures: the former to the west, not far from Joppa; the latter north of Jericho, near Gilgal.

11. *That prepare a table for that troop—*"Who set in order a table for Gad." The disquisitions and conjectures of the learned concerning Gad and Meni are infinite and uncertain; perhaps the most probable may be that Gad means good fortune, and Meni the moon.

12. *Therefore will I number you.* Referring to *Meni*, which signifies "number."

15. *Shall slay thee—*"Shall slay you."

17. *I create new heavens and a new earth.* This has been variously understood. Some Jews and some Christians understand it literally. God shall change the state of the atmosphere and render the earth more fruitful. Some refer it to what they call the millennium; others, to a glorious state of religion; others, to the re-creation of the earth after it shall have been destroyed by fire. I think it refers to the full conversion of the Jews ultimately, and primarily to the deliverance from the Babylonish captivity.

18. *Rejoice for ever in that which I create—* "Exult in the age to come which I create."

22. *They shall not build, and another inhabit.*

The reverse of the curse denounced on the disobedient, Deut. xxviii. 30: "Thou shalt build an house, and thou shalt not dwell therein: thou shalt plant a vineyard, and shalt not gather the grapes thereof." *For as the days of a tree.* It is commonly supposed that the oak, one of the most long-lived of the trees, lasts about a thousand years.

23. *They shall not labour in vain*—"My chosen shall not labor in vain." *Nor bring forth for trouble*—"Neither shall they generate a short-lived race."

CHAPTER 66

This chapter treats of the same subject with the foregoing. God, by His prophet, tells the Jews, who valued themselves much on their Temple and pompous worship, that the Most High dwelleth not in temples made with hands; and that no outward rites of worship, while the worshippers are idolatrous and impure, can please Him who looketh at the heart, 1-3. This leads to a threatening of vengeance for their guilt, alluding to their making void the law of God by their abominable traditions, their rejection of Christ, persecution of His followers, and consequent destruction by the Romans. But as the Jewish ritual and people shadow forth the system of Christianity and its professors, so, in the prophetical writings, the idolatries of the Jews are frequently put for the idolatries afterwards practiced by those bearing the Christian name. Consequently, if we would have the plenitude of meaning in this section of prophecy which the very context requires, we must look through the type into the antitype, viz., the very gross idolatries practiced by the members of Antichrist, the pompous heap of human inventions and traditions with which they have encumbered the Christian system, their most dreadful persecution of Christ's spiritual and true worshippers, and the awful judgments which shall overtake them in the great and terrible day of the Lord, 4-6. The mighty and sudden increase of the Church of Jesus Christ at the period of Antichrist's fall represented by the very strong figure of Sion being delivered of a man-child before the time of her travail, the meaning of which symbol the prophet immediately subjoins in a series of interrogations for the sake of greater force and emphasis, 7-9. Wonderful prosperity and unspeakable blessedness of the world when the posterity of Jacob, with the fullness of the Gentiles, shall be assembled to Messiah's standard, 10-14. All the wicked of the earth shall be gathered together to the battle of that great day of God Almighty, and the slain of Jehovah shall be many, 15-18. Manner of the future restoration of the Israelites from their several dispersions throughout the habitable globe, 19-21. Perpetuity of this new economy of grace to the house of Israel, 22. Righteousness shall be universally diffused in the earth, and the memory of those who have transgressed against the Lord shall be had in continual abhorrence, 23-24. Thus this great prophet, after tracing the principal events of time, seems at length to have terminated his views in eternity, where all revolutions cease, where the blessedness of the righteous shall be unchangeable as the new heavens, and the misery of the wicked as the fire that shall not be quenched.

This chapter is a continuation of the subject of the foregoing. The Jews valued themselves much upon their Temple, and the pompous system of services performed in it, which they supposed were to be of perpetual duration; and they assumed great confidence and merit to themselves for their strict observance of all the externals of their religion. These two chapters manifestly relate to the calling of the Gentiles, the establishment of the Christian dispensation, and the reprobation of the apostate Jews, and their destruction executed by the Romans.

2. *And all those things have been*—"And all these things are Mine." A word absolutely necessary to the sense is here lost out of the text: "Mine." It is preserved by the Septuagint and Syriac.

3. *He that killeth an ox is as if he slew a man*—"He that slayeth an ox killeth a man." These are instances of wickedness joined with hypocrisy, of the most flagitious crimes committed by those who at the same time affected great strictness in the performance of all the external services of religion. God, by the prophet Ezekiel, upbraids the Jews with the same practices: "When they had slain their children to their idols, then they came the same day into my sanctuary to profane it," chap. xxiii. 39. Of the same kind was the hypocrisy of the Pharisees in our Saviour's time, who "devour widows' houses, and for a pretence make long prayers," Matt. xxiii. 14. *He that offereth an oblation, as if he offered swine's blood*—"That maketh an oblation offereth swine's blood."

5. *Your brethren that hated you . . . said*—"Say to your brethren that hate you."

6. *A voice of noise from the city, a voice from the temple, a voice of the Lord.* It is very remarkable that similar words were spoken by Jesus, son of Ananias, previously to the destruction of Jerusalem. See his very affecting history related by Josephus *War,* B. vi, chap. v.

11. *With the abundance of her glory*—"From her abundant stores."

12. *Like a river, and . . . like a flowing stream*—"Like the great river, and like the overflowing stream." That is, the Euphrates.

15. *The Lord will come with fire*—"Jehovah shall come as a fire." For *baesh,* "in fire," the Septuagint had in their copy *kaesh,* "as a fire." *To render his anger with fury*—"To breathe forth His anger in a burning heat." Instead of *lehashib,* as pointed by the Masoretes, "to render," I understand it as *lehashshib,* "to breathe."

17. *Behind one tree*—"After the rites of Achad." The Syrians worshipped a god called Adad, Plin. *Nat. Hist.* xxxvii. 11. They held him to be the highest and greatest of the gods, and to be the same with Jupiter and the sun.

18. *For I know their works.* The concluding verses of this chapter refer to the complete restoration of the Jews, and to the destruction of all the enemies of the gospel of Christ, so that the earth shall be filled with the knowledge and glory of the Lord. *It shall come*—"And I come."

19. *That draw the bow.* I much suspect that the words "that draw the bow" are a corruption of the word "Moschi," the name of a nation situated between the Euxine and Caspian seas. *That have not heard my fame*—"Who never heard My name." For *shimi,* "my fame," I read, with the Septuagint and Syriac, *shemi,* "My name."

24. *For their worm shall not die.* These words of the prophet are applied by our blessed Saviour, Mark ix. 44, to express the everlasting punishment of the wicked in Gehenna, or in hell. Gehenna, or the Valley of Hinnom, was very near to Jerusalem to the southeast. It was the place where the idolatrous Jews celebrated that horrible rite of making their children pass through the fire, that is, of burning them in sacrifice to Moloch. To put a stop to this abominable practice, Josiah defiled, or desecrated, the place, by filling it with human bones, 2 Kings xxiii. 10, 14; and probably it was the custom afterwards to throw out the carcasses of animals there, when it also became the common burying place for the poorer people of Jerusalem.

The Book of

JEREMIAH

The Prophet Jeremiah, son of Hilkiah, was of the sacerdotal race, and a native of Anathoth, a village in the tribe of Benjamin, within a few miles of Jerusalem, which had been appointed for the use of the priests, the descendants of Aaron, Josh. xxi. 18. He was called to the prophetic office when very young; probably when he was fourteen years of age, and in the thirteenth of the reign of Josiah, 629 B.C. He continued to prophesy till after the destruction of Jerusalem by the Chaldeans, and it is supposed that about two years afterward he died in Egypt. Thus it appears that he discharged the arduous duties of the prophetic office for upwards of forty years.

His attachment to his country was strong and fervent; he foresaw by the light of prophecy the ruin that was coming upon it. He might have made terms with the enemy, and not only saved his life, but gained ease and plenty; but he chose rather to continue with his people, and take his part in all the disasters that befell them.

After the destruction of Jerusalem, Nebuchadnezzar having made Gedaliah governor of Judea, the fractious Jews rose up against him, and put him to death. They then escaped to Tahpanhes in Egypt, carrying Jeremiah with them, who, continuing to testify against their wickedness and idolatry, at length fell a victim to his faithfulness. They filled up the measure of their iniquity, as tradition reports, by stoning the prophet to death. God marked this murderous outrage by His peculiar displeasure; for in a few years after they were almost all miserably destroyed by the Chaldean armies which had invaded Egypt; and even this destruction had been foretold by the prophet himself, chap. xliv: "They shall be consumed by the sword and by the famine, until there be an end of them," a small remnant only escaping, vv. 14, 27-28.

It has often been remarked that, although several of the prophecies in this book have their dates distinctly noted, and most of the rest may be ascertained from collateral evidence, yet there is a strange disorder in the arrangement.

CHAPTER 1

General title to the whole book, 1-3. Jeremiah receives a commission to prophesy concerning nations and kingdoms, a work to which in the divine purpose he had been appointed before his birth, 4-10. The vision of the rod of an almond tree and of the seething pot, with their signification, 11-16. Promises of divine protection to Jeremiah in the discharge of the arduous duties of his prophetical office, 17-19.

1-3. *The words of Jeremiah.* These three verses are the title of the book, and were probably added by Ezra when he collected and arranged the sacred books, and put them in that order in which they are found in Hebrew Bibles in general. *Eleventh year of Zedekiah.* That is, the last year of his reign; for he was made prisoner by the Chaldeans in the fourth month of that year, and the carrying away of the inhabitants of Jerusalem was in the fifth month of the same year.

4. *The word of the Lord came unto me.* Then I first felt the inspiring influence of the Divine Spirit, not only revealing to me the subjects which He would have me to declare to the people, but also the words which I should use in these declarations.

5. *Before I formed thee.* I had destined you to the prophetic office before you were born. I had formed My plan, and appointed you to be My envoy to his people. St. Paul speaks of his own call to preach the gospel to the Gentiles in similar terms, Gal. i. 15-16.

6. *I cannot speak.* Being very young, and wholly inexperienced, I am utterly incapable of conceiving aright, or of clothing these divine subjects in suitable language. Those who are really called of God to the sacred ministry are such as have been brought to a deep acquaintance with themselves, feel their own ignorance, and know their own weakness. They know also the awful responsibility that attaches to the work, and nothing but the authority of God can induce such to undertake it.

7. *Whatsoever I command thee.* It is My words and message, not your own, that you shall deliver. I shall teach you; therefore your youth and inexperience can be no hindrance.

8. *Be not afraid of their faces.* That is, the Jews, whom he knew would persecute him because of the message which he brought. To be forewarned is to be half armed. He knew what he was to expect from the disobedient and the rebellious, and must now be prepared to meet it.

10. *I have . . . set thee over the nations.* God represents His messengers the prophets as doing what He commanded them to declare should be done. In this sense they rooted up, pulled down, and destroyed—declared God's judgments;

they builded up and planted—declared the promises of His mercy. Thus God says to Isaiah, chap. vi. 10: "Make the heart of this people fat . . . and shut their eyes." Show them that they are stupid and blind; and that, because they have shut their eyes and hardened their hearts, God will in His judgments leave them to their hardness and darkness.

11. *A rod of an almond tree. Shaked,* from *shakad,* "to be ready," "to hasten," "to watch for an opportunity to do a thing," to awake; because the almond tree is the first to flower and bring forth fruit.

12. *I will hasten my word.* Here is a paronomasia. What do you see? I see *shaked,* "an almond," the hastening tree, that which first awakes. *Thou hast well seen, for [shoked] I will hasten my word.* I will awake, or watch over My word for the first opportunity to inflict the judgments which I threaten.

13. *A seething pot . . . toward the north.* We find, from Ezek. xxiv. 3, etc., that a boiling pot was an emblem of war, and the desolations it produces. Some have thought that by the seething pot Judea is intended, agitated by the invasion of the Chaldeans, whose land lay north of Judea. But Dr. Blayney contends that *mippeney tsaphonah* should be translated, "From the face of the north," as it is in the margin; for, from the next verse, it appears that the evil was to come from the north; and therefore the steam, which was designed as an emblem of that evil, must have arisen from that quarter also. The pot denotes the empire of the Babylonians and Chaldeans lying to the north of Judea, and pouring forth its multitudes like a thick vapor, to overspread the land. Either of these interpretations will suit the text.

14. *Shall break forth.* "Shall be opened." The door shall be thrown abroad, that these calamities may pass out freely.

15. *Shall set every one his throne at the entering of the gates.* As the gates of the cities were the ordinary places where justice was administered, so the enemies of Jerusalem are here represented as conquering the whole land, assuming the reins of government, and laying the whole country under their own laws; so that the Jews should no longer possess any political power. They should be wholly subjugated by their enemies.

16. *I will utter my judgments.* God denounced His judgments. The conquest of their cities and the destruction of the realm were the facts to which these judgments referred; and these facts prove that the threatening was fulfilled. *Worshipped the works of their own hands.* Idolatry was the source of all their wickedness, and was the cause of all their desolations.

17. *Gird up thy loins.* Take courage and be ready, lest I confound you; take courage and be resolute, *pen,* lest by their opposition you be terrified and confounded. God is often represented as doing or causing to be done what He only permits or suffers to be done. Or, Do not fear them; I will not suffer you to be confounded.

18. *I have made thee this day a defenced city, and an iron pillar, and brazen walls.* Though you shall be exposed to persecutions and various indignities, they shall not prevail against you.

To their attacks you shall be as an impregnable city, as unshaken as an iron pillar, and as imperishable as a wall of brass. The issue proved the truth of this promise; he outlived all their insults, and saw Jerusalem destroyed, and his enemies, and the enemies of his Lord, carried into captivity. Instead of *chomoth, walls,* many MSS. and editions read *chomath,* "a wall," which corresponds with the singular nouns preceding.

19. *They shall not prevail against thee.* Because I am determined to defend and support you against all your enemies.

CHAPTER 2

God expresses His continued regard for His people, long since chosen, 1-3. He then expostulates with them on their ungrateful and worse than heathen return to His regard, 4-11; at which even the inanimate creation must be astonished, 12-13. After this their guilt is declared to be the sole cause of the calamities which their enemies had power to inflict on them, 14-17. They are upbraided for their alliances with idolatrous countries, 18-19; and for their strong propensity to idolatry, notwithstanding all the care and tender mercy of God, 20-29. Even the chastenings of the Almighty have produced in this people no repentance, 30. The chapter concludes with compassionately remonstrating against their folly and ingratitude in revolting so deeply from God, and with warning them of the fearful consequences, 31-37.

2. *I remember thee.* The *youth* here refers to their infant political state when they came out of Egypt; they just then began to be a people. Their *espousals* refer to their receiving the law at Mount Sinai, which they solemnly accepted, Exod. xxiv. 6-8, and which acceptance was compared to a betrothing or espousal. *Wentest after me.* Received My law, and were obedient to it. The kindness was that which God showed them by taking them to be His people, not their kindness to Him.

3. *Israel was holiness unto the Lord.* Fully consecrated to His service. *The firstfruits of his increase.* They were as wholly the Lord's as the firstfruits were the property of the priests according to the law, Num. xviii. 13. *All that devour him shall offend.* As they were betrothed to the Lord, they were considered His especial property; they therefore who injured them were considered as laying violent hands on the property of God.

6. *Through the wilderness.* Egypt was the house of their bondage: the *desert* through which they passed after they came out of Egypt was a place where the means of life were not to be found, where no one family could subsist, much less a company of 600,000 men. God mentions these things to show that it was by the bounty of an especial providence that they were fed and preserved alive. Previously to this, it was a *land that no man passed through, and where no man dwelt.* And why? Because it did not produce the means of life; it was the *shadow of death* in its appearance, and the grave to those who committed themselves to it.

7. *And I brought you into a plentiful country.* The land of Canaan. *My land.* The particular property of God, which He gave to them as an inheritance.

8. *They that handle the law.* "They that draw out the law"; they whose office it is to explain it, draw out its spiritual meanings, and show to what its testimonies refer. *The pastors also.* Kings, political and civil rulers.

9. *I will yet plead with you.* I will maintain My "process," vindicate My own conduct, and prove the wickedness of yours.

10. *The isles of Chittim.* This is the island of Cyprus, according to Josephus. *Send unto Kedar.* The name of an Arabian tribe. See if nations either near or remote, cultivated or stupid, have acted with such fickleness and ingratitude as you have done! They have retained their gods to whom they had no obligation; you have abandoned your God, to whom you owe your life, breath, and all things!

12. *Be astonished, O ye heavens.* Or, "The heavens are astonished." The original will admit either sense. The conduct of this people was so altogether bad that, among all the iniquities of mankind, neither heaven nor earth had witnessed anything so excessively sinful and profligate.

13. *Two evils.* First, they forsook God, the Fountain of life, light, prosperity, and happiness. Secondly, they hewed out broken cisterns; they joined themselves to idols, from whom they could receive neither temporal nor spiritual good! Their conduct was the excess of folly and blindness. What we call here *broken cisterns* means more properly such vessels as were ill made, not staunch. ill put together, so that the water leaked through them.

14. *Is Israel a servant?* Is he a slave purchased with money, or a servant born in the family? He is a son himself. If so, then, *why is he spoiled?* Not because God has not shown him love and kindness, but because he forsook God, turned to and is joined with idols.

15. *The young lions roared upon him.* The Assyrians, who have sacked and destroyed the kingdom of Israel, with a fierceness like that of pouncing upon their prey.

16. *The children of Noph and Tahapanes.* Noph and Tahapanes were two cities of Egypt, otherwise called Memphis and Daphni. It is well-known that the good king was defeated by the Egyptians. and slain in battle. Thus was the crown of Judah's head broken.

18. *What hast thou to do in the way of Egypt?* Why do you make alliances with Egypt? *To drink the waters of Sihor?* This means the Nile. See Isa. xxiii. 3. *The way of Assyria.* Why make alliances with the Assyrians? All such connections will only expedite your ruin. *To drink the waters of the river?* The Euphrates, as *nahar* or *hannahar* always means Euphrates. The country between the Tigris and Euphrates is termed to this day "the country beyond the river," i.e., Mesopotamia. Instead of cleaving to the Lord, they joined affinity and made alliances with those two nations, who were ever jealous of them and sought their ruin. Egypt was to them a broken reed instead of a staff; Assyria was a leaky cistern, from which they could derive no help.

20. *Of old time I have broken thy yoke.* It is thought by able critics that the verbs should be read in the second person singular, "Thou hast broken thy yoke, thou hast burst thy bonds"; and thus the Septuagint, the Vulgate, and the Arabic. But the Chaldee gives it a meaning which removes the difficulty: "I have broken the yoke of the people from thy neck; I have cut your bonds asunder." And when this was done, they did promise fair; for *thou saidst,*

I will not transgress. But still they played *the harlot*—committed idolatrous acts in the high places, where the heathen had built their altars.

21. *I had planted thee a noble vine.* I gave you the fullest instruction, the purest ordinances, the highest privileges; and reason would that I should expect you to live suitably to such advantages. But instead of this you have become degenerate; the tree is deteriorated, and the fruit is bad.

22. *For though thou wash thee with nitre.* It should be rendered *natar* or *natron,* a substance totally different from our *nitre.* It comes from the root *nathar,* "to dissolve, loosen," because a solution of it in water is abstersive, taking out spots from clothes. It is still used in the East for the purpose of washing. *Thine iniquity is marked before me.* No washing will take out your spots; the marks of your idolatry and corruption are too deeply rooted to be extracted by any human means.

23. *See thy way in the valley.* The Valley of Hinnom, where they offered their own children to Moloch, an idol of the Ammonites.

24. *Snuffeth up the wind.* In a high fever from the inward heat felt at such times, these animals open their mouths and nostrils as wide as possible, to take in large draughts of fresh air, in order to cool them.

26. *As the thief is ashamed.* As the pilferer is confounded when he is caught in the act, so shall you, your kings, princes, priests, and prophets, be confounded, when God shall arrest you in your idolatries, and deliver you into the hands of your enemies.

28. *According to the number of thy cities are thy gods.* Among heathen nations every city had its tutelary deity. Judah, far sunk in idolatry, had adopted this custom.

31. *Have I been a wilderness unto Israel?* Have I ever withheld from you any of the blessings necessary for your support? *A land of darkness.* Have you, since you passed through the wilderness, and came out of the darkness of Egypt, ever been brought into similar circumstances? *We are lords.* We wish to be our own masters.

32. *Can a maid forget her ornaments?* This people has not so much attachment to Me as young females have to their dress and ornaments. *Days without number.* That is, for many years; during the whole reign of Manasses, which was fifty-five years, the land was deluged with idolatry, from which the reform by good King Josiah, his grandson, had not yet purified it.

33. *Why trimmest thou thy way?* You have used a multitude of artifices to gain alliances with the neighboring idolatrous nations. *Hast thou also taught the wicked ones thy ways?* You have made even these idolaters worse than they were before.

34. *The blood of the souls of the poor innocents.* We find from the sacred history that Manasseh had filled Jerusalem with innocent blood; see 2 Kings xxi. 16 and Ezek. xxxiv. 10. *I have not found it by secret search, but upon all these.* Such deeds of darkness and profligacy are found only in Israel.

35. *Because I am innocent.* They continued to assert their innocence, and therefore expected that God's judgments would be speedily

removed! *I will plead with thee.* I will maintain My process, follow it up to conviction, and inflict the deserved punishment.

36. *Why gaddest thou about?* When they had departed from the Lord, they sought foreign alliances for support. (1) The Assyrians, 2 Chron. xxviii. 13-21; but they injured instead of helping them. (2) The Egyptians; but in this they were utterly disappointed, and were ashamed of their confidence. See chap. xxxvii. 7-8, for the fulfilment of this prediction.

37. *Thou shalt go forth from him, and thine hands upon thine head.* The hand being placed on the head was the evidence of deep sorrow, occasioned by utter desolation. See the case of Tamar, when ruined and abandoned by her brother Amnon, 2 Sam. xiii. 19.

CHAPTER 3

The first five verses of this chapter allude to the subject of the last; and contain earnest exhortations to repentance, with gracious promises of pardon, notwithstanding every aggravation of guilt, 1-5. At the sixth verse a new section of prophecy commences, opening with a complaint against Judah for having exceeded in guilt her sister Israel, already cast off for her idolatry, 6-11. She is cast off, but not forever; for to this same Israel, whose place of captivity (Assyria) lay to the north of Judea, pardon is promised on her repentance, together with a restoration to the Church of God, along with her sister Judah, in the latter days, 12-20. The prophet foretells the sorrow and repentance of the children of Israel under the gospel dispensation, 21. God renews His gracious promises, 22; and they again confess their sins. In this confession their not deigning to name the idol Baal, the source of their calamities, but calling him in the abstract shame, or a thing of shame, is a nice touch of the pencil, extremely beautiful and natural, 22-25.

1. *If a man put away his wife.* It was ever understood, by the law and practice of the country, that if a woman were divorced by her husband, and became the wife of another man, the first husband could never take her again. Now Israel had been married unto the Lord, joined in solemn covenant to Him to worship and serve Him only. Israel turned from following Him, and became idolatrous. On this ground, considering idolatry as a *spiritual whoredom*, and the precept and practice of the law to illustrate this case, Israel could never more be restored to the divine favor. But God, this first Husband, in the plenitude of His mercy, is willing to receive this adulterous spouse, if she will abandon her idolatries and return unto Him. And this and the following chapters are spent in affectionate remonstrances and loving exhortations addressed to these sinful people, to make them sensible of their own sin, and God's tender mercy in offering to receive them again into favor.

2. *As the Arabian in the wilderness.* They were as fully intent on the practice of their idolatry as the Arab in the desert is in lying in wait to plunder the caravans.

3. *There hath been no latter rain.* The former rain, which prepared the earth for tillage, fell in the beginning of November, or a little sooner; and the latter rain fell in the middle of April, after which there was scarcely any rain during the summer.

4. *Wilt thou not ... cry unto me, My father?* Will you not allow Me to be your Creator and Preserver, and cease thus to acknowledge idols?

5. *Will he reserve his anger for ever?* Why should not wrath be continued against you, as you continue transgression against the Lord?

6. *The Lord said also unto me in the days of Josiah the king.* This is a new discourse, and is supposed to have been delivered after the eighteenth year of the reign of Josiah. Here the prophet shows the people of Judah the transgressions, idolatry, obstinacy, and punishment of their brethren, the ten tribes, whom he calls to return to the Lord, with the most gracious promises of restoration to their own country, their reunion with their brethren of Judah, and every degree of prosperity in consequence. He takes occasion also to show the Jews how much more culpable they were than the Israelites, because they practiced the same iniquities while they had the punishment and ruin of the others before their eyes. He therefore exhorts them to return to God with all their hearts, that they might not fall into the same condemnation.

7. *And I said.* By the prophets Elijah, Elisha, Hosea, Amos; for all these prophesied to that rebellious people, and exhorted them to return to the Lord.

8. *I had put her away.* Given them up into the hands of the Assyrians.

9. *The lightness of her whoredom.* The grossness of her idolatry: worshipping objects the most degrading, with rites the most impure.

11. *Backsliding Israel hath justified herself more.* She was less offensive in My eyes, and more excusable, than treacherous Judah. So it is said, Luke xviii. 14, the humbled publican went down to his house justified rather than the boasting Pharisee.

12. *Proclaim these words toward the north.* The countries where the ten tribes were then in captivity, Mesopotamia, Assyria, Media, see 2 Kings xvii. 6; these lay north of Judea. How tender and compassionate are the exhortations in this and the following verses! Could these people believe that God had sent the prophet and yet prefer the land of their bondage to the blessings of freedom in their own country, and the approbation of their God?

14. *I will take you one of a city, and two of a family.* If there should be but one of a city left, or one willing to return, and two only of a whole tribe, yet will I receive these, and bring them back from captivity into their own land.

15. *I will give you pastors according to mine heart.* The pastor means either the king or the prophet; and the pastors here promised may be either kings or prophets, or both. These shall be according to God's own heart; they shall be of His own choosing and shall be qualified by himself: and in consequence they shall *feed* the people with *knowledge, deah,* that divine truth concerning the true God and the best interests of man which was essentially necessary to their salvation; *and understanding, haskeil,* the full interpretation of every point, that in receiving the truth they might become wise, holy, and happy.

16. *The ark of the covenant of the Lord.* This symbol of the Divine Presence, given to the Jews as a token and pledge of God's dwelling among them, shall be no longer necessary, and shall no longer exist; for in the days of the Messiah, to which this promise seems to relate, God's worship shall not be confined either to one place or to one people. The temple of God

shall be among men, and everywhere God be adored through Christ Jesus. *Neither shall that be done any more.* The ark shall be no more established, nor carried from place to place; nor shall men go to visit it. All its ceremonies and importance shall cease; and, if lost, shall never be rebuilt.

17. *They shall call Jerusalem the throne of the Lord.* The new Jerusalem, the universal Church of Christ, shall be God's throne; and wherever He is acknowledged as the Lamb of God who takes away the sin of the world, there God sits on His throne, and holds His court.

18. *The house of Judah shall walk with the house of Israel.* That is, in those days in which the Jews shall be brought in with the fullness of the Gentiles. *Out of the land of the north.* From Chaldea. This prophecy has two aspects: one refers to the return from the Babylonish captivity; the other, to the glorious days of Christianity. But the words may refer to that gathering together of the Jews, not only from Chaldea, but from the countries of their dispersion over the face of the whole earth, and uniting them in the Christian Church.

19. *How shall I put thee among the children?* As if He had said, How can you be accounted a holy seed, who are polluted? How can you be united to the people of God, who walk in the path of sinners? How can you be taken to heaven, who are unholy within and unrighteous without? *And I said, Thou shalt call me, My Father.* This is the answer to the above question. They could not be put among the children unless they became legal members of the heavenly family; and they could not become members of this family unless they abandoned idolatry, and took the Lord for their Portion. Nor could they be continued in the privileges of the heavenly family unless they no more turned away from their Heavenly Father.

21. *A voice was heard upon the high places.* Here the Israelites are represented as assembled together to bewail their idolatry and to implore mercy. While thus engaged, they hear the gracious call of Jehovah—

22. *Return, ye backsliding children.* This they gladly receive, and with one voice make their confession to him: *"Behold, we come unto thee, for thou art Jehovah our God";* and thence to the end of the chapter, show the reasons why they return unto God. (1) Because He is the true God. (2) Because the idols did not profit them; they could give no help in time of trouble. (3) Because it is the prerogative of God alone to give salvation. (4) Because they had no kind of prosperity since they had abandoned the worship of their Maker. And this was not only their case, but it was the case of their forefathers, who all suffered in consequence of their idolatry and disobedience. (5) These reasons are concluded with a hearty confession of sin, at the thought of which they are confounded; for the remembrance of their sin was grievous to them, and the burden was intolerable. This confession ended, God appears in the next chapter with gracious promises, and proper directions how they are to return, and how to conduct themselves in future.

24. *For shame hath devoured.* The word *shame,* here and in chap. xi. 13; Hos. ix. 10, is supposed to signify Baal, the idol which they worshipped.

CHAPTER 4

Sequel of the exhortations and promises addressed to Israel in the preceding chapter, 1-2. The prophet then addresses the people of Judah and Jerusalem, exhorting to repentance and reformation, that the dreadful visitation with which they were threatened might be averted, 3-4. He then sounds the alarm of war, 5-6. Nebuchadnezzar, like a fierce lion, is, from the certainty of the prophecy, represented to be on his march; and the disastrous event to have been already declared, 7-9. And as the lying prophets had flattered the people with the hopes of peace and safety, they are now introduced (when their predictions are falsified by the event), excusing themselves; and, with matchless effrontery, laying the blame of the deception upon God ("And they said," etc., so the text is corrected by Kennicott), 10. The prophet immediately resumes his subject; and, in the person of God, denounces again those judgments which were shortly to be inflicted by Nebuchadnezzar, 11-18. The approaching desolation of Jerusalem lamented in language amazingly energetic and exquisitely tender, 19-21. The incorrigible wickedness of the people the sole cause of these calamities, 22. In the remaining verses the prophet describes the sad catastrophe of Jerusalem by such a beautiful assemblage of the most striking and afflictive circumstances as form a picture of a land "swept with the besom of destruction." The earth seems ready to return to its original chaos; every ray of light is extinguished, and succeeded by a frightful gloom; the mountains tremble, and the hills shake, under the dreadful apprehension of the wrath of Jehovah; all is one awful solitude, where not a vestige of the human race is to be seen. Even the fowls of heaven, finding no longer whereon to subsist, are compelled to migrate; the most fruitful places are become a dark and dreary desert, and every city is a ruinous heap. To complete the whole, the dolorous shrieks of Jerusalem, as of a woman in peculiar agony, break through the frightful gloom; and the appalled prophet pauses, leaving the reader to reflect on the dreadful effects of apostasy and idolatry, 23-31.

1. *Shalt thou not remove.* This was spoken before the Babylonish captivity; and here is a promise that, if they will return from their idolatry, they shall not be led into captivity. So, even that positively threatened judgment would have been averted had they returned to the Lord.

2. *Thou shalt swear, The Lord liveth.* You shall not bind yourself by any false god; you shall acknowledge Me as the Supreme. Bind yourself by Me, and to Me; and do this *in truth, in judgment, and in righteousness. The nations shall bless themselves in him.* They shall be so fully convinced of the power and goodness of Jehovah in seeing the change wrought on you, and the mercies heaped upon you, that their usual mode of benediction shall be, "May the God of Israel bless thee!"

3. *Break up your fallow ground.* Fallow ground is either that which, having been once tilled, has lain long uncultivated; or, ground slightly ploughed, in order to be ploughed again previously to its being sown. You have been long uncultivated in righteousness; let true repentance break up your fruitless and hardened hearts; and when the seed of the word of life is sown in them, take heed that worldly cares and concerns do not arise, and, like thorns, choke the good seed.

4. *Circumcise yourselves.* Put away everything that has a tendency to grieve the Spirit of God, or to render your present holy resolutions unfruitful.

5. *Blow ye the trumpet.* Give full information to all parts of the land, that the people may assemble together and defend themselves against their invaders.

6. *I will bring evil from the north.* From the land of Chaldea.

7. *The lion is come up.* Nebuchadnezzar, king of Babylon. *The destroyer of the Gentiles.* Of the "nations," of all the people who resisted his authority.

8. *Lament and howl. Heililu.* The aboriginal Irish had a funeral song, still continued among their descendants, one part of which is termed the *ulaloo*. This is sung responsively or alternately, and is accompanied with a full chorus of sighs and groans. It has been thought that Ireland was originally peopled by the Phoenicians; if so, this will account for the similiarity of many words and customs among both these people.

9. *The heart of the king shall perish.* Shall lose all courage.

10. *Ah, Lord God! surely thou hast greatly deceived this people.* The prophet could not reconcile this devastation of the country with the promises already made; and he appears to ask the question, Hast Thou not then deceived this people in saying there shall be peace, i.e., prosperity? *Whereas the sword reacheth unto the soul.* That is, the life, the people being generally destroyed.

11-13. *A dry wind . . . a full wind . . . as clouds . . . as a whirlwind.* All these expressions appear to refer to the pestilential winds, suffocating vapors, and clouds and pillars of sand collected by whirlwinds, which are so common and destructive in the East (see on Isa. xxi. 1); and these images are employed here to show the overwhelming effect of the invasion of the land by the Chaldeans.

13. *Woe unto us!* The people, deeply affected with these threatened judgments, interrupt the prophet with the lamentation—*Woe unto us! for we are spoiled.* The prophet then resumes:

14. *O Jerusalem, wash thine heart.* Why do you not put away your wickedness, that you may be saved from these tremendous judgments? *How long shall thy vain thoughts of safety and prosperity lodge within thee?* While you continue a rebel against God, and provoke Him daily by your abominations!

15. *For a voice declareth from Dan.* Dan was a city in the tribe of Dan, north of Jerusalem; the first city in Palestine, which occurs in the way from Babylon to Jerusalem. *Affliction from mount Ephraim.* Between Dan and Jerusalem are the mountains of Ephraim. These would be the first places attacked by the Chaldeans, and the rumor from thence would show that the land was invaded.

16. *Watchers come from a far country.* Persons to besiege fortified places.

17. *As keepers of a field.* In the Eastern countries grain is often sown in the open country; and, when nearly ripe, guards are placed at different distances round about it to preserve it from being plundered. Jerusalem was watched, like one of these fields, by guards all round about it; so that none could enter to give assistance, and none who wished to escape were permitted to go out.

19. *My bowels.* From this to the twenty-ninth verse the prophet describes the ruin of Jerusalem and the desolation of Judea by the Chaldeans in the language and imagery scarcely paralleled in the whole Bible. At the sight of misery the bowels are first affected; pain is next felt by a sort of stricture in the pericardium; and then, the heart becoming strongly affected by irregular palpitations, a gush of tears, accompanied with wailings, is the issue.

20. *Destruction upon destruction.* Cities burnt, and their inhabitants destroyed. *My tents spoiled.* Even the solitary dwellings in the fields and open country do not escape.

23. *I beheld the earth* (the land), *and, lo, it was without form, and void. Tohu vabohu;* the very words used in Genesis to denote the formless state of the chaotic mass before God had brought it into order.

24. *The mountains . . . hills.* Princes, rulers were astonished and fled.

25. *The birds of the heavens were fled.* The land was so desolated that even the fowls of heaven could not find meat, and therefore fled away to another region. How powerfully energetic is this description!

30. *Though thou rentest thy face with painting.* This probably refers to the custom of introducing *stibium*, a preparation of antimony, between the eye and the lids, in order to produce a fine lustre, which occasions a distension of the eyelid in the time of the operation. In order to heighten the effect from this, some may have introduced a more than ordinary quantity, so as nearly to rend the eyelid itself. Though you make use of every means of address, of cunning, and of solicitation, to get assistance from the neighboring states, it will be all in vain. Reference is here particularly made to the practice of harlots to allure men.

31. *Bringeth forth her first child.* In such a case the fear, danger, and pain were naturally the greatest. *Spreadeth her hands.* The gesture indicated by nature to signify distress and implore help. We have met with this figure in other parts, and among the classic writers it is frequent.

CHAPTER 5

The prophet, having described the judgments impending over his countrymen, enlarges on the corruptions which prevailed among them. Their profession of religion was all false and hypocritical, 1-2. Though corrected, they were not amended, but persisted in their guilt, 3. This was not the case with the low and ignorant only, 4; but more egregiously so with those of the higher order, from whose knowledge and opportunities better things might have been expected, 5. God therefore threatens them with the most cruel enemies, 6; and appeals to themselves if they should be permitted to practice such sins unpunished, 7-9. He then commands their enemies to raze the walls of Jerusalem, 10; that devoted city, whose inhabitants added to all their other sins the highest contempt of God's word and prophets, 11-13. Wherefore His word, in the mouth of His prophet, shall be as fire to consume them, 14; the Chaldean forces shall cruelly afflict them, 15-17; and further judgments await them as the consequence of their apostasy and idolatry, 18-19. The chapter closes with a most melancholy picture of the moral condition of the Jewish people at that period which immediately preceded the Babylonish captivity, 20-31.

1. *Broad places.* Marketplaces, and those where there was most public resort. *If ye can find a man.* A certain philosopher went through the streets of Athens with a lighted lamp in his hand; and being asked what he sought, answered, "I am seeking to find a man." So in Jerusalem none was found, on the most diligent search, who acted worthy the character of a rational being. *I will pardon it.* I will spare the city for the sake of one righteous person. So at the intercession of Abraham, God would have spared Sodom if there had been ten righteous persons found in it, Gen. xviii. 26.

2. *The Lord liveth.* Though they profess to bind themselves by Jehovah, as if they acknowledged Him their God and only Lord, yet they swore falsely. For not believing in Him,

they took a false oath; one by which they did not believe themselves bound, not acknowledging Him as their Lord.

4. *These are poor.* They are ignorant; they have no education; they know no better.

5. *I will get me unto the great men.* Those whose circumstances and rank in life gave them opportunities of information which the others could not have, for the reasons already given. *These have altogether broken the yoke.* These have cast aside all restraint, have acted above law, and have trampled all moral obligations under their feet.

6. *Wherefore a lion.* Nebuchadnezzar, according to the general opinion; who is called here a *lion* for his courage and violence, a bear for his rapaciousness, and a *leopard* for his activity.

7. *In the harlots' houses.* In places consecrated to idolatry. In the language of the prophets, adultery generally signifies idolatry.

8. *After his neighbour's wife.* This may have been literally true, as the abominations of idolatry, in which they were so deeply practiced, would necessarily produce such a state of things as that here mentioned.

10. *Go ye up upon her walls.* This is the permission and authority given to the Chaldeans to pillage Jerusalem. *Take away her battlements.* Some translate "branches"; others, "vines." Destroy the branches, cut down the stem; but do not damage the root. Leave so many of the people that the state may be regenerated. The Septuagint, Syriac, and Arabic read, "Leave her foundations, for they are the Lord's"; and this agrees with "Destroy, but make not a full end."

12. *They have belied the Lord.* They have "denied" or disavowed the Lord. *It is not he. Lo hu,* "He is not"; there is no such being; therefore this evil shall not come upon us. On their premises, this conclusion was just. There is no Judge; therefore there shall be no judgment.

13. *And the prophets shall become wind.* What are the prophets? Empty persons. Their words are wind; we hear the sound of their threatenings, but of the matter of the threatenings we shall hear no more. *And the word is not in them.* There is no inspirer, but may their own predictions fall on their own heads!

14. *Because ye speak this word.* Because you thus treat My message, *I will make my words in thy mouth fire.* They have said, "They are but air"; but I will make them fire, and a fire too that shall devour them. And how this was to be done, and by whom, is mentioned in the next verse.

15. *I will bring a nation.* The Babylonians, whose antiquity was great, that empire being founded by Nimrod. *Whose language thou knowest not.* The Chaldee, which, though a dialect of the Hebrew, is so very different in its words and construction that in hearing it spoken they could not possibly collect the meaning of what was said.

16. *Their quiver is an open sepulchre.* They are such exact archers as never to miss their mark; every arrow is sure to slay one man.

18. *I will not make a full end.* There are more evils in store for you. You shall not only be spoiled, and all your property destroyed,

but you shall be carried into captivity; and you shall "serve strangers in a land that is not yours," v. 19.

23. *They are revolted and gone.* They have abandoned Me, and are gone farther and farther into transgression.

24. *Giveth rain, both the former and the latter.* See the note on chap. iii. 3. *The appointed weeks of the harvest.* As the early rains fell in the northern parts of Judea about the end of September, in the civil year of the Hebrews, so the latter rains fell before harvest, in the months of March and April. The appointed weeks of the harvest were those which fell between the Passover and Pentecost. In the southern parts the harvest was earlier than in the northern. If the word *weeks* be read with a *sin* instead of a *shin,* it will signify "fulness" or "sufficiency"; and thus the Septuagint and Vulgate have read it. I think the present reading is much to be preferred. God appoints a harvesttime, and in His good providence He generally gives harvest weather.

25. *Your iniquities have turned away these things.* When these appointed weeks of harvest do not come, should we not examine and see whether this be not in God's judgments? Have not our iniquities turned away these good things from us?

26. *They lay wait, as he that setteth snares.* A metaphor taken from fowlers, who, having fixed their nets, lie down and keep out of sight, that when birds come, they may be ready to draw and entangle them.

27. *As a cage is full of birds.* There is no doubt that the reference here is to a decoy or trap-cage; in these the fowlers put several tame birds, which when the wild ones see, they come and light on the cage, and fall into the snare.

28. *They judge not the cause . . . yet they prosper.* Perhaps we might be justified in translating, "And shall they prosper?"

31. *The prophets prophesy falsely.* The false prophets predict favorable things, that they may please both the princes and the people. *The priests bear rule by their means.* The false prophets affording them all that their influence and power can procure, to enable them to keep their places, and feed on the riches of the Lord's house. *And my people love to have it so.* Are perfectly satisfied with this state of things, because they are permitted to continue in their sins without reproof or restraint. The prophets and the priests united to deceive and ruin the people. The prophets gave out false predictions; by their means the priests got the government of the people into their own hands; and so infatuated were the people that they willingly abandoned themselves to those blind guides, and would not hearken to the voice of any reformer.

CHAPTER 6

Jeremiah, in the spirit of prophecy, seeing the Chaldeans on their march, bids his people set up the usual signals of distress, and spread the general alarm to betake themselves to flight, 1. Then, by a beautiful allusion to the custom of shepherds moving their flocks to the richest pastures, Jerusalem is singled out as a place devoted to be eaten up or trodden down by the armies of the Chaldeans, who are called up against her, and whose ardor and impatience are so great that the soldiers, when they arrive in the evening, regret they have no more day, and desire to begin the attack without waiting for the light of the morning, 2-5. God is then represented as animating and directing the besiegers against this guilty city, which sinned as incessantly as a fountain flows, 6-7, although warned of the fatal consequence, 8. He intimates also, by the gleaning of the grapes, that one invasion should carry away the remains of another, till their disobedience, hypocrisy, and other sins should end in their total overthrow, 9-15. And to show that God is clear when He judgeth, He mentions His having in vain admonished and warned them, and calls upon the whole world to witness the equity of His proceedings, 16-18, in punishing this perverse and hypocritical people, 19-20, by the ministry of the cruel Chaldeans, 21-23. Upon this a chorus of Jews is introduced expressing their fears and alarm, 24-25; to which the prophet echoes a response full of sympathy and tenderness, 26. The concluding verses, by metaphors taken from the process of refining gold and silver, represent all the methods hitherto used to amend them as wholly ineffectual, 27-30.

1. *O ye children of Benjamin, gather yourselves to flee.* As the invading armies are fast approaching, the prophet calls on the inhabitants of Jerusalem to sound an alarm, and collect all the people to arm themselves and go against the invaders. They are called the children of Benjamin, because Jerusalem was in the tribe of Benjamin. *Tekoa.* Was a city about twelve miles to the south of Jerusalem. *Beth-haccerem.* Was the name of a small village situated on an eminence between Jerusalem and Tekoa. On this they were ordered to set up a beacon, or kindle a large *fire*, which might be seen at a distance, and give the people to understand that an enemy was entering the land. *Out of the north.* From Babylon.

3. *The shepherds with their flocks.* The chiefs and their battalions. The invading army is about to spoil and waste all the fertile fields round about the city, while engaged in the siege.

4. *Prepare ye war against her.* The words of the invaders exciting each other to the assault, and impatient lest any time should be lost; lest the besieged should have time to strengthen themselves, or get in supplies.

5. *Arise, and let us go by night.* Since we have lost the day, let us not lose the night; but, taking advantage of the darkness, let us make a powerful assault while they are under the impression of terror.

6. *Hew ye down trees.* To form machines. *And cast a mount.* That may overlook the city, on which to place our engines. *This is the city to be visited.* We are sure of success, for their God will deliver it into our hands; for it is full of oppression, and He has consigned it to destruction.

7. *As a fountain casteth out her waters.* The inhabitants are incessant in their acts of iniquity; they do nothing but sin.

8. *Be thou instructed.* Still there is respite. If they would even now return unto the Lord with all their heart, the advancing Chaldeans would be arrested on their march and turned back.

9. *They shall throughly glean the remnant of Israel as a vine: turn back thine hand.* The Chaldeans are here exhorted to *turn back* and glean up the remnant of the inhabitants that were left after the capture of Jerusalem; for even that remnant did not profit by the divine judgments that fell on the inhabitants at large.

10. *The word of the Lord is unto them a reproach.* It is an object of derision; they despise it.

11. *I am full of the fury of the Lord.* God has given me a dreadful revelation of the judgments He intends to inflict: my soul is burdened with this prophecy. I have endeavored to suppress it, but I must pour it forth.

14. *They have healed also the hurt of the daughter of my people slightly.* "Of the daughter" is not in the text, and is here improperly added.

16. *Thus saith the Lord, Stand ye in the ways, and see.* Let us observe the metaphor. A traveller is going to a particular city. He comes to a place where the road divides into several paths; he is afraid of going astray. He stops short—endeavors to find out the right path; he cannot fix his choice. At last he sees another traveller; he inquires of him, gets proper directions—proceeds on his journey—arrives at the desired place—and reposes after his fatigue. There is an excellent sermon on these words in the works of our first poet, Geoffrey Chaucer; it is among *The Canterbury Tales*, and is called "Chaucer's Tale."

17. *I set watchmen.* I have sent prophets to warn you.

20. *Incense from Sheba.* Sheba was in Arabia, famous for the best incense. It was situated towards the southern extremity of the peninsula of Arabia; and was, in respect of Judea, *a far country.*

23. *They shall lay hold on bow and spear.* Still pointing out the Chaldeans.

27. *I have set thee for a tower and a fortress.* The words refer to the office of an assayer of silver and gold. The people are here represented under the notion of "alloyed silver." They are full of impurities; and they are put into the hands of the prophet, the assayer, to be purified. The "bellows" are placed, the "fire" is lighted up, but all to no purpose; so intensely commixed is the alloy with the silver that it cannot be separated.

CHAPTER 7

Here begins another section of prophecy, ending with the ninth chapter. It opens with exhorting to amendment of life, without which the confidence of the Jews in their Temple is declared vain, 1-11. God bids them take warning from the fate of their brethren the Israelites, who had been carried away captive on account of their sins, without any regard to that sacred place (Shiloh) where the ark of God once resided, 12-15. The iniquities of Judah are so great in the sight of God that the prophet is commanded not to intercede for the people, 16; the more especially as they persisted in provoking God by their idolatrous practices, 17-20. The Jewish sacrifices, if not accompanied with obedience to the moral law, are of no avail, 21-24. Notwithstanding the numerous messages of mercy from the time of the Exodus, the people revolted more and more; and have added to their other sins this horrible evil, the setting up of their abominations in the temple of Jehovah; or, in other words, they have encumbered the Mosaic economy, which shadowed forth the glorious truths of Christianity, with a heterogeneous admixture of the idolatrous, impure, and cruel rites of heathenism; consequently, the whole land shall be utterly desolated, 25-34.

1. *The word that came to Jeremiah.* This prophecy is supposed to have been delivered in the first year of the reign of Jehoiakim, son of Josiah, who, far from following the example of his pious father, restored idolatry, maintained bad priests and worse prophets, and filled Jerusalem with abominations of all kinds.

2. *Stand in the gate of the Lord's house.* There was a show of public worship kept up. The Temple was considered God's residence; the usual ceremonies of religion restored by Josiah were still observed; and the people were led to consider the Temple and its services as

sacred things, which would be preservatives to them in case of the threatened invasion.

4. *The temple of the Lord.* They seem to express the conviction which the people had, that they should be safe while their Temple service continued; for they supposed that God would not give it up into profane hands. But sacred places and sacred symbols are nothing in the sight of God when the heart is not right with Him.

5. *If ye throughly amend your ways.* Literally, "If in making good you fully make good your ways." God will no longer admit of half-hearted work.

12. *But go ye now unto my place which was in Shiloh.* See what I did to My tabernacle and ark formerly. After a long residence at Shiloh, for the iniquity of the priests and the people, I suffered it to fall into the hands of the Philistines, and to be carried captive into their land, and to be set up in the house of their idols. And because of *your* iniquities, I will deal with you and this Temple in the same way; for as I spared not Shiloh, though My ark was there, but made it a victim of My wrath, so will I do to Jerusalem and her Temple.

15. *The whole seed of Ephraim.* Taken here for all the ten tribes, that of Ephraim being the principal.

16. *Therefore pray not thou for this people.* They have filled up the measure of their iniquity, and they must become examples of My justice. How terrible must the state of that place be, where God refuses to pour out the spirit of supplication on His ministers and people in its behalf!

18. *The children gather wood.* Here is a description of a whole family gathered together, and acting unitedly in idolatrous worship. *The queen of heaven;* most probably the moon.

21. *Put your burnt offerings unto your sacrifices, and eat flesh.* I will receive neither sacrifice nor oblation from you; therefore you may take the beasts intended for sacrifice, and slay and eat them for your common nourishment.

23. *This thing commanded I them. . . . Obey my voice.* It was not sacrifices and oblations which I required of your fathers in the wilderness, but obedience.

29. *Cut off thine hair.* "Shear thy Nazarite." The Nazarite was one who took upon him a particular vow, and separated himself from all worldly connections for a certain time, that he might devote himself without interruption to the service of God; and during all this time no razor was to pass on his head. After the vow was over, he shaved his head and beard, and returned to society. See Num. vi. 2, etc. Jerusalem is here considered under the notion of a Nazarite, by profession devoted to the service of God. But that profession was empty; it was not accompanied with any suitable practice. God tells them here to cut off their hair; to make no vain pretensions to holiness or religion; to throw off the mask, and attempt no longer to impose upon themselves and others by their hypocritical pretensions.

31. *Tophet . . . in the valley of the son of Hinnom.* Tophet was the place in that valley where the continual fires were kept up, in and through which they consecrated their children to Moloch.

32. *The valley of slaughter.* The place where the slaughtered thousands of this rebellious people shall be cast, in order to their being burnt, or becoming food for the beasts of the field and the fowls of the air, v. 33. These words are repeated, and their meaning more particularly explained, chap. xix. 6-15.

34. *Then will I cause to cease . . . the voice of mirth.* There shall no longer be in Jerusalem any cause of joy; they shall neither marry nor be given in marriage, for the land shall be totally desolated. Such horrible sins required such a horrible punishment.

CHAPTER 8

The judgments threatened in the last chapter are here declared to extend to the very dead, whose tombs should be opened, and the carcasses treated with every mark of indignity, 1-3. From this the prophet returns to reprove them for their perseverance in transgression, 4-6; and for their thoughtless stupidity, which even the instinct of the brute creation, by a beautiful contrast, is made to upbraid, 7-9. This leads to further threatenings, expressed in a variety of striking terms, 10-13. Upon which a chorus of Jews is introduced, expressing their terror on the news of the invasion, 14-15; which is greatly heightened in the next verse by the prophet's hearing the snorting of Nebuchadnezzar's horses even from Dan, and then seeing the devastation made by his army, 16, whose cruelties God himself declares no entreaties will soften, 17. On this declaration the prophet laments most bitterly the fate of the daughter of his people, changing the scene unawares to the place of her captivity, where she is introduced, answering in mournful responses to the prophet's dirge, 18-22. The variety of images and figures used to diversify the same subject is equally pleasing and astonishing. The dress is generally new, always elegant.

1-2. *They shall bring out the bones.* This and the following two verses are a continuation of the preceding prophecy, and should not have been separated from the foregoing chapter. In order to pour the utmost contempt upon the land, the victorious enemies dragged out of their graves, caves, and sepulchres, the bones of kings, princes, prophets, priests, and the principal inhabitants, and exposed them in the open air; so that they became, in the order of God's judgments, a reproach to them in the vain confidence they had in the *sun, moon,* and the *host of heaven*—all the planets and stars, whose worship they had set up in opposition to that of Jehovah. This custom of raising the bodies of the dead, and scattering their bones about, seems to have been general. It was the highest expression of hatred and contempt.

4. *Moreover thou shalt say.* Dr. Blayney very properly observes, "In that part of the prophecy which follows next, the difference of speakers requires to be attended to; the transition being quick and sudden, but full of life and energy. The prophet at first, in the name of God, reproves the people's incorrigibility; he charges their wise ones with folly, and threatens them with grievous calamities, vv. 4-13. In the three next verses he seems to apostrophize his countrymen in his own person, and as one of the people that dwelt in the open towns, advising those that were in the like situation to retire with him into some of the fortified cities, and there wait the event with patience, since there was nothing but terror abroad, and the noise of the enemy, who had already begun to ravage the country, vv. 14-16. God speaks, v. 17, and threatens to bring foes against them that should be irresistible. The prophet appears

again in his own person, commiserating the daughter of his people, who is heard bewailing her forlorn case in a distant land; while the voice of God, like that of conscience, breaks in upon her complaints, and shows her that all this ruin is brought upon her by her own infidelities, vv. 18-20. The prophet once more resumes his discourse; he regrets that no remedy can be found to close up the wounds of his country, and pathetically weeps over the number of her slain, v. 21; chap. ix. 1."

Shall they fall, and not arise? shall he turn away, and not return? That is, It is as possible for sinners to return from their sin to God, for His grace is ever at hand to assist, as it is for God, who is pouring out His judgments, to return to them on their return to Him. But these held fast deceit, and refused to return; they would not be undeceived.

6. *As the horse rusheth into the battle.* This strongly marks the unthinking, careless desperation of their conduct.

7. *The stork in the heaven.* The birds of passage know the times of their going and return, and punctually observe them; they obey the dictates of nature, but My people do not obey My law.

8. *The pen of the scribes is in vain.* The "deceitful pen" of the scribes. They have written falsely, though they had the truth before them.

10. *Therefore will I give their wives.* From this to the end of v. 15 is repeated from chap. vi. 13-15.

16. *The snorting of his horses was.* From this to the end of v. 15 is repeated from Babylon to Jerusalem; and it was by this city, after the battle of Carchemish, that Nebuchadnezzar, in pursuing the Egyptians, entered Palestine. *The whole land trembled at the sound of the neighing of his strong ones.* Of his war horses. This is a fine image; so terrible was the united neighing of the cavalry of the Babylonians that the reverberation of the air caused the ground to tremble.

17. *I will send serpents.* These were symbols of the enemies that were coming against them, a foe that would rather slay them and destroy the land than get booty and ransom.

20. *The harvest is past.* The siege of Jerusalem lasted two years; for Nebuchadnezzar came against it in the ninth year of Zedekiah, and the city was taken in the eleventh; see 2 Kings xxv. 1-3.

22. *Is there no balm in Gilead?* The Israelites are represented as a man dying through disease; and a disease for the cure of which the balm of Gilead was well-known to be a specific, when judiciously applied by a physician. But though there be balm and a physician, the people are not cured; neither their spiritual nor political evils are removed.

CHAPTER 9

The prophet bitterly laments the terrible judgments about to be inflicted upon his countrymen, and points out some of the evils which have provoked the Divine Majesty, 1-9. Judea shall be utterly desolated, and the inhabitants transplanted into heathen countries, 10-17. In allusion to an ancient custom, a band of mourning women is called to lament over the ruins of Jerusalem, 17-18; and even the funeral dirge is given in terms full of beauty, elegance, and pathos, 19-22. God is the Fountain of all good; man, merely an instrument by which a portion of this good is distributed in the earth; therefore none should glory in his wisdom, might, or riches, 23-24. The judgments of God shall fall, not upon the land of Judea only, but also upon many heathen nations, 25-26.

1. *Oh that my head were waters.* "Who will give to my head waters?" My mourning for the sins and desolations of my people has already exhausted the source of tears: I wish to have a fountain opened there, that I may *weep day and night for the slain . . . of my people.* This has been the sorrowful language of many a pastor who has preached long to a hardened, rebellious people, to little or no effect. This verse belongs to the preceding chapter.

2. *Oh that I had in the wilderness.* Several interpreters suppose this to be the speech of God. I cannot receive this. I believe this verse to be spoken by the prophet, and that God proceeds with the next verse, and so on to the ninth inclusive.

3. *They bend their tongues like their bow for lies.* And their lies are such that they as fully take away life as the keenest arrow shot from the best-strung bow. The false prophets told the people that there was no desolation at hand; the people believed them, made no preparation for their defense, did not return to the Lord; and the sword came and destroyed them.

7. *Behold, I will melt them.* I will put them in the furnace of affliction, and see if this will be a means of purging away their dross.

10. *Both the fowl of the heavens and the beast are fled.* The land shall be so utterly devastated that neither beast nor bird shall be able to live in it.

11. *A den of dragons.* "Jackals."

12. *Who is the wise man?* To whom has God revealed these things? He is the truly wise man.

15. *I will feed them . . . with wormwood.* They shall have the deepest sorrow and heaviest affliction. They shall have poison instead of meat and drink.

17. *Call for the mourning women.* Those whose office it was to make lamentations at funerals, and to bewail the dead, for which they received pay. This custom continues to the present in Asiatic countries.

20. *Teach your daughters.* This is not a common dirge that shall last only till the body is consigned to the earth; it must last longer. Teach it to your children, that it may be continued through every generation, till God turn again your captivity.

21. *For death is come up into our windows.* Here death is personified, and represented as scaling their wall; and after having slain the playful children without, and the vigorous youth employed in the labors of the field, he is now come into the private houses, to destroy the aged and infirm; and into the palaces, to destroy the king and the princes.

22. *And as the handful after the harvestman.* The reapers, after having cut enough to fill their hand, threw it down; and the binders, following after, collected those handfuls, and bound them in sheaves. Death is represented as having cut down the inhabitants of the land, as the reapers do the corn. But so general was the slaughter that there was none to bury the dead, to gather up these handfuls; so that they

lay in a state of putrescence, *as dung upon the open field.*

23. *Let not the wise man glory in his wisdom.* Because God is the Fountain of all good, neither wisdom, nor might, nor riches, nor prosperity can come but from or through Him.

24. *But let him that glorieth.* To glory in a thing is to depend on it as the means or cause of procuring happiness.

25. *I will punish all them which are circumcised with the uncircumcised.* Do not imagine that you, because of your crimes, are the only objects of My displeasure; the circumcised and the uncircumcised, the Jew and the Gentile, shall equally feel the stroke of My justice. In like manner, other nations also were delivered into the hands of Nebuchadnezzar; these he immediately enumerates: Egypt and Edom, and the Moabites and the Ammonites, and the Arabians of the desert.

CHAPTER 10

The Jews, about to be carried into captivity, are here warned against the superstition and idolatry of that country to which they were going. Chaldea was greatly addicted to astrology, and therefore the prophet begins with warning them against it, 1-2. He then exposes the absurdity of idolatry in short but elegant satire; in the midst of which he turns, in a beautiful apostrophe, to the one true God, whose adorable attributes repeatedly strike in view, as he goes along, and lead him to contrast His infinite perfections with those despicable inanities which the blinded nations fear, 3-16. The prophet again denounces the divine judgments, 17-18; upon which Jerusalem laments her fate, and supplicates the divine compassion in her favor, 19-25.

1. *Hear ye the word which the Lord speaketh unto you.* Dr. Dahler supposes this discourse to have been delivered in the fourth year of the reign of Jehoiakim. It contains an invective against idolatry, showing its absurdity, and that the Creator alone should be worshipped by all mankind.

2. *Learn not the way of the heathen.* These words are more particularly addressed to the ten tribes scattered among the heathen by the Assyrians, who carried them away captive; they may also regard those in the land of Israel, who still had the customs of the former heathen settlers before their eyes. *Be not dismayed at the signs of heaven; for the heathen are dismayed.* The Chaldeans and Egyptians were notoriously addicted to astrology; and the Israelites here are cautioned against it.

3. *The customs of the people are vain.* The statutes and principles of the science are vain, empty, and illusory. *One cutteth a tree out of the forest.* See the notes on Isa. xl. 19 and xliv. 9, etc., which are all parallel places and where this conduct is strongly ridiculed.

5. *They are upright as the palm tree.* As straight and as stiff as the trees out of which they are hewn.

7. *Who would not fear thee?* Who would not worship Thee as the Author and Giver of all good? The fear of God is often taken for the whole of true religion.

8. *The stock is a doctrine of vanities.* Dr. Blayney translates, "The wood itself is a rebuker of vanities." The very tree out of which the god is hewn demonstrates the vanity and folly of the idolaters.

9. *Brought from Tarshish.* Some suppose this to be Tartessus in Spain, from which the

Phoenicians brought much silver. *Blue and purple is their clothing.* These were the most precious dyes; very rare, and of high price.

10. *But the Lord.* The original word should be preserved; however we agree to pronounce it: "Yehovah is the true God." He is without beginning, and without end. This is true of no being else. *He is the living God.* His being is underived, and He gives life to all.

11. *Thus shall ye say unto them.* This is the message you shall deliver to the Chaldean idolaters. *The gods that have not made the heavens and the earth, even they shall perish.* Both they and their worshippers shall be destroyed, and idolatry shall finally be destroyed from the earth.

13. *When he uttereth his voice, there is a multitude of waters.* This is a plain allusion to a storm of thunder and lightning, and the abundance of rain which is the consequence. This verse and the three following are the same in substance, and nearly in words, as chap. li. 16, and following.

14. *Every man is brutish. Nibar,* is a boor, acts as a brute, who may suppose that a stock of a tree, formed like a man, may be an intellectual being; and therefore shuns the form as though it had life. See Isa. xliv. 10-11.

16. *The portion of Jacob is not like them.* Every nation had its tutelary god; this was its "portion." *The portion,* i.e., the God, *of Jacob is not like them: for he is the former of all things,* and they are formed by their foolish worshippers.

17. *Gather up thy wares.* Pack up your goods, or what necessaries of life your enemies will permit you to carry away; for,

18. *I will sling out the inhabitants of the land.* I will project you with violence from your country. I will send you all into captivity. This discourse, from v. 17, is supposed to have been delivered in the eleventh year of Jehoiakim.

19. *This is a grief, and I must bear it.* Oppressive as it is, I have deserved it, and worse.

20. *My tabernacle is spoiled.* The city is taken, and all our villages ruined and desolated.

21. *The pastors are become brutish.* The king and his counsellors, who, by refusing to pay the promised tribute to Nebuchadnezzar, had kindled a new war.

22. *The noise of the bruit is come.* How this silly French word *bruit,* which signifies "noise," got in here, I cannot imagine. The simple translation is this: "The voice of the report! behold, it is come; yea, great commotion from the land of the north [Chaldea], to make the cities of Judea a desolation, a habitation of wild beasts." That is, the report we had heard of the projected invasion of Judea by Nebuchadnezzar is confirmed. He has entered the land; the Chaldeans are at the doors, and the total desolation of Judea is their sole object.

25. *Pour out thy fury upon the heathen.* Even those who are now the executors of Thy justice upon us will, in their turn, feel its scourge. This was fulfilled in the Chaldeans. Nebuchadnezzar was punished with madness, his son was slain in his revels, and the city was taken and sacked by Cyrus; and the Babylonish empire was finally destroyed!

CHAPTER 11

The prophet proclaims the tenor of God's covenant with the Jews of old, 1-5; and then reproves them for their hereditary disobedience, 6-10. In consequence of this the Almighty is introduced, declaring He will show them no pity, 11-13; forbidding Jeremiah to intercede, 14; rejecting their sacrifices, 15; and in a word, condemning this fair but unfruitful tree to the fire, 16-17. In what remains of the chapter the prophet predicts evil to his neighbors of Anathoth, who had conspired against him, 18-23. "Let us," said they, "destroy the tree with the fruit thereof," etc., alluding to what Jeremiah had said in the sixteenth verse.

1. *The word that came to Jeremiah.* This discourse is supposed to have been delivered in the first year of the reign of Zedekiah.

2. *Hear ye the words of this covenant.* It is possible that the prophet caused the words of the covenant made with their fathers in the desert (Exod. xxiv. 4-8) to be read to them on this occasion; or, at least, the blessings and the cursings which Moses caused to be pronounced to the people as soon as they had set foot in Canaan, Deuteronomy xxvii—xxviii.

3. *Cursed be the man that obeyeth not.* After the reading, the prophet appears to sum up the things contained in what was read to them; as if he had said, "You hear what the Lord saith unto you: remember, the sum of it is this: The man is cursed who obeyeth not; and he is blessed who obeys."

5. *So be it, O Lord.* Let Thy promises be fulfilled; and let the incorrigible beware of Thy threatenings!

6. *Proclaim all these words.* Let the same covenant, with the blessings and cursings, be read in every city of Judah, and in all the streets of Jerusalem, that all the people may know their duty, their privileges, and their danger.

10. *They are turned back to the iniquities of their forefathers.* A great reformation had taken place under the reign of Josiah, and the public worship of idols had been abolished, and most of the high places destroyed. But under the reign of his son and his successors, they had turned back again to idolatry, and were become worse than ever. It required a captivity to cure them of this propensity, and God sent one; after that, there was no idolatry among the Jews.

14. *Therefore pray not thou for this people.* I am determined to give them up into the hands of their enemies; I will neither hear your intercession, nor regard their prayers. Their measure is full.

15. *What hath my beloved to do in mine house?* This is an endearing expression, which properly belonged to the Israelites. When God took them into covenant with himself, they were espoused to Him, and therefore His *beloved.* But now that they have forsaken Him, and joined themselves to another, what have they to do with His house or its ordinances, which they wish now to frequent with vows and sacrifices, when they see the evil fast coming upon them?

16. *The Lord called thy name, A green olive tree.* That is, He made you like a green olive—fair, flourishing, and fruitful; but you are degenerated, and God has given the Chaldeans permission to burn you up.

18. *The Lord hath given me knowledge of it.* The men of Anathoth had conspired against his life, because he reproved them for their sins, and denounced the judgments of God against them. Of this God had given him a secret warning, that he might be on his guard.

19. *I was like a lamb or an ox.* "Like the familiar lamb"—the lamb bred up in the house, in a state of friendship with the family. The people of Anathoth were Jeremiah's townsmen; he was born and bred among them; they were his familiar friends; and now they lay wait for his life! *Let us destroy the tree with the fruit.* Let us slay the prophet, and his prophecies will come to an end.

20. *Let me see thy vengeance on them.* Rather, "I shall see Thy punishment inflicted on them."

22. *Behold, I will punish them.* And the punishment is, *Their young men shall die by the sword* of the Chaldeans; and *their sons and their daughters shall die by famine* that shall come on the land through the desolations occasioned by the Chaldean army.

CHAPTER 12

This chapter is connected with the foregoing. The prophet expostulates with God concerning the ways of Providence in permitting the wicked to prosper, 1-4. It is intimated to him that he must endure still greater trials, 5, from his false and deceitful brethren, 6; but that still heavier judgments awaited the nation for their crimes, 7-13. That God, however, would at length have compassion on them; restore them to their land; and turn His judgments against those that oppressed them, if not prevented by their becoming converts to the true religion, 14-17.

1. *Righteous art thou, O Lord, when I plead with thee.* The prophet is grieved at the prosperity of the wicked; and he wonders how, consistently with God's righteousness, vice should often be in affluence, and piety in suffering and poverty. He knows that God is righteous, that everything is done well; but he wishes to inquire how these apparently unequal and undeserved lots take place. On this subject he wishes to reason with God, that he may receive instruction.

2. *Thou art near in their mouth.* They have no sincerity; they have something of the form of religion, but nothing of its power.

3. *But thou, O Lord, knowest me.* I know that the very secrets of my heart are known to Thee; and I am glad of it, for Thou knowest that my heart is towards Thee—is upright and sincere.

4. *How long shall the land mourn?* These hypocrites and open sinners are a curse to the country; pull them out, Lord, that the land may be delivered of that which is the cause of its desolation.

5. *If thou hast run with the footmen.* If the smallest evils to which you are exposed cause you to make so many bitter complaints, how will you feel when, in the course of your prophetic ministry, you shall be exposed to much greater, from enemies much more powerful? *And if in the land of peace, wherein thou trustedst.* I believe the meaning is this, "If in a country now enjoying peace you scarcely think yourself in safety, what will you do in *the swelling of Jordan?* in the time when the enemy, like an overflowing torrent, shall deluge every part of the land?" The overflowing of Jordan, which generally happened in harvest, drove the lions and other beasts of prey from

their coverts among the bushes that lined its banks; who, spreading themselves through the country, made terrible havoc, slaying men, and carrying off the cattle.

6. *For even thy brethren, and the house of thy father.* You have none to depend on but God; even your brethren will betray you when they have it in their power.

7. *I have forsaken mine house.* I have abandoned My temple. *I have given the dearly beloved of my soul.* The people once in covenant with Me, and inexpressibly dear to Me while faithful. *Into the hand of her enemies.* This was a condition in the covenant I made with them; if they forsook Me, they were to be abandoned to their enemies, and cast out of the good land I gave to their fathers.

8. *Mine heritage is unto me as a lion.* The people are enraged against Me; they roar like a furious lion against their God.

10. *Many pastors have destroyed my vineyard.* My people have had many kinds of enemies which have fed upon their richest pastures: the Philistines, Moabites, Ammonites, Assyrians, Egyptians, and now the Chaldeans.

11. *No man layeth it to heart.* Notwithstanding all these desolations, from which the land everywhere mourns, and which are so plainly the consequences of the people's crimes, no man layeth it to heart, or considereth that these are God's judgments; and that the only way to have them removed is to repent of their sins, and turn to God with all their hearts.

12. *The sword of the Lord shall devour.* It is the sword of the Lord that has devoured, and will devour; this is what no man layeth to heart. They think these things come in the course of events.

14. *Against all mine evil neighbours.* All the neighboring nations who have united in desolating Judea shall be desolated in their turn; they also are wicked, and they shall be punished.

15. *I will return, and have compassion on them.* This is a promise of restoration from the Captivity, and an intimation also that some of their enemies would turn to the true God with them; learn the ways of His people; that is, would abjure idols, and take Jehovah for their God; and be built in the midst of His people, that is, Jew and Gentile forming one Church of the Most High.

17. *I will . . . destroy that nation.* Several of them did not obey, and are destroyed. Of the Moabites, Ammonites, and Chaldeans not one vestige remains. The sixteenth verse is supposed to be a promise of the conversion of the Gentiles. See Eph. ii. 13-22.

From the thirteenth verse to the end is a different discourse, and Dahler supposes it to have been delivered in the seventh or eighth year of the reign of Jehoiakim.

CHAPTER 13

This chapter contains an entire prophecy. The symbol of the linen girdle, left to rot for a considerable time, was a type of the manner in which the glory of the Jews should be marred during the course of their long captivity, 1-11. The scene of hiding the girdle being laid near the Euphrates intimated that the scene of the nation's distress should be Chaldea, which that river waters. The next three verses, by another emblem frequently used to represent the judgments of God, are designed to show that the calamities threatened should

be extended to every rank and denomination, 12-14. This leads the prophet to a most affectionate exhortation to repentance, 15-17. But God, knowing that this happy consequence would not ensue, sends him with an awful message to the royal family particularly, and to the inhabitants of Jerusalem in general, declaring the approaching judgments in plain terms, 18-27. The ardent desire for the reformation of Jerusalem, with which the chapter concludes, beautifully displays the compassion and tender mercy of God.

1. *Thus saith the Lord unto me.* This discourse is supposed to have been delivered under the reign of Jeconiah, the son and successor of Jehoiakim, who came to the throne in the eighteenth year of his age; when the Chaldean generals had encamped near to Jerusalem, but did not besiege it in form till Nebuchadnezzar came up with the great body of the army. In these circumstances the prophet predicts the captivity; and, by a symbolical representation of a rotten girdle, shows the people their totally corrupt state; and by another of bottles filled with wine, shows the destruction and madness of their counsels, and the confusion that must ensue.

Go and get thee a linen girdle. This was either a vision or God simply describes the thing in order that the prophet might use it in the way of illustration. *Put it not in water.* After having worn it, let it not be washed, that it may more properly represent the uncleanness of the Israelites; for they were represented by the girdle. "For as the girdle cleaveth to the loins of a man, so have I caused to cleave unto me the whole house of Israel and the whole house of Judah."

4. *Go to Euphrates, and hide it there.* Intending to point out, by this distant place, the country into which they were to be carried away captive.

7. *And, behold, the girdle was marred, it was profitable for nothing.* This symbolically represented the state of the Jews. They were corrupt and abominable; and God, by sending them into captivity, marred "the pride of Judah, and the great pride of Jerusalem," v. 9.

13. *Behold, I will fill all the inhabitants of this land . . . with drunkenness.* You, and your kings, and priests, and prophets are represented by these bottles. The wine is God's wrath against you, which shall first be shown by confounding your deliberations, filling you with foolish plans of defense, causing you from your divided counsels to fall out among yourselves, so that like so many drunken men you shall reel about and jostle each other; defend yourselves without plan, and fight without order, till you all fall an easy prey into the hands of your enemies. The ancient adage is here fulfilled: "Those whom God determines to destroy, He first renders foolish."

16. *Give glory to . . . God.* Confess your sins and turn to Him, that these sore evils may be averted. *While ye look for light.* While you expect prosperity, He turned *it into the shadow of death*—sent you adversity of the most distressing and ruinous kind. *Stumble upon the dark mountains.* Before you meet with those great obstacles, which, having no light, no proper understanding in the matter, you shall be utterly unable to surmount.

18. *Say unto the king and to the queen.* Probably Jeconiah and his mother, under whose tutelage, being young when he began to reign, he was left, as is very likely.

19. *The cities of the south shall be shut up.* Not only the cities of the north, the quarter at which the Chaldeans entered, but the cities of the south also; for he shall proceed from one extremity of the land to the other, spreading devastation everywhere, and carrying off the inhabitants.

20. *Where is the flock . . . thy beautiful flock?* Jerusalem is addressed. Where are the prosperous multitudes of men, women, and children? Alas! are they not driven before Babylonians, who have taken them captive?

21. *Thou hast taught them to be captains, and as chief over thee.* This is said of their enemies, whether Assyrians or Chaldeans; for ever since Ahaz submitted himself to the king of Assyria, the kings of Judah never regained their independence. Their enemies were thus taught to be their lords and masters.

22. *Are thy skirts discovered.* Your defense-less state is everywhere known; you are not only weak, but ignominiously so.

23. *Can the Ethiopian change his skin?* Can a *black*, at his own pleasure, change the color of his skin? Can the *leopard* at will change the variety of *his* spots? These things are natural to them, and they cannot be altered; so sin, and especially your attachment to idolatry, is become a second nature; and we may as well expect the Ethiopian to change his skin, and the leopard his spots, as you to do good, who have been accustomed to do evil.

24. *The wind of the wilderness.* Some strong, tempestuous wind, proverbially severe, coming from the desert to the south of Judea.

25. *Trusted in falsehood.* In idols, and in lying prophets.

27. *I have seen thine adulteries.* Your idola-tries of different kinds, practiced in various ways; no doubt often accompanied with gross debauchery. *Woe unto thee, O Jerusalem! wilt thou not be made clean?* We see from this that, though the thing was difficult, yet it was not impossible, for these Ethiopians to change their skin, for these leopards to change their spots. It was only their obstinate refusal of the grace of God that rendered it impossible.

CHAPTER 14

This chapter begins with foretelling a drought that should greatly distress the land of Judea, the effects of which are described in a most pathetic manner, 1-6. The prophet then, in the people's name, makes a confession of sins, and supplication for pardon, 7-9. But God declares His purpose to punish, forbidding Jeremiah to pray for the people, 10-12. False prophets are then complained of, and threatened with destruction, as are also those who attend to them, 13-16. The prophet, therefore, bewails their misery, 17-18; and though he had just now been forbidden to intercede for them, yet, like a tender pastor, who could not cease to be concerned for their welfare, he falls on the happy expedient of introducing themselves as supplicating in their own name that mercy which he was not allowed to ask in his, 19-22.

1. *The word . . . that came . . . concerning the dearth.* This discourse is supposed to have been delivered after the fourth year of Jehoi-akim.

2. *The gates thereof languish.* The gates be-ing the places of public resort, they are put here for the people. *They are black unto the ground.* Covered from head to foot with a black garment, the emblem of sorrow and calamity.

3. *Their nobles have sent their little ones.* So general was this calamity that the servants no longer attended to their lords, but everyone was interested alone for himself; and the nobles of the land were obliged to employ their own children to scour the land, to see if any water could be found in the tanks or the pits. In the dearth in the time of Elijah, Ahab, the king, and Obadiah, his counsellor, were obliged to traverse the land themselves in order to find out water to keep their cattle alive. This and the following three verses give a lively but distressing picture of this dearth and its effects.

4. *The ground is chapt.* The cracks in the earth before the descent of the rains are in some places a cubit wide, and deep enough to receive the greater part of a human body.

7. *O Lord, though our iniquities testify against us.* We deeply acknowledge that we have sinned, and deserve nothing but death. Yet act for Thy name's sake—work in our behalf, that we perish not.

8. *O the hope of Israel.* O Thou who art the only Object of the *hope* of this people. *The saviour thereof in time of trouble.* Who hast never yet abandoned them that seek Thee. *Why shouldest thou be as a stranger in the land?* As one who has no interest in the prosperity and safety of the country. *And as a wayfaring man.* A traveller on his journey. *That turneth aside to tarry for a night.* Who stays the shortest time he can; and takes up his lodging in a tent or caravanserai, for the dead of the night, that he may pursue his journey by break of day. Instead of dwelling among us, Thou hast scarcely paid the most transient visit to Thy land. Oh, come once more, and dwell among us.

11. *Pray not for this people.* They are ripe for destruction; intercede not for them.

13. *Ah, Lord God! behold, the prophets say unto them.* True, Lord, they are exceedingly wicked; but the false prophets have deceived them; this is some mitigation of their offense. This plea God does not admit; and why? The people believed them, without having any proof of their divine mission.

14. *The prophets prophesy lies.* They say they have visions, but they have them by divination, and they are false. The people should know their character, and avoid them; but they love to have it so, and will not be undeceived.

15. *By sword and famine shall those prophets be consumed.* Jeremiah had told Jehoiakim that, if he rebelled against Nebuchadnezzar, he should be overthrown, and the land wasted by *sword* and *famine;* the false prophets said there should be neither sword nor famine, but peace and prosperity. The king believed *them,* and withheld the tribute. Nebuchadnezzar, being incensed, invaded and destroyed the land; and the false prophets fell in these calamities. See 2 Kings xxv. 3; Lam. ii. 11-19.

17. *For the virgin daughter of my people is broken.* First, the land was sadly distressed by Pharaoh-necho, king of Egypt. Secondly, it was laid under a heavy tribute by Nebuchadnezzar. And, thirdly, it was nearly desolated by a famine afterwards. In a few years all these calamities fell upon them; these might be well called *a great breach . . . a very grievous blow.*

19. *We looked for peace.* We expected pros-perity when Josiah purged the land of idolatry.

20. *We acknowledge, O Lord, our wickedness,*

This the prophet did in behalf of the people; but, alas! they did not join him.

21. *Do not disgrace the throne of thy glory.* The Temple. Let not this sacred place be profaned by impious and sacrilegious hands. *Break not thy covenant.* See Exod. xxiv. 7-8; xix. 5. They had already broken the covenant, and they wish God to fulfil His part.

CHAPTER 15

God declares to Jeremiah that not even Moses and Samuel, whose prayers had been so prevalent, could divert Him from His purpose of punishing so wicked a people, 1. Accordingly their captivity is again announced in a variety of images so full of terror, 2-9, that the prophet complains of his own hard fate in being obliged to deliver such unwelcome messages, 10: for which too he is reproved, 11-14. Immediately he appeals to God for his sincerity, and supplicates pardon, 15-18; and God tempers His reproof with promising again to protect him in the faithful discharge of his duty, 19-21.

1. *Though Moses and Samuel. Moses* had often supplicated for the people, and in consequence they were spared. See Exod. xxxii. 11 and following verses; Num. xiv. 13. *Samuel* also had prayed for the people, and God heard him, 1 Sam. vii. 9. But if these or the most holy men were now to supplicate for this people, He would not spare them.

2. *Whither shall we go forth? . . . Such as are for death, to death.* Some shall be destroyed by the pestilence, here termed *death.* See chap. xviii. 21. Others shall be slain by the *sword* in battle, and in the sackage of cities. Others shall perish by *famine,* shall be starved to death through the mere want of the necessaries of life; and the rest shall go into *captivity.*

3. *I will appoint over them four kinds.* There shall appear four instruments of My justice: (1) *The sword to slay.* (2) *The dogs to tear* what is slain. (3) *The fowls of the heaven to* feed on the dead carcasses. And (4) *The wild beasts to destroy* all that the fowls have left.

4. *I will cause them to be removed into all kingdoms of the earth.* This seems to have respect to the succeeding state of the Jews in their different generations; never was there a prophecy more literally fulfilled, and it is still a standing monument of divine truth.

6. *I am weary with repenting.* With repeatedly "changing My purpose."

7. *I will fan them with a fan.* There is no pure grain; all is chaff. *In the gates of the land.* The places of public justice; and there it shall be seen that the judgments that have fallen upon them have been highly merited. And from these places of fanning they shall go out into their captivity.

8. *The mother of the young men.* The metropolis or mother city, Jerusalem.

9. *She that hath borne seven.* She that hath had a numerous offspring; Jerusalem, the parent of so many cities, villages, and families in the land. *Seven* signifies a complete or full number.

10. *A man of contention to the whole earth!* To the whole "land," to all his countrymen, though he had done nothing to merit their displeasure.

11. *I will cause the enemy to entreat thee well in the time of evil.* This was literally fulfilled; see chap. xxxix. 11, etc. Nebuchadnezzar had given strict charge to Nebuzar-adan, commander in chief, to look well to Jeremiah,

to do him no harm, and to grant him all the privileges he was pleased to ask.

12. *Shall iron break the northern iron and the steel?* Shall our weak forces be able to oppose and overcome the powers of the Chaldeans? *Nechasheth,* which we here translate *steel,* properly signifies brass or copper united with tin, which gives it much hardness, and enables it to bear a good edge.

13. *Thy substance . . . will I give to the spoil without price.* Invaluable property shall be given up to your adversaries. Or *without price* —you shall have nothing for it in return.

15. *O Lord . . . remember me, and visit me.* Let me not be carried away into captivity; and it does not appear that he had ever been taken to Babylon. After the capture of the city he went into Egypt and either died there or was put to death by his countrymen.

16. *Thy word was . . . the joy and rejoicing of mine heart.* When I did receive the prophetic message, I did rejoice in the honor Thou hadst done me; and I faithfully testified Thy will to them. They have become mine enemies; not because there was any evil in me, but because I was faithful to Thee.

21. *I will deliver thee out of the hand of the wicked.* From the power of this evil people. *And I will redeem thee out of the hand of the terrible.* Out of the power of the Chaldean armies. Everything took place as God had promised, for no word of His can ever fall to the ground.

CHAPTER 16

On account of the evils which threatened his country, the prophet is forbidden to encumber himself with a wife and family, or to bear any share in the little joys and sorrows of his neighbors, which were to be forgotten and absorbed in those public calamities, 1-9, which their sins should draw on them, 10-13. A future restoration however is intimated, 14-15, after those calamities should be endured, 16-18; and the conversion of the Gentiles is foretold, 19-21.

1. *The word of the Lord came also unto me.* This discourse Dahler supposes to have been delivered sometime in the reign of Jehoiakim.

2. *Thou shalt not take thee a wife.* As it would be very inconvenient to have a family when the threatened desolations should come on the place. The reason is given in the following verses.

4. *They shall die of grievous deaths.* All prematurely; see chap. xiv. 16. *As dung upon the face of the earth.* See chap. viii. 2. *Be meat for the fowls.* See chap. vii. 33.

5. *Enter not into the house of mourning.* The public calamities are too great to permit individual losses to come into consideration.

6. *Nor cut themselves.* A custom of the heathen forbidden to the Jews, Lev. xix. 28; Deut. xiv. 1, and which appears now to have prevailed among them; because, having become idolaters, they conformed to all the customs of the heathen.

8. *Thou shalt not also go into the house of feasting.* Funeral banquets were made to commemorate the dead, and comfort the surviving relatives; and the cup of consolation, strong mingled wine, was given to those who were deepest in distress, to divert their minds and to soothe their sorrows.

12. *And ye have done worse than your fathers.* The sins of the fathers would not have been visited on the children, had they not followed their example, and become even worse than they.

13. *Will I cast you out of this land.* See chap. vii. 15 and ix. 15.

14. *The Lord liveth, that brought up.* See Isa. xliii. 18.

15. *The land of the north.* Chaldea; and their deliverance thence will be as remarkable as the deliverance of their fathers from the land of Egypt.

16. *I will send for many fishers . . . for many hunters.* I shall raise up enemies against them, some of whom shall destroy them by wiles, and others shall ruin them by violence. This seems to be the meaning of these symbolical *fishers* and *hunters.*

18. *The carcases of their detestable . . . things.* Either meaning the idols themselves, which were only carcasses without life, or the sacrifices which were made to them.

19. *The Gentiles shall come.* Even the days shall come when the Gentiles themselves, ashamed of their confidence, shall renounce their idols, and acknowledge that their fathers had believed lies and worshipped vanities. This may be a prediction of the calling of the Gentiles by the gospel of Christ.

21. *Therefore, behold, I will this once.* I will not now change My purpose. They shall be visited and carried into captivity; nothing shall prevent this. *And they shall know that My name is Jehovah.* Since they would not receive the abundance of My mercies, they shall know what the true God can do in the way of judgment.

CHAPTER 17

This chapter begins with setting forth the very strong bias which the people of Judah had to idolatry, with the total consequences, 1-4. The happiness of the man that trusteth in Jehovah is then beautifully contrasted with the opposite character, 5-8. God alone knows the deceitfulness and wretchedness of the heart of man. 9-10. The comparison of a bird's hatching the eggs of another of a different species, which will soon forsake her, is highly expressive of the vanity of ill-acquired riches, which often disappoint the owner, 11. The prophet continues the same subject in his own person, appeals to God for his sincerity, and prays that the evil intended him by his enemies may revert on their own heads, 12-18. The remaining part of the chapter is a distinct prophecy relating to the due observance of the Sabbath, enforced by both promises and threatenings, 19-27.

1. *The sin of Judah.* Idolatry. *Is written with a pen of iron.* It is deeply and indelibly written in their hearts, and shall be as indelibly written in their punishment.

2. *Whilst their children remember.* Even the rising generation have their imagination stocked with idol images, and their memories with the frantic rites and ceremonies which they saw their parents observe in this abominable worship.

3. *O my mountain in the field.* The prophet here addresses the land of Judea, which was a mountainous country, Deut. iii. 25; but Jerusalem itself may be meant, which is partly built upon hills which, like itself, are elevated above the rest of the country.

5. *Cursed be the man that trusteth in man.* This reprehends their vain confidence in trusting in Egypt, which was too feeble itself to help,

and, had it been otherwise, too ill disposed towards them to help them heartily. An arm of flesh is put here for a weak and ineffectual support.

6. *He shall be like the heath in the desert.* Or like a blasted tree, without moisture, parched and withered. *Shall not see when good cometh.* Shall not be sensible of it, the previous drought having rendered it incapable of absorbing any more vegetable juices. *A salt land.* Barren, and therefore unfit to be inhabited.

8. *As a tree planted by the waters.* Which is sufficiently supplied with moisture, though the heat be intense, and there be no rain; for the roots being spread out by the river, they absorb from it all the moisture requisite for the flourishing vegetation of the tree.

9. *The heart is deceitful.* Akob halleb, "The heart is supplanting—tortuous—full of windings—insidious." *And desperately wicked.* And is "wretched" or "feeble"; distressed beyond all things, in consequence of the wickedness that is in it. *Who can know it?* It even hides itself from itself, so that its owner does not know it. A corrupt heart is the worst enemy the fallen creature can have.

10. *I the Lord search the heart.* The Lord is called by His apostles, Acts i. 24, the Knower of the heart. To Him alone can this epithet be applied; and it is from Him alone that we can derive that instruction by which we can in any measure know ourselves.

11. *As the partridge. Kore.* It is very likely that this was a bird different from our partridge. The text Dr. Blayney translates thus: "(As) the koré that hatcheth what it doth not lay, (so is) he who getteth riches, and not according to right." *And at his end shall be a fool.* Shall be reputed as such. He was a fool all the way through; he lost his soul to get wealth, and this wealth he never enjoyed.

13. *Written in the earth.* They shall never come to true honor. Their names shall be written in the dust, and the first wind that blows over it shall render it illegible.

14. *Heal me . . . and I shall be healed.* That is, I shall be thoroughly healed, and effectually saved, if Thou undertake for me.

15. *Where is the word of the Lord?* Where is the accomplishment of His threatenings? You have said that the city and the Temple should both be destroyed. No such events have yet taken place. But they did take place, and every tittle of the menace was strictly fulfilled.

16. *I have not hastened from being a pastor.* Dr. Blayney translates thus: "But I have not been in haste to outrun thy guidance." I was obliged to utter Thy prediction, but I have not hastened the evil day. For the credit of my prophecy I have not desired the calamity to come speedily; I have rather pleaded for respite.

17. *Be not a terror unto me.* Do not command me to predict miseries, and abandon me to them and to my enemies.

18. *Let them be confounded.* They shall be confounded. These words are to be understood as simple predictions, rather than as prayers.

19. *The gate of the children of the people.* I suppose the most public gate is meant, that through which there was the greatest thoroughfare.

21. *Take heed to yourselves, and bear no burden.* From this and the following verses we find the ruin of the Jews attributed to the breach of the Sabbath; as this led to a neglect of sacrifice, the ordinances of religion, and all public worship, so it necessarily brought with it all immorality. This breach of the Sabbath was that which let in upon them all the waters of God's wrath.

24. *If ye diligently hearken unto me.* So we find that, though their destruction was positively threatened, yet still there was an unexpressed proviso that, if they did return to the Lord, the calamities should be averted, and a succession of princes would have been continued on the throne of David, vv. 25-26.

CHAPTER 18

The type of the potter's vessel, and its signification, 1-10. The inhabitants of Judah and Jerusalem exhorted to repentance, 11; but on their refusal (which is represented to be as unnatural as if a man should prefer the snowy Lebanon or barren rock to a fruitful plain, or other waters to the cool stream of the fountain) their destruction is predicted, 12-17. In consequence of these plain reproofs and warnings of Jeremiah, a conspiracy is formed against him, 18. This leads him to appeal to God for his integrity, 19-20; who puts a most dreadful curse in the mouth of His prophet, strongly indicative of the terrible fate of his enemies, 21-23.

1. *The word which came to Jeremiah.* This discourse is supposed to have been delivered sometime in the reign of Jehoiakim, probably within the first three years.

2. *Go down to the potter's house.* By this similitude God shows the absolute state of dependence on himself in which He has placed mankind. They are as clay in the hands of the potter; and in reference to everything here below, He can shape their destinies as He pleases. Again, though while under the providential care of God they may go morally astray and pervert themselves, yet they can be reclaimed by the almighty and all-wise Operator, and become such vessels as seemeth good for Him to make. In considering this parable we must take heed that in running parallels we do not destroy the free agency of man, nor disgrace the goodness and supremacy of God.

4. *The vessel . . . was marred in the hand of the potter.* It did not stand in the working; it got out of shape; or some gravel or small stone, having been incorporated with the mass of clay, made a breach in that part where it was found, so that the potter was obliged to knead up the clay afresh, place it on the wheel, and form it anew; and then it was such a vessel as seemed good to the potter to make it.

6. *Cannot I do with you as this potter?* Have I not a right to do with a people whom I have created as reason and justice may require? If they do not answer My intentions, may I not reject and destroy them; and act as this potter, make a new vessel out of that which at first did not succeed in his hands?

7-10. *At what instant I shall speak concerning a nation.* These verses contain what may be called God's decree by which the whole of His conduct towards man is regulated. If He purpose destruction against an offending person, if that person repent and turn to God, he shall live and not die.

12. *There is no hope.* See chap. ii. 25.

14. *Will a man leave the snow of Lebanon?* Lebanon was the highest mountain in Judea.

Would any man in his senses abandon a farm that was always watered by the melted snows of Lebanon, and take a barren rock in its place? How stupid therefore and absurd are My people, who abandon the everlasting God for the worship of idols!

16. *A perpetual hissing.* A "shrieking, hissing"; an expression of contempt.

18. *Come, and let us devise devices.* Let us form a conspiracy against him, accuse him of being a false prophet, and a contradicter of the words of God; for God has promised us protection, and *he* says we shall be destroyed, and that God will forsake His people. *Let us smite him with the tongue.* On the tongue; so it should be rendered. Lying and false testimony are punished in the Eastern countries, to the present day, by smiting the person on the mouth with a strong piece of leather like the sole of a shoe.

20. *They have digged a pit for my soul.* For my "life." *Stood before thee to speak good for them.* I was their continual intercessor.

21. *Therefore deliver up their children.* The execrations in these verses should be considered as simply prophetic declarations of the judgments which God was about to pour out on them.

CHAPTER 19

By the significant type of breaking a potter's vessel, Jeremiah is directed to predict the utter desolation of Judah and Jerusalem, 1-15. The prophets taught frequently by symbolic actions as well as by words.

1. *Go and get a potter's earthen bottle.* This discourse was also delivered sometime in the reign of Jehoiakim. Under the type of breaking a potter's earthen bottle or jug, Jeremiah shows his enemies that the word of the Lord should stand, that Jerusalem should be taken and sacked, and they all carried into captivity.

5. *Offerings unto Baal.* A general name for all the popular idols: Baal, Moloch, Ashtaroth, etc.

7. *I will make void the counsel of Judah.* Probably this refers to some determination made to proclaim themselves independent, and pay no more tribute to the Chaldeans.

9. *I will cause them to eat the flesh of their sons.* This was literally fulfilled when Jerusalem was besieged by the Romans.

11. *Even so will I break this people and this city.* The breaking of the bottle was the symbolical representation of the destruction of the city and of the state. *That cannot be made whole again.* This seems to refer rather to the final destruction of Jerusalem by the Romans, than to what was done by the Chaldeans. Jerusalem was healed after seventy years: but nearly eighteen hundred years have elapsed since Jerusalem was taken and destroyed by the Romans; and it was then so broken that it could not be made whole again.

12. *And even make this city as Tophet.* A place of slaughter and destruction.

15. *Because they have hardened their necks.* A metaphor taken from unruly and unbroken oxen, who resist the yoke, break and run away with their gears. So this people had broken and destroyed the yoke of the law.

CHAPTER 20

Jeremiah, on account of his prophesying evil concerning Judah and Jerusalem, is beaten and imprisoned by Pashur, chief governor of the Temple, 1-2. On the following day the prophet is released, who denounces the awful judgments of God which should fall upon the governor and all his house, as well as upon the whole land of Judah, in the approaching Babylonish captivity, 3-6. Jeremiah then bitterly complains of the reproaches continually heaped upon him by his enemies; and, in his haste, resolves to speak no more in the name of Jehovah; but the word of the Lord is in his heart as a burning flame, so that he is not able to forbear, 7-10. The prophet professes his trust in God, whom he praises for his late deliverance, 11-13. The remaining verses, which appear to be out of their place, contain Jeremiah's regret that he was ever born to a life of so much sorrow and trouble, 14-18. This complaint resembles that of Job; only it is milder and more dolorous. This excites our pity, that our horror. Both are highly poetical, and embellished with every circumstance that can heighten the coloring. But such circumstances are not always to be too literally understood or explained. We must often make allowances for the strong figures of Eastern poetry.

3. *The Lord hath not called thy name Pashur.* —Security on all sides. *But Magor-missabib*— Fear on every side. This name has God given you because, in the course of His providence, you shall be placed in the circumstances signified by it; you shall be a terror to yourself.

6. *And thou, Pashur . . . shall go into captivity.* You shall suffer for the false prophecies which you have delivered, and for your insults to My prophet.

7. *O Lord, thou hast deceived me.* I think our translation of this passage is very exceptionable. The original word is *pittithani*, "Thou hast persuaded me," i.e., to go and prophesy to this people. I went, faithfully declared Thy message, and now I am likely to perish by their cruelty. As the root *pathah* signifies to "persuade" and "allure," as well as to "deceive," the above must be its meaning in this place. Taken as in our version, it is highly irreverent. It is used in the same sense here as in Gen. ix. 27; "God shall enlarge ['persuade,' margin] Japheth, and he shall dwell in the tents of Shem."

8. *I cried violence and spoil.* This was the burden of the message Thou didst give me.

9. *I will not make mention of him.* I will renounce the prophetic office, and return to my house.

10. *Report . . . and we will report it.* Let us spread calumnies against him everywhere; or let us spread reports of dangers coming upon him, that we may intimidate him, and cause him to desist.

11. *But the Lord is with me as a mighty terrible one.* Thus was he, by his strong confidence in the strong God, delivered from all his fears, and enabled to go on comfortably with his work.

13. *Sing unto the Lord.* He was so completely delivered from all fear that, although he remained in the same circumstances, yet he exults in the divine protection, and does not fear the face of any adversary.

14. *Cursed be the day wherein I was born.* If we take these words literally, and suppose them to be in their proper place, they are utterly inconsistent with that state of confidence in which he exulted a few minutes before. If they are the language of Jeremiah, they must have been spoken on a prior occasion, when probably he had given way to a passionate hastiness. They might well comport with the state he was in in v. 9. I really believe these

verses have got out of their proper place, which I conjecture to be between the eighth and ninth verses. There they will come in very properly, and might have been a part of his complaint in those moments when he had purposed to flee from God as did Jonah, and prophesy no more in His name. Transpositions in this prophet are frequent; therefore place these five verses after the eighth, and let the chapter end with the thirteenth, and the whole will form a piece of exquisite poetry. See Job iii. 3. The two passages are very similar.

CHAPTER 21

Nebuchadnezzar being come up against Jerusalem, Zedekiah sends Pashur and Zephaniah to the prophet to request him to intercede with God in behalf of His people, 1-2. But He is declared to be against Jerusalem, and the whole land of Judah; and the only mitigation of their punishment must proceed from their surrendering to the king of Babylon, 3-10. Prophecy concerning the house of the king of Judah, 11-12. Notwithstanding the amazing fortifications round about Jerusalem, in which the people vainly trust, the Lord will most assuredly visit them for their iniquities; the city shall be taken by the Chaldeans, 13-14.

1. *The word which came unto Jeremiah.* The chapters in the remaining parts of this prophecy seem strangely interchanged. The discourse here was delivered about the ninth year of the reign of Zedekiah. This chapter, observes Dr. Blayney, contains the first of those prophecies which were delivered by Jeremiah subsequent to the revolt of Zedekiah and the breaking out of the war thereupon; and which are continued on to the taking of Jerusalem, related in chap. xxix, in the following order: ch. xxi; xxxiv; xxxvii; xxxii; xxxiii; xxxviii; xxxix. *Pashur the son of Melchiah.* There can be little doubt that this Pashur was a different person from him who was called the son of Immur in the preceding chapter.

2. *Enquire, I pray thee.* See whether God intends to deliver us into or out of the hand of the Chaldeans.

4. *I will turn back the weapons.* Every attempt you make to repel the Chaldeans shall be unsuccessful. *I will assemble them into the midst of this city.* I will deliver the city into their hands.

6. *They shall die of a great pestilence.* The sword may appear to be that of man, though I have given the Chaldeans their commission; but the pestilence shall appear to be the immediate act of God.

7. *Nebuchadrezzar.* This name is spelt as above in twenty-six places of this book; and in ten places it is spelt Nebuchadnezzar, which is the common orthography.

8. *Behold, I set before you the way of life, and the way of death.* Meaning escape or destruction in the present instance. This is explained in the next verse.

10. *He shall burn it with fire.* What a heavy message to all; and especially to them who had any fear of God, or reverence for the Temple and its sacred services!

12. *Execute judgment in the morning.* Probably the time for dispensing the judgment was the morning, when the people were going to their work; but the words may mean, Do justice promptly, do not delay.

13. *O inhabitant of the valley, and rock of the plain.* Jerusalem itself, though partly on two hills, was also extended in the valley; and Zion, the city of David, was properly a rock, strongly fortified by both nature and art; and by its ancient possessors, the Jebusites, was deemed impregnable. *Who shall come down against us?* Probably the words of those courtiers who had persuaded Zedekiah to rebel against the king of Babylon.

14. *I will kindle a fire in the forest thereof.* I will send destruction into its center, that shall spread to every part of the circumference, and so consume the whole.

CHAPTER 22

This section of prophecy, extending to the end of the eighth verse of the next chapter, is addressed to the king of Judah and his people. It enjoins on them the practice of justice and equity, as they would hope to prosper, 1-4; but threatens them, in case of disobedience, with utter destruction, 5-9. The captivity of Shallum, the son of Josiah, is declared to be irreversible, 10-12; and the miserable and unlamented end of Jeconiah, contemptuously called Coniah, is foretold, 13-19. His family is threatened with the like captivity, and his seed declared to be forever excluded from the throne, 20-30.

1. *Go down to the house of the king of Judah, and speak there this word.* This is supposed by Dahler to have been published in the first year of the reign of Zedekiah.

2. *O king of Judah . . . thou, and thy servants.* His ministers are here addressed, as chiefly governing the nation, and who had counselled Zedekiah to rebel.

6. *Thou art Gilead unto me, and the head of Lebanon.* Lebanon was the highest mountain in Israel, and *Gilead* the richest and most fertile part of the country; and were, therefore, proper emblems of the reigning family. Though you are the richest and most powerful, I, who raised you up, can bring you down and make you a *wilderness.*

7. *They shall cut down thy choice cedars.* The destruction of the country is expressed under the symbol of the destruction of a fine forest.

8. *Many nations shall pass.* These words seem borrowed from Deut. xxix. 22, etc.

10. *Weep ye not for the dead.* Josiah, dead in consequence of the wound he had received at Megiddo, in a battle with Pharaoh-necho, king of Egypt; but he died in peace with God. *But weep sore for him that goeth away.* Namely, Jehoahaz, the son of Josiah, called below Shallum, whom Pharaoh-necho had carried captive into Egypt, from which it was prophesied he should never return, 2 Kings xxiii. 30-34. He was called Shallum before he ascended the throne, and Jehoahaz afterwards; so his brother Eliakim changed his name to Jehoiakim, and Mattaniah to Zedekiah.

13. *Woe unto him that buildeth his house.* These evils, charged against Jehoiakim, are nowhere else circumstantially related. We learn from 2 Kings xxiii. 35-37 that he taxed his subjects heavily, to give to Pharaoh-necho, king of Egypt: "He exacted the silver and gold of the people of the land," and "did that which was evil in the sight of the Lord." The mode of taxation is here intimated; he took the wages of the hirelings, and caused the people to work without wages in his own buildings.

15. *Shalt thou reign?* Do you think you are a great king, because you dwell in a splendid palace?

19. *With the burial of an ass.* Cast out, and left unburied, or buried without any funeral solemnities, and without such lamentations as the above.

20. *Go up to Lebanon.* Probably Anti-Libanus, which, together with Bashan and Abarim, which we here translate "passages," were on the way by which the captives should be led out of their own country.

21. *I spake unto thee in thy prosperity.* In all states and circumstances I warned you by My prophets; and you will be ashamed of your conduct only when you shall be stripped of all your excellencies, and reduced to poverty and disgrace, v. 22.

22. *The wind shall eat up all thy pastors.* A blast from God's mouth shall carry off your kings, princes, prophets, and priests.

23. *How gracious shalt thou be!* A strong irony.

24. *Though Coniah.* Called Jeconiah, probably on ascending the throne. See on v. 10. *The signet upon my right hand.* The most precious seal, ring, or armlet. Though dearer to Me than the most splendid gem to its possessor.

26. *I will cast thee out, and thy mother.* See all this fulfilled, 2 Kings xxiv. 12-13. All were carried by Nebuchadnezzar into captivity together.

28. *Is this man Coniah a despised broken idol?* These are probably the exclamations of the people, when they heard those solemn denunciations against their king and their country.

29. *O earth.* These are the words of the prophet in reply: O land! unhappy land! desolate land! Hear the judgment of the Lord!

30. *Write ye this man childless.* Though he had seven sons, 1 Chron. iii. 17, yet, having no successor, he is to be entered on the genealogical tables as one without children, for none of his posterity ever sat on the throne of David.

CHAPTER 23

Sequel of the discourse which commenced in the preceding chapter. The prophet denounces vengeance against the pastors of Israel who have scattered and destroyed the flock of the Lord, 1-2. He concludes with gracious promises of deliverance from the Babylonish captivity, and of better times under the Messiah, when the converts to Christianity, who are the true Israel of God, shadowed forth by the old dispensation, shall be delivered, by the glorious light of the gospel, from worse than Chaldean bondage, from the captivity of sin and death. But this prophecy will not have its fullest accomplishment till that period arrives which is fixed in the divine counsel for the restoration of Israel and Judah from their various dispersions, of which their deliverance from the Chaldean domination was a type; when Jesus, the Christ, the righteous Branch, the Root and Offspring of David, and the only legitimate Heir to the throne, shall take unto himself His great power, and reign gloriously over the whole house of Jacob, 3-8. At the ninth verse a new discourse commences. Jeremiah expresses his horror at the great wickedness of the priests and prophets of Judah, and declares that the divine vengeance is hanging over them. He exhorts the people not to listen to their false promises, 9-22; and predicts the utter ruin that shall fall upon all pretenders to inspiration, 23-32, as well as upon all scoffers at true prophecy, 33-40.

1. *Woe be unto the pastors!* There shall a curse fall on the kings, princes, priests, and prophets; who, by their vicious conduct and example, have brought desolation upon the people.

2. *Ye have scattered my flock.* The bad

government in both church and state was a principal cause of the people's profligacy.

5. *I will raise unto David a righteous Branch.* As there has been no age, from the Babylonish captivity to the destruction of Jerusalem by the Romans, in which such a state of prosperity existed, and no king or governor who could answer at all to the character here given, the passage has been understood to refer to our blessed Lord, Jesus Christ, who was a Branch out of the stem of Jesse; a righteous King; by the power of His Spirit and influence of His religion reigning, prospering, and executing judgment and justice in the earth.

6. *In his days Judah shall be saved.* The real Jew is not one who has his circumcision in the flesh, but in the spirit. The real Israel are true believers in Christ Jesus; and the genuine Jerusalem is the Church of the First-born, made free, with all her children, from the bondage of sin, Satan, death, and hell. *And this is his name whereby he shall be called, THE LORD OUR RIGHTEOUSNESS.* Dr. Blayney seems to follow the Septuagint; he translates thus, "And this is the name by which Jehovah shall call him, Our Righteousness." I prefer the translation of Blayney to all others.

9. *Mine heart within me is broken because of the prophets.* The first word of this clause is *lannebiim*, which we incorporate with the whole clause, and translate, *because of the prophets.* But as a new prophecy begins here, it is evident that the word is the title to this prophecy; and is thus distinguished by both Blayney and Dahler, "Concerning the Prophets." This discourse was delivered probably in the reign of Jehoiakim. *All my bones shake.* He was terrified even by his own message, and shocked at the profanity of the false prophets.

10. *The land is full of adulterers.* Of idolaters. Of persons who break their faith to Me, as an impure wife does to her husband. *The pleasant places of the wilderness are dried up.* He speaks here, most probably, in reference to dearth. Profane oaths, false swearing, evil courses, violence, etc., had provoked God to send this among other judgments; see v. 19.

11. *In my house.* They had even introduced idolatry into the temple of God!

13. *I have seen folly in the prophets of Samaria.* This was not to be wondered at, for their religion was a system of corruption.

14. *I have seen also in the prophets of Jerusalem.* That is, the prophets of Jerusalem, while professing a pure faith, have followed the ways of, and become as corrupt as, the prophets of Samaria. *They are all of them unto me as Sodom.* Incorrigible, brutish sinners, who will as surely be destroyed as Sodom and Gomorrah were.

16. *Harken not unto the words of the prophets.* That is, of those who promise you safety, without requiring you to forsake your sins and turn unto the Lord; see v. 17.

18. *Who hath stood in the counsel of the Lord?* Who of them has ever received a word of prophecy from Me?

23. *Am I a God at hand, . . . and not a God afar off?* You act as if you thought I could not see you! Am I not omnipresent? "Do not I fill heaven and earth?" (v. 24)

27. *By their dreams.* Dreams were anciently reputed as a species of inspiration; see Num. xii. 6; 1 Sam. xxviii. 6; Joel iii. 1; Dan. vii. 1.

28. *What is the chaff to the wheat? saith the Lord.* Do not mingle these equivocal matters with positive revelations.

29. *Is not my word like as a fire?* It enlightens, warms, and penetrates every part. When it is communicated to the true prophet, it is like a fire shut up in his bones. He cannot retain it; he must publish it. And when published, it is *like a hammer that breaketh the rock in pieces.* It is ever accompanied by a divine power that causes both sinner and saint to feel its weight and importance.

33. *What is the burden of the Lord?* The word *massa*, here used, signifies "burden, oracle, prophetic discourse," and is used by almost every prophet. But the persons in the text appear to have been mockers. "Where is this burden of the Lord?"—"What is the burden now?" To this insolent question the prophet answers in the following verses. *I will even forsake you.* I will punish the prophet, the priest, and the people, that speak thus, v. 34. Here are burdens.

36. *Every man's word shall be his burden.* You say that all God's messages are burdens, and to you they shall be such; whereas, had you used them as you ought, they would have been blessings to you. *For ye have perverted the words of the living God.* And thus have sinned against your own souls.

39. *I will utterly forget you, and I will forsake you, and the city.* Dr. Blayney translates: "I will both take you up altogether, and will cast you off together with the city." You are a burden to Me; but I will take you up, and then cast you off. I will do with you as a man weary with his burden will do: cast it off his shoulders, and bear it no more.

40. *I will bring an everlasting reproach upon you.* And this reproach of having rebelled against so good a God, and rejected so powerful a Saviour, follows them to this day through all their dispersions, in every part of the habitable earth. The word of the Lord cannot fail.

CHAPTER 24

Under the emblem of the good and bad figs is represented the fate of the Jews already gone into captivity with Jeconiah, and of those that remained still in their own country with Zedekiah. It is likewise intimated that God would deal kindly with the former, but that His wrath would still pursue the latter, 1-10.

1. *The Lord shewed me, and, behold, two baskets of figs.* Besides the transposition of whole chapters in this book, there is not infrequently a transposition of verses, and parts of verses. Of this we have an instance in the verse before us, the first clause of which should be the last. Thus: "After that Nebuchadrezzar king of Babylon had carried away captive Jeconiah the son of Jehoiakim king of Judah . . . with the carpenters and smiths, from Jerusalem, and had brought them to Babylon, the Lord shewed me, and, behold, two baskets of figs were set before the temple of the Lord." This prophecy was undoubtedly delivered in the first year of the reign of Zedekiah.

2. Under the type of good and bad figs, God represents the state of the persons who had already been carried captives into Babylon, with their king, Jeconiah, compared with the state

of those who should be carried away with Zedekiah. Those already carried away, being the choice of the people, are represented by the bad figs, that were good for nothing. The state also of the former in their captivity was vastly preferable to the state of those who were now about to be delivered into the hand of the king of Babylon. The latter would be treated as double rebels; the former, being the most respectable of the inhabitants, were treated well; and even in captivity, a marked distinction would be made between them, God ordering it so. But the prophet sufficiently explains his own meaning. "Set before the temple"—as an offering of the firstfruits of that kind. *Very good figs.* Or figs of the early sort. The fig trees in Palestine, says Dr. Shaw, produce fruit thrice each year. The first sort, called *boccore,* those here mentioned, come to perfection about the middle or end of June. The second sort, called *kermez,* or summer fig, is seldom ripe before August. And the third, which is called the winter fig, which is larger and of a darker complexion than the preceding, hangs all the winter on the tree, ripening even when the leaves are shed, and is fit for gathering in the beginning of spring. *Could not be eaten,* The "winter fig"—then in its crude or unripe state, the spring not being yet come.

5. *Like these good figs, so will I acknowledge.* Those already carried away into captivity, I esteem as far more excellent than those who still remain in the land. They have not sinned so deeply, and they are now penitent; and, therefore, "I will set mine eyes upon them for good," v. 6. I will watch over them by an especial providence, and they shall be restored to their own land.

7. *They shall be my people.* I will renew My covenant with them, *for they shall return unto me with their whole heart.*

8. *So will I give Zedekiah.* I will treat these as they deserve. They shall be carried into captivity, and scattered through all nations. Multitudes of those never returned to Judea; the others returned at the end of seventy years.

10. *I will send the sword.* Many of them fell by sword and famine in the war with the Chaldeans, and many more by such means afterwards. The first received their captivity as a correction, and turned to God; the latter still hardened their hearts more and more, and probably very many of them never returned— perhaps they are now amalgamated with heathen nations.

CHAPTER 25

This chapter contains a summary of the judgments denounced by Jeremiah against Judah, Babylon, and many other nations. It begins with reproving the Jews for disobeying the calls of God to repentance, 1-7; on which account their captivity, with that of other neighboring nations, during seventy years, is foretold, 8-11. At the expiration of that period (computing from the invasion of Nebuchadnezzar in the fourth year of Jehoiakim, to the famous edict of the first year of Cyrus) an end was to be put to the Babylonian empire, 12-14. All this is again declared by the emblem of that cup of wrath which the prophet, as it should seem in a vision, tendered to all the nations which he enumerates, 15-29. And for further confirmation, it is a third time repeated in a very beautiful and elevated strain of poetry, 30-38. The talent of diversifying the ideas, images, and language, even when the subject is the same, or nearly so, appears nowhere in such perfection as among the sacred poets.

1. *The word that came to Jeremiah . . . in the fourth year.* This prophecy, we see, was delivered in the fourth year of Jehoiakim, and the chapter that contains it is utterly out of its place. It should be between chapters xxxv and xxxvi. The defeat of the Egyptians by Nebuchadnezzar at Carchemish, and the subsequent taking of Jerusalem, occurred in this year. *The first year of Nebuchadrezzar.* This king was associated with his father two years before the death of the latter. The Jews reckon his reign from this time, and this was the first of those two years; but the Chaldeans date the commencement of his reign two years later, viz., at the death of his father.

7. *That ye might provoke.* You would not hearken, but chose to provoke Me with anger.

9. *Behold, I will send.* At this time Nebuchadrezzar had not invaded the land, according to this version. But the Hebrew may be translated, "Behold, I am sending, and have taken all the families"; that is, all the allies of the king of Babylon.

10. *I will take from them.* See chap. vii. 34 and xvi. 9. *The sound of the millstones, and the light of the candle.* These two are conjoined, because they generally ground the corn before day, by the light of the candle. Sir J. Chardin has remarked that everywhere in the morning may be heard the noise of the mills, for they generally grind every day just as much as is necessary for the day's consumption. Where then the noise of the mill is not heard, nor the light of the candle seen, there must be desolation.

11. *Shall serve the king of Babylon seventy years.* As this prophecy was delivered in the fourth year of Jehoiakim, and in the first of Nebuchadnezzar, and began to be accomplished in the same year (for then Nebuchadnezzar invaded Judea and took Jerusalem), seventy years from this time will reach down to the first year of Cyrus, when he made his proclamation for the restoration of the Jews, and the rebuilding of Jerusalem.

14. *Many nations and great kings.* The Medes and the Persians, under Cyrus; and several princes, his vassals or allies.

15. *Take the wine cup of this fury.* For an ample illustration of this passage and simile, see Isa. li. 21.

17. *Then took I the cup . . . and made all the nations to drink.* This cup of God's wrath is merely symbolical, and simply means that the prophet should declare to all these people that they shall fall under the Chaldean yoke, and that this is a punishment inflicted on them by God for their iniquities. *Then took I the cup;* I declared publicly the tribulation that God was about to bring on Jerusalem, the cities of Judah, and all the nations.

19. *Pharaoh king of Egypt.* This was Pharaoh-necho, who was the principal cause of instigating the neighboring nations to form a league against the Chaldeans.

20. *All the mingled people.* The strangers and foreigners; Abyssinians and others who had settled in Egypt. *Land of Uz.* A part of Arabia near to Idumea. See Job i. 1.

22. *Tyrus, and . . . Zidon.* The most ancient of all the cities of the Phoenicians. *Kings of the isles which are beyond the sea.* As the

Mediterranean Sea is most probably meant, and the Phoenicians had numerous colonies on its coasts, I prefer the marginal reading, "the kings of the region by the sea side."

23. *Dedan* was the son of Abraham by Keturah, Gen. xxv. 3. *Tema* was one of the sons of Ishmael, in the north of Arabia, Gen. xxxvi. 15. *Buz.* Brother of *Uz*, descendants of Nahor, brother of Abraham, settled in Arabia Deserta, Gen. xxii. 21.

25. *Zimri.* Descendants of Abraham, by Keturah, Gen. xxv. 2, 6. *Elam.* On the south frontier of Media, not far from Babylon.

26. *The kings of the north, far and near.* The first may mean Syria; the latter, the Hyrcanians and Bactrians. *And the king of Sheshach shall drink after them.* Sheshach was an ancient king of Babylon, who was deified after his death. Here it means either Babylon, or Nebuchadnezzar, the king of it. After it has been the occasion of ruin to so many other nations, Babylon itself shall be destroyed by the Medo-Persians.

27. *Be drunken, and spue.* Why did we not use the word vomit, less offensive than the other, and yet of the same signification?

29. *The city which is called by my name.* Jerusalem, which should be first given up to the destruction.

32. *Evil shall go forth from nation to nation.* One nation after another shall fall before the Chaldeans.

33. *From one end of the earth.* From one end of the "land" to the other. All Palestine shall be desolated by it.

34. *Howl, ye shepherds.* You kings and chiefs of the people. *Ye shall fall like a pleasant vessel.* As a fall will break and utterly ruin a precious vessel of crystal, agate, etc., so your overthrow will be to you irreparable ruin.

38. *As the lion.* Leaving the banks of Jordan when overflowed, and coming with ravening fierceness to the champaign country.

CHAPTER 26

Jeremiah, by the command of God, goes into the court of the Lord's house; and foretells the destruction of the Temple and city, if not prevented by the speedy repentance of the people, 1-7. By this unwelcome prophecy his life is in great danger; although saved by the influence of Ahikam, the son of Shaphan, who makes a masterly defense for the prophet, 8-19. Urijah is condemned, but escapes to Egypt; whence he is brought back by Jehoiakim, and slain, 20-23. Ahikam befriends Jeremiah, 24.

1. *In the beginning of the reign of Jehoiakim.* As this prophecy must have been delivered in the first or second year of the reign of Jehoiakim, it is totally out of its place here.

4. *If ye will not hearken.* This and several of the following verses are nearly the same with those in chap. vii. 13, etc.

8. *And all the people.* That were in company with the priests and the prophets.

10. *The princes of Judah.* The king's court; his cabinet counsellors.

12. *The Lord sent me to prophesy.* My commission is from Him, and my words are His own. I sought not this painful office. I did not run before I was sent.

13. *Therefore now amend your ways.* If you wish to escape the judgment which I have predicted, turn to God, and iniquity shall not be your ruin.

14. *As for me, behold, I am in your hand.* I am the messenger of God; you may do with me what you please. But if you slay me, you will bring innocent blood upon yourselves.

16. *This man is not worthy to die.* The whole court acquitted him.

17. *Certain of the elders.* This is really a fine defense, and the argument was perfectly conclusive. Some think that it was Ahikam who undertook the prophet's defense.

18. *Micah the Morasthite.* The same as stands among the prophets. Now all these prophesied as hard things against the land as Jeremiah has done; yet they were not put to death, for the people saw that they were sent of God.

20. *Urijah . . . who prophesied.* The process against Jeremiah is finished at the nineteenth verse; and the case of Urijah is next brought on, for he was also to be tried for his life; but hearing of it, he fled to Egypt. He was however condemned in his absence; and the king sent to Egypt, and brought him thence and slew him, and caused him to have an ignominious burial, vv. 21-23.

24. *The hand of Ahikam . . . was with Jeremiah.* And it was probably by his influence that Jeremiah did not share the same fate with Urijah. The Ahikam mentioned here was probably the father of Gedaliah, who, after the capture of Jerusalem, was appointed governor of the country by Nebuchadnezzar, chap. xl. 5. Of the Prophet Urijah we know nothing but what we learn from this place. *That they should not give him into the hand of the people.* Though acquitted in the supreme court, he was not out of danger; there was a popular prejudice against him, and it is likely that Ahikam was obliged to conceal him, that they might not put him to death.

CHAPTER 27

Ambassadors being come from several neighboring nations to solicit the king of Judah to join in a confederacy against the king of Babylon, Jeremiah is commanded to put bands and yokes upon his neck (the emblems of subjection and slavery), and to send them afterwards by those ambassadors to their respective prince; intimating by this significant type that God had decreed their subjection to the Babylonian empire, and that it was their wisdom to submit. It is further declared that all the conquered nations shall remain in subjection to the Chaldeans during the reign of Nebuchadnezzar, and those of his son and grandson, even till the arrival of that period in which the Babylonians shall have filled up the measure of their iniquities; and that then the mighty Chaldean monarchy itself, for a certain period the paramount power of the habitable globe, shall be visited with a dreadful storm of divine wrath, through the violence of which it shall be dashed to pieces like a potter's vessel, the fragments falling into the hands of many nations and great kings, 1-11. Zedekiah, particularly, is admonished not to join in the revolt against Nebuchadnezzar, and warned against trusting to the suggestions of false prophets, 12-18. The chapter concludes with foretelling that what still remained of the sacred vessels of the Temple should be carried to Babylon, and not restored till after the destruction of the Chaldean empire, 19-22.

1. *In the beginning of the reign of Jehoiakim.* It is most evident that his prophecy was delivered about the fourth year of Zedekiah, and not *Jehoiakim*, as in the text. See chap. xxviii. 1. And it is clear from the third and twelfth verses, where Zedekiah is expressly mentioned, that this is the true reading.

2. *Make thee bonds and yokes.* Probably yokes with straps, by which they were attached

to the neck. This was a symbolical action, to show that the several kings mentioned below should be brought under the dominion of the Chaldeans.

5. *I have made the earth.* I am the Creator and Governor of all things, and I dispose of the several kingdoms of the world as seemeth best to Me.

6. *And now have I given.* These kingdoms are at My sovereign disposal; and at present, for the punishment of their rulers and people, I shall give them into the hands of Nebuchadnezzar, king of Babylon.

7. *And all nations shall serve him* (Nebuchadnezzar), *and his son* (Evil-merodach, chap. lii. 31), *and his son's son* (Belshazzar, Dan. v. 11)—all which was literally fulfilled.

9. *Therefore hearken not ye to your prophets.* Who pretend to have a revelation from heaven. *Nor to your diviners.* Persons who guessed at futurity by certain signs in the animate or inanimate creation.

13. *Why will ye die?* If you resist the king of Babylon, to whom I have given a commission against you, you shall be destroyed by the sword and by famine; but if you submit, you shall escape all these evils.

16. *The vessels of the Lord's house.* Which had been carried away by Nebuchadnezzar under the reigns of Jehoiakim and Jeconiah, 2 Chron. xxxvi. 7-10. *Shall now shortly be brought again.* This is a lie. They shall not be restored till I bring them up, v. 22, which was after the Captivity, when they were sent back by Cyrus, the Lord inclining his heart to do it, Ezra i. 7 and vii. 19.

19. *Concerning the pillars.* Two brazen columns placed by Solomon in the portico of the Temple, eighteen cubits high, and twelve in circumference, 1 Kings vii. 15-22; Jer. lii. 11. *The sea.* The brazen sea, ten cubits in diameter. It contained water for different washings in the divine worship, and was supported on twelve brazen oxen. Perhaps these are what are called the bases here.

22. *They shall be carried to Babylon.* Far from those already taken being brought back, those which now remain shall be carried thither, unless ye submit to the Chaldeans. They did not submit, and the prophecy was literally fulfilled; see chap. lii. 17-23; 2 Kings xxv. 13.

CHAPTER 28

One of those pretended prophets spoken of in the preceding chapter, having contradicted and opposed Jeremiah, receives an awful declaration that, as a proof to the people of his having spoken without commission, he should die in the then current year; which accordingly came to pass in the seventh month, 1-17.

1. *And it came to pass the same year . . . the fifth month.* Which commenced with the first new moon of August, according to our calendar. This verse gives the precise date of the prophecy in the preceding chapter; and proves that Zedekiah, not Jehoiakim, is the name that should be read in the first verse of that chapter. *Hananiah the son of Azur the prophet.* One who called himself a prophet; who pretended to be in commerce with the Lord, and to receive revelations from Him. He was probably a priest; for he was of Gibeon, a sacerdotal city in the tribe of Benjamin.

2. *Thus speaketh the Lord.* What awful impudence, when he knew in his conscience that God had given him no such commission!

3. *Within two full years.* Time sufficient for the Chaldeans to destroy the city, and carry away the rest of the sacred vessels; but he did not live to see the end of this short period.

6. *Amen: the Lord do so.* Oh, that it might be according to your word! May the people find this to be true!

8. *The prophets that have been before me.* Namely, Joel, Amos, Hosea, Micah, Zephaniah, Nahum, Habakkuk, and others—all of whom denounced similar evils against a corrupt people.

9. *When the word of the prophet shall come to pass.* Here is the criterion. He is a true prophet who specifies things that he says shall happen, and also fixes the time of the event; and the things do happen, and in that time. You say that Nebuchadnezzar shall not overthrow this city; and that in two years from this time, not only the sacred vessels already taken away shall be restored, but also that Jeconiah and all the Jewish captives shall be restored, and the Babylonish yoke broken (see vv. 2-4). Now I say that Nebuchadnezzar will come this year, and destroy this city, and lead away the rest of the people into captivity, and the rest of the sacred vessels; and that there will be no restoration of any kind till seventy years from this time.

10. *Then Hananiah . . . took the yoke . . . and brake it.* He endeavored by this symbolical act to persuade them of the truth of his prediction.

13. *Yokes of iron.* Instead of Nebuchadnezzar's yoke being broken, this captivity shall be more severe than the preceding. All these nations shall have a yoke of iron on their neck. He shall subdue them, and take all their property, even the beasts of the field.

15. *Hear now, Hananiah; the Lord hath not sent thee.* This was a bold speech in the presence of those priests and people who were prejudiced in favor of this false prophet, who prophesied to them smooth things.

16. *This year thou shalt die.* By this shall the people know who is the true prophet. You have taught rebellion against the Lord, and God will cut you off; and this shall take place, not within seventy years, or two years, but in this very year, and within two months from this time.

17. *So Hananiah . . . died the same year in the seventh month.* The prophecy was delivered in the fifth month (v. 1), and Hananiah died in the seventh month. And thus God, in mercy, gave him about two months in which he might prepare to meet his Judge.

CHAPTER 29

This chapter contains the substance of two letters sent by the prophet to the captives in Babylon. In the first he recommends to them patience and composure under their present circumstances, which were to endure for seventy years, 1-14; in which, however, they should fare better than their brethren who remained behind, 15-19. But, finding little credit given to this me·sage, on account of the suggestions of the false prophets, Ahab, the son of Kolaiah, and Zedekiah, the son of Maaseiah, who flattered them with the hopes of a speedy end to their captivity, he sends a second, in which he denounces heavy judgments against those false prophets that deceived them, 20-23; as he did afterwards against

Shemaiah the Nehelamite, who had sent a letter of complaint against Jeremiah, in consequence of his message, 24-32.

1. *Now these are the words of the letter.* This transaction took place in the first or second year of Zedekiah. It appears that the prophet had been informed that the Jews who had already been carried into captivity had, through the instigations of false prophets, been led to believe that they were to be brought out of their captivity speedily. Jeremiah, fearing that this delusion might induce them to take some hasty steps, ill comporting with their present state, wrote a letter to them, which he entrusted to an embassy which Zedekiah had sent on some political concerns to Nebuchadnezzar. The letter was directed to the elders, priests, prophets, and people who had been carried away captives to Babylon.

4. *Thus saith the Lord of hosts.* This was the commencement of the letter.

5. *Build ye houses.* Prepare for a long continuance in your present captivity. Provide yourselves with the necessaries of life, and multiply in the land, that you may become a powerful people.

7. *Seek the peace of the city.* Endeavor to promote, as far as you can, the "prosperity" of the places in which you sojourn.

8. *Neither hearken to your dreams.* Rather, "dreamers"; for it appears there was a class of such persons, who not only had acquired a facility of dreaming themselves, but who undertook to interpret the dreams of others.

10. *For thus saith the Lord.* It has been supposed that a very serious transposition of verses has taken place here; and it has been proposed to read after v. 9 the sixteenth to the nineteenth inclusive; then the tenth, and on to the fourteenth inclusive; then the twentieth, the fifteenth, the twenty-first, and the rest regularly to the end.

14. *I will gather you from all the nations.* A quotation from Deut. xxx. 8, and see also Deut. iv. 7.

15. *Because ye have said.* The Septuagint very properly insert this verse between the twentieth and the twenty-first, and thus the connection here is not disturbed, and the connection below is completed.

17. *Behold, I will send upon them the sword.* Do not envy the state of Zedekiah, who sits on the throne of David, nor that of the people who are now in the land whence ye have been carried captive (v. 16). For I will send the *sword,* the *pestilence,* and the *famine* upon them; and afterwards shall cause them to be carried into a miserable captivity in all nations (v. 18). But you see the worst of your own case, and you have God's promise of enlargement when the proper time is come. The reader will not forget that the prophet is addressing the captives in Babylon.

21. *He shall slay them before your eyes.* Nebuchadnezzar would be led by political reasons to punish these pretended prophets, as their predictions tended to make his Israelitish subjects uneasy and disaffected, and might excite them to rebellion. He therefore slew them; two of them, it appears, he burnt alive, viz., Ahab and Zedekiah.

24. *Speak to Shemaiah.* Zephaniah was the second priest, *sagan,* or chief priest's deputy, and Seraiah, high priest, when Jerusalem was taken. See chap. lii. 24. Shemaiah directs his letter to the former, and tells him that God had appointed him to supply the place of the high priest, who was probably then absent. His name was either Azariah or Seraiah, his son, but called Jehoiada from the remarkable zeal and courage of that pontiff. After the taking of Jerusalem, Zephaniah was put to death by Nebuchadnezzar at Riblah; see chap. xxxvii. 3. The history of Jehoiada may be seen in 2 Kings xi. 3, etc.

26. *For every man that is mad, and maketh himself a prophet. Mad,* "in ecstatic rapture"; such as appeared in the prophets, whether true or false, when under the influence, the one of God, the other of a demon. See 2 Kings ix. 11; Hos. ix. 7.

CHAPTER 30

This and the following chapter must relate to a still future restoration of the posterity of Jacob from their several dispersions, as no deliverance hitherto afforded them comes up to the terms of it. For, after the return from Babylon, they were again enslaved by the Greeks and Romans, contrary to the prediction in the eighth verse; in every papistical country they have labored under great civil disabilities, and in some of them have been horribly persecuted; upon the ancient people has this mystic Babylon very heavily laid her yoke; and in no place in the world are they at present their own masters; so that this prophecy remains to be fulfilled in the reign of David, i.e., the Messiah; the type, according to the general structure of the prophetical writings, being put for the antitype. The prophecy opens by an easy transition from the temporal deliverance spoken of before, and describes the mighty revolutions that shall precede the restoration of the descendants of Israel, 1-9, who are encouraged to trust in the promises of God, 10-11. They are, however, to expect corrections; which shall have a happy issue in a future period, 12-17. The great blessings of Messiah's reign are enumerated, 18-22; and the wicked and impenitent declared to have to share in them, 23-24.

1. *The word that came to Jeremiah from the Lord.* This prophecy was delivered about a year after the taking of Jerusalem; so Dahler.

2. *Write thee all the words that I have spoken unto thee in a book.* The book here recommended I believe to be the thirtieth and thirty-first chapters; for among the Hebrews any portion of writing, in which the subject was finished, however small, was termed *sepher,* a "book," a treatise or discourse.

3. *The days come.* First, after the conclusion of the seventy years. Secondly, under the Messiah. *That I will bring again the captivity of . . . Israel.* The ten tribes, led captive by the king of Assyria, and dispersed among the nations. *And Judah.* The people carried into Babylon at two different times: first, under Jeconiah; and, secondly, under Zedekiah, by Nebuchadnezzar.

5. *We have heard a voice of trembling.* This may refer to the state and feelings of the people during the war which Cyrus carried on against the Babylonians. Trembling and terror would no doubt affect them, and put an end to peace and all prosperity; as they could not tell what would be the issue of the struggle, and whether their state would be better or worse should their present masters fall in the conflict. This is well described in the next verse, where men are represented as being, through pain and anguish, like women in travail. See the same comparison in Isa. xiii. 6-8.

7. *Alas! for that day is great.* When the Medes

and Persians with all their forces shall come on the Chaldeans, it will be the day *of Jacob's trouble*—trial, dismay, and uncertainty; but he shall be delivered out of it—the Chaldean empire shall fall, but the Jews shall be delivered by Cyrus.

8. *I will break his yoke.* That is, the yoke of Nebuchadnezzar. *Of him.* Of Jacob (v. 7), viz., the then captive Jews.

9. *But they shall serve the Lord their God, and David their king.* This must refer to the times of the Messiah; and hence the Chaldee has, "They shall obey the Lord their God, and they shall obey the Messiah, the Son of David." This is a very remarkable version; and shows that it was a version, not according to the letter, but according to their doctrine and their expectation.

Christ is promised under the name of His progenitor, David, Isa. lv. 3-4; Ezek. xxxiv. 23-24; xxxvii. 24-25; Hos. iii. 5.

11. *Though I make a full end of all nations.* Though the Persians destroy the nations whom they vanquish, yet they shall not destroy *thee.*

12. *Thy bruise is incurable. Anush,* "desperate," not *incurable;* for the cure is promised in v. 17, "I will restore health unto thee, and I will heal thee of thy wounds."

13. *There is none to plead thy cause.* All your friends and allies have forsaken you.

15. *Thy sorrow is incurable.* "Desperate." See v. 12.

16. *They that devour thee,* the Chaldeans. *Shall be devoured,* by the Medes and Persians. *All that prey upon thee will I give for a prey.* The Assyrians were destroyed by the Babylonians; the Babylonians, by the Medes and Persians; the Egyptians and Persians were destroyed by the Greeks, under Alexander.

18. *The city shall be builded upon her own heap.* See the Book of Nehemiah. *And the palace shall remain.* Meaning, the king's house shall be restored; or, more probably, the Temple shall be rebuilt; which was true, for after the Babylonish captivity it was rebuilt by Nehemiah, etc. By the *tents,* distinguished from the *dwellingplaces* of Jacob, we may understand all the minor dispersions of the Jews, as well as those numerous synagogues found in large cities.

21. *Their nobles shall be of themselves.* Strangers shall not rule over them; *and their governor shall proceed from the midst of them.* Both Nehemiah and Zerubbabel, their nobles and governors after the return from Babylon, were Jews.

22. *Ye shall be my people.* The old covenant shall be renewed.

23. *The whirlwind of the Lord.* A grievous tempest of desolation *shall fall with pain upon the head of the wicked,* on Nebuchadnezzar and the Chaldeans.

24. *In the latter days ye shall consider it.* By the *latter days* is generally meant; and that restoration which is the principal topic in this and the succeeding chapter refers to this time.

CHAPTER 31

This chapter continues the subject of the preceding in a beautiful vision represented at a distant period. God is introduced expressing His continual regard for Israel, and promising to restore them to their land and liberty, 1-5. Immediately heralds appear, proclaiming on Mount Ephraim the arrival of the great year of jubilee, and summoning the people to gather unto Zion, 6. Upon which God resumes the speech; and makes such gracious promises both of leading them tenderly by the way, and making them happy in their own land, that all the nations of the world are called upon to consider with deep attention this great salvation, 7-14. The scene is then diversified by a very happy invention. Rachel, the mother of Joseph and Benjamin, is represented as risen from her tomb, in a city of Benjamin near Jerusalem, looking about for her children, and bitterly lamenting their fate, as none of them are to be seen in the land of their fathers, 15. But she is consoled with the assurance that they are not lost, and that they shall in due time be restored, 16-17. To this another tender and beautiful scene immediately succeeds. Ephraim (often put for the ten tribes) comes in view. He laments his past errors, and expresses the most earnest desires of reconciliation; upon which God, as a tender Parent, immediately forgives him, 18-20. The virgin of Israel is then directed to prepare for returning home, 21-22; and the vision closes with a promise of abundant peace and security to Israel and Judah in the latter days, 23-26. The blessed condition of Israel under the Messiah's reign is then beautifully contrasted with their afflicted state during the general dispersion, 27-28. In the remaining part of the chapter the promises to the posterity of Jacob of the impartial administration of justice, increasing peace and prosperity, the universal diffusion of righteousness, and stability in their own land after a general restoration in gospel times, are repeated, enlarged on, and illustrated by a variety of beautiful figures, 29-40.

1. *At the same time.* This discourse was delivered at the same time with the former; and, with that, constitutes the book which God ordered the prophet to write. *Will I be the God of all the families of Israel.* I shall bring back the ten tribes, as well as their brethren the Jews. The restoration of the Israelites is the principal subject of this chapter.

2. *The people which were left of the sword.* Those of the ten tribes that had escaped death by the sword of the Assyrians. *Found grace in the wilderness.* The place of their exile; a wilderness, compared to their own land. See Isa. xl. 3.

3. *I have loved thee with an everlasting love.* I still bear to the Jewish people that love which I showed to their fathers in Egypt, in the wilderness, and in the Promised Land. *Therefore with lovingkindness have I drawn thee.* The exiles, who had not for a long time received any proofs of the divine protection, are represented as deploring their state. But God answers that, though this may seem to be the case, He has always loved them; and this continued love He will show by bringing them out of their captivity.

4. *O virgin of Israel.* Israelites in general; now called virgin, because restored to their ancient purity. *With thy tabrets.* Women in general played on these; they were used in times of rejoicing, and accompanied with dancing.

5. *Thou shalt yet plant vines upon the mountains of Samaria.* This was the regal city of the Israelites, as Jerusalem was of the Jews. *Shall eat them as common things.* By the law of Moses no man was permitted to eat of the fruit of his vineyard till the fifth year after planting. For the first three years it was considered uncircumcised, unclean, not fit to be eaten. In the fourth year it was holy to the Lord; the fruit belonged to Him. In the fifth year he might use it for himself, Lev. xix. 23-25. But in the time here mentioned the fruit should be considered *common*—lawful at all times to be eaten.

6. *For there shall be a day.* Literally, "for this is the day," or "the day is come." The *watchmen*—the prophets. *Arise ye, and let us*

go up to Zion. Let both Israelites and Jews join together in the worship of the Lord.

8. *I will bring them from the north country.* From Babylon. *From the coasts of the earth.* The ten tribes were carried away partly into Assyria by Tiglath-pileser, and partly into Mesopotamia and Media by Shalmaneser, 2 Kings xv. 29; xvii. 6. Assyria and Media, being very distant from Palestine, might have been called, in prophetic language, *the coasts of the earth.* *The blind and the lame.* I will so effectually remove all difficulties out of the way, so provide for them on the journey, so supernaturally support their bodies and minds, that the veriest invalids shall safely proceed to, and happily arrive at, the end of their journey.

9. *They shall come with weeping.* Duly penetrated with a sense of their sins, they shall deeply deplore them; and, while weeping for them, earnestly supplicate God to have mercy upon them. *By the rivers of waters.* I will so guide and provide for them in the arid deserts that they shall find streams of water whenever necessary. *Ephraim is my firstborn.* Ephraim, being the most considerable, is often put for the whole of the ten tribes.

12. *And shall flow together.* Perhaps this may refer to their assembling at the three great national feasts: the Passover, Pentecost, and Tabernacles.

14. *And I will satiate the soul of the priests.* The worship of God being restored, they shall have their proper share of the victims brought to the Temple.

15. *A voice was heard in Ramah.* The Ramah mentioned here (for there were several towns of this name) was situated in the tribe of Benjamin, about six or seven miles from Jerusalem. Near this place Rachel was buried; who is here, in a beautiful figure of poetry, represented as coming out of her grave, and lamenting bitterly for the loss of her children, none of whom presented themselves to her view, all being slain or gone into exile. St. Matthew, who is ever fond of accommodation, applies these words, chap. ii. 17-18, to the massacre of the children at Bethlehem. That is, they were suitable to that occasion, and therefore he so applied them, but they are not a prediction of that event.

16. *They shall come again from the land of the enemy.* This could not be said of the murdered innocents at Bethlehem; they never came again. But the Jews, who had gone into captivity, did come again from the land of their enemy to their own border.

18. *I have surely heard Ephraim bemoaning himself.* The exiled Israelites are in a state of deep repentance. *Thou hast chastised me, and I was chastised.* I was at first like an unbroken steer; the more I was chastised, the more I rebelled. But now I have benefited by Thy correction. *Turn thou me.* I am now willing to take Thy yoke upon me, but I have no power.

19. *After that I was turned.* Converted from my sin, folly, and idolatry. *I repented.* To conviction of sin, I now added contrition for sin. Conviction, in this sense of the word, must precede contrition or repentance. *I smote upon my thigh.* My sorrow grew deeper and deeper; I smote upon my thigh through the extremity of my distress. This was a usual sign of deep affliction. See Ezek. xxi. 12.

20. *Is Ephraim my dear son?* It is impossible to conceive anything more tenderly affectionate than this.

21. *Set thee up waymarks.* Alluding to stones, or heaps of stones, which travellers in the desert set up to ascertain the way, that they may know how to return. Mark the way to Babylon: thither you shall certainly go; but from it you shall as certainly return.

22. *A woman shall compass a man.* "A weak woman shall compass or circumvent a strong man." I think it likely that the Jews in their present distressed circumstances are represented under the similitude of a weak, defenseless female; and the Chaldeans under that of a fierce, strong man, who had prevailed over and oppressed this weak woman. But, notwithstanding the disparity between them, God would cause the *woman*—the weak, defenseless Jews, to *compass*—to overcome, the strong *man*—the powerful Babylonians.

23. *The Lord bless thee, O habitation of of justice.* After their return they shall be remarkably prosperous.

26. *Upon this I awaked.* It appears that the prophecy, commencing with chap. xxx. 2 and ending with v. 25 of this chapter, was delivered to the prophet in a dream.

27. *I will sow . . . with the seed of man, and with the seed of beast.* I will multiply both men and cattle.

29. *The fathers have eaten a sour grape.* A proverbial expression for "The children suffer for the offenses of their parents." This is explained in the next verse: "Every one shall die for his own iniquity." No child shall suffer divine punition for the sin of his father; only so far as he acts in the same way can he be said to bear the sins of his parents.

31. *A new covenant.* The Christian dispensation.

33. *After those days.* When vision and prophecy shall be sealed up, and Jesus have assumed that body which was prepared for Him, and have laid down His life for the redemption of a lost world, and, having ascended on high, shall have obtained the gift of the Holy Spirit to purify the heart, then God's *law* shall, by it, be put *in their inward parts,* and written on their *hearts,* so that all within and all without shall be holiness to the Lord. Then God will be truly *their God,* received and acknowledged as their Portion, and the sole Object of their devotion; and they shall be His people, filled with holiness, and made partakers of the divine nature, so that they shall perfectly love Him and worthily magnify His name.

34. *And they shall teach no more.* It shall be a time of universal light and knowledge; all shall know God in Christ, from the least to the greatest. The children shall be taught to read the new covenant, and to understand the terms of their salvation.

36. *If those ordinances.* As sure as the sun shall give light to the day, and the moon to the night, so surely shall the Jews continue to be a distinct people.

38. *The city shall be built to the Lord.* This cannot mean the city built after the return from Babylon, for two reasons: (1) This is to be much greater in extent; (2) It is to be permanent, never to be thrown down, v. 40.

It must therefore mean, if taken literally at all, the city that is to be built by them when they are brought in with the fullness of the Gentiles. *The tower of Hananeel.* This stood in the northeast part of the city; from thence the wall proceeded to the corner gate.

39. *Upon the hill Gareb.* Gareb and Goath are out of the limits of this city. The latter is supposed to be Golgotha; that is, the heap of Gotha, which, being the place where our Lord was crucified, was without the city. These hills were a little to the northwest of the old city walls, but are destined to be within the new city.

40. *The whole valley of the dead bodies.* The valley of the son of Hinnom. *And all the fields unto the brook of Kidron, unto the corner of the horse gate toward the east.* All these places, the fuller's field, etc., shall be consecrated to the Lord, and become a part of this new city; so that this will appear to be a city much more extensive than the city of Jerusalem ever was.

CHAPTER 32

Jeremiah, now confined for his faithful admonitions, foretells the fate of the king and city, 1-5. According to the direction of God, he buys of his cousin Hanameel a field in Anathoth; the contract, or deed of sale, being subscribed, sealed, and witnessed, and delivered to Baruch together with a duplicate not sealed, who is commanded to put them into an earthern vessel, that they may remain there for many days, 6-14. This transaction of the prophet, which is entered and subscribed in the public register, God constitutes a sign or pledge of the Jews' return from the Babylonish captivity, and of their again possessing houses, fields, and vineyards in their own land, and by their own right, according to their tribes and families, 15. Jeremiah's prayer, in which he recounts God's marvellous acts towards the children of Israel, and deeply deplores the lamentable state of the country, and the numerous provocations which have led to it, 16-25. After which God is introduced declaring His purpose of giving His people into the hands of their enemies, 26-35; promising, however, to restore them in due time to their ancient possessions, and to make with them an everlasting covenant, 36-44.

1. *The word that came.* This prophecy bears its own date: it was delivered in the tenth year of Zedekiah, which answered to the eighteenth of Nebuchadnezzar.

2. *Then the king of Babylon's army besieged Jerusalem.* The siege had commenced the year before, and continued a year after, ending in the fifth month of the following year; consequently the siege must have lasted about eighteen months and twenty-seven days. See 2 Kings xxv. 18.

7. *The right of redemption is thine.* The law had established that the estates of a family should never be alienated. If, therefore, a man through poverty was obliged to sell his patrimony, the nearest relative had a right to purchase it before all others, and even to redeem it, if it had been sold to another. This is what is called the right of goel, or "kinsman," Lev. xxv. 25. And in the year of jubilee the whole reverted to its ancient master, Lev. xxv. 13.

8. *This was the word of the Lord.* It was by His appointment that I was to make this purchase. The whole was designed as a symbolical act, to show the people that there would be a return from Babylon, that each family should reenter on its former possessions, and that a man might safely purchase on the certainty of this event.

9. *Weighed him the money.* It does not appear that there was any coined or stamped money

among the Jews before the Captivity; the Scripture, therefore, never speaks of counting money, but of weighing it.

10. *I subscribed the evidence.* We have here all the circumstances of this legal act: (1) An offer is made of the reversion of the ground, till the jubilee, to him who would then of right come into possession. (2) The price is agreed on, and the silver weighed in the balances. (3) A contract or deed of sale is drawn up, to which both parties agreeing, (4) Witnesses are brought forward to see it signed and sealed, for the contract was both subscribed and sealed. (5) A *duplicate* of the deed was drawn, which was not to be sealed, but to lie open for the inspection of those concerned, in some public place where it might be safe, and always to be seen. (6) The original, which was sealed up, was put in an earthen pitcher, in order to be preserved from accidents. (7) This was delivered by the purchaser into the hands of a third party, to be preserved for the use of the purchaser, and witnesses were called to attest this delivery. (8) They subscribed the book of the purchase, perhaps a town book, or register, where such purchases were entered. Baruch was a scribe by profession; and the deeds were delivered into his hands, before witnesses, to be preserved as above. Perhaps the law, in this case, required that the instrument should be thus lodged. But, in the present case, both the deeds, the original and the duplicate, were put into the earthen pitcher, because the city was about to be burnt; and, if lodged as usual, they would be destroyed in the general conflagration.

15. *Houses and fields . . . shall be possessed again.* That is, this is an evidence that the Captivity shall not last long; houses, etc., shall here be possessed again, either by their present owners or by immediate descendants.

24. *Behold the mounts.* The huge terraces raised up to plant their engines on, that they might throw darts, stones, etc., into the city. *Because of the sword, and of the famine, and of the pestilence.* The city was now reduced to extreme necessity; and from the siege continuing nearly a year longer, we may conclude that the besieged made a noble defense.

29. *With the houses, upon whose roofs.* As it is most probable that Baal was the sun, they might have chosen the tops of the houses, which were always flat, with battlements around, to offer incense and sacrifice to him at his rising, and while he was in sight above the horizon.

30. *For the children of Israel and the children of Judah have only done evil.* They have all been transgressors from their earliest history. *For the children of Israel.* The ten tribes. *Have only provoked me to anger with the work of their hands.* They have been sinners beyond all others, being excessive idolaters. Their hands have formed the objects of their worship.

37. *Behold, I will gather them out of all countries.* A promise often repeated. See chap. xxix. 14 and chap. xxxi. 8, etc.

44. *Men shall buy fields for money.* This is a reference to the symbolical purchase mentioned at the beginning of the chapter; *that* may be considered by them as a sure sign of their restoration, not only to the same land, but to their respective inheritances in that land. This the power of God could alone perform.

CHAPTER 33

In this chapter the prophet predicts a restoration of Israel and Judah to the favor of God, attended with such glorious circumstances as shall astonish all the world, 1-9. Their prosperity from that period is then described by a beautiful enumeration of circumstances. 10-13. This leads to the promise of the Messiah, the grand subject of the prophetical writings, and the happiness and stability which the children of Israel shall enjoy under His government; promises which, insofar as they respect the great body of the Jews, remain still to be fulfilled, 14-26.

1. *Moreover the word of the Lord.* This was in the eleventh year of the reign of Zedekiah, Jeremiah being still shut up in prison. But he was now *in the court of the prison,* where the elders and the king's officers, etc., might consult him with the greater ease. For they continued to inquire, foolishly thinking that if he would but prophesy good things these must come; or that he had sufficient power with God to induce Him to alter His mind—destroy the Chaldeans, and deliver the city.

2. *Thus saith the Lord the maker thereof.* The Doer of it. That is, He who is to perform that which He is now about to promise.

3. *Call unto me, and I will answer thee.* To Me alone it belongs to reveal what is future, and the stupendous things which are now coming are known only to myself.

4. *Thus saith the Lord.* This is a new confirmation of what has already been said, viz., The city shall fall, a number of the inhabitants shall perish, the rest shall be carried into captivity; but the nation shall be preserved, and the people return from their captivity.

7. *The captivity of Judah and the captivity of Israel.* This must respect the latter times, for the ten tribes did not return with the Jews at the termination of the seventy years.

8. *I will cleanse them.* These promises of pardon and holiness must be referred to their state under the gospel, when they shall have received Jesus as the promised Messiah.

11. *The voice of them that shall say, Praise the Lord of hosts.* That is, the voice of the Levites in the sacred service, intimating that the Temple should be rebuilt and the public service restored.

12. *An habitation of shepherds.* See chap. xxxi. 12.

14. *Behold, the days come.* See chap. xxiii. 5 and xxxi. 31. *That good thing which I have promised.* By My prophets; for those who have predicted the Captivity have also foretold its conclusion, though not in such express terms as Jeremiah did. See Hos. i. 10, etc.; ii. 15, etc.; vi. 11, etc.; Amos ix. 14, etc.; and Jer. iii. 12. etc. The end of the Captivity has been foretold by Micah, chap. vii. 9, etc.; Zephaniah, iii. 10, etc.; and by Jeremiah, chap. xvi. 15; xxiii. 3; xxix. 10; xxxii. 37.

16. *And this is the name wherewith she shall be called, The Lord our righteousness.* See what has been said on chap. xxiii. 6, which is generally supposed to be a strictly parallel passage; but they are very different, and I doubt whether they mean exactly the same thing. As to our translation here, it is ignorant, and almost impious; it says that Jerusalem, for that is the antecedent, shall be called "The Lord our righteousness." I will give the original, "And this One who shall call to her is the Lord our Justification"; that is, the salvation of the Jews shall take place when Jesus Christ is proclaimed to them as their Justifier, and they receive Him as such.

18. *Neither shall the priests the Levites want a man.* This is a repetition of the promise made to Phinehas, Num. xxv. 13.

22. *So will I multiply the seed of David.* This must be understood of the spiritual David, Jesus Christ, and His progeny, genuine Christians. The two families which God chose for the priesthood, that of Aaron and Phinehas, or, on its being taken away from him, that of Ithamar, 1 Sam. ii. 35, are both extinct. Nor has the office of high priest, or priest of any kind offering sacrifice, been exercised among the Jews for nearly eighteen hundred years. Therefore what is said here of the priesthood must refer to the spiritual priesthood, at the head of which is Jesus Christ.

CHAPTER 34

This chapter contains two prophecies: the first, delivered during the siege of Jerusalem, predicts to Zedekiah the taking and burning of the city, with his own peaceful death and honorable burial, 1-7. The second was delivered when the Chaldeans had for some time broken up the siege. It reproves the Jews for their conduct towards their brethren of the poorer sort, whom they released, by a solemn covenant, from bondage, in the extremity of their danger; but compelled to return to it when they thought that danger over, 8-11. For this God threatens them with the sword, pestilence, and famine; and with the return of the Chaldeans, who should take the city, destroy it and the other cities by fire, and make an utter desolation of the whole land of Judea, 12-22.

1. *The word which came unto Jeremiah.* This discourse was delivered in the tenth year of the reign of Zedekiah. The chapter contains two discourses; one, vv. 1-7, which concerns the taking of the city, and Zedekiah's captivity and death; the other, vv. 8-22, which is an invective against the inhabitants of Jerusalem for having Hebrew male and female slaves. These, having been manumitted at the instance of the prophet, were afterwards brought back by their old masters, and put in the same thraldom; for which God threatens them with severe judgments.

2. *He shall burn it with fire.* This was a newly added circumstance.

3. *Thou shalt not escape.* This, however, he had attempted, but was taken in his flight. See chap. xxxix. 4 and lii. 7, etc.

5. *Thou shalt die in peace.* You shall not die a violent death; and at your death you shall have all those funereal solemnities which were usual at the demise of kings. See 2 Chron. xvi. 14.

6. *Spake all these words unto Zedekiah.* He delivered this message at the hazard of his life. Jeremiah feared God, and had no other fear.

7. *Against Lachish, and against Azekah.* These were two cities of Judah of considerable importance; they had been strongly fortified by Rehoboam, 2 Chron. xi. 9-11; xxxii. 9.

8. *The word that came unto Jeremiah.* Here the second discourse begins, which was delivered probably a short time, even a few days, after the former. *Zedekiah had made a covenant.* We find no account elsewhere of this covenant: "Every man should let his manservant, and . . . his maidservant . . . go free"; i.e., as we learn from v. 14, on the sabbatical

year, for the seventh year was the year of release. See Deut. xv. 12.

11. *But afterward they turned.* They had agreed to manumit them at the end of the seventh year; but when the seventh year was ended, they recalled their engagement, and detained their servants.

17. *I proclaim a liberty for you.* You proclaimed liberty to your slaves, and afterward resumed your authority over them; and I had in consequence restrained the sword from cutting you off. But now I give liberty *to the sword, to the pestilence, and to the famine,* and to the captivity, to destroy and consume you, and enslave you; for you shall *be removed into all the kingdoms of the earth.* The prophet loves to express the conformity between the crime and its punishment.

18. *When they cut the calf in twain, and passed between the parts thereof.* This was the ancient and most solemn way of making a covenant. (1) A calf as sacrifice was offered to God to secure His approbation and support. (2) The victim was then exactly divided from the nose to the rump. (3) These divided parts were laid opposite to each other, a passage being left between them. (4) The contracting parties entered this passage at each end, met in the middle, and there took the covenant oath, adjudging themselves to death should they break this covenant. (5) Then they both feasted on the victim. In reference to this last circumstance, God says He will give their "bodies . . . for meat unto the fowls of heaven, and to the beasts." This is a further conformity between the crime and the punishment.

21. *The king of Babylon's army, which are gone up from you.* Nebuchadnezzar, hearing that there was an Egyptian army coming to the relief of Jerusalem, raised the siege, went out, and met and defeated the Egyptians. It was in the interim this prophecy was delivered.

22. *I will . . . cause them to return.* They did return; reinvested the city; and, after an obstinate defense, took it, plundered it, and burned it to the ground, taking Zedekiah and his princes captive.

CHAPTER 35

Jeremiah is commanded to go to the Rechabites, who, on the approach of the Chaldean army, took refuge in Jerusalem; and to try their obedience to the command of Jonadab (or Jehonadab, 2 Kings x. 15-16), their great progenitor, who lived in the reign of Jehu, king of Israel, upwards of two hundred and fifty years before this time; offers them wine to drink, which they refuse, 1-11. Hence occasion is taken to upbraid the Jews with their disobedience to God, their Heavenly Father, 12-17; and a blessing is pronounced on the Rechabites, 18-19.

1. *The word which came . . . in the days of Jehoiakim.* What strange confusion in the placing of these chapters! Who could have expected to hear of Jehoiakim again, whom we have long ago buried? And we have now arrived in the history at the very last year of the last Jewish king. This discourse was probably delivered in the fourth or fifth year of Jehoiakim's reign.

2. *The house of the Rechabites.* The Rechabites were not descendants of Jacob; they were Kenites, 1 Chron. ii. 55, a people originally settled in the land of Midian; and most probably the descendants of Jethro, the father-in-law of Moses. Compare Num. x. 29-32 with Judg. i. 16; iv. 11. Those mentioned here seem to have

been a tribe who fed their flocks in the deserts of Judea; they preserved the simple manners of their ancestors, considering the life of the inhabitants of cities and large towns as the death of liberty; believing that they would dishonor themselves by using that sort of food that would oblige them to live a sedentary life. Jonadab, one of their ancestors, had required his children and descendants to abide faithful to the customs of their forefathers; to continue to live in tents, and to nourish themselves on the produce of their flocks; to abstain from the cultivation of the ground, and from that particularly of the vine and its produce. His descendants religiously observed this rule, till the time when the armies of the Chaldeans had entered Judea; when, to preserve their lives, they retired within the walls of Jerusalem. But even there we find, from the account in this chapter, they did not quit their frugal manner of life, but most scrupulously observed the law of Jonadab, their ancestor, and probably of this family.

3. *The whole house of the Rechabites.* That is, the family—the chiefs of which are here specified.

4. *Igdaliah, a man of God.* A prophet or holy man, having some office in the Temple.

6-7. *We will drink no wine.* The reason is given above. Their whole religious and political institution consisted in obedience to three simple precepts, each of which has an appropriate spiritual meaning: (1) *Ye shall drink no wine.* You shall preserve your bodies in temperance. (2) *Neither shall ye build house.* You shall not become residents in any place; you shall not court earthly possessions. (3) *But . . . ye shall dwell in tents.* You shall imitate your forefathers, Abraham, Isaac, and Jacob, and the rest of the patriarchs, who dwelt in tents, being strangers and pilgrims upon earth, looking for a heavenly country, and being determined to have nothing here that would indispose their minds towards that place of endless rest.

11. *But . . . when Nebuchadrezzar . . . came up.* If at present we appear to be acting contrary in any respect to our institutions, in being found in the city, necessity alone has induced us to take this temporary step. We have sought the shelter of the city for the preservation of our lives; so [now] we dwell *at Jerusalem.*

14. *The words of Jonadab . . . are performed . . . but ye hearkened not unto me.* The Lord, knowing the fidelity of this people, chose to try them in this way, that He might, by their conscientious obedience to the precepts of their forefathers, show the Jews, to their confusion, their ingratitude to Him, and their neglect of His precepts, which if a man do, he shall live by them.

CHAPTER 36

God commands Jeremiah to write down in one roll or volume all the predictions he had uttered against Israel and Judah, and all the surrounding nations, from the day of his vocation to the prophetic office, that the house of Judah might have abundant warning of the dreadful calamities with which their country was about to be visited, if not prevented by a timely repentance, 1-3. The prophet employs Baruch, the scribe, the son of Neriah, to write from his mouth all the words of the Lord, and then to read them publicly upon a fast day in the Lord's house, 4-8. A general fast is proclaimed in the following year, viz., the fifth year of the reign of Jehoiakim; upon which occasion Baruch, in obedience to the prophet's command, reads the words of Jeremiah to all the people at the entry of the new gate of the Temple, 9-10. The princes, hearing of this, send for Baruch, who reads the roll to them; at the contents of which they are greatly alarmed, and solemnly resolve to give information to the king, at the same time advising both the prophet and his scribe to hide themselves, 11-19. Jehoiakim likewise having sent for the roll, Jehudi reads to him a part; and then the king, though advised to the contrary by some of his princes, having cut the leaves, throws the whole into the fire, 20-25, and orders Jeremiah and Baruch to be seized; but they could not be found, because a special providence of God had concealed them, 26. Jeremiah is commanded to rewrite his prophecies, and to denounce the judgments of God against the king who had destroyed the first roll, 27-31. Baruch accordingly writes from the mouth of Jeremiah a new copy, with numerous additions, 32.

1. *And it came to pass in the fourth year.* About the end of this year; see v. 9. This discourse also bears its own date, and was probably delivered at a time when the people enjoyed peace, and were about to celebrate one of their annual fasts.

2. *Take thee a roll of a book.* Take a sufficient quantity of parchment; cut and stitch it together, that it may make a roll on which to write the words that I have already spoken, that they may serve for a testimony to future generations. The Jewish rolls were made of vellum, or of sheepskins dressed in the half-tanned manner. These were cut into certain lengths, and those parts were all stitched together, and rolled upon a roller. The matter was written on these skins in columns. Sometimes two rollers are used, that as the matter is read from the roll in the left hand, the reader may coil it on the roller in his right. In this form the Pentateuch is written which is read in the synagogues.

3. *It may be that the house of Judah will hear.* It was yet possible to avert the judgments which had been so often denounced against them.

4. *Then Jeremiah called Baruch.* This man, so useful to the prophet, and so faithfully attached to him, was by office a scribe; which signifies, not only a writer, but also a man in office; a chancellor, secretary, etc., a learned man; one acquainted with laws and customs.

6. *Upon the fasting day.* A day when multitudes of people would be gathered together from all parts to implore the mercy of God. This was a favorable time to read these tremendous prophecies.

9. *In the ninth month.* Answering to a part of our December.

10. *In the chamber of Gemariah.* He was one of the princes of Judah. See v. 12.

17. *How didst thou write all these words? At his mouth?* So the text should be pointed. They wished to know whether he had not copied them, or whether he wrote as Jeremiah prophesied.

19. *Go, hide thee, thou and Jeremiah.* They saw that the king would be displeased, and most probably seek their lives; and as they believed the prophecy was from God, they wished to save both the prophet and his scribe; but they were obliged to inform the king of what they had heard.

22. *Winterhouse.* A warm apartment suited to the season of the year (December) when in Palestine there is often snow upon the ground, though it does not last long. *A fire on the hearth*—a pan or brazier of burning coals.

23. *When Jehudi had read three or four leaves.* Rather columns; for the law, and the sacred Hebrew books, are written in columns of a certain breadth. *He cut it with the penknife.* "The knife of the scribe." *And cast it into the fire.* To show his contempt for God's words.

25. *Elnathan and Delaiah and Gemariah.* Three of the princes wished to save the roll, and entreated the king that it might not be burnt. They would have saved it out of the fire, but the king would not permit it to be done.

26. *But the Lord hid them.* They had, at the counsel of some of the princes, hidden themselves, v. 19. And now, though a diligent search was made, the Lord did not permit them to be found.

28. *Take thee again another roll.* There was no duplicate of the former preserved; and now God inspired the prophet with the same matter that He had given him before; and there is to be added the heavy judgment that is to fall on Jehoiakim and his courtiers.

30. *He shall have none to sit upon the throne of David.* He shall have no successor, and himself shall have an untimely end, and shall not even be buried, but his body be exposed to the open air, both night and day.

CHAPTER 37

Zedekiah succeeds Coniah, the son of Jehoiakim, in the Jewish throne, and does that which is evil in the sight of the Lord, 1-2. The king sends a message to Jeremiah, 3-5. God suggests an answer; and foretells the return of the Chaldean army, who should most assuredly take and burn the city, 6-10. Jeremiah, in attempting to leave this devoted city, and retire to his possession in the country, is seized as a deserter, and cast into a dungeon, 11-15. The king, after a conference with him, abates the rigor of his confinement, 16-21.

1. *And king Zedekiah the son of Josiah.* Of the siege and taking of Jerusalem referred to here, and the making of Zedekiah king instead of Jeconiah, see 2 Kings xxiv. 1, etc.

3. *Zedekiah . . . to the prophet Jeremiah.* He was willing to hear a message from the Lord, provided it were according to his own mind. He did not fully trust in his own prophets.

4. *Now Jeremiah came in and went out.* After the siege was raised, he had a measure of liberty; he was not closely confined, as he afterwards was. See v. 16.

5. *Then Pharaoh's army.* This was Pharaoh-hophra, who then reigned in Egypt in place of his father, Necho. See Ezek. xxix. 6, etc. Nebuchadnezzar, hearing that the Egyptian army, on which the Jews so much depended, were on their march to relieve the city, suddenly raised the siege, and went to meet them. In the interim Zedekiah sent to Jeremiah to inquire of the Lord to know whether they might consider themselves in safety.

7. *Pharaoh's army . . . shall return to Egypt.* They were defeated by the Chaldeans; and, not being hearty in the cause, returned immediately to Egypt, leaving Nebuchadnezzar unmolested to recommence the siege.

10. *For though ye had smitten the whole army.* Strong words; but they show how fully God was determined to give up this city to fire and sword, and how fully He had instructed His prophet on this point.

12. *Jeremiah went forth.* At the time that Nebuchadnezzar had raised the siege, and gone to meet the Egyptian army. *Go into the land of Benjamin.* To Anathoth, his native city. *To separate himself thence.* The Chaldee: "He went that he might divide the inheritance which he had there among the people."

13. *Thou fallest away to the Chaldeans.* You are a deserter, and a traitor to your country. As he had always declared that the Chaldeans should take the city, etc., his enemies took occasion from this to say he was in the interest of the Chaldeans, and that he wished now to go to them, and betray the place.

15. *And smote him.* Without any proof of the alleged treachery, without any form of justice. *In prison in the house of Jonathan.* In Asiatic countries there is an apartment in the houses of the officers of the law, to confine all the accused that are brought before them. Jonathan was a scribe or secretary, and had a prison of this kind in his house.

16. *Entered into the dungeon, and into the cabins.* The dungeon was probably a deep pit; and *the cabins* or cells, niches in the sides, where different malefactors were confined.

17. *Is there any word from the Lord?* Is there any further revelation? *There is: . . . thou shalt be delivered.* What bold faithfulness! And to a king, in whose hands his life now lay.

19. *Where are now your prophets?* They told you that the Chaldeans should not come; I told you they would. According to my word the Chaldeans are come, and are departed only for a short time.

20. *Cause me not to return to the house of Jonathan.* He had been ill used in this man's custody, so as to endanger his life, the place being cold, and probably unhealthy.

21. *Then Zedekiah . . . the court of the prison.* Was contiguous to the king's house, where the prisoners could readily see their friends. *Give him daily a piece of bread out of the bakers' street.* From the public stores, which he received till all the provisions were spent.

CHAPTER 38

The princes of Judah, taking offense at Jeremiah on account of his predicting the destruction of Jerusalem and the Temple by the Chaldeans, cause him to be cast into a deep and miry dungeon, 1-6. Ebed-melech, an Ethiopian, gets the king's permission to take him out, 7-13. Jeremiah advises the king, who consulted him privately, to surrender to the Chaldeans, 14-23. The king promises the prophet that he will not put him to death, and requires him not to reveal what had passed to the princes; to whom he accordingly gives an evasive answer, telling them only so much of the conference as related to his request for his life, 24-28.

1. *Then Shephatiah.* This was the faction who were enemies to Jeremiah, and sought his life.

3. *This city shall surely be given.* This was a testimony that he constantly bore; he had the authority of God for it. He knew it was true, and he never wavered nor equivocated.

4. *Let this man be put to death.* And they gave their reasons plain enough, but the proof was wanting.

6. *So Jeremiah sunk in the mire.* Their obvious design was that he might be stifled in that place.

7. *Ebed-melech.* "The servant of the king," one of the eunuchs who belonged to the palace.

Perhaps it should be read, "Now, a servant of the king, a Cushite, one of the eunuchs." *The king then sitting in the gate of Benjamin.* To give audience, and to administer justice.

9. *My lord the king, these men have done evil.* He must have been much in the king's confidence, and a humane and noble-spirited man, thus to have raised his voice against the powerful cabal already mentioned.

10. *Take from hence thirty men.* The king was determined that he should be rescued by force, if the princes opposed.

22. *All the women . . . brought forth.* I think this place speaks of a kind of defection among the women of the harem; many of whom had already gone forth privately to the principal officers of the Chaldean army, and made the report mentioned in the end of this verse. These were the concubines or women of the second rank.

23. *They shall bring out all thy wives and thy children.* These were the women of the first rank, by whom the king had children. These had no temptation to go out to the Chaldeans, nor would they have been made welcome; but the others being young, and without children, would be well received by the Chaldean princes.

26. *I presented my supplication.* This was telling the truth, and nothing but the truth, but not the whole truth. The king did not wish him to defile his conscience, nor did he propose anything that was not consistent with the truth.

CHAPTER 39

This chapter gives an account of the siege and taking of Jerusalem; the flight, capture, and punishment of Zedekiah; the burning of the city; and the carrying away of the people (a few of the meanest excepted) to Babylon, 1-10; also of the release of Jeremiah, and the special orders of Nebuchadnezzar concerning him, 11-14. The remaining verses relate to the subject of the preceding chapter; and contain promises of personal safety to Ebed-melech the Ethiopian amidst the public calamities, on account of his piety, and his humanity to the prophet, 15-18.

1. *In the ninth year of Zedekiah . . . in the tenth month.* This month is called Tebeth in Esther ii. 16. It began with the first new moon of our January, and it was on the tenth day of this month that Nebuchadnezzar invested the city.

2. *The eleventh year . . . in the fourth month.* This month in the Hebrew calendar is called Thammuz, and commences with the first new moon of our July. The siege had lasted just eighteen months. *The city was broken up.* A breach was made in the wall by which the Chaldeans entered.

3. *Sat in the middle gate.* The city of Jerusalem stood upon two hills, Sion to the south, and Acra to the north, with a deep valley between them. The "gate of the center," as the term seems plainly to import, was a gate of communication in the middle of the valley, between the two parts of the city, sometimes called the higher and the lower city. The Chaldeans entered the city on the north side by a breach in the walls, ind rushing forward and posting themselves in this gate, in the very heart or center of the city, became thereby masters at will of the whole. Zedekiah with his troop, perceiving this, fled out of the opposite gate on the south side. *Nergal-sharezer.* These were the principal commanders; but Dr.

Blayney thinks that instead of six persons, we have in reality but three, as the name that follows each is a title of office.

4. *Went forth out of the city by night.* Probably there was a private passage underground, leading without the walls, by which Zedekiah and his followers might escape unperceived, till they had got some way from the city. *The way of the plain.* There were two roads from Jerusalem to Jericho. One passed over the mount of Olives; but, as this might have retarded his flight, he chose the way of the plain, and was overtaken near Jericho, perhaps about sixteen or eighteen miles from Jerusalem. He had probably intended to pass the Jordan, in order to escape to Egypt, as the Egyptians were then his professed allies.

5. *To Riblah.* This city was situated on the northern frontier of Palestine, and Hamath was a large city belonging also to Syria. See Gen. x. 18.

9. *Those that fell away.* That deserted to the Chaldeans during the siege.

10. *Left of the poor of the people.* The very refuse of the inhabitants, who were not worthy of being carried away; and among them he divided the fields and vineyards of those whom he took away.

12. *Take him ... look well to him.* Nebuchadnezzar had heard that this prophet had foretold his capture of the city, and had frequently used all his influence to induce Zedekiah to pay the tribute, and not rebel against him; and on this account would be inclined to show the prophet especial favor.

CHAPTER 40

This and the following four chapters contain a distinct account of what passed in the land of Judah from the taking of Jerusalem to the retreat of the remnant of the people to Egypt; together with the prophecies of Jeremiah concerning that place, whither he himself accompanied them. In this chapter we have an account of the enlargement of Jeremiah by Nebuzar-adan, the captain of the guard, who advises him to put himself under the jurisdiction of Gedaliah, the son of Ahikam, whom the king of Babylon had made governor over the land of Judea, 1-5. The prophet and many of the dispersed Jews repair to Gedaliah, 6-12. Johanan acquaints the governor of a conspiracy against him, but is not believed, 13-16.

1. *The word that came to Jeremiah.* This and the following four chapters contain a particular account of what passed in the land of Judea from the taking of the city to the retreat of the people into Egypt, and the prophecies of Jeremiah concerning them there.

2. *The Lord thy God hath pronounced.* I know that you are a true prophet, for what you have predicted from your God is come to pass.

4. *Come; and I will look well unto thee.* You are now at full liberty to do as you please, either to come to Babylon or to stay in your own land.

5. *Go back also to Gedaliah.* If you will stay in your own land, you had best put yourself under the protection of your countryman Gedaliah, whom the king of Babylon has made governor of the land.

8. *Ishmael the son of Nethaniah.* This is he who afterwards murdered Gedaliah. He had been employed to do this by Baalis, king of the Ammonites, with whom he appears to have taken refuge during the siege. See v. 14.

14. *But Gedaliah the son of Ahikam believed them not.* The account given of this man proves him to have been a person of uncommon greatness of soul. Conscious of his own integrity and benevolence, he took the portrait of others from his own mind; and therefore believed evil of no man, because he felt none towards any in his own breast. He may be reproached for being too credulous and confident, but anything of this kind that may be justly charged against him serves only to show the greatness of his mind.

CHAPTER 41

Ishmael executes his conspiracy against Gedaliah, the governor, and his companions, and attempts to carry away the Jews who were with him captives to the Ammonites, 1-10; but Johanan recovers them, and purposes to flee into Egypt, 11-18.

1. *Now ... in the seventh month.* Answering to the first new moon in our month of October. *There they did eat bread together.* This was the same as making a solemn covenant, for he who ate bread with another was ever reputed a friend.

2. *Smote Gedaliah.* See the preceding chapter, v. 14.

5. *Having their beards shaven.* All these were signs of deep mourning, probably on account of the destruction of the city.

6. *Weeping all along as he went.* This felonious hypocrite pretended that he also was deeply afflicted, and wished to bear them company in their sorrow. *Come to Gedaliah.* He will appoint you vineyards and fields.

7. *Slew them.* He kept the murder of Gedaliah secret, and no doubt had a band of his assassins lodged in Mizpah; and he decoyed these fourscore men thither that he might have strength to slay them. He kept ten alive because they told him they had treasures hidden in a field, which they would show him. Whether he kept his word with them is not recorded. He could do nothing good or great; and it is likely that, when he had possessed himself of those treasures, he served them as he had served their companions.

9. *Now the pit ... was it which Asa the king had made for fear of Baasha.* See 1 Kings xv. 22. Asa made this cistern as a reservoir for water for the supply of the place; for he built and fortified Mizpah at the time that he was at war with Baasha, king of Israel.

10. *Carried them away captive.* He took all these that he might sell them for slaves among the Ammonites.

14. *Went unto Johanan.* They were weary of the tyranny of Ishmael, and were glad of an opportunity to abandon him.

16. *The women ... children, and the eunuchs.* These were all, most probably, persons who belonged to the palace and harem of Zedekiah: some of them his own concubines, and their children.

17. *Dwelt in the habitation of Chimham.* The estate that David gave Chimham, the son of Barzillai. See 2 Sam. xix. 37, etc. He took this merely as a resting place; as he designed to carry all into Egypt, fearing the Chaldeans, who would endeavor to revenge the death of Gedaliah.

CHAPTER 42

Johanan and the remnant of the people desire Jeremiah to ask counsel of God what they should do, 1-3. The prophet assures them of safety in Judea, but destruction in Egypt, 4-18; and reproves their hypocrisy in asking counsel with which they had no intention to comply, 19-22.

1. *The captains of the forces.* The different leaders of the small bands or companies, collected from different parts of the land. The principal are those here named.

3. *That the Lord thy God may shew us.* They all thought there was no safety in Jerusalem or in Judea, and therefore determined to leave the land. But they did not know which might be the safest direction to take; for though they inclined to Egypt, yet they wished to know the mind of God on that point.

5. *The Lord be a true and faithful witness.* The Lord is such; and as you have bound yourselves to obey His voice, He will register the covenant, and bless or curse according as you shall conduct yourselves in this matter.

7. *After ten days.* All this time he was waiting upon God; for it is evident the prophets could not prophesy when they pleased, any more than the disciples of our Lord could work miracles when they wished. The gift of prophecy and the gift of miracles were both dependent on the will of the Most High, and each of them was given only for the moment; and when the necessity was over, the influence ceased.

10. *For I repent me of the evil.* The meaning is, As I have punished you only because you continued to be rebellious, I will arrest this punishment as soon as you become obedient to My word. You need not fear the king of Babylon if you have Me for your Helper; and I will so show mercy to you that he shall see it, and cease from afflicting you, as he shall see that I am on your side.

15. *If ye . . . set your faces to enter into Egypt,* etc. Every evil that you dreaded by staying in your own land shall come upon you in Egypt.

16. *The sword . . . and the famine . . . shall follow close after you.* Shall be at your heels, shall overtake and destroy you; for *there ye shall die.*

19. *Go ye not into Egypt.* Why? Because God knew, such was their miserable propensity to idolatry, that they would there adopt the worship of the country, and serve idols.

CHAPTER 43

The leading men, discrediting Jeremiah's prophecy, carry the people into Egypt, 1-7. Jeremiah, by a type, foretells the conquest of Egypt by Nebuchadnezzar, 8-13. This mode of conveying instruction by actions was very expressive, and frequently practiced by the prophets. The image of Nebuchadnezzar arraying himself with Egypt, as a shepherd puts on his garment, is very noble. Egypt at this time contended with Babylon, for the empire of the East; yet this mighty kingdom, when God appoints the revolution, shifts its owner with as much ease as a shepherd removes his tent or garment, which the new proprietor has only to spread over him. See v. 12.

2. *Thou speakest falsely.* They had no other color for their rebellion than flatly to deny that God had spoken what the prophet related.

6. *Men, and women, and children, and the king's daughters.* See chap. xli. 10. It is truly surprising that the Chaldeans should have left behind any of the royal family of Judah! But (1) Perhaps they knew not there were any. (2) If they did know, they might think, being children of concubines, they could not inherit. Or, (3) That, being females, they were not eligible. And they had taken care to seize all Zedekiah's sons, and slay them before his eyes.

7. *Came they even to Tahpanhes.* This city was called Daphne by the Greeks, and was situated at the extremity of Lower Egypt, near to Heliopolis. It was called Daphne Pelusiaca. They halted at this place, most probably for the purpose of obtaining the king's permission to penetrate farther into Egypt. It was at this place that, according to St. Jerome, tradition says the faithful Jeremiah was stoned to death by these rebellious wretches; for whose welfare he had watched, prayed, gone through many indignities, and suffered every kind of hardship. And now he sealed the truth of his divine mission with his blood.

9. *Take great stones.* This discourse seems to have been delivered about a year after the destruction of Jerusalem. They pretended that they dared not stay in Judea for fear of the Chaldeans. The prophet here assures them that Nebuchadnezzar shall come to Egypt, extend his conquests in that kingdom, and place his tent over the very place where these stones were laid up, and destroy them. How these prophecies were fulfilled, see at the end of chap. xliv.

11. *Such as are for death to death.* See chap. xv. 2.

12. *He shall burn them, and carry them away captives.* Some of these gods, such as were of wood, he will burn; those of metal he will carry away. Some of them were of gold. *Shall array himself with the land of Egypt.* Shall take all its wealth and all its grandeur, shall take all its spoils. *As a shepherd putteth on his garment.* With as much ease, and with as little opposition, and with as full a confidence that it is now his own. *He shall go forth from thence in peace.* He shall suffer no interruption, nor endure any disaster in his return from his Egyptian expedition.

13. *He shall break also the images of Beth-shemesh. Beith shemesh* is, literally, "the house or temple of the sun"; which was worshipped here, and whose images are said to have been of solid gold. These Nebuchadnezzar was to break and carry away; *and the houses of the gods*—all the temples of Egypt, he was to burn with fire. Beth-shemesh is the same as Heliopolis.

CHAPTER 44

Jeremiah reproves the Jews in Egypt for continuing in idolatry after the exemplary judgments inflicted by God on their nation for that sin, 1-14; and, upon their refusing to reform, denounces destruction to them, and to that kingdom wherein they sought protection, 15-30.

1. *The word that came to Jeremiah concerning all the Jews.* Dahler supposes this discourse to have been delivered in the seventeenth or eighteenth year after the taking of Jerusalem. *Which dwell at Migdol.* A city of Lower Egypt, not far from Pelusium. *Noph.* Memphis, a celebrated city of Middle Egypt, and the capital of its district. *The country of Pathros.* A district of Upper Egypt, known by the name of the Thebais. Thus we find that the

Jews were scattered over the principal parts of Egypt.

2. *No man dwelleth therein.* The desolation of the land of Judea must have been exceedingly great when this, in almost any sense, could be spoken of it.

4. *Oh, do not this abominable thing.* A strong specimen of affectionate entreaty. One of the finest figures of poetry, when judiciously managed, the anthropopathia, the ascribing human passions to God, is often used by this prophet; so God is said to grieve, to mourn, to repent, to be angry, etc. Here He is represented as tenderly expostulating: "Oh, do not"; or, "I entreat you, do not that abominable thing which I hate."

7. *This great evil against your souls.* Will not self-interest weigh with you? See what ruin your conduct has brought upon your country. Your fathers sinned as you are doing; and where are they now? Either destroyed, or in captivity. And you are now taking the same way to your own destruction.

9. *Have ye forgotten the wickedness of your fathers?* It seems that the women were principal agents in idolatrous practices; for the queens— the wives, of rulers and of common people, burnt incense to the queen of heaven (the moon), v. 17, and poured out drink offerings to her.

15. *Then all the men . . . and all the women.* We have not seen the women in determined rebellion before. Here they make a common cause with their idolatrous husbands.

19. *And when we burned incense to the queen of heaven.* The moon seems to have been called *melecheth*, as the sun was called *molech*.

22. *Therefore is your land a desolation.* I grant that you and your husbands have joined together in these abominations; and what is the consequence? *The Lord could no longer bear, because of your evil doings; and therefore is your land a desolation, and an astonishment, and a curse, without an inhabitant, . . . this day.*

30. *Behold, I will give Pharoah-hophra.* That is, Pharaoh Apries. How this and the prophecies in the preceding chapter were fulfilled, we learn from ancient historians. The sum of such information is this: The subjects of Pharaoh Apries rebelling, he sent Amasis, one of his generals, to reduce them to their duty. But no sooner had Amasis begun to make his speech than they fixed a helmet on his head, and proclaimed him king. Amasis accepted the title, and confirmed the Egyptians in their revolt; and the greater part of the nation declaring for him, Apries was obliged to retire into Upper Egypt; and the country being thus weakened by intestine war, was attacked and easily overcome by Nebuchadnezzar, who on quitting it left Amasis his viceroy. After Nebuchadnezzar's departure, Apries marched against Amasis; but, being defeated at Memphis, was taken prisoner, carried to Sais, and was strangled in his own palace, thus verifying this prophecy.

Thus Nebuchadnezzar made an easy conquest of the land. He conquered it as easily as "a shepherd puts on his cloak: he went thence in peace," having clothed himself with its spoils; and left all quiet under a viceroy of his own choosing. The rebellion of Pharaoh's subjects was the fire that God kindled in Egypt, chap.

xliii. 12. And thus was he delivered into the hands of his enemies, his revolted people; and into the hand of him who sought his life, i.e., Amasis, his general. And thus the whole prophecy was literally fulfilled.

CHAPTER 45

This chapter is evidently connected with the subject treated of in the thirty-sixth. Baruch, who had written the prophecies of Jeremiah, and read them publicly in the Temple, and afterwards to many of the princes, is in great affliction because of the awful judgments with which the land of Judah was about to be visited; and also on account of the imminent danger to which his own life was exposed, in publishing such unwelcome tidings, 1-3. To remove Baruch's fear with respect to this latter circumstance, the prophet assures him that, though the total destruction of Judea was determined because of the great wickedness of the inhabitants, yet his life should be preserved amidst the desolation, 4-5.

1. *The word that Jeremiah . . . spake unto Baruch.* This is another instance of shameless transposition. This discourse was delivered in the fourth year of Jehoiakim, several years before Jerusalem was taken by the Chaldeans. It is a simple appendage to chap. xxxvi, and there it should have been inserted.

3. *Thou didst say, Woe is me now!* All that were the enemies of Jeremiah became his enemies too, and he needed these promises of support. *The Lord hath added grief to my sorrow.* He had mourned for the desolations that were coming on his country, and now he mourns for the dangers to which he feels his own life exposed; for we find, from chap. xxxvi. 26, that the king had given commandment to take both Baruch and Jeremiah, in order that they might be put to death at the instance of his nobles.

4. *Behold, that which I have built.* I most certainly will fulfil all those threatenings contained in the roll you have written, for I will destroy this whole land.

5. *And seekest thou great things for thyself?* Nothing better can be expected of this people; your hopes in reference to them are vain. Expect no national amendment, till national judgments have taken place.

But thy life will I give unto thee for a prey. This is a proverbial expression. We have met with it before, chap. xxi. 9, xxxviii. 2, xxxix. 18; and it appears to have this meaning. As a prey or spoil is that which is gained from a vanquished enemy, so it is preserved with pleasure as the proof and reward of a man's own valor. So Baruch's life should be doubly precious unto him, not only on account of the dangers through which God had caused him to pass safely, but also on account of those services he had been enabled to render, the consolations he had received, and the continual and very evident interposition of God in his behalf. All these would be dearer to him than the spoils of a vanquished foe to the hero who had overcome in battle.

CHAPTER 46

The difference between the preceding and the subsequent prophecies in point of composition is very remarkable, the last excelling much in majesty and elegance. This chapter (of which the first verse forms a general title to this and the five chapters following) contains two distinct prophecies relating to Egypt. The first was delivered previous to an engagement between Pharaohnecho, king of Egypt, and Nebuchadnezzar, king of Babylon; in which the Egyptians were routed in Carchemish with great slaughter, as here predicted. The prophet sees the mighty preparations; but they are all declared to be of no avail, as God had decreed their fall, 1-6. The king of Egypt, however, is represented as marching with all the confidence of victory, like a river overflowing its banks, and threatening all around with its inundation, 7-8. But this immense armament of Pharaoh-necho, consisting of various nations, shall, by a righteous judgment of God, receive such a signal overthrow near the river Euphrates that the political consequence of Egypt shall be thereby irretrievably ruined, and its remaining power become contemptible in the sight of the nations, 9-12. The other prophecy, beginning at the thirteenth verse, relates to the memorable overthrow of the Egyptians by Nebuchadnezzar, subsequent to his siege of Tyre, in the sixteenth year after the destruction of Jerusalem, 13-26. The promise, in the conclusion of the chapter, of preservation to the Jews (who have for many ages continued a distinct people, when the various nations of antiquity who oppressed them, or with whom they had any intercourse, have long ago ceased to have any separate and visible existence), has been most remarkably fulfilled; and is a very signal act of Providence, and a pledge of the restoration of Israel to the divine favor, when the time of the Gentiles shall be fulfilled, 27-28.

1. *The word of the Lord . . . against the Gentiles.* This is a general title to the following collection of prophecies, written concerning different nations, which had less or more connection with the Jews, either as enemies, neighbors, or allies. They were not written at the same time; and though some of them bear dates, yet it would be difficult to give them any chronological arrangement.

2. *Pharaoh-necho.* This was the person who defeated the army of Josiah, in which engagement Josiah received a mortal wound, of which he died, greatly regretted, soon after at Megiddo. After this victory he defeated the Babylonians, and took Carchemish; and, having fortified it, returned to his own country. Nabo-polassar sent his son, Nebuchadnezzar, with an army against him, defeated him with immense slaughter near the river Euphrates, retook Carchemish, and subdued all the revolted provinces, according to the following prophecies.

3. *Order ye the buckler.* This is the call to the general armament of the people against the Chaldeans.

6. *Let not the swift flee away.* Even the swiftest shall not be able to escape. *They shall . . . fall toward the north.* By the Euphrates, which was northward of Judea. Here the Egyptian army was routed with great slaughter.

7. *Who is this that cometh up as a flood?* The vast concourse of people is here represented as a river; for instance, the Jordan, suddenly swollen with the rains in harvest, rolling its waters along, and overflowing the whole country. A fine image to represent the incursions of vast armies carrying all before them. Such was the army of Pharaoh-necho in its march to Carchemish.

9. *The Ethiopians.* Hebrew, *Cush, Phut,* and the *Ludim.* This army was composed of many nations. *Cush,* which we translate "Ethiopians," almost invariably means the Arabians; and here, those Arabs that bordered on Egypt near the Red Sea. *Phut* probably means the "Libyans"; for Phut settled in Libya, according to Josephus. Phut and Cush were two of the sons of Ham, and brothers to Mitsraim, the father of the Egyptians, Gen. x. 6; and the Ludim were descended from Mitsraim; see Gen. x. 13.

10. *For this is the day of the Lord God of hosts.* The prophet represents this as a mighty sacrifice, where innumerable victims were slain.

11. *Go up into Gilead, and take balm.* An irony. Egypt is so completely enfeebled by this overthrow that her political wound is utterly incurable. This figure is used with the more propriety here, as the Egyptians have been celebrated from the remotest antiquity for their knowledge of medicine.

12. *The nations have heard of thy shame.* Of your disgrace, by this prodigious slaughter of your troops.

13. *How Nebuchadrezzar . . . should come and smite the land of Egypt.* See on chap. xliv. This was after Amasis had driven Pharaohnecho into Upper Egypt. See chap. xliv. 30.

15. *They stood not, because the Lord did drive them.* The Lord panic-struck them, and drove them back.

16. *One fell upon another.* In their terror and confusion ranks fell on ranks, and overturned each other. *Let us go again to our own people.* Let us flee to our own country with all possible speed. These were the auxiliaries.

17. *They did cry there.* These allies sent their excuse to Pharaoh that the disasters they had met with had prevented them from joining him as they had intended.

18. *As Tabor is among the mountains.* This mountain is situated in the plain of Esdraelon in Galilee, on the confines of the tribes of Zebulun and Issachar, Josh. xix. 22. It stood by itself, separated from all the other mountains by deep valleys, and is the highest of the whole. *And as Carmel by the sea.* Carmel is a mountain on the coast of the Mediterranean Sea, on the southern frontier of the tribe of Asher. Were the Egyptians as distinguished for valor and strength as the mountains Tabor and Carmel are for height among the other mountains in their vicinity, they should not be able to stand the shock of the Chaldean army.

19. *Furnish thyself to go into captivity.* The thing is unavoidable; prepare for this calamity.

20. *Egypt is like a very fair heifer.* Fruitful and useful; but destruction cometh out of the north, from Chaldea. It may be that there is an allusion here to Isis, worshipped in Egypt under the form of a beautiful cow.

22. *The voice . . . shall go like a serpent.* See Isa. xxix. 4.

23. *They shall cut down her forest.* Supposed to mean her cities, of which Egypt had no fewer than 1,020.

24. *The hand of the people of the north.* The Chaldeans.

25. *The multitude of No.* Amon minno, the Amon of No, called by the Greeks "Jupiter's city." It was the famous Thebes, celebrated anciently for its hundred gates. *Amon* was the name by which the Egyptians called Jupiter, who had a famous temple at Thebes.

26. *Afterward it shall be inhabited.* That is, within forty years, as Ezekiel had predicted, chap. xxix. 13.

27. *Fear not . . . my servant Jacob.* In the midst of wrath God remembers mercy. Though Judah shall be destroyed, Jerusalem taken, the Temple burnt to the ground, and the people carried into captivity, yet the nation shall not be destroyed. A seed shall be preserved, out of which the nation shall revive.

CHAPTER 47

Among the nations doomed to suffer from the hostilities of Nebuchadnezzar are the Philistines (see chap. xxv. 20). And the calamities predicted in this chapter befell them probably during the long siege of Tyre, when their country was desolated to prevent their giving Tyre or Sidon any assistance, 1-5. The whole of this chapter is remarkably elegant. The address to the sword of Jehovah, at the close of it, is particularly a very beautiful and bold personification, 6-7.

1. *The word of the Lord . . . against the Philistines.* The date of this prophecy cannot be easily ascertained. *Before that Pharaoh smote Gaza.* We have no historical relation of any Egyptian king smiting Gaza. It was no doubt smitten by some of them; but when, and by whom, does not appear from either sacred or profane history.

2. *Waters rise up out of the north.* Waters is a common prophetic image for a multitude of people. The *north* here, as in other places of this prophecy, means Chaldea.

3. *The stamping of the hoofs.* At the "galloping sound." *The fathers shall not look back.* Though their children are left behind, they have neither strength nor courage to go back to bring them off.

4. *To spoil all the Philistines.* These people, of whom there were five seignories, occupied the coast of the Mediterranean Sea, to the south of the Phoenicians. *Tyrus and Zidon.* Places sufficiently remarkable in both the Old and New Testament, and in profane history. They belonged to the Phoenicians; and at this time were depending on the succor of their allies, the Philistines. But their expectation was cut off. *The remnant of the country of Caphtor.* Crete, or Cyprus. Some think it was a district along the coast of the Mediterranean, belonging to the Philistines.

5. *Baldness is come upon Gaza.* They have cut off their hair in token of deep sorrow and distress. *Ashkelon is cut off.* Or "put to silence," another mark of the deepest sorrow. Askelon was one of the five seignories of the Philistines; Gaza was another. *The remnant of their valley.* Or "plain"; for the whole land of the Philistines was a vast plain, which extended along the coast of the Mediterranean Sea from Phoenicia to the frontiers of Egypt. The whole of this plain, the territory of the Philistines, shall be desolated.

6. *O thou sword of the Lord.* This is a most grand prosopopoeia—a dialogue between the sword of the Lord and the prophet. Nothing can be imagined more sublime. *Put up thyself into thy scabbard, rest, and be still.* Shed no more blood, destroy no more lives, erase no more cities, desolate no more countries.

7. *How can it be quiet?* This is the answer of the sword. I am the officer of God's judgments, and He has given me a commission against Ashkelon, and against the seashore, all the coast where the Philistines have their territories. The measure of their iniquities is full, and these God hath appointed this sword to ravage. The Philistines were ever the implacable enemies of the Jews, and the basest and worst of all idolaters. On these accounts the sword of the Lord had its commission against them, and it did its office most fearfully and effectually by the hand of the Chaldeans.

CHAPTER 48

The following prophecy concerning the Moabites is supposed to have had its accomplishment during the long siege of Tyre in the reign of Nebuchadnezzar. The whole of this chapter is poetry of the first order. The distress of the cities of Moab, with which it opens, is finely described. The cries of one ruined city resound to those of another, 1-3. The doleful, helpless cry of the children is heard, 4; the highways, on either hand, resound with the voice of weeping, 5; and the few that remain resemble a blasted tree in the wide, howling waste, 6. Chemosh, the chief god of the Moabites, and the capital figure in the triumph, is represented as carried off in chains, with all his trumpery of priests and officers, 7. The desolation of the country shall be so general and sudden that, by a strong figure, it is intimated that there shall be no possibility of escape, except it be in the speediest flight, 8-9. And some idea may be formed of the dreadful wickedness of this people from the consideration that the prophet, under the immediate inspiration of the Almighty, pronounces a curse on those who do the work of the Lord negligently, in not proceeding to their utter extermination, 10. The subject is then diversified by an elegant and well-supported comparison, importing that the Moabites increased in insolence and pride in proportion to the duration of their prosperity, 11; but this prosperity is declared to be nearly at an end; the destroyer is already commissioned against Moab, and his neighbors called to sing the usual lamentation at his funeral, 12-18. The prophet then represents some of the women of Aroer and Ammon (the extreme borders of Moab) standing in the highways, and asking the fugitives of Moab, What intelligence? They inform him of the complete discomfiture of Moab, 19-24, and of the total annihilation of its political existence, 25. The divine judgments about to fall upon Moab are further represented under the expressive metaphor of a cup of intoxicating liquor, by which he should become an object of derision because of his intolerable pride, his magnifying himself against Jehovah, and his great contempt for the children of Israel in the day of their calamity, 26-27. The prophet then points out the great distress of Moab by a variety of striking figures, viz., by the failure of the customary rejoicings at the end of harvest, by the mournful sort of music used at funerals, by the signs which were expressive among the ancients of deep mourning, as shaving the head, clipping the beard, cutting the flesh, and wearing sackcloth; and by the methods of catching wild beasts in toils, and by the terror and pitfall, 28-46. In the close of the chapter it is intimated that a remnant shall be preserved from this general calamity whose descendants shall be prosperous in the latter days, 47.

1. *Against Moab.* This was delivered some time after the destruction of Jerusalem. The Moabites were in the neighborhood of the Ammonites, and whatever evils fell on the one would naturally involve the other. See Isa. xv and xvi on this same subject. *Woe unto Nebo! for it is spoiled.* This was a city in the tribe of Reuben, afterwards possessed by the Moabites. It probably had its name from Nebo, one of the principal idols of the Moabites. *Kiriathaim.* Another city of the Moabites. *Misgab is confounded.* There is no place of this name known; and therefore several learned men translate *hammisgab,* literally, "the high tower," or "fortress," which may apply to Kiriathaim, or any other high and well-fortified place.

2. *No more praise of Moab.* Dr. Blayney translates: "Moab shall have no more glorying in Heshbon; they have devised evil against her (saying.)" And this most certainly is the best translation of the original.

3. *Horonaim.* Another city of Moab, near to Luhith. At this latter place the hill country of Moab commenced.

6. *Flee, save your lives.* The enemy is in full pursuit of you. *Be like the heath.* Caaroer, "like Aroer," which some take for a city, others for a blasted or withered tree. It is supposed that a place of this name lay towards the north, in the land of the Ammonites, on a branch of the river Jabbok, surrounded by deserts. Save yourselves by getting into the wilderness, where the pursuing foe will scarcely think it worth his while to follow you, as the wilderness itself must soon destroy you.

7. *Chemosh shall go forth into captivity.* The grand national idol of the Moabites, Num. xxi. 29; Judg. xi. 24. Ancient idolaters used to take their gods with them to the field of battle.

9. *Give wings unto Moab.* There is no hope in resistance, and to escape requires the speediest flight.

10. *Cursed be he that doeth the work of the Lord deceitfully.* Moab is doomed to destruction, and the Lord pronounces a curse on their enemies if they do not proceed to utter extirpation. God is the Author of life, and has a sovereign right to dispose of it as He pleases, and these had forfeited theirs long ago by their idolatry and other crimes.

11. *Moab hath been at ease.* The metaphor here is taken from the mode of preserving wines. They let them rest upon their lees for a considerable time, as this improves them in both strength and flavor; and when this is sufficiently done, they pour them off into other vessels. Moab had been very little molested by war since he was a nation; he had never gone out of his own land. Though some had been carried away by Shalmaneser forty years before this, he has had neither wars nor captivity. *Therefore his taste remained in him.* Still carrying on the allusion to the curing of wines; by resting long upon the lees, the taste and smell are both improved.

13. *Beth-el their confidence.* Alluding to the golden calves which Jeroboam had there set up, and commanded all the Israelites to worship.

17. *How is the strong staff broken!* The sceptre. The sovereignty of Moab is destroyed.

18. *That dost inhabit Dibon.* This was anciently a city of the Reubenites, afterwards inhabited by the Moabites, about two leagues north of the river Arnon, and about six to the east of the Dead Sea.

19. *O inhabitant of Aroer.* See the note on v. 6. This place, being at a greater distance, is counselled to watch for its own safety, and inquire of every passenger, *What is done?* that it may know when to pack up and be gone.

20. *Tell ye it in Arnon.* Apprise the inhabitants there that the territories of Moab are invaded, and the country about to be destroyed, that they may provide for their own safety.

21. *Upon Holon,* etc. All these were cities of the Moabites, but several of them are mentioned in no other place.

25. *The horn of Moab is cut off, and his arm is broken.* His political and physical powers are no more.

27. *Was not Israel a derision unto thee?* Did you not mock My people, and say their God was no better than the gods of other nations? See Ezek. xxv. 8. *Was he found among thieves?* Did the Israelites come to rob and plunder you? Why then mock them, and rejoice at their desolation, when their enemies prevailed over them? This the Lord particularly resents.

28. *Dwell in the rock.* Go to the most inaccessible places in the mountains. *The hole's mouth.* And into the most secret caves and holes of the earth.

29. *The pride of Moab.* See Isa. xvi. 1.

32. *O vine of Sibmah.* See Isa. xvi. 8.

34. *As an heifer of three years old.* Which

runs lowing from place to place in search of her calf, which is lost or taken from her.

37. *For every head shall be bald.* These, as we have seen before, were signs of the deepest distress and desolation.

40. *He shall fly as an eagle.* The enemy will pounce upon him, carry him off, and tear him to pieces.

42. *Moab shall be destroyed from being a people.* They shall not have a king or civil governor, and I doubt whether there be any evidence that they were ever reinstated in their national character.

45. *They that fled stood under the shadow of Heshbon.* Heshbon being a fortified place, they who were worsted in the fight fled to it, and rallied under its walls; but, instead of safety, they found themselves disappointed, betrayed, and ruined. See v. 2. *But a fire shall come forth out of Heshbon.* Jeremiah has borrowed this part of his discourse from an ancient poet quoted by Moses, Num. xxi. 28. *The crown of the head.* The choicest persons of the whole nation.

46. *The people of Chemosh* The Moabites, who worshipped Chemosh as their supreme god.

47. *Will I bring again the captivity of Moab in the latter days.* That many of them returned on the edict of Cyrus, by virtue of which the Jews were restored, I doubt not; but neither the Ammonites, Moabites, Philistines, nor even the Jews themselves, were ever restored to their national consequence. Perhaps the restoration spoken of here, which was to take place in the latter days, may mean the conversion of these people, in their existing remnants, to the faith of the gospel.

CHAPTER 49

This chapter is a collection of prophecies relating to several nations in the neighborhood of Judea; and, like those preceding, are supposed to have been fulfilled by the ministry of Nebuchadnezzar during the thirteen years' siege of Tyre. The chapter opens with a prophecy concerning the Ammonites, whose chief city, Rabbah, shall be destroyed; and Malcom, the supreme divinity of the people, with all his retinue of priests and officers, carried into captivity, 1-5. Promise that the Ammonites shall be restored to their liberty, 6. Prophecy against the Edomites (very like that most dreadful one in the thirty-fourth chapter of Isaiah against the same people), who shall be utterly exterminated, after the similitude of Sodom and Gomorrah, 7-22. Prophecy against Damascus, 23-27; and against Kedar, 28-29. Utter desolation of the kingdoms of Hazor foretold, 30-33. The polity of the Elamites shall be completely dissolved, and the people dispersed throughout the nations, 34-38. The Elamites shall be delivered from their captivity in the latter days, 39. It will be proper here to observe that these predictions should not be so explained as if they admitted of merely a private interpretation; for, as Bishop Lowth remarks upon Isaiah's prophecy concerning the Idumeans, "by a figure very common in the prophetical writings, any city or people, remarkably distinguished as enemies of the people and kingdom of God, is put for those enemies in general." Therefore it is under the gospel dispensation that these prophecies shall be accomplished to their fullest extent upon all the antichristian nations that have sinned after the similitude of the ancient enemies of the people of God under the Mosaic economy.

1. *Concerning the Ammonites.* This prophetic discourse was also delivered after the capture of Jerusalem. *Hath Israel no sons? . . . no heir?* The Ammonites, it appears, took advantage of the depressed state of Israel, and invaded their territories in the tribe of Gad, hoping to make them their own forever. But the prophet intimates that God will preserve the descendants of Israel, and will bring them back to their

forfeited inheritances. *Why then doth their king? Malcom* or *Milcom,* the chief idol of the Ammonites. That the idol Milcom is here meant is sufficiently evident from v. 3.

3. *Run to and fro by the hedges.* It is supposed that this may refer to the women making lamentations for the dead, that were in general buried by the walls of their gardens. But others think that it refers to the smaller cities or villages, called here the daughters of *Rabbah,* the metropolis, the inhabitants of which are exhorted to seek safety somewhere else, as none can be expected from them, now that the enemy is at hand.

6. *Afterward I will bring again.* The Ammonites are supposed to have returned with the Moabites and Israelites, on permission given by the edict of Cyrus.

7. *Concerning Edom.* This is a new and separate discourse. *Teman.* A part of Idumea, put here for the whole country.

8. *Dwell deep.* An allusion to the custom of the Arabs, who, when about to be attacked by a powerful foe, strike their tents, pack up their utensils, lade their camels, and set off to the great desert, and so bury themselves in it that no enemy either will or can pursue. *Dedan.* Was a city of Idumea, not far from Teman.

9. *If grapegatherers.* Both in vintage and in harvest every grape and every stalk are not gathered; hence the gleaners get something for their pains. But your enemies shall not leave one of you behind; all shall be carried into captivity.

10. *I have made Esau bare.* I have stripped him of all defense, and have discovered his hiding places to his enemies.

11. *Leave thy fatherless children.* The connection of this with the context is not easy to be discerned; but, as a general maxim, it is of great importance. Widows and orphans are the peculiar care of God. He is as the best of fathers to the one, and the most loving of husbands to the other. Even the widows and orphans of Esau, who escape the general destruction, shall be taken by the Lord.

12. *Art thou he that shall altogether go unpunished?* A similar form of speech appears in chap. xxv. 29. Others, less wicked than you, have been punished; and can you expect to escape? You shall not escape.

13. *Bozrah shall become a desolation.* Bozrah, a city of Idumea, is here put for the whole country.

14. *I have heard a rumour.* The Lord has revealed to me what He is about to do to the Edomites. *An ambassador is sent.* I believe this means only that God has given permission, and has stirred up the hearts of these nations to go against those whom He has doomed to destruction.

16. *O thou that dwellest.* All Idumea is full of mountains and rocks, and these rocks and mountains full of caves, where, in time of great heats, and in time of war, the people take shelter.

18. *As in the overthrow of Sodom.* The destruction of Sodom and Gomorrah and the neighboring cities was so terrible that, when God denounces judgments against incorrigible sinners, He tells them they shall be like Sodom and Gomorrah. *No man shall abide there.* It shall be so desolate as not to be habitable. Travellers may lodge on the ground for a night, but it cannot become a permanent dwelling.

19. *Behold, he shall come up like a lion.* See chap. xii. 5. The similitude used here is well illustrated by Dr. Blayney: "When I shall occasion a like commotion in her (Idumea) as a fierce and strong lion may be supposed to do in the sheep-folds, then I will cause him (the man of whom it is said in the preceding verse that he should not dwell in it) to run away from her as the affrighted shepherds and their flocks run from the lion." *A chosen man.* Nebuchadnezzar. That is, God has chosen this man, and given him a commission against Idumea.

20. *The inhabitants of Teman.* Taken here for the whole of Idumea. These are a kind of synonyms which prevent monotony, and give variety to the poet's versification. *Surely the least of the flock shall draw them out.* They shall be like timid sheep; the weakest foe shall overcome them.

21. *The earth is moved.* The whole state is represented here as a vast building suddenly thrown down, so as to cause the earth to tremble, and the noise to be heard at a great distance.

22. *He shall come up and fly as the eagle.* Nebuchadnezzar. See chap. xlviii. 40.

23. *Concerning Damascus.* This is the head or title of another prophecy. Damascus was one of the principal cities of Syria. It was taken by David, 2 Sam. viii. 6, was retaken in the reign of Solomon, 1 Kings xi. 24, etc., and regained its independence. Its kings were often at war with the ten tribes, and once it joined with them for the destruction of Judah. To defend himself against these powerful enemies Ahaz made a league with the king of Assyria, who besieged Damascus, took, and demolished it. From that time we hear nothing of Damascus till we meet with it in this prophecy. It appears to have been rebuilt and restored to some consequence. It made an obstinate resistance to Nebuchadnezzar, but was at last taken and sacked by him. At present it is both a large and populous city, with considerable commerce. *Hamath is confounded.* This is a city of Syria, on the Orontes. *Arpad.* Not far from Damascus. *Sorrow on the sea.* They are like the troubled sea, that cannot rest.

25. *How is the city of praise not left!* Damascus is so ruined that she can no more be called a praiseworthy or happy city.

27. *The palaces of Ben-hadad.* Damascus was a seat of the Syrian kings, and Ben-hadad was a name common to several of its kings.

28. *Concerning Kedar, and concerning the kingdoms of Hazor.* This is the title of another new prophecy. *Kedar* was the name of one of the sons of Ishmael (Gen. xxv. 13) who settled in Arabia, and who gave name to a powerful tribe of Arabs who used to traffic with the Tyrians in cattle. It appears from this prophecy that Nebuchadnezzar got a commission to go against and reduce them to great misery.

30. *Dwell deep.* Retire into the depths of the desert. See on v. 8.

31. *The wealthy nation.* "The peaceable nation." *Have neither gates nor bars.* The Arabs,

who had nothing but their tents; no cities, nor even permanent villages.

32. *The utmost corners.* Even in these utmost, inaccessible recesses the sword and pillage shall reach them.

33. *Hazor shall be a dwelling for dragons.* Shall be turned into a wilderness. *A desolation for ever.* Never to be repeopled.

34. *The word . . . against Elam.* Another new head of prophecy. As this was delivered in the beginning of the reign of Zedekiah, it can have no natural nor historical connection with the other prophecies in this various chapter. Some think that, by Elam, Persia is always meant; but this is not at all likely. It was a part of the Babylonian empire in the time of Daniel (chap. viii. 2) and is most probably what is called Elymais by the Greeks.

35. *I will break the bow of Elam.* They were eminent archers, and had acquired their power and eminence by their dexterity in the use of the bow. See Isa. xxii. 6. Strabo, Livy, and others speak of their eminence in archery.

36. *Will I bring the four winds.* Nebuchadnezzar and his armies, gathered out of different provinces, and attacking this people at all points in the same time.

38. *I will set my throne in Elam.* This is spoken of either Nebuchadnezzar or Cyrus. It is certain that Cyrus did render himself master of Elymais and Media, which are in the land of Elam.

39. *I will bring again the captivity of Elam.* As this is to be in *the latter days,* probably it may mean the spiritual freedom which these people would receive under the gospel dispensation. Under Cyrus, the Elamites, collected out of all quarters, were united with the Persians, their neighbors, and became, with them, masters of the East.

CHAPTER 50

This and the following chapter contain a prophecy relating to the fall of Babylon, interspersed with several predictions relative to the restoration of Israel and Judah, who were to survive their oppressors, and, on their repentance, to be pardoned and brought to their own land. This chapter opens with a prediction of the complete destruction of all the Babylonish idols, and the utter desolation of Chaldea, through the instrumentality of a great northern nation, 1-3. Israel and Judah shall be reinstated in the land of their forefathers after the total overthrow of the great Babylonish empire, 4-5. Very oppressive and cruel bondage of the Jewish people during the Captivity, 6-7. The people of God are commanded to remove speedily from Babylon, because an assembly of great nations are coming out of the north to desolate the whole land, 8-10. Babylon, the hammer of the whole earth, the great desolater of nations, shall itself become a desolation on account of its intolerable pride, and because of the iron yoke it has rejoiced to put upon a people whom a mysterious Providence had placed under its domination, 11-34. The judgments which shall fall upon Chaldea, a country addicted to the grossest idolatry, and to every species of superstition, shall be most awful and general, as when God overthrew Sodom and Gomorrah, 35-40. Character of the people appointed to execute the divine judgments upon the oppressors of Israel, 41-45. Great sensation among the nations at the very terrible and sudden fall of Babylon, 46.

1. *The word that the Lord spake against Babylon.* This is also a new head of discourse. The prophecies contained in this and the following chapter were sent to the captives in Babylon in the fourth year of the reign of Zedekiah. They are very important; they predict the total destruction of the Babylonish empire, and the return of the Jews from their captivity. These chapters were probably composed, with several additions, out of the book that was then sent by Jeremiah to the captives by the hand of Seraiah. See chap. li. 59-64.

2. *Declare ye among the nations.* God's determination relative to this empire. *Set up a standard.* Show the people where they are to assemble. *Say, Babylon is taken.* It is a thing so firmly determined that it is as good as already done. *Bel,* the tutelar deity of Babylon, *is confounded,* because it cannot save its own city. *Merodach,* another of their idols, *is broken in pieces;* it was not able to save itself, much less the whole empire.

3. *Out of the north there cometh up a nation.* The Medes, who formed the chief part of the army of Cyrus, lay to the north or northeast of Babylon. *Shall make her land desolate.* This war, and the consequent taking of the city, began those disasters that brought Babylon in process of time to complete desolation; so that now it is not known where it stood, the whole country being a total solitude.

4. *In those days, and in that time.* In the times in which Babylon shall be opposed by the Medes and Persians, both Israel and Judah, seeing the commencement of the fulfilling of the prophecies, shall begin to seek the Lord with much prayer, and broken and contrite hearts. When the decree of Cyrus comes, they shall be ready to set off for their own country, deploring their offenses, yet rejoicing in the mercy of God which has given them this reviving in their bondage.

5. *Let us join ourselves to the Lord in a perpetual covenant.* All our former covenants have been broken; let us now make one that shall last forever. He shall be the Lord our God, and we will no more worship idols. This covenant they have kept to the present day; whatever their present moral and spiritual state may be, they are no idolaters, in the gross sense of the term.

6. *My people hath been lost sheep.* He pities them; for their pastors, kings, and prophets have caused them to err. *They have gone from mountain to hill.* In all high places they have practiced idolatry.

7. *Their adversaries said, We offend not.* God has abandoned them; we are only fulfilling His designs in plaguing them.

8. *Remove out of the midst of Babylon.* The sentence of destruction is gone out against it; prepare for your flight, that you be not overwhelmed in its ruin. *Be as the he goats before the flocks.* Who always run to the head of the flock, giving the example for others to follow. This may be addressed to the elders and persons of authority among the people.

9. *An assembly of great nations.* The army of Cyrus was composed of Medes, Persians, Armenians, Caducians, etc. Though all these did not come *from the north,* yet they were arranged under the Medes, who did come from the north, in reference to Babylon. *Their arrows.* They are such expert archers that they shall never miss their mark.

10. *Chaldea shall be a spoil.* She has been a spoiler, and she shall be spoiled. They had destroyed Judea, God's heritage; and now God shall cause her to be destroyed.

11. *As the heifer at grass.* You were wanton in the desolations you brought upon Judea.

12. *Your mother.* Speaking to the Chaldeans; Babylon, the metropolis, or mother city, shall be a wilderness, a dry land, a desert, fit for neither man nor beast.

15. *Shout against her round about.* Encompass her with lines and with troops; let none go in with relief, none come out to escape from her ruin.

16. *Cut off the sower.* Destroy the gardens and the fields, that there may be neither fruits nor tillage.

17. *Israel.* All the descendants of Jacob have been harassed and spoiled, first by the Assyrians, and afterwards by the Chaldeans. They acted towards them as a lion to a sheep which he has caught; first he devours all the flesh, next he breaks all the bones to extract the marrow.

18. *As I have punished the king of Assyria.* The Assyrians were overthrown by the Medes and the Chaldeans. The king is here taken for all their kings, generals, etc.: Tiglath-pileser, Shalmaneser, Sennacherib, Esar-haddon, etc. To them succeeded the Chaldean or Babylonish kings. Nebuchadnezzar came against Judea several times, and at last took the city and burnt it, profaned and demolished the Temple, wasted the land, and carried the princes and people into captivity.

19. *I will bring Israel again.* This seems to refer wholly to the ten tribes; for Carmel, Bashan, Mount Ephraim, and Gilead were in their territories.

20. *In those days, and in that time.* This phrase appears to take in the whole of an epoch, from its commencement to its end. See v. 4. *I will pardon them.* So as to deliver them from their captivity, and exact no more punishment from them whom I reserve, namely, the remnant left in the Babylonish captivity.

21. *Go up against the land of Merathaim . . . and against the inhabitants of Pekod.* No such places as these are to be found anywhere else, and it is not likely that places are at all meant. The ancient versions agree in rendering the first as an appellative, and the last as a verb, except the Chaldee, which has *Pekod* as a proper name. Dr. Dahler renders thus: "March against the country doubly rebellious, and against its inhabitants worthy of punishment." The words are addressed to the Medes and Persians; and the country is Chaldea, doubly rebellious by its idolatry and its insufferable pride. In these two it was exceeded by no other land.

23. *The hammer of the whole earth.* Nebuchadnezzar dashed to pieces the nations against whom he warred. He was the scourge of the Lord.

24. *I have laid a snare for thee.* It was not by storm that Cyrus took the city. The Euphrates ran through it; he dug a channel for the river in another direction, to divert its stream. He waited for that time in which the inhabitants had delivered themselves up to dabauchery; in the dead of the night he turned off the stream, and he and his army entered by the old channel, now void of its waters. This was the snare of which the prophet here speaks. See Herodotus, lib. i., c. 191.

26. *Open her storehouses.* At the time that Cyrus took the city, it was full of provisions and treasures of all kinds; the walls had suffered no injury; and when the inhabitants heard that the enemy was within, they thought they must have arisen out of the earth in the center of the city!

27. *Slay all her bullocks.* Princes, magistrates.

28. *Declare in Zion the vengeance of the Lord.* Zion was desolated by Babylon; tell Zion that God hath desolated the desolator. *The vengeance of his temple.* Which Nebuchadnezzar had pillaged, profaned, and demolished, transporting its sacred vessels to Babylon, and putting them in the temple of his god Bel.

29. *Call together the archers.* The preceding verses are the prediction; here God calls the Medes and Persians to fulfil it.

31. *O thou most proud.* "Pride" in the abstract; proudest of all people.

32. *And the most proud.* Here "pride" is personified and addressed, as if possessing a being and rational powers.

34. *Their Redeemer is strong.* And it was not that He wanted power, and that Nebuchadnezzar had much, that Jerusalem was taken; but because the people had sinned, and would not return; and therefore national sins called for national punishments. These have taken place, and now the Lord of Hosts shows them that the power of the Chaldeans is mere weakness against His might.

35. *A sword.* War and its calamities, or any grievous plague; and so in the following verses.

38. *A drought is upon her waters.* May not this refer to the draining of the channel of the Euphrates, by which the army of Cyrus entered the city. See on v. 24. The original is, however, *chereb,* "a sword," as in the preceding verses, which signifies war, or any calamity by which the thing on which it falls is ruined.

40. *As God overthrew Sodom.* As the very ground on which these cities stood, with all the plain, now lies under the Dead Sea, so Babylon and the adjacent country shall be rendered totally barren and unfruitful, and utterly incapable of being inhabited. And this is the fact concerning both countries.

41. *Behold, a people shall come from the north.* This and the two following verses are nearly the same with chap. vi. 22-24. But here, destroyers against Babylon are intended; there, destroyers against Jerusalem.

44. *Behold, he shall come up like a lion.* The same words as in chap. xlix. 19, etc.

46. *At the noise of the taking of Babylon.* See the parallel place, chap. xlix. 21. In the forty-ninth chapter, these words are spoken of Nebuchadnezzar; here, of Cyrus. The taking of Babylon was a wonder to all the surrounding nations. It was thought to be impregnable.

CHAPTER 51

Sequel of the prophecies of Jeremiah against Babylon. The dreadful, sudden, and final ruin that shall fall upon the Chaldeans, who have compelled the nations to receive their idolatrous rites (see an instance in the third chapter of Daniel), set forth by a variety of beautiful figures; with a command to the people of God (who have made continual intercession for the conversion of their heathen rulers) to flee from the impending vengeance, 1-14. Jehovah, Israel's God, whose infinite power, wisdom, and understanding are everywhere visible in the works of creation, elegantly contrasted with the utterly contemptible objects of the Chaldean worship, 15-19. Because of their great oppression of God's people, the Babylonians shall be visited with cruel enemies from the north, whose innumerable hosts shall fill the land, and utterly extirpate the original inhabitants, 20-44. One of the figures by which this formidable invasion is represented is awfully sublime. "The sea is come up upon Babylon; she is covered with the multitude of the waves thereof." And the account of the sudden desolation produced by this great armament of a multitude of nations (which the prophet, dropping the figure, immediately subjoins) is deeply afflictive. "Her cities are a desolation, a dry land, and a wilderness, a land wherein no man dwelleth, neither doth any son of man pass thereby." The people of God a third time admonished to escape from Babylon, lest they be overtaken with her plagues, 45-46. Other figures setting forth in a variety of lights the awful judgments with which the Chaldeans shall be visited on account of their very gross idolatries, 47-58. The significant emblem with which the chapter concludes, of Seraiah, after having read the book of the Prophet Jeremiah against Babylon, binding a stone to it, and casting it into the river Euphrates, thereby prefiguring the very sudden downfall of the Chaldean city and empire, 59-64, is beautifully improved by the writer of the Apocalypse, chap. xviii. 21, in speaking of Babylon the Great, of which the other was a most expressive type; and to which many of the passages interspersed throughout the Old Testament Scriptures relative to Babylon must be ultimately referred, if we would give an interpretation in every respect equal to the terrible import of the language in which these prophecies are conceived.

1. *Thus saith the Lord.* This chapter is a continuation of the preceding prophecy. *A destroying wind.* Such as the pestilential winds in the East; and here the emblem of a destroying army, carrying all before them, and wasting with fire and sword.

2. *And will send ... fanners.* When the corn is trodden out with the feet of cattle, or crushed out with a heavy wheel armed with iron, with a shovel they throw it up against the wind, that the chaff and broken straw may be separated from it. This is the image used by the Prophet; these people shall be trodden, crushed, and fanned by their enemies.

5. *For Israel hath not been forsaken.* God still continued His prophets among them; He had never cast them wholly off. Even in the midst of wrath—highly deserved and inflicted punishment—He has remembered mercy; and is now about to crown what He has done by restoring them to their own land. I conceive *asham*, which we translate *sin*, as rather signifying "punishment," which meaning it often has.

7. *Made all the earth drunken.* The cup of God's wrath is the plenitude of punishment that He inflicts on transgressors. It is represented as intoxicating and making them mad.

8. *Babylon is suddenly fallen and destroyed.* These appear to be the words of some of the spectators of Babylon's misery.

9. *We would have healed Babylon.* Had it been in our power, we would have saved her, but we could not turn away the judgment of God.

10. *The Lord hath brought forth our righteousness.* This is the answer of the Jews. God has vindicated our cause.

11. *Make bright the arrows.* This is the prophet's address to Babylon.

12. *Set up the standard.* A call to the enemies of Babylon to invest the city and press the siege.

13. *O thou that dwellest upon many waters.* You who have an abundant supply of waters. It was built on the confluence of the Tigris and Euphrates, the latter running through the city. But the *many waters* may mean the many nations which belonged to the Babylonish empire; nations and people are frequently so called in Scripture.

14. *I will fill thee with men.* By means of these very waters through the channel of your boasted river, you shall be filled with men, suddenly appearing as an army of "locusts"; and, without being expected, shall lift up a terrific cry, as soon as they have risen from the channel of the river.

15. *He hath made the earth by his power.* The omnipotence of God is particularly manifested in the works of creation. *He hath etablished the world by his wisdom.* The omniscience of God is particularly seen in the government of *tebel,* the inhabited surface of the globe. What a profusion of wisdom and skill is apparent in that wondrous system of providence by which He governs and provides for every living thing!

16. *When he uttereth his voice.* Sends thunder.

17. *Every man is brutish by his knowledge.* He is brutish for want of real knowledge, and he is brutish when he acknowledges that an idol is anything in the world. These verses, from fifteen to nineteen, are transcribed from chap. x. 12-16.

20. *Thou art my battle ax.* I believe Nebuchadnezzar is meant, who is called, chap. l. 23, "the hammer of the whole earth." Others think the words are spoken of Cyrus. All the verbs are in the past tense: "With thee have I broken in pieces," etc., etc.

25. *O destroying mountain.* An epithet which He applies to the Babylonish government; it is like a burning mountain, which, by vomiting continual streams of burning lava, inundates and destroys all towns, villages, fields in its vicinity. *And roll thee down from the rocks.* I will tumble you from the rocky base on which you rest. The combustible matter in your bowels being exhausted, you shall appear as an extinguished crater; and the stony matter which you cast out shall not be of sufficient substance to make a foundation stone for solidity, or a cornerstone for beauty, v. 26. Under this beautiful and most expressive metaphor, the prophet shows the nature of the Babylonish government; setting the nations on fire, deluging and destroying them by its troops, till at last, exhausted, it tumbles down, is extinguished, and leaves nothing as a basis to erect a new form of government on; but is altogether useless, like the cooled lava, which is, properly speaking, fit for no human purpose.

27. *Set ye up a standard.* Another summons to the Medes and Persians to attack Babylon. *Ararat, Minni.* The Greater and Lesser Armenia. *And Ashchenaz.* A part of Phrygia, near the Hellespont.

29. *And the land shall tremble.* It is represented here as trembling under the numerous armies that are passing over it, and the prancing of their horses.

30. *The mighty men ... have forborn to fight.* They were panic-struck when they found the Medes and Persians within their walls, and at once saw that resistance was useless.

31. *One post shall run to meet another.* As the city was taken by surprise, in the manner already related, so now messengers, one after another, were dispatched to give the king information of what was done; viz., that the city was taken at one end. Herodotus tells us that

the extreme parts of the city were taken before those of the center knew anything of the invasion. Herodot., lib. i, c. 191.

32. *That the passages are stopped.* Either the bridges or slips for boats, by which the inhabitants passed from one side to the other, and may mean the principal gates or passes in the city, which the victorious army would immediately seize, that they might prevent all communication between the inhabitants.

33. *The daughter of Babylon is like a threshingfloor.* The threshing wheel is gone over her; she is trodden underfoot.

34. *Nebuchadrezzar . . . hath devoured me.* These are the words of Judea; he has taken away all my riches. *He hath cast me out.* He shall vomit all up; i.e., they shall be regained.

35. *The violence done to me . . . be upon Babylon, . . . and my blood upon the inhabitants of Chaldea.* Zion begins to speak, v. 34, and ends with this verse. The answer of Jehovah begins with the next verse. Though the Chaldeans have been the instrument of God to punish the Jews, yet in return they, being themselves exceedingly wicked, shall suffer for all the carnage they have made, and for all the blood they have shed.

36. *I will dry up her sea.* Exhaust all her treasures.

37. *Without an inhabitant.* See chap. i. 39.

39. *In their heat I will make their feasts.* It was on the night of a feast day, while their hearts were heated with wine and revelry, that Babylon was taken; see Dan. v. 1-3. This feast was held in honor of the goddess Sheshach (or perhaps of Bel), who is mentioned, v. 41, as being taken with her worshippers. As it was in the night the city was taken, many had retired to rest, and never awoke; slain in their beds, they slept a perpetual sleep.

41. *How is Sheshach taken!* Perhaps the city is here called by the name of its idol. *The praise of the whole earth.* One of the seven wonders of the world; superexcellent for the height, breadth, and compass of its walls, its hanging gardens, the temple of Belus.

42. *The sea is come up.* A multitude of foes have inundated the city.

44. *I will punish Bel in Babylon.* Bel was their supreme deity. *That which he hath swallowed up.* The sacred vessels of the Temple of Jerusalem, which were taken thence by Nebuchadnezzar, and dedicated to him in his temple at Babylon. *The wall of Babylon shall fall.* It shall cease to be a defense, and shall molder away until, in process of time, it shall not be discernible.

45. *My people, go ye out.* A warning to all the Jews in Babylon to leave the city, and escape for their lives.

46. *A rumour shall . . . come one year.* A year before the capture of the city there shall be a rumor of war—and in that year Belshazzar was defeated by Cyrus. In the following year the city was taken.

48. *The heaven and the earth . . . shall sing for Babylon.* Its fall shall be a subject of universal rejoicing.

50. *Ye that have escaped the sword.* The Jews. *Let Jerusalem come into your mind.*

Pray for its restoration, and embrace the first opportunity offered of returning thither.

51. *Strangers are come into the sanctuaries.* The lamentation of the pious Jews for the profanation of the Temple by the Chaldeans.

53. *Though Babylon should mount up to heaven.* Though it were fortified even to the skies, it shall fall by the enemies that I will send against it.

55. *The great voice.* Its pride and insufferable boasting.

56. *The Lord God of recompences.* The fall of Babylon is an act of divine justice; whatever it suffers, it is in consequence of its crimes.

57. *I will make drunk her princes.* See. v. 39.

58. *The broad walls of Babylon.* Herodotus, who saw these walls, says, "The city was a regular square, each side of which was one hundred and twenty stadia, the circumference four hundred and eighty stadia. It was surrounded by a wall fifty cubits broad, and two hundred cubits high; and each side had twenty-five brazen gates."—Herod., lib. i, c. 178. Had not Cyrus resorted to stratagem, humanly speaking, he could not have taken this city. For the destruction of this wall and its very vestiges, see Isa. xiii. 19.

59. *The word which Jeremiah.* On account of the message sent by Jeremiah to the Jewish captives in Babylon.

60. *Wrote in a book.* Whether this book contained any more than is recorded in this place we do not know; probably it contained no more than what is found in vv. 62-64. A *book, sepher,* signifies, in Hebrew, any writing, great or small.

64. *Thus shall Babylon sink.* This is the emblem of its overthrow and irretrievable ruin. See Rev. xviii. 21, where we find that this is an emblem of the total ruin of mystical Babylon.

Thus far are the words of Jeremiah. It appears that the following chapter is not the work of this prophet; it is not his style. The author of it writes "Jehoachin"; Jeremiah writes him always "Jeconiah" or "Coniah." It is merely historical, and is very similar to 2 Kings xxiv. 18 —xxv. 30. The author, whoever he was, relates the capture of Jerusalem, the fate of Zedekiah, the pillage and burning of the city and the Temple. He mentions also certain persons of distinction who were slain by the Chaldeans. He mentions the number of the captives that were carried to Babylon at three different times, and concludes with the deliverance of King Jehoiachin from prison in Babylon, in which he had been for thirty-seven years.

CHAPTER 52

This chapter was added after Jeremiah's time probably by Ezra, after the return from the Captivity, of which it gives a short account, nearly the same as in 2 Kings xxiv. 18-20 and xxv. It is very properly subjoined to the preceding prophecies, in order to show how exactly they were fulfilled. It likewise forms a proper introduction to the following Lamentations, as it gives an account of the mournful events which gave rise to them. Zedekiah's evil reign and rebellion against Nebuchadnezzar, 1-3. Jerusalem is taken by the Chaldeans after a siege of eighteen months, 4-7. Zedekiah pursued and taken in the plains of Jericho, and his whole army dispersed, 8-9. The king's sons and all the princes of Judah slain in Riblah, 10. Zedekiah has his eyes put out by order of the Chaldean monarch; and is afterward bound in chains, carried to Babylon, and imprisoned for life, 11. Nebuzaradan, the captain of the guard, burns and spoils the city and Temple, 12-19. The two pillars of the Temple, with their dimensions and ornaments, 20-23. The officers of the Temple, and several others, carried away captives into Babylon, and then slain by order of Nebuchadnezzar, 24-27. The number of Jews that Nebuchadnezzar carried away captive in the seventh year of his reign, 28; in his eighteenth year, 29; and in his twenty-third year, 30. Evil-merodach, the son of Nebuchadnezzar, in the year of his accession to the throne of Babylon (which was in the thirty-seventh year of the captivity, and the one hundred and ninety-first from the building of Rome, according to the computation of Varro), orders Jehoiachin to be taken out of prison, and treats him kindly for the remainder of his life, 31-34.

1. *Zedekiah was one and twenty years old.* See 2 Kings xxiv. 18.

2. *And he did . . . evil.* This and the following verse are the same as 2 Kings xxiv. 19.

3. *Through the anger of the Lord.* Here is a king given to a people in God's anger, and taken away in His displeasure.

4. *Ninth year . . . tenth month.* Answering nearly to our January.

5. *So the city was besieged.* It held out one year and six months.

6. *And in the fourth month.* See chap. xxxix. 1, etc. The fourth month answers nearly to our July.

8. *The army of the Chaldeans pursued.* See 2 Kings xxv. 5.

9. *King of Babylon to Riblah.* See chap. xxxix. 5.

11. *He put out the eyes of Zedekiah.* See chap. xxxix. 7.

12. *Now in the fifth month.* Answering nearly to our August.

13. *And burned the house of the Lord.* Thus perished this magnificent structure, after it had stood 424 years, 3 months, and 8 days.

15. *Those that fell away.* The deserters to the Chaldeans during the siege.

16. *The poor of the land.* See chap. xxxix. 1.

17. *Also the pillars.* See chap. xxvii. 19.

24. *The second priest.* See 2 Kings xxv. 18. *The three keepers.* The priests who stood at the door to receive the offerings of the people; see 2 Kings xx. 9 and xxiii. 4.

25. *Seven men . . . that were near the king's person.* These were privy counsellors.

28-30. On these verses Dr. Blayney has some sensible remarks; I will extract the substance. These verses are not inserted in 2 Kings xxv. Here then we have three deportations, and those the most considerable ones, in the first, in the eighth, and nineteenth years of Neb-

uchadnezzar, sufficiently distinguished from those in the seventh, eighteenth, and twenty-third years. So that it seems most reasonable to conclude that by the latter three the historian meant to point out deportations of a minor kind, not elsewhere noticed in direct terms in Scripture.

The first of these, said to have been in the seventh year of Nebuchadnezzar, was one of those that had been picked up in several parts of Judah by the band of Chaldeans, Syrians, and others, whom the king of Babylon sent against the land previously to his own coming, 2 Kings xxiv. 2.

That in the eighteenth year corresponds with the time when the Chaldean army broke off the siege before Jerusalem, and marched to meet the Egyptian army, at which time they might think it proper to send off the prisoners that were in camp, under a guard to Babylon.

And the last, in the twenty-third year of Nebuchadnezzar, was when that monarch, being engaged in the siege of Tyre, sent off Nebuzaradan against the Moabites, Ammonites, and other neighboring nations, who at the same time carried away the gleanings of Jews that remained in their own land, amounting in all to no more than 745.

31. *Lifted up the head of Jehoiachin.* This phrase is taken from Gen. xl. 13. It is founded on the observation that those who are in sorrow hold down their heads, and when they are comforted, or the cause of their sorrow removed, they lift up their heads. The Hebrew phrase "lift up the head" signifies to "comfort, cheer, make happy."

32. *Spake kindly.* Conversed freely with him. *Set his throne.* Gave him a more respectable seat than any of the captive princes, or better than even his own princes had, probably near his person.

33. *And changed his prison garments.* That is, Jehoiachin changed his own garments, that he might be suited in that respect to the state of his elevation. Kings also, in token of favor, gave caftans or robes to those whom they wish to honor. *And he did continually eat bread before him.* Was a constant guest at the king's table.

34. *And . . . there was a continual diet given him.* This was probably a ration allowed by the king for the support of Jehoiachin's household. For other particulars, see 2 Kings xxv. 30.

The Book of
LAMENTATIONS

This book, like the several books of the Pentateuch, is denominated in Hebrew *eicah,* "how," from its first word; and sometimes *kinnoth,* "lamentations," from its subject. It is one of the books of the *Megilloth,* or Roll, among the Jews; and because it relates to the ruin of their affairs, and contains promises of restoration, it is peculiarly prized, and frequently read. The five Megilloth are: Ecclesiastes, Canticles, Lamentations, Ruth, and Esther.

There has been little difference among learned men concerning the author of this book. The whole current of antiquity and modern times has pointed out Jeremiah as the writer; of this the style is a sufficient evidence.

There has been more difference of opinion relative to the subject and occasion. Some have thought the book was composed on the death of Josiah; others, that it was composed on occasion of the destruction of Jerusalem, and the various desolations connected with it. To this all its parts and its general phraseology seem best to apply, and this is the sentiment most generally embraced at present. This will receive much proof from a minute consideration of the book itself.

The composition of this poem is what may be called very technical. Every chapter, except the last, is an acrostic. Of the first two, each verse begins with a several letter of the Hebrew alphabet, in the order of the letters, with this exception that in the second, third, and fourth chapters, the *phe* is put before the *ain;* whereas in all the acrostic psalms the latter preceded the former, as it does in all grammars of the Hebrew language. In the first and second chapters each verse is composed of three hemistichs or half-verses, except the seventh verse of the first and the nineteenth of the second chapter, which have each four hemistichs.

The third chapter contains sixty-four verses, each, as before, formed of three hemistichs, but with this difference that each hemistich begins with the same letter, so that the whole alphabet is thrice repeated in this chapter.

The fourth chapter is made up of twenty-two verses, according to the number of the Hebrew letters; but the composition is different from all the rest, for each verse consists of only two hemistichs, and those much shorter than any in the preceding chapters.

I have called this an inimitable poem; better judges are of the same opinion. "Never," says Bishop Lowth, "was there a more rich and elegant variety of beautiful images and adjuncts arranged together within so small a compass, nor more happily chosen and applied."

CHAPTER 1

The prophet begins with lamenting the dismal reverse of fortune that befell his country, confessing at the same time that her calamities were the just consequence of her sins, 1-6. Jerusalem herself is then personified and brought forward to continue the sad complaint, and to solicit the mercy of God, 7-22.

In all copies of the Septuagint the following words are found as a part of the text: "And it came to pass after Israel had been carried away captive, and Jerusalem was become desolate, that Jeremiah sat weeping: and he lamented with this lamentation over Jerusalem; and he said." I subjoin another taken from the first printed edition of the English Bible, that by Coverdale, 1535. "And it came to passe, (after Israel was brought into captyvitie, and Jerusalem destroyed;) that Jeremy the prophet sat weeping, mournynge, and makinge his mone in Jerusalem; so that with an hevy herte he sighed and sobbed, sayenge."

1. *How doth the city sit solitary!* Sitting down, with the elbow on the knee, and the head supported by the hand, without any company, unless an oppressor near—all these were signs of mourning and distress. The coin struck by Vespasian on the capture of Jerusalem, on the obverse of which there is a palm tree, the emblem of Judea, and under it a woman, the emblem of Jerusalem, sitting, leaning as before described, with the legend *Judea capta,* illustrates this expression as well as that in Isa. xlvii. 1. *Become as a widow.* Having lost her king. Cities are commonly described as the mothers of their inhabitants, the kings as husbands, and the princes as children. When therefore they are bereaved of these, they are represented as widows, and childless.

2. *Among all her lovers.* Her allies; her friends, instead of helping her, have helped her enemies. Several who sought her friendship when she was in prosperity, in the time of David and Solomon, are now among her enemies.

3. *Between the straits.* She has been brought into such difficulties that it was impossible for her to escape. Has this any reference to the circumstances in which Zedekiah and the princes of Judah endeavored to escape from

Jerusalem, "by the way of the gate between the two walls" Jer. lii. 7?

4. *The ways of Zion do mourn.* The ways in which the people trod coming to the sacred solemnities, being now no longer frequented, are represented as shedding tears; and the gates themselves partake of the general distress.

7. *Did mock at her sabbaths. Mishbatteha.* Some contend that *sabbaths* are not intended here. The Septuagint has "her habitation."

11. *They have given their pleasant things.* Jerusalem is compared to a woman brought into great straits, who parts with her jewels and trinkets in order to purchase by them the necessaries of life.

12. *Is it nothing to you, all ye that pass by?* The desolations and distress brought upon this city and its inhabitants had scarcely any parallel. Excessive abuse of God's accumulated mercies calls for singular and exemplary punishment.

14. *The yoke of my transgressions.* I am now tied and bound by the chain of my sins; and it is so wreathed, so doubled and twisted around me, that I cannot free myself. A fine representation of the miseries of a penitent soul, which feels that nothing but the pitifulness of God's mercy can loose it.

15. *Called an assembly.* The Chaldean army, composed of various nations, which God commissioned to destroy Jerusalem.

17. *Zion spreadeth forth her hands.* Extending the hands is the form in supplication. *Jerusalem is as a menstruous woman.* To whom none dared to approach, either to help or comfort, because of the law, Lev. xv. 19-27.

19. *I called for my lovers.* My allies; the Egyptians and others.

20. *Abroad the sword bereaveth.* War is through the country, *and at home . . . death;* the pestilence and famine rage in the city; calamity in every shape is fallen upon me.

21. *They have heard that I sigh.* My affliction is public enough, but no one comes to comfort me. *They are glad that thou hast done it.* On the contrary, they exult in my misery; and they see that Thou hast done what they were incapable of performing. *Thou wilt bring the day that thou hast called, and they shall be like unto me.* Babylon shall be visited in her turn, and Thy judgments poured out upon her shall equal her state with my own. See the last six chapters of the preceding prophecy for the accomplishment of this prediction.

22. *Let all their wickedness come before thee.* That is, Thou wilt call their crimes also into remembrance; and Thou wilt do unto them by siege, sword, famine, and captivity what Thou hast done to me. Though Thy judgments, because of Thy long-suffering, are slow, yet because of thy righteousness they are sure. Imprecations in the sacred writings are generally to be understood as declarative of the evils they indicate, or that such evils will take place. No prophet of God ever wished desolation on those against whom he was directed to prophesy.

CHAPTER 2

The prophet shows the dire effects of the divine anger in the miseries brought on his country; the unparalleled calamities of which he charges, in a great measure, on the false prophets, 1-14. In this desperate condition, the astonishment and byword of all who see her, Jerusalem is directed to sue earnestly for mercy and pardon, 15-22.

1. *How hath the Lord covered the daughter of Zion with a cloud!* The women in the Eastern countries wear veils, and often very costly ones. Here Zion is represented as being veiled by the hand of God's judgment. And what is the veil? A dark cloud, by which she is entirely obscured. *The beauty of Israel.* His temple. *His footstool.* The ark of the covenant, often so called.

2. *The Lord hath swallowed up.* It is a strange figure when thus applied, but Jehovah is here represented as having swallowed down Jerusalem and all the cities and fortifications in the land; that is, He has permitted them to be destroyed. See v. 5.

3. *The horn of Israel.* His power and strength. It is a metaphor taken from cattle, whose principal strength lies in their horns. *Hath drawn back his right hand.* He did not support us when our enemies came against us.

4. *He hath bent his bow . . . he stood with his right hand.* This is the attitude of the archer. He first bends his bow; then sets his arrow upon the string; and, lastly, placing his right hand on the lower end of the arrow, in connection with the string, takes his aim, and prepares to let fly.

7. *They have made a noise in the house of the Lord.* Instead of the silver trumpets of the sanctuary, nothing but the sounds of warlike instruments are to be heard.

8. *He hath stretched out a line.* The line of devastation, marking what was to be pulled down and demolished.

9. *Her gates are sunk into the ground.* The consequence of their being long thrown down and neglected. From this it appears that the Captivity had already lasted a considerable time. *Her king and her princes are among the Gentiles.* Zedekiah and many of the princes were then prisoners in Babylon, another proof that the Captivity had endured some time, unless all this be spoken prophetically of what should be done.

10. *Sit upon the ground.* See the note on chap. i. 1. *Keep silence.* No words can express their sorrows; small griefs are eloquent, great ones dumb.

11. *Swoon in the streets of the city.* Through the excess of the famine.

12. *When their soul was poured out into their mothers' bosom.* When, in endeavoring to draw nourishment from the breasts of their exhausted mothers, they breathed their last in their bosoms! How dreadfully afflicting was this!

13. *What thing shall I take?* Or, rather, as Dr. Blayney, "What shall I urge to thee?" How shall I comfort you? *Thy breach is great like the sea.* You have a flood of afflictions, a sea of troubles, an ocean of miseries.

14. *They have not discovered thine iniquity.* They did not reprove for sin; they flattered you in your transgressions; and instead of turning away your captivity, by turning you from your sins, they have pretended visions of good in your favor, and false burdens for your enemies.

15. *The perfection of beauty.* This probably applied only to the Temple. Jerusalem never was a fine or splendid city, but the Temple was most assuredly the most splendid building in the world.

16. *This is the day that we looked for.* Jerusalem was the envy of the surrounding nations; they longed for its destruction, and rejoiced when it took place.

17. *The Lord hath done that.* This and the sixteenth verse should be interchanged, to follow the order of the letters in the Hebrew alphabet; as the sixteenth has *phe* for its acrostic letter, and the seventeenth has *ain*, which should precede the other in the order of the alphabet.

18. *O wall of the daughter of Zion.* These words are probably those of the passengers, who appear to be affected by the desolations of the land; and they address the people, and urge them to plead with God day and night for their restoration. *Let not the apple of thine eye cease.* Bath ayin means either the pupil of the eye or the tears. Tears are the produce of the eye, and are here elegantly termed "the daughter of the eye." Let not your tears cease.

19. *Arise, cry out in the night.* This seems to refer to Jerusalem besieged. You who keep the night watches, pour out your hearts before the Lord, instead of calling the time of night, etc.; or, when you call it, send up a fervent prayer to God for the safety and relief of the place.

20. *Consider to whom thou hast done this.* Perhaps the best sense of this difficult verse is this: "Thou art our Father, we are Thy children. Wilt Thou destroy Thy own offspring? Was it ever heard that a mother devoured her own child, a helpless infant of a span long?" That it was foretold that there should be such distress in the siege that mothers should be obliged to eat their own children is evident enough from Lev. xxvi. 29; Deut. xxviii. 53, 56-57; but the former view of the subject seems the most natural, and is best supported by the context. *The priest and the prophet* are slain; "the young and old lie on the ground in the streets"; the "virgins and . . . young men are fallen by the sword; thou hast slain them in the day of thine anger; thou hast killed, and not pitied." See chap. iv. 10.

22. *Thou hast called as in a solemn day.* It is by Thy influence alone that so many enemies are called together at one time; and they have so hemmed us in that none could escape, and none remained unslain or uncaptivated. Perhaps the figure is the collecting of the people in Jerusalem on one of the solemn annual festivals.

CHAPTER 3

The prophet, by enumerating his own severe trials, 1-20, and showing his trust in God, 21, encourages his people to the like resignation and trust in the divine and never-failing mercy, 22-27. He vindicates the goodness of God in all His dispensations, and the unreasonableness of murmuring under them, 28-39. He recommends self-examination and repentance; and then, from their experience of former deliverances from God, encourages them to look for pardon for their sins, and retribution to their enemies, 40-66.

1. *I am the man that hath seen affliction.* Either the prophet speaks here of himself or he is personating his miserable countrymen. This

and other passages in this poem have been applied to Jesus Christ's passion but, in my opinion, without any foundation.

2. *He hath . . . brought me into darkness.* In the sacred writings, *darkness* is often taken for calamity; *light,* for prosperity.

5. *He hath builded against me.* Perhaps there is a reference here to the mounds and ramparts raised by the Chaldeans in order to take the city.

7. *He hath hedged me about.* This also may refer to the lines drawn round the city during the siege. But these and similar expressions in the following verses may be merely metaphorical, to point out their straitened, oppressed, and distressed state.

9. *He hath inclosed my ways with hewn stone.* He has put insuperable obstacles in my way, and confounded all my projects of deliverance and all my expectations of prosperity.

13. *The arrows of his quiver.* "The sons of his quiver." Arrows that issue from a *quiver* are here termed "the sons of the quiver."

16. *He hath also broken my teeth with gravel stones.* What a figure to express disgust, pain, and the consequent incapacity of taking food for the support of life; a man, instead of bread, being obliged to eat small pebbles, till all his teeth are broken to pieces by endeavoring to grind them! *He hath covered me with ashes. Hichphishani beepher,* "He hath plunged me into the dust." To be thrown into a mass or bed of perfect dust, where the eyes are blinded by it, the ears stopped, and the mouth and lungs filled at the very first attempt to respire after having been thrown into it—what a horrible idea of suffocation!

17. *Thou hast removed my soul.* Prosperity is at such an utter distance from me that it is impossible I should ever reach it; and as to happiness, I have forgotten whether I have ever tasted of it.

20. *My soul . . . is humbled in me.* It is evident that in the preceding verses there is a bitterness of complaint against the bitterness of adversity that is not becoming to man when under the chastising hand of God; and, while indulging this feeling, all hope fled. Here we find a different feeling; he humbles himself under the mighty hand of God, and then his hope revives, v. 21.

22. *It is of the Lord's mercy that we are not consumed.* Being thus humbled, and seeing himself and his sinfulness in a proper point of view, he finds that God, instead of dealing with him in judgment, has dealt with him in mercy; and that though the affliction was excessive, yet that it was less than his iniquity deserved. If, indeed, any sinner be kept out of hell, it is because God's compassion faileth not.

23. *They are new every morning.* Day and night proclaim the mercy and compassion of God. Who could exist throughout the day if there were not a continual superintending Providence? Who could be preserved in the night if the Watchman of Israel ever slumbered or slept?

26. *It is good that a man should both hope.* Hope is essentially necessary to faith. He that hopes not cannot believe; if there be no expectation, there can be no confidence.

27. *That he bear the yoke in his youth.* He who has not got under wholesome restraint in youth will never make a useful man, a good man, nor a happy man.

51. *Mine eye affecteth mine heart.* What I see I feel. I see nothing but misery; and I feel, in consequence, nothing but pain. *The daughters of my city.* The villages about Jerusalem.

52. *Mine enemies chased me.* From this to the end of the chapter the prophet speaks of his own personal sufferings, and especially of those which he endured in the dungeon. See Jer. xxxviii. 6, etc.

66. *Persecute and destroy them.* Thou wilt pursue them with destruction. These are all declaratory, not imprecatory. *From under the heavens of the Lord.* This verse seems to allude to the Chaldaic prediction in Jer. x. 11. By their conduct they will bring on themselves the curse denounced against their enemies.

CHAPTER 4

The present deplorable state of the nation is now contrasted with its ancient prosperity, 1-12; and the unhappy change ascribed, in a great degree, to the profligacy of the priests and prophets, 13-16. The national calamities are tenderly lamented, 17-20. The ruin of the Edomites also, who had insulted the Jews in their distress, is ironically predicted, 21. See Ps. cxxxvii. 7 and Obad. 10-12. The chapter closes with a gracious promise of deliverance from the Babylonish captivity, 22.

1. *How is the gold become dim!* The prophet contrasts, in various affecting instances, the wretched circumstances of the Jewish nation with the flourishing state of their affairs in former times. Here they are compared to *gold, zahab,* native gold from the mine, which, contrary to its nature, is *become dim,* is tarnished; and even the *fine,* the "sterling," *gold, kethem,* that which is stamped to make it current, is *changed* or "adulterated," so as to be no longer passable. *The stones of the sanctuary.* "The holy stones."

2. *The precious sons of Zion.* The Jewish priests and Jewish believers. *Comparable to fine gold.* Who were of the pure standard of holiness; holy, because God who called them is holy; but now esteemed no better than *earthen pitchers*—vessels of dishonor in comparison of what they once were.

3. *Even the sea monsters draw out the breast.* The whales give suck to their young ones. *Like the ostriches in the wilderness.* For her carelessness about her eggs, and her inattention to her young, the ostrich is proverbial.

4. *The tongue of the sucking child.* See chap. ii. 12.

5. *Embrace dunghills.* Lie on straw or rubbish, instead of the costly carpets and sofas on which they formerly stretched themselves.

6. *For the punishment.* He thinks the punishment of Jerusalem far greater than that of Sodom. That was destroyed in a moment, while all her inhabitants were in health and strength. Jerusalem fell by the most lingering calamities, her men partly destroyed by the sword, and partly by the famine.

7. *Her Nazarites were purer than snow. Nazir* does not always signify a person separated under a religious vow; it sometimes denotes what is chief or eminent.

10. *The hands of the pitiful women have sodden their own children.* See chap. ii. 20.

But here there is a reference to mothers eating their own children; and this was done, not by mothers cruel and brutal, but by the "compassionate," the "tenderhearted" mothers.

12. *The kings of the earth.* Jerusalem was so well fortified, by both nature and art, that it appeared as a miracle that it should be taken at all.

13. *For the sins of her prophets, and the iniquities of her priests.* These most wretched beings, under the pretense of zeal for the true religion, persecuted the genuine prophets, priests, and people of God, and caused their blood to be shed in the midst of the city, in the most open and public manner.

14. *They have wandered as blind men in the streets.* Rather, "They ran frantic through the streets; they were stained with blood." This was in their pretended zeal for their cause.

15. *When they fled away.* These priests and prophets were so bad that the very heathen did not like to permit them to sojourn among them. The prophet now resumes the history of the siege.

17. *We have watched for a nation.* Viz., the Egyptians, who were their pretended allies, but were neither able nor willing to help them against the Chaldeans.

18. *We cannot go in our streets.* Supposed to refer to the darts and other missiles cast from the mounds which they had raised on the outside of the walls, by which those who walked in the streets could not shield themselves.

19. *They pursued us upon the mountains.* They hunted down the poor Jews like wild beasts in every part of the country by their marauding parties, whilst the great army besieged Jerusalem. But this may apply to the pursuit of Zedekiah. See what follows.

20. *The breath of our nostrils, the anointed of the Lord.* That is, Zedekiah, the king, who was as the life of the city, was taken in his flight by the Chaldeans, and his eyes were put out; so that he was wholly unfit to perform any function of government; though they had fondly hoped that, if they surrendered and should be led captives, yet they should be permitted to live under their own laws and king in the land of their bondage.

21. *Rejoice and be glad, O daughter of Edom.* A strong irony. *The cup also shall pass through unto thee.* You who have triumphed in our disasters shall shortly have enough of your own. They had joined themselves to the Chaldeans (see Ps. cxxxvii. 7) and therefore they should share in the desolations of Babylon.

CHAPTER 5

This chapter is, as it were, an epiphonema, or conclusion to the four preceding, representing the nation as groaning under their calamities, and humbly supplicating the divine favor, 1-22.

1. *Remember, O Lord.* In the Vulgate, Syriac, and Arabic, this is headed, "The prayer of Jeremiah." Though this chapter consists of exactly twenty-two verses, the number of letters in the Hebrew alphabet, yet the acrostic form is no longer observed. Perhaps anything so technical was not thought proper when in agony and distress (under a sense of God's displeasure on account of sin) they prostrated themselves

before Him to ask for mercy. Be this as it may, no attempt appears to have been made to throw these verses into the form of the preceding chapters. It is properly a solemn prayer of all the people, stating their past and present sufferings, and praying for God's mercy.

2. *Our inheritance is turned to strangers.* The greater part of the Jews were either slain or carried away captive; and even those who were left under Gedaliah were not free, for they were vassals to the Chaldeans.

4. *We have drunken our water for money.* I suppose the meaning of this is that everything was taxed by the Chaldeans, and that they kept the management in their own hands, so that wood and water were both sold, the people not being permitted to help themselves. They were now so lowly reduced by servitude that they were obliged to pay dearly for those things which formerly were common and of no price.

5. *Our necks are under persecution.* We feel the yoke of our bondage; we are driven to our work like the bullock, which has a yoke upon his neck.

6. *We have given the hand to the Egyptians.* We have sought alliances with both the Egyptians and the Assyrians, and made covenants with them in order to get the necessaries of life.

7. *Our fathers have sinned, and are not.* Nations, as such, cannot be punished in the other world; therefore national judgments are to be looked for only in this life. The punishment which the Jewish nation had been meriting for a series of years came now upon them, because they copied and increased the sins of their fathers, and the cup of their iniquity was full.

8. *Servants have ruled over us.* Perhaps he here alludes to the Chaldean soldiers, whose will the wretched Jews were obliged to obey.

9. *We gat our bread with the peril of our lives.* They could not go into the wilderness to feed their cattle, or to get the necessaries of life, without being harassed and plundered by marauding parties, and by these were often exposed to the peril of their lives. This was predicted by Moses, Deut. xxviii. 31.

10. *Our skin was black . . . because of the terrible famine.* Because of the searching winds

that burnt up every green thing, destroying vegetation, and in consequence producing a famine.

11. *They ravished the women in Zion, and the maids in the cities of Judah.* The evil mentioned here was predicted by Moses, Deut. xxviii. 30, 32, and by Jeremiah, chap. vi. 12.

12. *Princes are hanged up by their hand.* It is very probable that this was a species of punishment. They were suspended from hooks in the wall by their hands till they died through torture and exhaustion. The body of Saul was fastened to the wall of Beth-shan, probably in the same way; but his head had already been taken off. They were hung in this way that they might be devoured by the fowls of the air.

13. *They took the young men to grind.* This was the work of female slaves. See Isa. xlvii. 2.

14. *The elders have ceased from the gate.* There is now no more justice administered to the people; they are under military law, or disposed of in every sense according to the caprice of their masters.

16. *The crown is fallen from our head.* At feasts, marriages, etc., they used to crown themselves with garlands of flowers; all festivity of this kind was now at an end. Or it may refer to their having lost all sovereignty, being made slaves.

18. *The foxes walk upon it.* Foxes are very numerous in Palestine; see Judg. xv. 4. It was usual among the Hebrews to consider all desolated land to be the resort of wild beasts; which is, in fact, the case everywhere when the inhabitants are removed from a country.

19. *Thou, O Lord, remainest for ever.* Thou sufferest no change. Thou didst once love us; oh, let that love be renewed towards us!

21. *Renew our days as of old.* Restore us to our former state. Let us regain our country, our Temple, and all the divine offices of our religion; but, more especially, Thy favor.

22. *But thou hast utterly rejected us.* It appears as if Thou hadst sealed our final reprobation, because Thou showest against us exceeding great wrath. But "convert us, O Lord, unto thee, and we shall be converted." He heard the prayer, and at the end of seventy years they were restored to their own land.

The Book of
EZEKIEL

Ezekiel, the prophet, was the son of Buzi; and was of the sacerdotal race, as himself informs us, chap. i. 3. He was carried captive by Nebuchadnezzar into Babylon, with Jeconiah, king of Judah, and 3,000 other captives of the principal inhabitants, and was sent into Mesopotamia, where he received the prophetic gift; which is supposed, from an obscure expression in his prophecies, chap. i. 1, to have taken place in the thirtieth year of his age. He had then been in captivity five years, and continued to prophesy about twenty-two years, to the fourteenth year after the destruction of Jerusalem.

About three months and ten days after this conquest of Jerusalem, Nebuchadnezzar made another descent, and again besieged the city; and Jechoiachin, who succeeded his father, Jehoiakim, was obliged to surrender. The victorious Chaldeans carried off all the inhabitants of note into Babylon, leaving none behind but the very poorest of the people. See 2 Kings xxiv. 8-16. These captives were fixed at Tel-abib, and other places on the river Chebar, which flows into the east side of the Euphrates at Carchemish, nearly two hundred miles northward of Babylon. There he was present in body, though in visionary representation he was sometimes taken to Jerusalem.

The principal design of this prophet was to comfort his companions in tribulation during their captivity, and to render it light by the most positive promises of their restoration to their own land, the rebuilding of the Temple, and the reestablishment of the divine worship, all their enemies being finally destroyed.

CHAPTER 1

This chapter contains that extraordinary vision of the divine glory with which the prophet was favored when he received the commission and instructions respecting the discharge of his office, which are contained in the two following chapters. The time of this divine manifestation to the prophet, 1-3. The vision of the four living creatures, and of the four wheels, 4-25. Description of the firmament that was spread over them, and of the throne upon which one sat in appearance as a man, 26-28. This vision, proceeding in a whirlwind from the north, seems to indicate the dreadful judgments that were coming upon the whole land of Judah through the instrumentality of the cruel Chaldeans, who lay to the north of it. See Jer. i. 14; iv. 6; and vi. 1.

1. *In the thirtieth year.* We know not what this date refers to. Some think it was the age of the prophet; others think the date is taken from the time that Josiah renewed the covenant with the people, 2 Kings xxii. 3. *Fourth month.* Thammuz, answering nearly to our July. *I saw visions of God.* Emblems and symbols of the Divine Majesty. He particularly refers to those in this chapter.

2. *Jehoiachin's captivity.* Called also Jeconiah and Coniah; see 2 Kings xxiv. 12. He was carried away by Nebuchadnezzar; see 2 Kings xxiv. 14.

3. *The hand of the Lord.* I was filled with His power, and with the influence of the prophetic spirit.

4. *A whirlwind came out of the north.* Nebuchadnezzar, whose land, Babylonia, lay north of Judea. Chaldea is thus frequently denominated by Jeremiah. *A great cloud, and a fire infolding itself.* A mass of fire concentrated in a vast cloud, that the flames might be more distinctly observable, the fire never escaping from the cloud, but issuing, and then

returning in upon itself. It was in a state of powerful agitation; but always involving itself, or returning back to the center whence it appeared to issue. *A brightness was about it.* A fine tinge of light surrounded the cloud, in order to make its limits the more discernible, beyond which verge the turmoiling fire did not proceed. *The colour of amber.* This was in the center of the cloud, and this amber-color substance was the center of the laboring flame. The word which we translate *amber* was used to signify a compound metal, very bright, made of gold and brass.

5. *Also out of the midst thereof came . . . four living creatures.* As the amber-colored body was the center of the fire, and this fire was in the center of the cloud; so out of this amber-colored igneous center came the living creatures just mentioned.

6. *Every one had four faces.* There were four several figures of these living creatures, and each of these figures had four distinct faces. But as the face of the man was that which was presented to the prophet's view, so that he saw it more plainly than any of the others, hence it is said, v. 5, that each of these figures had the likeness of a man; and the whole of this compound image bore a general resemblance to the human figure.

7. *Their feet were straight feet.* There did not seem to be any flexure at the knee, nor were the legs separated in that way as to indicate progression by walking. *Like the sole of a calf's foot.* Before it is stated to be a straight foot, one that did not lay down a flat horizontal sole, like that of the human foot. *And they*

sparkled like the colour of burnished brass.
I suppose this refers rather to the hoof of the calf's foot than to the whole appearance of the leg. There is scarcely anything that gives a higher lustre than highly polished or burnished brass. Our blessed Lord is represented with legs like burnished brass, Rev. i. 15.

9. *Their wings were joined one to another.*
When their wings were extended, they formed a sort of canopy level with their own heads or shoulders; and on this canopy was the throne, and the "likeness of the man" upon it, v. 26. *They turned not when they went.* The wings did not flap in flying; as they glided in reference to their feet, so they soared in reference to their wings.

10. *As for the likeness of their faces.* There was but one body to each of those compound animals, but each body had four faces: the faces of a man and of a lion on the right side; the faces of an ox and an eagle on the left side.

12. *They went every one straight forward.*
Not by progressive stepping, but by gliding. *Whither the spirit was to go.* Whither that whirlwind blew, they went, being borne on by the wind; see v. 4.

13. *Like burning coals of fire.* The whole substance appeared to be of flame; and among them frequent coruscations of fire, like vibrating lamps, often emitting lightning, or rather sparks of fire, as we have seen struck out of strongly ignited iron in a forge.

14. *The living creatures ran and returned.*
They had a circular movement; they were in rapid motion, but did not increase their distance from the spectator.

15. *One wheel upon the earth.* Most probably the wheel within means merely the nave in which the spokes are inserted, in reference to the ring, rim, or periphery, where these spokes terminate from the center or nave.

18. *As for their rings.* The rim or periphery. *They were dreadful.* They were exceedingly great in their diameter, so that it was tremendous to look from the part that touched the ground to that which was opposite above. *Were full of eyes.* Does not this refer to the appearance of nails keeping the spokes upon the rim?

19. *When the living creatures went, the wheels went.* The wheels were attached to the living creatures, so that, in progress, they had the same motion.

20. *The spirit of the living creature was in the wheels.* That is, the wheels were instinct with a vital spirit. Here then is the chariot of Jehovah. There are four wheels, on each of which one of the compound animals stands. The four compound animals form the body of the chariot, their wings spread horizontally above, forming the canopy or covering of this chariot; on the top of which, or upon the extended wings of the four living creatures, was the throne, on which was the appearance of a man, v. 26.

22. *The colour of the terrible crystal.* Like a crystal, well-cut and well-polished, with various faces, by which rays of light were refracted, assuming either a variety of prismatic colors or an insufferably brilliant splendor.

23. *Every one had two, which covered on this side.* While they employed two of their wings to form a foundation for the firmament to rest on, two other wings were let down to cover the lower part of their bodies; but this they did only when they stood, v. 24.

24. *The noise of their wings.* When the whirlwind drove the wheels, the wind rustling among the wings was like the noise of many waters. *As the voice of the Almighty.* Like distant thunder; for this is termed the voice of God, Ps. xviii. 13; Exod. ix. 23, 28-29; xx. 18.

26. *A sapphire.* The pure Oriental sapphire—a large, well-cut specimen of which is now before me—is one of the most beautiful and resplendent blues that can be conceived. I have sometimes seen the heavens assume this illustrious hue. The human form above this canopy is supposed to represent Him who, in the fullness of time, was manifested in the flesh.

27. *The colour of amber.* There are specimens of amber which are very pure and beautifully transparent. One which I now hold up to the light gives a most beautiful bright yellow color. Such a splendid appearance had the august Being who sat upon this throne from the reins upward; but from thence downward He had the appearance of fire, burning with a clear and brilliant flame.

28. *As the appearance of the bow.* Over the canopy on which this glorious personage sat there was a fine rainbow, which, from the description here, had all its colors vivid, distinct, and in perfection—red, orange, yellow, green, blue, indigo, and violet. And *this*, as above described, *was the appearance of the likeness of the glory of the Lord.* Splendid and glorious as it was, it was only *the appearance of the likeness,* a faint representation of the real thing.

CHAPTER 2

The prophet, having been overwhelmed with the glorious vision in the preceding chapter, is here strengthened and comforted, 1-2; and then commissioned to declare to the rebellious house of Israel the terrible judgments that would very shortly come upon the whole land, if they repented not; with a gracious assurance to Ezekiel that God would be constantly with him while executing the duties of his office, 3-5. The prophet is also commanded to be fearless, resolute, and faithful in the discharge of it, 6-8, as he must be the messenger of very unpleasing tidings, which will expose him to great persecution, 9-10.

1. *And he said unto me.* In the last verse of the preceding chapter we find that the prophet was so penetrated with awe at the sight of the glory of God in the mystical chariot that he fell upon his face; and, while he was in this posture of adoration, he heard the voice mentioned here.

2. *And the spirit entered into me.* This spirit was different to that mentioned above, by which the wheels, etc., were moved. The spirit of prophecy is here intended, whose office was not merely to enable him to foresee and foretell future events, but to purify and refine his heart, and qualify him to be a successful preacher of the word of life. *And set me upon my feet.* That he might stand as a servant before his master, to receive his orders.

3. *Son of man.* This appellative, so often mentioned in this book, seems to have been given first to this prophet, afterwards to Daniel, and after that to the Man Christ Jesus. Perhaps it was given to the two former to remind them

of their frailty, and that they should not be exalted in their own minds by the extraordinary revelations granted to them, and that they should feel themselves of the same nature with those to whom they were sent. To the latter it might have been appropriated merely to show that, though all His actions demonstrated Him to be God, yet that He was also really man; and that in the Man Christ Jesus dwelt "all the fulness of the Godhead bodily." *I send thee to the children of Israel.* To those who were now in captivity, in Chaldea particularly; and to the Jews in general, both far and near.

4. *Thou shalt say unto them, Thus saith the Lord.* Let them know that what you have to declare is the message of the Lord, that they may receive it with reverence.

5. *Yet shall know that there hath been a prophet among them.* By this time they shall be assured of *two* things: (1) That God in His mercy had given them due warning. (2) That themselves were inexcusable for not taking it.

6. *Be not afraid of them.* They will maltreat you for your message, but let not the apprehension of this induce you to suppress it. Though they be rebels, fear them not; I will sustain and preserve you.

7. *Whether they will hear.* Whether they receive the message or persecute you for it, declare it to them, that they may be without excuse.

9. *A roll of a book. Megillath sepher.* All ancient books were written so as to be rolled up; hence *volumen,* a "volume," from *volve,* "I roll."

10. *It was written within and without.* Contrary to the state of rolls in general, which are written on the inside only. *There was written therein lamentations, and mourning, and woe.* What an awful assemblage! "Lamentations, and a groan, and alas!"

CHAPTER 3

This chapter contains more particular instructions to the prophet. It begins with repeating his appointment to his office, 1-3. Ezekiel is then informed that his commission is, at this time, to the house of Israel exclusively, 4-6; that his countrymen would pay little regard to him, 7; that he must persevere in his duty notwithstanding such great discouragement; and he is endued with extraordinary courage and intrepidity to enable him fearlessly to declare to a disobedient and gainsaying people the whole counsel of God, 8-11. The prophet is afterwards carried by the spirit that animated the cherubim and wheels, and by which he received the gift of prophecy, to a colony of his brethren in the neighborhood, where he remained seven days overwhelmed with astonishment, 12-15. He is then warned of the awful importance of being faithful in his office, 16-21; commanded to go forth into the plain, that he may have a visible manifestation of the Divine Presence, 22; and is again favored with a vision of that most magnificent set of symbols described in the first chapter, by which the glorious majesty of the God of Israel was in some measure represented, 23. See also Isa. vi. 1-18; Dan. x. 5-19; and Rev. i. 10-16; iv. 1-11, for other manifestations of the divine glory, in all of which some of the imagery is very similar. The prophet receives directions relative to his future conduct, 24-27.

1. *Eat this roll, and go speak.* This must have passed in vision, but the meaning is plain. Receive My word—let it enter into your soul; digest it—let it be your nourishment.

3. *It was in my mouth as honey.* It was joyous to me to receive the divine message, to be thus let into the secrets of the divine counsel, and I promised myself much comfort in that intimate acquaintance with which I was favored

by the Supreme Being. In Rev. x. 10 we find St. John receiving a little book, which he ate, and found it sweet as honey in his mouth; but after he had eaten it, it made his belly bitter, signifying that a deep consideration of the awful matter contained in God's word against sinners, which multitudes of them will turn to their endless confusion, must deeply afflict those who know anything of the worth of an immortal spirit.

7. *Impudent and hardhearted.* "Stiff of forehead, and hard of heart" (margin).

14. *I went in bitterness.* Being filled with indignation at the wickedness and obstinacy of my people, I went, determining to speak the word of God without disguise, and to reprove them sharply for their rebellion; and yet I was greatly distressed because of the heavy message which I was commanded to deliver.

15. *Tel-abib.* "A heap of corn."

20. *When a righteous man doth turn from his righteousness.* From these passages we see that a righteous man may fall from grace, and perish everlastingly. *And I lay a stumblingblock before him.* That is, I permit him to be tried, and he fall in the trial. God is repeatedly represented as doing things which He only permits to be done. He lays a stumbling block, i.e., he permits one to be laid.

22. *Arise, go forth into the plain.* Into a place remote from observation and noise; a place where the glory of God might have sufficient room to manifest itself, that the prophet might see all its movements distinctly.

24. *The spirit . . . said unto me, Go, shut thyself within thine house.* Hide yourself for the present. The reason is immediately subjoined.

25. *They shall put bands upon thee.* Your countrymen will rise up against you and, to prevent your prophesying, will confine you.

26. *I will make thy tongue cleave to the roof of thy mouth.* I will not give you any message to deliver to them. They are so rebellious, it is useless to give them further warning.

CHAPTER 4

Ezekiel delineates Jerusalem, and lays siege to it, as a type of the manner in which the Chaldean army should surround that city, 1-3. The prophet commanded to lie on his left side 390 days, and on his right side 40 days, with the signification, 4-8. The scanty and coarse provision allowed the prophet during his symbolical siege, consisting chiefly of the worst kinds of grain, and likewise ill-prepared, as he had only cow's dung for fuel, tended all to denote the scarcity of provision, fuel, and every necessary of life which the Jews should experience during the siege of Jerusalem, 9-17.

1. *Take thee a tile.* A "brick" is most undoubtedly meant; yet even the larger dimensions here will not help us through the difficulty, unless we have recourse to the ancients, who have spoken of the dimensions of the bricks commonly used in building. Palladius is very particular on this subject: "Let the bricks be two feet long, one foot broad, and four inches thick." On such a surface as this the whole siege might be easily portrayed. But the tempered clay out of which the bricks were made might be meant here; of this substance he might spread out a sufficient quantity to receive all his figures.

2. *Battering rams.* This is the earliest account

we have of this military engine. It was a long beam with a head of brass, like the head and horns of a ram, whence its name. It was hung by chains or ropes, between two beams, or three legs, so that it could admit of being drawn backward and forward some yards. Several stout men, by means of ropes, pulled it as far back as it could go; and then, suddenly letting it loose, it struck with great force against the wall which it was intended to batter and bring down. This machine was not known in the time of Homer, as in the siege of Troy there is not the slightest mention of such. And the first notice we have of it is here, where we see that it was employed by Nebuchadnezzar in the siege of Jerusalem.

3. *Take thou unto thee an iron pan.* A "flat plate" or slice, as the margin properly renders it; such as are used in some countries to bake bread on, called a *griddle,* being suspended above the fire, and kept in a proper degree of heat for the purpose. The Chaldeans threw such a wall round Jerusalem, to prevent the besieged from receiving any succors, and from escaping from the city. *This shall be a sign to the house of Israel.* This shall be an emblematical representation of what shall actually take place.

4. *Lie thou also upon thy left side.* It appears that all that is mentioned here and in the following verses was done, not in idea, but in fact. The prophet lay down on his left side upon a couch to which he was chained, v. 5, for 390 days; and afterwards he lay in the same manner, upon his right side, for 40 days. And thus was signified the state of the Jews, and the punishment that was coming upon them. The days signify years, a day for a year; during which they were to bear their iniquity, or the temporal punishment due to their sins. The "three hundred and ninety days," during which he was to lie on his left side, and bear the iniquity of the house of Israel, point out two things: first, the duration of the siege of Jerusalem; second, the duration of the Captivity of the ten tribes, and that of Judah.

6. *Forty days.* Reckon, says Archbishop Newcome, near fifteen years and six months in the reign of Manasseh, two years in that of Amon, three months in that of Jehoahaz, eleven years in that of Jehoiakim, three months and ten days in that of Jehoiachin, and eleven years in that of Zedekiah; and there arises a period of forty years during which gross idolatry was practiced in the kingdom of Judah. *Forty days* may have been employed in spoiling and desolating the city and the Temple.

9. *Take thou also unto thee wheat.* In times of scarcity, it is customary in all countries to mix several kinds of coarser grain with the finer, to make it last the longer. This which the prophet is commanded to take, of wheat, barley, beans, lentils, millet, and fitches, was intended to show how scarce the necessaries of life should be during the siege.

10. *Twenty shekels a day.* The whole of the above grain, being ground, was to be formed into one mass, out of which he was to make 390 loaves, one loaf for each day; and this loaf was to be of 20 shekels in weight. Now a shekel, being in weight about half an ounce, this would be 10 ounces of bread for each day; and with this water to the amount of one-sixth part of a hin, which is about a pint and a half of our

measure. All this shows that so reduced should provisions be during the siege that they should be obliged to eat the meanest sort of aliment, and that by weight, and their water by measure.

12. *Thou shalt bake it with dung.* Dried ox and cow dung is a common fuel in the East; and with this, for want of wood and coals, they are obliged to prepare their food. Here the prophet is to prepare his bread with dry human excrement. And when we know that this did not come in contact with the bread, and was only used to warm the plate on which the bread was laid over the fire, it removes all the horror and much of the disgust. This was required to show the extreme degree of wretchedness to which they should be exposed; for, not being able to leave the city to collect the dried excrements of beasts, the inhabitants during the siege would be obliged, literally, to use dried human ordure for fuel. However, we find that the prophet was relieved from using this kind of fuel, for cows' dung was substituted at his request. See v. 15.

16. *I will break the staff of bread.* They shall be besieged till all the bread is consumed; see 2 Kings xxv. 3: "And on the ninth day of the fourth month, the famine prevailed in the city, and there was no bread for the people of the land." All this was accurately foretold, and as accurately fulfilled.

CHAPTER 5

In this chapter the prophet shows, under the type of hair, the judgments which God was about to execute on the inhabitants of Jerusalem by famine, sword, and dispersion, 1-4. The type or allegory is then dropped, and God is introduced declaring in plain terms the vengeance that was coming on the whole nation which had proved so unworthy of those mercies with which they had hitherto been distinguished, 5-17.

1-4. *Take thee a sharp knife.* It is likely that only one kind of instrument is here intended, a *knife* to be employed as a *razor.* Here is a new emblem produced, in order to mark out the coming evils. The prophet represents the Jewish nation; his hair, the people; the razor, the Chaldeans; the cutting the beard and hair, the calamities, sorrows, and disgrace coming upon the people. Cutting off the hair was a sign of mourning; see on Jer. xlv. 5; xlviii. 37; and also a sign of great disgrace; see 2 Sam. x. 4. He is ordered to divide the hair, v. 2, into three equal parts, to intimate the different degrees and kinds of punishment which should fall upon the people. The *balances,* v. 1, were to represent the divine justice, and the exactness with which God's judgments should be distributed among the offenders. This hair, divided into three parts, is to be disposed of thus: (1) A third part is to be burnt in the midst of the city, to show that so many should perish by famine and pestilence during the siege. (2) Another third part he was to cut in small portions about the city (that figure which he had portrayed upon the brick) to signify those who should perish in different sorties, and in defending the walls. (3) And the remaining third part he was to scatter in the wind, to point out those who should be driven into captivity. The sword following them was intended to show that their lives should be at the will of their captors, and that many of them should perish by the *sword* in their dispersions. The few hairs which he was to take in his skirts, v. 3, were intended to represent those few Jews that should be left in the land under Gedaliah, after the taking of the city. The throwing a part of these last into the fire, v. 4, was intended to show the miseries that these suffered in Judea, in Egypt, and finally in their being also carried away into Babylon on the conquest of Egypt by Nebuchadnezzar.

6. *She hath changed my judgments.* God shows the reason why He deals with Jerusalem in greater severity than with the surrounding nations, because she was more wicked than they.

9. *I will do in thee that which I have not done.* The destruction of Jerusalem by Nebuchadnezzar was one of the greatest calamities that ever fell on any nation or place before, and that by the Romans under Titus exceeded all that has taken place since.

CHAPTER 6

In this chapter, which forms a distinct section, the prophet denounces the judgments of God against the Jews for their idolatry, 1-7; but tells them that a remnant shall be saved, and brought to a sense of their sins by their severe afflictions, 8-14.

2. *Set thy face toward the mountains of Israel.* This is a new prophecy, and was most probably given after the 430 days of his lying on his left and right sides were accomplished. By *Israel* here, Judea is simply meant; not the ten tribes, who had long before been carried into captivity. Ezekiel uses this term in reference to the Jews only. *The mountains* may be addressed here particularly because it was on them the chief scenes of idolatry were exhibited.

5. *Will scatter your bones round about your altars.* This was literally fulfilled by the Chaldeans. According to Baruch, chap. ii. 24-25, they opened the sepulchres of the principal people, and threw the bones about on every side.

9. *They that escape of you shall remember me.* Those that escape the sword, the pestilence, and the famine, and shall be led into captivity, shall plainly see that it is God who has done this; and shall humble themselves on account of their abominations, leave their idolatry, and worship Me alone. And this they have done from the Babylonish captivity to the present day.

11. *Smite with thine hand, and stamp with thy foot.* Show the utmost marks of your astonishment and indignation, and dread of the evils that are coming upon them.

14. *And make the land . . . more desolate than the wilderness toward Diblath.* Diblath is situated in the land of Moab. It is mentioned in Num. xxxiii. 46 and in Jer. xlviii. 22. It was a part of that horrible wilderness mentioned by Moses, Deut. viii. 15, "wherein were fiery serpents, and scorpions, and drought."

CHAPTER 7

This chapter, which also forms a distinct prophecy, foretells the dreadful destruction of the land of Israel, or Judah (for after the captivity of the ten tribes these terms are often used indiscriminately for the Jews in general), on account of the heinous sins of its inhabitants, 1-15; and the great distress of the small remnant that should escape, 16-19. The Temple itself, which they had polluted with idolatry, is devoted to destruction, 20-22; and the prophet is directed to make a chain, as a type of that captivity, in which both king and people should be led in bonds to Babylon, 23-27. The whole chapter abounds in bold and beautiful figures, flowing in an easy and forcible language.

2. *The end is come upon the four corners of the land.* This is not a partial calamity; it shall cover and sweep the whole land. This whole chapter is poetical.

5. *An evil, an only evil.* The great, the sovereign, the last exterminating evil, is come: the sword, the pestilence, the famine, and the captivity.

6. *An end is come, the end is come: it watcheth for thee.* This is similar to the second verse; but there is a paronomasia, or play upon letters and words, which is worthy of note. *Kets ba, ba hakkets, hekits elayich.* *Katsah* signifies to make an end or extremity, by cutting off something, and *yakats* signifies to awake from sleep. The *end* or final destruction is here personified; and represented as an executioner who has arisen early from his sleep, and is waiting for his orders to execute judgment upon these offenders. Hence it is said—

7. *The morning is come unto thee.* Every note of time is used in order to show the certainty of the thing. *And not the sounding again of the mountains.* The hostile troops are advancing! You hear a sound, a tumultuous noise; do not suppose that this proceeds from festivals upon the mountains; from the joy of harvestmen or the treaders of the winepress. It is the noise of those by whom you and your country are to fall. "Now will I shortly pour out," v. 8. Here they come!

10. *Behold the day.* The same words are repeated, sometimes varied, and pressed on the attention with new figures and new circumstances, in order to alarm this infatuated people. Look at the day! It is come! *The morning is gone forth.* It will wait no longer. The *rod* that is to chastise you *hath blossomed;* it is quite ready. *Pride hath budded.* Your insolence, obstinacy, and daring opposition to God have brought forth their proper fruits.

11. *Violence is risen up into a rod of wickedness.* The prophet continues his metaphor: "Pride has budded."—And what has it brought forth? Violence and iniquity. To meet these, the rod of God cometh.

12. *Let not the buyer rejoice, nor the seller mourn.* Such is now the state of public affairs that he who through want has been obliged to sell his inheritance need not mourn on the account, as of this the enemy would soon have deprived him. And he who has bought it need not rejoice in his bargain, as he shall soon be stripped of his purchase, and either fall by the sword or be glad to flee for his life.

13. *For the seller shall not return.* In the sale of all heritages among the Jews, it was always understood that the heritage must return to the family on the year of jubilee, which was every fiftieth year; but in this case the seller should not return to possess it, as it was not likely that he should be alive when the next jubilee should come; and if he were even to live till that time, he could not possess it, as he would then be in captivity.

14. *They have blown the trumpet.* Vain are all the efforts you make to collect and arm the people, and stand on your own defense;

for all shall be dispirited, and none go to the battle.

15. *The sword is without.* War through all the country, and *pestilence* and *famine* within the city, shall destroy the whole, except a small remnant. He who endeavors to flee from the one shall fall by the other.

16. *They . . . shall be on the mountains like doves of the valleys.* Rather, "like mourning doves" chased from their dovecotes, and separated from their mates.

19. *They shall cast their silver in the streets.* Their riches can be of no use, as in a time of famine there is no necessary of life to be purchased, and gold and silver cannot fill their bowels. *It is the stumblingblock of their iniquity.* They loved riches, and placed in the possession of them their supreme happiness. Now they find a pound of gold not worth an ounce of bread.

20. *As for the beauty of his ornament.* Their beautiful Temple was their highest ornament, and God made it majestic by His presence. But they have even taken its riches to make their idols, which they have brought into the very courts of the Lord's house; and therefore God hath *set it,* the Temple, *from them,* given it up to pillage.

22. *The robbers shall enter into it.* The Chaldeans shall not only destroy the city, but they shall enter the Temple, deface it, plunder it, and burn it to the ground.

23. *Make a chain.* Point out the Captivity; show them that it shall come, and show them the reason: Because *the land is full of bloody crimes,* etc.

24. *The worst of the heathen.* The Chaldeans, the most cruel and idolatrous of all nations.

25. *They shall seek peace.* They see now that their ceasing to pay the tribute to the king of Babylon has brought the Chaldeans against them, and now they sue for peace in vain. He will not hear; he is resolved on their destruction.

CHAPTER 8

Here begins a section of prophecy extending to the twelfth chapter. In this chapter the prophet is carried in vision to Jerusalem, 1-4; and there shown the idolatries committed by the rulers of the Jews, even within the Temple. In the beginning of this vision, by the noblest stretch of an inspired imagination, idolatry itself is personified, and made an idol; and the image sublimely called, from the provocation it gave God, the "image of jealousy," 5. The prophet then proceeds to describe the three principal superstitions of this unhappy people: the Egyptian, 6-12, the Phoenician, 13-14, the Persian, 15-16; giving the striking features of each, and concluding with a declaration of the heinousness of their sins in the sight of God, and the consequent greatness of their punishment, 17-18.

1. *In the sixth year, in the sixth month, in the fifth day of the month.* This, according to Archbishop Ussher, was the sixth year of Ezekiel's captivity. The sixth day of the fifth month of the ecclesiastical year, which answers to August. This chapter and the three following contain but one vision, of which I judge it necessary to give a general idea, that the attention of the reader may not be too much divided. The prophet, in the visions of God, is carried to Jerusalem, to the northern gate of the Temple, which leads by the north side to the Court of the Priests. There he sees the glory of the Lord in the same manner as he did by the river Chebar. At one side he sees the "image of jealousy." Going thence to the Court of the People, he sees through an opening in the wall seventy elders of the people, who were worshipping all sorts of beasts and reptiles, which were painted on the wall. Being brought thence to the gate of the door of the house, he saw women weeping for "Tammuz" or Adonis. As he returned to the court of the priests, between the porch and the altar, he saw twenty-five men with their backs to the sanctuary and their faces towards the east, worshipping the rising sun. This is the substance of the vision contained in the *eighth* chapter. About the same time he saw six men come from the higher gate with swords in their hands, and among them, one with an inkhorn. Then the Divine Presence left the cherubim, and took post at the entrance of the Temple, and gave orders to the man with the inkhorn to put a mark on the foreheads of those who sighed and prayed because of the abominations of the land; and then commanded the men with the swords to go forward, and slay every person who had not this mark. The prophet, being left alone among the dead, fell on his face, and made intercession for the people. The Lord gives him the reason of his conduct; and the man with the inkhorn returns, and reports to the Lord what was done. These are the general contents of the *ninth* chapter. The Lord commands the same person to go in between the wheels of the cherubim, and take his hand full of live coals, and scatter them over the city. He went as commanded, and one of the cherubim gave him the coals; at the same time the glory of the Lord, that had removed to the threshold of the house, now returned, and stood over the cherubim. The cherubim, wheels, wings, etc., are here described as in the first chapter. This is the substance of the *tenth* chapter. The prophet then finds himself transported to the east gate of the Temple, where he saw twenty-five men, and among them "Jaazaniah the son of Azur, and Pelatiah the son of Benaiah, princes of the people," against whom the Lord commands him to prophesy, and to threaten them with the utmost calamities because of their crimes. Afterwards God himself speaks, and shows that the Jews who should be left in the land should be driven out because of their iniquities, and that those who had been led captive, and who acknowledged their sins and repented of them, should be restored to their own land. Then the glory of the Lord arose out of the city, and rested for a time on one of the mountains on the east of Jerusalem, and the prophet being carried in vision by the Spirit to Chaldea, lost sight of the chariot of the divine glory, and began to show to the captivity what the Lord had shown to him. This is the substance of the *eleventh* chapter.

3. *The image of jealousy.* We do not know certainly of what form this image was, nor what god it represented. Some say it was the image of Baal, which was placed in the Temple by Manasses; others, that it was the image of Tammuz. The prophet being returned towards the northern gate, where he had seen the image of jealousy, v. 14, there saw the women lamenting for Tammuz.

4. *The vision that I saw in the plain.* See the note on chap. iii. 23; see also chap. i. 3.

10. *And saw . . . every form of creeping things.* It is very likely that these images portrayed on the wall were the objects of Egyptian adoration.

11. *Jaazaniah the son of Shaphan.* Shaphan was a scribe, or what some call comptroller of the Temple, in the days of Josiah; and Jaazaniah, his son, probably succeeded him in this office. He was at the head of this band of idolaters.

14. *There sat women weeping for Tammuz.* This was Adonis, and so the Vulgate here translates. He is fabled to have been a beautiful youth beloved by Venus, and killed by a wild boar in Mount Lebanon. The women of Phoenicia, Assyria, and Judea worshipped him as dead with deep lamentation. *Tammuz* signifies "hidden" or "obscure," and hence the worship of his image was in some secret place.

16. *Five and twenty men.* These most probably represented the twenty-four courses of the priests, with the high priest for the twenty-fifth. This was the Persian worship, as their turning their faces to the east plainly shows they were worshipping the rising sun.

17. *They put the branch to their nose.* This is supposed to mean some branch or branches, which they carried in succession in honor of the idol, and with which they covered their faces, or from which they inhaled a pleasant smell, the branches being odoriferous.

CHAPTER 9

The vision in this chapter seems intended to denote the general destruction of the inhabitants of Jerusalem, excepting a few pious individuals that were distressed at the abominations that were committed in the land; who, in order to be delivered from the general calamity, were marked, in allusion, perhaps, to the custom of Eastern princes, who marked their servants in the forehead, or rather to the custom very frequent among the pagan worshippers, of indelibly imprinting on different parts of their body the marks of their idols. To indicate, likewise, that God was soon to forsake the Temple, the Shekinah, or glorious symbol of His presence, is seen to remove from the inner sanctuary to the threshold or door of the Temple, 1-7. The prophet intercedes for his people; but God, on account of the greatness of their sins, will not be entreated, 8-11.

1. *Cause them that have charge over the city.* By those six men with destroying weapons the Chaldeans are represented, who had received commission to destroy the city; and when the north is mentioned in such cases, Chaldea and the Chaldean armies are generally intended. There appear to have been six men with a sort of slaughter-bills, and one man with an inkhorn. These may represent the seven counsellors of the Eastern monarchs, who always saw the king's face, and knew all the secrets of the government. This person with the inkhorn might be termed, in our phrase, the recorder.

2. *Stood beside the brasen altar.* To signify that the people against whom they had their commission were, for their crimes, to be sacrificed to the demands of divine justice.

3. *And he called to the man.* The person here who called was that who sat on the chariot of the divine glory. See chap. i. 26.

4. *Set a mark upon the foreheads of the men that sigh.* This is in allusion to the ancient, everywhere-used custom of setting marks on servants and slaves, to distinguish them from others. It was also common for the worshippers of particular idols to have their idol's mark upon their foreheads, arms, etc.

6. *Begin at my sanctuary.* Let those who have sinned against most mercy, and most privileges, be the first victims of justice. Those who know their Lord's will, and do it not, shall be beaten with many stripes. The unfaithful members of Christ's Church will be first visited and most punished.

9. *For they say, The Lord hath forsaken the earth. Eth haarets,* "this land." He has no more place in Israel; He has quite abandoned it; He neither sees nor cares, and He can be no longer the Object of worship to any man in Israel. This seems to be the meaning; and God highly resents it, because it was bringing Him on a level with idols and provincial deities, who had, according to supposition, regency only in some one place.

10. *Mine eye shall not spare.* They say, "The Lord seeth not." This is false; I have seen all their iniquities, and do see all their abominations; and I will bring deserved judgment upon them, and then that eye which now sees will neither *pity* nor *spare.*

CHAPTER 10

The same august vision which appeared to the prophet at first is repeated here, and coals of fire are scattered over the city to intimate that it was to be burned. The symbol of the Divine Presence is likewise represented as removing farther and farther from the Temple, to signify that God's protection was about to be withdrawn from it, 1-22. It may not be improper to remark that whatever is particularly intended by the cherubim, wheels, firmament, throne, etc., described in this and the first chapter, the prophet several times informs us (chap. i. 28; iii. 25; viii. 4; x. 4, 18) that his vision was a manifestation or similitude of the glory of Jehovah; or, in other words, consisted of a set of hieroglyphics by which this glory was in some measure represented. It is also worthy of observation that the faces of the living creatures, of which we have an account in the fourth chapter of the Apocalypse, are precisely the same with those of Ezekiel's cherubim; and we may readily collect, as Mr. Mede remarks, the quarter of the heavens in which each cherub was situated in reference to the other three, from the consideration that, as Ezekiel saw the vision proceeding from the north (see chap. i. 4, 10), the human face of the cherubim was towards him, or the south; on his right hand, or the east, was the face of a lion; on his left hand, or the west, the face of an ox; and towards the north, the face of an eagle.

1. *As it were a sapphire stone.* See the note on chap. i. 22, 26. The chariot, here mentioned by the prophet, was precisely the same as that which he saw at the river Chebar, as himself tells us, v. 15, of which see the description in chap. i.

2. *Coals of fire.* These were to signify the burning of the city by the Chaldeans. It seems that the space between the four wheels, which was all on fire, was that from which those coals were taken.

3. *On the right side of the house.* The right hand always marked the south among the Hebrews.

4. *The glory of the Lord went up.* This is repeated from chap. ix. 3. *The house was filled with the cloud.* This is a fact similar to what occurred frequently at the Tabernacle in the wilderness, and in the dedication of the Temple by Solomon. What is mentioned here was the divine Shekinah, the symbolical representation of the majesty of God.

5. *As the voice of the Almighty God.* That is, as thunder; for this was called the voice of God.

9. *The colour of a beryl stone. Eben Tarshish,* "the stone of Tarshish." The Vulgate translates it "chrysolith"; Symmachus, the "jacinct"; the Septuagint, the "carbuncle." The *beryl* is a gem of a green color, passing from one side into blue, on the other side into yellow.

13. *As for the wheels, it was cried unto them . . . O wheel.* Never was there a more unfortunate and unmeaning translation. The word *haggalgal* may signify, simply, "the roller, or a chariot, or roll on, or the swift roller." Any of these will do: "And as to the wheels, they were called in my hearing the chariot."

20. *And I knew that they were the cherubims.* This formation of the plural is quite improper. In general, Hebrew nouns of the masculine gender end in *im* in the plural; the *s,* therefore should never be added to such. *Cherub* is singular; *cherubim* is plural.

CHAPTER 11

This chapter denounces the judgments of God against those wicked persons who remained in Jerusalem, and made a mock of the types and predictions of the prophets, 1-13; compare v. 3 with Jer. i. 13. God promises to favor those who were gone into captivity, and intimates their restoration from the Babylonish yoke, 14-21. Then the Shekinah, or symbol of the Divine Presence, is represented forsaking the city, as in the foregoing chapter it did the Temple, 22-23; and the prophet returns in vision to the place from which he set out (chap. viii. 1, etc.), in order to communicate his instructions to his brethren of the Captivity, 24-25.

1. *At the door of the gate five and twenty men.* The same persons, no doubt, who appear, chap. viii. 16, worshipping the sun. *Jaazaniah the son of Azur.* In chap. viii. 11, we find a "Jaazaniah the son of Shaphan." If Shaphan was also called Azur, they may be the same person. But it is most likely that there were two of this name, and both chiefs among the people.

3. *It is not near.* That is, the threatened invasion. *This city is the caldron, and we be the flesh.* See the vision of the seething pot, Jer. i. 13. These infidels seem to say: "We will run all risks, we will abide in the city. Though it be the caldron, and we the flesh, yet we will share its fate: if it perish, we will perish with it."

7. *Your slain . . . they are the flesh.* Jerusalem is the caldron, and those who have been slain in it, they are the flesh; and though you purpose to stay and share its fate, you shall not be permitted to do so; you shall be carried into captivity.

9. *And deliver you into the hands of strangers.* This seems to refer chiefly to Zedekiah and his family.

11. *I will judge you in the border of Israel.* Though Riblah was in Syria, yet it was on the very frontiers of Israel; and it was here that Zedekiah's sons were slain, and his own eyes put out.

13. *Pelatiah the son of Benaiah died.* Most probably he was struck dead the very hour in which Ezekiel prophesied against him. His death appears to have resembled that of Ananias and Sapphira, Acts v. 1, etc.

15. *Get you far from the Lord.* These are the words of the inhabitants of Jerusalem, against those of Israel who had been carried away to Babylon with Jeconiah. Go ye far from the Lord; but as for us, the land of Israel

is given to us for a possession. We shall never be removed from it, and they shall never return to it.

16. *Yet will I be to them as a little sanctuary.* Though thus exiled from their own land, yet not forgotten by their God. While in their captivity, I will dispense many blessings to them; and I will restore them to their own land, v. 17, from which they shall put away all idolatry, v. 18.

23. *The glory of the Lord went up from the midst of the city.* This vision is no mean proof of the long-suffering of God. He did not abandon this people all at once; He departed by little and little. First, He left the Temple. Secondly, He stopped a little at the gate of the city. Thirdly, He departed entirely from the city and went to the Mount of Olives, which lay on the east side of the city. Having tarried there for some time to see if they would repent and turn to Him—fourthly, He departed to heaven. The vision being now concluded, the prophet is taken away by the Spirit of God into Chaldea, and there announces to the captive Israelites what God had showed him in the preceding visions, and the good that He had spoken concerning them; who at first did not seem to profit much by them, which the prophet severely reproves.

CHAPTER 12

The prophet proceeds, by a variety of types and parables, to convince those of the Captivity that their brethren who were left behind to sustain the miseries of a siege and the insults of a conqueror would be in a much worse condition than they who were already settled in a foreign land. In the beginning of this chapter he foretells the approaching captivity of Judah by action instead of words, 1-7. He predicts particularly the flight, capture, captivity, and sufferings of Zedekiah and his followers, 8-16, compared with Jer. lii. 11. He is to eat his food with trembling and signs of terror, as an emblem of the consternation of the Jews when surrounded by their enemies, 17-20; and then he answers the objections and bywords of scoffers and infidels, who either disbelieved his threatenings or supposed the accomplishment of them very distant, 21-28. Josephus (*Antiq.* xi. 10) tells us that Zedekiah thought the prophecy of Ezekiel in the thirteenth verse inconsistent with that of Jeremiah (chap. xxxiv. 3) and resolved to believe neither. Both, however, were literally fulfilled; and the event convinced him that they were not irreconcilable. Thus, blinded by infidelity, sinners rush on to that destruction against which they are sufficiently warned.

2. *Which have eyes to see, and see not.* It is not want of grace that brings them to destruction. They have eyes to see, but they will not use them. No man is lost because he had not sufficient grace to save him, but because he abused that grace.

3. *Prepare thee stuff for removing.* Get carriages to transport your goods to another place, signifying by this the captivity that was at hand.

5. *Dig thou through the wall.* This refers to the manner in which Zedekiah and his family would escape from the city. They escaped by night through a breach in the wall. See Jer. xxxix. 2-4 and 2 Kings xxv. 4.

6. *Thou shalt cover thy face, that thou see not the ground.* Referring to the blinding of Zedekiah. Even the covering of the face might be intended to signify that in this way Zedekiah should be carried to Babylon on men's shoulders in some sort of palanquin, with a cloth tied over his eyes, because of the recent wounds made by extracting them. All the prophecies

from this to the twentieth chapter are supposed to have been delivered in the sixth year of Zedekiah, five years before the taking of Jerusalem.

10. *This burden.* By this I point out the capture, misery, and ruin of Zedekiah.

13. *I will bring him to Babylon . . . yet shall he not see it.* Because Nebuchadnezzar caused him to have his eyes put out at Riblah. To Babylon he was carried in his blind state, and there he died.

18. *Eat thy bread with quaking.* Assume the manner of a person who is every moment afraid of his life, who has nothing but a morsel of bread to eat and a little water to drink, thus signifying the siege, and the straits to which they should be reduced.

22. *The days are prolonged, and every vision faileth.* These are the words of the infidels and scoffers, who, because vengeance was not speedily executed on an evil work, set their heart to do iniquity. "These predictions either will not come in our days, or will wholly fail; why then should we disquiet ourselves about them?" Strange that the very means used by the most gracious God to bring sinners to repentance, should be made by them the very instruments of their own destruction! See 2 Pet. iii. 4.

23. *The days are at hand.* Far from failing or being prolonged, time is posting on, and the destruction threatened is at the door.

25. *In your days . . . will I say the word, and will perform it.* Even these mockers shall live to see and feel this desolation. This is more particularly intimated in the following verses.

CHAPTER 13

This chapter denounces heavy judgments against the lying prophets who flattered the people, in the midst of their sin and danger, with false hopes of peace and security, 1-9. The work of these deceivers is beautifully compared to a frail and insufficient piece of building, which can never stand against the battering elements of heaven (the Chaldean forces) which God will commission against it, 10-16. In the remaining part of the chapter woes are denounced against false prophetesses who practiced vain rites and divinations, with the view of promoting their own gain by deceiving the people, 17-23.

4. *Thy prophets are like the foxes in the deserts.* These false prophets are represented as the foxes who, having got their prey by great subtlety, run to the desert to hide both themselves and it. So the false prophets, when the event did not answer to their prediction, got out of the way, that they might not be overwhelmed with the reproaches and indignation of the people.

5. *Ye have not gone up into the gaps.* Far from opposing sinners, who are bringing down the wrath of God upon the place, you prevent their repentance by your flattering promises and false predictions.

9. *They shall not be in the assembly of my people.* They shall not be reputed members of My Church. They shall not be reckoned in the genealogy of true Israelites that return from captivity, and they shall never have a possession in the land; they shall be exheredited and expatriated. They shall all perish in the siege, by the sword, the famine, and the pestilence.

10. *One built up a wall.* A true prophet is as a wall of defense to the people. These false prophets pretend to be a wall of defense; but their wall is bad, and their mortar is worse. One gives a lying vision; another pledges himself that it is true; and the people believe what they say, and trust not in God, nor turn from their sins.

11. *There shall be an overflowing shower* that shall wash off this bad mortar, sweep away the ground on which the wall stands, and level it with the earth. In the Eastern countries, where the walls are built with unbaked bricks, desolations of this kind are often occasioned by tempestuous rains.

17. *Set thy face against the daughters of thy people, which prophesy.* From this it appears that there were prophetesses in the land of Israel that were really inspired by the Lord; for false prophetesses necessarily imply true ones, whom they endeavored to imitate.

18. *That sew pillows to all armholes.* I believe this refers to those cushions which are so copiously provided in the Eastern countries for the apartments of women, on which they sit, lean, rest their heads, and prop up their arms. I have several drawings of Eastern ladies who are represented on sofas, and often with their arm thrown over a pillow, which is thereby pressed close to their side, and against which they thus recline. The prophet's discourse seems to point out that state of softness and effeminacy to which the predictions of those false prophetesses allured the inhabitants of Jerusalem. A careless, voluptuous life is that which is here particularly reprehended. *And make kerchiefs.* Probably some kind of ornamental dress which rendered women more enticing, so that they could the more successfully hunt or inveigle souls (men) into the worship of their false gods.

20. *The souls that ye hunt to make them fly.* These false prophetesses decoyed men into gardens, where probably some impure rites of worship were performed, as in that of Asherah or Venus.

22. *With lies ye have made the heart of the righteous sad.* Here is the ministry of these false prophetesses, and its effects. They told lies: they would speak, and they had no truth to tell, and therefore spoke falsities. They "saddened the souls of the righteous, and strengthened the hands of the wicked." They promised them life, and prevented them from repenting and turning from their sins.

23. *Ye shall see no more vanity.* They pretended visions, but they were empty of reality. *Nor divine divinations.* As God would not speak to them, they employed demons.

CHAPTER 14

Here God threatens those hypocrites who pretended to worship Him, while they loved and practiced idolatry, 1-11. He declares His irreversible purpose of punishing so guilty a nation, in behalf of which no intercession of the people of God shall be of any avail. The gross idolaters of Jerusalem and Judah shall be visited with God's four sore judgments: famine, 12-14; wild beasts, 15-16; the sword, 17-18; and pestilence, 19-21. A remnant shall be delivered from the wrath coming upon the whole land, 22-23.

1. *Then came certain of the elders of Israel unto me.* These probably came to tempt him, or get him to say something that would embroil him with the government. They were bad men, as we shall see in the third verse.

3. *These men have set up their idols in their heart.* Not only in their houses, in the streets, but they had them in their hearts. These were stumbling blocks of iniquity; they fell over them, and broke the neck of their souls.

4. *According to the multitude of his idols.* I will treat him as an idolater, as a flagrant idolater.

7. *And cometh to a prophet.* Generally supposed to mean a false prophet. *I the Lord will answer him by myself.* I shall discover to him, by My own true prophet, what shall be the fruit of his ways. So, while their false prophets were assuring them of peace and prosperity, God's prophets were predicting the calamities that afterwards fell upon them. Yet they believed the false prophets in preference to the true.

9. *I the Lord have deceived that prophet.* That is, he ran before he was sent; he willingly became the servant of Satan's illusions; and I suffered this to take place, because he and his followers refused to consult and serve Me. I have often had occasion to remark that it is common in the Hebrew language to state a thing as done by the Lord which He only suffers or permits to be done, for so absolute and universal is the government of God that the smallest occurrence cannot take place without His will or permission.

10. *The punishment of the prophet.* They are both equally guilty; both have left the Lord, and both shall be equally punished.

13. *By trespassing grievously.* Having been frequently warned, and having refused to leave their sin, and so filled up the measure of their iniquity.

14. *Though . . . Noah, Daniel, and Job.* The intercession even the holiest of men shall not avert My judgments. Noah, though a righteous man, could not by his intercession preserve the old world from being drowned. Job, though a righteous man, could not preserve his children from being killed by the fall of their house. Daniel, though a righteous man, could not prevent the captivity of his country. Daniel must have been contemporary with Ezekiel. He was taken captive in the third year of Jehoiakim, Dan. i. 1. After this Jehoiakim reigned eight years, 2 Kings xxiii. 36. And this prophecy, as appears from chap. viii. 1, was uttered in the sixth year of Jehoiachin's captivity, who succeeded Jehoiakim, and reigned only three months, 2 Kings xxiv. 6, 8. Therefore at this time Daniel had been fourteen years in captivity. Even at this time he had gained much public celebrity. From this account we may infer that Job was as real a person as Noah or Daniel, and of their identity no man has pretended to doubt. When God, as above, has determined to punish a nation, no intercession shall avail.

21. *My four sore judgments. Sword,* war. *Famine,* occasioned by drought. *Pestilence* epidemic diseases which sweep off a great part of the inhabitants of a land. The *noisome beast,* the multiplication of wild beasts in consequence of the general destruction of the inhabitants.

22. *Behold, they shall come forth unto you.* Though there shall be great desolations in the land of Judea, yet a remnant shall be left that shall come here also as captives, and their account of the abominations of the people shall prove to you with what propriety I have acted in abandoning them to such general destruction. This speech is addressed to those who were already in captivity; i.e., those who had been led to Babylon with their king Jeconiah.

CHAPTER 15

The Jewish nation, about to be destroyed by the Chaldeans, compared to a barren vine which is fit for nothing but to be cast into the fire, 1-8.

2. *What is the vine tree more than any tree?* It is certain that the vine is esteemed only on account of its fruit. In some countries, it is true, it grows to a considerable size and thickness; but, even then, it is not of a sufficient density to work into furniture. But whatever may be said of the stock of the vine, it is the branch that the prophet speaks of here; and I scarcely know the branch of any tree in the forest more useless than is the branch of the vine. Out of it who can even make "a pin" to drive into a mud wall, or hang any vessel on? A vine would never be cultivated for the sake of its wood; it is really worthless but as it bears fruit. What is Israel? Good for nothing, but as God influenced them to bring forth fruit to His glory. But now that they have ceased to be fruitful, they are good for nothing, but, like a withered branch of the vine, to be burnt.

4. *The fire devoureth both the ends of it, and the midst of it is burned.* Judea is like a vine branch thrown into the fire, which seizes on both the ends, and scorches the middle. So both the extremities of the land are wasted; and the middle, Jerusalem, is now threatened with a siege, and by and by will be totally destroyed.

6. *Therefore thus saith the Lord.* As surely as I have allotted such a vine branch, or vine branches, for fuel, so surely have I appointed the inhabitants of Jerusalem to be consumed.

7. *They shall go out from one fire, and another fire shall devour them.* If they escape the sword, they shall perish by the famine; if they escape the famine, they shall be led away captives. To escape will be impossible.

CHAPTER 16

In this chapter the mercy of God to Jerusalem (or the Jewish church and nation) is set forth by the emblem of a person that should take up an exposed infant, bring her up with great tenderness, and afterwards marry her, 1-14. She is then upbraided with her monstrous ingratitude in departing from the worship of God, and polluting herself with the idolatries of the nations around her, under the figure of a woman that proves false to a tender and indulgent husband, 15-52. But, notwithstanding these her heinous provocations, God promises, after she should suffer due correction, to restore her again to His favor, 53-63. The mode of describing apostasy from the true religion to the worship of idols under the emblem of adultery (a figure very frequent in the sacred canon) is pursued with great force, and at considerable length, in both this and the twenty-third chapters; and is excellently calculated to excite in the Church of God the highest detestation of all false worship.

2. *Cause Jerusalem to know her abominations.* This chapter contains God's manifesto against this most abominable people; and although there are many metaphors here, yet all is not metaphorical. Where there was so much idolatry, there must have been adulteries, fornications, prostitutions, and lewdness of every description. For its key, see on the thirteenth and sixty-third verses.

3. *Thy birth and thy nativity is of the land of Canaan.* It would dishonor Abraham to say that you sprang from him; you are rather Canaanites than Israelites. The Canaanites were accursed; so are you. *Thy father was an Amorite, and thy mother an Hittite.* These tribes were the most famous, and probably the most corrupt, of all the Canaanites. So Isaiah calls the princes of Judah "rulers of Sodom," chap. i. 10; and John the Baptist calls the Pharisees a "generation [or brood] of vipers," Matt. iii. 7.

4. *As for thy nativity.* This verse refers to what is ordinarily done for every infant on its birth. The umbilical cord, by which it received all its nourishment while in the womb, being no longer necessary, is cut at a certain distance from the abdomen; on this part a knot is tied, which firmly uniting the sides of the tubes, they coalesce, and incarnate together. The extra part of the cord on the outside of the ligature, being cut off from the circulation by which it was originally fed, soon drops off, and the part where the ligature was is called the navel. In many places, when this was done, the infant was plunged into cold water; in all cases washed, and sometimes with a mixture of salt and water, in order to give a greater firmness to the skin, and constringe the pores. The last process was swathing the body, to support mechanically the tender muscles till they should acquire sufficient strength to support the body.

5. *Thou wast cast out in the open field.* This is an allusion to the custom of some heathen and barbarous nations, who exposed those children in the open fields to be devoured by wild beasts who had any kind of deformity, or whom they could not support.

6. *I said . . . Live.* I received the exposed child from the death that awaited it, while in such a state as rendered it at once an object of horror and also of compassion.

8. *Was the time of love.* You were marriageable. *I spread my skirt over thee.* I espoused you. This was one of their initiatory marriage ceremonies. See Ruth iii. 9. *I . . . entered into a covenant with thee.* Married you. Espousing preceded marriage.

10. *I clothed thee also with broidered work.* Cloth on which various figures, in various colors, were wrought by the needle.

12. *I put a jewel on thy forehead.* "Upon your nose." This is one of the most common ornaments among ladies in the East. European translators, not knowing what to make of a ring in the nose, have rendered it, *a jewel on thy forehead* or mouth.

13. *Thou didst prosper into a kingdom.* Here the figure explains itself: By this wretched infant, the low estate of the Jewish nation in its origin is pointed out; by the growing up of this child into woman's estate, the increase and multiplication of the people; by her being decked out and ornamented, her Tabernacle service and religious ordinances; by her betrothing and consequent marriage, the covenant which God made with the Jews; by her fornication and adulteries, their apostasy from God, and the establishment of idolatrous worship, with all its abominable rites; by her fornication and whoredoms with the Egyptians and Assyrians, the sinful alliances which the Jews made with those nations, and the incorporation of their idolatrous worship with that of Jehovah; by her lovers being brought against her, and stripping her naked, the delivery of the Jews into the hands of the Egyptians, Assyrians, and Chaldeans, who stripped them of all their excellencies, and at last carried them into captivity. This is the key to the whole of this long chapter of metaphors, and the reader will do well to forget the figures and look at the facts. The language and figures may in many places appear to us exceptionable, but these are quite in conformity to those times and places, and to every reader and hearer would appear perfectly appropriate, nor would engender either a thought or passion of an irregular or improper kind. Among naked savages irregular passions and propensities are not known to predominate above those in civilized life. And why? Because such sights are customary, and therefore in themselves innocent. And the same may be said of the language by which such states and circumstances of life are described. Had Ezekiel spoken in such language as would have been called chaste and unexceptionable among us, it would have appeared to his auditors as a strange dialect, and would have lost at least one-half of its power and effect. Let this be the prophet's apology for the apparent indelicacy of his metaphors; and mine, for not entering into any particular discussion concerning them.

24. *Thou hast also built* unto thee an eminent place. Gab, "a brothel."

26. *Great of flesh.* The most extensive idolaters.

27. *Have diminished thine ordinary. Chukkech* means here the household provision made for a wife—food, clothing, and money.

39. *They shall strip thee also of thy clothes . . . thy fair jewels.* Alluding to a lot common enough to prostitutes, their maintainers in the end stripping them of all they had given them.

42. *I will be quiet, and will be no more angry.* I will completely abandon you, have nothing more to do with you, think no more of you. When God in judgment ceases to reprehend, this is the severest judgment.

46. *Thine elder sister is Samaria, she and her daughters that dwell at thy left.* It is supposed that the prophet by Sodom in this place means the Israelites that dwelt beyond Jordan, in the land of the Moabites and Ammonites, or rather of the Moabites and Ammonites themselves. Literally, Sodom could not be called the younger sister of Jerusalem, as it existed before Jerusalem had a name. In looking east from Jerusalem, Samaria was on the left, and Sodom on the right hand; that is, the first was on the north, the second on the south of Jerusalem.

52. *They are more righteous than thou.* "They shall be justified more than you." They are less guilty in the sight of God, for their crimes were not accompanied with so many aggravations.

60. *I will remember my covenant.* That is, the covenant I made with Abraham in the day of your youth, when in him you began to be a nation.

61. *Thy sisters, thine elder and thy younger.* The Gentiles, who were before the Jews were called, and after the Jews were cast off, are here termed the elder and younger sister. These were to be given to Jerusalem for daughters; the latter should be converted to God by the ministry of men who should spring out of the Jewish church.

63. *When I am pacified toward thee.* This intimates that the Jews shall certainly share in the blessings of the gospel covenant, and that they shall be restored to the favor and image of God. And when shall this be? Whenever they please.

CHAPTER 17

This chapter begins with a new allegory or parable, 1-10, to which an explanation is immediately subjoined, 11-21. In the remaining verses the prophet, by a beautiful metaphor, makes an easy and natural transition to the Messiah, and predicts the security, increasing prosperity, and ultimate universality of His kingdom, 22-24. From the beauty of its images, the elegance of its composition, the perspicuity of its language, the rich variety of its matter, and the easy transition from one part of the subject to another, this chapter forms one of the most beautiful and perfect pieces of its kind that can possibly be conceived in so small a compass; and then the unexpected change from objects that presented nothing to the view but gloom and horror, to a prospect of ineffable glory and beauty, has a most happy effect. Every lowering cloud is dispelled, and the fields again smile in the beams of midday. The traveller, who this moment trembled as he looked around for shelter, now proceeds on his way rejoicing.

2. *Son of man, put forth a riddle.* An instrument formerly used for divination. This is not far removed from the Hebrew *chidah,* from *chad,* "to penetrate"; not that which penetrates the mind, but which we must penetrate to find out the sense.

3. *A great eagle.* Nebuchadnezzar. See Jer. xlviii. 40; xlix. 22; Dan. vii. 4. And see here, v. 12, where it is so applied. *Great wings.* Extensive empire. *Long-winged.* Rapid in his conquests. *Full of feathers.* Having multitudes of subjects. *Divers colours.* People of various nations. *Came unto Lebanon.* Came against Judea. *The highest branch.* King Jehoiachin he took captive to Babylon. *The cedar.* The Jewish state and king.

4. *The top of his young twigs.* The princes of Judah. *A land of traffic.* Chaldea. *A city of merchants.* Babylon, for which this city was the most celebrated of all the cities of the East. Its situation procured it innumerable advantages; its two rivers, the Tigris and Euphrates, and the Persian Gulf, gave it communication with the richest and the most distant nations.

5. *The seed of the land.* Zedekiah, brother of Jehoiachin. *Planted it in a fruitful field.* Made him king of Judea in place of his brother. *Placed it by great waters.* Put him under the protection of Babylon, situated on the confluence of the Tigris and Euphrates. *And set it as a willow tree.* Made him dependent on this city of great waters, as the willow is on humidity.

6. *A spreading vine of low stature.* The Jewish state having then no height of dominion, it must abide under the wings or branches of the Chaldean king. *Whose branches turned toward him, and the roots . . . under him.* Zedekiah was wholly dependent on Nebuchadnezzar, for both his elevation to the throne and his support on it.

7. *Another great eagle.* Pharaoh-hophra, or Apries, king of Egypt. *With great wings.* Extensive dominion. *And many feathers.* Numerous subjects. *Did bend her roots.* Looked to him for support in her intended rebellion against Nebuchadnezzar.

8. *It was planted in a good soil.* Though he depended on Babylon, he lived and reigned as Nebuchadnezzar's vicegerent in the land of Judea.

9 *Shall it prosper?* Shall Zedekiah succeed in casting off the yoke of the king of Babylon, to whom he had sworn fealty? *Shall he not pull up the roots?* Nebuchadnezzar will come and dethrone him. *And cut off the fruit.* The children of Zedekiah. *The leaves.* All the nobles; all shall perish with Zedekiah.

10. *Shall . . . utterly wither.* The regal government shall be no more restored. Zedekiah shall be the last king, and the monarchy shall finally terminate with him.

12. *Know ye not what these things mean?* They are explained in this and the following verses.

15. *Sending his ambassadors into Egypt.* Zedekiah must have sent his ambassadors into Egypt between the sixth month of his sixth year and the fifth month of his seventh year. Compare chap. viii. 1 with chap. xx. 1.

16. *In the midst of Babylon he shall die.* His eyes were put out; he was carried to Babylon, and never returned.

18. *Seeing he despised the oath.* This God particularly resents. He had bound himself by oath, in the presence of Jehovah, to be faithful to the covenant that he made with Nebuchadnezzar, and he took the first opportunity to break it; therefore he shall not escape.

21. *All his fugitives.* All who attempted to escape with him, and all that ran to Egypt shall fall by the sword.

22. *I will also take of the highest branch of the high cedar.* I will raise up another monarchy, which shall come in the line of David, namely, the Messiah; who shall appear as a tender plant, as to His incarnation; but He shall be high and eminent; His Church, the royal city, the highest and purest ever seen on the face of the earth.

23. *In the mountain of the height of Israel.* He shall make His appearance at the Temple, and found His Church at Jerusalem. *Shall bring forth boughs.* Apostles, evangelists, and their successors in the gospel ministry. *And bear fruit.* Multitudes of souls shall be converted by their preaching. *And under it shall dwell all fowl of every wing.* All the nations of the earth shall receive His gospel. *In the shadow of the branches thereof shall they dwell.* Trust in Him alone for salvation, and be saved in their trusting.

24. *All the trees of the field shall know.* All the people of Israel and of Chaldea. *I the Lord have brought down the high tree.* Have dethroned Jehoiachin. *Have exalted the low tree.* Put Zedekiah, brother of Jehoiachin, in his place. *Have dried up the green tree.* Zedekiah, who had numerous children, but who were all slain before his eyes at Riblah. *And have made the dry tree to flourish.* Have raised up a rod out of the stem of Jesse, the family of David being then apparently dried up and extinct. This was the promised Messiah, of the increase and government of whose Kingdom

and "peace there shall be no end, upon the throne of David, and upon his kingdom, to order it and to establish it with judgment and justice from henceforth even for ever."

CHAPTER 18

The Jews, in Ezekiel's time, complained of God's dealing hardly with them in punishing them for the sins of their forefathers, 1-2; their temporal calamities having been long threatened as the consequence of the national guilt (Jer. xv. 4, etc.), and from the general complexion of this chapter, it appears that the Jews so interpreted the second commandment of the Decalogue and other passages of like import, as if the sins of the forefathers were visited upon the children, independently of the moral conduct of the latter, not only in this world, but in that which is to come. To remove every foundation for such an unworthy idea of the divine government, God assures them, with an oath, that He had no respect of persons, 3-4; strongly intimating that the great mysteries in providence (mysterious only on account of the limited capacity of man) are results of the most impartial administration of justice; and that this would be particularly manifested in the rewards and punishments of another life, when every ligament that at present connects societies and nations together shall be dissolved, and each person receive according to his work, and bear his own burden. This is illustrated by a variety of examples: such as that of a just or righteous man, 5-9; his wicked son, 10-13; and again the just son of this wicked person, 14-20. Then a wicked man repenting, and finding mercy, whose former wickedness shall be no impediment to his salvation, 21-23; and a righteous man revolting, and dying in his sins, whose former righteousness shall be of no avail, 24. The conduct of the divine providence is then vindicated, 25-29; and all persons, without any exception, most earnestly exhorted to repentance, 30-31; because the Lord hath no pleasure in the death of the sinner, 32. As the whole of this chapter is taken up with the illustration of a doctrine nearly connected with the comfort of man, and the honor of the divine government, the prophet, with great propriety, lays aside his usual mode of figure and allegory, and treats his subject with the utmost plainness and perspicuity.

2. *The fathers have eaten sour grapes, and the children's teeth are set on edge.* We have seen this proverb already, Jer. xxxi. 29, etc., and have considered its general meaning. But the subject is here proposed in greater detail, with a variety of circumstances, to adapt it to all those cases to which it should apply. It refers simply to these questions: How far can the moral evil of the parent be extended to his offspring? And, Are the faults and evil propensities of the parents, not only transferred to the children, but punished in them? Do parents transfer their evil nature, and are their children punished for their offenses?

3. *As I live, saith the Lord, God, ye shall not have occasion any more to use this proverb in Israel.* I will now, by this present declaration, settle this question forever.

4. *All souls are mine.* Equally so; I am the Father of the spirits of all flesh, and shall deal impartially with the whole. *The soul that sinneth, it shall die.* None shall die for another's crimes; none shall be saved by another's righteousness.

5. *If a man be just, and do that which is lawful and right.* What is meant by this is immediately specified.

6. (1) *Hath not eaten upon the mountains.* Idolatrous worship was generally performed on mountains and hills; and those who offered sacrifices feasted on the sacrifice, and thus held communion with the idol. (2) *Neither hath lifted up his eyes to the idols.* Has paid them no religious adoration; has trusted in them for nothing, and has not made prayer nor supplication before them. (3) *Neither hath defiled his neighbour's wife.* Has had no adulterous connection with any woman, to which idolatrous

feasts and worship particularly led. (4) *Neither hath come near to a menstruous woman.* Has abstained from the use of the marriage-bed during the periodical indisposition of his wife, Lev. xx. 18.

7. (5) *Hath not oppressed any.* Has not used his power or influence to oppress, pain, or injure another. (6) *Hath restored to the debtor his pledge.* Has carefully surrendered the pawn or pledge when its owner came to redeem it. As the pledge is generally of more worth than that for which it is pledged, an unprincipled man will make some pretense to keep it, which is highly abominable in the sight of God. (7) *Hath spoiled none by violence.* Either by robbery or personal insult, for a man may be spoiled both ways. (8) *Hath given his bread to the hungry.* Has been kindhearted and charitable, especially to them that are in the deepest want. (9) *Hath covered the naked with a garment.* Has divided both his bread and his clothing with the necessitous.

8. (10) *Hath not given forth upon usury.* Nasach signifies "to bite"; usury is properly so termed, because it bites into and devours the principal. (11) *Neither hath taken any increase.* In lending has not required more than was lent. (12) *That hath withdrawn his hand from iniquity.* Never associates with those who act contrary to justice and equity. (13) *Hath executed true judgment between man and man.* Being swayed by neither prejudice, fear, nor favor. These thirteen points concern his social and civil relations.

10. *If he beget a son.* Who is the reverse of the above righteous character, according to the thirteen articles already specified and explained.

17. *He shall not die for the iniquity of his father.* He shall no more be affected by his father's crimes than his father was benefited by his grandfather's righteousness.

CHAPTER 19

This chapter contains two beautiful examples of the parable kind of writing: the one lamenting the sad catastrophe of Jehoahaz and Jehoiakim, 1-9, and the other describing the desolation and captivity of the whole people, 10-14. In the first parable, the lioness is Jerusalem. The first of the young lions is Jehoahaz, deposed by the king of Egypt; and the second lion is Jehoiakim, whose rebellion drew on himself the vengeance of the king of Babylon. In the second parable the vine is the Jewish nation, which long prospered, its land being fertile, its princes powerful, and its people flourishing; but the judgments of God, in consequence of their guilt, had now destroyed a great part of the people, and doomed the rest to captivity.

1. *Moreover take thou up a lamentation.* Declare what is the great subject of sorrow in Israel. Compose a funeral dirge. Show the melancholy fate of the kings who proceeded from Josiah. The prophet deplores the misfortune of Jehoahaz and Jehoiakim, under the figure of two lion whelps, which were taken by hunters, and confined in cages. Next he shows the desolation of Jerusalem under Zedekiah, which he compares to a beautiful vine pulled up by the roots, withered, and at last burned.

2. *What is thy mother? A lioness.* Judea may here be the mother; the lioness, Jerusalem. *She lay down among lions,* having confederacy with the neighboring kings; for *lion* here means king.

3. *She brought up one of her whelps.* Jehoahaz, son of Josiah, whose father was conquered and slain by Pharaoh-necho, king of Egypt. It learned to catch the prey. His reign was a reign of oppression and cruelty. He made his subjects his prey, and devoured their substance.

4. *The nations also heard of him.* The king of Egypt, whose subjects were of divers nations, marched against Jerusalem, took Jehoahaz prisoner, and brought him to Egypt.

5. *When she saw that she had waited.* Being very weak, the Jews found that they could not resist with any hope of success; so the king of Egypt was permitted to do as he pleased. *She took another of her whelps.* Jehoiakim. *And made him a young lion.* King of Judea.

6. *And he went up and down among the lions.* He became a perfect heathen, and made Judea as idolatrous as any of the surrounding nations. He reigned eleven years, a monster of iniquity, 2 Kings xxiii. 30, etc.

8. *The nations set against him.* The Chaldeans, Syrians, Moabites, and Ammonites, and the king of Babylon—king of many nations. *He was taken.* The city was taken by Nebuchadnezzar; and Jehoiakim was taken prisoner, and sent in chains to Babylon.

9. *That his voice should no more be heard.* He continued in prison many years, till the reign of Evil-merodach, who set him at liberty, but never suffered him to return to the mountains of Israel.

10. *Thy mother* (Jerusalem) *is like a vine in thy blood.* Of this expression I know not what to make. Some think the meaning is, "A vine planted by the waters to produce the blood of the grape." See Deut. xxxii. 14. Calmet reads *carmecha*, "thy vineyard," instead of *bedamecha*, "in thy blood." Here is no change but a *resh* for a *daleth*. This reading is supported by one of Kennicott's and one of De Rossi's MSS.: "Thy mother is like a vine in thy vineyard, planted by the waters." Of the textual reading no sense can be made. There is a corruption somewhere. *Full of branches.* Many princes. See next verse.

11. *She had strong rods.* Zedekiah and his many sons. *Her stature was exalted.* Zedekiah grew proud of his numerous offspring and prosperity; and although he copied the example of Jehoiakim, yet he thought he might safely rebel against the king of Babylon.

12. *But she was plucked up in fury.* Jerusalem, taken after a violent and most destructive siege, Nebuchadnezzar being violently enraged against Zedekiah for breaking his oath to him. *She was cast down to the ground.* Jerusalem was totally ruined by being burned to the ground. *Her strong rods were broken.* The children of Zedekiah were slain before his eyes, and after that his own eyes pulled out; and he was laden with chains, and carried into Babylon.

13. *And now she is planted in the wilderness.* In the land of Chaldea, whither the people have been carried captives; and which, compared with their own land, was to them a dreary wilderness.

14. *Fire is gone out.* A vindictive and murderous disposition has taken hold—*of a rod of her branches.* Ishmael, son of Nethaniah, who was of the blood-royal of Judah—*hath devoured her fruit.* Hath assassinated Gedaliah, slain many people, and carried off others into the country of the Ammonites. But he was pursued by Jonathan, the son of Kareah, who slew many of his adherents, and delivered much of the people. *She hath no strong rod.* None of the blood-royal of Judah left. And from that time not one of her own royal race ever sat upon the throne of Israel. *This is a lamentation.* This is a most lamentable business. *And shall be so punctually fulfilled, and the catastrophe shall be so complete, that it shall ever remain as a lamentation, as this state of Jerusalem shall never be restored.

CHAPTER 20

A deputation of the elders of Israel, as usual, in their distress, came to request Ezekiel to ask counsel of God, 1. In reply to this, God commands the prophet to put them in mind of their rebellion and idolatry: in Egypt, 2-9, in the wilderness, 10-27, and in Canaan, 28-32. Notwithstanding which the Lord most graciously promises to restore them to their own land, after they should be purged from their dross, 33-44. The last five verses of this chapter ought to begin the next, as they are connected with the subject of that chapter, being a prophecy against Jerusalem, which lay to the south of Chaldea, where the prophet then was, and which here and elsewhere is represented under the emblem of a forest doomed to be destroyed by fire, 45-49.

1. *In the seventh year.* Of the captivity of Jeconiah, and the seventh of the reign of Zedekiah. *Certain of the elders of Israel.* What these came to inquire about is not known. They were doubtless hypocrites and deceivers, from the manner in which God commands the prophet to treat them. It seems to have been such a deputation of elders as those mentioned chap. viii. 1 and xiv. 1.

3. *I will not be enquired of by you.* I will not hear you. I will have nothing to do with you.

4. *Wilt thou judge them?* The whole chapter is a consecutive history of the unfaithfulness, ingratitude, rebellion, and idolatry of the Jews, from the earliest times to that day; and vindicates the sentence which God had pronounced against them, and which He was about to execute more fully in delivering them and the city into the hands of the Chaldeans.

5. *I chose Israel.* They did not choose Me for their God till I had chosen them to be My people. *I lifted up mine hand.* I bound myself in a covenant to them to continue to be their God, if they should be faithful, and continue to be My people. Among the Jews the juror lifted up his right hand to heaven; which explains Ps. cxliv. 8: "Their right hand is a right hand of falsehood."

6. *To bring them forth of the land of Egypt.* When they had been long in a very disgraceful and oppressive bondage.

7. *Cast ye away . . . the abominations.* Put away all your idols, these incentives to idolatry that you have looked on with delight.

8. *They did not . . . cast away.* They continued attached to the idolatry of Egypt; so that, had I consulted My justice only, I should have consumed them even in Egypt itself. This is a circumstance that Moses has not mentioned, namely, their provoking God by their idolatry, after He had sent Moses and Aaron to them in Egypt.

9. *But I wrought for my name's sake.* I bare with them and did not punish them, lest the heathen, who had known My promises made to them, might suppose that I had either broken them through some caprice or was not able to fulfill them.

10. *I caused them to go forth.* Though greatly oppressed and degraded, they were not willing to leave their house of bondage. I was obliged to force them away.

11. *I gave them my statutes.* I showed them what they should do in order to be safe, comfortable, wise, and happy and what they should avoid in order to be uninjured in body, mind, and possessions. Had they attended to these things, they should have lived by them. They would have been holy, healthy, and happy.

12. *I gave them my sabbaths.* The religious observance of the Sabbath was the first statute or command of God to men. This institution was a sign between God and them, to keep them in remembrance of the creation of the world, of the rest that he designed them in Canaan, and of the eternal inheritance among the saints in light.

13. *But the house of Israel rebelled.* They acted in the wilderness just as they had done in Egypt, and He spared them there for the same reason. See v. 9.

15. *I lifted up my hand.* Their provocations in the wilderness were so great that I vowed never to bring them into the Promised Land. I did not consume them, but I disinherited them.

18. *But I said unto their children.* These I chose in their fathers' stead, and to them I purposed to give the inheritance which their fathers by disobedience lost.

22. *I withdrew mine hand.* I had just lifted it up to crush them as in a moment; for they also were idolatrous, and walked in the steps of their fathers.

25. *I gave them also statutes that were not good.* The simple meaning of this place and all such places is that, when they had rebelled against the Lord, despised His statutes, and polluted His Sabbaths—in effect cast Him off, and given themselves wholly to their idols— then He abandoned them, and they abandoned themselves to the customs and ordinances of the heathen.

26. *I polluted them in their own gifts.* I permitted them to pollute themselves by the offerings which they made to their idols.

29. *What is the high place?* What is it good for? Its being a place shows it to be a place of idolatry.

31. *Ye pollute yourselves.* This shows the sense in which God says, v. 26, "I polluted them in their own gifts." They chose to pollute themselves, and I permitted them to do so.

32. *And that which cometh into your mind.* You wish to be naturalized among idolaters. But this shall not be at all; you shall be preserved as a distinct people. You shall not be permitted to mingle yourselves with the people of those countries; even they, idolaters as they are, will despise and reject you.

35. *I will bring you into the wilderness of the people.* I will bring you out of your captivity, and bring you into your own land, which

you will find to be a wilderness, the consequence of your crimes. *There will I plead with you.* There I will be your King, and rule you with a sovereign rule; and the dispensations of My justice and mercy shall either end you or mend you.

37. *I will cause you to pass under the rod.* This alludes to the custom of tithing the sheep. I take it from the rabbins. The sheep were all penned; and the shepherd stood at the door of the fold, where only one sheep could come out at once. He had in his hand a rod dipped in vermillion; and as they came out, he counted one, two, three, four, five, six, seven, eight, nine; and as the tenth came out, he marked it with the rod, and said, "This is the tenth"; and that was set apart for the Lord. *I will bring you into the bond of the covenant.* You shall be placed under the same obligations as before, and acknowledge yourselves bound; you shall feel your obligation, and live according to its nature.

38. *I will purge out from among you the rebels.* The incorrigibly wicked I will destroy, those who will not receive Him whom I have appointed for this purpose as the Saviour of Israel.

39. *Go ye, serve ye every one his idols.* Thus God gave them statutes that were not good, and judgments whereby they could not live, by thus permitting them to take their own way, serve their gods, and follow the maxims and rites of that abominable worship.

40. *For in mine holy mountain.* The days shall come in which all true Israelites shall receive Him whom I have sent to be the true Sacrifice for the life of the world; and shall bring to Jerusalem, the pure Christian Church, their offerings, which I will there accept, for they will give Me thanks for My unspeakable Gift.

42. *And ye shall know.* "Shall acknowledge" *that I am* Jehovah.

43. *And there shall ye remember your ways.* You shall be ashamed of your past conduct, and of your long opposition to the gospel of your salvation. These promises may, in a certain limited sense, be applied to the restoration from the Babylonish captivity; but they must have their proper fulfilment when the Jews shall accept Jesus as their Saviour, and in consequence be brought back from all their dispersions to their own land.

46. *Set thy face toward the south.* Towards Judea, which lay south from Babylon, or Mesopotamia, where the prophet then dwelt. *The forest of the south field.* The city of Jerusalem, as full of inhabitants as the forest is of trees.

47. *I will kindle a fire.* I will send war, *and it shall devour every green tree,* the most eminent and substantial of the inhabitants; *and every dry tree,* the lowest and meanest also. *The flaming flame shall not be quenched.* The fierce ravages of Nebuchadnezzar and the Chaldeans shall not be stopped till the whole land is ruined. *All faces from the south to the north shall be burned.* From the one end of the land to the other there shall be nothing but fear, dismay, terror, and confusion, occasioned by the wide-wasting violence of the Chaldeans. Judea lay in length from north to south.

48. *All flesh.* All the people shall see that this war is a judgment of the Lord. *It shall not be quenched.* Till the whole land shall be utterly ruined.

CHAPTER 21

The prophet goes on to denounce the fate of Jerusalem and Judea, using signs of vehement grief to denote the greatness of the calamity, 1-7. He then changes the emblem to that of a sharp and bright sword, still denoting the same sad event, 8-17; and, becoming yet more explicit, he represents the king of Babylon, who was to be employed by God in this work, as setting out to take vengeance on both the Jews and the Ammonites, for joining with Egypt in a confederacy against him. He is described as standing at the parting of the roads leading to the respective capitals of the Jews and Ammonites; and doubting which to attack first, he commits the decision of the matter to his arts of divination, performed by mingling arrows inscribed with the names of the different nations or cities, and then marching against that whose name was written on the arrow first drawn from the quiver. In this case the name Jerusalem comes forward; and therefore he proceeds against it, 18-24. History itself could scarcely be more explicit than this prophecy. The profane prince Zedekiah is then declared to be given up by God, and his kingdom devoted to utter destruction, for that breach of oath of which the prophet foretells he should be guilty, 25-27. The remaining verses form a distinct prophecy rel ting to the destruction of the Ammonites, which was fulfilled about five years after the destruction of Jerusalem, 28-32.

2. *Set thy face toward Jerusalem.* This is a continuation of the preceding prophecy; and in this chapter the prophet sets before them, in the plainest language, what the foregoing metaphors meant, so that they could not complain of his parables.

3. *Behold, I am against thee.* Dismal news! When God is against us, who can be for us? *And will draw forth my sword.* War. *And will cut off from thee.* The land of Judea.

4. *From the south to the north.* The whole land shall be ravaged from one end to the other.

5. *It shall not return any more.* That is, till all the work that I have designed for it is done. Nor did it; for Nebuchadnezzar never rested till he had subdued all the lands from the south to the north, from the Euphrates to the Nile.

6. *Sigh . . . with the breaking of thy loins.* Let your mourning for this sore calamity be like that of a woman in the pains of travail.

7. *Wherefore sighest thou?* The prophet was a sign unto them. His sighing and mourning showed them how they should act.

10. *It contemneth the rod of my son.* It, the sword of Nebuchadnezzar, *contemneth the rod,* despises the power of influence, *of my son* —Israel, the Jewish people.

13. *Because it is a trial.* This will be a trial of strength and skill between the Chaldeans and the Jews, and a trial of faith and patience to the righteous. *And what if the sword* (Nebuchadnezzar) *contemn even the rod?* Overthrow Zedekiah? It will do so, for the regal government of Judea shall be no more. Or, "it is tried"; that is, the sword. Nebuchadnezzar has already shown himself strong and skillful.

14. *Let the sword be doubled the third time.* The sword has been doubled, and it shall come the third time. Nebuchadnezzar came against Judea thrice: (1) against Jehoiakim, (2) against Jeconiah, (3) against Zedekiah. The sword had already been doubled; it is to come now the third time, i.e., against Zedekiah. *The sword of the slain.* "The sword of the soldiers" of the Chaldeans. So in the next clause, "It is the sword of that great soldier," that eminent king and conqueror.

15. *Wrapped up.* It is not a blunt sword; it is carefully sharpened and preserved for the slaughter.

16. *Go thee one way or other.* You shall prosper, O sword, whithersoever you turn— against Ammon, or Judea, or Egypt.

19. *Appoint thee two ways.* Set off from Babylon, and lay down two ways, either of which you may take: that to the right, which leads to Jerusalem; or that to the left, which leads to Rabbath of the Ammonites, v. 20. But why against the Ammonites? Because both they and the Moabites were united with Zedekiah against the Chaldeans (see Jer. xxvii. 3), though they afterwards fought against Judea, chap. xii. 6.

21. *For the king of Babylon stood at the parting of the way.* He was in doubt which way he should first take, whether to humble the Ammonites by taking their metropolis, Riblath, or to go at once against Jerusalem. In this case of uncertainty he made use of divination. And this was of three kinds: (1) by *arrows,* (2) by *images* or talismans, (3) by inspecting the entrails of a sacrifice offered on the occasion.

22. *At his right hand was the divination for Jerusalem.* He had probably written on two arrows: one, Jerusalem; the other, Riblath; the third, left blank. He drew, and that on which Jerusalem was written came to his hand, in consequence of which he marched immediately against that city. It was ripe for destruction, and had he marched before or after, it would have fallen; but he never considered himself as sure of the conquest till now.

23. *To them that have sworn oaths.* To Zedekiah and his ministers, who had bound themselves by the oath of the Lord to be faithful to the Chaldeans, and to pay them the promised tribute. The oaths may refer, further, to the alliances formed with the Egyptians, Ammonites, and others. They will not believe that Nebuchadnezzar shall succeed against them, while they expect the powerful assistance of the Egyptians.

25. *And thou, profane wicked prince of Israel.* Zedekiah, called here *profane,* because he had broken his oath; and *wicked,* because of his opposition to God and His prophet.

26. *Exalt him that is low.* Give Gedaliah the government of Judea. *Abase him that is high.* Depose Zedekiah—remove his diadem, and take off his crown.

27. *I will overturn.* I will utterly destroy the Jewish government. *Until he come whose . . . is.* I.e., till the coming of the Son of David, the Lord Jesus, who, in a mystic and spiritual sense, shall have the throne of Israel, and *whose right it is.* See the famous prophecy, Gen. xlix. 10, and Luke i. 32. The *overturn* is thrice repeated here to point out, say the rabbins, the three conquests of Jerusalem, in which Jehoiakim, Jeconiah, and Zedekiah were overthrown.

28. *Concerning the Ammonites.* They had reproached and insulted Judea in its low estate; see chap. xxv. This prophecy against them was fulfilled about five years after the taking of Jerusalem. See Joseph. *Ant.,* lib. x; c. 11; and Jeremiah xxvii; xlviii; xlix; Ezekiel xxv.

30. *I will judge thee.* This seems to refer to Nebuchadnezzar, who, after his return from Jerusalem, became insane, and lived like a beast for seven years; but was afterwards restored, and acknowledged the Lord.

CHAPTER 22

This chapter contains a recital of ths sins of Jerusalem, 1-12; for which God threatens it with severe judgments, 13-16, in order to purify it from the dross, 17-22. And as the corruption is general, pervading prophets, priests, princes, and people, so, it is declared, shall be the punishment, 23-31.

2. *Wilt thou judge the bloody city?* Pronounce the sentence of death against the murderers. *Shew her all her abominations.* And a most revolting and dreadful catalogue of these is in consequence exhibited.

3. *Her time may come.* Till now, it was My long-suffering; she has fulfilled her days—completed the time of her probation; has not mended, but is daily worse; therefore her judgment can linger no longer.

5. *Those that be near.* Both distant as well as neighboring provinces consider you the most abandoned of characters, and through you many have been involved in distress and ruin.

6. *Behold, the princes.* You are a vile and murderous people, and your princes have been of the same character.

7. *In thee have they set light.* The children do not reverence their parents. The stranger is not only not succored, but he is oppressed. The widows and fatherless are vexed by wrongs and exactions.

8. *Thou hast despised.* All My ordinances are not only neglected, but treated with contempt, and My Sabbaths profaned. There is not only no power of godliness among you, but there is no form.

9. *In thee are men that carry tales.* Witnesses that will swear anything, even where life is concerned. *They eat upon the mountains.* Sacrifice to idols, and celebrate their festivals.

10. *In thee have they discovered.* They are guilty of the most abominable incest and unnatural lust. *In thee have they humbled.* In their unholy and unnatural connections, they have not abstained from those set apart because of their infirmities. The catalogue of crimes that follow is too plain to require comment.

18. *The house of Israel is to me become dross.* You must be put in the furnace, and subjected to the most intense fire, till your impurities are consumed away.

19. *I will gather you.* Jerusalem is represented here as the fining pot; all the people are to be gathered together in it, and the Chaldean fire is to melt the whole. And God will increase your sufferings; as the refiner blows the fire with his bellows, so God will blow upon you with the fire of His wrath, v. 21.

25. *There is a conspiracy.* The false prophets have united together to say and support the same things; and have been the cause of the destruction of souls, and the death of many, so that widows, through their means, are multiplied in you.

26. *Her priests.* Even they whose lips should preserve knowledge have not instructed the people; they have violated My law, not only in their private conduct, but in their careless and corrupt manner of serving in My temple.

27. *Her princes.* Are as bad as her priests; they are rapacious, and grievously oppress the people by unjust impositions in order to increase their revenues.

28. *Her prophets.* Even those who profess themselves to be My prophets have been unfaithful in the discharge of their office; have soothed the people in their sins, and pretended to have oracles of peace and safety when I had not spoken to them.

30. *I sought for a man.* I saw that there was a grievous breach made in the moral state of the people, and I sought for a man that would *stand in the gap;* that would faithfully exhort, reprove, and counsel, with all long-suffering and doctrine. But none was to be found!

CHAPTER 23

The idolatries of Samaria and Jerusalem are represented in this chapter by the bad practices of two common harlots, for which God denounces severe judgments against them, 1-49. See the sixteenth chapter, where the same metaphor is enlarged upon as here, it being the prophet's view to excite the utmost detestation of the crime against which he inveighs.

2. *Son of man, there were two women.* All the Hebrews were derived from one source, Abraham and Sarah; and, till the schism under Rehoboam, formed but one people. But as these ten tribes and a half separated from Judah and Benjamin, they became two distinct people under different kings, called the kingdom of Judah, and the kingdom of Israel. They are called here, because of their consanguinity, two sisters. The elder, Samaria, was called *Aholah,* "a tent." The younger, Judah, was called *Aholibah,* "my tent is in her," because the temple of God was in Jerusalem, the seat of the government of the kingdom of Judah.

5. *And Aholah played the harlot.* Without entering into detail here, or following the figures, they both became idolatrous, and received the impure rites of the Egyptians, Assyrians, and Chaldeans, of which connection the prophet speaks here as he did in chap. xvi.

In this chapter there are many of what we would call indelicate expressions, because a parallel is run between idolatry and prostitution, and the circumstances of the latter illustrate the peculiarities of the former. In such cases, perhaps, the matter alone was given to the prophet, and he was left to use his own language and amplify as he saw good. Ezekiel was among the Jews what Juvenal was among the Romans—a rough reprover of the most abominable vices. They both spoke of things as they found them; stripped vice naked, and scourged it publicly.

6. *Clothed with blue.* The "purple" dye was highly valued among the ancients, and at first was used only by kings; at last it was used among the military, particularly by officers of high rank in the country.

14. *Men pourtrayed upon the wall.* See chap. viii. 10.

23. *Pekod, and Shoa, and Koa.* These names have been thought to designate certain people bordering on the Chaldeans, but no geographer has ever been able to find them out. In our old translations these names were considered

appellatives—"rulers, mighty men, and tyrants." Others, following the literal import of the words, have translated, "visiting, shouting, and retreating."

25. *Shall take away thy nose.* A punishment frequent among the Persians and Chaldeans, as ancient authors tell.

32. *Thou shalt drink of thy sisters' cup.* You shall be ruined and desolated as Samaria was.

38. *They have defiled my sanctuary.* By placing idols there.

41. *And satest upon a stately bed.* Hast raised a stately altar to your idols, probably alluding to that which Ahaz ordered to be made, after the similitude of that which he saw at Damascus. The *bed* here is in allusion to the sofas on which the ancients were accustomed to recline at their meals, or to the couches on which they place Asiatic brides, with incense pots and sweetmeats on a table before them.

42. *And a voice of a multitude.* This seems to be an account of an idolatrous festival, where a riotous multitude was assembled, and fellows of the baser sort, with bracelets on their arms and chaplets on their heads, performed the religious rites.

45. *And the righteous men.* The Chaldeans, thus called because they are appointed by God to execute judgment on these criminals.

47. *Shall stone them with stones.* As they did adulteresses under the law. See Lev. xx. 10; Deut. xxii. 22, compared with John viii. 3.

48. *Thus will I cause lewdness to cease.* Idolatry; and from that time to the present day the Jews never relapsed into idolatry.

49. *Ye shall bear the sins of your idols.* The punishment due to your adultery; your apostasy from God, and setting up idolatry in the land.

CHAPTER 24

The prophet now informs those of the Captivity of the very day on which Nebuchadnezzar was to lay siege to Jerusalem (compare Jer. lii. 4,) and describes the fate of that city and its inhabitants by a very apt similitude, 1-14. As another sign of the greatness of those calamities, the prophet is forbidden to mourn for his wife, of whom he is to be deprived; intimating thereby that the sufferings of the Jews should be so astonishing as to surpass all expressions of grief; and that private sorrow, however affectionate and tender the object, ought to be absorbed in the public calamities, 15-18. The prophet, having further expressed his prediction in plain terms, intimates that he was to speak to them no more till they should have the news of these prophecies having been fulfilled, 19-27.

1. *The ninth year.* This prophecy was given in the ninth year of Zedekiah, the very day in which the king of Babylon commenced the siege of Jerusalem.

3. *Set on a pot.* The pot was Jerusalem; the flesh, the inhabitants in general; "every good piece, the thigh, and the shoulder," King Zedekiah and his family; the "bones," the soldiers; and the setting on the pot, the commencement of the siege. The prophet was then in Mesopotamia; and he was told particularly to mark the day, that it might be seen how precisely the spirit of prophecy had shown the very day in which the siege took place. Under the same image of a boiling pot, Jeremiah had represented the siege of Jerusalem, chap. i. 13. Ezekiel was a priest; the action of boiling pots was familiar to him, as these things were much in use in the Temple service.

5. *Make it boil well.* Let it boil over, that its own scum may augment the fire, that the *bones*—the soldiers—may be seethed therein. Let its contentions, divided counsels, and disunion be the means of increasing its miseries.

6. *Let no lot fall upon it.* Pull out the flesh indiscriminately; let no piece be chosen for king or priest, thus showing that all should be involved in one indiscriminate ruin.

7. *For her blood is in the midst of her.* She gloried in her idol sacrifices; she offered them upon a rock, where the blood should remain evident; and she poured none upon the ground to cover it with dust, in horror of that moral evil that required the blood of an innocent creature to be shed, in order to the atonement of the offender's guilt. To cover the blood of the victim, was a command of the law, Lev. xvii. 13; Deut. xii. 24.

8. *That it might cause fury.* This very blood shall be against them, as the blood of Abel was against Cain.

10. *Heap on wood.* Let the siege be severe, the carnage great, and the ruin and catastrophe complete.

13. *In thy filthiness is lewdness.* Zimmah, a word that denominates the worst kinds of impurity; adultery, incest, and the purpose, wish, design, and ardent desire to do these things.

16. *Behold, I take away from thee the desire of thine eyes.* Here is an intimation that the stroke he was to suffer was to be above all grief, that it would be so great as to prevent the relief of tears.

17. *Make no mourning.* As a priest, he could make no public mourning, Lev. xxi. 1, etc. *Bind the tire of thine head.* This seems to refer to the high priest's bonnet, or perhaps one worn by the ordinary priests. It might have been a black veil to cover the head. *Put on thy shoes upon thy feet.* Walking barefoot was a sign of grief. *Cover not thy lips.* Mourners covered the under part of the face, from the nose to the bottom of the chin. *Eat not the bread of men.* "the bread of miserable men," i.e., mourners; probably, the funeral banquet.

18. *At even my wife died.* The prophet's wife was a type of the city, which was to him exceedingly dear. The death of his wife represented the destruction of the city by the Chaldeans; see v. 21, where the Temple is represented to be the desire of his eyes, as his wife was, v. 16.

19. *Wilt thou not tell us?* In the following verses he explains and applies the whole of what he had done and said.

27. *In that day shall thy mouth be opened.* That is, When someone who shall have escaped from Jerusalem, having arrived among the captives, shall inform them of the destruction of the city, the Temple, the royal family, and the people at large, till then he might suppress his tears and lamentations. And we find from chap. xxxiii. 21 that one did actually escape from the city, and informed the prophet and his brethren in captivity that the city was smitten. Thus he was not only a prophet to foretell such things, but he was also a sign or portent, shadowing them out by circumstances in his own person and family; and thus the prediction,

agreeing so perfectly with the event, proved that the previous information was from the Lord.

CHAPTER 25

This chapter contains threatenings of the heavy judgments of God against the Ammonites, 1-7; Moabites, 8-11; Edomites, 12-14; and Philistines, 15-17; on account of their hatred to His people, and their insulting them in the time of their distress. These prophecies were fulfilled by the instrumentality of Nebuchadnezzar, about five years after the destruction of Jerusalem. The same events were predicted by several of the other prophets, as may be seen from the citation of parallel texts in the margin.

1. *The word of the Lord.* The chronological order of this chapter is after chap. xxxiii. 21, etc.

2. *Set thy face against the Ammonites.* We have already seen, chap. xxi. 19, etc., that when Nebuchadnezzar left Babylon, he was in doubt whether he should besiege Riblath, the capital of the Ammonites, or Jerusalem, the capital of the Jews, first; and having used his divination, he was determined, by the result, to attack Jerusalem the first. He did so; and the Ammonites, seeing the success of his arms, made friends with him, and exulted in the ruin of the Jews. God resents this, and predicts their downfall with that of Edom, Moab, and the Philistines. The fulfillment of this prediction is not noted in Scripture, but Josephus tells us that, about five years after the taking of Jerusalem, Nebuchadnezzar turned his arms against the Ammonites and Moabites, and afterwards against Egypt; and having subdued those nations, he returned to Babylon (Joseph. *Antiq.* l. x., c. ii).

7. *I will cause thee to perish.* Except in history, the name of the Ammonites does not now exist.

8. *Moab and Seir do say. Seir* means the Idumeans. It appears that both these, with the Ammonites, had made a league with Zedekiah, Jer. xxvii. 3, which they did not keep; and it is supposed that they even joined with the Chaldeans.

9. *I will open the side. Ketheph,* the shoulder, the strongest frontier place. *Beth-jeshimoth, Baal-meon, and Kiriathaim* were strong frontier towns of Moab.

12. *Because that Edom hath dealt.* The Edomites were the most inveterate enemies of the Jews from the very earliest times, and ever did all that they could to annoy them.

13. *I will make it desolate from Teman.* Teman and Dedan were both cities of the Moabites, and apparently at each extremity of the land.

14. *I will lay my vengeance upon Edom.* God will not allow men to insult those whom He has cast down. His judgment is sufficient; to add more is an insult to God. *By the hand of my people Israel.* This was fulfilled by the Maccabees, who not only defeated them and brought them under complete subjection, but obliged them to receive circumcision (Joseph. *Antiq.* l. xiii., c. 17; 1 Macc. v. 65).

15. *Because the Philistines.* They were as inimical to the Jews as the Ammonites were. Nebuchadnezzar punished them because they had assisted the Tyrians during the time he was besieging their city.

16. *I will cut off the Cherethims.* See 2 Sam. viii. 18. *The remnant of the sea coast.* The different seignories of the Philistines inhabited the coast of the Mediterranean Sea, from Judea to Egypt. For other matters relative to these prophecies, see the passages in the margin.

CHAPTER 26

This prophecy, beginning here and ending in the twentieth verse of the twenty-eighth chapter, is a declaration of the judgments of God against Tyre, a very famous commercial city of antiquity, which was taken by Nebuchadnezzar after an arduous siege of thirteen years. The prophet begins with introducing Tyre insulting Jerusalem, and congratulating herself on the prospect of accession to her commerce now that this city was no more, 1-2. Upon which God denounces utter destruction to Tyre, and the cities depending on her, 3-6. We have then a particular account of the person raised up in the course of the divine providence to accomplish this work. We see, as it were, His mighty hosts (which are likened to the caves of the sea for their multitude) raising the mounds, setting the engines, and shaking the walls; we hear the noise of the horsemen, and the sound of their cars; we see the clouds of smoke and dust; we see the sword bathed in blood, and hear the groans of the dying. Tyre (whose buildings were very splendid and magnificent, and whose walls were 150 feet in height, with a proportionable breadth) immediately disappears; her strong (and as she thought impregnable) towers are thrown down; and her very dust is buried in the sea. Nothing remains but the bare rock, 7-14. The scene is then varied. The isles and adjacent regions, by a very strong and beautiful figure, are represented to be shaken, as with a mighty earthquake by violent concussion occasioned by the fall of Tyre. The groans of the dying reach the ears of the people inhabiting these regions. Their princes, alarmed for themselves and grieved for Tyre, descend from their thrones, lay aside their robes, and clothe themselves with—sackcloth?—no, but with trembling! Arrayed in this astonishing attire, the prophet introduces them as a chorus of mourners, lamenting Tyre in a funeral song or dirge, as customary on the death of renowned personages. And pursuing the same image still further, in the person of God, He performs the last sad office for her. She is brought forth from her place in solemn pomp; the pit is dug for her; and she is buried, to rise no more, 15-21. Such is the prophecy concerning Tyre, comprehending both the city on the continent and that on the island, and most punctually fulfilled in regard to both. That on the continent was razed to the ground by Nebuchadnezzar, 572 B.C., and that on the island by Alexander the Great, 332 B.C. And at present, and for ages past, this ancient and renowned city, once the emporium of the world, and by her great naval superiority the center of a powerful monarchy, is literally what the prophet has repeatedly foretold it should be, and what in his time was, humanly speaking, so highly improbable—a bare rock, a place to spread nets on!

1. *The eleventh year.* This was the year in which Jerusalem was taken; the eleventh of the captivity of Jeconiah, and the eleventh of the reign of Zedekiah.

2. *Tyrus hath said.* From this it would appear that Jerusalem had been taken, which was on the fourth month of this year; but it is possible that the prophet speaks of the event beforehand. *She is broken that was the gates of the people.* Jerusalem, a general emporium. *I shall be replenished.* The merchandise that went to Jerusalem will come to me (to Tyre).

3. *Will cause many nations to come up against thee.* We have already seen that the empire of the Chaldeans was composed of many different provinces, and that Nebuchadnezzar's army was composed of soldiers from different nations. These may be the people meant, but I doubt whether this may not refer to the different nations which in successive ages fought against Tyre. It was at last finally destroyed in the sixteenth century of the Christian era.

4. *I will also scrape her dust from her.* I will totally destroy her fortifications, and leave her nothing but a barren rock, as she was before. This cannot refer to the capture of Tyre by

Nebuchadnezzar. It flourished long after his time.

5. *A place for the spreading of nets.* A place for the habitation of some poor fishermen, who spent the fishing season there, and were accustomed to dry their nets upon the rocks. See v. 11.

6. *And her daughters.* The places dependent on Tyre. As there were two places called Tyre, one on the mainland, and the other on a rock in the sea, opposite to that on the mainland, sometimes the one seems to be spoken of, and sometimes the other. That on the land was soon taken; but that in the sea cost Nebuchadnezzar thirteen years of siege and blockade. The two formed only one city, and one state.

7. *Nebuchadrezzar . . . king of kings.* An ancient title among those proud Asiatic despots.

8. *Thy daughters in the field.* This seems to be spoken of Tyre on the mainland.

12. *And they shall lay thy stones and thy timber and thy dust in the midst of the water.* This answers to the taking of Tyre by Alexander; he actually took the timbers, stones, rubbish, etc., of old Tyre, and filled up the space between it and new Tyre, and thus connected the latter with the mainland; and this he was obliged to do before he could take it.

14. *Thou shalt be built no more.* If this refer to Nebuchadnezzar's capture of the city, old Tyre must be intended; that was destroyed by him, and never rebuilt. But I doubt whether the whole of this prophecy do not refer to the taking of Tyre by Alexander, 300 years after its capture by Nebuchadnezzar.

15. *The isles shake at the sound of thy fall.* All those which had traded with this city, which was the grand mart, and on which they all depended. Her ruin involved them all, and caused general wailing.

17. *Wast strong in the sea.* The strength of Tyre was so great that Alexander despaired of being able to reduce it unless he could fill up that arm of the sea that ran between it and the mainland. And this work cost his army seven months of labor.

20. *And I shall set glory in the land of the living.* Judea so called, the land of the living God.

CHAPTER 27

This chapter may be considered as the second part of the prophecy concerning Tyre. The prophet pursues his subject in the manner of those ancient lamentations or funeral songs, in which the praeficiae or mourning women first recounted whatever was great or praiseworthy in the deceased, and then mourned his fall. Here the riches, glory, and extensive commerce of Tyre are enlarged upon, 1-25. Her downfall is then described in a beautiful allegory, executed in a few words, with astonishing brevity, propriety, and perspicuity, 26; upon which all the maritime and commercial world are represented as grieved and astonished at her fate, and greatly alarmed for their own, 27-36. Besides the view which this chapter gives of the conduct of Providence, and the example with which it furnishes the critic and man of taste of a very elegant and highly finished piece of composition, it likewise affords the antiquary a very curious and interesting account of the wealth and commerce of ancient times. And to the mind that looks for "a city that hath foundations," what a picture does the whole present of the mutability and inanity of all earthly things! Many of the places mentioned in ancient history have, like Tyre, long ago lost their political consequence; the geographical situation of others cannot be traced; they have sunk in the deep waters of oblivion; the east wind hath carried them away.

2. *Take up a lamentation for Tyrus.* This is a singular and curious chapter. It gives a very circumstantial account of the trade of Tyre with different parts of the world, and the different sorts of merchandise in which she trafficked. The places and the imports are as regularly entered here as they could have been in a European customhouse.

3. *The entry of the sea.* Tyre was a small island, or rather rock, in the sea, at a short distance from the mainland. We have already seen that there was another Tyre on the mainland, but they are both considered as one city.

4. *Thy builders have perfected thy beauty.* Under the allegory of a beautiful ship, the prophet, here and in the following verses, paints the glory of this ancient city.

5. *Fir trees of Senir. Senir* is a mountain which the Sidonians called Sirion, and the Hebrews "Hermon," Deut. iii. 9. It was beyond Jordan, and extended from Libanus to the mountains of Gilead.

6. *Of the oaks of Bashan.* Some translate "alder," others the "pine." *The company of the Ashurites.* The word *asherim* is by several translated "boxwood." The "seats" or *benches* being made of this wood inlaid with *ivory. Isles of Chittim.* The Italian islands; the islands of Greece; Cyprus.

8. *Zidon and Arvad.* Two powerful cities on the Phoenician coast, in the neighborhood of Tyre, from which Tyre had her sailors; and the best instructed of her own inhabitants were her pilots or steersmen.

9. *The ancients of Gebal.* This was a city of Phoenicia, near Mount Libanus, Josh. xiii. 5. It was called Biblos by the Greeks. *Thy calkers.* Those who repaired their vessels.

10. *They of Persia. Lud,* the Lydians; *Phut,* a people of Africa—see Gen. x. 6. From these places they had auxiliary troops; for as they traded with the then known world, were rich, and could afford to give good pay, they no doubt had soldiers and sailors from every part.

11. *The Gammadims were in thy towers.* Some think these were a people of Phoenicia; others, that tutelar images are meant; others, that the word expresses strong men, who acted as guards.

12. *Tarshish was thy merchant.* After having given an account of the naval and military equipment of this city, he now speaks of the various places and peoples with whom the Tyrians traded, and the different kinds of merchandise imported from those places.

13. *Javan, Tubal, and Meshech.* The Ionians, the Tybarenians, and the Cappadocians, or Muscovites. *They traded the persons of men.* That is, they trafficked in slaves. The bodies and souls of men were bought and sold in those days, as in our degenerate age. With these also they traded in brazen vessels.

15. *The men of Dedan.* Dedan was one of the descendants of Abraham by Keturah, and dwelt in Arabia, Gen. xxv. 3. Ivory and ebony might come from that quarter. By way of distinction ivory is called both in Hebrew *shen,* and in Arabic *shen,* the "tooth," as that beautiful substance is the tooth of the elephant.

16. *Syria.* These were always a mercantile

people. For the precious stones mentioned here see Exod. xxviii. 17.

17. *Judah, and the land of Israel . . . traded in thy market wheat.* The words have been understood as articles of merchandise, not names of places. So the Jews traded with the Tyrians in wheat, stacte, balsam, honey, oil, and resin.

18. *Damascus . . . wine of Helbon.* Now called by the Turks Haleb, and by us Aleppo. *White wool.* Very fine wool, wool of a fine quality.

19. *Dan also and Javan.* It is probable that both these words mean some of the Grecian islands. *Going to and fro.* They both imported and exported; but *meuzal* may be a proper name.

20. *Dedan.* Possibly the descendants of Dedan, son of Raamah; see Gen. x. 7. *In precious clothes for chariots.* Either fine carpets, or rich housings for horses, camels, etc., used for riding.

22. *Sheba and Raamah.* Inhabitants of Arabia Felix, at the entrance of the Persian Gulf, who were famous for their riches and spices.

23. *Haran.* In Mesopotamia; well-known in Scripture. *Canneh.* It is supposed to be a cape or port of Arabia Felix, on the Indian Sea. *Eden.* Equally famous; supposed to have been situated near the confluence of the Tigris and Euphrates. *Sheba.* Different from that in v. 22. This was probably near the country of the Edomites. *Asshur.* Perhaps the Assyrians.

24. *These were thy merchants in all sorts of things.* The above people traded with the Tyrians in a great variety of the most valuable merchandise.

26. *Thy rowers have brought thee into great waters.* Tyre is still considered under the allegory of a ship; and all the vessels of different nations trading with her are represented as towing her into deep waters—bringing her into great affluence. But while in this state, a stormy *east wind*, or a destructive wind, meaning the Chaldeans, arises, and dashes her to pieces!

27. *Thy riches.* This vast ship, laden with all kinds of valuable wares, and manned in the best manner, being wrecked, all her valuables, sailors, officers, went to the bottom.

28. *The cry of thy pilots.* When the ship was dashed against the rocks by the violence of the winds and the waves, and all hope of life was taken away, then a universal cry was set up by all on board.

CHAPTER 28

The first part of this chapter relates to a king of Tyre, probably the same who is called in the Phoenician annals Ithobalus. He seems to have been a vain man, who affected divine honors. The prophet treats his foolish pretensions with severe irony, and predicts his doom, 1-10. He then takes up a funeral dirge and lamentation over him, in which his former pomp and splendor are finely contrasted with his fall, in terms that seem frequently to allude to the fall of Lucifer from heaven (Isa. xiv), 11-19. The overthrow of Sidon, the mother city of Tyre, is next announced, 20-23; and the chapter concludes with a promise to the Jews of deliverance from all their enemies, and particularly of their restoration from the Babylonish captivity, 24-26.

2. *Say unto the prince of Tyrus.* But who was this prince of Tyrus? Some think Hiram; some, Sin; some, the devil. *I am a god.* That is, I am absolute, independent, and accountable

to none. He was a man of great pride and arrogance.

3. *Thou art wiser than Daniel.* Daniel was at this time living, and was reputable for his great wisdom. This is said ironically. See chap. xiv. 14; xxvi. 1.

5. *By thy great wisdom.* He attributed everything to himself; he did not acknowledge a divine providence. As he got all by himself, so he believed he could keep all by himself, and had no need of any foreign help.

7. *I will bring strangers upon thee.* The Chaldeans.

9. *Wilt thou yet say before him that slayeth thee?* Will you continue your pride and arrogance when the sword is sheathed in you, and still imagine that you are self-sufficient and independent?

12. *Thou sealest up.* This has been translated, "Thou drawest thy own likeness." "Thou formest a portrait of thyself; and hast represented thyself the perfection of wisdom and beauty." I believe this to be the meaning of the place.

13. *Thou hast been in Eden.* This also is a strong irony. Thou art like Adam, when in his innocence and excellence he was in the Garden of Eden!

14. *Thou art the anointed cherub that covereth.* The irony is continued; and here he is likened to the cherub that guarded the gates of paradise, and kept the way of the tree of life; or to one of the cherubs whose wings, spread out, covered the mercy seat. *Thou wast upon the holy mountain of God.* The irony is still continued; and now he is compared to Moses, and afterwards to one of the chief angels, who has walked up and down among the stones of fire; that is, your floors have been paved with precious stones, that shone and sparkled like fire.

15. *Thou wast perfect in thy ways.* The irony seems still to be kept up. You have been like the angels, like Moses, like the cherubs, like Adam, like God, till your iniquity was found out.

16. *I will cast thee as profane.* You shall be cast down from your eminence. *From the midst of the stones of fire.* Some, supposing that *stones of fire* means the stars, have thought that the whole refers to the fall of Satan.

18. *Thou hast defiled thy sanctuaries.* Irony continued. As God, as the angels, as the cherubim, you must have had your sanctuaries, but you have defiled them; and as Adam, you have polluted your Eden, and have been expelled from paradise.

19. *Thou shalt be a terror.* Instead of being an object of adoration you shall be a subject of horror, and at last be destroyed with your city, so that nothing but your name shall remain. It was entirely burnt by Alexander the Great, as it had been before by Nebuchadnezzar.

22. *I am against thee, O Zidon.* Sidon for a long time had possessed the empire of the sea and of all Phoenicia, and Tyre was one of its colonies; but in process of time the daughter became greater than the mother. It seems to have been an independent place at the time in which Tyre was taken, but it is likely that

it was taken by the Chaldeans soon after the former.

23. *And the wounded.* Chalal, "the soldiery." All its supports shall be taken away, and its defenders destroyed.

24. *There shall be no more a pricking brier.* Nothing to excite Israel to idolatry when restored from their captivity. Sidon being destroyed, there would come no encourager of idolatry from that quarter.

CHAPTER 29

This and the three following chapters foretell the conquest of Egypt by Nebuchadnezzar, which he accomplished in the twenty-seventh year of Jehoiachin's captivity. The same event is foretold by Jeremiah, chap. xlvi. 13, etc. The prophecy opens with God's charging the king of Egypt (Pharaoh-hophra) with the same extravagant pride and profanity which were in the preceding chapter laid to the charge of the prince of Tyre. He appears, like him, to have affected divine honors; and boasted so much of the strength of his kingdom that, as an ancient historian (Herodotus) tells us, he impiously declared that God himself could not dispossess him. Wherefore the prophet, with great majesty, addresses him under the image of one of those crocodiles or monsters which inhabited that river, of whose riches and revenue he vaunted; and assures him that, with as much ease as a fisherman drags the fish he has hooked, God would drag him and his people into captivity, and that their carcasses should fall a prey to the beasts of the field and to the fowls of heaven, 1-7. The figure is then dropped; and God is introduced denouncing, in plain terms, the most awful judgments against him and his nation, and declaring that the Egyptians should be subjected to the Babylonians till the fall of the Chaldean empire, 8-12. The prophet then foretells that Egypt, which was about to be devastated by the Babylonians, and many of the people carried into captivity, should again become a kingdom, but that it should never regain its ancient political importance; for, in the lapse of time, it should be even the basest of the kingdoms, a circumstance in the prophecy most literally fulfilled, especially under the Christian dispensation, in its government by the Mameluke slaves, 13-16. The prophecy, beginning at the seventeenth verse, is connected with the foregoing, as it relates to the same subject, though delivered about seventeen years later. Nebuchadnezzar and his army, after the long siege of Tyre, which made every head bald by constantly wearing their helmets, and wore the skin off every shoulder by carrying burdens to raise the fortifications, were disappointed of the spoil which they expected, by the retiring of the inhabitants to Carthage. God, therefore, promises him Egypt for his reward, 17-20. The chapter concludes with a prediction of the return of the Jews from the Babylonish captivity, 21.

1. *In the tenth year.* Of Zedekiah; and tenth of the captivity of Jeconiah.

2. *Set thy face against Pharaoh king of Egypt.* This was Pharaoh-hophra or Pharaoh-apries, whom we have so frequently met with in the prophecies of Jeremiah, and much of whose history has been given in the notes.

3. *The great dragon.* The original signifies any large animal. *The midst of his rivers.* This refers to the several branches of the Nile by which this river empties itself into Mediterranean. The crocodile was the emblem of Egypt.

4. *I will put hooks in thy jaws.* Amasis, one of this king's generals, being proclaimed king by an insurrection of the people, dethroned Apries, and seized upon the kingdom; and Apries was obliged to flee to Upper Egypt for safety.

5. *I will leave thee thrown into the wilderness.* Referring to his being obliged to take refuge in Upper Egypt. But he was afterwards taken prisoner, and strangled by Amasis. Herod., lib. ii. x. 169.

6. *They have been a staff of reed.* An inefficient and faithless ally. The Israelites expected assistance from them when Nebuchadnezzar came against Jerusalem; and they made

a feint to help them, but retired when Nebuchadnezzar went against them. Thus were the Jews deceived and ultimately ruined; see v. 7.

10. *From the tower of Syene. Mimmigdol seveneh,* "from Migdol to Syene." Syene was the last city in Egypt, going towards Ethiopia. It was famous for a well into which the rays of the sun fell perpendicularly at midday.

12. *Shall be desolate forty years.* The country from Migdol, which was on the isthmus between the Mediterranean and the Red Sea, was so completely ruined that it might well be called desert; and it is probable that this desolation continued during the whole of the reign of Amasis, which was just forty years. See Herod., lib. iii, c. 10.

13. *Will I gather the Egyptians.* It is probable that Cyrus gave permission to the Egyptians brought to Babylon by Nebuchadnezzar to return to their own country. And if we reckon from the commencement of the war against Pharaoh-hophra by Nebuchadnezzar to the third or fourth year of Cyrus, the term will be about forty years.

14. *Into the land of Pathros.* Supposed to mean the Delta, a country included between the branches of the Nile. It may mean the *Pathrusim,* in Upper Egypt, near to the Thebaid. This is most likely.

17. *The seven and twentieth year.* That is, of the captivity of Jeconiah, fifteen years after the taking of Jerusalem. The preceding prophecy was delivered one year before the taking of Jerusalem; this, sixteen years after; and it is supposed to be the last which this prophet wrote.

18. *Caused his army to serve a great service against Tyrus.* He was thirteen years employed in the siege. See Joseph. *Antiq.,* lib. x, c. 11. In this siege his soldiers endured great hardships. Being continually on duty, their heads became bald by wearing their helmets; and their shoulders bruised and peeled by carrying baskets of earth to the fortifications, and wood, to build towers. *Yet had he no wages, nor his army.* The Tyrians, finding it at last impossible to defend their city, put all their wealth aboard their vessels, sailed out of the port, and escaped for Carthage; and thus Nebuchadnezzar lost all the spoil of one of the richest cities in the world.

20. *I have given him the land of Egypt for his labour.* Because he fulfilled the designs of God against Tyre, God promises to reward him with the spoil of Egypt.

21. *Will I cause the horn of the house of Israel to bud.* This may refer generally to the restoration; but particularly to Zerubbabel, who became one of the leaders of the people from Babylon.

CHAPTER 30

This chapter describes, with great force and elegance the ruin of Egypt and all her allies by the Chaldeans under Nebuchadnezzar, 1-11; with an amplification of the distress of the principal cities of Egypt on that occasion, 12-19. The remaining verses are a short prophecy relating to the same event, and therefore annexed to the longer one preceding, although this was predicted sooner, 20-26.

2. *Howl ye, Woe worth the day! Heylilu, hah laiyom!* "Howl ye, Alas for the day!" The expressions signify that a most dreadful calamity was about to fall on Egypt and the neighboring

countries, called here the "time of the heathen," or of the "nations," the day of calamity to them. They are afterwards specified: Ethiopia, Libya, Lydia, and Chub, and the "mingled people," probably persons from different nations, who had followed the ill fortune of Pharaoh-hophra or Pharaoh-apries, when he fled from Amasis, and settled in Upper Egypt.

5. *Lydia.* This place is not well-known. The Ludim were contiguous to Egypt, Gen. xi. 13. *Chub.* Probably instead of *vechub,* "and Chub," we should read *vechol,* "and all the men of the land," etc.

7. *Shall be desolate.* All these countries shall be desolated, and the places named shall be chief in these desolations.

9. *Messengers go forth from me in ships.* Ships can ascend the Nile up to Syene or Essuan, by the cataracts; and when Nebuchadnezzar's vessel went up, they struck terror into the Ethiopians. They are represented here as the "messengers of God."

12. *I will make the rivers dry.* As the overflowing of the Nile was the grand cause of fertility to Egypt, the drying it up, or preventing that annual inundation, must be the cause of dearth, famine, etc. By *rivers* we may understand the various canals cut from the Nile to carry water into the different parts of the land. When the Nile did not rise to its usual height; these canals were quite dry.

13. *Their images to cease out of Noph.* Afterwards Memphis, and now Cairo. This was the seat of Egyptian idolatry, the place where Apis was particularly worshipped.

14. *I will make Pathros desolate.* See the preceding chapter, v. 14. *Zoan.* Tanis, the ancient capital of Egypt. *No.* Thebes, the city of Jupiter.

15. *My fury upon Sin.* Pelusium, a strong city of Egypt, on the coast of the Mediterranean Sea.

16. *Noph.* Cairo; see v. 13.

17. *Aven.* Or On, the famous Heliopolis, or city of the sun.

18. *Tehaphnehes.* Called also Tahapanes, Jer. ii. 16. *Break there the yokes.* The sceptres. Nebuchadnezzar broke the sceptre of Egypt when he confirmed the kingdom to Amasis, who had rebelled against Apries.

20. *In the eleventh year, in the first month, in the seventh day.* This was the eleventh year of the captivity of Jeconiah; a prophecy anterior by several years to that already delivered. In collecting the writings of Ezekiel, more care was taken to put all that related to one subject together than to attend to chronological arrangement.

21. *I have broken the arm of Pharaoh.* Perhaps this may refer to his defeat by Nebuchadnezzar when he was coming with the Egyptian army to succor Jerusalem.

22. *I will cause the sword to fall out of his hand.* When the arm is broken, the sword will naturally fall. But these expressions show that the Egyptians would be rendered wholly useless to Zedekiah, and should never more recover their political strength. This was the case from the time of the rebellion of Amasis.

26. *I will scatter the Egyptians.* Several fled

with Apries to Upper Egypt; and when Nebuchadnezzar wasted the country, he carried many of them to Babylon. See chap. xxix. 12.

CHAPTER 31

This very beautiful chapter relates also to Egypt. The prophet describes to Pharaoh the fall of the king of Nineveh (see the books of Nahum, Jonah, and Zephaniah) under the image of a fair cedar of Lebanon, once exceedingly tall, flourishing, and majestic, but now cut down and withered, with its broken branches strewed around, 1-17. He then concludes with bringing the matter home to the king of Egypt by telling him that this was a picture of his approaching fate, 18. The beautiful cedar of Lebanon, remarkable for its loftiness, and in the most flourishing condition, but afterwards cut down and deserted, gives a very lively painting of the great glory and dreadful catastrophe of both the Assyrian and Egyptian monarchies. The manner in which the prophet has embellished his subject is deeply interesting; the coloring is of that kind which the mind will always contemplate with pleasure.

1. *In the eleventh year.* A month before Jerusalem was taken by the Chaldeans.

3. *Behold, the Assyrian was a cedar.* Why is the *Assyrian* introduced here, when the whole chapter concerns Egypt? Bishop Lowth has shown that *ashshur erez* should be translated "the tall cedar," "the very stately cedar." Hence there is reference to his lofty top; and all the following description belongs to Egypt, not to Assyria. But see on v. 11.

4. *The waters made him great.* Alluding to the fertility of Egypt by the overflowing of the Nile. But *waters* often mean peoples. By means of the different nations under the Egyptians, that government became very opulent. These nations are represented as fowls and beasts, taking shelter under the protection of this great, political Egyptian tree, v. 6.

8. *The cedars in the garden of God.* Egypt was one of the most eminent and affluent of all the neighboring nations.

11. *The mighty one of the heathen.* Nebuchadnezzar. It is worthy of notice that Nebuchadnezzar, in the first year of his reign, rendered himself master of Nineveh, the capital of the Assyrian empire. This happened about twenty years before Ezekiel delivered this prophecy; on this account, *Ashshur*, v. 3, may relate to the Assyrians, to whom it is possible the prophet here compares the Egyptians. But see on v. 3.

13. *Upon his ruin shall all the fowls.* The fall of Egypt is likened to the fall of a great tree; and as the fowls and beasts sheltered under its branches before, v. 6, so they now feed upon its ruins.

14. *To the end that none of all the trees.* Let this ruin, fallen upon Egypt, teach all the nations that shall hear of it to be humble, because, however elevated, God can soon bring them down; and pride and arrogance, in either states or individuals, have the peculiar abhorrence of God.

15. *I caused Lebanon to mourn for him.* All the confederates of Pharaoh are represented as deploring his fall, vv. 16-17.

17. *They also went down into hell with him.* Into remediless destruction.

18. *This is Pharaoh.* All that I have spoken in this allegory of the lofty cedar refers to Pharaoh, king of Egypt, his princes, confederates, and people.

CHAPTER 32

The prophet goes on to predict the fall of the king of Egypt, under the figure of an animal of prey, such as a lion or crocodile, caught, slain, and his carcass left a prey to the fowls and wild beasts, 1-6. The figure is then changed; and the greatness of his fall (described by the darkening of the sun, moon, and stars) strikes terror into all the surrounding nations, 7-10. The prophet adds that the overthrow of the then reigning Egyptian dynasty was to be effected by the instrumentality of the king of Babylon, who should leave Egypt so desolate that its waters, (alluding to the metaphor used in the second verse) should run as pure and smooth as oil, without the foot of man or the hoof of a beast to disturb them, 11-16. A beautiful, nervous, and concise description of a land ruined and left utterly desolate. In the remaining part of the chapter the same event is portrayed by one of the boldest figures ever attempted in any composition, and which at the same time is executed with astonishing perspicuity and force. God is introduced ordering a place in the lower regions for the king of Egypt and his host, 17-18. The prophet delivers his message, pronounces their fate, and commands those who bury the slain to drag him and his multitudes to the subterraneous mansions, 19-20. At the tumult and commotion which this mighty work occasions, the internal shades are represented as roused from their couches to learn the cause. They see and congratulate the king of Egypt, on his arrival among them, 21. Pharaoh being now introduced into this immense subterraneous cavern (see the fourteenth chapter of Isaiah, where a similar imagery is employed), the prophet leads him all around the sides of the pit; shows him the gloomy mansions of former tyrants, tells their names as he goes along; beautifully contrasts their former pomp and destructive ambition, when they were a terror to the surrounding states, with their present most abject and helpless condition; declares that all these oppressors of mankind have not only been cut off out of the land of the living, but have borne down into the grave uncircumcised—that is, they have died in their sins, and therefore shall have no resurrection to eternal life; and concludes with showing Pharaoh the place destined for him in the midst of the uncircumcised, and of them that have been slain by the sword, 22-32. This prophetic ode may be considered as a finished model in that species of writing which is appropriated to the exciting of terror. The imagery throughout is sublime and terrible; and no reader of sensibility and taste can accompany the prophet in this funeral procession, and visit the mansions of Hades, without being impressed with a degree of awe nearly approaching to horror.

1. *In the twelfth year, in the twelfth month, in the first day of the month.* The *twelfth year* of the captivity of Jeconiah.

2. *Thou art like a young lion . . . and thou art as a whale in the seas.* You may be likened to two of the fiercest animals in the creation: to a lion, the fiercest on the land; to a "crocodile," *tannim,* the fiercest in the waters. It may, however, point out the hippopotamus, as there seems to be a reference to his mode of feeding. He walks deliberately into the water over head, and pursues his way in the same manner; still keeping on his feet, and feeding on the plants, etc., that grow at the bottom. Thus he fouls the water with his feet.

6. *The land wherein thou swimmest.* Egypt; so called because intersected with canals, and overflowed annually by the Nile.

7. *I will cover the heaven.* Destroy the empire. *Make the stars thereof dark.* Overwhelm all the dependent states. *I will cover the sun.* The king himself. *And the moon shall not give her light.* The queen may be meant, or some state less than the kingdom.

8. *And set darkness upon thy land.* As I did when a former king refused to let My people go to the wilderness to worship Me. I will involve you, and your house, and your people, and the whole land, in desolation and woe.

9. *I will also vex the hearts.* Even the remote nations, who had no connection with you, shall be amazed at the judgments which have fallen upon you.

14. *Cause their rivers to run like oil.* Bring

the whole state into quietness, there being no longer a political hippopotamus to foul the waters—to disturb the peace of the country.

17. *In the twelfth year.* This prophecy concerns the people of Egypt.

18. *Cast them down.* Show them that they shall be cast down.

21. *Out of the midst of hell.* Sheol, the place of burial. There is something here similar to Isa. xiv. 9, where the descent of the king of Babylon to the state of the dead is described.

22. *Asshur is there.* The mightiest conquerors of the earth have gone down to the grave before you; there they and their soldiers lie together, all slain by the sword.

23. *Whose graves are set in the sides of the pit.* Alluding to the niches in the sides of the subterranean caves or burying places, where the bodies are laid. These are numerous in Egypt.

24. *There is Elam.* The Elamites, not far from the Assyrians; others think that Persia is meant. It was invaded by the joint forces of Cyaxares and Nebuchadnezzar.

26. *There is Meshech, Tubal.* See chap. xxvii. 13.

27. *Gone down to hell with their weapons of war.* Are buried in their armor, and with their weapons lying by their sides. It was a very ancient practice, in different nations, to bury a warrior's weapons in the same grave with himself.

29. *There is Edom.* All the glory and pomp of the Idumean kings, who also helped to oppress the Israelites, are gone down into the grave. Their kings, princes, and all their mighty men lie mingled with the *uncircumcised,* not distinguished from the common dead.

30. *There be the princes of the north.* The kings of Media and Assyria, *and all the Zidonians*—the kings of Tyre, Sidon, and Damascus.

31. *Pharaoh shall see them.* Pharaoh also, who said he was a god, shall be found among the vulgar dead. *And shall be comforted.* Shall console himself, on finding that all other proud boasters are in the same circumstances with himself. Here is a reference to a consciousness after death.

CHAPTER 33

The prophet, after having addressed several other nations, returns now to his own; previously to which he is told, as on a former occasion, the duty of a watchman, the salvation or ruin of whose soul depends on the manner in which he discharges it. An awful passage indeed; full of important instruction both to such as speak and to such as hear the word of God, 1-9. The prophet is then directed what answer to make to the cavils of infidelity and impiety; and to vindicate the equity of the divine government by declaring the general terms of acceptance with God to be (as told before, chap. xviii) without respect of persons, so that the ruin of the finally impenitent must be entirely owing to themselves, 10-20. The prophet receives the news of the destruction of Jerusalem by the Chaldeans, about a year and four months after it happened, according to the opinion of some, who have been led to this conjecture by the date given to this prophecy in the twenty-first verse, as it stands in our common version. But some of the manuscripts of this prophet consulted by Dr. Kennicott have in this place the eleventh year, which is probably the genuine reading. To check the vain confidence of those who expected to hold out by possessing themselves of its other fastnesses, the utter desolation of all Judea is foretold, 21-29. Ezekiel is informed that among those that attended his instructions were a great number of hypocrites, against whom he delivers a most awful message. When the Lord is destroying these hypocrites, then shall they know that there hath been a prophet among them, 30-33.

2. *Son of man . . . if the people of the land take a man.* The first ten verses of this chapter are the same with chap. iii. 17-22; and to what is said there on this most important and awful subject I must refer the reader. Here the people choose the watchman; there the Lord appoints him. When God chooses, the people should approve.

11. *As I live, saith the Lord God, I have no pleasure in the death of the wicked.* From this to the twentieth verse inclusive is nearly the same with chap. xviii, on which I wish the reader to consult the notes.

19. *He shall live thereby.* "The wages of sin is death"; "the gift of God is eternal life." It is a miserable trade by which a man *cannot live; such a trade is sin.*

21. *One that had escaped out of Jerusalem.* After it had been taken by the Chaldeans. *Came unto me, saying, The city is smitten.* This very message God had promised to the prophet, chap. xxiv. 26.

22. *My mouth was opened.* They had now the fullest evidence that I had spoken from the Lord. I therefore spoke freely and fully what God delivered to me, chap. xxiv. 27.

24. *Abraham was one.* If he was called to inherit the land when he was alone, and had the whole to himself, why may we not expect to be established here, who are his posterity, and are many? They wished to remain in the land and be happy after the Chaldeans had carried the rest away captives.

25. *Ye eat with the blood.* Abraham was *righteous;* ye are *unrighteous.* Eating of blood, in any way dressed, or of flesh from which the blood had not been extracted, was and is in the sight of God abominable. All such practices He has absolutely and forever forbidden.

26. *Ye stand upon your sword.* You live by plunder, rapine, and murder.

27. *They that are in the wastes.* He seems to speak of those Jews who had fled to rocks, caves, and fortresses in the mountains; whose death he predicts, partly by the sword, partly by wild beasts, and partly by famine.

30. *Thy people still are talking against thee.* Bach should be rather translated, "concerning thee," than "against thee"; for the following verses show that the prophet was much respected.

32. *As a very lovely song.* They admired the fine voice and correct delivery of the prophet; this was their religion, and this is the whole of the religion of thousands to the present day.

CHAPTER 34

The prophet is commanded to declare the dreadful judgments of God against the covetous shepherds of Israel, who feed themselves, and not their flocks; by which emblem the priests and Levites are intended, who in Ezekiel's time were very corrupt, and the chief cause of Israel's apostasy and ruin, 1-10. From this gloomy subject the prophet passes to the blessedness of the true Israel of God under the reign of David, the Great Shepherd of the sheep, our Lord Jesus Christ being named after this prince by a figure exceedingly frequent in the sacred oracles, of putting the type for the antitype, 11-31.

2. *Prophesy against the shepherds of Israel.* The *shepherds* include, first, the priests and Levites; secondly, the kings, princes, and magis-

trates. The *flocks* mean the whole of the people; the "fat" and the "wool," the tithes and offerings, the taxes and imposts.

5. *And they were scattered.* There was no discipline kept up; and the flock, the Church, became disorganized, and separated from each other, in both affection and fellowship. And the consequence was, the grievous wolves, false and worldly interested teachers, seized on and made a prey of them.

6. *My sheep wandered through all the mountains.* They all became idolaters, and lost the knowledge of the true God.

16. *I will destroy the fat and the strong.* I will destroy those cruel and imperious shepherds who abuse their authority, and tyrannize over the flock.

17. *And as for you, O my flock.* After having spoken to the shepherds, he now addresses the flock. *I judge between cattle and cattle.* Between false and true professors.

18. *Have eaten up the good pasture.* Arrogate to yourselves all the promises of God, and will hardly permit the simple believer to claim or possess any token of God's favor.

20. *I will judge between the fat cattle and between the lean cattle.* Between the rich and the poor, those who fare sumptuously every day and those who have not the necessaries of life.

23. *I will set up one Shepherd . . . my servant David.* From the texts marked in the margin we understand that Jesus Christ alone is meant, as both Old and New Testaments agree in this. And from this one Shepherd all Christian ministers must derive their authority to teach, and their grace to teach effectually.

25. *I will make with them a covenant of peace.* The original is emphatic: "And I will cut with them the peace covenant"; that is, a covenant sacrifice, procuring and establishing peace between God and man, and between man and his fellows. I need not tell the reader that the cutting refers to the ancient mode of making covenants. The blood was poured out; the animal was divided from mouth to tail, exactly in two; the divisions placed opposite to each other; the contracting parties entered into the space, going in at each end, and met in the middle, and there took the covenant oath. *And will cause the evil beasts to cease.* These false and ravenous pastors. Christ purges them out of His Church, and destroys that power by which they lorded it over God's heritage.

26. *The shower to come down.* The Holy Spirit's influence. *There shall be showers of blessing.* Light, life, joy, peace, and power shall be manifest in all the assemblies of Christ's people.

29. *I will raise up . . . a plant of renown.* "A plantation to the name"; to the name of Christ. A Christian Church composed of men who are Christians, who have the spirit of Christ in them, and do not bear His name in vain.

CHAPTER 35

The prophet having formerly predicted the ruin of Edom, the same with Seir (chap. xxv. 12), now resumes and pursues the subject at greater length, intimating, as did also Isaiah (chap. xxi. 11-12), that though other nations should recover their liberty after the fall of the Babylonian monarchy, the Edomites should continue in bondage for their very despiteful behavior towards the children of Israel in the day of their calamity, 1-15.

2. *Set thy face against mount Seir.* That is, against the Edomites. This prophecy was probably delivered about the time of the preceding, and before the destruction of Idumea by Nebuchadnezzar, which took place about five years after. Calmet supposes that two destructions of Idumea are here foretold: one by Nebuchadnezzar, and the other by the Jews after their return from their captivity.

3. *Most desolate.* Literally, "A desolation and a wilderness."

5. *A perpetual hatred.* The Edomites were the descendants of Esau; the Israelites, the descendants of Jacob. Both these were brothers; and between them there was contention even in the womb, and they lived generally in a state of enmity. Their descendants kept up the ancient feud. But the Edomites were implacable; they had not only a rooted but perpetual enmity to the Israelites, harassing and distressing them by all possible means; and they seized the opportunity, when the Israelites were most harassed by other enemies, to make inroads upon them, and cut them off wherever they found them.

9. *Perpetual desolations.* You shall have perpetual desolation for your perpetual hatred.

10. *These two nations.* Israel and Judah. The Idumeans thought of conquering and possessing both; and they would have succeeded, but only the Lord was there; and this spoiled their projects, and blasted their hopes.

12. *They are laid desolate, they are given us to consume.* They exulted in seeing Judea overrun; and they rejoiced in the prospect of completing the ruin, when the Chaldeans had withdrawn from the land.

13. *Thus with your mouth ye have boasted against me.* You have said you would enter into those lands, and take them for your inheritance, though you knew that God had promised them to the Israelites, and that you should never have them for your portion.

14. *When the whole earth rejoiceth.* When the whole land shall rejoice in the restoration of the Jews, I will make you desolate.

15. *So will I do unto thee.* Others shall rejoice in your downfall as you have rejoiced at their downfall.

CHAPTER 36

The Edomites or Idumeans, during the Babylonish captivity, took possession of the mountainous parts of Judea, and the fortresses which commanded the country, intending to exclude the Jews if ever they should return from their captivity. The prophet therefore, by a beautiful personification, addresses the mountains of Israel; and, ascribing to them passions and emotions similar to those of his own breast, consoles them with the prospect of being soon rid of those usurping foes; of being freed from the dishonor of idols under which they groaned; and of flourishing again in their ancient glory under their rightful owners, 1-15. The idolatry and other sins of the Jews are then declared to be the cause of their captivity and dispersion, 16-20; from which however they are promised a deliverance in terms of great force and beauty, 21-38. This chapter contains also, under the type of the happy condition of the Israelites after their restoration from the Babylonish captivity, a glorious prophecy of the rich blessings of the gospel dispensation.

1. *Prophesy unto the mountains of Israel.* This is a part of the preceding prophecy, though

it chiefly concerns the Jews. In it they are encouraged to expect a glorious restoration, and that none of the evil wishes of their adversaries should take place against them.

2. *Because the enemy hath said.* The Idumeans thought they would shortly be put in possession of all the strong places of Israel.

4. *Therefore . . . thus saith the Lord God to the mountains.* They shall possess neither mountain nor valley, hill nor dale, fountain nor river; for though in My justice I made you desolate, yet they shall not profit by your disasters. See vv. 5-7.

8. *For they are at hand to come.* The restoration of the Jews is so absolutely determined that you may rest assured it will take place, and be as confident relative to it as if you saw the different families entering into the Israelitish borders. It was near at hand in God's determination, though there were about fifty-eight of the seventy years unelapsed.

9. *Ye shall be tilled and sown.* The land shall be cultivated as it formerly was, when best peopled and at peace.

25. *Then* (at the time of this great restoration) *will I sprinkle clean water upon you*—the truly cleansing water; the influences of the Holy Spirit typified by *water*, whose property it is to cleanse, whiten, purify, refresh, render healthy and fruitful. *And from all your idols.* False gods, false worship, false opinions, and false hopes.

26. *A new heart also will I give you.* I will change the whole of your infected nature; and give you new appetites, new passions; or, at least, the old ones purified and refined. The *heart* is generally understood to mean all the affections and passions.

29. *I will also save you from all your uncleannesses.* I repeat it, "I will save you from all your sins."

CHAPTER 37

This chapter treats of the same subject with the preceding, in a beautiful and significant vision. Under the emblem of the open valley being thickly strewed with very dry bones is represented the hopeless state of the Jews when dispersed throughout the provinces of the Chaldean empire. But God, contrary to every human probability, restores these bones to life, thereby prefiguring the restoration of that people from the Babylonish captivity, and their resettlement in the land of their forefathers, 1-14. The prophet then makes an easy and elegant transition to the blessedness of the people of God under the gospel dispensation, in the plenitude of its manifestation; when the genuine converts to Christianity, the spiritual Israel, shall be no longer under the domination of heathen and antichristian rulers, but shall be collected together into one visible Kingdom, and constitute but one flock under one Shepherd, 15-28. The vision of the dry bones reviving is considered by some as having a remote view to the general resurrection.

1. *The hand of the Lord was upon me.* The prophetic influence was communicated. *And carried me out in the spirit.* Or, And the Lord brought me out in the spirit; that is, a spiritual vision, in which all these things were doubtless transacted. *The valley which was full of bones.* This vision of the dry bones was designed, first, as an emblem of the then wretched state of the Jews; secondly, of the general resurrection of the body.

3. *Can these bones live?* Is it possible that the persons whose bones these are can return to life?

4. *Prophesy upon these bones.* Declare to your miserable countrymen the gracious designs of the Lord; show them that their state, however deplorable, is not hopeless.

5. *Behold, I will cause breath. Ruach* signifies both "soul, breath, and wind," and sometimes the "Spirit of God." "Soul" is its proper meaning in this vision, where it refers to the bones: "I will cause the soul to enter into you."

9. *Prophesy unto the wind. Ruach.* Address yourself to the "soul," and command it to enter into these well-organized bodies, that they may live. *Come from the four winds.* Souls, come from all parts where you are scattered, and reanimate these bodies from which you have been so long separated. *The four winds* signify all parts—in every direction. Literally it is, "Souls, come from the four souls"; "Breath, come from the four breaths"; or, "Wind, come from the four winds." But here *ruach* has both of its most general meanings, "wind" or "breath," and "soul."

11. *These bones are the whole house of Israel.* That is, their state is represented by these bones, and their restoration to their own land is represented by the revivification of these bones.

12. *I will open your graves.* Here is a pointed allusion to the general resurrection; a doctrine properly credited and understood by the Jews, and to which our Lord refers, John v. 25, 28-29: "The hour is coming, in the which all that are in the graves shall hear his voice, and shall come forth." *And cause you to come up out of your graves.* I am determined that you shall be restored; so that were you even in your graves, as mankind at the general resurrection, yet My all-powerful voice shall call you forth.

13. *When I have opened your graves.* When I shall have done for you what was beyond your hope, and deemed impossible, then you shall know that I am Jehovah.

14. *And shall put my spirit. Ruchi.* Here *ruach* is taken for the Holy Ghost.

Three degrees or processes have been remarked in this mystic vision. When the prophet was commanded to prophesy—to foretell, on the authority of God, that there should be a restoration to their own land—(1) There was a noise, which was followed by a general shaking, during which the bones became arranged and united. (2) The flesh and skin came upon them, so that the dry bones were no longer seen. (3) The spirit or soul came into them, and they stood up perfectly vivified.

Perhaps these might be illustrated by three periods of time, which marked the regeneration of the Jewish polity. (1) The publication of the edict of Cyrus in behalf of the Jews, which caused a general shaking or stir among the people, so that the several families began to approach each other, and prepare for their return to Judea, Ezra i. 2-3. (2) The edict published by Darius in the second year of his reign, Ezra iv. 23-24, which removed the impediments thrown in the way of the Jews, Ezra vi. 6-7, etc. (3) The mission of Nehemiah, with orders from Artaxerxes to complete the building of the Temple and the city, Neh. ii. 7, etc. Then the Jews became a great army, and found themselves in sufficient force to defend themselves and city against all their enemies.

16. *Son of man, take thee one stick.* The two sticks mentioned in this symbolical transaction represented, as the text declares, the two kingdoms of Israel and Judah, which were formed in the days of Rehoboam, and continued distinct till the time of the Captivity. The kingdom of Judah was composed of the tribes of Judah and Benjamin, with the Levites; all the rest went off in the schism with Jeroboam, and formed the kingdom of Israel. Though some out of those tribes did rejoin themselves to Judah, yet no whole tribe ever returned to that kingdom.

19. *The stick of Joseph, which is in the hand of Ephraim.* Jeroboam, the first king of the ten tribes, was an Ephraimite. Joseph represents the ten tribes in general; they were *in the hand of Ephraim,* that is, under the government of Jeroboam.

22. *I will make them one nation.* There was no distinction after the return from Babylon.

24. *And David my servant shall be king.* That this refers to Jesus Christ, see proved, chap. xxxiv. 23.

25. *The land that I have given unto Jacob my servant.* Jacob means here the twelve tribes; and the land given to them was the whole land of Palestine; consequently the promise states that, when they return, they are to possess the whole of the Promised Land.

26. *Covenant of peace.* See this explained, chap. xxxiv. 25.

27. *My tabernacle.* Jesus Christ, the true Tabernacle, in whom dwelt all the fullness of the Godhead bodily.

CHAPTER 38

The sublime prophecy contained in this and the following chapter relates to Israel's victory over Gog, and is very obscure. It begins with representing a prodigious armament of many nations combined together under the conduct of Gog, with the intention of overwhelming the Jews, after having been for some time resettled, in their land subsequent to their return from the Babylonish captivity, 1-9. These enemies are further represented as making themselves sure of the spoil, 10-13. But in this critical conjuncture when Israel, to all human appearance, was about to be swallowed up by her enemies, God most graciously appears, to execute by terrible judgments the vengeance threatened against these formidable adversaries of His people, 14-16. The prophet, in terms borrowed from human passions, describes, with awful emphasis, the fury of Jehovah as coming up to His face; and the effects of it so dreadful as to make all the animate and inanimate creation tremble, and even to convulse with terror the whole frame of nature, 17-23.

2. *Son of man, set thy face against Gog, the land of Magog.* This is allowed to be the most difficult prophecy in the Old Testament. It is difficult to us, because we know not the king nor people intended by it; but I am satisfied they were well-known by these names in the time that the prophet wrote. Rev. David Martin, pastor of the Walloon Church at Utrecht, concludes, after examining all previous opinions, that Antiochus Epiphanes, the great enemy of the Israelites, is alone intended here; and that *Gog,* which signifies "covered," is an allusion to the well-known character of Antiochus, whom historians describe as an artful, cunning, and dissembling man. See Dan. viii. 23, 25; xi. 23, 27, 32. *Magog* he supposes to mean the country of Syria. Of this opinion the following quotation from Pliny, *Hist. Nat.,* lib. v, c. 23, seems a proof; who, speaking of Coele-Syria, says: "Coele-Syria has Apamia separated from the

tetrarchy of the Nazarenes by the river Marsyia; and Bambyce, otherwise called Hierapolis; but by the Syrians, Magog." I shall at present examine the text by this latter opinion. *Chief prince of Meshech and Tubal.* These probably mean the auxiliary forces, over whom Antiochus was supreme; they were the Muscovites and Cappadocians.

4. *I will turn thee back.* Your enterprise shall fail.

5. *Persia.* That a part of this country was tributary to Antiochus, see 1 Macc. iii. 31. *Ethiopia, and Libya.* That these were auxiliaries of Antiochus is evident from Dan. xi. 43: "The Libyans and Ethiopians shall be at his steps."

9. *Thou shalt ascend and come like a storm.* It is observable that Antiochus is thus spoken of by Daniel, chap. xi. 40: "The king of the north"—Antiochus, "shall come against him" ("the king of the south" is the king of Egypt) "like a whirlwind."

10. *Shall things come into thy mind, and thou shalt think an evil thought.* Antiochus purposed to invade and destroy Egypt, as well as Judea; see Dan. xi. 31-32, 36.

12. *To take a spoil . . . and a prey.* When Antiochus took Jerusalem he gave the pillage of it to his soldiers, and spoiled the Temple of its riches, which were immense. See Joseph. *War,* lib. 1, c. 1.

13. *Sheba, and Dedan.* The Arabians, anciently great plunderers; and Tarshish, the inhabitants of the famous isle of Tartessus, the most noted merchants of the time. They are here represented as coming to Antiochus before he undertook the expedition, and bargaining for the spoils of the Jews. *Art thou come to take a spoil . . . to carry away silver and gold . . . cattle and goods?*

16. *When I shall be sanctified in thee, O Gog.* By the defeat of his troops under Lysias, his general, 1 Mac. iii. 32-33, etc., and chap. vi. 6.

21. *I will call for a sword against him.* Meaning Judas Maccabeus, who defeated his army under Lysias, making a horrible carnage.

22. *Great hailstones, fire, and brimstone.* These are probably figurative expressions, to signify that the whole tide of the war should be against him, and that his defeat and slaughter should be great.

CHAPTER 39

The prophet goes on to denounce the divine judgments against Gog and his army, 1-7; and describes their dreadful slaughter, 8-10, and burial, 11-16, in terms so very lofty and comprehensive as must certainly denote some very extraordinary interposition of Providence in behalf of the Jews. And to amplify the matter still more the prophet, with peculiar art and propriety, delays the summoning of all the birds and beasts of prey in nature to feast on the slain (in allusion to the custom of feasting on the remainder of sacrifices) till after the greater multitudes are buried; to intimate that even the remainder, and as it were the stragglers of such mighty hosts, would be more than sufficient to satisfy their utmost rapacity, 17-20. The remaining verses contain a prediction of the great blessedness of the people of God in gospel times, and of the stability of the kingdom of Christ, 21-29. It will be proper to remark that the great northern expedition against the natural Israel, described in this and the preceding chapter, is, from its striking resemblance in the main particulars, put by the writer of the Apocalypse (chap. xx. 7-10) for a much more formidable armament of a multitude of nations in the four quarters of the earth against the pure Christian Church, the mystical Israel; an event still extremely remote, and which it is thought shall immediately precede the destruction of the world by fire, and the general judgment.

2. *And leave but the sixth part of thee.* The margin has, "strike thee with six plagues; or, draw thee back with an hook of six teeth."

3. *I will smite thy bow out of thy left hand.* The Persians whom Antiochus had in his army, chap. xxxviii. 5, were famous as archers, and they may be intended here.

6. *I will send a fire on Magog.* On Syria. I will destroy the Syrian troops. *And among them that dwell carelessly in the isles.* The auxiliary troops that came to Antiochus from the borders of the Euxine Sea.

7. *In the midst of my people Israel.* This defeat of Gog is to be in Israel; and it was there, according to this prophecy, that the immense army of Antiochus was so completely defeated. *And I will not let them pollute my holy name any more.* See on 1 Macc. i. 11, etc., how Antiochus had profaned the Temple, insulted Jehovah and His worship, etc. God permitted that as a scourge to His disobedient people; but now the scourger shall be scourged, and he shall pollute the sanctuary no more.

9. *And shall set on fire . . . the weapons.* The Israelites shall make bonfires and fuel of the weapons, tents, etc., which the defeated Syrians shall leave behind them, as expressive of the joy which they shall feel for the destruction of their enemies. *They shall burn them with fire seven years.* These may be figurative expressions, after the manner of the Asiatics, whose language abounds with such descriptions. But as the slaughter was great, and the bows, arrows, quivers, shields, bucklers, hand staves, and spears were in vast multitudes, it must have taken a long time to gather them up in the different parts of the fields of battle, and the roads in which the Syrians had retreated, throwing away their arms as they proceeded; so there might have been a long time employed in collecting and burning them. Mariana, in his *History of Spain,* lib. xi, c. 24, says that after the Spaniards had given that signal overthrow to the Saracens, A.D. 1212, they found such a vast quantity of lances, javelins, and suchlike that they served them for four years for fuel.

11. *The valley of the passengers on the east of the sea.* That is, of Gennesareth, according to the Targum. *There shall they bury Gog and all his multitude.* Some read, "There shall they bury Gog, that is, all his multitude." Not Gog, or Antiochus himself, for he was not in this battle; but his generals, captains, and soldiers, by whom he was represented. As to *Hamon-gog,* we know no valley of this name but here. But we may understand the words thus: The place where this great slaughter was, and where the multitudes of the slain were buried, might be better called *Hamon-gog,* the "valley of the multitude of Gog," than the "valley of passengers."

12. *And seven months.* It shall require a long time to bury the dead. This is another figurative expression; which, however, may admit of a good deal of literal meaning. Many of the Syrian soldiers had secreted themselves in different places during the pursuit after the battle, where they died of their wounds, of hunger, and of fatigue, so that they were not all found and buried till seven months after the defeat of the Syrian army. This slow process of burying is distinctly related in the

following three verses, and extended even to a bone, v. 15; which, when it was found by a passenger, the place was marked, that the buriers might see and inter it. Seven months was little time enough for all this work; and in that country putrescency does not easily take place, the scorching winds serving to desiccate the flesh and preserve it from decomposition.

17. *Gather yourselves . . . to my sacrifice.* This is an allusion to a custom common in the East: when a sacrifice is made, the friends and neighbors of the party sacrificing are invited to come and feast on the sacrifice.

19. *And ye shall eat fat . . . and drink blood.* Who shall eat and drink, etc.? Not the Jews. It is the fowls and the beasts that God invites, v. 17: "Speak unto every feathered fowl, and to every beast of the field, Assemble yourselves . . . that ye may eat flesh, and drink blood"; nor are the persons altered in all these verses, 17-20.

25. *Now will I bring again the captivity of Jacob.* Both they and the heathen shall know that it was for their iniquity that I gave them into the hands of their enemies; and now I will redeem them from those hands in such a way as to prove that I am a merciful God, as well as a just God.

26. *After that they have borne their shame.* After they shall have borne the punishment due to a line of conduct which is their shame and reproach, viz., idolatry.

27. *When I have . . . gathered them.* Antiochus had before captured many of the Jews, and sold them for slaves; see Dan. xi. 33.

28. *And have left none of them any more there.* All that chose had liberty to return, but many remained behind. This promise may therefore refer to a greater restoration, when not a Jew shall be left behind. This, the next verse intimates, will be in the gospel dispensation.

29. *For I have poured out my spirit.* That is, I will pour out My Spirit; see the notes on chap. xxxvi. 25-29, where this subject is largely considered. This Spirit is to enlighten, quicken, purify, and cleanse their hearts; so that, being completely changed, they shall become God's people, and be a praise in the earth.

CHAPTER 40

The prophecy or vision, which begins here, continues to the end of the book. The Temple of Jerusalem lying in ruins when Ezekiel had this vision (for its date is the fourteenth year after the destruction of Jerusalem by Nebuchadnezzar), the Jews needed consolation. If they were not promised a restoration of the Temple, they would not feel so great an interest in returning home. It is thought by some that no model of Solomon's Temple had remained. To direct them, therefore, in the dimensions, parts, order, and rules of their new Temple might be one reason why Ezekiel is so particular in the description of the old; to which the new was conformable in figure and parts, though inferior in magnificence, on account of the poverty of the nation at the time. Whatever was august or illustrious in the prophetic figures, and not literally fulfilled in or near their own times, the ancient Jews properly considered as belonging to the time of the Messiah. Accordingly, upon finding that the latter Temple fell short of the model of the Temple here described by Ezekiel, they supposed the prophecy to refer, at least in part, to the period now mentioned. And we, who live under the gospel dispensation, have apostolical authority for the assertion that the Temple and Temple worship were emblematic of Christ's Church, frequently represented in the New Testament under the metaphor of a temple, in allusion to the symmetry, beauty, and firmness of that of Solomon; to its orderly worship; and to the manifestations it

had of the Divine Presence. This chapter commences with the time, manner, and end of the vision, 1-5. We have next a description of the east gate, 6-19, the north gate, 20-23, and the south gate, 24-31. A further description of the east gate, 32-34, and of the north gate, 35-38. Account of the eight tables, 39-43; of the chambers, 44-47; and of the porch of the Temple, 48-49.

1. *In the five and twentieth year of our captivity.* In the twenty-fifth year of the captivity of Jeconiah, and fourteen years after the taking of Jerusalem.

The Temple here described by Ezekiel is, in all probability, the same which he saw before his captivity, and which had been burned by the Chaldeans fourteen years before this vision. On comparing the Books of Kings and Chronicles with this prophet, we shall find the same dimensions in the parts described by both; for instance, the Temple, or place which comprehended the sanctuary, the holy place, and the vestibule or porch before the Temple, is found to measure equally the same in both Ezekiel and the Kings. Compare 1 Kings vi. 3-16 with chap. xli. 2, etc. The inside ornaments of the Temple are entirely the same; in both we see two courts; an inner one for the priests, and an outer one for the people. Compare 1 Kings vi. 29-36; 2 Chron. iv. 9; and Ezek. xli. 16-17 and xlviii. 7-10. So that there is room to suppose that, in all the rest, the Temple of Ezekiel resembled the old one; and that God's design in retracing these ideas in the prophet's memory was to preserve the remembrance of the plan, the dimensions, the ornaments, and whole structure of this divine edifice; and that at the return from captivity the people might more easily repair it, agreeably to this model. The prophet's applying himself to describe this edifice was a motive of hope to the Jews of seeing themselves one day delivered from captivity, the Temple rebuilt, and their nation restored to its ancient inheritance. Ezekiel touches very slightly upon the description of the Temple or house of the Lord, which comprehended the holy place or sanctuary, and which are so exactly described in the Books of Kings. He dwells more largely upon the gates, the galleries, and apartments of the Temple, concerning which the history of the kings had not spoken, or only just taken notice of by the way.

As the prophet knew that the Chaldeans had utterly destroyed the Temple, he thought it necessary to preserve an exact description of it, that on their restoration the people might build one on the same model.

2. *Set me upon a very high mountain.* Mount Moriah, the mount on which Solomon's Temple was built, 2 Chron. iii. 1.

3. *A man, whose appearance was like . . . brass.* Like bright polished brass, which strongly reflected the rays of light.

4. *Declare all that thou seest to the house of Israel.* That they may know how to build the second Temple, when they shall be restored from their captivity.

CHAPTER 41

In this chapter the prophet gives us a circumstantial account of the measures, parts, chambers, and ornaments of the Temple, 1-26.

1. *To the temple.* He had first described the courts and the porch. See chap. xl.

2. *The breadth of the door.* This was the door, or gate, of the sanctuary and this doorway

was filled up with folding gates. The measurements are exactly the same as those of Solomon's Temple. See 1 Kings vi. 2, 17.

4. *The length thereof, twenty cubits.* This is the measurement of the sanctuary, or holy of holies. This also was the exact measurement of Solomon's Temple; see 1 Kings vi. 20. This and the other resemblances here sufficiently prove that Ezekiel's Temple and that of Solomon were on the same plan, and that the latter Temple was intended to be an exact resemblance of the former.

6. *The side chambers were three.* We find, by Joseph. *Antiq.* viii. 3. 2, that around Solomon's Temple were chambers three stories high, each story consisting of thirty chambers. *Entered into the wall.* The beams were admitted into the outer wall, but they rested on projections of the inner wall.

7. *An enlarging, and a winding about.* Perhaps a winding staircase that widened upward as the inner wall decreased in thickness, this wall being six cubits thick as high as the first story, five from the floor of the second story to that of the third, and four from the floor to the ceiling of the third story; and thus there was a rest of one cubit in breadth to support the stories.

18. *A palm tree was between a cherub and a cherub.* That is, the palm trees and the cherubs were alternated, and each cherub had two faces, one of a lion and the other of a man; one of which was turned to the palm tree on the right, and the other to the palm tree on the left.

22. *The altar of wood.* This was the altar of incense, and was covered with plates of gold.

CHAPTER 42

This chapter gives us a description of the priests' chambers and their use, with the dimensions of the holy mount on which the Temple stood, 1-20.

1. *He brought me forth into the utter court.* He brought him out of the Temple into the court of the priests. This, in reference to the Temple, was called the outer court; but the court of the people was beyond this.

4. *A walk of ten cubits breadth inward.* This seems to have been a sort of parapet.

14. *They shall lay their garments wherein they minister.* The priests were not permitted to wear their robes in the outer court. These vestments were to be used only when they ministered; and when they had done, they were to deposit them in one of the chambers mentioned in the thirteenth verse.

20. *It had a wall round about . . . to make a separation between the sanctuary and the profane place.* The holy place was that which was consecrated to the Lord, into which no heathen, nor stranger, nor any in a state of impurity might enter. *The profane place* was that in which men, women, Gentiles, pure or impure, might be admitted. Josephus says (*War,* lib. vi, c. 14) that in his time there was a wall built before the entrance three cubits high, on which there were posts fixed at certain distances, with inscriptions on them in Latin and Greek, containing the laws which enjoined purity on those that entered, and forbidding all strangers to enter, on pain of death.

CHAPTER 43

The glory of the Lord is represented as returning to the Temple, 1-6; where God promises to fix His residence, if the people repent and forsake those sins which caused Him to depart from them, 7-12. Then the measures of the altar, and the ordinances relating to it, are set down, 13-27.

2. *The glory of the God of Israel came from the way of the east.* This was the chariot of cherubim, wheels, etc., which he saw at the river Chebar. And this glory, coming from the east, is going to enter into the eastern gate of the Temple, and thence to shine out upon the whole earth.

7. *Son of man, the place of my throne.* The throne refers to His majesty; the soles of His feet, to His condescension in dwelling among men. *Where I will dwell in the midst of the children of Israel.* The Tabernacle and Temple were types of the incarnation of Jesus Christ.

8. *In their setting of their threshold.* They had even gone so far as to set up their idol altars by those of Jehovah, so that their abominable idols were found in the very house of God! Therefore, He *consumed them in His anger.*

9. *Now let them put away their whoredom.* Their idolatry. *And the carcases of their kings.* It appears that God was displeased with their bringing their kings so near His temple. David was buried in the city of David, which was on Mount Zion, near to the Temple; and so were almost all the kings of Judah. But God requires that the place of His temple and its vicinity shall be kept unpolluted; and when they put away all kinds of defilement, then will He dwell among them.

10. *Shew the house to the house of Israel.* Show them this holy house where the holy God dwells, that they may be ashamed of their iniquities. Their name, their profession, their Temple, their religious services, all bound them to a holy life; all within them, all without them, should have been holiness unto the Lord. But alas! they have been bound by no ties, and they have sinned against all their obligations. Nevertheless, *let them measure the pattern,* let them see the rule by which they should have walked, and let them measure themselves by this standard, and walk accordingly.

11. *And if they be ashamed.* If, in a spirit of true repentance, they acknowledge their past transgressions, and purpose in His help never more to offend their God, then teach them everything that concerns My worship, and their profiting by it.

12. *This is the law of the house.* From the top of the mountain on which it stands, to the bottom, all round about, all shall be holy. No buildings shall be erected in any part, nor place nor spot be appropriated to a common use; all shall be considered as being most holy.

15. *So the altar.* Hahharel, "the mount of God." *And from the altar.* "And from the lion of God." Perhaps the first was a name given to the altar when elevated to the honor of God, and on which the victims were offered to Him; and the second, the "lion of God," may mean the hearth, which might have been thus called because it devoured and consumed the burnt offerings, as a lion does his prey. See Isa. xxix. 1.

17. *And the settle.* The "ledge" on which the priests walked round the altar; see v. 14. By these settles or ledges the altar was narrowed towards the top.

19. *The priests . . . that be of the seed of Zadok.* It was this Zadok that was put in the place of Abiathar by Solomon, 1 Kings ii. 35, in whose family the priesthood had continued ever since.

CHAPTER 44

This chapter gives an account of the glory of God having returned to the Temple, 1-4. The Jews reproved for suffering idolatrous priests to pollute it with their ministrations, 5-8. Ordinances respecting the conduct of the priests, and the maintenance due to them, 9-31.

1. *The outward sanctuary.* In opposition to the Temple itself, which was the inner sanctuary.

2. *This gate shall be shut.* It was not to be opened on ordinary occasions, nor at all on the weekdays, but only on the Sabbaths and the new moons.

5. *Mark well, and behold.* Take notice of everything; register all so fully that you shall be able to give the most minute information to the children of Israel.

7. *The fat and the blood.* These never went into common use; they were wholly offered to God. The *blood* was poured out; the *fat* consumed.

10. *And the Levites that are gone away far from me.* This refers to the schism of Jeroboam, who, when he set up a new worship, got as many of the priests and Levites to join him in his idolatry as he could. These, on the return from the Captivity, should not be permitted to perform the functions of priests in the new Temple; but they might be continued as keepers of all the charge of the house—be treasurers, guards of the Temple, porters, etc.; see vv. 11-15. The whole of these passages refer to the period of time when the second Temple was built.

16. *Come near to my table.* To place the shewbread there, and to burn incense on the golden altar in the holy of holies.

17. *No wool shall come upon them.* The reason is plain. Wool is more apt than linen to contract dirt and breed insects; linen breeds none; besides, this is a vegetable and the other an animal substance. It was an ancient maxim that whatever was taken from a dead body was impure in matters of religion, and should not be permitted to enter into the Temple. The Egyptian priests always wore linen on their bodies, and shoes of matting or rushes on their feet.

22. *Neither shall they take for their wives a widow.* This was prohibited to the high priest only, by Moses, Lev. xxi. 13-14.

CHAPTER 45

The several portions of land appointed for the sanctuary, 1-5, the city, 6, and the prince, 7-8. Regulations concerning the weights and measures, 9-12; with ordinances respecting the provisions for the ordinary and extraordinary sacrifices, 13-25.

1. *When ye shall divide by lot.* That is, when on your repossessing your land every family settles according to the allotment which it formerly had, for it is certain that the land was not divided afresh by lot after the Babylonish captivity. The allotment mentioned and described here was merely for the service of the Temple, the use of the priests, and the prince or governor of the people. A division of the whole land is not intended.

7. *A portion shall be for the prince. Nasi,* he who had the authority of chief magistrate; for there was neither king nor prince among the Jews after the Babylonish captivity.

8. *My princes shall no more oppress my people.* By exorbitant taxes to maintain profligate courts, or subsidize other powers to help to keep up a system of tyranny in the earth. The former princes even robbed the temple of God to give subsidies to other states.

16. *All . . . this oblation for the prince.* A present or offering to the prince.

18. *Thou shalt take a young bullock . . . and cleanse the sanctuary.* There is nothing of this in the Mosaic law; it seems to have been a new ceremony. An annual purification of the sanctuary may be intended.

20. *For him that is simple.* That wants understanding to conduct himself properly.

CHAPTER 46

Ordinances of worship prescribed for the prince and for the people, 1-15; and the gifts he may bestow on his sons and servants, 16-18. A description of the courts appointed for boiling or baking any part of the holy oblations, 19-24.

4. *The burnt offering that the prince shall offer.* The chief magistrate was always obliged to attend the public worship of God, as well as the priest, to show that the civil and ecclesiastical states were both under the same government of the Lord; and that no one was capable of being prince or priest who did not acknowledge God in all his ways.

9. *He that entereth in by the way of the north.* As the north and the south gates were opposite to each other, he that came in at the north must go out at the south; he that came in at the south must go out at the north. No person was to come in at the east gate, because there was no gate at the west; and the people were not permitted to turn round and go out at the same place by which they came in, for this was like turning their backs on God, and the decorum and reverence with which public worship was to be conducted would not admit of this. Besides, returning by the same way must have occasioned a great deal of confusion, where so many people must have jostled each other in their meetings in different parts of this space.

10. *And the prince in the midst of them.* Even he shall act in the same way; he must also go straight forward, and never turn his back to go out at the same gate by which he entered. The prince and the people were to begin and end their worship at the same time.

13. *Thou shalt prepare it every morning.* The evening offering is entirely omitted, which makes an important difference between this and the old laws. See Exod. xxix. 31-46.

17. *To the year of liberty.* That is, to the year of jubilee, called the "year of liberty" because there was then a general release. All

servants had their liberty, and all alienated estates returned to their former owners.

20. *The trespass offering.* Part of this, and of the sin offering, and the flour offering, was the portion of the priests, See Num. xviii. 9-10.

CHAPTER 47

The vision of the holy waters issuing out of the Temple, and their virtue; an emblem of the power of God's grace under the gospel, capable of healing all but the incorrigibly impenitent, represented by the marshy ground that cannot be healed, 1-12. Also a description of the several divisions of the Holy Land indiscriminately shared betwixt Jews and proselytes, to denote that in after times the privileges now enjoyed by the Jews should be also extended to the Gentiles, 13-23.

1. *Behold, waters issued out from under the threshold.* Ezekiel, after having made the whole compass of the court of the people, is brought back by the north gate into the courts of the priests; and, having reached the gate of the Temple, he saw waters which had their spring under the threshold of that gate, that looked towards the east; and which, passing to the south of the altar of burnt offerings on the right of the Temple, ran from the west to the east, that they might fall into the brook Kidron, and thence be carried into the Dead Sea. Literally, no such waters were ever in the Temple; and because there were none, Solomon had what is called the brazen sea made, which held water for the use of the Temple. It is true that the water which supplied this sea might have been brought by pipes to the place; but a fountain producing abundance of water was not there, and could not be there, on the top of such a hill; and consequently these waters, as well as those spoken of in Joel iii. 18 and in Zech. xiv. 8, are to be understood spiritually or typically; and indeed the whole complexion of the place here shows that they are thus to be understood. Taken in this view, I shall proceed to apply the whole of this vision to the effusion of light and salvation by the outpouring of the Spirit of God under the gospel dispensation, by which the knowledge of the true God was multiplied in the earth; and have only one previous remark to make, that the farther the waters flowed from the Temple, the deeper they grew. With respect to the phraseology of this chapter, it may be said that St. John had it particularly in view while he wrote his celebrated description of the paradise of God, Revelation xxii. The prophet may therefore be referring to the same thing which the apostle describes, viz., the grace of the gospel, and its effects in the world.

2. *There ran out waters.* The waters seem to have been at first in small quantity, for the words imply that they *oozed* or "dropped out."

3-5. *He measured a thousand cubits, . . . the waters were to the ancles; a thousand more . . . the waters were to the knees . . . a thousand more . . . they became a river that could not be forded. the waters were risen, and they were waters to swim in.*

A. This may be applied to the gradual discoveries of the plan of salvation—(1) in the patriarchal ages, (2) in the giving of the law, (3) in the ministry of John the Baptist, and, (4) in the full manifestation of Christ by the communication of the Holy Ghost.

B. This vision may be applied also to the growth of a believer in the grace and knowledge of God. There is—(1) the seed of the Kingdom,

(2) the blade from that seed, (3) the ear out of that blade, and (4) the full corn in that ear.

C. It may be applied to the discoveries a penitent believer receives of the mercy of God in his salvation. (1) He is a little child, born of God, born from above, and begins to taste the bread of life, and live on the heavenly food. (2) He grows up and increases in stature and strength, and becomes a young man. (3) He becomes matured in the divine life, and has his spiritual senses exercised so as to become a father in Christ. (4) In thus following on to know the Lord he finds a continual increase of light and life, till at last he is carried by the streams of grace to the ocean of eternal mercy.

D. These waters may be considered as a type of the progress which Christianity shall make in the world. (1) There were only a few poor fishermen. (2) Afterwards many Jews. (3) Then the Gentiles of Asia Minor and Greece. (4) The continent and isles of Europe. And, (5) now spreading through Africa, Asia, and America, at present these waters are no longer a river, but an immense sea; and the gospel fishers are daily bringing multitudes of souls to Christ.

9. *Every thing . . . whithersoever the rivers shall come, shall live.* Life and salvation shall continually accompany the preaching of the gospel; the death of sin being removed, the life of righteousness shall be brought in. *There shall be a very great multitude of fish.* On the above plan this must refer to genuine converts to the Christian faith; true believers, who have got life and salvation by the streams of God's grace. The apostles were fishers of men; converts were the fish caught.

10. *The fishers shall stand upon it.* On the above plan of interpretation these must mean— (1) the apostles of our Lord Jesus, (2) the preachers of the everlasting gospel. *From Engedi.* At the southern extremity of the Dead Sea. *Unto En-eglaim.* At the northern extremity of the same.

12. *The leaf thereof for medicine.* See Rev. xxii. 1-5.

13. *Joseph shall have two portions.* That is, in Ephraim and Manasseh, his two sons, who each had a separate inheritance.

17. *The border from the sea.* The north border eastward is ascertained, vv. 15-16; here it is shown how far it extends itself northward.

18. *The east sea.* The same as the Dead Sea.

19. *Tamar.* Called Hazazon-tamar, or Engedi, 2 Chron. xx. 2. *The river.* Besor, which runs into the sea near Gaza.

20. *The great sea.* The Mediterranean. *From the border.* The southern border, mentioned in v. 19.

CHAPTER 48

This chapter contains a description of the several portions of the land belonging to each tribe, together with the portion allotted to the sanctuary, city, suburb, and prince, 1-29; as also the measure and gates of the new city, 30-35.

1. *Now these are the names of the tribes.* See the division mentioned Num. xxxiv. 7-12, which casts much light upon this.

9. *The oblation.* This was a portion of land 25,000 cubits in length, by 10,000 broad; in the

center of which was the Temple, which must be destined for the use of the priests, the Levites, and the prince.

15. *And the five thousand, that are left.* The territory of the Levites was 25,000 square cubits, v. 20. But their city was only 4,500 square cubits; see vv. 13 and 16. There remained, therefore, 10,000 cubits square to be divided, of which 5,000 cubits in breadth by 25,000 in length, on the east and west sides, were reserved for a sort of second city; or for suburbs where laymen might dwell who were employed by those priests and Levites who lodged in the Temple and in the city, v. 18. And another space of 1,000 cubits in breadth by 25,000 in length, which extended only from north to south, was for fields and gardens appointed for the support of those lay servants. On which we may remark, there was no cultivated land between the portion of the Levites and that of the prince, but only on the east and west sides.

21. *And the residue . . . for the prince.* His portion was alongside that of the Levites, from west to east; these were on each side 25,000 cubits in length, from the east to the west, by 12,500 cubits in breadth from north to south. The space both above and below was equal, between the tribe of Judah and that of Benjamin to north and south, and the portion of the Levites, which had Judah and Benjamin to the north and south, and the portion of the prince to the east and to the west.

28. *From Tamar . . . in Kadesh.* The former was on the south of the Dead Sea; and the latter, or Kadesh-barnea, was still farther south, and at the extremity of the portion of Gad, which was the most southern tribe, as Dan was the most northern.

30. *These are the goings out.* Each of the four sides of the city was 4,500 cubits long. There were three gates on each side, as mentioned below; and the whole circumference of the city was 18,000 cubits.

The Book of
DANIEL

Daniel is said to have descended from the royal family of David; and he appears to have been carried into Babylon when very young, in the fourth year of Jehoiakim king of Judah, 606 B.C. He and his three fellow captives, *Hananiah, Mishael,* and *Azariah,* being likely youths, were chosen to be about the king's court, and were appointed to have an education suitable to the employments for which they were destined. As they had been carefully bred up in the Mosaic institutions, they regulated their conduct by them, even in the court of a heathen king, where they were in the capacity of *slaves.* Hence, though ordered to be fed from the royal table, they would not touch that food, because the Chaldeans ate of meat forbidden by the Mosaic law, and probably even that which might be denominated clean became defiled by having been sacrificed to idols before it was prepared for common use. At their earnest request, the officer under whose care they were placed permitted them to use vegetables only; and finding that they grew healthy and strong by this aliment, did not oblige them to use the portion sent from the king's table.

Daniel appears to have been instructed in all the wisdom of the Chaldeans, which was at that time greatly superior to the learning of the ancient Egyptians; and he was soon distinguished in the Babylonish court, as well for his wisdom and strong understanding as for his deep and steady piety. His interpretation of Nebuchadnezzar's dream of the variously compounded metallic image raised his credit so high at the court that he was established governor of the province of Babylon, and made chief of all the Magians, or wise men in that country.

This book divides itself into two parts. Part I is historical, and is contained in the six former chapters. Part II is prophetical, and occupies the other six.

CHAPTER 1

This chapter begins with giving a short account of Nebuchadnezzar's conquest of Judea, when Jehoiakim became tributary to him; and consequently the seventy years' captivity and vassalage began, 1-2. On this expedition (taking Egypt in his way) the king of Babylon set out towards the end of the third year of Jehoiakim, but did not take Jerusalem before the ninth month of the year following. Hence the seeming discrepancy between Daniel and Jeremiah (chap. xxv. 1), the one computing from the time of his setting out on the expedition, and the other from the time in which the purpose of it was accomplished. We have next an account of the manner in which Daniel and his companions were brought up at the king's court, 3-7. They reject the daily provision of meat granted by the king, lest they should be defiled, and are allowed to live on pulse, 8-16. Their great proficiency in the wisdom of that time, 17-20. Daniel flourishes till the reign of Cyrus the Persian, 21.

1. *In the third year of the reign of Jehoiakim.* This king was raised to the throne of Judea in the place of his brother Jehoahaz, by Pharaoh-necho, king of Egypt, 2 Kings xxiii. 34-36, and continued tributary to him during the first three years of his reign. But in the fourth, which was the first of Nebuchadnezzar, Jer. xxv. 1, Nebuchadnezzar completely defeated the Egyptian

army near the Euphrates, Jer. xlvi. 2; and this victory put the neighboring countries of Syria, among which Judea was the chief, under the Chaldean government. Thus Jehoiakim, who had first been tributary to Egypt, became now the vassal of the king of Babylon, 2 Kings xxiv. 1. At the end of three years Jehoiakim rebelled against Nebuchadnezzar, who, then occupied with others wars, did not proceed against Jerusalem till three years after, which was the eleventh and last of Jehoiakim, 2 Kings xxiii. 36. There are some difficulties in the chronology of this place. Calmet takes rather a different view of these transactions. He connects the history thus: Nabopolassar, king of Babylon, finding that one of his lords whom he had made governor of Coelesyria and Phoenicia had revolted from him and formed an alliance with the king of Egypt, sent Nebuchadnezzar, his son, whom he invested with the authority of king, to reduce those provinces, as was customary among the easterns when the heir presumptive was sent on any important expedition or embassy. This young prince, having quelled the insurrection in those parts, marched against Jerusalem about the end of the third or beginning of the fourth year of the reign of Jehoiakim, king of Judah. He soon took the city, and put Jehoiakim in chains with the design of carrying him to Babylon; but, changing his mind, he permitted him to resume the reins of government under certain oppressive conditions. At this year, the seventy years of the Babylonish captivity commence. Nabopolassar dying in the interim, Nebuchadnezzar was obliged to return speedily to Babylon, leaving his generals to conduct the Jewish captives to Babylon, among whom were Daniel and his companions.

2. *Part of the vessels of the house of God.* He took the richest and finest of them for the service of his god Bel, and left what were necessary for carrying on the public worship of Jehovah; for leaving Jehoiakim on the throne, he only laid the land under tribute. *The land of Shinar.* This was the ancient name of Babylon. See Gen. xi. 2. *The treasure house of his god.* This was Bel, who had a splendid temple in Babylon, and was the tutelar god of the city and empire.

3. *Master of his eunuchs.* This word *eunuchs* signifies officers about or in the palace, whether literally eunuchs or not.

4. *Children.* "Youths, young men"; and so the word should be rendered throughout this book. *Skilful in all wisdom.* Rather, persons capable of every kind of literary accomplishment, that they might be put under proper instruction.

6. *Now among these.* There were no doubt several noble youths from other provinces; but the four mentioned here were Jews, and are supposed to have all been of royal extraction.

7. *Unto whom the prince of the eunuchs gave names.* This change of names was a mark of dominion and authority. It was customary for masters to impose new names upon their slaves; and rulers often, on their ascending the throne, assumed a name different from that which they had before. *Daniel* signifies "God is my Judge." This name they changed into *Belteshatstsar*; in Chaldee, "The treasure of Bel." *Hananiah* signifies "The Lord has been gracious to me," or "He to whom the Lord is gracious." This name was changed into *Shadrach*, Chaldee, which has

been variously translated: "The inspiration of the sun"; "God, the author of evil, be propitious to us"; "Let God preserve us from evil." *Mishael* signifies "He who comes from God." Him they called *Meshach*, which in Chaldee signifies "He who belongs to the goddess Sheshach," a celebrated deity of the Babylonians, mentioned by Jeremiah, chap. xxv. 26. *Azariah*, which signifies "The Lord is my Helper" they changed into *Abed-nego*, which in Chaldee is "The servant of Nebo," who was one of their divinities.

11. *Then said Daniel to Melzar.* Melzar was an officer under Ashpenaz, whose office it was to attend to the food, clothing, etc., of these royal captives.

12. *Give us pulse to eat.* Seeds or grain, such as barley, wheat, rye, peas, etc. Though a vegetable diet might have produced that healthiness of the system in general, and of the countenance particularly, as mentioned here, yet we are to understand that there was an especial blessing of God in this, because this spare diet was taken on a religious account.

21. *The first year of king Cyrus.* That is, to the end of the Chaldean empire. And we find Daniel alive in the third year of Cyrus; see chap. x. 1.

CHAPTER 2

Nebuchadnezzar, in the second year of his reign (or in the fourth, according to the Jewish account, which takes in the first two years in which he reigned conjointly with his father), had a dream which greatly troubled him, but of which nothing remained in the morning but the uneasy impression. Hence the diviners, when brought in before the king, could give no interpretation, as they were not in possession of the dream, 1-13. Daniel then, having obtained favor from God, is made acquainted with the dream and its interpretation, 14-19; for which he blesses God in a lofty and beautiful ode, 20-23; and reveals both unto the king, telling him first the particulars of the dream, 24-35, and then interpreting it of the four great monarchies. The then existing Chaldean empire, represented by the head of gold, is the first; the next is the Medo-Persian; the third, the Macedonian or Grecian; the fourth, the Roman, which should break every other kingdom in pieces, but which in its last stage should be divided into ten kingdoms, represented by the ten toes of the image, as they are in another vision (chap. vii) by the ten horns of the fourth beast. He likewise informs the king that in the time of this last monarchy, viz., the Roman, God would set up the kingdom of the Messiah; which, though small in its commencement, should ultimately be extended over the whole earth, 36-45. Daniel and his three friends, Hananiah, Mishael, and Azariah (named by the prince of the eunuchs Shadrach, Meshach, and Abed-nego), are then promoted by the king to great honor, 46-49.

1. *The second year of the reign of Nebuchadnezzar.* That is, the second year of his reigning alone, for he was king two years before his father's death. This was therefore the fifth year of his reign, and the fourth of the captivity of Daniel. *Nebuchadnezzar dreamed dreams, wherewith his spirit was troubled.* The dream had made a deep and solemn impression upon his mind; and, having forgotten all but general circumstances, his mind was distressed.

2. *The Chaldeans.* Who these were is difficult to be ascertained. They might be a college of learned men, where all arts and sciences were professed and taught.

4. *Then spake the Chaldeans to the king in Syriack. Aramith,* the language of Aram or Syria. What has been generally called the Chaldee. *O king, live for ever.* With these words the Chaldee part of Daniel commences; and continues to the end of the seventh chapter.

5. *Ye shall be cut in pieces.* This was arbitrary and tyrannical in the extreme; but, in the order of God's providence, it was overruled to serve the most important purpose.

14. *Captain of the king's guard.* Chief of the king's executioners or slaughter men.

19. *Then was the secret revealed . . . in a night vision.* Daniel either dreamed it or it was represented to his mind by an immediate inspiration.

20. *Wisdom and might are his.* He knows all things, and can do all things.

24. *Destroy not the wise men.* The decree was suspended till it should be seen whether Daniel could tell the dream and give its interpretation.

27. *Cannot the wise men.* Cannot your own able men, aided by your gods, tell you the secret? This question was necessary in order that the king might see the foolishness of depending on the one or worshipping the other. *The soothsayers.* One of our old words: "The tellers of truth."

28. *There is a God in heaven.* To distinguish Him from those idols, the works of men's hands, and from the false gods in which the Chaldeans trusted. *In the latter days.* A phrase which, in the prophets, generally means the times of the Messiah.

31. *A great image.* Representing the four great monarchies.

32. *Head was of fine gold.* The Babylonish empire, the first and greatest. *Breast and his arms of silver.* The Medo-Persian empire, under Cyrus, etc. *His belly and his thighs of brass.* The Macedonian empire, under Alexander the Great, and his successors.

33. *His legs of iron.* The Roman government. *His feet part of iron and part of clay.* The same, mixed with the barbaric nations, and divided into ten kingdoms.

34. *A stone was cut out.* The fifth monarchy; the spiritual kingdom of the Lord Jesus, which is to last forever, and diffuse itself over the whole earth.

37. *The God of heaven.* Not given by your own gods, nor acquired by your own skill and prowess; it is a divine gift. *Power.* To rule this kingdom. *And strength.* To defend it against all foes. *And glory.* Great honor and dignity.

44. *A kingdom, which shall never be destroyed.* The extensive and extending empire of Christ. *Shall not be left to other people.* All the preceding empires have swallowed up each other successively, but this shall remain to the end of the world.

45. *The dream is certain.* It contains a just representation of things as they shall be. *And the interpretation thereof sure.* The parts of the dream being truly explained.

46. *The king . . . fell upon his face.* Prostrated himself; this was the fullest act of adoration among the ancients. *Worshipped Daniel.* Supposing him to be a god, or divine being. No doubt Daniel forbade him, for to receive this would have been gross idolatry.

47. *Your God is a God of gods.* He is greater than all others. *And a Lord of kings.* He governs in both heaven and earth.

48. *Made Daniel a great man.* (1) By giving him many rich gifts, (2) By making him governor over the whole province of Babylon, and (3) By making him the chief or president over all the wise men.

49. *Daniel requested of the king, and he set Shadrach, Meshach, and Abed-nego, over the affairs of the province of Babylon.* He wished his three companions promoted who had shared his anxieties and helped him by their prayers. They all had places of trust, in which they could do much good, and prevent much evil. *Daniel sat in the gate of the king.* That is, was the chief officer in the palace, and the greatest confidant and counsellor of the king.

CHAPTER 3

Nebuchadnezzar, having erected an image, whose height (including probably a very high pedestal) was sixty cubits, and the breadth six, ordered a numerous assembly, which he had convened, to fall down and worship it; threatening, at the same time, that whosoever refused should be cast into a fiery furnace, a punishment not uncommon in that country (see Jer. xxix. 22), 1-7. Daniel's three companions, Shadrach, Meshach, and Abed-nego, who were present, being ob-erved to refrain from this idolatrous worship, were accused before the king; who, in great wrath, commanded them to comply with his orders on pain of death, 8-15. But these holy men, with the greatest composure and serenity, expressed their firm resolution not to worship his gods or his images, whatever might be the consequence, 16-18. Upon which the king, unaccustomed to having his will opposed, in the height of his wrath, ordered the furnace to be made seven times hotter than usual, and these men to be cast into it, bound by the most mighty of his army, who were killed by the flame in the execution of this service, 19-23. On this occasion God literally performed His promise by Isaiah (chap. xliii. 2:) "When thou walkest through the fire, thou shalt not be burned; neither shall the flame kindle upon thee." For an angel of God, appearing in the furnace, protected these young men, and counteracted the natural violence of the fire; which, only consuming the cords with which they were bound, left them to walk at liberty, and in perfect safety, in the midst of the furnace. The king, astonished at this prodigy, called to them to come out of the furnace, and blessed God for sending an angel to deliver His servants; and commanded all his subjects, upon pain of death, not to speak irreverently of the God of Shadrach, Meshach, and Abed-nego, who were promoted to great power and honor, 24-30. A striking example of the interposition of Providence in favor of true and inflexible piety.

1. *Nebuchadnezzar the king made an image of gold.* It is supposed that the history given here did not occur till the close, or near the end, of Nebuchadnezzar's reign. For it was after his insanity, as we see chap. iv. 33-36, and this happened near the close of his reign. A few observations on this image may be necessary: (1) It is not likely that this image was in human form—the dimensions show the improbability of this. (2) It is not likely that this image was all of gold. (3) It might have been a pillar on which an image of the god *Bel* was erected. The image itself might be of gold, or more probably gilt, that is, covered with thin plates of gold, and on this account it might be called the golden image. *The plain of Dura.* The situation of this place is not exactly known; there was a town or city called *Dura,* or *Doura,* in Mesopotamia, near the Tigris.

2. *Sent to gather together the princes.* It is not easy to show what these different offices were, as it is difficult to ascertain the meaning of the Chaldee words.

4. *Then a herald cried aloud.* "A crier called with might."

5. *The sound of the cornet.* There is not less difficulty in ascertaining the precise meaning of these musical instruments than there is in the offices in v. 2.

6. *Shall the same hour.* This is the first place in the Old Testament where we find the division of time into hours. The Greeks say that Anaxi-

mander was the inventor. He had it probably from the Chaldeans, among whom this division was in use long before Anaximander was born.

8. *Accused the Jews.* That is, Shadrach, Meshach, and Abed-nego. The other Jews were left unnoticed, and probably at this time Daniel was too high to be touched, but we may rest assured that he was not found among these idolaters.

16. *We are not careful.* We have no need to put you to any further trouble; we have made up our minds on this subject, and have our answer ready: "Be it known unto thee . . . we will not serve thy gods." This was as honest as it was decisive.

20. *The most mighty men.* The generals, or chief officers of his army.

21. *Their hats.* This word "hat" is found only in this place in the Old Testament. The word *sarbal* properly means an outer garment.

25. *Is like the Son of God.* A most improper translation. What notion could this idolatrous king have of the Lord Jesus Christ? for so the place is understood by thousands. *Bar elahin* signifies "a son of the gods," that is, a divine person or angel; and so the king calls him in v. 28: "God . . . hath sent his angel, and delivered his servants."

28. *Blessed be the God of Shadrach.* Here is a noble testimony from a heathen. And what produced it? The intrepidly pious conduct of these three noble Jews.

29. *Speak any thing amiss.* Though by the decree the king does not oblige the people to worship the true God, yet he obliges them to treat Him with reverence.

30. *Then the king promoted.* He restored them to the offices which they held before the charge of disobedience and treason was brought against them.

At the end of this verse the Septuagint add, "And he advanced them to be governors over all the Jews that were in his kingdom." This may be the meaning of the latter verse. They were more likely to be set over the Jews than over the Chaldeans.

CHAPTER 4

Nebuchadnezzar, after having subdued all the neighboring countries, and greatly enriched and adorned his own, became so intoxicated with his prosperity as to draw down upon himself a very remarkable judgment, of which this chapter gives a particular account, in the very words of the edict or proclamation which the Babylonish monarch issued on his restoration to the throne. This state document begins with Nebuchadnezzar's acknowledging the hand of God in his late malady, 1-3. It then gives an account of the dream of Nebuchadnezzar, which portended the loss of his kingdom and reason for seven years, on account of his pride and arrogance, 4-18. So it was explained by Daniel, 19-27, and so it was verified by the event, 28-33. It then recites how, at the end of the period fixed by the God of heaven for the duration of his malady, the Chaldean monarch became sensible of his dependence on the Supreme Being, and lifted up his eyes to heaven in devout acknowledgment of the sovereign majesty of the King of Kings, the Ruler of the earth, whose dominion alone is universal, unchangeable, and everlasting, 34-37.

1. *Nebuchadnezzar the king, unto all people.* This is a regular decree, and is one of the most ancient on record, and no doubt was copied from the state papers of Babylon. Daniel has preserved it in the original language.

2. *I thought it good to shew.* A part of the decree was a recital of the wonders wrought by the hand of the true God in his kingdom and on his person.

4. *I . . . was at rest.* I had returned to my palace in Babylon after having subdued Syria, Phoenicia, Judea, Egypt, and Arabia. It was probably these great conquests that puffed him up with pride, and brought that chastisement upon him which he afterwards describes.

10. *I saw . . . a tree.* This vision Nebuchadnezzar says made him afraid. What a mercy it is that God has hidden futurity from us! Were he to show every man the lot that is before him, the misery of the human race would be complete. Great men and princes are often represented, in the language of the prophets, under the similitude of trees; see Ezek. xvii. 5-6; xxxi. 3, etc.; Jer. xxii. 15; Ps. i. 3; xxxvii. 35.

13. *A watcher and an holy one.* These are both angels but, according to the Chaldean oracles, of different orders. They appear, according to their opinions, to be a kind of judges of human actions who had the power of determining the lot of men; see v. 17.

14. *Hew down the tree.* As the tree was to be cut down, the beasts are commanded to flee away from under his branches. His courtiers, officers, all abandoned him as soon as his insanity appeared; but he soon fled from the society of men.

15. *Leave the stump.* Let him not be destroyed, nor his kingdom alienated.

16. *Let his heart be changed.* Let him conceive himself to be a beast, and act as such, herding among the beasts of the field. *Let seven times pass over him.* Let him continue in this state for seven years.

19. *Daniel . . . was astonied for one hour.* He saw the design of the dream, and he felt the great delicacy of interpreting it. He was not puzzled by the difficulties of it. He felt for the king, and for the nation; and with what force and delicacy does he express the general portent: "The dream . . . to them that hate thee, and the interpretation thereof to thine enemies"!

20. *The tree that thou sawest.* The dream is so fully interpreted in the following verses that it needs no comment.

26. *Thy kingdom shall be sure unto thee.* No new king was set up; Evil-merodach, his son, was regent during his father's insanity.

30. *Is not this great Babylon?* Here his heart was inflated with pride; he attributed everything to himself, and acknowledged God in nothing. The walls, hanging gardens, temple of Bel, and the royal palace, all built by Nebuchadnezzar, made it the greatest city in the world.

31. *While the word was in the king's mouth.* How awful to a victorious and proud king: "The kingdom is departed from thee"! All your goods and gods are gone in a moment!

36. *My reason returned.* Everything was fulfilled that was exhibited by the dream and its interpretation. It is very likely that this unfortunate king had so concealed himself that the place of his retreat was not found out; and the providence of God had so watched over everything that, on his return to his palace, he found his counsellors and his lords, who received him gladly, and cleaved to and served him as they had formerly done.

CHAPTER 5

In the commencement of this chapter we are informed how Belshazzar, the grandson of Nebuchadnezzar, when rioting in his palace, and profaning the sacred vessels of the Temple, 1-4, was suddenly terrified with the appearance of the fingers of a man's hand, which wrote a few words on the wall before him, 5-6. The wise men and astrologers were immediately called in to show the king the interpretation; but they could not so much as read the writing, because (as Houbigant and others have conjectured), though the words are in the Chaldee tongue, yet they were written in the Samaritan or ancient Hebrew characters, with which the wise men of Babylon were very probably unacquainted, as the Jews were at that time a despised people, and the knowledge of their language not a fashionable attainment, 7-9. Daniel, who had been so highly esteemed by Nebuchadnezzar for his superior wisdom, appears to have been altogether unknown to Belshazzar, till the queen (the same who had been the wife of Nebuchadnezzar according to the general opinion, or the queen consort according to others) had informed him, 10-12. Upon the queen's recommendation, Daniel is called in, 13-16; who boldly tells this despotic king that, as he had not benefited by the judgments inflicted on his grandfather, but gave himself up to pride and profanity, and had added to his other sins an utter contempt for the God of the Jews by drinking wine out of the sacred vessels of Jehovah in honor of his idols, 17-23, the Supreme Being, the Ruler of heaven and earth, had written his condemnation in three words, *Mene, Tekel, Peres,* 24-25; the first of which is repeated in the copies containing the Chaldean original; but all the ancient Versions, except the Syriac, are without this repetition. Daniel then gives the king and his lords the fearful import of the writing, viz., that the period allotted for the duration of the Chaldean empire was now completed (see Jer. xxv. 12-14), and that the kingdom was about to be transferred to the Medes and Persians, 26-28. However unwelcome such an interpretation must have been to Belshazzar, yet the monarch, overwhelmed with its clearness and certainty, commanded the prophet to be honored, 29. And that very night the prediction was fulfilled, for the king was slain, 30, and the city taken by the Medes and Persians, 31. This great event was also predicted by Isaiah and Jeremiah, and the manner in which it was accomplished is recorded by Herodotus and Xenophon.

1. *Belshazzar the king made a great feast.* After the death of Nebuchadnezzar, Evil-merodach, his son, ascended the throne of Babylon. Having reigned about two years, he was slain by his brother-in-law, Neriglissar. He reigned four years, and was succeeded by his son Leborosoarchod, who reigned only nine months. At his death Belshazzar, the son of Evil-merodach, was raised to the throne, and reigned seventeen years, and was slain, as we read here, by Cyrus, who surprised and took the city on the night of this festivity. But the Scripture mentions only Nebuchadnezzar, Evil-merodach, and Belshazzar, by name; and Jeremiah, chap. xxvii. 7, expressly says, "All nations shall serve him [Nebuchadnezzar], and his son [Evil-merodach], and his son's son [Belshazzar] until the very time of his land come"; i.e., till the time in which the empire should be seized by Cyrus. Here there is no mention of Neriglissar nor Laborosoarchod; but as they were usurpers, they might have been purposely passed by. But there remains one difficulty still: Belshazzar is expressly called the son of Nebuchadnezzar by the queen mother, v. 11. The solution of this difficulty is that in Scripture the name of "son" is indifferently given to sons and grandsons, and even to great-grandsons. *To a thousand of his lords.* Perhaps this means lords or satraps, that were each over 1,000 men.

8. *They could not read the writing.* Because it was in the pure Hebrew, not the Chaldean, character.

10. *The queen . . . came.* This is generally allowed to have been the widow of Nebuchadnezzar.

16. *Dissolve doubts.* Untie knots—unbind what is bound. An expression used in the East to signify a judge of eminent wisdom and skill.

17. *Let thy gifts be to thyself.* They could be of little use to any, as the city was in a few hours to be taken and pillaged.

18. *Nebuchadnezzar thy father.* Or "grandfather." See the notes on v. 1.

19. *Whom he would he slew.* The genuine character of a despot, whose will is the only rule of his conduct.

20. *He was deposed from his kingly throne.* Became insane, and the reins of government were taken out of his hands.

22. *Hast not humbled thine heart.* These judgments and mercies have had no good effect upon thee.

23. *But hast lifted up thyself against the Lord.* And the highest evidence of this rebellion was the profaning the sacred vessels of the Lord's house.

24. *Then was the part of the hand sent.* This was the filling up of the cup of your iniquity; this last act made you ripe for destruction.

25. It should be observed that each word stands for a short sentence: *mene* signifies "numeration"; *tekel,* "weighing"; and *peres,* "division." All the ancient versions, except the Syriac, read the words simply *Mene, Tekel, Phares,* as they are explained in the following verses, without the repetition of *Mene.*

29. *Clothed Daniel with scarlet.* More probably with "purple." The gold chain about the neck was an emblem of magisterial authority. It is often thus mentioned in Scripture.

30. *In that night was Belshazzar . . . slain.* Xenophon says he was dispatched by two lords, Gadatas and Gobrias, who went over to Cyrus to avenge themselves of certain wrongs which Belshazzar had done them. We have already seen that Cyrus entered the city by the bed of the Euphrates, which he had emptied, by cutting a channel for the waters and directing them into the marshy country.

31. *Darius the Median took the kingdom.* This is supposed to be the same as Cyaxares, son of Astyages and maternal uncle of Cyrus, to whom he gave the throne of Babylon after himself had had the honor of taking the city.

Daniel speaks nothing of the war that raged between the Babylonians and the Medes; but Isaiah speaks particularly of it, chaps. xiii—xiv; xlv—xlvli; and so does Jeremiah, chaps. l—li. I need not add that it is largely spoken of by profane authors. The Medes and Persians were confederates in the war; the former under Darius, the latter under Cyrus. Both princes are supposed to have been present at the taking of this city.

CHAPTER 6

Darius the Median, who succeeded Belshazzar in the kingdom of Babylon, having heard of Daniel's extraordinary wisdom and understanding, constituted him the chief of the three presidents who were over the whole empire, and purposed also to make him prime minister or viceroy, 1-3. This great partiality of the king towards a stranger of Jewish extraction, and who had been carried captive into Chaldea, raised up a great many enemies to Daniel; and a scheme was even contrived by the presidents and princes to ruin him, 4-15; which succeeded so far that he was cast into a den of lions, but was miraculously delivered, 16-23. Darius, who was greatly displeased with himself for having been entrapped by the governors of the provinces to the prejudice of his faithful minister, was pleased and astonished at this deliverance; punished Daniel's enemies with the same kind of death which they had designed for the prophet; and made a decree that, throughout his dominions, the God of Daniel should be had in the greatest veneration, 24-38.

1. *An hundred and twenty princes.* A chief or satrap over every province which belonged to the Medo-Persian empire. Afterwards we find it enlarged to 127 provinces, by the victories of Cambyses and Darius Hystaspes. See Esther i. 1.

2. *Three presidents.* Each having forty of these presidents accountable to him for their administration. *Daniel was first.* As being established over that part where was the seat of government. He was confirmed in his offices by Darius.

3. *The king thought to set him over the whole realm.* Intended to make him grand vizier. This partiality of the king made Daniel the object of the other presidents, and the grandees of the kingdom.

4. *Sought to find occasion against Daniel.* But they found no blemish in his administration, for he was faithful to his king; this was a virtue. But he was also faithful to his God; this they hoped to construe into a crime, and make it the cause of his ruin.

7. *Whosoever shall ask a petition.* What pretense could they urge for so silly an ordinance? Probably to flatter the ambition of the king, they pretend to make him a god for thirty days, so that the whole empire should make prayer and supplication to him, and pay him divine honors! This was the bait; but their real object was to destroy Daniel.

10. *Now when Daniel knew that the writing was signed.* He saw what was designed, and he knew whom he served. *His windows being open.* He would not shut them to conceal himself, but "kneeled down with his face turned toward Jerusalem, and prayed thrice each day, giving thanks to God as usual." When the Jews were in distant countries, in prayer they turned their faces towards Jerusalem; and when in Jerusalem, they turned their faces towards the Temple. Solomon, in his prayer at the dedication of the Temple, 1 Kings viii. 48, had entreated God to hear the prayers of those who might be in strange lands, or in captivity, when they should turn their faces towards their own land, which God gave unto their fathers; and towards the city which He had chosen, and the house which was dedicated to His name. It was in reference to this that Daniel turned his face towards Jerusalem when he prayed.

14. *The king . . . was sore displeased with himself.* And well he might, when through his excessive folly he passed a law that, for its ostensible object, would have been a disgrace almost to an idiot. *And set his heart on Daniel.* He strove by every means to get the law annulled. He had no doubt spoken to several of his lords in private, and had gone from one to another till the going down of the sun.

15. *Then these men assembled.* Having got favorable answers, as we may presume, from many individuals, he called a parliament; but they now collectively joined to urge the execution of the law, not its repeal.

16. *Then the king commanded.* With a heavy heart he was obliged to warrant this murderous conspiracy. But when passing sentence his last words were affecting: "Thy God whom thou servest continually, he will deliver thee."

17. *A stone was brought.* All this *precaution* served the purposes of the Divine Providence. There could be no trick nor collusion here; if Daniel be preserved, it must be by the power of the Supreme God. The same precaution was taken by the Jews in the case of the burial of our blessed Lord; and this very thing has served as one of the strongest proofs of the certainty of His resurrection and their unmixed wickedness.

18. *Passed the night fasting.* He neither ate nor drank, had no music to solace, nor sweet odors burnt or brought before him, and he passed the night without sleep. All this points out his great sincerity; and when it is considered that Darius could not be less than sixty-two or sixty-three years of age at this time, it shows more fully the depth of his concern.

22. *My God hath sent his angel.* Such a one as that who attended Shadrach, Meshach, and Abed-nego in the fiery furnace, and blew inside the flames, so that they could not hurt them. *Before him innocency was found in me.* Because I was innocent God has preserved me; and now that I am preserved, my innocence is fully proved.

26. *I make a decree, That . . . man tremble and fear before the God of Daniel.* As in the case of the three Hebrews, chap. iii. 29. The true God was known by His servants, and by the deliverances He wrought for them.

28. *So this Daniel prospered.* He had served five kings: Nebuchadnezzar, Evil-merodach, Belshazzar, Darius, and Cyrus. Few courtiers have had so long a reign, served so many masters without flattering any, been more successful in their management of public affairs, been so useful to the states where they were in office, been more owned of God, or have left such an example to posterity.

CHAPTER 7

The prophet having, in the preceding chapters of this book, related some remarkable events concerning himself and his brethren in the Captivity, and given proof of his being enabled by divine assistance to interpret the dreams of others, enters now into a detail of his own visions, returning to a period prior to the transactions recorded in the last chapter. The first in order of the prophet's visions is that of the four beasts, which arose out of a very tempestuous ocean, 1-9; and of One like the Son of Man who annihilated the dominion of the fourth beast, because of the proud and blasphemous words of one of its horns, 9-14. An angel deciphers the hieroglyphics contained in this chapter, declaring that the four beasts, diverse one from another, represent the four paramount empires of the habitable globe, which should succeed each other; and are evidently the same which were shadowed forth to Nebuchadnezzar by another set of hieroglyphics (see the second chapter), 15-26. But for the consolation of the people of God it is added that, at the time appointed in the counsel of Jehovah, "the kingdom and dominion, and the greatness of the kingdom under the whole heaven, shall be given to . . . the saints of the most High"; and that this kingdom shall never be destroyed or transferred to another people, as all the preceding dominations have been, but shall itself stand forever, 27-28. It will be proper to remark that the period of a time, times, and a half, mentioned in the twenty-fifth verse as the duration of the dominion of the little horn that made war with the saints (generally supposed to be a symbolical representation of the papal power), had most probably its commencement in A.D. 755 or 756, when Pepin, king of France, invested the pope with temporal power. This hypothesis will bring the conclusion of the period to about the year of Christ 2000, a time fixed by Jews and Christians for some remarkable revolution; when the world, as they suppose, will be renewed, the wicked cease from troubling the Church, and the saints of the Most High have dominion over the whole habitable globe. But this is all hypothesis.

1. *In the first year of Belshazzar.* This is the same Belshazzar who was slain at the taking of Babylon, as we have seen at the conclusion of chap. v.

2. *The four winds of the heaven strove upon the great sea.* The idea of strife is taken here

from the effects that must be produced were the east, the west, the north, and the south winds to rise tempestuously, and meet on the surface of the sea. By the great sea, the Mediterranean is meant. This dream is the same in meaning, under different emblems, as that of Nebuchadnezzar's metallic image; but in Daniel's dream several circumstances are added. It is supposed that Daniel had this dream about forty-eight years after Nebuchadnezzar had the vision of the great image.

3. *Four great beasts came up from the sea.* The term *sea*, in Hebrew *yam*, from *hamah*, "to be tumultuous, agitated," seems to be used here to point out the then known globe, because of its generally agitated state; and the four winds striving point out those predatory wars that prevailed almost universally among men, from the days of Nimrod, the founder of the Assyrian or Babylonish monarchy, down to that time, and in the end gave birth to the four great monarchies which are the subject of this vision.

4. *The first was like a lion, and had eagle's wings.* The beast like a lion is the kingdom of the Babylonians; and the king of Babylon is compared to a lion, Jer. iv. 7; Isa. v. 29; and is said to fly as an eagle, Jer. xlviii. 40; Ezek. xvii. 3, 7. The lion is considered the king of the beasts, and the eagle the king of the birds; and therefore the kingdom of Babylon, which was signified by the golden head of the great image, was the first and noblest of all the kingdoms; and was the greatest then in being. The wings of the eagle denote the rapidity with which the lion, Nebuchadnezzar, made his conquests. For in a few years, by his own arms, he brought his empire to such an extent, and raised it to such a degree of eminence, as was truly surprising; and all tended to show with what propriety this eagle-winged lion is here made his emblem. *The wings thereof were plucked.* Lydia, Media, and Persia, which had been provinces of the Babylonish empire, cast off the yoke, and put themselves under kings of their own. Besides, the rapidity of its conquests was stopped by its wars with the Medes and Persians; by whom it was at last conquered, and divided between Darius the Mede and Cyrus the Persian. *And made stand upon the feet as a man.* This I think refers to the taming of Nebuchadnezzar's pride. He had acted like a fierce and ravening lion. God struck him with insanity; he then lived the life of a beast, and had a beast's heart—disposition and habits. At last God restored him. *And a man's heart was given to it.* He became humane, humble, and pious; and in this state he appears to have died.

5. *Another beast . . . like to a bear.* This was the Medo-Persian empire, represented here under the symbol of the bear, as the largest species of these animals was found in *Media*, a mountainous, cold, and rough country, covered with woods. The Medes and Persians are compared to a *bear* on account of their *cruelty* and *thirst after blood,* a bear being a most voracious and cruel animal. The bear is termed by Aristotle an all-devouring animal; and the Medo-Persians are known to have been great robbers and spoilers. See Jer. li. 48-56. The Persians were notorious for the cruelty of their punishments. *Raised up itself on one side.* Cyrus arose on the borders of Chaldea, and thus the bear appeared to put itself in the position to attack the lion. *It had three ribs in the mouth of it.* The ribs

being between the teeth of the bear may show how Babylon, Lydia, and Egypt were ground and oppressed by the bear—the Persians; though, as ribs strengthen the body, they were a powerful support to their conquerors.

6. *Another, like a leopard . . . four wings . . . four heads.* This was the Macedonian or Greek empire, and Alexander the Great its king. *Four wings of a fowl.* The Babylonian empire was represented with two wings; and they sufficiently marked the rapidity of Nebuchadnezzar's conquests. But the Macedonian has here four wings; for nothing, in the history of the world, was equal to the conquests of Alexander, who ran through all the countries from Illyricum and the Adriatic Sea to the Indian Ocean and the River Ganges; and in twelve years subdued part of Europe and all Asia. *The beast had also four heads.* Signifying the empire after the death of Alexander, divided between his four generals: Cassander reigning over Macedon and Greece; Lysimachus, over Thrace and Bithynia; Ptolemy, over Egypt; and Seleucus, over Syria. *Dominion was given to it.* It was not owing to the skill, courage, or valor of Alexander and his troops that he made those wondrous conquests; the nations were given to him. For, as Bishop Newton says, had he not been assisted by the mighty power of God, how could he, with only 30,000 men, have overcome Darius with 600,000; and in so short a time have brought the countries from Greece as far as India into subjection?

7. *I saw . . . a fourth beast . . . it had great iron teeth.* This is allowed, on all hands, to be the Roman empire. It was dreadful, terrible, and exceeding strong; *it devoured and brake in pieces, and stamped the residue,* that is, the remains of the former kingdoms, with its feet. It reduced Macedon into a Roman province about one hundred and sixty-eight years before Christ; the kingdom of Pergamos, about one hundred and thirty-three years; Syria, about sixty-five; and Egypt, about thirty years before Christ. And, besides the remains of the Macedonian empire, it subdued many other provinces and kingdoms; so that it might, by a very usual figure, be said to devour the whole earth, to tread it down, and break it to pieces; and became in effect, what the Roman writers delight to call it, "the empire of the whole world." *It had ten horns.* The ten kingdoms into which the Roman empire was afterwards divided.

8. *Another little horn.* Among Protestant writers this is considered to be the popedom.

10. *A fiery stream issued.* This is not spoken of the final judgment; but of that which He was to execute upon this fourth beast, the Roman empire; and the little boasting horn, which is a part of the fourth beast, and must fall when the other falls.

11. *I beheld then because of the voice* (or, *the beast will be destroyed because*) *of the great words which the horn spake . . . his body destroyed.* When the dominion was taken from the rest of the beasts, their bodies were not destroyed, but suffered to continue still in being; but when the dominion shall be taken away from this beast, his body shall be totally destroyed; because other kingdoms succeeded to those, but no other earthly kingdom shall succeed to this (Bishop Newton).

13. *One like the Son of man came with the clouds of heaven.* This most certainly points

out the Lord Jesus, who took our nature upon Him that He might redeem us unto himself. To prove himself to be the Messiah, He applies, before the high priests, these words of the Prophet Daniel to himself, Matt. xxiv. 30.

14. *And there was given him dominion.* This also is applied to our Lord Jesus by himself after His resurrection, Matt. xxviii. 18. *His dominion is an everlasting dominion.* Christianity shall increase, and prevail to the end of the world. See the parallel passages in the margin.

15. *I Daniel was grieved.* The words in the original are uncommonly emphatic. "My spirit was grieved (or sickened) within its sheath (or scabbard)."

19. *His nails of brass.* This is not mentioned in the seventh verse, where the description of the beast is given.

21. *The same horn made war with the saints, and prevailed against them.* Those who make Antiochus the little horn make the saints the Jewish people. Those who understand the popedom by it see this as referring to the cruel persecutions of the popes of Rome against the Waldenses and Albigenses, and the Protestant church in general.

25. *He shall speak great words against the most High.* "He shall speak as if he were God." So St. Jerome quotes from Symmachus. To none can this apply so well or so fully as to the popes of Rome. They have assumed infallibility, which belongs only to God. They profess to forgive sins, which belongs only to God. They profess to open and shut heaven, which belongs only to God. They profess to be higher than all the kings of the earth, which belongs only to God. And they go beyond God in pretending to loose whole nations from their oath of allegiance to their kings, when such kings do not please them! *And shall wear out the saints.* By wars, crusades, massacres, inquisitions, and persecutions of all kinds. What in this way have they not done against all those who have protested against their innovations, and refused to submit to their idolatrous worship? Witness the exterminating crusades published against the Waldenses and Albigenses. Witness John Huss, and Jerome of Prague. *And think to change times and laws.* Appointing fasts and feasts; canonizing persons whom he chooses to call saints; granting pardons and indulgences for sins; instituting new modes of worship utterly unknown to the Christian Church; new articles of faith; new rules of practice; and reversing, with pleasure, the laws both of God and man (Dodd). *Until a time and times and the dividing of time.* In prophetic language a *time* signifies a "year"; and a prophetic year has a year for each day. Three years and a half (a day standing for a year, as in chap. ix. 24) will amount to 1,260 years, if we reckon 30 days to each month, as the Jews do. If the papal power, as a horn or temporal power, be intended here, which is most likely (and we know that that power was given in 755 to Pope Stephen II by *Pepin,* king of France), counting 1,260 years from that, we are brought to A.D. 2015. But I neither lay stress upon nor draw conclusions from these dates. If the church of Rome will reform itself, it will then be the true Christian Church, and will never be destroyed. Let it throw aside all that is ritually Jewish, all that is heathen, all that which pretends to be of God and which is only

of man, all doctrines that are not in the Bible, and all rites and ceremonies which are not of the appointment of Christ and His apostles; and then, all hail the once Roman, but now, after such a change, the holy, Catholic Church! Every true Protestant would wish rather the reform than the extinction of this church.

CHAPTER 8

This chapter contains Daniel's vision of the ram and he-goat, 1-14; referring, as explained by the angel, to the Persian and Grecian monarchies, 15-26. The little horn mentioned in the ninth verse (or fierce king, as interpreted in the twenty-third) is supposed by some to denote Antiochus Epiphanes; but seems more properly to apply to the Roman power in general, by which the polity and Temple of the Jews were destroyed, on account of the great transgressions of these ancient people of God; and particularly because of their very obstinate and unaccountable rejection of the glorious doctrines of Christianity, which had been preached among them by Jesus Christ and His apostles, and the truth of which God had attested "by signs and wonders, and by divers miracles and gifts of the Holy Ghost." Daniel is then informed of the 2,300 prophetic days (that is, years) which must elapse before the sanctuary be cleansed; or, in other words, before righteousness shall prevail over the whole earth. This period is supposed, with considerable probability, to have had its commencement when Alexander the Great invaded Asia, in the year before Christ 334. This will bring the close of it to about the end of the sixth chiliad of the world; when, as already observed, some astonishing changes are expected to take place in the moral condition of the human race; when power of Antichrist, both papal and Mohammedan, shall be totally annihilated, and universal dominion given to the saints of the Most High. The chapter concludes with the distress of Daniel on account of the fearful judgments with which his country should be visited in after ages, 27.

1. *In the third year of the reign of . . . Belshazzar.* We now come once more to the Hebrew, the Chaldee part of the book being finished. As the Chaldeans had a particular interest in both the history and prophecies from chap. ii. 4 to the end of chap. vii, the whole is written in Chaldee. But as the prophecies which remain concern times posterior to the Chaldean monarchy, and principally relate to the Church and people of God generally, they are written in the Hebrew language, this being the tongue in which God chose to reveal all His counsels given under the Old Testament relative to the New.

2. *I saw in a vision.* Daniel was at this time in Shushan, which appears to have been a strong place, where the kings of Persia had their summer residence. It was the capital of the province of Elam, which was most probably added to the Chaldean territories by Nebuchadnezzar; see Jer. xlix. 34-35. Here was Daniel's ordinary residence; and though here at this time, he, in vision, saw himself on the banks of the river Ulai. This is the same as the river Euleus, which divided Shushan or Susiana from Elymais.

3. *A ram which had two horns.* In the former vision there were four beasts, pointing out four empires; in this we have but two, as only two empires are concerned here, viz., the Grecian and the Persian. The Babylonish empire is not mentioned; its fate was before decided, and it was now at its close. By the *ram,* the empire of the Medes and Persians was pointed out, as explained by the angel Gabriel, v. 20; and particularly Cyrus, who was the founder of that empire. A *ram* was the symbol of the Persians; and a ram's head with two horns, one higher than the other, appears as such in different parts of the ruins of Persepolis. This ram had two horns; that is, two kingdoms, viz., Media and Persia; but one was higher than the other, and

the higher came up last. Media, signified by the shorter horn, was the more ancient of the two kingdoms. Persia, the higher horn, had come up but lately, and was of little historic or political consequence till the time of Cyrus. But in the reigns of this prince and his immediate successors, Persia attained a political consequence greatly superior to that possessed at any time by the kingdom of Media; therefore it is said to have been the higher, and to have come up last.

4. *I saw the ram pushing westward.* The Persians, who are signified by the ram, as well as their founder, Cyrus, pushed their conquests west, north, and south. The principal theatre of their wars, says Calmet, was against the Scythians, northward; against the Greeks, westward; and against the Egyptians, southward. *He did according to his will.* There was no other nation at that time that could stay the progress of the Persian arms.

5. *Behold an he goat.* This was Alexander the Great; and a goat was a very proper symbol of the Grecian or Macedonian people. *Came from the west.* Europe lies westward of Asia. *On the face of the whole earth.* Carrying everything before him. *Touched not the ground.* Seemed to fly from conquest to conquest. By the time Alexander was thirty years of age he had conquered all Asia: and, because of the rapidity of his conquests, he is represented as a leopard with four wings, in the preceding vision.

6. *And he came to the ram.* This and the following verse give an account of the overthrow of the Persian empire by Alexander and ran unto him in the fury of his power. The conflicts between the Greeks and the Persians were excessively severe. Alexander first vanquished the generals of Darius, at the river Granicus, in Phrygia; he next attacked and totally routed Darius, at the straits of Issus, in Cilicia; and afterwards at the plains of Arbela, in Assyria.

7. *And brake his two horns.* Subdued Persia and Media; sacked and burnt the royal city of Persepolis, the capital of the Persian empire and, even in its ruins, one of the wonders of the world to the present day. This he did because "he was moved with choler" against Darius, who had endeavored to draw off his captains with bribes, and had labored to induce some of his friends to assassinate him. Alexander, finding this, would listen to no proposals of peace, and was determined never to rest till he had destroyed Darius and his whole empire. In Media, Darius was seized and made prisoner by some of his own treacherous subjects, and afterwards basely murdered. *He cast him down to the ground, and stamped upon him.* Totally destroyed the family, and overturned the whole monarchy.

8. *The he goat waxed very . . . strong.* He had subdued nearly the whole of the then known world. *The great horn was broken.* Alexander died in the height of his conquests, when he was but about thirty-three years of age. His natural brother, Philip Aridaeus, and his two sons, Alexander Aegus and Hercules, kept up the show and name of the Macedonian kingdom for a time, but they were all murdered within fifteen years; and thus the great horn, the Macedonian kingdom, was broken, Alexander's family being now cut off. *And for it came up four notable ones.* The regal family being

all dead, the governors of provinces usurped the title of kings; and Antigonus, one of them, being slain at the battle of Ipsus, they were reduced to four, as we have already seen: (1) Seleucus, who had Syria and Babylon, from whom came the *Seleucidae*, famous in history; (2) Lysimachus, who had Asia Minor; (3) Ptolemy, son of Lagus, who had Egypt; and (4) Cassander, who had Greece and the neighboring countries. These held dominion towards the four winds of heaven. Cassander had the western parts, Lysimachus had the northern regions, Ptolemy possessed the southern countries, and Seleucus had the eastern provinces.

9. *Out of one of them came forth a little horn.* Some think that Antiochus Epiphanes is meant. *Toward the pleasant land.* Judea, so called in Ps. cvi. 24; Jer. iii. 19; Dan. xi. 16, 41.

10. *The host of heaven.* The Jewish hierarchy. *The stars*, the priests and Levites. The powers or *host of heaven* are probably intended by our Lord, Matt. xxiv. 29, to signify the whole Jewish hierarchy.

14. *Unto two thousand and three hundred days.* Though literally it be 2,300 evenings and mornings, yet I think the prophetic day should be understood here, as in other parts of this prophet, and must signify so many years. If we date these years from the vision of the he-goat (Alexander's invading Asia) this was 334 B.C.; and 2,300 years from that time will reach to A.D. 1966.

CHAPTER 9

Daniel, understanding from the prophecies of Jeremiah that the 70 years' captivity was now terminating, pours out his soul in fervent prayer to God, and earnestly supplicates pardon and restoration for his captive people, 1-19. When he is thus supplicating God in behalf of Israel, the angel Gabriel is sent to inform him of the 70 prophetic weeks, or 490 natural years, which should elapse from the date of the edict to rebuild Jerusalem and the Temple to the death of the Messiah, 20-27; a prophecy most exactly fulfilled by the event, according to the computation of the best chronologers. Dean Prideaux states the commencement of these 70 prophetic weeks to have been in the month Nisan, in the year of the Julian period 4256, which corresponds with A.M. 3546, B.C. 458, according to the Ussherian account. How awfully are the Jews blinded who, in contradiction to so clear a prophecy, still expect the Messiah, who was cut off, and, after suffering, is entered into His glory!

1. *In the first year of Darius.* This is the same Darius the Mede spoken of before, who succeeded Belshazzar, king of the Chaldeans. See chap. v. 31.

2. *I Daniel understood by books.* The prophecy referred to here is found Jer. xxv. 12; xxix. 10. The people must have been satisfied of the divine inspiration of Jeremiah or his prophecies would not have been so speedily collected nor so carefully preserved. It appears that there was a copy of them then in Daniel's hands.

3. *I set my face . . . to seek by prayer.* He found that the time of the promised deliverance could not be at any great distance; and as he saw nothing that indicated a speedy termination of their oppressive captivity, he was very much afflicted, and earnestly besought God to put a speedy end to it; and how earnestly he sought, his own words show. He prayed, he supplicated, he fasted, he put sackcloth upon his body, and he put ashes upon his head. He used that kind of prayer prescribed by Solomon in his prayer at the dedication of the Temple. See 1 Kings viii. 47-48.

4. *Keeping the covenant.* Fidelity and truth are characteristics of God. He had never yet broken His engagements to His followers, and was ever showing mercy to men.

7. *All Israel, that are near, and that are far off.* He prays both for Judah and Israel. The latter were more dispersed, and had been much longer in captivity.

9. *Mercies and forgivenesses.* From God's goodness flow God's mercies; from His mercies, forgivenesses.

11. *Therefore the curse is poured upon us.* It is probable that he alludes here to the punishment of certain criminals by pouring melted metal upon them; therefore he uses the word *tittach,* "it is poured out," like melted metal.

14. *The Lord watched upon the evil.* In consequence of our manifold rebellions He hath now watched for an opportunity to bring these calamities upon us.

17. *And cause thy face to shine.* Give us proof that Thou art reconciled to us.

19. *Thy city and thy people are called by thy name.* The Holy City, the city of the great King. I think it scarcely possible for any serious man to read these impressive and pleading words without feeling a measure of the prophet's earnestness.

21. *The man Gabriel.* Or the angel Gabriel, who had appeared to me as a "man." *Being caused to fly swiftly.* God hears with delight such earnest, humble, urgent prayers; and sends the speediest answer. Gabriel himself was ordered on this occasion to make more than usual speed.

24. *Seventy weeks are determined.* This is a most important prophecy, and has given rise to a variety of opinions relative to the proper mode of explanation; but the chief difficulty, if not the only one, is to find out the time from which these seventy weeks should be dated. What is here said by the angel is not a direct answer to Daniel's prayer. He prays to know when the seventy weeks of the Captivity are to end. Gabriel shows him that there are seventy weeks determined relative to a redemption from another sort of captivity, which shall commence with the going forth of the edict to restore and rebuild Jerusalem, and shall terminate with the death of Messiah, the Prince, and the total abolition of the Jewish sacrifices. In the following four verses he enters into the particulars of this most important determination, and leaves them with Daniel for his comfort, who has left them to the Church of God for the confirmation of its faith, and a testimony to the truth of divine revelation. Of all the writers I have consulted on this most noble prophecy, Dean Prideaux appears to me the most clear and satisfactory. I shall therefore follow his method in my explanation, and often borrow his words. *Seventy weeks are determined*—The Jews had sabbatic years, Lev. xxv. 8, by which their years were divided into weeks of years, as in this important prophecy, each week containing 7 years. The 70 weeks therefore here spoken of amount to 490 years. In v. 24 there are six events mentioned which should be the consequences of the incarnation of our Lord: (I) *To finish* ("to restrain") *the transgression,* which was effected by the preaching of the gospel, and pouring out of the Holy Ghost among men.

(II) *To make an end of sins;* rather "to make an end of sin offerings," which our Lord did when He offered His spotless soul and body on the Cross once for all. (III) *To make reconciliation* ("to make atonement or expiation") *for iniquity.* (IV) *To bring in everlasting righteousness,* "the righteousness, or righteous One, of ages." (V) *To seal up* ("to finish or complete") *the vision and prophecy;* that is, to put an end to the necessity of any further revelations, by completing the canon of Scripture, and fulfilling the prophecies which related to His person, sacrifice, and the glory that should follow. (VI) *And to anoint the most Holy, kodesh kodashim,* "the holy of holies." *Mashach,* "to anoint" (from which comes *mashiach,* "the Messiah," the Anointed One), signifies in general to consecrate or appoint to some special office. Here it means the consecration or appointment of our blessed Lord, the Holy One of Israel, to be the Prophet, Priest, and King of mankind.

The above 70 weeks, or 490 years, are divided in v. 25 into three distinct periods, to each of which particular events are assigned. The 3 periods are—(I) *Seven weeks,* that is, 49 years. (II) *Sixty-two weeks,* that is, 434 years. (III) *One week,* that is, 7 years. To the first period of 7 weeks the restoration and repairing of Jerusalem are referred; and so long were Ezra and Nehemiah employed in restoring the sacred constitutions and civil establishments of the Jews, for this work lasted 49 years after the commission was given by Artaxerxes. From the above 7 weeks the second period of 62 weeks, or 434 years more, commences, at the end of which the prophecy says *Messiah the Prince* should come. That is, 7 weeks, or 49 years, should be allowed for the restoration of the Jewish state; from which time till the public entrance of the Messiah on the work of the ministry should be 62 weeks, or 434 years—in all, 483 years. From the coming of our Lord, the third period is to be dated, viz., "He shall confirm the covenant with many for one week," that is, *seven years,* v. 27. This confirmation of the covenant must take in the ministry of John the Baptist with that of our Lord, comprehending the term of 7 years, during the whole of which He might be well said to confirm or ratify the new covenant with mankind. Our Lord says, "The law was until John"; but from his first public preaching the kingdom of God, or gospel dispensation, commenced. Dean Prideaux thinks that the whole refers to our Lord's preaching connected with that of the Baptist. *Vachatsi,* says he, signifies in the "half part" of the week; that is, in the latter 3½ years in which He exercised himself in the public ministry, He caused, by the sacrifice of himself, all other sacrifices and oblations to cease, which were instituted to signify His. In the latter parts of vv. 26 and 27 we find the third part of this great prophecy, which refers to what should be done after the completion of these 70 weeks.

26. *And the people of the prince that shall come shall destroy the city and the sanctuary.* By the "prince" Titus, the son of Vespasian, is plainly intended; and "the people" of that prince are no other than the Romans, who, according to the prophecy, destroyed the sanctuary, *hakkodesh,* "the holy place" or Temple, and, as a flood, swept away all, till the total destruction of that obstinate people finished the war.

27. *And for the overspreading of abomina-tions he shall make it desolate.* This clause is remarkably obscure. "And upon the wing of abominations causing amazement." This is a literal translation of the place; but still there is no determinate sense. A Hebrew MS., written in the thirteenth century, has preserved a very remarkable reading here, which frees the place from all embarrassment. Instead of the above reading, this valuable MS. has, "And in the temple [of the Lord] there shall be abomina-tion." This makes the passage plain, and is strictly conformable to the facts themselves, for the Temple was profaned; and it agrees with the prediction of our Lord, who said that the abomination that maketh desolate should stand in the holy place, Matt. xxiv. 15, and quotes the words as spoken by Daniel, the prophet. That the above reading gives the true sense, there can be little doubt, because it is counten-anced by the most eminent ancient versions. The Vulgate reads, "And in the temple there shall be abomination." The Septuagint, "And upon the temple there shall be the abomination of desolation."

CHAPTER 10

This and the two following chapters give an account of Daniel's last vision, wherein the succession of the Persian and Grecian monarchies is described, together with the wars that should take place between Syria and Egypt under the latter monarchy. The last part of the vision (from chap. xi. 36) seems to relate chiefly to the persecutions of the Church in the times of Antichrist, till it be purified from all its pollutions; after which will follow that glorious Kingdom of the saints spoken of in the seventh and eighth chapters. This chapter begins with an account of Daniel's fasting and humiliation, 1-3. Then we have a description of the Divine Person who appeared to the prophet, not unlike him who appeared to the apostle in the isle of Patmos, 4-21. See Rev. i. 10-16.

1. *In the third year of Cyrus.* Which answers to the first year of Darius the Mede. *The time appointed was long.* But the "warfare long"; there will be many contentions and wars before these things can be accomplished.

2. *I . . . was mourning three full weeks.* The weeks are most probably dated from the time of the termination of the last vision.

3. *I ate no pleasant bread.* This fast was rather a general abstinence, living all the while on coarse and unsavory food, drinking nothing but water, not using the bath, and most probably wearing haircloth next the skin, during the whole of the time.

4. *By the side of . . . Hiddekel.* The same as the Tigris, the great river of Assyria.

5. *Clothed in linen.* The description is in-tended to point out the splendor of the garments. *Gold of Uphaz.* The same as Ophir.

6. *His body also was like the beryl.* The description of this person is very similar to that of our Lord in Rev. i. 13-15.

7. *The men that were with me saw not the vision.* An exactly parallel case with what oc-curred at the conversion of Saul of Tarsus, Acts ix. 7. There was a divine influence which they all felt, but only Daniel saw the corporeal ap-pearance.

9. *Was I in a deep sleep.* I fell into a swoon.

10. *An hand touched me.* Nothing was appar-ent or palpable but a hand. A hand had written Belshazzar's fate upon the wall, and the hand is frequently mentioned when the power or maj-esty of God is intended. Perhaps by "hand" God himself may be meant.

12. *I am come for thy words.* On account of your prayers I am sent to comfort and instruct you.

13. *But the prince of the kingdom of Persia withstood me.* I think it would go far to make a legend or a precarious tale of this important place to endeavor to maintain that either a good or evil angel is intended here. Cyrus alone was the *prince of Persia,* and God had destined him to be the deliverer of his people; but there were some matters, of which we are not informed, that caused him to hesitate for some time. Fear-ing, probably, the greatness of the work, and not being fully satisfied of his ability to execute it, he therefore for a time resisted the secret in-spirations which God had sent him. The opposi-tion might be in reference to the building of the Temple. *But, lo, Michael.* Gabriel, who speaks, did not leave Cyrus till Michael came to take his place. Michael, "he who is like God," some-times appears to signify the Messiah, at other times the highest or chief archangel. Indeed there is no archangel mentioned in the whole Scrip-ture but this one. See Jude 9; Rev. xii. 7.

14. *For yet the vision is for many days.* There are many things which remain yet to be re-vealed, and the time of their accomplishment is very distant.

15. *I set my face toward the ground.* He was standing upright, v. 11, and he now bent his body in reverence, and looked down upon the ground.

16. *Like the similitude of the sons of men.* I think Gabriel is here meant, who appeared to Daniel in a human form; and so in v. 18, and see also chap. ix. 21. *Touched my lips.* Before this he was unable to speak. *By the vision.* The vision that I have already had, and of which I have not a proper knowledge, has greatly af-flicted me, because I see it intimates grievous calamities to my people. See chap. ix. 26.

17. *Neither is there breath.* He could not breathe freely; he was almost suffocated with sorrow.

19. *O man greatly beloved.* "Man of delights." *Let my lord speak.* I am now so strengthened and encouraged that I shall be able to bear any revelation that you may make.

20. *Knowest thou wherefore I come?* So high are you in the favor of God that He hath sent me unto you to give you further satisfaction, though I was elsewhere employed upon a most important mission, and I must speedily return to accomplish it, viz., *To fight with the prince of Persia.* To remove all the scruples of Cyrus, and to excite him to do all that God designs him to do for the restoration of my people, and the rebuilding of the city and Temple of Jerusalem. Nothing less than a supernatural agency in the mind of Cyrus can account for his decree in favor of the Jews. He had no natural, no politi-cal inclination to it; and his reluctance to obey the heavenly motions is here represented as a fight between him and the angel. *The prince of Grecia shall come.* I believe this refers to Alexander the Great, who was to destroy the Persian empire. See the second and third verses of the following chapter.

21. *Noted in the scripture of truth.* Perhaps this refers to what he had already written down.

See the preceding visions, which Daniel did not fully understand, though a general impression from them had filled his heart with sorrow. *Michael your prince.* The archangel mentioned before, v. 13, and who has been always supposed to be appointed by God as the guardian of the Jewish nation. It appears that God chose to make use of the ministry of angels in this work; that angels, as they could be in only one place at one time, could not produce influence where they were not; and that, to carry on the operation on the mind of the Persian king, it was necessary that either Gabriel or Michael should be present with him, and when one went on another commission another took his place; see v. 13. But we know so little of the invisible world that we cannot safely affirm anything positively.

CHAPTER 11

This chapter gives a more particular explanation of those events which were predicted in the eighth chapter. The prophet had foretold the partition of Alexander's kingdom into four parts. Two of these, in which were included Egypt and Syria, the one to the north, the other to the south, in respect of Judea, appear to take up the chief attention of the prophet, as his people were particularly concerned in their fate; these being the countries in which by far the greatest number of the Jews were, and still are, dispersed. Of these countries he treats (according to the views of the most enlightened expositors) down to the conquest of Macedon, A.M. 3836, B.C. 168, when he begins to speak of the Romans, 1-30; and then of the Church under that power, 31-35. This leads him to speak of Antichrist, who was to spring up in that quarter, 36-39; and of those powers which at the time of the end, or the latter days of the Roman monarchy (as this term is generally understood) were to push at it, and overthrow many countries, 40-43. By the king of the south, in the fortieth verse, the dominion of the Saracens, or Arabs, is supposed to be intended, which was an exceeding great plague to the Roman empire in the east, and also to several papistical countries, for the space of 150 years, i.e. from A.D. 612, when Mohammed and his followers first began their depredations, to A.D. 762, when Bagdad was built, and made the capital of the caliphs of the house of Abbas, from which epoch the Saracens became a more settled people. By the king of the north in the same verse the prophet is supposed by some to design that great scourge of Eastern Christendom, the Ottoman or Othman empire, by which, after about a hundred and fifty years of almost uninterrupted hostilities, the Roman empire in the East was completely overturned, A.D. 1453. The chapter concludes with a prediction of the final overthrow of this northern power, and of the manner in which this great event shall be accomplished, 44-45. But it should be observed that, notwithstanding the very learned observations of Bishop Newton and others upon this chapter, their scheme of interpretation presents very great and insurmountable difficulties; among which the very lengthy detail of events in the Syrian and Egyptian histories, comprising a period of less than two hundred years, and the rather uncouth transition to the incomparably greater transactions in Antichristian times, and of much longer duration, which are passed over with unaccountable brevity, are not the least. On all these subjects, however, the reader must judge for himself. See the notes.

1. *In the first year of Darius the Mede.* This is a continuation of the preceding discourse.

2. *There shall stand up yet three kings.* Gabriel had already spoken of Cyrus, who was now reigning; and after him three others should arise. These were: Cambyses, the son of Cyrus; Smerdis, the Magian, who was an impostor, who pretended to be another son of Cyrus; and Darius, the son of Hystaspes, who married Mandane, the daughter of Cyrus. *The fourth shall be far richer than they all.* This was Xerxes, the son of Darius, of whom Justin says: "He had so great an abundance of riches in his kingdom, that although rivers were dried up by his numerous armies, yet his wealth remained unexhausted."

3. *A mighty king shall stand up.* This was Alexander the Great. It is not said that this mighty king shall stand up against Xerxes, for he was not born till one hundred years after that monarch; but simply that he should "stand up," i.e., that he should reign in Greece.

4. *His kingdom shall be broken.* Shall, after his death, be divided among his four chief generals, as we have seen before. See chap. viii. 22. *And not to his posterity.* The family of Alexander had a most tragical end, so that in fifteen years after his death not one of his family or posterity remained alive! "Blood calls for blood." He (Alexander) was the great butcher of men. He was either poisoned or killed himself by immoderate drinking when he was only thirty-two years and eight months old; and a retributive Providence destroyed all his posterity, so that neither root nor branch of them was left on the face of the earth. Thus ended Alexander, the great butcher; and thus ended his family and posterity.

5. *The king of the south.* This was Ptolemy Lagus, one of his generals, who had the government of Egypt, Libra, etc., which are on the south of Judea. He was strong, for he had added Cyprus, Phoenicia, Caria, etc., to his kingdom of Egypt. *And one of his princes . . . shall be strong above him.* This was Seleucus Nicator, who possessed Syria, Babylon, Media, and the neighboring countries. This was "the king of the north," for his dominions lay north of Judea.

6. *In the end of years.* Several historical circumstances are here passed by. *The king's daughter of the south.* Berenice, daughter of Ptolemy Philadelphus, king of Egypt, was married to Antiochus Theos, king of Syria. These two sovereigns had a bloody war for some years; and they agreed to terminate it by the above marriage, on condition that Antiochus would put away his wife, Laodice, and her children, which he did; and Berenice having brought an immense fortune to her husband, all things appeared to go on well for a time. *But she shall not retain the power of the arm.* "Her posterity" shall not reign in that kingdom. *But she shall be given up.* Antiochus recalled his former wife, Laodice, and her children; and she, fearing that he might recall Berenice, caused him to be poisoned and her to be murdered, and set her son Callinicus upon the throne. *And they that brought her.* Her Egyptian women, striving to defend their mistress, were many of them killed. *And he that begat her.* Or, as the margin, "he whom she brought forth"; the son being murdered, as well as the mother, by order of Laodice. *And he that strengthened her.* Probably her father, Ptolemy, who was excessively fond of her, and who had died a few years before.

7. *But out of a branch of her roots.* A branch from the same root from which she sprang. This was Ptolemy Euergetes, her brother, who, to avenge his sister's death, marched with a great army against Seleucus Callinicus, took some of his best places, indeed all Asia, from Mount Taurus to India, and returned to Egypt with an immense booty, 40,000 talents of silver, precious vessels, and 2,500 images of their gods, without Callinicus daring to offer him battle.

8. *He shall continue more years.* Seleucus Callinicus died (an exile) by a fall from his horse, and Ptolemy Euergetes survived him four or five years.

9. *So the king of the south*—Ptolemy Euergetes—*shall come into his kingdom*—that of Seleucus Callinicus. *And shall return.* Having heard that a sedition had taken place in Egypt, Ptolemy Euergetes was obliged to return speedily in order to repress it; else he had wholly destroyed the kingdom of Callinicus.

10. *But his sons shall be stirred up.* That is, the sons of Callinicus, who were Seleucus Ceraunus and Antiochus, afterwards called the Great. *Shall assemble a multitude.* Seleucus Ceraunus did assemble a multitude of forces in order to recover his father's dominions; but, not having money to pay them, they became mutinous, and he was poisoned by two of his own generals. His brother Antiochus was then proclaimed king; so that one only of the sons did *certainly come, and overflow, and pass through;* he retook Seleucia, and regained Syria. He then returned, and overcame Nicolaus, the Egyptian general; and seemed disposed to invade Egypt, as he came even to his fortress, to the frontiers of Egypt.

11. *The king of the south.* Ptolemy Philopater, who succeeded his father, Euergetes. *Shall come forth and fight with him.* He did come forth to Raphia, where he was met by Antiochus, when a terrible battle was fought between these two kings. *And he* (Antiochus, the king of the north) *shall set forth a great multitude.* Amounting to 62,000 foot, 6,000 horse, and 102 elephants; but yet the multitude was *given into his hand,* the hand of the king of the south; for Ptolemy gained a complete victory. Raphia and other neighboring towns declared for the victor, and Antiochus was obliged to retreat with his scattered army to Antioch, from which he sent to solicit a peace. See Polybius. lib. v.

12. *His heart shall be lifted up.* Had Ptolemy improved his victory, he might have dispossessed Antiochus of his whole empire; but giving way to pride, and a criminally sensual life, he made peace on dishonorable terms; and though he had gained a great victory, yet his kingdom was not *strengthened by it,* for his subjects were displeased and rebelled against him, or at least became considerably disaffected.

13. *The king of the north shall return . . . after certain years.* In about fourteen years Antiochus did return, Philopater being dead, and his son Ptolemy Epiphanes being then a minor. He brought a much larger army and more riches; these he had collected in a late eastern expedition.

14. *Many stand up against the king of the south.* Antiochus, and Philip, king of Macedon, united together to overrun Egypt. *Also the robbers of thy people.* The Jews, who revolted from their religion, and joined Ptolemy, under Scopas. *Shall exalt themselves to establish the vision.* That is, to build a temple like that of Jerusalem, in Egypt, hoping thereby to fulfill a prediction of Isaiah, chap. xxx. 18-25, which seemed to intimate that the Jews and the Egyptians should be one people. They now revolted from Ptolemy and joined Antiochus, and this was the means of contributing greatly to the accomplishment of prophecies that foretold the calamities that should fall upon the Jews. *But they shall fall.* For Scopas came with a great army from Ptolemy and, while Antiochus was engaged in other parts, reduced Caelesyria and Palestine, subdued the Jews, placed guards on the coasts of Jerusalem, and returned with great spoils to Egypt.

15. *So the king of the north.* Antiochus came to recover Judea. Scopas was sent by Ptolemy to oppose him; but he was defeated near the fountains of Jordan, and was obliged to take refuge in Sidon with 10,000 men. Antiochus pursued and besieged him, and he was obliged by famine to surrender at discretion, and their lives only were spared. Antiochus afterwards besieged several of the fenced cities and took them; in short, carried all before him; so that the king of the south, Ptolemy, and *his chosen people,* his ablest generals, were not able to oppose him.

16. *He shall stand in the glorious land.* Judea. For he reduced Palestine; and the Jews supplied him with provisions, and assisted him to reduce the garrison that Scopas had left in the citadel of Jerusalem. *Which by his hand shall be consumed.* Or, "which shall be perfected in his hand." For Antiochus showed the Jews great favor: he brought back those that were dispersed, and reestablished them in the land; freed the priests and Levites from all tribute.

17. *He shall also set his face to enter.* Antiochus purposed to have marched his army into Egypt; but he thought it best to proceed by fraudulence, and therefore proposed a treaty of marriage between him and his daughter Cleopatra, called here *the daughter of women,* because of her great beauty and accomplishments. And this he appeared to do, having *upright ones with him.* Or, as the Septuagint have it, "And he will make all things straight with him"; that is, he acted as if he were influenced by nothing but the most upright views. But he intended his daughter to be a snare to Ptolemy, and therefore purposed to corrupt her that she might betray her husband. *But she shall not stand on his side.* On the contrary, her husband's interests became more dear to her than her father's, and by her means Ptolemy was put upon his guard against the intentions of Antiochus.

18. *Shall he turn his face unto the isles.* Antiochus had fitted out a great fleet of 100 large ships and 200 smaller, and with this fleet subdued most of the maritime places on the coast of the Mediterranean, and took many of the isles, Rhodes, Samos, Eubaea, Colophon, and others. *But a prince for his own behalf.* Or, "a captain." The consul Acilius Glabrio caused *the reproach . . . to cease* beat and routed his army at the straits of Thermopylae, and expelled him from Greece. So he obliged him to pay the tribute which he hoped to impose on others, for he would grant him peace only on condition of paying the expense of the war, 15,000 talents. *Without his own reproach.* Without losing a battle, or taking a false step, Acilius caused the reproach which he was bringing upon the Romans to turn upon himself.

19. *He shall turn his face toward the fort of his own land.* After this shameful defeat, Antiochus fled to Sardis, thence to Apamea, and the next day got into Syria, and to Antioch, his own fort, whence he sent ambassadors to treat for peace; and was obliged to engage to pay the immense sum of money mentioned above. *But he shall stumble and fall.* Being under the greatest difficulties how to raise the stipulated sums, he marched into his eastern provinces to

exact the arrears of taxes; and, attempting to plunder the temple of Jupiter Belus at Elymais, he was opposed by the populace, and he and his attendants slain. This is the account that Diodorus Siculus, Strabo, and Justin give of his death.

20. *Then shall stand up in his estate a raiser of taxes.* Seleucus Philopater succeeded his father, Antiochus. He sent his treasurer, Heliodorus, to seize the money deposited in the Temple of Jerusalem, which is here called *the glory of the kingdom;* see 2 Macc. ix. 23. He was so cramped to pay the annual tax to the Romans that he was obliged to burden his subjects with continual taxes. *He shall be destroyed, neither in anger*—fighting against an enemy, *nor in battle*—at the head of his troops; but basely and treacherously by the hand of Heliodorus, his treasurer, who hoped to reign in his stead.

21. *In his estate shall stand up a vile person.* This was Antiochus, surnamed Epiphanes—"the Illustrious." They did not give him the honor of the kingdom; he was at Athens, on his way from Rome, when his father died; and Heliodorus had declared himself king, as had several others. But Antiochus came in peaceably, for he obtained the kingdom by flatteries. He flattered Eumenes, king of Pergamus, and Attalus, his brother, and got their assistance. He flattered the Romans, and sent ambassadors to court their favor, and pay them the arrears of the tribute. He flattered the Syrians, and gained their concurrence; and as he flattered the Syrians, so they flattered him, giving him the epithet of Epiphanes—"the Illustrious." But that he was what the prophet here calls him, *a vile person,* is fully evident from what Polybius says of him, from *Athenaeus,* lib. v: "He was every man's companion: he resorted to the common shops, and prattled with the workmen: he frequented the common taverns, and ate and drank with the meanest fellows, singing debauched songs." On this account a contemporary writer, and others after him, instead of *Epiphanes,* called him *Epimanes*—"the Madman."

22. *And with the arms of a flood. The arms* which were *overflown . . . before him* were his competitors for the crown. They were vanquished by the forces of Eumenes and Attalus, and were dissipated by the arrival of Antiochus from Athens, whose presence disconcerted all their measures. *The prince of the covenant.* This was Onias, the high priest, whom he removed, and put Jason in his place, who had given him a great sum of money; and then put wicked Menelaus in his room, who had offered him a larger sum. Thus he acted deceitfully in the league made with Jason.

23. *He shall come up.* From Rome, where he had been a hostage for the payment of the tax laid on his father. *Shall become strong with a small people.* At first he had but few to espouse his cause when he arrived at Antioch, the people having been greatly divided by the many claimants of the crown; but being supported by Eumenes and Attalus, his few people increased, and he became strong.

24. *He shall enter peaceably even upon the fattest places.* The very richest provinces—Coelesyria and Palestine. *He shall do that which his fathers have not done, nor his fathers' fathers.* He became profuse in his liberalities, and scattered among them the prey of his enemies,

the spoil of temples, and the riches of his friends, as well as his own revenues. He spent much in public shows, and bestowed largesses among the people. We are told in 1 Macc. iii. 30, that "in the liberal giving of gifts he abounded above all the kings that went before him." These are nearly the words of the prophet. *He shall forecast his devices.* As Eulaeus and Lenaeus, who were the guardians of the young Egyptian king Ptolemy Philometor, demanded from Antiochus the restitution of Coelesyria and Palestine, which he refused, he foresaw that he might have a war with that kingdom; and therefore "he forecast devices"—fixed a variety of plans to prevent this, visited the strongholds and frontier places to see that they were in a state of defense. And this he did *for a time*—he employed some years in hostile preparations against Egypt.

25. *He shall stir up his power.* Antiochus marched against Ptolemy, *the king of the south* (Egypt), with a great army; and the Egyptian generals had raised a mighty force. *Stirred up to battle.* The two armies met between Pelusium and Mount Casius; but he (the king of the south) could not stand—the Egyptian army was defeated. The next campaign he had greater success; he routed the Egyptian army, took Memphis, and made himself master of all Egypt, except Alexandria; see 1 Macc. i. 16-19. And all these advantages he gained by "forecasting devices," probably by corrupting his ministers and captains. Ptolemy Macron gave up Cyprus to Antiochus; and the Alexandrians were led to renounce their allegiance to Ptolemy Philometor, and took Euergetes, or Physcon, his younger brother, and made him king in his stead. All this was doubtless by the corruptions of Antiochus.

26. *Yea, they that feed of the portion of his meat.* This is the proof of what has been last noted, that the intrigues of Antiochus, corrupting the ministers and officers of Ptolemy, were the cause of all the disasters that fell on the Egyptian king. *They that feed of the portion of his meat*—who were in his confidence and pay, and possessed the secrets of the state—betrayed him; and these were the means of destroying him and his army, so that he was defeated, as was before observed.

27. *And both these kings' hearts shall be to do mischief.* That is, Antiochus and Ptolemy Philometor, who was nephew to the former, and whose interest he now pretended to have much at heart, since the Alexandrians had renounced their allegiance to him, and set his younger brother, Euergetes, upon the throne. When Antiochus came to Memphis, he and Philometor had frequent conferences at the same table; and at these times they spoke lies to each other, Antiochus professing great friendship to his nephew and concern for his interests, yet in his heart designing to ruin the kingdom by fomenting the discords which already subsisted between the two brothers. On the other hand, Philometor professed much gratitude to his uncle for the interest he took in his affairs, and laid the blame of the war upon his minister, Eulaeus; while at the same time he spoke lies, determining as soon as possible to accommodate matters with his brother, and join all their strength against their deceitful uncle. *But it shall not prosper.* Neither succeeded in his ob-

ject, for the end of the appointed time was not yet come.

28. *Then shall he return into his land with great riches.* Antiochus did return, laden with riches, from the spoils that he took in Egypt; see 1 Macc. i. 19-20. And hearing that there had been a report of his death, at which the citizens of Jerusalem had made great rejoicings—*his heart shall be against the holy covenant.* He was determined to take a severe revenge, and he had an ostensible pretext for it; for Jason, who had been deprived of the high priesthood, hearing the report of the death of Antiochus, raised forces, marched against Jerusalem, took it, and obliged Menelaus, the high priest, to shut himself up in the castle. Antiochus brought a great army against Jerusalem; took it by storm; slew 40,000 of the inhabitants; sold as many more for slaves; boiled swine's flesh, and sprinkled the Temple and the altar with the broth; broke into the holy of holies; took away the golden vessels and other sacred treasures, to the value of 1,800 talents; restored Menelaus to his office; and made one Philip, a Phrygian, governor of Judea (1 Macc. i. 24; 2 Macc. v. 21).

29. *At the time appointed he shall return.* Finding that his treachery was detected, and that the two brothers had united their counsel and strength for their mutual support, he threw off the mask; and having collected a great army early in the spring, he passed through Coelesyria; entered Egypt; and the inhabitants of Memphis having submitted to him, he came by easy marches to Alexandria. But, says the prophet, *it shall not be as the former, or as the latter.* He had not the same success as the former, when he overthrew the Egyptian army at Pelusium; nor as the latter, when he took Memphis, and subdued all Egypt, except Alexandria.

30. *For the ships of Chittim shall come against him.* Chittim is well known to mean the Roman empire. Antiochus, being now in full march to besiege Alexandria, and within seven miles of that city, heard that ships were arrived there from Rome, with legates from the senate. He went to salute them. They delivered to him the letters of the senate, in which he was commanded, on pain of the displeasure of the Roman people, to put an end to the war against his nephews. Antiochus said he would go and consult his friends; on which Popilius, one of the legates, took his staff, and instantly drew a circle round Antiochus on the sand where he stood, and commanded him not to pass that circle till he had given a definitive answer. Antiochus, intimidated, said, he would do whatever the senate enjoined; and in a few days after began his march, and returned to Syria. *Therefore he shall be grieved.* "Grieving and groaning," says Polybius; both mortified, humbled, and disappointed. *Have indignation against the holy covenant.* For he vented his rage against the Jews; and he sent his general, Apollonius, with 22,000 men against Jerusalem, plundered and set fire to the city, pulled down the houses round about it, slew much of the people, and built a castle on an eminence that commanded the Temple, and slew multitudes of the poor people who had come up to worship, polluted every place, so that the Temple service was totally abandoned, and all the people fled from the city. And when he returned to Antioch

he published a decree that all should conform to the Grecian worship; and the Jewish worship was totally abrogated, and the Temple itself consecrated to Jupiter Olympius. How great must the wickedness of the people have been when God could tolerate this! In the transacting of these matters he had *intelligence with them that forsake the holy covenant;* with wicked Menelaus, the high priest; and the apostate Jews united with him, who gave from time to time such information to Antiochus as excited him against Jerusalem, the Temple, and the people. See 1 Macc. i. 41, 62; confirmed by Josephus, *War,* book i, chap. 1, s. 1.

31. *And arms shall stand on his part.* After Antiochus, *arms,* that is, the Romans, *shall stand* up: for "arms" in this prophecy everywhere denote military power; and "standing up," the power in activity and conquering.

36. *And the king shall do according to his will.* This may apply to Antiochus, who exalted himself above every god, called himself a god, sported with all religion, profaned the Temple. But others think an antichristian power in the Church is intended; for in the language of this prophecy *king* is taken for power, a kingdom, etc. That such a power did spring up in the Church that acted in an arbitrary manner against all laws, human and divine, is well-known. This power showed itself in the Greek emperors in the East, and in the bishops of Rome in the West.

CHAPTER 12

The proper conclusion to the great revolutions predicted in this and the following chapters is the general resurrection, of which the beginning of this chapter (if to be literally understood) gives some intimation, 1-3. Daniel is then commanded to shut up the words and to seal the book to the time of the end, 4; and is informed of the three grand symbolical periods of a time, times, and a half, 1,290 days, 1,335 days, 4-12; at the end of the last of which Daniel shall rest and stand in his lot, 13. It is generally thought by commentators that the termination of the last period is the epoch of the first resurrection. See Rev. xx. 4-5.

1. *And at that time Michael shall stand up.* Michael, the archangel, as has already been observed, was ever reputed the guardian of the Jewish people. *Every one that shall be found written in the book.* All that truly fear, love, and obey the Lord.

2. *Many of them that sleep in the dust of the earth.* This prophecy has been referred to the future restoration of the Jews. It will be also true of the state of mankind at the general judgment.

3. *And they that be wise.* Those who are thoroughly instructed in Christ's word and doctrine *shall shine*—shall be eminently distinguished in the Christian Church by the holiness of their lives and the purity of their creed. *And they that turn many to righteousness.* They who, by preaching Christ crucified among their brethren, shall be the means of converting them to the Christian faith, shall be *as the stars* —bright luminaries in the gospel kingdom of Jesus Christ.

4. *Shut up the words, and seal the book.* When a prophet received a prediction concerning what was at a considerable distance of time, he shut his book, did not communicate his revelation for some time after. This Daniel was commanded to do, chap. viii. 26. See also Isa.

xxix. 10-11; Rev. xxii. 10. Among the ancients, those were said to "seal" who in the course of their reading stamped the places of which they were yet doubtful, in order to keep them in memory, that they might refer to them again, as not yet fully understood. *Many shall run to and fro.* Many shall endeavor to search out the sense, *and knowledge shall be increased* by these means, though the meaning shall not be fully known till the events take place. Then the seal shall be broken, and the sense become plain. This seems to be the meaning of this verse, though another has been put on it, viz., "Many shall run to and fro preaching the Gospel of Christ, and therefore religious knowledge and true wisdom shall be increased." This is true in itself, but it is not the meaning of the prophet's words.

5. *Behold, there stood other two.* Probably two angels. We know no more of them, unless they be the same as those called "saints," chap. viii. 13, which see. The *river* was most likely the Tigris.

6. *The man clothed in linen.* Gabriel, in a human form. Thus he is represented, chap. x. 5.

7. *Which was upon the waters.* By this description, he was standing on the water. This is very similar to the description of the angel, Rev. x. 5-6, and in the seventh verse there seems to be a reference to this prophecy, *a time, times, and an half.* See the note on chap. vii. 25.

9. *The words are closed up.* The prophecy shall not be understood, but in its accomplish-ment; and then the depth of the wisdom and providence of God will be clearly seen in these matters. See on v. 4. We must wait *till the time of the end.*

10. *Many shall be purified.* During the interim the great work of God's providence and grace shall be carried on in the salvation of men; who, in the midst of trials, temptations, and difficulties, shall be *purified, and made white*—be fully saved from their sins. *None of the wicked shall understand.* Because they are wicked, and will continue in their sins, the eyes of their understanding shall be closed, and their hearts hardened, so that they shall not see the light of the glorious gospel. *But the wise.* Those who open their hearts to God, that He may pour in His light, *shall understand* the things that make for their peace.

12. *Blessed is he that waiteth.* He who implicitly depends on God, expecting, as His truth cannot fail, that these predictions shall be accomplished in due time. *And cometh to the thousand three hundred and five and thirty days.* This is 75 days more than what is included in the 3½ years, or the time, times, and a half in the seventh verse; and as we have met with so many instances of prophetical days and years, this undoubtedly is another instance; and as a day stands for a year, this must mean a period of 1,335 years, which period is to bring all these wonders to an end, v. 6. But we are left totally in the dark relative to the time from which these 1,335 years are to be reckoned.

The Book of
HOSEA

Hosea, the son of Beeri, is the first of the minor prophets. This prophet lived in the kingdom of Samaria; and his prophecies for the most part have a view to this state, though there are likewise some particular things which concern the kingdom of Judah.

We read, in the introduction to his prophecy, that he prophesied under the kings of *Judah*, Uzziah, Jotham, Ahaz, and Hezekiah, and under Jeroboam II, king of *Israel*.

St. Jerome and many others believe Hosea to be the oldest prophet, whose writings are in our possession; and he was witness to the first captivity of the four tribes carried away by Tiglath-pileser, and the extinction of the kingdom of Samaria by Shalmaneser. The first verses of chap. i have a view to the death of Zechariah, king of Israel, and son of Jeroboam II. From the sixth verse of the first chapter to the third chapter is a prediction of the captivity of Israel; but after he has foretold this captivity, he declares the return and end of it. He inveighs strongly against the disorders which prevailed in the kingdom of the ten tribes. It appears that in his time there were idols; not only at Dan, Bethel, and Samaria, but likewise at Gilgal, upon Tabor, at Sichem, Beersheba, and upon the mountains of Gilead. He speaks of the Israelites as of a people entirely corrupted, and the measure of whose sins was filled up; he foretells that their golden calves should be pulled down, cast upon the ground, and carried into Assyria.

He reflects, with the same severity, upon the irregularities which reigned in Judah. He stands up against those who went to worship false gods at Gilgal. He speaks of Sennacherib's invading the territories of Judah. He foretells that the people of Judah should still continue some time in their country after the captivity of the ten tribes; but that after this they themselves should likewise be carried captives beyond the Euphrates, from whence the Lord would bring them back after a certain number of years.

In the beginning of Hosea's prophecy, we read that the Lord directed him "to take unto thee a wife of whoredoms and children of whoredoms"; that is, to marry a woman who, before her marriage, had lived a debauched life, but who, after her marriage, should retire from all bad conversation, and whose children should be legitimate, notwithstanding that, by reason of the blemish which their mother had contracted by her former life, they were called "the children of whoredoms." This prostitute woman, and the children who were to be born of her, were a figure and a kind of real prophecy which described the idolatry and infidelity of Samaria and the ten tribes, formerly the Lord's spouse, but who afterwards became idolatrous and corrupt.

The children of this faithless woman are children of prostitution, since they imitate the idolatry of their mother. God gives these children the names of *Jezreel,* "God will disperse"; *Lo-rechamah,* or "Without mercy"; and *Lo-ammi,* "Thou art no longer my people"; to show —(1) That God was going to revenge upon the house of Jehu, king of Israel, the sins which he had committed at Jezreel, when he usurped the kingdom of the ten tribes. (2) That the Lord would treat His idolatrous and sinful people without mercy. (3) That He would reject them, and no more look upon them as His people.

CHAPTER 1

Under the figure of a wife proving false to her marriage vows, and bearing children that would follow her example, the prophet represents the shameful idolatry of the ten tribes, which provoked God to cast them off. The whole passage is information by action instead of words. The names of the children are all emblematical. The first is intended to put Israel in mind of their unrepented guilt, and the acts of cruelty committed in their palace of Jezreel (1 Kings xxi. 1). The second and third, signifying "not finding mercy" and "not my people," denote that, in consequence of their guilt, they were to be rejected of God, 1-9. God promises, however, to repair the loss to His Church by calling in the Gentiles, 10; and by uniting all the children of God under one Head, the Messiah, in the latter days, 11.

2. *A wife of whoredoms.* That is, says Newcome, a wife from among the Israelites, who were remarkable for spiritual fornication, or idolatry. God calls himself the Husband of Israel; and this chosen nation owed Him the fidelity of a wife. See Exod. xxxiv. 15; Deut. xxxi. 16; Judge. ii. 17; Isa. liv. 5; Jer. iii. 14; xxxi. 32; Ezek. xvi. 17; xxiii. 5, 27; Hos. ii. 2, 5; Rev. xvii. 1-2. He therefore says, with indignation, Go join thyself in marriage to one of those who have committed fornication against Me, and raise up children who, by the power of example, will themselves swerve to idolatry.

3. *He went and took Gomer.* All this appears to be a real transaction, though having a typical meaning.

4. *Call his name Jezreel.* That is, "God will disperse." This seems to intimate that a dispersion or sowing of Israel shall take place; which happened under Shalmaneser, king of Assyria, 2 Kings xvii. 5-6. But the word refers also to the name of a city, where Jehu slew Jezebel and all the children of Ahab, 2 Kings ix. 10, 36 and x. 6. *The blood of Jezreel.* Not Jehu's vengeance on Ahab's family, but his acts of cruelty while he resided at Jezreel, a city in the tribe of Issachar, Josh. xix. 18, where the kings of Israel had a palace, 1 Kings xxi. 1. *Will cause to cease the kingdom.* Either relating to the cutting off of the kingdom of Israel by the Assyrians, see v. 6, or to the ceasing of the kingdom of Israel from the house of Jehu, 2 Kings x. 30, and which was fulfilled, 2 Kings xv. 10.

5. *In the valley of Jezreel.* This also is supposed to relate either to some signal defeat of the Israelites by the Assyrians, which took place in the valley of Jezreel; or to the death of Zechariah, the fourth lineal descendant of Jehu, which may have happened here. See 2 Kings xv. 10.

6. *Call her . . . Lo-ruhamah.* "Not having obtained mercy." This also was a prophetic or typical name; and the reason of its imposition is immediately given: *For I will no more have mercy.* "For I will no more add to have mercy upon the house of Israel." This refers to the total destruction of that kingdom.

7. *But I will have mercy upon the house of Judah.* I will spare them as a kingdom after Israel has been carried away into captivity by the Assyrians. *And will save them by the Lord their God.* Remarkably fulfilled in the supernatural defeat of the army of the Assyrians, see 2 Kings xix. 35; and so they were saved, not by *bow,* nor by *sword,* nor by *battle,* nor by *horses,* nor by *horsemen.*

9. *Call his name Lo-ammi.* "Not My people."

10. *Yet the number of the children of Israel.* God had promised that the children of Israel should be as the sand of the sea. See Gen. xxxii. 12; Rom. ix. 25-26. And though for their iniquities He had thinned and scattered them, yet the spirit and design of His promise and covenant shall be fulfilled. An Israel there shall be. In the place of the reprobated people, who were now no longer His people, there shall be found an Israel that shall be the children "of the living God." See the above scriptures, and 1 Pet. ii. 10. This must mean either the Israelites after their conversion to Christianity, or even the Gentiles themselves converted to God, and now become the true Israel.

11. *The children of Judah and the children of Israel.* After the return from Babylon, the distinction between Israel and Judah was entirely destroyed; and those of them that did return were all included under one denomination, "Jews." The one *head* may refer to Zerubbabel, their leader, and afterwards under Ezra and Nehemiah. In the more extensive view of the prophet the "one head" may mean Jesus Christ, under whom the true Israel, Jews and Gentiles, shall be finally gathered together; so that there shall be one flock, and one Shepherd over that flock. *They shall come up out of the land.* Assyria and Chaldea in particular, but also from the various places of their dispersions in general. *Great shall be the day of Jezreel.* He alludes to the meaning of the word, the "seed of God." God, who has dispersed—sown—them in different lands, shall gather them together; and that day of God's power shall be great and glorious. It was a wonderful seedtime in the divine justice; it shall then be a wonderful

harvest in the divine mercy. He sowed them among the nations in His wrath; He shall reap them and gather them in His bounty.

CHAPTER 2

The prophet exhorts his people to speak and to act as becomes those who obtained mercy of God; and to remonstrate strongly against the conduct of their mother (Samaria), whose captivity is threatened on account of her forsaking God, and ascribing her prosperity to idols, 1-5. As an amplification of this threatening, the prophet enumerates a series of afflictions which were to befall her to bring her to a sense of her duty to God; and of her folly in seeking after idols, and falsely ascribing to them the blessings of Providence, 6-13. After these corrections, however, God promises to conduct Israel safely to their own land; perhaps alluding to their restoration from the Babylonish captivity, for this prophecy is supposed to have been delivered about two hundred and fifty years prior to this event, 14-15. He further engages to deal with them as a tender Husband, and not as a severe master, as were the idols which they served, 16-17. The rest of the chapter promises the people of God, the true Israel, security from every evil, with the possession of every blessing, under a new covenant; and that in terms full of beauty, energy, and consolation. Heaven and earth, and whatever they contain; all nature, and the God of nature, are represented as uniting to make the people of God happy; so that if they only breathe a wish, one part of nature, animate or inanimate, echoes it to another, and all join in sweet harmony to transmit it to the ear of the Almighty. "I will hear, saith the Lord, I will hear the heavens, and they shall hear the earth; and the earth shall hear the corn, and the wine, and the oil; and they shall hear Jezreel."

1. *Say ye unto your brethren, Ammi.* I prefer the interpretation of these proper names. *Say ye unto your brethren,* "My people"; *and to your sisters,* who have "obtained mercy."

2. *Plead with your mother.* People of Judah, accuse your mother (Jerusalem), who has abandoned My worship and is become idolatrous; convince her of her folly and wickedness, and let her return to Him from whom she has so deeply revolted.

3. *Lest I strip her naked.* Lest I expose her to infamy, want, and punishment. The punishment of an adulteress among the ancient Germans was this: "They shaved off her hair, stripped her naked in the presence of her relatives, and in this state drove her from the house of her husband." See on Isa. iii. 17; and see also Ezek. xvi. 39; xxiii. 26. *And set her like a dry land.* The Israelites, if obedient, were promised a land flowing with milk and honey; but, should they be disobedient, the reverse. And this is what God here threatens against disobedient Israel.

4. *They be the children of whoredoms.* They are all idolaters; and have been consecrated to idols, whose marks they bear.

5. *That give me my bread.* See the note on Jer. xliv. 17-18, where nearly the same words are found and illustrated.

6. *I will hedge up thy way with thorns.* I will put it out of your power to escape the judgments I have threatened; and, in spite of all your attachment to your idols, you shall find that they can give you neither bread, nor water, nor wool, nor flax, nor oil, nor drink. And he shall be brought into such circumstances that the pursuit of your expensive idolatry shall be impossible. And she shall be led so deep into captivity as never to find the road back to her own land. And this is the fact; for those who were carried away into Assyria have been lost among the nations, few of them having ever returned to Judea. And, if in being, where they are now is utterly unknown.

8. *For she did not know that I gave her corn.* How often are the gifts of God's immediate bounty attributed to fortuitous causes—to any cause but the right one! *Which they prepared for Baal.* And how often are the gifts of God's bounty perverted into means of dishonoring Him! God gives us wisdom, strength, and property; and we use them to sin against Him with the greater skill, power, and effect!

9. *Therefore will I return, and take away.* In the course of My providence I will withhold those benefits which she has prostituted to her idolatrous services. And I will neither give the land rain nor fruitful seasons.

10. *In the sight of her lovers.* Her idols, and her faithful or faithless allies.

12. *These are my rewards.* They attributed all the blessings of Providence as rewards received from the idols which they worshipped.

13. *Days of Baalim.* To *visit* signifies to "inflict punishment"; *the days* are taken for the acts of idolatrous worship committed on them; and *Baalim* means the multitude of false gods worshipped by them. *Baal* was a general name for a male idol, as *Astarte* was for a female. *Baalim* includes all the male idols, as *Ashtaroth* all those that were female. *Her earrings.* *Nizmah* signifies rather a "nose jewel." These are worn by females in the East to the present day, in great abundance. *And her jewels.* Rings, armlets, bracelets, ankle rings, and ornaments of this kind.

14. *I will allure her, and bring her into the wilderness, and speak comfortably unto her.* After inflicting many judgments upon her, I will restore her again. I will deal with her as a very affectionate husband would do to an unfaithful wife. Instead of making her a public example, he takes her in private, talks to and reasons with her; puts her on her good behavior; promises to pass by all, and forgive all, if she will now amend her ways. In the meantime he provides what is necessary for her wants and comfortable support; and thus, opening a door of hope for her, she may be fully reconciled; rejoice as at the beginning, when he first took her by the hand, and she became his bride.

15. *She shall sing there.* There she shall sing the responsive song, as on high festival occasions, and in marriage ceremonies. The Book of Canticles is of this sort.

16. *Thou shalt call me Ishi.* That is, "My Man," or, "My Husband," a title of love and affection; *and not Baali,* "My master," a title exciting fear and apprehension; which, howsoever good in itself, was now rendered improper to be applied to Jehovah, having been prostituted to false gods. This intimated that they should scrupulously avoid idolatry; and they had such a full proof of the inefficacy of their idolatrous worship that, after their captivity, they never more served idols.

18. *Will I make a covenant for them.* I will make an agreement between them and the birds, beasts, and reptiles, so that they shall not be injured by those; their flocks shall not be destroyed, nor their crops spoiled. I will also prevent every species of war, that they may no more have the calamities that arise from that source. They shall also be safe from robbers and nightly alarms; for *I will make them to lie down* in safety.

19. *I will betroth thee unto me.* The people are always considered under the emblem of a wife unfaithful to her husband. *In righteousness.* According to law, reason, and equity. *In judgment.* According to what is fit and becoming. *In lovingkindness.* Having the utmost affection and love for you. *In mercies.* Forgiving and blotting out all past miscarriages.

20. *In faithfulness.* You shalt no more prostitute yourself to idols, but be faithful to Him who calls himself your Husband. *Thou shalt know the Lord.* There shall be no more infidelity on your part nor divorce on Mine.

21. *I will hear, saith the Lord.* The sentence is repeated, to show how fully the thing was determined by the Almighty, and how implicitly they might depend on the divine promise.

22. *Shall hear the corn, and the wine.* When they seem to express a desire to supply the wants of man. *And they shall hear Jezreel.* The destitute people who are in want of the necessaries of life.

23. *I will sow her.* Alluding to the import of the name *Jezreel*, "the seed of God." Then shall it appear that God has shown mercy to them that had not obtained mercy. Then the covenant of God will be renewed; for He will call them His people who were not His people; and they shall call Jehovah their God, who before had Him not for the object of their worship.

The sentences in the latter part of this verse are very abrupt, but exceedingly expressive; leaving out those words supplied by the translators and which unnerve the passage, it stands thus: "I will say to not my people, Thou my people; and they shall say, My God."

CHAPTER 3

By the prophet's taking back his wife, for whom he (her friend or husband) still retained his affection, though she had proved unfaithful; by his entering into a new contract with her; and by his giving her hopes of reconciliation, after she should for some time prove, as in a state of widowhood, the sincerity of her repentance; is represented the gracious manner in which God will restore the Jews from the Babylonish captivity, 1-4. It is also very strongly intimated that the whole house of Israel will be added to the Church of Christ in the latter days, 5.

1. *Go yet, love a woman.* This is a different command from that mentioned in the first chapter. That denoted the infidelity of the kingdom of Israel and God's divorce of them. He gave them up to their enemies, and caused them to be carried into captivity. The *woman* mentioned here represents one who was a lawful wife joining herself to a paramour; then divorced by her husband; afterwards repenting, and desirous to be joined to her spouse; ceasing from her adulterous commerce, but not yet reconciled to him. This was the state and disposition of the Jews under the Babylonish captivity. Though separated from their own idols, they continued separated from their God. He is still represented as having affectionate feelings towards them; awaiting their full repentance and contrition, in order to renew the marriage covenant. These things are pointed out by the symbolical actions of the prophet.

Beloved of her friend. Or "a lover of evil." *According to the love of the Lord.* This woman,

who had proved false to her husband, was still beloved by him, though he could not acknowledge her; as the Israelites were beloved by the Lord, while they were looking after other gods. The *flagons of wine* were probably such as were used for libations, or drunk in idol feasts.

2. *Fifteen pieces of silver.* If they were shekels, the price of this woman was about two pounds five shillings. *An homer* of barley. As the homer was about eight bushels, the homer and half was about twelve or thirteen bushels.

3. *Thou shalt abide for me many days.* He did not take her home, but made a contract with her that, if she would abstain from her evil ways, he would take her to himself after a sufficient trial. In the meantime he gave her the money and the barley to subsist upon, that she might not be under the temptation of becoming again unfaithful. *So will I also be for thee.* That is, if you, Israel, will keep yourself separate from your idolatry, and give Me proof, by your total abstinence from idols, that you will be My faithful worshipper, I will receive you again, and in the meantime support you with the necessaries of life while you are in the land of your captivity.

4. *Many days without a king.* Hitherto this prophecy has been literally fulfilled. Since the destruction of the Temple by the Romans they have had neither king nor prince. *Without an image . . . ephod . . . teraphim.* The Septuagint, "Without a sacrifice, without an altar, without a priesthood, and without oracles."

5. *Afterward shall the children of Israel return.* Shall repent of their iniquities, *and seek the Lord;* lay aside their mock worship, and serve the true God in spirit and in truth. *And David their king.* Or as the Targum, "They shall obey the Messiah, the Son of David, their King"; and thus look believingly upon Him whom they have pierced, and mourn.

CHAPTER 4

The prophet charges his people with their enormous sins, 1-2; in consequence of which they are threatened with heavy judgments, 3-5. God himself is then introduced complaining of the ignorance and obstinacy of Israel; and as their priests had a large share in the common guilt, it is declared that they shall be visited with a proportionable share of the common ruin, 6-11. The sins of idolatry and divination are then particularly reproved, 12-14; and Judah admonished to beware of these sins, which would leave her rebellious sister Israel helpless and desolate as a lamb in a desert, 15-16. In the remaining verses the style is varied, but the subject is the same. Ephraim is given up to idolatry, and the necessary consequence declared to be a bitter draught! Immediately we see him bound in the wings of a mighty tempest, and driven as chaff before the wind, to either destruction or captivity, 17-19.

1. *The Lord hath a controversy.* What we should call a "lawsuit," in which God is Plaintiff, and the Israelites defendants. It is Jehovah *versus* Israel and Judah.

2. *Blood toucheth blood.* Murders are not only frequent, but assassinations are mutual.

4. *Yet let no man strive.* Or, "No man contendeth." All these evils stalk abroad unreproved, for all are guilty. *For thy people are.* The *people* and the *priest* are alike rebels against the Lord, the priests having become idolaters as well as the people. Bishop Newcome renders this clause, "And as is the provocation of the priest, so is that of my people."

5. Therefore shalt thou fall in the day. In the most open and public manner. *And the prophet also shall fall . . . in the night.* The false prophet, when employed in taking prognostications from stars. *And I will destroy thy mother.* The metropolis or mother city. Jerusalem or Samaria is meant.

7. Will I change their glory into shame. As the idolaters at Dan and Bethel have changed My glory into the similitude of an ox that eateth grass (Rom. i. 23), so will I change their glory into shame or ignominy.

8. They eat up the sin of my people. Chattath, the "sin offering."

12. At their stocks. They consult their wooden gods. *And their staff declareth.* They use divination by rods; see Ezekiel xxi.

13. The shadow thereof is good. Their "*daughters* committed *whoredom,* and their *spouses* committed *adultery.*" (1) Their deities were worshipped by prostitution. (2) They *drank* much in their idol worship, v. 11, and thus their passions became inflamed. (3) The *thick groves* were favorable to the whoredoms and adulteries mentioned here. In imitation of these, some nations have their public gardens.

14. I will not punish. "Why should ye be stricken any more? ye will revolt more and more." When God, in judgment, removes His judgments, the case of that people is desperate. While there is *hope,* there is *correction. Themselves are separated.* There is a reference here to certain debaucheries which should not be described. The state of the people at this time must have been abominable beyond all precedent—animal, sensual, bestial, diabolical: women consecrating themselves to serve their idols by public prostitution; boys dismembered like the *Galli* or priests of Cybele; men and women acting unnaturally; and all conjoining to act diabolically.

15. Let not Judah offend. Israel was totally dissolute; Judah was not so. Here she is exhorted to maintain her integrity. If the former will go to what was once Bethel, the "house of God," now *Beth-aven,* the "house of iniquity," because Jeroboam has set up his calves there, let not Judah imitate them. *Gilgal* was the place where the covenant of circumcision was renewed when the people passed over Jordan; but was rendered infamous by the worship of idols, after Jeroboam had set up his idolatry.

16. Israel slideth back. They are untractable, like an unbroken *heifer* or steer, that pulls back, rather than draw in the yoke. *Will feed them as a lamb in a large place.* A species of irony. You shall go to Assyria, and be scattered among the nations; you may sport yourselves in the extensive empire, whither you shall be carried captives.

17. Ephraim. The ten tribes. *Let him alone.* They are irreclaimable; leave them to the consequences of their vicious conduct.

18. Their drink is sour. Or rather, "He is gone after their wine." The enticements of idolatry have carried them away. *Her rulers with shame do love.* Rather, "have loved shame"; they glory in their abominations. *Give ye.* Perhaps it would be better to read, "Her rulers have committed, etc. They have loved gifts. What a shame!"

CHAPTER 5

This chapter begins with threatening the Israelites for ensnaring the people to idolatry by their sacrifices and other rites on Mizpah and Tabor, 1-5. Their sacrifices, however costly, are declared to be unacceptable, 6; and their substance is devoted to the locust, 7. Nor is judgment to stop here. The cities of Judah are called upon, in a very animated manner, to prepare for the approach of enemies. Benjamin is to be pursued; Ephraim is to be desolate; and all this is intimated to Israel, that they may by repentance avert the judgment, 8-9. The following verses contain further denunciations, 10-13, expressed in terms equally terrible and sublime, 14. The Lord afflicts them not willingly the children of men; He visits them with temporal calamities that He may heal their spiritual malady, 15.

1. Hear ye this, O priests. A process is instituted against the priests, the Israelites, and the *house of the king;* and they are called on to appear and defend themselves. The accusation is that they have ensnared the people, caused them to practice idolatry, at both *Mizpah* and *Tabor.* Mizpah was situated beyond Jordan, in the mountains of Gilead; see Judg. xi. 29. And Tabor was a beautiful mountain in the tribe of Zebulum. Both these places are said to be eminent for hunting, and hence the natural occurrence of the words *snare* and *net* in speaking of them.

2. The revolters are profound to make slaughter. Here may be a reference to the practice of hunters making deep pits in the ground, and lightly covering them over, that the beasts, not discovering them, might fall in, and become a prey. *Though I have been a rebuker.* "I will bring chastisement on them all."

6. They shall go with their flocks. They shall offer many sacrifices, professing to seek and be reconciled to the Lord, but they shall not find Him. As they still retain the spirit of their idolatry, He has withdrawn himself from them.

7. Now shall a month devour them. In a month's time the king of Assyria shall be upon them, and oblige them to purchase their lives and liberties by a grievous tax of fifty shekels per head. This Menahem, king of Israel, gave to Pul, king of Assyria, 2 Kings xv. 16-20. Instead of *month,* some translate the original "locust." "The locusts shall devour them."

8. Blow ye the cornet in Gibeah. Gibeah and *Ramah* were cities of Judah, in the tribe of Benjamin. *After thee, O Benjamin.* An abrupt call of warning. "Benjamin, fly for your life! The enemy is just behind you!" This is a prediction of the invasion of the Assyrians and the captivity of the ten tribes.

9. Among the tribes of Israel have I made known. They have got sufficient warning; it is their own fault that they have not taken it.

10. Like them that remove the bound. As execrable as they who remove the landmark. They have leaped over law's enclosure, and scaled all the walls of right; they have despised and broken all laws, human and divine.

11. Walked after the commandment. Jeroboam's commandment to worship his calves at Dan and Bethel. Many of them were not forced to do this; they did it willingly.

12. Unto Ephraim as a moth. I will consume them by little and little, as a moth frets a garment.

13. When Ephraim saw his sickness. When both Israel and Judah felt their own weakness to resist their enemies, instead of calling upon and trusting in Me, they sought sinful alliances, and trusted in their idols. *King Jareb.* This name occurs nowhere in Scripture but here and in chap. x. 6. The Vulgate and Targum render *yareb,* an "avenger," a person whom they thought able to save them from their enemies. It is well-known that Menahem, king of Israel, sought alliance with Pul and Tiglath-pileser, kings of Assyria, and Ahaz, king of Judah. These were the protectors that Ephraim sought after. See 2 Kings xv and xvi. But far from healing them by making them tributary, the Assyrians made their wound more dangerous.

15. *I will go and return to my place.* I will abandon them till they acknowledge their offenses. This had the wished-for effect, as we shall see in the following chapter; for they repented and turned to God, and He had mercy upon them.

CHAPTER 6

The prophet earnestly exhorts to repentance, 1-3. God is then introduced as very tenderly and pathetically remonstrating against the backslidings of Ephraim and Judah, 4-11.

1. *Come, and let us return unto the Lord.* When God had purposed to abandon them, and they found that He had returned to His place— to His temple, where alone He could be successfully sought—they, feeling their weakness, and the fickleness, weakness, and unfaithfulness of their idols and allies, now resolve to *return unto the Lord;* and referring to what He said, chap. v. 14: "I will tear and go away," they say, He "hath torn," but "he will heal us." Their allies had torn, but they gave them no healing.

2. *After two days will he revive.* Such is His power that in two or three days He can restore us. He can realize all our hopes, and give us the strongest token for good. *In the third day he will raise us up.* In so short a time can He give us complete deliverance. These words are supposed to refer to the death and resurrection of our Lord; and it is thought that the apostle refers to them, 1 Cor. xv. 4: Christ "rose again the third day according to the scriptures"; and this is the only place in the Scriptures, i.e., of the Old Testament, where His resurrection on the third day seems to be hinted at. The original, *yekimenu,* has been translated, "He will raise him up."

3. *Then shall we know.* We shall have the fullest evidence that we have not believed in vain. *If we follow on to know the Lord.* If we continue to be as much in earnest as we now are. *His going forth.* The manifestation of His mercy to our souls is as certain as the rising of the sun at the appointed time. *And he shall come unto us as the rain.* As surely as the early and the latter rain come. The first, to prepare the earth for the seed—this fell in autumn; the second, to prepare the full ear for the harvest— this fell in spring.

4. *O Ephraim, what shall I do unto thee?* This is the answer of the Lord to the above pious resolutions; sincere while they lasted, but frequently forgotten, because the people were fickle. Their *goodness* was like the *morning cloud* that fadeth away before the rising sun, or like *the early dew* which is speedily evaporated by heat.

5. *Therefore have I hewed them by the prophets.* I have sent My prophets to testify against their fickleness. They have smitten them with the most solemn and awful threatenings; they have, as it were, *slain them by the words of my mouth.* But to what purpose? *Thy judgments are as the light that goeth forth.* The proper reading is, most probably, "And My judgment is as the light going forth." It shall be both evident and swift.

7. *But they like men (keadam,* "like Adam") *have transgressed the covenant.* They have sinned against light and knowledge as he did. This is sense; the other is scarcely so. There was a striking similarity in the two cases. Adam, in paradise, transgressed the commandment, and I cast him out; Israel, in possession of the Promised Land, transgressed My covenant, and I cast them out, and sent them into captivity.

8. *Gilead is a city of them that work iniquity.* In this place Jacob and Laban made their covenant, and set up a heap of stones, which was called *Galeed,* the "heap of testimony"; and most probably idolatry was set up here. Perhaps the very heap became the object of superstitious adoration.

9. *As troops of robbers.* What a sad picture is this of the state of the priesthood! The country of Gilead was infamous for its robberies and murders. The idolatrous priests there formed themselves into companies, and kept possession of the roads and passes; and if they found any person going to Jerusalem to worship the true God, they put him to death.

10. *I have seen an horrible thing.* That is, the idolatry that prevailed in *Israel* to such a degree that the whole land was *defiled.*

11. *O Judah, he hath set an harvest for thee.* You also have transgressed; your harvest will come; you shall be reaped down and sent into captivity. *When I returned the captivity of my people.* Bishop Newcome translates, "Among those who lead away the captivity of my people."

CHAPTER 7

Here God complains that, though He had employed every means for reforming Israel, they still persisted in their iniquity, without fearing the consequences, 1-2; that those who ought to check their crimes were pleased with them, 3; and that they all burned with adultery, as an oven when fully heated, and ready to receive the kneaded dough, 4. The fifth verse alludes to some recent enormities; the sixth charges them with dividing their time between inactivity and iniquity; the seventh alludes to their civil broils and conspiracies (see 2 Kings xv. 10, 14, 25); the eighth, to their joining themselves with idolatrous nations; and the ninth describes the sad consequence. The tenth verse reproves their pride and open contempt of God's worship; the eleventh reproves their foolish conduct in applying for aid to their enemies (see 2 Kings xv. 19 and xvii. 4); the twelfth and thirteenth threaten them with punishments; the fourteenth charges them with hypocrisy in their acts of humiliation; the fifteenth, with ingratitude; and the image of the deceitful bow, in the sixteenth verse, is highly expressive of their frequent apostasies; and their hard speeches against God shall be visited upon them by their becoming a reproach in the land of their enemies.

1. *When I would have healed Israel.* As soon as one wound was healed, another was discovered. Scarcely was one sin blotted out till another was committed. *The thief cometh in.* Their own princes spoil them. *The troop of robbers spoileth without.* The Assyrians, under different leaders, waste and plunder the country.

3. *They make the king glad.* They pleased Jeroboam by coming readily into his measures, and heartily joining with him in his idolatry.

4. *As an oven heated by the baker.* Calmet's paraphrase on this and the following verses expresses pretty nearly the sense: Hosea makes a twofold comparison of the Israelites: to an *oven,* and to *dough.* Jeroboam set fire to his own oven—his kindgom—and put the leaven in his dough; and afterwards went to rest, that the fire might have time to heat his oven, and the leaven to raise his dough, that the false principles which he introduced might infect the whole population. This fire spread very rapidly, and the dough was very soon impregnated by the leaven. All Israel was seen running to this feast, and partaking in these innovations. But what shall become of the oven—the kingdom; and the bread—the people? The *oven* shall be consumed by these flames; the king, the princes, and the people shall be enveloped in the burning, v. 7. Israel was put under the ashes, as a loaf well-kneaded and leavened; but not being carefully turned, it was burnt on one side before those who prepared it could eat of it; and enemies and strangers came and carried off the loaf. See vv. 8-9. Their lasting captivity was the consequence of their wickedness and their apostasy from the religion of their fathers.

7. *All their kings are fallen.* There was a pitiful slaughter among the idolatrous kings of Israel; four of them had fallen in the time of this prophet. Zechariah was slain by Shallum; Shallum, by Menahem; Pekahiah, by Pekah; and Pekah, by Hoshea, 2 Kings xv. All were idolaters, and all came to an untimely death.

8. *A cake not turned.* In the East, having heated the hearth, they sweep one corner, put the cake upon it, and cover it with embers; in a short time they turn it, cover it again, and continue this several times, till they find it sufficiently baked.

9. *Gray hairs are here and there upon him, yet he knoweth not.* The kingdom is grown old in iniquity; the time of their captivity is at hand, and they are apprehensive of no danger.

11. *Ephraim also is like a silly dove without heart.* A bird that has little understanding, that is easily snared and taken. *They call to Egypt, they go to Assyria.* They strive to make these their allies and friends. But in this they showed that they were without heart, had not a sound understanding; for these were rival nations, and Israel could not attach itself to the one without incurring the jealousy and displeasure of the other. Thus, like the silly dove, they were constantly falling into snares; sometimes of the Egyptians, at others of the Assyrians. By the former they were betrayed; by the latter, ruined.

12. *When they shall go*—to those nations for help—*I will spread my net upon them.* I will cause them to be taken by those in whom they trusted.

13. *Though I have redeemed them.* Out of Egypt; and given them the fullest proof of My love and power. *Yet they have spoken lies against me.* They have represented Me as rigorous and cruel, and My service as painful and unprofitable.

16. *They return, but not to the most High.* They go to their idols. *They are like a deceitful bow.* Which, when it is reflexed, in order to be strung, suddenly springs back into its quiescent curve. This bending of the bow requires both strength and skill; and if not properly done, it

will fly back, and regain its former position; and in this recoil endanger the archer—may even break an arm. I have been in this danger myself in bending the Asiatic bow. *Shall fall by the sword. Their tongue* has been enraged against Me; the *sword* shall be enraged against them. They have *mocked* Me (v. 5) and their fall is now a subject of *derision in the land of Egypt.* What they have sown, that do they now reap.

CHAPTER 8

This chapter begins with threatening some hostile invasion in short and broken sentences, full of rapidity, and expressive of sudden danger and alarm: "The trumpet to thy mouth. He shall come as an eagle," 1. And why? For their hypocrisy, 2; iniquity, 3; treason (see 2 Kings xv. 13, 17) and idolatry, 4; particularly the worshipping of the calves of Dan and Bethel, 5-6. The folly and unprofitableness of pursuing evil courses is then set forth in brief but very emphatic terms. The labor of the wicked is vain, like sowing of the wind; and the fruit of it destructive as the whirlwind. Like corn blighted in the bud, their toil shall have no recompense; or if it should have a little, their enemies shall devour it, 7. They themselves, too, shall suffer the same fate, and shall be treated by the nations of Assyria and Egypt as the vile sherds of a broken vessel, 8-9. Their incorrigible idolatry is again declared to be the cause of their approaching captivity under the king of Assyria. And as they delighted in idolatrous altars, there they shall have these in abundance, 10-14. The last words contain a prediction of the destruction of the fenced cities of Judah, because the people trusted in these for deliverance, and not in the Lord their God.

1. *Set the trumpet to thy mouth.* Sound another alarm. Let them know that an enemy is fast approaching. *As an eagle against the house of the Lord.* Shalmaneser, king of Assyria, who, for his rapidity, avarice, rapacity, and strength, is fitly compared to this royal bird. He is represented here as hovering over the house of God, as the eagle does over the prey which he has just espied, and on which he is immediately to pounce.

2. *Israel shall cry.* The rapidity of the eagle's flight is well imitated in the rapidity of the sentences in this place. *My God, we know thee.* The same sentiment, from the same sort of persons, under the same feelings, as that in the Gospel of St. Matthew, chap. vii. 22-23: "Lord, have we not prophesied in thy name? and in thy name have cast out devils? . . . then will I profess unto them, I never knew you."

4. *They have set up kings, but not by me.* Properly speaking, not one of the kings of Israel, from the defection of the ten tribes from the house of David, was the anointed of the Lord. *I knew it not.* It had not My approbation. In this sense the word "know" is frequently understood. *That they may be cut off.* That is, They shall be cut off in consequence of their idolatry.

5. *Thy calf, O Samaria, hath cast thee off.* Bishop Newcome translates: "Remove far from thee thy calf, O Samaria!" Abandon your idolatry; for My anger is kindled against you.

7. *They have sown the wind, and they shall reap the whirlwind.* As the husbandman reaps the same kind of grain which he has sown, but in far greater abundance, so he who sows the wind shall have a whirlwind to reap. *It hath no stalk.* Nothing that can yield a blossom. If it have a blossom, that blossom shall not yield fruit; if there be fruit, the sower shall not enjoy it, for strangers shall eat it. The meaning is, the labors of this people shall be utterly unprofitable and vain.

8. *Now shall they be among the Gentiles.* They shall be carried into captivity, and there be as a vessel wherein there is no pleasure; one soiled, unclean, infectious, to be despised, abhorred, not used. The allusion is to a rotten, corrupted skin-bottle.

9. *They are gone up to Assyria.* For succor. *A wild ass alone by himself.* Like that animal, jealous of its liberty, and suffering no rival. *Ephraim hath hired lovers.* Hath subsidized the neighboring heathen states.

10. *For the burden of the king of princes.* The exactions of the Assyrian king, and the princes of the provinces.

11. *Many altars to sin.* Though it does not appear that the Jews in Babylon were obliged to worship the idols of the country except in the case mentioned by Daniel, yet it was far otherwise with the Israelites in Assyria, and the other countries of their dispersion. Because they had made many altars to sin while they were in their own land, they were obliged to continue in the land of their captivity a similar system of idolatry against their will. Thus they felt and saw the evil of their idolatry, without power to help themselves.

13. *They sacrifice flesh.* Bishop Newcome translates thus: "They sacrifice gifts appointed unto me, and eat flesh." They offer to their idols the things which belong to Jehovah; or, while pretending to offer unto the Lord, they eat and drink idolatrously; and therefore the Lord will not accept them. *They shall return to Egypt.* Many of them did return to Egypt after the conquest of Palestine by Shalmaneser, and many after the ruin of Jerusalem by Nebuchadnezzar; but they had in effect returned to Egypt by setting up the worship of the golden calves, which were in imitation of the Egyptian Apis.

CHAPTER 9

The prophet reproves the Israelites for their sacrifices and rejoicings on their corn-floors, by which they ascribed to idols, as the heathen did, the praise of all their plenty, 1. For which reason they are threatened with famine and exile, 2-3, in a land where they shall be polluted, and want the means of worshipping the God of their fathers, or observing the solemnities of His appointment, 4-5. Nay, more; they shall speedily fall before the destroyer, be buried in Egypt, and leave their own pleasant places desolate, 6-9. God is then introduced, declaring His early favor for His people, and the delight He took in their obedience; but now they had so deeply revolted, all their glory will take wing, God will forsake them, and their offspring be devoted to destruction, 10-17.

1. *Rejoice not.* Do not imitate the heathen, nor serve their idols. Do not prostitute your soul and body in practicing their impurities. Hitherto you have acted as a common harlot, who goes even to the common threshing places; connects herself with the meanest, in order to get a hire even of the grain there threshed out.

4. *As the bread of mourners.* By the law, a dead body, and everything that related to it, the house where it lay, and the persons who touched it, were all polluted and unclean, and whatever they touched was considered as defiled. See Deut. xxvi. 14; Num. xix. 11, 13-14.

5. *What will ye do in the solemn day?* When ye shall be despoiled of everything by the Assyrians; for the Israelites who remained in the land after their subjection to the Assyrians did worship the true God, and offer unto Him the sacrifices appointed by the law, though in an imperfect and schismatic manner; and it was a

great mortification to them to be deprived of their religious festivals in a land of strangers.

6. *For, lo, they are gone.* Many of them fled to Egypt to avoid the destruction, but they went there only to die. *The pleasant places for their silver.* The fine estates or villas which they had purchased by their money, being now neglected and uninhabited, are covered with *nettles*; and even *in their tabernacles,* thorns and brambles of different kinds grow.

7. *The days of visitation.* Of punishment. *The prophet is a fool.* Who has pretended to foretell, on divine authority, peace and plenty; for, behold, all is desolation. *The spiritual man. Ish haruach,* "the man of spirit," who was ever pretending to be under a divine afflatus. *Is mad.* He is now enraged to see everything falling out contrary to his prediction.

8. *The watchman of Ephraim.* The true prophet, *was with,* faithful to, God. *The prophet.* The false prophet is the *snare of a fowler;* is continually deceiving the people, and leading them into snares.

9. *They have deeply corrupted themselves, as in the days of Gibeah.* This relates to that shocking rape and murder of the Levite's wife mentioned in Judg. xix. 16, etc.

10. *I found Israel like grapes in the wilderness.* While they were faithful, they were as acceptable to Me as ripe grapes would be to a thirsty traveller in the desert. *And their abominations were according as they loved.* Or, "They became as abominable as the object of their love."

11. *Their glory shall fly away.* It shall suddenly spring away from them, and return no more. *From the birth.* "So that there shall be no birth, no carrying in the womb, no conception."—Newcome.

13. *Ephraim, as I saw Tyrus.* Tyre was strongly situated on a rock in the sea; Samaria was on a mountain, both strong and pleasant. But the strength and beauty of those cities shall not save them from destruction. *Ephraim shall bring forth his children to the murderer.* The people shall be destroyed, or led into captivity by the Assyrians.

14. *Give them, O Lord: what wilt thou give?* There is an uncommon beauty in these words. The prophet, seeing the evils that were likely to fall upon his countrymen, begins to make intercession for them; but when he had formed the first part of his petition, "Give them, O Lord," the prophetic light discovered to him that the petition would not be answered, and that God was about to give them something widely different. Then changing his petition, which the Divine Spirit had interrupted, by signifying that he must not proceed in his request, he asks the question, then, "What wilt Thou give them?" and the answer is, "Give them a miscarrying womb and dry breasts." And this he is commanded to announce. It is probable that the Israelites had prided themselves in the fruitfulness of their families and the numerous population of their country. God now tells them that this shall be no more; their wives shall be barren, and their land cursed.

15. *All their wickedness is in Gilgal.* Though we are not directly informed of the fact, yet we have reason to believe they had been guilty of

some scandalous practices of idolatry in *Gilgal*. See chap. iv. 15.

16. *Ephraim is smitten.* The thing being determined, it is considered as already done. *Their root is dried up.* They shall nevermore be a kingdom. And they never had any political form from their captivity by the Assyrians to the present day. *Yea, though they bring forth.* See the note on vv. 11-12.

17. *My God will cast them away.* Here the prophet seems to apologize for the severity of these denunciations; and to vindicate the divine justice, from which they proceeded. It is *because they did not hearken unto him* that *my God,* the Fountain of mercy and kindness, *will cast them away. And they shall be wanderers among the nations.* And where they have wandered to, who can tell? and in what nations to be found, no man knows.

CHAPTER 10

This chapter treats of the same subject, but elegantly varied. It begins with comparing Israel to a fruitful vine but corrupted by too much prosperity, 1. It next reproves and threatens them for their idolatry, 2; anarchy, 3; and breach of covenant, 4. Their idolatry is then enlarged on, and its fatal consequences declared in terms full of sublimity and pathos, 5-8. God is now introduced complaining of their excessive guilt; and threatening them with captivity in terms that bear a manifest allusion to their favorite idolatry, the worshipping the similitude of a calf or heifer, 9-11. Upon which the prophet, in a beautiful allegory suggested by the preceding metaphors, exhorts them to repentance; and warns them of the dreadful consequences of their evil courses, if obstinately persisted in, 12-15.

1. *Israel is an empty vine.* Or, "a vine that casteth its grapes." *He bringeth forth fruit.* Or, "He laid up fruit for himself." He abused the blessings of God to the purposes of idolatry. He was prosperous, but his prosperity corrupted his heart. *According to the multitude of his fruit.* He became idolatrous in proportion to his prosperity; and in proportion to their wealth was the costliness of their images, and the expensiveness of their idol worship.

2. *Their heart is divided.* They wish to serve God and mammon, Jehovah and Baal; but this is impossible.

4. *They have spoken words.* Vain, empty, deceitful words. *Swearing falsely.* This refers to the alliances made with strange powers, to whom they promised fidelity without intending to be faithful.

5. *The inhabitants of Samaria shall fear.* According to Calmet, shall worship the calves of Beth-aven; those set up by Jeroboam at Bethel. *Fear* is often taken for religious reverence. *The people thereof shall mourn.* On seeing the object of their worship carried into captivity, as well as themselves. *And the priests thereof.* *Kemarim.* The priests of Samaria, says Calmet, are here called *kemarim,* that is, "black coats" or "shouters," because they made loud cries in their sacrifices.

6. *A present to king Jareb.* See on chap. v. 13. If this be a proper name, the person intended is not known in history: but it is most likely that Pul, king of Assyria, is intended, to whom Menahem, king of Israel, appears to have given one of the golden calves, to insure his assistance.

7. *Her king is cut off as the foam.* As lightly as a puff of wind blows off the foam that is formed below by a fall of water, so shall the kings of Israel be cut off. We have already seen that not less than four of them died by assassination in a very short time. See on chap. vii. 7.

8. *The high places.* Idol temples. *Of Aven.* Beth-aven. *The thorn and the thistle shall come up on their altars.* Owing to the uncultivated and unfrequented state of the land, and of their places of idol worship, the people being all carried away into captivity. *And they shall say to the mountains, Cover us; and to the hills, Fall on us.* "This sublime description of fear and distress our Lord had in view, Luke xxiii. 30, which may be a reference, and not a quotation. However, the Septuagint, in the Codex Alexandrinus, has the same order of words as occurs in the evangelist" (Newcome).

9. *Thou hast sinned from the days of Gibeah.* This is another reference to the horrible rape and murder of the Levite's wife, Judg. xix. 13-14. *There they stood.* Only one tribe was nearly destroyed, viz., that of Benjamin. They were the criminals, *the children of iniquity;* the others were faultless, and stood only for the rights of justice and mercy.

10. *When they shall bind themselves in their two furrows.* "When they are chastised for their two iniquities," i.e., the calves in Dan and Bethel (Newcome). But this double iniquity may refer to what Jeremiah says, chap. ii. 13: "My people have committed two evils"—(1) "They have forsaken me"; (2) They have joined themselves to idols.

11. *Ephraim is as an heifer that is taught.* One thoroughly broken in to the yoke. *Loveth to tread out.* Goes peacably in the yoke; and is pleased because, not being muzzled, she eats of the corn. *I passed over upon her fair neck.* I brought the yoke upon it, that she should not tread out the corn merely, but draw the plough and drag the harrow. *Jacob shall break his clods.* Harrow.

12. *Break up your fallow ground.* Do not be satisfied with a slight furrow; let the land that was fallowed (slightly ploughed) be broken up again with a deep furrow.

13. *Ye have ploughed wickedness.* You have labored sinfully. *Ye have reaped iniquity.* The punishment due to your iniquity. *Ye have eaten the fruit of lies.* Your false worship and your false gods have brought you into captivity and misery. *Because thou didst trust in thy way.* Didst confide in your own counsels, and in *thy mighty men,* and not in the God who made you.

14. *Shall a tumult arise.* The enemy shall soon fall upon your people, and take all your fortified places. *As Shalman spoiled Beth-arbel.* Some think that an allusion is made here to the destruction of Arbela, a city of Armenia, by Shalmaneser, here called *Shalman;* and this while he was only general of the Assyrian forces, and not yet king. I think the history to which this refers is unknown.

15. *So shall Beth-el do unto you.* This shall be the consequence of your idolatry. *In a morning shall the king of Israel be cut off.* Suddenly, unexpectedly. Hoshea, the king of Israel, shall be cut off by the Assyrians.

CHAPTER 11

This chapter gives a very pathetic representation of God's tender and affectionate regard for Israel, by metaphors chiefly borrowed from the conduct of mothers toward their tender offspring. From this, occasion is taken to reflect on their ungrateful return to the divine goodness, and to denounce against them the judgments of the Almighty, 1-7. But suddenly and unexpectedly the prospect changes. Beams of mercy break from the clouds just now fraught with vengeance. God, to speak in the language of men, feels the relentings of a tender parent; His bowels yearn; His mercy triumphs; His rebellious child shall yet be pardoned. As the Lion of the tribe of Judah, He will employ His power to save His people; He will call His children from the land of their captivity; and, as doves, they will fly to Him, a faithful and a holy people, 8-12.

1. *When Israel was a child.* In the infancy of his political existence.

3. *I taught Ephraim also to go.* An allusion to a mother or nurse teaching a child to walk, directing it how to lift and lay its feet, and supporting it in the meantime by the arms, that it may use its feet with the greater ease. This is a passage truly pathetic.

4. *I drew them with cords of a man.* This is a reference to leading strings, one end of which is held by the child, the other by the nurse, by which the little one, feeling some support, and gaining confidence, endeavors to walk. *That take off the yoke on their jaws.* There appears to be here an allusion to the moving and pulling forward the collar or yoke of beasts which have been hard at work, to let in the cool air between it and their neck, so as to refresh them, and prevent that heat which with the sweat would scald their necks. I have often done this at the land ends, in ploughing. *And I laid meat unto them.* Giving them at the same time a bite of grass or hay, to encourage them to go on afresh.

5. *He shall not return into . . . Egypt.* I have brought them thence already, with the design that the nation should never return thither again. But as they have sinned, and forfeited My favor and protection, they shall go to Assyria; and this because they refused to return to Me.

6. *The sword shall abide on his cities.* Israel was agitated with external and intestine wars from the time of Jeroboam II. Although Zechariah, his son, reigned twelve years, yet it was in continual troubles; and he was at last slain by the rebel Shallum, who, having reigned one month, was slain by Menahem. Pekahiah succeeded his father, Menahem, and reigned two years, and was killed by Pekah, son of Remaliah. He joined Rezin, king of Syria, and made an irruption into the land of Judah. But Ahaz having obtained succor from Tiglath-pileser, king of Assyria, Pekah was defeated, and the tribes of Reuben, Gad, Naphtali, and the half-tribe of Manasseh were carried away captives by the Assyrian king. In a short time after, Hoshea, son of Elah, slew Pekah, and usurped the kingdom, which he could not possess without the assistance of Shalmaneser, who for his services imposed a tribute on the Israelitish king. Wishing to rid himself of this yoke, he applied to the king of Egypt; but this being known to Shalmaneser, he came against Samaria and after a three years' siege took and destroyed it. Thus the sword rested on their cities; it continued in the land till all was ruined.

7. *Though they called them to the most High.* Newcome is better: "And though they call on him together because of the yoke, he will not raise it. He shall receive no refreshment." See the metaphor, v. 4.

8. *How shall I give thee up?* See the notes on chap. vi. 4, where we have similar words from similar feeling. *Mine heart is turned within me.* Justice demands your punishment; Mercy pleads for your life. As you change, Justice resolves to destroy, or Mercy to save. My heart is oppressed, and I am weary with repenting—with so frequently changing My purpose. All this, though spoken after the manner of men, shows how merciful, compassionate, and loath to punish, the God of heaven is.

9. *I will not execute.* Here is the issue of this conflict in the divine mind. Mercy triumphs over Judgment; Ephraim shall be spared. He is God, and not man. He cannot be affected by human caprices. They are now penitent, and implore mercy; He will not, as *man* would do, punish them for former offenses, when they have fallen into His hand.

10. *They shall walk after the Lord.* They shall discern the operations of His providence, when *he shall roar like a lion.* When He shall utter His majestic voice, Cyrus shall make his decree. *The people shall tremble*—be in a state of commotion, everyone hurrying to avail himself of the opportunity to return to his own land.

11. *They shall tremble as a bird.* Those of them that are in Egypt shall also be called thence, and shall speed hither *as a bird.* Those in Assyria shall also be called to return, and they shall flee as doves to their windows.

12. *Ephraim compasseth me about with lies.* I think this verse does not well unite with the above; it belongs to another subject, and should begin the following chapter, as in the Hebrew. *Judah yet ruleth with God.* There is an allusion here to Gen. xxxii. 24, where Jacob, having wrestled with the Angel, had his name changed to Israel, one that "rules with God." That glory the Israelites had lost by their idolatry; but Judah still retained the true worship, and alone deserved the name of Israel.

CHAPTER 12

The prophet, in very pointed terms, describes the unprofitableness and destruction attending vicious courses; particularly such as Ephraim pursued, who forsook God, and courted the alliance of idolatrous princes, 1. Judah is also reproved, 2. He is reminded of the extraordinary favor of God to his father, Jacob, in giving him the birthright; and exhorted, after his example, to wrestle with God (the Angel of the covenant, the same unchangeable Jehovah) for a blessing; and to love mercy and execute justice, 3-6. Ephraim is accused of pursuing practices that are deceitful, although pretending to integrity, 7-8. God then threatens to deprive this people of their possessions, 9, as they had rejected every means of reformation, 10, and given themselves up to gross impieties, 11. And, as an aggravation of their guilt, they are reminded from what humble beginnings they had been raised, 12-13. The divine judgments about to fall upon Israel are declared to be the result of great provocation, 14.

1. *Ephraim feedeth on wind.* He forms and follows empty and unstable counsels. *Followeth after the east wind.* They are not only empty, but dangerous and destructive. The *east wind* was a parching, wasting, injurious wind. *He daily increaseth lies.* He promises himself safety from foreign alliances. He made *a covenant with the Assyrians,* and sent a subsidy of oil to Egypt. The latter abandoned him; the former oppressed him.

2. *The Lord hath also a controversy with Judah.* The rest of the prophecy belongs to both Judah and Israel. He reproaches both with their ingratitude, and threatens them with God's anger.

3. *He took his brother by the heel.* See on Gen. xxv. 26 and xxxii. 24, etc.

4. *He had power over the angel.* Who represented the invisible Jehovah. *He wept, and made supplication.* He entreated with tears that God would bless him, and he prevailed. The circumstance of his weeping is not mentioned in Genesis. *He found him in Beth-el.* It was there that God made those glorious promises to Jacob relative to his posterity. See in Gen. xxviii. 13-15.

5. *The Lord is his memorial.* He is the same God as when Jacob so successfully wrestled with Him.

6. *Therefore turn thou to thy God.* Because He is the same and cannot change. Seek Him as faithfully and as fervently as Jacob did, and you will find Him the same merciful and compassionate Being.

7. *He is a merchant.* Or a "Canaanite," referring to the Phoenicians, famous for their traffic. Ephraim is as corrupt as those heathenish traffickers were. He kept, as many in all ages have done, a weight and a weight—a heavy one to buy with and a light one to sell by.

8. *I am become rich.* They boasted in their riches, notwithstanding the unjust manner in which they were acquired.

9. *And I . . . the Lord thy God.* I, who brought you out of the land of Egypt, will again make you *to dwell in tabernacles.* This appears to be a threatening. I will reduce you to as miserable a state in the land of your captivity as you often were through your transgressions in the wilderness.

10. *I have also spoken.* I have used every means and employed every method to instruct and save you. I have sent *prophets,* who spoke plainly, exhorting, warning, and beseeching you to return to Me. They have had divine *visions,* which they have declared and interpreted. They have *used similitudes,* "symbols, metaphors, allegories," in order to fix your attention and bring you back to your duty and interest.

11. *Iniquity in Gilead.* Gilgal and Gilead are equally iniquitous and equally idolatrous. Gilead, which was beyond Jordan, had already been brought under subjection by Tiglath-pileser. Gilgal, which was on this side Jordan, shall share the same fate, because it is now as idolatrous as the other. *Their altars are as heaps.* They occur everywhere. The whole land is given to idolatry.

12. *Served for a wife.* Seven years for Rachel. *For a wife he kept sheep.* Seven years for Leah, having been cheated by Laban, who gave him first Leah instead of Rachel, and afterwards made him serve seven years more before he would confirm his first engagement. Critics complain of want of connection here. Why is this isolated fact predicted? Thus, in a detached sentence, the prophet speaks of the low estate of their ancestors and how amply the providence of God had preserved and provided for them. This is all the connection the place requires.

13. *By a prophet* (Moses) *the Lord brought Israel out of Egypt, and by a prophet* (Joshua) *was he preserved.* Joshua succeeded Moses, and brought the Israelites into the Promised Land; and when they passed the Jordan at Gilgal, he received the covenant of circumcision—and yet

this same place was now made by them the seat of idolatry!

14. *Therefore shall he leave his blood upon him.* He will not remove his guilt.

CHAPTER 13

This chapter begins with observing that the fear of God leads to prosperity, but sin to ruin; a truth most visibly exemplified in the sin and punishment of Ephraim, 1-3. As an aggravation of their guilt, God reminds them of His former favors, 4-5; which they had shamefully abused, 6; and which now expose them to dreadful punishments, 7-8. He, however, tempers these awful threatenings with gracious promises; and, on their repentance, engages to save them, when no other could protect them, 9-11. But, alas! instead of repenting, Ephraim is filling up the measure of his iniquity, 12-13. Notwithstanding this, God promises to put forth His almighty power in behalf of His people, and, as it were, raise them from the dead, 14; although, in the meantime, they must be visited with great national calamities, compared first to the noxious and parching east wind, 15, and described immediately after in the plainest terms, 16.

1. *When Ephraim spake trembling.* When he was meek and humble, of a broken heart and contrite spirit. *He exalted himself in Israel.* He became great in God's sight; he rose in the divine esteem in proportion as he sank in his own. *He offended in Baal.* He became an idolater. *He died.* The sentence of death from the divine justice went out against him.

3. *Therefore they shall be as the morning cloud . . . as the early dew . . . as the chaff . . . as the smoke.* Four things, most easy to be driven about and dissipated, are employed here to show how they should be scattered among the nations, and dissipated by captivity.

4. *I am the Lord thy God.* This was the first discovery I made of myself to you, and the first commandment I gave; and I showed you that besides Me there was *no saviour.*

5. *I did know thee.* I approved of you.

7. *Will I observe them.* The *leopard,* tiger, and panther will hide themselves in thick bushwood, near where they expect any prey to pass; and as soon as it comes near, spring suddenly upon it.

8. *As a bear . . . bereaved.* This is a figure to denote excessive ferocity. See 2 Sam. xvii. 8. *And will rend the caul of their heart.* Every savage beast goes first to the seat of the blood when it has seized its prey, as in this fluid they delight more than in the most delicate parts of the flesh.

10. *Give me a king and princes.* Referring to the time in which they cast off the divine theocracy and chose Saul in the place of Jehovah.

11. *I gave thee a king in mine anger.* Such was Saul, for they highly offended God when they clamored to have a king like the heathen nations that were around them. *Took him away in my wrath.* Permitted him and the Israelites to fall before the Philistines.

12. *The iniquity of Ephraim is bound up.* It is registered in My court of justice; the death warrant is in store, and will be produced in due time.

13. *The sorrows of a travailing woman.* These judgments shall come suddenly and unavoidably.

14. *I will ransom them from the power of the grave.* In their captivity they are represented as dead and buried, which is a similar view to that taken of the Jews in the Babylonish captivity by

Ezekiel in his vision of the valley of dry bones. *O grave, I will be thy destruction. Sheol,* which we translate *grave,* is the "state of the dead." *Maveth,* which we translate *death,* is the "principle of corruption" that renders the body unfit to be longer the tenement of the soul, and finally decomposes it. *Sheol* shall be destroyed, for it must deliver up all its dead. *Maveth* shall be annihilated, for the body shall be raised incorruptible. See the use which the apostle makes of this passage, 1 Cor. xv. 54-55. *Repentance shall be hid from mine eyes.* On these points I will not "change my purpose"; this is the signification of repentance when attributed to God.

15. *Though he be fruitful. Yaphri;* a paronomasia on the word *ephrayim,* which comes from the same root, *parah,* "to be fruitful, to sprout, to bud." *An east wind shall come.* As the east wind parches and blasts all vegetation, so shall Shalmaneser blast and destroy the Israelitish state.

16. *Samaria shall become desolate.* This was the capital of the Israelitish kingdom. What follows is a simple prophetic declaration of the cruelties which should be exercised upon this hapless people by the Assyrians in the sackage of the city.

CHAPTER 14

By the terrible denunciation of vengeance which concludes the preceding chapter, the prophet is led to exhort Israel to repentance, furnishing them with a beautiful

form of prayer, very suitable to the occasion, 1-3. Upon which God, ever ready to pardon the penitent, is introduced making large promises of blessings, in allusion to those copious dews which refresh the green herbs, and which frequently denote, not only temporal salvation, but also the rich and refreshing comforts of the gospel, 4-7. Their reformation from idolatry is foretold, and their consequent prosperity, under the emblem of a green, flourishing fir tree, 8; but these promises are confined to those who may bring forth the fruits of righteousness, and the wicked are declared to have no share in them, 9.

1. *O Israel, return unto the Lord.* These words may be considered as addressed to the people now in captivity; suffering much, but having still much more to suffer if they did not repent. But it seems all these evils might yet be prevented, though so positively predicted, if the people would repent and return; and the very exhortation to this repentance shows that they still had power to repent, and that God was ready to save them and avert all these evils.

3. *We will not ride upon horses*—We shall no more fix our hopes on the proud Egyptian cavalry, to deliver us out of the hands of enemies to whom Thy divine justice has delivered us.

4. *I will heal their backsliding.* Here is the answer of God to these prayers and resolutions.

8. *What have I to do any more with idols?* The conversion of Ephraim is now as complete as it was sincere. God hears and observes this. *I am like a green fir tree.* Perhaps these words should be joined to the preceding, as Newcome has done, and be a part of God's speech to Ephraim. "I have heard him; and I have seen him as a flourishing fir tree."

The Book of

JOEL

Joel, the son of Pethuel, was of the tribe of Reuben, and city of Beth-horan, or rather Beth-haran. Joel prophesied in the kingdom of Judah, and it is the opinion of some critics that he did not appear there till after the removal of the ten tribes and the destruction of the kingdom of Israel. We do not know distinctly the year wherein he began to prophesy, nor that in which he died. He speaks of a great famine, and an inundation of locusts, which ravaged Judea; but as these are evils not uncommon in that country we can infer nothing from thence towards fixing the particular period of Joel's prophecy.

The Hebrews maintain that Joel prophesied under Manasseh, and collateral circumstances seem to preponderate in favor of this hypothesis. Under the idea of an enemy's army, the prophet represents a cloud of locusts, which in his time fell upon Judea and caused great desolation. This, together with the caterpillars and the drought, brought a terrible famine upon the land. God, being moved with the calamities and prayers of His people, scattered the locusts, and the wind blew them into the sea. These misfortunes were succeeded by plenty and fertility. After this the prophet foretold the day of the Lord, and the vengeance He was to exercise in the valley of Jezreel. He speaks of the teacher of righteousness, whom God was to send; and of the Holy Spirit, who was to descend upon all flesh. He says that Jerusalem will be inhabited forever, that salvation will come out from thence, and that whosoever shall call upon the name of the Lord shall be saved. All this relates to the new covenant and the time of the Messiah.

CHAPTER 1

This and the beginning of the next chapter contain a double prophecy, applicable in its primary sense to a plague of locusts which was to devour the land, and to be accompanied with a severe drought and famine; and

in its secondary sense it denotes the Chaldean invasion. Both senses must be admitted. For some of the expressions will apply only to the dearth by insects; others, to the desolation by war. The contexture of both is beautiful and well-conducted. In this chapter the distress of every order of people is strongly painted; and not only does the face of nature languish when the God of nature is displeased, 1-19; but the very beasts of the field, by a bold figure, are represented as supplicating God in their distress, and reproaching the stupidity of man, 20.

2. *Hath this been in your days?* He begins very abruptly; and before he proposes his subject, excites attention and alarm by intimating that he is about to annnounce disastrous events, such as the oldest man among them has never seen, nor any of them learned from the histories of ancient times.

3. *Tell ye your children of it.* To heighten the effect, he still conceals the subject, and informs them that it is such as should be handed down from father to son through all generations.

4. *That which the palmerworm hath left.* Here he begins to open his message, and the words he chooses show that he is going to announce a devastation of the land by locusts, and a famine consequent on their depredations. What the different insects may be which he specifies is not easy to determine. I shall give the words of the original, with their etymology. The *palmerworm, gazam,* from the same root, "to cut short"; probably the caterpillar, from its cutting the leaves of the trees into pieces for its nourishment. The *locust, arbeh,* from *rabah,* "to multiply," from the immense increase and multitude of this insect. *Cankerworm, yelek,* from *lak,* "to lick or lap" with the tongue. *Caterpillar, chasil,* from *chasal,* "to consume, to eat up"; the consumer. Bishop Newcome translates the first "grasshopper"; the second, "locust"; the third, "devouring locust"; and the fourth, "consuming locust." After all that has been said by interpreters concerning these four animals, I am fully of opinion that the *arbeh,* or locust himself, is the *gazam,* the *yelek,* and the *chasil;* and that these different names are used here by the prophet to point out the locust in its different states, or progress from embryo to full growth. See the note on chap. ii. 2.

5. *Awake, ye drunkards.* The general destruction of vegetation by these devouring creatures has totally prevented both harvest and vintage. It is well-known that the ruin among the vines by locusts prevents the vintage for several years after.

6. *A nation is come up upon my land.* That real locusts are intended there can be little doubt; but it is thought that this may be a double prophecy, and that the destruction by the Chaldeans may also be intended, and that the four kinds of locusts mentioned above may mean the four several attacks made on Judea by them: the first in the last year of Nabonassar (father of Nebuchadnezzar), which was the third of Jehoiakim; the second when Jehoiakim was taken prisoner in the eleventh year of his reign; the third in the ninth year of Zedekiah; and the fourth three years after, when Jerusalem was destroyed by Nebuchadnezzar. Others say that they mean four powers which have been enemies of the Jews: (1) The *palmerworm,* the Assyrians and Chaldeans. (2) The *locust,* the Persians and Medes. (3) The *cankerworm,* the Greeks, and particularly Antiochus Epiphanes. (4) The *caterpillar,* the Romans.

7. *He hath laid my vine waste.* The locusts have eaten off both leaves and bark. *Chasoph chasaphah, he hath made it clean bare; suddad sadeh,* "the field is laid waste," v. 10; and *kesod mishshaddai, a destruction from the Al-*

mighty, v. 15, are all paronomasias, in which this prophet seems to delight.

8. *Lament like a virgin . . . for the husband of her youth. Virgin* is a very improper version here. The original is *bethulah,* which signifies a young woman or bride, not a virgin.

9. *The meat offering and the drink offering is cut off.* The crops and the vines being destroyed by the locusts, the total devastation in plants, trees, corn, etc., is referred to and described with a striking variety of expression in this and the following verses.

14. *Call a solemn assembly.* The clause should be translated—"Consecrate a fast, proclaim a time of restraint"; that is, of total abstinence from food, and from all secular employment. All the elders of the land and the representatives of the people were to be collected at the Temple to cry unto the Lord, to confess their sins, and pray for mercy. The Temple was not yet destroyed. This prophecy was delivered before the captivity of Judah.

18. *How do the beasts groan!* How do the horses *neigh!* How do the asses *bray!*

19. *O Lord, to thee will I cry.* Let this calamity come as it may, we have sinned, and should humble ourselves before God. *The fire hath devoured the pastures.* This may refer either to a drought or to the effects of the locusts.

20. *The beasts of the field cry also unto thee.* Even the cattle, wild and tame, are represented as supplicating God to have mercy upon them and send them provender! There is a similar affecting description of the effects of a drought in Jeremiah, chap. xiv. 6.

CHAPTER 2

The prophet sounds the alarm of a dreadful calamity, the description of which is most terribly worked up, 1-11. Exhortation to repentance, fasting, and prayer, that the divine judgments may be averted, 12-17. God will in due time take vengeance on all the enemies of pure and undefiled religion, 18-20. Great prosperity of the Jews subsequent to their return from the Babylonish captivity, 21-27. Joel then makes an elegant transition to the outpouring of the Holy Ghost on the Day of Pentecost, 28-30; for so these verses are explained by one of the twelve apostles of the Lamb. See Acts ii. 16-21. Prophecy concerning the destruction of Jerusalem, which was shortly to follow the opening of the gospel dispensation, 31. Promises of safety to the faithful and penitent; promises afterwards remarkably fulfilled to the Christians in their escape to Pella from the desolating sword of the Roman army, 32.

1. *Blow ye the trumpet in Zion.* This verse also shows that the Temple was still standing. All assemblies of the people were collected by the sound of the trumpet. *The day of the Lord cometh.* This phrase generally means a day of judgment or punishment.

2. *A day of darkness, etc.* The depredations of the locusts are described from the second to the eleventh verses, and their destruction in the twentieth. Dr. Shaw, who saw locusts in Barbary in 1724 and 1725, thus describes them: "Those which I saw in 1724 and 1725 were much bigger than our common grasshopper; and had brown spotted wings, with legs and bodies of a bright yellow. Their first appearance was toward the latter end of March, the wind having been for some time south. In the middle of April their numbers were so vastly increased that, in the heat of the day, they formed themselves into large and numerous swarms; flew in the air like a succession of clouds; and as the

prophet Joel expresses it (ii. 10), they darkened the sun. In the month of May, when the ovaries of those insects were ripe and turgid, each of these swarms began gradually to disappear; and retired into the plains, where they deposited their eggs. These were no sooner hatched in June than each of these broods collected itself into a compact body of a furlong or more square; and, marching immediately forward in the direction of the sea, they let nothing escape them; eating up everything that was green and juicy, not only the lesser kinds of vegetables, but the vine likewise; the fig tree, the pomegranate, the palm, and the apple tree, even all the trees of the field, Joel i. 12; in doing which they kept their ranks like men of war; climbing over, as they advanced, every tree or wall that was in their way. Nay, they entered into our very houses and bedchambers, like so many thieves. The inhabitants, to stop their progress, made a variety of pits and trenches all over their fields and gardens, which they filled with water; or else they heaped up in them heath, stubble, and suchlike combustible matter, which were severally set on fire upon the approach of the locusts. But this was all to no purpose, for the trenches were quickly filled up, and the fires extinguished, by infinite swarms succeeding one another; while the front was regardless of danger, and the rear pressed on so close that a retreat was altogether impossible. A day or two after one of these broods was in motion, others were already hatched to march and glean after them; gnawing off the very bark, and the young branches, of such trees as had before escaped with the loss only of their fruit and foliage. So justly have they been compared by the prophet Joel (chap. ii. 3) to a great army; who further observes, that 'the land is as the garden of Eden before them, and behind them a desolate wilderness.' " *A day of darkness.* They sometimes obscure the sun. *As the morning spread upon the mountains.* They appeared suddenly, as the sun, in rising behind the mountains, shoots his rays over them.

3. *A fire devoureth before them.* They consume like a general conflagration. "They destroy the ground, not only for the time, but burn trees for two years after" (Sir Hans Sloane, *Nat. Hist. of Jamaica,* I., 29). *Behind them a flame burneth.* "Wherever they feed," says Ludolf, in his *History of Ethiopia,* "their leavings seem as if parched with fire." *Nothing shall escape them.* "After devouring the herbage," says Adanson, "with the fruits and leaves of trees, they attacked even the buds and the very bark; they did not so much as spare the reeds with which the huts were thatched."

4. *The appearance of horses.* The head of the locust is remarkably like that of the horse. On this account the Italians call them *cavaletta,* cavalry.

5. *Like the noise of chariots.* Bochart remarks: "The locusts fly with a great noise, so as to be heard six miles off, and while they are eating the fruits of the earth, the sound of them is like that of a flame driven by the wind."

6. *All faces shall gather blackness.* Universal mourning shall take place, because they know that such a plague is irresistible.

7. *Like mighty men . . . like men of war (and as horsemen,* v. 4). The prophet does not say they are such, but they resemble. *They shall not break their ranks.* See the account on v. 2, from Dr. Shaw.

8. *They shall not be wounded.* They have hard scales like a coat of mail; but the expression refers to the utter uselessness of all means to prevent their depredations. See Shaw's account above.

10. *The earth shall quake . . . the heavens shall tremble.* Poetical expressions, to point out universal consternation and distress. *The sun and the moon shall be dark.* Bochart relates that "their multitude is sometimes so immense as to obscure the heavens for the space of twelve miles!"

11. *The Lord shall utter his voice.* Such a mighty force seems as if summoned by the Almighty, and the noise they make in coming announces their approach, while yet afar off.

12. *Turn ye even to me.* Three means of turning are recommended: *fasting, weeping, mourning,* i.e., continued sorrow.

13. *Rend your heart.* Let it not be merely a rending of your garments, but let your hearts be truly contrite. *And repenteth him of the evil.* Is ever ready to "change His purpose" to destroy, when He finds the culprit willing to be saved.

14. *Who knoweth if he will return?* He may yet interpose and turn aside the calamity threatened, and so far preserve the land from these ravagers that there will be food for men and cattle, and a sufficiency of offerings for the Temple service. Therefore—

15. *Blow the trumpet.* Let no time be lost, let the alarm be sounded.

16. *Gather the children.* Let all share in the humiliation, for all must feel the judgment, should it come. Let no state nor condition among the people be exempted. The elders, the young persons, the infants, the bridegroom, and the bride; let all leave their houses, and go to the temple of God.

17. *Let the priests . . . weep between the porch and the altar.* The altar of burnt offerings stood before the porch of the Temple, 1 Chron. viii. 12, and between them there was an open space of fifteen or twenty cubits. It was there that the priests prostrated themselves on such occasions. *Let them say.* The following was the form to be used on this occasion, *Spare thy people.* And if this be done with a rent heart, "then will the Lord be jealous for his land, and pity his people," v. 18. He will surely save if you seriously return to and penitently seek Him.

20. *I will remove far off from you the northern army.* "That is, the *locusts;* which might enter Judea by the *north.* Or the locusts may be thus called, because they spread terror like the *Assyrian* armies, which entered Judea by the *north.* See Zeph. ii. 13."—Newcome. Syria, which was northward of Judea, was infested with them; and it must have been a northern wind that brought them into Judea in the time of Joel; as God promises to change this wind, and carry them into a barren and desolate land, Arabia Deserta. *His face toward the east sea,* i.e., the Dead Sea, which lay eastward of Jerusalem. *His hinder part toward the utmost sea,* the western sea, i.e., the Mediterranean. and his stink shall come up. After having been drowned by millions in the Mediterranean,

the reflux of the tide has often brought them back and thrown them in heaps upon the shore, where they putrefied in such a manner as to infect the air and produce pestilence, by which both men and cattle have died in great multitudes. See Bochar, *Hieroz.*, ii, 481. Livy, and St. Augustine after him, relate that there was such an immense crowd of locusts in Africa that, having eaten up every green thing, a wind arose that carried them into the sea, where they perished; but being cast upon the shore, they putrefied, and bred such a pestilence that 80,000 men died of it in the kingdom of Massinissa, and 30,000 in the garrison of Utica, in which only 10 remained alive. See Livy, lib. xc, and August. *De Civitate Dei*, lib. iv, c. 31. *Because he hath done great things.* Or, *ki*, "although" he have done great things, or, "after" he has done them, i.e., in almost destroying the whole country.

21. *Fear not . . . for the Lord will do great things.* The words are repeated from the preceding verse; Jehovah will do great things in driving them away, and supernaturally restoring the land to fertility.

23. *The former rain moderately. Hammoreh litsedakah*, "the former rain in righteousness," that is, in due time and in just proportion. This rain fell after autumn, the other in spring. See Hos. vi. 3. *In the first month. Barishon*, "as aforetime."

25. *I will restore . . . the years.* It has already been remarked that the locusts not only destroyed the produce of that year, but so completely ate up all buds, and barked the trees, that they did not recover for some years. Here God promises that He would either prevent or remedy that evil; for He would restore the years that the locusts, cankerworm, caterpillar, and palmerworm had eaten.

26. *Praise the name of the Lord your God, that hath dealt wondrously with you.* In so destroying this formidable enemy; and so miraculously restoring the land to fertility, after so great a devastation.

28. *Shall come to pass afterward.* "After this"; the same, says Kimchi, as "in the latter days," which always refers to the "days of the Messiah"; and thus this prophecy is to be interpreted. We have the testimony of St. Peter, Acts ii. 17, that this prophecy relates to that mighty effusion of the Holy Spirit which took place after the Day of Pentecost. *Your sons and your daughters shall prophesy.* Shall "preach"—exhort, pray, and instruct, so as to benefit the Church.

29. *And also upon the servants and upon the handmaids.* The gifts of teaching and instructing men shall not be restricted to any one class or order of people. And this God has done, and is still doing. He left the line of Aaron, and took His apostles indiscriminately from any tribe. He passed by the regular order of the priesthood, and the public schools of the most celebrated doctors, and took His evangelists from among fishermen, tentmakers, and even the Roman taxgatherers. And He, lastly, passed by the Jewish tribes, and took the Gentile converts, and made them preachers of righteousness to the inhabitants of the whole earth.

30. *Wonders in the heavens and in the earth.* This refers to those dreadful sights, dreadful portents, and destructive commotion by which

the Jewish polity was finally overthrown, and the Christian religion established in the Roman empire. See how our Lord applies this prophecy, Matt. xxiv. 29.

31. *The sun shall be turned into darkness.* The Jewish polity, civil and ecclesiastical, shall be entirely destroyed. *Before the great and the terrible day of the Lord come.* In the taking and sacking of Jerusalem, and burning of the Temple, by the Romans, under Titus, the son of Vespasian.

32. *For in Mount Zion and in Jerusalem.* Our blessed Lord first began to preach the gospel in Mount Zion, in the Temple, and throughout Jerusalem. There He formed His Church, and thence He sent His apostles and evangelists to every part of the globe.

CHAPTER 3

The prophecy in this chapter is thought by some to relate to the latter times of the world, when God shall finally deliver His people from all their adversaries; and it must be confessed that the figures employed are so lofty as to render it impossible to restrain the whole of their import to any events prior to the commencement of the Christian era. The whole prophecy is delivered in a very beautiful strain of poetry, but what particular events are referred to is at present very uncertain, 1-21.

1. *For, behold, in those days.* According to the preceding prophecy, these days should refer to gospel times, or to such as should immediately precede them. *I shall bring again the captivity of Judah and Jerusalem.* This may refer to the return from the Babylonish captivity.

2. *The valley of Jehoshaphat.* There is no such valley in the land of Judea, and hence the word must be symbolical. It signifies the "judgment of God," or "Jehovah judgeth"; and may mean someplace where Nebuchadnezzar should gain a great battle, which would utterly discomfit the ancient enemies of the Jews, and resemble the victory which Jehoshaphat gained over the Ammonites, Moabites, and Edomites, 2 Chron. xx. 22-26. *And parted my land.* The above nations had frequently entered into the territories of Israel, and divided among themselves the lands they had thus overrun. While the Jews were in captivity, much of the land of Israel was seized on, and occupied by the Philistines and other nations that bordered on Judea.

3. *Have given a boy for an harlot.* To such wretched circumstances were the poor Jews reduced in their captivity that their children were sold by their oppressors, and both males and females used for the basest purposes. Or this may refer to the issue of the Chaldean war in Judea, where the captives were divided among the victors. And being set in companies, they *cast lots* for them. And those to whom they fell sold them for various purposes: the boys to be slaves and catamites, the girls to be prostitutes; and in return for them they got *wine* and such things. I think this is the meaning of the text.

4. *What have ye to do with me?* Why have the Tyrians and Sidonians joined their other enemies to oppress My people? *Will ye render me a recompence?* Do you think by this to avenge yourselves upon the Almighty? to retaliate upon God!

5. *Ye have taken my silver and my gold.* The Chaldeans had spoiled the Temple, and carried

away the sacred vessels, and put them in the temple of their own god in Babylon.

6. *Sold unto the Grecians.* These were the descendants of Javan, Gen. x. 2-5. And with them the Tyrians trafficked, Ezek. xxvii. 19. *That ye might remove them far from their border.* Intending to send them as far off as possible, that it might be impossible for them to get back to reclaim the land of which you had dispossessed them.

7. *I will raise them.* I shall find means to bring them back from the place whither you have sold them, and they shall retaliate upon you the injuries they have sustained. It is said that Alexander and his successors set at liberty many Jews that had been sold into Greece. And it is likely that many returned from different lands, on the publication of the edict of Cyrus.

8. *I will sell your sons.* When Alexander took Tyre, he reduced into slavery all the lower people, and the women.

9. *Prepare war.* Let all the enemies of God and of His people join together; let them even call all the tillers of the ground to their assistance, instead of laboring in the field; let every peasant become a soldier. Let them turn their agricultural implements into offensive weapons, so that the weak, being well-armed, may confidently say, "I am strong." Yet, when thus collected and armed, "Jehovah will bring down *thy mighty ones";* for so the clause in v. 11 should be rendered.

12. *Let the heathen be wakened.* The heathen "shall be wakened." *The valley of Jehoshaphat.* Any place where God may choose to display His judgments against His enemies.

13. *Put ye in the sickle.* The destruction of His enemies is represented here under the metaphor of reaping down the harvest; and of gathering the grapes, and treading them in the winepresses.

14. *Multitudes, multitudes. Hamonim, hamonim,* "crowds upon crowds," *in the valley of decision*—the same as the valley of Jehoshaphat, the place where God is to execute judgment on His enemies.

15. *The sun and the moon shall be darkened.* High and mighty states shall be eclipsed, and brought to ruin, and the *stars*—petty states, princes, and governors—*shall withdraw their shining;* withhold their influence and tribute from the kingdoms to which they have belonged, and set up themselves as independent governors.

16. *The Lord also shall roar, out of Zion.* His temple and worship shall be reestablished there, and He will thence denounce His judgments against the nations. *The heavens and the earth shall shake.* There shall be great commotions in powerful empires and their dependencies; but in all these things His own people shall be unmoved, for God shall be their *hope* and *strength.*

17. *So shall ye know.* By the judgments I execute on your enemies, and the support I give to yourselves, that I am the all-conquering Jehovah, and that I have again taken up My residence in Jerusalem. All this may refer, ultimately, to the restoration of the Jews to their land; when "holiness to the Lord" shall be their motto; and no strange god, nor impure people, shall be permitted to enter the city, or even pass through it. This, I think, must refer to gospel times.

18. *In that day.* After their return from their captivities. *The mountains shall drop down new wine.* A poetic expression for great fertility. *And all the rivers of Judah,* far from being generally dry in the summer, shall have their channels always full of water.

And a fountain shall come forth of the house of the Lord. See the account of the typical waters in Ezekiel, chap. xlvii, to which this seems to have a reference. At least the subject is the same, and seems to point out the grace of the gospel, the waters of salvation, that shall flow from Jerusalem, and *water the valley of Shittim.* Shittim was in the plains of Moab beyond Jordan (Num. xxxiii. 49; Josh. iii. 1); but as no stream of water could flow from the Temple, pass across Jordan, or reach this plain, *the valley of Shittim* must be considered symbolical, as the valley of Jehoshaphat. But as *Shittim* may signify "thorns," it may figuratively represent the most uncultivated and ferocious inhabitants of the earth receiving the gospel of Christ, and being civilized and saved by it. We know that briers and thorns are emblems of bad men; see Ezek. ii. 6. Thus all the figures in this verse will point out the happy times of the gospel.

19. *Egypt shall be a desolation.* While peace, plenty, and prosperity of every kind shall crown My people, all their enemies shall be as a *wilderness;* and those who have used *violence* against the saints of God, and shed the blood of innocents (of the holy martyrs) in their land, when they had political power, these and all such shall fall under the just judgments of God.

20. *But Judah shall dwell for ever.* The true Church of Christ shall be supported, while all false and persecuting churches shall be annihilated. The promise may also belong to the full and final restoration of the Jews, when they dwell at Jerusalem as a distinct people professing the faith of our Lord Jesus Christ.

21. *For I will cleanse their blood.* "I will avenge" the slaughter and martyrdom of My people, which I have not yet avenged.

The Book of
AMOS

Amos was of the little town of Tekoa, in the tribe of Judah, about four leagues southward of Jerusalem. There is no good proof, however, that he was a native of this place, but only that he retired thither when he was driven from Bethel, which was in the kingdom of the ten tribes. It is very probable that he was born within the territories of Israel, and that his mission was directed principally to this kingdom.

As he was prophesying in Bethel, where the golden calves were, in the reign of Jeroboam II, before the birth of Jesus Christ, 783, Amaziah, the high priest of Bethel, accused him before King Jeroboam, saying, "Amos hath conspired against thee in the midst of the house of Israel: the land is not able to bear all his words. For thus Amos saith, Jeroboam shall die by the sword, and Israel shall surely be led away captive out of their own land." Amaziah said therefore unto Amos, "O thou seer, go, flee thee away into the land of Judah, and there eat bread, and prophesy there: but prophesy not again any more at Beth-el; for it is the king's chapel, and it is the king's court."

Amos answer Amaziah, "I was no prophet, neither was I a prophet's son; but I was an herdman, and a gatherer of sycomore fruit: and the Lord took me as I followed the flock, and the Lord said unto me, Go, prophesy unto my people Israel." After this the prophet retired into the kingdom of Judah, and dwelt in the town of Tekoa, where he continued to prophesy. He complains in many places of the violence offered him by endeavoring to oblige him to silence, and bitterly exclaims against the disorders of Israel.

He began to prophesy the second year before the earthquake, which happened in the reign of King Uzziah; and which Josephus, with most of the ancient and modern commentators, refers to this prince's usurpation of the priest's office, when he attempted to offer incense to the Lord. The first of his prophecies, in order of time, are those of the seventh chapter. The others he pronounced in the town of Tekoa, whither he retired. His first two chapters are against Damascus, the Philistines, Tyrians, Edomites, Ammonites, Moabites, the kingdom of Judah, and that of the ten tribes. The evils with which he threatens them refer to the times of Shalmaneser, Tiglath-pileser, Sennacherib, and Nebuchadnezzar, who did so much mischief to these provinces, and at last led the Israelites into captivity.

He foretold the misfortunes into which the kingdom of Israel should fall after the death of Jeroboam II, who was then living. He foretold the death of King Zechariah; the invasion of the lands belonging to Israel by Pul and Tiglath-pileser, kings of Assyria; and speaks of the captivity of the ten tribes, and of their return into their own country. He makes sharp invective against the sins of Israel; against their effeminacy and avarice, their harshness to the poor, the splendor of their buildings, and the delicacy of their tables. He reproves the people of Israel for going to Bethel, Dan, Gilgal, and Beersheba, which were the most famous pilgrimages of the country; and for swearing by the gods of these places.

CHAPTER 1

This chapter denounces judgments against the nations bordering on Palestine, enemies to the Jews, viz., the Syrians, 1-5; Philistines, 6-8; Tyrians, 9-10; Edomites, 11-12, and Ammonites, 13-15. The same judgments were predicted by other prophets, and fulfilled, partly by the kings of Assyria, and partly by those of Babylon; though, like many other prophecies, they had their accomplishment by degrees, and at different periods. The prophecy against the Syrians, whose capital was Damascus, was fulfilled by Tiglath-pileser, king of Assyria; see 2 Kings xvi. 9. The prophecy against Gaza of the Philistines was accomplished by Hezekiah, 2 Kings xviii. 8; by Pharaoh, Jer. xlvii. 1; and by Alexander the Great; see Quintius Curtius, lib. iv, c. 6. The prophecy against Ashdod was fulfilled by Uzziah, 2 Chron. xxvi. 6; and that against Ashkelon by Pharaoh, Jer. xlvii. 5. All Syria was also subdued by Pharaoh-necho; and again by Nebuchadnezzar, who also took Tyre, as did afterwards Alexander. Nebuchadnezzar also subdued the Edomites, Jer. xxv. 9, 21 and xxvii. 3, 6. Judas Maccabeus routed the remains of them, 1 Macc. v. 3; and Hyrcanus brought them under entire subjection. The Ammonites were likewise conquered by Nebuchadnezzar. The earthquake, which the prophet takes for his era, is perhaps referred to in Zech. xiv. 5 and also in Isa. v. 25. Josephus ascribes it to Uzziah's invasion of the priestly office; see 2 Chron. xxvi. 16.

1. *The words of Amos*. This person and the father of Isaiah, though named alike in our translation, were as different in their names as in their persons. The father of Isaiah, *Amots;* the prophet before us, *Amos*. The first, *aleph, mem, vau, tsaddi;* the second, *ain, mem, vau, samech. Among the herdmen*. He seems to have been among the very lowest orders of life, a herdsman, one who tended the flocks of *others* in the open fields, and "a gatherer of sycomore fruit." Of whatever species this was, whether a kind of fig, it is evident that it was wild fruit; and he probably collected it for his own subsistence, or to dispose of either for the service of his employer, or to increase his scanty wages.

Before the earthquake. Probably the same as that referred to in Zech. xiv. 5.

2. *The Lord will roar from Zion*. It is a pity that our translators had not followed the hemistich form of the Hebrew:

Jehovah from Zion shall roar,
And from Jerusalem shall give forth his
   voice;
And the pleasant dwellings of the shepherds
   shall mourn,
And the top of mount Carmel shall wither.

Carmel was a very fruitful mountain in the tribe of Judah, Josh. xv. 55; Isa. xxxv. 2. This introduction was natural in the mouth of a herdsman who was familiar with the roaring of lions, the bellowing of bulls, and the lowing of kine. The roaring of the lion in the forest is one of the most terrific sounds in nature; when near, it strikes terror into the heart of both man and beast.

3. *For three transgressions of Damascus, and for four.* These expressions of *three* and *four*, so often repeated in this chapter, mean repetition, abundance, and anything that goes towards excess. "Very, very exceedingly"; and so it was used among the ancient Greek and Latin poets. See the passionate exclamation of Ulysses, in the storm, *Odyss.*, lib. v, v. 306.

THRICE *happy Greeks! and* FOUR *times who*
   were slain
In Atreus' cause, upon the Trojan plain.
Damascus was the capital of Syria.

4. *Ben-hadad.* He was son and successor of Hazael. See the cruelties which they exercised upon the Israelites, 2 Kings x. 32; xiii. 7, etc.; and see especially 2 Kings xiii. 12, where these cruelties are predicted. The *fire* threatened here is the war so successfully carried on against the Syrians by Jeroboam II, in which he took Damascus and Hamath, and reconquered all the ancient possessions of Israel. See 2 Kings xiv. 25-26, 28.

5. *The bar of Damascus.* The gates, whose long traverse bars, running from wall to wall, were their strength. I will throw it open; and the gates were forced, and the city taken, as above. *The plain of Aven . . . the house of Eden.* The *plain of Aven*, or *Birkath-Aven*, Calmet says, is a city of Syria, at present called Baal-Bek, and by the Greeks Heliopolis; and is situated at the end of that long valley which extends from south to north, between Libanus and Anti-Libanus. *The people of Syria shall go into captivity unto Kir.* Kir is supposed to be the country of Cyrene in Albania, on the river Cyrus, which empties itself into the Caspian Sea. The fulfillment of this prophecy may be seen in 2 Kings xvi. 1-9.

6. *They carried away captive.* Gaza is well know to have been one of the five lordships of the Philistines; it lay on the coast of the Mediterranean Sea, near to Egypt. The *captivity* mentioned here may refer to inroads and incursions made by the Philistines in times of peace. See 2 Chron. xxi. 16.

9. *Tyrus.* See Ezekiel xxvi; xxvii; and xxviii. *The brotherly covenant.* This possibly refers to the very friendly league made between Solomon and Hiram, king of Tyre, 1 Kings v. 12; but some contend that the brotherly covenant refers to the two people having descended from the two brothers, Jacob and Esau.

10. *I will send a fire on the wall of Tyrus.* The destructive fire or siege by Nebuchadnezzar, which lasted thirteen years, and ended in the destruction of this ancient city; see Ezekiel,

chap. xxvi. 7-14. It was finally ruined by Alexander.

11. *For three transgressions of Edom.* That the Edomites were always implacable enemies of the Jews is well-known; but most probably that which the prophet has in view was the part they took in distressing the Jews when Jerusalem was besieged, and finally taken, by the Chaldeans. See Obad. 11-14; Ezek. xxv. 12; xxxv. 5; Ps. cxxxvii. 7.

12. *Teman . . . Bozrah.* Principal cities of Idumea.

13. *The children of Ammon.* The country of the Ammonites lay to the east of Jordan, in the neighborhood of Gilead. *Rabbah* was its capital. *Because they have ripped up.* This refers to some barbarous transaction well-known in the time of this prophet, but of which we have no distinct mention in the sacred historians.

14. *With shouting in the day of battle.* They shall be totally subdued. This was done by Nebuchadnezzar. See Jer. xxvii. 3, 6.

15. *Their king shall go into captivity.* Probably *malcham* should be Milcom, who was a chief god of the Ammonites; and the following words, *he and his princes,* may refer to the body of his priesthood. See 1 Kings xi. 33. All these countries were subdued by Nebuchadnezzar.

CHAPTER 2

The prophet goes on to declare the judgments of God against Moab, 1-3; against Judah, 4-5; and then against Israel, the particular object of his mission. He enumerates some of their sins, 6-8, aggravated by God's distinguishing regard to Israel, 9-12; and they are in consequence threatened with dreadful punishments, 13-16. See 2 Kings xv. 19 and xvii. 6.

1. *For three transgressions of Moab, and for four.* See an explanation of this form, chap. i. 2. The land of the Moabites lay to the east of the Dead Sea. For the origin of this people, see Gen. xix. 37. *He burned the bones of the king of Edom into lime.* Possibly referring to some brutality, such as opening the grave of one of the Idumean kings, and calcining his bones. It is supposed by some to refer to the fact mentioned in 2 Kings iii. 26, when the kings of Judah, Israel, and Idumea joined together to destroy Moab. The king of it, despairing to save his city, took 700 men, and made a desperate sortie on the quarter where the king of Edom was; and, though not successful, took prisoner the son of the king of Edom; and, on their return into the city, offered him as a burnt offering upon the wall, so as to terrify the besieging armies, and cause them to raise the siege. Others understand the son that was sacrificed to be the king of Moab's own son.

2. *The palaces of Kirioth.* This was one of the principal cities of the Moabites. *Moab shall die with tumult.* All these expressions seem to refer to this city's being taken by storm, which was followed by a total slaughter of its inhabitants.

3. *I will cut off the judge.* Shophet may signify the chief magistrate.

4. *For three transgressions of Judah.* We may take the *three* and *four* here to any latitude; for this people lived in continual hostility to their God, from the days of David to the time of Uzziah, under whom Amos prophesied. Their iniquities are summed up under three general heads: (1) They *despised,* or rejected, *the law of the*

Lord. (2) They kept not His statutes. (3) They followed *lies*, were idolaters, and followed false prophets rather than those sent by Jehovah.

5. *I will send a fire upon Judah.* This fire was the war made upon the Jews by Nebuchadnezzar, which terminated with the sackage and burning of Jerusalem and its palace, the Temple.

6-8. *For three transgressions of Israel.* To be satisfied of the exceeding delinquency of this people, we have only to open the historical and prophetic books in any part, for the whole history of the Israelites is one tissue of transgression against God. Their crimes are enumerated under the following heads: (1) Their judges were mercenary and corrupt. (2) They were unmerciful to the poor generally. They *pant after the dust of the earth on the head of the poor;* or, to put it on the head of the poor; or, they bruise the head of the poor against the dust of the earth. (3) They *turn aside the way of the meek.* They are peculiarly oppressive to the weak and afflicted. (4) They were licentious to the uttermost abomination; for in their idol feasts, where young women prostituted themselves publicly in honor of Astarte, the father and son entered into impure connections with the same female. (5) They were cruel in their oppressions of the poor; for the garments or beds which the poor had pledged they retained contrary to the law, Exod. xxii. 7-26, which required that such things should be restored before the setting of the sun. (6) They punished the people by unjust and oppressive fines, and served their tables with wine bought by such fines. Or it may be understood of their appropriating to themselves that wine which was allowed to criminals to mitigate their sufferings in the article of death.

12. *But ye gave the Nazarites wine.* This was expressly forbidden in the laws of their institution. See Num. vi. 1-3.

13. *Behold, I am pressed under you.* The marginal reading is better: "Behold, I will press your place, as a cart full of sheaves presseth."

15. *Neither shall he that rideth the horse deliver himself.* I believe all these sayings, from verse 13 to 16 inclusive, are proverbs, to show the inutility of all attempts, even in the best circumstances, to escape the doom now decreed, because the cup of their iniquity was full.

CHAPTER 3

This chapter begins with reproving the twelve tribes in general, 1-2; and then particularly the kingdom of Israel, whose capital was Samaria. The prophet assures them that, while they were at variance with God, it would be unreasonable in them to expect His presence or favor. Other neighboring nations are then called upon to take warning from the judgments about to be inflicted upon the house of Israel, which would be so general that only a small remnant should escape them, 9-15. The image used by the prophet on this occasion (see verse 12), and borrowed from his former calling, is very natural and significant, and not a little dignified by the inspired writer's lofty air and manner.

1. *Against the whole family.* That is, all, both the kingdoms of Israel and Judah. In this all the twelve tribes are included.

2. *You only have I known.* I have taken no other people to be My own people. I have approved of you, loved you, fed, sustained, and defended you; but because you have forsaken Me, have become idolatrous and polluted, therefore will I punish you. And the punishment

shall be in proportion to the privileges you have enjoyed, and the grace you have abused.

5. *Can a bird fall in a snare?* Can you, as a sinful people, fall into calamities which I have not appointed? *Shall one take up a snare . . . and have taken nothing?* Will the snare be removed before it has caught the expected prey? Shall I remove My judgments till they are fully accomplished?

6. *Shall a trumpet be blown?* The sign of alarm and invasion. *Shall there be any evil in a city?* Shall there be any public calamity on the wicked that is not an effect of My displeasure? The word does not mean moral evil, but punishment for sin.

8. *The lion hath roared.* God hath sent forth a terrible alarm. *Who will not fear?* Can any hear such denunciations of divine wrath and not tremble? *Who can but prophesy?* Who can help proclaiming at large the judgment threatened against the nation? But I think *naba*, here, is to be taken in its natural and ideal signification, to "pray, supplicate." The Lord hath spoken of punishment—who can help supplicating His mercy, that His judgments may be averted?

12. *As the shepherd taketh out of the mouth of the lion.* Scarcely any of you shall escape; and those that do shall do so with extreme difficulty, just as a shepherd, of a whole sheep carried away by a lion, can recover no more than two of its legs or a piece of its ear, just enough to prove by the marks on those parts that they belonged to a sheep which was his own. *So shall the children of Israel be taken out.* Those of them that escape these judgments shall escape with as great difficulty, and be of as little worth, as the two legs and piece of an ear that shall be snatched out of the lion's mouth. *In the corner of a bed.* The *corner* is the most honorable place in the East, and a *couch* in the corner of a room is the place of the greatest distinction.

13. *Hear ye.* This is an address to the prophet.

14. *In the day that I shall visit.* When Josiah made a reformation in the land he destroyed idolatry, pulled down the temples and altars that had been consecrated to idol worship, and even burnt the bones of the priests of Baal and the golden calves upon their own altars. See 2 Kings xxiii. 15-16, etc.

15. *I will smite the winter house with the summer house.* I will not only destroy the poor habitations and villages in the country, but I will destroy those of the nobility and gentry; as well the lofty palaces in the fortified cities in which they dwell in the winter season, as those light and elegant seats in which they spend the summer season. *And the houses of ivory.* Those remarkable for their magnificence and their ornaments, not built of ivory, but in which ivory vessels, ornaments, and inlaying abounded.

CHAPTER 4

Israel reproved for their oppression, 1-3; idolatry, 4-5; and for their impenitence under the chastising hand of God, 6-11. The omniscience and uncontrollable power of God, 12-13.

1. *Hear this word, ye kine of Bashan.* Such an address was quite natural from the herdsman of Tekoa. *Bashan* was famous for the fertility of

its soil, and its flocks and herds; and the prophet here represents the iniquitous, opulent, idle, lazy drones, whether men or women, under the idea of fatted bullocks, which were shortly to be led out to the slaughter.

2. *He will take you away with hooks.* Two modes of fishing are here alluded to: (1) angling with rod, line, and baited hook; (2) that with the gaff, eel-spear, harpoon, or suchlike—the first used in catching small fish, by which the common people may be here represented; the second, for catching large fish. Some understand the latter word as meaning a sort of fishnets.

3. *And ye shall go out at the breaches.* Probably the metaphor is here kept up. They shall be caught by the hooks, or by the nets; and though they may make breaches in the latter by their flouncing, when caught they shall be taken out at these very breaches.

4. *Come to Beth-el, and transgress.* Spoken ironically. Go on to worship your calves at Bethel; and multiply your transgressions at Gilgal, the very place where I rolled away the reproach of your fathers, by admitting them there into My covenant by circumcision—a place that should have ever been sacred to Me, but you have now desecrated it by enormous idolatries. Let your morning and evening sacrifices be offered still to your senseless gods, and continue to support your present vicious priesthood by the regular triennial tithes which should have been employed in My service.

5. *Offer a sacrifice of thanksgiving.* To the senseless metal, from which ye never did and never could receive any help. Proceed yet further, and bring freewill offerings; testify superabundant gratitude to your metallic gods, to whom ye are under such immense imaginary obligations! *Proclaim and publish these offerings,* and set forth the perfections of the subjects of your worship; and see what they can do for you, when I, Jehovah, shall send drought, and blasting, and famine, and pestilence, and the sword among you.

6. *Cleanness of teeth.* Scarcity of bread, as immediately explained. *Yet have ye not returned unto me, saith the Lord.* This reprehension is repeated five times in this chapter; and in it are strongly implied God's long-suffering, His various modes of fatherly chastisement, the ingratitude of the people, and their obstinate wickedness.

7. *When there were yet three months to the harvest.* St. Jerome says, from the end of April, when the latter rain falls, until harvest, there are three months, May, June, and July, in which no rain falls in Judea. The rain, therefore, that God had withheld from them was that which was usual in the spring months, particularly in April. *I caused it to rain upon one city.* To prove to them that this rain did not come fortuitously or of necessity, God was pleased to make these most evident distinctions.

12. *Therefore thus will I do unto thee.* I will continue My judgments, I will fight against you; and, because I am thus determined, *prepare to meet thy God, O Israel.* This is a military phrase, and is to be understood as a challenge to come out to battle. As if the Lord had said, I will attack you immediately. Throw yourselves into a posture of defense, summon your idols to your help, and try how far your strength, and

that of your gods, will avail you against the unconquerable arm of the Lord of hosts!

13. *He that formeth the mountains.* Here is a powerful description of the majesty of God. He formed the earth; He created the wind; He knows the inmost thoughts of the heart; He is the Creator of darkness and light; He steps from mountain to mountain, and has all things under His feet! Who is He who hath done and can do all these things? *JEHOVAH ELOHIM TSEBAOTH,* that is His name. (1) Being. (2) The God who is in covenant with mankind. (3) The universal Commander of all the hosts of earth and heaven. This name is further illustrated in the following chapter.

CHAPTER 5

This chapter opens with a tender and pathetic lamentation, in the style of a funeral song, over the house of Israel, 1-2. The prophet than glances at the awful threatenings denounced against them, 3; earnestly exhorting them to renounce their idols, and seek Jehovah, of whom He gives a very magnificent description, 4-9. He then reproves their injustice and oppression with great warmth and indignation; exhorts them again to repentance; and enforces his exhortation with the most awful threatenings, delivered with great majesty and authority, and in images full of beauty and grandeur, 10-24. The chapter concludes with observing that their idolatry was of long standing, that they increased the national guilt by adding to the sins of their fathers; and that their punishment, therefore, should be great in proportion, 25-27. Formerly numbers of them were brought captive to Damascus, 2 Kings x. 32-33; but now they must go beyond it to Assyria, 2 Kings xv. 29; xvii. 6.

1. *Hear ye this word.* Attend to this doleful song which I make for the house of Israel.

2. *The virgin of Israel.* The kingdom of Israel, or the ten tribes, which were carried into captivity, and are now totally lost in the nations of the earth.

3. *The city that went out by a thousand.* The city that could easily have furnished, on any emergency, 1,000 fighting men, can now produce scarcely 100; and now of the 100 scarcely 10 remain. So reduced was Israel when Shalmaneser besieged and took Samaria, and carried the residue into captivity.

4. *Seek ye me, and ye shall live.* Cease your rebellion against Me; return to Me with all your heart; and though consigned to death, you shall be rescued and live.

5. *But seek not Beth-el.* There was one of Jeroboam's golden calves, and at *Gilgal* were carved images; both were places in which idolatry was triumphant. The prophet shows them that all hope from those quarters is utterly vain; *for Gilgal shall . . . go into captivity, and Beth-el be brought to nought.* There is a play or paronomasia on the letters and words in this clause: *haggilgal galoh yigleh, ubeith el yiheyeh leaven.* "This Gilgal shall go captive into captivity; and Beth-el [the house of God] shall be for Beth-aven" (the house of iniquity).

6. *Seek the Lord, and ye shall live.* Repeated from v. 4. *In the house of Joseph.* The Israelites of the ten tribes, of whom Ephraim and Manasseh, sons of Joseph, were the chief.

7. *Ye who turn judgment to wormwood.* Who pervert judgment; causing him who obtains his suit to mourn sorely over the expenses he has incurred in gaining his right.

8. *That maketh the seven stars and Orion.* See Job. ix. 9 and xxxviii. 32.

9. *That strengtheneth the spoiled.* Who takes the part of the poor and oppressed against the oppressor; and, in the course of His providence, sets up the former and depresses the latter.

10. *They hate him that rebuketh in the gate.* They cannot bear an upright magistrate, and will not have righteous laws executed.

11. *Your treading is upon the poor.* You tread them under your feet. *Ye take from him burdens of wheat.* You will have his bread for doing him justice.

12. *I know your manifold transgressions.* I have marked the multitude of your smaller crimes, as well as your mighty offenses.

13. *The prudent shall keep silence.* A wise man will consider that it is useless to complain. He can have no justice without bribes; and he has no money to give: consequently, in such an evil time, it is best to keep silence.

16. *They shall call the husbandman to mourning.* Because the crops have failed, and the ground has been tilled in vain.

17. *And in all vineyards shall be wailing.* The places where festivity especially used to prevail. *I will pass through thee.* As I passed, by the ministry of the destroying angel, through Egypt, not to spare, but to destroy.

18. *Woe unto you that desire the day of the Lord!* The prophet had often denounced the coming of God's day, that is, of a time of judgment; and the unbelievers had said, "Let His day come, that we may see it." Now the prophet tells them that that day would be to them *darkness,* calamity, *and not light,* not prosperity.

19. *As if a man did flee from a lion, and a bear met him.* The Israelites, under their king Menahem, wishing to avoid a civil war, called in Pul, king of Assyria, to help them. This led to a series of evils inflicted by the Syrian and Assyrian kings, till at last Israel was ravaged by Shalmaneser, and carried into captivity. Thus, in avoiding one evil they fell into another still more grievous.

21. *I hate, I despise your feast days.* I abominate those sacrificial festivals where there is no piety, and I despise them because they pretend to be what they are not.

23. *The noise of thy songs . . . the melody of thy viols.* They had both vocal and instrumental music in those sacrificial festivals, and God hated the noise of the one and shut His ears against the melody of the other.

24. *Let judgment run down.* Let the execution of justice be everywhere like the showers that fall upon the land to render it fertile; and *let righteousness* in heart and life be like a mighty river, or the Jordan, that shall wind its course through the whole nation, and carry every abomination into the Dead Sea.

25. *Have ye offered unto me sacrifices?* Did you offer to Me, during forty years in the wilderness, sacrifices in such a way as was pleasing to Me? Ye did not; for your hearts were divided, and ye were generally in a spirit of insurrection or murmuring.

26. *But ye have borne.* The preceding verse spoke of their fathers; the present verse speaks of the Israelites then existing, who were so grievously addicted to idolatry that they not only worshipped at stated public places the idols set up by public authority, but they carried their gods about with them everywhere. *The tabernacle of your Moloch.* Probably a small portable shrine, with an image of their god in it, such as *Moloch;* and the star or representative of their god *Chiun* (see Acts vii. 42).

27. *Will I cause you to go into captivity beyond Damascus.* That is, into Assyria, the way to which from Judea was by Damascus.

CHAPTER 6

The prophet reproves his people for indulging themselves in luxurious ease, and forming alliances with their powerful, idolatrous neighbors, 1. He asks if their lands or their lot be better than their own, 2; that they should choose to worship the gods of the heathen, and forsake Jehovah. Then follows an amplification of the sin which the prophet reproves, 3-6; to which he annexes very awful threatenings, confirmed by the oath of Jehovah, 7-8. He next particularly specifies the punishment of their sins by pestilence, 9-11; by famine, or a drought that should harden the earth so that it could not be tilled, 12; and by the sword of the Assyrians, 13-14.

1. *Woe to them that are at ease in Zion!* For *hashshaanannim,* "who dwell at ease," it has been proposed to read *hashshaanannim,* "who confidently lean," the two words differing in only one letter, an *ain* for an *aleph.* They leaned confidently on Zion, supposing that, notwithstanding their iniquities, they should be saved for Zion's sake. Thus the former clause will agree better with the latter, "leaning upon Zion," and "trusting in the mountain of Samaria." *Are named chief.* See Isa. xliv. 5. They call themselves not after their ancestors, but after the chief of the idolatrous nations with whom they intermarry, contrary to the law.

2. *Pass ye unto Calneh.* This is, says Calmet, the Ctesiphon on the river Tigris. *Hamath.* A city on the Orontes, in Syria. *Gath.* A well-known town, and head of one of the five seignories of the Philistines. *Be they better?* You have no more reason to expect exemption from the consequences of your sins than they had. They have been punished; so shall you.

4. *That lie upon beds of ivory.* The *beds* mentioned here may be either sofas to recline on at table or beds to sleep on, and these among the ancients were ornamented with ivory inlaid.

7. *With the first that go captive.* The house of Israel shall be carried into captivity before the house of Judah.

9. *Ten men . . . they shall die.* All shall be cut off by the sword, or by captivity, or by famine.

10. *A man's uncle shall take him up.* Bishop Newcome says this obscure verse seems to describe the effects of famine and pestilence during the siege of Samaria. The carcass shall be burnt, and the bones removed with no ceremony of funeral rites, and without the assistance of the nearest kinsman. Solitude shall reign in the house; and if one is left, he must be silent (see chap. viii. 3) and retired, lest he be plundered of his scanty provision!

11. *He will smite the great house with breaches.* The great and small shall equally suffer; no distinction shall be made; rich and poor shall fall together. Death has received his commission, and he will spare none.

12. *Shall horses run upon the rock?* First, they could not do it, because they were unshod;

for the shoeing of horses with iron was not then known. Secondly, if they did run on the rock, it would be useless to their owner, and hurtful to themselves. Thirdly, and it would be as useless to plough on the rock with oxen, for there it would be impossible to sow with any advantage.

13. *Ye which rejoice in a thing of nought.* In your idols, for an idol is nothing in the world. *Have we not taken to us horns?* We have arrived to power and dignity by our strength. *Horns* were the symbols of power and authority.

14. *I will raise up against you a nation.* The Assyrians under Pul, Tiglath-pileser, and Shalmaneser, who subdued the Israelites at various times, and at last carried them away captive in the days of Hoshea, the last king of Israel in Samaria. *From the entering in of Hemath* (on the north) *unto the river of the wilderness.* Besor, which empties itself into the sea, not far from Gaza, and was in the southern part of the tribe of Simeon.

CHAPTER 7

In this chapter God represents to Amos, by three several visions, the judgments He is about to bring on Israel. The first is a plague of locusts, threatening to cut off the hopes of the harvest by attacking it in the time of the second growth, the first luxuriances of the crop being probably mowed for the king's horses, 1-3. The next vision threatens a judgment by fire, which would consume a great part, 4-6; and the third a total overthrow of Israel, levelling it as it were by a line, 7-9. The rest of the chapter is a denunciation of heavy judgments against Amaziah, priest of Bethel, who had brought an accusation to the king against the prophet, 10-17.

1. *Behold, he formed grasshoppers.* "Locusts." *The shooting up of the latter growth.* The early crop of grass had been already mowed and housed. The second crop was not yet begun. By *the king's mowings* we may understand the first crop, a portion of which the king probably claimed as being the better hay.

2. *By whom shall Jacob arise?* The locusts, the symbols of the many enemies that had impoverished Jerusalem, having devoured much of the produce of the land, were proceeding, till, at the intercession of the prophet, they were removed.

3. *The Lord repented.* Changed His purpose of destroying them by the locusts. See v. 6.

4. *The Lord God called to contend by fire.* Permitted war, both civil and foreign, to harass the land, after the death of Jeroboam II. These wars would have totally destroyed it had not the prophet interceded.

7. *With a plumbline in his hand.* This appears to be intended as an emblem of strict justice, and intimated that God would now visit them according to their iniquities.

8. *I will set a plumbline.* I will visit them by justice without any mixture of mercy.

9. *And the high places of Isaac shall be desolate.* Their total destruction is at hand. The *high place of Isaac* was Beersheba, where Isaac had built an altar to the Lord, Gen. xxvi. 25. This high place, which had been abused to idolatrous uses, was demolished by Josiah, king of Judah, as we read in 2 Kings xxiii. 8, for he "defiled the high places . . . from Geba to Beersheba." *I will rise against the house of Jeroboam.* The Lord had promised to Jehu, the ancestor of Jeroboam, that his family should sit

on the throne of Israel to the fourth generation. Zechariah, the son of Jeroboam, was the fourth in order after Jehu; and on him the threatening in this verse fell; for he was murdered by Shallum after he had reigned six months, and in him the family became extinct. See 2 Kings x. 30 and xv. 8-10.

10. *Amaziah the priest of Beth-el.* The idolatrous priest who had been established by the king to maintain the worship of the golden calves which Jeroboam the elder had set up at this place. *Amos hath conspired against thee.* This was truly a lying prophet; there is not one word of truth in this message which he sent to Jeroboam. Amos had not conspired against the king—had not said that Jeroboam should die by the sword—and had not said that Israel should be carried away captive, though this last was implied in God's threatenings, and afterwards delivered by this prophet; see v. 17.

16. *Now therefore hear thou the word of the Lord.* While he was speaking in his own vindication, God seems to have inspired him with the awful prediction which he immediately delivers.

17. *Thy wife shall be an harlot.* As this was the word of the Lord, so it was fulfilled; but as we have no further account of this idolatrous priest, so we cannot tell in what circumstances these threatenings were executed. *Israel shall surely go into captivity.* He now declares fully what he had not declared before, though Amaziah had made it a subject of accusation. This particular was probably revealed at this instant, as well as those which concerned Amaziah and his family.

CHAPTER 8

This chapter begins with a fourth vision denoting the certainty and nearness of the destruction of Israel, 1-3. The prophet then proceeds to reprove their oppression and injustice, 4-7. Strong and beautiful figures, by which is represented the complete dissolution of the Israelitish polity, 8-10. The people threatened with a most awful judgment, a famine of the word of God, 11-14.

1. *A basket of summer fruit.* As summer fruit was not proper for preserving, but must be eaten as soon as gathered, so the Lord intimates by this symbol that the kingdom of Israel was now ripe for destruction, and that punishment must descend upon it without delay.

2. *A basket of summer fruit.* Kelub *kayits*; *the end is come—*bahakkets; here is a paronomasia or play upon the words *kayits*, "summer fruit," and *kets*, "the end," both coming from similar roots. See Ezek. vii. 2, where there is a similar play on the same word.

5. *Making the ephah small, and the shekel great.* Giving short measure, and taking full price; or buying with a heavy weight, and selling with one that was light.

6. *That we may buy the poor for silver.* Buying their services for such a time, with just money enough to clear them from other creditors. *And the needy for a pair of shoes.* See chap. ii. 6. *And sell the refuse of the wheat.* Selling bad wheat and damaged flour to poor people as good, knowing that such cannot afford to prosecute them.

7. *By the excellency of Jacob.* By the state of eminence to which He had raised the descendants of Jacob; or by the "excellent One of Jacob," that is, himself. The meaning is: "As surely as

I have raised you to such a state of eminence, so surely will I punish you in proportion to your advantages and your crimes."

12. *They shall wander from sea to sea.* From the Mediterranean to the Dead Sea or from west to east, and from north to south, *to seek the word of the Lord;* to find a prophet, or any person authorized by God to show them the end of their calamities. In this state they shall continue, because they have rejected Him who is the Bread of Life.

14. *By the sin of Samaria.* Baal, who was worshipped here. *Thy god, O Dan.* The golden calf, or ox, the representative of the Egyptian god Apis, or Osiris. *The manner of Beer-sheba.* The worship or object of worship. Another of the golden calves which Jeroboam had set up there.

CHAPTER 9

The first part of this chapter contains another vision, in which God is represented as declaring the final ruin of the kingdom of Israel, and the general dispersion of the people, 1-10. The prophet then passes to the great blessedness of the people of God under the gospel dispensation, 11-15. See Acts xv. 15-16.

1. *I saw the Lord standing upon the altar.* As this is a continuation of the preceding prophecy, the *altar* here may be one of those at either Dan or Beersheba. *Smite the lintel.* Either the piece of timber that binds the wall above the door or the upper part of the doorframe.

3. *Though they hide themselves.* All these are metaphorical expressions, to show the impossibility of escape.

4. *I will set mine eyes upon them for evil.* I will use that very providence against them which before worked for their good.

7. *Children of the Ethiopians.* Or Cushites. Cush was the son of Ham, Gen. x. 6; and his descendants inhabited a part of Arabia Petraea and Arabia Felix. All this stock was universally despised. *The Philistines from Caphtor.* The island of Crete, the people of which were the Cherethim. See 1 Sam. xxx. 14; Ezek. xxv. 16; Zeph. ii. 5. *The Syrians from Kir.* Perhaps a city of the Medes, Isa. xxii. 6. Aram, from whom Syria had its name, was the son of Shem, Gen. x. 22. The meaning of the verse is this: Do not presume on My having brought you out of the land of Egypt and house of bondage into a land flowing with milk and honey. I have brought other nations, and some of your neighbors, who are your enemies, from comparatively barren countries into fruitful territories.

8. *The eyes of the Lord God are upon the sinful kingdom.* The kingdom of Israel, peculiarly sinful; and therefore to be signally destroyed by the Assyrians.

11. *Will I raise up the tabernacle of David.* It must refer to their restoration under the gospel, when they shall receive the Lord Jesus as their Messiah, and be by Him restored to their own land. See these words quoted by James, Acts xv. 17. Then indeed it is likely that they shall possess the "remnant of Edom," and have the whole length and breadth of Immanuel's land, v. 12.

The Book of
OBADIAH

God is here represented as summoning the nations against Edom, and declaring that his strongholds should not save him, 1-4; that not a remnant, not a gleaning, should be left of him, 5; that the enemy would search out his people, and totally subdue them; and that none of their allies should stand by them, 6-9. He then enlarges on their particular offense, and threatens them with a speedy recompense, 10-16. The Babylonians accordingly subdued the Edomites, and expelled them from Arabia Petraea, of which they never afterwards recovered possession. The remaining verses contain a prophecy of the restoration of the Jews from the Babylonish captivity and of their victory over all their enemies, 17-21. Some commentators think that these last verses were fulfilled by the conquests of the Maccabees over the Edomites. See 1 Macc. v. 3-5, 65, etc.

Who was this prophet? where born? of what country? at what time did he prophesy? who were his parents? when and where did he die? are questions which have been asked from the remotest antiquity; and which, to this day, have received no answer worthy of recording. All that seems probable is that, as he prophesied concerning the destruction of Edom, he flourished a little before, or a little after, the taking of Jerusalem by Nebuchadnezzar, which happened about five hundred and eight-eight years before Christ; and the destruction of Idumea by the same monarch, which took place a short time after; probably between 588 B.C. and 575 B.C., in the interval of the thirteen years which Nebuchadnezzar employed in the siege of Tyre, which he undertook immediately after the capture of Jerusalem.

Obadiah foretells the subduction of the Idumeans by the Chaldeans, and finally by the Jews, whom they had used most cruelly when brought low by other enemies. These prophecies have been literally fulfilled, for the Idumeans, as a nation, are totally extinct.

Whoever will be at the trouble to collate this short prophecy with the forty-ninth chapter of Jeremiah will find a remarkable similarity, not only in the sentiments and words, but also in whole verses. In the above chapter Jeremiah predicts the destruction of the Idumeans. Whether he copied Obadiah, or Obadiah copied him, cannot be determined; but it would be very strange if two prophets, unacquainted with each other, should speak of the same event precisely in the same terms.

1. *We have heard a rumour.* See Jer. xlix. 14, where the same expressions are found. The prophet shows that the enemies of Idumea had confederated against it, and that Jehovah is now summoning them to march directly against it.

3. *The pride of thine heart.* St. Jerome observes that all the southern part of Palestine, from Eleutheropolis to Petra and Aialath, was full of caverns hewn out of the rocks, and that the people had subterranean dwellings similar to ovens. Here they are said to dwell *in the clefts of the rock,* in reference to the caverns above mentioned. Some think that by *sena,* "rock," Petra, the capital of Idumea, is intended.

4. *Though thou exalt thyself as the eagle.* Though like this bird you get into the highest cliff of the highest rock, it will not avail you. See Jer. xlix. 16.

5. *If thieves came to thee.* That is, if *thieves* entered your dwellings, they would not have taken everything; they would have laid hold on your wealth, and carried off as much as they could escape with conveniently. If *grapegatherers* entered your vineyards, they would not have taken every bunch; some gleanings would have been left. But the Chaldeans have stripped you bare; they have searched out all your "hidden things," v. 6; they have left you nothing.

7. *All the men of thy confederacy.* The Chaldeans are here intended, to whom the Idumeans were attached, and whose agents they became in exercising cruelties upon the Jews. *Have brought thee even to the border.* Have hemmed you in on every side, and reduced you to distress. Or, they have driven you to your border; cast you out of your own land into the hands of your enemies. *The men that were at peace with thee.* The men of your covenant, with whom you had made a league. *That eat thy bread.* That professed to be your firmest friends.

8. *Shall I not . . . destroy the wise men?* It appears, from Jer. xlix. 7, that the Edomites were remarkable for wisdom, counsel, and prudence.

9. *Thy mighty men, O Teman.* This was one of the strongest places in Idumea; and is put here, as in Amos i. 2, and elsewhere, for Idumea itself. *Mount of Esau.* Mount Seir.

10. *For thy violence against thy brother Jacob.* By this term the Israelites in general are understood; for the two brothers—Jacob, from whom sprang the Jews; and Esau, from whom sprang the Idumeans or Edomites—are here put for the whole people or descendants of both.

11. *Thou stoodest on the other side.* You not only did not help your brother when you might, but you did assist his foes against him. *And cast lots.* When the Chaldeans cast lots on the spoils of Jerusalem, you did come in for a share of the booty; *thou wast as one of them.*

12. *Thou shouldest not have looked.* The Edomites triumphed when they saw the judgments of God fall upon the Jews. This the Lord severely reprehends in vv. 12-15.

14. *Neither shouldest thou have stood in the crossway.* They are represented here as having stood in the passes and defiles to prevent the poor Jews from escaping from the Chaldeans. By stopping these passes, they threw the poor fugitives back into the teeth of their enemies. They had gone so far in this systematic cruelty as to deliver up the few that had taken refuge among them.

17. *But upon mount Zion shall be deliverance.* Here is a promise of the return from the Babylonish captivity. They shall come to Zion, and there they shall find safety; and it is remarkable that after their return they were greatly befriended by the Persian kings, and by Alexander the Great and his successors; so that, whilst they ravaged the neighboring nations, the Jews were unmolested. *And there shall be holiness.* They shall return to God, separate themselves from their idols, and become a better people than they were when God permitted them to be carried into captivity.

18. *The house of Jacob shall be a fire.* After their return from captivity, the Jews, called here the *house of Jacob* and the *house of Joseph,* did break out as *a flame* upon the Idumeans; they reduced them into slavery, and obliged them to receive circumcision, and practice the rites of the Jewish religion. See 1 Macc. v. 3, etc,; and Joseph. *Antiq.,* lib. xiii, c. 17. *There shall not be any remaining.* As a people and a nation they shall be totally destroyed. This is the meaning; it does not signify that every individual shall be destroyed.

19. *They of the south.* The Jews who possessed the southern part of Palestine should render themselves masters of the mountains of Idumea which were contiguous to them. *They of the plain.* From Eleutheropolis to the Mediterranean Sea. In this and the following verse the prophet shows the different districts which should be occupied by the Israelites after their return from Babylon. *The fields of Samaria.* Alexander the Great gave Samaria to the Jews, and John Hyrcanus subdued the same country after his wars with the Syrians. See Josephus, *contra. App.* lib. ii, and *Antiq.* lib. xiii, c. 18. *Benjamin shall possess Gilead.* Edom lay to the south, the Philistines to the west, Ephraim to the north, and Gilead to the east. Those who returned from Babylon were to extend themselves everywhere. See, for the fulfilment, 1 Macc. v. 9, 35, 45 and ix. 35-36.

20. *Zarephath.* Sarepta, a city of the Sidonians, 1 Kings xvii. 9. That is, they should possess the whole city of Phoenicia, called here *that of the Canaanites. Which is in Sepharad.* This is a difficult word.

21. *And saviours shall come up.* Certain persons whom God may choose to be deliverers of His people; such as Zerubbabel, Ezra, Nehemiah, and the Maccabees.

The Book of

JONAH

Jonah, the son of Amittai, was a Galilean, a native of Gath-hepher, which is believed to be the same as Jotapata, celebrated for the siege which Josephus, the historian, there maintained against the Roman army, a little before the destruction of Jerusalem. Gath-hepher was situated in the land of Zebulon. St. Jerome places it two miles from Sepphoris, in the way towards Tiberias.

What we know with certainty of Jonah is that, God having commanded him to go to Nineveh, and there proclaim that the cry of the inhabitants' sins was come up to heaven, and they were threatened with approaching ruin; instead of obeying these orders, he resolved to flee away. For this purpose he embarked at Joppa. But the Lord having sent a violent tempest while he was upon the sea, the mariners, with great fear, cried each of them to his god. In the meantime Jonah slept in the hold; whereupon the pilot wakened him, and they who were in the ship cast lots to know how this tempest was occasioned. The lot falling upon Jonah, they asked him who he was, and what he had done to bring upon them such a storm. He told them he was a Hebrew; that he worshipped the God of heaven, was one of His prophets, and fled from His presence to avoid going to Nineveh, whither he was sent. They asked him what was to be done to secure them from shipwreck. He replied: "Throw me into the sea, and the tempest will cease."

God prepared a great fish to swallow up Jonah. The prophet continued in the fish three days and three nights. He cried unto the Lord, and the Lord heard him, and commanded the fish to cast him upon the shore.

After this the word of the Lord came a second time to Jonah, and directed him to go to Nineveh. When he came into the city, which was three days' journey in extent, about twenty-five leagues in circumference, Jonah walked up and down a whole day, crying out, "In forty days Nineveh shall be destroyed." The Ninevites believed his word; they appointed a public fast to be observed; and, from the meanest of the people to the greatest, covered themselves with sackcloth. The king of Nineveh descended from his throne, and covered himself with sackcloth, and sat down upon ashes. God suffered himself to be moved with their repentance, and did not execute the sentence which He had pronounced against them.

Jonah was afflicted at this; and complained to God, saying that he had always questioned whether, as being a God of clemency and mercy, He would not be flexible to their prayers. After this, in all probability, Jonah returned from Nineveh into Judea.

We do not know when it was that Jonah foretold how Jeroboam II, king of Israel, should restore the kingdom of Samaria to its former extent, from the entrance of Hamath to the Dead Sea. Whether this was before or after his going to Nineveh, we cannot tell.

Our Saviour makes mention of Jonah in the Gospels. He says that the Ninevites shall one day rise in judgment against the Jews, and condemn them, because they repented at the preaching of Jonah, and the Jews would not hearken to Him who was greater than Jonah. And when the Pharisees required a sign of Him to prove His mission, He said He would give them no other than that of the prophet Jonah, that is to say, of His resurrection.

CHAPTER 1

Jonah, sent to Nineveh, flees to Tarshish, 1-3. He is overtaken by a great tempest, 4-14; thrown into the sea, 15-16; and swallowed by a fish, in the belly of which he is miraculously preserved alive three days and three nights, 17.

1. *Now the word of the Lord came unto Jonah.* He was of Gath-hepher, in the tribe of Zebulun, in lower Galilee, Josh. xix. 13; and he prophesied in the reigns of Jeroboam II and Joash, kings of Israel. Jeroboam came to the throne 823 years before the Christian era, and reigned in Samaria 41 years, 2 Kings xiv. 23-25. As a prophet, it is likely that he had but this one mission.

2. *Go to Nineveh.* This was the capital of the Assyrian empire, and one of the most ancient cities of the world, Gen. x. 10; and one of the largest, as it was three days' journey in circumference. It is reported to have had walls 100 feet high, and so broad that three chariots might run abreast upon them. It was situated on the Tigris, or a little to the west, or on the west side of that river. It was well peopled, and had at this time 120,000 persons in it reputed to be in a state of infancy, which on a moderate computation would make the whole number 600,000 persons.

3. *To flee unto Tarshish.* Tartessus, in Spain, near the straits of Gibraltar. *And went down*

to Joppa. The nearest port to Jerusalem on that side of the Mediterranean. *And he found a ship.* The Phoenicians carried on a considerable trade with Tartessus, Ezek. xxvii. 12, and it was probably in one of their ships that Jonah embarked.

7. *Come, and let us cast lots.* This was a very ancient mode of endeavoring to find out the mind of Divine Providence; and in this case it proves that they supposed the storm to have arisen on account of some hidden crime of some person aboard. *The lot fell upon Jonah.* In this case God directed the lot.

9. *I fear the Lord.* In this Jonah was faithful. He gave an honest testimony concerning the God he served, which placed Him before the eyes of the sailors as infinitely higher than the objects of their adoration.

17. *Now the Lord had prepared a great fish.* This could not have been a whale, for the throat of that animal can scarcely admit a man's leg; but it might have been a shark, which abounds in the Mediterranean, and whose mouth and stomach are exceedingly capacious. In several cases they have been known to swallow a man when thrown overboard. That days and nights do not, among the Hebrews, signify complete days and nights of twenty-four hours, see Esther iv. 16, compared with chap. v. 1; Judg. xiv. 17-18. Our Lord lay in the grave one natural day, and part of two others; and it is most likely that this was the precise time that Jonah was in the fish's belly.

CHAPTER 2

This chapter (except the first verse and the last, which make a part of the narrative) contains a beautiful prayer or hymn, formed of those devout thoughts which Jonah had in the belly of the great fish, with a thanksgiving for his miraculous deliverance.

1. *Then Jonah prayed . . . out of the fish's belly.* It may be asked, "How could Jonah either pray or breathe in the stomach of the fish?" Very easily, if God willed it. And let the reader keep this constantly in view; the whole is a miracle, from Jonah's being swallowed by the fish till he was cast ashore by the same animal. It was God that had prepared the great fish. It was the Lord that spake to the fish, and caused it to vomit Jonah upon the dry land. All is miracle.

2. *Out of the belly of hell.* Among the Hebrews *sheol* means the "grave," and deep pit, the place of separate spirits. Here the prophet represents himself as in the bottom of the sea, for so *sheol* must be understood in this place.

3. *All thy billows and thy waves passed over me.* This may be understood literally; while the fish, in whose belly he was, sought its pleasure or sustenance in the paths of the deep, the waves and billows of the sea were rolling above. This line seems borrowed from Ps. xlii. 7.

4. *I am cast out of thy sight.* See Ps. xxxi. 22.

5. *The waters compassed me about, even to the soul.* So as to seem to deprive me of life. I had no hope left. *The weeds were wrapped about my head.* This may be understood literally also. He found himself in the fish's stomach, together with seaweeds, and suchlike marine substances, which the fish had taken for its aliment.

6. *Yet hast thou brought up my life.* The substance of this poetic prayer was composed while in the fish's belly. But afterwards the prophet appears to have thrown it into its present poetic form, and to have added some circumstances, such as that before us; for he now speaks of his deliverance from this imminent danger of death. Thou hast *brought up my life from corruption.*

10. *And the Lord spake unto the fish.* That is, by His influence the fish swam to shore, and cast Jonah on the dry land.

CHAPTER 3

Jonah is sent again to Nineveh, a city of three days' journey (being sixty miles in circumference, according to Diodorus Siculus), 1-4. The inhabitants, in consequence of the prophet's preaching, repent in dust and ashes, 5-9. God, seeing that they were deeply humbled on account of their sins, and that they turned away from all their iniquities, repents of the evil with which He had threatened them, 10.

1. *And the word of the Lord.* The same oracle as that before given; and which, from what he had felt and seen of the justice and mercy of the Lord, he was now prepared to obey.

2. *And preach unto it the preaching.* "And cry the cry that I bid you." Be My herald, and faithfully deliver My message.

3. *Nineveh was an exceeding great city, of three days' journey.* See on chap. i. 2. Strabo says, lib. xvi, "It was much larger than Babylon"; and Ninus, the builder, not only proposed to make it the largest city of the world, but the largest that could be built by man. See Diodor. Sic. Bib. l. ii. And as we find, from the lowest computation, that it was at least fifty-four or sixty English miles in circumference, it would take the prophet three days to walk round and announce the terrible message, "Yet forty days, and Nineveh will be destroyed!"

8. *Let man and beast be covered.* This was done that every object which they beheld might deepen the impression already made, and cause them to mourn after a godly sort. Virgil tells us that the mourning for the death of Julius Caesar was so general that the cattle neither ate nor drank.

10. *And God saw their works.* They repented, and brought forth fruits meet for repentance, works which showed that they did most earnestly repent. He therefore changed His purpose, and the city was saved. The purpose was: If the Ninevites do not return from their evil ways, and the violence that is in their hands, within forty days I will destroy the city. The Ninevites did return, and therefore escaped the threatened judgment. Thus we see that the threatening was conditional.

CHAPTER 4

Jonah, dreading to be thought a false prophet, repines at God's mercy in sparing the Ninevites, whose destruction he seems to have expected, from his retiring to a place without the city about the close of the forty days. But how does he glorify that mercy which he intends to blame! And what an amiable picture does he give of the compassion of God, 1-5! This attribute of the Deity is still further illustrated by His tenderness and condescension to the prophet himself, who, with all his prophetic gifts, had much of human infirmity, 6-11.

1. *But it displeased Jonah exceedingly.* This hasty, and indeed inconsiderate prophet, was

vexed because his prediction was not fulfilled. He had more respect to his high sense of his own honor than he had to the goodness and mercy of God. *And he was very angry.* Because the prediction was not literally fulfilled, for he totally lost sight of the condition.

3. *Take, I beseech thee, my life from me.* "Take, I beseech Thee, even my soul."

4. *Doest thou well to be angry?* "Is anger good for you?" Dr. Taylor renders the clause, "Art thou very much grieved?"

5. *So Jonah went out of the city.* I believe this refers to what had already passed; and I therefore agree with Bishop Newcome, who translates, "Now Jonah had gone out of the city, and had sat."

6. *And the Lord God prepared a gourd.* I believe this should be rendered in the preter-pluperfect tense. The Lord had prepared this plant.

7. *But God prepared a worm.* By being eaten through the root, the plant, losing its nourish-ment, would soon wither; and this was the case in the present instance.

8. *A vehement east wind.* Which was of itself of a parching, withering nature; and the sun, in addition, made it intolerable. These winds are both scorching and suffocating in the East, for deserts of burning sand lay to the east or south-east, and the easterly winds often brought such a multitude of minute particles of sand on their wings as to add greatly to the mischief.

9. *I do well to be angry, even unto death.* Many persons suppose that the gifts of prophecy and working miracles are the highest that can be conferred on man; but they are widely mistaken, for the gifts change not the heart. Jonah had the gift of prophecy, but had not received that grace which destroys the old man.

11. *And should not I spare Nineveh?* In v. 10 it is said, "Thou hast had pity on the gourd," *attah chasta;* and here the Lord uses the same word, *veani lo achus,* "And shall not I have pity upon Nineveh?" How much is the city better than the shrub?

The Book of

MICAH

Micah, the Morasthite, or of Moresa, a village in the southern part of Judah, prophesied under Jotham, Ahaz, and Hezekiah, kings of Judah, for about fifty years. This prophet appeared almost at the same time with Isaiah, and has even borrowed some expressions from him. Compare Isa. ii. 2 with Mic. iv. 1, and Isa. xli. 15 with Mic. iv. 13.

The prophecy of Micah contains but seven chapters. He foretells the calamities of Samaria, which was taken by Shalmaneser, and reduced to a heap of stones. Afterwards he prophesies against Judah, and declares the troubles that Sennacherib should bring upon it under the reign of Hezekiah. Then he declaims against the iniquities of Samaria. He foretells the captivity of the ten tribes, and their return into their own country. The third chapter contains a pathetic invective against the princes of the house of Jacob, and the judges of the house of Israel; which seems levelled against the chief of the kingdom of Judah, the judges, the magistrates, the priests, the false prophets. He upbraids them with their avarice, their injustice, and falsehood; and tells them they will be the occasion that Jerusalem shall be reduced to a heap of rubbish, and the mountain of the Temple shall be as a forest. We are informed, Jer. xxvi. 18-19, that this prophecy was pronounced in the reign of Hezekiah, and that it saved Jeremiah from death.

After these terrible denunciations, Micah speaks of the reign of the Messiah, and of the establishment of the Christian Church. Micah speaks in particular of the birth of the Messiah, that he was to be born at Bethlehem, and that His dominion was to extend to the utmost parts of the earth.

The last two chapters of Micah contain, first, a long invective against the iniquities of Samaria. Then he foretells the fall of Babylon, the reestablishment of the cities of Israel, the greatness of the country possessed by the Israelites, their happiness, the graces wherewith God will favor them; and all this in such lofty terms that they chiefly agree with the Christian Church.

Bishop Newcome observes that Micah was of the kingdom of Judah, as he makes mention only of kings who reigned over that country. It is supposed that he prophesied further on in the reign of Hezekiah than Hosea did, although chap. v. 5 was written before the captivity of the ten tribes, which happened in the sixth year of Hezekiah. It is plain from chap. i. 1, 5, 9, 12-13 that he was sent to both Israel and Judah. Like Amos and Hosea, he reproves and threatens, with great spirit and energy, a corrupt people. See chap. ii. 1-3, 8-10; iii. 2-6, 10-16; vii. 2-4. And, like Hosea, he inveighs against the princes and prophets with the highest indignation. See chap. iii. 5-7, 9-12; vii. 3. The reader will observe that these similar topics are treated of by each prophet with remarkable variety and copiousness of expression.

CHAPTER 1

The prophet begins with calling the attention of all people to the awful descent of Jehovah, coming to execute His judgments against the kingdoms of Israel and Judah, 1-5; first against Samaria, whose fate the prophet laments in the dress of mourners, and with the doleful cries of the fox or ostrich, 6-8; and then against Jerusalem, which is threatened with the invasion of Sennacherib. Other cities of Judah are likewise threatened; and their danger represented to be so great as to oblige them to have recourse for protection even to their enemies the Philistines, from whom they desired at first to conceal their situation. But all resources are declared to be vain; Israel and Judah must go into captivity, 9-16.

1. *In the days of Jotham, Ahaz, and Hezekiah.* These three kings reigned about threescore years, and Micah is supposed to have prophesied about forty or fifty years; but no more of his prophecies have reached posterity than what are contained in this book, nor is there any evidence that any more was written. His time appears to have been spent chiefly in preaching and exhorting, and he was directed to write those parts only that were calculated to profit succeeding generations.

2. *Hear, all ye people.* The very commencement of this prophecy supposes preceding exhortations and predictions. *Hearken, O earth. Arets,* here, should be translated "land," the country of the Hebrews being only intended.

3. *For, behold, the Lord cometh forth.* See this clause, Amos iv. 13. He represents Jehovah as a mighty Conqueror, issuing from His pavilion, stepping from mountain to mountain, which rush down and fill the valleys before Him; a consuming fire accompanying Him, that melts and confounds every hill and dale, and blends all in universal confusion. *And why is all this mighty movement?* Verse 5, "For the transgression of Jacob is all this, and for the sins of the house of Israel."

5. *What is the transgression of Jacob?* Is it not something extremely grievous? Is it not that of *Samaria?* Samaria and Jerusalem, the chief cities, are infected with idolatry. Each has its high places and its idol worship, in opposition to the worship of the true God. That there was idolatry practiced by the elders of Israel, even in the temple of Jehovah, see Ezek. viii. 1, etc. As the royal cities in both kingdoms gave the example of gross idolatry, no wonder that it spread through the whole land of both Israel and Judah.

6. *I will make Samaria.* I will bring it to desolation: and, instead of being a royal city, it shall be a place for vineyards. *I will discover the foundations thereof.* I will cause its walls and fortifications to be razed to the ground.

7. *All the hires thereof shall be burned.* Multitudes of women gave the money they gained by their public prostitution at the temples for the support of the priesthood, the ornamenting of the walls, altars, and images. So that these things, and perhaps several of the images themselves, were literally the hire of the harlots. God threatens here to deliver all into the hands of enemies who should seize on this wealth, and literally spend it in the same way in which it was acquired; so that *to the hire of an harlot* these things should *return.*

9. *Her wound is incurable.* Nothing shall prevent their utter ruin, for they have filled up the measure of their iniquity. *He is come . . . even to Jerusalem.* The desolation and captivity of Israel shall first take place; that of Judah shall come after.

10. *Declare ye it not at Gath.* Do not let this prediction be known among the Philistines, else they will glory over you. *House of Aphrah.* Or "Beth-aphrah." This place is mentioned in Josh. xviii. 23, as in the tribe of Benjamin. There is a paronomasia, or play on words, here: *bebeith leaphrah aphar,* "Roll thyself *in the dust* in the house of dust."

11. *Inhabitant of Saphir. Sapher,* "Sephoris." *Zaanan.* Another city in the tribe of Judah, Josh. xv. 13. *Beth-ezel.* A place near Jerusalem, Josh. xiv. 5. Some think that Jerusalem itself is intended by this word.

12. *The inhabitant of Maroth.* There was a city of a similar name in the tribe of Judah, Josh. xv. 59.

13. *Inhabitant of Lachish.* This city was in the tribe of Judah, Josh. xv. 39, and was taken by Sennacherib when he was coming against Jerusalem, 2 Kings xviii. 13, etc., and it is supposed that he wished to reduce this city first, that, possessing it, he might prevent Hezekiah's receiving any help from Egypt. *She is the beginning of the sin.* This seems to intimate that Lachish was the first city in Judah which received the idolatrous worship of Israel.

14. *Give presents to Moresheth-gath.* Calmet says that Moresa or Morashti, and *Achzib,* were cities not far from Gath. It is possible that when Ahaz found himself pressed by Pekah, king of Israel, he might have sent to these places for succor, that by their assistance he might frustrate the hopes of the king of Israel; and this may be the meaning of *The houses of Achzib shall be a lie to the kings of Israel.* In these verses there are several instances of the paronomasia. See v. 10, *aphar,* "dust," and *aphrah,* the name of the city. Verse 11, *tsaanan,* the city, and *yatsah,* "to go out." Verse 13, *lachish,* the city, and *rechesh,* "the swift beast." Verse 14, *achzib,* the city, and *achzab,* "a lie." Such paronomasias were reputed ornaments by the prophets. They occur in Isaiah with great effect. See Isa. v. 7.

15. *Yet will I bring an heir unto thee, O . . . Mareshah.* Here is another instance, *haiyeresh,* "to bring an heir," and *mareshah,* the city, the name of which signifies "heirship." *Adullam the glory of Israel.* This was a fenced city in the south of Judah (see 2 Chron. xi. 7) towards the Dead Sea.

16. *Make thee bald.* Cutting off the hair was a sign of great distress, and was practiced on the death of near relatives; see Amos viii. 10. The desolation should be so great that Israel should feel it to her utmost extent, and the mourning should be like that of a mother for the death of her most delicate children. *Enlarge thy baldness as the eagle.* Referring to the molting of this bird, when in casting its feathers and breeding new ones it is very sickly, and its strength wholly exhausted. *They are gone into captivity.* This is a prediction of the captivity by Shalmaneser. Samaria, the chief city, is called on to deplore it, as then fast approaching.

CHAPTER 2

Here the prophet denounces a woe against the plotters of wickedness, the covetous, and the oppressor, 1-2. God is represented as devising their ruin, 3. An Israelite is then introduced as a mourner, personating his people, and lamenting their fate, 4. Their total expulsion is now threatened on account of their very numerous offenses, 5-10. Great infatuation of the people in favor of those pretenders to divine inspiration who prophesied to them peace and plenty, 11. The chapter concludes with a gracious promise of the restoration of the posterity of Jacob from captivity; possibly alluding to their deliverance from the Chaldean yoke, an event which was about two hundred years in futurity at the delivery of this prophecy, 12-13.

1. *Woe to them that devise iniquity!* Who lay schemes and plans for transgressions; and make these things their nocturnal meditations, that, having fixed their plan, they may begin to execute it as soon as it is light in the morning.

2. *They covet fields.* These are the rich and mighty in the land; and, like Ahab, they will take the vineyard or inheritance of any poor Naboth on which they may fix their covetous eye, so that they take away even the heritage of the poor.

3. *Against this family* (the Israelites) *do I devise an evil.* You have devised the evil of plundering the upright; I will devise the evil to you of punishment for your conduct; you shall have your *necks* brought under the yoke of servitude. Tiglath-pileser ruined this kingdom, and transported the people to Assyria, under the reign of Hezekiah, king of Judah; and Micah lived to see this catastrophe. See on v. 9.

4. *Take up a parable against you.* Your wickedness and your punishment shall be subjects of common conversation, and a "funeral dirge" shall be composed and sung for you as for the dead. The lamentation is that which immediately follows: *We be utterly spoiled;* and ends, "Are these his doings?" v. 7

5. *None that shall cast a cord.* You will no more have your inheritance divided to you by lot, as it was to your fathers; you shall have neither fields nor possessions of any kind.

6. *Prophesy ye not.* Do not predict any more evils—we have as many as we can bear. We are utterly ruined—shame and confusion cover our faces. The original is singular, and expressive of sorrow and sobbing. Literally, "Do not cause it to rain; they will cause it to rain; they cannot make it rain sooner than this; confusion shall not depart from us." To "rain" often means to "preach," to "prophesy"; Ezek. xxv. 46; xxi. 2; Amos vii. 16; Deut. xxxii. 2; Job xxix. 22; Prov. v. 3. The last line Bishop Newcome translates, "For he shall not remove from himself reproaches"; and paraphrases, "The true prophet will subject himself to public disgrace by exercising his office."

8. *My people is risen up as an enemy.* You are not only opposed to Me, but are enemies to each other. You rob and spoil each other. You plunder the peaceable passenger, depriving him of both his upper and under garment.

9. *The women of my people.* These two verses may probably relate to the war made on Ahaz by Rezin, king of Syria, and Pekah, king of Israel. They fell suddenly upon the Jews; killed in one day 120,000, took 200,000 captive, and carried away much spoil. Thus they rose up against them as enemies, when there was peace between the two kingdoms; spoiled them of their goods, carried away men, women, and children, till at the remonstrances of the prophet Oded they were released. See 2 Chron. xxviii. 6, etc. Micah lived in the days of Ahaz, and might have seen the barbarities which he here describes.

10. *Arise ye, and depart.* Prepare for your captivity; you shall have no resting place here. The very land is *polluted* by your iniquities, and shall vomit you out, and it shall be destroyed; and the destruction of it shall be great and sore. Some think this is an exhortation to the godly to leave a land that was to be destroyed so speedily.

11. *If a man walking in the spirit and falsehood.* The meaning is: If a man who professes to be divinely inspired do lie, by prophesying of plenty, then such a person shall be received as a true prophet by this people.

12. *I will surely assemble.* This is a promise of the restoration of Israel from captivity. He compares them to a flock of sheep rushing together to their fold, the hoofs of which make a wonderful noise or clatter.

13. *The breaker is come up.* He who is to give them deliverance, and lead them out on the way of their return. He who takes down the hurdles, or makes a gap in the wall or hedge, to permit them to pass through. This may ap v to those human agents that shall permit and order their return. And Jehovah being at their *head* may refer to their final restoration, when the Lord Jesus shall become their Leader, they having returned unto Him as the Shepherd and Bishop of their souls, and they and the Gentiles forming one fold under one Shepherd, to go no more out into captivity forever.

CHAPTER 3

In this chapter the prophet inveighs with great boldness and spirit against the princes and prophets of Judah; and foretells the destruction of Jerusalem as the consequence of their iniquity, 1-12. The last verse was fulfilled to a certain extent by Nebuchadnezzar, but most fully and literally by the Romans under Titus. See Josephus.

1. *Hear . . . O heads of Jacob.* The metaphor of the flock is still carried on. The chiefs of Jacob, and the princes of Israel, instead of taking care of the flocks, defending them, and finding them pasture, oppressed them in various ways. They are like wolves, who tear the skin of the sheep and the flesh off their bones. This applies to all unjust and oppressive rulers. Suetonius tells us, in his *Life of Tiberius,* that when the governors of provinces wrote to the emperor, entreating him to increase the tributes, he wrote back: "It is the property of a good shepherd to shear his sheep, not to skin them."

4. *Then shall they cry.* When calamity comes upon these oppressors, they shall cry for deliverance: but they shall not be heard because, in their unjust exactions upon the people, they went on ruthlessly, and would not hear the cry of the oppressed.

5. *That bite with their teeth.* That eat to the full; that are well provided for, and as long as they are so, prophesy smooth things, and cry, *Peace;* i.e., You shall have nothing but peace and prosperity. Whereas the true prophet, who *putteth not into their mouths,* who makes no provision for their evil propensities, they *prepare war against him.*

6. *Night shall be unto you.* You shall have no spiritual light, nor will God give you any revelation of His will. *The sun shall go down over the prophets.* They prospered for a while, causing the people to err; but they shall also be

carried into captivity, and then the sun of their prosperity shall go down forever.

7. *Shall the seers be ashamed.* For the false visions of comfort and prosperity which they pretended to see. *And the diviners confounded.* Who pretended to foretell future prosperity; for they themselves are now enthralled in that very captivity which the true prophets foretold, and which the false prophets said should not happen.

10. *They build up Zion with blood.* They might cry out loudly against that butchery practiced by Pekah, king of Israel, and Pul, coadjutor of Rezin, against the Jews. See on chap. ii. 9. But these were by no means clear themselves; for if they strengthened the city, or decorated the Temple, it was by the produce of their exactions and oppressions of the people.

12. *Therefore shall Zion . . . be plowed as a field.* Thus did the Romans treat Jerusalem when it was taken by Titus. Turnus Rufus caused a plough to be drawn over all the courts of the Temple to signify that it should never be rebuilt, and the place serve only for agricultural purposes. See Matt. xxiv. 2. Thus *Jerusalem* became *heaps,* an indiscriminate mass of ruins and rubbish; and *the mountain of the house,* Mount Moriah, on which the Temple stood, became so much neglected after the total destruction of the Temple that it soon resembled the *high places of the forest.* What is said here may apply also to the ruin of the Temple by Nebuchadnezzar in the last year of the reign of Zedekiah, the last king of the Jews.

CHAPTER 4

In the commencement of this chapter we have a glorious prophecy of the establishment and prosperity of the Messiah's kingdom; its peaceful character, increasing spiritual and political influence, ultimate universality, and everlasting duration, 1-4. Then breaks in a chorus of His people declaring their peculiar happiness in being members of His kingdom, 5. The prophet resumes the subject; predicts the restoration and future prosperity of Israel, 6-8; and exhorts them not to be discouraged at their approaching captivity, as they should in due time not only be delivered from it, but likewise be victorious over all their enemies, 9-13. These last verses, which evidently contain a prediction of the final triumph of Christianity over every adversary, have been applied to the conquests of the Maccabees; but the character and beneficial results of their military exploits, as far as we have any account of them, correspond but in a very faint degree to the beautiful and highly wrought terms of the prophecy. The first three verses of this chapter are very similar to the commencement of the second chapter of Isaiah, and the fourth, for beauty of imagery and elegance of expression, is not unworthy of that prophet.

1-4. *But in the last days it shall come to pass.* These four verses contain, says Bishop Newcome, a prophecy that was to be fulfilled by the coming of the Messiah, when the Gentiles were to be admitted into covenant with God, and the apostles were to preach the gospel, beginning at Jerusalem, Luke xxiv. 47; Acts ii. 14, etc.; when Christ was to be the spiritual Judge and King of many people, was to convince many nations of their errors and vices, and was to found a religion which had the strongest tendency to promote peace. See Isa. ii. 2, etc.

4. *Under his vine and under his fig tree.* A proverbial expression, indicative of perfect peace, security, and rural comfort. See on Isa. ii. 1. This verse is an addition to the prophecy as it stands in Isaiah.

5. *Every one in the name of his god.* This shall be the state of the Gentile world; but after the Captivity, the Jews walked in the name of Jehovah alone.

6-7. *Will I assemble her that halteth . . . driven out . . . afflicted.* Under these epithets, the state of the Jews, who were to be gathered into the Christian Church, is pointed out. They *halted* between the true God and idols; they were *driven out* into captivity, because of this idolatry; and they were variously *afflicted,* because they would not return unto the Lord that bought them.

8. *O tower of the flock.* I think the Temple is meant, or Jerusalem; the place where the *flock,* the whole congregation of the people, assembled to worship God. *Even the first dominion.* The divine theocracy under Jesus Christ; this former, this *first dominion,* was to be restored.

11. *Many nations are gathered against thee.* The Chaldeans, who were composed of many nations. And, we may add, all the surrounding nations were their enemies; and rejoiced when the Chaldean army had overthrown Jerusalem, destroyed the Temple, and led the people away captive. *Let her be defiled.* Let Jerusalem be laid as low as she can be, like a thing defiled and cast away with abhorrence; that their eyes might look upon Zion with scorn, contempt, and exultation.

12. *But they know not the thoughts of the Lord.* These think that God has utterly rejected His people, and they shall have a troublesome neighbor no more. But this is not His design. He will afflict them for a time; but these, the enemies of His people, He will gather as *sheaves* into the threshing floor, there to be trodden, and the wheel to go over them. This is the *counsel,* the "purpose" of God, which these do not understand. The persons here referred to are not only the Chaldeans, which were threshed by the Persians and Medes; but the Idumeans, Ammonites, Moabites, and Philistines, which the Jews afterwards subdued.

13. *Arise and thresh, O daughter of Zion.* This refers to the subject of the preceding verse. When God shall have gathered together all your enemies, as into the threshing floor, He will give you commission and power to get a complete victory over them, and reduce them to servitude. And that you may be able to do this, He will be on your side as a powerful Helper; here signified by the metaphors, iron horns, and brazen hoofs. You shall have power, authority, and unconquerable strength. *I will consecrate their gain unto the Lord.* What they have taken from you in the way of spoil shall be restored, and again consecrated unto the service of Him who will show himself to be *the Lord,* the Supreme Governor of the *whole earth.* Was not this prediction fulfilled when Cyrus gave the Jews permission to return to their own land, and gave them back the sacred vessels of the Temple which Nebuchadnezzar had carried away?

CHAPTER 5

This chapter begins, according to the opinion of some commentators, with a prophecy concerning the siege of Jerusalem by Nebuchadnezzar, and the great indignities which Zedekiah should suffer from the Babylonians, 1. We have next a most famous prediction concerning the birthplace of the Messiah, "whose goings forth have been from of old, from everlasting," 2. See Matt. ii. 6. The Jews obstinately persisting in their opposition to the

Messiah, God will there give them up into the hands of their enemies till the times of the Gentiles be fulfilled; and then all the posterity of Jacob, both Israel and Judah, shall be converted to the faith of our Lord Jesus Christ, and, along with the Gentiles, be brought into the large and peaceful pastures of this Great Shepherd of the sheep, 3-4. After this illustrious prophecy, the prophet goes on to foretell the downfall of the Assyrians, by whom are meant the enemies of the Church in general, the type being probably put for the antitype; the miraculous discomfiture of the great Assyrian army in the reign of Sennacherib strongly shadowing forth the glorious and no less miraculous triumphs of Christianity in the latter times, 5-6. See Isa. xi. 16. Some understand this prophecy of Antiochus and the seven famous Maccabees, with their eight royal successors, from Aristobulus to Antigonus; and it is not impossible that these people may be also intended, for we have often had occasion to remark that a prophecy of the Old Testament Scriptures has frequently more than one aspect. The seventh verse was fulfilled by the Jews spreading the knowledge of the true God during their captivity, and so paving the way for the gospel; but it will be more signally fulfilled after their conversion and restoration. See Rom. xi. 12-15. The remaining verses contain a prophecy of the final overthrow of all the enemies of pure and undefiled religion, and of the thorough purification of the Church of God from the corruptions of Antichrist, 8-15.

1. *O daughter of troops.* The Chaldeans, whose armies were composed of troops from various nations. *He* (Nebuchadnezzar) *hath laid siege against us* (Jerusalem): *they shall smite the judge of Israel* (Zedekiah) *with a rod upon the cheek.* They shall offer him the greatest indignity. They slew his sons before his face; and then put out his eyes, loaded him with chains, and carried him captive to Babylon.

2. *But thou, Beth-lehem Ephratah.* To distinguish it from another Bethlehem, which was in the tribe of Zebulun, Josh. xix. 15. *Thousands of Judah.* The tribes were divided into small portions called "thousands." *From everlasting.* "From the days of all time"; from time as it came out of eternity. That is, there was no time in which He has not been going forth—coming in various ways to save men.

3. *Therefore will he give them up.* Jesus Christ shall give up the disobedient and rebellious Jews into the hands of all the nations of the earth, till "she which travaileth hath brought forth"; that is, till the Christian Church, represented in Rev. xii. 1 under the notion of a woman in travail, shall have had the fullness of the Gentiles brought in. *Then the remnant of his brethren shall return.* The Jews also shall be converted unto the Lord; and thus "all Israel shall be saved," according to Rom. xi. 26.

4. *He shall stand and feed.* The Messiah shall remain with His followers, supporting and governing them in the strength and majesty of the Lord. *For now shall he be great.* The Messiah shall be *great,* as bringing salvation to *the ends of the earth.* All nations shall receive His religion, and He shall be universal King.

5. *And this man shall be the peace.* This clause should be joined to the preceding verse, as it finishes the prophecy concerning our blessed Lord, who is the Author and Prince of Israel; and shall finally give peace to all nations, by bringing them under His yoke. *When the Assyrian shall come.* This is a new prophecy, and relates to the subversion of the Assyrian empire. *Then shall we raise against him seven shepherds.* Supposed to mean the seven Maccabees, Mattathias, and his five sons, and Hyrcanus, the son of Simon. *Eight principal men.* "Eight princes, the Asmonean race; beginning with Aristobulus, and ending with Herod, who was married to Mariamme."—Sharpe. Perhaps *seven*

and *eight* are a definite for an indefinite number, as Eccles. xi. 2; Job v. 19.

6. *The land of Nimrod.* Assyria, and Nineveh, its capital; and Babylon, which was also built by Nimrod, who was its first king, Gen. x. 11-12, in the margin. *In the entrances thereof.* At its water gates; for it was by rendering themselves masters of the Euphrates that the Medes and Persians took the city, according to the prediction of Jeremiah, chap. li. 32, 36.

7. *The remnant of Jacob.* "From the reign of Darius Hystaspes (Ahasuerus, husband of Esther) the Jews were greatly favoured. Those who continued in Persia and Chaldea were greatly honoured under the protection of Mordecai and Esther."—Calmet. But others consider this as applying to the Maccabees. *As a dew from the Lord.* Even during their captivity many of the Jews were the means of spreading the knowledge of the one true God; see Dan. ii. 47; iii. 29; iv. 34; vi. 26. This may be the *dew from the Lord* mentioned here. When the Messiah appeared, the gospel was preached by them; and it shall again be propagated by their future glorious restoration, Rom. xi. 12, 25. *The grass, that tarrieth not for man.* Which grass springs up without the attention and culture of man. *Nor waiteth for the sons of men.* Libney adam, for the "sons of Adam," the first transgressor. The *dew* and the *showers* descend on the earth and water it, in order to render it fruitful; and the *grass* springs up independently of either the worth or the wickedness of man.

8. *As a lion.* In this and the following verse the victories of the Maccabees are supposed to be foretold.

9. *All thine enemies shall be cut off.* The Assyrians, who had destroyed Israel; and the Babylonians, who had ruined Judah.

10. *I will cut off thy horses.* You shall have no need of cavalry in your armies; God will fight for you.

11. *I will . . . throw down all thy strong holds.* You shall have no need of fortified cities; I will be your Defense.

12. *I will cut off witchcrafts.* You shall seek help only in Jehovah, your God. They have had neither soothsayers, images, groves, nor high places from the Captivity to the present day.

13. *Thy graven images also will I cut off.* You shall be no more an idolatrous people.

15. *I will execute vengeance . . . upon the heathen.* And He did so; for the empires of the Assyrians, Chaldeans, and others, the sworn enemies of the Jews, have long since been utterly destroyed.

CHAPTER 6

This chapter reproves and threatens. The manner of raising the attention by calling on man to urge his plea in the face of all nature, and on the inanimate creation to hear the expostulation of Jehovah with His people, is awakening and sublime, 1-2. The words of Jehovah follow, 3-5. And God's mercies having been set forth to His people, one of them is introduced, in a beautiful, dramatic form, asking what his duty is towards a God so gracious, 6-7. The answer follows in the words of the prophet, 8; who goes on to upbraid the people of his charge with their injustice and idolatry, to which he ascribes want of success in their lawful undertakings, and those heavy calamities which are now impending, 9-15.

1. *Arise, contend thou.* This chapter is a sort of dialogue between God and the people. God speaks the first five verses, and convicts the people of sin, righteousness, and judgment. The people, convinced of their iniquity, deprecate God's judgments, in the sixth and seventh verses. In the eighth verse God prescribes the way in which they are to be saved; and then the prophet, by the command of God, goes on to remonstrate from the ninth verse to the end of the chapter.

2. *Hear ye, O mountains.* Micah, as God's advocate, summons this people into judgment, and makes an appeal to inanimate creation against them.

4. *I brought thee up out of the land of Egypt.* Where you were slaves, and grievously oppressed; from all this I redeemed you. *I sent before thee Moses,* My chosen servant, and instructed him that he might be your leader and lawgiver. I sent with him *Aaron,* that he might be your priest. I sent *Miriam,* to whom I gave the spirit of prophecy, that she might be the director of your females.

5. *Remember now what Balak king of Moab consulted.* He sent for Balaam to curse your fathers, but by My influence he was obliged to bless them. See Numbers xxii and xxiii. *From Shittim unto Gilgal.* From the encampment at Shittim, Num. xxv. 1, on the way to that of Gilgal, Josh. iv. 19. Balaam gave different answers in the interval between these places.

6. *Wherewith shall I come before the Lord?* Now the people, as defendants, appear; but instead of vindicating themselves, or attempting to dispute what has been alleged against them, they seem at once to plead guilty; and now anxiously inquire how they shall appease the wrath of the Judge, how they shall make atonement for the sins already committed.

7. *Shall I give my firstborn for my transgression?* See some cases of such offerings, 2 Kings iii. 27; Lev. xx. 27. *The fruit of my body for the sin of my soul?* Shall I make the firstborn *chattah,* a "sin offering," for my soul?

9. *The Lord's voice crieth unto the city.* No man is found to hear; but the *man of wisdom* will hear, *tushiyah;* a word frequent in the writings of Solomon and Job, signifying wisdom, wealth, substance, reason, essence, happiness—anything that is complete; or that which is substantial, in opposition to vanity, emptiness, mere show, unsubstantiality. When God speaks, the man of common sense, who has any knowledge of God or his own soul, will *see thy name;* but instead of *yireh,* "will see," the Septuagint, Syriac, Vulgate, and Arabic have read *yirey,* "they that fear." The Vulgate reads: "And thou shalt be salvation to them that fear thy name." The Septuagint, "And he shall save those who fear his name."

13. *Will I make thee sick in smiting thee.* Perhaps better, "I also am weary with smiting you, in making you desolate for your sins."

14. *Thou shalt eat, but not be satisfied.* All your possessions are cursed, because of your sins; and you have no real good in all your enjoyments.

16. *The statutes of Omri are kept.* Omri, king of Israel, the father of Ahab, was one of the worst kings the Israelites ever had; and Ahab followed in his wicked father's steps. The *statutes* of those kings were the very grossest idolatry.

CHAPTER 7

The prophet begins this chapter with lamenting the decay of piety and the growth of ungodliness, using a beautiful allegory to imply (as explained in v. 2) that the good man is as seldom to be met with as the early fig of best quality in the advanced season, or the cluster after the vintage, 1-2. He then reproves and threatens in terms so expressive of great calamities as to be applied in the New Testament to times of the hottest persecution, 3-6. See Matt. x. 35-36. Notwithstanding which a Jew is immediately introduced declaring, in the name of his captive people, the strongest faith in the mercy of God, the most submissive resignation to His will, and the firmest hope in His favor in future times, when they should triumph over their enemies, 7-10. The prophet upon this resumes the discourse, and predicts their great prosperity and increase, 11-12; although the whole land of Israel must first be desolated on account of the great wickedness of its inhabitants, 13. The prophet intercedes in behalf of his people, 14. After which God is introduced promising, in very ample terms, their future restoration and prosperity, 15-17. And then, to conclude, a chorus of Jews is introduced, singing a beautiful hymn of thanksgiving, suggested by the gracious promises which precede, 18-20.

1. *Woe is me!* This is a continuation of the preceding discourse. And here the prophet points out the small number of the upright to be found in the land. He desired to see *the firstripe fruit*—distinguished and eminent piety; but he found nothing but a very imperfect or spurious kind of godliness.

2. *The good man is perished out of the earth.* A similar sentiment may be found in Ps. xii. 1; Isa. lvii. 1.

3. *That they may do evil with both hands.* That is, *earnestly,* greedily, to the uttermost of their power. *The prince asketh a bribe,* to forward claims in his court. *The judge asketh for a reward.* That he may decide the cause in favor of him who gives most money, whether the cause be good or evil. *The great man, he uttereth his mischievous desire.* Such consider themselves above law, and they make no secret of their unjust determinations. And *so they wrap it up*—they all conjoin in doing evil in their several offices, and oppressing the poor.

4. *The best of them is as a brier.* They are useless in themselves, and cannot be touched without wounding him that comes in contact with them. *The day of thy watchmen.* The day of vengeance, which the prophets have foreseen and proclaimed, is at hand.

6. *For the son dishonoureth the father.* See the use our Lord has made of these words, where He quotes them, Matt. x. 21, 25, 36.

8. *Rejoice not against me, O mine enemy.* The captive Israelites are introduced as speaking here and in the preceding verse. The *enemy* are the Assyrians and Chaldeans; the *fall* is their idolatry and consequent captivity; the *darkness,* the calamities they suffered in that captivity; their rise and *light,* their restoration and consequent blessedness.

9. *I will bear the indignation of the Lord.* The words of the penitent captives, acknowledging their sins and praying for mercy.

10. *Then she that is mine enemy.* This may refer particularly to the city of Babylon. *Shall she be trodden down.* Literally fulfilled in the sackage of that city by the Persians, and its consequent total ruin.

11. *In the day that thy walls are to be built.* This refers to Jerusalem; *the decree,* to the purpose of God to deliver the people into captivity. The restoration of Jerusalem is certainly what the prophet describes.

12. *In that day also he shall come.* The Israel-

ites were to return from their captivity, and reoccupy their ancient country from Assyria to Egypt; that is, from the river Euphrates to the river Nile, and from the Mediterranean Sea to the ocean, and from Mount Libanus to the mountains of Arabia Petraea, or Mount Seir. See Amos viii. 12. This prediction was literally fulfilled under the Asmoneans. The Jewish nation was greatly extended and very powerful under Herod, at the time that our Lord was born.

13. *Notwithstanding the land shall be desolate.* This should be translated in the preter tense, "Though the land had been desolate"; that is, the land of Israel had been desolate during the Captivity.

14. *Feed thy people with thy rod.* "With thy crook." The shepherd's crook is most certainly designed, as the word *flock* immediately following shows. No rod of correction or affliction is here intended, nor does the word mean such. *Solitarily.* They have been long without a shepherd or spiritual governor. *In the midst of*

Carmel. Very fruitful in vines. *Bashan and Gilead.* Proverbially fruitful in pasturages.

15. *According to the days.* This is the answer to the prophet's prayer; and God says He will protect, save, defend, and work miracles for them in their restoration, such as He wrought for their fathers in their return from Egypt to the Promised Land.

16. *The nations shall see and be confounded.* Whether the words in these verses (15-17) be applied to the return from the Babylonish captivity or to the prosperity of the Jews under the Maccabees, they may be understood as ultimately applicable to the final restoration of this people, and their lasting prosperity under the gospel.

20. *Thou wilt perform the truth to Jacob.* The promises which He has made to Jacob and His posterity. Not one of them can ever fall to the ground. *And the mercy to Abraham, which thou hast sworn;* viz., that in his Seed all the families of the earth should be blessed, that the Messiah should come from Abraham.

The Book of
NAHUM

Nahum was a native of Elkoshai, a little village of Galilee, whose ruins were still in being in the time of St. Jerome.

The particular circumstances of the life of Nahum are altogether unknown. His prophecy consists of three chapters, which make up but one discourse, wherein he foretells the destruction of Nineveh. He describes it in so pathetic a manner that he seems to have been upon the spot to declare to the Ninevites the destruction of their city.

We are inclined to be of St. Jerome's opinion, that he foretold the destruction of Nineveh in the time of Hezekiah, and after the war of Sennacherib in Egypt. Nahum speaks plainly of the taking of No-Ammon, a city of Egypt; of the haughtiness of Rabshakeh; of the defeat of Sennacherib; and he speaks of them as things that were past. He supposes that the Jews were still in their own country, and that they there celebrated their festivals. He speaks of the Captivity, and of the dispersion of the ten tribes. All these evidences convince us that Nahum cannot be placed before the fifteenth year of Hezekiah, since the expedition of Sennacherib against this prince was in the fourteenth year of his reign.

CHAPTER 1

This chapter opens the prophecy against the Assyrians and their metropolis with a very magnificent description of the infinite justice, tender compassion, and uncontrollable power of God, 1-8. To this succeeds an address to the Assyrians; with a lively picture of their sudden overthrow, because of their evil device against Jerusalem, 9-11. Then appears Jehovah himself, proclaiming deliverance to His people from the Assyrian yoke, and the destruction of the Assyrian idols, 12-14; upon which the prophet, with great emphasis, directs the attention of Judah to the approach of the messenger who brings such glad tidings; and exultingly bids his people to celebrate their solemn feasts, and perform their vows, as a merciful Providence would not suffer these enemies of the Jewish state to prevail against them, 15.

1. *The burden of Nineveh. Massa* not only signifies a *burden,* but also a thing "lifted up, pronounced, or proclaimed"; also a "message." It is used by the prophets to signify the revelation which they have received from God to deliver to any particular people: the "oracle"— the prophecy. Here it signifies the declaration

from God relative to the overthrow of Nineveh, and the commission of the prophet to deliver it. As the Assyrians under Pul, Tiglath-pileser, and Shalmaneser, three of their kings, had been employed by a just God for the chastisement His disobedient people, the end being now accomplished by them, God is about to burn the rod wherewith He corrected Israel; and Nineveh, the capital of the Assyrian empire, is to be destroyed. This prediction appears to have been accomplished a short time after this by Nebuchadnezzar and Cyaxares, the Ahasuerus of Scripture. *Nahum* signifies "comforter." The name was very suitable, as he was sent to comfort the people, by showing them that God was about to destroy their adversaries.

3. *The clouds are the dust of his feet.* This is spoken in allusion to a chariot and horses going on with extreme rapidity; they are all enveloped in a cloud of dust. So Jehovah is

represented as coming through the circuit of the heavens as rapidly as lightning, the clouds surrounding Him as the dust does the chariot and horses.

4. *He rebuketh the sea,* the Red Sea, and *the rivers;* probably an allusion to the passage of the Red Sea and Jordan. The description of the coming of Jehovah, from the third to the sixth verse, is dreadfully majestic.

8. *But with an overrunning flood.* Bishop Newcome thinks this may refer to the manner in which Nineveh was taken. The Euphrates overflowed its banks, deluged a part of the city, and overturned twenty stadia of the wall; in consequence of which the desponding king burned himself, and his palace, with his treasures. *Darkness shall pursue.* All kinds of calamity shall pursue them till they are destroyed.

9. *Affliction shall not rise up the second time.* There shall be no need to repeat the judgment; with one blow God will make a full end of the business.

11. *Imagineth evil against the Lord.* Such were Pul, 2 Kings xv. 10; Tiglath-pileser, 2 Kings xv. 29; Shalmaneser, 2 Kings xvii. 6; and Sennacherib, 2 Kings xviii. 17 and xix. 23. *A wicked counsellor.* Sennacherib and Rabshakeh.

12. *Though they be . . . many.* Sennacherib invaded Judea with an army of nearly 200,000 men. *Thus shall they be cut down.* The angel of the Lord (a suffocating wind) slew of them in one night 185,000, 2 Kings xix. 35.

13. *Now will I break his yoke from off thee.* This refers to the tribute which the Jews were obliged to pay to the Assyrians, 2 Kings xvii. 14.

14. *No more of thy name be sown.* No more of you shall be carried away into captivity. *I will make thy grave; for thou art vile.* I think this is an address to the Assyrians, and especially to Sennacherib. The house of his gods is to be his grave; and we know that while he was worshipping in the house of his god Nisroch, his two sons, Adrammelech and Sharezer, smote him there that he died, 2 Kings xix. 37.

15. *Behold upon the mountains.* Borrowed probably from Isa. lii. 7, but applied here to the messengers who brought the good tidings of the destruction of Nineveh. Judah might then keep her solemn feasts, for the wicked Assyrian should pass through the land no more, being entirely cut off, and the imperial city razed to its foundations.

CHAPTER 2

Nineveh is now called upon to prepare for the approach of her enemies, the instruments of Jehovah's vengeance, 1; and the military array and muster, the very arms and dress, of the Medes and Babylonians in the reigns of Cyaxares and Nabopolassar; their rapid approach to the city; the process of the siege, and the inundation of the river; the capture of the place; the captivity, lamentation, and flight of the inhabitants; the sacking of this immense, wealthy, and exceedingly populous city; and the consequent desolation and terror, are all described in the pathetic, vivid, and sublime imagery of Hebrew poetry, 2-10. This description is succeeded by a very beautiful and expressive allegory, 11-12; which is immediately explained, and applied to the city of Nineveh, 13. It is thought by some commentators that the metropolitan city of the Assyrian empire is also intended by the tender and beautiful simile, in the seventh verse, of a great princess led captive, with her maids of honor attending her, bewailing her and their own condition, by beating their breasts, and by other expressions of sorrow.

1. *He that dasheth in pieces.* Or "scattereth." The Chaldeans and Medes. *Keep the munition.* Guard the fenced places, From this to the end of the fifth verse, the preparations made at Nineveh to repel their enemies are described. The description is exceedingly picturesque. *Watch the way.* By which the enemy is most likely to approach. *Make thy loins strong.* Take courage. *Fortify thy power.* Muster your troops; call in all your allies.

4. *The chariots shall rage.* Those of the besiegers and the besieged, meeting in the streets, producing universal confusion and carnage.

5. *He shall recount his worthies.* Muster up his most renowned warriors and heroes. *Shall make haste to the wall.* Where they see the enemies making their most powerful attacks, in order to get possession of the city.

6. *The gates of the rivers shall be opened.* The account given by Diodorus Siculus, lib. ii, is very surprising. He begins thus: "There was a prophecy received from their forefathers, that Nineveh should not be taken till the river first became an enemy to the city. It happened in the third year of the siege, that the Euphrates [query, Tigris] being swollen with continued rains, overflowed part of the city, and threw down twenty stadia of the wall. The king, then imagining that the oracle was accomplished, and that the river was now manifestly become an enemy to the city, casting aside all hope of safety, and lest he should fall into the hands of the enemy, built a large funeral pyre in the palace, and having collected all his gold and silver and royal vestments, together with his concubines and eunuchs, placed himself with them in a little apartment built in the pyre; burnt them, himself, and the palace together. When the death of the king was announced by certain deserters, the enemy entered in by the breach which the waters had made, and took the city."

7. *And Huzzab shall be led away captive.* Perhaps *Huzzab* means the queen of Nineveh, who had escaped the burning mentioned above by Diodorus. As there is no account of the queen being burnt, but only of the king, the concubines, and the eunuchs, we may therefore naturally conclude that the queen escaped; and is represented here as *brought up* and delivered to the conqueror, her maids at the same time bewailing her lot. Some think *Huzzab* signifies Nineveh itself.

8. *But Nineveh is of old like a pool of water.* Bishop Newcome translates the line thus: "And the waters of Nineveh are a pool of waters." *Stand, stand.* Consternation shall be at its utmost height; the people shall flee in all directions; and though quarter is offered, and they are assured of safety if they remain, yet not one looketh back.

9. *Take ye the spoil.* Though the king burnt his treasures, vestments, he could not totally destroy the silver and the gold. Nor did he burn the riches of the city; these fell a prey to the conquerors; and there was no end of the store of glorious garments, and the most costly vessels and furniture.

10. *She is empty, and void, and waste.* The original is strongly emphatic. The words are of the same sound, and increase in their length as they point out great, greater, and greatest deso-

lation. *Bukah, umebukah, umebullakah.* "She is void, empty, and desolate."

11. *Where is the dwelling of the lions?* Nineveh, the habitation of bold, strong, and ferocious men. *The feedingplace of the young lions.* Whither her victorious and rapacious generals frequently returned to consume the produce of their success. Here they walked at large, *and none made them afraid.* Wheresoever they turned their arms they were victors, and all nations were afraid of them.

12. *The lion did tear.* This verse gives us a striking picture of the manner in which the Assyrian conquests and depredations were carried on. How many people were spoiled to enrich his *whelps*—his sons, princes, and nobles! How many women were stripped and slain, whose spoils went to decorate his *lionesses* —his queen, concubines, and mistresses! And they had even more than they could assume; their *holes* and *dens*—treasure-houses, palaces, and wardrobes—were filled *with ravin*, the riches which they got by plunder.

13. *Behold, I am against thee.* Assyria, and Nineveh, its capital. I will deal with you as you have dealt with others. *The voice of thy messengers.* Announcing your splendid victories, and the vast spoils taken.

CHAPTER 3

The prophet denounces a woe against Nineveh for her perfidy and violence. He musters up before our eyes the number of her chariots and cavalry; points to her burnished arms, and to the great and unrelenting slaughter which she spreads around her, 1-3. Because Nineveh is a city wholly given up to the grossest superstition, and is an instructress of other nations in her abominable rites, therefore she shall come to a most ignominious and unpitied end, 3-7. Her final ruin shall be similar to that of No, a famous city of Egypt, 8-11. The prophet then beautifully describes the great ease with which the strongholds of Nineveh should be taken, 12, and her judicial pusillanimity during the siege, 13; declares that all her preparation, her numbers, opulence, and chieftains, would be of no avail in the day of the Lord's vengeance, 14-17; and that her tributaries would desert her, 18. The whole concludes with stating the incurableness of her malady, and the dreadful destruction consequently awaiting her; and with introducing the nations which she had oppressed as exulting at her fall, 19.

1. *Woe to the bloody city!* Nineveh, the threatenings against which are continued in a strain of invective, astonishing for its richness, variety, and energy. One may hear and see the whip cracking, the horses prancing, the wheels rumbling, the chariots bounding after the galloping steeds; the reflection from the drawn and highly polished swords; and the hurled spears, like flashes of lightning, dazzling the eyes; the slain lying in heaps, and horses and chariots stumbling over them!

4. *Because of the multitude of the whoredoms.* Above, the Ninevites were represented under the emblem of a lion tearing all to pieces; here they are represented under the emblem of a beautiful harlot or public prostitute, enticing all men to her, inducing the nations to become idolatrous; and, by thus perverting them, rendering them also objects of the divine wrath. *Mistress of witchcrafts, that selleth nations through her whoredoms.* Using every means to excite to idolatry; and being, by menace or wiles, successful in all.

8. *Art thou better than populous No?* No-Ammon, in the Delta, on one branch of the Nile, which had been lately destroyed, probably by the Chaldeans. *The waters round about it.* Being situated in the Delta, it had the fork of two branches of the Nile to defend it by land; and its barrier or *wall* was the *sea*, the Mediterranean, into which these branches emptied themselves: so that this city, and the place it stood on, were wholly surrounded by the waters.

9. *Put and Lubim.* A part of Africa and Libya, which were all within reach of forming alliances with No-Ammon.

10. *They cast lots for her honourable men.* This refers still to the city called "populous No." And the custom of casting *lots* among the commanders, for the prisoners which they had taken, is here referred to. *Great men were bound in chains.* These were reserved to grace the triumph of the victor.

12. *Thy strong holds.* The effects of the consternation into which the Ninevites were cast by the assault on their city are here pointed out by a very expressive metaphor. The *firstripe figs*, when at full maturity, fell from the tree with the least shake; and so, at the first shake or consternation, all the fortresses of Nineveh were abandoned; and the king, in despair, burnt himself and household in his own palace.

13. *Thy people . . . are women.* They lost all courage, and made no resistance.

14. *Draw thee waters for the siege.* The Tigris ran near to Nineveh, and here they are exhorted to lay in plenty of fresh water, lest the siege should last long, and lest the enemy should cut off this supply. *Go into clay, and tread the morter.* This refers to the manner of forming bricks anciently in those countries; they digged up the clay, kneaded it properly by treading, mixed it with straw or coarse grass, molded the bricks, and dried them in the sun.

16. *Thou hast multiplied thy merchants.* Like Tyre, this city was a famous resort for merchants; but the multitudes which were there previously to the siege, like the locusts, took the alarm, and fled away.

17. *Thy crowned are as the locusts.* You have numerous princes and numerous commanders. *Which camp in the hedges in the cold day.* The locusts are said to lie in shelter about the hedges of fertile spots when the weather is cold, or during the night; but as soon as the sun shines out and is hot, they come out to their forage, or take to their wings.

18. *Thy shepherds slumber.* That is, the rulers and tributary princes, who, as Herodotus informs us, deserted Nineveh in the day of her distress, and came not forward to her succor.

19. *There is no healing of thy bruise.* You shall never be rebuilt. *All that hear the bruit of thee.* The report or acccount. *Shall clap the hands.* Shall exult in your downfall. *For upon whom hath not thy wickedness passed?* You have been a universal oppressor, and therefore all nations rejoice at your fall and utter desolation.

The Book of

HABAKKUK

CHAPTER 1

The prophet enters very abruptly on his subject, his spirit being greatly indignant at the rapid progress of vice and impiety, 1-4. Upon which God is introduced threatening very awful and sudden judgments to be inflicted by the ministry of the Chaldeans, 5-10. The Babylonians attribute their wonderful successes to their idols, 11. The prophet then, making a sudden transition, expostulates with God (probably personating the Jews) for permitting a nation much more wicked than themselves, as they supposed, to oppress and devour them, as fishers and foulers do their prey, 12-17.

We know little of this prophet. He was probably of the tribe of Simeon, and a native of Beth-zacar. It is very likely that he lived after the destruction of Nineveh, as he speaks of the Chaldeans, but makes no mention of the Assyrians. And he appears also to have prophesied before the Jewish captivity; see chap. i. 5; ii. 1; iii. 2, 16-19; and therefore Archbishop Newcome thinks he may be placed in the reign of Jehoiakim, between the years 606 B.C. and 598 B.C.

As a poet, Habakkuk holds a high rank among the Hebrew prophets. The beautiful connection between the parts of his prophecy, its diction, imagery, spirit, and sublimity, cannot be too much admired; and his hymn, chap. iii, is allowed by the best judges to be a masterpiece of its kind.

1. *The burden.* The word signifies an "oracle" or revelation in general; but chiefly one relative to future calamities.

2. *O Lord, how long shall I cry!* The prophet feels himself strongly excited against the vices which he beheld; and which, it appears from this verse, he had often declaimed against, but in vain. The people continued in their vices, and God in His long-suffering.

3. *And cause me to behold grievance. Amal,* labor, toil, distress, misery—the common fruits of sin.

5. *Behold ye among the heathen.* Instead of *baggoyim,* among the "nations" or *heathen,* some critics think we should read *bogedim,* "transgressors"; and to the same purpose the Septuagint, Syriac, and Arabic have read; and thus it is quoted by St. Paul, Acts xiii. 41. Newcome translates, "See, ye transgressors, and behold a wonder, and perish." *I will work a work in your days.* As he is speaking of the desolation that should be produced by the Chaldeans, it follows that the *Chaldeans* invaded Judah whilst those were living whom the prophet addressed.

6. *That bitter and hasty nation.* Cruel and oppressive in their disposition, and prompt and speedy in their assaults and conquests.

7. *Their judgment . . . shall proceed of themselves.* By revolting from the Assyrians, they have become a great nation. Thus their judgment and excellence were the result of their own valor. Other meanings are given to this passage.

8. *Their horses also are swifter than the leopards.* The Chaldean cavalry are proverbial for swiftness, courage, etc. In Jeremiah, chap. iv. 13, it is said, speaking of Nebuchadnezzar, "His chariots shall be as a whirlwind; his horses are swifter than eagles."

10. *They shall scoff at the kings.* No power shall be able to stand before them. They will have no need to build formidable ramparts; by sweeping the *dust* together they shall make mounts sufficient to pass over the walls and take the city.

11. *Then shall his mind change.* This is thought to relate to the change which took place in Nebuchadnezzar, when "a beast's heart was given to him," and he was "driven from the dwellings of men." And this was because of his offending—his pride and arrogance—and his attributing all his success to his idols.

12. *Art thou not from everlasting?* The idols change, and their worshippers change and fail; but Thou, Jehovah, art eternal; Thou canst not change, and they who trust in Thee are safe. Thou art infinite in Thy mercy; therefore, *we shall not die,* shall not be totally exterminated. *Thou hast ordained them for judgment.* Thou hast raised up the Chaldeans to correct and punish us, but Thou hast not given them a commission to destroy us totally.

13. *Thou art of purer eyes.* Seeing Thou art so pure, and *canst not look on iniquity*—it is so abominable—how canst Thou bear with them who *deal treacherously, and holdest thy tongue when the wicked devoureth the . . . righteous?"* All such questions are easily solved by a consideration of God's ineffable mercy, which leads Him to suffer long and be kind. He has no pleasure in the death of a sinner.

14. *Makest men as the fishes of the sea.* Easily are we taken and destroyed. We have no leader to guide us, and no power to defend ourselves. Nebuchadnezzar is here represented as a fisherman, who is constantly casting his nets into the sea, and enclosing multitudes of fishes; and, being always successful, he sacrifices to his own net—attributes all his conquests to his own power and prudence; not considering that he is only like a net that, after having been used for a while, shall at last be thrown by as useless, or burnt in the fire.

CHAPTER 2

The prophet, waiting for a return to his expostulation, is answered by God that the time for the destruction of the Jewish polity by the Chaldeans is not only fixed in the divine counsel, but is awfully near; and he is therefore commanded to write down the vision relative to this appalling subject in the most legible characters, and in the plainest language, that all who read it with attention (those just persons who exercise an unwavering faith in the declaration of God respecting the violent irruption of the merciless Babylonians) may flee from the impending vengenace, 1-4. The fall of the Chaldeans and of their ambitious monarch is then predicted, 5-10; and, by a strong and bold personification, the very stone and wood of those magnificent buildings, which the Babylonish king had raised by oppression and bloodshed, pronounce his woe, and in responsive taunts upbraid him, 11-12. The prophet then beautifully sets forth the absolute impotence of every effort, however well conducted, which is not in concert with the divine counsel. For though the wicked rage, and threaten the utter extermination of the people of God, yet when the set time to favor Zion is come, the destroyers of God's heritage shall themselves be destroyed, and "the earth shall be filled with the knowledge of the glory of God, as the waters cover the sea," 13-14. See Ps. cii. 13-16. For the cup of idolatry which Babylon has given to many nations, she will receive of the Lord's hand the cup of fury by the insurrection of mighty enemies (the Medes and Persians) rushing like wild beasts to destroy her, 15. In the midst of this distress the prophet very opportunely asks in what the Babylonians had profited by their idols, exposes the absurdity of trusting in them, and calls upon the whole world to stand in awe of the everlasting Jehovah, 16-19.

1. *I will stand upon my watch.* The prophets are always represented as watchmen, watching constantly for the comfort, safety, and welfare of the people; and watching also to receive information from the Lord. *What he will say unto me.* "In me"—in my understanding and heart. *And what I shall answer when I am reproved.* What I shall say to God in behalf of the people, and what the Lord shall command me to say to the people. Some translate, "And what he will answer for my conviction." Or, "what shall be answered to my pleading."

2. *Write the vision.* Carefully take down all that I shall say. *That he may run that readeth it.* That he who attentively peruses it may speed to save his life from the irruption of the Chaldeans, by which so many shall be cut off. The prophet does not mean that the words are to be made so plain that a man running by may easily read them, and catch their meaning.

3. *The vision is yet for an appointed time.* The Chaldeans, who are to ruin Judea, shall afterwards be ruined themselves. But they must do this work before they receive their wages; therefore the vision is for an appointed time. *But at the end it shall speak.* When his work of devastation is done, his day of retribution shall take place. *Though it tarry.* Though it appear to be long, do not be impatient; *it will surely come, it will not tarry* longer than the prescribed time, and this time is not far distant. *Wait for it.*

4. *Behold, his soul which is lifted up.* He that presumes on his safety without any special warrant from God is a proud man; and whatever he may profess, or think of himself, his mind *is not upright in him.* But he that is "just by faith shall live"—he that believes what God hath said relative to the Chaldeans besieging Jerusalem shall make his escape from the place, and consequently shall save his life. The words in the New Testament are accommodated to the salvation which believers in Christ shall possess.

5. *Because he transgresseth by wine.* Nebuchadnezzar is here represented in his usual character, proud, haughty, and ambitious; inebriated with his successes, and determined on more extensive conquests; and, like the "grave," can never have enough. Yet, after the subjugation of many peoples and nations, he shall be brought down, and become so despicable that he shall be a proverb or reproach, and be taunted and scorned by all those whom he had before enslaved.

6. *Shall not all these take up a parable against him?* His ambition, derangement, and the final destruction of his mighty empire by the Persians shall form the foundation of many sententious sayings among the people.

7. *Shall they not rise up suddenly?* Does not this refer to the sudden and unexpected taking of Babylon by Cyrus, whose troops entered into the city through the bed of the Euphrates, whose waters they had diverted by another channel; so that the Babylonians knew nothing of the matter till they saw the Persian soldiers rise up as in a moment, in the very heart of their city?

8. *For the violence of the land.* Or "for the violence done to the land" of Judea, and to *the city* of Jerusalem.

9. *An evil covetousness to his house.* Nebuchadnezzar wished to aggrandize his family, and make his empire permanent; but both family and empire were soon cut off by the death of his son Belshazzar, and the consequent destruction of the Chaldean empire.

10. *Hast sinned against thy soul.* Your life is forfeited by your crimes.

11. *The stone shall cry out of the wall, and the beam out of the timber shall answer it.* This appears to refer to the ancient mode of building walls: two or three courses of stone, and then one course of timber. See 1 Kings vi. 36; thus was the palace of Solomon built. The splendid and costly buildings of Babylon have been universally celebrated. But how were these buildings erected? By the spoils of conquered nations, and the expense of the blood of multitudes; therefore the stones and the timber are represented as calling out for vengeance against this ruthless conqueror.

12. *Woe to him that buildeth a town with blood!* At the expense of much slaughter. This is the answer of the *beam* to the *stone*.

13. *The people shall labour in the very fire.* All these superb buildings shall be burnt down. See the parallel passage, Jer. li. 58. *Shall weary themselves for very vanity.* For the gratification of the wishes of ambition, and in buildings which shall be brought to naught.

14. *For the earth shall be filled.* This is a singular and important verse. It may be first applied to Babylon. God's power and providence shall be widely displayed in the destruction of this city and empire. Secondly, it may be applied to the glorious days of the Messiah. Thirdly, it may be applied to the universal spread of the gospel over the habitable globe.

15. *Woe unto him that giveth his neighbour drink!* This has been considered as applying to Pharaoh-hophra, king of Egypt, who enticed his neighbors Jehoiachin and Zedekiah to rebel against Nebuchadnezzar, whereby the nakedness and imbecility of the poor Jews was soon discovered; for the Chaldeans soon took Jerusalem, and carried its kings, princes, and people into captivity.

16. *The cup of the Lord's right hand.* Among the ancients, all drank out of the same cup; it was passed from hand to hand, and each drank as much as he chose. The Chaldeans gave to the neighboring nations the cup of idolatry and

of deceitful alliance, and in return they received from the Lord the cup of His fury.

17. *For the violence of Lebanon.* Or the violence done to Lebanon; to men, to cattle, to Judea, and to Jerusalem. See the parallel place, v. 8. This may be a threatening against Egypt, as the former was against Chaldea.

18. *What profiteth the graven image?* This is against idolatry in general, and every species of it, as well as against those princes, priests, and people who practice it, and encourage others to do the same. *Dumb idols? Elilim illemim,* "dumb nothings." This is exactly agreeable to St. Paul, 1 Cor. viii. 4, who says, "An idol is nothing in the world."

CHAPTER 3

The prophet, being apprized of the calamities which were to be brought on his country by the ministry of the Chaldeans, and the punishments which awaited the Chaldeans themselves, partly struck with terror, and partly revived with hope and confidence in the divine mercy, beseeches God to hasten the redemption of His people, 1-2. Such a petition would naturally lead his thoughts to the astonishing deliverance which God vouchsafed to the same people of old; and the inference from it was obvious, that He could with the same ease deliver their posterity now. But, hurried on by the fire and impetuosity of his spirit, he disdains to wait the process of connecting these ideas, and bounds at once into the midst of his subject: "God came from Teman," etc., 3. He goes on to describe the majesty and might which God displayed in conducting His people to the land of promise, selecting the most remarkable circumstances, and clothing them in the most lofty language. As he goes along, his fancy becomes more glowing, till at length he is transported to the scene of action, and becomes an eyewitness of the wonders he describes. "I saw the tents of Cushan in affliction," 4-7. After having touched on the principal circumstances of that deliverance which he celebrates, he returns to what passed before them in Egypt, his enthusiasm having led him to begin in the midst of his subject, 8-15. And at last he ends the hymn as he began it, with expressing his awe of the divine judgments, and his firm trust in the mercy and goodness of God while under them; and that in terms of such singular beauty, elegance, and sublimity as to form a very proper conclusion to this admirable piece of divinely inspired composition, 16-19. It would seem from the title, and the note appended at the end, that it was set to music and sung in the service of the Temple.

1. *A prayer of Habakkuk . . . upon Shigionoth.* See the note on the title of Psalm vii, where the meaning of *Shiggaion* is given.

2. *In the midst of the years.* "As the years approach." The nearer the time, the clearer and fuller is the prediction; and the signs of the times show that the complete fulfilment is at hand.

3. *Teman.* This was a city, the capital of a province of Idumea, to the south of the land of Canaan, Num. xx. 21; Jer. xlix. 7. *Paran* was a city which gave its name to a province in Arabia Petraea, Gen. xxi. 21; Deut. xxxiii. 2. *Selah.* This word is not well-known; probably it means a pause or alteration in the music. See it in the Psalms.

4. *He had horns coming out of his hand.* "Rays." *His hand*—His power—was manifested in a particular place, by the sudden issuing out of rays, which diverged in coruscations of light, so as to illuminate the whole hemisphere. Yet *there was the hiding of his power.* His majesty could not be seen, nor any kind of image, because of the insufferable splendor.

5. *Before him went the pestilence.* This plague was several times inflicted on the disobedient Israelites in the wilderness; see Num. xi. 33; xiv. 37; xvi. 46; and was always the proof that the just God was then manifesting His

power among them. *Burning coals went forth at his feet.* Newcome translates, "And flashes of fire went forth after him." The disobedient Israelites were consumed by a fire that went out from Jehovah; see Lev. x. 2; Num. xi. 1; xvi. 35. And the burnt offering was consumed by a fire which came out from before Jehovah, Lev. xi. 24.

6. *He stood, and measured the earth. Erets,* "the land"; He divided the Promised Land among the twelve tribes. *He beheld, and drove asunder the nations.* The nations of Canaan, the Hittites, Hivites, Jebusites, etc., and all who opposed His people. Even His look dispersed them. *The everlasting mountains were scattered.* Or "broken asunder." This may refer to the convulsions on Mount Sinai, and to the earthquake which announced the descent of the Most High. See Exod. xix. 18.

7. *I saw the tents of Cushan in affliction. Cush* is Arabia. The Arabians dwelt in *tents.* When the Lord appeared on Mount Sinai, the Arabs of the Red Sea abandoned their tents, being terror-struck; and the Midianites also were seized with fear.

8. *Was the Lord displeased against the rivers?* Floods; here is a reference to the passage of the Red Sea. The Lord is represented as heading His troops, riding in His chariot, and commanding the sea to divide, that a free passage might be left for His army to pass over.

9. *Thy bow was made quite naked.* That is, it was drawn out of its case; as the arrows had their quiver, so the bows had their cases. This verse appears to be an answer to the questions in the preceding: "Was the Lord displeased?" The answer is, All this was done *according to the oaths of the tribes;* the covenant of God, frequently repeated and renewed, which He made with the tribes, to give them the land of the Canaanites for their inheritance. *Thou didst cleave the earth with rivers.* Or, "Thou didst cleave the streams of the land." Or, "Thou cleavedst the dry land into rivers." This may be a reference to the passage of Jordan, and transactions at Arnon and the brook Jabbok. See Num. xxi. 13-15.

10. *The mountains saw thee.* This is the continued answer to the questions in v. 8. These are figures highly poetic, to show with what ease God accomplished the most arduous tasks in behalf of His people. As soon as the *mountains* saw Him, they trembled, they were in pangs. When He appeared, the sea fled to right and left, to give Him a passage.

11. *The sun and moon stood still.* This was at the prayer of Joshua, when he fought against the Amorites. See Josh. x. 11-12. *At the light of thine arrows they went.* I think we should translate:

> *By their light, thine arrows went abroad;*
> *By their brightness, the lightning of Thy spear.*

Calvin very justly remarks that the arrows and spears of the Israelites are called those of God, under whose auspices the people fought. The meaning is that, by the continuation of the course, the Israelites saw how to continue the battle, till their enemies were all defeated.

12. *Thou didst march through the land.* This refers to the conquest of Canaan. God is repre-

sented as going at the head of His people as general in chief; and leading them on from conquest to conquest—which was the fact. *Thou didst thresh the heathen in anger.* Thou didst tread them down, as the oxen do the sheaves on the threshing floor.

13. *Thou wentest forth for the salvation of thy people.* Their deliverance would not have been effected but through Thy interference. *For salvation with thine anointed.* That is, with Joshua, whom God had anointed, or solemnly appointed to fill the place of Moses, and lead the people into the Promised Land. *Thou woundedst the head out of the house of the wicked.* This alludes to the slaying of the first-born through all the land of Egypt. *By discovering the foundation unto the neck.* The general meaning of this clause is sufficiently plain: the government of these lands should be utterly subverted; the very foundations of it should be razed. "Thou hast wounded the head even unto the neck, in the house of the wicked, by laying bare the foundation." There was no hope left to the Egyptians, because the firstborn of every family was cut off, so that the very foundation was laid bare, no firstborn being left to continue the heirship of families.

14. *Thou didst strike through.* The Hebrew will bear this sense: "Thou hast pierced amidst their tribes the head of their troops," referring to Pharaoh and his generals, who came like a whirlwind to fall upon the poor Israelites when they appeared to be hemmed in by sea, and no place for their escape.

16. *When I heard, my belly trembled.* The prophet, having finished his account of the wonders done by Jehovah, in bringing their fathers from Egypt into the Promised Land, now returns to the desolate state of his countrymen, who are shortly to be led into captivity, and suffer the most grievous afflictions. *When he* (Nebuchadnezzar) *cometh up unto the people*

(the Jews), *he will invade them* (overpower and carry them away captive) *with his troops.*

17. *Although the fig tree shall not blossom.* "Shall not flourish," shall not put forth its young figs, for the fig tree does not blossom.

These two verses give the finest display of resignation and confidence that I have ever met with. He saw that evil was at hand, and unavoidable; he submitted to the dispensation of God, whose Spirit enabled him to paint it in all its calamitous circumstances. He knew that God was merciful and gracious. He trusted to His promise, though all appearances were against its fulfillment; for he knew that the word of Jehovah could not fail, and therefore his confidence is unshaken.

19. *The Lord God is my strength.* This is an imitation, if not a quotation, from Ps. xviii. 32-33. *Will make me to walk upon mine high places.* This last verse is spoken in the person of the people, who seem to anticipate their restoration, and that they shall once more rejoice in the hills and mountains of Judea. *To the chief singer on my stringed instruments.* This line, which is evidently a superscription, leads me to suppose that, when the prophet had completed his short ode, he folded it up, with the above direction to the master singer, or leader of the choir, to be sung in the Temple service. Many of the psalms are directed in the same way. "To the master singer" or "chief musician"; to be sung, according to their nature, on different kinds of instruments, or with particular airs or tunes. *Neginoth,* which we translate "stringed instruments," means such as were struck with a plectrum, or excited by some kind of friction or pulsation; as violins and cymbals, or tambourines are. I do not think that the line makes any part of the prophecy, but merely the superscription or direction of the work when it was finished. The ending will appear much more dignified, this line being separated from it.

The Book of

ZEPHANIAH

CHAPTER 1

This chapter begins with denouncing God's judgments against Judah and Jerusalem, 1-3. Idolaters, and sinners of several other denominations, are then particularly threatened; and their approaching visitation enlarged on, by the enumeration of several circumstances which tend greatly to heighten its terrors, 4-18.

1. *The word of the Lord which came unto Zephaniah.* Though this prophet has given us so large a list of his ancestors, yet little concerning him is known, because we know nothing certain relative to the persons of the family whose names are here introduced. He prophesied *in the days of Josiah the son of Amon, king of Judah;* and from the description which he gives of the disorders which prevailed in Judea in his time, it is evident that he must have prophesied before the reformation made

by Josiah, which was in the eighteenth year of his reign. And as he predicts the destruction of Nineveh, chap. ii. 13, which could not have taken place before the sixteenth of Josiah, allowing with Berosus twenty-one years for the reign of Nabopolassar over the Chaldeans; we must, therefore, place this prophecy about the beginning of the reign of Josiah, or from 640 B.C. to 609 B.C.

2. *I will utterly consume all things.* All being now ripe for destruction, I will shortly bring a universal scourge upon the land. He speaks particularly of the idolaters.

3. *I will consume man and beast.* By *war,* and by *pestilence.* Even the waters shall be infected, and the fish destroyed; the air become contaminated, and the fowls die.

4. *I will cut off the remnant of Baal.* I think he refers here, partly at least, to the reformation which Josiah was to bring about. See the account, 2 Kings xxiii. 5. *The Chemarims.* The black-robed priests of different idols. See 2 Kings xxiii. 5. These were put down by Josiah.

5. *The host of heaven.* Sun, moon, planets, and stars. This worship was one of the most ancient and the most common of all species of idolatry; and it had a greater semblance of reason to recommend it. See 2 Kings xxiii. 5, 12; Jer. xix. 13; xxxii. 29. *That swear by the Lord, and that swear by Malcham.* Associating the name of an idol with that of the Most High. For *Malcham,* see Hos. iv. 15 and Amos v. 26.

6. *Them that are turned back.* Who have forsaken the true God, and become idolaters. *Nor enquired for him.* Have not desired to know His will.

7. *Hold thy peace at the presence of the Lord God.* Remonstrances are now useless. *The Lord hath prepared a sacrifice.* A slaughter of the people. *He hath bid his guests.* The Babylonians, to whom He has given a commission to destroy you.

8. *I will punish the princes, and the king's children.* After the death of Josiah the kingdom of Judah saw no prosperity, and every reign terminated miserably; until at last King Zedekiah and the king's children were cruelly massacred at Riblah, when Nebuchadnezzar had taken Jerusalem. *Strange apparel.* I really think this refers more to their embracing idolatrous customs and heathen usages than to their changing their dress.

9. *That leap on the threshold.* Or "that leap over the threshold." It is most probable that the Philistines are here meant. After the time that Dagon fell before the ark, and his hands were broken off on the threshold of his temple, his worshippers would no more set a foot upon the threshold, but stepped or leaped over it, when they entered into his temple.

10. *A cry from the fish gate.* This gate, which is mentioned in Neh. iii. 3, was opposite to Joppa; and perhaps the way in which the news came of the irruption of the Chaldean army, the *great crashing from the hills.* The second, or second city, may here mean a part of Jerusalem, mentioned in 2 Kings xxii. 14; 2 Chron. xxxiv. 22.

11. *Maktesh.* Calmet says this signifies a "mortar," or a rock in form of a mortar, and was the name of a quarter of Jerusalem where they hulled rice, corn, etc., according to St. Jerome. Some think the city of Jerusalem is meant, where the inhabitants should be beat and pounded to death as grain is pounded in a mortar.

12. *I will search Jerusalem with candles.* I will make a universal and thorough search. *That are settled on their lees.* Those who are careless, satisfied with the goods of this life.

14. *The great day of the Lord is near.* It commenced with the death of the good king Josiah, who was slain by Pharaoh-necho at Megiddo, and continued to the destruction of Jerusalem by Nebuchadnezzar.

15. *That day is a day of wrath.* From the fourteenth to the sixteenth verse inclusive

there is amplification of the disasters that were coming on Jerusalem; the invasion, incursion, attack, carnage, confusion, horrible din occasioned by the sound of the trumpet, the cries of the people, and the shrieks and groans of the dying, are pointed out with great force and mighty effect.

17. *They shall walk like blind men.* Be in the most perplexing doubt and uncertainty; and while in this state, have their blood poured out by the sword of their enemies, and their flesh trodden underfoot.

CHAPTER 2

The prophet, having declared the judgments which were ready to fall on his people, earnestly exhorts them to repentance, that these judgments may be averted, 1-3. He then foretells the fate of other neighboring and hostile nations: the Philistines, 4-7; Moabites and Ammonites, 8-11; Ethiopians, 12; and Assyrians, 13. In the close of the chapter we have a prophecy against Nineveh. These predictions were accomplished chiefly by the conquests of Nebuchadnezzar.

1. *Gather yourselves.* The Israelites are addressed.

3. *Ye meek of the earth.* Ye oppressed and humbled of the land. *It may be ye shall be hid.* The sword has not a commission against you. Ask God, and He will be a Refuge to you from the storm and from the tempest.

4. *Gaza shall be forsaken.* This prophecy is against the Philistines. They had been greatly harassed by the kings of Egypt; but were completely ruined by Nebuchadnezzar, who took all Phoenicia from the Egyptians; and about the time of his taking Tyre, devastated all the seignories of the Philistines.

5. *The sea coast, the nation of the Cherethites.* The *sea coast* means all the country lying on the Mediterranean coast from Egypt to Joppa and Gaza. The *Cherethites*—the Cretans, who were probably a colony of the Phoenicians. See 1 Sam. xxx. 14 and Amos ix. 7.

6. *And the sea coast shall be dwellings.* Newcome considers *keroth* as a proper name, not *cottages* or *folds.* The Septuagint have "Crete," and so has the Syriac.

7. *The coast shall be for the remnant.* Several devastations fell on the Philistines. Gaza was ruined by the army of Alexander the Great, and the Maccabees finally accomplished all that was predicted by the prophets against this invariably wicked people. They lost their polity, and were at last obliged to receive circumcision.

8. *I have heard the reproach of Moab.* God punished them for the curel part they had taken in the persecutions of the Jews; for when they lay under the displeasure of God, these nations insulted them in the most provoking manner. See Amos i. 13.

11. *He will famish all the gods of the earth.* They shall have no more sacrifices; their worship shall be entirely destroyed.

12. *Ye Ethiopians also.* Nebuchadnezzar subdued these. See Jer. xlvi. 2, 9; Ezek. xxx. 4, 10. See also Amos ix. 17.

13. *He will . . . destroy Assyria.* He will overthrow the empire, and Nineveh, their metropolitan city. See on Jonah and Nahum.

CHAPTER 3

The prophet reproves Jerusalem, and all her guides and rulers, for their obstinate perseverance in impiety, notwithstanding all the warnings and corrections which they had received from God, 1-7. They are encouraged, however, after they shall have been chastised for their idolatry, and cured of it, to look for mercy and restoration, 8-13; and excited to hymns of joy at the glorious prospect, 14-17. After which the prophet concludes with large promises of favor and prosperity in the days of the Messiah, 18-20. We take this extensive view of the concluding verses of this chapter because an apostle has expressly assured us that in every prophetical book of the Old Testament Scriptures are contained predictions relative to the gospel dispensation. See Acts iii. 24.

1. *Woe to her that is filthy!* This is a denunciation of divine judgment against Jerusalem.

2. *She obeyed not the voice.* Of conscience, of God, and of His prophets. *She received not correction.* Did not profit by His chastisements.

3. *Her princes . . . are roaring lions.* Tearing all to pieces without shadow of law, except their own despotic power. *Her judges are evening wolves.* Being a little afraid of the lionlike princes, they practice their unjust dealings from evening to morning, and take the day to find their rest. *They gnaw not the bones till the morrow.* They devour the flesh in the night, and gnaw the bones and extract the marrow afterwards.

4. *Her prophets are light and treacherous persons.* They betray the souls of the people for the sake of worldly honor, pleasure, and profit.

5. *The just Lord is in the midst thereof.* He sees, marks down, and will punish all these wickednesses. *Every morning doth he bring his judgment to light.* The sense is, says Bishop Newcome, "Not a day passes but we see instances of his goodness to righteous men, and of his vengeance on the wicked."

6. *I have cut off the nations.* Syria, Israel, and those referred to, Isa. xxxvi. 18, 20.

7. *Surely thou wilt fear me.* After so many displays of My sovereign power and judgments. *But they rose early.* And instead of returning to God, they practiced every abomination. They were diligent to find out times and places for their iniquity. This is the worst state of man.

8. *Wait ye upon me.* Expect the fulfillment of all My promises and threatenings; I am God, and change not. *For all the earth.* All the land of Judah.

9. *Will I turn to the people.* This promise must refer to the conversion of the Jews under the gospel. The *pure language* may here mean the form of religious worship. They had been before idolaters; now God promises to restore His pure worship among them.

10. *From beyond the rivers of Ethiopia.* This may denote both Africa and southern Arabia.

14. *Sing, O daughter of Zion.* Here is not only a gracious prophetic promise of their restoration from captivity, but of their conversion to God through Christ.

15. *The king of Israel, even the Lord, is in the midst of thee.* They have never had a king since the death of Zedekiah, and never shall have one till they have the King Messiah to reign among them; and this promise refers to that event.

16. *Fear thou not.* You shall have no more captivities nor national afflictions. *Let not thine hands be slack.* This may refer, first, to the rebuilding of the Temple of God, after the return from Babylon; and, secondly, to their diligence and zeal in the Christian Church.

17. *The Lord thy God.* Yehovah Eloheycha, "The self-existent and eternal Being, who is in covenant with you"; the character of God in reference to the Jews when standing in the nearest relation to them. *Is mighty.* Gibbor, is the "prevailing One," the "all-conquering Hero." The character which is given to Christ, Isa. ix. 6: "His name shall be called *El gibbor,* the prevailing Almighty God." *He will save.* "Deliver" you from all the power, from all the guilt, and from all the pollution of your sins; and when thus saved, *he will rejoice over thee with joy,* with peculiar gladness. *He will rest in his love*—He will renew His love. He will show the same love to you that He did of old to Abraham, Isaac, and Jacob.

18. *I will gather . . . sorrowful.* This may refer to those who, during the Captivity, mourned for their former religious assemblies; and who were reproached by their enemies because they could not enjoy their religious solemnities. See Psalm cxxxvii: "By the rivers of Babylon, there we sat down, yea, we wept, when we remembered Zion. . . . For there they that carried us away captive required of us a song," etc. This very circumstance may be the reference here.

19. *I will undo all that afflict thee.* They who have persecuted you shall be punished for it. It shows much malignity and baseness of mind to afflict or reproach those who are lying under the chastising hand of God. This was the conduct of the Edomites, Moabites, and Ammonites when the Jews were in adversity; and how severely did the Lord punish them for it! *I will save her that halteth.* See Mic. iv. 6, where there is a parallel place.

20. *At that time.* First, when the seventy years of the Babylonish captivity shall terminate. I will *bring you again* to your own land; and this restoration shall be a type of their redemption from sin and iniquity; and, at this time, and at this only, will they have *a name and a praise among all people of the earth,* not only among the Jews, but the Gentiles.

The Book of
HAGGAI

We know of the parentage of Haggai. He was probably born in Babylon during the Captivity, and appears to have been the first prophet sent to the Jews after their return to their own land. He was sent particularly to encourage the Jews to proceed with the building of the Temple, which had been interrupted for about fourteen years. Cyrus, who had published an edict empowering the Jews to return to Jerusalem and rebuild their city and Temple, revoked this edict in the second year of his reign, through the evil advice of his courtiers and other enemies of the Jews. After his death Cambyses renewed the prohibition; but after the death of Cambyses, Darius, the son of Hystaspes, renewed the permission; and Haggai was sent to encourage his countrymen to proceed with the work. Darius came to the throne about the year 521 B.C., and published his edict of permission for the Jews to rebuild the city and Temple in the second year of his reign, which was the sixteenth of their return from Babylon.

CHAPTER 1

The prophet reproves the people, and particularly their ruler and high priest, for negligence and delay in rebuilding the Temple; and tells them that their neglect was the cause of their having been visited with unfruitful seasons, and other marks of the divine displeasure, 1-11. He encourages them to set about the work, and on their doing so, promises that God will be with them, 12-15.

1. *In the sixth month.* Called *Elul* by the Hebrews. It was the sixth month of the ecclesiastical year, and the last of the civil year, and answered to a part of our September. *Zerubbabel the son of Shealtiel.* Who was son of Jeconiah, king of Judah, and of the family of David, and exercised the post of a governor among the people, but not over them, for both he and they were under the Persian government. But they were permitted to have Zerubbabel for their own governor, and Joshua for their high priest; and these regulated all matters relative to their peculiar political and ecclesiastical government. *Joshua the son of Josedech.* And son of Seraiah, who was high priest in the time of Zedekiah, and was carried into captivity by Nebuchadnezzar, 1 Chron. vi. 15. But Seraiah was slain at Riblah, by order of Nebuchadnezzar, 2 Kings xxv. 18-21.

2. *The time is not come.* They thought that the seventy years spoken of by Jeremiah were not yet completed, and it would be useless to attempt to rebuild until that period had arrived.

4. *Is it time for you?* If the time be not come to rebuild the Temple, it cannot be come for you to build yourselves comfortable houses. The foundation of the Temple had been laid fourteen years before, and some considerable progress made in the building, and it had been lying waste in that unfinished state to the present time.

5. *Consider your ways.* Is it fit that you should be building yourselves elegant houses, and neglect a place for the worship of that God who has restored you from captivity?

6. *Ye have sown much.* God will not bless you in any labor of your hands unless you rebuild His temple and restore His worship. This verse contains a series of proverbs, no less than five in the compass of a few lines.

8. *Go up to the mountains, and bring* wood. Go to Lebanon, and get timber. In the second year of the return from the Captivity, they had procured cedar trees from Lebanon, and brought them to Joppa, and had hired masons and carpenters from the Tyrians and Sidonians; but that labor had been nearly lost by the long suspension of the building. Ezra iii. 7.

9. *Ye looked for much.* You made great pretensions at first, but they have come to nothing. You did a little in the beginning, but so scantily and unwillingly that I could not but reject it. *Ye run every man unto his own house.* To rebuild and adorn it; and God's house is neglected!

10. *Therefore the heaven over you is stayed from dew.* It appears from the following verse that God had sent a drought upon the land, which threatened them with scarcity and famine.

12. *Then Zerubbabel.* The threatening of Haggai had its proper effect. The civil governor, the high priest, and the whole of the people united together to do the work. When the authority of God is acknowledged, His words will be carefully obeyed.

13. *Then spake Haggai.* He was the *Lord's messenger,* and he came with *the Lord's message,* and consequently he came with authority. *I am with you, saith the Lord.* Here was high encouragement. What may not a man do when God is his Helper?

15. *In the four and twentieth day.* Haggai received his commission on the first day of this month, and by the twenty-fourth day he had so completely succeeded that he had the satisfaction of seeing the whole people engaged heartily in the Lord's work; they left their own houses to build that of the Lord.

CHAPTER 2

When this prophecy was uttered, about four years before the Temple was finished, and sixty-eight after the former one was destroyed, it appears that some old men among the Jews were greatly dispirited on account of its being so much inferior in magnificence to that of Solomon. Compare Ezra iii. 12. To raise the spirits of the people, and encourage them to proceed with the work, the prophet assures them that the glory of the second Temple should be greater than that of the first, alluding perhaps to the glorious doctrines which should be preached in it by Jesus Christ and His apostles, 1-9. He then shows the people that the oblations brought by their priests could not sanctify them while they were unclean by their neglect of the Temple; and to convince them that the difficult times they had experienced during that neglect proceeded from that cause, he promises fruitful seasons from that day forward, 10-19. The concluding verses contain a prediction of the mighty revolutions that should take place by the setting up of the kingdom of Christ under the type of Zerubbabel, 20-23. As the time which elapsed between the date of the prophecy and the dreadful concussion of nations is termed, in v. 6, "a little while," the words may likewise have reference to some temporal revolutions then near, such as the commotions of Babylon in the reign of Darius, the Macedonian conquests in Persia, and the wars between the successors of Alexander. But the aspect of the prophecy is more directly to the amazing victories of the Romans, who, in the time of Haggai and Zechariah, were on the very eve of their successful career, and in the lapse of a few centuries subjugated the whole habitable globe; and therefore, in a very good sense, God may be said by these people to have shaken the heavens, and the earth, and the sea, and the dry land, and thus to have prepared the way for the opening of the gospel dispensation. See Heb. xii. 25-29. Others have referred this prophecy to the period of our Lord's second advent, to which there is no doubt it is also applicable, and when it will be in the most signal manner fulfilled. That the convulsion of the nations introducing this most stupendous event will be very great and terrible is sufficiently plain from Isaiah xxxiv—xxxv, as well as from many other passages of Holy Writ.

1. *In the seventh month.* This was a new message, and intended to prevent discouragment, and excite them to greater diligence in their work.

3. *Who is left among you that saw this house in her first glory?* Who of you has seen the Temple built by Solomon? The foundation of the present house had been laid about fifty-three years after the destruction of the Temple built by Solomon, and though this prophecy was uttered fifteen years after the foundation of this second Temple, yet there might still survive some of those who had seen the Temple of Solomon. *Is it not in your eyes?* Most certainly the Jews at this time had neither men nor means to make any such splendid building as that erected by Solomon. The present was as nothing when compared with the former.

4. *Yet now be strong.* Do not let this discourage you. The chief glory of the Temple is not its splendid building, but My presence; and as I covenanted to be with you when you came out of Egypt, so I will fulfill My covenant, for "my spirit remaineth among you: fear ye not," v. 5.

6. *Yet once, it is a little while, and I will shake the heavens.* "The political or religious revolutions which were to be effected in the world, or both," says Archbishop Newcome, "are here referred to; compare vv. 21-22; Matt. xxiv. 29; Heb. xii. 26-28."

7. *And the desire of all nations shall come.* This is a difficult place if understood of a person; but *chemdath,* "desire," cannot well agree with *bau,* "they shall come." It is true that some learned men suppose that *chemdoth,* "desirable things," may have been the original reading; but this is supported by no MS. It is generally understood of the desirable or valuable things which the different nations should bring into the Temple, and it is certain that many rich presents were brought into this Temple. All are puzzled with it. But the principal difficulty lies in the verb *ubau,* "they shall come." God says He will *shake* or stir up *all nations;* that these nations shall bring their desirable things; that the house shall be filled with God's glory; that the silver and gold, which these nations are

represented as bringing by way of gifts, are the Lord's; and that the glory of this latter house shall exceed the former. I cannot see how the words can apply to Jesus Christ, even if the construction were less embarrassed than it is, because I cannot see how He could be called the Desire of all nations. The whole seems to be a metaphorical description of the Church of Christ, and of His filling it with all the excellences of the Gentile world, when the fullness of the Gentiles shall be brought in.

9. *And in this place will I give peace.* Shalom, "a peace offering," as well as *peace* itself; or Jesus Christ, who is called the "Prince of Peace," through whom peace is proclaimed between God and man. But it is said that *the glory of this latter house shall be greater than of the former,* because under it the grand scheme of human salvation was exhibited, and the redemption price paid down for a lost world. As all probably applies to the Christian Church, the real house of God, its glory was most certainly greater than any glory which was ever possessed by that of the Jews.

10. *In the four and twentieth day of the ninth month.* Three months after they had begun to rebuild the Temple, Haggai is ordered to go and put two questions to the priests. (1) "If one bear holy flesh in the skirt of his garment," and he touch anything with his skirt, is that thing made holy? The priests answered, No! v. 12. (2) If one has touched a dead body, and thereby become unclean, does he communicate his uncleanness to whatever he may touch? And the priests answered, Yes! v. 13.

14. *Then answered Haggai . . . So is this people.* As an unclean man communicates his uncleanness to everything he touches, so are you unclean, and whatever you have hitherto done is polluted in the sight of God.

16. *Since those days were.* I have shown My displeasure against you, by sending blasting and mildew; and so poor have been your crops that *an heap of corn* which should have produced *twenty measures* produced only *ten;* and that quantity of grapes which in other years would have produced *fifty* measures, through their poverty, smallness, etc., produced only *twenty.* And this has been the case ever since the first stone was laid in this Temple; for your hearts were not right with Me, and therefore I blasted you "in all the labours of your hands; yet ye turned not to me," v. 17.

18. *Consider now from this day.* I will now change My conduct towards you; *from this day* that you have begun heartily to rebuild My temple and restore My worship, I will bless you. Whatever you sow, whatever you plant, shall be blessed; your land shall be fruitful, and you shall have abundant crops of all sorts.

20. *Again the word of the Lord came.* This was a second communication in the same day.

23. *And will make thee as a signet.* I will exalt you to high dignity, power, and trust, of which the seal was the instrument or sign in those days. You shall be under My peculiar care, and shall be to Me very precious. See Jer. xxii. 24; Cant. viii. 6. *For I have chosen thee.* He had an important and difficult work to do, and it was necessary that he should be assured of God's especial care and protection during the whole.

The Book of
ZECHARIAH

Zechariah was son of Berechiah, and grandson of Iddo. He returned from Babylon with Zerubbabel; and began to prophesy in the second year of the reign of Darius, son of Hystaspes, in the year before Christ, 516; in the eighth month of the holy years, two months after Haggai had begun to prophesy. These two prophets, with united zeal, encouraged at the same time the people to go on with the work of the Temple, which had been discontinued for some years.

Zechariah is the longest and the most obscure of all the twelve minor prophets. His style is interrupted, and without connection. His prophecies concerning the Messiah are more particular than those of the other prophets. The prophet Zechariah exactly foretold the siege of Babylon by Darius, son of Hystaspes. This prince laid siege to that rebellious city at the beginning of the fifth year of his reign, and reduced it at the end of twenty months. The prophets Isaiah and Jeremiah had foretold this calamity, and had admonished the Jews that inhabited there to make their escape when they perceived the time draw nigh. Isaiah says to them, "Go ye forth of Babylon, flee ye from the Chaldeans." And Jeremiah says, "Remove out of the midst of Babylon, and go forth out of the land of the Chaldeans, and be as the he goats before the flocks." And elsewhere, "Flee out of the midst of Babylon, and deliver every man his soul: be not cut off in her iniquity; for this is the time of the Lord's vengeance; he will render unto her a recompence." Lastly, Zechariah, a little before the time of her fall, writes thus to the Jews that were still in this city: "Ho, ho, come forth, and flee from the land of the north, saith the Lord; for I have spread you abroad as the four winds of heaven, saith the Lord. Deliver thyself, O Zion, that dwellest with the daughter of Babylon."

CHAPTER 1

The prophet earnestly exhorts the people to repentance, that they may escape such punishments as had been inflicted on their fathers, 1-6. The vision of the horses, with the signification, 7-11. The angel of the Lord successfully intercedes in behalf of Jerusalem, 12-17. The vision of the four horns, and of the four carpenters, 18-21.

1. *In the eighth month, in the second year of Darius.* This was Darius Hystaspes, and from this date we find that Zechariah began to prophesy just two months after Haggai.

3. *Turn ye unto me.* This shows that they had power to return, if they would but use it.

5. *Your fathers, where are they?* Israel has been destroyed and ruined in the bloody wars with the Assyrians; and Judah, in those with the Chaldeans. *The prophets, do they live for ever?* They also, who spoke unto your fathers, are dead; but their predictions remain; and the events which have taken place according to those predictions prove that God sent them.

6. *Did they not take hold of your fathers?* Everything happened according to the predictions, and they were obliged to acknowledge this; and yet they would not turn from their evil way.

7. *Upon the four and twentieth day of the eleventh month.* This revelation was given about three months after the former, and two months after they had recommenced the building of the Temple. *Sebat* answers to a part of our February. See Hag. ii. 18.

8. *I saw by night.* The time was emblematical of the affliction under which the Jews groaned. *A man.* An angel in the form of a man; sup-

posed to have been the Lord Jesus, who seems to have appeared often in this way, as a prelude to His incarnation; see Josh. v. 13; Ezek. i. 26; Dan. vii. 13; and x. 5. The same, probably, that appeared to Joshua with a drawn sword, as the captain of the Lord's host, Josh. v. 13-15. *A red horse.* An emblem of war and bloodshed. *Among the myrtle trees.* This tree was an emblem of peace, intimating that all war was shortly to end.

9. *O my lord, what are these?* The angel here mentioned was distinct from those mentioned in the eighth verse; he who talked with the prophet, v. 13.

10. *The man that stood among the myrtle trees.* The angel of the covenant, as above, v.

11. *Whom the Lord hath sent.* Who are constituted guardians of the land.

11. *All the earth sitteth still, and is at rest.* There is general peace through the Persian empire, and other states connected with Judea; but the Jews are still in affliction; their city is not yet restored, nor their Temple built.

12. *Then the angel of the Lord.* He who was among the myrtles—the Lord Jesus. *O Lord of hosts, how long?* Jesus Christ was not only the "Lamb slain from the foundation of the world," but was always the sole Mediator and Intercessor between God and man. *These threescore and ten years.* The time that had elapsed from the destruction of the Temple to the time in which the angel spoke.

13. *The Lord answered the angel.* And the angel told the prophet that the answer was gracious and comfortable. This answer is given in the next verse.

14. *I am jealous for Jerusalem.* I have for them a strong affection, and indignation against their enemies.

15. *I was but a little displeased.* I was justly displeased with My people, and I gave their enemies a commission against them; but they carried this far beyond My design by oppression and cruelty, and now they shall suffer in their turn.

16. *I am returned to Jerusalem with mercies.* Before, He came to them in judgments; and the principal mercy is, the house of the Lord shall be rebuilt, and the ordinances of the Lord re-established. *And a line shall be stretched forth.* The circuit shall be determined, and the city built according to the line marked out.

17. *My cities . . . shall yet be spread abroad.* The whole land of Judea shall be inhabited, and the ruined cities restored.

18. *And behold four horns.* Denoting four powers by which the Jews had been oppressed: the Assyrians, Persians, Chaldeans, and Egyptians.

20. *Four carpenters.* Four other powers, who should defeat the powers intended by the horns. These are the same as the four chariots mentioned in chap. vi. 1-3, 6-7. The first was Nabopolassar, father of Nebuchadnezzar, who overturned the empire of the Assyrians. The second was Cyrus, who destroyed the empire of the Chaldeans. The third was Alexander the Great, who destroyed the empire of the Persians. And the fourth was Ptolemy, who rendered himself master of Egypt.

21. *These are come to fray them.* To break, pound, and reduce them to powder. *Charashim* signifies either "carpenters" or "smiths"; probably the latter is here intended, who came with hammers, files, and suchlike, to destroy these horns, which no doubt seemed to be of iron.

CHAPTER 2

The vision with which this chapter opens portended great increase and prosperity to Jerusalem. Accordingly Josephus tells us (*Wars* v. iv. 2) that "the city, overflowing with inhabitants, extended beyond its walls," as predicted in the fourth verse, and acquired much glory during the time of the Maccabees; although these promises, and particularly the sublime image in the fifth verse, have certainly a still more pointed reference to the glory and prosperity of the Christian Church in the latter days, 1-5. See Revelation xxi—xxii. In consequence of these promises, the Jews, still inhabiting Babylon and the regions round about, are called upon to hasten home, that they might not be involved in the fate of their enemies, who were destined to fall a prey to the nations which they had formerly subdued, God's great love and zeal for his people moving Him to glorify them by humbling all their adversaries, 6-9. The most gracious promises of God's presence with His Church, and her consequent increase and prosperity, set forth in the remaining verses, 10-13, were to a certain extent fulfilled in the great number of proselytes made to Judaism after the return from the Captivity; but shall be more fully accomplished after the restoration of the Jews to the favor of God under the gospel. "For if the casting away of them [the natural Israel] be the reconciling of the world, what shall the receiving of them be, but life from the dead?"

1. *A man with a measuring line in his hand.* Probably a representation of Nehemiah, who got a commission from Artaxerxes Longimanus to build up the walls of Jerusalem; for hitherto it had remained without being enclosed.

4. *Run, speak to this young man.* Nehemiah must have been a *young man* when he was cupbearer to Artaxerxes. *As towns without walls.* It shall be so numerously inhabited as

not to be contained within its ancient limits. Josephus, speaking of this time, says, *Wars* v. iv. 2, "The city, overflowing with inhabitants, by degrees extended itself beyond its walls."

5. *I . . . will be unto her a wall of fire.* Her safety shall consist in My defense. I shall be as *fire round about* her. No adversary shall be permitted to touch her. Much of this must refer to the New Jerusalem.

6. *Flee from the land of the north.* From Chaldea, Persia, and Babylon, where several of the Jews still remained. See v. 7.

8. *After the glory.* After your glorious deliverance from the different places of your dispersion. He hath *sent me unto the nations which spoiled you,* that they may fall under grievous calamities, and be punished in their turn. On Babylon a great calamity fell, when besieged and taken by the Persians.

9. *I will shake mine hand upon them.* I will threaten first, and then stretch out My hand of judgment against them. *A spoil to their servants.* To those whom they had formerly subjected to their sway. As the Babylonians to the Medes and Persians; and so of the rest in the subversion of empires.

10. *I will dwell in the midst of thee, saith the Lord.* This must chiefly refer to the Christian Church, in which God ever dwells by the power of His Spirit, as He had done by the symbol of His presence in the first Jewish temple.

11. *Many nations shall be joined to the Lord.* This most certainly belongs to the Christian Church. No nation or people ever became converts to the Jewish religion, but whole nations have embraced the faith of our Lord Jesus Christ.

12. *The Lord shall inherit Judah his portion in the holy land.* This is a promise of the final restoration of the Jews, and that they should be God's portion in their own land.

13. *Be silent, O all flesh.* Let all the nations of the world be astonished at this. God will arise, and deliver this ancient people, and bring them into the glorious liberty of the sons of God.

CHAPTER 3

While the Jews were rebuilding their Temple, their adversaries endeavored to stop the work, Ezra v. This vision is therefore calculated to give them the strongest encouragement that God, after plucking them as brands out of the fire (or captivity of Babylon), would not now give them up, but would continue to prosper and favor them; and that notwithstanding the interruptions they should meet with, the work should be finished under the gracious superintendence of Providence; and their high priest, clothed in his pontifical robes, would soon officiate in the holy of holies, 1-7. The subject is then, by an easy transition, applied to a much greater future deliverance and restoration, of which Joshua and his companions, delivered now, are declared to be figures or types; for that the Messiah or Branch, the great High Priest typified by Joshua, would be manifested; and, like the principal stone represented in the vision, become the Chief Cornerstone of His Church; that the all-seeing eye of God would constantly guard it; and that by His atonement He would procure for it peace and pardon, 8-10.

1. *And he shewed me Joshua the high priest.* The Angel of the Lord is the Messiah, as we have seen before. Joshua, the high priest, may here represent the whole Jewish people; and *Satan,* the grand accuser of the brethren. There is a paronomasia here: *Satan* standing at his *right hand to resist him.* Satan signifies an

"adversary." *Lesiteno,* "to be his adversary," or accuser.

2. *Is not this a brand plucked out of the fire?* The Jews were nearly destroyed because of their sins; a remnant of them is yet left, and God is determined to preserve them. He has had mercy upon them, and forgiven them their sins. Would you have them destroyed?

3. *Joshua was clothed with filthy garments.* The Jewish people were in a most forlorn, destitute, and to all human appearance despicable, condition; and besides all, they were sinful, and the priesthood defiled by idolatry; and nothing but the mercy of God could save them.

4. *Take away the filthy garments.* The Jews wore sackcloth in times of public calamity; probably the filthy garments refer to this. Let their clothing be changed. I have turned again their captivity; I will fully restore them, and blot out all their iniquities.

5. *A fair mitre upon his head.* To signify that he had renewed to him the office of the high priesthood, which had been defiled and profaned before. The *mitre* was the bonnet which the high priest put on his head when he entered into the sanctuary, Exod. xxviii. 4, etc. *Clothed him with garments.* Referring to the vestments of the high priest.

9. *For behold the stone that I have laid.* Alluding no doubt to the foundation stone of the Temple. But this represented Christ Jesus: "Behold, I lay in Zion for a foundation a stone, a tried stone, a precious corner stone, a sure foundation," Isa. xxviii. 16. *Upon one stone shall be seven eyes.* This is supposed to mean the providence of God, as under it all the work should be completed. *I will engrave the graving thereof.* This is an allusion to engraving precious stones, in which the ancients greatly excelled. But what was *this* engraving? Was it not the following words? "I will remove the iniquity of that land in one day"; and was not this when Jesus Christ expired upon the Cross?

10. *Shall ye call every man his neighbour.* See Isa. xxxvi. 16. Everyone shall be inviting and encouraging another to believe on the Lord Jesus Christ, and thus taste and see that God is good. See Isa. ii. 2-3. And there shall be the utmost liberty to preach, believe on, and profess the faith of our Lord Jesus Christ.

CHAPTER 4

The prophet, overpowered by his last vision, is roused by the angel to behold another, 1; intended also to assure the Jews of the success of Joshua and Zerubbabel in building the Temple, and surmounting every obstacle in the way; till at length, by the good providence of God, it should be finished, amidst the joyful acclamations of the spectators, 2-10. The angel's explanation of the golden candlestick and of the two olive trees, 11-14.

1. *The angel . . . came again, and waked me.* Archbishop Newcome considers this vision as represented on the same night, chap. i. 8, with the preceding ones. See the latter part of v. 10 compared with chap. iii. 9. After some interval the prophet, overpowered with the vision which had been presented to him, was awakened from his prophetic trance as from a sleep.

2-3. *A candlestick all of gold.* This candlestick is formed in some measure after that of the sanctuary, Exod. xxv. 31-32. The *two olive trees* were to supply the bowl with oil; the *bowl* was to communicate the oil to the *seven pipes;*

and the seven pipes were to supply the *seven lamps.* In general, the candlestick, its bowl, pipes, lamps, and olive trees, are emblems of the pure service of God, and the grace and salvation to be enjoyed by His true worshippers.

6. *This is the word of the Lord unto Zerubbabel.* This prince was in a trying situation, and he needed especial encouragement from God; and here it is: *Not by might* (of your own), *nor by power* (authority from others), *but by my spirit*—the providence, authority, power, and energy of the Most High. In this way shall My temple be built; in this way shall My Church be raised and preserved.

7. *O great mountain.* The hindrances which were thrown in the way, the regal prohibition to discontinue the building of the Temple. *Before Zerubbabel . . . a plain.* The sovereign power of God shall remove them. March on, Zerubbabel; all shall be made plain and smooth before you. *He shall bring forth the headstone.* As he has laid the foundation stone, so shall he put on the headstone; as he has begun the building, so shall he finish it!

10. *Who hath despised the day of small things?* The poverty, weakness, and unbefriended state of the Jews. *And shall see the plummet in the hand of Zerubbabel.* He is master builder under God, the grand Architect. *Those seven . . . are the eyes of the Lord.* Either referring to His particular and especial providence or to those ministering spirits whom He has employed in behalf of the Jews, to dispense the blessings of that providence.

14. *These are the two anointed ones.* Joshua, the high priest; and Zerubbabel, the governor. These are *anointed*—appointed by the Lord; and *stand by* Him, the one to minister in the ecclesiastical, the other in the civil state.

CHAPTER 5

The vision of the large flying roll, with the angel's explanation, 1-4. The vision of the ephah, and of the woman sitting in it, with the signification, 5-11.

1. *Behold a flying roll.* This was twenty cubits long, and ten cubits broad; the prophet saw it expanded, and flying. Itself was the catalogue of the crimes of the people, and the punishment threatened by the Lord. Some think the crimes were those of the Jews; others, those of the Chaldeans. The *roll* is mentioned in allusion to those large rolls on which the Jews write the Pentateuch. One now lying before me is 153 feet long, by 21 inches wide, written on fine brown goatskin; some time since brought from Jerusalem, supposed to be 400 years old.

3. *Every one that stealeth . . . and every one that sweareth.* It seems that the roll was written on both the front and back. Stealing and swearing are supposed to be two general heads of crimes: the former comprising sins against men; the latter, sins against God. It is supposed that the roll contained the sins and punishments of the Chaldeans.

4. *Into the house of him.* Babylon, the house or city of Nebuchadnezzar, who was a public plunderer, and a most glaring idolater.

6. *This is an ephah that goeth forth.* This, among the Jews, was the ordinary measure of grain. The woman in the *ephah* is supposed to represent Judea, which shall be visited for its sins; the talent of lead on the ephah, within

which the woman was enclosed, the wrath of God, bending down this culprit nation, in the measure of its sins. For the angel said, "This is wickedness"; that is, the woman represents the mass of iniquity of this nation.

9. *There came out two women.* As the one woman represented the impiety of the Jewish nation, so these two women who were to carry the ephah, in which the woman "iniquity" was shut up, under the weight of a talent of lead, may mean the desperate unbelief of the Jews in rejecting the Messiah; and that impiety, or universal corruption of manners, which was the consequence of their unbelief, and brought down the wrath of God upon them. The strong *wings,* like those of *a stork,* may point out the power and swiftness with which Judea was carried on to fill up the measure of her iniquity, and to meet the punishment which she deserved. *Between the earth and the heaven.* Sins against God and man, sins which heaven and earth contemplated with horror. Or the Babylonians and Romans may be intended by the two women who carried the Jewish ephah to its final punishment. The Chaldeans ruined Judea before the advent of our Lord; the Romans, shortly after.

11. *To build it an house in the land of Shinar.* The land of *Shinar* means Babylon; and Babylon means Rome, in the Apocalypse. The building the house for the woman imprisoned in the ephah may signify that there should be a long captivity under the Romans, as there was under that of Shinar or Babylon.

CHAPTER 6

The vision of the four chariots drawn by several sorts of horses, 1-8. The other vision in this chapter may refer in its primary sense to the establishment of the civil and religious polity of the Jews under Joshua and Zerubbabel; but relates, in a fuller sense, to the Messiah, and to that spiritual Kingdom of which He was to be both King and High Priest. In Him all these types and figures were verified; in Him all the promises are yea and amen, 9-15.

1. *There came four chariots.* Four monarchies or empires. This is supposed to mean the same with the vision of the four horns, in chap. i. *Mountains of brass.* The strong barriers of God's purposes, which restrained those powers within the times and limits appointed by Jehovah.

2. *In the first chariot were red horses.* The empire of the Chaldeans, which overthrew the empire of the Assyrians. *The second chariot black horses.* The empire of the Persians, founded by Cyrus, which destroyed the empire of the Chaldeans.

3. *The third chariot white horses.* The empire of the Greeks, founded by Alexander the Great, which destoyed the empire of the Persians. *The fourth chariot grisled and bay horses.* That is, party-colored horses; or with horses, some grisled and some bay. The empire of the Romans or of the Greeks. The Greeks divided after the death of Alexander: one part pointing out the Lagidae, who attacked and subdued Egypt; and the other, the Seleucidae, who subdued Syria under Seleucus.

5. *The four spirits of the heavens.* Ministers of God's wrath against the sinful nations of the world.

6. *The black horses.* This refers to the second chariot; of the first the angel makes no mention,

because the empire designed by it had ceased to exist. This had red horses, to show the cruelty of the Chaldeans towards the Jews, and the carnage they committed in the land of Judea. *The black.* Cyrus, at the head of the Persians and Medes, bringing devastation and death among the Chaldeans, called the "north" in many parts of Scripture. *The white.* Alexander, who was splendid in his victories, and mild towards all that he conquered. *The grisled.* The Lagidae or Ptolemies, who founded an empire in Egypt; of these some were good, some bad, some despotic, some moderate, some cruel, and some mild; represented by the party-colored horses.

7. *And the bay went forth.* The Seleucidae, who conquered Syria and the upper provinces, and who wished to extend their conquests, and *sought to go, that they might walk to and fro through the earth,* were of unbounded ambition, and sought universal empire; such as Antiochus the Great. *So they walked to and fro,* did extend their conquests, and harassed many countries by their vexatious and almost continual wars.

8. *Have quieted my spirit in the north country.* They have fulfilled my judgments on Assyria and Chaldea. Nabopolassar and Cyrus first, against the Assyrians and Chaldeans; and Alexander next, against the Persians.

10. *Take of them of the captivity.* The names that follow were probably those to whom the silver and golden vessels of the Temple were instrusted. *The house of Josiah.* Probably an artificer in silver, gold, etc.

12. *Behold the man whose name is The BRANCH.* I cannot think that Zerubbabel is here intended; indeed, he is not so much as mentioned in chap. iii. 8. Joshua and his companions are called "figurative" or "typical" men. The crowning therefore of Joshua in this place, and calling him the branch, was most probably in reference to that glorious Person, the Messiah, of whom he was the type or figure. *And he shall grow up out of his place.* That is, out of David's root, tribe, and family. *And he shall build the temple of the Lord.* This cannot refer to the building of the Temple then in hand, for Zerubbabel was its builder; but to that temple, the Christian Church, that was typified by it. For Zerubbabel is not named here, and only "Joshua" or Jesus (the name is the same) is the Person who is to be crowned and to build this spiritual temple.

13. *Even he shall build the temple.* Joshua, not Zerubbabel. *He shall bear the glory.* Have all the honor of it, for none can do this but himself. The Messiah is still intended. *And shall sit and rule upon his throne.* For the government of the Church shall be upon His shoulder. *And he shall be a priest upon his throne.* He shall, as the great High Priest, offer the only available offering and atonement; and so He shall be both King and Priest, a royal King and a royal Priest, for even the *priest* is here stated to sit *upon his throne. And the counsel of peace shall be between them both.* The purpose to establish peace between heaven and earth must be between the Father and the Son.

15. *And they that are far off shall come.* The Gentiles shall come to the Saviour of the world; and *build*—become a part of this new

temple; for they, as living stones, shall become "an holy temple . . . an habitation of God through the Spirit." *Ye shall know that the Lord of hosts hath sent me.* These predictions, relative to the regal and sacerdotal offices of the Messiah, shall be so circumstantially fulfilled that you, Jews, shall be obliged to acknowledge that the Lord of hosts hath sent me with this message.

CHAPTER 7

Some Jews being sent from those who remained at Babylon to inquire of the priests and prophets at Jerusalem whether they were still bound to observe those fasts which had been appointed on occasion of the destruction of Jerusalem, and kept during the Captivity, the prophet is commanded to take this opportunity of enforcing upon them the weightier matters of the law, judgment and mercy, that they might not incur such calamities as befell their fathers. He also intimates that in their former fasts they had regarded themselves more than God; and that they had rested too much on the performance of external rites, although the former prophets had largely insisted on the superior excellence of moral duties, 1-14.

1. *The fourth year of King Darius.* Two years after they began to rebuild the Temple, see chap. i. 1. *The ninth month, even in Chisleu.* This answers to a part of our November and December. The names of the month appear only under and after the Captivity.

2. *When they had sent . . . Sherezer and Regem-melech.* To inquire whether the fasts should be continued, which they had hitherto observed on account of their ruined Temple; and the reason why they inquired was that they were rebuilding that Temple, and were likely to bring it to a joyful issue.

5. *When ye fasted and mourned in the fifth . . . month.* This they did in the remembrance of the burning of the Temple, on the tenth day of that month; and in the seventh month, on the third of which month they observed a fast for the murder of Gedaliah, and the dispersion of the remnant of the people which were with him. See Jer. xli. 1 and 2 Kings xxv. 25.

7. *The words which the Lord hath cried by the former prophets. Nebiim harishonim* is the title which the Jews give to Joshua, Judges, the two Books of Samuel, and the two Books of Kings. The "latter prophets," *nebiim acharonim,* are Isaiah, Jeremiah, Ezekiel, and the twelve minor prophets. *The south and the plain.* The *south* was the wilderness and mountainous parts of Judea; and the *plain,* the plains of Jericho.

11. *Pulled away the shoulder.* From under the yoke of the law, like an unbroken or restive bullock in the plough.

14. *I scattered them with a whirlwind.* This refers to the swift victories and cruel conduct of the Chaldeans towards the Jews. They came upon them like a whirlwind; they were tossed to and fro, and up and down, everywhere scattered and confounded.

CHAPTER 8

In this chapter God promises the continuance of His favor to those who are returned from the Captivity; so that, upon the removal of His judgments, the fasts they had observed during the Captivity may now be converted to so many occasions of rejoicing. He likewise promises in due time a general restoration of His people, and the enlargement of the Church by the accession of the Gentiles, 1-20. The conclusion of the chapter intimates further that the Jews, after their restoration, will be instrumental in converting many other nations, 21-23. Compare Rom. xi. 15-16.

2. *I was jealous.* Some refer this to the Jews themselves. They were as the spouse of Jehovah; but they were unfaithful, and God punished them as an injured husband might be expected to punish an unfaithful wife. Others apply it to the enemies of the Jews. Though I gave them a commission to afflict you, yet they exceeded their commission. I will therefore deal with them in *fury*—in vindictive justice.

3. *I am returned unto Zion.* I have restored her from her captivity. I will dwell among them. The Temple shall be rebuilt, and so shall Jerusalem; and instead of being false, unholy, and profligate, it shall be the *city of truth,* and My *holy mountain.*

6. *If it be marvellous.* You may think that this is impossible, considering your present low condition. But suppose it be impossible in your eyes, should it be so in Mine? *saith the Lord of hosts.*

7. *I will save my people from the east country, and from the west.* From every land in which any of them may be found. But these promises principally regard the Christian Church, or the bringing in the Jews with the fullness of the Gentiles.

9. *By the mouth of the prophets.* The day or time of the foundation was about two years before, as this discourse of the prophet was in the fourth year of Darius.

19. *The fast of the fourth month.* To commemorate the taking of Jerusalem, 2 Kings xxv. 3; Jer. xxxix. 2; and lii. 6-7. *The fast of the fifth.* In memory of the ruin of the Temple, 2 Kings xxv. 8; Jer. lii. 12-13. *The fast of the seventh.* For the murder of Gedaliah, Jer. xli. 1-17. *The fast of the tenth.* In commemoration of the siege of Jerusalem, which began on the tenth day of the tenth month, 2 Kings xxv. 1; Jer. lii. 4; Ezek. xxiv. 1-2; and see on chap. vii. 3, 5.

20. *There shall come people.* Similar promises to those in Isa. ii. 3 and in Mic. iv. 1-2.

23. *Ten men . . . shall take hold of the skirt of him that is a Jew.* The converts from among the Gentiles shall be to the Jews as ten to one. But *ten* may here signify a great number, without comparison.

CHAPTER 9

Syria, Phoenicia, and Palestine were conquered by Nebuchadnezzar, and afterwards by Alexander. Some apply the beginning of this chapter (1-7) to the one event, and some to the other. The close of the seventh verse relates to the number of Philistines that would become proselytes to Judaism (see Joseph. *Antiq.* xiv. 15, 4); and the eighth, to the watchful providence of God over His temple in those troublesome times. From this the prophet passes on to that most eminent instance of God's goodness to His Church and people, the sending of the Messiah, with an account of the peaceable tendency and great extent of His kingdom, 9-10. God then declares that He has ratified His covenant with His people, delivered them from their captivity, and restored them to favor, 11-12. In consequence of this, victory over their enemies is promised them in large and lofty terms, with every other kind of prosperity, 13-17. Judas Maccabeus gained several advantages over the troops of Antiochus, who was of Grecian or Macedonian descent. But without excluding these events, it must be allowed that the terms of this prophecy are much too strong to be confined to them; their ultimate fulfillment must therefore be referred to gospel times.

1. *The burden of the word of the Lord.* The oracle contained in the word which Jehovah now speaks. This is a prophecy against Syria, the Philistines, Tyre, and Sidon, which were to be subdued by Alexander the Great. After

this the prophet speaks gloriously concerning the coming of Christ, and redemption by Him.

Most learned men are of opinion that this and the succeeding chapters are not the work of Zechariah, but rather of Jeremiah, Hosea, or someone before the Captivity. It is certain that chap. xi. 12-13 is quoted in Matt. xxvii. 9-10, as the language of Jeremiah, the prophet. The first eight chapters appear by the introductory parts to be the prophecies of Zechariah. They stand in connection with each other, are pertinent to the time when they were delivered, are uniform in style and manner, and constitute a regular whole. But the last six chapters are not expressly assigned to Zechariah, and are unconnected with those that precede. The first three of them are unsuitable in many parts to the time when Zechariah lived; all of them have a more adorned and poetical turn of composition than the first eight chapters, and they manifestly break the unity of the prophetical book.

I conclude, from internal marks, that these three chapters (ix; x; xi) were written much earlier than the time of Jeremiah, and before the captivity of the ten tribes. They seem to suit Hosea's age and manner; but whoever wrote them, their divine authority is established by the two quotations from them, chap. ix. 9 and xi. 12-13.

The twelfth, thirteenth, and fourteenth chapters form a distinct prophecy, and were written after the death of Josiah, chap. xii. 11; but whether before or after the Captivity, and by what prophet, is uncertain, although I incline to think that the author lived before the destruction of Jerusalem by the Babylonians. See on chap. xiii. 2-6. They are twice quoted in the New Testament, chap. xii. 10 and xiii. 7 (Newcome).

My own opinion is that these chapters form not only a distinct work, but belong to a different author. If they do not belong to Jeremiah, they form a thirteenth book in the minor prophets, but the inspired writer is unknown.

The land of Hadrach. The valley of Damascus, or a place near to Damascus. Alexander the Great gained possession of Damascus, and took all its treasures; but it was without blood; the city was betrayed to him. *Damascus shall be the rest thereof.* The principal part of this calamity shall fall on this city. God's anger "rests" on those whom He punishes, Ezek. v. 13; xvi. 42; xxiv. 13. *When the eyes of man.* Newcome translates thus: "For the eye of Jehovah is over man, and over all the tribes of Israel." This is an easy sense, and is followed by the versions.

2. *And Hamath also shall border thereby.* Hamath on the river Orontes; and Tyre and Sidon, notwithstanding their political wisdom, address, and cunning, shall have a part in the punishment. These prophecies are more suitable to the days of Jeremiah than to those of Zechariah; for there is no evidence—although Alexander did take Damascus, but without bloodshed —that it was destroyed from the times of Zechariah to the advent of our Lord. And as Tyre and Sidon were lately destroyed by Nebuchadnezzar, it is not likely that they could soon undergo another devastation.

3. *And Tyrus did build herself.* The rock on which Tyre was built was strongly fortified; and that she had abundance of riches has been already seen, Ezek. xxviii. 1, etc.

4. *Will smite her power in the sea.* See Ezek. xxvi. 17. Though Alexander did take Tyre, Sidon, Gaza, etc., yet it seems that the prediction relative to their destruction was fulfilled by Nebuchadnezzar. See Amos i. 6-8; Zeph. ii. 4, 7.

5. *Ashkelon shall see it, and fear.* All these prophecies seem to have been fulfilled before the days of Zechariah—another evidence that these last chapters were not written by him. *Her expectation shall be ashamed.* The expectation of being succored by Tyre.

7. *I will take away his blood out of his mouth.* The Philistines, when incorporated with the Israelites, shall abstain from blood, and everything that is abominable. *And Ekron as a Jebusite.* As an inhabitant of Jerusalem. Many of the Philistines became proselytes to Judaism, and particularly the cities of Gaza and Ashdod. See Joseph. *Antiq.* lib. xiii, c. 15, s. 4.

8. *I will encamp about mine house.* This may apply to the conquests in Palestine by Alexander, who, coming with great wrath against Jerusalem, was met by Jaddua, the high priest, and his fellows in their sacred robes, who made intercession for the city and the Temple; and, in consequence, Alexander spared both, which he had previously purposed to destroy. He showed the Jews also much favor, and remitted the tax every seventh year, because the law on that year forbade them to cultivate their ground. See this extraordinary account in Joseph. *Antiq.,* lib. xi, c. 8, s. 5.

9. *Rejoice greatly, O daughter of Zion.* See this prophecy explained on Matt. xxi. 5. *Behold, thy King cometh.* Not Zerubbabel, for he was never king; nor have they had a king, except Jesus, the Christ, from the days of Zedekiah to the present time. *He is just.* The righteous One, and the Fountain of righteousness. *Riding upon an ass.* God had commanded the kings of Israel not to multiply horses. The kings who broke this command were miserable themselves, and scourgers to their people. Jesus came to fulfil the law. Had He in His title of King ridden upon a horse, it would have been a breach of a positive command of God; therefore He rode upon an ass, and thus fulfilled the prophecy, and kept the precept unbroken.

10. *I will cut off the chariot from Ephraim, and the horse from Jerusalem.* No wars shall be employed to spread the kingdom of the Messiah; for it shall be founded and established, "not by might, nor by power," but by the Spirit of the Lord of hosts, chap. iv. 6.

11. *As for thee also* (Jerusalem), *by the blood of thy covenant.* The covenant made with Abraham, Isaac, Jacob, and the Israelites in general, and ratified by the blood of many victims; until the time should come in which the Messiah should shed His blood, as typified by the ancient sacrifices. *I have sent forth thy prisoners.* Those who were under the arrest of God's judgments; the human race, fast bound in sin and misery, and who by the pitifulness of His tender mercy were loosed, He dying in their stead.

12. *Turn you to the strong hold.* Ye who feel your sins, and are shut up under a sense of your guilt, look up to Him who was delivered for your offenses, and rose again for your justification. *I will render double unto thee.* Give you an abundance of peace and salvation.

13. *When I have bent Judah.* Judah is the bow, and Ephraim is the arrows, and these are to be shot against the Greeks.

14. *The Lord shall be seen over them.* Shadowing and refreshing them, as the cloud did the camp in the wilderness.

16. *Shall save them in that day.* They are His flock, and He is their Shepherd; and, as His own, He shall save and defend them. *As the stones of a crown.* "Crowned stones erecting themselves"; i.e., being set up by themselves, as monuments of some deliverance, they seem to be lifting themselves up, offering themselves to the attention of every passenger.

CHAPTER 10

The promise of prosperity and plenty in the close of the preceding chapter leads the prophet to suggest, next, the means of obtaining them: supplication to Jehovah, and not to idols, whose worship had already proved a fertile source of calamities, 1-3. The rest of the chapter (like the preceding) promises to the Jews a restoration to their own land under rulers and governors, victory over their enemies, and much increase and prosperity; and this in a manner so miraculous that it is described, 4-12, by allusions to the deliverance from Egypt.

2. *The idols have spoken vanity.* This is spoken of the Jews, and must refer to their idolatry practiced before the Captivity, for there were no idols after. *Therefore they went their way.* They were like a flock that had no shepherd, shifting from place to place.

3. *Mine anger was kindled against the shepherds.* Bad kings and bad priests. *I punished the goats;* these were the wicked priests, who were shepherds by their office, and goats by the impurity of their lives.

4. *Out of him came forth the corner.* This is spoken of the tribe of Judah; all strength, counsel, and excellence came from that tribe. The cornerstone, the ornament and completion of the building; *the nail,* by which the tents were fastened, and on which they hung their clothes, armor, etc.; *the battle bow,* the choicest archers. *Every oppressor together.* Those heroes and generals by whom, under God, their foes should be totally routed. Perhaps all this is spoken of the Messiah.

5. *They shall be as mighty men.* The Maccabees and their successors. *Riders on horses.* The Macedonians, who opposed the Maccabees, and had much cavalry; whereas the Jews had none, and even few weapons of war, yet they overcame these horsemen.

6. *I will strengthen the house of Judah.* I doubt whether the sixth, seventh, eighth, and ninth verses are not to be understood of the future ingathering of the Jews in the times of the gospel. See Jer. iii. 14; xxiii. 6; Hos. i. 2; vi. 11.

7. *Ephraim shall be like a mighty man.* This tribe was always distinguished for its valor.

8. *I will hiss for them.* "I will shriek for them"; call them with such a shrill, strong voice that they shall hear Me, and find that it is the voice of their redemption.

11. *And he shall pass through the sea.* Here is an allusion to the passage of the Red Sea on their coming out of Egypt, and to their crossing Jordan when they went into the Promised Land. The waves or waters of both were dried up, thrown from side to side, till all the people passed safely through. When they shall return from the various countries in which they now sojourn, God will work, if necessary, similar miracles to those which He formerly worked for their forefathers; and the people shall be glad to let them go, however much they may be profited by their operations in the state. Those that oppose, as Assyria and Egypt formerly did, shall be brought down, and their sceptre broken.

CHAPTER 11

The commencement of this chapter relates to the destruction of Jerusalem and the Jewish polity, probably by the Babylonians; at least in the first instance, as the fourth verse speaks of the people thus threatened as the prophet's charge, 1-6. The prophet then gives an account of the manner in which he discharged his office, and the little value that was put on his labors. And this he does by symbolical actions, a common mode of instruction with the ancient prophets, 7-14. After the prophet, on account of the unsuccessfulness of his labors, had broken the two crooks which were the true badges of his pastoral office (to denote the annulling of God's covenant with them, and their consequent divisions and dispersions), he is directed to take instruments calculated to hurt and destroy, perhaps an iron crook, scrip, and stones, to express by these symbols the judgments which God was about to inflict on them by wicked rulers and guides, who should first destroy the flock, and in the end be destroyed themselves, 15-17. Let us now view this prophecy in another light, as we are authorized to do by Scripture, Matt. xxvii. 7. In this view the prophet, in the person of the Messiah, sets forth the ungrateful returns made to Him by the Jews, when He undertook the office of shepherd in guiding and governing them; how they rejected Him, and valued Him and His labors at the mean and contemptible price of thirty pieces of silver, the paltry sum for which Judas betrayed Him. Upon which He threatens to destroy their city and Temple, and to give them up to the hands of such guides and governors as should have no regard to their welfare.

1. *Open thy doors, O Lebanon.* Lebanon signifies the Temple, because built of materials principally brought from that place.

2. *Howl, fir tree.* This seems to point out the fall and destruction of all the mighty men.

3. *Young lions.* Princes and rulers. By *shepherds,* kings or priests may be intended.

4. *Feed the flock of the slaughter.* This people resemble a flock of sheep fattened for the shambles; *feed,* instruct, this people who are about to be slaughtered.

5. *Whose possessors.* Governors and false prophets, *slay them,* by leading them to those things that will bring them to destruction. *And they that sell them.* Give them up to idolatry.

6. *For I will no more pity.* I have determined to deliver them into the hands of the Chaldeans.

7. *And I will feed the flock of slaughter.* I showed them what God had revealed to me relative to the evils coming upon the land; and I did this the more especially for the sake of the poor of the flock. *Two staves.* Two shepherd's crooks. *One I called Beauty*—that probably by which they marked the sheep, dipping the end into vermillion, or some red liquid. And this was done when they were to mark every tenth sheep, as it came out of the field, when the tithe was to be set apart for the Lord. *The other I called Bands.* Probably that with the hook or crook at the head of it, by which the shepherd was wont to catch the sheep by the horns or legs when he wished to bring any to hand. *And I fed the flock.* These two rods show the beauty and union of the people, while under God as their Shepherd.

8. *Three shepherds also I cut off in one month.* Perhaps three orders may be intended: (1) The priesthood. (2) The dictatorship, including the scribes, Pharisees, etc. (3) The magistracy, the great Sanhedrin, and the smaller councils.

These were all annihilated by the Roman conquest.

10. *I took my staff . . . Beauty, and cut it asunder.* And thus I showed that I determined no longer to preserve them in their free and glorious state. And thus I brake My covenant with them, which they had broken on their part already.

11. *So the poor of the flock.* The pious, who attended to My teaching, saw that this was *the word*—the "design," of God.

12. *If ye think good, give me my price.* "Give me my hire." And we find they rated it contemptuously, thirty pieces of silver being the price of a slave, Exod. xxi. 32.

13. *And the Lord said unto me, Cast it unto the potter.* Jehovah calls the price of His prophet His own price; and commands that it should not be accepted, but given to a potter, to foreshadow the transaction related in Matt. xxvii. 7.

17. *Woe to the idol shepherd!* "The worthless" or "good for nothing" shepherd. The shepherd in name and office, but not performing the work of one. See John x. 11. *The sword shall be upon his arm.* Punishment shall be executed upon the wicked Jews, and especially their wicked kings and priests. See v. 16. *Arm*—the secular power; *right eye*—the ecclesiastical state. *His arm shall be clean dried up.* The secular power shall be broken, and become utterly inefficient. *His right eye shall be utterly darkened.* Prophecy shall be restrained; and the whole state, ecclesiastical and civil, shall be so completely eclipsed that none of their functions shall be performed.

CHAPTER 12

The first part of this chapter, with several passages in chap. xiv, relates to an invasion that shall be made on the inhabitants of Judea and Jerusalem in the latter ages of the world, some time after the restoration and settlement of the Jews in their own land. It also describes, in very magnificent terms, the signal interposition of God in their favor. From this the prophet proceeds in the latter part of the chapter, 10-14, to describe the spiritual mercies of God in converting His people; and gives a very pathetic and affecting account of the deep sorrow of that people when brought to a sense of their great sin in crucifying the Messiah, comparing it to the sorrow of a parent for his firstborn and only son, or to the lamentations made for Josiah in the valley of Megiddon, 2 Chron. xxxv. 24-25. A deep, retired sorrow, which will render the mourners for a season insensible to all the comforts and enjoyments of the most endearing society.

1. *The burden of the word of the Lord.* This is a new prophecy. It is directed to both Israel and Judah, though Israel alone is mentioned in this verse.

2. *Jerusalem a cup of trembling.* The Babylonians, who captivated and ruined the Jews, shall in their turn be ruined. I incline to think that what is spoken in this chapter about the Jews and Jerusalem belongs to the "glory of the latter times."

5. *The governors of Judah.* This supposes a union between the two kingdoms of Israel and Judah.

6. *Jerusalem shall be inhabited again.* This seems to refer to the future conversion of the Jews, and their return to their own land.

7. *The Lord also shall save the tents of Judah first.* This, I suppose, refers to the same thing. The gospel of Christ shall go from the least to the greatest. Eminent men are not the first that are called; the poor have the gospel preached to them. And this is done in the wise

providence of God, that the *glory of the house of David,* etc., that secular influence may appear to have no hand in the matter; and that God does not send His gospel to a great man because he is such.

10. *I will pour upon the house of David.* This is the way in which the Jews themselves shall be brought into the Christian Church.

11. *A great mourning.* A universal repentance. *As the mourning of Hadad-rimmon.* They shall mourn as deeply for the crucified Christ as their forefathers did for the death of Josiah, who was slain at *Hadad-rimmon in the valley of Megiddon.* See 2 Chron. xxxv. 24-25.

CHAPTER 13

After the humiliation and conversion of the Jews, foretold in the preceding chapter, they are here promised the full pardon of their sins, and a deliverance from idolatry and false prophets, 1-6. Prophecy concerning the death of the Messiah, and the persecution of His disciples, 7. The remaining verses may refer to those Jewish converts to Christianity who survived the calamities which their country suffered from the Romans, 8-9.

1. *In that day there shall be a fountain opened.* This chapter is a continuation of the preceding, and should not have been separated from it. *A fountain.* The source of mercy in Christ Jesus; perhaps referring to the death He should die, and the piercing of His side, when blood and water issued out. *To the house of David.* To David's family, and suchlike persons as it included. *Inhabitants of Jerusalem.* Suchlike persons as the Jews were in every part of their history. *For sin and for uncleanness.* For the removal of the guilt of sin, and for the purification of the soul from the uncleanness or pollution of sin.

2. *I will cut off the names of the idols.* There shall not only be no idolatry, but the very *names of the idols* shall be forgotten, or be held in such abhorrence that no person shall mention them. This prophecy seems to be ancient, and to have been delivered while idolatry had prevalence in Israel and Judah. *I will cause the prophets.* All false teachers.

4. *Neither shall they wear a rough garment.* A *rough garment* made of goats' hair, coarse wool, or the coarse pile of the camel, was the ordinary garb of God's prophets. And the false prophets wore the same; for they pretended to the same gifts, and the same spirit, and therefore they wore the same kind of garments. John Baptist had a garment of this kind.

6. *What are these wounds in thine hands?* Marks which he had received in honor of his idols. But he shall excuse himself by stating that he had received these marks in his own family; when, most probably, they had been dedicated to some of those idols. I do not think that these words are spoken at all concerning Jesus Christ. I have heard them quoted in this way, but I cannot hear such an application of them without horror. In quoting from the Old Testament in reference to the New, we cannot be too cautious. We may wound the truth instead of honoring it.

7. *Awake, O sword, against my shepherd.* This is generally understood of Jesus Christ. The sword is that of divine justice, which seemed to have been long asleep, and should long ago have struck either man or his Substitute, the Messiah. Jesus is here called God's *shepherd,* because He had appointed Him to feed

and govern, as well as to save, the whole lost world. *The man that is my fellow.* "Upon the strong man" or "the hero that is with me"; my neighbor. *Smite the shepherd, and the sheep shall be scattered.* This is quoted by our Lord, Matt. xxvi. 31, in relation to His disciples, who should be scattered on His crucifixion. And they were so; for every one, giving up all for lost, went to his own house. *And I will turn mine hand upon the little ones.* I will take care of the little flock, and preserve them from Jewish malice and Gentile persecution. And so this little flock was most wondrously preserved, and has been increasing from year to year from that time to the present day.

8. *Two parts therein shall be cut off.* In the war with the Romans. *But the third shall be left.* Those who believe on the Lord Jesus Christ shall be preserved alive; and not one of these perished in the siege, or afterwards, by those wars.

9. *I will bring the third part through the fire.* The Christian Church shall endure a great fight of afflictions, by which they shall be refined— not consumed. *I will say, It is my people.* The Church that I have chosen.

CHAPTER 14

The commencement of this chapter relates to the destruction of Jerusalem by the Romans, and to the calamities consequent on that event, 1-2. From this great Jewish tragedy the prophet immediately passes to the utter extermination of the enemies of Christianity in the latter days. God will display His power in behalf of His people in a manner so astonishing and miraculous that even they themselves, and much more their enemies, shall be struck with terror, 3-5. The national prosperity of the Jews shall then be permanent and unmixed, 6-7; and these people shall be made the instruments of converting many to the faith of the Messiah, 8-9. The great increase and prosperity of the Christian Church, the New Jerusalem, is then described in terms accommodated to Jewish ideas; and the most signal vengeance denounced against all her enemies, 10-19. From that happy period God's name will be honored in everything, and His worship everywhere most reverently observed, 20-21.

1. *Behold, the day of the Lord cometh.* This appears to be a prediction of that war in which Jerusalem was finally destroyed, and the Jews scattered all over the face of the earth, and of the effects produced by it.

2. *I will gather all nations.* The Romans, whose armies were composed of all the nations of the world. In this verse there is a pitiful account given of the horrible outrages which should be committed during the siege of Jerusalem and at its capture. *The residue of the people shall not be cut off.* Many were preserved for slaves, and for exhibition in the provincial theatres.

3. *Then shall the Lord go forth, and fight against those nations.* Against the Romans, by means of the northern nations, who shall destroy the whole empire of this once mistress of the world. But this is an obscure place.

4. *And his feet shall stand.* He shall appear in full possession of the place, as a mighty Conqueror. *And the mount of Olives shall cleave.* God shall display His miraculous power as fully in the final restoration of the Jews as He did when He divided the Red Sea, that their forefathers might pass through dry-shod. Some refer this to the destruction of the city by the Romans. It was on the Mount of Olives that Titus posted his army to batter Jerusalem. *And half of the mountain shall remove.* I really think that these words refer to the intrenchments, redoubts, etc., which the Romans made while carrying on the siege of this city; and particularly the lines or trenches which the army made on Mount Olivet itself.

5. *Ye shall flee to the valley.* Some think this refers to the valley through which Zedekiah and others endeavored to escape when Nebuchadnezzar pressed the siege of Jerusalem, but it appears to speak only of the Jewish wars of the Romans. *Azal.* This, as a place, is not known. If a place, it was most probably near to Jerusalem, and had its name from that circumstance.

6. *The light shall not be clear, nor dark.* Metaphorically, there will be a mixture of justice and mercy in all this.

7. *At evening time it shall be light.* At the close of this awful visitation, there shall be light.

8. *Living waters shall go out.* There shall be a wide diffusion of divine knowledge, and of the plan of human salvation, which shall go out by apostles and preachers, first from Jerusalem. *The former sea, and . . . the hinder sea.* The Dead Sea and the Mediterranean; see Joel ii. 20. These are metaphors. *In summer.* In time of drought; or in the countries where there was no knowledge of God, there shall these waters flow. The stream shall never cease; it shall run in *summer* as well as *winter*.

9. *And the Lord shall be king.* When this universal diffusion of divine knowledge shall take place. Wherever it goes, the laws of God shall be acknowledged; and, consequently, He shall be King over the whole earth.

10. *All the land shall be turned as a plain.* Or rather, "He shall encompass the whole land as a plain." He shall cast His defense all around it; from *Geba,* in Benjamin, north of Jerusalem (Josh. xxi. 17), to *Rimmon* in Judah, to the *south of Jerusalem,* Josh. xv. 32. *It shall be lifted up.* The city shall be exalted. *And inhabited in her place.* Jerusalem shall be rebuilt in the very place in which it originally stood. *From Benjamin's gate,* which was probably on the north side of Jerusalem, *unto the place of the first gate,* supposed to be that called "the old gate," Neh. iii. 6; xii. 39, placed by Lightfoot towards the southwest. *Unto the corner gate.* See 2 Kings xiv. 13. *The tower of Hananeel.* This tower and the corner gate seem to be placed as two extremities of the city.

16. *Shall even go up from year to year.* The Jews had three grand original festivals, which characterized different epochs in their history, viz.: (1) The Feast of the Passover, in commemoration of their departure from Egypt. (2) The Feast of Pentecost, in commemoration of the giving of the law upon Mount Sinai. (3) The Feast of Tabernacles, in commemoration of their wandering forty years in the wilderness. This last feast is very properly brought in here to point out the final restoration of the Jews, and their establishment in the light and liberty of the gospel of Christ, after their long wandering in vice and error.

20. *Holiness unto the Lord.* As the gospel is a holy system, preaching holiness and producing holiness in those who believe, so all without, as well as within, shall bear this impress; and even a man's labor shall be begun and continued and ended in the Lord; yea, and the animals He uses, and the instruments He works with, shall be all consecrated to God through Christ.

The Book of
MALACHI

CHAPTER 1

This chapter begins with showing the great and free favor which God had manifested to the Israelites, above what He had done to the Edomites, who are threatened with further marks of the divine displeasure; alluding, perhaps, to the calamities which they suffered from Judas Maccabeus and John Hyrcanus (see 1 Macc. v. 65 and Joseph. *Antiq.* xiii. 9), 1-5. God then reproaches His people, and especially their priests, for their ungrateful returns to His distinguished goodness, 6. They are particularly charged with sacrificing the refuse of beasts, 7-9, for which God threatens to reject them, 10, and choose other nations who will show more reverence to His name and worship, 11-14.

1. *The burden of the word of the Lord to Israel by Malachi.* This prophet is undoubtedly the *last* of the Jewish prophets. He lived after Zechariah and Haggai; for we find that the Temple, which was begun in their time, was standing complete in his. See chap. iii. 10. Some have thought that he was contemporary with Nehemiah; indeed, several have supposed that Malachi is no other than Ezra under the feigned name of "angel of the Lord" or "my angel." John the Baptist was the link that connected Malachi with Christ. According to Archbishop Ussher, he flourished in 416 B.C.; but the Authorized Version, which we have followed in the margin, states this even to have happened nineteen years later.

2. *Was not Esau Jacob's brother?* Have I not shown a greater partiality to the Israelites than I have to the Edomites? *I loved Jacob.* My love to Jacob has been proved by giving him greater privileges and a better inheritance than what I have given to Esau.

3. *And I hated Esau.* I have shown him less love, Gen. xxix. 30-31. I comparatively hated him by giving him an inferior lot. And now I have not only laid waste the dwelling place of the Edomites, by the incursions of their enemies, but (v. 4) they shall remain the perpetual monuments of My vengeance.

4. *They shall build, but I will throw down.* We have already seen enough of the wickedness of the Edomites to justify the utmost severity of divine justice against them. The pulling down predicted here was by Judas Maccabeus; see 1 Macc. v. 65; and by John Hyrcanus; see Joseph. *Antiq.*, lib. xiii, c. 9, x. 1. *They shall call them, The border of wickedness.* A wicked land. Among this people scarcely any trace of good could ever be noted.

5. *Your eyes.* You Israelites shall see, in your succeeding generations, that *the Lord will be magnified.* By His kindness in Israel, and His judgments beyond.

6. *A son honoureth his father.* I am your Father—*where,* then, *is mine honour?* Where your filial obedience? *If I be a master, where is my fear?* The respect due to Me.

7. *Ye offer polluted bread.* The priests, probably to ingratiate themselves with the people, took the refuse beasts, etc., and offered them to God; and thus the sacrificial ordinances were rendered *contemptible.*

11. *From the rising of the sun.* The total abolition of the Mosaic sacrifices, and the establishment of a spiritual worship over the whole earth, is here foretold.

12. *Ye have profaned it.* You have desecrated God's worship; is it any wonder that God should cast you off, and follow you with His judgments?

13. *Ye have snuffed at it.* A metaphor taken from cattle which do not like their fodder. They blow strongly through their noses upon it, and after this neither they nor any other cattle will eat it.

CHAPTER 2

The priests reproved for their unfaithfulness in their office, for which they are threatened to be deprived of their share of the sacrifice (the shoulder) and rewarded only with ignominy and ordure, 1-3. The degeneracy of the order is then complained of, and they are again threatened, 4-9. The rest of the chapter reproves the people for marrying strange and idolatrous women; and multiplying divorces, with all their consequent distress, in order to make way for such illicit alliances, 10-17. See Neh. x. 30 and xiii. 33, etc.

2. *Yea, I have cursed them already.* This may refer, generally, to unfruitful seasons; or, particularly, to a dearth that appears to have happened about this time. See Hag. i. 6-11.

3. *Behold, I will corrupt your seed.* So as to render it unfruitful.

4. *This commandment.* That in the first verse; to drive such priests from His presence and His service. *That my covenant might be with Levi.* I gave the priesthood and the service of My altar to that tribe.

5. *My covenant was with him of life and peace.* These are the two grand blessings given to men by the new covenant, which was shadowed by the Old. To man, excluded from the favor of God, and sentenced to death because of sin, God gave *berith,* a "covenant sacrifice," and this secured *life*—exemption from the death deserved by transgressors; communication of that inward spiritual life given by Christ, and issuing in that eternal life promised to all His faithful disciples. And, as it secured life, so it gave *peace,* prosperity, and happiness; peace between God and man, between man and man, and between man and his own conscience.

8. *But ye are departed out of the way.* You have become impure yourselves, and you have led others into iniquity.

9. *Therefore have I also made you contemptible.* The people despised you because they saw that you acted contrary to your functions.

10. *Have we not all one father?* From this to v. 16 the prophet censures the marriages of Israelites with strange women, which the law had forbidden, Deut. vii. 3. And also divorces, which seem to have been multiplied for the purpose of contracting these prohibited marriages. *Why do we deal treacherously?* Gain the affections of the daughter of a brother Jew, and then profane the covenant of marriage, held sacred among our fathers, by putting away this same wife and daughter!

11. *Daughter of a strange god.* Of a man who worships an idol.

12. *The master and the scholar.* He who teaches such doctrine, and he who follows this teaching, the Lord will cut off both the one and the other.

13. *Covering the altar of the Lord with tears.* Of the poor women who, being divorced by cruel husbands, come to the priests, and make an appeal to God at the altar; and you do not speak against this glaring injustice.

14. *Ye say, Wherefore?* Is the Lord angry with us? Because you have been *witness* of the contract made between the parties; and when the lawless husband divorced his wife, the wife of his youth, his companion, and the wife of his covenant, you did not execute on him the discipline of the law.

15. *And did not he make one?* One of each kind, Adam and Eve. *Yet had the residue of the spirit;* He could have made millions of pairs, and inspired them all with living souls. Then wherefore one? He made one pair from whom all the rest might proceed, that He might have a holy offspring; that children being a marked property of one man and one woman, proper care might be taken that they should be brought up in the discipline of the Lord. Perhaps the holy or *godly seed, zera Elohim,* "a seed of God," may refer to the Messiah.

16. *For the Lord . . . hateth putting away.* He abominates all such divorces, and him that makes them. *Covereth violence with his garment.* And He also notes those who frame idle excuses to cover the violence they have done to the wives of their youth, by putting them away, and taking others in their place, whom they now happen to like better, when their own wives have been worn down in domestic services.

17. *Ye have wearied the Lord.* He has borne with you so long, and has been provoked so often, that He will bear it no longer. It is not fit that He should.

CHAPTER 3

In allusion to the custom of sending pioneers to prepare the way for the march of an Eastern monarch, the coming of Christ's forerunner is described, and then the coming of Christ himself, 1; with the terrible judgments which were to accompany that event, in order to refine and purify His people and His priests, 2-6. The following verses reprehend them for withholding the legal tithes and offerings, with large promises in case of their repentance and amendments, 7-12. The prophet expostulates with the people for their hard and profane speeches against the conduct of Providence, and declares God will one day make a fearful and final distinction between the righteous and the wicked, whose different characters are in the meantime carefully recorded, 13-18.

1. *Behold, I will send my messenger.* Malachi, the very name of the prophet. But this speaks of John the Baptist. I, the Messiah, the Seed of God, mentioned above, *will send my messenger,* John the Baptist. *And the Lord, whom ye seek.* The Messiah, whom ye expect, from the account given by the prophet Daniel, chap. ix. 24. *Shall suddenly come to his temple.* Shall soon be presented before the Lord in His temple, cleanse it from its defilement, and fill it with His teaching and His glory. *The messenger of the covenant.* He that comes to fulfill the great design, in reference to the covenant made with Abram, that in his seed all the families of the earth should be blessed.

3. *He shall sit as a refiner.* Alluding to the case of a refiner of metals, sitting at his fire; increasing it when he sees necessary, and watching the process of his work. *The sons of Levi.* Those who minister in their stead under the new covenant, for the old Levitical institutions shall be abolished.

6. *I am the Lord, I change not.* The new dispensation of grace and goodness, which is now about to be introduced, is not the effect of any change in My counsels. It is, on the contrary, the fulfillment of My everlasting purposes; as is also the throwing aside of the Mosaic ritual, which was intended only to introduce the great and glorious gospel of My Son. And because of this ancient covenant, you Jews are not totally consumed; but you are now, and shall be still, preserved as a distinct people—monuments of both My justice and mercy.

8. *Will a man rob God?* Here is one point on which you are guilty; you withhold the *tithes* and *offerings* from the temple of God, so that the divine worship is neglected.

9. *Ye are cursed with a curse.* The whole nation is under My displeasure. The curse of God is upon you.

10. *Bring ye all the tithes.* They had so withheld these that the priests had not food enough to support life, and the sacred service was interrupted. See Neh. xiii. 10.

16. *They that feared the Lord.* There were a few godly in the land, who, hearing the language and seeing the profligacy of the rebels above, concluded that some signal mark of God's vengeance must fall upon them; they, therefore, as the corruption increased, cleaved the closer to their Maker. There are three characteristics given of this people: (1) They *feared the Lord.* They had that reverence for Jehovah that caused them to depart from evil, and to keep His ordinances. (2) They *spake often one to another.* They kept up the communion of saints. By mutual exhortation they strengthened each each other's hands in the Lord. (3) They *thought upon his name.* His name was sacred to them; it was a fruitful source of profound and edifying meditation.

17. *They shall be mine.* I will acknowledge them as My subjects and followers; in the day, especially, when I come to punish the wicked and reward the righteous. *When I make up my jewels.* My peculium, my "proper treasure"; that which is a man's own, and most prized by him.

CHAPTER 4

God's awful judgments on the wicked, 1. Great blessedness of the righteous, 2-3. The prophet then, with a solemnity becoming the last of the prophets, closes the Sacred Canon with enjoining the strict observance of the law till the forerunner already promised should appear, in the spirit of Elijah, to introduce the Messiah, and begin a new and everlasting dispensation. 4-6.

1. *Behold, the day cometh, that shall burn as an oven.* The destruction of Jerusalem by the Romans. *And all the proud.* This is in reference to v. 15 of the preceding chapter. *The day that cometh shall burn them up.* Either by famine, by sword, or by captivity. All those rebels shall be destroyed. *It shall leave them neither root nor branch.* A proverbial expression for total destruction.

2. *You that fear my name.* The persons mentioned in the sixteenth verse of the preceding chapter; you that look for redemption through the Messiah. *The Sun of righteousness.* The Lord Jesus, the promised Messiah, the Hope of Israel. *With healing in his wings.* As the sun, by the rays of light and heat, revives, cheers, and fructifies the whole creation, giving, through God, light and life everywhere; so Jesus Christ, by the influences of His grace and Spirit, shall quicken, awaken, enlighten, warm, invigorate, heal, purify, and refine every soul that believes in Him; and, by His wings or rays, diffuse these blessings from one end of heaven to another.

5. *Behold, I will send you Elijah the prophet.* This is meant alone of John the Baptist, as we learn from Luke i. 17, in whose spirit and power he came.

6. *And he shall turn* (convert) *the heart of the fathers to the children.* Or, together with the children; both old and young. *Lest I come and,* finding them unconverted, *smite the earth with a curse, cherem,* "utter extinction." So we find that, had the Jews turned to God, and received

the Messiah at the preaching of John the Baptist and that of Christ and His apostles, the awful *cherem* of final excision and execration would not have been executed upon them.

There are three remarkable predictions in this chapter: (1) The advent of John Baptist, in the spirit and authority of Elijah. (2) The manifestation of Christ in the flesh, under the emblem of the Sun of righteousness. (3) The final destruction of Jerusalem, represented under the emblem of a burning oven, consuming everything cast into it.

In most of the Masoretic Bibles the fifth verse is repeated after the sixth—"Behold, I send unto you Elijah the prophet, before the great and terrible day of Jehovah come"; for the Jews do not like to let their sacred book end with a *curse;* and hence, in reading, they immediately subjoin the above verse, or else the fourth—"Remember ye the law of Moses my servant."

In most MSS. and printed Masoretic Bibles there are only three chapters in this prophet, the fourth being joined to the third, making it twenty-four verses. In the Jewish reckonings the Twelve Minor Prophets make but one book.

I have this day completed this commentary, on which I have labored above thirty years; and which, when I began, I never expected to live long enough to finish. May it be a means of securing glory to God in the highest, and peace and goodwill among men upon earth! Amen, Amen.

ADAM CLARKE

Heydon Hall, Middlesex,
Monday, March 28, A.D. 1825.

THE NEW TESTAMENT

OF OUR LORD AND SAVIOUR JESUS CHRIST

The Gospel According to
MATTHEW

The general title of this latter collection of sacred books, which, as well as the former, all Christians acknowledge to have been given by immediate inspiration from God, is in the Greek *He Kaine Diatheke,* which we translate The New Testament, but which should rather be translated The New Covenant. Paul, 2 Cor. iii. 14, calls the sacred books before the time of Christ, *He Palaia Diatheke,* The Old Covenant. This apostle evidently considers the Old Testament and the New as two covenants, Gal. iv. 24, and in comparing these two together he calls one the old covenant, the other the new; one the first, the other that which is recent. In opposition to the old covenant, which was to terminate in the new, he calls this better, more excellent, Heb. vii. 22; 8:6; and everlasting, Heb. viii. 20, because it is never to be changed nor terminate in any other, and is to endure endlessly itself. The word covenant, from *con,* "together," and *venio,* "I come," signifies a contract or agreement made between two parties, to fulfill the conditions of which they are mutually bound.

The term *new covenant,* as used here, seems to mean that grand plan of agreement or reconciliation which God made between himself and mankind by the death of Jesus Christ; in consequence of which all those who truly repent and unfeignedly believe in the great atoning sacrifice are purified from their sins and united to God. Christ is called the Mediator of the new covenant, Heb. vii. 15. And referring to the ratification of this new covenant or agreement, by means of His own death, in the celebration of His last supper, Christ says, "This cup is the new testament [covenant] in my blood"; i.e., an emblem or representation of the new covenant ratified by His blood. See Luke xxii. 20.

The particular title to each of the following four books, in most Greek MSS. and printed editions, is the Gospel according to Matthew—Mark—Luke—John; i.e., the gospel or history of our blessed Lord as written and transmitted to posterity by each of these writers. Our word *gospel* comes from the Anglo-Saxon *godspel,* and is compounded of *god,* "good," and *spel,* "history, narrative, doctrine, mystery, or secret"; and was applied by our ancestors to signify the revelation of that glorious system of truth which had been in a great measure hidden or kept secret from the foundation of the world.

The Greek word *evangelion*—from *ev,* "good," and *anyelia,* a "message"—signifies good news, or glad tidings in general; and is evidently intended to point out, in this place, the good message or the glad tidings of great joy which God has sent to all mankind, preaching peace and reconciliation by Christ Jesus, who is Lord of all; proclaiming that He, as the promised Messiah, has, by the grace of God, tasted death for every man—for He has died for their offenses, and risen again for their justification—and that, through His grace, every sinner under the whole heaven may turn to God and find mercy.

CHAPTER 1

The genealogy of Christ, 1, divided into three classes of fourteen generations each: the first fourteen, from Abraham to David, 2-6; the second fourteen, from Solomon to Jechonias, 7-10; the third fourteen, from Jechonias to Christ, 11-16. The sum of these generations, 17. Christ is conceived by the Holy Ghost, and born of the Virgin Mary, when she was espoused to Joseph, 18. Joseph's anxiety and doubts are removed by the ministry of an angel, 19-20, by whom the Child is named Jesus, 21. The fulfillment of the prophecy of Isaiah relative to this, 22-23. Joseph takes home his wife, Mary, and Christ is born, 24-25.

1. *The book of the generation of Jesus Christ.* I suppose these words to have been the original title to this Gospel; and that they signify, according to the Hebrew phraseology, not only the account of the genealogy of Christ, but the history of His birth, acts, sufferings, death, resurrection, and ascension.

The phrase, "book of the generation," *sepher toledoth,* is frequent in the Jewish writings, and is translated by the Septuagint, *biblos geneseos,*

as here, by the Evangelist; and regularly conveys the meaning given to it above. E.g., "This is the book of the generations of Adam," Gen. v. 1; that is, the account of the life of Adam and certain of his immediate descendants. Again, "These are the generations of Jacob," Gen. xxxvii. 2; that is, the account or history of Jacob, his son Joseph, and the other remarkable branches of the family. And again, "These are the generations of Aaron and Moses," Num. 3:1; that is, the history of the life and acts of these persons and some of their immediate descendants. The same form of expression is also used in Gen. ii. 4, when giving the history of the creation of heaven and earth. *The son of David, the son of Abraham.* No person ever born could boast, in a direct line, a more illustrious ancestry than Jesus Christ. David, the most renowned of sovereigns, was king and prophet; Abraham, the most perfect character in all antiquity, was priest and prophet. But the three offices were never united except in the person of Christ; He alone was Prophet, Priest, and King. This threefold office Christ executes not only in a general sense, in the world at large, but in a particular sense, in every Christian soul. He is first a Prophet, to teach the heart of man the will of God. He is next a Priest, to apply that atonement to the guilty conscience, the necessity of which, as a Priest, He had previously made known. And lastly, as a King, He leads captivity captive, subdues and destroys sin, and reigns Lord over all the powers and faculties of the human soul. It is remarkable that the Evangelist names David before Abraham, though the latter was many generations older. The reason seems to be this, not only that David was not only the most illustrious of our Lord's predecessors, as being both king and prophet, but that promise which at first was given to Abraham was at last determined and restricted to the family of David. Son of David was an epithet by which the Messiah was afterwards known among the Jews.

8. *Joram begat Ozias.* Ozias was not the immediate son of Joram; there were three kings between them, Ahaziah, Joash, and Amaziah, which swell the fourteen generations to seventeen. But it is observed that omissions of this kind are not uncommon in the Jewish genealogies. Matthew took up the genealogies just as he found them in the public Jewish records, which, though they were in the main correct, yet were deficient in many particulars.

11. *Josias begat Jechonias.* There are three considerable difficulties in this verse: (1) Josias was not the father of Jechonias; he was only the grandfather of that prince, I Chron. iii. 14-16. (2) Jechonias had no brethren; at least, none are on record. (3) Josias died twenty years before the Babylonish captivity took place, and therefore Jechonias and his brethren could not have been begotten about the time they were carried away to Babylon. To this may be added a fourth difficulty, viz., there are only thirteen in this second class of generations; or forty-one, instead of forty-two, in the whole. But all these difficulties disappear by adopting a reading found in many manuscripts: And Josias begat Jehoiakim (or Joakim), and Joakim begat Jechonias.

12. *Jechonias begat Salathiel.* After Jechonias was brought to Babylon, he was put in prison by Nebuchadnezzar, where he continued till the death of this prince and the accession of Evil-merodach, who brought him out of prison, in which he had been detained thirty-seven years, and restored him to such favor that his throne (seat) was exalted above all the kings which were with him in Babylon, Jer. 3:31-32. But though he thus became a royal favorite, he was never restored in his kingdom. The term "carrying away to Babylon" would be more properly translated by the word transportation, which is here peculiarly appropriate. The change was not voluntary; they were forced away.

16. *Jesus, who is called Christ.* As the word *Christos*, Christ, signifies "the anointed or anointer," from *chrio*, "to anoint," it answers exactly to the Hebrew *mashiach*, which we pronounce Messiah or Messias. As the same Person is intended by both the Hebrew and Greek appellation, it should be regularly translated the Messiah, or the Christ.

17. *Fourteen generations.* The Jews had a sort of technical method of summing up generations in this way. In Synopsis, *Sohar*, p. 132, n. 18, we have the following words, "From Abraham to Solomon were fifteen generations and then the moon was at the full. From Solomon to Zedekiah were other fifteen generations; the moon was then in the wane, and Zedekiah's eyes were put out." That is, the regal state came to its zenith of light and glory in the time of Solomon, but decreased gradually, till it became nearly extinct in the days of Zedekiah.

18. *Espoused to Joseph.* The word refers to the previous marriage agreement, in which the parties mutually bound themselves to each other, without which no woman was ever married among the Jews. *Before they came together.* The woman was espoused at her own or her father's house, and generally some time elapsed before she was taken home to the house of her husband, Deut. xxii. 7; Judg. xiv. 7-8. Among the Jews the espousal, though the marriage had not been consummated, was considered as perfectly legal and binding on both sides; and hence a breach of this contract was considered as a case of adultery, and punished exactly in the same way. See Deut. xxii. 25-28. *She was found with child.* Her situation was the most distressing and humiliating that can be conceived. Nothing but the fullest consciousness of her own integrity and the strongest confidence in God could have supported her in such trying circumstances, where her reputation, her honor, and her life were at stake. What conversation passed between her and Joseph on this discovery we are not informed; but the issue proves that it was not satisfactory to him, nor could he resolve to consider her as his wife till God had sent His angel to bear the most unequivocal testimony to the Virgin's innocence. His whole conduct, on this occasion, was exceedingly benevolent and humane. He might at once have taken the advantage of the law, Deut. xxii. 23-24, and had her stoned to death.

19. *To make her a publick example.* Though Joseph was a righteous man, and knew that the law required that such persons as he supposed his wife to be should be put to death, yet, as righteousness is ever directed by mercy, he determined to put her away or divorce her privately, i.e., without assigning any cause, that her life might be saved. And as the offense was against himself, he had a right to pass it by if he chose.

20. *That which is conceived* (or formed) *in her.* It appears that the human nature of Jesus Christ was a real creation in the womb of the Virgin by the power of the Holy Spirit. *The angel of the Lord* mentioned here was probably the angel Gabriel, who six months before had been sent to Zacharias and Elisabeth to announce the birth of Christ's forerunner, John the Baptist. See Luke i. 36.

21. *Jesus.* The same as Joshua, *Yehoshua*, from *yasha*, "he saved, delivered, put to a state of safety." *He shall save his people from their sins.* This shall be His great business in the world, the great errand on which He is come, viz., to make an atonement for, and to destroy, sin. Deliverance from all the power, guilt, and pollution of sin is the privilege of every believer in Christ Jesus. The perfection of the gospel system is not that it makes allowances for sin,

but that it makes an atonement for it; not that it tolerates sin, but that it destroys it.

23. *Behold, a virgin shall be with child.* Both the divine and human nature of our Lord, as well as the miraculous conception, appear to be pointed out in the prophecy quoted here by the Evangelist: He shall be called *Im-Menu-El;* literally, "The strong God with us." "The Word" which "was God . . . was made flesh, and dwelt among us . . . full of grace and truth," John i. 1-14. So that we are to understand "God with us" to imply God incarnated—God in human nature. This seems further evident from the words of the prophet, Isa. 7:15, "Butter and honey shall he eat"—He shall be truly man, grow up and be nourished in a human, natural way; which refers to His being "with us," i.e., incarnated. To which the prophet adds, "That he may know to refuse the evil, and choose the good"—or rather, "According to His knowledge, reprobating the evil, and choosing the good." This refers to Him as God. Now this union of the divine and human nature is termed a sign or miracle, i.e., something which exceeds the power of nature to produce. And this miraculous union was to be brought about in a miraculous way: "Behold, a virgin shall conceive"—the only one that ever was, or ever shall be, a mother in this way. In what sense, then, is Christ "God with us"? Jesus is called Immanuel, or God with us, in His incarnation—God united to our nature, God with man, God in man; God with us by His continual protection; God with us by the influences of His Holy Spirit—in the Holy Sacrament—in the preaching of His Word—in private prayer; and God with us through every action of our lives that we begin, continue, and end in His name. He is God with us to comfort, enlighten, protect, and defend us in every time of temptation and trial, in the hour of death, in the day of judgment; and God with us and in us, and we with and in Him, to all eternity.

25. *Her firstborn son.* Literally, "That Son of hers, the firstborn One." That Mary might have had other children, any person may reasonably and piously believe; that she had others, many think exceedingly probable, and that this text is at least an indirect proof of it. *He knew her not.* Had no matrimonial intercourse with her— till she had brought forth that Son of hers of whom the Evangelist had been just speaking, the firstborn, the eldest of the family, to whom the birthright belonged, and who was miraculously born before she knew any man, being yet in a state of virginity. *He called his name Jesus.* This name was given by the command of God, see v. 16, and was imposed on Christ when eight days old; for then, according to the Jewish law, He was circumcised. The goodness of God is manifested, not only in His giving His Son to save a lost world, but also in the choice of the persons who were His progenitors; among whom we find, first, saints, to excite our courage: Abraham, remarkable for his faith; Isaac, for his obedience; and Jacob, for his fervor and constancy. Secondly, penitent sinners, to excite our confidence, such as David, Manasses, etc. Thirdly, sinners, of whose repentance and salvation we hear nothing, to put us on our guard. Four women are mentioned in this genealogy; two of these were adulteresses, Tamar and Bathsheba; and two were Gentiles, Rahab and Ruth,

and strangers to the covenant of promise; to teach us that Jesus Christ came to save sinners, and that, though strangers to His people, we are not on that account excluded from a salvation which God has designed for all men. He is not the God of the Jews only; He is also the God of the Gentiles.

CHAPTER 2

Wise men come from the East to worship Christ, 1-2. Herod, hearing of the birth of our Lord, is greatly troubled, 3; and makes inquiry of the chief priests and scribes where the Christ should be born, 4. They inform him of the prophecy relative to Bethlehem, 5-6. The wise men, going to Bethlehem, are desired by Herod to bring him word when they have found the Child, pretending that he wished to do Him homage, 7-8. The wise men are directed by a star to the place where the young Child lay, adore Him, and offer Him gifts, 9-11. Being warned of God not to return to Herod, they depart into their own country another way, 12. Joseph and Mary are divinely warned to escape into Egypt, because Herod sought to destroy Jesus, 13-14. They obey, and continue in Egypt till the death of Herod, 15. Herod, finding that the wise men did not return, is enraged, and orders all the young children in Bethlehem, under two years of age, to be massacred, 16-18. Herod dies, and Joseph is divinely warned to return to the land of Israel, 19-21. Finding that Archelaus reigned in Judea in place of his father, Herod, Joseph goes to Galilee and takes up his residence at Nazareth, 22-23.

1. *Bethlehem of Judaea.* This city is mentioned in Judg. xvii. 7. It is situated on the declivity of a hill about six miles from Jerusalem. *Beth-lechem* in Hebrew signifies "the house of bread." The name may be considered as very properly applied to that place where Jesus, the Messiah, the True Bread that came down from heaven, was manifested to give life to the world. *In the days of Herod the king.* This is Herod, improperly denominated "the Great," the son of Antipater, an Idumean. He reigned thirty-seven years in Judea, reckoning from the time he was created king of that country by the Romans. Our blessed Lord was born in the last year of his reign; and at this time the sceptre had literally departed from Judah, a foreigner being now upon the throne. *There came wise men from the east.* Or Magi "came from the Eastern countries." That many Jews were mixed with this people there is little doubt; and that these Eastern Magi, or philosophers, astrologers, or whatever else they were, might have been originally of that class there is room to believe. These, knowing the promise of the Messiah, were now probably, like other believing Jews, waiting for "the consolation of Israel." It is very probable that the persons mentioned by the Evangelist were a sort of astrologers, probably of Jewish extraction, that they lived in Arabia Felix, and came to worship their newborn Sovereign.

2. *We have seen his star.* Having discovered an unusual luminous appearance or meteor in the heavens, supposing these persons to have been Jews, and knowing the prophecies relative to the redemption of Israel, they probably considered this to be the star mentioned by Balaam, Num. xiv. 17. *In the east.* "At its rise." *To worship him.* Or "to do Him homage." The word signifies to crouch and fawn like a dog at his master's feet. It means to prostrate oneself to another, according to the Eastern custom which is still in use. As to what is here called a *star,* some make it a meteor, others a luminous appearance like an aurora borealis, others a comet. There is no doubt the appearance was very striking, but it seems to have been a simple meteor provided for the occasion.

3. *When Herod . . . heard these things, he was troubled.* Herod's consternation was probably occasioned by the agreement of the account of the Magi with an opinion predominant throughout the East, and particularly in Judea, that some great personage would soon make his appearance for the deliverance of Israel from their enemies, and would take upon himself universal empire.

4. *The chief priests.* Not only the high priest for the time being, and his deputy, with those who had formerly borne the high priest's office —but also the chiefs or heads of the twenty-four sacerdotal families, which David distributed into so many courses, 1 Chronicles xxiv. *Scribes.* The word in the Septuagint is used for a political officer, whose business it was to assist kings and civil magistrates, and to keep an account in writing of public acts and occurrences. Such an officer is called in Hebrew the king's scribe or secretary. See the Septuagint, II Kings 7:10. The word is often used by the Septuagint for a man of learning, especially for one skilled in the Mosaic law; and in the same sense it is used by the New Testament writers. It is therefore to be understood as always implying a man of letters, or learning, capable of instructing the people. The word is used in Acts xix. 35 for a civil magistrate at Ephesus, probably such a one as we would term recorder. It appears that Herod at this time gathered the whole Sanhedrin, in order to get the fullest information on a subject by which all his jealous fears had been alarmed.

6. *And thou Bethlehem, in the land of Juda.* To distinguish it from Bethlehem in the tribe of Zebulon, Josh. xix. 15. *Among the princes of Juda.* In Mic. v. 2 it is "the thousands of Judah." There is reason to believe that each tribe was divided into small portions called thousands. These thousands being petty governments, Matthew renders them by the word *hegemosin*, because the word princes or governors was more intelligible in the Greek tongue than thousands, though in this case they both signify the same. *That shall rule my people Israel.* Who shall feed My people—that is, as a shepherd feeds his flock. Among the Greeks, kings are called, by Homer, shepherds of the people.

8. *That I may come and worship him also.* See v. 2, and on Gen. xvii. 3 and Exod. iv. 31. What exquisite hypocrisy was here! He only wished to find out the Child that he might murder Him; but see how that God who searches the heart prevents the designs of wicked men from being accomplished!

9. *In the east.* Or "at its rise."

11. *They presented unto him gifts.* The people of the East never approach the presence of kings and great personages without a present in their hands. *Gold, and frankincense, and myrrh.* Some will have these gifts to be emblematic of the divinity, regal office, and manhood of Christ. "They offered Him incense as their God; gold as their King; and myrrh as united to a human body, subject to suffering and death." Rather, they offered Him the things which were in most esteem among themselves and which were productions of their own country. The gold was probably a very providential supply, as on it, it is likely, they subsisted while in Egypt.

13. *Flee into Egypt.* Many Jews had settled in Egypt; not only those who had fled thither

in the time of Jeremiah, see chap. 48, but many others who had settled there also on account of the temple which Onias IV had built at Heliopolis.

15. *Out of Egypt have I called my son.* This is quoted from Hos. 11:1, where the deliverance of Israel, and that only, is referred to. But as that deliverance was extraordinary, it is very likely that it had passed into a proverb, so that "Out of Egypt have I called my son" might have been used to express any signal deliverance.

16. *Slew all the children.* This cruelty of Herod seems alluded to in very decisive terms by Macrobius, who flourished toward the conclusion of the fourth century: "When he heard that among those male infants about two years old, which Herod, the king of the Jews, ordered to be slain in Syria, one of his sons was also murdered, he said: 'It is better to be Herod's hog than his son.'"

18. *In Rama was there a voice heard.* These words, quoted from Jer. xxxi. 15, were originally spoken concerning the captivity of the ten tribes, but are here elegantly applied to the murder of the innocents at Bethlehem. As Rachel might be said to weep over her children which were slaughtered or gone into captivity, so in Bethlehem the mothers bitterly lamented their children because they were slain.

20. *They are dead.* Both Herod and Antipater, his son; though some think the plural is here used for the singular, and that the death of Herod alone is here intended. But as Herod's son Antipater was at this time heir apparent to the throne, and he had cleared his way to it by procuring the death of both his elder brothers, he is probably alluded to here, as doubtless he entered into his father's designs. *They are dead* —Antipater was put to death by his father's command, five days before this execrable tyrant went to his own place.

22. *When he heard that Archelaus did reign.* This son partook of the cruel and bloodthirsty disposition of his father. At one of the Passovers he caused 3,000 of the people to be put to death in the Temple and city. For his tyranny and cruelty Augustus deprived him of the government and banished him. His character considered, Joseph, with great propriety, forbore to settle under his jurisdiction. He turned aside into the parts of Galilee. Here Antipas governed, who is allowed to have been of comparatively mild disposition. He was besides in a state of enmity with his brother Archelaus.

23. *That it might be fulfilled which was spoken by the prophets.* It is difficult to ascertain by what prophets this was spoken. The margin usually refers to Judg. 13:5, where the angel, foretelling the birth of Samson, says, "No razor shall come on his head: for the child shall be a Nazarite [*nezir*] unto God from the womb." The second passage usually referred to is Isa. 11:1: "There shall come forth a rod out of the stem of Jesse, and a Branch [*netser*] shall grow out of his roots." That this refers to Christ, there is no doubt. Jer. xxiii. 5 is supposed to speak in the same language, "I will raise unto David a righteous Branch." But here the word is *tsemach*, not *netser;* and it is the same in the parallel place, Zech. iii. 8; vi. 12. Therefore these two prophets cannot be referred to. But the passages in Judges and Isaiah may have been in the eye of the Evangelist, as

well as the whole institution relative to the Nazarite. Gusset, Wolf, Rosenmuller, and others give four rules according to which the phrase *that it might be fulfilled* may be applied in the New Testament: (1) When the thing predicted is literally accomplished; (2) When that is done, of which the Scripture has spoken, not in a literal sense, but in a spiritual sense; (3) When a thing is done neither in a literal nor spiritual sense, according to the fact referred to in the Scripture, but is similar to that fact; (4) When that which has been mentioned in the Old Testament as formerly done is accomplished in a larger and more extensive sense in the New Testament. Matthew seems to quote according to all these rules, and it will be useful to the reader to keep them constantly in view.

CHAPTER 3

John the Baptist begins to preach, 1. The subject of his preaching, 2-3. Description of his clothing and food, 4. The success of his ministry, 5-6. His exhortation to the Pharisees, 7-9. He denounces the judgments of God against the impenitent, 10. The design of his baptism and that of Christ, 11-12. He baptizes Christ in Jordan, 13-15; who is attested to be the Messiah by the Holy Spirit, and a voice from heaven, 16-17.

1. *John the Baptist.* John, surnamed the Baptist because he required those to be baptized who professed to be contrite because of their sins, was the son of a priest named Zacharias, and his wife, Elisabeth, and was born about six months before our blessed Lord. *Came . . . preaching.* *Kerysson,* "proclaiming," as a herald, a matter of great and solemn importance to men; the subject not his own, nor of himself, but from that God from whom alone he had received his commission. *The wilderness of Judaea.* That is, the country parts, as distinguished from the city.

2. *Repent.* This was the matter of the preaching. The sinner is led to understand that the way he has walked in is the way of misery, death, and hell. *The kingdom of heaven is at hand.* Referring to the prophecy of Daniel (vii. 13-14) where the reign of Christ among men is expressly foretold. This phrase and "the kingdom of God" mean the same thing—the dispensation of infinite mercy and manifestation of eternal truth by Christ Jesus, producing the true knowledge of God, accompanied with that worship which is pure and holy, worthy of that God who is its Institutor and its Object. But why is this called a Kingdom? Because it has its laws, all the moral precepts of the gospel; its subjects, all who believe in Christ Jesus; and its King, the Sovereign of heaven and earth. Jesus Christ never saved a soul which He did not govern, nor is this Christ precious or estimable to any man who does not feel a spirit of subjection to the divine will. But why is it called the kingdom of Heaven? Because God designed that His kingdom of grace here should resemble the Kingdom of glory above. It is further added, This Kingdom *is at hand.* The dispensation of the glorious gospel was now about to be fully opened, and the Jews were to have the first offers of salvation. This Kingdom is also at hand to us; and wherever Christ crucified is preached, there is salvation to be found.

3. *The voice of one crying in the wilderness.* Or a voice of a crier in the wilderness. This is quoted from Isa. xi. 3, which clearly proves that John the Baptist was the person of whom the prophet spoke. The idea is taken from the practice of Eastern monarchs, who, whenever they entered upon an expedition or took a journey through a desert country, sent harbingers before them to prepare all things for their passage; and pioneers to open the passes, to level the ways, and to remove all impediments. The Jewish church was that desert country to which John was sent to announce the coming of the Messiah. It was destitute at that time of all religious cultivation, and of the spirit and practice of piety; and John was sent to prepare the way of the Lord, by preaching the doctrine of repentance.

4. *His raiment of camel's hair.* A sort of coarse or rough covering, which it appears was common to the prophets, Zech. xiii. 4. In such a garment we find Elijah clothed, 2 Kings 1:8. And as John had been designed under the name of this prophet, Mal. iv. 5, whose spirit and qualifications he was to possess, Luke i. 17, he took the same habit and lived in the same state of self-denial. *His meat was locusts.* May either signify the insect called the locust, which still makes a part of the food in the land of Judea, or the top of a plant. Many eminent commentators are of the latter opinion, but the first is the most likely. *Wild honey.* Such as he got in the rocks and hollows of trees, and which abounded in Judea; see 1 Sam. xiv. 26. It is most likely that the dried locusts, which are an article of food in Asiatic countries to the present day, were fried in the honey, or compounded in some manner with it.

6. *Were baptized.* Were the people dipped or sprinkled? Those who are dipped or immersed in water, in the name of the Holy Trinity, I believe to be evangelically baptized; those who are washed or sprinkled with water in the name of the Father, and of the Son, and of the Holy Ghost, I believe to be equally so. *Confessing their sins.* Earnestly acknowledging that their sins were their own, thus taking the whole blame upon themselves, and laying nothing to the charge of God or man. This is essential to true repentance; and till a man take the whole blame on himself, he cannot feel the absolute need he has of casting his soul on the mercy of God, that he may be saved.

7. *Pharisees.* A very numerous sect among the Jews, who, in their origin, were very probably a pure and holy people. It is likely that they got the name of Pharisees, i.e., Separatists (from *pharash,* "to separate"), from their separating themselves from the pollution of the Jewish national worship. But in process of time, like all religious sects and parties, they degenerated; they lost the spirit of their institution. They ceased to recur to first principles, and had only the form of godliness, when Jesus Christ preached in Judea; for He bore witness that they did make the outside of the cup and platter clean—they observed the rules of their institution but the spirit was gone. *Sadducees.* A sect who denied the existence of angels and spirits, consequently all divine influence and inspiration, and also the resurrection of the dead. The Sadducees of that time were the materialists and deists of the Jewish nation. When the sect of the Pharisees arose cannot be distinctly ascertained, but it is supposed to have been some time after the Babylonish captivity. The

sect of the Sadducees were the followers of one Sadok, a disciple of Antigonus Sochaeus, who flourished about three centuries before Christ. *O generation of vipers.* A terribly expressive speech. A serpentine brood, from a serpentine stock. As their fathers were, so were they, children of the wicked one. This is God's estimate of a sinner, whether he wade in wealth or soar in fame. *The wrath to come.* The desolation which was about to fall on the Jewish nation for their wickedness, and threatened in the last words of their own Scriptures. See Mal. iv. 6. "Lest I come and smite the earth with a curse." This wrath or curse was coming; they did not prevent it by turning to God, and receiving the Messiah, and therefore the wrath of God came upon them to the uttermost.

10. *And now also the ax is laid.* Or, Even now the ax lieth. As if he had said, There is not a moment to spare—God is about to cut off every impenitent soul—you must therefore either turn to God immediately or be utterly and finally ruined. It was customary with the prophets to represent the kingdoms, nations, and individuals, whose ruin they predicted, under the notion of forests and trees doomed to be cut down. See Jer. xlvi. 22-23; Ezek. xxxi. 3, 11-12. The Baptist follows the metaphor; the Jewish nation is the tree, and the Romans the ax which, by the just judgment of God, was speedily to cut it down.

11. *But he that cometh after me,* or, is coming after me, who is now on His way, and will shortly make His appearance. Jesus Christ began His ministry when He was thirty years of age, Luke 3:23, which was the age appointed by the law, Num. iv. 3. John the Baptist was born about six months before Christ; and as he began his public ministry when thirty years of age, then this coming after refers to six months after the commencement of John's public preaching, at which time Christ entered upon His. *Whose shoes I am not worthy to bear.* This saying is expressive of the most profound humility and reverence. To put on, take off, and carry the shoes of their masters was not only among the Jews but also among the Greeks and Romans the work of the vilest slaves. *With the Holy Ghost, and with fire.* That the influences of the Spirit of God are here designed needs but little proof. Christ's religion is to be a spiritual religion, and was to have its seat in the heart. Outward precepts, however well they might describe, could not produce inward spirituality. This was the province of the Spirit of God, and of Him alone; therefore He is represented here under the similitude of fire, because He was to illuminate and invigorate the soul, penetrate every part, and assimilate the whole to the image of the God of glory.

12. *Whose fan is in his hand.* The Romans are here termed God's fan, as in v. 10 they were called His ax, and as in 12:7, they are termed His troops or armies. *His floor.* Does not this mean the land of Judea, which had been long, as it were, the threshing floor of the Lord? God says He will now, by the winnowing fan (viz., the Romans), throughly cleanse this floor. The *wheat,* those who believe in the Lord Jesus, He *will gather* into His *garner,* either take to heaven from the evil to come, or put in a place of safety, as He did the Christians by sending them to Pella previously to the destruc-

tion of Jerusalem. *But he will burn up the chaff*—the disobedient and rebellious Jews, who would not come unto Christ, that they might have life. *Unquenchable fire.* That cannot be extinguished by man.

14. *John forbad him.* Earnestly and pressingly opposed Him; this is the proper import of the words.

15. *To fulfil all righteousness.* That is, "every righteous ordinance"; so I think the words should be translated. But was this an ordinance? Undoubtedly; it was the initiatory ordinance of the Baptist's dispensation. Now as Christ had submitted to circumcision, which was the initiatory ordinance of the Mosaic dispensation, it was necessary that He should submit to this, which was instituted by no less an authority, and was the introduction to His own dispensation of eternal mercy and truth. But it was necessary on another account. Our Lord represented the high priest, and was to be the High Priest over the house of God. As the high priest was initiated into his office by washing and anointing, so must Christ; and hence He was baptized, washed, and anointed by the Holy Ghost. Thus He fulfilled the righteous ordinance of His initiation into the office of High Priest, and thus was prepared to make an atonement for the sins of mankind.

16. *The heavens were opened unto him.* That is, to John the Baptist—*and he,* John, *saw the Spirit of God . . . lighting upon him,* i.e., Jesus. This passage affords no mean proof of the doctrine of the Trinity. That three distinct Persons are here represented there can be no dispute: (1) The person of Jesus Christ, baptized by John in Jordan; (2) The person of the Holy Ghost in a bodily shape (Luke iii. 22) like a dove; (3) The person of the Father—a voice came out of heaven, saying, "This is my beloved Son." The voice is here represented as proceeding from a different place to that in which the persons of the Son and Holy Spirit were manifested; and merely, I think, more forcibly to mark this divine Personality.

17. *In whom I am well pleased.* "In whom I have delighted"—though it is supposed that the past tense is here used for the present. By this voice, and overshadowing of the Spirit, the mission of the Lord Jesus was publicly and solemnly accredited, God intimating that He had before delighted in Him; the law, in all its ordinances, having pointed Him out, for they could not be pleasing to God but as they were fulfilled in, and showed forth, the Son of Man, till He came.

CHAPTER 4

Jesus, in the wilderness, is tempted by Satan, 1-11. He goes into Galilee, 12; and Capernaum, 13. The prophecy which was thus fulfilled, 14-16. He begins to preach publicly, 17. Calls Simon Peter, and his brother Andrew, 18-20. Calls also James and John, the sons of Zebedee, 21-22. Preaches and works miracles throughout Galilee, 23. Becomes famous in Syria, and is followed by multitudes from various quarters, among whom he works a great variety of miracles, 24-25.

1. *Then was Jesus led up of the spirit.* This transaction appears to have taken place immediately after Christ's baptism; and this bringing up of Christ was through the influence of the Spirit of God, that Spirit which had rested upon Him in His baptism. *To be tempted.* The first act of the ministry of Jesus Christ was a

combat with Satan. Does not this receive light from Gen. iii. 15: "I will put enmity between" the woman's Seed and thy seed; "it shall bruise thy head, and thou shalt bruise his heel."

2. *And when he had fasted forty days.* It is remarkable that Moses, the great lawgiver of the Jews, previous to his receiving the law from God, fasted forty days in the mount; that Elijah, the chief of the prophets, fasted also forty days; and that Christ, the Giver of the new covenant, should act in the same way. Was not all this intended to show that God's kingdom on earth was to be spiritual and living? That it should not consist "in meat and drink; but righteousness, and peace, and joy in the Holy Ghost," Rom. xiv. 17?

3. *And when the tempter.* This onset of Satan was made (speaking after the manner of men) judiciously; he came when Jesus, after having fasted forty days and forty nights, was hungry. Now as hunger naturally diminishes the strength of the body, the mind gets enfeebled, and becomes easily irritated; and if much watching and prayer be not employed, the uneasiness which is occasioned by a lack of food may soon produce impatience, and in this state of mind the tempter has great advantages. *Command that these stones.* The meaning of this temptation is: "Distrust the divine providence and support, and make use of illicit means to supply Thy necessities."

4. *But by* (or upon,) *every word. Rhema* in Greek answers to *dabar* in Hebrew, which means not only "a word spoken" but also "thing, purpose, appointment." Our Lord's meaning seems to be this: God purposes the welfare of His creatures—all His appointments are calculated to promote this end. Some of them may appear to man to have a contrary tendency; but even *fasting* itself, when used in consequence of a divine injunction, becomes a means of supporting that life which it seems naturally calculated to impair or destroy.

5. *Pinnacle of the temple.* It is very likely that this was what was called the king's gallery; which, as Josephus says, "deserves to be mentioned among the most magnificent things under the sun: for upon a stupendous depth of a valley, scarcely to be fathomed by the eye of him that stands above, Herod erected a gallery of a vast height, from the top of which if any looked down, he would grow dizzy, his eyes not being able to reach so vast a depth."

6. *Cast thyself down.* Our Lord had repelled the first temptation by an act of confidence in the power and goodness of God, and now Satan solicits Him to make trial of it. Through the unparalleled subtlety of Satan, the very means we made use of to repel one temptation may be used by him as the groundwork of another. *He shall give his angels charge.* This is a mutilated quotation of Ps. xci. 11. The clause "to keep thee in all thy ways," Satan chose to leave out, as quite unsuitable to his design. That God has promised to protect and support His servants admits of no dispute; but as the path of duty is the way of safety, they are entitled to no good when they walk out of it. *In their hands they shall bear thee up.* This quotation from Ps. xci. 11 is a metaphor taken from a nurse's management of her child. In teaching it to walk, she guides it along plain ground; but when stones or other obstacles occur, she lifts up the child and carries it over them, and then sets it down to walk again.

7. *Thou shalt not tempt.* To expose myself to any danger naturally destructive, with the vain presumption that God will protect and defend me from the ruinous consequences of my imprudent conduct, is to tempt God.

8. *An exceeding high mountain, and sheweth him.* If the words *all the kingdoms of the world* be taken in a literal sense, then this must have been a visionary representation, as the highest mountain on the face of the globe could not suffice to make evident even one hemisphere of the earth, and the other must of necessity be in darkness. But if we take *the world* to mean only the land of Judea and some of the surrounding nations, as it appears sometimes to signify, then the mountain described by the Abbe Mariti (*Travels Through Cyprus,* etc.) could have afforded the prospect in question. Speaking of it, he says, "Here we enjoyed the most beautiful prospect imaginable. This part of the mountain overlooks the mountains of Arabia, the country of Gilead, the country of the Amorites, the plains of Moab, the plains of Jericho, the river Jordan, and the whole extent of the Dead Sea. It was here that the devil said to the Son of God, 'All these kingdoms will I give thee, if thou wilt fall down and worship me.'"

9. *If thou wilt fall down and worship me.* As if he had said, "The whole of this land is now under my government; do me homage for it, and I will deliver it into Thy hand."

10. *Get thee hence.* This temptation savoring of nothing but diabolical impudence, Jesus did not treat it as the others, but with divine authority commanded the tempter to return to his own place. In the course of this trial it appears that our blessed Lord was tempted: (1) to distrust—"command that these stones be made bread"; (2) to presumption, "Cast thyself down"; (3) to worldly ambition, "All these things will I give thee"; and (4) to idolatry, "Fall down and worship me," or do me homage. There is probably not a temptation of Satan but is reducible to one or other of these four articles. From the whole we may learn that: (1) No man, howsoever holy, is exempted from temptation; for God manifested in the flesh was tempted by the devil. (2) The best way to foil the adversary is by "the sword of the Spirit, which is the word of God," Eph. vi. 17. (3) To be tempted even to the greatest abominations (while a person resists) is not sin, for Christ was tempted to worship the devil. (4) There is no temptation which is from its own nature, or favoring circumstances, irresistible. God has promised to bruise even Satan under our feet. As I wish to speak what I think most necessary on every subject when I first meet it, and once for all, I would observe: (1) That the fear of being tempted may become a most dangerous snare; (2) That when God permits a temptation or trial to come, He will give grace to bear or overcome it; (3) That our spiritual interests shall be always advanced in proportion to our trials and faithful resistance; (4) That a more than ordinary measure of divine consolation shall be the consequence of every victory.

11. *Behold, angels came and ministered unto him.* That is, brought that food which was necessary to support nature.

13. *And leaving Nazareth.* Or entirely leaving Nazareth. It seems that, from this time, our blessed Lord made Capernaum His ordinary place of residence and utterly forsook Nazareth, because they had wholly rejected His word, and even attempted to take away His life (see Luke iv. 29). Galilee was bounded by Mount Lebanon on the north, by the river Jordan and the Sea of Galilee on the east, by Chison on the south, and by the Mediterranean on the west. *Nazareth,* a little city in the tribe of Zebulun, in lower Galilee, with Tabor on the east and Ptolemais on the west. It is supposed that this city was the usual residence of our Lord for the first thirty years of His life. *Capernaum,* a city famous in the New Testament but never mentioned in the Old. Probably it was one of those cities which the Jews built after their return from Babylon. Capernaum is well known to have been the principal scene of our Lord's miracles during the three years of His public ministry. *Zabulon,* the country of this tribe, in which Nazareth and Capernaum were situated, bordered on the Lake of Gennesaret, stretching to the frontiers of Sidon, Gen. xlix. 13. *Nepthalim* was contiguous to it, and both were on the east side of Jordan, Josh. 19:34.

15. *Galilee of the Gentiles.* Or of the nations. So called because it was inhabited by Egyptians, Arabians, and Phoenicians, according to the testimony of Strabo and others. The Hebrew *goyim* and the Greek *ethnon* signify "nations," and in the Old and New Testaments mean those people who were not descendants of any of the twelve tribes. The word *Gentiles,* from *gens,* "a nation," signifies the same. It was a regular tradition among the ancient Jews that the Messiah should begin His ministry in Galilee.

16. *The people which sat in darkness.* This is quoted from Isa. ix. 2, where, instead of sitting, the prophet used the word "walked." The Evangelist might change the term on purpose, to point out the increased misery of the state of these persons. Sitting in darkness expresses a greater degree of intellectual blindness than walking in darkness does. In the time of Christ's appearing the people were in a much worse state than in the time of the prophet, nearly seven hundred years before. *The region and shadow of death.* These words are amazingly descriptive. A region of death—death's country, where, in a peculiar manner, Death lived, reigned, and triumphed, subjecting all the people to his sway. *Shadow of death.* Used only here and in Luke 1:79, but often in the old covenant. As in the former clause death is personified, so here. Death is here represented as standing between the land above mentioned and the light of light, or Sun of righteousness; in consequence of which all the inhabitants were involved in a continual cloud of intellectual darkness, misery, and sin. The heavenly Sun was continually eclipsed to them till this glorious time when Jesus Christ, the true Light, shone forth in the beauty of holiness and truth. Christ began His ministry in Galilee, and frequented this uncultivated place more than He did Jerusalem and other parts of Judea; here His preaching was peculiarly needful, and by this was the prophecy fulfilled.

17. *Jesus began to preach, and to say, Repent.* Every preacher commissioned by God to proclaim salvation to a lost world begins his work with preaching the doctrine of repentance. This was the case with all the prophets, John the Baptist, Jesus Christ, all the apostles, and all their genuine successors in the Christian ministry.

18. *Simon called Peter, and Andrew his brother.* Why did not Jesus Christ call some of the eminent scribes or Pharisees to publish His gospel, and not poor, unlearned fishermen, without credit or authority? Because it was the kingdom of Heaven they were to preach, and their teaching must come from above. Besides, the conversion of sinners, though it be effected instrumentally by the preaching of the gospel, yet the Grand Agent in it is the Spirit of God.

19. *Follow me.* Come after Me. Receive My doctrines, imitate Me in My conduct—in every respect be My disciples. Following a person, in the Jewish phrase, signifies being his disciple or scholar.

20. *They straightway left their nets.* A change, as far as it respected secular things, every way to their disadvantage.

22. *Left the ship and their father.* By *the ship* we are to understand the fishing boat used for extending their nets in the water and bringing the hawser or rope of the farther end to shore, by which the net was pulled to land.

23. *Teaching in their synagogues.* Synagogue, from *syn,* "together," and *ago,* "I bring," a public assembly of persons, or the place where such persons publicly assembled. Synagogues, among the Jews, were probably not older than the return from the Babylonish captivity. They were erected not only in cities and towns, but in the country, and especially by rivers, that they might have water for the convenience of their frequent washings. Not less than ten persons of respectability composed a synagogue, as the rabbins supposed that this number of persons, of independent property and well-skilled in the law, were necessary to conduct the affairs of the place and keep up the divine worship. The chief things belonging to a synagogue were: (1) the ark or chest, made after the mode of the ark of the covenant, containing the Pentateuch; (2) the pulpit and desk, in the middle of the synagogue, on which he stood who read or expounded the law; (3) the seats or pews for the men below, and the galleries for the women above; (4) the lamps to give light in the evening service, and at the Feast of the Dedication; (5) apartments for the utensils and alms-chests. The synagogue was governed by a council or assembly, over whom was a president, called in the Gospels the ruler of the synagogue. These are sometimes called chiefs of the Jews, the rulers, the priests or elders, the governors, the overseers, the fathers of the synagogue. Service was performed in them three times a day—morning, afternoon, and night. *Preaching the gospel of the kingdom.* Or proclaiming the glad tidings of the Kingdom. Behold here the perfect pattern of an evangelical preacher: (1) He goes about seeking sinners on every side, that he may show them the way to heaven. (2) He proclaims the glad tidings of the Kingdom, with a freedom worthy of the King whom he serves. (3) He makes his reputation and the confidence of the people subservient not to his own interest, but to the salva-

tion of souls. (4) To his preaching he joins, as far as he has ability, all works of mercy and temporal assistance to the bodies of men. (5) He takes care to inform men that diseases and all kinds of temporal evils are the effects of sin, and their hatred to iniquity should increase in proportion to the evils they endure through it. (6) And that nothing but the power of God can save them from sin and its consequences.

24. *Possessed with devils* (demoniacs). Persons possessed by evil spirits. This is certainly the plain, obvious meaning of *demoniac* in the Gospels. Our common version, which renders the word "those . . . possessed with devils," is not strictly correct, as the word devil is not found in the plural in any part of the Sacred Writings when speaking of evil spirits; for though there are multitudes of demons (Mark v. 9), yet it appears there is but one devil, who seems to be supreme, or head, over all the rest. *Diabolos* signifies an accuser or slanderer (1 Tim. iii. 11; 2 Tim. iii. 3; Titus ii. 3). Perhaps Satan was called so (1) because he accused or slandered God in paradise (Gen. iii. 5), and (2) because he is the accuser of men (Rev. vii. 9-10). See also Job i. 2. *He healed them.* Either with a word or a touch; and thus proved that all nature was under His control.

25. This verse is immediately connected with the fifth chapter, and should not be separated from it. *Great multitudes.* This, even according to the Jews, was one proof of the days of the Messiah. *Decapolis.* A small country situated between Syria and Galilee of the nations. It was called *Decapolis* (from *deka,* "ten," and *polis,* a "city") because it contained only ten cities, the metropolis and most ancient of which was Damascus. *From beyond Jordan.* Or from the side of Jordan. Probably this was the country which was occupied anciently by the two tribes of Reuben and Gad, and the half-tribe of Manasseh.

CHAPTER 5

Christ begins His sermon on the mount. 1-2. The Beatitudes, 3-12. The disciples the salt of the earth, and light of the world, 13-16. Christ is not come to destroy, but confirm and fulfill, the law and the prophets, 17-19. Of the righteousness of the scribes and Pharisees, 20. Interpretation of the precepts relative to murder, anger, and injurious speaking, 21-22. Of reconciliation, 23-26. Of impure acts and propensities, and the necessity of mortification, 27-30. Of divorce, 31-32. Of oaths and profane swearing, 33-37. Of bearing injuries and persecution, 38-41. Of borrowing and lending, 42. Of love and hatred, 43-46. Of civil respect, 47. Christ's disciples must resemble their Heavenly Father, 48.

1. *And seeing the multitudes.* These *multitudes,* viz., those mentioned in the preceding verse, which should make the first verse of this chapter. *He went up into a mountain.* That He might have the greater advantage of speaking, so as to be heard by that great concourse of people which followed Him. Probably nothing more is meant here than a small hill or eminence. *And when he was set.* The usual posture of public teachers among the Jews, and among many other people. *His disciples.* Literally, a scholar. Those who originally followed Christ, considered Him in the light of a divine Teacher.

3. *Blessed.* Or, happy. Homer, *Iliad* i. 339, calls the supreme gods *theon makaron,* "the ever happy and immortal gods," and opposes them to mortal men. *Poor in spirit.* One who is deeply sensible of his spiritual poverty and wretchedness. In the original this means someone who

trembles or shrinks with fear. Being destitute of the true riches, he is tremblingly alive to the necessities of his soul, shrinking with fear lest he should perish without the salvation of God. Such Christ pronounces happy, because there is but a step between them and that Kingdom which is here promised. *Kingdom of heaven.* Or, "of the heavens." A participation of all the blessings of the new covenant here, and the blessings of glory above. See this phrase explained, chap. iii. 2.

4. *Blessed are they that mourn.* That is, those who, feeling their spiritual poverty, mourn after God, lamenting the iniquity that separates them from the Fountain of blessedness.

5. *Blessed are the meek.* Happy are those who are of a quiet, gentle spirit, in opposition to the proud and supercilious scribes and Pharisees, and their disciples. *For they shall inherit the earth.* Or "the land." Under this expression, which was commonly used by the prophets to signify the land of Canaan, in which all temporal good abounded, Judg. xviii. 9-10, Jesus Christ points out that abundance of spiritual good which was provided for men in the gospel. Besides, Canaan was a type of the kingdom of God; and who is so likely to inherit glory as the man in whom the meekness and gentleness of Jesus dwell?

6. *They which do hunger and thirst.* As the body has its natural appetites of hunger and thirst for the food and drink suited to its nourishment, so has the soul. When the soul is awakened to a sense of its wants, and begins to hunger and thirst after righteousness or holiness, which is its proper food, we know that it must be purified by the Holy Spirit, and be made a partaker of that living bread, John viii. 48, or perish everlastingly. Now, as God never inspires a prayer but with a design to answer it, he who hungers and thirsts after the full salvation of God may depend on being speedily and effectually blessed or satisfied, well-fed. *Righteousness* here is taken for all the blessings of the new covenant—all the graces of the Messiah's kingdom—a full restoration to the image of God!

7. *The merciful.* The word *mercy,* among the Jews, signified two things: the pardon of injuries, and almsgiving. Our Lord undoubtedly takes it in its fullest latitude here. *They shall obtain mercy.* Mercy is not purchased but at the price of mercy itself, and even this price is a gift of the mercy of God.

8. *Pure in heart.* In opposition to the Pharisees, who affected outward purity, while their hearts were full of corruption and defilement. A principal part of the Jewish religion consisted in outward washings and cleansings; on this ground they expected to *see* God, to enjoy eternal glory. But Christ here shows that a purification of the *heart* from all vile affections and desires is essentially requisite in order to enter into the kingdom of God. He whose soul is not delivered from all sin, through the Blood of the covenant, can have no scriptural hope of ever being with God. *Shall see God.* This is a Hebraism which signifies "possess God, enjoy His felicity," as seeing a thing was used among the Hebrews for possessing it.

9. *The peacemakers.* A peacemaker is a man who, being endowed with a generous public spirit, labors for the public good, and feels his

own interest promoted in promoting that of others. Therefore, instead of fanning the fire of strife, he uses his influence and wisdom to reconcile the contending parties, adjust their differences, and restore them to a state of unity.

10. *They which are persecuted.* They who are hard pressed upon, and pursued with repeated acts of enmity. They are happy who suffer seems a strange saying; and that the righteous should suffer merely because they are such seems as strange. But such is the enmity of the human heart to everything of God and goodness that all those who live godly in Christ Jesus shall suffer persecution in one form or other. *For theirs is the kingdom of heaven.* That spiritual Kingdom, explained in chap. iii. 2, and that Kingdom of glory which is its counterpart and consequence.

11. *When men shall revile you, and persecute.* The persecution mentioned in the preceding verse comprehends all outward acts of violence —all that the hand can do. This comprehends also all calumny, slander, etc.—all that the tongue can effect.

12. *Rejoice.* In the testimony of a good conscience; for, without this, suffering has nothing but misery in it. *Be exceeding glad.* "Leap for joy." There are several cases on record where this was literally done by martyrs.

13. *Ye are the salt of the earth.* Our Lord shows here what the preachers of the gospel, and what all who profess to follow Him, should be: the *salt,* to preserve the world from putrefaction and destruction. *But if the salt have lost his savour.* A preacher, or private Christian, who has lost the life of Christ, and the witness of His Spirit, out of his soul may be likened to such salt. He may have the sparks and glittering particles of true wisdom, but without its unction or comfort. Only that which is connected with the Rock, the soul that is in union with Christ Jesus by the Holy Spirit, can preserve its *savor,* and be instrumental of good to others.

14. *Ye are the light of the world.* That is, the instruments which God chooses to make use of to illuminate the minds of men, as He uses the sun to enlighten the world.

15. *Neither do men light a candle, and put it under a bushel.* A measure among both Greeks and Romans, containing a little more than a peck. From some ancient writers we learn that only those who had bad designs hid a candle under a bushel; that, in the dead of the night, when all were asleep, they might rise up, and have light at hand to help them to effect their horrid purposes of murder, etc.

16. *Let your light so shine.* Or more literally, "Thus let your light shine." As the sun is lighted up in the firmament of heaven to diffuse its light and heat freely to every inhabitant of the earth; and as the lamp is not set under the bushel, but placed upon the lampstand, that it may give light to all in the house, thus let every follower of Christ, and especially every preacher of the gospel, diffuse the light of heavenly knowledge and the warmth of divine love through the whole circle of their acquaintance.

17. *Think not that I am come to destroy the law.* "Do not imagine that I am come to violate the law." I am not come to make the law of none effect—to dissolve the connection which

subsists between its several parts, or the obligation men are under to have their lives regulated by its moral precepts; nor am I come to dissolve the connecting reference it has to the promised. But I am come to complete— to perfect its connection and reference, to accomplish everything shadowed forth in the Mosaic ritual, to fill up its great design; and to give grace to all My followers, "to fill up, or complete" every moral duty. Christ completed the law: (1) *In itself,* it was only the shadow, the typical representation, of good things to come; and He added to it that which was necessary to make it perfect, His own sacrifice, without which it could neither satisfy God nor sanctify men. (2) He completed it *in himself,* by submitting to its types with an exact obedience, and verifying them by His death upon the Cross. (3) He completes this law, and the sayings of His prophets, *in his members,* by giving them grace to love the Lord with all their heart, soul, mind, and strength, and their neighbor as themselves; for this is all the *law* and the *prophets.*

18. *Till heaven and earth pass away.* From the very beginning of His ministry, Jesus Christ teaches the instability of all visible things. *One jot or one tittle.* One *yod,* the smallest letter in the Hebrew alphabet. One *tittle* or "point," meaning either those points which serve for vowels in this language, if they then existed, or the points of certain letters. *Till all be fulfilled.* Or "accomplished." Though all earth and hell should join together to hinder the accomplishment of the great designs of the Most High, yet it shall all be in vain—even the sense of a single letter shall not be lost. The words of God, which point out His designs, are as unchangeable as His nature itself.

19. *Whosoever therefore shall break one of these least commandments.* The Pharisees were remarkable for making a distinction between weightier and lighter matters in the law, and between what has been called, in a corrupt part of the Christian Church, *mortal* and *venial sins.*

20. *Except your righteousness shall exceed.* "Unless your righteousness abound more"—unless it take in not only the letter but the spirit and design of the moral and ritual precept (the one directing you how to walk so as to please God; the other pointing out Christ, the great Atonement, through and by which a sinner is enabled to do so)—more than that *of the scribes and Pharisees,* who only attend to the letter of the law, and had indeed made even that of no effect by their traditions—*ye shall not enter into the kingdom of heaven.*

21. *Ye have heard that it was said by them of old time.* "To or by the ancients." By the "ancients" we may understand those who lived before the law, and those who lived under it. *Thou shalt not kill.* Murder was, in the most solemn manner, forbidden before, as well as under, the law, Gen. xi. 5-6.

22. *Whosoever is angry with his brother without a cause.* What our Lord seems here to prohibit is not merely that miserable facility which some have of being angry at every trifle, continually taking offense against their best friends, but that anger which leads a man to commit outrages against another. *Shall be in danger of the judgment.* "Shall be liable to the judgment." *Raca.* From the Hebrew *rak,* "to be

empty." It signifies a "vain, empty, worthless fellow, shallow brains." a term of great contempt. *The council.* The famous council, known among the Jews by the name of Sanhedrin. It was composed of seventy-two elders. This grand Sanhedrin not only received appeals from the inferior Sanhedrins, or court of twenty-three, but could alone take cognizance, in the first instance, of the highest crimes, and alone inflict the punishment of stoning. *Thou fool. Moreh,* probably from *marah,* "to rebel," a "rebel against God," apostate from all good. This term implied, among the Jews, the highest enormity and most aggravated guilt. *Shall be in danger of hell fire.* Our Lord here alludes to the valley of the son of Hinnom. This place was near Jerusalem, and had been formerly used for those abominable sacrifices, in which the idolatrous Jews had caused their children to pass through the fire to Molech. See 2 Kings xxiii. 10; 2 Chron. xxviii. 3; Jer. vii. 31-32. From the circumstance of this valley having been the scene of those infernal sacrifices, the Jews, in our Saviour's time, used the word for "hell," the place of the damned. There are *three* kinds of offences here, which exceed each other in their degrees of guilt: (1) *Anger* against a man, accompanied with some injurious act. (2) *Contempt,* expressed by the opprobrious epithet *raka, or shallow brains.* (3) *Hatred and mortal enmity,* expressed by the term *moreh,* or apostate, where such apostasy could not be proved. Now, proportioned to these *three* offenses were *three* different degrees of punishment, each exceeding the other in its severity, as the offenses exceeded each other in their different degrees of guilt: (1) The *judgment,* the council of *twenty-three,* which could inflict the punishment of *strangling.* (2) The *Sanhedrin,* or great council, which could inflict the punishment of *stoning.* (3) The being *burnt alive* in the valley of the son of Hinnom. This appears to be the meaning of our Lord.

23. *Therefore if thou bring thy gift.* Evil must be nipped in the bud. An unkind thought of another may be the foundation of that which leads to actual murder.

24. *Leave there thy gift before the altar.* This is as much as to say, "Do not attempt to bring any offering to God while you are in a spirit of enmity against any person; or have any difference with your neighbor, which you have not used your diligence to get adjusted." It is our duty and interest, both to bring our gift and offer it too; but God will not accept any act of religious worship from us while any enmity subsists in our hearts towards any soul of man, or while any subsists in our neighbor's heart towards us which we have not used the proper means to remove.

25. *Agree with thine adversary quickly.* *Adversary,* properly a plaintiff in law—a perfect law term. Our Lord enforces the exhortation given in the preceding verses, from the consideration of what was deemed prudent in ordinary lawsuits. A good use of this very prudential advice of our Lord is this: You are a sinner; God has a controversy with you. There is but a step between you and death. Now is the accepted time. You are invited to return to God by Christ Jesus. Come immediately at His call, and He will save your soul.

26. *The uttermost farthing.* This was the smallest coin among the Romans.

28. *Whosoever looketh on a woman to lust after her.* "Earnestly to covet her." The verb is undoubtedly used here by our Lord in the sense of coveting through the influence of impure desire. *Hath committed adultery with her already in his heart.* It is the earnest wish or desire of the soul which, in a variety of cases, constitutes the good or evil of an act. If a man earnestly wish to commit an evil, but cannot because God puts time, place, and opportunity out of his power, he is fully chargeable with the iniquity of the act by that God who searches and judges the heart. If voluntary and deliberate looks and desires make adulterers and adulteresses, how many persons are there whose whole life is one continued crime!

29. *And if thy right eye offend thee.* The *right eye* and the *right hand* are used here to point out those sins which appear most pleasing and profitable to us; from which we must be separated, if we desire ever to see the kingdom of God.

29-30. *Pluck it out . . . cut it off.* We must shut our senses against dangerous objects to avoid the occasions of sin, and deprive ourselves of all that is most dear and profitable to us in order to save our souls, when we find that these dear and profitable things, however innocent in themselves, cause us to sin against God. *It is profitable for thee that one of thy members.* Men often part with some members of the body, at the discretion of a surgeon, that they may preserve the trunk, and die a little later; and yet they will not deprive themselves of a look, a touch, a small pleasure, which endanger the eternal death of the soul.

31. *Whosoever shall put away his wife.* The Jewish doctors gave great license in the matter of divorce. Among them a man might divorce his wife if she displeased him even in the dressing of his victuals!

32. *Saving for the cause of fornication.* As fornication signifies no more than the unlawful connection of unmarried persons, it cannot properly be used when speaking of those who are married. I have therefore translated "on account of whoredom." It does not appear that there is any other case in which Jesus Christ admits of divorce. A real Christian ought rather to beg of God the grace to bear patiently and quietly the imperfections of his wife than to think of the means of being parted from her.

33. *Thou shalt not forswear thyself.* They dishonor the great God and break this commandment who use frequent oaths and imprecations, even in reference to things that are true; and those who make vows and promises which they either cannot perform or do not design to fulfill are not less criminal. *Perform unto the Lord thine oaths.* The morality of the Jews on this point was truly detestable; they maintained that a man might swear with his lips and annul it in the same moment in his heart.

34. *Swear not at all.* Much has been said in vindication of the propriety of swearing in civil cases before a magistrate, and much has been said against it. The best way is to have as little as possible to do with oaths. An oath will not bind a dishonest person nor a liar; and an honest man needs none, for his character and conduct swear for him.

34-35. Neither by heaven . . . nor by the earth. It was a custom among the ancient Scythians, when they wished to bind themselves in the most solemn manner, to swear by the king's throne; and if the king was at any time sick, they believed it was occasioned by someone's having taken the oath falsely.

36. Neither shalt thou swear by thy head. For these plain reasons: (1) God commands you not to do it. (2) You have nothing which is your own, and you should not pledge another's property. (3) It never did, and never can, answer any good purpose. (4) Being a breach of the law of God, it is the way to everlasting misery.

37. Let your communication be, Yea, yea; Nay, nay. That is, a positive and forthright affirmation or negation, according to your knowledge of the matter concerning which you are called to testify. Do not equivocate; mean what you assert, and adhere to your assertion. *Whatsoever is more than these.* That is, more than a bare affirmation or negation, according to the requirements of Eternal Truth, cometh of evil; or "is of the wicked one", i.e., the devil, the father of superfluities and lies.

38. An eye for an eye. Our Lord refers here to the law of retaliation mentioned in Exod. xxi. 24, which obliged the offender to suffer the same injury he had committed. The Greeks and Romans had the same law.

39. Resist not evil. Or "the evil person." Our Lord's meaning is, "Do not repel one outrage by another." *Turn to him the other also.* That is, rather than avenge yourself, be ready to suffer patiently a repetition of the same injury. But these exhortations belong principally to those who are persecuted for righteousness' sake.

40. And if any man will sue thee at the law. Everywhere our blessed Lord shows the utmost disapprobation of such litigations as tended to destroy brotherly kindness and charity. It is evident He would have His followers to suffer rather the loss of all their property than to have recourse to such modes of redress at so great a risk. *Coat.* See on Luke vi. 29.

41. Shall compel thee to go a mile, go with him twain. This derives its meaning from reference to the Persians. The Persian messengers had the royal authority for pressing horses, ships, and even men to assist them in the business on which they were employed. We are here exhorted to patience and forgiveness: (1) when we receive in our persons all sorts of insults and affronts, v. 39; (2) when we are despoiled of our goods, v. 40; (3) when our bodies are forced to undergo all kinds of toils, vexations, and torments, v. 41. The proper way to face the injustice of man is to exercise under it meekness, gentleness, and long-suffering, without which disposition of mind no man can be happy either here or hereafter; for he that avenges himself must lose the mind of Christ, and thus suffer an injury ten thousand times greater than he can ever receive from man. Revenge at such an expense is dear indeed.

42. Give to him that asketh thee, and from him that would borrow. To give and lend freely to all who are in need is a general precept from which we are excused only by our inability to perform it.

43. Thou shalt love thy neighbour, and hate thine enemy. You shall love your friend and hate your enemy. This was certainly the meaning which the Jews put on it; for neighbor, with them, implied those of the Jewish race, and all others were considered by them as natural enemies.

44. Love your enemies. This is the most sublime piece of morality ever given to man. But who can obey it? None but he who has the mind of Christ. *Bless them that curse you.* "Give them good words" for their bad words. *Do good to them that hate you.* Give your enemy every proof that you love him. We must not love in tongue, but in deed and in truth. *Pray for them which despitefully use you.* Those who constantly harass and slander you. *Pray for them.* I cannot change that wicked man's heart, and while it is unchanged he will continue to harass me, God alone can change it. Then I must implore Him to do that which will at once secure the man's salvation and contribute so much to my own peace. *And persecute you.* Those who "press hard on" and "pursue" you with hatred and malice accompanied with repeated acts of enmity. In this verse our Lord shows us that a man may be our enemy in *three* different ways: (1) in his heart, by hatred; (2) in his words, by cursing or using direful imprecations against us; (3) in his actions, by continually harassing and abusing us. He shows us also how we are to behave to those. The hatred of the first we are to meet with love. The cursings or evil words of the second we are to meet with good words and blessings. And the repeated injurious acts of the third we are to meet with continual prayer to God for the man's salvation.

45. That ye may be the children of your Father. As a man's child is called his, because a partaker of his own nature, so a holy person is said to be a child of God, because he is a partaker of the divine nature. If God had not loved us while we were His enemies, we could never have become His children, and we shall cease to be such as soon as we cease to imitate Him.

46. For if ye love them which love you. He who loves only his friends does nothing for God's sake. He who loves for the sake of pleasure or interest pays himself. God has no enemy which He hates but sin; we should have no other. *The publicans.* That is, "taxgatherers." A farmer or collector of the taxes or public revenues. This class of men were detestable among the Romans, the Greeks, and the Jews for their intolerable rapacity and avarice. They were abhorred in an especial manner by the Jews, to whom the Roman government was odious. These, assisting in collecting the Roman tribute, were considered as betrayers of the liberties of their country, and abettors of those who enslaved it.

47. And if ye salute your brethren only. Instead of *brethren,* upwards of one hundred MSS., and several of them of great authority and antiquity, have "friends." As *brother* is more conformable to the Jewish mode of address, it should be retained in the text.

48. Be ye therefore perfect, even as your Father. God himself is the only Pattern of the perfection which He recommends to His children. The words are very emphatic: "Ye shall be therefore *perfect*"—you shall be filled with the spirit of that God whose name is Mercy, and whose nature is love. These words of our Lord include both a *command* and a *promise*. Can we be fully saved from sin in this world? This is an important question, to which this text gives a satisfactory answer: "Ye shall be perfect, as your Father, who is in heaven, is perfect." As in His infinite nature there is no sin, nothing but goodness and love, so in your finite nature there shall dwell no sin, for the law of the spirit of life in Christ Jesus shall make you free from the law of sin and death, Rom. viii. 2. God shall live in, fill, and rule your hearts; and, in what He fills and influences, neither Satan nor sin can have any part. But where is the person thus saved? Wherever he is found who loves God with all his heart, soul, mind, and strength, and his neighbor as himself.

CHAPTER 6

Of almsgiving, 1-5. Of prayer, 6-8. The Lord's Prayer, or model according to which Christians whould pray, 9-13. Of forgiveness, 14-15. Of fasting, 16-17. Of laying up treasures, 18-21. Of the single eye, 22-23. The impossibility of serving two masters, 24. Of contentment and confidence in the divine providence, 25-32. Directions about seeking the kingdom of God, 33-34.

1. *That ye do not your alms.* "Perform not your acts of righteousness"—such as almsgiving, fasting, and prayer, mentioned immediately after. "Righteousness" was a common word for *alms* among the Jews. Dr. Lightfoot shows that it was thus commonly used among the Jewish writers: "It is questioned," says he, "whether *Matthew* writ *alms* or *righteousness*. I answer: That our Saviour certainly said *righteousness*, I make no doubt at all; but that that word could not be otherwise understood by the common people than of *alms*, there is as little doubt to be made." *Before men.* Our Lord does not forbid public almsgiving, fasting, and prayer, but simply censures those vain and hypocritical persons who do these things publicly in order that they may be seen of men, and receive from them the reputation of saints.

2. *Therefore when thou doest thine alms.* In the first verse the exhortation is general: "Take heed." In this verse the address is pointed—*thou. Do not sound a trumpet.* It may be that this was literally practiced among the Pharisees, who seemed to live on the public esteem, and were excessively self-righteous and vain. Having something to distribute by way of alms, it is very probable they caused this to be published by blowing a trumpet or horn, under pretense of collecting the poor, though with no other design than to gratify their own ambition. It must be granted that in the Jewish writings there is no such practice referred to. *They have their reward.* That is, the honor and esteem of men, which they sought. God is under no obligation to them—they did nothing with an eye to His glory, and from Him they can expect no recompense. They had their recompense in this life, and could expect none in the world to come.

3. *Let not thy left hand know.* In many cases, works of charity must be hidden from even our nearest relatives, who, if they knew, would hinder us from doing what God has given us power and inclination to perform. We must go even further and conceal them as far as is possible from ourselves, by not thinking of them, or eyeing them with complacency.

4. *Which seeth in secret.* We should ever remember that the eye of the Lord is upon us, and that He sees not only the act, but also every motive that led to it.

5. *And when thou prayest.* Signifies "to pour out prayers or vows," probably alluding to the offerings or libations which were poured out before, or on, the altar. A proper idea of prayer is a pouring out of the soul unto God, as a freewill offering (solemnly and eternally dedicated to Him), accompanied with the most earnest desire that it may know, love, and serve Him alone. He that comes thus to God will ever be heard and blessed. Prayer is the language of dependence; he who prays not is endeavoring to live independently of God. This was the first curse, and continues to be the great curse of mankind. *Thou shalt not be as the hypocrites.* Properly a stage-player who acts under a mask, personating a character different from his own; a counterfeit, a dissembler; one who would be thought to be different from what he really is. A person who wishes to be taken for a follower of God but who has nothing of religion except the outside. *Love to pray standing in the synagogues and in the corners of the streets.* The Jewish phylacterical prayers were long, and the canonical hours obliged them to repeat these prayers wherever they happened to be; and the Pharisees, who were full of vainglory, contrived to be overtaken in the streets at the canonical hour, that they might be seen by the people and be applauded for their great and conscientious piety.

6. *But thou, when thou prayest.* Prayer is the most secret intercourse of the soul with God, and as it were the conversation of one heart with another. The world is too profane and treacherous to be of the secret. We must *shut the door* against it; endeavor to forget it, with all the affairs which busy and amuse it. Prayer requires retirement, at least of the heart; for this may be fitly termed the *closet* in the house of God, which house the body of every real Christian is, I Cor. iii. 16.

7. *Use not vain repetitions.* Prayer requires more of the heart than of the tongue. The eloquence of prayer consists in the fervency of desire and the simplicity of faith. Our trust and confidence ought to proceed from that which God is able to do in us, and not from that which we can say to Him.

8. *Your Father knoweth what things ye have need of.* Prayer is not designed to inform God, but to give man a sight of his misery; to humble his heart, to excite his desire, to inflame his faith, to animate his hope, to raise his soul from earth to heaven, and to put him in mind that there is his Father, his country, and inheritance. In the preceding verses we may see three faults which our Lord commands us to avoid in prayer: (1) Hypocrisy. *Be not as the hypocrites,* v. 5. (2) Dissipation. *Enter into thy closet,* v. 6. (3) Much speaking, or unmeaning repetition. *Be not like the heathen,* v. 7.

9. *After this manner therefore pray ye.* Forms of prayer were frequent among the Jews, and every public teacher gave one to his disciples. Some forms were drawn out to a considerable length, and from these abridgments were made. To the latter sort the following prayer belongs, and consequently, besides its own very important use, it is a plan for a more extended devotion. *Our Father.* It was a maxim of the Jews that a man should not pray alone, but

join with the church; by which they particularly meant that he should, whether alone or with the synagogue, use the plural number as comprehending all the followers of God. The word *Father,* placed here at the beginning of this prayer, includes two grand ideas which should serve as a foundation to all our petitions: (1) That tender and respectful love which we should feel for God, such as that which children feel for their fathers; (2) That strong confidence in God's love to us, such as fathers have for their children. Thus all the petitions in this prayer stand in strictest reference to the word *Father,* the first three referring to the love we have for God, and the last three to that confidence which we have in the love He bears to us.

Which art in heaven. The phrase, *Our Father which art in heaven* was very common among the ancient Jews, and was used by them precisely in the same sense as it is used here by our Lord. This phrase in the Scriptures seems used to express: (1) His omnipresence. "The . . . heaven of heavens cannot contain thee," 1 Kings viii. 27. (2) His majesty and dominion over His creatures. "Art not thou God in heaven? and rulest not thou over all the kingdoms of the heathen?" 2 Chron. xx. 6 (3) His power and might. "Art not thou God in heaven? . . . and in thine hand is there not power and might, so that none is able to withstand thee?" 2 Chron. xx. 6 (4) His omniscience. "The Lord's throne is in heaven: his eyes behold, his eyelids try, the children of men," Ps. xi. 4. (5) His infinite purity and holiness. Thou art "the high and lofty One that inhabiteth eternity, whose name is Holy," Isa. lvii. 15. *Hallowed.* *Hagiazo* from a negative, and *ge, the earth,* a thing *separated from the earth,* or from earthly purposes and employments. As the word *sanctified* or *hallowed,* in Scripture, is frequently used for the consecration of a thing or person to a holy use or office, as the Levites, firstborn, Tabernacle, Temple, and their utensils, which were all set apart from every earthly, common, or profane use, and employed wholly in the service of God, so the Divine Majesty may be said to be sanctified by us, in analogy to those things, viz., when we separate Him from, and in our conceptions and desires exalt Him above, earth and all things. *Thy name.* That is, God himself, with all the attributes of His divine nature—His power, wisdom, justice, mercy. We hallow God's name: (1) with our *lips,* when all our conversation is holy, and we speak of those things which are meet to minister grace to the hearers; (2) in our *thoughts,* when we suppress every rising evil, and have our tempers regulated by His grace and Spirit; (3) in our *lives,* when we begin, continue, and end our works to His glory; (4) in our *families,* when we endeavor to bring up our *children* in the discipline and admonition of the Lord; (5) in a particular *calling* or *business,* when we separate the falsity, deception, and lying, commonly practiced, from it, buying and selling as in the sight of the holy and just God.

10. *Thy kingdom come.* The ancient Jews scrupled not to say: "He prays not at all, in whose prayers there is no mention of the kingdom of God." *Thy will be done.* This petition is properly added to the preceding; for when the Kingdom of righteousness, peace, and joy, in the Holy Spirit, is established in the heart, there is then an ample provision made for the fulfillment of the divine will. *As it is in heaven.* The Jews maintained that they were the angels of God upon earth, as those pure spirits were angels of God in heaven; hence they said, "As the angels sanctify the divine name in heaven, so the Israelites sanctify the divine name upon earth." Observe: (1) The salvation of the soul is the result of two wills conjoined: the will of God and the will of man. If God will not the salvation of man, he cannot be saved. If man will not the salvation God has prepared for him, he cannot be delivered from his sins. (2) This petition certainly points out a deliverance from all sin. For nothing that is unholy can consist with the divine will; and if this be fulfilled in man, surely sin shall be banished from his soul. (3) This is further evident from these words, *as it is in heaven;* i.e., as the angels do it, that is, with all zeal, diligence, love, delight, and perseverance. (4) Does not the petition plainly imply we may live without sinning against God?

11. *Give us this day our daily bread.* The word *epiousion* has greatly perplexed critics and commentators. I find upwards of thirty different explanations of it. It is found in no Greek writer before the Evangelists. The interpretation of Theophylact, one of the best of the Greek fathers, has ever appeared to me to be the most correct, "Bread, sufficient for our substance and support," i.e., that quantity of food which is necessary to support our health and strength, by being changed into the substance of our bodies.

12. *And forgive us our debts.* Sin is represented here under the notion of a debt, and as our sins are many, they are here called *debts.* God made man that he might live to His glory, and gave him a law to walk by; and if, when he does anything that tends not to glorify God, he contracts a debt with divine justice, how much more is he debtor when he breaks the law by actual transgression! *Forgive us.* Man has nothing to pay; if his debts are not forgiven, they must stand charged against him forever, as he is absolutely insolvent. Forgiveness, therefore, must come from the free mercy of God in Christ. *As we forgive our debtors.* It was a maxim among the ancient Jews that no man should lie down in his bed without forgiving those who had offended him. That man condemns himself to suffer eternal punishment who makes use of this prayer with revenge and hatred in his heart.

13. *And lead us not into temptation.* That is, "Bring us not into sore trial." *Peirasmon,* which may be here rendered "sore trial," comes from *peiro,* "to pierce through," as with a spear, or spit, used so by some of the best Greek writers. The word not only implies violent assaults from Satan, but also sorely afflictive circumstances, none of which we have as yet grace or fortitude sufficient to bear. "Bring us not in," or *lead us not into.* This is a mere Hebraism. God is said to do a thing which He only permits or suffers to be done. The process of *temptation* is often as follows: (1) a simple evil thought; (2) a strong imagination, or impression made on the imagination, by the thing to which we are tempted; (3) delight in viewing it; (4) consent of the will to perform it. A man may be tempted without entering *into* the temptation:

entering into it implies giving way, closing in with, and embracing it. *But deliver us from evil.* "From the wicked one." Satan is expressly called "the wicked one." *Deliver us.* A very expressive word—"Break our chains, and loose our bands"—snatch, pluck us from the evil, and its calamitous issue. *For thine is the kingdom . . . forever. Amen.* The whole of this doxology is rejected by Wetstein, Griesbach, and the most eminent critics. It is variously written in several MSS., and omitted by most of the fathers, both Greek and Latin. *For ever.* "To the for evers." Well-expressed by our common translation "for ever and ever"—the first *ever* in our ancient use of the word taking in the whole duration of time, and the second *ever* the whole of eternity. *Amen.* This word is Hebrew and signifies "faithful" or "true." The word itself implies a confident resting of the soul in God, with the fullest assurance that all these petitions shall be fulfilled to everyone who prays according to the directions given before by our blessed Lord.

14. *If ye forgive men.* He who shows mercy to men receives mercy from God.

15. *But if ye forgive not.* A vindictive man excludes himself from all hope of eternal life, and himself seals his own damnation. *Trespasses. Paraptomata,* from *para* and *pipto,* "to fall off." What a remarkable difference there is between this word and "debts" in v. 12! Men's sins against us are only their stumblings, or fallings off from the duties they owe us, but ours are debts to God's justice, which we can never discharge.

16. *When ye fast.* A total abstinence from food for a certain time. Abstaining from flesh, and living on fish, vegetables, etc., is no fast, but may be rather considered a burlesque on fasting. *As the hypocrites, of a sad countenance.* A hypocrite has always a difficult part to act. When he wishes to appear as a penitent, not having any godly sorrow at heart, he is obliged to counterfeit it the best way he can, by a gloomy and austere look.

17. *Anoint thine head, and wash thy face.* These were forbidden in the Jewish canon on days of fasting and humiliation; and hypocrites availed themselves of this ordinance, that they might appear to fast.

18. *Thy Father which seeth in secret.* Let us not be afraid that our hearts can be concealed from God; but let us fear lest He perceive them to be more desirous of the praise of men than they are of that glory which comes from Him.

19. *Lay not up for yourselves treasures upon earth.* What blindness is it for a man to lay up that as a treasure which must necessarily perish! *Rust.* This word cannot be properly applied to rust, but to anything that consumes or cankers clothes or metals. *Where thieves do not break through.* Literally "dig through," i.e., the wall, in order to get into the house. This was not a difficult matter, as the house was generally made of mud and straw.

20. *Lay up . . . treasures in heaven.* It is certain we have not the smallest portion of temporal good but what we have received from the unmerited bounty of God; and if we give back to Him all we have received, yet still there is no merit that can fairly attach to the act, as the goods were the Lord's; for I am not to suppose that I can purchase anything from a man by his own property. On this ground the doctrine of human merit is one of the most absurd that ever was published among men or credited by sinners.

21. *Where your treasure is.* If God be the Treasure of our souls, our hearts—i.e., our affections and desires—will be placed on things above. An earthly-minded man proves that his treasure is below; a heavenly-minded man shows that his treasure is above.

22. *The light of the body is the eye.* That is, the eye is to the body what the sun is to the universe in the daytime, or a lamp or candle to a house at night. *If therefore thine eye be single.* "Simple, uncompounded," i.e., so perfect in its structure as to see objects distinctly and clearly.

23. *Evil,* i.e., "diseased or defective." An evil eye was a phrase in use among the ancient Jews to denote an envious, covetous man or disposition; a man who repined at his neighbor's prosperity, loved his own money, and would do nothing in the way of charity for God's sake. Our blessed Lord, however, extends and sublimes this meaning, and uses the sound eye as a metaphor to point out that simplicity of intention and purity of affection with which men should pursue the supreme good.

24. *No man can serve two masters.* The master of our heart may be fitly termed the *love* that reigns in it. We serve that only which we love supremely. *He will hate the one, and love the other.* The word *hate* has the same sense here as it has in many places of Scripture; it merely signifies to love less. *Mammon* is used for *money.*

25. *Therefore.* "On this account," namely, that you may not serve mammon, but have unshaken confidence in God, *I say unto you. Take no thought.* Be not anxiously careful. Prudent care is never forbidden by our Lord, but only that anxious, distracting solicitude which, by dividing the mind and drawing it different ways, renders it utterly incapable of attending to any solemn or important concern. In this and the following verses our Lord lays down several reasons why men should not disquiet themselves about the wants of life or concerning the future. The *first* is the experience of greater benefits already received. *Is not the life more than meat, and the body than raiment?* Can He who gave us our bodies, and breathed into them the breath of life, before we could ask them from Him, refuse us that which is necessary to preserve both, and when we ask it in humble confidence?

26. *Behold the fowls of the air.* The *second* reason why we should not be anxiously concerned about the future is the example of the smaller animals, which the providence of God feeds without their own labor, though He be not their father.

27. *Which of you by taking thought can add one cubit unto his stature?* The *third* reason against these carking cares is the unprofitableness of human solicitude, unless God vouchsafe to bless it. What can our uneasiness do but render us still more unworthy of the divine care? *Add one cubit unto his stature.* I think *helikian* should be rendered "age" here, and so

our translators have rendered the word in John ix. 21, "He is of age."

28. *And why take ye thought for raiment?* Or, "why are ye anxiously careful about raiment?" The *fourth* reason against such inquietudes is the example of inanimate creatures. The herbs and flowers of the field have their being, nourishment, exquisite flavors, and beautiful hues from God himself. They are not only without anxious care, but also without care or thought of every kind. *Consider.* Diligently consider this, "lay it earnestly to heart," and let your confidence be unshaken in the God of infinite bounty and love.

29. *Solomon in all his glory.* Some suppose that, as the robes of state worn by the Eastern kings were usually white, as were those of the nobles among the Jews, therefore the lily was chosen for the comparison.

30. *If God so clothe the grass of the field.* Christ confounds both the luxury of the rich in their superfluities and the distrust of the poor as to the necessaries of life. Let man, who is made for God and eternity, learn from a flower of the field how low the care of Providence stoops. All our inquietudes and distrusts proceed from lack of faith. *To morrow is cast into the oven.* The inhabitants of the East, to this day, make use of dry straw, withered herbs, and stubble, to heat their ovens.

31. *What shall we eat? or, What shall we drink?* These three inquiries engross the whole attention of those who are living without God in the world. The belly and back of a worldling are his compound god; and these he worships in the lust of the flesh, in the lust of the eye, and in the pride of life.

32. *For after all these things do the Gentiles seek.* The *fifth* reason against solicitude about the future is that to concern ourselves about these wants with anxiety, as if there was no such thing as a providence in the world; with great affection towards earthly enjoyments, as if we expected no other; and without praying to God or consulting His will, as if we could do anything without Him—this is to imitate the worst kind of heathens, who live without hope, and without God in the world. *Seek.* "To seek intensely, earnestly, again and again." The true characteristic of the worldly man; his soul is never satisfied—Give! give! is the ceaseless language of his earth-born heart. *Your heavenly Father knoweth.* The *sixth* reason against this anxiety about the future is—because God, our Heavenly Father, is infinite in wisdom and knows all our wants.

33. *His righteousness.* That holiness of heart and purity of life which God requires of those who profess to be subjects of that spiritual Kingdom mentioned above. The *seventh* reason against these worldly cares and fears is—because the business of our salvation ought to engross us entirely; hither all our desires, cares, and inquiries ought to tend. Grace is the way to glory —holiness, the way to happiness.

34. *Take therefore no thought.* That is, "Be not therefore anxiously careful." The *eighth* and last reason against this preposterous conduct is that carking care is not only useless in itself, but renders us miserable beforehand. *Sufficient unto the day is the evil thereof.* "Sufficient for each day is its own calamity." Each

day has its peculiar trials; we should meet them with confidence in God. As we should live but a day at a time, so we should take care to suffer no more evils in one day than are necessarily attached to it. He who neglects the present for the future is acting opposite to the order of God, his own interest, and to every dictate of sound wisdom. Let us live for eternity, and we shall secure all that is valuable in time.

CHAPTER 7

Our Lord warns men against rash judgment and uncharitable censures, 1-5. Shows that holy things must not be profaned, 6; gives encouragement to fervent, persevering prayer, 7-11. Shows how men should deal with each other, 12. Exhorts the people to enter in at the strait gate, 13-14; to beware of false teachers, who are to be known by their fruits, 15-20. Shows that no man shall be saved by his mere profession of Christianity, however specious, 21-23. The parable of the wise man who built his house upon a rock, 24-25. Of the foolish man who built his house, without a foundation, on the sand, 26-27. Christ concludes His sermon, and the people are astonished at His doctrine, 28-29.

1. *Judge not, that ye be not judged.* These exhortations are pointed against rash, harsh, and uncharitable judgments, the thinking evil, where no evil seems, and speaking of it accordingly.

2. *For with what judgment.* He who is severe on others will naturally excite their severity against himself.

3. *And why beholdest thou the mote?* Might be translated the "splinter"; for "splinter" bears some analogy to *beam*, but *mote* does not. It often happens that the faults which we consider as of the first enormity in others are, to our own iniquities, as a chip is when compared to a large beam.

4. *Or how wilt thou say?* That man is utterly unfit to show the way of life to others who is himself walking in the way of death.

5. *Thou hypocrite.* A hypocrite, who professes to be what he is not (viz., a true Christian), is obliged, for the support of the character he has assumed, to imitate all the dispositions and actions of a Christian; consequently he must reprove sin, and endeavor to show an uncommon affection for the glory of God.

6. *Give not that which is holy.* "The holy or sacred thing"; i.e., anything, especially, of the sacrificial kind, which had been consecrated to God. As a general meaning of this passage, we may just say: The sacrament of the Lord's Supper, and other holy ordinances which are instituted only for the genuine followers of Christ, are not to be dispensed to those who are continually returning like the snarling, ill-natured dog to their easily predominant sins of rash judgment, barking at and tearing the characters of others by evil speaking, backbiting, and slandering; nor to him who, like the swine, is frequently returning to wallow in the mud of sensual gratifications and impurities.

7. *Ask . . . seek . . . knock.* These three words include the ideas of want, loss, and earnestness. *Ask:* turn beggar at the door of mercy. You are destitute of all spiritual good, and it is God alone who can give it to you; and you have no claim but what His mercy has given you on itself. *Seek:* You have lost your God, your paradise, your soul. Look about you—leave no stone unturned. There is no peace, no final salvation for you till you get your soul restored to the favor and image of God. *Knock:* Be in earnest—

be importunate. Eternity is at hand! And, if you die in your sins, where God is you shall never come. *Ask* with confidence and humility. *Seek* with care and application. *Knock* with earnestness and perseverance.

8. *For every one that asketh receiveth.* Prayer is always heard after one manner or other. No soul can pray in vain that prays as directed above.

9. *Or what man is there . . . whom if his son?* Men are exhorted to come unto God with the persuasion that He is a most gracious and compassionate Parent, who possesses all heavenly and earthly good, knows what is necessary for each of His creatures, and is infinitely ready to communicate that which they need most. *Will he give him a stone?* Will he not readily give him bread if he have it? This was a proverb in other countries; a benefit grudgingly given by an avaricious man is called by Seneca stony bread.

11. *If ye, then, being evil.* Who are radically and diabolically depraved, yet feel yourselves led, by natural affection, to give those things to your children which are necessary to support their lives, how much more will your Father who is in heaven, whose nature is infinite goodness, mercy, and grace, *give good things*—His grace and Spirit (the Holy Ghost, Luke xi. 13)—*to them that ask him?*

12. *Therefore all things whatsoever ye would that men.* The general meaning of it is this: "Guided by justice and mercy, do unto all men as you would have them to do to you, were your circumstances and theirs reversed."

13. *Enter ye in at the strait gate.* The words in the original are very emphatic: Enter in (to the kingdom of Heaven) through this strait gate, i.e., of doing to everyone as you would he should do unto you; for this alone seems to be the *strait gate* which our Lord alludes to. *For wide is the gate.* And very "broad"; a spacious, roomy place that leadeth forward into that *destruction*, meaning eternal misery.

14. *Because strait is the gate.* Instead of *because*, I should prefer "how," which reading is supported by a great majority of the best MSS., versions, and fathers. How strait is that gate! This mode of expression more forcibly points out the difficulty of the way to the Kingdom. *Few there be that find it.* The strait gate signifies literally what we call a wicket, i.e., a little door in a large gate. *Gate*, among the Jews, signifies, metaphorically, the entrance, introduction, or means of acquiring anything. So they talk of the gate of repentance, the gate of prayers and the gate of tears. When God, say they, shut the gate of paradise against Adam, He opened to him the gate of repentance.

15. *Beware of false prophets.* By f a l s e prophets we are to understand teachers of erroneous doctrines, who come professing a commission from God, but whose aim is not to bring the heavenly treasure to the people, but rather to rob them of their earthly good.

16. *Ye shall know them by their fruits.* Fruits, in the Scripture and Jewish phraseology, are taken for "works" of any kind.

17. *So every good tree.* As the *thorn* can produce only thorns, not grapes; and the thistle, not figs, but prickles, so an unregenerate heart will produce fruits of degeneracy. As we perfectly know that a good tree will not produce bad fruit, and the bad tree will not, cannot produce good fruit, so we know that the profession of godliness, while the life is ungodly, is imposture, hypocrisy, and deceit. A man cannot be a saint and a sinner at the same time.

18. *A good tree cannot bring forth evil fruit.* Love to God and man is the root of the good tree, and from this principle all its fruit is found.

19. *Every tree that bringeth not forth good fruit.* What a terrible sentence is this against Christless pastors and Christless hearers!

20. *Wherefore by their fruits.* This truth is often repeated, because our eternal interests depend so much upon it. Not to have good fruit is to have evil; there can be no innocent sterility in the invisible tree of the heart.

21. *Not every one.* The sense of this verse seems to be this: No person, by merely acknowledging My authority, believing in the divinity of My nature, professing faith in the perfection of My righteousness, and the infinite merit of My atonement, *shall enter into the kingdom of heaven*—shall have any part with God in glory; but *he that doeth the will of my Father*—he who gets the bad tree rooted up, the good tree planted, and continues to bring forth fruit to the glory and praise of God.

22. *Many will say to me in that day.* "In that very day," viz., the day of judgment—*Have we not prophesied,* taught, publicly preached, *in thy name;* acknowledging Thee to be the only Saviour, and proclaiming Thee as such to others; *cast out demons,* impure spirits, who had taken possession of the bodies of men; *done many wonderful works,* miracles, being assisted by supernatural agency to invert even the course of nature, and thus prove the truth of the doctrine we preached?

23. *Will I profess.* I will fully and plainly tell them, *I never knew you*—I never "approved" of you; for so the word is used in many places, in both the Old and New Testaments. You held the truth in unrighteousness, while you preached My pure and holy doctrine; and for the sake of My own truth, and through My love to the souls of men, I blessed your preaching. But yourselves I could never esteem, because you were destitute of the spirit of My gospel, unholy in your hearts, and unrighteous in your conduct. *Depart from me.* What a terrible word! What a dreadful separation! Depart from Me, from the very Jesus whom you have proclaimed, in union with whom alone eternal life is to be found! For, united to Christ, all is heaven; separated from Him, all is hell.

24. *Therefore whosoever heareth these sayings of mine.* That is, the excellent doctrines laid down before in this and the preceding two chapters. *I will liken him unto a wise man.* To a prudent man, a man of sense and understanding, who, foreseeing the evil, hideth himself, who proposes to himself the best end, and makes use of the proper means to accomplish it. True wisdom consists in getting the building of our salvation completed. To this end we must build on the Rock, Christ Jesus, and make the building firm, by keeping close to the maxims of His gospel, and having our tempers and lives conformed to its word and spirit; and

when, in order to this, we lean on nothing but the grace of Christ, we then build upon a solid rock.

25. *And the rain descended, and the floods came, and the winds blew.* There are three general kinds of trials to which the followers of God are exposed, and to which, some think, our Lord alludes here: *First,* those of temporal afflictions, coming in the course of divine providence; these may be likened to the torrents of *rain. Second,* those which come from the passions of men, and which may be likened to the impetuous *rivers. Third,* those which come from Satan and his angels, and which, like tempestuous *whirlwinds,* threaten to carry everything before them. He alone whose soul is built on the Rock of ages stands all these shocks; and not only stands in, but profits by them.

26. *And every one that heareth . . . and doeth them not.* Was there ever a stricter system of morality delivered by God to man than in this sermon? He who reads or hears it and does not look to God to conform his soul and life to it, and notwithstanding is hoping to enter into the kingdom of Heaven, is like the fool who *built his house upon the sand.* When the rain, the rivers, and the winds come, his building must fall, and his soul be crushed into the nethermost pit by its ruins.

27. *And the rain descended, and the floods came.* A fine illustration of this may be seen in the case of the fishermen in Bengal, who, in the dry season, build their huts on the beds of sand from which the river has retired. But when the rain sets in suddenly, as it often does, accompanied with violent northwest winds, and the waters pour down in torrents from the mountains, in one night multitudes of these buildings are swept away, and the place where they stood is on the next morning indiscoverable.

28. *The people were astonished.* "The multitudes," for vast crowds attended the ministry of this most popular and faithful of all preachers. They *were astonished at his doctrine.* They heard the law defined in such a manner as they had never thought of before, and this sacred system of morality urged home on their consciences with such clearness and authority as they had never felt under the teaching of their scribes and Pharisees.

29. *Having authority.* They felt a commanding power and authority in His word, i.e., His doctrine. His statements were perspicuous, His exhortations persuasive, His doctrine sound and rational, and His arguments irresistible.

CHAPTER 8

Great multitudes follow Christ, 1. He heals a leper, 2-4. Heals the centurion's servant, 5-13. Heals Peter's wife's mother, 14-15; and several other diseased persons, 16-17. Departs from that place, 18. Two persons offer to be His disciples, 19-22. He and His disciples are overtaken with a tempest, which He miraculously stills, 23-27. He cures demoniacs, and the demons which were cast out enter into a herd of swine, which, rushing into the sea, perish, 28-32. The swineherds announce the miracle to the Gergesenes, who request Christ to depart from their country, 33-34.

1. *From the mountain.* That mountain on which He had delivered the preceding inimitable sermon. *Great multitudes followed him.* Having been deeply impressed with the glorious doctrines which they had just heard.

2. *And, behold, there came a leper.* The leprosy was an inveterate cutaneous disease, appearing in dry, thin, white, scurfy scales or scabs, either on the whole body or on some part of it, usually attended with violent itching and often with great pain. The various symptoms of this dreadful disorder, which was a striking emblem of sin, may be seen in Leviticus xiii—xiv, where also may be read the legal ordinances concerning it. *Lord, if thou wilt, thou canst make me clean.* As this leper may be considered as a fit emblem of the corruption of man by sin, so may his cure, of the redemption of the soul by Christ. A sinner, truly penitent, seeks God with a respectful faith; approaches Him in the spirit of adoration; humbles himself under His mighty hand, acknowledging the greatness of his fall and the vileness of his sin. His prayer, like that of the leper, should be humble, plain, and full of confidence in that God who can do all things, and of dependence upon His will or mercy, from which all good must be derived. It is peculiar to God that He need only *will* what He intends to perform. His power is His will.

3. *Jesus put forth his hand . . . I will; be thou clean.* The most sovereign authority is assumed in this speech of our blessed Lord— *I will.* There is here no supplication of any power superior to His own; and the event proved to the fullest conviction, and by the clearest demonstration, that His authority was absolute and His power unlimited. *And immediately his leprosy was cleansed.* What an astonishing sight! A man whose whole body was covered over with the most loathsome disease cleansed from it in a moment of time! Was it possible for any soul to resist the evidence of this fact?

4. *Jesus saith unto him, See thou tell no man.* Had our Lord, at this early period, fully manifested himself as the Messiah, the people in all likelihood would have proclaimed Him King. This, however, refused by Him, must have excited the hatred of the Jewish rulers and the jealousy of the Roman government; and, speaking after the manner of men, His further preachings and miracles must have been impeded. This alone seems to be the reason why He said to the leper, *See thou tell no man. Shew thyself to the priest.* This was to conform to the law instituted in this case, Lev. xiv. 1, etc. *Offer the gift.* This gift was two living, clean birds, some cedarwood, with scarlet and hyssop, Lev. xiv. 4, which were to be brought for his cleansing; and, when clean, two he lambs, one ewe lamb, three tenth deals of flour, and one log of oil, v. 10. But if the person were poor, then he was to bring one lamb, one tenth deal of flour, one log of oil, and two turtledoves or young pigeons, vv. 21-22.

Now all this was to be done *for a testimony unto them,* to prove that this leper, who was doubtless well-known in the land, had been thoroughly cleansed; and thus, in this private way, to give full proof to the priesthood that Jesus was the true Messiah. The Jewish rabbins allowed that curing the lepers should be a characteristic of the Messiah; therefore the obstinacy of the priests in rejecting Christ was utterly inexcusable.

5. *A centurion.* A Roman military officer who had the command of 100 men.

6. *Lord.* Rather, "Sir," for so the word should always be translated when a Roman is the speaker. *Lieth at home.* "Lieth all along"; intimating that the disease had reduced him to a state of the utmost impotence, through the grievous torments with which it was accompanied. *Sick of the palsy.* Or "paralytic."

7. *I will come and heal him.* "I am coming, and will heal him." Jesus did not positively say, *I will come and heal him;* this could not have been strictly true, because our Lord healed him without going to the house. Foreseeing the exercise of the centurion's faith, He promises that while He is coming, ere He arrives at the house, He will heal him, and this was literally done, v. 13.

8. *But speak the word only.* Or, "Speak by word or command." Jesus can will away the palsy, and speak away the most grievous torments.

9. *For I am a man under authority.* That is, "under the authority of others." The argument of the centurion seems to run thus. If I, who am a person subject to the control of others, yet have some so completely subject to myself that I can say to one, *Come, and he cometh;* to another, *Go, and he goeth;* and to my slave, *Do this, and he doeth it;* how much more then canst Thou accomplish whatsoever Thou willest, being under no control, and having all things under Thy command!

10. *I have not found so great faith, no, not in Israel.* That is, I have not found so great an instance of confidence and faith in My power, even among the Jews, as this Roman, a Gentile, has shown himself to possess.

11. *Many shall come from the east and west.* Men of every description, of all countries, and of all professions; *and shall sit down,* that is, to meat, for this is the proper meaning. The rabbins represent the blessedness of the kingdom of God under the notion of a banquet. *With Abraham, and Isaac, and Jacob.* In the closest communion with the most eminent followers of God. But if we desire to inherit the promises, we must be followers of them who through faith and patience enjoy them. Let us therefore imitate Abraham in his faith, Isaac in his obedience unto death, and Jacob in his hope and expectation of good things to come.

12. *Shall be cast out into outer darkness.* As the enjoyment of that salvation which Jesus Christ calls the kingdom of Heaven is here represented under the notion of a nuptial festival, at which the guests sat down in a reclining posture with the master of the feast, so the state of those who were excluded from the banquet is represented as deep darkness, because the nuptial solemnities took place at night. And because they who were shut out were not only exposed to shame, but also to hunger and cold, therefore it is added, *There shall be weeping and gnashing of teeth.*

13. *As thou hast believed; so be it done.* "According to your faith be it done unto you," is a general measure of God's dealings with mankind. God is the same in the present time which He was in ancient days; and miracles of healing may be wrought on our own bodies and souls, and on those of others, by the instrumentality of our faith. But, alas! where is faith to be found! *And his servant was healed in the*

selfsame hour. "In that very hour." Faith is never exercised in the power and goodness of God till it is needed; and, when its is exercised, God works the miracle of healing.

14. *Peter's house.* That Peter lived at Capernaum, and that Christ lodged with him, is fully evident from this verse compared with chap. xvii. 24. *Peter's . . . wife's mother.* Learn hence, says Theophylact, that marriage is no hindrance to virtue, since the chief of the apostles had his wife. Marriage is one of the first of divine institutions, and is a positive command of God. He says the state of celibacy is not good, Gen. ii. 18. Those who pretend to say that the single state is more holy than the other slander their Maker, and say in effect, "We are too holy to keep the commandments of God."

15. *He touched her hand.* Can anything on this side the unlimited power of God effect such a cure with only a touch? If the Scriptures had not spoken of the divinity of Christ, these proofs of His power must have demonstrated it to the common sense of every man whose creed had not previously blinded him.

16. *When the even was come.* The Jews kept their Sabbath from evening to evening, according to the law, Lev. xxiii. 32, "From even unto even, shall ye celebrate your sabbath." Hence it was that the sick were not brought out to our Lord till after sunset, because then the Sabbath was ended. *Many that were possessed with devils.* Dr. Lightfoot gives two sound reasons why Judea, in our Lord's time, abounded with demoniacs. First, because they were then advanced to the very height of impiety. See what Josephus, their own historian, says of them: There was not (said he) a nation under heaven more wicked than they were. Secondly, because they were then strongly addicted to magic, and so, as it were, invited evil spirits to be familiar with them. *And healed all that were sick.* Not a soul did the Lord Jesus ever reject who came to Him soliciting His aid. Need any sinner despair who comes to Him, conscious of his spiritual malady, to be healed by His merciful hand?

17. *Himself took our infirmities.* The quotation is taken from Isa. liii. 4, where the verb *nasa* signifies to "bear sin," so as to "make atonement for it." And the rabbins understand this place to speak of the sufferings of the Messiah for the sins of Israel; and say that all the diseases, all the griefs, and all the punishments due to Israel shall be borne by Him. Christ fulfills the prophecies in all respects, and is himself the completion and truth of them, as being the Lamb and Victim of God, which bears and takes away the sin of the world. The text in Isaiah refers properly to the taking away of sin; and this in the Evangelist, to the removal of corporeal afflictions. But as the diseases of the body are the emblems of the sin of the soul, Matthew, referring to the prediction of the prophet, considered the miraculous healing of the body as an emblem of the soul's salvation by Christ Jesus.

18. *Unto the other side.* Viz., of the Lake of Genesareth, whence He proceeded to the country of the Gergesenes, v. 28.

19. *A certain scribe.* Few of this class came to the Lord Jesus for instruction or salvation. *Master.* Rather, "teacher," the person who shows

or points out a particular way or science. *I will follow thee whithersoever thou goest.* Every teacher among the Jews had disciples, and some especially that followed or accompanied them wherever they went, that they might have some person at hand with whom they might converse concerning the divine law.

20. *The foxes have holes.* Reader! are you a poor man? and do you fear God? Then what comfort must you derive from the thought that you so nearly resemble the Lord Jesus! *Son of man.* A Hebrew phrase, expressive of humiliation and debasement; and, on that account, applied emphatically to himself by the meek and lowly Jesus. Besides, it seems here to be used to point out the incarnation of the Son of God, according to the predictions of the prophets, Ps. viii. 5; Dan. vii. 13. And as our Lord was now showing forth His eternal divinity in the miracles He wrought, He seems studious to prove to them the certainty of His incarnation, because on this depended the atonement for sin. Indeed our Lord seems more intent on giving the proofs of His *humanity* than of His *divinity*, the latter being necessarily manifested by the miracles which He was continually working.

21 *Another of his disciples.* This does not mean any of the twelve, but one of those who were constant hearers of our Lord's preaching, the name of *disciple* being common to all those who professed to believe in Him, John vi. 66. *Bury my father.* Probably his father was old, and apparently near death; but it was a maxim among the Jews that, if a man had any duty to perform to the dead, he was, for that time, free from the observance of any other precept or duty.

22. *Let the dead bury their dead.* It was usual for the Jews to consider a man as *dead* who had departed from the precepts of the law; and, on this ground, every transgressor was reputed a dead man. Our Lord's saying, being in common use, had nothing difficult in it to a Jew. Natural death is the separation of the body and soul; spiritual death, the separation of God and the soul. Men who live in sin are dead to God. Leave the *spiritually* dead to bury their *natural* dead.

25. *Lord, save us: we perish.* One advantage of trials is to make us know our weakness, so as to oblige us to have recourse to God by faith in Christ. It is by faith alone that we may be said to approach Him; by love we are united to Him, and by prayer we awake Him.

26. *Why are ye fearful, O ye of little faith?* Faith is ever bold—incredulity always timid. When faith fails in temptation, there is the utmost danger of shipwreck. *Then he arose, and rebuked the winds,* as the agitation of the sea was only the effect of the wind, it was necessary to remove the cause of the disturbance, that the effect might cease. *There was a great calm.* One word of Christ can change the face of nature; one word of His can restore calm and peace to the most troubled and disconsolate soul.

27. *The men marvelled.* Every part of the creation (man excepted) hears and obeys the Creator's voice. *What manner of man is this?* "How great is this Person!" Here was God fully manifest; but it was in the flesh—there were the hidings of His power.

28. *The country of the Gergesenes.* This word is variously written in the MSS. and versions: Gergasenes, Gerasenes, Gadarenes. *Two possessed with devils.* Mark and Luke mention only one demoniac, probably the fiercer of the two.

29. *What have we to do with thee?* The literal translation is, "What is it to us and to Thee?" which perhaps might be understood to imply their disclaiming any design to interfere with the work of Christ, and that He should not therefore meddle with them; for it appears they exceedingly dreaded His power. *What have we to do with thee?* is a Jewish phrase which often occurs in the Old Testament, signifying an abrupt refusal of some request, or a wish not to be troubled with the company or importunity of others. *Art thou come hither to torment us before the time?* From this it appears that a greater degree of punishment awaited these demons than they at that time endured; and that they knew there was a time determined by the divine Judge when they should be sent unto greater torments.

33. *And they that kept them fled.* Terrified at what had happened to the swine.

34. *The whole city came out.* Probably with the intention to destroy Jesus for having destroyed their swine; but, having seen Him, they were awed by His presence, and only besought Him to depart from their borders. Many rather choose to lose Jesus Christ than those temporal goods by which they gratify their passions at the expense of their souls. They love even their swine better than their salvation.

CHAPTER 9

Christ heals a paralytic person at Capernaum, 1-8. Calls Matthew, 9-10. Eats with publicans and sinners, at which the Pharisees are offended, and He vindicates His conduct, 11-13. The disciples of John come to Him and inquire about fasting, 14-17. A ruler requests Him to heal his daughter, 18-19. On His road to the ruler's house, He heals a diseased woman, 20-22. Arriving at the ruler's house, He restores the young woman to life, 23-26. Heals two blind men, 27-31. Casts out a dumb demon, 32-34. Preaches and works miracles in all the cities and villages, 35. Is greatly affected at the desolate and dark state of the Jewish people, 36. Exhorts His disciples to pray to God to send them proper instructors, 37-38.

1. *He . . . came into his own city.* Viz., Capernaum, where He seems to have had His common residence at the house of Peter. This verse properly belongs to the preceding chapter.

2. *Lying on a bed.* A "couch" or "sofa," such as they reclined on at meals. *Seeing their faith.* The faith of the paralytic person, and the faith of those who brought him. *Be of good cheer.* "Son, take courage!" Probably he began to despond, and Christ spoke thus to support his faith. *Thy sins be forgiven thee.* Moral evil has been the cause of all the natural evil in the world. Christ goes to the source of the malady, which is sin. It is probable that this paralytic person had, in the earnest desires of his heart, entreated the cure of his soul, leaving his body to the care of others, as the first miracle of healing is wrought on his soul. It may be necessary to be observed that it was a maxim among the Jews that no diseased person could be healed till all his sins were blotted out. Hence our Lord first forgives the sins and then heals the body of the paralytic person. This appears to have been founded on Ps. ciii. 3. "Who forgiveth all thine iniquities; who healeth all thy dis-

eases." See also Ps. xli. 3-4. It may be observed, also, that most people are more in earnest about their souls when in sickness than in health, and therefore are more earnest in prayer for salvation.

3. *This man blasphemeth.* Wherever it is used in reference to God, it simply signifies "to speak impiously" of His nature, or attributes, or works. "Injurious speaking" is its proper translation when referred to man.

4. *Jesus knowing their thoughts.* In telling them what the thoughts of their hearts were (for they had expressed nothing publicly), He gave them the fullest proof of His power to forgive sins; because only God can forgive sins, and only God can search and know the heart.

5. *For whether is easier, to say, Thy sins be forgiven thee; or to say, Arise, and walk?* Both are equally easy, and equally difficult, for both require unlimited power to produce them. And everything is equally easy to that power which is unlimited. A universe can be as easily produced by a single act of the divine will as the smallest elementary part of matter.

6. *But that ye may know.* External miracles are the proofs of internal ones. Three miracles are wrought in this case: (1) The remission of the poor man's sins. (2) The discernment of the secret thoughts of the scribes. (3) The restoring of the paralytic, in an instant, to perfect soundness. Thus one miracle becomes the proof and establishment of another. Never was a clearer proof of omnipotent energy and mercy brought under the senses of man. Here is an absolutely perfect miracle wrought, and here are absolute incontestable proofs that the miracle *was* wrought; and the conclusion is the fullest demonstration of the divinity of the ever-blessed Jesus. *Arise, take up thy bed.* Being enabled to obey this command was the public proof that the man was made whole.

9. *Named Matthew.* Generally supposed to be the same who wrote this history of our blessed Lord. *Mathai* signifies a "gift" in Syriac; probably so named by his parents as implying a "gift from God." *The receipt of custom.* The customhouse, the place where the taxes levied by the Romans of the Jews were collected. *Follow me.* That is, Become My disciple. *And he arose, and followed him.* How blessed it is to be obedient to the first call of Christ—how much happiness and glory are lost by delays, though conversion at last may have taken place!

10. *Sat at meat in the house.* Viz., of Matthew, who it appears, from Luke v. 29, made a great feast on the occasion, thus testifying his gratitude for the honor done him; and that his friends and acquaintances might profit by the teaching of his new Master, he invites them to the entertainment that was honored by the presence of Christ. His companions, it appears, were not of the most creditable kind. They were "taxgatherers and sinners."

11. *When the Pharisees saw it.* The self-righteous Pharisees considered it equal to legal defilement to sit in company with taxgatherers and heathens.

12. *They that be whole need not a physician.* A common proverb, which none could either misunderstand or misapply.

13. *I will have mercy, and not sacrifice.* Quoted from 1 Sam. xv. 22. These are remarkable words. We may understand them as implying: (1) That God prefers an act of mercy, shown to the necessitous, to any act of religious worship to which the person might be called at that time. (2) That the whole sacrificial system was intended only to point out the infinite mercy of God to fallen man, in his redemption by the Blood of the new covenant. (3) That we should not rest in the sacrifices, but look for the mercy and salvation prefigured by them. *Go ye and learn.* A form of speech in frequent use among the rabbins, when they referred to any fact or example in the Sacred Writings.

14. *Thy disciples fast not.* Probably meaning that they did not fast so frequently as the others did, or for the same purposes, which is very likely, for the Pharisees had many superstitious fasts. They fasted in order to have lucky dreams, to obtain the interpretation of a dream, or to avert the evil import of a dream. They also fasted often in order to obtain the things they wished for. The tract *taanith* is full of these fasts, and of the wonders performed thus by the Jewish doctors.

15. *Can the children of the bridechamber?* These persons were the companions of the bridegroom, who accompanied him to the house of his father-in-law when he went to bring the bride to his own home. The marriage feast among the Jews lasted seven days, but the new-married woman was considered to be a bride for thirty days.

16. *No man putteth a piece of new cloth.* "No man putteth a patch of unscoured cloth upon an old garment."
That which is put in . . . taketh from the garment. Instead of closing up the rent, it makes a larger, by tearing away with it the whole breadth of the cloth over which it was laid; "it taketh its fulness or whole breadth from the garment."

17. *New wine into old bottles.* It is still the custom, in the Eastern countries, to make their bottles of goatskins. If these happened to be old, and new wine were put into them, the violence of the fermentation must necessarily burst them; and therefore newly made bottles were employed for the purpose of putting that wine in which had not yet gone through its state of fermentation. The institutes of Christ, and those of the Pharisees, could never be brought to accord; an attempt to combine the two systems would be as absurd as it would be destructive. The old covenant made way for the new, which was its completion and its end; but with that old covenant the new cannot be incorporated.

18. *A certain ruler.* There were two officers in the synagogue: *chazan,* the bishop or overseer of the congregation; and *rosh,* the head or ruler of the congregation. The *chazan* takes the book of the law and gives it to the *rosh,* or ruler, and he appoints who shall read the different sections. Jairus, who is the person intended here, was, in this latter sense, the ruler or governor of one of the synagogues, probably at Capernaum. *My daughter is even now dead.* Or, "My daughter was just now dying"; or "is by this time dead"; i.e., as Mr. Wakefield properly observes, She was so ill when I left home that she must be dead by this time. This turn of the expression reconciles the account given here with that in Mark and Luke. To be successful in our applications to God by prayer, four things

are requisite; and this ruler teaches us what they are. *First*, A man should place himself in the presence of God—he came unto Him. *Secondly*, He should humble himself sincerely before God—*he fell* down before Him—*at his feet*, Mark v. 22. *Thirdly*, He should lay open his wants with a holy earnestness—*he besought him* greatly, Mark v. 23. *Fourthly*, He should have unbounded confidence in the power and goodness of Christ, that his request shall be granted —*lay thy hand upon her, and she shall live*. Imposition of hands was a rite anciently used by the servants of God, through which heavenly influences were conveyed to the bodies and souls of men.

19. *Jesus arose, and followed him.* Our blessed Lord could have acted as well at a distance as present; but He goes to the place, to teach His ministers not to spare either their steps or their pains when the salvation of a soul is in question.

20. *The hem of his garment.* The "fringes," which the Jews were commanded to wear on their garments. See Num. xv. 38.

21. *She said within herself, If I may but touch his garment.* Her disorder was of that delicate nature that modesty forbade her to make any public acknowledgment of it, and therefore she endeavored to transact the whole business in private.

22. *Daughter, be of good comfort.* "Take courage, Daughter." *Thy faith hath made thee whole.* "This thy faith hath saved thee"; i.e., your faith in My power has interested that power in your behalf, so that you are saved from your disorder, and from all its consequences.

23. *Saw the minstrels and the people making a noise.* "Pipers." That pipes were in use among the Jews, in times of calamity or death, is evident from Jer. xlviii. 36. And among the Greeks and Romans, as well as among the Jews, persons were hired on purpose to follow the funeral processions with lamentations. See Jer. ix. 17-21; Amos v. 16. Even the poorest among the Jews were required to have two pipers and one mourning woman.

24. *The maid is not dead, but sleepeth.* That is, she is not dead so as to continue under the power of death; but shall be raised from it as a person is from natural sleep. *They laughed him to scorn.* "They ridiculed Him"—"they grinned a ghastly smile," expressive of the contempt they felt for His person and knowledge.

25. *He . . . took her by the hand, and the maid arose.* The fountain of life thus communicating its vital energy to the dead body. Where death has already taken place, no power but that of the great God can restore to life; in such a case, vain is the help of man. So the soul that is dead in trespasses and sins—that is, sentenced to death because of transgression—and is thus dead in law, can be restored to spiritual life only by the mighty power of the Lord Jesus, because He alone has made the atonement, and He alone can pardon transgression.

26. *And the fame thereof went abroad.* In this business Jesus himself scarcely appears, but the work effected by His sovereign power is fully manifested; to teach us that it is the business of a successful preacher of the gospel to conceal himself as much as possible, that God alone may have the glory of His own grace.

27. *Son of David.* This was the same as if they had called Him "Messiah." Two things here are worthy of remark: (1) That it was a generally received opinion at this time in Judea that the Messiah should be Son of David, John vii. 42 (2) That Jesus Christ was generally and incontestably acknowledged as coming from this stock, Matt. xii. 23.

28. *When he was come into the house.* That is, the house of Peter at Capernaum, where He ordinarily lodged. *Believe ye that I am able to do this?* Without faith Jesus does nothing to men's souls now, no more than He did to their bodies in the days of His flesh. *They said unto him, Yea, Lord.* Under a sense of our spiritual blindness we should have: (1) A lively faith in the almighty grace of Christ. (2) A fervent, incessant cry for the communication of this grace. (3) A proper view of His incarnation, because it is through His union with our nature, and by His sufferings and death, we are to expect salvation.

29. *According to your faith.* See on chap. viii. 13.

30. *Straitly charged them.* He charged them severely; He charged them, on pain of His displeasure, not to make it as yet public. See the reasons, chap. viii. 4.

31. *But they . . . spread abroad his fame.* They should have held their peace, for "to *obey* is better than *sacrifice*," 1 Sam. xv. 22; but man must always be wiser than God.

32. *A dumb man possessed with a devil.* Some demons rendered the persons they possessed paralytic, some blind, others dumb. It was the interest of Satan to hide his influences under the appearance of natural disorders.

33. *And when the devil was cast out, the dumb spake.* The very miracle which was now wrought was to be the demonstrative proof of the Messiah's being manifested in the flesh. See Isa. xxxv. 5-6. *It was never so seen in Israel.* The greatest of the prophets has never been able to do such miracles as these.

34. *He casteth out devils through the prince of the devils.* It is a consummate piece of malice to attribute the works of God to the devil. Envy cannot suffer the approbation which is given to the excellencies of others. Those whose hearts are possessed by this vice speak the very language of the devil.

35. *Jesus went about all the cities and villages.* Of Galilee. See on chap. iv. 23-24. A real minister of Jesus Christ, after His example, is neither detained in one place by a comfortable provision made by some nor discouraged from pursuing his work by the calumny and persecution of others.

36. *Moved with compassion.* From *splanchnon*, "a bowel." The Jews esteemed the bowels to be the seat of sympathy and the tender passions, and so applied the organ to the sense. *And were scattered abroad.* "Thrown down, or, all along." They were utterly neglected as to the interests of their souls, and rejected by the proud and disdainful Pharisees.

37. *The harvest.* The souls who are ready to receive the truth are very numerous, *but the labourers are few*. There are multitudes of scribes, Pharisees, and priests, of reverend and right reverend men; but there are few that

work. Jesus wishes for laborers, not gentlemen who are either idle drones or slaves to pleasure and sin.

38. *That he will send forth labourers.* "That He would thrust forth laborers." It is God's province to thrust out such preachers as shall labor; and it is our duty to entreat Him to do so. A minister of Christ is represented as a day laborer. He comes into the harvest, not to become lord of it, not to live on the labor of others but to work, and to labor his day. Though the work may be very severe, yet, to use a familiar expression, there are good wages in the harvest home; and the day, though hot, is but a short one.

CHAPTER 10

Jesus calls, commissions, and names His twelve disciples, 1-4. Gives them particular instructions relative to the objects of their ministry, 5-6. Mode of preaching, etc., 7-15. Foretells the afflictions and persecutions they would have to endure, and the support they should receive, 16-25. Cautions them against betraying His cause in order to procure their personal safety, 26-39. And gives especial promises to those who should assist His faithful servants in the execution of their work, 40-42.

1. *Twelve disciples.* Our Lord seems to have had the twelve patriarchs, heads of the congregation of Israel, in view in His choosing twelve disciples. That He had the plan of the ancient Jewish church in His eye is sufficiently evident from chap. xix. 28; and from Luke x. 1; xxii. 30; John xvii. 1, etc.; and Rev. xxi. 12-14. *He gave them power against unclean spirits.* Here we find the first call to the Christian ministry, and the end proposed by the commission given. He whose ministry is not accompanied with healing to diseased souls was never called of God. But let it be observed that, though the spiritual gifts requisite for the ministry must be supplied by God himself, yet this does not preclude the importance of *human learning.* No man can have his mind too well cultivated, to whom a dispensation of the gospel is committed. The influence of the Spirit of God was no more designed to render human learning useless than that learning should be considered as superseding the necessity of divine inspiration.

2. *Apostles.* This is the first place where the word is used. *Apostolos,* an "apostle," comes from *apostello,* "I send a message." The word was anciently used to signify a person commissioned by a king to negotiate any affair between him and any other power or people. It is worthy of notice that those who were Christ's *apostles* were first His *disciples;* to intimate that men must be first *taught* of God before they be *sent* of God. These twelve apostles were chosen: (1) That they might be with our Lord, to see and witness His miracles, and hear His doctrine; (2) That they might bear testimony of the former, and preach His truth to mankind. *The first, Simon, who is called Peter, and Andrew his brother.* We are not to suppose that the word *first* refers to any kind of dignity, as some have imagined; it merely signifies the "first in order"—the person first mentioned.

3-4. *Bartholomew.* Many are of opinion that this was Nathanael, mentioned in John i. 46, whose name was probably *Nathanael bar Talmai,* Nathanael, the son of Talmai. Here his own name is repressed, and he is called *Bar Talmai,* or *Bartholomew,* from his father. *Matthew the publi-*

can. The writer of this history. *James the son of Alphaeus.* This person was also called Cleopas, or Clopas, Luke xxiv. 18; John xix. 25. He had married Mary, sister to the blessed Virgin, John xix. 25. *Simon.* He was third son of Alphaeus, and brother of James and Jude, or Judas, Matt. xiii. 55. *The Canaanite.* This word is not put here to signify a particular people, as it is elsewhere used in the Sacred Writings; but it is formed from the Hebrew *kana,* which signifies "zealous," literally translated by Luke, chap. vi. 15, *Zelotes,* or the "zealous," probably from his great fervency in preaching the gospel of his Master. But see Luke vi. 15. *Judas Iscariot.* Probably from the Hebrew *ish kerioth,* a "man of Kerioth," which was a city in the tribe of Judah, Josh. xv. 25, where it is likely this man was born. As *iscara* signifies "strangulation," and Judas hanged himself after he had betrayed our Lord, Dr. Lightfoot seems inclined to believe that he had his name from this circumstance, and that it was not given him till after his death. *Who also betrayed him.* Rather, "even he who betrayed Him, or delivered Him up."

5. *These twelve Jesus sent forth, and commanded.* To be properly qualified for a minister of Christ, a man must be, (1) filled with the Spirit of holiness; (2) called to this particular work; (3) instructed in its nature; and (4) commissioned to go forth and testify the gospel of the grace of God. These are four different gifts which a man must receive from God by Christ Jesus. To these let him add all the human qualifications he can possibly attain, as in his arduous work he will require every gift and every grace. *Go not into the way of the Gentiles.* Our Lord only intended that the *first* offers of salvation should be made to the Jewish people, and that the heathen should not be noticed in this first mission, that no stumbling block might be cast in the way of the Jews. *Into any city of the Samaritans enter ye not.* The Samaritans afterwards had the gospel preached to them by Christ himself, John iv. 4, etc., for the reason assigned above. Such as God seems at first to pass by are often those for whom He has designed His greatest benefits (witness the Samaritans, and the Gentiles in general), but He has His own proper time to discover and reveal them. The history of the *Samaritans* is sufficiently known from the Old Testament. Properly speaking, the inhabitants of the city of Samaria should be termed Samaritans; but this epithet belongs chiefly to the people sent into that part of the Promised Land by Shalmaneser, king of Assyria, when he carried the Israelites that dwelt there captives beyond the Euphrates, and sent a mixed people, principally Cuthites, to dwell in their place. These were altogether heathens at first, but they afterwards incorporated the worship of the true God with that of their idols. See the whole account, 2 Kings xvii. 5, etc. From this time they feared Jehovah, and served other gods till after the Babylonish captivity. From Alexander the Great, Sanballat, their governor, otained permission to build a temple upon Mount Gerizim, which the Jews conceiving to be in opposition to their temple at Jerusalem, hated them with a perfect hatred, and would have no fellowship with them. The Samaritans acknowledge the divine authority of the law of Moses, and carefully preserve it in their own characters, which are probably the genuine ancient Hebrew. The Samaritan Pentateuch is printed in the London Polyglott.

6. *But go rather to the lost sheep.* The Jewish church was the ancient fold of God; but the sheep had wandered from their Shepherd, and were lost. Our blessed Lord sends these under-shepherds to seek, find, and bring them back to the Shepherd and Overseer of their souls.

7. *And as ye go, preach.* "As you proceed, proclaim like heralds"—make this proclamation wherever you go, and while you are journeying. Preach and travel; and, as you travel, preach—proclaim salvation to all you meet. Wherever the ministers of Christ go, they find lost, ruined souls; and wherever they find them, they should proclaim Jesus, and His power to save. For an explanation of the word "proclaim" or *preach,* see on chap. iii. 1. From this commission we learn what the grand subject of apostolic preaching was—*The kingdom of heaven is at hand!*

8. *Raise the dead.* This is wanting in the MSS. marked EKLMS of *Griesbach,* and in those marked BHV of *Mathai,* and in upwards of *one hundred* others. It is also wanting in the *Syriac* (Vienna edition), latter *Persic, Sahidic, Armenian, Slavonic,* and in one copy of the *Itala;* also in *Athanasius, Basil,* and *Chrysostom.* There is no evidence that the disciples raised any dead person previously to the resurrection of Christ. The words should certainly be omitted, unless we could suppose that the authority now given respected not only their present mission, but comprehended also their future conduct. *Freely ye have received, freely give.* A rule very necessary, and of great extent. A minister or laborer in the gospel vineyard, though worthy of his comfortable support while in the work, should never preach for hire, or make a secular traffic of a spiritual work.

9. *Provide neither gold, nor silver, nor brass in your purses.* "In your girdles." It is supposed that the people of the East carry their money in a fold of their girdles. This is scarcely correct; they carry it in a purse in the bosom, under the girdles. This I have often observed. "Have no money in your purse" is a command, obedience to which was secured by the narrow circumstances of most of the primitive genuine preachers of the gospel.

10. *Nor scrip for your journey.* To carry provisions. It was a leathern pouch hung about their necks, in which they put their victuals. This was, properly, the shepherd's bag. *Neither two coats.* Nothing to encumber you. *The workman is worthy of his meat.* "Of his maintenance." It is a maintenance, and that only, which a minister of God is to expect, and that he has a divine right to; but not to make a fortune, or lay up wealth. Besides, it is the *workman,* he that labors in the Word and doctrine, that is to get even this.

11. *Into whatsoever city or town ye shall enter.* In the commencement of Christianity, Christ and His preachers were all itinerant. *Enquire who in it is worthy.* That is, of a good character; for a preacher of the gospel should be careful of his reputation, and lodge only with those who are of a regular life. *There abide till ye go thence.* "Go not from house to house," Luke x. 7. Acting contrary to this precept has often brought a great disgrace on the gospel of God. Stay in your own lodging as much as possible, that you may have time for prayer and study. Seldom frequent the tables of the rich and great; if you do, it will unavoidably prove a snare to you.

12. *Salute it.* Saying, "Peace be to this house."

13. *If the house be worthy.* If that family be proper for a preacher to lodge in, and the master be ready to embrace the message of salvation. *Your peace.* The blessings you have prayed for shall come upon the family; God will prosper them in their bodies, souls, and substance. *Let your peace.* The blessings prayed for, return to you. "It shall turn back upon yourselves." They shall get nothing, and you shall have an increase.

14. *Shake off the dust of your feet.* The Jews considered themselves defiled by the dust of a heathen country, which was represented by the prophets as a polluted land, Amos vii. 17, when compared with the land of Israel, which was considered as a holy land, Ezek. xlv. 1. Therefore, to shake the dust of any city of Israel from off one's clothes or feet was an emblematical action, signifying a renunciation of all further connection with them, and placing them on a level with the cities of the heathen. See Amos ix. 7.

15. *In the day of judgment.* Or, "punishment." Perhaps not meaning the day of general judgment, nor the day of the destruction of the Jewish state by the Romans, but a day in which God should send punishment on that particular city, or on that person, for their crimes. So the day of judgment of Sodom and Gomorrah was the time in which the Lord destroyed them by fire and brimstone.

16. *Behold, I send you forth as sheep in the midst of wolves.* He who is called to preach the gospel is called to embrace a state of constant labor and frequent suffering. He who gets ease and pleasure in consequence of embracing the ministerial office neither preaches the gospel nor is sent of God. If he did the work of an evangelist, wicked men and demons would both oppose him. *Wise* ("prudent") *as serpents, and harmless as doves.* This is a proverbial saying; so in *Shir hashirim Rabba,* fol. 16, "The holy blessed God said to the Israelites, Ye shall be towards me as upright as the doves; but, towards the Gentiles, as cunning as serpents."

17. *But beware of men.* Or, Be on your guard against men, these men; i.e. your countrymen; those from whom you might have reasonably expected comfort and support; and especially those in power, who will abuse that power to oppress you. *Councils* ("sanhedrins") and *synagogues.* See on chap. v. 22. "By *synagogues* we may understand here, not the places of public worship, but assemblies where *three* magistrates, chosen out of the principal members of the synagogue, presided to adjust differences among the people: these had power, in certain cases, to condemn to the *scourge,* but not to *death.* See Acts xxii. 19; 2 Cor. xi. 24, compared with Luke xii. 11." See Lightfoot.

18. *Ye shall be brought before governors.* By governors and kings we may understand the Roman proconsuls, governors of provinces, and the kings who were tributary to the Roman government, and the emperors themselves, before whom many of the primitive Christians were brought. *For a testimony against them and* *the Gentiles.* That is, to render testimony to both Jews and Gentiles of the truth and power of My gospel.

19. *Take no thought how or what he shall speak.* Be not anxiously careful, because such anxiety argues distrust in God, and infallibly produces a confused mind. In such a state, no person is fit to proclaim or vindicate the truth. This promise, *It shall be given you,* banishes all distrust and inquietude on dangerous occasions; but without encouraging sloth and negligence, and without dispensing with the obligation we are under to prepare ourselves by the meditation of sacred truths, by the study of the Holy Scriptures, and by prayer.

20. *For it is . . . the Spirit of your Father.* This was an extraordinary promise, and was literally fulfilled to those first preachers of the gospel; and to them it was essentially necessary, because the New Testament dispensation was to be fully opened by their extraordinary inspiration. In a certain measure it may be truly said that the Holy Spirit animates the true disciples of Christ and enables them to *speak.* *Your Father.* This is added to excite and increase their confidence in God.

21. *And the brother shall deliver up the brother.* What an astonishing enmity is there in the soul of man against God and goodness!

22. *Ye shall be hated of all men for my name's sake.* Because ye are attached to Me, and saved from the corruption that is in the world, therefore the world will hate you. "The laws of Christ condemn a vicious world, and gall it to revenge." *He that endureth to the end shall be saved.* He who holds fast faith and a good conscience *to the end,* till the punishment threatened against this wicked people be poured out, he *shall be saved,* preserved from the destruction that shall fall upon the workers of iniquity.

23. *But when they persecute you.* It is prudence and humility (when charity or righteousness obliges us not to the contrary) to avoid persecution. *Ye shall not have gone over* ("ended" or finished," margin) *the cities.* The word here is generally understood as implying "to go over or through," intimating that there should not be time for the disciples to travel over the cities of Judea before the destruction predicted by Christ should take place. But this is very far from being the truth, as there were not less than forty years after this was spoken before Jerusalem was destroyed. Some contend that the passage should be translated, "Ye shall not have instructed, i.e., preached the gospel in the cities of Israel, till the Son of man be come." *Till the Son of man be come* may refer either to the outpouring of the Spirit on the Day of pentecost or to the subversion of the Jewish state.

24. *The disciple is not above his master.* Or in plainer terms, "A scholar is not above his teacher." Jesus is the great Teacher; we profess to be His scholars. He who keeps the above saying in his heart will never complain of what he suffers.

25. *It is enough for the disciple that he be as his master.* Can any man who pretends to be a scholar or disciple of Jesus Christ expect to be treated well by the world? Will not the world love its own, and them only? Why, then, so much impatience under sufferings, such an excessive sense of injuries, such delicacy? Can you expect anything from the world better than you receive? *Beelzebub.* This name is variously written in the MSS. *Beelzeboul, Beelzeboun, Beelzebud,* but there is a vast majority in favor of the reading *Beelzebul,* which should, by all means, be inserted in the text instead of *Beelzebub.* It is supposed that this idol was the same with *Baalzebub* the *god fly,* worshipped at Ekron, 2 Kings i. 2, etc., who had his name changed afterwards by the Jews to *Baal zebul,* the *dung god,* a title expressive of the utmost contempt.

26. *Fear them not.* A general direction to all the persecuted followers of Christ. Fear them not, for they can make you suffer nothing worse than they have made Christ suffer; and under all trials He has promised the most ample support. *For there is nothing covered.* God sees everything; this is consolation to the upright, and dismay to the wicked. And He will bring into judgment every work, and every secret thing, whether good or bad, Eccles. xii. 14.

27. *What I tell you in darkness.* A man ought to preach that only which he has learned from God's Spirit, and His testimonies; but let him not pretend to bring forth anything new or mysterious. There is nothing that concerns our salvation that is newer than the new covenant; and in that there are, properly speaking, no mysteries. What was secret before is now made manifest in the gospel of the ever-blessed God. See Eph. iii. 1-12. *What ye hear in the ear.* The doctor who explained the law in Hebrew had an interpreter always by him, in whose ears he softly whispered what he said; this interpreter spoke aloud what had been thus whispered to him. The spirit of our Lord's direction appears to be this: Whatever I speak to you is for the benefit of mankind—keep nothing from them; declare explicitly the whole counsel of God; *preach ye* (proclaim) *upon the housetops.* The houses in Judea were flat-roofed, with ballustrades round about, which were used for the purpose of taking the air, prayer, meditation, and it seems, from this place, for announcing things in the most public manner.

28. *Fear not them which kill the body.* Those who slay with acts of cruelty, alluding probably to the cruelties which persecutors should exercise on His followers in their martyrdom. *But are not able to kill the soul.* Hence we find that the body and the soul are distinct principles, for the body may be slain and the soul escape; and, secondly, that the soul is immaterial, for the murderers of the body are not able, have it not in their power, to injure it. *Fear him.* It is not hellfire we are to fear, but it is God, without the stroke of whose justice hell itself would be no punishment, and whose frown would render heaven itself insupportable.

29. *Are not two sparrows sold for a farthing?* The word *assarion,* which we translate *farthing,* is found among the rabbins in the word *aisar,* which is used among them to express a thing of the lowest or almost no value. The doctrine intended to be inculcated is this: The providence of God extends to the minutest things; everything is continually under the government and care of God, and nothing occurs without His will or permission. If then He regards *sparrows,* how

much more man, and how much more still the soul that trusts in Him! *Without your Father.* Without the will of your Father. All things are ordered by the *counsel* of God. This is a great consolation to those who are tried and afflicted.

30. *But the very hairs of your head are all numbered.* Nothing is more astonishing than the care and concern of God for His followers. The least circumstances of their lives are regulated, not merely by that general providence which extends to all things, but by a particular providence which fits and directs all things to the design of their salvation, causing them all to cooperate for their present and eternal good.

31. *Fear ye not therefore, ye are of more value.* None can estimate the value of a soul, for which Christ has given His blood and life! Have confidence in His goodness, for He who so dearly purchased you will miraculously preserve and save you.

32. *Whosoever therefore shall confess me before men.* That is, whosoever shall acknowledge Me to be the Messiah, and have his heart and life regulated by My spirit and doctrine. It is not merely sufficient to have the heart right before God; there must be a firm, manly, and public profession of Christ before men.

33. *Whosoever shall deny me.* Whosoever prefers his worldly interest to his duty to God sets a greater value on earthly than on heavenly things, and prefers the friendship of men to the approbation of God. Let it be remembered that to be renounced by Christ is to have Him for neither Mediator nor Saviour. To appear before the tribunal of God without having Christ for our Advocate, and, on the contrary, to have Him there as our Judge, and a Witness against us—how can a man think of this and not die with horror!

34. *Think not that I am come to send peace.* The meaning of this difficult passage will be plain when we consider the import of the word *peace,* and the expectation of the Jews. The word *shalom* was used among the Hebrews to express all possible blessings, temporal and spiritual, but especially the former. The import of our Lord's teaching here is this: Do not imagine, as the Jews in general vainly do, that I am come to *send forth,* by forcing out the Roman power, that temporal prosperity which they long for. I am not come for this purpose, but to send forth the Roman sword, to cut off a disobedient and rebellious nation, the cup of whose iniquity is already full, and whose crimes cry aloud for speedy vengeance.

35. *I am come to set a man at variance.* The spirit of Christ can have no union with the spirit of the world. Even a father, while unconverted, will oppose a godly child. Thus the spirit that is in those who sin against God is opposed to that spirit which is in the followers of the Most High.

36. *A man's foes shall be they of his own household.* Our Lord refers here to their own traditions. So *Sota,* fol. 49. "A little before the coming of the Messiah, the son shall insult the father, the daughter rebel against her mother, the daughter-in-law against her mother-in-law; and each man shall have his own household for his enemies."

37. *He that loveth father or mother more than me.* He whom we love the most is he whom we study most to please, and whose will and interests we prefer in all cases. If, in order to please a father or mother who is opposed to vital godliness, we abandon God's ordinances and followers, we are unworthy of anything but hell.

38. *He that taketh not his cross,* i.e., he who is not ready, after My example, to suffer death in the cause of My religion, *is not worthy of me,* does not deserve to be called My disciple.

39. *He that findeth his life,* i.e., he who, for the sake of his temporal interest, abandons his spiritual concerns, shall lose his soul; and he who, in order to avoid martyrdom, abjured the pure religion of Christ, shall lose his soul, and perhaps his life too.

40. *He that receiveth you,* treats you kindly, *receiveth me.* I will consider the kindness as shown to myself, for he who receiveth Me as the true Messiah receiveth that God by whose counsels and through whose love I am come.

41. *He that receiveth a prophet.* A "teacher," not a "foreteller of future events," for this is not always the meaning of the word, but one commissioned by God to teach the doctrines of eternal life. It is no small honor to receive into one's house a minister of Jesus Christ. Many sayings of this kind are found among the rabbins, and this one is common: "He who receives a learned man, or an elder, into his house, is the same as if he had received the *Shekinah.*" And again: "He who speaks against a faithful pastor, it is the same as if he had spoken against God himself."

42. *Little ones.* My apparently mean and generally despised disciples. *Verily . . . he shall in no wise lose his reward.* The rabbins have a similar saying: "He that gives food to one that studies in the law, God will bless him in this world, and give him a lot in the world to come." Love heightens the smallest actions, and gives a worth to them which they cannot possess without it.

CHAPTER 11

Christ, having finished His instructions to His disciples, departs to preach in different cities, 1. John sends two of his disciples to Him to inquire whether He were the Christ, 2-6. Christ's testimony concerning John, 7-15. He upbraids the Jews with their capriciousness, 16-19. The condemnation of Chorazin, and Bethsaida, and Capernaum, for their unbelief and unpenitence, 20-24. Praises the divine wisdom for revealing the gospel to the simple-hearted, 25-26. Shows that none can know God but by the revelation of His Son, 27. Invites the distressed to come unto Him, and gives them the promise of rest for their souls, 28-30.

1. This verse properly belongs to the preceding chapter, from which it should on no account be separated, as with that it has the strictest connection, but with this it has none. *Their cities.* The cities of the Jews.

2. *John had heard in the prison.* John was cast into prison by order of Herod Antipas, chap. xiv. 3, etc., a little after our Lord began His public ministry, chap. iv. 12; and after the first Passover, John iii. 24.

3. *Art thou he that should come?* "He that cometh" seems to have been a proper name of the Messiah; to save or deliver is necessarily implied. There is some difficulty in what is here spoken of John. Some have thought he was utterly ignorant of our Lord's divine mission, and that he sent merely for his own

information; but this is certainly inconsistent with his own declaration, Luke iii. 15, etc.; John i. 15, 26, 33; iii. 28, etc. Others suppose he sent the message merely for the instruction of his disciples; that, as he saw his end approaching, he wished them to have the fullest conviction that Jesus was the Messiah, that they might attach themselves to Him. A third opinion takes a middle course between the two former, and states that, though John was at first perfectly convinced that Jesus was the Christ, yet, entertaining some hopes that He would erect a secular kingdom in Judea, wished to know whether this was likely to take place speedily. It is very probable that John now began, through the length of his confinement, to entertain doubts relative to His kingdom, which perplexed and harassed his mind; and he took the most reasonable way to get rid of them at once, viz., by applying to Christ himself.

4. *Go and shew John again those things which ye do hear and see.* Christ would have men to judge only of Him and of others by their works. This is the only safe way of judging. A man is not to be credited because he professes to know such and such things, but because he demonstrates by his conduct that his pretensions are not vain.

5. *The lame walk.* They "walk about," to give the fullest proof to the multitude that their cure was real. These miracles were not only the most convincing proofs of the supreme power of Christ, but were also emblematic of that work of salvation which He effects in the souls of men. (1) Sinners are *blind;* their understanding is so darkened by sin that they see not the way of truth and salvation. (2) They are *lame*—not able to walk in the path of righteousness. (3) They are *leprous*—their souls are defiled with sin, the most loathsome and inveterate disease. (4) They are *deaf* to the voice of God, His Word, and their own consciences. (5) They are *dead* in trespasses and sins, God, who is the Life of the soul, being separated from it by iniquity. Nothing less than the power of Christ can redeem from all this; and from all this, that power of Christ actually does redeem every penitent, believing soul. Giving sight to the blind and raising the dead are allowed by the ancient rabbins to be works which the Messiah should perform when He should manifest himself in Israel. *The poor have the gospel preached to them.* And what was this gospel? Why, the glad tidings that Jesus Christ came into the world to save sinners; that He opens the eyes of the blind; enables the lame to walk with an even, steady, and constant pace in the way of holiness; cleanses the lepers from all the defilement of their sins; opens the ears of the deaf to hear His pardoning words; and raises those who were dead in trespasses and sins to live in union with himself to all eternity.

6. *Blessed is he, whosoever shall not be offended in me.* Or, "Happy is he who will not be stumbled at Me."

7. *What went ye out into the wilderness to see?* The purport of our Lord's design, in this and the following verses, is to convince the scribes and Pharisees of the inconsistency of their conduct in acknowledging John the Baptist for a divinely authorized teacher and not believing in the very Christ which he pointed out to them. He also shows, from the excellencies of John's character, that their confidence in him was not misplaced, and that this was a further argument why they should have believed in Him, whom the Baptist proclaimed as being far superior to himself. *A reed shaken with the wind?* An emblem of an irresolute, unsteady mind, which believes and speaks one thing today and another tomorrow. Christ asks these Jews if they had ever found anything in John like this: Was he not ever steady and uniform in the testimony he bore to Me?

8. *A man clothed in soft raiment?* A second excellency in John was his sober and mortified life. A preacher of the gospel should have nothing about him which savors of effeminacy and worldly pomp. *Are in kings' houses.* A third excellency in John was, he did not affect high things. He was contented to live in the desert, and to announce the solemn and severe truths of his doctrine to the simple inhabitants of the country.

9. *A prophet? yea . . . and more than a prophet.* That is, one more excellent than a prophet; one greatly beyond all who had come before him, being the immediate forerunner of Christ, and who was especially commissioned to prepare the way of the Lord. This was a fourth excellency.

10. *Behold, I send my messenger.* A fifth excellency of the Baptist was his preparing the way of the Lord, being the instrument, in God's hand, of preparing the people's hearts to receive the Lord Jesus; and it was probably through his preaching that so many thousands attached themselves to Christ immediately on His appearing as a public Teacher.

11. *A greater than John the Baptist.* A sixth excellency of the Baptist—he was greater than any prophet from the beginning of the world till that time: (1) Because he was prophesied of by them, Isa. xl. 3; Mal. iii. 1. (2) Because he had the privilege of showing the fulfilment of their predictions, by pointing out that Christ has now come, which they foretold should come. (3) Because he saw and enjoyed that salvation which they could only foretell. *Notwithstanding he that is least in the kingdom of heaven.* By the kingdom of Heaven in this verse is meant the fullness of the blessings of the gospel of peace, which fullness was not known till after Christ had been crucified, and had risen from the dead. Now the least in this Kingdom, the meanest preacher of a crucified, risen, and glorified Saviour, was greater than John, who was not permitted to live to see the plenitude of gospel grace in the pouring out of the Holy Spirit.

12. *The kingdom of heaven suffereth violence.* The taxgatherers and heathen, whom the scribes and Pharisees think have no right to the kingdom of the Messiah, filled with holy zeal and earnestness, seize at once on the proffered mercy of the gospel, and so take the Kingdom as by force from those learned doctors who claimed for themselves the chiefest places in that Kingdom. He that will take, get possession of, the Kingdom of righteousness, peace, and spiritual joy must be in earnest. All hell will oppose him in every step he takes; and if a man be not absolutely determined to give up his sins and evil companions, and have his soul saved at all

hazards, and at every expense, he will surely perish everlastingly. This requires a violent earnestness.

14. *This is Elias, which was for to come.* This should always be written Elijah, that as strict a conformity as possible might be kept up between the names in the Old Testament and the New. The prophet Malachi, who predicted the coming of the Baptist in the spirit and power of Elijah, gave the *three* following distinct characteristics of him. First, That he should be the forerunner and messenger of the Messiah: "Behold, I will send my messenger . . . before me," Mal. iii. 1. Secondly, That he should appear before the destruction of the second Temple: "And the Lord, whom ye seek, shall suddenly come to his temple," *ibid.* Thirdly, That he should preach repentance to the Jews; and that, some time after, the great and terrible day of the Lord should come, and the Jewish land be smitten with a curse, chap. iv. 5-6. Now these three characters agree perfectly with the conduct of the Baptist and what shortly followed his preaching, and have not been found in anyone else, which is a convincing proof that Jesus was the promised Messiah.

15. *He that hath ears to hear, let him hear.* As if our Lord had said, These things are so clear and manifest that a man has only to hear them to be convinced and fully satisfied of their truth.

16. *But whereunto shall I liken this generation?* That is, the Jewish people—"this race." *In the markets.* Or "places of concourse." *Calling unto their fellows.* Or "companions."

17. *We have piped unto you, and ye have not danced.* We have begun the music, which should have been followed by the dance, but you have not attended to it. *We have mourned . . . and ye have not lamented.* "You have not smote the breast."

18. *For John came neither eating nor drinking.* Leading a very austere and mortified life, and yet you did not receive him. *He hath a devil.* He is a vile hypocrite, influenced by a demon to deceive and destroy the simple.

19. *The Son of man came eating and drinking.* That is, went wheresoever He was invited to eat a morsel of bread, and observed no rigid fasts. *They say, Behold a man gluttonous.* Whatever measures the followers of God may take, they will not escape the censure of the world; the best way is not to be concerned at them. *But wisdom is justified of her children.* *Of,* here and in many places of our translation, ought to be written "by" in modern English. It is likely that by *children* our Lord simply means the fruits or effects of wisdom, according to the Hebrew idiom, which denominates the fruits or effects of a thing as its children.

20. *Then began he to upbraid the cities.* The more God has done to draw men unto himself, the less excusable are they if they continue in iniquity.

21. *Woe unto thee, Chorazin . . . Bethsaida!* It would be better to translate "alas for thee" than *woe unto thee.* The former is an exclamation of pity; the latter, a denunciation of wrath. *Tyre and Sidon* were two heathen cities situated on the shore of the Mediterranean Sea,

into which it does not appear that Christ ever went, though He was often very nigh to them.

23. *Thou, Capernaum, which art exalted unto heaven.* A Hebrew metaphor expressive of the utmost prosperity and the enjoyment of the greatest privileges. This was properly spoken of this city because that in it our Lord dwelt, and wrought many of His miraculous works. *Shalt be brought down to hell.* Perhaps not meaning here the place of torment, but rather a state of desolation. The original word is *Hades* —the invisible receptacle or mansion of the dead, answering to *sheol,* in Hebrew; and implying, often, (1) the grave; (2) the state of separate souls, or unseen world of spirits, whether of torment, Luke xvi. 23, or in general, Rev. i. 18; vi. 8; xx. 13-14. The word *hell,* used in the common translation, conveys now an improper meaning of the original word, because *hell* is used only to signify the place of the damned.

24. *Day of judgment* may either refer to that particular time in which God visits for iniquity or to that great day in which He will judge the world by the Lord Jesus Christ.

25. *I thank thee.* "I fully agree with Thee"—I am perfectly of the same mind. Thou hast acted in all things according to the strictest holiness, justice, mercy, and truth.

27. *No man knoweth the Son, but the Father; neither knoweth any man.* None can fully comprehend the nature and attributes of God but Christ; and none can fully comprehend the nature, incarnation, etc., of Christ but the Father.

28. *Come unto me.* This phrase in the new covenant implies, simply, believing in Christ and becoming His disciple or follower. *All ye that labour and are heavy laden.* The Jews, heavily laden with the burdensome rites of the Mosaic institution, rendered still more oppressive by the additions made by the scribes and Pharisees, who, our Lord says (chap. xxiii. 4), bound on "heavy burdens"; and laboring, by their observance of the law, to make themselves pleasing to God, are here invited to lay down their load, and receive the salvation procured for them by Christ. Sinners, wearied in the ways of iniquity, are also invited to come to this Christ and find speedy relief. Penitents, burdened with the guilt of their crimes, may come to this Sacrifice and find instant pardon. Believers, sorely tempted, and oppressed by the remains of the carnal mind, may come to this Blood that cleanseth from all unrighteousness; and, purified from all sin, and powerfully succored in every temptation, they shall find uninterrupted *rest* in this complete Saviour.

29. *Take my yoke upon you.* Strange paradox! that a man already weary and overloaded must take a new weight upon him, in order to be eased and find rest! *I am meek and lowly in heart.* Wherever pride and anger dwell, there is nothing but mental labor and agony; but where the meekness and humility of Christ dwell, all is smooth, even, peaceable, and quiet. For "the work of righteousness is peace; and the effect of righteousness quietness and assurance for ever," Isa. xxxii. 17.

30. *For my yoke is easy.* My gospel imposes nothing that is difficult; on the contrary, it provides for the complete removal of all that which oppresses and renders man miserable, viz., sin.

CHAPTER 12

Jesus and His disciples go through the cornfields on the Sabbath, and the latter pluck and eat some of the ears, at which the Pharisees take offense, 1-2. Our Lord vindicates them, 3-8. The man with the withered hand cured, 9-13. The Pharisees seek His destruction, 14. He heals the multitudes, and fulfills certain prophecies, 15-21. Heals the blind and dumb demoniac, 22-23. The malice of the Pharisees reproved by our Lord, 24-30. The sin against the Holy Ghost, 31-32. Good and bad trees known by their fruits—evil and good men by their conduct, 33-37. Jonah, a sign of Christ's death and resurrection, 38-40. The men of Nineveh and the queen of the south shall rise up in the judgment against the Jews, 41-42. Of the unclean spirit, 43-45. Christ's mother and brethren seek Him, 46-50.

3. *Have ye not read what David did?* The original history is in 1 Sam. xxi. 1-6.

4. *He entered into the house of God.* Viz., the house of Ahimelech, the priest, who dwelt at Nob, with whom the Tabernacle then was, in which the Divine Presence was manifested. *And did eat the shewbread.* "Bread of the presence," or faces, because this bread was to be set continually before the face of Jehovah. See the notes on Exod. xxv. 23 and 30.

5. *The priests . . . profane the sabbath.* Profane, i.e., put it to what might be called a common use, by slaying and offering up sacrifices, and by doing the services of the Temple.

6. *In this place is one greater than the temple.* Does not our Lord refer here to Mal. iii. 1? Compare this with Heb. iii. 3. The Jews esteemed nothing greater than the Temple, except God, who was worshipped in it. Christ, by asserting He is *greater than the temple,* asserts that He is God.

8. *The Son of man is Lord even of the sabbath day.* The change of the Jewish into the Christian Sabbath, called the "Lord's day," Rev. i. 10, shows that Christ is not only the Lord, but also the truth and completion of it. For it seems to have been by an especial providence that this change has been made and acknowledged all over the Christian world.

10. *A man which had his hand withered.* Probably through a partial paralysis. The man's hand was withered; but God's mercy had still preserved to him the use of his feet. He uses them to bring him to the public worship of God, and Jesus meets and heals him there.

12. *How much then is a man better than a sheep?* There are many persons who call themselves Christians who do more for a beast of burden or pleasure than they do for a man for whom Christ died!

13. *Stretch forth thine hand.* The bare command of God is a sufficient reason of obedience. Faith disregards apparent impossibilities, where there are a command and a promise of God. The effort to believe is often that faith by which the soul is healed. It is worthy of remark that as the man was healed with a word, without even a touch, the Sabbath was unbroken, even according to their most rigid interpretation of the letter of the law.

14. *Held a council against him.* Nothing sooner leads to utter blindness and hardness of heart than envy.

15. *Jesus . . . withdrew himself from thence.* It is the part of prudence and Christian charity not to provoke, if possible, the blind and the hardened. *Great multitudes followed him, and he healed them all.* The rejection of the gospel in one place has often been the means of sending it to and establishing it in another.

18. *Behold my servant.* This title was given to our blessed Lord in several prophecies. See Isa. xlii. 1; liii. 2. Christ assumes it, Ps. xl. 7-9. Compare these with John xvii. 4 and Phil. ii. 7. God required an acceptable and perfect service from man; but man, being sinful, could not perform it. Jesus, taking upon Him the nature of man, fully performed the whole will of God. *And he shall shew judgment to the Gentiles.* That is, He will publish the gospel to the heathen; for the word here answers to the word *mishpat* of the prophet, and it is used among the Hebrews to signify laws, precepts, and a whole system or body of doctrine.

19. *He shall not strive, not cry.* The spirit of Christ is not a spirit of contention, murmuring, clamor, or litigiousness. He who loves these does not belong to Him. Christ therefore fulfilled a prophecy by withdrawing from this place, on account of the rage of the Pharisees.

20. *A bruised reed shall he not break.* A reed is, in Scripture, the emblem of weakness, Ezek. xxix. 6; and a *bruised* reed must signify that state of weakness that borders on dissolution and death. *And smoking flax shall he not quench.* Linos means the wick of a lamp, and *typhomenon* is intended to point out its expiring state, when the oil has been all burnt away from it, and nothing is left but a mere snuff, emitting smoke. Some suppose the Jewish state, as to ecclesiastical matters, is here intended, the prophecy declaring that Christ would not destroy it, but leave it to expire of itself, as it already contained the principles of its own destruction. Others have considered it as implying that great tenderness with which the blessed Jesus should treat the weak and the ignorant, whose good desires must not be stifled, but encouraged. The *bruised reed* may recover itself, it permitted to vegetate under the genial influences of heaven; and the life and light of the expiring lamp may be supported by the addition of fresh oil. Jesus therefore quenches not faint desires after salvation, even in the worst and most undeserving of men; for even such desires may lead to the fullness of the blessing of the gospel of peace. *Judgment unto victory.* See v. 18. By *judgment* understand the gospel, and by *victory* its complete triumph over Jewish opposition and Gentile impiety. He will continue by these mild and gentle means to work till the whole world is Christianized and the universe filled with His glory.

21. *And in his name shall the Gentiles trust.* "They shall hope."

22. *One possessed with a devil, blind, and dumb.* A person from whom the indwelling demon took away both sight and hearing. Satan makes himself master of the heart, the eyes, and the tongue of the sinner. His heart he fills with the love of sin; his eyes he blinds that he may not see his guilt, and the perdition which awaits him; and his tongue he hinders from prayer and supplication, though he gives it increasing liberty in blasphemies, lies, slanders, etc. None but Jesus can redeem from this threefold captivity.

23. *Is not this the son of David?* Is not this the true Messiah? Do not these miracles sufficiently prove it?

24. *Beelzebub.* See chap. x. 25.

27. *By whom do your children cast them out? Children,* or sons, of the prophets means the disciples of the prophets; and children or sons of the Pharisees, disciples of the Pharisees. From Acts xix. 13-14, it is evident there were *exorcists* among the Jews, and from our Lord's saying here, it is also evident that the disciples of the Pharisees did cast out demons, or at least those who educated them wished to have it believed that they had such a power. Our Lord's argument here is extremely conclusive: If the man who casts our demons proves himself thereby to be in league with and influenced by Satan, then your disciples, and you who taught them, are all of you in league with the devil.

28. *But if I cast out devils by the Spirit* of *God.* Perhaps the *Spirit of God* is here mentioned by way of opposition to the magical incantations of the Jews; for it is well-known that by fumigations and magical washings they professed to cast out devils. *Then the kingdom of God.* For the destruction of the kingdom of Satan plainly implies the setting up of the kingdom of God. *Is come unto you.* Is come unexpectedly upon you.

29. *Else how can one enter into a strong man's house?* Men, through sin, are become the very house and dwelling place of Satan, having of their own accord surrendered themselves to this unjust possessor; for whoever gives up his soul to sin gives it up to the devil. It is Jesus, and Jesus alone, who can deliver from the power of this bondage. When Satan is cast out, Jesus purifies and dwells in the heart.

30. *He that is not with me is against me.* There is no medium between loving the Lord and being His enemy—between belonging to Christ or to Satan. If we be on the side of the devil, we must expect to go to the devil's hell; if we be on the side of Christ, we may expect to go to His heaven.

Scattereth abroad. This seems to have been a proverbial form of speech, and may be a metaphor taken from shepherds. He who does not help the true shepherd to gather his flock into the fold, is, most likely, one who wishes to scatter them, that he may have the opportunity of stealing and destroying them.

31. *All manner of sin and blasphemy.* Injurious or impious speaking, mocking, and deriding speech. *But the blasphemy against the Holy Ghost,* i.e., when the person obstinately attributed those works to the devil which he had the fullest evidence could be wrought only by the Spirit of God. That this, and nothing else, is the sin against the Holy Spirit is evident from the connection in this place, and more particularly from Mark iii. 28-30. Here the matter is made clear beyond the smallest doubt—the "unpardonable sin," as some term it, is neither less nor more than ascribing the miracles Christ wrought, by the power of God, to the spirit of the devil. Many sincere people have been grievously troubled with apprehensions that they had committed the unpardonable sin; but let it be observed that no man who believes the divine mission of Jesus Christ ever can commit this sin.

32. *Neither in this world, neither in the world to come.* Neither in this dispensation, viz., the Jewish, nor in that which is to come, viz., the Christian. *The world to come* is a constant phrase for the times of the Messiah in the Jewish writers.

33. *Either make the tree good.* The works will resemble the heart. Nothing good can proceed from an evil spirit; no good fruit can proceed from a corrupt heart. Before the heart of man can produce any good, it must be renewed and influenced by the Spirit of God.

34. *O generation of vipers.* These are apparently severe words, but they were extremely proper in reference to that execrable people to whom they were addressed. The whole verse is an inference from what was spoken before. *Out of the abundance* (the overflowings) *of the heart.* Wicked words and sinful actions may be considered as the overflowings of a heart that is more than full of the spirit of wickedness; and holy words and righteous deeds may be considered as the overflowings of a heart that is filled with the Holy Spirit, and running over with love to God and man.

35. *A good man out of the good treasure of the heart.* The good heart is the good treasury, and the treasure that is in it is the love of God, and of all mankind. The bad heart is the bad treasury, and its treasure is the carnal mind, which is enmity against God, and ill will to man.

36. *Every idle word.* A word that does nothing, that neither ministers grace nor instruction to them who hear it. The word corresponds to the Hebrew *shave,* which signifies not only vain or empty, but also wicked and injurious, such as a false testimony against a neighbor.

37. *By thy words thou shalt be justified.* That is, the whole tenor of your conversation will be an evidence for or against you in the great day. "Lord, put a watch before the door of my lips!" is a prayer proper for all men.

39. *An evil and adulterous generation.* Or "race of people." Our Lord terms the Jews an adulterous race. Under the old covenant, the Jewish nation was represented as in a marriage contract with the Lord of hosts, as believers in the new covenant are represented as the spouse of Christ. All unfaithfulness and disobedience was considered as a breach of this marriage contract; hence the persons who were thus guilty are denominated adulterers and adulteresses.

40. *Three days and three nights.* Our Lord rose from the grave on the day but one after His crucifixion: so that, in the computation in this verse, the part of the day on which He was crucified, and the part of that on which He rose again, are severally estimated as an entire day; and this, no doubt, exactly corresponded to the time in which Jonah was in the belly of the fish. The very same quantity of time which is here termed three days and three nights, and which, in reality, was only one whole day, a part of two others, and two whole nights, is termed three days and three nights, in the Book of Esther: "Go . . . neither eat nor drink three days, night or day . . . and so will I go in unto the king," chap. iv. 16 Afterwards it follows, chap v. 1: "On the third day . . . Esther . . . stood in the inner court of the king's house." Thus, then, three days and three nights, according to this Jewish method of reckoning, included any part of the first day, the whole of the following night, the next day and its night, and any part of the

succeeding or third day. *In the whale's belly.* A fish of the shark kind, and not a *whale,* is here meant. It is well-known that the throat of a *whale* is capable of admitting little more than the arm of an ordinary man; but many of the shark species can swallow a man whole, and men have been found whole in the stomachs of several.

41. *The men of Nineveh shall rise in judgment.* The voice of God, threatening temporal judgments, caused a whole people to repent who had neither Moses nor Christ, neither the law nor the prophets, and who perhaps never had but this one preacher among them. What judgment may not we expect, if we continue impenitent, after all that God has bestowed upon us? *A greater than Jonas is here.* "Something more." The evidence offered by Jonah sufficed to convince and lead the Ninevites to repentance, but here was more evidence, and a greater Person; and yet so obstinate are the Jews that all is ineffectual. (1) Christ, who preached to the Jews, was infinitely greater than Jonah, in His nature, person, and mission. (2) Jonah preached repentance in Nineveh only forty days, and Christ preached among the Jews for several years. (3) Jonah wrought no miracles to authorize his preaching; but Christ wrought miracles every day, in every place where He went, and of every kind. And (4) Notwithstanding all this, the people of Judea did not repent, though the people of Nineveh did.

42. *The queen of the south.* In 1 Kings x. 1, this queen is said to be of Saba, which was a city and province of Arabia Felix, to the south, or southeast, of Judea. *Uttermost parts of the earth.* A form of speech which merely signifies "a great distance."

43. *When the unclean spirit.* If there had been no reality in demoniacal possessions, our Lord would have scarcely appealed to a case of this kind here to point out the real state of the Jewish people, and the desolation which was coming upon them.

44. *Into my house.* The soul of that person from whom he had been expelled by the power of Christ, and out of which he was to have been kept by continual prayer, faith, and watchfulness. *He findeth it empty.* "Unoccupied," empty of the former inhabitant, and ready to receive a new one, denoting a soul that has lost the life and power of godliness and the testimony of the Holy Spirit. *Swept, and garnished.* Idle, or unemployed, it may refer here to the person as well as to his state. His affections and desires are no longer busied with the things of God, but gad about, like an idle person, among the vanities of a perishing world. *Swept,* from love, meekness, and all the fruits of the Spirit; and *garnished,* "adorned, decorated," with the vain, showy trifles of folly and fashion.

45. *Seven other spirits more wicked. Seven* was a favorite number with the Jews, implying frequently, with them, something "perfect, completed, filled up," for such is the proper import of the Hebrew word *sheva* or *shevang,* nearly allied in sound to our *seven. The last state of that man is worse than the first.* His soul, before influenced by the Spirit of God, dilated and expanded under its heavenly influences, becomes more capable of refinement in iniquity, as its powers are more capacious than formerly. Evil habits are formed and strengthened by relapses; and relapses are multiplied, and become more incurable, through new habits. *So shall it be also unto this wicked generation.* And so it was, for they grew worse and worse, as if totally abandoned to diabolic influence, till at last the besom of destruction swept them and their privileges, national and religious, utterly away. What a terrible description of a state of apostasy is contained in these verses!

46. *His mother and his brethren.* These are supposed to have been the cousins of our Lord, as the word *brother* is frequently used among the Hebrews in this sense. But there are others who believe Mary had other children beside our Lord and that these were literally His brothers who are spoken of here. And although it be possible that these were the sons of Mary, the wife of Cleopas or Alpheus, his mother's sister, called his "relations," Mark iii. 21, yet it is as likely that they were the children of Joseph and Mary, and brethren of our Lord, in the strictest sense of the word.

48. *Who is my mother? and who are my brethren?* The reason of this seeming disregard of His relatives was this: They came to seize upon Him, for they thought He was distracted. See Mark iii. 21.

50. *Whosoever shall do the will of my Father.* Those are the best-acknowledged relatives of Christ who are united to Him by spiritual ties, and who are become one with Him by the indwelling of His Spirit. We generally suppose that Christ's relatives must have shared much of His affectionate attention, and doubtless they did; but here we find that whosoever does the will of God is equally esteemed by Christ as His *brother, sister,* or even His *mother.* What an encouragement for fervent attachment to God!

CHAPTER 13

Christ teaches the multitudes out of a ship, they standing on the shore, 1-2. The parable of the sower, 3-9. He gives His reasons for speaking in parables, 10-17. Explains the parable of the sower, 18-23. Parable of the tares and the wheat, 24-30. Of the grain of mustard seed, 31-32. Of the leaven, 33. The prophecy fulfilled by this mode of teaching, 34-35. He explains the parable of the tares and the wheat, 36-43. Parable of the treasure hid in a field, 44. Of the pearl merchant, 45-46. Of the dragnet, 47-50. His application of the whole, 51-52. He teaches in His own country, and His neighbors take offense, 53-56. Our Lord's observations on this, 57. He works no miracle among them because of their unbelief, 58.

1. *The same day.* Our Lord scarcely ever appears to take any rest. He is incessant in His labors, and instant in season and out of season; and in this He has left all His successors in the ministry an example, that they should follow His steps. *Went Jesus out of the house.* This was the house of Peter. *Sat by the sea side.* The Sea of Galilee, on the borders of which the city of Capernaum was situated.

2. *Into a ship.* It probably belonged to some of the fishermen (see chap. iv. 22).

3. *He spake many things unto them in parables.* A comparison or similitude, in which one thing is compared with another, especially spiritual things with natural, by which means these spiritual things are better understood, and make a deeper impression on an attentive mind. Under the parable of the *sower,* our Lord intimates

(1) That of all the multitudes then attending His ministry, few would bring forth fruit to perfection; and (2) That this would be a general case in preaching the gospel among men.

4. *Some seeds fell by the way side.* The hard-beaten path, where no plough had broken up the ground.

5. *Stony places.* Where there was a thin surface of earth and a rock at the bottom.

7. *Among thorns.* Where the earth was ploughed up, but the brambles and weeds had not been cleared away.

8. *Good ground.* Where the earth was deep, the field well-ploughed, and the brambles and weeds all removed.

9. *Who hath ears to hear.* Let every person who feels the necessity of being instructed in the things which concern his soul's welfare pay attention to what is spoken, and he shall become wise unto salvation.

11. *It is given unto you to know the mysteries.* By *mysteries,* here, we may understand not only things concerning the scheme of salvation, which had not yet been revealed, but also the prophetic declarations concerning the future state of the Christian Church, expressed in the ensuing parables. *To them it is not given* to know the purport and design of these things—they are gross of heart, earthly, and sensual, and do not improve the light they have received.

12. *Whosoever hath, to him shall be given.* This is an allusion to a common custom in all countries. He who possesses much or is rich, to such a person presents are ordinarily given. *Whosoever hath not, from him shall be taken away even that he hath.* That is, the poor man; he that has little may be easily made a prey of, and so lose his little.

13. *Therefore speak I to them in parables.* On this account, viz., to lead them into a proper knowledge of God. I speak to them in parables, natural representations of spiritual truths, that they may be allured to inquire, and to find out the spirit which is hidden under the letter; *because . . . seeing* the miracles which I have wrought, they *see not,* i.e., the end for which I have wrought them; *and hearing* My doctrines, *they hear not,* so as to profit by what is spoken. *Neither do they understand;* they do not lay their hearts to it.

14. *In them is fulfilled.* "Is again fulfilled"; this proper meaning of the Greek word has been generally overlooked. The Evangelist means that as these words were fulfilled in the Jews, in the time of the prophet Isaiah, so they are now *again* fulfilled in these their posterity, who exactly copy their fathers' example. These awful words may be *again* fulfilled in us if we take not warning by the things which these disobedient people have suffered. *By hearing ye shall hear.* Jesus Christ shall be sent to you; His miracles you shall fully see; and His doctrines you shall distinctly hear—but God will not force you to receive the salvation which is offered.

15. *Heart is waxed gross.* "Is become fat"—inattentive, stupid, insensible. They hear heavily with their ears—are half asleep while the salvation of God is preached unto them. *Their eyes they have closed.* Totally and obstinately resisted the truth of God, and shut their eyes against the light. *Lest . . . they should see.* Lest they

should see their lost estate, and be obliged to turn unto God and seek His salvation. His state is truly deplorable who is sick unto death and yet is afraid of being cured. The fault is here totally in the people, and not at all in that God whose name is Mercy and whose nature is love.

16. *But blessed are your eyes.* You improve the light which God has given you, and you receive an increase of heavenly wisdom by every miracle and by every sermon.

17. *Many prophets and righteous men.* These lived by and died in the faith of the promised Messiah; the fullness of the time was not then come for His manifestation in the flesh.

19. *When any one heareth the word of the kingdom.* Viz., the preaching of the gospel of Christ. *And understandeth it not.* Perhaps more properly, "regardeth it not," does not lay his heart to it. *The wicked one.* He who distresses and torments the soul. Mark, chap. iv. 15, calls him *Satan,* the "adversary" or "opposer," because he resists men in all their purposes of amendment, and to the utmost of his power opposes, in order to frustrate, the influences of divine grace upon the heart. In the parallel place in Luke, viii. 12, he is called *the devil.* It is worthy of remark that the three Evangelists should use each a different appellative of this mortal enemy of mankind; probably to show that the devil, with all his powers and properties, opposes everything that tends to the salvation of the soul. *Catcheth away.* Makes the utmost haste to pick up the good seed, lest it should take root in the heart. A careless, inattentive hearer is compared to the *way side*—his heart is an open road, where evil affections and foolish and hurtful desires continually pass and repass without either notice or restraint.

20. *But he that received the seed into stony places, the same is he.* That is, is a fit emblem of that man who, hearing the gospel, is affected with its beauty and excellency, and immediately receiveth it *with joy*—is glad to hear what God has done to make man happy.

21. *Yet hath he not root in himself.* His soul is not deeply convinced of its guilt and depravity; the fallow ground is not properly ploughed up, nor the rock broken. *When tribulation or persecution ariseth,* which he did not expect, "he is soon stumbled"—seeks some pretext to abandon both the doctrine and the followers of Christ.

22. *He also that received seed among the thorns.* In land ploughed, but not properly cleared and weeded. *Is he*—represents that person *that heareth the word; and the care,* rather "the anxiety" the whole system of anxious, carking cares. *The deceitfulness of riches.* Which promise peace and pleasure, but can never give them. *Choke the word.* Or "together choke the word," meaning either that these grow up together with the word, overtop, and choke it, or that these united together, viz., carking, worldly cares, with the delusive hopes and promises of riches, cause the man to abandon the great concerns of his soul and seek, in their place, what he shall eat, drink, and wherewithal he shall be clothed. Dreadful stupidity of man, thus to barter spiritual for temporal good—a heavenly inheritance for an earthly portion! The seed of the Kingdom can never produce much fruit in any heart till the thorns and thistles of vicious affections and impure desires be plucked up by the roots and burned.

23. *Good ground.* That which had depth of mold, was well-ploughed and well-weeded. *Is he that heareth.* Who diligently attends the ministry of *the word. And understandeth it.* Lays the subject to heart, deeply weighing its nature, design, and importance. *Which also beareth fruit.* His fruitfulness being an almost necessary consequence of his thus laying the divine message to heart. Let it be observed that to *hear,* to *understand,* and to *bring forth fruit* are the three grand evidences of a genuine believer. He who does not *hear* the word of wisdom cannot *understand* what makes for his peace; and he who does not *understand* what the gospel requires him to be and to perform cannot *bring forth fruit;* and he who is not fruitful, very fruitful, cannot be a disciple of Christ, see John xv. 8; and he who is not Christ's disciple cannot enter into the kingdom of God. From the different portions of fruit produced by the good ground, a *hundred, sixty,* and *thirty,* we may learn that all sound believers are not equally fruitful. All hear, understand, and bring forth fruit, but not in the same degrees—occasioned partly by their situation and circumstances not allowing them such extensive opportunities of receiving and doing good; and partly by lack of mental capacity—for every mind is not equally improvable. Let it be further observed that the unfruitfulness of the different lands was not owing to bad seed or an unskillful sower—the same sower sowed the same seed in all, and with the same gracious design—but it is unfruitful in many because they are careless, inattentive, and worldly-minded.

24. *The kingdom of heaven.* God's method of managing the affairs of the world and the concerns of His Church. *Is likened unto a man which sowed good seed in his field.* In general, the world may be termed the field of God; and in particular, those who profess to believe in God through Christ are His field or farm, among whom God sows nothing but the pure, unadulterated word of His truth.

25. *But while men slept.* When the professors were lukewarm and the pastors indolent, *his enemy came and sowed tares,* degenerate wheat. The righteous and the wicked are often mingled in the Visible Church.

26. *When the blade was sprung up . . . then appeared the tares also.* Satan has a shoot of iniquity for every shoot of grace; and when God revives His work, Satan revives his also. No marvel, therefore, if we find scandals arising suddenly to discredit a work of grace where God has begun to pour out His Spirit.

27. *So the servants . . . said unto him, Sir, didst not thou sow good seed?* A faithful and vigilant minister of Christ fails not to discover the evil, to lament it, and to address himself to God by prayer, in order to find out the cause of it, and to receive from Him proper information how to behave on the occasion.

28. *An enemy hath done this.* It is the interest of Satan to introduce hypocrites and wicked persons into religious societies, in order to discredit the work of God, and to favor his own designs. *Wilt thou then that we go and gather them up?* A zeal which is rash and precipitate is as much to be feared as the total lack of strict discipline.

29. *But he said, Nay.* God judges quite otherwise than men of this mixture of good and evil in the world; He knows the good which He intends to produce from it, and how far His patience towards the wicked should extend in order to their conversion, or the further sanctification of the righteous.

30. *Let both grow together.* Though every minister of God should separate from the Church of Christ every incorrigible sinner, yet he should proceed no further. The man is not to be persecuted in his body or goods because he is not sound in the faith—God tolerates him; so should men.

31. *The kingdom of heaven is like to a grain of mustard seed.* This parable is a representation of the progress of the gospel in the world, and of the growth of grace in the soul. That grace which leads the soul to the fullness of glory may begin, and often does, in a single good desire—a wish to escape hell, or a desire to enjoy God in heaven.

32. *Which indeed is the least of all seeds.* That is, of all those seeds which produce plants, whose stems and branches, according to the saying of the botanists, are apt *arborescere,* to grow into a ligneous or *woody* substance. *Becometh a tree.* That is, it is not only the largest of plants which are produced from such small seeds, but partakes, in its substance, the close, woody texture, especially in warm climates, where we are informed it grows to an almost incredible size.

33. *The kingdom of heaven is like unto leaven.* On the nature and effects of *leaven,* see the note on Exod. xii. 8. As the property of *leaven* is to change, or assimilate to its own nature, the meal or dough with which it is mixed, so the property of the grace of Christ is to change the whole soul into its own likeness; and God intends that this principle should continue in the soul till all is leavened—till the whole bear the image of the heavenly, as it before bore the image of the earthly. Both these parables are prophetic, and were intended to show principally how, from very small beginnings, the gospel of Christ should pervade all the nations of the world and fill them with righteousness and true holiness.

35. *By the prophet.* As the quotation is taken from Ps. lxxviii. 2, which is attributed to Asaph, he must be the *prophet* who is meant in the text; and, indeed, he is expressly called a prophet, 1 Chron. xx. v. 2.

36. *Jesus . . . went into the house: and his disciples came.* Those who attend only to the public preaching of the gospel of God are not likely to understand fully the mysteries of the kingdom of Heaven. To understand clearly the purport of the divine message, a man must come to God by frequent, fervent, secret prayer.

44. *The kingdom of heaven is like unto treasure hid in a field.* "To a hidden treasure." We are not to imagine that the *treasure* here mentioned, and to which the gospel salvation is likened, means a pot or chest of money hidden in the field, but rather a gold or silver mine, which he who found out could not get at, or work, without turning up the field, and for this purpose he bought it. *He hideth,* i.e., "he kept secret," told the discovery to no person, till he had bought the field.

Our Lord's meaning seems to be this: *The kingdom of heaven*—the salvation provided by the gospel—*is like unto treasure*—something of inestimable worth—*hid in a field*. It is a rich mine, the veins of which run in all directions in the sacred Scriptures; therefore the field must be dug up, the records of salvation diligently and carefully turned over, and searched. *Which when a man hath found*—when a sinner is convinced that the promise of life eternal is to him, "he kept secret"—pondered the matter deeply in his heart; he examines the preciousness of the treasure, and counts the cost of purchase. *For joy thereof*—finding that this salvation is just what his needy soul requires, and what will make him presently and eternally happy, *goeth and selleth all that he hath*—renounces his sins, abandons his evil companions, and relinquishes all hope of salvation through his own righteousness; *and buyeth that field*—not merely buys the Book for the sake of the salvation it describes, but, by the Blood of the covenant, buys gold tried in the fire, white raiment, etc.; in a word, pardon and purity, which he receives from God for the sake of Jesus.

45. *A merchant man, seeking goodly pearls.* The meaning of this parable is the same with the other; and both were spoken to impress more forcibly this great truth on the souls of the people—eternal salvation from sin and its consequences is the supreme good of man, should be sought after above all things, and prized beyond all that God has made.

47. *Is like unto a net.* A "dragnet." As this is dragged along it keeps gathering all in its way, both good and bad, small and great; and when it is brought to the shore, those which are proper for use are preserved, and those which are not are either destroyed or thrown back into the water. By the *net* may be understood the preaching of the gospel of the Kingdom, which keeps drawing men into the profession of Christianity and into the fellowship of the Visible Church of Christ.

52. *Every scribe.* Minister of Christ; *which is instructed*—taught of God; *unto the kingdom of heaven*—in the mysteries of the gospel of Christ; *out of his treasure*—his granary or storehouse; *things new and old*—a Jewish phrase for "great plenty." A small degree of knowledge is not sufficient for a preacher of the gospel. The sacred writings should be his treasure, and he should properly understand them. Some have thought that old and new things here, which imply the produce of the past and the produce of the present year, may also refer to the *old* and *new* covenants—a proper knowledge of the Old Testament Scriptures and of the doctrines of Christ as contained in the New.

54. *And when he was come into his own country.* Probably Nazareth, where His parents lived, and where He had continued till His thirtieth year, though it appears He had a lodging in Peter's house at Capernaum.

55. *Is not this mother called Mary? and his brethren, James . . . ?* This insulting question seems to intimate that our Lord's family was a very obscure one; and that they were of small repute among their neighbors, except for their piety. It is possible that *brethren* and *sisters* may mean here "near relations," as the words are used among the Hebrews in this lati-

tude of meaning; but I confess it does not appear to me likely. Why should the children of another family be brought in here to share a reproach which it is evident was designed for Joseph, the carpenter; Mary, his wife; Jesus, their son; and their other children?

57. *And they were offended in him.* They took offense at Him, making the meanness of His family the reason why they would not receive Him as a prophet, though they were astonished at His wisdom and at His miracles, v. 54. *A prophet is not without honour.* This seems to have been a proverbial mode of speech, generally true, but not without some exceptions.

CHAPTER 14

Herod, having heard the fame of Christ, supposes Him to be John the Baptist, risen from the dead, 1-2. A circumstantial account of the beheading of John the Baptist, 3-12. Five thousand men, besides women and children, fed with five loaves and two fishes, 13-21. The disciples take ship, and Jesus stays behind, and goes privately into a mountain to pray, 22-23. A violent storm arises, by which the lives of the disciples are endangered, 24. In their extremity Jesus appears to them, walking upon the water, 25-27. Peter, at the command of his Master, leaves the ship and walks on the water to meet Christ, 28-31. They both enter the ship and the storm ceases, 32-33. They come into the land of Gennesaret, and He heals many diseased people, 34-36.

1. *Herod the tetrarch.* This was Herod Antipas, the son of Herod the Great. The word *tetrarch* properly signifies a person who rules over the fourth part of a country; but it is taken in a more general sense by the Jewish writers, meaning sometimes simply a governor, or a king; see v. 9. The estates of Herod the Great were not, at his death, divided into four tetrarchies, but only into three. One was given by the Emperor Augustus to Archelaus; the second to Herod Antipas, the person in the text; and the third to Philip: all three, sons of Herod the Great.

3. *For Herodias' sake.* This infamous woman was the daughter of Aristobulus and Berenice, and granddaughter of Herod the Great. Her first marriage was with Herod Philip, her uncle, by whom she had Salome. Some time after, she left her husband, and lived publicly with Herod Antipas, her brother-in-law, who had been before married to the daughter of Aretas, king of Arabia Petraea. As soon as Aretas understood that Herod had determined to put away his daughter, he prepared to make war on him. The two armies met, and that of Herod was cut to pieces by the Arabians; and this, Josephus says, was supposed to be a judgment of God on him for the murder of John the Baptist. See the account in Josephus, *Antiq., lib. xviii, c. 7.*

4. *For John said unto him, It is not lawful for thee to have her.* Here is an instance of zeal, fidelity, and courage highly worthy of imitation.

5. *He feared the multitude.* Miserable prince, who fears more to offend his people than to sin against his God by shedding innocent blood!

6. *Herod's birthday.* Either the day in which he was born or the day on which he began to reign, for both were termed birthdays. See 1 Sam. xiii. 1; Hos. vii. 5. The kings of Persia were accustomed to reject no petition that was preferred to them during the entertainment. *The daughter.* This was Salome, mentioned before.

8. *Give me here John Baptist's head in a charger.* The word *charger* formerly signified a

large dish, bowl, or drinking cup; anything is better than *charger*, which never conveyed much meaning, and now conveys none.

9. *The king was sorry.* He knew John to be a righteous man. *Nevertheless for the oath's sake.* "The oaths"—he had probably sworn again and again—one sin begets many.

11. *His head was . . . given to the damsel: and she brought it to her mother.* There is no person so revengeful as a lascivious woman when reproved and blamed. A preacher of the gospel has most to fear from this quarter.

13. *When Jesus heard of it, he departed thence.* Had the blessed Jesus continued in that place, it is probable the hand of this impure female murderer would have been stretched out against Him also. He withdrew therefore, not through fear, but to teach His messengers rather to yield to the storm than expose themselves to destruction, where, from circumstances, the case is evidently hopeless. *The people . . . followed him on foot.* Or "by land," which is a common acceptation of the word in the best Greek writers.

14. *Jesus . . . was moved with compassion.* He was moved with "tender compassion," so I think the word should in general be translated.

15. *Send the multitude away, that they may go . . . and buy.* The disciples of Christ are solicitous for the people's temporal as well as spiritual welfare; and he is not worthy to be called a minister of Christ who does not endeavor to promote both to the uttermost of his power.

16. *They need not depart.* He that seeks first the kingdom of Heaven is sure to have every temporal requisite.

17. *We have here but five loaves, and two fishes.* When we are deeply conscious of our own necessities, we shall be led to depend on Jesus with a firmer faith. God often permits His servants to be brought low, that they may have repeated opportunities of proving the kindness and mercy of their gracious Lord and Master.

19. *And took the five loaves.* This was the act of the father of a family among the Jews—his business it was to take the bread into his hands, and render thanks to God, before any of the family was permitted to taste of it. *Looking up to heaven.* To teach us to acknowledge God as the Supreme Good, and Fountain of all excellence. *He blessed.* The word "God" should, I think, be rather inserted here than the word "them," because it does not appear that it was the loaves which Christ blessed, but that God who had provided them; and this indeed was the Jewish custom, not to bless the food, but the God who gave it. However, there are others who believe the loaves are meant, and that He blessed them in order to multiply them. *And brake.* The Jews made their bread broad and thin like cakes, and to divide such, being very brittle, there was no need of a knife.

20. *They did all eat, and were filled.* Here was an incontestable miracle—5,000 men, besides women and children, fed with 5 cakes and 2 fishes! But did not this creation of bread prove the unlimited power of Jesus? Undoubtedly; and nothing less than eternal power and Godhead could have effected it. *They took up . . . twelve baskets.* It was customary for many of

the Jews to carry a basket with them at all times, and Wakefield's conjecture here is very reasonable: "By the number here particularized, it should seem that each apostle filled his own bread basket." The simple reason why the Jews carried baskets with them appears to be this: When they went into Gentile countries, they carried their own provision with them, as they were afraid of being polluted by partaking of the meat of heathens.

22. *Jesus constrained his disciples to get into a ship.* Either they were afraid to return into the jurisdiction of Herod or they were unwilling to embark without their Lord and Protector, and would not enter their boat till Christ had commanded them to embark. *Unto the other side.* Towards Capernaum, v. 34; John vi. 16-17; or Bethsaida—see on Mark vi. 45.

23. *He went up into a mountain apart, to pray.* Some make this part of our Lord's conduct emblematic of the spirit and practice of prayer, and observe that the proper dispositions and circumstances for praying well are: (1) retirement from the world, (2) elevation of the heart to God, (3) solitude, and (4) the silence and quiet of the night. It is certain in this also Christ has left us an example that we should follow His steps.

24. *Tossed with waves.* "Grievously agitated."

25. *The fourth watch.* Anciently the Jews divided the night into three watches, consisting of four hours each. The first watch is mentioned, Lam. ii. 19; the second, Judg. vii. 19; and the third, Exod. xiv. 24; but a fourth watch is not mentioned in any part of the Old Testament. This division the Romans had introduced in Judea, as also the custom of dividing the day into twelve hours; see John xi. 9. The first watch began at six o'clock in the evening, and continued till nine; the second began at nine, and the fourth began at three, and continued twelve, and continued till three next morning; and the fourth began at three, and continued till six. It was, therefore, between the hours of three and six in the morning that Jesus made His appearance to His disciples. *Walking on the sea.* Thus suspending the laws of gravitation was a proper manifestation of unlimited power. Jesus did this by His own power; therefore Jesus showed forth His Godhead.

27. *It is I; be not afraid.* Nothing but this voice of Christ could, in such circumstances, have given courage and comfort to His disciples. Those who are grievously tossed with difficulties and temptations require a similar manifestation of His power and goodness. When He proclaims himself in the soul, all sorrow and fear and sin are at an end.

29. *Peter . . . walked on the water.* However impossible the thing commanded by Christ may appear, it is certain He will give power to accomplish it to those who receive His word by faith; but we must take care never to put Christ's power to the proof for the gratification of a vain curiosity, or even for the strengthening of our faith, when the ordinary means for doing that are within our reach.

30. *When he saw the wind boisterous, he was afraid.* It was by faith in the power of Christ he was upheld; when that faith failed by which the laws of gravitation were suspended, no wonder that those laws returned to their wonted

action, and that he began to sink. It was not the violence of the winds nor the raging of the waves which endangered his life, but his littleness of faith.

31. *Jesus stretched forth his hand.* Every moment we stand in need of Christ. While we stand, we are upheld by His power only; and when we are falling, or have fallen, we can be saved only by His mercy.

32. *The wind ceased.* Jesus is the Prince of Peace, and all is peace and calm where He condescends to enter and abide.

34. *The land of Gennesaret.* It was from this country that the sea or lake of Gennesaret had its name.

35. *The men of that place had knowledge of him,* i.e., "They knew Him again." They had already seen His miracles; and now they collect all the diseased people they can find, that He may have the same opportunity of showing forth His marvellous power, and they of being the instruments of relieving their friends and neighbors.

36. *That they might only touch the hem of his garment.* What mighty influence must the grace and Spirit of Christ have in the soul when even the border or *hem of his garment* produced such wonders in the bodies of those who touched it!

CHAPTER 15

The Pharisees accuse the disciples of eating with unwashed hands, 1-2. Our Lord answers, and convicts them of gross hypocrisy, 3-9. Teaches the people and the disciples what it is that renders men unclean, 10-20. Heals the daughter of a Canaanitish woman, 21-28. Heals many diseased people on a mountain of Galilee, 29-31. With seven loaves and a few little fishes, He feeds 4,000 men, besides women and children, 32-38. Having dismissed the multitudes, He comes to the coast of Magdala, 39.

1. *Scribes and Pharisees . . . of Jerusalem.* Our Lord was now in Galilee, chap. xiv. 34.

2. *Elders.* Rulers and magistrates among the Jews. *The tradition of the elders.* The word tradition has occupied a most distinguished place, in both the Jewish and the Christian Church. Man is ever fond of mending the work of his Maker, and hence he has been led to put his finishing hand even to divine revelation! The Latin term, *tradition,* is from *trado,* to "deliver," especially "from one to another—to hand down." Among the Jews, *tradition* signifies what is also called the *oral* law, which they distinguish from the *written* law. This last contains the Mosaic precepts, as found in the Pentateuch; the former, the traditions of the elders, i.e., traditions, or doctrines, that had been successively handed down from Moses through every generation, but not committed to writing. The Jews feign that, when God gave Moses the written law, He gave him also the oral law, which is the interpretation of the former. This law Moses at first delivered to Aaron, then to his sons Eleazar and Ithamar, and after these to the seventy-two elders, who were six of the most eminent men chosen out of each of the twelve tribes. These seventy-two, with Moses and Aaron, delivered it again to all the heads of the people, and afterwards to the congregation at large. They say also that before Moses died he delivered his oral law, or system of traditions, to Joshua, and Joshua to the elders which suc-

ceeded him—they to the prophets, and the prophets to each other, till it came to Jeremiah, who delivered it to Baruch, his scribe, who repeated it to Ezra, who delivered it to the men of the great synagogue.

3. *Why do ye also transgress the commandment?* Ye accuse My disciples of transgressing the traditions of the elders—I accuse you of transgressing the commands of God and that too in favor of your own tradition, thus preferring the inventions of men to the positive precepts of God. Pretenders to zeal often prefer superstitious usages to the divine law, and human inventions to the positive duties of Christianity.

4. *Honour thy father and mother.* This word was taken in great latitude of meaning among the Jews; it not only meant respect and submission, but also "to take care of a person, to nourish and support him, to enrich." See Num. xxii. 17; Judg. xiii. 17; 1 Tim. v. 17. And that this was the sense of the law, as it respected parents, see Deut. xxvii. 16, and see the note on Exod. xx. 12.

5. *It is a gift.* Corban (Mark vii. 11), an offering of approach; something consecrated to the service of God in the Temple, by which a man had the privilege of approaching his Maker.

7. *Hypocrites, well did Esaias prophesy of you.* In every place where the proper names of the Old Testament occur in the New, the same mode of orthography should be followed: I therefore write *Isaiah* with the Hebrew, not *Esaias,* with the Greek. This prophecy is found in chap. xxix. 13.

8. *Their heart is far from me.* The true worship of God consists in the union of the heart to Him—where this exists not, a particle of the spirit of devotion cannot be found.

9. *In vain they do worship me.* By the traditions of the elders, not only the word of God was perverted, but His worship also was greatly corrupted. But the Jews were not the only people who have acted thus; whole Christian churches, as well as sects and parties, have acted in the same way.

10. *Hear, and understand.* Hear—make it a point of conscience to attend to the ministry of the Word. Understand—be not satisfied with attending places of public worship merely; see that the teaching be of God, and that you lay it to heart.

11. *Not that which goeth into the mouth defileth.* This is an answer to the carping question of the Pharisees mentioned in v. 2: "Why do Thy disciples eat with unwashed hands?"
That which cometh out of the mouth. That is, what springs from a corrupt, unregenerate heart—a perverse will and impure passions—these defile, i.e., make him a sinner.

12. *The Pharisees were offended.* None so liable to take offense as formalists and hypocrites, when you attempt to take away the false props from the one and question the sincerity of the other. Besides, Pharisees must never be suspected of ignorance, for they are the men, and wisdom must die with them!

13. *Every plant.* "Every plantation." The Pharisees, as a religious body, were now a plantation of trees which God did not plant, water, nor own; therefore, they should be *rooted up.*

14. *Let them alone.* "Give them up, or leave them." Our blessed Lord meant "give them up," have no kind of religious connection with them, and the strong reason for which He immediately adds, because they are *blind leaders.* Probably the words may be understood as a sort of proverbial expression for "Don't mind them: pay no regard to them. They are altogether unworthy of notice."

16. *Are ye also yet without understanding?* The word which we translate *yet* should be here rendered "still": Are ye still void of understanding? The word is used in this sense by several Greek writers.

19. *Evil thoughts.* "Wicked dialogues"—for in all evil surmisings the heart holds a conversation, or dialogue, with itself. For *murders,* two MSS. have "envyings," and three others have both. Envy and murder are nearly allied; the former has often led to the latter.

20. *These . . . defile a man.* Our Lord's argument is very plain. What goes into the mouth descends into the stomach and other intestines; part is retained for the nourishment of the body, and part is ejected, as being improper to afford nourishment. Nothing of this kind defiles the soul, because it does not enter into it; but the evil principles that are in it, producing evil thoughts, murders, etc., these defile the soul, because they have their seat and operation in it.

21. *Departed into the coasts of Tyre and Sidon.* "Towards" the coasts, or confines. It is not clear that our Lord ever left the land of the Hebrews. Tyre and Sidon are usually joined together, principally because they are but a few miles distant from each other.

22. *A woman of Canaan.* Matthew gives her this name because of the people from whom she sprung—the descendants of Canaan, Judg. i. 31-32; but Mark calls her a "Syrophenician," because of the country where she dwelt. The Canaanites and Phoenicians have often been confounded. This is frequently the case in the Septuagint. Compare Gen. xlvi. 10 with Exod. vi. 15, where the same person is called a Phoenician in the one place and a Canaanite in the other. *Have mercy on me.* How proper is this prayer for a penitent! There are many excellencies contained in it; (1) It is short, (2) humble, (3) full of faith, (4) fervent, (5) modest, (6) respectful, (7) rational, (8) relying only on the mercy of God, (9) persevering. *Son of David.* An essential character of the true Messiah.

23. *He answered her not a word.* Seemed to take time to consider her request, and to give her the opportunity of exercising her faith, and manifesting her fervor.

24. *I am not sent but unto the lost sheep.* By the divine appointment I am come to preach the gospel to the Jews only.

25. *Lord, help me.* Let me also share in the deliverance afforded to Israel.

26. *The children's bread.* The salvation provided for the Jews, who were termed "the children of the kingdom." And cast it to the "little dogs"; such the Gentiles were reputed by the Jewish people, and our Lord uses that form of speech which was common among His countrymen.

27. *Truth, Lord.* Yes Lord. This appears to be not so much an assent as a bold reply to our Lord's reason for apparently rejecting her suit. The little dogs share with the children, for they eat the crumbs which fall from their masters' table. I do not desire what is provided for these highly favored children, only what they leave. A single exertion of Thy almighty power, in the healing of my afflicted daughter, is all that I wish for; and this the highly favored Jews can well spare without lessening the provision made for themselves. Is not this the sense of this noble woman's reply?

28. *O woman, great is thy faith.* The hindrances thrown in this woman's way only tended to increase her faith. Her faith resembles a river which becomes enlarged by the dykes opposed to it, till at last it sweeps them entirely away with it. *Her daughter was made whole.* Persevering faith and prayer are next to omnipotent.

29. *Went up into a mountain.* "The mountain." "Meaning," says Wakefield, "some particular mountain which he was accustomed to frequent."

33. *Whence should we have so much bread in the wilderness?* This world is a desert, where nothing can be found to satisfy the soul of man but the salvation which Christ has procured.

37. *They did all eat, and were filled.* "They were satisfied." The husks of worldly pleasures may *fill* the man, but cannot *satisfy* the soul.

38. *Four thousand.* Let the poor learn from these miracles to trust in God for support. Whatever His ordinary providence denies, His miraculous power will supply.

39. *He sent away the multitude.* But not before He had instructed their souls, and fed and healed their bodies. *The coasts of Magdala.* In the parallel place, Mark viii. 10, this place is called Dalmanutha. Either Magdala was formed by a transposition of letters from Dalman, to which the Syriac termination *atha* had been added, or the one of these names refers to the country and the other to a town in that neighborhood.

CHAPTER 16

The Pharisees insidiously require our Lord to give them a sign, 1. They are severely rebuked for their hypocrisy and wickedness, 2-5. The disciples are cautioned to beware of them and their destructive doctrine, 6-12. The different opinions formed by the people of Christ, 13-14. Peter's confession, and our Lord's discourse on it, 15-20. He foretells His sufferings, and reproves Peter, 21-23. Teaches the necessity of self-denial and shows the reasons on which it is founded, 24-26. Speaks of a future judgment, 27. And promises the speedy opening of the glory of His own kingdom on earth, 28.

1. *Shew them a sign.* These sects, however opposed among themselves, most cordially unite in their opposition to Christ and His truth. *Tempting . . . him.* Feigning a desire to have His doctrine fully proved to them, that they might credit it, and become His disciples, but having no other design than to betray and ruin Him.

2. *When it is evening.* There are certain signs of fair and foul weather, which you are in the constant habit of observing, and which do not fail.

3. *The sky is red and lowering.* The signs of fair and foul weather were observed in a similar manner among the Romans, and indeed among most other people.

4. *Wicked and adulterous generation.* The Jewish people are represented in the Sacred Writings as married to the Most High; but, like a disloyal wife, forsaking their true Husband, and uniting themselves to Satan and sin. *Seeketh after a sign,* "seeketh sign upon sign," or still "another sign." Our blessed Lord had already wrought miracles sufficient to demonstrate both His divine mission and His divinity; only one was further necessary to take away the scandal of His cross and death, to fulfill the Scriptures, and to establish the Christian religion; and that was His resurrection from the dead, which, He here states, was typified in the case of Jonah.

5. *Come to the other side.* Viz., the coast of Bethsaida, by which our Lord passed, going to Caesarea, for He was now on His journey thither. See v. 13, and Mark viii. 22, 27.

6. *Beware of the leaven.* Bad doctrines act in the soul as leaven does in meal; they assimilate the whole spirit to their own nature. A man's particular creed has a greater influence on his tempers and conduct than most are aware of. Pride, hypocrisy, and worldly-mindedness, which constituted *the leaven of the Pharisees* and Sadducees, ruin the major part of the world.

7. *They reasoned.* For, as Lightfoot observes, the term leaven was very rarely used among the Jews to signify doctrine, and therefore the disciples did not immediately apprehend His meaning.

9-10. *Do ye not yet understand . . . the five loaves . . . Neither the seven?* How astonishing is it that these men should have any fear of lacking bread, after having seen the two miracles which our blessed Lord alludes to above!

12. They now perceived that He warned them. against the superstition of the Pharisees, which produced hypocrisy, pride, envy, etc., and the false doctrine of the Sadducees, which denied the existence of a spiritual world, the immortality of the soul, the resurrection of the body, and the providence of God.

13. *Caesarea Philippi.* A city, in the tribe of Naphtali, near to Mount Libanus, in the province of Iturea. Its ancient name was *Dan,* Gen. xiv. 14; afterwards it was called *Lais,* Judg. xviii. 7. But Philip the tetrarch, having rebuilt and beautified it, gave it the name of Caesarea, in honor of Tiberius Caesar, the reigning emperor; but to distinguish it from another Caesarea, which was on the coast of the Mediterranean Sea, and to perpetuate the fame of him who rebuilt it, it was called Caesarea Philippi, or Caesarea of Philip. *Whom do men say?* He asked His disciples this question, not because He was ignorant what the people thought and spoke of Him, but to have the opportunity, in getting an express declaration of their faith from themselves, to confirm and strengthen them in it; but see on Luke ix. 20. *Some . . . John the Baptist.* By this and other passages we learn that the Pharisaic doctrine of the transmigration of souls was pretty general; for it was upon this ground that they believed that the soul of the Baptist, or of Elijah, Jeremiah, or some of the prophets, had come to a new life in the body of Jesus.

16. *Thou art the Christ, the Son of the living God.* Every word here is emphatic—a most concise, and yet comprehensive, confession of faith. *The Christ,* or "Messiah," points out His divinity, and shows His office; *the Son* designates His person. On this account it is that both are joined together so frequently in the new covenant. *Of the living God*—literally, of God the Living One. *Living.* A character applied to the Supreme Being, not only to distinguish Him from the dead idols of paganism, but also to point Him out as the Source of life, present, spiritual, and eternal. Probably there is an allusion here to the great name *Yehovah,* which properly signifies being or existence.

17. *Blessed art thou, Simon Bar-jona.* Or "Simon, son of Jonah." *Flesh and blood. I.e.,* "Man"; no human being hath revealed this.

18. *Thou art Peter.* This was the same as if He had said "I acknowledge you for one of My disciples"—for this name was given him by our Lord when He first called him to the apostleship. *Peter* signifies a stone, or fragment of a "rock"; and our Lord, whose constant custom it was to rise to heavenly things through the medium of earthly, takes occasion from the name, the metaphorical meaning of which was "strength" and "stability," to point out the solidity of the confession, and the stability of that cause which should be founded on "the Christ, the Son of the living God."

"Upon this very rock," this true confession of yours—that I am the Messiah, that am come to reveal and communicate the living God, that the dead, lost world may be saved—upon this very Rock, myself, thus confessed, will I build My Church, "my assembly, or congregation," i.e., of persons who are made partakers of this precious faith. That Peter is not designed in our Lord's words must be evident to all who are not blinded by prejudice. Peter was only one of the builders in this sacred edifice, who himself tells us was built on this living Foundation Stone: 1 Pet. ii. 4-5. Therefore Jesus Christ did not say, "On you, Peter, will I build My Church," but changes immediately the expression and says, "Upon that very rock," to show that He addressed neither Peter nor any other of the apostles. So the supremacy of Peter and the infallibility of the Church of Rome must be sought in some other scripture, for they certainly are not to be found in this. *The gates of hell,* i.e., the "machinations and powers" of the invisible world. In ancient times the gates of fortified cities were used to hold councils in, and were usually places of great strength. Our Lord's expression means that neither the plots, stratagems, nor strength of Satan and his angels should ever so far prevail as to destroy the sacred truths in the above confession.

19. *The keys of the kingdom.* By the *kingdom of heaven* we may consider the true Church, that house of God, to be meant; and by the *keys,* the power of admitting into that house, or of preventing any improper person from coming in. In other words, the doctrine of salvation and the full declaration of the way in which God will save sinners, and who they are that shall be finally excluded from heaven, and on what account. When the Jews made a man a doctor of the law, they put into his hand the key of the closet in the Temple where the sacred books were kept, and also tablets to write upon, signifying by this that they gave him authority to teach, and to explain the Scriptures to the people. This prophetic declaration of our Lord was

literally fulfilled to Peter, as he was made the first instrument of opening, i.e., preaching the doctrines of the kingdom of Heaven to the Jews, Acts ii. 41; and to the Gentiles, Acts x. 44-47; xi. 1; xv. 7. *Whatsoever thou shalt bind on earth.* This mode of expression was frequent among the Jews; they considered that everything that was done upon earth, according to the order of God, was at the same time done in heaven. Hence they were accustomed to say that when the priest, on the Day of Atonement, offered the two goats upon earth, the same were offered in heaven. As one goat, therefore, is permitted to escape on earth, one is permitted to escape in heaven; and when the priests cast the lots on earth, the priest also casts the lots in heaven. The disciples of our Lord, from having the *keys*, i.e., the true knowledge of the doctrine of the kingdom of Heaven, should be able at all times to distinguish between the clean and the unclean, and pronounce infallible judgment; and this "binding" and "loosing," or pronouncing fit or unfit for fellowship with the members of Christ, being always according to the doctrine of the gospel of God, should be considered as proceeding immediately from heaven, and consequently as divinely ratified. "Binding" and "loosing" were terms in frequent use among the Jews, and they meant bidding and forbidding, granting and refusing, declaring lawful or unlawful.

20. *Then charged he his disciples.* "He strictly charged them."

21. *From that time forth began Jesus.* Before this time our Lord had spoken of His death only in a vague and obscure manner (see chap. xii. 40), because He would not afflict His disciples with this matter sooner than necessity required. But now, as the time of His crucifixion drew nigh, He spoke of His sufferings and death in the most express and clear terms. Three sorts of persons, our Lord intimates, should be the cause of His death and passion: the *elders,* the *chief priests,* and the *scribes.*

22. *Then Peter took him.* "Took Him up"—suddenly interrupted Him, as it were calling Him to order. *Be it far from thee, Lord.* "Be merciful to thyself, Lord." Peter knew that Christ had power sufficient to preserve himself from all the power and malice of the Jews, and wished Him to exert that in His own behalf which He had often exerted in the behalf of others.

23. *Get thee behind me, Satan.* "Get behind Me, you adversary." This is the proper translation of the Hebrew word *Satan,* from which the Greek word is taken. Our blessed Lord certainly never designed that men should believe He called Peter "devil" because he, through erring affection, had wished Him to avoid that death which He predicted to himself. This translation, which is literal, takes away that harshness which before appeared in our Lord's words. *Thou art an offence unto me.* You are a stumbling block in My way, to impede Me in the accomplishment of the great design. *Thou savourest not.* That is, "do not relish," or, do not "understand or discern" the things of God—you are wholly taken up with the vain thought that My kingdom is of this world. He who opposes the doctrine of the atonement is an adversary and offense to Christ, though he be as sincere in his profession as Peter himself was.

24. *Will come after me.* I.e., to be My disciple. *Let him deny himself.* "Let him deny, or renounce, himself fully—in all respects—perseveringly." A man's *self* is to him the prime cause of most of his miseries.

25. *For whosoever will save his life.* That is, "shall wish to save his life"—at the expense of his conscience, and casting aside the cross, he, *shall lose it*—the very evil he wishes to avoid shall overtake him; and he shall lose his soul in the bargain. See then how necessary it is to renounce oneself!

26. *Lose his own soul.* Or "lose his life." On what authority many have translated the word *psyche* in the twenty-fifth verse "life," and in this verse *soul,* I know not, but am certain it means "life" in both places. If a man should gain the whole world, its riches, honors, and pleasures, and lose his life, what would all these profit him, seeing they can be enjoyed only during life?

27. *For the Son of man shall come in the glory of his Father.* This seems to refer to Dan. vii. 13-14. "Behold, one like the Son of man came . . . to the Ancient of days . . . And there was given him dominion, and glory, and a kingdom, that all people, nations, and languages, should serve him." This was the glorious mediatorial Kingdom which Jesus Christ was now about to set up, by the destruction of the Jewish nation and polity, and the diffusion of His gospel through the whole world. If the words be taken in this sense, the *angels* or messengers may signify the apostles and their successors in the sacred ministry, preaching the gospel in the power of the Holy Ghost. It is very likely that the words do not apply to the final judgment, to which they are generally referred, but to the wonderful display of God's grace and power after the Day of Pentecost.

28. *There be some . . . which shall not taste of death.* This verse seems to confirm the above explanation, as our Lord evidently speaks of the establishment of the Christian Church after the Day of Pentecost, and its final triumph after the destruction of the Jewish polity; as if He had said, "Some of you, My disciples, shall continue to live until these things take place." The destruction of Jerusalem and the Jewish economy, which our Lord here predicts, took place about forty years after this; and some of the persons now with Him doubtless survived that period, and witnessed the extension of the Messiah's kingdom. Our Lord told them these things before, that when they came to pass they might be confirmed in the faith, and expect an exact fulfillment of all the other promises and prophecies which concerned the extension and support of the kingdom of Christ.

CHAPTER 17

The transfiguration of Christ, 1-8. Christ's discourse with His disciples on the subject, 9-13. He heals a lunatic, 14-18. His discourse with His disciples on this subject also, 19-21. He foretells His own sufferings and death, 22-23. He is required to pay tribute at Capernaum, 24-26; and provides the money by a miracle, 27.

1. *After six days.* Mark ix. 2 has the same number; but Luke says, ix. 28, after "eight" days. The reason of this difference seems to be the following: Matthew and Mark reckon the days from that mentioned in the preceding chapter to that mentioned in this; Luke includes

both days, as well as the six intermediate. Hence the one makes eight, the other six, without any contradiction. *Peter, James, and John.* He chose those that they might be witnesses of His transfiguration, two or three witnesses being required by the Scripture to substantiate any fact. The same three were made witnesses of His agony in the garden, chap. xxvi. 37. *An high mountain.* This was one of the mountains of Galilee, but whether Mount Tabor or not is uncertain. Some think it was Mount Hermon. St. Luke says Christ and His disciples went up into the mountain to pray, chap. ix. 28.

2. *Was transfigured.* That fullness of the Godhead which dwelt bodily in Christ now shone forth through the human nature, and manifested to His disciples not only that divinity which Peter had before confessed, chap. xvi. 16, but also the glorious resurrection body, in which they should exist in the presence of God to eternity.

3. *Moses and Elias.* Elijah came from heaven in the same body which he had upon earth, for he was translated, and did not see death, 2 Kings ii. 11. And the body of Moses was probably raised again as a pledge of the resurrection. It was a constant and prevalent tradition among the Jews that both Moses and Elijah should appear in the times of the Messiah, and to this very tradition the disciples refer, v. 10. We may conceive that the law in the person of Moses, the great Jewish legislator, and the prophets in the person of Elijah, the chief of the prophets, came now to do homage to Jesus Christ, and to render up their authority into His hands, as He was the End of the law and the grand Subject of the predictions of the prophets. This appears more particularly from what Luke says, chap. ix. 31, that Moses and Elijah conversed with our Lord on His death, which He was about to accomplish, because in it all the rites, ceremonies, and sacrifices of the law, as well as the predictions of the prophets, were fulfilled.

4. *Then answered Peter . . . let us make here three tabernacles.* That is, when he saw Moses and Elijah ready to depart from the mount, Luke ix. 33, he wished to detain them, that he might always enjoy their company with that of his Lord and Master, still supposing that Christ would set up a temporal kingdom upon earth.

5. *A bright cloud overshadowed them.* A *cloud* was frequently the symbol of the Divine Presence. *This is my beloved Son.* "This is My Son, the beloved One, in whom I have delighted," or "been well pleased." God adds His testimony of approbation to what was spoken of the sufferings of Christ by Moses and Elijah, thus showing that the sacrificial economy of the old covenant was in itself of no worth, but as it referred to the grand atonement which Jesus was about to make. Therefore He says, "In Him have I delighted," intimating that it was in Him alone, as typified by those sacrifices, that He had delighted through the whole course of the legal administration; and that it was only in reference to the death of His Son that He accepted the offerings and oblations made to Him under the old covenant. *Hear . . . him.* The disciples wished to detain Moses and Elijah that they might hear them, but God shows that the law which had been in force, and the prophets which had prophesied, until now, must all give place to Jesus; and He alone must now be at-

tended to, as "the way, the truth, and the life," for no man could now come unto the Father but through Him.

6. *Fell on their face.* Dismayed by the voice, and dazzled by the glory of the cloud. So Daniel, chap. viii. 17, and Saul of Tarsus, Acts ix. 4.

7. *Jesus came and touched them.* Exactly parallel to this account is Dan. viii. 18, "I was in a deep sleep [i.e., a trance] on my face toward the ground: but he touched me, and set me upright." It is very likely that this transfiguration took place in the night, which was a more proper season to show forth its glory than the daytime. Luke, chap. ix. 37, expressly says that it was on the next day after the Transfiguration that our Lord came down from the mount.

9. *Tell the vision to no man.* See the note on chap. xvi. 20; and further observe that, as this Transfiguration was intended to show forth the final abolition of the whole ceremonial law, it was necessary that a matter which could not fail to irritate the Jewish rulers and people should be kept secret till Jesus had accomplished vision and prophecy by His death and resurrection.

10. *Why then say the scribes that Elias must first come?* As the disciples saw that Elijah returned to heaven, knowing the tradition of the elders, and the prophecy on which the tradition was founded, Mal. iv. 5-6, "Behold, I will send you Elijah the prophet before . . . the great and dreadful day of the Lord [shall come]: and he shall turn the hearts," it was natural enough for them to inquire what the meaning of the tradition and the intention of the prophecy were.

11. *Elias truly shall first come, and restore all things.* Or "will reform." No fanciful restoration of all men, devils, and damned spirits is spoken of as either being done or begun by the ministry of John, but merely that he should preach a doctrine tending to universal reformation of manners, and should be greatly successful. See Matt. iii. 1-7 and especially Luke iii. 3-15, where we find that a general reformation had taken place: (1) among the common people; (2) among the taxgatherers, and (3) among the soldiers. And as John announced the coming Christ, who was to baptize with the Holy Ghost, i.e., to enlighten, change, and purify the heart, that the reform might be complete, both outward and inward, he may be said, in the strictest sense of the word, to have fulfilled the prophecy. And that he was the Elijah mentioned by Malachi, the words of Gabriel to the Virgin Mary prove, Luke i. 17—"And he [John] shall go before him [Christ] in the spirit and power of Elias, to turn the hearts of the fathers to the children, and the disobedient to the wisdom of the just."

12. *Knew him not.* "They have not acknowledged him." That is, the Jewish rulers have not acknowledged him, did not receive him as the forerunner of the Messiah.

14. *When they were come to the multitude.* It appears that a congregation had been collected during our Lord's stay on the mount. *Kneeling down to him.* Or falling at His knees.

15. *My son . . . is lunatick.* One who was most affected with this disorder at the change and full of the moon. But this lunacy was occasioned by a demon. *Ofttimes he falleth into the fire, and oft into the water.* Those who are under the influence of the devil are often driven

to extremes in everything. Such are often driven into the *fire* of presumption or the *waters* of despair. Satan takes advantage of our natural temper, state of health, and outward circumstances to plague and ruin our souls.

17. *O faithless and perverse generation.* These and the following words may be considered as spoken: (1) To the disciples, because of their unbelief, v. 20. (2) To the father of the possessed, who should have brought his son to Christ. (3) To the whole multitude, who were slow of heart to believe in Him as the Messiah, notwithstanding the miracles which He wrought.

20. *As a grain of mustard seed.* Our Lord means a thriving and increasing faith; which like the grain of mustard seed, from being the least of seeds, becomes the greatest of all herbs, even a tree in whose branches the fowls of the air take shelter.

21. *This kind goeth not out but by prayer.* The whole verse is wanting in the famous Vatican MS., one of the most ancient and most authentic perhaps in the world. It is wanting also in the Coptic, Ethiopic, Syriac, Hieros., and one copy of the Itala. But all the MSS. acknowledge it in the parallel place, Mark ix. 29, only the Vatican MS. leaves out *fasting.* I strongly suspect it to be an interpolation; but, if it be, it is very ancient, as Origen, Chrysostom, and others of the primitive fathers acknowledged it.

23. *They were exceeding sorry.* Since the conversation on the mount with Moses and Elijah, Peter, James, and John could have no doubt that their Lord and Master must suffer, and that it was for this end He came into the world. But while they submitted to the counsel of God, their affection for Him caused them to feel exquisite distress.

24. *They that received tribute.* This was not a tax to be paid to the Roman government, but a tax for the support of the Temple. The law, Exod. xxx. 13, obliged every male among the Jews to pay half a shekel yearly for the support of the Temple.

25. *He saith, Yes.* From this reply of Peter it is evident that our Lord customarily paid all taxes, tributes, etc., which were common among the people wherever He came. The children of God are subject to all civil laws in the places where they live—and should pay the taxes levied on them by public authority.

26. *Then are the children free.* As this money is levied for the support of that Temple of which I am the Lord, then I am not obliged to pay the tax; and My disciples, like the priests that minister, should be exempted from the necessity of paying.

CHAPTER 18

The disciples inquiring who should be greatest in Christ's kingdom, 1, He takes occasion to recommend humility, simplicity, and disinterestedness, 2-6. Warns them against offenses, 7. Recommends mortification and self-denial, 8-9. Charges them to avoid giving offense, 10-11. Parable of him who had lost one sheep out of his flock consisting of 100, 12-14. How to deal with an offending brother, 15-18. A gracious promise to social prayer, 19-20. How often an offending brother who expresses sorrow, and promises amendment, is to be forgiven, 21-22. The parable of the king who called his servants to account, and finds one who owed him 10,000 talents, who, being unable to pay, and imploring mercy, was forgiven, 23-27. Of the same person, who treated his fellow servant unmercifully, who owed him but a small sum. 28-30. Of the punishment inflicted on this unmerciful servant, 31-35.

1. *Who is the greatest?* Could these disciples have viewed the kingdom of Christ in any other light than that of a temporal one? Hence they wished to know whom He would make His prime minister—whom His general—whom His chief chancellor—whom supreme judge. The disciples having lately seen the keys delivered to Peter, and found that he, with James and John, had been privileged with being present at the Transfiguration, it is no wonder if a measure of jealousy and suspicion began to work in their minds. From this inquiry we may also learn that the disciples had no notion of Peter's supremacy.

3. *Except ye be converted.* Unless you are saved from those prejudices which are at present so baneful to your nation (seeking a temporal and not a spiritual kingdom), unless you are clothed with the spirit of humility, you cannot enter into the spirit, design, and privileges of My spiritual and eternal kingdom. *And become as little children.* I.e., be as truly without worldly ambition, and the lust of power, as little children are, who act among themselves as if all were equal.

5. *One such little child.* As our Lord in the preceding verses considers a little child an emblem of a genuine disciple, so by the term in this verse He means a disciple only. *Whoso shall receive,* i.e., show unto such a childlike, unambitious disciple of Mine any act of kindness for My sake, I will consider it as done to myself.

6. *But whoso shall offend one of these little ones.* But, on the contrary, whosoever shall cause one of the least of those who believe in Me to be stumbled—to go into the spirit of the world, or give way to sin—such a one shall meet with the most exemplary punishment. *A millstone.* "An ass's millstone," because in ancient times, before the invention of wind and water mills, the stones were turned sometimes by slaves, but commonly by asses or mules.

7. *Woe!* or "Alas!" It is the opinion of some eminent critics that this word is ever used by our Lord to express sympathy and concern. *Because of offences.* Scandals, stumbling blocks, persecutions, etc.

10. *One of these little ones.* One of My simple, loving, humble disciples. *Their angels . . . always behold.* Our Lord here not only alludes to, but in my opinion establishes, the notion received by almost all nations, viz., that every person has a guardian angel; and that these have always access to God, to receive orders relative to the management of their charge. See Ps. xxxiv. 7; Heb. i. 14. *Always behold the face.* Hence, among the Jews, the angels were styled "angels of the face," and Michael is said to be "the prince of the face." This is an allusion to the privilege granted by Eastern monarchs to their chief favorites and privy counsellors of Ahasuerus, are said to see the king's face. Esther i. 14.

11. *For the Son of man.* This is added as a second reason why no injury should be done to His followers. The Son of Man has so loved them as to come into the world to lay down His life for them.

14. *It is not the will of your Father.* If any soul be finally lost, it is not because God's will or counsel was against its salvation, or that a proper provision had not been made for it; but that, though light came into the world, it pre-

ferred darkness to light, because of its attachment to its evil deeds.

15. *If thy brother*—any who is a member of the same religious society—*trespass against thee,* (1) *Go and* reprove him *alone*—it may be in person; if that cannot be so well done, by your messenger, or in writing (which in many cases is likely to be the most effectual). Observe, our Lord gives no liberty to omit this, or to exchange it for either of the following steps. If this do not succeed,

16. (2) *Take with thee one or two more.* Men whom he esteems, who may then confirm and enforce what you say; and afterwards, if need require, bear witness of what was spoken. If even this do not succeed, then, and not before,

17. (3) *Tell it unto the church.* Lay the whole matter before the congregation of Christian believers in that place of which he is a member, or before the minister and elders, as the representatives of the church or assembly. If all this avail not, then, *Let him be unto thee as an heathen man and a publican.* To whom you are, as a Christian, to owe earnest and persevering goodwill and acts of kindness; but have no religious communions with him till, if he have been convicted, he acknowledge his fault. Whosoever follows this threefold rule will seldom offend others, and never be offended himself (Rev. J. Wesley). Reproving a brother who had sinned was a positive command under the law. See Lev. xix. 17. And the Jews have a saying that one of the causes of the ruin of their nation was, "No man reproved another."

18. *Whatsoever ye shall bind.* Whatever determinations you make, in conformity to these directions for your conduct to an offending brother, will be accounted just, and ratified by the Lord. Binding signified, and was commonly understood by the Jews at that time to be, a declaration that anything was unlawful to be done; and loosing signified, on the contrary, a declaration that anything may be lawfully done. The words *bind* and *loose* are used in a declaratory sense, of things, not of persons.

19. *If two of you shall agree.* "Symphonize, or harmonize." It is a metaphor taken from a number of musical instruments set to the same key and playing the same tune. Here it means a perfect agreement of the hearts, desires, wishes, and voices of two or more persons praying to God.

20. *For where two or three are gathered together.* There are many sayings among the Jews almost exactly similar to this, such as, "Wherever even two persons are sitting in discourse concerning the law, the Divine Presence is among them." *In my name* seems to refer particularly to a public profession of Christ and His gospel. *There am I in the midst.* None but God could say these words, to say them with truth, because God alone is everywhere present, and these words refer to His omnipresence.

21. *Till seven times?* Though *seven* was a number of perfection among the Hebrews, and often meant much more than the units in it imply, yet it is evident that Peter uses it here in its plain literal sense, as our Lord's words sufficiently testify. It was a maxim among the Jews never to forgive more than thrice. Peter enlarges this charity more than one-half, and our

Lord makes even his enlargement septuple; see v. 22. Revenge is natural to man; i.e., man is naturally a vindictive being, and, in consequence, nothing is more difficult to him than forgiveness of injuries.

22. *Seventy times seven.* There is something very remarkable in these words, especially if collated with Gen. iv. 24, where the very same words are used—If any man kill Lamech, he shall be avenged seventy times seven. The just God punishes sin in an exemplary manner. Sinful man, who is exposed to the stroke of divine justice, should be abundant in forgiveness, especially as only the merciful shall find mercy.

24. *Ten thousand talents.* "A myriad of talents," the highest number known in Greek arithmetical notation.

25. *He had not to pay.* That is "not being able to pay." *Commanded him to be sold . . . his wife and children.* Our Lord here alludes to an ancient custom among the Hebrews of selling a man and his family to make payment of contracted debts. See Exod. xxii. 3; Lev. xxv. 39, 47; 2 Kings iv. 1.

26. *Fell down, and w o r s h i p p e d   him.* "Crouched as a dog before him," with the greatest deference, submission, and anxiety. *Have patience with me.* "Be long-minded towards me —give me longer space."

27. *Moved with compassion.* Or with "tender pity." This is the source of salvation to a lost world, the tender pity, the eternal mercy of God.

30. *And he would not.* To the unmerciful, God will show no mercy; this is an eternal purpose of the Lord, which never can be changed. God teaches us what to do to a fellow sinner by what He does to us. Our fellowservant's debt to us, and ours to God, are as 100 denarii to 10,000 talents! When we humble ourselves before Him, God freely forgives us all this mighty sum! And shall we exact from our brother recompense for the most trifling faults?

34. *Delivered him to the tormentors.* Not only continued captivity is here intended, but the tortures to be endured in it.

35. *So likewise shall my heavenly Father do also unto you.* The goodness and indulgence of God towards us are the pattern we should follow in our dealings with others.

CHAPTER 19

Jesus leaves Galilee, and comes into the coasts of Judea, and is followed by great multitudes, whom He heals, 1-2. The question of the Pharisees concerning divorce answered, and the doctrine of marriage explained, 3-9. The inquiry of the disciples on this subject, 10. Our Lord's answer, explaining the case of eunuchs, 11-12. Little children brought to Christ for His blessing, 13-15. The case of the young man who wished to obtain eternal life, 16-22. Our Lord's reflections on this case, in which He shows the difficulty of a rich man's salvation, 23-26. What they shall possess who have left all for Christ's sake and the gospel, 27-29. How many of the first shall be last, and the last first, 30.

1. *Beyond Jordan.* Or "by the side of Jordan." Matthew begins here to give an account of Christ's journey (the only one he mentions) to Jerusalem, a little before the Passover, at which He was crucified. See Mark x. 1; Luke ix. 51.

3. *Tempting him.* "Trying" what answer He would give to a question which, however decided by Him, would expose Him to censure. *Is it lawful . . . for every cause?* What made

our Lord's situation at present so critical in respect to this question was: At this time there were two famous divinity and philosophical schools among the Jews, that of Shammai, and that of Hillel. On the question of divorce, the school of Shammai maintained that a man could not legally put away his wife except for whoredom. The school of Hillel taught that a man might put away his wife for a multitude of other causes, and when she did not "find grace in his sight"; i.e., when he saw any other woman that pleased him better.

5. *For this cause.* Being created for this very purpose, that they might glorify their Maker in a matrimonial connection. *Shall a man leave* (wholly give up) *father and mother*—the matrimonial union being more intimate and binding than even paternal or filial affection—and shall be "closely united, shall be firmly cemented" to his wife. A beautiful metaphor, which most forcibly intimates that nothing but death can separate them, as a well-glued board will break sooner in the whole wood than in the glued joint. *And they twain shall be one flesh.* Not only meaning that they should be considered as one body, but also as two souls in one body, with a complete union of interests, and an indissoluble partnership of life and fortune, comfort and support, desires and inclinations, joys and sorrows.

6. *What therefore God hath joined together.* "Yoked together," as oxen in the plough, where each must pull equally, in order to bring it on. Among the ancients, when persons were newly married, they put a yoke upon their necks or chains upon their arms to show that they were to be one, closely united, and pulling equally together in all the concerns of life.

7. *Why did Moses then command to give a writing of divorcement?* It is not an unusual case for the impure and unholy to seek for a justification of their conduct from the law of God itself, and to wrest scripture to their own destruction.

8. *Moses because of the hardness of your hearts.* Moses perceived that if divorce were not permitted, in many cases, the women would be exposed to great hardships through the "cruelty" of their husbands.

9. *Except it be for fornication.* The grand subject of dispute between the two schools mentioned above was the word in Deut. xxiv. 1, "When a man hath taken a wife, and she find no grace in his sight, because of some uncleanness." This the school of Shammai held to mean whoredom or adultery; but the school of Hillel maintained that it signified any corporeal defect which rendered the person deformed, or any bad temper which made the husband's life uncomfortable.

10. *If the case of the man.* "Of a husband," so I think the word should be translated here. Our word "husband" comes from the Anglo-Saxon *hus* and *band*: the "bond" of the house, anciently spelled "housebond"—so in my old MS. Bible. It is a lamentable case when the husband, instead of being the bond and union of the family, scatters and ruins it by dissipation, riot, and excess. *It is not good to marry.* That is, if a man have not the liberty to put away his wife when she is displeasing to him. God had said,

Gen. ii. 18, It is not good for man to be alone, i.e., unmarried. The disciples seem to say that, if the husband have not the power to divorce his wife when she is displeasing to him, it *is not good for him to marry.* Here was a flat contradiction to the decision of the Creator.

12. *Eunuchs.* "To have the care of the bed or bedchamber," this being the principal employment of *eunuchs* in the Eastern countries, particularly in the apartments of queens and princesses. These are they whom our Lord says are *made eunuchs of men,* merely for the above purpose. *So born from their mother's womb.* Such as are naturally incapable of marriage, and consequently should not contract any. *For the kingdom of heaven's sake.* I believe our Lord here alludes to the case of the Essenes, one of the most holy and pure sects among the Jews. These abstained from all commerce with women, hoping thereby to acquire a greater degree of purity, and be better fitted for the kingdom of God. They had no children of their own, but constantly adopted those of poor people, and brought them up in their own way. *He that is able to receive.* These words are variously translated: he who can "take, let him take it"; "comprehend, let him comprehend it"; "admit, let him admit it." The meaning seems to be, Let the man who feels himself capable of embracing this way of life embrace it; but none can do it but he to whom it is given, who has it as a gift from his mother's womb.

13. *Then were there brought unto him little children.* These are termed by Luke, chap. xviii. 15, "infants," very young children; and it was on this account, probably, that the disciples rebuked the parents, thinking them too young to receive good. *That he should put his hands.* It was a common custom among the Jews to lay their hands on the heads of those whom they blessed or for whom they prayed. This seems to have been done by way of dedication or consecration to God—the person being considered as the sacred property of God ever after.

14. *Of such is the kingdom of heaven.* Or, "The kingdom of heaven is composed of such." A great part of God's kingdom is composed of such literally, and those only who resemble little children shall be received into it; see on chap. xviii. 3. Christ loves little children because He loves simplicity and innocence; He has sanctified their very age by passing through it himself—the holy Jesus was once a little child.

16. *One came.* Much instruction may be had from seriously attending to the conduct, spirit, and question of this person. (1) He came running, Mark x. 17, and he was deeply convinced of the importance of his business, and seriously determined to seek so as to find. (2) He kneeled, or caught Him by the knees, thus evidencing his humility, and addressing himself only to mercy. (3) He came in the spirit of a disciple, or scholar, desiring to be taught a matter of the utmost importance to him—Good teacher. (4) He came in the spirit of obedience; he had worked hard to no purpose, and he is still willing to work, provided he can have a prospect of succeeding—*What good thing shall I do?* (5) His question was the most interesting and important that any soul can ask of God—How shall I be saved?

17. *Why callest thou me good?* Or, "Why do

you question Me concerning that good thing?" The whole passage therefore may be read thus: "O Teacher! what good thing shall I do that I may have eternal life? And He said unto him, Why do you question Me concerning that good thing? There is One that is good." *Keep the commandments.* From this we may learn that God's great design in giving His law to the Jews was to lead them to the expectation and enjoyment of eternal life. But as all the law referred to Christ, and He became "the end of the law for righteousness" (justification) to all that believe, so He is to be received, in order to have the end accomplished which the law proposed.

19. *Thou shalt love thy neighbour as thyself.* Self-love, as it is generally called, has been grievously declaimed against, even by religious people, as a most pernicious and dreadful evil. But they have not understood the subject on which they spoke. They have denominated that intense propensity which unregenerate men feel to gratify their carnal appetites and vicious passions self-love, whereas it might be more properly termed self-hatred or self-murder. If I am to love my neighbor as myself, and this "love worketh no ill to his neighbour," then self-love, in the sense in which our Lord uses it, is something excellent.

20. *All these things have I kept.* I have made these precepts the rule of my life. There is a difference worthy of notice between this and our Lord's word. He says, v. 17, *keep,* earnestly, diligently, as with watch and ward, probably referring not only to the letter but to the spirit. The young man modestly says, All these have I "observed"; I have paid attention to, and endeavored to regulate my conduct by them. I have "kept them in custody." *What lack I yet?* He felt a troubled conscience, and a mind unassured of the approbation of God; and he clearly perceived that something was wanting to make him truly happy.

21. *If thou wilt be perfect.* "Be complete," have the business "finished," and all hindrances to your salvation removed, *go and sell that thou hast*—go and dispose of your possessions, to which it is evident his heart was too much attached, *and give to the poor*—for your goods will be a continual snare to you if you keep them; *and thou shalt have treasure in heaven*—the loss, if it can be called such, shall be made amply up to you in that eternal life about which you inquired; *and come and follow me*—be My disciple, and I will appoint you to preach the kingdom of God to others.

22. *Went away sorrowful.* Men undergo great agony of mind while they are in suspense between the love of the world and the love of their souls. *He had great possessions.* And what were these in comparison of peace of conscience and mental rest?

23. *A rich man shall hardly enter.* That is, into the spirit and privileges of the gospel in this world, and through them into the Kingdom of glory.

24. *A camel.* It was a mode of expression common among the Jews, and signified a thing impossible. Hence this proverb: "No man sees a palm tree of gold, nor an elephant passing through the eye of a needle."

26. *With men this is impossible.* God alone can take the love of the world out of human heart. Therefore the salvation of the rich is represented as possible only to Him.

27. *What shall we have therefore?* "What reward shall we get?"

28. *The regeneration.* Some refer this to the time in which the new heavens and the new earth shall be created, and the soul and body united. *Judging the twelve tribes.* From the parallel place, Luke xxii. 28-30, it is evident that sitting on thrones and judging the twelve tribes means simply obtaining eternal salvation, and the distinguishing privileges of the Kingdom of glory, by those who continued faithful to Christ in His sufferings and death. *Judging.* "Governing, presiding, holding the first or most distinguished place."

29. *Shall receive an hundredfold.* Viz., in this life, in value, though perhaps not in kind; and in the world to come *everlasting life.*

30. *But many that are first.* The Jews, who have been the first and most distinguished people of God, will in general reject the gospel of My grace, and be consequently rejected by Me. The Gentiles, who have had no name among the living, shall be brought to the knowledge of the truth, and become the first, the chief, and most exalted people of God.

CHAPTER 20

The similitude of the householder hiring laborers into his vineyard, to show that the Gentiles should be preferred to the Jews, according to what was hinted at the close of the last chapter, 1-16. On the way going up to Jerusalem He predicts His sufferings and death, 17-19. The mother of Zebedee's children requests dignities for her sons, 20-21. Christ, by His answer, shows that sufferings, not worldly honors, are to be the lot of His most faithful followers, and that seats in glory can be given only to those who are prepared for them, 22-23. From this our Lord takes occasion to teach the necessity of humility, and to show that those who wished to be chief must be servants of all, 24-28. On His coming to Jericho, He restores sight to two blind men, who, being restored, follow Him, 29-34.

1. *For the kingdom of heaven is like unto a man . . . an householder.* The manner of God's proceeding under the gospel dispensation resembles a householder who went out at "daybreak," "together with the morning." This was what was called, among the Jews and Romans, the first hour, answering to six o'clock in the morning. *To hire labourers.* "Some workmen," for he had not got all that was necessary, because we find him going out at other hours to hire more.

3. *The third hour.* Nine o'clock in the morning. *Marketplace.* Where laborers usually stood till they were hired.

5. *The sixth hour.* "Twelve o'clock." *Ninth hour.* Three o'clock in the afternoon.

6. *Eleventh.* Five o'clock in the evening, when there was only one hour before the end of the Jewish day, which, in matters of labor, closed at six.

8. *When even was come.* Six o'clock, the time they ceased from labor, and the workmen came to receive their wages. *Steward.* "A manager of the household concerns" under the master.

13. *Friend, I do thee no wrong.* The salvation of the Gentiles can in itself become no impediment to the Jews; there is the same Jesus both for the Jew and for the Greek. Eternal life is

offered to both through the Blood of the Cross, and there is room enough in heaven for all.

15. *Is it not lawful for me?* As eternal life is the free gift of God, He has a right to give it in whatever proportions, at whatever times, and on whatever conditions He pleases. *Is thine eye evil?* An evil eye among the Jews meant a malicious, covetous, or envious person.

17. *And Jesus going up.* From Jericho to Jerusalem, chap. xix. 15.

18. *The Son of man shall be betrayed.* Or "will be delivered up." This is the third time that our Lord informed His disciples of His approaching sufferings and death. This was a subject of the utmost importance, and it was necessary they should be well prepared for such an awful event.

19. *Deliver him to the Gentiles to mock.* This was done by Herod and his Roman soldiers. See Luke xxiii. 11. *To scourge, and to crucify.* This was done by Pilate, the Roman governor. The punishment of the cross was Roman, not Jewish; but the chief priests condemned Him to it, and the Romans executed the sentence.

20. *The mother of Zebedee's children.* This was Salome.

21. *Grant that these my two sons.* James and John. See Mark xv. 40. In the preceding chapter, v. 28, our Lord had promised His disciples that they should sit on twelve thrones, judging the twelve tribes. Salome, probably hearing of this, and understanding it literally, came to request the chief dignities in this new government for her sons. And it appears it was at their instigation that she made this request, for Mark, chap. x. 35, informs us that these brethren themselves made the request, i.e., they made it through the medium of their mother.

22. *Ye know not what ye ask.* How strange is the infatuation in some parents which leads them to desire worldly or ecclesiastical honors for their children! He must be much in love with the Cross who wishes to have his child a minister of the gospel; for, if he be such as God approves of in the work, his life will be a life of toil and suffering.

23. *Is not mine to give, but it shall be given to them for whom it is prepared of my Father.* The true construction of the words is this: "To sit on My right hand and on My left is not mine to give, except to them for whom it is prepared of My Father." According to the prediction of Christ, these brethren did partake of His afflictions. James was martyred by Herod, Acts xii. 2; and John was banished to Patmos for the testimony of Christ, Rev. i. 9.

25. *Exercise dominion . . . and . . . authority upon them.* They "tyrannized" and "exercised arbitrary power" over the people.

26. *It shall not be so among you.* Every kind of lordship and spiritual domination over the Church of Christ, like that exercised by the Church of Rome, is destructive and antichristian. *Your minister.* Or "deacon." I know no other word which could at once convey the meaning of the original and make a proper distinction between it and *servant*, in v. 27. The office of a deacon, in the primitive Church, was to serve in the love feasts, to distribute the bread and wine to the communicants; to proclaim different parts and times of worship in the churches;

and to take care of the widows, orphans, prisoners, and sick, who were provided for out of the revenues of the Church. Thus we find it was the very lowest ecclesiastical office.

27. *Your servant.* The lowest secular office, as deacon was the lowest ecclesiastical office.

28. *A ransom for many.* Or "a ransom instead of many,"—one Ransom, or Atonement, instead of the many prescribed in the Jewish law.

30. *Two blind men.* Mark x. 46 and Luke xviii. 35 mention only one blind man, Bartimaeus. Probably he was mentioned by the other Evangelists as being a person well-known before and after his cure. *Sitting by the way side.* In the likeliest place to receive alms, because of the multitudes going and coming between Jerusalem and Jericho. *Cried out.* Though God had deprived them, for wise reasons, of their eyes, He left them the use of their speech. It is never so ill with us but it might be much worse; let us therefore be submissive and thankful.

33. *That our eyes may be opened.* He who feels his own sore, and the plague of his heart, has no great need of a prompter in prayer. A hungry man can easily ask bread; he has no need to go to a book to get expressions to state his wants in. His hunger tells him he wants food, and he tells this to the person from whom he expects relief.

34. *So Jesus had compassion on them.* "He was moved with tender pity." The tender pity of Christ met the earnest cry of the blind men, and their immediate cure was the result. *They followed him.* As a proof of the miracle that was wrought, and of the gratitude which they felt to their Benefactor.

CHAPTER 21

Christ rides into Jerusalem upon an ass, and the multitude receive Him joyfully, 1-11. He enters the Temple, and expels the money changers, 12-13. The blind and the lame come to Him and are healed, 14. The chief priests and scribes are offended, 15. Our Lord confounds them, and goes to Bethany, 16-17. The barren fig tree blasted, 18-22. While He is teaching in the Temple, the chief priests and elders question His authority; He answers and confutes them, 23-27. The parable of the man and his two sons, 28-32. The parable of a vineyard let out to husbandmen, 33-42; applied to the priests and Pharisees, 43-45; who wish to kill Him, but are restrained by the fear of the people, who acknowledge Christ for a prophet, 46.

1. *Bethphage.* A place on the west declivity of Mount Olivet, from which it is thought the whole declivity and part of the valley took their name. It is supposed to have derived its name from the fig trees which grew there.

2. *Ye shall find an ass tied, and a colt.* Asses and mules were in common use in Palestine; horses were seldom to be met with.

5. *Tell ye the daughter of Sion.* The quotation is taken from Zech. ix. 9, but not in the precise words of the prophet. This entry into Jerusalem has been termed the triumph of Christ. It was indeed the triumph of humility over pride and worldly grandeur, of poverty over affluence, and of meekness and gentleness over rage and malice. He is coming now meek, full of kindness and compassion to those who were plotting His destruction! He comes to deliver up himself into their hands; their King comes to be murdered by His subjects, and to make His death a ransom price for their souls!

7. *And put on them their clothes.* Thus acknowledging Him to be their King, for this was a custom observed by the people when they found that God had appointed a man to the kingdom.

8. *Cut down branches from the trees.* Carrying palm and other branches was emblematical of victory and success, Rev. vii. 9.

9. *Hosanna to the son of David.* When persons applied to the king for help, or for a redress of grievances, they used the word *hosanna.* "Save now!" or "Save, we beseech thee!" *Son of David.* A well-known epithet of the Messiah. *He that cometh in the name.* He who comes in the name and authority of the Most High. *Hosanna in the highest.* Either meaning, Let the heavenly hosts join with us in magnifying this august Being!—or, let the utmost degrees of hosanna, of salvation, and deliverance, be communicated to Thy people! Probably there is an allusion here to the custom of the Jews in the Feast of Tabernacles. During the first seven days of that feast they went once round the altar, each day, with palm and other branches in their hands, singing hosanna. But on the eighth day of that feast they walked seven times round the altar, singing the hosanna; and this was termed the "great hosanna"; i.e., "Assist with the greatest succor."

10. *All the city was moved.* Or, "The whole city was in motion." Was in a tumult—they saw and heard plainly that the multitude had proclaimed Christ as King and Messiah. *Who is this?* Who is accounted worthy of this honor?

11. *This is Jesus the prophet.* That Prophet of whom Moses spoke in Deut. xviii. 18.

12. *Moneychangers.* Persons who furnished the Jews and proselytes who came from other countries with the current coin of Judea, in exchange for their own.

13. *My house shall be called the house of prayer.* This is taken from Isa. lvi. 7. *But ye have made it a den of thieves.* This is taken from Jer. vii. 11. Our Lord alludes here to those dens and caves in Judea in which the public robbers either hid or kept themselves fortified.

14. *The blind and the lame came.* Having condemned the profane use of the Temple, He now shows the proper use of it. It is a house of prayer, where God is to manifest His goodness and power in giving sight to the spiritually blind, and feet to the lame.

15. *The chief priests . . . were sore displeased.* Or "were incensed." Incensed at what? At the purification of the profaned Temple! This was a work they should have done themselves, but for which they had neither grace nor influence; and their pride and jealousy will not suffer them to permit others to do it. Strange as it may appear, the priesthood itself, in all corrupt times, has been ever the most forward to prevent a reform in the Church.

16. *Out of the mouth of babes.* The eighth psalm, out of which these words are quoted, is applied to Jeuss Christ in three other places in the new covenant, 1 Cor. xv. 27; Eph. i. 22; Heb. ii. 6. It was a common thing among the Jews for the children to be employed in public acclamations, and thus they were accustomed to hail their celebrated rabbins. This shouting of the children was therefore no strange thing in the land; only they were exasperated because a Person was celebrated against whom they had a rooted hatred.

17. *And he left them* (finally leaving them), *and went . . . into Bethany; and he lodged there.* Bethany was a village about two miles distant from Jerusalem, by Mount Olivet, John xi. 18; and it is remarkable that from this day till His death, which happened about six days after, He spent not one night in Jerusalem, but went every evening to Bethany, and returned to the city each morning. See Luke xxi. 37; xxii. 39; John viii. 1-2. They were about to murder the Lord of glory; and the true Light, which they had rejected, is now departing from them.

18. *Now in the morning as he returned into the city.* Which was His custom from the time He wholly left Jerusalem, spending only the daytime teaching in the Temple; see v. 17. This was probably on Thursday, the twelfth day of the month *Nisan. He hungered.* Probably neither He nor His disciples had anything but what they got from public charity, and the hand of that seems to have been cold at this time.

19. *He saw a fig tree in the way.* "By the roadside." As this fig tree was by the wayside, it was no private property; and on this account our Lord, or any other traveller, had a right to take of its fruit. For a full explanation of this difficult passage, relative to this emblematic fig tree, see on Mark xi. 13.

21. *If ye have faith, and doubt not.* "Removing mountains," and "rooting up of mountains" are phrases very generally used to signify the removing or conquering great difficulties—getting through perplexities. So, many of the rabbins were termed "rooters up of mountains," because they were dexterous in removing difficulties, solving cases of conscience. In this sense our Lord's words are to be understood. He that has faith will get through every difficulty and perplexity; mountains shall become molehills or plains before him.

23. *By what authority doest thou these things?* The things which the chief priests allude to were His receiving the acclamations of the people as the promised Messiah, His casting the traders out of the Temple, and His teaching the people publicly in it.

25. *The baptism of John.* Had John a divine commission or not for his baptism and preaching? Our Lord here takes the wise in their own cunning. He knew the estimation John was in among the people, and He plainly saw that if they gave any answer at all they must convict themselves; and so they saw, when they came to examine the question.

27. *We cannot tell,* said they; which, in the words of truth, should have been, "We will not tell," for we will not have this man for the Messiah; because, if we acknowledge John as His forerunner, we must, of necessity, receive Jesus as the Christ.

28. *A certain man had two sons.* Under the emblem of these two sons—one of whom was a libertine, disobedient, and insolent, but who afterwards thought on his ways, and returned to his duty; and the second, a hypocrite, who promised all, and did nothing;—our Lord points out, on the one hand, the taxgatherers and

sinners of all descriptions, who, convicted by the preaching of John and that of Christ, turned away from their iniquities and embraced the gospel; and, on the other hand, the scribes, Pharisees, and self-righteous people, who, pretending a zeal for the law, would not receive the salvation of the gospel.

29. *I will not.* This is the general reply of every sinner to the invitations of God, and in it the Most High is treated without ceremony or respect.

30. *I go, sir.* This is all respect, complaisance, and professed obedience. But he *went not;* he promised well, but did not perform. What a multitude of such are in the world, professing to know God but denying Him in their works! Alas! what will such professions avail, when God comes to take away the soul?

31. *The publicans and the harlots.* In all their former conduct they had said no. Now they yield to the voice of truth when they hear it, and enter into the Kingdom, embracing the salvation brought to them in the gospel. The others, who had always been professing the most ready and willing obedience, and who pretended to be waiting for the kingdom of God, did not receive it when it came, but rather chose, while making the best professions, to continue members of the synagogue of Satan.

32. *John came unto you in the way of righteousness.* Proclaiming the truth, and living agreeably to it. Or, "John came unto you, who are in the way of righteousness." This seems rather to be the true meaning and construction of this passage. The Jews are here distinguished from the Gentiles. The former were in *the way of righteousness,* had the revelation of God, and the ordinances of justice established among them.

33. *There was a certain householder.* Let us endeavor to find out a general and practical meaning for this parable. A *householder*—the Supreme Being. The *family*—the Jewish nation. The *vineyard*—the city of Jerusalem. The *fence*—the divine protection. The *winepress*—the law and sacrificial rites. The *tower*—the Temple, in which the Divine Presence was manifested. The *husbandmen*—the priests and doctors of the law. *Went from home*—entrusted the cultivation of the vineyard to the priests, with the utmost confidence, as a man would do who had the most trusty servants, and was obliged to absent himself from home for a certain time. Our Lord takes this parable from Isa. v. 1. *Digged a winepress.* Mark has the pit under the press, into which the liquor ran, when squeezed out of the fruit by the press.

34. *He sent his servants.* Prophets, which, from time to time, He sent to the Jewish nation to call both priests and people back to the purity of His holy religion. *Receive the fruits of it.* Alluding to the ancient custom of paying the rent of a farm in kind; that is, by a part of the produce of the farm.

35. *Beat one.* "Took his skin off, flayed him," probably alluding to some who had been excessively scourged.

36. *Other servants.* There is not a moment in which God does not shower down His gifts upon men, and require the fruit of them. *More than the first.* Or more honorable.

37. *Last of all he sent . . . his son.* This requires no comment. Our Lord plainly means himself. *They will reverence.* They will reflect upon their conduct and blush for shame because of it, when they see my son.

38. *Said among themselves.* Alluding to the conspiracies which were then forming against the life of our blessed Lord, in the councils of the Jewish elders and chief priests. See chap. xxvii. 1.

39. *Cast him out of the vineyard.* Utterly rejected the counsel of God against themselves, and would neither acknowledge the authority of Christ nor submit to His teaching.

41. *He will miserably destroy those wicked men.* So, according to this Evangelist, our Lord caused them to pass that sentence of destruction upon themselves which was literally executed about forty years after.

42. *The stone.* R. Solom. Jarchi, on Micah v, says this *stone* means the Messiah. This seems to have been originally spoken of David, who was at first rejected by the Jewish rulers, but was afterwards chosen by the Lord to be the great ruler of His people, Israel. The quotation is taken from Ps. cxviii. 22. *The builders.* The chief priests and elders of the people, with the doctors of the law. *Rejected.* An expression borrowed from masons, who, finding a stone, which being tried in a particular place, and appearing improper for it, is thrown aside, and another taken; however, at last, it may happen that the very stone which had been before rejected may be found the most suitable as the headstone of the corner.

44. The forty-fourth verse should certainly come before v. 43; otherwise the narration is not consecutive. This is an allusion to the punishment of stoning among the Jews. The place of stoning was twice as high as a man. While standing on this, one of the witnesses struck the culprit on the loins, so that he fell over this scaffold; if he died by the stroke and fall, well; if not, the other witness threw a stone upon his heart, and dispatched him. The stone thrown on the culprit was, in some cases, as much as two men could lift up.

43. *Therefore say I.* Thus showing them that to them alone the parable belonged. *The kingdom of God shall be taken from you*—the gospel shall be taken from you, and given to the Gentiles, who will receive it, and bring forth fruit to the glory of God. *Bringing forth the fruits.* As in verse 34 an allusion is made to paying the landlord in kind, so here the Gentiles are represented as paying God thus. The returns which He expects for His grace are the fruits of grace; nothing can ever be acceptable in the sight of God that does not spring from himself.

45. *The chief priests . . . perceived that he spake of them.* The most wholesome advice passes for an affront with those who have shut their hearts against the truth. When that which should lead to repentance only kindles the flame of malice and revenge, there is but little hope of the salvation of such persons.

CHAPTER 22

A lawyer questions Him concerning the greatest commandment in the law, 34-40. He asks them their opinion
of the Christ, and confounds them, 41-46.

2. *The kingdom of heaven.* It appears from
Luke xiv. 15 that it was at an entertainment
that this parable was originally spoken. It was a
constant practice of our Lord to take the subjects
of His discourses from the persons present, or
from the circumstances of times, persons, and
places. See chap. xvi. 6; John iv. 7-10; vi. 26-27;
vii. 37. A preacher that can do so can never be
at a loss for text or sermon. *A marriage for his
son.* "A marriage feast." Or a feast of inauguration, when his son was put in possession of the
government, and thus he and his new subjects
became married together. See 1 Kings i. 5-9,
19, 25, where such a feast is mentioned. From
this parable it appears plain that: (1) the king
means the great God; (2) his son, the Lord
Jesus; (3) the marriage, His incarnation, or espousing human nature, by taking it into union
with himself; (4) the marriage feast, the economy of the gospel, during which men are invited
to partake of the blessings purchased by, and
consequent on, the incarnation and death of our
blessed Lord; (5) by those who had been bidden,
or "invited," v. 3, are meant the Jews in general,
who had this union of Christ with human nature,
and His sacrifice for sin, pointed out by various
rites, ceremonies, and sacrifices under the law,
and who by all the prophets had been constantly
invited to believe in and receive the promised
Messiah; (6) by the servants, we are to understand the first preachers of the gospel, proclaiming salvation to the Jews—John the Baptist
and the seventy disciples, Luke x. 1 may be
here particularly intended; (7) by the other servants, v. 4, the apostles seem to be meant, who,
though they were to preach the gospel to the
whole world, yet were to begin at Jerusalem,
Luke xxiv. 47, with the first offers of mercy;
(8) by their making light of it, v. 5, is pointed
out their neglect of this salvation, and their
preferring secular enjoyments to the kingdom
of Christ; (9) by injuriously using some and
slaying others of his servants, v. 6, is pointed
out the persecution raised against the apostles
by the Jews, in which some of them were
martyred; (10) by sending forth his troops, v. 7,
is meant the commission given to the Romans
against Judea; and by the burning of their city,
the total destruction of Jerusalem by Titus, the
son of Vespasian, which happened about forty
years after.

4. *Fatlings.* Properly, "fatted rams," 2 Sam.
vi. 13; 1 Chron. xv. 26.

8. *Were not worthy.* Among the Mohammedans, refusal to come to a marriage feast, when
invited, is considered a breach of the law of God.
Anyone that shall be invited to a dinner and
does not accept the invitation disobeys God and
His messenger; and anyone who comes unin-
vited, you may say is a thief, and returns a
plunderer. It was probably considered in this
light among all the Oriental nations. This observation is necessary in order to point out more
forcibly the iniquity of the refusal mentioned in
the text.

9. *Go ye therefore into the highways.* "Cross-
or by-paths"; the places where two or more roads
met in one, leading into the city, where people
were coming together from various quarters of
the country. Luke adds "hedges," to point out

the people to whom the apostles were sent, as
either miserable vagabonds or the most indigent
poor, who were wandering about the country, or
sitting by the sides of the ways and hedges,
imploring relief. This verse points out the final
rejection of the Jews and the calling of the
Gentiles. It was a custom among the Jews, when
a rich man made a feast, to go out and invite
in all destitute travellers. *As many as ye shall
find, bid to the marriage.* God sends His salvation to every soul, that all may believe and be
saved.

10. *Gathered together all . . . both bad and
good.* By the preaching of the gospel, multitudes
of souls are gathered into what is generally
termed the visible Church of Christ.

11. *When the king came.* When God shall
come to judge the world. *Wedding garment.*
Among the Orientals, long white robes were
worn at public festivals; and those who appeared
on such occasions with any other garments were
esteemed, not only highly culpable, but worthy
of punishment. This marriage feast or dinner
(the communication of the graces of the gospel
in this life) prepares for the marriage supper
of the Lamb, Rev. xix. 7-9, the enjoyment of
eternal blessedness in the Kingdom of glory.
Now as without holiness no man can see the
Lord, we may at once perceive what our Lord
means by the *wedding garment*—it is holiness of
heart and life. The text last quoted asserts that
the fine, white, and clean linen (alluding to the
marriage garment above mentioned) was an
emblem of the righteousness of the saints.

12. *He saith unto him, Friend.* Rather, "companion." As this man represents the state of a
person in the visible Church who neglects to
come unto the Master of the feast for a marriage
garment, for the salvation which Christ has
procured, he cannot be with any propriety called
a *friend,* but may well be termed a "companion,"
as being a member of the Visible Church. *He
was speechless.* He was "muzzled" or "gagged."
He had nothing to say in vindication of his
neglect. There was a garment provided, but he
neither put it on nor applied for it. His conduct, therefore, was in the highest degree insulting and indecorous.

13. *Cast him into outer darkness.* The Jewish
marriages were performed in the night season,
and the hall where the feast was made was
superbly illuminated. The *outer darkness*
means, therefore, the darkness on the outside of
this festal hall, rendered still more gloomy to
the person who was suddenly thrust out into it
from such a profusion of light.

15. *In his talk.* "By discourse," intending to
ask Him subtle and ensnaring questions, His
answers to which might involve Him either with
the Roman government or with the great Sanhedrin.

16. *The Herodians.* The preceding parable had
covered the Pharisees with confusion. When it
was ended they went out, not to humble themselves before God and deprecate the judgments
with which they were threatened, but to plot
afresh the destruction of their Teacher. The
depth of their malice appears (1) in their mode
of attack. They had often questioned our Lord
on matters concerning religion, and His answers
only served to increase His reputation and their
confusion. They now shift their ground, and

question Him concerning state affairs, and the question is such as must be answered; and yet the answer, to all human appearance, can be none other than what may be construed into a crime against the people or against the Roman government. (2) Their profound malice appears further in the choice of their companions in this business, viz., the Herodians. Herod himself was extremely attached to the Roman emperor, and made a public profession of it. All these considerations engaged the Pharisees to unite with the Herodians, who, as the Syriac intimates, were the domestics of Herod, in this infernal plot. (3) Their profound malice appears further in the praises they gave our Lord. "Teacher, *we know that thou art true, and teachest the way of God.*" This was indeed the real character of our blessed Lord; and now they bear testimony to the truth, merely with the design to make it subserve their bloody purposes. (4) Their malice appears still further in the question they propose. *Is it lawful to give tribute unto Caesar, or not?*—v. 17. The constitution of the Jewish republic rendered an answer to this question extremely difficult: (1) In the presence of the people, who professed to have no other king but God, and looked on their independence as an essential point of their religion; (2) In the presence of the Pharisees, who were ready to stir up the people against Him if His decision could be at all construed to be contrary to their prejudices or to their religious rights. (3) In the presence of the Herodians, who, if the answer should appear to be against Caesar's rights, were ready to inflame their master to avenge, by the death of our Lord, the affront offered to his master, the emperor.

20. *Whose is this image and superscription?* He knew well enough whose they were, but He showed the excellency of His wisdom in making them answer to their own confusion. They came to ensnare our Lord in His discourse, and now they are ensnared in their own. He who digs a pit for his neighbor ordinarily falls into it himself.

21. *They say unto him, Caesar's.* The *image* was the head of the emperor; the *superscription,* his titles. Tiberius was emperor at this time. *Render therefore unto Caesar.* The conclusion is drawn from their own premises. You acknowledge this to be Caesar's coin; this coin is current in your land; the currency of this coin shows the country to be under the Roman government; and your acknowledgment that it is Caesar's proves you have submitted. Do not, therefore, be unjust; but render to Caesar the things which you acknowledge to be his; at the same time, be not impious, but render unto God the things which belong to God. The image of princes stamped on their coin denotes that temporal things belong all to their government. The image of God stamped on the soul denotes that all its faculties and powers belong to the Most High, and should be employed in His service.

22. *When they had heard these words, they marvelled.* And well they might—"Never man spake like this man." By this decision Caesar is satisfied—he gets his own to the uttermost farthing. God is glorified—His honor is in every respect secured. And the people are edified—one of the most difficult questions that could

possibly come before them is answered in such a way as to relieve their consciences and direct their conduct.

24. *Raise up seed unto his brother.* This law is mentioned in Deut. xxv. 5. The meaning of the expression is that the children produced by this marriage should be reckoned in the genealogy of the deceased brother and enjoy his estates. The word *seed* should be always translated "children" or "posterity."

25. *Seven brethren.* It is very likely that the Sadducees increased the number, merely to make the question the more difficult.

29. *Ye do err.* Or, "Ye are deceived"—by your impure passions, *not knowing the scriptures,* which assert the resurrection, *nor the* miraculous *power of God* by which it is to be effected.

31. *Have ye not read?* This quotation is taken from Exod. iii. 6, 16; and as the five books of Moses were the only part of Scripture which the Sadducees acknowledged as divine, our Lord, by confuting them from those books, proved the second part of His assertion, "You are ignorant of those very Scriptures which you profess to hold sacred."

32. *I am the God of Abraham.* Let it be observed that Abraham was dead upwards of three hundred years before these words were spoken to Moses; yet still God calls himself the *God of Abraham.* Now Christ properly observes that God *is not the God of the dead* (that word being equal, in the sense of the Sadducees, to an eternal annihilation), *but of the living.* It therefore follows that, if He be the *God of Abraham . . . Isaac, and . . . Jacob,* these are not dead, but alive; alive with God, though they had ceased, for some hundreds of years, to exist among mortals.

33. *The multitude . . . were astonished at his doctrine.* God uses the infidelity of some for the edification of others. Truth always gains by being opposed.

34. *They were gathered together.* "They came together with one accord," or, "for the same purpose"; i.e., of ensnaring Him in His discourse, as the Sadducees had done, v. 23.

35. *A lawyer.* "A teacher of the law." What is called *lawyer* in the common translation conveys a wrong idea to most readers. These teachers of the law were the same as the scribes.

36. *Which is the great commandment?* We see here three kinds of enemies and false accusers of Christ and His disciples, and three sorts of accusations brought against them: (1) The Herodians, or politicians and courtiers, who formed their questions and accusations on the rights of the prince, and matters of state, v. 16; (2) The Sadducees, or libertines, who founded theirs upon matters of religion, and articles of faith, which they did not credit, v. 23. (3) The Pharisees, lawyers, scribes, hypocritical pretenders to devotion, who founded theirs on that vital and practical godliness (the love of God and man) of which they wished themselves to be thought the sole proprietors.

37. What is implied in loving God with all the heart, soul, mind, strength, and when may a man be said to do this? (1) He loves God *with all* his *heart* who loves nothing in comparison of Him and nothing but in reference to Him, who is ready to give up, do, or suffer anything in

order to please and glorify Him. (2) He loves God *with all* his *soul,* or rather, "with all his life," who is ready to give up life for His sake— to endure all sorts of torments, and to be deprived of all kinds of comforts, rather than dishonor God—who employs life with all its comforts and conveniences to glorify God in, by, and through all. (3) He loves God with all his strength, Mark xii. 30; Luke x. 27, who exerts all the powers of his body and soul in the service of God; who, for the glory of his Maker, spares neither labor nor cost; who sacrifices his time, body, health, ease, for the honor of God, his divine Master; who employs in His service all his goods, his talents, his power, credit, authority, and influence. (4) He loves God *with all* his *mind* (intellect) who applies himself only to know God and His holy will; who receives with submission, gratitude, and pleasure the sacred truths which God has revealed to man.

39. *Thou shalt love thy neighbour.* The love of our neighbor springs from the love of God as its Source; is found in the love of God as its principle, pattern, and end; and the love of God is found in the love of our neighbor as its effect, representation, and infallible mark.

40. *On these two commandments hang all the law and the prophets.* They are like the first and last links of a chain; all the intermediate ones depend on them. True religion begins and ends in love to God and man. These are the two grand links that unite God to man, man to his fellows, and men again to God.

41. *While the Pharisees were gathered together.* Jesus asks a question in His turn, utterly to confound them, and to show the people that the source of all the captious questions of his opponents was their ignorance of the prophecies relative to the Messiah.

42. *What think ye of Christ?* Or, What are your thoughts concerning "the Christ"—the Messiah? For to this title the emphatic article should always be added. *Whose son is he?* From what family is He to spring? *They say unto him, The son of David.* This was a thing well-known among the Jews, and universally acknowledged; see John vii. 42; and is a most powerful proof against them that the Messiah is come. Is it not evident that God designed that the Messiah should come at a time when the public genealogies might be inspected, to prove that it was He who was prophesied of, and that no other was to be expected? The Evangelists, Matthew and Luke, were so fully convinced of the conclusiveness of this proof that they had recourse to the public registers; and thus proved to the Jews, from their own records, that Jesus was born of the family mentioned by the prophets. Nor do we find that a scribe, Pharisee, or any other ever attempted to invalidate this proof, though it would have essentially subserved their cause, could they have done it.

43. *How then doth David in spirit* (or by the Spirit—by the inspiration of the Spirit of God) *call him Lord? saying,*

44. *The Lord* (Jehovah) *said unto my Lord.* (Adonai, my Prop, Stay, Master, Support), *Sit thou on my right hand.* Take the place of the greatest eminence and authority. *Till I make thine enemies thy footstool.* Till I subdue both Jews and Gentiles under Thee, and cause them to acknowledge Thee as their Sovereign and Lord. This quotation is taken from **Ps. cx. 1;** and from it these two points are clear: (1) That David wrote it by the inspiration of God; and (2) That it is a prophetic declaration of the Messiah.

45. *How is he his son?* As the Jews did not attempt to deny the conclusion of our Lord's question—which was, The Messiah is not only the Son of David according to the flesh, but He is the Lord of David according to His divine nature—then it is evident they could not. Indeed there was no other way of invalidating the argument but by denying that the prophecy in question related to Christ. But it seems the prophecy was so fully and so generally understood to belong to the Messiah that they did not attempt to do this; for it is immediately added, "No man was able to answer him a word." They were completely nonplussed and confounded.

46. *Neither durst any . . . ask him any more questions.* The Pharisees and Herodians were defeated, vv. 15-22. The Sadducees were confounded, vv. 29-33; the lawyers, nonplussed, vv. 37-40; and the Pharisees, finally routed, vv. 41-46. Thus did the wisdom of God triumph over the cunning of men.

CHAPTER 23

The character of the scribes and Pharisees, and directions to the people and the disciples to receive the law from them, but not to follow their bad example, 1-7. The disciples exhorted to humility, 8-12. Different woes pronounced against the scribes and Pharisees for their intolerance, 13; rapacity, 14; false zeal, 15; superstition in oaths and tithes, 16-23; hypocrisy, 24-28. Their cruelty, 29-32. Their persecution of the apostles, their destruction foretold, 33-36. Christ's lamentation over Jerusalem, 37-39.

2. *The scribes and the Pharisees sit in Moses' seat.* They "sat" there formerly by divine appointment; they *sit* there now by divine permission. What our Lord says here refers to their expounding the Scriptures, for it was the custom of the Jewish doctors to *sit* while they expounded the law and prophets, chap. v. 1; Luke iv. 20-22, and to stand up when they read them. By the *seat* of Moses we are to understand authority to teach the law. Moses was the great teacher of the Jewish people, and the scribes are here represented as his successors.

3. *All therefore whatsoever.* That is, all those things which they read out of the law and prophets, and all things which they teach consistently with them. This must be our Lord's meaning. He could not have desired them to do everything without restriction which the Jewish doctors taught, because himself warns His disciples against their false teaching, and testifies that they had made the word of God of none effect by their traditions. See chap. xv. 6.

4. *They bind heavy burdens.* They are now so corrupt that they have added to the ceremonies of the law others of their own invention, which are not only burdensome and oppressive, but have neither reason, expediency, nor revelation, to countenance them. In a word, like all their successors in spirit to the present day, they were severe to others but very indulgent to themselves.

5. *Phylacteries.* These were small slips of parchment or vellum on which certain portions of the law were written. The Jews tied these about their foreheads and arms, for three differ-

ent purposes: (1) To put them in mind of those precepts which they should constantly observe; (2) To procure their reverence and respect in the sight of the heathen; And (3) To act as amulets or charms to drive away evil spirits. An original phylactery lies now before me. It is a piece of fine vellum, about eighteen inches long, and an inch and a quarter broad. It is divided into four unequal compartments. In the first is written, in a very fair character, with many *apices,* after the mode of the German Jews, the first ten verses of Exodus xiii; in the second compartment is written from the eleventh to the sixteenth verse of the same chapter, inclusive; in the third, from the fourth to the ninth verse, inclusive, of Deuteronomy vi, beginning with *Hear, O Israel;* in the fourth, from the thirteenth to the twenty-first verse, inclusive, of Deuteronomy xi.

7. *To be called of men, Rabbi, Rabbi.* "My teacher! My teacher!" The second *rabbi* is omitted by several excellent MSS., by most of the ancient versions, and by some of the fathers. There are three words used among the Jews as titles of dignity which they apply to their doctors —Rabh, Rabbi, and Rabban. They may be considered as three degrees of comparison: *Rabh,* great; *Rabbi,* greater; and *Rabban,* greatest.

8. *But be not ye called Rabbi.* None of the prophets had ever received this title, nor any of the Jewish doctors before the time of Hillel and Shammai, which was about the time of our Lord.

9. *Call no man your father.* Our Lord probably alludes to the AB, or father of the Sanhedrin, who was the next after the *nasi,* or president. By which He gives His disciples to understand that He would have no second, after himself, established in His Church, of which He alone was the Head; and that perfect equality must subsist among them.

10. *Neither be ye called masters.* "Leaders." God is in all these respects jealous of His honor. To Him alone it belongs to guide and "lead" His Church, as well as to govern and defend it.

12. *Whosoever shall exalt himself.* The way to arrive at the highest degree of dignity, in the sight of God, is by being willing to become the servant of all. Nothing is more hateful in His sight than pride.

13-14. *Woe unto you, scribes!* I think these two verses should be transposed. This transposition is authorized by some of the best MSS., versions, and fathers. The fifteenth reads best after the thirteenth.

13. *Ye shut up the kingdom.* As a key by opening a lock gives entrance into a house, so knowledge of the sacred testimonies, manifested in expounding them to the people, may be said to open the way into the kingdom of Heaven. But where men who are termed teachers are destitute of this knowledge themselves, they may be said to *shut* this Kingdom, because they occupy the place of those who should teach, and thus prevent the people from acquiring heavenly knowledge. *The kingdom of heaven* here means the gospel of Christ; the Pharisees would not receive it themselves, and hindered the common people as far as they could.

15. *Compass sea and land.* A proverbial expression, similar to ours, "You leave no stone unturned"; intimating that they did all in their power to gain converts, not to God, but to their sect. *Proselyte.* "A stranger" or "foreigner"; one who is come from his own people and country to sojourn with another. *Twofold more.* The Greek word which has generally been translated "twofold," *kypke,* has been demonstrated to mean "more deceitful." *The child of hell.* A Hebraism for an excessively wicked person, such as might claim hell for his mother and the devil for his father.

23. *Ye pay tithe of mint.* They were remarkably scrupulous in the performance of all the rites and ceremonies of religion, but totally neglected the soul, spirit, and practice of godliness. *Judgment.* Acting according to justice and equity towards all mankind. *Mercy*—to the distressed and miserable. And *faith* in God as the Fountain of all righteousness, mercy, and truth. *These ought ye to have done.* Our Lord did not object to their paying tithe even of common potherbs—this did not affect the spirit of religion. But while they did this and suchlike, to the utter neglect of justice, mercy, and faith, they showed that they had no religion, and knew nothing of its nature.

24. *Blind guides, which strain at a gnat, and swallow a camel.* This clause should be thus translated: "You strain out the gnat, but you swallow down the camel." In the common translation, *strain at a gnat* conveys no sense. Indeed it is likely to have been at first an error of the press, "at" for "out," which, on examination, I find escaped in the edition of 1611, and has been regularly continued since.

25. *Ye make clean the outside.* The Pharisees were exceedingly exact in observing all the washings and purifications prescribed by the law, but paid no attention to that inward purity which was typified by them. A man may appear clean without who is unclean within; but outward purity will not avail in the sight of God, where inward holiness is wanting. *Extortion and excess.* "Rapine and intemperance."

27. *For ye are like.* "Ye exactly resemble"— the parallel is complete. *Whited sepulchres.* "Whitewashed tombs." As the law considered those unclean who had touched anything belonging to the dead, the Jews took care to have their tombs whitewashed each year, that, being easily discovered, they might be consequently avoided.

30. *We would not have been partakers.* They imagined themselves much better than their ancestors; but our Lord, who knew what they would do, uncovers their hearts, and shows them that they are about to be more abundantly vile than all who had ever preceded them.

31. *Ye be witnesses.* There are many who think that, had they lived in the time of our Lord, they would not have acted towards Him as the Jews did. But we can scarcely believe that they who reject His gospel, trample underfoot His precepts, do despite to the Spirit of His grace, love sin and hate His followers, would have acted otherwise to Him than the murdering Jews, had they lived in the same times.

32. *Fill ye up then.* Notwithstanding the profession you make, you will fill up the measure of your fathers—will continue to walk in their way, accomplish the fullness of every evil purpose by murdering Me; and then, when the measure of your iniquity is full, vengeance shall come upon you to the uttermost, as it did on

your rebellious ancestors. The thirty-first verse should be read in a parenthesis, and then the thirty-second will appear to be, what it is, an inference from the thirtieth. You will fill up, or *fill ye up.* But it is manifest that the imperative is put here for the future, a thing quite consistent with the Hebrew idiom, and frequent in the Scriptures.

34. *Wherefore.* To show how My prediction, "You will fill up the measure of your fathers," shall be verified, *Behold, I send* (I am just going to commission them) *prophets . . . and some of them ye shall kill* (with legal process) and some of them you will crucify, pretend to try and find guilty, and deliver them into the hands of the Romans, who shall, through you, thus put them to death. By *prophets, wise men, and scribes,* our Lord intends the Evangelists, apostles, deacons, who should be employed in proclaiming His gospel—men who should equal the ancient prophets, their wise men, and scribes, in all the gifts and graces of the Holy Spirit.

35. *Upon the earth.* "Upon this land," meaning probably the land of Judea, for thus the word is often to be understood. The national punishment of all the innocent *blood* which had been shed in the land shall speedily come upon you, *from the blood of . . . Abel,* the just, the first prophet and preacher of righteousness, Heb. xi. 4; 2 Pet. ii. 5, *unto the blood of Zacharias son of Barachias.* It is likely that our Lord refers to the murder of Zechariah, mentioned in 2 Chron. xxiv. 20-22, who said to the people, "Why transgress ye the commandments of the Lord, [so] that ye cannot prosper? because ye have forsaken the Lord, he hath also forsaken you. And they conspired against him, and stoned him . . . at the commandment of the king in the court of the house of the Lord. . . . And when he died, he said, The Lord look upon it, and require it." But it is objected that this Zechariah was called the son of Jehoiada, and our Lord calls this one the son of Barachiah. Let it be observed: (1) that double names were frequent among the Jews, and sometimes the person was called by one, sometimes by the other; (2) that Jerome says that in the Gospel of the Nazarenes it was Jehoiada, instead of Barachiah; (3) that Jehoiada and Barachiah have the very same meaning, the "praise or blessing of Jehovah"; (4) that as the Lord required the blood of Zechariah so fully that in a year all the princes of Judah and Jerusalem were destroyed by the Syrians, and Joash, who commanded the murder, was slain by his own servants, 2 Chron. xxiv. 23-25, and their state grew worse and worse, till at last the Temple was burned, and the people carried into captivity by Nebuzaradan—so it should also be with the present race. The Lord would, after the crucifixion of Christ, visit upon them the murder of all those righteous men, that their state should grow worse and worse, till at last the Temple should be destroyed, and they finally ruined by the Romans. *Between the temple and the altar.* That is, between the sanctuary and the altar of burnt offerings.

36. *Shall come upon this generation.* "Upon this race of men," viz., the Jews. This phrase often occurs in this sense in the Evangelists.

38. *Behold, your house.* "The Temple"; this is certainly what is meant.

39. *Ye shall not see me.* I will remove My gospel from you, and withdraw My protection.

Till ye shall say, Blessed. Till after the fullness of the Gentiles is brought in, when the word of life shall again be sent unto you; then will you rejoice, and bless, and praise Him *that cometh in the name of the Lord,* with full and final salvation for the lost sheep of the house of Israel. See Rom. xi. 26-27.

CHAPTER 24

Christ foretells the destruction of the Temple, 1-2. His disciples inquire when and what shall be the signs of this destruction, 3. Our Lord answers, and enumerates them —false Christs, 4-5. Wars, famines, pestilences, and earthquakes, 6-8. Persecution of His followers, 9. Apostasy from the truth, 10-13. General spread of the gospel, 14. He foretells the investment of the city by the Romans, 15-18. The calamities of those times, 19-22. Warns them against seduction by false prophets, 23-26. The suddenness of these calamities, 27-28. Total destruction of the Jewish polity, 29-31. The whole illustrated by the parable of the fig tree, 32-33. The certainty of the event, though the time is concealed, 34-36. Careless state of the people, 37-41. The necessity of watchfulness and fidelity illustrated by the parable of the two servants: one faithful, the other wicked, 42-51.

This chapter contains a prediction of the utter destruction of the city and Temple of Jerusalem, and the subversion of the whole political constitution of the Jews; and is one of the most valuable portions of the new covenant Scriptures, with respect to the evidence which it furnishes of the truth of Christianity. Everything which our Lord foretold should come on the Temple, city, and people of the Jews has been fulfilled in the most correct and astonishing manner; and witnessed by a writer who was present during the whole, who was himself a Jew, and is acknowledged to be a historian of indisputable veracity in all those transactions which concern the destruction of Jerusalem. Without having designed it, he has written a commentary on our Lord's words, and shown how every tittle was punctually fulfilled, though he knew nothing of the scripture which contained this remarkable prophecy.

1. *And Jesus went out, and departed from the temple.* Or, "And Jesus, going out of the Temple, was going away." This is the arrangement of the words in several eminent manuscripts, versions, and fathers, and is much clearer than that in the common translation. The Jews say the Temple was built of white and green-spotted marble. Josephus says the stones were white and strong; fifty feet long, twenty-four broad, and sixteen thick. *Antiq,* b. 15, c. xi.

2. *There shall not be left here one stone.* These seem to have been the last words He spoke as He left the Temple, into which He never afterwards entered; and when He got to the Mount of Olives, He renewed the discourse. From this mount, on which our Lord and His disciples now sat, the whole of the city and particularly the Temple were clearly seen. This part of our Lord's prediction was fulfilled in the most literal manner. Josephus says, *War,* b. vii, c. 1; "Caesar gave orders that they should now demolish the whole city and temple, except the three towers, Phaselus, Hippicus, and Mariamne, and a part of the western wall, and these were spared; but, for all the rest of the wall, it was laid so completely even with the ground, by those who dug it up to the foundation, that there was left nothing to make those that came thither believe it had ever been inhabited."

3. *Tell us, when shall these things be?* There appear to be three questions asked here by the

disciples. (1) *"When shall these things be?"* viz., the destruction of the city, Temple, and Jewish state. (2) *"What shall be the sign of thy coming?"* viz., to execute these judgments upon them, and to establish Thy own Church. (3) *When shall this world end?* When wilt Thou come to judge the quick and the dead? But there are some who maintain that these are but three parts of the same question, and that our Lord's answers refer only to the destruction of the Jewish state, and that nothing is spoken here concerning the last or judgment day. *End of the world.* Or "of the age," viz., the Jewish economy, which is a frequent accommodated meaning of the word.

4. *Take heed that no man deceive you.* The world is full of deceivers, and it is only by taking heed to the counsel of Christ that even His followers can escape being ruined by them. From this to v. 31, our Lord mentions the signs which should precede His coming. The *first* sign is false christs.

5. *For many shall come in my name.* Josephus says (*War*, b. ii, c. 13) that there were many who, pretending to divine inspiration, deceived the people, leading out numbers of them to the desert, pretending that God would there show them the signs of liberty, meaning redemption from the Roman power, and that an Egyptian false prophet led 30,000 men into the desert, who were almost all cut off by Felix. See Acts xxi. 38. It was a just judgment for God to deliver up that people into the hands of false christs who had rejected the true one. About twelve years after the death of our Lord, when Cuspius Fadus was procurator of Judea, arose an impostor of the name of Theudas, who said he was a prophet, and persuaded a great multitude to follow him with their best effects to the river Jordan, which he promised to divide for their passage; and saying these things, says Josephus, "he deceived many"—almost the very words of our Lord. A few years afterwards, under the reign of Nero, while Felix was procurator of Judea, impostors of this stamp were so frequent that some were taken and killed almost every day (Josephus *Ant.*, b. xx, cc. 4 and 7).

6. The *second* sign given by our Lord is *wars and rumours of wars.* These may be seen in Josephus (*Ant.*, b. xviii, c. 9; *War*, b. ii, c. 10), especially as to the *rumours of wars,* when Caligula ordered his statue to be set up in the Temple of God, which the Jews having refused, had every reason to expect a war with the Romans, and were in such consternation on the occasion that they even neglected to till their land.

7. *Nation shall rise against nation.* This portended the dissensions, insurrections, and mutual slaughter of the Jews and those of other nations who dwelt in the same cities together; as particularly at Caesarea, where the Jews and Syrians contended about the right of the city, which ended there in the total expulsion of the Jews, above 20,000 of whom were slain. The whole Jewish nation, being exasperated at this, flew to arms, and burned and plundered the neighboring cities and villages of the Syrians, making an immense slaughter of the people. The Syrians, in return, destroyed not a less number of the Jews. At Scythopolis they murdered upwards of 13,000. At Ascalon they killed

2,500. At Ptolemais they slew 2,000, and made many prisoners. The Tyrians also put many Jews to death, and imprisoned more. The people of Gadara did likewise; and all the other cities of Syria, in proportion as they hated or feared the Jews. At Alexandria the Jews and heathens fought, and 50,000 of the former were slain. The people of Damascus conspired against the Jews of that city, and assaulting them unarmed, killed 10,000 of them. *Kingdom against kingdom.* This portended the open wars of different tetrarchies and provinces against each other. The *third* sign, pestilence and famine— *There shall be famines, and pestilences.* There was a famine foretold by Agabus, Acts xi. 28, which is mentioned by Suetonius, Tacitus, and Eusebius, "which came to pass in the days of Claudius Caesar," and was so severe at Jerusalem that Josephus says (*Ant.*, b. xx, c. 2) many died for lack of food. *Pestilences* are the usual attendants of famines, as the scarcity and badness of provisions generally produce epidemic disorders. The *fourth* sign, *earthquakes, in divers places.* It means particularly those popular commotions and insurrections which have already been noted; but if we confine it to *earthquakes,* there were several in those times to which our Lord refers. The *fifth* sign, fearful portents. To these Luke adds that there shall be "fearful sights and great signs . . . from heaven," chap. xxi. 11.

8. *All these are the beginning of sorrows.* "Travailing pains." The whole land of Judea is represented under the notion of a woman in grievous travail; but our Lord intimates that all that had already been mentioned were only the first pangs and throes, and nothing in comparison of that hard and death-bringing labor which should afterwards take place. From the calamities of the nation in general, our Lord passes to those of the Christians; and, indeed, the sufferings of His followers were often occasioned by the judgments sent upon the land, as the poor Christians were charged with being the cause of these national calamities and were cruelly persecuted on that account.

9. *Then shall they deliver you up to be afflicted.* Rather, "Then they will deliver you up to affliction."

10. *Then shall many be offended, and shall betray one another.* To illustrate this point, one sentence out of Tacitus (*Annal.* l. xv) will be sufficient, who, speaking of the persecution under Nero, says, "At first several were seized, who confessed, and then by their discovery a great multitude of others were convicted and executed."

12. *The love of many shall wax cold.* By reason of these trials and persecutions from without, and those apostasies and false prophets from within, the love of many to Christ and His doctrine, and to one another, shall grow cold. Some openly deserting the faith, as v. 10; others corrupting it, as v. 11; and others growing indifferent about it, as v. 12. Even at this early period there seems to have been a very considerable defection in several Christian churches; see Gal. iii. 1-4; 2 Thess. iii. 1; 2 Tim. i. 15.

13. *But he that shall endure* the persecutions that shall come—*unto the end,* to the destruction of the Jewish polity, without growing cold or apostatizing—*shall be saved,* shall be delivered

in all imminent dangers, and have his soul at last brought to an eternal glory. It is very remarkable that not a single Christian perished in the destruction of Jerusalem, though there were many there when Cestius Gallus invested the city; and had he persevered in the siege, he would soon have rendered himself master of it. But when he unexpectedly and unaccountably raised the siege, the Christians took that opportunity to escape. See Eusebius, *Hist. Eccles.*, lib. iii, c. 5.

14. *And this gospel of the kingdom shall be preached in all the world.* But, notwithstanding these persecutions, there should be a universal publication of the glad tidings of the Kingdom *for a witness [testimony] to all nations.* God would have the iniquity of the Jews published everywhere before the heavy stroke of His judgments should fall upon them, that all mankind, as it were, might be brought as witnesses against their cruelty and obstinacy in crucifying and rejecting the Lord Jesus. *In all the world.* Perhaps no more is meant here than the Roman empire. Tacitus informs us (*Annal.* l. xv) that, as early as the reign of Nero, the Christians were grown so numerous at Rome as to excite the jealousy of the government, and in other parts they were in proportion. *Then shall the end come.* When this general publication of the gospel shall have taken place, then a period shall be put to the whole Jewish economy, by the utter destruction of their city and Temple.

15. *The abomination of desolation, spoken of by Daniel.* This *abomination of desolation* (Luke xxi. 20-21) refers to the Roman army; and this abomination standing *in the holy place* is the Roman army besieging Jerusalem. This, our Lord says, is what was spoken of by Daniel the prophet, in the ninth and eleventh chapters of his prophecy, and so let everyone who reads these prophecies understand them; and in reference to this very event they are understood by the rabbins. The Roman army is called an *abomination* for its ensigns and images, which were so to the Jews. Josephus says (*War*, b. vi, c. 6) the Romans brought their ensigns into the Temple, and placed them over against the eastern gate, and sacrificed to them there. The Roman army is therefore fitly called the *abomination,* and "the abomination that maketh desolate," as it was to desolate and lay waste Jerusalem; and this army besieging Jerusalem is called by Mark (chap. xiii. 14) "standing where it ought not," that is, as in the text here, *the holy place,* as not only the city, but a considerable compass of ground about it, was deemed holy, and consequently no profane persons should stand on it.

16. *Then let them which be in Judea flee into the mountains.* This counsel was remembered afterwards and wisely followed by the Christians afterwards. Eusebius and Epiphanius say that at this juncture, after Cestius Gallus had raised the siege and Vespasian was approaching with his army, all who believed in Christ left Jerusalem and fled to Pella, and other places beyond the river Jordan; and so they all marvellously escaped the general shipwreck of their country—not one of them perished. See on v. 13.

17. *Let him which is on the house top.* The houses of the Jews, as well as those of the ancient Greeks and Romans, were flat-roofed, and had stairs on the outside, by which persons might ascend and descend without coming into the house. In the Eastern walled cities, these flat-roofed houses usually formed continued terraces from one end of the city to the other, which terraces terminated at the gates. He therefore who is walking on the housetop, let him *not come down to take any thing out of his house;* but let him instantly pursue his course along the tops of the houses, and escape out at the city gate as fast as he can.

18. *Neither let him which is in the field return back.* Because when once the army of the Romans sits down before the city, there shall be no more any possibility of escape, as they shall never remove till Jerusalem be destroyed.

19. *And woe unto them* (alas! for them) *that are with child!* For such persons are not in a condition to make their escape; neither can they bear the miseries of the siege. Josephus says the houses were full of women and children that perished by the famine, and that the mothers snatched the food even out of their own children's mouths. See *War*, b. v, c. 10.

20. *But pray ye that your flight be not in the winter.* For the hardness of the season, the badness of the roads, the shortness of the days, and the length of the nights will all be great impediments to your flight. *Neither on the sabbath day.* That you may not raise the indignation of the Jews by travelling on that day, and so suffer that death out of the city which you had endeavored to escape from within. Besides, on the Sabbath days the Jews not only kept within doors, but the gates of all the cities and towns in every place were kept shut and barred; so that if their flight should be on a Sabbath, they could not expect admission into any place of security in the land. Our Lord had ordered His followers to make their escape from Jerusalem when they should see it encompassed with armies; but how could this be done? God took care to provide amply for this. In the twelfth year of Nero, Cestius Gallus, the president of Syria, came against Jerusalem with a powerful army. He might, says Josephus, *War*, b. ii, c. 19, have assaulted and taken the city, and thereby put an end to the war; but without any just reason, and contrary to the expectation of all, he raised the siege and departed. Josephus remarks that, after Cestius Gallus had raised the siege, "many of the principal Jewish people, forsook the city, as men do a sinking ship." Vespasian was deputed in the room of Cestius Gallus, who, having subdued all the country, prepared to besiege Jerusalem, and invested it on every side. But the news of Nero's death, and soon after that of Galba, and the disturbances that followed, and the civil wars between Otho and Vitellius, held Vespasian and his son Titus in suspense. Thus the city was not actually besieged in form till after Vespasian was confirmed in the empire and Titus was appointed to command the forces in Judea. It was in those incidental delays that the Christians, and indeed several others, provided for their own safety, by flight.

21. *For then shall be great tribulation.* No history can furnish us with a parallel to the calamities and miseries of the Jews: rapine, murder, famine, and pestilence within; fire and sword, and all the horrors of war, without. Our Lord wept at the foresight of these calamities, and it is almost impossible for any humane

person to read the relation of them in Josephus without weeping also. Luke, chap. xxi. 22, calls these the "days of vengeance, that all things which are written may be fulfilled."

22. *Except those days should be shortened.* Josephus computes the number of those who perished in the siege at eleven hundred thousand, besides those who were slain in other places, *War,* b. vi, c. 9; and if the Romans had gone on destroying in this manner, the whole nation of the Jews would, in a short time, have been entirely extirpated. But, for the sake of the elect, the Jews, that they might not be utterly destroyed, and for the Christians particularly, the days were shortened. These, partly through the fury of the zealots on one hand and the hatred of the Romans on the other, and partly through the difficulty of subsisting in the mountains, without houses or provisions, would in all probability have all been destroyed, by either the sword or famine, if the days had not been shortened. The besieged themselves helped to shorten those days by their divisions and mutual slaughters, and by fatally deserting their strongholds, where they never could have been subdued but by famine alone. So well-fortified was Jerusalem, and so well-provided to stand a siege, that the enemy without could not have prevailed had it not been for the factions and seditions within. When Titus was viewing the fortifications after the taking of the city, he could not help ascribing his success to God. "We have fought," said he, "with God on our side; and it is God who pulled the Jews out of these strong holds: for what could machines or the hands of men avail against such towers as these?" (*War,* b. vi, c. 9.)

23-24. *Then if any man shall say unto you, Lo, here is Christ.* Our Lord had cautioned His disciples against false Christs and prophets before, v. 11; but He seems here to intimate that there would be especial need to attend to this caution about the time of the siege. And in fact many such impostors did arise about that time, promising deliverance from God; and the lower the Jews were reduced, the more disposed they were to listen to such deceivers. Like a man drowning, they were willing to catch even at a straw, while there was any prospect of being saved. But as it was to little purpose for a man to take upon him the character of the Christ, without miracles to avouch his divine mission, so it was the common artifice of these impostors to show *signs* and *wonders*—the very words used by Christ in this prophecy, and by Josephus in his history, *Ant.* b. xx, c. 7.

26. *If they shall say unto you, Behold, he is in the desert.* Is it not worthy of remark that our Lord not only foretold the appearance of these impostors, but also the manner and circumstances of their conduct? Some He mentions as appearing in the desert. Josephus says (*Ant.* b. xx, c. 7, and *War,* b. ii, c. 13): That many impostors and cheats persuaded the people to follow them to the desert, promising to show them signs and wonders done by the providence of God, is well-attested. An Egyptian false prophet, mentioned by Josephus, *Ant.* b. xx, c. 7, and in the Acts, chap. xxi. 38, "leddest out into the wilderness four thousand men that were murderers," but these were all taken or destroyed by Felix. Another promised salvation to the people if they would follow him to the

desert, and he was destroyed by Festus, *Ant.* b. xx, c. 7. Also, one Jonathan, a weaver, persuaded a number to follow him to the desert, but he was taken and burnt alive by Vespasian. See *War,* b. vii, c. 11. As some conducted their deluded followers to the desert, so did others to the *secret chambers.* Josephus mentions a false prophet, *War,* b. vi, c. 5, who declared to the people in the city that God commanded them to go up into the Temple and there they should receive the signs of deliverance. A multitude of men, women, and children went up accordingly; but, instead of deliverance, the place was set on fire by the Romans, and 6,000 perished miserably in the flames, or in attempting to escape them.

27. *For as the lightning cometh out of the east, and shineth even unto the west.* It is worthy of remark that our Lord, in the most particular manner, points out the very march of the Roman army. They entered into Judea on the east, and carried on their conquest westward, as if not only the extensiveness of the ruin, but the very route which the army would take, were intended in the comparison of the lightning issuing from the east and shining to the west.

28. *For wheresoever the carcase is.* "The dead carcass." The Jewish nation, which was morally and judicially dead. *There will the eagles.* The Roman armies, called so partly from their strength and fierceness and partly from the figure of these animals which was always wrought on their ensigns, or even in brass, placed on the tops of their ensign-staves. It is remarkable that the Roman fury pursued these wretched men wheresoever they were found. They were a dead carcass doomed to be devoured, and the Roman eagles were the commissioned devourers. See the pitiful account in Josephus, *War,* b. vii, cc. 2—3, 6, 9—11.

29. *Immediately after the tribulation.* Commentators generally understand this, and what follows, of the end of the world and Christ's coming to judgment; but the word *immediately* shows that our Lord is not speaking of any distant event, but of something immediately consequent on calamities already predicted—and that must be the destruction of Jerusalem.

30. *Then shall appear the sign of the Son of man.* The plain meaning of this is that the destruction of Jerusalem will be such a remarkable instance of divine vengeance and such a signal manifestation of Christ's power and glory that all the Jewish *tribes* shall mourn, and many will, in consequence of this manifestation of God, be led to acknowledge Christ and His religion. By "of the land," in the text, is evidently meant here, as in several other places, the land of Judea and its tribes, either its the inhabitants or the Jewish people wherever found.

31. *He shall send his angels.* "His messengers," the apostles, and their successors in the Christian ministry. *With a great sound of a trumpet.* Or "a loud-sounding trumpet"—the earnest, affectionate call of the gospel of peace, life, and salvation. *Shall gather together his elect.* The Gentiles, who were now chosen or elected, in place of the rebellious, obstinate Jews, according to our Lord's prediction, Matt. viii. 11-12 and Luke xiii. 28-29. To Matthew's account, Luke adds, chap. xxi. 24, "They shall fall by the edge of the sword, and shall be led

away captive into all nations: and Jerusalem shall be trodden down of the Gentiles, until the times of the Gentiles be fulfilled." The number of those who fell by the sword was very great. Eleven hundred thousand perished during the siege. Many were slain at other places and at other times. Many also were led away captives into all nations. Josephus says the number of the captives taken in the whole war amounted to 97,000. Those above seventeen years of age were sent to the works in Egypt; but most were distributed through the Roman provinces, to be destroyed in their theaters by the sword and by the wild beasts; and those under seventeen years of age were sold for slaves. Jerusalem also was, according to the prediction of our Lord, to be "trodden down of the Gentiles." Accordingly it has never since been in the possession of the Jews.

32. *Learn a parable of the fig tree.* That is, These signs which I have given you will be as infallible a proof of the approaching ruin of the Jewish state as the budding of the trees is a proof of the coming summer.

34. *This generation shall not pass.* "This race"; i.e., the Jews shall not cease from being a distinct people till all the counsels of God relative to them and the Gentiles be fulfilled. Some translate *this generation* as meaning the persons who were then living, that they should not die before these signs took place. But though this was true as to the calamities that fell upon the Jews, and the destruction of their government and Temple, yet as our Lord mentions Jerusalem's continuing to be under the power of the Gentiles till the fulness of the Gentiles should come in, i.e., till all the nations of the world should receive the gospel of Christ, after which the Jews themselves should be converted unto God, Rom. xi. 25. I think it more proper not to restrain its meaning to the few years which preceded the destruction of Jerusalem, but to understand it of the care taken by divine providence to preserve them as a distinct people, and yet to keep them out of their own land and from their Temple service. See on Mark xiii. 30. But still it is literally true in reference to the destruction of Jerusalem. John probably lived to see these things come to pass. The war began, as Josephus says, *Ant.* b. xx, c. 11, s. 1, in May, A.D. 66. The Temple was burnt August 10, A.D. 70, the same day and month on which it had been burnt by the king of Babylon, Josephus, *Ant.* b. xx, c. 11, s. 8. The city was taken September 8, in the second year of the reign of Vespasian, or the year of Christ 70, *Ant.* b. vi, c. 10.

36. *But of that day and hour. Hora* here is translated "season" by many eminent critics, and is used in this sense by both sacred and profane authors. As the *day* was not known in which Jerusalem should be invested by the Romans, therefore our Lord advised His disciples to pray that it might not be on a Sabbath; and as the "season" was not known, therefore they were to pray that it might not be in the winter, v. 20. See on Mark xiii. 32.

37-38. *As the days of Noe . . . they were eating and drinking.* The design of these verses seems to be that the desolation should be as general as it should be unexpected.

39. *And knew not.* "They considered not"— did not lay Noah's warning to heart, till it was too late to profit by it: *so shall* it *be*—and so it was in this coming of the Son of Man.

40-41. *Then shall two* men . . . *two women . . . one shall be taken, and the other left.* The meaning seems to be that so general should these calamities be that no two persons, wheresoever found, or about whatsoever employed, should be both able to effect their escape; and that captivity and the sword should have a complete triumph over this unhappy people. *Two women shall be grinding.* Women alone are still employed in grinding the corn in the East; and it is only when dispatch is required, or the uppermost millstone is heavy, that a second woman is added.

42. *Watch therefore.* Be always on your guard, that you may not be taken unawares, and that you may be properly prepared to meet God in the way of either judgment or mercy, whensoever He may come.

45. *Who then is a faithful and wise servant?* All should live in the same expectation of the coming of Christ which a servant has with respect to the return of his master, who, in departing for a season, left the management of his affairs to him, and of which management he is to give an exact account on his master's return.

51. *Cut him asunder.* This refers to an ancient mode of punishment used in several countries. Isaiah is reported to have been sawed asunder. That it was an ancient mode of punishment is evident from what Herodotus says: that Sabacus, king of Ethiopia, had a vision in which he was commanded to cut in two all the Egyptian priests.

CHAPTER 25

The parable of the ten virgins, five of whom were wise, and five foolish, 1-12. The necessity of being constantly prepared to appear before God, 13. The parable of the talents, 14-30. The manner in which God shall deal with the righteous and the wicked in the judgment of the great day, 31-46.

1. *Then shall the kingdom of heaven.* The state of Jews and professing Christians—or the state of the Visible Church at the time of the destruction of Jerusalem, and in the day of judgment, for the parable appears to relate to both those periods. And particularly at the time in which Christ shall come to judge the world, it shall appear what kind of reception His gospel has met with. *Virgins.* Denoting the purity of the Christian doctrine and character. In this parable the *bridegroom* is generally understood to mean Jesus Christ. The *feast,* that state of felicity to which He has promised to raise His genuine followers. The *wise,* or "prudent," and *foolish virgins,* those who truly enjoy, and those who only profess, the purity and holiness of His religion. The *oil,* the grace and salvation of God, or that faith which works by love. The *vessel,* the heart in which this oil is contained. The *lamp,* the profession of enjoying the burning and shining light of the gospel of Christ. *Going forth,* the whole of their sojourning upon earth.

2. *Five of them were wise.* Or "provident"— they took care to make a proper provision beforehand, and left nothing to be done in the last moment. *Five were foolish.* "Careless." *Moros* is thus defined, "he who sees not what

is proper or necessary." These did not see that it was necessary to have "oil in their vessels" (the salvation of God in their souls), as well as a burning lamp of religious profession, vv. 3-4.

4. *Took oil in their vessels.* They not only had a sufficiency of oil in their lamps, but they carried a vessel with oil to recruit their lamps, when it should be found expedient. This the foolish or improvident neglected to do; hence, when the oil that was in their lamps burned out, they had none to pour into the lamps to maintain the flame.

5. *The bridegroom tarried.* The coming of the bridegroom to an individual may imply his death, His coming to the world—the final judgment. The delay—the time from a man's birth till his death, in the first case; in the second, the time from the beginning to the end of the world. *Slumbered and slept.* Or, "They became drowsy and fell asleep." As sleep is frequently used in the sacred writings for death, so drowsiness, which precedes sleep, may be considered as pointing out the decays of the constitution, and the sicknesses which precede death.

6. *At midnight there was a cry.* The Jewish weddings were generally celebrated in the night, yet they usually began at the rising of the evening star; but in this case there was a more than ordinary delay.

8. *Our lamps are gone out.* "Are going out." So then it is evident that they were once lighted. They had once hearts illuminated and warmed by faith and love; but they had backslidden from the salvation of God, and now they are excluded from heaven, because, through their carelessness, they have let the light that was in them become darkness, and have not applied in time for a fresh supply of the salvation of God.

9. *Lest there be not enough for us and you.* These had all been companions in the Christian course, and there was a time when they might have been helpful to each other; but that time is now past forever—none has a particle of grace to spare, not even to help the soul of the dearest relative! The grace which every man receives is just enough to save his own soul; he has no merits to bequeath to the church, no work of supererogation which can be placed to the account of another. *Go ye rather to them that sell, and buy.* "Rather go to them that sell, and buy for yourselves, lest there be not enough for us and you."

10. *While they went to buy, the bridegroom came.* What a dismal thing it is not to discover the emptiness of one's heart of all that is good till it is too late to make any successful application for relief! God alone knows how many are thus deceived. *And they that were ready.* "They who were prepared"—who had not only a burning *lamp* of an evangelical profession, but had *oil* in their *vessels,* the faith that works by love in their hearts, and their lives adorned with all the fruits of the Spirit. *The door was shut.* Dreadful and fatal words! No hope remains. Nothing but death can shut this door; but death may surprise us in our sins, and then despair is our only portion.

11. *Afterwards came also the other virgins, saying, Lord, Lord.* Earnest prayer when used in time may do much good; but it appears, from this parable, that there may come a time when

prayer even to Jesus may be too late!—viz., when the door is shut—when death has separated the body and the soul.

13. *Watch therefore.* If to *watch* be to employ ourselves chiefly about the business of our salvation, alas! how few of those who are called Christians are there who do *watch!*

15. *He gave . . . to every man according to his several ability.* The talent which each man has suits his own state best, and it is only pride and insanity which lead him to desire and envy the graces and talents of another. The man who improves the grace he has received, however small, will as surely get to the kingdom of God as he who has received most from his Master and improved all.

In this parable of our Lord, four things may be considered:

I. *The master who distributes the talents.*
(1) The master's *kindness.* The servants have nothing—deserve nothing—have no claim on their master; yet he, in his kindness, delivers unto them his goods, not for his advantage, but for their comfort and salvation. (2) The master distributes these goods *diversely*—giving to one five, to another two, and to another one. No person can complain that he has been forgotten; the master gives to each. (3) The master distributes his talents with *wisdom.* He gave to each *according to his several ability,* i.e., to the power he had to improve what was given.

II. *The servants who improved their talents.* These persons are termed slaves, such as were the property of the master, who might dispose of them as he pleased. *Then he that had received the five talents went and traded,* v. 16. (1) The work was *speedily* begun—as soon as the master gave the talents and departed, so soon they began to labor. There is not a moment to be lost—every moment has its grace, and every grace has its employment, and everything is to be done for eternity. (2) The work was *perseveringly* carried on; *after a long time the Lord of those servants cometh,* v. 19. The master was long before he returned, but they did not relax. Many begin well, and continue faithful for a time—but how few persevere to the end! (3) Their work was crowned with *success.* They doubled the sum which they had received. Every grace of God is capable of great improvement. (4) They were ready to give in a *joyful* account when their master came and called for them. (5) Their *recompense* from their gracious master. (*a*) They receive *praise. Well done, thou good and faithful servant* v. 21. What a glorious thing to have the approbation of God, and the testimony of a good conscience! They were good, pure, and upright within—*faithful,* using to God's glory the blessings He had given. (*b*) They receive gracious promises. "You have been faithful over a little; I will set you over much." These promises refer not only to a future here; for the more faithfully a man improves what God has already given him, the more he shall have from his gracious Master. For He giveth more grace, till He fills the faithful soul with His own fullness. (*c*) They receive glory. *Enter thou into the joy of thy Lord.* As you were partakers of My nature on earth, be sharers of My glory in heaven. The joy, the happiness wherewith I am happy, shall be your eternal portion!

III. *The servant who buried his talent.* He

that had received one went and digged in the earth, and hid his Lord's money, v. 18. (1) See the *ingratitude* of this servant. His master gave him a talent, capable of being improved to his own present and eternal advantage; but he slights the mercy of his lord. (2) See his *idleness.* Rather than exert himself to improve what he has received, he goes and hides it. (3) See his gross *error.* He digs to hide it—puts himself to more trouble to render the mercy of God to him of none effect than he would have had in combating and conquering the world, the devil, and the flesh. (4) See his *injustice.* He takes his master's money, and neither improves nor designs to improve it, even while he is living on and consuming that bounty which would have been sufficient for a faithful servant. (5) Hear the *absurdity* of his *reasoning. Lord, I knew thee that thou art an hard* (or avaricious) *man, reaping where thou hast not sown,* v. 24. The wicked excuse of this faithless servant confuted itself and condemned him.

IV. *The awful punishment of this faithless servant.* (1) He is *reproached. Thou wicked and slothful servant! Wicked*—in your heart; *slothful*—in your work. *Thou knewest that I reap where I sowed not.* You are condemned by your own mouth—whose is the unemployed talent? Did I not give you this? And did I require the improvement of two when I gave you but one? You know I did not. (2) He is *stripped* of what he *possessed. Take therefore the talent from him.* Oh, terrible word! Remove the candlestick from that slothful, worldly-minded church; take away the inspirations of the Holy Spirit from that lukewarm, Christless Christian, who lives only to resist them and render them of none effect. (3) He is *punished* with an everlasting *separation* from God and the glory of His power. *Cast forth the unprofitable servant,* v. 30. Let him have nothing but darkness who refused to walk in the light; let him have nothing but misery—*weeping and gnashing of teeth,* who has refused the happiness which God provided for him.

27. *With usury.* "With its produce," not *usury;* for that is unlawful interest, more than the money can properly produce.

31. *When the Son of man shall come.* This must be understood of Christ's coming at the last day, to judge mankind, though all the preceding part of the chapter may be applied also to the destruction of Jerusalem.

32. *All nations.* Literally, "all the nations"—all the Gentile world; the Jews are necessarily included, but they were spoken of in a particular manner in the preceding chapter. *He shall separate them.* Set each kind apart by themselves. *As a shepherd divideth.* It does not appear that *sheep* and *goats* were ever penned or housed together, though they might feed in the same pasture; yet even this was not done but in separate flocks; so Virgil, *Eclog.* vii. v. 2.

33. *He shall set the sheep.* The *right hand* signifies, among the rabbins, approbation and eminence; the *left hand,* rejection, and disapprobation. *Sheep,* which have ever been considered as the emblems of mildness, simplicity, patience, and usefulness, represent here the genuine disciples of Christ. *Goats,* which are naturally quarrelsome, lascivious, and excessively ill-scented, were considered as the symbols

of riotous, profane, and impure men. They here represent all who have lived and died in their sins. See Ezek. xxxiv. 17 and Zech. x. 3.

34. *Ye blessed of my Father.* This is the King's address to his followers, and contains the reason why they were found in the practice of all righteousness, and were now brought to this state of glory—they were blessed—came as children, and received the benediction of the *Father,* and became, and continued to be, members of the heavenly family. *Inherit.* The inheritance is only for the children of the family—"if sons, then heirs," Gal. iv. 7, but not otherwise. *Prepared for you.* That is, The Kingdom of glory is designed for such as you. *From the foundation of the world.* It was God's purpose and determination to admit none into His heaven but those who were made partakers of His holiness, Heb. xii. 14.

35. *I was an hungred, and ye gave me meat.* Everything which is done to a follower of Christ, whether it be good or evil, He considers as done to himself; see v. 40; Acts ix. 4-5; Heb. vi. 10. Of all the fruits of the Spirit, none are mentioned here but those that spring from love, or mercy, because these give men the nearest conformity to God. Jesus had said, "Blessed are the merciful: for they shall obtain mercy"; and He here shows how this promise shall be fulfilled. The rabbins say: "As often as a poor man presents himself at thy door, the holy blessed God stands at his right hand: if thou give him alms, know that he who stands at his right hand will give thee a reward. But if thou give him not alms, he who stands at his right hand will punish thee." A *stranger, and ye took me in.* "You entertained Me."

36. *I was sick, and ye visited me.* Relieving the strangers and visiting the sick were in high estimation among the Jews. One of their sayings on this head is worthy of notice: "He who neglects to visit the sick is like him who has shed blood," That is, as he has neglected, when it was in his power, to preserve life, he is as guilty in the sight of the Lord as he is who has committed murder.

37. *Lord, when saw we thee an hungred.* This barbarous expression, *an hungred,* should be banished out of the text, wheresoever it occurs, and the simple word "hungry" substituted for it. Whatever is done for Christ's sake is done through Christ's grace; and he who does the work attributes to Jesus both the will and the power by which the work was done, and seeks and expects the kingdom of Heaven, not as a reward, but as a gift of pure, unmerited mercy.

40. *Inasmuch as ye have done it unto one of the least of these my brethren.* The meanest follower of Christ is acknowledged by Him as His *brother!*

41. *Depart from me, ye cursed.* Or, "Ye cursed! depart." These words are the address of the King to the sinners, and contain the reason why they are to be separated from blessedness: You are cursed, because you have sinned, and would not come unto Me that you might have life. *Into everlasting fire.* This is the punishment of sense. You shall not only be separated from Me, but you shall be tormented—awfully, everlastingly tormented in that place of separa-

tion. *Prepared for the devil and his angels.* The devil and his angels sinned before the creation of the world, and the place of torment was *then* prepared for them. It never was designed for human souls; but as the wicked are partakers with the devil and his angels in their iniquities, in their rebellion against God, so it is right that they should be sharers with them in their punishment.

42. *I was an hungred, and ye gave me no meat.* I put it in your power to do good, and you would not. A variety of occasions offered themselves to you, but you neglected them all, so that My blessings in your hands, not being improved, according to My order, became a curse to you.

43. *I was a stranger.* If men were sure that Jesus Christ was actually somewhere in the land, in great personal distress, hungry, thirsty, naked, and confined, they would doubtless run unto and relieve Him. Now Christ assures us that a man who is hungry, thirsty, naked is His representative, and that whatever we do to such a one He will consider as done to himself.

44. *Lord, when saw we thee an hungred?* It is want of faith which in general produces hardheartedness to the poor. The man who sees only with eyes of flesh is never likely to discover Christ in the person of a man destitute of the necessaries of life.

46. *And these shall go away into everlasting punishment.* No appeal, no remedy, to all eternity! No end to the punishment of those whose final impenitence manifests in them an eternal will and desire to sin. By dying in a settled opposition to God, they cast themselves into a necessity of continuing in an eternal aversion from Him. But some are of the opinion that this punishment shall have an end. This is as likely as that the glory of the righteous shall have an end, for the same word is used to express the duration of the punishment as is used to express the duration of the state of glory. I have seen the best things that have been written in favor of the final redemption of damned spirits, but I never saw an answer to the argument against that doctrine drawn from this verse but what sound learning and criticism should be ashamed to acknowledge. Some have gone a middle way, and think that the wicked shall be annihilated. This, I think, is contrary to the text; if they *go into . . . punishment,* they continue to exist; for that which ceases to be ceases to suffer.

CHAPTER 26

Christ predicts His being betrayed and crucified, 1-2. The chief priests, scribes, and elders consult about His death, 3-5. A woman anoints His head at Bethany, at which the disciples are offended, but Christ vindicates her conduct, 6-13. Judas, for thirty pieces of silver, engages with the chief priests to betray Him, 14-16. He eats a Passover with His disciples, and assures them of His approaching death, and that one of them would betray Him, 17-21. On each asking, Is it I? Christ asserts that Judas is the traitor, 22-25. Having eaten His last supper, He institutes the Eucharist, to be observed in His Church as a memorial of His sacrificial death, 26-29. They sing a hymn, go to the Mount of Olives, and He again announces His approaching death and resurrection, 30-32. Peter asserts His resolution to be faithful to his Master, and Christ foretells his denial and apostasy, 33-35. He goes to Gethsemane; the transactions there, 36-46. Judas comes with the high priest's mob and betrays Him with a kiss, 47-50. Peter cuts off the ear of the high priest's servant; Christ discourses with the multitude, 51-55. The disciples flee, and He is led to Caiaphas, 56-57. Peter follows at a distance, 58. They seek false witnesses, and question our Lord, who de-

clares himself to be the Christ, 59-64. They accuse Him of blasphemy, and abuse Him, 65-68. Peter's denial and repentance, 69-75.

1. *When Jesus had finished all these sayings.* He began these sayings on Mount Olivet, chap. xxiv. 1, and continued them till He entered into Bethany, whither He was going.

2. *The passover.* A feast instituted in Egypt to commemorate the destroying angel's passing over the houses of the Israelites, when he slew the firstborn of the Egyptians. See the whole of this business largely explained in the notes on Exod. xii. 1-27. This feast began on the fourteenth day of the first moon, in the first month, Nisan, and it lasted only one day; but it was immediately followed by the days of unleavened bread, which were seven, so that the whole lasted eight days, and all the eight days are sometimes called the feast of *the passover,* and sometimes the "feast or days of unleavened bread." See Luke xxii. 1-7. *The Son of man is betrayed* (rather "delivered up") *to be crucified.* With what amazing calmness and precision does our blessed Lord speak of this awful event! What a proof does He here give of His prescience in so correctly predicting it, and of His love in so cheerfully undergoing it! These two verses have no proper connection with this chapter, and should be joined to the preceding.

3. *Then assembled together the chief priests.* That is, during the two days that preceded the Passover.

4. *And consulted that they might take Jesus by subtilty.* The providence of God frustrated their artful machinations; and that event which they wished to conduct with the greatest privacy and silence was transacted with all possible celebrity, amidst the thousands who resorted to Jerusalem at this season for the keeping of the Passover.

5. *Not on the feast day, lest there be an uproar.* It was usual for the Jews to punish criminals at the public festivals; but in this case they were afraid of an insurrection, as our Lord had become very popular. The providence of God directed it thus, for the reason given in the preceding note.

6. *Simon the leper.* This was probably no more than a surname, as Simon the Canaanite, chap. x. 4, and Barsabas Justus, Acts i. 23, and several others. Yet it might have been some person that Christ had healed of this disease.

7. *There came unto him a woman.* There is much contention among commentators about the transaction mentioned here and in John xii. 14, some supposing them to be different, others to be the same. Some think that the *woman* mentioned here was Mary, the sister of Lazarus; others, Mary Magdalene; but against the former opinion it is argued that it is not likely, had this been Mary the sister of Lazarus, that Matthew and Mark would have suppressed her name. Besides, say they, we should not confound the repast which is mentioned here with that mentioned by John, chap. xii. 3. This one was made only *two* days before the Passover, and that one *six* days before; the one was made at the house of Simon the leper, the other at the house of Lazarus, John xii. 1-2. At this, the woman poured the oil on the *head* of Christ;

at the other, Mary anointed Christ's *feet* with it.

9. *And given to the poor.* How often does charity serve as a cloak for covetousness! God is sometimes robbed of His right under the pretense of devoting what is withheld to some charitable purpose, to which there was no intention ever to give it.

10. *Why trouble ye the woman?* Or, "Why do you put the woman to pain?" A generous mind is ever pained when it is denied the opportunity of doing good, or when its proffered kindness is refused.

11. *Ye have the poor always with you.* And, consequently, have the opportunity of doing them good at any time. *But me ye have not always;* My bodily presence is about to be removed from you forever. The woman, under a presentiment of My death, is preparing Me for My burial.

12. *She did it for my burial.* Or, "She hath done it to embalm Me." Our Lord took this opportunity to tell them once more that He was shortly to die.

13. *Wheresoever this gospel shall be preached.* Another remarkable proof of the prescience of Christ. *For a memorial of her.* As embalming preserves the body from corruption, and she has done this good work to embalm and preserve this body, so will I order everything concerning this transaction to be carefully recorded, to preserve her memory to the latest ages. The actions which the world blames, through the spirit of envy, covetousness, or malice, God takes delight to distinguish and record.

14. *Then . . . Judas.* After this supper at Bethany, Judas returned to Jerusalem and made his contract with the chief priests.

16. *He sought opportunity.* "A convenient or fit opportunity." Men seldom leave a crime imperfect. When once sin is conceived, it meets, in general, with few obstacles, till it brings forth death. How deceitful, how deeply damning, is the love of money!

17. *Now the first day of the feast of unleavened bread.* As the Feast of Unleavened Bread did not begin till the day after the Passover, the fifteenth day of the month (Lev. xxiii. 5-6; Num. xxviii. 16-17), this could not have been, properly, the first day of that feast. But as the Jews began to eat unleavened bread on the fourteenth (Exod. xii. 18), this day was often termed the first of unleavened bread. The Evangelists use it in this sense, and call even the paschal day by this name. See Mark xiv. 12; Luke xxii. 7. *Where wilt thou that we prepare?* How astonishing is this, that He who created all things, whether visible or invisible, and by whom all things were upheld, should so empty himself as not to be Proprietor of a single house in His whole creation, to eat the last Passover with His disciples! It is worthy of note what the Talmudists say, that the inhabitants of Jerusalem did not let out their houses to those who came to the annual feasts, but afforded all accommodations of this kind gratis. A man might, therefore, go and request the use of any room, on such an occasion, which was as yet unoccupied.

18. *Go . . . to such a man.* It is probable that this means some person with whom Christ was well-acquainted, and who was known to the disciples. Grotius observes that the Greeks use this form when they mean some particular person who is so well-known that there is no need to specify him by name. *My time is at hand.* That is, the time of My crucifixion.

19. *And the disciples did.* The disciples that were sent on this errand were Peter and John. See Luke xxii. 9. *They made ready the passover.* That is, they provided the lamb, etc., which were appointed by the law for this solemnity.

20. *Now when the even was come, he sat down with the twelve.* It is a common opinion that our Lord ate the Passover some hours before the Jews ate it; for the Jews, according to custom, ate theirs at the end of the fourteenth day, but Christ ate His the preceding even, which was the beginning of the same sixth day, or Friday. The Jews begin their day at sunsetting, we at midnight. Thus Christ ate the Passover on the same day with the Jews, but not on the same hour. Christ kept this Passover the beginning of the fourteenth day, the precise day and hour in which the Jews had eaten their first Passover in Egypt. See Exod. xii. 6-12. And in the same part of the same day in which the Jews had sacrificed their first paschal lamb, viz., "between the two evenings," about the ninth hour, or three o'clock, Jesus Christ, our Passover, was sacrificed for us. For it was at this hour that He yielded up His last breath; and then it was that, the sacrifice being completed, Jesus said, "It is finished."

21. *One of you shall betray me.* Or "will deliver Me up." Judas had already *betrayed* Him, v. 15, and he was now about to deliver Him into the hands of the chief priests, according to the agreement he had made with them.

22. *They were exceeding sorrowful.* That is, the eleven who were innocent; and the hypocritical traitor, Judas, endeavored to put on the appearance of sorrow.

23. *He that dippeth his hand.* As the Jews ate the Passover a whole family together, it was not convenient for them all to dip their bread in the same dish. They therefore had several little dishes or plates, in which was the juice of the bitter herbs, mentioned Exod. xii. 8, on different parts of the table; and those who were nigh one of these dipped their bread in it. As Judas is represented as dipping in the same dish with Christ, it shows that he was either near or opposite to Him. If this man's heart had not been hardened, and his conscience seared beyond all precedent, by the deceitfulness of his sin, would he have showed his face in this sacred assembly, or have thus put the seal to his own perdition by eating of this sacrificial lamb?

24. *The Son of man goeth.* That is, is about to die. "Going, going away, departing" are frequently used in the best Greek and Latin writers for "death" or "dying." The same words are often used in the Scriptures in the same sense. *It had been good for that man.* Can this be said of any sinner, in the common sense in which it is understood, if there be any redemption from hell's torments? Can the doctrine of the non-eternity of hell's torments stand in the presence of this saying? Or can the doctrine of the annihilation of the wicked consist with this declaration? It was common for the Jews to

say of any flagrant transgressor, "It would have been better for him had he never been born."

25. *Judas . . . said, Master, is it I?* What excessive impudence! He knew, in his conscience, that he had already betrayed his Master, and was waiting now for the servants of the chief priests, that he might deliver Him into their hands; and yet he says (hoping that he had transacted his business so privately that it had not yet transpired), *Master, is it I?* It is worthy of remark that each of the other disciples said, *Lord, is it I?* But Judas dares not, or will not, use this august title, but simpy say, "Teacher, is it I?" *Thou hast said.* "Ye have said" was a common form of expression for "Yes. It is so."

26. *As they were eating.* Either an ordinary supper, or the paschal lamb, as some think. This is the first institution of what is termed the Lord's Supper. *Jesus took bread.* Of what kind? Unleavened bread, certainly, because there was no other kind to be had in all Judea at this time; for this was the first day of unleavened bread (v. 17), i.e., the fourteenth of the month Nisan, when the Jews, according to the command of God (Exod. xii. 15-20; xxiii. 15; and xxxiv. 25), were to purge away all leaven from their houses. For he who sacrificed the Passover, having leaven in his dwelling, was considered to be such a transgressor of the divine law as could no longer be tolerated among the people of God, and therefore was to be cut off from the congregation of Israel. Now if any respect should be paid to the primitive institution, in the celebration of this divine ordinance, then unleavened, unyeasted bread should be used. *And blessed it.* Both Matthew and Mark use the word *blessed* instead of "gave thanks," which is the word used by Luke and Paul. The terms, in this case, are nearly of the same import, as both blessing and giving thanks were used on these occasions. But what was it that our Lord blessed? Not the bread, though many think the contrary, being deceived by the word *it*, which is improperly supplied in our version. In all the four places referred to above, whether the word *blessed* or *gave thanks* is used, it refers not to the bread, but to God, the Dispenser of every good. Our Lord here conforms himself to that constant Jewish custom, viz., of acknowledging God as the Author of every good and perfect gift, by giving thanks or taking the bread and taking the cup at their ordinary meals. The Jewish form of blessing, probably that which our Lord used on this occasion is: "Blessed be thou, our God, King of the universe who bringest forth bread out of the earth!" "Likewise, on taking the cup, they say: "Blessed be our God, the King of the universe, the Creator of the fruit of the vine!"

And brake it. We often read in the Scriptures of breaking bread, but never of cutting it. The breaking of the bread I consider essential to the proper performance of this solemn and significant ceremony, because this act was designed by our Lord to shadow forth the wounding, piercing, and breaking of His body upon the Cross. *And gave it to the disciples.* Not only the breaking, but also the distribution, of the bread are necessary parts of this rite. *This is my body.* Here it must be observed that Christ had nothing in His hands at this time but part of that unleavened bread which He and His disciples had been eating at supper, and therefore He could mean no more than this, viz., that the bread which He was now breaking *represented* His body, which in the course of a few hours was to be crucified for them. The truth is, there is scarcely a more common form of speech in any language than "This is" for "This represents or signifies." And as our Lord refers in the whole of this transaction to the ordinance of the Passover, we may consider Him as saying: "This bread is now My body in that sense in which the paschal lamb has been My body hitherto; and this cup is My blood of the New Testament in the same sense as the blood of bulls and goats has been My blood under the Old (Exodus xxiv; Hebrews ix). That is, the paschal lamb and the sprinkling of blood represented My sacrifice to the present time; this bread and this wine shall represent My body and blood through all future ages. Therefore, "Do this in remembrance of Me."

28. *For this is my blood of the new testament.* This is the reading both here and in Mark; but Luke and Paul say, "This cup is the new testament in my blood." This passage has been strangely mistaken. By *new testament*, many understand nothing more than the Book commonly known by this name, containing the four Gospels, Acts of the Apostles, apostolical Epistles, and Book of the Revelation; and they think that the cup of the new testament means no more than merely that cup which the Book called the New Testament enjoins in the sacrament of the Lord's Supper. The original which we translate *the new testament* and which is general title of all the contents of the Book already described simply means "the new covenant." *Covenant* signifies an agreement, contract, or compact between two parties by which both are mutually bound to do certain things on certain conditions and penalties. It answers to the Hebrew *berith*, which often signifies, not only the covenant or agreement, but also the sacrifice which was slain on the occasion, by the blood of which the covenant was ratified; and the contracting parties professed to subject themselves to such a death as that of the victim in case of violating their engagements. In this place our Lord terms His blood "the blood of the new covenant"; by which He means that grand plan of agreement, or reconciliation, which God was now establishing between himself and mankind, by the passion and death of His Son, through whom alone men could draw nigh to God. *Which is shed* (poured out) *for many.* Often used in a sacrificial sense in the Septuagint, to "pour out" or "sprinkle" the blood of the sacrifices before the altar of the Lord, by way of atonement. See 2 Kings xvi. 15; Lev. viii. 15; ix. 9; Exod. xxix. 12; Lev. iv. 7, 14, 17, 30, 34; and in various other places. Our Lord, by this very remarkable mode of expression, teaches us that, as His body was to be broken or crucified, "in our stead," so here the Blood was to be poured out to make an atonement, as the words *remission of sins* sufficiently prove; for "without shedding of blood [there] is no remission," Heb. ix. 22. The whole of this passage will receive additional light when collated with Isa. liii. 11-12. "By his knowledge shall my righteous servant justify many; for he shall bear their iniquities . . . because he hath poured out his soul unto death . . . and he bare the sin of many." The pouring out of the soul unto death in the prophet answers to "This is the blood of the new covenant which is poured out for you," in the Evangelists. *For the remission of sins.* "For [or in reference to] the taking away of sins." For although the Blood is shed and the atonement made, no man's sins are taken away until as a true penitent he returns to God and, feeling his utter incapacity to save himself, believes in Christ Jesus, who is the Justifier of the ungodly. The phrase *remission of sins* (frequently used by the Septuagint), being thus explained by our Lord, is often used by the Evangelists and the apostles, and does not mean merely the pardon of sins, as it is generally understood, but the removal or taking away of sins—not only the guilt, but also the very nature of sin, and the pollution of the soul through it; and comprehends all that is generally understood by the terms justification and sanctification. Both Luke and Paul add that, after giving the bread, our Lord said, "This do in remembrance of me." And after giving the cup, Paul alone adds, "This do ye, as oft as ye drink it, in remembrance of me." The account as given by Paul should be carefully followed, being fuller, and received, according to his own declaration, by especial revelation from God. See 1 Cor. xi. 23, *For I have received of the Lord that which also I delivered unto you.*

29. *I will not drink henceforth of this fruit of the vine.* These words seem to intimate no more than this: We shall not have another opportunity of eating this bread and drinking this wine together, as in a few hours My crucifixion shall take place. *Until that day when I drink it new with you.* That is, I shall no more drink of the produce of the vine with you; but shall drink *new* wine—wine of a widely different nature from this—a wine which the kingdom of God alone can afford. The term *new* in Scripture is often taken in this sense. So the "new heaven," and "new earth," the "new covenant," the "new man" mean a heaven, earth, covenant, man of a very different nature from the former. From what our Lord says here, we learn that the sacrament of His supper is a type and a pledge to genuine Christians of the felicity they shall enjoy with Christ in the Kingdom of glory.

30. *And when they had sung an hymn.* Probably no more than a kind of recitative reading or chanting. As to the hymn itself, we know, from the universal consent of Jewish antiquity, that it was composed of Psalms 113—118, termed by the Jews *halel*, from *halelu-yah*, the first word in Psalm 113. These six psalms were always sung at every paschal solemnity. They sung this great hallel on account of the five great benefits referred to in it; viz., (1) The Exodus from Egypt, Ps. cxiv. 1, "When Israel went out of Egypt." (2) The miraculous division of the Red Sea, v. 3, "The sea saw it, and fled." (3) The promulgation of the law, v. 4, "The mountains skipped like ... lambs." (4) The resurrection of the dead, Ps. cxvi. 9, "I will walk before the Lord in the land of the living." (5) The passion of the Messiah, Ps. cxv. 1, "Not unto us, O Lord, not unto us."

31. *All ye shall be offended.* Or rather, "You will all be stumbled"—you will all forsake Me, and lose in a great measure your confidence in Me. *This night.* The time of trial is just at hand. *I will smite the shepherd.* It will happen to you as to a flock of sheep whose shepherd has been slain—the leader and guardian being removed, the whole flock shall be scattered, and be on the point of becoming a prey to ravenous beasts.

32. *But after I am risen again.* Do not lose your confidence; for though I shall appear for a time to be wholly left to wicked men, and be brought under the power of death, yet I will rise again, and triumph over all your enemies and mine. *I will go before you.* Still alluding to the case of the shepherd and his sheep. Though the shepherd have been smitten and the sheep scattered, the shepherd shall revive again, collect the scattered flock, and *go before* them, and lead them to peace, security, and happiness.

33. *Peter . . . said unto him, Though all men shall be offended . . . yet will I never.* The presumptuous person imagines he can do everything, and can do nothing; thinks he can excel all, and excels in nothing; promises everything, and performs nothing. The humble man acts a quite contrary part. There is nothing we know so little of as ourselves—nothing we see less of than our own weakness and poverty.

34. *Jesus said.* Our Lord's answer to Peter is very emphatic and impressive. *Verily*—I speak a solemn, weighty truth, you will not only be stumbled, fall off and forsake your Master, but you will even *deny* that you have, or ever had, any knowledge of or connection with Me; and this you will do, not by little and little, through a long process of time, till the apostasy, daily gathering strength, shall be complete; but you will do it *this* very *night,* and that not once only, but *thrice.*

35. *Though I should die with thee, yet will I not deny thee.* He does not take the warning which his Lord gave him—he trusts in the warm, sincere attachment to Christ which he now feels, not considering that this must speedily fail unless supported by the power of God.

36. *A place called Gethsemane.* A garden at the foot of the Mount of Olives. The name seems to be formed from *gath,* "a press," and *shemen,* "oil"; probably the place where the produce of the mount of Olives was prepared for use. The garden of the oil press, or olive press.

37. *And he took with him Peter and the two sons of Zebedee.* That is, James and John, the same persons who had beheld His transfiguration on the mount—that they might contemplate this agony in the light of that glory which they had there seen, and so be kept from being stumbled by a view of His present humiliation. *And very heavy.* "Overwhelmed with anguish." This word is used by the Greeks to denote the most extreme anguish which the soul can feel—excruciating anxiety and torture of spirit.

38. *My soul is exceeding sorrowful* (or "is surrounded with exceeding sorrow"), *even unto death.* This latter word explains the two former: My soul is so dissolved in sorrow, My spirit is filled with such agony and anguish, that, if speedy succor be not given to My body, death must be the speedy consequence.

39. *This cup.* The word *cup* is frequently used in the Sacred Writings to point out sorrow, anguish, terror, death. It seems to be an allusion to a very ancient method of punishing criminals. A cup of poison was put into their hands, and they were obliged to drink it. Socrates was killed thus, being obliged by the magis-

trates of Athens to drink a cup of the juice of hemlock.

40. *He . . . saith unto Peter.* He addressed himself more particularly to this apostle because of the profession he had made, v. 33; as if He had said: "Is this the way you testify your affectionate attachment to Me? You all said you were ready to die with Me; *what,* then, cannot you *watch . . . one hour?"*

41. *That ye enter not into temptation. Watch* —that you be not taken unawares; *and pray*— that when it comes you may be enabled to bear it.

42. *O my Father, if this cup may not pass away from me.* If it be not possible to redeem fallen man unless I drink this cup, unless I suffer death for them; *thy will be done*—I am content to suffer whatever may be requisite to accomplish the great design. In this address the humanity of Christ most evidently appears, for it was His humanity alone that could suffer.

44. *Prayed the third time.* So Paul wrote: "I besought the Lord thrice, that it might depart from me" (2 Cor. xii. 8). This *thrice* repeating the same petition argues deep earnestness of soul.

45. *Sleep on now, and take your rest.* Perhaps it might be better to read these words interrogatively, and paraphrase them thus: "Do you sleep on still?" My *hour*—in which I am to be delivered up, *is at hand;* therefore, now think of your own personal safety. *The Son of man is betrayed into the hands of sinners.* Viz., the Gentiles or heathens, who were generally distinguished by this appellation from the Jews.

46. *Rise, let us be going.* That is, to meet them, giving thereby the fullest proof that I know all their designs and might have, by flight or otherwise, provided for My own safety. But I go willingly to meet that death which their malice designs Me, and through it provide for the life of the world.

47. *Judas, one of the twelve.* More deeply to mark his base ingratitude and desperate wickedness. *A great multitude with swords and staves.* They did not come as officers of justice but as a desperate mob.

48. *Gave them a sign.* How coolly deliberate is this dire apostate! The man whom *I shall kiss*—how deeply hypocritical! That is He; *hold him fast,* "seize Him"—how diabolically malicious!

49. *Hail, master.* A usual compliment among the Jews. Judas pretends to wish our Lord continued health while he is meditating His destruction! *And kissed him.* "And tenderly kissed Him"—this is the proper meaning of the original word. He kissed Him again and again— still pretending the most affectionate attachment to Him, though our Lord had before unmasked him.

50. *Jesus said unto him, Friend* (rather, "companion"), *wherefore art thou come?* How must these words have cut his very soul, if he had any sensibility left! Surely you, who have so long been My companion, are not come against Me, your Lord, Teacher, and Friend! What is the human heart not capable of, when abandoned by God, and influenced by Satan and the love of money!

51. *One of them which were with Jesus.* This was Peter—*struck a servant of the high priest's* (the servant's name was Malchus, John xviii. 10), *and smote off his ear.* In Luke xxii. 51 it is said, Jesus touched and healed it. Here was another miracle, and striking proof of the divinity of Christ.

52. *Put up again thy sword into his place.* Neither Christ nor His religion is to be defended by the secular arm. *Shall perish with the sword.* The general meaning of this verse is, they who contend in battle are likely, on both sides, to become the sacrifices of their mutual animosities. But it is probably a prophetic declaration of the Jewish and Roman states. The Jews put our Lord to death under the sanction of the Romans—both took the sword against Christ, and both perished by it. But how came Peter to have a sword? Judea was at this time so infested with robbers and cutthroats that it was not deemed safe for any person to go unarmed. He probably carried one for his mere personal safety.

53. *More than twelve legions of angels.* As if He had said, Instead of you twelve, one of whom is a traitor, My Father can give me *more than twelve legions of angels* to defend Me. A legion, at different times, contained different numbers; 4,200, 5,000, and frequently 6,000 men.

54. *But how then*—had I such a defense— *shall the scriptures be fulfilled,* which say *that thus it must be?* That is, that I am to suffer and die for the sin of the world. Probably the scriptures to which our Lord principally refers are Psalms xxii; lxix; and especially Isaiah liii and Dan. ix. 24-27. Christ shows that they had no power against Him but what He permitted, and that He willingly gave up himself into their hands.

56. *But all this was done.* This is probably the observation of the Evangelist. *Then all the disciples forsook him, and fled.* He had but twelve who professed inviolable attachment to Him. One of these betrayed Him; another denied Him with oaths; and the rest ran away and utterly abandoned Him to His implacable enemies!

57. *They . . . led him away to Caiaphas.* John says, chap. xviii. 13, that they led him first to Annas; but this appears to have been done merely to do him honor as the father-in-law of Caiaphas, and his colleague in the high priesthood. But as the Sanhedrin was assembled at the house of Caiaphas, it was there He must be brought to undergo His mock trial.

58. *Peter followed him afar off.* Poor Peter! This is the beginning of his dreadful fall. His fear kept him from joining the company and publicly acknowledging his Lord, and his affection obliged him to follow at a distance that he might see the end. *And sat with the servants, to see the end.* When a man is weak in faith and can as yet only follow Christ at a distance, he should avoid all dangerous places and the company of those who are most likely to prove a snare to him.

59. *All the council, sought false witness.* What a prostitution of justice! They first resolve to ruin Him, and then seek the proper means of effecting it; they declare Him criminal, and after that do all they can to fix some crime upon Him, that they may appear to have some shadow

of justice on their side when they put Him to death.

61. *I am able to destroy the temple of God.* (1) These words were not fairly quoted. Jesus had said, John ii. 19, "Destroy this temple, and in three days I will raise it up." (2) The innuendo which they produce, applying these words to a pretended design to destroy the temple at Jerusalem, was utterly unfair; for these words He spoke of the temple of His body.

63. *I adjure thee by the living God.* I put Thee to Thy oath. To this solemn adjuration Christ immediately replies, because He is now called on, in the name of God, to bear another testimony to the truth.

64. *Thou hast said.* That is, I am the Christ, the promised Messiah (see on v. 25) and *you* and this whole nation shall shortly have the fullest proof of it. For *hereafter,* in a few years, *shall ye see the Son of man sitting on the right hand of power,* fully invested with absolute dominion, *and coming in the clouds of heaven,* to execute judgment upon this wicked race. Our Lord appears to refer to Dan. vii. 13: "One like the Son of man came with the clouds of heaven." This may also refer to the final judgment.

65. *The high priest rent his clothes.* This rending of the high priest's garments was expressly contrary to the law, Lev. x. 6 and xxi. 10. But it was a common method of expressing violent grief, Gen. xxxvii. 29, 34; Job i. 20, and horror at what was deemed blasphemous or impious, 2 Kings xviii. 37; xix. 1; Acts xiv. 14. All that heard a blasphemous speech were obliged to rend their clothes, and never to sew them up again.

66. *He is guilty of death.* "He is liable to death." All the forms of justice are here violated. The judge becomes a party and accuser, and proceeds to the verdict without examining whether all the prophecies concerning the Messiah and the innumerable miracles which He wrought did not justify Him.

67. *Then did they spit in his face.* This was done as a mark of the most profound contempt. See Job xvi. 10 and xxx. 10; Isa. l. 6; Mic. v. 1. The judges now delivered Him into the hands of the mob. *And buffeted him.* Smote Him with their fists. "Beat with the hand, the fingers being clenched." *Smote him with the palms of their hands.* "Smite the cheek with the open hand."

68. *Prophesy unto us, thou Christ.* Their conduct toward Him now was expressly prophesied of, by a man whose divine mission they did not pretend to deny; see Isa. l. 6. It appears that, before they buffeted Him, they bound up His eyes; see Mark xiv. 65.

69. *A damsel came unto him.* "A maidservant." *Thou also wast with Jesus.* What a noble opportunity had Peter now to show his zeal for the insulted cause of truth and his attachment to his Master!

72. *And again he denied with an oath.* He has told a lie, and he swears to support it. A liar has always some suspicion that his testimony is not credited, for he is conscious of his own falsity, and is therefore naturally led to support his assertions by oaths.

73. *Thy speech.* "Your manner of speech," "that dialect of yours"—his accent being differ-

ent from that of Jerusalem. *Bewrayeth thee.* "Makes you manifest."

74. *Then began he to curse and to swear.* Rather, "Then he began positively to affirm." *The cock crew.* This animal becomes, in the hand of God, the instrument of awaking the fallen apostle at last to a sense of his fall, danger, and duty.

75. *Peter remembered the word of Jesus.* Luke says, chap. xxii. 61, "The Lord turned, and looked upon Peter." *And wept bitterly.* Felt bitter anguish of soul, which evidenced itself by the tears of contrition which flowed plentifully from his eyes. "Let him that standeth take heed lest he fall." Where the mighty have been slain, what shall support the feeble? Only the grace of the almighty God. This transaction is recorded by the inspired penmen: (1) That all may watch unto prayer, and shun the occasions of sin. (2) That if a man be unhappily overtaken in a fault, he may not despair, but cast himself immediately with a contrite heart on the infinite tenderness and compassion of God.

CHAPTER 27

In the morning, Christ is bound and delivered to Pontius Pilate, 1-2. Judas, seeing his Master condemned, repents, acknowledges his transgression to the chief priests, attests Christ's innocence, throws down the money, and goes and hangs himself, 3-5. They buy the potter's field with the money, 6-10. Christ, questioned by Pilate, refuses to answer, 11-14. Pilate, while inquiring of the Jews whether they would have Jesus or Barabbas released, receives a message from his wife to have nothing to do in this wicked business, 15-19. The multitude, influenced by the chief priests and elders, desire Barabbas to be released, and Jesus to be crucified, 20-23. Pilate attests his innocence, and the people make themselves and their posterity responsible for His blood, 24-25. Barabbas is released, and Christ is scourged, 26. The soldiers strip Him, clothe Him with a scarlet robe, crown Him with thorns, mock, and variously insult Him, 27-31. Simon compelled to bear His cross, 32. They bring Him to Golgotha, give Him vinegar mingled with gall to drink, crucify Him, and cast lots for His raiment, 33-36. His accusation, 37. Two thieves are crucified with Him, 38. He is mocked and insulted while hanging on the Cross, 39-44. The awful darkness, 45. Jesus calls upon God, is offered vinegar to drink, expires, 46-50. Prodigies that accompanied and followed His death, 51-53. He is acknowledged by the centurion, 54. Several women behold the Crucifixion, 55-56. Joseph of Arimathea begs the body of Pilate, and deposits it in his own new tomb, 57-60. The women watch the sepulchre, 61. The Jews consult with Pilate how they may prevent the resurrection of Christ, 62-64. He grants them a guard for the sepulchre, and they seal the stone that stopped the mouth of the tomb where He was laid, 65-66.

1. *When the morning was come.* As soon as it was light. *Took counsel against Jesus.* They had begun this counsel the preceding evening; see chap. xxvi. 59. But as it was contrary to all forms of law to proceed against a person's life by night, they seem to have separated for a few hours, and then, at the break of day, came together again, pretending to conduct the business according to the forms of law. *To put him to death.* They had already determined His death, and pronounced the sentence of death on Him; chap. xxvi. 66. And now they assemble under the pretense of reconsidering the evidence and deliberating on it, to give the greater appearance of justice to their conduct.

3. *Judas . . . when he saw that he was condemned, repented.* There is much of the wisdom and goodness of God to be seen in this part of Judas' conduct. Had our Lord been condemned to death on the evidence of one of His own disciples, it would have furnished infidels with a strong argument against Christ and the Christian religion.

4. *Innocent blood.* A Hebraism for an "innocent man." *What is that to us?* What is it? A great deal. You should immediately go and reverse the sentence you have pronounced, and liberate the innocent Person.

5. *In the temple* signifies, properly, the Temple itself, into which none but the priests were permitted to enter. "Near the Temple," by the Temple door, where the boxes stood to receive the freewill offerings of the people, for the support and repairs of the sacred edifice. *Hanged himself.* Or was "strangled." Some eminent critics believe that he was only suffocated by excessive grief, and thus they think the account here given will agree with that in Acts i. 18. I have my doubts. The old method of reconciling the two accounts appears to me quite plausible—he went and strangled himself, and the rope breaking, he fell down; and by the violence of the fall his body was burst, and "his bowels gushed out."

6. *The treasury.* The place whither the people brought their freewill offerings for the service of the Temple.

7. *To bury strangers in.* "The strangers," probably meaning, as some learned men conjecture, the Jewish strangers who might have come to Jerusalem, either to worship or on some other business, and died there during their stay.

8. *The field of blood.* In vain do the wicked attempt to conceal themselves; God makes them instrumental in discovering their own wickedness. Judas, by returning the money, and the priests, by laying it out, raise to themselves an eternal monument—the one of his treachery, the others of their perfidiousness, and both of the innocence of Jesus Christ.

9. *Jeremy the prophet.* The words quoted here are not found in the prophet Jeremiah, but in Zech. xi. 13. It was ancient custom among the Jews, says Dr. Lightfoot, to divide the Old Testament into three parts. The first beginning with the law was called The Law; the second beginning with the Psalms was called The Psalms; the third beginning with the prophet in question was called Jeremiah. Thus, then, the writings of Zechariah and the other prophets being included in that division that began with Jeremiah, all quotations from it would go under the name of this prophet. If this be admitted, it solves the difficulty at once.

12. *He answered nothing.* An answer to such accusations was not necessary; they sufficiently confuted themselves.

14. *Marvelled greatly.* Silence under calumny manifests the utmost magnanimity. The chief priests did not admire this because it confounded them; but Pilate, who had no interest to serve by it, was deeply affected. This very silence was predicted, Isa. liii. 7.

15. *The governor was wont to release.* Whence this custom originated among the Jews is not known; probably it was introduced by the Romans themselves, or by Pilate, merely to oblige the Jews, by showing them this public token of respect.

16. *A notable prisoner called Barabbas.* This person had, a short time before, raised an insurrection in Jerusalem, in which it appears, from Mark xv. 7, some lives were lost. In some MSS. this man has the surname of *Jesus.*

18. *For envy.* "Through malice." Then it was his business, as an upright judge, to disperse this mob, and immediately release Jesus. Seeing malice is capable of putting even Christ himself to death, how careful should we be not to let the least spark of it harbor in our breasts! Let it be remembered that malice as often originates from *envy* as it does from anger.

19. *I have suffered many things . . . in a dream.* There is no doubt that God had appeared unto this woman, testifying the innocence of Christ, and showing the evils which should pursue Pilate if this innocent blood should be shed by his authority.

20. *Ask Barabbas.* Who had raised an insurrection and committed murder—and to *destroy Jesus,* who had, during the space of three years and a half, gone about unweariedly, from village to village, instructing the ignorant, healing the diseased, and raising the dead.

22. *What shall I do then with Jesus?* Showing, hereby, that it was his wish to release Him.

23. *What evil hath he done?* Pilate plainly saw that there was nothing laid to His charge for which, consistently with the Roman laws, he could condemn Him. *But they cried out the more.* What strange fury and injustice! They could not answer Pilate's question, *What evil hath he done?* He had done none, and they knew He had done none; but they were determined on His death.

24. *Pilate . . . took water, and washed his hands.* Thus signifying his innocence. It was a custom among the Hebrews, Greeks, and Latins to wash the hands in token of innocence, and to show that they were pure from any imputed guilt. In case of an undiscovered murder, the elders of that city which was nearest to the place where the dead body was found were required by the law, Deut. xxi. 1-10, to wash their hands over the victim which was offered to expiate the crime, and thus make public protestation of their own innocence.

25. *His blood be on us, and on our children.* If this Man be innocent, and we put Him to death as a guilty person, may the punishment due to such a crime be visited upon us, and upon our children after us! What a dreadful imprecation! and how literally fulfilled! They were visited with the same kind of punishment; for the Romans crucified them in such numbers when Jerusalem was taken that there was found a deficiency of crosses for the condemned and of places for the crosses.

26. *Scourged Jesus.* This is allowed to have been a very severe punishment of itself among the Romans, the flesh being generally cut by the whips used for this purpose. It has been thought that Pilate might have spared this additional cruelty of whipping, but it appears that it was a common custom to scourge those criminals which were to be crucified (see Josephus De Bello, lib. ii, c. 25), and lenity in Christ's case is not to be allowed; He must take all the misery in full tale. *Delivered him to be crucified.* Tacitus, the Roman historian, mentions the death of Christ in very remarkable terms: "Nero put those who commonly went by the name of Christians to the most exquisite tortures. The author of this name was Christ, who was capitally punished in the reign of Tiberius, by Pontius Pilate the Procurator."

27. *The common hall.* Or *praetorium.* Called so from the *praetor,* a principal magistrate among the Romans, whose business it was to administer justice in the absence of the consul.

28. *Stripped him.* Took off His mantle, or upper garment. *A scarlet robe.* Or, according to Mark and John, a purple robe, such as emperors and kings wore.

29. *A crown of thorns.* It does not appear that this crown was intended to be an instrument of punishment or torture to His head, but rather to render Him ridiculous; for which cause also they put a *reed* in His hand, by way of sceptre, and bowed their knees, pretending to do Him homage. The crown was not probably of thorns in our sense of the word; there are eminently learned men who think that the crown was formed of the herb *acanthus.* This, however, is a prickly plant, though nothing like *thorns* in the common meaning of that word. Painters, the worst of all commentators, frequently represent Christ with a crown of long thorns, which one standing by is striking into His head with a stick. These representations engender ideas both false and absurd.

32. *A man of Cyrene . . . him they compelled to bear his cross.* In John, chap. xix. 16-17, we are told Christ himself bore the Cross, and this it is likely He did for a part of the way; but, being exhausted with the scourging and other cruel usage which He had received, He was found incapable of bearing it alone. Therefore they obliged Simon, not, I think, to bear it entirely, but to assist Christ, by bearing a part of it. It was a constant practice among the Romans to oblige criminals to bear their crosses to the place of execution, insomuch that Plutarch makes use of it as an illustration of the misery of vice. "Every kind of wickedness produces its own particular torment, just as every malefactor, when he is brought forth to execution, carries his own cross."

33. *A place called Golgotha.* From the Hebrew *golgoleth,* "a skull," probably so called from the many skulls of those who had suffered crucificion and other capital punishments scattered up and down in the place. It is the same as Calvary, *Calvaria,* i.e., *calvi capitis area,* the place of bare skulls. Some think the place was thus called because it was in the form of a human skull. It is likely that it was the place of public execution.

34. *They gave him vinegar to drink mingled with gall.* Perhaps *gall* signifies no more than bitters of any kind. It was a common custom to administer a stupefying potion compounded of sour wine, which is the same as vinegar, frankincense, and myrrh to condemned persons to help to alleviate their sufferings or so disturb their intellect that they might not be sensible of them. Some person, out of kindness, appears to have administered this to our blessed Lord; but He, as in all other cases, determining to endure the fullness of pain, refused to take what was thus offered to Him, choosing to tread the winepress alone.

35. *And they crucified him.* Crucifixion properly means the act of nailing or tying to a cross. The cross was made of two beams, either crossing at the top at right angles, like a *T,* or in the middle of their length, like an *X.* There was, besides, a piece on the center of the transverse beam, to which the accusation or statement of the crime of the culprit was attached, and a piece of wood which projected from the middle, on which the person sat, as on a sort of saddle, and by which the whole body was supported. It was probably the Romans who introduced it among the Jews. Before they became subject to the Romans, they used hanging or gibbeting, but not the cross. This punishment was the most dreadful of all others, for both the shame and the pain of it; and so scandalous that it was inflicted as the last mark of detestation upon the vilest of people. It was the punishment of robbers and murderers, provided they were slaves; but if they were free, it was thought too infamous a punishment for such, let their crimes be what they might. The body of the criminal was fastened to the upright beam, by nailing or tying the feet to it, and on the transverse piece by nailing, and sometimes tying the hands to it. The anguish occasioned by crucifixion was so intense that *crucio,* among the Romans, was the common word by which they expressed suffering and torment in general. *And parted his garments, casting lots.* These were the Roman soldiers who had crucified Him; and it appears from this circumstance that in those ancient times the spoils of the criminal were claimed by the executioners, as they are to the present day. It appears that they divided a part, and cast lots for the rest; viz., for His seamless coat, John xix. 23-24. *That it might be fulfilled which was spoken by the prophet, [saying], They parted my garments among them, and upon my vesture did they cast lots.* The whole of this quotation should be omitted, as making no part originally of the genuine text of this Evangelist. It is omitted by almost every MS. of worth and importance, by almost all the versions, and the most reputable of the primitive fathers, who have written or commented on the place. The words are plainly an interpolation, borrowed from John xix. 24, in which place they will be properly noticed.

36. *They watched him.* To prevent His disciples or relatives from taking away the body or affording any relief to the Sufferer.

37. *His accusation.* It was a common custom to affix a label to the cross, giving a statement of the crime for which the person suffered. It is with much propriety that Matthew calls this *accusation,* for it was false that Christ ever pretended to be King of the Jews in the sense the inscription held forth. He was accused of this, but there was no proof of the accusation; however it was affixed to the Cross. From John xix. 21 we find that the Jews wished this to be a little altered: "Write," said they, "that he said, I am King of the Jews," thus endeavoring by the addition of a vile lie to countenance their own conduct in putting Him to death. But this Pilate refused to do. Both Luke, chap. xxiii. 38, and John, chap. xix. 20, say that this accusation was written in Greek, Latin, and Hebrew.

38. *Two thieves.* "Robbers," or cutthroats, men who had committed robbery and murder; for it does not appear that persons were crucified for robbery only. Thus was our Lord "numbered" (His name enrolled, placed as it were in the death warrant) "with the transgressors," according to the prophetic declaration, Isa. liii. 12, and the Jews placed Him between these two, perhaps to intimate that He was the worst felon of the three.

39. *Wagging their heads.* In token of contempt.

40. *Thou that destroyest.* Who pretended that you could have destroyed the Temple, and built it up again in three days. Cruelty is obliged to take refuge in lies in order to vindicate its infamous proceedings. *If thou be the Son of God.* Or rather, "a son of God," i.e., a peculiar favorite of the Most High.

42. *He saved others; himself he cannot save.* Or, "Cannot He save himself?"

43. *If he will have him.* Or "if He delight in Him."

44. *The thieves also . . . cast the same in his teeth.* That is, one of the robbers; for one, we find, was a penitent, Luke xxiii. 39-40.

45. *There was darkness over all the land.* I am of opinion that does not mean all the world but only the land of Judea. So the word is used chap. xxiv. 30; Luke ix. 25, and in other places.

46. *My God, my God, why hast thou forsaken me?* These words are quoted by our Lord from Ps. xxii. 1; they are of very great importance, and should be carefully considered. Some suppose "that the divinity had now departed from Christ, and that his human nature was left unsupported to bear the punishment due to men for their sins." But this is by no means to be admitted, as it would deprive His sacrifice of its infinite merit, and consequently leave the sin of the world without an atonement. Take deity away from any redeeming act of Christ and redemption is ruined. Others imagine that our Lord spoke these words to the Jews only, to prove to them that He was the Messiah. "The Jews," say they, "believed this psalm to speak of the Messiah. They quoted the eighth verse of it against Christ—'He trusted on the Lord that he would deliver him; let him deliver him, seeing he delighted in him.' (See this chap., v. 43.) To which our Lord immediately answers, *My God, my God,* thus showing that He was the Person of whom the Psalmist prophesied." I have doubts concerning the propriety of this interpretation. The words might be thus translated: "My God! My God! to what sort of persons hast Thou left Me?" The words thus understood are rather to be referred to the wicked Jews than to our Lord, and are an exclamation indicative of the obstinate wickedness of His crucifiers, who steeled their hearts against every operation of the Spirit and power of God. Through the whole of the Sacred Writings, God is represented as *doing* those things which, in the course of His providence, he only *permits to be done.* Therefore the words, "To whom hast Thou left or given Me up?" are only a form of expression for "How astonishing is the wickedness of those persons into whose hands I am fallen!" If this interpretation be admitted, it will free this celebrated passage from much embarrassment, and make it speak a sense consistent with itself, and with the dignity of the Son of God. The words of Mark, chap. xv. 34, agree pretty nearly with this translation of the Hebrew: "To what [sort of persons, understood] has Thou left me?" But whatever may be thought of the above mode of interpretation, one thing is certain, viz., that the words could not be used by our Lord in the sense in which they are generally understood. This is sufficiently evident, for He well knew why He was come *unto that hour;* nor could He be forsaken of God, in whom dwelt all the fullness of the Godhead bodily. The Deity, however, might restrain so much of its consolatory support as to leave the human nature fully sensible of all its sufferings, so that the consolations might not take off any part of the keen edge of His passion; and this was necessary to make His sufferings meritorious. And it is probable that this is all that is intended by our Lord's quotation from the twenty-second psalm. Taken in this view, the words convey an unexceptionable sense, even in the common translation.

47. *This man calleth for Elias.* Probably these were Hellenistic Jews, who did not fully understand the meaning of our Lord's words. Elijah was daily expected to appear as the forerunner of the Messiah, whose arrival, under the character of a mighty prince, was generally supposed to be at hand throughout the East. See Mal. iii. 23; Matt. ii. 2-4; xvii. 10-12.

48. *Took a spunge.* This being the most convenient way to reach a liquid to His mouth; tied it *on a reed,* that they might be able to reach His lips with it. This reed, as we learn from John, was a stalk of hyssop, which in that country must have grown to a considerable magnitude. This appears also to have been done in mercy, to alleviate His sufferings. See v. 34.

50. *Yielded up the ghost.* "He dismissed the spirit." He himself willingly gave up that life which it was impossible for man to take away. It is not said that He hung on the Cross till He died through pain and agony; nor is it said that His bones were broken, the sooner to put Him out of pain, and to hasten His death. But that He himself "dismissed the soul," that He might thus become, not a forced sacrifice, but a freewill Offering for sin. Now, as our English word *ghost,* from the Anglo-Saxon *gast,* an "inmate, inhabitant, guest" (a casual visitant), also a "spirit," is now restricted among us to the latter meaning, always signifying the immortal spirit or soul of man, the guest of the body; and as giving up the spirit, ghost, or soul, is an act not proper to man, though commending it to God, in our last moments, is both an act of faith and piety; and as giving up the ghost, i.e., dismissing His spirit from His body, is attributed to Jesus Christ, to whom alone it is proper. I therefore object against its use in every other case. Every man, since the Fall, has not only been liable to death, but has deserved it, as all have forfeited their lives because of sin. Jesus Christ, as born immaculate, and having never sinned, had not forfeited His life, and therefore may be considered as naturally and properly immortal. "No man," says He, "taketh it," My life, "from me, but I lay it down of myself. I have power to lay it down, and I have power to take it again . . . Therefore doth my Father love me, because I lay down my life, that I might take it again," John x. 18, 17. Hence we rightly translate Matt. xxvii. 50. "He gave up the ghost"; i.e., He "dismissed His spirit," that He might die for the sin of the world. The Evangelist John, xix. 30, makes use of an expression to the same import, which we translate in the same way: "He de-

livered up His spirit." We translate Mark xv. 37 and Luke xxiii. 46, "He gave up the ghost," but not correctly, because the word in both these places is very different—"He breathed His last," or "expired"; though in the latter place, Luke xxiii. 46, there is an equivalent expression —"Father, into thy hands I commend my spirit"; i.e., "I place My soul in Thy hand," proving that the act was His own, that no man could take His life away from Him, that He did not die by the perfidy of His disciple or the malice of the Jews, but by His own free act. Thus He laid down his life for the sheep. Of Ananias and Sapphira, Acts v. 5, 10, and of Herod, Acts xii. 23, our translation says, they "gave up the ghost"; but the word in both places is simply to "breathe out," to "expire," or "die." But in no case, either by the Septuagint in the Old, or any of the sacred writers in the New Testament, is "He dismissed his spirit," or "delivered up his spirit," spoken of any person but Christ. Abraham, Isaac, Ishmael, Jacob, and others "breathed their last"; Ananias, Sapphira, and Herod "expired"; but none, Jesus Christ excepted, "gave up the ghost, dismissed, or delivered up his own spirit."

51. *The veil of the temple was rent.* That is, the veil which separated the holy place, where the priests ministered, from the holy of holies, into which the high priest only entered, and that once a year, to make a general expiation for the sins of the people. This rending of the veil was emblematical, and pointed out that the separation between Jews and Gentiles was now abolished, and that the privilege of the high priest was now communicated to all mankind. All might henceforth have access to the throne of grace, through the one great Atonement and Mediator, the Lord Jesus. See this beautifully illustrated in Heb. x. 19-22.

52. *And the graves were opened.* By the earthquake; *and many bodies of saints which slept,* i.e., were dead, sleep being a common expression for death in the Scriptures.

53. *And came out of the graves after his resurrection.* Not before, as some have thought, for Christ was himself the Firstfruits of them, who slept, 1 Cor. xv. 20. The *graves* were opened at His death by the earthquake, and the bodies came out at His *resurrection. And appeared unto many.* Thus establishing the truth of our Lord's resurrection in particular, and of the resurrection of the body in general, by many witnesses.

54. *The centurion.* The Roman officer who superintended the execution, called *centurio,* from *centum,* a hundred, because he had the command of 100 men. *Truly this was the Son of God.* An innocent, holy, and divine Person; and God thus shows His disapprobation of this bloody tragedy. It is not likely that this centurion had any knowledge of the expectation of the Jews relative to the Messiah, and did not use the words in this sense. "A son of God," as the Romans used the term, would signify no more than a very eminent or divine person, a hero.

55. *Many women.* To their everlasting honor, these women evidenced more courage and affectionate attachment to their Lord and Master than the disciples did, who had promised to die with Him rather than forsake Him. *Beholding afar off.* "At a distance."

56. *Mary Magdalene.* She probably had her name from Magdala, a village or district in Lower Galilee. See chap. xv. 39. *Mary the mother of James.* She was mother of him called James the lesser, or junior, who was son of Alphaeus or Cleopas; see chap. x. 3; Mark xv. 40; John xix. 25; and she was sister to the Holy Virgin. Thus it appears that there were four remarkable Marys mentioned in the Gospels: (1) Mary the Virgin, wife of Joseph. (2) Mary Salome, her sister, wife of Cleopas, John xix. 25. (3) Mary Magdalene, or Mary of Magdala; and (4) Mary, the sister of Martha and Lazarus, John xi. 1.

57. *When the even.* This must have been about three o'clock or a little after; for our Lord having expired about three o'clock, v. 46, and the Jewish Passover beginning about four, it was necessary that Joseph, who would not fail to eat the Passover at the usual time, should have obtained and buried the body of Christ some time before four o'clock. But such was the general consternation, occasioned by the prodigies that took place on this most awful occasion, that we may safely conjecture that nothing was done in order, and perhaps the Passover itself was not eaten at the usual hour, if at all, that day. *A rich man.* He was a counsellor of the great Sanhedrin, Luke xxiii. 50; and, from the accounts given of him by the Evangelists, we learn that he was a man of the greatest respectability. He now acted a more honorable part than all the disciples of our Lord. He was of Arimathaea, or Rama, in the tribe of Benjamin, Matt. ii. 17, but lived ordinarily in Jerusalem as being a member of the great council.

58. *Begged the body.* That he might bury it honorably; otherwise, by the Jewish customs, He would have either been burned, or buried in the common place appointed for executed criminals.

59. *Wrapped it in a clean linen cloth.* The Jews, as well as the Egyptians, added spices to keep the body from putrefaction, and the linen was wrapped about every part to keep the aromatics in contact with the flesh. From John xix. 39-40 we learn that a mixture of myrrh and aloes of 100 pounds' weight had been applied to the body of Jesus when He was buried. And that a second embalmment was intended, we learn from Luke xxiii. 56 and xxiv. 1, as the hurry to get the body interred before the Sabbath did not permit them to complete the embalming in the first instance.

60. *Laid it in his own new tomb.* To all human appearance the body of Christ must have had the same burial place with those of the two robbers, as "he was numbered with the transgressors," and suffered with them; for then He was a Sacrifice, bearing the sin of the world in His own body on the tree. But now the Sacrifice is offered, the atonement made and accepted; He is no longer to be enrolled with the transgressors, and, according to a prophecy delivered nearly seven hundred years before that time, He is to have the burying place of a rich man. See Isa. liii. 9-10. Had our Lord been buried in the common burial ground of the malefactors, His resurrection could not have been so distinctly remarked, as the chief priests would never have thought of sealing the stone there or setting a watch. But now that the body is given into the hands of a friend, they

judge it necessary to make use of these precautions, in order, as they said, to prevent imposture; and from this very circumstance the resurrection of Christ had its fullest evidence, and was put beyond the power of successful contradiction.

61. *Mary Magdalene, and the other Mary.* The mother of James and Joses, v. 56. The mother of our Lord had probably, by this time, been taken home to the house of John. See John xix. 26-27. *Sitting over against the sepulchre.* These holy women, filled with that love to their Lord which death cannot destroy, cleaved to Him in life, and in death were not divided. They came to the grave to see the end, and overwhelmed with sorrow and anguish, sat down to mourn.

62. *The next day.* This was the seventh, or Saturday, and might be what we should term the evening of the sixth, or Friday, because the Jews always ended their day when the sun set, and then began the next. *That followed the day of the preparation.* That is, of the Sabbath. The victuals which were to be used on the Sabbath by the Jews were always prepared the preceding evening before the sun set. It is of this *preparation* that the Evangelist speaks here, and it is the same which is mentioned by Mark, chap. xv. 42; by Luke, chap. xxiii. 54; and by John, chap. xix. 31. But there was another preparation which happened in the same day, viz., the preparation of the Passover. This began about twelve o'clock, and continued till four, the time in which they ate the paschal lamb. See John xix. 14.

63. *Sir, we remember.* While these wicked men are fulfilling their own vicious counsels, they are subserving the great cause of Christianity. Everything depended on the resurrection of Christ. If it did not appear that He rose from the dead, then the whole system was false, and no atonement was made. It was necessary, therefore, that the chief priests should make use of every precaution to prevent an imposture, that the resurrection of Christ might have the fullest evidence to support it. See on v. 60. The word *kyrie* is here very properly translated "Sir," which, in many other places, is as improperly translated *Lord.* When a Roman is the speaker or the person addressed, *kyrie* should always be translated "sir"; when strangers address our Lord, the word is a title of civil respect, and should, in general, be translated in the same way. *After three days I will rise again.* This they probably took from His saying, "Destroy this temple, and in three days I will raise it up." If so, they destroyed, by their own words, the false accusation they brought against Him to put Him to death. Then they perverted the meaning; now they declare it. Thus the wise are taken in their own craftiness.

65. *Ye have a watch.* The Jews had a corps of Roman troops, consisting of several companies, as a guard for the Temple, Acts iv. 1. These companies mounted guard by turns; see Luke xxii. 4. Some of these companies, which were not then on duty, Pilate gave them leave to employ to watch the tomb.

66. *Made the sepulchre sure, sealing the stone, and setting a watch.* Or rather, "made the tomb secure by the guard, and by sealing the stone." The guard was to take care that the disciples should not steal him away; and the seal, which was probably the seal of the governor, was to

prevent the guards from being corrupted so as to permit the theft. So everything was done which human policy and prudence could to prevent a resurrection, which these very precautions had the most direct tendency to authenticate and establish. How wonderful are the wisdom and goodness of God!

CHAPTER 28

The resurrection of Christ declared by an angel to the two Marys at the sepulchre, 1-6. They are commissioned to announce this to the disciples, 7. They go, and are met by Christ himself, who promises to meet the disciples in Galilee, 8-10. The watch go into the city, and report to the chief priests what had taken place, 11. They give them money, to say that His disciples had stolen the body by night, while they slept, 12-15. Christ meets the eleven disciples in a mountain of Galilee, 16-17. He gives them a commission to preach the gospel throughout the earth; to baptize in the name of the Father, and of the Son, and of the Holy Ghost; and promises to be with them to the end of the world, 18-20.

1. *In the end of the sabbath.* "After the end of the week." In general the Jews divided their natural day, which consisted of twenty-four hours, into day and night. Their artificial day began at the rising and ended at the setting of the sun; all the rest of the time, from the setting to the rising of the sun, they termed night. Hence the same word, in Hebrew, signifies both evening and night, Gen. i. 5; Mark vi. 47. Matthew has employed the word in this extensive sense here, pointing out the latter part of the Jewish night, that which immediately preceded the rising of the sun, and not that first part which we call the evening. The transaction mentioned here evidently took place early on the morning of the third day after our Lord's crucifixion; what is called our Sunday morning, or first day of the next week. *Came . . . to see the sepulchre.* That is, they set out at this time in order to visit the tomb of our Lord, and also to weep there, John xi. 31, and to embalm the body of our Lord, Luke xxiv. 1. Matthew omits Mary Salome, mentioned by Mark; and Joanna, the wife of Chuza, Herod's steward, mentioned by Luke. The other Mary was the wife of Cleopas, and the mother of James and Joses, mentioned before, chap. xxvii. 56. Were not Mary and Salome two distinct persons?

2. *A great earthquake.* A "shaking" or "commotion" of any kind; probably the word means no more than the confusion caused among the guards by the angel's appearance. All this had taken place before the women reached the sepulchre. *The angel of the Lord descended from heaven.* Matthew is very particular in this to show that the word *angel* is not to be taken in the sense of an ordinary messenger, who might have come from Joseph of Arimathaea, or from any other; but in the sense of an extraordinary messenger, who descended from God out of heaven for this very purpose. It is likely that the angel had descended, rolled away the stone, and was sitting on it, before the women reached the tomb.

3. *His countenance.* "His appearance" or "his face," for so the word is used in some of the best Greek writers. It seems, from Mark xvi. 5, that this angel had assumed the appearance of a young man. *Like lightning.* Coruscations of glory continually flaming from his face. This might produce the confusion mentioned in v. 2. *His raiment white as snow.* He was clothed in garments emblematical of the glad tidings which

he came to announce. It would have been inconsistent with the message he brought had the angel appeared in black robes, such as those preposterously wear who call themselves his successors in the ministry of a once suffering, but now risen and highly exalted, Saviour.

4. *The keepers . . . became as dead men.* God can, by one and the same means, comfort His servants and terrify His enemies. The resurrection of Christ is a subject of terror to the servants of sin and a subject of consolation to the sons of God, because it is proof of the resurrection of both—the one to shame and everlasting contempt—the other to eternal glory and joy.

5. *I know that ye seek Jesus.* Speaking after the manner of men, these women deserved to be the first witnesses of the resurrection of Christ. During life they ministered to Him, and in death they were not divided. They attended Him to the Cross, notwithstanding their attachment to Him exposed them to the most imminent danger; and now they come to watch and weep at His tomb. The common opinion is that women are more fickle and less courageous than men. The reverse of this I believe to be the truth in those who are thoroughly converted to God; and who, previously to conversion, whether man or woman, can be trusted in any case?

6. *Come, see the place.* The tomb in which our Lord was laid was no doubt like the rest of the Jewish burying places, a receptacle for the several dead of a whole family, divided into separate niches, where each had his place. *Come, see the place* was tantamount to, Come and see the niche in which He was laid—it is now empty. Nor was there any other body in the place, for the tomb was a *new* one, in which no man had ever been laid, John xix. 41; so there could be no deception in the case.

7. *Go quickly, and tell his disciples.* Thus these faithful women proclaim the gospel to those who were afterwards to be the teachers of the whole human race! *That he is risen from the dead.* There is a remarkable saying of R. Judah Hakkodesh, which some critics quote on this subject: "After three days the soul of the Messiah shall return to its body, and he shall go out of that stone in which he shall be buried." *Goeth before you into Galilee.* As himself promised, chap. xxvi. 32.

8. *They departed quickly from the sepulchre.* At the desire of the angel they went into the tomb, to have the fullest certainty of the Resurrection. *Fear and great joy. Fear* produced by the appearance of this glorious messenger of God, and *great joy* occasioned by the glad tidings of the resurrection of their Lord and Master. At the mention of unexpected good news, fear and joy are generally intermingled.

9. *All hail.* "Be safe, rejoice."

10. *Be not afraid.* They were seized with fear at the sight of the angel, and this was now renewed by this unexpected appearance of Christ. *Go tell my brethren.* This is the first time our Lord called His disciples by this endearing name. They no doubt thought that their Lord would reproach them with their past cowardice and infidelity; but, in speaking thus, He gives them a full assurance, in the most tender terms, that all that was past was as buried forever.

11. *Some of the watch.* Or "guards." Probably the rest still remained at the tomb, waiting for orders to depart, and had sent these to intimate to their employers the things that had taken place.

12. *With the elders.* That is, the "senators" of the great Sanhedrin or Jewish council of state, elsewhere called "the elders of the people"; they could now meet, as the Sabbath was over.

13. *His disciples came by night.* This was as absurd as it was false. On one hand, the terror of the disciples, the smallness of their number (only eleven), and their almost total want of faith; on the other, the great danger of such a bold enterprise, the number of armed men who guarded the tomb, the authority of Pilate and of the Sanhedrin, must render such an imposture as this utterly devoid of credit. *Stole him away while we slept.* Here is a whole heap of absurdities. (1) Is it likely that so many men would all fall asleep, in the open air, at once? (2) Is it at all probable that a Roman guard should be found off their watch, much less asleep, when it was instant death, according to the Roman military laws, to be found in this state? (3) Could they be so sound asleep as not to awake with all the noise which must be necessarily made by removing the great stone and taking away the body? (4) Is it at all likely that these disciples could have had sufficient time to do all this, and to come and return, without being perceived by any person? And (5), If they were asleep, how could they possibly know that it was the *disciples* that stole Him, or indeed that any person or persons stole Him? For, being asleep, they could see no person.

14. *If this come to the governor's ears.* Pilate. *We will persuade him* that it is for his own interest and honor to join in the deception; and we will render you *secure*—we will take care that you shall not suffer that punishment for this pretended breach of duty which otherwise you might expect.

15. *Until this day.* That is to say, the time in which Matthew wrote his Gospel.

16. *Then the eleven disciples went.* When the women went and told them that they had seen the Lord, and that He had promised to meet them in Galilee. From the eleventh to the fifteenth verse inclusive should be read in a parenthesis, as the sixteenth verse is the continuation of the subject mentioned in the tenth.

17. *But some doubted.* That is, Thomas only at first doubted. The expression simply intimates that they did not all believe at that time.

18. *And Jesus came and spake unto them.* It is supposed by some that the reason why any doubted was that, when they saw Jesus at first, He was at a distance; but when He came up, drew near to them, they were fully persuaded of the identity of His person. *All power is given unto me.* Or, "All authority in heaven and upon earth is given unto Me." One fruit of the sufferings and resurrection of Christ is represented to be His having authority or right *in heaven* to send down the Holy Spirit—to raise up His followers thither—and to crown them in the Kingdom of an endless glory; *in earth,* to convert sinners; to sanctify, protect, and perfect His Church; to subdue all nations to himself;

and, finally, to judge all mankind. If Jesus Christ were not equal with the Father, could He have claimed this equality of power without being guilty of impiety and blasphemy? Surely not; and does He not, in the fullest manner, assert His Godhead, and His equality with the Father, by claiming and possessing all the authority in heaven and earth?—i.e., all the power and authority by which both empires are governed?

19. *Go ye therefore.* Because I have the authority aforesaid, and can send whomsoever I will to do whatsoever I please. *Teach,* "make disciples of all nations," bring them to an acquaintance with God who bought them, and then baptize *them in the name of the Father.* It is natural to suppose that adults were the first subjects of baptism; for as the gospel was, in a peculiar manner, sent to the Gentiles, they must hear and receive it before they could be expected to renounce their old prejudices and idolatries and come into the bonds of the Christian covenant. But certainly no argument can be drawn from this concession against the baptism of children. When the Gentiles and Jews had received the faith and blessings of the gospel, it is natural enough to suppose they should wish to get their children incorporated with the Visible Church of Christ; especially if, as many pious and learned men have believed, baptism succeeded to circumcision, which I think has never yet been disproved. The apostles knew well that the Jews not only circumcised the children of proselytes, but also baptized them; and as they now received a commission to teach and proselyte all the nations, and baptize them in the name of the Holy Trinity, they must necessarily understand that infants were included. Nor could they, the custom of their country being considered, have understood our Lord differently unless He had, in the most express terms, said that they were not to baptize children, which neither He nor His apostles ever did. And as to the objection that the baptized were obliged to profess their faith, and that, therefore, only adults should be baptized, there is no weight at all in it; because what is spoken of such refers to those who, only at that period

of life, heard the gospel, and were not born of parents who had been Christians; therefore they could not have been baptized into the Christian faith, forasmuch as no such faith was at their infancy preached in the world. *In the name of the Father.* Baptism, properly speaking, whether administered by dipping or sprinkling, signifies a full and eternal consecration of the person to the service and honor of that Being in whose name it is administered. But this consecration can never be made to a creature; therefore the *Father,* and the *Son,* and the *Holy Spirit* are not creatures. Again, baptism is not made in the name of a quality or attribute of the divine nature; therefore the *Father,* and the *Son,* and the *Holy Spirit* are not qualities or attributes of the divine nature. The orthodox, as they are termed, have generally considered this text as a decisive proof of the doctrine of the Holy Trinity, and what else can they draw from it? Is it possible for words to convey a plainer sense than do these? And do they not direct every reader to consider the *Father,* the *Son,* and the *Holy Spirit* as three distinct Persons?

20. *Teaching them to observe all things.* Men are ignorant of divine things and must be taught. Only those can be considered as proper teachers of the ignorant who are thoroughly instructed in whatsoever Christ has commanded. Persons who are entrusted with the public ministry of the Word should take care that they teach not human creeds and confessions of faith in place of the Sacred Writings but those things, and those only, which Jesus has commanded. *And, lo, I am with you alway.* Literally, "Behold, I am with you every day." *Unto the end of the world.* Some translate, "to the end of this age," meaning the apostolic age, or Jewish dispensation; and then they refer the promise of Christ's presence to the working of miracles, and explain this by Mark xvi. 17-19, "In my name shall they cast out devils." But though the words are used in this sense in several places, see chap. xiii. 39-40, 49 and xxiv. 3, yet it is certain they were repeatedly used among the primitive ecclesiastical writers to denote the "consummation of all things"; and it is likely that this is the sense in which they are used here.

The Gospel According to

MARK

This person, the second in the commonly received order of the four Evangelists, was named John Mark, and was the son of a pious woman called Mary, who dwelt at Jerusalem. She was an early believer, and the disciples often met at her house. Peter, having been delivered out of prison by an angel, "came to the house of Mary the mother of John, whose surname was Mark; where many were gathered together praying," Acts xii. 12. This very first mention of John Mark assures us of Peter's intimacy in that family. It is almost universally allowed that Mark, mentioned by Peter, 1 Epist., chap. v. 13, is this Evangelist, and that he is the same with him who is called "sister's son to Barnabas," Col. iv. 10, and is supposed to have been converted by Peter to the Christian faith. He travelled from Jerusalem to Antioch with Paul and Barnabas, Acts xii. 25, and some short time after he accompanied them to other countries as their "minister," Acts xiii. 5. When they returned to the continent, and came on shore at Perga in Pamphylia, he departed from them and returned to Jerusalem, v. 13. Afterwards he would have gone with Paul and Barnabas, but the former refused to take him because of his having left them at Pamphylia. Paul and Barnabas then separated, and Mark accompanied his uncle Barnabas to Cyprus, Acts xv. 36-41. Afterwards Paul and he were fully reconciled, as evidently appears from 2 Tim. iv. 11: "Take Mark, and bring him with thee: for he is profitable to me for the ministry." This appears also from Philemon, v. 24, where Mark is styled Paul's fellow labourer; and from Col. iv. 10, where we find the apostle recommending him in a particular manner to the church of God at that place. He is generally supposed to have been particularly intimate with Peter, to have written his Gospel at Rome, A.D. 64, and to have died at Alexandria in Egypt, in the eighth year of the reign of Nero.

How Mark composed his Gospel is a question not yet decided among learned men. Many of the primitive fathers, such as Papias, Clemens Alexandrinus, Irenaeus, Tertullian, Origen, Eusebius, etc., believed that he was only the amanuensis of Peter; that this apostle, through modesty, would not put his name to the work, but dictated the whole account, and Mark wrote it down from his mouth. Augustine appears to have been the first who maintained that Mark abridged St. Matthew's Gospel, and that it is not to be considered as an original work. Others suppose that Mark compiled it, partly out of Matthew's Gospel and partly out of the Gospel of Luke. But most of these are conjectures which appear to have very little foundation. Critics are also divided concerning the language in which it was written, and the people to whom it was sent. Some have contended for a Latin original, because of several Latin words found in it. But such words are better accounted for by supposing that his Gospel was written for the use of the Roman people; and that it is on this account that he wholly passes by the genealogy of our Lord, as being a point of no consequence to Gentile converts, though very necessary for the Jews, and especially the Jews of Palestine. That it was originally written in Greek is a point now acknowledged by almost all learned men.

CHAPTER 1

The mission, preaching, and success of John Baptist, 1-5. His manner of life, 6. Proclaims Christ, and baptizes Him in Jordan, 7-11. The temptation of Christ, 12-13. John being put in prison, Christ begins to preach, 14-15. He calls Andrew and Simon, 16-18; James and John, 19-20. Teaches in Capernaum, 21-22. Casts out a demon, 23-28. Goes into the house of Simon, and heals his mother-in-law, 29-31. Heals many diseased persons, 32-34. Goes to the desert, and is followed by His disciples, 35-37. Preaches in different towns and synagogues of Galilee, and casts out devils, 38-39. Cleanses a leper, who publishes abroad his miraculous cure, 40-45.

1. *The beginning of the gospel.* With utmost propriety Mark begins the Gospel dispensation by the preaching of John the Baptist, the forerunner of Jesus Christ and the first proclaimer of the incarnated Messiah. *Son of God.* Mark thus points out Jesus' divine origin, and thus glances at His miraculous conception. This was an essential character of the Messiah. See Matt. xvi. 16; xxvi. 63; Luke xxii. 67, etc.

2. *As it is written in the prophets.* Rather, "As it is written by Isaiah the prophet." I think this reading should be adopted, instead of that in the common text. It is the reading of several MSS. and versions of great repute, and in several of the Fathers. As this prophecy is found both in Isaiah and Malachi, early scribes probably changed the reading to *the prophets,* that it might comprehend both.

3. *The voice of one crying.* See on Matt. iii. 1-3.

4. *John.* The original name is *Yehochanan,* compounded of *Yehovah chanan,* the "grace or mercy of Jehovah"—a most proper and significant name for the forerunner of the "God of all grace." It was John's business to proclaim the gospel of the grace of God, and to point out that Lamb or sacrifice of God which takes away the sin of the world. *For the remission of sins.* Or "toward the remission." They were to repent, and be baptized with reference to the remission of sins. Repentance prepared the

soul for it, and baptism was the type or pledge of it.

5. *All the land.* See on Matt. iii. 4-6. *Confessing their sins.* It was an invariable custom among the Jews to admit no proselyte to baptism till he had in the most solemn manner declared that he had renounced forever all idolatrous worship, all heathen superstitions, and promised an entire and unreserved submission to the law of Moses.

6. *John was clothed . . .* See the note on Matt. iii. 4.

7. *The latchet of whose shoes.* The shoe of the ancients was properly only a sole tied round the foot and ankle with strings or thongs.

8. *I indeed have baptized you with water.* As if he had said: This baptism is not to be rested in; it is only an emblem of that which you must receive from Him who is mightier than I. It is He only who can communicate the Holy Spirit; and water baptism is nothing, but as it points out, and leads to, the baptism of the Holy Ghost.

12. *The spirit driveth him.* "Pulleth Him forth." Matthew says, chap. iv. 1, "was . . . led up."

13. *With the wild beasts.* This is a curious circumstance, which is mentioned by none of the other Evangelists, and seems to intimate that He was in the most remote, unfrequented, and savage part of the desert; which, together with the diabolic influence, tended to render the whole scene the more horrid.

15. *The time is fulfilled.* That is, the time appointed for sending the Messiah; and particularly the time specified by Daniel, chap. ix. 24-27.

16. *Andrew his brother.* Instead of the common reading, *his brother,* the best MSS. and versions have "the brother of Simon," which should be received into the text.

22. *As one that had authority.* From God, to do what He was doing, and to teach a pure and beneficent system of truth. *And not as the scribes.* Who had no such authority, and whose teaching was not accompanied by the power of God to the souls of the people: (1) because the matter of the teaching did not come from God, and (2) because the teachers themselves were not commissioned by the Most High.

23. *A man with an unclean spirit.* This demoniac is mentioned only by Mark and Luke, chap. iv. 31. It seems the man had lucid intervals; else he could not have been admitted into the synagogue. *Unclean [or impure] spirit* —a common epithet for those fallen spirits; but here it may mean one who filled the heart of him he possessed with lascivious thoughts, images, desires, and propensities.

24. *What have we to do with thee?* Or, "What is it to us and to Thee?" or, What business hast Thou with us? There is a phrase exactly like it in 2 Sam. xvi. 10, "What have I to do with you, ye sons of Zeruiah?" The Septuagint translate the Hebrew just as the Evangelist does here; it is the same idiom in both places. *Art thou come to destroy us?* We may suppose this spirit to have felt and spoken thus: "Is this the time of which it hath been predicted that in it the Messiah should destroy all that power which we have usurped and exercised over the bodies and souls of men? Alas! it is so: I now plainly see *who thou art, the Holy One of God,* who art come to destroy unholiness, in which we have our residence, and through which we have our reign in the souls of men." An unholy spirit is the only place where Satan can have his full operation, and show forth the fullness of his destroying power.

25. *And Jesus rebuked him.* A spirit of this cast will yield only to the sovereign power of the Son of God.

26. *And when the unclean spirit had torn him.* "And . . . had thrown him [down] in the midst," Luke iv. 35, and "convulsed" him.

27. *For with authority.* They had never heard such a gracious doctrine, and had never seen any teaching supported by miracles before. How much must this Person be superior to men! They are brought into subjection by unclean spirits; this Person subjects unclean spirits to himself.

28. *And immediately his fame spread abroad.* The word *immediately* is used more frequently by this Evangelist than by any other writer of the new covenant. It is very often superfluous, and may often be omitted in the translation without any prejudice to the sense of the passage in which it is found.

29. See this account of the healing of Peter's mother-in-law explained at large, Matt. viii. 14-17.

32. *When the sun did set.* See on Matt. viii. 16.

35. *In the morning . . . a great while before day.* By *the morning* is to be understood the whole space of three hours which finished the fourth watch of the night. *And there prayed.* Not that He needed anything, for in Him dwelt "all the fulness of the Godhead bodily," but that He might be a Pattern to us.

Everything that our blessed Lord did He performed either as our Pattern or as our Sacrifice.

36. *And Simon . . . followed after him.* "Followed Him eagerly."

37. *All men seek for thee.* Some to hear; some to be healed; some to be saved; and some, perhaps, through no good motive.

38. *The next towns.* Properly signifies such towns as resembled cities for magnitude and number of inhabitants, but which were not walled, as were cities. *For therefore came I forth.* For this purpose am I come forth—to preach the gospel to every creature, that all might hear, and fear, and return unto the Lord. The towns and the villages will not come to the preacher—the preacher must go to them, if he desires their salvation.

39. *And he preached.* "He continued preaching." This is the proper meaning of the words. He never slackened His pace—He continued proclaiming the glad tidings of salvation to all. There was no time to be lost—immortal souls were perishing for lack of knowledge; and the grand adversary was prowling about, seeking whom he might devour.

40. *There came a leper.* See the notes on Matt. vii. 2, etc. Should any be inclined to preach on this cleansing of the leper, Mark is the best Evangelist to take the account from, because he is more circumstantial than either Matthew or Luke.

45. *Began to publish it much.* Began to publish "many things"; probably all that he had heard about our Lord's miraculous works. *Jesus could no more openly enter into the city.* A city of Galilee, probably Chorazin or Bethsaida, in which He did not appear, for fear of exciting the jealousy of the secular government or the envy and malice of the Jewish rulers.

CHAPTER 2

Christ preaches in Capernaum, 1-2. A paralytic person is brought to Him, whose sins are pronounced forgiven, 3-5. The scribes accuse Him of blasphemy, 6-7. He vindicates himself, and proves His power to forgive sins, by healing the man's disease, 8-11. The people are astonished and edified, 12. He calls Levi from the receipt of custom, 13-14. Eats in his house with publicans and sinners, at which the Pharisees murmur, 15-16. He vindicates His conduct, 17. Vindicates His disciples, who are accused of not fasting, 18-22; and for plucking the ears of corn on the Sabbath day, 23-26; and teaches the right use of the Sabbath, 27-28.

1. *In the house.* The house of Peter, with whom Christ lodged when at Capernaum.

2. *So much as about the door.* Meaning the yard or court before the house. *Preached the word.* The doctrine of the kingdom of God.

3. *One sick of the palsy.* "A paralytic person." See Matt. ix. 1. *Borne of four.* Four men, one at each corner of the sofa or couch on which he lay. This sick man appears to have been too feeble to come himself, and too weak to be carried in any other way.

4. *They uncovered the roof.* The houses in the East are generally made flat-roofed, that the inhabitants may have the benefit of taking the air on them. They are also furnished with battlements round about, Deut. xxii. 8; Judg. xvi. 27; and 2 Sam. xi. 2, to prevent persons from falling off; and have a trapdoor by which to descend into the house. This door, it appears, was too narrow to let down the sick man and

his couch; so *they uncovered the roof,* removed a part of the tiles, and having *broken it up,* taken away the laths or timber to which the tiles had been attached, they then had room to let down the afflicted man.

7. *Why doth this man thus speak blasphemies?* See this explained, Matt. ix. 3.

14. *Levi.* The same as Matthew; he appears to have been a Jew, though employed in the odious office of a taxgatherer. For an account of his call, see his Gospel, chap. ix. 9.

16. *Sinners.* The Gentiles or heathens are generally to be understood in the Gospels, for this was a term the Jews never applied to any of themselves. See the note on Matt. ix. 10.

17. *To repentance.* This is omitted by many manuscripts and versions, and many authorities approve of the omission.

21. *No man . . . seweth.* See Matt. ix. 16. "No man seweth a piece of unscoured cloth upon an old garment."

23. *Went through the corn fields.* See on Matt. xii. 1.

26. *The days of Abiathar the high priest.* It appears from 1 Sam. xxi. 1, which is the place referred to here, that Ahimelech was then high priest at Nob. And from 1 Sam. xxii. 20; xxiii. 6; and 1 Chron. xviii. 16, it appears that Abiathar was the son of Ahimelech. Some suggest that Abiathar was the *priest,* and Ahimelech or Abimelech the *high priest,* and thus endeavor to reconcile both the sacred historians. Others reconcile the accounts thus: Ahimelech was called *Ahimelech Abiathar, ab,* "father," understood; and Abiathar was called *Abiathar Ahimelech, ben,* "son," understood. Probably they both officiated in the high priesthood, and the name of the office was indifferently applied to either. *Shewbread.* See Matt. xii. 4.

27. *The Sabbath was made for man.* That he might have the seventh part of his whole time to devote to the purposes of bodily rest and spiritual exercises. And in these respects it is of infinite use to mankind. Where no Sabbath is observed, there disease, poverty, and profligacy generally prevail. Had we no Sabbath, we should soon have no religion.

28. *The Son of man is Lord.* See on Matt. xii. 7-8. Some have understood this as applying to men in general, and not to Christ. It was made for man, for his ease, comfort, and use, and to these purposes he is to apply it. But this is a very harsh, and at the same time a very lax, mode of interpretation; for it seems to say that a man may make what use he pleases of the Sabbath; and were this true, the moral obligation of the Sabbath would soon be annihilated. God ordained the Sabbath not only to be a type of that rest which remains for the people of God, but also to be a means of promoting the welfare of men in general.

CHAPTER 3

The man with the withered hand healed, 1-5. The Pharisees plot our Lord's destruction, 6. Christ withdraws, and is followed by a great multitude, 7-9. He heals many, and goes to a mountain to pray, 10-13. He ordains twelve disciples, and gives them power to preach and work miracles, 14-15. Their names, 16-19. The multitudes throng Him, and the scribes attribute His miracles to Beelzebub, 20-22. He vindicates himself by a parable, 23-27. Of the blasphemy against the Holy Ghost, 28-30. His mother and brethren send for Him,

31-32. And He takes occasion from this to show that they who do the will of God are to Him as His brother, sister, and mother, 33-35.

1. *A man there which had a withered hand.* See this explained on Matt. xii. 10, etc., and on Luke vi. 6, 10.

2. *They watched him.* "They maliciously watched Him." See on Luke xiv. 1.

4. *To do good . . . or . . . evil? to save life, or to kill?* It was a maxim with the Jews, as it should be with all men, that he who neglects to preserve life when it is in his power is to be reputed a murderer.

5. *With anger, being grieved for the hardness of their hearts.* These words are not found in any of the other Evangelists. For *hardness,* some manuscripts read "deadness"; and others, "blindness." Join all these together, and they will scarcely express the fullness of this people's wretchedness. By a long resistance to the *grace* and Spirit of God, their hearts had become *callous;* they were past feeling. By a long opposition to the light of God, they became dark in their understanding, were *blinded* by the deceitfulness of sin, and thus were past seeing. By a long continuance in the practice of every evil work, they were cut off from all union with God, the Fountain of spiritual life; and, becoming *dead* in trespasses and sins, they were incapable of any resurrection but through a miraculous power of God. *With anger.* The anger which our Lord felt proceeded from excessive grief, which was occasioned by their obstinate stupidity and blindness. *Whole as the other.* This is omitted by the best MSS. and versions.

6. *Herodians.* For an account of these, see the note on Matt. xvi. 1; xxii. 16.

7. *Galilee.* See Matt. iv. 13, 15.

8. *Tyre and Sidon.* See Matt. xi. 21. *When they had heard what great things he did, came unto him.* So if Christ be persecuted and abandoned by the wicked, there are a multitude of pious souls who earnestly seek and follow Him. He who labors for God will always find more than he loses, in the midst of all his contradictions and persecutions.

9. *A small ship.* It was doubtless a boat, which probably belonged to some of the disciples. Our Lord was at this time teaching by the Sea of Galilee. The word *ship* is utterly improper in many places of our translation, and tends to mislead the people.

10. *They pressed upon him.* "Rushed upon Him," through eagerness to have their spiritual and bodily maladies immediately removed. *Plagues.* Properly such "disorders" as were inflicted by the Lord. The word *plague* tends to mislead.

14. *He ordained twelve.* He "made" twelve. Here is nothing of what we call *ordaining.* Christ simply appointed them to be with Him, and that He might send them occasionally to preach.

15. *To have power to heal . . . and to cast out devils.* The business of a minister of Christ is: (1) to preach the gospel, (2) to be the physician of souls, and (3) to wage war with the devil and destroy his kingdom.

16. *Simon.* See on Matt. x. 2, etc.

17. *Sons of thunder.* Probably so named because of their zeal and power in preaching the

gospel. Some think that our Lord gave this appellative to the sons of Zebedee because of their desire to bring fire down from heaven, i.e., a storm of thunder and lightning, to overturn and consume a certain Samaritan village, the inhabitants of which would not receive their Master. See the account in Luke ix. 53-54. It was a very usual thing among the Jews to give to their rabbins surnames which signified some particular quality or excellence.

19. *Into an house.* As Christ was now returned to Capernaum, this was probably the house of Peter, mentioned in chap. ii. 1.

20. *Eat bread.* Had no time to take any necessary refreshment.

21. *His friends.* Or "relations." *They said, He is beside himself.* The enemies of Christ raised this report; and His relatives, probably thinking that it was true, went to confine Him. Let a Christian but neglect the care of his body for a time, in striving to enter in at the strait gate; let a minister of Christ but impair his health by his pastoral labors—presently "he is distracted"; he has "not the least conduct nor discretion." But let a man forget his soul, let him destroy his health by debaucheries, let him expose his life through ambition, and he may, notwithstanding, pass for a very prudent and sensible man!

22. *He hath Beelzebub.* See on Matt. xii. 24-26.

27-30. *No man.* For an explanation of these verses, and a definition of the sin against the Holy Ghost, see Matt. xii. 29-33.

29. *Eternal damnation.* Or "everlasting judgment." But instead, BL and two others read *hamartematos*, "sin." The *Codex Bezae*, two others, and some of the fathers read *hamartias*, a word of the same import. Grotius, Mill, and Bengel prefer this latter reading. *Sin* or *trespass* is the reading of the Coptic, Armenian, Gothic, Vulgate, and all the Itala but two. *Everlastinge trespas* is the translation in my old MSS. English Bible.

31. *His brethren and his mother.* Or rather, "his mother and his brethren." This is the arrangement of the best and most ancient MSS.; and this clause, *and thy sisters,* should be added to verse 32 on the authority of numerous manuscripts and some editions and marginal renderings. Griesbach has received this reading into the text.

CHAPTER 4

The parable of the sower, 1-9. Its interpretation, 10-20. The use we should make of the instructions we receive, 21-25. The parable of the progressively growing seed, 26-29. Of the mustard seed, 30-34. Christ and His disciples are overtaken by a storm, 35-38. He rebukes the wind and the sea, and produces fair weather, 39-41.

2. *He taught them many things by parables.* See every part of this parable of the sower explained on Matt. xiii. 1.

4. *The fowls.* "Of the air" is the common reading; but it should be omitted, on the authority of many MSS. and almost all the versions. Bengel and Griesbach have left it out of the text. It seems to have been inserted in Mark from Luke viii. 5.

10. *They that were about him.* None of the other Evangelists intimate that there were any besides the twelve with Him: but it appears there were several others present; and though they were not styled disciples, yet they appear to have seriously attended to His public and private instructions.

13. *Know ye not this parable?* The scope and design of which is so very obvious. *How then will ye know all parables?* Of which mode of teaching you should be perfect masters, in order that you may be able successfully to teach others. This verse is not found in any of the other Evangelists.

15. *These are they.* Probably our Lord here refers to the people to whom He had just now preached, and who, it is likely, did not profit by the word spoken.

21. *Is a candle . . . put under a bushel?* The design of My preaching is to enlighten men; My parables are not designed to hide the truth, but to make it more manifest.

22. *For there is nothing hid.* Probably our Lord means that all that had hitherto been secret relative to the salvation of a lost world, or only obscurely pointed out by types and sacrifices, shall now be uncovered and made plain by the everlasting gospel. See on Matt. v. 15; x. 26.

25. *He that hath.* See on Matt. xiii. 12.

26. *So is the kingdom of God.* This parable is mentioned only by Mark, a proof that Mark did not abridge Matthew.

27. *And should sleep, and rise night and day.* That is, he should sleep by night and rise by day, for so the words are obviously to be understood. *He knoweth not how.* How a plant grows is a mystery in nature which the wisest philosopher in the universe cannot fully explain.

28. *Bringeth forth . . . of herself.* By its own energy, without either the influence or industry of man. *The full corn.* "Full wheat"; the perfect, full-grown, or ripe head of grain. The kingdom of God, which is generated in the soul by the word of life, under the influence of the Holy Spirit, is first very small; there is only a *blade,* but this is full of promise, for a good blade shows there is a good seed at bottom, and that the soil in which it is sown is good also. *Then the ear*—the strong stalk grows up, and the ear is formed at the top. The faith and love of the believing soul increase abundantly; it is justified freely through the redemption that is in Christ. It has the *ear* which is shortly to be filled with the ripe grain, the outlines of the whole image of God. *Then the full corn.* The soul is purified from all unrighteousness; and, having escaped the corruption that is in the world, it is made a partaker of the divine nature, and is filled with all the fullness of God.

29. *He putteth in the sickle.* "He sendeth out the sickle," i.e., the reapers—the instrument, by a metonomy, being put for the persons who use it. This is a common figure. It has been supposed that our Lord intimates here that, as soon as a soul is made completely holy, it is taken into the kingdom of God. But certainly the parable does not say so. When the corn is ripe, it is reaped for the benefit of him who sowed it, for it can be of little or no use till it be ripe. So when a soul is saved from all sin, it is capable of being fully employed in the work of the Lord; it is then, and not

till then, fully fitted for the Master's use. God saves men to the uttermost, that they may here perfectly love Him and worthily magnify His name. To take them away the moment they are capable of doing this would be, so far, to deprive the world and the Church of the manifestation of the glory of His grace.

31. *A grain of mustard seed.* See on Matt. xiii. 31-32.

33. *With many such parables. Many* is omitted by L, sixteen others; the Syriac, both the Persic, one Arabic, Coptic, Armenian, Aethiopic, and two of the Itala. Mill approves of the omission, and Griesbach leaves it doubtful. It is probably an interpolation. The text reads better without it. *As they were able to hear.* Or to "understand," always suiting His teaching to the capacities of His hearers. I have always found that preacher most useful who could adapt his phrase to that of the people to whom he preached.

34. *He expounded all things to his disciples.* That they might be capable of instructing others. Outside hearers, those who do not come into close fellowship with the true disciples of Christ, have seldom more than a superficial knowledge of divine things. In the fellowship of the saints, where Jesus the Teacher is always to be found, everything is made plain—for the secret of the Lord is with them who fear Him.

35. *Let us pass over unto the other side.* Our Lord was now by the Sea of Galilee.

36. *They took him even as he was in the ship.* The construction of this verse is exceedingly difficult. The meaning appears to be this: The disciples sailed off with Him just as He was in the boat out of which He had been teaching the people, and they did not wait to provide any accommodations for the passage. This I believe to be the meaning of the inspired penman.

37. *A great storm of wind.* See on Matt. viii. 24.

39. *Peace, be still.* "Be silent! Be still!" There is uncommon majesty and authority in these words. Who but God could act thus? Perhaps this saving of His disciples in the boat might be designed to show forth that protection and deliverance which Christ will give to His followers, however violently they may be persecuted by earth or hell.

40. *Why are ye so fearful?* Having Me with you. *How is it that ye have no faith?* Having already had such proofs of My unlimited power and goodness.

41. *What manner of man is this?* They were astonished at such power proceeding from a Person who appeared to be only like one of themselves.

CHAPTER 5

The man possessed with a legion of demons cured, 1-20. He raises Jairus' daughter to life, and cures the woman who had an issue of blood, 21-43.

1. *The Gadarenes.* Some of the MSS. have *Gergasenes,* and some of them *Gerasenes.* The Gadarenes were included within the limits of the Gergasenes. Dr. Lightfoot supposes that, of the two demoniacs mentioned here, one was of Gadara, and consequently a heathen, the other

was a Gergesenian, and consequently a Jew; and he thinks that Mark and Luke mention the Gadarene demoniac because his case was a singular one, being the only heathen cured by our Lord except the daughter of the Syrophoenician woman.

2. *A man with an unclean spirit.* There are two mentioned by Matthew, who are termed "demoniacs."

3. *Who had his dwelling among the tombs.* See Matt. viii. 28.

4. *With fetters and chains.* His strength, it appears, was supernatural, no kind of chains being strong enough to confine him.

5. *Crying, and cutting himself with stones.* In this person's case we see a specimen of what Satan could do in all the wicked if God should permit him. But even the devil himself has his chain, and he who often binds others is always bound himself.

6. *Worshipped him.* "Did Him homage," compelled thereto by the power of God. How humiliating to Satan thus to be obliged to acknowledge the superiority of Christ!

7. *What have I to do with thee?* Or, "What is it to Thee and me?" or, "Why dost Thou trouble thyself with me?" See on chap. i. 24 and Matt. viii. 29, where the idiom and meaning are explained.

10. *Out of the country.* Strange that these accursed spirits should find it any mitigation of their misery to be permitted to exercise their malevolence in a particular district! But as this is supposed to have been a heathen district, therefore the demons might consider themselves in their own territories; and probably they could act there with less restraint than they could do in a country where the worship of God was established.

20. *Decapolis.* See on Matt. iv. 25.

23. *My little daughter.* "That little daughter of mine." The words express much tenderness and concern. Luke observes, chap. viii. 42, that she was his "only daughter," and was about "twelve years of age." *At the point of death.* "In the last extremity, the last gasp." See on Matt. ix. 18.

25. *A certain woman.* See Matt. ix. 20.

26. *Had suffered many things of many physicians . . . and was nothing bettered, but rather grew worse.* No person will wonder at this account when he considers the therapeutics of the Jewish physicians in reference to hemorrhages, especially of the kind with which this woman was afflicted. From some of these nostrums it is evident the woman could not be *bettered,* and from some others it is as evident that she must be made *worse;* and from all together it is indubitably certain that she must have *suffered many things*—and from the persons employed, the expense of the medicaments, and the number of years she was afflicted, as she was not a person of great opulence, it is most perfectly credible that she *spent all that she had.* She was therefore a fit patient for the Great Physician. It has been said, and the saying is a good one, "Man's extremity is God's opportunity." Never could the power and goodness of God be shown in a more difficult and distressful case. And now Jesus comes, and she is healed.

27. *Came in the press behind.* She had formed her resolution in faith; she executes it, notwithstanding her weakness, with courage; and now she finds it crowned with success.

31. *Thou seest the multitude thronging thee.* Many touch Jesus who are not healed by Him; the reason is, they do it not by faith, through a sense of their wants, and a conviction of His ability and willingness to save them. Faith conveys the virtue of Christ into the soul, and spiritual health is the immediate consequence of this received virtue.

34. *Be whole of thy plague.* Rather, "Continue whole," not, *Be whole,* for she was already healed. But this contains a promise, necessary to her encouragement, that her disorder should afflict her no more.

35. *Why troublest thou the Master?* These people seem to have had no other notion of our Lord than that of an eminent physician, who might be useful while there was life, but afterwards could do nothing.

36. *Jesus . . . saith.* These words were spoken by our Lord to the afflicted father, immediately on his hearing of the death of his child, to prevent that distress which he otherwise must have felt on finding that the case was now, humanly speaking, hopeless.

38. *He cometh.* But *they come* is the reading of a number of MSS. and several versions.

40. *The father and the mother.* Prudence required that they should be present, and be witnesses of the miracle. *And them that were with him.* That is, Peter, James, and John, v. 37. It is remarkable that our Lord gave a particular preference to these three disciples, beyond all the rest, on three very important occasions. They were present (1) at the Transfiguration, (2) at the raising of Jairus' daughter, and (3) at His agony in the Garden of Gethsemane.

43. *Something should be given her to eat.* For though He had employed an extraordinary power to bring her to life, He wills that she should be continued in existence by the use of ordinary means. "When the miraculous power of God is necessary, let it be resorted to; when it is not necessary, let the ordinary means be used." To act otherwise would be to tempt God.

CHAPTER 6

Our Lord's countrymen are astonished at His wisdom and mighty works, and are offended at Him, 1-4. He works few miracles there, because of their unbelief, 5-6. He sends forth His disciples by two and two to preach, etc., 7-11. They depart, preach, and work miracles, 12-13. Different opinions of Christ, 14-16. Account of the beheading of John Baptist, 17-29. The disciples return, and give an account of their mission, 30. Jesus departs with them to a place of privacy, and the people follow Him, 31-33. He has compassion on them, and miraculously feeds 5,000 with 5 loaves and 2 fishes, 34-44. He sends the disciples by sea to Bethsaida, and himself goes into a mountain to pray, 45-46. The disciples meet with a storm, and He comes to them walking upon the water, and appeases the winds and the sea, 47-52. They come into the land of Gennesaret, and He works many miracles, 53-56.

1. *And he went out from thence.* That is, from Capernaum.

3. *Is not this the carpenter?* Among the ancient Jews, every father was bound to do four things for his son: (1) to circumcise him, (2) to redeem him, (3) to teach him the law, (4) to teach him a trade. And this was founded on the following just maxim: "He who teaches not his son to do some work is as if he taught him robbery!" It is therefore likely that Joseph brought up our Lord to his own trade.

7. *By two and two.* That they might encourage and support each other, and to show that union among the ministers of the gospel is essential to the promotion of the cause of truth.

8. *A staff only.* It is likely He desired them to take only one with every two, merely for the purpose of carrying any part of their clothes on, when they should be obliged to strip them off by reason of the heat; for walking staves, or things of this kind, were forbidden—see Matt. x. 10. But probably no more is designed than simply to state that they must not wait to make any provision for the journey, but go off just as they were, leaving the provision necessary in the present case to the care of Divine Providence.

9. *Shod with sandals.* The sandal seems to have been similar to the Roman *solea,* which covered only the sole of the foot, and was fastened about the foot and ankle with straps. *Sandals* were originally a part of the woman's dress; ancient authors represent them as worn only by women. In Matt. x. 10 the disciples are commanded to take no *shoes,* which word is nearly of the same import with *sandals;* but, as our Lord intimates to them that they should be free from all useless incumbrances, that they might fulfill His orders with the utmost diligence and dispatch, so we may suppose that the sandal was a lighter kind of wear than the shoe; and indeed the word *sandal* might be properly translated a "light shoe."

11. *And whosoever shall not receive you.* "Whatsoever place will not receive you" is the reading of some versions. *Verily.* All this clause is omitted in several MSS. and versions. Mill and Beza approve of the omission, and Griesbach leaves it out of the text. It has probably been transferred here from Matt. x. 15.

13. *Anointed with oil many that were sick.* This is spoken of only here and in Jas. v. 14. This ceremony was in great use among the Jews, and in certain cases it might be profitable. But in the cases mentioned here, which were merely miraculous, it could avail no more of itself than the imposition of hands. It was used symbolically, as an emblem of that ease, comfort, and joy which they prayed God to impart to the sick.

15. *Or as one of the prophets.* Or is omitted by many MSS. Bengel, Wetstein, and Griesbach leave it out of the text. The omission of it mends the sense much.

19. *Would have killed.* "Sought to kill him." See the whole of this account, from v. 17 to v. 29, explained on Matt. xiv. 2-12.

21. *Lords.* Probably governors of particular districts. *High captains.* Literally, "chiefs" or "captains" over 1,000 men, military chiefs. *Chief estates.* Probably such as might be called nobles by title only, having no office civil or military; probably magistrates.

23. *Unto the half of my kingdom.* A noble price for a dance! This extravagance in favor of female dancers has the fullest scope in the East, even to the present day.

26. *For their sakes which sat with him.* Prob-

ably these persons joined in with the request, and were glad of this opportunity to get this light of Israel extinguished, he being a public reprover of all their vices.

30. *The apostles gathered themselves together.* For they went different ways before, by two and two, v. 7; and now they return and meet Christ at Capernaum.

31. *Rest a while.* Rest is necessary for those who labor, and a zealous preacher of the gospel will as often stand in need of it as a galley slave.

33. *The people.* Or "the multitudes." This is wanting in many MSS., but it seems necessary to make the sense clear. There is scarcely a verse in the whole New Testament that has suffered so much from transcribers as this verse. Amidst the abundance of various readings, one can scarcely tell what its original state was.

34. *Much people.* See this miracle explained on Matt. xiv. 14, etc.

41. *And blessed.* I think the word *God* should be inserted here, as in Matt. xiv. 19. See the note there. The food we receive from God is already blessed, and does not stand in need of being blessed by man; but God, who gives it, deserves our warmest thanksgivings, as frequently as we are called to partake of His bounty.

43. *Twelve baskets.* These were either the baskets used by the disciples, see Matt. xiv. 20, or baskets belonging to some of the multitude, who might have brought some with them to carry provisions, or other things necessary for the sick, whom they brought to Christ to be healed.

44. *Were about five thousand.* This miracle is mentioned by all the four Evangelists. It is one of the most astonishing that Christ has wrought. It is a miracle whch could not be counterfeited, and a full proof of the divinity of Christ.

45. *To the other side before unto Bethsaida.* John says, chap. vi. 17, to "Capernaum." It is probable our Lord ordered them to steer to one or other of these two places, which were about four miles distant, and on the same side of the Sea of Galilee.

47. *The ship was in the midst of the sea.* See all the parts of this wonderful transaction considered on Matt. xiv. 22-33.

49. *They supposed it had been a spirit.* That is, by whom the storm had been raised.

52. *Their heart was hardened.* See this explained, Matt. xiv. 33.

53. *The land of Gennesaret.* This country lay on the coast of the Sea of Galilee: it is described by Josephus as being exceedingly pleasant and fertile. It had its name of Gennesaret from *gen*, a "garden," and *sar*, a "prince," either because the king had a garden there or because of its great fertility.

54. *They knew him.* "They recollected Him," for He had before preached and wrought miracles in different places of the same country.

56. *Villages.* Probably small towns near cities. *Country.* Villages at a distance from cities and large public towns.

CHAPTER 7

The Pharisees find fault with the disciples for eating with unwashen hands, 1-5. Christ exposes their hypocrisy, and shows that they had made the word of God of no effect by their traditions, 6-13. He shows what things defile men, 14-16; and teaches His disciples in private that the sin of the heart alone, leading to vicious practices, defiles the man, 17-23. The account of the Syrophoenician woman, 24-30. He heals a man who was dumb, and had an impediment in his speech, 31-37.

1. *Came from Jerusalem.* Probably for the express purpose of disputing with Christ, that they might entangle Him in His talk.

2. *They found fault.* This is wanting in many MSS. and several versions; Mill and Bengel approve the omission, and Griesbach rejects the word. If the third and fourth verses be read in a parenthesis, the second and fifth verses will appear to be properly connected, without the above clause.

3. *Except they wash their hands.* The hand to the wrist—"Unless they wash the hand up to the wrist, *eat not*." This sort of washing was, and still continues to be, an act of religion in the Eastern countries. It is particularly commanded in the Koran, Surat, v, v. 7, "O believers, when ye wish to pray, wash your faces, and your hands up to the elbows—and your feet up to the ankles," which custom it is likely Mohammed borrowed from the Jews. The Jewish doctrine is this: "If a man neglect the washing, he shall be eradicated from this world."

4. *Except they wash.* Or "dip." But instead of the word in the text, the famous Codex Vaticanus (B), eight others, and Euthymius have *sprinkle.* However the Jews sometimes washed their hands previously to their eating; at other times they simply dipped or plunged them into the water. *Of cups.* Any kind of earthen vessels. *Pots.* "Of measures," a measure for liquids, formed from the Latin *sextarius,* equal to a pint and a half English. *Of brasen vessels.* These, if polluted, were only to be washed or passed through the fire, whereas the earthen vessels were to be broken. *And of tables.* "Beds, couches." This is wanting in some MSS.

8. *Washing of pots and cups.* This whole clause is wanting in some MSS. and versions.

9. *Full well.* A strong irony. How noble is your conduct! From conscientious attachment to your own traditions you have annihilated the commandments of God! *That ye may keep.* God's law was nothing to these men in comparison of their own; hear a case in point. "Rabba said, How foolish are most men! They observe the precepts of the divine law, and neglect the statutes of the rabbins!"

10. *For Moses said.* See all these verses, from this to the twenty-third, explained on Matt. xv. 3-20.

14. *When he had called all the people.* But instead of *all*, "again" is the reading of some MSS. and versions. Mill and Griesbach approve of this reading.

19. *Purging all meats.* For what is separated from the different aliments taken into the stomach, and thrown out of the body, is the innutritious parts of all the meats that are eaten; and thus they are purged, nothing being left behind but what is proper for the support of the body.

24. *Into the borders of Tyre and Sidon.* Or "into the country between Tyre and Sidon."

25. *A certain woman.* See this account of the Syrophoenician woman explained at large, Matt. xv. 21-28.

26. *The woman was a Greek.* All heathen or idolaters were called *Greeks* by the Jews. Jews and Greeks divided the whole world at this period.

30. *Laid upon the bed.* The demon having tormented her so that her bodily strength was exhausted, and she was now laid upon the couch to take a little rest.

32. *They bring unto him one that was deaf, and had an impediment in his speech.* Though from the *letter* of the text, it does not appear that this man was absolutely deprived of speech (for *mogilalos* literally signifies one that cannot speak plainly, a stammerer), yet it is certain also that the word means a dumb person; and it is likely that the person in question was dumb, because he was deaf; and it is generally found that he who is totally deaf is dumb also.

33. *And he spit, and touched his tongue.* This place is exceedingly difficult. There is scarcely an action of our Lord's life but one can see an evident reason for, except this. Various interpretations are given of it—none of them satisfies my mind. After all, it is possible that what is attributed here to Christ belongs to the person who was cured. I will give my sense of the place in a short paraphrase: And Jesus *took him aside from the multitude: and* (the deaf man) *put his fingers into his ears,* intimating thereby to Christ that they were so stopped that he could not hear; *and having spat out,* that there might be nothing remaining in his mouth to offend the sight when Christ should look at his tongue, *he touched his tongue,* showing to Christ that it was so bound that he could not speak; *and he looked up to heaven,* as if to implore assistance from above; *and he groaned,* being distressed because of his present affliction, and thus implored relief. For, not being able to *speak,* he could only *groan* and *look up,* expressing by these signs, as well as he could, his afflicted state, and the desire he had to be relieved. Then Jesus, having compassion upon him, *said, Be opened: and immediately his ears were opened,* so that he could hear distinctly; and the impediment to his speaking was removed, so that *he spake properly.* The original will admit of this interpretation; and this, I am inclined to believe, is the true meaning of this otherwise (to me and many others) unaccountable passage.

35. *He spake plain.* "Distinctly, without stammering."

36. *Tell no man.* See on Matt. viii. 4. This miracle is not mentioned by any other of the Evangelists—another proof that Mark did not abridge Matthew.

37. *He hath done all things well.* This has been, and ever will be, true of every part of our Lord's conduct. In creation, providence, and redemption He hath done all things well.

CHAPTER 8

Asks His disciples what the public thought of Him, 27-30. Acknowledges himself to be the Christ, and that He must suffer, 31-33. And shows that all His genuine disciples must take up their cross, suffer in His cause, and confess Him before men, 34-38.

1. *The multitude being very great.* Or rather, "There was again a great multitude." Instead of *very great,* I read *again a great,* which is the reading of many MSS. and versions. There had been such a multitude gathered together once before, who were fed in the same way. See chap. vi. 34, etc.

2. *Have nothing to eat.* If they had brought any provisions with them, they were now entirely expended, and they stood in immediate need of a supply.

3. *For divers of them came from far.* And they could not possibly reach their respective homes without perishing, unless they got food.

7. *And they had a few small fishes.* This is not noticed in the parallel place, Matt. xv. 36.

10. *Dalmanutha.* See the note on Matt. xv. 39.

12. *And he sighed deeply in his spirit.* Or "having deeply groaned"—so the word properly means. He was exceedingly affected at their obstinacy and hardness of heart. See Matt. xvi. 1-4.

14. *Now the disciples had forgotten to take bread.* See all this, to v. 21, explained at large on Matt. xvi. 4-12.

23. *And he took the blind man by the hand.* Giving him proof of His readiness to help him, and thus preparing him for the cure which He was to work. *Led him out of the town.* Thus showing the inhabitants that He considered them unworthy of having another miracle wrought among them. *When he had spit on his eyes.* There is a similar transaction to this mentioned in John ix. 6. It is likely this was done merely to separate the eyelids, as in certain cases of blindness they are found always gummed together. It required a miracle to restore the sight, and this was done in consequence of Christ having laid His hands upon the blind man. It required no miracle to separate the eyelids, and therefore natural means only were employed—this was done by rubbing them with spittle, but whether by Christ or by the blind man is not absolutely certain. See on chap. vii. 33.

24. *I see men as trees, walking.* His sight was so imperfect that he could not distinguish between men and trees, only by the motion of the former.

25. *And saw every man clearly.* Our Lord could have restored this man to sight in a moment; but He chose to do it in the way mentioned in the text, to show that He is a Sovereign of His own graces; and to point out that, however insignificant means may appear when He chooses to work by them; and that, however small the first manifestations of mercy may be, they are nevertheless the beginnings of the fullness of the blessings of the gospel of peace.

26. *He sent him away to his house.* So it appears that this person did not belong to Bethsaida, for in going to his house he was not to enter into the village. This miracle is not mentioned by any other of the Evangelists. It affords another proof that Mark did not abridge Matthew's Gospel.

27. *And Jesus went out.* See on Matt. xvi. 13-20.

32. *And he spake that saying.* Concerning the certainty and necessity of His sufferings—*openly*: "with great plainness, confidence, or emphasis," so that the disciples now began fully to understand Him. This is an additional observation of Mark. For Peter's reproof, see on Matt. xvi. 22, etc.

34. *Whosoever will come after me.* It seems that Christ formed, on the proselytism of the Jews, the principal qualities which He required in the proselytes of His covenant. The *first* condition of proselytism among the Jews was that he that came to embrace their religion should come voluntarily and that neither force nor influence should be employed in this business. This is also the first condition required by Jesus Christ, and which He considers as the foundation of all the rest: "If a man is willing to come after Me." The *second* condition required in the Jewish proselyte was that he should perfectly renounce all his prejudices, his errors, his idolatry, and everything that concerned his false religion; and that he should entirely separate himself from his most intimate friends and acquaintances. It was on this ground that the Jews called proselytism a "new birth," and proselytes "newborn" and "new men"; and our Lord requires men to be born again, not only of water, but by the Holy Ghost. See John iii. 5. All this our Lord includes in this word, *Let him deny himself.* To this the following scriptures refer: Matt. x. 33; John iii. 3, 5; 2 Cor. v. 17. The *third* condition on which a person was admitted into the Jewish church as a proselyte was that he should submit to the yoke of the Jewish law and bear patiently the inconveniences and sufferings with which a profession of the Mosiac religion might be accompanied. Christ requires the same condition; but, instead of the ycke of the law, He brings in His own doctrine, which He calls His yoke, Matt. xi. 29; and His *cross*, the *taking up* of which not only implies a bold profession of Christ crucified, but also a cheerful submitting to all the sufferings and persecutions to which He might be exposed, and even to death itself. The *fourth* condition was that he should solemnly engage to continue in the Jewish religion, faithful even unto death. This condition Christ also requires; and it is comprised in this word, *Let him . . . follow me.*

35. *For whosoever will save his life.* On this and the following verses, see Matt. xvi. 24, etc.

38. *Whosoever therefore shall be ashamed of me.* Our Lord hints here at one of the principal reasons of the incredulity of the Jews—they saw nothing in the person of Jesus Christ which corresponded to the pompous notions which they had formed of the Messiah. *And of my words.* This was another subject of offense to the Jews: the doctrine of the Cross must be believed; a suffering Messiah must be acknowledged; and poverty and affliction must be borne; and death, perhaps, suffered in consequence of becoming His disciples.

CHAPTER 9

The transfiguration of Christ, and the discourse occasioned by it, 1-13. He casts out a dumb spirit which His disciples could not, 14-29. He foretells His death, 30-32. The disciples dispute about supremacy, and Christ corrects them, 33-37. Of the person who cast out demons in Christ's name but did not follow Him, 38-40. Every kind office done to the disciples of Christ shall be rewarded by Him, and all injuries done to them shall be punished, 41-42. The necessity of mortification and self-denial, 43-48. Of the salting of sacrifices, 49; and the necessity of having union among the disciples of Christ, 50.

1. *There be some.* This verse properly belongs to the preceding chapter, and to the preceding discourse. It is in this connection in Matt. xvi. 27-28. See the notes there.

2. *And after six days Jesus taketh with him Peter.* For a full account of the nature and design of the Transfiguration, see on Matt. xvii. 1, etc. *An high mountain.* I have conjectured, Matt. xvii. 1, that this was one of the mountains of Galilee; some say Hermon, some Tabor.

12. *And how it is written.* Rather, "as also it is written."

15. *Were greatly amazed.* Probably because He came so unexpectedly.

17. *A dumb spirit.* That is, a demon who afflicted those in whom it dwelt with an in capacity of speaking.

18. *Pineth away.* By these continual torments; so he was not only deaf and dumb, but sorely tortured besides.

20. *When he saw him . . . the spirit tare him; and he fell on the ground,* etc. When this demon saw Jesus, he had great rage, knowing that his time was short; and hence the extraordinary convulsions mentioned above.

22. *If thou canst do any thing.* I have already tried Thy disciples, and find they can do nothing in this case; but if *thou* hast any power, in mercy use it in our behalf.

23. *If thou canst believe.* This was an answer to the inquiry above. I can furnish a sufficiency of power, if *you* can but bring faith to receive it. Why are not our souls completely healed? Why is not every demon cast out? Why are not pride, self-will, love of the world, lust, anger, peevishness, with all the other bad tempers and dispositions which constitute the mind of Satan, entirely destroyed? Alas! it is because we do not *believe.* Jesus is able; more, Jesus is willing; but we are not willing to give up our idols; we give not credence to His word; therefore has sin a being in us, and dominion over us.

24. *Lord, I believe.* The word *Lord* is omitted by many MSS. and versions. Griesbach leaves it out. The omission, I think, is proper, because it is evident the man did not know our Lord, and therefore could not be expected to accost Him with a title expressive of that authority which he doubted whether He possessed, unless we grant that he used the word *kyrie* after the Roman custom, for "Sir." *Help thou mine unbelief.* That is, assist me against it. Give me a power to believe.

25. *I charge thee.* Considerable emphasis should be laid on the pronoun: You resisted the command of My disciples; now *I* command you to come out.

29. *Prayer and Fasting.* See on Matt. xvii. 21. This case is related by both Matthew and Luke, but it is greatly amplified in Mark's account, and many new circumstances related—another proof that Mark did not abridge Matthew.

30. *They . . . passed through Galilee.* See on Matt. xvii. 22-27.

32. *But they understood not.* It does not

appear likely, from Matthew's account, that three of the disciples, Peter, James, and John, could be ignorant of the reasons of Christ's death and resurrection, after the Transfiguration. On the contrary, from that time they must have had at least a general understanding of this important subject. But the other nine might have been ignorant of this matter, who were not present at the Transfiguration; probably it is of these that the Evangelist speaks here.

33. *And being in the house.* That is, Peter's house, where He ordinarily lodged.

34. *Who should be the greatest.* See on Matt. xviii. 1-5.

38. *We saw one casting out devils in thy name.* It can scarcely be supposed that a man who knew nothing of Christ, or who was only a common exorcist, could be able to work a miracle in Christ's name. We may therefore safely imagine that this was either one of John the Baptist's disciples, who, at his master's command, had believed in Jesus, or one of the seventy whom Christ had sent out, Luke x. 1-7, who, after he had fulfilled his commission, had retired from accompanying the other disciples. But as he still held fast his faith in Christ and walked in good conscience, the influence of his Master still continued with him, so that he could cast out demons as well as the other disciples. *We forbad him.* I do not see that we have any right to attribute any other motive to John than that which he himself owns—*because he followeth not us*—because he did not attach himself constantly to Thee, as we do, we thought he could not be in a proper spirit.

39. *Forbid him not.* If you meet him again, let him go on quietly in the work in which God owns him. If he were not of God, the demons would not be subject to him, and his work could not prosper. A spirit of bigotry has little countenance from these passages. There are some who are so outrageously wedded to their own creed and religious system that they would rather let sinners perish than suffer those who differ from them to become the instruments of their salvation.

40. *He that is not against us is on our part.* Or rather, "Whosoever is not against you is for you."

There is a parallel case to this mentioned in Num. xi. 26-29. The reader will easily observe that Joshua and John were of the same bigoted spirit, and that Jesus and Moses acted from the spirit of candor and benevolence.

43. *The fire that never shall be quenched.* That is, "the inextinguishable fire." The same clause in v. 45 is omitted in BCL, seven others, Syriac, later Persic, Coptic, and one Itala. "Eternal fire" is the expression of Matthew.

44. *Where their worm dieth not.* The bitter reflection, "I might have avoided sin, but I did not; I might have been saved, but I would not," must be equal to ten thousand tormentors. What intolerable anguish must this produce in a damned soul! *Their worm.* It seems everyone has his *worm*, his peculiar remorse for the evils he did, and for the grace he rejected; while the *fire*, the state of excruciating torment, is common to all. Reader! may the living God save you from this *worm* and from this *fire*! *The fire is not quenched.* The state of punishment is continual; there is no respite, alleviation, nor end!

49. *For every one shall be salted with fire.* Every one of those who shall live and die in sin; but there is great difficulty in this verse. The Codex Bezae and some other MSS. have omitted the first clause; and several MSS. keep the first and omit the last clause—*and every sacrifice shall be salted with salt.* Some take the whole in a good sense, as referring to the influence of the Spirit of God in the hearts of believers, which shall answer the same end to the soul, in preserving it from the contagion that is in the world, as salt did in the sacrifices offered to God to preserve them from putrefaction. Old Trapp's note on the place pleases me as much as any I have seen: "The *Spirit*, as *salt*, must dry up those bad *humors* in us which breed the never-dying worm; and, as fire, must waste our corruptions, which else will carry us on to the unquenchable fire." Perhaps the whole is an allusion to the purification of vessels, and especially such metallic vessels as were employed in the service of the sanctuary. Probably the following may be considered as a parallel text: "Every thing that may abide the fire, ye shall make it go through the fire, and it shall be clean . . . and all that abideth not the fire ye shall make go through the water," Num. xxxi. 23. You disciples are the Lord's sacrifice; you shall go through much tribulation, in order to enter into My kingdom. But you are salted, you are influenced by the Spirit of God, and are immortal till your work is done; and should you be offered up, martyred, this shall be a means of establishing more fully the glad tidings of the Kingdom. And this Spirit shall preserve all who believe on Me from the corruption of sin, and from eternal perdition. That converts to God are represented as His offering, see Isa. lxvi. 20, the very place which our Lord appears to have here in view.

50. *Have salt in yourselves.* See that you have at all times the preserving principle of divine grace in your hearts, and give that proof of it which will satisfy your own minds and convince or silence the world. Live in brotherly kindness and peace with each other.

CHAPTER 10

The Pharisees question our Lord concerning divorce, 1-12. Little children are brought to Him, 13-16. The person who inquired how he might inherit eternal life, 17-22. How difficult it is for a rich man to be saved, 23-27. What they shall receive who have left all for Christ and His gospel, 28-31. He foretells His death, 32-34. James and John desire places of preeminence in Christ's kingdom, 35-41. Christ shows them the necessity of humility, 42-45. Blind Bartimaeus healed, 46-52.

1. *He arose.* "He departed thence." Many transactions took place between those mentioned in the preceding chapter and these that follow, which are omitted by Matthew and Mark; but they are related by both Luke and John.

2. *Is it lawful for a man to put away his wife?* See this question about divorce largely explained on Matt. xix. 3-12.

12. *And if a woman shall put away her husband.* From this it appears that in some cases the wife assumed the very same right of divorcing her husband that the husband had of divorcing his wife; and yet this is not recorded anywhere in the Jewish laws, as far as I can find, that the women had such a right.

13. *And they brought young children.* See on Matt. xix. 13-15.

16. *And he took them up in his arms.* Jesus Christ loves little children, and they are objects of His most peculiar care. *And blessed them.* Then, though little children, they were capable of receiving Christ's blessing. If Christ embraced them, why should not His Church embrace them?

17. *There came one running.* See the case of this rich young man largely explained on Matt. xix. 16, etc.

21. *Then Jesus beholding him.* "Looking earnestly" or "affectionately upon him," *loved him,* because of his youth, his earnestness, and his sincerity. *One thing thou lackest.* What was that? A heart disengaged from the world, and a complete renunciation of it and its concerns, that he might become a proper and successful laborer in the Lord's vineyard.

22. *And he was sad at that saying.* This young man had perhaps been a saint, and an eminent apostle, had he been poor! From this, and a multitude of other cases, we may learn that it is oftentimes a misfortune to be rich. But who is aware of this?—and who believes it?

29. *And the gospel's.* Read, "for the sake of the gospel," on the authority of most MSS. and almost all the versions.

30. *In this time.* "In this very time." Though Jews and Gentiles have conspired together to destroy both Me and you, My providence shall so work that nothing shall be lacking while anything is necessary. Those who have left all for the sake of Christ do find, among genuine Christians, spiritual relatives, which are as dear to them as fathers, mothers, etc. Yet they have the promise of *receiving an hundredfold* often literally fulfilled; for wherever a Christian travels among Christians, the shelter of their houses and the product of their lands are at his service as far as they are requisite. *With persecutions.* For while you meet with nothing but kindness from true Christians, you shall be despised, and often afflicted, by those who are enemies to God and goodness. But, for your comfort, you shall have in *the world to come,* "the coming world" (that world which is on its way to meet you), *eternal life.*

32. *And he took again the twelve.* Or thus: "For having again taken the twelve." I translate *kai* "for," which signification it often bears; see Luke i. 22; John xii. 35, and elsewhere. This gives the reason of the wonder and fear of the disciples, for He *began to tell them,* on the way, what was to befall Him.

35. *And James and John . . . come unto him.* The request here mentioned, Matthew says, chap. xx. 20, was made by Salome, their mother. The two places may be easily reconciled thus: The mother introduced them, and made the request as if from herself; Jesus, knowing whence it had come, immediately addressed himself to James and John, who were standing by; and the mother is no further concerned in the business.

38. *And be baptized.* "Or be baptized." Instead of *and,* "or" is the reading of many versions and MSS.

41. *When the ten heard it.* See Matt. xx. 24-28.

46. *Blind Bartimaeus. Bar* in Syriac signifies "son." It appears that he was thus named because Timeus, *Talmeus* or *Talmai,* was the name of his father, and thus the son would be called Bar-talmeus, or *Bartholomew.* It was because he was the most remarkable that this Evangelist mentions him by name, as a person probably well-known in those parts.

50. *And he, casting away his garment.* He cast off his outward covering, a blanket, or loose piece of cloth, the usual upper garment of an Asiatic mendicant, which kept him from the inclemency of the weather, that he might have nothing to hinder him from getting speedily to Christ. If every penitent were as ready to throw aside his self-righteousness and sinful encumbrances as this blind man was to throw aside his garment, we should have fewer delays in conversions than we now have.

52. *Followed Jesus in the way.* Instead of *Jesus,* several eminent critics read *him.*

CHAPTER 11

Christ rides triumphantly into Jerusalem, 1-11. The barren fig tree cursed, 12-14. He cleanses the Temple, 15-17. The scribes and chief priests are enraged, 18. Reflections on the withered fig tree, 19-23. Directions concerning prayer and forgiveness, 24-26. The chief priests, etc., question Him by what authority He did His works, 27-28. He answers, and confounds them, 29-33.

1. *He sendeth forth two of his disciples.* This was done but a few days before the Passover. See our Lord's entry into Jerusalem illustrated, on Matt. xxi. 1-17.

2. *Whereon never man sat.* No animal was allowed to be employed in sacred uses, even among the heathen, that had previously been used for any domestic or agricultural purpose; and those which had never been yoked were considered as sacred.

3. *And straightway he will send him hither.* From the text I think it is exceedingly plain that our Lord did not beg, but borrow, the colt; therefore the latter clause of this verse should be understood as the promise of *returning* him. Is not the proper translation the following? "And if anyone say to you, Why do ye this? Say, The Lord hath need of him, and will speedily send him back hither."

6. *And they let them go.* Having a full assurance that the beast should be safely and speedily restored.

10. *In the name of the Lord.* Omitted by some MSS. and several versions. *Hosanna in the highest.* See on Matt. xxi. 9.

11. *When he had looked round about upon all things.* He examined everything, to see if the matters pertaining to the divine worship were properly conducted, to see that nothing was wanting, nothing superfluous. *And now the eventide was come.* The time in which He usually left Jerusalem to go to Bethany.

13. *For the time of figs was not yet.* Rather, "For it was not the season of gathering figs yet." When our Lord saw this fig tree by the wayside, apparently flourishing, he went to it to gather some of the figs. Being on the wayside, it was not private but public property, and any traveller had an equal right to its fruit. As it was not as yet the time for gathering in the fruits, and yet about the time when they were

ready to be gathered, our Lord with propriety expected to find some. This tree was intended to point out the state of the Jewish people. (1) They made a profession of the true religion. (2) They considered themselves the peculiar people of God, and despised and reprobated all others. (3) They were only hypocrites, having nothing of religion but the profession—*leaves,* and no *fruit.* Our Lord's conduct towards this tree is to be considered as emblematical of the treatment and final perdition which was to come upon this hypocritical and ungodly nation. (1) It was a proper time for them to have borne fruit. Jesus had been preaching the doctrine of repentance and salvation among them for more than three years; the choicest influences of Heaven had descended upon them; and everything was done in this vineyard that ought to be done, in order to make it fruitful. (2) The time was now at hand in which God would require fruit, good fruit; and, if it did not produce such, the tree should be hewn down by the Roman axe. Therefore (1) The *tree* is properly the Jewish nation; (2) Christ's *curse,* the sentence of destruction which had now gone out against it; and (3) *Its withering away,* the final and total ruin of the Jewish state by the Romans. His cursing the fig tree was not occasioned by any resentment at being disappointed at not finding fruit on it, but to point out unto His disciples the wrath which was coming upon a people who had now nearly filled up the measure of their iniquity.

15. *And they come.* This was the next day after our Lord's triumphant entry into Jerusalem; for on the evening of that day He went to Bethany and lodged there, v. 11, and returned the next morning to Jerusalem.

19. *He went out of the city.* To go to Bethany.

22. *Have faith in God.* "Have the faith of God," i.e., Have strong faith, or the strongest faith, for thus the Hebrews expressed the superlative degree.

25. *When ye stand praying.* This expression may mean no more than, "When ye are disposed or have a mind, to pray," i.e., whenever you perform that duty. But the Pharisees loved to pray standing, that they might be seen of men.

26. The verse is wanting in some MSS. and editions.

27-33. See on Matt. xxi. 23-27.

32. *They feared the people.* Or rather, "We fear," etc.

CHAPTER 12

The parable of the vineyard let out to wicked husbandmen, 1-12. The Pharisees and Herodians question Him about paying tribute to Caesar, 13-17. The Sadducees question Him about the resurrection, 18-27. A scribe questions Him concerning the chief commandment of the law, 28-34. Christ asks the scribes why the Messiah is called David's Son, 35-37. He warns His disciples against the scribes, 38-40. Of the widow that cast two mites into the treasury, 41-44.

1. *A certain man planted a vineyard.* See this parable explained, Matt. xxi. 33-41.

4. *At him they cast stones, and wounded him in the head.* Or rather, "they made short work of it." We have followed the Vulgate in translating the original, *wounded him in the head,* in which signification, I believe, the word is found in no Greek writer. [It] signifies to "sum up, to comprise," and is used in this sense by Paul, Rom. xiii. 9.

9. *And will give the vineyard unto others.* I will give it into the care of new vinedressers, the Evangelists and apostles. And under their ministry, multitudes were brought to God before the destruction of Jerusalem.

13. *And they send unto him.* See this, and to v. 17, largely explained on Matt. xxii. 15-22.

18. See this question, concerning the resurrection, explained in detail on Matt. xxii. 23-32.

23. *When they shall rise.* This clause is wanting in several MSS.

27. *But the God of the living.* God is left out by many MSS.

30. *Thou shalt love the Lord.* On the nature and properties of the love of God and man, and the way in which this commandment is fulfilled, see the notes on Matt. xxii. 37, etc.

32. *And the scribe said.* The answer of the scribe, contained in verses 32-34, is not found in either Matthew or Luke. This is another proof against Mark's supposed abridgment.

34. *Thou art not far from the kingdom of God.* This scribe appears to have been a prudent, sensible, and pious man; almost a Christian—so near the kingdom of God that he might have easily stepped in.

35. *How say the scribes?* See Matt. xxii. 41, etc.

37. *The common people heard him gladly.* And doubtless many of them were brought to believe and receive the truth. By the comparatively poor the gospel is still best received.

38. *Beware of the scribes.* See on Matt. xxiii. 1, etc.

41. *Cast money into the treasury.* It is worthy of observation that the money put into the treasury, even by the rich, is termed by the Evangelist "brass money," probably that species of small brass coin which was called *prutah* among the Jews, two of which make a farthing. We call this *mite,* from the French, *miete,* which signifies a crumb or very small morsel. The *prutah* was the smallest coin in use among the Jews, and there is a canon among the rabbins that no person shall put less than two *prutahs* into the treasury. This poor widow would not give less, and her poverty prevented her from giving more. And whereas it is said that *many . . . rich* persons *cast in much* (many), this may only refer to the number of the *prutahs* which they threw in, and not to the value. What opinion should we form of a rich man who, in a collection for a public charity, threw in only a handful of halfpence? The whole of this account is lacking in Matthew —another proof that Mark did not abridge him.

CHAPTER 13

Jesus predicts the destruction of the Temple, 1-2. His disciples inquire when this shall be, and what previous sign there shall be of this calamity, 3-4; which questions He answers very solemnly and minutely, 5-27; illustrates the whole by a parable, 28-29; asserts the absolute certainty of the events, 30-31; shows that the precise time cannot be known by man, 32; and inculcates the necessity of watchfulness and prayer, 33-37.

1. *See what manner of stones.* Josephus says (*Ant.* b. xv, c. xi) "that these stones were white and strong, fifty feet long, twenty-four broad, and sixteen in thickness." If this account can

be relied on, well might the disciples be struck with wonder at such a superb edifice, and formed by such immense stones! The principal contents of this chapter are largely explained in the notes on Matthew xxiv.

9. *Councils.* "Sanhedrins." The grand Sanhedrin consisted of seventy-two elders (this was the national council of state), and the small Sanhedrins, which were composed of twenty-three counsellors. *Synagogues.* Courts of justice for villages, etc., consisting of three magistrates, chosen out of the principal directors of the synagogue in that place. *Rulers.* Or "governors." The Roman deputies, such as Pontius Pilate. *Kings.* The tetrarchs of Judea and Galilee, who bore this name.

11. *Neither do ye premeditate.* This is wanting in some MSS. and versions. On this verse see Matt. x. 19.

15. *House top.* See on Matt. xxiv. 17.

30. *This generation.* "This very race of men." It is certain that this word has two meanings in the Scriptures: that given in the text, and that above. *Generation* signifies a period of a certain number of years, sometimes more, sometimes less. In Deut. i. 35 and ii. 14, Moses uses the word to point out a term of thirty-eight years, which was precisely the number in the present case; for Jerusalem was destroyed about thirty-eight years after our Lord delivered this prediction. But as there are other events in this chapter which certainly look beyond the destruction of Jerusalem, and which were to take place before the Jews should cease to be a distinct people, I should therefore prefer the translation given above. See Matt. xxiv. 34.

34. *Left his house.* "Family." Our blessed Lord and Master, when He ascended to heaven, commanded His servants to be faithful and watchful.

35. *Watch ye therefore.* The more the master is expected, the more diligent ought the servants to be in working, watching, and keeping themselves in readiness.

36. *He find you sleeping.* A porter asleep exposes the house to be robbed, and well deserves punishment.

CHAPTER 14

The Jews conspire against Christ, 1-2. He is anointed in the house of Simon the leper, 3-9. Judas Iscariot sells Him to the chief priests for thirty pieces of money, 10-11. He orders His disciples to prepare the Passover, 12-16. Predicts His approaching death, 17-21. Institutes the holy Eucharist, 22-26. Foretells the unfaithfulness of His disciples in general, 27-28, and Peter's denial, 29-31. His agony in the garden, 32-36. The disciples overcome by sleep, 37-42. Judas comes with a mob from the chief priests, and betrays Him with a kiss; they seize Him, 43-49. The disciples flee, 50. A young man following, and about to be apprehended, makes his escape, 51-52. Jesus is brought before the chief priests, and Peter follows at a distance, 53-54. He is examined, insulted, and abused, and condemned on false evidence, 55-65. Peter thrice denies Him, reflects on his wickedness, and repents of his sin, 66-72.

1. *Unleavened bread.* After they began to eat unleavened bread; see on Matt. xxvi. 2.

3. *Spikenard.* Or "nard." An Indian plant, whose root is very small and slender. It puts forth a long and small stalk, and has several ears or spikes even with the ground, which has given it the name of spikenard. *Very precious.* Or rather, "unadulterated." Theophylact gives this interpretation of the passage: "Unadulterated nard, and prepared with fidelity."

8. *To anoint my body to the burying.* "Against," or "in reference to," its embalmment, thus pointing out My death and the embalmment of My body, for the bodies of persons of distinction were wrapped up in aromatics to preserve them from putrefaction.

9. *For a memorial of her.* See on Matt. xxvi. 13.

11. *They were glad.* The joy that arises from the opportunity of murdering an innocent person must be completely infernal.

14. *Say ye to the good man of the house.* "Say ye to the master of the house."

15. *Furnished.* "Spread" with carpets—so this word is often used. But it may also signify the couches on which the guests reclined when eating. It does not appear that the Jews ate the Passover now, as their fathers did formerly, standing, with their shoes on and their staves in their hands.

19. *And another said, Is it I?* This clause is wanting in several MSS. and versions.

20. *That dippeth with me in the dish.* In the East persons never eat together from one dish, except when a strong attachment subsists between two or more persons of the same caste; in such a case one invites another to come and sit by him and eat from the same dish. This custom seems to have existed among the Jews; and the sacred historian mentions this notice of our Lord's, *It is one of the twelve, that dippeth with me in the dish,* to mark more strongly the perfidy of the character of Judas.

21. *Goeth.* That is, to die.

30. *That . . . thou.* Su is added by most MSS. and versions. It adds much to the energy of the passage, every word of which is deeply emphatical. "Verily I say unto you that you, this day, in this very night, before the cock shall crow twice, you will deny Me."

36. *Abba, Father.* This Syriac word, which intimates filial affection and respect and parental tenderness, seems to have been used by our blessed Lord, merely considered as man, to show His complete submission to His Father's will, and the tender affection which He was conscious His Father had for Him. *Abba,* Syriac, is here joined to *pater,* Greek, both signifying "father"; so Paul, Rom. viii. 15; Gal. iv. 6. The reason is that from the time in which the Jews became conversant with the Greek language, by means of the Septuagint version and their commerce with the Roman and Greek provinces, they often intermingled Greek and Roman words with their own language.

51. *A certain young man.* Probably raised from his sleep by the noise which the rabble made who came to apprehend Jesus, having wrapped the sheet or some of the bedclothing about him, became thereby the more conspicuous. On his appearing, he was seized; but as they had no way of holding him but only by the cloth which was wrapped round him, he disengaged himself from that, and so escaped out of their hands. This circumstance is not related by any other of the Evangelists.

54. *Peter followed.* On Peter's denial, see Matt. xxvi. 57, etc. *At the fire.* Literally, "at the light," i.e., a fire that cast considerable light,

in consequence of which the maidservant was the better able to distinguish him; see v. 67.

72. *And when he thought thereon, he wept.* Or "he fell a weeping."

CHAPTER 15

Jesus is brought before Pilate, examined, and accused, but makes no answer, 1-5. The multitude clamor for the release of Barabbas, and the crucifixion of Christ, 6-14. Pilate consents, and He is led away, mocked, insulted, and nailed to the Cross, 15-26. Two thieves are crucified with Him, 27-28. While hanging on the Cross, He is mocked and insulted, 29-32. The miraculous darkness and our Lord's death, 33-37. The rending of the veil, and the confession of the centurion, 38-39. Several women attend, and behold His death, 40-41. Joseph of Arimathaea begs the body from Pilate, and buries it, 42-46. Mary Magdalene and Mary the mother of Joses note the place of His burial, 47.

1. *In the morning.* See Matt. xxvii. 1, etc.

8. *The multitude crying aloud.* The word itself strongly marks the vociferations or, to come nearer the original word, the bellowing of the multitude. It signifies, properly, a loud and long cry, such as Christ emitted on the Cross. See the whole history of these proceedings against our Lord treated at large on Matthew xxvii.

17. *And platted a crown of thorns.* In the note on Matt. xxvii. 29, I have ventured to express a doubt whether our Lord was crowned with *thorns,* in our sense of the word, this crown being designed as an instrument of torture. I am still of the same opinion, having considered the subject more closely since writing that note.

21. *A Cyrenian.* One of Cyrene, a celebrated city in Libya. *The father of Alexander and Rufus.* It appears that these two persons were well-known among the first disciples of our Lord. It is not unlikely that this is the same *Alexander* who is mentioned, Acts xix. 33, and that the other is the *Rufus* spoken of by Paul, Rom. xvi. 13.

25. *The third hour.* It has been before observed that the Jews divided their night into four watches, of three hours each. They also divided the day into four general parts. The first began at sunrise; the second, three hours after; the third, at midday; the fourth, three hours after, and continued till sunset. Christ having been nailed to the Cross a little after midday, John xix. 14-17, and having expired about three o'clock, Mark xv. 33, the whole business of the Crucifixion was finished within the space of this third division of the day, which Mark calls here the *third hour.* Commentators and critics have found it very difficult to reconcile this *third* hour of Mark, with the *sixth* hour of John, chap. xix. 14. It is supposed that the true reading, in John xix. 14, should be the *third* instead of the *sixth.*

28. *The scripture was fulfilled.* All this verse is wanting in many MSS., some versions, and several of the fathers.

37. *Gave up the ghost.* This was about three o'clock, or what was termed by the Jews the ninth hour, about the time that the paschal lamb was usually sacrificed. The darkness mentioned here must have endured about two hours and a half.

42. *The day before the sabbath.* What we would call Friday evening. As the law of Moses had ordered that no criminal should continue hanging on a tree or gibbet till the setting of the sun, Joseph, fearing that the body of our Lord might be taken down and thrown into the common grave with the two robbers, came and earnestly entreated Pilate to deliver it to him, that he might bury it in his own new tomb.

43. *Went in boldly unto Pilate.* It needed no small measure of courage to declare now for Jesus, who had been a few hours ago condemned as a blasphemer by the Jews and as a seditious person by the Romans; and this was the more remarkable in Joseph because hitherto, for fear of the Jews, he had been only a secret disciple of our Lord. See John xix. 38.

47. *Beheld where he was laid.* The courage and affection of these holy women cannot be too much admired. The strength of the Lord is perfected in weakness; for here a timid man and a few weak women acknowledge Jesus in death, when the strong and the mighty utterly forsook Him.

CHAPTER 16

Early in the morning after the Sabbath, the three Marys come to the sepulchre, bringing sweet spices to embalm the body, 1-4. They see an angel, who announces the resurrection of our Lord, 5-8. Jesus appears to Mary Magdalene, who goes and tells the disciples, 9-11. He appears also to the two disciples who were going into the country, who also tell it to the rest, 12-13. Afterwards He appears unto the eleven, and commissions them to preach the gospel to all mankind, 14-16. And promises to endue them with power to work miracles, 17-18. He is received up into heaven, 19. And they go forth to preach and work miracles, 20.

1. *And anoint him.* Rather "to embalm Him." This is a proof that they had not properly understood what Christ had so frequently spoken, viz., that He would rise again the third day. And this inattention or unbelief of theirs is a proof of the truth of the Resurrection.

2. *Very early in the morning.* This was the time they left their own houses, and by the rising of the sun they got to the tomb. As the preceding day was the Sabbath, they could not, consistently with the observances of that day, approach the tomb.

6. *Jesus of Nazareth.* The Jews had given this name to Christ by way of reproach, Matt. ii. 23; but as it was under this name that He was crucified, John xix. 19, the angel here, and the apostles after, have given Him the same name, Acts iv. 10, etc. Names which the world in derision fixes on the followers of God often become the general appellatives of religious bodies; thus *Quakers, Puritans, Pietists,* and *Methodists* have in their respective times been the *nicknames* given in derision by the world to those who separated themselves from its corruptions.

7. *Tell his disciples and Peter.* Why is not Peter included among the disciples? For this plain reason—he had forfeited his discipleship, and all right to the honor and privileges of an apostle, by denying his Lord and Master. However he is now a penitent; tell him that Jesus is risen from the dead, and is ready to heal his backsliding, and love him freely; so that, after being converted, he may strengthen his brethren.

9. *Now when Jesus was risen,* etc.—This, to the conclusion of the Gospel, is wanting in the famous Codex Vaticanus, and has anciently been wanting in many others. In the margin of the later Syriac version there is a remarkable addition after this verse; it is as follows: "And

they declared briefly all that was commanded, to them that were with Peter. Afterward Jesus himself published by them, from east to west, the holy and incorruptible preaching of eternal salvation. Amen." *Mary Magdalene.* It seems likely that, after this woman had carried the news of Christ's resurrection to the disciples, she returned alone to the tomb; and that it was then that Christ appeared to her, John xx. 1-12; and a little after, He appeared to all the women together, Matt. xxviii. 9; Luke xxiv. 10.

10. *Them that had been with him.* Not only the eleven disciples, but several others who had been the occasional companions of Christ and the apostles. *Mourned and wept.* Because they had lost their Lord and Master, and had basely abandoned Him in His extremity.

12. *He appeared . . . unto two of them.* These were the two who were going to Emmaus. The whole account is given by Luke, chap. xxiv. 13-34, where see the notes.

14. *And upbraided them with their unbelief.* Never were there people so difficult to be persuaded of the truth of spiritual things as the disciples. It may be justly asserted that people of so skeptical a turn of mind would never credit anything till they had the fullest evidence of its truth. The unbelief of the disciples is a strong proof of the truth of the gospel of God.

15. *Go ye into all the world.* See on Matt. xxviii. 19. *And preach the gospel to every creature.* "Proclaim the glad tidings"—of Christ crucified, and raised from the dead—"to all the creation"—to the Gentile world.

16. *He that believeth.* He that credits this gospel as a revelation from God; *and is baptized*—takes upon him the profession of it, obliging himself to walk according to its precepts; *shall be saved*—redeemed from sin here, and brought at last to the enjoyment of My eternal glory. *But he that believeth not shall be damned*—because he rejects the only provision that could be effectual to his soul's salvation.

17. *These signs shall follow.* Or rather, "accompany." *Them that believe.* "The believers," as we express it; i.e., the apostles, and all those who in those primitive times were endued with miraculous powers, for the confirmation of the doctrines they preached. *In my name.* That is, by the authority and influence of the almighty Jesus. *Cast out devils.* Whose kingdom Jesus Christ was manifested to destroy. *Speak with new tongues.* This was most literally fulfilled on the Day of Pentecost, Acts ii. 4-12.

18. *Take up serpents.* This also was literally fulfilled in the case of Paul, Acts xxviii. 5. *If they drink any deadly thing.* Being understood —if they should through mistake or accident drink any poisonous matter, their constant Preserver will take care that it shall not injure them. See a similar promise, Isa. xliii. 2. *They shall lay hands on the sick.* And I will convey a healing power by their hands, so that the sick shall recover, and men shall see that these are sent and acknowledged by the Most High. Several instances of this kind are found in the Acts of the Apostles.

19. *After the Lord had spoken* these things, and conversed with them for forty days, *he was received up into heaven,* there to appear in the presence of God for us.

20. *The Lord working with them.* This cooperation was twofold, internal and external. Internal, illuminating their minds, convincing them of the truth, and establishing them in it. External, conveying their word to the souls that heard it, by the demonstration of the Holy Ghost; convincing them of sin, righteousness, and judgment; justifying them by His blood, and sanctifying them by His Spirit. Though miraculous powers are not now requisite, because the truth of the gospel has been sufficiently confirmed, yet this cooperation of God is indispensably necessary, without which no man can be a successful preacher, and without which no soul can be saved. *With signs following.* "The accompanying signs"; viz., those mentioned in the seventeenth and eighteenth verses, and those others just now spoken of, which still continue to be produced by the energy of God, accompanying the faithful preaching of His unadulterated Word. *Amen.* This is added here by many MSS. and versions, but is supposed not to have made a part of the text originally.

The Gospel According to

LUKE

There is little certain known of this Evangelist. From what is spoken in the Scriptures, and by the best informed of the primitive fathers, the following probable account is collected.

Luke was, according to Dr. Lardner, a Jew by birth, and an early convert to Christianity; but Michaelis thinks he was a Gentile, and brings Col. iv. 10-11, 14 in proof, where Paul distinguished Aristarchus, Marcus, and Jesus, who was called Justus, from Epaphras, Lucas, and Demas, who were of the *circumcision,* i.e. *Jews.* Some think he was one of our Lord's seventy disciples. It is worthy of remark that he is the only Evangelist who mentions the commission given by Christ to the seventy, chap. x. 1-20. It is likely he is the Lucius mentioned in Rom. xvi. 21, and if so he was related to the Apostle Paul, and that it is the same Lucius of Cyrene who is mentioned in Acts xiii. 1, and in general with others, Acts xi. 20. Some of the ancients, and some of the most learned and judicious among the moderns, think he was one of the two whom our

Lord met on the way to Emmaus on the day of His resurrection, as related in Luke xxiv. 13-35; one of these was called Cleopas, v. 18; the other is not mentioned, the Evangelist himself being the person and the relator.

Paul styles him his fellow laborer, Philemon, v. 24. It is barely probable that he is the person mentioned in Col. iv. 14, "Luke, the beloved physician." All the ancients of repute, such as Eusebius, Gregory Nyssen, Jerome, Paulinus, Euthalius, Euthymius, and others, agree that he was a physician, but where he was born and where he exercised the duties of his profession are not known. Many moderns have attributed to him the most profound skill in the science of painting. This is justly esteemed fabulous.

He accompanied Paul when he first went into Macedonia, Acts xvi. 8-40; xx; xxvii; and xxviii. Whether he went with him constantly afterwards is not certain; but it is evident he accompanied him from Greece through Macedonia and Asia to Jerusalem, where he is supposed to have collected many particulars of the evangelic history. From Jerusalem he went with Paul to Rome, where he stayed with him the two years of his imprisonment in that city. This alone makes out the space of five years, and upwards. It is probable that he left Paul when he was set at liberty, and that he then went into Greece, where he finished and published this Gospel, and the Book of Acts, which he dedicated to Theophilus, an honorable Christian friend of his in that country. It is supposed that he died in peace about the eightieth or eighty-fourth year of his age. Some suppose he published this Gospel fifteen (others, twenty-two) years after the ascension of Christ.

Some learned men think that Luke has borrowed considerably from Matthew. It is allowed that there is considerable diversity in the order of time between Matthew and Luke, which is accounted for thus: Matthew deduces the facts related in his history in chronological order. Luke, on the contrary, appears to have paid little attention to this order, because he proposed to make a classification of events, referring each to its proper class, without paying any attention to chronological arrangement.

CHAPTER 1

The preface, or Luke's private epistle to Theophilus, 1-4. The conception and birth of John the Baptist foretold by the angel Gabriel, 5-17. Zacharias doubts, 18. The angel declares he shall be dumb till the accomplishment of the prediction, 19-25. Six months after, the angel Gabriel appears to the Virgin Mary, and predicts the miraculous conception and birth of Christ, 26-38. Mary visits her cousin Elisabeth, 39-45. Mary's song of exultation and praise, 46-56. John the Baptist is born, 57-66. The prophetic song of his father, Zacharias, 67-79. John is educated in the desert, 80.

1. *Many have taken in hand.* Great and remarkable characters always have many biographers. So it appears it was with our Lord. But as most of these accounts were inaccurate, recording as facts things which had not happened, and through ignorance or design mistaking others, especially in the place where Luke wrote, it seemed good to the Holy Spirit to inspire this holy man with the most correct knowledge of the whole history of our Lord's birth, preaching, miracles, sufferings, death, resurrection, and ascension, that the sincere, upright followers of God might have a sure foundation on which they might safely build their faith. *Most surely believed among us.* "Facts confirmed by the fullest evidence." Everything that had been done or said by Jesus Christ was so public, so plain, and so accredited by thousands of witnesses, who could have had no interest in supporting an imposture, as to carry the fullest conviction to the hearts of those who heard and saw Him of the divinity of His doctrine and the truth of His miracles.

2. *Even as they delivered them unto us which from the beginning were eyewitnesses.* Probably this alludes to the Gospels of Matthew and Mark, which it is likely were written before Luke wrote his, and on the models of which he professes to write his own; and *from the beginning* must mean from the time that Christ first began to proclaim the glad tidings of the Kingdom. *Eyewitnesses* must necessarily signify those who had been with Him from the beginning, and consequently had the best opportunities of knowing the truth of every fact.

3. *Having had perfect understanding.* "Having accurately traced up"—entered into the very spirit of the work, and examined everything to the bottom; in consequence of which investigation I am completely convinced of the truth of the whole. Though God gives His Holy Spirit to all them who ask Him, yet this Gift was never designed to set aside the use of those faculties with which He has already endued the soul, and which are as truly His gifts as the Holy Spirit itself is. The nature of inspiration, in the case of Luke, we at once discover: he set himself by impartial inquiry and diligent investigation to find the whole truth and to relate nothing but the truth; and the Spirit of God presided over and directed his inquiries, so that he discovered the whole truth and was preserved from every particle of error. *From the very first.* "From their origin." Some think *anothen* should, in this place, be translated "from above"; and that it refers to the inspiration by which Luke wrote. I prefer our translation, or "from the origin," which several good critics contend for, and which meaning it has in some of the best Greek writers. *Theophilus.* As the literal import of this word is "friend of God," some have supposed that under this name Luke comprised all the followers of Christ, to whom, as "friends of God," he dedicated this faithful history of the life, doctrine, death, and resurrection of our Lord. But this interpretation appears to have little solidity in it; for if all the followers of Christ are addressed, why is the singular number used? and what good end could there be accomplished by using a feigned name? Besides, *most excellent* could never be applied in this way, for it evidently designates a particular person, and one probably distinguished by his situation in life; though this does not necessarily follow from the title, which was often given in the way of friendship. *Theophilus* appears to

have been some very reputable Greek or Roman who was one of Luke's disciples.

4. *Wherein thou hast been instructed.* In which you have been "catechized." It appears that Theophilus had already received the first elements of the Christian doctrine, but had not as yet been completely grounded in them. That he might know the certainty of the things in which he had been thus catechized, by having all the facts and their proofs brought before him *in order,* the Evangelist sent him this faithful and divinely inspired narrative.

5. *In the days of Herod, the king.* This was Herod, surnamed the Great, the son of Antipater, an Idumean by birth, who had professed himself a proselyte to the Jewish religion, but regarded no religion further than it promoted his secular interests and ambition. Thus, for the first time, the throne of Judah was filled by a person not of Jewish extraction, who had been forced upon the people by the Roman government. Hence it appears plain that the prophecy of Jacob, Gen. xlix. 10, was now fulfilled, for the sceptre had departed from Judah; and now was the time, according to another prophecy, to look for the Governor from Bethlehem, who should rule and feed the people of Israel, Mic. v. 1-2. *The course of Abia.* When the sacerdotal families grew very numerous, so that all could not officiate together at the Tabernacle, David divided them into twenty-four classes, that they might minister by turns, 1 Chron. xxiv. 1, etc., each family serving a whole week, 2 Kings xi. 7; 2 Chron. xxiii. 8. *Abia* was the eighth in the order in which they had been originally established, 1 Chron. xxiv. 10. These dates and persons are particularly mentioned as a full confirmation of the truth of the facts themselves; because any person, at the time this Gospel was written, might have satisfied himself by applying to the family of John the Baptist, the family of our Lord, or the surrounding neighbors. What a full proof of the Gospel history! It was published immediately after the time in which these facts took place; and among the very people, thousands of whom had been eyewitnesses of them; and among those, too, whose essential interest it was to have discredited them if they could. And yet, in all that age, in which only they could have been contradicted with advantage, no man ever arose to call them in question! What an absolute proof was this that the thing was impossible, and that the truth of the Gospel history was acknowledged by all who paid any attention to the evidences it produced! *Of the daughter of Aaron.* That is, she was of one of the sacerdotal families. This shows that John was most nobly descended. His father was a priest, and his mother the daughter of a priest; and thus by both father and mother he descended from the family of Amram, of whom came Moses, Aaron, and Miriam, the most illustrious characters in the whole Jewish history.

6. *They were both righteous.* Upright and holy in all their outward conduct in civil life. *Before God.* Possessing the spirit of the religion they professed; exercising themselves constantly in the presence of their Maker, whose eye they knew was upon all their conduct, and who examined all their motives. *Walking in all the commandments and ordinances of the Lord blameless.* None being able to lay any evil to

their charge. They were as exemplary and conscientious in the discharge of their religious duties as they were in the discharge of the offices of civil life. Perhaps *commandments* may here mean the Decalogue; and *ordinances,* the ceremonial and judicial laws which were delivered after the Decalogue, as all the precepts delivered from Exodus xxi to xxiv are termed *ordinances.*

7. *Both were now well stricken in years.* By the order of God, sterility and old age both met in the person of Elisabeth to render the birth of a son (humanly speaking) impossible. This was an exact parallel to the case of Sarah and Abraham, Gen. xi. 30; xvii. 17. Christ must (by the miraculous power of God) be born of a virgin; whatever was connected with or referred to His incarnation must be miraculous and impressive. Isaac was his grand type, and therefore must be born miraculously—contrary to the common course and rule of nature. John the Baptist was to be the forerunner of Christ; his birth, like that of Isaac, must be miraculous, because, like the other, it was to be a representation of the birth of Christ. Therefore his parents were both far advanced in years, and besides, Elisabeth was naturally barren. The birth of these three extraordinary persons was announced nearly in the same way. God himself foretells the birth of Isaac, Gen. xvii. 16. The angel of the Lord announces the birth of John the Baptist, Luke i. 13; and six months after, the angel Gabriel, the same angel, proclaims to Mary the birth of Christ!

8. *Before God.* In the Temple, where God used to manifest His presence, though long before this time He had forsaken it; yet on this important occasion the angel of His presence had visited it.

9. *His lot was.* We are informed in the Talmud that it was the custom of the priests to divide the different functions of the sacerdotal office among themselves by *lot;* and in this case the decision of the lot was that Zacharias should at that time burn the incense before the Lord in the holy place.

10. *The whole multitude . . . were praying.* The incense was itself an emblem of the prayers and praises of the people of God; see Ps. cxli. 2; Rev. viii. 1. While therefore the rite is being performed by the priest, the people are employed in the thing signified. Happy the people who attend to the spirit as well as the letter of every divine institution! Incense was burnt twice a day in the Temple, in the morning and in the evening, Exod. xxx. 7-8; but the Evangelist does not specify the time of the day in which this transaction took place. It was probably in the morning.

11. *There appeared unto him an angel of the Lord.* There had been neither prophecy nor angelic ministry vouchsafed to this people for about four hundred years. But now, as the Sun of Righteousness is about to arise upon them, the dayspring from on high visits them, that they may be prepared for that kingdom of God which was at hand.

12. *Zacharias . . . was troubled.* Or "confounded" at his sudden and unexpected appearance; *and fear fell upon him,* lest this heavenly messenger were come to denounce the judgments of God against a faithless and disobedient

people, who had too long and too well merited them.

13. *Thy prayer is heard.* This probably refers, first, to the frequent prayers which he had offered to God for a son; and second, to those which he had offered for the deliverance and consolation of Israel. They are all heard—you shall have a son, and Israel shall be saved. If fervent, faithful prayers be not immediately answered, they should not be considered as lost; all such are heard by the Lord, are registered in heaven, and shall be answered in the most effectual way and in the best time. Answers to prayer are to be received by faith; but faith should not only accompany prayer while offered on earth, but follow it all its way to the throne of grace, and stay with it before the throne till dismissed with its answer to the waiting soul. *Thou shalt call his name John.* For the proper exposition of this name, see on Mark i. 4.

14. *Thou shalt have joy.* "He will be joy and gladness to you." A child of prayer and faith is likely to be a source of comfort to his parents. *Many shall rejoice at his birth.* He shall be the minister of God for good to multitudes, who shall, through his preaching, be turned from the error of their ways and converted to God, their Saviour.

15. *He shall be great in the sight of the Lord.* That is, before Jesus Christ, whose forerunner he shall be; or he shall be a "truly great person," for so this form of speech may imply. *Neither wine nor strong drink.* I.e., all fermented liquors which have the property of intoxicating, or producing drunkenness. The original word, *sikera,* comes from the Hebrew, *shakar,* "to inebriate." "Any inebriating liquor," says Jerome, "is called *sicera,* whether made of *corn, apples, honey, dates,* or any other fruits." *Shall be filled with the Holy Ghost.* Shall be divinely designated to this particular office, and qualified for it, *from his mother's womb*—from the instant of his birth.

16. *Many of the children of Israel shall he turn.* See this prediction fulfilled, chap. iii. 10-18.

17. *He shall go before him.* Jesus Christ, *in the spirit and power of Elias;* he shall resemble Elijah in his retired and austere manner of life, and in his zeal for the truth, reproving even princes for their crimes; compare 1 Kings xxi. 17-24 with Matt. xiv. 4. It was on these accounts that the Prophet Malachi, chap. iv. 6, had likened John to this prophet. See also Isa. xl. 3 and Mal. iv. 5-6. *To turn the hearts of the fathers.* By a very expressive figure of speech Abraham, Isaac, and Jacob, and the rest of the patriarchs are represented here as having their hearts alienated from the Jews, their children, because of their unbelief and disobedience; but that the Baptist should so far succeed in converting them to the Lord their God that these holy men should again look upon them with delight and acknowledge them for their children. *The disobedient.* Or "unbelieving," the persons who would no longer credit the predictions of the prophets relative to the manifestation of the Messiah. Unbelief and disobedience are so intimately connected that the same word in the sacred writings often serves for both.

19. *I am Gabriel.* This angel is mentioned in Dan. viii. 16; ix. 21. The original is exceedingly expressive; it is compounded of *geburah* and

el, "the might of the strong God." An angel with such a name was exceedingly proper for the occasion, as it pointed out that all-prevalent power by which the strong God could accomplish every purpose and subdue all things to himself. *That stand in the presence of God.* This is an allusion to the case of the prime minister of an Eastern monarch, who alone has access to his master at all times and is therefore said, in the Eastern phrase, "to see the presence," or "to be in the presence." From the allusion we may conceive the angel Gabriel to be in a state of high favor and trust before God.

20. *Thou shalt be dumb.* "Silent"; this translation is literal; the angel immediately explains it, You shall not be *able to speak.* Dumbness ordinarily proceeds from a natural imperfection or debility of the organs of speech. In this case there was no natural weakness or unfitness in those organs; but for his rash and unbelieving speech, silence is imposed upon him by the Lord, and he shall not be able to break it till the Power that has silenced him gives him again the permission to speak! Let those who are intemperate in the use of their tongues behold here the severity and mercy of the Lord: nine months' silence for one intemperate speech! Many, by giving way to the language of unbelief, have lost the language of praise and thanksgiving for months, if not years!

21. *The people waited.* The time spent in burning the incense was probably about half an hour, during which there was a profound silence as the people stood without engaged in mental prayer. To this there is an allusion in Rev. viii. 1-5. Zacharias had spent not only the time necessary for burning the incense, but also that which the discourse between him and the angel took up.

22. *They perceived that he had seen a vision.* As the sanctuary was separated from the court by a great veil, the people could not see what passed; but they understood this from Zacharias himself, who "made signs," or "nodded" unto them to that purpose. Signs are the only means by which a dumb man can convey his ideas to others.

23. *As soon as the days of his ministration were accomplished.* Each family of the priesthood officiated one whole week, 2 Kings xi. 17.

24. *Hid herself five months.* That she might have the fullest proof of the accomplishment of God's promise before she appeared in public, or spoke of her mercies.

25. *To take away my reproach.* As fruitfulness was a part of the promise of God to His people, Gen. xvii. 6, and children, on this account, being considered as a particular blessing from Heaven, Exod. xxiii. 26; Lev. xxvi. 9; Ps. cxxvii. 3, so barrenness was considered among the Jews as a reproach, and a token of the disapprobation of the Lord, 1 Sam. i. 6.

26. *A city of Galilee.* As Joseph and Mary were both of the family of David, the patrimonial estate of which lay in Bethlehem, it seems as if the family residence should have been in that city, and not in Nazareth; for we find that, even after the return from the Captivity, the several families went to reside in these cities to which they originally belonged. See Neh. xi. 3. But it is probable that the Holy Family removed to Galilee for fear of exciting

the jealousy of Herod, who had usurped that throne to which they had an indisputable right.

28. *And the angel came in unto her.* Some think that all this business was transacted in a vision, and that there was no personal appearance of the angel. When divine visions were given, they are announced as such in the sacred writings; nor can we with safety attribute anything to a vision where a divine communication is made, unless it is specified as such in the text. *Hail.* Analogous to, "Peace be to you"—May you enjoy all possible blessings! *Highly favoured.* As being chosen in preference to all the women upon earth to be the mother of the Messiah. Not the "mother of God," for that is blasphemy. *The Lord is with thee.* You are about to receive the most convincing proofs of God's peculiar favor toward you. *Blessed art thou among women.* That is, you are favored beyond all others.

29. *She was troubled at his saying.* The glorious appearance of the heavenly messenger filled her with amazement, and she was puzzled to find out the purport of his speech.

31. *Thou . . . shalt call his name JESUS.* See on Matt. i. 20-21; here; chap. ii. 21; and John i. 29.

33. *The house of Jacob.* All who belong to the twelve tribes, the whole Israelitish people.

34. *Seeing I know not a man.* Or "husband." As she was only contracted to Joseph, and not as yet married, she knew that this conception could not have yet taken place; and she modestly inquires by what means the promise of the angel is to be fulfilled in order to regulate her conduct accordingly.

35. *The Holy Ghost shall come upon thee.* This conception shall take place suddenly, and the Holy Spirit himself shall be the grand Operator. *The power,* the miracle-working power, *of the Highest shall overshadow thee,* to accomplish this purpose, and to protect you from danger. As there is a plain allusion to the Spirit of God brooding over the face of the waters, to render them prolific, Gen. i. 2, I am the more firmly established in the opinion advanced on Matt. i. 20, that the rudiments of the human nature of Christ were a real creation in the womb of the Virgin, by the energy of the Spirit of God. *Therefore also that holy thing (or Person) . . . shall be called the Son of God.* We may plainly perceive here that the angel does not give the appellation of *Son of God* to the divine nature of Christ, but to that holy person or thing which was to be born of the Virgin by the energy of the Holy Spirit. The divine nature could not be born of the Virgin; the human nature was born of her. The divine nature had no beginning; it was God manifested in the flesh, 1 Tim. iii. 16; it was that Word which, being in the beginning (from eternity) with God, John i. 2, was afterwards made flesh (became manifest in human nature), and tabernacled among us, John i. 14. Of this divine nature the angel does not particularly speak here, but of the tabernacle or shrine which God was now preparing for it, viz., the *holy thing* that was to be born of the Virgin. Two natures must ever be distinguished in Christ: the human nature, in reference to which He is the Son of God and inferior to Him, Mark xiii. 32; John v. 19; xiv. 28; and the divine nature, which was from eternity, and equal to God, John i. 1; x. 30; Rom. ix. 5; Col. i. 16-18. It is true that to Jesus the Christ, as He appeared among men, every characteristic of the divine nature is sometimes attributed without appearing to make any distinction between the divine and human natures. But is there any part of the Scriptures in which it is plainly said that the divine nature of Jesus was *the Son of God?* Here, I trust, I may be permitted to say, with all due respect for those who differ from me, that the doctrine of the eternal sonship of Christ is in my opinion anti-scriptural and highly dangerous.

36. *Thy cousin Elisabeth.* "Thy kinswoman." As Elisabeth was of the tribe of Levi, v. 5, and Mary of the tribe of Judah, they could not be relatives but by the mother's side. *She hath also conceived.* And this is wrought by the same power and energy through which you shall conceive. Thus God has given you a proof and pledge, in what He has done for Elisabeth, of what He will do for you; therefore, have faith in God. *Who was called barren.* It is probable that Elisabeth got this appellative by way of reproach; or to distinguish her from some other Elisabeth, also well-known, who had been blessed with children. Perhaps this is the reproach which Elisabeth speaks of in v. 25, her common name among men, among the people who knew her, being "Elisabeth the barren."

37. *For with God nothing shall be impossible.* Words of the very same import with those spoken by the Lord to Sarah, when He foretold the birth of Isaac, Gen. xviii. 14, "Is any thing too hard for the Lord?" As there can be no doubt that Mary perceived this allusion to the promise and birth of Isaac, so she must have had her faith considerably strengthened by reflecting on the intervention of God in that case.

38. *Behold the handmaid of the Lord.* I fully credit what thou sayest, and am perfectly ready to obey thy commands, and to accomplish all the purposes of thy grace concerning me. It appears that at the instant of this act of faith, and purposed obedience, the conception of the immaculate humanity of Jesus took place; and it was done unto her according to his word.

39. *In those days.* As soon as she could conveniently fit herself out for the journey. *With haste.* This probably refers to nothing else than the earnestness of her mind to visit her relative Elisabeth, and to see what the Lord had wrought for her.

41. *Elisabeth was filled with the Holy Ghost.* This seems to have been the accomplishment of the promise made by the angel, v. 15, "He shall be filled with the Holy Ghost, even from his mother's womb." The mother is filled with the Holy Spirit, and the child in her womb becomes sensible of the divine influence.

42. *Blessed art thou among women.* Repeating the words of the angel, v. 28, of which she had probably been informed by the holy Virgin, in the present interview.

43. *The mother of my Lord.* The prophetic spirit, which appears to have overshadowed Elisabeth, gave her a clear understanding in the mystery of the birth of the promised Messiah.

45. *Blessed is she that believed; for there shall be.* Or, "Blessed is she who hath believed that there shall be." This I believe to be the

proper arrangement of the passage, and is thus noticed in the marginal reading. Faith is here represented as the foundation of true happiness, because it receives the fulfillment of God's promises.

46. *And Mary said.* Two copies of the Itala, and some books mentioned by Origen, give this song to Elisabeth. It is a counterpart of the song of Hannah, as related in 1 Sam. ii. 1-10. *My soul doth magnify the Lord.* The verb signifies "to celebrate with words, to extol with praises." This is the only way in which God can be magnified, or made great; for, strictly speaking, nothing can be added to God, for He is infinite and eternal. Therefore the way to magnify Him is to show forth and celebrate those acts in which He has manifested His greatness.

47. *My spirit hath rejoiced.* "Exulted." These words are uncommonly emphatical—they show that Mary's whole soul was filled with the divine influence, and wrapped up in God.

48. *He hath regarded.* "Looked favorably." In the most tender and compassionate manner He has visited me in my humiliation, drawing the reasons of His conduct, not from any excellence in me, but from His own eternal kindness and love. *All generations shall call me blessed.* This was the character by which alone she wished to be known, viz., "The blessed or happy virgin." What dishonor do those do to this holy woman who give her names and characters which her pure soul would abhor, and which properly belong to God, her *Saviour!* By her votaries she is addressed as "Queen of Heaven," "Mother of God," titles both absurd and blasphemous.

49. *He that is mighty hath done to me great things!* Or "miracles." *Holy is his name.* Probably the word which Mary used was *chesed,* which though we sometimes translate *holy,* see Ps. lxxxvi. 2; cxlv. 17, yet the proper meaning is "abundant goodness, exuberant kindness"; and this well agrees with the following clause.

50. *His mercy is on them that fear him.* His exuberant kindness manifests itself in acts of mercy to all those who fear or reverence His name; and this is continued *from generation to generation,* because He is abundant in goodness, and because He delights in mercy. This is a noble, becoming, and just character of the God of the Christians; a Being who delights in the salvation and happiness of all His creatures, because His name is mercy, and His nature love.

51. *He hath shewed strength.* Or, "He hath gained the victory." The word is used for "victory," by Homer, Hesiod, Sophocles, Euripides, and others. *With his arm.* Grotius has well observed that God's efficacy is represented by His finger, His great power by His hand, and His omnipotence by His arm. The plague of lice was the "finger" of God, Exod. vii. 18. The plagues in general were wrought by His "hand," Exod. iii. 20. And the destruction of Pharaoh's host in the Red Sea, which was effected by the omnipotence of God, is called the act of His "arm," Exod. xv. 16. *He hath scattered.* "Hath scattered abroad"; as a whirlwind scatters dust and chaff. *The proud.* Or "haughty"—the haughty men, who wish to be noticed in preference to all others, and feel sovereign contempt for all but themselves. These God scatters

abroad—instead of being in His sight, as in their own, the most excellent of the earth, He treats them as straw, stubble, chaff, and dust. *In the imagination of their hearts.* While they are forming their insolent, proud, and oppressive projects —laying their plans, and imagining that accomplishment and success are waiting at their right hand—the whirlwind of God's displeasure blows, and they and their machinations are dissipated together.

52. *He hath put down the mighty from their seats.* Or, "He hath taken down potentates from their thrones." This probably alludes to the removal of Saul from the throne of Israel, and the establishment of the kingdom in the person and family of David. And as Mary spoke prophetically, this saying may also allude to the destruction of the kingdom of Satan and his allies, and the final prevalence of the kingdom of Christ.

53. *Filled the hungry . . . the rich he hath sent empty away.* God is here represented under the notion of a Person of unbounded benevolence, who is daily feeding multitudes at His gates. The poor man comes through a sense of his want to get his daily support, and God feeds him; the rich man comes through the lust of gain, to get more added to his abundance, and God sends him away empty— not only gives him nothing more, but often deprives him of that which he has, because he has not improved it to the honor of the Giver.

54. *He hath holpen [supported] his servant Israel.* Israel is here represented as falling, and the Lord comes speedily in and props him up. The house of David was now ready to fall and rise no more; Jesus, being born of the very last branch of the regal line, revived the family, and restored the dominion. *In remembrance of his mercy.* By *mercy,* the covenant which God made with Abraham, Gen. xv. 18, as intended; which covenant proceeded from God's eternal mercy, as in it salvation was promised to all the nations of the earth. See Gen. xvii. 19 and xxii. 18; and this promise was, one form or other, given to all the fathers, v. 55. This song properly consists of three parts. (1) In the *first* part Mary praises God for what He had done for *herself,* vv. 46-50. (2) In the *second,* she praises Him for what He had done, and would do, against the oppressors of *His people,* vv. 51-53. (3) In the *third,* she praises Him for what He had done, and would do, for His *Church,* vv. 53-56.

56. *And Mary abode with her about three months.* According to some, the departure of Mary from Hebron must have been but a few days before the birth of John, as nine months had now elapsed since Elisabeth's conception; see v. 36.

57. *Now Elisabeth's full time came.* But, according to others, we are to understand the three months of Mary's visit as preceding the birth of John, which would complete the time of Elisabeth's pregnancy, according to v. 36, and the only difficulty is to ascertain whether Mary went immediately to Hebron after her salutation or whether she tarried nearly three months before she took the journey.

58. *And her neighbours and her cousins . . . rejoiced with her.* Because sterility was a reproach; and they now rejoiced with their relative, from whom that reproach was now rolled away.

59. *On the eighth day they came to circum-*

cise. See an account of this institution in the note on Gen. xvii. 10-14. Had circumcision been essential to an infant's salvation, God would not have ordered it to be delayed to the eighth day, because in all countries multitudes die before they arrive at that age. Baptism, which is generally allowed to have been substituted for circumcision, is no more necessary to the salvation of an infant than circumcision was. Both are signs of the covenant—circumcision, of the putting away the impurity of the flesh; and baptism, of the "washing of regeneration, and renewing of the Holy Ghost." *They called him Zacharias.* Among the Jews, the child was named when it was circumcised, and ordinarily the name of the father was given to the firstborn son.

60. *Not so; but he shall be called John.* This is the name which the angel desired should be given him, v. 13, and of which Zacharias by writing had informed his wife. There is something very remarkable in the names of this family: *Zacharias,* the "memory or memorial of Jehovah"; *Elisabeth,* the "Sabbath or rest of my strong God"—names probably given them by their parents, to point out some remarkable circumstance in their conception or birth; and *John,* which should always be written *Jehochanan* or *Yehochanan,* the "grace or mercy of Jehovah"—so named because he was to go before and proclaim the "God of all grace," and the mercy granted through Him to a lost world.

61. *None of thy kindred.* As the Jewish tribes and families were kept sacredly distinct, it appears the very names of the ancestors were continued among their descendants, partly through reverence for them and partly to avoid confusion in the genealogical tables, which, for the sake of distinguishing the inheritances, were carefully preserved in each of the families.

62. *They made signs to his father.* Who, it appears from this, was deaf as well as dumb; otherwise they might have asked him and obtained his answer in this way.

63. *A writing table.* "A "tablet," diminutive of a "table."

64. The latter clause of the preceding verse should be joined with the beginning of this, as follows: *And they marvelled all, for his mouth was opened.* The people did not wonder because Zacharias said, *He shall be called John,* but because he himself was that instant restored to the use of his speech. *And he spake, and praised God.* In his nine months' silence he had learned the proper use of his tongue; and God, whose power was discredited by it, is now magnified.

65. *And fear came.* Seeing what they might have thought a paralytic affection so suddenly and effectually healed. This word certainly means in several places "religious fear or reverence"; and in this sense it is used in Acts ix. 31; Rom. iii. 18; xiii. 7; 1 Pet. i. 17; ii. 18; iii. 2.

66. *What manner of child shall this be!* As there have been so many extraordinary things in his conception and birth, surely God has designed him for some extraordinary purpose. These things they *laid . . . up in their hearts,* patiently waiting to see what God would work. *The hand of the Lord was with him.* God

defended and prospered him in all things, and the prophetic spirit began to rest upon him.

67. *Zacharias . . . prophesied.* The word *prophesy* is to be taken here in its proper acceptation, for the "predicting or foretelling future events." Zacharias spoke not only of what God had already done, but also of what He was about to do in order to save a lost world.

68. *Blessed be the Lord God of Israel; for.* Zacharias praises God for two grand benefits which He had granted to His people. (1) He has *visited* them. (2) He has *ransomed* them. God visits His people in the incarnation of Jesus Christ; therefore this Christ is called by Him "Jehovah the God of Israel." Here the highest and most glorious character of the Supreme Being is given to Christ. *He hath . . . redeemed.* "He hath made a ransom"—laid down the ransom price. *Lytroo* signifies particularly to "ransom a captive from the enemy, by paying a price." The following remarkable passage from Josephus, *Ant.,* b. xiv, c. 14, sect. 1, fully illustrates this meaning of the original. "Herod, not knowing what had happened to his brother, hastened to ransom him from the enemy, and was willing to pay a ransom for him, to the amount of three hundred talents." Sinners are fallen into the hands of their enemies, and are captives to sin and death. Jesus ransoms them by His own blood, and restores them to life, liberty, and happiness.

69. *And hath raised up an horn of salvation.* That is, a "mighty and glorious Saviour," a quotation from Ps. xviii. 2. Horns are the well-known emblems of strength, glory, and power, in both sacred and profane writers, because the strength and beauty of horned animals consist in their horns. It is likely that the allusion is here made to the horns of the altar; and as the altar was a place of refuge and safety, and those who laid hold on its horns were considered to be under the protection of the Lord, so, according to the expression of Zacharias, Jesus Christ is a new Altar, to which whosoever flees shall find refuge. *In the house of his servant David.* Or "in the family"; so the word *house* is often used in the Sacred Writings. In v. 32 the angel states that Mary was of the family of David; and Zacharias, who from the nature of his office must have been well acquainted with the public genealogical tables, attests the same thing. This is a matter of considerable importance, because it shows forth the truth of all the prophetic declarations, which uniformly state that the Messiah should come from the family and sit on the throne of David.

71. *That we should be saved* (literally, *a salvation*) *from our enemies.* As Zacharias spoke by the inspiration of the Holy Spirit, the salvation which he mentions here must necessarily be understood in a spiritual sense. Satan, death, and sin are the enemies from whom Jesus came to deliver us. Sin is the most dangerous of all, and is properly the only enemy we have to fear.

74-75. *Being delivered.* The salvation brought by Jesus Christ consists in the following things: (1) We are to be *delivered out of the hand of our enemies,* so that sin shall neither have dominion over us nor existence in us. (2) We are to *serve* (worship) God, to render Him that service and adoration which the letter and spirit of His religion require. (3) We are to live *in holiness,* a strict inward conformity to the mind of Christ—*and righteousness,* a full outward conformity to the precepts of the gospel. (4) This is to be done *before* God, under the continual influence and support of His grace, and with a constant evidence of His presence and approbation. (5) This state is a state of true happiness—it is *without fear.* Sin is all cast out; holiness is brought in. God's power upholds and His approbation cheers and comforts the believing heart. (6) This blessedness is to continue as long as we exist—*all the days of our life,* in all ages, in all situations, and in all circumstances.

76-79. *And thou, child, etc.* Zacharias proclaims the dignity, employment, doctrine, and success of his son, and the ruin and recovery of the Jews and the Gentiles. (1) His dignity. *Thou . . . shalt be called* (constituted) *the prophet of the Highest. Prophet* has two acceptations: first, a person who foretells future events; and, second, a teacher of men in the things of God, 1 Cor. xiv. 3. John was a prophet in both senses. He had the honor of being the last and clearest prophet of the old covenant and the first of the new. (2) His employment. *Thou shalt go before the face of the Lord to prepare his ways.* He should be the immediate forerunner of Jesus Christ, none being capable of succeeding him in his ministry but Christ himself. He was to *prepare his ways,* to be the honored instrument, in the hands of God, of disposing the hearts of multitudes of the Israelites to believe in and follow the Lord Jesus. (3) Zacharias points out the doctrine or teaching of John. It should be the science of *salvation.* (4) Zacharias predicts the success of his son's ministry. Under his preaching the people should be directed to that *tender mercy* of God through which they might obtain *the remission of their sins,* vv. 77-78. (5) Zacharias points out the wretched state in which the inhabitants of Judea and the Gentile world were then found. Their *feet* had wandered out of *the way of peace* (v. 79), of temporal and spiritual prosperity. They had got into a state of *darkness*—they were blind concerning the things of God, and the things which belonged to their salvation. They had become contented inhabitants of this land of intellectual darkness—they had sat down in it, and were not concerned to get out of it. They were about to perish in it—*death* had his dominion there; and his swift approaches to them were now manifested to the prophet by seeing his *shadow* cast upon them. Ignorance of God and salvation is *the shadow of death;* and the substance, eternal ruin, is essentially connected with the projected shadow. See these phrases explained at large on Matt. iv. 16. (6) Zacharias proclaims the recovery of a lost world. As the removal of this darkness and redemption from this death were now at hand, John is represented as being a *dayspring from on high,* a "morning star," that foretold the speedy approach of the day, for the rising of the Sun of Righteousness. That these words should be applied to John, and not to Christ, I am fully satisfied.

80. *The child grew.* Increased in stature and bodily vigor. *And waxed strong in spirit*—had his understanding divinely illuminated and confirmed in the truths of God. *And was in the deserts*—the city of Hebron, the circumjacent hill country, and in or near Nazareth. *Till the day of his shewing,* or "manifestation"—till he was thirty years of age, before which time the law did not permit a man to enter into the public ministry, Num. iv. 3.

CHAPTER 2

The decree of Augustus to enroll all the Roman empire, 1-2. Joseph and Mary go to their own city to be enrolled, 3-5. Christ is born, 6-7. His birth is announced to the shepherds, 8-14. They go to Bethlehem, and find Joseph, Mary, and Christ, 15-20. Christ is circumcised, 21. His parents go to present Him in the Temple, 22-24. Simeon receives Him; his song, 25-35. Anna the prophetess, 36-38. The Holy Family return to Nazareth, 39-40. They go to Jerusalem at the Feast of the Passover, and leave Jesus behind in Jerusalem, 41-44. They return seeking Him, and find Him in the midst of the doctors, 45-47. His mother chides Him, 48. His defense of His conduct, 49-50. They all return to Nazareth, 51-52.

1. *Caesar Augustus.* This was Caius Caesar Octavianus Augustus, who was proclaimed emperor of Rome in the twenty-ninth year before our Lord, and died A.D. 14. *That all the world should be taxed.* "The whole of that empire." It is agreed, on all hands, that this cannot mean the *whole world,* as in the common translation, for this very sufficient reason, that the Romans had not the dominion of the whole earth, and therefore could have no right to raise levies or taxes in those places to which their dominion did not extend.

7. *Laid him in a manger.* Many have thought that this was a full proof of the meanness and poverty of the Holy Family, that they were obliged to take up their lodging in a stable; but such people overlook the reason given by the inspired penman, *because there was no room for them in the inn.* As multitudes were going now to be enrolled, all the lodgings in the inn had been occupied before Joseph and Mary arrived.

8. *There were . . . shepherds abiding in the field.* It was a custom among the Jews to send out their sheep to the deserts, about the Passover, and bring them home at the commencement of the first rain; during the time they were out, the shepherds watched them night and day. As the Passover occurred in the spring, and the first rain began early in the month of *Marchesvan,* which answers to part of our October and November, we find that the sheep were kept out in the open country during the whole of the summer. And as these shepherds had not yet brought home their flocks, it is a presumptive argument that October had not yet commenced, and that, consequently, our Lord was not born on the twenty-fifth of December, when no flocks were out in the fields.

9. *The angel of the Lord came upon them.* Or "stood over them." It is likely that the angel appeared in the air at some little distance above them, and that from him the rays of *the glory of the Lord shone round about them,* as the rays of light are projected from the sun. *They were sore afraid.* Terrified with the appearance of so glorious a being, and probably fearing that he was a messenger of justice, coming to announce divine judgments or punish them immediately for sins with which their consciences would not fail, on such an occasion, to reproach them.

10. *Behold, I bring you good tidings.* I am not come to declare the judgments of the Lord, but His merciful loving-kindness, the subject being a matter of *great joy.* He then declares his

message. *Unto you*—to the Jews first, and then to the human race.

11. *A Saviour, which is Christ the Lord. A Saviour,* the same as *Jesus,* from to "make safe, to deliver, preserve, to make alive." *Which is Christ.* "The anointed," the same as Messiah. This name points out the Saviour of the world in His prophetic, regal, and sacerdotal offices, as in ancient times prophets, kings, and priests were anointed with oil when installed into their respective offices. Anointing was the same with them as consecration is with us. It appears from Isa. lxi. 1 that anointing with oil in consecrating a person to any important office, whether civil or religious, was considered as an emblem of the communication of the gifts and graces of the Holy Spirit. *The Lord.* The supreme, eternal Being, the Ruler of the heavens and the earth. The Septuagint generally translate *Yehovah* by *Kyrios.* This Hebrew word, from *hayah, he was,* properly points out the eternity and self-existence of the Supreme Being. Jesus is a *Prophet,* to reveal the will of God, and instruct men in it. He is a *Priest,* to offer up sacrifice, and make atonement for the sin of the world. He is *Lord,* to rule over and rule in the souls of the children of men.

12. *This shall be a sign* (or token) *unto you; Ye shall find* this glorious Person, however strange it may appear, *wrapped in swaddling clothes, lying in a manger.* It is by humility that Christ comes to reign; and this is the only way into His kingdom! Pride is the character of all the children of Adam; humility, the mark of the Son of God, and of all His followers. Christ came in the way of humility to destroy that pride which is the root of evil in the souls of men.

13. *Suddenly there was with the angel.* This multitude of the heavenly host had just now descended from on high, to honor the newborn Prince of Peace, to give His parents the fullest conviction of His glory and excellence, and to teach the shepherds, who were about to be the first proclaimers of the gospel, what to think and what to speak of Him who, while He appeared as a helpless Infant, was the Object of worship to the angels of God.

14. *Glory to God in the highest.* The design of God, in the Incarnation, was to manifest the hidden glories of His nature, and to reconcile men to each other and to himself. The angels therefore declare that this Incarnation shall manifest and promote the *glory of God,* not only in the *highest* heavens, among the *highest* orders of beings, but in the *highest* and most exalted degrees. *Peace, good will toward men.* Men are in a state of hostility with Heaven and with each other. The carnal mind is enmity against God. He who sins wars against his Maker. When men become reconciled to God, through the death of His Son, they love one another. They have *peace* with God, *peace* in their own consciences, and *peace* with their neighbors; *good will* dwells among them, speaks in them, and works by them.

15. *Let us now go even unto Bethlehem.* Let us go across the country at the nearest, that we may lose no time, that we may speedily see this glorious Reconciler of God and man.

17. *They made known abroad the saying.* These shepherds were the first preachers of the gospel of Christ; and what was their text? Why, *Glory to God in the highest heavens,* and *on earth peace and goodwill among men.*

19. *And pondered them in her heart.* "Weighing them in her heart." "Weighing" is an English translation of our word "pondering," from the Latin *ponderare.* Every circumstance relative to her Son's birth, Mary treasured up in her memory; and every new circumstance she weighed, or compared with those which had already taken place, in order to acquire the fullest information concerning the nature and mission of her Son.

20. *The shepherds returned, glorifying and praising*—These simple men, having satisfactory evidence of the truth of the good tidings, and feeling a divine influence upon their own minds, returned to the care of their flocks, glorifying God for what He had shown them, and for the blessedness which they felt.

21. *When eight days were accomplished.* The law had appointed that every male should be circumcised at eight days old, or on the eighth day after its birth, Gen. xvii. 12; and our blessed Lord received circumcision in token of His subjection to the law, Gal. iv. 4; v. 3.

22. *Days of her purification.* That is, thirty-three days after what was termed the seven days of her uncleanness—forty days in all; for that was the time appointed by the law, after the birth of a male child. See Lev. xii. 2, 6. The MSS. and versions differ much in the pronoun in this place: some reading *her purification;* others, *his purification;* others, *their purification.* Two versions and two of the fathers omit the pronoun. *Their* and *his* have the greatest authorities in their support, and the former is received into most of the modern editions. The purification of every mother and child, which the law enjoined, is a powerful argument in proof of that original corruption and depravity which every human being brings into the world. The woman to be purified was placed in the east gate of the court, called Nicanor's gate, and was there sprinkled with blood; thus she received the atonement.

24. *And to offer a sacrifice.* Neither mother nor child was considered as in the Lord's covenant or under the divine protection till these ceremonies prescribed by the law had been performed. *A pair of turtledoves.* One was for a burnt offering and the other for a sin offering; see Lev. xii. 8. The rich were required to bring a lamb; but the poor and middling classes were required to bring either two *turtledoves* or two *pigeons.* This is a proof that the Holy Family were not in affluence. Jesus sanctified the state of poverty, which is the general state of man, by passing through it. Therefore the poor have the gospel preached unto them, and the poor are they who principally receive it.

25. *And, behold, there was a man in Jerusalem.* This man is distinguished because of his singular piety. There can be no doubt that there were many persons in Jerusalem named *Simeon,* besides this man; but there was none of the name who merited the attention of God so much as he in the text. *The same man was just.* He steadily regulated all his conduct by the law of his God; *and devout*—he had fully consecrated himself to God, so that he added a pious heart to a righteous conduct. The original word

signifies also a person of good report—one well received among the people, or one cautious and circumspect in matters of religion. *Waiting for the consolation of Israel.* That is, the Messiah, who was known among the pious Jews by this character; He was to be the *consolation of Israel* because He was to be its Redemption. *The Holy Ghost was upon him.* He was a man divinely inspired, overshadowed, and protected by the power and influence of the Most High.

26. *It was revealed unto him.* He was "divinely informed"—he had an express communication from God concerning the subject. "The secret of the Lord is with them that fear him." The soul of a righteous and devout man is a proper habitation for the Holy Spirit. *The Lord's Christ.* Rather, "the Lord's anointed": that Prophet, Priest, and King who was typified by so many anointed persons under the old covenant.

27. *He came by the Spirit into the temple.* Probably he had in view the prophecy of Malachi, chap. iii. 1, "The Lord, whom ye seek, shall suddenly come to his temple." Now the prophecy was just going to be fulfilled; and the Holy Spirit, who dwelt in the soul of this righteous man, directed him to go and see its accomplishment. Those who come, under the influence of God's Spirit, to places of public worship will undoubtedly meet with Him who is the Comfort and Salvation of Israel. *After the custom of the law.* To present Him to the Lord, and then redeem Him by paying five shekels, Num. xviii. 15-16, and to offer those sacrifices appointed by the law.

28. *Then took he him up in his arms.* What must the holy soul of this man have felt in this moment!

29. *Lord, now lettest thou thy servant depart in peace.* "Now Thou dismissest," "loosest" him from life, having lived long enough to have the grand end of life accomplished. *According to thy word.* It was promised to him that he should not die till he had seen the Lord's Anointed, v. 26; and now, having seen Him, he expects to be immediately dismissed in peace into the eternal world, having a full assurance and enjoyment of the salvation of God.

30. *Thy salvation.* That Saviour which it became the goodness of God to bestow upon man, and which the necessities of the human race required. Christ is called our *salvation*, as He is called our Life, our Peace, our Hope; i.e., He is the Author of all these to them who believe.

31. *Which thou hast prepared.* Which Thou hast "made ready" *before the face*, in the presence, *of all people.* Here salvation is represented under the notion of a feast which God himself has provided for the whole world, and to partake of which He has invited all the nations of the earth. There seems a direct allusion here to Isa. xxv. 6, "In this mountain shall the Lord of hosts make unto all people a feast of fat things." Salvation is properly the food of the soul, by which it is nourished unto eternal life; he that receiveth not this must perish forever.

32. *A light to lighten the Gentiles.* "A light of the Gentiles, for revelation." By Moses and the prophets, a "light of revelation" was given to the Jews, in the blessedness of which the Gentiles did not partake. By Christ and His apostles a luminous revelation is about to be given unto the Gentiles, from the blessedness of which the Jews in general, by their obstinacy and unbelief, shall be long excluded. But to all true Israelites it shall be a *glory*, an evident fulfillment of all the predictions of the prophets, relative to the salvation of a lost world; and the first offers of it shall be made to the Jewish people, who may see in it the truth of their own Scriptures indisputably evinced.

33. *Joseph and his mother marvelled.* For they did not as yet fully know the counsels of God relative to the salvation which Christ was to procure, nor the way in which the purchase was to be made.

34. *This child is set for the fall.* This seems an allusion to Isa. viii. 14-15: Jehovah, God of hosts, shall be "for a stone of stumbling and for a rock of offence to both the houses of Israel . . . And many among them shall stumble, and fall." As Christ did not come as a temporal deliverer, in which character alone the Jews expected Him, the consequence should be, they would reject Him, and so fall by the Romans. See Rom. xi. 11-12 and Matthew xxiv. But in the fullness of time there shall be a *rising again of many in Israel.* See Rom. xi. 26. *And for a sign.* A "mark" to shoot at—a metaphor taken from archers. Or perhaps Simeon refers to Isa. xi. 10-12. "There shall be a root of Jesse, which shall stand for an ensign of the people; to it shall the Gentiles seek"—intimating that the Jews would reject it, while the Gentiles should flock to it as their ensign of honor, under which they were to enjoy a glorious rest.

35. *Yea, a sword shall pierce through thy own soul also.* Probably meaning, You *also*, as well as your Son, shall die a martyr for the truth. But as this is a metaphor used by the most respectable Greek writers to express the most pungent sorrow, it may here refer to the anguish Mary must have felt when standing beside the cross of her tortured Son, John xix. 25.

36. *Anna, a prophetess.* It does not appear that this person was a *prophetess* in the strict sense of the word, i.e., one who could foretell future events, but rather a holy woman who, from her extensive knowledge and deep experience in divine things, was capable of instructing others—according to the use of the word *propheteuo*, 1 Cor. xiv. 3: "He that prophesieth, speaketh unto men to edification, and exhortation, and comfort." So we find this holy widow proclaiming Jesus to all who looked "for redemption in Jerusalem," v. 38. *The tribe of Aser.* This was one of the ten tribes of the kingdom of Israel, several families of which had returned from their idolatry unto God, in the time that Hezekiah proclaimed the Passover in Jerusalem, which is mentioned in 2 Chron. xxx. 1-11. *Seven years.* She was a pure virgin when married, was favored with her husband but *seven* years, and was now in all, taking in the time of her virginity, marriage, and widowhood, eighty-four years of age. At such an age it might be supposed she was reasonably exempted from performing the severer duties of religion, but her spirit of piety continued still to burn with a steady and undiminished flame.

37. *Departed not from the temple.* Attended constantly at the hours of prayer, which were nine in the morning and three in the afternoon.

See Acts ii. 15; iii. 1. It does not appear that women had any other functions to perform in that holy place. *With fastings.* She accompanied her devotion with frequent fastings, probably not oftener than twice in the week, for this was the custom of the most rigid Pharisees; see chap. xviii. 12.

38. *Coming in that instant.* "At that very time"—while Simeon held the blessed Redeemer in his arms, and was singing his departing and triumphal song. *Gave thanks likewise.* She, as well as Simeon, returned God public thanks for having sent this Saviour to Israel. *Spake of him.* Of the nature and design of His mission, and the glory that should take place in the land. *To all them that looked for redemption.* As Daniel's seventy weeks were known to be now completed, the more pious Jews were in constant expectation of the promised Messiah. *In Jerusalem.* It is probable she went about from house to house, testifying the grace of God.

40. *The child grew.* As to His body—being in perfect health. *Waxed strong in spirit.* His rational soul became strong and vigorous. *Filled with wisdom.* The divinity continuing to communicate itself more and more in proportion to the increase of the rational principle. The reader should never forget that Jesus was perfect man as well as God. *And the grace of God was upon him.* The word not only means *grace* in the common acceptation of the word (some blessing granted by God's mercy to those who are sinners, or have no merit), but it means also "favor" or "approbation"; and this sense I think most proper for it here when applied to the human nature of our blessed Lord; and thus our translators render the same word, v. 52. Even Christ himself, who knew no sin, grew in the favor of God, and as to His human nature, increased in the graces of the Holy Spirit.

41. *His parents went . . . every year.* This was their constant custom, because positively enjoined by the law, Exod. xxiii. 17. But it does not appear that infants were obliged to be present; and yet all the men-children are positively ordered to make their appearance at Jerusalem thrice in the year, Exod. xxxiv. 23. And our Lord, being now *twelve years old*, v. 42, accompanies His parents to the feast. Probably this was the very age at which the male children were obliged to appear before the Lord at the three public festivals—the Feast of Unleavened Bread, of Weeks, and of Tabernacles. According to the Jewish canons, it was the age at which they were obliged to begin to learn a trade.

43. *Had fulfilled the days.* Eight days in the whole: one was the Passover, and the other seven the days of unleavened bread.

44. *Supposing him to have been in the company.* Some have supposed that the men and women marched in separate companies on these occasions, which is very likely; and that sometimes the children kept company with the men, sometimes with the women. This might have led to what otherwise seems to have been inexcusable carelessness in Joseph and Mary. Joseph, not seeing Jesus in the men's company, might suppose He was with His mother in the women's company, and Mary, not seeing Him with her, might imagine He was with Joseph. *And they sought him.* "They earnestly sought Him." They are now both duly affected with a

sense of their great loss and great negligence. *Kinsfolk and acquaintance.* Those of the same family and neighborhood went up to Jerusalem together on such occasions.

45. *Seeking him.* Or rather, "seeking Him diligently." This is the reading of several MSS., Vulgate, and nine copies of the Itala.

46. *Sitting in the midst of the doctors.* The rabbins, who were explaining the law and the ceremonies of the Jewish religion to their disciples. *Asking them questions.* Not as a scholar asks his teacher, to be informed; but as a teacher, who proposes questions to his scholars in order to take an occasion to instruct them.

47. *Answers.* The word seems not to mean *answers* only, but what Jesus said by way of question to the doctors, v. 46.

48. *Why hast thou thus dealt with us?* It certainly was not His fault, but theirs. Men are very apt to lay on others the blame of their own misconduct.

49. *How is it that ye sought me?* Is not this intended as a gentle reproof? *My Father's business.* "My Father's concerns." Some think that these words should be translated, "In My Father's house," which was a reason that they should have sought Him in the Temple only. As if He had said, Where should a child be found, but in his father's house?

51. *Was subject unto them.* Behaved towards them with all dutiful submission. Probably His working with His hands at His reputed father's business is here also implied; see on v. 41. No child among the Jews was ever brought up in idleness.

52. *Jesus increased in wisdom.* See on v. 40.

CHAPTER 3

The time in which John the Baptist began to preach, 1-3. The prophecies which were fulfilled in him, 4-6. The matter and success of his preaching, 7-9; among the people, 10-11; among the publicans, 12-13; among the soldiers, 14. His testimony concerning Christ, 15-18. The reason why Herod put him afterwards in prison, 19-20. He baptizes Christ, on whom the Spirit of God descends, 21-22. Our Lord's genealogy, 23-38.

1. *Fifteenth year.* This was the fifteenth of his principality and thirteenth of his monarchy; for he was two years joint emperor, previously to the death of Augustus. *Tiberius Caesar.* This emperor succeeded Augustus, in whose reign Christ was born. He began his reign August 19, A.D. 14, reigned twenty-three years, and died March 16, A.D. 37, aged seventy-eight years. He was a most infamous character. During the latter part of his reign especially, he did all the mischief he possibly could; and that his tyranny might not end with his life, he chose Caius Caligula for his successor, merely on account of his bad qualities. *Herod.* This was Herod Antipas, the son of Herod the Great, who murdered the innocents. It was the same Herod who beheaded John Baptist, and to whom our Lord was sent by Pilate. *Ituraea and . . . Trachonitis.* Two provinces of Syria, on the confines of Judea. *Abilene.* Another province of Syria, which had its name from Abila, its chief city. These estates were left to Herod Antipas and his brother *Philip* by the will of their father, Herod the Great, and were confirmed to them by the decree of Augustus.

That Philip was tetrarch of *Trachonitis* in the fifteenth year of Tiberius we are assured by

Josephus, who says that Philip the brother of Herod died in the twentieth year of Tiberius, after he had governed Trachonitis, Batanea, and Gaulonitis thirty-seven years, *Antiq.,* b. xviii, c. 5, s. 6. And Herod continued tetrarch of Galilee till he was removed by Caligula, the successor of Tiberius, *Antiq.,* b. xviii, c. 8, s. 2. That *Lysanias* was tetrarch of *Abilene* is also evident from Josephus. He continued in this government till the Emperor Claudius took it from him, A.D. 42, and made a present of it to Agrippa. See *Antiq.,* b. xix, c. 5, s. 1. *Tetrarch* signifies the "ruler of the fourth part of a country." See the note on Matt. xiv. 1.

2. *Annas and Caiaphas being the high priests.* Caiaphas was the son-in-law of Annas or Ananias, and it is supposed that they exercised the high priest's office by turns. *The word of God came unto John.* That is, the Holy Spirit revealed to him this doctrine of salvation. This *came* upon him in the desert, where he was living in such a state of austerity as gave him full right to preach all the rigors of penitence to others.

3. *The baptism of repentance.* See on Matt. iii. 4-6, and Mark i. 1 and xvi at the end.

4. *Prepare ye the way.* It was customary for the Hindoo kings, when on journeys, to send a certain class of the people two or three days before them, to command the inhabitants to clear the ways—a very necessary precaution where there are no public roads.

5. *Every valley shall be filled.* All hindrances shall be taken out of the way. A quotation from the Greek version of Isa. xl. 4, containing an allusion to the preparations made in rough countries to facilitate the march of mighty kings and conquerors.

7-9. On this account of the Baptist's mode of preaching, see the notes on Matt. iii. 7-11.

10. *What shall we do then?* The preaching of the Baptist had been accompanied with an uncommon effusion of that Spirit which convinces of sin, righteousness, and judgment. The people who heard him now earnestly begin to inquire what they must do to be saved. They are conscious that they are exposed to the judgments of the Lord, and they wish to escape from the coming wrath.

11. *He that hath two coats.* He first teaches the great mass of the people their duty to each other. They were uncharitable and oppressive, and he taught them not to expect any mercy from the hand of God while they acted towards others in opposition to its dictates. If men be unkind and uncharitable towards each other, how can they expect the mercy of the Lord to be extended towards themselves?

12. *Then came also publicans.* He next instructs the taxgatherers in the proper discharge of their duty, though it was an office detested by the Jews at large, yet the Baptist does not condemn it. It is only the abuse of it that he speaks against. If taxes be necessary for the support of a state, there must be collectors of them; and the collector, if he properly discharge his duty, is not only a useful, but also a respectable, officer. But it seems the Jewish taxgatherers exacted much more from the people than government authorized them to do, v. 13, and the surplus they pocketed. For an account of the *publicans,* see the note on Matt. v. 46.

14. *The soldiers likewise demanded of him.* He, thirdly, instructs those among the military. They were either Roman soldiers or the soldiers of Herod or Philip. Use no violence to any; do not extort money or goods by force or violence from any. *Neither accuse any falsely.* Or "on a frivolous pretense"—"be not sycophants," like those who are base flatterers of their masters, who to ingratiate themselves into their esteem, malign, accuse, and impeach the innocent. *Be content with your wages.* The word signifies not only the money which was allotted to a Roman soldier, which was two *oboli,* about three halfpence per day, but also the necessary supply of wheat, barley, etc.

15. *Whether he were the Christ.* So general was the reformation which was produced by the Baptist's preaching that the people were ready to consider him as the promised Messiah. Thus John came in the spirit and power of Elijah, and reformed all things; showed the people, the taxgatherers, and the soldiers their respective duties, and persuaded them to put away the evil of their doings. See the note on Matt. xvii. 11.

16-17. On these verses see Matt. iii. 11-12 and Mark i. 7-8, and particularly the note on John iii. 5.

19. *Herod the tetrarch.* See this subject explained at large, Matt. xiv. 1, etc., and Mark vi. 21, 23.

21. *Jesus also being baptized.* See on Matt. iii. 16-17.

23, etc. *Thirty years of age.* This was the age required by the law, to which the priests must arrive before they could be installed in their office; see Num. iv. 3. *Being (as was supposed) the son of Joseph.* This same phrase is used by Herodotus to signify one who was only reputed to be the son of a particular person. Much learned labor has been used to reconcile this genealogy with that in Matthew, chap. i, and there are several ways of doing it; the following, which appears to me to be the best, is also the most simple and easy. Matthew, in *descending* from Abraham to Joseph, the spouse of the blessed Virgin, speaks of sons properly such, by way of natural generation: *Abraham begat Isaac, and Isaac begat Jacob,* etc. But Luke, in *ascending* from the Saviour of the world to God himself, speaks of *sons* either properly or improperly such; on this account he uses an indeterminate mode of expression. *And Jesus himself began to be about thirty years of age, being (as was supposed) the son of Joseph . . . of Heli . . . of Matthat,* etc. After this observation it is next necessary to consider that, in the genealogy described by Luke, there are two sons improperly such: i.e., two sons-in-law instead of two sons. The two sons-in-law who are to be noticed in this genealogy are Joseph, the son-in-law of Heli, whose own father was Jacob, Matt. i. 16; and Salathiel, the son-in-law of Neri, whose own father was Jechonias, 1 Chron. iii. 17 and Matt. i. 12. This remark alone is sufficient to remove every difficulty. Thus it appears that Joseph, son of Jacob, according to Matthew, was son-in-law of Heli, according to Luke. And Salathiel, son of Jechonias, according to the former, was son-in-law of Neri, according to the latter. Mary therefore appears to have been the daughter of Heli, so called by abbreviation for *Heliachim,* which is the same in Hebrew with *Joachim.* Joseph, son of Jacob, and Mary, daughter of Heli, were of the same family. Both came from Zerubbabel: Joseph from Abiud, his eldest son, Matt. i. 13; and Mary by Rhesa, the youngest. See v. 27. It is worthy of being remarked that Matthew, who wrote principally for the Jews, extends his genealogy to Abraham, through whom the promise of the Messiah was given to the Jews; but Luke, who wrote his history for the instruction of the Gentiles, extends his genealogy to Adam, to whom the promise of the Redeemer was given in behalf of himself and of all his posterity.

36. *Of Cainan.* This *Cainan,* the son of *Arphaxad,* and father of *Sala,* is not found in any other Scripture genealogy.

CHAPTER 4

Christ's temptation, 1-13. Teaches in the synagogues of Galilee, 14-15. He preaches in a synagogue at Nazareth, 16-28. They attempt to kill him, 29-30. He preaches in Capernaum, 31-32, and casts out a demon, 33-37. Heals Peter's mother-in-law, and various others, 38-41. He goes to the desert, and preaches afterwards in the synagogues of Galilee, 42-44.

1. *Was led by the Spirit.* Or, "And was carried about." Matthew says, "he was brought up." Mark says, "the Spirit driveth him"—"putteth Him forth." But each of the Evangelists attributes this to the Holy Ghost, not to Satan.

7. *If thou therefore wilt worship me.* This temptation is the last in order, as related by Matthew; and it is not reasonable to suppose that any other succeeded to it. Luke has here told the particulars, but not in the order in which they took place. See every circumstance of this temptation considered and explained in the notes on Matt. iv. 1-11.

14. *Returned in the power of the Spirit.* "In the mighty power of the Spirit." Having now conquered the grand adversary, he comes in the miracle-working energy of the Spirit to show forth His power, Godhead, and love to the people, that they might believe and be saved. He who, through the grace of God, resists and overcomes temptation is always bettered by it. This is one of the wonders of God's grace, that those very things which are designed for our utter ruin He makes the instruments of our greatest good.

15. *And he taught in their synagogues.* We do not find even the persecuting Jews ever hindered Christ or His disciples from preaching in their synagogues. *Glorified of all.* All felt the power of His preaching, and acknowledged the divinity of His mission. The scandal of the Cross had not yet taken place.

16. *To Nazareth, where he had been brought up.* It is likely that our Lord lived principally in this city till the thirtieth year of His age; but after He entered on His public ministry, His usual place of residence was at the house of Peter, in Capernaum. *As his custom was.* Our Lord regularly attended the public worship of God in the synagogues, for there the Scriptures were read. To worship God publicly is the duty of every man, and no man can be guiltless who neglects it. If a person cannot get such public worship as he likes, let him frequent such as he can get. Better to attend the most indifferent than to stay at home, especially on the Lord's day. *Stood up for to read.* The

Jews, in general, sat while they taught or commented on the Sacred Writings or the traditions of the elders; but when they *read* either the law or the prophets, they invariably *stood up;* it was not lawful for them even to lean against anything while employed in reading.

17. *And when he had opened the book.* "When He had unrolled it." The Sacred Writings used to this day, in all the Jewish synagogues, are written on skins of parchment or vellum, sewed end to end, and rolled on two rollers, beginning at each end; so that, in reading from right to left, they roll off with the left, while they roll on with the right. Probably the place in the Prophet Isaiah here referred to was the lesson for that day; and Jesus unrolled the manuscript till He came to the place. Then, after having read, He rolled it up again, and returned it to the officer, v. 20, the ruler of the synagogue, or his servant, whose business it was to take care of it.

18. *The Spirit of the Lord.* This is found in Isa. lxi. 1; but our Lord immediately adds to it v. 7 of chap. xlii. The proclaiming of liberty to the captives and the acceptable year (or year of acceptance) of the Lord is a manifest allusion to the proclaiming of the year of jubilee by sound of trumpet; see Lev. xxv. 9, etc., and the notes there. This was a year of general release of debts and obligations, of bond men and women, of lands and possessions which had been sold from the families and tribes to which they belonged. Our Saviour, by applying this text to himself, a text so manifestly relating to the institution above mentioned, plainly declares the typical design of that institution. *He hath anointed me.* I have been designed and set apart for this very purpose; My sole business among men is to proclaim glad tidings *to the poor.* All the functions of this new Prophet are exercised on the hearts of men; and the grace by which He works in the heart is a grace of healing, deliverance, and illumination.

20. *Were fastened on him.* Were "attentively fixed on Him."

22. *At the gracious words.* "To the words of grace," or the doctrines of grace, which He then preached.

23. *Physician, heal thyself.* That is, heal the brokenhearted in Thine own country, as the latter clause of the verse explains it; but they were far from being in a proper spirit to receive the salvation which He was ready to communicate, and therefore they were not healed.

24. *No prophet is accepted.* See on Matt. xiii. 55-57.

25. *In the days of Elias.* See this history, 1 Kings xvii. 1-9, compared with chap. xviii. 1-45. This was evidently a miraculous interference, as no rain fell for three years and six months, even in the rainy seasons.

26. *Unto none of them was Elias sent, save unto Sarepta.* The sentence is elliptical, and means this: To *none of them* was Elias sent; he was not sent except to *Sarepta;* for the widow at Sarepta was a Sidonian, not a widow of Israel.

27. *None of them was cleansed.* This verse is to be understood as the twenty-sixth; for Naaman, being a Syrian, was no leper in Israel.

28. *Were filled with wrath.* They seem to have drawn the following conclusion from what our Lord spoke: "The Gentiles are more precious in the sight of God than the Jews; and to them His miracles of mercy and kindness shall be principally confined." This was pretty near the truth, as the event proved. Those who profit not by the light of God, while it is among them, shall have their candle extinguished.

30. *Passing through the midst of them.* Either He shut their eyes so that they could not see Him or He so overawed them by His power as to leave them no strength to perform their murderous purpose. The man Christ Jesus was immortal till His time came, and all His messengers are immortal till their work is done.

31. *Came down to Capernaum.* Which it is likely He made His ordinary place of residence from this time.

32. *His word was with power.* "With authority." He assumed the tone and manner of a new Lawgiver; and uttered all His doctrines, not in the way of exhortation or advice, but in the form of precepts and commands, the unction of the Holy Spirit accompanying all He said.

33. *A spirit of an unclean devil.* As "demon" was used in both a good and a bad sense before and after the time of the Evangelists, the word *unclean* may have been added here by Luke merely to express the quality of *this* spirit. But it is worthy of remark that the inspired writers never use the word *demon* in a good sense.

35. *And hurt him not.* Though he "convulsed" him, Mark i. 26, and threw him down in the midst of them, probably with the design to take away his life, yet our Lord permitted it not; and this appears to be the meaning of the place. The spirit was not permitted essentially to injure him at that time.

37. *The fame.* The "sound." This is a very elegant metaphor. The people are represented as struck with astonishment, and the "sound" goes out through all the coasts, in allusion to the propagation of sound by a smart stroke upon any substance, by which the air is suddenly agitated and conveys the report made by the stroke to distant places.

38. *Simon's wife's mother.* See on Matt. viii. 14-17. As soon as Peter began to follow Christ, his family began to benefit by it.

40. *When the sun was setting.* And consequently the Sabbath ended, for before this it would have been unlawful to bring their sick to be healed.

42. *And the people sought him.* Rather "Sought Him earnestly." This reading is supported by many MSS. The people had tasted the good word of God, and now they cleave to Christ with their whole hearts. Hearing the words of Christ and feeling the influence of His Spirit upon the soul will attract and influence the heart; and indeed nothing else can do it. *And stayed him.* Strove "to detain Him"; "they caught hold of Him," thus showing their great earnestness to be further instructed.

43. *I must preach the kingdom of God to other cities.* To proclaim the kingdom of God was the Messiah's great work; healing the diseases of the people was only an emblematical and secondary work, a work that was to be the proof of His goodness, and the demonstration of His authority to preach the gospel, and open the kingdom of Heaven to all believers.

CHAPTER 5

The miraculous draught of fishes at the Lake of Gennesaret, 1-11. Christ heals a leper, 12-14. His fame being published abroad, He withdraws to the desert, 15-16. He heals a paralytic person, at which the scribes and Pharisees murmur, but the people glorify God, 17-26. He calls the publican Levi, who makes a feast for Christ, to which he invites a great number of publicans and others, at which the scribes and Pharisees murmur, and our Lord vindicates His conduct, 27-32. The question about fasting answered, 33-35. The parable of the new piece of cloth put on the old garment, and the new wine in old bottles, 36-39.

1. *The people pressed upon him.* There was a glorious prospect of a plentiful harvest, but how few of these blades came to full corn in the ear! To hear with diligence and affection is well; but a preacher of the gospel may expect that, out of crowds of hearers, only a few, comparatively, will fully receive the truth and hold out to the end. *The lake of Gennesaret.* Called also the "sea of Galilee," Matt. iv. 18 and Mark i. 16; and the "sea of Tiberias," John vi. 1. No synagogue could have contained the multitudes who attended our Lord's ministry, and therefore He was obliged to preach in the open air.

2. *Two ships.* "Two vessels." It is highly improper to term these *ships.* They appear to have been only such small boats as are used to manage nets on flat, smooth beaches.

3. *And taught . . . out of the ship.* They pressed so much upon Him on the land, through their eagerness to hear the doctrine of life, that He could not conveniently speak to them, and so was obliged to get into one of the boats; and, having pushed a little out from the land, He taught them. The smooth, still water of the lake must have served excellently to convey the sounds to those who stood on the shore.

5. *Simon . . . said unto him, Master. Epistota.* This is the first place where this word occurs; it is used by none of the inspired penmen but Luke, and he applies it only to our blessed Lord. It properly signifies a *praefect,* or one who is *set over* certain affairs or persons; it is used also for an instructor or teacher. Peter considered Christ, from what he had heard, as Teacher of a divine doctrine, and as having authority to command. He seems to comprise both ideas in this appellation; he listened attentively to His teaching, and readily obeyed His orders. *We have toiled all the night.* They had cast the net several times in the course of the night, and drew it to shore without success, and were now greatly disheartened. *At thy word I will let down the net.* He who assumes the character of a fisher of men, under any authority that does not proceed from Christ, is sure to catch nothing; but he who labors by the order and under the direction of the great Shepherd and Bishop of souls cannot labor in vain.

6. *Their net brake.* Or "began to break," or was "likely to be broken." Had it broken, as our version states, they could have caught no fish.

7. *They beckoned unto their partners.* Had not these been called in to assist, the net must have been broken and all the fish lost. What a

pity there should be such envious separation among the different sects that profess to believe in Christ Jesus! Did they help each other in the spirit of Christian fellowship, more souls would be brought to the knowledge of the truth. Some will rather leave souls to perish than admit of partners in the sacred work. It is an intolerable pride to think nothing well done but what we do ourselves, and a diabolic envy to be afraid lest others should be more successful than we are. *They . . . filled both the ships.* Both the boats had as many as they could carry, and were so heavily laden that they were ready to sink. As one justly observes, "There are fish plenty to be taken, were there skillful hands to take, and vessels to contain them. Many are disputing about the size, capacity, and goodness of their nets and their vessels, while the fish are permitted to make their escape."

8. *Depart from me; for I am a sinful man.* "Go out from" me, i.e., from my boat. Peter was fully convinced that this draught of fish was a miraculous one; and that God himself had particularly interfered in this matter, whose presence and power he reverenced in the person of Jesus. But as he felt himself a sinner, he was afraid the divine purity of Christ could not possibly endure him; therefore he wished for a separation from that power, which he was afraid might break forth and consume him. It seems to have been a received maxim among the Jews that whoever had seen a particular manifestation of God should speedily die.

10. *Thou shalt catch men.* "You shall catch men alive"; this is the proper signification of the word. *Fear not.* These discoveries of God tend to life, not to death; and you shall become the instruments of life and salvation to a lost world.

11. *They forsook all, and followed him.* God expects this from every person, and especially from those in whose hearts, or in whose behalf, He has wrought a miracle of grace or of providence.

12. *A certain city.* This was some city of Galilee, probably Chorazin or Bethsaida.

16. *And he withdrew himself into the wilderness.* Or rather, "He frequently withdrew into the desert." He made it a frequent custom to withdraw from the multitudes for a time, and pray, teaching hereby the ministers of the gospel that they are to receive fresh supplies of light and power from God by prayer, that they may be the more successful in their work; and that they ought to seek frequent opportunities of being in private with God and their books. A man can give nothing unless he first receive it; and no man can be successful in the ministry who does not constantly depend upon God, for the excellence of the power is all from Him. Why is there so much preaching, and so little good done? Is it not because the preachers mix too much with the world, keep too long in the crowd, and are so seldom in private with God?

17. *On a certain day.* This was when He was at Capernaum. See Mark ii. 1. *The power of the Lord.* The "mighty" or "miraculous" power of the Lord, i.e., of Jesus, was there *to heal them*—as many as were diseased in either body or soul. Where the teaching of Christ is, there also is the power of Christ to redeem and save.

18. *A man which was taken with a palsy.* See

this case described on Matt. ix. 1, etc., and Mark ii. 1, etc.

21. *Who can forgive sins, but God alone?* If Jesus were not God, He could not forgive sins; and His arrogating this authority would have been blasphemy against God, in the most proper sense of the word. That these scribes and Pharisees might have the fullest proof of His Godhead, He works in their presence three miracles, which from their nature could be effected only by an omniscient and omnipotent Being. The miracles are: (1) the remission of the poor man's sins, (2) the discernment of the secret thoughts of the scribes, (3) the restoration of the paralytic in an instant to perfect soundness.

26. *Strange things.* "Paradoxes." A paradox is something that appears false and absurd, but is not really so, or something contrary to the commonly received opinion.

27. *Levi.* See on Matt. ix. 9; Mark ii. 14.

28. *And he left all.* "Completely abandoning" his office, and everything connected with it. He who wishes to preach the gospel, like the disciples of Christ, must have no earthly entanglement.

29. *A great feast.* "A splendid entertainment." The word refers more properly to the number of the guests, and the manner in which they were received, than to the quality or quantity of the fare. A great number of his friends and acquaintance were collected on the occasion, that they might be convinced of the propriety of the change he had made, when they had the opportunity of seeing and hearing his heavenly Teacher.

37. *The new wine will burst the bottles.* These old bottles would not be able to stand the fermentation of the new wine, as the old sewing would be apt to give way. It is scarcely necessary to remark that the Eastern bottles are made of skins, generally those of goats.

39. *The old is better.* Is more "agreeable to the taste or palate." The "old wine," among the rabbins, was "the wine of three leaves"— that is, wine three years old—because, from the time that the vine had produced that wine, it had put forth its leaves three times.

CHAPTER 6

The disciples pluck and eat the ears of corn on the Sabbath day, and the Pharisees find fault, 1-2. Our Lord shows the true use of the Sabbath, 3-5. He heals the man with the withered hand, 6-11. He goes into a mountain to pray, and calls twelve disciples, 12-16. Multitudes are instructed and healed, 17-19. Pronounces four blessings, 20-23, and four woes, 24-26. Gives various instructions about loving our enemies, being patient, gentle, kind, grateful, and merciful, 27-36. Harsh judgments censured, and charity recommended, 37-38. The parable of the blind leading the blind, 39. Of the mote in a brother's eye, 40-42. Of the good and corrupt tree, 43-44. The good and evil treasure of the heart, 45. The parable of the two houses, one builded on the rock, and the other on the sand, 46-49.

1. *On the second sabbath after the first.* "In the first Sabbath after the second." What does this mean? In answering this question, commentators are greatly divided. By this Sabbath seems meant that which immediately followed the two great feasts, the first and last day of the Passover, and was, therefore, the *second* after the proper Passover day. The words in the Greek seem to signify the "second first Sabbath"; and, in the opinion of some, the Jews had three first Sabbaths: viz., the first Sabbath after the Pass-

over, that after the Feast of Pentecost, and that after the Feast of Tabernacles. According to this opinion, this "second first Sabbath" must have been the first Sabbath after Pentecost. This was the second day after the Passover, the day in which they were forbidden to labor, Lev. xxiii. 6, and for this reason was termed *sabbath*, Lev. xxiii. 15. But here it is marked by the name "second first Sabbath," because, being the day after the Passover, it was in this respect the *second;* and it was also the *first*, because it was the first day of unleavened bread, Exod. xii. 15-16. I think, with many commentators, that this transaction happened on the first Sabbath of the month Nisan; that is, after the second day of the Feast of Unleavened Bread. We may well suppose that our Lord and His disciples were on their way from Jerusalem to Galilee, after having kept the Passover. The word "the second first," is omitted by some MSS. and versions and the verse is read thus: "It came to pass, that he walked through the corn fields on a Sabbath day." I suppose they omitted the above word because they found it difficult to fix the meaning, which has been too much the case in other instances.

2. *Which is not lawful.* See on Matt. xii. 2-8.

3. *What David did.* See on Mark ii. 26-27.

4. After this verse, the Codex Bezae and two ancient MSS. have the following extraordinary addition: *On the same day, seeing one working on the Sabbath, he said unto him, Man, if indeed thou knowest what thou dost, blessed art thou; but if thou knowest not, thou art cursed, and art a transgressor of the law.* Whence this strange addition proceeded, it is hard to tell. The meaning seems to be this: If you now work on the Jewish Sabbath, from a conviction that that Sabbath is abolished, and a new one instituted in its place, then happy are you, for you have received divine instruction in the nature of the Messiah's kingdom; but if you do this through a contempt for the law of God, then you are accursed, forasmuch as you are a transgressor of the law.

6. *Whose right hand was withered.* See on Matt. xii. 10, etc.

7. *Watched him.* "They maliciously watched Him." This is the import of the word, chap. xiv. 1; xx. 20, and in the parallel place, Mark iii. 2.

9. *I will ask you one thing.* I will put a question to you. See on Mark iii. 4-5.

12. *In prayer to God.* Or "in the prayer of God"; i.e., "very fervent and earnest prayer."

13. *He chose twelve.* "He chose twelve out of them." Our Lord at this time had several disciples, persons who were converted to God under His ministry; and out of these converts He chose twelve, whom He appointed to the work of the ministry; and called them *apostles*, i.e., persons "sent" or commissioned by himself to preach that gospel to others by which they had themselves been saved.

15. *Called Zelotes.* Some Jews gave this name to themselves according to Josephus (*War*, b. iv, c. iii, s. 9 and vii, c. vii, s. 1), "because they pretended to be more than ordinarily *zealous* for religion, and yet practiced the very worst of actions." It is very probable that this name was first given to certain persons who were *more zealous* for the cause of pure and undefiled religion than the rest of their neighbors.

17. *And stood in the plain.* In Matt. v. 1, which is supposed to be the parallel place, our Lord is represented as delivering this sermon on the mountain; and this has induced some to think that the sermon mentioned here by Luke, though the same in substance with that in Matthew, was delivered in a different place, and at another time. But, as Dr. Priestly justly observes, Matthew's saying that Jesus was "sat down" after He had gone up to the mountain, and Luke's saying that He *stood on the plain* when He healed the sick, before the discourse, are no inconsistencies. Jesus ascends a mountain, employs the night in prayer; and, having thus solemnly invoked the divine blessing, authoritatively separates the twelve apostles from the mass of His disciples. He then descends, and heals in the plain all the diseased among a great multitude, collected from various parts by the fame of His miraculous power. Having thus created attention, He likewise satisfied the desire of the people to hear His doctrine, retiring first to the mountain whence He came, that His attentive hearers might follow Him and might better arrange themselves before Him.

20. *Blessed be ye poor.* See the Sermon on the Mount paraphrased and explained, Matthew v; vi; vii.

22. *They shall separate you.* Meaning, They will excommunicate you, or "separate you from their communion." Luke, having spoken of their separating or excommunicating them, continues the same idea in saying that they would *cast out* their *name* likewise, as a thing evil in itself. By *your name* is meant their name as His disciples. As such, they were sometimes called "Nazarenes," and sometimes "Christians"; and both these names were matter of reproach in the mouths of their enemies. So James (ii. 7) says to the converts, "Do not they blaspheme that worthy name by the which ye are called"? So when Paul (in Acts xxiv. 5) is called "a ringleader of the sect of the Nazarenes," the character of "a pestilent fellow" and that of "a mover of sedition" are joined to it; and in Acts xxviii. 22 the Jews say to Paul, "As concerning this sect, we know that every where it is spoken against"; and this is implied in 1 Pet. iv. 14, when he says, "If ye be reproached for the name of Christ," i.e., as "Christians," agreeably to what follows there in v. 16, "If any man suffer as a Christian." In after times we find Pliny, *Epist.* x. 97, consulting the Emperor Trajan whether or not he should "punish the name itself (of Christian), though no evil should be found in it."

23. *Did their fathers unto the prophets.* See 1 Kings xviii. 4; xix. 20; 2 Chron. xxiv. 21; xxxvi. 16; Neh. ix. 26.

24-26. *But woe unto you that are rich!* The Pharisees, who were laden with the spoils of the people which they received in gifts. These three verses are not found in the sermon as recorded by Matthew. They seem to be spoken chiefly to the scribes and Pharisees, who, in order to be pleasing to all, spoke to everyone what he liked best; and by finesse, flattery, and lies found out the method of gaining and keeping the good opinion of the multitude.

29. *Thy cloak . . . thy coat.* Coat. chiton,

signifies "undergarment"; and *cloak, himation,* means "upper garment."

30. *Ask them not again.* Or, "Do not beg them off." It is probable that what is here spoken relates to requiring a thing speedily that had been lent, while the reason for borrowing it still continues. In Ecclus. xx. 15, it is a part of the character of a very bad men "that to-day he lendeth, and to-morrow will he ask it again."

32. *For sinners also love those that love them.* I believe the word is used by Luke in the same sense in which "taxgatherers" is used by Matthew, chap. v. 46-47, and signifies "heathens"; not only men who have no religion, but men who acknowledge none.

34. *Of whom ye hope to receive.* Or "whom ye expect to return it."

35. *Love ye your enemies.* This is the most sublime precept ever delivered to man. A false religion durst not give a precept of this nature, because, without supernatural influence, it must be forever impracticable. In these words of our blessed Lord we see the tenderness, sincerity, extent, disinterestedness, pattern, and issue of the love of God dwelling in man. *Lend, hoping for nothing again.* The rabbins say that he who lends without usury, God shall consider him as having observed every precept.

36. *Be ye therefore merciful.* Or "compassionate." A merciful or compassionate man easily forgets injuries; pardons them without being solicited; and does not permit repeated returns of ingratitude to deter him from doing good, even to the unthankful and the unholy. See on Matt. v. 7.

37. *Judge not.* See on Matt. vii. 1. *Forgive.* The mercy and compassion which God recommends extend to the forgiving of all the injuries we have received, or can receive.

38. *Bosom.* Or "lap." Almost all ancient nations wore long, wide, and loose garments; and when about to carry anything which their hands could not contain, they used a fold of their robe in nearly the same way as women here use their aprons. The phrase is continually occurring in the best and purest Greek writers. See also Ps. cxxix. 7; Prov. vi. 27; xvii. 23. *The same measure that ye mete withal it shall be measured to you again.* The same words we find in the Jerusalem Targum on Gen. xxxviii. 26. Our Lord, therefore, lays down a maxim which themselves allowed.

39. *Can the blind lead the blind?* This appears to have been a general proverb, and to signify that a man cannot teach what he does not understand. This is strictly true in spiritual matters. A man who is not illuminated from above is utterly incapable of judging concerning spiritual things, and wholly unfit to be a guide to others.

40. *Every one that is perfect.* Or "thoroughly instructed." The noun is used by the Greek medical writers to signify the reducing a disjointed limb. It sometimes signifies to "repair" or "mend," and in this sense it is applied to broken nets, Matt. iv. 21; Mark i. 19; but in this place, and in Heb. xiii. 21; 2 Tim. iii. 17, it means "complete instruction and information." Everyone who is "thoroughly instructed" in divine things, who has his heart united to God, whose disordered tempers and passions are purified and "restored to harmony and order"; everyone

who has in him the mind that was in Christ, though he cannot be above, yet will be *as*, his Teacher—"holy, harmless, undefiled, separate from sinners."

41. *And why beholdest thou the mote?* See this explained on Matt. vii. 3-5.

43. *Corrupt fruit.* Literally, *rotten fruit;* but here it means such fruit as is unfit for use. See on Matt. vii. 17-20.

45. *A good man.* See on Matt. xii. 35.

46. *Lord, Lord.* God judges of the heart, not by *words,* but by *works.*

47. *I will shew you.* "I will show you plainly." I will enable you fully to comprehend My meaning on this subject by the following parable.

48. *He is like a man.* See on Matt. vii. 24-27.

CHAPTER 7

Christ heals the servant of a centurion, who is commended for his faith, 1-10. Raises a widow's son to life at Nain, 11-17. John Baptist hears of His fame, and sends two of his disciples to inquire whether He was the Christ, 18-23. Christ's character of John, 24-30. The obstinate blindness and capriciousness of the Jews, 31-35. A Pharisee invites Him to his house, where a woman anoints His head with oil, and washes His feet with her tears, 36-38. The Pharisee is offended 39. Our Lord reproves him by a parable, and vindicates the woman, 40-46; and pronounces her sins forgiven, 47-50.

2. *A certain centurion's servant.* See this miracle explained on Matt. viii. 5-13.

3. *Elders of the Jews.* These were either "magistrates" in the place, or the *elders* of the synagogue which the centurion had built, v. 5. He sent these, probably, because he was afraid to come to Christ himself, not being a Jew, by either nation or religion. In the parallel place in Matthew he is represented as coming to Christ himself; but it is a usual form of speech in all nations to attribute the act to a person which is done, not by himself, but by his authority.

10. *Found the servant whole.* This cure was the effect of the faith, prayer, and humility of the centurion, through which the almighty energy of Jesus Christ was conveyed to the sick man. But these very graces in the centurion were the products of grace. It is God himself who, by the gifts of His mercy, disposes the soul to receive its cure; and nothing can contribute to the reception of His grace but what is the fruit of grace itself. The apostle says, "The grace of God that bringeth salvation hath appeared to all men," Titus ii. 11. It should therefore be our concern, not to resist the operations of this grace: for though we cannot endue ourselves with any gracious disposition, yet we can quench the Spirit, by whose agency these are produced in the soul. The centurion had not received the grace of God in vain.

11. *Nain.* A small city of Galilee, in the tribe of Issachar. According to Eusebius, it was two miles from Mount Tabor, southward; and near to Endor.

12. *Carried out.* The Jews always buried their dead without the city, except those of the family of David.

18. *The disciples of John shewed him.* It is very likely that John's disciples attended the ministry of our Lord at particular times.

19. *Art thou he that should come?* Are you the promised Messiah? See on Matt. xi. 3.

Some have thought that this character of our Lord, "he who cometh," refers to the prophecy of Jacob, Gen. xlix. 10, where He is called *Shiloh*, which Grotius and others derive from *shalach*, "he sent." Hence, as the time of the fulfillment of the prophecy drew nigh, He was termed, "He who cometh," i.e., He who is just now ready to make His appearance in Judea. In Zech. ix. 9, a similar phrase is used, "Behold, thy King cometh unto thee . . . having salvation." This is meant of the Messiah only; therefore I think the words "to save" are necessarily implied.

21. *Unto many that were blind he gave sight.* Rather, "He kindly gave sight"; or, "He graciously gave sight." This is the proper meaning of the original words. In all His miracles, Jesus showed the tenderest mercy and kindness; not only the cure, but the manner in which He performed it, endeared Him to those who were objects of His compassionate regards.

22-28. See these verses explained at large on Matt. xi. 4-15.

29. *Justified God.* Or "declared God to be just." The sense is this: John preached that the divine wrath was coming upon the Jews, from which they might flee by repentance, chap. iii. 7. The Jews, therefore, who were baptized by Him, with the baptism of repentance, did thereby acknowledge that it is but *justice* in God to punish them for their wickedness unless they repented, and were baptized in token of it. This is the sense in which the word is used here and in Ps. li. 4, compared with Job xxxii. 2, and by this Evangelist again in chap. x. 29 and xvi. 15.

30. *Rejected the counsel of God.* Or "frustrated the will of God." Kypke says the verb has two meanings: (1) to "disbelieve"; (2) "despise, or disobey," and that both senses may be properly conjoined here. The will of God was that all the inhabitants of Judea should repent at the preaching of John, be baptized, and believe in Christ Jesus. Now as they did not repent at John's preaching, so they did not believe his testimony concerning Christ. Thus the will, gracious counsel, or design of God relative to their salvation was annulled or frustrated. They *disbelieved* His promises, *despised* the Messiah, and *disobeyed* His precepts.

31. *And the Lord said.* Almost every MS. of authority and importance, with most of the versions, omits these words. As the *Evangelistaria* (the books which contained those portions of the Gospels which were read in the churches) began at this verse, the words were probably at first used by them to introduce the following parable. There is the fullest proof that they never made a part of Luke's text.

32. *They are like unto children.* See on Matt. xi. 16-19. It is probable that our Lord alludes here to some play or game among the Jewish children, no account of which is now on record.

35. *Wisdom is justified.* Probably the *children of wisdom* is a mere Hebraism here for the "products or fruits of wisdom"; hence the Vatican MS., one other, and some versions have "works," instead of "sons," in the parallel place, Matt. xi. 19.

36. *One of the Pharisees.* Called Simon, v. 40. This account is considered by many critics and commentators to be the same with that in Matt. xxvi. 6, etc.; Mark xiv. 3; and John xii. 3. This subject is considered pretty much at large in the notes on Matt. xxvi. 6, etc., to which the reader is requested to refer.

37. *A woman . . . which was a sinner.* Many suppose that this woman had been a notorious public prostitute. My own opinion is that she had been a mere heathen who dwelt in this city (probably Capernaum) who, through the ministry of Christ, had been before this converted to God, and came now to give this public testimony of her gratitude to her gracious Deliverer from the darkness and guilt of sin. I am inclined to think that the original word is used for "heathen" or "Gentile" in several places of the sacred writings. I am fully persuaded that this is its meaning in Matt. ix. 10-11, 13; xi. 19; and xxvi. 45—*The Son of man is betrayed into the hands of sinners*, i.e., is delivered into the hands of the "heathens," viz., the Romans, who alone could put Him to death. I think also it has this meaning in Luke vi. 32-34; xv. 1-2, 7, 10; xix. 7; John ix. 31. I think no other sense can be justly assigned to it in Gal. ii. 15: "We who are Jews by nature, and not sinners of the Gentiles." It is, I think, likely that the grand subject of the self-righteous Pharisee's complaint was her being a "heathen." As those who were touched by such contracted a legal defilment, he could not believe that Christ was a conscientious Observer of the law, seeing He permitted her to touch Him, knowing who she was; or, if He did not know that she was a heathen, it was a proof that He was no prophet, v. 39, and consequently had not the discernment of spirits which prophets were supposed to possess. Many suppose this person to be the same as Mary Magdalene, but of this there is no solid proof.

38. *Stood at his feet behind him.* In taking their meals the Eastern people reclined on one side; the loins and knees being bent to make the more room, the feet of each person were turned outwards behind him. This is the meaning of standing behind at His feet. *Began to wash his feet with tears.* She began to water His feet—to let a shower of tears fall on them. As the Jews wore nothing like our shoes (theirs being a mere sole, bound about the foot and ankle with thongs), their feet being so much exposed had frequent need of washing, and this they ordinarily did before taking their meals. *Kissed his feet.* With affectionate tenderness, or "kissed them again and again." See on Matt. xxvi. 49. The kiss was used in ancient times as the emblem of love, religious reverence, subjection, and supplication. It has the meaning of supplication, in the way of adoration, accompanied with subjection. See 1 Kings xix. 18, "Every mouth which hath not kissed him [Baal]"; and Job xxxi. 27, "My mouth hath [not] kissed my hand"—I have paid no sort of adoration to false gods; and Ps. ii. 12, "Kiss the Son, lest he be angry"—close in with Him, embrace affectionately, the offers of mercy made unto you through Christ Jesus, "lest he [the Lord] be angry [with you], and ye perish"—which commandment this woman seems to have obeyed, in both the literal and the spiritual sense. Kissing the feet was practiced also among the heathens to express subjection of spirit and earnest supplication. Kissing the feet is a further proof that this

person had been educated a heathen. This was no part of a Jew's practice.

41. *A certain creditor.* It is plain that in this parable our Lord means, by the *creditor,* God; and, by the *two debtors,* Simon and the woman who was present. Simon, who had the light of the law, and who in consequence of his profession as a Pharisee was obliged to abstain from outward iniquity, might be considered as the debtor who owed only *fifty* pence, or *denarii.* The woman, whom I have supposed to be a heathen, not having these advantages, having no rule to regulate her actions, and no curb on her evil propensities, may be considered as the debtor who owed *five hundred pence,* or *denarii.* And when both were compared, Simon's debt to God might be considered, in reference to hers, as *fifty* to *five hundred.* However we find, notwithstanding this great disparity, both were insolvent. Simon, the religious Pharisee, could no more pay his *fifty* to God than this poor heathen her *five hundred;* and if both be not freely forgiven by the divine mercy, both must finally perish. Having *nothing to pay, he* kindly *forgave them both.*

42. *Which of them will love him most?* Which is under the greater obligation and should love him most?

43. *He to whom he forgave most.* By this acknowledgment he was, unknowingly to himself, prepared to receive our Lord's reproof.

44. *Thou gavest me no water.* In this respect Simon was sadly deficient in civil respect, whether this proceeded from forgetfulness or contempt. The custom of giving water to wash the guest's feet was very ancient. See instances in Gen. xviii. 4; xxiv. 32; Judg. xix. 21; 1 Sam. xxv. 41.

46. *My head with oil thou didst not anoint.* Anointing the head with oil was as common among the Jews as washing the face with water is among us. See Ruth iii. 3; 2 Sam. xii. 20; xiv. 2; 2 Kings iv. 2; and Ps. xxiii. 5, where the author alludes to the Jewish manner of receiving and entertaining a guest.

47. *For she loved much.* Or, "Therefore she loved much." It appears to have been a consciousness of God's forgiving love that brought her at this time to the Pharisee's house. In the common translation her forgiveness is represented to be the consequence of her loving much, which is causing the tree to produce the root, and not the root the tree. I have considered *hoti* here as having the sense of *dioti,* "therefore"; because, to make this sentence suit with the foregoing parable, vv. 42-43, and with what immediately follows here, *but to whom little is forgiven, the same loveth little,* we must suppose her love was the *effect* of her being pardoned, not the *cause* of it. *Hoti* seems to have the sense of "therefore" in Matt. xiii. 13; John viii. 44; 1 Cor. x. 17; and in the Septuagint, in Deut. xxxiii. 52; Isa. xlix. 19; Hos. ix. 15; and Eccles. v. 6. Both these particles are often interchanged in the New Testament.

48. *Thy sins are forgiven.* He gave her the fullest assurance of what He had said before to Simon (v. 47). While the Pharisee murmured, the poor penitent rejoiced.

50. *Thy faith hath saved thee.* Thy faith hath been the instrument of receiving the salvation which is promised to those who repent.

Go in peace. Though peace of conscience be the inseparable consequence of the pardon of sin, yet here it seems to be used as a valediction or farewell; as if He had said, May goodness and mercy continue to follow you! In this sense it is certainly used in Judg. xviii. 6; 1 Sam. i. 17; xx. 42; xxix. 7; 2 Sam. xv. 9; Jas. ii. 16.

CHAPTER 8

Jesus preaches through every city and village, 1. Women minister to Him, 2-3. Instructs the multitudes by the parable of the sower, 4-8. Explains it at large to His disciples, 9-15. Directions how to improve by hearing the gospel, 16-18. His mother and brethren seek Him, 19-21. He and His disciples go upon the lake, and are taken in a storm, 22-25. They arrive among the Gadarenes, 26. He cures a demoniac, 27-39. He returns from the Gadarenes, and is requested by Jairus to heal his daughter, 40-42. On the way He cures a diseased woman, 43-48. Receives information that the daughter of Jairus is dead, 49. Exhorts the father to believe; arrives at the house, and raises the dead child to life, 50-56.

1. *Throughout every city and village.* That is, of Galilee.

2. *Out of whom went seven devils.* Who had been possessed in a most extraordinary manner; probably a case of inveterate lunacy, brought on by the influence of evil spirits. The number *seven* may here express the superlative degree. Mary Magdalene is commonly thought to have been a prostitute before she came to the knowledge of Christ, and then to have been a remarkable penitent. So historians and painters represent her: but neither from this passage nor from any other of the New Testament can such a supposition be legitimately drawn. I conclude, therefore, that the common opinion is a vile slander on the character of one of the best women mentioned in the gospel of God, and a reproach cast on the character and conduct of Christ and His disciples. From the whole account of Mary Magdalene it is highly probable that she was a person of great respectability in that place; such a person as the wife of Chuza, Herod's steward, could associate with, and a person on whose conduct or character the calumniating Jews could cast no aspersions.

3. *Herod's steward.* Though the original word signifies sometimes the "inspector" or "overseer" of a province, and sometimes a "tutor of children," yet here it seems to signify the "overseer of Herod's domestic affairs," the "steward of his household." *Unto him.* Instead of *unto him,* meaning Christ, many of the best MSS. and versions have *to them,* meaning both our Lord and the twelve apostles; see v. 1. This is unquestionably the true meaning.

5. *A sower went out to sow.* See all this parable largely explained on Matt. xiii. 1-23.

15. *With patience.* Rather, "with perseverance." The Greek word which our translators render *patience* properly signifies here, and in Rom. ii. 7, "perseverance." The *good ground,* because it is *good,* strong and vigorous, continues to bear; bad or poor ground cannot produce a good crop, and besides it is very soon exhausted. The persons called the *good ground* in the text are filled with the power and influence of God and therefore continue to bring forth fruit; i.e., they persevere in righteousness. From this we may learn that the "perseverance of the saints," as it is termed, necessarily implies that they continue to bring forth fruit to the glory of God. Those who are not fruitful are not in a state of perseverance.

16. *Lighted a candle.* This is a repetition of a part of our Lord's Sermon on the Mount. See the notes on Matt. v. 15; x. 26; and on Mark iv. 21-22.

17. *For nothing is secret.* Whatever I teach you in private, you shall teach publicly; and you shall illustrate and explain every parable now delivered to the people.

18. *Even that which he seemeth to have.* Or rather, "even what he hath." *What he seemeth to have* seems to me to contradict itself. Let us examine this subject a little. (1) To *seem* to have a thing is only to have it in appearance and not in reality; but what is possessed in appearance only can only be taken away in appearance; therefore on the one side there is no gain, and on the other side no loss. On this ground, the text speaks just nothing. (2) It is evident that *what he seemeth to have,* here, is equivalent to *what he hath,* in the parallel places, Mark iv. 25; Matt. xiii. 12; xxv. 29; and in Luke xix. 26. (3) It is evident also that these persons had something which might be taken away from them. (4) The word *dokein* is often an expletive; so Xenophon in *Hellen,* vi. "Because he seemed to be" (i.e., was) "their father's friend." So in his *Oecon,* "Among the cities that seemed to be" (actually were) "at war." So *Athenaeus,* lib. vi, ch. 4, "They who seemed to be" (who really were) "the most opulent, drank out of brazen cups." (5) It often *strengthens* the sense, and is thus used by the very best Greek writers.

19. *His mother and his brethren.* See the notes on Matt. xii. 46, etc., and on Mark iii. 31, etc.

22. *Let us go over.* See on Matt. viii. 24, etc., and Mark iv. 36-41.

23. *There came down a storm of wind . . . and they . . . were in jeopardy.* This is a parallel passage to that in Jon. i. 4, "There was a mighty tempest in the sea, so that the ship was like to be broken." The word *jeopardy,* an inexpressive French term, is properly the exclamation of a disappointed gamester, *Jeu perdu!* "The game is lost!"

25. *Where is your faith?* You have a power to believe, and yet do not exercise it! You have "little faith" (Matt. viii. 26) because you do not use the grace which I have already given you. Many are looking for *more* faith without using that which they have.

26. *The country of the Gadarenes.* Or, according to several MSS., *Gerasenes* or *Gergasenes.* See on Matt. viii. 28 and Mark v. 1.

27. *A certain man.* See the case of this demoniac considered at large on the parallel places, Matt. viii. 28-34; Mark v. 1-20.

33. *Then went the devils out of the man, and entered into the swine.* Some critics and commentators would have us to understand all this of the man himself, who, they say, was a most outrageous maniac; and that, being permitted by our Lord, he ran after the swine, and drove them all down a precipice into the sea! This is solemn trifling indeed; or, at least, trifling with solemn things. It is impossible to read over the account, as given here by Luke, and admit this mode of explanation.

34. *They fled, and went and told it. They . . . went* is omitted by almost every MS. of repute and by the best of the ancient versions.

40. *Gladly received him.* This is the proper import of the word; therefore our translators needed not to have put *gladly* in italics, as though it were not expressed in the text.

41. *A man named Jairus.* See these two miracles—the raising of Jairus' daughter and the cure of the afflicted woman—considered and explained at large on Matt. ix. 18-26 and Mark v. 22-43.

42. *The people thronged him.* Almost "suffocated Him"—so great was the throng about Him.

43. *Spent all her living upon physicians.* See the note on Mark v. 26.

46. *I perceive that virtue. Dynamin,* divine or miraculous power.

54. *He put them all out.* That is, the pipers and those who made a noise, weeping and lamenting. See Matt. ix. 23; Mark v. 38.

55. *And he commanded to give her meat.* Though she was raised to life by a miracle, she was not to be preserved by a miracle. Nature is God's great instrument, and He delights to work by it; nor will He do anything by His sovereign power, in the way of miracle, that can be effected by His ordinary providence.

CHAPTER 9

Christ sends His apostles to preach and work miracles, 1-6. Herod, hearing of the fame of Jesus, is perplexed; some suppose that John Baptist is risen from the dead; others, that Elijah or one of the old prophets was come to life, 7-9. The apostles return and relate the success of their mission. He goes to a retired place, and the people follow Him, 10-11. He feeds 5,000 men with 5 loaves and 2 fishes, 12-17. He asks His disciples what the public think of Him, 18-21. Foretells His passion, 22. Shows the necessity of self-denial, and the importance of salvation, 23-25. Threatens those who deny Him before men, 26. The Transfiguration, 27-36. Cures a demoniac, 37-43. Again foretells His passion, 44-45. The disciples contend who shall be greatest, 46-48. Of the person who cast out devils in Christ's name, but did not associate with the disciples, 49-50. Of the Samaritans who would not receive Him, 51-56. Of the man who wished to follow Jesus, 57-58. He calls another disciple, who asks permission first to bury his father, 59. Our Lord's answer, 60-62.

1. *Power and authority.* The words properly mean here the power to work miracles, and that authority by which the whole demoniac system was to be subjected to them. The reader will please to observe: (1) Luke mentions both *devils* (demons) and *diseases;* therefore he was either mistaken or demons and diseases are not the same. (2) The treatment of these two was not the same; the demons were to be cast out, the diseases to be healed. See Matt. x. 1.

2. *To preach the kingdom of God.* For an explication of this phrase, see on Matt. iii. 2.

3. *Take nothing.* See on Mark vi. 7-8. *Neither money.* See on Matt. x. 9.

7. *Herod the tetrarch.* See on Matt. xiv. 1. *By him.* This is omitted by some MSS. and versions. It is probable that Luke might have written, "Herod, hearing of all the things that were done"; but Matthew says particularly that it was the fame of Jesus of which he heard, chap. xiv. 1. *He was perplexed.* "He was greatly perplexed." It is a metaphor taken from a traveller who in his journey meets with several paths, only one of which leads to the place whither he would go; and, not knowing which to take, he is distressed with perplexity and doubt.

10. *Told him all.* "Related distinctly."

11. *The people . . . followed him.* Observe here five grand effects of divine grace. (1) The people are drawn to *follow* Him. (2) He kindly *receives* them. (3) He *instructs* them in the things of God. (4) He *heals* all their diseases. (5) He *feeds* their bodies and their souls.

12. *Send the multitude away.* See this miracle explained at large on the parallel places, Matt. xiv. 15-21; Mark vi. 36-44.

18. *Whom say the people?* "The common people," i.e., the mass of people.

23. *If any man will come after me.* See on Matt. xvi. 24 and on Mark viii. 34, where the nature of proselytism among the Jews is explained.

24. *Will save his life.* See on Matt. xvi. 24, etc.

25. *Lose himself.* That is, his "life" or "soul." See the parallel places, Matt. xvi. 25; Mark viii. 35, and especially the note on the former. *Or be cast away.* "Or receive [spiritual] damage." I have added the word "spiritual" here, which I conceive to be necessarily implied. Because if a man received only temporal damage in some respect or other, yet gaining the whole world must amply compensate him. But if he should receive spiritual damage—hurt to his soul in the smallest degree—the possession of the universe could not indemnify him.

26. *Ashamed of me.* See on Mark viii. 38.

28. *About an eight days after.* See the whole of this important transaction explained at large on Matt. xvii. 1-13.

31. *His decease.* "That going out [or death] of His." That peculiar kind of death—its nature, circumstances, and necessity being considered.

35. *This is my beloved Son.* Instead of "the beloved One," some MSS. and versions have "the chosen One"; and the Aethiopic translator, as in several other cases, to be sure of the true reading, retains both.

39. *A spirit taketh him.* This very phrase is used by heathen writers when they speak of supernatural influence.

42. *The devil threw him down, and tare him.* See this case considered at large on Matt. xvii. 15-18 and on Mark ix. 14-27.

43. *The mighty power.* This "majesty" of God. They plainly saw that it was a case in which any power inferior to that of God could be of no avail, and they were deeply struck with the majesty of God manifested in the conduct of the blessed Jesus.

44. *Let these sayings sink down into your ears.* Or "put these words into your ears." To other words you may lend occasional attention —but to what concerns My sufferings and death you must ever listen. Let them constantly occupy a place in your most serious meditations and reflections.

45. *But they understood not.* See the note on Mark ix. 32.

46. *There arose a reasoning.* "A dialogue took place"—one inquired, and another answered, and so on.

49. *We forbad him.* See this subject considered on Mark ix. 38, etc.

52. *Sent messengers.* "Angels," literally; but this proves that the word "angel" signifies a messenger of any kind, whether divine or hu-

man. The messengers in this case were probably James and John.

53. *His face was.* They saw He was going up to Jerusalem to keep the feast (it was the Feast of Tabernacles, John vii. 2); and knowing Him thereby to be a Jew, they would afford nothing for His entertainment; for in religious matters the Samaritans and Jews had no dealings; see John iv. 9. The Samaritans were a kind of mongrel heathens; they feared Jehovah, and served other gods, 2 Kings xvii. 34.

54. *That we command fire.* Vengeance belongs to the Lord. What we suffer for His sake should be left to himself to reprove or punish. The insult is offered to Him, not to us.

55. *Ye know not what manner of spirit ye are of.* Ye do not consider that the present is a dispensation of infinite mercy and love, and that the design of God is not to destroy sinners, but to give them space to repent, that He may save them unto eternal life. And ye do not consider that the zeal which you feel springs from an evil principle, being more concerned for your own honor than for the honor of God. The disciples of that Christ who died for His enemies should never think of avenging themselves on their persecutors. The words, *Ye know not what manner of spirit ye are of. For the Son of man is not come to destroy men's lives, but to save them,* are wanting in many MSS.

57. *A certain man.* He was a scribe. See on Matt. viii. 19-22. It is probable that this took place when Christ was at Capernaum, as Matthew represents it, and not on the way to Jerusalem through Samaria.

61. *Another also said.* This circumstance is not mentioned by any of the other Evangelists; and Matthew alone mentions the former case, vv. 57-58. *Let me first go bid them farewell, which are at home.* "Permit me to set in order my affairs at home." Those who understand the Greek text will see at once that it will bear this translation well, and that this is the most natural. This person seems to have had in view the case of Elisha, who made a similar request to the Prophet Elijah, 1 Kings xix. 19-20, which request was granted by the prophet. But our Lord, seeing that this person had too much attachment to the earth, and that his return to worldly employments, though for a short time, was likely to become the means of stifling the good desires which he now felt, refused to grant him that permission.

62. *Put his hand to the plow.* Can any person properly discharge the work of the ministry who is engaged in secular employments? A farmer and a minister of the gospel are incompatible characters. As a person who holds the plow cannot keep on a straight furrow if he look behind him, so he who is employed in the work of the ministry cannot do the work of an evangelist if he turn his desires to worldly profits. Such a person is not *fit*, "properly disposed," has not his mind properly directed towards the heavenly inheritance, and is not *fit* to show the way to others. In both these verses there is a plain reference to the call of Elisha.

CHAPTER 10

give account of their mission, 17-20. Christ rejoices that the things which were hidden from the wise and prudent had been revealed unto babes, and shows the great privileges of the gospel, 21-24. A lawyer inquires how he shall inherit eternal life, and is answered, 25-29. The story of the Good Samaritan, 30-37. The account of Martha and Mary, 38-42.

1. *The Lord appointed other seventy.* Rather, "seventy others," not *other seventy,* as our translation has it, which seems to intimate that he had appointed seventy before this time, though probably the word *other* has a reference to the twelve chosen first. He not only chose twelve disciples to be constantly with Him, but He chose seventy others to go before Him. Our blessed Lord formed everything in His Church on the model of the Jewish church; and why? Because it was the pattern shown by God himself, the divine form, which pointed out the heavenly substance which now began to be established in its place. As He before had chosen twelve apostles, in reference to the twelve patriarchs, who were the chiefs of the twelve tribes, He now "publicly appointed" (for so the word means) *seventy* others, as Moses did the seventy elders whom he associated with himself to assist him in the government of the people; see Exod. xviii. 19; xxiv. 1-9. These Christ sent by *two and two:* (1) to teach them the necessity of concord among the ministers of righteousness; (2) that in the mouths of two witnesses everything might be established; and (3) that they might comfort and support each other in their difficult labor. See on Mark vi. 7. Several MSS. and versions have *seventy-two.* Sometimes the Jews chose six out of each tribe; this was the number of the great Sanhedrin.

2. *That he would send forth.* There seems to be an allusion here to the case of reapers who, though the harvest was perfectly ripe, yet were in no hurry to cut it down. News of this is brought to *the Lord of the harvest,* the farmer, and he is entreated to exert his authority, and hurry them out; and this he does because the harvest is spoiling for want of being reaped and gathered in. See the notes on Matt. ix. 37-38.

4. *Carry neither purse, nor scrip.* See on Matt. x. 9, etc., and Mark vi. 8, etc.

6. *The son of peace.* In the Jewish style, a man who has any good or bad quality is called the *son* of it. Thus, wise men are called "the children of wisdom," Matt. xi. 19; Luke vii. 35. So, likewise, what a man is doomed to, he is called *the son* of, as in Eph. ii. 3, wicked men are styled the "children of wrath"; so Judas is called "the son of perdition," John xvii. 12; and a man who deserves to die is called, 2 Sam. xii. 5, a "son of death." *Son of peace* in the text not only means a peaceable, quiet man, but one also of good report for his uprightness and benevolence.

7. *The labourer is worthy.* See on Matt. x. 8. *Go not from house to house.* See on Matt. x. 11.

9. *The kingdom of God is come nigh unto you.* "Is just upon you." This was the general text on which they were to preach all their sermons. See it explained, Matt. iii. 2.

11. *Even the very dust of your city.* See on Matt. x. 14-15.

13. *Woe unto thee, Chorazin!* See on Matt. xi. 21-24.

15. *To hell.* To hades. See this explained, Matt. xi. 23.

18. *I beheld Satan.* Or "Satan himself"—"The very Satan, the supreme adversary"—falling *as lightning,* with the utmost suddenness, as a flash of lightning falls from the clouds, and at the same time in the most observable manner. The fall was both very sudden and very apparent.

19. *To tread on serpents.* It is possible that by *serpents and scorpions* our Lord means the scribes and Pharisees, whom He calls "serpents" and a "brood of vipers," Matt. xxiii. 33, because through the subtilty and venom of the old *serpent,* the devil, they opposed Him and His doctrine. And by trampling on these, it is likely that He means they should get a complete victory over such; as it was an ancient custom to trample on the kings and generals who had been taken in battle, to signify the complete conquest which had been gained over them. See Josh. x. 24. See also Rom. xvi. 20.

20. *Because your names are written in heaven.* This form of speech is taken from the ancient custom of writing the names of all the citizens in a public register, that the several families might be known, and the inheritances properly preserved. This custom is still observed even in these kingdoms, though not particularly noticed. Every child that is born in the land is ordered to be *registered,* with the names of its parents, and the time when born, baptized, or registered; and this register is generally kept in the parish church, or in some public place of safety. Such a register as this is called in Phil. iv. 3; Rev. iii. 5, "the book of life," i.e., the book or register where the persons were enrolled as they came into life.

21. *Rejoiced in spirit.* Was truly and heartily joyous, felt an inward triumph. But *the Holy Spirit* is the reading here of numerous MSS. and versions. These might be considered sufficient authority to admit the word into the text. *I thank thee.* Bishop Pearce justly observes the thanks are meant to be given to God for revealing them to babes, not for hiding them from the others. *Thou hast hid.* That is, Thou hast not revealed them to the scribes and Pharisees, who idolized their own wisdom; but Thou *hast revealed them* to the simple and humble of heart.

27. *Thou shalt love the Lord.* See this important subject explained at large on Matt. xxii. 37-40. *Thy neighbour as thyself.* See the nature of *self-love* explained on Matt. xix. 19.

29. *Willing to justify himself.* Wishing to make it appear that he was a righteous man, and that consequently he was in the straight road to the kingdom of God, said, *Who is my neighbour?* supposing our Lord would have at once answered, "Every Jew is to be considered as such, and the Jews only." Now as he imagined he had never been deficient in his conduct to any person of his own nation, he thought he had amply fulfilled the law. This is the sense in which the Jews understood the word *neighbour,* as may be seen from Lev. xxix. 15-18. But our Lord shows here that the acts of kindness which a man is bound to perform to his neighbor when in distress, he should perform to any person, of whatever nation, religion, or kindred, whom he finds in necessity. As the word signifies one who is "near," this very circumstance makes any person our neighbor whom we know; and, if in distress, an object of our most compassionate regard.

30. *And Jesus answering.* Rather, "Then Jesus took him up." This I believe to be the meaning of the word; he threw out a challenge, and our Lord "took him up" on his own ground. *A certain man went down from Jerusalem.* This was the most public road in all Judea, as it was the grand thoroughfare between these two cities for the courses of priests, 12,000 of whom are said to have resided at Jericho. *Fell among thieves.* At this time the whole land of Judea was much infested with hordes of banditti, and it is not unlikely that many robberies might have been committed on that very road to which our Lord refers.

31. *And by chance.* Properly means the "coincidence of time and circumstance." At the time in which the poor Jew was half dead, through the wounds which he had received, a priest came where he was.

31-32. *Priest* and *Levite* are mentioned here, partly because they were the most frequent travellers on this road, and partly to show that these were the persons who, from the nature of their office, were most obliged to perform works of mercy, and from whom a person in distress had a right to expect immediate succor and comfort; and their inhuman conduct here was a flat breach of the law, Deut. xxii. 1-4.

33. *Samaritan* is mentioned merely to show that he was a person from whom a Jew had no right to expect any help or relief, because of the enmity which subsisted between the two nations.

34. *Pouring in oil and wine.* These, beaten together, appear to have been used formerly as a common medicine for fresh wounds. Bind up a fresh cut immediately in a soft rag or lint, moistened with pure olive oil, and the parts will heal by what is called the first intention, and more speedily than by any other means.

35. *Two pence.* Two denarii.

36. *Which . . . was neighbour?* Which fulfilled the duty which one neighbor owes to another?

37. *He that shewed mercy.* Or "so much mercy." His prejudice would not permit him to name the Samaritan, yet his conscience obliged him to acknowledge that he was the only righteous person of the three. *Go, and do thou likewise.* Be even to your enemy in distress as kind, humane, and merciful as this Samaritan was.

38. *Received him.* "Kindly received." She received Him in a friendly manner, under her roof, and entertained Him hospitably. So the word is used in the best Greek writers. Martha is supposed by some to have been a widow, with whom her brother, Lazarus, and sister, Mary, lodged.

39. *Sat at Jesus' feet.* This was the posture of the Jewish scholars while listening to the instructions of the rabbins. It is in this sense that Paul says he was "brought up at the feet of Gamaliel," Acts xxii. 3.

40. *Martha was cumbered.* "Perplexed." She was harassed with different cares and employments at the same time, one drawing one way, and another, another—a proper description of a worldly mind. But in Martha's favor it may be justly said that all her anxiety was to provide suitable and timely entertainment for our Lord and His disciples. And we should not, on the merest supposition, attribute earthly-mindedness to a woman whose character stands unimpeachable in the gospel; and who, by entertaining Christ and His disciples, and providing liberally for them, gave the highest proof that she was influenced by liberality and benevolence, and not by parsimony or covetousness. *Dost thou not care?* Dost Thou not think it wrong that my sister thus leaves me to provide and prepare this supper, *alone?*

41. *Thou art careful and troubled.* "You are distracted, your mind is divided," in consequence of which "you are disturbed," your spirit is thrown into a tumult. *About many things.* Getting a variety of things ready for this entertainment, much more than are necessary on such an occasion.

42. *One thing is needful.* This is the end of the sentence, according to Bengel. "Now Mary hath chosen . . ." begins a new one. One single dish, the simplest and plainest possible, is such as best suits Me and My disciples, whose meat and drink it is to do the will of our Heavenly Father. *Mary hath chosen that good part.* That is, of hearing My word, of which she shall not be deprived, it being at present of infinitely greater importance to attend to My teaching than to attend to any domestic concerns. While you are busily employed in providing that portion of perishing food for perishing bodies, Mary has chosen that spiritual *portion* which endures forever, and which *shall not be taken away from her.* Therefore I cannot command her to leave her present employment, and go and help you bring forward a variety of matters which are by no means necessary at this time. The words *one thing is needful,* on which we lay so much stress, are wanting in some of the most ancient MSS., and are omitted by some of the fathers, who quote all the rest of the passage—a plain proof that the meaning which we take out of them was not thought of in very ancient times; and in other MSS., versions, and fathers there is an unusual variety of readings where even the thing, or something like it, is retained. Some have it thus: "Martha, Martha, thou laborest much, and yet a little is sufficient, yea, one thing only." Others: "And only one thing is required." Others: "Thou art anxious and embarrassed about many things, when that which is needful is very small." Others: "But here there need only a few things." Others: "But a few things, or one only, is necessary." Now these are the readings of almost all the ancient versions; and we plainly perceive by them that what we term the *one thing needful* is not understood by one of them as referring to the salvation of the soul, but to the provision then to be made. In short, I wonder how the present most exceptionable mode of interpretation ever obtained, as having no countenance in the text, ancient MSS. or versions, and as being false in itself. For even Christ himself could not say that sitting at His feet and hearing His word was the one thing needful. Repentance, faith, prayer, obedience, and a thousand other things are necessary to our salvation, besides merely hearing the doctrines of Christ, even with the humblest heart.

CHAPTER 11

Christ teaches His disciples to pray, 1-4. Shows the necessity of importunity in prayer, 5-13. Casts out a dumb demon, 14. The Jews ascribe this to the power of Beelzebub; our Lord vindicates His conduct, 15-23. Miserable state of the Jews, 24-26. Who they are that are truly blessed, 27-28. He preaches to the people, 29-36. A Pharisee invites Him to dine with him, who takes offense because He washed not His hands, 37-38. Our Lord exposes their hypocrisy, 39-44. He denounces woes against the lawyers, 45-52. The scribes and Pharisees are greatly offended, and strive to entangle Him in His words, 53-54.

1-5. *Teach us to pray.* See the nature of prayer, with an ample explanation of the different parts of the Lord's Prayer, treated of in Matt. vi. 5-15. The prayer related here by Luke is not precisely the same as that mentioned by Matthew; and indeed it is not likely that it was given at the same time. There are many variations in the MSS. in this prayer, but they seem to have proceeded principally from the desire of rendering this similar to that in Matthew. Attempts of this nature have given birth to multitudes of the various readings in the MSS. of the New Testament. It should be remarked also that there is no vestige of the doxology found in Matthew in any copy of Luke's Gospel.

4. *Deliver us from evil.* Literally, "Deliver us from the wicked one."

6. *In his journey is come.* Or perhaps more literally, "A friend of mine is come to me out of his way," which renders the case more urgent— a friend of mine, benighted, belated, and who has lost his way, is come unto me.

9. *And* [or, therefore] *I say unto you, Ask,* Be importunate with God, not so much to prevail on Him to save you, as to get yourselves brought into a proper disposition to receive that mercy which He is ever disposed to give. He who is not importunate for the salvation of his soul does not feel the need of being saved; and were God to communicate His mercy to such they could not be expected to be grateful for it, as favors are prized and esteemed only in proportion to the sense men have of their necessity and importance.

13. *The Holy Spirit.* Or, as several MSS. have it, *the good spirit.* See on Matt. vii. 11.

14. *Casting out a devil.* See on Matt. xii. 22.

19. *Beelzebub.* See on Matt. x. 25.

20. *Finger of God.* See on Exod. viii. 19.

27. *A certain woman . . . lifted up her voice, and said.* It was very natural for a *woman,* who was probably a mother, to exclaim thus. She thought that the happiness of the woman who was mother to such a Son was great indeed; but our blessed Lord shows her that even the holy Virgin could not be benefited by her merely being the mother of His human nature, and that only they were happy who carried Christ in their hearts. True happiness is found in *hearing* the glad tidings of salvation by Christ Jesus, and *keeping* them in a holy heart, and *practicing* them in an unblamable life.

29. *This is an evil generation.* Or, "This is a wicked race of men." See on Matt. xii. 38-42.

33. *No man, when he hath lighted.* See on Matt. v. 15. Our Lord intimates that if He worked a miracle among such an obstinate people, who were determined to disbelieve every evidence of His messiahship, He should act as a man who lighted a candle and then covered it

with a bushel, which must prevent the accomplishment of the end for which it was lighted.

34. *The light of the body is the eye.* Or, "The eye is the lamp of the body." See on Matt. vi. 22.

36. *The whole shall be full of light.* Or "altogether enlightened"; i.e., when the eye is perfect, it enlightens the whole body. Every object within the reach of the eye is as completely seen as if there was an eye in every part. So the eye is to every part of the body what the lamp is to every part of the house. When the light of Christ dwells fully in the heart, it extends its influence to every thought, word, and action, and directs its possessor how he is to act in all places and circumstances.

37. *To dine.* The word signifies the *first* eating of the day. The Jews made but two meals in the day; their *ariston* may be called their "breakfast" or their "dinner," because it was both, and was but a slight meal. Their chief meal was their supper, after the heat of the day was over; and the same was the principal meal among the Greeks and Romans.

38. *First washed.* See on Mark vii. 2-4.

40. *Did not he that made that which is without?* God has made you such, both as to your bodies and souls, as He intended should show forth His praise. But can you think that the purpose of God can be accomplished by you while you attend only to external legal purifications, your hearts being full of rapine and wickedness?

41. *Give alms of such things as ye have.* Meaning either what was within the dishes spoken of before, or what was within their houses or power, or what they had "at hand." Far from spoiling the poor by wicked exactions, rather *give* them *alms* of everything you possess; and when a part of everything you *have* is sincerely consecrated to God for the use of the poor, then all that remains will be *clean* unto you. You will have the blessing of God in your basket and store, and everything will be sanctified to you. These verses are very difficult, and are variously translated and interpreted by critics and divines. I have given what I believe to be our Lord's meaning, in the preceding paraphrase.

42. *Ye tithe mint and rue.* See on Matt. xxiii. 23.

43. *Ye love the uppermost seats.* Every one of them affected to be a ruler in the synagogues.

44. *Ye are as graves which appear not.* In Matt. xxiii. 27 our Lord tells them that they exactly resembled whitewashed tombs; they had no fairness but on the outside. But here He says they are like hidden tombs, graves which were not distinguished by any outward decorations, and were not elevated above the ground, so that those who walked over them did not consider what corruption was within. So they, under the veil of hypocrisy, covered their iniquities, so that those who had any intercourse or connection with them did not perceive what accomplished knaves they had to do with.

45. *Thou reproachest us.* He alone who searches the heart could unmask these hypocrites; and He did it so effectually that their own consciences acknowledged the guilt, and re-echoed their own reproach.

46. *Ye lade men with burdens.* By insisting on the observance of the traditions of the elders, to which it appears, by the way, they paid no great attention themselves. See on Matt. xxiii. 4.

47. *Ye build the sepulchres.* That is, you rebuild and beautify them.

48. *Truly ye bear witness.* You acknowledge that those of old who killed the prophets were your *fathers,* and you are about to show, by your conduct towards Me and My apostles, that you are as capable of murdering a prophet now as they were of old.

49. *The wisdom of God.* These seem to be Luke's words, and to mean that Jesus, *the wisdom of God* (as He is called, 1 Cor. i. 24), added the words which follow here, on that occasion; and this interpretation of the words is agreeable to that of Matthew, who makes Jesus speak in His own person: "Wherefore, behold, I send unto you prophets," Matt. xxiii. 34.

50. *That the blood.* That the particle may be translated "so that," pointing out the event only, nor the design or intention, Bishop Pearce has well shown in his note on this place, where he refers to a like use of the word in chap. ix. 45; xiv. 20; John x. 17; Rom. v. 20; xi. 11; 1 Cor. i. 15, 31.

51. *From the blood of Abel.* See this subject explained at large on Matt. xxiii. 35. *Required.* May be translated either by the word "visited" or "revenged," and the latter word evidently conveys the meaning of our Lord. They are here represented as having this blood among them; and it is intimated that God will come by and by to *require* it, and to inquire how it was shed, and to punish those who shed it.

52. *Ye have taken away the key of knowledge.* By your traditions you have taken away the true method of interpreting the prophecies; you have given a wrong meaning to those scriptures which speak of the kingdom of the Messiah, and the people are thereby hindered from entering into it.

53. *Began to urge him vehemently.* They "began to be furious." They found themselves completely unmasked in the presence of a vast concourse of people. They therefore questioned Him on a variety of points, and hoped by the multitude and impertinence of their questions to puzzle or irritate Him, so as to induce Him to "speak rashly" (for this is the import of the word), that they might find some subject of accusation against Him.

CHAPTER 12

Christ preaches to His disciples against hypocrisy, and against timidity in publishing the gospel, 1-5. Excites them to have confidence in divine providence, 6-7. Warns them against denying Him or betraying His cause, 8-9. Of the blasphemy against the Holy Ghost, 10. Promises direction and support in persecution, 11-12. Warns the people against covetousness, 13-15. Parable of the rich man who pulled down his granaries to build greater, 16-21. Cautions against carking cares and anxieties, 22-32. The necessity of living to God, and in reference to eternity, 33-40. At the request of Peter, He further explains the preceding discourse, 41-48. The effects that should be produced by the preaching of the gospel, 49-53. The signs of the times, 54-57. The necessity of being prepared to appear before the judgment seat of God, 58-59.

1. *An innumerable multitude of p e o p l e.* "Myriads of people." A myriad is 10,000, and myriads must, at the very lowest, mean 20,000. But the word is often used to signify a crowd or multitude which cannot be readily numbered. There was doubtless a vast crowd assembled on this occasion, and many of them were deeply instructed by the very important discourse which our Lord delivered. *Leaven of the Pharisees.* See Matt. xvi. 1-12. *Which is hypocrisy.* These words are supposed by some to be an addition to the text, because it does not appear that it is their *hypocrisy* to which Christ alludes, but their false doctrines. They had, however, a large proportion of both.

2. *There is nothing covered.* See the notes on Matt. v. 15; x. 26-27; Mark iv. 22.

5. *Fear him.* Even the friends of God are commanded to fear God, as a Being who has authority to send both body and soul into hell. Therefore it is proper even for the most holy persons to maintain a fear of God, as the Punisher of all unrighteousness.

6. *Are not five sparrows sold for two farthings?* See this explained on Matt. x. 29, from which place we learn that two sparrows were sold for one farthing, and here that *five* were sold for *two farthings.*

7. *Fear not therefore.* Want of faith in the providence and goodness of God is the source of all human inquietudes and fears. He has undertaken to save and defend those to the uttermost who trust in Him.

8. *Shall confess.* See on Matt. x. 32-33.

10. *Him that blasphemeth.* See the sin *against the Holy Ghost* explained, Matt. xii. 32.

11. *Unto magistrates, and powers.* See Matt. x. 17-20. *Take ye no thought.* See Matt. vi. 25; x. 19.

13. *Speak to my brother, that he divide.* Among the Jews, the children had the inheritance of their fathers divided among them; the eldest had a double portion, but all the rest had equal parts. It is likely the person complained of in the text was the elder brother, and he wished to keep the whole to himself—a case which is far from being uncommon.

14. *A judge.* Without some judgment given in the case, no division could be made; therefore Jesus added the word *judge.* A minister of Christ ought not to concern himself with secular affairs any further than charity and the order of discipline require it. Better to leave all these things to the civil magistrate, unless where a lawsuit may be prevented, and the matter decided to the satisfaction or acquiescence of both parties.

15. *Beware of covetousness.* Or rather, "Beware of all inordinate desires." I add "all," on the authority of many MSS., versions, and several of the primitive fathers. Inordinate desires—from *pleion,* "more," and *echein,* "to have"; the desire to have *more* and *more,* let a person possess whatever he may—such a disposition of mind is never satisfied; for as soon as one object is gained, the heart goes out after another. *Consisteth not in the abundance.* That is, "dependeth not on the abundance." It is not superfluities that support man's life, but necessaries. What is necessary, God gives liberally; what is superfluous, He has not promised. Nor can a man's life be preserved by the abundance of his possessions; to prove this Jesus spoke the following parable.

16. *The ground of a certain rich man.* He had generally what is called good luck in his farm and this was a remarkably plentiful year.

17. *He thought within himself.* Began to be puzzled in consequence of the increase of his goods. Riches, though ever so well acquired, produce nothing but vexation and embarrassment.

18. *I will pull down.* The rich are full of designs concerning this life, but in general take no thought about eternity till the time that their goods and their lives are both taken away.

19. *Soul, thou hast much goods.* Great possessions are generally accompanied with pride, idleness, and luxury; and these are the greatest enemies to salvation.

20. *Thou fool.* To imagine that a man's comfort and peace can depend upon temporal things, or to suppose that these can satisfy the wishes of an immortal spirit! *This night.* What a dreadful awakening of a soul, long asleep in sin! He is now hurried into the presence of his Maker; none of his worldly goods can accompany him, and he has not a particle of heavenly treasure!

21. *So is he.* That is, "thus will it be." This is not an individual case; all who make this life their portion, and who are destitute of the peace and salvation of God, shall, sooner or later, be surprised in the same way. *Layeth up treasure for himself.* This is the essential characteristic of a covetous man. He desires riches; he gets them; he lays them up, not for the necessary uses to which they might be devoted, but *for himself*—to please himself, and to gratify his avaricious soul. Such a person is commonly called a "miser," i.e., literally, a wretched, "miserable" man.

22. *Take no thought.* Be not anxiously careful. See on Matt. vi. 25.

25. *To his stature one cubit?* See on Matt. vi. 27.

28. *Into the oven.* See the note on Matt. vi. 30.

29. *Neither be ye of doubtful mind.* Or "in anxious suspense."

30. *The nations of the world seek after.* Or "earnestly seek"; to seek one thing after another, to be continually and eagerly coveting. This is the employment of the nations of this world, utterly regardless of God and eternity! It is the essence of heathenism to live only for this life; and it is the property of Christianity to lead men to live here in reference to another and better world.

32. *Fear not, little flock.* Or "very little flock." This is what some term a double diminutive, and, literally translated, is "little, little flock." Though this refers solely to the apostles and first believers, of whom it was literally true, yet we may say that the number of genuine believers has been, and is still, small in comparison of heathens and false Christians. *It is your Father's good pleasure.* "It hath pleased," though this tense joined with an infinitive has often the force of the present. Our Lord intimates, God has already given you that Kingdom which consists in righteousness, peace, and joy in the Holy Ghost, and has undertaken to protect and save you to the uttermost. Therefore, fear not; the smallness of your number cannot hurt you, for Omnipotence itself has undertaken your cause.

33. *Sell that ye have.* Dispose of your goods. Be not like the foolish man already mentioned, who laid up the produce of his fields, without permitting the poor to partake of God's bounty. Turn the fruits of your fields (which are beyond what you need for your own support) into money, and give it in alms; and the treasure thus *laid out* shall be as *laid up* for yourselves and families in heaven.

34. *Where your treasure is.* Men fix their hearts on their treasures, and often resort to the place where they have deposited them, to see that all is safe and secure. Let God be the Treasure of your soul, and let your heart go frequently to the place where His honor dwelleth.

35. *Let your loins.* Be active, diligent, determined, ready; let all hindrances be removed out of the way, and let the candle of the Lord be always found burning brightly in your hand.

37. *He shall gird himself.* Alluding to the long garments which were worn in the Eastern countries; and which, in travelling and serving, were tucked up in their belts. That those among the Romans who waited on the company at table were *girded,* and had their clothes tucked up, appears from what Horace says, "He runs about like a girded waiter."

38. *If he shall come in the second watch.* See the note on Matt. xiv. 25.

42. *Faithful and wise steward.* Those appear to have been stewards among the Jews whose business it was to provide all the members of a family, not only with food, but with raiment.

46. *With the unbelievers.* Or, rather, "the unfaithful." Persons who had the light and knowledge of God's Word, but made an improper use of the privileges they received.

47. *Shall be beaten with many stripes.* Criminals among the Jews could not be beaten with more than forty stripes; and as this was the sum of the severity to which a whipping could extend, it may be all that our Lord here means. But, in some cases, a man was adjudged to receive fourscore stripes! How could this be, when the law had decreed only forty? Answer: By doubling the crime. He received forty for each crime; if he were guilty of two offenses, he might receive fourscore.

48. *Shall be beaten with few.* For petty offenses the Jews in many cases inflicted so few as four, five, and six stripes.

From this and the preceding verse we find that it is a crime to be ignorant of God's will, because to everyone God has given less or more of the means of instruction.

49. *I am come to send fire.* See this subject largely explained on Matt. x. 34, etc. From the connection in which these words stand, both in this place and in Matthew, it appears as if our Lord intended by the word *fire,* not only the consuming influence of the Roman sword, but also the influence of His own Spirit in the destruction of sin. In both these senses this *fire* was *already kindled.* As yet, however, it appeared but as a spark, but was soon to break out into an all-consuming flame.

50. *But I have a baptism.* The fire, though already kindled, cannot burn up till after the Jews have put Me to death. Then the Roman sword shall come, and the Spirit of judgment, burning, and purification shall be poured out.

51. *To give peace.* See Matt. x. 34.

52. *Five in one house divided.* See on Matt. x. 35-36.

54. *A cloud rise.* See on Matt. xvi. 2-3.

56. *This time?* Can you not discover from the writings of the prophets and from the events which now take place that this is the time of the Messiah, and that I am the very Person foretold by them?

57. *And why . . . judge ye?* Even without the express declarations of the prophets, you might, from what you see and hear yourselves, discern that God has now visited His people in such a manner as He never did before.

58. *When thou goest with thine adversary.* This and the next verse are a part of our Lord's Sermon on the Mount. See them explained, Matt. v. 25-26. *Give diligence.* "Give labor," do everything in your power to get free before a suit commences. *The officer.* Properly signifies such an officer as was appointed to levy the fines imposed by the law for a violation of any of its precepts.

59. *Till thou hast paid the very last mite.* And when can this be, if we understand the text spiritually? Can weeping, wailing, and gnashing of teeth pay to divine justice the debt a sinner has contracted? This is impossible. Let him who readeth understand.

CHAPTER 13

Christ preaches the necessity of repentance, from the punishment of the Galileans massacred by Pilate, 1-3. And by the death of those on whom the tower in Siloam fell, 4-5. The parable of the barren fig tree, 6-9. Christ cures a woman who had been afflicted eighteen years, 10-13. The ruler of the synagogue is incensed and is reproved by our Lord, 14-17. The parable of the mustard seed, 18-19; of the leaven, 20-21. He journeys towards Jerusalem, and preaches, 22. The question, Are there few saved? and our Lord's answer, with the discourse thereon, 23-30. He is informed that Herod purposes to kill Him, 31-32. Predicts His own death at Jerusalem, and denounces judgments on that impenitent city, 33-35.

1. *At that season.* At what time this happened is not easy to determine, but it appears that it was now a piece of news which was told to Christ and His disciples for the first time. *Whose blood Pilate had mingled.* This piece of history is not recorded (as far as I can find) by Josephus; however, he states that the Galileans were the most seditious people in the land. They belonged properly to Herod's jurisdiction; but, as they kept the great feasts at Jerusalem, they probably, by their tumultuous behavior at some one of them, gave Pilate, who was a mortal enemy to Herod, a pretext to fall upon and slay many of them and thus, perhaps, sacrifice the people to the resentment he had against the prince.

4. *The tower in Siloam.* This tower was probably built over one of the porticoes near the pool, which is mentioned in John ix. 7. See also Neh. iii. 15. "Debtors," a Jewish phrase for *sinners.* Persons professing to be under the law are bound by the law to be obedient to all its precepts; those who obey not are reckoned "debtors" to the law, or rather to that divine justice from which the law came.

5. *Ye shall all likewise perish.* "In a like way, in the same manner." This prediction of our Lord was literally fulfilled. When the city was taken by the Romans, multitudes of the priests, who were going on with their sacrifices, were slain, and their blood mingled with the blood of their victims; and multitudes were buried under the ruins of the walls, houses, and Temple. See Josephus, *War,* b. vi, cc. iv—vi.

6. *A certain man.* Many meanings are given to this parable, and divines may abound in them. The sense which our Lord designed to convey by it appears to be the following: (1) *A person,* God Almighty. (2) *Had a fig tree,* the Jewish church. (3) *Planted in his vineyard*—established in the land of Judea. (4) *He came seeking fruit*—He required that the Jewish people should walk in righteousness, in proportion to the spiritual culture He bestowed on them. (5) *The vinedresser*—the Lord Jesus, for God hath committed all judgment to the Son, John v. 22. (6) *Cut it down*—let the Roman sword be unsheathed against it. (7) *Let it alone*—Christ is represented as Intercessor for sinners, for whose sake the day of their probation is often lengthened; during which time He is constantly employed in doing everything that has a tendency to promote their salvation. (8) *Thou shalt cut it down*—a time will come that those who have not turned at God's invitations and reproofs shall be cut off, and numbered with the transgressors.

7. *Behold these three years.* From this circumstance in the parable it may be reasonably concluded that Jesus had been, at the time of saying this, exercising His ministry for three years past; and from what is said in v. 8 of letting it alone this year also, it may be concluded likewise that this parable was spoken about a *year* before Christ's crucifixion. *Why cumbereth it the ground?* Or in other words, "Why should the ground be also useless?" The tree itself brings forth no fruit; let it be cut down that a more profitable one may be planted in its place.

18-19. *The kingdom . . . is like a grain of mustard seed.* See on Matt. xiii. 31.

21. *Like leaven.* See this explained, Matt. xiii. 33.

22. *Journeying toward Jerusalem.* Luke represents all that is said, from chap. ix. 51, as having been done and spoken while Christ was on His last journey to Jerusalem.

24. *Many . . . will seek.* They *seek*—wish and desire; but they do not *strive.* Therefore, because they will not "agonize"—will not be in earnest—they shall not get in.

25. *And hath shut to the door.* See the notes on Matt. vii. 22-23 and xxv. 10-41.

28. *Abraham, and Isaac.* See on Matt. viii. 11, where the figures and allusions made use of here are particularly explained.

29. *They shall come.* That is, the Gentiles, in every part of the world, shall receive the gospel of the grace of God, when the Jews shall have rejected it.

30. *There are last which shall be first.* See on Matt. xix. 30.

31. *Depart hence.* It is probable that the place from which Christ was desired to depart was Galilee or Perea, for beyond this Herod had no jurisdiction. *Herod will kill thee.* Lactantius says that this Herod was the person who chiefly instigated the Jewish rulers to put our Lord to death—fearing lest himself should be expelled from the kingdom, if Christ should be permitted to set up His.

32. *Tell that fox.* Herod was a very vicious prince, and lived in public incest with his sister-in-law, Mark vi. 17. A fox among the Jews appears to have been the emblem of a wicked ruler who united cunning with cruelty, and was always plotting how he might aggrandize himself by spoiling the people. *To day and to morrow.* I am to work miracles for two days more, and on the third day I shall be put to death. But it is probable that this phrase only means that He had but a short time to live, without specifying its duration. *Perfected.* Or "finished." I shall then have accomplished the purpose for which I came into the world, leaving nothing undone which the counsel of God designed Me to complete. Hence, in reference to our Lord, the word implies His dying, as the plan of human redemption was not finished till He bowed His head and gave up the ghost on the Cross; see John xix. 30, where the same word is used. It is used also in reference to Christ's *death*, Heb. ii. 10; v. 9; see also Acts xx. 24 and Heb. xii. 23.

33. *I must walk.* I must continue to work miracles and teach for a short time yet, and then I shall die in Jerusalem. Therefore I cannot depart, according to the advice given Me (v. 31), nor can a hair of My head fall to the ground till My work be all done. *Perish out of Jerusalem.* A man who professes to be a *prophet* can be tried on that ground only by the grand Sanhedrin, which always resides at Jerusalem; and as the Jews are about to put Me to death, under the pretense of My being a false prophet, therefore My sentence must come from this city and My death take place in it.

35. *Your house.* The Temple—called here *your house,* not "My house"—I acknowledge it no longer; I have abandoned it, and will dwell in it no more forever. So He said, 2 Chron. xxxvi. 17, when He delivered the Temple into the hands of the Chaldeans—*the house of their sanctuary.* A similar form of speech is found, Exod. xxxii. 7, where the Lord said to Moses, "Thy people," to intimate that He acknowledged them no longer for His followers. But some think that our Lord means, not the Temple, but the whole commonwealth of the Jews.

CHAPTER 14

Christ heals a man ill of the dropsy, on a Sabbath day, 1-6. He inculcates humility by a parable, 7-11. The poor to be fed, and not the rich, 12-14. The parable of the great supper, 15-24. How men must become disciples of Christ, 25-27. The parable of the prudent builder, who estimates the cost before he commences his work, 28-30. And of the provident king, 31-32. The use of these parables, 33. The utility of salt while in its strength and perfection, and its total uselessness when it has lost its savor, 34-35.

1. *Chief Pharisees.* Or "one of the rulers of the Pharisees." A man who was of the sect of the Pharisees, and one of the rulers of the people. *To eat bread on the sabbath day.* But why is it that there should be an invitation or dinner given on the Sabbath day? Answer: The Jews purchased and prepared the best viands they could procure for the Sabbath day, in order to do it honor. As the Sabbath is intended for the benefit of both the body and soul of man, it should not be a day of austerity or fasting, especially among the laboring poor. The most wholesome and nutritive food should be then procured if possible, that both body and soul may feel the influence of this divine appointment,

and give God the glory of His grace. On this blessed day let every man eat his bread with gladness and singleness of heart, praising God. *They watched him.* Or "were maliciously watching." The conduct of this Pharisee was most execrable. Professing friendship and affection, he invited our blessed Lord to his table, merely that he might have a more favorable opportunity of watching His conduct, that he might accuse Him and take away His life. In eating and drinking people feel generally less restraint than at other times and are apt to converse more freely. The man who can take such an advantage over one of his own guests must have a baseness of soul of which we would have thought that devils alone were capable.

2. *The dropsy.* "Dropsical." Probably the insidious Pharisee had brought this dropsical man to the place, not doubting that our Lord's eye would affect His heart, and that He would instantly cure him; and then he could most plausibly accuse Him for a breach of the Sabbath. If this were the case, and it is likely, how deep must have been the perfidy and malice of the Pharisee!

4. *They held their peace.* They could not answer the question but in the affirmative; and as they were determined to accuse Him if He did heal the man, they could not give an answer but such as would condemn themselves, and therefore they were silent.

7. *They chose out the chief rooms.* When custom and law have regulated and settled places in public assemblies, a man who is obliged to attend may take the place which belongs to him, without injury to himself or to others. When nothing of this nature is settled, the law of humility and the love of order are the only judges of what is proper. To take the highest place when it is not our due is public vanity; obstinately to refuse it when offered is another instance of the same vice, though private and concealed. Humility takes as much care to avoid the ostentation of an affected refusal as the open seeking of a superior place. In this parable our Lord only repeats advices which the rabbins had given to their pupils, but were too proud to conform to themselves. Rabbi Akiba said, "Go two or three seats lower than the place that belongs to thee, and sit there till they say unto thee, 'Go up higher'; but do not take the uppermost seat, lest they say unto thee, 'Come down': for it is better that they should say unto thee, 'Go up, go up'; than that they should say, 'Come down, come down.'"

11. *For whosoever exalteth himself.* This is the unchangeable conduct of God. He is ever abasing the proud, and giving grace, honor, and glory to the humble.

12. *Call not thy friends.* Our Lord certainly does not mean that a man should not entertain, at particular times, his friends. But what He inculcates here is charity to the poor; and what He condemns is those entertainments which are given to the rich either to flatter them or to procure a similar return.

14. *For they cannot recompense thee.* Because you have done it for God's sake only, and they cannot make you a recompense, therefore God will consider himself your Debtor, and will recompense you in the resurrection of the righteous.

16-24. *A certain man made a great supper.* See a similar parable to this, though not spoken on the same occasion, explained, Matt. xxii. 1-14.

23. *Compel them to come in.* "Prevail" on them by the most earnest entreaties. The word is used by Matthew, chap. xiv. 22, and by Mark, chap. vi. 45; in both places when Christ is said to "constrain" His disciples to get into the vessel, nothing but His commanding or persuading them to do it can be reasonably understood.

26. *And hate not.* Matthew, chap. x. 37, expresses the true meaning of this word, when he says, "He that loveth father or mother more than me." In chap. vi. 24 he uses the word *hate* in the same sense. When we read, Rom. ix. 13, "Jacob have I loved, but Esau have I hated," the meaning is simply, I have loved Jacob, the Israelites, more than Esau, the Edomites. That this is no arbitrary interpretation of the word *hate*, but one agreeable to the Hebrew idiom, appears from what is said on Gen. xxix. 30-31, where Leah's being *hated* is explained by Rachel's being loved more than Leah.

28. *To build a tower.* Probably this means no more than a dwelling house, on the top of which, according to the Asiatic manner, battlements were built, both to take the fresh air on, and to serve for refuge from and defense against an enemy. It was also used for prayer and meditation. This parable represents the absurdity of those who undertook to be disciples of Christ without considering what difficulties they were to meet with, and what strength they had to enable them to go through with the undertaking. He that will be a true disciple of Jesus Christ shall require no less than the mighty power of God to support him, as both hell and earth will unite to destroy him.

33. *Whosoever he be of you.* This seems to be addressed particularly to those who were then, and who were to be, preachers of His gospel, and who were to travel over all countries publishing salvation to a lost world.

CHAPTER 15

Publicans and sinners draw near to hear our Lord, at which the Pharisees are offended, 1-2. Christ vindicates His conduct in receiving them by the parable of the lost sheep, 3-7. The parable of the lost piece of money, 8-10; and the affecting parable of the prodigal son, 11-32.

1. *Publicans and sinners.* "Taxgatherers and heathens"; persons who believed neither in Christ nor in Moses. See the note on chap. vii. 36. Concerning the "taxgatherers," see the note on Matt. v. 46.

2. *Receiveth sinners.* He "receives them cordially, affectionately," takes them to His bosom, for so the word implies.

4. *What man of you?* Our Lord spoke this and the following parable to justify His conduct in receiving and conversing with sinners. *An hundred sheep.* Parables similar to this are frequent among the Jewish writers. The whole flock of mankind, both Jews and Gentiles, belongs unto this divine Shepherd; and it is but reasonable to expect that the gracious Proprietor will look after those who have gone astray, and bring them back to the flock. The lost sheep is an emblem of a heedless, thoughtless sinner, one who follows the corrupt dictates of his own heart without ever reflecting upon his conduct or considering what will be the issue of his unholy course of life. No creature strays more easily than a sheep; none is more heedless; and none so incapable of finding its way back to the flock, when once gone astray. It will bleat for the flock, and still run on in an opposite direction to the place where the flock is; this I have often noticed. No creature is more defenseless than a sheep, and more exposed to be devoured by dogs and wild beasts. Even the fowls of the air seek its destruction. I have known ravens often attempt to destroy lambs by picking out their eyes, in which, when they have succeeded, as the creature does not see whither it is going, it soon falls an easy prey to its destroyer.

7. *Just persons, which need no repentance.* Who do not require "such a change of mind and purpose" as these do—who are not so profligate, and cannot repent of sins they have never committed. Distinctions of this kind frequently occur in the Jewish writings. There are many persons who have been brought up in a sober and regular course of life, attending the ordinances of God and being true and just in all their dealings; these most materially differ from the heathens mentioned in v. 1, because they believe in God, and attend the means of grace. They differ also essentially from the taxgatherers mentioned in the same place, because they wrong no man and are upright in their dealings. Therefore they cannot repent of the sins of a heathen, which they have not practiced; nor of the rapine of a taxgatherer, of which they have never been guilty. As, therefore, these *just persons* are put in opposition to the taxgatherers and heathens, we may at once see the scope and design of our Lord's words. These needed no repentance in comparison of the others, as not being guilty of their crimes. And as these belonged, by outward profession at least, to the flock of God, and were sincere and upright according to their light, they are considered as being in no danger of being *lost*; and as they fear God, and work righteousness according to their light, He will take care to make those further discoveries to them of the purity of His nature, the holiness of His law, and the necessity of the atonement, which He sees to be necessary. On this ground, the owner is represented as feeling more joy in consequence of finding *one sheep* that was *lost*, there having been almost no hope of its recovery, than he feels at seeing ninety and nine still safe under his care.

8. *Ten pieces of silver.* "Ten drachmas." I think it always best to retain the names of these ancient coins, and to state their value in English money. Every reader will naturally wish to know by what names such and such coins were called in the countries in which they were current. The Grecian *drachma* was worth about the same as the Roman *denarius*. The *drachma* that was lost is also a very expressive emblem of a sinner who is estranged from God, and enslaved to habits of iniquity. The longer a piece of money is lost, the less probability is there of its being again found. So the sinner sinks deeper and deeper into the impurities of sin and gets the image and superscription of his Maker defaced from his heart.

12. *Give me the portion of goods.* It may seem strange that such a demand should be made, and that the parent should have acceded to it, when he knew that it was to minister to his debauches that his profligate son made the demand here specified. But the matter will appear plain when it is considered that it has been an immemorial custom in the East for sons to demand and receive their portion of the inheritance during their father's lifetime; and the parent, however aware of the dissipated inclinations of the child, could not legally refuse to comply with the application.

13. *Riotous living.* In a course of life that led him to *spend all.*

15. *To feed swine.* The basest and vilest of all employments and, to a Jew, peculiarly degrading. Shame, contempt, and distress are wedded to sin, and can never be divorced. No character could be meaner in the sight of a Jew than that of a swineherd. Herodotus informs us that in Egypt they were not permitted to mingle with civil society, nor to appear in the worship of the gods, nor would the very dregs of the people have any matrimonial connections with them.

16. *With the husks.* Bochart, I think, has proved that *keratia* does not mean *husks.* He shows also that the original word means the fruit of the *charub* tree, which grows plentifully in Syria. This kind of pulse was made use of to feed *swine.*

17. *When he came to himself.* A state of sin is represented in the sacred writings as a course of folly and madness, and repentance is represented as a restoration to sound sense. *I perish with hunger!* "Here" is added by some MSS. and most of the versions.

18. *Against heaven.* That is, "against God." The Jews often make use of this periphrasis in order to avoid mentioning the name of God, which they have ever treated with the utmost reverence. But some contend that it should be translated "even unto heaven"; a Hebraism for, I have sinned exceedingly, beyond all description.

20. *And kissed him.* Or "kissed him again and again." The father thus showed his great tenderness towards him, and his great affection for him.

22. *Bring forth the best robe.* "Bring out that chief garment," the garment which was laid by, to be used only on birthdays or festival times. *Put a ring on his hand.* Giving a ring was in ancient times a mark of honor and dignity. See Gen. xli. 42; 1 Kings xxi. 8; Esther viii. 2; Dan. vi. 17; Jas. ii. 2. *Shoes on his feet.* Formerly those who were captivated had their shoes taken off, Isa. xx. 1; and when they were restored to liberty their shoes were restored. See 2 Chron. xxviii. 15.

23. *The fatted calf, and kill it.* "Sacrifice it." In ancient times the animals provided for public feasts were first sacrificed to God. The blood of the beast being poured out before God, by way of atonement for sin, the flesh was considered as consecrated, and the guests were considered as feeding on divine food.

24. *Was dead.* Lost to all good—given up to all evil. In this figurative sense the word is used by the best Greek writers.

25. *His elder son.* Meaning probably persons of a regular moral life, who needed no repentance in comparison of the prodigal already described. *In the field.* Attending the concerns of the farm. *He heard music. Symphonias,* a number of sounds mingled together, as in a con-

cert. *Dancing.* But Le Clerc denies that the word means *dancing* at all, as it properly means a "choir of singers." The "symphony" mentioned before may mean the musical instruments which accompanied the choirs of singers.

28. *He was angry.* This refers to the indignation of the scribes and Pharisees, mentioned in vv. 1-2. In every point of view, the anger of the old son was improper and unreasonable. He had already received his part of the inheritance (see v. 12), and his profligate brother had received no more than what was his just dividend. Besides, what the father had acquired since that division he had a right to dispose of as he pleased, even to give it all to one son; nor did the ancient customs of the Asiatic countries permit the other children to claim any share in such property thus disposed of.

29. *Never gavest me a kid.* It is evident from v. 12 that the father gave him his portion when his profligate brother claimed his, for he divided his whole substance between them. And though he had not claimed it, so as to separate from, and live independently of, his father, yet he might have done so whenever he chose; and therefore his complaining was both undutiful and unjust.

30. *This thy son.* "This son of thine"—words expressive of supreme contempt. *This son*—he would not condescend to call him by his name, or to acknowledge him for his brother; and at the same time bitterly reproaches his amiable father for his affectionate tenderness, and readiness to receive his once undutiful, but now penitent, child!

31. *All that I have is thine.* See on v. 28.

32. *This thy brother.* Or "this brother of thine." To awaken this ill-natured, angry, inhumane man to a proper sense of his duty, to both his parent and his brother, this amiable father returns him his own unkind words, but in a widely different spirit. This son of mine to whom I show mercy is *your brother,* to whom you should show tenderness and affection, especially as he is no longer the person he was. He was dead in sin—he is quickened by the power of God; he was *lost* to you, to me, to himself, and to our God, but now he is *found.* This, as well as the two preceding parables, was designed to vindicate the conduct of our blessed Lord in receiving taxgatherers and heathens. And as the Jews, to whom it was addressed, could not but approve of the conduct of this benevolent father, and reprobate that of his elder son, so they could not but justify the conduct of Christ towards those outcasts of men, and at least in the silence of their hearts pass sentence of condemnation upon themselves.

CHAPTER 16

The parable of the unjust steward, 1-8. Christ applies this to His hearers, 9-13. The Pharisees take offense, 14. Our Lord reproves them, and shows the immutability of the law, 15-17. Counsels against divorce, 18. The story of the rich man and the beggar, commonly called Dives and Lazarus, 19-31.

1. *A steward.* One who superintends domestic concerns, and ministers to the support of the family, having the products of the field and business put into his hands for this very purpose. *Wasted his goods.* Had been profuse and profligate, and had embezzled his master's substance.

2. *Give an account of thy.* Produce your books of receipts and disbursements, that I may see whether the accusation against you is true or false. The original may be translated, "Give up the business of the stewardship."

3. *I cannot dig.* He could not submit to become a common day laborer, which was both a severe and base employment. *To beg I am ashamed.* And as these were the only honest ways left him to procure a morsel of bread, and he would not submit to either, he found he must continue the system of knavery, in order to provide for his idleness and luxury, or else starve.

4. *They may receive me.* That is, the debtors and tenants, who paid their debts and rents, not in money, but in kind; such as wheat, oil, and other produce of their lands.

6. *An hundred measures of oil.* "A hundred baths." The *bath* was the largest measure of capacity among the Hebrews, except the *homer*, of which it was the tenth part: see Ezek. xlv. 11, 14. It is equal to the *ephah*, i.e., to seven gallons and a half of our measure. *Take thy bill.* "Your account." The writing in which the debt was specified, together with the obligation to pay so much, at such and such times. This appears to have been in the handwriting of the debtor, and probably signed by the steward, and this precluded imposition on each part. To prevent all appearance of forgery in this case, he is desired to write it over again, and to cancel the old engagement.

7. *An hundred measures of wheat.* "A hundred cors." *Koros,* from the Hebrew *cor,* was the largest measure of capacity among the Hebrews, whether for solids or liquids. As the *bath* was equal to the *ephah*, so the *cor* was equal to the *homer*. It contained about seventy-five gallons and five pints English.

8. *The lord commended.* Viz., the master of this unjust steward. He spoke highly of the address and cunning of his iniquitous servant. He had, on his own principles, made a very prudent provision for his support; but his master no more approved of his conduct in this than he did in his wasting his substance before. From the ambiguous and improper manner in which this is expressed in the common English translation, it has been supposed that our blessed Lord commended the conduct of this wicked man; but the word there translated *lord* simply means the "master" of the unjust steward. *The children of this world.* Such as mind worldly things only, without regarding God or their souls. A phrase by which the Jews always designate the Gentiles. *Children of light.* Such as are illuminated by the Spirit of God, and regard worldly things only as far as they may subserve the great purposes of their salvation, and become the instruments of good to others. But ordinarily the former evidence more carefulness and prudence in providing for the support and comfort of this life than the latter do in providing for another world.

9. *The mammon of unrighteousness.* Literally, "the mammon of injustice." Riches promise much, and perform nothing; they excite hope and confidence, and deceive both. In making a man depend on them for happiness, they rob him of the salvation of God and of eternal glory. For these reasons they are represented as unjust and deceitful. *When ye fail.* That is, when ye

"die." The Septuagint use the word in this very sense, Jer. xlii. 17, 22. So does Josephus, *War,* chap. iv. 1, 9. *They may receive you.* The expression seems to be a mere Hebraism: *they may receive you,* for "ye shall be received"; i.e., God shall admit you, if you make a faithful use of His gifts and graces. He who does not make a faithful use of what he has received from his Maker has no reason to hope for eternal felicity.

10. *He that is faithful in that which is least.* He who has the genuine principles of fidelity in him will make a point of conscience of carefully attending to even the smallest things; and it is by habituating himself to act uprightly in little things that he acquires the gracious habit of acting with propriety, fidelity, honor, and conscience in matters of the greatest concern. On the contrary, he who does not act uprightly in small matters will seldom feel himself bound to pay much attention to the dictates of honor and conscience, in cases of high importance. Can we reasonably expect that a man who is continually falling by little things has power to resist temptations to great evils?

12. *That which is another man's.* Or rather "another's." That is, worldly riches, called another's: (1) Because they belong to God, and He has not designed that they should be any man's portion; (2) Because they are continually changing their possessors, being in the way of commerce, and in providence going from one to another. *That which is your own.* Grace and glory, which God has particularly designed for you.

13. *No servant can serve two masters.* The heart will be either wholly taken up with God or wholly engrossed with the world.

14. *They derided him.* Or rather, "They treated Him with the utmost contempt." So we may translate the original words, which literally signify, "They turned up their noses at Him."

15. *Ye . . . justify yourselves.* "You declare yourselves to be just."

16. *The law and the prophets were until John.* The law and the prophets continued to be the sole teachers till John came, who first began to proclaim the glad tidings of the kingdom of God. And now, he who wishes to be made a partaker of the blessings of that Kingdom must "rush speedily" into it, as there will be but a short time before an utter destruction shall fall upon this ungodly race. They who wish to be saved must imitate those who take a city by storm—rush into it, without delay, as the Romans are about to do into Jerusalem.

18. *Putteth away* (or divorceth) *his wife.* See on Matt. v. 31-32; xix. 9-10; Mark x. 12, where the question concerning divorce is considered at large.

19. *There was a certain rich man.* This account of the rich man and Lazarus is either a parable or a real history. If it be a parable, it is what may be; if it be a history, it is that which has been. Either a man may live as is here described, and go to perdition when he dies; or some have lived in this way, and are now suffering the torments of an eternal fire. The account is equally instructive in whichsoever of these lights it is viewed. *There was a certain rich man.* Here is the *first* degree of his reprobation—he got all he could, and kept

all to himself. He *was clothed in purple and fine linen.* Purple was a very precious and costly stuff; but our Lord does not say that in the use of it he exceeded the bounds of his income, nor of his rank in life. Yet our Lord lays this down as a *second* cause of his perdition. He *fared sumptuously every day.* Now let it be observed that the law of Moses, under which this man lived, forbade nothing on this point but excess in eating and drinking. Besides, this rich man is not accused of having eaten food which was prohibited by the law, or of having neglected the abstinences and fasts prescribed by it. It is true, he is said to have feasted *sumptuously every day;* but our Lord does not intimate that this was carried to excess, or that it ministered to debauch. What are his crimes? (1) He was *rich.* (2) He was *finely clothed.* And (3) he *feasted well.* No other evil is spoken of him. In comparison of thousands he was not only blameless, but he was a virtuous man.

20. *There was a certain beggar named Lazarus.* His name is mentioned because his character was good and his end glorious, and because it is the purpose of God that the righteous shall be had in everlasting remembrance. *Lazarus,* a contraction of the word *Eliezar,* which signifies the "help or assistance of God"—a name properly given to a man who was both poor and afflicted, and had no help but that which came from heaven.

22. *Abraham's bosom,* an allusion to the custom at Jewish feasts, when three persons reclining on their left elbows on a couch, the person whose head came near the breast of the other was said to lie in his bosom. So it is said of the beloved disciple, John xiii. 25. *Abraham's bosom* was a phrase used among the Jews to signify the paradise of God. *The rich man also died, and was buried.* There is no mention of this latter circumstance in the case of Lazarus. He was buried, no doubt—necessity required this; but he had the burial of a pauper, while the pomp and pride of the other followed him to the tomb.

23. *And seeth Abraham afar off, and Lazarus in his bosom.* He sees Lazarus clothed with glory and immortality—this is the first circumstance in his punishment. What a contrast! What a desire does he feel to resemble him, and what rage and despair because he is not like him!

25. *Son, remember that thou in thy lifetime receivedst thy good things.* The remembrance of the good things possessed in life, and now to be enjoyed no more forever, together with the remembrance of grace offered or abused, will form a circumstance in the perdition of the ungodly.

26. *Beside all this, between us and you there is a great gulf.* The eternal purpose of God, formed on the principles of eternal reason, separates the persons and the places of abode of the righteous and the wicked, so that there can be no intercourse: *They which would pass from hence to you cannot; neither can they pass to us, that would come from thence.* The iniquitous conduct of relatives and friends, who have been perverted by the bad example of those who are lost, is a source of present punishment to them; and if they come also to the same place of torment, must be, to those who were the instruments of bringing them thither, an eternal

source of anguish. "Send Lazarus to my father's family, for I have five brothers, that he may earnestly testify to them, that they come not to this place of torment." These brothers had probably been influenced by his example to content themselves with an earthly portion, and to neglect their immortal souls. Those who have been instruments of bringing others into hell shall suffer the deeper perdition on that account.

29. *They have Moses and the prophets.* This plainly supposes they were all Jewish believers; they had these writings in their hands, but they did not permit them to influence their lives.

30. *If one went to them from the dead.* Many are desirous to see an inhabitant of the other world, and converse with him, in order to know what passes there. Make way! Here is a damned soul, which Jesus Christ has evoked from the hell of fire! Hear him! Hear him tell of his torments! Hear him utter his regrets!

31. *If they hear not Moses.* This answer of Abraham contains two remarkable propositions: (1) That the Sacred Writings contain such proofs of a divine origin that, though all the dead were to arise to convince an unbeliever of the truths therein declared, the conviction could not be greater nor the proof more evident of the divinity and truth of these sacred records than that which themselves afford; (2) That to escape eternal perdition and get at last into eternal glory, a man is to receive the testimonies of God and to walk according to their dictates.

CHAPTER 17

Christ teaches the necessity of avoiding offenses, 1-2. How to treat an offending brother, 3-4. The efficacy of faith, 5-6. No man by his services or obedience can profit his Maker, 7-10. He cleanses ten lepers, 11-19. The Pharisees inquire when the kingdom of God shall commence; Christ answers them, and corrects their improper views of the subject, 20-37.

1. *It is impossible but that offences will come.* Such is the corrupt state of the human heart that, notwithstanding all the influences of grace and the promises of glory, men will continue to sin against God; and His justice must continue to punish.

2. *A millstone.* To have a millstone hanged about the neck was a common proverb.

3-4. *If thy brother trespass.* See the notes on Matt. xviii. 21-22.

5. *Increase our faith.* This work of pardoning every offense of every man, and that continually, seemed so difficult, even to the disciples themselves, that they saw, without an extraordinary degree of faith, they should never be able to keep this command.

6. *As a grain of mustard seed.* A faith that increases and thrives as that is described to do. *This sycamine.* The words seem to intimate that they were standing by such a tree. The *sycamine* is probably the same as the "sycamore." Jerome, who was well-acquainted with these countries, translates the word "mulberry tree." *Be thou plucked up by the root.* See the note on Matt. xxi. 21, where it is shown that this mode of speech refers to the accomplishment of things very difficult, but not impossible.

7-9. *Which of you, having a servant?* It is never supposed that the master waits on the servant—the servant is bound to wait on his master, and to do everything for him to the uttermost of his power. Nor does the former expect thanks for it, for he is bound by his agreement to act thus because of the stipulated reward, which is considered as being equal in value to all the service that he can perform.

10. *We are unprofitable servants.* This text has often been produced to prove that no man can live without committing sin against God. But let it be observed the text says *unprofitable servants,* not sinful servants.

12. *Which stood afar off.* They kept at a distance, because forbidden by law and custom to come near to those who were sound, for fear of infecting them. See Lev. xiii. 46; Num. v. 2; 2 Kings xv. 5.

13. *They lifted up their voices.* They cried with one accord—they were all equally necessitous, and there was but one voice among them all, though ten were engaged in crying at the same time. As they were companions in suffering, they were also companions in prayer.

14. *Shew yourselves unto the priests.* According to the direction, Lev. xiii. 2, etc.; xiv. 2, etc. Our Lord intended that their cure should be received by faith. They depended on His goodness and power; and though they had no promise, yet they went at His command to do that which those only were required by the law to do who were already healed. *And ... as they went,* in this spirit of implicit faith, *they were cleansed.* God highly honors this kind of faith, and makes it the instrument in His hand of working many miracles. He who will not believe till he receives what he calls a reason for it is never likely to get his soul saved. The highest, the most sovereign reason that can be given for believing is that God has commanded it.

15. *One of them, when he saw that he was healed.* It seems that he did not wait to go first to the priest, but turned immediately back, and gave public praise to the kind hand from which he had received his cure.

16. *He was a Samaritan.* One who professed a very corrupt religion, and from whom much less was to be expected than from the other nine, who probably were Jews.

18. *This stranger.* Often God receives more praise and affectionate obedience from those who had long lived without His knowledge and fear than from those who were bred up among His people and who profess to be called by His name. The simple reason is, Those who have much forgiven will love much, chap. vii. 47.

19. *Thy faith hath made thee whole.* Your faith has been the means of receiving that influence by which you have been cleansed.

20. *Cometh not with observation.* "With scrupulous observation."

21. *Lo here! or, lo there!* Perhaps those Pharisees thought that the Messiah was kept secret, in some private place, known only to some of their rulers; and that by and by He should be proclaimed in a similar way to that in which Joash was by Jehoiada the priest. See the account, 2 Chron. xxiii. 1-11.

22. *When ye shall desire to see one of the days.* As it was our Lord's constant custom to support and comfort the minds of His disciples, we cannot suppose that He intimates here that they shall be left destitute of those blessings

necessary for their support in a day of trial. When He says, *Ye shall desire to see one of the days of the Son of man,* He either means, you of this nation, you Jews, and addresses His disciples as if they should bear witness to the truth of the declaration, intimating that heavy calamities were about to fall upon them, and that they should desire in vain to have those opportunities of returning to God which now they rejected; or He means that such should the distressed state of this people be that the disciples would through pity and tenderness desire the removal of those punishments from them which could not be removed because the cup of their iniquity was full. But the former is more likely to be the sense of the place.

24. *As the lightning, that lighteneth.* See this particularly explained, Matt. xxiv. 27-28.

25. *But first must he suffer many things.* As the cup of the iniquity of this people shall not be full till they have finally rejected and crucified the Lord of life and glory, so this desolation cannot take place till after My death.

26. *As it was in the days of Noe.* See on Matt. xxiv. 38.

27. *They did eat, they drank.* They spent their whole lives in reference to this world, and made no sort of provision for their immortal souls. So it was when the Romans came to destroy Judea; there was a universal carelessness, and no one seemed to regard the warnings given by the Son of God.

31. *He which shall be upon the house top.* See this explained on Matt. xxiv. 17.

32. *Remember Lot's wife.* Relinquish everything, rather than lose your souls. She "looked back," Gen. xix. 26; probably she turned back also to carry some of her goods away—for so much the preceding verse seems to intimate—and became a monument of the divine displeasure, and of her own folly and sin.

33. *Whosoever shall seek to save his life.* These or similar words were spoken on another occasion. See on Matt. x. 39; xvi. 25-26.

34 and 36. On the subject of these verses see Matt. xxiv. 40-41. The thirty-sixth verse is, without doubt, an interpolation. It was probably borrowed from Matt. xxiv. 40. The whole verse is wanting in most MSS. and versions and in many of the fathers.

37. *Where, Lord?* In what place shall all these dreadful evils fall? The answer our Lord gives in a figure, the application of which they are to make themselves. Where the "dead carcass" is, there will be the "birds of prey"—where the sin is, there will the punishment be. *Thither will the eagles* (or vultures) *be gathered together.*

CHAPTER 18

The parable of the importunate widow, 1-8. Of the Pharisee and the publican, 9-14. Infants brought to Christ, 15-17. The ruler who wished to know how he might inherit eternal life, 18-23. Our Lord's reflections on his case, 24-27. What they shall receive who follow Christ, 28-30. He foretells His approaching passion and death, 31-34. He restores a blind man to sight at Jericho, 35-43.

1. *Men ought always to pray.* Therefore the plain meaning and moral of the parable are evident; viz., that as afflictions and desolations were coming on the land, and they should have

need of much patience and continual fortitude, and the constant influence and protection of the Almighty, therefore they should be instant in prayer. It states, further, that men should never cease praying for that the necessity of which God has given them to feel till they receive a full answer to their prayers. No other meaning need be searched for in this parable; Luke, who perfectly knew his Master's meaning, has explained it as above.

2. *A judge, which feared not God, neither regarded man.* It is no wonder that our Lord calls this person an "unrighteous judge," v. 6. Because this person *feared not God,* he paid no attention to the calls of justice; and because he respected not *man,* he was unmoved at the complaint of the widow.

3. *Avenge me of mine adversary.* The original had better be translated, "Do me justice against, or vindicate me from, my adversary." If the woman had come to get revenge, as our common translation intimates, I think our blessed Lord would never have permitted her to have the honor of a place in the sacred records. She desired to have justice, and that only; and by her importunity she got that which the unrighteous judge had no inclination to give, but merely for his own ease.

4. *He said within himself.* How many actions which appear good have neither the love of God nor that of our neighbor, but only self-love of the basest kind, for their principle and motive!

5. *She weary me.* "Stun me." A metaphor taken from boxers, who bruise each other, and by beating each other about the face "blacken the eyes." See 1 Cor. ix. 27.

6. *Hear what the unjust judge saith.* Our blessed Lord intimates that we should reason thus with ourselves: "If a person of such an infamous character as this judge was could yield to the pressing and continual solicitations of a poor widow, for whom he felt nothing but contempt, how much more ready must God be, who is infinitely good and merciful, and who loves His creatures in the tenderest manner, to give His utmost salvation to all them who diligently seek it!"

7. *And shall not God avenge his own elect?* And will not God, the righteous Judge, "do justice for His chosen?" As God has graciously promised to give salvation to every soul that comes unto Him through His Son, and has put His Spirit in their hearts, inducing them to cry unto Him incessantly for it, the goodness of His nature and the promise of His grace bind Him to hear the prayers they offer unto Him, and to grant them all that salvation which He has led them by His promise and Spirit to request. *Which cry day and night unto him.* This is a genuine characteristic of the true elect or disciples of Christ. They feel they have neither light, power, nor goodness but as they receive them from Him; and, as He is the Desire of their souls, they incessantly seek that they may be upheld and saved by Him. *Though he bear long with them.* Rather, "and He is compassionate towards them," and consequently not at all like to the unrighteous judge.

8. *He will avenge them speedily.* Or, "He will do them justice speedily"—"instantly, in a trice." (1) Because He has promised it; and (2) Because He is inclined to do it. *When the Son of man cometh.* To require the produce of the seed of the Kingdom sown among this people. *Shall he find faith on the earth?* Or rather, "Shall He find fidelity in this land?" Shall He find that the soil has brought forth a harvest proportioned to the culture bestowed on it?

9. *Despised.* "Disdained, made nothing of others, treated them with sovereign contempt." Our Lord grants that the Pharisees made clean the outside; but, alas! what pride, vainglory, and contempt for others, were lodged within!

10. *Publican.* See an account of these on Matt. v. 46. Both these persons *went up into the temple to pray,* i.e., to worship God. They were probably both Jews, and felt themselves led by different motives to attend at the Temple, at the hour of prayer: the one to return thanks for the mercies he had received; the other to implore that grace which alone could redeem him from his sins.

11. *Stood and prayed thus with himself.* Or "stood by himself and prayed," as some would translate the words. *God, I thank thee.* In Matt. v. 20, our Lord says, "Unless your righteousness abounds more than that of the scribes and Pharisees, you shall not enter into the kingdom of God." Now the righteousness of the scribes and Pharisees is described here by a Pharisee himself. We find it was twofold: (1) It consisted in doing no harm to others, (2) In attending all the ordinances of God, then established in the Jewish economy; and in these things they were not like *other men,* the bulk of the inhabitants of the land paying little or no attention to them. That the Pharisees were in their origin a pure and holy people can admit of little doubt, but that they had awfully degenerated before our Lord's time is sufficiently evident. They had lost the spirit of their institution, and retained nothing else than its external regulations. This Pharisee did no harm to others—I am not rapacious, nor unjust, nor an adulterer.

12. He observed the ordinances of religion—*I fast twice in the week.* The Jewish days of fasting, in each week, were the second and fifth, what we call Monday and Thursday. These were instituted in remembrance of Moses' going up to the mount to give the law, which they suppose to have been on the fifth day; and of his descent, after he had received the two tables, which they suppose was on the second day of the week. *I give tithes of all that I possess.* Or "of all I acquire."

13. *The publican, standing afar off.* Not because he was a heathen and dared not approach the holy place (for it is likely he was a Jew), but because he was a true penitent, and felt himself utterly unworthy to appear before God. *Would not lift up . . . his eyes.* Holding down the head, with the eyes fixed upon the earth, was (1) a sign of deep distress, (2) of a consciousness and confession of guilt, and (3) it was the very posture that the Jewish rabbins required in those who prayed to God. So the Pharisee appears to have forgotten one of his own precepts. *But smote upon his breast.* Smiting the breast was a token of excessive grief, commonly practiced in all nations. It seems to intimate a desire in the penitent to punish that heart through the evil propensities of which the sin deplored had been committed. *God be merciful to me.* "Be propitious toward me through sacrifice"—or, Let an atonement be

made for me. I am a sinner, and cannot be saved but in this way. The Greek word often signifies to make expiation for sin. We see then, at once, the reason why our blessed Lord said that the taxgatherer "went down to his house justified rather than the other"; he sought for mercy through an atonement for sin, which was the only way in which God had from the beginning purposed to save sinners. As the Pharisee depended on his doing no harm and observing the ordinances of religion for his acceptance with God, according to the economy of grace and justice, he must be rejected. For as all had sinned and come short of the glory of God, and no man could make an atonement for his sins, so he who did not take refuge in that which God's mercy had provided must be excluded from the kingdom of Heaven.

14. *Went down to his house justified.* His sin blotted out, and himself accepted. *Rather than the other.* That is, the other was not accepted, because he exalted himself—he made use of the mercies which he acknowledged he owed to God, to make claims on the divine approbation, and to monopolize the salvation of the Most High!

15-17. *They brought unto him also infants.* On these verses the reader is requested to consult the notes on Matt. xix. 13-14 and on Mark x. 16.

18-23. *A certain ruler.* See the case of this person largely explained on Matt. xix. 16-22 and Mark x. 21-22.

24. *How hardly shall they that have riches.* See the notes on this discourse of our Lord, on Matt. xix. 24-30 and Mark x. 30.

28. *We have left all.* Our trades, our houses, and families. The reader is desired to consult the notes on Matt. iv. 20; xix. 27, etc.

29. *That hath left house, or parents.* See on Matt. xix. 28-29 and Mark x. 29-30.

31. *Behold, we go up to Jerusalem.* See the notes on this discourse, Matt. xx. 17-19 and Mark x. 32.

33. *And the third day he shall rise again.* See Hos. vi. 2; and let the reader observe that the passage should be read thus: "In the third day He will raise Him up, and we shall live before Him"; His resurrection shall be the pledge, token, and cause of ours.

34. *They understood none of these things.* Notwithstanding all the information which Christ had given them concerning this awful subject, they could not as yet fully comprehend how the Messiah should suffer; or how their Master, whose power they knew was unlimited, should permit the Jews and Gentiles to torment and slay Him as He here intimates they would.

35. *A certain blind man.* Bartimaeus. See this transaction explained at large on Matt. xx. 29-34 and Mark x. 46, etc.

CHAPTER 19

The conversion of Zacchaeus, 1-10. The parable of the nobleman, his ten servants, and the ten pounds, 11-27. Christ sends His disciples for a colt, on which He rides into Jerusalem, 28-40. He weeps over the city, and foretells its destruction, 41-44. Goes into the Temple, and casts out the buyers and sellers, 45-46. The chief priests and the scribes seek to destroy Him, but are afraid of the people, who hear Him attentively, 47-48.

1. *Entered and passed through.* "Was passing through." Our Lord had not as yet passed *through Jericho*—He was only "passing" through it; for the house of Zacchaeus, in which He was to lodge, v. 5, was in it.

2. *Zacchaeus.* It is not unlikely that this person was a Jew by birth; see v. 9. But because he had engaged in a business so infamous, in the eyes of the Jews, he was considered as a mere heathen, v. 7. *Chief among the publicans.* Either a farmer-general of the taxes, who had subordinate collectors under him, or else the most respectable and honorable man among that class at Jericho. *He was rich.* And therefore the more unlikely to pay attention to an impoverished Messiah, preaching a doctrine of universal mortification and self-denial.

3. *And he sought to see Jesus who he was.* So the mere principle of curiosity in him led to his conversion and salvation, and to that of his whole family, v. 9.

4. *He ran before.* The shortness of his stature was amply compensated by his agility and invention. Had he been as tall as the generality of the crowd, he might have been equally unnoticed with the rest. His getting into the tree made him conspicuous; had he not been so low of stature he would not have done so. Even the imperfections of our persons may become subservient to the grace of God in our eternal salvation. As the Passover was at hand, the road was probably crowded with people going to Jerusalem, but the fame of the cure of the blind man was probably the cause of the concourse at this time.

6. *Received him joyfully.* He had now seen who He was, and he wished to hear what He was; and therefore he rejoiced in the honor that God had now conferred upon him. How often does Christ make the proposal of lodging, not only in our house, but in our heart, without its being accepted!

7. *To be guest with a man that is a sinner.* Meaning either that he was a heathen or, though by birth a Jew, yet as bad as a heathen, because of his unholy and oppressive office.

8. *If I have taken any thing . . . by false accusation.* Esychophantesa, from *sychon*, "a fig," and *phaino*, "I show or declare"; for among the primitive Athenians, when the use of that fruit was first found out, or in the time of a dearth when all sorts of provisions were exceedingly scarce, it was enacted that no figs should be exported from Attica; and this law (not being actually repealed when a plentiful harvest had rendered it useless by taking away the reason of it) gave occasion to ill-natured and malicious fellows to accuse all persons they found breaking the letter of it; and from them all busy informers have ever since been branded with the name of "sycophants." *I restore him fourfold.* This restitution the Roman laws obliged the taxgatherers to make, when it was proved they had abused their power by oppressing the people. See the observations at the end of Genesis xlii and Num. v. 7.

11. *Immediately appear.* Perhaps the generality of His followers thought that on His arrival at Jerusalem He would proclaim himself king.

12. *A certain nobleman.* In the following parable there are two distinct morals intended: (1) the behavior of the *citizens* to the nobleman, and (2) the behavior of his own *servants* to him. (1) By the behavior of the *citizens*, and

their punishment (verses 14, 27), we are taught that the Jews, who were the people of Christ, would reject Him, and try to prevent His reigning over them in His spiritual kingdom, and would for that crime be severely punished by the destruction of their state. And this moral is all that answers to the introductory words, v. 11, "They thought that the kingdom of God should immediately appear." (2) The other moral extends itself through the whole of the parable, viz., that the disciples of Christ, who are His *servants*, and who made a good improvement of the favors granted them by the gospel, should be rewarded in proportion to the improvement made under the means of grace. The meaning of the different parts of this parable appears to be as follows. *A certain nobleman*—The Lord Jesus, who was shortly to be crucified by the Jews. *Went into a far country.* Ascended to the right hand of the Divine Majesty. *To receive . . . a kingdom.* To take possession of the mediatorial Kingdom, the right to which, as Messiah, He had acquired by His sufferings; see Phil. ii. 8-9; Heb. i. 3, 8-9. In these words there is an allusion to the custom of those days, when they who had kingdoms or governments given unto them went to Rome to receive that dignity from the emperors. In proof of this, see Josephus, *Ant.,* 1. xiv, c. xiv, where we find Herod went to Rome to receive the sanction and authority of the Roman emperor. And, from lib. xvii, c. 3, we learn that his successors acted in the same way. *And to return.* To judge and punish the rebellious Jews.

13. *Ten servants.* All those who professed to receive His doctrine. *Ten* was a kind of sacred number among the Hebrews, as well as *seven*. *Ten pounds.* Ten minas. It appears from Ezek. xlv. 12 to have been equal to sixty shekels in money.

14. *His citizens.* Or "countrymen"—the Jewish people, who professed to be subjects of the kingdom of God. *Hated him.* Despised Him for the meanness of His birth, His crucifixion to the world, and for the holiness of His doctrine. Neither mortification nor holiness suits the dispositions of the carnal mind. *Sent a message after him.* As, in v. 12, there is an allusion to a person's going to Rome, when elected to be ruler of a province or kingdom, to receive that dignity from the hand of the emperor, so it is here intimated that, after the person went to receive this dignity, some of the discontented citizens took the opportunity to send an embassy to the emperor to prevent him from establishing the object of their hatred in the government. *We will not have this man.* The Jews rejected Jesus Christ, would not submit to His government, and a short time after this preferred even a murderer to Him.

15. *When he was returned.* When He came to punish the disobedient Jews, and when He shall come to judge the world. See the parable of the *talents*, Matt. xxv. 14, etc.

16. *Lord, thy pound hath gained ten.* The principal difference between this parable and that of the talents above referred to is that the *mina* given to each seems to point out the gift of the gospel, which is the same to all who hear it; but the talents distributed in different proportions according to each man's ability seem to intimate that God has given different capacities and advantages to men, by which this one gift of the gospel may be differently improved.

17. *Over ten cities.* This is to be understood as referring to the new kingdom which the nobleman had just received. His former trustiest and most faithful servants he now represents as being made governors under him over a number of cities, according to the capacity he found in each, which capacity was known by by the improvement of the minas.

20. *Lord, behold, here is thy pound.* See Matt. xxv. 18.

23. *With usury.* "With its produce," i.e., what the loan of the money is fairly worth, after paying the person sufficiently for using it.

26. *And from him that hath not.* See this particularly explained, Matt. xiii. 12.

27. *Those mine enemies . . . bring hither.* The Jews, whom I shall shortly slay by the sword of the Romans.

28. *He went before.* Perhaps it means that He walked at the head of His disciples, and that He and His disciples kept on the road before other companies who were then also on their way to Jerusalem, in order to be present at the feast.

29-38. See this Triumphal Entry into Jerusalem explained at large on Matt. xxi. 1-11 and Mark xi. 1-10.

40. *If these should hold their peace, the stones would immediately cry out.* Of such importance is My present conduct to you and to others, being expressly predicted by one of your own prophets, Zech. ix. 9, as pointing out the triumph of humility over pride, and of meekness over rage and malice, as signifying the salvation which I bring to the lost souls of men, that, if this multitude were silent, God would give even to the stones a voice, that the advent of the Messiah might be duly celebrated.

41. *And wept over it.* See Matt. xxiii. 37.

42. *The things which belong unto thy peace!* It is very likely that our Lord here alludes to the meaning of the word Jerusalem, *yereh,* "he shall see," and *shalom,* "peace or prosperity." Now, because the inhabitants of it had not "seen" this "peace" and salvation, because they had refused to open their eyes, and behold this glorious light of heaven which shone among them, therefore He said, *Now they are hid from thine eyes,* still alluding to the import of the name.

43. *Cast a trench about thee.* This was literally fulfilled when this city was besieged by Titus. Josephus gives a very particular account of the building of it, this wall, which he says was effected in three days, though it was not less than thirty-nine furlongs in circumference; and that, when this wall and trench were completed, the Jews were so enclosed on every side that no person could escape out of the city, and no provision could be brought in, so that they were reduced to the most terrible distress by the famine which ensued. The whole account is well worth the reader's attention. See Josephus, *War,* book v, chap. xii, secs. 1-3.

44. *The time of thy visitation.* That is, the time of God's gracious offers of mercy to you. This took in all the time which elapsed from the preaching of John the Baptist to the coming of the Roman armies, which included a period of above forty years.

45. *Went into the temple.* See all this transaction explained, Matt. xxi. 12-16.

47. *And he taught daily in the temple.* This He did for five or six days before His crucifixion. Some suppose that it was on Monday in the Passion Week that He thus entered into Jerusalem and purified the Temple; and on Thursday He was seized late at night. During these four days He taught in the Temple, and lodged each night at Bethany.

48. *Were very attentive to hear him.* Or, "They heard Him with the utmost attention"; literally, "They hung upon Him, hearing." The same form of speech is used often by both Greek and Latin writers of the best repute.

CHAPTER 20

The question concerning the authority of Christ and the baptism of John, 1-8. The parable of the vineyard let out to wicked husbandmen, 9-18. The chief priests and scribes are offended, and lay snares for Him, 19-20. The question about tribute, 21-26. The question about the resurrection of the dead, and our Lord's answer, 27-40. How Christ is the Son of David, 41-44. He warns His disciples against the hypocrisy of the scribes, whose condemnation He points out, 45-47.

1. *One of those days.* Supposed to have been one of the four last days of His life, mentioned in chap. xix. 47, probably Tuesday before the Passover.

2. *By what authority.* See the note on Matt. xxi. 23-27.

9. *A certain man planted a vineyard.* See this parable largely explained, Matt. xxi. 33-46. See also on Mark xii. 4-9.

16. *God forbid.* Or, "Let it not be." Our phrase, *God forbid*, answers pretty well to the meaning of the Greek, but it is no translation.

18. *Grind him to powder.* See on Matt. xxi. 44.

20. *They watched him.* "Insidiously watching." See on chap. xiv. 1. *Spies.* One who crouches in some secret place to spy, listen, catch, or hurt. Hesychius explains the word by "those who lie in wait," or in "ambush," to surprise and slay. Josephus uses the word to signify a person bribed for a particular purpose. No doubt the persons mentioned in the text were men of the basest principles and were hired by the malicious Pharisees to do what they attempted in vain to perform.

22. *Is it lawful for us to give tribute unto Caesar?* See this insidious but important question considered at large on Matt. xxii. 16-22.

29. *There were therefore seven brethren.* See on Matt. xxii. 23-33.

34. *The children of this world.* Men and women in their present state of mortality and probation, procreation being necessary to restore the waste made by death, and to keep up the population of the earth.

36. *Equal unto the angels.* Who neither marry nor die.

38. *All live unto him.* There is a remarkable passage in Josephus' account of the Maccabees, chap. xvi, which proves that the best informed Jews believed that the souls of righteous men were in the presence of God in a state of happiness. "They who lose their lives for the sake of God, live unto God, as do Abraham, Isaac, and Jacob, and the rest of the patriarchs." So the resurrection of the dead, and the immortality and immateriality of the soul, were not strange or unknown doctrines among the Jews.

40. *They durst not ask.* Or "did not venture" to ask any other question, for fear of being again confounded, as they had already been.

41. *How say they?* See the note on Matt. xxii. 42-46.

43. *Thy footstool.* Literally, "the footstool of Thy feet." They shall not only be so far humbled that the feet may be set on them; but they shall be actually subjected, and put completely under that Christ whom they now despise and are about to crucify.

46. *Beware of the scribes.* Take heed that you are not seduced by those who should show you the way of salvation. See on Matt. xxiii. 4-14.

CHAPTER 21

The poor widow casting two mites into the treasury, 1-4. The destruction of the Temple foretold, 5-6. The signs of this desolation, 7. False Christs, 8. Wars, 9-10. Earthquakes and fearful sights, 11. Persecutions against the godly, 12-19. Directions how to escape, 20-22. The tribulation of those times, 23-28. The parable of the fig tree, illustrative of the time when they may expect these calamities, 29-33. The necessity of sobriety and watchfulness, 34-36. He teaches by day in the Temple, and lodges by night in the Mount of Olives, and the people come early to hear Him, 37-38.

1. *The rich men casting their gifts into the treasury.* See all this, vv. 1-4, explained on Mark xii. 41-44.

2. *A certain poor widow.* A widow "miserably poor," and her being miserably poor heightened the merit of the action. *Two mites.* Which Mark says, chap. xii. 42, make a "farthing," or *quadrans*, the fourth part of an *as*, or "penny," as we term it. In Plutarch's time we find the smallest piece of brass coin in use among the Romans was the *quadrans*, but it appears that a smaller piece of money was in circulation among the Jews in our Lord's time, called here, and in Mark, chap. xii. 42, a *lepton*, i.e., "small, diminished." In ancient times our penny used to be marked with a deep indented cross, dividing the piece into four equal parts, which, when broken in two, made the halfpenny, and, when broken into four, made the "fourthing," what we have corrupted into *farthing*. Probably the Roman *quadrans* was divided in this way for the convenience of the poor.

5. *Goodly stones.* Or "costly stones." It has been thought by some that this relates not so much to the stones of which the Temple was built as to the precious stones with which it was decorated. For an account of the stones of the Temple, see on Mark xiii. 1. *And gifts.* Or "consecrated things," "consecrated to sacred uses."

6. *One stone upon another.* This was literally fulfilled. See Matt. xxiv. 2.

8. *Many shall come in my name.* Usurping My name; calling themselves the Messiah. See Matt. xxiv. 5. Concerning this prediction of the destruction of Jerusalem and its literal accomplishment, see the notes on Matt. xxiv. 1-42.

9. *Commotions.* Seditions and civil dissensions, with which no people were more agitated than the Jews.

11. *Fearful sights.* What these were the reader will find in detail on Matt. xxiv. 7.

12. *Synagogues.* Or "assemblies." See these all explained on Mark xiii. 9.

13. *It shall turn to you for a testimony.* That is, it shall turn out on your part for a testimony to them (your persecutors) that you are thoroughly persuaded of the truth of what you teach and that you are no impostors.

14. *Settle it therefore.* See on Matt. x. 19.

15. *I will give you a mouth and wisdom.* A mouth must appear plain to every person to be used here for a "ready utterance" or "eloquence" in speaking. They shall have an abundance of wisdom to know what to say, and they shall have an irresistible eloquence to say what they ought.

18. *But there shall not an hair of your head perish.* A proverbial expression for, You shall not suffer any essential injury. Every genuine Christian shall escape when this desolation comes upon the Jewish state.

19. *In your patience.* Rather, "your perseverance," your faithful continuance in My word and doctrine. *Possess ye your souls.* You will preserve your souls. You shall escape the Roman sword, and not one of you shall perish in the destruction of Jerusalem. Instead of "possess, or preserve ye," I read "ye shall preserve." This reading is supported by many of the MSS., versions, and fathers.

22. *These be the days of vengeance.* See on Matt. xxiv. 21.

24. *They shall fall by the edge of the sword.* Those who perished in the siege are reckoned to be not less than eleven hundred thousand. See Matt. xxiv. 22. *And shall be led away captive.* To the number of ninety-seven thousand. See Josephus, *War,* b. vi, c. ix, s. 2-3, and on Matt. xxiv. 31. *Trodden down of the Gentiles.* Judea was so completely subjugated that the very land itself was sold by Vespasian; the Gentiles possessing it, while the Jews were either nearly all killed or led away into captivity. *Of the Gentiles be fulfilled.* Till the different nations of the earth, to whom God shall have given the dominion over this land, have accomplished all that which the Lord hath appointed them to do; and till the time of their conversion to God take place.

25. *The sea and the waves roaring.* Figuratively pointing out the immense Roman armies by which Judea was to be overrun and destroyed.

26. *Men's hearts failing them for fear.* Or "men fainting away through fear, being ready to die." *Coming on the earth.* Or "coming upon this land."

29. *He spake to them a parable.* Illustrated all these predicted facts by the simile of a fig tree. See this explained on Matt. xxiv. 32.

31. *The kingdom of God is nigh at hand.* After the destruction of the Jewish state, the doctrine of Christ crucified shall be preached everywhere, and everywhere prevail.

32. *This generation.* This race of men; but see on Matt. xxiv. 34 and Mark xiii. 30.

34. *Take heed to yourselves.* See our Lord's parable relative to this matter explained, Mark xiii. 34. *Be overcharged.* Literally, "be made heavy," as is generally the case with those who have eaten or drunk too much.

35. *The face of the whole earth.* Or "of this whole land." The land of Judea, on which these heavy judgments were to fall.

36. *Watch ye therefore, and pray always.* Perhaps we should connect "continually" with *watch,* as it appears to be the most natural order. Indeed the word "continually" belongs equally to both *watch* and *pray;* and no man is safe, at any time, who does not attend to this advice as literally as possible. *That shall come to pass.* That is, the tribulations which are on their way to overwhelm and destroy the Jewish people. These are sufficiently stated in the preceding verses. *To stand before the Son of man.* To be *acquitted* and to be *condemned* are expressed, in Rom. xiv. 4, by "standing" and "falling." Those who were faithful to the grace they had received were not only not destroyed in the destruction of Jerusalem, but became heralds of the grace and mercy of God to the nations. Thus they were counted worthy *to stand before the Son of man*—to minister salvation in His name.

37. *And in the day time.* Or "every day." This probably relates to the last four days of His life already mentioned. *Abode in the mount.* He taught all day in the Temple, and withdrew every evening and lodged in Bethany, a town at the foot or on the declivity of the Mount of Olives.

CHAPTER 22

The chief priests and scribes plot our Lord's destruction, 1-2. Judas, at the instigation of the devil, betrays Him, 3-6. He eats His last supper with His disciples, 7-18. Institutes the Eucharist, 19-20. Announces one of His disciples as the traitor, 21-23. The contention which should be greatest, 24-30. Warns Peter against Satan's devices, 31-32. Peter's resolution, 33. His denial foretold, 34. Tells His disciples to make prudent provision for their own support, 35-37. The two swords, 38. He goes to the Mount of Olives, and has His agony in the garden, 39-46. Judas comes with a mob, 47-48. Peter cuts off the ear of the high priest's servant, which Christ heals by a touch, 49-51. He addresses the chief priests and captains of the Temple, 52-53. They lead Him to the high priest's house, and Peter follows and denies His Master, 54-60. Christ looks upon him; he is stung with remorse, and weeps bitterly, 61-62. Jesus is mocked, and variously insulted, 63-65. The next morning He is questioned before the council, 66-67. He acknowledges himself to be the Son of God, 68-70. They condemn Him, 71.

1. *The feast of unleavened bread.* See this largely explained, Exod. xxiii. 14; xxiii. 2-40; and on Matt. xxvi. 2.

2. *They feared the people.* The great mass of the people seem to have been convinced that Christ was at least a prophet sent from God, and it is likely they kept steady in their attachment to Him. The multitude, who are represented as clamoring for His blood at the Crucifixion, appear to have been a mere mob, formed out of the creatures of the chief priests and Pharisees.

3. *Then entered Satan into Judas.* The devil filled the heart of Judas with avarice, and that infamous passion led him to commit the crime here specified. This at once accounts for the whole of this most unprincipled and unnatural transaction.

4. *And captains.* Among the priests who were in waiting at the Temple, some were appointed for a guard to the Temple, and over these were "commanding officers."

5. *They . . . covenanted to give him money.* Matthew says thirty pieces, or staters, of silver, the common price of the meanest slave.

6. *And he promised.* That is, to do it—or he accepted the proposal.

7. *The passover.* That on which they feasted, viz., the sacrificed paschal lamb.

8-13. *He sent Peter and John.* See the subject of these verses largely explained on Matt. xxvi. 17-19 and Mark xiv. 13, 15.

14. *And when the hour was come.* That is, the evening. See Matt. xxvi. 20 and Mark xiv. 17.

15. *With desire I have desired.* A Hebraism for "I have desired most earnestly." Our Lord's meaning seems to be that, having purposed to redeem a lost world by His blood, He ardently longed for the time in which He was to offer himself up. Such love did the holy Jesus bear to the human race. This eucharistic Passover was celebrated once, by way of anticipation, before the bloody sacrifice of the Victim of salvation, and before the deliverance it was appointed to commemorate, as the figurative Passover had been likewise once celebrated before the going out of Egypt and the deliverance of God's chosen people.

16. *Until it be fulfilled in the kingdom of God.* That is, until that of which the Passover is a type is fulfilled in My death, through which the kingdom of God, or of Heaven (see Matt. iii. 2), shall be established among men.

17. *He took the cup.* This was not the sacramental cup, for that was taken after supper, v. 20, but was the cup which was ordinarily taken before supper. *Divide it among yourselves.* Pass the cup from one to another; thus the cup which Christ gave to the first person on His right hand continued to be handed from one to another till it came to the last person on His left.

18. *I will not drink of the fruit of the vine.* That is, before the time of another Passover the Holy Ghost shall descend, the gospel of the Kingdom be established, and the sacramental supper shall take place of the paschal lamb; for in a few hours His crucifixion was to take place.

19. *Took bread.* See the nature and design of the Lord's Supper explained in the notes on Matt. xxvi. 26-29. *This do in remembrance of me.* That the Jews in eating the Passover did it to represent the sufferings of the Messiah is evident from the tract *Pesachim*, fol. 119.

20. *This cup is the new testament in my blood.* Perhaps it might be better to paraphrase the passage thus: "This cup which is poured out for you signifies the blood of the new covenant, which is shortly to be ratified in (or by) the shedding of My blood." Or, "This cup is the new covenant, poured out for you with My blood"; that is, the paschal sacrifice and My sacrifice happen together.

22. *The Son of man goeth.* That is, He is about to die. "Going, going away, and departing" are used, by the best Greek and Latin writers, for "death" and "dying."

23. *They began to inquire among themselves.* See the notes on Matt. xxvi. 23-24.

25. *Are called benefactors.* The very Greek word used by the Evangelist was the surname of some of the Ptolemies of Egypt: *Ptolemy Euergetes,* i.e., "the Benefactor." It was a custom among the ancient Romans to distribute part of the lands which they had conquered on the frontiers of the empire to their soldiers. Those

who enjoyed such lands were called *beneficiarii,* beneficed persons; and the lands themselves were termed *beneficia,* benefices, as being held on the *beneficence* of the sovereign. And it is no wonder that such sovereigns, however tyrannical or oppressive they might have been in other respects, were termed *benefactors* by those who were thus dependent on their bounty.

26. *Let him be as the younger.* Dr Lightfoot justly conjectures that Peter was the eldest of all the disciples; and he supposes that the strife was kindled between him and the sons of Zebedee, James and John. These three disciples were those whom Christ had distinguished by peculiar marks of His favor; and therefore it is natural to conclude that the strife lay between these three, the two brothers and Peter. Shall we or Peter be at the head? Neither, says our Lord. *Let him,* Peter, *who is chief* (the eldest) *among you, be as John, the younger.*

29. *I appoint unto you a kingdom, as my Father hath appointed unto me.* Our Lord is probably to be understood as promising that they should get a Kingdom, a state of blessedness, as He should get it—they must go through much tribulation in order to enter into the kingdom of God.

31. *Simon, Simon.* When a name is thus repeated in the sacred writings, it appears to be always intended as an expression of love, manifested by a warning voice. As if He had said, While you and the others are contending for supremacy, Satan is endeavoring to destroy you all; but I have prayed for you, as being in most danger. *Satan hath desired to have you.* That is, all the apostles but particularly the three contenders; the plural pronoun sufficiently proves that these words were not addressed to Peter alone. Satan had already got one, Judas; he had nearly got another, Peter; and he wished to have all. But we see by this that the devil cannot even tempt a man unless he receive permission. He desires to do all evil; he is permitted only to do some.

32. *I have prayed for thee.* From the natural forwardness and impetuosity of your own spirit, you will be brought into the most imminent danger; "but I have supplicated for you, that your faith may not utterly fail"—"fall utterly or entirely off." Peter's faith did *fail,* but not utterly; he did *fall,* but he did not fall off, apostatize, or forsake his Master and His cause finally, as Judas did. Everybody sees, from Peter's denial of his Lord, that his faith did fail, and his great courage too; and yet they read, in the common translation, that Christ prayed that it might *not fail.* Can they then conceive that our Lord's prayer was heard? The translation which I have given above removes this embarrassment and apparent contradiction. *When thou art converted.* Restored to a sense of your folly and sin, and to Me and My cause—establish these *thy brethren.* All the disciples forsook Jesus and fled, merely through fear of losing their lives; Peter, who continued for a while near Him, denied his Master with oaths, and repeated this thrice. Our Lord seems to intimate that, after this fall, Peter would become more cautious and circumspect than ever; and that he should become uncommonly strong in the faith, which was the case; and that, notwithstanding the baseness of his past conduct, he should be a proper instrument for strength-

ening the feebleminded, and supporting the weak. His two Epistles to the persecuted Christians show how well he was qualified for this important work.

34. The cock shall not crow this day. Matt. xxvi. 34 and Mark xiv. 30 say "this night"; both expressions are right, because the Jewish day, of twenty-four hours, began with the evening, and ended at the evening of the following day. On Peter's denial, see the notes on Matt. xxvi. 31-35.

35. When I sent you without purse. See the notes on Matt. x. 9-10.

36. He that hath no sword. The word stands rather oddly in the passage. The verse, translated in the order in which it stands, is as follows: "And he who hath none, let him sell his garment and buy—a sword." [Some] think that it was a proverbial expression, intimating a time of great difficulty and danger, and that now the disciples had need to look to themselves, for His murderers were at hand. The reader will observe that these words were spoken to the disciples just before He went to the Garden of Gethsemane, and that the danger was now so very near that there could be no time for any of them to go and sell his garment in order to purchase a sword to defend himself and his Master from the attack of the Jewish mob. Judea was at this time, as we have already noticed, much infested by robbers; while our Lord was with His disciples, they were perfectly safe, being shielded by His miraculous power. Shortly they must go into every part of the land and would need weapons to defend themselves.

37. Must yet be accomplished. Probably meaning that, though this prophecy did refer to some particular matter in the time of the prophet, yet it "farther" related to Christ, and could not have its complete accomplishment but in His crucifixion as a criminal. *For the things concerning me have an end.* As if He had said: My work is now almost done; yours is only beginning. I am now about to be crucified and numbered with the transgressors. Think what will be done to you, and what ought to be done by you; and then think if this be a time for you to be contending with each other.

38. Lord, behold, here are two swords. And he said unto them, It is enough. These words cannot be well understood as being an answer to the supposed command of Christ for everyone who had no sword to go and sell his garment and buy one, for in this case they were not *enough,* or "sufficient," as nine of the disciples must be without any instrument of defense. But they may be understood as pointing out the readiness and determination of Peter, and perhaps some others, to defend our Lord: "Thou shalt not be treated as a transgressor; here are two swords, and we will fight for Thee." In v. 33, Peter had said he was ready to go with Christ either to prison or death which showed his strong resolution to stand by and defend his Master, even at the expense of his life. But, alas, he depended too much on himself! *It is enough.* The meaning probably is, There is enough said on the subject; as immediately after this He entered into His agony. I must here confess that the matter about the *swords* appears to me very obscure. I am afraid I do not understand it, and I know of none who does. Schoettgen and Lightfoot have said much

on the subject; others have endeavored to get rid of the difficulty by translating a "knife," which was necessary on long journeys for providing forage and fuel, as they were to depend wholly on their own industry, under God, for all the necessaries of life while going through the nations of the earth, preaching the gospel to Jews and Gentiles. I cannot say which sense the reader should prefer.

40. When he was at the place. Viz., Gethsemane. On this agony of our Lord see the notes on Matt. xxvi. 36-46.

43. There appeared an angel . . . from heaven. It was as necessary that the fullest evidence should be given, not only of our Lord's divinity, but also of His humanity. His miracles sufficiently attested the former; His hunger, weariness, and agony in the garden, as well as His death and burial, were proofs of the latter. As man, He needs the assistance of an angel to support His body, worn down by fatigue and suffering. See at the end of v. 44.

44. Prayed more earnestly. With greater emphasis and earnestness than usual, with strong crying and tears, Heb. v. 7; the reason given for which is that He was *in an agony. Drops of blood.* Some have thought that the meaning of the words is that the sweat was so profuse that every drop was as large as a drop of blood, not that the sweat was blood itself, but this does not appear likely. There have been cases in which persons in a debilitated state of body, through horror of soul, have had their sweat tinged with blood. Dr. Mead from Galen observes, "Cases sometimes happen in which, through mental pressure, the pores may be so dilated that the blood may issue from them; so that there may be a bloody sweat."

48. Betrayest thou the Son of man with a kiss? Do you attempt to kiss Me as a friend, while you are delivering Me up into the hands of My enemies? We need not wonder at all this, as Satan himself had entered into the heart of this traitor; see v. 3. Consequently we can expect nothing from him but what is fell, deceitful, and cruel.

51. Suffer ye thus far. Or, "Suffer Me to go thus far." As they had now a firm hold of Christ, Matt. xxvi. 50, He wished them to permit Him to go as far as Malchus, whose ear was cut off, that He might heal it. However, the words may be understood as an address to His disciples: "Let them proceed"; make no resistance; for in this way only are the Scriptures to be fulfilled.

53. I was daily with you in the temple. Alluding to the four preceding days, during the whole of which He taught in the Temple, see chap. xxi. 37 and Matt. xxi. 17. *This is your hour, and the power of darkness.* That is, the time in which you are permitted to unrein your malice, which you could not do before, because God did not permit you; and so perfectly are you under His control that neither you nor the prince of darkness can proceed a hair's breadth against Me but through this permission. What a comfortable thought is it to the followers of Christ that neither men nor demons can act against them but by the permission of their Heavenly Father, and that He will not suffer any of those who trust in Him to be tried above what they are able to bear, and will make the trial issue in their greater salvation and in His glory!

56. A certain maid beheld him. Or "attentively beholding him." And this she did by the help of the light of the fire at which Peter sat.

57. And he denied him. See the notes on Matt. xxvi. 58, 69, etc.

62. And Peter went out. The word Peter is omitted by many good MSS., and some of the ancient versions.

63. Mocked him, and smote him. This and the following verses are placed by Matthew and Mark before the relation of Peter's denial. For their explanation, see on Matt. xxvi. 67-68.

68. And if I also ask you. Concerning the Christ, in case you cannot give Me such an answer as may prove I am not the Christ, you will not let Me go; for I know you are determined to put Me to death.

69. Hereafter. "From this very time." The kingdom of God is now going to be set up. See the note on Matt. xvi. 27-28.

70. Art thou then the Son of God? They all insisted on an answer to this question, and the high priest particularly put it to Him, Matt. xxvi. 63.

71. We ourselves have heard. We have heard Him profess himself the Son of God; He is therefore guilty of blasphemy, and, as an impious pretender to a divine mission, we must proceed against and condemn Him to death. See the note on Matt. xxvi. 66. Thus they proceeded as far as they could; He must now be brought before Pilate, as the Jews had no power to put Him to death. His trial before Pilate is related in the subsequent chapter.

On our Lord's agony in the garden, related in the forty-third and forty-fourth verses, much has been written, but to little purpose. The cause of this agony seems not to have been well understood, and there have been many wild conjectures concerning it. Some think it was occasioned by "the Divine wrath pressing in upon him; for, as he was bearing the sin of the world, God looked on and treated him as if he were a sinner." There is something very shocking in this supposition; and yet it is truly astonishing how general it is. The ministry of the angel, in this case, is a sufficient refutation of this opinion; for what sort of strength could an angel give Christ against God's indignation? Indeed the ministry of the angel, who must have been sent from God, and sent in love too, is a full proof that God's wrath was not poured out on our blessed Redeemer at this time. What renders this circumstance more difficult is that there is no mention of it in any of the other Evangelists; and it is worthy of remark that, among many of the ancients, the authenticity of these two verses, the forty-third and forty-fourth, has been doubted, and in consequence they are omitted in several MSS. and in some versions and fathers. The Codex Alexandrinus and the Codex Vaticanus omit both verses; in some other very ancient MSS. they stand with an *asterisk* before them, as a mark of dubiousness. They are, however, extant in such a vast number of MSS., versions, and fathers as to leave no doubt with most critics of their authenticity. After all that has been said or perhaps can be said on this subject there will remain mysteries which only the bright light of the eternal world

can sufficiently illustrate. That Christ was now suffering, "the just for the unjust, that he might bring us to God," and that He was bearing in His body the punishment due to their sins, I have no doubt; and that the agony of His mind in these vicarious sufferings caused the effusion of the bloody sweat from His body may be easily credited without supposing Him to be at all under the displeasure of His Heavenly Father. For as God can see nothing but as it is, He could not see Him as a sinner who was purity itself. In every act Jesus was that beloved Son in whom the Father was ever well pleased.

CHAPTER 23

Christ is led to Pilate, and accused by the Jews, 1-2. Pilate examines, and pronounces Him innocent, 3-4. The Jews virulently accuse Him, 5. Pilate, understanding that He was of Galilee, sends Him to Herod, by whom He is examined, 6-9. The chief priests and scribes vehemently accuse Him, and Herod and his soldiers mock Him, 10-11. Pilate and Herod become friends, 12. Pilate, before the chief priests, rulers, and people, pronounces Christ to be innocent, and offers to release Him, 13-20. The Jews clamor for His condemnation, and Pilate gives Him up to their will, 21-25. Simon bears His cross, 26. The people bewail Him, and He foretells the destruction of the Jewish state, 27-31. He and two malefactors are brought to Calvary, and are crucified, 32-33. He prays for His crucifiers, 34. He is derided, mocked, and insulted by the rulers, and by the soldiers, 35-37. The superscription on the Cross, 38. The conduct of the two malefactors, to one of whom He promises paradise, 39-43. The great darkness, 44-45. He gives up the ghost, 46. The centurion and many others are greatly affected at His death, 47-49. Joseph of Arimathaea begs the body, and puts it in his own new tomb, 50-53. The women prepare spices and ointments to embalm Him, 54-56.

1. *The whole multitude.* It seems most probable that the chief priests, elders, scribes, and captains of the Temple, together with their servants, dependents, and other persons hired for the purpose, made up the multitude mentioned here. The common people were generally favorers of Christ; and for this reason the Jewish rulers caused Him to be apprehended in the night and in the absence of the people, chap. xxii. 6, and it was now but just the break of day, xxii. 66.

2. *Perverting the nation.* The Greek word signifies "stirring up to disaffection and rebellion." Many MSS. and versions add "our" *nation.* They intimated that He not only preached corrupt doctrine, but that He endeavored to make them disaffected towards the Roman government, for which they now pretended to feel a strong affection! *Forbidding to give tribute to Caesar.* These were the falsest slanders that could be invented. The whole of our Lord's conduct disproved them. And His decision in the case of the question about the lawfulness of paying tribute to Caesar, Matt. xxii. 21, was so fully known that we find Pilate paid not the least attention to such evidently malicious and unfounded accusations. Neither Christ nor any of His followers, from that day until now, ever forbade the paying tribute to Caesar; that is, constitutional taxes to a lawful prince.

7. *Herod's jurisdiction.* The city of Nazareth, in which Christ had continued till He was thirty years of age, and that of Capernaum, in which He principally resided the last years of His life, were both in lower Galilee, of which Herod Antipas was tetrarch. Pilate was probably glad of this opportunity to pay a little respect to Herod, whom it is likely he had irritated, and with whom he now wished to be friends. See v. 12.

10. *The chief priests . . . vehemently accused him.* Corrupt priests and teachers are generally the most implacable enemies of Christ and His truth. Evil passions betray those who are slaves to them. An affected moderation would have rendered these accusers less suspected, their accusations more probable, and the envy less visible than this vehemence. But envy seldom or never consults prudence, and God permits this to be so for the honor of truth and innocence.

11. *A gorgeous robe.* It probably means a "white robe," for it was the custom of the Jewish nobility to wear such. Hence in Rev. iii. 4 it is said of the saints, "They shall walk with me in white [garments]: for they are worthy." In such a robe Herod, by way of mockery, caused our Lord to be clothed; but the nobility among the Romans wearing purple for the most part, Pilate's soldiers, who were Romans, put on Jesus a "purple robe," Mark xv. 17; John xix. 2—both of them following the custom of their own country, when, by way of mocking our Lord as a King, they clothed Him in robes of state.

12. *Pilate and Herod were made friends.* I do not find any account of the cause of the enmity which subsisted between Herod and Pilate given by ancient authors, and the conjectures of the moderns on the subject should be considered as mere guesses. It is generally supposed that this enmity arose from what is related in chap. xiii of the Galileans whose blood Pilate had mingled with that of their sacrifices. These were Herod's subjects, and Pilate seems to have fallen on them at the time they were offering sacrifices to God at the Temple.

15. *No, nor yet Herod: for I sent you to him.* That is, to see whether he could find that Christ had ever attempted to raise any disaffection or sedition among the Galileans, among whom He had spent the principal part of His life; and yet Herod has not been able to find out any evil in His conduct. Your own accusations I have fully weighed, and find them frivolous to the last degree. Instead of *for I sent you to him,* many MSS., with some versions, read, "For he hath sent Him to us." As if he had said, "Herod had sent Him back to us, which is a sure proof that he had found no blame in Him." *Nothing worthy of death is done unto him.* Or rather, "Nothing worthy of death is committed by Him," not *done unto him.*

17. *For of necessity he must release one.* That is, he was under the necessity of releasing one at this feast. The custom, however it originated, had now been so completely established that Pilate was obliged to attend to it.

18. *Away with this man.* That is, "Put Him to death"—literally, "Take this One away," i.e., to punishment, to death.

22. *I have found no cause of death in him.* "I find no crime worthy of death in Him." There is nothing proved against Him that can at all justify me in putting Him to death. So here our blessed Lord was in the most formal manner justified by His judge. Now as this decision was publicly known, and perhaps registered, it is evident that Christ died as an innocent Person, and not as a malefactor. On the fullest conviction of His innocence, His judge pronounced Him guiltless, after having patiently heard everything that the inventive malice of these wicked men could allege against Him; and when he wished to dismiss Him, a violent mob took and murdered Him.

26. *Simon, a Cyrenian.* See on Matt. xxvii. 32.

27. *Bewailed and lamented him.* "Beat their breasts."

28. *Weep not for me.* Many pious persons have been greatly distressed in their minds because they could not weep on reading or hearing of the sufferings of Christ. For the relief of all such let it be forever known that no human spirit can possibly take any part in the passion of the Messiah. His sufferings were such as only God manifested in the flesh could bear; and as they were all of an expiatory nature, no man can taste of or share in them.

30. *Mountains, fall on us.* As this refers to the destruction of Jerusalem, and as the same expressions are used in Rev. vi. 16, Dr. Lightfoot conjectures that the whole of that chapter may relate to the same event.

31. *If they do these things in a green tree.* This seems to be a proverbial expression, the sense of which is: If they spare not a tree which, by the beauty of its foliage, abundance and excellence of its fruits, deserves to be preserved, then the tree which is dry and withered will surely be cut down. If an innocent Man be put to death in the very face of justice, in opposition to all its dictates and decisions, by a people who profess to be governed and directed by divine laws, what desolation, injustice, and oppression may not be expected when anarchy and confusion sit in the place where judgment and justice formerly presided? Our Lord alludes prophetically to those tribulations which fell upon the Jewish people about forty years after.

32. *Two other, malefactors.* Should certainly be translated "two others, malefactors," as in the Bibles published by the King's printer, Edinburgh. As it now stands in the text, it seems to intimate that our blessed Lord was also a *malefactor.*

33. *The place which is called Calvary.* See on Matt. xxvii. 33. *They crucified him.* See the nature of this punishment explained, Matt. xxvii. 35.

34. *They know not what they do.* If ignorance does not excuse a crime, it at least diminishes the atrocity of it. However, these persons well knew that they were crucifying an innocent man; but they did not know that by this act of theirs they were bringing down on themselves and on their country the heaviest judgments of God. In the prayer, *Father, forgive them,* that word of prophecy was fulfilled, "He made intercession for the transgressors," Isa. liii. 12.

35. *Derided him.* "Treated Him with the utmost contempt," in the most infamous manner. See the meaning of this word explained, chap. xvi. 14.

36. *Offering him vinegar.* See on Matt. xxvii. 34. Vinegar or small sour wine was a common drink of the Roman soldiers; and it is supposed that wherever they were on duty they had a vessel of this liquor standing by. It appears that at least two cups were given to our Lord: one before He was nailed to the Cross, viz., of wine mingled with myrrh; and another of vine-

gar, while He hung on the Cross. Some think there were three cups: one of wine mixed with myrrh; the second, of vinegar mingled with gall; and the third, of simple vinegar. Allow these three cups, and the different expressions in all the Evangelists will be included.

38. *A superscription.* See Matt. xxvii. 37. *In letters of Greek, and Latin, and Hebrew.* The inscription was written in all these languages, which were the most common, that all might see the reason why He was put to death. The inscription was written in Greek, on account of the Hellenistic Jews, who were then at Jerusalem because of the Passover; it was written in Latin, that being the language of the government under which He was crucified; and it was written in Hebrew, that being the language of the place in which this deed of darkness was committed. But, by the good providence of God, the inscription itself exculpated Him and proved the Jews to be rebels against, and murderers of, their King. See the note on Matt. xxvii. 37. It is not to be wondered at that they wished Pilate to alter this inscription, John xix. 21, as it was a record of their infamy.

39. *One of the malefactors which were hanged.* It is likely that the two robbers were not nailed to their crosses, but only tied to them by cords, and thus they are represented in ancient paintings. If not nailed, they could not have suffered much, and therefore they were found still alive when the soldiers came to give the *coup de grace,* which put a speedy end to their lives, John xix. 31-33.

40. *Dost not thou fear God?* The sufferings of this person had been sanctified to him, so that his heart was open to receive help from the hand of the Lord. He is a genuine penitent, and gives the fullest proof he can give of it, viz., the acknowledgment of the justice of his sentence. He had sinned, and he acknowledges his sin; his heart believes unto righteousness, and with his tongue he makes confession unto salvation. While he condemns himself, he bears testimony that Jesus was innocent. Bishop Pearce supposes that these were not robbers in the common sense of the word, but Jews who took up arms on the principle that the Romans were not to be submitted to and that their levies of tribute money were oppressive, and therefore they made no scruple to rob all the Romans they met with. These Jews Josephus calls "robbers," the same term used by the Evangelists. This opinion gains some strength from the penitent thief's confession: *We receive the due reward of our deeds*—we rose up against the government, and committed depredations in the country; *but this man hath done nothing amiss*—"out of place, disorderly," nothing calculated to raise sedition or insurrection.

42. *Lord, remember me.* It is worthy of remark that this man appears to have been the first who believed in the intercession of Christ.

43. *In paradise.* The Garden of Eden, mentioned in Gen. ii. 8, is also called, from the Septuagint, the "garden of Paradise." The word *Eden* signifies "pleasure" and "delight." Several places were thus called; see Gen. iv. 16; 2 Kings xix. 12; Isa. xxxvii. 12; Ezek. xxvii. 23; and Amos i. 5—and such places probably had this name from their "fertility, pleasant situation." In this light the Septuagint have viewed Gen.

ii. 8, as they render the passage thus: "God planted a paradise in Eden." Hence the word has been transplanted into the New Testament, and is used to signify a place of exquisite pleasure and delight.

Paradise was in the beginning the habitation of man in his state of innocence, in which he enjoyed that presence of his Maker which constituted his supreme happiness. Our Lord's words intimate that this penitent should be immediately taken to the abode of the spirits of the just, where he should enjoy the presence and approbation of the Most High.

44. *Darkness over all the earth.* See the note on Matt. xxvii. 45. The darkness began at the sixth hour, about our twelve o'clock at noon, and lasted till the ninth hour, which answered to our three o'clock in the afternoon.

45. *The veil . . . was rent.* See Matt. xxvii. 51.

46. *Into thy hands I commend my spirit.* Or, "I will commit My spirit"—"I deposit My soul in Thy hands." Another proof of the immateriality of the soul, and of its separate existence when the body is dead.

48. *And all the people.* All were deeply affected except the priests, and those whom they had employed to serve their base purposes. The darkness, earthquake, etc., had brought terror and consternation into every heart.

50-51. *Joseph . . . of Arimathaea.* See the notes on Matt. xxvii. 57-60 and those especially on Mark xv. 43.

54. *And the sabbath drew on.* Or, "The Sabbath was lighting up," i.e., with the candles which the Jews light just before six in the evening, when the Sabbath commences. The same word is used for the dawning of the day, Matt. xxviii. 1.

55. *The women also, which came.* These were Mary of Magdala, Joanna, and Mary the mother of James, chap. xxiv. 10. To these three, Mark, in chap. xvi. 1, adds, Salome; but some think that this was only a surname of one of these Marys.

56. *Prepared spices and ointments.* This was in order to embalm Him, which sufficiently proves that they had no hope of His resurrection the third day. *And rested the sabbath day.* For though the Jewish canons allowed all works necessary for the dead to be done, even on the Sabbath, such as washing and anointing, provided they moved not a limb of the dead person, yet, as the Jews had put Christ to death under the pretense of His being a malefactor, it would not have been either prudent or safe to appear too forward in the present business; and therefore they rested on the Sabbath.

CHAPTER 24

The women coming early to the sepulchre on the first day of the week, bringing their spices, find the stone rolled away and the tomb empty, 1-3. They see a vision of angels, who announce Christ's resurrection, 4-8. The women return and tell this to the eleven, 9-10. They believe not, but Peter goes and examines the tomb, 11-12. Christ, unknown, appears to two of the disciples who are going to Emmaus, and converses with them, 13-29. While they are eating together, He makes himself known, and immediately disappears, 30-31. They return to Jerusalem, and announce His resurrection to the rest of the disciples 32-35. Jesus himself appears to them, and gives them the fullest proof of the reality of His resurrection, 36-43. He preaches to them, and gives them the promise of the Holy Spirit, 44-49. He takes them to Bethany, and ascends to heaven in their sight, 50-51. They worship Him, and return to Jerusalem, 52-53.

1. *Bringing the spices.* To embalm the body of our Lord; but Nicodemus and Joseph of Arimathaea had done this before the body was laid in the tomb. See John xix. 39-40. But there was a second embalming found necessary. The first must have been hastily and imperfectly performed; the spices now brought by the women were intended to complete the preceding operation. *And certain others with them.* This clause is wanting in some MSS. and versions. Dionysius Alexandrinus and Eusebius also omit it. The omission is approved by Mill, Bengel, Wetstein, Griesbach, and others.

2. *They found the stone rolled away.* An angel from God had done this before they reached the tomb, Matt. xxviii. 2. On this case we cannot help remarking that when persons have strong confidence in God obstacles do not hinder them from undertaking whatever they have reason to believe He requires; and the removal of them they leave to Him.

3. *And found not the body of the Lord.* His holy soul was in paradise, chap. xxiii. 43; and the Evangelist mentions the body particularly, to show that this only was subject to death.

5. *Why seek ye the living among the dead?* This was a common form of speech among the Jews and seems to be applied to those who were foolishly, impertinently, or absurdly employed. As places of burial were unclean, it was not reasonable to suppose that the living should frequent them; or that if any was missing, he was likely to be found in such places.

7. *Sinful men.* Or "heathens," i.e., the Romans by whom only He could be put to death, for the Jews themselves acknowledged that this power was now vested in the hands of the Roman governor alone. See John xix. 15.

8. *They remembered his words.* Even the simple recollection of the words of Christ becomes often a source of comfort and support to those who are distressed or tempted, for His words are the words of eternal life.

10. *And Joanna.* She was the wife of Chuza, Herod's steward. See chap. viii. 3.

12. *Then arose Peter.* John went with him, and got to the tomb before him. See John xx. 2-3. *The linen clothes laid by themselves.* Or "the linen clothes only." This was the fine linen which Joseph of Arimathaea bought, and wrapped the body in, Mark xv. 46. Small as this circumstance may at first view appear, it is, nevertheless, no mean proof of the resurrection of our Lord. Had the body been stolen away, all that was wrapped about it would have been taken away with it, as the delay which must have been occasioned by stripping it might have led to the detection of the theft; nor would the disciples have run such a risk if they had stolen Him, when stripping the body could have answered no end. This circumstance is related still more particularly by John, chap. xx. 5-7. Peter "saw the linen clothes lying . . . and the napkin, that was about his head, not lying with the linen clothes, but wrapped together in a place by itself."

13. *Behold, two of them.* This long and interesting account is not mentioned by Matthew nor John, and is only glanced at by Mark, chap. xvi. 12-13. One of these disciples was Cleopas, v. 18, and the other is supposed by many learned men, both ancient and modern, to have been Luke himself. See the sketch of his life prefixed to these notes. *Threescore furlongs.* Some MSS. say 160 furlongs, but this is a mistake, for Josephus assigns the same distance to this village from Jerusalem as the Evangelist does. "Ammaus is sixty stadia distant from Jerusalem," about 7 English miles and three-quarters. A *stadium* was about 243 yards.

15. *And reasoned.* Concerning the probability or improbability of Christ being the Messiah, or of His resurrection from the dead. It was a laudable custom of the Jews, and very common also, to converse about the law in all their journeyings; and now they had especial reason to discourse together, of both the law and the prophets, from the transactions which had recently taken place.

16. *Their eyes were holden.* It does not appear that there was anything supernatural here, for the reason why these persons (who were not apostles, see v. 33) did not recollect our Lord is given by Mark, chap. xvi. 12, who says that Christ appeared to them in another form.

18. *Cleopas.* The same as Alphaeus, father of the Apostle James, Mark iii. 18, and husband of the sister of the Virgin, John xix. 25. *Art thou only a stranger?* As if he had said, What has been done in Jerusalem within these few days has been so public, so awful, and so universally known that, if you had been but a lodger in the city for a single night, I cannot conceive how you could miss hearing of these things. Indeed, you appear to be the *only* person unacquainted with them.

19. *Which was a prophet.* "A man prophet," a genuine prophet; but this has been considered as a Hebraism: "for, in Exod. ii. 14, a *man prince* is simply a *prince;* and in 1 Sam. xxxi. 3, *men archers* mean no more than *archers.*" But my own opinion is that this word is often used to deepen the signification; so in the above quotations: *Who made thee a man prince* (i.e., a mighty sovereign) *and a judge over us?* Exod. ii. 14. And, *The battle went sore against Saul, and the men archers* (i.e., the stout, or well-aiming archers) *hit him,* 1 Sam. xxxi. 3. So *aner prophetes* here signifies, He was a "genuine prophet," nothing like those false ones by whom the people have been so often deceived; and He has proved the divinity of His mission by His heavenly teaching and astonishing miracles. *Mighty in deed and word.* Irresistibly eloquent. "Powerful in deed," working incontrovertible miracles.

21-24. Cleopas paints the real state of his own mind in these verses. In his relation there is scarcely anything well connected. Important points are referred to, and not explained, though he considered the person to whom he spoke as entirely unacquainted with these transactions. His own hopes and fears he cannot help mixing with the narration, and throwing over the whole that confusion that dwells in his own heart. The narration is not at all in Luke's style; but as it is probable he was the other disciple who was present, and had heard the words of Cleopas, he gave them in that simple, natural, artless manner in which they were spoken. Had the account been forged, those simple, natural touches would not have appeared. *To day is the third day.* Our Lord had often said that He would rise again the third day; and though Alphaeus had little hope of this resurrection, yet he could not help recollecting the words he had heard, especially as they seemed to be confirmed by the relation of the women, vv. 22-24.

25. *O fools, and slow of heart to believe.* "Inconsiderate" men, justly termed such because they had not properly attended to the description given of the Messiah by the prophets, nor to His teaching and miracles, as proofs that He alone was the Person they described. *Slow of heart.* "Backward," not easy to be persuaded of the truth, always giving way to doubtfulness and distrust. This very imperfection in them is a strong evidence of the truth of the doctrine which they afterwards believed, and proclaimed to the world. Had they not had the fullest assurance of these things, they never would have credited them; and it is no small honor to the new-covenant Scriptures that such persons were chosen, first to believe them; secondly, to proclaim them in the world; and, thirdly, to die on the evidence of those truths, the blessed influence of which they felt in their own hearts and fully exemplified in their lives.

26. *Ought not Christ to have suffered?* "Was it not necessary that the Christ should suffer?" This was the way in which sin must be expiated and without this no soul could have been saved. The suffering Messiah is He alone by whom Israel and the world can be saved.

27. *Beginning at Moses.* What a sermon this must have been, where all the prophecies relative to the incarnation, birth, teaching, miracles, sufferings, death, and resurrection of the blessed Jesus were all adduced, illustrated, and applied to himself, by an appeal to the well-known facts which had taken place during His life! We are almost irresistibly impelled to exclaim, What a pity this discourse has not been preserved! No wonder their hearts burned within them while hearing such a sermon from such a Preacher! The law and the prophets had all borne testimony, either directly or indirectly, to Christ; and we may naturally suppose that these prophecies and references were those which our Lord at this time explained and applied to himself. See v. 32.

28. *He made as though he would have gone further.* That is, "He was going on, as though He intended to go farther"; and so He doubtless would had they not earnestly pressed Him to lodge with them. His preaching had made a deep impression upon their hearts, v. 32, and now they feel it their greatest privilege to entertain the Preacher.

29. *For it is toward evening.* And consequently both inconvenient and unsafe to proceed to another village. *And he went in.* And so He will to you, you penitent soul! Therefore take courage, and be not faithless but believing.

30. *He took bread.* This was the office of the master and father of a family, and this was our Lord's usual custom among His disciples. Those whom Christ lodges with He feeds, and feeds too with bread that He has blessed, and this feeding not only strengthens but also enlightens the soul.

31. *Their eyes were opened.* But we are not to imagine that He administered the holy Eucharist at this time; there is not the most distant evidence of this. It was a mere family meal, and ended before it was well begun. *They knew him.* His acting as father of the family, in taking, blessing, and distributing the bread among them,

caused them to recollect those lips which they had often heard speak, and those hands by which they had often been fed. Perhaps He also threw off the disguise which He had before assumed, and now appeared in His own person. *He vanished out of their sight.* Probably, during their surprise, He took the opportunity of withdrawing from the place, leaving them to reflect and meditate on what they had heard and seen.

32. *Did not our heart burn within us?* His word was in our heart as a burning fire, Jer. xx. 9. Our hearts waxed hot within us, and while we were musing the fire burned, Ps. xxxix. 3. In some such way as this the words of the disciples may be understood.

34. *Saying, The Lord is risen indeed.* The meaning here is that these two disciples found the apostles, and those who were with them, unanimously testifying that Christ had risen from the dead. It is not the two disciples to whom we are to refer the word *saying,* but to the body of the disciples.

35. *And they.* The two disciples who were just come from Emmaus "related what had happened to them on the way," going to Emmaus, "and how He had been known unto them in the breaking of bread," while supping together at the above village.

36. *And as they thus spake.* While the two disciples who were going to Emmaus were conversing about Christ, He joined himself to their company. Now while they and the apostles are confirming each other in their belief of His resurrection, Jesus comes in, to remove every doubt, and to give them the fullest evidence of it. And it is ever true that wherever two or three are gathered together in His name He is in the midst of them. *Peace be unto you.* The usual salutation among the Jews. "May you prosper in body and soul, and enjoy every heavenly and earthly good!"

37-39. *And supposed that they had seen a spirit.* But if there be no such thing as a disembodied spirit, would not our Lord have shown them their error? Instead of this, He confirms them in their opinion, by saying, *A spirit hath not flesh and bones, as ye see me have;* therefore He says, *Handle me, and see me.* They probably imagined that it was the soul only of our blessed Lord which they saw; but they were soon fully convinced of the identity of His person and the reality of His resurrection; for (1) they saw His body, (2) they heard Him speak, (3) they handled Him, (4) they saw Him eat a piece of broiled fish and honeycomb, which they gave Him. In these things it was impossible for them to have been deceived.

41. *They yet believed not for joy.* They were so overcome with the joy of His resurrection that they did not, for some time, properly receive the evidence that was before them—as we phrase it, they thought the news too good to be true.

44. *The law . . . the prophets, and . . . the psalms.* The common Jewish division of the writings of the old covenant is the following. and indeed seems to be the same to which our Lord alludes: (1) The law, *thorah,* including Genesis, Exodus, Leviticus, Numbers, and Deuteronomy. (2) The prophets, *nabiaim,* or "teachers," including Joshua, Judges, the two Books of Samuel, and the two Books of Kings; these were

termed the "former prophets." Isaiah, Jeremiah, Ezekiel, Hosea, Joel, Amos, Obadiah, Jonah, Micah, Nahum, Habakkuk, Zephaniah, Haggai, Zechariah, and Malachi—these were termed the "latter prophets." (3) The hagiographa (*holy writings*), *kethuvim*, which comprehended the Psalms, Proverbs, Job, Canticles, Ruth, Lamentations, Ecclesiastes, Esther, Daniel, Ezra, Nehemiah, and the two Books of Chronicles. The Jews made anciently only twenty-two books of the whole, to bring them to the number of the letters in the Hebrew alphabet; and this they did by joining Ruth to Judges, making the two Books of Samuel only one, and so of Kings and Chronicles, joining the Lamentations to Jeremiah, and making the twelve minor prophets only one book.

45. *Then opened he their understanding.* "He fully opened." They had a measure of light before, so that they discerned the Scriptures to be the true *Word* of God, and to speak of the Messiah; but they had not light sufficient to enable them to apply these Scriptures to their Lord and Master. But now, by the influence of Christ, they see not only the prophecies which pointed out the Messiah, but also the Messiah who was pointed out by these prophecies. The Book of God may be received in general as a divine Revelation, but the proper meaning, reference, and application of the Scriptures can be discerned only by the light of Christ. Even the very plain Word of God is a dead letter to those who are not enlightened by the grace of Christ. And why? Because this Word speaks of spiritual and heavenly things, and the carnal mind of man cannot discern them. They who receive not this inward teaching continue dark and dead while they live.

47. *Remission of sins.* The "taking away"—removal of *sins,* in general—everything that relates to the destruction of the power, the pardoning of the guilt, and the purification of the heart from the very nature of sin. *Should be preached in his name.* See the office of a proclaimer, herald, or preacher explained in the note on Matt. iii. 1. *In his name.* On His authority, and in virtue of the atonement made by Him. For on what other ground could the inhabitants of the earth expect *remission of sins? Among all nations.* Because God wills the salvation of all, and Jesus Christ by His grace has tasted death for every man, Heb. ii. 9. *Beginning at Jerusalem.* Making the first overtures of mercy to My murderers! If, then, the sinners of Jerusalem might repent, believe, and be saved, none on this side of hell need despair.

48. *Ye are witnesses of these things.* He gave them a full commission to proclaim these glad tidings of peace and salvation to a lost world. The disciples were *witnesses* not only that Christ had suffered and risen again from the dead, but also that He opens the understanding by the inspiration of His Spirit, that He gives repentance, that He pardons sin and purifies from all unrighteousness, and that He is not willing that any should perish, but that all should come unto the knowledge of the truth and be saved.

49. *The promise of my Father.* That is, the *Holy Ghost,* promised, John xv. 26. See Acts i. 4; ii. 33.

51. *Carried up into heaven.* Into that heaven from which He had descended, John i. 18; iii. 13. This was forty days after His resurrection, Acts i. 3, during which time He had given the most convincing proofs of that resurrection, not only to the apostles, but to many others, to upwards of five hundred at one time, 1 Cor. xv. 6. As in His life they had seen the way to the Kingdom, and in His death the price of the Kingdom, so in His ascension they had the fullest proof to the immortality of the soul, the resurrection of the human body, and of His continual intercession at the right hand of God. There are some remarkable circumstances relative to this ascension mentioned in Acts i. 4-12.

53. *Were continually in the temple.* Especially till the Day of Pentecost came, when they received the promise mentioned, v. 49. *Praising and blessing God.* Magnifying His mercy and speaking good of His name. Thus the days of their mourning were ended, and they began that life upon earth in which they still live in the kingdom of God.

I cannot close these observations with a more profitable word than what is contained in that truly apostolic and sublime prayer for the second *Sunday in Advent;* and may he who reads it weigh every word in the spirit of faith and devotion! "Blessed God! who hast caused all holy scriptures to be written for our learning; grant that we may in such wise *hear* them, *read, mark, learn,* and *inwardly digest* them, that, by patience and comfort of thy holy word, we may embrace and ever hold fast the blessed hope of everlasting life, which thou hast given us in our Saviour Jesus Christ!"

Now "unto him that loved us, and washed us from our sins in his own blood, and hath made us kings and priests unto God and his Father; to him be glory and dominion for ever and ever. Amen."

The Gospel According to

JOHN

John, the writer of this Gospel, was the son of a fisherman named Zebedee, and his mother's name was Salome. Compare Matt. xxvii. 56 with Mark xv. 40 and xvi. 1. His father, Zebedee, was probably of Bethsaida, and with his sons James and John followed his occupation on the Sea of Galilee. The call of these two brothers to the apostleship is related in Matt. iv. 21-22; Mark i. 19-20; Luke v. 1-10. John is generally supposed to have been about twenty-five years of age when he began to follow our Lord.

John was with our Lord in His transfiguration on the mount, Matt. xvii. 2; Mark ix. 2; Luke ix. 28; during His agony in the garden, Matt. xxvi. 37; Mark xiv. 33; and when He was crucified, John xix. 26.

He saw our Lord expire upon the Cross, and saw the soldier pierce His side with a spear, John xix. 34-35. Our Lord tenderly committed to him the care of His mother, Mary.

He was one of the first of the disciples that visited the sepulchre after the resurrection of Christ; and was present with the other disciples, when Jesus showed himself to them on the evening of the same day on which He arose; and likewise eight days after, chap. xx. 19-29.

In conjunction with Peter he cured a man who had been lame from his mother's womb, for which he was cast into prison, Acts iii. 1-10. He was afterwards sent to Samaria, to confer the Holy Ghost on those who had been converted there by Philip the deacon, Acts viii. 5-25. Paul informs us, Galatians ii, that John was present at the Council of Jerusalem, of which an account is given, Acts xv.

It is evident that John was present at most of the things related by him in his Gospel; and that he was an eye and ear witness of our Lord's labors, journeyings, discourses, miracles, passion, crucifixion, resurrection, and ascension. After the Ascension he returned with the other apostles from Mount Olivet to Jerusalem and took part in all transactions previously to the Day of Pentecost; at which time he, with the rest, partook of the mighty outpouring of the Holy Spirit, by which he was eminently qualified for the place he afterwards held in the apostolic Church.

Irenaeus, Eusebius, Origen, and others assert that he was a long time in Asia, continuing there till Trajan's time, who succeeded Nerva, A.D. 98. And Polycrates, bishop of Ephesus, A.D. 196, asserts that John was buried in that city. Jerome confirms this testimony, and says that John's death happened in the sixty-eighth year after our Lord's passion.

Tertullian and others say that Domitian having declared war against the Church of Christ, in the fifteenth year of his reign, A.D. 95, John was banished from Ephesus and carried to Rome, where he was immersed in a caldron of boiling oil, out of which however he escaped unhurt; and that afterwards he was banished to the isle of Patmos, in the Aegean Sea, where he wrote the Apocalypse. Domitian having been slain in A.D. 96, his successor, Nerva, recalled all the exiles who had been banished by his predecessor; and John is supposed to have returned the next year to Ephesus, being then about ninety years of age. He is thought to have been the only apostle who died a natural death, and to have lived upwards of one hundred years. This Gospel is supposed by learned men to have been written about A.D. 68 or 70; by others, A.D. 86; and, by others, A.D. 97; but the most probable opinion is that it was written at Ephesus about the year 86.

Jerome, in his comment on Galatians vi, says that John continued preaching when he was so enfeebled with old age that he was obliged to be carried into the assembly; and that, not being able to deliver any long discourse, his custom was to say, in every meeting, "My dear children, love one another!" Mary lived under his care till the day of her death.

Besides the Gospel before us, John is generally reputed to have been the author of the three Epistles which go under his name, and of the Apocalypse. The former certainly breathe the genuine spirit of this apostle, and are invaluable monuments of his spiritual knowledge and deep piety, as well as of his divine inspiration. As the Gospel and the Epistles prove him to have been an *evangelist* and *apostle,* his Book of Revelation ranks him among the profoundest of the *prophets.*

Learned men are not wholly agreed about the *language* in which this Gospel was originally written. Some think John wrote it in his own native tongue, the Aramean or Syriac, and that it was afterwards translated, by rather an unskillful hand, into Greek. This opinion is not supported by strong arguments. That it was originally written in Greek is the general and most likely opinion.

What the *design* of John was in writing this Gospel has divided and perplexed many critics and learned divines. Some suppose that it was to refute the errors taught by one Cerinthus, who rose up at that time, and asserted that Jesus was not born of a virgin, but was the real son of Joseph and Mary; that, at His baptism, the Christ, what we term the divine nature, descended into Him in the form of a dove, by whose influence He worked all His miracles; and that when He was about to suffer, this Christ, or divine nature, departed from Him and left the man Jesus to suffer death.

Others suppose he wrote with the prime design of confuting the heresy of the Gnostics, who derived their existence from Simon Magus, and who formed their system out of heathenism, Judaism, and Christianity. Concerning the person of our Lord, they held opinions similar to those of Cerinthus, and they arrogated to themselves the highest degrees of knowledge and spirituality. Though it is likely that the Gnostics held all these strange doctrines, and that many parts in John's Gospel may be successfully quoted against them, yet I must own I think the Evangelist had a more general end in view than the confutation of their heresies. It is more likely that he wrote for the express purpose of giving the Jews, his countrymen, proper notions of the Messiah and His kingdom; and to prove that Jesus, who had lately appeared among them, was this Christ. His own words sufficiently inform us of his motive, object, and design, in writing this Gospel: "These [things] are written, that ye might believe that Jesus is the Christ, the Son of God; and that believing ye might have life through his name," chap. xx. 31.

CHAPTER 1

The eternity of the Divine Logos, or Word of God, the Dispenser of light and life, 1-5. The mission of John the Baptist, 6-13. The incarnation of the Logos or Word of God, 14. John's testimony concerning the Logos, 15-18. The priests and Levites question Him concerning His mission and His baptism, 19-22. His answer, 23-28. His further testimony on seeing Christ, 29-34. He points Him out to two of his disciples, who thereupon follow Jesus, 35-37. Christ's address to them, 38-39. Andrew invites his brother, Simon Peter; Christ's address to him, 40-42. Christ calls Philip, and Philip invites Nathanael, 43-46. Christ's characterization of Nathanael, 47. A remarkable conversation between Him and His disciple, 48-51. John's introduction is from v. 1 to v. 18 inclusive. It contains a reason why the *Logos* or "Word" was made flesh.

1. *In the beginning.* That is, before anything was formed—ere God began the great work of creation. This is the meaning of the word in Gen. i. 1, to which the Evangelist evidently alludes. This phrase fully proves, in the mouth of an inspired writer, that Jesus Christ was no part of the creation, as He existed when no part of that existed; and that consequently He is no creature, as all created nature was formed by Him; for "without him was not any thing made that was made," v. 3. Now as what was before creation must be eternal, and as what gave being to all things could not have borrowed or derived its being from anything, therefore Jesus, who was before all things and who made all things, must necessarily be the eternal God. *Was the Word.* Or "existed the Logos." This term "Logos" should be left untranslated, for the very same reason the names *Jesus* and *Christ* are left untranslated. And as it would be highly improper to say, "the Deliverer, the Anointed," instead of "Jesus Christ," so I deem it improper to say, "the Word," instead of *the Logos.* But as every appellative of the Saviour of the world was descriptive of some excellence in His person, nature, or work, so the epithet *Logos,* which signifies "a word spoken, speech, eloquence, doctrine, reason, or the faculty of reasoning," is very properly applied to Him who is the "true Light, which lighteth every man that cometh into the world," v. 9; who is the Fountain of all wisdom; who giveth being, life, light, knowledge, and reason to all men; who is the grand Source of revelation, who has declared

God unto mankind; who spake by the prophets, "for the testimony of Jesus is the spirit of prophecy," Rev. xix. 10; who has illustrated life and immortality by His gospel, 2 Tim. i. 10; and who has fully made manifest the deep mysteries which lay hidden in the bosom of the invisible God from all eternity, John i. 18. The apostle does not borrow this mode of speech from the writings of Plato, as some have imagined; he took it from the scriptures of the Old Testament, and from the subsequent style of the ancient Jews. *And the Word was God.* Or "God was the Logos"; therefore no subordinate being, no second to the Most High, but the supreme, eternal Jehovah.

3. *All things were made by him.* That is, by this Logos. In Gen. i. 1, God is said to have created all things; in this verse, Christ is said to have created all things. The same unerring Spirit spoke in Moses and in the Evangelists; therefore Christ and the Father are One.

4. *In him was life.* This expression is not to be understood of natural life, but of that life eternal which He revealed to the world, 2 Tim. i. 10; to which He taught the way, chap. xiv. 6; which He promised to believers, chap. x. 28; which He purchased for them, chap. vi. 51, 53-54; which He is appointed to give them, chap. xvii. 2; and to which He will raise them up, v. 29, because He hath the life in himself, v. 26.

5. *And the light shineth in darkness.* By *darkness* here may be understood: (1) the heathen world, Eph. v. 8; (2) the Jewish people; (3) the fallen spirit of man. *Comprehended it not.* "Prevented it not—hindered it not."

6. *Whose name was John.* This was John the Baptist; see his name and the nature of his office explained, Mark i. 4 and Matt. iii. 1-3.

7. *That all men through him might believe.* He testified that Jesus was the *true Light*—the true Teacher of the way to the Kingdom of glory, and the Lamb or Sacrifice of God, which was to bear away the sin of the world, v. 29, and invited men to believe in Him for the remission of their sins, that they might receive the baptism of the Holy Ghost, vv. 32-34.

9. *Which lighteth every man.* As Christ is the Spring and Fountain of all wisdom, so all the wisdom that is in man comes from Him. The human intellect is a ray from His brightness; and reason itself springs from this Logos, the eternal Reason. Some of the most eminent rabbins understand Isa. lx. 1, "Arise, shine; for thy light is come," of the Messiah, who was to illuminate Israel. *That cometh into the world.* Or "coming into the world." This heavenly light shines into the soul of every man, to convince of sin, righteousness, and judgment; and it is through this light, which no man brings into the world with him, but which Christ mercifully gives to him on his coming into it, that what is termed conscience among men is produced. No man could discern good from evil were it not for this light thus supernaturally and graciously restored.

10. *He was in the world.* From its very commencement—He governed the universe—regulated His Church—spake by His prophets—and often, as the Angel or Messenger of Jehovah, appeared to them and to the patriarchs. *The world knew him not.* "Did not acknowledge Him"; for the Jewish rulers *knew* well enough that He was "a teacher come from God," but they did not choose to acknowledge Him as such.

11. *He came unto his own.* "To those of His own family, city, country"; "and His own people"—His own citizens, brethren, subjects. *Received him not.* Would not acknowledge Him as the Messiah, nor believe in Him for salvation.

12. *Gave he power.* "Privilege, honor, dignity, or right." He who is made a child of God enjoys the greatest "privilege" which the Divine Being can confer on this side of eternity. Those who accept Jesus Christ as He is offered to them in the gospel have, through His blood, a "right" to this sonship; for by that sacrifice this blessing was purchased, and the fullest promises of God confirm it to all who believe. And those who are engrafted in the heavenly family have the highest "honor" and "dignity" to which it is possible for a human soul to arrive.

13. *Which were born, not of blood.* Who were regenerated, "not of bloods"—the union of father and mother, or of a distinguished or illustrious ancestry, for the Hebrew language makes use of the *plural* to point out the dignity or excellence of a thing; and probably by this the Evangelist intended to show his countrymen that having Abraham and Sarah for their parents would not entitle them to the blessings of the new covenant, as no man could lay claim to them but in consequence of being born of God. Therefore neither *the will of the flesh* (anything that the corrupt heart of man could purpose or determine in its own behalf) nor *the will of man* (anything that another may be disposed to do in our behalf) can avail here. This new birth must come through the *will of God*—through His own unlimited power and boundless mercy, prescribing salvation by Christ Jesus alone.

14. *And the Word was made flesh.* That very Person who was in the beginning—who was with God—and who was God, v. 1, in the fullness of time became flesh—became incarnated by the power of the Holy Ghost, in the womb of the Virgin. Allowing this apostle to have written by divine inspiration, is not this verse, taken in connection with v. 1, an absolute and incontest-able proof of the proper and eternal Godhead of Christ Jesus? *And dwelt among us.* "And tabernacled among us," the human nature which He took of the Virgin being as the shrine, house, or temple in which His immaculate deity condescended to dwell. The word is probably an allusion to the divine Shekinah in the Jewish Temple; and as God has represented the whole gospel dispensation by the types and ceremonies of the old covenant, so the Shekinah in the Tabernacle and Temple pointed out this manifestation of God in the flesh. The word is thus used by the Jewish writers; it signifies with them a manifestation of the divine Shekinah. *We beheld his glory.* This refers to the Transfiguration, at which John was present, in company with Peter and James. *The glory as of the only begotten.* That is, such a glory as "became," or was "proper to," the Son of God; for thus the particle *hos* should be here understood. There is also here an allusion to the manifestations of God above the ark in the Tabernacle (see Exod. xxv. 22; Num. vii. 89); and this connects itself with the first clause, "He tabernacled," or "fixed His tent among us." While God dwelt in the Tabernacle, among the Jews, the priests saw His glory; and while Jesus dwelt among men His glory was manifested in His gracious words and miraculous acts. *The only begotten of the Father.* That is, the only Person born of a woman whose human nature never came by the ordinary way of generation, it being a mere creation in the womb of the Virgin by the energy of the Holy Ghost. *Full of grace and truth.* Full of favor, kindness, and mercy to men; teaching the way to the kingdom of God, with all the simplicity, plainness, dignity, and energy of *truth.*

15. *Of him.* The glorious Personage before mentioned. John the Baptist, whose history was well-known to the persons to whom this Gospel came in the beginning, *bare witness . . . and* [*he*] *cried*—being deeply convinced of the importance and truth of the subject, he delivered his testimony with the utmost zeal and earnestness, saying, *This was he of whom I spake, He that cometh after me*—for I am no other than the voice of the crier in the wilderness, Isa. xl. 3, the forerunner of the Messiah. *Was before me.* Speaking by the prophets, and warning your fathers to repent and return to God, as I now warn you; *for he was before me*—He was from eternity, and from Him I have derived both my being and my ministry.

16. *And of his fulness.* Of the plenitude of His grace and mercy, by which He made an atonement for sin, and of the plenitude of His wisdom and truth, by which the mysteries of heaven have been revealed and the science of eternal truth taught, *have all we received.* All we apostles have received *grace* or mercy to pardon our sins, and *truth* to enable us so to write and speak concerning these things, that those who attend to our testimony shall be unerringly directed in the way of salvation, and with us continue to receive "grace upon grace," one blessing after another, till they are filled with all the fullness of God. It is only necessary to add that John seems here to refer to the gospel as succeeding the law. The law was certainly a dispensation of both *grace* and *truth,* for it pointed out the gracious design of God to save men by Christ Jesus. But the gospel, which had now taken place, introduced that plenitude

of *grace* and *truth* to the whole world, which the law had only shadowed forth to the Jewish people, and which they imagined should have been restrained to themselves alone. In the most gracious economy of God, one dispensation of mercy and truth is designed to make way for, and to be followed by, another and a greater. Thus the law succeeded the patriarchal dispensation, and the gospel the law; more and more of the plenitude of the grace of the gospel becomes daily manifest to the genuine followers of Christ; and to those who are faithful unto death, a heaven full of eternal glory will soon succeed to the grace of the gospel.

17. *The law was given by Moses.* Moses received the law from God, and through him it was given to the Jews, Acts vii. 38. *But grace and truth.* Which he had already mentioned, and which were to be the subject of the book which he was now writing, *came* to all mankind "through Jesus Christ," who is the Mediator of the new covenant, as Moses was of the old, Heb. viii. 6; ix. 15; Gal. iii. 19. *Jesus Christ.* "Jesus the Christ, the Messiah," or anointed Prophet, Priest, and King, sent from heaven.

18. *No man hath seen God at any time.* Moses and others heard His voice, and saw the cloud and the fire, which were the symbols of His presence; but such a manifestation of God as had now taken place, in the person of Jesus Christ, had never before been exhibited to the world. It is likely that the word *seen,* here, is put for "known," as in chap. iii. 32; 1 John iii. 2, 6; and 3 John, v. 11; and this sense the latter clause of the verse seems to require—*No man,* how highly soever favored, "hath fully known God, at any time," in any nation or age. *The only begotten Son, which is in the bosom of the Father,* who was intimately acquainted with all the counsels of the Most High, *he hath declared him,* hath announced the divine oracles unto men; for in this sense the word is used by the best Greek writers. "Lying in the bosom" is spoken of in reference to the Asiatic custom of reclining while at meals. The person who was next the other was said to "lie in his bosom"; and he who had this place in reference to the master of the feast was supposed to share his peculiar regards, and to be in a state of the utmost favor and intimacy with him.

19. *And this is the record of John.* He persisted in this assertion, testifying to the Jews that this Jesus was *the Christ.*

20. *He confessed, and denied not; but confessed.* A common mode of Jewish phraseology. John renounces himself, that Jesus may be All in All.

21. *Art thou Elias?* The scribes themselves had taught that Elijah was to come before the Messiah. See Matt. xvii. 10; and this belief of theirs supported by a literal construction of Mal. iv. 5. *Art thou that prophet?* The prophet spoken of by Moses, Deut. xviii. 15, 18. This text they had also misunderstood, for the prophet or teacher promised by Moses was no other than the Messiah himself. See Acts iii. 22. But the Jews had a tradition that Jeremiah was to return to life, and restore the pot of manna, the ark of the covenant, etc., which he had hidden that the Babylonians might not get them. Besides this, they had a general expectation that all the prophets should come to life in the days of the Messiah. *I am not.* I am not the prophet which you expect, nor Elijah—though he was the Elijah that was to come; for in the spirit and power of that eminent prophet he came, proclaiming the necessity of reformation in Israel. See Matt. xi. 14; xvii. 10-13.

22. *That we may give an answer to them that sent us.* These Pharisees were probably a deputation from the grand Sanhedrin, the members of which, hearing of the success of the Baptist's preaching, were puzzled to know what to make of him, and seriously desired to hear from himself what he professed to be.

23. *I am the voice of one crying.* See the notes on Matt. iii. 3; Mark i. 4-5.

25. *Why baptizest thou then?* Baptism was a very common ceremony among the Jews, who never received a proselyte into the full enjoyment of a Jew's privileges till he was both baptized and circumcised. But such baptisms were never performed except by an ordinance of the Sanhedrin, or in the presence of three magistrates. Besides, they never baptized any Jew or Jewess, nor even those who were the children of their proselytes; for, as all these were considered as born in the covenant, they had no need of baptism, which was used only as an introductory rite. Now, as John had in this respect altered the common custom so very essentially, admitting to his baptism the Jews in general, the Sanhedrin took it for granted that no man had authority to make such changes, unless especially commissioned from on high; and that only *the prophet,* or *Elijah,* or the *Messiah* himself could have authority to act as John did.

26. *I baptize with water.* See on Mark i. 8. I use the common form, though I direct the baptized to a different end, viz., that they shall repent of their sins and believe in the Messiah. *There standeth one among you.* That is, the Person whose forerunner I am is now dwelling in the land of Judea and will shortly make His appearance among you. Christ was not present when John spoke thus, as may be seen from v. 29.

27. *Is preferred before me.* "Who was before me." This clause is wanting in a few of the MSS. and versions, and in some of the primitive fathers.

28. *These things were done in Bethabara.* It is very probable that the word *Bethany* should be inserted here instead of *Bethabara.* This reading, in the judgment of the best critics, is the genuine one. It is supported by many authorities, including some of the most eminent of the primitive fathers, before the time of Origen, who is supposed to have first changed the reading. *Bethabara* signifies literally "the house of passage," and is thought to be the place where the Israelites passed the river Jordan under Joshua. There was a place called *Bethany,* about two miles from Jerusalem, at the foot of the Mount of Olives. But there was another of the same name, beyond Jordan, in the tribe of Reuben. It was probably of this that the Evangelist speaks; and Origen, not knowing of this second Bethany, altered the reading to *Bethabara.*

29. *The next day.* The day after that on which the Jews had been with John, v. 19. *Behold the Lamb of God.* This was said in allusion to what was spoken in Isa. liii. 7. Jesus was the

true Lamb or Sacrifice required and appointed by God, of which those offered daily in the Tabernacle and Temple, Exod. xxix. 38-39, and especially the paschal lamb, were only the types and representatives. See Exod. xii. 4-5; 1 Cor. v. 7. The continual morning and evening sacrifice of a lamb, under the Jewish law, was intended to point out the continual efficacy of the blood of atonement; for even at the throne of God, Jesus Christ is ever represented as a Lamb newly slain, Rev. v. 6. But John, pointing to Christ, calls Him emphatically *the Lamb of God.* All the lambs which had been hitherto offered had been furnished by men; this was provided by God, as the only sufficient and available Sacrifice for the sin of the world.

31. *And I knew him not.* John did not know our Lord personally, and perhaps had never seen Him, at the time he spoke the words in v. 15. Nor is it any wonder that the Baptist should have been unacquainted with Christ, as he had spent thirty years in the hill country of Hebron, and our Lord remained in a state of great privacy in the obscure city of Nazareth, in the extreme borders of Galilee. *But that he should be made manifest to Israel.* One design of My publicly baptizing Jesus was that He, coming to my baptism, should be shown to be what He is, by some extraordinary sign from heaven.

32. *I saw the Spirit descending.* See the notes on Matt. iii. 16-17.

33. *He that sent me . . . said unto me.* From this we may clearly perceive that John had a most intimate acquaintance with the Divine Being; and received not only his call and mission at first, but every subsequent direction, by immediate, unequivocal inspiration.

35. *The next day.* After that mentioned in v. 29. *Two of his disciples.* One of them was Andrew, v. 40, and it is very likely that John himself was the other; in everything in which he might receive honor he studiously endeavors to conceal his own name.

36. *And looking upon Jesus.* "Attentively beholding"—to view with steadfastness and attention. He who desires to discover the glories and excellencies of this Lamb of God must thus look on Him. At first sight He appears only as a man among men, and as dying in testimony to the truth, as many others have died. But on a more attentive consideration He appears to be no less than God manifest in the flesh, and by His death making an atonement for the sin of the world. *Behold the Lamb of God!* By this the Baptist designed to direct the attention of his own disciples to Jesus, not only as the great Sacrifice for the sin of the world, but also as the complete Teacher of heavenly truth.

38. *What seek ye?* These disciples might have felt some embarrassment in addressing our blessed Lord, after hearing the character which the Baptist gave of Him; to remove or prevent this, He graciously accosts them, and gives them an opportunity of explaining themselves to Him. Such questions, we may conceive, the blessed Jesus still puts to those who in simplicity of heart desire an acquaintance with Him. A question of this nature we may profitably ask ourselves: *What seek ye?* In this place? In the company you frequent? In the conversation in which you engage? In the affairs with which you are occupied? In the works which you

perform? *Rabbi.* "Teacher." Behold the modesty of these disciples—we wish to be scholars; we are ignorant—we desire to be taught; we believe Thou art a Teacher come from God. *Where dwellest thou?* That we may come and receive Thy instructions.

39. *Come and see.* If those who know not the salvation of God would *come* at the command of Christ, they should soon *see* that with Him is the fountain of life, and in His light they should see light. *The tenth hour.* Generally supposed to be about what we call four o'clock in the afternoon. According to chap. xi. 9, the Jews reckoned twelve hours in the day; and of course each hour of the day, thus reckoned, must have been something longer or shorter, according to the different times of the year in that climate. The sixth hour with them answered to our twelve o'clock, as appears from what Josephus says in his life, chap. liv. "That on the Sabbath day it was the rule for the Jews to go to dinner at the sixth hour." Dr. Macknight, however, is of opinion that the Evangelist is to be understood as speaking of the Roman hour, which was ten o'clock in the morning; and, as the Evangelist remarks, *They . . . abode with him that day,* it implies that there was a considerable portion of time spent with our Lord. But had it been the Jewish tenth hour, it would have been useless to remark their abiding with Him that day, as there were only two hours of it still remaining.

41. *Findeth his own brother Simon.* Every man who has been brought to an acquaintance with God should endeavor to bring at least another with him; and his first attention should be fixed upon those of his own household.

42. *Cephas, which is by interpretation, A stone.* The reason why this name was given to Simon, who was ever afterwards called Peter, may be seen in the notes on Matt. xvi. 18-19.

43. *Philip.* This apostle was a native of Bethsaida in Galilee. He must not be confounded with Philip the deacon, spoken of in Acts vi. 5.

45. *Nathanael.* This apostle is supposed to be the same with *Bartholomew,* which is very likely, for these reasons: (1) That the Evangelists who mention Bartholomew say nothing of Nathanael; and that John, who speaks of Nathanael, says nothing of Bartholomew. (2) No notice is taken anywhere of Bartholomew's vocation, unless his and that of Nathanael mentioned here be the same. (3) The name of Bartholomew is not a proper name; it signifies the "son of Ptolomy"; and Nathanael might have been his own name. (4) John seems to rank Nathanael with the apostles when he says that Peter and Thomas, the two sons of Zebedee, Nathanael, and two other disciples, being gone a fishing, Jesus showed himself to them, John xxi. 2-4. *Moses in the law.* See Gen. iii. 15; xxii. 18; xlix. 10; Deut. xviii. 18. *And the prophets.* See Isa. iv. 2; vii. 14; ix. 5; xl. 10; liii. 1, etc.; Jer. xxiii. 5; xxxiii. 14-15; Ezek. xxiv. 23; xxxvii. 24; Dan. ix. 24; Mic. v. 2; Zech. vi. 12; ix. 9; xii. 10.

46. *Can there any good thing come out of Nazareth?* Bishop Pearce supposes that the *ti anathon* of the Evangelist has some particular force in it: for, in Jer. xxxiii. 14, God says, "I will perform *that good thing* which I have promised"; and this, in v. 15, is explained to mean his causing "the Branch of righteousness

[i.e., the Messiah] to grow up unto David," from whom Jesus was descended. In this view, Nathanael's question seems to imply that not Nazareth, but Bethlehem, was to be the birthplace of the Messiah, according to what the chief priests and scribes had determined, Matt. ii. 4-6. If this conjecture be not thought solid, we may suppose that Nazareth, at this time, was become so abandoned that no good could be expected from any of those who dwelt in it, and that its wickedness had passed into a proverb: Can anything good be found in Nazareth? *Come and see.* He who candidly examines the evidences of the religion of Christ will infallibly become a believer. No history ever published among men has so many external and internal proofs of authenticity as does this.

47. *Behold an Israelite indeed.* A worthy descendant of the patriarch Jacob, who not only professes to believe in Israel's God, but who worships Him in sincerity and truth, according to his light. *In whom is no guile!* To find a man, living in the midst of so much corruption, walking in uprightness before his Maker, was a subject worthy the attention of God himself. Behold this man! and, while you see and admire, imitate his conduct.

48. *Whence knowest thou me?* He was not yet acquainted with the divinity of Christ, could not conceive that He could search his heart, and therefore asks how He could acquire this knowledge of him, or who had given him that character. *Under the fig tree.* Probably engaged in prayer with God for the speedy appearing of the salvation of Israel; and the shade of this fig tree was perhaps the ordinary place of retreat for this upright man. It is not "a fig tree," but *the fig tree,* one particularly distinguished from the others.

49. *Rabbi.* That is, "Teacher!" and so this word should be translated. *Thou art the Son of God.* The promised Messiah. *Thou art the King of Israel.* The real Descendant of David, who was to sit on that spiritual throne of which the throne of David was the type.

50. *Because I said unto thee, I saw thee.* As you have credited My divine mission on this simple proof, that I saw you when and where no human eye, placed where Mine was, could see you, your faith shall not rest merely upon this, *for you shall see greater things than these*—more numerous and express proofs of My eternal power and Godhead.

51. *Verily, verily.* Amen, amen. The doubling of this word probably came from this circumstance: that it was written both in Hebrew and in Greek, signifying, "It is true." *Heaven open.* This seems to be a figurative expression. (1) Christ may be understood by this saying to mean that a clear and abundant revelation of God's will should now be made unto men; that heaven itself should, as it were, be laid *open,* and all the mysteries which had been shut up and hidden in it from eternity, relative to the salvation and glorification of man, should be now fully revealed. (2) That by the *angels of God ascending and descending* is to be understood that a perpetual intercourse should now be opened between heaven and earth through the medium of Christ, who was God manifested in the flesh. Our blessed Lord represented in His mediatorial capacity as the Ambassador of God to men; and *the angels ascending and descending upon the Son of man* is a metaphor taken from the custom of dispatching couriers or messengers from the prince to his ambassador in a foreign court, and from the ambassador back to the prince. This metaphor will receive considerable light when compared with 2 Cor. v. 19-20: "God was in Christ, reconciling the world unto himself . . . we are ambassadors for Christ, as though God did beseech you by us: we pray you in Christ's stead, be ye reconciled to God."

CHAPTER 2

The miracle at Cana in Galilee, where our Lord changed water into wine, 1-11. He goes to Capernaum, 12. He purges the Temple at the Feast of the Passover, 13-17. The Jews require a miracle, as a proof that He had authority to do these things, 18. In answer He refers to His own death and resurrection, 19-22. Many believe on Him while at the Feast of the Passover, to whom Jesus would not trust himself, 23-25.

1. *Cana of Galilee.* This was a small city in the tribe of Asher, Josh. xix. 28, and by saying this was Cana of *Galilee,* the Evangelist distinguishes it from another Cana which was in the tribe of Ephraim, in the Samaritan country. See Josh. xvi. 8; xvii. 9. Some suppose that the *third day* mentioned here refers to the third day of the marriage feast, such feasts lasting among the Jews seven days. See Judg. xiv. 12, 17-18.

3. *They have no wine.* Though the blessed Virgin is supposed never to have seen her Son work a miracle before this time, yet she seems to have expected Him to do something extraordinary on this occasion, as from her acquaintance with Him she must have formed some adequate idea of His power and goodness.

4. *Woman, what have I to do with thee?* "O woman, what is this to you and Me?" This is an abrupt denial, as if He had said: "We are not employed to provide the necessaries for this feast; this matter belongs to others, who should have made a proper and sufficient provision for the persons they had invited." The words seem to convey a reproof to the Virgin for meddling with that which did not particularly concern her. But here indeed there appears to be no blame. It is very likely the bride or bridegroom's family were relatives of the blessed Virgin; and she would naturally suppose that our Lord would feel interested for the honor and comfort of the family, and knowing that He possessed extraordinary power, made this application to Him to come forward to their assistance. Our Lord's answer to His mother, if properly translated, is far from being disrespectful. He addresses the Virgin as He did the Syrophoenician woman, Matt. xv. 28; as He did the Samaritan woman, John iv. 21; as He addressed His disconsolate mother when He hung upon the Cross, chap. xix. 26; as He did His most affectionate friend Mary Magdalene, chap. xx. 15, and as the angels had addressed her before, v. 13; and as Paul does the believing Christian woman, 1 Cor. vii. 16—in all which places the same term which occurs in this verse is used, and where certainly no kind of disrespect is intended. *Mine hour is not yet come.* Or my "time," for in this sense the word is often taken. My time for working a miracle is not yet fully come. What I do, I do when necessary, and not before. Nature is unsteady, full of haste, and ever blundering in consequence. It

is the folly and sin of men that they are ever finding fault with the divine providence. According to them, God never does anything in due time—He is too early or too late; whereas it is utterly impossible for the divine wisdom to forestall itself or for the divine goodness to delay what is necessary.

5. *His mother saith.* The Virgin seems to have understood our Lord as hinted above. It was not yet time to grant them a supply, because the want had not as yet been generally felt. But, silently receiving the respectful caution, she saw that miracle should be wrought when it best suited the purposes of the divine wisdom.

6. *After the manner of the purifying of the Jews.* Or "for the purpose of the purifying of the Jews." The preposition which I have translated "for the purpose" often denotes in the best Greek writers the final cause of a thing. These six vessels were set in a convenient place, for the purpose of the Jews washing their hands before they sat down to meat, and probably for other purposes of purification. See this custom referred to in Matt. xv. 2. *Containing two or three firkins apiece.* "Measures" or *metretes.* [Some] make each *metretes* to contain ten gallons and two pints.

8. *Governor of the feast.* The original word signifies one who is "chief or head over three couches, or tables." In the Asiatic countries, they take their meals reclining on small, low couches. And when many people are present, so that they cannot all eat together, three of these low tables or couches are put together in form of a crescent, and one of the guests is appointed to take charge of the persons who sit at these tables. Hence the appellation of *architriclinus,* the "chief over three couches or tables," which in process of time became applied to the *governor* or "steward" of a feast, let the guests be many or few; and such person, having conducted the business well, had a festive crown put on his head by the guests at the conclusion of the feast. *And they bare it.* A question has been asked, "Did our Lord turn all the water into wine which the six measures contained?" To which I answer: There is no proof that He did; and I take it for granted that He did not. It may be asked, "How could a part be turned into wine, and not the whole?" To which I answer: The water, in all likelihood, was changed into wine *as it was drawn out,* and not otherwise. "But did not our Lord by this miracle minister to vice, by producing an excess of inebriating liquor?" No; for the following reasons: (1) The company was a select and holy company, where no excess could be permitted. And (2) our Lord does not appear to have furnished any extra quantity, but only what was necessary. "But it is intimated in the text that the guests were nearly intoxicated before this miraculous addition to their wine took place; for the Evangelist says, 'when they have become intoxicated.' " I answer: (1) It is not intimated, even in the most indirect manner, that *these* guests were at all intoxicated. (2) The words are not spoken of the persons at *that* wedding at all; the governor of the feast only states that such was the common custom at feasts of this nature, without intimating that any such custom prevailed there. (3) The original word bears a widely different meaning from that which the objection forces upon it. The verbs signify not

only "to inebriate" but "to take wine, to drink wine, to drink enough"; and in this sense the verb is evidently used in the Septuagint, Gen. xliii. 34; Cant. v. 1; Hag. i. 6.

10. *The good wine until now.* That which our Lord now made being perfectly pure and highly nutritive.

11. *This beginning of miracles.* It was probably the first He ever wrought; at any rate, it was the first He wrought after His baptism and the first He wrought publicly. *His glory.* His supreme divinity, chap. i. 14. *His disciples believed on him.* Were more abundantly confirmed in their faith that He was either the promised Messiah or a most extraordinary prophet, in the fullest intercourse with the ever blessed God.

13. *And the Jews' passover was at hand.* This was the reason why He stayed but a few days at Capernaum, v. 12, as He wished to be present at the celebration of this feast at Jerusalem. This was the *first* passover after Christ's baptism. The *second* is mentioned in Luke vi. 1; the *third,* in John vi. 4; and the *fourth,* which was that at which He was crucified, in chap. xi. 55. From which it appears: (1) that our blessed Lord continued His public ministry about three years and a half, according to the prophecy of Daniel, chap. ix. 27; and (2) that, having been baptized about the beginning of His thirtieth year, He was crucified precisely in the middle of His thirty-third.

14. *Found in the temple those that sold oxen.* This is a *similar* fact to that mentioned in Matt. xxi. 12; Mark xi. 15; Luke xix. 45. If it be the *same* fact, then John anticipates three years of time in relating it here, as that cleansing of the Temple mentioned by the other Evangelists took place in the last week of our Lord's life. Mr. Mann, Dr. Priestley, and Bishop Pearce contend that our Lord cleansed the Temple only *once,* and that was at the last Passover. Calvin, Dr. Lardner, Bishop Hurd, and Bishop Newcome contend that He purged the Temple *twice;* and that this mentioned by John was the *first* cleansing, which none of the other Evangelists have mentioned. The vindication of God's house from profanation was the *first* and the *last* care of our Lord, and it is probable He began and finished His public ministry by this significant act. It certainly appears that John directly asserts an early cleansing of the Temple by the series of His history, as the other three Evangelists assert a later cleansing of it. And though the act mentioned here seems to be nearly the same with that mentioned by the other Evangelists, yet there are some differences. John alone mentions the "scourge of rushes" and the casting out of the "sheep and oxen." Besides, there is a considerable difference in our Lord's manner of doing it. In the cleansing mentioned by the three Evangelists, He assumes a vast deal of authority and speaks more pointedly concerning himself than He appears to do in this cleansing mentioned by John. The reason which has been given is, In the first cleansing He was just entering upon His public ministry, and therefore avoided (as much as was consistent with the accomplishment of His work) the giving any offence to the Jewish rulers; but in the last cleansing He was just concluding His ministry, being about to offer up His life for the salvation of the world, in consequence of which He speaks fully and without reserve.

17. *The zeal of thine house.* See Ps. lix. 10. Zeal to promote Thy glory, and to keep Thy worship pure.

18. *What sign shewest thou?* When Moses came to deliver Israel he gave signs, or miracles, that he acted under a divine commission. What miracle dost Thou work to show us that Thou art vested with similar authority?

19. *Destroy this temple.* "This very temple," perhaps pointing to His body at the same time.

20. *Forty and six years was this temple in building.* The Temple of which the Jews spoke was begun to be rebuilt by Herod the Great in the eighteenth year of his reign (see Josephus). But though he finished the main work in nine years and a half, yet some additional buildings or repairs were constantly carried on for many years afterwards. Herod began the work sixteen years before the birth of our Lord; the transactions which are here related took place in the thirtieth year of our Lord, which make the term exactly forty-six years. Josephus has told us that the whole of the buildings belonging to the Temple were not finished till Nero's reign, when Albinus, the governor of Judea, was succeeded by Gessius Florus, which was eighty years after the eighteenth year of Herod's reign.

21. *Of the temple of his body.* Rather, "the temple, His body." His body had no particular temple; but it was the temple of His divinity— the place in which, as in the ancient Temple, His Godhead dwelt. See how the Jews perverted these words, Matt. xxvi. 60, and the notes there.

22. *Remembered that he had said this unto them.* *Unto them* is wanting in many MSS. and versions. *They believed the scripture.* The scripture which the Evangelist immediately refers to may have been Ps. xvi. 10. Compare this with Acts ii. 31-32 and with chap. xiii. 35-37. See also Ps. ii. 7, and compare it with Heb. i. 5, and chap. v. 5, and with Acts xiii. 33. They understood these scriptures in a sense in which they never before understood them.

23. *Many believed in his name.* They believed Him to be the promised Messiah, but did not believe in Him to the salvation of their souls; for we find from the following verse that their hearts were not at all changed, because our blessed Lord could not trust himself to them.

CHAPTER 3

The conversation between Nicodemus and our Lord, about the new birth and faith in His testimony, 1-15. The love of God, the source of human salvation, 16. Who are condemned, and who are approved, 17-21. Jesus and His disciples come to Judea, and baptize, 22. John baptizes in Aenon, 23-24. The disciples of John and the Pharisees dispute about purifying, 25. The discourse between John and his disciples about Christ, in which the excellence, perfection, and privileges of the Christian dispensation are pointed out, 26-36.

1. *Nicodemus, a ruler of the Jews.* One of the members of the grand Sanhedrin, for such were ordinarily styled *rulers* among the Jews.

2. *Came to Jesus by night.* He had matters of the utmost importance on which he wished to consult Christ; and he chose the *night* season, perhaps less through the fear of man than through a desire to have Jesus alone, as he found Him all the day encompassed with the multitude, so that it was impossible for him to get an opportunity to speak fully on those weighty affairs concerning which he intended to consult Him. *Rabbi.* "My Master" or "Teacher," a title of respect given to the Jewish doctors, something like our "Doctor of Divinity," i.e., teacher of divine things. But as there may be many found among us who, though they bear the title, are no teachers, so it was among the Jews; and perhaps it was in reference to this that Nicodemus uses the word *didaskalos* immediately after, by which, in chap. i. 39, John translates the word rabbi. *Rabbi,* teacher, is often no more than a title of respect; *didaskalos* signifies a person who not only has the name of teacher but who actually does teach. *We know that thou art a teacher come from God. We,* all the members of the grand Sanhedrin, and all the rulers of the people, who have paid proper attention to Thy doctrine and miracles. We are all convinced of this, though we are not all candid enough to own it. It is possible, however, that *we know* signifies no more than "it is known, it is generally acknowledged and allowed," *that thou art a teacher come from God. No man can do these miracles.* It is on the evidence of Thy miracles that I ground my opinion of Thee. No man can do what Thou dost unless the omnipotence of God be with him.

3. *Jesus answered.* Not in the language of compliment; He saw the state of Nicodemus' soul, and He immediately addressed himself to him on a subject the most interesting and important. But what connection is there between our Lord's reply and the address of Nicodemus? Probably our Lord saw that the object of his visit was to inquire about the Messiah's kingdom; and in reference to this He immediately says, *Except a man be born again.* The repetition of *amen,* or *verily, verily,* among the Jewish writers, was considered of equal import with the most solemn oath. *Be born again.* Or "from above"; different to that new birth which the Jews supposed every baptized proselyte enjoyed; for they held that the Gentile who became a proselyte was like a newborn child. This birth was of water from below; the birth for which Christ contends is "from above"—by the agency of the Holy Spirit. Every man must have two births: one from heaven, the other from earth—one of his body, the other of his soul. Without the first he cannot see nor enjoy this world; without the last he cannot see nor enjoy the kingdom of God. As there is an absolute necessity that a child should be born into the world, that he may see its light, contemplate its glories, and enjoy its good, so there is an absolute necessity that the soul should be brought out of its state of darkness and sin, through the light and power of the grace of Christ, that it may be able to *see,* or to "discern," the glories and excellencies of the kingdom of Christ here, and be prepared for the enjoyment of the Kingdom of glory hereafter. The Jews had some general notion of the new birth; but, like many among Christians, they put the acts of proselytism, baptism, etc., in the place of the Holy Spirit and His influence. They acknowledged that a man must be born again; but they made that new birth to consist in profession, confession, and external washing. The new birth which is here spoken of comprehends not only what is termed justification or pardon but also sanctification or holiness. Sin must be pardoned and the impurity of the heart washed away before any soul can possibly enter into

the kingdom of God. As this new birth implies the renewing of the whole soul in righteousness and true holiness, it is not a matter that may be dispensed with. Heaven is a place of holiness, and nothing but what is like itself can ever enter into it.

4. *How can a man be born when he is old?* It is probable that Nicodemus was pretty far advanced in age at this time; and from his answer we may plainly perceive that, like the rest of the Jews, and like multitudes of Christians, he rested in the letter, without paying proper attention to the spirit. The shadow, without the thing signified, had hitherto satisfied him. Our Lord knew him to be in this state, and this was the cause of His pointed address to him.

5. *Of water and of the Spirit.* To the baptism of water a man was admitted when he became a proselyte to the Jewish religion; and, in this baptism, he promised in the most solemn manner to renounce idolatry, to take the God of Israel for his God, and to have his life conformed to the precepts of the divine law. But the water which was used on the occasion was only an emblem of the Holy Spirit. The soul was considered as in a state of defilement because of past sin. Now, as by that water the body was washed, cleansed, and refreshed, so, by the influences of the Holy Spirit, the soul was to be purified from its defilement and strengthened to walk in the way of truth and holiness. When John came baptizing with water, he gave the Jews the plainest intimations that this would not suffice; that it was only typical of that baptism of the Holy Ghost, under the similitude of fire, which they must all receive from Jesus Christ. See Matt. iii. 11. Therefore our Lord asserts that a man must be *born of water and of the Spirit,* i.e., of the Holy Ghost, which, represented under the similitude of *water,* cleanses, refreshes, and purifies the soul. Though baptism by water into the Christian faith was necessary to every Jew and Gentile that entered into the kingdom of the Messiah, it is not necessary that by water and the Spirit (in this place) we should understand two different things. It is probably only an elliptical form of speech for the Holy Spirit under the similitude of water; as, in Matt. iii. 3, "the Holy Ghost and fire" do not mean two things, but one, viz., the Holy Ghost under the similitude of fire—pervading every part, refining and purifying the whole.

6. *That which is born of the flesh is flesh.* This is the answer to the objection made by Nicodemus in v. 4. "Can a man enter the second time into his mother's womb, and be born?"

8. *The wind bloweth.* Though the manner in which this new birth is effected by the Divine Spirit be incomprehensible to us, yet we must not on this ground suppose it to be impossible. The wind blows in a variety of directions—we hear its sound, perceive its operation in the motion of the trees, etc., and feel it on ourselves —but we cannot discern the air itself; we only know that it exists by the effects which it produces. *So is every one that is born of the Spirit;* the effects are as discernible and as sensible as those of the wind, but itself we cannot see. But he who is born of God knows that he is thus born. "The Spirit itself," the grand Agent in this new birth, "beareth witness with our spirit," that he is born of God, Rom. viii. 16; for "he that believeth . . . hath the

witness in himself," 1 John iv. 13 and v. 10; Gal. iv. 6. And so does this Spirit work in and by him that others, though they see not the principle, can easily discern the change produced; for "whatsoever is born of God overcometh the world," 1 John v. 4.

9. *How can these things be?* Our Lord had very plainly told him how these things could be, and illustrated the new birth by one of the most proper similes that could be chosen; but so intent was this great man on making everything submit to the testimony of his senses that he appears unwilling to believe anything unless he can comprehend it. This is the case with many—they profess to believe because they comprehend, but they are impostors who speak thus. There is not a man in the universe that can fully comprehend one operation, either of God or of His instrument nature; and yet they must believe, and do believe, though they never did nor ever can fully comprehend, or account for, the objects of their faith.

10. *Art thou a master of Israel?* Have you taken upon you to guide the blind into the way of truth, and yet know not that truth yourself? Do you command proselytes to be baptized with water as an emblem of a new birth, and are you unacquainted with the cause, necessity, nature, and effects of that new birth? "But I am taught to believe that this baptism is regeneration." Then you are taught to believe a falsity. Whereby are such persons made the children of grace? Not by the water, but by the "death unto sin," and the "new birth unto righteousness"; i.e., through the agency of the Holy Ghost sin is destroyed and the soul filled with holiness.

11. *We speak that we do know.* I and My disciples do not profess to teach a religion which we do not understand nor exemplify in our conduct. A strong but delicate reproof to Nicodemus, who, though a master of Israel, did not understand the very rudiments of the doctrine of salvation.

12. *If I have told you earthly things.* If after I have illustrated this new birth by a most expressive metaphor taken from earthly things, and after all you believe not, how can you believe should I tell you of *heavenly things,* in such language as angels use, where earthly images and illustrations can have no place? Or if you, a teacher in Israel, do not understand the nature of such an earthly thing, or custom of the kingdom established over the Jewish nation, as being born of baptism, practiced every day in the initiation of proselytes, how will you understand such heavenly things as the initiation of My disciples by the baptism of the Holy Ghost and fire from heaven, if I should proceed further on the subject?

13. *No man hath ascended.* This seems a figurative expression for "No man hath known the mysteries of the kingdom of God," as in Deut. xxx. 12; Ps. lxxiii. 17; Prov. xxx. 4; Rom. xi. 34. And the expression is founded upon this generally received maxim: That to be perfectly acquainted with the concerns of a place, it is necessary for a person to be on the spot. But our Lord probably spoke to correct a false notion among the Jews, viz., that Moses had ascended to heaven in order to get the law. It is not Moses who is to be heard now, but Jesus; Moses did not ascend to heaven, but the

Son of Man is come down from heaven to reveal the divine will. *That came down.* The incarnation of Christ is represented under the notion of His *coming down* from heaven to dwell upon earth.

14. *As Moses lifted up.* He shows the reason why He descended from heaven, that He might be lifted up, i.e., crucified, for the salvation of mankind, and be, by the appointment of God, as certain a Remedy for sinful souls as the brazen serpent elevated on a pole, Num. xxi. 9, was for the bodies of the Israelites which had been bitten by the fiery serpents in the wilderness.

16. *For God so loved the world.* Such a love as that which induced God to give His only begotten Son to die for the world could not be described; Jesus Christ does not attempt it. He has put an eternity of meaning in the particle *so* and left a subject for everlasting contemplation, wonder, and praise, to angels and to men. The same Evangelist uses a similar mode of expression, 1 Epist. iii. 1: "Behold, what manner of love the Father hath bestowed upon us."

17. *For God sent not.* It was the opinion of the Jews that the Gentiles, whom they often term "the world," and "nations of the world," were to be destroyed in the days of the Messiah. Christ corrects this false opinion and teaches here a contrary doctrine. God, by giving His Son and publishing His design in giving Him, shows that He purposes the salvation, not the destruction, of the world—the Gentile people. Nevertheless, those who will not receive the salvation He had provided for them, whether Jews or Gentiles, must necessarily perish; for this plain reason, there is but one remedy, and they refuse to apply it.

18. *He that believeth.* As stated before on v. 16. *Is not condemned.* For past sin, that being forgiven on his believing in Christ. *But he that believeth not.* When the gospel is preached to him, and the way of salvation made plain. *Is condemned already.* Continues under the condemnation which divine justice has passed upon all sinners; and has this superadded, *He hath not believed in the name of the only begotten Son of God,* and therefore is guilty of the grossest insult to the divine majesty in neglecting, slighting, and despising the salvation which the infinite mercy of God had provided for him.

19. *This is the condemnation.* That is, this is the reason why some shall finally perish, not that they came into the world with a perverted and corrupt nature, which is true; nor that they lived many years in the practice of sin, which is also true; but because they refused to receive the salvation which God sent to them. *Light is come.* That is, Jesus, the Sun of righteousness, the Fountain of light and life, diffusing His benign influences everywhere, and favoring men with a clear and full revelation of the divine will. *Men loved darkness.* Have preferred sin to holiness, Belial to Christ, and hell to heaven. *Chashac,* "darkness," is frequently used by the Jewish writers for the angel of death and for the devil. *Because their deeds were evil.* An allusion to robbers and cutthroats, who practice their abominations in the night season for fear of being detected.

20. *For every one that doeth evil hateth the light.* He who doth vile or abominable things,

alluding to the subject mentioned in the preceding verse. *Lest his deeds should be reproved.* Or "discovered." To "manifest" or "discover" is one sense of the original word in the best Greek writers, and is evidently its meaning in this place.

21. *Wrought in God.* In His presence, and through His assistance. This is the end of our Lord's discourse to Nicodemus; and though we are not informed here of any good effects produced by it, yet we learn from other scriptures that it had produced the most blessed effects in his mind, and that from this time he became a disciple of Christ. He publicly defended our Lord in the Sanhedrin, of which he was probably a member, chap. vii. 50; and, with Joseph of Arimathaea, gave Him an honorable funeral, chap. xix. 39, when all His bosom friends had deserted Him.

22. *Came . . . into the land of Judaea.* Jerusalem itself, where Christ held the preceding discourse with Nicodemus, was in Judea; but the Evangelist means that our Lord quitted the city and its suburbs and went into the country parts. The same distinction between Jerusalem and Judea is made in Acts i. 8; x. 39; and in 1 Macc. iii. 34; 2 Macc. i. 1, 10. *And baptized.* It is not clear that Christ did baptize with water, but His disciples did—chap. iv. 2; and what they did, by His authority and command, is attributed to himself. It is a common custom, in all countries and in all languages, to attribute the operations of those who are under the government and direction of another to him by whom they are directed and governed.

23. *In Aenon.* This place was eight miles southward from Scythopolis, between Salim and Jordan. *There was much water.* And this was equally necessary where such multitudes were baptized, whether the ceremony was performed by dipping or sprinkling. But as the Jewish custom required the persons to stand in the water, and, having been instructed, and entered into a covenant to renounce all idolatry, and take the God of Israel for their God, then plunge themselves under the water, it is probable that the rite was thus performed at Aenon.

25. *John's disciples and the Jews.* Instead of *Jews,* some versions and fathers read, "a Jew." The *person* here spoken of was probably one who had been baptized by the disciples of our Lord, and the subject of debate seems to have been whether the baptism of John or that of Christ was the most efficacious towards *purifying.*

26. *And they came unto John.* That he might decide the question.

27. *A man can receive nothing.* Or, "A man can receive nothing from heaven, unless it be given him." I have received, not only my commission, but the power also by which I have executed it, from above. As I took it up at God's command, so I am ready to lay it down when He pleases. I have told you from the beginning that I was only the forerunner of the Messiah; and was sent, not to form a separate party, but to point out to men that Lamb of God which takes away the sin of the world, v. 28.

29. *He that hath the bride.* The congregation of believers. *Is the bridegroom.* The Lord Jesus, the Head of the Church. *The friend of the*

bridegroom. The person whom the Greeks called the *paranymph*. There were two at each wedding: one waited on the bride, the other on the bridegroom. Their business was to serve them, to inspect the concerns of the bridechamber, and afterwards to reconcile differences between husband and wife, when any took place. John considers himself as standing in this relation to the Lord Jesus, while espousing human nature and converting souls to himself; this is the meaning of "standeth by," i.e., ready to serve.

30. *He must increase.* His present success is but the beginning of a most glorious and universal spread of righteousness, peace, truth, and goodwill among men. *I must decrease.* My baptism and teaching, as pointing out the coming Messiah, must *cease;* because the Messiah is now come, and has entered publicly on the work of His glorious ministry.

31. *Is above all.* This blessed Bridegroom, who has descended from heaven, v. 13, is above all, superior to Moses, the prophets, and me. *He that is of the earth.* John himself, who was born in the common way of man. *Speaketh of the earth.* Cannot speak of heavenly things as Christ can do, and only represents divine matters by these earthly ordinances, for the spirit and meaning of which you must all go to the Messiah himself.

32. *And no man receiveth his testimony.* Or, "And this his testimony no man taketh up." That is, the testimony which John had borne to the Jews that Jesus was the promised Messiah. *No man taketh up.* No person is found to tread in my steps and to publish to the Jews that this is the Christ, the Saviour of the world.

33. *Hath set to his seal.* That is, hath hereby confirmed the truth of the testimony which he has borne. As a testator sets his seal to an instrument in order to confirm it, and such instrument is considered as fully confirmed by having the testator's seal affixed to it, so I, by taking up this testimony of Christ and proclaiming it to the Jews, have fully confirmed it, as I know it to be a truth; which knowledge I have from the immediate inspiration of the Holy Spirit.

34. *For God giveth not the Spirit by measure.* He is the most perfect of all teachers, as having received the Holy Spirit as none before Him ever did. Without measure—not for a particular time, people, purpose, etc., but for the whole compass of time, and in reference to all eternity. It is worthy of remark that this was fully done after the outpouring of the Spirit on the Day of Pentecost, Acts ii. 1, as may be clearly seen in all the apostolic Epistles. The Jews observe that the Holy Spirit was given only in certain measures to the prophets; some writing only cne book, others two.

35. *All things into his hand.* See on Matt. xi. 27. A principal design of John is to show that Christ was infinitely above every teacher, prophet, and divine messenger that had ever yet appeared. The prophets had various gifts: some had visions, other dreams; some had the gift of *teaching,* others of comforting, etc. But none possessed all these gifts; Christ alone possessed their plenitude, and is all things in all.

36. *Hath everlasting life.* He has already the seed of this life in his soul, having been made a partaker of the grace and spirit of Him in whom he has believed. *He that believeth not.* Or "obeyeth not." *Shall not see life.* Shall never enjoy it, there being no way to the kingdom of God but through Christ Jesus, Acts iv. 12. And none can expect to enter into this Kingdom but those who obey Him; for to such only He is the Author of eternal salvation, Heb. v. 9. *But the wrath of God abideth on him.* The "displeasure" of God. I should prefer "displeasure" to *wrath,* because the common acceptation of the latter (*fury, rage*) is not properly applicable here. Perhaps the original word is used in the same sense here as in Rom. ii. 5; iii. 5; xiii. 4-5; Eph. v. 6; 1 Thess. i. 10; v. 9, where it evidently means "punishment," which is the effect of irritated justice. Taken in this sense, we may consider the phrase as a Hebraism: "punishment of God," i.e., the most heavy and awful of all punishments—such as sin deserves, and such as it becomes divine justice to inflict. And this *abideth on him*—endures as long as his unbelief and disobedience remain!

CHAPTER 4

Jesus, finding that the Pharisees took offense at His making many disciples, leaves Judea to pass into Galilee, 1-3. And passing through Samaria comes to Sychar, and rests at Jacob's Well, 4-6. While His disciples were gone to the city to buy meat, a woman of Samaria comes to draw water, with whom our Lord discourses at large on the spiritual nature of His religion, the perfection of the divine nature, and the purity of His worship, 7-24. On His informing her that He was the Messiah, she leaves her pitcher, and goes to inform her townsmen, 25-30. His discourse with His disciples in her absence, 31-38. Many of the Samaritans believe on Him, 39-42. He stays two days with them, and goes into Galilee, 43-45. He comes to Cana, and heals the son of a nobleman, in consequence of which he believes on Him, with his whole family, 46-54.

1. *Jesus made and baptized.* These seem to be quoted as the very words which were brought to the Pharisees; and, from our Lord's conduct after this information, we may take it for granted that they were so irritated that they were determined to seek an occasion to take away His life; in consequence of which, leaving Judea, He withdrew into Galilee.

2. *Jesus himself baptized not.* See chap. iii. 22.

4. *And he must needs go through Samaria.* Or, "It was necessary for Him to pass through Samaria." From Jerusalem to Galilee through Samaria, according to Josephus, was three days' journey.

5. *A city . . . called Sychar.* This city was anciently called Shechem. It seems to have been situated at the foot of Mount Gerizim, in the province of Samaria, on which the temple of the Samaritans was built. After the ruin of Samaria by Salmanezer, Sychar, or Shechem, became the capital of the Samaritans; and it continued so, according to Josephus, *Ant.* l. xi, c. 8, in the time of Alexander the Great. It was about ten miles from Shiloh, forty from Jerusalem, and fifty-two from Jericho. It probably got the name of Sychar, which signifies "drunken," from the drunkenness of its inhabitants. With this crime the Prophet Isaiah (ch. xxviii. 1, 3, 7-8) solemnly charges the Ephraimites, within whose limits the city stood. This place is remarkable in the Scriptures: (1) As being that where Abram first stopped on his coming from Haran to Canaan; (2) Where God first appeared to that patriarch, and promised to give the land to his seed; (3) The place where Abram first built an altar

to the Lord, and called upon His name, Gen. xii. 7. *That Jacob gave to his son Joseph.* Jacob had bought this field from the children of Hamor, the father of Shechem, for a hundred pieces of silver, or lambs, Gen. xxxiii. 19; and in it he built an altar, which he dedicated to *El Elohey Yishrael,* the strong God, the covenant God of Israel, v. 19. This, Jacob left as a private or overplus inheritance to Joseph and his children. See Gen. xlviii. 21-22 and Josh. xxiv. 32.

6. *The sixth hour.* About twelve o'clock; see the notes on chap. i. 30. The *time* is noted here: (1) To account for Christ's *fatigue*—He had already travelled several hours. (2) To account for His *thirst*—the sun had at this time waxed hot. (3) To account for the disciples going to *buy food,* v. 8, because this was the ordinary time of *dinner* among the Jews. See the note referred to above. Dr. Macknight thinks the *sixth hour* to be the Roman six o'clock in the afternoon.

7. *There cometh a woman of Samaria to draw water.* That this was the employment of the females, we see in different parts of the Sacred Writings. See Gen. xxiv. 11, etc.; Exod. ii. 16. The Jews say that those who wished to get wives went to the wells where young women were accustomed to come and draw water; and it is supposed that women of ill fame frequented such places also.

9. *That thou, being a Jew.* Probably the inhabitants of Judea distinguished themselves from those of Samaria by some peculiar mode of dress, and by this the Samaritan woman might have known Christ. But it is likely that our Lord spoke the Galilean dialect, by which we find, from Mark xiv. 70, a Jew of that district might easily be known. *The Jews have no dealings with the Samaritans.* Perhaps better, "Jews have no communion with Samaritans." These words appear to be added by the Evangelist himself, in explanation of the woman's question. The original word has been variously translated and understood. It has been understood to mean the Jews will be "under no kind of obligation" to the Samaritans—will borrow nothing from them—will not drink out of the same cup or well with them—will not sit down to meals with them, nor eat out of the same vessel—will have no religious connection, no commercial dealings with them. The word "communion," I think, fully expresses the sense of the original; and, being as extensive in its meaning as our word *dealings,* is capable of as general an interpretation. The deadly hatred that subsisted between these two nations is known to all. The Jews cursed them, and believed them to be accursed. Their most merciful wish to the Samaritans was that they might have no part in the resurrection; or, in other words, that they might be annihilated.

10. *If thou knewest the gift of God.* "Free gift." A *gift* is anything that is given for which no equivalent has been or is to be returned; a "free gift" is that which has been given without asking or entreaty. Such a gift of kindness was Jesus Christ to the world, chap. iii. 16; and through Him comes the gift of the Spirit, which those who believe on His name were to receive. *Living water.* By this expression, which was common to the inhabitants both of the East and of the West, is always meant "spring water," in opposition to dead, stagnant water contained in ponds, pools, tanks, or cisterns; and what our Lord means by it is evidently the Holy Spirit, as may be seen from chap. vii. 38-39. As water quenches the thirst, refreshes and invigorates the body, purifies things defiled, and renders the earth fruitful, so it is an apt emblem of the gift of the Holy Ghost, which so satisfies the souls that receive it that they thirst no more for earthly good; it purifies also from all spiritual defilement, on which account it is emphatically styled the *Holy* Spirit; and it makes those who receive it fruitful in every good word and work.

11. *Thou hast nothing to draw with.* "Thou hast no bucket." Good water is not plentiful in the East; and travellers are often obliged to carry leathern bottles or buckets with them, and a line also, to let them down into the deep wells, in order to draw up water. If the well was in our Lord's time, as it was found by Mr. Maundrell, thirty-five yards deep, it would require a considerable line to reach it; and with such it is not likely that even the disciples of our Lord were provided. The woman might well say, *The well is deep,* and *thou hast nothing to draw with . . . whence then hast thou that living water?*

12. *Our father Jacob.* The *ancient* Samaritans were undoubtedly the descendants of Jacob, for they were the ten tribes that revolted in the reign of Rehoboam. But those in our Lord's time were not genuine Israelites, but a corrupted race, sprung from a mixture of different nations sent thither by Salmanezer, king of the Assyrians. See 2 Kings xvii.

14. *Springing up into everlasting life.* On this account he can never thirst; for how can he lack water who has in himself a living, eternal spring?

15. *Give me this water.* She did not as yet comprehend our Lord's meaning; but her curiosity was much excited, and this was the design of our Lord, that He might have her mind properly prepared to receive the great truths which He was about to announce.

16. *Call thy husband.* Our Lord appears to have spoken these words for two purposes: (1) To make the woman consider her own state; (2) To show her that He knew her heart and the secret actions of her life, and was therefore well qualified to teach her heavenly truths.

18. *Thou hast had five husbands.* It is not clear that this woman was a prostitute. She might have been legally married to those five, and might have been divorced through some misbehavior of her own, not amounting to adultery; for the adulteress was to be put to death, by both the Jewish and the Samaritan law, not divorced. Or she might have been cast off through some caprice of her husband; for, in the time of our Lord, divorces were very common among the Jews, so that a man put away his wife for any fault. See the note on Matt. v. 31. *He whom thou now hast is not thy husband.* Bishop Pearce would translate this clause in the following manner: "There is no husband whom thou now hast"—or, less literally, "Thou hast no husband now." Probably the meaning is, Thou art contracted to another, but not yet brought home; therefore he is not yet thy husband.

19. *I perceive that thou art a prophet.* And therefore thought Him well qualified to decide

the grand question in dispute between the Jews and the Samaritans; but she did not perceive Him to be the Messiah.

20. *Worshipped in this mountain.* Probably pointing to Mount Gerizim, at the foot of which Sychar was situated. The patriarchs had worshipped here—Jacob builded an altar on this mountain, and worshipped the true God; see Gen. xxii. 2; xxxiii. 20. Thus she could say, *Our fathers worshipped in this mountain.* On this mountain Sanballat had built them a temple, about 332 years before our Lord's incarnation. See Joseph., *Antiq.* xi, c. viii, s. 4, and 2 Macc. vi. 2.

21. *The hour cometh.* The time was now at hand in which the spiritual worship of God was about to be established in the earth, and all the Jewish rites and ceremonies entirely abolished. *Worship the Father.* This epithet shows the mild, benignant, and tender nature of the gospel dispensation. Men are called to worship their Heavenly Father, and to consider themselves as His children. In reference to this, our Lord's prayer begins, *Our Father which art in heaven.* See v. 23.

22. *Ye worship ye know not what.* The Samaritans believed in the same God with the Jews; but, as they rejected all the prophetical writings, they had but an imperfect knowledge of the Deity. Besides, as they incorporated the worship of idols with His worship, they might be justly said to worship Him whom they did not properly know. See the account of their motley worship, 2 Kings xvii. 26-34. But after Sanballat had built the temple on Mount Gerizim, the idolatrous worship of the Cutheans and Sepharvites, etc., was entirely laid aside, the same religious service being performed in the Samaritan temple which was performed in that at Jerusalem. *We know what we worship.* We Jews acknowledge all the attributes of His nature, and offer to Him only the sacrifices prescribed in the law. *Salvation is of the Jews.* "Salvation is from the Jews." *Salvation* seems here to mean the Saviour, the Messiah, as it does in Luke ii. 30; Acts iv. 12; and so the woman appears to have understood it, v. 25. The Messiah was to spring from the Jews—from them, the preaching of the gospel and the knowledge of the truth were to go to all the nations of the world. It was to the Jews that the promises were made; and it was in their prophetic Scriptures, which the Samaritans rejected, that Jesus Christ was proclaimed and described. See Isa. xi. 3.

23. *The true worshippers shall worship the Father in spirit.* The worship of the Samaritans was a defective worship—they did not receive the prophetical writings. That of the Jews was a carnal worship, dealing only in the letter, and referring to the spirit and design, which were at a distance, by types and ceremonies.

24. *God is a Spirit.* This is one of the first, the greatest, the most sublime, and necessary truths in the compass of nature! There is a God, the Cause of all things—the Fountain of all perfection—without parts or dimensions, for He is eternal—filling the heavens and the earth—pervading, governing, and upholding all things, for He is an infinite Spirit! A man worships God in *spirit* when, under the influence of the Holy Ghost, he brings all his affections, appetites, and desires to the throne of God; and he worships Him in *truth* when every purpose and passion of his heart, and when every act of his religious worship, is guided and regulated by the word of God.

25. *I know that Messias cometh.* Though they did not receive the prophetic writings, yet the tradition of the advent of the Messiah, which was common among the Jews, and founded on promises contained even in the books of Moses, was generally received among the Samaritans also. *Which is called Christ.* This appears to be the Evangelist's explanation of the Hebrew word, according to his custom; chap. i. 38, 41-42; ix. 7, etc. For we cannot suppose that the woman understood Greek, so as to translate the Hebrew word to our Lord; or that she should suppose that a person who was a Jew, v. 9, and a prohpet, v. 19, could stand in need of this interpretation. *He will tell us all things.* Relative to the nature of God, the nature of His worship, and the proper place to adore Him in.

26. *Jesus saith unto her, I . . . am he.* Our Lord never spoke in such direct terms concerning himself to His own countrymen; nor even to His own disciples, till a little before His death. The reason given by Bishop Pearce is the following: The woman being alone when Jesus said it and being a Samaritan, He had no reason to apprehend that the Samaritans, if they knew His claim, would disturb His ministry before the time of His suffering came—which seems to have been the reason why He concealed it so long from His own countrymen.

27. *Came his disciples.* From the town, whither they went to buy food, v. 8. *Marvelled that he talked with the woman.* Because it was contrary to the custom of the Eastern countries; and there are many canons, among the rabbins, against it. To the present time, if a man meet even his own wife in the street, he does not speak to her; and this is done to keep up the appearance of a chastity and temperance of which the Eastern world knows nothing. *Yet no man said.* They were awed by His majesty, and knew that He must have sufficient reasons to induce Him to act a part to which He was not at all accustomed.

28. *Left her waterpot.* She was so penetrated with the great truths which Jesus had announced that she forgot her errand to the well, and returned to the city without the water for which she came out!

29. *All things that ever I did.* The Jews believed that one essential characteristic of the Messiah would be that He should be able to tell the secrets of all hearts. This they believed was predicted, Isa. xi. 2-3.

30. *They went out of the city.* Such effect had the simple testimony of the woman on their minds. *And came unto him.* Or "were coming to Him"; for they did not reach Him immediately, all that discourse between Him and His disciples mentioned in vv. 31-39 inclusive having taken place before the people of Sychar got to the well.

31. *Master, eat.* They knew that He was greatly spent both with hunger and fatigue.

32. *I have meat to eat that ye know not of.* Our blessed Lord seizes every opportunity to raise the minds of His apostles to heavenly things through the medium of earthly matters.

33. *Hath any man brought him ought to eat?*

Has He got food in any preternatural way? They could not help remembering the miraculous interventions of divine providence in feeding Elijah by the ravens, at the brook Cherith, 1 Kings xvii. 4-6, and by the ministry of an angel, chap. xix. 5-8, and our Lord's preternatural repast in the wilderness, after His victory over Satan, Matt. iv. 11.

34. *My meat is to do the will of him that sent me.* In these words our blessed Lord teaches a lesson of zeal and earnestness to His apostles, and to all their successors in the Christian ministry. Let the salvation of souls lie nearer your heart then life itself. Let eating and drinking, labor and rest, reading, thinking, study, prayer, and all things be directed to the accomplishment of this great work.

35. *There are yet four months, and then cometh harvest?* In Palestine the harvest did not begin till after the Passover, which was fixed on the fourteenth of the month Nisan, which answers to our March, and sometimes extends into April. The barley harvest was the first, after that the wheat; and both were finished by Pentecost. For in the Feast of Pentecost the firstfruits of all the harvest were carried to the Temple and waved before the Lord. See Lev. xxiii. 11. *Lift up your eyes, and look on the fields,* over which it is likely the Samaritans were then coming in troops, guided by the woman who had already received the light of the gospel of peace. *The fields . . . are white already to harvest.* Multitudes of Samaritans are coming to believe on Me, and to be saved unto eternal life. Probably they had a kind of white raiment.

36. *And he that reapeth receiveth wages.* Or, "And already the reaper receiveth wages." By making the word "already" the beginning of this verse, on the authority of some excellent MSS. and versions, a more consistent sense is obtained than from the common arrangement, where "already" terminates the preceding verse.

37. *Herein is that saying true, One soweth, and another reapeth.* Or, "One is the sower, and another is the reaper." In what respects you, of this business, this proverb is true—*One is the sower;* for I have sent you to reap, to preach My gospel and gain converts, where you have not labored—have not sown the first seeds of eternal life.—Others have labored—the patriarchs and prophets—and you are entered into the fruits of their labors.

39. *Many of the Samaritans . . . believed on him for the saying of the woman.* This woman was the first apostle of Christ in Samaria! She went and told her fellow citizens that the Messiah was come, and gave for proof that He had told her the most secret things she had ever done; see on v. 29. This word, which is twice repeated, in v. 29 and here, strongly intimates that a more particular conversation had taken place between our Lord and the Samaritan woman than what is here related.

40. *He abode there two days.* We are not told that He wrought any miracles among them. This does not appear to have been necessary; they were a simplehearted, teachable people, and they credited Him on the evidence of His own eternal truth. Why are not miracles wrought now? Miracles were only for the establishment of the doctrines of Christianity where they were first preached. We profess to

believe these doctrines; therefore, to us, miracles would be useless. Where the doctrine is credited, no miracle is necessary; the Samaritans believed, and no miracle was wrought among them, for the simple reason that it was not necessary.

42. *We have heard him ourselves.* On seeing and hearing our Lord, the faith of those who had already believed on the woman's testimony was abundantly confirmed; and, besides those, many others believed who had not heard the woman speak. *This is indeed the Christ.* The promised Messiah. *The Saviour of the world.* Not of the Jews only, but of the Samaritans, and of the whole Gentile world.

44. *Jesus himself testified.* He bore testimony to the general truth of the following proverb. See on Matt. xiii. 57.

45. *The Galilaeans received him.* They received Him as the promised Messiah because of the miracles which they had seen Him perform at Jerusalem, at the Passover. See chap. ii. 23.

46. *Where he made the water wine.* See the notes on chap. ii. 1, etc. Cana was on the road from Nazareth to Capernaum and the Sea of Tiberias. *A certain nobleman.* An officer of the king's court, for this is the meaning of the original word. This officer belonged to Herod Antipas, who was then tetrarch of Galilee. This officer, whoever he was, appears to have had his ordinary abode at Capernaum; and hearing that Christ was at Cana, he came expressly from Capernaum thither to entreat Him to heal his child.

48. *Except ye see signs and wonders.* Our Lord did not tell this man that he had no faith, but that he had not enough. If he had had none, he would not have come from Capernaum to Cana to beg Him to heal his son. If he had had enough, he would have been contented with recommending his son to our Lord, without entreating Him to go to Capernaum to heal him, which intimates that he did not believe our Lord could do it at a distance. But the words are not addressed to the nobleman alone, but to all the Galilean Jews in general; for our Lord uses the plural number, which He never does when addressing an individual. These people differed widely from the people of Sychar; they had neither a love of the truth nor simplicity of heart, and would not believe anything from heaven unless forced on their minds by the most striking miracles. They were favored with the ministry of John Baptist; but, as that was not accompanied with miracles, it was not generally credited. They required the miracles of Christ in order that they might credit the advent of the Messiah.

49. *Sir, come down.* He did not think our Lord could cure him without being present, and seems here to feel himself hurt because our Lord did not come at his first entreaty. It is difficult for a proud man, or a man in office, to humble himself or to treat even God Almighty with proper respect.

50. *Go thy way; they son liveth.* Had our Lord gone with him, as he wished, his unbelief could not have been fully removed, as he would have still thought that our Lord's power could not reach from Cana to Capernaum. In order to destroy his unbelief at once, and bring him into the fullness of the faith of His supreme

power, He cures him, being apparently absent, by that energy through which He fills both the heavens and the earth. Here it may be observed that our blessed Lord did what this man requested Him to do, but not in the way in which he wished it to be done. God will save all to the uttermost who call upon Him, but not in the way in which they may desire. Eternal life is the free gift of God, and He has a right to give it as He pleases; and He always gives His gifts in that way in which His glory is best promoted, and our eternal interest secured. *The man believed the word.* And yet it appears that he had suspended his faith upon a certain condition: "If I find on my return that my son is healed, I will believe that Jesus is the Messiah."

52. *Then enquired he of them the hour.* The servants, overjoyed to find their master's son so suddenly restored, set off to meet him, that they might impart to him tidings which they knew would be so very agreeable; and he, intent on having his faith settled, began immediately to inquire what time it was when the fever left him, to see whether his cure was the effect of some natural cause or whether it was done by the power of Christ. *Yesterday at the seventh hour.* At the time we would call one o'clock.

53. *So the father knew.* He had the fullest proof that his son's cure was supernatural, and that it was wrought by the Lord Jesus. *Himself believed, and his whole house.* He and his whole family became true converts to the doctrine of the manifested Messiah. The whole family, impressed with the great kindness of God in sending health to the child, were the more easily led to believe in the Lord Jesus. The sickness of the child became the means of salvation to all the household. They no doubt thought at first that God was dealing hardly with them, when threatening to remove the child; but now they see that in very faithfulness God had afflicted them. Let us learn never to murmur against God, or think that He does not act kindly towards us.

54. *This is again the second miracle.* The first miracle which Christ performed was in this same city of Cana, just after His baptism; and this second took place after His arrival here from Jerusalem, whence, we have seen, He was driven by the persecution raised against Him by the scribes and Pharisees. By construing the word *again,* with *he came,* that confusion which is evident in the common version is entirely removed.

CHAPTER 5

The man who had been diseased thirty-eight years healed on the Sabbath day, 1-9. The Jews cavil, persecute Christ, and seek to kill Him, because He had done this cure on the Sabbath, 10-16. Our Lord vindicates His conduct, and shows, from the testimony of the Father, the Scriptures, John the Baptist, and His own works, that He came from God, to be the Light and Salvation of the world, 17-39. He reproves the Jews for their obstinacy, 40; hatred to God, 41-42; pride, 43-44; and disbelief of their own law, 45-47.

1. *A feast.* This is generally supposed, by the best critics, to have been the Feast of the Passover, which was the most eminent feast among the Jews. In several excellent MSS. the article is added, *the feast,* the grand, the principal festival. Petavius supposes that the feast of *Purim* is here meant; and one MS. reads the feast of *Tabernacles.* Several of the primitive fathers believe *Pentecost* to be intended; and they are followed by many of the moderns, because, in chap. vii. 2, mention is made of the feast of *Tabernacles,* which followed *Pentecost,* and was about the latter end of our September. Lightfoot has observed that the other Evangelists speak very sparingly of our Lord's acts in Judea. They mention nothing of the Passovers, from our Lord's baptism till His death, excepting the very last; but John points at them all. The *first* he speaks of in chap. ii. 13; the *third,* in chap. vi. 4; the *fourth,* in chap. xii. 1; and the *second,* in this place. For although he does not call it the Passover, but a *feast* in general, yet the circumstances agree best with this feast; and our Lord's words, chap. iv. 35, seem to cast light on this subject.

2. *There is.* This is thought by some to be a proof that John wrote his Gospel before the destruction of Jerusalem, and that the pool and its porticoes were still remaining. Though there can be little doubt that Jerusalem was destroyed many years before John wrote, yet this does not necessarily imply that the pool and its porticoes must have been destroyed too. It, or something in its place, is shown to travellers to the present day. But instead of *is,* both the Syriac, all the Arabic, Persic, Armenian, and Nonnus read "was," which is to me some proof that it did not exist when these versions were made, and that the pool which is shown now is not the original. *By the sheep market.* Rather, "gate"; see Neh. iii. 1, 32; xii. 39. This was in all probability the gate through which the sheep were brought which were offered in sacrifice in the Temple. *Bethesda.* This word is variously written in the MSS. and versions, but this reading is the genuine one. Bethesda, or according to the Hebrew *Bethchasdah,* signifies literally "the house of mercy." It got this name probably from the cures which God mercifully performed there. It is likely the porticoes were built for the more convenient reception of the poor and distressed, who came hither to be healed.

3. *Waiting for the moving of the water.* This clause, with the whole of the fourth verse, is wanting in some MSS. and versions; but I think there is no sufficient evidence against their authenticity.

4. *Certain season.* This probably refers to the time of the feast, during which only this miraculous virtue lasted. It is not likely that the angel appeared to the people—his descent might be only known by the ebullition caused in the waters. Was not the whole a type of Christ? See Zech. xiii. 1. He is the true *Bethesda,* or "house of mercy," the "fountain opened to the house of David and to the inhabitants of Jerusalem for sin and for uncleanness," unto which all the diseased may come, and find health and life eternal.

5. *Had an infirmity thirty and eight years.* The length of the time he had been afflicted makes the miracle of his cure the greater. There could have been no collusion in this case. As his affliction had lasted thirty-eight years, it must have been known to multitudes; therefore he could not be a person prepared for the occasion. All Christ's miracles have been wrought in such a way and on such persons and occasions as abolutely to preclude all possibility of the suspicion of imposture.

6. *Wilt thou be made whole?* Christ, by asking this question, designed to excite in this person faith, hope, and a greater desire of being healed. He wished him to reflect on his miserable state, that he might be the better prepared to receive a cure, and to value it when it came.

8. *Rise, take up thy bed, and walk.* Jesus speaks here as God. He speaks in no name but His own, and with an authority which belongs to God alone. And what is the consequence? The man became whole immediately; and this sudden restoration to health and strength was an incontestable proof of the omnipotence of Christ. It has been remarked that our Lord, after having performed a miracle, was accustomed to connect some circumstance with it which attested its truth. After the miracle of the five loaves, He ordered the fragments to be collected, which were more in quantity than the loaves themselves, though several thousands had been fed. When He changed the water into wine, He ordered some to be taken first to the steward of the feast, that he might taste and bear testimony to its genuineness and excellency. When He cured the lepers, He commanded them to show themselves to the priests, whose business it was to judge of the cure. So here, He judged it necessary, after having cured this infirm man, to order him not only to *arise,* but to *take up his bed,* and *walk,* which sufficiently attested the miracle which He had wrought.

11. *He that made me whole.* The poor man reasoned conclusively: He who could work such a miracle must be at least the best of men. Now a good man will neither do evil himself nor command others to do it. But he who cured me ordered me to carry my bed; therefore there can be no evil in it.

13. *Jesus had conveyed himself away.* Or "had withdrawn himself." And this He might easily do, as there was a crowd in the place. Some think the words indicate that Jesus withdrew on seeing a multitude in the place, i.e., raising a tumult, because of the man's carrying his bed. He had not yet finished His work and would not expose himself to the envy and malice of the Jewish rulers.

14. *Jesus findeth him in the temple.* The man being conscious that it was through the mercy of God that he was restored (though he did not as yet know distinctly who Christ was) went to the Temple to return thanks to God for his cure. Whether this was on the same day or some other does not distinctly appear; it was probably the same day, after he had carried home his couch. *Sin no more, lest a worse thing come unto thee.* Our Lord, intending to disclose to this man who He was, gave him two proofs of the perfection of His knowledge. (1) He showed him that He knew the secret of the past—*sin no more,* thereby intimating that his former sins were the cause of his long affliction. (2) He showed him that He knew the future—*lest a worse thing come unto thee;* if your iniquity be repeated, your punishment will be increased.

15. *The man departed, and told the Jews.* He did not say it was Jesus who had ordered him to carry his bed, but it was Jesus who had cured him; and he left them to draw the inference, viz., that this Jesus must have the miraculous power of God.

17. *My Father worketh hitherto, and I work.* Or, "As My Father worketh until now." God created the world in six days; on the seventh He rested from all creating acts and set it apart to be an everlasting memorial of His work. But though He rested from creating, He never ceased from preserving and governing that which He had formed. In this respect He can keep no sabbaths; for nothing can continue to exist or answer the end proposed by the divine wisdom and goodness without the continual energy of God. So *I work*—I am constantly employed in the same way, governing and supporting all things, comforting the wretched, and saving the lost; and to Me, in this respect, there is no Sabbath.

18. *Making himself equal with God.* This the Jews understood from the preceding verse, nor did they take a wrong meaning out of our Lord's words; for He plainly stated that, whatever was the Father's work, His was the same, thus showing that He and the Father were one. They had now found out two pretenses to take away His life. One was that He had broken the Sabbath—"dissolved," as they pretended, the obligation of keeping it holy. The other was that He was guilty of blasphemy, in *making himself equal with God.* For both of these crimes a man, according to the law, must suffer death. See Num. xv. 32; Lev. xxiv. 11, 14, 16.

19. *The Son can do nothing of himself.* Because of His inseparable union with the Father; nor can the Father do anything of *himself,* because of His infinite unity with the Son. *What things soever he doeth, these also doeth the Son.* The conclusion from our Lord's argument is: If I have broken the Sabbath, so has God also, for I can do nothing but what I see Him doing.

20. *Greater works than these.* Two of these He immediately mentions: *raising the dead,* v. 21; and *judging the world,* v. 22. *That ye may marvel.* Or "so as to make you wonder." Our Lord sometimes speaks of himself as God, and sometimes as the Ambassador of God. As He had a human and a divine nature, this distinction was essentially necessary.

21. *As the Father raiseth up the dead.* This He did in the case of the widow's son at Sarepta, I Kings xvii. 22, by the ministry of the Prophet Elijah. And again, in the case of the Shunammite's son, 2 Kings iv. 32-35, by the ministry of the Prophet Elisha. *The Son quickeneth whom he will.* He raiseth from death to life whomsoever He pleases. So He did, for He raised the ruler's daughter, Mark v. 35-42; the widow's son at Nain, Luke vii. 11-15; and Lazarus, at Bethany, John xi. 14-44. *Whom he will.* Here our Lord points out His sovereign power and independence; He gives life according to His own will—not being obliged to supplicate for the power by which it was done, as the prophets did, His own will being absolute and sufficient in every case.

22. *The Father judgeth no man.* This confirms what He had said before, vv. 17, 19, that the Father acts not without the Son, nor the Son without the Father; their acts are common, their power equal.

23. *That all men should honour the Son.* If then the Son is to be honored, even as the Father is honored, then the Son must be God, as receiving that worship which belongs to God alone. To worship any creature is idolatry. Christ is to be honored even as the Father is honored; therefore Christ is not a creature, and, if not a creature, consequently the Creator. *He that honoureth not the Son.* God will not receive that man's adoration who refuses to honor Jesus, *even as* He honors Him. The Jews expected the Messiah as a great and powerful prince; but they never thought of a person coming in that character enrobed with all the attributes of Godhead. To lead them off from this error our Lord spoke the words recorded in these verses.

24. *He that heareth my word*—My doctrine—*and believeth on him that sent me*—he who credits My divine mission, that I am come to give light and life to the world by My doctrine and death—*hath everlasting life*—the seed of this life is sown in his heart the moment he believes—*and shall not come into condemnation,* "into judgment"—that which will speedily come on this unbelieving race, and that which shall overwhelm the wicked in the great day. *But is passed from death unto life.* Has "changed his country, or place of abode." Death is the country where every Christless soul lives. The man who knows not God lives a dying life or a living death; but he who believes in the Son of God passes over from the empire of death to the empire of life.

25. *The dead shall hear the voice.* Three kinds of death are mentioned in the Scriptures: *natural, spiritual,* and *eternal.* The *first* consists in the separation of the body and soul; the *second,* in the separation of God and the soul; the *third,* in the separation of body and soul from God in the other world. Answerable to these three kinds of death, there is a threefold life: *natural* life, which consists in the union of the soul and body; *spiritual* life, which consists in the union of God and the soul, by faith and love; *eternal* life, which consists in the communion of the body and soul with God, by holiness, in the realms of bliss.

27. *Because he is the Son of man.* Because He is the Messiah; for in this sense the phrase *Son of man* is often to be understood.

30. *I can of mine own self do nothing.* Because of My intimate union with God. See on v. 19. *I seek not mine own will.* I do not, I cannot attempt to do anything without God. This, that is, the Son of Man, the human nature which is the temple of My divinity, chap. i. 14, is perfectly subject to the deity that dwells in it. In this respect our blessed Lord is the perfect Pattern of all His followers. In everything their wills should submit to the will of their Heavenly Father.

.31. *If I bear witness.* If I had no proof to bring of My being the Messiah, and equal to God, common sense would direct you to reject My testimony; but the mighty power of God, by which I work My miracles, sufficiently attests that My pretensions are well-founded.

32. *There is another.* God the Father, who by His Spirit in your prophets described My person, office, and miracles. You read these Scriptures, and you cannot help seeing that they testify of Me. No person ever did answer the description there given but myself, and I answer to that description in the fullest sense of the word.

33. *Ye sent unto John.* I am not without human testimony of the most respectable kind. *Ye sent unto John, and he bare witness.*

34. *But I receive not testimony from man* (only). I have no need of John's testimony; the works that I do bear sufficient testimony to Me, v. 36. *But these things I say.* You believed John to be a prophet. A prophet cannot lie; he bore testimony that I am the Lamb of God, that beareth away the sin of the world, chap. i. 29. Therefore, that you may be saved by believing in Me as such, I have appealed to John's testimony.

35. *He was a burning and a shining light.* "He was a burning and a shining lamp." The expression of "lamp" our Lord took from the ordinary custom of the Jews, who termed their eminent doctors "the lamps of Israel." *Burning* may refer to the zeal with which John executed his message; and *shining* may refer to the clearness of the testimony which he bore concerning Christ. He who wishes to save souls must both *burn* and *shine;* the clear light of the knowledge of the sacred records must fill his understanding, and the holy flame of loving zeal must occupy his heart. Zeal without knowledge is continually blundering, and knowledge without zeal makes no converts to Christ. *For a season.* The time between his beginning to preach and his being cast into prison. *To rejoice.* "To jump for joy," as we would express it. They were exceedingly rejoiced to hear that the Messiah was come, because they expected Him to deliver them out of the hands of the Romans. But when a spiritual deliverance, of infinitely greater moment, was preached to them, they rejected both it and the light which made it manifest.

36. *But I have greater witness.* However decisive the judgment of such a man as John may be, nevertheless I am not obliged to depend on his testimony alone; for I have a greater one, that of Him whom you acknowledge to be your God. And how do I prove that this God bears testimony to Me? By My *works:* these miracles, which attest My mission and prove by themselves that nothing less than unlimited power and boundless love could ever produce them.

37. *The Father himself . . . hath borne witness.* That is, by His prophets. *Ye have neither heard his voice.* I make these words, with Bishop Pearce, a parenthesis. The sense is—"Not that My Father ever appeared visibly or spake audibly to any of you; but He did it by the mouths of His prophets." Lately, however, He had added to their testimony His own voice from heaven on the day of Christ's baptism. See Matt. iii. 17.

38. *Ye have not his word abiding in you.* Though you believe the Scriptures to be of God, yet you do not let them take hold of your hearts—His word is in your mouth, but not in your mind.

39. *Search the scriptures.* This should be translated, not in the imperative, but in the indicative mood—thus, "You search the Scriptures diligently." That these words are commonly read in the imperative mood is sufficiently known; but this reading can never accord well with the following verse, nor can the force and energy of the words be perceived by this version. The rabbins strongly recommend the study of the Scriptures. The *Talmud, Tract. Shabbath,* fol. 30, brings in God thus addressing

David: "I am better pleased with one day in which thou sittest and studiest the law, than I shall be with a thousand sacrifices which thy son Solomon shall offer upon my altar." The word which might be translated, "You search diligently," is very expressive. Homer, *Il.* xviii. l. 321, applies it to a *lion* deprived of his whelps, who "scours the plains, and *traces* the *footsteps* of the man." And in *Odyss.* xix. l. 436, to *dogs tracing* their game by the *scent* of the *foot.* In the Septuagint the verb answers to the Hebrew *chapash,* "to search by uncovering"; to *chakar,* "to search minutely, to explore"; to *chashaph,* "to strip, make bare"; and to *mashash,* "to feel, search by feeling." It is, says Chrysostom, "a metaphor taken from those who dig deep, and search for metals in the bowels of the earth. They look for the bed where the metal lies, and break every clod, and sift and examine the whole, in order to discover the ore."

40. *And ye will not come to me.* Though you thus search the Scriptures, in hopes of finding the Messiah and eternal life in them, yet *ye will not come to me,* believe in Me, and be My disciples, though so clearly pointed out by them, that you may have that eternal life, which can come only through Me.

41. *I receive not honour from men.* I do not stand in need of you or your testimony. I act through neither self-interest nor vanity. Your salvation can add nothing to Me, nor can your destruction injure Me. I speak only through My love for your souls, that you may be saved.

42. *But I know you, that ye have not.* Do not say that you oppose Me through zeal for God's honor and love for His name, because I make myself equal to Him; no, this is not the case. I know the dispositions of your souls; and I know you have neither *love* for His name nor zeal for His glory. You read the Scriptures, but you do not enter into their meaning.

43. *I am come in my Father's name.* With all His influence and authority. Among the rabbins it was essential to a teacher's credit that he should be able to support his doctrine by the authority of some eminent persons who had gone before. *If another shall come in his own name.* Having no divine influence and no other authority than his own, *him ye will receive.* For an account of these false Christs, see the notes on Matt. xxiv. 5.

44. *How can ye believe, which receive honour?* The grand obstacle to the salvation of the scribes and Pharisees was their pride, vanity, and self-love. They lived on each other's praise. If they had acknowledged Christ as the only Teacher, they must have given up the good opinion of the multitude; and they chose rather to lose their souls than to forfeit their reputation among men! *From God only.* Or "from the only God."

45. *Do not think that I will accuse you.* You have accused Me with a breach of the Sabbath, which accusation I have demonstrated to be false. I could, in return, accuse you, and substantiate the accusation, with the breach of the whole law; but this I need not do, for *Moses, in whom ye trust,* accuses you. You read his law, acknowledge you should obey it, and yet break it both in the letter and in the spirit.

46. *He wrote of me.* For instance, in reciting the prophecy of Jacob, Gen. xlix. 10: "The sceptre shall not depart from Judah, nor a lawgiver from between his feet, until Shiloh come; and unto him shall the gathering of the people be." And in Deut. xviii. 18: "I will raise them up a Prophet from among their brethren, like unto thee, and will put my words in his mouth." Compare this with Acts iii. 22 and vii. 37.

47. *But if ye believe not his writings.* If you lay them not to heart—if you draw not those conclusions from them which their very letter, as well as their spirit, authorizes you to draw—*how shall ye believe my words,* against which you have taken up the most ungrounded prejudice?

CHAPTER 6

Jesus passes the Sea of Tiberias, and a great multitude follow Him, 1-4. He feeds 5,000 with 5 loaves and 2 fishes, 5-13. They acknowledge Him to be the Prophet that should come into the world, 14. They purpose to force Him to become their King, and He withdraws from the multitude, 15. The disciples take ship and go towards Capernaum, and are overtaken with a storm, 16-18. Christ comes to them, walking upon the water, 19-21. The people take boats and follow Him, 22-24. He reproves their fleshly motives, 25-27. They profess a desire to be instructed, 28. Christ preaches to them, and shows them that He is the Bread of Life, and that they who reject Him are without excuse, 29-40. They are offended and cavil, 41-42. He asserts and illustrates His foregoing discourse, 43-51. They again cavil, and Christ gives further explanations, 52-59. Several of the disciples are stumbled at His assertion that unless they ate His flesh and drank His blood they could not have life, 60. He shows them that His words are to be spiritually understood, 61-65. Several of them withdraw from Him, 66. He questions the twelve whether they also were disposed to forsake Him, and Peter answers for the whole, 67-69. Christ exposes the perfidy of Judas, 70-71.

1. *After these things.* This is a sort of indefinite expression, from which we can gather nothing relative to the time in which these things happened. *Jesus went over the sea of Galilee.* Or, as some translate the words, "by the side of the sea of Galilee." From Luke, chap. ix. 10, we learn that this was a desert place in the vicinity of Bethsaida. The sea of *Galilee, Gennesaret,* and *Tiberias* are the same in the New Testament with the sea of *Cinnereth* in the Old. *Tiberias* was a city in Galilee, situated on the western side of the lake.

2. *They saw his miracles which he did.* John does not mention these miracles but Matthew details them, from chap. xii. 2 to chap. xiv. 13. John seems more intent on supplying the deficiencies of the other Evangelists than in writing a connected history himself.

3. *Went up into a mountain.* This mountain must have been in the desert of Bethsaida, in the territories of Philip, tetrarch of Galilee. Our Lord withdrew to this place for a little rest; for He and His disciples had been so thronged with the multitudes, continually coming and going, that they had not time to take necessary food. See Mark vi. 31.

4. *And the passover . . . was nigh.* This happened about ten or twelve days before the third Passover which Christ celebrated after His baptism. For a particular account of our Lord's four Passovers see the note on chap. ii. 13. For thirty days before the Passover there were great preparations made by the Jews, but especially in the last nineteen days, in order to celebrate the feast with due solemnity.

5. *Saw a great company.* See this miracle explained at large on Matt. xiv. 13, etc.; Mark vi. 31, etc.; Luke ix. 10, etc. In speaking of the

Passovers and various other matters it does not appear that John follows any strict chronological order. *Saith unto Philip.* This, with what follows to the end of the seventh verse, is not mentioned by any of the other Evangelists. *Philip* was probably the provider for the disciples, as Judas was the treasurer. *Whence shall we buy bread?* Instead of *shall we buy,* I should read "may we buy," which is the reading of many MSS. As Philip was of Bethsaida, chap. i. 44; xii. 21, he must have been much better acquainted with the country in which they then were than any other of the disciples.

6. *This he said to prove him.* To try his faith, and to see whether he and the other apostles had paid proper attention to the miracles which they had already seen Him work; and to draw their attention more particularly to that which He was now about to perform. This is an observation of the Evangelist himself, who often interweaves his own judgment with the facts he relates, which Matthew rarely ever does.

8. *Andrew, Simon Peter's brother, saith.* The other Evangelists attribute this answer to the apostles in general. See the passages referred to above.

9. *There is a lad here.* A "little boy," or "servant," probably one who carried the apostles' provisions, or who came on purpose to sell his bread and fish. *Five barley loaves.* Barley bore scarcely one-third of the value of wheat in the East; see Rev. vi. 6. That it was a very mean fare appears from Ezek. xiii. 19, where the false prophetesses are said to pollute the name of God "for handfuls of barley," i.e., for the meanest reward. And Plutarch, in *Apoph.,* p. 174, speaking concerning the flight of Artaxerxes Mnemon, says he was reduced to such distress as to be obliged to eat barley bread. *Two small fishes.* The word signifies "whatever is eaten with bread," to perfect the meal, or to help the digestion.

10. *There was much grass in the place.* Perhaps newly mown grass, or hay, is meant (so the Vulgate *foenum*), and this circumstance marks out more particularly that the Passover was at hand. In Palestine the grass is ready for mowing in March, and this miracle seems to have been wrought only a few days before the commencement of that festival.

11. *Jesus took the loaves.* See the notes on Matt. xiv. 19-21. As there were 5 loaves and 5,000 people, so there was one loaf to every thousand men, independently of the women and children.

12. *Gather up the fragments.* Among the Jews the *peah,* or residue after a meal, was the property of the servitors.

14. *This is of a truth that prophet.* Spoken of in Deut. xviii. 15, viz., the Messiah. How near were these people at this time to the kingdom of Heaven!

15. *Take him by force, to make him a king.* The Jews had often suffered by famine in those times in which their enemies were permitted to prevail over them; but, finding that Jesus had such power as to multiply a few loaves to feed thousands, they took it for granted that while He was at their head no evil could possibly happen to them and therefore were determined immediately to proclaim Him king and rid themselves at once of Herod and the Romans. Our Lord perceiving this, either by some words which they had dropped or by His penetration of their hearts, retired before the project had been fully formed or could be put into execution. It was not till a considerable time afterwards that even the disciples fully understood that His kingdom was not of this world. *Into a mountain.* That on which He was with His disciples previously to His working this miracle; see v. 3. Matthew, chap. xiv. 22-23, and Mark, vi. 45-46, say that before this Jesus constrained His disciples to embark in the vessel and go along the seacoast towards Capernaum, or Bethsaida—see here v. 17, and the note on Mark vi. 45; and that after they were gone He dismissed the multitudes, having no doubt given them such advices as the nature of the case required, after which He went into the mountain to pray.

17. *Toward Capernaum.* Mark says, chap. vi. 45, that our Lord commanded them to go along to Bethsaida; and in the course of the history we find they got neither to Bethsaida nor Capernaum, but landed in the country of Gennesaret, Matt. xiv. 34. Our Lord seems to have desired them to go to either Bethsaida or Capernaum, which were only a very few miles distant, and on the same side of the sea. The reason why they could reach neither was the storm which the Evangelists say rose at the time, and the wind being contrary.

19. *Had rowed.* Their vessel was a small one only, something of the boat kind. As to sails, if they had any they could not now venture to carry them because of the storm. *Five and twenty or thirty furlongs.* Between three and four miles.

21. *Immediately the ship was at the land.* How far they were from the place at which they landed when our Lord came to them, we know not. But the Evangelist seems to speak of their sudden arrival there as extraordinary and miraculous.

23. *There came other boats.* After Jesus and His disciples had departed. *From Tiberias.* Herod Antipas built this city near the lake of Gennesaret, in the best parts of Galilee, and called it *Tiberias,* in honor of Tiberius, the Roman emperor; see Jos., *Ant.,* book xviii, chap. 2, sec. 3.

24. *They also took shipping.* That is, as many of them as could get accommodated with boats took them, and thus got to Capernaum. But many others doubtless went thither on foot, as it is not at all likely that five or six thousand persons could get boats enough to carry them.

25. *On the other side of the sea.* That is, on the seacoast, to the northward of it, where Capernaum lies in the land of Gennesaret. It was in one of the synagogues of Capernaum that He delivered the following discourse; see v. 59.

26. *Ye seek me, not because ye saw.* Though the miracle of the loaves was one of the most astonishing that ever was wrought upon earth; and though this people had, by the testimony of all their senses, the most convincing proof of its reality; yet we find many of them paid little attention to it, and regarded the omnipotent hand of God in it no further than it went to satisfy the demands of their appetite! Most men are willing to receive temporal good from the hands of God; and there are few, very few, who are willing to receive spiritual blessings.

27. *Labour not for the meat.* That is, for that "only," but "also for the bread." *Him hath God the Father sealed.* By this expression our Lord points out the commission which, as the Messiah, He received from the Father, to be Prophet and Priest to an ignorant, sinful world. As a person who wishes to communicate his mind to another who is at a distance writes a letter, seals it with his own seal, and sends it directed to the person for whom it was written, so Christ, who lay in the bosom of the Father, came to interpret the divine will to man, bearing the image, superscription, and seal of God in the immaculate holiness of His nature, the unsullied truth of His doctrine, and in the astonishing evidence of His miracles. But He came also as a Priest, to make an atonement for sin; and the bread which nourishes unto eternal life, He tells us, v. 51, is His body, which He gives for the life of the world; and to this sacrifice of himself the words *him hath God the Father sealed* seem especially to relate. It certainly was a custom, among nations contiguous to Judea, to set a seal upon the victim which was deemed proper for sacrifice.

28. *That we might work the works of God.* That is, divine works, or such as God can approve.

29. *This is the work of God, that ye believe.* There is nothing you can be employed in more acceptable to God than in yielding to the evidence set before you, and acknowledging Me as your Messiah and the Saviour of a lost world.

30. *What sign?* "What miracle?" So the word is evidently used in John ii. 11, 23, and in many other places. *That we may see, and believe thee.* That, having *seen* the miracle, we may *believe* Thee to be the promised Messiah. They had already seen the miracle of the five loaves, and did not believe; and it was impossible for them to see anything more descriptive of unlimited power and goodness.

31. *Our fathers did eat manna in the desert.* Their argument seems to run thus: Thou hast, we grant, fed 5,000 men with 5 loaves and 2 small fishes, but what is this in comparison of what Moses did in the desert, who for forty years fed more than a million of persons with bread from heaven? Do something like this, and then we will believe in Thee, as we have believed in Moses.

32. *Moses gave you not that bread from heaven.* Our Lord refutes the argument of the Jews by proving: (1) That it was not Moses, but God, who gave the manna; (2) That this bread was not the *true* bread, but was merely a type of it; (3) That God had given them now a Bread infinitely more excellent; (4) That himself is that heavenly nourishment of which He spake, and who was typified by the manna in the desert.

34. *Lord, evermore give us this bread.* Either meaning, "Let the miracle of the manna be renewed, and continue among us forever"; or, "Let that Bread of which Thou hast spoken become our constant nourishment." The Jews expected that when the Messiah should come He would give them all manner of delicacies, and, among the rest, manna, wine, and spicy oil.

35. *I am the bread of life.* That is, the Bread which gives *life*, and preserves from death. *He that cometh to me.* The person who receives My doctrine and believes in Me as the great atoning Sacrifice shall be perfectly satisfied and never more feel misery of mind. All the guilt of his sins shall be blotted out, and his soul shall be purified unto God; and, being enabled to love Him with all his heart, he shall rest, fully, supremely, and finally happy, in his God.

37. *All that the Father giveth me.* The neuter gender, *pan,* is probably used here for the masculine, *pas. Shall come to me.* All that are drawn by the Father, v. 44, i.e., all those who are influenced by His Spirit, and yield to those influences. "For as many as are led [not driven or dragged] by the Spirit of God, they are the sons [children] of God," Rom. viii. 14. God sent His prophets to proclaim His salvation to this people; and He accompanied their preaching with the influence of His Spirit. Those who yielded were saved; those who did not yield to these drawings were lost. *I will in no wise cast out.* The words are exceedingly emphatic— "I will by no means thrust out of doors." Our blessed Lord alludes to the case of a person in deep distress and poverty who comes to a nobleman's house, in order to get relief. The person appears; and the owner, far from treating the poor man with asperity, welcomes, receives him kindly, and supplies his wants. So does Jesus. Never did He reject the suit of a penitent, however grievous his crimes might have been.

38. *Not to do mine own will.* I am come, not to act according to human motives, passions, or prejudices; but according to infinite wisdom, goodness, and mercy. Jewish passions and prejudices would reject publicans and sinners as those alluded to, and shut the gate of heaven against the Gentiles; but God's mercy receives them, and I am come to manifest that mercy to men.

39. *I should lose nothing.* It is the will of God that every soul who believes should continue in the faith, and have a resurrection unto life eternal. But He wills this continuance in salvation without purposing to force the persons so to continue. God may will a thing to be without willing that it *shall be.* Judas was given to Christ by the Father, chap. xvii. 12. The Father willed that this Judas should continue in the faith, and have a resurrection unto life eternal; but Judas sinned and perished. Now it is evident that God willed that Judas *might be* saved, without willing that he *must* be saved infallibly and unconditionally. When a man is a worker together with the grace of God, he is saved; when he receives that grace of God in vain, he is lost—not through a lack of will or mercy in God, but through lack of his cooperation with divine grace. God saves no man as a stock or a stone, but as a reasonable being and free agent. "That which thou hast heard, thou mayest hold fast, and persevere in, if thou wilt," says Augustine. *Raise it up again at the last day.* The Jews believed that the wicked should have no resurrection; and that the principle that led to the resurrection of the body, in the righteous, was the indwelling Spirit of God.

40. *This is the will of him that sent me.* Lest they should take a wrong meaning out of His words, as many have done since, He tells them that, far from any person being excluded from His mercy, it was the will of God that everyone who saw Him might believe and be saved. The power without which they could not

believe He freely gave them, but the use of that power was their own. God gives the grace of repentance and faith to every man, but He neither repents nor believes for any man. Each must repent for his own sins, and believe in the Lord Jesus, through the grace given, or perish.

41. *The Jews then murmured.* Because the whole of His discourse went to prove that He was infinitely greater than Moses, and that He alone could give present peace and eternal glory to men.

44. *Except the Father . . . draw him.* But how is a man drawn? Augustine answers from the poet, "A man is attracted by that which he delights in." Show green herbage to a sheep; he is drawn by it. Show nuts to a child, and he is drawn by them. They run wherever the person runs who shows these things. They run after him, but they are not forced to follow; they run through the desire they feel to get the things they delight in. So God draws man. He shows him his wants—He shows the Saviour whom He has provided for him. The man feels himself a lost sinner; and, through the desire which he finds to escape hell and get to heaven, he comes unto Christ, that he may be justified by His blood. Unless God thus draw, no man will ever come to Christ; because none could, without this drawing, ever feel the need of a Saviour. Drawing, or alluring, not dragging, is here to be understood. The best Greek writers use the verb in the same sense of "alluring, inciting."

45. *It is written in the prophets.* Isa. liv. 13; Jer. xxxi. 34. *They shall be all taught of God.* This explains the preceding verse. God teaches a man to know himself, that, finding his need of salvation, he may flee to lay hold on the hope which his Heavenly Father has set before him in the gospel. God draws men by His *love,* and by showing them what His love has done for them. *Fear* repels, but *love* attracts. He who is ever preaching the terrors of the law, and representing God as a vindictive judge, will never bring sinners to Him. They are afraid of this terrible God; but they love Him who "so loved the world, that he gave his only begotten Son, that whosoever believeth in him should not perish, but have everlasting life."

46. *Not that any man hath seen the Father.* He does not teach men by appearing personally before them, or by any other outward voice than that of His Word and messengers; but He teaches by His Spirit. *He which is of God.* That is, Christ alone. Neither Moses nor any of the prophets had ever seen God. Jesus, who lay in the bosom of the Father, saw and revealed Him, chap. i. 18.

49. *Your fathers did eat manna . . . and are dead.* That bread neither preserved their bodies alive nor entitled them to life eternal; but those who receive My salvation shall not only be raised again in the last day, but shall inherit eternal life. It was an opinion of the Jews themselves that their fathers who perished in the wilderness should never have a resurrection. Our Lord takes them on their own ground: You acknowledge that your fathers who fell in the wilderness shall never have a resurrection, and yet they ate of the manna. Therefore that manna is not the bread that preserves to everlasting life, according even to your own concession.

50. *This is the bread.* I am come for this very purpose, that men may believe in Me and have eternal life.

51. *Is my flesh, which I will give.* Our Lord explains His meaning more fully in these words than He had done before. Having spoken so much of the bread which feeds and nourishes the soul and preserves from death, the attention of His hearers was fixed upon His words, which to them appeared inexplicable; and they desired to know what their meaning was. He then told them that the bread meant His *flesh* (His life), which He was about to give up to save the life of the world. Here our Lord plainly declares that His death was to be a vicarious sacrifice and atonement for the sin of the world; and that as no human life could be preserved unless there was *bread* (proper nourishment) received, so no soul could be saved but by the merit of His death.

52. *How can this man give us his flesh to eat?* Our Lord removes this difficulty, and answers the question in v. 63.

53. *Except ye eat the flesh of the Son of man.* Unless you be made partakers of the blessings about to be purchased by My blood, passion, and violent death, you cannot be saved. Bishop Pearce justly observes that the ideas of eating and drinking are here borrowed to express "partaking of" and "sharing in." Thus spiritual happiness on earth, and even in heaven, is expressed by eating and drinking; instances of which may be seen in Matt. viii. 11; xxvi. 29; Luke xiv. 15; xxii. 30; and Rev. ii. 17. Those who were made partakers of the Holy Spirit are said by Paul, 1 Cor. xii. 13, to be "made to drink into [or of] one Spirit." This, indeed, was a very common mode of expression among the Jews.

54. *Hath eternal life.* This can never be understood of the sacrament of the Lord's Supper: (1) Because this was not instituted till a year after, at the last Passover; (2) It cannot be said that those who do not receive that sacrament must perish everlastingly; (3) Nor can it be supposed that all those who do receive it are necessarily and eternally saved. On the contrary, Paul intimates that many who received it at Corinth perished because they received it unworthily, not discerning the Lord's body, not distinguishing between it and a common meal, and not properly considering that Sacrifice for sin of which the sacrament of the Lord's Supper was a type; see 1 Cor. xi. 30.

55. *My flesh is meat indeed, and my blood is drink indeed.* Or rather, "My flesh is the true meat." In both clauses of this verse, instead of the *adverb* I read the *adjective,* agreeing with *brosis.* This reading is supported by many MSS. Our Lord terms His flesh the "true meat," and His blood the "true drink," because those who received His grace merited by His death would be really nourished and supported thereby unto eternal life.

56. *Dwelleth in me, and I in him.* Of all connections and unions, none is so intimate and complete as that which is effected by the digestion of aliments, because they are changed into the *very substance* of him who eats them; and this our Lord makes the model of that union which subsists between himself and genuine believers. He lives in them, and they in Him; for they are made partakers of the divine nature, 2 Pet. i. 4.

57. *So he that eateth me, even he shall live by me.* From which we learn that the union between Christ and His followers shall be similar to that which subsists between God and Christ.

59. *In the synagogue . . . in Capernaum.* From v. 26 to this verse the Evangelist gives us the discourse which our Lord preached in the synagogue, in which He was repeatedly interrupted by the Jews; but this gave Him the fuller opportunity to proclaim the whole truth relative to His passion and death, to edify the disciples, and confute these gainsayers.

60. *Many therefore of his disciples.* So it appears that He had many more than the twelve who constantly accompanied Him. *This is an hard saying; who can hear it?* Who can digest such doctrine as this? It is intolerable; it is impracticable.

62. *If ye shall see the Son of man ascend.* You need not be stumbled at what I say concerning eating My flesh and drinking My blood, for you shall soon have the fullest proof that this is *figuratively* spoken, for I shall ascend with the same body with which I shall arise from the dead; therefore My flesh and blood, far from being eaten by men, shall not even be found among them.

63. *It is the spirit that quickeneth.* It is the spiritual sense only of My words that is to be attended to, and through which life is to be attained, 2 Cor. iii. 6. Such only as eat and drink what I have mentioned, in a spiritual sense, are to expect eternal life. *The words that I speak.* Instead of *I speak,* I read, "I have spoken," on the authority of many MSS. This is an important reading, and plainly shows that our Lord's words here do not refer to any new point of doctrine which He was then inculcating, but to what He had spoken concerning His being the living Bread, and concerning the eating of His flesh and drinking of His blood, in the preceding verses. *Are spirit, and they are life.* As My words are to be spiritually understood, so the life they promise is of a spiritual nature.

64. *But there are some of you that believe not.* This is addressed to Judas, and to those disciples who left Him, v. 66. *And who should betray him.* Or "who would deliver Him up."

65. *Therefore said I unto you.* V. 44; see the note there. *Except it were given unto him.* None can come at first unless he be drawn by the Father; and none can continue unless he continue under those sacred influences which God gives only to those who do not receive His first graces in vain. Augustine himself grants that it was the sole fault of these disciples that they did not believe and were saved. "If I be asked why these could not believe, I immediately answer, because they would not."

66. *Many of his disciples went back.* They no longer associated with Him nor professed to acknowledge Him as the Messiah. None of these were of the twelve.

67. *Will ye also go away?* Or, "Do ye also desire?" These words are very emphatic. Will you abandon Me?—you, whom I have distinguished with innumerable marks of My affection—you, whom I have chosen out of the world to be My companions—you, to whom I have revealed the secrets of the eternal world—you, who have been witnesses of all My miracles—you, whom I intend to seat with Me on My throne in glory; will you go away?

68. *Simon Peter answered.* With his usual zeal and readiness, speaking in behalf of the whole, *To whom shall we go?* Where shall we find a more gracious master—a more powerful redeemer—a more suitable saviour? *Thou [alone] hast the words of eternal life.*

69. *We believe.* On the authority of Thy word; *and are sure*—"have known," by the evidence of Thy miracles, *that thou art that Christ,* the promised Messiah. Instead of *Christ, the Son of the living God,* some excellent MSS. read "the holy one of God."

70. *Have not I chosen you twelve?* Have I not, in an especial manner, called you to believe in My name, and chosen you to be My disciples, and the propagators of My doctrine? *Nevertheless, one of you is a devil,* or "accuser," enlisted on the side of Satan, who was a murderer from the beginning.

71. *He spake of Judas . . . for he it was that should betray him.* "He who was about to deliver Him up." By referring to this matter so often, did not our blessed Lord intend to warn Judas? Was not the evil fully exposed to his view? And who dare say that it was impossible for him to avoid what he had so often been warned against?

CHAPTER 7

Jesus continues in Galilee, 1. He is desired to go to the Feast of Tabernacles, 2-5. His answer, 6-9. He goes up, and the Jews seek Him at the feast, 10-13. He teaches in the Temple, 14-24. The Jews are confounded by His preaching, 25-27. He continues to teach; they wish to slay Him, 28-30. Many of the people believe on Him, 31. The Pharisees murmur, and our Lord reasons with them, 32-36. His preaching on the last day of the feast, 37-39. The people are greatly divided in their opinions concerning Him, 40-44. The officers, who were sent by the Pharisees to take Him, return, and because they did not bring Him their employers are offended, 45-49. Nicodemus reasons with them, 50-53.

1. *After these things.* John passes from the preceding discourse of our Lord, which He delivered a little before the Passover, chap. vi. 4, to the Feast of Tabernacles, which happened six months after, and thus omits many things mentioned by the other Evangelists which our blessed Lord said and did during that time. He had already gone over Galilee four or five times; and He continued there, because He found that the hatred of the Jews was such that they would kill Him if they could meet with Him in Judea; and His time to suffer was not yet come. *For he would not walk in Jewry.* He found greater scope for the exercise of His important ministry in Galilee than in Judea, as the chief priests were continually plotting His death.

2. *Feast of tabernacles.* This feast was celebrated on the fifteenth day of the month *Tisri,* answering to the last half of our September and the first half of October. This month was the seventh of the ecclesiastical, and first of the civil, year. The feast took its name from the tents which were erected about the Temple, in public places, in courts, on the flat roofs of their houses, and in gardens; in which the Jews dwelt for eight days, in commemoration of the forty years during which their fathers dwelt in the wilderness. It was one of the three solemn annual feasts in which all the males were obliged, by the law, to appear at Jerusalem. This feast was celebrated in the following manner. All the people cut down branches of palm trees, willows, and myrtles (and tied them together with gold and silver cords, or with ribbons), which they carried with them all day, took them into their synagogues and kept them by them while at prayers. On the other days of the feast they carried them with them into the Temple and walked round the altar with them in their hands, singing, "Hosanna!" i.e., "Save, we beseech Thee!" —the trumpets sounding on all sides. To this feast John seems to refer, Rev. vii. 9-10, where he represents the saints standing before the throne, with palm branches in their hands, singing, "Salvation to God." On the seventh day of the feast, they went seven times round the altar, and this was called the "great Hosanna." But the ceremony at which the Jews testified most joy was that of pouring out the water, which was done on the eighth day of the feast. A priest drew some water out of the Pool of Siloam, in a golden vessel, and brought it into the Temple; and at the time of the morning sacrifice, while the members of the sacrifice were on the altar, he went up and poured this water mingled with wine upon it, the people all the while singing, with transports of joy, Isaiah xii, especially v. 6: "With joy shall ye draw water out of the wells of salvation." To this part of the ceremony our Lord appears to allude in v. 37 of this chapter.

3. *His brethren . . . said.* It is generally supposed that these were the children of the sisters of his mother, Mary; but some of the ancients have stated that Joseph had several children by a former wife. No solid proof can be alleged against this, nor can we pretend to say that these were not the children of Joseph and Mary. Our blessed Lord, it is true, was her Firstborn, while she was yet a virgin; but no man can prove that He was her last.

4. *No man that doeth any thing in secret.* They took it for granted that Christ was influenced by the same spirit which themselves felt, and that therefore He should use every opportunity of exhibiting himself to the public, that He might get into repute; and they hoped that a part of His honor would be reflected back upon themselves, as being His near relations.

5. *Neither did his brethren believe in him.* They did not receive Him as the promised Messiah; but, having seen so many of His miracles, they could not but consider Him as an eminent prophet. They supposed that if He were the Messiah He would wish to manifest himself as such to the world; and because He did not do so they did not believe that He was the Salvation of Israel.

6. *My time is not yet come.* It is probable our Lord meant no more than this, that He had some business to transact before He could go to Jerusalem; but His brethren, having nothing to hinder them, might set off immediately. Others think He spoke of His passion: My time of suffering is not yet come. as you are still in friendship with the world, you need not be under any apprehension of danger; you may go when you please. The first sense I think is the best.

7. *The world cannot hate you.* The Jews will not persecute you, because you are in their sentiments and interests. *But me it hateth.* Be-

cause I condemn its injustice, its pride, its ambition, and its maxims by My life and doctrine. It is very likely that the term *world* means here the Jewish people only.

8. *I go not up yet unto this feast.* Porphyry accuses our blessed Lord of falsehood, because He said here, I will not go to this feast, and yet afterwards He went; and some interpreters have made more ado than was necessary in order to reconcile this seeming contradiction. To me the whole seems very simple and plain. Our Lord did not say, "I will not go to this feast"; but merely, I go not yet or am not "going," i.e., at present; because, as He said in v. 6 and repeats here, His time was not yet come—He had other business to transact before He could go.

11. *Then the Jews sought him.* By Jews here are to be understood the scribes, Pharisees, and rulers of the people, and not the inhabitants of the province of Judea.

12. *Some said, He is a good man.* The multitude were divided in their opinions concerning Him. Those who knew Him best said, *He is a good man.* Those who spoke according to the character given Him by the priests said, *Nay; but he deceiveth the people.*

15. *How knoweth this man letters, having never learned?* The Jewish learning consisted in the knowledge of their own Scriptures and the traditions of their elders. As these branches of learning were taught at the Jewish schools, and our Lord had never attended there, they were astonished to find Him excelling in that sort of learning of which they themselves professed to be the sole teachers.

16. *My doctrine is not mine.* Our blessed Lord, in the character of Messiah, might as well say, *My doctrine is not mine,* as an ambassador might say, I speak not my own words, but his who sent me.

17. *If any man will do his will.* I will give you a sure rule by which you may judge of My doctrine: If you really wish to do the will of God, begin the practice of it; and take My doctrine and apply it to all that you know God requires of man.

18. *He that speaketh of himself.* I will give you another rule whereby you shall know whether I am from God or not: If I speak so as to procure My own glory, to gratify vanity, or to secure and promote My secular interests, then reject Me as a deceiver and as a false prophet. *And no unrighteousness is in him.* Or, "There is no falsehood in him."

19. *Did not Moses give you the law?* The scribes and Pharisees announced our Lord to the multitude as a deceiver; and they grounded their calumny on this, that He was not an exact observer of the law, for He had healed a man on the Sabbath day, chap. v. 9-10, and consequently must be a false prophet. Now they insinuated that the interests of religion required Him to be put to death (1) as a violator of the law and (2) as a false prophet and deceiver of the people. To destroy this evil reasoning our Lord speaks in this wise; If I deserve death for curing a man on the Sabbath and desiring him to carry home his bed, which you consider a violation of the law, you are more culpable than I am, for you circumcise a child on the Sabbath, which requires much more bustle and is of so

much less use than what I have done to the infirm man.

21. *I have done one work.* That of curing the impotent man, already referred to. See chap. v. 9. *And ye all marvel.* Or, "You all marvel because of this."

22. *But of the fathers.* That is, it came "from the patriarchs." Circumcision was not, properly speaking, one of the laws of the Mosaic institution, it having been given at first to Abraham, and continued among his posterity till the giving of the law, Gen. xvii. 9-10, etc. Ye . . . *circumcise a man.* That is, a male child, for every male child was circumcised when eight days old; and if the eighth day after its birth happened to be a Sabbath, it was nevertheless circumcised, that the law might not be broken which had enjoined the circumcision to take place at that time, Lev. xii. 3.

23. *Every whit whole.* Some think that the original words should be translated "the whole man"; and that the meaning is that the blessed Saviour made him whole in both body and soul. This makes the miracle the greater, and shows still more forcibly the necessity of doing it without delay.

24. *Judge not according to the appearance.* Attend to the law, not merely in the letter, but in its spirit and design. Learn that the law which commands men to rest on the Sabbath day is subordinate to the law of mercy and love, which requires them to be ever active to promote God's glory in the comfort and salvation of their fellow creatures. And endeavor to judge of the merit or demerit of an action, not from the first impression it may make upon your prejudices, but from its tendency, and the motives of the person, as far as it is possible for you to acquaint yourselves with them, still believing the best where you have no certain proof to the contrary.

26. *That this is the very Christ.* In most of the common printed editions *alethos* is found, *the very Christ;* but the word is wanting in many MSS. and several editions. Calmet observes that the multitude which heard our Lord at this time was composed of three different classes of persons: (1) The rulers, priests, and Pharisees, declared enemies of Christ; (2) The inhabitants of Jerusalem, who knew the sentiments of their rulers concerning Him; (3) The strangers, who from different quarters had come up to Jerusalem to the feast, and who heard Christ attentively, being ignorant of the designs of the rulers against Him. Our Lord addresses himself in this discourse principally to His enemies. The strange Jews were those who were astonished when Christ said, v. 20, that they sought to kill Him. And the Jews of Jerusalem were those who, knowing the disposition of the rulers, and seeing Christ speak openly, no man attempting to seize Him, addressed each other in the foregoing words, *Do the rulers know indeed that this is the Christ?* imagining that the chief priests had at last been convinced that Jesus was the Messiah.

27. *No man knoweth whence he is.* The generality of the people knew very well that the Messiah was to be born in Bethlehem, in the city, and of the family, of David; see v. 42. But from Isaiah liii. 8, "Who shall declare his generation?" they probably thought that there should be something so peculiarly mysterious in His birth, or in the manner of His appearing, that no person could fully understand.

28. *Ye both know me, and ye know whence I am.* Perhaps they should be read interrogatively: "Do you both know Me, and know whence I am?" Our Lord takes them up on their own profession and argues from it. Since you have got so much information concerning Me, add this to it, to make it complete; viz., that *I am not come of myself,* am no self-created or self-authorized prophet. I came from God; the testimony of John the Baptist, the descent of the Holy Ghost, the voice from heaven, the purity and excellence of My doctrine, and the multitude of My miracles sufficiently attest this. Now God is *true,* who has borne testimony to Me. But you know Him not; therefore it is that this testimony is disregarded.

31. *Will he do more miracles?* It was the belief of the Jews, and they founded it upon Isa. xxxv. 5, that, when the Messiah came, He would do all kinds of miracles. And in order that they might have the fullest proof of the divine mission of Christ, it had pleased God to cause miracles to cease for between four and five hundred years, and that John the Baptist himself had not wrought any. His miracles, therefore, were a full proof of His divine mission.

32. *The people murmured such things.* The people began to be convinced that He was the Messiah; and this being generally whispered about, the Pharisees thought it high time to put Him to death, lest the people should believe on Him. Therefore they *sent officers to take him.*

33. *Yet a little while am I with you.* As He knew that the Pharisees had designed to take and put Him to death, and that in about six months from this time, as some conjecture, He should be crucified, He took the present opportunity of giving this information to the common people, who were best disposed towards Him, that they might lay their hearts to His teaching and profit by it while they had the privilege of enjoying it. The word *autois,* "to them," in the beginning of this verse, is wanting in many MSS. Our Lord did not speak these words to the officers who came to apprehend Him, as *autois* here implies, but to the common people, merely to show that He was not ignorant of the designs of the Pharisees, though they had not yet been able to put them into practice.

34. *Ye shall seek me, and shall not find me.* When the Roman armies come against you, you will vainly seek for a deliverer. But you shall be cut off in your sins, because you did not believe in Me. And *where I am*—in the Kingdom of glory—*ye cannot come,* for nothing that is unholy shall enter into the New Jerusalem.

35. *The dispersed among the Gentiles.* Or "Greeks." By the *dispersed* are meant here the Jews who were scattered through various parts of that empire which Alexander the Great had founded in Greece, Syria, Egypt, and Asia Minor, where the Greek language was used and where the Jewish Scriptures in the Greek version of the Septuagint were read.

37. *In the last day, that great day of the feast.* This was the eighth day, and was called the *great day* because of certain traditional observances, and not on account of any excellence which it derived from the original institution.

On the seven days they professed to offer sacrifices for the seventy nations of the earth, but on the eighth day they offered sacrifices for Israel; therefore the eighth day was more highly esteemed than any of the others. See the account of the Feast of Tabernacles, in the note on v. 2. It was probably when they went to draw water from the Pool of Siloam, and while they were pouring it out at the foot of the altar, that our Lord spoke these words.

38. *He that believeth on me, as the scripture hath said.* He who receives Me as the Messiah, according to what the Scripture has said concerning Me—My person, birth, conduct, preaching, and miracles being compared with what is written there, as ascertaining the true Messiah. *Out of his belly*—"from his heart and soul"; for in his soul shall this Spirit dwell. *Living water.* As a true spring is ever supplied with water from the great deep with which it has communication, so shall the soul of the genuine believer be supplied with light, life, love, and liberty, and all the other graces of the indwelling Spirit from the indwelling Christ. The Jews frequently compare the gifts and influences of the Holy Spirit to water in general. The Scriptures abound in this metaphor. See Ps. xxxvi. 8-9; Isa. xliv. 3-4; Joel ii. 23.

39. *Was not yet given.* "Given" is added by many MSS. and several of the primitive fathers. The word seems necessary to the completion of the sense.

40. *Of a truth this is the Prophet.* The great prophet or "teacher" spoken of by Moses, Deut. xviii. 15, which they improperly distinguished from the Messiah, v. 41.

41. *Shall Christ come out of Galilee?* As the prophets had declared that the Messiah was to come from the tribe of Judah and from the family of David, and should be born in the city of Bethlehem, these Jews, imagining that Christ had been born in Galilee, concluded that He could not be the Messiah.

42. *Where David was?* That is, where he was born, 1 Sam. xvi. 1, 4, and where he was before he became king in Israel.

43. *There was a division.* A "schism"; they were divided in sentiment and separated into parties.

44. *Would have taken him.* Or "they wished to seize Him." And this they would have done, and destroyed Him too at that time, had they been unanimous; but their being divided in opinion, v. 43, was the cause, under God, why His life was at that time preserved. How true are the words of the prophet: "The wrath of man shall praise thee: the remainder of wrath shalt thou restrain," Ps. lxxvi. 10!

45. *Then came the officers.* They had followed Him for several days, seeking for a proper opportunity to seize on Him, when they might fix some charge of sedition upon Him; but the more they listened, the more they were convinced of His innocence, purity, and consummate wisdom.

46. *Never man spake like this man.* Though these officers had gone on the errand of their masters, they had not entered into their spirit. They were sent to apprehend a seditious man and a false prophet. They came where Jesus taught; they found Him to be a different Person

to the description they received from their masters, and therefore did not attempt to touch or molest Him. No doubt they expected when they told their employers the truth that they would have commended them and acknowledged their own mistake, but these simple people were not in the secret of their masters' malice.

48. *Have any of the rulers . . . believed on him?* Very few. But is this a proof that He is not of God? No, truly. If He were of the world, the world would love its own. The religion of Christ has been in general rejected by the rulers of this world.

49. *This people.* "This rabble." The common people were treated by the Pharisees with the most sovereign contempt. They were termed *am ha-arets,* "people of the earth," and were not thought worthy to have a resurrection to eternal life.

50. *Nicodemus . . . being one of them.* That is, a Pharisee, and a ruler of the Jews; see on chap. iii. 1.

51. *Doth our law judge any man?* "The man," i.e., who is accused. Perhaps Nicodemus did not refer so much to anything in the law of Moses as to what was commonly practiced among them. Josephus says, *Ant.,* b. xiv, c. 9, s. 3, "That the law has forbidden any man to be put to death, though wicked, unless he be first condemned to die by the Sanhedrin." It was probably to this law that Nicodemus here alludes. See laws relative to this point in Deut. xvii. 8, etc.; xix. 15.

52. *Art thou also of Galilee?* They knew very well that he was not, but they spoke this by way of reproach. As if they had said, You are no better than He is, as you take His part. *Search, and look.* Examine the Scriptures, search the public registers, and you will see that out of Galilee there arises no prophet. This conclusion, says Calmet, was false, because Jonah was of Gath-hepher, in Galilee; see 2 Kings xiv. 25, compared with Josh. xix. 13. The Prophet Nahum was also a Galilean, for he was of the tribe of Simeon.

53. *And every man went.* The authority and influence of Nicodemus, in this case, was so great that the Sanhedrin broke up without being able to conclude anything. As the feast was now ended, they were not obliged to continue any longer in or about Jerusalem, and therefore all returned to their respective dwellings. This verse and the first eleven verses of the following chapter are wanting in several MSS. Some of those which retain the paragraph mark it with obelisks, as a proof of spuriousness. Those which do retain it have it with such a variety of reading as is nowhere else found in the sacred writings. Professor Griesbach leaves the whole paragraph in the text with notes of doubtfulness. Most of the modern critics consider it as resting on no solid authority.

CHAPTER 8

The story of the woman taken in adultery, 1-11. Jesus declares himself the Light of the World, 12. The Pharisees cavil, 13. Jesus answers, and shows His authority, 14-20. He delivers a second discourse, in which He convicts them of sin, and foretells their dying in it because of their unbelief, 21-24. They question Him; He answers, and foretells His own death, 25-29. Many believe on Him in consequence of this last discourse, 30. To whom He gives suitable advice, 31-32. The Jews again cavil, and plead the nobility and advantages of their birth, 33. Jesus shows the vanity of their pretensions and the wickedness of their hearts, 34-47. They blaspheme, and Christ convicts and reproves them, and asserts His divine nature, 48-58. They attempt to stone Him, 59.

3. *A woman taken in adultery.* It is allowed that adultery was exceedingly common at this time, so common that they had ceased to put the law in force against it. The waters of jealousy were no longer drunk, the culprits, or those suspected of this crime, being so very numerous; and the men who were guilty themselves dared not try their suspected wives, as it was believed the waters would have no evil effect upon the wife if the husband himself had been criminal. See the whole of the process on the waters of jealousy in the notes on Num. v. 14.

5. *That such should be stoned.* It is not strictly true that Moses ordered adultery in general to be punished by stoning. The law simply says that the adulterer and the adulteress shall be "put to death," Lev. xx. 10; Deut. xxii. 22. The rabbins say they were strangled. This they affirm was the ordinary mode of punishment where the species of death was not marked in the law. If the person guilty of an act of this kind had been betrothed, but not married, she was to be stoned, Deut. xxii. 23. But if she was the daughter of a priest, she was to be burned alive, Lev. xxi. 9. It appears from Ezek. xvi. 38, 40 that adulteresses in the time of that prophet were stoned and pierced with a sword.

6. *That they might have to accuse him.* Had our Lord condemned the woman to death, they might have accused Him to Pilate, as arrogating to himself the power of life and death, which the Romans had taken away from the Jews. Besides, the Roman laws did not condemn an adulteress to be put to death. On the other hand, if He had said she should not be put to death, they might have represented Him to the people as One who decided contrary to the law and favored the crime of which the woman was accused. *With his finger wrote.* Several MSS. add *their sins who accused her, and the sins of all men.* There are many idle conjectures concerning what our Lord wrote on the ground. We never find that Christ wrote anything before or after this, and what He wrote at this time we know not.

7. *He that is without sin.* Meaning the same kind of sin, adultery, fornication. *Let him first cast a stone at her.* Or "upon her." The Jewish method of stoning, according to the rabbins, was as follows: The culprit, half naked, the hands tied behind the back, was placed on a scaffold, ten or twelve feet high. The witnesses, who stood with her, pushed her off with great force. If she was killed by the fall, there was nothing further done; but if she was not, one of the witnesses took up a very large stone, and dashed it upon her breast, which generally was the *coup de grace,* or finishing stroke.

9. *Being convicted by their own conscience.* So it is likely they were all guilty of similar crimes. *Their own* is not in the original, and is needless; *being convicted by conscience* is expressive enough. *Beginning at the eldest, even unto the last.* "From the most honorable to those of the least repute." In this sense the words are undoubtedly to be understood. *The woman standing in the midst.* But if they all went out, how could she be in the midst? It is not said that all the people whom our Lord had

been instructing went out, but only her accusers; see v. 2. The rest undoubtedly continued with their Teacher.

11. *Neither do I condemn thee.* After weighing what has been adduced in favor of its authenticity and seriously considering its state in the MSS., I must confess the evidence in its favor does not appear to me to be striking. Yet I by no means would have it expunged from the text. It may however be necessary to observe that a very perfect connection subsists between v. 52 of chap. vii and v. 12 of this chapter—all the intermediate verses having been omitted by MSS. of the first antiquity and authority. In some MSS. it is found at the end of this Gospel; in others a vacant place is left in this chapter; and in others it is placed after the twenty-first chapter of Luke.

12. *Then spake Jesus again unto them.* Allowing the story about the woman taken in adultery to be authentic and to stand here in its proper place, we may consider that our Lord, having begun to teach the people in the Temple, was interrupted by the introduction of this woman by the scribes and Pharisees; and now, having dismissed them and the woman also, He resumes His discourse. *I am the light of the world.* The Fountain whence all intellectual light and spiritual understanding proceed; without Me all is darkness, misery, and death. The Divine Being was by the rabbins denominated *The light of the world.* So in *Bamidbar Rabbi:* "The Israelites said to God, O Lord of the universe, thou commandest us to light lamps to thee, yet thou art the light of the world: and with thee the light dwelleth." Our Lord, therefore, assumes here a well-known character of the Supreme Being, and with this we find the Jews were greatly offended. *Shall not walk in darkness.* He shall be saved from ignorance, infidelity, and sin. He *shall have the light of life*—such a light as brings and supports life. The sun, the fountain of light, is also the fountain of life; by its vivifying influences, all things live—neither animal nor vegetative life could exist were it not for its influence. Jesus, the Sun of Righteousness, Mal. iv. 2, is the Fountain of all spiritual and eternal life. His light brings life with it, and they who walk in His light live in His life. Some suppose our Lord alludes to the custom of lighting lamps or torches on the first day of the Feast of Tabernacles. But as these words seem to have been spoken the day after that last and great day of the feast, mentioned in chap. vii. 37, they may rather be considered as referring to the following custom. It has already been observed that the Jews added a ninth day to this feast, which day they termed "the feast of joy for the law"; and on that day they were accustomed to take all the sacred books out of the chest where they had been deposited, and put a lighted candle in their place, in allusion to Prov. vi. 23: "For the commandment is a lamp [or candle]; and the law is light"; or to Ps. cxix. 105: "Thy word is a lamp unto my feet, and a light unto my path." If this custom existed in the time of our Lord, it is most likely that it is to it He here alludes, as it must have happened about the same time in which these words were spoken. As the Messiah was frequently spoken of by the prophets under the emblem of light (see Isa. lx. 1; xlix. 6; ix. 2), the Pharisees must at once

perceive that He intended to recommend himself to the people as the Messiah, when He said, *I am the light of the world.*

13. *Thou bearest record.* As if they had said, Dost Thou imagine that we shall believe Thee, in a matter so important, on Thy bare assertion? Had these people attended to the teaching and miracles of Christ, they would have seen that His pretensions to the Messiahship were supported by the most irrefragable testimony.

14. *I know whence I came.* I came from God, and am going to God, and can neither do nor say anything but what leads to and glorifies Him.

15. *Ye judge after the flesh.* Because I appear in the form of man, judging from this appearance, you think I am but a mere man—pay attention to My teaching and miracles, and you shall then see that nothing less than infinite wisdom and unlimited power could teach and do what I have taught and performed.

19. *Ye neither know me.* You know neither the Messiah nor the God that sent Him. *If ye had known me.* If you had received My teaching, you would have got such an acquaintance with the nature and attributes of God as you never could have had and never can have any other way. That is a true saying, "No man hath seen God at any time; the only begotten Son, which is in the bosom of the Father, he hath declared him." The nature and perfections of God never can be properly known but in the light of the gospel of Jesus Christ.

20. *The treasury.* Lightfoot observes, from the rabbins, that the treasury was in what was called the "court of the women"—that there were thirteen chests in it; in the thirteenth only the women were permitted to put their offerings. Probably the other twelve were placed there in reference to the twelve tribes, each perhaps inscribed with the name of one of Jacob's twelve sons. *His hour was not yet come.* The time was not arrived in which He had determined to give himself up into the hands of His crucifiers.

21. *Then said Jesus again unto them.* He had said the same things to them the day before. See chap. vii. 34. *Ye shall seek me.* When your calamities come upon you, you shall in vain seek for the help of the Messiah, whom you now reject and whom you shall shortly crucify.

22. *Will he kill himself?* They now understood that He spoke concerning His death; but before, chap. vii. 35, they thought He spoke of going to some of the Grecian provinces to preach to the dispersed Jews.

23. *Ye are from beneath.* You are capable of murder, and of self-murder too, because you have nothing of God in you. They verified this character in murdering the Lord Jesus; and many of them afterwards, to escape famine, put an end to their own lives.

25. *Who art thou?* This marks the indignation of the Pharisees—as if they had said: Who art Thou that takest upon Thee to deal out threatenings in this manner against us? *Jesus saith unto them, Even the same that I said unto you from the beginning.* Rather, "Just what I have already told you," i.e., that "I am the light of the world"—the Christ—the Saviour of mankind.

26. *I have many things to say and to judge of you.* Or "to speak and to condemn."

28. *When ye have lifted up.* When you have crucified Me, and thus filled up the measure of your iniquities, you shall know that I am the Christ by the signs that shall follow; and you shall know that what I spoke is true by the judgments that shall follow. To be lifted up is a common mode of expression among the Jewish writers for "to die" or "to be killed."

29. *The Father hath not left me alone.* Though you shall have power to put Me to death, yet this shall not be because He has abandoned Me. No—He is ever with Me, because I do that which pleases Him; and it is His pleasure that I should lay down My life for the salvation of the world.

30. *As he spake these words, many believed on him.* The same sun that hardens the clay softens the wax. This discourse, which proved the savor of death unto death to the obstinate Pharisees, became the savor of life unto life to many of the simplehearted people.

31. *If ye continue in my word.* Or "in this doctrine of Mine." It is not enough to receive God's truth—we must retain and walk in it. And it is only when we receive the truth, love it, keep it, and walk in it, that we are the genuine disciples of Christ.

32. *Ye shall know the truth.* Shall have a constant experimental knowledge of its power and efficacy. *And the truth shall make you free.* It was a maxim of the Jews "that no man was free, but he who exercised himself in the meditation of the law." No man is truly free but he in whose heart the power of sin is destroyed, and who has received the Spirit of adoption, through which he cries, "Abba! Father!" See Rom. viii. 15. The bondage of sin is the most grievous bondage, and freedom from its guilt and influence is the greatest liberty.

33. *They answered.* That is, the other Jews who had not believed—the carping, cavilling Pharisees already mentioned; for the words cannot be spoken of the simple people who had already believed. *Were never in bondage to any man.* This assertion was not only false, but it was ridiculous in the extreme, seeing their whole history, sacred and profane, is full of recitals of their servitude in Egypt, in Chaldea, under the Persians, under the Macedonians, and under the Romans.

34. *Whosoever committeth sin is the servant of sin.* Or "is the slave of sin." This was the slavery of which Christ spoke, and deliverance from it was the liberty which He promised.

35. *And the servant abideth not in the house.* Or, rather, "Now the slave abideth not in the family." As if Jesus had said: And now that I am speaking of a *slave,* I will add one thing more, viz., a slave has no right to any part of the inheritance in the family to which he belongs; but the *son,* the legitimate son, has a right.

37. *My word hath no place in you.* Or, "This doctrine of Mine has no place in you." You hear the truths of God but you do not heed them; the word of life has no influence over you. And how can it when you seek to kill Me because I proclaim this truth to you? From what is here said it is manifest, says Dr. Lightfoot, that the whole tendency of our Saviour's discourse is to show the Jews that they are the seed of that serpent which was to bruise the heel of the Messiah. Else what could that

mean, v. 44: "Ye are of your father the devil"; i.e., "Ye are the seed of the serpent"?

38. *I speak that which I have seen.* I speak nothing but that unchangeable, eternal truth which I have received from the bosom of God. *Ye do that which ye have seen.* Instead of *ye have seen* I think we should read "ye have heard," on the authority of some MSS. Jesus saw the Father, for He was the Word that was with God from eternity. The Jews did not see; they only felt and heard their father the devil.

39. *If ye were Abraham's children.* Griesbach reads *ye are* instead of *ye were*, on the authority of some MSS. *Ye would do the works of Abraham.* As the son has the nature of his father in him, and naturally imitates him, so if you were the children of Abraham you would imitate him in his faith, obedience, and uprightness. But this you do not, for you seek to kill Me merely because I tell you the truth. Abraham never did anything like this; therefore you have no spiritual relationship to him.

41. *Ye do the deeds of your father.* You have certainly another father than Abraham—one who has instilled his own malignant nature into you; and as you seek to murder Me for telling you the truth, you must be the offspring of him who was a murderer from the beginning, and stood not in the truth, v. 44. *We be not born of fornication.* We are not a mixed, spurious breed —our tribes and families have been kept distinct—we are descended from Abraham by his legal wife, Sarah. *We have one Father, even God.* In the spiritual sense of father and son we are not a spurious, that is, an *idolatrous* race; because we acknowledge none as our spiritual father, and worship none as such, but the true God.

42. *If God were your Father, ye would love me.* I came from God, and it would be absurd to suppose that you would persecute Me if you were under the influence of God. The children of the same father should not murder each other.

43. *Why do ye not understand my speech?* "This My mode of speaking"—when illustrating spiritual by natural things. *Because ye cannot hear my word.* That is, you cannot bear My doctrine. It comes too close to you; it searches your hearts, detects your hypocrisy, and exposes your iniquitous intentions and designs. And as you are determined not to leave your sins, so you are purposed not to hear My doctrine.

44. *Ye are of your father the devil.* You are the seed of the old serpent. See on v. 37. *The lusts of your father.* Like father, like son. What Satan desires, you desire, because you are filled with his nature. *He was a murderer from the beginning.* It was through him that Adam transgressed, in consequence of which death entered into the world, and slew him and all his posterity. *Abode not in the truth.* "He stood not in the truth"—was once in a state of glorious felicity, but fell from it; and, being deprived of all good himself, he could not endure that others should enjoy any. *He speaketh of his own.* "He speaketh of his own offspring," or, "from his own disposition," for he is the father and fountain of all error and falsity; and all who are deceived by him, and partake of his disposition, falsity, and cruelty are his offspring.

For he is a liar, and the father of it—literally, "his father also."

46. *Which of you convinceth me of sin?* Do you pretend to reject the truths which I announce, because My life does not correspond to the doctrines I have taught? But can any of you prove Me guilty of any fault? But it is probable that *sin* is put here in opposition to *truth* in the same verse, and then it should be rendered "falsehood." The very best Greek writers use the word in the same sense.

48. *Thou art a Samaritan.* This is the only time in which the Jews gave our Lord this title of reproach, and they probably grounded it on His having preached among them and lodged in their villages. See the account in chap. iv; but *Samaritan,* among them, meant a person unworthy of any credit. *Hast a devil.* Art possessed by an evil spirit and art, in consequence, deranged.

49. *I have not a devil.* The first part of the charge was too futile; if taken literally, it was both absurd and impossible. They did not believe it themselves, and therefore our Lord does not stop a moment to refute it; but He answers to the second with the utmost meekness and conclusiveness: I honor God. This is what no demon can do nor any man who is under such influence.

50. *I seek not mine own glory.* Another proof that I am not influenced by any spirit but that which proceeds from God. But there is *one that seeketh*—i.e., My glory—*and judgeth*—will punish you for your determined obstinacy and iniquity.

51. *Shall never see death.* He shall never come under the power of the death of the soul, but shall live eternally with Me in glory.

54. *Your God.* Many MSS. and most of the versions read *our* instead of *your.* The variation is of very little consequence. They called God their God, while enemies to Him in both their spirit and conduct.

56. *Abraham rejoiced to see my day.* Or "he earnestly desired to see My day"; his soul "leaped" forward in earnest hope and strong expectation that he might see the incarnation of Jesus Christ. *And he saw it.* Not only in the first promise, Gen. iii. 15, for the other patriarchs saw this as well as he; and not only in that promise which was made particularly to himself, Gen. xii. 7; xxii. 18 (compared with Gal. iii. 16), that the Messiah should spring from his family. But he saw this day especially when Jehovah appeared to him in a human form, Gen. xviii. 2, 17, which many suppose to have been a manifestation of the Lord Jesus.

59. *Then took they up stones.* It appears that the Jews understood Him as asserting His Godhead; and, supposing Him to be a blasphemer, they proceeded to stone Him, according to the law, Lev. xxiv. 16. *But Jesus hid himself.* In all probability He rendered himself invisible— though some will have it that He conveyed himself away from those Jews who were His enemies, by mixing himself with the many who believed on Him (vv. 30-31) and who, we may suppose, favored His escape. *Going through the midst of them, and so passed by.* These words are wanting in the Codex Bezae, and in several

editions and versions. Erasmus, Grotius, Beza, Pearce, and Griesbach think them not genuine.

CHAPTER 9

Account of the man who was born blind, 1-5. Christ heals him, 6-7. The man is questioned by his neighbors, 8-12. He is brought to the Pharisees, who question him, 13-17, and then his parents, 18-23. They again interrogate the man, who, vindicating the conduct of Christ, is excommunicated by them, 24-34. Jesus, hearing of the conduct of the Pharisees, afterwards finds the man, and reveals himself to him, 35-38. He passes sentence on the obduracy and blindness of the Pharisees, 39-41.

1. *And as Jesus passed by.* This chapter is a continuation of the preceding, and therefore the word *Jesus* is not in the Greek text; it begins simply thus—"And passing along." Having left the Temple, where the Jews were going to stone Him (chap. viii. 59), it is probable our Lord went, according to His custom, to the Mount of Olives. The next day, which was the Sabbath, v. 14, He met a man who had been born blind, sitting in some public place, and asking alms from those who passed by, v. 8.

2. *Who did sin, this man, or his parents?* The doctrine of the transmigration of souls appears to have been an article in the creed of the Pharisees, and it was pretty general among both the Greeks and the Asiatics. The Pythagoreans believed the souls of men were sent into other bodies for the punishment of some sin which they had committed in a pre-existent state. This seems to have been the foundation of the disciples' question to our Lord.

3. *Neither hath this man sinned, nor his parents.* That is, the blindness of this person is not occasioned by any sin of his own, nor of his parents; but has happened in the ordinary course of divine providence, and shall now become the instrument of salvation to his soul, edification to others, and glory to God. Many of the Jews thought that marks on the body were proofs of sin in the soul.

4. *While it is day.* Though I plainly perceive that the cure of this man will draw down upon Me the malice of the Jewish rulers, yet I must accomplish the work for which I came into the world while it is day—while the term of this life of Mine shall last. It was about six months after this that our Lord was crucified. It is very likely that the day was now declining and night coming on, and He took occasion from this circumstance to introduce the elegant metaphor immediately following. By this we are taught that no opportunity for doing good should be omitted—*day* representing the opportunity: *night*, the loss of that opportunity.

5. *I am the light of the world.* Like the sun, it is My business to dispense light and heat everywhere, and to neglect no opportunity that may offer to enlighten and save the bodies and souls of men. See chap. viii. 12.

6. *Anointed the eyes of the blind man.* It would be difficult to find out the reason which induced our Lord to act thus. It is certain this procedure can never be supposed to have been any likely medical means to restore sight to a man who was born blind; this action, therefore, had no tendency to assist the miracle. The Jews believed that there was some virtue in spittle to cure the diseases of the eye, but then they always accompanied this with some charm. Per-

haps the best lesson we can learn from this is that God will do His own work in His own way; and, to hide pride from man, will often accomplish the most beneficial ends by means not only simple or despicable in themselves, but by such also as appear entirely contrary, in their nature and operation, to the end proposed to be effected by them.

7. *By interpretation, Sent.* From the Hebrew *shalach*, "he sent"; either because it was looked upon as a gift sent from God, for the use of the city, or because its waters were directed or sent by canals or pipes, into different quarters, for the same purpose.

8. *That he was blind.* Instead of this, "when he begged," or "was a beggar," is the reading of many MSS. This is in all probability the true reading.

9. *Some said, This is he.* This miracle was not wrought in private—nor before a few persons—nor was it lightly credited. Those who knew him before were divided in their opinion concerning him—not whether the man who sat there begging was blind before, for this was known to all; nor whether the person now before them saw clearly, for this was now notorious; but whether this was the person who was born blind, and who used to sit begging in a particular place. *Others said, He is like him.* This was very natural, for certainly the restoration of his sight must have given him a very different appearance to what he had before.

11. *A man that is called Jesus.* The whole of this relation is simple and artless in the highest degree. The blind man had never seen Jesus, but he had heard of His name—he felt that He had put something on his eyes, which he afterwards found to be clay—but how this was made he could not tell, because he could not see Jesus when He did it. Therefore he does not say, "He made clay of spittle"—but simply, "He made clay, and spread it upon my eyes."

12. *Where is he?* They had designed to seize and deliver Him up to the Sanhedrin, as a violator of the law, because He had done this on the Sabbath day.

13. *They brought to the Pharisees.* These had the chief rule, and determined all controversies among the people; in every case of religion, their judgment was final. The people, now fully convinced that the man had been cured, brought him to the Pharisees, that they might determine how this was done and whether it had been done legally.

14. *It was the sabbath.* Some of the ancient rabbins taught, and they have been followed by some moderns not much better skilled in physic than themselves, that the saliva is a cure for several disorders of the eyes; but the former held this to be contrary to the law if applied on the Sabbath.

16. *This man is not of God.* He can neither be the Messiah nor a prophet, for He has broken the Sabbath. The Jews always argued falsely on this principle. The law relative to the observation of the Sabbath never forbade any work but what was of the servile and unnecessary kind. Works of necessity and mercy never could be forbidden on that day by Him whose name is Mercy, and whose nature is love; for the Sabbath was made for man, and not

man for the Sabbath. Were it otherwise, the Sabbath would be rather a curse than a blessing. *How can a man that is a sinner?* They knew very well that, though magicians and impostors might do things apparently miraculous, yet nothing really good could be performed by them. *And there was a division among them.* Schisma, "a schism," a decided difference of opinion, which caused a separation of the assembly.

17. *He is a prophet.* They had intended to lay snares for the poor man, that, getting him to acknowledge Christ for the Messiah, they might put him out of the synagogue, v. 22, or put him to death, that such a witness to the divine power of Christ might not appear against them. But, as the mercy of God had given him his sight, so the wisdom of God taught him how to escape the snares laid for his ruin. If they allow that Jesus was a prophet, then, even in their sense, He might break the law of the Sabbath, and be guiltless. Or if they did not allow Him to be a prophet, they must account for the miracle some other way than by the power of God; as from Satan or his agents no good can proceed—to do this it was impossible. So the wisdom of God taught the poor man to give them such an answer as put them into a complete dilemma, from which they could not possibly extricate themselves.

18. *But the Jews did not believe.* All the subterfuge they could use was simply to sin against their conscience, by asserting that the man had not been blind. But out of this subterfuge they were soon driven by the testimony of the parents, who, if tried further on this subject, might have produced as witness, not only the whole neighborhood, but nearly the whole city; for it appears the man got his bread by publicly begging, v. 8.

21. *He is of age.* Literally, "he has stature," i.e., he is a full-grown man; and in this sense the phrase is used by the best Greek writers. Mature age was fixed among the Jews at thirty years.

22. *Put out of the synagogue.* That is, "excommunicated"—separated from all religious connection with those who worshipped God. This was the lesser kind of excommunication among the Jews and was against the followers of Christ till after the Resurrection.

24. *Give God the praise.* Having called the man a second time, they proceeded to deal with him in the most solemn manner; and therefore they put him to his oath; for the words above were the form of an oath, proposed by the chief magistrate to those who were to give evidence to any particular fact, or to attest anything, as produced by or belonging to the Lord. But while they solemnly put him to his oath, they endeavored to put their own words in his mouth, viz., he *is a sinner*—a pretender to the prophetic character, and a transgressor of the law of God; assert this, or you will not please us.

25. *Whereas I was blind, now I see.* He pays no attention to their cavils, nor to their perversion of justice; but in the simplicity of his heart speaks to the fact of the reality of which he was ready to give them the most substantial evidence.

27. *I have told you already.* So he did, v. 15.

And did you not hear? You certainly did. Why then do you wish to *hear it again?* Is it because you wish to become His disciples? The poor man continued steady in his testimony; and by putting this question to them, he knew he should soon put an end to the debate.

28. *Then they reviled him.* They spoke "cutting, piercing" words. Solomon talks of some who spoke "like the piercings of a sword," Prov. xiii. 18. And the Psalmist speaks of words that are like "drawn swords," Ps. lv. 21, words which show that the person who speaks them has his heart full of murderous intentions; and that, if he had the same power with a sword as he has with his tongue, he would destroy him whom he thus reproaches.

29. *We know not from whence he is.* As if they had said: We have the fullest assurance that the commission of Moses was divine, but we have no proof that this Man has such a commission: and should we leave Moses, and attach ourselves to this Stranger? No.

30. *Why herein is a marvellous thing.* As if he had said, "This is wonderful indeed!" Is it possible that such persons as you are, whose business it is to distinguish good from evil, and who pretend to know a true from a false prophet, cannot decide in a case so plain? Has not the Man opened my eyes? Is not the miracle known to all the town; and could anyone do it who was not endued with the power of God?

31. *God heareth not sinners.* I believe the word signifies "heathens," or persons not proselyted to the Jewish religion; and therefore it is put in opposition to "a worshipper of [the true] God." But in what sense may it be said, following our common version, that *God heareth not sinners?* When they regard iniquity in their heart—when they wish to be saved, and yet abide in their sins—when they will not separate themselves from the workers and works of iniquity.

32. *Since the world began.* "From the age"—probably meaning from the commencement of time. Neither Moses nor the prophets have ever opened the eyes of a man who was born blind. If this Person then were not the best of beings, would God grant Him a privilege which He has hitherto denied to His choicest favorites? *Opened the eyes of one that was born blind.* That there are cases in which a person who was born blind may be restored to sight by surgical means we know, but no such means were used by Christ. And it is worthy of remark that from the foundation of the world no person *born blind* has been restored to sight, even by surgical operation, till about the year of our Lord 1728, when the celebrated Dr. Cheselden, by couching the eyes of a young man, fourteen years of age, who had been born blind, restored him to perfect soundness. This was the effect of well-directed surgery; that performed by Christ was a miracle.

33. *If this man were not of God.* A very just conclusion: God is the Fountain of all good. All good must proceed from Him, and no good can be done but through Him. If this Person were not commissioned by the good God, He could not perform such beneficent miracles as these.

34. *Thou wast altogether born in sins.* You have not only been a vile wretch in some other

preexistent state, but your parents also have been grossly iniquitous; therefore you and they are punished by this blindness. *And they cast him out.* They immediately "excommunicated" him, as the margin properly reads—drove him from their assembly with disdain, and forbade his further appearing in the worship of God. Thus a simple man, guided by the Spirit of truth, and continuing steady in his testimony, utterly confounded the most eminent Jewish doctors.

35. *Dost thou believe on the Son of God?* This was the same with, "Dost thou believe on the Messiah?" for these two characters were inseparable.

36. *Who is he, Lord?* It is very likely that the blind man did not know that it was Jesus the Christ who now spoke to him, for it is evident he had never seen Him before this time; and he might now see Him without knowing that He was the Person by whom he was cured, till our Lord made that discovery of himself mentioned in the following verse.

38. *And he said, Lord, I believe.* That is, I believe Thou art the Messiah; and, to give the fullest proof of the sincerity of his faith, he fell down before and adored Him. Never having seen Jesus before, but simply knowing that a person of that name had opened his eyes, he had only considered Him as a holy man and a prophet. But now that he sees and hears Him, he is convinced of His divinity, and glorifies Him as his Saviour. The word *kyrie* has two meanings; it signifies "Lord," or Sovereign Ruler, and "Sir," a title of civil respect. In the latter sense it seems evidently used in the thirty-sixth verse, because the poor man did not then know that Jesus was the Messiah; in the former sense it is used in this verse—now the healed man knew the quality of his Benefactor.

39. *For judgment I am come.* I am come to manifest and execute the just judgment of God: (1) By giving sight to the blind and light to the Gentiles, who sit in darkness, (2) By removing the true light from those who, pretending to make a proper use of it, only abuse the mercy of God. In a word, salvation shall be taken away from the Jews, because they reject it; and the kingdom of God shall be given to the Gentiles.

40. *Are we blind also?* These Pharisees understood Christ as speaking of blindness in a spiritual sense, and wished to know if He considered them in that state.

41. *If ye were blind.* If you had not had sufficient opportunities to have acquainted yourselves with My divine nature, by the unparalleled miracles which I have wrought before you and the holy doctrine which I have preached, then your rejecting Me could not be imputed to you as sin. But because you say, *We see*—we are perfectly capable of judging between a true and false prophet, and can from the Scriptures point out the Messiah by His works—on this account you are guilty. And your sin is of no common nature; it *remaineth;* i.e., it shall not be expiated. As you have rejected the Lord from being your Deliverer, so the Lord has rejected you from being His people. When the Scripture speaks of sin "remaining," it is always put in opposition to

pardon; for pardon is termed the "taking away of sin," chap. i. 29; Ps. xxxii. 5.

CHAPTER 10

Christ speaks the parable of the sheepfold, 1-6. Proclaims himself the Door of the sheepfold, 7-10, and the Good Shepherd who lays down His life for the sheep, 11-18. The Jews are again divided, and some revile and some vindicate our Lord, 19-21. His discourse with the Jews at the Temple, on the Feast of Dedication, 22-29. He having asserted that He was one with the Father, the Jews attempt to stone Him, 30-31. He vindicates His conduct, and appeals to His works, 32-38. They strive to apprehend Him; He escapes, and retires beyond Jordan, 39-40. Many resort to and believe on Him there, 41-42.

1. *Verily, verily.* Our Lord introduces this discourse in a most solemn manner, *Verily, verily*—Amen, amen!—"It is true, it is true!"—a Hebraism for, This is a most important and interesting truth, a truth of the utmost concern to mankind. *He that entereth not by the door.* Christ assures us, v. 7, that he is *the door;* whoever, therefore, enters not by Jesus Christ into the pastoral office is no other than *a thief and a robber* in the sheepfold. And he enters not by Jesus Christ who enters with a prospect of any other interest besides that of Christ and His people. Ambition, avarice, love of ease, a desire to enjoy the conveniences of life, to be distinguished from the crowd, to promote the interests of one's family, and even the whole design of providing against want—these are all ways by which thieves and robbers enter into the Church. Acting through motives of self-interest and with the desire of providing for himself and his family are innocent, yea, laudable, in a secular business; but to enter into the ministerial office through motives of this kind is highly criminal before God.

2. *He that entereth in by the door.* Observe here the marks, qualities, and duties of a good pastor. The *first* mark is that he has a lawful entrance into the ministry by the internal call of Christ, namely, by an impulse proceeding from His Spirit, upon considerations which respect only His glory, and upon motives which aim at nothing but the good of His Church, the salvation of souls, the doing the will of God, and the sacrificing himself entirely to His service, and to that of the meanest of His flock.

3. *To him the porter openeth.* In the porter opening the door to the true shepherd we may discover the *second* mark of a true minister—his labor is crowned with success. The Holy Spirit opens his way into the hearts of his hearers and he becomes the instrument of their salvation. See Col. iv. 3; 2 Cor. ii. 12; 1 Cor. xvi. 9; Rev. iii. 8. *The sheep hear his voice.* A *third* mark of a good shepherd is that he speaks so as to instruct the people—*the sheep hear his voice.* A man who preaches in such a language as the people cannot comprehend may do for a stage-player or a mountebank, but not for a minister of Christ. *He calleth his own sheep by name.* A *fourth* mark of a good pastor is that he is well acquainted with his flock; he knows them by name—he takes care to acquaint himself with the spiritual states of all those that are entrusted to him. *And leadeth them out.* A *fifth* mark of a good shepherd is, he *leads* the flock, does not lord it over God's heritage, nor attempt by any rigorous discipline not founded on the gospel of Christ to drive men into the way of life; nor drive them out of it, which

many do, by a severity which is a disgrace to the mild gospel of the God of peace and love. He leads them out of themselves to Christ, *out of the follies*, diversions, and amusements of the world, into the path of Christian holiness.

4. *He goeth before them.* A *sixth* mark of a true pastor is, he gives them a good example; he not only preaches, but he lives, the truth of the gospel. He enters into the depths of the salvation of God. The minister who is in this state of salvation *the sheep*, genuine Christians, will *follow . . . for they know his voice.* It was the custom in the Eastern countries for the shepherd to go at the head of his sheep, and they followed him from pasture to pasture.

5. *And a stranger will they not follow.* That is, a man who, pretending to be a shepherd of the flock of God, is a *stranger* to that salvation which he professes to preach.

7. *I am the door of the sheep.* It is through Me only that a man can have a lawful entrance into the ministry; and it is through Me alone that mankind can be saved.

8. *All that ever came before me.* Or, as some translate, "all that came instead of Me," i.e., all that came as the Christ, or Messiah, such as Theudas, and Judas the Gaulonite, who are mentioned, Acts v. 36-37; and who were indeed no other than thieves, plundering the country wherever they came; and murderers, not only slaying the simple people who resisted them, but leading the multitudes of their followers to the slaughter. But our Lord probably refers to the scribes and Pharisees, who pretended to show the way of salvation to the people—who in fact stole into the fold, and clothed themselves with the fleece, and devoured the sheep. The thief and the robber should be properly distinguished; one takes by cunning and stealth, the other openly and by violence.

9. *I am the door: by me if any man enter.* Those who come for salvation to God, through Christ, shall obtain it. *He shall be saved*—he shall have his sins blotted out, his soul purified, and himself preserved unto eternal life. *Go in and out.* This phrase, in the style of the Hebrews, points out all the actions of a man's life and the liberty he has of acting or not acting. A good shepherd conducts his flock to the fields where good pasturage is to be found, watches over them while there, and brings them back again and secures them in the fold.

10. *But for to steal, and to kill, and to destroy.* Those who enter into the priesthood that they may enjoy the revenues of the Church are the basest and vilest of thieves and murderers. Their ungodly conduct is a snare to the simple, and the occasion of much scandal to the cause of Christ. Their doctrine is deadly; they are not commissioned by Christ, and therefore they cannot profit the people. Their character is well pointed out by the Prophet Ezekiel, chap. xxxiv. 2, etc.: "Woe be to the shepherds of Israel that do feed themselves! . . . Ye eat the fat, and ye clothe you with the wool, ye kill them that are fed: but ye feed not the flock." *That they might have life.* My doctrine tends to life, because it is the true doctrine—that of the false and bad shepherds tends to death, because it neither comes from nor can lead to that God who is the Fountain of life.

11. *I am the good shepherd.* Whose character is the very reverse of that which has already been described. In vv. 7 and 9, our Lord had called himself "the door of the sheep," as being the sole Way to glory, and Entrance into eternal life. Here He changes the thought, and calls himself the *shepherd*, because of what He was to do for them that believe in Him, in order to prepare them for eternal glory. *Giveth his life for the sheep.* That is, gives up His soul as a sacrifice to save them from eternal death.

14. *I . . . know my sheep.* I know "them that are Mine."

16. *Other sheep I have.* The Gentiles and Samaritans. As if our Lord had said, Do not imagine that I shall lay down My life for the Jews, exclusively of all other people. No, I shall die also for the Gentiles; and, though they *are not of this fold* now, those among them that believe shall be united with the believing Jews, and made one fold under one Shepherd, Eph. ii. 13-17.

17. *Therefore doth my Father love me.* As I shall be shortly crucified by you, do not imagine that I am abandoned by My Heavenly Father and therefore fall thus into your hands. The Father loveth Me particularly on this account, because I am going to *lay down my life* for the life of the world. Again, do not suppose that I shall be put to death by your rulers because I have not strength to resist them. *I lay down my life* voluntarily and cheerfully. No one can *take* it away from Me; see v. 18. And I shall give you the fullest proof of My supreme power by raising, in three days, that very crucified, wounded body from the grave.

18. *I have power.* Or "authority."

19. *There was a division.* "A schism." They were divided in their opinions; one part received the light, and the other resisted it. *Again.* There was a dissension of this kind before among the same people; see chap. ix. 16.

20. *He hath a devil, and is mad.* So, then, a demoniac and a madman were not exactly the same in the apprehension of the Jews; no more than the effect is the same with the cause which produces it. Some will have it that, when the Jews told our Lord that He had a demon, they meant no more than that He was deranged; but here these matters are evidently distinguished. They believed Him to be possessed by a demon, who deranged His faculties, and that He must have been a wicked man, and a deceiver, thus to be put under the power of such a spirit.

21. *These are not the words of him that hath a devil.* If He were deranged by an unclean spirit, His words would bear a similitude to the spirit that produced them; but these are words of deep sense, soberness, and piety. Besides, could a demoniac open the eyes of blind men? This is not the work of a demon. Now we have seen that this Man has restored a man who was born blind. Therefore it is demonstrably evident that He is neither a madman nor a demoniac.

22. *The feast of the dedication.* This was a feast instituted by Judas Maccabaeus in commemoration of his purifying the Temple after it had been defiled by Antiochus Epiphanes. This feast began on the twenty-fifth of the month, *Cisleu* (which answers to the eighteenth of our December), and continued for eight days. When

Antiochus had heard that the Jews had made great rejoicings on account of a report that had been spread of his death, he hastened out of Egypt to Jerusalem, took the city by storm, and slew of the inhabitants in three days 40,000 persons; and 40,000 more he sold for slaves to the neighboring nations. Not contented with this, he sacrificed a great sow on the altar of burnt offerings; and, broth being made by his command of some of the flesh, he sprinkled it all over the Temple, that he might defile it to the uttermost. After this, the whole of the Temple service seems to have been suspended for three years; see 1 Macc. iv. 36, etc. Judas Maccabaeus restored the Temple service and cleansed it from pollution. *It was winter.* Or, "It was stormy or rainy weather." And this is the reason, probably, why our Lord is represented as walking in "Solomon's porch," or portico, v. 23. Though it certainly was in *winter* when this feast was held, yet it does not appear that the word above refers so much to the time of the year as to the state of the weather.

23. *Solomon's porch.* By what we find in Josephus, a portico built by Solomon, on the east side of the outer court of the Temple, was left standing by Herod when he rebuilt the Temple. This portico was 400 cubits long and was left standing, probably, because of its grandeur and beauty. But when Agrippa came to Jerusalem, a few years before the destruction of the city by the Romans, and about eighty years after Herod had begun his building (till which time what Herod had begun was not completed), the Jews solicited Agrippa to repair this portico at his own expense, using for argument not only that the building was growing ruinous but that otherwise 18,000 workmen, who had all of them, until then, been employed in carrying on the works of the Temple, would be all at once deprived of a livelihood.

24. *How long dost thou make us to doubt?* Or, "How long dost Thou kill us with suspense?" The Jews asked this question through extreme perfidiousness. They wished to get Him to declare himself king of the Jews, that they might accuse him to the Roman governor; and by it they insolently insinuated that all the proofs He had hitherto given them of His divine mission were good for nothing.

25. *I told you.* That is, I told you before what I tell you now again, that "the works which I do bear testimony to Me."

27. *My sheep hear my voice;* but you will not hear. My sheep *follow me;* but you will neither follow nor acknowledge Me. Any person who reads without prejudice may easily see that our Lord does not at all insinuate that these persons could not believe because God had made it impossible to them, but simply because they did not hear and follow Christ, which the whole of our blessed Lord's discourse proves that they might have done. The sheep of Christ are not those who are included in any eternal decree, to the exclusion of others from eternal mercy; but they are those who hear, believe in, follow, and obey the Saviour of the world.

28. *They shall never perish.* Why? Because they hear My voice, and follow Me; therefore I know, I approve of and love them, and *give unto them eternal life.* They who continue to hear

Christ's voice, and to follow Him, shall never perish. They give themselves up to God—believe so on Jesus that He lives in their hearts. God hath given unto them "eternal life, and this life is in his Son. He that hath the Son hath life," 1 John v. 11-12. Now it is evident that only those who have Christ living in and governing their souls, so that they possess the mind that was in Him, are His sheep—are those that shall never perish, because they have this eternal life abiding in them. Therefore to talk of a man's being one of the elect—one that shall never perish—one who shall have eternal life—who shall never be plucked out of the hand of God, while he lives in sin, has no Christ in his heart, has either never received or fallen away from the grace of God, is as contrary to common sense as it is to the nature and testimonies of the Most High. Final perseverance implies final faithfulness—he that endures to the end shall be saved—he that is faithful unto death shall have a crown of life. And will any man attempt to say that he who does not endure to the end and is unfaithful shall ever enter into life?

30. *I and my Father are one.* If Jesus Christ were not God, could He have said these words without being guilty of blasphemy? It is worthy of remark that Christ does not say, *I and my Father,* which *my* our translation very improperly supplies, and which in this place would have conveyed a widely different meaning; for then it would imply that the human nature of Christ, of which alone, I conceive, God is ever said to be the Father in Scripture, was equal to the Most High. But He says, speaking then as God over all, "I and the Father"—the Creator of all things, the Judge of all men, the Father of the spirits of all flesh—*are one,* one in nature, one in all the attributes of Godhead, and one in all the operations of those attributes; and so it is evident the Jews understood Him.

31. *The Jews took up stones.* To stone Him as a blasphemer, Lev. xxiv. 14-16, because He said He was one with God. The Evangelist adds the word *again,* because they had attempted to do this before; see chap. viii. 59. But it seems they were prevented from doing this now by the following discourse.

32. *Many good works have I shewed you.* I have healed your sick, delivered those of you who were possessed from the power of demons; I have fed multitudes of your poor, and I have taught you in all places, at all times, without expense, with patience; and is this My reward? To "show good works or good things" is a Hebraism which signifies to do them really, to give good things liberally.

33. *But for blasphemy.* I have elsewhere shown that the original word, when applied to men, signifies "to speak injuriously" of their persons, character, connections, etc.; but when applied to God it signifies "to speak impiously," i e., contrary to His nature, perfections, the wisdom of His providence, or goodness of His works. *Thou, being a man.* That is, only a man—*makest thyself God.* When Christ said before, v. 30, "I and the Father are one," had the Jews understood Him as only saying He had a unity of sentiments with the Father, they would not have attempted to treat Him for this as a blasphemer; because in this sense Abraham, Isaac, Moses, David, and all the

prophets were one with God. But what irritated them so much was that they understood Him as speaking of a unity of nature. Therefore they say here, *Thou makest thyself God;* which word they understood, not in a figurative, metaphorical, or improper sense, but in the most literal meaning of the term.

34. *Is it not written in your law?* The words which our Lord quotes are taken from Ps. lxxxii. 6, which shows that under the word *law* our Lord comprised the Jewish sacred writings in general. *Ye are gods.* That is, "judges," who are called *elohim.* That judges are here meant appears from Ps. lxxxii. 2, etc., and also from what follows here.

35. *And the scripture cannot be broken.* "Dissolved," rendered of none effect; i.e., it cannot be gainsaid or set aside. Every man must believe this, because it is the declaration of God. If those were termed *gods* who were only earthly magistrates, fallible mortals—and that they are termed gods is evident from that Scripture which cannot be gainsaid—what greater reason then have I to say, *I am the Son of God,* and one with God, when, as Messiah, I have been "consecrated," sent into the world, to instruct and save men; and when, as God, I have wrought miracles which could be performed by no power less than that of omnipotence?

37. *If I do not the works.* I desire you to believe only on the evidence of My works; if I do not do such works as God only can perform, then believe Me not.

38. *Believe the works.* Though you do not now credit what I have said to you, yet consider My works, and then you will see that these works prove that "I am in the Father, and the Father in me"; and, consequently, that I and the Father are one.

39. *They sought again to take him.* They could not reply to His arguments but by stones. The evidence of the truth could not be resisted, and they endeavored to destroy the Person who spoke it. *But he escaped.* In such a way as we know not, for the Evangelist has not specified the manner of it.

40. *Where John at first baptized.* That is, at Bethabara; see chap. i. 28. Afterwards, John baptized at Aenon, chap. iii. 23.

42. *Many believed on him there.* The people believed on Him: (1) because of the testimony of John the Baptist, whom they knew to be a good and a wise man, and a prophet of the Lord; and (2) because of the miracles which they saw Jesus work. These fully proved that all that John had said of Him was true.

CHAPTER 11

Account of the sickness of Lazarus, 1. His sisters, Martha and Mary, send for Christ, 2. Our Lord's discourse with His disciples on this sickness and consequent death, 3–16. He arrives at Bethany four days after the burying of Lazarus, 17–18. Martha meets Christ—their conversation, 19–27. She returns and Mary goes out to meet Him, in great distress, 28–33. Christ comes to the grave—His conversation there, 34–42. He raises Lazarus from the dead, 43–46. The priests and Pharisees, hearing of this, hold a council, and plot His destruction, 47–48. The remarkable prophecy of Caiaphas, and the consequent proceedings of the Jews, 49–53. Jesus withdraws into a city called Ephraim, 54. They lay wait for Him at the Passover, 55–57.

1. *Lazarus, of Bethany.* John, who seldom relates anything but what the other Evangelists

have omitted, does not tell us what gave rise to that familiar acquaintance and friendship that subsisted between our Lord and this family. It is surprising that the other Evangelists have omitted so remarkable an account as this, in which some of the finest traits in our Lord's character are exhibited. The conjecture of Grotius has a good deal of weight. He thinks that the other three Evangelists wrote their histories during the life of Lazarus, and that they did not mention him for fear of exciting the malice of the Jews against him. And indeed we find, from chap. xii. 10, that they sought to put Lazarus to death also, that our Lord might not have one monument of His power and goodness remaining in the land. Probably both Lazarus and his sisters were dead before John wrote. *Bethany* was situated at the foot of the Mount of Olives, about two miles from Jerusalem.

2. *It was that Mary which anointed.* There is much disagreement between learned men relative to the two anointings of our Lord, and the persons who performed these acts. The various conjectures concerning these points the reader will find in the notes on Matt. xxvi. 7, etc. Some think that the anointing of which the Evangelist speaks is that mentioned in chap. xii. 1, etc., and which happened about six days before the Passover. John, therefore, is supposed to *anticipate* the account, because it served more particularly to designate the person of whom he was speaking.

3. *He whom thou lovest is sick.* Nothing could be more simple, nor more modest, than this prayer. They do not say, Come and heal him; or, Command the disease to depart even where Thou art, and it will obey Thee. They content themselves with simply stating the case and using an indirect but a most forcible argument to induce our Lord to show forth His power and goodness.

4. *This sickness is not unto death.* Not to final privation of life at this time; but a temporary death shall be now permitted, that the glory of God may appear in the miracle of his resurrection. It is very likely that this verse contains the message which Christ sent back by the person whom the afflicted sisters had sent to Him.

5. *Now Jesus loved Martha, and her sister, and Lazarus.* Therefore His staying two days longer in Bethabara was not through lack of affection for this distressed family, but merely that He might have a more favorable opportunity of proving to them how much He loved them. Christ never denies a less favor but in order to confer a greater. God's delays in answering prayers offered to Him by persons in distress are often proofs of His purpose to confer some great kindness; and they are also proofs that His wisdom finds it necessary to permit an increase of the affliction, that His goodness may be more conspicuous in its removal.

8. *The Jews of late sought to stone thee.* It was but a few weeks before that they were going to stone Him in the Temple, on the day of the Feast of the Dedication, chap. x. 31.

9. *Are there not twelve hours in the day?* Our Lord alludes to the case of a traveller who has to walk the whole day. The *day* points out

the time of life—the *night,* that of death. He has already used the same mode of speech in chap. ix. 4: "I must work the works of him that sent me, while it is day: the night cometh, when no man can work." Here He refers to what the apostles had just said—"The Jews were but just now going to stone Thee." *Are there not,* said He, *twelve hours in the day?* I have not travelled these twelve hours yet—My last hour is not yet come; and the Jews, with all their malice and hatred, shall not be able to bring it a moment sooner than God has purposed. *If any man walk in the day, he stumbleth not.* A traveller should use the day to walk in, and not the night. During the day he has the sun, the light of this world; he sees his way, and does not stumble. But if he walk in the night, he stumbleth, because there is no light "in it," v. 10; i.e., there is no sun above the horizon. The words *en auto,* v. 10, refer not to the man, but to the world, the sun, its light, not being above the horizon.

11. *Lazarus sleepeth.* It was very common among the Jews to express death by sleep; and the expressions "falling asleep," "sleeping with their fathers" were in great use among them. The Hebrews probably used this form of speech to signify their belief in the immortality of the soul and the resurrection of the body. It is certain that our Lord received no intimation of Lazarus' death from any person, and that He knew it through that power by which He knows all things.

12. *If he sleep, he shall do well.* That is, "if he sleep only." Though the word sleep frequently meant death (see Acts vii. 60; 1 Cor. xi. 30; xv. 18, 20), yet, as it was an ambiguous term, the disciples appear here to have mistaken its meaning. *If he sleep, he shall do well,* or "recover," became a proverbial form of speech among the Jews. In most diseases sleep is a very favorable prognostic.

15. *I am glad for your sakes that I was not there.* "I tell you plainly, Lazarus is dead; and I am glad I was not there—if I had been, I should have been prevailed on to heal him almost as soon as he fell sick, and I should not have had so striking an occasion to manifest the glory of God to you, and to establish you in the faith."

16. *Thomas, which is called Didymus. Thomas,* or Thaom, was his Hebrew name, and signifies a "twin." *Didymus* is a literal translation of the Hebrew word into Greek. *Let us also go, that we may die with him.* That is, "Seeing we cannot dissuade our Lord from going, and His death is likely to be the inevitable consequence, let us give Him the fullest proof we can of our love, by going and suffering death with Him." Some think Thomas spoke these words peevishly, and that they should be translated thus, "Must we also go, and expose ourselves to destruction with Him?" But I think the first sense is to be preferred. When a matter is spoken which concerns the moral character of a person and which may be understood in a good and a bad sense, that sense which is most favorable to the person should certainly be adopted.

17. *He had lain in the grave four days already.* Our Lord probably left Bethabara the day, or the day after, Lazarus died. He came to Bethany three days after; and it appears that Lazarus had been buried about four days and consequently that he had been put in the grave the day or day after he died. Though it was the Jewish custom to embalm their dead, yet we find, from v. 39, that he had not been embalmed; and God wisely ordered this, that the miracle might appear the more striking.

18. *Fifteen furlongs.* About two miles, for the Jewish miles contained about seven furlongs and a half.

19. *Many of the Jews came.* Bethany being so nigh to Jerusalem, many of the relatives and friends of the family came, according to the Jewish custom, to mourn with the afflicted sisters. Mourning, among the Jews, lasted about thirty days. The first three days were termed days of weeping; then followed seven of lamentation. During the three days the mourner did no servile work; and if anyone saluted him, he did not return the salutation. During the seven days he did no servile work, except in private—lay with his bed on the floor—did not put on his sandals—did not wash nor anoint himself—had his head covered. All the thirty days he continued unshaven, wore no white or new clothes, and did not sew up the rents which he had made in his garments.

20. *Martha . . . went and met him.* Some suppose she was the eldest of the two sisters—she seems to have had the management of the house. See Luke x. 40. *Mary sat still in the house.* It is likely that by this circumstance the Evangelist intended to convey the idea of her sorrow and distress, because anciently afflicted persons were accustomed to put themselves in this posture, as expressive of their distress, their grief having rendered them as it were immovable.

21. *If thou hadst been here, my brother had not died.* Mary said the same words to him a little after, v. 32, which proves that these sisters had not a complete knowledge of the omnipotence of Christ. They thought He could cure at hand, but not at a distance; or they thought that it was because He did not know of their brother's indisposition that He permitted him to die.

22. *I know, that even now.* She durst not ask so great a favor in direct terms; she only intimated modestly that she knew He could do it.

23. *Thy brother shall rise again.* That is, directly; for it was by raising him immediately from the dead that He intended to comfort her.

24. *I know that he shall rise again in the resurrection.* The doctrine of the resurrection of the dead was then commonly received; and though it was our Lord who fully exemplified it by His own resurrection, yet the opinion was common, not only among God's people, but among all those who believed in the God of Israel. The Jewish writings after the Captivity are full of this doctrine. See 2 Macc. vii. 9, 14, 23, 36; xii. 43; xiv. 46; Wisd. v. 1, 7, 17; vi. 6-7.

25. *I am the resurrection, and the life.* You say that your brother shall rise again in the resurrection at the last day; but by whom shall he arise if not by Me, who am the Author of the resurrection and the Source of life? And is it not as easy for Me to raise him now as to raise him then? *Though he were dead.* Every man who has believed or shall believe in Me,

though his believing shall not prevent him from dying a natural death, yet his body shall be reanimated, and he shall live with Me in an eternal glory. And everyone who is now dead, dead to God, dead in trespasses and sins, if he believe in Me, trust on Me as his sole Saviour, he shall *live*, shall be quickened by My Spirit, and live a life of faith, working by love.

26. *Shall never die*. Or "shall not die forever." Though he die a temporal death, he shall not continue under its power forever, but shall have a resurrection to life eternal. *Believest thou this?* God has determined to work in the behalf of men only in proportion to their faith in Him. It was necessary, therefore, that these persons should be well instructed concerning His nature, that they might find no obstacles to their faith.

27. *Yea, Lord: I believe.* "I have believed." Either meaning that she had believed this for some time past or that, since He began to teach her, her faith had been considerably increased. Martha here acknowledges Christ for the Messiah promised to their fathers; but her faith goes no further; and, having received some hope of her brother's present resurrection, she waited for no further instruction, but ran to call her sister.

28. *The Master is come.* This was the appellation which He had to the family; and from these words it appears that Christ had inquired for Mary, desiring to have her present, that He might strengthen her faith, previously to His raising her brother.

30. *Jesus was not yet come into the town.* As the Jewish burying places were without their cities and villages, it appears that the place where our Saviour was, when Martha met Him, was not far from the place where Lazarus was buried.

31. *She goeth unto the grave to weep there.* It appears that it was the custom for the nearest relatives of the deceased to go at times during the three days of weeping, accompanied by their friends and neighbors, to mourn near the graves of the deceased. They supposed that for three days the spirit hovered about the place where the body was laid, to see whether it might be again permitted to enter; but when it saw the face change, it knew that all hope was now past. It was on this ground that the seven days of lamentation succeeded the three days of weeping, because all hope was now taken away.

33. *He groaned in the spirit.* Here the blessed Jesus shows himself to be truly man; and a Man, too, who, notwithstanding His amazing dignity and excellence, did not feel it beneath Him to sympathize with the distressed, and weep with those who wept. After this example of our Lord, shall we say that it is weakness, folly, and sin to weep for the loss of relatives?

35. *Jesus wept.* The least verse in the Bible, yet inferior to none.

37. *Could not this man, which opened the eyes?* Through the maliciousness of their hearts these Jews considered the tears of Jesus as a proof of His weakness.

38. *It was a cave.* It is likely that several of the Jewish burying places were made in the sides of rocks.

39. *Take ye away the stone.* He desired to convince all those who were at the place, and especially those who took away the stone, that Lazarus was not only dead, but that putrescency had already taken place, that it might not afterwards be said that Lazarus had only fallen into a lethargy, but that the greatness of the miracle might be fully evinced. *He stinketh.* The body is in a state of putrefaction. The Greek word signifies simply "to smell," whether the scent be good or bad; but the circumstances of the case sufficiently show that the latter is its meaning here. *For he hath been dead four days.* "This is the fourth day," i.e., since his interment. Christ himself was buried on the same day on which He was crucified, see chap. xix. 42, and it is likely that Lazarus was buried also on the same day on which he died.

40. *If thou wouldest believe.* So it appears that it is faith alone that interests the miraculous and saving power of God in behalf of men.

41. *Where the dead was laid.* These words are wanting in some MSS. *Father, I thank thee.* As it was a common opinion that great miracles might be wrought by the power and in the name of the devil, Jesus lifted up His eyes to heaven, and invoked the supreme God before these unbelieving Jews, that they might see that it was by His power, and by His only, that this miracle was done.

43. *He cried with a loud voice.* In chap. v. 25, our Lord had said that the time was coming in which the dead should hear the voice of the Son of God and live. He now fulfills that prediction and cries aloud, that the people may take notice, and see that even death is subject to the sovereign command of Christ.

44. *Bound hand and foot with graveclothes.* "Swathed about with rollers." These were long slips of linen a few inches in breadth with which the body and limbs of the dead were swathed, and especially those who were embalmed, that the aromatics might be kept in contact with the flesh. But as it is evident that Lazarus had not been embalmed, it is probable that his limbs were not swathed together, as is the constant case with those who are embalmed, but separately, so that he could come out of the tomb at the command of Christ, though he could not walk freely till the rollers were taken away. *Loose him, and let him go.* He would have the disciples and those who were at hand take part in this business, that the fullest conviction might rest on every person's mind concerning the reality of what was wrought. He whom the grace of Christ converts and restores to life comes forth at His call from the dark, dismal grave of sin, in which his soul has long been buried. He walks, according to the command of Christ, in newness of life; and gives, by the holiness of his conduct, the fullest proof to all his acquaintance that he is alive from the dead.

45. *Many of the Jews . . . believed on him.* They saw that the miracle was incontestable, and they were determined to resist the truth no longer. Their friendly visit to these distressed sisters became the means of their conversion.

47. *Then gathered the chief priests and the Pharisees a council.* The Pharisees, as such, had no power to assemble councils; and therefore only those are meant who were scribes or elders of the people, in conjunction with Annas and his son-in-law, Caiaphas, who were the

high priests here mentioned. See chap. xviii. 13, 24. *What do we?* This last miracle was so clear, plain, and incontestable that they were driven now to their wits' end. Their own spies had come and borne testimony of it.

48. *All men will believe on him.* If we permit Him to work but a few more miracles like these last two (the cure of the blind man and the resurrection of Lazarus), He will be universally acknowledged for the Messiah; the people will proclaim Him king; and the Romans, who can suffer no government here but their own, will be so irritated that they will send their armies against us and destroy our Temple and utterly dissolve our civil and ecclesiastical existence. *Both our place and nation.* Literally, "this place," but that the Temple only is understood is clear from Acts vi. 13-14; 2 Macc. i. 14; ii. 18; iii. 18; v. 16-17; x. 7; where it is uniformly called "the place," or "the holy place," because they considered it the most glorious and excellent place in the world. When men act in opposition to God's counsel, the very evils which they expect thereby to avoid will come upon them. They said, If we do not put Jesus to death, the Romans will destroy both our Temple and nation. Now it was because they put Him to death that the Romans burned and razed their Temple to the ground and put a final period to their political existence. See Matt. xxii. 7 and the notes on chap. xxiv.

49. *Caiaphas being the high priest that same year.* By the law of Moses, Exod. xl. 15, the office of high priest was for life, and the son of Aaron's race always succeeded his father. But at this time the high priesthood was almost annual. The Romans and Herod put down and raised up whom they pleased, and when they pleased, without attending to any other rule than merely that the person put in this office should be of the sacerdotal race. According to Josephus, *Ant.* xviii, c. 3, the proper name of this person was Joseph, and Caiaphas was his surname. He possessed the high priesthood for eight or nine years and was deposed by Vitellius, governor of Judea. *Ye know nothing.* Of the perilous state in which you stand.

50. *Nor consider.* Instead of ye do not *consider,* which properly conveys the idea of "conferring" or "talking together," *neither do ye reason* or *consider rightly* is the reading of several MSS. and some of the primitive fathers. *That one man should die for the people.* In saying these remarkable words Caiaphas had no other intention than merely to state that it was better to put Jesus to death than to expose the whole nation to ruin on His account. His maxim was, It is better to sacrifice one man than a whole nation.

51. *This spake he not of himself.* Wicked and worthless as he was, God so guided his tongue that, contrary to his intention, he pronounced a prophecy of the death of Jesus Christ. I have already remarked that the doctrine of a vicarious atonement had gained, long before this time, universal credit in the world. Words similar to these of Caiaphas are, by the prince of all the Roman poets, put in the mouth of Neptune, when promising Venus that the fleet of Aeneas should be preserved, and his whole crew should be saved, one only excepted, whose death he speaks of in these remarkable words: "One life shall fall, that many may be saved."

This victim the poet informs us was Palinurus, the pilot of Aeneas' own ship, who was precipitated into the deep by a divine influence.

52. *And not for that nation only.* These, and the preceding words in v. 51, are John's explication of what was prophetic in the words of Caiaphas; as if John had said, He is indeed to die for the sins of the Jewish nation, but not for theirs alone, but for the sins of the whole world. See His own words afterwards, 1 John ii. 1-2. *Gather together in one.* That He should "collect into one body"; form one Church out of the Jewish and Gentile believers. *Children of God that were scattered abroad.* Probably John meant only the Jews who were dispersed among all nations since the conquest of Judea by the Romans (these are called "the dispersed," chap. vii. 35, and Jas. i. 1); and it is because he refers to these only that he terms them here *the children of God,* which was an ancient character of the Jewish people; see Deut. xxxii. 5; Isa. xliii. 6; xlv. 11; Jer. xxxii. 1. Taking his words in this sense, then his meaning is this: that Christ was to die, not only for the then inhabitants of Judea, but for all the Jewish race wheresoever scattered; and that the consequence would be that they should be all collected from their various dispersions and made one body. This comports with the predictions of Paul, Rom. xi. 1-32.

53. *They took counsel together.* They were of one accord in the business, and had fully made up their minds on the subject; they waited only for a proper opportunity to put Him to death.

54. *Walked no more openly.* He did not go as before through the cities and villages, teaching, preaching, and healing the sick. *A city called Ephraim.* Variously written in the MSS., Ephraim, Ephrem, Ephram, and Ephratha. This was a little village situated in the neighborhood of Bethel; for the scripture (2 Chron. xiii. 19) and Josephus join them both together. Eusebius and Jerome say it was about twenty miles north of Jerusalem.

55. *The Jews' passover was nigh at hand.* It is not necessary to suppose that this verse has any particular connection with the preceding. Most chronologists agree that our Lord spent at least two months in Ephraim. This was the last Passover which our Lord attended, and it was at this one that He suffered death for the salvation of a lost world. As the Passover was nigh, many of the inhabitants of Ephraim and its neighborhood went up to Jerusalem, some time (perhaps seven or eight days, for so much time was required to purify those who had touched the dead) before the feast, that they might purify themselves, and not eat the Passover otherwise than prescribed in the law. Many of the country people, in the time of Hezekiah, committed a trespass by not attending to this; see 2 Chron. xxx. 18-19. Those mentioned in the text wished to avoid this inconvenience.

56. *Then sought they for Jesus.* Probably those of Ephraim, in whose company Christ is supposed to have departed for the feast, but, having stayed behind, perhaps at Jericho, or its vicinity, the others had not missed Him till they came to the Temple, and then inquired among each other whether He would not attend the feast. Or the persons mentioned in the text

might have been the agents of the high priest, and hearing that Christ had been at Ephraim, came and inquired among the people that came from that quarter whether Jesus would not attend the festival, knowing that He was punctual in His attendance on all the Jewish solemnities.

57. *Had given a commandment.* Had given order; "positive order," or "injunction," and perhaps with a grievous penalty, that no one should keep the place of His residence a secret. This was their hour, and the power of darkness; and now they were fully determined to take away His life. The order here spoken of was given in consequence of the determination of the council, mentioned in vv. 48-53.

CHAPTER 12

Jesus sups in the house of Lazarus, and Mary anoints His feet, 1-3. Judas Iscariot finds fault, and reproves her, 4-6. Jesus vindicates Mary and reproves Judas, 7-8. The chief priests consult to put Lazarus to death, because that through him many believed on Jesus, 9-11. He enters Jerusalem in triumph; the people meet Him, and the Pharisees are troubled, 12-19. Greeks inquire after Jesus, 20-22. Our Lord's discourse on the subject, 23-26. Speaks of His passion, and is answered by a voice from heaven, 27-28. The people are astonished at the voice, and Jesus explains it to them, and foretells His death, 29-33. They question Him concerning the perpetuity of the Messiah, and He instructs them, 34-36. Many believe and in them the saying of Isaiah is fulfilled, 37-41. Some of the chief rulers believe, but are afraid to confess Him, 42-43. He proclaims himself the Light of the world, and shows the danger of rejecting His words, 44-50.

1. *Six days before the passover.* Reckoning the day of the Passover to be the last of the six.

5. *Three hundred pence.* Or denarii.

6. *Not that he cared for the poor.* There should be a particular emphasis laid on the word *he*, as the Evangelist studies to show the most determined detestation to his conduct. *And bare what was put therein.* Or rather, as some eminent critics contend, "and stole what was put in it." This seems the proper meaning of *ebastazen;* and in this sense it is used, chap. xx. 15: "If thou hast stolen Him away." In the same sense the word is used by Josephus, *Ant.,* b. xii, c. 5, s. 4, where, speaking of the pillage of the Temple by Antiochus, he says, "He carried off, or stole, also the vessels of the Lord." If stealing were not intended by the Evangelist, the word itself must be considered as superfluous; for when we are told that he had the *bag,* we need not be informed that he had what was *in* it. But the apostle says *he was a thief,* and because he was a thief and had the common purse in his power, therefore he stole as much as he conveniently could without subjecting himself to detection. And as he saw that the death of Christ was at hand, he wished to secure a provision for himself before he left the company of the apostles. The *bag* meant originally the little box, or sheath, in which the tongues or reeds used for pipes were carried. The Greek word is used in Hebrew letters by the Talmudists to signify a "purse, scrip, chest, coffer." As our Lord and His disciples lived on charity, a bag or scrip was provided to carry those pious donations by which they were supported. And Judas was steward and treasurer to this holy company.

7. *Let her alone: against the day of my burying hath she kept this.* Several MSS. and versions read thus: "Let her alone, that she may keep it to the day of my embalming." This reading, which has the approbation of Mill, Bengel, Griesbach, Pearce, and others, intimates that only a part of the ointment was then used, and that the rest was kept till the time that the women came to embalm the body of Jesus, Luke xxiv. 1.

9. *Much people of the Jews.* John, who was a Galilean, often gives the title of *Jews* to those who were inhabitants of Jerusalem.

10. *Consulted that they might put Lazarus also to death.* As long as he lived they saw an incontestable proof of the divine power of Christ; therefore they wished to put Him to death, because many of the Jews, who came to see him through curiosity, became converts to Christ through his testimony.

13. *Took branches.* See on Matt. xxi. 1, etc., and Mark xi. 1-6, where this transaction is largely explained.

16. *Then remembered they.* After the ascension of Christ, the disciples saw the meaning of many prophecies which referred to Christ, and applied them to Him, which they had not fully comprehended before. Indeed it is only in the light of the new covenant that the old is to be fully understood.

17. *When he called.* It appears that these people who had seen Him raise Lazarus from the dead were publishing abroad the miracle, which increased the popularity of Christ and the envy of the Pharisees.

19. *Ye prevail nothing.* By either your threatenings or excommunications. *The world is gone after him.* The whole mass of the people are becoming His disciples. This is a very common form of expression among the Jews, and simply answers to the French, *tout le monde,* and to the English, "everybody"—the bulk of the people.

20. *Certain Greeks.* There are three opinions concerning these: (1) That they were proselytes of the gate or covenant, who came up to worship the true God at this feast; (2) That they were real Jews, who lived in Grecian provinces, and spoke the Greek language; (3) That they were mere Gentiles, who never knew the true God; and, hearing of the fame of the Temple or the miracles of our Lord, came to offer sacrifices to Jehovah and to worship Him according to the manner of the people of that land. Of these opinions the reader may choose, but the first seems best founded.

22. *Andrew and Philip tell Jesus.* How pleasing to God is this union when the ministers of His gospel agree and unite together to bring souls to Christ!

23. *The hour is come, that the Son of man.* The time is just at hand in which the gospel shall be preached to all nations, the middle wall of partition broken down, and Jews and Gentiles united in one fold. But this could not be till after His death and resurrection, as the succeeding verse teaches.

24. *Except a corn of wheat fall into the ground and die.* Our Lord compares himself to a grain of wheat; His death, to a grain sown and decomposed in the ground; His resurrection, to the blade which springs up from the dead grain, which grain, thus dying, brings forth

an abundance of fruit. I must die to be glorified; and, unless I am glorified, I cannot establish a glorious Church of Jews and Gentiles upon earth.

25. *He that loveth his life.* See on Matt. x. 39; Luke xiv. 26. I am about to give up My life for the salvation of men; but I shall speedily receive it back with everlasting honor, by My resurrection from the dead. In this I should be imitated by My disciples, who should, when called to it, lay down their lives for the truth; and if they do, they shall receive them again with everlasting honor.

26. *If any man serve me.* To such a person a twofold promise is given: (1) He shall be with Christ, in eternal fellowship with Him; and (2) He shall be honored by the Lord; he shall have an abundant recompense in glory.

27. *Now is my soul troubled.* Our blessed Lord took upon Him our weaknesses, that He might sanctify them to us. As a man He was *troubled* at the prospect of a violent death. Nature abhors death. God has implanted that abhorrence in nature, that it might become a principle of self-preservation; and it is to this that we owe all that prudence and caution by which we avoid danger. When we see Jesus working miracles which demonstrate His omnipotence, we should be led to conclude that He was not man were it not for such passages as these. The reader must ever remember that it was essentially necessary that He should be man, for without being such He could not have died for the sin of the world. *And what shall I say? Father, save me from this hour.* Which may be paraphrased thus: "And why should I say, Father, save Me from this hour, when for this cause I am come to this hour?" The common version makes our blessed Lord contradict himself here, by not attending to the proper punctuation of the passage, and by translating the particle *ti* as *what*, instead of *why* or *how*.

28. *Father, glorify thy name.* By the *name* of God is to be understood himself, in all His attributes: His wisdom, truth, mercy, justice, holiness, which were all more abundantly glorified by Christ's death and resurrection (i.e., shown forth in their own excellence) than they had ever been before. Christ teaches here a lesson of submission to the divine will.

29. *The people . . . said that it thundered: others said, An angel spake to him.* Bishop Pearce says, Probably there was thunder as well as a voice, as in Exod. xix. 16-17, and some persons, who were at a small distance, might hear the thunder without hearing the voice, while others heard the voice too; and these last said, "An angel hath spoken to Him."

30. *This voice came not because of me, but for your sakes.* Probably meaning those Greeks who had been brought to Him by Philip and Andrew. The Jews had frequent opportunities of seeing His miracles and of being convinced that He was the Messiah; but these Greeks, who were to be a firstfruits of the Gentiles, had never any such opportunity. For their sakes, therefore, to confirm them in the faith, this miraculous voice appears to have come from heaven.

31. *Now is the judgment of this world.* The judgment spoken of in this place is applied by some to the punishment which was about to

fall on the Jewish people for rejecting Christ. And the ruler or *prince of this world* is understood to be Satan, who had blinded the eyes of the Jews and hardened their hearts, that they might not believe on the Son of God. But his kingdom, not only among the Jews, but in all the world, was about to be destroyed by the abolition of idolatry and the vocation of the Gentiles.

32. *I . . . will draw all men unto me.* After I shall have died and risen again, by the preaching of My Word and the influence of My Spirit, I shall attract and illuminate both Jews and Gentiles. It was one of the peculiar characteristics of the Messiah that unto Him should the "gathering of the people be," Gen. xlix. 10. And probably our Lord refers to the prophecy, Isa. xi. 10, which peculiarly belonged to the Gentiles: "There shall be a root of Jesse, which shall stand for an ensign of the people; to it shall the Gentiles seek: and his rest shall be glorious." There is an allusion here to the ensigns or colors of commanders of regiments, elevated on high places on long poles, that the people might see where the pavilion of their general was and so flock to his standard.

34. *We have heard out of the law.* That is, out of the sacred writings. The words here are quoted from Ps. cx. 4; but the Jews called every part of the sacred writings by the name *The Law*, in opposition to the words or sayings of the scribes. *That Christ abideth for ever.* There is no part of the law nor of the Scripture that said the Messiah should not die; but there are several passages that say as expressly as they can that Christ must die, and die for the sin of the world, too. See especially Isa. liii. 1, etc.; Dan. ix. 24, 27. But as there were several passages that spoke of the perpetuity of His reign, as Isa. ix. 7; Ezek. xxxvii. 25; Dan. vii. 14, they probably confounded the one with the other, and thus drew the conclusion, The Messiah cannot die; for the Scripture hath said, His throne, kingdom, and reign shall be eternal. The prophets, as well as the Evangelists and apostles, speak sometimes of the *divine*, sometimes of the *human* nature of Christ. When they speak of the former, they show forth its glory, excellence, omnipotence, omniscience, and eternity; when they speak of the latter, they show forth its humiliations, afflictions, sufferings, and death. And those who do not make the proper distinction between the two natures of Christ, the human and the divine, will ever make blunders as well as the Jews.

35. *Yet a little while is the light with you.* In answer to their objection, our Lord compares himself to a light which was about to disappear for a short time and afterwards to shine forth with more abundant luster; but not to their comfort, if they continued to reject its present beamings. He exhorts them to follow this light while it is among them. The Christ shall abide forever, it is true; but He will not always be visible. When He shall depart from you, you shall be left in the thickest darkness, in impenitence and hardness of heart. Then shall you wish to see one of the days of the Son of Man, and shall not see it, Luke xvii. 22. Then shall ye seek Me, but shall not find Me, John vii. 34. For the kingdom of God shall be taken from you, and given to the Gentiles, Matt. xxi. 43. If you do not believe in Me now, **you shall**

then wish you had done it, when wishing shall be forever fruitless. Instead of *with you,* "among you" is the reading of some MSS.

36. *Children of light.* Let the light, the truth of Christ, so dwell in and work by you that you may be all light in the Lord; that as truly as a child is the produce of his own parent and partakes of his nature, so you may be children of the light, having nothing in you but truth and righteousness. *Did hide himself from them.* Either by rendering himself invisible or by suddenly mingling with the crowd, so that they could not perceive Him. See chap. viii. 59. Probably it means no more than that He withdrew from them and went to Bethany, as was His custom, a little before His crucifixion; and concealed himself there during the night, and taught publicly every day in the Temple. It was in the night season that they endeavored to seize upon Him, in the absence of the multitude.

37. *Yet they believed not on him.* Though the miracles were wrought for this very purpose, that they might believe in Christ, and escape the coming wrath, and every evidence was given that Jesus was the Messiah, yet they did not believe; but they were blinded by their passions, and obstinately hardened their hearts against the truth.

38. *That the saying of Esaias.* Or, "Thus the word of Isaiah was fulfilled." *Our report.* The testimony of the prophets concerning the person, office, sufferings, death, and sacrifice of the Messiah. See Isa. liii. 1, etc. *The arm of the Lord.* The power, strength, and miracles of Christ.

39. *Therefore they could not believe.* Why? Because they did not believe the report of the prophets concerning Christ; therefore they credited not the miracles which He wrought as a proof that He was the Person foretold by the prophets, and promised to their fathers. The prophecy of Isaiah was neither the cause nor the motive of their unbelief; it was a simple prediction, which imposed no necessity on them to resist the offers of mercy. Thus then saith Augustine: "If I be asked why they could not believe? I immediately answer, Because they would not. And God, having foreseen their bad will, foretold it by the prophet."

40. *And I should heal them.* This verse is taken from Isa. vi. 9, and perhaps refers more to the judgments that should fall upon them as a nation, which God was determined should not be averted, than it does to their eternal state. To suppose that the text meant that God was unwilling that they should turn unto Him, lest He should be obliged to save them, is an insupportable blasphemy.

41. *When he saw his glory.* Isa. vi. 1, etc. "I saw also the Lord [Jehovah] sitting upon a throne, high and lifted up, and his train filled the temple. Above it stood the seraphims . . . And one cried unto another, and said, Holy, holy, holy, is the Lord of hosts: the whole earth is full of his glory."

42. *Among the chief rulers also many believed on him.* We know the names of only two of them, Nicodemus and Joseph of Arimathaea. *But . . . they did not confess him.* Or "it." They were as yet weak in the faith, and could not bear the reproach of the cross of Christ. Besides, the principal rulers had determined to excommunicate every person who acknowledged Christ for the Messiah; see chap. ix. 22.

43. *They loved the praise of men.* The "glory" or honor that cometh from men.

44. *Jesus cried and said.* This is our Lord's concluding discourse to this wicked people. Probably this and the following verses should be understood as a part of the discourse which was left off at the thirty-sixth verse. *Jesus cried*—He spoke these words aloud, and showed His earnest desire for their salvation. *Believeth not on me* (only), *but on him that sent me.* Here He asserts again His indivisible unity with the Father. He who believes on the Son believes on the Father; he who hath seen the Son hath seen the Father; he who honors the Son honors the Father. Though it was for asserting this (His oneness with God) that they were going to crucify Him, yet He retracts nothing of what He had spoken, but strongly reasserts it in the very jaws of death!

46. *I am come a light into the world.* Probably referring to what His forerunner had said, chap. i. 5. Before the coming of this Saviour, this Sun of Righteousness, into the world, all was darkness. At His rising the darkness is dispersed; but it profits only those whose eyes are open to receive the rays of this Sun of Righteousness.

47. *And believe not.* "And keep them not," is the reading of some MSS. A man must *hear* the words of Christ in order to *believe* them; and he must *believe* in order to keep them; and he must keep them in order to his salvation. *I judge him not.* I need not to do it; the words of Moses and the prophets judge and condemn him.

48. *The word that I have spoken, the same shall judge him.* You shall be judged according to My doctrine. The maxims which you have heard from My mouth shall be those on which you shall be tried in the great day; and you shall be condemned or acquitted according as you have believed or obeyed them, or according as you have despised and violated them. See this proved, Matt. xxv. 35, etc.

49. *Gave me a commandment.* Or "commission." Christ, as the Messiah, received His "commission" from God: what He should command—everything that related to the foundation and establishment of the Christian institution; and what He should speak—all His private conversations with His disciples or others, He, as man, commanded and spoke through the constant inspiration of the Holy Spirit.

50. *I know that his commandment is life everlasting.* These words of our Lord are similar to that saying in John's First Epistle, chap. v. 11-12. "This is the record, that God hath given to us eternal life, and this life is in his Son. He that hath the Son hath life." God's *commandment* or "commission" is, Preach salvation to a lost world, and give thyself a Ransom for all; and whoever believes on Thee shall not perish, but have everlasting life. The public work of our Lord was now done; and the remnant of His time, previously to His crucifixion, He spent in teaching His disciples—instructing them in the nature of His kingdom, His intercession, and the mission of the Holy Spirit; and in that heavenly life which all true believers live with the Father, through faith in the Son, by the operation of the Holy Ghost.

CHAPTER 13

Christ washes the feet of His disciples, and gives them instructions concerning humility and charity, 1-17. He tells them that one of themselves will betray Him, 18-20. The disciples doubting of whom He spoke, Peter desires John to ask Him, 21-25. Jesus shows that it is Judas Iscariot, 26. Satan enters into Judas, and he rises up and leaves the company, 27-30. Christ shows His approaching death, and commands His disciples to love one another, 31-35. Peter, professing strong attachment to Christ, is informed of His denial, 36-38.

1. *Now before the feast of the passover, when Jesus knew.* Or, as some translate, "Now Jesus having known, before the feast of the passover, that his hour was come." The supper mentioned in v. 2 is supposed to have been that on the Thursday evening, when the Feast of the Passover began; and though, in our common translation, this passage seems to place the supper *before* that feast, yet, according to the amended translation, what is here said is consistent with what we read in the other Evangelists. *Having loved his own.* His disciples. *Which were in the world.* Who were to continue longer in its troubles and difficulties. *He loved them unto the end.* Continued His fervent affection towards them to His latest breath, and gave them that convincing proof of it which is mentioned in v. 5. That the disciples alone are meant here every man must see.

2. *And supper being ended.* Rather, "while supper was preparing." To support this new translation of the words, it may be remarked that, from vv. 26 and 30, it appears that the supper was not then *ended.* Nay, it is probable that it was not then begun; because the washing of feet (v. 5) was usually practiced by the Jews before they entered upon their meals, as may be gathered from Luke vii. 44, and from the reason of the custom. I think that John wrote, not *genomenou,* but *ginomenou,* as in some MSS., which latter reading is approved by several eminent critics, and should be translated as above. By the *supper* I suppose to be meant, not only the eating of it, but the preparing and dressing of it, and doing all things necessary previously to the eating of it. The devil had, before this time of the supper, put it into Judas' heart to betray his Master. See Matt. xxvi. 14, etc.; Mark xiv. 10-11; and Luke xxii. 3, etc. Calmet observes that John, designing only to supply what was omitted by the other Evangelists, passes over all the transactions of the Tuesday, Wednesday, and Thursday before the Passion, and at once goes from Monday evening to Thursday evening. It is remarkable that John says nothing about the institution of the Holy Sacrament, which Matthew (xxvi. 26, etc.), Mark (xiv. 22, etc.), and Luke (xxii. 19, etc.) describe so particularly. No other reason can be assigned for this than that he found it completely done by the others, and that he designed only to supply their defects. *The devil having now put into the heart.* Judas formed his plot six days before this, on occasion of what happened at the house of Simon the leper.

3. *Knowing that the Father had given.* Our Lord, seeing himself almost at the end of His race, and being about to leave His apostles, thought it necessary to leave them a lesson of humility exemplified by himself, to deliver them from the bad influence of those false ideas which they formed concerning the nature of His kingdom.

4. *He riseth from supper.* Not from eating, as Bishop Pearce has well observed, but from His place at table; probably the dishes were not as yet laid down, though the guests were seated. According to the custom of the Jews and other Asiatics, this washing must have taken place before the supper. *Laid aside his garments.* That is, His gown or upper coat, with the girdle wherewith it was girded close to his tunic or undercoat; and, instead of this girdle, He tied a *towel* about Him: (1) that He might appear in the character of a servant; and (2) that He might have it in readiness to dry their feet after He had washed them.

5. *Poureth water into a bason.* This was the office of the meanest slaves. When David sent to Abigail, to inform her that he had chosen her for wife, she arose and said: "Behold, let thine handmaid be a servant to wash the feet of the servants of my lord," 1 Sam. xxv. 41. Some of the ancients have supposed that our Lord began with washing the feet of Judas, to inspire him with sentiments of compunction and remorse, to melt him down with kindness, and to show all His disciples how they should act towards their enemies.

6. *Lord, dost thou wash my feet?* Every word here is exceedingly emphatic. Peter had often seen the great humility of his Lord, but never saw His condescension so particularly marked as in this instance.

7. *What I do thou knowest not now.* As if our Lord had said, Permit Me to do it now, and I will shortly explain to you the nature of this action, and My motives for doing it. *Thou shalt know hereafter.* After this business is finished. And so we find He explained the whole to them as soon as He had finished the washing; see vv. 12-17.

10. *He that is washed.* That is, he who has been in the bath, as probably all the apostles had lately been, in order to prepare themselves the better for the paschal solemnity; for on that occasion it was the custom of the Jews to bathe twice. *Needeth not save to wash his feet.* To cleanse them from any dirt or dust that might have adhered to them, in consequence of walking from the bath to the place of supper. The washing, therefore, of the *feet* of such persons was all that was necessary, previously to their sitting down to table. *Ye are clean, but not all.* Eleven of you are upright and sincere; the twelfth is a traitor. So it appears He had washed the feet of all the twelve; but as no external ablutions can purify a hypocrite or a traitor, therefore Judas still remained unclean.

12. *Know ye what I have done?* Our Lord had told Peter, in the presence of the rest, v. 7, that he should afterwards know what was the intent and meaning of this washing; and now He begins to fulfill His promise. Therefore I think it more likely that He gives a *command,* here, than asks a *question,* as He knew himself that they did not comprehend His design. On this account *ginoskete* might be translated in the imperative mood, "Consider what I have done."

13. *Ye call me Master and Lord.* Similar to *Rabbi,* and *Mar,* titles very common among the Jewish doctors. This double title was not given except to the most accredited teachers.

14. *Ye also ought to wash one another's feet.* That is, you should be ready, after My example,

to condescend to all the weakness of your brethren, to be willing to do the meanest offices for them, and to prefer the least of them in honor to yourselves.

16. *The servant is not greater than his lord.* Christ has ennobled the acts of humility by practicing them himself. The true glory of a Christian consists in being, in his measure, as humble as his Lord. *Neither he that is sent.* "Nor an apostle." As I think these words were intended for the suppression of all worldly ambition and lordly conduct in the apostles and their successors in the ministry, therefore I think the original word *apostolos* should be translated "apostle," rather than *he that is sent,* because the former rendering ascertains and determines the meaning better.

17. *If ye know these things, happy.* True happiness consists in the knowledge of God, and in obedience to Him. A man is not happy because he knows much; but because he receives much of the divine nature and is, in all his conduct, conformed to the divine will.

18. *I speak not of you all.* This is a continuation of that discourse which was left off at the tenth verse. The preceding verses may be read in a parenthesis. *I know whom I have chosen.* I am not deceived in My choice; I perfectly foresaw everything that has happened, or can happen. I have chosen Judas, not as a wicked man, nor that he should become such; but I plainly foresaw that he would abuse My bounty, give way to iniquity, deliver Me into the hands of My enemies, and bring ruin upon himself. *That the scripture may be fulfilled.* Or, "Thus the scripture is fulfilled." Christ applies to Judas what David had said of his rebellious son Absalom, Ps. xli. 9, who was one of the most express emblems of this traitor. *He that eateth bread with me.* That is, he who was in habits of the utmost intimacy with Me. *Hath lifted up his heel.* An illusion to a restive, ill-natured horse, that sometimes kicks even the person who feeds and takes care of him.

19. *That . . . ye may believe.* These frequent predictions of His death, so circumstantial in themselves, had the most direct tendency to confirm the disciples, not only in the belief of His being the Messiah, but also in that of His omniscience.

20. *He that receiveth whomsoever I send.* See similar words, Matt. x. 40. Our Lord spoke this to comfort His disciples. He showed them that, although they should be rejected by many, they would be received by several; and that whoever received them should reap the utmost benefit by it.

21. *Was troubled in spirit.* See the note on chap. xi. 33. *And testified.* Spoke with great earnestness. *Shall betray me.* "Will deliver Me up." Judas had already betrayed our blessed Lord, and he was now on the point of delivering Him up into the hands of the chief priests. By all these warnings, did not our Lord intend that Judas should be benefited—that he should repent of his iniquity, and turn and find mercy?

22. *Looked one on another, doubting of whom he spake.* See the notes on Matt. xxvi. 20-25. Everyone but Judas, conscious of his own innocence, looked about upon all the rest, wondering who in that company could be such a traitor. Even Judas himself is not suspected. Is not this a proof that his general conduct had been such as to subject him to no suspicion?

23. *Now there was leaning on Jesus' bosom.* The Jews of those days at their suppers reclined, supported by their left arms, on couches placed round the table, as the Greeks and Romans did. On each couch there were two or three persons; and the head of one of them came near to the bosom of him who reclined above him on the same couch. The person here mentioned was John, the writer of this history, who, being more tenderly loved by Christ than the rest, had always that place at table which was nearest to his Lord.

25. *He then lying on Jesus' breast.* Laying his head against the breast of Christ, in a loving, respectful manner. As the expressions in the text are different here from those in the preceding verse, it shows that John altered his position at table, in order to ask the question which Peter suggested, which he probably did by whispering to our Lord. For from v. 28 we may learn that the other disciples had not heard what John said; and it is likely that the following words—"It is he to whom I shall give the morsel when I have dipped it," were whispered back by Christ to John.

26. *And when he had dipped the sop.* Dr. Lightfoot observes that it was no unusual thing to dip a sop and give it to any person; and it is probable that the rest of the disciples considered it as given to Judas that he might hurry to do some work on which He wished to employ him, and not wait to finish his supper in a regular manner.

27. *Satan entered into him.* He had entered into him before, and now he enters again, to strengthen him in his purpose of delivering up his Master. But the morsel was not the cause of this entering in; the giving of it only marks the time in which the devil confirmed Judas in his traitorous purpose. Some have thought that this morsel was the sacrament of the Lord's Supper, but this is an utter mistake. *That thou doest, do quickly.* As if He had said: "You are past all counsel; you have filled up the measure of your iniquity, and have wholly abandoned yourself to Satan. What you are determined to do, and I to permit, do directly; delay not. I am ready."

29. *Give something to the poor.* It is well-known that our Lord and His disciples lived on public charity, and yet they gave alms out of what they had thus received. From this we learn that even those who live on charity themselves are expected to divide a little with those who are in deeper distress and want.

31. *Now is the Son of man glorified.* "Hath been glorified." Now it fully appears that I am the Person appointed to redeem a lost world by My blood. I have already been glorified by this appointment, and am about to be further glorified by My death, resurrection, and ascension.

32. *And shall straightway glorify him.* Or "glorify Him immediately"; as He did, not only in the miracles wrought at His death, but also in that remarkable case mentioned, chap. xviii. 6, when the whole crowd that came to seize Him were driven back with a word of His mouth, and fell to the ground.

33. *Little children.* Or, rather, "beloved children"—a word frequently used by this apos-

tle in his Epistles. It is an expression which implies great tenderness and affection, and such as a fond mother uses to her most beloved babes. Now that Judas was gone out, He could use this epithet without any restriction of meaning. *Yet a little while.* The end of My life is at hand; Judas is gone to consummate his treason; I have but a few hours to be with you, and by and by you shall be scattered. *Ye shall seek me.* For a few days you shall feel great distress because of My absence. *Whither I go, ye cannot come.* Your time is not up.

34. *A new commandment I give unto you.* In what sense are we to understand that this was a *new* commandment? "Thou shalt love thy neighbour as thyself," was a positive precept of the law, Lev. xix. 18, and it is the very same that Christ repeats here; how then was it *new?* Our Lord answers this question, Even *as I have loved you.* Now Christ more than fulfilled the Mosaic precept; He not only loved His neighbor as himself, but He loved him more than himself, for He laid down His life for men. In this He calls upon the disciples to imitate Him, to be ready on all occasions to lay down their lives for each other.

35. *By this shall all men know.* From this time forward, this mutual and disinterested love shall become the essential and distinctive mark of all My disciples. When they love one another with pure hearts, fervently, even unto death, then shall it fully appear that they are disciples of that Person who laid down His life for His sheep, and who became, by dying, a Ransom for all. The disciples of different teachers were known by their habits, or some particular creed or rite, or point of austerity, which they had adopted; but the disciples of Christ were known by this love which they bore to each other. The primitive Christians were particularly known by this among the Gentiles. Tertullian, in his *Apology,* gives us their very words: "See, said they, how they love one another, and are ready to lay down their lives for each other."

36. *Thou canst not follow me now.* You have not faith strong enough to die for Me, nor is your work yet done; but hereafter you shall suffer for My sake, and die in defense of My truth. See chap. xxi. 18.

37. *Why cannot I follow thee now?* Peter probably thought that our Lord intended to go on some long journey, which would necessarily subject Him to many inconveniences and fatigue; and he felt disposed to follow Him in this supposed journey, at all hazards. He saw no reason, because he did not see our Lord's meaning, why he could not follow Him *now. I will lay down my life for thy sake.* Poor Peter! You were sincere, but you did not know your own strength. You were at this time willing to die, but when the time came were not able. Christ must first die for Peter, before Peter can die for Him. Let no man think he can do anything good without the immediate assistance of God. Peter's denial should be an eternal warning to all self-confident persons; though there be sincerity and goodwill at the bottom, yet in the trial these cannot perform that office which belongs to the power of God. We should *will,* and then look to God for *power* to execute; without Him we can do nothing.

CHAPTER 14

Christ comforts His disciples, on the event of His removal from them, by the consideration of His going to prepare a place for them in heaven, 1-4. Thomes questions Him concerning the way to the Father, and is answered, 5-7. Philip proposes a difficulty, and Christ shows that He and the Father are one; that He is Mediator between God and man; and that whatsoever is asked in His name shall be obtained, 8-14. He promises them the Holy Spirit as the Comforter and Spirit of truth, 15-18. Shows them that He is shortly to leave them, and that those who love Him should be loved of the Father, 19-21. Jude asks a question, how Christ is to manifest himself to the disciples, and not to the Jews, 22. Christ answers, and shows that the manifestation is to be made to those who love God, and to them the Holy Spirit is to be an infallible Teacher, 23-26. He bequeaths His peace to them, and fortifies them against discouragements, 27-29. Foretells His approaching death, 30-31.

1. *Let not your heart be troubled.* After having answered Peter's question, He addresses himself again to His disciples, and tells them not to be afflicted at His leaving them, nor to lose courage because of what He said concerning Peter's denying Him; that if they reposed their confidence in God, He would protect them; and that, howsoever they might see Him treated, they should believe in Him more firmly, as His sufferings, death, and resurrection should be to them the most positive proof of His being the Messiah, the Saviour of the world. *Ye believe in God, believe also in me.* It is best to read both the verbs in the imperative mood—Place your confidence in God, and in Me as the Mediator between God and man, vv. 12-14; expect the utmost support from God, but expect it all through Me. The disciples began to lose all hope of a secular kingdom, and were discouraged in consequence. Christ promises them a spiritual and heavenly inheritance, and thus lifts up their drooping hearts.

2. *In my Father's house.* The Kingdom of glory. *Many mansions.* Though I have said before that where I am going you cannot come now, yet do not think that we shall be forever separated. I am going to that state of glory where there is not only a place of supreme eminence for myself, but also places for all My disciples—various degrees of glory suited to the various capacities and attainments of My followers. Our Lord alludes here to the Temple, which was called the "house of God," in the precincts of which there were a great number of chambers, 1 Kings vi. 5; Ezra viii. 29; Jer. xxxv. 2, 4; xxxvi. 10. *If it were not so, I would have told you.* If your places were not prepared in the kingdom of God, I would not have permitted you to have indulged a vain hope concerning future blessedness.

3. *And if I go.* And when I shall have gone and prepared a place for you—opened the Kingdom of an eternal glory for your reception, and for the reception of all that shall die in the faith—*I will come again,* after My resurrection, and give you the fullest assurances of this state of blessedness; and confirm you in the faith, by My grace and the effusion of My Spirit.

4. *And whither I go ye know.* I have told you this so often and so plainly that you must certainly have comprehended what I have said.

5. *Lord, we know not.* Thomas, perhaps, thought that our Lord only spoke of His going some distance from the place where He then was.

6. *I am the way* that leads to the Father; *the truth* that teaches the knowledge of God,

and directs in the way; *the life* that animates all those who seek and serve Him, and which is to be enjoyed eternally at the end of the way.

7. *If ye had known me, ye should have known my Father.* Because I and the Father are one, chap. x. 30. Or, If you had properly examined the intention and design of the law, you would have been convinced that it referred to Me; and that all that I have done and instituted was according to the design and intention of the Father, as expressed in that law.

8. *Shew us the Father.* As if he had said, We have seen and adored Thee, and our happiness will be complete if Thou show us the Father. The demand of Philip was similar to that made by Moses, Exod. xxxiii. 18. He wished to see the glory of God. In Peter, James, or John, this would have been inexcusable; but Philip had not seen the Transfiguration on the mount.

9. *He that hath seen me hath seen the Father.* Could any *creature* say these words? Do they not evidently imply that Christ declared himself to His disciples to be the everlasting God?

10. *I am in the Father, and the Father in me.* We are essentially one, and those who have seen Me have seen Him who sent me. *He doeth the works.* We are not only one in nature, but one also in operation. The works which I have done bear witness of the infinite perfection of My nature. Such miracles as I have wrought could be performed only by unlimited power.

12. *And greater works than these.* The miracles which I have wrought could not have been wrought but by the omnipotence of God, but that omnipotence can work *greater*. And those who believe on My name shall, through My almighty power, be enabled to work *greater* miracles than those which I have ordinarily wrought. Perhaps the *greater works* refer to the immense multitudes that were brought to God by the ministry of the apostles. *Because I go unto my Father.* Where I shall be an Intercessor for you, that—

13. *Whatsoever ye shall ask in my name.* To enable you to perform these miracles, and to convert souls, may be granted you. Besides, by going unto the Father, I shall receive the Holy Spirit, and send down His abundant *influences* into the hearts of those who believe.

15. *If ye love me, keep my commandments.* Do not be afflicted at the thought of My being separated from you; the most solid proof you can give of your attachment to and affection for Me is to keep My commandments. This I shall receive as a greater proof of your affection than your tears.

16. *I will pray the Father.* After having made an atonement for the sin of the world, I will become the Mediator between God and man; and through My mediation and intercession shall all the blessings of grace and glory be acquired. *Another Comforter.* The word *paracletos* signifies not only a *comforter*, but also an "advocate," a "defender" of a cause, a "counsellor, patron, mediator." Christ is thus termed, 1 John ii. 1, where the common translation renders the word "advocate." Christ is thus called because He is represented as transacting the concerns of our souls with God; and for this cause, He tells us, He goes unto the Father, v. 12. The Holy Spirit is thus called because He transacts the cause of God and Christ with us, explains to us the nature and importance of the great atonement, shows the necessity of it, counsels us to receive it, instructs us how to lay hold on it, vindicates our claim to it, and makes intercessions in us with unutterable groanings. As Christ acted with His disciples while He sojourned with them, so the Holy Ghost acts with those who believe in His name. *For ever.* As the death and atonement of Christ will be necessary to man till the conclusion of the world, so the office of the Holy Spirit must be continued among men till the end of time. Therefore says Christ, "He shall continue with you forever," teaching, comforting, advising, defending, and interceding for you and for all My followers to the end of time.

17. *The Spirit of truth.* The Spirit, or Holy Ghost, whose essential office is to manifest, vindicate, and apply the *truth. The world cannot receive.* By the *world*, John means those who are influenced only by the desire of the flesh, the desire of the eye, and the pride of life, 1 John ii. 16. Now these cannot receive the Spirit of truth, because they see *him not*, have no spiritual discernment, attend to nothing but the dictates of their corrupt passions and affections, and will admit of no influence but what can be an object of their senses. *But ye know him.* You have already received a measure of the truth, and you believe in this Spirit. Probably our Lord refers to the knowledge which they should afterwards attain; in this sense the passage has been understood by the *Vulgate*—"Ye shall know him." *For he dwelleth with you.* Or, "He shall dwell with you"; and this, it is very evident, is the meaning of the Evangelist, who not unfrequently uses the present for the future tense.

18. *I will not leave you comfortless.* Literally, "orphans." The disciples of a particular teacher among the Hebrews called him "father"; his scholars were called his *children*, and, on his death, were considered as orphans. Christ calls His disciples "children, beloved children," chap. xiii. 33; and now that He is about to be removed from them by death, He assures them that they shall not be left fatherless, or without a teacher; for in a little time He should come again (rise from the dead), and after His ascension they should be made partakers of that Spirit which would be their Comforter, Advocate, Teacher, and Guide forever.

19. *Because I live.* As surely as I shall rise from the dead, so shall you. My resurrection shall be the proof and pledge of yours. And *because I live* a life of intercession for you at the right hand of God, you shall live a life of grace and peace here, and a life of glory hereafter.

20. *That I am in my Father.* After My resurrection, you shall be more fully convinced of this important truth, that I and the Father are one; for I will live in you by the energy of My Spirit, and you shall live in Me by faith, love, and obedience.

21. *He it is that loveth me.* See on v. 15. *And will manifest myself to him.* All My faithful disciples shall see Me after My resurrection; and I will manifest My power and goodness to all those who believe in and obey Me, even to the end of the world.

22. *Judas.* The same as Thaddeus and Leb-

beus, the brother of James, and author of what is called the Epistle of Jude. *How is it?* Or, "How can it be?"—"What is to happen?"—On what account is it? Judas, who was probably thinking that the kingdom of Christ should extend over all the earth, wonders how this can be, and yet Christ manifest himself only to His disciples and not to the world, v. 19. To this our Lord, in a more express manner than He had done before, answers:

23. *If a man.* Not only My present disciples, but all those who shall believe on Me through their word, or that of their successors. *Love me.* Receive me as his Saviour, and get the love of God shed abroad in his heart by the Holy Ghost. *He will keep my words.* Observe all My sayings, and have his affections and conduct regulated by My Spirit and doctrine. *My Father will love him.* Call him His child; support, defend, and preserve him as such. *And we will come unto him.* God the Father, through His Son, will continue to pour out His choicest blessings upon his head and upon his heart. *And make our abode with him.* Will make his heart our temple, where God, the Father, Son, and Spirit, shall rest, receive homage, and dwell to eternity.

24. *He that loveth me not.* Hence we learn that the man who is not obedient to the testimonies of Christ does not love Him.

26. *He shall teach you all things.* If in the things which I have already spoken to you there appear to you any obscurity, the Holy Spirit, the Advocate, Counsellor, and Instructor, will take away all your doubts, free you from all embarrassment, and give you a perfect understanding in all things; and this Spirit ye shall shortly receive. *And bring all things to your remembrance.* Here Christ promises them that inspiration of the Holy Spirit which enabled them not only to give a true history of His life and death, but also gave them the most perfect recollection of all the words which He had spoken to them, so that they have been able to transmit to posterity the identical words which Jesus uttered in His sermons, and in His different discourses with them, the Jews, and others.

27. *Peace I leave with you.* The Jewish form of salutation and benediction. A wish of peace among them is thus to be understood. "May you prosper in body and soul, and enjoy every earthly and heavenly good!" *My peace I give unto you.* Such tranquillity of soul, such uninterrupted happiness of mind, such everlasting friendship with God as I enjoy, may ye all enjoy! And such blessedness I bequeath unto you; it is My last, My best, My dying legacy. *Not as the world giveth.* Not as the Jews, in empty wishes; not as the people of the world, in empty compliments. Their salutations and benedictions are generally matters of custom and polite ceremony, given without desire or design; but I mean what I say. What I wish you, that I will give you. To His followers Jesus gives peace, procures it, preserves it, and establishes it. He is the Author, Prince, Promoter, and Keeper of peace. *Neither let it be afraid.* Let not your heart "shrink back" through fear of any approaching evil. This is the proper meaning of the word. In a few hours you will be most powerfully assaulted, but stand firm. The evil will fall only upon Me;

and this evil will result in your comfort and salvation, and in the redemption of a lost world.

28. *I go away.* To the Father by My death. *And come again unto you.* By My resurrection. *Ye would rejoice.* Because, as the Messiah, I am going to receive a Kingdom, and power, and glory, forever. Therefore as My friends you should rejoice in My elevation, though for a while it may put you to the pain of being separated from Me. Besides, I am going that I may send you the Holy Spirit, who shall fill you with the fullness of God. On your own account, therefore, you should have rejoiced and not mourned. *My Father is greater than I.* In v. 24, Christ tells His disciples that the Father had sent Him; i.e., in His quality of Messiah, He was sent by the Father to instruct and to save mankind. Now, as the sender is greater than the sent, chap. xiii. 16, so in this sense is the Father greater than the Son; and in this sense was the passage understood by Origen, Jerome, Novatian, and Vigilius, who read the text thus: "The Father, who sent me, is greater than I."

29. *I have told you before it come to pass.* Lest My death should be a stumbling block to you, I have spoken of it beforehand, and showed you the necessity of it, that when it happens you may believe that, as I could predict it so clearly and so circumstantially, so all the good which I have promised shall be the result may be confidently expected by you; and that your sorrow, if not entirely removed, may at least be much mitigated.

30. *The prince of this world. Of this* is omitted by many MSS. I rather think the omission of the pronoun makes the sense more general; for had He said *this world,* the words might have been restrained to the Jewish state or to the Roman government. But who is the person called here the *prince of the world?* Mr. Wakefield thinks that Christ speaks here of himself, as He does in chap. xii. 31, and translates this verse and the following thus: "For the ruler of this world is coming; and I have nothing now to do, but to convince the world that I love the Father, and do as he commanded me." Others think that our Lord refers to the Roman government, the ruler of the world, who, by its deputy, Pilate, was going to judge Him, but who should "find nothing" (which is the reading found in some excellent MSS. and versions, and is followed by almost all the primitive fathers) as a just cause of death in Him; and this indeed Pilate witnessed in the most solemn manner. See chap. xviii. 38; xix. 4, 12; see also Luke xxiii. 4, etc., and Matt. xxvii. 24. But the most general opinion is that Satan is meant, who is called the "prince of the power of the air," Eph. ii. 2; and who is supposed to be the same that is called "the god of this world," 2 Cor. iv. 4; and who at his last and most desperate trial, the agony in the garden, should be convinced that there was nothing of his nature in Christ, nothing that would coincide with his solicitations, and that he should find himself completely foiled in all his attacks, and plainly foresee the impending ruin of his kingdom. It is very difficult to ascertain the real meaning here; of the different opinions proposed above, the reader must take that which he deems the most likely.

31. *Arise, let us go hence.* Calmet supposes that Christ, having rendered thanks to God,

and sung the usual hymn, Matt. xxvi. 30; Mark xiv. 26, rose from the table, left the city, and went towards the Garden of Olives, or Garden of Gethsemane, on the road to which a part of the following discourse was delivered. It was now about midnight, and the moon was almost full, it being the fourteenth day of her age, about the time in which the Jewish Passover was to be slain.

CHAPTER 15

The union of Jesus Christ with His followers, represented by the parable of a vine and its branches, 1-11. He exhorts them to mutual love, 12. Calls them His friends, and promises to lay down His life for them, 13-15. Appoints them their work, and promises them success in it, 16. Renews the exhortation to mutual love, 17, and foretells the opposition they would meet with from the world, 18-21. The sin of the Jews in rejecting Christ, 22-25. The Holy Spirit is promised as a Witness for Christ, and the Comforter of the disciples, 26-27.

2. *Every branch in me.* I stand in the same relation to My followers, and they to Me, as the vine to the branches, and the branches to the vine. *He taketh away.* As the vinedresser will remove every unfruitful branch from the vine, so will My Father remove every unfruitful member from My mystical body—such as Judas, the unbelieving Jews, the apostatizing disciples, and all false and merely nominal Christians, who are attached to the vine by faith in the word and divine mission of Christ, while they live not in His life and Spirit and bring forth no fruit to the glory of God. *He purgeth it.* "He pruneth." The branch which bears not fruit, the husbandman "taketh it away." But the branch that beareth fruit, "He taketh away from it"; i.e., He prunes away excrescences, and removes everything that might hinder its increasing fruitfulness. The verb "I take away" signifies ordinarily to "cleanse, purge, purify," but is certainly to be taken in the sense of "pruning," or "cutting off," in this text.

3. *Now ye are clean.* "Ye are pruned." As our Lord has not changed the metaphor, it would be wrong to change the expression. *Through the word.* "Through that word"—that doctrine of holiness which I have incessantly preached unto you, and which you have received. Perhaps our Lord more immediately refers here to the words which He had spoken concerning Judas, chap. xiii. 21-30, in consequence of which Judas went out and finished his bargain with the chief priests. He being gone off, the body of the apostles was purified; and thus he might say, *Now ye are clean through the word which I have spoken unto you.*

4. *Abide in me.* Hold fast faith and a good conscience; and let no trials turn you aside from the truth. *And I will abide in you*—you shall receive every help and influence from Me that your souls can require in order to preserve and save them to eternal life.

5. *Without me ye can do nothing.* "Separated from Me, ye can do nothing at all." God can do without man, but man cannot do without God. Following the metaphor of our Lord, it would be just as possible to do any good without Him as for a branch to live, thrive, and bring forth fruit while cut off from that tree from which it not only derives its juices but its very existence also.

6. *If a man abide not in me.* Our Lord in the plainest manner intimates that a person

may as truly be united to Him as the branch is to the tree that produces it, and yet be afterwards cut off and cast into the fire, because he has not brought forth fruit to the glory of his God. No man can cut off a branch from a tree to which that branch was never united; it is absurd, and contrary to the letter and spirit of the metaphor, to talk of being "seemingly" in Christ—because this means nothing. If there was only a seeming union, there could be only a seeming excision. So the matter is just where it began; nothing is done on either side, and nothing said to any purpose. *He is cast forth.* Observe that person who abides not in Christ, in a believing, loving, obedient spirit, (1) Is *cut off* from Jesus, having no longer any right or title to Him or to His salvation. (2) He is *withered*—deprived of all the influences of God's grace and Spirit. (3) He is *gathered*—becomes (through the judgment of God) again united with backsliders like himself and other workers of iniquity. And, being abandoned to his own heart and Satan, he (4) is *cast into the fire*—separated from God's people, from God himself, and from the glory of His power. And (5) he is *burned*—is eternally tormented with the devil and his angels, and with all those who have lived and died in their iniquity.

7. *If ye abide in me.* Observe, (1) That in order to have influence with God, we must be united to Christ—*if ye abide in me.* (2) That in order to be preserved in this union, we must have our lives regulated by the doctrine of Christ—*and my words abide in you.* (3) That to profit by this union and doctrine, we must pray—*ye shall ask.* (4) That every heavenly blessing shall be given to those who continue in this union with a loving, obedient, praying spirit—*ye shall ask what ye will.*

8. *Herein is my Father glorified.* Or "honored." It is the honor of the husbandman to have good, strong, vigorous vines, plentifully laden with fruit. So it is the honor of God to have strong, vigorous, holy children, entirely freed from sin, and perfectly filled with His love.

10. *If ye keep my commandments.* Hence we learn that it is impossible to retain a sense of God's pardoning love without continuing in the obedience of faith.

11. *That my joy may remain in you.* That the joy which I now feel, on account of your steady, affectionate attachment to Me, may be lasting, I give you both warnings and directions, that you may abide in the faith. *That your joy might be full.* Or "complete"—"filled up"; a metaphor taken from a vessel into which water or any other thing is poured till it is full to the brim.

12. *That ye love one another.* See on chap. xiii. 34. So deeply was this commandment engraven on the heart of this Evangelist that Jerome says that in his extreme old age, when he used to be carried to the public assemblies of the believers, his constant saying was, "Little children, love one another." His disciples, wearied at last with the constant repetition of the same words, asked him why he constantly said the same thing. "Because [said he] it is the commandment of the Lord, and the observation of it alone is sufficient."

13. *That a man lay down his life for his friends.* No man can carry his love for his friend farther than this; for when he gives up his life, he gives up all that he has. This proof of My love for you I shall give in a few hours, and the doctrine which I recommend to you I am just going to exemplify myself.

15. *Henceforth I call you not servants.* Which He at least indirectly had done, chap. xiii. 16; Matt. x. 24-25; Luke xvii. 10. *I have called you friends.* I have admitted you into a state of the most intimate fellowship with myself, and have made known unto you whatsoever I have heard from the Father which, in your present circumstances, it was necessary for you to be instructed in.

16. *Ye have not chosen me.* You have not elected Me as your Teacher; I have called you to be My disciples, witnesses and depositories of the truth. It was customary among the Jews for every person to choose his own teacher. *And ordained you.* "I have appointed you." The word is *etheka*, "I have put or placed you," i.e., in the vine.

18. *If the world hate you.* As the followers of Christ were to be exposed to the hatred of the world, it was no small consolation to them to know that that hatred would be only in proportion to their faith and holiness; and that, consequently, instead of being troubled at the prospect of persecution, they should rejoice because that should always be a proof to them that they were in the very path in which Jesus himself had trod.

19. *Ye are not of the world . . . therefore.* On this very account, because you do not join in fellowship with those who know not God, therefore they hate you.

20. *If they have kept my saying.* Or "doctrine." Whosoever acknowledges Me for the Christ will acknowledge you for My ministers. Some translate the passage thus: "If they have watched My sayings," i.e., with an intent to accuse Me for something which I have said, "they will watch yours also"; therefore be on your guard. *Paraterein* has this sense, as we have had occasion to observe before; and perhaps *terein* has the same sense here, as it is much more agreeable to the context.

21. *Because they know not him that sent me.* This is the foundation of all religious persecution; those who are guilty of it, whether in church or state, know nothing about God.

22. *But now they have no cloke for their sin.* They are without "excuse." See the margin, and see the note on chap. ix. 41. Christ had done such works as demonstrated Him to be the Messiah—yet they rejected Him; here lay their sin. And this sin, and the punishment to which it exposed them, still remain; for they still continue to reject the Lord that bought them.

25. *Written in their law.* See on chap. x. 34. These words are taken from Ps. lxix. 4. This psalm is applied to Christ, chap. ii. 17; xix. 28; to the vengeance of God against Judea, Acts i. 20. The psalm seems entirely prophetic of Christ.

26. *But when the Comforter is come.* See on chap. xiv. 16.

26-27. *He shall testify . . . and ye also shall bear witness.* He shall bear His testimony in

your souls, and you shall bear this testimony to the world. Our Lord appears to reason thus: In every respect the unbelief of the Jews is inexcusable. They believe not My doctrine, notwithstanding its purity and holiness. They believe not in the Father who sent Me, notwithstanding I have confirmed My mission by the most astonishing miracles. One thing only remains now to be done, i.e., to send them the Holy Spirit, to convince them of sin, righteousness, and judgment; and this He shall do, not only by His influence upon their hearts, but also by your words. And when they shall have resisted this Spirit, then the cup of their iniquity shall be filled, and wrath shall come upon them to the uttermost.

CHAPTER 16

Christ warns His disciples, and foretells the persecutions they should receive from the Jews, 1-4. Foretells His death, and promises them the Comforter, 5-7. Points out His operations among the Jews, and in the world, 8-11. His peculiar influences on the souls of the disciples, 12-15. Speaks figuratively of His death and resurrection, at which His disciples are puzzled, 16-18. He explains and illustrates the whole by a similitude, 19-22. Shows himself to be the Mediator between God and man, and that all prayers must be put up in His name, 23-28. The disciples clearly comprehend His meaning, and express their strong faith in Him, 29-30. He again foretells their persecution, and promises them His peace and support, 31-33.

1. *These things have I spoken.* Particularly what is mentioned in the two last chapters. *Be offended.* "That ye should not be stumbled." May not fall away from the faith, nor receive any injury to your souls, as that man does to his body who stumbles or falls over a stone or block in the way which he has not discovered.

2. *They shall put you out of the synagogues.* They will "excommunicate" you. In these excommunications they were spoiled of all their substance; see Ezra x. 8 and Heb. x. 34, and deprived of their character, their influence, and every necessary of life. *That whosoever killeth you.* This Paul found; for more than forty Jews bound themselves under a curse that they would neither eat nor drink till they had killed him, Acts xxiii. 12-13; and agreeably to this, it is said, in that Tract of the Talmud which is entitled *Bammidbar*, R. xxi. ad. Num. xxv. 13: "He who sheds the blood of the ungodly, is equal to him who brings an offering to God."

3. *Because they have not known the Father.* Ignorance of the benevolence of God, and of the philanthropy of Christ, is the grand fountain whence all religious persecution and intolerance proceed.

4. *At the beginning.* I would not trouble you by speaking of these things pointedly at first, when I chose you to be My disciples, but have referred them to the present time, lest you should be discouraged, and now declare them only because it is absolutely necessary that you should be put upon your guard.

5. *None of you asketh me, Whither goest thou?* In chap. xiii. 36, Peter had asked, "Lord, whither goest thou?"—and Thomas much the same in chap. xiv. 5, both of whom had received an answer. But now, at the time when Jesus was speaking this, none of them asked this question, because their hearts were filled with sorrow, v. 6.

7. *It is expedient for you that I go away.* In other places He had shown them the ab-

solute necessity of His death for the salvation of men; see Matt. xx. 19; xxvi. 2; Mark ix. 31; x. 33; Luke ix. 44; xviii. 32. This He does not repeat here, but shows them that, by the order of God, the Holy Spirit cannot come to them, nor to the world, unless He first die; and consequently men cannot be saved but in this way.

8. *He will reprove.* He will demonstrate these matters so clearly as to leave no doubt on the minds of those who are simple of heart, and so fully as to confound and shut the mouths of those who are gainsayers. *The world.* The Jewish nation first, and afterwards the Gentile world; for His influences shall not be confined to one people, place, or time.

9. *Of sin.* Of the sin of the Jews in not receiving Me as the Messiah, though My mission was accredited by the very miracles which the prophets foretold; see Isa. xxxv. 3-6. This was literally fulfilled on the Day of Pentecost, when the Spirit was given; for multitudes of Jews were then convinced of this sin, and converted to God. See Acts ii. 37.

10. *Of righteousness.* Of My innocence and holiness, because I go away to My Father, of which My resurrection from the dead and My ascension to heaven shall be complete proofs.

11. *Of judgment.* Of the false judgment of the Jews in condemning the Lord Jesus, who, as some think, is intended here by the ruler *of this world.* Others think that Satan is meant, whose usurped power over the world was now to be greatly restrained, and by and by totally destroyed; see chap. xii. 31; Col. ii. 15; Rev. xi. 15; xii. 10-11. Perhaps our Lord's meaning is that, as a most astonishing judgment or punishment was now about to fall upon the Jews in consequence of their obstinate infidelity, the Holy Ghost by the ministry of the apostles should demonstrate that this judgment, severe as it might seem, was amply merited by this worst of all people. One general exposition may be given of these three verses. The Holy Spirit will convince the world of *sin* committed, and guilt and condemnation thereby incurred; of *righteousness*—of the necessity of being pardoned, and made righteous through the blood of the Lamb, who, after being offered up for sin, went to the Father, ever to appear in His presence as our intercessor; and of *judgment*—of the great day thereof, when none shall be able to stand but those whose sins are pardoned and whose souls are made righteous. In all that our Lord says here, there seems to be an allusion to the office of an advocate in a cause, in a court of justice; who, by producing witnesses and pleading upon the proof, convicts the opposite party of sin, demonstrates the righteousness of his client, and shows the necessity of passing judgment upon the accuser.

13. *He will guide you.* He will consider your feeble infant state; and, as a father leads his child by the hand, so will the Holy Spirit lead and guide you.

15. *All things that the Father hath are mine.* If Christ had not been equal to God, could He have said this without blasphemy? *And shew it unto you.* As Christ is represented as the Ambassador of the Father, so the Holy Spirit is represented as the Ambassador of the Son, coming vested with His authority, as the Interpreter and Executor of His will.

16. *A little while.* He had but a few hours to live. *And ye shall not see me.* I shall be hidden from your view in the grave. *Again, a little while.* In three days after My death. *Ye shall see me.* I will rise again, and show myself to you. Or, As I am going by My ascension to the Father, in a short time, you shall see Me personally no more; but in a little while I shall pour out My Spirit upon you, and others through your ministry; and you shall see Me virtually in the great and wonderful work which shall then take place in the hearts and lives of men.

18. *What is this that he saith?* They knew from what He had said that He was to die, but knew not what He meant by their seeing Him again in a little time.

20. *Ye shall weep and lament.* To see Me crucified and laid in the grave. *But the world shall rejoice.* The chief priests, scribes, Pharisees, and persecuting Jews in general will triumph, hoping that their bad cause is crowned with success. *But your sorrow shall be turned into joy.* When you see Me risen from the dead. It is very evident that our Lord uses the word *world* in several parts of this discourse of His to signify the unbelieving and rebellious Jews.

21. *For joy that a man is born.* Anthropos is put here for a "human creature," whether male or female, as *homo* among the Romans denoted either man or woman.

22. *Your joy no man taketh from you.* Or "shall take away." Some excellent MSS. and versions read the verb in the future tense. Our Lord's meaning appears to have been this: that His resurrection should be so *completely demonstrated* to them that they should never have a doubt concerning it; and consequently that their joy should be great and permanent, knowing that the atonement was made, the victory gained, and the kingdom of Heaven opened to all believers.

23. *Ye shall ask me nothing.* Ye shall then be led, by that Spirit which guides into all truth, to consider Me in the character of Mediator in the kingdom of God, and to address your prayers to the Father in *my name*—in the name of Jesus, the Saviour, because I have died to redeem you —in the name of Christ, the Anointed, because I have ascended to send down the gift of the Holy Ghost.

24. *Hitherto have ye asked nothing in my name.* You have not as yet considered Me the great Mediator between God and man; but this is one of the truths which shall be more fully revealed to you by the Holy Spirit. *Ask.* In My name; and *ye shall receive*—all the salvation you thus request; the consequence of which shall be *that your joy* shall be *full*—you shall be thoroughly happy in being made completely holy.

25. *In proverbs.* That is, words which, besides their plain, literal meaning, have another, viz., a spiritual or figurative one. I have represented heavenly things to you through the medium of earthly. *The time cometh.* Viz., the interval from His resurrection to His ascension, which consisted of forty days, during which He instructed His disciples in the most sublime mysteries and truths of His kingdom, Acts. i. 3.

26. *I say not unto you, that I will pray the*

Father for you. I need not tell you that I will continue as your Intercessor; I have already given you so many proofs of My love that you cannot possibly doubt this. Besides, the Father himself needs no entreaty to do you good, for He loves you, and is graciously disposed to save you to the uttermost, because "you have loved Me and believed in Me as coming from God," for the salvation of the world.

28. *I came forth from the Father.* With whom I existed from eternity in glory. *Am come into the world.* By my incarnation. *I leave the world.* By My death. *And go to the Father.* By My ascension. These four words contain the whole economy of the gospel of man's salvation, and a consummate abridgment of the Christian faith. This gave the disciples a key to the whole of our Lord's discourse; and especially to that part, v. 16, that had so exceedingly embarrassed them, as appears by vv. 17-18.

29. *Lo, now speakest thou plainly.* The disciples received more light now on the nature of Christ's person and office than they had ever done before.

30. *Now are we sure that thou knowest all things.* Is not the following the meaning of the disciples? We believe that Thou art not only the Messiah who came out from God, but that Thou art that God who searchest the heart and triest the reins, and needest not to be asked in order to make Thee acquainted with the necessities of Thy creatures; for Thou perfectly knowest their wants, and art infinitely disposed to relieve them.

31. *Do ye now believe?* And will you continue to believe? You are now fully convinced; and will you in the hour of trial retain your conviction, and prove faithful and steady?

32. *The hour cometh.* You shall shortly have need of all the faith you profess. You now believe Me to be the Omniscient; but you will find difficulty to maintain this faith when you see Me seized, condemned, and crucified as a malefactor. Yes, your faith will be then so shaken that you shall run away, each striving to save himself at his "own home," or among his "kindred."

33. *That in me ye might have peace.* I give you this warning as another proof that I know all things, and to the end that you may look to Me alone for peace and happiness. The peace of God is ever to be understood as including all possible blessedness—light, strength, comfort, support, a sense of the divine favor, unction of the Holy Spirit, purification of heart, and all these to be enjoyed *in Christ. In the world ye shall have tribulation.* Or, as most of the very best MSS. read, "ye have"—the tribulation is at hand; you are just about to be plunged into it. *But be of good cheer.* Do not despond on account of what I have said. The world shall not be able to overcome you, how severely soever it may try you. *I have overcome the world.* I am just now going by My death to put it and its god to the rout. My apparent weakness shall be My victory; My ignominy shall be My glory; and the victory which the world, the devil, and My adversaries in general shall appear to gain over Me shall be their own lasting defeat and My eternal triumph.

CHAPTER 17

Christ prays the Father to glorify Him, 1. In what eternal life consists, 2-3. Shows that He has glorified His Father by fulfilling His will upon earth and revealing Him to the disciples, 4-8. Prays for them, that they may be preserved in unity and kept from evil, 9-16. Prays for their sanctification, 17-19. Prays also for those who should believe on Him through their preaching, that they all might be brought unto a state of unity, and finally brought to eternal glory, 20-26.

1. *These words spake Jesus.* That is, what is related in the preceding chapters.

I. Our Lord's Prayer for Himself, vv. 1-5

Father. Here our Lord addresses the whole divine nature, as He is now performing His last acts in His state of humiliation. *Glorify thy Son.* Cause Him to be acknowledged as the promised Messiah by the Jewish people, and as the universal Saviour by the Gentile world; and let such proofs of His Godhead be given as shall serve to convince and instruct mankind. *That thy Son also may glorify thee.* That by dying He may magnify Thy law and make it honorable, respected among men—show the strictness of Thy justice, and the immaculate purity of Thy nature.

2. *As thou hast given him power.* As the Messiah, Jesus Christ, received from the Father *universal dominion. All flesh,* i.e., all the "human race," was given unto Him, that by one sacrifice of himself He might reconcile them all to God, having by His grace tasted death for every man, Heb. ii. 9. *That he should give eternal life.* As all were delivered into His power, and He poured out His blood to redeem all, then the design of God is that all should have eternal life, because all are given for this purpose to Christ.

3. *This is life eternal.* It is called *eternal life* to show that it reaches beyond the limits of time, and that it necessarily implies: (1) the immortality of the soul; (2) the resurrection of the body; and (3) that it is never to end, hence called "a life ever living." *The only true God.* The way to attain this eternal life is to acknowledge, worship, and obey, the one only true God, and to accept as Teacher, Sacrifice, and Saviour, the Lord Jesus, the one and only true Messiah.

4. *I have glorified thee.* Our Lord, considering himself as already sacrificed for the sin of the world, speaks of having completed the work which God had given Him to do; and He looks forward to that time when, through the preaching of His gospel, His sacrifice should be acknowledged, and the true God should be known and worshipped by the whole world.

5. *Before the world was.* That is, from eternity, before there was any creation—so the phrase, and others similar to it, are taken in the sacred writings; see v. 24; Ps. xc. 2; Eph. i. 4. See chap. i. 1.

II. Our Lord's Prayer for His Disciples, vv. 6-19

6. *I have manifested thy name.* I have brought it into light, and caused it to shine in itself, and to illuminate others. A little of the divine nature was known by the works of creation; a little more was known by the Mosaic revelation. But the full manifestation of God, His nature, and His attributes, came only through the revelation of Christ. *The men which thou gavest me.* That is, the apostles, who, having received this

knowledge from Christ, were by their preaching and writings to spread it through the whole world. *Out of the world.* From among the Jewish people; for in this sense is the word *kosmos* to be understood in various parts of our Lord's last discourses. *Thine they were.* Objects of Thy choice; *and thou gavest them me* from among this very unbelieving people, that they might be My disciples and the heralds of My salvation. *And they have kept thy word.* Though their countrymen have rejected it; and they have received Me as Thy well-beloved Son in whom Thou delightest.

8. *I have given unto them the words.* I have delivered Thy doctrine to them, so that they have had a pure teaching immediately from heaven. *And have known surely.* Are fully convinced and acknowledge that I am the promised Messiah, and that they are to look for none other, and that My mission and doctrine are all divine.

9. *I pray not for the world.* I am not yet come to that part of My intercession; see v. 20. I am now wholly employed for My disciples, that they may be properly qualified to preach My salvation to the ends of the earth. Jesus here imitates the high priest, the second part of whose prayer, on the day of expiation, was for the *priests, the sons of Aaron.* These words may also be understood as applying to the rebellious Jews. God's wrath was about to descend upon them, and Christ prays that His own followers might be kept from the evil, v. 15. But He does not thus pray for the *world,* the rebellious Jews, because the cup of their iniquity was full, and their judgment slumbered not.

10. *I am glorified in them.* Christ speaks of the things which were not, but which should be, as though they were. He anticipates the glorifying of His name by the successful preaching of the apostles.

11. *I am no more in the world.* I am just going to leave the world, and therefore they shall stand in need of peculiar assistance and support. They have need of all the influence of My intercession, that they may be preserved in Thy truth. *Keep through thine own name those whom thou hast given me.* Instead of *those whom thou hast given me,* many MSS. read *ho,* which refers to *thy name,* immediately preceding. The whole passage should be read thus: "Holy Father, keep them through Thy own name which Thou hast given me, that they may be one." By the *name,* here, it is evident that the doctrine or knowledge of the true God is intended; as if our Lord had said, Keep them in that doctrine which Thou hast given Me, that they may be one. This reading is supported by the most ample evidence and indisputable authority. *That they may be one.* That they and all that believe through their word (the doctrine which I have given them) may be one body, united by one Spirit to Me, their living Head. The union which Christ recommends here and prays for is so complete and glorious as to be fitly represented by that union which subsists between the Father and the Son.

12. *I kept them in thy name.* In Thy doctrine and truth. *But the son of perdition.* So we find that Judas, whom all account to have been lost, and whose case at best is extremely dubious, was first given by God to Christ. But why was he lost? Because, says Augustine, he would

not be *saved;* and he further adds, After the commission of his crime, he might have returned to God and have found mercy. *Perdition* or "destruction" is personified; and Judas is represented as being her *son,* i.e., one of the worst of men. *That the scripture might be fulfilled.* Or, "Thus the scripture is fulfilled"; see Ps. xli. 9; cix. 8, compared with Acts i. 20.

13. *My joy fulfilled in themselves.* See on chap. xv. 11.

14. *I have given them thy word.* Or "Thy doctrine." *And the world hath hated them.* The Jewish rulers have hated them.

15. *That thou shouldest take them out of the world.* They must not yet leave the land of Judea; they had not as yet borne their testimony here, concerning Christ crucified and risen again from the dead.

17. *Sanctify them. Hagiason,* from *a,* negative, and *ge,* "the earth." This word has two meanings: (1) It signifies to "consecrate," to "separate" from earth and common use, and to "devote" or "dedicate" to God and His service. (2) It signifies to "make holy" or "pure." The prayer of Christ may be understood in both these senses. He prayed (1) that they might be fully consecrated to the work of the ministry, and separated from all worldly concerns; (2) that they might be holy, and patterns of all holiness to those to whom they announced the salvation of God. *Through thy truth.* It is not only according to the truth of God that ministers are to be set apart to the sacred work; but it is from that truth, and according to it, that they must preach to others. That doctrine which is not drawn from the truth of God can never save souls.

18. *As thou hast sent me . . . so have I also sent them.* The apostles had the same commission which Christ had, considered as man—they were endued with the same Spirit, so that they could not err, and their word was accompanied with the same success.

19. *I sanctify myself.* I "consecrate" and "devote" myself to death—that I may thereby purchase eternal salvation for them. There seems to be here an allusion to the entering of the high priest into the holy of holies, when, having offered the sacrifice, he sprinkled the blood before the ark of the covenant. So Jesus entered into the holiest of all by His own blood, in order to obtain everlasting redemption for men; see Heb. ix. 11-13. The word *hagiazo,* to "consecrate" or "sanctify," is used in the sense of devoting to death, in Jer. xii. 3, both in the Hebrew and in the Septuagint; the Hebrew signifies also to "sacrifice."

III. OUR LORD'S PRAYER FOR HIS CHURCH, and for all who would believe on His name, through the preaching of the apostles and their successors

20. *Neither pray I for these alone.* This prayer extends itself through all ages, and takes in every soul that believes in the Lord Jesus. And what is it that Christ asks in behalf of His followers? The greatest of blessings: unity, peace, love, and eternal glory.

21. *That they all may be one.* This prayer was literally answered to the first believers, who were all of one heart and of one soul, Acts iv. 32. And why is it that believers are not in the same spirit now? Because they neither

attend to the example nor to the truth of Christ. *That the world may believe.* We have already seen that the word *cosmos, world,* is used in several parts of this last discourse of our Lord to signify the "Jewish people" only.

22. *And the glory which thou gavest me I have given them.* As Christ, according to His human nature, is termed the Son of God, He may be understood as saying: "I have communicated to all those who believe, or shall believe, in Me the glorious privilege of becoming sons of God; that, being all adopted children of the same Father, they may abide in peace, love, and unity."

23. *That the world may know.* That the Jewish people first, and secondly the Gentiles, may acknowledge Me as the true Messiah, and be saved unto life eternal.

24. *That they may behold my glory.* That they may enjoy eternal felicity with Me in Thy kingdom. So the word is used, chap. iii. 3; Matt. v. 8.

25. *The world hath not known thee.* Has not acknowledged Me. See on chap. i. 11-12. *And these have known.* Here our Lord, returning to the disciples, speaks: (1) of their having received Him as the Messiah; (2) of His making the Father known unto them; (3) of His purpose to continue to influence them by the Spirit of truth, that they might be perfectly united to God by an indwelling Saviour forever.

26. *I have declared unto them thy name.* I have taught them the true doctrine. *And will declare it.* This He did: (1) by the conversations He had with His disciples after His resurrection, during the space of forty days; (2) by the Holy Spirit, who was poured out upon them on the Day of Pentecost.

Our Lord's sermon, which He concluded by the prayer recorded in this chapter, begins at v. 13 of chap. xiii and is one of the most excellent that can be conceived. His Sermon on the Mount shows men what they should *do,* so as to please God; this sermon shows them *how* they are to do the things prescribed in the other. In the former the reader sees a strict morality which he fears he shall never be able to perform. In this he sees all things are possible to him who believes; for that very God who made him shall dwell in his heart, and enable him to do all that He pleases to employ him in.

CHAPTER 18

Jesus passes the brook Cedron, and goes to the Garden of Gethsemane, 1. Judas, having betrayed Him, comes to the place with a troop of men to take Him, 2-3. Jesus addresses them, and they fall to the ground, 4-6. He addresses them again, and Peter smites Malchus, 7-11. They seize Him and lead Him away to Caiaphas, 12-14. Peter follows to the palace of the high priest, 15-18. The high priest questions Christ concerning His doctrine, and Jesus answers, and is smitten, 19-23. Peter denies his Lord twice, 24-27. Jesus is led to the judgment hall, and Pilate and the Jews converse about Him, 28-32. Pilate converses with Jesus, who informs him of the spiritual nature of His kingdom, 33-37. Pilate returns to the Jews, and declares Christ to be innocent, 38. He seeks to discharge Him, and the Jews clamor for His condemnation, 39-40.

1. *Over the brook Cedron.* Having finished the prayer related in the preceding chapter, our Lord went straight to the Garden of Gethsemane, Matt. xxvi. 36, which was in the Mount of Olives, eastward of Jerusalem. This mount was separated from the city by a very

narrow valley, through the midst of which the brook Cedron ran. Cedron is a very small rivulet, about six or seven feet broad, nor is it constantly supplied with water, being dry all the year except during the rains. It is mentioned in the Old Testament: 2 Sam. xv. 23; 1 Kings xv. 13; 2 Kings xxiii. 4. And it appears the Evangelist mentions it here only to call to remembrance what happened to David when he was driven from Jerusalem by his son Absalom, and he and his followers obliged to pass the brook Cedron on foot; see 2 Sam. xv. 23. All this was a very expressive figure of what happened now to this Second David by the treachery of one of His own disciples. *A garden.* Gethsemane; see on Matt. xxvi. 36. John mentions nothing of the agony in the garden; probably because he found it so amply related by all the other Evangelists. As that account should come in here, the reader is desired to consult the notes on Matt. xxvi. 36-47. See also Mark xiv. 30-36 and Luke xxii. 40-44.

2. *Judas . . . knew the place.* As many had come from different quarters to celebrate the Passover at Jerusalem, it could not be an easy matter to find lodging in the city. Jesus therefore chose to pass the night in the garden with His disciples, which, from this verse and from Luke xxii. 39, we find was His frequent custom, though He often lodged in Bethany. But as He had supped in the city this evening, Judas took it for granted that He had not gone to Bethany, and therefore was to be met with in the garden; and having given this information to the priests, they gave him some soldiers and others that he might be the better enabled to seize and bring Him away.

3. *A band.* "The band" or "troop." Some think that the *spira* was the same as the Roman *cohort,* and was the tenth part of a legion, which consisted sometimes of 4,200 and sometimes of 5,000 foot. But Raphelius, on Matt. xxvii. 27, has clearly proved, from Polybius, that the *spira* was no more than a tenth of the fourth part of a legion. And as the number of the legions was uncertain, and their divisions not at all equal, no person can tell how many the band or *spira* contained. This band was probably those Roman soldiers given by the governor for the defense of the Temple, and the *officers* were those who belonged to the Sanhedrin. *With lanterns and torches.* With these they had intended to search the corners and caverns, provided Christ had hidden himself; for they could not have needed them for any other purpose, it being now the fourteenth day of the moon's age, in the month Nisan, and consequently it appeared full and bright. The *weapons* mentioned here were probably no other than clubs, staves, and instruments of that kind, as we may gather from Matt. xxvi. 55; Mark xiv. 48; Luke xxii. 52. The swords mentioned by the other Evangelists were probably those of the Roman soldiers; the clubs and staves belonged to the chief priest's officers.

4. *Jesus therefore, knowing all things.* He had gone through all His preaching, working of miracles, and passion, and had nothing to do now but to offer up himself on the Cross; He therefore went forth to meet them, to deliver himself up to death.

5. *Jesus of Nazareth.* They did not say this till after Judas kissed Christ, which was the

sign which he had agreed with the soldiers to give them that they might know whom they were to seize; see Matt. xxvi. 48.

6. *They went backward, and fell to the ground.* None of the other Evangelists mentions this very important circumstance. Our Lord chose to give them this proof of His infinite power that they might know that their power could not prevail against Him if He chose to exert His might, seeing that the very breath of His mouth confounded, drove back, and struck them down to the earth. Thus by the blast of God they might have perished, and by the breath of His nostrils they might have been consumed, Job. iv. 9.

8. *Let these go their way.* These words are rather words of authority than words of entreaty. I voluntarily give myself up to you, but you must not molest one of these My disciples.

10. *Having a sword.* See the note on Luke xxii. 36. *Cut off his right ear.* He probably designed to have cut his skull in two, but God turned it aside, and only permitted the ear to be taken off; and this He would not have suffered, but only that He might have the opportunity of giving them a most striking proof of His divinity in working an astonishing miracle on the occasion. See the notes on Matt. xxvi. 51-56. The other three Evangelists mention this transaction; but neither gives the name of Peter nor of Malchus, probably because both persons were alive when they wrote; but it is likely both had been long dead before John published his history.

11. *The cup which my Father hath given me.* The cup sometimes signifies the lot of life, whether prosperous or adverse: here it signifies the final sufferings of Christ.

12. *The captain.* The *chiliarch*, or "chief over one thousand men." He was probably the prefect, or captain, of the Temple guard.

13. *To Annas.* This man must have had great authority in his nation: (1) Because he had been a long time high priest; (2) Because he had no less than five sons who successively enjoyed the dignity of the high priesthood; and (3) Because his son-in-law Caiaphas was at this time in possession of that office. It is likely that Annas was chief of the Sanhedrin and that it was to him in that office that Christ was first brought. *That same year.* The office was now no longer during life as formerly. See the note on chap. xi. 49. What is related in the twenty-fourth verse, "Now Annas had sent him bound unto Caiaphas," comes properly in after the thirteenth verse. See the margin.

14. *Caiaphas was he, which gave counsel.* Therefore he was an improper person to sit in judgment on Christ, whom He had prejudged and precondemned; see on chap. xi. 50-52. But Christ must not be treated according to the rules of justice; if He had, He could not have been put to death.

15. *And . . . another disciple.* There are many conjectures who this disciple was. Jerome, Chrysostom, Theophylact, Nonnus, Lyra, Erasmus, Piscator, and others say it was John. It is true John frequently mentions himself in the third person; but then he has always "whom Jesus loved," as in chap. xiii. 23; xix. 26; xxi. 7, 20, except in chap. xix. 35, where he has plainly pointed out himself as writer of this Gospel. But in the place before us he has mentioned no circumstance by which that disciple may be known to be John. To this may be added that John being not only a Galilean, but a fisherman by trade, it is not likely that he should have been known to the high priest, as it is here said of that disciple who followed Jesus with Peter. The conjecture of Grotius is the most likely, viz., that it was the person at whose house Jesus had supped. Augustine, *Tract* 113, speaks like a man of sound sense: We should not decide hastily, says he, on a subject concerning which the Scripture is silent.

18. *Servants and officers.* These belonged to the chief priests; the Roman soldiers had probably been dismissed after having conducted Christ to Annas.

19. *Asked Jesus of his disciples, and of his doctrine.* He probably asked Him by what authority, or in virtue of what right, He collected disciples, formed a different sect, preached a new doctrine, and set himself up for a public Reformer? As religion was interested in these things, the high priest was considered as being the proper judge. But all this, with what follows, was transacted by night, and this was contrary to established laws. For the *Talmud* states that "criminal processes can neither commence nor terminate, but during the course of the day. If the person be acquitted, the sentence may be pronounced during that day; but, if he be condemned, the sentence cannot be pronounced till the next day. But no kind of judgment is to be executed, either on the eve of the Sabbath, or the eve of any festival." Nevertheless, to the lasting infamy of this people, Christ was judicially interrogated and condemned during the night; and on the night, too, of the Passover, or, according to others, on the eve of that feast. Thus all the forms of justice were insulted and outraged in the case of our Lord. In this "his humiliation his judgment was taken away," Acts viii. 33.

20. *I spake openly to the world.* To every person in the land indiscriminately—to the people at large. This is another proof that John uses the term *world* to mean the Jewish people only, for it is certain our Lord did not preach to the Gentiles. The answer of our Lord, mentioned in this and the following verse, is such as became a Person conscious of His own innocence and confident in the righteousness of His cause. I have taught in the Temple, in the synagogues, in all the principal cities, towns, and villages, and through all the country. I have had no secret school. You and your emissaries have watched Me everywhere. No doctrine has ever proceeded from My lips but what was agreeable to the righteousness of the law and the purity of God. Ask those who have attended our public ministrations and hear whether they can prove that I or My disciples have preached any false doctrines, have ever troubled society, or disturbed the state. Attend to the ordinary course of justice, call witnesses, let them make their depositions, and then proceed to judge according to the evidence brought before you.

22. *One of the officers . . . struck Jesus.* This was an outrage to all justice. For a prisoner, before he is condemned, is ever considered to be under the especial protection of justice; nor has anyone a right to touch him but according

to the direction of the law. But it has been observed before that if justice had been done to Christ He could have neither suffered nor died.

24. *Now Annas had sent him.* It has been observed before that the proper place of this verse is immediately after the thirteenth; and if it be allowed to stand here it should be read in a parenthesis and considered as a recapitulation of what had been done before.

27. *And immediately the cock crew.* Peter denied our Lord three times. His first denial took place when he was without, or beneath, in the hall of Caiaphas' house. He was not in the higher part where Christ stood before the high priest, but without that division of the hall and in the lower part with the servants and officers, at the fire kindled in the midst of the hall, vv. 16, 18; and the girl who kept the door had entered into the hall, where she charged Peter. His second denial was a short time after the first, Luke xxii. 58. Having once denied his Master, he naturally retired from the place where his accuser was to the vestibule of the hall, Matt. xxvi. 71, and it was the time of the first cock-crowing, or soon after midnight. After his remaining here a short time, perhaps an hour, another girl saw him and said to them who were standing by in the vestibule that he was one of them. Peter, to avoid this charge, withdrew into the hall and warmed himself. The girl, and those to whom she had spoken, followed him, the communication between the two places being immediate. Here a man enforced the charge of the girl, according to Luke; and others urged it, according to John; and Peter denied Jesus vehemently. His third denial was in the hall within sight of Jesus, though at such a distance from Him that Jesus could not know what passed but in a supernatural way. And about an hour after his second denial those who stood by founded a third charge against him, on his being a Galilean, which Luke says, chap. xxii. 59, one in particular strongly affirmed; and which, according to John, v. 26, was supported by one of Malchus' relations. This occasioned a more vehement denial than before, and immediately the cock crew the second time. The first denial may have been between our twelve and one, and the second between our two and three. The time of Peter's denials happened during the space of the third Roman watch, or that division of the night between twelve and three, which is called "cock-crowing," Mark xiii. 35.

28. *The hall of judgment.* To the praetorium. This was the house where Pilate lodged; hence called in our margin *Pilate's house.* The praetorium is so called from being the dwelling place of the *praetor,* or chief of the province. It was also the place where he held his court and tried causes. John has omitted all that passed in the house of Caiaphas—the accusations brought against Christ, the false witnesses, the insults which He received in the house of the high priest, and the assembling of the grand council, or Sanhedrin. These he found amply detailed by the other three Evangelists, and for this reason it appears that he omitted them. John's is properly a supplementary Gospel. Lest *they should be defiled.* The Jews considered even the touch of a Gentile as a legal defilement, and therefore would not venture into the

praetorium for fear of contracting some impurity, which would have obliged them to separate themselves from all religious ordinances till the evening, Lev. xv. 10-11, 19-20. *That they might eat the passover.* Some maintain that *to pascha* here does not mean the paschal lamb but the other sacrifices which were offered during the paschal solemnity—for this had been eaten the evening before; and that our Lord was crucified the day after the Passover. Others have maintained that the paschal lamb is here meant, that this was the proper day for sacrificing it, that it was on the very hour in which it was offered that Christ expired on the Cross, and that therefore our Lord did not eat the paschal lamb this year, or that He ate it some hours before the common time. That Jesus ate a Passover this last year of His life is sufficiently evident from Matt. xxvi. 17-19; Mark xiv. 12-18; Luke xxii. 8-15; and that He ate this Passover some hours before the ordinary time and was himself slain at that hour in which the paschal lamb was ordered by the law to be sacrificed is highly probable, if not absolutely certain.

29. *Pilate then went out.* This was an act of condescension; but, as the Romans had confirmed to the Jews the free use of all their rites and ceremonies, the governor could not do less then comply with them in this matter. He went out to them, that they might not be obliged to come into the hall and thus run the risk of being defiled.

30. *If he were not a malefactor.* So they did not wish to make Pilate the judge, but the executor of the sentence which they had already illegally passed.

31. *It is not lawful for us to put any man to death.* They might have judged Jesus according to their law, as Pilate bade them do, but they could only excommunicate or scourge Him. They might have voted Him worthy of death, but they could not put Him to death, if anything of a secular nature were charged against Him. The power of life and death was in all probability taken from the Jews when Archelaus, king of Judea, was banished to Vienna, and Judea was made a Roman province; and this happened more than fifty years before the destruction of Jerusalem. But the Romans suffered Herod, mentioned in Acts xii, to exercise the power of life and death during his reign. After all, I think it probable that, though the power of life and death was taken away from the Jews as far as it concerned affairs of state, yet it was continued to them in matters which were wholly of an ecclesiastical nature; and that they only applied thus to Pilate to persuade him that they were proceeding against Christ as an enemy of the state, and not as a transgressor of their own peculiar laws and customs. Hence, though they assert that He should die according to their law, because He made himself the Son of God, chap. xix. 7, yet they lay peculiar stress on His being an enemy to the Roman government; and when they found Pilate disposed to let Him go, they asserted that if he did he was not Caesar's friend, v. 12. It was this that intimidated Pilate and induced him to give Him up, that they might crucify Him.

32. *That the saying of Jesus might be fulfilled.* Or, "Thus the word was fulfilled." God permitted the Jews to lose the power of life

and death, in the sense before stated, that according to the Roman laws, which punished sedition with the cross, Christ might be crucified, according to His own prediction, chap. xii. 32 and iii. 14.

33. *Art thou the King of the Jews?* Luke says expressly, xxiii. 2, that when the Jews brought Him to Pilate they began to accuse Him as a rebel, who said He was King of the Jews, and forbade the people to pay tribute to Caesar. It was in consequence of this accusation that Pilate asked the question mentioned in the text.

34. *Sayest thou this thing of thyself?* That is, Is it because My enemies thus accuse Me or because you have any suspicion of Me that you ask this question?

35. *Am I a Jew?* That is, I am not a Jew, and cannot judge whether Thou art what is called the Christ, the King of the Jews. It is Thine own countrymen, and their spiritual rulers, who delivered Thee up to me with the above accusation. *What hast thou done?* If Thou dost not profess thyself King over this people, and an enemy to Caesar, what is it that Thou hast done for which they desire Thy condemnation?

36. *My kingdom is not of this world.* It is purely spiritual and divine. If it had been of a secular nature, then My servants would have contended—they would have opposed force with force, as the kingdoms of this world do in their wars; but as *my kingdom is not of this world*, therefore no resistance has been made.

37. *Thou sayest.* A common form of expression for "Yes, it is so." I was born into the world that I might set up and maintain a spiritual government, but this government is established in and by truth. All that love truth hear My voice and attend to the spiritual doctrines I preach. It is by *truth* alone that I influence the minds and govern the manners of My subjects.

38. *What is truth?* Among the sages of that time there were many opinions concerning *truth*, and some had even supposed that it was a thing utterly out of the reach of men. Pilate perhaps might have asked the question in a mocking way; and his not staying to get an answer indicated that he either despaired of getting a satisfactory one or that he was indifferent about it. *I find in him no fault.* Having asked the above question, and being convinced of our Lord's innocence, he went out to the Jews to testify his conviction, and to deliver Him, if possible, out of their hands.

39. *But ye have a custom.* Nothing relative to the origin or reason of this custom is known. Commentators have swum in an ocean of conjecture on this point.

40. *Barabbas was a robber.* See Matt. xxvii. 16.

CHAPTER 19

Jesus is scourged, crowned with thorns, and mocked by the soldiers, 1-3. He is brought forth by Pilate, wearing the purple robe; and the Jews clamor for His death, 4-8. Conversation between our Lord and Pilate, 9-11. Pilate expostulates with the Jews on their barbarous demands; but they become more inveterate, and he delivers Christ into their hands, 12-16. He, bearing His cross, is led to Golgotha, and crucified, 17-22. The soldiers cast lots for His raiment, 23-24. Jesus commends His mother to the care of John, 25-27. Jesus thirsts, receives vinegar, and

dies, 28-30. The Jews request that the legs of those who were crucified might be broken; the soldiers break those of the two thieves, and pierce the side of Christ; the Scriptures fulfilled in these acts, 31-37. Joseph of Arimathaea begs the body of Christ, and Nicodemus brings spices to embalm it, 38-40. He is laid in a new sepulchre, 41-42.

1. *Pilate therefore took Jesus, and scourged him.* That is, caused Him to be scourged. As our Lord was scourged by order of Pilate, it is probable He was scourged in the Roman manner, which was much more severe than that of the Jews. The latter never gave more than thirty-nine blows; for the law had absolutely forbidden a man to be abused, or his flesh cut in this chastisement, Deut. xxv. 3. Though it was customary to scourge the person who was to be crucified, yet it appears that Pilate had another end in view by scourging our Lord. He hoped that this would satisfy the Jews, and that he might then dismiss Jesus. This appears from Luke xxiii. 16.

2. *Platted a crown of thorns.* See on Matt. xxvii. 29.

7. *We have a law.* In Lev. xxiv. 14-16 we find that blasphemers of God were to be put to death; and the chief priests having charged Jesus with blasphemy, they therefore voted that He deserved to die. They might refer also to the law against false prophets, Deut. xviii. 20. *The Son of God.* It is certain that the Jews understood this in a very peculiar sense. When Christ called himself *the Son of God*, they understood it to imply positive equality to the Supreme Being; and, if they were wrong, our Lord never attempted to correct them.

8. *He was the more afraid.* While Jesus was accused only as a disturber of the peace of the nation, which accusation Pilate knew to be false, he knew he could deliver Him, because the judgment in that case belonged to himself. But when the Jews brought a charge against Him of the most capital nature, from their own laws, he then saw that he had everything to fear if he did not deliver Jesus to their will. The Sanhedrin must not be offended—the populace must not be irritated. From the former a complaint might be sent against him to Caesar; the latter might revolt, or proceed to some acts of violence, the end of which could not be foreseen. Pilate was certainly to be pitied. He saw what was right and he wished to do it, but he had not sufficient firmness of mind. Some suppose that Pilate's fear arose from hearing that Jesus had said He was *the Son of God;* because Pilate, who was a polytheist, believed that it was possible for the offspring of the gods to visit mortals; and he was afraid to condemn Jesus, for fear of offending some of the supreme deities. Perhaps the question in the succeeding verse refers to this.

9. *Whence art thou?* This certainly does not mean, From what country art Thou? for Pilate knew this well enough; but it appears he made this inquiry to know who were the parents of Christ; what were His pretensions, and whether He really were a demigod, such as the heathens believed in. To this question we find our Lord gave no answer. He had already told him that His kingdom was not of this world; and that He came to erect a spiritual Kingdom, not a temporal one, chap. xviii. 36-37. This answer He deemed sufficient; and He did not choose to satisfy a criminal curiosity, nor to enter

into any debate concerning the absurdity of the heathen worship.

11. *Hath the greater sin.* It is a sin in you to condemn Me, while you are convinced in your conscience that I am innocent; but the Jews who delivered Me to you, and Judas, who delivered Me to the Jews, have the greater crime to answer for.

12. *Pilate sought to release him.* Pilate made five several attempts to release our Lord, as we may learn from Luke xxiii. 4, 15, 20, 22; John xix. 4, 12-13. *Thou art not Caesar's friend.* You do not act like a person who has the interest of the emperor at heart. This insinuation determined Pilate to make no longer resistance; he was afraid of being accused, and he knew Tiberius was one of the most jealous and distrustful princes in the world. During his reign accusations of conspiracies were much in fashion; they were founded on the silliest pretenses, and punished with excessive rigor.

13. *The Pavement.* Literally, "a stone pavement." Probably it was that place in the open court where the chair of justice was set, for the prefects of provinces always held their courts of justice in the open air, and which was paved with stones of various colors, like that of Ahasuerus, Esther i. 6, of red, blue, white, and black marble; what we still term Mosaic work, or something in imitation of it. *Gabbatha.* That is, "an elevated place"; from *gabah,* "high, raised up." It is very likely that the judgment seat was considerably elevated in the court, and that the governor went up to it by steps; and perhaps these very steps were what was called *the Pavement.* The place was probably called *Lithostroton,* or *the Pavement;* the seat of judgment, *Gabbatha,* the "raised or elevated" place.

14. *It was the preparation of the passover.* That is, the time in which they were just preparing to kill the paschal lamb. Critics differ widely concerning the time of our Lord's crucifixion, and this verse is variously understood. Some think it signifies merely the preparation of the Sabbath, and that it is called *the preparation of the passover* because the preparation of the Sabbath happened that year on the eve of the Passover. Others think that the preparation of the Sabbath is distinctly spoken of in v. 31, and was different from what is here mentioned. Contending nations may be more easily reconciled than contending critics. *Behold your King!* This was probably intended as an irony; and by thus turning their pretended serious apprehensions into ridicule, he hopes still to release Him.

15. *Away with him.* Probably this means, "Kill Him."

16. *Then delivered he him.* This was not till after he had washed his hands, Matt. xxvii. 24, to show by that symbolical action that he was innocent of the death of Christ. John omits this circumstance, together with the insults which Christ received from the soldiers. See Matt. xxvii. 26, etc.; Mark xv. 16, etc.

17. *Bearing his cross.* He bore it all alone first. When He could no longer carry the whole through weakness, occasioned by the ill usage He had received, Simon, a Cyrenian, helped Him to carry it; see the note on Matt. xxvii. 32. *Golgotha.* See on Matt. xxvii. 33.

18. *Two other.* Matthew and Mark in the parallel places calls them robbers or murderers; they probably belonged to the gang of Barabbas.

19. *Pilate wrote a title.* See on Matt. xxvii. 37.

20. *Hebrew, and Greek, and Latin.* See on Luke xxiii. 38.

22. *What I have written I have written.* That is, I will not alter what I have written. The Roman laws forbad the sentence to be altered when once pronounced; and as this inscription was considered as the sentence pronounced against our Lord, therefore it could not be changed. But this form of speech is common in the Jewish writings, and means simply, What is done shall continue. Pilate seems to speak prophetically. This is the King of the Jews; they shall have no other Messiah forever.

23. *To every soldier a part.* So it appears there were four soldiers employed in nailing Him to and rearing up the Cross. Our Lord was now in the grand office of High Priest, and was about to offer the expiatory Victim for the sin of the world. And it is worthy of remark that the very dress He was in was similar to that of the Jewish high priest. The following is the description given of his dress by Josephus: "Now this coat (*chiton*) was not composed of two pieces, nor was it sewed together upon the shoulders and sides, but it was one long vestment, so woven as to have an opening for the neck; not an oblique one, but parted all along the back and breast: it was also parted where the hands were to come out."

24. *That the scripture might be fulfilled.* The words are taken from Ps. xxii. 18, where it appears they were spoken prophetically of this treatment which Jesus received, upwards of a thousand years before it took place! But it should be remarked that this form of speech, which frequently occurs, often means no more than that the thing so fell out that such a portion of Scripture may be exactly applied to it.

25. *Mary the wife of Cleophas.* She is said, in Matt. xxvii. 56 and Mark xv. 40, to have been the mother of James the Less and of Joses; and this James, her son, is said, in Matt. x. 3, to have been the son of Alphaeus; hence it seems that Alphaeus and Cleophas were the same person. To which may be added that Hegesippus is quoted by Eusebius as saying that Cleophas was the brother of Joseph, the husband of the Virgin. In many cases it is very difficult to distinguish the different Marys mentioned by the Evangelists.

26. *The disciple . . . whom he loved.* John, the writer of this Gospel. *Woman, behold thy son!* This is a remarkable expression, and has been much misunderstood. It conveys no idea of disrespect, nor of unconcern, as has been commonly supposed. "Man" and "woman" were titles of as much respect among the Hebrews as "sir" and "madam" are among us. But why did not Jesus call her "Mother"? Probably because He wished to spare her feelings; He would not mention a name the very sound of which must have wrung her heart with additional sorrow. On this account He said, *Behold thy son!* This was the language of pure natural affection. It is probable that it was because the keeping of the blessed Virgin was entrusted to him that he was the only disciple of our Lord who died a

natural death, God having preserved him for the sake of the person whom He gave him in charge. It is very likely that Joseph was dead previously to this, and that this was the reason why the desolate Virgin is committed to the care of the beloved disciple.

28. *I thirst.* The scripture that referred to His drinking the vinegar is Ps. lxix. 21. The fatigue which He had undergone, the grief He had felt, the heat of the day, and the loss of blood were the natural causes of this thirst.

29. *A vessel full of vinegar.* This was probably that tart small wine which we are assured was the common drink of the Roman soldiers. Our word *vinegar* comes from the French *vin aigre, sour* or "tart wine." This vinegar must not be confounded with the "vinegar and gall" mentioned in Matt. xxvii. 34 and Mark xv. 23. That, being a stupefying potion, intended to alleviate His pain, He refused to drink; but of this He took a little, and then expired, v. 30. *And put it upon hyssop.* Or, according to others, "putting hyssop about it."

30. *It is finished.* As if He had said: "I have executed the great designs of the Almighty—I have satisfied the demands of His justice—I have accomplished all that was written in the prophets, and suffered the utmost malice of My enemies; and now the way to the holy of holies is made manifest through My blood." An awful, yet a glorious finish!

31. *It was the preparation.* Every Sabbath had a preparation which began at the ninth hour (that is, three o'clock) the preceding evening. Josephus, *Ant.,* b. xvi, c. 6, s. 2, recites an edict of the Emperor Augustus in favor of the Jews, which orders "that no one shall be obliged to give bail or surety on the Sabbath day, nor on the preparation before it, after the ninth hour." The time fixed here was undoubtedly in conformity to the Jewish custom, as they began their preparation at three o'clock on the Friday evening. *That the bodies should not remain.* For the law, Deut. xxi. 22-23, ordered that the bodies of criminals should not hang all night; and they did not wish to have the Sabbath profaned by either taking them down on that day or letting them hang to disturb the joy of that holy time. *For that sabbath day was an high day.* (1) Because it was the Sabbath. (2) Because it was the day on which all the people presented themselves in the Temple according to the command, Exod. xxiii. 17. (3) Because that was the day on which the sheaf of the firstfruits was offered, according to the command, Lev. xxiii. 10-11. So that upon this day there happened to be three solemnities in one. It might be properly called a high day because the Passover fell on that Sabbath. *Their legs might be broken.* Lactantius says that it was a common custom to break the legs or other bones of criminals upon the cross; and this appears to have been a kind of *coup de grace,* the sooner to put them out of pain.

34. *With a spear pierced his side.* The soldier who pierced our Lord's side has been called by the Roman Catholic writers *Longinus,* which seems to be a corruption of *lonche,* a *spear* or "dart." They moreover tell us that this man was converted—that it was he who said, "Truly this was the Son of God"—that he travelled into Cappadocia, and there preached the gospel of

Christ, and received the crown of martyrdom. But this deserves the same credit as the other legends of the Popish church. *Blood and water.* It may be naturally supposed that the spear went through the pericardium and pierced the heart; that the water proceeded from the former, and the blood from the latter. Ambrose, Augustine, and Chrysostom make the *blood* an emblem of the Eucharist, and the *water* an emblem of baptism. Others represent them as the emblem of the old and new covenants. Protestants have thought them the emblems of justification, which is through the *blood* of the Lamb, and sanctification, which is through the *washing* of regeneration; and it is in reference to the first notion that they mingle the wine with water in the sacrament of the Lord's Supper. The issuing of the blood and water appears to be only a natural effect of the above cause, and probably nothing mystical or spiritual was intended by it. However it affords the fullest proof that Jesus *died* for our sins.

35. *He that saw it.* Most probably John himself, who must have been pretty near the Cross to have been able to distinguish between the blood and the water as they issued from the side of our blessed Lord. *And he knoweth.* This appears to be an appeal to the Lord Jesus for the truth of the testimony which he had now delivered. But why such a solemn appeal unless there was something miraculous in this matter? It might appear to him necessary: (1) because the other Evangelists had not noticed it; (2) because it contained the most decisive proof of the *death* of Christ, as a wound such as this was could not have been inflicted (though other causes had been wanting) without occasioning the death of the person, and on His *dying* for men depended the salvation of the world; and (3) because two important prophecies were fulfilled by this very circumstance, both of which designated more particularly the person of the Messiah. "A bone of him shall not be broken," Exod. xii. 46; Num. ix. 12; Ps. xxxiv. 20. "They shall look upon me whom they have pierced," Zech. xii. 10; Ps. xxii. 16.

38. *Joseph of Arimathaea.* See on Matt. xxvii. 57-60; and particularly Mark xv. 42-43.

39. *Nicodemus.* See on chap. iii. 1. *Myrrh and aloes.* Which drugs were used to preserve bodies from putrefaction.

41. *There was a garden.* It was an ancient custom for particular families to have burying places in their gardens. See 2 Kings xxi. 18, 26. *New sepulchre.* See on Matt. xxvii. 60.

42. *Because of the Jews' preparation.* From this it may be conjectured that they had designed to put Him in a more magnificent tomb, or that they intended to make one expressly for himself after the Passover, or that they had designed to put Him somewhere else, but could not do it for want of time; and that they put Him here because the tomb *was nigh.* It appears plainly, from embalming, that none of these persons had any hope of the resurrection of Christ. They considered Him as a great and eminent prophet, and treated Him as such.

CHAPTER 20

Mary Magdalene, coming early to the sepulchre, finds it empty, and runs and tells Peter, 1-2. Peter and John run to the tomb, and find all as Mary had reported, 3-10. Mary sees a vision of angels in the tomb, 11-13.

Jesus himself appears to her, and sends her with a message to the disciples, 14-18. He appears to the disciples, gives the fullest proof of the reality of His resurrection, and communicates to them a measure of the Holy Spirit, 19-23. The determined incredulity of Thomas, 24-25. Eight days after, Jesus appears again to the disciples, Thomas being present, to whom He gives the proofs he had desired, 26-27. Thomas is convinced, and makes a noble confession, 28. Our Lord's reflections on his case, 29. Various signs done by Christ, not circumstantially related, 30. Why others are recorded, 31.

All that John relates concerning the resurrection of our Lord he has collected partly from the account given by Mary Magdalene, and partly from his own observations. From Mary he derived the information given in vv. 1-2, and from vv. 11-18; from his own actual knowledge, what he relates in vv. 3-10, 19-29, and the whole of chap. xxi. It is supposed that he details the account given by Mary without altering any circumstance and without either addition or retrenchment.

1. *The first day of the week.* On what we call Sunday morning, the morning after the Jewish Sabbath. As Christ had been buried in haste, these holy women had bought aromatics, Mark xvi. 1; Luke xxiv. 1, to embalm Him afresh, and in a more complete manner than it could have been done by Joseph and Nicodemus. John mentions only Mary of Magdala, because he appears to wish to give a more detailed history of her conduct than of any of the rest. But the other Evangelists speak of three persons who went together to the tomb, viz., Mary of Magdala, Mary the mother of James, and Salome, Matt. xxviii. 1; Mark xvi. 1.

2. *Then she runneth.* This was after the women had seen the angels, who said He was risen from the dead, Luke xxiv. 4. She told not only Peter and John but the other apostles also, Matt. xxviii. 8; but only the two disciples above mentioned went to the tomb to see whether what she had said was true. *They have taken away the Lord.* She mentions nothing of what the angels had said, in her hurry and confusion; she speaks things only by halves; and probably the vision of angels might have appeared to her only as an illusion of her own fancy, and not to be any further regarded.

4. *Outrun Peter.* Not because he had a greater desire to see into the truth of these things, but because he was younger and lighter of foot.

6. *Seeth the linen clothes lie.* To "look steadily" at anything, so as to discover what it is and to be satisfied with viewing it.

7. *Wrapped together in a place by itself.* The providence of God ordered these very little matters, so that they became the fullest proofs against the lie of the chief priests that the body had been stolen away by the disciples. If the body had been stolen away, those who took it would not have stopped to strip the clothes from it and to wrap them up and lay them by in separate places.

8. *That other disciple.* John. *Saw.* That the body was not there. *And believed.* That it had been taken away, as Mary had said; but he did not believe that He was risen from the dead. See what follows.

9. *They knew not the scripture.* Viz., Ps. xvi. 9-10: "Thou wilt not leave my soul in hell" —For Thou wilt not abandon My life to the grave, nor "suffer thine Holy One to see corruption." It was certainly a reproach to the disciples that they had not understood this prophecy, when our Lord had often given them the most direct information concerning it. However, this ingenuous confession of John in a matter so dishonorable to himself is a full proof of his sincerity and of the truth of his narration.

10. *Unto their own home.* Either to their own houses, if they still had any, or to those of their friends, or to those where they had a hired lodging, and where they met together for religious purposes.

11. *But Mary stood without.* She remained some time after Peter and John had returned to their own homes.

12. *Seeth two angels.* She knew these to be angels by their white and glistering robes. Matthew and Mark mention but one angel— probably that one only that spoke, v. 13. *One at the head, and the other at the feet.* So were the cherubim placed at each end of the mercy seat, Exod. xxv. 18-19.

13. *They have taken away my Lord.* It was conjectured, on chap. xix. 42, that the body of our Lord was put here only for the time being, that, after the Sabbath, they might carry it to a more proper place. Mary seems to refer to this: *They have taken away my Lord, and I know not where they have laid him.* This removal she probably attributed to some of our Lord's disciples or to some of His friends.

14. *She turned herself back.* Or "she was turned back," i.e., to go again with the other women to Jerusalem, who had already departed; but she had not as yet gone so far as to be out of the garden. *Knew not that it was Jesus.* John has here omitted what the angels said to the women about Christ's being risen, probably because it was so particularly related by the other Evangelists: Matt. xxviii. 5-7; Mark xvi. 6-7; Luke xxiv. 5-7. Mary was so absorbed in grief that she paid but little attention to the person of our Lord, and therefore did not at first discern it to be He; nor could she imagine such an appearance possible, as she had no conception of His resurrection from the dead. She was therefore in every way unprepared to recognize the person of our Lord.

15. *Supposing him to be the gardener.* The inspector or overseer of the garden, the person who had the charge of the workmen, and who care of the produce of the garden, and who rendered account to the owner. *And I will take him away.* How true is the proverb, "Love feels no load"! Jesus was in the prime of life when He was crucified, and had a hundred pounds' weight of spices added to His body; and yet Mary thinks of nothing less than carrying Him away with her if she can but find where He is laid!

16. *Mary.* This word was no doubt spoken with uncommon emphasis; and the usual sound of Christ's voice accompanied it, so as immediately to prove that it must be Jesus. What transports of joy must have filled this woman's heart! Let it be remarked that Mary Magdalene sought Jesus more fervently and continued more affectionately attached to Him than any of the rest; therefore to her first Jesus is pleased to show himself, and she is made the first herald of the gospel of a risen Saviour.

17. *Touch me not.* "Cling not to Me." *Aptomai* has this sense in Job xxxi. 7, where the Septuagint use it for the Hebrew *dabak,* which signifies to "cleave, cling, stick, or be glued to." From Matt. xxviii. 9, it appears that some of the women "held him by the feet, and worshipped him." This probably Mary did; and our Lord seems to have spoken to her to this effect:

"Spend no longer time with Me now. I am not going immediately to heaven—you will have several opportunities of seeing Me again. But go and tell My disciples that I am, by and by, to ascend to My Father and God, who is your Father and God also. Therefore, let them take courage."

18. *Told the disciples . . . that he had spoken these things.* Mark says, chap. xvi. 11, that the afflicted apostles could not believe what she had said. They seem to have considered it as an effect of her troubled imagination.

19. *The doors were shut . . . for fear of the Jews.* We do not find that the Jews designed to molest the disciples; but, as they had proceeded so far as to put Christ to death, the faith of the disciples not being very strong, they were led to think that they should be the next victims if found. Some think, therefore, that they had the doors not only *shut* but barricaded. Nevertheless Jesus came in, the doors being shut, i.e., while they continued shut. But how? By His almighty power; and further we know not. Yet it is quite possible that no miraculous influence is here intended. The doors might be shut for fear of the Jews; and Jesus might open them, and enter in the ordinary way. Where there is no need for a miracle, a miracle is never wrought. The Evangelist has omitted the appearing of our Lord to the other women who came from the tomb, Matt. xxviii. 9, and that to the two disciples who were going to Emmaus, Luke xxiv. 13, etc., which all happened in the course of this same day. *Peace be unto you.* His usual salutation and benediction. May every blessing of heaven and earth which you need be granted unto you!

20. *He shewed unto them his hands and his side.* So it appears that His body bore the marks of the nails and the spear; and these marks were preserved that the disciples might be the more fully convinced of the reality of His resurrection.

21. *Even so send I you.* As I was sent to proclaim the truth of the Most High, and to convert sinners to God, I send you for the very same purpose, clothed with the very same authority, and influenced by the very same Spirit.

22. *He breathed on them.* Intimating, by this, that they were to be made new men, in order to be properly qualified for the work to which He had called them. For in this breathing He evidently alluded to the first creation of man, when God breathed into him the breath of lives, and he became a living soul, the breath or Spirit of God (*ruach Elohim*) being the grand principle and cause of his spiritual and divine life. *Receive ye the Holy Ghost.* From this act of our Lord, the influences of the Holy Spirit on the souls of men have been termed His "inspiration"; from *in*, "into," and *spiro*, "I breathe." Every word of Christ which is received in the heart by faith comes accompanied by this divine breathing; and without this there is neither light nor life.

23. *Whose soever sins ye remit.* See the note on Matt. xvi. 19 and xviii. 18. It is certain God alone can forgive sins; and it would be not only blasphemous but grossly absurd to say that any creature could remit the guilt of a transgression which had been committed against the Creator. The apostles received from the Lord the doctrine of reconciliation and the doctrine of condemnation. They who believed on the Son of God, in consequence of their preaching, had their sins remitted; and they who would not believe were declared to lie under condemnation.

24. *Thomas . . . called Didymus.* See this name explained, chap. xi. 16. *Was not with them.* And by absenting himself from the company of the disciples he lost this precious opportunity of seeing and hearing Christ, and of receiving (at this time) the inestimable blessing of the Holy Ghost. Where two or three are assembled in the name of Christ, He is in the midst of them. Christ had said this before; Thomas should have remembered it, and not have forsaken the company of the disciples. What is the consequence? His unbelief becomes (1) Utterly *unreasonable.* Ten of his brethren witnessed that they had seen Christ, v. 15; but he rejected their testimony. (2) His unbelief became *obstinate.* He was determined not to believe on any evidence that it might please God to give him; he would believe according to his own prejudices, or not at all. (3) His unbelief became *presumptuous.* A view of the person of Christ will not suffice; he will not believe that it is He unless he can put his finger into the holes made by the nails in his Lord's hand, and thrust his hand into the wound made by the spear in His side. Thomas had lost much good, and gained much evil, and yet was insensible of his state. Behold the consequences of forsaking the assemblies of God's people! Jesus comes to the meeting—a disciple is found out of his place, who might have been there; and he is not only not blessed, but his heart becomes hardened and darkened through the deceitfulness of sin. It was through God's mere mercy that Thomas ever had another opportunity of being convinced of his error.

26. *After eight days.* It seems likely that this was precisely on that day on which Christ had appeared to them before, and from this we may learn that this was the weekly meeting of the apostles; and though Thomas was not found at the former meeting, he was determined not to be absent from this. According to His custom, Jesus came again; for He cannot forget His promise—two or three are assembled in His name, and He was engaged to be among them.

27. *Then saith he to Thomas.* Through His infinite compassion He addressed him in a particular manner, condescending in this case to accommodate himself to the prejudices of an obstinate, though sincere, disciple. *Reach hither thy finger.* And it is very probable that Thomas did so, for his unbelief was too deeply rooted to be easily cured.

28. *Thomas answered.* Those who deny the Godhead of Christ would have us to believe that these words are an exclamation of Thomas, made through surprise, and that they were addressed to the Father and not to Christ. However, a man must do violence to every rule of construction who can apply the address here to any but Christ. The text is plain: Jesus comes in—sees Thomas, and addresses him, desiring him to come to Him and put his finger into the print of the nails. Thomas, perfectly satisfied of the reality of our Lord's resurrection, *said unto him, My Lord and my God.* Thomas

was the first who gave the title of *God* to Jesus; and by this glorious confession made some amends for his former obstinate incredulity.

29. *Thomas.* This word is omitted by almost every MS., version, and ancient commentator of importance. *Blessed are they.* You have seen, and therefore you have believed, and now you are blessed; you are now happy—fully convinced of My resurrection. Yet no less blessed shall all those be who believe in My resurrection without the evidence you have had.

30. *Many other signs truly did Jesus.* That is, besides the two mentioned here, vv. 19 and 26, viz., Christ's entering into the house in a miraculous manner twice, notwithstanding the doors were fast shut; see on v. 19. The other miracles which our Lord did, and which are not related here, were such as were necessary to the disciples only, and therefore not revealed to mankind at large.

31. *That ye might believe.* What is here recorded is to give a full proof of the divinity of Christ; that He is the promised Messiah; that He really suffered and rose again from the dead; and that through Him every believer might have eternal life.

CHAPTER 21

Jesus shows himself to the disciples at the Sea of Tiberias, 1-5. The miraculous draught of fishes, 6-11. He dines with His disciples, 12-14. Questions Peter concerning his love to Him, and gives him commission to feed His sheep, 15-17. Foretells the manner of Peter's death; 18-19. Peter inquires concerning John, and receives an answer that was afterwards misunderstood, 20-23. John's concluding testimony concerning the authenticity of his Gospel, and the end for which it was written, 24-25.

1. *Jesus shewed himself again.* After that our Lord had appeared several times to the women, and to the apostles at Jerusalem, and at the tomb, He bade them go into Galilee, giving them the promise of meeting them there, Matt. xxviii. 7; Mark xvi. 7. This promise we find He fulfilled in the way John relates here. This was the seventh appearance of our Lord after the Resurrection. Matthew, chap. xxviii. 16, has but just mentioned it; of it the rest of the Evangelists say nothing, and this is the reason why John gives it so particularly.

3. *Peter saith . . . I go a fishing.* Previously to the crucifixion of our Lord, the temporal necessities of himself and His disciples appear to have been supplied by the charity of individuals, Luke viii. 3. As it is probable that the scandal of the Cross had now shut up this source of support, the disciples, not fully knowing how they were to be employed, purposed to return to their former occupation of fishing in order to gain a livelihood; and therefore the seven, mentioned in v. 2, embarked on the Sea of Tiberias, otherwise called the Sea of Galilee. *That night they caught nothing.* God had so ordered it that they might be the more struck with the miracle which He afterwards wrought.

4. *Knew not that it was Jesus.* Probably because it was either not light enough, or He was at too great a distance, or He had assumed another form, as in Mark xvi. 12.

5. *Children.* A term of familiarity and affectionate kindness; it literally signifies "little children" or "beloved children." *Any meat.* Anything that is eaten with bread, or suchlike solid substances, to make the deglutition the more easy. Here it evidently means any kind of fish; and our Lord seems to have appeared at first in the character of a person who wished to purchase a part of what they had caught.

6. *For the multitude of fishes.* This was intended as an emblem of the immense number of souls which should be converted to God by their ministry, according to the promise of Christ, Matt. iv. 19.

7. *His fisher's coat.* Or "his upper coat." *He was naked.* He was only in his "vest." *Naked* is often used to signify the absence of this upper garment only. In 1 Sam. xix. 24, when Saul had put off his upper garments, he is said to have been "naked"; and David, when girded only with a linen ephod, is said to have been "uncovered," in 2 Sam. vi. 14, 20. *Cast himself into the sea.* It is likely that they were in very shallow water; and, as they were only 200 cubits from the land, it is possible that Peter only stepped into the water that he might assist them to draw the boat to land, which was now heavily laden.

8. *Dragging the net.* It is probable that this was that species of fishing in which the net was stretched from the shore out into the sea. The persons who were in the boat, and who shot the net, fetched a compass, and bringing in a hawser, which was attached to the other end of the net, those who were on shore helped them to drag it in. As the net was sunk with weights to the bottom, and the top floated on the water by corks, or pieces of light wood, all the fish that happened to come within the compass of the net were of course dragged to shore. The sovereign power of Christ had in this case miraculously collected the fish to that part where He ordered the disciples to cast the net.

9. *They saw a fire.* This appears to have been a new miracle. It could not have been a fire which the disciples had there, for it is remarked as something new. Besides, they had caught no fish, v. 5, and here was a small fish upon the coals, and a loaf of bread provided to eat with it. The whole appears to have been miraculously prepared by Christ.

12. *Come and dine.* Though this is the literal translation of the word, yet it must be observed that it was not dinner time, being as yet early in the morning, v. 4; but Kypke has largely shown that the original word is used by Homer, Xenophon, and Plutarch to signify "breakfast," or any early meal, as well as what we term "dinner." It might perhaps appear singular; otherwise it would be as agreeable to the use of the Greek word to have translated it, "Come and breakfast." *Durst ask him.* Ever since the confession of Thomas, a proper awe of the deity of Christ had possessed their minds.

13. *And giveth them.* Eating likewise with them, as Luke expressly says, chap. xxiv. 43.

14. *This is now the third time.* That is, this was the third time He appeared unto the apostles when all or most of them were together. He appeared to ten of them, chap. xx. 19; again to eleven of them, v. 26; and at this time to seven of them, v. 2 of this chapter. But when the other Evangelists are collated we shall find that this was the seventh time in which He

had manifested himself after He arose from the dead. (1) He appeared to Mary of Magdala, Mark xvi. 9; John xx. 15-16. (2) To the holy women who came from the tomb, Matt. xxviii. 9. (3) To the two disciples who went to Emmaus, Luke xxiv. 13, etc. (4) To Peter alone, Luke xxiv. 34. (5) To the ten, in the absence of Thomas, chap. xx. 19. (6) Eight days after to the eleven, Thomas being present, v. 26. (7) To the seven, mentioned in v. 2 of this chapter, which was between the eighth and fortieth day after His resurrection. Besides these *seven* appearances, He showed himself (8) to the disciples on a certain mountain in Galilee, Matt. xxviii. 16. If the appearance mentioned by Paul, 1 Cor. xv. 6, to upwards of 500 brethren at once—if this be not the same with His appearance on a mountain in Galilee, it must be considered the ninth. According to the same apostle, He was seen of James, 1 Cor. xv. 7, which may have been the tenth appearance. And after this to all the apostles when, at Bethany, He ascended to heaven in their presence. See Mark xvi. 19-20; Luke xxiv. 50-53; Acts i. 3-12; 1 Cor. xv. 7. This appears to have been the eleventh time in which He distinctly manifested himself after His resurrection. But there might have been many other manifestations which the Evangelists have not thought proper to enumerate, as not being connected with anything of singular weight or importance.

15. *Simon . . . lovest thou me?* Peter had thrice denied his Lord, and now Christ gives him an opportunity in some measure to repair his fault by a triple confession. *More than these?* This was a kind of reproach to Peter. He had professed a more affectionate attachment to Christ than the rest; he had been more forward in making professions of friendship and love than any of the others; and no one (Judas excepted) had treated his Lord so basely. As he had before intimated that his attachment to his Master was *more* than that of the rest, our Lord now puts the question to him, "Dost thou love Me more than these?" To which Peter made the most modest reply—*Thou knowest that I love thee,* but no longer dwells on the strength of his love, nor compares himself with even the meanest of his brethren. He had before cast the very unkind reflection on his brethren, "Though all . . . be offended because of thee, yet will I never be offended," Matt. xxvi. 33. But he had now learned, by dreadful experience, that he who trusts his own heart is a fool; and that a man's sufficiency for good is of the Lord alone. The words *more than these,* Bishop Pearce thinks refer to the provisions they were eating, or to their secular employments. But it appears to me that our Lord refers to the profession made by Peter, which I have quoted above. It is remarkable that in these three questions our Lord uses the verb *agapao,* which signifies to "love affectionately, ardently, supremely, perfectly"; and that Peter always replies using the verb *phileo,* which signifies to "love," to "like," to "regard," to "feel friendship" for another. As if our Lord had said, "Peter, do you love Me ardently and supremely?" To which Peter answers, "Lord, I feel an affection for Thee—I do esteem Thee—but dare, at present, say no more." There is another remarkable change of terms in this place. In vv. 15 and 17 our Lord uses the verb

bosko, "to feed"; and in v. 16 He uses the word *poimaino,* which signifies to "tend a flock"—not only to "feed," but to "take care of, guide, govern, defend"—by which He seems to intimate that it is not sufficient merely to offer the Bread of Life to the congregation of the Lord, but he must take care that the sheep be properly collected, attended to, regulated, guided. Every spiritual shepherd of Christ has a flock, composed of lambs—"young converts"—and sheep—"experienced Christians"—to feed, guide, regulate, and govern. To be properly qualified for this, his wisdom and holiness should always exceed those of his flock.

18. *Thou shalt stretch forth thy hands.* Wetstein observes that it was a custom at Rome to put the necks of those who were to be crucified into a yoke, and to stretch out their hands and fasten them to the end of it; and having thus led them through the city they were carried out to be crucified. Thus then Peter was girded, chained, and carried whither he would not—not that he was unwilling to die for Christ, but he was a man—he did not love death, but he loved his life less than he loved his God.

19. *Should glorify God.* Ancient writers state that, about thirty-four years after this, Peter was crucified; and that he deemed it so glorious a thing to die for Christ that he begged to be crucified with his head downwards, not considering himself worthy to die in the same posture in which his Lord did. *Follow me.* Whether our Lord meant by these words that Peter was to walk with Him a little way for a private interview, or whether He meant that he was to imitate His example, or be conformed to Him in the manner of His death, is very uncertain.

22. *If I will that he tarry till I come.* Augustine, Bede, and others understood the passage thus: If I will that he remain till I come and take him away by a natural death, what is that to you? Follow Me to your crucifixion. On this it may be observed that all antiquity agrees that John, if he did die, was the only disciple who was taken away by a natural death. Others imagine that our Lord was only now taking Peter aside to speak something to him in private, and that Peter, seeing John following, wished to know whether he should come along with them; and that our Lord's answer stated that John should remain in that place till Christ and Peter returned to him—and to this meaning of the passage many eminent critics incline. I rather lean to this opinion.

24. *This is the disciple.* It is, I think, very likely that these two verses were added by some of the believers at that time, as a testimony to the truth of the preceding narration; and I allow, with Bishop Pearce and others, that it is possible that John may mean himself when he says *we know;* yet I think that it is very unlikely.

25. *Could not contain.* Origen's signification of the word is to "admit of" or "receive favorably." As if he had said, The miracles of Christ are so many, and so astonishing, that if the whole were to be detailed the world would not receive the account with proper faith; but enough is recorded that men may believe that Jesus is the Son of God, and that in believing they may have life through His name, chap. xx. 31. We have already seen that this apostle often uses the term world to designate the Jewish people only; and if it have this sense here, which is possible, it will at once vindicate the above exposition. As if he had said, Were I to detail all the signs and miracles which Jesus did among His disciples, and in the private families where He sojourned, the Jewish people themselves would not receive nor credit these accounts; but enough is written to prove that this Christ was the promised Messiah.

The Book of
THE ACTS

The Book of the *Acts of the Apostles* forms the fifth and last of the historical books of the New Testament. And on this account it has been generally placed at the end of the four Gospels, though in several MSS. and versions it is found at the end of Paul's Epistles, as many circumstances in them are referred to by the narrative contained in this book, which is carried down almost to the apostle's death.

This book has had a variety of names: "Acts of the Apostles" is the title it bears in the Codex Bezae. "Acts of the Holy Apostles" is its title in the Codex Alexandrinus, and several others, as well as in several of the ancient versions, and in the Greek and Latin fathers. One or other form of the above title is followed by almost all the editors of the Greek Testament, and translators and commentators in general. By some it has been reckoned a fifth Gospel; and by Oecumenius it is termed "The Gospel of the Holy Spirit."

All antiquity is unanimous in ascribing this book to Luke as the author. From the commencement of it we see plainly that it can be attributed to no other; and it seems plain that Luke intended it as a continuation of his Gospel, being dedicated to Theophilus, to whom he had dedicated the former, and to which in the introduction to this he expressly refers. Indeed he has taken up the narrative in this book precisely in the place where he dropped it in the other: "The former treatise have I made, O Theophilus, of all that Jesus began both to do and teach, until the day in which he was taken up." From this we may form a safe conjecture that the two books were written at no greater a distance from each other than the time of the last occurrence recorded in this book. Some have supposed that this book was written from Alexandria, but this does not appear to be probable. The conjecture of Michaelis is much more likely, viz., that it was written from Rome, at which place Luke mentions his arrival, in company with Paul, shortly before the close of the book. See Acts xxviii. 16.

Luke's long attendance upon Paul, and his having been himself eyewitness to many of the facts which he has recorded, independently of his divine inspiration, render him a most respectable and credible historian. His medical knowledge, for he is allowed to have been a physician, enabled him both to form a proper judgment of the miraculous cures which were performed by Paul and to give an account and authentic detail of them.

The object of Luke appears to have been twofold: (1) To relate in what manner the gifts of the Holy Spirit were communicated on the Day of Pentecost, and the subsequent miracles performed by the apostles, by which the truth of Christianity was confirmed; (2) To deliver such accounts as proved the claim of the Gentiles to admission into the Church of Christ, a claim disputed by the Jews, especially at the time when the Acts of the Apostles was written. Hence we see the reason why he relates, chap. viii, the conversion of the Samaritans; and chaps. x—xi, the story of Cornelius, and the determination of the council in Jerusalem relative to the Levitical law; and for the same reason he is more diffuse in his account of Paul's conversion, and his preaching to the Gentiles, than he is on any other subject.

Luke's narration bears every evidence of truth and authenticity. It is not a *made-up* history. The language and manner of every speaker are different, and the same speaker is different in his manner according to the audience he addresses. The speeches of Stephen, Peter, Cornelius, Tertullus, and Paul are all different, and such as we might naturally expect from the characters in question and the circumstances in which they were at the time of speaking. Paul's speeches are also suited to the occasion, and to the persons before whom he spoke.

In the Book of the Acts we see how the Church of Christ was formed and settled. The apostles simply proclaim the truth of God relative to the passion, death, resurrection, and ascension of Christ, and God accompanies their testimony with the demonstration of His Spirit. What is the consequence? Thousands acknowledge the truth, embrace Christianity, and openly profess it at the most imminent risk of their lives.

CHAPTER 1

Luke's prologue, containing a repetition of Christ's history from His passion till His ascension, 1-9. Remarkable circumstances in the Ascension, 10-11. The return of the disciples to Jerusalem, and their employment there, 12-14. Peter's discourse concerning the death of Judas Iscariot, 15-20, and the necessity of choosing another apostle in his place, 21-22. Barsabas and Matthias being set apart by prayer, the apostles having given their votes, Matthias is chosen to succeed Judas, 23-26.

1. *The former treatise.* The Gospel according to Luke, which is here most evidently intended. *O Theophilus.* See the note on Luke i. 3. *To do and teach.* These two words comprise His miracles and sermons.

3. *To whom . . . he shewed himself alive . . . by many infallible proofs.* By many proofs of such a nature, and connected with such circumstances, as to render them indubitable; for this is the import of the Greek word. *Pertaining to the kingdom of God.* Whatever concerned the doctrine, discipline, and establishment of the Christian Church.

4. *And, being assembled together.* Instead of "being assembled together," several good MSS. and versions read "living or eating together," which refers the conversation reported here to some particular time when He sat at meat with His disciples. *The promise of the Father.* The Holy Spirit, which indeed was the grand promise of the New Testament, as Jesus Christ was of the Old. How properly do we still pray, and how necessary is the prayer, "Cleanse the thoughts of our hearts by the inspiration of thy Holy Spirit, that we may perfectly love thee, and worthily magnify thy name, through Jesus Christ our Lord! Amen."—Communion Service. *Ye have heard of me.* In His particular conversations with His disciples, such as those related in John xiv. 16-26; xv. 26; xvi. 7-15.

5. *Ye shall be baptized with the Holy Ghost not many days hence.* John baptized with water, which was a sign of penitence, in reference to the remission of sin; but Christ baptizes with the Holy Ghost, for the destruction of sin, the illumination of the mind, and the consolation of the heart.

6. *At this time restore again the kingdom.* That the disciples, in common with the Jews, expected the Messiah's kingdom to be at least in part secular, I have often had occasion to note. In this opinion they continued less or more till the Day of Pentecost, when the mighty outpouring of the Holy Spirit taught them the spiritual nature of the kingdom of Christ. The Kingdom had now for a considerable time been taken away from Israel; the Romans, not the Israelites, had the government. The object of the disciples' question seems to have been this: to gain information, from their all-knowing Master, whether the time was now fully come in which the Romans should be thrust out and Israel made, as formerly, an independent kingdom.

7. *The times or the seasons. Times* here may signify any large portion of a period, era, or century; and *seasons,* the particular part, season, or opportunity in that period in which it might be proper to do any particular work.

8. *But ye shall receive power.* Translating different terms of the original by the same English word is a source of misapprehension and error. We must not understand *dynamis,* which we translate *power* in this verse, as we

do *exousia,* translated by the same word in the preceding verse. In the latter, God's infinite "authority" over all times and seasons, and His uncompellable liberty of acting or not acting in any given case, are particularly pointed out. In the other, the "energy" communicated by Him to His disciples through which they were enabled to work miracles is particularly intended; and *dynamis,* in general, signifies such power. The disciples were to be made instruments in the establishment of the kingdom of Christ, but this must be by the *energy* of the Holy Ghost sent down from heaven. *Ye shall be witnesses.* Though the word *earth* is often used to denote Judea alone, yet here it is probable it is to be taken in its largest extent. All the inhabitants of the globe might at that period be considered divisible into three classes: (1) The Jews, who adhered to the law of Moses and the prophetic writings, worshipping the true God only and keeping up the Temple service as prescribed in their law; (2) The Samaritans, a mongrel people who worshipped the God of Israel in connection with other gods, 2 Kings xvii. 5, etc., and who had no kind of religious connection with the Jews; and (3) the Gentiles, the heathens through all other parts of the world, who were addicted to idolatry alone and had no knowledge of the true God. By the terms in the text we may see the extent to which this commission of instruction and salvation was designed to reach: to the Jews, to the Samaritans, and to *the uttermost part of the earth,* i.e., to the Gentile nations. Thus, to the *whole human race* the gospel of the Kingdom was to be proclaimed.

9. *He was taken up.* He was speaking face-to-face with them, and *while they beheld, he was taken up.* He began to ascend to heaven, and they continued to look after Him till *a cloud received him out of their sight*—till He had ascended above the region of the clouds, by the density of which all further distinct vision was prevented.

10. *Looked stedfastly.* Keeping their eyes intensely fixed on their ascending Lord, continuing to look even after He had ascended above the region of the inferior clouds. *Two men stood by them.* Doubtless angels in human shape. *In white apparel.* As emblematical of their purity, happiness, and glory.

13. *They went up into an upper room.* This was either a room in the Temple or in the house of one of the disciples, where this holy company was accustomed to meet. In Luke xxiv. 53, it is said that, after their return from Mount Olivet, "they were continually in the temple, praising and blessing God." It is probable, therefore, that the *upper room* mentioned in this verse is that apartment of the Temple mentioned above. But still it is not certain that this place should be so understood, as we have the fullest proofs that the *upper rooms* in private houses were used for the purpose of reading the law and conferring together on religious matters. Add to this that the room here mentioned seems to have been the place where all the apostles lodged, and therefore most probably a private house.

14. *These . . . continued . . . in prayer and supplication.* Waiting for the promise of the Father, according to the direction of our Lord, Luke xxiv. 49. The words *and supplication* are omitted by some MSS. *With the women.* Prob-

ably those who had been witnesses of His resurrection, with the immediate relatives of the apostles. Peter we know was married, Matt. viii. 14, and so might others of the disciples; and therefore the wives of the apostles, as well as of other pious men, may be here intended.

15. *In the midst of the disciples.* But instead of this, *brethren* is the reading of some MSS. This seems the best reading because of what immediately follows; for it was not among the *disciples* merely that He stood, but among the whole company, which amounted to 120. It is remarkable that this was the number which the Jews required to form a council in any city; and it is likely that in reference to this the disciples had gathered together, with themselves, the number of 120, chosen out of the many who already had been converted by the ministry of our Lord, the 12 disciples, and the 70 whom He had sent forth to preach, Luke x. 1, etc. Thus they formed a complete council in presence of which the important business of electing a person in the place of Judas was to be transacted.

16. *The Holy Ghost by the mouth of David.* This is a strong attestation to the divine inspiration of the Book of Psalms. They were dictated by the Holy Spirit and spoken by the mouth of David.

17. *Obtained part of this ministry.* "He obtained the lot of this ministry"—not that he or any of the twelve apostles were chosen to this ministry by lot; but as "lot" signifies the portion a man has in life, what comes to him in the course of the divine providence, or as an especial gift of God's goodness, it is used here, as in many other parts of the sacred writings, to signify office or station.

18. *Purchased a field with the reward of iniquity.* Probably Judas did not purchase the field himself, but the money for which he sold his Lord was thus applied; see Matt. xxvii. 6-8. It is possible, however, that he might have designed to purchase a field or piece of ground with this reward of his iniquity, and might have been in treaty for it, though he did not close the bargain, as his bringing the money to the treasury proves. The priests, knowing his intentions, might have completed the purchase, and, as Judas was now dead, applied the field thus bought for the burial of strangers, i.e., Jews from foreign parts, or others who, visiting Jerusalem, had died there. Though this case is possible, yet the passage will bear a very consistent interpretation without the assistance of this conjecture; for in ordinary conversation we often attribute to a man what is the consequence of his own actions, though such consequence was never designed nor wished for by himself. Thus we say of a man embarking in a hazardous enterprise, "He is gone to seek his death"; of one whose conduct has been ruinous to his reputation, "He has disgraced himself"; of another who has suffered much in consequence of his crimes, "He has purchased repentance at a high price." All these, though undesigned, were consequences of certain acts, as the buying of the field was the consequence of Judas' treason. *And falling headlong, he burst asunder.* It is very likely that the eighteenth and nineteenth verses are not the words of Peter, but of the historian Luke, and should be read in a paren-

thesis; then the seventeenth and twentieth verses will make a connected sense.

19. *It was known unto all the dwellers at Jerusalem.* The repentance of Judas, his dying testimony in behalf of our Lord's innocence, and his tragic death were publicly known, as was also the transaction about the purchase of the field; and hence arose the name by which it was publicly known. *That field is called in their proper tongue, Aceldama.* This *proper tongue* was not the Hebrew; that had long ceased to be the proper tongue in Palestine. It was a sort of Chaldaio-Syriac which was commonly spoken.

20. *For it is written in the book of Psalms.* The places usually referred to are Ps. lxix. 25: "Let their habitation be desolate; and let none dwell in their tents"; and Ps. cix. 8: "Let his days be few; and let another take his office," *pekudato,* "his overseership, his charge of visitation or superintendence"—translated by the Septuagint, *ten episcopen,* and Vulgate, *episcopatum;* and we, following both, *bishopric,* but not with sufficient propriety. For surely the office or charge of Judas was widely different from what we call *bishopric,* the diocese, estate, and emoluments of a bishop. *Episcopos,* which was corrupted by our Saxon ancestors into *biscop,* and by us into "bishop," signifies literally an "overseer or superintendent."

21. *Which have companied with us.* They judged it necessary to fill up this blank in the apostolate by a person who had been an eyewitness of the acts of our Lord. *Went in and out.* A phrase which includes all the actions of life.

22. *Beginning from the baptism of John.* From the time that Christ was baptized by John in Jordan, for it was at that time that His public ministry properly began. *Must one be ordained.* This translation misleads every reader who cannot examine the original text. There is no term for *ordained* in the Greek; "to be" is the only word in the verse to which this interpretation can be applied. The New Testament printed at London, by Robert Barker, the king's printer, in 1615, renders this and the preceding verse more faithfully and more clearly than our common version: "Wherefore of these men who have companied with us, all the time that the Lord Jesus was conversant among us, beginning from the baptism of John unto the day he was taken up from us, must one of them be made a witness with us of his resurrection." The word *ordained* would naturally lead most readers to suppose that some ecclesiastical rite was used on the occasion, such as imposition of hands, although nothing of the kind appears to have been employed.

23. *They appointed two.* These two were probably of the number of the seventy disciples, and in this respect well fitted to fill up the place. It is likely that the disciples themselves were divided in opinion which of these two was the most proper person, and therefore laid the matter before God, that He might decide it by the lot. No more than two candidates were presented, probably because the attention of the brethren had been drawn to those two alone, as having been most intimately acquainted with our Lord, or in being better qualified for the work than any of the rest.

24. *Thou, Lord, which knowest the hearts.* "Searcher of hearts" seems to be used here as

an attribute of God; He knows the hearts, the most secret purposes, intentions, and dispositions of all men. And because He is the Knower of hearts, He knew which of these men He had qualified the best, by natural and gracious dispositions and powers, for the important work to which one of them was now to be appointed.

25. *That he may take part of this ministry.* Instead of "the lot," which we translate *part*, "the place" is the reading of some MSS. and from them the verse may be read thus, "That he may take the place of this ministry and apostleship (from which Judas fell), and go to his own place." Some of the best critics assert that the words belong to Matthias—*his own place* being the office to which he was about to be elected. Should any object that this could not be called *his own place* because he was not yet appointed to it, but hell might be properly called Judas' own place because by treason and covetousness he was fully prepared for that place of torment, it may be answered that the *own* or proper *place* of a man is that for which he is eligible from being qualified for it, though he may not yet possess such a place.

26. *They gave forth their lots.* In what manner this or any other question was decided by lot, we cannot precisely say. The most simple form was to put two stones, pieces of board, metal, or slips of parchment, with the names of the persons inscribed on them, into an urn; and after prayer, sacrifice, etc., to put in the hand and draw out one of the lots, and then the case was decided. *He was numbered with the eleven apostles.* The word comes from "together with," "according to," and a "pebble or small stone," used for lots, and as a means of enumeration among the Greeks, Romans, and Egyptians; hence the words "calculate, calculation," from *calculus*, a small stone or pebble. From this use of the word, though it signifies in general to sum up, associate, we may conjecture that the calculus or pebble was used on this occasion.

CHAPTER 2

The Day of Pentecost having arrived, and the disciples being assembled, the Holy Spirit descended as a mighty rushing wind, and in the likeness of fiery tongues sat upon them; in consequence of which they were all enabled to speak different languages, which they had never learned, 1-4. An account of persons from various countries who were present, and were astonished to hear the apostles declare the wonderful works of God in their respective languages, 5-12. Some cavil, 13, and are confounded by Peter, who asserts that this work is of God; and that thereby a most important prophecy was fulfilled, 14-21. He takes occasion from this to preach Jesus to them, as the true Lord and only Messiah, 22-36. The people are alarmed and convinced, and inquire what they shall do, 37. He exhorts them to repent and be baptized in the name of Jesus, that they may receive remission of sins and the gift of the Holy Spirit, 38-40. They gladly receive his word, about three thousand are baptized and added to the Church in one day; they continue steadfast in the apostles' doctrine and fellowship, 41-42. The apostles work many miracles; and the disciples have all things in common, and live in a state of great happiness and Christian fellowship, 43-47.

1. *When the day of Pentecost was fully come.* The Feast of Pentecost was celebrated fifty days after the Passover, and has its name from *penteconta,* "fifty." It commenced on the fiftieth day, reckoned from the first day of unleavened bread, i.e., on the morrow after the paschal lamb was offered. The law relative to this feast is found in Lev. xxiii. 15-16, in these words: "And ye shall count unto you from the morrow after the sabbath, from the day that ye brought the sheaf of the wave offering; seven sabbaths shall be complete: even unto the morrow after the seventh sabbath shall ye number fifty days." This feast was instituted in commemoration of the giving the law on Mount Sinai, and is therefore sometimes called by the Jews "the joy of the law," and frequently the Feast of Weeks. There is a correspondence between the giving of the law, which is celebrated by this Feast of Pentecost, together with the crucifixion of our Lord, which took place at the Passover, and this descent of the Holy Spirit, which happened at this Pentecost. At the Passover, the Israelites were delivered from Egyptian bondage; this was a type of the thraldom in which the human race were to Satan and sin. At the Passover, Jesus Christ, who was typified by the paschal lamb, was sacrificed for the sin of the world, and by this sacrifice redemption from sin and Satan is now procured and proclaimed. On Pentecost, God gave His law on Mount Sinai, accompanied with thunderings and lightnings. On Pentecost, God sent down His Holy Spirit, like a rushing mighty wind; and tongues of fire sat upon each disciple, in order that, by His influence, that new law of light and life might be promulgated and established. *They were all with one accord in one place.* It is probable that the *all* here mentioned means the 120 spoken of in chap. i. 15, who were all together at the election of Matthias. *In one place.* Where this place was we cannot tell. It was probably in the Temple, as seems to be intimated in v. 46, where it is said they were "daily with one accord in the temple"; and as this was the third hour of the day, v. 15, which was the Jewish hour of morning prayer, it is most probable that the Temple was the place in which they were assembled.

2. *A sound from heaven.* Probably thunder is meant, which is the harbinger of the Divine Presence. *Rushing mighty wind.* There is a good deal of similarity between this account and that of the appearance of God to Elijah, 1 Kings xix. 11-12, where the strong wind, the earthquake, and the fire were harbingers of the Almighty's presence, and prepared the heart of Elijah to hear the small still voice. So this *sound* and the *mighty rushing wind* prepared the apostles to receive the influences and gifts of the Holy Spirit. In both cases the *sound, strong wind,* and *fire,* although *natural* agents, were *supernaturally* employed.

3. *Cloven tongues like as of fire.* The *tongues* were the emblem of the languages they were to speak. The *cloven tongues* pointed out the diversity of those languages; and the *fire* seemed to intimate that the whole would be a spiritual gift, and be the means of bringing light and life to the souls who should hear them preach the everlasting gospel in those languages. *Sat upon each of them.* That unusual appearances of fire were considered emblems of the presence and influence of God both the Scriptures and the Jewish writings amply prove. Thus God manifested himself to Moses when He appointed him to deliver Israel, Exod. iii. 2-3; and thus He manifested himself when He delivered the law on Mount Sinai, Exod. xix. 16-20. *It sat upon each.* That is, one of those tongues, like flames, sat upon the head of each disciple; and the continuance of the appearance, which is indicat-

ed by the word *sat,* shows that there could be no illusion in the case. I still think that in all this case the agent was natural, but supernaturally employed.

4. *To speak with other tongues.* At the building of Babel the language of the people was confounded, and in consequence of this they became scattered over the face of the earth. At this foundation of the Christian Church, the gift of various languages was given to the apostles that the scattered nations might be gathered, and united under one Shepherd and Superintendent of all souls. *As the Spirit gave them utterance.* The word seems to imply such utterance as proceeded from immediate inspiration and included oracular communications.

5. *Devout men, out of every nation.* Either by these we are simply to understand Jews who were born in different countries and had now come up to Jerusalem to be present at the Passover, and for purposes of traffic, or proselytes to Judaism who had come up for the same purpose; for I cannot suppose that the term *devout men* can be applied to any other.

6. *When this was noised abroad.* If we suppose that there was a considerable peal of thunder, which produced the mighty rushing *wind* already noticed in v. 2, then the whole city must have been alarmed; and as various circumstances might direct their attention to the Temple, having flocked thither they were further astonished and confounded to hear the disciples of Christ addressing the mixed multitude in the languages of the different countries from which these people had come. *Every man heard them speak in his own language.* We may naturally suppose that, as soon as any person presented himself to one of these disciples, he, the disciple, was immediately enabled to address him in his own language, however various this had been from the Jewish or Galilean dialects.

7. *Are not all these . . . Galilaeans?* Persons who know no other dialect, save that of their own country. Persons wholly uneducated, and consequently naturally ignorant of those languages which they now speak so fluently.

8. *How hear we every man in our own tongue?* Some have supposed from this that the miracle was not so much wrought on the disciples as on their hearers; imagining that, although the disciples spoke their own tongue, yet every man so understood what was spoken as if it had been spoken in the language in which he was born. Though this is by no means so likely as the opinion which states that the disciples themselves spoke all these different languages, yet the miracle is the same howsoever it be taken.

9. *Parthians.* Parthia anciently included the northern part of modern Persia; it was situated between the Caspian Sea and Persian Gulf, rather to the eastward of both. *Medes.* Media was a country lying in the vicinity of the Caspian Sea, having Parthia on the east, Assyria on the south, and Mesopotamia on the west. *Elamites.* Probably inhabitants of that country now called Persia; both the *Medes* and *Elamites* were a neighboring people, dwelling beyond the Tigris. *Mesopotamia.* Situated between the Tigris and Euphrates rivers. *Judaea.* This word has exceedingly puzzled commentators and critics, and most suspect that it is

not the true reading. *Cappadocia* was an ancient kingdom of Asia, comprehending all that country that lies between Mount Taurus and the Euxine Sea. *Pontus* was anciently a very powerful kingdom of Asia, originally a part of Cappadocia. *Asia.* Meaning probably Asia Minor.

10. *Phrygia.* A country in Asia Minor, southward of Pontus. *Pamphylia.* The ancient name of the country between Lycia and Cilicia, near the Mediterranean Sea. *Egypt.* A very extensive country of Africa. *Libya.* In a general way, among the Greeks, signified Africa; but the northern part, in the vicinity of Cyrene, is here meant. *Cyrene.* A country in Africa on the coast of the Mediterranean Sea, southward of the most western point of the Island of Crete. *Strangers of Rome.* Persons dwelling at Rome and speaking the Latin language, partly consisting of regularly descended *Jews* and *proselytes* to the Jewish religion.

11. *Cretes.* Natives of Crete, a large and noted island in the eastern part of the Mediterranean Sea. *Arabians.* Natives of Arabia, a wellknown country of Asia, having the Red Sea on the west, the Persian Gulf on the east, Judea on the north, and the Indian Ocean on the south. *The wonderful works of God.* Such as the incarnation of Christ; His various miracles, preaching, death, resurrection, and ascension; and the design of God to save the world through Him. From this one circumstance we may learn that all the people enumerated above were either *Jews* or *proselytes;* and that there were probably none that could be, strictly speaking, called heathens among them.

13. *These men are full of new wine.* Rather "sweet wine"; cannot mean the *mustum,* or *new wine,* as there could be none in Judea so early as Pentecost.

14. *Peter, standing up with the eleven.* They probably spoke by turns, not all together; but Peter began the discourse. *All ye that dwell at Jerusalem.* Would be better translated by the word "sojourn," because they were not inhabitants of Judea, but the strangers mentioned in vv. 9-11, who had come up to the feast.

15. *But the third hour of the day.* That is, about nine o'clock in the morning, previously to which the Jews scarcely ever ate or drank, for that hour was the hour of prayer. This custom appears to have been so common that even the most intemperate among the Jews were not known to transgress it.

16. *Spoken by the prophet Joel.* The prophecy which he delivered so long ago is just now fulfilled; and this is another proof that Jesus, whom you have crucified, is the Messiah.

17. *In the last days.* The time of the Messiah; and so the phrase was understood among the Jews. *Your sons and your daughters shall prophesy.* The word *prophesy* is not to be understood here as implying the knowledge and discovery of future events, but signifies to teach and proclaim the great truths of God, especially those which concerned redemption by Jesus Christ. *Your young men shall see visions.* These were two of the various ways in which God revealed himself under the Old Testament. Sometimes He revealed himself by a symbol, which was a sufficient proof of the Divine Presence; fire was the most ordinary, as it was the most expressive, symbol. Thus He

appeared to Moses on Mount Horeb, and afterwards at Sinai; to Abraham, Genesis xv; to Elijah, 1 Kings xix. 11-12. At other times He revealed himself by angelic ministry; this was frequent, especially in the days of the patriarchs, of which we find many instances in the Book of Genesis. By *dreams* He discovered His will in numerous instances. See the remarkable case of Joseph, Gen. xxxvii. 5, 9; of Jacob, Gen. xxviii. 1 ff.; xlvi. 2 ff.; of Pharaoh, Gen. xli. 1-7; of Nebuchadnezzar, Dan. iv. 10-17.

18. *On my servants and on my handmaidens.* This properly means persons of the lowest condition, such as male and female slaves. As the Jews asserted that the spirit of prophecy never rested upon a poor man, these words are quoted to show that, under the gospel dispensation, neither bond nor free, male nor female, is excluded from sharing in the gifts and graces of the Divine Spirit.

19. *I will shew wonders.* It is likely that both the prophet and the apostle refer to the calamities that fell upon the Jews at the destruction of Jerusalem, and the fearful signs and portents that preceded those calamities. *Blood, and fire, and vapour of smoke.* Skirmishes and assassinations over the land, and wasting the country with fire and sword.

20. *The sun shall be turned into darkness, and the moon into blood.* These are figurative representations of *eclipses*, intended most probably to point but the fall of the *civil* and *ecclesiastical* state in Judea.

21. *Whosoever shall call on the name of the Lord shall be saved.* The predicted ruin is now impending, and only such as receive the gospel of the Son of God shall be saved. And that none but the *Christians* did escape, when God poured out these judgments, is well-known; and that all the Christians did escape, not one of them perishing in these devastations, stands attested by the most respectable authority. See the note on Matt. xxiv. 13.

22. *A man approved of God.* "Celebrated, famous." The sense of the verse seems to be this: "Jesus of Nazareth, a Man sent of God, and celebrated among you by miracles, wonders, and signs," and all these done in such profusion as had never been done by the best of your most accredited prophets. And these signs were such as demonstrated His Divine mission.

23. *By the determinate counsel;* that counsel of God which "defined the time, place, and circumstance," according to His foreknowledge. *By wicked hands have crucified and slain.* I think this refers to the Romans, and not to the Jews, the former being the agents to execute the evil purposes of the latter. It is well-known that the punishment of the cross was not a Jewish, but a Roman, punishment. Hence we may infer that by *the hands of the wicked,* the Romans are meant, being called *anomoi,* "without law," because they had no revelation from God.

24. *Whom God hath raised up.* For as God alone gave Him up to death, so God alone raised Him up from death. *Having loosed the pains of death.* "Removed the pains or sufferings of death." Instead of *death,* several MSS. have "hell," or the "place of separate spirits"; and perhaps it was on no better authority than this various reading, supported but by slender evidence, that "He descended into hell" became an article in what is called the Apostles' Creed. And on this article many a popish legend has been builded, to the discredit of sober sense and true religion.

25. *For David speaketh concerning him.* The quotation here is made from Psalm xvi, which contains a most remarkable prophecy concerning Christ, every word of which applies to Him, and to Him exclusively.

26. *And my tongue was glad.* In the Hebrew it is, "And my glory was glad"; but the Evangelist follows the Septuagint. And what is to be understood by "glory" here? Why, the "soul," certainly, and not the *tongue.*

27. *Thou wilt not leave my soul in hell.* "In hades," that is, the state of separate spirits, or the state of the dead. *To see corruption.* "Dust thou art, and unto dust thou shalt return," was a sentence pronounced on man after the Fall; therefore this sentence could be executed on none but those who were fallen. But Jesus, being conceived without sin, neither partook of human corruption nor was involved in the condemnation of fallen human nature; consequently it was impossible for His body to *see corruption;* and it could not have undergone the temporary death, to which it was not naturally liable, had it not been for the purpose of making an atonement.

28. *Thou hast made known to me the ways of life.* That is, the way from the region of death, or state of the dead and separate spirits; so that I shall resume the same body, and live the same kind of life, as I had before I gave up My life for the sin of the world.

29. *Let me freely speak . . . of the patriarch David.* Dr. Lightfoot: "That this passage, *Thou shalt not leave my soul in hell,* is not to be applied to David himself appears in that I may confidently aver concerning him, that he was *dead* and *buried,* and never rose again; but his soul was left in the state of the dead, and he saw corruption, for his sepulchre is with us to this day."

30. *According to the flesh, he would raise up Christ.* This whole clause is wanting in some MSS.

31. *That his soul was not left in hell.* The words *his soul* are omitted by some MSS.

32. *Whereof we all are witnesses.* That is, the whole 120 saw Him after He rose from the dead, and were all ready, in the face of persecution and death, to attest this great truth.

34. *David is not ascended.* Consequently he has not sent forth this extraordinary gift; but it comes from his Lord, of whom he said, *The Lord said unto my Lord.*

35. *Until I make thy foes thy footstool.* It was usual with conquerors to put their feet on the necks of vanquished leaders, as emblematical of the state of subjection to which they were reduced, and the total extinction of their power.

36. *Both Lord and Christ.* Not only the Messiah, but the supreme Governor of all things and all persons, Jews and Gentiles, angels and men. In the preceding discourse, Peter assumes a fact which none would attempt to deny, viz., that Jesus had been lately crucified by them. He then proves (1) His resurrection, (2) His ascension, (3) His exaltation to the right hand

of God, (4) the effusion of the Holy Spirit, which was the fruit of His glorification, and which had not only been promised by himself but foretold by their own prophets; in consequence of which it was indisputably proved (5) that this same Jesus whom they had crucified was the promised Messiah; and if so, (6) the Governor of the universe, from whose power and justice they had everything to dread, as they refused to receive His proffered mercy and kindness.

38. *Peter said unto them, Repent.* Humble yourselves before God, and deeply deplore the sins you have committed; pray earnestly for mercy, and deprecate the displeasure of incensed justice. For a definition of repentance, see on Matt. iii. 2. *And be baptized every one of you.* Take on you the public profession of the religion of Christ, by being baptized in His name, and thus acknowledge yourselves to be His disciples and servants. *For the remission of sins.* "In reference to the remission or removal of sins," baptism pointing out the purifying influences of the Holy Spirit. *Ye shall receive the gift of the Holy Ghost.* Receive the baptism, in reference to the removal of sins, and you shall receive the Holy Ghost, by whose agency alone the efficacy of the blood of the covenant is applied, and by whose refining power the heart is purified.

39. *For the promise is unto you.* Jews of the land of Judea. Not only the fulfillment of the *promise* which he had lately recited from the prophecy of Joel was made to them, but in this promise was also included the purification from sin, with every gift and grace of the Holy Spirit. *To all that are afar off.* To the Jews wherever dispersed, and to all the Gentile nations. *Even as many as the Lord our God shall call,* i.e., all to whom, in the course of His providence and grace, He shall send the preaching of Christ crucified.

40. *Save yourselves from this untoward generation.* Separate yourselves from them. "Be saved." The power is present with you; make a proper use of it, and you shall be delivered from their obstinate unbelief, and the punishment that awaits it in the destruction of them and their city by the Romans.

41. *They that gladly received his word.* The word which signifies "joyfully, readily, willingly" implies that they approved of the doctrine delivered, that they were glad to hear of this way of salvation, and that they began immediately to act according to its dictates. The word is however omitted by some MSS. *Were baptized.* That is, in the name of Jesus, v. 38, for this was the criterion of a Jew's conversion. This baptism was a very powerful means to prevent their apostasy; they had, by receiving baptism in the name of Jesus, renounced Judaism and all the political advantages connected with it. Dr. Lightfoot has well remarked that the Gentiles who received the Christian doctrine were baptized in the "name of the Father, and the Son, and the Holy Ghost"; whereas the Jewish converts, for the reasons already given, were baptized in the "name of the Lord Jesus." *Were added . . . three thousand souls.* They went over from one party to another. The Greek writers make use of this verb to signify that act by which cities, towns, or provinces changed their masters, and put themselves under another

government. So these 3,000 persons left the scribes and Pharisees, and put themselves under the teaching of the apostles, professing the Christian doctrine, and acknowledging that Christ was come, and that He who was lately crucified by the Jews was the promised and only Messiah; and in this faith they were baptized. These 3,000 were not converted under one discourse, nor in one place, nor by one person. All the apostles preached, some in one language, and some in another; and not in one house—for where was there one at that time that could hold such a multitude of people? For, out of the multitudes that heard, 3,000 were converted. The truth seems to be this: All the apostles preached in different parts of the city during the course of that day; and "in that day" 3,000 converts were the fruits of the conjoint exertions of these holy men.

42. *They continued stedfastly in the apostles' doctrine.* They received it, retained it, and acted on its principles. *And fellowship. Koinonia,* "community," meaning association for religious and spiritual purposes. *And in breaking of bread.* Whether this means the holy Eucharist or their common meals, it is difficult to say. *Breaking of bread* was that act which preceded a feast or meal, and which was performed by the master of the house when he pronounced the blessing—what we would call "grace" before meat.

44. *And all that believed.* "The believers," i.e., those who conscientiously credited the doctrine concerning the incarnation, crucifixion, resurrection, and ascension of Jesus Christ, and had, in consequence, received redemption in His blood. *Were together.* "These words signify either, in one time, chap. iii. 1; or in one place, chap. ii. 1; or in one thing. The last of these three senses seems to be the most proper here; for it is not probable that the believers, who were then 3,000 in number, v. 41, besides the 120 spoken of in chap. i. 15, were used all to meet at one time, or in one place, in Jerusalem." *And had all things common.* Perhaps this has not been understood. At all the public religious feasts in Jerusalem there was a sort of community of goods. No man at such times hired houses or beds in Jerusalem; all were lent *gratis* by the owners. Also, provisions of water were made for them at the public expense. Therefore a sort of community of goods was no strange thing at Jerusalem at such times as these. It appears, however, that this community of goods was carried further; for we are informed, v. 45, that they *sold their possessions and goods, and parted them to all men, as every man had* need. But this probably means that, as in consequence of this remarkable outpouring of the Spirit of God and their conversion they were detained longer at Jerusalem than they had originally intended, they formed a kind of community for the time being, that none might suffer want on the present occasion; as no doubt the unbelieving Jews, who were mockers, v. 13, would treat these new converts with the most marked disapprobation.

46. *They, continuing daily with one accord in the temple.* They were present at all the times of public worship, and joined together in prayers and praises to God; for it is not to be supposed that they continued to offer any of the sacrifices prescribed by the law. *Breaking*

bread from house to house. This may signify that select companies, who were contiguous to each other, frequently ate together at their respective lodgings on their return from public worship. But *kat'oikon,* which we translate *from house to house,* is repeatedly used by the Greek writers for "at home" (see margin); for though they had all things in common, each person lived at his own table. *Breaking bread* is used to express the act of taking their meals. The bread of the Jews was thin, hard, and dry, and was never cut with the knife as ours is, but was simply broken by the hand. *With gladness and singleness of heart.* A true picture of genuine Christian fellowship. They ate their bread; they had no severe fasts. The Holy Spirit had done in their souls, by His refining influence, what others vainly expect from bodily austerities. It may also be said that, if they had no severe fasts, they had no splendid feasts; all was moderation, and all was contentment. They were full of *gladness,* spiritual joy and happiness; and *singleness of heart,* every man worthy of the confidence of his neighbor.

47. *And the Lord added to the church daily such as should be saved.* Though many approved of the life and manners of these primitive Christians, yet they did not become members of this holy Church, God permitting none to be *added* to it but those who were "saved" from their sins and prejudices. Our translation *such as should be saved* is improper and insupportable. The original means simply and solely those who were then saved; those who were redeemed from their sins, and baptized into the faith of Jesus Christ.

CHAPTER 3

Peter and John go to the Temple at the hour of prayer, and heal a man who had been lame from his mother's womb, 1-8. The people are astonished, and the apostles inform them that it was not by their own power they had healed the man, but through the power of Jesus of Nazareth, whom they had crucified, 9-16. Peter both excuses and reproves them, and exhorts them to repentance, 17-21. Shows that in Jesus Christ the prophecy of Moses was fulfilled; that all the prophets testified of Jesus and His salvation, 22-24; that in Him the covenant made with Abraham is fulfilled; and that Christ came to bless them by turning them away from their iniquities, 25-26.

1. Peter and John went up together. The words which we translate *together,* and which are the first words in this chapter in the Greek text, are added by several MSS. and versions to the last verse of the preceding chapter. But they do not make as good a sense there as they do here; and should be translated, not *together,* which really makes no sense here, but "at that time"; intimating that this transaction occurred about the same time as those which are mentioned at the close of the former chapter. *At the hour of prayer.* This, as is immediately added, was the *ninth* hour, which answers, in a general way, to our three o'clock in the afternoon. It appears that there were *three* hours of the day destined by the Jews to public prayer; perhaps they are referred to by David, Ps. lv. 17: "Evening, and morning, and at noon, will I pray, and cry aloud." There are three distinct times marked in the Book of the Acts. The third hour, chap. ii. 15, answering, as we have already seen, to nearly our nine o'clock in the morning; the sixth hour, chap. x. 9, answering to about twelve with us; and the ninth hour, mentioned in this verse, and answer-

ing to our three in the afternoon. I should be glad to know that every Christian in the universe observed the same rule. It is the most natural division of the day; and he who conscientiously observes these three stated times of prayer will infallibly grow in grace and in the knowledge of Jesus Christ our Lord.

2. *A . . . man lame from his mother's womb.* The case of this man must have been well-known: (1) from the long standing of his infirmity; (2) from his being daily exposed in a place so public. It appears that he had no power to walk, and was what we term a "cripple," for he was carried to the gate of the Temple, and laid there in order to excite compassion. These circumstances are all marked by Luke, the more fully to show the greatness and incontestable nature of the miracle. *The gate . . . which is called Beautiful.* There are different opinions concerning this gate. Josephus observes (Bell, *Jud.,* l. v, c. 5, s. 3) that the Temple had nine gates, which were on every side covered with gold and silver; but there was one gate which was without the holy house, and was of Corinthian brass, and greatly excelled those which were only covered with gold and silver. The magnitudes of the other gates were equal one to another; but that of the Corinthian gate, which opened on the east, over against the gate of the holy house itself, was much larger. "For its height was fifty cubits, and its doors were forty cubits, and it was adorned after a most costly manner, as having much richer and thicker plates of silver and gold upon them than upon the other." This last was probably the gate which is here called *Beautiful;* because it was on the outside of the Temple, to which there was an easy access, and because it was evidently the most costly, according to the account in Josephus.

4. *Look on us.* He wished to excite and engage his attention that he might see what was done to produce his miraculous cure, and, it is likely, took this occasion to direct his faith to Jesus Christ. Peter and John probably felt themselves suddenly drawn by the Holy Spirit to pronounce the healing name in behalf of this poor man.

5. *Expecting to receive something of them.* Because it was a constant custom for all who entered the Temple to carry money with them to give to the treasury, or to the poor, or to both. It was on this ground that the friends of the lame man laid him at the gate of the Temple, as this was the most likely place to receive alms.

6. *Silver and gold have I none.* Though it was customary for all those who entered the Temple to carry some money with them, for the purposes mentioned above, yet so poor were the apostles that they had nothing to give, either to the sacred treasury or to the distressed. The popish writers are very dexterous at forming analogies between Peter and the pope, but it is worthy of note that they have not attempted any here. Thomas Aquinas, surnamed the angelical doctor, who was highly esteemed by Pope Innocent IV, going one day into the pope's chamber, where they were reckoning large sums of money, the pope, addressing himself to Aquinas, said: "You see that the Church is no longer in an age in which she can say, *Silver and gold have I none?*" "It is true, holy father,"

replied the angelical doctor, "nor can she now say to the lame man, *Rise up and walk!"*. .

7. *Immediately his feet and ancle bones received strength.* The suddenness of the cure was the proof of the miracle; his walking and leaping were the evidences of it.

8. *Walking, and leaping, and praising God.* These actions are very naturally described. *He walked* in obedience to the command of the apostle to rise up and walk; *he leaped,* to try the strength of his limbs, and to be convinced of the reality of the cure; *he praised God,* as a testimony of the gratitude he felt for the cure he had received. Now was fulfilled, in the most literal manner, the words of the Prophet Isaiah, chap. xxxv. 6: "Then shall the lame man leap as an hart."

9. *And all the people saw him.* The miracle was wrought in the most public manner, and in the most public place, and in a place where the best judgment could be formed of it. For, as it was a divine operation, the priests were the most proper persons to judge of it; and under their notice it was now wrought.

11. *Held Peter and John.* He felt the strongest affection for them, as the instruments by which the divine influence was conveyed to his diseased body. *In the porch that is called Solomon's.* On this portico see Bishop Pearce's note, inserted in this work, John x. 23.

12. *As though by our own power.* "Miraculous energy." *Or holiness.* Meaning "religious attachment to the worship of God." Do not think that we have wrought this miracle by any power of our own; or that any supereminent piety in us should have induced God thus to honor us, by enabling us to work it.

13. *The God of Abraham.* This was wisely introduced, to show them that He whom they called their God had acknowledged Jesus Christ for His Son, and wrought this miracle in His name; and by thus honoring Jesus, whom they slew, He had charged home the guilt of that murder upon them. *Denied him in the presence of Pilate.* You have renounced Him as your King, and denounced Him to death as a malefactor, when Pilate, convinced of His perfect innocense, was *determined,* "judged" it proper and just, to let Him go. Pilate wished to act according to justice; you acted contrary to justice and equity in all their forms.

14. *Ye denied the Holy One.* A manifest reference to Ps. xvi. 10: "Thou wilt not . . . suffer thine Holy One to see corruption." *And desired a murderer.* Barabbas. The case must have been fresh in their own remembrance. Like cleaves to like, and begets its like; they were murderers themselves, and so Christ calls them, Matt. xxii. 7, and they preferred a murderer to the holy and righteous One of God.

15. *And killed the Prince of life.* "The author of this life," not only implying that all life proceeds from Jesus Christ as its Source, but that the life-giving influence of that religion which they were now proclaiming came all through Him. *Archegos* signifies a "prime leader or author, a captain." In Heb. ii. 10, Christ is called the "captain of . . . salvation." He teaches the doctrine of life and salvation, leads the way in which men should walk, and has purchased the eternal life and glory which are to be enjoyed at the end of the way. So the Jews

preferred a son of death, a destroyer of life, to the Author and Procurer of life and immortality!

16. *And his name.* Jesus, the Saviour; *through faith in his name,* as the Saviour, and Author of life, and all its concomitant blessings, such as health.

17. *I wot.* "I know." Wot is from Anglo-Saxon; and hence "wit," science or understanding. *Through ignorance ye did it.* This is a very tender excuse for them; and one which seems to be necessary in order to show them that their state was not utterly desperate. For if all that they did to Christ had been through absolute malice (they well knowing who He was), if any sin could be supposed to be unpardonable, it must have been theirs. Peter, foreseeing that they might be tempted thus to think, and consequently to despair of salvation, tells them that their offense was extenuated by their ignorance of the Person they had tormented and crucified.

18. *But those things . . . he hath so fulfilled.* Your ignorance and malice have been overruled by the sovereign wisdom and power of God, and have become the instruments of fulfilling the divine purpose, that Christ must suffer in order to make an atonement for the sin of the world. *All his prophets* had declared this; some of them in express terms, others indirectly and by symbols.

19. *Repent ye therefore.* Now that you are convinced that this was the Messiah, let your minds be changed and your hearts become contrite for the sins you have committed. *And be converted.* Turn to God through this Christ, deeply deploring your transgressions and believing on His name; *that your sins may be blotted out,* which are not only recorded against you, but for which you are condemned by the justice of God; and the punishment due to them must be executed upon you, unless prevented by your repentance, and turning to Him whom you have pierced. The blotting *out of* sins may refer to the ceremony of the waters of jealousy, where the curse that was written in the book was to be *blotted out* with the bitter water. See the note on Num. v. 23. *When the times of refreshing shall come.* "That the times of refreshing may come." *Anapsyxis* signifies a "breathing time, or respite," and may be here applied to the space that elapsed from this time till the destruction of Jerusalem by the Romans. This was a time of respite, which God gave them to repent of their sins, and be converted to himself. Taking the word in the sense of refreshment in general, it may mean the whole reign of the Kingdom of grace, and the blessings which God gives here below to all genuine believers, peace, love, joy, and communion with himself. See on v. 21.

20. *Which before was preached unto you.* Instead of *before . . . preached,* some MSS. have, who was "before designed, or appointed"; and this is without doubt the true reading. Christ crucified was the Person whom God had from the beginning "appointed" or "designed" for the Jewish people.

21. *Whom the heaven must receive.* He has already appeared upon earth, and accomplished the end of His appearing; He has ascended unto heaven to administer the concerns of His kingdom, and there He shall continue till He comes again to judge the quick and the dead.

The times of restitution of all things. The word *apokatastasis* from *apo*, which signifies "from," and *kathistanein*, to "establish or settle" anything, viz., in a good state; and, when *apo* is added to it, then this preposition implies that this good state in which it is settled was preceded by a bad one, from which the change is made to a good one. So in chap. i. 6, when the disciples said to Christ, "Wilt thou at this time restore again the kingdom to Israel?" they meant, as the Greek word implies, Wilt Thou take the kingdom from the Romans, and give it back to the Jews? Now as the word is here connected with *which God hath spoken by the mouth of all his holy prophets*, it must mean the accomplishment of all the prophecies and promises contained in the Old Testament relative to the kingdom of Christ upon earth, the whole reign of grace, from the ascension of our Lord till His coming again, for of all these things have the holy prophets spoken; and as the grace of the gospel was intended to destroy the reign of sin, its energetic influence is represented as restoring all things, destroying the bad state, and establishing the good—taking the kingdom out of the hands of sin and Satan, and putting it into those of righteousness and truth. This is done in every believing soul; all things are restored to their primitive order. Therefore the words are to be applied to this, and no other meaning. *All his holy prophets. All* is omitted by some MSS. *Since the world began. Ap'aionos;* as *aion* signifies complete and ever-during existence or eternity, it is sometimes applied, by way of accommodation, to denote the whole course of any one period, such as the Mosaic dispensation. See the note on Gen. xxi. 33. It may therefore here refer to that state of things from the giving of the law; and as Moses is mentioned in the next verse, and none before him, it is probable that the phrase should be so understood here. But if we apply it to the commencement of time, the sense is still good.

22. *Moses truly said unto the fathers.* From this appeal to Moses it is evident that Peter wished them to understand that Jesus Christ was come, not as an ordinary prophet, to exhort to repentance and amendment, but as a Legislator, who was to give them a new law, and whose commands and precepts they were to obey, on pain of endless destruction.

25. *Ye are the children of the prophets.* As you are the children or disciples of the prophets, you are bound to believe their predictions, and obey their precepts; and not only so, but you are entitled to their promises. Your duty and your interest go hand in hand; and there is not a blessing contained in the covenant which was made with your fathers but belongs to you. Now as this covenant respected the blessings of the gospel, you must believe in Jesus Christ, in order to be put in possession of all those blessings.

26. *Unto you first God, having raised up.* As you are the children of the prophets and of the covenant, the first offers of salvation belong to you, and God thus makes them to you. God designs to *bless you;* but it is by *turning away every one of you from his iniquities.* The salvation promised in the covenant is a salvation from sin, not from the Romans; and no man can have his sin blotted out who does not turn away from it.

CHAPTER 4

The priests and Sadducees are incensed at the apostles' teaching, and put them in prison, 1-3. The number of those who believed, 4. The rulers, elders, and scribes call the apostles before them, and question them concerning their authority to teach, 5-7. Peter, filled with the Holy Ghost, answers, and proclaims Jesus, 8-12. They are confounded at his discourse and the miracle wrought on the lame man, yet command them not to preach in the name of Jesus, 13-18. Peter and John refuse to obey, 19-20. They are further threatened and dismissed, 21-22. They return to their own company, who all join in praise and prayer to God, 23-30. God answers, and fills them with the Holy Spirit, 31. The blessed state of the primitive disciples, 32-35. The case of Joses, who sells his estate, and brings the money to the common stock, 36-37.

1. *The priests.* These persons had evidenced the most implacable enmity against Christ from the beginning. *The Sadducees.* Whose whole system was now in danger by the preaching of the resurrection of Christ; for they believed not in the immortality of the soul nor in any future world.

2. *Being grieved.* They were "thoroughly fatigued" with the continuance of this preaching; their minds suffered more labor, through vexation at the success of the apostles, than the bodies of the apostles did in their fatiguing exercise of preaching during the whole day.

4. *The number . . . was about five thousand.* That is, as I understand the passage, the 120 which were converted before Pentecost, the 3,000 converted at Pentecost, and 1,880 converted since the conversion of the 3,000, making in the whole 5,000, or *about* that number.

5. *Their rulers, and elders, and scribes.* Those with the high priest, Annas, formed the Sanhedrin, or grand council of the Jews.

6. *Annas.* Though this man was not now actually in the office of high priest, yet he had possessed it for eleven years, bore the title all his life, and had the honor of seeing five of his sons fill that eminent place after him—an honor that never happened to any other person from the commencement of the Mosaic institution. *And Caiaphas.* He was son-in-law to Annas, John xviii. 13; was now high priest, and the same who, a short time before, condemned Christ to be crucified. *And John.* Dr. Lightfoot conjectures, with great probability, that this was Jochanan ben Zaccai, who was very famous at that time in the Jewish nation. *And Alexander.* This was probably Alexander Lysimachus, one of the richest Jews of his time, who made great presents to the Temple and was highly esteemed by King Agrippa. *Of the kindred of the high priest.* Or rather, "of the race of the high priests," i.e., of the family out of which the high priests were chosen. It may, however, comprehend those who belonged to the families of Annas and Caiaphas, and all who were connected with the sacerdotal family. Luke distinctly mentions all these to show how formidable the enemies were against whom the infant Church of Christ had to contend.

7. *By what power, or by what name, have ye done this?* It seems that this council were convinced that the lame man was miraculously healed, but it is very likely that they believed the whole to be the effect of magic; and as all intercourse with familiar spirits, and all spells, charms, etc., were unlawful, they probably hoped that on examination this business would come out, and that then these disturbers of

their peace would be put to death. Hence they inquired *by what power,* by what supernatural energy; or *in what name,* by what mode of incantation; and who is the spirit you invoke, in order to do these things?

8. *Then Peter, filled with the Holy Ghost.* Who guided him into all truth, and raised him far above the fear of man, placing him in a widely different state of mind to that in which he was found when, in the hall of Caiaphas, he denied his Master through fear of a servant girl. But now was fulfilled the promise of Christ, Matt. x. 18-20: "And ye shall be brought before governors and kings for my sake . . . but . . . take no thought how or what ye shall speak . . . For it is not ye that speak, but the Spirit of your Father which speaketh in you."

10. *By the name of Jesus Christ of Nazareth.* This was a very bold declaration in the presence of such an assembly, but he felt he stood on good ground. The cure of the lame man the day before was notorious. His long infirmity was well-known; his person could be easily identified; and he was now standing before them whole and sound. They themselves therefore could judge whether the miracle was true or false. But the reality of it was not questioned, nor was there any difficulty about the instruments that were employed; the only question was, *How* have you done this? and in *whose name?* Peter immediately answers, We have done it in the name of Jesus of Nazareth, whom *ye crucified,* and whom God hath *raised from the dead.*

11. *This is the stone which was set at nought of you builders.* By your rejection and crucifixion of Jesus Christ you have fulfilled one of your own prophecies, Ps. cxviii. 22; and as one part of this prophecy is now so literally fulfilled, you may rest assured, so shall the other; and this rejected *stone* shall speedily become *the head stone of the corner.*

12. *For there is none other name.* Not only no other person, but no *name* except that divinely appointed one, Matt. i. 21, by which salvation from sin can be expected—*none* given *under heaven*—no other means ever devised by God himself for the salvation of a lost world.

13. *The boldness of Peter and John.* The "freedom and fluency" with which they spoke; for they spoke now from the immediate influence of the Holy Ghost, and their word was with power. *That they were unlearned and ignorant men. Agrammatoi,* persons without literature, not brought up in nor given to literary pursuits—*and ignorant, idiotai,* persons in private life, brought up in its occupations alone. It does not mean ignorance in the common acceptation of the term, and our translation is very improper. In no sense of the word could any of the apostles be called *ignorant men;* for though their spiritual knowledge came all from heaven, yet in all other matters they seem to have been men of good, sound, strong common sense. *They took knowledge of them* may imply that they got information that they had been disciples of Christ, and probably they might have seen them in our Lord's company. *That they had been with Jesus.* Had they not had His teaching, the present company would soon have confounded them; but they spoke with so much power and authority that the whole Sanhedrin was confounded.

14. *They could say nothing against it.* They could not gainsay the apostolic doctrine, for that was supported by the miraculous fact before them. If the doctrine be false, the man cannot have been miraculously healed; if the man be miraculously healed, then the doctrine must be true that it is by the name of Jesus of Nazareth that he has been healed.

16. *A notable miracle hath been done.* A miracle has been wrought, and this miracle is "known," and acknowledged to be such. All Jerusalem knew that he was lame—lame from his birth, and that he had long begged at the Beautiful Gate of the Temple; and now all Jerusalem knew that he was healed, and there was no means by which such a self-evident fact could be disproved.

17. *But that it spread no further.* Not the news of the miraculous healing of the lame man, but the doctrine and influence which these men preached and exerted. More than a thousand people had already professed faith in Christ in consequence of this miracle (see v. 4); and if this teaching should be permitted to go on, probably accompanied with similar miracles, they had reason to believe that all Jerusalem (themselves excepted, who had steeled their hearts against all good) should be converted to the religion of Him whom they had lately crucified. *Let us straitly threaten them.* "Let us threaten them with threatening," a Hebraism, and a proof that Luke has translated the words of the council into Greek, just as they were spoken. *That they speak . . . to no man in this name.* Nothing so ominous to them as the name of Christ crucified, because they themselves had been His crucifiers. On this account they could not bear to hear salvation preached to mankind through Him of whom they had been the betrayers and murderers, and who was soon likely to have no enemies but themselves.

21. *When they had further threatened them.* When they had added to their former threatenings, repeating the former menaces and adding new penalties. *Because of the people.* The people saw the miracle, confessed the finger of God, believed on the Lord Jesus, and thus became converts to the Christian faith; and the converts were now so numerous that the Sanhedrin was afraid to proceed to any extremities, lest an insurrection should be the consequence.

22. *The man was above forty years old.* The disease was of long standing, and consequently the more inveterate; but all difficulties, small or great, yield equally to the sovereign power of God.

23. *They went to their own company.* This was properly the first persecution that had been raised up against the Church since the resurrection of Christ; and as the rest of the disciples must have known that Peter and John had been cast into prison, and that they were to be examined before the Sanhedrin, and knowing the evil disposition of the rulers toward their brethren, they doubtless made joint supplication to God for their safety. In this employment it is likely Peter and John found them on their return from the council, and repeated to them all their treatment, with the threats of the chief priests and elders.

24. *Lord, thou art God.* "Thou, God, art the sovereign Lord." Thy rule is universal, and Thy power unlimited.

26. *Against the Lord, and against his Christ* should be translated "against His Anointed," because it particularly agrees with "whom thou hast anointed," in the succeeding verse.

27. There is a parenthesis in this verse that is not sufficiently noticed. It should be read in connection with v. 28, thus: "For of a truth against thy holy child Jesus, whom thou hast anointed (for to do whatsoever thy hand and thy counsel determined before to be done), both Herod, and Pontius Pilate, with the Gentiles, and the people of Israel, were gathered together." It is evident that what God's *hand and . . . counsel determined before to be done* was not that which Herod, Pontius Pilate, the Gentiles (Romans) and the people of Israel had done and were doing; for then their rage and vain counsel would be such as God himself had determined should take place, which is both impious and absurd. But these gathered together to hinder what God had before determined that His Christ or Anointed should perform; and thus the passage is undoubtedly to be understood. *Were gathered together.* "In this very city" is added by some MSS. This makes the words much more emphatic; in this Thy own city, these different and in all other cases dissentient powers are leagued together against Thine Anointed, and are determined to prevent the accomplishment of Thy purpose.

29. *And now, Lord, behold their threatenings.* It is not against us, but against Thee, that they conspire; it is not to prevent the success of our preaching, but to bring to nought Thy counsel. The whole of their enmity is against Thee. Now, Lord, look upon it; consider this. *And grant unto thy servants.* While we are endeavoring to fulfill Thy counsels, and can do nothing without Thee, sustain our courage, that we may proclaim Thy truth with boldness and irresistible power.

30. *By stretching forth thine hand to heal.* Show that it is Thy truth which we proclaim, and confirm it with miracles, and show how highly Thou hast magnified Thy Son, Jesus, whom they have despised and crucified, by causing signs and wonders to be wrought in His name. *Thy holy child Jesus* should be translated "Thy holy Servant," as in v. 25, "thy servant David," not "Thy child David." The word is the same in both places.

31. *The place was shaken.* This earthquake was an evidence of the presence of God, and a most direct answer to their prayer, as far as that prayer concerned themselves. The earthquake proclaimed the stretched-out arm of God, and showed them that resistance against His counsels and determinations must come to nought. *And they were all filled with the Holy Ghost.* And in consequence of this, *they spake the word of God with boldness*—a pointed answer to a second part of their request, v. 29. Though these disciples had received the Holy Spirit on the Day of Pentecost, yet they were capable of larger communications; and what they had then received did not preclude the necessity of frequent supplies on emergent occasions. Neither apostle nor private Christian can subsist in the divine life without frequent influences from on high.

32. *The multitude of them that believed.* The whole 5,000, mentioned in v. 4, and probably many others who had been converted by the ministry of the other apostles since that time. *Were of one heart and of one soul.* Were in a state of the most perfect friendship and affection. *They had all things common.* See the notes on chap. ii. 44. See below, v. 34.

33. *With great power gave the apostles witness.* This power they received from the Holy Spirit, who enabled them, "with striking miracles," to give proof of *the resurrection of the Lord Jesus;* for this is the point that was particularly to be proved. That He was slain and buried, all knew; that He rose again from the dead, many knew; but it was necessary to give such proofs as should convince and confound all. *Great grace was upon them all.* They all received much of the favor or grace of God, and they had much favor with all who feared God. In both these ways this clause may be understood.

34. *Neither was there any among them that lacked.* It was customary with the Jews to call the poor together to eat of the sacrifices; but as the priests were incensed against Christ and Christianity, consequently the Christian poor could have no advantage of this kind. Therefore by making a common stock for the present necessity the poor were supplied; so there was none among them that lacked. This provision therefore of the community of goods, which could be but temporary, was made both suitably and seasonably.

36. *The son of consolation.* As *paraclesis* signifies "exhortation," as well as *consolation,* and is indeed distinguished from the latter, 1 Cor. xiv. 3, the original name was probably *Bar naba,* or *Bar nebia,* which signifies the "son of prophecy or exhortation." This is certainly one sense which prophecy has in the New Testament; and in this way Barnabas distinguished himself among the apostles. See chap. xi. 23. Barnabas "exhorted them all, that with purpose of heart they would cleave unto the Lord." *A Levite, and of the country of Cyprus.* Cyprus is an island in the Mediterranean Sea, off Cilicia, and not very distant from the Jewish coast. The Jews were very numerous in that island. Though he was a Levite, he might have had land of his own by private purchase. The Levites, as a tribe, had no land in Israel; but the individuals certainly might make purchases anywhere.

It is worthy of remark that the two apostles of the Gentiles, though of Jewish extraction, were both born in Gentile countries; Paul in Cilicia, Barnabas in Cyprus. This gave them many advantages: served to remove prejudices from the heathens; and gave them no doubt much facility in the Greek tongue, without which they could have done but little in Asia Minor, nor in most parts of the Roman Empire where they travelled. How admirably does God determine even the place of our birth and the bounds of our habitation! The man whom He calls to His work He will take care to endue with every necessary qualification. And is it too much to say that God never did call a man to preach the gospel whom He did not qualify in such a manner that both the workman and the work should appear to be of God? Some have said that "ignorance is the mother of devotion." Devotion and religion are both scandalized by the saying. Every genuine minister of Christ has an enlightened heart; and to this it is his duty to add a well-cultivated mind. A block-head never did, and never can, make a minister.

CHAPTER 5

The hypocrisy of Ananias and his wife, Sapphira, and their awful death, 1-11. The apostles work many miracles, and the Church of God is increased, 12-16. The high priest and the Sadducees, being incensed against the apostles, seize and put them in prison, 17-18. The angel of God delivers them, and commands them to go to the Temple, and proclaim the gospel, 19-20. The high priest, having gathered the council together in the morning, sends to the prison to have the apostles brought before him, 21. The officers return and report that they found the prison shut and the watch set, but that the men were gone, 22-23. A messenger arrives in the meanwhile and says that the apostles are preaching in the Temple, 24-25. The captain and officers go and bring them before the council, who expostulate with them, 26-28. The apostles defend themselves, and charge the council with the murder of Christ, and assert His resurrection from the dead and ascension to the right hand of God, 29-32. The council are confounded and purpose to slay the apostles, 33. Gamaliel gives them seasonable and prudent advice, 34-39. The council agree to it, but before they discharge the apostles, beat them, and command them not to teach in the name of Jesus, 40. They depart rejoicing in their persecution, and continue to preach Jesus Christ, 41-42.

1. *But a certain man named Ananias.* The import of his name, *chananiyah*, the "grace or mercy of the Lord," agrees very ill with his conduct.

2. *Kept back part of the price.* Ananias and Sapphira evidently were persons who professed faith in Christ with the rest of the disciples. While all were making sacrifices for the present necessity, they came forward among the rest, pretending to bring all the money they had received for a possession (of what kind we know not) which they had sold. A *part* of this price, however, they kept back, not being willing to trust entirely to the bounty of Providence, as the others did.

3. *Why hath Satan filled thine heart?* The verb which we translate *to fill*, Kypke has showed by many examples to signify to "in-stigate, excite, impel," and it was a common belief, as well among the heathens as among the Jews and Christians, that when a man did evil he was excited to it by the influence and malice of an evil spirit. *To lie to the Holy Ghost.* "To deceive the Holy Spirit." Every lie is told with the intention to deceive; and they wished to deceive the apostles, and, in effect, that Holy Spirit under whose influence they professed to act. Lying against the Holy Ghost is in the next verse said to be lying against God; therefore the Holy Ghost is *God. To keep back part of the price.* The verb is used by the Greek writers to signify "purloining part of the public money." The word is used here with great propriety, as the money for which the estate was sold was public property, as it was for this purpose alone that the sale was made.

5. *Fell down, and gave up the ghost.* "Fall-ing down, he expired, breathed his last." "Gave up the ghost" is a very improper translation here.

6. *The young men arose.* Some of the stout young men belonging to the disciples then present, who were the fittest to undertake a work of this kind, which required considerable bodily exertion. *Buried him.* This was on the same day in which he died. It was a clear case that he was dead, and dead by a judgment of God that would not be revoked.

10. *Yielded up the ghost.* It was not by Peter's words, nor through Peter's prayers, nor through shame, nor through remorse, that this guilty pair died, but by an immediate judgment of God. It was right in this infant state of the Church to show God's displeasure against deceit, fraud, and hypocrisy. Had this guilty pair been permitted to live after they had done this evil, this long-suffering would have been infallibly abused by others; and instead of leading them who had sinned to repentance might have led them to hardness of heart by causing them to presume on the mercy of God. That hypocrisy may be afraid to show her face, God makes these two an example of His justice.

11. *Great fear came upon all the church.* This judgment answered the end for which it was inflicted; a deeply religious fear occupied every mind, and hypocrisy and deception were banished from this holy assembly.

12. *Solomon's porch.* See the note on John x. 23.

13. *And of the rest durst no man join himself to them.* Who were these called the *rest?* Calmet observes that the Jewish nation was then divided into many different sects, who entertained widely different opinions on various articles. The apostles adopted none of these jarring sentiments, and none of the different sects dared to join themselves to them; neither Pharisees, Sadducees, nor Herodians, as such, were found in this simple, holy Church.

15. *That . . . the shadow of Peter passing by.* I cannot see all the miraculous influence here that others profess to see. The people who had seen the miracles wrought by the apostles pressed with their sick to share the healing benefit. As there must have been many dis-eased people, it is not likely that the apostles, who generally addressed such persons, prayed, and used imposition of hands, could reach all those that were brought to them as fast as the solicitude of their friends could wish. As there-fore they could not get Peter or the other apostles personally to all their sick, they thought if they placed them on that side of the way where the shadow was projected (the sun probably now declining, and consequently the shadow lengthening) they should be healed by the *shadow* of the man passing over them, in whose person such miraculous powers were lodged. But it does not appear that the persons who thus thought and acted were of the number of those converts already made to the faith of Christ, nor does it appear that any person was healed in this way.

16. *Sick folks, and them which were vexed with unclean spirits.* Here it is evident that *sick people* are distinguished from those who were *vexed with unclean spirits;* and therefore they were not one and the same thing. The same distinction is made in Matt. iv. 24; x. 1; Mark i. 32, 34; xvi. 17-18; and Luke iv. 40-41 and vii. 21.

17. *The high priest . . . and . . . the sect of the Sadducees.* "The heresy of the Sad-ducees." In this place, as well as in several others, the word *hairesis*, "heresy," has no evil meaning in itself. It signifies a "sect" or "party," whether good or bad, distinguished from any other sect. *Hairesis, heresy,* comes from *haireo,* "I choose," and was anciently applied to the different "sects" of the heathen philosophers,

the members of each sect having chosen their own in preference to all the others. *Were filled with indignation.* With "zeal." *Zelos* signifies a vehement affection or disposition of the mind, which, according to its object, is either good or bad, laudable or blamable. Its meaning in this place is easily discerned, and not improperly translated *indignation* in our version.

19. *But the angel of the Lord . . . opened the prison doors.* This was done: (1) To increase the confidence of the apostles, by showing them that they were under the continual care of God; and (2) To show the Jewish rulers that they were fighting against God while persecuting His followers and attempting to prevent them from preaching the gospel.

20. *All the words of this life.* This is another periphrasis for "gospel." *Go to the temple*—the most public place, and *speak . . . to the people*—who come there to worship according to the law, *the words of this life*—the whole doctrine of salvation from sin and death; and show that the law is fulfilled in the sacrifice of Jesus, and that by His resurrection He has brought life and immortality to light.

21. *Called the council together.* The "Sanhedrin."

23. *The prison truly found we shut.* All the doors were properly bolted and the keepers at their post; *but when we had opened,* for it appears they were alone in possession of the keys. How much this must have increased their astonishment when they found that the doors were not broken open, the guards properly posted, and everything as they left it!

24. *They doubted of them whereunto this would grow.* They did not know what to think of the apostles, whether they had saved themselves by magic or whether they were delivered by a real miracle; and they were at a loss to tell what the issue of these things would be.

26. *Brought them without violence.* On receiving the information mentioned above, proper officers were sent to seize and bring them before the council. The officers, on reaching the Temple, found the multitude gladly receiving the doctrine of the apostles and so intent on hearing all the words of this life that they were afraid to show any hostility to the apostles, lest the people should stone them. We may therefore conclude that the officers entreated them to accompany them to the council; and that they felt it their duty to obey every ordinance of man for the Lord's sake and so cheerfully went with them, trusting in the Lord their God.

28. *Did not we straitly command you?* "With commanding did we not command you?"; a Hebraism—another proof of the accuracy and fidelity of Luke, who seems always to give every man's speech as he delivered it—not the substance, but the very words. See chap. iv. 17. *Not teach in this name.* That is, of Jesus as the Christ or Messiah. *Intend to bring this man's blood upon us.* You speak in such a way of Him to the people as to persuade them that we have crucified an innocent Man.

29. *We ought to obey God rather than men.* The same answer they gave before, chap. iv. 19, founded on the same reason, which still stood good. We have received our commission from God; we dare not lay it down at the desire or command of *men.*

30. *The God of our fathers raised up Jesus.* It was well to introduce this, that the council might at once see that they preached no strange God; and that He who so highly honored the patriarchs, Moses, and the prophets had yet more highly honored Jesus Christ in raising Him from the dead and seating Him at His right hand, and proclaiming Him as the only Giver of salvation and the repentance which leads to it. *Whom ye slew.* They charge them again with the murder of Christ, as they had done before, chap. iv. 10-12.

31. *Him hath God exalted with his right hand.* By a supereminent display of His "almighty power," for so the *right hand* of God often means. *A Prince.* The Leader or Director in the way. See the notes on chap. iii. 15 and 19. *And a Saviour.* "A Deliverer or Preserver." The word *soter* comes from *sozo,* to "save, deliver, preserve, escape from death or danger, bring into a state of security or safety." *Jesus* and *Saviour* are nearly of the same import. He alone delivers from sin, death, and hell; by Him alone we escape from the snares and dangers to which we are exposed: and it is by and in Him, and in connection with Him, that we are preserved blameless and harmless. He alone can save the soul from sin and preserve it in that state of salvation. *Forgiveness of sins.* The "taking away of sins." This is not to be restrained to the mere act of justification; it implies the removal of sin, whether its power, guilt, or impurity be considered. Through Jesus we have the destruction of the power, the pardon of the guilt, and the cleansing from the pollution, of sin. The two words in italics in this text, *to be,* are impertinently introduced; it reads much better without them.

32. *We are his witnesses.* The word *his* is omitted by several MSS. It does not seem to be necessary. *Of these things.* "Of these transactions"; i.e., of Christ's life and miracles, and of your murderous proceedings against Him. *To them that obey him.* We obey God, not you; and therefore God gives us this Spirit, which is in us a Fountain of light, life, love, and power.

33. *They were cut to the heart.* Literally, "they were sawn through." They were stung to the heart, not with compunction nor remorse, but with spite, malice, and revenge. For, having the murder of Christ thus brought home to their consciences, in the first feelings of their malice and revenge they thought of destroying the persons who had witnessed their nefarious conduct.

34. *A Pharisee, named Gamaliel, a doctor of the law.* "This," says Dr. Lightfoot, "was Rabban Gamaliel the first; commonly, by way of distinction, called Rabban Gamaliel the elder. He was president of the council after the death of his own father, Rabban Simeon, who was the son of Hillel. He was Paul's master, and the thirty-fifth receiver of the traditions, and on this account might not be improperly termed *a doctor of the law,* because he was one that kept and handed down the Cabala received from Mount Sinai. He died eighteen years before the destruction of Jerusalem, his son *Simeon* succeeding him in the chair, who perished in the ruins of the city." Though probably no favorer of Christianity, yet for a Pharisee he

seems to have possessed a more liberal mind than most of his brethren; the following advice was at once humane, sensible, candid, and enlightened.

35. *What ye intend to do.* "What you are about to do." They had already intended to destroy them; and they were now about to do it.

36. *Rose up Theudas.* Josephus, *Ant.*, l. xx, c. 4, s. 1, mentions one named *Theudas* who was the author of an insurrection, about whom there has been much controversy whether he were the person spoken of here by Gamaliel. Every circumstance, as related by Josephus, agrees well enough with what is referred to here except the chronology; for the Theudas mentioned by Josephus made his insurrection when Fadus was governor of Judea, which was at least ten years after the time in which the apostles were brought before this council. Much labor has been thrown away in unsuccessful attempts to reconcile the historian and the Evangelist, when it is very probable they speak of different transactions. Dr. Lightfoot thinks that "Josephus has made a slip in his chronology." I confess the matter does not appear to me of so much consequence. *Boasting himself to be somebody.* "Saying that he was a great personage," i.e., according to the supposition of Bishop Pearce, setting himself up to be king of the Jews.

37. *Judas of Galilee.* Josephus mentions the insurrection made by Judas of Galilee, *Ant.*, l. xviii, c. 1, and says it was when Cyrenius was governor of Syria. Pearce supposes that there were two "taxations" or "enrollments"; and that the one mentioned here took place ten years after that mentioned in Luke ii.

38. *Refrain from these men.* Do not molest them; leave them to God. For if this counsel and work be of man it will come to nought, like the rebellion of Theudas, and that of Judas of Galilee.

40. *To him they agreed.* That is, not to stay the apostles nor to attempt any further to imprison them. But their malevolence could not be thus easily satisfied, and therefore they beat them—probably gave each of them thirty-nine stripes; and having commanded them not to speak in the name of Jesus, they let them go.

41. *Rejoicing that they were counted worthy.* The whole verse may be read thus: "But they departed rejoicing from the presence of the Sanhedrin, because they were deemed worthy to be dishonored on account of the name." The word *his* is omitted by some MSS. The name probably by this time distinguished both the Author of salvation and the sacred system of doctrine which the apostles preached.

42. *Daily in the temple.* That is, at the hours of morning and evening prayer; for they felt it their duty to worship God in public, and to help others to make a profitable use of the practice. Every man that professes Christianity should in this respect also copy their conduct; nor can any man be considered to have any religion who does not attend on the public worship of his Maker. *They ceased not to teach and preach Jesus.* Far from desisting, they became more zealous, yea, incessant, in their work. They took advantage of the public assemblies in the Temple, as well as of all private opportunities, to *teach* all the truths of their holy religion;

and to *preach,* proclaim Jesus as the only Messiah, that He who was crucified rose from the dead and was exalted a Prince and a Saviour at the right hand of God.

CHAPTER 6

The Hellenistic Jews complain against the Hebrews, that their widows were neglected in the daily ministration, 1. To remedy the evil complained of, the apostles appoint seven deacons to superintend the temporal affairs of the Church, 2-6. The progress of the Word of God in Jerusalem, 7. Stephen, one of the deacons, becomes very eminent, and confounds various Jews of the synagogues of the Libertines, 8-10. They suborn false witnesses against him, to get him put to death, 11-14. He appears before the council with an angelic countenance, 15.

1. *A murmuring of the Grecians against the Hebrews.* Those who are here termed Grecians, or Hellenists, were Jews who sojourned now at Jerusalem but lived in countries where the Greek language was spoken, and probably in general knew no other. They are distinguished here from those called *Hebrews,* by which we are to understand native Jews, who spoke what was then termed the Hebrew language, a sort of Chaldaio-Syriac. The foreign or Hellenistic Jews began to be jealous that their widows were neglected in the daily ministration, that they either had not the proportion or were not duly served, the Palestine Jews being partial to those of their own country. This shows that the community of goods could never have been designed to become general. Indeed, it was no ordinance of God; and, in any state of society, must in general be impracticable.

2. *It is not reason.* "It is not pleasing, proper, or fitting," *that we should leave the word of God,* that we should give up ourselves or confide to others the doctrine of salvation which God has commanded us to preach unto the people. *And serve tables.* Become providers of daily bread for your widows and poor. Others can do this, to whom our important office is not intrusted.

3. *Wherefore . . . look ye out among you seven men.* Choose persons in whom you can all confide, who will distribute the provisions impartially and in due time; and let these persons be the objects of the choice of both the Hebrews and the Hellenists, that all cause of murmuring and discontent may be done away. Probably the *seven* men were to take each his day of service, and then there would be a superintendent for these widows for each day of the week. *Of honest report.* Persons to whose character there is authentic "testimony," well-known and accredited. *Full of the Holy Ghost.* Saved into the spirit of the gospel dispensation, and made partakers of that Holy Ghost by which the soul is sanctified, and endued with those graces which constitute the mind that was in Christ. *And wisdom.* Prudence, discretion, and economy; for mere piety and uprightness could not be sufficient where so many must be pleased, and where frugality, impartiality, and liberality, must ever walk hand in hand. *Whom we may appoint.* Instead of *we may appoint,* "we shall appoint" is the reading of several MSS. It makes, however, very little difference in the sense.

4. *We will give ourselves continually to prayer.* "We will steadfastly and invariably attend," we will carefully keep our hearts to this work. The word is very emphatic.

5. *Stephen, a man full of faith and of the Holy Ghost.* A person every way properly fitted for his work, and thus qualified to be the first martyr of the Christian Church. *Nicolas a proselyte of Antioch.* A heathen Greek, who had not only believed in the God of Israel but had also received circumcision, and consequently was a "proselyte of the covenant." As this is the only proselyte mentioned here, we may presume that all the rest were native Jews.

6. *And when they had prayed.* The apostles prayed for these persons, that they might in every respect be qualified for their office and be made successful in it. And when they had done this they *laid their hands* upon them, and by this rite appointed them to their office.

7. *The word of God increased.* By such preachers as the apostles and these deacons, no wonder the doctrine of God increased—became widely diffused and generally known; in consequence of which the number of the disciples must be greatly multiplied—for God will ever bless His own Word when ministered by those whom He has qualified to proclaim it. *A great company of the priests were obedient to the faith.* This was one of the greatest miracles wrought by the grace of Christ; that persons so intent on the destruction of Christ, His apostles, and His doctrine should at last espouse that doctrine is astonishing, and that they who had withstood the evidence of the miracles of Christ should have yielded to the doctrine of His death and resurrection is worthy of note. And from this we may learn that it is not by miracles that sinners are to be converted unto God, but by the preaching of Christ dying for their offenses and rising again for their justification.

8. *Stephen, full of faith and power.* Instead of *faith,* "grace" is the reading of some MSS.

9. *The synagogue . . . of the Libertines.* That Jews and proselytes from various countries had now come up to Jerusalem to bring offerings and to attend the Feast of Pentecost we have already seen, chap. ii. The persons mentioned here were foreign Jews, who appear to have had a synagogue peculiar to themselves at Jerusalem, in which they were accustomed to worship when they came to the public festivals.

10. *They were not able to resist the wisdom.* He was wise, well-exercised, and experienced in divine things; and, as appears by his defense in the following chapter, well-versed in the Jewish history. The spirit by which he spake was the Holy Spirit, and its power was irresistible.

11. *Then they suborned men.* They made "underhand" work; got associated to themselves profligate persons, who for money would swear anything. *Blasphemous words against Moses, and against God.* This was the most deadly charge they could bring against him. We have already seen, Matt. ix. 4, that *blasphemy,* when against *God,* signifies speaking impiously of His nature, attributes, or works; and when against *men,* it signifies speaking injuriously of their character, blasting their reputation. These false witnesses came to prove that he had blasphemed Moses by representing him as an impostor, or the like; and God, by either denying His being, His providence, **or the justice of His government.**

12. *And they*—the Libertines, etc., mentioned before, *stirred up the people*—raised a mob against him, and to assist and countenance the mob got the *elders* and *scribes* to conduct it, who thus made themselves one with the basest of the people whom they collected; and then altogether, without law or form of justice, rushed on the good man, seized him, and brought him to a council who, though they sat in the seat of judgment, were ready for every evil work.

13. *Against this holy place.* The Temple, that it shall be destroyed. *And the law.* That it cannot give life, nor save from death. It is very likely that they had heard him speak words to this amount, which were all as true as the spirit from which they proceeded; but they gave them a very false coloring, as we see in the succeeding verse.

15. *Saw his face as it had been the face of an angel.* It appears that the light and power of God which dwelt in his soul shone through his face, and God gave them this proof of the falsity of the testimony which was now before them; for as the face of Stephen now shone as the face of Moses did when he came down from the mount, it was the fullest proof that he had not spoken blasphemous words either against Moses or God, else this splendor of heaven had not rested upon him.

CHAPTER 7

Stephen, being permitted to answer for himself relative to the charge of blasphemy brought against him by his accusers, gives a circumstantial relation of the call of Abraham, when he dwelt in Mesopotamia, in Charran, etc., 1-8. The history of Jacob and Joseph, 9-17. The persecution of their fathers in Egypt, 18-19. The history of Moses and his acts till the exodus from Egypt, 20-37. The rebellion and idolatry of the Israelites in the wilderness, 38-43. The erection of the Tabernacle of witness, which continued till the time of David, 44-46. Of the Temple built by Solomon for that God who cannot be confined to temples built by hands, 47-50. Being probably interrupted in the prosecution of his discourse, he urges home the charge of rebellion against God, persecution of His prophets, the murder of Christ, and neglect of their own law against them, 51-53. They are filled with indignation, and proceed to violence, 54. He sees the glory of God, and Christ at the right hand of the Father, and declares the glorious vision, 55-56. They rush upon him, drag him out of the city, and stone him, 57-58. He invokes the Lord Jesus, prays for his murderers, and expires, 59-60.

1. *Are these things so?* Have you predicted the destruction of the Temple? And have you said that Jesus of Nazareth shall change our customs, abolish our religious rites and Temple service? Have you spoken these blasphemous things against Moses and against God? Here was some color of justice, for Stephen was permitted to defend himself. And in order to do this he thought it best to enter into a detail of their history from the commencement of their nation, and thus show how kindly God had dealt with them, and how ungraciously they and their fathers had requited Him. And all this naturally led him to the conclusion that God could no longer bear with a people the cup of whose iniquity had been long overflowing, and therefore they might expect to find wrath, without mixture of mercy. But how could Luke get all this circumstantial account? He might have been present and heard the whole; or, more probably, he had the account from Paul, whose companion he was, and who was certainly present when Stephen was judged and stoned, for **he was consenting to his death and kept the**

clothes of them who stoned him. See chap. vii. 58; viii. 1; and xxii. 20.

2. *Men, brethren, and fathers.* Rather, "brethren and fathers." Literally it is "men-brethren," a very usual form in Greek. *The God of glory appeared.* As Stephen is now vindicating himself from the false charges brought against him, he shows that he had uttered no blasphemy against either God, Moses, or the Temple; but states that his accusers, and the Jews in general, were guilty of the faults with which they charged him, that they had from the beginning rejected and despised Moses and had always violated his laws. He proceeds to state that there is no blasphemy in saying that the Temple shall be destroyed—they had been without a temple till the days of David, nor does God ever confine himself to temples built by hands, seeing He fills both heaven and earth; that Jesus is the Prophet of whom Moses spoke, and whom they had persecuted, condemned, and at last put to death; that they were wicked and uncircumcised in heart and in ears, and always resisted the Holy Ghost, as their fathers did. This is the substance of Stephen's defense as far as he was permitted to make it, a defense which they could not confute, containing charges which they most glaringly illustrated and confirmed by adding the murder of this faithful disciple to that of his all-glorious Master. *Was in Mesopotamia.* In that part of it where Ur of the Chaldees was situated, near to Babel, and among the rivers (Tigris and Euphrates) which gave the name of Mesopotamia to the country. *Before he dwelt in Charran.* This is called Haran in our translation of Gen. xi. 31; this place also belonged to Mesopotamia, as well as Ur, but is placed west of it on the maps. It seems most probable that Abraham had two calls, one in Ur and the other in Haran. He left Ur at the first call and came to Haran; he left Haran at the second call and came into the Promised Land.

5. *Gave him none inheritance.* Both Abraham and Jacob had small parcels of land in Canaan; but they had them by purchase, not by God's gifts; for as Abraham was obliged to buy a burying place in Canaan, Genesis xxiii, it is obvious he had no inheritance there.

6. *That his seed should sojourn in a strange land.* See Gen. xv. 13-14. *Four hundred years.* Moses says, Exod. xii. 40, that the sojourning of the children of Israel in Egypt was 430 years. Paul has the same number, Gal. iii. 17; and so has Josephus. Stephen uses the round number of 400.

7. *Will I judge.* "I will punish," for in this sense the Greek word is frequently taken.

8. *He gave him the covenant of circumcision.* That is, he instituted the rite of circumcision as a sign of that covenant which He had made with him and his posterity. See Gen. xvii. 10. *And so Abraham begat Isaac.* "And thus," in this covenant, he begat Isaac; and as a proof that he was born under this covenant, was a true son of Abraham and inheritor of the promises, he circumcised him the eighth day.

9. *And the patriarchs.* The twelve sons of Jacob, thus called because each was chief or head of his respective family or tribe. *Moved with envy.* We translate *zelos* variously: "zeal" or "fervent affection," whether its object be

good or bad, is its general meaning; and *zeloo* signifies to be "indignant, envious." See the note on chap. v. 17. The brethren of Joseph, hearing of his dreams, and understanding them to portend his future advancement, filled with envy, sold Joseph into the land of Egypt, hoping by this means to prevent his future grandeur; *but God,* from whom the portents came, *was with him,* and made their envy the direct means of accomplishing the great design.

10. *Gave him favour and wisdom in the sight of Pharaoh.* God gave him much *wisdom,* in consequence of which he had *favour* with the king of Egypt. See the whole of this remarkable history explained at large, Genesis xli—xlv.

14. *Threescore and fifteen souls.* There are several difficulties here, which it is hoped the reader will find satisfactorily removed in the note on Gen. xlvi. 20. It is well-known that in Genesis xlvi and Deut. x. 22 their number is said to be "threescore and ten"; but Stephen quotes from the Septuagint, which adds five persons to the account which are not in the Hebrew text.

16. *And were carried over to Sychem.* "It is said, Gen. l. 13, that Jacob was buried in the cave of the field of Machpelah before Mamre. And in Josh. xxiv. 32 and Exod. xiii. 19, it is said that the bones of Joseph were carried out of Egypt by the Israelites, and buried in Shechem, which Jacob bought from the sons of Hamor, the father of Shechem. As for the eleven brethren of Joseph, we are told by Josephus, *Ant.,* l. ii, c. 8, s. 2, that they were buried in Hebron, where their father had been buried. But, since the books of the Old Testament say nothing about this, the authority of Stephen (or of Luke here) for their being buried in Sychem is at least as good as that of Josephus for their being buried in Hebron."—Bishop Pearce. We have the uniform consent of the Jewish writers that all the patriarchs were brought out of Egypt and buried in Canaan, but none, except Stephen, mentions their being buried in Sychem. As Sychem belonged to the Samaritans, probably the Jews thought it too great an honor for that people to possess the bones of the patriarchs, and therefore have carefully avoided making any mention of it. *That Abraham bought for a sum of money.* Two accounts seem here to be confounded: (1) The purchase made by Abraham of the cave and field of Ephron, which was in the field of Machpelah; this purchase was made from the children of Heth, Gen. xxiii. 3, 10, 17. (2) The purchase made by Jacob, from the sons of Hamor or Emmor, of a sepulchre in which the bones of Joseph were laid; this was in Sychem or Shechem, Gen. xxxiii. 19; Josh. xxiv. 32. The word *Abraham,* therefore, in this place is certainly a mistake; and the word *Jacob,* which some have supplied, is doubtless more proper. Bishop Pearce supposes that Luke originally wrote, "which he bought for a sum of money"; i.e., which Jacob bought, who is the last person of the singular number spoken of in the preceding verse. Those who saw that the word *bought* had no nominative case joined to it, and did not know where to find the proper one, seem to have inserted *Abraham* in the text for that purpose, without sufficiently attending to the different circumstances of his purchase from that of Jacob's.

19. *The same dealt subtilly.* A word borrowed from the Septuagint, who thus translate the Hebrew, "Let us deal wisely with it"; i.e., with cunning and deceit, as the Greek word implies, and which is evidently intended by the Hebrew. See Gen. xxvii. 35, "Thy brother came with subtilty." For this the Egyptians were so remarkable that "to Egyptize" signified "to act cunningly" and "to use wicked devices." *To the end they might not live.* Might not grow up and propagate, and thus build up the Hebrew nation.

20. *Moses . . . was exceeding fair.* "Was fair to God"; i.e., was divinely beautiful. See the note on Exod. ii. 2.

22. *In all the wisdom of the Egyptians.* Who were, at that time, the most intelligent and best instructed people in the universe. Philo says Moses was taught arithmetic, geometry, poetry, music, medicine, and the knowledge of hieroglyphics. In *Sohar Cadash,* fol. 46, it is said "that, of the ten portions of wisdom which came into the world, the Egyptians had nine, and that all the inhabitants of the earth had only the remaining portion." *Was mighty in words and in deeds.* This may refer to the glorious doctrines he taught and the miracles he wrought in Egypt.

23. *When he was full forty years old.* This was a general tradition among the Jews: "Moses was forty years in Pharaoh's court, forty years in Midian, and forty years he served Israel." *To visit his brethren.* Probably on the ground of trying to deliver them from their oppressive bondage. This desire seems to have been early infused into his mind by the Spirit of God; and the effect of this desire to deliver his oppressed countrymen was his refusing to be called the son of Pharoah's daughter—(see Heb. xi. 24) and thus renouncing all right to the Egyptian crown, "choosing rather to endure affliction with the people of God, than to enjoy the pleasures of sin for a season."

24. *Smote the Egyptian.* See this explained, Exod. ii. 11-12.

25. *He supposed his brethren would have understood.* He probably imagined that, as he felt from the divine influence he was appointed to be their deliverer, they would have his divine appointment signified to them in a similar way; and the act of justice which he now did in behalf of his oppressed countryman would be sufficient to show them that he was now ready to enter upon his office, if they were willing to concur.

26. *Unto them as they strove.* Two Hebrews. See on Exod. ii. 13, etc.

30. *In a flame of fire in a bush.* See this and the following verses largely explained in the notes on Exod. iii. 1-8.

36. *He brought them out, after that he had shewed wonders.* Thus the very person whom they had rejected, and in effect delivered up into the hands of Pharaoh that he might be slain, was the person alone by whom they were redeemed from their Egyptian bondage. And does not Stephen plainly say by this that the very Person, Jesus Christ, whom they had rejected and delivered up into the hands of Pilate to be crucified was the Person alone by whom they could be delivered out of their spiritual bondage

and made partakers of the inheritance among the saints in light?

37. *This is that Moses, which said . . . A prophet.* This very Moses, so highly esteemed and honored by God, announced that very Prophet whom you have lately put to death.

38. *With the angel which spake to him.* Stephen shows that Moses received the law by the ministry of angels, and that he was only a mediator between the angel of God and them. *The lively oracles.* The "living oracles." The doctrines of life, those doctrines obedience to which entitled them, by the promise of God, to a long life upon earth, which spoke to them of that spiritual life which every true believer has in union with his God, and promised that eternal life which those who are faithful unto death shall enjoy with Him in the realms of glory. The Greek word which we translate *oracle* signifies a "divine revelation, a communication from God himself," and is here applied to the Mosaic law; to the Old Testament in general, Rom. iii. 2; Heb. v. 12; and to divine revelation in general, 1 Pet. iv. 11.

42. *Then God turned, and gave them up.* He left them to themselves, and then they deified and worshipped the sun, moon, planets, and principal stars. *In the book of the prophets.* As this quotation is found in Amos, chap. v. 25, by the *book of the prophets* is meant the twelve minor prophets, which in the ancient Jewish division of the sacred writings formed only one book. *Have ye offered to me slain beasts.* It is certain that the Israelites did offer various sacrifices to God while in the wilderness, and it is as certain that they scarcely ever did it with an upright heart.

43. *Ye took up the tabernacle of Moloch, and the star of your god Remphan, figures which ye made to worship them.* This is a literal translation of the place, as it stands in the Septuagint; but in the Hebrew text it stands thus: "But ye have borne the tabernacle of your Molech, and Chiun, your images, the star of your god which ye made to yourselves." This is the simple version of the place, unless we should translate "ye took Sikuth your king" (instead of "ye took up the tabernacle of your Molek"), as some have done. The place is indeed very obscure, and the two texts do not tend to cast light on each other. The rabbins say *siccuth,* which we translate "tabernacle," is the name of an idol. Molech is generally understood to mean the sun; and several persons of good judgment think that by *Remphan* or "Raiphan" is meant the planet Saturn. It will be seen above that instead of *Remphan,* or, as some of the best MSS. have it, *Rephan,* the Hebrew text has *Chiun,* which might possibly be a corruption of *Reiphan.* This emendation would bring the Hebrew, Septuagint, and the text of Luke, nearer together; but there is no authority either from MSS. or versions for this correction. However, as *Chiun* is mentioned in no other place, though *Molech* often occurs, it is the more likely that there might have been some very early mistake in the text, and that the Septuagint has preserved the true reading. It was customary for the idolaters of all nations to carry images of their gods about them in their journeys, military expeditions; and these, being very small, were enclosed in little boxes, perhaps some of them in the shape of temples,

called "tabernacles"; or, as we have it, chap. xix. 24, "shrines." Such images as these I suppose the idolatrous Israelites, in imitation of their neighbors, the Moabites, Ammonites, etc., to have carried about with them; and to such the prophet appears to me unquestionably to allude. *I will carry you away beyond Babylon.* You have carried your idolatrous images about; and I will carry you into captivity, and see if the gods in whom you have trusted can deliver you from My hands. Instead of *beyond Babylon,* Amos, from whom the quotation is made, says, "I will carry you beyond Damascus." Where they were carried was into Assyria and Media, not Damascus, but beyond Babylon itself; and as Stephen knew this to be the fact, he states it here, and thus more precisely fixes the place of their captivity. The Holy Spirit, in His further revelations, has undoubted right to extend or illustrate those which He had given before. This case frequently occurs when a former prophecy is quoted in later times.

44. *Our fathers had the tabernacle of witness in the wilderness.* That is, the Tabernacle in which the two tables of stone written by the finger of God were laid up, as a testimony that He had delivered these laws to the people, and that they had promised to obey them. As one great design of Stephen was to show the Jews that they placed too much dependence on outward privileges, and had not used the law, the Tabernacle, the Temple, nor the Temple service for the purpose of their institution, he labors to bring them to a due sense of this, that conviction might lead to repentance and conversion. And he further shows that God did not confine His worship to one place or form. He was worshipped without any shrine in the times of the patriarchs, Abraham, Isaac, Jacob. He was worshipped with a Tabernacle, or portable temple, in the wilderness. He was worshipped also in the fixed Temple projected by David but built by Solomon. He asserts farther that His infinite majesty cannot be confined to temples made by human hands; and where there is neither Tabernacle nor Temple (in any part of His vast dominions), He may be worshipped acceptably by the upright in heart. Thus he proves that neither Tabernacle nor Temple is essentially requisite for the true worship of the true God. *Speaking unto Moses.* "Who spake," as in the margin; signifying the angel of God who spake to Moses, or God himself. See Exod. xxv. 40.

45. *Brought in with Jesus.* That is, with Joshua, whom the Greek version, quoted by Stephen, always writes *Iesous,* Jesus, but which should constantly be written "Joshua" in such cases as the present, in order to avoid ambiguity and confusion. *Possession of the Gentiles.* "Of the heathens," whom Joshua conquered, and gave their land to the children of Israel.

46. *Desired to find a tabernacle.* This was in David's heart, and it met with the divine approbation; see 2 Sam. vii. 2, etc., and see the purpose, Ps. cxxxii. 2-5. But as David had been a man of war, and had shed much blood, God would not permit him to build the Temple; but he laid the plan and made provision for it, and Solomon executed the design.

48. *The most High dwelleth not in temples made with hands.* Here Stephen evidently refers to Solomon's speech, 1 Kings viii. 27. "But will

God indeed dwell on the earth? behold, the heaven and heaven of heavens cannot contain thee; how much less this house that I have builded?" Both Solomon and Stephen mean that the majesty of God could not be contained, not even in the whole vortex of nature, much less in any temple which human hands could erect. *As saith the prophet.* The place referred to is Isa. lxvi. 1-2: "Thus saith the Lord, The heaven is my throne, and the earth my footstool: where is the house that ye build unto me? and where is the place of my rest?" with which the quotation by Stephen agrees.

50. *Hath not my hand made all these things?* Stephen certainly had not finished his discourse nor drawn his inferences from the facts already stated; but it is likely that, as they perceived he was about to draw conclusions unfavorable to the Temple and its ritual, they immediately raised up a clamor against him, which was the cause of the following very cutting address.

51. *Ye stiffnecked.* A metaphor taken from untoward oxen who cannot be broken into the yoke, and whose strong necks cannot be bent to the right or the left. *Uncircumcised in heart and ears.* This was a Jewish mode of speech, often used by the prophets. Circumcision was instituted, not only as a sign and seal of the covenant into which the Israelites entered with their Maker, but also as a type of that purity and holiness which the law of God requires; and by this cutting off, the propensity to that crime which ruins the body, debases the mind, and was generally the forerunner of idolatry was happily lessened. *Ye do always resist the Holy Ghost.* Because they were uncircumcised in *heart,* they always resisted the influences of the Holy Spirit, bringing light and conviction to their minds; in consequence of which they became hardened through the deceitfulness of sin, and neither repented at the preaching of John nor credited the glad tidings told them by Christ and the apostles. Because they were uncircumcised in *ears,* they would neither hear nor obey Moses, the prophets, Christ, nor the apostles. *As your fathers did, so do ye.* They were disobedient children, of disobedient parents; in all their generations they had been disobedient and perverse. This whole people, as well as this text, are fearful proofs that the Holy Spirit, the almighty energy of the living God, may be resisted and rendered of none effect.

52. *Which of the prophets have not your fathers persecuted?* You have not only resisted the Holy Ghost, but you have *persecuted* all those who have spoken to you in His name and by His influence: thus you prove your opposition to the Spirit himself, by your opposition to everything that proceeds from Him. *They have slain them.* Isaiah, *who shewed before of the coming of* Christ, the Jews report, was sawn asunder at the command of Manasseh. *The coming of the Just One.* Meaning Jesus Christ; emphatically called the *just* or "righteous" Person, not only because of the unspotted integrity of His heart and life, but because of His plenary acquittal when tried at the tribunal of Pilate: *I find in him no fault at all.* The mention of this circumstance served greatly to aggravate their guilt. The character of *Just One* is applied to our Lord in three other places of Scripture: chap. iii. 14; xxii. 14; and

Jas. v. 6. *The betrayers and murderers.* You first delivered Him up into the hands of the Romans, hoping they would have put Him to death; but when they acquitted Him, then, in opposition to the declaration of His innocence and in outrage to every form of justice, you took and murdered Him. This was a most terrible charge, and one against which they could set up no sort of defense. No wonder, then, that they were instigated by the spirit of the old destroyer, which they never resisted, to add another murder to that of which they had been so recently guilty.

53. *By the disposition of angels.* After all that has been said on this difficult passage, perhaps the simple meaning is that there were "ranks" of angels attending on the Divine Majesty when He gave the law, a circumstance which must have added greatly to the grandeur and solemnity of the occasion; and to this Ps. lxviii. 17 (marg.) seems to me most evidently to allude: "The chariots of God are twenty thousand, even many thousands of angels: the Lord is among them, as in Sinai, in the holy place." It was not then by the mouths nor by the hands of angels as prime agents that Moses, and through him the people, received the law; but God himself gave it, accompanied with many thousands of those glorious beings. As it is probable they might be assisting in this most glorious solemnity, therefore Paul might say, Gal. iii. 19, that it was "ordained by angels in the hand of a mediator." And as they were the only persons that could appear, for no man hath seen God at any time, therefore the apostle might say further (if indeed he refers to the same transaction; see the note there), "The word spoken by angels was stedfast," Heb. ii. 2.

54. *They were cut to the heart.* They *were* "sawn through." See the note on chap. v. 33. *They gnashed on him with their teeth.* They were determined to hear him no longer; were filled with rage against him, and evidently thirsted for his blood.

55. *Saw the glory of God.* The Shekinah, the splendor or manifestation of the Divine Majesty. *And Jesus standing on the right hand of God.* In his official character, as Mediator between God and man.

57. *They . . . stopped their ears.* As a proof that he had uttered blasphemy, because he said he saw Jesus standing at the right hand of God. This was a fearful proof against them; for if Jesus was at the *right hand of God,* then they had murdered an innocent Person, and they must infer that God's justice must speedily avenge His death. They were determined not to suffer a man to live any longer who could say he saw the heavens opened and Jesus Christ standing at the right hand of God.

58. *Cast him out of the city, and stoned him.* They did not however wait for any sentence to be pronounced upon him; it seems they were determined to stone him first, and then prove, after it had been done, that it was done justly. For the manner of stoning among the Jews, see the note on Lev. xxiv. 23.

59. *And they stoned Stephen, calling upon God.* The word God is not found in any MS. or version, nor in any of the primitive fathers except Chrysostom. It is not genuine, and should not be inserted here. The whole sentence literally reads thus: "And they stoned Stephen,

invoking and saying, Lord Jesus, receive my spirit!" Here is a most manifest proof that prayer is offered to Jesus Christ, and that in the most solemn circumstances in which it could be offered, viz., when a man was breathing his last. This is, properly speaking, one of the highest acts of worship which can be offered to God; and if Stephen had not conceived Jesus Christ to be God, could he have committed his soul into His hands?

60. *He kneeled down.* That he might die as the subject of his heavenly Master—acting and suffering in the deepest submission to His divine will and permissive providence; and at the same time showing the genuine nature of the religion of his Lord, in pouring out his prayers with his blood in behalf of his murderers! *Lay not this sin to their charge.* That is, do not impute it to them so as to exact punishment. How much did the servant resemble his Lord, "Father, forgive them; for they know not what they do"! This was the cry of our Lord in behalf of His murderers; and the disciple, closely copying his Master, in the same spirit and with the same meaning, varies the expression, crying with a loud voice, *Lord, lay not this sin to their charge!* Christ had given what some have supposed to be an impossible command, "Love your enemies . . . pray for them which despitefully use you, and persecute you." And Stephen shows here, in his own person, how practicable the grace of his Master had made this sublime precept. *He fell asleep.* This was a common expression among the Jews to signify death, and especially the death of good men. But this sleep is, properly speaking, not attributable to the soul, but to the body; for he had commended his spirit to the Lord Jesus, while his body was overwhelmed with the shower of stones cast on him by the mob. The first clause of the next chapter should come in here, *And Saul was consenting unto his death.* Never was there a worse division than that which separated it from the end of this chapter. This should be immediately altered, and the amputated member restored to the body to which it belongs.

CHAPTER 8

A general persecution is raised against the Church, 1. Stephen's burial, 2. Saul greatly oppresses the followers of Christ, 3-4. Philip the deacon goes to Samaria, preaches, works many miracles, converts many persons, and baptizes Simon the sorcerer, 5-13. Peter and John are sent by the apostles to Samaria; they confirm the disciples, and by prayer and imposition of hands they confer the Holy Spirit, 14-17. Simon the sorcerer, seeing this, offers them money, to enable him to confer the Holy Spirit, 18-19. He is sharply reproved by Peter and exhorted to repent, 20-23. He appears to be convinced of his sin, and implores an interest in the apostle's prayers, 24. Peter and John, having preached the gospel in the villages of Samaria, return to Jerusalem, 25. An angel of the Lord commands Philip to go towards Gaza, to meet an Ethiopian eunuch, 26. He goes, meets, and converses with the eunuch, preaches the gospel to him, and baptizes him, 27-38. The Spirit of God carries Philip to Azotus, passing through which, he preaches in all the cities till he comes to Caesarea, 39-40.

1. *Saul was consenting unto his death.* The word signifies "gladly consenting," being pleased with his murderous work! It has already been remarked that this clause belongs to the conclusion of the preceding chapter; so it stands in the Vulgate, and so it should stand in every version. *There was a great persecution.* The Jews could not bear the doctrine of Christ's resurrection, for this point being proved demonstrated His innocence and their enormous guilt

in His crucifixion. As therefore the apostles continued to insist strongly on the resurrection of Christ, the persecution against them became hot and general. *They were all scattered abroad . . . except the apostles.* Their Lord had commanded them, when persecuted in one city, to flee to another. This they did, but wherever they went they proclaimed the same doctrines, though at the risk and hazard of their lives. It is evident, therefore, that they did not flee from persecution, or the death it threatened, but merely in obedience to their Lord's command. That the apostles were not also exiled is a very remarkable fact. They continued in Jerusalem, to found and organize the infant Church, and it is marvellous that the hand of persecution was not permitted to touch them. Why this should be we cannot tell, but so it pleased the great Head of the Church.

2. *Devout men carried Stephen to his burial.* The Greek word signifies not only to "carry," or rather to "gather up," but also to do everything necessary for the interment of the dead. Among the Jews, and indeed among most nations of the earth, it was esteemed a work of piety, charity, and mercy to bury the dead.

3. *Saul . . . made havock of the church.* The word signifies the act of ferocious animals, such as bears, wolves, and the like, in seeking and devouring their prey. This shows with what persevering rancor this man pursued the harmless Christians, and thus we see in him what bigotry and false zeal are capable of performing. *Haling men and women.* The word signifies "dragging" them before the magistrates or dragging them to justice. *Committed them to prison.* For, as the Romans alone had the power of life and death, the Sanhedrin, by whom Saul was employed, chap. xxvi. 10, could do no more than arrest and imprison, in order to inflict any punishment short of death. It is true Paul himself says that some of them were put to death (see chap. xxvi. 10); but this was done either by Roman authority or by what was called the "judgment of zeal," i.e., when the mob took the execution of the laws into their own hands, and massacred those whom they pretended to be blasphemers of God. For these sanctified their murderous outrage under the specious name of zeal for God's glory, and quoted the example of Phineas as a precedent. Such persons as these formed a sect among the Jews, and are known in ecclesiastical history by the appellation of *Zealots* or *Sicarii.*

4. *They that were scattered . . . went every where preaching.* Thus the very means devised by Satan to destroy the Church became the very instruments of its diffusion and establishment.

5. *Then Philip.* One of the seven deacons, chap. vi. 5, called afterwards "Philip the evangelist," chap. xxi. 8. *The city of Samaria.* At this time there was no city of Samaria existing; according to Josephus, *Ant.,* l. xiii, c. 10, s. 3, Hyrcanus had so utterly demolished it as to leave no vestige of it remaining. Herod the Great did afterwards build a city on the same spot of ground, but he called it *Sebaste,* i.e., *Augusta,* in compliment to the Emperor Augustus, as Josephus tells us, *Ant.,* l. xv, c. 8, s. 5; *War,* l. i, c. 2, s. 7; and by this name of *Sebaste,* or *Augusta,* that city, if meant here, would in all probability have been called. As Sychem was

the very heart and seat of the Samaritan religion, and Mount Gerizim the cathedral church of that sect, it is more likely that it should be intended than any other. As the Samaritans received the same law with the Jews, as they also expected the Messiah, as Christ had preached to and converted many of that people, John iv, it was very reasonable that the earliest offers of salvation should be made to them, before any attempt was made to evangelize the Gentiles. The Samaritans, indeed, formed the connecting link between the Jews and the Gentiles; for they were a mongrel people, made up of both sorts, and holding both Jewish and pagan rites. See the account of them on Matt. x. 5.

6. *The people with one accord gave heed.* He had fixed their attention, not only with the gravity and importance of the matter of his preaching, but also by *the miracles which he did.*

7. *For unclean spirits, crying with a loud voice, came out of many that were possessed.* Hence it is evident that these *unclean spirits* were not a species of diseases, as they are here distinguished from the *paralytic* and the *lame.* There is nothing more certain than that the New Testament writers mean real diabolic possessions by the terms "unclean spirits," "devils," etc., which they use.

9. *And bewitched the people of Samaria.* "Astonishing, amazing, or confounding" the judgment of the people, from *existemi,* to "remove out of a place or state, to be transported beyond oneself, to be out of one's wits."

10. *This man is the great power of God.* That is, he is invested with it and can command and use it. They certainly did not believe him to be God, but they thought him to be endued with a great supernatural power. There is a remarkable reading here in several MSS. which should not pass unnoticed. The passage reads thus, "This person is that power of God which is called the Great." This appears to be the true reading; but what the Samaritans meant by that power of God which they termed "the Great," we know not.

12. *But when they believed Philip.* So it is evident that Philip's word came with greater power than that of Simon, and that his miracles stood the test in such a way as the feats of Simon could not.

13. *Simon himself believed also.* He was struck with the doctrine and miracles of Philip —he saw that these were real; he knew his own to be fictitious. He believed therefore that Jesus was the Messiah, and was in consequence baptized. *Continued with Philip, and wondered.* He was as much "astonished" and "confounded" at the miracles of Philip as the people of Samaria were at his *legerdemain.*

14. *The word of God.* The doctrine of the Lord Jesus Christ. *They sent unto them Peter and John.* There was no individual ruler among the apostles—there was not even a president of the council; and Peter, far from being chief of the apostles, is one of those sent, with the same commission and authority as John, to confirm the Samaritans in the faith.

15. *When they were come down.* The very same mode of speaking, in reference to Jerusalem formerly, obtains now in reference to London. The metropolis in both cases is con-

sidered as the center; and all parts, in every direction, no matter how distant, or how situated, are represented as below the metropolis. *Prayed for them, that they might receive the Holy Ghost.* It seems evident, from this case, that even the most holy deacons, though full of the Holy Ghost themselves, could not confer this heavenly Gift on others. This was the prerogative of the apostles, and they were only instruments; but they were those alone by which the Lord chose to work. They prayed and laid their hands on the disciples, and God sent down the Gift; so the blessing came from God by the apostles, and not from the apostles to the people. But for what purpose was the Holy Spirit thus given? Certainly not for the sanctification of the souls of the people; this they had on believing in Christ Jesus, and this the apostles never dispensed. It was the miraculous gifts of the Spirit which were thus communicated.

17. *Then laid they their hands on them.* Probably only on some select persons, who were thought proper for public use in the church. They did not lay hands on *all,* for certainly no hands in this way were laid on Simon.

18. *When Simon saw.* By hearing these speak with different tongues and work miracles. *He offered them money.* Supposing that the dispensing of this Spirit belonged to them—that they could give it to whomsoever they pleased; and imagining that, as he saw them to be poor men, they would not object to taking money for their gift; and it is probable that he had gained considerably by his juggling, and therefore could afford to spare some, as he hoped to make it all up by the profit which he expected to derive from this new influence.

20. *Thy money perish with thee.* This is an awful declaration, and imports thus much, that if he did not repent, he and his ill-gotten goods would perish together; his money should be dissipated and his soul go into perdition. *That the gift of God may be purchased.* Peter takes care to inform not only Simon, but all to whom these presents may come, that the Spirit of God is the Gift of God alone, and consequently cannot be purchased with money.

21. *Thou hast neither part nor lot in this matter.* You have no part among the faithful and no lot in this ministry. That the word which we translate *lot* is to be understood as implying a "spiritual portion, office," see proved in the note on Num. xxvi. 55. *Thy heart is not right.* It is not through motives of purity, benevolence, or love to the souls of men that you desired to be enabled to confer the Holy Ghost; it is through pride, vainglory, and love of money. You would now give a little money that you might, by your new gift, gain much.

22. *Repent therefore of this thy wickedness.* Peter did not suppose his case to be utterly hopeless, though his sin, considered in its motives and objects, was of the most heinous kind. *If perhaps the thought of thine heart may be forgiven thee.* His sin as yet existed only in thought and purpose; and therefore it is said, *if perhaps the thought of thine heart may be forgiven.*

23. *The gall of bitterness.* A Hebraism for "excessive bitterness." Gall, wormwood, and suchlike were used to express the dreadful effects of sin in the soul: the bitter repentance, bitter regret, bitter sufferings, bitter death which it produces. In Deut. xxix. 18, idolatry and its consequences are expressed by having among them "a root that beareth gall and wormwood." And in Heb. xii. 15, some grievous sin is intended when the apostle warns them, "lest any root of bitterness springing up trouble you, and thereby many be defiled." *Bond of iniquity.* An allusion to the mode in which the Romans secured their prisoners, chaining the right hand of the prisoner to the left hand of the soldier who guarded him; as if the apostle had said, You are tied and bound by the chain of your sin; justice has laid hold upon you, and you have only a short respite before your execution, to see if you will repent.

24. *Pray ye to the Lord for me.* The words of Peter certainly made a deep impression on Simon's mind, and he must have had a high opinion of the apostle's sanctity and influence with God when he thus commended himself to their prayers.

26. *Gaza, which is desert.* "This is the desert" or "this is in the desert." Gaza was a town about two miles and a half from the seaside; it was the last town which a traveller passed through when he went from Phoenicia to Egypt, and was at the entrance into a wilderness. Schoettgen thinks that *desert* should be referred, not to Gaza, but to the *way,* and that it signifies a road that was less frequented. If there were two roads to Gaza from Jerusalem, as some have imagined, the eunuch might have chosen that which was desert, or less frequented, for the sake of privacy in his journeying religious exercises.

27. *An eunuch.* The term eunuch was given to persons in authority at court, to whom its literal meaning did not apply. Potiphar was probably a eunuch only as to his office, for he was a married man. See Gen. xxxvii. 36; xxxix. 1. And it is likely that this Ethiopian was of the same sort. *Of great authority.* Her treasurer, for it is here said, he *had the charge of all her treasure.* It does not appear, as some have imagined, that the Abyssinians were converted to the Christian faith by this eunuch, nor by any of the apostles, as there is strong historic evidence that they continued Jews and pagans for more than three hundred years after the Christian era. Their conversion is with great probability attributed to Frumentius, sent to Abyssinia for that purpose by Athanasius, bishop of Alexandria, about A.D 330.

28. *Sitting in his chariot, read Esaias the prophet.* He had gone to Jerusalem to worship; he had profited by his religious exercises; and even in traveling he is improving his time. God sees his simplicity and earnestness and provides him an instructor who should lead him into the great truths of the gospel, which without such a one he could not have understood. Many, after having done their duty, as they call it, in attending a place of worship, forget the errand that brought them thither, and spend their time, on their return, rather in idle conversation than in reading or conversing about the Word of God. It is no wonder that such should be always learning and never able to come to the knowledge of the truth.

29. *Then the Spirit said unto Philip.* This holy man having obeyed the first direction he

received from God, and gone southward without knowing the reason why, it was requisite that he should now be informed of the object of his mission. The *Spirit said unto* him, *Go near, and join thyself.* The angel who had given him the first direction had departed, and the influence of the Holy Spirit now completed the information. It is likely that what the Spirit did in this case was by a strong impression on his mind, which left him no doubt of its being from God.

30. *Heard him read the prophet Esias.* The eunuch, it seems, was reading aloud, and apparently in Greek, for that was the common language in Egypt; and, indeed, almost in every place it was understood. And it appears that it was the Greek version or the Septuagint that he was reading, as the quotation below is from that version.

32. *The place of the scripture.* The "section" or "paragraph."

33. *In his humiliation his judgment was taken away.* He who was the Fountain of judgment and justice had no justice shown Him *in his humiliation,* viz., that time in which He emptied himself and appeared in the form of a servant. *Who shall declare his generation?* Answering to the Hebrew *doro,* which Bishop Lowth understands as implying his "manner of life." It was the custom among the Jews, when they were taking away any criminal from judgment to execution, to call out and inquire whether there was any person who could appear in behalf of the character of the criminal—whether there was any who, from intimate acquaintance with his manner *of life,* could say anything in his favor? In our Lord's case, this benevolent inquiry does not appear to have been made; and perhaps to this breach of justice, as well as of custom, the prophet refers.

35. *Began at the same scripture.* He did not confine himself to this one scripture, but made this his text and showed, from the general tenor of the sacred writings, that Jesus was the Christ, or Messiah; and that in His person, birth, life, doctrine, miracles, passion, death, and resurrection the scriptures of the Old Testament were fulfilled. This preaching had the desired effect, for the eunuch was convinced of the truth of Philip's doctrine and desired to be baptized in the name of Jesus.

36. *See, here is water.* He was not willing to omit the first opportunity that presented itself of his taking upon *himself* the profession of the gospel. By this we may see that Philip had explained the whole of the Christian faith to him, and the *way* by which believers were brought into the Christian Church.

37. *I believe that Jesus Christ is the Son of God.* This whole verse is omitted by several MSS.; almost all the critics declare against it as spurious.

38. *And they went down.* They "alighted from the chariot into the water." While Philip was instructing him and he professed his faith in Christ, he probably plunged himself under the water, as this was the plan which appears to have been generally followed among the Jews in their baptisms; but the person who had received his confession of faith was he to whom the baptism was attributed, as it was administered by his authority.

39. *The Spirit of the Lord caught away Philip.* Perhaps this means no more than that the Holy Spirit suggested to the mind of Philip that he should withdraw abruptly from the eunuch and thus leave him to pursue his journey, reflecting on the important incidents which had taken place.

40. *Philip was found at Azotus.* From the time he left the eunuch he was not heard of till he got to Azotus, which, according to Dr. Lightfoot, was about thirty-four miles from Gaza, and probably it was near Gaza that Philip met the eunuch. The Azotus of the New Testament is the Ashdod of the Old. It was given by Joshua to the tribe of Judah, Josh. xv. 47. It was one of the five lordships which belonged to the Philistines, and is a seaport town on the Mediterranean Sea, between Gaza on the south, and Joppa or Jaffa on the north. *Preached in all the cities, till he came to Caesarea.* This was Caesarea in Palestine, formerly called Strato's Tower, built by Herod the Great in honor of Augustus. There was an excellent harbor here made by Herod; and after the destruction of Jerusalem, it became the capital of the whole land of Judea. It must be always distinguished from Caesarea Philippi, which was an inland town not far from the springs of Jordan. Whenever the word Caesarea occurs without Philippi, the former is intended. As Philip preached in all the cities of Palestine till he came to Caesarea, he must have preached in the different cities of the Philistine country, Ashdod, Akkaron, and Jamnia. It appears, from chap. xxi. 8, that Philip settled at Caesarea, where he had a house and family, four of his unmarried daughters being prophetesses.

CHAPTER 9

Saul, bent on the destruction of the Christians, obtains letters from the high priest, authorizing him to seize those whom he should find at Damascus, and bring them bound to Jerusalem, 1-2. On his way to Damascus he has a divine vision, is convinced of his sin and folly, is struck blind, and remains three days without sight, and neither eats nor drinks, 3-9. Ananias, a disciple, is commanded in a vision to go and speak to Saul, and restore his sight, 10-16. Ananias goes and lays his hands on him, and he receives his sight, and is baptized, 17-19. Saul, having spent a few days with the Christians at Damascus, goes to the synagogues, proclaims Christ, and confounds the Jews, 20-22. The Jews lay wait to kill him, but the disciples let him down over the walls of the city in a basket by night, and he escapes to Jerusalem, 23-25. Having wished to associate with the disciples there, they avoid him; but Barnabas takes and brings him to the apostles, and declares his conversion, 26-27. He continues in Jerusalem preaching Christ, and arguing with the Hellenistic Jews, who endeavor to slay him; but the disciples take him to Caesarea, and send him thence to his own city, Tarsus, 28-30. About this time the churches, being freed from persecution, are edified and multiplied, 31. Peter heals Aeneas at Lydda, who had been afflicted with the palsy eight years, in consequence of which miracle all the people of Lydda and Saron are converted, 32-35. Account of the sickness and death of a Christian woman named Tabitha, who dwelt at Joppa, and her miraculous restoration to life by the ministry of Peter, 36-41. Gracious effects produced among the inhabitants of Lydda by this miracle, 42-43.

1. *Saul, yet breathing out threatenings and slaughter.* The original text is very emphatic and points out how determinate Saul was to pursue and accomplish his fell purpose of totally destroying the infant Church of Christ. The mode of speech introduced above is very frequent in the Greek writers, who often express any vehement and *hostile* affection of the mind by the verb *pneein,* to "breathe," to "pant"; so Theocritus, *Idyll.* xxii, v. 82: "They came into the assembly, breathing mutual slaughter."

Euripides has the same form, *breathing out fire, and slaughter* (Iphig. in Taur.).

Luke, who was master of the Greek tongue, chose such terms as best expressed a heart desperately and incessantly bent on accomplishing the destruction of the objects of its resentment. Such at this time was the heart of Saul of Tarsus; and it had already given full proof of its malignity, not only in the martyrdom of Stephen, but also in making havoc of the Church, and in forcibly entering every house, and dragging men and women whom he suspected of Christianity, and committing them to prison. See chap. viii. 3. *Went unto the high priest.* As the high priest was chief in all matters of an ecclesiastical nature, and the present business was pretendedly religious, he was the proper person to apply to for letters by which this virulent persecutor might be accredited. The letters must necessarily be granted in the name of the whole Sanhedrin, but the *high priest* was the proper organ through whom this business might be negotiated.

2. *Letters to Damascus to the synagogues.* Damascus, anciently called *Damask,* was once the metropolis of all Syria. It was situated at fifty miles' distance from the sea, from which it is separated by lofty mountains. It is washed by two rivers, Amara or Abara, which ran through it, and Pharpar, called by the Greeks the golden stream, which ran on the outside of its walls. It is one of the most ancient cities in the world, for it existed in the time of Abraham, Gen. xiv. 15, and how long before is not known. The city of Damascus is at present a place of considerable trade, owing to its being the rendezvous for all the pilgrims from the north of Asia on their road to and from the temple of Mecca. It is surrounded with pretty strong walls, which have *nine* gates, and is between four and five miles in circumference. In the time of Paul it was governed by Aretas, whose father, Obodas, had been governor of it under Augustus. Damascus is 112 miles south of Antioch, 130 N.N.E. of Jerusalem. The silks and linens, known by the name of "damasks," were probably first manufactured by the inhabitants of this ancient city. *Any of this way.* That is, this "religion," for so *derec* in Hebrew and *hodos* in Hellenistic Greek are often to be understood. *Derec Yehovah,* the way of the Lord, implies the whole of the worship due to Him and prescibed by himself; the way or path in which He wills men to walk, that they may get safely through life and finally attain everlasting felicity. *Whether they were men or women.* Provided they were Jews, for no converts had as yet been made among the Gentiles, nor did the power of the high priest and Sanhedrin extend to any but those who belonged to the synagogues. In every country where there were Jews and synagogues, the power and authority of the Sanhedrin and high priest were acknowledged, just as papists in all countries acknowledge the authority of the pope.

4. *And he fell to the earth.* Being struck down with the lightning. Many persons suppose he was on horseback, and painters thus represent him; but this is utterly without foundation. Painters are in almost every case wretched commentators.

5. *Who art thou, Lord?* "Who art thou, Sir?" He had no knowledge who it was that addressed him, and would only use the term *Kyrios,* as any Roman or Greek would, merely as a term of civil respect. *I am Jesus whom thou persecutest.* "Your enmity is against Me and My religion; and the injuries which you do to My followers I consider as done to myself." The following words, making twenty in the original, and thirty in our version, are found in no Greek MS. The words are, "It is hard for thee to kick against the pricks. And he trembling and astonished said, Lord, what wilt thou have me to do? And the Lord said unto him." It is not very easy to account for such a large addition, which is not only not found in any Greek MS. yet discovered, but is wanting in the Itala, Erpen's Arabic, the Syriac, Coptic, Sahidic, and most of the Slavonian. It is found in the Vulgate; and was probably borrowed from chap. xxvi. 14, and some marginal notes. *It is hard for thee.* This is a proverbial expression, which exists, not only in substance, but even in so many words, both in the Greek and Latin writers. *Kentron* signifies an ox goad, a piece of pointed iron stuck in the end of a stick, with which the ox is urged on when drawing the plough. The origin of the proverb seems to have been this: Sometimes it happens that a restive stubborn ox kicks back against the goad and thus wounds himself more deeply; hence it has become a proverb to signify the fruitlessness and absurdity of rebelling against lawful authority, and the getting into greater difficulties by endeavoring to avoid trifling sufferings.

6. *Trembling.* Under a strong apprehension of meeting the judgment he deserved. *And astonished.* At the light, the thunder, and the voice. *Lord, what wilt thou have me to do?* The word *Kyrie, Lord,* is here to be understood in its proper sense, as expressing authority and dominion; in the fifth verse it appears to be equivalent to our word "sir." *Go into the city, and it shall be told thee.* Jesus could have informed him at once what was His will concerning him; but He chose to make one of those very disciples whom he was going to bring in bonds to Jerusalem the means of his salvation.

7. *Stood speechless, hearing a voice, but seeing no man.* The men were "stupefied," hearing *the voice* or thunder, but not distinguishing the words, which were addressed to Saul alone; and which were spoken out of the thunder, or in a small, still voice, after the peal had ceased. The remarkable case, 1 Kings xix. 11-13, may serve to illustrate that before us. The thunder must have been heard by all; the small, still voice by Saul alone. This consideration amply reconciles the passage in the text with that in chap. xxii. 9, where Paul says, "They that were with me saw indeed the light, and were afraid; but they heard not the voice of him that spake to me." They had heard the thunder which followed the escape of the lightning, but they heard not the *voice* of Him that spake to Saul; they did not hear the words, "I am Jesus whom thou persecutest"; but they saw and heard enough to convince them that the whole was supernatural, for they were all struck down to the earth with the splendor of the light and the sound of the thunder, which I suppose took place on this occasion. It has been a question among

divines whether Jesus Christ did really appear to Saul on this occasion. Ananias, it seems, was informed that there had been a real appearance, for in addressing Saul, v. 17, he says, "The Lord . . . Jesus, that appeared unto thee in the way as thou camest." And Barnabas intimated as much when he brought him before the apostles at Jerusalem, for he "declared unto them how he had seen the Lord in the way, and that he had spoken to him." But Paul's own words, 1 Cor. ix. 1, put the subject out of dispute: "Am I not an apostle? am I not free? have I not seen Jesus Christ our Lord?" To which may be added, 1 Cor. xv. 8, "And last of all he was seen of me also, as of one born out of due time."

9. *Neither did eat nor drink.* The anxiety of his mind and the anguish of his heart were so great that he had no appetite for food; and he continued in total darkness and without food for *three days*, till Ananias proclaimed salvation to him in the name of the Lord Jesus.

11. *Arise, and go into the street which is called Straight.* How very particular is this direction! And it was necessary that it should be so, that he might see the whole to be a divine communication; the house was probably one in which Saul was accustomed to reside when at Damascus, and where he was known as a native of Tarsus. Tarsus was a city of Cilicia, seated on the Cydnus, and now called Tarasso. It was, at one period, the capital of all Cilicia, and became a rival to Alexandria and Athens in the arts and sciences. The inhabitants, in the time of Julius Caesar, having shown themselves friendly to the Romans, were endowed with all the privileges of Roman citizens; and it was on this account that Paul claimed the rights of a Roman citizen—a circumstance which on different occasions was to him, and the cause in which he was engaged, of considerable service. *Behold, he prayeth.* He is earnestly seeking to know My will, and to find the salvation of his soul; therefore go speedily and direct him.

12. *Hath seen in a vision.* While God prepares Ananias by a vision to go and minister to Saul, He at the same time prepares Saul by another vision to profit by this ministry.

13. *Lord, I have heard by many of this man.* This was all done in a dream, else this sort of reasoning with his Maker would have been intolerable in Ananias. *Thy saints.* That is, the Christians, or followers of Christ. *Hagioi* signifies not only holy persons but also consecrated persons; from *a*, negative, and *ge*, the "earth"; persons who are separated from all earthly uses, and consecrated to the service of God alone.

14. *And here he hath authority.* Ananias had undoubtedly heard of Saul's coming, and the commission he had received from the chief priests; and he was about to urge this as a reason why he should have no connection with so dangerous a man.

15. *Go thy way.* He was thus prevented from going further in his reasoning on this subject. *Chosen vessel.* Properly a Hebraism for an "excellent or well-adapted instrument." Every reader of the Bible must have noticed how often the word *chosen* is used there to signify excelling or eminent. So we use the word *choice*—"choice men," eminent persons; "choice things," excellent articles. So in Jer. xxii. 7; "They shall cut down thy choice cedars." Whoever considers the character of Paul, his education,

attainments in natural knowledge, the distinguished part he took—first against Christianity, and afterwards, on the fullest conviction, the part he took in its favor—will at once perceive how well he was every way qualified for the great work to which God had called him. *To bear my name before the Gentiles.* To carry the ensign of the Cross among the Greeks and Romans. Hence he was emphatically called "the apostle of the Gentiles," 1 Tim. ii. 7; 2 Tim. i. 11. See also Gal. ii. 7-8 and Eph. iii. 8.

16. *How great things he must suffer.* Instead of proceeding as a persecutor and inflicting sufferings on others, I will show him how many things he himself must suffer for preaching that very doctrine which he has been hitherto employed in persecuting. Strange change indeed! And with great show of reason, as with incontrovertible strength of argument, has a noble writer, Lord Lyttleton, adduced the conversion of Saul of Tarsus and his subsequent conduct as an irrefragable proof of the truth of Christianity.

17. *Brother Saul.* As he found that the Head of the Church had adopted Saul into the heavenly family, he made no scruple to give him the right hand of fellowship, and therefore said, *Brother Saul. The Lord, even Jesus.* Of what use is this intrusive word *even* here? It injures the sense. Luke never wrote it; and our translators should not have inserted it. *The Lord . . . Jesus*, the sovereign Jesus who *appeared unto thee in the way . . . hath sent me, that thou mightest receive thy sight, and be filled with the Holy Ghost.* Christ could have cured him as miraculously by His own power, without human means, as He had enlightened his heart without them; but He will honor man by making him His agent, even in working miracles. *And be filled with the Holy Ghost.* So appears that the Holy Spirit was given to him at this time, and probably by the imposition of the hands of Ananias.

18. *And arose, and was baptized.* That he was baptized by Ananias there is every reason to believe, as he appears to have been the chief Christian at Damascus.

19. *When he had received meat, he was strengthened.* His mind must have been greatly worn down under his three days' conviction of sin and the awful uncertainty he was in concerning his state, but when he was baptized and had received the Holy Ghost, his soul was divinely invigorated; and now by taking food his bodily strength, greatly exhausted by three days' fasting, was renewed also. *Then was Saul certain days with the disciples.* Doubtless under instructions relative to the doctrines of Christianity, which he must learn particularly in order to preach them successfully.

20. *Preached Christ in the synagogues.* Instead of *Christ*, "Jesus" is the reading of some MSS. The great question to be determined for the conviction of the Jews was that Jesus was the Son of God. Saul was now convinced that Jesus, whom they had crucified, and who had appeared to him on the way, was the *Son of God*, or Messiah; and therefore as such he proclaimed Him. The word *Christ* should be changed for "Jesus," as the latter is, without doubt, the genuine reading.

21. *Is not this he that destroyed them?* The verb has three acceptations in the Greek writers: (1) "To treat one as an enemy, to spoil him of

his goods"; (2) "To lead away captive, to imprison"; (3) "To slay." Paul was properly "a destroyer" in all these senses. (1) He acted as the most determined enemy of the Christians: "Being exceedingly mad against them," he "persecuted them even unto strange cities," chap. xxvi. 11. (2) He shut up many of the saints in prison, chap. viii. 3; ix. 14; xxvi. 10. (3) He persecuted them unto death—gave his voice against them, that they might be destroyed, and was a principal instrument in the martyrdom of Stephen. He breathed "threatenings and slaughter." See chap. vii. 58; viii. 1; ix. 1; xxvi. 10-11. Therefore these three meanings of the original word are all exemplified in the conduct of Saul.

22. *Confounded the Jews.* Overwhelmed them so with his arguments that they were obliged to "blush" for the weakness of their own cause. *Proving that this.* This Person, viz., Jesus, *is very Christ;* "Is the Christ, or Messiah." See on v. 20.

23. *And after that many days were fulfilled.* What follows relates to transactions which took place about three years after his conversion, when he had come a second time to Damascus, after having been in Arabia. See Gal. i. 17-18.

24. *They watched the gates day and night to kill him.* At this time Damascus was under the government of Aretas, king of Arabia, who was now at war with Herod, his son-in-law, who had put away his daughter in order to marry Herodias, his brother Philip's wife. As Herod was supported by the Romans, Saul's enemies might intimate that he was in league with them or Herod; and as the gates of the city were constantly watched and shut, that no spy might enter and no fugitive get away, they thought it would be easy to apprehend him, and doubtless got orders for the different officers at the gates to be on the lookout that he might not be permitted to escape.

25. *Let him down by the wall.* Favored probably by a house built against or upon the wall, through the window of which they could lower him in a basket, and by this means he made his escape. His escape was something similar to that of the spies at Jericho, Josh. ii. 15.

26. *He assayed to join himself to the disciples.* "He endeavored to get closely united to them," to be in religious fellowship with them. *Believed not that he was a disciple.* They did not suppose it possible that such a person could be converted to the faith of Christ. The full power of divine grace in the conversion of the soul was not yet completely known.

27. *Barnabas . . . brought him to the apostles.* That is, to Peter and James; for others of the apostles he saw none, Gal. i. 19. It appears that he went up at this time to Jerusalem merely to see Peter, with whom he abode fifteen days, Gal. i. 18.

28. *He was with them coming in and going out.* Freely conversing and associating with them; but this seems to have continued only fifteen days. See Gal. i. 18.

29. *Disputed against the Grecians.* That is, the Hellenistic Jews, viz., those who lived in Grecian cities, spoke the Greek language, and used the Septuagint version for their Scriptures.

30. *Sent him forth to Tarsus.* This was his own city, and it was right that he should proclaim to his own countrymen and relatives that

gospel through which he was become wise to salvation.

31. *Then had the churches rest.* Instead of *the churches,* some MSS. have "the Church." Every assembly of God's people was "a church"; the aggregate of these assemblies was "the Church." The word which we translate *rest,* and which literally signifies "peace," evidently means, in this place, "prosperity"; and in this sense both it and the Hebrew *shalom* are repeatedly used. But what was the cause of this *rest* or success? Some say, the conversion of Saul, who before made havoc of the Church; but this is not likely, as he could not be a universal cause of persecution and distress, however active and virulent he might have been during the time of his enmity to the Christian Church. Besides his own persecution, related above, shows that the opposition to the gospel continued with considerable virulence three years after his conversion; therefore it was not Saul's ceasing to be a persecutor that gave this rest to the churches. Dr. Lardner, with a greater show of probability, maintains that this rest was owing to the following circumstance: In the third year of Caligula, A.D. 39, Petronius, who was made president of Syria in the place of Vitellius, was sent by the emperor to set up his statue in the Temple at Jerusalem. This was a thunderstroke to the Jews and so occupied them that they had no time to think of anything else, apprehending that their Temple must be defiled and the national religion destroyed or themselves run the risk of being exterminated if they rebelled against the imperial decree. It appears therefore that, as these transactions took place about the time mentioned in the text, their persecution from the Romans diverted them from persecuting the Christians; and *then had the churches rest throughout all Judaea and Galilee and Samaria,* the terror occasioned by the imperial decree having spread itself through all those places.

Were edified. A metaphor taken from a building. All this is beautifully pointed out by Peter, 1 Pet. chap. ii. 4-5: "To whom [Jesus Christ] coming, as unto a living stone . . . chosen of God, and precious, ye also, as lively [living] stones, are built up a spiritual house, an holy priesthood, to offer up spiritual sacrifices . . . to God by Jesus Christ." And Paul goes through the whole figure at large, in the following inimitable words: "Ye are . . . the household of God; and are built upon the foundation of the apostles and prophets, Jesus Christ himself being the chief corner stone; in whom all the building fitly framed together groweth unto an holy temple in the Lord: in whom ye also are builded together for an habitation of God through the Spirit," Eph. ii. 19-22. *Walking in the fear of the Lord.* Keeping a continually tender conscience, abhorring all sin, having respect to every divine precept, dreading to offend Him from whom the soul has derived its being and its blessings. Without this salutary *fear* of God there never can be any circumspect walking. *In the comfort of the Holy Ghost.* In a consciousness of their acceptance and union with God, through His Spirit, by which solid peace and happiness are brought into the soul, the truly religious man knowing and feeling that he is of God by the Spirit which is given him. Nothing less can be implied in the *comfort of the Holy Ghost.* Were *multiplied.* No wonder that the Church of God increased when such lights as these shone among men. This is a short but full and forcible description of the righteousness, purity, and happiness of the primitive Church.

32. *As Peter passed throughout all quarters.* The churches having rest, the apostles made use of this interval of quiet to visit the different congregations, in order to build them up on their most holy faith. Of Saul we hear no more till chap. xi. 30, which is supposed to be about five years after this time—eight in all from his conversion. Peter, it seems, had continued in Jerusalem all the time that the churches were in a state of persecution throughout the whole land. Great as he was, he never evidenced that steady, determinate courage by which Paul was so eminently distinguished; nor did he ever suffer half so much for God and His truth. *To the saints.* The Jews who had been converted to Christianity. *Which dwelt at Lydda.* A town in the tribe of Ephraim, almost on the border of Judea, and nigh unto Joppa.

33. *A certain man named Aeneas.* This name has been celebrated in the annals of heathen poetry in that beautiful work of the poet Virgil, called the "Aeneid," which gives an account of the misfortunes, travels, wars, of a Trojan prince of this name, after the destruction of his native city, Troy. *Had kept his bed eight years.* This was occasioned by a palsy, and now inveterate and hopeless through its long standing.

34. *Jesus Christ maketh thee whole.* Not Peter, for he had no power but what was given him from above. And, as an instrument, any man could heal with this power as well as Peter; but God chose to put honor upon those primitive preachers of His Word, that men might see that they were commissioned from heaven. *Arise, and make thy bed.* Give now full proof that Jesus Christ has made you whole by arising and by making your bed. He was at home, and therefore was not commanded, as the paralytic person, to take up his bed; but he was ordered to make it—strew it afresh, that all might see that the cure was perfect.

35. *All that dwelt in Lydda and Saron saw him.* Saron was that country that lay between Joppa and Lydda. The long affliction of this man had been well-known; and his cure, consequently, became a subject of general examination. It was found to be real. It was known to have been performed by the grace and mercy of Christ, and the consequence of all this conviction was that all these people became Christians.

36. *Now there was at Joppa.* This was a seaport town on the coast of the Mediterranean Sea, about a day's journey from Jerusalem. It is at present called Jaffa, and is still a place of considerable note. *A certain disciple named Tabitha.* This word is more properly Syriac than Hebrew. The word *tabio* and the feminine *tabitho* have the same meaning as the Greek *Dorcas*, and signify the "gazel" or "antelope"; and it is still customary in the East to give the names of beautiful animals to young women. The comparison of fine eyes to those of the antelope is continually occurring in the writings of the Arabic and Persian poets. The person in the text probably had her name in the same way. She was very beautiful, and was therefore called *Tabitha* and *Dorcas. This woman was full*

of good works. She spent her life in acts of kindness and charity, Her soul was *full* of love to God and man, and her whole time was filled up with works of piety and mercy.

37. *She was sick, and died.* Even her holiness and usefulness could not prevent her from sickness and death. "Dust thou art, and unto dust shalt thou return," is a decree that must be fulfilled, even on the saints; for "the body is dead," sentenced to death, "because of sin," though "the Spirit is life because of righteousness." *Whom when they had washed.* Having the fullest proof that she was dead, they prepared for her interment. In most nations of the world it was customary to wash their dead before they buried them and before they laid them out to lie in state.

38. *Sent unto him . . . desiring . . . that he would not delay to come.* Tabitha died at Joppa, and Peter was at Lydda. But why did they send for Peter? We cannot tell. It is not likely that they had any expectation that he should raise her from the dead, for none of the apostles had as yet raised any; and if God did not choose to restore Stephen to life, this favor could not be reasonably expected in behalf of inferior persons. However they might hope that he who cured Aeneas at Lydda might cure Dorcas, for it is probable that they had sent for Peter before she died.

39. *Shewing the coats and garments.* These, it appears, she had made for the poor, and more particularly for poor *widows*, in whose behalf she had incessantly labored.

40. *Peter put them all forth, and kneeled down, and prayed.* It was not even known to Peter that God would work this miracle: therefore he put all the people out, that he might seek the will of God by fervent prayer and during his supplications be liable to neither distraction nor interruption, which he must have experienced had he permitted this company of weeping widows to remain in the chamber. *Said, Tabitha, arise.* During his wrestling with God he had, undoubtedly, received confidence that she would be raised at his word.

41. *Saints and widows.* In primitive times the *widows* formed a distinct part of the Christian Church.

42. *Many believed in the Lord.* That is, in Christ Jesus, in whose name and through whose power they understood this miracle to be wrought.

43. *He tarried many days in Joppa.* Taking advantage of the good impression made on the people's minds by the miracle, he preached to them the great truths of Christianity and thus established them in the faith. *Simon a tanner.* Whether the original word signifies a *tanner* or a "currier" is of little consequence. The person who dealt in the hides, whether of clean or unclean animals. could not be in high repute among the Jews. Even in Joppa the trade appears to have been reputed unclean; and therefore this Simon had his house by the sea side. See chap. x. 6.

CHAPTER 10

An angel appears to Cornelius, a centurion, and directs him to send to Joppa, for Peter, to instruct him in the way of salvation, 1-6. He sends accordingly, 7-8. While the messengers are on their way to Joppa, Peter has a remarkable vision, by which he is taught how he should treat the Gentiles, 9-16. The messengers arrive at the house of Simon the tanner, and deliver their message, 17-22. They lodge there that night, and on the morrow Peter accompanies them to Caesarea, where they find Cornelius and his friends assembled, waiting the coming of Peter, 23-24. Peter makes an apology for his coming, and inquires for what purpose Cornelius had sent for him, 25-29. Cornelius answers, 30-33. Peter preaches unto him Jesus, as the Saviour of the world, and the Judge of quick and dead, 34-43. While he speaks, the Holy Ghost descends on Cornelius and his company; and they speak with new tongues, and magnify God, 44-46. Peter commands them to be baptized in the name of the Lord, 47-48.

1. *There was a certain man in Caesarea.* This was Caesarea of Palestine, called also Strato's Tower, as has been already noted, and the residence of the Roman procurator. *A centurion.* The chief or captain of 100 men, as both the Greek and Latin words imply. *The band called the Italian band.* The word which we translate *band* signifies the same as "cohort" or "regiment," which sometimes consisted of 555 infantry and 66 cavalry. A Roman legion consisted of 10 cohorts. When in former times the Roman legion contained 6,000, each cohort consisted of 600.

2. *A devout man.* A person who worships the true God and is no idolater. *One that feared God.* One who was acquainted with the true God, by means of His Word and laws; who respected these laws, and would not dare to offend his Maker and his Judge. *With all his house.* He took care to instruct his family in the knowledge which he himself had received, and to establish the worship of God in his house. *Gave much alms.* His love to God led him to love men, and this love proved its sincerity by acts of beneficence and charity. *Prayed to God alway.* Was ever in the spirit of prayer and frequently in the act. What an excellent character is this! And yet the man was a Gentile! He was what a Jew would repute common and unclean; see v. 28.

3. *He saw in a vision evidently.* The text is as plain as it can be that an angel of God did appear to Cornelius. This was in a *vision,* i.e., "a supernatural representation"; and it was "manifestly, evidently" made, and at such a time too as precluded the possibility of his being asleep; for it was *about the ninth hour of the day,* answering to our three o'clock in the afternoon, the time of public prayer, according to the custom of the Jews, and while Peter was engaged in that sacred duty.

4. *Thy prayers and thine alms are come up for a memorial.* Being all performed in simplicity and godly sincerity, they were acceptable to the Most High. *Come up for a memorial.* This form of speech is evidently borrowed from the sacrificial system of the Jews. Pious and sincere prayers are high in God's estimation; and therefore are said to ascend to Him, as the smoke and flame of the burnt offering appeared to ascend to heaven. These prayers and alms came up for a *memorial* before God. This is a manifest allusion to the meat offering, which, in Lev. ii. 16, is said to be a memorial (speaking after the manner of men) to put God in remembrance that such a person was His worshipper and needed His protection and help.

6. *Simon a tanner.* See the note on chap. ix. 43. *He shall tell thee what thou oughtest to do.* This clause, so explanatory, is wanting in almost every MS. and version of note.

7. *And a devout soldier.* It has already been remarked that Cornelius had taken care to instruct his family in divine things, and it appears also that he had been attentive to the spiritual interests of his regiment. We do not find that it was then, even among the Romans, considered a disgrace for a military officer to teach his men lessons of morality and piety towards God, whatever it may be in some Christian countries in the present time.

8. *He sent them to Joppa.* It has been properly remarked that, from Joppa, Jonah was sent to preach to the Gentiles of Nineveh; and from the same place Peter was sent to preach the gospel to the Gentiles at Caesarea.

9. *On the morrow, as they went on their journey.* The messengers could not have left the house of Cornelius till about two hours before sunset; therefore they must have travelled a part of the night in order to arrive at Joppa the next day, towards noon. Cornelius sent two of his household servants, by way of respect to Peter; probably the soldier was intended for their defense, as the roads in Judea were by no means safe. *Peter went up upon the house top to pray.* It has often been remarked that the houses in Judea were built with flat roofs, on which people walked, conversed, meditated, prayed. The housetop was the place of retirement, and thither Peter went for the purpose of praying to God.

10. *He became very hungry.* It seems that this happened about dinnertime, for it appears that they were making ready, "dressing the victuals" for the family. The dinner among the ancients was a very slight meal, and they had no breakfast; their supper was their principal meal. *He fell into a trance.* "An ecstasy fell upon him." A person may be said to be in an ecstasy when transported with joy or admiration, so that he is insensible to every object but that on which he is engaged.

11. *And saw heaven opened.* His mind now entirely spiritualized and absorbed in heavenly contemplation, was capable of discoveries of the spiritual world. *A great sheet knit at the four corners.* Perhaps intended to be an emblem of the universe and its various nations, to the four corners of which the gospel was to extend and to offer its blessings to all the inhabitants, without distinction of nation.

12. *All manner of fourfooted beasts.* Every species of quadrupeds, whether wild or domestic; all reptiles, and all fowls. Consequently both clean and unclean were present in this visionary representation, those that the Jewish law allowed to be sacrificed to God, or proper for food, as well as those which that law had prohibited in both cases.

13. *Rise, Peter; kill, and eat.* "Sacrifice and eat." Though this verb is sometimes used to signify the slaying of animals for food, yet as the proper notion is to slay for the purpose of sacrifice it appears to me to be better to preserve that meaning here.

14. *Common or unclean.* By *common* whatever was in general use among the Gentiles is to be understood; by *unclean,* everything that was forbidden by the Mosaic law. However the one word may be considered as explanatory of the other. The rabbins themselves, and many of the primitive fathers, believed that by the unclean animals forbidden by the law the Gentiles were meant.

15. *What God hath cleansed.* God, who made at first the distinction between Jews and Gentiles, has a right to remove it whenever and by whatever means He pleases. He, therefore, who made the distinction, for wise purposes, between the clean and the unclean now pronounces all to be clean.

16. *This was done thrice.* For the greater certainty, and to make the deeper impression on the apostle's mind. *And the vessel was received up again into heaven.* Both Jews and Gentiles came equally from God; and to Him, both, by the preaching of the gospel, shall again return.

17. *While Peter doubted . . . the men . . . stood before the gate.* In all this we find an admirable display of the economy of providence. Cornelius prays and has a vision which prepares him to receive instruction from Peter; Peter prays and has a vision which prepares and disposes him to give instruction to Cornelius. While he is in doubts and perplexity what the full meaning of the vision might be, the messengers, who had been dispatched under the guidance of an especial providence, came to the door; and the Holy Spirit gives him information that his doubts should be all cleared up by accompanying the men who were now inquiring for him.

21. *Which were sent unto him from Cornelius.* This clause is wanting in almost every MS. of worth and in almost all the versions. *What is the cause wherefore ye are come?* He still did not know the full import of the vision; but being informed by the Holy Spirit that three men were seeking him and that he should go with them, without scruple, he instantly obeyed.

22. *Cornelius the centurion.* They gave him the simple relation which they had received from their master. *To hear words of thee.* But of what kind they could not as yet tell.

23. *Then called he them in.* They had already walked a long journey in a short time and needed refreshment; and it was thought expedient they should rest that night with Simon the tanner. *Certain brethren from Joppa.* They were six in number, as we learn from chap. xi. 12. It was necessary that there should be several witnesses of the important transactions which were about to take place, as on no slight evidence would even the converted Jews believe that repentance unto life and the Holy Spirit should be granted to the Gentiles.

24. *His kinsmen and near friends.* His "relatives," and his "necessary friends." It appears that he had collected the whole circle of his intimate acquaintance, that they also might profit by a revelation which he expected to come immediately from heaven, and these amounted to many persons; see v. 27.

25. *Fell down at his feet, and worshipped him.* As Peter's coming was announced by an angel, Cornelius might have supposed that Peter himself was an angel, and of a superior order, seeing he came to announce what the first angel was not employed to declare. It was probably in consequence of this thought that he prostrated himself before Peter, offering him the highest act of civil respect; for there was nothing in the act, as performed by Cornelius, which belonged to the worship of the true God.

28. *Ye know how that it is an unlawful thing.* He addressed the whole company, among whom, it appears, there were persons well acquainted with Jewish customs. *But God hath shewed me.* He now began to understand the import of the vision which he saw at Joppa. A Gentile is not to be avoided because he is a Gentile; God is now taking down the partition wall which separated them from the Jews.

29. *I ask . . . for what intent ye have sent for me?* Peter had been informed of this by the servants of Cornelius, v. 22; but as all the company might not have been informed of the circumstances, he, as it were, invites him to tell his story afresh, that his friends might be the better prepared to receive the truth which he was about to dispense in obedience to his divine commission.

30. *Four days ago I was fasting until this hour.* The word fasting is wanting in some MSS.

31. *Thy prayer is heard.* See the note on v. 4. Cornelius prayed, fasted, and gave alms. It was in this way he looked for salvation, not to purchase it; a thought of this kind does not appear to have entered into his mind. But these were the means he used to get his soul brought to the knowledge of the truth.

33. *Are we all here present before God.* The people were all waiting for the preacher, and every heart was filled with expectation; they waited as *before God,* from whose messenger they were about to hear the words of life.

34. *God is no respecter of persons.* He does not esteem a Jew because he is a Jew; nor does he detest a Gentile because he is a Gentile. It was a long and deeply rooted opinion among the Jews that God never would extend His favor to the Gentiles, and that the descendants of Jacob only should enjoy His peculiar favor and benediction. Of this opinion was Peter previously to the heavenly vision mentioned in this chapter. He was now convinced that *God is no respecter of persons,* that as all must stand before His judgment seat to be judged according to the deeds done in the body, so no one nation or people or individual could expect to find a more favorable decision than another who was precisely in the same moral state; for the phrase "respect of persons" is used in reference to unjust decisions in a court of justice, where through favor or interest or bribe a culprit is acquitted and a righteous or innocent person condemned. See Lev. xix. 15; Deut. i. 16-17; and xvi. 19.

35. *But in every nation he that feareth him.* In every nation he who, according to his light and privileges, fears God, worships Him alone (for this is the true meaning of the word), *and worketh righteousness,* abstains from all evil, gives to all their due, injures neither the body, soul, nor reputation of his neighbor, *is accepted with him.*

36. *The word which God sent.* Few verses in the New Testament have perplexed critics and divines more than this. The ancient copyists seem also to have been puzzled with it, as the great variety in the different MSS. sufficiently proves. A foreign critic makes a good sense by connecting this with the preceding verse, thus: "In every nation he that feareth him and worketh righteousness is accepted with him, according to that doctrine which God sent unto the children of Israel, by which he published peace (i.e., reconciliation between Jews and Gentiles) by Jesus Christ, who is Lord of all"; and because "Lord of all," both of Jews

and Gentiles, therefore He must be impartial; and because impartial, or "no respecter of persons," therefore, "in every nation," whether Judea, Greece, or Italy, "he that feareth him [God], and worketh righteousness, is accepted with him." I believe *the word* should be translated, "that doctrine." The whole may be literally read thus: "As to the doctrine sent to the children of Israel, preaching the glad tidings of peace by Jesus Christ, He is Lord of all, ye know what was done through all Judea, beginning after the baptism which John preached. Jesus, who was from Nazareth, whom God anointed with the Holy Ghost, and with mighty power went about doing good, and healing all that were tyrannically oppressed by the devil, for God was with him."

37. *That word . . . ye know.* This account of Jesus of Nazareth you cannot be unacquainted with, because it has been proclaimed throughout all Judea and Galilee from the time that John began to preach. You have heard how He was anointed with the Holy Ghost, and of the miracles which He performed; how He went about doing good and healing all kinds of demoniacs and by these mighty and beneficent acts giving the fullest proof that God was with Him. This was the exordium of Peter's discourse, and thus he begins from what they knew to teach them what they did not know.

38. *God anointed Jesus of Nazareth.* Here the apostle refers to Christ as the promised Messiah; for as Messiah signifies "the Anointed One," and "Christ" has the same signification in Greek, and the Messiah, according to the prophets and the expectation of the Jews, was to work miracles, Peter proclaims Jesus as the Messiah, and refers to the miracles which He wrought as the proof of it. This delicate but forcible allusion is lost by most readers.

39. *We are witnesses of all.* In this speech Peter may refer not only to the twelve apostles but to the six brethren whom he had brought with him. *Whom they slew.* As the truth of the resurrection must depend on the reality of the death of Christ, it was necessary that this should be stated and shown to rest on the most indubitable evidence.

40. *Him God raised up the third day.* He lay long enough under the power of death to prove that He was dead; and not too long, lest it should be supposed that His disciples had time sufficient to practice some deceit or imposture; and to prevent this the Jews took care to have the tomb well-guarded during the whole time which He lay there.

41. *Not to all the people.* In the order of divine providence the public were no longer to be instructed by Jesus Christ personally, but it was necessary those who were to preach redemption in His name should be thoroughly furnished to this good and great work; therefore the time He spent on earth after His resurrection was devoted to the instruction of His disciples. *Witnesses chosen before of God.* That is, God chose such men to attest this fact as were in every way best qualified to give evidence on the subject. The first preachers of the gospel must be the witnesses of its facts.

42. *And he commanded us to preach.* By thus assuring them that Jesus Christ was appointed to judge the world he at once showed them the necessity of subjection to Him, that

they might stand in the day of His appearing. *The Judge of quick and dead.* The word *quick* we retain from our ancient mother tongue, the Saxon, "to live." By *quick and dead* we are to understand: (1) all that had lived from the foundation of the world till that time, and all that were then alive; (2) all that should be found alive at the day of judgment, as well as all that had died previously.

43. *To him give all the prophets witness.* See Isa. ix. 6; lii. 7; liii, 5-6; lix. 20; Jer. xxxi, 34; Dan. ix. 24; Mic. vii. 18, etc.; and Zech. xiii. 1. As Jesus Christ was the sum and substance of the law and the Mosaic dispensation, so all the prophets bore testimony, either directly or indirectly, to Him; and indeed without Him and the salvation He has promised there is scarcely any meaning in the Mosaic economy nor in most of the allusions of the prophets. *Remission of sins.* The phrase means simply the "taking away of sins"; and this does not refer to the guilt of sin merely, but also to its power, nature, and consequences. All that is implied in pardon of sin, destruction of its tyranny, and purification from its pollution is here intended; and it is wrong to restrict such operations of mercy to pardon alone.

44. *While Peter yet spake.* It is not very likely that the words recorded by Luke are all that the apostle spoke on this occasion; but while he continued to discourse with them on this subject, *the Holy Ghost fell on all them which heard the word,* and His descent was known by their being enabled to speak with different kinds of tongues. In what manner this gift was bestowed we cannot tell; probably it was in the same way in which it had been given on the Day of Pentecost. For as they spake with tongues, which was the effect of the descent of the Spirit as flaming tongues on the heads of the disciples on the Day of Pentecost, it is very likely that the same appearance now took place.

45. *They of the circumcision . . . were astonished.* Because it was a maxim with them that the Shekinah or divine influence could not be revealed to any person who dwelt beyond the precincts of the Promised Land. Nor did any of them believe that the Divine Spirit could be communicated to any Gentile. It is no wonder, therefore, that they were amazed when they saw the Spirit of God so liberally given as He was on this occasion.

46. *And magnify God.* They had got new hearts as well as new tongues, and having believed with the heart unto righteousness, their tongues made confession unto salvation; and God was magnified for the mercy which He had imparted.

47. *Can any man forbid water?* These had evidently received the Holy Ghost and consequently were become members of the mystical body of Christ; and yet Peter requires that they shall receive baptism by water, that they might become members of the Christian Church. In other cases they received baptism first and the Spirit afterwards by the imposition of hands; see chap. xix. 4-6, where the disciples who had received only the baptism of John were baptized again with water in the name of the Lord Jesus; and after even this the apostles prayed and laid their hands on them before they were made partakers of the Holy Ghost. So we find

that Jesus Christ had His water baptism as well as John, and that even He who gave the baptism of the Holy Ghost required the administration of water baptism also.

48. *To be baptized in the name of the Lord.* That is, in the name of Jesus Christ, which implied their taking upon them the public profession of Christianity, and believing on Christ Jesus as their Saviour and Sovereign; for as they were baptized in His name, they professed thereby to be His disciples and followers. *Then prayed they him to tarry certain days.* They felt the necessity of further instruction, and prayed him to continue his ministry a little longer among them; and to this he no doubt consented. This was, properly speaking, the commencement of the Christian Church, as composed of Jews and Gentiles, partaking of the same baptism, united under the same Head, made partakers of the same Spirit, and associated in the same aggregate body. Now was the middle wall of partition broken down, and the Gentiles admitted to the same privileges with the Jews.

CHAPTER 11

Peter returns to Jerusalem, and is accused of having associated with the Gentiles, 1-3. He defends himself, by relating at large the whole business concerning Cornelius, 4-17. His defense is accepted, and the whole Church glorifies God for having granted unto the Gentiles repentance unto life, 18. An account of the proceedings of those who were scattered abroad by the persecution that was raised about Stephen; and how they had spread the gospel among the circumcision, in Phenice, Cyprus, and Antioch, 19-21. The church at Jerusalem, hearing of this, sends Barnabas to confirm them in the faith, 22-23. His character, 24. He goes to Tarsus to seek Saul, whom he brings to Antioch, where the disciples are first called Christians, 25-26. Certain prophets foretell the dearth which afterwards took place in the reign of the Emperor Claudius, 27-28. The disciples send relief to their poor brethren in Judea, by the hands of Barnabas and Saul, 29-30.

1. *And the apostles and brethren that were in Judaea.* According to Calmet, Judea is here put in opposition to Caesarea, which, though situated in Palestine, passed for a Greek city, being principally inhabited by pagans, Greeks, or Syrians.

2. *Contended with him.* A manifest proof this that the primitive church at Jerusalem had no conception of Peter's supremacy or of his being prince of the apostles. He is now called to account for his conduct, which they judged to be reprehensible.

3. *Thou wentest in to men uncircumcised.* In a Jew, this was no small offense; and as they did not know the reason of Peter's conduct, it is no wonder they should call him to account for it, as they considered it to be a positive transgression of the law and custom of the Jews.

4. *But Peter rehearsed the matter from the beginning, and expounded it by order.* To remove their prejudice and to give them the fullest reasons for his conduct, he thought it best to give them a simple relation of the whole affair; which he did, as we have seen in the preceding chapter, with a few additional circumstances here.

12. *These six brethren.* Probably pointing to them, being present, as proper persons to confirm the truth of what he was delivering.

14. *Thou and all thy house shall be saved.* This is an additional circumstance. Before, it was said, chap. x. 6, Peter "shall tell thee what thou oughtest to do"; and, in v. 32, "who, when he cometh, shall speak unto thee." But in Peter's relation the matter is more explicitly declared: He *shall tell thee words, whereby thou and all thy house shall be saved.* He shall announce to you all the doctrine of salvation.

16. *Ye shall be baptized with the Holy Ghost.* These words are very remarkable. The words of our Lord, as quoted in chap. i. 5, to which Peter refers here, have been supposed by many to be referred to the apostles alone; but here it is evident that Peter believed they were a promise made to all Christians, i.e., to all, whether Jews or Gentiles, who should believe on Jesus Christ. Therefore when he saw that the Holy Ghost fell upon those Gentiles, he considered it a fulfillment of our Lord's promise.

17. *God gave them the like gift.* Viz., the Holy Spirit, and His various gifts and graces, in the same way and in the same measure in which He gave them to us Jews. *What was I, that I could withstand God?* It was not I who called them to salvation; it was God; and the thing is proved to be from God alone, for none other could dispense the Holy Spirit.

18. *They held their peace.* Their prejudices were confounded; they considered the subject, and saw that it was from God. Then they glorified Him, because they saw that He had granted unto the *Gentiles repentance unto life.* As the word which we translate *repentance* signifies literally "a change of mind," it may be here referred to a change of religious views. And as *repentance* signifies a change of life and conduct, from evil to good, so the word may be used here to signify a change from a false religion to the true one, from idolatry to the worship of the true God. The Christians who were present were all satisfied with Peter's account and apology; but it does not appear that all were ultimately satisfied, as we know there were serious disputes in the Church afterwards on this very subject. See chap. xv. 5, where Christian believers from among the Pharisees insisted that it was necessary to circumcise the converted Gentiles and cause them to keep the law of Moses. This opinion was carried much further in the church at Jerusalem afterwards, as may be seen at large in chap. xxi.

19. *The persecution that arose about Stephen.* That is, those who were obliged to flee from Jerusalem at the time of that persecution in which Stephen lost his life. See chap. viii. 1. *Phenice.* Phoenicia, a country between Galilee and Syria, along the coast of the Mediterranean Sea, including Tyre, Sidon, etc. It is often mentioned as a part of Syria. *Cyprus.* An island of the Mediterranean Sea, over against Syria. *Antioch.* A city of Syria, built by Antiochus Seleucus, near the Orontes River, at that time one of the most celebrated cities of the East. *Unto the Jews only.* For they knew nothing of the vision of Peter, and did not believe that God would open the door of faith to the Gentiles. The next verse informs us that there were others who were better instructed.

20. *Men of . . . Cyrene.* The metropolis of the Cyrenaica, a country of Africa, bounded on the north by the Mediterranean and on the south by the Sahara. *Spake unto the Grecians.* "The Hellenists." Who these were, we have already seen, chap. vi and ix. 29, viz., Jews living in

Greek cities and speaking the Greek language. But instead of *Grecians,* "Greeks" is the reading of several MSS. On this evidence Griesbach has admitted it into the text, and few critics entertain any doubt of the genuineness of the reading. This intimates that, besides preaching the gospel to the Hellenistic Jews, some of them preached it to heathen Greeks.

21. *The hand of the Lord was with them.* By the *hand, arm,* and *finger* of God, in the Scripture, different displays or exertions of His power are intended. Here it means that the energy of God accompanied them and applied their preaching to the souls of all attentive hearers. *A great number believed.* That Jesus was the Christ, and that He had died for their offenses and risen again for their justification. Because the apostles preached the truth, and the hand of God was with them, therefore *a great number believed, and turned unto the Lord,* becoming His disciples.

22. *The church which was in Jerusalem.* This was the original, the mother church of Christianity, not the church of Rome. A Christian church means a company of believers in Christ Jesus, united for the purposes of Christian fellowship and edification in righteousness. *They sent forth Barnabas.* It seems, then, that the church collectively had power to commission and send forth any of its own members whom it saw God had qualified for a particular work. There must have been, even at that time, an acknowledged superiority of some members of the church beyond others. The apostles held the first rank; the deacons (probably the same as those called prophets, as being next chosen), the second; and perhaps those called evangelists, simply preachers of the truth, the third rank.

23. *Had seen the grace of God.* That is, had seen the effects produced by the grace of God. *Was glad.* Not envious because God had blessed the labors of others of his Master's servants, but rejoiced to find that the work of salvation was carried on by such instruments as God chose and condescended to use. They who cannot rejoice in the conversion of sinners because they have not been the means of it, or because such converts or their ministers have not precisely the same views of certain doctrines which they have themselves, show that they have in them little, if anything, of the mind that was in Christ. *With purpose of heart they would cleave unto the Lord.* These converts had begun well; they must continue and persevere. God gave them the grace, the principle of life and action; it was their business to use this. Barnabas therefore exhorted them with "determination" of heart, with "set, fixed purpose and resolution," that *they would cleave unto the Lord:* "to remain with the Lord"; to continue in union and fellowship with Him; to be faithful in keeping His truth, and obedient in the practice of it. It is absurd to talk of being children of God and of absolute, final perseverance when the soul has lost its spiritual union. There is no perseverance but in cleaving to the Lord; he who in his works denies Him does not cleave to Him.

24. *For he was a good man.* Here is a proper character of a minister of the gospel. (1) He is *a good man.* His bad heart is changed, his evil dispositions rooted out; and the mind that was in Christ implanted in him. (2) He is *full of the*

Holy Ghost. He is holy, because the Spirit of holiness dwells in him. (3) He is full *of faith.* He implicitly credits his Lord; he knows that He could not lie—that His word could not fail.

25. *To Tarsus, for to seek Saul.* The persecution raised against him obliged him to take refuge in his own city, where, as a Roman citizen, his person was in safety. See chap. ix. 29-30.

26. *He brought him unto Antioch.* As this city was the metropolis of Syria and the third city for importance in the whole Roman Empire, Rome and Alexandria alone being more eminent, Barnabas might think it expedient to have for his assistance a person of such eminent talents as Saul, and who was especially appointed by Christ to proclaim the gospel to the Gentiles. Saul appears also to have been a thorough master of the Greek tongue, and consequently the better qualified to explain the gospel to the Greek philosophers, and to defend it against their cavils. Barnabas, also being a native of Cyprus, chap. iv. 36, where the Greek language was spoken, was judged to be proper for this mission, perhaps on this account, as well as on account of his disinterestedness, holiness, and zeal.

And the disciples were called Christians first in Antioch. It is evident they had the name *Christians* from *Christ,* their Master, as the Platonists and Pythagoreans had their name from their masters, Plato and Pythagoras. Now as these had their name from those great masters because they attended their teaching and credited their doctrines, so the disciples were called *Christians* because they took Christ for their Teacher, crediting His doctrines and following the rule of life laid down by Him. It has been a question, By whom was this name given to the disciples? Some think they assumed it; others, that the inhabitants of Antioch gave it to them; and others, that it was given by Saul and Barnabas. The word in our common text which we translate *were called* signifies, in the New Testament, to "appoint, warn, or nominate," by divine direction. In this sense the word is used in Matt. ii. 12; Luke ii. 26; and in the preceding chapter of this book, v. 22. If, therefore, the name was given by divine appointment, it is most likely that Saul and Barnabas were directed to give it; and that therefore the name *Christian* is from God, as well as that grace and holiness which are so essentially required and implied in the character. Before this time the Jewish converts were simply called, among themselves, *disciples,* i.e., scholars; *believers, saints, the church,* or *assembly;* and, by their enemies, *Nazarenes, Galileans,* the *men of this way* or *sect;* and perhaps by other names which are not come down to us. They considered themselves as one family, and hence the appellation of *brethren* was frequent among them. A Christian, therefore, is the highest character which any human being can bear upon earth; and to receive it from God, as those appear to have done—how glorious the title! It is however worthy of remark that this name occurs in only three places in the New Testament: here, and in chap. xxvi. 28, and in 1 Pet. iv. 16.

27. *Came prophets from Jerusalem.* Though the term prophet is used in the New Testament simply to signify a "teacher," yet here it evidently means also such as were under divine

inspiration, and foretold future events. This was certainly the case with Agabus, v. 28, though perhaps his ordinary character was that of a "teacher" or "preacher." It seems from various scriptures, Romans xii; 1 Corinthians xiii and xiv, that the prophets of the New Testament were: (1) teachers or preachers in general; (2) persons who on special occasions were under the influence of the Divine Spirit, and then foretold certain future events; (3) persons who recited hymns to the honor of God in the public assemblies of the Christians; (4) persons who prayed in those assemblies, having sometimes the gift of tongues, at other times not. From Ephes. ii. 20 and iii. 5, we learn that the *prophets* of the Christian Church were inferior to the apostles; but, from v. 11 of Eph. iv, we see that they were superior to all other teachers, even to evangelists and pastors.

28. *Agabus.* This prophet, of whom we know nothing, is once more mentioned, chap. xxi. 10. He was probably a Jew, but whether converted now to Christianity we cannot tell. *Great dearth throughout all the world.* The words probably here mean the land of Judea, though sometimes by this phrase the whole Roman Empire is intended. In the former sense the disciples appear to have understood it, as the next verse informs us; for they determined to send relief to their brethren in Judea, which they could not have done had the famine been general. It does not appear that they expected it to extend even to Antioch in Syria, where they then were, else they would have thought of making provision for themselves.

It is well-known from history that there were several famines in the reign of Claudius. Dion Cassius, lib. lx, mentions a severe famine in the first and second year of the reign of Claudius, which was sorely felt in Rome itself. A second famine happened about the fourth year of this reign, which continued for several years, and greatly afflicted the land of Judea. Several authors notice this, but particularly Josephus, *Ant.,* l. xx, c. 5, s. 2, where, having mentioned Tiberius Alexander as succeeding to the procuratorship in the place of Cuspius Fadus, he says that, "during the government of these procurators, a great famine afflicted Judea." A third famine is mentioned by Eusebius, in *An. Abrahami,* which commences with the calends of October, A.D. 48, which was so powerful "in Greece that a modius [about half a bushel of grain] was sold for six drachmas." A fourth famine, which took place in the eleventh year of Claudius, is mentioned by Tacitus, *Annal.,* l. xii, s. 43, in which there was so great a dearth of provisions, and famine in consequence, that it was esteemed a divine judgment.

It may now be inquired, To which of these famines in the reign of Claudius does the prophecy of Agabus refer? Most learned men are of opinion that the famine of which Agabus prophesied was that mentioned above which took place in the fourth year of this emperor, A.D. 47. This famine is particularly mentioned by Josephus, *Ant.,* l. xx, c. 2, s. 5, who describes it as "a very great famine, in which many died for want of food."

29. *Then the disciples . . . determined to send relief.* These were probably Gentile converts; and as they considered themselves receiving the spiritual blessings, which they now so happily enjoyed, through the means of the Christians in Judea, they resolved to communicate to them a portion of their temporal goods; and every man did this *according to his ability,* i.e., he gave a certain proportion of the property with which the providence of God had entrusted him.

CHAPTER 12

Herod persecutes the Christians. 1. Kills James, 2. And casts Peter into prison, 3-4. The church makes incessant prayer for his deliverance, 5. An angel of God opens the prison doors and leads him out, 6-10. Peter rejoices, and comes to the house of Mary, where many were praying, and declares how he was delivered, 11-17. The soldiers who kept the prison are examined by Herod, and he commands them to be put to death, 18-19. Herod is enraged against the people of Tyre, but is appeased by their submission, 20. He makes an oration to the people, receives idolatrous praises, and an angel of the Lord smites him, and he dies a miserable death, 21-23. The word of God increases, 24. Barnabas and Saul, having fulfilled their ministry, return from Jerusalem accompanied by John Mark, 25.

1. *Herod the king.* This was Herod Agrippa, the son of Aristobulus, and grandson of Herod the Great; he was nephew to Herod Antipas, who beheaded John the Baptist, and brother to Herodias. He was made king by the Emperor Caligula, and was put in possession of all the territories formerly held by his uncle Philip and by Lysanias; viz., Iturea, Trachonitis, Abilene, with Gaulonitis, Batanaea, and Penias. To these the Emperor Claudius afterwards added Judea and Samaria; which were nearly all the dominions possessed by his grandfather, Herod the Great.

2. *He killed James the brother of John with the sword.* This was James the Greater, son of Zebedee, and must be distinguished from James the Less, son of Alphaeus. This latter was put to death by Ananias, the high priest, during the reign of Nero. This James with his brother John were those who requested to sit on the right and left hand of our Lord, see Matt. xx. 23; and our Lord's prediction was now fulfilled in one of them, who by his martyrdom drank of our Lord's cup and was baptized with His baptism. By the death of James, the number of the apostles was reduced to eleven; and we do not find that ever it was filled. The apostles never had any successors; God has continued their doctrine, but not their order. By killing with the sword we are to understand beheading. Among the Jews there were four kinds of deaths: (1) stoning; (2) burning; (3) killing with the sword, or beheading; and (4) strangling. The third was a Roman as well as a Jewish mode of punishment. Killing with the sword was the punishment which, according to the Talmud, was inflicted on those who drew away the people to any strange worship, *Sanhedr.,* fol. iii. James was probably accused of this, and hence the punishment mentioned in the text.

3. *He proceeded . . . to take Peter also.* He supposed that these two were pillars on which the infant cause rested; and that, if these were removed, the building must necessarily come down. *The days of unleavened bread.* About the latter end of March or beginning of April.

4. *Four quaternions of soldiers.* That is, sixteen, or four companies of four men each, who had the care of the prison, each company taking in turn one of the four watches of the night. *Intending after Easter to bring him forth.* "After the Passover." Perhaps there never was a more unhappy, not to say absurd, translation than that in our text. But before I come to explain the word, it is necessary to observe that our term called Easter is not exactly the same with the Jewish Passover. This festival is always held on the fourteenth day of the first vernal full moon; but the Easter of the Christians, never till the next Sabbath after said full moon. The first vernal moon is that whose fourteenth day is either on the day of the vernal equinox or the next fourteenth day after it. The vernal equinox, according to a decree of the council of Nice, is fixed to the twenty-first day of March; and therefore the first vernal moon is that whose fourteenth day falls upon the twenty-first of March or the first fourteenth day after. The earliest Paschal term being the twenty-first of March, the twenty-second of March is the earliest Easter possible; and the eighteenth of April being the latest Paschal term, the seventh day after, that is, the twenty-fifth of April, is the latest Easter possible. The term *Easter*, inserted here by our translators, they borrowed from the ancient Anglo-Saxon service books, or from the version of the Gospels which always translates the *to pascha* of the Greek by this term. Wycliffe used the word *paske*, i.e., Passover; but Tyndale, Coverdale, following the old Saxon mode of translation, insert *Easter;* the Geneva Bible very properly renders it the Passover.

5. *Prayer was made without ceasing.* The Greek word signifies both "fervor" and "earnestness," as well as "perseverance." These prayers of the church produced that miraculous interference mentioned below, and without which Peter could not have thus escaped from the hands of this ruthless king.

6. *Sleeping between two soldiers, bound with two chains.* Two soldiers guarded his person, his right hand being bound to the left hand of one, and his left hand bound to the right hand of the other. This was the Roman method of guarding their prisoners and appears to be what is intimated in the text.

7. *Smote Peter on the side.* He struck him in such a way as was just sufficient to awake him from his sleep.

8. *Gird thyself.* It seems Peter had put off the principal part of his clothes, that he might sleep with more comfort. His resuming all that he had thrown off was a proof that everything had been done leisurely. It appears that the two soldiers were overwhelmed by a deep sleep, which fell upon them from God.

9. *He . . . wist not.* He "knew" not. He supposed himself to be in a dream.

10. *The first and the second ward.* It is supposed that ancient Jerusalem was surrounded by three walls. If so, then passing through the gates of these three walls successively is possibly what is meant by the expression in the text. The prison in which he was confined might have been that which was at the outer wall. *Iron gate.* This was the innermost wall of the three, and was strongly plated over with iron, for the greater security. Perhaps this is all that is meant by the *iron gate.* One of the quaternions of soldiers was placed at each gate. *Which opened . . . of his own accord.* Influenced by the unseen power of the angel. *The angel departed from him.* Having brought him into a place in which he no longer needed his assistance. What is proper to God He always does; what is proper to man He requires him to perform.

11. *When Peter was come to himself.* Everything he saw astonished him; he could scarcely credit his eyes. He was in a sort of ecstasy; and it was only when the angel left him that he was fully convinced that all was real. *And . . . all the expectation of the . . . Jews.* It seems they had built much on the prospect of having him sacrificed, as they already had James.

12. *And when he had considered.* When he had weighed everything and was fully satisfied of the divine interposition, he went to the house of Mary, the mother of John Mark, the author of the Gospel, where it appears many were gathered together making prayer and supplication, probably for Peter's release.

13. *As Peter knocked.* The door was probably shut for fear of the Jews; and as most of the houses in the East have an area before the door, it might have been at this outer gate that Peter stood knocking. *A damsel came to hearken, named Rhoda.* She came to inquire who was there. Rhoda signifies a "rose"; and it appears to have been customary with the Jews to give the names of flowers and trees to their daughters.

15. *It is his angel.* It was a common opinion among the Jews that every man has a guardian angel, and in the popish church it is an article of faith. As *angelos* signifies in general "a messenger," whether divine or human, some have thought that the angel or messenger here means a servant or person which the disciples supposed was sent from Peter to announce something of importance to the brethren.

17. *Declared . . . how the Lord had brought him out of the prison.* He still persisted in the belief that his deliverance was purely supernatural. It seems that some modern critics could have informed him of his mistake. *Shew these things unto James, and to the brethren.* That is, in one word, show them to the church, at the head of which James undoubtedly was, as we may clearly understand by the part he took in the famous council held at Jerusalem, relative to certain differences between the believing Jews and Gentiles. See chap. xv. 13-21. There is still no supremacy for Peter. He who was bishop or overseer of the church at Jerusalem was certainly at the head of the whole Church of God at this time; but James was then bishop or inspector of the church at Jerusalem, and, consequently, was the only visible head then upon earth. *He departed . . . into another place.* Where he went we know not, but it is probable that he withdrew for the present into a place of privacy, till the heat of the inquiry was over relative to his escape from the prison, for he saw that Herod was intent on his death.

19. *Commanded that they should be put to death.* He believed, or pretended to believe, that the escape of Peter was owing to the negligence of the keepers. Jailers, watchmen, etc., ordinarily suffered the same kind of punishment which should have been inflicted on the prisoner whose escape they were supposed to have favored. *He went down from Judaea to Caesarea.* How soon he went down and how long he stayed there we do not know.

20. *Highly displeased with them of Tyre.* On what account Herod was thus displeased is not related by any historian, as far as I have been able to ascertain. Josephus, who speaks of this journey of Herod to Caesarea, says nothing of it; and it is useless for *us* to conjecture. *Having made Blastus . . . their friend.* Blastus was probably a eunuch, and had considerable influence over his master, Herod; to reach the master, it is likely they bribed the chamberlain. *Desired peace.* The Tyrians and Sidonians being equally subjects of the Roman government with the inhabitants of Galilee, Herod could not go to war with them; but, being irritated against them, he might prevent their supplies. They therefore endeavored to be on peaceable, i.e., friendly, terms with him. *Their country was nourished by the king's country.* That is, they had all their supplies from Galilee; for Tyre and Sidon, being places of trade and commerce, with little territory, were obliged to have all their provisions from the countries under Herod's jurisdiction. This had been the case even from the days of Solomon, as we learn from 1 Kings v. 11, where it is said that "Solomon gave Hiram twenty thousand measures of wheat for food to his household, and twenty measures of pure oil: thus gave Solomon to Hiram year by year." See also Ezek. xxvii. 17.

21. *Upon a set day.* A day on which games were exhibited in honor of the Roman emperor. What this refers to, we learn from Josephus. "Herod, having reigned three years over all Judea (he had reigned over the tetrarchy of his brother Philip four years before this), went down to Caesarea, and there exhibited shows and games in honour of Claudius, and made vows for his health. On the second day of these shows, he put on a garment made wholly of silver, and of a contexture most truly wonderful, and came into the theatre early in the morning; at which time the silver of his garment, being illuminated by the first reflection of the sun's rays, shone out after a surprising manner, and was so resplendent as to spread a horror over those who looked intently upon him; and presently his flatterers cried out, one from one place and another from another, 'He is a god:' and they added, 'Be thou merciful to us, for although we have hitherto reverenced thee only as a man, yet shall we henceforth own thee as superior to mortal nature.' Nor did the king rebuke them, nor reject their impious flattery. But, looking up, he saw an owl on a certain rope over his head, and immediately conceived that this bird was to him a messenger of ill tidings; and he fell into the deepest sorrow; a severe pain also arose in his bowels, and he died after five days' severe illness." This is the sum of the account given by Josephus, *Ant.*, l. xix, c. 8, s. 2.

23. *The angel of the Lord smote him.* His death was most evidently a judgment from God. *Because he gave not God the glory.* He did not rebuke his flatterers, but permitted them to give him that honor that was due to God alone. *And gave up the ghost.* That is, he died of the disorder by which he was then seized, after having lingered in excruciating torments for five days, as Josephus has stated. Antiochus Epiphanes and Herod the Great died of the same kind of disease.

24. *But the word of God.* The Christian doctrine preached by the apostles *grew and multiplied*—became more evident, and had daily accessions; for the spirit of revelation rested on those men, and God was daily adding to that word as circumstances required, in order to complete that testimony of His which we now find contained in the New Testament. As there is in the original an allusion to the vegetation of grain (it *grew,* as corn grows, the stalk and the ear; it was *multiplied,* as the corn is in the full ear), there is probably a reference to the parable of the sower and his seed; for the seed is the Word of God and the doctrine of the Kingdom. It was liberally sown; it grew vigorously, and became greatly multiplied.

25. *Returned from Jerusalem.* That is, to Antioch, after the death of Herod. *When they had fulfilled their ministry.* When they had carried the alms of the Christians at Antioch to the poor saints at Jerusalem, according to what is mentioned, chap. xi. 29-30, to support them in the time of the coming famine. *And took with them John, whose surname was Mark.* This was the son of Mary, mentioned in v. 12. He accompanied the apostles to Cyprus and afterwards in several of their voyages, till they came to Perga in Pamphylia. Finding them about to take a more extensive voyage, he departed from them. See the case, chap. xiii. 13 and xv. 37-40.

CHAPTER 13

Of the prophets and teachers in the church of Antioch, 1. By command of the Holy Spirit the church appoints Saul and Barnabas to a particular work, 2-3. They depart, and travel to Seleucia, Cyprus, and Salamis, preaching in the Jewish synagogues, 4-5. At Paphos they meet with Bar-Jesus or Elymas, a Jewish sorcerer, who endeavors to prevent the deputy of the island from receiving the Christian faith, 6-8. Saul, for the first time called Paul, denounces the judgments of God upon him, and he is struck blind, 9-11. The deputy, seeing this, is confirmed in the faith, 12. Paul and his company leave Paphos and come to Pamphylia, where John Mark leaves them, and returns to Jerusalem, 13. Paul and Barnabas proceed to Antioch; and, coming into a synagogue of the Jews, are requested by the rulers of it to preach to the people, 14-15. Paul preaches, and proves that Jesus is the Christ, 16-41. The Gentiles desire the sermon to be preached to them the next Sabbath, and many of the Jews and proselytes receive the Christian faith, 42-43. The next Sabbath the whole city attend; and the Jews, filled with envy, contradict and blaspheme, 44-45. Paul and Barnabas with great boldness show that, by the order of God, the gospel was to be preached first to them; but, seeing they had rejected it, it should now be taken from them and sent to the Gentiles, 46-47. The Gentiles rejoice and receive the truth, 48-49. The Jews raise a persecution against the apostles and expel them, 50. They come to Iconium, full of joy and the Holy Ghost, 51-52.

1. *Certain prophets and teachers.* It is probable that these were not distinct offices, both might be vested in the same persons. By *prophets* we are to understand, when the word is taken simply, persons who were frequently inspired to predict future events; and by *teachers,* persons whose ordinary office was to instruct the people in the Christian doctrine. These also, to be properly qualified for the office, must have been endued with the influence of the Holy Spirit; for, as but a very small portion of the Scriptures of the New Testament could have as yet been given, it was necessary that the teachers should derive much of their own teaching by immediate revelation from God. *Barnabas.* Of whom see before, chap. xi. 22-24. *Simeon . . . Niger.* Or "Simeon the Black," because of either his complexion or his hair. *Lucius of Cyrene.* See chap. xi. 20. *Manaen, which had been brought up with Herod.* Our margin has given the proper meaning of the original word "a foster-brother"; i.e., Manaen was the son of the woman who nursed Herod Antipas. Of a person whose name was Manaen or Menahem, and who was in the court of Herod, we read several things in the Jewish writers. They say that this man had the gift of prophecy, and that he told Herod, when he was but a child, that he would be king. When Herod became king he sent for him to his court, and held him in great estimation. It might have been the son of this Menahem of whom Luke here speaks.

2. *As they ministered to the Lord, and fasted.* On Mondays and Thursdays it was usual with the more pious Jews to attend the public service in their synagogues, and to fast; the former is what we are to understand by ministering to the Lord. On the Sabbaths they attended the service in the synagogue, but did not fast. The Greek word signifies "performing the office of praying, supplicating, rendering thanks." *The Holy Ghost said.* A revelation of the divine will was made to some person then present. *Separate me Barnabas and Saul.* Consecrate, or set them apart, for the particular work whereunto I have called them. How this was done we find in the next verse.

3. *And when they had fasted and prayed, and laid their hands on them.* (1) They *fasted;* this was probably done by the whole church. (2) They *prayed* that God would bless and prosper them in their work. (3) They *laid . . . hands upon them,* thus solemnly appointing them to that particular work. But was it by this fasting, praying, and imposition of hands that these men were qualified for this work? No. God had already called them to it, v. 2, and He who called them had qualified them. Both their call and their qualification came from God, but He chose that they should have also the sanction of that church of which they had been members; and therefore He said, "Separate me." The ordination of elders among the Jews was by three persons; and here we find three, Simeon, Lucius, and Manaen, ordaining two others, Barnabas and Saul. But how did the Jews ordain? Not by imposition of hands. This is strictly forbidden; see Maimon. Sanh., chap. 4. "After what manner is the ordaining of elders for ever? Not that they should lay their hands on the head of an elder; but only that they should call him Rabbi, and say to him, Behold, thou art ordained, and hast power of judging." The church at Antioch, however, did depart from this custom: they put their hands on the heads of Barnabas and Saul, thus designating them to be the persons whom they, under the direction of the Holy Spirit, sent to preach the gospel of Christ to the heathen.

4. *Being sent forth by the Holy Ghost.* By His influence, authority, and under His continual direction. Without the first, they were not qualified to go; without the second, they had no authority to go; and without the third, they could not know where to go. *Departed unto Seleucia.* Near the place where the Orontes River pours itself into the sea. *They sailed to Cyprus.* A well-known island in the Mediterranean Sea.

5. *Salamis.* The capital of the island of Cyprus, situated on the eastern part of the island. *They preached the word of God.* The

doctrine of God, the Christian religion, emphatically so called. *They had also John to their minister.* This was John Mark, of whom we heard, chap. xii. 25; for their *minister,* to assist them in minor offices, as deacon or servant, that they might give themselves wholly to the doctrine of the Lord.

6. *Gone through the isle.* The "whole" *isle* is added here by some MSS. *Unto Paphos.* This town, next in importance to Salamis, was situated on the western part of the isle; and having gone from Salamis to this place is a proof that they had gone through the whole island from east to west, according to the reading noticed above. There was probably no town in the universe more dissolute than Paphos. Here Venus had a superb temple; here she was worshipped with all her rites; and from this place she was named the "Paphian Venus," the "queen of Paphos." This temple and whole city were destroyed by an earthquake, so that a vestige of either does not now remain. *A certain sorcerer.* "A magician," one who used magical arts and pretended to have commerce with supernatural agents. *A false prophet.* A deceiver, one who pretended to have a divine commission, a fortune-teller. *Bar-Jesus.* That is, "the son of Jesus."

7. *The deputy of the country.* The "proconsul." In those days the Romans sent two different kinds of governors into the provinces. Some of the provinces were *imperial,* and into those they sent *propretors;* others belonged to the *senate* and people of Rome, and into those they sent *proconsuls.* Cyprus had formerly been an imperial province; but Augustus, who made the distinction, had given it to the people, whence it was governed by a proconsul. *A prudent man.* A man of "good sense," of a sound understanding, and therefore wished to hear the doctrine taught by these apostles; he did not persecute the men for their preaching, but sent for them that he might hear for himself.

8. *But Elymas the sorcerer (for so is his name by interpretation).* That is, Elymas is the interpretation of the word *magos,* or *sorcerer;* not of the word Bar-Jesus, as some have imagined.

9. *Saul, (who also is . . . Paul).* This is the first time the name Paul occurs and the last time in which this apostle is called Saul as his common or general name. *Saul, Shaül,* was the name of the first Israelitish king, and signifies "asked, sought"; from *shaal,* "he asked, inquired." *Paul, Paulus,* if derived from the Latin, signifies "little, dwarfish." It is well-known that the Jews in the apostolic age had frequently two names: one Hebrew, the other Greek or Roman. Saul was born of Jewish parents, a Hebrew of the Hebrews; he had therefore his first name from that language, *Shaül,* "asked or begged," as it is possible he might have been a child for whom his parents had addressed their fervent petitions to God. The case of Samuel is one in point. See 1 Sam. i. 9-18. As he was born in Tarsus, in Cilicia, he was consequently born a free Roman citizen; and hence his parents would naturally give him, for cognomen, some name borrowed from the Latin tongue; and Paulus, which signifies "little," might indicate that he was at his birth a small child. It is very likely that he was low in stature all his days; and that it is to this he refers himself, 2 Cor. x. 10, "For . . . his bodily

presence is weak, and his speech contemptible." If he were small in stature, his voice would be naturally low and feeble; and the Greeks, who were fond of a thundering eloquence, would despise him on this very account. *Filled with the Holy Ghost.* Therefore the sentence he pronounced was not from himself, but from God. And indeed, had he not been under a divine influence, it is not likely he would have ventured thus to accost this sorcerer in the presence of the governor, who no doubt had greatly admired him.

10. *O full of all subtilty.* "Deceit," pretending to supernatural powers without possessing any, and having only cunning and deceit as their substitutes. *And . . . mischief.* From *rhadios,* "easy," and *ergon,* "a work"; one who is ready at his work; a word which excellently well defines a juggler, one who is expert at sleight of hand, though it is often employed to signify an abandoned and accomplished villain. *Child of the devil.* "Son of the devil," possessing his nature, filled with his cunning, and in consequence practicing deceit. *Enemy of all righteousness.* Opposed in your heart to all that is just, true, and good.

Wilt thou not cease to pervert? "Will you not cease perverting?" He had probably labored in this bad work from the beginning of Paul's ministry in the place, and God in His mercy had borne with him; and no doubt the apostle had warned him, for thus much seems implied in the reproof. *The right ways of the Lord.* "The ways of the Lord, the straight ways." This saying is very emphatical. The ways of Elymas were crooked and perverse; *the ways of the Lord,* the doctrine taught by Him, plain and straight. What is here said of the conduct and teaching of Elymas, for he was a false prophet, is true of all false doctrine. It is complex, devious, and tortuous; while the doctrine of God is simple, plain, and straight, directing in the way, the sure way, that leads to present peace and everlasting happiness. From the phraseology which the apostle employs in this terrible address to Elymas we may learn, as well as from his name Bar-Jesus, that he was by birth and education a Jew. On this account he was the greater enemy to Christianity, and on this same account he was the less excusable.

11. *The hand of the Lord is upon thee.* The power of God is now about to deal with you in the way of justice. *Thou shalt be blind.* Every word here proves the immediate inspiration of Paul. He was full of the Holy Ghost when he began this address; by the light of that Spirit he discerned the state of Elymas and exposed his real character; and by the prophetic influence of that same Spirit he predicted the calamity that was about to fall upon him, while as yet there was no sign of his blindness. *Not seeing the sun for a season.* In the midst of judgment God remembers mercy. This blindness was not to be perpetual; it was intended to be the means of awakening and softening the hard heart of this poor sinner. There is an ancient tradition, and it is mentioned by both Origen and Chrysostom, that Elymas, in consequence of this, became a sincere convert to the religion of Christ. Origen says: "And Paul by a word striking him blind, who was with the proconsul, Sergius Paul, by anguish converted him to godliness." *There fell on him a mist and darkness.* *Achlus* is a disordered state of the eye in which

the patient sees through a thick mist. This thick mist, or perturbed state of the eye, took place first; it increased, and thick, positive *darkness* was the issue. *He went about.* Not knowing how to take a right step, he groped about in great uncertainty; and not being able to find his way, he sought for some persons to lead him by the hand.

12. *The deputy . . . believed.* This was a proof that the doctrine was true; and that the power of God, from which nothing could be concealed and which nothing could resist, was with these preachers. *Being astonished.* Being struck with astonishment, as Elymas was struck with blindness.

13. *Paul and his company loosed from Paphos.* They sailed away from this island, leaving, it may be presumed, Elymas a sincere and deeply humbled penitent; and Sergius Paul, a thorough and happy believer in the doctrine of Christ. Previously to this time Luke always mentions Barnabas before Paul; but after this he mentions Paul always first, probably after seeing how God had distinguished him in the late proceedings at Cyprus, as much of the Holy Spirit now rested upon him. *They came to Perga in Pamphylia.* As Perga was not a maritime town, it is conjectured that the apostles sailed up the river Cestrus, in order to come to this place, which, according to Strabo, was situated about sixty leagues up this river, and near to which was a famous temple dedicated to Diana. *And John departing from them.* Why John Mark left his brethren at this place we are not informed; probably he went to visit his pious mother, Mary, at Jerusalem, and to see Peter, to whom he is supposed to have been much attached. It certainly was not with the approbation of Paul that he left them at this place as we learn from chap. xv. 38; yet his departure does not seem to have merited the displeasure of Barnabas. For John Mark having met these apostles at Antioch when Paul purposed to revisit the various places where they had planted the word of God, Barnabas was willing to take him with them; but Paul would not consent, because he had "departed from them from Pamphylia, and went not with them to the work," chap. xv. 35-39; and this occasioned a separation between Barnabas and Paul. It does not appear that John Mark was under any obligation to accompany them any longer or any farther than he pleased. He seems to have been little else than their servant, and certainly was not divinely appointed to this work, as they were; and consequently might leave them innocently, though not kindly, if they could not readily supply his place.

14. *They came to Antioch in Pisidia.* This place is mentioned thus to distinguish it from Antioch in Syria, with which it had nothing in common but the name. There were several cities and towns in various districts of these countries called Antioch; some have reckoned up not less than twelve. *Into the synagogue on the sabbath day.* Though Paul was now on a special mission to the Gentiles, yet he availed himself of every opportunity, in every place, of making the first offer of salvation to the Jews.

15. *After the reading of the law and the prophets.* A certain portion of the *law* and another of the *prophets* were read every Sabbath, and the law was so divided as to be read over once every year. It has been a question

in what language were the law and prophets read in a synagogue of Pisidia, for in that district Strabo informs us that four languages were spoken, viz., the Pisidian, the Solyman, the Greek, and the Lydian. Dr. Lightfoot conjectures, with great probability, that the Scriptures were read in the original Hebrew, and that an interpreter rendered the reading to the people in their mother tongue. *The rulers of the synagogue.* These were the persons whose business it was to read the appointed sections, to take care of the synagogue and its concerns, and to see that all was done decently and in order. *Sent unto them.* Seeing them to be Jews, they wished them to give some suitable address to the people, i.e., to the Jews who were then engaged in divine worship; for the whole of the following discourse, which greatly resembles that of Stephen, chap. vii, is directed to the Jews alone; and this was probably spoken in either Hebrew or Greek. *Ye men and brethren.* "Men brethren," a Hebraism for, "You men who are our brethren," i.e., Jews, as we ourselves are. *If ye have any word of exhortation.* "If you have any subject of consolation," any word of comfort to us, who are sojourners in this strange land, speak it. The "Consolation of Israel" was an epithet of the Messiah among the Jews, and it is probable that it was in reference to Him that the rulers of the synagogue spoke.

16. *Men of Israel, you that are Jews by birth; and ye that fear God*—you that are proselytes to the Jewish religion. In this discourse Paul proves that Jesus Christ is the Messiah, sent from God, for the salvation not only of the Jews, but of the whole human race. And this he does, not with the rhetorician's arts, but in a plain, simple detail of the history of Christ and the most remarkable transactions of the people of God, which referred to His manifestation in the flesh.

17. *The God of . . . our fathers.* The apostle begins his discourse with the Egyptian bondage and their deliverance from it, as points the most remarkable and striking in their history, in which the providence and mighty power of God, exerted so frequently in their behalf, were peculiarly conspicuous. *Exalted the people.* Even when they were strangers in the land and greatly oppressed, God exalted them; made them a terror to their enemies, and multiplied them greatly. *With an high arm.* A literal translation of the Hebrew phrase, "with a lifted-up arm," to protect them and destroy their enemies. The meaning of the phrase is "a manifest display of the divine power."

18. *About the time of forty years.* The space of time between their coming out of Egypt and going into the Promised Land. *Suffered he their manners.* He dealt indulgently with them; howsoever they behaved toward Him, He mercifully bore with and kindly treated them. But instead of *etropophoresen*, some MSS. read *etrophophoresen*, which signifies, "He nourished and fed them, or bore them about in His arms as a tender nurse does her child." This reading agrees excellently with the scope of the place and is a reading of at least equal value with that in the commonly received text. Both, when rightly understood, speak nearly the same sense; but the latter is the most expressive, and agrees best with Paul's discourse and the history to which he alludes. See the same form of ex-

pression, Num. xi. 12; Exod. xix. 4; Isa. xlvi. 3-4; and lxiii. 9.

19. *Destroyed seven nations.* The Canaanites, Hittites, Girgasites, Amorites, Hivites, Peresites, and Jebusites.

20. *And after that he gave unto them judges about the space of four hundred and fifty years.* This is a most difficult passage. The apostle seems here to contradict the account in 1 Kings vi. 1: "And it came to pass in the four hundred and eightieth year after the children of Israel were come out of the land of Egypt, in the fourth year of Solomon's reign . . . he began to build the house of the Lord." Calmet has paraphrased these passages nearly to the same sense. The text may be thus connected; v. 19: "And having destroyed seven nations in the land of Canaan, He divided their land to them by lot, about one hundred and fifty years after. And afterwards He gave them judges, to the time of Samuel the prophet." The paraphrase of Calmet is the following: "*The God of this people of Israel chose our fathers* in the person of Abraham; he promised him the land of Canaan; and four hundred and fifty years after this promise, and the birth of Isaac, who was the son and heir of the promise, he put them in possession of that land which he had promised so long before." As this view of the subject removes all the principal difficulties, I shall not trouble my reader with other modes of interpretation.

21. *Saul the son of Cis.* In all proper names quoted from the Old Testament, we should undoubtedly follow, as nearly as possible, the same orthography: "Kish" was the name of this king's father, and so we spell it in the Old Testament. *The space of forty years.* Reckoning from the time of his anointing by Samuel to the time of his death.

22. *David . . . a man after mine own heart.* That is, a man who would rule the kingdom according to God's will.

23. *Of this man's seed hath God . . . raised . . . a Saviour.* That the Messiah was promised to come from the family of David, see Isa. xi. 1-2 and Jer. xxiii. 5-6.

25. *As John fulfilled his course.* "As John was fulfilling his race, he said." It has been supposed that the word "course," or "race," is used here to point out the short duration of the Baptist's ministry, and the fervent zeal with which he performed it. It signifies properly his ministry, or life.

26. *Men and brethren.* This should have been translated simply "brethren." See the note on chap. vii. 2. *Children of the stock of Abraham.* All you that are Jews. *And whosoever among you feareth God.* That is, all you who are Gentiles, and are now proselytes to the Jewish religion. *The word of this salvation.* The doctrine that contains the promise of deliverance from sin and the means by which it is brought about.

27. *Because they knew him not.* A gentle excuse for the persecuting high priests. They did not know that Jesus was the Christ, because they did not know the prophets; and only did they not know the prophets which were read every Sabbath day? Because they did not desire to know His will, and therefore they knew not the doctrine of God; nor did they know that, in condemning Christ, they fulfilled

those very Scriptures which were read every Sabbath day in their synagogues.

30. *But God raised him from the dead.* And thus gave the fullest proof of His innocence.

31. *He was seen many days.* The thing was done but a very short time since; and many of the witnesses are still alive, and ready to attest the fact of this Resurrection in the most unequivocal manner.

32. *We declare unto you glad tidings.* We proclaim that gospel to you which is the fulfillment of the promise made unto the fathers.

33. *Thou art my Son, this day have I begotten thee.* It has been disputed whether this text should be understood of the incarnation or of the resurrection of our Lord. If understood of His incarnation, it can mean no more than this, that the human nature of our blessed Lord was begotten by the energy of the Holy Spirit in the womb of the blessed Virgin; for as to His divine nature, which is allowed to be God, it could be neither created nor begotten. But the doctrine of the eternal sonship of Christ is absolutely irreconcilable to reason and contradictory to itself. Eternity is that which has had no beginning nor stands in any reference to time; Son supposes time, generation, and Father, and time also antecedent to such a generation. Therefore the rational conjunction of these two terms, "Son" and "eternity," is absolutely impossible, as they imply essentially different and opposite ideas. If the passage in question be understood of the resurrection of Christ, it points out that the human nature, which was produced by the power of God in the womb of the Virgin and which was the Son of God, could see no corruption; and therefore, though it died for sin, must be raised from the dead before it saw corruption. Thus God owned that human nature to be peculiarly His own; and therefore Jesus Christ was "declared to be the Son of God with power . . . by the resurrection from the dead," Rom. i. 4.

34. *No more to return to corruption.* To the grave, to death, the place and state of corruption. *The sure mercies of David.* These words are quoted literatim from the Septuagint version of Isa. lv. 3, and which Paul considers as being fulfilled in the resurrection of Christ. From this application of the words it is evident that the apostle considered the word *David* as signifying the Messiah; and then the *sure* or faithful *mercies,* being such as relate to the new covenant and the various blessings promised in it, are evidently those which are sealed and confirmed to mankind by the resurrection of Christ.

36. *David . . . fell on sleep . . . and saw corruption.* David died, was buried, and never rose again; therefore David cannot be the person spoken of here. These words can be applied to Jesus Christ only, and in Him they are most exactly fulfilled.

38. *Be it known unto you therefore.* This is the legitimate conclusion: Seeing the word of God is true, and He has promised an endless succession to the seed of David; seeing David and all his family have failed in reference to the political kingdom, a spiritual Kingdom and a spiritual succession must be intended, that the sure covenant and all its blessings may be continued. Again: Seeing the person by whom this is to be done is to see no corruption;

seeing David has died, and has seen (fallen under the power of) corruption; seeing Jesus the Christ has wrought all the miracles which the prophets said He should work; seeing He has suffered all the indignities which your prophets said He must suffer; seeing after His death He has most incontestably risen again from the dead, and has not fallen under the power of corruption—then He must be the very Person in whom all the predictions are fulfilled, and the Person through whom all the blessings of the covenant must come. *Through this man is preached unto you the forgiveness of sins.* See the notes on chap. v. 30-31. Remission of sins—the removal of the power, guilt, and pollution of sin—comes alone through this Man whom you crucified and who is risen from the dead.

39. *And by him.* On His account, and through Him, *all that believe* in His divine mission and the end for which He has been manifested, namely, to put away sin by the sacrifice of himself, *are justified from all things,* from the guilt of all transgressions committed against God, *from which ye could not be justified by the law of Moses;* because it is impossible that "the blood of bulls and of goats, and the ashes of an heifer sprinkling the unclean," or any other rite or service of this kind, could take away sin from the soul, cancel its guilt in the conscience, or make an atonement to the divine justice.

40. *Beware . . . lest that come upon you.* If you reject these benefits, now freely offered to you in this preaching of Christ crucified, you may expect such judgments from the hand of God as your forefathers experienced, when, for their rebellion and their contempt of His benefits, their city was taken, their Temple destroyed, and themselves either slain by the sword or carried into captivity. It is evident that Paul refers to Hab. i. 5-10.

41. *Behold, ye despisers.* There is a remarkable difference here between the Hebrew text in Habakkuk and that in the Septuagint, which is a little abridged here by Paul. It may now be necessary to inquire how Luke and the Septuagint should substitute *ye despisers,* for "ye among the heathen," in the Hebrew text. Without troubling myself or my readers with laborious criticisms on these words, I will simply state my opinion, that the prophet, instead of *bagoyim,* "among the heathen," wrote *bogadim,* "despisers," or *transgressors*—a word which differs only in a single letter, *daleth,* for *vau.* It seems as evident as it can be that this was the word which the Septuagint found in the copy from which they translated. Their evidence, and that of the apostle, joined to the consideration that the interchange of the two letters mentioned above might have been easily made, is quite sufficient to legitimate the reading for which I contend. The word which we translate *perish* signifies more properly "disappear, or hide yourselves"; as people, astonished and alarmed at some coming evil, betake themselves to flight, and hide themselves in order to avoid it.

42. *When the Jews were gone out.* That part of them in whom the words of the prophet were fulfilled, viz., those who, though they had the clearest relation of so interesting a history, would not believe it; they shut their eyes against the light and hardened their hearts

against the truth. There were other Jews in the assembly that did believe and were saved. *The Gentiles besought.* There is some doubt whether the original should be translated *the Gentiles besought* or "they besought the Gentiles"; for the words will bear either, but the latter sense more naturally. When the Jews retired, determining not to credit what was spoken, the apostle, seeing the Gentiles of a better mind, requested them to come and hear those words, or doctrines, the next Sabbath. On this verse there is a great number of various readings: instead of, "when the Jews were going out of the synagogue," some MSS. read, "As they were going out, they entreated that these words should be preached unto them the next Sabbath." The most eminent critics approve of this reading; indeed it stands on such authority as to render it almost indubitable. We are therefore to understand the words thus: that, "as they were going out on the breaking up of the assembly, some of them desired that they might have these doctrines preached to them on the ensuing week or Sabbath." And thus all the ambiguity of the verse vanishes.

43. *Many of the Jews.* Direct descendants from some of the twelve tribes, and religious proselytes, heathens who had been converted to Judaism, and, having submitted to circumcision, had become *proselytes* of the covenant; though some think that the expression means persons who believed in one God, like the Jews, but who had not received circumcision.

44. *The next sabbath day.* The good news had spread far and wide, by means of the converted Jews and proselytes. *Almost the whole city.* Jews, proselytes, and Gentiles came together to hear "this doctrine of God," this divine teaching, by which so many of their kindred and acquaintance had become so wise and happy.

45. *The Jews . . . were filled with envy.* See on chap. v. 17. These could not bear the Gentiles, who believed in Christ, to be equal with them; and yet, according to the gospel, it was really the case. *Contradicting.* The arguments and statements brought forward by the disciples; *and blaspheming,* speaking impiously and injuriously of Jesus Christ.

46. *Waxed bold.* Having great liberty of speech; a strong, persuasive, and overpowering eloquence. They had eternal truth for the basis of this discourse, a multitude of incontestable facts to support it, an all-persuading eloquence to illustrate and maintain what they had asserted. *Ye put it from you.* "Ye disdain" this doctrine, and consider it "contemptible"; so the word is frequently used.

47. *For so . . . the Lord commanded us.* The apostles could quote a pertinent scripture for everything they did, because the outlines of the whole gospel dispensation are founded in the law and the prophets, and they were now building the Church of God according to the pattern shown them in the mount. *I have set thee to be a light of the Gentiles.* This quotation is from Isa. xlix. 6 and was most fully in point. *For salvation unto the ends of the earth.* The very name of the Messiah, viz., Jesus, announced the design and end of His mission. He is the "Saviour," and is to be proclaimed as such to *the ends of the earth,* to all mankind.

48. *As many as were ordained to eternal life believed.* This text has been most pitifully misunderstood. Many suppose that it simply means that those in that assembly who were foreordained, or predestinated by God's decree to eternal life, believed under the influence of that decree. Now we should be careful to examine what a word means before we attempt to fix its meaning. Whatever *tetagmenoi* may mean, which is the word we translate *ordained,* it includes no idea of *preordination* or *predestination* of any kind. The verb *tasso* signifies to "place, set, order, appoint, dispose"; hence it has been considered here as implying the disposition or readiness of mind of several persons in the congregation, such as the religious proselytes mentioned in v. 43, who possessed the reverse of the disposition of those Jews who spake against those things, contradicting and blaspheming, v. 45. Though the word in this place has been variously translated, yet, of all the meanings ever put on it, none agrees worse with its nature and known signification than that which represents it as intending those who were predestinated to eternal life; this is no meaning of the term and should never be applied to it.

49. *The word of the Lord was published.* Those who had come from different parts and were converted carried the glad tidings to their respective neighborhoods.

50. *Devout and honourable women.* It is likely that these were heathen matrons who had become proselytes to the Jewish religion; and as they were persons of affluence and respectability, they had considerable influence with the civil magistracy of the place, and probably their husbands were of this order; and it is likely that they used that influence, at the instigation of the Jews, to get the apostles expelled from the place.

51. *They shook off the dust of their feet against them.* This was a very significant rite; by it they in effect said: "You are worse than the heathen; even your very land is accursed for your opposition to God, and we dare not permit even its dust to cleave to the soles of our feet; and we shake it off, in departing from your country, according to our Lord's command (Matt. x. 14), for a testimony against you, that we offered you salvation, but you rejected it and persecuted us." The Jews, when travelling in heathen countries, took care, when they came to the borders of their own, to shake off the dust of their feet, lest any of the unhallowed ground should defile the sacred land of Israel. *Came unto Iconium.* According to Strabo, Iconium was a small fortified town, the capital of Lycaonia.

52. *The disciples were filled with joy, and with the Holy Ghost.* Though in the world they had tribulation, yet in Christ they had peace. The happiness of a genuine Christian lies far beyond the reach of earthly disturbances, and is not affected by the changes and chances to which mortal things are exposed. The martyrs were more happy in the flames than their persecutors could be on their beds of down.

CHAPTER 14

Paul and Barnabas, having preached at Iconium with great success, are persecuted, and obliged to flee to Lystra and Derbe, 1-6. Here they preach, and heal a cripple; on which, the people, supposing them to be gods, are about to offer them sacrifices, and are with difficulty prevented by these apostles, 7-18. Certain Jews from

Antioch and Iconium, coming thither, induce the people to stone Paul; who, being dragged out of the city as dead, while the disciples stand around him, rises up suddenly, and returns to the city, and the next day departs to Derbe, 19-20. Having preached here, he and Barnabas return to Lystra, Iconium, and Antioch, confirming the disciples, and ordaining elders in every church, 21-23. They pass through Pisidia and Pamphylia, 24. Through Perga and Attalia, 25; and sail to Antioch in Syria, 26. When, having called the disciples together, they inform them of the door of faith opened to the Gentiles, and there abide a long time with the church, 27-28.

1. *So spake,* with such power and demonstration of the Spirit, *that a great multitude both of the Jews,* genuine descendants of one or other of the twelve tribes, *and also of the Greeks,* probably such as were proselytes, believed, received the Christian religion as a revelation from God, and confided in its Author for salvation, according to the apostles' preaching.

2. *Evil affected.* "Irritated or exasperated their minds against the brethren," the disciples of Christ.

3. *Long time therefore abode they.* Because they had great success, therefore they continued a long time, gaining many converts, and building up in their most holy faith those who had believed, notwithstanding the opposition they met with from both the unbelieving Jews and the heathens. *Speaking boldly.* Having great liberty of speech, a copious and commanding eloquence, springing from a consciousness of the truth which they preached.

4. *The multitude of the city was divided.* The Jews treated the apostles as false teachers, and their miracles as impositions, and many of the people held with them; while the others, who had not hardened their hearts against the truth, felt the force of it and, being without prejudice, could easily discern the miracles to be the work of God, and therefore held with the apostles.

5. *An assault made.* A "desperate attempt" was made by *their ruler,* i.e., by the heathen rulers of the people, and the synagogue.

9. *That he had faith to be healed.* How did this faith come to this poor heathen? Why, by hearing the Word of God preached; for it is said, *The same heard Paul speak.* And it appears that he credited the doctrine he heard, and believed that Jesus could, if He would, make him whole. Besides, he must have heard of the miracles which the apostles had wrought (see v. 3), and this would raise his expectation of receiving a cure.

10. *He leaped and walked.* Giving the fullest proof of his restoration; his leaping, however, might have been through joy of having received his cure.

12. *They called Barnabas, Jupiter; and Paul, Mercurius.* The heathens supposed that Jupiter and Mercury were the gods who most frequently assumed the human form, and Jupiter was accustomed to take Mercury with him on such expeditions. Jupiter was the supreme god of the heathens, and Mercury was by them considered the god of eloquence. As the ancients usually represented Jupiter as rather an aged man, large, noble, and majestic; and Mercury young, light, and active, the conjecture of Chrysostom is very probable, that Barnabas was a large, noble, well-made man, and probably in years; and Paul, young, active, and eloquent; on which account they termed the former Jupi-

ter, and the latter Mercury. That Mercury was eloquent and powerful in his words is allowed by the heathens; and the very epithet that is applied here to Paul, "He was the chief or leader of the discourse," was applied to Mercury.

13. *Then the priest of Jupiter, which was before their city.* Many cities were put under the protection of a particular deity, and the image of that deity placed at the entrance, to signify that he was the guardian and protector. To this Luke, everywhere as accurate as he is circumstantial, refers. Lystra, it appears, was under the guardianship of *Jupiter Propulaius,* which Luke translates "the Jupiter that was before the city," which is another term for *Jupiter Custos,* or Jupiter the Guardian. All these deities, according to the attributes they sustained, had their peculiar priests, rites, and sacrifices. Hence we can see with what accuracy Luke wrote. The person who was going to offer them sacrifices was the priest of *Jupiter Custos,* under whose guardianship the city of Lystra was, and whom the priest supposed had visited the city in a human form. *Oxen and garlands.* That is, oxen adorned with flowers, their horns gilded, and necks bound about with fillets, as was the custom in sacrificial rites. They also crowned the gods themselves, the priests, and gates of the temples, with flowers.

15. *We also are men of like passions with you.* This saying of the apostles has been most strangely perverted. A pious commentator, taking the word *passion* in its vulgar and most improper sense (a bad temper, an evil propensity) and supposing that these holy men wished to confess that they also had many sinful infirmities and wrong tempers, endeavors to illustrate this sense of the word by appealing to the contention of Paul and Barnabas. But the expression means no more than, "We are truly *human beings,* with the same powers and appetites as your own; need food and raiment as you do; and are all mortal like yourselves." *That ye should turn from these vanities.* That is, from these idols and false gods. How often false gods and idolatry are termed *vanity* in the Scriptures, no careful reader of the Bible needs to be told. What a bold saying was this in the presence of a heathen mob, intent on performing an act of their superstitious worship, in which they no doubt thought the safety of the state was concerned! The ancient fable related by Ovid, *Metam., l. i.* vv. 211-239, will cast some light on the conduct of the Lystrians in this case. The following is its substance: "Jupiter, having been informed of the great degeneracy of mankind, was determined himself to survey the earth. Coming to this province [*Lycaonia*], disguised in human shape, he took up his residence at the palace of *Lycaon,* then kind of that country: giving a sign of his godhead, the people worship him: Lycaon sneers, doubts his divinity, and is determined to put it to the trial. Some ambassadors from the Molossian state having just arrived, he slew one of them, boiled part of his flesh, and roasted the rest, and set it before Jupiter: the god, indignant at the insult, burnt the palace, and turned the impious king into a *wolf.*" From this time, or rather from this fable, the whole province was called Lycaonia. The simple people now seeing such proofs of supernatural power, in the miracles wrought by Barnabas and Paul, thought that Jupiter had again visited them; and fearing lest they should

meet with his indignation, should they neglect duly to honor him, they brought oxen and garlands, and would have offered them sacrifice, had they not been prevented by the apostles themselves. This circumstance will account for their whole conduct, and shows the reason why Jupiter was the tutelar god of the place. *The living God.* Widely different from those stocks and stones which were objects of their worship. *Which made heaven, and earth.* And as all things were made by His power, so all subsist by His providence; and to Him alone all worship, honor, and glory are due.

16. *Who in times past suffered all nations.* The words *all nations* should be rendered "all the Gentiles," merely to distinguish them from the Jewish people, who, having a revelation, were not left *to walk in their own ways.*

17. *He left not himself without witness.* Though He gave the Gentiles no revelation of His will, yet He continued to govern them by His gracious providence, doing them *good* in general, giving them rain to fertilize their grounds, and *fruitful seasons* as the result.

19. *There came thither certain Jews from Antioch.* Those were, no doubt, the same who had raised up persecution against Paul and Barnabas at Iconium and Antioch before. They followed the apostles with implacable malice; and what they could not do themselves they endeavored to do by others, whose minds they first perverted, and then irritated to deeds of fell purpose. *Supposing he had been dead.* They did not leave stoning him till they had the fullest evidence that he was dead; and so, most probably, he was.

20. *The disciples stood round about him.* No doubt in earnest prayer, entreating the Author of life that his soul might again return to its battered tenement. *He rose up.* Miraculously restored, not only to life, but to perfect soundness; so that he was able to walk into the city, that his persecutors might see the mighty power of God in his restoration, and the faith of the young converts be confirmed in the truth and goodness of God.

21. *Preached the gospel to that city.* Derbe, a city in the same province. *They returned again to Lystra, and to Iconium.* Behold the courage of these Christian men! They counted not their lives dear to them, and returned to do their Master's work in the very places in which they had been so grievously persecuted, and where one of them had been apparently stoned to death!

23. *When they had ordained them elders.* *Elder* seems to be here the name of an office. These were all young or new converts, and yet among them the apostles constitute *elders.* They appointed persons the most experienced, and the most advanced in the divine life, to watch over and instruct the rest. But what is the meaning of the word *cheirotonesantes,* which we translate *ordained?* The word *ordain* we use in an ecclesiastical sense and signify by it the appointment of a person to an office in the church by the imposition of the hands of those who are rulers in that church. But *cheirotonia* signifies the "holding up" or "stretching out the hand," as approving of the choice of any person to a particular work, whereas *cheirothesia* signifies the "imposition of hands." I believe the simple truth to be this, that in

ancient times the people chose by the *cheirotonia* (lifting up of hands) their spiritual pastor; and the rulers of the church, whether apostles or others, appointed that person to his office by the *cheirothesia,* or "imposition of hands"; and perhaps each of these was thought to be equally necessary, the church agreeing in the election of the person, and the rulers of the church appointing, by imposition of hands, the person thus elected. *And had prayed with fasting.* This was to implore God's special assistance, as they well knew that without His influence even their appointment could avail nothing. *Commended them to the Lord.* To His especial care and protection.

25. *They went down into Attalia.* This was a seaport town in Pamphylia.

26. *And thence sailed to Antioch.* This was Antioch in Syria, to reach which, by sea, they were obliged to coast a part of the Mediterranean Sea, steering between Cyprus and Cilicia. *Whence they had been recommended . . . for the work which they fulfilled.* The reader will recollect that it was from this Antioch they had been sent to preach the gospel to the heathen in Asia Minor (see chap. xiii. 1-2), and that they *fulfilled* that *work.*

27. *Had gathered the church together.* The church by which they had been sent on this very important, successful mission. *They rehearsed all that God had done with them.* Not what they had done themselves, but what God made them the instruments of working. *And how he had opened the door of faith.* How God by His providence and grace had made a way for preaching Christ crucified among the heathen; and how the heathen had received that gospel, which, through faith in Christ Jesus, was able to save their souls.

CHAPTER 15

Certain teachers from Judea insist on the necessity of the converted Gentiles being circumcised, 1. Paul and Barnabas are sent to Jerusalem to consult the apostles on this subject, 2. They come to Jerusalem, and inform the apostles of the conversion of the Gentiles, and of the trouble which certain Pharisees had occasioned concerning circumcision, 3-5. The apostles having assembled to consider the question, Peter delivers his opinion, 6-11. Barnabas and Paul relate their success among the Gentiles, 12. James delivers his judgment, 13-21. The apostles and elders agree to what he proposes, and send Judas and Silas with Paul and Barnabas to the converted Gentiles, 22; and send an epistle containing their decree to the churches of Antioch, Syria, and Cilicia, 23-29. Paul and his company return, and read the epistle to the brethren at Antioch, which produces great joy; and Judas and Silas preach to them, 30-32. Judas returns to Jerusalem, but Silas continues with Paul and Barnabas, teaching and preaching, 33-35. Paul proposes to Barnabas to visit the churches where they had preached; on the latter determining to take John Mark with them, Paul refuses, 36-38. They disagree; and Barnabas, taking John Mark, sails to Cyprus, 39. And Paul, taking Silas, goes through Syria and Cilicia, confirming the churches, 40-41.

1. *Except ye be circumcised.* The persons who taught this doctrine appear to have been converts to Christianity; but supposing that the Christian religion was intended to perfect the Mosaic, and not to supersede it, they insisted on the necessity of circumcision, because by that a man was made debtor to the whole law, to observe all its rites and ceremonies. This question produced great disturbance in the apostolic Church; and, notwithstanding the decree mentioned in this chapter, the apostles were frequently obliged to interpose their authority in order to settle it; and we find a whole

church, that at Galatia, drawn aside from the simplicity of the Christian faith by the subtilty of Judaizing teachers among themselves, who insisted on the necessity of the converted Gentiles being circumcised. *Ye cannot be saved.* Ye can enjoy neither God's blessing in time nor His glory in eternity. Such an assertion as this, from any reputable authority, must necessarily shake the confidence of young converts.

2. *No small dissension and disputation.* Paul and Barnabas were fully satisfied that God did not design to bring the converted Gentiles under the yoke of circumcision. They knew that Jesus Christ was "the end of the law for righteousness [justification] to every one that believeth," and therefore they opposed the Judaizing teachers. *And certain other of them.* If this be the journey to which Paul alludes, Gal. ii. 1-5, then he had Titus with him; and how many others went from the church of Antioch we cannot tell. This journey was fourteen years after Paul's conversion, and was undertaken by express revelation, as he informs us in Gal. ii. 2, which revelation appears to have been given to certain persons in the church of Antioch, as we learn from this verse, and not to Paul and Barnabas themselves.

3. *Being brought on their way by the church.* That is, the members of the church provided them with all necessaries for their journey. *Declaring the conversion of the Gentiles.* Much stress is laid on this. It was a miracle of God's mercy that the Gentiles should be received into the Church of God; and they had now the fullest proof that the thing was likely to become general, by the conversion of Cornelius, the conversion of the people of Antioch, of Cyprus, Pisidia, Pamphylia, Lycaonia.

4. *They were received of the church.* The whole body of Christian believers. *The apostles.* We read of none but John, Peter, and James. See Gal. ii. 9. *And elders.* Those who were officers in the church, under the apostles. *They declared.* To this council they gave a succinct account of the great work which God had wrought by them among the Gentiles. This was Paul's third journey to Jerusalem after his conversion. See an account of his first journey, chap. ix. 26, and of his second in chap. xi. 30.

5. *But there rose up certain of the sect of the Pharisees.* This verse appears to be part of the declaration made by Paul and Barnabas to this council; for, having stated how God blessed their ministry among the Gentiles, they proceed to declare how all the good work was likely to be destroyed by certain Pharisees who, having received the Christian faith, came down to Antioch and began to teach the necessity of circumcision.

6. *The apostles and elders came together.* This was the first council ever held in the Christian Church, and we find that it was composed simply of the apostles and elders.

7. *When there had been much disputing.* By those of the sect of the believing Pharisees, for they strongly contended for the circumcision. Though the apostles and elders were under the inspiration of the Almighty, and could by this inspiration have immediately determined the question, yet it was highly necessary that the objecting party should be permitted to come forward and allege their reasons for the doctrines they preached; and that these reasons should be fairly met by argument, and the thing proved to be useless in itself, inexpedient in the present case, and unsupported by any express authority from God. *Peter rose up, and said.* This was after the matters in dispute had been fully debated; and now the apostles, like judges, after hearing counsel on both sides, proceed to give judgment on the case. *A good while ago.* "From the days of old," a phrase which simply signifies "some years ago."

8. *And God, which knoweth the hearts.* We had this epithet of the Divine Being once before; see chap. i. 24, and the note there: "It occurs nowhere else in the New Testament." *Bare them witness.* Considered them as proper or fit to receive the gospel of Christ. It is properly remarked by learned men that "to bear witness to any person" signifies to "approve," to "testify in behalf of." Here it signifies that, as God evidently sent the gospel to the Gentiles and by the preaching of it conveyed the Holy Spirit to them who believed, and as He who knows all hearts and their secrets can make no improper judgment of any, therefore what He had done was right.

9. *Put no difference between us and them.* Giving them the Holy Spirit, though uncircumcised, just as He had given Him to us who were circumcised; an evident proof that, in the judgment of God, circumcision was no preparation to receive the gospel of Christ. And as the purification of the heart by the Holy Spirit was the grand object of the religion of God, and that alone by which the soul could be prepared for a blessed immortality, and the Gentiles had received that without circumcision, consequently the shadow could not be considered of any worth, now the substance was communicated.

10. *Now therefore why tempt ye God?* As God, by giving the Holy Spirit to the Gentiles, evidently shows He does not design them to be circumcised in order to become debtors to the law, to fulfill all its precepts, why will you provoke Him to displeasure by doing what He evidently designs shall not be done? *A yoke . . . which neither our fathers nor we were able to bear.* This does not refer to the moral law—that was of eternal obligation—but to the ritual law, which, through the multitude of its sacrifices and ordinances, was exceedingly burdensome to the Jewish people.

11. *Through the grace of the Lord Jesus Christ we shall be saved.* This seems to be an answer to an objection, "Has not God designed to save us, the Jews, by an observance of the law; and them, the Gentiles, by the faith of the gospel?" No, for we Jews can be saved no other way than through the grace of the Lord Jesus Christ, and this is the way in which the Gentiles in question have been saved.

12. *Gave audience to Barnabas and Paul.* These apostles came forward next to corroborate what Peter had said, by showing the miracles and wonders which God had by them wrought among the Gentiles. Peter stated facts; Paul and Barnabas confirmed the statement.

13. *James answered.* He was evidently president of the council, and is generally called bishop of Jerusalem. The rest either argued

on the subject or gave their opinion; James alone pronounced the definitive sentence. Had Peter been prince and head of the apostles, and of the Church, he would have appeared here in the character of judge, not of mere counsellor or disputant.

14. *Simeon hath declared.* It is remarkable that James does not give him even the title which he received from our Lord at the time in which he is supposed to have been made head of the Church, and vicar of Christ upon earth; so that it is evident James did not understand our Lord as giving Peter any such preeminence, and therefore he does not even call him "Peter," but simply *Simeon. To take out of them a people for his name.* To form among the Gentiles, as he had among the Jews, a people called by His name and devoted to His honor.

15. *And to this agree the words of the prophets.* Peter had asserted the fact of the conversion of the Gentiles, and James shows that that fact was the fulfillment of declarations made by the prophets.

16. *After this I will return, and will build again.* These two verses, sixteenth and seventeenth, are quoted from Amos ix. 11-12, nearly as they now stand in the best editions of the Septuagint, and evidently taken from that version, which differs considerably from the Hebrew text. As James quoted them as a prophecy of the calling of the Gentiles into the Church of God, it is evident the Jews must have understood them in that sense; otherwise they would have immediately disputed his application of them to the subject in question and have rejected his conclusion by denying the premises.

17. *That the residue of men might seek.* Instead of this the Hebrew has, "That they may possess the remnant of Edom." Now it is evident that in the copy from which the Seventy translated they found *yidreshu,* "they might seek," instead of *yireshu,* "they may possess," where the whole difference between the two words is the change of the *yod* for a *daleth,* which might be easily done; and *Edom,* the "Idumeans," which differs from the other letters. It shows that even in Jerusalem and in the early part of the apostolic age the Septuagint version was quoted in preference to the Hebrew text. But God was evidently preparing the way of the gospel by bringing this venerable version into general credit and use, which was to be the means of conveying the truths of Christianity to the whole Gentile world. How precious should this august and most important version be to every Chritsain, and especially to every Christian minister! A version without which no man ever did or ever can critically understand the New Testament!

18. *Known unto God are all his works from the beginning.* As if he had said, This is not a new counsel of God; He had purposed, from the time He called the Israelites, to make the Gentiles partakers of the same grace and mercy. The whole of this verse is very dubious; the principal part of it is omitted by the most ancient MSS.

19. *Wherefore my sentence is.* "Wherefore I judge." There is an authority here that does not appear in the speech of Peter; this authority was felt and bowed to by all the council, and the decree proposed by James adopted.

20. *But that we write unto them.* Four things are prohibited in this decree: (1) *Pollutions of idols;* (2) *fornication;* (3) *things strangled;* (4) *blood.* By the first, *pollutions of idols,* or as it is in v. 29, "meats offered to idols," not only all idolatry was forbidden, but eating things offered in sacrifice to idols, knowing that they were thus offered, and joining with idolaters in their sacred feasts. By the second, *fornication,* all uncleanness of every kind was prohibited; for *porneia* not only means *fornication,* but "adultery," and especially the prostitution which was so common at the idol temples. By the third, *things strangled,* we are to understand the flesh of those animals which were strangled for the purpose of keeping the blood in the body, as such animals were esteemed a greater delicacy. By the fourth, *blood,* we are to understand, not only the thing itself, but also all cruelty, manslaughter, and murder, as some of the ancient fathers have understood it.

21. *Moses of old time hath in every city.* The sense of this verse seems to be this: As it was necessary to write to the Gentiles what was strictly necessary to be observed by them, relative to these points, it was not so to the converted Jews; for they had Moses—that is, the law—preached to them, "in the city"—that is, Antioch; and by the reading of the law in the synagogues every Sabbath day they were kept in remembrance of those institutions which the Gentiles, who had not the law, could not know.

22. *Then pleased it the apostles and elders, with the whole church.* James determined what ought to be done; and the whole assembly resolved how that should be done. *Chosen men of their own company.* Paul and Barnabas were to return. They could have witnessed to the church at Antioch what was done at the council at Jerusalem; but as it was possible that their testimony might be suspected, from the part they had already taken in this question at Antioch, it was necessary that a deputation from the council should accompany them. Accordingly, Judas and Silas are sent to corroborate by their oral testimony what was contained in the letters sent from the council.

23. *Send greeting unto the brethren . . . of the Gentiles.* There was no occasion to send such a letter to the brethren which were of the Jews, because that law which had been so long read in their synagogues taught them all those things, and therefore the epistle is sent exclusively to the Gentiles. The word *greeting* is in the original *chairein,* "to be well, to be safe"—a very usual form in Greek epistles.

24. *Certain which went out from us.* So the persons who produced these doubtful disputations at Antioch had gone out from the apostles at Jerusalem and were of that church; persons zealous for the law and yet, strange to tell, so conscientiously attached to the gospel that they risked their personal safety by professing it. *To whom we gave no such commandment.* As, therefore, they went out from that church, they should have taught nothing which was not owned and taught by it; much less should they have taught in opposition to it.

27. *Judas and Silas . . . shall . . . tell you the same things.* These were proofs that the testimony of Paul and Barnabas was true, and that the letter was not forged, as they could

witness the same things which the letter contained.

28. *For it seemed good to the Holy Ghost, and to us.* The whole council had met under His direction, had consulted under His influence; and gave forth their decree from His especial inspiration.

29. *Fare . . . well.* An old English form of expressing "good wishes" and "goodwill"—"Go well, go prosperously!" The Greek word *errhosthe*, here used, from "to strengthen, make strong," has nearly the same signification: "be strong, courageous, active, be in health, and be prosperous!"

31. *They rejoiced for the consolation.* It was not a matter of small moment to have a question on which such stress was laid decided by an apostolic council, over which the Spirit of God presided.

33. *They were let go.* That is, both had liberty to depart; but Silas chose to stay a little longer with the brethren.

34. *Notwithstanding it pleased Silas.* This whole verse is wanting in some MSS. It does not appear to have been originally in the text.

36. *Let us go . . . and visit our brethren in every city.* This heavenly man projected a journey to Cyprus, Perga, Iconium, Lystra, Derbe, Antioch in Pisidia; for in all these places he had preached and founded churches in the preceding year. He saw it was necessary to water the seed he had planted; for these were young converts, surrounded with impiety, opposition, and superstition, and had few advantages among themselves.

39. *The contention was so sharp between them.* For all this sentence there is only in the Greek text: "There was therefore a paroxysm," an incitement, a stirring up. But does this imply anger or ill will on either side? Certainly not. Here, these two apostles differed, and were strenuous, each in support of the part he had adopted. "Paul," as an ancient Greek commentator has it, "being influenced only with the love of righteousness; Barnabas being actuated by love to his relative." John Mark had been tried in trying circumstances, and he failed; Paul therefore would not trust him again. The affection of Barnabas led him to hope the best, and was therefore desirous to give him another trial. Barnabas would not give up; Paul would not agree. They therefore agreed to depart from each other, and take different parts of the work. Each had an attendant and companion at hand. So Barnabas took John Mark and sailed to Cyprus; Paul took Silas, and went into Syria. To all human appearance it was best that they separated, as the churches were more speedily visited, and the work of God more widely and more rapidly spread. And why is it that this is brought in as a proof of the sinful imperfection of these holy apostles? because those who thus treat the subject can never differ with another without feeling wrong tempers; and then, as destitute of good breeding as they are of humility, they attribute to others the angry, proud, and wrathful dispositions which they feel in themselves; and because they cannot be angry and sin not, they suppose that even apostles themselves cannot. Should any man say there was sin in this contention between Paul and Barnabas, I answer, there is no

evidence of this in the text. Should he say the word *paroxysm* denotes this, I answer, "It does not." And the verb is often used in a good sense. So Isocrates ad Demosth. cap. xx: "But thou wilt be the more *stirred up* to the love of good works." And such persons forget that this is the very form used by the apostle himself, Heb. x. 24: which these objectors would be highly displeased with me were I to translate, "Let us consider one another to an angry contention of love and good works." From these examples it appears that the word is used to signify "incitement" of any kind; it is taken to express a strong excitement to the love of God and man, and to the fruits by which such love can be best proved; and, in the case before us, there was certainly nothing contrary to this pure principle in either of those heavenly men.

40. *Being recommended . . . unto the grace of God.* Much stress has been laid upon this to show that Barnabas was in the wrong and Paul in the right, because "the brethren recommended Paul and Silas to the grace of God, but they did not recommend Barnabas and John Mark; this proves that the church condemned the conduct of Barnabas, but approved that of Paul." Now there is no proof that the church did not recommend Barnabas to the grace of God, as well as Paul; but as Luke had for the present dropped the story of Barnabas, and was now going on with that of Paul and Silas, he begins it at this point, viz., his being recommended by the brethren to the grace of God; and then goes on to tell of his progress in Syria, Derbe, and Lystra. See the next chapter. With this verse the following chapter should begin; and this is the division followed by the most correct copies of the Greek text.

41. *Confirming the churches.* This was the object of his journey. They were young converts, and had need of establishment; and there is no doubt but by showing them the decision made at the late council of Jerusalem their faith was greatly strengthened, their hope confirmed, and their love increased.

CHAPTER 16

Paul, coming to Derbe and Lystra, meets with Timothy, the son of a Jewess by a Greek father, whom he circumcises, and takes with him into his work, 1-3. As they pass through the different cities, they deliver the apostles' decrees to the churches; and they are established in the faith, and daily increase in numbers, 4-5. They travel through Phrygia, Galatia, Mysia, and to Troas, 6-8. Where Paul has a vision relative to his preaching in Macedonia, 9-10. Leaving Troas, he sails to Samothracia and Neapolis, and comes to Philippi in Macedonia, 11-12. Lydia, a seller of purple, receives the apostles' teaching; and she and her family are baptized, 13-15. A young woman with a spirit of divination is dispossessed by Paul, 16-18. Her masters, finding their gain by her soothsaying gone, make an attack upon Paul and Silas, drag them before the magistrates, who command them to be beaten, thrust into the closest prison, and their feet made fast in the stocks, 19-24. Paul and Silas singing praises at midnight, the prison doors are miraculously opened, and all the bonds of the prisoners loosed, 25-26. The keeper being alarmed, supposing that the prisoners were fled, is about to kill himself, but is prevented by Paul, 27-28. He inquires the way of salvation, believes, and he and his whole family are baptized, 29-34. The next morning the magistrates order the apostles to be dismissed, 35-36. Paul pleads his privilege as a Roman, and accuses the magistrates of injustice, who, being alarmed, come themselves to the prison, deliver them, and beg them to depart from the city, 37-39. They leave the prison, enter into the house of Lydia, comfort the brethren, and depart, 40.

1. *A certain disciple.* This Timothy was the same person to whom Paul wrote those two noble Epistles which are still extant. His moth-

er's name was Eunice, as we learn from 2 Tim. i. 5. What his father's name was we know not.

2. *Which was well reported of.* These words are spoken of Timothy, and not of his father. At this time Timothy must have been very young; for, several years after, when appointed to superintend the church at Crete, he appears to have been then so young that there was a danger of its operating to the prejudice of his ministry: 1 Tim. iv. 12, "Let no man despise thy youth." He had a very early religious eudcation from his godly mother, Eunice, and his not less pious grandmother, Lois; and from his religious instructions was well-prepared for the work to which God now called him.

3. *Took and circumcised him.* For this simple reason that the Jews would neither have heard him preach and would have any connection with him had he been otherwise. Besides, Paul himself could have had no access to the Jews in any place had they known that he associated with a person who was uncircumcised; they would have considered both to be unclean.

5. *And so were the churches established.* The disputations at Antioch, relative to circumcision, had no doubt spread far and wide among other churches and unhinged many. The decrees of the apostles came in good time and prevented further mischief. The people, saved from uncertainty, became established in the faith; and the Church had a daily accession of converted souls.

6. *Were forbidden of the Holy Ghost to preach the word in Asia.* The Asia mentioned here could not be Asia Minor in general, but it was what was called Proconsular Asia. The apostles were not suffered to visit these places at this time; but they afterwards went thither, and preached the gospel with success, for it was in this Proconsular Asia that the seven churches were situated.

7. *After they were come to Mysia.* They passed through Phrygia into Mysia, which lay between Bithynia on the north, Phrygia on the east, Aeolia on the south, and the Mediterranean on the west. *But the Spirit suffered them not.* God saw that that was not the most proper time to preach the Word at Bithynia, as He willed them to go immediately to Macedonia, the people there being ripe for the Word of Life. Instead of *the Spirit*, "the Spirit of Jesus," is the reading of some MSS. The reading is undoubtedly genuine, and should be immediately restored to the text.

8. *Came down to Troas.* The part of Phrygia Minor in which the celebrated city of Troy was formerly situated.

9. *A vision appeared to Paul in the night.* Whether this was in a dream or whether a representation made to the senses of the apostle, we cannot tell.

10. *We endeavoured to go into Macedonia.* This is the first place that the historian Luke refers to himself: *we endeavoured.* And from this it has been supposed that he joined the company of Paul, for the first time, at Troas. *Assuredly gathering.* Drawing an inference from the vision that had appeared. *That the Lord had called us for to preach.* That is, they inferred that they were called to *preach the gospel* in Macedonia, from what the vision had said, "Come over . . . and help us"; the *help*

meaning, "Preach to us the gospel." Instead of *the Lord,* meaning Jesus, several MSS. have "God."

11. *Loosing from Troas.* Setting sail from this place. *With a straight course to Samothracia.* This was an island of the Aegean Sea, contiguous to Thrace, and hence called Samothracia, or the Thracian Samos. It is about twenty miles in circumference. *And the next day to Neapolis.* There were many cities of this name, but this was a seaport town of Macedonia, a few miles eastward of Philippi. *Neapolis* signifies the "new city."

12. *And from thence to Philippi.* This was a town of Macedonia, on the confines of Thrace, situated on the side of a steep eminence. It took its name from Philip II, king of Macedon. *The chief city of that part of Macedonia.* This passage has greatly puzzled both critics and commentators. It is well-known that when Paulus Aemilius had conquered Macedonia he divided it into four parts and that he called the country that lay between the rivers Strymon and Nessus the first part and made Amphipolis its chief city or metropolis; Philippi, therefore, was not its chief city. But Bishop Pearce has, with great show of reason, argued that though Amphipolis was made the chief city of it by Paulus Aemilius, yet Philippi might have been the chief city in the days of Paul, which was 220 years after the division by P. Aemilius. Besides, as it was at this place that Augustus gained that victory which put him in possession of the whole Roman Empire, might not he have given to it that dignity which was before enjoyed by Amphipolis? *And a colony.* That is, a colony of Rome; for it appears that a colony was planted here by Julius Caesar, and afterwards enlarged by Augustus. The people, therefore, were considered as freemen of Rome and from this called themselves Romans, v. 21. The Jewish definition of *kolonia* is "a free city, which does not pay tribute."

13. *By a river side, where prayer was wont to be made.* "Where it was said there was a *proseucha.*" The *proseucha* was a "place of prayer," or a place used for worship, where there was no synagogue. It was a large building uncovered, with seats, as in an amphitheatre. Buildings of this sort the Jews had by the seaside and by the sides of rivers. *Spake unto the women.* Probably this was before the time of their public worship, and while they were waiting for the assembling of the people in general; and Paul improved the opportunity to speak concerning Christ and salvation to the women that resorted thither.

14. *Lydia, a seller of purple.* She probably had her name from the province of Lydia, in which the city of Thyatira was situated. The Lydian women have been celebrated for their beautiful purple manufactures. *Which worshipped God.* That is, she was a proselyte to the Jewish religion, as were probably all the women that resorted hither. *Whose heart the Lord opened.* As she was a sincere worshipper of God, she was prepared to receive the heavenly truths spoken by Paul and his companions; and as she was faithful to the grace she had received, so God gave her more grace, and gave her now a divine conviction that what was spoken by Paul was true. Therefore *she attended unto the things*—she believed them and

received them as the doctrines of God; and in this faith she was joined by her whole family, and in it they were all baptized.

16. *As we went to prayer.* "Into the *proseucha*"; see on v. 13. The article is added here by some MSS. This makes the place more emphatic, and seems to determine the above meaning to be right—not the act of prayer or praying to God, but the place in which these proselytes assembled for the purpose of praying, reading the law and the prophets, and suchlike exercises of devotion. *Possessed with a spirit of divination.* "Having a spirit of Python." Pytho was, according to fable, a huge serpent that had an oracle at Mount Parnassus, famous for predicting future events. Apollo slew this serpent, and hence he was called *Pythius*, and became celebrated as the foreteller of future events; and all those who either could or pretended to predict future events were influenced by the spirit of Apollo Pythius. *Brought her masters much gain by soothsaying.* "By divination," or what we call telling fortunes. Our term *soothsaying* coming from the Anglo-Saxon "truth"; and "to say," i.e., "truth saying." For as it was supposed among the heathen that such persons spoke by the inspiration of their god, consequently what they said must be true.

17. *These men are the servants.* It is astonishing how such a testimony could be given in such a case; every syllable of it true, and at the same time full, clear, and distinct. But mark the deep design and artifice of this evil spirit. He well knew that the Jewish law abhorred all magic, incantations, magical rites, and dealings with familiar spirits. He therefore bore what was in itself a true testimony to the apostles, that by it he might destroy their credit and ruin their usefulness.

18. *I command thee in the name of Jesus.* Jesus is the "Saviour"; Satan is Apollyon, the "destroyer." The sovereign Saviour says to the destroyer, Come out of her. *And he came out in the same hour.*

19. *When her masters saw.* It appears she was maintained by some men who received a certain pay from every person whose fortune she told. *The hope of their gains was gone.* "This hope"; viz., the spirit. So completely was this spirit cast out that the girl could divine no more, and yet she continued a heathen still, for we do not hear a word of her conversion. *Drew them into the marketplace.* This was the place of public resort, and by bringing them here they might hope to excite a general clamor against them; and probably those who are here called *the rulers* were civil magistrates, who kept offices in such public places for the preservation of the peace of the city.

20. *Brought them to the magistrates.* The "commanders of the army," who, very likely, as this city was a Roman colony, possessed the sovereign authority. The civil magistrates, therefore, having heard the case, as we shall soon find, in which it was pretended that the safety of the state was involved, would naturally refer the business to the decision of those who had the supreme command. *Exceedingly trouble our city.* They are destroying the public peace, and endangering the public safety.

21. *And teach customs.* Religious opinions and religious rites. *Which are not lawful for us*

to *receive.* The Romans were very jealous of their national worship. Cicero, *De Legibus*, lib. ii, c. 8, says: "No person shall have any separate *gods*, nor new *ones*; nor shall he privately worship any strange *gods*, unless they be publicly allowed." It was on such laws as these that the people of Philippi pleaded against the apostles. These men bring new gods, new worship, new rites; we are Romans, and the laws forbid us to worship any new or strange god, unless publicly allowed.

22. *The multitude rose up together.* There was a general outcry against them; and the magistrates tore off their clothes, and delivered them to the mob, commanding the lictors to beat them with rods. This was the Roman custom of treating criminals.

23. *Laid many stripes upon them.* The Jews never gave more than thirty-nine stripes to any criminal, but the Romans had no law relative to this. They gave as many as they chose; and the apostles had, undoubtedly, the fullest measure. And perhaps Paul refers to this where he says, 2 Cor. xi. 23, "In stripes beyond measure."

24. *The inner prison.* Probably what we would call the dungeon; the darkest and most secure cell. *Made their feet fast in the stocks.* The *stocks* is supposed to mean two large pieces of wood, pierced with holes like our stocks, and fitted to each other, that when the legs were in they could not be drawn out. The holes being pierced at different distances, the legs might be separated to a great extent, which must produce extreme pain.

25. *At midnight Paul and Silas . . . sang praises.* Though these holy men felt much and had reason to fear more, yet they were undismayed and even happy in their sufferings; they were so fully satisfied that they were right and had done their duty that there was no room for regret or self-reproach. At the same time, they had such consolations from God as could render any circumstances not only tolerable but delightful. They *prayed*, first, for grace to support them, and for pardon and salvation for their persecutors; and then, secondly, *sang praises unto God*, who had called them to such a state of salvation, and had accounted them worthy to suffer shame for the testimony of Jesus. And although they were in the inner prison, they sang so loudly and so heartily that the prisoners heard them.

26. *There was a great earthquake.* Thus God bore a miraculous testimony of approbation to His servants, and by the earthquake and loosing the bonds of the prisoners showed, in a symbolical way, the nature of that religion which they preached. While it shakes and terrifies the guilty, it proclaims deliverance to the captives and the opening of the prison doors to them that are bound, and sets at liberty them that are bruised. *Every one's bands were loosed.* And yet so eminently did God's providence conduct everything that not one of the prisoners made his escape, though the doors were open and his bolts off!

27. *The keeper of the prison . . . would have killed himself.* Every jailer was made responsible for his prisoner, under the same penalty to which the prisoner himself was exposed. The jailer, awaking and finding the prison doors open, taking it for granted that all the prisoners had made their escape and that he must lose

his life on the account, chose rather to die by his own hand than by that of others. For it was customary among the heathens when they found death inevitable to take away their own lives.

29. *He called for a light.* That he might see how things stood and whether the words of Paul were true; for on this his personal safety depended. *Came trembling.* Terrified by the earthquake and feeling the danger to which his own life was exposed.

31. *Believe on the Lord Jesus.* Receive the religion of Christ, which we preach, and let your household also receive it, and all of you shall be placed in the sure way to final salvation.

32. *And they spake unto him the word of the Lord.* Thus, by teaching him and all that were in his house the doctrine of the Lord, they plainly pointed out to them the way of salvation. And it appears that he and his whole family who were capable of receiving instructions embraced this doctrine and showed the sincerity of their faith by immediately receiving baptism.

33. *Washed their stripes.* "He washed from the stripes"; i.e., he washed the blood from the wounds.

34. *He set meat before them.* They were sufficiently exhausted, and needed refreshment; nor had the apostles any such inherent miraculous power as could prevent them from suffering through hunger, or enable them to heal their own wounds. As they were the instruments of bringing health to his soul, he became the instrument of health to their bodies.

35. *The magistrates sent the serjeants.* The original word means the *lictors,* persons who carried before the consul the *fasces,* which was a hatchet, round the handle of which was a bundle of rods tied. Why the magistrates should have sent an order to dismiss the apostles, whom they had so barbarously used the preceding evening, we cannot tell, unless we receive the reading of the Codex Bezae as genuine, viz., "And when it was day, the magistrates came together into the court, and remembering the earthquake that had happened, they were afraid, and they sent the serjeants." The Itala version of this same MS. has the same reading; so has also the margin of the later Syriac. If this MS. be correct, the cause of the dismissal of the apostles is at once evident. The earthquake had alarmed the magistrates; and taking it for granted that this was a token of the divine displeasure against them for their unprincipled conduct towards those good men, they wished to get as quietly rid of the business as they could, and therefore sent to dismiss the apostles. Whether this reading be genuine or not, it is likely that it gives the true cause of the magistrates' conduct.

37. *They have beaten us openly . . . being Romans.* Paul well knew the Roman laws, and on their violation by the magistrates he pleads. The Valerian law forbade any Roman citizen to be bound. The Porcian law forbade any to be beaten with rods. And the illegality of the proceedings of these magistrates was further evident in their condemning and punishing them unheard. This was a gross violation of a common maxim in the Roman law. Cicero: "Many who are accused of evil may be absolved, when the cause is heard; but unheard, no man can be condemned." *Let them come themselves and*

fetch us out. The apostles were determined that the magistrates should be humbled for their illegal proceedings, and that the people at large might see that they had been unjustly condemned and that the majesty of the Roman people was insulted by the treatment they had received.

38. *They feared, when they heard that they were Romans.* They feared because the Roman law was so constituted that an insult offered to a citizen was deemed an insult to the whole Roman people. There is a remarkable addition here, in both the Greek and the Latin of the Codex Bezae. It is as follows: "And when they were come with many of their friends to the prison, they besought them to go out, saying: We were ignorant of your circumstances, that ye were righteous men. And, leading them out, they besought them, saying, Depart from this city, lest they again make an insurrection against you, and clamour against you."

40. *Entered into the house of Lydia.* This was the place of their residence while at Philippi; see v. 15. *They comforted them, and departed.* The magistrates were sufficiently humbled and the public at large, hearing of this circumstance, must be satisfied of the innocency of the apostles.

CHAPTER 17

Paul and his company, passing through Amphipolis and Apollonia, come to Thessalonica, where they preach the gospel to the Jews, several of whom believe, 1-4. Others raise a mob and bring Jason, who had received the apostles, before the magistrates, who, having taken bail of him and his companions, dismiss them, 5-9. Paul and Silas are sent away by night unto Berea, where they preach to the Jews, who gladly receive the gospel, 10-12. Certain Jews from Thessalonica, hearing that the Bereans had received the gospel, come thither and raise up a persecution, 13. Paul is sent away by the brethren to Athens, where he preaches to the Jews, 14-17. He is encountered by the Epicureans and Stoics, who bring him to the Areopagus, and desire him to give a full explanation of his doctrine, 18-20. The character of the Athenians, 21. Paul preaches to them, and gives a general view of the essential principles of theology, 22-31. Some mock, some hesitate, and some believe, and among the latter, Dionysius and Damaris, 32-34.

1. *Passed through Amphipolis.* This city was the metropolis of the first division of Macedonia, as made by Paulus Aemilius; see the note on chap. xvi. 10. It was built by Cimon, the Athenian general who sent 10,000 Athenians thither as a colony. It stood in an island in the river Strymon and had its name of Amphipolis because included between the two grand branches of that river where they empty themselves into the sea, the river being on "both sides of the city." *Apollonia.* This was another city of Macedonia, between Amphipolis and Thessalonica. It does not appear that Paul stopped at any of these cities, and they are only mentioned by the historian as places through which the apostles passed on their way to Thessalonica. It is very likely that in these cities there were no Jews, and that might have been the reason why the apostles did not preach the gospel there, for we find them almost constantly beginning with the Jews; and the Hellenist Jews living among the Gentiles became the medium through which the gospel of Christ was conveyed to the heathen world. *Thessalonica.* This was a celebrated city of Macedonia, situated on what was called the Thermaic Gulf. According to Stephanus Byznatinus, it was embellished and enlarged by Philip, king of Macedon, who called it *Thessalonica,* "the victory of Thessalia," on ac-

count of the victory he obtained there over the Thessalians; but prior to this it was called Thermae. But Strabo, Tzetzes, and Zonaras say that it was called *Thessalonica* from Thessalonica, wife of Cassander and daughter of Philip.

2. *As his manner was.* He constantly offered salvation first to the Jews, and for this purpose attended their Sabbath days' meetings at their synagogues.

3. *Opening and alleging.* "Proving by citations." His method seems to have been this: (1) He collected the scriptures that spoke of the Messiah. (2) He applied these to Jesus Christ, showing that in Him all these scriptures were fulfilled, and that He was the Saviour of whom they were in expectation. He showed also that the *Christ*, or Messiah, *must needs have suffered*—that this was predicted, and was an essential mark of the true Messiah. By proving this point he corrected their false notion of a triumphant Messiah and thus removed the scandal of the Cross.

4. *The devout Greeks.* That is, Gentiles who were proselytes to the Jewish religion, so far as to renounce idolatry and live a moral life, but probably had not received circumcision.

5. *Certain lewd fellows of the baser sort.* This is not a very intelligible translation. These were probably a low kind of lawyers, or *attorneys* without principle, who gave advice for a trifle and fomented disputes and litigations among the people. They were such as always attended forensic litigations, waiting for a job and willing to defend any side of a question for money. They were wicked men of the forensic tribe. *Gathered a company, and set all the city on an uproar.* And after having made this sedition and disturbance, charged the whole on the peaceable and innocent apostles! This is precisely the same way that persecution against the truth and followers of Christ is still carried on. *Assaulted the house of Jason.* This was the place where the apostles lodged, and therefore his goods were clear spoil and his person fair game.

7. *These all do contrary to the decrees of Caesar.* Persecutors always strive to affect the lives of the objects of their hatred by accusing them of sedition or plots against the state. *That there is another king, one Jesus.* How malevolent was this saying! The apostles proclaimed Jesus as King—that is true; but never once insinuated that His kingdom was of this world.

8. *And they troubled the people and the rulers.* It is evident that there was no disposition in either the people or the rulers to persecute the apostles. But these wicked Jews, by means of the unprincipled, wicked lawyers, those "lewd fellows of the baser sort," threw the subject into the form of law, making it a state question, in which form the rulers were obliged to notice it. But they showed their unwillingness to proceed in a matter which they saw proceeded from malice by letting Jason and his companions go off on bail.

9. *Taken security.* "Having taken what was sufficient." Sufficient for the present, to prove that the apostles were upright, peaceable, and loyal men; and that Jason and his friends were the like, and would be at any time forthcoming to answer for their conduct.

10. *Sent away Paul and Silas by night.* Fearing some farther machinations of the Jews and their associates. *Berea.* This was another city of Macedonia, on the same gulf with Thessalonica, and not far from Pella, the birthplace of Alexander the Great.

11. *These were more noble than those in Thessalonica.* "Were of a better race, extraction, or birth" than those at Thessalonica; but the word refers more to their conduct as a proof of their better disposition than to their birth or any peculiar lineal nobility. It was a maxim among the Jews that "none was of a noble spirit who did not employ himself in the study of the law." It appears that the Bereans were a better educated and more polished people than those at Thessalonica.

12. *Therefore many of them believed.* From the manner in which they heard, received, and examined the Word preached to them, it was not likely they could be deceived. And as it was the truth that was proclaimed to them, it is no wonder that they apprehended, believed, and embraced it. *Of honourable women which were Greeks.* Probably mere heathens are meant; and these were some of the chief families in the place. Thus we find that the preaching of Paul at Berea was made the instrument of converting both Jews and Gentiles.

14. *To go as it were to the sea.* This passage is generally understood to mean that the disciples took Paul towards the sea, as if he had intended to embark and return to Troas, but with the real design to go to Athens. By taking a vessel at that part of the sea nearest to Berea they might have coasted it to Athens, which was quite a possible case; and as we do not hear of his stopping at any place on his journey to preach, it is very probable that he went by sea to this city. *Silas and Timotheus abode there still.* The persecution, it seems, was directed principally against Paul. Silas and Timotheus, holy men, were left behind to water the seed which Paul had planted.

15. *Brought him unto Athens.* This was one of the most celebrated cities in the world, whether we consider its antiquity, its learning, its political consequence, or the valor of its inhabitants. About thirteen or fourteen hundred years before Christ it was called Athens, from *Athene*, a name of Minerva, to whom it was dedicated and who was always considered the protectress of the city. The whole city at first was built upon a hill or rock, in the midst of a spacious plain; but in process of time the whole plain was covered with buildings, which were called the lower city, while the ancient was called Acropolis, or the upper city. In its most flourishing state this city was not less than twenty-two Roman miles in circumference. The buildings of Athens were the most superb and best executed in the world. The greatest men that ever lived, scholars, lawyers, statesmen, and warriors, were Athenians. Its institutions, laws, and literature were its own unrivalled boast and the envy of the world. The city still exists; the Acropolis in a state of comparative repair.

16. *He saw the city wholly given to idolatry.* "Full of idols." Bishop Pearce produces a most apposite quotation from Pausanias, which confirms the observation: "There was no place where so many idols were to be seen." Petronius, who was contemporary with Paul, in his

Satyr, chap. xvii, makes Quartilla say of Athens: "Our region is so *full of deities* that you may more frequently meet with a *god* than a *man*."

17. *Disputed he in the synagogue with the Jews*, proving that Jesus was the Messiah; *and with the devout persons,* probably heathens, proselyted to the Jewish religion. *And in the market;* I suppose the *agora* here means some such place as our exchange, where people of business usually met and where the philosophers conversed and reasoned.

18. *Certain philosophers of the Epicureans.* These were the followers of Epicurus, who acknowledged no gods except in name, and absolutely denied that they exercised any government over the world or its inhabitants; and that the chief good consisted in the gratification of the appetites of sense. *And of the Stoicks.* These did not deny the existence of the gods, but they held that all human affairs were governed by fate. They did not believe that any good was received from the hands of their gods; and considered, as Seneca asserts, that any good and wise man was equal to Jupiter himself. Both these sects agreed in denying the resurrection of the body, and the former did not believe in the immortality of the soul. Epicurus, the founder of the Epicurean sect, was born at Athens, 341 B.C. Zeno, the founder of the Stoic sect, was born in the isle of Cyprus about thirty years before Christ. His disciples were called Stoics from the *Stoa*, a famous portico at Athens where they studied. *What will this babbler say?* The word which we translate *babbler* signifies literally "a collector of seeds," and is the "name of a small bird that lives by picking up seeds on the road." The epithet became applied to persons who collected the sayings of others, without order or method, and detailed them among their companions in the same way. *A setter forth of strange gods.* "Of strange or foreign demons." That this was strictly forbidden, at both Rome and Athens, see on chap. xvi. 21. There was a difference in the heathen theology between *god* and *demon.* The *theoi* were such as were gods by nature; the *daimonia* were men who were deified. This distinction seems to be in the mind of these philosophers when they said that the apostles seemed to be setters forth of "strange demons" because they preached unto them Jesus, whom they showed to be a man, suffering and dying, but afterwards raised to the throne of God. This would appear to them tantamount with the deification of heroes who had been thus honored for their especial services to mankind.

19. *They took him, and brought him unto Areopagus.* The Areopagus was a hill not far from the Acropolis, already described, where the supreme court of justice was held—one of the most sacred and reputable courts that had ever existed in the Gentile world. It had its name, *Areopagus,* or the "Hill of Mars," or "Ares," from the circumstance, according to poetic fiction, of Mars being tried there by a court of twelve gods for the murder of Halirrhothius, son of Neptune.

20. *Thou bringest . . . strange things to our ears.* The doctrine of the apostles was different from any they had ever heard. It was wholly spiritual and divine; thus it was *strange.* It was contrary to their customs and manners, and thus it was strange also. As it spoke much of the

exaltation and glory of Jesus Christ, they supposed Paul to be a "setter forth of strange gods"; and therefore, on the authority of the laws which forbade the introduction of any new deities or modes of worship, he was called before the Areopagus.

21. *All the Athenians and strangers which were there.* As Athens was renowned for its wisdom and learning, it became a place of public resort for philosophers and students from different parts of the then civilized world. The flux of students was in consequence great; these, having much leisure time, would necessarily be curious to know what was passing in the world and would frequently assemble together in places of public resort to meet with strangers just come to the city, and either, as Luke says, to tell or to hear some new thing.

22. *Paul stood in the midst of Mars' hill.* That is, in the midst of the judges who sat in the Areopagus. *Ye are too superstitious.* I perceive that in all respects you are greatly addicted to religious practices; and as a religious people you will candidly hear what I have to say in behalf of that worship which I practice and recommend.

23. *Beheld your devotions.* "The objects of your worship"; the different images of their gods which they held in religious veneration, sacrificial instruments, altars, etc. *To the unknown God.* That there was an altar at Athens thus inscribed we cannot doubt after such a testimony, though Jerome questions it in part; for he says Paul found the inscription in the plural number, but because he would not appear to acknowledge a plurality of gods, he quoted it in the singular. This is a most foolish saying. Had Paul done so, how much would such a begging of the question have prejudiced his defense in the minds of his intelligent judges! Pausanias says that at Athens there are "altars of gods which are called, The unknown ones." Now though in these last passages both gods and altars are spoken of in the plural number, yet it is reasonable to suppose that on each or upon some one of them the inscription "To the unknown god" was actually found. *Whom therefore ye ignorantly worship.* There is here a fine paronomasia or play on the words. The apostle tells them that (on their system) they were a very religious people—that they had an altar inscribed, *Agnosto theo,* "To the unknown God." Him therefore, says he, whom *agnoountes,* "ye unknowingly" worship, I proclaim to you—assuming it as a truth that, as the true God was *not known* by them and there was an altar dedicated "to the unkown God," this God was that God whose nature and operations he now proceeded to declare. By this fine turn he eluded the force of that law which made it a capital offense to introduce any new god into the state, and of the breach of which he was charged, v. 18; and thus he showed that he was bringing neither new god nor new worship among them, but only explaining the worship of one already acknowledged by the state, though not as yet known.

24. *God that made the world.* Paul assumes that this God could not be confined within temples made with hands, as He was the Lord or Governor of heaven and earth. That by fair consequence the gods whom they worshipped,

which were shut up in their temples, could not be this God; and they must be less than the places in which they were contained. This was a strong, decisive stroke against the whole system of the Grecian idolatry.

25. *Neither is worshipped with men's hands.* This is an indirect stroke against making of images and offering of sacrifices. He is not worshipped with human hands, as if He needed anything. Nor has He required victims for His support; for it is impossible that He should need anything who himself gives being, form, and life to all creatures. *Giveth . . . life, and breath, and all things.* These words are elegantly introduced by Paul. God gives *life*, because He is the Fountain of it. He gives *breath*, the faculty of breathing or respiration, by which this life is preserved. But as much more is necessary to keep the animal machine in a state of repair, God gives all the other things which are requisite for this great and important purpose, that the end for which life was given may be fully answered.

26. *Hath made of one blood.* In some MSS. the word *blood* is omitted. *He hath made of one* (meaning Adam) *all nations of men . . . and hath determined the times before appointed.* Instead of *the times before appointed*, several MSS. read "the appointed times"; that is, the times appointed by His providence, on which the several families should go to those countries where His wisdom designed they should dwell. *And the bounds of their habitation.* Every family being appointed to a particular place, that their posterity might possess it for the purposes for which infinite wisdom and goodness gave them their being and the place of their abode. Every nation had its lot thus appointed by God, as truly as the Israelites had the land of Canaan.

27. *That they should seek the Lord.* This is a conclusion drawn from the preceding statement. God, who is infinitely great and self-sufficient, has manifested himself as the Maker of the world, the Creator, Preserver, and Governor of men. He has assigned them their portion and dispensed to them their habitations and the various blessings of His providence, to the end that they should seek Him in all His works. *Feel after him.* That they might grope after Him, as a person does his way who is blind or blindfolded. The Gentiles, who had not a revelation, must grope after God as the principle of spiritual life, that they might find Him to be a Spirit and the Source of all intellectual happiness; and the apostle seems to state that none need despair of finding this fountain of goodness, because He is *not far from every one of us.*

28. *For in him we live, and move, and have our being.* He is the very Source of our existence. The principle of life comes from Him; the principle of motion also comes from Him—one of the most difficult things in nature to be properly apprehended, and a strong proof of the continual presence and energy of the Deity. *And have our being.* "And we are"; we live in Him, move in Him, and are in Him. Without Him we not only can do nothing, but without Him we are nothing. "We are," i.e., we continue to be, because of His continued, present, all-pervading, and supporting energy. *As certain also of your own poets.* Probably he means not only Aratus, in whose poem, entitled *Phae-*

nomena, the words quoted by Paul are to be found literatim, but also Cleanthus, in whose "Hymn to Jupiter" the same words occur. But the sentiment is found in several others, being very common among the more enlightened philosophers. By saying *your own poets* he does not mean poets born at Athens, but merely Grecian poets, Aratus and Cleanthus being chief. Aratus was a Cilician, one of Paul's own countrymen, and with his writings Paul was undoubtedly well-acquainted, though he had flourished about three hundred years before that time.

29. *Forasmuch then as we are the offspring of God.* This inference of the apostle was very strong and conclusive, and his argument runs thus: "If we are the offspring of God, He cannot be like those images of gold, silver, and stone which are formed by the art and device of man, for the parent must resemble his offspring. Seeing therefore that we are living and intelligent beings, He from whom we have derived that being must be living and intelligent. It is necessary also that the object of religious worship should be much more excellent than the worshipper; but a man is, by innumerable degrees, more excellent than an image made out of gold, silver, or stone. And yet it would be impious to worship a man; how much more so to worship these images as gods!" Every man in the Areopagus must have felt the power of this conclusion; and, taking it for granted that they had felt it, he proceeds.

30. *The times of this ignorance God winked at.* He who has an indisputable right to demand the worship of all His creatures has mercifully overlooked those acts of idolatry which have disgraced the world and debased man. But *now*, as He has condescended to give a revelation of himself, He *commands*, as the Sovereign, *all men every where*, over every part of His dominions, *to repent*, "to change their views"; *because he hath appointed a day, in the which he will judge the world in righteousness.* And as justice will then be done, no sinner, no persevering idolater, shall escape punishment. The word which we translate *wink at* signifies simply "to look over," and seems to be here used in the sense of passing by, not particularly noticing it. So God overlooked, or passed by, the times of heathenish ignorance.

31. *He hath appointed a day.* He has fixed the time in which He will judge the world, though He has not revealed this time to man. *By that man whom he hath ordained.* He has also appointed the Judge by whom the inhabitants of the earth are to be tried. *Whereof he hath given assurance.* "Having given to all this indubitable proof" that Jesus Christ shall judge the world, by raising Him from the dead. The sense of the argument is this: "Jesus Christ, whom we preach as the Saviour of men, has repeatedly told His followers that He would judge the world, and has described to us at large the whole of the proceedings of that awful time, Matt. xxv. 31, etc.; John v. 25. Though He was put to death by the Jews, and thus He became a Victim for sin, yet God raised Him from the dead. By raising Him from the dead, God has set His seal to the doctrines He has taught. One of these doctrines is that He shall *judge the world.* His resurrection, established by the most incontrovertible evidence, is there-

fore a proof, an incontestable proof, that He shall judge the world according to His own declaration."

32. *When they heard of the resurrection.* Paul undoubtedly had not finished his discourse; it is likely that he was about to proclaim salvation through Christ crucified. But on hearing of the resurrection of the body, the assembly instantly broke up—the Epicureans mocking, "began to laugh," and the Stoics saying they would take another opportunity to hear him on that subject.

33. *So Paul departed from among them.* He could not be convicted of having done anything contrary to the law, and when the assembly broke up he was permitted to go about his own business.

34. *Certain men clave unto him.* Became affectionately united to him *and believed* the doctrines he had preached. *Dionysius the Areopagite.* There can be no doubt that this man was one of the judges of this great court, but whether the president or otherwise we cannot tell. Humanly speaking his conversion must have been an acquisition of considerable importance to the Christian religion; for no person was a judge in the Areopagus who had not borne the office of *archon*, or chief governor of the city, and none bore the office of judge in this court who was not of the highest reputation among the people for his intelligence and exemplary conduct.

CHAPTER 18

Paul, leaving Athens, comes to Corinth, meets with Aquila and Priscilla, and labors with them at tent making, 1-3. He preaches, and proves that Jesus was the Christ, 4-5. The Jews oppose and blaspheme, and he purposes to go to the Gentiles, 6. Justus, Crispus, and several of the Corinthians believe, 7-8. Paul has a vision, by which he is greatly comforted, 9-10. He continues there a year and six months, 11. Gallio being deputy of Achaia, the Jews make insurrection against Paul, and bring him before the deputy, who dismisses the cause; whereupon the Jews commit a variety of outrages, 12-17. Paul sails to Syria, and from thence to Ephesus, where he preaches, 18-20. He leaves Ephesus—goes to Caesarea, visits Antioch, Galatia, and Phrygia, 21-23. Account of Apollos and his preaching, 24-28.

1. *Paul departed from Athens.* How long he stayed here we cannot tell; it is probable it could not be less than three months. But finding that the gospel made little progress among the Athenians, he resolved to go to Corinth. Corinth was situated on the isthmus that connects Peloponnesus to Attica, and was the capital of all Achaia. It was most advantageously situated for trade; for by its two ports, the Lecheum and Cenchreae, it commanded the commerce of both the Ionian and the Aegean Sea. It was destroyed by the Romans under Mummius about one hundred and forty-six years before Christ, in their wars with Attica; but was rebuilt by Julius Caesar, and became one of the most considerable cities of Greece. It is about forty-six miles west of Athens.

2. *Claudius had commanded all Jews to depart from Rome.* This edict of the Roman emperor is not mentioned by Josephus; but it is probably the same to which Suetonius refers in his life of Claudius, where he says, "He expelled the Jews from Rome, as they were making continual insurrections, under their leader Chrestus." Who this Chrestus was we cannot tell; probably Suetonius meant "Christ," but this I confess does not appear to me likely.

There might have been a Jew of the name of Chrestus who had made some disturbances, and in consequence Claudius thought proper to banish all Jews from the city. But how could he intend Christ, who was never at Rome?

3. *He abode with them, and wrought.* It was a custom among the Jews, even of such as had a better education than ordinary, which was Paul's case, to learn a trade, that wherever they were they might provide for themselves in case of necessity. And though Paul in some cases lived on the bounty of his converts, yet he chose not to do so at Ephesus, chap. xx. 34; nor at Corinth or other places, 1 Cor. iv. 12; 2 Cor. ix. 8-9; 2 Thess. iii. 8; and this Paul did for a reason which he gives in 2 Cor. xi. 9-12.

4. *He reasoned in the synagogue every sabbath.* Discoursed at large concerning Jesus as the Messiah, proving this point from their own Scriptures, collated with the facts of our Lord's life. *And persuaded the Jews and the Greeks.* Many, both Jews and proselytes, were convinced of the truth of his doctrine. Among his converts was Epenetus, the firstfruit of his labor in Achaia, Rom. xvi. 5; and the family of Stephanas was the next; and then Crispus and Caius, or Gaius—all of whom the apostle himself baptized, 1 Cor. i. 14-16.

5. *When Silas and Timotheus were come.* We have seen, chap. xvii. 13, that when Paul was obliged to leave Berea because of the persecution raised up against him in that place, he left Silas and Timotheus behind, to whom he afterwards sent word to rejoin him at Athens with all speed. It appears, from 1 Thess. iii. 10, that on Timothy's coming to Athens, Paul immediately sent him, and probably Silas with him, to comfort and establish the church at Thessalonica. How long they labored here is uncertain, but they did not rejoin him till some time after he came to Corinth. It appears that he was greatly rejoiced at the account which Timothy brought of the church at Thessalonica; and it must have been immediately after this that he wrote his First Epistle to that church, which is probably the first, in order of time, of all his Epistles. *Paul was pressed in the spirit.* Or he was "constrained by the Spirit" of God, in an extraordinary manner, to testify *to the Jews that Jesus was Christ.* Instead of *in the spirit,* "in the word" is the reading of several MSS. Bishop Pearce thus paraphrases the verse: "And when Silas and Timotheus were come from Macedonia, Paul set himself, together with them, wholly *to the word;* i.e., he was fully employed, now that he had their assistance, in preaching the gospel, called *the word* in chap. iv. 6; xvi. 6, 32; and xvii. 11." This appears to be the true sense of the word, and that *to logo* is the genuine reading there can be no doubt. From this time we hear no more of Silas; probably he died in Macedonia.

6. *When they opposed.* Systematically opposing, putting themselves "in warlike order" against him; so the word implies. *He shook his raiment.* This was an action similar to that of shaking the dust off the feet; see on Matt. x. 14. *Your blood be upon your own heads.* That is, you alone are the cause of the destruction that is coming upon yourselves and upon your country. *I am clean.* "I am pure or innocent" of your death and ruin. I have proposed to you the gospel of Jesus Christ, the only means by

which you can be saved, and you have utterly rejected it. I shall labor no more with you, and from henceforth shall confine my labors to the Gentiles. Paul must refer to the Jews and Gentiles of Corinth particularly, for he preached to the Jews occasionally in other places (see chap. xix. 8-9), and several were brought to the knowledge of the truth.

7. *And he departed thence.* From his former lodging, or that quarter of the city where he had dwelt before with Aquila and Priscilla; and went to lodge with *Justus,* apparently a proselyte. This person is called Titus, and Titus Justus, in several MSS. and versions.

8. *Crispus, the chief ruler of the synagogue.* This person held an office of considerable consequence, and therefore his conversion to Christianity must have been very galling to the Jews. It belonged to the chief or ruler of the synagogue to preside in all the assemblies, interpret the law, decide concerning things lawful and unlawful, punish the refractory, excommunicate the rebellious, solemnize marriages, and issue divorces. It is likely that, on the conversion of Crispus, Sosthenes was chosen to succeed him. *Many of the Corinthians.* Those to whom the sacred historian refers were probably Gentiles and were the fruits of the apostle's labors after he had ceased to preach among the Jews.

9. *Then spake the Lord to Paul in the night by a vision.* It is likely that Paul was at this time much discouraged by the violent opposition of the Jews, and probably was in danger of his life (see v. 10), and might have been entertaining serious thoughts of ceasing to preach, or leaving Corinth. To prevent this, and comfort him, God was pleased to give him this vision. *Be not afraid.* That this comfort and assurance were necessary himself shows us in his First Epistle to these Corinthians, chap. ii. 3: "I was with you in weakness, and in fear, and in much trembling."

10. *No man shall set on thee.* No man shall be permitted to "lay violent hands" upon you. It is very likely that the Jews had conspired his death, and his preservation was an act of the especial interposition of Divine Providence. *I have much people in this city.* "In this very city." There are many here who have not resisted My Spirit, and consequently are now under its teachings and are ready to embrace My gospel as soon as you shall declare it unto them.

11. *He continued there a year and six months.* He was now confident that he was under the especial protection of God and therefore continued *teaching the word,* "the doctrine" *of God.* It is very likely that it was during his stay here that he wrote his First Epistle to the Thessalonians, and the Second not long after.

12. *When Gallio was the deputy of Achaia.* The Romans comprehended under the name of Achaia all that part of Greece which lay between Thessaly and the southernmost coasts of Peloponnesus. Pausanias, in *Attic.* vii. 16, says that the Romans were accustomed to send a governor into that country, and that they called him the "governor of Achaia," not of Greece; because the Achaeans, when they subdued Greece, were the leaders in all the Grecian affairs. *Gallio.* This proconsul was eldest brother to the celebrated Seneca, the stoic phi-

losopher, preceptor of Nero, and who is so well-known among the learned by his works. Gallio and Annaeus Mela, his brother, shared in the disgrace of their brother Seneca; and by this tyrant, Nero, whose early years were so promising, the three brothers were put to death. It was to this *Gallio* that Seneca dedicates his book *De Ira.* Seneca describes him as a man of the most amiable mind and manners. *And brought him to the judgment seat.* They had no power to punish any person in the Roman provinces, and therefore were obliged to bring their complaint before the Roman governor. "The powers that be are ordained of God." Had the Jews possessed the power here, Paul had been put to death!

13. *Persuadeth men to worship God contrary to the law.* This accusation was very insidious. The Jews had permission from the Romans to worship their own God in their own way; this the laws allowed. The Roman worship was also established by the law. The Jews probably intended to accuse Paul of acting contrary to both laws. "He is not a Jew, for he does not admit of circumcision; he is not a Gentile, for he preaches against the worship of the gods. He is setting up a worship of his own, in opposition to all laws, and persuading many people to join with him. He is therefore a most dangerous man, and should be put to death."

14. *Paul was now about to open his mouth.* He was about to enter on his defense; but Gallio, perceiving that the prosecution was through envy and malice, would not put Paul to any further trouble, but determined the matter as follows. *If it were a matter of wrong.* Of "injustice"; anything contrary to the rights of the subject. *Or wicked lewdness.* "Destructive mischief." *Reason would that I should bear with you.* "According to reason, or the merit of the case, I should patiently hear you."

15. *But if it be a question of words.* Concerning "doctrine" *and names*—whether the person called Jesus be the Person you call the Messiah. *And of your law*—any particular nicety concerning that law which is peculiar to yourselves. *Look ye to it*—settle the business among yourselves; the Roman government does not meddle with such matters; and I will not take upon me to decide in a case that does not concern my office.

16. *And he drave them from the judgment seat.* He saw that their accusation was both frivolous and vexatious, and he ordered them to depart, and the assembly to disperse. The word which we translate *he drave* does not signify here any act of violence on the part of Gallio or the Roman officers, but simply an authoritative dismission.

17. *Then all the Greeks took Sosthenes.* As this man is termed the chief ruler of the synagogue, it is probable that he had lately succeeded Crispus in that office (see v. 8); and that he was known either to have embraced Christianity or to have favored the cause of Paul. He is supposed to be the same person whom Paul associates with himself in the First Epistle to the Corinthians, chap. i. 1. But why should the Greeks beat Sosthenes? I have in the above note proceeded on the supposition that this outrage was committed by the Jews; and my reason for it is this: *The Greeks is*

omitted by several MSS., and it is much more likely that the Jews beat one of their own rulers through envy at his conversion than that the Greeks should do so. *And Gallio cared for none of those things.* "And Gallio did not concern himself," did not intermeddle with any of these things. It is not very likely, however, that Gallio saw this outrage; for, though it was before the judgment seat, it probably did not take place till Gallio had left the court; and though he might be told of it, he left the matter to the lictors and would not interfere. The conduct of Gallio has been, in this case, greatly censured, and I think with manifest injustice. In the business brought before his tribunal, no man could have followed a more prudent or equitable course. His whole conduct showed that it was his opinion that the civil magistrate had nothing to do with religious opinions or the concerns of conscience, in matters where the safety of the state was not implicated. He therefore refused to make the subject a matter of legal discussion.

18. *And Paul . . . tarried there yet a good while.* The persecuting Jews plainly saw from the manner in which the proconsul had conducted this business that they could have no hope of raising a state persecution against the apostles, and the laws provided so amply for the personal safety of every Roman citizen that they were afraid to proceed any further in their violence. It could not be unknown that Paul was possessed of the right of Roman citizenship, and therefore his person was sacred as long as he did nothing contrary to the laws. *Having shorn his head in Cenchrea.* But who was it that had shorn his head? Paul or Aquila? Some think the latter, who had bound himself by the Nazarite vow, probably before he became a Christian; and being under that vow, his conscience would not permit him to disregard it. There is nothing in the text that absolutely obliges us to understand this action as belonging to Paul. It seems to have been the act of Aquila alone; and therefore both Paul and Priscilla are mentioned before Aquila; and it is natural to refer the vow to the latter. Yet there are certainly some weighty reasons why the vow should be referred to Paul, and not to Aquila; I cannot help leaning to the latter opinion. *Cenchrea.* This was a port on the east side of the isthmus of Corinth, opposite to the Lecheum, which was the other port on the west. And it is likely that it was at Cenchrea that Paul took shipping for Syria, as it would be more convenient for him and a shorter passage to embark at Cenchrea in order to go by the Aegean Sea to Syria than to embark at the Lecheum and sail down into the Mediterranean.

19. *He came to Ephesus.* Where it appears he spent but one Sabbath. It is supposed that Paul left Aquila and Priscilla at this place, and that he went on alone to Jerusalem, for it is certain they were at Ephesus when Apollos arrived there. See vv. 24 and 26. Ephesus was, at the time in which Paul visited it, one of the most flourishing cities of Asia Minor. It abounded with the most eminent orators and philosophers in the world, and was adorned with the most splendid buildings. Here was that famous temple of Diana, reputed one of the seven wonders of the world. This city is now under the dominion of the Turks and is in a state of almost entire ruin.

21. *I must . . . keep this feast.* Most likely the Passover, at which he wished to attend for the purpose of seeing many of his friends and having the most favorable opportunity to preach the gospel to thousands who would attend at Jerusalem on that occasion. The whole of this clause, *I must by all means keep this feast that cometh in Jerusalem,* is wanting in some MSS. Without this clause the verse will read thus: "But he bade them farewell, saying, I will return again unto you, if God will." And this he did before the expiration of that same year, chap. xix. 1, and spent three years with them, chap. xx. 31, extending and establishing the church at that place.

22. *Landed at Caesarea.* This must have been Caesarea in Palestine. *Gone up.* To Jerusalem, though the name is not mentioned; but this is a common form of speech in the Evangelists, Jerusalem being always meant when this expression was used. For the word "to go up" is often used absolutely to signify "to go to Jerusalem"; e.g., "Go ye up unto this feast: I go not up yet," John vii. 8; "But when his brethren were gone up, then went he also up unto the feast," v. 10; "There were certain Greeks . . . that came up to worship," John xii. 20. *Saluted the church.* That is, the church at Jerusalem, called emphatically *The church* because it was the first church—the mother or apostolic church; and from it all other Christian churches proceeded. *Went down to Antioch.* That is, Antioch in Syria, as the word is generally to be understood when without addition; so Caesarea is always to be understood Caesarea in Palestine when without the addition of "Philippi."

23. *In order. Kathexes,* a word peculiar to Luke. See his Gospel, chap. i. 1; viii. 1; and his history of the Acts, chap. iii. 24; xi. 4, and the place above—the only places where this word occurs in the New Testament. It properly signifies "in order, distinctly, particularly." If Paul went up to Jerusalem at this time, which we are left to infer, for Luke has not expressed it (v. 22), it was his fourth journey thither.

24. *A certain Jew named Apollos.* It is strange that we should find a Jew, not only with a Roman name, as *Aquila,* an "eagle," but with the name of one of the false gods, as *Apollos. Born at Alexandria.* This was a celebrated city of Egypt built by Alexander the Great, from whom it took its name. It was seated on the Mediterranean Sea. It was in this city that Ptolemy Soter founded the famous academy called the Museum, in which a society of learned men devoted themselves to philosophical studies. Some of the most celebrated schools of antiquity flourished here; and here was the Tower of Pharos, esteemed one of the seven wonders of the world. *An eloquent man.* Having strong rhetorical powers; highly cultivated, no doubt, in the Alexandrian schools. *Mighty in the scriptures.* Thoroughly acquainted with the law and prophets, and well skilled in the Jewish method of interpreting them.

25. *This man was instructed in the way of the Lord.* He was "catechized," initiated, in the way, the "doctrine," of Jesus as the Christ. *Being fervent in the spirit.* Being full of zeal to propagate the truth of God, he taught diligently, "accurately" (so the word should be translated), the things of Christ as far as he could know them through the ministry of John

the Baptist; for it appears he knew nothing more of Christ than what John preached.

26. *They took him unto them.* This "eloquent man, and mighty in the scriptures," who was even a public teacher, was not ashamed to be indebted to the instructions of a Christian woman, in matters that concerned not only his own salvation but also the work of the ministry in which he was engaged.

27. *When he was disposed to pass into Achaia.* There is a very long and important addition here in the Codex Bezae, of which the following is a translation: "But certain Corinthians, who sojourned at Ephesus, and heard him, entreated him to pass over with them to their country. Then, when he had given his consent, the Ephesians wrote to the disciples at Corinth, that they should receive this man. Who, when he was come . . ." *Which had believed through grace.* These words may refer either to Apollo or to the people at Corinth. It was through grace that they had believed, and it was through grace that Apollo was enabled to help them much.

28. *He mightily convinced the Jews.* "He vehemently confuted" the Jews; *and that publickly,* not in private conferences, but in his public preaching; *shewing by the scriptures* of the Old Testament, which the Jews received as divinely inspired, *that Jesus,* who had lately appeared among them and whom they had crucified, *was the Christ,* the promised Messiah, and that there was salvation in none other; and that they must receive Him as the Messiah in order to escape the wrath to come.

CHAPTER 19

Paul, coming to Ephesus, finds certain disciples who had not received the gift of the Holy Ghost, knowing only the baptism of John, but who receive it through the imposition of his hands, 1-7. He preaches for three months in the synagogues, 8. Many being hardened, he leaves the synagogues and teaches daily in the school of Tyrannus for two years, 9-10. He works many miracles, 11-12. Account of the vagabond exorcist Jews, and the seven sons of Sceva, 13-17. Many are converted, and burn their magical books, 18-20. Paul purposes to pass through Macedonia and Achaia, to go to Jerusalem, and afterwards to Rome; but having sent Timotheus and Erastus to Macedonia, continues a little longer in Asia, 21-22. Demetrius, a silversmith of Ephesus, raises an uproar against Paul, which, after some tumultuous proceedings, is appeased by the town clerk, 23-41.

1. *Paul having passed through the upper coasts.* That is, through those parts of Asia Minor that lay eastward of Ephesus, such as Galatia, Phrygia, and probably Lycaonia and Lydia; and it is in reference to Ephesus that these are called the *upper* coasts.

2. *Have ye received the Holy Ghost?* It is likely that these were Asiatic Jews, who, having been at Jerusalem about twenty-six years before this, had heard the preaching of John and received his baptism, believing in the coming Christ, whom John had proclaimed; but it appears that till this time they had got no further instruction in the Christian religion. Paul, perceiving this, asked them if they had received the Holy Ghost since they believed. For it was the common privilege of the disciples of Christ to receive not only the ordinary graces but also the extraordinary gifts of the Holy Spirit, and thus the disciples of Christ differed from those of John and of all others. John baptized with water; Jesus baptized with the Holy Ghost. *We have not so much as heard whether.* That is, they had not heard that there were particular

gifts and graces of the Holy Spirit to be received. They could not mean that they had not heard of the Holy Spirit; for John, in his baptism, announced Christ as about to baptize with the Holy Ghost, Matt. iii. 11; Luke iii. 16. But they simply meant that they had not heard that this Spirit, in His gifts, had been given to or received by anyone.

4. *That they should believe on him which should come after.* John baptized them with the baptism of repentance; this was common to all the baptisms administered by the Jews to proselytes. But telling them that they should believe on Him who was coming was peculiar to John's baptism.

5. *When they heard this.* As there is no evidence in the New Testament of persons being rebaptized, unless this be one, many criticisms have been hazarded to prove that these persons were not rebaptized. I see no need of this. To be a Christian a man must be baptized in the Christian faith; these persons had not been baptized into that faith, and therefore were not Christians; they felt this, and were immediately baptized into *the name of the Lord Jesus.*

6. *They spake with tongues, and prophesied.* They received the miraculous gift of different languages, and in those languages they taught to the people the great doctrines of the Christian religion; for this appears to be the meaning of the word *prophesied,* as it is used above.

8. *Spake boldly . . . three months.* We have often remarked that Paul in every place made his first offers of salvation to the Jews, and it was only when they rejected it that he turned to the Gentiles; see chap. xviii. 6. And the same line of conduct he pursues here; he goes to the school of Tyrannus, at least a public place to which all might resort, when they obstinately rejected the gospel in the synagogue. *Disputing and persuading.* Holding conversations with them in order to persuade them of the truth of the doctrine of Christ.

9. *When divers were hardened.* When "some" of them were hardened; several no doubt felt the power of divine truth, and yielded consent. Our term *divers,* one of the most bald in our language, has too general a meaning for this place. *Separated the disciples.* Paul and those converted under his ministry had doubtless been in the habit of attending public worship in the synagogue, but on the persecuting conduct of these Jews, he and his converts wholly withdrew from the synagogue and took a place for themselves; and constantly afterwards held their own meetings at a schoolroom, which no doubt they hired for the purpose.

10. *By the space of two years.* The schoolhouse of Tyrannus was Paul's regular chapel; and it is likely that in it he taught Christianity, as Tyrannus taught languages or sciences. *All they . . . in Asia heard the word.* Meaning probably the Proconsular Asia. *Jews and Greeks.* For, although he ceased preaching in the synagogues of the Jews, yet they continued to hear him in the school of Tyrannus.

11. *God wrought special miracles.* Miracles of no "ordinary" kind, i.e., extraordinary miracles.

12. *Handkerchiefs or aprons.* Probably the *sudaria* were a sort of handkerchiefs, which in travelling were always carried in the hand for the convenience of wiping the face; and the

simikinthia were either the sashes or girdles that went about the loins. These, borrowed from the apostle and applied to the bodies of the diseased, became the means in the hand of God of their restoration to health. *The diseases departed from them, and the evil spirits went out of them.* Here there is a most evident distinction made between the *diseases* and the *evil spirits;* hence they were not one and the same thing.

13. *Certain of the vagabond Jews, exorcists.* "Certain of the Jews who went about practicing exorcisms." *Vagabond* has a very bad acceptation among us; but literally *vagabundus* signifies a "wanderer," one that has no settled place of abode.

14. *Seven sons of one Sceva.* It has been often remarked that in our Lord's time there were many of the Jews that professed to cast out demons; and perhaps to this our Lord alludes, Matt. xii. 27.

15. *Jesus I know, and Paul I know.* In the answer of the demoniac, the verb is varied: I "acknowledge" Jesus, and "am acquainted with" Paul; but of whom are ye?

16. *And the man in whom the evil spirit was.* Thus we find that one man was more powerful than these seven brothers, so that he stripped them of their upper garments and beat and wounded the whole! Was not this a proof that he derived his strength from the evil spirit that dwelt in him?

17. *The name of the Lord Jesus was magnified.* They saw that there was a sovereign power in the name of Jesus which could not be imitated by these lying exorcists; they therefore reverenced this name, and despised those pretenders.

19. *Which used curious arts.* From the use of this word in the Greek writers we know that it signified "magical arts, sorceries, incantations." Ephesus abounded with these. *Brought their books together.* When it is said they brought their books together, we are to understand the books which treated of these curious arts. *And burned them before all.* These must have been thoroughly convinced of the truth of Christianity and of the unlawfulness of their own arts.

20. *So mightily grew the word of God and prevailed.* It is probable that it was about this time that Paul had that conflict which he mentions in 1 Cor. xv. 32, "If after the manner of men I have fought with [wild] beasts at Ephesus." See the note there. It means some severe trials not here mentioned, unless we may suppose him to refer to the ferocious insurrection headed by Demetrius, mentioned at the end of this chapter.

21. *Paul purposed in the spirit.* Previously to this he appears to have concerted a journey to Macedonia and a visit to Corinth, the capital of Achaia, where he seems to have spent a considerable time (see 1 Cor. xvi. 5-6), and afterwards to go to Jerusalem. But it is likely that he did not leave Ephesus till after Pentecost (1 Cor. xvi. 8). And he resolved if possible to see Rome, which had been the object of his wishes for a considerable time. See Rom. i. 10, 13; xvi. 23. It is generally believed that during this period, while at Ephesus, he wrote his First Epistle to the Corinthians.

22. *So he sent into Macedonia.* He desired Timothy to go as far as Corinth, 1 Cor. iv. 18, and after that to return to him at Ephesus, 1 Cor. xvi. 11; but he himself continued in Asia some time longer, probably to make collections for the poor saints in Jerusalem. *Erastus,* mentioned here for the first time, appears to have been the chamberlain of either Ephesus or Corinth; see Rom. xvi. 23. He was one of Paul's companions and is mentioned as being left by the apostle at Corinth, 2 Tim. iv. 20.

23. *No small stir about that way.* Concerning the gospel, which the apostles preached; and which is termed "this way," chap. ix. 2.

24. *Silver shrines for Diana.* It is generally known that the temple of Diana at Ephesus was deemed one of the seven wonders of the world and was a most superb building. It appears that the *silver shrines* mentioned here were small, portable representations of this temple, which were bought by strangers as matters of curiosity and probably of devotion. *Brought no small gain.* There were many made, many sold, and probably at considerable prices.

25. *By this craft we have our wealth.* The word signifies not only "wealth," but also "abundance." It was a most lucrative trade; and he plainly saw that, if the apostles were permitted to go on thus preaching, the worship of Diana itself would be destroyed, and consequently all the gain that he and his fellows derived from it would be brought to nought.

26. *This Paul hath persuaded and turned away much people.* From the mouth of this heathen we have in one sentence a most pleasing account of the success with which God had blessed the labors of the apostles: *not alone at Ephesus, but almost throughout all Asia,* they had *persuaded* and converted *much people.* For they had insisted that they could be no gods which are made with hands, and this the common sense of the people must at once perceive.

29. *The whole city was filled with confusion.* Thus we find the peace of the whole city was disturbed, not by an apostle preaching the gospel of Christ, but by one interested, unprincipled knave who did not even plead conscience for what he was doing; but that it was by this craft he and his fellows got their wealth, and he was afraid to lose it. *Rushed . . . into the theatre.* The theatres, being very spacious and convenient places, were often used for popular assemblies and public deliberation, especially in matters which regarded the safety of the state.

31. *Certain of the chief of Asia.* Some of the "Asiarchs." The Asiarchs were those to whom the care and regulation of the public games were entrusted; they were a sort of high priests, and were always persons of considerable riches and influence. These could not have been Christians, but they were what the sacred text states them to have been, *his friends;* and foreseeing that Paul would be exposed to great danger if he went into the theatre amidst such a tumultuous assembly, they sent a message to him, entreating him not to go into danger so apparent.

32. *Some . . . cried one thing, and some another.* This is an admirable description of a tumultuous mob, gathered together without law or reason; getting their passions inflamed, and looking for an opportunity to commit outrages, without why or wherefore—principle or object.

For the assembly was confused. Ecclesia, the same word which we translate "church"; and thus we find that it signifies any assembly, and that only the circumstances of the case can determine the precise nature of the assembly to which this word is applied.

33. *They drew Alexander out of the multitude, the Jews putting him forward.* From this and the following verses it is pretty evident that this Alexander was brought forward on this occasion by the Jews, that he might make an oration to the multitude, in order to exculpate the Jews, who were often by the heathens confounded with the Christians; and cast the whole blame of the uproar upon Paul and his party. He was probably chosen because he was an able speaker; and when he beckoned with his hand to gain an audience, the Greeks, knowing that he was a Jew and consequently as much opposed to the worship of Diana as Paul was, would not hear him.

35. *When the townclerk.* L i t e r a l l y, the "scribe." *Is a worshipper of the great goddess Diana.* The word *neocoros*, which we translate "worshipper," signified at first, among the ancient Greeks, no more than "sweeper of the temple," and answered nearly to our "sexton." In process of time the care of the temple was entrusted to this person. At length the *neocori* became persons of great consequence, and were those who offered sacrifices for the life of the emperor. Whole cities took this appellation, as appears on many ancient coins and medals; and Ephesus is supposed to have been the first that assumed this title. *Of the image which fell down from Jupiter.* The original image of the Ephesian Diana was supposed to have descended from heaven, which intimates that it was so old that no person knew either its maker or the time in which it was formed; and it was the interest of the priests to persuade the people that this image had been sent to them as a present from Jupiter himself.

37. *These men . . . are neither robbers of churches.* "Spoilers of sacred places." As his design evidently was to appease and conciliate the people, he fixed first on a most incontrovertible fact: These men have not spoiled your temples, nor is there any evidence that they have even blasphemed your goddess.

38. *If Demetrius . . . have a matter against any man.* If it be any breach of law, in reference to Demetrius and the artists, *the law is open,* or rather, "the judges are now sitting"; so the words may be understood. *And there are deputies,* "proconsuls," appointed to guard the peace of the state, and to support every honest man in his right. *Let them implead one another;* let the one party bring forward his action of assault or trespass, and the other put in his defense; the laws are equal and impartial, and justice will be done to him who is wronged.

39. *But if ye enquire any thing concerning other matters,* in which the safety of the state or the national worship is concerned, know that such a matter is not the business of the mob; it must be heard and determined *in a lawful assembly,* one legally constituted and properly authorized to hear and determine on the subject.

40. *For we are in danger.* Popular commotions were always dreaded by the Roman government. One of the Roman laws made all such commotions of the people capital offenses against those who raised them. "He who raises a mob shall forfeit his life." If such a law existed at Ephesus—and it probably did, from this reference to it in the words of the town clerk or recorder—then Demetrius must feel himself in great personal danger, and that his own life lay now at the mercy of those whom he had accused, concerning whom he had raised such an outcry and against whom nothing disorderly could be proved.

41. *He dismissed the assembly.* Another proof that the word *ecclesia*, which we generally translate "church," signifies an *assembly* of any kind.

CHAPTER 20

Paul retires to Macedonia, 1. He goes into Greece, where he tarries three months; and, purposing to sail to Syria, he returns through Macedonia, 2-3. Several persons accompany him into Asia, and then go before and tarry for him at Troas, 4-5. Paul and Luke sail from Philippi, and in five days reach Troas, where they meet their brethren from Asia, and abide there seven days, 6. On the first day of the week, the disciples coming together to break bread, Paul preaching to them and continuing his speech till midnight, a young man of the name of Eutychus, being in a deep sleep, fell from the third loft and was killed, 7-9. Paul restores him to life, resumes his discourse, and continuing it till daybreak, then departs, 10-12. Luke and his companions sail to Assos, whither Paul comes by land, 13. He embarks with them at Assos, comes to Mitylene, 14. Sails thence, and passes by Chios, arrives at Samos, tarries at Trogyllium, and comes to Miletus, 15. Purposing to get as soon as possible to Jerusalem, he sends from Miletus, and calls the elders of the church of Ephesus, to whom he preaches a most affecting sermon, gives them the most solemn exhortations, kneels down and prays with them, takes a very affecting leave of them, and sets sail for Caesarea, in order to go to Jerusalem, 16-38.

1. *After the uproar was ceased.* The tumult excited by Demetrius apparently induced Paul to leave Ephesus sooner than he had intended. He had written to the Corinthians that he should leave that place after Pentecost, 1 Cor. xvi. 8; but it is very probable that he left it sooner.

2. *He came into Greece.* Into "Hellas," Greece properly so called, the regions between Thessaly and Propontis, and the country of Achaia. He did not, however, go there immediately. He passed through Macedonia, v. 1, in which he informs us, 2 Cor. vii. 5-7, that he suffered much, from both believers and infidels; but was greatly comforted by the arrival of Titus, who gave him a very flattering account of the prosperous state of the church at Corinth. A short time after this, being still in Macedonia, he sent Titus back to Corinth, 2 Cor. viii. 16-17, and sent by him the Second Epistle which he wrote to that church, as Theodoret and others suppose. Some time after, he visited Corinth himself, according to his promise, 1 Cor. xvi. 5. This was his third voyage to that city, 2 Cor. xii. 14; xiii. 1.

3. *Abode three months.* Partly, as we may suppose, at Corinth; from which place he is supposed to have sent his Epistle to the Romans, because he continued longer here than at any other place, and mentions several of the Corinthians in his salutations to the believers of Rome. *When the Jews laid wait for him.* Paul had determined to go by sea to Syria, and from thence to Jerusalem. This was the first object of his journey, and this was the readiest road he could take; but, hearing that the Jews had *laid wait* for him, probably to attack his ship on the

voyage, seize his person, sell him for a slave, and take the money which he was carrying to the poor saints at Jerusalem, he resolved to go as much of the journey as he conveniently could by land. Therefore he returned through Macedonia and from thence to Troas, where he embarked to sail for Syria on his way to Jerusalem. The whole of his journey is detailed in this and the following chapter.

4. *And there accompanied him.* Rather, says Bishop Pearce, "there followed him as far as to Asia"; for they were not in his company till he set sail from Philippi and came to them at Troas, in Asia, whither they had gone before and where they tarried for him, v. 5. *Into Asia.* These words are wanting in two MSS. Some think that they embarrass this place; for how these could "accompany" him into Asia, and "go before him," and "tarry for him" at Troas, v. 6, is not so very clear. Mr. Wakefield gets rid of the difficulty by reading the verse thus: "Now Sopater of Berea accompanied him; but Aristarchus and Secundus of Thessalonica, Gaius of Derbe, Timothy (of Lystra), and Tychicus and Trophimus of Asia, went before, and tarried for us at Troas."

Sopater of Berea. Sopater seems to be the same as *Sosipater,* whom Paul mentions as his kinsman, Rom. xvi. 21. Some MSS. add *Pyrrhou,* "Sopater the son of Pyrrhus." *Aristarchus* of Thessalonica. This person occurs in chap. xix. 29, and is mentioned there as a Macedonian. He attended Paul in his journey to Rome, chap. xxvii. 2, and was his fellow laborer, Philemon, v. 24, and his fellow prisoner, Col. iv. 10-11. Secundus is mentioned nowhere but in this place. *Gaius of Derbe.* This is supposed to be the same who is mentioned in chap. xix. 26, and who is there called "a man of Macedonia," of which some suppose he was a native, but descended from a family that came from Derbe; but as Gaius, or Caius, was a very common name, these might have been two distinct persons. One of this name was baptized by Paul at Corinth, 1 Cor. i. 14, and entertained him as his host while he abode there, Rom. xvi. 23. *And Timotheus.* This was the same person of whom mention is made, chap. xvi. 1, and to whom Paul wrote the two Epistles which are still extant; and who was a native of Lystra, as we learn from the above place. *Tychicus . . . of Asia.* This person was high in the confidence of Paul. He styles him "a beloved brother and faithful minister in the Lord," whom he sent to the Ephesians, that he might know their affairs, and comfort their hearts, Eph. vi. 21-22. He sent him for the same purpose, and with the same commendations, to the Colossians, Col. iv. 7-8. Paul seems also to have designed him to superintend the church at Crete in the absence of Titus; see Titus ii. 12. He seems to have been the most intimate and confidential friend that Paul had. *Trophimus.* Was an Ephesian. He accompanied Paul from Ephesus into Greece, as we see here; and from thence to Jerusalem, chap. xxi. 29. He had no doubt travelled with him on other journeys, for we find, by 2 Tim. iv. 20, that he was obliged to leave him sick at Miletus, being then, as it is likely, on his return to his own kindred at Ephesus.

6. *Days of unleavened bread.* The seven days of the Passover, in which they ate unleavened bread. See the account of this festival in the notes on Exodus xii. It is evident, from the manner in which Luke writes here, that he had not been with Paul since the time he accompanied him to Philippi, chap. xvi. 10-12; but he now embarks at Philippi with the apostle and accompanies him to Troas and continues with him through the rest of his journey.

7. *Upon the first day of the week.* What was called "the Lord's day," the Christian Sabbath, in which they commemorated the resurrection of our Lord, and which among all Christians afterwards took the place of the Jewish Sabbath. *To break bread.* To break the Eucharist, as the Syriac has it; intimating by this that they were accustomed to receive the Holy Sacrament on each Lord's day. It is likely that, besides this, they received a common meal together. Some think the *agape,* or "love feast," is intended. *Continued his speech until midnight.* At what time he began to preach we cannot tell, but we hear when he concluded. He preached during the whole night, for he did not leave off till the break of the next day, v. 11, though about midnight his discourse was interrupted by the fall of Eutychus. Paul must have preached a sermon not less than six hours long. But it is likely that a good part of this time was employed in hearing and answering questions.

8. *Upper chamber.* The pious Quesnel supposes that the smoke issuing from the many lamps in this upper chamber was the cause of Eutychus falling asleep; and this, he says, the apostle mentions in charity to excuse the young man's appearing negligent.

9. *There sat in a window.* This was probably an opening in the wall, to let in light and air, for there was no glazing at that time; and it is likely that Eutychus fell backward through it down to the ground, on the outside.

10. *And Paul . . . fell on him.* Stretched himself upon him, in the same manner as Elisha did on the Shunammite's son, 2 Kings iv. 33-35; though the action of lying on him, in order to communicate warmth to the flesh, might not have been continued so long as in the above instance.

11. *Had broken bread.* Had taken some refreshment, in order to their journey. *And talked a long while.* Having "familiarly conversed," for this is the import of the word, which is very different from the *dielezeto,* of the seventh verse, and the *dialegonmenou,* of the ninth, which imply solemn, grave discourse.

13. *Sailed unto Assos.* Assos, according to Pausanias, *Eliac.* ii. 4, and Pliny, *Hist. Nat.* xxxvi. 27, was a maritime town of Asia. The passage by sea to this place was much longer than by land; and therefore Paul chose to go by land, while the others went by sea. *Intending to take in Paul.* "To take him in again," for it appears he had already been aboard that same vessel, probably the same that had carried them from Philippi to Troas, v. 6.

14. *Came to Mitylene.* This was a seaport town in the isle of Lesbos.

15. *Over against Chios.* This was a very celebrated island between Lesbos and Samos, famous in antiquity for its extraordinary wines. At this island the apostle did not touch. *Arrived at Samos.* This was another island of the Aegean Sea. It does not appear that they landed at Samos; they passed close by it, and anchored

at Trogyllium. This was a promontory of Ionia, which gave name to some small islands in the vicinity of Samos. *Came to Miletus.* Miletus is famous for being the birthplace of Thales, one of the seven wise men of Greece. Anaximander was also born here, and several other eminent men.

16. *To sail by Ephesus.* Not to touch there at this time. *To be at Jerusalem the day of Pentecost.* That he might have the opportunity of preaching the kingdom of God to multitudes of Jews from different places, who would come up to Jerusalem at that feast; and then he no doubt expected to see there a renewal of that Day of Pentecost in which the Spirit was poured out on the disciples and in consequence of which so many were converted to God.

17. *He sent to Ephesus, and called the elders of the church.* These are called *episcopoi,* "bishops," v. 28. By the *presbyteroi,* "presbyters or elders," here we are to understand all that were in authority in the church, whether they were bishops or overseers, or seniors in years, knowledge, and experience. The *elders* were probably the first order in the church; an order which was not so properly constituted, but which rose out of the state of things. From these *presbuteroi* the *episcopoi,* overseers or superintendents, were selected. Those who were eldest in years, Christian knowledge, and experience would naturally be preferred to all others as overseers of the Church of Christ. From the Greek word come the Latin *presbyterus,* the English "presbyter," the French *prestre,* and our own term "priest"; and all, when traced up to their original, signify merely an elderly or aged person, though it soon became the name of an office rather than of a state of years. Now as these *elders* are called "bishops," in v. 28, we may take it for granted that they were the same order; or rather, that these superintendents of the Church were indifferently called either "presbyters" or "bishops."

19. *Serving the Lord with all humility.* This relates not only to his zealous and faithful performance of his apostolic functions, but also to his private walk as a Christian, and shows with what carefulness this apostle himself was obliged to walk in order to have his calling and election as a Christian ratified and made firm.

20. *I kept back nothing.* Notwithstanding the dangers to which he was exposed and the temptations he must have had to suppress those truths that were less acceptable to the unrenewed nature of man, or to the particular prejudices of the Jews and the Gentiles, he fully and faithfully, at all hazards, declared what he terms, v. 27, the whole counsel of God.

21. *Testify both to . . . Jews, and . . . Greeks.* He always began with the *Jews;* and in this case he had preached to them alone for three months, chap. xix. 8-10, and left their synagogues only when he found, through their obstinacy, he could do them no good. *Repentance toward God.* As all had sinned against God, so all should humble themselves before Him against whom they have sinned. But humiliation is no atonement for sin; therefore repentance is insufficient unless faith in our Lord Jesus Christ accompany it. Repentance disposes and prepares the soul for pardoning mercy, but can never be considered as making compensation for past acts of transgression. This *repentance*

and *faith* were necessary to the salvation of both Jews and Gentiles, for all had sinned and come short of God's glory.

22. *I go bound in the spirit.* Either meaning the strong influence of the Divine Spirit upon his mind or the strong propensity in his own will, wish, and desire to visit Jerusalem; and in this sense "to bind" is sometimes used. But it appears more consistent with the mind of the apostle, and with that influence under which we find that he constantly acted, to refer it to the influence of the Holy Ghost.

24. *None of these things move me.* I consider them as nothing; I value them not a straw; they weigh not with me. *Neither count I my life dear.* I am not my own; my life and being are the Lord's. He requires me to employ them in His service; I act under His direction, and am not anxious about the issue. *Finish my course with joy.* "My ministerial function." We have already met with this word in application to the same subject, chap. xiii. 25. And the apostle here adds, by way of explanation, even that "ministry, which I have received of the Lord." The words *with joy* are omitted by several MSS. *To testify.* "Earnestly, solemnly, and strenuously to assert, vindicate, and prove the gospel of the grace of God," not only to be in itself what it professes to be, but to be also the power of God for salvation to everyone that believes.

25. *Ye all . . . shall see my face no more.* This probably refers simply to the persons who were now present, concerning whom he might have had a divine intimation that they should not be found in life when he should come that way again. Or it may refer only to Ephesus and Miletus. From the dangers to which he was exposed it was, humanly speaking, unlikely that he should ever return; and this may be all that is implied. But that he did revisit those parts, though probably not Miletus or Ephesus, appears likely from Phil. i. 25-27; ii. 24; Philemon 22; Heb. xiii. 19-23. But in all these places he speaks with a measure of uncertainty: he had not an absolute evidence that he should not return, but in his own mind it was a matter of uncertainty. The Holy Spirit did not think proper to give him a direct revelation on this point.

26. *I am pure from the blood of all.* If any man, Jew or Gentile, perish in his sins, his blood shall be upon him; he alone shall be accessory to his own perdition. I am blameless, because I have fully shown to both the way to escape from every evil.

27. *I have not shunned to declare.* "I have not suppressed or concealed" anything, through fear or favor, that might be beneficial to your souls. This is properly the meaning of the original word. *All the counsel of God.* All that God has "determined" and revealed concerning the salvation of man—the whole doctrine of Christ crucified, with repentance towards God, and faith in Jesus as the Messiah and great atoning Priest. In Isa. ix. 6, Jesus Christ is called the *wonderful Counsellor,* which the Septuagint translate "the messenger of the great counsel." To this the apostle may have referred, as we well know that this version was constantly under his eye. Declaring therefore to them the whole counsel of God, the whole of that counsel or design of God, was in effect

declaring the whole that concerned the *Lord Jesus*, who was the *Messenger of this counsel.*

28. *Made you overseers.* "Appointed you bishops," for so we translate the original word in most places where it occurs: but "overseers" or "inspectors" is much more proper. The persons who examine into the spiritual state of the flock of God, and take care to lead them in and out and to find them pasture, are termed "superintendents." That "bishop" and "presbyter," or "elder," were at this time of the same order, and that the word was indifferently used of both, see noticed on v. 17. *Feed the church of God.* This verse has been the subject of much controversy, particularly in reference to the term *of God*, in this place, and concerning it there is great dissension among the MSS. and versions. Three readings exist in them, in reference to which critics and commentators have been much divided; viz., "the church of God," "of the Lord," "of the Lord and God."

29. *After my departing.* Referring most likely to his death, for few of these evils took place during his life. *Grievous wolves.* Persons professing to be teachers; Judaizing Christians, who, instead of feeding the flock, would feed themselves, even to the oppression and ruin of the church.

30. *Also of your own selves.* From out of your own assembly *shall men arise, speaking perverse things*, teaching for truth what is erroneous in itself and perversive of the genuine doctrine of Christ crucified. *To draw away disciples.* To make schisms or rents in the church, in order to get a party to themselves.

31. *Therefore watch, and remember.* The only way to abide in the truth is to *watch* against evil, and for good; and to "keep in mind" the heavenly doctrines originally received. *By the space of three years.* The Greek word here does not necessarily mean three whole years; it may be months more or less. In chap. xix. 8 and 10, we have an account of his spending "two years and three months" among them; probably this is all that is intended.

32. *I commend you to God.* Instead of *to God*, several MSS. have "to the Lord"; neither reading makes any difference in the sense. *And to the word of his grace.* The doctrine of salvation by Christ Jesus. Being made children of God by faith in Christ Jesus, and *sanctified* by His Spirit, they have a right to the heavenly *inheritance*; for only the children of the family can possess the celestial estate. Thus we find they must be saved by grace and be made thereby children of God; be *sanctified* by His Spirit; and then, being prepared for, they are removed in due time into the heavenly inheritance.

33. *I have coveted no man's silver.* And from this circumstance they would be able to discover the grievous wolves and the perverters; for these had nothing but their own interests in view, whereas the genuine disciples of Christ neither coveted nor had worldly possessions. Paul's account of his own disinterestedness is very similar to that given by Samuel of his, 1 Sam. xii. 3-5.

34. *These hands have ministered.* It was neither "sin nor discredit" for the apostle to work to maintain himself, when the circumstances of the church were such that it could not support

him. Still many eminent ministers of God are obliged to support themselves and their families, at least in part, in the same way, while indefatigably testifying the gospel of the grace of God.

35. *I have shewed you all things.* The clause should be read thus—"I have showed you in all things." *It is more blessed to give than to receive.* That is, the giver is more "happy" than the receiver. Where or on what occasion our Lord spake these words we know not, as they do not exist in any of the four Evangelists. But that our Lord did speak them Paul's evidence is quite sufficient to prove. The sentiment is worthy of Christ.

37. *Fell on Paul's neck.* Leaned their heads against his shoulders and kissed his neck. This was not an unusual custom in the East.

38. *That they should see his face no more.* This was a most solemn meeting, and a most affecting parting. The man who had first pointed out to them the Lord Jesus Christ, by whom they had been brought into so glorious a state of salvation, is now going away, in all likelihood to be seen no more till the day in which the quick and dead shall stand before the throne of judgment.

As the disciples are stated to have come together on *the first day of the week*, we may learn from this that ever since the apostolic times the "Lord's day," now the Christian Sabbath, was set apart for religious exercises, such as the preaching of God's holy Word and celebrating the sacrament of the Lord's Supper. Besides its being the day on which our blessed Lord rose from the dead, the practice of the apostles and the primitive Church is an additional reason why we should religiously celebrate this first day of the week. They who, professing the Christian religion, still prefer the Jewish Sabbath have little to support them in the New Testament.

CHAPTER 21

Paul and his company sail from Miletus, and come to Coos, Rhodes, and Patara, 1. Finding a Phoenician ship at Patara, they go on board, sail past Cyprus, and land at Tyre, 2-3. Here they find disciples, stay seven days, and are kindly entertained, 4-5. Having bade the disciples farewell, they take ship and sail to Ptolemais, salute the brethren, stay with them one day, come to Caesarea, and lodge with Philip, one of the seven deacons, 6-9. Here they tarry a considerable time, and Agabus, the prophet, foretells Paul's persecution at Jerusalem, 10-11. The disciples endeavor to dissuade him from going: but he is resolute, and he and his company depart, 12-16. They are kindly received by James and the elders, who advise Paul, because of the Jews, to show his respect for the law of Moses by purifying himself, with certain others that were under a vow, with which advice he complies, 17-26. Some of the Asiatic Jews, finding him in the Temple, raise an insurrection against him, and would have killed him had he not been rescued by the chief captain, who orders him to be bound and carried into the castle, 27-36. Paul requests liberty to address the people, and is permitted, 37-40.

1. *Came with a straight course.* Having had, as is necessarily implied, wind and tide in their favor. *Coos.* An island in the sea. It was famous for being the birthplace of Hippocrates, the most eminent of physicians, and Apelles, the most celebrated of painters. *Rhodes.* Another island in the same sea, celebrated for its Colossus, which was one of the seven wonders of the world. This was a brazen statue of Apollo, so high that ships in full sail could pass between its legs. It was the work of Chares, a pupil of Lysippus, who spent 12 years in making it. It

was 106 feet high and so great that few people could fathom its thumb. It was thrown down by an earthquake about 224 years before Christ, after having stood 66 years. *Patara.* One of the chief seaport towns of Syria.

2. *Phoenicia.* A part of Syria.

3. *Cyprus.* See the note on chap. iv. 36. *Tyre.* A city of Phoenicia, one of the most celebrated maritime towns in the world. *There the ship was to unlade her burden.* The freight that she had taken in at Ephesus she was to unlade at Tyre, to which place she was bound.

4. *Who said to Paul through the Spirit.* We cannot understand this as a command from the Holy Spirit not to go up to Jerusalem, else Paul must have been highly criminal to have disobeyed it. *Through the Spirit* must either refer to their own great earnestness to dissuade him from taking a journey which they plainly saw would be injurious to him—or if it refer to the Holy Spirit, it must mean that if he regarded his personal safety he must not at this time go up to Jerusalem. The Spirit foretold Paul's persecutions, but does not appear to have forbidden his journey; and Paul was persuaded that in acting as he was about to do, whatever personal risk he ran, he should bring more glory to God by going to Jerusalem than by tarrying at Tyre or elsewhere. The purport of this divine communication was, "If you go up to Jerusalem, the Jews will persecute you, and you will be imprisoned." As he was apprised of this, he might have desisted, for the whole was conditional. Paul might or might not go to Jerusalem; if he did go, he would be persecuted and be in danger of losing his life.

5. *When we had accomplished those days.* That is, the seven days mentioned in the preceding verse. *And they all brought us on our way, with wives and children.* It is not likely that Paul, Silas, and Luke had either wives or children with them; and it is more natural to suppose that the brethren of Tyre with their wives and children are those that are meant. These, through affection to the apostles, accompanied them from their homes to the ship; and the coming out of the husbands, wives, and children shows what a general and affectionate interest the preaching and private conversation of these holy men had excited. *Kneeled down on the shore, and prayed.* As God fills heaven and earth, so He may be worshipped everywhere: as well, when circumstances require it, on the seashore as in the temple. We have already seen, in the case of Lydia, that the Jews had *proseuchas* by the riversides; and an observation in Tertullian seems to intimate that they preferred such places, and in the open air offered their petitions to God by the seashore.

6. *Taken . . . leave.* "Having given each other the kiss of peace," as was the constant custom of the Jews and primitive Christians.

7. *We came to Ptolemais.* This was a seaport town of Galilee, not far from Mount Carmel, between Tyre and Caesarea, where the river Belus empties itself into the sea. It was at first called Accho, and belonged to the tribe of Asher, Judg. i. 31. It was enlarged and beautified by the first of the Egyptian Ptolemies, from whom it was called *Ptolemais.* This place terminated St. Paul's voyage.

8. *We that were of Paul's company.* This clause is wanting in some MSS. *Philip the evangelist.* One of the seven deacons, who seems to have settled here after he had baptized the eunuch. See on chap. viii. 40.

9. *Four daughters, virgins, which did prophesy.* Probably these were no more than teachers in the church, for we have already seen that this is a frequent meaning of the word *prophesy;* and this is undoubtedly one thing intended by the prophecy of Joel, quoted in chap. ii. 17-18 of this book.

10. *Agabus.* See the note on chap. xi. 28.

11. *Took Paul's girdle, and bound his own hands.* This was no doubt a *prophet* in the commonly received sense of the term; and his mode of acting was like that of the ancient prophets, who often accompanied their predictions with significant emblems. Jeremiah was commanded to bury his girdle by the river Euphrates, to mark out the captivity of the Jews, Jer. xiii. 4. For more examples of this figurative or symbolical prophesying, see Isaiah xx; Jer. xxvii. 2-3; xxviii. 4; Ezekiel iv; xii. *Into the hands of the Gentiles.* That is, the Romans, for the Jews had not, properly speaking, the power of life and death. And as Agabus said he should be delivered into the hands of the Gentiles he showed thereby that they would attempt to destroy his life. This prediction of Agabus was literally fulfilled; see v. 33.

12. *Besought him not to go up to Jerusalem.* For they all understood the prophecy to be conditional and contingent, and that it was in Paul's power to turn the scale.

13. *I am ready not to be bound only.* He was resolute and determined, but was under no constraining necessity.

14. *The will of the Lord be done.* May that which is most for His glory take place! They plainly saw from the prophecy what would take place if Paul went to Jerusalem, and everyone saw that he had power to go or not to go.

15. *Took up our carriages.* We made ourselves ready, packed up our things, got our baggage in order.

16. *And brought with them one Mnason.* It is not very likely that they would bring a man *with* them with whom they were to *lodge* in Jerusalem. Therefore the text should perhaps be read as Bishop Patrick proposes: "There went with us certain of the disciples of Caesarea, bringing us to one Mnason, with whom we were to lodge." This is most likely, as the text will bear this translation. But it is possible that Mnason, formerly of Cyprus, now an inhabitant of Jerusalem, might have been down at Caesarea, met the disciples, and invited them to lodge with him while they were at Jerusalem; and having transacted his business at Caesarea, might now accompany them to Jerusalem. His being an *old disciple* may either refer to his having been a very early convert, probably one of those on the Day of Pentecost, or to his being now an old man.

18. *Went in with us unto James.* This was James the Less, son of Mary and cousin to our Lord. He appears to have been bishop of the church in Jerusalem and perhaps the only apostle who continued in that city. We have already seen what a very important character he sustained in the council. See chap. xv. 13. *All the elders were present.* It appears that they had

been convened about matters of serious and important moment; and some think it was relative to Paul himself, of whose arrival they had heard, and well knew how many of those that believed were disaffected towards him.

19. *Declared particularly.* He no doubt had heard that they were prejudiced against him, and by declaring what God had done by him among the Gentiles, showed how groundless this prejudice was; for were he a bad man, or doing anything that he should not do, God would not have made him such a singular instrument of so much good.

20. *How many thousands.* "How many myriads," how many times 10,000. This intimates that there had been a most extraordinary and rapid work even among the Jews; but what is here spoken is not to be confined to the Jews of Jerusalem, but to all that had come from different parts of the land to be present at this Pentecost. *They are all zealous of the law.* The Jewish economy was not yet destroyed, nor had God as yet signified that the whole of its observances was done away. He continued to tolerate that dispensation which was to be in a certain measure in force till the destruction of Jerusalem, and from that period it was impossible for them to observe their own ritual. Thus God abolished the Mosaic dispensation by rendering, in the course of His providence, the observance of it impossible.

21. *Thou teachest . . . to forsake Moses.* From anything that appears in the course of this book to the contrary, this information was incorrect; we do not find Paul preaching thus to the Jews. It is true that in his Epistles, some of which had been written before this time, he showed that circumcision and uncircumcision were equally unavailable for the salvation of the soul, and that by the deeds of the law no man could be justified; but he had not yet said to any Jew, "Forsake Moses, and do not circumcise your children." He told them that Jesus Christ had delivered them from the yoke of the law; but they had, as yet, liberty to wear that yoke if they pleased. He had shown them that their ceremonies were *useless* but not *destructive;* that they were dangerous only when they depended on them for salvation.

22. *The multitude must needs come together.* Whether this refers to a regular convocation of the church or to a tumult that would infallibly take place when it was heard that the apostle was come, we cannot pretend to say; but it is evident that James and the elders wished some prudent steps to be taken in order to prevent an evil that they had too much reason to fear.

23. *We have four men which have a vow.* From the shaving of the head, mentioned immediately after, it is evident that the four men in question were under the vow of Nazariteship, and that the days of their vow were nearly at an end, as they were about to shave their heads; for during the time of the Nazariteship the hair was permitted to grow, and shaven off only at the termination of the vow. Among the Jews it was common to make vows to God on extraordinary occasions, and that of the Nazarite appears to have been one of the most common; and it was permitted by their law for any person to perform this vow by proxy. See the law produced in my note on Num. vi. 21. "It was also customary for the richer sort to bestow

their charity on the poorer sort for this purpose; for Josephus, *Ant.,* lib. xix, c. 6, s. 1, observes that Agrippa, on his being advanced from a prison to a throne by the Emperor Claudius, came to Jerusalem; and there, among other instances of his religious thankfulness shown in the Temple, *he ordered very many Nazarites to be shaven,* he furnishing them with money for the expenses of that, and of the sacrifices necessarily attending it."

24. *Be at charges with them.* Or rather, "be at charges for them"; help them to bear the expense of that vow. Eight lambs, four rams, besides oil, flour, etc., were the expenses on this occasion. See the notes on Numbers vi. *Thou . . . walkest orderly, and keepest the law.* Perhaps this advice meant no more than, Show them, by such means as are now in your power, that you are not an enemy to Moses; that you do still consider the law to be holy, and the commandment holy, just, and good. Paul did so, and bore the expenses of those who, from a scruple of conscience, had made a vow, and perhaps were not well able to bear the expense attending it. Had they done this in order to acquire justification through the law, Paul could not have assisted them in any measure with a clear conscience. But as he did assist them, it is a proof that they had vows rather referred to a sense of obligation and the gratitude due to God for mercies already received than to the procuring of future favors of any kind.

25. *As touching the Gentiles.* See the notes on chap. xv.

26. *To signify the accomplishment.* "Declaring" the accomplishment. As this declaration was made to the priest, the sense of the passage is the following, if we suppose Paul to have made an offering for himself, as well as the four men: "The next day Paul, taking the four men, began to purify, set himself apart, or consecrate himself with them. Entering into the Temple, he publicly declared to the priests that he would observe the separation of a Nazarite, and continue it for seven days, at the end of which he would bring an offering for himself and the other four men, according to what the law prescribed in that case." But it is likely that Paul made no offering for himself, but was merely at the expense of theirs. However we may consider this subject, it is exceedingly difficult to account for the conduct of James and the elders, and of Paul on this occasion. There seems to have been something in this transaction which we do not fully understand.

27. *The Jews which were of Asia.* These pursued him with the most deliberate and persevering malice in every place, and it appears that it was through them that the false reports were sent to and circulated through Jerusalem.

28. *This is the man, that teacheth.* As much as if they had said: This is the man concerning whom we wrote to you, who in every place endeavors to prejudice the Gentiles against the Jews, against the Mosaic law, and against the Temple and its services. *Brought Greeks also into the temple.* This was a most deliberate and malicious untruth. Paul could accomplish no purpose by bringing any Greek or Gentile into the Temple; and their having seen Trophimus, an Ephesian, with him, *in the city* only, was no ground on which to raise a slander that must so materially affect both their lives. Josephus in-

forms us, *War,* lib. v, c. 5, s. 2, that on the wall which separated the court of the Gentiles from that of the Israelites was an inscription in Greek and Latin letters which stated that no stranger was permitted to come within the holy place on pain of death. With such a prohibition as this before his eyes, was it likely that Paul would enter into the Temple in company with an uncircumcised Greek? The calumny refutes itself.

30. *They took Paul.* They tumultuously seized on him; *and drew him out of the temple,* out of the court of the Israelites, where he was worshipping. *And . . . the doors were shut;* the doors of the court of the Gentiles, probably to prevent Paul from getting any succor from his friends in the city, for their whole proceedings show that they purposed to murder him. They brought him out of the court of the Israelites, that court being peculiarly holy, that it might not be defiled by his blood; and they shut the court of the Gentiles, that they might have the opportunity unmolested of killing him in that place, for the court of the Gentiles was reckoned to be less holy than that of the Israelites.

31. *The chief captain of the band.* The Roman tribune, who had a troop of soldiers under him which lodged in general in the castle of Antonia, which was built at the angle where the northern and western porticoes of the outer court of the Temple were joined together. This castle was built by John Hyrcanus, high priest of the Jews. It was at first called Baris, and was the royal residence of the Asmoneans, as long as they reigned in Jerusalem. It was beautified by Herod the Great and called Antonia, in honor of his friend Mark Antony. By this castle the Temple was commanded, as it stood on higher ground. Josephus describes this castle, *War,* b. v. c. 5, s. 8, "as having four towers, from one of which the whole temple was overlooked; and that one of the towers was joined to the porticoes of the temple, and had a double pair of stairs from it, by which soldiers in the garrison were used to come down with their arms to the porticoes, on the festival days, to keep the people quiet; for, as the temple was a guard to the city, so this castle was a guard to the temple." The name of this chief captain, or tribune, was Claudius Lysias, as we learn from chap. xxiii. 26.

32. *Ran down unto them.* Ran down the stairs to the porticoes mentioned above.

33. *To be bound with two chains.* To be bound between two soldiers, his right hand chained to the left hand of the one, and his left hand to the right of the other.

36. *Away with him.* That is, Kill him; dispatch him! for so much this phrase always means in the mouth of a Jewish mob.

38. *Art not thou that Egyptian?* The history to which Claudius Lysias refers is taken from Josephus, *Ant.,* l. xx, c. 7, s. 6, and *War,* l. ii, c. 13, s. 5, and is in substance as follows: An Egyptian, whose name is not known, pretended to be a prophet, and told his followers that the walls of Jerusalem would fall down before them if they would assist him in making an attack on the city. He had address enough to raise a rabble of 30,000 men, and with these advanced as far as the Mount of Olives. But Felix, the Roman governor, came suddenly upon him with a large body of Roman troops, both infantry and cavalry. The mob was speedily dispersed, 400

killed, 200 taken prisoners, and the Egyptian himself, with some of his most faithful friends, escaped, of whom no account was ever afterwards heard. As Lysias found such an outcry made against Paul, he supposed that he must be some egregious malefactor, and probably that Egyptian who had escaped, as related above. Learned men agree that Luke refers to the same fact of which Josephus speaks; but there is a considerable difference between the numbers in Josephus and those in Luke, the former having 30,000, the latter only 4,000. The small number of killed and prisoners, only 600 in all according to Josephus, leads us to suspect that his number is greatly exaggerated, as 600 in killed and prisoners of a mob of 30,000, routed by regular infantry and cavalry, is no kind of proportion; but it is a sufficient proportion to a mob of 4,000. Dean Aldridge has supposed that the number in Josephus was originally 4,000, but that ancient copyists, mistaking the Greek delta, "four," for lambda, "thirty," wrote 30,000, instead of 4,000. There is another way of reconciling the two historians, which is this: When this Egyptian impostor at first began to make great boasts and large promises, a multitude of people, to the amount at least of 30,000 weary of the Roman yoke, from which he promised them deliverance, readily arranged themselves under his banners. As he performed nothing that he promised, 26,000 of these had melted away before he reached Mount Olivet; this remnant the Romans attacked and dispersed. Josephus speaks of the number he had in the beginning; Luke, of those that he had when he arrived at Mount Olivet. *That were murderers? Sicarii,* "assassins." They derived their name from *sica,* a sort of crooked knife, which they concealed under their garments, and privately stabbed the objects of their malice.

39. *I am a man which am a Jew.* A periphrasis for "I am a Jew." *Of Tarsus . . . no mean city.* In the notes on chap. ix. 11, I have shown that Tarsus was a city of considerable importance, and in some measure a rival to Rome and Athens; and that, because of the services rendered to the Romans by the inhabitants, Julius Caesar endowed them with all the rights and privileges of Roman citizens. When Paul calls it *no mean city* he speaks a language that was common to those who have had occasion to speak of Tarsus. Xenophon calls it "a great and flourishing city."

40. *Paul stood on the stairs.* Where he was out of the reach of the mob and was surrounded by the Roman soldiers. *Beckoned with the hand.* Waving the hand, which was the sign that he was about to address the people. *He spake unto them in the Hebrew tongue.* What was called then the Hebrew, viz., the Chaldaeo-Syriac; very well expressed by the *Codex Bezae,* "in their own dialect."

Never was there a more unnatural division than that in this chapter; it ends with a single comma! The best division would have been at the end of the twenty-fifth verse.

CHAPTER 22

Paul, in his address to the people, gives an account of his birth and education, 1-3. His prejudices against Christianity, 4-5. And of his miraculous conversion, and call to the apostleship, 6-21. The Jews, hearing him say that God had sent him to preach the gospel to the Gentiles, become exceedingly outrageous and clamor for his life,

22-23. The chief captain orders him to be examined by scourging; but he, pleading his privilege as a Roman citizen, escapes the torture, 24-29. The next day the chief captain brings Paul before the chief priests and their council, 30.

1. *Men, brethren, and fathers.* A Hebrew form of expression for "brethren and fathers," for two classes only are addressed. *Hear ye my defence.* "This apology of mine." In this sense the word "apology" was anciently understood; hence the "Apologies" of the primitive fathers, i.e., their defenses of the Christian religion. And this is its proper literal meaning; but it is now used only as implying an excuse for improper conduct.

2. *When they heard that he spake in the Hebrew tongue.* He had probably been traduced by the Jews of Asia as a mere Gentile, distinguished only by his virulence against the Jewish religion.

3. *I am verily a man which am a Jew.* A periphrasis for "I am really a Jew." He shows that he could not be ignorant of the Jewish religion, as he had had the best instructer in it which Jerusalem could produce. *Feet of Gamaliel.* See a full account of this man in the note on chap. v. 34. It has been generally supposed that the phrase *brought up at the feet* is a reference to the Jewish custom, viz., that the disciples of the rabbins sat on low seats, or on the ground, whilst the rabbin himself occupied a lofty chair. But we rather learn, from Jewish authority, that the disciples of the rabbins stood before their teachers. Kypke therefore contends that *at the feet* means the same as "near," or "before," which is not an unfrequent mode of speech among both sacred and profane writers. *According to the perfect manner.* That is, according to that strict interpretation of the law, and especially the traditions of the elders, for which the Pharisees were remarkable. That it is Pharisaism that the apostle has in view when he says he was taught "according to the most exact manner" is evident; and hence, in chap. xxvi. 5, he calls Pharisaism "the most exact system," and under it he was zealous towards God, scrupulously exact in every part of his duty, accompanying this with reverence to the Supreme Being.

4. *I persecuted this way.* This doctrine, this way of worshipping God and arriving at a state of blessedness. *Binding and delivering into prisons.* See on chap. viii. 3; ix. 2.

5. *The high priest doth bear me witness.* He probably referred to the letters of authority which he had received from the high priest and the whole *estate of the elders,* "the whole of the presbytery," that is, the Sanhedrin; and it is likely that he had those letters to produce. This zeal of his against Christianity was an ample proof of his sincerity as a Pharisaical Jew.

6-13. *As I made my journey.* See the whole of this account and all the particular circumstances considered at large in the notes on chap. ix. 1, etc.

14. *And see that Just One.* The Lord Jesus, called the *Just One* in opposition to the Jews, who crucified Him as a malefactor; see the note on chap. vii. 52. This is an additional proof that Jesus Christ did actually appear unto Saul of Tarsus.

15. *Thou shalt be his witness unto all.* You shall proclaim Christ crucified to both Jews and Gentiles.

16. *Arise, and be baptized.* Take now the profession of Christ's faith most solemnly upon you by being baptized in the name of Father, Son, and Holy Spirit. *Wash away thy sins.* Let this washing of your body represent to you the washing away of your sins, and know that this washing away of sin can be received only by invoking the name of the Lord.

17. *When I was come again to Jerusalem.* It is likely that he refers to the first journey to Jerusalem, about three years after his conversion, chap. ix. 25-26 and Gal. i. 18. *I was in a trance.* This circumstance is not mentioned anywhere else, unless it be that to which himself refers in 2 Cor. xii. 2-4, when he conceived himself transported to the third heaven; and if the case be the same, the appearance of Jesus Christ to him and the command given are circumstances related only in this place.

19. *I imprisoned and beat in every synagogue.* This shows what an active instrument Saul of Tarsus was in the hands of this persecuting priesthood, and how very generally the followers of Christ were persecuted, and how difficult it was at this time to profess Christianity.

20. *When the blood of thy martyr Stephen was shed.* See on chap. vii. 58; viii. 1. All these things Paul alleged as reasons why he could not expect to be received by the Christians; for how could they suppose that such a persecutor could be converted?

21. *I will send thee far hence unto the Gentiles.* This was the particular appointment of Paul; he was the apostle of the Gentiles. For though he preached frequently to the Jews, yet to preach the gospel to the Gentiles and to write for the conversion and establishment of the Gentile world were his peculiar destination. Hence we find him and his companions travelling everywhere. None of the apostles travelled, none preached, none labored as this man; and, we may add, none was so greatly owned of God. Next to Jesus Christ, Paul is the glory of the Christian Church. Jesus is the Foundation; Paul, the master builder.

22. *They gave him audience unto this word.* Namely, that God had sent him to the Gentiles. Not that they refused to preach the law to the Gentiles and make them proselytes, for this they were fond of doing, so that our Lord says they compassed sea and land to make a proselyte; but they understood the apostle as stating that God had rejected *them* and called the Gentiles to be His peculiar people in their place, and this they could not bear. *Away with such a fellow.* According to the law of Moses, he who attempted to seduce the people to any strange worship was to be stoned, Deut. xiii. 15. The Jews wished to insinuate that the apostle was guilty of this crime and that therefore he should be stoned, or put to death.

23. *Cast off their clothes.* Bishop Pearce supposes that shaking their upper garments is all that is meant here, and that it was an ancient custom for men to do so when highly pleased or greatly irritated; but it is likely that some of them were now actually throwing off their clothes, in order to prepare to stone Paul. *Threw dust into the air.* In sign of contempt and by way of execration. Shimei acted so in order

to express his contempt of David, 2 Sam. xvi. 13, where it is said he "cursed [him] as he went, and threw stones at him"; or, as the margin, he "dusted him with dust." Their throwing dust in the air was also expressive of extraordinary rage and vindictive malice. The apostle, being guarded by the Roman soldiers, was out of the power of the mob; and their throwing dust in the air not only showed their rage, but also their vexation that they could not get the apostle into their power.

24. *Examined by scourging.* As the chief captain did not understand the Hebrew language, he was ignorant of the charge brought against Paul and ignorant also of the defense which the apostle had made. As he saw that they grew more and more outrageous, he supposed that Paul must have given them the highest provocation; and therefore he determined to put him to the torture, in order to find out the nature of his crime.

25. *And as they bound him.* They were going to tie him to a post, that they might scourge him. *Is it lawful?* The Roman law absolutely forbade the binding of a Roman citizen.

28. *With a great sum obtained I this freedom.* So it appears that the freedom, even of Rome, might be purchased and that it was sold at a very high price. *But I was free born.* It has been generally believed that the inhabitants of Tarsus, born in that city, had the same rights and privileges as Roman citizens in consequence of a charter or grant from Julius Caesar. Pliny tells us that Tarsus was a free city. And Appian says that Antony "made the people of Tarsus free, and discharged them from paying tribute." These testimonies are of weight sufficient to show that Paul, by being born at Tarsus, might have been *free born* and a Roman.

29. *After he knew that he was a Roman.* He who was going to scourge him durst not proceed to the torture when Paul declared himself to be a *Roman.* A passage from Cicero throws the fullest light on this place: "Whosoever he might be whom thou wert hurrying to the rack, were he even unknown to thee, if he said that he was a Roman citizen, he would necessarily obtain from thee, the Praetor, by the simple mention of Rome, if not an escape, yet at least a delay of his punishment."

30. *He . . . commanded . . . all their council to appear.* Instead of "to come," which we translate, *to appear,* "to assemble," or "meet together" is the reading of several MSS.; this reading is most probably the true one. As the chief captain wished to know the certainty of the matter, he desired the Jewish council, or Sanhedrin, to assemble and examine the business thoroughly, that he might know of what the apostle was accused. As the law would not permit him to proceed against a Roman in any judicial way but on the clearest evidence, and as he understood that the cause of their enmity was something that concerned their religion, he considered the Sanhedrin to be the most proper judge and therefore commanded them "to assemble."

This chapter should end with the twenty-ninth verse, and the following should begin with the thirtieth; this is the most natural division, and is followed by some of the most correct editions of the original text.

CHAPTER 23

Paul defending himself before the high priest, he commands him to be smitten on the mouth, 1-2. Paul sharply reproves him, and being reproved for this by one of the attendants, accounts for his conduct, 3-5. Seeing that the assembly is composed of Pharisees and Sadducees, and that he can expect no justice from his judges, he asserts that it was for his belief in the resurrection that he was called in question, on which the Pharisees declare in his favor, 6-9. A great dissension arises, and the chief captain, fearing lest Paul should be pulled to pieces, brings him into the castle, 10. He is comforted by a dream, 11. More than forty persons conspire his death, 12-15. Paul's sister's son, hearing of it, informs the captain of the guard, 16-22. He sends Paul by night, under a strong escort of horse and foot, to Caesarea, to Felix, and with him a letter, stating the circumstances of the case, 23-33. They arrive at Caesarea, and Felix promises him a hearing when his accusers shall come down, 34-35.

1. *I have lived in all good conscience.* Some people seem to have been unnecessarily stumbled with this expression. What does the apostle mean by it? Why, that, while he was a Jew, he was one from principle of conscience; that what he did while he continued Jew, he did from the same principle; that when God opened his eyes to see the nature of Christianity he became a Christian because God persuaded his conscience that it was right for him to become one—that, in a word, he was sincere through the whole course of his religious life and his conduct had borne the most unequivocal proofs of it.

2. *The high priest Ananias.* There was a high priest of this name who was sent a prisoner to Rome by Quadratus, governor of Syria, to give an account of the part he took in the quarrel between the Jews and the Samaritans; see Joseph., *Antiq.,* l. xx, c. 6, s. 8. Krebs has proved that this very Ananias, on being examined at Rome, was found innocent, returned to Jerusalem, and was restored to the high priesthood; see Joseph., *Antiq.,* l. xx, c. 9, s. 2. *To smite him on the mouth.* Because he professed to have a good conscience, while believing on Jesus Christ and propagating His doctrine.

3. *God shall smite thee, thou whited wall.* Thou hypocrite! who sittest on the seat of judgment, pretending to hear and seriously weigh the defense of an accused person, who must in justice and equity be presumed to be innocent till he is proved to be guilty; and instead of acting according to the law, *commandest me to be smitten contrary to the law,* which always has the person of the prisoner under its protection.

5. *I wist not, brethren, that he was the high priest.* After all the learned labor that has been spent on this subject, the simple meaning appears plainly to be this: Paul did not know that Ananias was high priest. He had been long absent from Jerusalem; political changes were frequent; the high priesthood was no longer in succession, and was frequently bought and sold; the Romans put down one high priest and raised up another as political reasons dictated. As the person of Ananias might have been wholly unknown to him, as the hearing was very sudden, and there was scarcely any time to consult the formalities of justice, it seems very probable that Paul, if he ever had known the person of Ananias, had forgotten him. And as in a council or meeting of this kind the presence of the high priest was not indispensably necessary, he did not know that the person who presided was not the *sagan,* or high priest's deputy, or some other person put in the seat

for the time being. *Thou shalt not speak evil of the ruler of thy people.* If I had known he was the high priest, I should not have publicly pronounced this execration, for respect is due to his person for the sake of his office. I do not see that Paul intimates that he had done anything through inadvertence, nor does he here confess any fault. He states two facts: (1) That he did not know him to be the high priest; (2) That such a one, or any ruler of the people, should be reverenced. But he neither recalls or makes an apology for his words; he had not committed a trespass, and he did not acknowledge one.

6. *I am a Pharisee, the son of a Pharisee.* Instead of "of a Pharisee," some MSS. have "of the Pharisees"; which, if acknowledged to be the genuine reading, would alter the sense thus, "I am a Pharisee, and a disciple of the Pharisees," for so the word *son* is frequently understood. *Of the hope and resurrection.* Concerning the hope of the resurrection. Paul had preached the resurrection of the dead, on the foundation and evidence of the resurrection of Christ. For this he and the apostles were some time before imprisoned by the high priest and elders, chap. iv. 1-3 and v. 17, because they preached through Jesus the resurrection of the dead. This they could not bear; for if Jesus Christ rose from the dead, their malice and wickedness in putting Him to death were incontrovertibly established.

7. *And the multitude was divided.* Paul, perceiving the assembly to consist of Sadducees and Pharisees, and finding he was not to expect any justice, thought it best thus to divide the council by introducing a question on which the Pharisees and Sadducees were at issue. He did so; and the Pharisees immediately espoused his side of the question, because in opposition to the Sadducees, whom they abhorred as irreligious men.

8. *The Sadducees say that there is no resurrection.* It is strange, since these denied a future state, that they observed the ordinances of the law; for they also believed the five books of Moses to be a revelation from God. Yet they had nothing in view but temporal good, and they understood the promises in the law as referring to these things alone.

9. *The scribes . . . arose, and strove.* They "contended forcibly"—they came to an open rupture with the Sadducees; and in order to support their own party against them, they even admitted as truth Paul's account of his miraculous conversion, and therefore they said, *If a spirit or an angel hath spoken to him.* He had previously mentioned that Jesus Christ had appeared to him when on his way to Damascus; and though they might not be ready to admit the doctrine of Christ's resurrection, yet they could, consistently with their own principles, allow that the soul of Christ might appear to him. They immediately caught at this, as furnishing a strong proof against the doctrine of the Sadducees, who neither believed in angel nor spirit, while the Pharisees confessed both. *Let us not fight against God.* These words are wanting in some MSS.

10. *The chief captain . . . commanded the soldiers to go down.* It appears that the chief captain was present during these transactions, and that he had a body of soldiers in readiness in the castle of Antonia; and it was from this that he commanded them to "come down," for the rescue and preservation of Paul.

11. *Be of good cheer, Paul.* It is no wonder if, with all these trials and difficulties, Paul was much dejected in mind; and especially as he had not any direct intimation from God what the end of the present trials would be. To comfort him and strengthen his faith, God gave him this vision. *So must thou bear witness also at Rome.* This was pleasing intelligence to Paul, who had long desired to see that city and preach the gospel of Christ there. He appears to have had an intimation that he should see it; but how, he could not tell. This vision satisfied him that he should be sent thither by God himself. This would settle every fear and scruple concerning the issue of the present persecution.

12. *That they would neither eat nor drink.* These forty Jews were no doubt of the class of the *sicarii* mentioned before (similar to those afterwards called "assassins"), a class of fierce zealots, who took justice into their own hand, and who thought they had a right to dispatch all those who, according to their views, were not orthodox in their religious principles. If these were in their bad way conscientious men, must they not all perish through hunger, as God put it out of their power to accomplish their vow? No, for the doctrine of sacerdotal absolution was held among the Jews as among the Papists. Hence it is said, in *Hieros. Avodah Zarah*, fol. 40: "He that hath made a vow not to eat any thing, woe to him, if he eat; and woe to him, if he do not eat. If he eat, he sinneth against his vow; and if he do not eat, he sinneth against his life." What must such a man do in this case? Let him go to the wise men, and they will loose him from his vow, as it is written in Prov. xii. 18: "The tongue of the wise is health." When vows were so easily dispensed with, they might be readily multiplied.

15. *And we, or ever he come near, are ready to kill him.* We shall lie in weight and dispatch him before he can reach the chief captain. The plan was well and deeply laid, and nothing but an especial providence could have saved Paul.

16. *Paul's sister's son.* This is all we know of Paul's family.

17. *Bring this young man unto the chief captain.* Though Paul had the most positive assurance from divine authority that he should be preserved, yet he knew that the divine providence acts by reasonable and prudent means; and that if he neglected to use the means in his power, he could not expect God's providence to work in his behalf. He who will not help himself, according to the means and power he possesses, has neither reason nor revelation to assure him that he shall receive any assistance from God.

23. *Two hundred soldiers.* "Infantry or foot soldiers." *Horsemen threescore and ten.* There was always a certain number of horse, or cavalry, attached to the foot. *Spearmen.* Persons who held a spear or javelin in their hand, from "taking or holding a thing in the right hand." *The third hour of the night.* About 9:00 p.m., for the greater secrecy, and to elude the cunning, active malice of the Jews.

24. *Provide them beasts.* One for Paul and some others for his immediate keepers. *Felix*

the governor. This Felix was a freed man of the Emperor Claudius and brother of Pallas, chief favorite of the emperor. Tacitus calls him Antonius Felix, and gives us to understand that he governed with all the authority of a king and the baseness and insolence of a slave. Drusilla, the sister of Agrippa, was his wife at this time; see chap. xxiv. 22. He was an unrighteous governor; a base, mercenary, and bad man; see chap. xxiv. 2.

25. *He wrote a letter after this manner.* It appears that this was not only the substance of the letter, but the letter itself. The whole of it is so perfectly formal as to prove this, and in this simple manner are all the letters of the ancients formed. In this also we have an additional proof of Luke's accuracy.

30. *I sent straightway to thee.* As the proper person before whom this business should ultimately come, and by whom it should be decided. *Farewell.* "Be in good health."

31. *Antipatris.* This place was rebuilt by Herod the Great and denominated *Antipatris* in honor of his father, Antipater. It was situated between Joppa and Caesarea, on the road from Jerusalem to this latter city. The distance between Jerusalem and Caesarea was about seventy miles.

32. *On the morrow they left the horsemen.* Being now so far from Jerusalem, they considered Paul in a state of safety from the Jews and that the 70 horsemen would be a sufficient guard; 400 footmen therefore returned to Jerusalem, and the horsemen went on to Caesarea with Paul. We need not suppose that all this troop reached Antipatris on the same night in which they left Jerusalem; therefore, instead of "They brought him by night to Antipatris," we may understand the text thus—"Then the soldiers took Paul by night, and brought him to Antipatris." And the thirty-second verse need not to be understood as if the footmen reached the castle of Antonia the next day (though all this was possible) but that, having reached Antipatris and refreshed themselves, they set out the same day on their march to Jerusalem. *On the morrow they . . . returned;* that is, they began their march back again to the castle. See on chap. xxiv. 1.

33. *Who.* That is, the seventy horsemen mentioned above.

35. *I will hear thee.* "I will give you a fair, full, and attentive hearing *when thine accusers are also come,* in whose presence you shall be permitted to defend yourself. *In Herod's judgment hall.* "In Herod's praetorium," so called because it was built by Herod the Great. The praetorium was the place where the Roman *praetor* had his residence; and it is probable that in or near this place there was a sort of guard-room where state prisoners were kept. Paul was lodged here till his accusers should arrive.

CHAPTER 24

After five days Ananias, the high priest, the elders, and one Tertullus, an orator, come to Caesarea to accuse Paul, 1. The oration of Tertullus, 2-9. Paul's defense, 10-21. Felix, having heard his defense, proposes to leave the final determination of it till Claudius Lysias should come down; and in the meantime orders Paul to be treated with humanity and respect, 22-23. Felix and Drusilla, his wife, hear Paul concerning the faith of Christ, and Felix is greatly affected, 24-25. On the expectation of obtaining money for his liberation, Felix keeps Paul in prison, 26, and being superseded in the government of Judea by Porcius Festus, in order to please the Jews he leaves Paul bound, 27.

1. *After five days.* These days are to be reckoned from the time in which Paul was apprehended at Jerusalem, and twelve days after he had arrived in that city; see v. 11. Calmet reckons the days thus: Luke says that Paul was apprehended at Jerusalem when the seven days of his vow were nearly ended, chap. xxi. 27; that is, at the end of the fifth day after his arrival. The next day, which was the sixth, he was presented before the Sanhedrin. The night following he was taken to Antipatris. The next day, the seventh, he arrived at Caesarea. Five days afterwards, that is, the twelfth day after his arrival at Jerusalem, the high priest and the elders, with Tertullus, came down to accuse him before Felix. *A certain orator named Tertullus.* This was probably a Roman proselyte to Judaism, yet he speaks everywhere as a Jew. Roman orators, advocates, were found in different provinces of the Roman Empire and they, in general, spoke both the Greek and Latin languages; and being well acquainted with the Roman laws and customs, were no doubt very useful.

2. *Tertullus began to accuse him.* There are three parts in this oration of Tertullus: (1) the exordium, (2) the proposition, (3) the conclusion. The exordium contains the praise of Felix and his administration, merely for the purpose of conciliating his esteem, vv. 2-4. The proposition is contained in v. 5. The narration and conclusion, in vv. 6-8. *By thee we enjoy great quietness.* As bad a governor as Felix most certainly was, he rendered some services to Judea. The country had long been infested with robbers; and a very formidable banditti of this kind, under one Eliezar, he entirely suppressed (Joseph., *Antiq.*, l. xx, c. 6; *Bell.*, l. ii, c. 22). He also suppressed the sedition raised by an Egyptian impostor who had seduced 30,000 men; see on chap. xxi. 38. He had also quelled a very afflictive disturbance which took place between the Syrians and the Jews of Caesarea. On this ground Tertullus said, "By you we enjoy great quietness, and illustrious deeds are done to this nation by your prudent administration." This was all true; but notwithstanding this, he is well-known from his own historians and from Josephus to have been not only a very bad man, but also a very bad governor. He was mercenary, oppressive, and cruel; and of all these the Jews brought proofs to Nero, before whom they accused him; and had it not been for the interest and influence of his brother Pallas, he had been certainly ruined.

3. *We accept it always, and in all places.* We have at all times a grateful sense of your beneficent administration, and we talk of it in all places, not only before your face, but behind your back.

4. *Hear us of thy clemency.* Give us this further proof of your kindness by hearkening to our present complaint. The whole of this exordium was artful enough, though it was lame. The orator had certainly a very bad cause, of which he endeavored to make the best. Felix was a bad man and bad governor, and yet he must praise him to conciliate his esteem. Paul was a very good man and nothing amiss could be proved against him, and yet he must endeavor to blacken him as much as possible in

order to please his unprincipled and wicked employers. His oration has been blamed as weak, lame, and imperfect; and yet perhaps few with so bad a cause could have made better of it.

5. *For we have found this man.* Here the proposition of the orator commences. He accuses Paul, and his accusation includes four particulars: (1) He is a pest, an exceedingly bad and wicked man. (2) He excites disturbances and seditions against the Jews. (3) He is the chief of the sect of the Nazarenes, who are a very bad people and should not be tolerated. (4) He has endeavored to pollute and profane the Temple, and we took him in the fact. *A pestilent fellow.* The word *loimos, pestis*—the plague or pestilence—is used by both Greek and Roman authors to signify a very bad and profligate man; we have weakened the force of the word by translating the substantive adjectively. Tertullus did not say that Paul was a *pestilent fellow*, but he said that he was the very pestilence itself. *A mover of sedition.* Instead of *sedition*, some MSS. read "commotions," which is probably the true reading. *Among all the Jews.* Bishop Pearce contends that the words should be understood thus—"one that stirreth up tumults against all the Jews"; for if they be understood otherwise, Tertullus may be considered as accusing his countrymen as if they, at Paul's instigation, were forward to make insurrections everywhere. On the contrary, he wishes to represent them as a persecuted and distressed people by means of Paul and his Nazarenes. *A ringleader.* This is a military phrase, and signifies the "officer who stands on the right of the first rank"; the "captain of the front rank" of the sect of the Nazarenes; "of the heresy of the Nazarenes." This word is used six times by Luke; viz., in this verse, and in v. 14, and in chap. v. 17; xv. 5; xxvi. 5; and xxviii. 22. But in none of them does it appear necessarily to include that bad sense which we generally assign to the word "heresy." See the note on chap. v. 17, where the subject is largely considered; and see further on v. 14.

6. *Hath gone about to profane the temple.* This was a heavy charge, if it could have been substantiated, because the Jews were permitted by the Romans to put any person to death who profaned their Temple. This charge was founded on the gross calumny mentioned in chap. xxi. 28-29; for as they had seen Trophimus, an Ephesian, with Paul in the city, they pretended that Paul had brought him into the Temple. *Would have judged according to our law.* He pretended that they would have tried the case fairly had not the chief captain taken him violently out of their hands; whereas, had not Lysias interfered, they would have murdered him on the spot.

7. *With great violence.* I rather think means "with an armed force." Tertullus intimates that Lysias interfered contrary to law and brought soldiers to support him in his infringement on their constitution. This is what he seems to say and complain of, for the Jews were vexed with Lysias for rescuing the apostle from their hands.

8-9. *Commanding his accusers to come.* Here Tertullus closes his opening and statement of the case, and now he proceeds to call and examine his witnesses; and they were no doubt examined one by one, though Luke sums the

whole up in one word—*The Jews also assented, saying that these things were so.*

10. *Then Paul . . . answered.* The apostle's defense consists of two parts: (I) The exordium, which has for its object the praise of his judge, whose qualifications to discern and decide on a question of this nature he fully allows, and expects from this circumstance to have a favorable hearing. (II) The tractation, which consists of two parts: (*a*) Refutation: (1) of the charge of polluting the Temple, (2) of stirring up sedition, (3) of being a leader of any sect who had a different worship from the God of their fathers; (*b*) Affirmation: (1) that he had lived so as to preserve a good conscience towards God and towards men; (2) that so far from polluting the Temple, he had been purified in it, and was found thus worshipping according to the law of God; (3) that what Tertullus and his companions had witnessed was perfectly false; and he defied them to produce a single proof, and appealed to those who had been witnesses of his conduct in Jerusalem, who should have been there could they have proved anything against him. *Thou hast been of many years a judge.* Cumanus and Felix were, for a time, joint governors of Judea. But after the condemnation of Cumanus the government fell entirely into the hands of Felix; and from Josephus we learn that this was now the sixth or seventh year of his administration, which might be called *many years* when the very frequent removals of the governors of the provinces are considered. *A judge.*—The same here in signification as the Hebrew *shophet*, which means a "ruler" or "governor." This was the title of the ancient governors of Israel. *The more cheerfully.* With a "better heart or courage" because, as your long residence among us has brought you to a thorough acquaintance with our customs, I may expect a proper decision in my favor, my cause being perfectly sound.

11. *There are yet but twelve days.* This is his reply to their charge of sedition, the improbability of which is shown from the short time he had spent in Jerusalem, quite insufficient to organize a sedition of any kind; nor could a single proof be furnished that he had attempted to seduce any man or unhinge any person from his allegiance by subtle disputations, in either the Temple, the synagogues, or the city. So that this charge necessarily fell to the ground self-confuted unless they could bring substantial proof against him, which he challenges them to do.

14. *That after the way which they call heresy.* See the explanation of this word in the note on chap. v. 17, and see before, v. 5, where what is here translated *heresy* is there rendered "sect." At this time the word had no bad acceptation in reference to religious opinions. The Pharisees themselves, the most respectable body among the Jews, are called a "sect"; for Paul, defending himself before Agrippa, says that he lived a Pharisee according to the strictest sect. And Josephus, who was a Pharisee, speaks of "the sect of the Pharisees," *Life*, chap. xxxviii. Therefore it is evident that the word heresy had no bad meaning among the Jews; it meant simply a "religious sect." Why then did they use it by way of degradation to Paul? This seems to have been the cause. They had already two accredited sects in the land, the

Pharisees and Sadducees. The interests of each of these were pretty well balanced, and each had a part in the government, for the council, or Sanhedrin, was composed of both Sadducees and Pharisees; see chap. xxiii. 6. They were afraid that the Christians, whom they called Nazarenes, should form a new sect and divide the interests of both the preceding; and what they feared, that they charged them with. On this account the Christians had both the Pharisees and the Sadducees for their enemies. *So worship, I the God of my fathers.* I bring in no new object of worship, no new religious creed. I believe all things as they profess to believe; I acknowledge *the law* and *the prophets* as divinely inspired books, and have never in the smallest measure detracted from the authority or authenticity of either.

15. *And have hope toward God.* I not only do not hold anything by which the general creed of this people might be altered, in reference to the present state, but also I hold nothing different from their belief in reference to a future state; for if I maintain the doctrine of the resurrection of the dead, it is what themselves allow.

16. *And herein do I exercise myself.* And this very tenet is a pledge for by good behavior; for as I believe there will be a resurrection, "both of the just and unjust," and that every man shall be judged for the deeds done in the body, so *I exercise myself* day and night that I may have *a conscience void of offence toward God, and toward men. Toward God.* In entertaining no opinion contrary to His truth and in offering no worship contrary to His dignity, purity, and excellence. *Toward men.* In doing nothing to them that I would not, on a change of circumstances, they would do to me, and in withholding nothing by which I might comfort and serve them.

17. *Now after many years.* And as a full proof that I act according to the dictates of this divine and beneficent creed, far from coming to disturb the peace of society or to injure any person, I have brought *alms to my nation,* the fruits of my own earning and influence among a foreign people, and *offerings* to my God and His temple, proving hereby my attachment to my country and my reverence for the worship of my country's God.

18. *Found me purified in the temple.* And the Jews of Asia, who stirred up the persecution against me in Jerusalem, found me purified in the Temple, regularly performing the religious vow into which I had entered, giving no cause for suspicion; for I made no *tumult,* nor had I any number of people with me by whom I could have accomplished any seditious purpose.

20. *Any evil doing in me, while I stood before the council.* The Jews of Asia, the most competent witnesses, though my declared enemies, and they who stirred up the persecution against me, should have been here. Why are they kept back? Because they could prove nothing against me. Let these therefore who are here depose, if they have found any evil in me or proved against me by my most virulent adversaries when examined before them in their council at Jerusalem.

21. *Except it be for this one voice.* The Sadducees who belong to that council, and who deny the resurrection of the dead, may indeed blame me for professing my faith in this doctrine. But as this is a doctrine credited by the nation in general, and as there can be nothing criminal in such a belief, and they can bring no accusation against me relative to anything else, this of course is the sum of all the charges to which I am called to answer before you this day.

22. *And when Felix heard these things.* There is considerable difficulty in this verse. Translators greatly vary concerning the sense, and the MSS. themselves read variously. Wakefield's translation appears to be as proper as most: "Now Felix, upon hearing these things, put them off by saying, When Lysias the captain is come down, after I have gained a more exact knowledge of this doctrine, I will inquire fully into your business."

23. *He commanded a centurion to keep Paul.* He gave him into the custody of a captain, by whom he was most likely to be well used. *And to let him have liberty;* he freed him from the chains with which he was bound to the soldiers, his keepers. *And that he should forbid none of his acquaintance,* of his "own people," his fellow apostles, and the Christians in general, *to minister or come unto him;* to furnish him with any of the conveniences and comforts of life, and visit him as often as they pleased. This was an ample proof that Felix found no evil in him; and he would certainly have dismissed him but for two reasons: (1) He wanted to please the Jews, who, he knew, could depose grievous things against his administration. (2) He hoped to get money from the apostle or his friends as the purchase of his liberty.

24. *His wife Drusilla.* Felix was thrice married. Two of his wives were named Drusilla; one was a Roman, the niece or granddaughter of Antony and Cleopatra, mentioned by Tacitus, l. v, c. 9. The other, the person in the text, was a Jewess, daughter of Herod Agrippa the Great. When she was but six years of age she was affianced to Epiphanes, son of Antiochus, king of Comagene, who had promised to embrace Judaism on her account. But as he did not keep his word, her brother Agrippa (mentioned in chap. xxv. 13) refused to ratify the marriage. About the year of our Lord 53 he married her to Azizus, king of the Emesenes, who received her on condition of being circumcised. Felix, having seen her, fell desperately in love with her and by means of a pretended Jewish magician, a native of Cyprus, persuaded her to leave her husband, on which Felix took her to wife. She appears on the whole to have been a person of indifferent character, though one of the finest women of that age. It is said that she and a son she had by Felix were consumed in an eruption of Mount Vesuvius. See Josephus, *Antiq.,* l. xx, c. 7. *Heard him concerning the faith in Christ.* For the purpose mentioned in the note on v. 21, that he might be the more accurately instructed in the doctrines and views of the Christians.

25. *As he reasoned of righteousness.* The principles and requisitions of justice and right between God and man, and between man and his fellows in all relations and connections of life. *Temperance.* "Chastity; self-government or moderation" with regard to a man's appetites, passions, and propensities of all kinds. *And judgment to come.* The day of retribution in

which the unjust, intemperate, and incontinent must give account of all the deeds done in the body. This discourse of Paul was most solemnly and pointedly adapted to the state of the person to whom it was addressed. Felix was tyrannous and oppressive in his government; lived under the power of avarice and unbridled appetites; and his incontinence, intemperance, and injustice appear fully in depriving the king of Emesa of his wife and in his conduct towards Paul and the motives by which that conduct was regulated. *Go thy way for this time.* His conscience had received as much terror and alarm as it was capable of bearing; and probably he wished to hide, by privacy, the confusion and dismay which by this time were fully evident in his countenance.

26. *He hoped also that money should have been given him.* Bishop Pearce asks, "How could St. Luke know this?" To which I answer: From the report of Paul, with whom Felix had frequent conferences and to whom he undoubtedly expressed this wish.

27. *After two years.* That is, from the time that Paul came prisoner to Caesarea.

CHAPTER 25

Porcius Festus being appointed governor of Judea instead of Felix, the Jews beseech him to have Paul brought up to Jerusalem, that he might be tried there, they lying in wait to kill him on the way, 1-3. Festus refuses, and desires those who could prove anything against him to go with him to Caesarea, 4-5. Festus, having tarried at Jerusalem about ten days, returns to Caesarea, and the next day Paul is brought to his trial, and the Jews of Jerusalem bring many groundless charges against him, against which he defends himself, 6-8. In order to please the Jews, Festus asks Paul if he is willing to go up to Jerusalem and be tried there, 9. Paul refuses, and appeals to Caesar, and Festus admits the appeal, 10-13. King Agrippa and Bernice, his wife, come to Caesarea to visit Festus, and are informed by him of the accusations against Paul, his late trial, and his appeal from them to Caesar, 14-21. Agrippa desires to hear Paul, and a hearing is appointed for the following day, 22. Agrippa, Bernice, the principal officers and chief men of the city being assembled, Paul is brought forth, 23. Festus opens the business with generally stating the accusations against Paul, his trial on these accusations, the groundless and frivolous nature of the charges, his own conviction of his innocence, and his desire that the matter might be heard by the king himself, that he might have something specifically to write to the emperor, to whom he was about to send Paul, agreeably to his appeal, 24-27.

1. *Now when Festus was come into the province.* By the province is meant Judea; for after the death of Herod Agrippa, Claudius thought it imprudent to trust the government in the hands of his son Agrippa, who was then but seventeen years of age; therefore Cuspius Fadus was sent to be procurator. And when afterwards Claudius had given to Agrippa the tetrarchate of Philip, that of Batanea and Abila, he nevertheless kept the province of Judea more immediately in his own hands, and governed it by procurators sent from Rome (Joseph., *Ant.*, l. xx, c. 7, s. 1). Felix being removed, Porcius Festus is sent in his place; and having come to Caesarea, where the Roman governor generally had his residence, after he had tarried three days he went up to Jerusalem to acquaint himself with the nature and complexion of the ecclesiastical government of the Jews; no doubt, for the purpose of the better administration of justice among them.

2. *The high priest . . . informed him against Paul.* They supposed that as Felix, to please them, on the resignation of his government had left Paul bound, so Festus, on the assumption of it, would, to please them, deliver him into their hand. But as they wished this to be done under the color of justice, they exhibited a number of charges against Paul, which they hoped would appear to Festus a sufficient reason why a new trial should be granted, and he be sent to Jerusalem to take this trial. Their motive is mentioned in the succeeding verse.

4. *Festus answered, that Paul should be kept at Caesarea.* It is truly astonishing that Festus should refuse this favor to the heads of the Jewish nation, which to those who were not in the secret must appear so very reasonable; and especially as, on his coming to the government, it might be considered an act that was likely to make him popular—and he could have no interest in denying their request. But God had told Paul that he should testify of Him at Rome, and He disposed the heart of Festus to act as he did, and thus disappointed the malice of the Jews and fulfilled His own gracious design. *He . . . would depart shortly.* So had the providence of God disposed matters that Festus was obliged to return speedily to Caesarea, and thus had not time to preside in such a trial at Jerusalem. And this reason must appear sufficient to the Jews; especially as he gave them all liberty to come and appear against him who were able to *prove* the alleged charges.

5. *Let them . . . which among you are able.* "Those who have authority"; for so is this word often used by good Greek authors, and by Josephus.

6. *When he had tarried . . . more than ten days.* The strangeness of this mode of expression suggests the thought that our printed text is not quite correct in this place, and this suspicion is confirmed by an examination of MSS. and versions. "Not more than eight or ten days" is the reading of several MSS.

7. *The Jews . . . laid many and grievous complaints against Paul.* As they must have perceived that the Roman governors would not intermeddle with questions of their law, they no doubt invented some new charges, such as sedition and treason, in order to render the mind of the governor evil affected towards Paul. But their malicious designs were defeated, for assertion would not go for proof before a Roman tribunal; this court required proof, and the bloodthirsty persecutors of the apostle could produce none.

8. *While he answered for himself.* In this instance Luke gives only a general account both of the accusations and of Paul's defense. But from the words in this verse the charges appear to have been threefold: (1) that he had broken the law, (2) that he had defiled the Temple, (3) that he had dealt in treasonable practices; to all of which he no doubt answered particularly, though we have nothing further here than this, *Neither against the law of the Jews, neither against the temple, nor yet against Caesar, have I offended any thing at all.*

9. *Willing to do the Jews a pleasure.* This was merely to please them and conciliate their esteem; for he knew that, as Paul was Roman citizen, he could not oblige him to take a new trial at Jerusalem.

10. *I stand at Caesar's judgment seat.* Every procurator represented the person of the emperor in the province over which he presided; and as the seat of government was at Caesarea,

and Paul was now before the tribunal on which the emperor's representative sat, he could say, with the strictest propriety, that he stood before *Caesar's judgment seat,* where, as a freeman of Rome, he should be tried. *As thou very well knowest.* The record of this trial before Felix was undoubtedly left for the inspection of Festus; for, as he left the prisoner to his successor, he must also leave the charges aaginst him and the trial which he had undergone. Besides, Festus must be assured of his innocence from the trial through which he had just now passed.

11. *For if I be an offender.* If it can be proved that I have broken the laws, so as to expose me to capital punishment, I do not wish to save my life by subterfuges. I am before the only competent tribunal; here my business should be ultimately decided. *No man may deliver me unto them.* The words of the apostle are very strong and appropriate. The Jews asked as a "favor," *charin,* from Festus, that he would send Paul to Jerusalem, v. 3. Festus, willing to do the Jews *charin,* this "favor," asked Paul if he would go to Jerusalem, and there be judged, v. 9. Paul says, I have done nothing amiss, either against the Jews or against Caesar. Therefore no man "can make a present of me to them"; that is, favor them so far as to put my life into their hands, and thus gratify them by my death. Festus, in his address to Agrippa, v. 16, admits this, and uses the same form of speech: "It is not the custom of the Romans gratuitously to give up anyone." Much of the beauty of this passage is lost by not attending to the original words. *I appeal unto Caesar.* A freeman of Rome who had been tried for a crime and sentence passed on him had a right to appeal to the emperor if he conceived the sentence to be unjust; but even before the sentence was pronounced, he had the privilege of an appeal, in criminal cases, if he conceived that the judge was doing anything contrary to the laws. This law was so very sacred and imperative that, in the persecution under Trajan, Pliny would not attempt to put to death Roman citizens who were proved to have turned Christians. Hence, in his letter to Trajan, l. x, Ep. 97, he says, "There were others guilty of similar folly, whom, finding them to be Roman citizens, I have determined to send to the city." Very likely these had appealed to Caesar.

12. *Conferred with the council.* From this circumstance we may learn that the appeal of Paul to Caesar was conditional, else Festus could not have deliberated with his council whether it should be granted; for he had no power to refuse to admit such an appeal. We may, therefore, understand Paul thus: "I now stand before a tribunal where I ought to be judged; if you refuse to hear and try this cause, rather than go to Jerusalem, I appeal to Caesar." Festus therefore consulted with the council, whether he should proceed to try the cause or send Paul to Rome; and it appears that the majority were of opinion that he should be sent to Caesar. *Hast thou appealed unto Caesar?* Rather, "Thou hast appealed unto Caesar, and to Caesar thou shalt go." The Jews were disappointed of their hope, and Festus got his hand creditably drawn out of a business with which he was likely to have been greatly embarrassed.

13. *King Agrippa.* This was the son of Herod Agrippa, who is mentioned in chap. xii. 1. Upon the death of his father's youngest brother, Herod, he succeeded him in the kingdom of Chalcis, by the favor of the Emperor Claudius (Jos., *Antiq.,* l. xx, c. 4, s. 2; and *Bell.,* l. ii, c. 12, s. 1. Afterwards Claudius removed him from that kingdom to a larger one, giving him the tetrarchy of Philip, which contained Trachonitis, Batanea, and Gaulonitis. He gave him, likewise, the tetrarchy of Lysanias, and the province which Varus had governed (Jos., *Antiq.,* l. xx, c. 6, s. 1; *Bell.,* l. ii, c. 12, s. 8. Nero made a further addition, and gave him four cities: Abila, Julias in Peraea, Tarichaea, and Tiberias in Galilee (Jos., *Antiq.,* l. xx, c. 7, 2. 4; *Bell.,* l. ii, c. 13, s. 2. Claudius gave him the power of appointing the high priest among the Jews (Joseph., *Antiq.,* l. xx, c. 1, s. 3); and instances of his exercising this power may be seen in Joseph., *Antiq.,* l. xx, c. 7, s. 8, 11. This king was strongly attached to the Romans and did everything in his power to prevent the Jews from rebelling against them; and when he could not prevail, he united his troops to those of Titus and assisted in the siege of Jerusalem. He survived the ruin of his country several years. Bernice, or as she is sometimes called, Berenice, was sister of this Agrippa and of the Drusilla mentioned in chap. xxiv. She was at first married to her uncle Herod, king of Chalcis (Joseph., *Antiq.,* l. xix, c. 9, s. 1); and on his death went to live with her brother Agrippa, with whom she was violently suspected to lead an incestuous life.

14. *Declared Paul's cause unto the king.* Festus knew that Agrippa was better acquainted with such matters than he, and he wished in some sort to make him a party in this business.

15. *Desiring to have judgment against him.* Instead of *judgment,* "condemnation, sentence of death" is the reading of several MSS., which is probably genuine. This is evidently the meaning of the place, whichever reading we prefer. Nothing could satisfy these men but the death of the apostle. It was not justice they wanted, but his destruction.

16. *It is not the manner of the Romans to deliver any man to die.* "To make a present of any man"; gratuitously to give up the life of any man, through favor or caprice. Here is a reference to the subject discussed on v. 11. *Before that he which is accused have the accusers face to face.* For this righteous procedure the Roman laws were celebrated over the civilized world. Appian says: "It is not their custom to condemn men before they have been heard."

19. *Questions . . . of their own superstition.* "Questions concerning their own religion." *Superstition* meant something as bad among the Romans as it does among us; and is it likely that Festus, only a procurator, should thus speak to Agrippa, a king, concerning his own religion? He could not have done so without offering the highest insult. The word must therefore simply mean "religion."

20. *I doubted of such manner of questions.* Such as whether he had broken their law, defiled their Temple; or whether this Jesus, who was dead, was again raised to life.

21. *Unto the hearing of Augustus.* "To the discrimination of the emperor."

22. *I would also hear the man myself.* A spirit of curiosity, similar to that of Herod, Luke xxiii. 8.

23. *With great pomp.* "With much phantasy," great splendor, great parade, superb attendance, or splendid retinue; in this sense the Greek word is used by the best writers. *The place of hearing.* A sort of audience chamber, in the palace of Festus. This was not a trial of Paul; there were no Jews present to accuse him, and he could not be tried but at Rome, as he had appealed to Caesar. These grandees wished to hear the man speak of his religion, and in his own defense, through a principle of curiosity.

26. *I have no certain thing to write.* Nothing alleged against him has been substantiated. *Unto my lord.* The title *Kyrios, Dominus, Lord,* both Augustus and Tiberius had absolutely refused; and forbade, even by public edicts, the application of it to themselves. Tiberius himself was accustomed to say that he was lord only of his slaves, emperor or general of the troops, and prince of the senate. The succeeding emperors were not so modest; they affected the title. Nero, the then emperor, would have it; and Pliny the younger is continually giving it to Trajan in his letters.

27. *For it seemeth to me unreasonable.* Every reader must feel the awkward situation in which Festus stood. He was about to send a prisoner to Rome to appear before Nero, though he had not one charge to support against him; and yet he must be sent, for he had appealed to Caesar. He hopes therefore that Agrippa, who was of the Jewish religion, would be able to discern more particularly the merits of this case; and might, after hearing Paul, direct him how to draw up those letters which, on sending the prisoner, must be transmitted to the emperor.

This chapter ends as exceptionally as the twenty-first. It should have begun at v. 13, and have been continued to the end of the twenty-sixth chapter, or both chapters have been united in one.

CHAPTER 26

Paul answers for himself before Agrippa, to whom he pays a true compliment, in order to secure a favorable hearing, 1-3; gives an account of his education from his youth up, 4-5; shows that the Jews persecuted him for his maintaining the hope of the resurrection, 6-8; states his persecution of the Christians, 9-11; gives an account of his miraculous conversion, 12-15; and of his call to the ministry, 16-18. His obedience to that call, and his success in preaching the doctrine of Christ crucified, 19-23. While he is thus speaking, Festus interrupts him, and declares him to be mad through his abundant learning, 24; which charge he modestly refutes with inimitable address, and appeals to King Agrippa for the truth and correctness of his speech, 25-27. On which Agrippa confesses himself almost converted to Christianity, 28. Paul's affectionate and elegant address to him on this declaration, 29. The council breaks up, and they all pronounce him innocent, 30-32.

1. *Then Paul stretched forth the hand.* This act, as we have already seen on chap. xxi. 40, was merely to gain attention; it was no rhetorical flourish, nor designed for one. From knowing, partly by descriptions and partly by ancient statues, how orators and others who address a concourse of people stood, we can easily conceive the attitude of Paul. When the right hand was stretched out, the left remained under the cloak, which being thrown off the right shoulder, to give the arm the fuller liberty, it then rested on the left. Under these circumstances, the hand could be stretched out gracefully.

2. *I think myself happy.* As if he had said, This is a peculiarly fortunate circumstance in my favor that I am called to make my defense before a judge so intelligent and so well acquainted with the laws and customs of our country. This Agrippa was king of Trachonitis, a region which lay on the north of Palestine, on the east side of Jordan, and south of Damascus.

4. *My manner of life.* The apostle means to state that, though born in Tarsus, he had a regular Jewish education, having been sent up to Jerusalem for that purpose, but at what age does not appear; probably about twelve, for at this age the male children were probably brought to the annual solemnities.

5. *After the most straitest sect.* That is, the Pharisees; who were reputed the strictest in their doctrines and in their moral practices of all the sects then among the Jews. The sects were the Pharisees, Sadducees, and Essenes.

6. *For the hope of the promise.* This does not appear to mean the hope of the Messiah, as some have imagined, but the hope of the resurrection of the dead, to which the apostle referred in chap. xxiii. 6, where he says to the Jewish council, "Of the hope and resurrection of the dead I am called in question."

8. *That God should raise the dead.* As Agrippa believed in the true God, and knew that one of His attributes was omnipotence, he could not believe that the resurrection of the dead was an impossible thing. To this belief of his the apostle appeals, and the more especially because the Sadducees denied the doctrine of the resurrection, though they professed to believe in the same God. *Two* attributes of God stood pledged to produce this resurrection: His truth, on which His promise was founded; and His power, by which the thing could be easily affected, as that power is unlimited. Some of the best critics think this verse should be read thus: "What! should it be thought a thing incredible with you, if God should raise the dead?"

10. *Many of the saints.* From what is said in this verse it seems that Paul, before his conversion, was invested with much power. He imprisoned the Christians; punished many in various synagogues; compelled them to blaspheme—to renounce and perhaps to execrate Christ, in order to save their lives; and *gave* his voice, exerted all his influence and authority, against them, in order that they might be put to death. And from this it would seem that there were other persons put to death besides Stephen, though their names are not mentioned.

12. *Whereupon as I went to Damascus.* See the whole account of the conversion of Saul of Tarsus explained at large in the notes on chap. ix. 2, etc.

16. *But rise.* The particulars mentioned here and in the following two verses are not given in chap. ix nor in chap. xxiii, where he gives an account of his conversion. He has detailed the different circumstances of that important event, as he saw it necessary; and perhaps there were several others which then took place that he had no opportunity of mentioning, because there was nothing in succeeding occurrences which rendered it necessary to produce them. *To make thee a minister.* "An under-rower"; that is, one who is under the guidance and authority of another; an assistant, or servant. So

Paul was to act solely under the authority of Jesus Christ. *And a witness. Martyra,* a "martyr." Though this word literally means a *witness,* yet we apply it only to such persons as have borne testimony to the truth of God at the hazard and expense of their lives. In this sense also ancient history states Paul to have been a *witness;* for it is said he was beheaded at Rome, by the command of Nero. *In the which I will appear.* Here Christ gives him to understand that he should have further communications from himself; and this may refer either to those interpositions of divine providence by which he was so often rescued from destruction, or to those encouragements which he received in dreams, visions, trances, or to that general inspiration under which he was enabled to apprehend and reveal the secret things of God for the edification of the Church.

17. *Delivering thee from the people.* From the Jews—*and from the Gentiles,* put here in opposition to the Jews; and both meaning mankind at large, wheresoever the providence of God might send him. But he was to be delivered from the malice of the Jews, that he might be sent with salvation to the Gentiles.

18. *To open their eyes.* To be the instrument of informing their understanding in the things of God. *To turn them from darkness to light.* From heathenism and superstition to the knowledge and worship of the true God. *From the power of Satan unto God.* From the "authority" and domination of Satan; for as the kingdom of darkness is his kingdom, so those who live in this darkness are under his dominion, and he has authority and right over them. *And inheritance.* By remission of sins, i.e., the removal of the guilt and pollution of sin, they become children of God; and, if children, then heirs. And as the inheritance is said to be *among them which are sanctified,* this is a further proof that *aphesis hamartion* signifies, not only the forgiveness of sins, but also the purification of the heart. *By faith that is in me.* By believing on Christ Jesus, as dying for their offenses and rising again for their justification. Thus we see not only that this salvation comes through Christ, but that it is to be received by faith; and consequently neither by the merit of works nor by that of suffering.

20. *That they should repent.* Be deeply humbled for their past iniquities, *and turn to God* as their Judge and Saviour, avoiding all idolatry and all sin, and thus do *works meet for repentance;* that is, show by their conduct that they had contrite hearts and that they sincerely sought salvation from God alone. For the meaning of the word *repentance,* see the note on Matt. iii. 2.

21. *For these causes the Jews . . . went about to kill me.* These causes may be reduced to four heads: (1) He had maintained the resurrection of the dead; (2) The resurrection of Christ, whom they had crucified and slain; (3) That this Jesus was the promised Messiah; (4) He had offered salvation to the Gentiles as well as to the Jews.

23. *That Christ should suffer.* That "the Christ," or "Messiah," should suffer. This, though fully revealed in the prophets, the prejudices of the Jews would not permit them to receive. They expected their Messiah to be a glorious secular prince; and, to reconcile Isaiah 53 with their system, they formed the childish notion of two Messiahs—*Messiah ben David,* who should reign, conquer, and triumph; and *Messiah ben Ephraim,* who should suffer and be put to death. As the apostle says, he preached "none other things than those which the prophets and Moses did say should come"; therefore he understood that both Moses and the prophets spoke of the resurrection of Christ. *That he should be the first that should rise from the dead.* That is, that He should be the first who should rise from the dead so as to die no more; and to give, in His own person, the proof of the resurrection of the human body, no more to return under the empire of death. In no other sense can Jesus Christ be said to be the first that rose again from the dead, for Elisha raised the son of the Shunammite. A dead man, put into the sepulchre of the Prophet Elisha, was restored to life as soon as he touched the prophet's bones. Christ himself had raised the widow's son at Nain; and He had also raised Lazarus and several others. All these died again; but the human nature of our Lord was raised from the dead, and can die no more. Thus He was the first who rose again from the dead to return no more into the empire of death. *And should shew light unto the people.* Should give the true knowledge of the law and the prophets to the Jews, for these are meant by the term *people,* as in v. 17. *And to the Gentiles,* who had no revelation, and who sat in the valley of the shadow of death. That the Messiah should be the Light of both the Jews and the Gentiles, the prophets had clearly foretold. See Isa. lx. 1: "Arise, shine [or be illuminated]; for thy light is come, and the glory of the Lord is risen upon thee." And again, Isa. xlix. 6: "I will also give thee for a light to the Gentiles, that thou mayest be my salvation unto the end of the earth." With such sayings as these Agrippa was well acquainted, from his education as a Jew.

24. *Paul, thou art beside thyself.* "Thou art mad, Paul!" "Thy great learning hath turned thee into a madman."

25. *I am not mad, most noble Festus.* The title *most noble,* or "most excellent," which he gives to Festus, shows at once that he was far above indulging any sentiment of anger or displeasure at Festus, though he had called him a madman. "Most excellent" was merely a title which belonged to the office of Festus. Paul hereby acknowledges him as the governor. *Speak forth the words of truth and soberness.* Words of "truth and of mental soundness."

26. *Before whom also I speak freely.* This is a further judicious apology for himself and his discourse. As if he had said: Conscious that the king understands all these subjects well, being fully versed in the law and the prophets, I have used the utmost freedom of speech, and have mentioned the tenets of my religion in their own appropriate terms. *This thing was not done in a corner.* The preaching, miracles, passion, death, and resurrection of Jesus Christ were most public and notorious; and of them Agrippa could not be ignorant. And indeed it appears from his own answer that he was not, but was now more fully persuaded of the truth than ever, and almost led to embrace Christianity.

27. *Believest thou the prophets?* Having made his elegant compliment and vindication to Festus, he turns to Agrippa; and with this strong

appeal to his religious feeling, says, *Believest thou the prophets?*—and immediately anticipates his reply, and with great address speaks for him, *I know that thou believest.* The inference from this belief necessarily was: "As you believe the prophets, and I have proved that the prophets have spoken about Christ, as suffering and triumphing over death, and that all they say of the Messiah has been fulfilled in Jesus of Nazareth, then you must acknowledge that my doctrine is true."

28. *Almost thou persuadest me to be a Christian.* This declaration was almost the necessary consequence of the apostle's reasoning and Agrippa's faith. If he believed the prophets, see vv. 22-23, and believed that Paul's application of their words to Christ Jesus was correct, he must acknowledge the truth of the Christian religion; but he might choose whether he would embrace and confess this truth or not. However, the sudden appeal to his religious faith extorts from him the declaration, "Thou hast nearly persuaded me to embrace Christianity." How it could have entered into the mind of any man who carefully considered the circumstances of the case to suppose that these words of Agrippa are spoken ironically is to me unaccountable.

29. *I would to God.* So fully am I persuaded of the infinite excellence of Christianity and so truly happy am I in possession of it that "I most ardently wish that not only you, but this whole council, were not only almost, but altogether, such as I am, these chains excepted."

32. *Then said Agrippa.* The king himself, who had participated in the strongest emotions on the occasion, feels himself prompted to wish the apostle's immediate liberation; but this was now rendered impracticable because he had appealed to Caesar. The appeal was no doubt registered, and the business must now proceed to a full hearing. Bishop Pearce conjectures, with great probability, that Agrippa, on his return to Rome, represented Paul's case so favorably to the emperor, or his ministers of state, that he was soon set at liberty there, as may be concluded from chap. xxviii. 30, that he dwelt two whole years in his own hired place. And to the same cause it seems to have been owing that Julius, who had the care of Paul as a prisoner in the ship, treated him courteously; see chap. xxvii. 3, 43. And the same may be gathered from chap. xxviii. 14, 16. So that this defense of the apostle before Agrippa, Bernice, and Festus was ultimately serviceable to his important cause.

CHAPTER 27

It being determined that Paul should be sent to Rome, he is delivered to Julius, a centurion, 1. They embark in a ship of Adramyttium, and come the next day to Sidon, 2-3. They sail thence and pass Cyprus, Cilicia, and Pamphylia, and come to Myra, 4-5. They are transferred there to a ship of Alexandria going to Italy; sail past Cnidus, Crete, Salmone, and come to the Fair Havens, 6-8. Paul predicts a disastrous voyage, 9-11. They sail from the Fair Havens, in order to reach Crete, and winter there; but, having a comparatively favorable wind, they sail past Crete, and meet with a tempest, and are brought into extreme peril and distress, 12-20. Paul's exhortation and prediction of the loss of the ship, 21-26. After having been tossed about in the Adriatic Sea for many days, they are at last shipwrecked on the island of Melita; and the whole crew, consisting of 276 persons, escape safe to land, on broken fragments of the ship, 27-44.

1. *And when it was determined.* That is, when the governor had given orders to carry Paul to Rome, according to his appeal, together with other prisoners who were bound for the same place. *We should sail.* By this it is evident that Luke was with Paul, and it is on this account that he was enabled to give such a circumstantial account of the voyage. *Julius, a centurion of Augustus' band.* Lipsius has found the name of this cohort on an ancient marble; see Lips. in *Tacit. Hist.,* l. ii. The same cohort is mentioned by Suetonius in his life of Nero, 20.

2. *A ship of Adramyttium.* There were several places of this name; and in different MSS. the name is variously written. The port in question appears to have been a place in Mysia, in Asia Minor. *Aristarchus, a Macedonian.* We have seen this person with Paul at Ephesus, during the disturbances there, chap. xix. 29, where he had been seized by the mob and was in great personal danger. He afterwards attended Paul to Macedonia, and returned with him to Asia, chap. xx. 4. Now, accompanying him to Rome, he was there a fellow prisoner with him, Col. iv. 10, and is mentioned in Paul's Epistle to Philemon, v. 24, who was probably their common friend. Luke and Aristarchus were certainly not prisoners at this time, and seem to have gone with Paul merely as his companions, through affection to him, and love for the cause of Christianity. How Aristarchus became his fellow prisoner, as is stated in Col. iv. 10, we cannot tell, but it could not have been at this time.

6. *A ship of Alexandria.* It appears, from v. 38, that this ship was laden with wheat, which she was carrying from Alexandria to Rome. We know that the Romans imported much corn from Egypt, together with different articles of Persian and Indian merchandise.

7. *Sailed slowly many days.* Partly because the wind was contrary and partly because the vessel was heavy-laden. *Over against Cnidus.* This was a city or promontory of Asia, opposite to Crete, at one corner of the peninsula of Caria. Some think that this was an island between Crete and a promontory of the same name.

8. *The fair havens.* This port still remains, and is known by the same name; it was situated towards the northern extremity of the island.

9. *Sailing was now dangerous, because the fast was now already past.* It is generally allowed that the fast mentioned here was that of the great Day of Atonement, which was always celebrated on the tenth day of the seventh month, which would answer to the latter end of our September; see Lev. xvi. 29; xxiii. 27, etc. As this was about the time of the autumnal equinox, when the Mediterranean Sea was sufficiently tempestuous, we may suppose this feast alone to be intended. To sail after this feast was proverbially dangerous among the ancient Jews.

10. *I perceive that this voyage will be with hurt.* Paul might either have had this intimation from the Spirit of God or from his own knowledge of the state of this sea after the autumnal equinox, and therefore gave them this prudent warning.

11. *The centurion believed the master.* The "pilot"; *and the owner of the ship,* the "captain" and "proprietor." This latter had the command of the ship and the crew; the pilot had the guidance of the vessel along those dangerous

coasts, under the direction of the captain; and the centurion had the power to cause them to proceed on their voyage or to go into port, as he pleased, as he had other state prisoners on board and probably the ship itself was freighted for government. Paul told them, if they proceeded, they would be in danger of shipwreck. The pilot and captain said there was no danger; and the centurion, believing them, commanded the vessel to proceed on her voyage.

12. *Might attain to Phenice.* It appears that the Fair Havens were at the eastern end of the island, and they wished to reach Phoenice, which lay farther towards the west. *Toward the south west and north west.* The *libs* certainly means the southwest, called *libs,* from Libya, from which it blows towards the Aegean Sea. The *chorus* means a northwest wind.

13. *When the south wind blew softly.* Though this wind was not very favorable, yet because it blew softly they supposed they might be able to make their passage. *They sailed close by Crete.* Kept as near the coast as they could.

14. *A tempestuous wind, called Euroclydon.* The reading of the Codex Alexandrinus is *eurakylon,* the "northeast" wind, which is the same with the *euro-aquilo* of the Vulgate.

15. *And when the ship was caught.* The ship was violently hurried away before this strong *levanter;* so that it was impossible for her to "face the wind," to "turn her prow to it," so as to shake it out, as I have heard sailors say, and have seen them successfully perform in violent tempests and squalls. *We let her drive.* We were obliged to let her go right before this tempestuous wind, whithersoever it might drive her.

16. *A certain island . . . called Clauda.* Called also *Gaudos;* situated at the southwestern extremity of the island of Crete. *Much work to come by the boat.* It was likely to have been washed overboard; or if the boat was in tow, at the stern of the vessel, which is probable, they found it very difficult to save it from being staved or broken to pieces.

17. *Undergirding the ship.* This method has been used even in modern times. It is called frapping the ship. A stout cable is slipped under the vessel at the prow, which they can conduct to any part of the ship's keel and then fasten the two ends on the deck, to keep the planks from starting; as many rounds as they please may be thus taken about the vessel. *The quicksands.* "Into the syrt." There were two famous Syrts, or quicksands, on the African coast: one called the *syrtis major,* lying near the coast of Cyrene; and the other, the *syrtis minor,* not far from Tripoli. Both these were proverbial for their multitude of shipwrecks.

18. *Lightened the ship.* Of what, we know not; but it was probably cumbrous wares, by which the deck was thronged, and which were prejudicial to the due trim of the vessel.

19. *The tackling of the ship.* All supernumerary anchors, cables, baggage, etc.

20. *Neither sun nor stars in many days appeared.* And consequently they could make no observation; and, having no magnetical needle, could not tell in what direction they were going.

21. *Have gained this harm and loss.* It seems strange to talk of gaining a loss, but it is a correct rendering of the original which expresses the idea of "acquisition," whether of good or evil.

22. *There shall be no loss of . . . life.* That must be joyous news to those from whom "all hope that we should be saved was . . . taken away," v. 20.

26. *We must be cast upon a certain island.* The angel which gave him this information did not tell him the name of the island. It turned out to be Melita, on which, by the violence of the storm, they were wrecked some days after.

28. *And sounded.* "Heaving the lead." *Twenty fathoms.* About forty yards in depth.

29. *Cast four anchors out of the stern.* By this time the storm must have been considerably abated, though the agitation of the sea could not have subsided much. The anchors were cast out of the stern to prevent the vessel from drifting ashore, as they found that, the farther they stood in, the shallower the water grew; therefore they dropped the anchor astern, as even one ship's length might be of much consequence.

30. *The shipman,* the sailors, *let down the boat.* Having lowered the boat from the deck into the sea, they pretended that it was necessary to carry some anchors ahead to keep her from being carried in a dangerous direction by the tide, but with the real design to make for shore, and so leave the prisoners and the passengers to their fate. This was timely noticed by the pious and prudent apostle, who, while simply depending on the promise of God, was watching for the safety and comfort of all.

31. *Except these abide in the ship, ye cannot be saved.* God, who has promised to save your lives, promises this on the condition that you make use of every means He has put in your power to help yourselves.

32. *The soldiers cut off the ropes.* These were probably the only persons who dared to oppose the will of the sailors; this very circumstance is an additional proof of the accuracy of Luke.

33. *While the day was coming on.* It was then apparently about daybreak. *This day is the fourteenth day that ye have . . . continued fasting.* You have not had one regular meal for these fourteen days past. Indeed we may take it for granted that during the whole of the storm very little was eaten by any man; for what appetite could men have for food who every moment had death before their eyes?

34. *An hair fall from the head.* A proverbial expression for "You shall neither lose your lives nor suffer any hurt in your bodies, if you follow my advice."

35. *Gave thanks to God.* Who had provided the food, and preserved their lives and health to partake of it.

38. *They lightened the ship.* They hoped that by casting out the lading the ship would draw less water, in consequence of which they could get nearer the shore.

39. *They knew not the land.* And therefore knew neither the nature of the coast nor where the proper port lay. *A . . . creek with a shore.* A bay, with a shore; a neck of land perhaps on either side, running out into the sea, and this little bay or gulf between them—though some think it was a tongue of land running out into

the sea, having the sea on both sides, at the point of which these "two seas met," v. 41. There is such a place as this in the island of Malta, where tradition says Paul was shipwrecked, and which is called la Cale de St. Paul.

40. *Taken up the anchors.* Weighed all the anchors that they had cast out of the stern. Some think the meaning of the word is they slipped their cables, and so left the anchors in the sea. *Loosed the rudder bands.* Or the bands of the rudders; for large vessels in ancient times had two or more rudders, one at the side, and another at the stern, and sometimes one at the prow. The bands were some kind of fastenings by which the rudders were hoisted some way out of the water; for as they could be of no use in the storm, and should there come fair weather, the vessel could not do without them, this was a prudent way of securing them from being broken to pieces by the agitation of the waves. These bands being loosed, the rudders would fall down into their proper places, and serve to steer the vessel into the creek which they now had in view. *Hoised up the mainsail.* Not the *mainsail,* but the *jib,* or triangular sail which is suspended from the foremast to the bowsprit; with this they might hope both to steer and to carry in the ship.

41. *Where two seas met.* The tide running down from each side of the tongue of land, mentioned in v. 39, and meeting at the point. *Ran the ship aground.* In striving to cross at this point of sea land they had not taken a sufficiency of sea room, and therefore ran aground. *The forepart stuck fast.* Got into the sands; and perhaps the shore here was very bold or steep, so that the stem of the vessel might be immersed in the quicksands, which would soon close round it, while the stern, violently agitated with the surge, would soon be broken to pieces.

43. *Willing to save Paul.* Had one fallen, for the reasons those cruel and dastardly soldiers gave, so must all the rest. The centurion saw that Paul was not only an innocent but an extraordinary and divine man, and therefore for his sake he prevented the massacre; and, unloosing every man's bonds, he commanded those that could to swim ashore and escape. It is likely that all the soldiers escaped in this way, for it was one part of the Roman military discipline to teach the soldiers to swim.

44. *And the rest.* That could not swim. *Some on boards,* planks, spars, etc., got *safe to land;* manifestly by an especial providence of God.

CHAPTER 28

Paul, and the rest of the crew, getting safely ashore, find that the island on which they were shipwrecked is called Melita, 1. They are received with great hospitality by the inhabitants, 2. A viper comes out of the bundle of sticks laid on the fire and seizes on Paul's hand, 3. The people, seeing this, suppose him to be a murderer, and thus pursued by divine vengeance, 4. Paul having shaken it off his hand without receiving any damage, they change their minds and suppose him to be a god, 5-6. Publius, the governor of the island, receives them courteously, and Paul miraculously heals his father, who was ill of a fever, 7-8. He heals several others also, who honor them much and give them presents, 9-10. After three months' stay they embark in a ship of Alexandria, land at Syracuse, stay there three days, sail thence, pass the straits of Rhegium, and land at Puteoli; find some Christians there, tarry seven days, and set forward for Rome, 11-14. They are met at Appii Forum by some Christians, and Paul is greatly encouraged, 15. They come to Rome, and Julius delivers his prisoners to the captain of the guard, who permits Paul to dwell by himself, attended only by the soldier that kept him, 16. Paul calls the chief Jews together and states his case

to them, 17-20. They desire to hear him concerning the faith of Christ, 21-22; and having appointed unto him a day, he expounds to them the kingdom of Christ, 23. Some believe and some disbelieve; and Paul informs them that, because of their unbelief and disobedience, the salvation of God is sent to the Gentiles, 24-29. Paul dwells two years in his own hired house, preaching the kingdom of God, 30-31.

1. *They knew that the island was called Melita.* Now called Malta. It is about fifty miles from the coast of Sicily; twenty miles long, twelve miles in its greatest breadth; and about sixty miles in circumference. It is one immense rock of white, soft freestone, with about one foot depth of earth on an average. It produces cotton, excellent fruits, and fine honey, from which it appears the island originally had its name; for *meli,* and in the genitive case, *melitos,* signifies "honey." Others suppose that it derived its name from the Phoenicians, who established a colony in it, and made it a place of "refuge" when they extended their traffic to the ocean, because it was furnished with excellent harbors. Hence in their tongue it would be called *Meliteh,* "escape or refuge."

2. *The barbarous people.* This island was peopled by the Phoenicians or Carthaginians. Their ancient language was no doubt in use among them at that time, though mingled with some Greek and Latin terms; and this language must have been unintelligible to the Romans and the Greeks. With these, as well as with other nations, it was customary to call those *barbarians* whose language they did not understand. Paul himself speaks after this manner in 1 Cor. xiv. 11: "If I know not the meaning of the voice, I shall be unto him that speaketh a barbarian, and he that speaketh shall be a barbarian unto me." *Because of the present rain, and . . . of the cold.* This must have been sometime in October; and when we consider the time of the year, the tempestuousness of the weather, and their escaping to shore on planks, spars, etc., wet of course to the skin, they must have been very *cold,* and have needed all the kindness that these well-disposed people showed them.

4. *The venomous beast.* The venomous animal; for *theria* is a general name among the Greek writers for serpents, vipers, scorpions, wasps, and suchlike creatures. *Vengeance suffereth not to live.* These heathens had a general knowledge of retributive justice, and they thought that the stinging of the serpent was a proof that Paul was a murderer.

6. *When he should have swollen.* When he should have been "inflamed." *Said that he was a god.* As Hercules was one of the gods of the Phoenicians, and was worshiped in Malta under the epithet of the "dispeller of evil," they probably thought that Paul was Hercules; and the more so because Hercules was famous for having destroyed, in his youth, two serpents that attacked him in his cradle.

7. *The chief man of the island.* The term *chief,* used here by Luke, was the ancient title of the governor of this island, as is evident from an inscription found in Malta. This title is another proof of the accuracy of Luke, who uses the very epithet by which the Roman governor of that island was distinguished.

8. *The father of Publius lay sick of a fever* and dysentery. *Paul . . . prayed.* That God would exert His power; *and laid his hands on him,* as the means which God ordinarily used

to convey the energy of the Holy Spirit, *and healed him,* God having conveyed the healing power by this means.

9. *Others . . . which had diseases.* Luke was a physician, yet we do not find him engaging in these cures. As a medical man, he might have been of use to the father of Publius, but he is not even consulted on the occasion.

10. *Honored us with many honors.* The word is often used to signify a pecuniary "recompense" or "present." In the sense of a pecuniary recompense, or price, paid for anything, the word is met with in I Cor. vi. 20 and vii. 23. *Such things as were necessary.* They had before given them many presents, and now they gave them a good sea stock, all that was necessary for their passage.

11. *After three months.* Supposing that they had reached Malta about the end of October, as we have already seen, then it appears that they left it about the end of January or the beginning of February; and, though in the depth of winter, not the worst time for sailing, even in those seas, the wind being then generally more steady, and, on the whole, the passage more safe. *Whose sign was Castor and Pollux.* These were two fabulous semi-deities, reported to be the sons of Jupiter and Leda, who were afterwards translated to the heavens, and made the constellation called *Gemini,* or the "Twins." This constellation was deemed propitious to mariners; and, as it was customary to have the images of their gods on both the head and the stern of their ships, we may suppose that this Alexandrian ship had these on either her prow or stern, and that these gave name to the ship.

12. *Landing at Syracuse.* In order to go to Rome from Malta, their readiest course was to keep pretty close to the eastern coast of Sicily, in order to pass through the straits of Rhegium and get into the Tyrrhenian Sea. *Syracuse* is one of the most famous cities of antiquity; it is the capital of the island of Sicily, and was built about 730 years before the Christian era. This was the birthplace of the illustrious Archimedes, who, when the city was besieged by the Romans, under Marcellus, about 212 years before Christ, defended the place with his powerful engines against all the valor and power of the assailants. He beat their galleys to pieces by huge stones projected from his machines.

13. *We fetched a compass.* "Whence we coasted about." *Rhegium.* A city and promontory in Italy, opposite to Sicily. It is now called *Reggio.* It had its name, *Rhegium,* from the Greek "to break off," because it appears to have been broken off from Sicily. *The south wind blew.* This was the fairest wind they could have from Syracuse, to reach the straits of Rhegium. *The next day to Puteoli.* This place, now commonly called Pozzuoli, is an ancient town of Naples.

14. *Where we found brethren.* That is, Christians; for there had been many in Italy converted to the faith of Christ some considerable time before this, as appears from Paul's Epistle to the Romans, written some years before this voyage. *We went toward Rome.* One of the most celebrated cities in the universe, the capital of Italy, and once of the whole world, situated on the river Tiber. This famous city was founded by Romulus, 753 years before the Christian era.

15. *When the brethren heard of us.* By whom the gospel was planted at Rome is not known; it does not appear that any apostle was employed in this work. It was probably carried thither by some of those who were converted to God on the Day of Pentecost; for there were then at Jerusalem, not only "devout men," proselytes to the Jewish religion, "from every nation under heaven," Acts ii. 5, but there were "strangers of Rome" also, v. 10. And it is most reasonable to believe, as we know of no other origin, that it was by these that Christianity was planted at Rome. *As far as Appii forum.* About fifty-two miles from Rome; a long way to come on purpose to meet the apostle! The Appii Forum, or "Market of Appius," was a town on the Appian Way, a road paved from Rome to Campania by the consul Appius Claudius. It was near the sea and was a famous resort for sailors and peddlers. *And The three taverns.* This was another place on the same road, and about thirty-three miles from Rome. Some of the Roman Christians had come as far as Appii Forum; others, to the Three Taverns. *Thanked God, and took courage.* He had longed to see Rome (see Rom. i. 9-15); and finding himself brought through so many calamities, and now so near the place that he was met by a part of that church to which, some years before, he had written an Epistle, he gave thanks to God, who had preserved him; and took fresh courage in the prospect of bearing there a testimony for his Lord and Master.

16. *The captain of the guard.* This word properly means the "commander of a camp"; but it signifies the prefect, or commander of the pretorian cohorts, or emperor's guards. *With a soldier that kept him.* That is, the soldier to whom he was chained, as has been related before, chap. xii. 6.

17. *Paul called the chief of the Jews together.* We have already seen, in chap. xviii. 2, that Claudius had commanded all Jews to depart from Rome, but it seems they were permitted to return very soon; and from this verse it appears that there were then chiefs, probably of synagogues, dwelling at Rome. *I have committed nothing.* Lest they should have heard and received malicious reports against him, he thought it best to state his own case.

20. *For the hope of Israel I am bound.* As if he had said: This, and this alone, is the cause of my being delivered into the hands of the Romans. I have proclaimed Jesus as the Messiah; have maintained that though He was crucified by the Jews, yet He rose again from the dead; and, through Him, I have preached the general resurrection of mankind. This all Israel professes to hope for, and yet it is on this account that the Jews persecute *me.* Both the Messiah and the Resurrection might be said to be the hope of Israel; and it is hard to tell which of them is here meant. See chap. xxiii. 6; xxiv. 15, 21; and xxvi. 6.

21. *We neither received letters.* This is very strange, and shows us that the Jews knew their cause to be hopeless, and therefore did not send it forward to Rome. They wished for an opportunity to kill Paul; and when they were frustrated by this appeal to the emperor, they permitted the business to drop.

22. *For as concerning this sect.* See the note on chap. xxiv. 14. A saying of Justin Martyr

casts some light on this saying of the Jews. He asserts that the Jews not only cursed them in their synagogues, but they sent out chosen men from Jerusalem to acquaint the world, and particularly the Jews everywhere, that the Christians were an atheistical and wicked sect, which should be detested and abhorred by all mankind (Justin Martyr, *Dial.*, p. 234).

23. *To whom he expounded . . . the kingdom of God.* To whom he showed that the reign of the Messiah was to be a spiritual reign; and that Jesus, whom the Jewish rulers had lately crucified, was the true Messiah, who should rule in this spiritual Kingdom. These two points were probably those on which he expatiated from morning to evening, proving both out of the law and out of the prophets.

24. *Some believed.* His message was there treated as his gospel is to the present day. Some believe and are converted; others continue in obstinate unbelief and perish. Could the Jews then have credited the spiritual nature of the Messiah's kingdom, they would have found little difficulty to receive Jesus Christ as the Messiah.

25. *Agreed not among themselves.* It seems that a controversy arose between the Jews themselves, in consequence of some believing and others disbelieving, and the two parties contested together; and in respect to the unbelieving party, the apostle quoted the following passage from Isa. vi. 9.

26. *Hearing ye shall hear.* See the notes on Matt. xiii. 14 and John xii. 39-40.

28. *The salvation of God is sent unto the Gentiles.* Paul had spoken to this effect twice before, chap. xiii. 46 and chap. xviii. 6, where see the notes. But here he uses a firmer tone, being out of the Jewish territories and under the protection of the emperor. By *the salvation of God,* all the blessings of the kingdom of Christ are intended. This salvation God could have sent unto the Gentiles independently of the Jewish disobedience; but He waited till they had rejected it, and then reprobated them, and elected the Gentiles. Thus the elect became reprobate, and the reprobate elect. *They will hear it.* That is, they will obey it; for *akouein* signifies not only "to hear" but also "to obey."

30. *Paul dwelt two whole years in his own hired house.* As a state prisoner, he might have had an apartment in the common prison; but peculiar favor was showed him, and he was permitted to dwell alone, with the soldier that guarded him, v. 16. Finding now an opportunity of preaching the gospel, he hired a house for the purpose. Here he received all that came unto him, and preached the gospel with glorious success; so that his bonds became the means of spreading the truth, and he became celebrated even in the palace of Nero, Phil. i. 12-13; and we find that there were several saints even in Caesar's household, Phil. iv. 22. While he was in captivity, the church at Philippi, to which he was exceedingly dear, sent him some pecuniary assistance by the hands of their minister, Epaphroditus, who, it appears, risked his life in the service of the apostle, and was taken with a dangerous malady. When he got well, he returned to Philippi and, it is supposed, carried with him that Epistle which is still extant. From it we learn that Timothy was then at Rome with Paul, and that he had the prospect of being shortly delivered from his captivity. See Phil. i. 12-13; ii. 25; iv. 15-16, 18, etc.

31. *Preaching the kingdom of God.* Showing the spiritual nature of the true Church, under the reign of the Messiah. *Those things which concern the Lord.* The Redeemer of the world was to be represented as the Lord, as Jesus, and as the Christ. As *the Lord,* the sole Potentate, the Maker and Upholder of all things, and the Judge of all men. As *Jesus*—the "Saviour"; He who saves, delivers, and preserves; and especially He who saves His people from their sins. As *Christ*—the same as Messiah, both signifying the "anointed"; He who was appointed by the Lord to this great and glorious work, who had the Spirit without measure, and who anoints, communicates the gifts and graces of that Spirit to all true believers. Paul taught the *things which concerned* or belonged to *the Lord Jesus Christ.* He proved Him to be the Messiah foretold by the prophets and expected by the Jews; he spoke of what He does as the Lord, what He does as Jesus, and what He does as Christ. *With all confidence.* "Liberty of speech"; perfect freedom to say all he pleased, and when he pleased. He had the fullest toleration from the Roman government to preach as he pleased and what he pleased, and the unbelieving Jews had no power to prevent him. It is supposed that it was during this residence at Rome he converted Onesimus, and sent him back to his master, Philemon, with the Epistle which is still extant. And it is from vv. 22 and 24 of that Epistle that we learn that Paul had then with him Epaphras, Marcus, Aristarchus, Demas, and Luke.

Here Luke's account of Paul's travels and sufferings ends, and it is probable that this history was written soon after the end of the two years mentioned in v. 30. That the apostle visited many places after this, suffered much in the great cause of Christianity, and preached the gospel of Jesus with amazing success, is generally believed. How he came to be liberated we are not told; but it is likely that, having been kept in this sort of confinement for about two years, and none appearing against him, he was released by the imperial order. Concerning the time, place, and manner of his death we have little certainty. It is commonly believed that, when a general persecution was raised against the Christians by Nero, about A.D. 64, under pretense that they had set Rome on fire, both Paul and Peter then sealed the truth with their blood, the latter being crucified with his head downward, the former being beheaded, in either A.D. 64 or 65.

The Epistle to the
ROMANS

This Epistle is directed to those who composed the Christian Church in the city of Rome. That there were among these Romans, properly such, that is, heathens who had been converted to the Christian faith, there can be no doubt; but the principal part of the church in that city seems to have been formed from Jews, sojourners at Rome, and from such as were proselytes to the Jewish religion.

When, or by whom, the gospel was first preached at Rome cannot be ascertained. Those who assert that Peter was its founder can produce no solid reason for the support of their opinion. Had this apostle first preached the gospel in that city, it is not likely that such an event would have been unnoticed in the Acts of the Apostles, where the labors of Peter are particularly detailed with those of Paul, which indeed form the chief subject of this book. Nor is it likely that the author of this Epistle should have made no reference to this circumstance, had it been true. Those who say that this church was founded by these two apostles conjointly have still less reason on their side; for it is evident, from chap. i. 8 ff., that Paul had never been at Rome previously to his writing this Epistle. It is most likely that no apostle was employed in this important work, and that the gospel was first preached there by some of those persons who were converted at Jerusalem on the Day of Pentecost; for we find, from Acts ii. 10, that there were at Jerusalem strangers of Rome, Jews, and proselytes; and these, on their return, would naturally declare the wonders they had witnessed, and proclaim that truth by which they themselves had received salvation.

The occasion of writing this Epistle may be easily collected from the Epistle itself. It appears that Paul had been made acquainted with all the circumstances of the Christians at Rome by Aquila and Priscilla (see chap. xvi. 3) and by other Jews who had been expelled from Rome by the decree of Claudius (mentioned in Acts xviii. 2). Finding that they consisted partly of heathens converted to Christianity, and partly of Jews who had, with many remaining prejudices, believed in Jesus as the true Messiah, and that many contentions arose from the claims of the Gentile converts to equal privileges with the Jews, and from the absolute refusal of the Jews to admit these claims unless the Gentile converts became circumcised, he wrote to adjust and settle these differences.

From a proper consideration of the design of the apostle in writing this Epistle, and from the nature and circumstances of the persons to whom it was directed, much light may be derived for a proper understanding of the Epistle itself. When the reader considers that the church at Rome was composed of heathens and Jews, that the latter had been taught to consider themselves the only people on earth to whom the divine favor extended; that these alone had a right to all the blessings of the Messiah's kingdom; that the giving them the law and the prophets, which had not been given to any other people, was the fullest proof that these privileges did not extend to the nations of the earth; and that, though it was possible for the Gentiles to be saved, yet it must be in consequence of their becoming circumcised, and taking on them the yoke of the law—when, on the other hand, the reader considers the Roman Gentiles, who formed the other part of the church at Rome, as educated in the most perfect contempt of Judaism and of the Jews, who were deemed to be haters of all mankind and degraded with the silliest superstitions, and now evidently rejected and abandoned by that God in whom they professed to trust; it is no wonder if, from these causes, many contentions arose, especially at a time when the spirit of Christianity was but little understood, and among a people, too, who do not appear to have had any apostolic authority established among them to settle religious differences.

That the apostle had these things particularly in his eye is evident from the Epistle itself. His first object is to confound the pride of the Jews and the Gentiles; and this he does by showing the former that they had broken their own law, and consequently forfeited all the privileges which the obedient had a right to expect. He shows the latter that, however they might boast of eminent men, who had been an honor to their country, nevertheless the Gentiles, as a people, were degraded by the basest of crimes and the lowest idolatry; that, in a word, the Gentiles had as little cause to boast in their philosophers as the Jews had to boast in the faith and piety of their ancestors; "for all have sinned, and come short of the glory of God." This subject is particularly handled in the first five chapters, and often referred to in other places.

Concerning the time in which this Epistle was written, there is not much difference of opinion. It is most likely that it was written when Paul was at Corinth; see chap. xvi. 23 compared with I Cor. i. 14; and Rom. xvi. 1 compared with 2 Tim. iv. 20. It appears, from chap. xvi. 22, that Paul did not write this Epistle with his own hand, but used a person called Tertius as his amanuensis; and that it was sent by the hands of Phoebe, a deaconess of the church of Cenchrea, which was the eastern port on the Isthmus of Corinth.

CHAPTER 1

Paul shows the Romans his divine call to the apostleship, and for what end he was thus called, 1-6. His salutation to the church at Rome, and his commendation of their faith, 7-8. His earnest desire to see them, that he might impart to them some spiritual gifts, 9-15. His description of the gospel of Christ, 16-17. The crimes and profligacy of the Gentile world, which called aloud for the judgments of God, 18-32.

1. *Paul, a servant of Jesus Christ.* The word here translated *servant* properly means a "slave," one who is the entire property of his master, and is used here by the apostle with great propriety. He felt he was not his own, and that his life and powers belonged to his heavenly Owner, and that he had no right to dispose of or employ them but in the strictest subserviency to the will of his Lord. In this sense, and in this spirit, he is the willing slave of Jesus Christ; and this is, perhaps, the highest character which any soul of man can attain on this side of eternity. *Called to be an apostle.* The word *apostle*, from *apostellein*, "to send," signifies simply a "messenger" or "envoy"; one sent on a confidential errand. But here it means an extraordinary messenger, one sent by God himself to deliver the most important message on behalf of his Maker—in a word, one sent by the divine authority to preach the gospel to the nations. The word *kletos, called,* signifies here the same as "constituted," and should be joined with *apostolos*, as it is in the Greek, and translated thus: "Paul, a servant of Jesus Christ, constituted an apostle." This sense the word *called* has in many places of the sacred writings; e.g., "Behold, what manner of love the Father hath bestowed on us, that we should be called [constituted, or made] the sons of God." As it is likely that no apostle had been employed in founding the church at Rome, and there was need of much authority to settle the matters that were there in dispute, it was necessary he should show them that he derived his authority from God, and was immediately delegated by Him to preach and write as he was now doing. *Separated unto the gospel.* Set apart and appointed to this work, and to this only; as the Israelites were separate from all the people of the earth, to be the servants of God.

2. *Which he had promised afore.* Both in the law and in the prophets God showed His purpose to introduce into the world a more perfect and glorious state of things; which state was to take place by and under the influence of the Messiah, who should bring life and immortality to light by His gospel.

3. *Concerning his Son.* That is, the gospel relates everything concerning the conception, birth, preaching, miracles, passion, death, resurrection, and ascension of Jesus Christ, who was of the seed-royal, being, as far as His humanity was considered, the Son of David, and then the only rightful Heir to the Israelitish throne.

4. *And declared to be the Son of God.* The word which we render "declared" comes from *horizo*, to "bound, define, determine, or limit," and hence our word "horizon," the line that determines the farthest visible part of the earth, in reference to the heavens. In this place the word signifies such a manifest and complete exhibition of the subject as to render it indubitable. The resurrection of Christ from the dead was such a manifest proof of our Lord's innocence, the truth of His doctrine, and the fulfillment of all that the prophets had spoken, as to leave no doubt on any considerate and candid mind. *With power.* With a miraculous display of divine energy; for how could His body be raised again but by the miraculous energy of God? *According to the spirit of holiness.* There are many differences of sentiment relative to the meaning of this phrase in this place; some supposing that the spirit of holiness implies the divine nature of Jesus Christ; others, His immaculate sanctity; etc. To me it seems that the apostle simply means that the Person called Jesus, lately crucified at Jerusalem, and in whose name salvation was preached to the world, was the Son of God, the very Messiah promised before in the Holy Scriptures; and that He was this Messiah was amply demonstrated. (1) By His resurrection from the dead, the irrefragable proof of His purity, innocence, and the divine approbation. (2) He was proved to be the Son of God, the promised Messiah, by the Holy Spirit (called here *the spirit of holiness*).

5. *Grace and apostleship.* The peculiar influence and the essential qualifications which such an office requires. *For obedience to the faith.* That by this office, which I have received from God, and the power by which it is accompanied, I might proclaim the *faith*, the gospel of Jesus; and show all nations the necessity of believing in it, in order to their salvation.

6. *Ye are also the called.* You Romans are all invited to believe in Christ Jesus, for the salvation of your souls; and to you, with the rest, my apostolical mission extends. This appears to be the most obvious sense of the word *called* in this place—to be called by the gospel is to be invited to believe in Christ Jesus, and become His disciples. The word sometimes means "constituted," or "made," as in v. 1.

7. *Called to be saints.* Invited to become holy persons, by believing the gospel and receiving the gifts of the Holy Ghost. Or, here, the word may have the meaning of "made" or "constituted," as above. *Grace to you.* May you be partakers of the divine favor, the source whence every blessing is derived. *And peace.* The same as *shalom* in Hebrew, generally signifying all kinds of blessing, but especially harmony and unity, and the bond of such unity. *From God our Father.* The apostle wishes them all the blessings which can flow from God, as the Fountain of grace, producing in them all the happiness which a heart filled with the peace of God can possess; all of which are to be communicated to them through the Lord Jesus Christ.

8. *First, I thank my God.* From this to the end of v. 17 belongs to the preface, in which the apostle endeavors to conciliate the good opinion of the Christians at Rome, and to prepare their minds for his reproofs and exhortations. *Your faith is spoken of,* is celebrated, *throughout the whole world*—in every place where the Christian religion is professed, through all parts of the Roman dominions; for in this sense we should understand the words *the whole world*.

9. *Whom I serve with my spirit.* Whom "I worship with the profoundest religious reverence," for so the original certainly means. I not only employ all the powers of my body in this service, but all those of my soul, being thoroughly convinced of the absolute truth of the religion I preach.

10. *Making request.* By this we see how earnestly the apostle longed to see Rome. It had long been a subject of continual prayer to God that he might have *a prosperous journey* to, or rather "meeting" with, them.

11. *Some spiritual gift.* This probably means some of the extraordinary gifts of the Holy Spirit, which, being given to them, might tend greatly to establish their faith in the gospel of Christ. It is very likely that such gifts were conferred only by means of apostles; and as the apostle had not yet been at Rome, consequently the Roman Christians had not yet received any of these miraculous gifts, and thus they differed widely from all the other churches which had been raised by the apostle's ministry.

13. *But was let hitherto.* The word *let,* from the Anglo-Saxon, *lettan,* to "hinder," signifies impediment or hindrance of any kind. But it is likely that the original word, "I was forbidden," refers to a divine prohibition; he would have visited them long before, but God did not see right to permit him.

14. *I am debtor both to the Greeks, and to the Barbarians.* All the nations of the earth, themselves excepted, were termed *Barbarians* by the Greeks.

15. *I am ready to preach.* I have a ready mind. I was prevented only by the providence of God from visiting you long ago.

16. *I am not ashamed of the gospel of Christ.* This text is best illustrated by Isa. xxviii. 16; xlix. 23, quoted by the apostle, chap. x. 11: "For the scripture saith, Whosoever believeth on him shall not be ashamed"; i.e., they shall neither be confounded nor disappointed of their hope. *It is the power of God unto salvation.* The almighty power of God accompanies this preaching to the souls of them that believe; and the consequence is they are saved; and what but the power of God can save a fallen, sinful soul? *To the Jew first.* Not only the Jews have the first offer of this gospel, but they have the greatest need of it; being so deeply fallen, and having sinned against such glorious privileges, they are much more culpable than the Gentiles, who never had the light of a divine revelation. *And also to the Greek.* Though the salvation of God has hitherto been apparently confined to the Jewish people, yet it shall be so no longer; for the gospel of Christ is sent to the Gentiles as well as the Jews, God having put no difference between them, and Jesus Christ having tasted death for every man.

17. *For therein.* In the gospel of Christ. *Is the righteousness of God.* God's method of saving sinners. *Revealed from faith to faith.* Shown to be by *faith,* and not by the works of any law. That *righteousness* signifies God's method of saving mankind by faith in Christ is fully evident from the use of the term in chap. ix. 30: "The Gentiles, which followed not after righteousness"—who had no knowledge, by revelation, of God's method of justifying and saving sinners, "have attained to righteousness"—have had imparted to them God's method of salvation by faith in Christ. V. 31: "But Israel," the Jews, "which followed after the law of righteousness"—that law, the end or object of which is Christ, and through Him justification to all that believe (chap. x. 4)—"hath not attained to the law of righteousness"—have not found out the genuine plan of salvation, even in that law

which so strongly and generally proclaims justification by faith. And why have they not found it? V. 32: "Because they sought it not by faith, but as it were by the works of the law"—they did not discern that even its works or prescribed religious observances were intended to lead to faith in that glorious Mediator of whom they were the types and representatives; but the Jews trusted in the observances themselves, hoping to acquire justification and final salvation by that means. "For they stumbled at that stumblingstone"—at the doctrine of Christ crucified as the only sure ground on which the expectation of future salvation can be founded. Therefore, "being ignorant of God's righteousness"—God's method of saving sinners—"and going about to establish their own righteousness" —their own method of salvation, by the observance of those rites and ceremonies which should have led them by faith to Christ—they did not submit "themselves unto the righteousness of God"—they would not submit to be saved in God's way, and therefore rejected, persecuted, and crucified the Lord Jesus; see chap. x. 3. This collation of passages most evidently shows that the word *righteousness* here means simply God's method of saving sinners, or God's way of salvation, in opposition to the ways and means invented by the fancies or prejudices of men. There are few words in the sacred writings which are taken in a greater variety of acceptations than the word *tsedakah* in Hebrew, and *dikaiosyne* in Greek, both of which we generally translate *righteousness.* Our English word was originally "rightwiseness," and thus the righteous man was a person who was allowed to understand the claims of justice and right, and who, knowing them, acted according to their dictates. Such a man is thoroughly wise; he aims at the attainment of the best end by the use of the best means. This is a true definition of wisdom, and the righteous man is he that knows most and acts best. The Hebtew *tsadak,* in its ideal meaning, contains the notion of a beam or scales in equipoise, what we call "even balance." *The just shall live by faith.* This has been understood two ways: (1) That the just or righteous man cannot live a holy and useful life without exercising continual faith in our Lord Jesus—which is strictly true. (2) It is contended by some able critics that the words of the original text should be: "The just by faith, shall live"; that is, he alone that is justified by faith shall be saved—which is also true, as it is impossible to get salvation in any other way. This last meaning is probably the true one, as the original text in Hab. ii. 4 speaks of those who believed the declarations of God when the Chaldeans besieged Jerusalem, and, having acted conformably to them, escaped with their lives.

18. *For the wrath of God is revealed.* The apostle has now finished his preface, and comes to the grand subject of the Epistle; namely, to show the absolute need of the gospel of Christ, because of the universal corruption of mankind, which was so great as to incense the justice of God and call aloud for the punishment of the world. (1) He shows that all the heathen nations were utterly corrupt, and deserved this threatened punishment. And this is the subject of the first chapter, from v. 18 to the end. (2) He shows that the Jews, notwithstanding the greatness of their privileges, were no better than the Gentiles; and therefore the wrath of God was

revealed against them also. This subject he treats in chap. ii. and chap. iii. 1-19. (3) He returns, as it were, on both, chap. iii. 20-31, and proves that, as the Jews and Gentiles were equally corrupt, they could not be saved by the deeds of any law; that they stood equally in need of that salvation which God had provided; that both were equally entitled to that salvation, for God was the God of the Gentiles as well as of the Jews. By *the wrath of God* we are not to understand any uneasy passion in the Divine Being; but the displeasure of His righteousness, which is expressed by the punishments inflicted on the ungodly, those who retain not God in their knowledge; and the unrighteous, those whose lives are profligate. As in the gospel the righteousness of God is *revealed* for the salvation of the ungodly, so is the wrath of God *revealed* against the workers of iniquity. Those who refuse to be saved in the way revealed by His mercy must be consumed in the way revealed by His justice. *Ungodliness.* Probably intended here to express atheism, polytheism, and idolatry of every kind. *Unrighteousness.* Everything contrary to strict morality; all viciousness and profligacy of conduct. *Who hold the truth in unrighteousness.* Some contend that the word here does not signify to *hold,* but to "hinder"; and that the place should be translated, "who through maliciousness hinder the truth"; i.e., prevent it from taking hold of their hearts, and from governing their conduct. This is certainly a very usual acceptation of the verb.

20. *The invisible things of him.* His invisible perfections are manifested by His visible works, and may be apprehended by what He has made; their immensity showing His omnipotence; their vast variety, His omniscience; and their adaptation to the most beneficent purposes, His infinite goodness. *His eternal power.* That all-powerful energy that ever was and ever will exist; so that, ever since there was a creation to be surveyed, there have been intelligent beings to make that survey. *And Godhead.* His acting as God in the government and support of the universe. His works prove His being.

21. *Because that, when they knew God.* When they thus acquired a general knowledge of the unity and perfections of the divine nature, *they glorified him not as God*—they did not proclaim Him to the people, but shut up His glory (as Bishop Warburton expresses it) in their mysteries, and gave the people, in exchange for an incorruptible God, an image made like to corruptible man. *They glorified him not.* They did not give Him that worship which His perfections required. *Neither were thankful.* They manifested no gratitude for the blessings they received from His providence but *became vain in their imagination,* "in their reasonings." This certainly refers to the foolish manner in which even the wisest of their philosophers discoursed about the divine nature, not excepting Socrates, Plato, or Seneca.

22. *Professing themselves to be wise.* This is most strikingly true of all the ancient philosophers, whether Greeks or Romans, as their works, which remain, sufficiently testify. The word signifies not merely the *professing* but the "assumption" of the philosophic character.

23. *They changed the glory.* The finest representation of their deities was in the human figure, and on such representative figures the sculptors spent all their skill. And when they

had formed their gods according to the human shape, they endowed them with human passions. *And to birds.* As the eagle of Jupiter among the Romans, and the ibis and hawk among the Egyptians, which were all sacred animals. *Four-footed beasts.* As the ox among the Egyptians, from which the idolatrous Israelites took their golden calf. The goat, the monkey, and the dog were also sacred animals among the same people. *Creeping things.* Such as the crocodile and *scarabeus,* or beetle, among the Egyptians.

24. *God . . . gave them up.* They had filled up the measure of their iniquities, and God, by permitting them to plunge into all manner of irregularities, thus, by one species of sin, inflicted punishment on another. *Dishonour their own bodies.* Probably alluding here to what is more openly expressed in vv. 26-27. *Between themselves.* "Of themselves," of their own free accord.

25. *Changed the truth of God into a lie.* In the place of the true worship of God, they established idolatry. In various places of Scripture idols are termed *lies,* Isa. xliv. 20; Jer. x. 14; and xiii. 25. The true God was known among the primitive inhabitants of the earth. Those who first became idolaters literally changed the truth of God into a lie; they did know the true God, but they put idols in His place.

26. *For this cause God gave them up.* Their system of idolatry necessarily produced all kinds of impurity. How could it be otherwise, when the highest objects of their worship were adulterers, fornicators, and prostitutes of the most infamous kind, such as Jupiter, Apollo, Mars, Venus?

28. *They did not like to retain God.* It would, perhaps, be more literal to translate, "They did not search to retain God in their knowledge." They did not examine the evidences before them (vv. 19-20) of His being and attributes; therefore *God gave them over to a reprobate mind,* to an "unsearching or undiscerning" mind, for it is the same word in both places. They did not reflect on the proofs they had of the divine nature, and God abandoned them to the operations of a mind incapable of reflection.

29. *Being filled with all unrighteousness.* Every vice contrary to justice and righteousness. *Fornication.* All commerce between the sexes out of the bounds of lawful marriage. Some of the best MSS. omit this reading. *Wickedness.* "Malignity," that which is oppressive to its possessor and to its object. *Covetousness.* The intense love or lust of gain, the determination to be rich, the principle of a dissatisfied and discontented soul. *Maliciousness.* "Malice, ill-will"; what is radically and essentially vicious. *Full of envy.* "Pain felt and malignity conceived at the sight of excellence or happiness in another." *Murder.* Taking away the life of another by any means; mortal hatred, for he that hates his brother in his heart is a murderer. *Debate.* "Contention, discord." Of this vile passion the Greeks made a goddess. *Deceit.* "Lying, falsity, prevarication, imposition." *Malignity.* Bad customs, founded in corrupt sentiment, producing evil habits, supported by general usage. It is generally interpreted a malignity of mind which leads its possessor to put the worst construction on every action, ascribing to the best deeds the worst motives.

Whisperers. Secret detractors; those who, under pretended secrecy, carry about accusations against their neighbors, whether true or false, blasting their reputation by clandestine tittle-tattle. This word should be joined to the succeeding verse. The whispering is well expressed by the Greek word *psithuristas.*

30. *Backbiters.* Those who speak against others; false accusers, slanderers. *Haters of God.* Atheists, contemners of sacred things, maligners of providence, scorners. All profligate deists are of this class; and it seems to be the finishing part of a diabolic character. *Despiteful.* Stormy, boisterous; abusing both the characters and persons of those over whom they can have any power. *Proud.* They who are continually exalting themselves and depressing others, magnifying themselves at the expense of their neighbors. *Boasters.* Self-assuming, vainglorious, and arrogant men. *Inventors of evil things.* Those who have invented destructive customs, rites, fashions; such as the different religious ceremonies among the Greeks and Romans—the orgies of Bacchus, the mysteries of Ceres. Multitudes of which evil things, destructive and abominable ceremonies, are to be found in every part of the heathen worship. *Disobedient to parents.* Though filial affection was certainly more recommended and cultivated than many other virtues, yet there are many instances on record of the grossest violation of this great branch of the law of nature.

31. *Without understanding.* Persons incapable of comprehending what was spoken; destitute of capacity for spiritual things. *Covenantbreakers.* Persons who could be bound by no oath because, properly speaking, they had no God to witness or avenge their misconduct. As every covenant or agreement is made as in the presence of God, so he that opposes the being and doctrine of God is incapable of being bound by any covenant; he can give no pledge for his conduct. *Without natural affection.* Without that attachment which nature teaches the young of all animals to have to their mothers, and the mothers to have for their young. The heathen, in general, have made no scruple to expose the children they did not think proper to bring up, and to dispatch their parents when they were grown old or past labor. *Implacable.* The word here shows a deadly enmity, the highest pitch of an unforgiving spirit; in a word, persons who would not make reconciliation to either God or man. *Unmerciful.* Those who were incapable, through the deep-rooted wickedness of their own nature, of showing mercy to an enemy when brought under their power.

32. *Who, knowing the judgment of God.* The grand rule of right which God has revealed to every man, the knowledge of which He has, more or less, given to every nation of the world, relative to honoring parents, taking care of their own offspring, keeping engagements. In the worst states of heathenism this great principle has been acknowledged; but through the prevalence of corruption in the heart, this law, though acknowledged, was not obeyed; and the corruption increased so that those were highest in repute who had cast off all restraints of this kind; so that they even delighted in them; highly applauded, and gladly associated with those transgressors—which argues the very highest pitch of moral depravity.

CHAPTER 2

The apostle shows that the Jew, who condemns the Gentiles, and considers them utterly unworthy of the blessings of the gospel, is inexcusable, because he is guilty of the same crimes, and therefore shall not escape the righteous judgment of God, 1-3. It is an awful thing to despise the goodness and long-suffering of God, which lead to repentance, 4-5. God, the impartial Judge, will render to every man according to his works, 6-11. The Jews and the Gentiles will be judged according to their respective advantages and disadvantages, 12-13. In some cases the Gentiles, who had no law, have shown a better disposition than the Jews, 14-16. The Jews, by their unfaithfulness, have been a stumbling block to the Gentiles, 17-24. Jewish rites and ceremonies of no advantage, unless productive of change of heart and conduct, 25. The Gentiles, who attend to the small light which they have received from God, are in a better state than the unfaithful Jews, with all their superior religious privileges, 26-27. What constitutes a real Jew in the sight of God, 28-29.

1. *That judgest.* "The judger"; you assume the character of a judge, and in that character condemn others who are less guilty than yourself.

2. *We are sure that the judgment of God.* God is impartial, and will punish sin wheresoever He finds it. Transgression in a Jew is not less criminal than iniquity in a Gentile.

4. *Or despisest thou the riches of his goodness?* Will you render of none effect that marked benevolence of God towards you which has given so many superior advantages, and that *forbearance* which has tolerated your many miscarriages, and that *longsuffering* which, after repeated provocations, still continues to bear with you? *Not knowing.* Not "acknowledging" that this goodness of God, which has so long manifested itself in forbearance and long-suffering, *leadeth thee to repentance*—was designed to accomplish this blessed end, which your want of consideration and acknowledgment has rendered, hitherto, ineffectual. This was a maxim among the Jews themselves; for, in *Synopsis Sohar,* it is said: "The holy blessed God delays his anger against the wicked, to the end that they may repent and be converted."

5. *But after thy hardness.* Occasioned by your long course of iniquity. *And impenitent heart*—produced by your hardness, through which you are callous to the calls and expostulations of conscience. *Treasurest up*—continue to increase your debt to the divine justice, which will infallibly inflict *wrath,* punishment, in *the day of wrath*—the judgment day, in which He will render to every man according to his works. The word *treasure* the Hebrew uses to express any kind of store or collection. So treasures of gold, silver, corn, wine, oil, etc., mean collections or an abundance of such things; the word is used by the Greek writers precisely in the same sense. By *wrath* we are to understand "punishment," as in chap. 1. 18; and it is used so by the very best Greek writers. The *treasure of wrath,* in this verse, is opposed to the *riches of goodness,* in the preceding. As surely as you despise or neglect to improve the riches of God's goodness, so surely you shall share in the treasures of His wrath. The punishment shall be proportioned to the mercy you have abused.

6. *Who will render.* Who, in the day of judgment, will reward and punish every man according as his life and conversation have been.

7. *To them.* In this manner will God, in the great day, dispense punishments and rewards: (1) He will give eternal life to them who, in all the trials and difficulties of the present state, have persevered *in well doing*—seeking for and expecting *glory, honour,* and *immortality.*

8. *But unto them.* (2) He will manifest His *indignation,* and inflict *wrath*—punishment, on all who are *contentious*—who obstinately dispute against the truth, and *obey unrighteousness* —who act under the influence of the principle of sin, and not under the influence of the Spirit of God.

9. *Tribulation and anguish.* Misery of all descriptions, without the possibility of escape, will this righteous Judge inflict upon every impenitent sinner. The Jew first, as possessing greater privileges, and having abused greater mercies; and also on the Gentile, who, though he had not the same advantages, had what God saw was sufficient for his state; and, having sinned against them, shall have punishment proportioned to his demerit.

10. *But glory, honour, and peace.* While the finally impenitent Jew and Gentile shall experience the fullest effects of the righteous indignation of the supreme Judge, every man that *worketh good*—that lives in a conscientious obedience to the known will of God—whether he be Jew or Gentile, shall have *glory, honour,* and *peace;* i.e., eternal blessedness.

11. *For there is no respect of persons with God.* The righteous Judge will not act according to any principle of partiality; the character and conduct alone of the persons shall weigh with Him. He will take no wicked man to glory, let his nation or advantages be what they may; and He will send no righteous man to perdition, though brought up in the very bosom of Gentilism.

12. *For as many as have sinned without law.* They, viz., the Gentiles, who shall be found to have transgressed against the mere light of nature, or rather, "that true Light, which lighteth every man that cometh into the world," John i. 9, shall not come under the same rule with those, the Jews, who have in addition to this enjoyed an extraordinary revelation, but they shall be dealt with according to the inferior dispensation under which they lived, while those, the Jews, who have *sinned in the law*—the positive, divine revelation granted to them, *shall be judged by the law,* and punished proportionably to the abuse of such an extraordinary advantage.

13. *For not the hearers of the law.* It does not follow, because one people are favored with a divine revelation, that therefore they shall be saved; while the others who have not had that revelation shall finally perish; this is not God's procedure. Where He has given a *law,* a divine revelation, He requires obedience to that law; and only those who have been *doers* of that law, who have lived according to the light and privileges granted in that revelation, *shall be justified*—shall be finally acknowledged to be such as are fit for the kingdom of God.

14. *For when the Gentiles, which have not the law.* Nor does it follow that the Gentiles, who have not had a divine revelation, shall either perish because they had it not or their unrighteous conduct pass unpunished because not having this revelation might be considered as an excuse for their sins. *Do by nature the things contained in the law.* Do, without this divine revelation, through that light which God imparts to every man, *the things contained in the law*—act according to justice, mercy, temperance, and truth, the practice of which the revealed law so powerfully enjoins; *these . . . are*

a law unto themselves—they are not accountable to any other law, and are not to be judged by any dispensation different from that under which they live.

15. *Which shew the work of the law.* In acting according to justice, mercy, temperance, and truth they show that the great object of the law, which was to bring men from injustice, cruelty, intemperance, and falsity, is accomplished so far in them; *their conscience also bearing witness*—that faculty of the soul, where that divine light dwells and works, shows them that they are right; and thus they have a comfortable testimony in their own souls of their own integrity. *Their thoughts the mean while accusing or else excusing one another;* or rather, "their reasonings between one another accusing or answering for themselves." As if the apostle had said: And this point, that they have a law and act according to it, is further proved from their conduct in *civil* affairs; and from that correct sense which they have of *natural justice* in their *debates,* either in their *courts of law* or in their *treatises on morality.* All these are ample proofs that God has not left them without light; and that, seeing they have such correct notions of right and wrong, they are accountable to God for their conduct in reference to these notions and principles. This seems to be the true meaning of this difficult clause. See below. Much stress has been laid on the words *by nature,* in v. 14, as if the apostle designed to intimate that nature, independently of the influence of divine grace, possessed such principles as were sufficient to guide a man to glory. But certainly the term cannot be so understood here. I rather think that "certainly, truly" is its sense here: "For when the Gentiles, which have not the law, *truly,* or in effect, *do* the things contained in the law." This seems to be its sense in Gal. iv. 8: "When ye knew not God, ye did service unto them which certainly are no gods"; i.e., are false gods. The passage in v. 15, *Their thoughts . . . accusing or else excusing one another,* certainly does not refer to any expostulations or operations of *conscience,* for this is referred to in the preceding clause. The words *accusing* and *excusing,* "answering or defending one another among themselves," are all forensic or law terms, and refer to the mode of conducting suits of law in courts of justice, where one is plaintiff, who produces his accusation; another is defendant, who rebuts the charge and defends himself; and then the business is argued before the judges. This process shows that they have a law of their own, and that to this law it belongs to adjust differences—to right those who have suffered wrong, and to punish the guilty. As to the phrase *written in their hearts,* it is here opposed to the Jewish laws, which were written on tables of stone. The Jews drew the maxims by which their conduct was regulated from a divine revelation; the Gentiles drew theirs from what God, in the course of His providence and gracious influence, had shown them to be right, useful, and necessary. And with them this law was "well known and affectionately regarded"; for this is one meaning of the phrase *written in their hearts.*

17. *Behold, thou art called a Jew.* What the apostle had said in the preceding verses being sufficient to enforce conviction on the conscience of the Jew, he now openly argues with him in the most plain manner, asserting that his

superior knowledge, privileges, and profession served only to aggravate his condemnation. *And restest in the law.* You trust in it for your endless salvation. The word implies the strongest confidence of safety and security. You "repose your whole trust and confidence" in this law. *And makest thy boast of God.* That you know His nature and attributes, which are not known to the Gentiles. The word implies the idea of "exulting" in anything, as being a proper object of hope and dependence; and when referred to God, it points out that He is the sure Cause of hope, dependence, joy, and happiness; and that it is the highest honor to be called to know His name, and be employed in His service. As if the apostle had said: You rejoice in God as the Object of your hope and dependence; you praise and magnify Him; you account it your greatest honor that He is your God, and that you worship Him.

18. *Knowest his will.* Have been favored with a revelation of His own will, immediately from himself. *The things that are more excellent.* "The things that differ"—that revelation which God has given of himself makes the nicest distinctions between right and wrong, between vice and virtue; showing how you should walk so as to please God, and, consequently, acquire the most excellent portion that human spirits can have on this side of heaven. For all these blessings you acknowledge to receive from your law, *being instructed,* being "catechized," from your infancy in the knowledge of divine things.

19. *And art confident.* In consequence of all these religious advantages, you believe that you are able to teach others, and to be guides and lights to the bewildered, darkened Gentiles, who may become proselytes to your religion.

20. *An instructor of the foolish.* You believe the Gentiles to be babes and fools when compared with yourselves; that you alone possess the only true knowledge; that you are the only favorites of Heaven; and that all nations must look up to you as possessing the only *form of knowledge,* the grand scheme and draught of all true science, of everything that is worthy to be learned: the system of eternal truth, derived from the law.

21. *Thou therefore.* That the Jewish priesthood was exceedingly corrupt in the time of the apostle, and that they were so long before, is fully evident from the sacred writings and from Josephus. The high priesthood was bought and sold like other commodities.

24. *For the name of God is blasphemed.* In *Debarim rabba* it is said: "The rulers destroy the influence of their own words among the people; and this is done when a rabbin, sitting and teaching in the academy, says, Do not take usury, and himself takes it; do not commit rapine, and himself commits it; do not steal, and himself steals." That they were exceedingly lax in their morals, the following fact proves: "Rabbi Ilai said, If a man see that his evil propensities are likely to prevail against him, let him go to some place where he is not known, and let him put on black clothes, and cover his head with a black veil; and then let him do whatsoever he pleases, lest the name of God should be publicly profaned."

25. *For circumcision verily profiteth.* It is a blessing to belong to the Church of God and wear the sign of the covenant, provided the terms of the covenant are complied with. *But if thou be a breaker of the law.* If you do not observe the conditions of the covenant, the outward sign is both without meaning and without effect. This was a maxim of the rabbins themselves; for they allowed that an apostate or ungodly Israelite must go to hell, notwithstanding his circumcision.

26. *Therefore if the uncircumcision.* If the Gentile be found to act according to the spirit and design of the law, his acting thus uprightly, according to the light which God has afforded him, will be reckoned to him as if he were circumcised and walked agreeably to the law.

27. *And shall not uncircumcision which is by nature?* And shall not the Gentile, who is according to the custom of his country—who is by birth not obliged to be circumcised? *If it fulfil the law.* If such a person act according to the spirit and design of the law. *Judge,* "condemn" *thee,* who, while you enjoy the letter, the written law, and bear in your body the proof of the circumcision which it requires, *dost transgress the law.*

28. *For he is not a Jew,* a genuine member of the Church of God, who has only an outward profession. *Neither is that circumcision.* Circumcision is a rite which represents a spiritual thing, viz., the change and purification of the heart, as may be seen from Jer. iv. 4, 6, 10; ix. 26; Ezek. xliv. 7, 9.

29. *But he is a Jew.* A true member of the Church of God. *Which is one inwardly.* Who has his heart purified, according to what God has uniformly prescribed by His prophets. For *circumcision is . . . of the heart, in the spirit,* "by the Spirit" of God, who is the Author of all spiritual affections and holy purposes; or everything here is to be understood spiritually, and not literally; for without holiness none can please God, and without holiness none can see Him. *Whose praise is not of men.* It has, with great probability, been conjectured that the apostle may here refer to the signification of the name Jew, or Judah, *Yehudah,* "Praise." Such a one is a true Israelite, who walks in a conformity to the spirit of his religion. His countrymen may praise him because he is a steady professor of the Jewish faith; but God praises him because he has entered into the spirit and design of the covenant made with Abraham, and has got the end of his faith, the salvation of his soul.

CHAPTER 3

The apostle points out the peculiar privileges of the Jews, 1-8. But shows that they also, as well as the Gentiles, had sinned and forfeited all right and title to both; and does not set aside, but establishes the law, God's especial favor, 9. The corrupt state of all mankind, 10-18. All the world is guilty before God, and none can be justified by the works of the law, 19-20. God's mercy in providing redemption for a lost world, by Jesus Christ, 21-26. This excludes boasting on the part both of Jew and Gentile; provides salvation through faith for both; and does not set aside, but establishes the law, 27-31.

As the first nine verses are a dialogue between the apostle and a Jew, I shall prefix the speakers to their respective questions and answers, to make the whole the more intelligible to the reader.

1. JEW. *What advantage then hath the Jew? or what profit is there of circumcision?* As if he had said: You lately allowed (chap. ii. 25) that "circumcision verily profiteth." But if cir-

cumcision, or our being in covenant with God, raises us no higher in the divine favor than the Gentiles; if the virtuous among them are as acceptable as any of us; nay, and condemn our nation too, as no longer deserving the divine regards; pray tell me, wherein lies the superior honor of the Jew; and what benefit can arise to him from his circumcision, and being vested in the privileges of God's peculiar people?

2. APOSTLE. *Much every way.* The Jews, in reference to the means and motives of obedience, enjoy many advantages beyond the Gentiles; and, principally, because *unto them were committed the oracles of God*—that revelation of His will to Moses and the prophets, containing a treasure of excellencies with which no other part of the world has been favored.

3. JEW. *For what?* "What then, *if some did not believe?*" If some of the Jewish nation have abused their privileges, and acted contrary to their obligations, shall their wickedness annul the promise which God made to Abraham that He would, by an everlasting covenant, be a God to him and to his seed after him? Gen. xvii. 7. Shall God, therefore, by stripping the Jews of their peculiar honor, as you intimate He will, falsify His promise to the nation, because some of the Jews are bad men?

4. APOSTLE. *God forbid.* "Let it not be, far from it, by no means." *Yea, let God be true, but every man a liar.* We must ever maintain that God is true, and that if, in any case, His promise appear to fail, it is because the condition on which it was given has not been complied with; which is the sense of what is written, Ps. li. 3: I acknowledge my sin, and condemn myself that the truth of Thy promise (2 Sam. vii. 15-16) to establish my house and throne forever may be vindicated when Thou shalt execute that dreadful threatening (2 Sam. xii. 10) that the sword shall never depart from my house, which I own I have brought upon myself by my own iniquity. Should any man say that the promise of God had failed toward him, let him examine his heart and his ways, and he will find that *he* has departed out of that way in which alone God could, consistently with His holiness and truth, fulfill the promise.

5. JEW. *But if our unrighteousness commend the righteousness of God.* May we not suppose that our unrighteousness may serve to commend and illustrate the mercy of God in keeping and fulfilling to us the promise which He made to our forefathers? The more wicked we are, the more His faithfulness to His ancient promise is to be admired. And if so, would not God appear unjust in taking vengeance and casting us off? *I speak as a man.* I feel for the situation of both myself and my countrymen, and it is natural for one to speak as I do.

6. APOSTLE. *God forbid.* "By no means." God cannot be unjust; were He unjust, He could not be qualified to judge the world, nor inflict that punishment on the unfaithful Jews to which I refer.

7. JEW. *For if the truth of God.* But to resume my reasoning (see v. 5): If the faithfulness of God in keeping His promise made to our fathers is, through our unfaithfulness, made far more glorious than it otherwise would have been, why should we then be blamed for that which must redound so much to the honor of God?

8. APOSTLE. *And not rather.* And why do you not say, seeing you assume this ground, that in all cases we should do wickedly, because God, by freely pardoning, can so glorify His own grace? This is a most impious sentiment, but it follows from your reasoning; it has, indeed, been most injuriously laid to the charge of us apostles, who preach the doctrine of free pardon, through faith, without the merit of works; but this is so manifest a perversion of the truth that a just punishment may be expected to fall on the propagators of such a slander.

9. JEW. *What then?* After all, have not we Jews a better claim to the privileges of the kingdom of God than the Gentiles have?

APOSTLE. *No, in no wise.* For I have already proved that both Jews and Gentiles are under the guilt of sin; that they are equally unworthy of the blessings of the Messiah's kingdom; and that they must both, equally, owe their salvation to the mere mercy of God. From this, to the end of the twenty-sixth verse, the apostle proceeds to prove his assertion that both Jews and Gentiles were all under sin; and, that he might enforce the conviction upon the heart of the Jew, he quotes his own Scriptures, which he acknowledged had been given by the inspiration of God, and consequently true.

10. *As it is written.* See Ps. xiv. 1-3, from which this and the following two verses are taken. *There is none righteous.* This is true, not only of the Jews, but of the Gentiles—of every soul of man, considered in his natural and practical state, previously to his receiving the mercy of our Lord Jesus Christ. There is no righteous principle in them, and consequently no righteous act can be expected from them; see on v. 12. God himself is represented as looking down from heaven to see if there were any that feared and sought after Him; and yet He, who cannot be deceived, could find none!

12. *They are all gone out of the way.* They have all "diverged" from the right way; they have either abandoned or corrupted the worship of God: the Jews, in forsaking the law and the prophets; and the Gentiles, in acting contrary to the law which God had written on their hearts. And the departure of both from the truth proves the evil propensity of human nature in general. *They are together become unprofitable.* They are "useless," good for nothing; or, as the Hebrew has it, "they are putrid." He views the whole mass of mankind as slain and thrown together, to putrefy in heaps. This is what is termed the corruption of human nature. *There is none that doeth good.* In v. 10 it is said, "There is none righteous"; here, *There is none that doeth good.* The first may refer to the want of a righteous principle; the second, to the necessary consequence of the absence of such a principle. If there be no righteousness within, there will be no acts of goodness without.

13. *Their throat is an open sepulchre.* This and all the following verses to the end of v. 18 are found in the Septuagint, but not in the Hebrew text. The verses in question, however, are not found in the Alexandrian MS. But they exist in the Vulgate, the Aethiopic, and the Arabic. As the most ancient copies of the Septuagint do not contain these verses, some contend that the apostle has quoted them from different parts of Scripture; and later transcribers of the Septuagint, finding that the tenth,

eleventh, and twelfth verses were quoted from Psalm xiv, imagined that the rest were found originally there too, and so incorporated them in their copies from the apostle's text. *Their throat is an open sepulchre*—By their malicious and wicked words they bury, as it were, the reputation of all men. The whole of this verse appears to belong to their habit of lying, defamation, slandering, by which they wounded, blasted, and poisoned the reputation of others.

14. *Whose mouth is full of cursing.* They never speak but in profane oaths, blasphemies, and malice.

15. *Their feet are swift to shed blood.* They make use of every means in their power to destroy the reputation and lives of the innocent.

16. *Destruction and misery are in their ways.* Destruction is their work, and *misery* to themselves and to the objects of their malice is the consequence of their impious and murderous conduct.

17. *And the way of peace have they not known.* They neither have peace in themselves nor do they suffer others to live in quiet; they are brooders and fomenters of discord.

18. *There is no fear of God before their eyes.* This completes their bad character; they are downright atheists, at least practically such. They fear not God's judgments, although His eye is upon them in their evil ways. There is not one article of what is charged against the Jews and Gentiles here that may not be found justified by the histories of both, in the most ample manner. And what was true of them in those primitive times is true of them still. With very little variation, these are the evils in which the vast mass of mankind delight and live.

19. *What things soever the law saith.* That the word *law* here does not mean the Pentateuch is evident from the preceding quotations, not one of which is taken from that work. The term *law* must here mean either the Jewish writings in general or that rule of moral conduct which God had given to both Jews and Gentiles: to the former in their own Scriptures; to the latter in that law written in their hearts by His own Spirit, and acknowledged in their written codes, and in their pleading in every civil case. Now, according to this great law, this rule of moral conduct, whether given in a written revelation, as to the Jews, or by the secret inspiration of His Spirit, as in certain cases to the Gentiles, *every mouth may be stopped, and all the world,* both Jews and Gentiles, stand convicted *before God;* for all mankind have sinned against this law.

20. *Therefore by the deeds of the law.* On the score of obedience to this moral law, *there shall no flesh,* "no human being," *be justified:* none can be accepted in the sight of God. And why? Because *by the law is the knowledge of sin.* It is that which ascertains what sin is, shows how men have deviated from its righteous demands, and sentences them to death because they have broken it.

21. *But now the righteousness of God.* God's method of saving sinners is now shown by the gospel to be through His own mere mercy, by Christ Jesus; *without the law*—without any right or claim which might result from obedience to the law; and is evidently that which was intended by God from the beginning, for it is *witnessed by the law and the prophets*—

the rites and ceremonies of the one, and the preachings and predictions of the others, all bearing testimony to the great design of God, and to the absolute necessity there was for the sacrifice and salvation which God had provided.

22. *Even the righteousness of God.* That method of saving sinners which is not of works, but by faith in Christ Jesus; and it is not restrained to any particular people, as the law and its privileges were, but is unto all mankind in its intention and offer, and becomes effectual to them that believe; for God hath now made *no difference* between the Jews and the Gentiles.

23. *For all have sinned.* And consequently are equally helpless and guilty; and, as God is no respecter of persons, all human creatures being equally His offspring, and there being no reason why one should be preferred before another, therefore His endless mercy has embraced all. *And come short of the glory of God.* These words have been variously translated. "Failed of attaining the glory of God"; stand in need of the glory, that is, the mercy of God." The simple meaning seems to be this: that all have sinned, and none can enjoy God's glory but they that are holy; consequently both Jews and Gentiles have failed in their endeavors to attain it, as by the works of any law no human being can be justified.

24. *Being justified freely by his grace.* So far from being able to attain the glory of God by their obedience, they are all guilty; and to be saved must be freely pardoned by God's grace, which is shown to them who believe, through the redemption, the "ransom price," which is in the sacrifice of Christ Jesus. The original properly means the price laid down for the redemption of a captive.

25. *Whom God hath set forth.* Appointed and published to be a *propitiation,* the "mercy seat," or "place of atonement"; because the blood of the sacrifice was sprinkled on and before that, in order to obtain remission of sin. The mercy seat was the lid or cover of the ark of the covenant, where God was manifest in the symbol of His presence between the cherubim; therefore the atonement that was made in this place was properly made to God himself. *Through faith in his blood.* This shows what we are to understand both by the *redemption* and by the *propitiation;* viz., that they refer to the sacrificial death of Jesus Christ, as the atonement made, and the *price* paid down, for the redemption of the souls of men. *To declare his righteousness.* "For the manifestation of His righteousness"; His mercy in saving sinners, by sending Jesus Christ to make an atonement for them; thereby declaring His readiness to remit all past transgressions committed by both Jews and Gentiles, during the time in which His merciful forbearance was exercised towards the world. And this applies to all who hear the gospel now; to them is freely offered remission of all *past sins.*

26. *To declare, I say, at this time.* To manifest now, by the dispensation of the gospel, *his righteousness,* His infinite mercy; and to manifest it in such a way that He might still appear to be the *just* God, and yet *the justifier,* the Pardoner, *of him which believeth in Jesus.* Here we learn that God designed to give the most evident displays of both His justice and mercy: of His justice, in requiring a sacrifice, and absolutely refusing to give salvation to a lost

world in any other way; and of His mercy, in providing the sacrifice which His justice required. Thus, because Jesus was an Atonement, a Ransom Price, for the sin of the world, therefore God can, consistently with His justice, pardon every soul that believeth in Jesus. This is the full discovery of God's righteousness, of His wonderful method of magnifying His law and making it honorable; of showing the infinite purity of His justice, and of saving a lost world. Hitherto, from the ninth verse, the apostle had gone on without interruption, proving that Jew and Gentile were in a state of guilt and condemnation, and that they could be saved only by the redemption that is in Christ Jesus. The Jew, finding his boasted privileges all at stake, interrupts him, and asks:

27. Jew. *Where is boasting then?* "This glorying" of ours. Have we nothing in which we can trust for our acceptance with God? No merit of our own? Nothing accruing to us from our circumcision and being in covenant with God?

Apostle. *It is excluded.* "It is shut out"; the door of heaven is shut against everything of this kind.

Jew. *By what law?* By what rule, doctrine, or reason is it shut out? by the law *of works?* The rule of obedience, which God gave to us, and by which obedience we are accepted by Him?

Apostle. *Nay.* Not by the law of works; glorying is not cut off or shut out by that; it stands in full force as the rule of life. But you have sinned and need pardon. The law of works grants no pardon; it requires obedience, and threatens the disobedient with death. But all glorying in the expectation of salvation through your own obedience is excluded by the law; the doctrine of faith, faith alone, in the mercy of God, through the propitiation made by the blood of Jesus (v. 25), is that by which you can be justified, pardoned, and taken into the divine favor.

28. *Therefore we conclude.* Seeing these things cannot be denied, viz., that all have sinned; that all are guilty; that all are helpless; that none can deliver his own soul; and that God, in His endless mercy, has opened "a new and living way" to the holiest by the blood of Jesus, Heb. x. 19-20; therefore we, apostles and Christian teachers, *conclude,* prove by fair, rational consequence, that *a man,* any man, *is justified,* has his sins blotted out, and is received into the divine favor, *by faith* in Christ's blood, *without the deeds of the law,* which never could afford, to either Jew or Gentile, a ground for justification; because both have sinned against the law which God has given them, and consequently forfeited all right and title to the blessings which the obedient might claim.

29. *Is he the God of the Jews only?* Do not begin to suppose that because you cannot be justified by the works of the law, and God has in His mercy found out a new method of saving you, that therefore this mercy shall apply to the Jews exclusively. Is not God the Maker, Preserver, and Redeemer *also of the Gentiles? Yes, of the Gentiles also,* as much as of the Jews. For all have equally sinned and there is no reason, if God be disposed to show mercy at all, that He should prefer the one to the other; since they are all equally guilty, sinful, and necessitous.

30. *Seeing it is one God.* This has been rendered, "Seeing God is one." It however makes little difference in the sense. The apostle's meaning most evidently is, It is one and the same God who made both Jews and Gentiles, who shall *justify,* pardon, *the circumcision,* the believing Jews, *by faith,* and the *uncircumcision,* the believing Gentiles, by the same faith; as there is but one Saviour and one atonement provided for the whole. It is fanciful to suppose that the apostle has one meaning when he says, *by faith,* and a different meaning when he says, *through faith.* Both the prepositions are to be understood in precisely the same sense; only the addition of the article in the last case extends and more pointedly ascertains the meaning. It is one and the same God who shall justify the believing Jews by faith and the believing Gentiles "by that same faith."

31. *Do we then make void the law through faith?* (1) By *law* here we may understand the whole of the Mosaic law, in its rites and ceremonies, of which Jesus Christ was the Subject and the End. (2) We may understand also the moral law, that which relates to the regulation of the manners or conduct of men. This law also was established by the doctrine of salvation by faith, because this faith works by love, and love is the principle of obedience: and whosoever receives salvation through faith in Christ receives power to live in holy obedience to every moral precept.

CHAPTER 4

Abraham was justified by faith, and not by the works of the law; for his faith was imputed to him for righteousness, 1-5. David also bears testimony to the same doctrine, 6-8. Abraham, the father of the Jewish race, was justified by faith, even before he was circumcised; therefore salvation must be of the Gentiles as well as the Jews, 9-12. And the promise that all the nations of the earth should be blessed in him was made to him while he was in an uncircumcised state; and therefore, if salvation were of the Jews alone, the law, that was given after the promise, would make the promise of no effect, 13-17. Description of Abraham's faith, and its effects, 18-22. This account is left on record for our salvation, that we might believe on Christ, "who was delivered for our offences, and was raised again for our justification," 23-25.

The apostle, having proved in the foregoing chapter that neither Jews nor Gentiles have a right to the blessing of God's peculiar kingdom otherwise than by grace, which is as free for the one as the other, in this chapter advances a new argument to convince the Jew, and to show the believing Gentile, in a clear light, the high value and strong security of the mercies freely bestowed on them in the gospel; and at the same time to display the scheme of divine providence, as laid in the counsel and will of God. His argument is taken from Abraham's case: Abraham was the father and head of the Jewish nation; he had been a heathen, but God pardoned him and took him and his posterity into his special covenant, and bestowed upon them many extraordinary blessings above the rest of mankind; and it is evident that Abraham was not justified by any obedience to law, or rule of right action, but, in the only way in which a sinner can be justified, by prerogative or the mercy of the Lawgiver. Now this is the very same way in which the gospel saves the believing Gentiles, and gives them a part in the blessings of God's covenant. Why then should the Jews oppose the Gentiles? especially as the Gentiles were actually included in the covenant made with Abraham; for the promise, Gen. xvii. 4, stated that he should be the "father of many nations." Consequently the covenant being made with Abraham, as the head or father of many nations, all in any nation who stood on the same religious principle with him were his *seed* and with him interested in the same covenant. But Abraham stood by faith in the mercy of God pardoning his idolatry; and upon this footing the believing Gentiles stand in the gospel; and therefore they are the "seed of Abraham," and included in the covenant and promise made to him.

To all this the apostle knew well it would be objected that it was not faith alone that gave Abraham a right to the blessings of the covenant, but his obedience to the law of circumcision; and this, being peculiar to the Jewish nation, gave them an interest in the Abrahamic covenant; and that, consequently, whoever among the Gentiles would be interested in that covenant ought to embrace Judaism, become circumcised, and thus come under obligation to the whole law. With this very objection the apostle very dexterously introduces his argument, vv. 1-2; shows that, according to the Scripture account, Abraham was justified by faith, vv. 3-5; explains the nature of that justification, by a quotation out of the Psalms, vv. 6-9; proves that Abraham was justified long before he was circumcised, vv. 9-11; that the believing Gentiles are his seed to whom the promise belongs, as well as the believing Jews, vv. 12-17; and he describes Abraham's faith, in order to explain the faith of the gospel, vv. 17-25. We may still suppose that the dialogue is carried on between the apostle and the Jew, and it will make the subject still more clear to assign to each his respective part. The Jew asks a single question, which is contained in the first and part of the second verses. And the apostle's answer takes up the rest of the chapter.

1. JEW. *What shall we then say that Abraham, our father as pertaining to the flesh, hath found?* The *pertaining to the flesh* must here refer to the sign in Abraham's flesh, viz., his circumcision, on which the Jew would found his right to peculiar blessings.

2. *For if Abraham were justified by works.* The JEW proceeds: I conclude, therefore, that Abraham was *justified by works,* or by his obedience to the law of circumcision; and, consequently, he has cause for glorying, to "exult" in something which he has done to entitle him to these blessings. Now it is evident that he has this glorying, and consequently that he was justified by works.

APOSTLE. *But not before God.* These seem to be the apostle's words, and contain the beginning of his answer to the arguments of the Jew, as if he had said: Allowing that Abraham might glory in being called from heathenish darkness into such marvellous light, and exult in the privileges which God had granted to him, yet this glorying was not before God as a reason why those privileges should be granted, the glorying itself being a consequence of these very privileges.

3. *For what saith the scripture?* The scriptural account of this transaction, Gen. xv. 6, is decisive; for there it is said, Abraham "believed" God, and it was counted, it was reckoned "to him for righteousness," for justification.

4. *Now to him that worketh is the reward not reckoned of grace, but of debt.* Therefore if Abraham had been justified by works, the blessings he received would have been given to him as a reward for those works, and consequently his believing could have had no part in his justification, and his faith would have been useless.

5. *But to him that worketh not.* Which was the case with Abraham, for he was called when he was ungodly, i.e., an idolater; and, on his believing, was freely justified. And as all men have sinned, none can be justified by works; and, therefore, justification, if it take place at all, must take place in behalf of the ungodly, forasmuch as all mankind are such. It is necessary to observe here, in order to prevent confusion and misapprehension, that although the verb *dikaioo* has a variety of senses in the New Testament, yet here it is to be taken as implying the "pardon of sin," "receiving a person into the favor of God." It is also necessary to observe that our translators render the verb *logizomai* differently in different parts of this chapter. It is rendered "counted," vv. 3, 5; "reckoned," vv. 4, 9-10; "imputed," vv. 6, 8, 11, 22-24. "Reckoned" is probably the best sense in all these places.

6. *Even as David also.* David, in Ps. xxxii. 1-2, gives us also the true notion of this way of justification, i.e., by faith, without the merit of works, where he says—

7. *Blessed are they whose iniquities are forgiven.* That is, the man is truly "happy" whose iniquities, whose transgressions of the law, are forgiven; for by these he was exposed to the most grievous punishment. *Whose sins,* his innumerable deviations from the strict rule of truth and righteousness, *are covered*—entirely removed out of sight, and thrown into oblivion.

8. *Blessed is the man to whom the Lord will not impute sin.* That man is truly happy to whose charge God does not reckon sin; that is, they alone are happy who are redeemed from the curse of the law and the consequence of their ungodly life, by having their sins freely forgiven, through the mercy of God.

9. *Cometh this blessedness . . . upon the circumcision only?* The word *only* is very properly supplied by our translators, and is here quite necessary to complete the sense. If this pardon, granted in this way, be essential to "happiness"—and David says it is so—then is it the privilege of the Jews exclusively? This cannot be; for it is by the mere mercy of God, through faith. But if God offer it to the circumcision, not because they have been obedient, for they also have sinned, but because of His mere mercy, then of course the same blessedness may be offered to the Gentiles who believe in the Lord Jesus. And this is evident; *for we say,* following our own Scriptures, *that faith was reckoned to Abraham for righteousness.* He had no merit; he was an idolater. But he believed in God, and his faith was reckoned to him "in reference to his justification."

10. *How was it then reckoned?* In what circumstances was Abraham when this blessing was bestowed upon him? When he was circumcised, or before? *Not in circumcision, but in uncircumcision.* Faith was reckoned to Abraham for justification, as we read in Gen. xv. 6, but circumcision was not instituted till about fourteen or fifteen years after, Gen. xvii. 1, etc.;

for faith was reckoned to Abraham for righteousness or justification at least one year before Ishmael was born; compare Genesis xv and xvi. At Ishmael's birth he was eighty-six years of age, Gen. xvi. 16; and at the institution of circumcision, Ishmael was thirteen, and Abraham ninety-nine years old.

11. *And he received the sign of circumcision, a seal.* So far was obedience to the law of circumcision from being the reason of his justification that he not only received this justification before he was circumcised, but he received the *sign* of circumcision as a *seal* of the pardon which he had before actually received. And thus he became the *father,* the great head and representative, of all them that believe; particularly the Gentiles, who are now in precisely the same state in which Abraham was when he received the mercy of God. The whole of the apostle's argument in this fourth chapter to the Romans proves that we believing Gentiles are the seed of Abraham, to whom, as well as to himself, the promise was made; and that the promise made to him is the same in effect as that promise which is now made to us. There is nothing more common in the Jewish writers than the words *sign* and *seal* as signifying the mark in the flesh by the rite of circumcision.

12. *And the father of circumcision.* He is also the head and representative of all the circumcision of all the Jews *who also walk in the steps of that faith;* who seek for justification by faith only, and not by the works of the law—for this was the faith that Abraham had before he received circumcision.

13. *For the promise, that he should be the heir of the world.* This promise intimated that he should be the medium through whom the mercy of God should be communicated to the *world,* to both Jews and Gentiles; and the manner in which he was justified, be the rule and manner according to which all men should expect this blessing. Abraham is here represented as having all the world given to him as his inheritance, because in him all nations of the earth are blessed.

14. *For if they which are of the law be heirs.* If the Jews only be heirs of the promise made to Abraham, and that on the ground of prior obedience to the law, then *faith is made void,* is entirely useless; *and the promise,* which was made to faith, is *made of none effect.*

15. *Because the law worketh wrath.* For *law,* any law, or rule of duty. No law makes provision for the exercise of mercy, for it *worketh wrath,* "punishment," for the disobedient. *Law* necessarily subjects the transgressor to punishment. But the Jews have a law, which they have broken, and now they are exposed to the penal sanctions of that law; and if the promises of pardon without the works of the law do not extend to them, they must be finally miserable, because they have all broken the law, and the law exacts punishment. This was a home stroke, and the argument is unanswerable.

16. *Therefore it is of faith, that it might be by grace.* On this account the promise is mercifully grounded, not on obedience to a law, but on the infinite goodness of God; and thus the promise is *sure to all the seed*—to all, both Jews and Gentiles, who, believing in Christ Jesus, have a right to all the blessings contained in the Abrahamic covenant. *All the seed* necessarily comprehends all mankind.

17. *As it is written, I have made thee a father.* That Abraham's being a father of many nations has relation to the covenant of God made with him may be seen, Gen. xvii. 4-5: "Behold my covenant is with thee, and thou shalt be a father of many nations. Neither shall thy name any more be called Abram, but thy name shall be Abraham; for a father of many nations have I made thee"; i.e., he was constituted the head of many nations, the Gentile world, by virtue of the covenant which God made then with him. *God, who quickeneth the dead.* God is the most proper Object of trust and dependence; for being almighty, eternal, and unchangeable, He can even raise the dead to life, and call *those things which be not as though they were.* He is the Creator; He gave being when there was none. He can as infallibly assure the existence of those things which are not as if they were already actually in being. And, on this account, He can never fail of accomplishing whatsoever He has promised.

19. *He considered not his own body now dead.* He showed at once the correctness and energy of his faith: God cannot lie; Abraham can believe. It is true that, according to the course of nature, he and Sarah were so old that they could not have children; but God is almighty, and can do whatsoever He will, and will fulfill His promise. This was certainly a wonderful degree of faith; as the promise stated that it was in *his* posterity that all the nations of the earth were to be blessed; that he had, as yet, no child by Sarah; that he was one hundred years old; that Sarah was ninety; and that, added to the utter improbability of her bearing at that age, she had ever been barren before. All these were so many reasons why he should not credit the promise; yet he believed. Therefore it might be well said, v. 20, that *he staggered not at the promise,* though everything was unnatural and improbable; *but was strong in faith,* and, by this almost inimitable confidence, gave *glory to God.* It was to God's honor that His servant put such unlimited confidence in Him; and he put this confidence in Him on the rational ground that God was *fully able* to perform what He had promised.

21. *And being fully persuaded.* His soul was "full of confidence" that the truth of God bound Him to fulfil His promise, and His power enabled Him to do it.

22. *And therefore it was imputed to him for righteousness.* Abraham's strong faith in the promise of the coming Saviour, for this was essential to his faith, was reckoned to him for justification. For it is not said that any righteousness, either his own or that of another, was imputed or reckoned to him for justification; but *it,* i.e., his faith in God.

23. *Now it was not written for his sake alone.* The fact of Abraham's believing and receiving salvation through that faith is not recorded as a mere circumstance in the patriarch's life, intended to do him honor.

24. *But for us also.* The mention of this circumstance has a much more extensive design than merely to honor Abraham. It is recorded as the model according to which God will save both Jews and Gentiles.

25. *Who was delivered for our offences.* Who was delivered up to death as a Sacrifice for our sins; for in what other way or for what other purpose could He, who is innocence itself, be *delivered for our offences? And was raised again for our justification.* He was raised that we might have the fullest assurance that the death of Christ had accomplished the end for which it took place, viz., our reconciliation to God. (1) From a careful examination of the divine oracles it appears that the death of Christ was an atonement or expiation for the sin of the world. (2) And as His death was an atonement for our sins, so His resurrection was the proof and pledge of our eternal life. (3) The doctrine of justification by faith, which is so nobly proved in the preceding chapter, is one of the grandest displays of the mercy of God to mankind. It is so very plain that all may comprehend it, and so free that all may attain it. (4) The doctrine of the imputed righteousness of Christ, as held by many, will not be readily found in this chapter, where it has been supposed to exist in all its proofs. It is repeatedly said that faith is imputed for righteousness, but in no place here that Christ's obedience to the moral law is imputed to any man. The truth is, the moral law was broken, and did not now require obedience. It required this before it was broken; but after it was broken, it required death. Either the sinner must die or someone in his stead; but there was none whose death could have been an equivalent for the transgressions of the *world* but Jesus Christ. Jesus therefore died for man; and it is through His blood, the merit of His passion and death, that we have redemption, and not by His obedience to the moral law in our stead. (5) This doctrine of the imputed righteousness of Christ is capable of great abuse. To say that Christ's personal righteousness is imputed to every true believer is not scriptural. To say that He has fulfilled all righteousness for us, or in our stead, if by this is meant His fulfillment of all moral duties, is neither scriptural nor true. That He has died in our stead is a great, glorious, and scriptural truth; that there is no redemption but through His blood is asserted beyond all contradiction in the oracles of God. But there are a multitude of duties which the moral law requires which Christ never fulfilled in our stead, and never could—in the relation of parents, husbands, wives, etc.

CHAPTER 5

The effects of justification by faith, peace with God, 1. The joyous hope of eternal glory, 2. Glorying in tribulation, 3. And gaining thereby patience, experience, and hope, 4. And having the love of God shed abroad in the heart by the Holy Spirit, 5. The state of the world when Christ died for it, 6-10. Jesus Christ is an Atonement, 11. Sin and death entered into the world by Adam's transgression, and all became guilty before God, 12-14. God's grace in sending Christ into the world to save fallen man, 15-19. The law is brought in to show the exceeding sinfulness of sin, 20. The grace of Christ is to be as extensive in its influences and reign, as sin has been in its enslaving and destructive nature, 21.

1. *Therefore being justified by faith.* The apostle takes it for granted that he has proved that justification is by faith, and that the Gentiles have an equal title with the Jews to salvation by faith. And now he proceeds to show the effects produced in the hearts of the believing Gentiles by this doctrine. We are justified, have all our sins pardoned by faith, as the instrumental cause; for, being sinners, we have no works of righteousness that we can plead. *We have peace with God.* Before, while sinners, we were in a state of enmity with God, which was sufficiently proved by our rebellion against his authority, and our transgression of his laws; but now, being reconciled, we have peace with God. *Peace* is generally the firstfruits of our justification. *Through our Lord Jesus Christ.* His passion and death being the sole cause of our reconciliation to God.

2. *By whom also.* We are not only indebted to our Lord Jesus Christ for the free and full pardon which we have received, but our continuance in a justified state depends upon His gracious influence in our hearts and His intercession before the throne of God. *We have access.* "We have received this access." It was only through Christ that we could at first approach God, and it is only through Him that the privilege is continued to us. And this access to God, or "introduction" to the Divine Presence, is to be considered as a lasting privilege. We are not brought to God for the purpose of an interview, but to remain with Him. *Into this grace.* This state of favor and acceptance. *Wherein we stand.* Having firm footing, and a just title through the blood of the Lamb to the full salvation of God. *And rejoice.* Have solid happiness, from the evidence we have of our acceptance with Him.

3. *And not only so.* We are not only happy from being in this state of communion with our God, and the prospect of being eternally with Him. *But we glory in tribulations also.* All the sufferings we endure for the testimony of our Lord are so sanctified to us by His grace that they become powerful instruments of increasing our happiness. *Tribulation worketh patience.* "Endurance" under trials, without sustaining loss or deterioration. It is a metaphor taken from refining metals. We do not speak thus from any sudden raptures or extraordinary sensations we may have of spiritual joy; for we find that the tribulations through which we pass are the means of exercising and increasing our patience, our meek forbearance of injuries received, or persecutions experienced, on account of the gospel.

4. *And patience, experience.* "Full proof, by trial," of the truth of our religion, the solidity of our Christian state, and the faithfulness of our God. In such cases we have the opportunity of putting our religion to the test; and by every such test it receives the deeper sterling stamp. The apostle uses here also a metaphor taken from the purifying, refining, and testing of silver and gold. *Experience, hope.* For we thus calculate, that He who has supported us in the past will support us in those which may yet come; and as we have received so much spiritual profiting by means of the sufferings through which we have already passed, we may profit equally by those which are yet to come. This *hope* prevents us from dreading coming trials; we receive them as means of grace, and find that all things work together for good to them that love God.

5. *And hope maketh not ashamed.* A hope that is not rationally founded will have its expectation cut off, and then shame and confusion will be the portion of its possessor. *Because the love of God is shed abroad in our hearts.* We have the most solid and convincing tes-

timony of God's love to us by that measure of it which He has communicated to our hearts. There it is "poured out" and diffused abroad, filling, quickening, and invigorating all our powers and faculties. The *Holy Ghost* comes with it; by His energy it is diffused and pervades every part.

6. *For when we were yet without strength.* The apostle, having pointed out the glorious state of the believing Gentiles, takes occasion to contrast this with their former state, and the means by which they were redeemed from it. Their former state he points out in four particulars, which may be applied to men in general. (1) They were *without strength;* in a weak, dying state; neither able to resist sin nor *do* any good; utterly devoid of power to extricate themselves from the misery of their situation. (2) They were *ungodly;* without either the worship or knowledge of the true God; they had not God in them; and, consequently, were not partakers of the divine nature. Satan lived in, ruled, and enslaved their hearts. (3) They were *sinners,* v. 8, aiming at happiness, but constantly "missing the mark," which is the ideal meaning of the Hebrew *chata* and the Greek *hamartano.* (4) They were *enemies,* v. 10, from *echthos,* "hatred, enmity," persons who hated God and holiness; and acted in continual hostility to both. What a gradation is here! *Died for the ungodly.* "He died instead of the ungodly"; see also v. 8; so Luke xxii. 19. The body of Christ, "which is given for you"; i.e., the life that is laid down in your stead. In this way the preposition *hyper* is used by the best Greek writers.

7. *For scarcely for a righteous man will one die.* The Jews divide men, as to their moral character, into four classes. The first class consists of those who say, "What is mine, is my own; and what is thine, is thy own." These may be considered the just, who render to every man his due; or rather, they who neither give nor take. The second class is made up of those who say, "What is mine, is thine; and what is thine, is mine." These are they who accommodate each other, who borrow and lend. The third class is composed of those who say, "What is mine, is thine; and what is thine, let it be thine." These are the pious, or good, who give up all for the benefit of their neighbor. The fourth class are those who say, "What is thine, is mine; and what is thine, shall be mine." These are the impious, who take all, and give nothing. Now, for one of the first class, who would die? *Peradventure for a good man some would even dare to die.* This is for one of the third class, who gives all he has for the good of others. This is the truly benevolent man, whose life is devoted to the public good; for such a person, peradventure, some who have had their lives perhaps preserved by his bounty would even dare to die.

8. *But God commendeth his love.* God "hath set" this act of infinite mercy in the most conspicuous light, so as to recommend it to the notice and admiration of all. *While we were yet sinners.* We were neither righteous nor good, but impious and wicked.

9. *Much more then, being now justified.* If Jesus Christ, in His endless compassion towards us, gave His life for ours, while we were yet enemies; being now justified *by his blood,* by

His death on the Cross, and thus reconciled to God, *we shall be saved from wrath,* from "punishment" for past transgression, *through him,* by what He has thus suffered for us.

10. *We were reconciled.* The enmity existing before rendered the reconciliation necessary. In every human heart there is a measure of enmity to holiness, and consequently to the Author of it. *We shall be saved by his life.* For, (1) as He died for our sins, so He rose again for our justification; and His resurrection to *life* is the grand proof that He has accomplished whatever He had purposed in reference to the salvation of man. (2) This may be also understood of His life of intercession: for it is written, "He ever liveth to make intercession for them," Heb. vii. 25. Through this life of intercession at the right hand of God we are spared and blessed. (3) And it will not be amiss to consider that, as our salvation implies the renovation of our nature, and our being restored to the image of God, so [it] may be rendered: "We shall be saved in His life." (4) The example also of the life of Christ is a means of salvation. He hath left us "an example" that we "should follow his steps"; and he that followeth Him "shall not walk in darkness, but shall have the light of life," John viii. 12.

11. *We also joy,* "we exult," or "glory" *in God.* We now feel that God is reconciled to us, and we are reconciled to Him. The enmity is removed from our souls; and He, for Christ's sake, through *whom we have received the atonement,* "the reconciliation," has remitted the wrath, the punishment which we deserved; and now, through this reconciliation, we expect an eternal glory. It was certainly improper to translate here *atonement,* instead of "reconciliation"; as *katallasso* signifies to "reconcile," and is so rendered by our translators in all the places where it occurs. It does not mean the *atonement* here, as we generally understand that word, viz., the sacrificial death of Christ, but rather the effect of that atonement, the removal of the enmity, and by this, the change of our condition and state; from *kata,* intensive, and *allasso,* "to change"—the thorough change of our state from enmity to friendship. God is reconciled to us and we are reconciled to Him by the death of His Son, and thus there is a glorious change from enmity to friendship; and we can exult in God through our Lord Jesus Christ, by whom we have received this "reconciliation."

12. *Wherefore, as by one man sin entered into the world.* From this verse to the conclusion of the chapter the apostle produces a strong argument to prove that, as all mankind stood in need of the grace of God in Christ to redeem them from their sins, so this grace has been afforded equally to all, both Jews and Gentiles. The order in which the apostle handles this argument is this: (1) He affirms that death passed upon all men by Adam's one transgression, v. 12. (2) He proves this, vv. 13-14. (3) He affirms there is a correspondence between Adam and Christ, or between the "offence" and the "free gift," v. 14. (4) This correspondence, so far as the two opposite parts answer to each other, is justly expressed in vv. 18-19; and there we have the main or fundamental position of the apostle's argument, in relation to the point which he has been arguing from the beginning of the Epistle, namely, the extensiveness of the

grace of the gospel, that it actually reaches to all men, and is not confined to the Jews. (5) But before he laid down this position, it was necessary that he should show that the correspondence between Adam and Christ, or between the "offence" and the "gift," is not to be confined strictly to the bounds specified in the position, as if the gift reached no further than the consequences of the offense, when in reality it extends vastly beyond them, vv. 15-17. (6) Having settled these points, as previously necessary to clear his fundamental position and fit to his argument, he then lays down that position in a diversified manner of speech, vv. 18-19, just as in 1 Cor. xv. 20-21, and leaves us to conclude, from the premises laid down, vv. 15-17, that the gift and the grace in their utmost extent are as free to all mankind who are willing to accept of them as in this particular instance, the resurrection from the dead. They *shall* all be raised from the dead hereafter; they *may* all be quickened by the Spirit here. (7) Having thus shown the extensiveness of the divine grace, in opposition to the dire effects of the law under which Adam was, that the Jews might not overlook what he intended they should particularly observe, he puts them in mind that the law given to Adam, Transgress and die, was introduced into the Jewish constitution by the ministry of Moses; and for this end, that "the offence," with the penalty of death annexed to it, "might abound," v. 20. But to illustrate the divine grace by setting it in contrast to the law, he immediately adds: Where sin, subjecting to death, "abounded, grace did much more abound"; that is, in blessings bestowed, it has stretched far beyond both Adam's transgression and the transgressions under the law of Moses, vv. 20-21. *Sin entered into the world.* There was neither sin nor death before the offense of Adam; after that there were both. Adam's transgression was therefore the cause of both. *And death by sin.* Natural evil is evidently the effect of moral evil; if man had never sinned, he had never suffered. *Death passed upon all men.* Hence we see that all human beings partook in the consequences of Adam's sin. *For that all have sinned.* All are born with a sinful nature; and the seeds of this evil soon vegetate, and bring forth corresponding fruits.

13. *For until the law sin was in the world.* As death reigned from Adam to Moses, so also did *sin.* Now, as there was no written *law* from Adam to that given to Moses, the death that prevailed could not be the breach of that law; for sin, so as to be punished with temporal death, *is not imputed when there is no law,* which shows the penalty of sin to be death. Therefore men are not subjected to death for their own personal transgressions, but for the sin of Adam, as through his transgression all come into the world with the seed of death and corruption in their own nature, superadded to their moral depravity.

14. *Who is the figure of him that was to come.* Adam was the *figure, typos,* the "type, pattern, or resemblance" *of him that was to come;* i.e., of the Messiah. The correspondence between them appears in the following particulars: (1) Through him, as its spring and fountain, sin became diffused through the world, so that every man comes into the world with sinful propensities. Through Christ, as its Spring and Fountain, righteousness becomes diffused through the earth, so that every man is made partaker of a principle of grace and truth. (2) "As in Adam all die, even so in Christ shall all be made alive," I Cor. xv. 22. "For since by man came death, by man came also the resurrection of the dead," v. 21. (3) As in or through Adam guilt came upon all men, so, through Christ, "the free gift came upon all men unto justification of life," v. 18. These alone seem to be the instances in which a similitude exists between Adam and Christ.

15. *For if through the offence of one many be dead.* That "the many" of the apostle here means all mankind needs no proof to any but that person who finds himself qualified to deny that all men are mortal. And if "the many"— that is, all mankind—have died through the offense of one, certainly the *gift by grace* which abounds unto "the many" by Christ Jesus must have reference to every human being. If the consequences of Christ's incarnation and death extend only to a few, or a select number of mankind, then the consequences of Adam's sin have extend only to a few, or a select number of man-number; and if only many and not all have fallen, only that many had need of a Redeemer. For it is most evident that the same persons are referred to in both clauses of the verse. *Hath abounded unto many.* That is, Christ Jesus died for every man; salvation is free for all; saving grace is tendered to every soul; and a measure of the divine light is actually communicated to every heart, John i. 9. And as the grace is offered, so it may be received; and hence the apostle says, v. 17: "They which receive abundance of grace and of the gift of righteousness shall reign in life by . . . Jesus Christ." By receiving is undoubtedly meant not only the act of receiving, but retaining and improving the grace which they receive; and as all may receive, so all may improve and retain the grace they do receive; and, consequently, all may be eternally saved. But of multitudes Christ still may say, "They will not come unto Me, that they might have life."

16. *And not as it was by one that sinned.* That is, the judicial act that followed Adam's sin (the sentence of death pronounced upon him, and his expulsion from paradise) took its rise from his one offense alone, and terminated in condemnation; but the free gift of God in Christ takes its rise also from the *many offences* which men, in a long course of life, have personally committed; and the object of this grace is to justify them freely, and bring them to eternal life.

17. *Death reigned by one.* Death is here personified, and is represented as reigning over the human race. *Shall reign in life.* Those who receive, retain, and improve the abundant grace offered by Jesus Christ shall be redeemed from the empire of death and exalted to the throne of God, to live and reign with Him ever, world without end. See Rev. i. 5-6; ii. 7, 10-11; iii. 21. If we carefully compare v. 15 with v. 17, we shall find that there is a correspondence between the abounding, v. 17, and *hath abounded,* v. 15; between the *gift of righteousness,* i.e., "justification," v. 17, and *the gift by grace,* v. 15. Therefore, if we understand the abounding of grace and the gift of justification, v. 17, we shall understand *the grace of God, and the gift by grace, which . . . hath abounded unto many,* v. 15.

But the abounding of grace, and the gift of justification, v. 17, are that *grace* and *gift* which are received by those who shall *reign in* (eternal) *life*. Reigning in life is the consequence of receiving the grace and gift. Therefore receiving the grace is a necessary qualification on our part for reigning in life; and this necessarily implies our believing in Christ Jesus as having died for our offenses, receiving the grace so freely offered us, using the means in order to get more grace, and bringing forth the fruits of the Spirit.

18. *Therefore as by the offence of one.* Literally, "Therefore, as by one offense unto all men, unto condemnation; so likewise, by one righteousness unto all men, to justification of life." This is evidently an elliptical sentence, and its full meaning can be gathered only from the context. He who had no particular purpose to serve would most probably understand it, from the context, thus: "Therefore as by one sin all men came into condemnation, so also by one righteous act all men came unto justification of life."

20. *The law entered, that the offence might abound.* After considering various opinions concerning the true meaning of this verse, I am induced to prefer my own as being the most simple. By *law* I understand the Mosaic law. By entering in, or, rather, "coming in privily," see Gal. ii. 4 (the only place where it occurs besides), I understand the temporary or limited use of that law, which was, as far as its rites and ceremonies are considered, confined to the Jewish people, and to them only till the Messiah should come. But considered as the moral law, or rule of conscience and life, it has in its spirit and power been slipped in, introduced into every conscience, that sin might abound, that the true nature, deformity, and extent of sin might appear; for by the law is the knowledge of sin. For how can the finer deviations from a straight line be ascertained without the application of a known straightedge? Without this rule of right, sin can be known only in a sort of general way. *But where sin abounded.* Whether in the world or in the heart of the individual, being discovered by this most pure and righteous law, *grace did much more abound;* not only pardon for all that is past is offered by the gospel, but also the Holy Spirit, in the abundance of His gifts and graces, is communicated, so as to prepare the receiver for an "exceeding and eternal weight of glory." Thus the grace of the gospel not only redeems from death and restores to life, but brings the soul into such a relationship with God, and into such a participation of eternal glory, as we have no authority to believe ever would have been the portion even of Adam himself had he even eternally retained his innocence.

21. *That as sin hath reigned unto death.* As extensively, as deeply, as universally, as *sin,* whether implying the act of transgression or the impure principle from which the act proceeds, or both. *Hath reigned,* subjected the whole earth and all its inhabitants; the whole soul, and all its powers and faculties. *Unto death,* temporal of the body, spiritual of the soul, and eternal of both. *Even so,* as extensively, deeply, and universally, *might grace reign*—filling the whole earth, and pervading, purifying, and refining the whole soul. *Through righteousness*—

through this doctrine of free salvation by the blood of the Lamb, and by the principle of holiness transfused through the soul by the Holy Ghost. *Unto eternal life*—the proper object of an immortal spirit's hope, the only sphere where the human intellect can rest, and be happy in the place and state where God is. *By Jesus Christ our Lord*—as the Cause of our salvation, the Means by which it is communicated, and the Source whence it springs. Thus we find that the salvation from sin here is as extensive and complete as the guilt and contamination of sin.

CHAPTER 6

We must not abuse the boundless goodness of God by continuing in sin, under the wicked persuasion that the more we sin the more the grace of God will abound, 1. For, having been baptized into Christ, we have professed thereby to be dead to sin, 2-4, and to be planted in the likeness of His resurrection, 5. For we profess to be crucified with Him, to die and rise again from the dead, 6-11. We should not, therefore, let sin reign in our bodies, but live to the glory of God, 12-14. The gospel makes no provision for living in sin, any more than the law did; and those who commit sin are the slaves of sin, 15-19. The degrading and afflictive service of sin, and its wages eternal death; the blessed effects of the grace of God in the heart, of which eternal life is the fruit, 20-23.

The apostle, having proved that salvation, to both Jew and Gentile, must come through the Messiah, and be received by faith only, proceeds in this chapter to show the obligations under which both were laid to live a holy life, and the means and advantages they enjoyed for that purpose. This he does, not only as a thing highly and indispensably necessary in itself—for without holiness none can see the Lord—but to confute a calumny which appears to have been gaining considerable ground even at that time, viz., that the doctrine of justification by faith alone, through the grace of Christ Jesus, rendered obedience to the moral law useless; and that the more evil a man did, the more the grace of God would abound to him in his redemption from that evil. That this calumny was then propagated we learn from chap. iii. 8; and the apostle defends himself against it in the thirty-first verse of the same by asserting that his doctrine, far from making void the law, served to establish it. But in this and the following two chapters he takes up the subject in a regular, formal manner, and shows both Jews and Gentiles that the principles of the Christian religion absolutely require a holy heart and a holy life and make the amplest provisions for both.

1. *Shall we continue in sin?* It is very likely that these were the words of a believing Gentile, who—having as yet received but little instruction, for he is but just brought out of his heathen state to believe in Christ Jesus—might imagine, from the manner in which God had magnified His mercy, in blotting out his sin on his simply believing on Christ, that, supposing he even gave way to the evil propensities of his own heart, his transgressions could do him no hurt now that he was in the favor of God.

2. *God forbid.* "Let it not be; by no means; far from it; let not such a thing be mentioned!" —any of these is the meaning of the Greek phrase, which is a strong expression of surprise and disapprobation; and is not properly rendered by our *God forbid!* for, though this may express the same thing, yet it is not proper to make the sacred name so familiar on such occasions. *How shall we, that are dead to sin?*

The phraseology of this verse is common among Hebrews, Greeks, and Latins. To die to a thing or person is to have nothing to do with it or him, to be totally separated from them; and to live to a thing or person is to be wholly given up to them, to have the most intimate connection with them.

3. *Know ye not?* Every man who believes the Christian religion, and receives baptism as the proof that he believes it, and has taken up the profession of it, is bound thereby to a life of righteousness. To be *baptized into Jesus Christ* is to receive the doctrine of Christ crucified, and to receive baptism as a proof of the genuineness of that faith, and the obligation to live according to its precepts. *Baptized into his death.* That, as Jesus Christ in His crucifixion died completely, so that no spark of the natural or animal life remained in His body, so those who profess His reliigon should be so completely separated and saved from sin that they have no more connection with it, nor any more influence from it, than a dead man has with or from his departed spirit.

4. *We are buried with him by baptism into death.* It is probable that the apostle here alludes to the mode of administering baptism by immersion, the whole body being put under the water, which seemed to say, The man is drowned, is dead; and when he came up out of the water, he seemed to have a resurrection to life. The man is risen again; he is alive! *Raised up from the dead by the glory of the Father.* From this we learn that, as it required the *glory of the Father,* that is, His glorious energy, to raise up from the grave the dead body of Christ, so it requires the same glorious energy to quicken the dead soul of a sinner and enable him to walk in newness of life.

5. *For if we have been planted together.* When the seed or plant is inserted in the ground, it derives from that ground all its nourishment and all those juices by which it becomes developed; by which it increases in size, grows firm, strong, and vigorous and puts forth its leaves, blossoms, and fruit. The *death* of Jesus Christ is represented as the cause whence His fruitfulness as the Author of eternal salvation to mankind is derived; and genuine believers in Him are represented as being *planted . . . in . . . his death,* and growing out of it; deriving their growth, vigor, firmness, beauty, and fruitfulness from it.

6. *Our old man is crucified with him.* This seems to be a further extension of the same metaphor. When a seed is planted in the earth, it appears as if the whole body of it perished. The *body* dies that the germ may live. How is the principle of life which Jesus Christ has implanted in us to be brought into full effect, vigor, and usefulness? By the destruction of the *body of sin.* Our *old man,* our wicked, corrupt, and fleshly self, is to be crucified, to be as truly slain as Christ was crucified, that our souls may as truly be raised from a death of sin to a life of righteousness as the body of Christ was raised from the grave, and afterwards ascended to the right hand of God. But how does this part of the metaphor apply to Jesus Christ? Plainly and forcibly. Jesus Christ took on Him a body, a body "in the likeness of sinful flesh," chap. viii. 3, and gave up that body to death; through which death alone an atonement was made for sin, and the way laid open for the vivifying Spirit to have the fullest access to, and the most powerful operation in, the human heart. Here the body of Christ dies that He may be a quickening Spirit to mankind. Our *body of sin* is destroyed by this quickening Spirit, that henceforth we should live unto Him who died and rose again. Thus the metaphor, in all its leading senses, is complete, and applies most forcibly to the subject in question. We find that the *old man,* used here and in Eph. iv. 22 and Col. iii. 9, is the same as "the flesh with the affections and lusts," Gal. v. 24; and "the body of the sins of the flesh," Col. ii. 11; and the very same which the Jewish writers term the "old Adam" and which they interpret by "evil concupiscence"; the same which we mean by indwelling sin, or the infection of our nature, in consequence of the Fall. From all which we may learn that the design of God is to counterwork and destroy the very spirit and soul of sin, that we shall no longer serve it, no longer be its slaves.

7. *He that is dead is freed from sin.* Literally, is "justified" from sin, or is freed or delivered from it. Does not this simply mean that the man who has received Christ Jesus by faith, and has been, through believing, made a partaker of the Holy Spirit, has had his "old man," all his evil propensities, destroyed; so that he is not only justified freely from all sin, but wholly sanctified unto God? The context shows that this is the meaning. Every instance of violence is done to the whole scope and design of the apostle by the opinion that "this text is a proof that believers are not fully saved from sin in this life, because only he that is dead is freed from sin." Then death is his justifier and deliverer! So then, the death of Christ and the influences of the Holy Spirit were only sufficient to depose and enfeeble the tyrant sin; but our death must come in to effect his total destruction! Thus our death is, at least partially, our Saviour; and thus, that which was an effect of sin (for sin entered into the world, and death by sin) becomes the means of finally destroying it! The divinity and philosophy of this sentiment are equally absurd. It is the blood of Christ alone that cleanses from all unrighteousness; and the sanctification of a believer is no more dependent on death than his justification.

9. *Christ being raised from the dead dieth no more.* So we, believing in Christ Jesus, and having a death unto sin and a life unto righteousness, should sin no more.

10. *He died unto sin once.* From the whole scope of the apostle's discourse it is plain that he considers the death of Christ is a death or sacrifice for sin, a sin offering. In this sense no man has ever died for sin, or ever can die.

11. *Reckon ye also yourselves to be dead.* Die as truly unto sin as He died for sin. Live as truly *unto* God as He lives *with* God. This seems to be the spirit of the apostle's meaning.

12. *Let not sin therefore reign.* This is a personification. Sin is represented as a king, ruler, or tyrant, who has the desires of the mind and the members of the body under his control, so that by influencing the passions he governs the body. Do not let sin reign, do not let him work; that is, let him have no place, no being in your souls; because, wherever he is he governs, less or more.

13. *Neither yield ye your members.* Do not yield to temptation. It is no sin to be tempted; the sin lies in yielding. While the sin exists only in Satan's solicitation, it is the devil's sin, not ours. When we yield, we make the devil's sin our own; then we enter into temptation. "Resist the devil, and he will flee from you." *Yield yourselves unto God.* Let God have your wills; keep them ever on His side. There they are safe, and there they will be active. Satan cannot force the will, and God will not. Indeed it would cease to be will were it forced by either; it is essential to its being that it is free. *And your members as instruments.* Let soul and body be employed in the service of your Maker; let Him have your hearts, and with them your heads, your hands, your feet. Think and devise what is pure; speak what is true, and to the use of edifying; work that which is just and good; and walk steadily in the way that leads to everlasting felicity. Be holy within and holy without.

14. *Sin shall not have dominion over you.* God delivers you from it; and if you again become subject to it, it will be the effect of your own choice or negligence. *Ye are not under the law.* That law which exacts obedience without giving power to obey, that condemns every transgression and every unholy thought without providing for the extirpation of evil or the pardon of sin. *But under grace.* You are under the merciful and beneficent dispensation of the gospel, that, although it requires the strictest conformity to the will of God, affords sufficient power to be thus conformed; and in the death of Christ has provided pardon for all that is past, and grace to help in every time of need.

15. *Shall we sin, because we are not under the law?* Shall we abuse our high and holy calling because we are not under that law which makes no provision for pardon, but are under that gospel which has opened the fountain to wash away all sin and defilement? Shall we sin because grace abounds? Shall we do evil that good may come of it? This be far from us!

16. *To whom ye yield yourselves.* Can you suppose that you should continue to be the *servants* of Christ if you give way to *sin?* Is he not the master who exacts the service, and to whom the service is performed? *Sin* is the service of Satan; *righteousness,* the service of Christ. If you sin, you are the servants of Satan, and not the servants of God. The word which we translate *servants* properly signifies "slaves"; and a slave among the Greeks and Romans was considered as his master's property, and he might dispose of him as he pleased. Under a bad master, the lot of the slave was most oppressive and dreadful: his ease and comfort were never consulted; he was treated worse than a beast; and in many cases his life hung on the mere caprice of the master. This state is the state of every poor, miserable sinner; he is the slave of Satan, and his own evil lusts and appetites are his most cruel taskmasters. The same word is applied to the servants of Christ, the more forcibly to show that they are their Master's property; and that, as He is infinitely good and benevolent, therefore His service must be perfect freedom. Indeed, He exacts no obedience from them which He does not turn to their eternal advantage, for this Master has no self-interest to secure.

17. *But God be thanked, that ye were the servants of sin.* This verse should be read thus: "But thanks be to God that, although you were the servants of sin, nevertheless you have obeyed from the heart that form of doctrine that was delivered unto you"; or, "that mold of teaching into which you were cast." The apostle does not thank God that they were sinners; but that, although they were such, they had now received and obeyed the gospel. The Hebrew phrase, Isa. xii. 1, is exactly the same as that of the apostle here: "In that day thou shalt say . . . I will praise thee . . . [for] thou wast angry with me": that is, "Although Thou wast angry with me, Thou hast turned away Thy wrath." *That form of doctrine.* Christianity is represented under the notion of a "mold," or "die," into which they were cast, and from which they took the impression of its excellence. The figure upon this die is the image of God, righteousness and true holiness, which was stamped on their souls in believing the gospel and receiving the Holy Ghost. The words may be literally translated, "into which mold of doctrine ye have been cast."

18. *Being then made free from sin.* A term that refers to the manumission of a slave. They were redeemed from the slavery of sin, and became the servants of righteousness. Both *sin* and *righteousness* are personified: *sin* can enjoin no good and profitable work; *righteousness* can require none that is unjust or injurious.

19. *I speak after the manner of men.* This phrase is often used by the Greek writers to signify what was easy to be comprehended; what was level with common understandings, delivered in a popular style; what was different from the high flights of the poets and the studied, sublime obscurity of the philosophers. *Because of the infirmity of your flesh.* As if he had said: I make use of metaphors and figures connected with well-known natural things. *Servants to uncleanness.* These different expressions show how deeply immersed in and enslaved by sin these Gentiles were before their conversion to Christianity. Several of the particulars are given in the first chapter of this Epistle.

20. *Ye were free from righteousness.* These two servitudes are incompatible; if we cannot serve God and mammon, surely we cannot serve Christ and Satan. We must be either sinners or saints, God's servants or the devil's slaves.

21. *What fruit had ye then in those things?* God designs that every man shall reap benefit by his service. What benefit have you derived from the service of sin? *Whereof ye are now ashamed.* You blush to remember your former life. It was scandalous to yourselves, injurious to others, and highly provoking to God. *The end of those things is death.* Whatever sin may promise of pleasure or advantage, the end to which it necessarily tends is the destruction of body and soul.

22. *But now being made free from sin.* As being free from righteousness is the finished character of a sinner, so being *made free from sin* is the finished character of a genuine Christian. *And become servants to God.* They were transferred from the service of one master to that of another; they were freed from the slavery of sin, and engaged in the service of

God. *Fruit unto holiness.* Holiness of heart was the principle, and righteousness of life the fruit.

23. *For the wages of sin is death.* The second death, everlasting perdition. Every sinner earns this by long, sore, and painful service. Oh, what pains do men take to get to hell! *But the gift of God is eternal life.* A man may merit hell, but he cannot merit heaven. The apostle does not say that the wages of righteousness is eternal life: no, but that this eternal life, even to the righteous, is the gracious "gift of God." And even this gracious gift comes *through Jesus Christ our Lord.* He alone has procured it; and it is given to all those who find redemption in His blood. A sinner goes to hell because he deserves it; a righteous man goes to heaven because Christ has died for him, and communicated that grace by which his sin is pardoned and his soul made holy. The word *wages* signified the daily pay of a Roman soldier. So every sinner has a daily pay, and this pay is death; he has misery because he sins. Sin constitutes hell; the sinner has a hell in his own bosom; all is confusion and disorder where God does not reign. Every indulgence of sinful passions increases the disorder, and consequently the misery, of a sinner. If men were as much in earnest to get their souls saved as they are to prepare them for perdition, heaven would be highly peopled, and devils would be their own companions.

CHAPTER 7

The law has power over a man as long as he lives, 1. And a wife is bound to her husband only as long as he lives, 2-3. Christian believers are delivered from the Mosaic law by Christ Jesus, and united to God, 4-7. By the law is the knowledge of sin, 8. But it gives no power over it, 9-11. Yet it is holy, just, and good, 12. How it convinces of sin, and brings into bondage, 13-24. No deliverance from its curse but by Jesus Christ, 25.

The apostle, having in the preceding chapter shown the converted Gentiles the obligations they were under to live a holy life, addresses himself here to the Jews who might hesitate to embrace the gospel, lest by this means they should renounce the law, which might appear to them as a renunciation of their allegiance to God. As they rested in the law as sufficient for justification and sanctification, it was necessary to convince them of their mistake. That the law was insufficient for their justification the apostle had proved, in chapters iii, iv, and v; that it is insufficient for their sanctification he shows in this chapter; and introduces his discourse by showing that a believing Jew is discharged from his obligations to the law, and is at liberty to come under another and much happier constitution, viz., that of the gospel of Christ, 1-4. In the fifth verse he gives a general description of the state of a Jew, in servitude to sin, considered as under mere law. In the sixth verse he gives a summary account of the state of a Christian, or believing Jew, and the advantages he enjoys under the gospel. Upon the fifth verse he comments, from verse 7 to the end of the chapter; and upon the sixth verse he comments, chap. viii. 1-11.

In explaining his position in the fifth verse he shows: (1) That the law reaches to all the branches and latent principles of sin, v. 7. (2) That it subjected the sinner to death, vv. 8-12, without the expectation of pardon. (3) He shows the reason why the Jew was put under

it, v. 13. (4) He proves that the law, considered as a rule of action, though it was spiritual, just, holy, and good in itself, yet was insufficient for sanctification, or for freeing a man from the power of inbred sin. For, as the prevalency of sensual appetites cannot wholly extinguish the voice of reason and conscience, a man may acknowledge the law to be holy, just, and good, and yet his passions reign within him, keeping him in the most painful and degrading servitude, while the law supplies no power to deliver him from them, vv. 14-24, as that power can be supplied only by the grace of Jesus Christ, v. 25.

1. *For I speak to them that know the law.* This is a proof that the apostle directs this part of his discourse to the Jews. *As long as he liveth.* Or "as long as it liveth"; law does not extend its influence to the dead, nor do abrogated laws bind. It is all the same whether we understand these words as speaking of a law abrogated, so that it cannot command, or of its objects being dead, so that it has none to bind. In either case the law has no force.

2. *For the woman which hath an husband.* The apostle illustrates his meaning by a familiar instance. A married woman is bound to her husband while he lives; but when her husband is dead, she is discharged from the law by which she was bound to him alone.

3. *So then if, while her husband liveth.* The object of the apostle's similitude is to show that each party is equally bound to the other, but that the death of either dissolves the engagement. *So . . . she is no adulteress, though she be married to another.* And do not imagine that this change would argue any disloyalty in you to your Maker; for as He has determined that this law of ordinances shall cease, you are no more bound to it than a woman is to a deceased husband, and are as free to receive the gospel of Christ as a woman in such circumstances would be to remarry.

4. *Wherefore, my brethren.* This is a parallel case. You were once under the law of Moses and were bound by its injunctions, but now you are become dead to that law—a modest, inoffensive mode of speech, for "the law, which was once your husband, is dead." God has determined that it shall be no longer in force; so that now, as a woman whose husband is dead is freed from the law of that husband, or from her conjugal vow, and may legally be married to another, so God, who gave the law under which you have hitherto lived, designed that it should be in force only till the advent of the Messiah. That advent has taken place; the law has consequently ceased, and now you are called to take on you the yoke of the gospel, and lay down the yoke of the law; and it is the design of God that you should do so. *That ye should be married to another . . . who is raised from the dead.* As "Christ is the end of the law for righteousness to every one that believeth," the object of God in giving the law was to unite you to Christ; and as He has died, He has not only abolished that law which condemns every transgressor to death, but He has also made that atonement for sin by His own death, which is represented in the sacrifices prescribed by the law. And as Jesus Christ is risen again from the dead, He has thereby given the fullest proof that by His death He has procured the resurrection of mankind and made that atonement required by the law. *That we should bring forth fruit unto God*—we, Jews, who believe in Christ, have, in consequence of our union with Him, received the gifts and graces of the Holy Spirit; so that we bring forth that fruit of holiness unto God which, without this union, it would be impossible for us to produce.

5. *For when we were in the flesh.* When we were without the gospel, in our carnal and unregenerated state, though believing in the law of Moses and performing the rites and offices of our religion. *The motions of sins, which were by the law.* "The passions of sins, the evil propensities to sins." To every particular sin there is a propensity; one propensity does not excite to all kinds of sinful acts. Hence the apostle uses the plural number, "the passions or propensities of sins," sins being not more various than their propensities in the unregenerate heart which excite to them. These "propensities" constitute the fallen nature; they are the disease of the heart, the pollution and corruption of the soul. *Did work in our members.* The evil propensity acts in the whole nervous and muscular system, applying that stimulus to every part which is necessary to excite them to action. *To bring forth fruit unto death.* To produce those acts of transgression which subject the sinner to death, temporal and eternal. When the apostle says the *motions of sins, which were by the law,* he points out a most striking and invariable characteristic of sin, viz., its rebellious nature; it ever acts against law, and the most powerfully against known law. Because the law requires obedience, therefore it will transgress. The law is equally against evil passions and evil actions, and both these exert themselves against it. So these motions which were by the law became roused into the most powerful activity by the prohibitions of the law. They were comparatively dormant till the law said, "Thou shalt not do this; thou shalt do that"; then the rebellious principle in the evil propensity became roused, and acts of transgression and omissions of duty were the immediate consequences.

6. *But now we are delivered from the law.* We who have believed in Christ Jesus are delivered from that yoke by which we were bound, which sentenced every transgressor to perdition, but provided no pardon even for the penitent and no sanctification for those who are weary of their inbred corruptions. *That being dead wherein we were held.* To us believers in Christ this commandment is abrogated; we are transferred to another constitution. That law which kills ceases to bind us; it is dead to us who have believed in Christ Jesus, who is "the end of the law" for justification and salvation to everyone that believes. *That we should serve in newness of spirit.* We are now brought under a more spiritual dispensation; now we know the spiritual import of all the Mosaic precepts. We see that the law referred to the gospel, and can be fulfilled only by the gospel. *The oldness of the letter.* The merely literal rites, ceremonies, and sacrifices are now done away; and the *newness of spirit,* the true intent and meaning of all, are now fully disclosed; so that we are got from an imperfect state into a state of perfection and excellence. We sought justification and sanctification, pardon and holiness, by the law, and have found that the law could not give them; we have sought these in the gospel scheme, and we have found them. We serve God now, not according to the old, literal sense, but in the true spiritual meaning.

7. *Is the law sin?* The apostle had said, v. 5: "The motions of sins, which were by the law, did . . . bring forth fruit unto death"; and now he anticipates an objection, "Is therefore the law sin?" To which he answers, as usual, "By no means." Law is only the means of disclosing this sinful propensity, not of producing it, as a bright beam of the sun introduced into a room shows millions of motes which appear to be dancing in it in all directions. But these were not introduced by the light; they were there before, only there was not light enough to make them manifest. So the evil propensity was there before, but there was not light sufficient to discover it. *I had not known sin, but by the law.* Mr. Locke and Dr. Taylor have properly remarked the skill used by Paul in dexterously avoiding, as much as possible, the giving offense to the Jews: and this is particularly evident in his use of the word *I* in this place. In the beginning of the chapter, where he mentions their knowledge of the law, he says "ye"; in the fourth verse he joins himself with them, and says "we"; but here, and so to the end of the chapter, where he represents the power of sin and the inability of the law to subdue it, he appears to leave them out, and speaks altogether in the first person, though it is plain he means all those who are under the law. So, chap. iii. 7, he uses the singular pronoun, "Why . . . am I . . . judged as a sinner?" when he evidently means the whole body of unbelieving Jews. There is another circumstance in which his address is peculiarly evident: his demonstrating the insufficiency of the law under color of vindicating it. He knew that the Jew would take fire at the least reflection on the law, which he held in the highest veneration; and therefore he very naturally introduces him catching at that expression, v. 5, "the motions of sins, which were by the law," or notwithstanding the law. "What!" says this Jew, "do you vilify the law, by charging it with favoring sin?" By no means, says the apostle; I am very far from charging the law with favoring sin. "The law is holy, and the commandment holy, and just, and good," v. 12. Thus he writes in vindication of the law; and yet at the same time shows: (1) That the law requires the most extensive obedience, discovering and condemning sin in all its most secret and remote branches, v. 7. (2) That it gives sin a deadly force, subjecting every transgression to the penalty of death, vv. 8-14. And yet, (3) supplies neither help nor hope to the sinner, but leaves him under the power of sin, and the sentence of death, v. 14. While the human heart is its own measure, it will rate its workings according to its own propensities, for itself is its highest rule. But when God gives a true insight of His own perfections, to be applied as a rule of both passion and practice, then sin is discovered, and discovered too to be exceedingly sinful. So strong propensities, because they appear to be inherent in our nature, would have passed for natural and necessary operations, and their sinfulness would not have been discovered if the law had not said, *Thou shalt not covet;* and thus determined that the propensity itself, as well as its outward operations, is sinful.

8. *Sin, taking occasion by the commandment.*
I think the pointing, both in this and in the
eleventh verse, to be wrong; the comma should
be after *occasion,* and not after *commandment.*
"But sin, taking occasion, wrought in me by this
commandment all manner of concupiscence."
There are different opinions concerning the
meaning of the word *occasion.* Dr. Waterland
translates the clause, "Sin, taking advantage."
Dr. Taylor contends that all commentators have
mistaken the meaning of it, and that it should
be rendered "having received force." For this
acceptation of the word I can find no adequate
authority except in its etymology. The word
appears to signify, in general, whatsoever is necessary for the completion or accomplishment
of any particular purpose. There is a personification in the text; sin is represented as a
murderer watching for life, and snatching at
every means and embracing every opportunity
to carry his fell purpose into effect. The miserable sinner has a murderer, sin, within him;
this murderer can destroy life only in certain
circumstances. Finding that the law condemns
the object of his cruelty to death, he takes occasion from this to work in the soul all manner
of concupiscence, evil and irregular desires and
appetites of every kind, and by thus increasing
the evil, exposes the soul to more condemnation; and thus it is represented as being slain,
v. 11. That is, the law, on the evidence of those
sinful dispositions and their corresponding practices, condemns the sinner to death, so that he is
dead in law. Thus the very prohibition, as we
have already seen in the preceding verse, becomes the instrument of exciting the evil propensity; for, although a sinner has the general
propensity to do what is evil, yet he seems to
feel most delight in transgressing known law.
For without the law sin was dead. Where there
is no law there is no transgression, "for sin is
the transgression of the law"; and no fault can
be imputed unto death where there is no
statute by which such a fault is made a capital
offense. Dr. Taylor thinks that *without the law*
means the time before the giving of the law
from Mount Sinai, which took in the space of
430 years, during which time the people were
under the Abrahamic covenant of grace; and
without the law that was given on Mount Sinai,
the sting of death, which is sin, had not power
to slay the sinner; the law was not reenacted
till it was given by Moses, chap. v. 13. The
Jew was then *alive,* v. 9, because he was not
under the law subjecting him to death for his
transgressions; *but when the commandment
came,* with the penalty of death annexed, *sin
revived,* and the Jew died. *All manner of concupiscence.* It showed what was evil and forbade it; and then the principle of rebellion,
which seems essential to the very nature of sin,
rose up against the prohibition, and he was the
more strongly incited to disobey in proportion
as obedience was enjoined. Thus the apostle
shows that the law had authority to prohibit,
condemn, and destroy; but no power to pardon
sin, root out enmity, or save the soul. The word
which we render *concupiscence* signifies simply
"strong desire" of any kind; but in the New
Testament it is generally taken to signify irregular and unholy desires. Sin in the mind is the
desire to do, or to be, what is contrary to the
holiness and authority of God. *For without the
law sin was dead.* This means, according to

Dr. Taylor's hypothesis, the time previous to the
giving of the law. But it seems also consistent
with the apostle's meaning to interpret the place
as implying the time in which Paul, in his unconverted Jewish state, had not the proper
knowledge of the law—while he was unacquainted with its spirituality. He felt evil desire,
but he did not know the evil of it.

10. *And the commandment,* meaning the law
in general. *Which was ordained to life,* the rule
of righteousness teaching those statutes "which
if a man do, he shall live in them," Lev. xviii. 5.
I found, by transgressing it, *to be unto death;*
for it only presented the duty and laid down the
penalty, without affording any strength to resist
sin or subdue evil propensities.

11. *Sin, taking occasion.* Sin, deriving
strength from the law, threatening death to the
transgressor, *deceived me,* drew me aside to
disobedience, promising me gratification, honor,
independence, as it promised to Eve; for to her
history the apostle evidently alludes, and uses
the very same expression, *deceived me.* See the
Septuagint, Gen. iii. 13. *And by it slew me.*
Subjected me to that death which the law denounced against transgressors, and rendered me
miserable during the course of life itself. It is
well-known to scholars that the verb signifies
not only "to slay" or "kill," but also to "make
wretched." Every sinner is only exposed to
death because he has sinned, and must sooner
or later die; but he is miserable in both body
and mind by the influence and the effects of sin.
He lives a dying life, or a living death.

12. *Wherefore the law is holy.* As if he had
said, to soothe his countrymen, to whom he had
been showing the absolute insufficiency of the
law either to justify or save from sin: I do not
intimate that there is anything improper or imperfect in the law as a rule of life. It prescribes
what is *holy, just,* and *good;* for it comes from
a holy, just, and good God. The *law,* which
is to regulate the whole of the outward conduct,
is holy; and the *commandment,* "Thou shalt not
covet," which is to regulate the heart, is not less
so. All is excellent and pure; but it neither
pardons sin nor purifies the heart; and it is
because it is holy, just, and good that it condemns transgressors to death.

13. *Was then that which is good made death
unto me?* This is the question of the Jew, with
whom the apostle appears to be disputing. "Do
you allow the law to be good, and yet say it is
the cause of our death?" The apostle answers:
God forbid. "By no means." It is not the law
that is the cause of your death, but sin. It was
sin which subjected us to death by the law,
justly threatening sin with death, which law
was given that sin might appear—might be set
forth in its own colors—when we saw it subjected us to death by a law perfectly holy, just,
and good; that sin, by the law, might be represented what it really is, an exceeding great and
deadly evil.

14. *For we know that the law is spiritual.*
This is a general proposition, and probably, in
the apostle's autograph, concluded the above
sentence. The law is not to be considered as a
system of external rites and ceremonies, nor
even as a rule of moral action. It is a spiritual
system; it reaches to the most hidden purposes,
thoughts, dispositions, and desires of the heart
and soul; and it reproves and condemns every-

thing, without hope of reprieve or pardon, that is contrary to eternal truth and rectitude. *But I am carnal, sold under sin.* This was probably, in the apostle's letter, the beginning of a new paragraph. I believe it is agreed, on all hands, that the apostle is here demonstrating the insufficiency of the law in opposition to the gospel; that by the former is the knowledge, by the latter the cure, of sin. Therefore by *I* here he cannot mean himself, nor any Christian believer. If the contrary could be proved, the argument of the apostle would go to demonstrate the insufficiency of the gospel as well as the law. It is difficult to conceive how the opinion could have crept into the Church, or prevailed there, that "the apostle speaks here of his *regenerate state;* and that what was, in such a state, true of himself, must be true of all others in the same state." This opinion has, most pitifully and most shamefully, not only lowered the standard of Christianity, but destroyed its influence and disgraced its character. It requires but little knowledge of the spirit of the gospel, and of the scope of this Epistle, to see that the apostle is here either personating a Jew under the law and without the gospel or showing what his own state was when he was deeply convinced that by the deeds of the law no man could be justified, and had not as yet heard those blessed words: "Brother Saul, the Lord . . . Jesus, that appeared unto thee in the way . . . hath sent me, that thou mightest receive thy sight, and be filled with the Holy Ghost," Acts ix. 17. In this and the following verses he states the contrariety between himself, or any Jew while without Christ, and the law of God. Of the latter he says, "It *is spiritual";* of the former, *I am carnal, sold under sin.* Of the carnal man, in opposition to the spiritual, never was a more complete or accurate description given. The expressions "in the flesh" and "after the flesh," in v. 5 and in chap. viii. 5, 8-9, etc., are of the same import with the word *carnal* in this verse. To be "in the flesh," or to be "carnally minded," solely respects the unregenerate. While unregenerate, a man is in a state of death and enmity against God, chap. viii. 6-9. This is Paul's own account of a carnal man. Those who are of another opinion maintain that by the word *carnal* here the apostle meant that corruption which dwelt in him after his conversion. But this opinion is founded on a very great mistake; for although there may be, after justification, the remains of the carnal mind, which will be less or more felt till the soul is completely sanctified, yet the man is never denominated from the inferior principle, which is under control, but from the superior principle which habitually prevails. Whatever epithets are given to corruption or sin in Scripture, opposite epithets are given to grace or holiness. By these different epithets are the unregenerate and regenerate denominated. From all this it follows that the epithet *carnal,* which is the characteristic designation of an unregenerate man, cannot be applied to Paul after his conversion; nor, indeed, to any Christian in that state. [But cf. I Cor. 3:3—Ed.] But the word *carnal,* though used by the apostle to signify a state of death and enmity against God, is not sufficient to denote all the evil of the state which he is describing; hence he adds, expressions which the Spirit of God uses in Scripture to describe the full depravity of fallen man. It implies a willing slavery; Ahab had sold

himself to work evil, I Kings xxi. 20. And of the Jews it is said, in their utmost depravity, "Behold, for your iniquities have you sold yourselves," Isa. l. 1. Now if the word *carnal* in its strongest sense had been sufficiently significant of all he meant, why add to this charge another expression still stronger? We must therefore understand the phrase *sold under sin* as implying that the soul was employed in the drudgery of sin; that it was "sold over" to this service, and had no power to disobey this tyrant, until it was redeemed by another. And if a man be actually sold to another, and he acquiesce in the deed, then he becomes the legal property of that other person. This state of bondage was well-known to the Romans. The sale of slaves they saw daily, and could not misunderstand the emphatical sense of this expression. Sin is here represented as a person, and the apostle compares the dominion which sin has over the man in question to that of a master over his legal slave. Universally through the Scriptures man is said to be in a state of bondage to sin until the Son of God make him free, but in no part of the sacred writings is it ever said that the children of God are sold under sin.

15. *For that which I do I allow not.* The first clause of this verse is a general assertion concerning the employment of the person in question in the state which the apostle calls *carnal* and *sold under sin.* The Greek word which is here translated *I do* means a work which the agent continues to perform till it is finished, and is used by the apostle, Phil. ii. 12, to denote the continued employment of God's saints in His service to the end of their lives, "Work out your own salvation." The word here denotes an employment of a different kind; and therefore the man who now feels the galling dominion of sin says, What I am continually laboring at *I allow not.* "I do not acknowledge" to be right, just, holy, or profitable. *But what I hate, that do I.* I am a slave, and under the absolute control of my tyrannical master; I hate his service, but am obliged to work his will. Who, without blaspheming, can assert that the apostle is speaking this of a man in whom the Spirit of the Lord dwells? From v. 7 to this one the apostle, says Dr. Taylor, denotes the Jew in the flesh by a single *I;* here he divides that *I* into two *I's,* or figurative persons, representing two different and opposite principles which were in him. The one *I,* or principle, assents to the law that it is good, and wills and chooses what the other does not practice, v. 16. This principle he expressly tells us, v. 22, is the "inward man"; "the law of my mind," v. 23; the "mind," or rational faculty, v. 25; for he could find no other inward man, or law of the mind, but the rational faculty, in a person who was carnal and sold under sin. The other *I,* or principle, transgresses the law, v. 23, and does those things which the former principle allows not. This principle he expressly tells us, v. 18, is the "flesh," the "law in my members," or sensual appetite, v. 23; and he concludes in the last verse that these two principles, residing and counteracting each other in the same person, are reason and lust, or sin that dwells in us. And it is very easy to distinguish these two *I's,* or principles. For instance, v. 17: "Now then it is no more I that do it, but sin that dwelleth in me." The *I* he speaks of here is opposed to indwelling or gov-

erning sin; and therefore plainly denotes the principle of reason, the "inward man," or "law of my mind"; in which, I add, a measure of the light of the Spirit of God shines, in order to show the sinfulness of sin. These two different principles he calls, one "flesh," and the other "Spirit," Gal. v. 17, where he speaks of their contrariety in the same manner that he does here. And we may give a probable reason why the apostle dwells so long upon the struggle and opposition between these two principles; it appears intended to answer a tacit but very obvious objection. The Jew might allege: "But the law is holy and spiritual; and I assent to it as good, as a right rule of action, which ought to be observed. Yea, I esteem it highly; I glory and rest in it, convinced of its truth and excellency. And is not this enough to constitute the law a sufficient principle of sanctification?" The apostle answers, "No; wickedness is consistent with a sense of truth. A man may assent to the best rule of action, and yet still be under the dominion of lust and sin, from which nothing can deliver him but a principle and power proceeding from the fountain of life."

16. *If then I do that which I would not,* knowing that the law condemns it and that therefore it must be evil, *I consent unto the law;* I show by this circumstance that I acknowledge the law to be good.

17. *Now then it is no more I.* It is not that I which constitutes reason and conscience. *But sin*—corrupt and sensual inclinations—*that dwelleth in me*—that has the entire domination over my reason, darkening my understanding, and perverting my judgment; for which there is condemnation in the law, but no cure. So we find here that there is a principle in the unregenerate man stronger than reason itself; a principle which is, properly speaking, not of the essence of the soul, but acts in it, as its lord, or as a tyrant. This is inbred and indwelling sin, the seed of the serpent, by which the whole soul is darkened, confused, perverted, and excited to rebellion against God.

18. *For I know that in me.* I have learned by experience that in an unregenerate man there is *no good.* There is no principle by which the soul can be brought into the light, no principle by which it can be restored to purity; fleshly appetites alone prevail, and the brute runs away with the man. *For to will is present with me.* When the apostle says, *To will is present with me,* he shows that the will is on the side of God and truth, so far that it consents to the propriety and necessity of obedience. There has been a strange clamor raised up against this faculty of the soul, as if the very essence of evil dwelt in it, whereas the apostle shows throughout this chapter that the will was regularly on God's side, while every other faculty appears to have been in hostility to Him. The truth is, men have confounded the will with the passions, and laid to the charge of the former what properly belongs to the latter. The will is right, but the passions are wrong. It discerns and approves, but is without ability to perform; it has no power over sensual appetites; in these the principle of rebellion dwells.

19. *For the good that I would I do not.* Here again is the most decisive proof that the will is on the side of God and truth. *But the evil which I would not.* And here is equally decisive proof

that the will is against or opposed to evil. It is not the will that leads men astray, but the corrupt passions which oppose and oppress the will. The plain state of the case is this: the soul is so completely fallen that it has no power to do good till it receive that power from on high. But it has power to see good, to distinguish between that and evil; to acknowledge the excellence of this good, and to will it, from a conviction of that excellence; but further it cannot go. Yet in various cases it is solicited and consents to sin; and because it is will, that is, because it is a free principle, it must necessarily possess this power; and although it can do no good unless it receive grace from God, yet it is impossible to force it to sin. Even Satan himself cannot do this; and before he can get it to sin, he must gain its consent. Thus God in His endless mercy has endued this faculty with a power in which, humanly speaking, resides the salvability of the soul; and without this the soul must have eternally continued under the power of sin, or been saved as an inert, absolutely passive machine. But does not this arguing destroy the doctrine of free grace? No! it establishes that doctrine. (1) It is through the grace, the unmerited kindness, of God that the soul has such a faculty, and that it has not been extinguished by sin. (2) This will, though a free principle, yet, properly speaking, has no power by which it can subjugate the evil or perform the good. We know that the eye has a power to discern objects, but without light this power is perfectly useless, and no object can be discerned by it. So of the person represented here by the apostle it is said, *To will is present with me,* v. 18; "To will is ever in readiness, it is ever at hand, it lies constantly before me"; *but how to perform that which is good I find not;* that is, the man is unregenerate, and he is seeking justification and holiness from the law. The law was never designed to give these—it gives the knowledge, not the cure, of sin. Here, then, the free agency of man is preserved, without which he could not be in a salvable state; and the honor of the grace of Christ is maintained, without which there can be no actual salvation.

20. *It is no more I.* My will is against it; my reason and conscience condemn it. *But sin that dwelleth in me*—the principle of sin, which has possessed itself of all my carnal appetites and passions, and thus subjects my reason and domineers over my soul. Thus I am in perpetual contradiction to myself. Two principles are continually contending in me for the mastery: my reason, on which the light of God shines, to show what is evil; and my passions, in which the principle of sin works, to bring forth fruit unto death.

21. *I find then a law.* I am in such a condition and state of soul, under the power of such habits and sinful propensities, *that when I would do good*—when my will and reason are strongly bent on obedience to the law of God and opposition to the principle of sin—*evil is present with me,* "evil is at hand; it lies constantly before me." As the will to do good is constantly at hand, v. 18, so the principle of rebellion exciting me to sin is equally present; but as the one is only will, wish, and desire, without power to do what is willed, to obtain what is wished, or to perform what is desired, sin continually prevails. The word *law* in this verse must be taken as implying any strong or confirmed habit, under

the influence of which the man generally acts; and in this sense the apostle most evidently uses it in v. 23.

22. *I delight in the law of God after the inward man.* Every Jew, and every unregenerate man, who receives the Old Testament as a revelation from God must acknowledge the great purity, excellence, and utility of its maxims, though he will ever find that without the grace of our Lord Jesus he can never act according to those heavenly maxims; and without the mercy of God, can never be redeemed from the curse entailed upon him for his past transgressions. To say that the *inward man* means the regenerate part of the soul is supportable by no argument. If it be said that it is impossible for an unregenerate man to *delight in the law of God*, the experience of millions contradicts the assertion. Every true penitent admires the moral law, longs most earnestly for a conformity to it, and feels that he can never be satisfied till he awakes up after this divine likeness; and he hates himself because he feels that he has broken it, and that his evil passions are still in a state of hostility to it.

23. *But I see another law in my members.* Though the person in question is more or less under the continual influence of reason and conscience, which offer constant testimony against sin, yet as long as help is sought only from the law, and the grace of Christ in the gospel is not received, the remonstrances of reason and conscience are rendered of no effect by the prevalence of sinful passions; which, from repeated gratifications, have acquired all the force of habit, and now *give law* to the whole carnal man. *Warring against the law of my mind.* There is an allusion here to the case of a city besieged, at last taken by storm, and the inhabitants carried away into captivity; carrying on a system of warfare; laying continual siege to the soul; repeating incessantly its attacks; harassing, battering, and storming the spirit; and, by all these assaults, reducing the man to extreme misery. Never was a picture more impressively drawn and more effectually finished; for the next sentence shows that this spiritual city was at last taken by storm, and the inhabitants who survived the sackage led into the most shameful, painful, and oppressive captivity. *Bringing me into captivity to the law of sin.* He does not here speak of an occasional advantage gained by sin; it was a complete and final victory gained by corruption, which, having stormed and reduced the city, carried away the inhabitants with irresistible force into captivity. This is the consequence of being overcome; he was now in the hands of the foe, as the victor's lawful captive. This is the import of the original word, and is the very term used by our Lord when speaking of the final ruin, dispersion, and captivity of the Jews. He says, "They . . . shall be led away captive into all nations," Luke xxi. 24. When all this is considered, who, in his right mind, can apply it to the holy soul of the apostle of the Gentiles? Is there anything in it that can belong to his gracious state? Surely nothing. The basest slave of sin, who has any remaining checks of conscience, cannot be brought into a worse state than that described here by the apostle. Sin and corruption have a final triumph; and conscience and reason are taken prisoners, laid in fetters, and sold for slaves. Can this ever be

said of a man in whom the Spirit of God dwells, and whom the law of the Spirit of life in Christ Jesus has made free from the law of sin and death? See chap. viii. 2.

24. *O wretched man that I am!* This affecting account is finished more impressively by the groans of the wounded captive. Having long maintained a useless conflict against innumerable hosts and irresistible might, he is at last wounded and taken prisoner; and to render his state more miserable, is not only encompassed by the slaughtered, but chained to a dead body; for there seems to be here an allusion to an ancient custom of certain tyrants, who bound a dead body to a living man, and obliged him to carry it about, till the contagion from the putrid mass took away his life! Virgil paints this in all its horrors in the account he gives of the tyrant Mezentius. We may naturally suppose that the cry of such a person would be, "Wretched man that I am, who shall deliver me from this dead body?" And how well does this apply to the case of the person to whom the apostle refers! A *body*—a whole mass of sin and corruption, was bound to his soul with chains which he could not break; and the mortal contagion, transfused through his whole nature, was pressing him down to the bitter pains of an eternal death. He now finds that the law can afford him no deliverance, and he despairs of help from any human being. But while he is emitting his last or almost expiring groan, the redemption by Christ Jesus is proclaimed to him; and, if the apostle refers to his own case, Ananias unexpectedly accosts him with— "Brother Saul, the Lord . . . Jesus, that appeared unto thee in the way . . . hath sent me [unto thee], that thou mightest receive thy sight, and be filled with the Holy Ghost." He sees then an open door of hope, and he immediately, though but in the prospect of this deliverance, returns God thanks for the well-grounded hope which he has of salvation "through Jesus Christ our Lord."

25. *I thank God through Jesus Christ.* Instead of *I thank God,* several excellent MSS., with the Vulgate, some copies of the Itala, and several of the fathers, read "the grace of God," or "the grace of our Lord Jesus Christ"; this is an answer to the almost despairing question in the preceding verse. The whole, therefore, may be read thus: "O wretched man that I am! who shall deliver me from the body of this death?" ANSWER—"The grace of God through our Lord Jesus Christ." Thus we find that a case of the kind described by the apostle in the preceding verses, whether it were his own before he was brought to the knowledge of Christ, particularly during the three days that he was at Damascus, without being able to eat or drink, in deep penitential sorrow, or whether he personates a Pharisaic yet conscientious Jew deeply concerned for his salvation—I say, we find that such a case can be relieved by the gospel of Christ only; or, in other words, that no scheme of redemption can be effectual to the salvation of any soul, whether Jew or Gentile, but that laid down in the gospel of Christ. *So then with the mind I myself serve the law of God.* That this clause contains the inference from the preceding train of argumentation appears evident from the *therefore* with which the apostle introduces it. As if he had said: "To conclude, the sum of what I have advanced concerning

the power of sin in the carnal man and the utter insufficiency of all human means and legal observances to pardon sin and expel the corruption of the heart is this: that the very same person, the 'the same I,' while without the gospel, under the killing power of the law, will find in himself two opposite principles, the one subscribing to and approving the law of God and the other, notwithstanding, bringing him into captivity to sin. His 'inward man,' his rational powers and conscience, will assent to the justice and propriety of the requisitions of the law; and yet, notwithstanding this, his fleshly appetites, the 'law in his members,' will 'war against the law of his mind,' and continue, till he receives the gospel of Christ, to keep him in the galling captivity of sin and death."

CHAPTER 8

The happy state of those who believe in Christ, and walk under the influence of His Spirit, 1-2. The design of God in sending His Son into the world was to redeem men from sin, 3-4. The miserable state of the carnally minded, 5-8. How Christ lives and works in His followers; their blessedness here, and their happiness hereafter, 9-17. Sufferings are the common lot of all men, and from which Gentiles and Jews have the hope of being finally delivered, 18-23. The use and importance of hope, 24-25. The Spirit makes intercession for the followers of Christ, 26-27. "All things work together for good to them that love God," and who act according to His gracious purpose in calling them, 28. The means used to bring men to eternal glory, 29-30. The great blessedness, confidence, and security of all genuine Christians, whom, while they hold fast faith and a good conscience, nothing can separate from the love of God, 31-39.

1. *There is therefore now no condemnation.* To do justice to Paul's reasoning, this chapter must be read in the closest connection with the preceding. There we have seen the unavailing struggles of an awakened Jew, who sought pardon and holiness from that law which he was conscious he had broken; and in which he could find no provision for pardon, and no power to sanctify. This conviction having brought him to the very brink of despair, and being on the point of giving up all hope, he hears of redemption by Jesus Christ, thanks God for the prospect he has of salvation, applies for and receives it, and now magnifies God for the unspeakable gift of which he has been made a partaker. Those who restrain the word *now,* so as to indicate by it the gospel dispensation only, do not take in the whole of the apostle's meaning. The apostle has not been dealing in general matters only, but also in those which are particular. He has not been pointing out merely the difference between the two dispensations, the Mosaic and the Christian; but he marks out the state of a penitent under the former and that of a believer under the latter. The last chapter closed with an account of his salvation. The *now,* therefore, in the text must refer more to the happy transition from darkness to light, from condemnation to pardon, which this believer now enjoys, than to the Christian dispensation taking the place of the Jewish economy. *Who walk not after the flesh.* In this one verse we find the power and virtue of the gospel scheme. It pardons and sanctifies; the Jewish law could do neither. By faith in our Lord Jesus Christ the penitent, condemned by the law, is pardoned; the carnal man, laboring under the overpowering influence of the sin of his nature, is sanctified. He is first freely justified; he feels no condemnation. He is fully sanctified; he walks not after the flesh, but after the spirit.

This last clause is wanting in the principal MSS., versions, and fathers. It was probably to make the thing more obvious that this explanatory clause was added by some copyist, for it does not appear to have made an original part of the text; and it is most likely that it was inserted here from the fourth verse.

2. *For the law of the Spirit of life.* The gospel of the grace of Christ, which is not only a law or rule of life, but affords that sovereign energy by which guilt is removed from the conscience, the power of sin broken, and its polluting influence removed from the heart. Most people allow that Paul is here speaking of his own state; and this state is so totally different from that described in the preceding chapter that it is absolutely impossible that they should have been the state of the same being at one and the same time.

3. *For what the law could not do.* The law could not pardon; the law could not sanctify; the law could not dispense with its own requisitions; it is the rule of unrighteousness, and therefore must condemn unrighteousness. This is its unalterable nature. Had there been perfect obedience to its dictates, instead of condemning it, it would have applauded and rewarded; but as the *flesh,* the carnal and rebellious principle, had prevailed, and transgression had taken place, it was rendered *weak,* inefficient to undo this work of the flesh, and bring the sinner into a state of pardon and acceptance with God. *God sending his own Son in the likeness of sinful flesh.* Did that which the law could not do; i.e., purchased pardon for the sinner, and brought every believer into the favor of God. And this is effected by the incarnation of Christ. He in whom dwelt the fullness of the Godhead bodily took upon Him the *likeness of sinful flesh,* that is, a human body like ours, but not sinful as ours; *and for sin,* "and as a sacrifice for sin" (this is the sense of the word in a multitude of places); *condemned sin in the flesh*—condemned that to death and destruction which had condemned us to both. *Condemned sin in the flesh.* The design and object of the incarnation and sacrifice of Christ was to condemn sin, to have it executed and destroyed; not to tolerate it as some think, or to render it subservient to the purposes of His grace, as others; but to annihilate its power, guilt, and being in the soul of a believer.

4. *That the righteousness of the law might be fulfilled in us.* That the guilt might be pardoned through the merit of that sacrifice; and that we might be enabled, by the power of His own grace and Spirit, to walk in newness of life; loving God with all our heart, soul, mind, and strength, and our neighbor as ourselves. And thus the righteousness, the spirit, design, and purpose of the law are fulfilled in us, through the *strength of the Spirit of Christ,* which is here put in opposition to *the weakness of the law through the flesh.*

5. *For they that are after the flesh.* Here is the great distinction between Jews and genuine Christians: the former are *after the flesh,* are under the power of the carnal, rebellious principle; and consequently *mind,* "relish," *the things of the flesh,* the things which appertain merely to the present life, having no relish for spiritual and eternal things. *But they that are after the Spirit.* They who are regenerated, who are born of the Spirit, being redeemed from the influ-

ence and law of the carnal mind; these relish *the things of the Spirit*—they are spiritually minded, and pass through things temporal, so as not to lose the things which are eternal.

6. *For to be carnally minded is death.* To live under the influence of the carnal mind is to live in the state of condemnation, and consequently liable to death eternal; whereas, on the contrary, he who is *spiritually minded* has the *life* and *peace* of God in his soul, and is in full prospect of life eternal.

7. *Because the carnal mind is enmity against God.* Because it is a *carnal mind,* and relishes earthly and sinful things, and lives in opposition to the pure and holy law of God, therefore, it *is enmity against God;* it is irreconcilable and implacable hatred. *It is not subject to the law of God.* It will come under no obedience, for it is sin, and the very principle of rebellion; and therefore it cannot be subject, nor subjected, for it is essential to sin to show itself in rebellion; and when it ceases to rebel, it ceases to be sin. From this we learn that the design of God in the economy of the gospel is not to weaken, curtail, or lay the carnal principle in bonds, but to destroy it. As it is *not subject,* and cannot be subject, *to the law of God,* it must be destroyed, else it will continue to rebel against God.

8. *So then.* Because this carnal mind is enmity against God, *they that are in the flesh,* who are under the power of the workings of this carnal mind (which every soul is that has not received redemption in the blood of the Lamb), *cannot please God,* because of the rebellious workings of this principle of rebellion and hatred. And if they cannot *please* God, they must be displeasing to Him, and consequently in the broad road to final perdition.

9. *But ye are not in the flesh.* You Christians, who have believed in Christ Jesus as the Sin Offering which has condemned sin in the flesh, and having been justified by faith and made partakers of the Holy Spirit, are enabled to walk in newness of life. *If so be that the Spirit of God dwell in you.* Or "seeing that" the Spirit of God dwelleth in you. The *flesh,* the sinful principle, dwelt in them before, and its motions were the proofs of its indwelling; but now the Spirit dwells in them, and His testimony in their conscience and His powerful operations in their hearts are the proofs of His indwelling.

10. *And if Christ be in you.* This is the criterion by which you may judge of the state of grace in which you stand. If Christ dwell in your hearts by faith, *the body is dead because of sin,* "in reference to sin"; the members of your body no more perform the work of sin than the body of a dead man does the functions of natural life. Or the apostle may mean that although *because of sin* the life of man is forfeited and the sentence, "Dust thou art, and unto dust shalt thou return," must be fulfilled on every human being, until the judgment of the great day, yet their souls being quickened by the indwelling Spirit of Christ, which enables them to live a life of righteousness, they receive a full assurance that their bodies, which are now condemned to death because of sin, shall be raised again to a life of immortal glory.

11. *But if the Spirit.* This verse confirms the sense given to the preceding. He who here receives the grace and Spirit of Christ, and continues to live under its influence a life of obedience to the divine will, shall have a resurrection.

12. *Therefore, brethren.* Dr. Taylor is of opinion that the apostle, having spoken separately to both Jews and Gentiles concerning holiness and the obligations to it, now addresses himself to both conjointly, and, (1) Draws the general conclusion from all his arguments upon this subject, v. 12. (2) Proves the validity of their claims to eternal life, vv. 14-17. (3) And as the affair of suffering persecution was a great stumbling block to the Jews, and might very much discourage the Gentiles, he introduces it to the best advantage, v. 17, and advances several arguments to fortify their minds under all trials: as (a) That they suffered with Christ; (b) In order to be glorified with Him in a manner which will infinitely compensate all sufferings, vv. 17-18. (c) All mankind are under various pressures, longing for a better state, vv. 19-22. (d) Many of the most eminent Christians are in the same distressed condition, v. 23. (e) According to the plan of the gospel, we are to be brought to glory after a course of patience exercised in a variety of trials, vv. 24-25. (f) The Spirit of God will supply patience to every upright soul under persecution and suffering, vv. 26-27. (g) All things, even the severest trials, shall work together for their good, v. 28. And this he proves by giving us a view of the several steps which the wisdom and goodness of God have settled in order to our complete salvation, vv. 29-30. Thence he passes to the affair of our perseverance, concerning which he concludes, from the whole of his preceding arguments, that as we are brought into a state of pardon by the free grace of God, through the death of Christ, who is now our Mediator in heaven, no possible cause, providing we continue to love and serve God, shall be able to pervert our minds or separate us from His love in Christ Jesus, vv. 31-39. *Therefore* is the grand inference from all that he has been arguing in relation to sanctity of life, both to the Gentiles, chap. vi, and to the Jews, chaps. vii and viii to this verse, where I suppose he begins to address himself to both, in a body, to the end of the chapter.

13. *But if ye through the Spirit*—if you seek that grace and spiritual help which the gospel of Christ furnishes—resist, and, by resisting, *mortify the deeds of the* flesh, against which the law gave you no assistance, *ye shall live* a life of faith, love, and holy obedience here, and a life of glory hereafter.

14. *For as many as are led by the Spirit.* No man who has not divine assistance can either find the way to heaven or walk in it when found. As Christ by His sacrificial offering has opened the kingdom of God to all believers, and as a Mediator transacts the concerns of their Kingdom before the throne, so the Spirit of God is the great Agent here below to enlighten, quicken, strengthen, and guide the true disciples of Christ; and all that are born of this Spirit are led and guided by Him, and none can pretend to be the children of God who are not thus guided.

15. *Ye have not received the spirit of bondage.* All that were under the law were under bondage to its rites and ceremonies; and as,

through the prevalence of that corrupt nature with which every human being is polluted, and to remove which the law gave no assistance, they were often transgressing, consequently they had forfeited their lives, and were continually, through fear of death, subject to bondage, Heb. ii. 15. The believers in Christ Jesus were brought from under that law and from under its condemnation, and consequently were freed from its bondage. *But ye have received the Spirit of adoption.* You are brought into the family of God by adoption; and the Agent that brought you into this family is the Holy Spirit; and this very Spirit continues to witness to you the grace in which you stand, by enabling you to call God your Father, with the utmost filial confidence and affection. *The Spirit of adoption.* Adoption was an act frequent among the ancient Hebrews, Greeks, and Romans, by which a person was taken out of one family and incorporated with another. Persons of property, who had no children of their own, adopted those of another family. The child thus adopted ceased to belong to his own family and was in every respect bound to the person who had adopted him, as if he were his own child, and in consequence of the death of his adopting father he possessed his estates. If a person after he had adopted a child happened to have children of his own, then the estate was equally divided between the adopted and real children. The Romans had regular forms of law by which all these matters were settled. *Whereby we cry, Abba, Father.* It has been remarked that slaves were not permitted to use the term *Abba,* father, or *Imma,* mother, in accosting their masters and mistresses. And from this some suppose that the apostle intimates that being now brought from under the spirit of bondage, in which they durst not call God their *Father,* they are not only brought into a new state, but have got that language which is peculiar to that state. Some have supposed that the apostle, by using the Syriac and Greek words which express *Father,* shows the union of Jewish and Gentile believers in those devotions which were dictated by a filial spirit. Others have thought that these were the first words which those generally uttered who were made partakers of the Holy Spirit. It is enough to know that it was the language of their sonship; and that it expressed the clear assurance they had of being received into the divine favor, the affection and gratitude they felt for this extraordinary blessing and their complete readiness to come under the laws and regulations of the family, and to live in the spirit of obedience.

16. *The Spirit itself beareth witness with our spirit.* "That same Spirit," the Spirit of adoption; that is, the Spirit who witnesses this adoption; which can be no other than the Holy Ghost himself, and certainly cannot mean any disposition or affection of mind which the adopted person may feel. *With our spirit.* In our understanding, the place or recipient of light and information, and the place or faculty to which such information can properly be brought. This is done that we may have the highest possible evidence of the work which God has wrought. As the window is the proper medium to let the light of the sun into our apartments, so the understanding is the proper medium of conveying the Spirit's influence to the soul. We therefore have the utmost evi-dence of the fact of our adoption which we can possibly have; we have the word and Spirit of God, and the word sealed on our spirit by the Spirit of God. And this is not a momentary influx. If we take care to walk with God and not grieve the Holy Spirit, we shall have an abiding testimony; and while we continue faithful to our adopting Father, the Spirit that witnesses that adoption will continue to witness it, and hereby we shall know that we are of God by the Spirit which He giveth us.

17. *And if children, then heirs.* For the legitimate children alone can inherit the estate. This is not an estate to which they succeed in consequence of the death of a former possessor; it is like the Promised Land, given by God himself, and divided among the children of the family. *Heirs of God.* It is neither an earthly portion nor a heavenly portion, but GOD himself, who is to be their Portion. It is not heaven they are to inherit; it is GOD, who is infinitely greater and more glorious than heaven itself. *Joint-heirs with Christ.* Partaking of the same eternal glory with the glorified human nature of Christ. *If so be that we suffer with him.* Observe, says Dr. Taylor, how prudently the apostle advances to the harsh affair of suffering. He does not mention it till he has raised up their thoughts to the highest object of joy and pleasure —the happiness and glory of a joint inheritance with the ever-blessed Son of God. We are *heirs; heirs of God, and joint-heirs with Christ; if so be that we suffer with him.* This, with the additional consideration that we suffer with Christ, or as He himself suffered, would greatly qualify the transitory afflictions of this world, and dispose them to attend to the other arguments He had to offer.

18. *For I reckon that the sufferings.* If the glory that is to be revealed be the enjoyment of God himself, then the sufferings of this life, which, when compared with eternity, are but as for a moment, are not worthy to be put in competition with this glory which shall be revealed in us.

19. *For the earnest expectation of the creature.* There is considerable difficulty in this and the following four verses, and the difficulty lies chiefly in the meaning of the word which we translate *the creature,* and *creation.* Some think that by it the brute creation is meant; others apply it to the Jewish people; others, to the godly; others, to the Gentiles; others, to the good angels; and others, to the fallen spirits, both angelic and human. Dr. Lightfoot's mode of explanation appears to me to be the best, on the whole. "There is," says he, "a twofold key hanging at this place, which may unlock the whole, and make the sense plain and easy. (1) The first is the phrase which we render 'the whole creation,' v. 22, and with which we meet twice elsewhere in the New Testament. Mark xvi. 15: 'Preach the gospel to every creature'; and Col. i. 23: The gospel 'was preached to every creature.' Now it is sufficiently apparent what is meant in both these places, viz. 'all nations.' For that which in Mark is, 'Preach the gospel to every creature,' is, in Matthew, 'Go . . . and teach all nations.' (2) The second key is the word, v. 20, which is not unfitly rendered *vanity;* but then this vanity is improperly applied to the vanishing, dying, changing state of the creation. For *vanity* does not so much de-

note the vanishing condition of the outward state as it does the inward vanity or emptiness of the mind. So the apostle, speaking of the Gentiles concerning whom he speaks here, tells us, They 'became vain in their imaginations,' chap. i. 21; and again, The 'Gentiles walk, in the vanity of their mind,' Eph. iv. 17. Throughout this whole place the apostle seems to allude to the bondage of the Israelites in Egypt and their deliverance from it, with a comparison made betwixt the Jewish and the Gentile church. When God would deliver Israel from his bondage, He challenges him for His Son, and His firstborn, Exod. iv. 22. And in like manner the Gentiles earnestly expect and wait for such a kind of manifestation of the sons of God within and among themselves. The Romans to whom the apostle writes knew well how many predictions and promises it had pleased God to publish by His prophets concerning gathering together and adopting sons to himself among the Gentiles; the *manifestation* of which *sons* the whole Gentile world with a 'neck' as it were 'stretched out,' as the word implies, doth now wait for."

20. *For the creature was made subject to vanity.* The Gentile world was subject to vanity of mind; but how? *Not willingly, but by reason of him who hath subjected the same.* May we not say it became vain willingly, but was made subject to vanity unwillingly?

21. *Because the creature.* This and the preceding verse should be thus connected: "in hope that the creature itself also shall be delivered." The word *phthora* denotes, very frequently, "sinful corruption." So 2 Pet. i. 4: "Corruption . . . through lust." 2 Cor. xi. 3: "Lest your minds should be corrupted." I Cor. xv. 33: "Evil communications corrupt good manners." The sense, therefore, of the apostle in this place seems to be: The Gentile world shall, in time, be delivered from the bondage of their "sinful corruption" (i.e., the bondage of their lusts and vile affections), and be brought into such a noble liberty as the sons of God enjoy.

22. *The whole creation groaneth and travaileth.* If it be inquired how the Gentile world groaned and travailed in pain, let them who explain this of the fabric of the material world tell us how that groans and travails. They must needs own it to be a borrowed and allusive phrase; but in the sense above given, the very literal construction may be admitted.

23. *And not only they, but ourselves also.* Neither the Gentiles only, but we Jews also, to whom God hath granted *the firstfruits of the Spirit.* We sigh among ourselves for their sakes, *waiting for the adoption;* that is, *the redemption of our* mystical *body,* whereof the Gentiles make a very great part.

24. *For we are saved by hope.* We are supported and are comfortable in the expectation we have of receiving from the hand of our God all the good we need in the troubles and adversities of this life, and of having our bodies raised from corruption and death at the general resurrection. *Hope that is seen is not hope.* As hope signifies "the expectation of future good," so it necessarily supposes that the object of it is not *seen,* i.e., not "enjoyed"; for to see in Scripture language sometimes signifies to enjoy, as in Job vii. 7: "Mine eye shall no more see [margin, 'enjoy'] good." The *hope that is seen,* that is, "enjoyed," is no longer hope; it is fruition; and a man cannot hope for that which he has in his possession.

25. *But if we hope for that we see not.* If we have a well-grounded expectation of our resurrection and final glorification, knowing that such things are necessarily future and must for a certain time be delayed, then do we patiently wait for them, continue patiently to endure the common ills of life and whatever tribulations we may be exposed to in consequence of our Christian profession.

26. *The Spirit also helpeth our infirmities.* The same Spirit mentioned before as bearing witness with ours that we are the children of God; and consequently it is not a disposition or frame of mind, for the disposition of our mind surely cannot help the infirmities of our minds. The word *synantilambanetai* is very inadequately expressed by *helpeth.* It is compounded of *syn,* "together," *anti,* "against," and *lambanomai,* "to support or help," and signifies such assistance as is afforded by any two persons to each other who mutually bear the same load or carry it between them. He who prays receives help from the Spirit of God; but he who prays not receives no such help. *For we know not what we should pray for as we ought.* And should therefore be liable to endless mistakes in our prayers if suitable desires were not excited by the Holy Spirit and power received to bring these desires, by prayer, before the throne of grace. *But the Spirit itself,* "the same Spirit," viz., the Spirit that witnesses of our adoption and sonship, vv. 15-16, *maketh intercession for us.* Surely if the apostle had designed to teach us that he meant our own sense and understanding by the *Spirit,* he never could have spoken in a manner in which plain common sense was never likely to comprehend his meaning.

27. *He maketh intercession for the saints.* The word *entynchano* signifies to apply oneself to a person in behalf of another, to "intercede" or "negotiate for." Our Lord makes intercession for us by negotiating and managing, as our Friend and Agent, all the affairs pertaining to our salvation. And the Spirit of God makes intercession for the saints, not by supplication to God on their behalf, but by directing and qualifying their supplications in a proper manner by His agency and influence upon their hearts; which, according to the gospel scheme, is the peculiar work and office of the Holy Spirit. *According to the will of God.* According to the mind, intention, or design of God. And thus the prayers which we offer up, and the desires which subsist in the unutterable groanings, are all such as are pleasing in the sight of God. So that God, whose is the Spirit, and who is acquainted with the mind of the Spirit, knows what He means when He leads the saints to express themselves in words, desires, groans, sighs, or tears. In each, God reads the language of the Holy Ghost, and prepares the answer according to the request.

28. *And we know that all things work together for good to them that love God.* To understand this verse aright, let us observe: (1) That the persons in whose behalf all things work for good are they who *love God* and, consequently, who live in the spirit of obedience. (2) It is not said that all things *shall* work for

good, but that they work now in the behalf of him who loveth now, for both verbs are in the present tense. (3) All these things *work together;* while they are working, God's providence is working, His Spirit is working, and they are working together with Him. *To them who are the called according to his purpose.* Dr. Taylor translates *the called,* "the invited," and observes that it is a metaphor taken from inviting guests or making them welcome to a feast. Our being *called* or "invited," according to God's purpose, proves that all things work for our good, on the supposition that we love God, and not otherwise. How is it evident and unquestionable that we are *called?* From our being in the Visible Church and professing the faith of the gospel. For always, in the apostolic writings, all that are in the Visible Church and profess the faith of the gospel are numbered among the *called* or "invited"; i.e., among the persons who are invited to feast on the covenant sacrifice.

29. *The firstborn among many brethren.* That He might be the Chief or Head of all the redeemed; for His human nature is the firstfruits of the resurrection from the dead; and He is the first human being that, after having passed through death, was raised to eternal glory.

30. *Whom he did predestinate.* The Gentiles, whom He determined to call into His Church with the Jewish people, *he called*—He invited by the preaching of the gospel, to believe on His Son, Jesus Christ. *He also justified.* Pardoned the sins of all those who with hearty repentance and true faith turned unto Him. *He also glorified.* He has honored and dignified the Gentiles with the highest privileges, and He has already taken many of them to the Kingdom of glory and many more are on their way thither; and all who love Him and continue faithful unto death shall inherit that glory eternally. Though the terms are here used in a more general sense, yet if we take them more restrictedly, we must consider that in the work of justification sanctification is implied, justification being the foundation and beginning of that work. From all this we learn that none will be *glorified* who have not been sanctified and *justified.* The word *doxa,* which we render "glory," and *doxazo,* to "glorify," both mean to "render illustrious, eminent," in various parts of the New Testament; and in this sense the verb is used in John xi. 4; xii. 23, 28; xiii. 31-32; xiv. 13; xv. 8; xxi. 19; Acts iii. 13; and in chap. xi. 13—in none of which places eternal beatification can be intended. Here it seems to mean that those whom God had called into a state of justification He had rendered illustrious by innumerable gifts, graces, and privileges, in the same manner as He had done to the Israelites of old. The whole of the preceding discourse will show that everything here is conditional, as far as it relates to the ultimate salvation of any person professing the gospel of Christ; for the promises are made to character, and not to persons, as some have most injudiciously affirmed. The apostle insists upon a character all along from the beginning of the chapter. V. 1: "There is . . . no condemnation to them which are in Christ Jesus, who walk not after the flesh, but after the Spirit." V. 13: "If ye live after the flesh, ye shall die." The absolute

necessity of holiness to salvation is the very subject of his discourse; this necessity he positively affirms, and establishes by the most solid arguments.

31. *What shall we then say to these things?* What conclusion should we draw from the above premises—from all that was already laid down in the preceding chapters, but especially in the preceding verses, from vv. 28 to 30 inclusive? As if he had said: What comfort may we derive from these doctrines? God has called us all to holiness, and to love to Him, which is the principle of holiness. *If God be for us, who can be against us?* He who is infinitely wise has undertaken to direct us; He who is infinitely powerful has undertaken to protect us; He who is infinitely good has undertaken to save us. What cunning, strength, or malice can prevail against His wisdom, power, and goodness?

32. *He that spared not his own Son.* And can we, His sincere followers, doubt of the safety of our state, or the certainty of His protection? No; for if He loved us, Gentiles and Jews, so intensely as to deliver up to death His own Son *for us all,* can He withhold from us any minor blessing? Nay, will He not, on the contrary, *freely give us all things?*

33. This and the following two verses contain a string of questions, most appropriately introduced and most powerfully urged, tending to show the safety of the state of those who have believed the gospel of the grace of God. I shall lay these verses down as they are pointed by the best Greek critics: "Who shall lay anything to the charge of God's elect?—God, who justifieth? Who is he that condemneth?—Christ, who died? or, rather, who is risen again? He who is at the right hand of God? He who maketh intercession for us? Who shall separate us from the love of Christ?—Tribulation? or distress? or persecution? or famine? or nakedness? or peril? or sword?" In all these questions the apostle intimates that if neither God nor Christ *would* bring any charge against them who love Him, none else *could.* And as God justifies through Christ, who died, consequently no charge can lie against these persons, as God alone could produce any; and He, so far from doing this, has justified them—freely forgiven their trespasses.

34. *Who is even at the right hand of God.* To which He has exalted our human nature, which He took in conjunction with His divinity; and there he *maketh intercession for us*—manages all the concerns of His own kingdom in general, and of every member of His Church in particular.

35. *Who shall separate us from the love of Christ?* I do think that this question has been generally misunderstood. The apostle is referring to the persecutions and tribulations to which genuine Christians were exposed through their attachment to Christ, and the gracious provision God had made for their support and final salvation. As in this provision God had shown His infinite love to them in providing Jesus Christ as their Sin Offering, and Jesus Christ had shown His love in suffering death upon the Cross for them, so, here, he speaks of the love of the followers of God to that Christ who had first loved them. Therefore the question is not, Who shall separate the love of Christ from us? or prevent Christ from loving us? but,

Who shall separate *us* from the love of Christ? Who or what shall be able to remove *our affection* from Him? And the questions that immediately follow show that this is the sense of the passage; for the *tribulation, distress,* etc., which he enumerates are things by which *they* might be affected, but by which *Christ* could not be affected. *Shall tribulation? Thlipsis,* grievous affliction, or distress of any kind; from *thlibo,* to "compress, oppress, straiten"; anything by which a man is rendered miserable. *Or distress?* A word of nearly the same import with the former, but more intense in its signification. It signifies "straitness," being hemmed in on every side, without the possibility of getting out or escaping. *Or persecution? Diogmos* from *dioko,* to "pursue, press upon, prosecute," signifies such pursuing as an enemy uses in order to overtake the object of his malice that he may destroy him. *Or famine?* The total want of bread, and all the necessaries of life. *Or peril?* A state of extreme and continued danger, perplexing and distressing with grievous forebodings and alarms. *Or sword?* "Slaughter"; the total destruction of life, and especially beheading, and suchlike, done by the order of the civil magistrate; for the word is used in this Epistle, chap. xiii. 4, to signify the authority and power which he has of judicially terminating life; i.e., of inflicting capital punishment.

36. *As it is written.* And these are no more than we may naturally expect from the present constitution of the world, and the positive predictions of the prophet, Ps. xliv. 22, who foresaw that a wicked world would always persecute and oppress the true followers of God.

37. *Nay.* As the prophet adds in the same place, "All this is come upon us; yet have we not forgotten thee, neither have we dealt falsely in thy covenant," vv. 17-18. So all these things may happen unto us, but *in all these things we are more than conquerors.* We abide faithful in the new covenant of our God; and He is faithful who has promised to support and make us more than conquerors; i.e., to give us a complete triumph over sin, and death, and hell, not leaving one enemy unsubdued.

38. *For I am persuaded,* after the blessed experience we have had of support by the grace and Spirit of Him that loved us, that neither fear of *death,* nor hope of *life,* nor evil *angels, nor principalities, nor powers,* persecuting us for Christ's sake; nor the *things* we endure at *present,* nor the *things to come,* whatever tribulation we may be called to suffer in future.

39. *Nor height* of honor, *nor depth* of ignominy, *nor any other creature* (nor any other thing whatever), *shall be able to separate us* who love God *from the love of God, which* He has vouchsafed to us *in Christ Jesus.*

CHAPTER 9

Paul expresses his great sorrow for the unbelief and obstinacy of the Jews, 1-3. Whose high privileges he enumerates, 4-5. Points out the manner in which God has chosen to communicate the knowledge of His name to both Jews and Gentiles; and how He deals, whether in judgment or mercy, with individuals; and produces the cases of Abraham, Isaac, Jacob, Esau, and Pharaoh, 6-17. God shows mercy and judgment as He thinks proper, and none have a right to find fault with His proceedings, 18-20. He has the same power over the human race as the potter has over the clay, 21-23. The prophets predicted the calling of the Gentiles, and the rejection of the Jews, 24-29. The Gentiles have attained to the knowledge of God's method of saving sinners,

while the Jews have not attained this knowledge, 30-31. The reason why the Jews have not attained the salvation provided for them in the gospel, 32-33.

1. *I say the truth in Christ, I lie not.* This is one of the most solemn oaths any man can possibly take. He appeals to Christ as the Searcher of hearts that he tells the truth; asserts that his conscience was free from all guile in this matter, and that the Holy Ghost bore him testimony that what he said was true.

3. *For I could wish that myself were accursed from Christ.* Very few passages in the New Testament have puzzled critics and commentators more than this. Every person saw the perfect absurdity of understanding it in a literal sense, as no man in his right mind could wish himself eternally damned in order to save another, or to save even the whole world. And the supposition that such an effect could be produced by such a sacrifice was equally absurd and monstrous. The Greek word *anathema* properly signifies anything devoted to God, so as to be destroyed; it answers to the Hebrew *cherem,* which the Septuagint translate by it, and means either a "thing or person separated from its former state or condition, and devoted to destruction." In this sense it is used, Deut. vii. 25-26; Josh. vi. 17-18; vii. 12. It is certain that the word, among both Hebrews and Greeks, was used to express a person devoted to destruction for the public safety. This one circumstance is sufficient to explain the word in this place. Paul desired to be devoted to destruction, as the Jews then were, in order to redeem his countrymen from this most terrible excision. He was willing to become a sacrifice for the public safety, and to give his life to redeem theirs.

4. *Who are Israelites.* Descendants of Jacob, a man so highly favored of God, and from whom he received his name *Israel*—"a prince of God," Gen. xxxii. 28, from which name his descendants were called *Israelites,* and separated unto God for His glory and praise. Their very name of *Israelites* implied their very high dignity; they were a royal nation, princes of the most high God. *The adoption.* The Israelites were all taken into the family of God, and were called His sons and firstborn, Exod. iv. 22; Deut. xiv. 1; Jer. xxxi. 9; Hos. xi. 1; and this adoption took place when God made the covenant with them at Horeb. *The glory.* The manifestation of God among them; principally by the cloud and pillar, and the Shekinah, or Divine Presence, appearing between the cherubim over the mercy seat. These were peculiar to the Jews; no other nation was ever thus favored. *The covenants.* The covenants made with Abraham, both that which relates to the spiritual seed and that which was peculiar to his natural descendants, Gal. iii. 16-17; which covenants were afterwards renewed by Moses, Deut. xxix. 1. *The giving of the law.* The revelation of God by God himself, containing a system of moral and political precepts. This was also peculiar to the Jews, for to no other nation had He ever given a revelation of His will. *The service.* The particular ordinances, rites, and ceremonies of their religious worship, and especially the sacrificial system, so expressive of the sinfulness of sin and the holiness of God. *The promises.* The land of Canaan, and the blessings of the Messiah and His kingdom, which promises had been made and often repeated to the patriarchs and to the prophets.

5. *Whose are the fathers.* Abraham, Isaac, Jacob, Joseph, the twelve patriarchs, Moses, Joshua, Samuel, David, etc., without controversy, the greatest and most eminent men that ever flourished under heaven. From these, in an uninterrupted and unpolluted line, the Jewish people had descended, and it was no small glory to be able to reckon, in their genealogy, persons of such incomparable merit and excellency. *And of whom as concerning the flesh Christ came.* These ancestors were the more renowned as being the progenitors of the human nature of the Messiah Christ; the Messiah "according to the flesh" sprang from them. But this Messiah was more than man; He is *God over all;* the very Being who gave them being, though He appeared to receive a being from them. Here the apostle most distinctly points out the twofold nature of our Lord—His eternal Godhead and His humanity.

6. *Not as though the word of God hath taken none effect.* A Jew might have objected, as in chap. iii. 3: "Is not God bound by His faithfulness to continue the Jews as His peculiar church and people, notwithstanding the infidelity of the major part of them?" To which it may be answered: This awful dispensation of God towards the Jews is not inconsistent with the veracity of the divine promise; for even the whole body of natural-born Jews are not the whole of the Israelites comprehended in the promise. Abraham is the father of many nations; and his seed is not only that which is of the *law,* but that also which is "of the faith of Abraham," chap. iv. 16-17. The Gentiles were included in the Abrahamic covenant as well as the Jews, and therefore the Jews have no exclusive right to the blessings of God's kingdom.

7. *Neither because they are the seed of Abraham.* Nor can they conclude, because they are the natural descendants of Abraham, that therefore they are all of them, without exception, the children in whom the promise is to be fulfilled. *But, In Isaac shall thy seed be called.* The promise is not confined to immediate natural descent, but may be accomplished in any part of Abraham's posterity. For Abraham had several sons besides Isaac, Gen. xxv. 1-2, particularly Ishmael, who was circumcised before Isaac was born, and in whom Abraham was desirous that the promise should be fulfilled, Gen. xvii. 18. In him God might have fulfilled the promise had He so pleased; and yet He said to Abraham, Gen. xxi. 12: Not in Ishmael, but "in Isaac shall thy seed be called."

8. *That is, They which are the children of the flesh.* Whence it appears that not the children who descend from Abraham's loins, nor those who were circumcised as he was, nor even those whom he might expect and desire, are therefore the Church and people of God; but those who are made children by the good pleasure and promise of God, as Isaac was, are alone to be accounted for the seed with whom the covenant was established.

9. *For this is the word of promise.* That is, this is evidently implied in the promise recorded in Gen. xviii. 10: "At this time I will come," saith God, "and exert My divine power, and Sarah, though fourscore and ten years old, shall have a son"; which shows that it is the sovereign will and act of God alone which singles out and constitutes the peculiar seed that was to inherit the promise made to Abraham.

11. *For the children being not yet born.* As the word *children* is not in the text, the word "nations" would be more proper; for it is of nations that the apostle speaks, as the following verses show, as well as the history to which he refers. *Neither having done any good.* To merit the distinction of being made the peculiar people of God. *Or evil,* to deserve to be left out of this covenant, and the distinguishing national blessings which it conferred. *That the purpose of God according to election might stand*—that such distinctions might appear to depend on nothing but God's free choice. *Not of works,* or any desert in the people or nations thus chosen; but of the mere purpose *of him that calleth* any people He pleases, to make them the depositories of His especial blessings, and thus to distinguish them from all others.

12-13. *The elder shall serve the younger.* These words, with those of Malachi, *Jacob have I loved, but Esau have I hated,* are cited by the apostle to prove, according to their typical signification, that the "purpose of God according to election" does and will stand, "not of *works,* but of *him that calleth*"; that is, that the purpose of God, which is the ground of that election which He makes among men, unto the honor of being Abraham's seed, might appear to remain unchangeable in Him, and to be even the same which He had declared unto Abraham. That these words are used in a *national* and not in a *personal* sense is evident from this: that, taken in the latter sense they are not true, for Jacob never did exercise any power over Esau, nor was Esau ever subject to him. Jacob, on the contrary, was rather subject to Esau, and was sorely afraid of him; and, first, by his messengers, and afterwards personally, acknowledged his brother to be his lord, and himself to be his servant; see Gen. xxxii. 4; xxxiii. 8, 13. And hence it appears that neither Esau nor Jacob, nor even their posterities, are brought here by the apostle as instances of any *personal* reprobation from eternity. For it is very certain that very many, if not the far greatest part, of Jacob's posterity were wicked, and rejected by God; and it is not less certain that some of Esau's posterity were partakers of the faith of their father Abraham. (1) It incontestably appears from these passages that the prophet does not speak at all of the *person* of Jacob or Esau, but of their respective *posterities.* (2) If neither the prophet nor the apostle speaks of the persons of Jacob or Esau, but of their posterity, then it is evident that neither the love of God to Jacob nor the hatred of God to Esau were such according to which the eternal states of men, in either happiness or misery, are to be determined; nor is there here any scriptural or rational ground for the decree of unconditional personal election and reprobation, which comparatively modern times have endeavored to build on these scriptures.

14. *What shall we say then?* To what conclusion shall we come on the facts before us? Shall we suggest that God's bestowing peculiar privileges in this unequal manner on those who otherwise are in equal circumstances is inconsistent with justice and equity? "By no means." Whatever God does is right, and He may dispense His blessings to whom and on what terms He pleases.

15. *For he saith to Moses, I will have mercy.* The words of God to Moses, Exod. xxxiii. 19, show that God has a right to dispense His blessings as He pleases; for, after He had declared that He would spare the Jews of old and continue them in the relation of His peculiar people, when they had deserved to have been cut off for their idolatry, He said: "I will make all my goodness pass before thee, and I will proclaim the name of the Lord before thee . . . and will shew mercy on whom I will shew mercy"; and I will have compassion on whom I will have compassion. As if He had said: I will make such a display of My perfections as shall convince you that My nature is kind and beneficent; but know that I am a debtor to none of My creatures. I will give My salvation in My own way and on My own terms. "He that believeth not shall be damned." This is God's ultimate design; this purpose He will never change, and this He has fully declared in the everlasting gospel. This is the grand decree of reprobation and election.

16. *So then it is not of him that willeth.* I conclude, therefore, from these several instances, that the making or continuing any body of men as the peculiar people of God is righteously determined, not by the judgment, hopes, or wishes of men, but by the will and wisdom of God alone.

17. *For the scripture saith unto Pharaoh.* Instead of showing the Israelites mercy, He might justly have suffered them to go on in sin, till He should have signalized His wisdom and justice in their destruction; as appears from what God in His Word declares concerning His dealings with Pharaoh and the Egyptians, Exod. ix. 15-16: "For now I had stretched forth my hand [in the plague of boils and blains], and I had smitten thee and thy people with the pestilence; and thou hadst [by this plague] been cut off from the earth [as thy cattle were by the murrain]; *but in very deed for this cause have I raised thee up*"—I have restored you to health by removing the boils and blains, and by respiting your deserved destruction to a longer day, that I may, in your instance, give such a demonstration of My power in your final overthrow that all mankind may learn that I am God, the righteous Judge of all the earth, the Avenger of wickedness.

18. *Therefore hath he mercy on whom he will.* This is the apostle's conclusion from the facts already laid down: that God, according to His own will and wisdom, in perfect righteousness, bestows *mercy*—that is to say, His blessings—upon one part of mankind (the Jews of old and the Gentiles of the present time) while He suffers another part (the Egyptians of old and the Jews of the present day) to go on in the abuse of His goodnsss and forbearance, hardening themselves in sin, till He brings upon them a most just and exemplary punishment, unless this be prevented by their deep repentance and general return to God through Jesus, the promised, the real *Messiah.*

19. *Why doth he yet find fault?* The question here is: If God's glory be so highly promoted and manifested by our obstinacy, and He suffers us to proceed in our hardness and infidelity, why does He find fault with us, or punish us for that which is according to His good pleasure?

20. *Nay but, O man, who art thou?* As if he had said: Weak, ignorant man, dare you retort on the infinitely good and righteous God? God has made, created, *formed* the Jewish nation, and shall the thing formed, when it hath corrupted itself, pretend to correct the wise and gracious Author of its being, and say, *Why hast thou made me thus?*

21. *Hath not the potter power over the clay?* The apostle continues his answer to the Jew. Has not God shown by the parable of the potter, Jer. xviii. 1 ff., that He may justly dispose of nations and of the Jews in particular according as He in His infinite wisdom may judge most right and fitting; even as the potter has a right, out of the same lump of clay, to make one vessel to a more honorable and another to a less honorable use, as his own judgment and skill may direct? The reference to this parable shows most positively that the apostle is speaking of men, not *individually*, but *nationally;* and it is strange that men should have given his words any other application with this scripture before their eyes.

22. *What if God, willing to shew his wrath?* The apostle refers here to the case of Pharaoh and the Egyptians, and to which he applies Jeremiah's parable of the potter, and from them to the then state of the Jews. Pharaoh and the Egypians were *vessels of wrath*—persons deeply guilty before God; and by their obstinate refusal of His grace and abuse of His goodness they had fitted themselves for that destruction which the *wrath*, the vindictive justice of God, inflicted, after He had *endured* their obstinate rebellion *with much longsuffering;* which is a most absolute proof that the hardening of their hearts and their ultimate punishment were the consequences of their obstinate refusal of His grace and abuse of His goodness, as the history in Exodus sufficiently shows. As the Jews of the apostle's time had sinned after the similitude of the Egyptians, hardening their hearts and abusing His goodness after every display of His long-suffering kindness, being now fitted for destruction, they were ripe for punishment; and that *power*, which God was making *known* for their salvation, having been so long and so much abused and provoked, was now about to show itself in their destruction as a nation. But even in this case there is not a word of their final damnation; much less that either they or any others were by a sovereign decree reprobated from all eternity; and that their very sins, the proximate cause of their punishment, were the necessary effect of that decree which had from all eternity doomed them to endless torments.

23. *And that he mght make known.* God "endured with much longsuffering the *vessels of wrath*": (1) "To *shew his wrath*, and to make his power known"; and also (2) *That he might make known the riches of his glory on the vessels of mercy.*

24. *Even us, whom he hath called.* All the Jews and Gentiles who have been "invited" by the preaching of the gospel to receive justification by faith in our Lord Jesus Christ, and have come to the gospel feast on this invitation.

25. *As he saith also in Osee.* It is a cause of not a little confusion that a uniformity in the orthography of the proper names of the Old and New Testaments has not been preserved. What stranger to our sacred books would suppose that the *Osee* above meant the Prophet Hosea,

from whom, chap. ii. 23, this quotation is taken: "I will have mercy on her that had not obtained mercy; and I will say to them which were not my people, Thou art my people"? The apostle shows that this calling of the Gentiles was no fortuitous thing, but a firm purpose in the divine mind, which He had largely revealed to the prophets; and by opposing the calling of the Gentiles, the Jews in effect renounced their prophets and fought against God.

26. *And it shall come to pass.* These quotations are taken out of Hosea, chap. i. 10: "Yet the number of the children of Israel shall be as the sand of the sea, which cannot be measured nor numbered; and it shall come to pass, that in the place where it was said unto them, Ye are not my people, there it shall be said unto them, Ye are the sons of the living God." As if he had said: The decrease of numbers in the Church, by God's utterly taking away the ten tribes (v. 6) shall be well supplied by what shall afterwards come to pass by calling the Gentiles into it.

28. *For he will finish the work, and cut it short.* These appear to be forensic terms, and refer to the conclusion of a judicial proceeding; the Lord has tried and found them guilty, and will immediately execute upon them the punishment due to their transgressions.

29. *And as Esaias said before.* What God designs to do with the Jews at present, because of their obstinacy and rebellion, is similar to what He has done before, to which the same prophet refers, chap. i. 9: "Except the Lord of hosts had left unto us a very small remnant, we should have been as Sodom, and we should have been like unto Gomorrah"; i.e., had not God, who commands and overrules all the powers in heaven and earth, in mercy preserved a very small remnant, to keep up the name and being of the nation, it had been quite cut off and extinct, as were Sodom and Gomorrah.

31. *But Israel, which followed after.* But the Jews, who have hitherto been the people of God, though they have been industrious in observing a rule by which they supposed they could secure the blessings of God's peculiar kingdom, yet have not come up to the true and only rule by which these blessings can be secured.

32. *Wherefore?* And where lies their mistake? Being ignorant of God's righteousness, of His method of saving sinners by faith in Christ, they went about to establish their own righteousness—their own method of obtaining everlasting salvation. They attend not to the Abrahamic covenant, which stands on the extensive principles of grace and faith; but they turn all their regards to the law of Moses. They imagine that their obedience to that law gives them a right to the blessings of the Messiah's kingdom. But finding that our gospel sets our special interest in God and the privileges of His Church on a different footing, they are offended, and refuse to come into it.

33. *As it is written, Behold, I lay in Sion.* Christ, the Messiah, is become "a stone of stumbling" to them, and thus what is written in the prophecy of Isaiah is verified in their case, Isa. viii. 14; xxviii. 16: *Behold, I lay in Sion,* i.e., I shall bring in My Messiah. But He shall be a widely different Person from him whom the Jews expect; for whereas they expect

the Messiah to be a mighty secular prince, and to set up a secular kingdom, He shall appear "a man of sorrows, and acquainted with grief"; and redeem mankind, not by His sword or secular power, but by His humiliation, passion, and death. Therefore they will be offended at Him and reject Him, and think it would be reproachful to trust in such a Person for salvation. *And whosoever believeth on him.* But so far shall any be from confusion or disappointment who believes in Christ that, on the contrary, every genuine believer shall find salvation—the remission of sins here, and eternal glory hereafter.

CHAPTER 10

The apostle expresses his earnest desire for the salvation of the Jews, 1. Having a zeal for God, but not according to knowledge, they sought salvation by works, and not by faith in Christ, 2-4. The righteousness which is of the law described, 5. That which is by faith described also, 6-10. He that believes and calls on the name of the Lord shall be saved, 11-13. What is necessary to salvation—believing, hearing, preaching, a divine mission, the gospel, and obedience to its precepts, 14-16. Faith comes by hearing, 17. The universal spread of the gospel predicted by the prophets, 18-20. The ingratitude and disobedience of the Israelites, 21.

1. *My heart's desire.* Though the apostle knew that the Jews were now in a state of rejection, yet he knew also that they were in this state through their own obstinacy, and that God was still waiting to be gracious, and consequently that they might still repent and turn to Him. Of his concern for their salvation he had already given ample proof, when he was willing to become a sacrifice for their welfare; see chap. ix. 3.

2. *They have a zeal of God.* They believe their law to have come immediately from God himself, and are jealous of its glory and excellence; they conscientiously observe its rites and ceremonies, but they do not consider the object and end of those rites. They sin more through ignorance than malice; and this pleads in their excuse. By this fine apology for them, the apostle prepares them for the harsher truths which he was about to deliver.

3. *For . . . being ignorant of God's righteousness*—not knowing God's method of saving sinners, which is the only proper and efficient method. *And going about to establish their own righteousness*—seeking to procure their salvation by means of their own contriving. They *have not submitted*—they have not bowed to the determinations of the Most High, relative to His mode of saving mankind, viz., through faith in Jesus Christ as the only available Sacrifice for sin, the end to which the law pointed.

4. *For Christ is the end of the law.* Where the law ends, Christ begins. The law ends with representative sacrifices; Christ begins with the real offering. The law is our schoolmaster to lead us to Christ; it cannot save, but it leaves us at His door, where alone salvation is to be found. Christ as an atoning Sacrifice for sin was the grand Object of the whole sacrificial code of Moses; His passion and death were the fulfillment of its great object and design. Separate this sacrificial death of Christ from the law, and the law has no meaning, for it is impossible that the blood of bulls and goats should take away sins. God never designed that the sacrifices of the law should be considered the atonement for sin, but a type or representative of

that atonement; and that the atonement was the sacrifice offered by Christ. Thus He was *the end of the law,* in respect to its sacrifices.

5. *For Moses describeth the righteousness which is of the law.* The place to which the apostle refers seems to be Lev. xviii. 5: "Ye shall therefore keep my statutes, and my judgments; which if a man do, he shall live in them." These words seem to be spoken in answer to an objection which might be made by a Jew: "Did not Moses give us a law, the observance of which would secure our salvation?" Such a law Moses undoubtedly gave, and that law promises life to those who perform it precepts; but who can plead for life on this ground who rejects that Christ who is "the end of the law"? No man ever did, nor ever can, fulfill that law so as to merit salvation by the performance of it. For as "all have sinned, and come short of the glory of God," they are all under the curse of the law, which says: "Cursed is every one that continueth not in all things which are written in the book of the law to do them," Deut. xxvii. 26; Gal. iii. 10. Therefore by the deeds of this law none can be justified, because all are in a state of condemnation for transgressions already committed against it.

6-7. *But the righteousness which is of faith.* As it is most evident that there can be no justification by works, as all are sinful and all in a guilty state, if God will grant salvation at all, it must be by *faith.* But faith must have an object and a reason for its exercise. The Object is Jesus Christ; the reason is the infinite merit of His passion and death. *Who shall ascend into heaven?* As Christ is "the end of the law" for justification to everyone that believes, no observance of the law can procure Him. Who by the practice of the law can bring Christ down from heaven? or, when brought down, and crucified and buried, as a Sacrifice for sin, who can bring Him up again from the dead? And both His death and resurrection are essentially necessary for the salvation of a lost world. Or the sense of the apostle may be this: They who will not believe in Christ crucified must in effect be seeking another Messiah to come down from heaven with a different revelation; or they who will not credit the doctrine that we preach concerning His resurrection seem in effect to say, Christ yet remains to be raised from the dead, and reign over the Jews as a mighty secular Sovereign, subjecting the Gentile world to the sway of His righteous sceptre.

8. *But what saith it? The word is nigh thee.* There is no occasion to seek high or low for the saving power; the word of reconciliation is nigh. The way of salvation is now both plain and easy. By the preaching of the gospel the doctrine of salvation is *nigh thee,* and the saving influence is at hand. It is *in thy mouth,* easy to be understood, easy to be professed; *and in thy heart,* if you are upright before God, sincerely desiring to be saved on His own terms.

9. *That if thou shalt confess.* Acknowledge the Lord Jesus Christ as the only Saviour. *Believe in thine heart* that He who died for your offenses has been raised for your justification, and depend solely on Him for that justification, and *thou shalt be saved.*

10. *For with the heart man believeth.* And be sincere in this. *For with the heart,* duly affected with a sense of guilt and of the suffi-

ciency of the sacrifice which Christ has offered, *man believeth unto righteousness,* believes to receive "justification"; for this is the proper meaning of the term here, and in many other parts of this Epistle. *And with the mouth confession is made unto salvation.* He who believes aright in Christ Jesus will receive such a full conviction of the truth, and such an evidence of his redemption, that his mouth will boldly confess his obligation to his Redeemer, and the blessed persuasion he has of the remission of all his sins through the blood of the Cross.

11. *For the scripture saith.* And however the Jews may despise this gospel, because it comes not unto them with pomp and ceremony, it puts those who receive it into possession of every heavenly blessing; and this is according to the positive declarations of the prophets, for it is written, Isa. xxviii. 16; xlix. 23: *Whosoever believeth on him shall not be ashamed.* He shall neither be disappointed of his hope nor ashamed of his confidence, because he has that faith which is "the evidence of things not seen," the subsistence "of things hoped for," Heb. xi. 1.

12. *For there is no difference between the Jew and the Greek.* All are equally welcome to this salvation. Here the Jew has no exclusive privilege, and from this the Greek is not rejected. One simple way of being saved is proposed to all, viz., faith in the Lord Jesus Christ.

13. *For whosoever shall call.* Nor shall anyone who hears this doctrine of salvation and credits it as he is commanded be permitted to pray or supplicate the throne of grace in vain. For the Prophet Joel hath declared, chap. ii. 32: *Whosoever shall call upon,* invoke, *the name of the Lord* Jesus Christ, the Saviour of sinners, *shall be saved*—shall have his guilt pardoned, his heart purified; and if he abide in the faith, rooted and grounded in Him, showing forth the virtues of Him who has called him out of darkness into His marvellous light, he shall be saved with all the power of an eternal life. It is evident that Paul understood the text of Joel as relating to our blessed Lord; and therefore his word *Kyrios* must answer to the prophet's word *Yehovah,* which is no mean proof of the Godhead of Jesus Christ.

16. *But they have not all obeyed the gospel.* This seems to be the objection of a Jew; as if he had said: A divine mission would be attended with success, whereas there are numbers who pay no attention to the glad tidings you preach. To this the apostle answers that the Spirit of God by Isaiah, chap. liii. 1, foretold it would be so, even in the case of the Jews themselves, when he said, Lord, *who hath believed our report?* For although God brings the message of salvation to men, He does not oblige them to embrace it.

17. *So then faith cometh by hearing.* Preaching the gospel is the ordinary means of salvation; faith in Christ is the result of hearing the *word,* the "doctrine" of God preached.

18. *But I say, Have they not heard?* But to return to the objection: You say they have not all believed; I ask: Have they not all heard? Have not the means of salvation been placed within the reach of every Jew in Palestine, and within the reach of all those who sojourn in the different Gentile countries where we have

preached the gospel, as well to the Jews as to the Gentiles themselves? Yes; for we may say of the preaching of the gospel what the Psalmist has said (Ps. xix. 4) of the heavenly bodies: *Their sound went into all the earth, and their words unto the ends of the world.* As the celestial luminaries have given testimony of the eternal power and Godhead of the Deity to the habitable world, the gospel of Christ has borne testimony to His eternal goodness and mercy to all the land of Palestine, and to the whole Roman Empire.

19. *But I say, Did not Israel know?* You object to this preaching among the Gentiles; but is not this according to the positive declaration of God? He, foreseeing your unbelief and rebellion, said by Moses, Deut. xxxii. 21, *I will provoke you to jealousy by them that are no people, and by a foolish nation I will anger you.* As you have provoked Me to jealousy with worshipping those that are no gods, I will provoke you to jealousy by those which are *no people.* This most evidently refers to the calling or inviting of the Gentiles to partake of the benefits of the gospel, and plainly predicts the envy and rage which would be excited in the Jews in consequence of those offers of mercy made to the Gentiles.

20. *But Esaias* (the Greek orthography for Isaiah) *is very bold.* Speaks out in the fullest manner and plainest language, chap. lxv. 1, notwithstanding the danger to which such a declaration exposed him among a crooked, perverse, and dangerous people: *I was found of them that sought me not;* I put my salvation in the way of those (the Gentiles) who were not seeking for it, and knew nothing of it; thus the "Gentiles, which followed not after righteousness, have attained to [the law of] righteousness," chap. ix. 30, and they have found that redemption which the Jews have rejected.

21. *But to Israel he saith.* In the very next verse (Isa. lxv. 2), *All day long have I stretched forth my hands,* manifesting the utmost readiness and willingness to gather them all together under My protecting care; but I stretched forth My hands in vain, for they are a disobedient and gainsaying people. They not only disobey My command, but they gainsay and contradict My prophets. Thus the apostle proves, in answer to the objection made, v. 16, that the infidelity of the Jews was the effect of their own obstinacy; that the opposition which they are now making to the gospel was foretold and deplored 700 years before; and that their opposition, far from being a proof of the insufficiency of the gospel, proved that this was the grand means which God had provided for their salvation; and having rejected this, they could expect no other.

CHAPTER 11

God has not universally nor finally rejected Israel; nor are they all at present rejecters of the gospel, for there is a remnant of true believers now, as there was in the days of the Prophet Elijah, 1-5. These have embraced the gospel, and are saved by grace, and not by the works of the law, 6. The body of the Israelites, having rejected this, are blinded, according to the prophetic declaration of David, 7-10. But they have not stumbled, so as to be finally rejected; but through their fall, salvation is come to the Gentiles, 11-14. There is hope of their restoration, and that the nation shall yet become a holy people, 15-16. The converted Gentiles must not exult over the fallen Jews; the latter having fallen by unbelief, the former stand by faith, 17-20.

The Jews, the natural branches, were broken off from the true olive, and the Gentiles having been grafted in, in their place, must walk uprightly, else they also shall be cut off, 21-22. The Jews, if they abide not in unbelief, shall be again grafted in; and when the fullness of the Gentiles is come in, the great Deliverer shall turn away ungodliness from Jacob, according to the covenant of God, 23-27. For the sake of their forefathers God loves them, and will again call them, and communicate His gifts to them, 28-29. The gospel shall be again sent to them, as it has now been sent to the Gentiles, 30-32. This procedure is according to the immensity of the wisdom, knowledge, and unsearchable judgments of God, who is the Creator, Preserver, and Governor of all things, and to whom all adoration is due, 33-36.

1. *I say then, Hath God cast away his people?* Has He utterly and finally rejected them? for this is necessarily the apostle's meaning, and is the import of the Greek word which signifies to "thrust" or "drive away." Has He thrust them off, and driven them eternally from Him? *God forbid*—"By no means." This rejection is neither *universal* nor *final. For I also am an Israelite*—I am a regular descendant from Abraham, through Israel or Jacob, and by his son Benjamin. And I stand in the Church of God, and in the peculiar covenant; for the rejection is only of the obstinate and disobedient; those who believe on Christ, as I have done, are continued in the Church.

2. *God hath not cast away his people which he foreknew.* God has not finally and irrecoverably rejected a people whom He has "loved (or approved) so long," for this is evidently the meaning of the word in this place. *Wot ye not what the scripture saith?* "Do you not know what the Scripture saith?" The reference is to 1 Kings xix. 10, 14. And the apostle's answer to the objecting Jew is to the following effect: God has not universally thrust away His people, for whom in the promise to Abraham He intended, and to whom decreed, to grant His special favor and blessing; but the case is now much as it was in the days of Elijah. That prophet, in his addresses to God, made his complaint against Israel thus:

3. *Lord, they have killed thy prophets.* They will not permit any person to speak unto them in Thy name; and they murder those who are faithful to the commission which they have received from Thee. *Digged down thine altars.* They are profligate and profane beyond example, and retain not the slightest form of religion. *I am left alone.* There is no prophet besides myself left, and they seek to destroy me.

4. *But what saith the answer of God?* The answer which God made assured him that there were *seven thousand,* that is, several or many thousands; for so we must understand the word *seven,* a certain for an uncertain number. These had continued faithful to God; but, because of Jezebel's persecution, they were obliged to conceal their attachment to the true religion; and God, in His providence, preserved them from her sanguinary rage. *Who have not bowed the knee.* Baal was the god of Jezebel; or, in other words, his worship was then the worship of the state. But there were several thousands of pious Israelites who had not acknowledged this idol, and did not partake in the idolatrous worship.

5. *Even so then at this present time.* As in the present day the irreligion of the Jews is very great, yet there is a remnant, a considerable number, who have accepted of the grace of the gospel. *According to the election of grace.* And these are saved just as God has saved all be-

lievers from the beginning. They are chosen by His *grace*, not on account of any worth or excellence in themselves, but through His goodness are they chosen to have a place in His Church, and continue to be His people, entitled to all the privileges of the new covenant. The *election of grace* simply signifies God's gracious design in sending the Christian system into the world, and saving under it all those who believe in Christ Jesus, and none else. Thus the believers in Christ are chosen to inherit the blessings of the gospel, while those who seek justification by the works of the law are rejected.

6. *And if by grace.* And let this very remnant of pious Jews who have believed in Christ Jesus know that they are brought in in precisely the same way as God has brought in the Gentiles, the one having no more worthiness to plead than the other, both being brought in and continued in by God's free grace, and not by any observance of the Mosaic law. And this is done according to the election of grace, or the rule of choosing any persons to be the people of God upon the footing of grace, which takes in all that believe in His Son, Jesus Christ. Some of the Jewish people did so believe; therefore those believing Jews are "a remnant according to the election of grace." They are saved in that way in which alone God will save mankind. *And if by grace.* Then let these very persons remember that their election and interest in the covenant of God has no connection with their old Jewish works; for were it of works, grace would lose its proper nature, and cease to be what it is—a free, undeserved gift. *But if it be of works.* On the other hand, could it be made to appear that they are invested in these privileges of the kingdom of Christ only by the observance of the law of Moses, then *grace* would be quite set aside; and if it were not, *work*, or the merit of obedience, would lose its proper nature, which excludes favor and free gift.

7. *What then?* What is the real state of the case before us? *Israel*, the body of the Jewish people, have not obtained that which they so earnestly desire, i.e., to be continued, as they have been hitherto, the peculiar people of God; *but the election hath obtained it*—as many of them as have believed in Jesus Christ and accepted salvation through Him. This is the grand scheme of the election by grace; God chooses to make those His peculiar people who believe in His Son, and none other shall enjoy the blessings of His kingdom. Those who would not receive Him are *blinded*; they have shut their eyes against the light, and are in the very circumstances of those mentioned by the Prophet Isaiah, chap. xxix. 10.

8. *God hath given them the spirit of slumber.* As they had willfully closed their eyes against the light, so God has, in judgment, given them up to the *spirit of slumber.*

9. *And David saith, Let their table.* And from their present disposition it is reasonable to conclude that the same evils will fall upon them as fell upon the disobedient in former times, as predicted by David, Ps. lxix. 22-23, that their very blessings should become curses to them, and their temporal mercies be their only recompense; and yet even these earthly blessings, by not being enjoyed in the Lord, should be a stumbling block over which they should fall, and, instead of being a blessing, should be the means of their punishment.

10. *Let their eyes be darkened.* All these words are declarative, and not imprecatory. God declares what will be the case of such obstinate unbelievers; "their table," their common providential blessings, will become "a snare, and a trap, and a stumblingblock," and the means of their punishment. Their eyes will be more and more darkened as they persist in their unbelief, and their "back shall be bowed down always." Far from becoming a great and powerful nation, they shall continue ever in a state of abject slavery and oppression, till they acknowledge Jesus as the promised Messiah, and submit to receive redemption in His blood.

11. *Have they stumbled that they should fall?* Have the Jews, now for their disobedience and unbelief rejected, so sinned against God as to be forever put out of the reach of His mercy? "By no means." Are they, as a nation, utterly irrecoverable? This is the sense of the place, and here the prophecy of the restoration of the Jewish nation commences. *But rather through their fall salvation is come.* The Church of God cannot fail; if the Jews have broken the everlasting covenant, Isa. xxiv. 5, the Gentiles shall be taken into it; and this very circumstance shall be ultimately the means of exciting them to seek and claim a share in the blessings of the new covenant. This is what the apostle terms provoking *them to jealousy*, i.e., exciting them to emulation, for so the word should be understood. We should observe here that the *fall* of the Jews was not in itself the cause or reason of the calling of the Gentiles. Whether the Jews had stood or fallen, whether they had embraced or rejected the gospel, it was the original purpose of God to take the Gentiles into the Church, for this was absolutely implied in the covenant made with Abraham; and it was in virtue of that covenant that the Gentiles were now called, and not because of the unbelief of the Jews.

12. *Now if the fall of them.* The English reader may imagine that because *fall* is used in both these verses the original word is the same. But *their fall* and *the fall of them* are *parastoma*, the same word which we render "offence," chap. v. 15, 17-18, and might be rendered "lapse." Whereas *that they should fall* (v. 11) is *hina pesosi*. Now *pipto*, "to fall," is used in a sense so very emphatical as to signify "being slain." It is well-known that to *fall* in battle means to be "killed." It is in such a sense as this that Paul used the word *fall* when he says, "Have they stumbled that they should fall?" *The riches of the world.* If in consequence of their unbelief the riches of God's grace and goodness be poured out on the whole Gentile world, how much more shall that dispensation of grace and mercy enrich and aggrandize the Gentiles, which shall bring the whole body of the Jews to the faith of the gospel! Here the apostle supposes, or rather predicts, that such a dispensation shall take place, and that therefore the Jews have not so stumbled as to be finally irrecoverable.

13. This and the following verse should be read in a parenthesis. Paul, as the apostle of the Gentiles, wished to show them the high pitch of glory and blessedness to which they had been called, that they might have a due sense of God's mercy in calling them to such a state of

salvation, and that they might be jealous over themselves, lest they should fall as the Jews had done before them; and he dwells particularly on the greatness of those privileges which the Gentiles had now received, that he might stir up the minds of his countrymen to emulation, and might be the means of saving some of them, as he states in the following verse. *I magnify mine office.* Literally, "I honor this my ministry."

14. *Might save some of them.* And yet all these were among the reprobate, or rejected; however, the apostle supposed that none of them were irrecoverably shut out from the divine favor and that *some* of them, by his preaching, might be disposed to receive salvation by Christ Jesus.

15. *But life from the dead.* If the rejection of the Jews became the occasion of our receiving the gospel, so that we can even glory in our tribulations, though they themselves became chief instruments of our sufferings, yet so far must we feel from exulting over them that we should esteem their full conversion to God as great and choice a favor as we would the restoration of a most intimate friend to life, who had been at the gates of death. The restoration of the Jews to a state of favor with God to which the apostle refers, and which is too plainly intimated by the spirit of prophecy to admit of a doubt, will be a most striking event. Their being preserved as a distinct people is certainly a strong collateral proof that they shall once more brought into the Church of God; and their conversion to Christianity will be an incontestable proof of the truth of divine revelation, and doubtless will become the means of converting multitudes of deists, who will see the prophecies of God, which had been delivered so long before, so strikingly fulfilled in this great event. We need not wonder if a whole nation should then be born as in a day.

16. *For if the firstfruit be holy.* As consecrating the firstfruits to God was the means of drawing down His blessing upon the rest, so the conversion of Abraham to the true faith. and the several Jews who have now embraced Christianity, are pledges that God will, in process of time, admit the whole Jewish nation into His favor again, so that they shall constitute a part of the Visible Church of Christ. *If the root be holy, so are the branches.* The word *holy* in this verse is to be taken in that sense which it has so frequently in the Old and New Testaments, viz., "consecrated, set apart to sacred uses." It must not be forgotten that the first converts to Christ were from among the Jews; these formed the *root* of the Christian Church. These were *holy,* "consecrated" to God, and those who among the Gentiles were converted by their means were also "consecrated." But the chief reference is to the ancestors of the Jewish people, Abraham, Isaac, and Jacob; and as these were devoted to God and received into His covenant, all their posterity, the *branches* which proceeded from this *root,* became entitled to the same privileges; and as the *root* still remains, and the *branches* also, the descendants from that root still remain. They still have a certain title to the blessings of the covenant, though because of their obstinate unbelief these blessings are suspended, as they cannot, even on the ground of the old covenant,

enjoy these blessings but through faith; for it was when Abraham believed God that it was accounted to him for righteousness, and thus he became an heir of the righteousness which is by faith.

17. *And if some of the branches*—if the present nation of the Jews, because of their unbelief, are cut off from the blessings of the Church of God, and the high honor and dignity of being His peculiar people. *And thou, being a wild olive*—ye Gentiles, being without the knowledge of the true God, and consequently bringing forth no fruits of righteousness. *Wert grafted in among them*—are now inserted in the original stock, having been made partakers of the faith of Abraham, and consequently of his blessings; and enjoy, as the people did who sprang from him, *the fatness of the olive tree,* the promises made to the patriarchs, and the spiritual privileges of the Jewish church.

18. *Boast not against the branches.* While you are ready to acknowledge that you were included in the covenant made with Abraham, and are now partakers of the same blessings with him, do not "exult over," much less insult, *the branches,* his present descendants, whose place you now fill up, according to the election of grace. For remember, you are not the *root,* nor do you bear the root, but the root bears you. You have not been the means of deriving any blessing on the Jewish people; but through that very people, which you may be tempted to despise, all the blessing and excellencies which you enjoy have been communicated to you.

19. *Thou wilt say then.* You may think that you have reason to exult over them, because it is a fact that God has been displeased with them, and therefore has *broken them off;* has cast them out of the Church and taken you into it in their place.

20. *Well; because of unbelief.* This statement is all true; but then, consider, why is it that they were cast out? Was it not because of their unbelief? And you stand by *faith;* you were made partakers of these blessings by faith. *Be not highminded;* let this humble, not exalt you in your own estimation.

21. *For if God spared not the natural branches.* If He, in His infinite justice and holiness, could not tolerate sin in the people whom He foreknew, whom He had so long loved, cherished, miraculously preserved, and blessed, *take heed lest he also spare not thee.* Be convinced that the same righteous principle in Him will cause Him to act towards you as He has acted towards them, if you sin after the similitude of their transgression; and to this, self-sufficiency and self-confidence will soon lead you.

22. *Behold therefore the goodness.* The exclamation, *Behold the goodness of God!* is frequent among the Jewish writers when they wish to call the attention of men to particular displays of God's mercy, especially towards those who are singularly unworthy. *And severity of God.* As *goodness* signifies the essential quality of the divine nature, the fountain of all good to men and angels, so *severity* signifies that particular exercise of His goodness and holiness which leads Him to sever from His mystical body whatsoever would injure, corrupt, or destroy it. The apostle, having adopted this metaphor as the best he could find to express that act of God's justice and mercy by which the

Jews were rejected and the Gentiles elected in their stead, and in order to show that though the Jewish tree was cut down, or its branches lopped off, yet it was not rooted up, he informs the Gentile believers that, as it is customary to insert a good scion in a bad or useless stock, they who were bad, contrary to the custom in such cases, were grafted in a good stock, and their growth and fruitfulness proclaimed the excellence and vegetative life of the stock in which they were inserted. This was the *goodness* of the heavenly Gardener to them; but it was *severity,* an act of "excision," to the Jews.

23. *If they abide not still in unbelief.* So we find that their rejection took place in consequence of their willful obstinacy, and that they may return into the fold, the door of which still stands open. *For God is able to graff them in again.* Fallen as they are and degraded, God can, in the course of His providence and mercy, restore them to all their forfeited privileges; and this will take place if *they abide not still in unbelief,* which intimates that God has furnished them with all the power and means necessary for faith, and that they may believe on the Lord Jesus whenever they will.

24. *The olive tree which is wild by nature.* Which is "naturally" wild and barren; for that the wild olive bore no fruit is sufficiently evident from the testimony of the authors who have written on the subject. Hence the proverb, "More unfruitful than the wild olive." *And wert graffed contrary to nature.* "Contrary to all custom"; for a scion taken from a barren or useless tree is scarcely ever known to be grafted into a good stock; but here the Gentiles, a fruitless and sinful race, are grafted on the ancient patriarchal stock. Now if it was possible to effect such a change in the state and disposition of the Gentiles, who were (Eph. ii. 12) "without God [atheists] in the world," how much more possible is it, speaking after the manner of men, to bring about a similar change in the Jews, who acknowledge the one, only, and true God, and receive the law and the prophets as a revelation from Him! This seems to be the drift of the apostle's argument.

25. *I would not . . . that ye should be ignorant of this mystery.* Mystery signifies anything that is hidden or covered, or not fully made manifest. In the New Testament it signifies, generally, "any thing or doctrine that has not, in former times, been fully known to men"; or "something that has not been heard of, or which is so deep, profound, and difficult of comprehension that it cannot be apprehended without special direction and instruction." Here it signifies the doctrine of the future restoration of the Jews, not fully known in itself, and not at all known as to the time in which it will take place. In chap. xvi. 25, it means the Christian religion, not known till the advent of Christ. *Lest ye should be wise in your own conceits.* It seems from this, and from other expressions in this Epistle, that the converted Gentiles had not behaved toward the Jews with that decorum and propriety which the relation they bore to them required. In this chapter the apostle strongly guards them against giving way to such a disposition. *Blindness in part is happened to Israel.* Partial blindness, or blindness to a part of them; for they were not all believers. Several thousands of them had been converted to the

Christian faith; though the body of the nation, and especially its rulers, civil and spiritual, continued opposed to Christ and His doctrine. *Until the fulness of the Gentiles be come in.* And this blindness will continue till the Church of the Gentiles be fully completed—till the gospel be preached through all the nations of the earth, and multitudes of heathens everywhere embrace the faith. By the *fulness* a "great multitude" may be intended, which should be so dilated on every hand as to fill various regions. The apostle, therefore, seems to give this sense of the mystery—that the Jews will continue in a state of blindness till such time as a "multitude of nations," or Gentiles, shall be converted to the Christian faith; and the Jews, hearing of this, shall be excited, by a spirit of emulation, to examine and acknowledge the validity of the proofs of Christianity and embrace the faith of our Lord Jesus Christ.

26. *And so all Israel shall be saved.* Shall be brought into the way of salvation by acknowledging the Messiah, for the word certainly does not mean eternal glory; for no man can conceive that a time will ever come in which every Jew then living shall be taken to the Kingdom of glory. The term *saved* as applied to the Israelites in different parts of the Scripture signifies no more than their being gathered out of the nations of the world, separated to God, and possessed of the high privilege of being His peculiar people. And we know that this is the meaning of the term by finding it applied to the body of the Israelites when this alone was the sum of their state. *As it is written.* The apostle supports what he advances on this head by a quotation from Scripture, which in the main is taken from Isa. lix. 20: *The Deliverer shall come out of Zion, and turn away ungodliness from Jacob.* Now this cannot be understood of the manifestation of Christ among the Jews or of the multitudes which were converted before, at, and for some time after, the Day of Pentecost; for these times were all past when the apostle wrote this Epistle. And as no remarkable conversion of that people has since taken place, therefore the fulfillment of this prophecy is yet to take place. In what manner Christ is to *come out of Sion,* and in what way or by what means He is to "turn away transgression from Jacob," we cannot tell; and to attempt to conjecture, when the time, occasion, means, etc., are all in mystery, would be more than reprehensible.

27. *For this is my covenant unto them, when I shall take away their sins.* The reader, on referring to Isa. lix. 20-21, will find that the words of the original are here greatly abridged. They are the following: "And the Redeemer shall come to Zion, and unto them that turn from transgression in Jacob, saith the Lord. As for me, this is my covenant with them, saith the Lord, My Spirit that is upon thee, and my words which I have put in thy mouth, shall not depart out of thy mouth, nor out of the mouth of thy seed, nor out of the mouth of thy seed's seed, saith the Lord, from henceforth and for ever."

It may not be amiss to subjoin here a collection of those texts in the Old Testament that seem to point out a restoration of the Jewish commonwealth to a higher degree of excellence than it has yet attained: Isa. ii. 2-5; xix. 24-25; xxv. 6 ff.; xxx. 18-19, 26; lx throughout; lxv. 17

to the end; Jer. xxxi. 10-12; xlvi. 27-28; Ezek. xx. 34, 40 ff.; xxviii. 25-26; xxiv. 20 ff.; xxxvi. 8-16; xxxvii. 21-28; xxxix. 25 ff.; Joel iii. 1-2, 17, 20-21; Amos ix. 9 to the end; Obad. vv. 17, 21; Mic. iv. 3-7; vii. 18-20; Zeph. iii. 19-20.

28. *As concerning the gospel.* The unbelieving Jews, with regard to the *gospel* which they have rejected, are at present *enemies* to God, **and aliens from His kingdom, under His Son, Jesus Christ.** But with regard to the original purpose of *election,* whereby they were chosen and separated from all the people of the earth to be the peculiar people of God, *they are beloved for the fathers' sakes;* He has still favor in store for them on account of their forefathers, the patriarchs.

29. *For the gifts and calling of God.* The *gifts* which God has bestowed upon them, and the *calling*—the invitation—with which He has favored them, He will never revoke. In reference to this point there is no "change of mind" in Him; and therefore the possibility and certainty of their restoration to their original privileges, of being the people of God, of enjoying every spiritual blessing with the fullness of the Gentiles, may be both reasonably and safely inferred. *Repentance,* when applied to God, signifies simply "change of purpose" relative to some declarations made subject to certain conditions.

30. *For as ye in times past.* The apostle pursues his argument in favor of the restoration of the Jews. *As ye,* Gentiles, *in times past,* for many ages back. *Have not believed.* Were in a state of alienation from God, yet not so as to be totally and forever excluded, *Have now obtained mercy.* For you are now taken into the kingdom of the Messiah; through *their unbelief* —by that method which, in destroying the Jewish peculiarity, and fulfilling the Abrahamic covenant, has occasioned the unbelief and obstinate opposition of the Jews.

31. *Even so have these also.* In like manner the Jews are, through their infidelity, shut out of the kingdom of God. *That through your mercy.* This exclusion will not be everlasting; but this will serve to open a new scene, when, through further displays of mercy to you Gentiles, *they also may obtain mercy*—shall be received into the kingdom of God again; and this shall take place whenever they shall consent to acknowledge the Lord Jesus, and see it their privilege to be fellow heirs with the Gentiles of the grace of life. As sure, therefore, as the Jews were once in the Kingdom, and the Gentiles were not; as sure as the Gentiles are now in the Kingdom, and the Jews are not; so surely will the Jews be brought back into that Kingdom.

32. *For God hath concluded them all in unbelief.* God hath "shut" or "locked" them all up under unbelief. This refers to the guilty state of both Jews and Gentiles. They had all broken God's law—the Jews, the written law; the Gentiles, the law written in their hearts. See chap. i. 19-20 and ii. 14-15. They are represented here as having been accused of their transgressions; tried at God's bar; found guilty on being tried; condemned to the death they had merited; remanded to prison, till the sovereign will relative to their execution should be announced; "shut" or "locked up," under the jailer, *un-*

belief; and there both continued in the same state, awaiting the execution of their sentence. But God, in His own compassion, moved by no merit in either party, caused a general pardon by the gospel to be proclaimed to *all.* The Jews have refused to receive this pardon on the terms which God has proposed it, and therefore continue locked up under unbelief. The Gentiles have welcomed the offers of grace, and are delivered out of their prison. But as the offers of mercy continue to be made to all indiscriminately, the time will come when the Jews, seeing the vast accession of the Gentile world to the kingdom of the Messiah, and the glorious privileges which they in consequence enjoy, shall also lay hold on the hope set before them, and thus become with the Gentiles one flock under one Shepherd and Bishop of all their souls. The same figure is used in Gal. iii. 22-23. "But the scripture hath concluded [locked up] all under sin, that the promise by faith of Jesus Christ might be given to them that believe. But before faith came, we were kept [we were guarded as in a stronghold] under the law, shut up [locked up together] unto the faith which should afterwards be revealed." It is a fine and well-chosen metaphor in both places, and forcibly expresses the guilty, helpless, wretched state of both Jews and Gentiles.

33. *O the depth of the riches both of the wisdom and knowledge of God!* This is a very proper conclusion of the whole preceding discourse. *Wisdom* may here refer to the designs of God; *knowledge,* to the means which He employs to accomplish these designs.

34. *For who hath known the mind of the Lord?* Who can pretend to penetrate the counsels of God, or fathom the reasons of His conduct? His designs and His counsels are like himself, infinite; and consequently, inscrutable.

35. *Or who hath first given to him?* Who can pretend to have any demands upon God? To whom is He indebted? Have either Jews or Gentiles any right to His blessings? May not He bestow His favors as He pleases, and to whom He pleases? Does He do any injustice to the Jews in choosing the Gentiles? And was it because He was under obligation to the Gentiles that He has chosen them in the place of the Jews? Let him who has any claim on God prefer it, and he shall be compensated.

36. *For of him.* This is far from being the case, *for of him,* as the original Designer and Author; *and through* (by) *him,* as the prime and efficient Cause; *and to him,* as the ultimate End for the manifestation of His eternal glory and goodness, *are all things* in universal nature, through the whole compass of time and eternity. *To whom be glory.* And let Him have the praise of all His works, from the hearts and mouths of all His intelligent creatures, *for ever*— throughout all the generations of men. *Amen*— "So be it!" Let this be established forever!

CHAPTER 12

Such displays of God's mercy as Jews and Gentiles have received should induce them to consecrate themselves to Him, and not be conformed to the world, 1-2. Christians are exhorted to think meanly of themselves, 3. And each to behave himself properly in the office which he has received from God, 4-8. Various important moral duties recommended, 9-18. We must not avenge ourselves, but overcome evil with good, 19-21.

The apostle, having now finished the *doctrinal* part of this Epistle, proceeds to the *practical*.

1. *I beseech you therefore, brethren.* This address is probably intended for both the Jews and the Gentiles; though some suppose that the Jews are addressed in the first verse, the Gentiles in the second. *By the mercies of God.* "By the tender mercies or compassions of God," such as a tender father shows to his refractory children; who, on their humiliation, is easily persuaded to forgive their offenses. *That ye present your bodies.* A metaphor taken from bringing sacrifices to the altar of God. The person offering picked out the choicest of his flock, brought it to the altar, and presented it there as an atonement for his sin. They are exhorted to give themselves up in the spirit of sacrifice; to be as wholly the Lord's property as the whole burnt offering was, no part being devoted to any other use. *A living sacrifice.* In opposition to those dead sacrifices which they were in the habit of offering while in their Jewish state; and that they should have the lusts of the flesh mortified, that they might live to God. *Holy.* Without spot or blemish, referring still to the sacrifice required by the law. *Acceptable unto God.* The sacrifice being perfect in its kind, and the intention of the offerer being such that both can be *acceptable* and well pleasing to God, who searches the heart. All these phrases are sacrificial, and show that there must be a complete surrender of the person—the *body*, the whole man, mind and flesh, to be given to God; and that he is to consider himself no more his own, but the entire property of his Maker. *Your reasonable service.* Nothing can be more consistent with reason than that the work of God should glorify its Author. We are not our own; we are the property of the Lord by the right of creation and redemption, and it would be as unreasonable as it would be wicked not to live to His glory, in strict obedience to His will. The *reasonable service* of the apostle may refer to the difference between the Jewish and Christian worship. The former religious service consisted chiefly in its sacrifices, which were of irrational creatures. The Christian service or worship is "rational," because performed according to the true intent and meaning of the law, the heart and soul being engaged in the service. He alone lives the life of a fool and a madman who lives the life of a sinner against God; for in sinning against his Maker he wrongs his own soul, loves death, and rewards evil unto himself.

2. *And be not conformed to this world.* By *this world* may be understood that present state of things among both the Jews and the Gentiles; the customs and fashions of the people who then lived, the Gentiles particularly, who had neither the power nor the form of godliness. The world that now is, this present state of things, is as much opposed to the spirit of genuine Christianity as the world then was. *Be ye transformed.* "Be ye metamorphosed, transfigured," appear as new persons, and with new habits; as God has given you a new form of worship, so that you serve in the newness of the spirit, and not in the oldness of the letter. The word implies a radical, thorough, and universal change, both outward and inward. *By the renewing of your mind.* Let the inward change produce the outward. Where the spirit, the

temper, and disposition of the *mind*, Eph. iv. 23, are not renewed, an outward change is of but little worth, and but of short standing. *That ye may prove.* That you may have practical proof and experimental knowledge of the *will of God*—of His purpose and determination, which is *good* in itself, infinitely so. *Acceptable*, "well pleasing to and well received by" every mind that is renewed and transformed. *And perfect.* Finished and complete. When the mind is renewed, and the whole life changed, then the will of God is perfectly fulfilled; for this is its grand design in reference to every human being.

3. *Through the grace given unto me.* By the grace given, Paul most certainly means his apostolic office, by which he had the authority, not only to preach the gospel, but also to rule the Church of Christ. This is the meaning of the word in Eph. iii. 8: "Unto me, who am less than the least of all saints, is this grace given [is conceded this office or employment immediately by God himself], that I should preach among the Gentiles the unsearchable riches of Christ." *Not to think . . . more highly.* "Not to act proudly"; to arrogate nothing to himself on account of any grace he had received, or of any office committed to him. *But to think soberly.* The reader will perceive here a sort of *paronomasia*, or play upon words: *phronein*, from *phren*, the "mind," signifies to "think, mind, relish, to be of opinion"; and *sophronein* signifies to be of a sound mind, to "think discreetly, modestly, humbly." Let no man think himself more or greater than God has made him; and let him know that whatever he is or has of good or excellence, he has it from God; and that the glory belongs to the Giver, and not to him who has received the gift. *Measure of faith.* It is very likely that the *faith* here used means the Christian religion; and the *measure*, the degree of knowledge and experience which each had received in it, and the power this gave him of being useful in the Church of God.

4. *For as we have many members.* As the human body consists of many parts, each having its respective office, and all contributing to the perfection and support of the whole; each being indispensably necessary in the place which it occupies, and each equally useful though performing a different function.

5. *So we, being many.* We who are members of the Church of Christ, which is considered the body of which He is the Head, have various offices assigned to us, according to the measure of grace, faith, and religious knowledge which we possess; and although each has a different office, and qualifications suitable to that office, yet all belong to the same body, and each has as much need of the help of another as that other has of his. Therefore let there be neither pride on the one hand, nor envy on the other.

6. *Having then gifts differing.* As the goodness of God, with this view of our mutual subserviency and usefulness, has endowed us with different gifts and qualifications, let each apply himself to the diligent improvement of his particular office and talent, and modestly keep within the bounds of it, not exalting himself or despising others. *Whether prophecy.* That *prophecy* in the New Testament often means the gift of "exhorting, preaching, or of expounding the Scriptures," is evident from many places in the Gospels, Acts, and Paul's Epistles;

see 1 Cor. xi. 4-5; and especially 1 Cor. xiv. 3: "He that prophesieth speaketh unto men to edification, and exhortation, and comfort." This was the proper office of a preacher; and it is to the exercise of this office that the apostle refers in the whole of the chapter from which the above quotations are made. I think the apostle uses the term in the same sense here—Let every man who has the gift of preaching and interpreting the Scriptures do it in proportion to the grace and light he has received from God and in no case arrogate to himself knowledge which he has not received; let him not esteem himself more highly on account of this gift, or affect to be wise above what is written, or indulge himself in fanciful interpretations of the Word of God. *The proportion of faith,* which some render the "analogy of faith," signifies in grammar "the similar declension of similar words"; but in scriptural matters it has been understood to mean the general and consistent plan or scheme of doctrines delivered in the Scriptures, where everything bears its due relation and proportion to another. Thus the death of Christ is commensurate in its merits to the evils produced by the fall of Adam. The doctrine of justification by faith bears the strictest analogy or proportion to the grace of Christ and the helpless, guilty, condemned state of man.

7. *Or ministry. Diakonia* simply means the office of a deacon. *Or he that teacheth.* The teacher was a person whose office it was to instruct others, whether by catechizing or simply explaining the grand truths of Christianity.

8. *Or he that exhorteth.* The person who admonished and reprehended the unruly or disorderly; and who supported the weak and comforted the penitents, and those who were under heaviness through manifold temptations. *He that giveth.* He who distributeth the alms of the church. *With simplicity,* being influenced by no partiality, but dividing to each according to the necessity of his case. *He that ruleth.* He that presides over a particular business; but as the verb also signifies to "defend or patronize," it is probably used here to signify receiving and providing for strangers, and especially the persecuted who were obliged to leave their own homes, and were destitute, afflicted, and tormented. It might also imply the persons whose business it was to receive and entertain the apostolical teachers who travelled from place to place, establishing and confirming the churches. *He that sheweth mercy.* Let the person who is called to perform any act of compassion or mercy to the wretched do it, not grudgingly nor of necessity, but from a spirit of pure benevolence and sympathy. The poor are often both wicked and worthless; and if those who are called to minister to them as stewards, overseers, etc., do not take care, they will get their hearts hardened with the frequent proofs they will have of deception, lying, idleness, etc. If whatever is done in this way be not done unto the Lord, it can never be done with *cheerfulness.*

9. *Let love be without dissimulation.* Have no "hypocritical" love; let not your love wear a mask; make no empty professions. *Abhor that which is evil.* Hate sin as you would hate that hell to which it leads. *Stygeo* signifies to "hate or detest with horror"; the preposition greatly strengthens the meaning. Styx was a feigned river in hell by which the gods were wont to swear, and if any of them falsified this oath he was deprived of his nectar and ambrosia for a hundred years; hence the river was reputed to be hateful, and *stygeo* signified "to be as hateful as hell." *Cleave to that which is good.* "Be cemented or glued to that which is good"; so the word literally signifies. Have an unalterable attachment to whatever leads to God and contributes to the welfare of your fellow creatures.

10. *Be kindly affectioned one to another with brotherly love.* It is difficult to give a simple translation of the original. The word *philadelphia* signifies that affectionate regard which every Christian should feel for another, as being members of the same mystical body; hence it is emphatically termed the "love of the brethren." When William Penn, of deservedly famous memory, made a treaty with the Indians in North America, and purchased from them a large woody tract, which, after its own nature and his name, he called Pennsylvania, he built a city on it, and peopled it with Christians of his own denomination, and called the city from the word in the text *Philadelphia.* The word *philostorgos,* which we translate *kindly affectioned,* signifies that tender and indescribable affection which a mother bears to her child, and which almost all creatures manifest towards their young. "Love a brother Christian with the affection of a natural brother." *In honour preferring one another.* The meaning appears to be this: Consider all your brethren as more worthy than yourself; and let neither grief nor envy affect your mind at seeing another honored and yourself neglected. This is a hard lesson, and very few persons learn it thoroughly. If we wish to see our brethren honored, still it is with the secret condition in our own minds that we be honored more than they. We have no objection to the elevation of others, providing we may be at the head. But who can bear even to be what he calls neglected? I once heard the following conversation between two persons. "I know not," said one, "that I neglect to do anything in my power to promote the interest of true religion in this place, and yet I seem to be held in very little repute, scarcely any person even noticing me." To which the other replied: "My good friend, set yourself down for nothing, and if any person takes you for something it will be all clear gain."

11. *Not slothful in business.* That God who forbade working on the seventh day has, by the same authority, enjoined it on the other six days. He who neglects to labor during the week is as culpable as he is who works on the Sabbath. An idle, slothful person can never be a Christian. *Fervent in spirit.* Do nothing at any time but what is to the glory of God, and do everything as unto Him; and in everything let your hearts be engaged. Be always in earnest, and let your heart ever accompany your hand. *Serving the Lord.* Ever considering that His eye is upon you, and that you are accountable to Him for all that you do, and that you should do everything so as to please Him. In order to this there must be simplicity in the intention and purity in the affections.

12. *Rejoicing in hope.* Of that glory of God that to each faithful follower of Christ shall shortly be revealed. *Patient in tribulation.* Re-

membering that what you suffer as Christians you suffer for Christ's sake; and it is to His honor, and the honor of your Christian profession, that you suffer it with an even mind. *Continuing instant in prayer.* Making the most fervent and intense application to the throne of grace for the light and power of the Holy Spirit; without which you can neither abhor evil, do good, love the brethren, entertain a comfortable hope, nor bear up patiently under the tribulations and ills of life.

13. *Distributing to the necessity of saints.* Relieve your poor brethren according to the power which God has given you. Do good unto all men, but especially to them which are of the household of faith. *Given to hospitality.* "Pursuing hospitality," or the duty of entertaining strangers. A very necessary virtue in ancient times, when houses of public accommodation were exceedingly scarce. This exhortation might have for its object the apostles, who were all itinerants; and in many cases the Christians, flying before the face of persecution.

14. *Bless them which persecute you.* Give good words, or pray for them that give you bad words, who make dire imprecations against you. *Bless* them, pray for them, and on no account curse them, whatever the provocation may be. Have the loving, forgiving mind that was in your Lord.

15. *Rejoice with them that do rejoice.* Take lively interest in the prosperity of others. Let it be a matter of rejoicing to you when you hear of the health, prosperity, or happiness of any brother. *Weep with them that weep.* Labor after a compassionate or sympathizing mind. Let your heart feel for the distressed; enter into their sorrows, and bear a part of their burdens.

16. *Be of the same mind.* Live in a state of continual harmony and concord, and pray for the same good for all which you desire for yourselves. *Mind not high things.* Be not ambitious; affect nothing above your station; do not court the rich nor the powerful; do not pass by the poor man to pay your court to the great man; do not affect titles or worldly distinctions, much less sacrifice your conscience for them. The attachment to high things and high men is the vice of little, shallow minds. *But condescend to men of low estate.* Be a companion of the humble, and pass through life with as little noise and show as possible. Let the poor, godly man be your chief companion; and learn from his humility and piety to be humble and godly. The term which we translate *condescend* signifies "to be led, carried, or dragged away to prison with another"; and points out the state in which the primitive Christians were despised and rejected of men, and often led forth to prison and death. *Be not wise in your own conceits.* Be not puffed up with an opinion of your own consequence, for this will prove that the consequence itself is imaginary. *Be not wise* "by yourselves"—do not suppose that wisdom and discernment dwell alone with you. Believe that you stand in need of both help and instruction from others.

17. *Recompense.* Do not take notice of every little injury you may sustain. Beware of too nice a sense of your own honor; intolerable pride is at the bottom of this. *Provide things honest.* Be prudent, be cautious; neither eat, drink, nor wear, but as you pay for everything.

18. *If it be possible.* To live in a state of peace with one's neighbors, friends, and even family, is often very difficult. But the man who loves God must labor after this, for it is indispensably necessary even for his own sake. A man cannot have broils and misunderstandings with others without having his own peace very materially disturbed: he must, to be happy, be at peace with all men, whether they will be at peace with him or not.

19. *Dearly beloved, avenge not yourselves.* You are the children of God, and He loves you; and because He loves you He will permit nothing to be done to you that He will not turn to your advantage. Never take the execution of the law into your own hands; rather suffer injuries. The Son of Man is come, not to destroy men's lives, but to save; be of the same spirit. When He was reviled, He reviled not again. It is the part of a noble mind to bear up under unmerited disgrace; little minds are litigious and quarrelsome. *Give place unto wrath.* Leave room for the civil magistrate to do his duty; he holds the sword for this purpose; and if he be unfaithful to the trust reposed in him by the state, leave the matter to God, who is the righteous Judge; for by avenging yourselves you take your cause both out of the hands of the civil magistrate and out of the hands of God. I believe this to be the meaning of *give place unto wrath,* "punishment"; the penalty which the law, properly executed, will inflict. *Vengeance is mine.* This fixes the meaning of the apostle, and at once shows that the exhortation, *Rather give place unto wrath,* or "punishment," means, Leave the matter to the judgment of God; it is His law that in this case is broken, and to Him the infliction of deserved punishment belongs. *I will repay.* In My own time and in My own way. But He gives the sinner space to repent, and this long-suffering leads to salvation.

20. *If thine enemy hunger, feed him.* Do not withhold from any man the offices of mercy and kindness. You have been God's enemy, and yet God fed, clothed, and preserved you alive; do to your enemy as God has done to you. If your enemy be hungry, feed him; if he be thirsty, give him drink—so has God dealt with you. And has not a sense of His goodness and long-suffering towards you been a means of melting down your heart into penitential compunction, gratitude, and love towards Him? How know you that a similar conduct towards your enemy may not have the same gracious influence on him towards you? Your kindness may be the means of begetting in him a sense of his guilt; and, from being your fell enemy, he may become your real friend. This I believe to be the sense of this passage, which many have encumbered with difficulties of their own creating. The whole is a quotation from Prov. xxv. 21-22, in the precise words of the Septuagint; and it is very likely that the latter clause of this verse, *Thou shalt heap coals of fire on his head,* is a metaphor taken from smelting metals. The ore is put into the furnace, and fire put both under and over, that the metal may be liquefied, and leaving the dross, may fall down pure to the bottom of the furnace. It is most evident from the whole connection of the place and the apostle's use of it that the heaping of the coals of fire upon the head of the enemy is intended to

produce, not an evil, but the most beneficial effect; and the following verse is an additional proof of this.

21. *Be not overcome of evil.* Do not, by giving place to evil, become precisely the same character which you condemn in another. *Overcome evil with good*—however frequently he may grieve and infuriate you, always repay him with kindness; your goodwill, in the end, may overcome his evil.

CHAPTER 13

Subjection to civil governors inculcated, from the consideration that civil government is according to the ordinance of God, and that those who resist the lawfully constituted authorities shall receive condemnation, 1-2. And those who are obedient shall receive praise, 3. The character of a lawful civil governor, 4. The necessity of subjection, 5. The propriety of paying lawful tribute, 6-7. Christians should love one another, 8-10. The necessity of immediate conversion to God proved from the shortness and uncertainty of time, 11-12. How the Gentiles should walk so as to please God, and put on Christ Jesus in order to their salvation, 13-14.

1. *Let every soul be subject unto the higher powers.* This is a very strong saying, and most solemnly introduced; and we must consider the apostle as speaking, not from his own private judgment, or teaching a doctrine of present expediency, but declaring the mind of God on a subject of the utmost importance to the peace of the world; a doctrine which does not exclusively belong to any class of people, order of the community, or official situations, but to every soul; and, on the principles which the apostle lays down, to every soul in all possible varieties of situation, and on all occasions. And what is this solemn doctrine? Let every man be obedient to the civil government under which the providence of God has cast his lot. *For there is no power but of God.* As God is the Origin of power, and the supreme Governor of the universe, He delegates authority to whomsoever He will; and though in many cases the governor himself may not be of God, yet civil government is of Him. For without this there could be no society, no security, no private property; all would be confusion and anarchy, and the habitable world would soon be depopulated.

2. *Whosoever . . . resisteth the power.* "He who sets himself in order against this order" of God; and *they who resist,* they who obstinately, and for no right reason, oppose the ruler, and strive to unsettle the constitution, and to bring about illegal changes, *shall receive to themselves damnation.* "Condemnation"; shall be condemned by both the spirit and the letter of that constitution, which, under pretense of defending or improving, they are indirectly laboring to subvert.

3. *For rulers are not a terror to good works.* Here the apostle shows the civil magistrate what he should be: he is clothed with great power, but that power is entrusted to him, not for the terror and oppression of the upright man, but to overawe and punish the wicked. It is, in a word, for the benefit of the community, and not for the aggrandizement of himself, that God has entrusted the supreme civil power to any man. *Wilt thou then not be afraid of the power?* If you would not live in fear of the civil magistrate, live according to the laws. You may expect that he will rule according to the laws; and consequently instead of incurring blame, you will have *praise.* This is said on the supposition that the ruler is himself a good man. Such the laws suppose him to be; and the apostle, on the general question of obedience and protection, assumes the point that the magistrate *is* such.

4. *For he is the minister of God to thee for good.* Here the apostle puts the character of the ruler in the strongest possible light. *He is the minister of God*—the office is by divine appointment. *He beareth not the sword in vain.* His power is delegated to him for the defense and encouragement of the good, and the punishment of the wicked; and he has authority to punish capitally, when the law so requires. This the term *sword* leads us to infer. *For he is the minister of God, a revenger.* "For he is God's vindictive minister." *To execute wrath;* to inflict "punishment" upon the transgressors of the law; and this according to the statutes of that law, for God's civil ministers are never allowed to pronounce or inflict punishment according to their own minds or feelings, but according to the express declarations of the law.

5. *Ye must needs be subject.* There is a necessity that you should be subject, not only for wrath, "on account of the punishment" which will be inflicted on evildoers, *but also for conscience sake;* not only to avoid punishment, but also to preserve a clear conscience.

6. *For this cause pay ye tribute also.* Because civil government is an order of God, and the ministers of state must be at considerable expense in providing for the safety and defense of the community, it is necessary that those in whose behalf these expenses are incurred should defray that expense; and hence nothing can be more reasonable than an impartial and moderate taxation, by which the expenses of the state may be defrayed and the various officers, whether civil or military, who are employed for the service of the public are adequately remunerated. By *God's ministers* are not meant here the ministers of religion, but the civil officers in all departments of the state.

7. *Render therefore to all their dues.* This is an extensive command. Be rigidly just; withhold from neither the king nor his ministers, nor his officers of justice and revenue, nor from even the lowest of the community, what the laws of God and your country require you to pay. *Tribute to whom tribute.* This word probably means such taxes as were levied on persons and estates. *Custom to whom custom.* This word probably means such duties as were laid upon goods, merchandise, etc., on imports and exports; what we commonly call *custom.* *Fear to whom fear.* It is likely that the word which we translate *fear* signifies that "reverence" which produces obedience. Treat all official characters with respect, and be obedient to your superiors. *Honour to whom honour.* The word may here mean that "outward respect" which the principle of reverence, from which it springs, will generally produce. Never behave rudely to any person; but behave respectfully to men in office. If you cannot even respect the man—for an important office may be filled by an unworthy person—respect the office, and the man on account of his office. If a man habituate himself to disrespect official characters, he will soon find himself disposed to

pay little respect or obedience to the laws themselves.

8. *Owe no man any thing, but to love one another.* In the preceding verses the apostle has been showing the duty, reverence, and obedience which all Christians, from the highest to the lowest, owe to the civil magistrate, whether he be emperor, king, proconsul, or other state officer; here he shows them their duty to each other. But this is widely different from that which they owe to the civil government. To the first they owe subjection, reverence, obedience, and tribute; to the latter they owe nothing but mutual love, and those offices which necessarily spring from it. Therefore the apostle says, *Owe no man;* as if he had said: You owe to your fellow brethren nothing but mutual love, and this is what the law of God requires, and in this the law is fulfilled.

9. *For this, Thou shalt not commit adultery.* He that loves another will not deprive him of his wife, of his life, of his property, of his good name; and will not even permit a desire to enter into his heart which would lead him to wish to possess anything that is the property of another; for the law, the sacred Scripture, has said: *Thou shalt love thy neighbour as thyself.* It is remarkable that *thou shalt not bear false witness* is missing from several MSS. The generality of the best critics think it a spurious reading.

10. *Love worketh no ill.* As he that loves another will act towards that person as, on a reverse of circumstances, he would that his neighbor should act towards him, therefore this love can never work ill towards another; and on this head, i.e., the duty we owe to our neighbor, *love is the fulfilling of the law.*

11. *And that, knowing the time.* Some think the passage should be paraphrased thus: We have now many advantages which we did not formerly possess. *Salvation* is *nearer*—the whole Christian system is more fully explained, and the knowledge of it more easy to be acquired than formerly; on which account a greater progress in religious knowledge and in practical piety is required of us, and we have for a long time been too remiss in these respects.

12. *The night is far spent.* If we understand this in reference to the heathen state of the Romans, it may be paraphrased thus: *The night is far spent*—heathenish darkness is nearly at an end. *The day is at hand*—the full manifestation of the Sun of Righteousness, in the illumination of the whole Gentile world, approaches rapidly. The manifestation of the Messiah is regularly termed by the ancient Jews *day,* because previously to this all is *night. Cast off the works of darkness*—prepare to meet this rising light, and welcome its approach, by throwing aside superstition, impiety, and vice of every kind; and *put on the armour of light*—fully receive the heavenly teaching, by which your spirits will be as completely armed against the attacks of evil as your bodies could be by the best weapons and impenetrable armor. This sense seems most suitable to the following verses, where the vices of the Gentiles are particularly specified; and they are exhorted to abandon them, and to receive the gospel of Christ. The common method of explanation is this: *The night is far spent*—our present imperfect life, full of afflictions, temptations, and

trials, is almost run out; *the day* of eternal blessedness *is at hand*—is about to dawn on us in our glorious resurrection unto eternal life. Therefore, *let us . . . cast off*—let us live as candidates for this eternal glory. But this sense cannot at all comport with what is said below, as the Gentiles are most evidently intended.

13. *Let us walk honestly, as in the day.* "Let us walk decently." Let our deportment be decent, orderly, such as we shall not be ashamed of in the eyes of the whole world. *Not in rioting and drunkenness. Rioting,* according to Hesychius, signifies "unclean and dissolute songs," banquets, and suchlike. *Methais* signifies "drunken festivals," such as were celebrated in honor of their gods, when after they had sacrificed they drank to excess, accompanied with abominable acts of every kind. *Not in chambering.* This is no legitimate word, and conveys no sense till, from its connection in this place, we force a meaning upon it. The original word signifies "whoredoms" and prostitution of every kind. *And wantonness.* All manner of "uncleanness." *Not in strife and envying.* Not in contentions and furious altercations, which must be the consequence of such practices as are mentioned above. Can any man suppose that this address is to the Christians at Rome? That they are charged with practices almost peculiar to the heathens? And practices of the most abandoned and dissolute sort? If those called Christians at Rome were guilty of such acts, there could be no difference, except in profession, between them and the most abominable of the heathens. But it is impossible that such things should be spoken to the followers of Christ, for the very grace that brings repentance enables the penitent to cast aside and abominate all such vicious and abominable conduct. The advices to the Christians may be found in the preceding chapter; those at the conclusion of this chapter belong solely to the heathens.

14. *Put ye on the Lord Jesus.* This is in reference to what is said, v. 13: "Let us put on decent garments"—let us make a different profession, unite with other company, and maintain that profession by a suitable conduct. Putting on or being clothed with Jesus Christ signifies receiving and believing the gospel; and consequently taking its maxims for the government of life, having the mind that was in Christ. The ancient Jews frequently use the phrase putting on the Shekinah, or divine majesty, to signify the soul's being clothed with immortality and rendered fit for glory. "To be clothed with a person" is a Greek phrase signifying to "assume the interests" of another—to enter into his views, to imitate him, and be wholly on his side. Chrysostom particularly mentions this as a common phrase, "such a one hath put on such a one"; i.e., he closely follows and imitates him. The mode of speech itself is taken from the custom of stage players; they assumed the name and garments of the person whose character they were to act, and endeavored as closely as possible to imitate him in their spirit, words, and actions. *And make not provision for the flesh.* By *flesh* we are here to understand not only the body, but all the irregular appetites and passions which led to the abominations already recited. No provision should be made for the encouragement and gratification of such a principle as this. *To fulfil the lusts thereof.* "In

reference to its lusts"; such as the rioting, drunkenness, prostitutions, and uncleanness, mentioned in v. 13, to make provision for which the Gentiles lived and labored, and bought and sold, and schemed and planned; for it was the whole business of their life to gratify the sinful lusts of the flesh. Their philosophers taught them little else; and the whole circle of their deities, as well as the whole scheme of their religion, served only to excite and inflame such passions and produce such practices.

CHAPTER 14

In things indifferent, Christians should not condemn each other, 1. Particularly with respect to different kinds of food, 2-4. And the observation of certain days, 5-6. None of us should live unto himself, but unto Christ, who lived and died for us, 7-9. We must not judge each other, for all judgment belongs to God, 10-13. We should not do anything by which a weak brother may be stumbled or grieved; lest we destroy him for whom Christ died, 14-16. The kingdom of God does not consist in outward things, 17-18. Christians should endeavor to cultivate peace and brotherly affection, and rather deny themselves of certain privileges than be the means of stumbling a weak brother, 19-21. The necessity of doing all in the spirit of faith, 22-23.

It seems very likely, from this and the following chapter, that there were considerable misunderstandings between the Jewish and Gentile Christians at Rome relative to certain customs which were sacredly observed by the one and disregarded by the other. The principal subject of dispute was concerning *meats* and *days*. The converted Jew, retaining a veneration for the law of Moses, abstained from certain meats and was observant of certain days; while the converted Gentile, understanding that the Christian religion laid him under no obligations to such ceremonial points, had no regard to either. It appears further that mutual censures and uncharitable judgments prevailed among them, and that brotherly love and mutual forbearance did not generally prevail. The apostle in this part of his Epistle exhorts that in such things, not essential to religion and in which both parties, in their different way of thinking, might have an honest meaning and serious regard to God, difference of sentiments might not hinder Christian fellowship and love; but that they would mutually forbear each other, make candid allowance, and especially not carry their gospel liberty so far as to prejudice a weak brother, a Jewish Christian, against the gospel itself, and tempt him to renounce Christianity.

1. *Him that is weak in the faith.* By this the apostle most evidently means the converted Jew, who must indeed be weak in the faith if he considered this distinction of meats and days essential to his salvation. *Receive ye.* Associate with him; receive him into your religious fellowship; but when there, let all religious altercations be avoided. *Not to doubtful disputations.* Do not reject any from your Christian communion because of their particular sentiments on things which are in themselves indifferent.

2. *One believeth that he may eat all things.* He believes that whatsoever is wholesome and nourishing, whether herbs or flesh, whether enjoined or forbidden by the Mosaic law, may be safely and conscientiously used by every Christian. *Another, who is weak, eateth herbs.* Certain Jews lately converted to the Christian faith and having as yet little knowledge of its doctrines believe the Mosaic law relative to

clean and unclean meats to be still in force; and therefore when they are in a Gentile country, for fear of being defiled, avoid flesh entirely and live on vegetables.

3. *Let not him that eateth,* the Gentile, who eats flesh, *despise him,* the Jew, who *eatest not* flesh but herbs. *And let not him,* the Jew, *which eateth not* indiscriminately, *judge*—condemn—*him,* the Gentile, *that eateth* indiscriminately flesh or vegetables. *For God hath received him.* Both being sincere and upright, and acting in the fear of God, are *received* as heirs of eternal life, without any difference on account of these religious scruples or prejudices.

4. *Who art thou that judgest another man's servant?* Who has ever given you the right to condemn the servant of another man, in things pertaining to his own master? *To his own master he standeth or falleth.* He is to judge him, not you; your intermeddling in this business is both rash and uncharitable. *Yea, he shall be holden up.* He is sincere and upright, and *God, who is able to make him stand,* will uphold him, and so teach him that he shall not essentially err. And it is the will of God that such upright though scrupulous persons should be continued members of His Church.

5. *One man esteemeth one day above another.* Perhaps the word *day* is here taken for "time, festival," and suchlike, in which sense it is frequently used. Reference is made here to the Jewish institutions and especially their festivals, such as the Passover, Pentecost, Feast of Tabernacles, new moons, jubilee. The converted Jew still thought these of moral obligation; the Gentile Christian not having been bred up in this way had no such prejudices. And as those who were the instruments of bringing him to the knowledge of God gave him no such injunctions, consequently he paid to these no religious regard. *Another.* The converted Gentile *esteemeth every day*—considers that all time is the Lord's, and that each day should be devoted to the glory of God, and that those festivals are not binding on him. We add here *alike*, and make the text say what I am sure was never intended, viz., that there is no distinction of days, not even of the Sabbath; and that every Christian is at liberty to consider even this day to be holy or not holy, as he happens to be persuaded in his own mind. That the Sabbath is of lasting obligation may be reasonably concluded from its institution (see the note on Gen. ii. 3) and from its typical reference. All allow that the Sabbath is a type of that rest in glory which remains for the people of God. Now all types are intended to continue in full force till the antitype or thing signified take place; consequently the Sabbath will continue in force till the consummation of all things. The word *alike* should not be added, nor is it acknowledged by any MS. or ancient version. *Let every man be fully persuaded.* With respect to the propriety or non-propriety of keeping the above festivals let every man act from the plenary conviction of his own mind. There is a sufficient latitude allowed; all may be fully satisfied.

6. *He that regardeth the day.* A beautiful apology for mistaken sincerity and injudicious reformation. Do not condemn the man for what is indifferent in itself; if he keep these

festivals, his purpose is to honor God by the religious observance of them. On the other hand, he who finds that he cannot observe them in honor of God, not believing that God has enjoined them, does not observe them at all. In like manner, he that eateth any creature of God which is wholesome and proper food gives thanks to God as the Author of all good. And he who cannot eat of all indiscriminately, but is regulated by the precepts in the Mosaic law relative to clean and unclean meats, also *giveth God thanks*. Both are sincere, both upright; both act according to their light. God accepts both, and they should bear with each other.

7. *None of us liveth to himself*. The Greek writers use the phrase to signify acting according to one's own judgment, following one's own opinion. Christians must act in all things according to the mind and will of God, and not follow their own wills. The apostle seems to intimate that in all the above cases each must endeavor to please God, for he is accountable to Him alone for his conduct in these indifferent things. God is our Master; we must live to Him, as we live under His notice and by His bounty; and when we cease to live among men, we are still in His hand. Therefore what we do, or what we leave undone, should be in reference to that eternity which is ever at hand.

9. *Christ both died, and rose*. That we are not our own, but are the Lord's in both life and death, is evident from this—that Christ lived, and died, and rose again, *that He might be Lord of the dead and living; for* His power extends equally over both worlds. Separate, as well as embodied, spirits are under His authority; and He it is who is to raise even the dead to life, and thus all throughout eternity shall live under His dominion. The clause *and rose* is wanting in several reputable MSS., and certainly is not necessary to the text.

10. *But why dost thou,* Christian Jew, observing the rites of the Mosaic law, *judge,* condemn, *thy brother,* the Christian Gentile, who does not think himself bound by this law? *Or why dost thou,* Christian Gentile, *set at nought* your Christian Jewish brother, as if he were unworthy of your regard, because he does not yet believe that the gospel has set him free from the rites and ceremonies of the law? *We shall all stand before the judgment seat of Christ.* Why should we then judge and condemn each other? We are accountable to God for our conduct, and shall be judged at His bar; and let us consider that whatever measure we mete, the same shall be measured unto us again.

12. *Every one of us shall give account of himself.* We shall not, at the bar of God, be obliged to account for the conduct of each other—each shall give account of himself; and let him take heed that he be prepared to give up his accounts with joy.

13. *Let us not therefore judge one another any more.* Let us abandon such rash conduct. It is dangerous; it is uncharitable. Judgment belongs to the Lord. *That no man put a stumblingblock.* Let both the converted Jew and Gentile consider that they should labor to promote each other's spiritual interests, and not be a means of hindering each other in their Christian course; or of causing them to abandon the gospel, on which, and not on questions of

rites and ceremonies, the salvation of their soul depends.

14. *I know, and am persuaded by the Lord Jesus.* After reasoning so long and so much with these contending parties on the subject of their mutual misunderstandings, without attempting to give any opinion, but merely to show them the folly and uncharitableness of their conduct, he now expresses himself fully and tells them that *nothing* is *unclean of itself,* and that he has the inspiration and authority of Jesus Christ to say so; for to such an inspiration he must refer in such words as *I know, and am persuaded by the Lord Jesus.* And yet, after having given them this decisive judgment, through respect to the tender, mistaken conscience of weak believers, he immediately adds: *But to him that esteemeth any thing to be unclean, to him it is unclean;* because if he act contrary to his conscience, he must necessarily contract guilt. For he who acts in opposition to his conscience in one case may do it in another, and thus even the plain declarations of the Word of God may be set aside on things of the utmost importance, as well as the erroneous though well-intentioned dictates of his conscience on matters which he makes of the last consequence, though others who are better taught know them to be indifferent. It is dangerous to trifle with conscience, even when erroneous; it should be borne with and instructed; it must be won over, not taken by storm. Its feelings should be respected because they ever refer to God, and have their foundation in His fear. He who sins against his conscience in things which everyone else knows to be indifferent will soon do it in those things in which his salvation is most intimately concerned. It is a great blessing to have a well-informed conscience; it is a blessing to have a tender conscience; and even a sore conscience is infinitely better than none.

15. *If thy brother be grieved.* If he thinks that you do wrong, and he is in consequence stumbled at your conduct. *Now walkest thou not charitably.* "According to love," for "love worketh no ill to his neighbour"; but by your eating some particular kind of meat on which neither your life nor well-being depends, you work ill to him by grieving and distressing his mind; and therefore you break the law of God in reference to him, while pretending that your Christian liberty raises you above his scruples. *Destroy not him with thy meat, for whom Christ died.* This puts the uncharitable conduct of the person in question in the strongest light, because it supposes that the weak brother may be so stumbled as to fall and perish finally, even the man *for whom Christ died.* To injure a man in his circumstances is bad; to injure him in his person is worse; to injure him in his reputation it still worse; and to injure his soul is worst of all. No wickedness, no malice, can go further than to injure and destroy the soul. Your uncharitable conduct may proceed thus far; therefore you are highly criminal before God. From this verse we learn that a man for whom Christ died may perish, or have his soul destroyed, and destroyed with such a destruction as implies perdition; the original is very emphatic. Christ died in his stead; do not destroy his soul. The sacrificial death is as strongly expressed as it can be, and there is no word in the New Testament that more forcibly implies

eternal ruin than the verb *apollyo,* from which is derived that most significant name of the devil, Apollyon, the "Destroyer," the great universal murderer of souls.

16. *Let not then your good be evil spoken of.* Do not make such a use of your Christian liberty as to subject the gospel itself to reproach. Whatsoever you do, do it in such a manner, spirit, and time as to make it productive of the greatest possible good. There are many who have such an unhappy method of doing their good acts as not only to do little or no good by them but a great deal of evil. It requires much prudence and watchfulness to find out the proper time of performing even a good action.

17. *For the kingdom of God.* That holy religion which God has sent from heaven, and which He intends to make the instrument of establishing a counterpart of the Kingdom of glory among men. *Is not meat and drink.* It consists not in these outward and indifferent things. *But righteousness.* Pardon of sin, and holiness of heart and life. *And peace.* In the soul, from a sense of God's mercy; peace regulating, ruling, and harmonizing the heart. *And joy in the Holy Ghost.* Solid spiritual happiness, a joy which springs from a clear sense of God's mercy, the love of God being shed abroad in the heart by the *Holy Ghost.* In a word, it is happiness brought into the soul by the Holy Spirit, and maintained there by the same influence. This is a genuine counterpart of heaven: *righteousness* without sin, *peace* without inward disturbance, *joy* without any kind of mental agony or distressing fear.

18. *For he that in these things.* The man, whether Jew or Gentile, who *in these things*—"righteousness, and peace, and joy in the Holy Ghost"—*serveth Christ,* acts according to His doctrine, is *acceptable to God.* For he has not only the form of godliness in thus serving Christ, but he has the power, the very spirit and essence of it, in having "righteousness, and peace, and joy in the Holy Ghost"; and therefore the whole frame of his mind, as well as his acts, must be acceptable to God. *And approved of men;* for although religion may be persecuted, yet the righteous man who is continually laboring for the public good will be generally esteemed.

19. *Let us therefore follow.* Far from contending about meats, drinks, and festival times, in which it is not likely that the Jews and Gentiles will soon agree, let us endeavor to the utmost of our power to promote peace and unanimity, that we may be instrumental in edifying each other, in promoting religious knowledge and piety instead of being stumbling blocks in each other's way.

20. *For meat destroy not the work of God.* Do not hinder the progress of the gospel either in your own souls or in those of others by contending about lawful or unlawful meats. And do not destroy the soul of your Christian brother, v. 15, by offending him so as to induce him to apostatize. *All things indeed are pure.* This is a repetition of the sentiment delivered in v. 14, in different words. Nothing that is proper for aliment is unlawful to be eaten; *but it is evil for that man who eateth with offence*—the man who either eats contrary to his own conscience or so as to grieve and stumble another does an evil act; and however lawful the

thing may be in itself, his conduct does not please God.

21. *It is good neither to eat flesh.* The spirit and self-denying principles of the gospel teach us that we should not only avoid everything in eating or drinking which may be an occasion of offense or apostasy to our brethren, but even to lay down our lives for them should it be necessary. *Whereby thy brother stumbleth. Proskoptei* from *pros,* "against," and *kopto,* "to strike, to hit the foot against a stone in walking, so as to halt, and be impeded in one's journey." It here means, spiritually, anything by which a man is so perplexed in his mind as to be prevented from making due progress in the divine life, anything by which he is caused to halt, to be undecisive, and undetermined; and under such an influence no man has ever yet grown in grace and in the knowledge of Jesus Christ. *Or is offended. Scandalizetai* from *scandalon,* a "stumbling block"; anything by which a person is caused to fall, especially into a snare, trap, or gin. Originally the word signified the piece of wood or key in a trap which, being trodden on, caused the animal to fall into a pit or the trap to close upon him. In the New Testament it generally refers to total apostasy from the Christian religion, and this appears to be its meaning in this place. *Or is made weak.* Without mental vigor; without power sufficiently to distinguish between right and wrong, good and evil, lawful and unlawful. The last two terms are omitted by two excellent MSS. and by some of the primitive fathers. It is very likely that they were added by some early hand by way of illustration.

22. *Hast thou faith?* The term *faith* seems to signify in this place a "full persuasion in a man's mind that he is right," that what he does is lawful, and has the approbation of God and his conscience. *Happy is he that condemneth not.* That man only can enjoy peace of conscience who acts according to the full persuasion which God has given him of the lawfulness of his conduct, whereas he must be miserable who allows himself in the practice of anything for which his conscience upbraids and accuses him. This is a most excellent maxim, and every genuine Christian should be careful to try every part of his conduct by it. If a man have not peace in his own bosom, he cannot be happy; and no man can have peace who sins against his conscience. If a man's passions or appetite allow or instigate him to a particular thing, let him take good heed that his conscience approve what his passions allow, and that he live not the subject of continual self-condemnation and reproach. Even the man who has the too scrupulous conscience had better, in such matters as are in question, obey its erroneous dictates than violate this moral feeling and live only to condemn the actions he is constantly performing.

23. *And he that doubteth.* This verse is a necessary part of the preceding, and should be read thus: "But he that doubteth is condemned if he eat, because he eateth not of faith." The meaning is sufficiently plain. He that feeds on any kind of meats prohibited by the Mosaic law with the persuasion in his mind that he may be wrong in so doing is condemned by his conscience for doing that which he has reason to think God has forbidden. *For whatsoever is*

not of faith is sin. Whatever he does, without a full persuasion of its lawfulness (see v. 22), is to him *sin,* for he does it under a conviction that he may be wrong in so doing. Therefore if he makes a distinction in his own conscience between different kinds of meats, and yet eats of all indifferently, he is a sinner before God. There are few readers who have not remarked that the last three verses of this Epistle (chap. xvi. 25-27) appear to stand in their present place without any obvious connection, and apparently after the Epistle is concluded. And it is well-known to critics that a number of MSS. and versions add those verses at the end of the fourteenth chapter. These words certainly connect better with the close of the fourteenth chapter and the beginning of the fifteenth than they do with the conclusion of the sixteenth, where they are now generally found. But I shall defer my observations upon them till I come to that place, with only this remark, that the *stablishing* mentioned in chap. xvi. 25 corresponds well with the *doubting* of chap. xiv. 23; and indeed the whole matter of these verses agrees so well with the subject so largely handled in the preceding chapter that there can be very little doubt of their being in their proper place if joined to the end of this chapter, as they are in some MSS. and versions.

CHAPTER 15

The strong should bear the infirmities of the weak, and each strive to please, not himself, but his neighbor, after the example of Christ, 1-3. Whatsoever was written in old times was written for our learning, 4. We should be of one mind, that we might with one mouth glorify God, 5-6. We should accept each other as Christ has accepted us, 7. Scriptural proofs that Jesus Christ was not only the Minister of the circumcision, but came also for the salvation of the Gentiles, 8-12. The God of hope can fill us with all peace and joy in believing, 13. Character of the church of Rome, 14. The reason why the apostle wrote so boldly to the church in that city—what God had wrought by him, and what he purposed to do, 15-24. He tells them of his intended journey to Jerusalem, with a contribution to the poor saints—a sketch of this journey, 25-29. He commends himself to their prayers, 30-33.

1. *We then that are strong.* The sense of this verse is supposed to be the following: We Gentile Christians who perfectly understand the nature of our gospel liberty not only lawfully may, but are bound in duty to, bear any inconveniences that may arise from the scruples of the weaker brethren, and to ease their consciences by prudently abstaining from such indifferent things as may offend and trouble them, and not take advantage from our superior knowledge to make them submit to our judgment.

2. *Let every one of us please his neighbour.* For it should be a maxim with each of us to do all in our power to please our brethren, and especially in those things in which their spiritual edification is concerned. Though we should not indulge men in mere whims and caprices, yet we should bear with their ignorance and their weakness, knowing that others had much to bear with from us before we came to our present advanced state of religious knowledge.

3. *For even Christ pleased not himself.* Christ never acted as One who sought His own ease or profit. He not only bore with the weakness, but with the insults, of His creatures; as it is written in Ps. lxix. 9: *The reproaches of them that reproached thee fell on me*—I not only bore their insults, but bore the punishment due

to them for their vicious and abominable conduct. That this psalm refers to the Messiah and His sufferings for mankind is evident, not only from the quotation here, but also from John xix. 28-29, when our Lord's receiving the vinegar during His expiatory suffering is said to be a fulfilling of the scripture, viz., of v. 21 of this very psalm; and His cleansing the Temple, John ii. 15-17, is said to be a fulfillment of v. 9, "For the zeal of thine house hath eaten me up," the former part of which verse the apostle quotes here.

4. *For whatsoever things were written aforetime.* This refers not only to the quotation from Psalms 69, but to all the Old Testament scriptures; for it can be to no other scriptures that the apostle alludes. And from what he says here of them, we learn that God had not intended them merely for those generations in which they were first delivered, but for the instruction of all the succeeding generations of mankind. *That we through patience and comfort of the scriptures*—that we, through those remarkable examples of *patience* exhibited by the saints and followers of God, whose history is given in those scriptures, and the *comfort* which they derived from God in their patient endurance of sufferings brought upon them through their faithful attachment to truth and righteousness —*might have hope* that we shall be upheld and blessed as they were, and our sufferings become the means of our greater advances in faith and holiness, and consequently our hope of eternal glory be the more confirmed. Some think that the word which we translate *comfort* should be rendered "exhortation"; but there is certainly no need here to leave the usual acceptation of the term, as the word comfort makes a regular and consistent sense with the rest of the verse.

5. *Now the God of patience and consolation.* May that God who endued them with *patience,* and gave them the *consolation* that supported them in all their trials and afflictions, *grant you to be likeminded*—give you the same mode of thinking and the same power of acting towards each other, *according* to the example of *Christ.*

6. *That ye*—Jews and Gentiles—*may with one mind.* Thinking the same things, and bearing with each other, after the example of Christ. *And one mouth,* in all your religious assemblies, without jarring or contentions. *Glorify God* for calling you into such a state of salvation, and showing himself to be your loving, compassionate Father, as he is *the Father of our Lord Jesus Christ.* It is very likely that the apostle refers here to religious acts in public worship which might have been greatly interrupted by the dissensions between the converted Jews and the converted Gentiles. These differences he labors to compose; and after having done all that was necessary in the way of instruction and exhortation, he now pours out his soul to God, who alone could rule and manage the heart, that He would enable them to think the same things, to be of the same judgment, and that all, feeling their obligation to Him, might join in the sweetest harmony in every act of religious worship.

7. *Wherefore receive ye one another.* Have the most affectionate regard for each other, and acknowledge each other as the servants and children of God Almighty. *As Christ*

also received us. In the same manner and with the same cordial affection as Christ has received us into communion with himself, and has made us partakers of such inestimable blessings, condescending to be present in all our assemblies. And as Christ has received us thus to the glory of God, so should we, Jews and Gentiles, cordially receive each other, that God's glory may be promoted by our harmony and brotherly love.

8. *Jesus Christ was a minister of the circumcision.* To show the Gentiles the propriety of bearing with the scrupulous Jews, he shows them here that they were under the greatest obligations to his people; to whom, in the days of His flesh, Jesus Christ confined His ministry, giving the world to see that He allowed the claim of the Jews as having the first right to the blessings of the gospel. And He confined His ministry thus to the Jews to *confirm the truth of God* contained in the *promises* made unto the patriarchs; for God had declared that thus it should be; and Jesus Christ, by coming according to the promise, has fulfilled this truth by making good the promises. Therefore salvation is of the Jews, as a kind of right conveyed to them through the promises made to their fathers. But this salvation was not exclusively designed for the Jewish people, as God by His prophets had repeatedly declared.

9. *And that the Gentiles might glorify God for his mercy.* As the Jews were to glorify God for His *truth,* so the Gentiles were to glorify God for His *mercy.* The Jews received the blessings of the gospel by right of promise, which promise God had most punctually and circumstantially fulfilled. The Gentiles had received the same gospel as an effect of God's mere mercy, having no right in consequence of any promise or engagement made with any of their ancestors, though they were originally included in the covenant made with Abraham. *I will confess to thee among the Gentiles.* This quotation is taken from Ps. xviii. 49, and shows that the Gentiles had a right to glorify God for His mercy to them.

13. *Now the God of hope.* "May the God of this hope"—that God who caused both Jews and Gentiles to hope that the gracious promises which He made to them should be fulfilled; and who, accordingly, has fulfilled them in the most punctual and circumstantial manner. *Fill you with all joy.* Give you true spiritual happiness: *peace* in your own hearts, and unity among yourselves; *in believing* not only the promises which He has given you, but believing in Christ Jesus, in whom all the promises are yea and amen.

14. *And I . . . am persuaded of you.* This is supposed to be an address to the Gentiles, and it is managed with great delicacy. He seems to apologize for the freedom he had used in writing to them, which he gives them to understand proceeded from the authority he had received by his apostolical office, the exercise of which office respected them particularly.

15. *Nevertheless . . . I have written.* Notwithstanding I have this conviction of your extensive knowledge in the things of God, I have made bold to write to you *in some sort,* "to a party" among you, as some learned men translate the words, who stand more in need of such instructions than the others; and I do this

because of the grace—because of the "office"—which I have received from God, namely, to be the apostle of the Gentiles.

16. *Ministering the gospel of God.* "Acting as a priest." Here is a plain allusion, says Dr. Whitby, to the Jewish sacrifices offered by the priest, and *sanctified* or made acceptable by the *libamen* offered with them; for he compares himself, in preaching the gospel, to the priest performing his sacred functions—preparing his sacrifice to be offered. The Gentiles, converted by him and dedicated to the service of God, are his sacrifices and oblation. The Holy Spirit is the *libamen* poured upon this sacrifice, by which it was sanctified and rendered *acceptable* to God. The words of Isa. lxvi. 20, "And they shall bring all your brethren for an offering unto the Lord out of all nations," might have suggested the above idea to the mind of the apostle.

17. *I have therefore whereof I may glory.* Being sent of God on this most honorable and important errand, I have matter of great exultation, not only in the honor which He has conferred upon me, but in the great success with which He has crowned my ministry.

18. *For I will not dare to speak.* If the thing were not as I have stated it, I would not dare to arrogate to myself honors which did not belong to me. But God has made me the apostle of the Gentiles; and the conversion of the Gentiles is the fruit of my ministry, Christ having *wrought by me* for this purpose. *By word and deed.* These words may refer to the doctrines which he taught and to the miracles which he wrought among them. So they became obedient to the doctrines, on the evidence of the miracles with which they were accompanied.

19. *Through mighty signs and wonders.* This more fully explains the preceding clause. Through the power of the Holy Ghost he was enabled to work among the Gentiles *mighty signs and wonders,* so that they were fully convinced that both his doctrine and mission were divine; and therefore they cheerfully received the gospel of the Lord Jesus. *Round about unto Illyricum.* It is a country of Europe, extending from the Adriatic gulf to Pannonia. From Jerusalem the apostle went round the eastern coast of the Mediterranean Sea. *I have fully preached the gospel.* "I have successfully preached"—I have not only proclaimed the Word, but made converts and founded churches.

20. *So have I strived to preach the gospel.* For I have considered it my "honor" to preach the gospel where that gospel was before unknown. This is the proper import of the word; from *philos,* a "friend," and *time,* "honor."

21. *But as it is written.* These words, quoted from Isa. lii. 15, the apostle applies to his own conduct; not that the words themselves predicted what Paul had done, but that he endeavored to fulfill such a declaration by his manner of preaching the gospel to the heathen.

22. *For which cause.* My considering it a point of honor to build on no other man's foundation; and, finding that the gospel has been long ago planted at Rome, I have been prevented from going thither, purposing rather to spend my time and strength in preaching where Christ has not yet been proclaimed.

23. *But . . . having no more place in these parts.* Having nothing further at present that I can do—for *topon echein* signifies not merely "to have a place of residence," or the like, but "convenience, opportunity," which is a frequent meaning of the phrase among the best Greek writers—having no large place or city where Christianity has not yet been planted, in which I can introduce the gospel. The apostle was then at Corinth; and having evangelized all those parts, he had no opportunity of breaking up any new ground.

24. *Whensoever I take my journey into Spain.* Where it is very likely the gospel had not been planted. *I will come to you.* These words are wanting in almost every MS. of note. If the first clause of this verse be read in connection with the latter clause of the preceding, it will fully appear that this rejected clause is useless. "Having a great desire these many years to come unto you whensoever I take my journey into Spain: for I trust to see you in my journey." *Somewhat filled with your company.* The word which we translate *filled* would be better rendered "gratified"; for it signifies to be "satisfied, to be gratified, and to enjoy." The apostle, though he had not the honor of having planted the church at Rome, yet expected much gratification from the visit which he intended to pay them.

25. *Now I go unto Jerusalem.* From this and the following two verses we learn that the object of his journey to Jerusalem was to carry a contribution made among the Gentile Christians of Macedonia and Achaia for the relief of the poor Jewish Christians at Jerusalem. About this affair he had taken great pains, as appears from 1 Cor. xvi. 1-4; 2 Corinthians vii and ix. His design in this affair is very evident from 2 Cor. ix. 12-13. The apostle was in hopes that this liberal contribution sent by the Gentile Christians who had been converted by Paul's ministry would engage the affections of the Jewish Christians, who had been much prejudiced against the reception of the Gentiles into the Church without being previously obliged to submit to the yoke of the law. He wished to establish a coalition between the converted Jews and Gentiles, being sensible of its great importance to the spread of the gospel; and his procuring this contribution was one laudable device to accomplish this good end. This shows why he so earnestly requests the prayers of the Christians at Rome, that his service which he had for Jerusalem might be accepted of the saints.

27. *For if the Gentiles have been made partakers.* It was through and by means of the Jews that the Gentiles were brought to the knowledge of God and the gospel of Christ. These were the *spiritual things* which they had received, and the pecuniary contribution was the *carnal things* which the Gentiles were now returning.

28. *When therefore I have performed this service, and have sealed,* faithfully delivered up, *to them this fruit,* of the success of my ministry and of your conversion to God, *I will come by you into Spain.* This was in his desire; he had fully purposed it, if God should see meet to permit him; but it does not appear that he ever went.

29. *In the fulness of the blessing of the gospel of Christ.* The words *of the gospel* are wanting in almost every MS. of importance. There is no doubt they should be omitted. "The fulness of the blessing of Christ" is really more than "the fulness of the blessing of the gospel of Christ."

30. *For the love of the Spirit.* By that love of God which the Holy Spirit sheds abroad in your hearts. *That ye strive together.* "That you agonize with me." He felt that much depended on the success of his present mission to the Christians at Jerusalem, and their acceptance of the charitable contribution which he was bringing with him, in order to conciliate them to the reception of the Gentiles into the Church of God without obliging them to submit to circumcision.

31. *That I may be delivered from them that do not believe.* He knew that his countrymen who had not received the gospel lay in wait for his life; and no doubt they thought they should do God service by destroying him, not only as an apostate, in their apprehension, from the Jewish religion, but as one who was laboring to subvert and entirely destroy it. *And that my service.* But several eminent MSS. read "the gift which I bear." This probably was a gloss, which in many MSS. subverted the word in the text; for *service* in its connection here could refer to nothing else but the contribution which he was carrying to the poor saints at Jerusalem.

32. *That I may come unto you with joy.* That his apprehensions of ill usage were not groundless, and the danger to which his life was exposed real, we have already seen in the account given of this visit, Acts xxi—xxiv; and that he had such intimations from the Holy Spirit himself appears from Acts xx. 23; xxi. 11; and xx. 38. Should his journey to Jerusalem be prosperous and his service accepted, so that the converted Jews and Gentiles should come to a better understanding, he hoped to see them at Rome with great joy; and if he got his wishes gratified through their prayers, it would be the full proof that this whole business had been conducted according to the will of God.

33. *The God of peace be with you.* The whole object of the Epistle is to establish peace between the believing Jews and Gentiles, and to show them their mutual obligations, and the infinite mercy of God to both; and now he concludes with praying that the God of peace— He from whom it comes and by whom it is preserved—may be forever with them. The word *Amen* at the end does not appear to have been written by the apostle; it is wanting in some of the most ancient MSS.

CHAPTER 16

The apostle commends to the Christians at Rome Phoebe, a deaconess of the church at Cenchrea, 1-2. Sends greetings to Aquila and Priscilla, of whom he gives a high character; and greets also the Church at their house, 3-5. Mentions several others by name, both men and women, who were members of the church of Christ at Rome, 6-16. Warns them to beware of those who cause dissensions and divisions, of whom he gives an awful character, 17-18. Extols the obedience of the Roman Christians, and promises them a complete victory over Satan, 19-20. Several persons send their salutations, 21-23. To whose good wishes he subjoins the apostolic blessing; commends them to God; gives an abstract of the doctrines of the gospel; and concludes with ascribing glory to the only wise God, through Christ Jesus, 24-27.

1. *I commend unto you Phebe.* As the apostle had not been at Rome previously to his writing this Epistle, he could not have had a personal acquaintance with those members of the church there to whom he sends these friendly salutations. It is likely that many of them were his own converts, who in different parts of Asia Minor and Greece had heard him preach the gospel and afterwards became settlers at Rome. Phoebe is here termed a *servant*, "a deaconess" *of the church . . . at Cenchrea*. There were deaconesses in the primitive Church, whose business it was to attend the female converts at baptism; to instruct the catechumens, or persons who were candidates for baptism; to visit the sick, and those who were in prison; and, in short, perform those religious offices for the female part of the Church which could not with propriety be performed by men. They were chosen in general out of the most experienced of the Church, and were ordinarily widows who had borne children. Some ancient constitutions required them to be forty, others fifty, and others sixty years of age. It is evident that they were ordained to their office by the imposition of the hands of the bishop, and the form of prayer used on the occasion is extant in the apostolical constitutions. In the tenth or eleventh century the order became extinct in the Latin church, but continued in the Greek church till the end of the twelfth century. *Cenchrea* was a seaport on the east side of the isthmus which joined the Morea to Greece, as Lechaeum was the seaport on the west side of the same isthmus.

2. *Succourer of many*. One who probably entertained the apostles and preachers who came to minister at Cenchrea, and who was remarkable for entertaining strangers.

3. *Greet Priscilla and Aquila*. This pious couple had been obliged to leave Rome, on the edict of Claudius, see Acts xviii. 2, and take refuge in Greece. It is likely that they returned to Rome at the death of Claudius, or whenever the decree was annulled. It seems they had greatly contributed to assist the apostle in his important labors. Instead of "Priscilla," the principal MSS. and versions have "Prisca," which most critics suppose to be the genuine reading.

4. *Who have for my life laid down their own necks*. What transaction this refers to we know not; but it appears that these persons had on some occasion hazarded their own lives to save that of the apostle, and that the fact was known to all the churches of God in that quarter, who felt themselves under the highest obligations to these pious persons for the important service which they had thus rendered.

5. *The church that is in their house*. In these primitive times no such places existed as those which we now term churches; the word always signifying the "congregation" or "assembly" of believers, and not the place they assembled in. *Epaenetus . . . the firstfruits of Achaia*. In 1 Cor. xvi. 15, the house or family of Stephanas is said to be the firstfruits of Achaia. How then can it be said here that Epenetus was the firstfruits, or first person who had received the gospel in that district? *Ans.*—Epenetus might have been one of the family of Stephanas; for it is not said that Stephanas was the firstfruits, but his house or family; and there can be no impropriety in supposing that one of that house or family was called Epenetus; and that this person, being the only one of the family now at Rome, might be mentioned as the first-

fruits of Achaia. This would rationally account for the apparent difficulty were we sure that *of Achaia* was the true reading; but this is more than doubtful, for *of Asia* is the reading of several MSS.

6. *Greet Mary, who bestowed much labour on us*. Who this *Mary* was or what the *labour* was which she bestowed upon the apostles, we know not. Her works, though hidden from man, are with God and her name is recorded with honor in this book of life.

7. *Andronicus and Junia, my kinsmen*. As the word signifies "relatives," whether male or female, and as *Junia* may probably be the name of a woman, the wife of Andronicus, it would be better to say "relatives" than *kinsmen*. But probably Paul means no more than that they were Jews; for in chap. ix. 3 he calls all the Jews his "kinsmen according to the flesh." *My fellowprisoners*. As Paul was in prison often, it is likely that these persons shared this honor with him on some occasion, which is not distinctly marked. *Of note among the apostles*. Whether this intimates that they were noted apostles or only highly reputed by the apostles is not absolutely clear, but the latter appears to me the most probable. They were well-known not only to Paul but also to the rest of the apostles. *In Christ before me*. That is, they were converted to Christianity before Paul was; probably at the Day of Pentecost, or by the ministry of Christ himself, or by that of the seventy disciples.

8. *Amplias my beloved in the Lord*. One who is my "particular friend," and also a genuine Christian.

9. *Urbane, our helper*. Who this Urbanus was we know not; what is here stated is that he had been a fellow laborer with the apostles. *Stachys my beloved*. One of my "particular friends."

10. *Apelles approved in Christ*. A man who, on different occasions, had given the highest proofs of the sincerity and depth of his religion. Some suppose that *Apelles* was the same with Apollos. Whoever he was, he had given every demonstration of being a genuine Christian. *Of Aristobulus' household*. It is doubted whether this person was converted, as the apostle does not salute him, but his *household;* or as the margin reads, "his friends." He might have been a Roman of considerable distinction who, though not converted himself, had Christians among his servants or his slaves. But whatever he was, it is likely that he was dead at this time, and therefore only those of his household are referred to by the apostle.

11. *Herodion my kinsman*. Probably another converted Jew. See on v. 7. *Of the household of Narcissus*. Probably dead also, as we have supposed Aristobulus to have been at this time. *Which are in the Lord*. This might intimate that some of this family were not Christians, those only of that family that were converted to the Lord being saluted.

12. *Tryphena and Tryphosa*. Two holy women, who it seems were assistants to the apostle in his work, probably by exhorting, visiting the sick, etc. *Persis* was another woman who it seems excelled the preceding; for of her it is said, She *laboured much in the Lord*. We learn from this that Christian women as well as men

labored in the ministry of the Word. In those times of simplicity all persons, whether men or women, who had received the knowledge of the truth believed it to be their duty to propagate it to the uttermost of their power.

13. *Rufus chosen in the Lord.* One of great excellence in Christianity; a "choice" man, as we would say. So the word often signifies. *His mother and mine.* It is not likely that the mother of Rufus was the mother of Paul; but while she was the natural mother of the former, she acted as a mother to the latter. We say of a person of this character that she is a "motherly" woman. Among the ancients, he or she who acted a kind, instructing, and indulgent part to another was styled the "father" or "mother" of such a one.

14. *Salute Asyncritus . . .* Who these were we know not. *Hermas* was probably the same to whom a work called the Shepherd is attributed; a work with this title is still extant, and may be found among the writings of the apostolical fathers. But it is in vain to look for identity of persons in similarity of names, for among the Greeks and Romans at this time there were many persons who bore the same names mentioned in this chapter.

15. *Salute Philologus.* Of these several persons, though much has been conjectured, nothing certain is known. Even the names of some are so ambiguous that we know not whether they were men or women. They were persons well-known to Paul, and undoubtedly were such as had gone from different places where the apostle had preached to sojourn or settle at Rome. One thing we may remark, that there is no mention of Peter, who, according to the Roman and papistical catalogue of bishops, must have been at Rome at this time. If he were not now at Rome, the foundation stone of Rome's ascendancy, of Peter's supremacy, and of the uninterrupted succession is taken away, and the whole fabric falls to the ground. But if Peter were at Rome at this time, Paul would have sent his salutations to him in the first place.

16. *Salute one another with an holy kiss.* In those early times the *kiss*, as a token of peace, friendship, and brotherly love, was frequent among all people; and the Christians used it in their public assemblies, as well as in their occasional meetings. This was at last laid aside, not because it was abused, but because, the Church becoming very numerous, the thing was impossible. In some countries the kiss of friendship is still common; and in such countries it is scarcely ever abused, nor is it an incentive to evil because it is customary and common. Shaking of hands is now substituted for it in almost all Christian congregations. *The churches of Christ salute you.* The word *all* is added here by some of the most reputable MSS. and principal versions. Paul must mean, here, that all the churches in Greece and Asia, through which he had passed, in which the faith of the Christians at Rome was known, spoke of them affectionately and honorably; and probably knowing the apostle's design of visiting Rome, desired to be kindly remembered to the church in that city.

18. *They . . . serve not our Lord Jesus.* They profess to be apostles, but they are not apostles of Christ; they neither do His will nor preach His doctrine. They serve *their own belly*—they have intruded themselves into the Church of Christ that they might get a secular support; it is for worldly gain alone that they take up the profession of the ministry. They have no divine credentials; they convert not the heathen nor the ungodly, for they have no divine unction. But *by good words and fair speeches* (for they have no miraculous nor saving powers) *deceive the hearts of the simple,* perverting Christian converts, that they may get their property, and thus secure a maintenance for themselves.

19. *For your obedience is come abroad.* The apostle gives this as a reason why they should continue to hear and heed those who had led them into the path of truth, and avoid those false teachers whose doctrines tended to the subversion of their souls. *Yet I would have you wise.* I would wish you carefully to discern the good from the evil, and to show your wisdom by carefully avoiding the one and cleaving to the other.

20. *The God of peace.* Who neither sends nor favors such disturbers of the tranquility of His Church. *Shall bruise Satan.* Shall give you the dominion over the great adversary of your souls, and over all his agents who, through his influence, endeavor to destroy your peace and subvert your minds. Several critics suppose that the word *Satan* is a sort of collective term here, by which all opposers and adversaries are meant, and especially those false teachers to whom he refers above. *The grace of our Lord.* That you may be truly wise, simple, obedient, and steady in the truth, may the favor or gracious influence of our Lord Jesus Christ be with you—without which you cannot be preserved from evil, nor do anything that is good.

Here the apostle appears to have intended to conclude his Epistle; but afterwards he added a postscript, if not two, as we shall see below. Several ancient MSS. omit the whole of this clause, probably thinking that it had been borrowed from v. 24. But on the ground that the apostle might have added a postscript or two, not having immediate opportunity to send the Epistle, there is no need for this supposition.

21. *Timotheus my workfellow.* This is on all hands allowed to be the same Timothy to whom Paul directs the two Epistles which are still extant. *Lucius.* This was probably Luke, the Evangelist, and writer of the book called the Acts of the Apostles. *Jason.* It is likely that this is the same person mentioned in Acts xvii. 7, who at Thessalonica received the apostles into his house, and befriended them at the risk of both his property and life. *Sosipater.* He was a Berean, the son of one Pyrrhus, a Jew by birth, and accompanied Paul from Greece into Asia, and probably into Judea. See Acts xx. 4.

22. *I Tertius, who wrote this epistle.* It appears that Paul dictated it to him, and he wrote it down from the apostle's mouth, and here introduces himself as joining with Paul in affectionate wishes for their welfare. *Salute you in the Lord.* I wish you well in the name of the Lord: or, I feel for you that affectionate respect which the grace of the Lord Jesus inspires. It is not clear whether the following two verses be the words of Tertius or of Paul.

23. *Gaius mine host.* Gaius in Greek is the same as *Caius* in Latin, which was a very com-

mon name among the Romans. Luke (Acts xix. 29) mentions one "Gaius of Macedonia," who was exposed to much violence at Ephesus in the tumult excited by Demetrius the silversmith against Paul and his companions; and it is very possible that this was the same person. He is here called not only the *host,* the "entertainer" of Paul, or Tertius (if he wrote this and the following verse), but also of *the whole church;* that is, he received and lodged the apostles who came from different places, as well as the messengers of the churches. *Erastus the chamberlain of the city.* "Treasurer of the city" of Corinth, from which Paul wrote this Epistle. This is supposed to be the same person as is mentioned in Acts xix. 22. He was one of Paul's companions, and, as appears from 2 Tim. iv. 20, was left about this time by the apostle at Corinth. He is called the *chamberlain,* which signifies the same as "treasurer," he to whom the receipt and expenditure of the public money were intrusted. Such persons were in very high credit; and if Erastus was at this time treasurer, it would appear that Christianity was then in considerable repute in Corinth. But if the Erastus of the Acts was the same with the Erastus mentioned here, it is not likely that he now held the office, for this could not at all comport with his travelling with Paul. Hence several, both ancients and moderns, who believe the identity of the persons, suppose that Erastus was not now treasurer, but that having formerly been so, he still retained the title. Chrysostom thought that he still retained the employment. *Quartus a brother.* Whether the brother of Erastus or of Tertius we know not; probably nothing more is meant than that he was a Christian—one of the heavenly family, a *brother* in the Lord.

24. *The grace of our Lord.* This is the conclusion of Tertius, and is similar to what Paul used above. Hence it is possible that Tertius wrote the whole of the twenty-second, twenty-third, and twenty-fourth verses without receiving any particular instructions from Paul, except the bare permission to add his own salutations with those of his particular friends. There is a great deal of disagreement among the MSS. and versions relative to this verse, some rejecting it entirely, and some of those which place the following verses at the end of chap. xiv inserting it at the end of the twenty-seventh verse in that place.

25. *Now to him.* In the note at the end of chap. xiv I have shown that this and the following verses are by the most reputable MSS. and versions placed at the end of that chapter, which is supposed by most critics to be their proper place. *Of power to stablish you.* To that God without whom nothing is wise, nothing strong; who is as willing to teach as He is wise, as ready to help as He is strong. *According to my gospel.* That gospel which explains and publishes God's purpose of taking the Gentiles to be His people under the Messiah, without subjecting them to the law of Moses. This is what he here calls the preaching of Jesus Christ.

Which was kept secret. This purpose of calling the Gentiles, and giving them equal privileges to the Jews without obliging them to submit to circumcision.

26. *But now is made manifest.* Now, under the New Testament dispensation, and by my preaching. *By the scriptures of the prophets.* Hints relative to this important work being scattered up and down through all their works, but no clear revelation that the Gentiles, who should be admitted into the Church, should be admitted without passing under the yoke of the Mosaic law. This was the point which was kept secret. As to the calling of the Gentiles, this was declared in general terms by the prophets, and the apostle quotes and makes a most important use of their predictions; but the other was a point on which the prophets gave no information, and it seems to have been peculiarly revealed to Paul, who received *the commandment of the everlasting God* to make it known to all the Gentiles—all the people of the earth that were not of Jewish extraction. And it was to be made known *for the obedience of faith,* that they might believe its doctrines and obey its precepts; its universal voice requiring repentance towards God, faith in our Lord Jesus Christ, and circumcision of the heart, in the place of all Jewish rites and ceremonies.

27. *To God only wise.* This comes in with great propriety. He alone who is the Fountain of wisdom and knowledge had all this mystery in himself; and He alone who knew the times, places, persons, and circumstances could reveal the whole; and He has revealed all in such a way as not only to manifest His unsearchable wisdom, but also His infinite goodness. Therefore to Him be *glory* for His wisdom in devising this most admirable plan, and His goodness in sending Christ Jesus to execute it; to Him, through Christ Jesus, be glory *for ever*—because this plan is to last forever, and is to have no issue but in eternal glory. *Written to the Romans from Corinthus.* That this Epistle was written from Corinth is almost universally believed. That *Phebe* was a deaconess of the church at Cenchrea, we have seen in the first verse of this chapter; and that the Epistle might have been sent by her to Rome is possible. This subscription, however, stands on very questionable grounds. It is wanting in almost all the ancient MSS.; and even of those which are more modern, few have it entirely, as in our common editions. The subscriptions to the sacred books are of little or no authority, all having been added in latter times, and frequently by injudicious hands. The word *Amen* was seldom added by the inspired writers, and here it is wanting in almost all the ancient MSS. As this was a word in frequent use in religious services, pious people would naturally employ it in finishing the reading or copying of this Epistle, as they would thereby express their conviction of the truth of its contents, and their desire that the promises contained in it might be fulfilled to them and to the Church at large.

The First Epistle to the

CORINTHIANS

Corinth, to which this and the following Epistle were sent, was one of the most celebrated cities of Greece. It was situated on a gulf of the same name, and was the capital of the Peloponnesus or Achaia, and was united to the continent by an isthmus or neck of land that had the port of Lecheum on the west and that of Cenchrea on the east, by which it commanded the navigation and commerce both of the Ionian and Aegean seas, consequently of Italy on the one hand and of all the Greek islands on the other. In a word, it embraced the commerce of the whole Mediterranean Sea, from the straits of Gibraltar on the west to the port of Alexandria on the east, with the coasts of Egypt, Palestine, Syria, and Asia Minor. It is supposed by some to have been founded 1,504 years before the Christian era. It was at first but a very inconsiderable town; but at last, through its extensive commerce, became the most opulent city of Greece, and the capital of a powerful state. It was destroyed by the Romans under Mummius, about 146 years before Christ, but was afterwards rebuilt by Julius Caesar.

Corinth exceeded all the cities of the world for the splendor and magnificence of its public buildings, such as temples, palaces, theatres, porticos, cenotaphs, baths, and other edifices; all enriched with a beautiful kind of columns, capitals, and bases, from which the Corinthian order in architecture took its rise. The temple of Venus was not only very splendid, but also very rich, and maintained, according to Strabo, not less than 1,000 courtesans, who were the means of bringing an immense concourse of strangers to the place. Thus riches produced luxury, and luxury a total corruption of manners; though arts, sciences, and literature continued to flourish long in it, and a measure of the martial spirit of its ancient inhabitants was kept alive in it by means of those public games which, being celebrated on the isthmus which connects the Peloponnesus to the mainland, were called the Isthmian games, and were exhibited once every five years. It is well-known that the apostle alludes to these games in different parts of his Epistles.

As we have seen that Corinth was well-situated for trade, and consequently very rich, it is no wonder that, in its heathen state, it was exceedingly corrupt and profligate. The inhabitants of it were as lascivious as they were learned. Public prostitution formed a considerable part of their religion; and they were accustomed in their public prayers to request the gods to multiply their prostitutes! And in order to express their gratitude to their deities for the favors they received, they bound themselves, by vows, to increase the number of such women; for commerce with them was esteemed neither sinful nor disgraceful. So notorious was this city for such conduct that the verb to "Corinthize" signified to act the prostitute.

CHAPTER 1

The salutation of Paul and Sosthenes, 1-2. The apostolical benediction, 3. Thanksgiving for the prosperity of the church at Corinth, 4. In what that prosperity consisted, 5-9. The apostle reproves their dissensions, and vindicates himself from being any cause of them, 10-17. States the simple means which God uses to convert sinners and confound the wisdom of the wise, etc., 18-21. Why the Jews and Greeks did not believe, 22. The matter of the apostle's preaching, and the reasons why that preaching was effectual to the salvation of men, 23-29. All should glory in God, because all blessings are dispensed by Him through Christ Jesus, 30-31.

1. *Paul, called to be an apostle.* The word *called* may be here used, as in some other places, for "constituted." As the apostle had many irregularities to reprehend in the Corinthian church, it was necessary that he should be explicit in stating his authority. *Through the will of God.* By a particular appointment from God alone; for, being an extraordinary messenger, he derived no part of his authority from man. *Sosthenes our brother.* Probably the same person mentioned in Acts xviii. 17.

2. *The church of God which is at Corinth.* This church was planted by the apostle himself.

Sanctified in Christ Jesus. "Separated" from the corruptions of their place and age. *Called to be saints.* "Constituted saints," or "invited" to become such; this was the design of the gospel, for Jesus Christ came to save men from their sins. *With all that in every place.* All who profess Christianity, both in Corinth, Ephesus, and other parts of Greece or Asia Minor; and by this we see that the apostle intended that this Epistle should be a general property of the universal Church of Christ, though there are several matters in it that are suited to the state of the Corinthians only.

4. *For the grace . . . which is given you.* Not only their calling to be saints, and to be sanctified in Christ Jesus, but for the various spiritual gifts which they had received, as specified in the succeeding verses.

5. *Ye are enriched—"ye abound." In all utterance.* "In all doctrine"; for so the word should certainly be translated and understood.

6. *As the testimony of Christ.* The testimony of Christ is the gospel which the apostle had

preached, and which had been confirmed by various gifts of the Holy Spirit and miracles wrought by the apostle.

7. *So that ye come behind in no gift.* Every gift and grace of God's Spirit was possessed by the members of that church, some having their gifts after this manner, others after that. *Waiting for the coming of our Lord.* It is difficult to say whether the apostle means the final judgment or our Lord's coming to destroy Jerusalem and make an end of the Jewish polity. (See 1 Thess. iii. 13.)

8. *Who shall . . . confirm you.* As the testimony of Christ was *confirmed* among you, so, in conscientiously believing and obeying, God will *confirm* you through that testimony. (See v. 6.) *In the day of our Lord Jesus.* In the day that He comes to judge the world, according to some; but in the day in which He comes to destroy the Jewish polity, according to others. While God destroys them who are disobedient, He can save you who believe.

9. *God is faithful.* The faithfulness of God is a favorite expression among the ancient Jews, and by it they properly understand the integrity of God in preserving whatever is entrusted to Him. *Unto the fellowship.* Into the communion or participation of Christ, in the graces of His Spirit and the glories of His future kingdom. God will continue to uphold and save you if you entrust your bodies and souls to Him. But can it be said that God will keep what is either not entrusted to Him or, after being entrusted, is taken away?

10. *Now I beseech you, brethren.* The apostle having finished his introduction comes to his second point, exhorting them to abstain from dissensions, that they might be of the same heart and mind, striving together for the hope of the gospel. *By the name of our Lord Jesus.* By His authority, and in His place, and on account of your infinite obligations to His mercy in calling you into such a state of salvation. *That ye all speak the same thing.* The members of the Church of God should labor to be of the *same mind,* and to *speak the same thing,* in order to prevent divisions, which always hinder the work of God. On every essential doctrine of the gospel all genuine Christians agree; why then need religious communion be interrupted?

11. *By them which are of the house of Chloe.* This was doubtless some very religious matron at Corinth whose family were converted to the Lord, some of whom were probably sent to the apostle to inform him of the dissensions which then prevailed in the church at that place. *Contentions.* "Altercations"; produced by the "divisions," mentioned above. When once they had divided, they must necessarily have contended, in order to support their respective parties.

12. *Every one of you saith.* It seems from this expression that the whole church at Corinth was in a state of dissension. The converts at Corinth were partly Jews and partly Greeks. The Gentile part, as Dr. Lightfoot conjectures, might boast the names of Paul and Apollos; the Jewish, those of Cephas and Christ. But these again might be subdivided; some probably considered themselves disciples of Paul, he being the immediate instrument of their conversion, while others might prefer Apollos for his extraordinary eloquence.

13. *Is Christ divided?* Can He be split into different sects and parties? Has He different and opposing systems? Or is the Messiah to appear under different persons? *Was Paul crucified for you?* As the gospel proclaims salvation through the *crucified* only, has Paul poured out his blood as an atonement for you? This is impossible, and therefore your being called by my name is absurd; for His disciples you should be, alone, who has bought you by His blood. *Were ye baptized in the name of Paul?* To be *baptized in,* or "into," the *name* of one implied that the baptized was to be the disciple of him into whose name, religion, etc., he was baptized. As if he said: Did I ever attempt to set up a new religion, one founded on my own authority, and coming from myself? On the contrary, have I not preached Christ crucified for the sin of the world; and called upon all mankind, both Jews and Gentiles, to believe on Him?

14. *I thank God that I baptized none of you.* None of those who now live in Corinth, except *Crispus,* the ruler of the synagogue, Acts xviii. 8. *And Gaius,* the same person probably with whom Paul lodged, Rom. xvi. 23, where see the notes.

15. *Lest any should say.* He was careful not to baptize, lest it should be supposed that he wished to make a party for himself; because superficial observers might imagine that he baptized them into his own name, to be his followers, though he baptized them into the name of Christ only. Instead of *I had baptized* the Codex Alexandrinus, the Codex Ephraim, and several others read "ye were baptized." And if we read "so that," instead of *lest,* the sentence will stand thus: "So that no one can say that ye were baptized into my name." This appears to be the true reading.

16. *The household of Stephanas.* From Rom. xvi. 15 we learn that the family of Stephanas were the first converts in Achaia, probably converted and baptized by the apostle himself. *I know not whether I baptized any other.* I do not recollect that there is any person now residing in Corinth, or Achaia, besides the above-mentioned, whom I have baptized. It is strange that the doubt here expressed by the apostle should be construed so as to affect his inspiration! What, does the inspiration of prophet or apostle necessarily imply that he must understand the geography of the universe, and have an intuitive knowledge of all the inhabitants of the earth, and how often and where they may have changed their residence! Nor was that inspiration ever given so to work on a man's memory that he could not forget any of the acts which he had performed during life. Inspiration was given to the holy men of old that they might be able to write and proclaim the mind of God in the things which concern the salvation of men.

17. *For Christ sent me not to baptize.* It appears sufficiently evident that baptizing was considered to be an inferior office; and though every minister of Christ might administer it, yet apostles had more important work. Preparing these adult heathens for baptism by the continual preaching of the Word was of much greater consequence than baptizing them when thus prepared to receive and profit by it. *Not with wisdom of words.* In several places in the

New Testament the term *logos* is taken not only to express a word, a speech, a saying, etc., but "doctrine," or the matter of teaching. Here, and in 1 Thess. i. 5, and several other places, it seems to signify "reason," or that mode of rhetorical argumentation so highly prized among the Greeks. The apostle was sent not to pursue this mode of conduct, but simply to announce the truth; to proclaim Christ crucified for the sin of the world; and to do this in the plainest and simplest manner possible, lest the numerous conversions which followed might be attributed to the power of the apostle's eloquence, and not to the demonstration of the Spirit of God.

18. *For the preaching of the cross.* "The doctrine of the Cross," or the doctrine that is of or concerning the Cross; that is, the doctrine that proclaims salvation to a lost world through the crucifixion of Christ. *Is to them that perish foolishness.* There are, properly speaking, but two classes of men known where the gospel is preached: the unbelievers and gainsayers, who are perishing; and the obedient believers, who are in a state of salvation.

19. *For it is written.* The place referred to is Isa. xxix. 14.

20. *Where is the wise . . . the scribe . . . the disputer of this world?* These words most manifestly refer to the Jews, as the places (Isa. xxix. 14; xxxiii. 18; and xliv. 25) to which he refers cannot be understood of any but the Jews. The *wise* man of the apostle is the *chakam* of the prophet, whose office it was to teach others. The *scribe* of the apostle is the *sopher* of the prophet; this signifies any man of learning, as distinguished from the common people, especially any master of the traditions. The *disputer* answers to the *derosh*, or *darshan*, the "propounder of questions"; the seeker of allegorical, mystical, and cabalistical senses from the Holy Scriptures. Now as all these are characters well-known among the Jews, and as the words *of this world* are a simple translation of *olam hazzeh*, which is repeatedly used to designate the Jewish republic, there is no doubt that the apostle has the Jews immediately in view.

21. *For after that in the wisdom of God.* The plain meaning of this verse is that the wise men of the world, especially the Greek philosophers, who possessed every advantage that human nature could have independently of a divine revelation, and who had cultivated their minds to the uttermost, could never, by their learning, wisdom, and industry, find out God; nor had the most refined philosophers among them just and correct views of the divine nature, nor of that in which human happiness consists. *By the foolishness of preaching.* By the preaching of Christ crucified, which the Gentiles termed *foolishness*, in opposition to their own doctrines, which they termed *wisdom*. It was not by the foolishness of preaching, literally, nor by the foolish preaching, that God saved the world; but by that gospel which they called *foolishness;* which was, in fact, *the wisdom of God*, and also the power of God to the salvation of them that believed.

22. *For the Jews require a sign.* Instead of *a sign*, several MSS., with many of the fathers, have "signs"; which reading, as undoubtedly genuine, Griesbach has admitted into the text. *And the Greeks seek after wisdom.* Such wisdom, or philosophy, as they found in the writings of Cicero, Seneca, Plato, etc., which was called philosophy, and which came recommended to them in all the beauties and graces of the Latin and Greek languages.

23. *But we.* Apostles, differing widely from these Gentile philosophers. *Preach Christ crucified.* Call on men, both Jews and Gentiles, to believe in Christ, as having purchased their salvation by shedding His blood for them. *Unto the Jews a stumblingblock.* Because Jesus came meek, lowly, and impoverished; not seeking worldly glory, nor affecting worldly pomp; whereas they expected the Messiah to come as a mighty prince and conqueror. Because Christ did not come so, they were offended at Him. *Unto the Greeks foolishness.* Because they could not believe that proclaiming supreme happiness through a man that was crucified at Judea as a malefactor could ever comport with reason and common sense; for both the matter and manner of the preaching were opposite to every notion they had formed of what was dignified and philosophic.

24. *But unto them which are called.* Those, of both Jews and Greeks, who were by the preaching of the gospel *called* or "invited" to the marriage feast, and have accordingly believed in Christ Jesus. The *called*, or "invited," is a title of genuine Christians, and is frequently used in the New Testament. "Saints" is used in the same sense.

25. *The foolishness of God is wiser.* The meaning of these strong expressions is that the things of God's appointment which seem to men *foolishness* are infinitely beyond the highest degree of human wisdom; and those works of God which appear to superficial observers weak and contemptible surpass all the efforts of human power. The means which God has appointed for the salvation of men are so wisely imagined and so energetically powerful that all who properly use them shall be infallibly brought to the end—final blessedness—which He has promised to them who believe and obey.

26. *Ye see your calling.* The state of grace and blessedness to which you are invited. I think *blepo* should be read in the imperative: "Take heed to, or consider, your calling, brethren; that not many of you are wise after the flesh, not many mighty, not many noble." *Men* is not in the original, and Paul seems to allude to the Corinthian believers in particular. This seems to have been said in opposition to the high and worldly notions of the Jews, who assert that the Divine Spirit never rests upon any man unless he be wise, powerful, and rich. Now this Divine Spirit did rest upon the Christians at Corinth, and yet these were, in the sense of the world, neither wise, rich, nor noble. We spoil, if not corrupt, the apostle's meaning by adding *are called*, as if God did not send His gospel to the wise, the powerful, and the noble, or did not will their salvation. The truth is, the gospel has an equal call to all classes of men; but the *wise*, the *mighty*, and the *noble* are too busy or too sensual to pay any attention to an invitation so spiritual and so divine; and therefore there are few of these in the Church of Christ in general.

27. *But God hath chosen the foolish things.* God has chosen by means of men who are esteemed rude and illiterate to confound the great-

est of the Greek philosophers and overturn their systems; and by means of men *weak*, without secular power or authority, to confound the scribes and Pharisees; and in spite of the exertions of the Jewish sanhedrin, to spread the doctrine of Christ crucified all over the land of Judea, and by such instruments as these to convert thousands of souls to the faith of the gospel.

28. *And base things . . . and things which are despised.* It is very likely that the apostle refers here to the Gentiles and to the Gentile converts, who were considered base and despicable in the eyes of the Jews, who counted them no better than dogs, and who are repeatedly called the *things that are not.* By these very people, converted to Christianity, God has brought *to nought* all the Jewish pretensions.

29. *That no flesh should glory.* God does His mighty works in such a way as proves that, though He may condescend to employ men as instruments, yet they have no part either in the contrivance or energy by which such works are performed.

30. *But of him are ye in Christ Jesus.* Even the good which you possess is granted by God, for it is by and through Him that, Christ Jesus comes, and all the blessings of the gospel dispensation. *And righteousness.* "Justification," as procuring for us that remission of sins which the law could not give, Gal. ii. 21; iii. 21. *And sanctification.* As procuring for and working in us not only an external and relative holiness, as was that of the Jews, but true and eternal holiness, Eph. iv. 24, wrought in us by the Holy Spirit.

31. *According as it is written.* In Jer. ix. 23-24: "Thus saith the Lord, Let not the wise man glory in his wisdom, neither let the mighty man glory in his might, let not the rich man glory in his riches: but let him that glorieth glory in this, that he understandeth and knoweth me, that I am the Lord which exercise lovingkindness, judgment, and righteousness, in the earth." So then, as all good is of and from God, let him that has either wisdom, strength, riches, pardon, holiness, or any other blessing, whether temporal or spiritual, acknowledge that he was nothing but what he has received.

CHAPTER 2

The apostle makes an apology for his manner of preaching, 1. And gives the reason why he adopted that manner, 2-5. He shows that this preaching, notwithstanding it was not with excellence of human speech or wisdom, yet was the mysterious wisdom of God, which the princes of this world did not know, and which the Spirit of God alone could reveal, 6-10. It is the Spirit of God only that can reveal the things of God, 11. The apostles of Christ know the things of God by the Spirit of God, and teach them, not in the words of man's wisdom, but in the words of that Spirit, 12-13. The natural man cannot discern the things of the Spirit, 14. But the spiritual man can discern and teach them, because he has the mind of Christ, 15-16.

1. *When I came to you.* Acting suitably to my mission, which was to preach the gospel, but not with human eloquence, chap. i. 17. I declared to you the *testimony*, the gospel, *of God, not with excellency of speech*, not with arts of rhetoric, used by your own philosophers, where the excellence of the speech recommends the matter, and compensates for the want of solidity and truth. On the contrary, the testimony concerning Christ and His salvation is so supremely excellent as to dignify any kind of language by which it may be conveyed.

2. *I determined not to know any thing among you.* Satisfied that the gospel of God could alone make you wise unto salvation, I determined to cultivate no other knowledge, and to teach nothing but *Jesus Christ, and him crucified*, as the foundation of all true wisdom, piety, and happiness.

3. *I was with you in weakness.* It is very likely that Paul had not only something in his speech very unfavorable to a ready and powerful elocution, but also some infirmity of body that was still more disadvantageous to him. A fine appearance and a fine voice cover many weaknesses and defects, and strongly and forcibly recommend what is spoken, though not remarkable for depth of thought or solidity of reasoning. Many popular orators have little besides their persons and their voice to recommend them. *In fear, and in much trembling.* An eminent divine has said that it requires three things to make a good preacher: study, temptation, and prayer. The latter, no man that lives near to God can neglect; the former, no man who endeavors rightly to divide "the word of truth" will neglect; and with the second every man will be more or less exercised whose whole aim is to save souls. Those of a different cast the devil permits to pass quietly on in their own indolent and prayerless way.

4. *And my speech.* My "doctrine"; the matter of my preaching. *And my preaching.* "My proclamation." *Was not with enticing words of man's wisdom.* "With persuasive doctrines of human wisdom"; in every case I left man out, that God might become the more evident. I used none of the means of which great orators avail themselves in order to become popular, and thereby to gain fame. *But in demonstration of the Spirit.* In the "manifestation." The doctrine that he preached was revealed by the Spirit. That it was a revelation of the Spirit, the holiness, purity, and usefulness of the doctrine rendered manifest; and the overthrow of idolatry and the conversion of souls, by the power and energy of the preaching, were the demonstration that all was divine. The greater part of the best MSS., versions, and fathers leave out the adjective *man's* before *wisdom.*

5. *That your faith should not stand.* That the illumination of your souls and your conversion to God might appear to have nothing human in it. Your belief, therefore, of the truths which have been proposed to you is founded, not in human wisdom, but in divine power.

6. *We speak wisdom among them that are perfect.* By *among them that are perfect* we are to understand Christians of the highest knowledge and attainments, those who were fully instructed in the knowledge of God through Christ Jesus. Nothing, in the judgment of Paul, deserved the name of *wisdom* but this. And though he apologizes for his not coming to them with excellency of speech or wisdom, yet he means what was reputed wisdom among the Greeks, and which, in the sight of God, was mere folly when compared with that wisdom that came from above.

7. *The wisdom of God in a mystery.* The gospel of Jesus Christ, which had been comparatively *hidden* from the foundation of the

world (the settling of the Jewish economy, as this phrase often means), though appointed from the beginning to be revealed in the fullness of time.

8. *Which none of the princes of this world knew.* Here it is evident that *this world* refers to the Jewish state, and to the degree of knowledge in that state, and the rulers, the priests, rabbins, etc., who were principally concerned in the crucifixion of our Lord. *The Lord of glory.* Or the "glorious Lord," infinitely transcending all the rulers of the universe, whose is eternal glory.

9. *But, as it is written.* The quotation is taken from Isa. lxiv. 4. The sense is continued here from verse the seventh, and "we speak" is understood—We do not speak or preach the wisdom of this world; but that mysterious wisdom of God, of which the prophet said: *Eye hath not seen, nor ear heard, neither have entered into the heart of man, the things which God hath prepared for them that love him.* These words have been applied to the state of glory in a future world; but they certainly belong to the present state, and express merely the wondrous light, life, and liberty which the gospel communicates to them that believe in the Lord Jesus Christ in that way which the gospel itself requires.

10. *But God hath revealed them unto us.* A manifest proof that the apostle speaks here of the glories of the gospel, and not of the glories of the future world. *Yea, the deep things of God.* It is only the Spirit of God who can reveal the counsels of God. These are the purposes which have existed in His infinite wisdom and goodness from eternity; and particularly what refers to creation, providence, redemption, and eternal glory, as far as men and angels are concerned in these purposes. The apostles were so fully convinced that the scheme of redemption proclaimed by the gospel was divine that they boldly asserted that these things infinitely surpassed the wisdom and comprehension of man. The apostles were as truly conscious of their own inspiration as they were that they had consciousness at all; and what they spoke, they spoke as they were moved by the Holy Ghost.

12. *Now we have received, not the spirit of the world.* We who are the genuine apostles of Christ have received this Spirit of God, by which we know the deep things of God; and through the teaching of that Spirit we preach Christ crucified. We have not therefore *received . . . the spirit of the world*—of the Jewish teachers, who are all looking for a worldly kingdom and a worldly Messiah, and interpret all the scriptures of the Old Testament which relate to Him in a carnal and worldly sense. *That we might know the things.* It is evident that, as the apostle means by "princes of the world" the rulers of the Jews, vv. 6-8, so by *spirit of the world* he here means Jewish wisdom, or their carnal mode of interpreting the sacred oracles and their carnal expectation of a worldly kingdom under the Messiah.

13. *Which things also we speak.* We dare no more use the language of the Jews and the Gentiles in speaking of those glorious things than we can indulge their spirit. The Greek orators affected a high and florid language, full of tropes and figures, which dazzled more than

it enlightened. The rabbins affected obscurity, and were studious to find out cabalistical meanings, which had no tendency to make the people wise unto salvation. The apostles could not follow any of these; they spoke the things of God in the words of God. *Comparing spiritual things with spiritual.* This is commonly understood to mean comparing the spiritual things under the Old Testament with the spiritual things under the New, but this does not appear to be the apostle's meaning. The word which we translate *comparing* rather signifies "conferring, discussing, or explaining"; and the word *pneumatikois* should be rendered "to spiritual men," and not be referred to *spiritual things.* The passage therefore should be thus translated: "Explaining spiritual things to spiritual persons." And this sense the following verse absolutely requires.

14. *But the natural man.* The animal man—the man who is in a mere state of nature, and lives under the influence of his animal passions. The person in question is not only one who either has had no spiritual teaching or has not profited by it, but one who lives for the present world, having no respect to spiritual or eternal things. This "animal man" is opposed to the "spiritual man"; and as this latter is one who is under the influence of the Spirit of God, so the former is one who is without that influence. *But the natural man*—The apostle appears to give this as a reason why he explained those deep spiritual things to spiritual men: because the "animal man"; the man who is in a state of nature, without the regenerating grace of the Spirit of God, *receiveth not the things of the Spirit*—neither apprehends nor comprehends them. He has no relish for them; he considers it the highest wisdom to live for this world.

15. *But he that is spiritual judgeth all things.* He who has the mind of Christ discerns and judges of all things spiritual, yet he himself is not discerned by the mere animal man. Some suppose that the word should be understood thus: "He examines, scrutinizes, convinces, reproves," which it appears to mean in chap. xiv. 24; and they read the verse thus: The *spiritual* man, the well-taught Christian, convinces, i.e., can easily convict, all men, every animal man, of error and vice; yet he himself is not convicted of no man. His mind is enlightened and his life is holy, and therefore the animal man cannot convict him of sin. This is a good sense, but the first appears the most natural.

16. *For who hath known the mind of the Lord?* Who that is still an animal man can know the mind of God? so as to *instruct him,* viz., the spiritual man, the same that is spoken of in v. 15. But the words may be better understood thus: How can the animal man know the mind of the Lord? And how can any man communicate that knowledge which he has never acquired, and which is foolishness to him, because it is spiritual and he is animal? This quotation is made from Isa. xl. 13. *But we have the mind of Christ.* He has endowed us with the same disposition, being born again by His Spirit; therefore we are capable of knowing His mind and receiving the teachings of His Spirit. The words *that he may instruct him* should be translated "that he may teach it"; that is, the mind of God—not instruct God, but teach His mind to others.

CHAPTER 3

Because of the carnal, divided state of the people at Corinth, the apostle was obliged to treat them as children in the knowledge of sacred things, 1-3. Some were for setting up Paul, others Apollos, as their sole teachers, 4. The apostle shows that himself and fellow apostles were only instruments which God used to bring them to the knowledge of the truth; and even their sowing and watering the seed was of no use unless God gave the increase, 5-8. The Church represented as God's husbandry, and as God's building, the Foundation of which is Christ Jesus, 9-11. Ministers must beware how and what they build on this foundation, 12-15. The Church of God is His temple, and he that defiles it shall be destroyed, 16-17. No man should depend on his own wisdom; for the wisdom of the world is foolishness with God, 18-20. None should glory in man as his teacher; God gives His followers every good, for both time and eternity, 21-23.

1. *I, brethren, could not speak unto you as unto spiritual.* This is a continuation of the preceding discourse. *But as unto carnal.* Persons under the influence of fleshly appetites, coveting and living for the things of this life. *Babes in Christ.* Just beginning to acquire some notion of the Christian religion, but as yet very incapable of judging what is most suitable to yourselves, and consequently utterly unqualified to discern between one teacher and another; so that your making the distinctions which you do make, so far from being a proof of mature judgment, is on the contrary a proof that you have no right judgment at all; and this springs from your want of knowledge in divine things.

2. *I have fed you with milk.* I have instructed you in the elements of Christianity—in its simplest and easiest truths; because from the low state of your minds in religious knowledge, you were incapable of comprehending the higher truths of the gospel; and in this state you will still continue. The apostle thus exposes to them the absurdity of their conduct in pretending to judge between preacher and preacher while they had but a very partial acquaintance even with the first principles of Christianity.

3. *There is among you envying, and strife, and divisions.* There are three things here worthy of note: these people were wrong in *thought, word,* and *deed. Envying* refers to the state of their souls; they had inward grudgings and disaffection towards each other. *Strife* or "contention" refers to their words; they were continually disputing and contending whose party was the best, each endeavoring to prove that he and his party were alone in the right. *Divisions* refers to their conduct; as they could not agree, they contended till they separated from each other, and thus rent the Church of Christ. Thus the *envying* and grudging led to *strife* and evil speaking, and this led to *divisions* and fixed parties. In this state well might the apostle say, *Are ye not carnal, and walk as men?* You act just as the people of the world, and have no more of the spirit of religion than they.

4. *For while one saith, I am of Paul.* It was notorious that both Paul and Apollos held the same creed; between them there was not the slightest difference. When, therefore, the dissentients began to prefer the one to the other, it was the fullest proof of their carnality, because in the doctrines of these apostles there was no difference, so that what the people were captivated by must be something in their outward manner, Apollos being probably more eloquent than Paul. Their preferring one to another on such an account proved that they were *carnal*

—led by their senses and mere outward appearances, without being under the guidance of either reason or grace.

5. *Ministers by whom ye believed.* The different apostles who have preached unto you the word of life are the means which God has used to bring you to the knowledge of Christ. No one of those has either preached or recommended himself; they all preach and recommend Christ Jesus the Lord.

6. *I have planted.* I first sowed the seed of the gospel at Corinth, and in the region of Achaia. *Apollos watered.* Apollos came after me, and by his preachings and exhortations watered the seed which I had sowed. *But God gave the increase.* The seed has taken root, has sprung up, and borne much fruit; but this was by the especial blessing of God.

7. *So then neither is he that planteth any thing.* God alone should have all the glory, as the seed is His, the ground is His, the laborers are His, and the produce all comes from himself.

8. *He that planteth and he that watereth are one.* Both Paul and Apollos have received the same doctrine, preach the same doctrine, and labor to promote the glory of God in the salvation of your souls. Why should you be divided with respect to Paul and Apollos while these apostles are intimately one in spirit, design, and operation? *According to his own labour.* God does not reward His servants according to the success of their labor, because that depends on himself; but He rewards them according to the quantum of faithful labor which they bestow on His work.

9. *For we are labourers together with God.* It would perhaps be more correct to translate, "We are fellow laborers of God"; i.e., we labor together in the work of God. Far from being divided among ourselves, we jointly labor, as oxen in the same yoke, to promote the honor of our Master. *Ye are God's husbandry, ye are God's building.* The word which we translate *husbandry* signifies properly an "arable field"; so Prov. xxiv. 30: "I went by the field of the slothful"; and chap. xxxi. 16: The wise woman "considereth a field, and buyeth it." It would be more literal to translate it, "You are God's farm." *Ye are God's building.* You are not only the field which God cultivates, but you are the house which God builds, and in which He intends to dwell. As no man in viewing a fine building extols the quarryman that dug up the stones, the hewer that cut and squared them, the mason that placed them in the wall, the woodman that hewed down the timber, the carpenter that squared and jointed it, but the architect who planned it, and under whose direction the whole work was accomplished; so no man should consider Paul or Apollos or Cephas anything but as persons employed by the great Architect to form a building which is to become a habitation of himself through the Spirit, and the design of which is entirely His own.

10. *As a wise masterbuilder.* The design or plan of the building is from God; all things must be done according to the pattern which He has exhibited. But the execution of this plan was entrusted chiefly to Paul; he was the wise or "experienced architect" which God used in order to lay the foundation; to ascertain the essential

and immutable doctrines of the gospel—those alone which came from God, and which alone He would bless to the salvation of mankind. *Let every man take heed how he buildeth thereupon.* Let him take care that the doctrines which he preaches be answerable to those which I have preached; let him also take heed that he enjoin no other practice than that which is suitable to the doctrine, and in every sense accords with it.

11. *Other foundation can no man lay.* I do not speak particularly concerning the *foundation* of this spiritual building; it can have no other foundation than Jesus Christ. There cannot be two opinions on this subject among the true apostles of our Lord. The only fear is lest an improper use should be made of this heavenly doctrine, lest a bad superstructure should be raised on this Foundation.

12. *If any man build . . . gold, silver.* By *gold, silver,* and *precious stones* the apostle certainly means pure and wholesome doctrines; by *wood, hay,* and *stubble,* false doctrines, such as at that time prevailed in the Corinthian church.

13. *The day shall declare it, because it shall be revealed by fire.* There is much difference of opinion relative to the meaning of the terms in this and the following two verses. That the apostle refers to the approaching destruction of Jerusalem I think very probable; and when this is considered, all the terms and metaphors will appear clear and consistent. The *day* is the time of punishment coming on this disobedient and rebellious people. And this day being *revealed by fire* points out the extreme rigor and totally destructive nature of that judgment. *And the fire shall try every man's work.* If the apostle refers to the Judaising teachers and their insinuations that the law, especially circumcision, was of eternal obligation, then the day of fire—the time of vengeance—which was at hand, would sufficiently disprove such assertions as, in the judgment of God, the whole Temple service should be destroyed; and the people, who fondly presumed on their permanence and stability, should be dispossessed of their land and scattered over the face of the whole earth.

14. *If any man's work abide.* Perhaps there is here an allusion to the purifying of different sorts of vessels under the law. All that could stand the fire were to be purified by the fire; and those which could not resist the action of the fire were to be purified by water, Num. xxxi. 23. The "gold," "silver," and "precious stones" could stand the fire; but the "wood," "hay," and "stubble" must be necessarily consumed. So, in that great and terrible day of the Lord, all false doctrine, as well as the system that was to pass away, should be made sufficiently manifest; and God would then show that the gospel, and that alone, was that system of doctrine which He should bless and protect, and none other.

15. *If any man's work shall be burned, he shall suffer loss.* If he have preached the necessity of incorporating the law with the gospel, or proclaimed as a doctrine of God anything which did not proceed from heaven, *he shall suffer loss*—all his time and labor will be found to be uselessly employed and spent. *But he himself shall be saved.* If he have sincerely and conscientiously believed what he preached, and

yet preached what was wrong, not through malice or opposition to the gospel, but through mere ignorance, *he shall be saved.* God in His mercy will pass by his errors, and he shall not suffer punishment because he was mistaken. Yet, as in most erroneous teachings there is generally a portion of willful and obstinate ignorance, the salvation of such erroneous teachers is very rare; and is expressed here, *yet so as by fire,* i.e., with great difficulty. The apostle obviously refers to the case of a man who, having builded a house and begun to dwell in it, the house happens to be set on fire, and he has warning of it just in time to escape with his life, losing at the same time his house, his goods, his labor, and almost his own life. So he who, while he holds the doctrine of Christ crucified as the only foundation on which a soul can rest its hopes of salvation, builds at the same time on that foundation Antinomianism or any other erroneous or destructive doctrine, he shall lose all his labor, his own soul scarcely escape everlasting perdition; nor even this unless sheer ignorance and inveterate prejudice, connected with much sincerity, be found in his case.

16. *Ye are the temple of God.* The apostle resumes here what he had asserted in v. 9: "Ye are God's building." As the whole congregation of Israel were formerly considered as the temple and habitation of God, because God dwelt among them, so here the whole church of Corinth is called *the temple of God,* because all genuine believers have the *Spirit* of God to dwell in them; and Christ has promised to be always in the midst even of two or three who are gathered together in His name. Therefore where God is, there is His temple.

17. *If any man defile the temple.* "If any man destroy the temple of God, him will God destroy." The verb is the same in both clauses. If any man injure, corrupt, or destroy the church of God by false doctrine, God will destroy him—will take away his part out of the book of life.

18. *If any man among you seemeth to be wise.* "If any pretend or affect to be wise." This seems to refer to some individual in the church of Corinth who had been very troublesome to its peace and unity. *Let him become a fool.* Let him divest himself of his worldly wisdom, and be contented to be called a *fool,* and esteemed one, that he may become wise unto salvation, by renouncing his own wisdom and seeking that which comes from God. But probably the apostle refers to him who, pretending to great wisdom and information, taught doctrines contrary to the gospel.

19. *The wisdom of this world,* whether it be the pretended deep and occult wisdom of the rabbins or the wire-drawn speculations of the Grecian philosophers, *is foolishness with God;* for as folly consists in spending time, strength, and pains to no purpose, so these may be fitly termed fools who acquire no saving knowledge by their speculations. *He taketh the wise in their own craftiness.* This is a quotation from Job. v. 13, and powerfully shows what the wisdom of this world is. It is a sort of craft, a subtle trade, which they carry on to wrong others and benefit themselves; and they have generally too much cunning to be caught by men, but God often overthrows them with their own devisings.

20. *The Lord knoweth the thoughts of the wise.* They are always full of schemes and plans for earthly good; and God knows that all this is *vain,* "empty," and unsatisfactory, and will stand them in no stead when He comes to take away their souls. This is a quotation from Ps. xciv. 11. What is here said of the vanity of human knowledge is true of every kind of wisdom that leads not immediately to God himself.

22. *Whether Paul, or Apollos.* As if he had said: God designs to help you by all things and persons; every teacher sent from Him will become a blessing to you if you abide faithful to your calling. *Or the world.* The word *cosmos* here means rather the inhabitants of the world than what we commonly understand by the world itself; and this is its meaning in John iii. 16-17; vi. 33; xiv. 31; xvii. 21. See particularly John xii. 19. The apostle's meaning evidently is: Not only Paul, Apollos, and Cephas are yours—appointed for and employed in your service—but every person besides with whom you may have any intercourse or connection, whether Jew or Greek, whether enemy or friend. *Or life,* with all its trials and advantages; every hour of it, every tribulation in it, the whole course of it, as the grand state of your probation, is a general blessing to you. *Or death.* That solemn hour, so dreadful to the wicked, and so hateful to those who live without God—that is yours. *Death* is your servant. He comes a special messenger from God for you; he comes to undo a knot that now connects body and soul, which it would be unlawful for yourselves to untie. He comes to take your souls to glory; and he cannot come before his due time to those who are waiting for the salvation of God. *Or things present.* Every occurrence in providence in the present life, for God rules in providence as well as in grace. *Or things to come.* The whole order and economy of the eternal world; all in heaven and all in earth are even now working together for your good.

23. *And ye are Christ's.* "You are of Christ"; all the light and life which you enjoy you have received through and from Him, and He has bought you with His blood. *And Christ is God's.* "And Christ is of God." Christ, the Messiah, is the Gift of God's eternal love and mercy to mankind.

CHAPTER 4

Ministers should be esteemed by their flocks as the stewards of God, whose duty and interest it is to be faithful, 1-2. Precipitate and premature judgments condemned, 3-5. The apostle's caution to give the Corinthians no offense, 6. We have no good but what we receive from God, 7. The worldly-mindedness of the Corinthians, 8. The enumeration of the hardships, trials, and sufferings of the apostles, 9-13. For what purpose Paul mentions these things, 14-16. He promises to send Timothy to them, 17. And to come himself shortly, to examine and correct the abuses that had crept in among them, 18-21.

1. *Let a man so account of us.* This is a continuation of the subject in the preceding chapter, and should not have been divided from it. The fourth chapter would have begun better at v. 6, and the third should have ended with the fifth verse. *As of the ministers of Christ.* The word means an "under-rower," or one who, in the trireme, quadrireme, or quinquereme galleys, rowed in one of the undermost benches; but it means also, as used by the Greek writers, any inferior officer or assistant. By the term

here the apostle shows the Corinthians that, far from being heads and chiefs, he and his fellow apostles considered themselves only as inferior officers, employed under Christ; from whom alone they received their appointment, their work, and their recompense. *Stewards of the mysteries of God.* "Economists" of the divine mysteries. The steward was the master's deputy in regulating the concerns of the family, providing food for the household, seeing it served out at the proper times and seasons, and in proper quantities. He received all the cash, expended what was necessary for the support of the family, and kept exact accounts, which he was obliged at certain times to lay before the master. The *mysteries,* the doctrines of God, relative to the salvation of the world by the passion and death of Christ; and the inspiration, illumination, and purification of the soul by the Spirit of Christ, constituted a principal part of the divine treasure intrusted to the hands of the stewards by their heavenly Master.

3. *It is a very small thing that I should be judged of you.* Those who preferred Apollos or Cephas before Paul would of course give their reasons for this preference; and these might, in many instances, be very unfavorable to his character as a man, a Christian, or an apostle. Of this he was regardless, as he sought not his own glory, but the glory of God in the salvation of their souls. *Or of man's judgment.* Literally, "or of man's day": any day set apart by a judge or magistrate to try a man on. *I judge not mine own self.* I leave myself entirely to God, whose I am, and whom I serve.

4. *For I know nothing by myself.* I am not conscious that I am guilty of any evil, or have neglected to fulfill faithfully the duty of a steward of Jesus Christ. The import of the verb is "to be conscious of guilt." *Yet am I not hereby justified.* I do not pretend to say that though I am not conscious of any offense towards God I must therefore be pronounced innocent. No. I leave those things to God; He shall pronounce in my favor, not I myself. By these words the apostle, in a very gentle yet effectual manner, censures those rash and precipitate judgments which the Corinthians were in the habit of pronouncing on both men and things—a conduct than which nothing is more reprehensible and dangerous.

5. *Judge nothing before the time.* God, the righteous Judge, will determine everything shortly; it is His province alone to search the heart, and *bring to light the hidden things of darkness.* If you are so pure and upright in your conduct, if what you have been doing in these divisions, etc., is right in His sight, then shall you *have praise* for the same; if otherwise, yourselves are most concerned. Some refer the praise to Paul and his companions: "Then shall every one of us apostles have praise of God."

6. *These things.* Which I have written, chap. iii. 5, etc. *I have in a figure transferred to myself and to Apollos.* I have written as if myself and Apollos were the authors of the sects which now prevail among you; although others, without either our consent or knowledge, have proclaimed us heads of parties.

7. *For who maketh thee to differ?* It is likely that the apostle is here addressing himself to some one of those *puffed up* teachers, who was

glorying in his gifts, and in the knowledge he had of the gospel, etc. As if he had said: If you have all that knowledge which you profess to have, did you not receive it from myself or some other of my fellow helpers who first preached the gospel at Corinth? Have you a particle of light that you have not received from our preaching? Why then do you glory, boast, and exult, as if God had first spoken by you, and not by us?

8. *Now we* (Corinthians) *are full* of secular wisdom; *now ye are rich,* in both wealth and spiritual gifts (chap. xiv. 26). *Ye have reigned as kings,* flourishing in the enjoyment of these things, in all tranquillity and honor, *without* any want of *us; and I would to God ye did reign,* in deed, and not in conceit only, *that we also,* poor, persecuted, and despised apostles, *might reign with you.*—Whitby. Though this paraphrase appears natural, yet I am of opinion that the apostle here intends a strong irony; and one which, when taken in conjunction with what he had said before, must have stung them to the heart. It is not an unusual thing for many people to forget, if not despise, the men by whom they were brought to the knowledge of the truth; and take up with others to whom, in the things of God, they owe nothing.

9. *God hath set forth us the apostles last.* Seneca speaks thus, Epist. vii: "In the morning men are exposed to lions and bears; at mid-day to their spectators; those that kill are exposed to one another; the victor is detained for another slaughter; the conclusion of the fight is death. The former fighting compared to this was mercy; now it is mere butchery: they have nothing to cover them; their whole body is exposed to every blow, and every stroke produces a wound." *We are made a spectacle.* We are exhibited on the "theatre" to the world; we are lawful booty to all mankind, and particularly to the men of the world, who have their portion in this life. *Angels* are astonished at our treatment, and so are the more considerate part of *men.* Who at that time would have coveted the apostolate?

10. *We are fools for Christ's sake.* Here he still carries on the allusion to the public spectacles among the Romans, where they were accustomed to hiss, hoot, mock, and variously insult the poor victims. To this Philo alludes, speaking of the treatment which the Jews received at Rome: "For, as if exhibited upon a theatre, we are hissed, most outrageously hooted, and insulted beyond all bounds." *Ye are wise in Christ.* Surely all these expressions are meant ironically. The apostles were neither *fools,* nor *weak,* nor contemptible; nor were the *Corinthians,* morally speaking, *wise,* and *strong,* and *honourable.* Change the persons, and then the epithets will perfectly apply.

11. *We both hunger, and thirst.* Who would then have been an apostle of Christ, even with all its spiritual honors and glories, who had not a soul filled with love to both God and man, and the fullest conviction of the reality of the doctrine he preached, and of that spiritual world in which alone he could expect rest? *Have no certain dwellingplace.* We are mere itinerant preachers, and when we set out in the morning know not where or whether we shall or not get a night's lodging.

12. *Working with our own hands.* They were obliged to labor in order to supply themselves with the necessaries of life while preaching the gospel to others. *Being reviled, we bless.* What a most amiable picture does this exhibit of the power of the grace of Christ! Man is naturally a proud creature, and his pride prompts him always to avenge himself in whatever manner he can, and repay insult with insult. It is only the grace of Christ that can make a man patient in bearing injuries, and render blessing for cursing, beneficence for malevolence. Blaspheming against men is anything by which they are injured in their persons, characters, or property.

13. *We are made as the filth of the world, and are the offscouring of all things.* The Greek word which we render *filth* is a "purgation, or lustrative sacrifice"; that which we translate *offscouring* is "a redemption sacrifice." To understand the full force of these words as applied by the apostle in this place we must observe that he alludes to certain customs among the heathens, who, in the time of some public calamity, chose out some unhappy men of the most abject and despicable character to be a public *expiation* for them. These they maintained a whole year at the public expense; and then they led them out, crowned with flowers, as was customary in sacrifices; and, having heaped all the curses of the country upon their heads, and whipped them seven times, they burned them alive, and afterwards their ashes were thrown into the sea, while the people said these words: "Be thou our propitiation." The apostle therefore means that he and his fellows were treated like those wretched beings who were judged to be fit for nothing but to be expiatory victims to the infernal gods, for the safety and redemption of others. Our words *filth* and *offscouring* convey no legitimate sense of the original.

14. *I write not these things to shame you.* It is not by way of finding fault with you for not providing me with the necessaries of life that I write thus; but I do it to warn you to act differently for the time to come; and be not so ready to be drawn aside by every pretender to apostleship, to the neglect of those to whom, under God, you owe your salvation.

15. *For though ye have ten thousand instructors.* "Myriads of leaders," that is, an indefinite multitude; for so the word is often used. The *paidagogos,* from which we have our word "pedagogue," which we improperly apply to a "schoolmaster," was, among the Greeks, the person or servant who attended a child, had the general care of him, and who led him to school for the purpose of being instructed by the teacher. It seems there were many at Corinth who offered their services to instruct this people, and who were not well-affected towards the apostle. *Not many fathers.* Many offer to instruct you who have no parental feeling for you; and how can they? You are not their spiritual children; you stand in this relation to me alone. *For in Christ Jesus*—by the power and unction of His Spirit—*I have begotten you*—I was the means of bringing you into a state of salvation, so that you have been born again. You are my children alone in the gospel.

16. *Wherefore, I beseech you, be ye followers of me.* It should rather be translated, "Be ye imitators of me"; *mimetai,* from which we have

our word "mimic," which, though now used only in a bad or ludicrous sense, simply signifies an imitator of another person, whether in speech, manner, habit, or otherwise. As children should imitate their parents in preference to all others, he calls on them to imitate him, as he claims them for his children.

17. *For this cause.* That you imitate me, and know in what this consists. *I sent unto you Timotheus.* The same person to whom he wrote the two Epistles that are still extant under his name, and whom he calls here his *beloved son,* one of his most intimate disciples, and whom he had been the means of bringing to God through Christ. *My ways which be in Christ.* This person will also inform you of the manner in which I regulate all the churches, and show to you that what I require of you is no other than what I require of all the churches of Christ which I have formed, as I follow the same plan of discipline in every place.

18. *Some are puffed up.* Some of your teachers act with great haughtiness, imagining themselves to be safe, because they suppose that I shall not revisit Corinth.

19. *But I will come to you shortly.* God being my Helper, I fully purpose to visit you; and then I shall put those proud men to the proof, not of their *speech*—eloquence, or pretensions to great knowledge and influence—but of their *power*—the authority they profess to have from God, and the evidences of that authority in the works they have performed.

20. *For the kingdom of God.* The religion of the Lord Jesus is *not in word*—in human eloquence, excellence of speech, or even in doctrines; *but in power,* in the mighty energy of the Holy Spirit, enlightening, quickening, converting, and sanctifying believers.

21. *Shall I come unto you with a rod, or in love?* Here he alludes to the case of the teacher and father, mentioned in v. 15. Shall I come to you with the authority of a teacher, and use the *rod* of discipline? or shall I come in the tenderness of a father, and entreat you to do what I have authority to enforce? Among the Jews, those who did not amend, after being faithfully admonished, were whipped, either publicly or privately, in the synagogue.

CHAPTER 5

Account of the incestuous person, or of him who had married his father's wife, 1. The apostle reproves the Corinthians for their carelessness in this matter, and orders them to excommunicate the transgressor, 2-5. They are reprehended for their glorying, while such scandals are among them, 6. They must purge out the old leaven, that they may properly celebrate the Christian Passover, 7-9. They must not associate with any who professing the Christian religion, are guilty of any scandalous vice, and must put away from them every evil person, 10-13.

1. *There is fornication among you.* The word which we translate *fornication* in this place must be understood in its utmost latitude of meaning as implying all kinds of impurity; for that the Corinthians were notoriously guilty of every species of irregularity and debauch we have already seen, and it is not likely that in speaking on this subject, in reference to a people so very notorious, he would refer to only one species of impurity. *That one should have his father's wife.* Commentators and critics have found great difficulties in this statement. One

part of the case is sufficiently clear, that a man who professed Christianity had illegal connections with his father's wife. But the principal question is, Was his father alive or dead? Most think the father was alive, and imagine that to this the apostle refers, 2 Cor. vii. 12, where, speaking of the person who did the wrong, he introduces also him who had suffered the wrong; which must mean the father, and the father then alive. After all that has been said on this subject, I think it most natural to conclude that the person in question had married the wife of his deceased father, not his own mother, but stepmother, then a widow. The word *named* is wanting in almost every MS. and version of importance and certainly makes no part of the text. The words should be read, "and such fornication as is not amongst the Gentiles," i.e., not allowed.

2. *Ye are puffed up.* Ye are full of strife and contention relative to your parties and favorite teachers, and neglect the discipline of the church. Had you considered the greatness of this crime, you would have rather *mourned,* and have put away this flagrant transgressor from among you. *Taken away from among you.* This is supposed by some to refer to the punishment of death, by others to excommunication. The Christian Church was at this time too young to have those forms of excommunication which were practiced in succeeding centuries. Probably no more is meant than a simple disowning of the person, accompanied with the refusal to admit him to the sacred ordinances, or to have any intercourse or connection with him.

3. *Absent in body, but present in spirit.* Perhaps Paul refers to the gift of the discernment of spirits, which it is very likely the apostles in general possessed on extraordinary occasions. He had already seen this matter so clearly that he had determined on that sort of punishment which should be inflicted for this crime.

4. *In the name of our Lord Jesus.* Who is the Head of the Church, and under whose authority every act is to be performed. *And my spirit.* My apostolical authority derived from Him; *with the power,* with the miraculous energy of the Lord Jesus, which is to inflict the punishment that you pronounce.

5. *To deliver such an one unto Satan.* There is no evidence that delivering to Satan was any form of excommunication known among either the Jews or the Christians. It was a species of punishment administered in extraordinary cases, in which the body and the mind of an incorrigible transgressor were delivered by the authority of God into the power of Satan, to be tortured with diseases and terrors as a warning to all. But while the body and mind were thus tormented, the immortal spirit was under the influence of the divine mercy; and the affliction, in all probability, was in general only for a season; though sometimes it was evidently unto death, as the *destruction of the flesh* seems to imply. But the soul found mercy at the hand of God.

6. *Your glorying is not good.* You are triumphing in your superior knowledge, and busily employed in setting up and supporting your respective teachers, while the church is left under the most scandalous corruptions—corruptions which threaten its very existence if not

purged away. *Know ye not?* With all your boasted wisdom, do you not know and acknowledge the truth of a common maxim, *A little leaven leaveneth the whole lump?* If this *leaven,* the incestuous person, be permitted to remain among you; if his conduct be not exposed by the most formidable censure, the floodgates of impurity will be opened on the church, and the whole state of Christianity ruined in Corinth.

7. *Purge out therefore the old leaven.* As it is the custom of the Jews previously to the Passover to search their houses in the most diligent manner for the old leaven, and throw it out, sweeping every part clean, so act with this incestuous person.

8. *Therefore let us keep the feast.* It is very likely that the time of the Passover was now approaching, when the Church of Christ would be called to extraordinary acts of devotion, in commemorating the passion, death, and resurrection of Christ; and of this circumstance the apostle takes advantage in his exhortation to the Corinthians. *Not with old leaven.* Under the Christian dispensation we must be saved equally from Judaism, heathenism, and sin of every kind. *Malice* and *wickedness* must be destroyed; and *sincerity* and *truth,* inward purity and outward holiness, take their place. *Sincerity,* such purity of affections and conduct that even the light of God shining upon them discovers no flaw, and *truth*—inwardly as well as outwardly what they profess to be.

10. *For then must ye needs go out of the world.* What an awful picture of the general corruption of manners does this exhibit! The Christians at Corinth could not transact the ordinary affairs of life with any others than with fornicators, covetous persons, extortioners, railers, drunkards, and idolaters because there were none others in the place! How necessary was Christianity in that city!

11. *But now I have written.* I not only write this, but I add more: If anyone who *is called a brother,* i.e., professes the Christian religion, be a *fornicator, covetous, idolater, railer, drunkard, or extortioner,* not even to *eat* with such— have no communion with such a one, in things either sacred or civil. You may transact your worldly concerns with a person that knows not God and makes no profession of Christianity, whatever his moral character may be; but you must not even thus far acknowledge a man professing Christianity who is scandalous in his conduct. Let him have this extra mark of your abhorrence of all sin; and let the world see that the Church of God does not tolerate iniquity.

12. *For what have I to do to judge them also that are without?* The term *without* signifies those who were not members of the church. The word *also,* which greatly disturbs the sense here, is wanting in several MSS. The sentence I think, with the omission of *also,* should stand thus: "Does it belong to me to pass sentence on those which are without"—which are not members of the church? "By no means. You pass sentence on them which are within"— which are members of the church: "those which are without"—which are not members of the church, "God will pass sentence on," in that way in which He generally deals with the heathen world. "But put away the evil from among yourselves." This is most evidently the apostle's

meaning, and renders all comments unnecessary. In the last clause there appears to be an allusion to Deut. xvii. 7, where the like directions are given to the congregation of Israel, relative to a person found guilty of idolatry: "Thou shalt put the evil away from among you"—where the version of the Septuagint is almost the same as that of the apostle.

CHAPTER 6

The Corinthians are reproved for their litigious disposition: brother going to law with brother, and that before the heathen, 1-6. They should suffer wrong rather than do any, 7-8. No unrighteous person can enter into the glory of God, 9-10. Some of the Corinthians had been grievous sinners, but God had saved them, 11. Many things may be lawful which are not at all times expedient, 12. Meats are for the belly, and the belly for meats; but the body is not for uncleanness, 13. Christ's resurrection a pledge of ours, 14. The bodies of Christians are members of Christ, and must not be defiled, 15-17. He that commits fornication sins against his own body, 18. Strong dissuasives from it, 19-20.

1. *Dare any of you?* From the many things that are here reprehended by the apostle, we learn that the Christian church at Corinth was in a state of great imperfection, notwithstanding there were very many eminent characters among them. Divided as they were among themselves, there was no one person who possessed any public authority to settle differences between man and man; therefore, as one party would not submit to the decisions of another, they were obliged to carry their contentions before heathen magistrates; and probably these very subjects of litigations arose out of their ecclesiastical divisions. *Before the unjust, and not before the saints.* The heathen judges were termed *dikastai* from their presumed righteousness in the administration of justice. Here the apostle, by a paronomasia, calls them *adikoi,* unrighteous persons; and it is very likely that at Corinth, where such corruption of manners reigned, there was a great perversion of public justice; and it is not to be supposed that matters relative to the Christians were fairly decided. The Christians the apostle terms *saints,* which they were all by profession; and doubtless many were so in spirit and in truth.

2. *The saints shall judge the world.* Nothing can be more evident than that the writers of the New Testament often use *ho cosmos, the world,* to signify the Jewish people; and sometimes the Roman Empire, and the Jewish state. In the former sense it is often used by our Lord. "When the Son of man shall sit in the throne of his glory, ye also shall sit upon twelve thrones, judging the twelve tribes of Israel," Matt. xix. 28. It is supposed that He refers to the same subject as that mentioned here—the saints judging the world; and that Paul has His words in view in what he says here to the Corinthians. By "judging the twelve tribes of Israel" some have imagined that having authority in the Church is merely intended; but Dr. Lightfoot contends that the words referred to the coming of our Lord to execute judgment on the Jews, and to destroy their state; and that the doctrine of the apostles, not themselves, was to judge and condemn that most disobedient people. I think, with Dr. Lightfoot, that these words of the apostle refer to the prediction of Dan. chap. vii. 18, 27, and such like prophecies, where the kingdoms of the earth are promised to the saints of the Most High; that is, that a time shall come when Christianity shall so far prevail that

the civil government of the world shall be administered by Christians, which, at that time, was administered by heathens.

4. *Things pertaining to this life.* They could examine all civil cases among themselves, which they were permitted to determine without any hindrance from the heathen governments under which they lived. *Who are least esteemed in the church.* Those who were in the lowest order of judges.

5. *Is it so, that there is not a wise man among you?* Have you none among yourselves that can be arbitrators of the differences which arise, that you go to the heathen tribunals?

6. *Brother goeth to law with brother.* One Christian sues another at law! This is almost as great a scandal as can exist in a Christian society. Those in a religious community who will not submit to a proper arbitration, made by persons among themselves, should be expelled from the Church of God.

7. *There is utterly a fault among you.* There is a most manifest "defect" among you: (1) Of peaceableness; (2) Of brotherly love; (3) Of mutual confidence; and (4) Of reverence for God, and concern for the honor of His cause. *Why do ye not rather take wrong?* Better suffer an injury than take a method of redressing yourselves which must injure your own peace and greatly dishonor the cause of God.

8. *Nay, ye do wrong.* Far from suffering, you are the aggressors; and defraud your pious, long-suffering brethren, who submit to this wrong rather than take those methods of redressing their grievances which the spirit of Christianity forbids. Probably the apostle refers to him who had taken his father's wife.

9. *The unrighteous shall not inherit the kingdom.* The unrighteous, those who act contrary to right, cannot *inherit*, for the inheritance is by right. He who is not a child of God has no right to the family inheritance, for that inheritance is for the children. "If children, then heirs; heirs of God, and joint-heirs with Christ," Rom. viii. 17. There are here ten classes of transgressors which the apostle excludes from the kingdom of God; and any man who is guilty of any one of the evils mentioned above is thereby excluded from this Kingdom, whether it imply the Church of Christ here below or the state of glory hereafter.

11. *And such were some of you.* It was not with the prospect of collecting saints that the apostles went about preaching the gospel of the Kingdom. None but sinners were to be found over the face of the earth; they preached that sinners might be converted unto God, made saints, and constituted into a church; and this was the effect as well as the object of their preaching. *But ye are washed.* Several suppose that the order in which the operations of the grace of God take place in the soul is inverted, but I am of a very different mind. Everything will appear here in its order when we understand the terms used by the apostle. *Ye are washed;* you have been baptized into the Christian faith, and you have promised in this baptism to put off all filthiness of the flesh and spirit; the washing of your bodies is emblematical of the purification of your souls. *Ye are sanctified.* From *a*, privative, and *ge*, "the earth"; you are separated from earthly things to be

connected with spiritual. You are separated from time to be connected with eternity. You are separated from idols to be joined to the living God. Separation from common, earthy, or sinful uses, to be wholly employed in the service of the true God, is the ideal meaning of this word, in both the Old and New Testaments. It was in consequence of their being separated from the world that they became a church of God. You were formerly workers of iniquity, and associated with workers of iniquity; but now you are separated from them, and united together to work out your salvation with fear and trembling before God. *Ye are justified.* You have been brought into a state of favor with God, your sins having been blotted out through Christ Jesus, the Spirit of God witnessing the same to your conscience, and carrying on by His energy the great work of regeneration in your hearts.

12. *All things are lawful unto me.* It is likely that some of the Corinthians had pleaded that the offense of the man who had his father's wife, as well as the eating the things offered to idols, was not contrary to the law, as it then stood. To this the apostle answers: Though such a thing be lawful, yet the case of fornication, mentioned in chap. v. 1, is not expedient—it is not agreeable to propriety, decency, order, and purity. It is contrary to the established usages of the best and most enlightened nations, and should not be tolerated in the Church of Christ.

13. *Meats for the belly.* God has provided different kinds of aliments for the appetite of man, and among others those which are generally offered to idols; and He has adapted the appetite to these aliments, and the aliments to the appetite. *But God shall destroy both it and them;* none of these is eternal; all these lower appetites and sensations will be destroyed by death and have no existence in the resurrection body. *Now the body is not for fornication.* Though God made an appetite for food, and provided food for that appetite, yet He has not made the body for any uncleanness nor indulgence in sensuality; but He has made it for Christ. And Christ was provided to be a Sacrifice for this body as well as for the soul, by taking our nature upon Him; so that now, as human beings, we have an intimate relationship to the Lord; and our bodies are made not only for His service but to be His temples.

14. *And God hath both raised up the Lord.* He has raised up the human nature of Christ from the grave, as a pledge of our resurrection; and will also raise us up by His own power, that we may dwell with Him in glory forever.

15. *Know ye not that your bodies are the members of Christ?* Because He has taken your nature upon Him, and thus, as believers in Him, you are the members of Christ. *Shall I then take?* Shall we who profess to be members of His body, of His flesh, and of His bones, connect ourselves with harlots, and thus dishonor and pollute the bodies which are members of Christ?

17. *Is one spirit.* He who is united to God, by faith in Christ Jesus, receives His Spirit, and becomes a partaker of the divine nature. Who can change such a relationship for communion with a harlot, or for any kind of sensual gratification?

18. *Flee fornication.* Abominate, detest, and

escape from every kind of uncleanness. Some sins, or solicitations to sin, may be reasoned with; in the above cases, if you parley you are undone; reason not but fly! *Sinneth against his own body.* Though sin of every species has a tendency to destroy life, yet none are so mortal as those to which the apostle refers; they strike immediately at the basis of the constitution. By the just judgment of God, all these irregular and sinful connections are married to death.

19. *Your body is the temple of the Holy Ghost.* What an astonishing saying is this! As truly as the living God dwelt in the Mosaic Tabernacle and in the Temple of Solomon, so truly does the Holy Ghost dwell in the souls of genuine Christians; and as the Temple and all its utensils were holy, separated from all common and profane uses and dedicated alone to the service of God, so the bodies of genuine Christians are holy, and all their members should be employed in the service of God alone. *And ye are not your own.* You have no right over yourselves, to dispose of either your body or any of its members as you may think proper or lawful; you are bound to God, and to Him you are accountable.

20. *Ye are bought with a price.* As the slave who is purchased by his master for a sum of money is the sole property of that master, so you, being bought with the price of the blood of Christ, are not your own; you are His property. As the slave is bound to use all his skill and diligence for the emolument of his master, so you should employ body, soul, and spirit in the service of your Lord; promoting, by every means in your power, the honor and glory of your God, whom you must also consider as your Lord and Master. *And in your spirit, which are God's* is wanting in some MSS. and in several of the primitive fathers. Almost every critic of note considers them to be spurious.

CHAPTER 7

A solution of several difficult cases concerning marriage and married persons, 1-6. God has given every man his proper gift, 7. Directions to the unmarried and widows, 8-9. Directions to the married 10-11. Directions to men married to heathen women, and to women married to heathen men, 12-16. Every man should abide in his vocation, 17-24. Directions concerning virgins, and single persons in general, 25-28. How all should behave themselves in the things of this life, in reference to eternity, 29-31. The trials of the married state, 32-35. Directions concerning the state of virginity or celibacy, 36-38. How the wife is bound to her husband during his life, and her liberty to marry another after his death, 39-40.

1. *The things whereof ye wrote unto me.* It is sufficiently evident that the principal part of this Epistle was written in answer to some questions which had been sent to the apostle in a letter from the Corinthian church; and the first question seems to be this: "Is it proper for a man to marry in the present circumstances of the church?" The question concerning the expediency or inexpediency of marriage was often agitated among the ancient philosophers; and many, though inclined to decide against it, because of the troubles and cares connected with it, tolerated it in their opinions because, though an evil, it was judged to be a necessary evil. But this was not the common opinion; the Jews absolutely required that every man should marry, and reputed those as murderers who did not. By the laws of Lycurgus unmarried per-

sons were prohibited from seeing the public games. By the laws of the Spartans bachelors were punished. And Plato declares all such unworthy of any honor.

2. *Let every man have his own wife.* Let every man have one woman, *his own;* and every woman one man, *her own.* Here, plurality of wives and husbands is most strictly forbidden; and they are commanded to marry for the purpose of procreating children.

3. *Let the husband render unto the wife due benevolence.* Though our version is no translation of the original, yet few persons are at a loss for the meaning, and the context is sufficiently plain. Some have rendered the words, not unaptly, the "matrimonial debt" or "conjugal duty"—that which a wife owes to her husband, and the husband to his wife; and which they must take care mutually to render, else alienation of affection will be the infallible consequence, and this in numberless instances has led to adulterous connections. In such cases the wife has to blame herself for the infidelity of her husband, and the husband for that of his wife. What miserable work has been made in the peace of families by a wife or a husband pretending to be wiser than the apostle, and too holy and spiritual to keep the commandments of God!

4. *The wife hath not power.* Her person belongs to her husband; her husband's person belongs to her. Neither of them has any authority to refuse what the other has a matrimonial right to demand. The woman that would act so is either a knave or a fool. It would be trifling to attribute her conduct to any other cause than weakness or folly. She does not love her husband; or she loves someone else better than her husband; or she makes pretensions to a fancied sanctity unsupported by Scripture or common sense.

5. *Defraud ye not one the other.* What you owe thus to each other never refuse paying, unless by mutual consent; and let that be only for a certain time, when prudence dictates the temporary separation, or when some extraordinary spiritual occasion may render it mutually agreeable, in order that you may fast and pray, and derive the greatest possible benefit from these duties by being enabled to wait on the Lord without distraction. *That Satan tempt you not for your incontinency.* It is most evident that the separations permitted by the apostle, for he enjoins none, are only for a season, on extraordinary occasions; and that the persons may *come together again,* lest Satan, taking advantage of their matrimonial abstinence, might tempt either party to illicit commerce. *Incontinency,* "want of strength" to regulate one's desires or appetites; from *a,* negative, and *kratos,* "strength." It is remarkable that the apostle supposes that even this temporary continence might produce incontinence; and universal observation confirms the supposition.

6. *I speak this by permission.* It was a constant custom of the more conscientious rabbins to make a difference between the things which they enjoined on their own judgment and those which they built on the authority of the law. Thus Rabbi Tancum: "The washing of hands before meat is in our own power; washing after meat is commanded." We may understand the

apostle here as saying that the directions already given were from his own judgment, and not from any divine inspiration; and we may take it for granted that where he does not make this observation he is writing under the immediate afflatus of the Holy Spirit.

7. *For I would that all men.* He wished that all that were then in the Church were, like himself, unmarried; but this was in reference to the necessities of the Church, or what he calls, v. 26, the "present distress." For it never could be his wish that marriage should cease among men, and that human beings should no longer be propagated upon earth. Nor could he wish that the Church of Christ should always be composed of single persons; this would have been equally absurd. But as the Church was then in straits and difficulties, it was much better for its single members not to encumber themselves with domestic embarrassments. *Every man hath his proper gift of God.* Continence is a state that cannot be acquired by human art or industry; a man has it from God, or not at all.

8. *The unmarried and widows.* It is supposed that the apostle speaks here of men who had been married but were now widowers; as he does of women who had been married, in the word *widows.* And when he says *even as I,* he means that he himself was a widower; for several of the ancients rank Paul among the married apostles.

9. *But if they cannot contain.* If they find it inconvenient and uncomfortable to continue as widowers and widows, let them remarry.

10. *I command, yet not I, but the Lord.* I do not give my own private opinion or judgment in this case; for the Lord Jesus commands that man shall not put asunder them whom God hath joined, Matt. v. 32; xix. 6. And God has said the same, Gen. ii. 24.

11. *But and if she depart.* He puts the case as probable, because it was frequent, but lays it under restrictions. *Let her remain unmarried.* She departs at her own peril, but she must not marry another; she must either continue unmarried or be reconciled to her husband. *And let not the husband put away his wife.* Divorces cannot be allowed but in the case of fornication. An act of this kind dissolves the marriage vow, but nothing else can.

12. *But to the rest speak I, not the Lord.* As if he had said: For what I have already spoken I have the testimony of the Lord by Moses, and of my own Lord and Master, Christ; but for the directions which I am now about to give there is no written testimony, and I deliver them now for the first time. These words do not intimate that the apostle was not now under the influences of the divine Spirit, but that there was nothing in the sacred writings which bore directly on this point. *If any brother,* a Christian man, *hath a wife that believeth not,* i.e., who is a heathen, not yet converted to the Christian faith, *and she be pleased to dwell with him,* notwithstanding his turning Christian since their marriage, *let him not put her away* because she still continues in her heathen superstition.

13. *And the woman,* converted from heathenism to the Christian faith, *which hath an husband,* who still abides in heathenism; *if he be*

pleased to dwell with her, notwithstanding she has become a Christian since their marriage, *let her not leave him* because he still continues a heathen.

14. *The unbelieving husband is sanctified by the wife.* Or rather, is to be reputed as sanctified on account of his wife. She being a Christian woman and he, though a heathen, being by marriage one flesh with her, her sanctity, as far as it refers to outward things, may be considered as imputed to him so as to render their connection not unlawful. The case is the same when the wife is a heathen and the husband a Christian. The word sanctification here is to be applied much more to the Christian state than to any moral change in the persons, for "saints" is a common term for Christians. *Else were your children unclean.* If this kind of relative sanctification were not allowed, the children of these persons could not be received into the Christian Church, nor enjoy any rights or privileges as Christians; but the Church of God never scrupled to admit such children as members, just as well as she did those who had sprung from parents both of whom were Christians. The Jews considered a child as born "out of holiness" whose parents were not proselytes at the time of the birth, though afterwards they became proselytes. On the other hand, they considered the children of heathens born "in holiness" provided the parents became proselytes before the birth. All the children of the heathens were reputed unclean by the Jews, and all their own children holy. This shows clearly what the apostle's meaning is.

15. *But if the unbelieving depart.* Whether husband or wife, if such obstinately depart and utterly refuse all cohabitation, *a brother or a sister,* a Christian man or woman, *is not under bondage* to any particular laws, so as to be prevented from remarrying. Such, probably, the law stood then; but it is not so now, for the marriage can be dissolved only by death or by the ecclesiastical court. *God hath called us to peace.* The refractory and disagreeing party should not be compelled to fulfill such matrimonial engagements as would produce continual jarring and discord. At the same time each should take care that he give no cause for disagreements and separations, for the Author of the Christian religion is the Author of *peace,* and has *called* us to it.

16. *For what knowest thou, O wife?* You that are Christians, and who have heathen partners, do not give them up because they are such, for you may become the means of saving them unto eternal life. Bear your cross and look up to God, and He may give your unbelieving husband or wife to your prayers.

17. *But as God hath distributed to every man.* Let every man fulfill the duties of the state to which God in the course of His providence has called him. *So ordain I in all churches.* I do not lay on you a burden which others are not called to bear; this is the general rule which, by the authority of God, I impose on every Christian society.

18. *Is any man called being circumcised?* Is any man who was formerly a Jew converted to Christianity? *Let him not become uncircumcised.* Let him not endeavor to abolish the sign of the old covenant, which he bears in his flesh. *Let him not be circumcised.* Let no man

who, being a Gentile, has been converted to the Christian faith submit to circumcision as something necessary to his salvation.

19. *Circumcision is nothing.* Circumcision itself, though commanded of God, is nothing of itself, it being only a sign of the justification which should be afterwards received by faith. At present, neither it nor its opposite either hinders or furthers the work of grace; and *keeping* the commandments of God, from His love shed abroad in a believing heart, is the sum and substance of religion.

20. *Let every man abide in the same calling.* As both the circumcised and uncircumcised, in Christ, have the same advantages, and to their believing the same facilities, so any situation of life is equally friendly to the salvation of the soul, if a man be faithful to the grace he has received. Therefore in all situations a Christian should be content, for all things work together for good to him who loves God.

21. *Art thou called being a servant?* Are you converted to Christ while you are a "slave"—the property of another person, and bought with his money? *Care not for it*—this will not injure your Christian condition. But if you can obtain your liberty, *use it rather,* prefer this state for the sake of freedom, and the temporal advantages connected with it.

22. *For he that is called.* The man who, being a "slave," is converted to the Christian faith is the Lord's freeman; his condition as a slave does not vitiate any of the privileges to which he is entitled as a Christian. On the other hand, all free men who receive the grace of Christ must consider themselves the "slaves of the Lord," i.e., His real property, to be employed and disposed of according to His godly wisdom, who, notwithstanding their state of subjection, will find the service of their Master to be perfect freedom.

23. *Ye are bought with a price.* As truly as your bodies have become the property of your masters, in consequence of their paying down a price for you, so sure you are now the Lord's property, in consequence of your being purchased by the blood of Christ. Some render this verse interrogatively: "Are you bought with a price" from your slavery? "Do not again become slaves of men." Never sell yourselves; prefer and retain your liberty now that ye have acquired it.

24. *Let every man . . . abide with God.* Let him live to God in whatever station he is placed by Providence. If he be a slave, God will be with him even in his slavery, if he be faithful to the grace which he has received. It is very likely that some of the slaves at Corinth, who had been converted to Christianity, had been led to think that their Christian privileges absolved them from the necessity of continuing slaves or, at least, brought them on a level with their Christian masters. A spirit of this kind might have soon led to confusion and insubordination, and brought scandals into the church. It was therefore a very proper subject for the apostle to interfere in; and to his authority the persons concerned would doubtless respectfully bow.

25. *Now concerning virgins.* This was another subject on which the church at Corinth had asked the advice of the apostle. The word virgin we take to signify a "pure, unmarried young woman"; but it is evident that the word

in this place means young unmarried persons of either sex, as appears from vv. 26-27, 32-34, and from Rev. xiv. 4. The word is frequently applied to men as well as to women. *I have no commandment of the Lord.* There is no thing in the sacred writings that directly touches this point. *Yet I give my judgment.* As every way equal to such commandments had there been any, seeing I have received the teaching of His own Spirit, and have obtained *mercy of the Lord to be faithful* to this heavenly gift, so that it abides with me to lead me into all truth. In this way I think the apostle's words may be safely understood.

26. *This is good for the present distress.* The word signifies "necessity, distress, tribulation, and calamity," as it does in Luke xxi. 23; 2 Cor. vi. 4; and xii. 10. In such times, when the people of God had no certain dwelling place, when they were lying at the mercy of their enemies without any protection from the state—the state itself often among the persecutors—he who had a family to care for would find himself in very embarrassed circumstances, as it would be much more easy to provide for his personal safety than to have the care of a wife and children. On this account it was much better for unmarried persons to continue for the present in their celibacy.

27. *Art thou bound unto a wife?* I.e., married; for the marriage contract was considered in the light of a bond. *Seek not to be loosed.* Neither regret your circumstances, notwithstanding the present distress, nor seek on this account for a dissolution of the marriage contract. But if you are under no matrimonial engagements, do not for the present enter into any.

28. *But and if thou marry.* As there is no law against this, even in the present distress, you have not sinned, because there is no law against this; and it is only on account of prudential reasons that I give this advice. *And if a virgin marry.* Both the man and the woman have equal privileges in this case; either of them may marry without sin. It is probable, as there were many sects and parties in Corinth, that there were among them those who forbade to marry, 1 Tim. iv. 3. *Trouble in the flesh.* From the simple circumstance of the incumbrance of a family while under persecution, because of the difficulty of providing for its comfort and safety while flying before the face of persecution. *But I spare you.* The evil is coming, but I will not press upon you the observance of a prudential caution which you might deem too heavy a cross.

29. *The time is short.* These persecutions and distresses are at the door, and life itself will soon be run out. Even then Nero was plotting those grievous persecutions with which he not only afflicted but devastated the Church of Christ. *They that have wives.* Let none begin to think of any comfortable settlement for his family; let him sit loose to all earthly concerns, and stand ready prepared to escape for his life or meet death, as the providence of God may permit. The husband will be dragged from the side of his wife to appear before the magistrates and be required to either abjure Christ or die.

30. *They that weep.* There will be shortly be such a complete system of distress and confusion that private sorrows and private joys

will be absorbed in the weightier and more oppressive public evils. Yet let every man still continue in his calling; let him buy and sell and traffic as usual, though in a short time, either by the coming persecution or by the levelling hand of death, he that had earthly property will be brought into the same circumstances with him who had none.

31. *And they that use this world.* Let them who have earthly property or employments discharge conscientiously their duties, from a conviction of the instability of earthly things. Make a right use of everything, and pervert nothing from its *use.* To *use* a thing is to employ it properly in order to accomplish the end to which it refers. To *abuse* a thing signifies to pervert it from that use. Pass through things' temporal so as not to lose those which are eternal. *For the fashion of this world.* The present state or constitution of things; the frame of the world, that is, the world itself. But often the term *world* is taken to signify the Jewish state and polity; the destruction of this was then at hand, and this the Holy Spirit might then signify to the apostle.

32. *Without carefulness.* Though all these things will shortly come to pass, yet do not be anxious about them. *He that is unmarried careth for the things that belong to the Lord.* He has nothing to do with a family, and therefore can give his whole time to the service of his Maker, having Him alone to please.

33. *But he that is married.* He has a family to provide for, and his wife to please, as well as to fulfill his duty to God and attend to the concerns of his own soul. The single man has nothing to attend to but what concerns his own salvation; the married man has all this to attend to, and besides to provide for his wife and family, and take care of their eternal interests also.

34. *There is a difference also between a wife and a virgin.* That is: There is this difference between a married and an unmarried woman. *The unmarried . . . careth* (only) *for the things of the Lord,* having no domestic duties to perform. *That she may be holy*—separated to divine employments, *both in body and in spirit.* Whereas *she that is married careth* (also) *for the things of the world, how she may please her husband,* having many domestic duties to fulfill, her husband being obliged to leave to her the care of the family and all other domestic concerns.

35. *This I speak for your own profit.* The advices belong to yourselves alone, because of the peculiar circumstances in which you are placed. Nothing spoken here was ever designed to be of general application; it concerned the church at Corinth alone, or churches in similar circumstances. *Not that I may cast a snare upon you.* Here is a manifest allusion to the retiarius among the Romans, who carried a small casting net, which he endeavored to throw over the head of his adversary and thus entangle him; or to a similar custom among the Persians, who made use of a noose called the *camand,* which they employed in the same way. The apostle therefore intimates that what he says was not intended absolutely to bind them, but to show them the propriety of following an advice which in the present case would be helpful to them in their religious connections, that they might *attend upon the Lord without distraction,* which

they could not do in times of persecution, when, in addition to their own personal safety, they had a wife and children to care for.

36. *Uncomely towards his virgin.* Different meanings have been assigned to this verse. I shall mention three of the principal. (1) "In those early times, both among the Hebrews and Christians, the daughters were wholly in the power of the father, so that he might give or not give them in marriage as he chose; and might bind them to perpetual celibacy if he thought proper; and to this case the apostle alludes. If the father had devoted his daughter to perpetual virginity, and he afterwards found that she had fixed her affections upon a person whom she was strongly inclined to marry, and was now getting past the prime of life; he, seeing from his daughter's circumstances that it would be wrong to force her to continue in her state of celibacy, though he had determined before to keep her single, yet he might in this case alter his purpose without sin, and let her and her suitor marry." (2) "The whole verse and its context speaks of young women dedicated to the service of God, who were called *virgins* in the primitive Church. And a case is put here, 'that circumstances might occur to render the breach of even a vow of this kind necessary, and so no sin be committed.' " (3) "The apostle does not mean a virgin, but the 'state of virginity' or celibacy, whether in man or woman." This last opinion seems to be the true sense of the apostle.

38. *Instead of he that giveth her in marriage,* I purpose to read "he who marrieth," which is the reading of the Codex Alexandrinus, the Codex Vaticanus, and of some others. *His own virgin* is added after the above by several very ancient and reputable MSS., but it seems so much like a gloss that Griesbach has not made it even a candidate for a place in the text. "He then who marrieth," though previously intending perpetual virginity, doeth well, as this is agreeable to laws both divine and human; and he "who marrieth not," *doeth better,* because of the present distress.

39. *The wife is bound by the law.* This seems to be spoken in answer to some other question of the Corinthians to this effect: "May a woman remarry whose husband is dead, or who has abandoned her?" To which he replies, in general, that as long as her husband is living the law binds her to him alone; but, if the husband die, she is free to remarry, but *only in the Lord.* That is, she must not marry a heathen nor an irreligious man; and she should not only marry a genuine Christian, but one of her own religious sentiments; for, in reference to domestic peace, much depends on this.

40. *But she is happier if she so abide.* If she continue in her widowhood because of the present distress. *After my judgment.* According to the view I have of the subject, which view I take by the light of the divine Spirit, who shows me the tribulations which are coming on the Church. *I think . . . I have the Spirit of God.* Might be translated, "I am certain that I have the Spirit of God." Ulpian, on Demosthen., *Olynth.* 1, says, "The word *dokein* is used by the ancients, not always to express what is doubtful, but often to express what is true and certain." The apostle cannot be understood as expressing any doubt of his being under the

inspiration of the divine Spirit, as this would have defeated his object in giving the above advices; for if they were not dictated by the Spirit of God, can it be supposed that, in the face of apparent self-interest and the prevalence of strong passions, they could have been expected to have become rules of conduct to this people? They must have understood him as asserting that he had the direction of the Spirit of God in giving those opinions, else they could not be expected to obey.

CHAPTER 8

The question of the Corinthians concerning meats offered to idols, and the apostle's preface to his instructions on that head, 1-3. The nature of idolatry, 4-5. Of genuine worship, 6. Some ate of the animals that had been offered to idols knowingly, and so defiled their consciences, 7. Neither eating nor abstinence in itself recommends us to God, 8. But no man should use his Christian liberty so as to put a stumbling block before a brother, 9-10. If he act otherwise, he may be the means of a brother's destruction, 11. Those who act so as to wound the tender conscience of a brother sin against Christ, 12. The apostle's resolution on this head, 13.

1. *As touching things offered unto idols.* This was another subject on which the Corinthians had asked the apostle's advice. *We know that we all have knowledge.* I am inclined to think that these are not Paul's words, but a quotation from the letter of the Corinthians to him, and a proof of what the apostle says below, *Knowledge puffeth up. Knowledge puffeth up, but charity edifieth.* This knowledge is very nearly allied to pride; it *puffeth up* the mind with vain conceit, makes those who have it bold and rash, and renders them careless of the consciences of others.

2. *He knoweth nothing yet.* The person who acts in this rash, unfeeling way, from the general knowledge which he has of the vanity of idolatry and the liberty which the gospel affords from Jewish rites, with all his knowledge does not know this, that though the first and greatest commandment says, "Thou shalt love the Lord thy God with all thy heart," yet the second is like unto it: "Thou shalt love thy neighbour as thyself." He then that can torment his neighbors' weak or tender conscience with his food or his conduct does not love him as himself, and therefore knows nothing as he ought to know.

3. *But if any man love God,* in that way which the commandment requires, which will necessarily beget love to his neighbor, *the same is known of him,* is approved of God, and acknowledged as His genuine follower.

5. *There be that are called gods.* There are many images that are supposed to be representations of divinities. But these divinities are nothing, the figments of mere fancy; and these images have no corresponding realities. *Whether in heaven or in earth.* As the sun, moon, planets, stars, the ocean, rivers, trees, etc. And thus there are, nominally, *gods many, and lords many.*

6. *But to us there is but one God, the Father.* Who produced all things, himself uncreated and unoriginated. *And we in him,* "and we for Him," all intelligent beings having been created for the purpose of manifesting His glory by receiving and reflecting His wisdom, goodness, and truth. *And one Lord Jesus.* Only one visible Governor of the world and the Church. *By whom are all things.* Who was the Creator,

as He is the Upholder, of the universe. *And we by him,* being brought to the knowledge of the true God by the revelation of Jesus Christ; for it is the only begotten Son alone that can reveal the Father. The "gods" of whom the apostle speaks were their divinities, or objects of religious worship; the "lords" were the rulers of the world, such as emperors, who were considered next to gods, and some of them were deified. In opposition to those "gods" he places *God, the Father,* the Fountain of plenitude and being; and in opposition to the "lords" he places *Jesus Christ,* who made and who governs all things.

7. *There is not in every man that knowledge.* This is spoken in reference to what is said, v. 4: "We know that an idol is nothing in the world." *For some with a conscience of the idol,* viz., that it is something, *eat it*—the flesh that was offered to the idol—as a thing thus offered, considering the feast as a sacred banquet by which they have fellowship with the idol. *And their conscience being weak,* not properly instructed in divine things, *is defiled*—he performs what he does as an act of religious worship, and thus his conscience contracts guilt through this idolatry.

8. *Meat commendeth us not to God.* No such feasts as these can be a recommendation of our souls or persons to the Supreme Being. As to the thing considered in itself, the eating gives us no spiritual advantage, and the eating not is no spiritual loss.

9. *But take heed.* Lest by frequenting such feasts and eating things offered to idols, under the conviction that an idol is nothing and that you may eat those things innocently, this liberty of yours should become a means of grievously offending a weak brother who has not your knowledge or inducing one who respects you for your superior knowledge to partake of these things with the conscience, the persuasion and belief, that an idol is something, and to conclude that, as you partake of such things, so he may also, and with safety. He is not possessed of your superior information on this point, and he eats to the idol what you take as a common meal.

10. *If any man see thee which hast knowledge.* Of the true God, and who are reputed for your skill in divine things. *Sit at meat in the idol's temple.* Is it not strange that any professing the knowledge of the true God should even enter one of those temples? And is it not more surprising that any Christian should be found to feast there? But by all this we may see that the boasted knowledge of the Corinthians had very little depth in things purely spiritual. *Be emboldened to eat.* Be "built up"— be confirmed and established in that opinion which before he doubtingly held, that on seeing you eat he may be led to think there is no harm in feasting in an idol temple nor in eating things offered to idols.

11. *Shall the weak brother perish?* Being first taught by thy conduct that there was no harm in thus eating, he grieves the Spirit of God, becomes again darkened and hardened, and sliding back into idolatry, dies in it, and so finally perishes. *For whom Christ died.* So we learn that a man may perish for whom Christ died; this admits of no quibble. If a man *for whom Christ died,* apostatizing from Christian-

ity (for he is called a *brother* though *weak*), returning again to and dying in idolatry, cannot go to heaven, then a man for whom Christ died may perish everlastingly. And if it were possible for a believer, whether strong or weak, to retrace his steps back to idolatry and die in it, surely it is possible for a man who had escaped the pollutions that are in the world to return to it, live and die in its spirit, and perish everlastingly also.

12. *But when ye sin so against the brethren.* Against Christians, who are called by the gospel to abhor and detest all such abominations. *Ye sin against Christ.* By sending to perdition, through your bad example, a soul for whom He shed His blood, and so far defeating the gracious intentions of His sacrificial death.

13. *Wherefore.* Rather than give any occasion to a Christian to sin against and so to harden his conscience that he should return to idolatry and perish, I would not only abstain from all meats offered to idols, but I would eat *no flesh,* should I exist through the whole course of time, but live on the herbs of the field, rather than cause my brother to stumble, and thus fall into idolatry and final ruin. The greater our reputation for knowledge and sanctity, the greater mischief we shall do by our influence and example if we turn aside from the holy commandment delivered unto us. Every man should walk so as either to light or lead his brother to heaven.

CHAPTER 9

Paul vindicates his apostleship, and shows that he has equal rights and privileges with Peter and the brethren of our Lord; and that he is not bound, while doing the work of an apostle, to labor with his hands for his own support, 1-6. He who labors should live by the fruit of his own industry, 7. For the law will not allow even the ox which treads out the corn to be muzzled, 8-10. Those who minister in spiritual things have a right to a secular support for their work, 11-14. He shows the disinterested manner in which he has preached the gospel, 15-18. How he accommodated himself to the prejudices of men, in order to bring about their salvation, 19-23. The way to heaven compared to a race, 24. The qualifications of those who may expect success in the games celebrated at Corinth, and what that success implies, 25. The apostle applies these things spiritually to himself; and states the necessity of keeping his body in subjection, lest, after having proclaimed salvation to others, he should become a castaway, 26-27.

1. *Am I not an apostle?* It is sufficiently evident that there were persons at Corinth who questioned the apostleship of Paul; and he was obliged to walk very circumspectly that they might not find any occasion against him. *Am I not an apostle? am I not free?* These questions are all designed as assertions of the affirmative: "I am an apostle, and I am free"—possessed of all the rights and privileges of an apostle. *Have I not seen Jesus Christ?* From whom in His personal appearance to me I have received my apostolic commission. This was judged essentially necessary to constitute an apostle. See Acts xxii. 14-15; xxvi. 16. *Are not ye my work?* Your conversion from heathenism is the proof that I have preached with the divine unction and authority.

2. *If I be not an apostle unto others.* If there be other churches which have been founded by other apostles, yet it is not so with you. *The seal of mine apostleship are ye.* Your conversion to Christianity is God's *seal* to my apostleship. Had not God sent me, I could not have profited your souls. The *seal* was a figure cut

in a stone, and that set in a ring, by which letters of credence and authority were stamped. The ancients, particularly the Greeks, excelled in this kind of engraving. *In the Lord.* The apostle shows that it was by the grace and influence of God alone that he was an apostle, and that they were converted to Christianity.

3. *Mine answer to them.* This is my defense against those who examine me. The words are forensic; and the apostle considers himself as brought before a legal tribunal, and questioned so as to be obliged to answer as upon oath. His defense therefore was this, that they were converted to God by his means. This verse belongs to the preceding two verses.

4. *Have we not power to eat and to drink?* Have we not "authority," or "right," to expect sustenance while we are laboring for your salvation? Meat and drink, the necessaries, not the superfluities, of life, were what those primitive messengers of Christ required; it was just that they who labored in the gospel should live by the gospel. They did not wish to make a fortune or accumulate wealth; a living was all they desired.

5. *Have we not power to lead about a sister, a wife?* When the apostle speaks of leading about a sister, a wife, he means, first, that he and all other apostles, and consequently all ministers of the gospel, had a right to marry. For it appears that our Lord's brethren, James and Jude, were married; and we have infallible evidence that Peter was a married man, not only from this verse, but from Matt. viii. 14, where his mother-in-law is mentioned as being cured of a fever by our Lord. And secondly, we find that their wives were persons of the same faith, for less can never be implied in the word *sister.*

6. *Or I only and Barnabas?* Have we alone of all the apostles no right to be supported by our converts? It appears from this: (1) That the apostles did not generally support themselves by their own labor; (2) That Paul and Barnabas did thus support themselves. Some of the others probably had not a business at which they could conveniently work, but Paul and Barnabas had a trade at which they could conveniently labor wherever they came.

7. *Who goeth a warfare . . . at his own charges?* These questions, which are all supposed from the necessity and propriety of the cases to be answered in the affirmative, tend more forcibly to point out that the common sense of man joins with the providence of God in showing the propriety of every man living by the fruits of his labor. The first question applies particularly to the case of the apostle. Does a soldier provide his own victuals? *Opsonion* is used by the Greek writers to express the military pay or wages, for the Roman soldiers were paid not only in money but in victuals.

8. *Say I these things as a man?* Is this only human reasoning? or does not God say in effect the same things?

9. *Thou shalt not muzzle the mouth of the ox.* See Deut. xxv. 4. *Doth God take care for oxen?* This question is to be understood thus: Is it likely that God should be solicitous for the comfort of oxen and be regardless of the welfare of man? In this divine precept the kindness and providential care of God are very forcibly pointed out. He takes care of oxen; He wills them

all that happiness of which their nature is susceptible; and can we suppose that He is unwilling that the human soul shall have that happiness which is suited to its spiritual and eternal nature?

10. *And he that thresheth in hope should be partaker of his hope.* Many of the best MSS. and versions read the passage thus: "And he who thresheth in hope of partaking."

11. *If we have sown unto you spiritual things.* If we have been the means of bringing you into a state of salvation by the divine doctrines which we have preached unto you, is it too much for us to expect a temporal support when we give ourselves up entirely to this work? Every man who preaches the gospel has a right to his own support and that of his family while thus employed.

12. *If others be partakers of this power.* If those who in any matter serve you have a "right" to a recompense for that service, surely we who have served you in the most essential matters have a right to our support while thus employed in your service. *We have not used this power.* Though we had this "right," we have not availed ourselves of it, but have worked with our hands to bear our own charges, lest any of you should think that we preached the gospel merely to procure a temporal support, and so be prejudiced against us, and thus prevent our success in the salvation of your souls.

13. *They which minister about holy things.* All the officers about the Temple, whether priests, Levites, Nethinim, etc., had a right to their support while employed in its service. The priests partook of the sacrifices; the others had their maintenance from tithes, firstfruits, and offerings made to the Temple, for it was not lawful for them to live on the sacrifices. Hence the apostle makes the distinction between those who *minister about holy things* and those who *wait at the altar.*

14. *Even so hath the Lord ordained.* This is evidently a reference to our Lord's ordination, Matt. x. 10: "The workman is worthy of his meat." And Luke x. 7: "For the labourer is worthy of his hire." And in both places it is the preacher of the gospel of whom he is speaking.

15. *Neither have I written.* Though I might plead the authority of God in the law, of Christ in the gospel, the common consent of our own doctors, and the usages of civil society, yet I have not availed myself of my privileges; nor do I now write with the intention to lay in my claims.

16. *For though I preach the gospel.* I have cause of glorying that I preach the gospel free of all charges to you; but I cannot glory in being a preacher of the gospel, because I am not such by either my own skill or power. I have received from God both the office and the grace by which I execute the office.

17. *For if I do this thing willingly.* If I be a cordial cooperator with God, *I have a reward,* an incorruptible crown, v. 25. Or, if I freely preach this gospel without being burdensome to any, I have a special reward. But if I do not, I have simply an office to fulfill, into which God has put me, and may fulfill it conscientiously, and claim my privileges at the same time; but then I lose that special reward which I have

in view by preaching the gospel without charge to any.

18. *That I abuse not my power.* I am inclined to think that *katachresasthai* is to be understood here, not in the sense of abusing, but of "using to the uttermost"—exacting everything that a man can claim by law.

19. *For though I be free.* Although I am under no obligation to any man, yet I act as if every individual had a particular property in me, and as if I were the "slave" of the public.

20. *Unto the Jews I became as a Jew.* In Acts xvi. 3, we find that for the sake of the unconverted Jews he circumcised Timothy. *To them that are under the law.* To those who considered themselves still under obligation to observe its rites and ceremonies, though they had in the main embraced the gospel, he became as if under the same obligations; and therefore purified himself in the Temple, as we find related in Acts xxi. 26. After the first clause, *to them that are under the law, as under the law,* the following words, "not being myself under the law," are added by several MSS.

21. *To them that are without law.* The Gentiles, who had no written law, though they had the law written in their hearts; see on Rom. ii. 15. *Being not without law to God.* Instead of *to God* and *to Christ,* the most important MSS. and versions have "of God" and "of Christ"; being not without the law of God, but under the law of Christ.

22. *To the weak became I as weak.* Those who were conscientiously "scrupulous," even in respect to lawful things. *I am made all things to all men.* I assumed every shape and form consistent with innocency and perfect integrity; giving up my own will, my own way, my own ease, my own pleasure, and my own profit, that I might save the souls of all. Let those who plead for the system of accommodation on the example of Paul attend to the end he had in view and the manner in which he pursued that end. It was not to get money, influence, or honor, but to save souls! It was not to get ease, but to increase his labors. It was not to save his life, but rather that it should be a sacrifice for the good of immortal souls!

23. *And this I do for the gospel's sake.* Instead of *this,* "all things" (I do all things for the gospel's sake), is the reading of many MSS. Several of the fathers have the same reading, and there is much reason to believe it to be genuine. *That I might be partaker thereof with you.* That I might attain to the reward of eternal life which it sets before me; and this is in all probability the meaning of *to evangelion,* which we translate "the gospel," and which should be rendered here "prize" or "reward"; this is a frequent meaning of the original word: "I do all this for the sake of the prize, that I may partake of it with you."

24. *They which run in a race run all.* It is sufficiently evident that the apostle alludes to the athletic exercises in the games which were celebrated every fifth year on the isthmus which joins the Peloponnesus to the mainland, and were thence termed the "Isthmian games." *But one receiveth the prize.* The apostle places the Christian race in contrast to the Isthmian games; in them, only one received the prize, though all ran; in this, if all run, all will receive the prize.

Therefore he says, *So run, that ye may obtain.* Be as much in earnest to get to heaven as others are to gain their prize; and, although only one of them can win, all of you may obtain.

25. *Is temperate in all things.* All those who contended in these exercises went through a long state and series of painful preparations. To this exact discipline Epictetus refers, cap. 35: "Do you wish to gain the prize at the Olympic games?—Consider the requisite preparations and the consequences: you must observe a strict regimen; must live on food which you dislike; you must abstain from all delicacies; must exercise yourself at the necessary and prescribed times both in heat and in cold; you must drink nothing cooling; take no wine as formerly; in a word, you must put yourself under the directions of a pugilist, as you would under those of a physician, and afterwards enter the lists. Here you may get your arm broken, your foot put out of joint, be obliged to swallow mouthfuls of dust, to receive many stripes, and after all be conquered." *They do it to obtain a corruptible crown.* The *crown* won by the victor in the Olympian games was made of the wild olive. These were all *corruptible,* for they began to wither as soon as they were separated from the trees or plucked out of the earth. In opposition to these, the apostle says, he contended for an incorruptible crown, the heavenly inheritance.

26. *I therefore so run, not as uncertainly.* In the foot-course in those games, how many soever ran, only one could have the prize, however strenuously they might exert themselves; therefore all ran uncertainly. But it was widely different in the Christian course; if everyone ran as he ought, each would receive the prize. *Not as one that beateth the air.* Kypke observes that there are three ways in which persons were said to beat the air: (1) When in practicing for the combat they threw their arms and legs about in different ways, thus practicing the attitudes of offense and defense. (2) Sometimes boxers were to aim blows at their adversaries which they did not intend to take place, and which the others were obliged to exert themselves to prevent as much as if they had been really intended. (3) Pugilists were said to beat the air when they had to contend with a nimble adversary, who, by running from side to side, stooping, and various contortions of the body, eluded the blows of his antagonist; who spent his strength on the air, frequently missing his aim, and sometimes overturning himself in attempting to hit his adversary, who by his agility had been able to elude the blow.

27. *But I keep under my body.* This is an allusion, not only to boxers, but also to wrestlers in the same games, as we learn from the word *hypopiazo,* which signifies to "hit in the eyes"; and *doulagogo,* which signifies to trip, and give the antagonist a fall, and then keep him down when he was down, and having obliged him to acknowledge himself conquered, make him a slave. The apostle considers his body as an enemy with which he must contend; he must mortify it by self-denial, abstinence, and severe labor. It must be the slave of his soul, and not the soul the slave of the body, which in all unregenerate men is the case. *Lest . . . when I have preached to others.* The word which we translate "having preached" refers to the office

of the "herald" at these games, whose business it was to proclaim the conditions of the games, display the prizes, exhort the combatants, excite the emulation of those who were to contend, declare the terms of each contest, pronounce the name of the victors, and put the crown on their heads. *Should be a castaway.* The word signifies such a person as the judges of the games reject as not having deserved the prize. So Paul himself might be rejected by the great Judge; and to prevent this he ran, he contended, he denied himself, and brought his body into subjection to his spirit, and had his spirit governed by the Spirit of God.

CHAPTER 10

Peculiar circumstances in the Jewish history were typical of the greatest mysteries of the gospel; particularly their passing through the Red Sea, and being overshadowed with the miraculous cloud, 1-2. The manna with which they were fed, 3. And Rock out of which they drank, 4. The punishments inflicted on them for their disobedience are warnings to us, 5. We should not lust as they did, 6. Nor commit idolatry, 7. Nor fornication as they did, in consequence of which 23,000 of them were destroyed, 8. Nor tempt Christ as they did, 9. Nor murmur, 10. All these transgressions and their punishments are recorded as warnings to us, that we may not fall away from the grace of God, 11-12. God never suffers any to be tempted above their strength, 13. Idolatry must be detested, 14. And the sacrament of the Lord's Supper properly considered and taken, that God may not be provoked to punish us, 15-22. There are some things which may be legally done which are not expedient; and we should endeavor so to act as to edify each other, 23-24. The question concerning eating things offered to idols considered, and finally settled, 25-30. e should do all things to the glory of God, avoid whatsoever might be the means of stumbling another, and seek the profit of others in spiritual matters rather than our own gratification, 31-33.

1. *I would not that ye should be ignorant.* It seems as if the Corinthians had supposed that their being made partakers of the ordinances of the gospel, such as baptism and the Lord's Supper, would secure their salvation, notwithstanding they might be found partaking of idolatrous feasts; as long, at least, as they considered an idol to be nothing in the world. To remove this destructive supposition, which would have led them to endless errors in both principle and practice, the apostle shows that the Jews had sacramental ordinances in the wilderness, similar to those of the Christians; and that, notwithstanding they had the typical baptism from the cloud, and the typical eucharist from the paschal lamb, and the manna that came down from heaven, yet, when they joined with idolaters and partook of idolatrous feasts, God was not only displeased with them but signified this displeasure by pouring out His judgments upon them, so that in one day 23,000 of them were destroyed.

2. *And were all baptized unto Moses.* Rather "into Moses", into the covenant of which Moses was the mediator; and by this typical baptism they were brought under the obligation of acting according to the Mosaic precepts, as Christians receiving Christian baptism are said to be baptized "into Christ," and are thereby brought under obligation to keep the precepts of the gospel.

3. *Spiritual meat.* The manna which is here called *spiritual:* (1) Because it was provided supernaturally; and, (2) Because it was a type of Christ Jesus, John vi. 31.

4. *Spiritual drink.* By the *spiritual meat* and *spiritual drink* the apostle certainly means both meat and drink which were furnished to the

Israelitish assembly miraculously, as well as typically. *The spiritual Rock that followed them.* It appears that the apostle does not speak about the rock itself, but of Him whom it represented; namely, Christ. This was the *Rock that followed them,* and ministered to them; and this view of the subject is rendered more probable by what is said, v. 9, that they tempted Christ, and were destroyed by serpents.

5. *They were overthrown in the wilderness.* And yet all these persons were "under the cloud," "all passed through the sea," all were "baptized unto Moses in the cloud and in the sea," all ate "the same spiritual meat," all drank "the same spiritual drink," for they were made partakers of the spiritual Rock, Christ. Nothing can be a more decisive proof than this that people who have every outward ordinance and are made partakers of the grace of our Lord Jesus may so abuse their privileges and grieve the Spirit of God as to fall from their state of grace and perish everlastingly.

6. *These things were our examples.* The punishments which God inflicted on them furnish us with evidences of what God will inflict upon us if we sin after the similitude of those transgressors. *We should not lust after evil things.* It is most evident that the apostle refers here to the history in Num. xi. 4, etc: "And the mixed multitude . . . fell a lusting . . . and said, Who shall give us flesh to eat?" Into the same spirit the Corinthians had most evidently fallen; they lusted after the flesh in the idol feasts, and therefore frequented them to the great scandal of Christianity. The apostle shows them that their sin was of the same nature as that of the murmuring, rebellious Israelites whom God so severely punished; and if He did not spare the natural branches, there was no likelihood that He should spare *them.*

7. *Neither be ye idolaters.* The apostle considers partaking of the idolatrous feasts as being the flesh to their gods considered them as feeding invisibly with them on the flesh thus offered, and that everyone that partook of the feast was a real participator with the god to whom the flesh or animal had been offered in sacrifice. *Rose up to play.* See the note on Exod. xxxii. 6. The Jews generally explain this word as implying idolatrous acts only. I have considered it as implying acts of impurity, with which idolatrous acts were often accompanied. It also means those dances which were practiced in honor of their gods.

8. *Fell in one day three and twenty thousand.* In Num. xxv. 9 the number is 24,000; and allowing this to be the genuine reading (and none of the Hebrew MSS. exhibit any various reading in the place), Moses and the apostle may be thus reconciled: In Num. xxv. 4, God commands Moses to "take all the heads [the rulers] of the people, and hang them up before the Lord against the sun"; these possibly amounted to 1,000, and those who fell by the plague were 23,000, so that the whole amounted to 24,000.

9. *Neither let us tempt Christ.* Instead of *Christ* several MSS. and a few versions have "the Lord."

10. *Neither murmur ye.* It appears from what the apostle says here that the Corinthians were murmuring against God and His apostle for prohibiting them from partaking of the idola-

trous feasts, just as the Israelites did in the wilderness in reference to a similar subject. *Destroyed of the destroyer.* The Jews suppose that God employed destroying angels to punish those rebellious Israelites; they were five in number, and one of them they call *the destroyer.*

11. *Upon whom the ends of the world are come.* The end of the times included within the whole duration of the Mosaic economy. For although the word *aion* means in its primary sense "endless being" or duration, yet in its accommodated sense it is applied to any round or duration that is complete in itself; and here it evidently means the whole duration of the Mosaic economy. We are to consider the apostle's words as referring to the end of the Jewish dispensation and the commencement of the Christian, which is the last dispensation which God will vouchsafe to man in the state of probation.

12. *Let him that thinketh he standeth.* "Let him who most confidently standeth"—him who has the fullest conviction in his own conscience that his heart is right with God, and that his mind is right in the truth—take heed lest he fall from his faith, and from the state of holiness in which the grace of God has placed him. I have already shown that the verb *dokein,* which we render "to seem, to think, to suppose," is used by the best Greek writers, not to lessen or weaken the sense, but to render it stronger and more emphatic. In a state of probation everything may change; while we are in this life we may stand or fall. Our standing in the faith depends on our union with God, and that depends on our watching unto prayer and continuing to possess that faith that worketh by love. The highest saint under heaven can stand no longer than he depends upon God and continues in the obedience of faith. He that ceases to do so will fall into sin and get a darkened understanding and a hardened heart, and he may continue in this state till God comes to take away his soul. Therefore "let him who most assuredly standeth take heed lest he fall"; not only partially, but finally.

13. *But such as is common to man.* Chrysostom has properly translated this word "small, short, moderate." Your temptations or trials have been but trifling in comparison of those endured by the Israelites; they might have been easily resisted and overcome. Besides, God will not suffer you to be tried above the strength He gives you; but as the trial comes, He will provide you with sufficient strength to resist it; as the trial comes in, He will make your way out. The words are very remarkable, "He will, with the temptation, make the deliverance, or way out." Satan is never permitted to block up our way without the providence of God making a way through the wall.

14. *Wherefore . . . flee from idolatry.* This is a trial of no great magnitude; to escape from so gross a temptation requires but a moderate portion of grace and circumspection.

15. *I speak as to wise men.* The Corinthians valued themselves not a little on their wisdom and various gifts; the apostle admits this and draws an argument from it against themselves. As you are so wise, surely you can see the propriety of abominating idolatry of every kind; for an idol is nothing in the world and can do nothing for you and nothing against you.

16. *The cup of blessing.* The apostle speaks here of the Eucharist, which he illustrates by *the cup of blessing,* over which thanks were expressed at the conclusion of the Passover. *The communion of the blood of Christ.* We who partake of this sacred cup in commemoration of the death of Christ are made partakers of His body and blood and thus have fellowship with Him, as those who partake of an idol feast thereby, as much as they can, participate with the idol to whom the sacrifice was offered.

17. *For we being many are one bread.* The original would be better translated thus: "Because there is one bread, or loaf, we, who are many, are one body." As only one loaf was used at the Passover, and those who partook of it were considered to be one religious body, so we who partake of the eucharistical bread and wine, in commemoration of the sacrificial death of Christ, are one spiritual society, because we are all made partakers of that one Christ whose blood was shed for us to make an atonement for our sins, as the blood of the paschal lamb was shed and sprinkled in reference to this of which it was the type.

18. *Behold Israel after the flesh.* The Jews not yet converted to Christianity, the latter being Israel after the Spirit. As the design of the apostle was to withdraw his converts at Corinth from all temptations to idolatry, he produces two examples to show the propriety of his endeavors. (1) All who join together in celebrating the Lord's Supper, and are partakers of that one bread, give proof by this that they are Christians and have fellowship with Christ. (2) All the Israelites who offer sacrifice and partake of those sacrifices give proof thereby that they are Jews, and are in fellowship with the object of their worship. So they who join in idol festivals and eat things which have been offered to idols give proof that they are in communion with those idolaters, and that they have fellowship with the demons they worship.

19. *What say I then?* A Jewish phrase for, "I conclude." And this is his conclusion: that although an idol is nothing, has neither power nor influence, nor are things offered to idols anything the worse for being thus offered, yet, as the things sacrificed by the Gentiles are sacrificed to demons and not to God, those who partake of them have fellowship with demons. Those who profess Christianity cannot have fellowship with both Christ and the devil.

21. *Ye cannot drink the cup of the Lord.* It is in vain that you who frequent these idol festivals profess the religion of Christ and commemorate His death and passion in the holy Eucharist; for you cannot have that fellowship with Christ which this ordinance implies while you are partakers of the table of demons.

22. *Do we provoke the Lord to jealousy?* All idolatry is represented as a sort of spiritual adultery. It is giving that heart to Satan that should be devoted to God; and He is represented as being jealous because of the infidelity of those who have covenanted to give their hearts to Him. *Are we stronger than he?* As He has threatened to punish such transgressors and will infallibly do it, can we resist His omnipotence? A sinner should consider, while he is in rebellion against God, whether he be able to resist that power whereby God will inflict vengeance.

23. *All things are lawful for me.* I may lawfully eat all kinds of food, *but all things are not expedient.* It would not be "becoming" in me to eat of all, because I should by this offend and grieve many weak minds.

24. *Let no man seek his own.* Let none for his private gratification or emolument disturb the peace or injure the soul of another. Let every man live, not for himself, but for every part of the great human family with which he is surrounded.

25. *Whatsoever is sold in the shambles, that eat.* The case to which the apostle refers is simply this: It was customary to bring the flesh of the animal to market, the blood of which had been poured out in sacrifice to an idol. Or, taken more particularly, the case was this: One part of the sacrifice was consumed on the altar of the idol; a second part was dressed and eaten by the sacrificer; and a third belonged to the priest, and was often sold in the shambles. To partake of the second share, or to feast upon the sacrifice, Paul absolutely forbids, because this was one part of the religious worship which was paid to the idol; it was sitting down as guests at his table, in token that they were in fellowship with him. This was utterly incompatible with receiving the sacrament of the Lord's Supper, which was the communion of the body and blood of Christ. But as to the third share, the apostle leaves them at liberty either to eat of it or forbear—except that, by eating, their weak brethren should be offended; in that case, though the thing was lawful, it was their duty to abstain.

26. *For the earth is the Lord's.* And because God made the earth and its fullness, all animals, plants, and vegetables, there can be nothing in it or them impure or unholy, because all are the creatures of God.

27. *If any . . . bid you to a feast.* The apostle means any common meal, not an idol festival; for to such no Christian could lawfully go. Whatsoever is set before you, eat. Do not act as the Jews generally do, torturing both themselves and others with questions.

28. *This is offered in sacrifice unto idols.* While they were not apprized of this circumstance they might lawfully eat; but when told that the flesh set before them had been offered to an idol, then they were not to eat, for the sake of his weak conscience who pointed out the circumstance. For the apostle still takes it for granted that even the flesh offered in sacrifice to an idol might be eaten innocently at any private table, as in that case they were no longer in danger of being partakers with devils, as this was no idol festival. *For the earth is the Lord's, and the fulness thereof.* This whole clause, which appears also in v. 26, is wanting here in a number of MSS. and in several of the fathers. It has scarcely any authority to support it.

29-30. *For why is my liberty judged of another man's conscience?* Though in the case of flesh offered to idols and other matters connected with idolatry (on which it appears there was much of a tender conscience among some of the Corinthians) it was necessary to sacrifice something to an overscrupulous conscience, yet the gospel of Christ did not lay any man under this general burden, that he must do nothing at which any weak brother might feel hurt or be stumbled; for the liberty of the gospel must not take for its rule the scrupulosity of any conscience. For if a man, by grace—by the allowance or authority of the gospel—partake of anything that God's bounty has sent and which the gospel has not forbidden and give thanks to God for the blessing, no man has right or authority to condemn such a person. This seems to be the meaning of these two verses; and they read a lesson of caution to rash judges, and to those who are apt to take offense.

31. *Whether therefore ye eat, or drink.* As no general rule can be laid down in reference to the above particulars, there is one maxim of which no Christian must lose sight—that whether he eats or drinks of this or the other kind of aliments, or whatever else he may do, he must do it so as to bring glory to God. This is a sufficient rule to regulate every man's conscience and practice in all indifferent things, where there are no express commands or prohibitions.

32. *Give none offence.* Scrupulously avoid giving any cause of offense either to the unconverted *Jews* or to the unconverted *Gentiles,* so as to prejudice them against Christianity; *nor to the church of God,* made up of converts from the above parties.

33. *Even as I please all men.* Act as I do. Forgetting myself, my own interests, convenience, ease, and comfort, I labor for the welfare of others, and particularly that they may be saved. How blessed and amiable were the spirit and conduct of this holy man!

CHAPTER 11

The apostle reprehends the Corinthians for several irregularities in their manner of conducting public worship: the men praying or prophesying with their heads covered, and the women with their heads uncovered, contrary to custom, propriety, and decency, 1-6. Reasons why they should act differently, 7-16. They are also reproved for their divisions and heresies, 17-19. And for the irregular manner in which they celebrated the Lord's Supper, 20-22. The proper manner of celebrating this holy rite laid down by the apostle, 23-26. Directions for a profitable receiving of the Lord's Supper, and avoiding the dangerous consequences of communicating unworthily, 27-34.

1. *Be ye followers of me.* This verse certainly belongs to the preceding chapter, and is here out of all proper place and connection.

2. *That ye remember me in all things.* It appears that the apostle had previously given them a variety of directions relative to the matters mentioned here; that some had paid strict attention to them, and that others had not; and that contentions and divisions were the consequences, which he here reproves and endeavors to rectify.

3. *The head of every man is Christ.* The apostle is speaking particularly of Christianity and its ordinances. Christ is the Head or Author of this religion and is the Creator, Preserver, and Lord of every man. The man also is the lord or head of the woman; and the Head or Lord of Christ, as Mediator between God and man, is God the Father. Here is the order—God sends His Son, Jesus Christ, to redeem man; Christ comes and lays down His life for the world; every man who receives Christianity confesses that Jesus Christ is Lord, to the glory of God the Father; and every believing woman will acknowledge, according to Gen. iii. 16, that God

has placed her in a dependence on the subjection to the man. So far there is no difficulty in this passage.

4. *Praying or prophesying.* Any person who engages in public acts in the worship of God, whether prayer, singing, or exhortation; for we learn from the apostle himself that "to prophesy" signifies to speak "unto men to edification, and exhortation, and comfort," chap. xiv. 3. And this comprehends all that we understand by exhortation, or even preaching. *Having his head covered,* with his cap or turban on, *dishonoureth his head,* because the head being covered was a sign of subjection; and while he was employed in the public ministration of the Word he was to be considered as a representative of Christ, and on this account his being veiled or covered would be improper. This decision of the apostle was in point-blank hostility to the canons of the Jews; for they would not suffer a man to pray unless he was veiled, for which they gave this reason: "He should veil himself to show that he is ashamed before God, and unworthy with open face to behold Him."

5. *But every woman that prayeth.* Whatever may be the meaning of praying and prophesying in respect to the man, they have precisely the same meaning in respect to the woman. So that some women at least, as well as some men, might speak to others to edification, and exhortation, and comfort. And this kind of prophesying or teaching was predicted by Joel, ii. 28, and referred to by Peter, Acts ii. 17. And had there not been such gifts bestowed on women, the prophecy could not have had its fulfillment. The only difference marked by the apostle was, the man had his head uncovered, because he was the representative of Christ; the woman had hers covered, because she was placed by the order of God in a state of subjection to the man, and because it was a custom, among both the Greeks and the Romans, and among the Jews an express law, that no woman should be seen abroad without a veil. This was a common custom through all the East, and none but public prostitutes went without veils. And if a woman should appear in public without a veil, she would dishonor, *her head*—her husband. And she must appear like to those women who had their hair shorn off as the punishment of whoredom, or adultery.

6. *For if the woman be not covered.* If she will not wear a veil in the public assemblies, *let her . . . be shorn*—let her carry a public badge of infamy; *but if it be a shame*—if to be shorn or shaven would appear, as it must, a badge of infamy, *then let her be covered*—let her by all means wear a veil.

7. *A man indeed ought not to cover his head.* He should not wear his cap or turban in the public congregation, for this was a badge of servitude, or an indication that he had a conscience overwhelmed with guilt; and besides, it was contrary to the custom that prevailed, among both the Greeks and the Romans. *He is the image and glory of God.* He is God's vicegerent in this lower world; and by the authority which he has received from his Maker he is His representative among the creatures and exhibits, more than any other part of the creation, the glory and perfections of the Creator. *But the woman is the glory of the man.* As the man is, among the creatures, the representative of the

glory and perfections of God, so that the fear of Him and the dread of Him are on every beast of the field, etc., so the woman is, in the house and family, the representative of the power and authority of the man. I believe this to be the meaning of the apostle; and that he is speaking here principally concerning power and authority, and skill to use them. It is certainly not the moral image of God, nor His celestial glory, of which he speaks in this verse.

8. *For the man is not of the woman.* His meaning is that the man does not belong to the woman, as if she were the principal; but the woman belongs to the man in that view.

9. *Neither was the man created.* For the man was not created upon the woman's account. The reason is plain from what is mentioned above; and from the original creation of woman she was made for the man, to be his proper or suitable helper.

10. *For this cause ought the woman to have power on her head because of the angels.* "And because of this superiority in the man, I conclude that the woman should have on her head a veil, the mark of her husband's power over her, especially in the religious assemblies, where the angels are supposed to be invisibly present." The custom of the Nazarite may cast some light upon this place. As Nazarite means one who has separated himself by vow to some religious austerity, wearing his own hair, etc., so a married woman was considered a Nazarite for life, i.e., separated from all others, and joined to one husband, who is her lord. And hence the apostle, alluding to this circumstance, says, *The woman ought to have power on her head,* i.e., wear her hair and veil; for her hair is a proof of her being a Nazarite, and of her subjection to her husband, as the Nazarite was under subjection to the Lord, according to the rule or law of his order.

11. *Neither is the man without the woman.* The apostle seems to say: I do not intimate any disparagement of the female sex, by insisting on the necessity of her being under the power or authority of the man, for they are both equally dependent on each other.

12. *For as the woman is of the man.* For as the woman was first formed out of the side of man, man has ever since been formed out of the womb of the woman; but they, as all other created things, are of God.

13. *Judge in yourselves.* Consider the subject in your own common sense, and then say whether it be decent for a woman to pray in public without a veil on her head. The heathen priestesses prayed or delivered their oracles bareheaded or with dishevelled hair; to be conformed to them would be very disgraceful to Christian women. And in reference to such things as these the apostle appeals to their sense of honor and decency.

14. *Doth not even nature itself teach you that if a man have long hair?* Nature certainly teaches us, by bestowing it, that it is proper for women to have long hair; and it is not so with men. The hair of the male rarely grows like that of a female, unless art is used, and even then it bears but a scanty proportion to the former. Hence it is truly womanish to have long hair, and it is a shame to the man who affects it. In ancient times the people of Achaia, the province in which Corinth stood, and the Greeks in general, were noted for their long hair; and hence called by Homer, in a great variety of places, "the long-haired Greeks." Long hair was certainly not in repute among the Jews. The Nazarites let their hair grow, but it was as a token of humiliation; and it is possible that Paul had this in view. There were consequently two reasons why the apostle should condemn this practice: (1) Because it was a sign of humiliation; (2) Because it was womanish. After all, it is possible that Paul may refer to dressed, frizzled, and curled hair, which shallow and effeminate men might have affected in that time, as they do in this.

15. *But if a woman have long hair.* The Author of their being has given a larger proportion of hair to the head of women than to that of men; and to them it is an especial ornament, and may in various cases serve as a veil.

16. *But if any man seem to be contentious.* If any person sets himself up as a wrangler, put himself forward as a defender of such points —that a woman may pray or teach with her head uncovered, and that a man may, without reproach, have long hair—let him know that we have no such custom as either, nor are they sanctioned by any of the churches of God, whether among the Jews or among the Gentiles.

17. *Now in this . . . I praise you not.* In the beginning of this Epistle the apostle did praise them for their attention in general to the rules he had laid down; see v. 2. But here he is obliged to condemn certain irregularities which had crept in among them, particularly relative to the celebration of the Lord's Supper. Through some false teaching which they had received, in the absence of the apostle, they appear to have celebrated it precisely in the same way the Jews did their Passover. That, we know, was a regular meal, only accompanied with certain peculiar circumstances and ceremonies. Two of these ceremonies were eating bread, solemnly broken, and drinking a cup of wine called the cup of blessing. Now it is certain that our Lord has taken these two things and made them expressive of the crucifixion of His body and the shedding of His blood as an atonement for the sins of mankind. The teachers which had crept into the Corinthian church appear to have perverted the whole of this divine institution, for the celebration of the Lord's Supper appears to have been made among them a part of an ordinary meal. The people came together and it appears brought their provisions with them. Some had much; others had less. Some ate to excess; others had scarcely enough to suffice nature. One was hungry, and the other was drunken, "was filled to the full"; this is the sense of the word in many places of Scripture.

18. *There be divisions among you.* They had "schisms" among them; the old parties were kept up, even in the place where they assembled to eat the Lord's Supper.

19. *There must be also heresies.* Not a common consent of the members of the church either in the doctrines of the gospel or in the ceremonies of the Christian religion. Their difference in religious opinion led to a difference in their religious practice, and thus the church of God, that should have been one body, was

split into sects and parties. The divisions and the heresies sprang out of each other.

20. *This is not to eat the Lord's supper.* They did not come together to eat the Lord's Supper exclusively, which they should have done and not have made it a part of an ordinary meal.

21. *Every one taketh before . . . his own supper.* They had a grand feast, though the different sects kept in parties by themselves; but all took as ample a supper as they could provide (each bringing his own provisions with him) before they took what was called the Lord's Supper.

22. *Have ye not houses to eat and to drink in?* They should have taken their ordinary meal at home, and have come together in the church to celebrate the Lord's Supper. *Despise ye the church of God?* You render the sacred assembly and the place contemptible by your conduct, and you show yourselves destitute of that respect which you owe to the place set apart for divine worship. *And shame them that have not.* "Them that are poor"; not them who had not victuals at that time, but those who are so poor as to be incapable of furnishing themselves as others had done.

23. *I have received of the Lord.* It is possible that several of the people at Corinth did receive the bread and wine of the Eucharist as they did the paschal bread and wine, as a mere commemoration of an event. And as our Lord had by this institution consecrated that bread and wine, not to be the means of commemorating the deliverance from Egypt and their joy on the account, but their deliverance from sin and death by His passion and cross, therefore the apostle states that he had received from the Lord what he delivered; viz., that the eucharistic bread and wine were to be understood of the accomplishment of that of which the paschal lamb was the type—the body broken for them, the blood shed for them.

26. *Ye do shew the Lord's death.* As in the Passover they showed forth the bondage they had been in and the redemption they had received from it, so in the Eucharist they showed forth the sacrificial death of Christ and the redemption from sin derived from it.

27. *Whosoever shall eat . . . and drink . . . unworthily.* To put a final end to controversies and perplexities relative to these words and the context, let the reader observe that to *eat* and *drink* the bread and wine in the Lord's Supper *unworthily* is to eat and drink as the Corinthians did, who ate it, not in reference to Jesus Christ's sacrificial death, but rather in such a way as the Israelites did the Passover, which they celebrated in remembrance of their deliverance from Egyptian bondage. Likewise these mongrel Christians at Corinth used it as a kind of historical commemoration of the death of Christ and did not, in the whole institution, discern the Lord's body and blood as a sacrificial offering for sin; and besides, in their celebration of it they acted in a way utterly unbecoming the gravity of a sacred ordinance. *Shall be guilty of the body and blood of the Lord.* If he use it irreverently, if he deny/ that Christ suffered unjustly (for of some such persons the apostle must be understood to speak), then he in effect joins issue with the Jews in their condemnation and crucifixion of the Lord Jesus, and renders

himself guilty of the death of our blessed Lord. Some, however, understand the passage thus: is guilty, i.e., eats and drinks unworthily, and brings on himself that punishment mentioned in v. 30.

28. *Let a man examine himself.* Let him try whether he has proper faith in the Lord Jesus, and whether he discerns the Lord's body, and whether he duly considers that the bread and wine point out the crucified body and spilt blood of Christ.

29. *Eateth and drinketh damnation.* "Judgment, punishment"; and yet this is not unto *damnation,* for the judgment or punishment inflicted upon the disorderly and the profane was intended for their emendation; for in v. 32 it is said, when we are "judged," we are chastened, corrected as a father does his children, "that we should not be condemned with the world."

30. *For this cause.* That they partook of this sacred ordinance without discerning the Lord's body. *Many are weak and sickly.* It is hard to say whether these words refer to the consequences of their own intemperance or to some extraordinary disorders inflicted immediately by God himself. That there were disorders of the most reprehensible kind among these people at this sacred supper, the preceding verses sufficiently point out; and after such excesses, many might be *weak* and *sickly* among them, and *many* might *sleep,* i.e., "die"; for continual experience shows us that many fall victims to their own intemperance. However, acting as they did in this solemn and awful sacrament, they might have "provoked God to plague them with divers diseases and sundry kinds of death."

31. *If we would judge ourselves.* If, having acted improperly, we condemn our conduct and humble ourselves, we shall not be *judged,* i.e., "punished" for the sin we have committed.

33. *When ye come together to eat* (the Lord's Supper), *tarry one for another*—do not eat and drink in parties as ye have done heretofore, and do not connect it with any other meal.

34. *And if any man hunger,* let him not come to the house of God to eat an ordinary meal; *let him eat at home*—take that in his own house which is necessary for the support of his body before he comes to that sacred repast, where he should have the feeding of his soul alone in view. *That ye come not together unto condemnation.* That you may avoid the curse that must fall on such worthless communicants as those above mentioned, and that you may get that especial blessing which everyone that discerns the Lord's body in the Eucharist must receive. *The rest will I set in order.* All the other matters relative to this business to which you have referred in your letter I will regulate when I come to visit you, as, God permitting, I fully design. The apostle did visit them about one year after this, as is generally believed.

CHAPTER 12

The apostle proceeds to the question of the Corinthians concerning spiritual gifts, 1. He calls to their remembrance their former state, and how they were brought out of it, 2-3. Shows that there are diversities of gifts which proceed from the Spirit, 4. Diversities of administrations which proceed from the Lord Jesus, 5. And diversities of operations which proceed from God, 6. What these gifts are, and how they are dispensed, 7-11. Christ is the Head, and the Church His members; and this is pointed out under the similitude of the human body.

12-13. The relation which the members of the body have to each other, and how necessary their mutual support, **14-26.** The members in the Church, or spiritual body, and their respective offices, **27-30.** We should earnestly covet the best gifts, **31.**

1. *Now concerning spiritual gifts.* This was a subject about which they appear to have written to the apostle, and concerning which there were probably some contentions among them. The words may as well be translated "concerning spiritual persons" as *spiritual gifts,* and indeed the former agrees much better with the context. *I would not have you ignorant.* I wish you fully to know whence all such gifts come, and for what end they are given, that each person may serve the church in the capacity in which God has placed him, that there may be no misunderstandings and no schism in the body.

2. *Ye were Gentiles.* Previously to your conversion to the Christian faith, you were heathens, *carried away,* not guided by reason or truth, but hurried by your passions into a senseless worship, the chief part of which was calculated only to excite and gratify animal propensities. *Dumb idols.* Though often supplicated, could never return an answer; so that not only the image could not speak, but the god or demon pretended to be represented by it could not speak—a full proof that an idol was nothing in the world.

3. *No man speaking by the Spirit of God.* It was granted on all hands that there could be no religion without divine inspiration, because God alone could make His will known to men. Hence heathenism pretended to this inspiration; Judaism had it in the law and the prophets; and it was the very essence of the Christian religion. Both Judaism and heathenism were full of expectations of a future teacher and deliverer; and to this person, especially among the Jews, the Spirit in all the prophets gave witness. This was the Messiah, who was manifested in the person of Jesus of Nazareth; and Him the Jews rejected, though He proved His divine mission both by His doctrines and by His miracles. But as the Holy Spirit through all the law and the prophets gave testimony to the Messiah, and as Jesus proved himself to be the Christ by both His miracles and His doctrines, no man under the inspiration of the divine Spirit could say to Him, "Anathema"—Thou art a deceiver, and a person worthy of death, etc., as the Jews did. Therefore the Jews were no longer under the inspiration of the Spirit of God. *And that no man can say that Jesus is the Lord.* Nor can we demonstrate this person to be the Messiah and the Saviour of men but by the Holy Ghost, He attesting the truth of our doctrines to them that hear, by enlightening their minds, changing their hearts, and filling them with the peace and love of God.

4. *There are diversities of gifts.* "Gracious endowments," leading to miraculous results.

5. *Differences of administrations.* Various offices in the Church, such as apostle, prophet, and teacher; the qualifications for such offices, as well as the appointments themselves, coming immediately from the one Lord Jesus Christ.

6. *Diversities of operations.* Miraculous influences exerted on others, such as the expulsion of demons, inflicting extraordinary punishments (as in the case of Ananias and Sapphira, Elymas the sorcerer, etc.), the healing of different diseases, raising the dead, etc. All these proceeded from God the Father, as the Fountain of all goodness and power, and the immediate Dispenser of every good and perfect gift.

In the preceding three verses we find more than an indirect reference to the doctrine of the sacred Trinity. Gifts are attributed to the Holy Spirit, v. 4; administrations to the Lord Jesus, v. 5; operations to God the Father, v. 6.

7. *The manifestation of the Spirit.* This is variably understood by the fathers, some of them rendering "illumination," others "demonstration," and others "operation." The apostle's meaning seems to be this: Whatever gifts God has bestowed, or in what various ways soever the Spirit of God may have manifested himself, it is all for the common benefit of the Church. God has given no gift to any man for his own private advantage or exclusive profit. He has it for the benefit of others as well as for his own salvation.

8. *Word of wisdom.* In all these places I consider that the proper translation of *logos* is "doctrine," as in many other places of the New Testament. It is very difficult to say what is intended here by the different kinds of gifts mentioned by the apostle; they were probably all supernatural, and were necessary at that time only for the benefit of the Church. By "doctrine of wisdom" we may understand the mystery of our redemption, in which the wisdom of God was most eminently conspicuous. By "the doctrine of knowledge" we may understand either a knowledge of the types, etc., in the Old Testament or what are termed "mysteries": the calling of the Gentiles, the recalling of the Jews, the mystery of iniquity, of the beast, etc., and especially the mystical sense or meaning of the Old Testament, with all its types, rites, ceremonies.

9. By *faith* we are to understand that miraculous faith by which they could remove mountains, chap. xiii. 2. *Gifts of healing* simply refers to the power which at particular times the apostles received from the Holy Spirit to cure diseases.

10. *The working of miracles.* This seems to refer to the same class as the "operations," v. 6, as the words are the same; and to signify those powers by which they were enabled at particular times to work miraculously on others, ejecting demons, inflicting punishments or judgments, as in the cases mentioned under v. 6. *Prophecy.* This seems to import two things: (1) The predicting future events such as then particularly concerned the state of the Church and the apostles—as the dearth foretold by Agabus, Acts xi. 28; and the binding of Paul, and delivering him to the Romans, Acts xxi. 10; and Paul's foretelling his own shipwreck on Malta, Acts xxvii. 25; and (2) As implying the faculty of teaching or expounding the Scriptures, which is also a common acceptation of the word. *Discerning of spirits.* A gift by which the person so privileged could discern a false miracle from a true one, or a pretender to inspiration from him who was made really partaker of the Holy Ghost. It probably extended also to the discernment of false professors from true ones as appears in Peter in the case of Ananias and his wife. *Divers kinds of tongues.* "Different languages," which they had never learned, and which God gave them for the immediate instruction of people of different countries who attended their ministry. *Interpretation of tongues.* It was necessary that while one was speaking the deep things of God in a company where several were present who did not understand, though the majority did, there should be a person who could immediately interpret what was said to that part of the congregation that did not understand the language. This power to interpret was also an immediate gift of God's Spirit and is classed here among the miracles.

11. *But all these worketh that one and the selfsame Spirit.* All these gifts are miraculously bestowed. They cannot be acquired by human art or industry, the different languages excepted; but they were given in such a way, and in such circumstances, as sufficiently proved that they also were miraculous gifts.

12. *For as the body is one.* Though the human body have many members and though it be composed of a great variety of parts, yet it is but one entire system, every part and member being necessary to the integrity or completeness of the whole. *So also is Christ.* That is, So is the Church the body of Christ, being composed of the different officers already mentioned, and especially those enumerated, v. 28, apostles, prophets, teachers, etc. It cannot be supposed that Christ is composed of many members, and therefore the term Church must be understood; unless we suppose, which is not probable, that the term *Christ* is used to express the Church or whole body of Christian believers.

13. *For by one Spirit are we all baptized.* As the body of man, though composed of many members, is informed and influenced by one soul, so the Church of Christ, which is His body, though composed of many members, is informed and influenced by one Spirit, the Holy Ghost; actuating and working by His spiritual body, as the human soul does in the body of man. *To drink into one Spirit.* We are to understand being made partakers of the gifts and graces of the Holy Ghost agreeably to the words of our Lord, John vii. 37, etc.: "If any man thirst, let him come unto me, and drink . . . this spake he of the Spirit, which they that believe on him should receive."

14. *For the body is not one member.* The mystical body, the Church, as well as the natural body, is composed of many members.

15. *If the foot shall say.* As all the members of the body are necessarily dependent on each other, and minister to the general support of the system, so is it in the Church.

21. *And the eye cannot say unto the hand, I have no need of thee.* The apostle goes on, with his principal object in view, to show that the gifts and graces with which their different teachers were endowed were all necessary for their salvation, and should be collectively used. For not one of them was unnecessary, nor could they dispense with the least of them; the body of Christ needed the whole for its nourishment and support.

22. *Those members . . . which seem to be more feeble.* These, and the less honorable and uncomely, mentioned in the next verses, seem to mean the principal viscera, such as the heart, lungs, stomach, and intestinal canal. These, when compared with the arms and limbs, are comparatively weak and some of them, considered in themselves, uncomely and less honorable; yet these are more essential to life than any of the others. A man may lose an eye by accident, and an arm or a leg may be amputated, and yet the body live and be vigorous; but let the stomach, heart, lungs, or any of the viscera be removed, and life becomes necessarily extinct.

25. *That there should be no schism in the body.* That there should be no unnecessary and independent part in the whole human machine, and that every part should contribute something to the general proportion, symmetry, and beauty of the body.

26. *And whether one member suffer.* As there is a mutual exertion for the general defense, so there is a mutual sympathy. If the eye, the hand, the foot be injured, the whole man grieves; and if by clothing, or anything else, any particular member or part is adorned, strengthened, or better secured, it gives a general pleasure to the whole man.

27. *Now ye are the body of Christ.* As the members in the human body, so the different members of the mystical body of Christ. All are intended by Him to have the same relation to each other, to be mutually subservient to each other, to mourn for and rejoice with each other. He has also made each necessary to the beauty, proportion, strength, and perfection of the whole. Not one is useless; not one, unnecessary. Paul, Apollos, Cephas, etc., with all their variety of gifts and graces, are "for the perfecting of the saints, for the work of the ministry, for the edifying to the body of Christ," Eph. iv. 12. Hence no teacher should be exalted above or opposed to another.

28. *God hath set some in the church.* As God has made evident distinctions among the members of the human body, so that some occupy a more eminent place than others, so has He in the Church. And to prove this, the apostle enumerates the principal offices, and in the order in which they should stand. *First apostles.* Persons immediately designated by Christ, and sent by Him to preach the gospel to all mankind. *Secondarily prophets.* A person who, under divine inspiration, predicts future events; but the word is often applied to those who preach the gospel. *Thirdly teachers.* Persons whose chief business it was to instruct the people in the elements of the Christian religion, and their duty to each other. *Miracles.* Persons endued with miraculous gifts. *Gifts of healings.* Such as laying hands upon the sick, and healing them. *Helps.* Dr. Lightfoot conjectures that these were the apostles' helpers; persons who accompanied them, baptized those who were converted by them, and were sent by them to such places as they could not attend to, being otherwise employed. The Levites are termed by the Talmudists "helps of the priests." The word occurs in Luke i. 54; Rom. viii. 26. *Governments.* Dr. Lightfoot contends that this word does not refer to the power of ruling, but to the case of a person endued with a deep and comprehensive mind, who is profoundly wise and prudent. *Diversities of tongues.* "Kinds of tongues"; that is, different kinds. The power to speak, on all necessary occasions, languages which they had not learned.

29. *Are all apostles?* That is: All are not apostles, all are not prophets, etc. God has distributed His various gifts among various persons, each of whom is necessary for the complete edification of the body of Christ.

31. *But covet earnestly.* To *covet* signifies to "desire earnestly." Some think that this verse should be read affirmatively, "You earnestly contend about the best gifts; but I show unto you a more excellent way"; i.e., get your hearts filled with love to God and man—love, which is the principle of obedience, which works no ill to its neighbor, and which is the fulfilling of the law. This is a likely reading, for there were certainly more contentions in the church of Corinth about the gifts than about the graces of the Spirit.

CHAPTER 13

Charity, or love to God and man, the sum and substance of all true religion; so that without it the most splendid eloquence, the gift of prophecy, the most profound knowledge, faith by which the most stupendous miracles might be wrought, benevolence the most unbounded, and zeal for the truth, even to martyrdom, would all be unavailing to salvation, 1-3. The description and praise of this grace, 4-7. Its durableness; though tongues, prophecies, and knowledge shall cease, yet this shall never fail, 8-10. Description of the present imperfect state of man, 11-12. Of all the graces of God in man, charity, or love, is the greatest, 13.

1. *Though I speak.* At the conclusion of the preceding chapter the apostle promised to show the Corinthians a "more excellent way" than that in which they were now proceeding. They were so distracted with contentions, divided by parties, and envious of each other's gifts that unity was nearly destroyed. This was a full proof that love to God and man was wanting, and that without this their numerous gifts and other graces were nothing in the eyes of God; for it was evident that they did not love one another, which is a proof that they did not love God, and consequently that they had not true religion. Before I proceed to the consideration of the different parts of this chapter, it may be necessary to examine whether the word *agape* be best translated by charity or "love." Wycliffe, translating from the Vulgate, has the word *charity;* and him our Authorized Version follows. But Coverdale, Matthews, Cranmer, and the Geneva Bible have "love," which is adopted by recent translators and commentators in general, among whom are Dodd and Wesley. All these strenuously contend that the word *charity,* which is now confined to "almsgiving," is utterly improper, and that the word "love" alone expresses the apostle's sense. *The tongues of men.* All human languages, with all the eloquence of the most accomplished orator. *And of angels.* I.e., though a man knew the language of the eternal world so well that he could hold conversation with its inhabitants, and find out the secrets of their Kingdom. Or probably the apostle refers to a notion that was common among the Jews that there was a language by which angels might be invoked, adjured, collected, and dispersed; and by the means of which many secrets might be found out, and curious arts and sciences known. *Sounding brass.* That is, like a trumpet made of brass. *Tinkling cymbal.* Though I possessed the knowledge of all languages, and could deliver even the truth of God in them in the most eloquent manner, and had not a heart full of love to God and man, my religion is no more to my salvation than the sounds emitted by the brazen trumpet, or the jingling of the cymbals could contribute intellectual pleasure to the instruments which produce them; and, in the sight of God, I am of no more moral worth than those sounds are.

I will quote Josiah Gregory: "People of little religion are always noisy; he who has not the love of God and man filling his heart is like an empty wagon coming violently down a hill: it makes a great noise, because there is nothing in it."

2. *And though I have the gift of prophecy.* Though I should have received from God the knowledge of future events, so that I could correctly foretell what is coming to pass in the world and in the Church; *and understand all mysteries.* The meaning of all the types and figures in the Old Testament, and all the unexplored secrets of nature; *and all knowledge*—every human art and science; *and though I have all faith*—such miraculous faith as would enable me even to remove mountains, or had such powerful discernment in sacred things that I could solve the greatest difficulties; *and have not charity*—this love to God and man, as the principle and motive of all my conduct, the characteristics of which are given in the following verses; *I am nothing*—nothing in myself, nothing in the sight of God, nothing in the Church, and good for nothing to mankind. Balaam and several others not under the influence of this love of God prophesied.

3. *And though I bestow all my goods to feed the poor.* This is a proof that *charity,* in our sense of the word, is not what the apostle means; for surely almsgiving can go no further than to give up all that a man possesses in order to relieve the wants of others. The word which we translate *to feed the poor* signifies to "divide into morsels, and put into the mouth," which implies carefulness and tenderness in applying the bounty thus freely given. *And though I give my body to be burned.* Mr. Wakefield renders this clause thus: "And though I give up my body so as to have cause of boasting"; in vindication of which he first refers to Dan. iii. 28; Acts xv. 26; Rom. viii. 32; Phil. i. 20. "That I may boast" is the reading of the Aethiopic and Coptic, and of the Codex Alexandrinus; several Greek and Latin MSS. referred to by Jerome; and of Jerome himself. who translates the passage thus: "If I deliver up my body that I may glory, or have cause of boasting." The charity or love which God recommends, the apostle describes in sixteen particulars, which are the following:

4. (1) *Charity suffereth long.* "Has a long mind"; to the end of which neither trials, adversities, persecutions, nor provocations can reach. The love of God, and of our neighbor for God's sake, is patient towards all man. It suffers all the weakness, ignorance, errors, and infirmities of the children of God, and all the malice and wickedness of the children of this world; and all this, not merely for a time, but *long,* without end. (2) *Is kind.* It is tender and compassionate in itself, and *kind* and obliging to others; it is mild, gentle, and benign; and if called to suffer, inspires the sufferer with the most amiable sweetness and the most tender affection. It is also submissive to all the dispensations of God, and creates trouble to no one. (3) *Charity envieth not.* Is not grieved because another possesses a greater portion of earthly, intellectual, or spiritual blessings. Those who have this pure love rejoice as much at the happiness, the honor, and comfort of others as they can do in their own. They are ever willing that others should be preferred before

them. (4) *Charity vaunteth not itself.* This word is variously translated; "acteth not rashly, insolently; is not inconstant." There is a phrase in our own language that expresses what I think to be the meaning of the original, does not "set itself forward"—does not desire to be noticed or applauded, but wishes that God may be All in All. (5) *Is not puffed up.* Is not "inflated" with a sense of its own importance; for it knows it has nothing but what it has received, and that it deserves nothing that it has got. Every man whose heart is full of the love of God is full of humility; for there is no man so humble as he whose heart is cleansed from all sin. True humility arises from a sense of the fullness of God in the soul; abasement from a sense of corruption is a widely different thing.

5. (6) *Doth not behave itself unseemly.* Love never acts out of its place or character; observes due decorum and good manners; is never rude, bearish, or brutish; and is ever willing to become all things to all men, that it may please them for their good to edification. No ill-bred man, or what is termed rude or unmannerly, is a Christian. A man may have a natural bluntness, or be a clown, and yet there be nothing boorish or hoggish in his manner. I must apologize for using such words; they best express the evil against which I wish both powerfully and successfully to declaim. I never wish to meet with those who affect to be called "blunt, honest men"; who feel themselves above all the forms of respect and civility, and care not how many they put to pain, or how many they displease. But let me not be misunderstood; I do not contend for ridiculous ceremonies and hollow compliments. There is surely a medium, and a sensible Christian man will not be long at a loss to find it out. (7) *Seeketh not her own.* Is not desirous of her own spiritual welfare only, but of her neighbor's also. For the writers of the Old and New Testaments do almost everywhere, agreeably to their Hebrew idiom, express a preference given to one thing before another by an affirmation of that which is preferred, and a negative of that which is contrary to it. Love is never satisfied but in the welfare, comfort, and salvation of all. That man is no Christian who is solicitous for his own happiness alone, and cares not how the world goes, so that himself be comfortable. (8) *Is not easily provoked.* "Is not provoked, is not irritated, is not made sour or bitter." How the word *easily* got into our translation it is hard to say; but, however it got in, it is utterly improper, and has nothing in the original to countenance it. The New Testament, printed in 1547, the first year of Edward VI, in English and Latin, has simply, "is not provokeed to angre." The edition published in English in the following year, 1548, has the same rendering, but the orthography better: "is not provoked to anger." The Bible in folio, with notes, published the next year, 1549, by Edmund Becke, preserves nearly the same reading, "is not provoketh to anger." The large folio printed by Richard Cardmarden, at Rouen, 1566, has the same reading. The translation made and printed by the command of King James I, in 1611, departs from all these, and improperly inserts the word *easily*, which might have been His Majesty's own. And yet this translation was not followed by some subsequent editions; for the quarto Bible printed at London four years after, 1615, not only retains this

original and correct reading, "it is not provoked to anger," but has the word "love" everywhere in this chapter instead of *charity*, in which all the preceding versions and editions agree. In short, this is the reading of Coverdale, Matthews, Cranmer, the Geneva, and others; and our own Authorized Version is the only one which I have seen where this false reading appears. The apostle's own words in v. 7 are a sufficient proof that love of which he speaks can never be provoked. When the man who possesses this love gives way to provocation, he loses the balance of his soul and grieves the Spirit of God. In that instant he ceases from loving God with all his soul, mind, and strength; and surely if he get embittered against his neighbor, he does not love him as himself. (9) *Thinketh no evil.* "Believes no evil where no evil seems." Never supposes that a good action may have a bad motive; gives every man credit for his profession of religion, uprightness, godly zeal, while nothing is seen in his conduct or in his spirit inconsistent with this profession. His heart is so governed and influenced by the love of God that he cannot think of evil but where it appears. The original implies that he does not "invent or devise" any evil, or does not "reason" on any particular act or word so as to infer evil from it, for this would destroy his love to his brother; it would be ruinous to charity and benevolence.

6. (10) *Rejoiceth not in iniquity.* "Rejoiceth not in falsehood." but on the contrary, *rejoiceth in the truth.* (11) *But rejoiceth in the truth.* Everything that is opposite to falsehood and irreligion. Those who are filled with the love of God and man rejoice in the propagation and extension of divine truth.

7. (12) *Beareth all things.* This word is also variously interpreted; to "endure, bear, sustain, cover, conceal, contain." But the true import must be found either in "cover" or "contain." Love conceals everything that should be concealed; betrays no secret; retains the grace given; and goes on to continual increase. A person under the influence of this love never makes the sins, follies, faults, or imperfections of any man the subject of either censure or conversation. He covers them as far as he can; and if alone privy to them, he retains the knowledge of them in his own bosom as far as he ought. (13) *Believeth all things.* Is ever ready to believe the best of every person, and will credit no evil of any but on the most positive evidence. (14) *Hopeth all things.* When there is no place left for believing good of a person, then love comes in with its hope, where it could not work by its faith; and begins immediately to make allowances and excuses, as far as a good conscience can permit; and further, anticipates the repentance of the transgressor, and his restoration to the good opinion of society and his place in the Church of God, from which he had fallen. 15) *Endureth all things.* Bears up under all persecutions and maltreatment from open enemies, and professed friends; bears adversities with an even mind, as it submits with perfect resignation to every dispensation of the providence of God; and never says of any trial, affliction, or insult, "This cannot be endured."

8. (16) *Charity never faileth.* "This love never falleth off," because it bears, believes, hopes, and endures all things; and while it does so it cannot fail. It is the means of preserving all

other graces; indeed, properly speaking, it includes them all; and all receive their perfection from it. Love to God and man can never be dispensed with. It is essential to social and religious life; without it no communion can be kept up with God, nor can any man have a preparation for eternal glory whose heart and soul are not deeply imbued with it. *Prophecies, they shall fail.* Whether the word imply predicting future events or teaching the truths of religion to men, all such shall soon be rendered useless. Though the accurate prophet and the eloquent, persuasive preacher be useful in their day, they shall not be always so, nor shall their gifts fit them for glory; nothing short of the love above described can fit a soul for the kingdom of God. *Tongues, they shall cease.* The miraculous gift of different languages shall also cease, as being unnecessary. *Knowledge, it shall vanish away.* All human arts and sciences, as being utterly useless in the eternal world, though so highly extolled and useful here.

9. *For we know in part.* We have here but little knowledge even of earthly, and much less of heavenly, things. He that knows most knows little in comparison of what is known by angels and the spirits of just men made perfect. And as we know so very little, how deficient must we be if we have not much love! *We prophesy in part.* Even the sublimest prophets have been able to say but little of the heavenly state, and the best preachers have left the Spirit of God very much to supply. When you have learned all you can from your ministers, remember you have much to learn from God; and for this you should diligently wait on Him by the reading of His Word and by incessant prayer.

10. *But when that which is perfect.* The state of eternal blessedness. *Then that which is in part,* that which is imperfect, *shall be done away;* the imperfect as well as the probationary state shall cease forever.

11. *When I was a child.* This future state of blessedness is as far beyond the utmost perfection that can be attained in this world as our adult state of Christianity is above our state of natural infancy, in which we understand only as children understand.

12. *Now we see through a glass, darkly.* Of these words some literal explanation is necessary. The word which we translate *a glass* literally signifies a mirror or reflector, and among the ancients mirrors were made of fine polished metal. The word here may signify anything by which the image of a person is reflected, as in our "looking, or look-in, glass." The word is not used for a glass to look through, nor would such an image have suited with the apostle's design. The word which we render *darkly* will help us to the true meaning of the place. "Now, in this life, we see by means of a mirror reflecting the images of heavenly and spiritual things, in an enigmatical manner, invisible things being represented by visible, spiritual by natural, eternal by temporal; but then, in the eternal world, face-to-face, everything being seen in itself, and not by means of a representative or similitude." *Now I know in part.* Though I have an immediate revelation from God concerning His great design in the dispensation of the gospel, yet there are lengths, breadths, depths, and heights of this design which even that revelation has not discovered; nor can they be known and apprehended in the present imperfect state.

Eternity alone can unfold the whole scheme of the gospel. *As also I am known.* In the same manner in which disembodied spirits know and understand.

13. *And now* (in the present life) *abideth faith, hope, charity.* These three supply the place of that direct vision which no human embodied spirit can have; these abide or "remain" for the present state. *Faith,* by which we apprehend spiritual blessings, and walk with God. *Hope,* by which we view and expect eternal blessedness, and pass through things temporal so as not to lose those which are eternal. *Charity* or "love," by which we show forth the virtues of the grace which we receive by faith in living a life of obedience to God and of goodwill and usefulness to man. *But the greatest of these is charity.* Without *faith* it is impossible to please God; and without it, we cannot partake of the grace of our Lord Jesus. Without *hope* we could not endure as seeing Him who is invisible, nor have any adequate notion of the eternal world, nor bear up under the afflictions and difficulties of life. But great and useful and indispensably necessary as these are, yet *charity* or "love" is greater; "love is the fulfilling of the law"; but this is never said of faith or hope. *Love* is properly the image of God in the soul; for "God is love." By *faith* we receive from our Maker; by *hope* we expect a future and eternal good; but by love we resemble God, and by it alone are we qualified to enjoy heaven and be one with Him throughout eternity. *Faith,* says one, is the foundation of the Christian life and of good works; *hope* rears the superstructure; but *love* finishes, completes, and crowns it in a blessed eternity. *Faith* and *hope* respect ourselves alone; *love* takes in both God and man. *Faith* helps, and *hope* sustains us; but *love* to God and man makes us obedient and useful. This one consideration is sufficient to show that love is greater than either faith or hope. Some say *love* is the greatest because it remains throughout eternity, whereas *faith* and *hope* proceed only through life; hence we say that there faith is lost in sight, and hope in fruition. But does the apostle say so? Or does any man inspired by God say so? I believe not. *Faith* and *hope* will as necessarily enter into eternal glory as *love* will. The perfections of God are absolute in their nature, infinite in number, and eternal in their duration. However high, glorious, or sublime the soul may be in that eternal state, it will ever, in respect to God, be limited in its powers, and must be improved and expanded by the communications of the Supreme Being. Hence it will have infinite glories in the nature of God to apprehend by *faith,* to anticipate by *hope,* and enjoy by *love.*

CHAPTER 14

We should earnestly desire spiritual gifts; but prophesying is to be preferred, because it is superior to the gift of tongues, 1-2. Prophesying defined. 3. How to regulate this supernatural gift of tongues, in teaching for the edification of the church, 4-13. In praying and giving thanks, 14-17. Those who speak with tongues should interpret that others may be edified, 18-22. What benefit may accrue from this in the public assemblies, 23-28. How the prophets or teachers should act in the church, 29-33. Women should keep silence in the church, 34-35. All should be humble, and everything should be done in love, 36-40.

1. *Follow after charity.* Most earnestly labor to be put in possession of that love which bear-

eth, believeth, hopeth, and endureth all things. It may be difficult to acquire and difficult to retain this blessed state, but it is essential to your present peace and eternal happiness. This clause belongs to the preceding chapter. *Desire spiritual gifts.* You are very intent on getting those splendid gifts which may add to your worldly consequence and please your carnal minds; but labor rather to get the gifts of God's Spirit, by which you may grow in grace and be useful to others; and particularly desire *that ye may prophesy*—that you may be able to teach and instruct others in the things of their salvation.

2. *For he that speaketh in an unknown tongue.* This chapter is crowded with difficulties. It is not likely that the Holy Spirit should in the church suddenly inspire a man with the knowledge of some foreign language which none in the church understood but himself; and lead him to treat the mysteries of Christianity in that language, though none in the place could profit by his teaching. Dr. Lightfoot's mode of reconciling these difficulties is the most likely I have met with. He supposes that by the unknown *tongue* the Hebrew is meant, and that God restored the true knowledge of this language when He gave the apostles the gift of tongues. As the Scriptures of the Old Testament were contained in this language, and it has beauties, energies, and depths in it which no verbal translation can reach, it was necessary, for the proper elucidation of the prophecies concerning the Messiah and the establishment of the Christian religion, that the full meaning of the words of this sacred language should be properly understood. *Speaketh not unto men, but unto God.* None present understanding the language, God alone knowing the truth and import of what he says. *In the spirit he speaketh mysteries.* Though his own mind (for so *pneumati* is understood here by many eminent critics) apprehends the mysteries contained in the words which he reads or utters; but if by *the spirit* we understand the Spirit of God, it only shows that it is by that Spirit that he is enabled to speak and apprehend these mysteries.

3. *But he that prophesieth.* The person who has the gift of teaching is much more useful to the church than he is who has only the gift of tongues, because he speaks to the profit of men: viz., to their *edification*, by the Scriptures he expounds; to their *exhortation*, by what he teaches; and to their *comfort*, by his revelation.

4. *He that speaketh in an unknown tongue*— in the Hebrew, for instance. The knowledge of the depth and power of which he has got by a divine revelation *edifieth himself* by that knowledge. *But he that prophesieth.* Has the gift of preaching. *Edifieth the church.* Speaketh unto men to edification, exhortation, and comfort, v. 3.

5. *I would that ye all spake with tongues.* The word *thelo* does not so much imply a wish or desire as a command or permission. As if he had said: I do not restrain you to prophesying or teaching, though I prefer that; but I give you full permission to speak in Hebrew whenever it is proper, and when one is present who can interpret for the edification of the church, provided yourselves have not that gift, though you understand the language. The apostle said "tongue," in the singular number, vv. 2, 4, because he spoke of a single man; now he says *tongues*, in the plural number, because he speaks of many speaking. But he has the same meaning in both places. *Greater is he that prophesieth.* A useful, zealous preacher, though unskilled in learned languages, is much *greater* in the sight of God, and in the eye of sound common sense, than he who has the gift of those learned tongues, *except he interpret;* and we seldom find great scholars good preachers. This should humble the scholar, who is too apt to be proud of his attainments and despise his less learned but more useful brother.

6. *Speaking with tongues.* Without interpreting. *What shall I profit you?* I.e., I shall not profit you, *except I shall speak to you either by revelation* of some secret thing; *or by knowledge* of some mystery; *or by prophesying*, foretelling some future event; *or by doctrine*, instructing you what to believe and practice.

7. *And even things without life.* As if he had said, I may illustrate this further by referring to a *pipe* or *harp;* if these were to utter mere *sounds* without order, harmony, or melody, though every tone of music might be in the sounds, surely no person could discern a tune in such sounds nor receive pleasure from such discords. Even so is the person who speaks in an unknown tongue, but does not interpret. His speech tends no more to edification than those discordant and unmeaning sounds do to pleasure and delight.

8. *If the trumpet give an uncertain sound.* If, when the soldier should prepare himself for the battle, the trumpet should give a different sound to that which is ordinarily used on such occasions, the soldier is not informed of what he should do, and therefore does not arm himself; consequently that vague, unintelligible sound of the trumpet is of no use.

9. *Likewise ye.* If you do not speak in the church so as to be understood, your labor is useless. *Ye shall speak into the air*—your speech will be lost and dissipated in the air, without conveying any meaning to any person; there will be a noise or sound, but nothing else.

10. *There are, it may be.* "For example." *So many kinds of voices.* So many different languages, each of which has its distinct articulation, pronunciation, emphasis, and meaning; or there may be so many different nations, each possessing a different language.

11. *If I know not the meaning of the voice.* The "power" and signification of the language. *I shall be unto him that speaketh a barbarian.* I shall appear to him, and he to me, as a person who had no distinct and articulate sounds which can convey any kind of meaning. This observation is very natural. When we hear persons speaking in a language of which we know nothing, we wonder how they can understand each other, as in their speech there appears to us no regular distinction of sounds or words.

12. *Forasmuch as ye are zealous.* Seeing you affect so much to have spiritual gifts, seek that you may get those by which you may excel in edifying the church.

13. *Pray that he may interpret.* Let him who speaks or reads the prophetic declarations in the Old Testament, in that tongue in which they were originally spoken and written, pray to God that he may so understand them himself and receive the gift of interpretation that he may

be able to explain them in all their depth and latitude to others.

14. *For if I pray in an unknown tongue.* If my prayers are composed of sentences and sayings taken out of the prophets and in their own language, *my spirit prayeth,* my heart is engaged in the work, and my prayers answer all the purpose of prayers to myself; but *my understanding is unfruitful* to all others, because they do not understand my prayers, and I either do not or cannot interpret them.

15. *I will pray with the spirit.* I will endeavor to have all my prayers influenced and guided by the Spirit of God, and to have my own heart deeply affected in and by the work. *And I will pray with the understanding also.* I will endeavor so to pray that others may understand me, and thus be edified and improved by my prayers. And therefore I will pray in a language in the public congregation that may be understood by all present, so that all may join not only in the act but in the spirit of devotion. *I will sing with the spirit.* It does appear that singing psalms or spiritual hymns was one thing that was implied in what is termed "prophesying" in the Old Testament, as is evident from 1 Sam. x. 5-6, 10. And when this came through an immediate afflatus or inspiration of God, there is no doubt that it was exceedingly edifying, and must have served greatly to improve and excite the devotional spirit of all who were present.

16. *He that occupieth the room of the unlearned.* One who is not acquainted with the language in which you speak, sing, or pray. *Say Amen.* Give his assent and ratification to what he does not understand. It was very frequent in primitive times to express their approbation in the public assemblies by *Amen.* This practice, soberly and piously conducted, might still be of great use in the Church of Christ.

17. *Thou verily givest thanks well.* Because he felt gratitude and, from a sense of his obligation, gave praise to God; but because this was in an unknown tongue, those who heard him received no edification.

18. *I speak with tongues more than ye all.* He understood more languages than any of them did; and this was indispensably necessary, as he was the apostle of the Gentiles in general, and had to preach to different provinces where different dialects, if not languages, were used. In the Hebrew, Syriac, Greek, and Latin, he was undoubtedly well-skilled from his education; and how many he might understand by miraculous gift we cannot tell. But even literally understood, it is very probable that he knew more languages than any man in the church of Corinth.

19. *Yet in the church.* As the grand object of public worship is the edification of those who attend, *five words* spoken so as to convey edification were of much more consequence than *ten thousand* which, not being understood, could convey none. By the word *tongue,* to which we add *unknown,* I suppose the apostle always means the Hebrew, for the reasons offered in the note on v. 1.

20. *Be not children in understanding.* There are three words here to which we must endeavor to affix the proper sense: (1) *paidia* signifies "children" in general, but particularly such as are grown up, so as to be fit to send to school

in order to receive instruction; (2) *nepios* signifies an "infant," one that cannot yet speak, and is in the lowest stage of infancy; (3) *teleioi,* from *teleo,* "I complete or perfect," signifies those who are arrived at perfect maturity, of both growth and understanding. We shall now see the apostle's meaning: *Brethren, be not* as "little children" just beginning to go to school, in order to learn the first elements of their mother tongue, and with an understanding sufficient only to apprehend those elements. *In malice.* "In wickedness be as infants," who neither speak, do, nor purpose evil. *But in understanding.* "Be perfect men," whose vigor of body and energy of mind show a complete growth and a well-cultivated understanding.

21. *In the law it is written.* But the passage quoted is in Isa. xxviii. 11. Here is no contradiction, for the term *torah,* law, was frequently used by the Jews to express the whole Scriptures, law, prophets, and hagiographa; and they used it to distinguish these sacred writings from the words of the scribes. *With men of other tongues.* Bishop Pearce paraphrases this verse as follows: "With the tongues of foreigners and with the lips of foreigners will I speak to this people; and yet, for all that, will they not hear me, saith the Lord." To enter into the apostle's meaning we must enter into that of the prophet. The Jewish people were under the teaching of the prophets who were sent from God; these instructed, reproved, and corrected them by this divine authority. They however became so refractory and disobedient that God purposed to cast them off, and abandon them to the Babylonians: then they had a people to teach, correct, and reprove them whose language they did not understand. The discipline that they received in this way was widely different from that which they received while under the teaching of the prophets and the government of God; and yet for all this they did not humble themselves before their Maker, that this affliction might be removed from them.

22. *Wherefore tongues are for a sign.* The miraculous gift of tongues was never designed for the benefit of those who have already believed, but for the instruction of unbelievers, that they might see from such a miracle that this is the work of God, and so embrace the gospel. But as in the times of the prophet the strange Babylonish tongues came in the way of punishment and not in the way of mercy, take heed that it be not the case now; that by dwelling on the gift ye forget the Giver, and what was designed for you as a blessing may prove to you to be a curse. For it, because you have the gift of tongues, you will choose for your own aggrandizement to use them in the public congregation where none understands them, God may curse your blessings. *Prophesying.* Teaching the things of God in a known language is of infinitely more consequence than speaking in all the foreign tongues in the universe.

23. *Will they not say that ye are mad?* So they well might, finding a whole assembly of people talking languages which those who had most need of instruction could not understand.

24. *But if all prophesy.* If all those who teach do it in the tongue which all understand, if an unbeliever, or one who knows nothing of the sacred language, come in and hear things

just suited to his own state, he is convicted by all and *he is judged* by all.

25. *And thus are the secrets of his heart.* As these who were the prophets or teachers had often the discernment of spirits, they were able in certain cases, and probably very frequently, to tell a man the *secrets* of his own heart; and where this was not directly the case, God often led His ministers to speak those things that were suitable to the case before them, though they themselves had no particular design. The sinner, therefore, convinced that God alone could uncover the secrets of his heart, would be often obliged to fall *down on his face,* abashed and confounded, and acknowledge that God was truly among them.

26. *How is it . . . every one of you hath a psalm?* When the whole church came together, among whom there were many persons with extraordinary gifts, each of them wished to put himself forward and occupy the time and attention of the congregation; hence confusion must necessarily take place, and perhaps not a little contention. This was contrary to that edifying which was the intention of these gifts.

27. *Speak in an unknown tongue.* The Hebrew, as has already been conjectured. Let it be *by two, or at the most by three, and that by course.* Let only two or three in one assembly act in this way, that too much time may not be taken up with one exercise; and let this be done *by course,* the one after the other, that two may not be speaking at the same time; *and let one interpret* for all that shall thus speak.

28. *But if there be no interpreter.* If there be none present who can give the proper sense of this Hebrew reading and speaking, then let him keep silence and not occupy the time of the church by speaking in a language which only himself can understand.

29. *Let the prophets.* Those who have the gift of speaking to men "to edification, and exhortation, and comfort," v. 3. *Two or three.* As prophesying implied psalmody, teaching, and exhortation, Dr. Lightfoot thinks that the meaning of the place is this: Let one sing who has a psalm; let another teach who has a doctrine; and let a third exhort, or comfort, who has a gift of that kind. *And let the other judge.* The other prophets or qualified persons judge of the propriety of what had been spoken; or let them "discern" how the revelation under the new covenant confirmed and illustrated the revelation granted under the Old Testament. It appears to have been taken for granted that a man might pretend to this spirit of prophecy who was not sent of God; and therefore it was the duty of the accredited teachers to examine whether what he spoke was according to truth and the analogy of faith.

30. *Be revealed to another that sitteth by.* Probably those who were teachers sat on a particular seat, or place, from which they might most readily address the people; and this may be the meaning of sitting by. If such a person could say, I have just received a particular revelation from God, then let him have the liberty immediately to speak it, as it might possibly relate to the circumstances of that time and place.

31. *For ye may all prophesy one by one.* The gifts which God grants are given for the purpose of edification, but there can be no edification where there is confusion; therefore let them speak one by one.

32. *And the spirits of the prophets.* Let no one interrupt another; let all be ready to prefer others before themselves, and let each feel a spirit of subjection to his brethren. God grants no ungovernable gifts.

33. *For God is not the author of confusion.* Let not the persons who act in the congregation in this disorderly manner say that they are under the influence of God; for He is not the Author of confusion. But two, three, or more praying or teaching in the same place at the same time is *confusion,* and God is not the Author of such work; and let men beware how they attribute such disorder to the God of order and peace. The apostle calls such conduct "tumult, sedition"; and such it is in the sight of God and in the sight of all good men. How often is a work of God marred and discredited by the folly of men! For nature will always, and Satan too, mingle themselves as far as they can in the genuine work of the Spirit, in order to discredit and destroy it. Nevertheless in great revivals of religion it is almost impossible to prevent wildfire from getting in among the true fire, but it is the duty of the ministers of God to watch against and prudently check this; but if themselves encourage it, then there will be confusion and every evil work.

34. *Let your women keep silence in the churches.* This was a Jewish ordinance; women were not permitted to teach in the assemblies, or even to ask questions. This was their condition till the time of the gospel, when, according to the prediction of Joel, the Spirit of God was to be poured out on the women as well as the men, that they might "prophesy," i.e., teach. And that they did prophesy or teach is evident from what the apostle says, chap. xi. 5, where he lays down rules to regulate this part of their conduct while ministering in the church. But does not what the apostle says here contradict that statement and show that the words in chap. xi should be understood in another sense? For here it is expressly said that they should *keep silence in the churches;* for it was *not permitted* to a woman *to speak.* Both places seem perfectly consistent. It is evident from the context that the apostle refers here to asking questions, and what we call "dictating" in the assemblies. It was permitted to any man to ask questions, to object, altercate, attempt to refute, etc., in the synagogue; but this liberty was not allowed to any woman. Paul confirms this in reference also to the Christian church. He orders them to *keep silence;* and, if they wished to "learn any thing, let them ask of their husbands at home," because it was perfectly indecorous for women to be contending with men in public assemblies, on points of doctrine, cases of conscience, etc. But this by no means intimated that when a woman received any particular influence from God to enable her to teach that she was not to obey that influence; on the contrary, she was to obey it, and the apostle lays down directions in chap. xi for regulating her personal appearance when thus employed. All that the apostle opposes here is their questioning, finding fault, disputing, in the Christian church, as the Jewish men were permitted to do in their synagogues; together with the attempts to usurp

any authority over the men by setting up their judgment in opposition to them, for the apostle has in view especially acts of disobedience, arrogance, etc., of which no woman would be guilty who was under the influence of the Spirit of God. *But . . . to be under obedience, as also saith the law.* This is a reference to Gen. iii. 16: "Thy desire shall be to thy husband, and he shall rule over thee." From this it is evident that it was the disorderly and disobedient that the apostle had in view, and not any of those on whom God had poured out his Spirit.

35. *For it is a shame for women to speak in the church.* The Jews would not suffer a woman to read in the synagogue, though a servant or even a child had this permission; but the apostle refers to irregular conduct, such conduct as proved that they were not under obedience, v. 34.

36. *Came the word of God out from you?* Was it from you that other churches received the gospel? Are you the mother church, that you should have rules, and orders, and customs, different from all others; and set yourselves up for a model to be copied by all the churches of Christ? *Or came it unto you only?* Are you the only church of God? Are there not many others founded before you that have no such customs and permit no such disorders?

37. *If any man think himself to be a prophet.* He who is really a *spiritual* man, under the influence of the Spirit of God and capable of teaching the divine will, he will acknowledge that what I now say is from the same Spirit; and that the things which I now write are the *commandments* of God, and must be obeyed on pain of His displeasure.

38. *But if any man be ignorant.* If he affect to be so, or pretend that he is ignorant, *let him be ignorant*—let him be so at his peril.

39. *Covet to prophesy.* Let it be your endeavor and prayer to be able to teach the way of God to the ignorant; this is the most valuable, because the most useful, gift of the Spirit. *And forbid not to speak with tongues.* Let every gift have its own place and operation; let none envy another; nor prevent him from doing that part of the work to which God, by giving the qualification, has evidently called him.

40. *Let all things be done decently.* In their proper forms with becoming reverence, according to their dignity and importance. Everything in the Church of God should be conducted with gravity and composure, suitable to the importance of the things, the infinite dignity of the object of worship, and the necessity of the souls in behalf of which those religious ordinances are instituted. *And in order.* Everything in its place, everything in its time, and everything suitably. *Let all things be done decently and in order* is a direction of infinite moment in all the concerns of religion, and of no small consequence in all the concerns of life. How much pain, confusion, and loss would be prevented were this rule followed!

CHAPTER 15

The gospel which the apostle preached to the Corinthians; viz., that Christ died for our sins, and rose again the third day, 1-4. The witnesses of His resurrection, Peter, James, and more than five hundred brethren, 5-7. Lastly, Paul himself saw him and was called by Him to the apostleship, 8-11. Objections against the resurrection of the dead answered, 12-34. The manner in which this great work shall be performed, 35-49. The astonishing events that shall take place in the last day, 50-57. The use we should make of this doctrine, 58.

It appears from this chapter that there were some false apostles at Corinth who denied the resurrection (see v. 12), in consequence of which Paul discusses three questions in this chapter: (1) Will there be a resurrection of the dead? vv. 1-35; (2) What will be the nature of the resurrection bodies? vv. 35-51; (3) What will become of those who are found alive in the day of judgment? vv. 51-57.

1. *The gospel which I preached unto you.* This gospel is contained in Christ dying for our sins, being buried, and rising again the third day.

2. *If ye keep in memory.* Your future salvation, or being brought finally to glory, will now depend on your faithfulness to the grace that you have received.

3. *For I delivered unto you first of all.* "As the chief things," or matters of the greatest importance; fundamental truths. *That which I also received.* By revelations from God himself, and not from man. *That Christ died for our sins.* The death of Jesus Christ, as a vicarious Sacrifice for sin, is among the things that are of chief importance, and is essential to the gospel scheme of salvation. *According to the scriptures.* It is not said anywhere in the Scriptures, in express terms, that Christ should rise on the third day; but it is fully implied in His types, as in the case of Jonah, who came out of the belly of the fish on the third day; but particularly in the case of Isaac, who was a very expressive type of Christ; for, as his being brought to the Mount Moriah, bound, and laid on the wood, in order to be sacrificed, pointed out the death of Christ, so his being brought alive on the third day from the mount was a figure of Christ's resurrection.

5. *That he was seen of Cephas, then of the twelve.* This refers to the journey to Emmaus, Luke xxiv. 13 and 34, and to what is related Mark xvi. 14. *Then of the twelve.* Perhaps the term *twelve* is used here merely to point out the society of the apostles, who, though at this time they were only eleven, were still called the *twelve* because this was their original number, and a number which was afterward filled up. See John xx. 24.

6. *Above five hundred brethren at once.* This was probably in Galilee, where our Lord had many disciples. See Matt. xxviii. 16. What a remarkable testimony is this to the truth of our Lord's resurrection! *Five hundred* persons saw Him at one time, the greater part of whom were alive when the apostle wrote, and he might have been confronted by many if he had dared to assert a falsity.

7. *After that, he was seen of James.* But where, and on what occasion, we are not told. But one thing is sufficiently evident from what is here said, that this James, of whom the apostle speaks, was still alive; for the apostle's manner of speaking justifies this conclusion.

8. *And last of all . . . of me also.* It seems that it was essential to the character of a primitive apostle that he had seen and conversed with Christ; and it is evident, from the history of Saul's conversion, Acts ix. 4-7, that Jesus Christ did appear to him; and he pleaded this ever after as a proof of his call to the apostleship. And it does not appear that, after this time, Jesus

ever did make any personal discovery of himself to anyone. *As of one born out of due time.* The apostle considers himself as coming after the time in which Jesus Christ personally conversed with His disciples; and that therefore, to see Him at all, he must see Him in this extraordinary way. The words signify not merely one *born out of due time,* but one born before his time; and consequently, not bidding fair for vigor, usefulness, or long life. But it is likely that the apostle had a different meaning; and that he refers to the original institution of the twelve apostles, in the rank of whom he never stood, being appointed, not to fill up a place among the twelve, but as an extra and additional apostle.

9. *I am the least of the apostles.* This was literally true in reference to his being chosen last, and chosen not in the number of the twelve, but as an extra apostle. How much pains do some men take to make the apostle contradict himself, by attempting to show that he was the very greatest of the apostles, though he calls himself the least! Taken as a man and a minister of Christ, he was greater than any of the twelve; taken as an apostle he was less than any of the twelve, because not originally in that body. *Am not meet to be called an apostle.* None of the twelve had ever persecuted Christ nor withstood His doctrine: Saul of Tarsus had been, before his conversion, a grievous persecutor; and therefore he says, "I am not proper to be called an apostle, because I persecuted the Church of God," i.e., of Christ, which none of the apostles ever did.

10. *But by the grace of God I am what I am.* God, by His mere grace and goodwill, has called me to be an apostle, and has denominated me such. *And his grace.* Nor have I been unfaithful to the divine call. I used the grace which He gave me; and when my labors, travels, and sufferings are considered, it will be evident that I have labored more abundantly than the whole twelve. This was most literally true. *Yet not I, but the grace of God.* It was not through my own power or wisdom that I performed these things, but through the divine influence which accompanied me.

11. *Whether it were I or they.* All the apostles of Christ agree in the same doctrines. We all preach one and the same thing; and, as we preached, *so ye believed,* having received from us the true apostolical faith, that Jesus died for our sins, and rose again for our justification, and that His resurrection is the pledge and proof of ours.

12. *Now if Christ be preached.* Seeing it is true that we have thus preached Christ, and you have credited this preaching, *how say some among you,* who have professed to receive this doctrine from us, *that there is no resurrection of the dead,* though we have shown that His resurrection is the proof and pledge of ours? That there was some false teacher, or teachers, among them, who was endeavoring to incorporate Mosaic rites and ceremonies with the Christian doctrines, and even to blend Sadduceeism with the whole, appears pretty evident. To confute this mongrel Christian and overturn his bad doctrine the apostle writes this chapter.

13. *If there be no resurrection of the dead.* As Christ was Partaker of the same flesh and

blood with us, and He promised to raise mankind from the dead through His resurrection, if the dead rise not, then Christ has had no resurrection. There seem to have been some at Corinth who, though they denied the resurrection of the dead, admitted that Christ had risen again. The apostle's argument goes therefore to state that, if Christ was raised from the dead, mankind may be raised; if mankind cannot be raised from the dead, then the body of Christ was never raised.

14. *Then is our preaching vain.* Our whole doctrine is useless and false.

15. *False witnesses.* As having testified the fact of Christ's resurrection, as a matter which ourselves had witnessed, when we knew that we bore testimony to a falsehood. But could 500 persons agree in this imposition? And if they did, is it possible that someone would not discover the cheat, when he could have no interest in keeping the secret, and might greatly promote his secular interest by making the discovery? Such a case can never occurred, and never can occur. The testimony, therefore, concerning the resurrection of Christ is incontrovertibly true.

17. *Ye are yet in your sins.* If Christ has not risen from the dead, there is a presumption that He has been put to death justly; and if so, consequently He has made no atonement; and *ye are yet in your sins*—under the power, guilt, and condemnation of them.

18. *They also which are fallen asleep.* All those who, by either martyrdom or natural death, have departed in the faith of our Lord Jesus Christ, *are perished;* their hope was without foundation, and their faith had not reason and truth for its object.

19. *If in this life only we have hope.* It would be better to translate and point this verse as follows: "And if in this life we have hoped in Christ only, we are more to be pitied than all men." If in this life we have no other hope and confidence but in Christ (and if He be still dead, and not yet risen), we are more to be pitied than any other men; we are sadly deceived.

20. *But now is Christ risen.* On the contrary, Christ is raised from the dead, and is become the *firstfruits of them that slept.* His resurrection has been demonstrated, and our resurrection necessarily follows; as sure as the firstfruits are the proof that there is a harvest, so surely the resurrection of Christ is a proof of ours.

21. *For since by man came death.* Mortality came by Adam, immortality by Christ; so sure as all have been subjected to natural death by Adam, so sure shall all be raised again by Christ Jesus.

24. *When he shall have delivered up the kingdom.* The mediatorial Kingdom, which comprehends all the displays of His grace in saving sinners and all His spiritual influence in governing the Church. *All rule and all authority and power.* As the apostle is here speaking of *the end* of the present system of the world, the rule, authority, and power may refer to all earthly governments, emperors, kings, princes, etc.; though angels, principalities, and powers, and the rulers of the darkness of this world, and all spiritual wickedness in high

places may be also intended. Our Lord Jesus is represented here as administering the concerns of the Kingdom of grace in this lower world during the time that this divine economy lasts; and when *the end*—the time determined by the wisdom of God—comes, then, as there is no longer any need of this administration, the Kingdom is delivered up unto the Father: an allusion to the case of Roman viceroys or governors of provinces, who, when their administration was ended, delivered up their kingdoms or governments into the hands of the emperor.

25. *For he must reign.* This is according to the promise, Ps. cx. 1: "The Lord said unto my Lord, Sit thou at my right hand, until I make thine enemies thy footstool." Therefore the Kingdom cannot be given up till all rule and government be cast down. So that while the world lasts, Jesus, as the Messiah and Mediator, must reign; and all human beings are properly His subjects, are under His government, and are accountable to Him.

26. *The last enemy,* Death, shall be destroyed; shall be "counterworked, subverted," and finally "overturned." But death cannot be *destroyed* by there being simply no further death; death can be destroyed and annihilated only by a general resurrection.

27. *For he hath put all things under his feet.* The Father hath put all things under the feet of Christ according to the prophecy, Psalms cx. *He is excepted.* I.e., The Father, who hath put all things under Him, the Son. This observation seems to be introduced by the apostle to show that he does not mean that the divine nature shall be subjected to the human nature. Christ, as Messiah, and Mediator between God and man, must ever be considered inferior to the Father; and His human nature, however dignified in consequence of its union with the divine nature, must ever be inferior to God. The whole of this verse should be read in a parenthesis.

28. *The Son also himself be subject.* When the administration of the Kingdom of grace is finally closed; when there shall be no longer any state of probation, and consequently no longer need of a distinction between the Kingdom of grace and the Kingdom of glory; then the Son, as being man and Messiah, shall cease to exercise any distinct dominion; and *God* shall *be all in all.*

29. *Else what shall they do which are baptized for the dead?* This is certainly the most difficult verse in the New Testament; for, notwithstanding the greatest and wisest men have labored to explain it, there are to this day nearly as many different interpretations of it as there are interpreters. The sum of the apostle's meaning appears to be this: If there be no resurrection of the dead, those who, in becoming Christians, expose themselves to all manner of privations, crosses, severe sufferings, and a violent death, can have no compensation, nor any motive sufficient to induce them to expose themselves to such miseries. But as they receive baptism as an emblem of "death" in voluntarily going under the water, so they receive it as an emblem of the resurrection unto eternal life in coming up out of the water; thus they are *baptized for the dead,* in perfect faith of the resurrection. The following three verses seem to confirm this sense.

30. *And why stand we in jeopardy every*

hour? Is there any reason why we should voluntarily submit to so many sufferings, and every hour be in danger of losing our lives, if the dead rise not? On the conviction of the possibility and certainty of the resurrection, we are thus baptized for the dead. We have counted the cost, despise sufferings, and exult at the prospect of death, because we know we shall have a resurrection unto eternal life.

31. *I protest by your rejoicing.* "By your exultation or boasting." *I die daily.* A form of speech for "I am continually exposed to death."

32. *If after the manner of men.* Much learned criticism has been employed on this verse, to ascertain whether it is to be understood literally or metaphorically. Does the apostle mean to say that he had literally fought with wild beasts at Ephesus? or, that he had met with brutish, savage men, from whom he was in danger of his life? That Paul did not fight with wild beasts at Ephesus may be argued: (1) From his own silence on this subject, when enumerating his various sufferings, 2 Cor. xi. 23 ff; (2) From the silence of his historian, Luke, who in the acts of this apostle gives no intimation of this kind; and it certainly was too remarkable a circumstance to be passed over, either by Paul in the catalogue of his own sufferings or by Luke in his history; (3) From similar modes of speech which are employed metaphorically and are so understood; (4) From the improbability that a Roman citizen, as Paul was, should be condemned to such a punishment when in other cases, by pleading his privilege, he was exempted from being scourged; and (5) From the positive testimony of Tertullian and Chrysostom, who deny the literal interpretation. *What advantageth it me, if the dead rise not?* I believe the common method of pointing this verse is erroneous; I propose to read it thus: "If, after the manner of men, I have fought with beasts at Ephesus, what doth it advantage me? If the dead rise not, let us eat and drink, for tomorrow we die."

What the apostle says here is a regular and legitimate conclusion from the doctrine that there is no resurrection: For if there be no resurrection, then there can be no judgment—no future state of rewards and punishments. Why, therefore, should we bear crosses, and keep ourselves under continual discipline? Let us eat and drink, take all the pleasure we can, for tomorrow we die; and there is an end of us forever. The words, *Let us eat and drink; for tomorrow we die,* are taken from Isa. xxii. 13, as they stand now in the Septuagint; and are a pretty smooth proverbial saying, which might be paralleled from the writings of several Epicurean heathens.

33. *Be not deceived.* Do not impose on yourselves, and do not permit others to do it. *Evil communications corrupt good manners.* There are many sayings like this among the Greek poets; but this of the apostle is generally supposed to have been taken from Menander's *lost* comedy of *Thais:* "Bad company good morals doth corrupt."

34. *Awake to righteousness.* Shake off your slumber; awake fully, thoroughly, "as ye ought to do"; so the word should be rendered, not *awake to righteousness. Sin not.* For this will lead to the destruction of both body and soul. Life is but a moment; improve it. Heaven has

blessings without end. *Some have not the knowledge of God.* The original is very emphatic: "Some have an ignorance of God"; they do not acknowledge God. To have an ignorance of God—a sort of substantial darkness, that prevents the light of God from penetrating the soul—is a worse state than to be simply in the dark or without the divine knowledge. The apostle probably speaks of those who were once enlightened, once had good morals, but were corrupted by bad company.

35. *But some man will say.* It is very likely that the apostle by *some man* means particularly the false apostle or teacher at Corinth who was chief in the opposition to the pure doctrine of the gospel, and to whom, in this covert way, he often refers. The second part of the apostle's discourse begins at this verse. What shall be the nature of the resurrection body? (1) The question is stated, v. 35. (2) It is answered: first, by a similitude, vv. 36-38; secondly, by an application, vv. 39-41; and thirdly, by explication, vv. 42-50.

36. *Thou fool.* If this be addressed, as it probably is, to the false apostle, there is a peculiar propriety in it, as this man seems to have magnified his own wisdom and set it up against both God and man; and none but a *fool* could act so. At the same time, it is folly in any to assert the impossibility of a thing because he cannot comprehend it. *That which thou sowest is not quickened, except it die.* A grain of wheat is composed of the body and the germ. The latter forms an inconsiderable part of the mass of the grain; the body forms nearly the whole. This body dies—becomes decomposed—and forms a fine earth, from which the germ derives its first nourishment; by the nourishment thus derived the germ is *quickened*, receives its first vegetable life, and through this means is rendered capable of deriving the rest of its nourishment and support from the grosser earth in which the grain was deposited. Whether the apostle would intimate here that there is a certain germ in the present body which shall become the seed of the resurrection body, this is not the place to inquire.

37. *Thou sowest not that body that shall be.* This is decomposed and becomes the means of nourishing the whole plant.

38. *But God giveth it a body.* And is there any other way of accounting for it by the miraculous working of God's power? For out of that one bare grain are produced a system of roots, a tall and vigorous stalk, with all its appendages of leaves, besides the full corn in the ear, the whole making several hundred times the quantum of what was originally deposited. There are no proofs that what some call "nature" can effect this; it will ever be a philosophical as well as a scriptural truth that *God giveth it a body as it hath pleased* [pleaseth] *him;* and so doth He manage the whole of the work that every seed shall have its *own body:* that the wheat germ shall never produce barley; nor the rye, oats.

39. *All flesh is not the same flesh.* Though the organization of all animals is in its general principles the same, yet there are no two different kinds of animals that have flesh of the same flavor, whether the animal be beast, fowl, or fish. And this is precisely the same with vegetables.

40. *There are also celestial bodies, and bodies terrestrial.* The apostle certainly does not speak of *celestial* and *terrestrial* bodies in the sense in which we use those terms. We invariably mean by the former the sun, moon, planets, and stars; by the latter, masses of inanimate matter. But the apostle speaks of human beings, some of which were clothed with *celestial*, others with *terrestrial*, bodies. It is very likely, therefore, that he means by the *celestial bodies* such as those refined human bodies with which Enoch, Elijah, and Christ himself appear to the realms of glory; to which we may add the bodies of those saints which arose after our Lord's resurrection and, after having appeared to many, doubtless were taken up to paradise. By *terrestrial* bodies we may understand those in which the saints now live. *But the glory of the celestial is one.* The *glory*—the excellence, beauty, and perfection. Even the present frail human body possesses an indescribable degree of contrivance, art, economy, order, beauty, and excellence; but the *celestial* body, that in which Christ now appears. and according to which ours shall be raised (Phil. iii. 21), will exceed the excellence of this beyond all comparison. A *glory* or "splendor" will belong to that which does not belong to this. Here there is a *glory* of excellence, for the bodies of the saints shall shine like "the sun in the kingdom of their Father." See Matt. xiii. 43.

41. *There is one glory of the sun.* As if he had said: This may be illustrated by the present appearance of the celestial bodies which belong to our system. The *sun* has a greater degree of splendor than the *moon;* the moon, than the planets; and the planets, than the *stars.*

42. *So also is the resurrection of the dead.* That is, the bodies of the dead, though all immortal, shall possess different degrees of splendor and glory, according to the state of holiness in which their respective souls were found. *It is sown in corruption.* The body is buried in a state of degradation, decay, and corruption. The apostle uses the word *sown* to intimate that the body shall rise again, as a seed springs up that has been sown in the earth. *It is raised in incorruption.* Being no more subject to corruption, dissolution, and death.

43. *It is sown in dishonour.* Being now stripped of all the glory it had as a machine, fearfully and wonderfully made by the hands of God, and also consigned to death and destruction because of sin. This is the most dishonorable circumstance. *It is raised in glory.* It is raised a glorious body, because immortal, and forever redeemed from the empire of death. *It is sown in weakness.* The principles of dissolution, corruption, and decay have prevailed over it; disease undermined it; and death made it his prey. *It is raised in power.* To be no more liable to weakness through labor, decay by age, wasting by disease, and dissolution by death.

44. *It is sown a natural body.* An "animal body." *It is raised a spiritual body.* One perfect in all its parts, no longer dependent on natural productions for its support, being built up on indestructible principles, and existing in a region where there shall be no more death. The body is spiritual and has a spiritual existence and spiritual support. As the seed which is sown in the earth rots, and out of the germ contained

in it God in His providence produces a root, stalk, leaves, ear, and a great numerical increase of grains, is it not likely that God, out of some essential parts of the body that now is, will produce the resurrection body; and will then give the soul a body as it pleaseth Him; and so completely preserve the individuality of every human being, as He does of every grain, giving to each its own body (v. 38)? So that as surely as the grain of wheat shall produce wheat after it is cast in the earth, corrupts, and dies, so surely shall our bodies produce the same bodies as to their essential individuality.

45. *The first man Adam was made a living soul.* These forms of expression are common among the Jews; hence we find "Adam the first" and "Adam the last." The apostle says this is written: *The first man Adam was made a living soul.* This is found in Gen. ii. 7, in the words "the breath of life," which the apostle translates *a living soul.* *The last Adam was made a quickening spirit.* This is also said to be *written;* but where? In the very same verse, and in these words: "And man [Adam] became a living soul," which the apostle translates a "quickening or life-giving spirit."

46. *That was not first which is spiritual.* The *natural* or "animal" body, described in v. 44, was the *first;* it was the body with which Adam was created. The *spiritual* body is the last, and is that with which the soul is to be clothed in the resurrection.

47. *The first man is of the earth.* That is, Adam's body was made out of the dust of the earth, and hence the apostle says he was "of the dust." *The second man is . . . from heaven.* The resurrection body shall be of a heavenly nature, and not subject to decay or death. What is formed of earth must live after an earthly manner, must be nourished and supported by the earth. What is from heaven is of a spiritual nature, and shall have no further connection with, nor dependence upon, earth. I conceive both these clauses to relate to man, and to point out the difference between the animal body and the spiritual body, or between the bodies which we now have and the bodies which we shall have in the resurrection. But can this be the meaning of the clause, *the second man is the Lord from heaven?* In the quotation I have omitted "the Lord," on the basis of many authorities. Some of the most eminent of modern critics leave out the word, and Tertullian says that it was put in by the heretic Marcion. I do think that the word is not legitimate in this place. The verse is read by the MSS., versions, and fathers referred to, thus: "The first man is of the earth, earthy; the second man is of heaven, heavenly." The *first man* and the *second man* of this verse are the same as the "first Adam" and the "second Adam" of v. 45, and it is not clear that Christ is meant in either place.

48. *As is the earthy.* As Adam was, who was formed from the earth, so are all his descendants: frail, decaying, and subject to death. *As is the heavenly.* As is the heavenly state of Adam and all glorified beings, so shall be the state of all those who at the resurrection are found fit for glory.

49. *And as we have borne the image of the earthy.* As being descendants from Adam we have all been born in his likeness and subject to the same kind of corruption, disgrace, and death, we shall also be raised to a life immortal such as he now enjoys in the kingdom of God. This interpretation proceeds on the ground that what is here spoken belongs to Adam in his twofold state, viz., of mortality and immortality, of disgrace and honour, of earth and heaven.

50. *Flesh and blood cannot inherit the kingdom.* This is a Hebrew periphrasis for "man," and man in his present state of infirmity and decay. Man in his present state cannot inherit the kingdom of God; his nature is not suited to that place; he could not, in his present weak state, endure an exceeding great and eternal weight of glory. Therefore it is necessary that he should die, or be changed, that he should have a celestial body suited to the celestial state.

51. *I shew you a mystery.* That is, a thing which you have never known before. But what is this *mystery?* Why, that *we shall not all sleep*—we shall not all die; *but we shall all be changed.* Of this the Jews had not distinct notions. For as flesh and blood cannot inherit glory, and all shall not be found dead at the day of judgment, then all must be *changed*— undergo such a change that their bodies may become spiritual, like the bodies of those who shall be raised from the dead.

52. *In a moment.* "In an atom"; that is, an indivisible point of time. *In the twinkling of an eye,* as soon as a man can wink, which expressions show that this mighty work is to be done by the almighty power of God, as He does all His works. The resurrection of all the dead from the foundation of the world to that time and the change of all the living then upon earth shall be the work of a single moment. *At the last trump.* This, as well as all the rest of the peculiar phraseology of this chapter, is merely Jewish. *For the trumpet shall sound.* By this the apostle confirms the substance of the tradition that there shall be the sound of a trumpet on this great day; and this other scriptures teach. See Zech. ix. 14; Matt. xxiv. 31; John v. 25; 1 Thess. iv. 16, in which latter place the apostle treats this subject among the Thessalonians as he does here among the Corinthians. *Shall be raised incorruptible.* Fully clothed with a new body, to die no more. *We shall be changed.* That is, those who shall then be found alive.

53. *For this corruptible.* Because flesh and blood cannot inherit glory, therefore there must be a refinement by death, or a change without it.

54. *Death is swallowed up in victory.* These words are a quotation from Isa. xxv. 8, where the Hebrew is: "He [God] hath swallowed up death in victory"; or "forever." These words in the Septuagint are thus translated: "Death having prevailed, or conquered, hath swallowed up." But in the version of Theodotion, the words are the same with those of the apostle. The Hebrew *lanetsach* the Septuagint sometimes translate "in victory," but most commonly "forever." Death is here personified and represented as a devouring being, swallowing up all the generations of men; and by the resurrection of the body and the destruction of the empire of death, God is represented as swallowing him up; or that eternity gulps him down, so that he is endlessly lost and absorbed in its illimitable waste.

55. *O death, where is thy sting? O grave, where is thy victory?* These words are generally supposed to be taken from Hos. xiii. 14, where the Hebrew stands thus: "O death, I will be thy plagues; O grave, I will be thy destruction"; and which the Septuagint translate very nearly as the apostle, "O death, where is thy revenge, or judicial process? O grave, where is thy sting?" Both Death and Hades are here personified. Death is represented as having a *sting*, "dagger, or goad," by which, like the driver of oxen, he is continually irritating and urging on (these irritations are the diseases by which men are urged on till they fall into Hades, the empire of Death;); to Hades, *victory* is attributed, having overcome and conquered all human life, and subdued all to its own empire. Hades, which we here translate *grave,* is generally understood to be the place of separate spirits.

56. *The sting of death is sin.* The apostle explains himself particularly here. Death could not have entered into the world if sin had not entered first; it was *sin* that not only introduced *death,* but has armed him with all his destroying force. The goad or dagger of death is sin; by this both body and soul are slain. *The strength of sin is the law.* The law of God forbids all transgression, and sentences those who commit it to temporal and eternal death. Sin has its controlling and binding power from the law. The law curses the transgressor and provides no help for him; and if nothing else intervene, he must, through it, continue ever under the empire of death.

57. *But thanks be to God.* What the law could not do, because it is law (and law cannot provide pardon), is done by the gospel of our Lord Jesus Christ. He has died to slay Death; He has risen again to bring mankind from under the empire of Hades. All this He has done through His mere unmerited mercy; and eternal thanks are due to God for this unspeakable gift. He has given us the *victory* over sin, Satan, death, the grave, and hell.

58. *Be ye stedfast.* "Be settled"; confide in the truth of this doctrine of the resurrection, and everything that pertains to it, as confidently as a man sits down on a seat which he knows to be solid, firm, and safe, and on which he has often sat. *Always abounding in the work of the Lord.* The *work of the Lord* is obedience to His holy Word; every believer in Christ is a workman of God. He that works not to bring glory to God and good to man is not acknowledged as a servant of Christ; and if he be not a servant, he is not a son; and if not a son, then not an heir. And he must not only work, but abound in that work, ever exceeding his former self; and this, not for a time, but *always;* beginning, continuing, and ending every act of life to God's glory and the good of his fellows. *Your labour is not in vain.* "Your labor in the Lord is not in vain"; you must not only work, but you must *labour*—put forth all your strength; and you must work and labor *in the Lord*—under His direction, and by His influence; for without Him ye can do nothing. And this labor cannot be *in vain;* you shall have a resurrection unto eternal life—not because you have labored, but because Christ died and gave you grace to be faithful. One remark I cannot help making: The doctrine of the resurrection appears to have been thought of much more consequence among the primitive Christians than it is now! How is this? The apostles were continually insisting on it, and exciting the followers of God to diligence, obedience, and cheerfulness through it. There is not a doctrine in the gospel on which more stress is laid, and there is not a doctrine in the present system of preaching which is treated with more neglect!

CHAPTER 16

The apostle exhorts the Corinthians to make a contribution for the relief of the poor Christians at Jerusalem, and directs to the best mode of doing it, 1-4. Promises to pay them a visit after Pentecost, 5-9. Gives directions about the treatment of Timothy and Apollos, 10-12. And concerning watchfulness, etc., 13-14. Commends the house of Stephanas, and expresses his satisfaction at the visit paid him by Stephanas, Fortunatus, and Achaicus, 15-18. Sends the salutations of different persons, 19-21. Shows the awful state of those who were enemies to Christ, 22. And concludes the Epistle with the apostolical benediction, 23-24.

1. *The collection for the saints.* The Christians living at Jerusalem, we may naturally suppose, were greatly straitened, as the enmity of their countrymen to the gospel of Christ led them to treat those who professed it with cruelty and spoil them of their goods (see Heb. x. 34; and Rom. xv. 26); and the apostle hereby teaches that it was the duty of one Christian congregation to help another when in distress.

2. *Upon the first day of the week.* It appears from the whole that *the first day of the week,* which is the Christian Sabbath, was the day on which their principal religious meetings were held in Corinth and the churches of Galatia, and consequently in all other places where Christianity had prevailed. This is a strong argument for the keeping of the Christian Sabbath. We may observe that the apostle follows here the rule of the synagogue; it was a regular custom among the Jews to make their collections for the poor on the Sabbath day, that they might not be without the necessaries of life, and might not be prevented from coming to the synagogue.

3. *Whomsoever ye shall approve by your letters.* Why should Paul require *letters* of approbation in behalf of certain persons when he himself should be among them and could have their characters *viva voce*? It is probable that he refers here to letters of recommendation which they had sent to him while he was away; and he now promises that, when he shall come to Corinth, he would appoint these persons whom they had recommended to carry the alms to Jerusalem. Some MSS. and several versions join *by letters* to the following words, and read the verse thus: "When I come, those whom ye shall approve I will send with letters to bring your liberality to Jerusalem." This seems most natural.

4. *And if it be meet.* If it be a business that requires my attendance, and it be judged proper for me to go to Jerusalem, I will take those persons for my companions.

5. *I will come unto you, when I shall pass through Macedonia.* Paul was now at Ephesus; for almost all allow, in opposition to the subscription at the end of this Epistle that states it was written from Philippi, that it was written from Ephesus. This is supported by many strong arguments; and the eighth verse here seems to put it past all question: "I will tarry at Ephesus"; i.e., I am in Ephesus, and here I purpose to remain until Pentecost. Though Macedonia was not in the direct way from Ephesus to Corinth, yet the apostle intended to make it in his way. And it was because it was not in the direct road, but lay at the upper end of the Aegean Sea, and very far out of his direct line, that he says, *I do pass through Macedonia*—I have purposed to go thither before I go to Corinth.

6. *Yea, and winter with you.* He purposed to stay till Pentecost at Ephesus; after that to go to Macedonia, and probably to spend the summer there; and come in the autumn to Corinth, and there spend the winter. *That ye may bring me on my journey.* That you may furnish me with the means of travelling. It appears that in most cases the different churches paid his expenses to other churches; where this was not done, then he labored at his business to acquire the means of travelling.

7. *I will not see you now by the way.* From Ephesus to Corinth was merely across the Aegean Sea, and a comparatively short passage.

8. *I will tarry at Ephesus.* And it is very probable that he did so, and that all these journeys were taken as he himself had projected.

9. *A great door and effectual is opened.* "A great and energetic door is opened to me"; that is, God has made a grand opening to me in those parts, which I perceive will require much labor; and besides, I shall have *many adversaries* to oppose me. *Door* often signifies occasion or opportunity; but here the apostle may allude to the throwing open of the great doors of the Circus Maximus before the chariot races began, and the *many adversaries* may refer to the numerous competitors in those races.

10. *Now if Timotheus come.* Of Timothy we have heard before, chap. iv. 17. And we learn from Acts xix. 22 that Paul sent him with Erastus from Ephesus to Macedonia. It is evident therefore, in opposition to the very exceptionable subscription at the end of this Epistle, that the Epistle itself was not sent by Timothy, as there stated. *That he may be with you without fear.* That he may be treated well, and not perplexed and harassed with your divisions and jealousies; *for he worketh the work of the Lord*—he is divinely appointed, as I also am.

11. *Let no man . . . despise him.* Let none pretend to say that he has not full authority from God to do the work of an evangelist. *But conduct him forth in peace.* I believe, with Bishop Pearce, that this clause should be translated and pointed thus: Accompany him upon his journey, *that he may come unto me in peace,* "in safety," as the word is used in Mark v. 34 and Luke vii. 50. *For I look for him with the brethren.* This clause should not be understood as if Paul was expecting certain brethren with Timothy, but it was the brethren that were with Paul that were looking for him; "I, with the brethren, am looking for him."

12. *As touching our brother Apollos.* It appears from this that the "brethren" of whom the apostle speaks in the preceding verse were then with him at Ephesus; "I, with the brethren, greatly desired to come." *But his will was not at all to come.* As there had been a faction set up in the name of Apollos at Corinth, he probably thought it not prudent to go thither at this time, lest his presence might be the means of giving it either strength or countenance.

13. *Watch ye.* You have many enemies; be continually on your guard. Be always circumspect: (1) Watch against evil; (2) Watch for opportunities to receive good; (3) Watch for opportunities to do good; (4) Watch over each other in love; (5) Watch that none may draw you aside from the belief and unity of the gospel. *Stand fast in the faith.* Hold in conscientious credence what you have already received as the truth of God, for it is the gospel by which you shall be saved and by which you are now put into a state of salvation. *Quit you like men.* Be not like "children, tossed to and fro . . . with every wind of doctrine." Let your understanding receive the truth; let your judgment determine on the absolute necessity of retaining it; and give up life rather than give up the testimony of God. *Be strong.* Put forth all the vigor and energy which God has given you in maintaining and propagating the truth, and your spiritual strength will increase by usage. The terms in this verse are all military. *Watch ye.* Watch, and be continually on your guard, lest you be surprised by your enemies; keep your scouts out, and all your sentinels at their posts, lest your enemies steal a march upon you. See that the place you are in be properly defended, and that each be alert to perform his duty. *Stand fast in the faith.* Keep in your ranks; do not be disorderly; be determined to keep your ranks unbroken; keep close together. On your unity your preservation depends; if the enemy succeed in breaking your ranks, and dividing one part of this sacred army from another, your rout will be inevitable. *Quit yourselves like men.* When you are attacked, do not flinch; maintain your ground; resist; press forward; strike home; keep compact; conquer. *Be strong.* If one company or division be opposed by too great a force of the enemy, strengthen that division and maintain your position; if an attack is to be made on any part or intrenchment of the foe, summon up all your courage, sustain each other. Fear not, for fear will enervate you. Your cause is good; it is *the faith,* the religion of Jesus. He is your Captain in the field; and should you even die in the contest, the victory is yours.

14. *Let all your things be done with charity.* Let "love" to God, to man, and to one another be the motive of all your conduct.

15. *Ye know the house of Stephanas.* You know that Stephanas and his "family" have addicted themselves to the help of the followers of Christ; they have been the chief instruments of supporting the work of God in Achaia, of which work they themselves have been the firstfruits.

16. *That ye submit yourselves unto such.* That you have due regard to them, and consider them as especial instruments in the hand of God for countenancing and carrying on His great work. The submission here recommended does not imply obedience, but kind and courteous demeanor.

17. *I am glad of the coming of Stephanas.* It was by these that the Corinthians had sent that letter to the apostle to answer which was a main part of the design of Paul in this Epistle. *Fortunatus.* This man is supposed to have survived Paul; to be the same mentioned by Clement in his epistle to the Corinthians, sec. 59, as the bearer of that epistle from Clement

at Rome to the Christians at Corinth. *For that which was lacking on your part.* This may refer either to additional communications besides those contained in the letter which the Corinthians sent to the apostle—which additional circumstances were furnished by the persons above; and from them Paul had a fuller account of their spiritual state than was contained in the letter—or to some contributions on their part for the support of the apostle in his peregrinations and labors.

18. *They have refreshed my spirit and yours.* They have been a means of contributing greatly to my comfort, and what contributes to my comfort must increase yours. This is probably the meaning of the apostle. *Therefore acknowledge ye them.* Pay them particular respect, and let all be held in esteem in proportion to their work and usefulness. When this is made the rule of respect and esteem, then foolish and capricious attachments will have no place. A man will then be honored in proportion to his merit, and his merit will be estimated by his usefulness among men.

19. *The churches of Asia salute you.* I.e., The churches in Asia Minor. *Aquila and Priscilla.* Of these eminent persons we have heard before; see Acts xviii. 2, 18, 26; and Rom. xvi. 3. *With the church that is in their house.* That is, the company of believers who generally worshipped there. There were no churches or chapels built at that time, and the assemblies of Christians were necessarily held in private houses. It appears that Aquila and Priscilla devoted their house to this purpose. The house of Philemon was of the same kind; Philemon v. 2. So was likewise the house of Nymphas, Col. iv. 15.

20. *With an holy kiss.* The ancient patriarchs, and the Jews in general, were accustomed to kiss each other whenever they met; and this was a token of friendship and peace with them, as shaking of hands is with us. The primitive Christians naturally followed this example of the Jews.

21. *The salutation of me Paul with mine own hand.* This should be rendered: "The salutation is written by the hand of me Paul." It is very likely that the apostle wrote this and the following verses with his own hand. The rest, though dictated by him, was written by an amanuensis.

22. *If any man love not the Lord Jesus.* This is directed immediately against the Jews. From chap. xii. 3, we find that the Jews, who pretended to be under the Spirit and teaching of God, called Jesus "accursed"; i.e., a person who should be devoted to destruction. In this place the apostle retorts the whole upon themselves, and says: *If any man love not the Lord Jesus Christ, let him be Anathema,* "accursed" and "devoted to destruction." This is not said in the way of a wish or imprecation, but as a prediction of what would certainly come upon them if they did not repent, and of what did come on them because they did not repent. It is generally allowed that the apostle refers here to some of the modes of excommunication among the Jews, of which there were three, viz.: *Niddui,* which signifies a simple separation or exclusion of a man from the synagogue, and from his wife and family, for thirty days. *Cherem,* which was inflicted on him who had borne the *niddui,* and who had not, in the thirty days, made proper compensation, in order to be reconciled to the synagogue. This was inflicted with dire execrations, which he was informed must all come upon him if he did not repent. *Shammatha.* This was the direst of all, and cut off all hope of reconciliation and repentance, after which the man was neither reconcilable to the synagogue nor acknowledged as belonging even to the Jewish nation. *Anathema, Maran-atha.* "Let him be accursed; our Lord cometh." I cannot see the reason why these words were left untranslated. The former is Greek, and has been already explained; the latter is Syriac, *maran-atha,* "Our Lord is coming"; i.e., to execute the judgment denounced. Does not the apostle refer to the last verse in their Bible? "Lest I come and smite the land with a curse"? And does he not intimate that the Lord was coming to smite the Jewish land with that curse? Which took place a very few years after. What the apostle has said was prophetic, and indicative of what was about to happen to that people. God was then coming to inflict punishment upon them; He came, and they were broken and dispersed.

23. *The grace of our Lord Jesus.* May the favor, influence, mercy, and salvation procured by Jesus Christ be *with you*—prevail among you, rule in you, and be exhibited by you, in your life and conversation!

24. *Amen.* So be it. But this word is wanting in most MSS. of repute, and certainly was not written by the apostle.

The Second Epistle to the
CORINTHIANS

It is a general opinion among learned men that this Epistle was written about a year after the former, and this seems to be supported by the words in chap. ix. 2: "Achaia was ready a year ago"; for the apostle having given instructions for that collection, to which he refers in these words at the close of the preceding Epistle, they would not have had the "forwardness" there mentioned till a year had elapsed. As the apostle had purposed to stay at Ephesus till Pentecost, 1 Cor. xvi. 8; and he stayed some time in Asia after his purpose to leave Ephesus and go to Macedonia, Acts ix. 21-22; and yet making here his apology for not wintering in Corinth, as he thought to do, 1 Cor. xvi. 6; this Epistle must have been written after the winter, and consequently when a new year was begun. It therefore seems to have been written after his second coming to Macedonia, mentioned in Acts xx. 3.

That the First Epistle had produced powerful effects among the Corinthians is evident from what the apostle mentions in this. Titus had met him in Macedonia, and told him of the reformation produced by this Epistle (see chap. vii. 5): that the church had excommunicated the incestuous man; that the Epistle had overwhelmed them with great distress; had led them to a close examination of their conduct and state; and had filled them with respect and affection for their apostle. Hearing this, Paul wrote this Second Epistle, to comfort, to commend them, and to complete the work which he had begun, by causing them to finish the contribution for the poor saints at Jerusalem; and also to vindicate his own apostolic character, and to unmask the pretended apostle who had led them so long astray.

Its principal divisions are—

I. The *preface*, chap. i. vv. 1-7.

II. The *narration*, comprehending an account of what had happened to himself; his answer to their questions concerning the incestuous person, with different other matters; among which, the following are the chief:

(1) The persecution which he had suffered in Asia, and from which he had been miraculously rescued, chap. i. 8-14.

(2) His purpose to pay them a visit, chap. i. 15-24.

(3) Concerning the sorrow which they had suffered on account of the excommunication of the incestuous person, chaps. ii. and vii.

(4) His own vindication against the false apostle; in which he gives an account of his doctrine, chap. iii. 6-18. His conduct, chap. iv. 1-6. His bodily infirmities, chap. iv. 7; and chap. v.

(5) Strongly exhorts them to a holy life, chaps. vi and vii.

III. Of the *alms* that had been collected, and were yet to be collected, chaps. viii. and ix.

IV. His *defense* against the false apostle and his caluminators in general, chaps. x—xii.

V. *Miscellaneous* matters, chap. xiii.

It may be remarked, once for all, that none of these or such artificial divisions are made by the apostle himself, no more than the divisions into chapters and verses. All these are the work of man. The apostle appears to have sat down and, under the influence of the Divine Spirit, he wrote on the different subjects treated of in the Epistle just in the order that these things occurred to his mind, without intending particular heads, divisions, or subdivisions. And as he probably wrote the whole with very little intermission of time, his sense will be best apprehended by those who carefully read over the whole at one sitting.

CHAPTER 1

Paul encourages them to trust in God in all adversities, from a consideration of the support which He had granted them already in times of afflictions; and expresses his strong confidence of their fidelity, 1-7. Mentions the heavy tribulation which he had passed through in Asia, as also his deliverance, 8-11. Shows in what the exultation of a genuine Christian consists, 12. Appeals to their own knowledge of the truth of the things which he wrote to them, 13-14. Mentions his purpose of visiting them, and how sincere he was in forming it; and the reason why he did not come, as he had purposed, 15-24.

1. *Paul, an apostle.* Paul, commissioned immediately by Jesus Christ himself, according to the will of God, to preach the gospel to the Gentiles. See on 1 Cor. i. 1. *In all Achaia.* The whole of the Peloponnesus, or that country separated from the mainland by the Isthmus of Corinth. From this we may learn that this Epistle was sent not only to the church at Corinth, but to all the churches in that country.

2. *Grace be to you and peace.* See Rom. i. 7.

3. *Blessed be God.* Let God have universal and eternal praise: (1) Because he is the *Father of our Lord Jesus Christ,* who is the Gift of His endless love to man, John i. 16. (2) Because

He is *the Father of mercies,* the Source whence all mercy flows, whether it respect the body or the soul, time or eternity; the Source of "tender mercy," for so the word implies. See on Rom. xii. 1. And (3) Because he is *the God of all comfort*—the Fountain whence all consolation, happiness, and bliss flow to angels and to men.

4. *Who comforteth us.* Who shows himself to be the God of tender mercy, by condescending to notice us, who have never deserved any good at His hand; and also the God of all consolation, by comforting *us in all our tribulation*—never leaving us a prey to anxiety, carking care, persecution, or temptation; but, by the comforts of his Spirit, bearing us up in, through, and above all our trials and difficulties. *That we may be able to comfort them.* Even spiritual comforts are not given us for our use alone; they, like all the gifts of God, are given that they may be distributed, or become the instruments of help to others.

5. *The sufferings of Christ.* Suffering endured for the cause of Christ: such as persecutions, hardships, and privations of different kinds. *Our consolation also aboundeth.* We stood as well, as firmly, and as easily in the heaviest trial as in the lightest, because the consolation was always proportioned to the trial and difficulty. Hence we learn that he who is upheld in a slight trial need not fear a great one; for if he be faithful, his consolation shall abound as his sufferings abound. Is it not as easy for a man to lift 100 pounds' weight as it is for an infant to lift a few ounces? The proportion of strength destroys the comparative difficulty.

6. *And whether we be afflicted.* See on v. 4. *Which is effectual.* There is a strange and unusual variation in the MSS. and versions in this passage. Perhaps the whole should be read thus: *For if we be afflicted, it is for your encouragement and salvation; and if we be comforted, it is also for your encouragement, which exerted itself by enduring the same sufferings which we also suffer.* This transposition of the middle and last clauses is authorized by the best MSS. and versions. The meaning seems to be this: While you abide faithful to God, no suffering can be prejudicial to you; on the contrary, it will be advantageous, God having your comfort and salvation continually in view by all the dispensations of His providence; and while you patiently endure, your salvation is advanced, sufferings and consolations all becoming energetic means of accomplishing the great design, for all things work together for good to them that love God.

8. *Our trouble which came to us in Asia.* To what part of his history the apostle refers we know not. Some think it is to the Jews' lying in wait to kill him, Acts xx. 3; others, to the insurrection raised against him by Demetrius and his fellow craftsmen, Acts xix. 23; others, to his fighting with beasts at Ephesus, 1 Cor. xv. 32, which they understand literally; and others think that there is a reference here to some persecution which is not recorded in any part of the apostle's history. *We were pressed out of measure, above strength.* The original is exceedingly emphatic; we were weighed down beyond what any natural strength could support.

9. *We had the sentence of death in ourselves.* The tribulation was so violent and overwhelming that he had no hope of escaping death. *That we should not trust in ourselves.* The tribulation was of such a nature as to take away all expectation of help but from God alone.

11. *Ye also helping together by prayer.* Even an apostle felt the prayers of the Church of God necessary for his comfort and support. What innumerable blessings do the prayers of the followers of God draw down on those who are the objects of them! *The gift bestowed . . . by the means of many persons.* The blessings communicated by means of their prayers. *Thanks may be given by many.* When they who have prayed hear that their prayers are so particularly answered, then all that have prayed will feel themselves led to praise God for His gracious answers. Thus the prayers of many obtain the *gift,* and the thanksgivings of many acknowledge the mercy. The *gift* which the apostle mentions was his deliverance from the dangers and deaths to which he was exposed.

12. *For our rejoicing is this.* Our "boasting, exultation, subject of glorying." *The testimony of our conscience.* That testimony or witness which conscience, under the light and influence of the Spirit of God, renders to the soul of its state, sincerity, safety. *In simplicity.* Not compounded, having one end in view, having no sinister purpose. In *godly sincerity.* "The sincerity of God"; that is, such a sincerity as comes from His work in the soul. "Sincerity" comes from the "splendor, or bright shining of the sun"; and here signifies such simplicity of intention and purity of affection as can stand the test of the light of God shining upon it, without the discovery being made of a single blemish or flaw. *Not with fleshly wisdom.* The cunning and duplicity of man who is uninfluenced by the Spirit of God and has his secular interest, ease, profit, pleasure, and worldly honor in view. *But by the grace of God.* Which alone can produce the simplicity and godly sincerity before mentioned and inspire the wisdom that comes from above. *We have had our conversation.* We have conducted ourselves. The word properly refers to the whole tenor of a man's life—all that he does, says, and intends; and the object or end he has in view, and in reference to which he speaks, acts, and thinks; and is so used by the best Greek writers. The word *conversation* is not an unapt Latinism for the Greek terms, as *conversatio* comes from *con,* "together," and *verto,* "I turn"; and is used by the Latins in precisely the same sense as the other is by the Greeks, signifying the whole of a man's conduct, the tenor and practice of his life. *In the world.* Both among Jews and Gentiles have we always acted as seeing Him who is invisible. *More abundantly to you-ward.* That is, We have given the fullest proof of this in our "conduct" towards you. You have witnessed the holy manner in which we have always acted; and God is Witness of the purity of the motives by which we have been actuated; and our conscience tells us that we have lived in uprightness before Him.

13. *Than what ye read.* Viz., in the First Epistle which he had sent them. *Or acknowledge.* To be the truth of God; and which he hoped they would continue to acknowledge, and not permit themselves to be turned aside from the hope of the gospel.

14. *Have acknowledged us in part.* May sig-

nify here not *in part,* but "some of you"; and it is evident, from the distracted state of the Corinthians and the opposition raised there against the apostle, that it was only a part of them that did acknowledge him and receive and profit by his Epistles and advice. *We are your rejoicing.* You boast of us as the ministers of Christ through whom you have believed, as we boast of you as genuine converts to the Christian faith and worthy members of the Church of God.

15. *And in this confidence.* Under the conviction or persuasion that this is the case; that you exult in us, as we do in you. *I was minded.* I had purposed *to come unto you before,* as he had intimated, 1 Cor. xvi. 5; for he had intended to call on them in his way from Macedonia, but this purpose he did not fulfill; and he gives the reason, v. 23. *A second benefit.* He had been with them once, and they had received an especial blessing in having the seed of life sown among them by the preaching of the gospel; and he had purposed to visit them again that they might have a *second* blessing, in having that seed watered.

17. *Did I use lightness?* When I formed this purpose, was it without due consideration? and did I abandon it through fickleness of mind? *That with me there should be yea.* That I should act as carnal men, who change their purposes and falsify their engagements according as may seem best to their secular interest?

18. *But as God is true.* Setting the God of truth before my eyes, I could not act in this way; and as sure as He is true, so surely were my purposes sincere; and it was only my uncertainty about your state that induced me to postpone my visit. See v. 23.

19. *For the Son of God.* If I could have changed my purpose through carnal or secular interest, then I must have had the same interest in view when I first preached the gospel to you, with Silvanus and Timotheus. But did not the whole of our conduct prove that we neither had nor could have such interest in view?

20. *For all the promises of God.* Had we been light, fickle, worldly-minded persons, persons who could be bound by our engagements only as far as comported with our secular interest, would God have confirmed our testimony among you? Did we not lay before you the promises of God? And did not God fulfill those promises by us—by our instrumentality, to your salvation and His own glory? *In him are yea, and in him Amen.* All the promises which God has made to mankind are *yea,* true in themselves, and *Amen,* faithfully fulfilled to them who believe in Christ Jesus. The *promises* are all made in reference to Christ; for it is only on the gospel system that we can have promises of grace, for it is only on that system that we can have mercy. Therefore the promise comes originally by Christ, and is *yea;* and it has its fulfillment through Christ, and is *Amen;* and this is to *the glory of God,* by the preaching of the apostles. From what the apostle says here, and the serious and solemn manner in which he vindicates himself, it appears that his enemies at Corinth had made a handle of his not coming to Corinth, according to his proposal, to defame his character and to depreciate his ministry; but he makes use of it as a means of exalting the truth and the mercy of God through Christ Jesus; and of showing that the promises of God not only come by him, but are fulfilled through him.

21. *Now he which stablisheth us with you.* It is God that has brought both us and you to this sure state of salvation through Christ; and He has anointed us, giving us the extraordinary influences of the Holy Ghost, that we might be able effectually to administer this gospel to your salvation. Through this unction we know and preach the truth, and are preserved by it from dissimulation and falsity of every kind.

22. *Who hath also sealed us.* Not only deeply impressed His truth and image upon our hearts but, by the miraculous gifts of the Holy Spirit, attested the truth of our extraordinary unction or calling to the ministry. *And given the earnest of the Spirit.* From this unction and sealing we have a clear testimony in our souls, the Divine Spirit dwelling constantly in us, of our acceptance with God, and that our ways please Him. The *arrabon* of the apostle is the same as the *erabon* of Moses, Gen. xxxviii. 17-18, 20, which we there translate "pledge." The word properly signifies an *earnest* of something promised; a "part of the price" agreed for between a buyer and seller, by giving and receiving of which the bargain was ratified; or a "deposit," which was to be restored when the thing promised was given. From the use of the term in Genesis, which the apostle puts here in Greek letters, we may at once see his meaning above and in Eph. i. 14, the Holy Spirit being an *earnest* in the *hearts;* and an "earnest of the promised inheritance" means a security given in hand for the fulfillment of all God's promises relative to grace and eternal life. We may learn from this that eternal life will be given in the great day to all who can produce the "pledge." He who is found then with the earnest of God's Spirit in his heart shall not only be saved from death but have that eternal life of which it is the pledge, the earnest, and the evidence.

23. *I call God for a record upon my soul.* The apostle here resumes the subject which he left in v. 16, and in the most solemn manner calls God to witness, and consequently to punish, if he asserted anything false, that it was through tenderness to them that he did not visit Corinth at the time proposed. As there were so many scandals among them, the apostle had reason to believe that he should be obliged to use the severe and authoritative part of his function in the excommunication of those who had sinned, and delivering them over to Satan for the destruction of the flesh; but to give them space to amend, and to see what effect his Epistle might produce (not having heard as yet from them), he proposed to delay his coming.

24. *Not for that we have dominion over your faith.* I will not come to exercise my apostolical authority in punishing them who have acted sinfully and disorderly, for this would be to several of you a cause of distress, the delinquents being friends and relatives; but I hope to come to promote your *joy,* to increase your spiritual happiness, by watering the seed which I have already sowed. This I think to be the meaning of the apostle. It is certain that the *faith* which they had already received was preached by the apostles; and therefore in a certain sense, according to our meaning of the term, they had a right to propound to them the articles which they ought to believe; and to forbid them, in the most solemn manner, to

believe anything else as Christianity which was opposed to those articles. In that sense they had *dominion over their faith;* and this dominion was essential to them as apostles.

CHAPTER 2

The apostle further explains the reasons why he did not pay his intended visit to the Corinthians, 1. And why he wrote to them in the manner he did, 2-5. He exhorts them also to forgive the incestuous person, who had become a true penitent; and therefore he had forgiven him in the name of Christ, 6-11. He mentions the disappointment he felt when he came to Troas in not meeting with Titus, from whom he expected to hear an account of the state of the Corinthian church, 12-13. Gives thanks to God for the great success he had in preaching the gospel, so that the influence of the name of Christ was felt in every place, 14. Shows that the gospel is a savor of life to them that believe, and of death to them that believe not, 15-16. And that he and his brethren preached the pure, unadulterated doctrine of God among the people, 17.

1. *But I determined this.* The apostle continues to give further reasons why he did not visit them at the proposed time. Because of the scandals that were among them he could not see them comfortably; and therefore he determined not to see them at all till he had reason to believe that those evils were put away.

2. *For if I make you sorry.* Should he have come and used his apostolical authority in inflicting punishment upon the transgressors, this would have been a common cause of distress. And though he might expect that the sound part of the church would be a cause of consolation to him, yet as all would be overwhelmed with trouble at the punishment of the transgressors, he could not rejoice to see those whom he loved in distress.

3. *And I wrote this same unto you.* This I particularly marked in my First Epistle to you; earnestly desiring your reformation, lest, if I came before this had taken place, I must have come with a rod and have inflicted punishment on the transgressors. See 1 Corinthians v.

4. *For out of much affliction.* It is very likely that the apostle's enemies had represented him as a harsh, austere, authoritative man, who was better pleased with inflicting wounds than in healing them. But he vindicates himself from this charge by solemnly asserting that this was the most painful part of his office, and that the writing of his First Epistle to them cost him *much affliction* and anguish of heart and *many tears.*

5. *But if any have caused grief.* Here he seems to refer particularly to the cause of the incestuous person. *Grieved me, but in part.* I cannot help thinking that the *ek merous* and *apo merous,* which we render *in part,* and which the apostle uses so frequently in these Epistles, are to be referred to the people. A *part* of them had acknowledged the apostle, chap. i. 14; and here, a *part* of them had given him cause of grief; and therefore he immediately adds, *that I may not overcharge you all.* As only a part of you have put me to pain (viz., the transgressor and those who had taken his part), it would be unreasonable that I should "load you all" with the blame which attaches to that party alone.

6. *Sufficient to such a man is this punishment.* That is, the man has already suffered sufficiently. Here he gives a proof of his parental tenderness towards this great transgressor. He had been disowned by the church; he had deeply repented; and now the apostle pleads for him.

7. *Ye ought rather to forgive him.* He had now suffered enough, for the punishment inflicted had answered the end for which it was inflicted; and there was some danger that, if this poor culprit were not restored to the bosom of the church, his distress and anguish would destroy his life or drive him to despair.

8. *That ye would confirm your love toward him.* You do love him, notwithstanding the reproach he has brought on the gospel; and notwithstanding your love to him, you were obliged to cut him off for the credit of the gospel. Now that he has repented, I beseech you to confirm, to "ratify," by a public act of the church, your love to him; give him the fullest proof that you do love him, by forgiving him and restoring him to his place in the church.

10. *To whom ye forgive any thing.* Here he further shows them that his sole object in the punishment inflicted on the transgressor was his amendment and therefore promises to ratify, in the name and authority of Christ, the free pardon which he exhorts them to dispense. *In the person of Christ.* As I believe Christ acts towards his penitent soul, so do I. Christ forgives his sin, and takes him to His favor; let us therefore forgive him his offense against the church and restore him to its communion.

11. *Lest Satan should get an advantage.* If the man who has given sufficient proof of the sincerity of his repentance be not restored, he may be overwhelmed with sorrow and sink into despair; and then the discipline of the church will be represented, not as emendatory, but as leading to destruction. Of this our enemies would most gladly avail themselves, as they wish to discredit this ministry; and there is always at hand a devil to suggest evil and prompt men to do it, for in this respect we have thorough acquaintance with *his devices.* Let us therefore be careful to remove, from both Satan and his partisans, all those occasions which might turn to the disadvantage or disparagement of the gospel of Christ.

12. *When I came to Troas.* After having written the former Epistle, and not having heard what effect it had produced on your minds, though the Lord had opened me a particular door to preach the gospel, in which I so especially rejoice and glory.

13. *I had no rest in my spirit.* I was so concerned for you, through the love I bear you, that I was greatly distressed because I did not find Titus returned to give me an account of your state. *But taking my leave of them.* I went thence into Macedonia, expecting to find him there; and thither he did come, and gave me a joyous account of your state. See chap. viii. 6-7.

14. *Now thanks be unto God.* His coming dispelled all my fears, and was the cause of the highest satisfaction to my mind; and filled my heart with gratitude to God, who is the Author of all good, and *who always causeth us to triumph in Christ;* not only gives us the victory, but such a victory as involves the total ruin of our enemies. A triumph among the Romans, to which the apostle here alludes, was a public and solemn honor conferred by them on a victorious general by allowing him a magnificent procession through the city. This was not granted by the senate unless the general had gained a very signal and decisive victory—conquered a

province, etc. On such occasions the general was usually clad in a rich purple robe interwoven with figures of gold, setting forth the grandeur of his achievements; his buskins were beset with pearls; and he wore a crown, which at first was of laurel, but was afterwards of pure gold. In one hand he had a branch of laurel, the emblem of victory; and in the other, his truncheon. He was carried in a magnificent chariot, adorned with ivory and plates of gold, and usually drawn by two white horses. Musicians led up the procession, and played triumphal pieces in praise of the general; and these were followed by young men, who led the victims which were to be sacrificed on the occasion, with their horns gilded, and their heads and necks adorned with ribbons and garlands. Next followed carts loaded with the spoils taken from the enemy, with their horses and chariots. These were followed by the kings, princes, or generals taken in the war, loaded with chains. Immediately after them came the triumphal chariot, before which, as it passed, the people strewed flowers and shouted, *"Io, triumphe!"* The triumphal chariot was followed by the senate; and the procession was closed by the priests and their attendants, with the different sacrificial utensils, and a white ox, which was to be the chief victim. They then passed through the triumphal arch, along the *via sacra* to the capitol, where the victims were slain. During this time all the temples were opened, and every altar smoked with offerings and incense.

The people at Corinth were sufficiently acquainted with the nature of a *triumph.* About two hundred years before this, Lucius Mummius, the Roman consul, had conquered all Achaia, destroyed Corinth, Thebes, and Chalcis; and, by order of the senate, had a grand triumph, and was surnamed "Achaicus." Paul had now a *triumph* (but of a widely different kind) over the same people; his triumph was in Christ, and to Christ he gives all the glory. His sacrifice was that of thanksgiving to his Lord; and the incense offered on the occasion caused the *savor* of the knowledge of Christ to be manifested in every place. As the smoke of the victims and incense offered on such an occasion would fill the whole city with their perfume, so the odor of the name and doctrine of Christ filled the whole of Corinth and the neighboring regions; and the apostles appeared as triumphing in and through Christ over devils, idols, superstition, ignorance, and vice, wherever they came.

15. *For we are unto God a sweet savour of Christ.* The apostle still alludes to the case of a triumph. The conqueror always represented the person of Jupiter, as even the heathens supposed that God alone could give the victory; and as the punishment of death was inflicted on some of the captives, who had often rebelled and broken leagues and covenants, so others were spared, made tributaries, and often became allies. Alluding to this, the apostle says: We are a *sweet savour* to God—we have fulfilled His will in faithfully proclaiming the gospel and fighting against sin. And as He has determined that those who believe shall be saved and those who believe not shall perish, we are equally acceptable to Him though we unsuccessfully preach the gospel to some who obstinately reject it and so *perish*, as we are in preaching to others who believe and are *saved*.

16. *To the one we are the savour of death unto death.* There are several sayings among the ancient Jewish writers similar to this. In *Debarim Rabba,* sec. i. fol. 248, it is said: "As the bee brings home honey to its owner, but stings others; so it is with the words of the law; They are a savour of lives to the Israelites: and a savour of death to the people of this world." The apostle's meaning is plain: Those who believe and receive the gospel are saved; those who reject it perish. *Who is sufficient for these things?* Is it the false apostle that has been laboring to pervert you? Or is it the men to whom God has given an extraordinary commission, and sealed it by the miraculous gifts of the Holy Ghost? That this is the apostle's meaning is evident from the following verse.

17. *For we are not as many, which corrupt the word of God.* God has made us sufficient for these things by giving us His own pure doctrine, the ministry of reconciliation, which we conscientiously preserve and preach; and we act, not like many among you, who, having received that doctrine, *corrupt* it, mingling with it their own inventions and explaining away its force and influence, so as to accommodate it to men of carnal minds. The word *kapelenontes,* from *kapelos,* a "tavern keeper," signifies acting like an unprincipled vintner; for this class of men have ever been notorious for adulterating their wines, mixing them with liquors of no worth, that thereby they might increase their quantity; and thus the mixture was sold for the same price as the pure wine. See Isa. i. 22. "Your vintners mix your wine with water"; that is, Your false prophets and corrupt priests adulterate the Word of God and render it of none effect by their explanations and traditions. The word has been used, among both the Greeks and the Latins, to signify a prostitution of what was right and just, for the sake of gain.

CHAPTER 3

The apostle shows, in opposition to his detractors, that the faith and salvation of the Corinthians were a sufficient testimony of his divine mission; that he needed no letters of recommendation, the Christian converts at Corinth being a manifest proof that he was an apostle of Christ, 1-3. He extols the Christian ministry as being infinitely more excellent than that of Moses, 4-12. Compares the different modes of announcing the truth under the law and under the gospel. In the former it was obscurely delivered; and the veil of darkness, typified by the veil which Moses wore, is still on the hearts of the Jews; but when they turn to Christ this veil shall be taken away, 13-16. On the contrary, the gospel dispensation is spiritual; leads to the nearest views of heavenly things; and those who receive it are changed into the glorious likeness of God by the agency of His Spirit, 17-18.

1. *Do we begin again to commend ourselves?* By speaking thus of our sincerity, divine mission, etc., is it with a design to conciliate your esteem or ingratiate ourselves in your affections? By no means. *Or need we . . . epistles of commendation.* Are we so destitute of ministerial abilities and divine influence that we need, in order to be received in different churches, to have letters of recommendation? Certainly not. God causes us to triumph through Christ in every place, and your conversion is such an evident seal to our ministry as leaves no doubt that God is with us. *Letters of commendation* were frequent in the primitive Church; and were also in use in the apostolic Church, as we learn from this place. But these were, in all probability, not used by the apostles.

Their helpers, successors, and those who had not the miraculous gifts of the Spirit needed such letters; and they were necessary to prevent the churches from being imposed on by false teachers. But when apostles came, they brought their own testimonials, the miraculous gifts of the Holy Spirit.

2. *Ye are our epistle.* I bear the most ardent love to you. I have no need to be put in remembrance of you by any Epistles or other means; *ye are . . . written in our hearts*—I have the most affectionate remembrance of you. *Known and read of all men.* For wherever I go I mention you, speak of your various gifts and graces, and praise your knowledge in the gospel.

3. *Manifestly declared to be the epistle of Christ.* You are in our hearts, and Christ has written you there; but yourselves are the *epistle of Christ.* The change produced in your hearts and lives, and the salvation which you have received, are as truly the work of Christ as a letter dictated and written by a man in his work. *Ministered by us.* You are the writing, but Christ used me as the pen. Christ dictated, and I wrote; and the divine characters are not made with *ink, but with the Spirit of the living God,* for the gifts and graces that constituted the mind that was in Christ are produced in you by the Holy Ghost. *Not in tables of stone.* Where men engrave contracts or record events; *but in fleshy tables of the heart*—the work of salvation taking place in all your affections, appetites, and desires, working that change within that is so signally manifested without.

5. *Not that we are sufficient of ourselves.* We do not arrogate to ourselves any power to enlighten the mind or change the heart; we are only instruments in the hand of God.

6. *Who . . . hath made us able ministers.* This is a more formal answer to the question, "Who is sufficient for these things?" chap. ii. 16. God, says the apostle, has made us *able ministers;* He has made us sufficient for these things; for the reader will observe that he uses the same word in both places. We apostles execute, under the divine influence, what God himself has devised. We are ministers of the new covenant; of this new dispensation of truth, light, and life, by Christ Jesus; a system which not only proves itself to have come from God, but necessarily implies that God himself by His own Spirit is a continual Agent in it, ever bringing its mighty purposes to pass. *Not of the letter, but of the spirit.* The apostle does not mean here, as some have imagined, that he states himself to be a minister of the New Testament, in opposition to the Old, and that it is the Old Testament that kills and the New that gives life; but that the New Testament gives the proper meaning of the Old, for the old covenant had its *letter* and its *spirit,* its "literal" and its "spiritual" meaning. The law was founded on the very supposition of the gospel; and all its sacrifices, types, and ceremonies refer to the gospel. The Jews rested in the *letter,* which not only afforded no means of life, but killed, by condemning every transgressor to death. They did not look at the *spirit,* did not endeavor to find out the spiritual meaning; and therefore they rejected Christ, who was "the end of the law" for justification, and so for redemption from death to everyone that believes. Every institution has its *letter* as well

as its *spirit,* as every word must refer to something of which it is the sign or significator. The gospel has both its *letter* and its *spirit;* and multitudes of professing Christians, by resting in the letter, receive not the life which it is calculated to impart. Water, in baptism, is the *letter* that points out the purification of the soul; they who rest in this letter are without this purification; and dying in that state, they die eternally. Bread and wine in the sacrament of the Lord's Supper are the *letter;* the atoning efficacy of the death of Jesus and the grace communicated by this to the soul of a believer are the *spirit.* Multitudes rest in this *letter,* simply receiving these symbols without reference to the atonement or to their guilt, and thus lose the benefit of the atonement and the salvation of their souls.

7. *The ministration of death.* Here the apostle evidently intends the law. It was a ministration or "service" of *death.* It was the province of the law to ascertain the duty of man, to assign his duties, to fix penalties for transgressions. As man is prone to sin, and is continually committing it, this law was to him a continual *ministration of death.* Yet this *ministration of death* (the Ten Commandments, written on stones; a part of the Mosaic institutions being put for the whole) *was glorious*—was full of splendor; for the apostle refers to the thunderings, and lightnings, and luminous appearances which took place in the giving of the law, so that the very body of Moses partook of the effulgence in such a manner that the children of Israel could not look upon his face; and he, to hide it, was obliged to use a veil. All this was intended to show the excellency of that law as an institution coming immediately from God: and the apostle gives it all its heightenings, that he may compare it to the gospel, and thereby prove that, glorious as it was, it had no glory that could be compared with that of the gospel; and that even the glory it had was a glory that was to be *done away*—to be absorbed, as the light of the stars, planets, and moon, is absorbed in the splendor of the sun.

8. *The ministration of the spirit.* The gospel dispensation, which gives the true spiritual sense of the law. *Be rather glorious.* Forasmuch as the thing signified is of infinitely more consequence than that by which it is signified.

9. *The ministration of condemnation.* The law, which ascertained sin, and condemned it to just punishment. *The ministration of righteousness.* The gospel, the grand business of which was to proclaim the doctrine "of justification," and to show how God could be just and yet the Justifier of him who believes in Jesus.

10. *For even that which was made glorious.* The law, which was exhibited for a time in great glory and splendor, partly when it was given and partly by the splendor of God in the Tabernacle and first Temple. But all this ceased and was done away; was intended to give place to the gospel, and has actually given place to that system, so that now in no part of the world is that law performed, even by the people who are attached to it and reject the gospel. *The glory that excelleth.* The gospel dispensation, giving supereminent displays of the justice, holiness, goodness, mercy, and majesty of God.

11. *For if that which is done away.* Here is another striking difference between the law and

the gospel. The former is termed that which is "counterworked and abolished"; the latter, that which "continues," which is not for a particular time, place, and people, as the law was, but for all times, all places, and all people.

12. *Seeing . . . we have such hope.* Such glorious prospects as those blessings which the gospel sets before us. *We use great plainness of speech.* We speak not only with all confidence, but with all imaginable *plainness.*

13. *And not as Moses.* The splendor of Moses' countenance was so great that the Israelites could not bear to look upon his face, and therefore he was obliged to veil his face. This, it appears, he did typically, to represent the types and shadows by which the whole dispensation of which he was the minister was covered. So that the Israelites *could not stedfastly look*—could not then have the full view or discernment of that in which the Mosaic dispensation should issue and terminate.

14. *But their minds were blinded.* By resting in the letter, shutting their eyes against the light that was granted to them, they contracted a hardness or stupidity of heart. And the veil that was on the face of Moses, which prevented the glory of his face from shining out, may be considered as emblematical of the veil of darkness and ignorance that is on their hearts, and which hinders the glory of the gospel from shining in. *In the reading of the old testament.* Here is an evident allusion to the conduct of the Jews in their synagogues. When they read the law they cover the whole head with a veil, which they term the *tallith*, "veil," from *talal*, "to cover"; and this voluntary usage of theirs, the apostle tells us, is an emblem of the darkness of their hearts while they are employed even in sacred duties. *Which veil is done away in Christ.* It is only by acknowledging *Christ* that the darkness is removed, and the end and spiritual meaning of the law discerned.

16. *When it shall turn to the Lord.* When the Israelitish nation shall turn to the Lord Jesus, the veil shall be taken away; the true light shall shine, and they shall see all things clearly. There is an evident allusion here to the case of Moses, mentioned in Exod. xxxiv. 34. When he came from the Lord and spoke to the Israelites, he put the veil over his face; but when he returned to speak with the Lord, then he took off the veil. So when the Israelitish nation shall return to speak with and pray to the Lord Jesus, the veil of darkness and ignorance shall be taken away from their hearts; but never before that time. The words seem to imply: (1) That there will be a conversion of the Jews to Christianity; and (2) That this conversion will be en masse; that a time will come when the whole nation of the Jews, in every place, shall turn to Christ; and then the Gentiles and Jews make one fold, under one Shepherd and Bishop of all souls.

17. *Now the Lord is that Spirit.* In vv. 6 and 8 the word *spirit* evidently signifies the gospel; so called because it points out the spiritual nature and meaning of the law, because it produces spiritual effects, and because it is especially the dispensation of the Spirit of God. Here Jesus Christ is represented as that *Spirit*, because He is "the end of the law" for justification to everyone that believes; and because the residue of the Spirit is with Him, and He is the

Dispenser of all its gifts, graces, and influences. *And where the Spirit of the Lord is.* Wherever this gospel is received, there the Spirit of the Lord is given; and wherever that Spirit lives and works, there is *liberty*, not only from Jewish bondage, but from the slavery of sin—from its power, its guilt, and its pollution.

18. *But we all, with open face.* The Jews were not able to look on the face of Moses, the mediator of the old covenant, and therefore he was obliged to veil it. But all we Christians, with face uncovered, behold, as clearly as we can see our own natural face in a "mirror," the glorious promises and privileges of the gospel of Christ; and while we contemplate, we anticipate them by desire and hope, and apprehend them by faith, and *are changed* from the glory there represented to the enjoyment of the thing which is represented, even the glorious image—righteousness and true holiness—of the God of glory. *As by the Spirit of the Lord.* By the energy of that Spirit of Christ which gives life and being to all the promises of the gospel; and thus we are made partakers of the divine nature and escape all the corruptions that are in the world. This appears to me to be the general sense of this verse; its peculiar terms may be more particularly explained. The word *katoptrizomenoi*, which we translate *beholding . . . in a glass*, comes from *kata*, "against," and *optomai*, "I look"; and properly conveys the sense of looking into a mirror, or discerning by reflected light. Now as mirrors, among the Jews, Greeks, and Romans, were made of highly polished metal (see the note on 1 Cor. xiii. 12), it would often happen, especially in strong light, that the face would be greatly illuminated by this strongly reflected light; and to this circumstance the apostle seems here to allude. So by earnestly contemplating the gospel of Jesus and believing on Him who is its Author, the soul becomes illuminated with His divine splendor, for this sacred mirror reflects back on the believing soul the image of Him whose perfections it exhibits; and thus we see the glorious form after which our minds are to be fashioned. And by believing and receiving the influence of His Spirit our form is *changed into the same image*, which we behold there; and this is the image of God, lost by our fall, and now recovered and restored by Jesus Christ.

CHAPTER 4

Paul shows the integrity with which he had preached the gospel of Christ, 1-2. And that, if it was unprofitable to any who had heard it, it was because their unbelieving hearts were blinded, 3-4. How he preached, and how he was qualified for the work, 5-7. The troubles and difficulties he met with in his labors, and the hope and consolations by which he was supported, 8-15. And the prospect he had of eternal blessedness, 16-18.

1. *Seeing we have this ministry.* The gospel, of which he gave that noble account which we read in the preceding chapter. *We faint not.* We meet with many tribulations, but are supported in and through all by the grace of the gospel. Instead of *ouk ekkakoumen*, we *faint not, enkakoumen,* "we act not wickedly," is the reading of some MSS. Wakefield thinks it the genuine reading; it certainly makes very good sense with what goes before and what follows. If we follow this reading the whole verse may be read thus: "Wherefore, as we have obtained mercy, or been graciously entrusted, with this

ministry, we do not act wickedly, but have renounced the hidden things of dishonesty."

2. *But have renounced.* We have disclaimed *the hidden things of dishonesty;* "the hidden things of shame." *Not walking in craftiness.* In "subtlety" and "clever cunning," as the false teachers did. *Nor handling the word of God deceitfully.* Not using the doctrines of the gospel to serve any secular or carnal purpose; not explaining away their force so as to palliate or excuse sin; not generalizing its precepts so as to excuse many in particular circumstances from obedience, especially in that which most crossed their inclinations. There were deceitful handlers of this kind in Corinth, and there are many of them still in the garb of Christian ministers; persons who disguise that part of their creed which, though they believe it is of God, would make them unpopular; affecting moderation in order to procure a larger audience and more extensive support; not attacking prevalent and popular vices; calling dissipation of mind "relaxation," and worldly and carnal pleasures "innocent amusements." *Commending ourselves to every man's conscience.* Speaking so that every man's conscience shall bear its testimony that we proclaim the truth of God. This is one characteristic of divine truth: even every man's *conscience* will acknowledge it, though it speak decidedly against his own practices.

3. *But if our gospel be hid.* "Veiled"; he refers to the subject that he had treated so particularly in the conclusion of the preceding chapter. If there be a veil on the gospel, it is only to the willfully blind; and if any man's heart be veiled that hears this gospel, it is a proof that he is among the *lost.* The word does not necessarily imply those that will perish eternally, but is a common epithet to point out a man without the gospel and without God in the world. Christ commands His disciples in preaching the gospel to go "to the lost sheep of the house of Israel," Matt. x. 6; for himself says, Matt. xviii. 11 and Luke xix. 10: "The Son of man is come to seek and to save that which was lost." The word more properly signifies, not those who are *lost,* but those who "are perishing"; and will perish, if not sought and saved.

5. *For we preach not ourselves.* We proclaim neither our own wisdom nor our own power; we have nothing but what we have received; we do not wish to establish our own authority nor to procure our own emolument. *But Christ Jesus the Lord.* We proclaim the Author of this glorious gospel as Christ, the same as *hammashiach,* the Messiah, the "Anointed One"; Him of whom the prophets wrote; and who is the Expectation, as He is the Glory, of Israel. We proclaim Him as Jesus, *Yehoshua,* the "Saviour" and "Deliverer," who saves men from their sins. And further, we proclaim this Jesus, the Messiah, to be the Lord, the great Ruler who has all power in heaven and earth, who made and governs the world, and who can save to the uttermost all that come to God through Him. *And ourselves your servants.* Laboring as fervently and as faithfully for your eternal interests as your most trusty slaves can do for your secular welfare. And we do this for Christ's sake. For although we by our labor show ourselves to be your *servants,* yea, your "slaves," yet it is a voluntary service; and we

are neither employed by you nor receive our wages from you. We belong to Jesus; and are your servants on His account, and by His order.

6. *For God, who commanded the light to shine out of darkness.* The apostle refers here to Gen. i. 3. For when God created the heavens and the earth, "darkness was upon the face of the deep. . . . And God said, Let there be light: and there was light." Thus He caused *the light to shine out of darkness. Hath shined in our hearts.* He has given our *hearts* the glorious light of the gospel, as He has given the world the glorious light of the sun. It is in the "appearance" and "person" of Jesus Christ that these blessings are communicated to us.

7. *But we have this treasure in earthen vessels.* The original signifies more literally *vessels* made of shells, which are very brittle. The word *ostracon* not only signifies a shell, or vessel made of shell, but also *earthen vessels* which have been burnt in the kiln, and earthen vessels or pottery in general. *That the excellency of the power may be of God, and not of us.* God keeps us continually dependent upon himself. The good therefore that is done is so evidently from the power of God that none can pretend to share the glory with Him.

8. *We are troubled on every side.* We have already seen, in the notes on the ninth chapter of the preceding Epistle, that Paul has made several allusions to those public games which were celebrated every fifth year at the Isthmus of Corinth. In this and the following three verses the apostle makes allusion to the contests at those games, and the terms which he employs in these verses cannot be understood but in reference to those agonistical exercises to which he alludes. Dr. Hammond has explained the whole on this ground, and I shall here borrow his help. There are four pairs of expressions taken from the customs of the *agones:* (1) *Troubled on every side, yet not distressed.* (2) *Perplexed, but not in despair.* (3) *Persecuted, but not forsaken.* (4) *Cast down, but not destroyed.* Three of these pairs belong to the customs of wrestling; the fourth, to that of running in the race. *Troubled on every side.* The word *thlibesthai* belongs clearly to wrestling. *Perplexed, but not in despair.* The word "to be in perplexity" is fit for the wrestler, who being puzzled by his antagonist's skill knows not what to do.

9. *Persecuted, but not forsaken.* The *pursued* (*diokomenoi*) is peculiar to the race, when one being foremost others pursue, and get up close after him, endeavoring to outstrip him, but cannot succeed. This is the meaning of not "outstripped," or "outgone," as the word implies. *Cast down, but not destroyed.* This also belongs to wrestlers, where he that throws the other first is conqueror. And then, the being not *destroyed* signifies that, although they were "thrown down"—cast into troubles and difficulties—yet they rose again, and surmounted them all.

10. *Always bearing about in the body.* Being every moment in danger of losing our lives in the cause of truth, as Jesus Christ was. There is probably an allusion here to the marks, wounds, and bruises which the contenders in those games got, and continued to carry throughout life.

11. *For we which live.* And yet, although we are preserved alive, we are in such continual dangers that we carry our life in our hands, and are constantly in the spirit of sacrifice. But the *life,* the preserving power, of Christ is manifest in our continual support.

12. *Death worketh in us.* We apostles are in continual danger, and live a dying life, while you who have received this gospel from us are in no danger.

13. *We having the same spirit of faith.* As David had when he wrote Ps. cxvi. 10: "I believed, therefore have I spoken." *We also believe* that we shall receive the fulfillment of all God's promises; and being fully convinced of the truth of the Christian religion, we *speak* and testify that our deliverance is from God.

14. *Knowing that he which raised up the Lord.* And though we shall at last seal this truth with our blood, we fear not, being persuaded that as the body of Christ was raised from the dead by the power of the Father, so shall our bodies be raised, and that we shall have an eternal life with Him in glory.

15. *For all things are for your sakes.* We proclaim all these truths and bear all these sufferings for your sakes. *That the abundant grace.* The "abounding benefit"—the copious outpouring of the gifts and graces of the Holy Spirit, by which you have been favored and enriched, may *through the thanksgiving of many redound to the glory of God;* i.e., that the gratitude of the multitudes which have been converted may keep pace with the blessings which they have received, and "abound," as these blessings have abounded.

16. *For which cause we faint not.* See on v. 1. Here we have the same various reading, "We do no wickedness"; and it is supported by a member of MSS. The common reading, *faint not,* appears to agree best with the apostle's meaning. *But though our outward man.* That is, our bodies, that part of us that can be seen, heard, and felt. *Perish*—be slowly consumed by continual trials and afflictions, and be martyred at last. *Yet the inward man.* Our soul, that which cannot be felt or seen by others, *is renewed,* is "revived," and receives a daily increase of light and life from God.

17. *For our light affliction.* "It is everywhere visible what influence Paul's Hebrew had on his Greek: *cabad* signifies to be 'heavy,' and to be 'glorious'; the apostle in his Greek unites these two significations, and says, *weight of glory.*"

18. *While we look not at the things which are seen.* While we "aim not" at the things which are seen, do not make them our object, are not striving to obtain them; for they are not worthy the pursuit of an immortal spirit, because they are seen, they are "temporary," they are to have a short duration. But the things which we make our scope and aim are *not seen;* they are spiritual, and therefore invisible to the eye of the body; and besides, they are *eternal,* things that are permanent, that can have no end. Afflictions may be means of preparing us for glory if, during them, we receive grace to save the soul; but afflictions of themselves have no spiritual nor saving tendency. On the contrary, they sour the unregenerated mind and cause murmurings against the dispensations of divine providence.

CHAPTER 5

The apostle's strong hope of eternal glory, and earnest longings after that state of blessedness, 1-4. The assurance that he had of it from the Holy Spirit, and his carefulness to be always found pleasing to the Lord, 5-9. All must appear before the judgment seat of Christ, 10. Knowing that this awful event must take place, he labored to convince men of the necessity of being prepared to meet the Lord, being influenced to this work by his love of Christ, 11-13. Jesus Christ having died for all is a proof that all were dead, 14. Those for whom He died should live to Him, 15. We should know no man after the flesh, 16. They who are in Christ are new creatures, 17. The glorious ministry of reconciliation, 18-21.

1. *If our earthly house of this tabernacle.* By *earthly house* the apostle most evidently means the body in which the soul is represented as dwelling or sojourning for a time, and from which it is to be liberated at death. The apostle also alludes here to the ancient Jewish Tabernacle, which, on all removals of the congregation, was *dissolved* and taken in pieces; and the ark of the covenant, covered with its own curtains, was carried by itself; and when they came to the place of rest, the dissolved parts of the Tabernacle were put together as before. When we consider this simile in connection with the doctrine of the resurrection, then we shall see that he intends to convey the following meaning: that as the Tabernacle was taken down in order to be again put together, so the body is to be *dissolved,* in order to be reedified; that as the ark of the covenant subsisted by itself, while the Tabernacle was down, so can the soul when separated from the body; that as the ark had then its own veil for its covering, Exod. xl. 21, so the soul is to have some vehicle in which it shall subsist till it receives its body at the resurrection.

2. *For in this we groan.* While in this state and in this body, we are encompassed with many infirmities and exposed to many trials. When the apostle says that they earnestly desired *to be clothed upon with our house which is from heaven,* he certainly means that the great concern of all the genuine followers of God was to be fully prepared to enjoy the beatific vision of their Maker and Redeemer.

3. *If so be that being clothed.* That is, fully prepared in this life for the glory of God; *we shall not be found naked.* Destitute in that future state of that divine image which shall render us capable of enjoying an endless glory.

4. *For we that are in this tabernacle.* We who are in this state of trial and difficulty *do groan, being burdened: not for that we would be unclothed.* We do not desire death; nor to die, even with the full prospect of eternal glory before our eyes, an hour before that time which God in His wisdom has assigned. *But clothed upon.* To have the fullest preparation for eternal glory. *That mortality might be swallowed up of life.* Being fully prepared for the eternal state, we shall scarcely be said to die, all that is mortal being absorbed and annihilated by immortality and glory.

5. *Now he that hath wrought us for the selfsame thing.* God has given us our being and our body for this very purpose, that both might be made immortal and both be glorified together. Or God himself has given us this insatiable hungering and thirsting after righteousness and immortality.

6. *We are always confident.* We are always "full of courage"; we never despond; we know

where our help lies; and, having the earnest of the Spirit, we have the full assurance of hope. *Whilst we are at home in the body.* The original words in this sentence are very emphatic: *endemein* signifies to "dwell among one's own people"; *ekdemein,* to "be a sojourner among a strange people." Heaven is the home of every genuine Christian, and is claimed by them as such; see Phil. i. 23. Yet while here below, the body is the proper home of the soul. We see plainly that the apostle gives no intimation of an intermediate state between being at home in the body and being present with the Lord. There is not the slightest intimation here that the soul sleeps.

7. *For we walk by faith.* While we are in the present state *faith* supplies the place of direct vision. In the future world we shall have *sight.*

8. *We are confident.* We are "of good courage," notwithstanding our many difficulties; because we have this earnest of the Spirit, and the unfailing testimony of God. And notwithstanding this, we are *willing rather to be absent from the body*—we certainly prefer a state of glory to a state of suffering, and the enjoyment of the beatific vision to even the anticipation of it by faith and hope; but, as Christians, we cannot desire to die before our time.

9. *Wherefore we labour.* From *philos,* "loving," and *time,* "honor." We act at all times on the principles of honor; we are, in the proper sense of the word, ambitious to do and say everything consistently with our high vocation. *We may be accepted of him.* "To be pleasing to Him." Through the love we have to God, we study and labor to please Him.

10. *For we must all appear before the judgment seat.* We labor to walk so as to please Him, because we know that we shall have to give a solemn account of ourselves before the judgment seat of Christ. *That every one may receive the things.* That "each may receive to himself, into his own hand," his own reward and his own wages. *The things done in his body.* That is, while he was in this lower state; for in this sense the term body is taken often in this Epistle. We may observe also that the soul is the grand agent; the body is but its instrument.

11. *Knowing therefore the terror of the Lord.* This, I think, is too harsh a translation; should be rendered, "knowing therefore the fear of the Lord"; which, strange as it may at first appear, often signifies the "worship" of the Lord, or that religious reverence which we owe to Him. As we know therefore what God requires of man, because we are favored with His own revelation, *we persuade men* to become Christians, and to labor to be acceptable to Him, because they must all stand before the judgment seat. *But we are made manifest unto God.* God, who searches the heart, knows that we are upright in our endeavors to please Him; and because we are fully persuaded of the reality of eternal things, therefore we are fully in earnest to get sinners converted to Him. *Manifest in your consciences.* We have reason to believe that you have had such proof of our integrity and disinterestedness, that your consciences must acquit us of every unworthy motive and of every sinister view.

12. *For we commend not ourselves.* I do not say these things to bespeak your good opinion, to procure your praise; but to *give you occasion to glory,* to exult on our behalf; and to furnish you with an answer to all those who either malign us or our ministry, and who only *glory in appearance.* Paul probably speaks here concerning the false apostle, who had been dividing the church and endeavoring to raise a party to himself by vilifying both the apostle and his doctrine.

13. *Beside ourselves.* Probably he was reputed by some to be deranged. Festus thought so: "Paul, thou art beside thyself; [too] much learning doth make thee mad." And his enemies at Corinth might insinuate not only that he was deranged, but attribute his derangement to a less worthy cause than intense study and deep learning. *It is to God.* If we do appear, in speaking of the glories of the eternal world, to be transported beyond ourselves, it is through the good hand of our God upon us, and we do it to promote His honor. *Whether we be sober,* speak of divine things in a more cool and dispassionate manner, it is that we may the better instruct and encourage you.

14. *For the love of Christ constraineth us.* We have the love of God shed abroad in our hearts, and this causes us to love God intensely, and to love and labor for the salvation of men. And it is the effect produced by this love which "bears us away with itself," which causes us to love after the similitude of that love by which we are influenced; and as God so loved the world as to give His Son for it, and as Christ so loved the world as to pour out His life for it, so we, influenced by the very same love, desire to spend and be spent for the glory of God and the salvation of immortal souls. *If one died for all, then were all dead.* The first position the apostle takes for granted; viz., that Jesus Christ died for all mankind. The second position he infers from the first, and justly too; for if all had not been guilty, and consigned to eternal death because of their sin, there could have been no need of His death.

15. *And that he died for all, that they which live.* This third position he draws from the preceding: If all were dead, and in danger of endless perdition; and if He died for all, to save them from that perdition; then it justly follows that they are not their own, that they are bought by His blood; and *should not . . . live unto themselves,* for this is the way to final ruin; *but unto him which died for them,* and thus made an atonement for their sins, *and rose again* for their justification.

16. *Know we no man after the flesh.* As we know that "all have sinned, and come short of the glory of God," therefore we esteem no man on account of his family relations or the stock whence he proceeded. *Yea, though we have known Christ after the flesh.* We know that the Jews valued themselves much in having Abraham for their father, and some of the Judaizing teachers at Corinth might value themselves in having seen Christ in the flesh, which certainly Paul did not; hence he takes occasion to say here that this kind of privilege availed nothing.

17. *If any man be in Christ, he is a new creature.* It is vain for a man to profess affinity to Christ according to the flesh while he is unchanged in his heart and life, and dead in trespasses and sins; for he that is in Christ,

that is, a genuine Christian, having Christ dwelling in his heart by faith, is a *new creature*. His old state is changed. He was a child of Satan; he is now a child of God. He was a slave of sin; he is now made free from sin. *Behold, all things are become new.* The man is not only mended, but he is new-made; he is *a new creature*, a "new creation."

18. *And all things are of God.* As the thorough conversion of the soul is compared to a new creation, and creation is the proper work of an all-wise, almighty Being; then this total change of heart, soul, and life, which takes place under the preaching of the gospel, is effected by the power and grace of God. *The ministry of reconciliation.* The "office or function" of this reconciliation; called, v. 19, "the word"; the "doctrine of this reconciliation." *Reconciliation* comes from "to change thoroughly"; and the grand object of the gospel is to make a complete change in men's minds and manners; but the first object is the removal of enmity from the heart of man, that he may be disposed to accept of the salvation God has provided for him, on the terms which God has promised. The enmity in the heart of man is the grand hindrance to his salvation.

19. *That God was in Christ.* This is the doctrine which this ministry of reconciliation holds out, and the doctrine which it uses to bring about the reconciliation itself.

20. *We are ambassadors for Christ.* "We execute the function of ambassadors in Christ's stead." He came from the Father to mankind on this important embassy. He has left the world, and appointed us in His place. *As though God did beseech you by us.* What we say to you we say on the authority of God; our entreaties are His entreaties; our warm love to you, a faint reflection of His infinite love. We pray you to return to God; it is His will that you should do so. We promise you remission of sins; we are authorized to do so by God himself. In Christ's stead we pray you to lay aside your enmity and *be reconciled to God*.

21. *For he hath made him to be sin for us.* "He made Him who knew no sin (who was innocent) a Sin Offering for us." The word *hamartia* occurs here twice. In the first place it means *sin*, i.e., transgression and guilt; and of Christ it is said, "He knew no sin," i.e., was innocent; for not to know sin is the same as to be conscious of innocence. In the second place it signifies a "sin offering," or "sacrifice for sin," and answers to the *chattaah* and *chattath* of the Hebrew text; which signifies both "sin" and "sin offering" in a great variety of places in the Pentateuch. The Septuagint translate the Hebrew word by *hamartia* in ninety-four places in Exodus, Leviticus, and Numbers, where a "sin offering" is meant; and where our version translates the word, not "sin," but an "offering for sin." Had our translators attended to their own method of translating the word in other places where it means the same as here, they would not have given this false view of a passage which has been made the foundation of a most blasphemous doctrine; viz., that our sins were imputed to Christ, and that He was a proper Object of the indignation of divine justice, because He was blackened with imputed sin; and some have proceeded so far in this blasphemous career as to say that Christ may be considered

as the greatest of sinners, because all the sins of mankind, or of the elect, as they say, were imputed to Him, and reckoned as His own. Thus they have confounded sin with the punishment due to sin. Christ suffered in our stead, died for us, bore our sins (the punishment due to them) in His own body upon the tree, for the Lord laid upon Him the iniquities of us all; that is, the punishment due to them; explained by making "his soul," His life, "an offering for sin," and healing us by His stripes. *That we might be made the righteousness of God in him. The righteousness of God* signifies here the "salvation" of God, as comprehending justification through the blood of Christ, and sanctification through His Spirit; or as the mountains of God, the hail of God, the wind of God mean exceeding high mountains, extraordinary hail, and most tempestuous wind, so here the righteousness of God may mean a thorough righteousness, complete justification, complete sanctification such as none but God can give, such as the sinful nature and guilty conscience of man require, and such as is worthy of God to impart. And all this righteousness, justification, and holiness we receive in, by, for, and through Him.

CHAPTER 6

We should not receive the grace of God in vain, having such promises of support from Him, 1-2. We should act so as to bring no disgrace on the gospel. 3. How the apostles behaved themselves, preached, suffered, and rejoiced, 4-10. Paul's affectionate concern for the Corinthians, 11-13. He counsels them not to be yoked with unbelievers, and advances several arguments why they should avoid them, 14-16. Exhorts them to avoid evil companions and evil practices, on the promise that God will be their Father and that they shall be His sons and His daughters, 17-18.

1. *We then, as workers together with him.* The last two words, *with him*, are not in the text, and some supply the place thus: "We then, as workers together with you." For my own part I see nothing wanting in the text if we only suppose the term "apostles"; *we* (i.e., apostles), "being fellow workers, also entreat you not to receive the grace of God in vain." By the *grace of God*, this grace or benefit of God, the apostle certainly means the grand sacrificial offering of Christ for the sin of the world, which He had just before mentioned in speaking of the ministry of reconciliation. We learn, therefore, that it was possible to *receive the grace of God* and not ultimately benefit by it; or in other words, to begin in the Spirit and end in the flesh.

2. *For he saith.* That is, God hath said it, by the prophet Isaiah, chap. xlix. 8; which place the apostle quotes *verbatim et literatim* from the Septuagint. And from this we may at once see what is *the accepted time*, and what *the day of salvation*. The advent of the Messiah was the time of God's pleasure or benevolence, of which all the faithful were in expectation; and the *day of salvation* was the time in which this salvation should be manifested and applied. I rather think that this second verse should be read immediately after the last verse of the preceding chapter, as where it now stands it greatly disturbs the connection between the first and the third verses. I will set down the whole in the order in which I think they should stand. "Now then we are ambassadors for Christ, as though God did beseech you by us: we pray

you in Christ's stead, be ye reconciled to God. For he hath made him . . . [a] sin [offering] for us, who knew no sin; that we might be made the righteousness of God in him. For he saith, I have heard thee in a time accepted, and in the day of salvation have I succoured thee: behold, now is the accepted time; behold, now is the day of salvation." Immediately after this, the sixth chapter will very properly commence, and we shall see that the connection will be then undisturbed: "We then, as fellow workers, beseech you also that ye receive not this grace of God in vain, giving no offence in any thing, that this ministry be not blamed." This change of the place of the second verse, which everyone allows must, if it stand here, be read in a parenthesis, preserves the whole connection of the apostle's discourse and certainly sets his argument before us in a stronger light.

3. *Giving no offence.* The word signifies a "stumbling block" in general, or anything over which a man stumbles or falls; and here means any transgression or scandal that might take place among the ministers, or the Christians themselves, whereby either Jews or Gentiles might take occasion of offense and vilify the gospel of Christ.

4. *But in all things approving ourselves.* The apostle now proceeds to show how conscientiously himself and his fellow laborers acted in order to render the ministry of reconciliation effectual to the salvation of men. They not only gave no offense in anything, but they labored to manifest themselves to be the genuine ministers of God, *in much patience*, bearing calmly up under the most painful and oppressive afflictions. *In afflictions.* This may signify the series of persecutions and distresses in general, the state of cruel suffering in which the Church of God and the apostles then existed. *In necessities.* "Straits" and "difficulties," including all that want and affliction which arose from the impoverished state of the Church. *In distresses.* Such straits and difficulties as were absolutely unavoidable and insurmountable. The word implies "being reduced to a narrow place, driven to a corner, hemmed in on every side," as the Israelites were at the Red Sea—the sea before them, Pharaoh and his host behind them, and Egyptian fortresses on either hand. God alone could bring them out of such difficulties, when their enemies themselves saw that the wilderness had shut them in. So was it often with the apostles; all human help failed, and their deliverance came from God alone.

5. *In stripes, in imprisonments.* Of these the history of the Acts of the Apostles gives ample testimony; and there were doubtless many instances of persecution in various forms which are not on record. *In tumults.* "Insurrections" raised against them because of the gospel. It is more natural to understand the word thus than of agitations or tossings to and fro in consequence of their unsettled state of life; or because of persecution, which obliged them to flee from place to place. *In labours.* Both with our own hands to provide for ourselves the necessaries of life, that we might not be chargeable to others, and in labors to spread the gospel of God through all countries where His providence opened our way. *In watchings.* Passing many nights without sleep or rest. *In fastings.* Partly constrained through want of

food and partly voluntary, as a means of obtaining an increase of grace both for ourselves and for the churches.

6. *By pureness.* In "simplicity" of intention, and "purity" of affection, together with that chastity and holinsss of life which the gospel enjoins. *By knowledge.* Of the divine mysteries. *By longsuffering.* Under all provocations. *By kindness.* To our most virulent persecutors, and to all men. *By the Holy Ghost.* The constant indwelling of the Holy Spirit, and with it the various gifts of the Holy Spirit by which he was enabled to work miracles. *By love unfeigned.* "Love without hypocrisy."

7. *By the word of truth.* The doctrine of truth received immediately from God, and faithfully and affectionately preached to men. *By the power of God.* Confirming this doctrine, not only by the miracles which we were enabled to work, but also by the application of that truth to the souls of the people by the energy of God. *By the armour of righteousness.* Such as that described by the apostle, Eph. vi. 13-17, which he calls there "the whole armour of God." *On the right hand and on the left.* Particularly the shield and the sword; the former on the left arm, the latter in the right hand.

8. *By honour and dishonour.* By going through both; sometimes respected, sometimes despised. *By evil report and good report.* Sometimes praised, at other times calumniated. *As deceivers.* Said to carry about a false doctrine for our secular emolument. *And yet true.* Demonstrated by the nature of the doctrine, as well as by our life and conversation, that we are true men, having nothing in view but God's glory and the salvation of the world.

9. *As unknown.* Persons who are to be suspected as harboring dark designs; persons of neither birth, parentage, nor respectable connections in life. *And yet well known.* Proved by our whole conduct to have no such designs, and demonstrated to be holy, upright, and useful. *As dying.* Through continual dangers, fatigues, and persecutions. *And, behold, we live.* We are preserved by the mighty power of God in the greatest dangers and deaths. *As chastened.* As though we were disobedient children. *And not killed.* Though we continue in the very same line of conduct that is supposed to bring on us those chastisements, and which, if it were criminal, would justly expose us to death for incorrigible obstinacy; but our preservation is a proof that we please God.

10. *As sorrowful.* Considerate men supposing from our persecuted state and laborious occupation (often destitute of the necessaries of life; seldom enjoying its conveniences, and scarcely ever its comforts) that we must be the most miserable of all men. *Yet always rejoicing.* Having the consolation of God's Spirit at all times, and a glorious prospect of a blessed immortality. *As poor.* Destitute of all worldly good and secular interest. *Yet making many rich.* By dispensing to them the treasures of salvation; making them rich in faith, and heirs of the Kingdom. *As having nothing.* Being the most abject of the poor. *And yet possessing all things* that are really necessary to the preservation of our lives. For the wants under which we labor for a time are supplied again by a bountiful Providence. The man who possesses a contented spirit possesses *all things*, for he is

satisfied with every dispensation of the providence of God; and "a contented mind is a continual feast."

11. *O ye Corinthians, our mouth is open unto you.* I speak to you with the utmost freedom and fluency because of my affection for you. *Our heart is enlarged.* It is expanded to take you and all your interests in, and to keep you in the most affectionate remembrance.

12. *Ye are not straitened in us.* That is, You have not a narrow place in our affections. The metaphor here is taken from the case of a person pent up in a small or narrow place, where there is scarcely room to breathe. *Ye are straitened in your own bowels.* I have not the same place in your affections which you have in mine. The *bowels* are used in Scripture to denote the most "tender affections."

13. *Now for a recompense in the same.* That you may, in some sort, repay me for my affection towards you. *I speak to you as unto my children,* whom I have a right to command. *Be ye also enlarged;* love me as I love you.

14-15. *Be ye not unequally yoked together with unbelievers.* This is a military term: keep in your own ranks; do not leave the Christian community to join in that of the heathens. The verb signifies to leave one's own rank, place, or order, and go into another; and here it must signify not only that they should not associate with the Gentiles in their idolatrous feasts, but that they should not apostatize from Christianity; and the questions which follow show that there was a sort of fellowship that some of the Christians had formed with the heathens which was both wicked and absurd, and if not speedily checked would infallibly lead to final apostasy. Some apply this exhortation to pious persons marrying with those who are not decidedly religious and converted to God. That the exhortation may be thus applied I grant, but it is certainly not the meaning of the apostle in this place. Nevertheless common sense and true piety show the absurdity of two such persons pretending to walk together in a way in which they are not agreed. A very wise and very holy man has given his judgment on this point: "A man who is truly pious, marrying with an unconverted woman, will either draw back to perdition, or have a cross during life." The same may be said of a pious woman marrying an unconverted man. Such persons cannot say this petition of the Lord's Prayer, "Lead us not into temptation." They plunge into it of their own accord. *For what fellowship?* As *righteousness* cannot have communion with *unrighteousness,* and *light* cannot dwell with *darkness,* so *Christ* can have no concord with *Belial,* nor can he that *believeth* have any with an *infidel.* All these points were self-evident; how then could they keep up the profession of Christianity, or pretend to be under its influence, while they associated with the unrighteous, had communion with darkness, concord with Belial, and partook with infidels?

16. *What agreement hath the temple of God with idols?* Nothing could appear more abominable to a Jew than an idol in the Temple of God. Here, then, could be no agreement; the worship of the two is wholly incompatible. *Ye are the temple of the living God.* God intends to make the heart of every believer His own house. *I will dwell in them, and walk in them.*

The words are very emphatic: "I will inhabit in them." *I will be their God.* They shall have no other God, they shall have none besides Me; and if they take Me for their God, I will be to them all that an infinite, eternal, and self-sufficient Being can be to His intelligent offspring. *They shall be my people.* If they take Me for their God, their supreme and eternal Good, I will take them for My people; and instruct, enlighten, defend, provide for, support, and bless them, as if I had none else to care for in the creation.

17. *Wherefore come out from among them.* Is it not plain from this and the following verse that God would be their God only on the ground of their taking Him for such, and that this depended on their being separated from the works and workers of iniquity?

18. *Will be a Father unto you.* I will act towards you as the most affectionate father can act towards his most tender and best beloved child. *And ye shall be my sons and daughters.* You shall all be of the household of God, the family of heaven; you shall be holy, happy, and continually safe. *Saith the Lord Almighty.* The Lord, the Governor of all things. Earthly fathers, however loving and affectionate, may fail to provide for their children because not everything is at their disposal; they may frequently lack both the power and the means, though to will may be present with them. But the Lord who made and who governs all things can never lack will, power, nor means. The promise is sure to the children, and the children are those who take the Almighty for their God. For the promise belongs to no soul that is not separate from sinful ways, works, and men. Those who touch the unclean thing, i.e., who do what God forbids, and hold communion with unrighteousness, can never stand in the endearing relation of children to God Almighty: and this is most forcibly stated by God himself in these verses, and in the beginning of the following chapter, the first verse of which should conclude this.

CHAPTER 7

The apostle's inference from the preceding exhortation, 1. He presses them to receive him with affection, because of his great love towards them, 2-4. He tells them what distress he felt on their account in Macedonia, till he had met with Titus, and heard of their prosperity, 5-7. He rejoices that his First Epistle was made the means of their reformation, 8-9. States how they were affected by his letter, and the process of their reformation, 10-11. Shows why he had written to them, 12. Rejoices that his boasting of them to Titus is found to be a truth; and takes occasion to mention the great affection of Titus for them, and his own confidence in them, 13-16.

1. *Having therefore these promises.* The promises mentioned in the last three verses of the preceding chapter, to which this verse should certainly be joined. *Let us cleanse ourselves.* Let us apply to Him for the requisite grace of purification; and avoid everything in spirit and practice which is opposite to the doctrine of God, and which has a tendency to pollute the soul. *Filthiness of the flesh.* The apostle undoubtedly means drunkenness, fornication, adultery, and all such sins as are done immediately against the body; and by *filthiness of the . . . spirit,* all impure desires, unholy thoughts, and polluting imaginations. If we avoid and abhor evil inclinations, and turn away our eyes from beholding vanity, incentives

to evil being thus lessened (for the eye affects the heart), there will be the less danger of our falling into outward sin. And if we avoid all outward occasions of sinning, evil propensities will certainly be lessened. All this is our work under the common aids of the grace of God. We may turn away our eyes and ears from evil, or we may indulge both in what will infallibly beget evil desires and tempers in the soul. How can those expect God to purify their hearts who are continually indulging their eyes, ears, and hands in what is forbidden, and in what tends to increase and bring into action all the evil propensities of the soul? *Perfecting holiness.* Getting the whole mind of Christ brought into the soul. This is the grand object of a genuine Christian's pursuit. The means of accomplishing this are: (1) Resisting and avoiding sin, in all its inviting and seducing forms. (2) Setting the *fear of God* before our eyes, that we may dread His displeasure, and abhor whatever might excite it, and whatever might provoke Him to withhold His manna from our mouths.

2. *Receive us.* This address is variously understood. *Receive us* into your affections—love us as we love you. *Receive us* as your apostles and teachers; we have given you full proof that God has both sent and owned us. *Receive,* "comprehend," what we now say to you, and carefully mark it. *We have wronged no man.* We have never acted contrary to the strictest justice. *We have corrupted no man.* With any false doctrine or pernicious opinion. *We have defrauded no man.* Of any part of his property. But what have your false teachers done? They have beguiled you from the simplicity of the truth, and thus corrupted your minds, chap. xi. 3. They have brought you into bondage; they have taken of you, devoured you, exalted themselves against you, and you have patiently suffered all this, chap. xi. 20. It is plain that he refers here to the false apostle or teacher which they had among them.

3. *I speak not this to condemn you.* I do not speak to reproach but to correct you. I wish you to open your eyes and see how you are corrupted, spoiled, and impoverished by those whom you have incautiously preferred to the true apostles of Jesus Christ. *I have said before, that ye are in our hearts.* He has in effect and substance said this in chap. i. 6-8; ii. 4, 12; iii. 2; and v. 13. *To die and live with you.* An expression which points out the strongest affection, as in cases where love blinds us to the faults of those whom we love, and causes us to prefer them to all others.

4. *Great is my boldness of speech.* He seems to refer to the manner in which he spoke of them to others. *Great is my glorying of you.* They had probably been very loving and affectionate previously to the time in which they were perverted by their false apostle. He therefore had boasted of them in all the churches. *I am filled with comfort.* My affection for you has still the most powerful ascendancy in my soul. Here we may see the affection of the most tender father to his children. *I am exceeding joyful.* "I superabound in joy"; I have a joy beyond expression—an extremely rare verb. I have not met with it in any Greek author; and it occurs nowhere in the New Testament but here and in Rom. v. 20. *In all our tribulation.* Perhaps *epi* here should be rendered "under"

instead of *in,* as it signifies, Mark ii. 26; Luke iii. 2; Acts xi. 28. "Under all our tribulations, I feel inexpressible joy on your account."

5. *When we were come into Macedonia.* Paul, having left Ephesus, came to Troas, where he stopped some time; afterwards he came to Macedonia, whence he wrote this Epistle. *Our flesh had no rest.* So exceedingly anxious was he to know the success of his First Epistle to them. *Without were fightings.* The oppositions of pagans, Jews, and false brethren. *Within were fears.* Uncertain conjectures relative to the success of his Epistle; fears lest the severity of it should alienate their affections utterly from him; fears lest the party of the incestuous person should have prevailed; fears lest the teaching of the false apostle should have perverted their minds from the simplicity of the truth. All was uncertainty, all apprehension; and the Spirit of God did not think proper to remove the causes of these apprehensions in any extraordinary way.

6. *Comforted us by the coming of Titus.* Who brought him a most satisfactory account of the success of his Epistle, and the good state of the Corinthian church.

7. *He told us your earnest desire.* To see me, and correct what was amiss among yourselves. *Your mourning.* Because you had sinned. *Your fervent mind.* The zeal you felt to testify your affectionate regard for me.

8. *I do not repent, though I did repent.* Though I had many doubts in my mind concerning the success of my letter, and though I grieved that I was obliged to write with so much severity, the case absolutely requiring it, yet now I am not sorry that I have written that letter, because I find it has completely answered the end for which it was sent.

9. *Ye sorrowed to repentance.* You had such a sorrow as produced a complete change of mind and conduct. We see that a man may sorrow and yet not repent. *Made sorry after a godly manner.* It was not a sorrow because you were found out, but a sorrow because you had sinned against God. *Damage by us in nothing.* Your repentance prevented that exercise of my apostolic duty which would have consigned your bodies to destruction, that your souls might be saved in the day of the Lord Jesus.

10. *For godly sorrow.* That which has the breach of God's holy law for its object. *Worketh repentance,* a thorough "change of mind" *unto salvation,* because the person who feels it cannot rest till he finds pardon through the mercy of God. *But the sorrow of the world worketh death.* Sorrow for lost goods, lost friends, death of relatives, when it is poignant and deep, produces diseases, increases those that already exist, and often leads men to lay desperate hands on themselves. This sorrow leads to destruction, the other leads to salvation; the one leads to heaven, the other to hell.

11. *What carefulness it wrought in you.* Carefulness of obeying my directions, v. 15; *yea, what clearing of yourselves* from guilt by inflicting censures on the guilty person, and putting away evil from among you, 1 Cor. xv. 18; *yea, what indignation* against him who had dishonored his profession, and defiled the church; *yea, what fear* of my displeasure, and the rod which I threatened, 1 Cor. iv. 21; *yea,*

what vehement desire to rectify what was amiss in this matter, v. 7; *yea, what zeal* for me; *yea, what revenge* in punishing the delinquent!

In all things. In the whole of your conduct in this affair since you have received my letter, *ye have approved yourselves to be clear;* not only to be clear of contumacy and obstinate persistence in your former conduct, but to have done all in the compass of your power to rectify the abuses which had crept in among you. The Corinthians were not *clear,* i.e., innocent or void of blame in the fact, but they were clear of all blame in their endeavors to remove the evil.

12. *Not for his cause that had done the wrong.* Viz., the incestuous person. *Nor for his cause that suffered wrong.* Some think the apostle means himself; others, that he means the church at Corinth, the singular being put for the plural; others, the family of the incestuous person; and others, the father of the incestuous person. If this latter opinion be adopted, it would seem to intimate that the father of this person was yet alive, which would make the transgression more flagrant; but these words might be spoken in reference to the father, if dead, whose cause should be vindicated; as his injured honor might be considered, like Abel's blood, to be crying from the earth. *But that our care for you . . . might appear.* It was not to get the delinquent punished, nor merely to do justice to those who had suffered in this business, that the apostle wrote his Epistle to them, but that they might have the fullest proof of his fatherly affection for them, and his concern for the honor of God.

13. *For the joy of Titus.* Titus, who had now met Paul in Macedonia, gave him the most flattering accounts of the improved state of the Corinthian church; and indeed their kind usage of Titus was a full proof of their affection for Paul.

14. *For if I have boasted.* The apostle had given Titus a very high character of this church, and of their attachment to himself, and doubtless this was the case previously to the evil teacher coming among them, who had succeeded in changing their conduct, and changing in a great measure their character also. But now they return to themselves, so that the good character which the apostle gave them before, and which they had for a time forfeited, is now as applicable to them as ever. Therefore his boasting of them is still found a truth.

15. *Whilst he remembereth the obedience of you all.* This is a very natural picture; he represents Titus as overjoyed even while he is delivering his account of the Corinthian church. He expatiated on it with extreme delight, and thereby showed at once both his love for Paul and his love for them. He loved them because they so loved the apostle; and he loved them because they had shown such kindness to himself; and he loved them because he found so many excellent and rare gifts, joined to so much humility, producing such an exemplary and holy life. *With fear and trembling ye received him.* You reverenced his authority; you were obedient to his directions; and you dreaded lest anything should be undone or ill done which he had delivered to you in the name of God.

16. *I have confidence in you in all things.* It appears that the apostle was now fully persuaded, from the accounts given by Titus, that every scandal had been put away from this church; that the faction which had long distracted and divided them was nearly broken; that all was on the eve of being restored to its primitive purity and excellence; and that their character was now so firmly fixed that there was no reason to apprehend that they should be again tossed to and fro with every wind of doctrine.

CHAPTER 8

The apostle stirs them up to make a collection for the poor Christians at Jerusalem, by the very liberal contributions of the people of Macedonia for the same purpose, who were comparatively a poor people, 1-5. He tells them that he had desired Titus to finish this good work among them which he had begun, hoping that, as they abounded in many excellent gifts and graces, they would abound in this also, 6-8. He exhorts them to this by the example of Jesus Christ, who, though rich, subjected himself to voluntary poverty, that they might be enriched, 9. He shows them that this contribution, which had been long ago begun, should have been long since finished, 10. And that they should do everything with a ready and willing mind, according to the ability which God had given them; that abundance should not prevail on one hand, while pinching poverty ruled on the other; but that there should be an equality, 11-14. He shows from the distribution of the manna in the wilderness that the design of God was that every member of His spiritual household should have the necessaries of life, 15. He tells them that he had now sent Titus, and another with him, to Corinth, to complete this great work, 16-22. The character which he gives of Titus and the others employed in this business, 23-24.

1. *Moreover, brethren, we do you to wit.* In all our dignified version very few ill-constructed sentences can be found; however here is one, and the worst in the book. *We do you to wit* is in the original, "We made known unto you." This is plain and intelligible, the other is not so; and the form is now obsolete. *The grace of God bestowed.* The charitable contribution made by the churches in Macedonia, to which they were excited by the grace or influence of God upon their hearts; not *bestowed on,* but "given in." That *charis* means "liberality" appears from v. 6: "We desired Titus, that as he had begun, so he would also finish" this charitable contribution. And v. 7: That "ye abound" in this liberal contribution. And v. 19: "Who was also chosen of the churches to travel with us" with this charitable contribution, "which is administered," which is to be dispensed, "by us." This charity is styled the *grace of God,* either from its exceeding greatness (as the "cedars of God" and "mountains of God" signify great cedars and great mountains, Ps. xxxvi. 6; lxxx. 10); or, rather, it is called so as proceeding from God, who is the Dispenser of all good, and the Giver of this disposition; for the motive of charity must come from Him. *The churches of Macedonia.* These were Philippi, Thessalonica, Berea.

2. *In a great trial of affliction.* The sense of this verse is the following: The Macedonians, though both poor and persecuted, rejoiced exceedingly that an opportunity was afforded them of doing good to their more impoverished and more persecuted brethren.

3. *For to their power.* In their liberality they had no rule but their ability; they believed they were bound to contribute all they could; and even this rule they transgressed, for they went *beyond their power*—they deprived themselves for a time of the necessaries of life, in order to give to others who were destitute even of necessaries.

4. *Praying us with much intreaty.* We had not to solicit them to this great act of kindness; they even entreated us to accept their bounty, and to take on ourselves the administration or application of it to the wants of the poor in Judea.

5. *Not as we hoped.* They far exceeded our expectations, for they consecrated themselves entirely to the work of God, giving themselves and all they possessed first unto the Lord; and then, as they saw that it was the will of God that they should come especially forward in this charitable work, they gave themselves to us to assist to the uttermost in providing relief for the suffering Christians in Judea.

6. *That we desired Titus.* Titus had probably laid the plan of this contribution when he was before at Corinth, according to the direction given by the apostle, 1 Cor. xvi. 1. *The same grace.* Liberality. See the note on v. 1.

7. *As ye abound in every thing.* In *faith,* crediting the whole testimony of God; in *utterance,* "in doctrine," knowing what to teach; *knowledge* of God's will, and prudence to direct you in teaching and doing it; in *diligence,* to amend all that is wrong among you, and to do what is right; *and in your love to us,* whom now you prize the apostles of the Lord, and your pastors in Him. *Abound in this grace also.* Be as eminent for your charitable disposition as you are for your faith, doctrine, knowledge, diligence, and love.

8. *I speak not by commandment.* I do not positively order this; I assume no right or authority over your property; what you devote of your substance to charitable purposes must be your own work, and a freewill offering. *The forwardness of others.* Viz., the churches of Macedonia, which had already exerted themselves so very much in this good work. And the apostle here intimates that he takes this opportunity to apprise them of the zeal of the Macedonians, lest those at Corinth, who excelled in every other gift, should be outdone in this.

9. *For ye know the grace of our Lord Jesus Christ.* This was the strongest argument of all; and it is urged home by the apostle with admirable address. *Ye know.* You are acquainted with God's ineffable love in sending Jesus Christ into the world; and you know the *grace*—the infinite benevolence of Christ himself. *That, though he was rich.* The Possessor, as He was the Creator, of the heavens and the earth. *For your sakes he became poor.* He emptied himself, and "made himself of no reputation, and took upon him the form of a servant, and . . . humbled himself . . . unto death, even the death of the cross." *That ye through his poverty*—through His humiliation and death, *might be rich*—might regain your forfeited inheritance, and be enriched with every grace of His Holy Spirit, and brought at last to His eternal glory.

10. *Herein I give my advice.* For I speak not by way of commandment, v. 8. *For this is expedient for you.* It is necessary you should do this to preserve a consistency of conduct; for you began this work a year ago, and it is necessary that you should complete it as soon as possible. *Not only to do, but also to be forward.* Literally, "to do and to will"; but as the will must be before the deed, *thelein* must be

taken here in the sense of "delight," as it frequently means in the Old and New Testaments. *A year ago.* It was about a year before this that the apostle, in his First Epistle, chap. xvi. 2, had exhorted them to make this contribution; and there is no doubt that they, in obedience to his directions, had begun to lay up in store for this charitable purpose. He therefore wishes them to complete this good work, and thus show that they were not led to it by the example of the Macedonians, seeing they themselves had been first movers in this business.

11. *A readiness to will, so there may be a performance.* You have willed and purposed this; now perform it. *Out of that which ye have.* Give as God has enabled you; and give as God has disposed you. He requires each man to do as he can, and accepts the will where the means are wanting to perform the deed.

12. *According to that a man hath.* According to his real property; not taking that which belongs to his own family, and is indispensably necessary for their support; and not taking that which belongs to others, viz., what he owes to any man.

13. *That other men be eased.* I do not design that you should impoverish yourselves in order that others may live affluently.

14. *But by an equality.* That you may do to those who are distressed now as, on a change of circumstances, you would wish them to do to you. And I only wish that of your *abundance* you would now minister to their wants; and it may be that *their abundance* may yet *supply* your wants; for so liable are all human affairs to change that it is as possible that you rich Corinthians should need the charitable help of others as it is that those Jews, who once had need of nothing, should now be dependent on your bounty. *That there may be equality.* That you may exert yourselves so in behalf of those poor people that there may be between you an *equality* in the necessaries of life, your abundance supplying them with that of which they are utterly destitute.

15. *He that had gathered much had nothing over.* On the passage to which the apostle alludes, Exod. xvi. 18, I have stated that, probably, every man gathered as much manna as he could, and when he brought it home and measured it by the omer (for this was the measure for each man's eating), if he had a surplus it went to the supply of some other family that had not been able to collect enough; the family being large, and the time in which the manna might be gathered, before the heat of the day, not being sufficient to collect a supply for so numerous a household, several of whom might be so confined as not to be able to collect for themselves. Thus there was an *equality* among the Israelites in reference to this thing, and in this light these words of Paul lead us to view the passage. To apply this to the present case: The Corinthians, in the course of God's providence, had gathered more than was absolutely necessary for their own support; by giving the surplus to the persecuted and impoverished Christian Jews there would be an *equality.*

16. *But thanks be to God.* He thanks God, who had already disposed the heart of Titus to attend to this business; and, with his usual address, considers all this as done in the behalf of the Corinthian church.

17. *He accepted the exhortation.* I advised him to visit you and excite you to this good work, and I found that he was already disposed in his heart to do it; God put this "earnest care into the heart of Titus for you," v. 16.

18. *The brother, whose praise is in the gospel.* Who this *brother* was we cannot tell; some suppose it was Luke, who wrote a Gospel, and who was the companion of Paul in several of his travels; others think it was Silas; others, Barnabas; others, Mark; and others, Apollos. Neither ancients nor moderns agree in either; but Luke, John, and Mark seem to have the most probable opinions in their favor. Whoever the person was, he was sufficiently known to the Corinthians, as we learn by what the apostle says of him in this place.

19. *Chosen of the churches to travel with us.* Appointed by a "show of hands." This appointment, by the suffrage of the churches, seems to refer more to Luke than anyone else. *With this grace.* Liberal contribution. See on v. 1. *Your ready mind.* Your willingness to relieve them. But, instead of *your*, "our" is the reading of almost all the best MSS. and all the versions. This is doubtless the true reading.

20. *Avoiding this, that no man should blame us.* Taking this prudent caution to have witnesses of our conduct, and such as were chosen by the churches themselves, that we might not be suspected of having either embezzled or misapplied their bounty.

21. *Providing for honest things.* Taking care to act so as not only to be clear in the sight of God, but also to be clear in the sight of all men, avoiding even the appearance of evil.

22. *We have sent with them.* Titus and probably Luke. *Our brother,* probably Apollos. *Now much more diligent.* Finding that I have the fullest confidence in your complete reformation and love to me, he engages in this business with alacrity, and exceeds even his former diligence.

23. *Whether any do enquire of Titus.* Should it be asked, "Who is this Titus?" I answer, He is my companion, and my fellow laborer in reference to you; chap. ii. 13; vii. 6-7. Should any inquire, Who are these *brethren,* Luke and Apollos? I answer, *They are* "apostles" *of the churches,* and intensely bent on promoting *the glory of Christ.*

24. *Wherefore shew ye to them, and before the churches.* Seeing they are persons every way worthy in themselves, and coming to you on such an important occasion, and so highly recommended, receive them affectionately; and let them thus see that the very high character I have given of you is not exaggerated, and that you are as ready in every work of charity as I have stated you to be. Act in this for your honor.

CHAPTER 9

Paul intimates that so ready were the Corinthians to make this charitable contribution that it was scarcely necessary for him to write, 1-2. But lest they should not be ready when he came, he had sent the brethren, Titus, etc., beforehand; lest if any of the Macedonians should come with him, they should find them not prepared, though he had boasted so much of their ready mind, 3-5. He gives them directions how they shall contribute; and the advantage to be gained by it, in the fulfillment of the promises of God, 6-11. He shows them that by this means the poor shall be relieved,

God glorified, their Christian temper manifested, and the prayers of many engaged in their behalf, 12-14. And concludes with giving thanks to God for His unspeakable gift, 15.

1. *It is superfluous for me to write to you.* I need not enlarge, having already said enough. See the preceding chapter.

2. *I know the forwardness of your mind.* You have already firmly purposed to contribute to the support of the poor and suffering saints. *That Achaia was ready a year ago.* The apostle means not only Corinth but other churches in different parts about Corinth; we know there was a church at Cenchrea, one of the ports on the Corinthian Isthmus. *Your zeal hath provoked very many.* Hearing that the Corinthians were so intent on the relief of the sufferers in Palestine, other churches, and especially they of Macedonia, came forward the more promptly and liberally.

3. *Yet have I sent the brethren.* Titus and his companions, mentioned in the preceding chapter. *That, as I said, ye may be ready.* And he wished them to be ready, that they might preserve the good character he had given them. This was for their honor; and if they did not take care to do so, he might be reputed a liar; and thus both they and himself be *ashamed* before the Macedonians, should any of them at this time accompany him to Corinth.

5. *Whereof ye had notice before.* Instead of "spoken of before," several MSS. and several of the fathers have "what was promised before." The sense is not very different; probably the latter reading was intended to explain the former. *Bounty, and not as of covetousness.* Had they been backward, strangers might have attributed this to a covetous principle.

6. *He which soweth sparingly.* This is a plain maxim; no man can expect to reap but in proportion as he has sowed. And here almsgiving is represented as a seed sown, which shall bring forth a crop. If the sowing be liberal and the seed good, the crop shall be so too. Sowing is used among the Jews to express almsgiving; so they understand Isa. xxxii. 20: "Blessed are ye that sow beside all waters"; i.e., who are ready to help everyone that is in need. And Hos. x. 12, they interpret: "Sow to yourselves almsgiving, and ye shall reap in mercy"—if you show mercy to the poor, God will show mercy to you.

7. *Not grudgingly, or of necessity.* The Jews had in the Temple two chests for alms: the one was of what was necessary, i.e., what the law required; the other was of the freewill offerings. To escape perdition some would grudgingly give what necessity obliged them; others would give cheerfully, for the love of God, and through pity to the poor. Of the first, nothing is said; they simply did what the law required. Of the second much is said; God loves them. The benefit of almsgiving is lost to the giver when he does it with a grumbling heart.

8. *God is able to make all grace abound.* We have already seen, chap. viii. 1, that the word *charis,* in the connection in which the apostle uses it in these chapters, signifies a "charitable gift"; here it certainly has the same meaning. God is able to give you, in His mercy, abundance of temporal good; that, having a sufficiency, you may abound in every good work. This refers to the sowing plenteously; those who

do so shall reap plenteously—they shall have an abundance of God's blessings.

9. *He hath dispersed abroad.* Here is still the allusion to the sower. He sows much, not at home merely, or among those with whom he is acquainted, but *abroad,* among the strangers, whether of his own or of another nation. The quotation is taken from Ps. cxii. 9. *He hath given to the poor.* This is the interpretation of "he hath scattered abroad"; and therefore it is said, *his righteousness remaineth for ever*—his good work is had in remembrance before God. By *righteousness* we have already seen that the Jews understand "almsgiving."

10. *Now he that ministereth seed to the sower.* The *sower,* as we have already seen, is he that gives alms of what he hath; and God, who requires him to give these alms, is here represented as providing him with the means. The word *he that ministereth* is very emphatic; it signifies "he who leads up the chorus"; it means also to "join to, associate, to supply or furnish one thing after another" so that there be no want or chasm. Thus God is represented, in the course of His providence, associating and connecting causes and effects; keeping everything in its proper place and state of dependence on another, and all upon himself; so that summer and winter, heat and cold, seedtime and harvest, regularly succeed each other. Thus God leads up this grand chorus of causes and effects. *The fruits of your righteousness.* Your beneficence.

11. *Being enriched in every thing.* Observe, Why does God give riches? That they may be applied to His glory and the good of men. Why does He increase riches? That those who have them may exercise all bountifulness. And if they be *enriched in every thing,* what will be the consequence if they do not exercise *all bountifulness?* Why, God will curse their blessings; the rust shall canker them, and the moth shall consume their garments. But if, on the other hand, they do thus apply them, then they cause *thanksgiving to God.* The ninth and tenth verses should be read in a parenthesis, for this verse connects with the eighth.

12. *For the administration of this service.* The poor are relieved, see the hand of God in this relief, and give God the glory for His grace.

13. *By the experiment of this ministration.* In this, and in the preceding and following verses, the apostle enumerates the good effects that would be produced by their liberal almsgiving to the poor saints at Jerusalem. (1) The wants of the saints would be supplied. (2) Many thanksgivings would thereby be rendered unto God. (3) The Corinthians would thereby give proof of their subjection to the gospel. And, (4) The prayers of those relieved will ascend up to God in behalf of their benefactors.

14. *The exceeding grace of God in you.* By the "superabounding" or "transcending grace" of God, which was in them, the apostle most evidently means the merciful and charitable disposition which they had towards the suffering saints.

15. *Thanks be unto God for his unspeakable gift.* Some contend that Christ only is here intended; others, that the almsgiving is meant. After all the difference of commentators and preachers, it is most evident that the *unspeak-able gift* is precisely the same with the "super-abounding grace or benefit" of the preceding verse. If therefore Jesus Christ, the Gift of God's unbounded love to man, be the meaning of the *unspeakable gift* in this verse, He is also intended by the superabounding grace in the preceding. But it is most evident that it is the work of Christ in them, and not Christ himself, which is intended in the fourteenth verse; and consequently that it is the same work, not the operator, which is referred to in this last verse.

CHAPTER 10

The apostle vindicates himself against the aspersions cast on his person by the false apostle; and takes occasion to mention his spiritual might and authority, 1-6. He shows them the impropriety of judging after the outward appearance, 7. Again refers to his apostolical authority, and informs them that when he again comes among them he will show himself in his deeds as powerful as his letters intimated, 8-11. He shows that these false teachers sat down in other men's labors, having neither authority nor influence from God to break up new ground, while he and the apostles in general had the regions assigned to them through which they were to sow the seed of life; and that he never entered into any place where the work was made ready to his hand by others, 12-16. He concludes with intimating that the glorying of those false apostles was bad; that they had nothing but self-commendation; and that they who glory should glory in the Lord, 17-18.

1. *I Paul myself beseech you by the meekness.* Having now finished his directions and advices relative to the collection for the poor, he resumes his argument relative to the false apostle, who had gained considerable influence by representing Paul as despicable in his person, his ministry, and his influence. Under this obloquy the apostle was supported by the meekness and gentleness of Christ; and through the same heavenly disposition he delayed inflicting that punishment which, in virtue of his apostolical authority, he might have inflicted on him who had disturbed and labored to corrupt the Christian Church. *Who in presence am base among you, but being absent am bold toward you.* He seems to quote these as the words of his calumniator, as if he had said: "This apostle of yours is a mere braggadocio; when he is among you, you know how base and contemptible he is; when absent, see how he brags and boasts." The word which we render *base* signifies "lowly," and, as some think, "short of stature." The insinuation is that, when there was danger or opposition at hand, Paul acted with great obsequiousness, fearing for his person and authority, lest he should lose his secular influence.

2. *Some, which think of us as if we walked according to the flesh.* As it is customary for cowards and overbearing men to threaten the weak and the timid when present, to bluster when absent, and to be very obsequious in the presence of the strong and courageous. This conduct they appear to have charged against the apostle, which he calls here walking after *the flesh*—acting as a man who had worldly ends in view and would use any means in order to accomplish them.

3. *Though we walk in the flesh.* That is: Although I am in the common condition of human nature, and must live as a human being, yet I do *not war after the flesh*—I do not act the coward, as they insinuate.

4. *The weapons of our warfare.* The apostle often uses the metaphor of a *warfare* to represent the life and trials of a Christian minister.

See Eph. vi. 10-17; 1 Tim. i. 18; 2 Tim. ii. 3-5. *Are not carnal.* Here he refers to the means used by the false apostle in order to secure his party. *But mighty through God.* Our doctrines are true and pure. They come from God and lead to Him, and He accompanies them with His mighty power to the hearts of those who hear them; and the *strong holds*—the apparently solid and cogent reasoning of the philosophers—we, by these doctrines, pull down.

5. *Casting down imaginations.* "Reasonings" or "opinions." The Greek philosophers valued themselves especially on their ethic systems, in which their reasonings appeared to be very profound and conclusive; but they were obliged to assume principles which were either such as did not exist or were false in themselves. *Every high thing.* Even the pretendedly sublime doctrines, for instance, of Plato, Aristotle, and the Stoics in general, fell before the simple preaching of Christ crucified. *The knowledge of God.* The doctrine of the unity and eternity of the divine nature, which was opposed by the plurality of their idols, and the generation of their gods, and their man-made deities. *The obedience of Christ.* Subjection to idols was annihilated by the progress of the gospel among the heathen.

6. *And having in a readiness to revenge all disobedience.* I am ready through this mighty armor of God to punish those opposers of the doctrine of Christ and the disobedience which has been produced by them. *When your obedience is fulfilled.* When you have in the fullest manner discountenanced those men, and separated yourselves from their communion. All the terms in these two verses are military. Allusion is made to a strongly fortified city, where the enemy had made his last stand: entrenching himself about the walls; strengthening all his redoubts and ramparts; raising castles, towers, and various engines of defense and offense upon the walls; and neglecting nothing that might tend to render his stronghold impregnable. The army of God comes against the place and attacks it; the "strong holds," all the "fortified places," are carried. The "imaginations," engines, and whatever the imagination or skill of man could raise, are speedily taken and destroyed. Every "high thing"—all the castles and towers are sapped, thrown down and demolished; the walls are battered into breaches; and the besieging army, carrying everything at the point of the sword, enter the city, storm and take the citadel. Everywhere defeated, the conquered submit, and are brought "into captivity," "are led away captives."

7. *Do ye look on things after the outward appearance?* Do not be carried away with appearances; do not be satisfied with show and parade. *If any man trust to himself that he is Christ's.* Here, as in several other places of this and the preceding Epistle, the *any,* or "certain," person most evidently refers to the false apostle who made so much disturbance in the church. And this man trusted to himself—assumed to himself that he was Christ's messenger. *Let him of himself.* Without any authority, certainly, from God; but as he arrogates to himself the character of a minister of Christ, let him acknowledge that even so we are Christ's ministers; and that I have, by my preaching and the miracles which I have wrought, given the

fullest proof that I am especially commissioned by Him.

8. *For though I should boast.* I have a greater authority and spiritual power than I have yet shown, both to edify and to punish; but I employ this for your *edification* in righteousness, and not for the *destruction* of any delinquent.

9. *That I may not seem.* This is an elliptical sentence, and may be supplied thus: "I have not used this authority; nor will I add any more concerning this part of the subject, lest I should seem, as my adversary has insinuated, to wish to terrify you by my letters."

10. *For his letters, say they, are weighty and powerful.* He boasts of high powers, and that he can do great things. See on vv. 1-2. *But his bodily presence is weak.* When you behold the man, you find him a feeble, contemptible mortal; and when you hear him speak, *his speech,* probably his "doctrine," is good for nothing. If we can credit some ancient writers, such as Nicephorus, we shall find the apostle thus described: "Paul was a little man, crooked, and almost bent like a bow; with a pale countenance, long and wrinkled; a bald head; his eyes full of fire and benevolence; his beard long, thick, and interspersed with grey hairs, as was his head." Perhaps there is not one of these statements correct. As to Nicephorus, he is a writer of the fourteenth century, weak and credulous, and worthy of no regard. That Paul could be no such diminutive person we may fairly presume from the office he filled under the high priest, in the persecution of the Church of Christ; and that he had not an impediment in his speech, but was a graceful orator, we may learn from his whole history, and especially from the account we have, Acts xiv. 12, where the Lycaonians took him for Mercury, the god of eloquence, induced thereto by his powerful and persuasive elocution.

11. *Such as we are in word.* A threatening of this kind would doubtless alarm the false apostle; and it is very likely that he did not await the apostle's coming, as he would not be willing to try the fate of Elymas.

12. *We dare not make ourselves.* As if he had said: I dare neither associate with, nor compare myself to, those who are full of self-commendation. *But they measuring themselves by themselves.* As they dare not compare themselves with the true apostles of Christ, they compare themselves with each other; and, as they have no perfect standard, they can have no excellence.

13. *Things without our measure.* By the *measure* mentioned here, it seems as if the apostle meant the commission he received from God to preach the gospel to the Gentiles; *a measure* or "district" that extended through all Asia Minor and Greece, down to Achaia, where Corinth was situated, *a measure to reach even unto you.* But the expressions in these verses are all agonistical, and taken from the stadium or racecourse in the Olympic and Isthmian games. The *measure* was the length of the course; the rule or line, vv. 15 and 16, was probably the same with the white line which marked out the boundaries of the stadium; and the verbs "reach unto," "stretch out," etc., are all references to the exertions made to win the race.

14. *For we stretch not ourselves beyond.* We

have not proceeded straight from Macedonia through Thessaly, and across the Adriatic Gulf into Italy, which would have led us *beyond* you westward; but knowing the mind of our God, we left this direct path, and came southward through Greece, down into Achaia, and there we planted the gospel. The false apostle has therefore got into our province, and entered into our labors, and there boasts as if the conversion of the heathen Achaians had been his own work.

15. *Not boasting of things without our measure.* We speak only of the work which God has done by us; for we have never attempted to enter into other men's labors, and we study to convert those regions assigned to us by the Holy Spirit. We enter the course lawfully, and run according to rule. *When your faith is increased.* When you receive more of the life and power of godliness, and when you can better spare me to go to other places. *We shall be enlarged by you.* Probably signifies here to be "praised" or "commended"; and the sense would be this: We hope that shortly, on your gaining an increase of true religion, after your long distractions and divisions, you will plainly see that we are the true messengers of God to you; and that in all your intercourse with your neighbors, or foreign parts, you will speak of this gospel preached by us as a glorious system of saving truth; and that, in consequence, the heathen countries around you will be the better prepared to receive our message, and thus our rule or district will be abundantly extended. This interpretation agrees well with the following verse.

16. *To preach the gospel in the regions beyond you.* He probably refers to those parts such as Sparta, that lay southward of them; and to Italy, which lay on the west. *Not to boast in another man's line.* So very scrupulous was the apostle not to build on another man's foundation that he would not even go to those places where other apostles were laboring.

17. *He that glorieth, let him glory in the Lord.* Instead of boasting or exulting even in your own success in preaching the gospel, as none can be successful without the especial blessing of God, let God, who gave the blessing, have the glory.

18. *Not he that commendeth himself.* Not the person who makes a parade of his own attainments; who preaches himself, and not Christ Jesus the Lord; and, far from being your servant for Christ's sake, affects to be your ruler—not such a one shall be approved of God by an especial blessing on his labors, *but whom the Lord commendeth,* by giving him the extraordinary gifts of the Holy Spirit and converting the heathen by his ministry. These were qualifications to which the false apostle at Corinth could not pretend.

CHAPTER 11

The apostle apologizes for expressing his jealousy relative to the true state of the Corinthians, still fearing lest their minds should have been drawn aside from the simplicity of the gospel, 1-3. From this he takes occasion to extol his own ministry, which had been without charge to them, having been supported by the churches of Macedonia while he preached the gospel at Corinth, 4-11. Gives the character of the false apostles, 12-15. Shows what reasons he has to boast of secular advantages of birth, education, divine call to the ministry, labors in that ministry, grievous persecutions, great sufferings, and extraordinary hazards, 16-33.

1. *Would to God ye could bear with me.* As the word *God* is not mentioned here, it would have been much better to translate the passage literally thus: "I wish ye could bear a little with me." The too frequent use of this sacred name produces a familiarity with it that is not at all conducive to reverence and godly fear. *In my folly.* In my seeming folly, for being obliged to vindicate his ministry, it was necessary that he should speak much of himself, his sufferings, and his success. And as this would appear like boasting, and boasting is always the effect of an empty, foolish mind, those who were not acquainted with the necessity that lay upon him to make this defense might be led to impute it to vanity.

2. *That I may present you as a chaste virgin.* There seems to be a reference to Lev. xxi. 14, that the high priest must not marry anyone that was not a pure virgin. Here then Christ is the High Priest, the Spouse or Husband; the Corinthian church, the pure virgin to be espoused; the apostle and his helpers had educated and prepared this virgin for her husband and espoused her to him.

3. *As the serpent beguiled Eve through his subtilty.* This is a strong reflection on the false apostle and his teaching. He was subtle, and by his subtlety he was enabled to corrupt the minds of the people from the simplicity of the gospel of Christ; or, to follow the metaphor, he had seduced the pure, chaste, well-educated virgin from her duty, affection, and allegiance to her one only true Husband, the High Priest, Jesus Christ.

4. *For if he that cometh.* The false apostle who came after Paul had left Corinth. *Preacheth another Jesus.* Who can save more fully and more powerfully than that Jesus whom I have preached. *Or if ye receive another spirit.* And if in consequence of believing in this new saviour you receive another *spirit,* the gifts, graces, and consolations of which are greater than those which you have received from the Holy Ghost, who has been given to you on your believing on the Christ whom we preached. *Or another gospel.* Containing more privileges, spiritual advantages, and stronger excitements to holiness than that which we have preached and which you have accepted, *ye might well bear with him.* This would be a sufficient reason why you should not only *bear with him,* but prefer him to me.

5. *I was not . . . behind the very chiefest apostles.* That is: The most eminent of the apostles have not preached Christ, ministered the Spirit, explained and enforced the doctrines of the gospel in a more powerful and effectual manner than I have done.

6. *But though I be rude in speech.* Though I speak like a common, unlettered man, in plain, unadorned phrase, studying none of the graces of eloquence, yet I am not unskilled in the most profound *knowledge* of God, of spiritual and eternal things, of the nature of the human soul, and the sound truths of the gospel system. You yourselves are witnesses of this, as in all these things I have been thoroughly manifested among you.

7. *Have I committed an offence in abasing myself?* Have I transgressed in laboring with my hands that I might not be chargeable to

you? and getting my deficiencies supplied by contributions from other churches, while I was employed in laboring for your salvation? Does your false apostle insinuate that I have disgraced the apostolic office by thus descending to servile labor for my support? Well, I have done this that you *might be exalted*—that you might receive the pure doctrines of the gospel, and be exalted to the highest pitch of intellectual light and blessedness. And will you complain that I preached the gospel gratis to you? Surely not. The whole passage is truly ironical.

8. *I robbed other churches.* This part of the sentence is explained by the latter, *taking wages . . . to do you service.* The word signifies the pay of money and provisions given daily to a Roman soldier. As if he had said: I received food and raiment, the bare necessaries of life, from other churches while laboring for your salvation. Will you esteem this a crime?

9. *And when I was present with you.* The particle which we translate *and* should be rendered "for" in this place: "For when I was with you, and was in want, *I was chargeable to no man.*" I preferred to be, for a time, even without the necessaries of life, rather than be a burden to you. To whom was this a reproach, to me or to you? *The brethren which came from Macedonia.* He probably refers to the supplies which he received from the church at Philippi, which was in Macedonia; of which he says, that "in the beginning of the gospel . . . no church communicated with me as concerning giving and receiving, but ye only. For even in Thessalonica ye sent once and again unto my necessity," Phil. iv. 15-16.

10. *As the truth of Christ is in me.* That is: I speak as becomes a Christian man, and as influenced by the gospel of Christ. It is a solemn form of asseveration, if not to be considered in the sense of an oath. *In the regions of Achaia.* The whole of the Peloponnesus, in which the city of Corinth stood. From this it appears that he had received no help from any of the other churches in the whole of that district.

11. *Wherefore.* Why have I acted thus? and why do I propose to continue to act thus? is it *because I love you not*, and will not permit you to contribute to my support? *God knoweth* the contrary; I do most affectionately love you.

12. *But what I do.* I act thus *that I may cut off occasion* of glorying, boasting, or calumniating *from them*—the false prophets and his partisans, "who seek occasion"—who would be glad that I should become chargeable to you, that it might in some sort vindicate them who exact much from you; for they "bring you into bondage" and "devour you," v. 20. Nothing could mortify these persons more than to find that the apostle did take nothing and was resolved to take nothing, while they were fleecing the people.

13. *For such are false apostles.* Persons who pretend to be apostles but have no mission from Christ. *Deceitful workers.* They do preach and labor, but they have nothing but their own emolument in view. *Transforming themselves.* Assuming as far as they possibly can, consistently with their sinister views, the habit, manner, and doctrine of the apostles of Christ.

14. *And no marvel.* And no wonder; it need not surprise you what the disciples do, when you consider the character of the master. *Satan himself is transformed into an angel of light.* As in v. 3 the apostle had the history of the temptation and fall of man particularly in view, it is very likely that here he refers to the same thing. In whatever form Satan appeared to our first mother, his pretensions and professions gave him the appearance of a good angel; and by pretending that Eve should get a great increase of light, that is, wisdom and understanding, he deceived her, and led her to transgress. It is generally said that Satan has three forms under which he tempts men: (1) the subtle serpent, (2) the roaring lion, (3) the angel of light. He often, as the angel of light, persuades men to do things under the name of religion which are subversive of it.

15. *Whose end shall be according to their works.* A bad way leads to a bad end. The way of sin is the way to hell.

16. *Let no man think me a fool.* See the note on v. 1. As the apostle was now going to enter into a particular detail of his qualifications, natural, acquired, and spiritual, and particularly of his labors and sufferings, he thinks it necessary to introduce the discourse once more as he did in v. 1.

17. *I speak it not after the Lord.* Were it not for the necessity under which I am laid to vindicate my apostleship, my present glorying would be inconsistent with my Christian profession of humility and knowing no one after the flesh.

18. *Seeing that many glory after the flesh.* Boast of external and secular things.

19. *Ye suffer fools gladly, seeing ye yourselves are wise.* A very fine irony. You are so profoundly *wise* as to be able to discern that I am a fool. Well, it would be dishonorable to you as *wise* men to fall out with a fool; you will therefore gladly bear with his impertinence and foolishness because of your own profound wisdom.

20. *For ye suffer.* As you are so meek and gentle as to submit to be brought into *bondage*, to have your property devoured, your goods taken away, yourselves laid in the dust, so that others may *exalt* themselves over you—yea, and will bear from those the most degrading indignity—then of course you will bear with one who has never insulted, defrauded, devoured, taken of you, exalted himself against you, or offered you any kind of indignity; and who only wishes you to bear his confident boasting concerning matters which he can substantiate. The expressions in this verse are some evidence that the false apostle was a Judaizing teacher. *Ye suffer*, says the apostle, *if a man bring you into bondage*, probably meaning to the Jewish rites and ceremonies, Gal. iv. 9; v. 1. *If he devour you;* as the Pharisees did the patrimony of the widows, and for a pretense made long prayers; *if a man take of you*, exact different contributions, pretendedly for the Temple at Jerusalem. *If he exalt himself*, pretending to be of the seed of Abraham, infinitely higher in honor and dignity than all the families of the Gentiles; *if he smite you on the face*, treat you with indignity, as the Jews did the Gentiles, considering them only as dogs, and not fit to be ranked with any of the descendants of Jacob.

22. *Are they Hebrews?* Speaking the sacred

language, and reading in the congregation from the Hebrew Scriptures? The same is my own language. *Are they Israelites?* Regularly descended from Jacob, and not from Esau? I am also one. *Are they the seed of Abraham?* Circumcised, and in the bond of the covenant? *So am I.* I am no proselyte, but I am a Hebrew of the Hebrews by both father and mother; and can trace my genealogy through the tribe of Benjamin, up to the father of the faithful.

23. *Are they ministers of Christ?* So we find that these were professors of Christianity; and that they were genuine Jews, and such as endeavored to incorporate both systems, and no doubt to oblige those who had believed to be circumcised; and this appears to have been the bondage into which they had brought many of the believing Christians. *I am more.* More of a minister of Christ than they are, and have given fuller proofs of it. I have suffered persecution for the cross of Christ, and of the Jews too; and had I preached up the necessity of circumcision, I should have been as free from opposition as these are. *In labours more abundant.* Far from sitting down to take my ease in a church already gathered into Christ, I travel incessantly, preach everywhere and at all risks, in order to get the heathen brought from the empire of darkness into the kingdom of God's beloved Son. *In stripes above measure.* Being beaten by the heathen, who had no particular rule according to which they scourged criminals; and we find, from Acts xvi. 22-23, that they beat Paul unmercifully with many stripes. *In prisons more frequent.* See Acts xxi. 11 and the whole of the apostle's history; and his long imprisonment of at least two years at Rome, Acts xxviii. It does not appear that there is any one instance of a false apostle having been imprisoned for the testimony of Christ; this was a badge of the true apostles. *In deaths oft.* That is, in the most imminent dangers. See 1 Cor. xv. 31; 2 Cor. iv. 11.

24. *Of the Jews five times received I forty stripes save one.* That is, he was five times scourged by the Jews, whose law (Deut. xxv. 3) allowed forty stripes; but they, pretending to be lenient, and to act within the letter of the law, inflicted but thirty-nine. To except one stripe from the forty was a very ancient canon among the Jews, as we learn from Josephus, *Antiq.,* l. iv, c. viii, s. 21, who mentions the same thing: "forty stripes, excepting one." The Mishna gives this as a rule, Mish., *Maccoth,* fol. 22, 10: "How often shall he, the culprit, be smitten? Ans. forty stripes, wanting one; i.e., with the number which is nighest to forty." They also thought it right to stop under forty, lest the person who counted should make a mistake, and the criminal get more than forty stripes, which would be injustice, as the law required only forty. The manner in which this punishment was inflicted is described in the Mishna, fol. 22, 2: "The two hands of the criminal are bound to a post, and then the servant of the synagogue either pulls or tears off his clothes till he leaves his breast and shoulders bare. A stone or block is placed behind him on which the servant stands; he holds in his hands a scourge made of leather, divided into four tails. He who scourges lays one third on the criminal's breast, another third on his right shoulder, and another third on his left. The man who receives the punishment is neither sitting nor standing, but all the while stooping; and the man smites with all his strength, with one hand."

25. *Thrice was I beaten with rods.* This was under the Roman government, as their lictors beat criminals in this way. We hear of the apostle's being treated thus once, namely, at Philippi, Acts xvi. 22. *Once was I stoned.* Namely, at Lystra, Acts xiv. 19, etc. *A night and a day I have been in the deep.* To what this refers we cannot tell; it is generally supposed that in some shipwreck not on record the apostle had saved himself on a plank, and was a whole day and night on the sea, tossed about at the mercy of the waves.

26. *In journeyings often.* He means the particular journeys which he took to different places, for the purpose of propagating the gospel. *In perils of waters.* Exposed to great dangers in crossing rivers; for of "rivers" the original must be understood. *Of robbers.* Judea itself, and perhaps every other country, was grievously infested by bandits of this kind; and no doubt the apostle in his frequent peregrinations was often attacked; but being poor and having nothing to lose, he passed unhurt, though not without great danger. *In perils by mine own countrymen.* The Jews had the most rooted antipathy to him, because they considered him an apostate from the true faith, and also the means of perverting many others. There are several instances of this in the Acts; and a remarkable conspiracy against his life is related, Acts xxiii. 12, etc. *In perils by the heathen.* In the heathen provinces whither he went to preach the gospel. Several instances of these perils occur also in the Acts. *In perils in the city.* The different seditions raised against him; particularly in Jerusalem, to which **Ephesus** and Damascus may be added. *Perils in the wilderness.* Uninhabited countries through which he was obliged to pass in order to reach from city to city. In such places it is easy to imagine many dangers from bandits, wild beasts, cold, starvation, etc. *Perils in the sea.* The different voyages he took in narrow seas, such as the Mediterranean, about dangerous coasts, and without compass. *False brethren.* Persons who joined themselves to the Church, pretending faith in Christ, but intending to act as spies, hoping to get some matter of accusation against him. He not doubt suffered much also from apostates.

27. *In weariness and painfulness.* Tribulations of this kind were his constant companions.

28. *Beside those things that are without.* Independently of all these outward things, I have innumerable troubles and mental oppressions. *Which cometh upon me.* This continual press of business; this insurrection of cases to be heard, solved, and determined, relative to the doctrine, discipline, state, persecution, and supply of all the churches. All his perils were little in comparison of what he felt relative to the peace, government, and establishment of all the churches among the Gentiles; for as he was the apostle of the Gentiles, the government of all the churches among these fell in some sort on him, whether they were of his own planting or of the planting of others. See Col. ii. 1. None but a conscientious minister, who has at heart the salvation of souls, can enter into the apostle's feelings in this place.

29. *Who is weak?* What church is there under persecution with which I do not immediately sympathize? or who from his weakness in the faith and scrupulousness of conscience is likely to be turned out of the way, to whom I do not condescend, and whose burden I do not bear? *Who is offended,* or likely to be turned out of the way, *and I burn not* with zeal to restore and confirm him?

30. *I will glory . . . which concern mine infirmities.* I will not boast of my natural or acquired power, neither in what God has done by me; but rather in what I have suffered for Him. Many persons have understood by *infirmities* what they call the indwelling sin of the apostle, and say that "he gloried in this, because the grace of Christ was the more magnified in his being preserved from ruin, notwithstanding this indwelling adversary." And to support this most unholy interpretation they quote those other words of the apostle, chap. xii. 9: "Most gladly therefore will I rather glory in my infirmities," my indwelling corruptions, "that the power of Christ," in chaining the fierce lion, "may rest upon me." But it would be difficult to produce a single passage in the whole New Testament where the word which we translate infirmity has the sense of sin or moral corruption.

31. *The God and Father of our Lord.* Here is a very solemn asseveration, an appeal to the ever blessed God for the truth of what he asserts. It is something similar to his asseveration or oath in v. 10 of this chapter; see also Rom. ix. 5 and Gal. i. 20.

32. *In Damascus the governor under Aretas.* For a description of Damascus see the note on Acts ix. 2. And for the transaction to which the apostle refers see Acts ix. 23. As to King Aretas, there were three of this name. The first is mentioned in 2 Maccab. v. 8; the second, by Josephus. The third, who is the person supposed to be referred to here, was the father-in-law of Herod Antipas, of whom see the notes, Acts ix. 23 ff. *The governor.* Who this ethnarch was we cannot tell. The word ethnarch signifies the governor of a province, under a king or emperor. *Desirous to apprehend me.* The enemies of the apostle might have represented him to the governor as a dangerous spy, employed by the Romans.

33. *Through a window in a basket.* Probably the house was situated on the wall of the city. See the notes on this history, Acts ix. 23-25.

CHAPTER 12

Paul mentions some wonderful revelations which he had received from the Lord, 1-5. He speaks of his sufferings in connection with these extraordinary revelations, that his character might be duly estimated, 6. That he might not be too much exalted, a messenger of Satan is sent to buffet him; his prayer for deliverance, and the divine answer, 7-9. He exults in sufferings and reproaches, and vindicates his apostleship, 10-13. Promises to come and visit them, 14-15. Answers some objections, 16-18. And expresses his apprehensions that when he visits them he shall find many evils and disorders among them, 19-21.

1. *It is not expedient for me.* There are several various readings on this verse which are too minute to be noticed here; they seem in effect to represent the verse thus: "If it be expedient to glory (which does not become me), I will proceed to visions," etc. The plain meaning of the apostle, in this and the preceding chapter, in reference to glorying is that, though to boast in any attainments or in what God did by him was in all possible cases to be avoided, as being contrary to the humility and simplicity of the gospel, yet the circumstances in which he was found in reference to the Corinthian church and his detractors there rendered it absolutely necessary; not for his personal vindication, but for the honor of the gospel, the credit of which was certainly at stake. *I will come to visions.* Symbolical representations of spiritual and celestial things, in which matters of the deepest importance are exhibited to the eye of the mind by a variety of emblems, the nature and properties of which serve to illustrate those spiritual things. *Revelations.* A manifestation of things not before known, and such as God alone can make known, because they are a part of His own inscrutable counsels.

2. *I knew a man in Christ.* I knew a Christian, or a Christian man. *Fourteen years ago.* On what occasion or in what place this transaction took place we cannot tell; there are many conjectures among learned men concerning it, but of what utility can they be when everything is so palpably uncertain? *Whether in the body, I cannot tell.* That the apostle was in an ecstasy or trance, something like that of Peter, Acts x. 9, etc., there is reason to believe; but we know that being carried literally into heaven was possible to the Almighty. *Caught up to the third heaven.* He appeared to have been carried up to this place; but whether bodily he could not tell, or whether the spirit were not separated for the time and taken up to the third heaven he could not tell. *The third heaven*—The Jews talk of seven heavens, and Mohammed has received the same from them; but these are not only fabulous but absurd. In the sacred writings three heavens only are mentioned. The first is the atmosphere, what appears to be intended by *rekia*, the firmament or expansion, Gen. i. 6. The second, the starry heaven; where are the sun, moon, planets, and stars; but these two are often expressed under the one term *shamayim*, the two heavens, or expansions; and in Gen. i. 17 they appear to be both expressed by *rekia hashshamayim*, the "firmament of heaven." And, thirdly, the place of the blessed, or the throne of the divine glory, probably expressed by the words *hashshamayim*, the "heavens of heavens." But on these subjects the Scripture affords us but little light, and on this distinction the reader is not desired to rely.

4. *Caught up into paradise.* The Jewish writers have no less than four paradises, as they have seven heavens: but it is needless to wade through their fables. Among Christian writers it generally means the place of the blessed, or the state of separate spirits. *Which it is not lawful for a man to utter.* The Jews thought that the divine name, the Tetragrammaton *Yehovah*, should not be uttered, and that it is absolutely unlawful to pronounce it; indeed they say that the true pronunciation is utterly lost, and cannot be recovered without an express revelation. Not one of them, to the present day, ever attempts to utter it; and when they meet with it in their reading always supply its place with *Adonai*, Lord. It is probable that the apostle refers to some communication concerning the divine nature and the divine economy, of which he was only to make a general use in his preaching and writing. No doubt what he

learned at this time formed the basis of all his doctrines.

5. *Of such an one will I glory.* Through modesty he does not mention himself, though the account can be understood of no other person; for did he mean any other, the whole account would be completely irrelevant.

6. *I shall not be a fool.* Who that had received such honor from God would have been fourteen years silent on the subject? *I will say the truth.* I speak nothing but truth; and the apostle seems to have intended to proceed with something else of the same kind, but, finding some reason probably occurring suddenly, says, *I forbear*—I will say no more on this subject. *Lest any man should think of me above.* The apostle spoke of these revelations for two purposes: first, lest his enemies might suppose they had cause to think meanly of him; and, secondly, having said thus much, he forbears to speak any further of them, lest his friends should think too highly of him. It is a rare gift to discern when to speak and when to be silent; and to know when enough is said on a subject, neither too little nor too much.

7. *And lest I should be exalted.* There were three evils to be guarded against: (1) the contempt of his gifts and call by his enemies, (2) the overweening fondness of his friends, and (3) self-exultation. *A thorn in the flesh.* The word signifies a "stake." Whatever it was, it was *in the flesh,* i.e., of an outward kind. It was neither sin nor sinfulness, for this could not be given him to prevent his being exalted above measure; for sin never had and never can have this tendency. What this *thorn in the flesh* might be has given birth to a multitude of conjectures: Tertullian thought it the earache; *Chrysostom,* the headache; *Cyprian,* many and grievous bodily torments. I believe the apostle to refer simply to the distresses he had endured through the opposition he met with at Corinth; which were as painful and grievous to him as *a thorn* in his *flesh,* or his being bound to a stake; for if he could have devoted himself to destruction, Rom. ix. 3, for his rebellious and unbelieving countrymen, what must he have suffered on account of an eminent church being perverted and torn to pieces by a false teacher? God permitted this to keep the apostle humble, and at last completely delivered the church out of the hands and influence of this deceiver; none, not even the incestuous person, having been turned finally out of the way by the false doctrines there preached. *The messenger of Satan.* Another mode of expressing what he calls the *thorn in the flesh;* and he seems most plainly to refer to the false apostle at Corinth. The apostle himself was, as he styles himself to this church, chap. i. 1, the "apostle of Jesus Christ." The person in question is styled here "the apostle or angel of Satan." It is almost impossible to mistake the apostle's meaning and reference. Jesus Christ sent Paul to proclaim His truth, and found a church at Corinth. Satan, the adversary of God's truth, sent a man to preach lies at the same place, and turn the church of God into his own synagogue; and by his teaching lies and calumnies the apostle was severely buffeted.

8. *I besought the Lord.* That is, Christ, as the next verse absolutely proves, and the Socinians themselves confess. And if Christ be an object of prayer in such a case as this, or indeed in

any case, it is a sure proof of His divinity; for only an omniscient Being can be made an object of prayer. *Thrice.* It is worthy of remark that our Lord in His agony acted in the same way. At three different times He applied to God that the cup might depart from Him; and in each application He spoke the same words, Matt. xxvi. 39-44. There is, therefore, a manifest allusion to our Lord's conduct in these words of the apostle.

9. *My grace is sufficient for thee.* Thou shalt not be permitted to sink under these afflictions. Your enemies shall not be able to prevail against you. *My strength is made perfect in weakness.* The more, and the more violently, you are afflicted and tried, being upheld by My power and prospered in all your labors, the more eminently will My power be seen and acknowledged. For the weaker the instrument I use, the more the power of My grace shall be manifested. *Will I rather glory in my infirmities.* Therefore his *infirmities* do not mean his corruptions, or sins, or sinfulness of any kind; for it would be blasphemous for any man to say, I will rather glory that God leaves my corruptions in me than that He should take them away. *That the power of Christ may rest upon me.* That it may "overshadow me as a tent" or tabernacle, affording me shelter, protection, safety, and rest. This expression is like that, John i. 14: "And the Word was made flesh," and made His tabernacle among us, "full of grace and truth." The same eternal Word promised to make His tabernacle with the apostle, and gives him a proof that He was still the same, "full of grace and truth," by assuring him that His grace should be sufficient for him. Paul, knowing that the promise of grace could not fail, because of the divine truth, says: *Most gladly therefore will I rather glory in my afflictions,* that such a power of Christ may overshadow and defend me. The words are also similar to those of the Prophet Isaiah, chap. iv. 5: "Upon all the glory shall be a defence."

10. *Therefore I take pleasure.* I not only endure them patiently, but am pleased when they occur; for I do it *for Christ's sake,* on His account; for on His account I suffer. *For when I am weak,* most oppressed with trials and afflictions, *then am I strong,* God supporting my mind with His most powerful influences, causing me to rejoice with joy unspeakable and full of glory.

11. *I am become a fool in glorying.* It is not the part of a wise or gracious man to boast; but *ye have compelled me*—I have been obliged to do it, in order to vindicate the cause of God. *I ought to have been commended of you.* You should have vindicated both myself and my ministry against the detractors that are among you. *Though I be nothing.* Though I have been thus set at nought by your false apostle, and though in consequence of what he has said some of you have been ready to consider me as nothing—what we call good for nothing.

12. *The signs of an apostle were wrought among you.* Though I have been reputed as nothing, I have given the fullest proof of my divine mission by various signs, wonders, and miracles, and by that patience which I have manifested towards you; though I had power from God to inflict punishment on the transgressors, I have in every case forborne to do it.

13. *For what is it wherein ye were inferior?* This is a fine, forcible, yet delicate stroke. It was your duty and your interest to have supported your apostle; other churches have done so. I did not require this from you; in this respect all other churches are superior to you. I am the cause of your inferiority, by not giving you an opportunity of ministering to my necessities; *forgive me* the *wrong* I have done you. It is the privilege of the churches of Christ to support the ministry of His gospel among them. Those who do not contribute their part to the support of the gospel ministry either care nothing for it or derive no good from it.

14. *The third time I am ready.* That is, this is the third time that *I am ready*—have formed the resolution—to visit you. He had formed this resolution twice before, but was disappointed. See 1 Cor. xvi. 5 and 2 Cor. i. 15-16. He now formed it a third time, having more probability of seeing them now than he had before. See chap. xiii. 2. *I seek not yours, but you.* I seek your salvation; I desire not your property. Others have sought your property, but not your salvation. *For the children ought not to lay up for the parents.* You may have many teachers, but you have but one Father; "for in Christ Jesus I have begotten you through the gospel"; see 1 Cor. iv. 15.

15. *And I will very gladly spend and be spent for you.* I will continue to act as a loving father, who spends all he has upon his children, and expends his own strength and life in providing for them the things necessary for their preservation and comfort. *Though the more abundantly I love you.* I will then act towards you with the most affectionate tenderness, though it happen to me, as it often does to loving fathers, that their disobedient children love them less in proportion as their love to them is increased. Does it not frequently happen that the most disobedient child in the family is that one on which the parents' tenderness is more especially placed? See the parable of the prodigal son. It is in the order of God that it should be so, else the case of every prodigal would be utterly deplorable. The shepherd feels more for the lost sheep than for the ninety-nine that have not gone astray.

16. *But be it so, I did not burden you.* That is: You grant that I did not burden you, that I took nothing from you, but preached to you the gospel freely. But you say that, being crafty, *I caught you with guile;* i.e., getting from you, by means of others, what I pretended to be unwilling to receive immediately from yourselves.

17. *Did I make a gain of you?* Did any person I ever sent to preach the gospel to you or help you in your Christian course ever get anything from you for me? Produce the proof if you can.

18. *I desired Titus.* I never sent any to you but Titus and another brother; chap. viii. 6, 18. *And did Titus make a gain of you?* Did he get anything from you, either for himself or for me? You know he did not. He was actuated by *the same spirit* and he *walked in the same steps.*

19. *Think ye that we excuse ourselves?* That we "make an apology" for our conduct; or that I have sent Titus and that brother to you because I was ashamed or afraid to come myself?

We speak before God in Christ. I have not done so. I speak the truth before God; He is Judge whether I was actuated in this way by any sinister or unworthy motive. *For your edifying.* Whatever I have done in this or any other way I have done it for your *edifying,* not for any emolument to myself or friends.

20. *I fear, lest, when I come.* I think the present time is used here for the past; the apostle seems most evidently to be giving them the reason why he had not come to them according to his former purposes, and why he sent Titus and his companion. He was afraid to come at that time lest he should find them perverted from the right way, and be obliged to make use of his apostolical rod, and punish the offenders. But, feeling towards them the heart of a tender father, he was unwilling to use the rod; and sent the First Epistle to them, and the messengers above mentioned, being reluctant to go himself till he had satisfactory evidence that their divisions were ended and that they had repented for and put away the evils that they had committed. *Debates, envyings.* From these different expressions, which are too plain to need interpretation, we see what a distracted and divided state the church at Corinth must have been in. Brotherly love and charity seem to have been driven out of this once heavenly assembly. These *debates,* etc., are precisely the opposites to that love which the apostle recommends and explains by its different properties in the thirteenth chapter of his First Epistle.

21. *Lest, when I come again.* And even after all that has been done for you, I fear that when I do come—when I pay you my second visit, *my God will humble me*—will permit me to be affected with deep sorrow through what I may see among you, as I have been by the buffetings of the apostle of Satan who has perverted you. Humiliation is repeatedly used for "affliction." *Have sinned already.* "Who have sinned before"; who were some of the first offenders, and have not yet repented. *Of the uncleanness.* There must have been a total relaxation of discipline, else such abominations could not have been tolerated in the Christian Church. And although what is here spoken could be the case of only a few, yet the many were ill disciplined, else these must have been cast out.

CHAPTER 13

The apostle again says that this is the third time he has purposed to come and see them; and threatens that he will, by the power of Christ, punish every incorrigible sinner, 1-4. Exhorts them to examine themselves, whether they be in the faith, 5-6. Prays that they may do no evil, 7. And shows how ardently he wishes their complete restoration to unity and purity, 8-9. Tells them for what reason he writes to them, 10. Bids them farewell, 11. Gives them some directions, and concludes with his apostolical benediction, 12-14.

1. *This is the third time I am coming to you.* These words are nearly the same with those in chap. xii. 14, and probably refer to the purpose which he had twice before formed of seeing them. But the latter clause seems to attach a different meaning to the passage; at least so it has been understood by some learned men.

3. *Since ye seek a proof of Christ.* The conversion of the Corinthians was to themselves a solid proof that Christ spoke by the apostle; and therefore he could, with great propriety,

say that this power of Christ, far from being *weak,* was *mighty* among them.

4. *For though he was crucified through weakness.* It is true Christ was crucified, and His crucifixion appeared to be the effect of His *weakness;* yet even this was not so. He gave up His life; none could take it away from Him. And in His last struggle, had He even been deficient in power, He could have had more than twelve legions of angels to support Him against the high priest's mob, Matt. xxvi. 53; but how then could the Scripture be fulfilled? And had He not died, how could the human race have been saved? *We also are weak in him.* Because we are on Christ's side we appear to you as weak as He did to the Jews; but it is not so, for *we . . . live with him,* under the same influence and partaking of the same life, manifesting by our preaching and miracles the *power of God toward you.* While I do not use the rod, I appear to you weak; I will use it, and then you shall find me to be strong.

5. *Examine yourselves, whether ye be in the faith.* "Try yourselves"; pierce your hearts; try yourselves by what I have written, and see whether you retain the true faith of the gospel. *Prove your own selves.* "Put yourselves to the test," as you would try gold or silver suspected of adulteration. No more take that for gospel which is not so than you would take adulterated money for sterling coin. This is a metaphor taken from testing or assaying adulterated metals. *Know ye not your own selves?* Are you not full of wisdom and understanding? And is it not as easy to find out a spurious faith as it is to detect a base coin? There is an assay and touchstone for both. Does Jesus Christ dwell in you? You have His Spirit, His power, His mind, if you are Christians; and the Spirit of Christ bears witness with your spirit that you are the children of God. And this is the case *except ye be reprobates;* "base counterfeit coin"; mongrel Christians.

6. *Ye shall know that we are not reprobates.* You have had, and you shall have, the fullest proof that I have preached the true faith among you, and that God has confirmed it by His testimony; and thus that I am proved and manifested to be what I ought to be, and shown to be approved of God.

7. *I pray to God that ye do no evil.* That you do not persist in that course which will oblige me to use the power of Christ, with which I am endued, to punish you. *Not that we should appear approved.* We do not wish to give this proof that we are approved of God, by inflicting this punishment on the transgressors. *But that ye should do that which is honest.* That you may do that which is "right" and "seemly," *though we* should *be,* in consequence of that, *as reprobates*—as persons "not approved" of God; because your reformation will prevent the exercise of this power which would otherwise have given an awful proof that we are approved of God.

8. *For we can do nothing against the truth, but for the truth.* As we are the apostles of God, we cannot bring to you any false doctrine; and as we profess to be under the influence of God's Spirit, we cannot do anything that is opposed to that truth, or which might be prejudicial to it. On the contrary, what we say

and do is *for* that *truth,* to propagate and establish it.

9. *For we are glad, when we are weak.* It will give me indescribable pleasure that I should still appear to be poor, despicable, and destitute of this extraordinary power with which God has clothed me, so that you be strong in all the gifts and graces of the Holy Spirit. *And this also we wish, even your perfection.* We cannot be satisfied that persons with such eminent endowments and who have once received the truth as it is in Jesus should be deficient in any of the graces that constitute the mind of Christ, such as brotherly love, charity, harmony, unity, and order. I have given the above paraphrase to this verse because of the last term, *perfection.* It signifies the reducing of a dislocated limb to its proper place; and hence, as Beza says on this passage: "The apostle's meaning is, that whereas the members of the church were all, as it were, dislocated and out of joint, they should be joined together in love; and they should endeavor to make perfect what was amiss among them, either in faith or morals." It is a metaphor, also, taken from a building; the several stones and timbers being all put in their proper places and situations, so that the whole building might be "complete," and be a proper habitation for the owner. The same figure, though not in the same terms, the apostle uses, Eph. ii. 20-22. The *perfection* or "rejointing" which the apostle wishes is that which refers to the state of the church in its fellowship, unity, order, etc. And *perfection* in the soul is the same, in reference to it, as perfection in the church is to its order and unity. The perfection or rejointing of the soul implies its purification, and placing every faculty, passion, and appetite in its proper place; so that the original order, harmony, unity, and purity of the soul may be restored; and the whole builded up to be a habitation of God through the Spirit, Eph. ii. 22.

10. *Therefore I write these things.* I only threaten you now, by this Epistle, to put you on your guard, and lead you to reformation before I visit you; that I may not then have to use *sharpness,* "a cutting off," employing thus my apostolical authority to inflict punishment—a *power* which God has given me rather to be employed in your *edification* than in your *destruction.*

11. *Finally.* All that "remains" for me now to write is to wish you all manner of happiness, and so to take my leave. *Farewell.* A good wish; go on prosperously! *Be perfect.* "Be compact"; get into joint again; let unity and harmony be restored. *Be of good comfort.* "Receive admonition," that you may receive *comfort.* If you take my advice, you shall have consolation; if you do not, you will have nothing but misery and woe. *Be of one mind.* "Think the same"; let there be no dissensions among you. *Live in peace.* "Cultivate peace"; or, as he says elsewhere, "Follow peace," and pursue it, Heb. xii. 14. Cultivate a peaceable disposition, and neither say nor do anything which has a tendency to irritate each other. *And the God of love and peace shall be with you.* While you are full of contentions, dissensions, and discord, *peace* can have no place among you; and as to *love,* the fulfiling of the law, that worketh no ill to its neighbor, it has necessarily taken its flight. *Love* cannot live, neither exist, where there are brawls, contentions, and divisions.

And where neither *peace* nor *love* is to be found, there God cannot be.

12. *Greet one another with an holy kiss.* Use every means by which a good understanding may be brought about. Let the spirit of friendship live among you, and encourage its continuance by every friendly act. See the note on Rom. xvi. 16.

13. *All the saints.* The Christians of Macedonia or Philippi, from which he wrote this Epistle. In the primitive Church a saint and a Christian were the same thing, for the Christian religion calls every man to be holy.

14. *The grace of the Lord Jesus Christ.* All the "favor" and "beneficence" that come from and through the Redeemer of the world; as the *Lord*, the Ruler and Governor of all things; as *Jesus*, the "Saviour" of all men by His passion and death; as *Christ*, the Distributer of all the divine unction which enlightens, comforts, harmonizes, and purifies the mind. May this most exalted, glorious, and all-sufficient Saviour be ever with you! *And the love of God.* God, your Maker, in that infinite love which induced Him to create the world, and form man in His own image and in His own likeness, that he might be capable of knowing, loving, and enjoying Him forever; and God in the fullest manifestations of that love which caused Him to give His only begotten Son, to the end that they who believe on Him should not perish but have everlasting life. May this God of love, and this *love of God*, be ever with you! *And the communion of the Holy Ghost.* May that Holy Spirit, that divine and eternal Energy which proceeds from the Father and the Son; that heavenly Fire that gives light and life, that purifies and refines, sublimes and exalts, comforts and invigorates, make you all "partakers" with himself! *Koinonia,* which we translate "fellowship" and *communion,* signifies properly "participation," having things in common, partaking with each other. This points out the astonishing privileges of true believers: they have *communion* with God's Spirit; share in all His gifts and graces; walk in His light; through Him they have the fullest confidence that they are of God, that He is their Father and Friend, and has blotted out all their iniquities; this they know by the Spirit whom He has given them. This text, as well as that of Matt. iii. 16-17, and that other, Matt. xxviii. 19, strongly marks the doctrine of the Holy Trinity. *Amen.* This word is wanting, as usual, in almost every MS. of authority. *Amen* seems to have been anciently added at the conclusion of books, exactly as we add the word *finis,* both merely signifying the end. As to the inscription, it is wanting, either in whole or in part, in almost all the ancient MSS.

The Epistle to the
GALATIANS

Galatia was anciently a part of Phrygia and the neighboring countries. It had its name from the Gauls, who, having in several bodies invaded Asia Minor, conquered this country and settled in it. Under the reign of Augustus Caesar, about twenty-six years before our Lord, it was reduced into the form of a Roman colony, and was governed by a propraetor, appointed by the emperor.

Paul was probably the first who had preached the gospel in this region, as appears pretty evident from Gal. i. 6: "I marvel that ye are so soon removed from him that called you into the grace of Christ"; and from chap. iv. 13: "Ye know how through infirmity of the flesh I preached the gospel unto you at the first."

As to the precise time in which this Epistle was written there have been various opinions among learned men. Some of the ancients believed it to be the very first written of all Paul's Epistles. Others have supposed that it was written after his second journey to Galatia, Acts xviii. 23; and others, with more probability, after his first journey, Acts xvi. 6. That it was written soon after one of the apostle's visits to that region seems evident from the following complaint: "I marvel that ye are so soon removed from him that called you," chap. i. 6; it has been therefore conjectured that only one or two years had elapsed from that time.

From the complexion of this Epistle it appears to have been written to the Jews who were dispersed in Galatia; see Acts ii. 9. And although in chap. iv. 8 it is said that the persons to whom the apostle writes did not know God, and "did service unto them which by nature are no gods," this must be understood of those who had been proselytes to the Jewish religion, as the nineteenth verse sufficiently shows; for after they had been converted to Christianity, they turned "again to the weak and beggarly elements."

These Galatians were doubtless converted by Paul; see Acts xvi. 6; xviii. 23. But after his departure from them, some teachers had got in among them who endeavored to persuade them, and successfully too, that they should be circumcised and keep the Mosaic law. See chap. i. 6; iv. 9-10, 21; v. 1-2; vi. 12. And the apostle labors to bring them back from the errors of these false teachers.

The arguments which the apostle uses to prove the truth of the Christian religion, as well as the nullity of the Mosaic institutions, are the following:

1. That himself, immediately after his conversion, without having any conference with any of the apostles, preached the pure doctrines of Christianity, doctrines strictly conformable to those preached by the genuine disciples of the Lord; and this was a proof that he had received them by immediate inspiration, as he could have known them no other way.

2. That he was led to oppose Peter because he had withdrawn himself from communion with the converted Gentiles, and thereby gave occasion to some to suppose that he considered the law as still binding on those who believed, and that the Gentiles were not to be admitted to an equality of religious privileges with the Jews.

3. That no rites or ceremonies of the Jewish law could avail anything in the justification of a sinner, and that faith in Christ was the only means of justification.

4. That their own works could avail nothing towards their justification: (1) For the Spirit of God was given them in consequence of receiving the Christian doctrine, chap. iii. 2-5. That the works of the law cannot justify, because Abraham was justified by faith long before the law of Moses was given, chap. iii. 6-7. (3) That the curse of the law, under which every sinner lives, is not removed but by the sacrifice of Christ, chap. iii. 8-9.

5. That it is absurd for the sons of God to become slaves to Mosaic rites and ceremonies.

The rest of the Epistle is of a practical nature. Although subjects of this kind may be gathered out of the Epistle, yet it is very evident that the apostle himself has observed no technical division or arrangement of his matter, his chief design being: (1) To vindicate his own apostleship, and to show that he was not inferior to Peter himself, whom their false teachers appear to have set up in opposition to Paul; (2) To assert and maintain justification by faith in opposition to all Judaizing teachers; (3) To call them back to the liberty of the gospel, from which, and its privileges, they had shamelessly apostatized; and (4) To admonish and exhort them to walk worthy of their vocation, by devoting themselves to the glory of God and the benefit of their brethren. Lastly, he asserts his own determination to be faithful, and concludes with his apostolical benediction.

CHAPTER 1

Paul shows that he was especially called of God to be an apostle, 1. Directs his Epistle to the churches through the regions of Galatia, 2. Commends them to the grace of Christ, who gave himself for their sins, 3-5. Marvels that they had so soon turned away from the grace of the gospel of Christ, to what falsely pretended to be another gospel, 6-7. Pronounces him accursed who shall preach any other doctrine than that which he had delivered to them, 8-9. Shows his own uprightness, and that he received his doctrine from God, 10-12. Gives an account of his conversion and call to the apostleship, 13-17. How three years after his conversion he went up to Jerusalem, and afterwards went through the regions of Syria and Cilicia, preaching the faith of Christ, to the great joy of the Christian churches in Judea, 18-24.

1. *Paul, an apostle, (not of men).* Not commissioned by any assembly or council of the apostles. *Neither by man.* Nor by any one of the apostles; neither by James, who seems to have been president of the apostolic council at Jerusalem; nor by Peter, to whom, in a particular manner, the keys of the Kingdom were entrusted. *But by Jesus Christ.* Having his mission immediately from Christ himself, and *God the Father, who raised him from the dead,* see Acts xxii. 14-15, and commanded him to go both to the Jews and to the Gentiles.

2. *And all the brethren which are with me.* It is very likely that this refers to those who were his assistants in preaching the gospel, and not to any private members of the church. *Churches of Galatia.* Galatia was a region or province of Asia Minor; there was neither city nor town of this name. But as in this province Paul had planted several churches, he directs the Epistle to the whole of them; for it seems they were all pretty nearly in the same state and needed the same instructions.

4. *Who gave himself for our sins.* Who became a Sin Offering to God in behalf of mankind, that they might be saved from their sins.

5. *To whom be glory for ever.* Let Him have the glory to whom alone it is due, for having delivered us from the present evil world, and from all bondage to Mosaic rites and ceremonies.

6. *I marvel that ye are so soon removed.* It was a matter of wonder to the apostle that a people so soundly converted to God should have so soon made shipwreck of their faith. *From him that called you.* The apostle seems here to mean himself. He called them *into the grace of Christ;* and they not only abandoned that grace, but their hearts became greatly estranged from him; so that, though at first they would have plucked out their eyes for him, they at last counted them their enemy, chap. iv. 14-16.

7. *Which is not another.* It is not gospel, i.e., "good tidings," for it loads you again with the burdens from which the genuine gospel had disencumbered you. Instead of giving you peace, it troubles you; instead of being a useful supplement to the gospel of Christ, it perverts that gospel. You have gained nothing but loss and damage by the change.

8. *But though we, or an angel.* That gospel which I have already preached to you is the only true gospel; were I to preach *any other,* I should incur the curse of God. If your false teachers pretend, as many in early times did, that they received their accounts by the ministry of an angel, let them be accursed; separate them from your company, and have no religious communion with them.

9. *Let him be accursed.* Perhaps this is not designed as an imprecation, but a simple direction; for the word here may be understood as implying that such a person should have no countenance in his bad work, but let him, as Theodoret expresses it, "be separated from the communion of the church." This, however, would also imply that unless the person repented the divine judgments would soon follow.

10. *Do I now persuade men, or God?* The words may be rendered to "court or solicit the favor of God," as the after clause sufficiently proves. While the apostle was a persecutor of the Christians, he was the servant of men and *pleased men.* When he embraced the Christian doctrine, he became the *servant* of God, and pleased Him.

11. *But I certify you, brethren.* I wish you fully to comprehend that the gospel which I preached to you is not after man; there is not a spark of human invention in it, nor the slightest touch of human cunning.

12. *I neither received it of man.* By means of any apostle, as was remarked on v. 1. No man taught me what I have preached to you. *But by the revelation of Jesus Christ.* Being commissioned by himself alone, receiving the knowledge of it from Christ crucified.

13. *Ye have heard of my conversation.* "My manner of life," the mode in which I conducted myself. *Beyond measure I persecuted the church.* For proofs of this the reader is referred to Acts ix. 1-2; xxii. 4. The apostle tells them that they had heard this, because, being Jews, they were acquainted with what had taken place in Judea relative to these important transactions.

14. *And profited in the Jews' religion.* The apostle does not mean that he became more exemplary in the love and practice of the pure law of God than any of his countrymen, but that he was more profoundly skilled in the *traditions* of the *fathers* than most of his contemporaries.

15. *Who separated me from my mother's womb.* Him whom I acknowledge as the God of grace; who preserved me by His providence when I was a helpless infant, and saved me by His grace when I was an adult persecutor.

16. *To reveal his Son in me.* To make me know Jesus Christ, and the power of His resurrection. *That I might preach him among the heathen.* For it was to the Gentiles, and the dispersed Jews among the Gentiles, that Paul was especially sent. Peter was sent more particularly to the Jews in the land of Judea; Paul, to those in the different Greek provinces. *I conferred not with flesh and blood.* I did not take counsel with men; "flesh and blood" is a periphrasis for "man," any man.

17. *Neither went I up to Jerusalem.* The aim of the apostle is to show that he had his call so immediately and pointedly from God himself that he had no need of the concurrence even of the apostles, being appointed by the same authority and fitted to the work by the same grace and Spirit as they were. *But I went into Arabia.* That part of Arabia which was contiguous to Damascus, over which Aretas was then king. Of this journey into Arabia we have no other account. As Luke was not then with him, it is not inserted in the Acts of the Apostles.

18. *After three years I went up to Jerusalem to see Peter.* These three years may be reckoned either from the departure of Paul from Jerusalem or from his return from Arabia to Damascus. *To see Peter.* To become "personally acquainted" with Peter; for this is the proper import of the verb from which we have the word "history," which signifies a "relation of

things from personal knowledge and actual acquaintance. *And abode with him fifteen days.* It was not, therefore, to get religious knowledge from him that he paid him this visit. He knew as much of the Jewish religion as Peter did, if not more; and as to the gospel, he received that from the same source and had preached it three years before this.

19. *James the Lord's brother* is mentioned thus to distinguish him from James the brother of John.

20. *Before God, I lie not.* This he speaks in reference to having seen only Peter and James at Jerusalem; and consequently to prove that he had not learned the gospel from the assembly of the apostles at Jerusalem, nor consequently received his commission from them.

22. *And was unknown by face.* I was not personally acquainted with any of the churches of Judea; I was converted in another place, and had not preached the gospel in any Christian congregation in that country. I knew only those at Jerusalem.

23. *They had heard only.* As a persecutor of the Church of Christ, I was well-known; and as a convert to Christ I was not less so. The fame of both was great, even where I was personally unknown.

24. *They glorified God in me.* Hearing now that I preached that faith which before I had persecuted and endeavored to destroy, they glorified God for the grace which had wrought my conversion. I owe nothing to them; I owe all to God—and they themselves acknowledge this. I received all from God, and God has all the glory.

CHAPTER 2

The apostle mentions his journey to Jerusalem with Barnabas and Titus, 1. Shows that he went thither by revelation, and what he did while there, and the persons with whom he had intercourse, 2-8. How the apostles gave him the right hand of fellowship, 9-10. How he opposed Peter at Antioch, and the reason why, 11-14. Shows that the Jews as well as the Gentiles must be justified by faith, 15-16. They who seek this justification should act with consistency, 17-18. Gives his own religious experience, and shows that through the law he was dead to the law and crucified with Christ, 19-20. Justification is not of the law, but by the faith of Christ, 21.

1. *Then fourteen years after.* There is a considerable difference among critics concerning the time specified in this verse; the apostle is however generally supposed to refer to the journey he took to Jerusalem about the question of circumcision, mentioned in Acts xv. 4. Others contend that the journey of which the apostle speaks is that mentioned in Acts xi. 27, when Barnabas and Saul were sent by the church of Antioch with relief to the poor Christians in Judea.

2. *I went up by revelation.* This either means that he went up at that time by an express *revelation* from God that it was his duty to do so, made either to the church of Antioch to send these persons to Jerusalem or to these persons to go according to the directions of that church, or the apostle here wishes to say that, having received the gospel *by revelation* from God, to preach Christ among the Gentiles, he went up "according" to that revelation, and told what God had done by him among the Gentiles. Or it may refer to the revelation made to "certain prophets" who came to Antioch, and

particularly "Agabus," who signified by the Spirit that there would be a dearth, in consequence of which the disciples purposed to send relief to their poor brethren at Jerusalem. See Acts xi. 27-30. *But privately to them which were of reputation.* To the "chief men"; those who were highest in reputation among the apostles, "the honorable." With these the apostle intimates that he had some private conferences. *Lest by any means.* And he held these private conferences with those more eminent men to give them information how, in consequence of his divine call, he had preached the gospel to the Gentiles, and the great good which God had wrought by his ministry; but they, not knowing the nature and end of his call, might be led to suppose he had acted wrong, and thus labored in vain. It was necessary, therefore, that he should give the apostolic council the fullest information that he had acted according to the divine mind in every respect, and had been blessed in his deed.

3. *But neither Titus, who was with me.* The apostle proceeds to state that his account was so satisfactory to the apostles that they not only did not require him to insist on the necessity of circumcision among the Gentiles, but did not even require him to have Titus, who was a Greek, circumcised; though that might have appeared expedient, especially at Jerusalem, to prevent false brethren from making a handle of his uncircumcision, and turning it to the prejudice of the gospel in Judea.

4. *To spy out our liberty.* The Judaizing brethren got introduced into the assembly of the apostles, in order to find out what was implied in the *liberty* of the gospel, that they might know the better how to oppose Paul and his fellows in their preaching Christ to the Gentiles and admitting them into the Church without obliging them to observe circumcision and keep the law.

5. *To whom we gave place by subjection.* So fully satisfied was he with his divine call, and that he had in preaching among the Gentiles acted in strict conformity to it, that he did not submit in the least to the opinion of those Judaizing teachers; and therefore he continued to insist on the exemption of the Gentiles from the necessity of submitting to Jewish rites. *That the truth of the gospel*—this grand doctrine that the Gentiles are admitted by the gospel of Christ to be fellow heirs with the Jews—*might continue;* and thus the same doctrine is continued with you Gentiles.

6. *These who seemed to be somewhat.* "Those who were of acknowledged reputation." The verb *dokein*, "to seem," is repeatedly used by the best Greek writers, not to call the sense in question or to lessen it, but to deepen and extend it. See the note on Luke viii. 18. Perhaps this verse had best be translated thus: "But there is no difference between those who were of acknowledged reputation and myself; God accepts no man's person; but in the conferences which I held with them they added nothing to me"—gave me no new light; did not attempt to impose on me any obligation, because they saw that God had appointed me my work, and that His counsel was with me.

7. *But contrariwise.* They were so far from wishing me to alter my plan, or to introduce anything new in my doctrine to the Gentiles, that they saw plainly that my doctrine was the same as their own, coming immediately from the same source; and therefore gave to me and to Barnabas the right hand of fellowship. *The gospel of the uncircumcision.* They saw to their utmost satisfaction that I was as expressly sent by God to preach the gospel to the Gentiles as Peter was to preach it to the Jews.

8. *For he that wrought effectually.* "He who wrought powerfully with Peter wrought powerfully also with me." He gave us both those talents which were suited to our work, and equal success in our different departments.

9. *James, Cephas, and John, who seemed to be pillars.* "Who were known to be very eminent, and acknowledged as chief men" among the apostles. Among the Jews, persons of great eminence and importance are represented as "pillars" and "foundations" of the world. *The right hands of fellowship.* Giving the right hand to another was the mark of confidence, friendship, and fellowship.

10. *Only they would that we should remember the poor.* they saw plainly that God had as expressly called Barnabas and me to go to the Gentiles as He had called them to preach to the Jews, and they did not attempt to give us any new injunctions, only wished us to remember the poor in Judea; but this was a thing to which we were previously disposed.

11. *When Peter was come to Antioch.* There had been a controversy whether Peter here should not be read "Kephas"; and whether this Kephas was not a different person from Peter the apostle. Instead of *Peter,* several MSS. and versions and several of the Greek fathers read *Kephas.* That Peter the apostle is meant, the most sober and correct writers of antiquity maintain.

12. *Before that certain came from James, he did eat with the Gentiles.* Here was Peter's fault. He was convinced that God had pulled down the middle wall of partition that had so long separated the Jews and Gentiles, and he acted on this conviction, associating with the latter and eating with them. But when certain Jews came from James, who it appears considered the law still to be in force, lest he should place a stumbling block before them he withdrew from all commerce with the converted Gentiles, and acted as if he himself believed the law to be still in force, and that the distinction between the Jews and the Gentiles should still be kept up.

13. *And the other Jews dissembled likewise.* That is: Those who were converted to Christianity from among the Jews, and who had also been convinced that the obligation of the Jewish ritual had ceased, seeing Peter act this part, and also fearing them that were of the circumcision, separated themselves from the converted Gentiles and acted so as to convince the Jews that they still believed the law to be of moral obligation; and so powerful was the torrent of such an example that the gentle, loving-hearted *Barnabas also was carried away with their dissimulation,* "with their hypocrisy," feigning to be what they really were not.

14. *That they walked not uprightly.* They did not walk "with a straight step"—they did not maintain a firm footing. *According to the truth of the gospel.* According to that true doctrine, which states that "Christ is the end of the law"

for justification "to every one that believeth"; and that such are under no obligation to observe circumcision and the other peculiar rites and ceremonies of the law. *If thou, being a Jew, livest.* This was a cutting reproof. He was a Jew and had been circumstantially scrupulous in everything relative to the law; and it required a miracle to convince him that the Gentiles were admitted on their believing in Christ to become members of the same Church and fellow heirs of the hope of eternal life; and in consequence of this he went in with the Gentiles and ate with them; i.e., associated with them as he would with Jews. But now, fearing them of the circumcision, he withdrew from this fellowship. *Why compellest thou the Gentiles?* You once considered that they were not under such an obligation, and now you act as if you did consider the law in full force; but you are convinced that the contrary is the case, yet act differently! This is "hypocrisy."

15. *We who are Jews by nature.* We who belong to the Jewish nation—who have been born, bred, and educated Jews. *And not sinners of the Gentiles.* Not without the knowledge of God, as they have been. Among the nations or Gentiles many Jews sojourned, who in Scripture are known by the name of Hellenists, and these were distinguished from those who were termed *sinners of the Gentiles*—"heathens."

16. *Knowing that a man is not justified.* Neither the works of the Jewish law, nor of any other law, could justify any man.

17. *But if, while we seek to be justified.* If, while we acknowledge that we must be justified by faith in Christ, *we ourselves also are found sinners,* enjoining the necessity of fulfilling the law, which is impossible, we thus constitute ourselves *sinners. Is therefore Christ the minister of sin?*—Christ, who has taught us to renounce the law, and expect justification through His death? *God forbid* that we should either act so or think so.

18. *For if I build again the things which I destroyed.* If I act like a Jew and enjoin the observance of the law on the Gentiles, which I have repeatedly asserted and proved to be abolished by the death of Christ, then I "build up what I destroyed" and thus *make myself a transgressor* by not observing the law in that way in which I appear to enjoin the observance of it upon others.

19. *For I through the law am dead to the law.* In consequence of properly considering the nature and requisitions of the law, I am dead to all hope and expectation of help or salvation from the law, and have been obliged to take refuge in the gospel of Christ.

20. *I am crucified with Christ.* The death of Christ on the Cross has showed me that there is no hope of salvation by the law; I am therefore as truly dead to all expectation of justification by the law as Christ was dead when He gave up the ghost upon the Cross. *Yet not I.* It is not of my natural life I speak, nor of any spiritual things which I myself have procured; *but Christ liveth in me.* But this *life* I have *by the faith of the Son of God*—by believing on Christ as a Sacrifice for sin; for he *loved me,* and because He did so He *gave himself for me*—made himself a Sacrifice unto death, that I might be saved from the bitter pains of death eternal.

21. *I do not frustrate.* I do not "contemn,

despise, or render useless" *the grace of God*—the doctrine of Christ crucified, which I must do if I preach the necessity of observing the law. *For if righteousness.* If "justification" and salvation *come by* an observance of *the law, then Christ is dead in vain.* His death is useless if an observance of the law can save us; but no observance of the law can save us, and therefore there was an absolute necessity for the death of Christ.

CHAPTER 3

The apostle inquires how they could be so foolish as to renounce the gospel of Christ and turn back to the law after having heard, received, and suffered so much for the gospel, 1-5. Asserts the doctrine of justification by faith, on the example of Abraham, 6-9. Shows that all who are under the law are under the curse, from which Christ alone redeems us; and the promise made to Abraham comes to the Gentiles who believe, 10-14. For the covenant is not by the works of the law, but by promise, 15-18. The law was given to show the sinfulness of sin, and to act as a schoolmaster till Christ should come, 19-25. It is by faith only that any become children of God, 26. And under the gospel all those distinctions which subsisted under the law are done away; and genuine believers, whether Jews or Gentiles, bond or free, are one in Christ Jesus, and accounted the genuine children of Abraham, 27-29.

1. *O foolish Galatians.* O infatuated people, you make as little use of reason as those who have none; you have acted in this business as those do who are "fascinated"—they are led blindly and unresistingly on to their own destruction. *That ye should not obey the truth.* This clause is wanting in some MSS., and in the most important of the Greek and Latin fathers. Of the clause Professor White says, "It should certainly be expunged." There are several various readings on this verse, from which it appears that the verse in the best ancient MSS. and versions was read thus: "O foolish Galatians, who hath bewitched you? Before whose eyes Jesus Christ crucified hath been plainly set forth." *Among you* is wanting in some MSS. and in several of the fathers. The words appear to disturb the sense.

2. *Received ye the Spirit by the works of the law.* This may refer to the miraculous gifts of the Spirit, which were very common in the apostolic Church. Did you receive these extraordinary gifts in consequence of your circumcision and observing the Mosaic precepts? or was it by the *hearing* of the gospel, prescribing *faith* in Christ crucified? It may also refer to the spirit of adoption, and consequently to their sonship.

3. *Having begun in the Spirit.* Having received a spiritual religion which refined and purified your hearts; and having received the Holy Spirit of God, by whom you were endued with various miraculous influences; and the spirit of adoption, by which you were assured of the remission of sins and incorporation with the family of God. *Are ye now made perfect by the flesh?* Are you seeking to complete that spiritual religion, and to perfect these spiritual gifts, by the carnal rite of circumcision? It appears that by the *Spirit,* here, not only the Holy Spirit, but His gifts, are to be understood; and by the *flesh,* by a metonymy, "circumcision" itself.

4. *Have ye suffered so many things in vain?* Have you received and lost so much good? The verb signifies to "suffer pain or loss" or to "possess and enjoy." Though it is possible that the Galatians had *suffered* some persecution for

the truth of Christ, yet it is as likely that the apostle refers to the benefits which they had received. You have received faith, the pardon of your sins, the gift of the Holy Spirit, and with it many extraordinary gifts and graces. Have you received all these *in vain? if . . . yet in vain*—if it be credible that you have sacrificed so many excellent benefits for an imaginary good.

5. *He therefore that ministereth to you the Spirit.* The apostle means himself; he had been the means of conveying the Holy Spirit to them, and by that *Spirit* he wrought miracles among them. And he did all this, not as a Jew (for as such he had no power), but he did all as a believer in Christ. The word which we translate *ministereth* is very emphatic and signifies "leading up the chorus," bringing up one after another, adding grace to grace, benefit to benefit; so that it appears that they had not only some, but many, benefits, God by means of His apostle having greatly enriched them with various spiritual blessings.

6. *Abraham believed God.* This is quoted from Gen. xv. 6; and Paul produces it, Rom. iv. 3-5. Abraham, while even uncircumcised, believed in God, and his faith was reckoned to him for justification; and Abraham is called the "father of the faithful" or "of believers." If then he was justified by faith long before the law was given, the law is not necessary to salvation. It is remarkable that the Jews themselves maintained that Abraham was saved by faith. Mehilta, in *Yalcut Simeoni*, p. 1, fol. 69, makes this assertion: "It is evident that Abraham could not obtain an inheritance either in this world or in the world to come but by faith."

8. *The scripture, foreseeing.* See the notes on Rom. iv. 3-16. As God intended to justify the heathen through faith, He *preached the gospel* that contains the grand display of the doctrine of salvation by faith, *before*, to *Abraham*, while he was in his heathen state; and thus he is called "the father of believers." Therefore it must refer to them who shall believe the same gospel among the Gentiles, consequently the promise was fulfilled: *In thee shall all nations [of the earth] be blessed.*

9. *They which be of faith.* All who believe, as Abraham has believed, are made partakers of Abraham's blessings.

10. *As many as are of the works of the law.* All that seek salvation by the performance of the works of the law are under the curse, because it is impossible for them to come up to the spiritual meaning and intent of the law; and the law pronounces them *cursed that continueth not in all things which are written in the book of the law to do them.* Hence every Jew is necessarily under the curse of God's broken law; and every sinner is under the same curse, though he be not a Jew, who does not take refuge in the salvation provided for him by the gospel.

11. *But that no man is justified by the law,* by the observance of the law, suppose he had even continued in all things that are written in it to do them, *is evident;* for the Prophet Habakkuk, chap. ii. 4, has declared, under the direct influence of the Spirit of God, *The just shall live by faith;* or, "He who is just by faith shall live." Therefore this justification comes not by works, or the observance of the law, but by faith.

12. *And the law is not of faith.* It promises no forgiveness to believing, but requires obedience. It is not, What do you believe? but, What have you done? *The man that doeth them perfectly at all times, and in all places, he shall live in them;* but if in any case he fails, he forfeits his life.

13. *Christ hath redeemed us.* "Hath bought us with a price"; viz., His blood, or life. *Being made a curse for us.* Being made an Atonement for our sins; for whatever was offered as an atonement for sin was considered as bearing the punishment due to sin, and the person who suffered for transgression was considered as bearing the curse in his body. Therefore in the same day in which a criminal was executed it was ordered that his body should be buried, that the land might not be polluted; because he that was hanged, which was the case with every heinous culprit, was considered accursed of God, Deut. xxi. 22-23.

14. *That the blessing of Abraham.* That is, justification or the pardon of sin, with all other blessings consequent on it, such as peace with God, spiritual life, and eternal glory. *Might come on the Gentiles through Jesus Christ.* So we find that He was made a curse for us that the blessings promised to Abraham might be given to them who believe on Him, as having been made a curse; i.e., an expiatory Victim for them. *The promise of the Spirit.* The spirit of adoption, sonship with God; and *Spirit* of God to attest that sonship. All this was *through faith.* Hence, from the beginning God had purposed that salvation should be *through faith,* and never expected that any soul of man should be justified by the works of the law; and gave that law only that the exceeding sinfulness of sin might appear, and that man might be prepared to welcome the gospel, which proclaimed salvation to a lost world through the atoning passion and death of Christ.

15. *I speak after the manner of men.* I am about to produce an example taken from civil transactions. *If it be confirmed*—if an agreement or bond be signed, sealed, and witnessed. *No man disannulleth.* It stands under the protection of the civil law, and nothing can be legally erased or added.

16. *Now to Abraham and his seed.* The promise of salvation by faith was made to Abraham and his posterity. *He saith not, And to seeds.* It was one particular kind of posterity which was intended: *but as of one . . . which is Christ;* i.e., to the spiritual Head, and all believers in Him, who are children of Abraham, because they are believers, v. 7. But why does the apostle say, Not of seeds, as of many? To this it is answered that Abraham possessed in his family two seeds: one natural, viz., the members of his own household; and the other spiritual, those who were like himself because of their faith. The promises were not of a temporal nature. Had they been so, they would have belonged to his natural seed. But they did not; therefore they must have belonged to the spiritual posterity.

17. *Confirmed before of God in Christ.* I.e., the promise of justification made to believers in Christ Jesus, who are the spiritual seed of Christ, as they are children of Abraham from

the similitude of their faith. Abraham believed in God and it was reckoned to him for justification; the Gentiles believed in Christ and received justification. *Four hundred and thirty years after.* God made a covenant with Abraham that the Messiah should spring from his posterity. This covenant stated that justification should be obtained by faith in the Messiah. The law was given 430 years after the covenant with Abraham; therefore the law could not possibly annul the Abrahamic covenant.

19. *Wherefore then serveth the law?* If the law does not annul the Abrahamic covenant, and cannot confer salvation on its votaries, why did God give it? This was a very natural objection, and must arise in the mind of any Jew who had paid attention to the apostle's reasoning. *It was added because of transgressions.* It was given that we might know our sinfulness, and the need we stood in of the mercy of God. *Till the seed should come.* The law was to be in force till the advent of the Messiah. After that it was to cease. *It was ordained by angels.* The ministry of angels was certainly used in giving the law; see Ps. lxviii. 17; Acts vii. 53; and Heb. ii. 2; but they were only instruments for transmitting. Moses was the mediator between God and the people, Deut. v. 5.

20. *A mediator is not a mediator of one.* As a mediator signifies a "middle person," there must necessarily be two parties between whom he stands and acts in reference to both, as he is supposed to have the interests of both equally at heart. Though Moses was the mediator between God and the Israelites, yet he was not the mediator between God and that one seed which was to come; viz., the Gentiles who should believe in Christ. *But God is one.* He is the one God, who is the Father of the spirits of all flesh, the God of the Gentiles as well a the God of the Jews. That this is Paul's meaning is evident from his use of the same words in other places, 1 Tim. ii. 5: "For there is one God, and one mediator between God and man"; that is, There is only one God and one Mediator for the whole human race. The sense of the whole is: Moses was the mediator of one part of Abraham's seed, viz., the Israelites; but of the other seed, the Gentiles, he was certainly not the mediator; for the Mediator of that seed, according to the promise of God and covenant made with Abraham, is Christ.

21. *Is the law then against the promises of God?* Is it possible that the intervention of the law, in reference to one part of the Abrahamic seed, should annul the promise made to the other? It is impossible. *For if there had been a law.* If any *law* or "rule" of life could have been found out that would *have given life*—saved sinners from death, and made them truly happy —then *righteousness,* "justification," *should have been by the law.*

22. *But the scripture hath concluded.* All the writings of the prophets have uniformly declared that men are all sinners, and the law declares the same by the continual sacrifices which it prescribes. All therefore have sinned and come short of the glory of God; and being tried and found guilty, "the Scripture hath shut them up"—put them in prison, and locked them up, till the time should come in which the sentence of the law should be executed upon them.

23. *But before faith came.* Before the gospel was published. *We were kept under the law, shut up.* "We were kept as in a stronghold, locked up, unto the faith," the religion of the Lord Jesus, *which should afterwards be revealed.*

24. *The law was our schoolmaster.* "The law was our pedagogue into Christ." The pedagogue is not the *schoolmaster,* but the servant who had the care of the children to lead them to and bring them back from school, and had the care of them out of school hours. Thus the law did not teach us the living, saving knowledge; but by its rites and ceremonies, and especially by its sacrifices, it directed us to Christ, that we might be justified by faith. This is a beautiful metaphor and highly illustrative of the apostle's doctrine.

25. *But after that faith is come.* When Christ was manifested in the flesh and the gospel was preached, we were no longer under the pedagogue; we came to Christ, learned of Him, became wise unto salvation. It is worthy of remark that "the law" is used by Paul to signify, not only the law properly so called, but the whole of the Mosaic economy; so "the faith" is used by him to express, not merely the act of believing in Christ, but the whole of the gospel.

26. *For ye,* who have believed the gospel, *are all the children of God by faith in Christ Jesus.* But no man is a child of God by circumcision nor by any observance of the Mosaic law.

27. *As many of you as have been baptized into Christ.* All of you who have believed in Christ as the promised Messiah, and received baptism as a public proof that you had received Christ as your Lord and Saviour, *have put on Christ*—have received His Spirit, entered into His interests, and copied His manners. To *put on* or to "be clothed with" one is to assume the person and character of that one; and they who do so are bound to act his part, and to sustain the character which they have assumed. The profession of Christianity is an assumption of the character of Christ. He has left us an example that we should follow His steps; and we should, as Christians, have that mind in us which was in Him.

28. *There is neither Jew nor Greek. Greek* is put here for "heathen." Under the gospel all distinctions are done away, as either helping or hindering; all are equally welcome to Christ, and all have an equal need of Him. All persons of all sects and conditions and sexes who believe in Him become one family through Him. They are one body, of which He is the Head. *Neither male nor female.* With great reason the apostle introduces this. Between the privileges of men and women there was a great disparity among the Jews. A man might shave his head and rend his clothes in the time of mourning; a woman was not permitted to do so. A man might betroth his daughter; a woman had no such power. A man might sell his daughter; a woman could not. In many cases women were treated more like children than adults. Under the blessed spirit of Christianity, they have equal rights, equal privileges, and equal blessings; and, let me add, they are equally useful.

29. *And if ye be Christ's.* Or, as several good MSS. read, "If ye be one in Christ." If you have all received justification through His blood, and the mind that was in Him, *then are ye Abra-*

ham's seed; you are that real, spiritual posterity of Abraham, that other seed, to whom the promises were made; and then *heirs according to the promise,* being fitted for the rest that remains for the people of God, that heavenly inheritance which was typified by the earthly Canaan.

CHAPTER 4

The apostle shows that, as an heir in nonage is under tutors and guardians, so were the Galatians while under the law; and, as the heir when he comes of age is no longer under guardians, so they, when the gospel came, arrived at full maturity, and were redeemed from the law, 1-3. He shows, further, that when the fullness of the time came God sent forth His Son, that we might obtain the adoption of sons, and have the strongest evidence of that adoption, 4-6. Those who are children of God are heirs of heaven, 7. He compares their former and latter state, and shows the reason he had to fear that his labor on their behalf was in vain, 8-11. He mentions his trials among them, and their kindness to him, 12-16. Shows his tender affection for them, and exhorts them to return to the gospel, 17-20. Shows the excellence of the gospel beyond that of the law, by the allegory of Mount Sinai and Jerusalem, 21-27. Shows also that the believing Gentiles are children of the promise, as Isaac was; and have been elected in the place of the Jews, who have been cast out according to the Scriptures, 28-31.

1. *The heir, as long as he is a child.* Though he be appointed by his father's will heir of all his possessions, yet till he arrive at the legal age he is master of nothing, and does not differ from one of the common domestics.

2. *But is under tutors,* "guardians," *and governors,* those who have the charge of the family. These words are nearly similar; but we may consider the first as "executor," the last as the person who superintends the concerns of the family and estate till the heir become of age, such as we call "trustee." *Until the time appointed of the father.* The time mentioned in the father's will or testament.

3. *Even so we.* The whole Jewish people were in a state of nonage while under the law. *The elements of the world.* A mere Jewish phrase, "the principles of this world"; that is, the rudiments or principles of the Jewish religion. The apostle intimates that the law was not the science of salvation; it was only the elements or alphabet of it; and in the gospel this alphabet is composed into a most glorious system of divine knowledge. But as the alphabet is nothing of itself unless compounded into syllables, words, sentences, and discourses, so the law, taken by itself, gives no salvation. It contains indeed the outlines of the gospel, but it is the gospel alone that fills up these outlines.

4. *When the fulness of the time was come.* The time which God in His infinite wisdom counted best, in which all His counsels were "filled up"; the time which His Spirit, by the prophets, had specified; and the time to which He intended the Mosaic institutions should extend, and beyond which they should be of no avail. *God sent forth his Son,* Him who came immediately from God himself, *made of a woman,* according to the promise, Gen. iii. 15; produced by the power of God in the womb of the Virgin Mary without any intervention of man. *Made under the law.* In subjection to it, that in Him all its designs might be fulfilled and by His death the whole might be abolished, the law dying when the Son of God expired upon the Cross.

5. *To redeem them.* To "pay down a price" for them, and thus "buy them off" from the necessity of observing circumcision, offering brute sacrifices, performing different ablutions, etc. *That we might receive the adoption of sons.* Which adoption we could not obtain by the law, for it is the gospel only that puts us among the children and gives us a place in the heavenly family.

6. *And because ye are sons.* By faith in Christ Jesus, being redeemed from both the bondage and the curse of the law. *God* the Father, called generally the First Person of the glorious Trinity, *hath sent forth the Spirit—* the Holy Ghost, the Second Person of that Trinity—*of his Son,* Jesus Christ, the Third Person of the Trinity, *crying, Abba, Father,* from the fullest and most satisfactory evidence that God, the Father, Son, and Spirit, had become their portion.

7. *Thou art no more a servant.* You who have believed in Christ are no longer a "slave," either under the dominion of sin or under obligation to the Mosaic ritual; *but a son* of God, adopted into the heavenly family. *And if a son, then an heir.* Having a right to the inheritance because one of the family, for none can inherit but the children. But this heirship is the most extraordinary of all. It is not an heirship of any tangible possession, either in heaven or on earth; it is not to possess a part or even the whole of either. It is to possess Him who made all things; not God's works, but God himself; heirs *of God through Christ.*

8. *When ye knew not God.* Though it is evident from the complexion of the whole of this Epistle that the great body of the Christians in the churches of Galatia were converts from among the Jews or proselytes to Judaism, yet from this verse it appears that there were some who had been converted from heathenism, unless we suppose that the apostle here particularly addresses those who had been proselytes to Judaism and thence converted to Christianity, which appears to be most likely from the following verses.

9. *Now, after that ye have known God.* After having been brought to the knowledge of God as your Saviour. *Or rather are known of God.* Are approved of Him, having received the adoption of sons. *To the weak and beggarly elements.* After receiving all this, will you turn again to the ineffectual rites and ceremonies of the Mosaic law—rites too weak to counteract your sinful habits, and too poor to purchase pardon and eternal life for you? If the Galatians were turning again to them, it is evident that they once had been addicted to them. And this they might have been, allowing that they had become converts from heathenism to Judaism and from Judaism to Christianity.

10. *Ye observe days.* You superstitiously regard the Sabbaths and particular days of your own appointment. *And months.* New moons. *Times*—festivals, such as those of Tabernacles, Dedication, Passover. *Years.* Annual atonements, sabbatical years, and jubilees.

11. *I am afraid of you.* I begin now to be seriously alarmed for you, and think you are so thoroughly perverted from the gospel of Christ that all my pains and labor in your conversion have been thrown away.

12. *Be as I am.* Thoroughly addicted to the Christian faith and worship, from the deepest conviction of its truth. *For I am as ye are.*

I was formerly a Jew, and as zealously addicted to the rites and ceremonies of Judaism as you are, but I am saved from that means and unprofitable dependence. "Be therefore as I am now, who was once as you now are." *Ye have not injured me at all.* I do not thus earnestly entreat you to return to your Christian profession because your perversion has been any loss to me, nor because your conversion can be to me any gain. You have not injured me at all; you injure only yourselves.

13. *Ye know how through infirmity.* The apostle seems to say that he was much afflicted in body when he first preached the gospel to them. And is this any strange thing, that a minister so laborious as Paul was should be sometimes overdone and overcome by the severity of his labors? Surely not. This might have been only an occasional affliction while laboring in that part of Asia Minor, and not a continual and incurable infirmity, as some have too hastily conjectured.

14. *And my temptation which was in my flesh.* On this verse there are a great many various readings, as there are various opinions. Instead of *my temptation,* a number of MSS. and versions and several of the primitive fathers have "your temptation." The word which we translate *temptation* signifies "trial" of any kind. The verse therefore may be read, "You despised not the trial which was in my flesh"; or, "You despised not your trial, which was in my flesh"; i.e., what my flesh suffered on your account, the afflictions I passed through in consequence of my severe labors on your account. They received him *as an angel of God,* as a messenger from heaven, and *as Christ Jesus* himself. This appears to me to be the simple meaning of the apostle, and that he alludes to neither a bodily nor a mental infirmity which generally or periodically afflicted him, as some have imagined. Nor does he appear at all to speak of the same case as that mentioned in 2 Cor. xii. 7.

15. *Where is then the blessedness ye spake of? Ye spake of* should be in italics, there being no corresponding word in the Greek text. Perhaps there is not a sentence in the New Testament more variously translated than this. "What was then your blessedness!" Or, "How great was your happiness at that time!" Or, "What blessings did ye then pour on me!" It is worthy of remark that, instead of *what,* several MSS. and some of the fathers have *where;* and *was* is omitted by some. According to these authorities the text should be read thus: "Where then is your blessedness?" Having renounced the gospel, you have lost your "happiness." What have your false teachers given you to compensate the loss of communion with God, or that Spirit of adoption, that Spirit of Christ, by which you cried, "Abba, Father"! If, however, we understand the words as implying the benedictions they then heaped on the apostle, the sense will be sufficiently natural, and agree well with the concluding part of the verse; *for I bear you record, that, if . . . possible, ye would have plucked out your own eyes, and have given them to me.* You had then the strongest affection for me; you loved God, and you loved me for God's sake, and were ready to give me the most unequivocal proof of your love. Dearer than one's eyes, or to profess to give one's eyes for the sake of a person, appears to have been a proverbial expression, intimating the highest tokens of the strongest affection.

16. *Am I therefore become your enemy?* How is it that you are so much altered towards me that you now treat me as an enemy, who formerly loved me with the most fervent affection? Is it *because I tell you the truth,* that very truth for which you at first so ardently loved me?

17. *They zealously affect you, but not well.* It is difficult for common readers to understand the meaning of these words; perhaps it would be better to translate: These false teachers "endeavor to conciliate your esteem, but not on honest or true principles." They work themselves into your good graces; they wish you to place all your affection upon themselves. *They would exclude you.* They wish to "shut you out" from the affection of your apostle, *that ye might affect them,* that you might love them alone, hear them alone, abide by their directions only, and totally abandon him who called you into the grace of the gospel of Christ. Some MSS. read "us" instead of *you;* they wish to shut us entirely out from among you, that you may receive and believe them alone. The sense is nearly the same but the former appears to be the more authentic reading.

18. *It is good to be zealously affected.* It is well to have a determined mind and an ardent heart in reference to things which are laudable and good. *Not only when I am present.* You were thus attached to me when I was among you, but now you have lost both your reverence and affection for me. Your false teachers pretended great concern for you, that you might put all your confidence in them. They have gained their end; they have estranged you from me, and got you to renounce the gospel, and have brought you again into your former bondage.

19. *My little children.* "My beloved children." As their conversion to God had been the fruit of much labor, prayers, and tears, so he felt them as his children and peculiarly dear to him because he had been the means of bringing them to the knowledge of the truth. Therefore he represents himself as suffering the same anxiety and distress which he endured at first when he preached the gospel to them, when their conversion to Christianity was a matter of great doubt and uncertainty. The metaphor which he uses needs no explanation. *Until Christ be formed in you.* Till you once more receive the Spirit and unction of Christ in your hearts, from which you are fallen by your rejection of the spirit of the gospel.

20. *I desire to be present with you.* I wish to accommodate my doctrine to your state; I know not whether you need stronger reprehension or to be dealt with more leniently. *I stand in doubt of you.* I have doubts concerning your state, the progress of error and conviction among you, which I cannot fully know without being among you. This appears to be the apostle's meaning, and tends much to soften and render palatable the severity of his reproofs.

21. *Ye that desire to be under the law.* You who desire to incorporate the Mosaic institutions with Christianity, and thus bring yourselves into bondage to circumcision and a great variety of oppressive rites. *Do ye not hear the law?* Do you not understand what is written

in the Pentateuch relative to Abraham and his children? It is evident that the word *law* is used in two senses in this verse. It first means the Mosaic institutions; secondly, the Pentateuch, where the history is recorded to which the apostle refers.

22. *For it is written.* Viz., in Gen. xvi. 15 and xxii. 1, *that Abraham had two sons,* Ishmael and Isaac: *the one,* Ishmael, *by a bondmaid,* Hagar; *the other,* Isaac, *by a freewoman,* Sarah.

23. *Was born after the flesh.* Ishmael was born according to the course of nature, his parents being both of a proper age, so that there was nothing uncommon or supernatural in his birth. This is the proper meaning of the apostle's *after* or "according to" *the flesh. By promise.* Both Abraham and Sarah had passed, that age in which the procreation of children was possible on natural principles. The birth, therefore, of Isaac was supernatural; it was the effect of an especial promise of God, and it was only on the ground of that promise that it was either credible or possible.

24. *Which things are an allegory.* They are to be understood spiritually, more being intended in the account than meets the eye. *Allegory* signifies a "thing that is a representative of another," where the literal sense is the representative of a spiritual meaning. *For these are the two covenants.* These signify two different systems of religion: the one by Moses, the other by the Messiah. *The one from the mount Sinai.* On which the law was published, which was typified by Hagar, Abraham's bond maid. *Which gendereth to bondage.* For as the bond maid or slave could only gender, "bring forth her children," in a state of slavery, so all that are born and live under those Mosaic institutions are born and live in a state of bondage— a bondage to various rites and ceremonies; under the obligation to keep the whole law, yet from its severity and their frailness obliged to live in the habitual breach of it, and in consequence exposed to the curse which it pronounces.

25. *For this Agar is mount Sinai in Arabia.* This is the common reading; but it is read differently in some of the most respectable MSS., versions, and fathers—thus: "For this Sinai is a mountain of Arabia," the word *Agar* being omitted. *Answereth to Jerusalem.* Hagar, the bond maid, bringing forth children in a state of slavery, *answereth to Jerusalem which now is,* "points out" or "bears a similitude" to Jerusalem in her present state of subjection; which, *with her children,* her citizens, is not only *in bondage* to the Romans, but in a worse bondage to the law, to its oppressive ordinances, and to the heavy curse which it has pronounced against all those who do not keep them.

26. *But Jerusalem which is above.* The apostle still follows the Jewish allegory, showing not only how the story of Hagar and Sarah, Ishmael and Isaac, was allegorized, but pointing out also that even Jerusalem was the subject of allegory. *Is free, which is the mother of us all.* There is a spiritual Jerusalem, of which this is the type; and this Jerusalem, in which the souls of all the righteous are, is free from all bondage and sin. Or by this, probably, the kingdom of the Messiah was intended; and this certainly answers best to the apostle's meaning, as the subsequent verse shows. There is an earthly Jerusalem, but this earthly Jerusalem

typifies a heavenly Jerusalem. The former, with all her citizens, is in bondage; the latter is a free city, and all her inhabitants are free also. And this Jerusalem is our *mother;* it signifies the Church of Christ, the metropolis of Christianity, or rather the state of liberty into which all true believers are brought. The word *panton, of . . . all,* is omitted by almost every MS. and version of antiquity and importance, and by the most eminent of the fathers who quote his place. It is undoubtedly spurious, and the text should be read thus: "But Jerusalem, which is above, is free, which is our mother."

27. *Rejoice, thou barren that bearest not.* This quotation is taken from Isa. liv. 1, and is certainly a promise which relates to the conversion of the Gentiles, as the following clause proves. *For the desolate,* the Gentile world, *hath many more children,* is a much larger and more numerous Church, *than she,* Jerusalem, the Jewish state, *which hath an husband,* has been so long in covenant with God, living under His continual protection and in possession of a great variety of spiritual advantages; and especially those offered to her by the gospel, which she has rejected, and which the Gentiles have accepted.

28. *Now we,* who believe in the Lord Jesus, *are the children of promise*—are the spiritual offspring of the Messiah, the Seed of Abraham, in whom the promise stated that all the nations of the earth should be blessed.

29. *But as then he,* Ishmael, *that was born after the flesh,* whose birth had nothing supernatural in it but was according to the ordinary course of nature, *persecuted him,* Isaac, *that was born after the Spirit*—who had a supernatural birth, according to the promise, and through the efficacy of the Holy Spirit giving effect to that promise, "Sarah shall have a son," Gen. xvii. 16-21; xxi. 1. *Persecuted him;* the persecution here referred to is that mentioned in Gen. xxi. 9. It consisted in mocking his brother, Isaac. *Even so it is now.* So the Jews in every place persecute the Christian, and show thereby that they are rather of the posterity of Hagar than of Sarah.

30. *What saith the scripture?* (In Gen. xxi. 10.) *Cast out the bondwoman and her son.* And what does this imply in the present case? Why, that the present Jerusalem and her children shall be cast out of the favor of God, and *shall not be heir with the son of the freewoman* —shall not inherit the blessings promised to Abraham, because they believe not in the promised Seed.

31. *So then . . . we,* Jews and Gentiles, who believe on the Lord Jesus, *are not children of the bondwoman,* are not in subjection to the Jewish law, *but of the free;* and consequently are delivered from all its bondage, obligation, and curse.

CHAPTER 5

flesh, which exclude from the kingdom of God those who bear them, 15-21. Enumerates also the fruits of the Spirit, which characterize the disciples of Christ, 22-24. Exhorts them to live in the Spirit, and not provoke each other, 25-26.

1. *Stand fast therefore in the liberty.* This is intimately connected with the preceding chapter, the apostle having said just before, "So then, brethren, we are not children of the bond-woman, but of the free," immediately adds, *Stand fast therefore in the liberty wherewith Christ hath made us free.* Hold fast your Christian profession; it brings spiritual liberty. On the contrary, Judaism brings spiritual bondage. The liberty mentioned by the apostle is freedom from Jewish rites and ceremonies, called properly here *the yoke of bondage;* and also liberty from the power and guilt of sin, which nothing but the grace of Christ can take away.

2. *If ye be circumcised.* By circumcision you take on you the whole obligation of the Jewish law, and consequently profess to seek salvation by means of its observances. Therefore Christ can profit you nothing; for by seeking justification by the works of the law you renounce justification by faith in Christ.

3. *He is a debtor to do the whole law.* Lays himself, by receiving circumcision, under the obligation to fulfill all its precepts and ordinances.

4. *Christ is become of no effect unto you.* It is vain for you to attempt to unite the two systems. You must have the law and no Christ or Christ and no law for your justification. *Ye are fallen from grace.* From the gospel. They had been brought into the grace of the gospel, and now, by readopting the Mosaic ordinance, they had apostatized from the gospel as a system of religion, and had lost the grace communicated to their souls, by which they were preserved in a state of salvation. The peace and love of God, received by Jesus Christ, could not remain in the hearts of those who had rejected Christ. They had therefore in every sense of the word *fallen from grace,* and whether some of them ever rose again is more than we can tell.

5. *For we,* Christians, *through the Spirit,* through the operation of the Holy Ghost, under this spiritual dispensation of the gospel, *wait for the hope of righteousness*—expect that which is the object of our hope, on our being justified by faith in Christ. *Righteousness* may here, as in many other places of Paul's Epistles, mean "justification." And the hope of justification, or the hope excited and inspired by it, is the possession of eternal glory; for, says the apostle, Rom. v. 1-2, "Being justified by faith, we have peace with God . . . and rejoice in hope of the glory of God." As this glory is necessarily future, it is to be waited for. But this waiting, in a thorough Christian, is not only a blessed expectation, but also a continual anticipation of it; and therefore the apostle says we "receive out of it." This is no fanciful derivation; it exists in the experience of every genuine Christian. He is continually anticipating or receiving foretastes of that glory the fullness of which he expects after death. Thus Christians are receiving the end of their faith, the salvation of their souls, 1 Pet. i. 9.

6. *For in Jesus Christ.* By the dispensation of the gospel all legal observances as essential to salvation are done away; and uncircumcision, or the Gentile state, contributes as much to salvation as circumcision or the Jewish state. They are both equally ineffectual; and nothing now avails in the sight of God but that faith "which is made active [or energetic] by love." God acknowledges no faith as of the operation of His Spirit that is not active or obedient. But the principle of all obedience to God and beneficence to man is *love;* therefore faith cannot work unless it be associated with love.

7. *Ye did run well.* You once had the faith that worked by love—you were genuine, active, useful Christians. *Who did hinder?* Who prevented you from continuing to obey the truth? You could be turned aside only by your own consent. Paul here, as in 1 Cor. ix. 24, compares Christianity to a race.

8. *This persuasion,* of the necessity of your being circumcised and obeying the law of Moses, is *not of him that calleth you.* I never preached such a doctrine to you; I called you out of bondage to liberty, from a galling yoke to a cheerful service.

9. *A little leaven leaveneth the whole lump.* A proverbial expression (see 1 Cor. v. 6) very aptly applied to those who receive the smallest tincture of false doctrine relative to the things essential to salvation, which soon influences the whole conduct so that the man becomes totally perverted. They might have argued, "It is a small thing, and should not be made a subject of serious controversy, whether we be circumcised or not." Granted that in itself it is a small matter; but as every man who is circumcised "is a debtor to do the whole law," v. 3, then your circumcision leads necessarily to your total perversion; as the little portion of leaven, mixed with the batch, soon leavens the whole lump.

10. *I have confidence in you.* I now feel a persuasion from the Lord that I shall not be permitted to expostulate with you in vain. *That ye will be none otherwise minded*—that you will be aware of the danger to which you are exposed, that you will retreat in time, and recover the grace which you have lost. *But he that troubleth you.* The false teacher who sowed doubtful disputations among you, and thus has troubled the repose of the whole church, *shall bear his judgment,* shall meet with the punishment he deserves for having sown his tares among God's wheat.

11. *If I yet preach circumcision.* It is very likely that some of the false apostles, hearing of Paul's having circumcised Timothy, Acts xvi. 3, which must have been done about this time, reported him as being an advocate for circumcision, and by this means endeavored to sanction their own doctrine. To this the apostle replies: Were it so, that I am a friend to this measure, is it likely that I should suffer persecution from the Jews? But I am everywhere persecuted by them, and I am persecuted because I am known to be an enemy to circumcision. Were I a friend to this doctrine, the *offence of the cross,* preaching salvation only through the sacrifice of Christ, would soon cease; because, to be consistent with myself, if I preached the necessity of circumcision I must soon cease to preach Christ crucified, and then the Jews would be no longer my enemies.

12. *I would they were even cut off which trouble you.* As the persons who were breeding all this confusion in the churches of Galatia were members of that church, the apostle ap-

pears to me to be simply expressing his desire that they might be *cut off* or "excommunicated" from the church.

13. *Ye have been called unto liberty.* A total freedom from all the burdensome rites and ceremonies of the Mosaic law. *Only use not that liberty for an occasion to the flesh.* By *flesh* here we may understand all the unrenewed desires and propensities of the mind, whatsoever is not under the influence and guidance of the Holy Spirit of God. Your liberty is from that which would oppress the spirit, not from that which would lay restraints on the flesh. The gospel proclaims liberty from the ceremonial law, but binds you still faster under the moral law. To be freed from the ceremonial law is the gospel liberty; to pretend freedom from the moral law is antinomianism. *By love serve one another.* Having that "faith which worketh by love," serve each other to the uttermost of your power; serve each other, when necessary, as "slaves" serve their masters.

14. *For all the law,* which respects our duty to our fellows, *is fulfilled,* is comprehended, *in one word: Thou shalt love thy neighbour as thyself.*

15. *If ye bite and devour one another.* These churches seem to have been in a state of great distraction; there were continual altercations among them. They had fallen from the grace of the gospel; and as Christ no longer dwelt in their hearts by faith, pride, anger, ill will, and all unkind and uncharitable tempers took possession of their souls, and they were in consequence alternately destroying each other. Nothing is so destructive to the peace of man and to the peace of the soul as religious disputes; where they prevail, religion in general has little place.

16. *Walk in the Spirit.* Get back that Spirit of God which you have grieved and lost; take up that spiritual religion which you have abandoned. *Ye shall not fulfil the lust of the flesh.* If the Spirit of God dwell in and rule your heart, the whole carnal mind will be destroyed; and then, not only carnal ordinances will be abandoned, but also the works and propensities of the flesh.

17. *For the flesh lusteth against the Spirit.* God still continues to strive with you, notwithstanding your apostasy, showing you whence you have fallen and exciting you to return to Him; but your own obstinacy renders all ineffectual; and through the influence of these different principles you are kept in a state of self-opposition and self-distraction, *so that ye cannot do the things that ye would.* You are convinced of what is right, and you wish to do it; but having abandoned the gospel and the grace of Christ, the law and its ordinances which you have chosen in their place afford you no power to conquer your evil propensities. It was on this ground that the apostle exhorted them, v. 16, to "walk in the Spirit," that they might not "fulfil the lust of the flesh," as without the grace of God they could do nothing.

18. *But if ye be led of the Spirit.* If you receive again the gospel and the grace of Christ, and permit yourselves to be influenced by the Holy Spirit, whom you are now grieving, *ye are not under the law,* you will not feel those evil propensities which now disgrace and tor-

ment you; but they must prevail while you are not under the influence of the grace and Spirit of Christ.

19. *Now the works of the flesh are manifest.* By *flesh* we are to understand the evil and fallen state of the soul, no longer under the guidance of God's Spirit and right reason, but under the animal passions; and they are rendered even more irregular and turbulent by the influence of sin, so that man is in a worse state than the brute. And so all-commanding is this evil nature that it leads men into all kinds of crimes, among them the following, which *are manifest*—known to all, and most prevalent; and though these are most solemnly forbidden by your law, the observance of its ordinances gives no power to overcome them, and provides no pardon for the guilt and condemnation produced by them. *Adultery.* Illicit connection with a married person. This word is wanting in this place in the best MSS., versions, and fathers, the next term often comprehending both. *Fornication.* Illicit connection between single or unmarried persons, yet often signifying adultery also. *Uncleanness.* Whatever is opposite to purity; probably meaning here, as in Rom. i. 24; 2 Cor. xii. 21, unnatural practices; sodomy, bestiality. *Lasciviousness.* Whatever is contrary to chastity; all lewdness.

20. *Idolatry.* Worshipping of idols; frequenting idol festivals; all the rites of Bacchus, Venus, etc., which were common among the Gentiles. *Witchcraft. Pharmaceia* from *pharmacon,* "a drug or poison"; because in all spells and enchantments, whether true or false, drugs were employed. *Hatred.* "Aversions" and "antipathies," when opposed to brotherly love and kindness. *Variance.* "Contentions," where the principle of hatred proceeds to open acts; hence contests, altercations, lawsuits, and disputes in general. *Emulations.* "Envies" or "emulations"; that is, strife to excel at the expense of another; lowering others to set up oneself; unholy zeal, fervently adopting a bad cause, or supporting a good one by cruel means. *Wrath.* Turbulent passions, disturbing the harmony of the mind, and producing domestic and civil broils and disquietudes. *Strife.* Disputations, janglings. *Seditions.* Divisions into separate factions; parties, whether in the church or state. *Heresies.* "Factions"; parties in the church separating from communion with each other, and setting up altar against altar. The word, which is harmless in itself, is here used in a bad sense.

21. *Envyings.* "Pain felt, and malignity conceived, at the sight of excellence or happiness," a passion the most base and the least curable of all that disgrace or degrade the fallen soul. *Murders.* Similarity of sound to the preceding seems to have suggested the word in this association; it is wanting in several MSS. Murder signifies the destruction of human life; and as he who hates his brother in his heart is ready to take away his life, so he is called a murderer. *Revellings.* Lascivious feastings, with obscene songs, music, etc. *And such like.* All that proceeds from the evil passions of a fallen spirit, besides those above specified; and all that the law of God specifies and condemns. *Of the which I tell you before.* When I first preached the gospel to you. *As I have also told you in time past.* When I paid my second visit to you, for the apostle did visit them twice. See

Acts xvi. 6 and xviii. 23. *Shall not inherit.* They are not children of God, and therefore cannot inherit the Kingdom which belongs only to the children of the divine family.

22. *But the fruit of the Spirit.* Both "flesh," the sinful dispositions of the human heart, and spirit, the changed or purified state of the soul by the grace and Spirit of God, are represented by the apostle as trees, one yielding good, the other bad fruit; the productions of each being according to the nature of the tree, as the tree is according to the nature of the seed from which it sprang. The bad seed produced a bad tree, yielding all manner of bad fruit; the good seed produced a good tree, bringing forth fruits of the most excellent kind. The tree of the flesh, with all its bad fruits, we have already seen; the tree of the Spirit with its good fruits, we shall now see. *Love.* An intense desire to please God, and to do good to mankind; the very soul and spirit of all true religion; the fulfilling of the law, and what gives energy to faith itself. *Joy.* The exultation that arises from a sense of God's mercy communicated to the soul in the pardon of its iniquities, and the prospect of that eternal glory of which it has the foretaste in the pardon of sin. *Peace.* The calm, quiet, and order which take place in the justified soul instead of the doubts, fears, alarms, and dreadful forebodings which every true penitent more or less feels, and must feel till the assurance of pardon brings peace and satisfaction to the mind. *Longsuffering.* Long-mindedness, bearing with the frailties and provocations of others, from the consideration that God has borne long with ours and that, if He had not, we should have been speedily consumed; bearing up also through all the troubles and difficulties of life without murmuring or repining; submitting cheerfully to every dispensation of God's providence, and thus deriving benefit from every occurrence. *Gentleness.* Benignity, affability; a very rare grace, often wanting in many who have a considerable share of Christian excellence. A good education and polished manners, when brought under the influence of the grace of God, will bring out this grace with great effect. *Goodness.* The perpetual desire and sincere study, not only to abstain from every appearance of evil, but to do good to the bodies and souls of men to the utmost of our ability. *Faith.* Here used for "fidelity"—punctuality in performing promises, conscientious carefulness in preserving what is committed to our trust, in restoring it to its proper owner, in transacting the business confided to us, neither betraying the secret of our friend nor disappointing the confidence of our employer.

23. *Meekness.* Mildness, indulgence toward the weak and erring, patient suffering of injuries without feeling a spirit of revenge, an even balance of all tempers and passions, the entire opposite to anger. *Temperance.* "Continence, self-government, or moderation," principally with regard to sensual or animal appetites. Moderation in eating, drinking, sleeping, etc. *Against such there is no law.* Those whose lives are adorned by the above virtues cannot be condemned by any law, for the whole purpose and design of the moral law of God is fulfilled in those who have the Spirit of God producing in their hearts and lives the preceding fruits.

24. *And they that are Christ's,* all genuine Christians, *have crucified the flesh*—are so far from obeying its dictates and acting under its influence that they have crucified their sensual appetites; they have nailed them to the cross of Christ, where they have expired with Him. Hence, says Paul, Rom. vi. 6, "our old man," the flesh, with its affections and lusts, "is crucified with him, that the body of sin might be destroyed, that henceforth we should not serve sin." By which we see that God has fully designed to save all who believe in Christ from all sin, whether outward or inward, with all the *affections,* irregular "passions," and *lusts,* disorderly "wishes" and "desires"—all that a man may feel contrary to love and purity, and all that he may desire contrary to moderation and that self-denial peculiar to the Christian character.

25. *If we live in the Spirit,* if we profess to believe a spiritual religion, *let us also walk in the Spirit*—let us show in our lives and conversation that the Spirit of God dwells in us.

26. *Let us not be desirous of vain glory.* "Let us not be vainglorious"—boasting of our attainments; vaunting ourselves to be superior to others; or seeking honor from those things which do not possess moral good, in birth, riches, or eloquence. *Provoking one another.* What this may refer to we cannot tell. Whether to the Judaizing teachers endeavoring to set themselves up beyond the apostle, and their attempts to lessen him in the people's eyes, that they might secure to themselves the public confidence and thus destroy Paul's influence in the Galatian churches, or whether to some other matter in the internal economy of the church, we know not. But the exhortation is necessary for every Christian, and for every Christian church. He who professes to seek the honor that comes from God should *not be desirous of vain glory.* He who desires to keep the unity of the Spirit in the bond of peace should not provoke another. He who knows that he never deserved any gift or blessing from God should not envy another those blessings which the divine goodness may have thought proper to bestow upon him.

CHAPTER 6

The apostle teaches them to be tender and affectionate towards any who, through surprise and the violence of temptation, have fallen into sin, and to bear each other's burdens, 1-2. To think humbly of themselves and to conclude concerning their own character rather from the evidence of their works than from anything else, 3-5. To minister to the support of those who instruct them in righteousness, 6. He warns them against self-deception, because whatever a man sows, that he shall reap, 7-8. Exhorts them not to be weary in well doing, and to embrace every opportunity to do good, 9-10. Intimates that his love to them led him to write this whole Epistle with his own hand, 11. Points out the object that those had in view who wished them to be circumcised, 12-13. He exults in the cross of Christ, and asserts that a new creation of the soul is essential to its salvation; and wishes peace to them who act on this plan, 14-16. States that he bears in his body the marks of the Lord Jesus, 17. And concludes with his apostolical benediction, 18.

1. *Brethren, if a man be overtaken.* If he be "surprised, seized on" without warning, "suddenly invaded, taken before he is aware"; all these meanings the word has in connections similar to this. *Ye which are spiritual.* You who still retain the grace of the gospel, and have wisdom and experience in divine things. *Restore such an one.* Bring the man "back into

his place." It is a metaphor taken from a dislocated limb, brought back into its place by the hand of a skillful and tender surgeon. *In the spirit of meekness.* Use no severity nor haughty carriage towards him; as the man was suddenly overtaken, he is already deeply humbled and distressed, and needs much encouragement and lenient usage. There is a great difference between a man who being suddenly assailed falls into sin and the man who transgressed in consequence of having walked in the counsel of the ungodly or stood in the way of sinners. *Considering thyself.* Looking to thyself; as he fell through a moment of unwatchfulness, look about, that you are not surprised. As he fell, so may you. You are now warned at his expense; therefore keep a good lookout. *Lest thou also be tempted.* And having had this warning, you will have less to plead in extenuation of your offense.

2. *Bear ye one another's burdens.* Have sympathy; feel for each other; and consider the case of a distressed brother as your own. *And so fulfil the law of Christ.* That law or commandment, "Ye shall love one another"; or that, "Do unto all men as ye would they should do unto you." We should be as indulgent to the infirmities of others as we can be consistently with truth and righteousness. Our brother's infirmity may be his burden; and if we do not choose to help him to bear it, let us not reproach him because he is obliged to carry the load.

3. *If a man think himself to be something.* I.e., to be a proper Christian man. *When he is nothing;* being destitute of that charity which beareth, hopeth, and endureth all things. See 1 Cor. xiii. 1, etc. Those who suppose themselves to excel all others in piety, understanding, etc., while they are harsh, censorious, and overbearing, prove that they have not the charity that "thinketh no evil," and in the sight of God are only "as sounding brass" and "a tinkling cymbal." There are no people more censorious or uncharitable than those among some religious people who pretend to more light and a deeper communion with God. They are generally carried away with a sort of sublime, high-sounding phraseology which seems to argue a wonderfully deep acquaintance with divine things; stripped of this, many of them are like Samson without his hair.

4. *Prove his own work.* Let him examine himself and his conduct by the words and example of Christ, and if he find that they bear this touchstone, then he shall have *rejoicing in himself alone,* feeling that he resembles his Lord and Master, *and not in another*—not derive his consolation from comparing himself with another who may be weaker or less instructed than himself. The only rule for a Christian is the word of Christ; the only pattern for his imitation is the example of Christ. He should not compare himself with others; they are not his standard. Christ has left us an example that we should follow His steps.

5. *Every man shall bear his own burden.* All must answer for themselves, not for their neighbors. And every man must expect to be dealt with by the divine Judge, as his character and conduct have been. The greater offenses of another will not excuse your smaller crimes. Every man must give account of himself to God.

6. *Let him that is taught in the word,* he who receives instructions in Christianity by the public preaching of the Word. *Communicate unto him that teacheth,* contribute to the support of the man who has dedicated himself to the work of the ministry, and who gives up his time and his life to preach the gospel. It appears that some of the believers in Galatia could receive the Christian ministry without contributing to its support. This is both ungrateful and base. We do not expect that a common schoolmaster will give up his time to teach our children their alphabet without being paid for it; and can we suppose that it is just for any person to sit under the preaching of the gospel in order to grow wise unto salvation by it, and not contribute to the support of the spiritual teacher? It is unjust.

7. *Be not deceived.* Neither deceive yourselves nor permit yourselves to be deceived by others. He seems to refer to the Judaizing teachers. *God is not mocked.* You cannot deceive Him, and He will not permit you to mock Him with pretended instead of real services. *Whatsoever a man soweth.* Whatsoever kind of grain a man sows in his field, of that shall he reap; for no other species of grain can proceed from that which is sown.

8. *He that soweth to his flesh.* In like manner, he that *soweth to the flesh,* who indulges his sensual and animal appetites, shall have *corruption* as the crop: you cannot expect to lead a bad life and go to heaven at last. According as your present life is, so will be your eternal life; whether your sowing be to the flesh or to the Spirit, so will your eternal reaping be. To sow here means transacting the concerns of a man's natural life. To reap signifies his enjoyment or punishment in another world. Probably by *flesh* and *Spirit* the apostle means Judaism and Christianity. Circumcision of the flesh was the principal rite of the former; circumcision in the heart, by the Spirit, the chief rite of the latter. Hence the one may have been called *flesh;* the other, *Spirit.* He who rejects the gospel, and trusts only in the rites and ceremonies of the law for salvation, will reap endless disappointment and misery. He who trusts in Christ, and receives the gifts and graces of the Holy Spirit, shall reap life everlasting.

9. *Let us not be weary.* Well doing is easier in itself than ill doing; and the danger of growing weary in the former arises only from the opposition to good in our own nature, or the outward hindrances we may meet with from a gainsaying and persecuting world. *In due season we shall reap.* As a husbandman, in ploughing, sowing, and variously laboring in his fields, is supported by the hope of a plentiful harvest, which he cannot expect before the right and appointed time, so every follower of God may be persuaded that he shall not be permitted to pray, weep, deny himself, and live in a conformity to his Maker's will without reaping the fruit of it in eternal glory. And although no man obtains glory because he has prayed, yet none can expect glory who do not seek it in this way. This is sowing to the Spirit; and the Spirit and the grace are furnished by Christ Jesus, and by Him the kingdom of Heaven is opened to all believers; but only those who believe, love, and obey shall enter into it.

10. *As we have therefore opportunity.* While

it is the time of sowing let us sow the good seed; and let our love be, as the love of Christ is, free, manifested to all. Let us help all who need help according to the uttermost of our power, but let the first objects of our regard be those *who are of the household of faith*—the members of the Church of Christ, who form one family, of which Jesus Christ is the Head. Those have the first claims on our attention; but all others have their claims also, and therefore we should *do good unto all.*

12. *A fair shew in the flesh.* The Jewish religion was general in the region of Galatia and was respectable. As it was then professed and practiced among the Jews, this religion had nothing very grievous to the old man; an unrenewed nature might go through all its observances with little pain or cross-bearing. On the other hand, Christianity could not be very popular; it was too strict. A Jew made a fair show there, according to his carnal system, and it was a temptation to a weak Christian to swerve into Judaism, that he might be exempted from persecution and be creditable among his countrymen.

13. *Neither they themselves who are circumcised.* They received circumcision and professed Judaism, not from a desire to be conformed to the will of God, but Judaism was popular, and the more converts the false teachers could make, the more occasion of glorying they had; and they wished to get those Christian converts to receive circumcision, that they might glory in their flesh.

14. *But God forbid that I should glory.* Whatever others may do, or whatever they may exult or glory in, God forbid that I should "exult" except *in the cross of our Lord Jesus Christ;* in the grand doctrine that justification and salvation are only through Christ crucified, He having made an atonement for the sin of the world by His passion and death. And I glory also in the disgrace and persecution which I experience through my attachment to this crucified Christ. *By whom the world is crucified unto me.* Jewish rites and Gentile vanities are equally insipid to me; I know them to be empty and worthless. If Jews and Gentiles despise me, I despise that in which they trust; through Jesus, all are *crucified unto me.*

15. *In Christ Jesus.* Under the dispensation of the gospel, of which He is Head and supreme, *neither circumcision,* nothing that the Jew can boast of, nothing that the Gentile can call excellent, *availeth any thing*—can in the least

contribute to the salvation of the soul. *But a new creature.* "But a new creation"; not a *new creature* merely (for this might be restrained to any new power or faculty), but a total renewal of the whole man, of all the powers and passions of the soul; and as creation could not be effected but by the power of the Almighty, so this change cannot be effected but by the same energy.

16. *As many as walk according to this rule.* "This canon"; viz., what is laid down in the preceding verses, that redemption is through the sacrifice of Christ, that circumcision and uncircumcision are equally unavailable, and that none can be saved without being created anew. This is the grand canon or "rule" in Christianity. *Peace be on them.* Those who act from this conviction will have the *peace* and *mercy* of God; for it is in this way that *mercy* is communicated and *peace* obtained. *The Israel of God.* The true Christians, called here *the Israel of God,* to distinguish them from Israel according to the flesh.

17. *From henceforth let no man trouble me.* Put an end to your contentions among yourselves; return to the pure doctrine of the gospel; abandon those who are leading you astray; separate from the church those who corrupt and disturb it; and let me be grieved no longer with your defections from the truth. *I bear in my body the marks of the Lord Jesus.* The *stigmata,* of which the apostle speaks here, may be understood as implying the scars of the wounds which he had received in the work of the ministry; and that he had such scars we may well conceive when we know that he had been scourged, stoned, and maltreated in a variety of ways. The writer could show such scars himself, received in the same way. Or the apostle may allude to the *stigmata* or *marks* with which servants and slaves were often impressed, in order to ascertain whose property they were. You glory in your mark of circumcision; I glory in the marks which I bear in my body for the testimony of the Lord; I am an open, professed Christian, and have given full proof of my attachment to the cause of Christianity.

18. *The grace,* favor, benevolence, and continual influence of the Lord Jesus, *be with your spirit*—may it live in your heart, enlighten and change your souls, and be conspicuous in your life!

Unto the Galatians, written from Rome. This, or the major part of it, is wanting in the best and most ancient MSS.

The Epistle to the

EPHESIANS

Ephesus was a city of Ionia, in Asia Minor, and once the metropolis of that part of the world. The ancient city was situated at the mouth of the river Cayster, on the shore of the Aegean Sea, about fifty miles south of Smyrna. The Ephesus in which Paul founded a church, which for a time flourished gloriously, was not the ancient Ephesus; for that was destroyed, and a new city of the same name was built by Lysimachus.

It is, however, a doubt with many learned men whether this Epistle was sent to the church at Ephesus. They think that the proper direction is, The Epistle of Paul to the Laodiceans; and suppose it to be the same which the apostle mentions, Col. iv. 16: "When this epistle is read among you, cause that it be read also in the church of the Laodiceans; and that ye likewise read the epistle from Laodicea."

It must be allowed that the arguments that this is the Epistle to the Laodiceans are both plausible and strong; and yet almost the whole of antiquity is in favor of the Epistle being sent originally to the church at Ephesus. Puzzled with these two considerations, some critics have pointed out a middle way. They suppose that several copies of this Epistle were directed to no particular church, but were intended for all the churches in Asia Minor; and that different copies might have different directions, from this circumstance, that Paul, in writing the first verse, "Paul, an apostle of Jesus Christ . . . to the saints which are," left a blank after "are," which was in some cases filled up with *at Ephesus;* in others, with *at Laodicea;* though there might be one copy expressly sent by him to the church of the Laodiceans, while he wished that others should be directed to the different churches through Asia Minor. That there were copies which had no place specified, we learn from **St. Basil.**

CHAPTER 1

The apostle's salutation to the church, 1-2. He blesses God for calling the Gentiles to the adoption of children by Jesus Christ, by whose sacrificial death both they and the Jews find redemption, 3-7. He shows that it was through the great abundance of God's wisdom and goodness that the Gentiles were called into a state of salvation, and that they should receive the Holy Spirit as the earnest of their inheritance, 8-15. He praises God for their conversion, and prays that they may be further enlightened, that they may see the glory of Christ, and partake of the blessings procured by His passion and exaltation, 16-23.

1. *To the saints which are at Ephesus.* By the term *saints* we are to understand those who in that place professed Christianity, and were members of the Christian Church. *Saint* properly signifies a "holy person," and such the gospel of Christ requires every man to be, and such every true believer is, in both heart and life; but *saint* appears to have been as ordinary a denomination of a believer in Christ in those primitive times as the term "Christian" is now. *The faithful in Christ Jesus.* The "believers"— the persons who received Christ as the promised Messiah and the Saviour of the world, and continued in the grace which they had received.

3. *Blessed be the God.* See the note on 2 Cor. i. 3, where the same form is used. *With all spiritual blessings.* With the pure doctrines of the gospel, and the abundant gifts and graces of the Holy Ghost, justifying, sanctifying, and building us up on our most holy faith. *In heavenly places.* "In heavenly things," such as those mentioned above; they were not yet in *heavenly places,* but they had abundance of

heavenly things to prepare them for heavenly places. Some think the word should be understood as signifying *blessings* of the most exalted or excellent kind, such as are *spiritual* in opposition to those that are earthly, such as are eternal in opposition to those that are temporal; and all these in, through, and by Christ. We have already seen, on Gal. iv. 26, that the heavenly Jerusalem, or "Jerusalem which is from above," is used by the Jews to signify the days of the Messiah, and that state of grace and glory which should follow the Levitical worship and ceremonies; and it is possible that Paul may use "heavenly things," in this sense: "God hath blessed us with all spiritual blessings in heavenly things, or in this heavenly state," in which life and immortality are brought to light by the gospel. This is apparently the preferable sense.

4. *According as he hath chosen us in him.* As He has decreed from "the beginning of the world," and has kept in view from the commencement of the religious system of the Jews (which the phrase sometimes means) to bring us Gentiles to the knowledge of the glorious state of salvation by Christ Jesus. The Jews considered themselves an elect or chosen people, and wished to monopolize the whole of the divine love and beneficence. The apostle here shows that God had the Gentiles as much in the contemplation of His mercy and goodness as He had the Jews; and the blessings of the gospel, now so freely dispensed to them, were the proof that God had thus chosen them, and that His end in giving them the gospel was the same which He had in view by giving the law to the

Jews, viz., that they might be holy and without blame before Him. And as His object was the same in respect to them both, they should consider that, as He loved them, so they should love one another. God having provided for each the same blessings, they should therefore be *holy*—fully separated from earth and sin, and consecrated to God; and *without blame*—having no spot nor imperfection, their inward holiness agreeing with their outward consecration. The words are a metaphor taken from the perfect and immaculate sacrifices which the law required the people to bring to the altar of God. But as *love* is the fulfilling of the law, and love the fountain whence their salvation flowed, therefore love must fill their hearts towards God and each other, and love must be the motive and end of all their words and works.

5. *Having predestinated us.* As the doctrine of eternal predestination has produced much controversy in the Christian world, it may be necessary to examine the meaning of the term, that those who do use it may employ it according to the sense it has in the oracles of God. The verb *proorizo*, from *pro,* "before," and *horizo,* "I define, finish, bound, or terminate," whence *horos,* "a boundary or limit," signifies to "define beforehand," and circumscribe by certain bounds or limits; and is originally a geographical term, but applied also to anything concluded, or determined, or demonstrated. Here the word is used to point out God's fixed purpose or predetermination to bestow on the Gentiles the blessing of the adoption of "sons" by Jesus Christ, which adoption had been before granted to the Jewish people; and without circumcision, or any other Mosaic rite, to admit the Gentiles to all the privileges of His Church and people. The apostle marks that all this was "foredetermined" by God, as He had foredetermined the bounds and precincts of the land which He gave them according to the promise made to their fathers; that the Jews had no reason to complain, for God had formed this purpose before He had given the law, or called them out of Egypt (for it was before the foundation of the world, v. 2); and that, therefore, the conduct of God in calling the Gentiles now—bringing them into His Church, and conferring on them the gifts and graces of the Holy Spirit—was in pursuance of His original design; and if He did not do so, His eternal purposes could not be fulfilled; and that, as the Jews were taken to be His peculiar people, not because they had any goodness or merit in themselves, so the Gentiles were called, not for any merit they had, but *according to the good pleasure of his will;* that is, according to His eternal benevolence, showing mercy and conferring privileges in this new creation, as He had done in the original creation.

6. *To the praise of the glory of his grace.* The glory of his grace, for "His glorious or illustrious grace," according to the Hebrew idiom. But the grace or mercy of God is peculiarly illustrated and glorified in the plan of redemption by Christ Jesus. By the giving of the law, God's justice and holiness were rendered most glorious; by the giving of the gospel, His grace and mercy are made equally conspicuous. *Wherein he hath made us accepted in the beloved.* This translation is not clear; "with which He has graciously favored us through the Be-loved" is at once more literal and more intelligible. *In the beloved* must certainly mean "in Christ," who is termed God's beloved Son, Matt. iii. 17.

7. *In whom we have redemption.* God has glorified His grace by giving us redemption by the blood of His Son, and this redemption consists in forgiving and delivering us from our sins; so then Christ's blood was the redemption price paid down for our salvation.

8. *Wherein he hath abounded.* That is, in the dispensation of mercy and goodness by Christ Jesus. *In all wisdom and prudence.* Giving us apostles the most complete instructions in heavenly things by the inspiration of His Spirit; and at the same time *prudence,* that we might know when and where to preach the gospel so that it might be effectual to the salvation of those who heard it. Nothing less than the Spirit of God could teach the apostles that *wisdom* by which they were to instruct a dark and sinful world; and nothing less than the same Spirit could inspire them with that *prudence* which was necessary to be exercised in every step of their life and ministry.

9. *Having made known unto us the mystery.* That the Gentiles should ever be received into the Church of God, and have all the privileges of the Jews, without being obliged to submit to circumcision and perform the rites and ceremonies of the Jewish law, was a *mystery*—a "hidden thing" which had never been published before; and now revealed only to the apostles. It was God's *will* that it should be so, but that will He kept hidden to the present time. A *mystery* signifies something hidden, but it ceases to be a mystery as soon as it is revealed. *Good pleasure.* "That benevolent design which He had purposed in himself," not being induced by any consideration from without.

10. *In the dispensation of the fulness of times.* The dispensation of the gospel, that plan by which God has provided salvation for a lost world; and according to which He intends to gather all believers, both Jews and Gentiles, into one Church under Jesus Christ, their Head and Governor. *The fulness of times*—By this phrase we are to understand either the gospel dispensation, which is the consummation of all preceding dispensations and the last that shall be afforded to man, or that advanced state of the world which God saw to be the most proper for the full manifestation of those benevolent purposes which He had formed in himself relative to the salvation of the world by Jesus Christ. *That he might gather together in one.* The gathering together both Jews and Gentiles, who have believed in Christ, into one Church and flock. *All things . . . which are in heaven, and which are on earth.* This clause is variously understood. Some think by *things . . . in heaven* the Jewish state is meant; and by *things . . . on earth,* the Christian. The Jews had been long considered a divine or heavenly people. But there are others who imagine the *things . . . in heaven* mean the angelical hosts; and the *things . . . on earth,* believers of all nations, who shall all be joined together at last in one assembly to worship God throughout eternity. And some think that the *things . . . in heaven* mean the saints who died before Christ's advent, and who are not to be made perfect till the resurrection.

And some think that, as the Hebrew phrase *shamayim vehaarets,* the "heavens and the earth," signifies all creatures, the words in the text are to be understood as signifying all mankind, without discrimination of peoples, kindreds, or tongues: Jews, Greeks, or barbarians —all that are saved of all nations (being saved in the same way, viz., by faith in Christ Jesus, without any distinction of nation or previous condition) and all gathered into one Church or assembly. I believe that the forming one Church out of both Jews and Gentiles is that to which the apostle refers. This agrees with what is said in chap. ii. 14-17.

11. *In whom,* Christ Jesus; *also we*—believing Jews; *have obtained an inheritance*—what was promised to Abraham and his spiritual seed, viz., the adoption of sons, and the kingdom of Heaven. *Being predestinated.* God having determined to bring both Jews and Gentiles to salvation, not by works nor by any human means or schemes, but by Jesus Christ; that salvation being defined and determined before in the divine mind, and the means by which it should be brought about all being according to His purpose, who consults not His creatures, but operates according to *the counsel of his own will,* that being ever wise, gracious, and good.

12. *That we.* Jews, now apostles and messengers of God, to whom the first offers of salvation were made, and who were the first that believed in Christ. *Should be to the praise of his glory.* By being the means of preaching Christ crucified to the Gentiles, and spreading the gospel throughout the world.

13. *In whom ye also trusted.* You Gentiles, having heard from us the *word,* the doctrine of the *truth,* which is *the gospel,* or glad tidings, *of your salvation,* have believed, as we Jews have done, and received similar blessings to those with which God has favored us. *In whom also,* Christ Jesus, *after that ye had believed,* viz., that He was the only Saviour, and that through His blood redemption might be obtained, *ye were sealed with that holy Spirit of promise.* It was customary among all nations, when a person purchased goods of any kind, to mark with his seal that which he had bought, in order that he might know it, and be able to claim it if mixed with the goods of others; to this custom the apostle may here allude. But it was also customary to set a seal upon what was dedicated to God, or what was to be offered to Him in sacrifice.

14. *Which is the earnest of our inheritance.* This Holy Spirit, sealing the soul with truth and righteousness, is the *earnest,* "foretaste," and "pledge" of the heavenly inheritance. And he who can produce this *earnest*—this witness of the Spirit—in the day of judgment shall have an abundant entrance into the holiest. *The redemption of the purchased possession.* That is, till the time when body and soul are redeemed from all their miseries and glorified in the kingdom of Heaven. *The redemption of the purchased possession.* All those who believe in Christ Jesus are considered as His peculiar people and property, and to them eternal glory is promised. The Spirit of promise, which is given them, is a pledge that they shall have a resurrection from the dead, and eternal blessedness; the *redemption,* or bringing to life of the body, cannot take place till the day of judgment, but

the Holy Spirit promises this redemption, and is now in their hearts an *earnest* or "pledge" of this complete restoration at the great day, which will then be, in an especial manner, *unto the praise of his glory,* viz., of Christ, who has bought them by His blood.

15. *Faith in the Lord Jesus.* Cordial reception of the Christian religion, amply proved by their *love unto all the saints*—to all the Christians. Perhaps *love* here implies not only the kind affection so called but also all the fruits of love —benevolence and kind offices of every description.

16. *Cease not to give thanks.* The apostle intimates, so fully satisfied was he of the genuineness of their conversion, and of their steadiness since their conversion, that it was to him a continual cause of thanksgiving to God, who had brought them into that state of salvation; and of prayer, that they might be preserved blameless to the end. *Making mention of you.* While praying for the prosperity of the Christian cause generally, he was led, from his particular affection for them, to mention them by name before God.

17. *That the God of our Lord Jesus.* Jesus Christ, as Man and Mediator, has the *Father* for His God and Father; and it is in reference to this that He himself says: "I ascend unto my Father, and your Father; and to my God, and your God," John xx. 17. *The Father of glory.* The Author and Giver of that glory which you expect at the end of your Christian race. This may be a Hebraism for "glorious Father," but the former appears to be the best sense. *The spirit of wisdom and revelation.* I pray that God may give you His Holy Spirit, by whom His will is revealed to men, that He may teach and make you wise unto salvation, that you may continue to acknowledge Him, Christ Jesus, as your only Lord and Saviour.

18. *The eyes of your understanding being enlightened.* Instead of *of your understanding,* "of your heart," is the reading of several MSS. "The eyes of your heart" is undoubtedly the true reading. *The hope of his calling.* That you may clearly discern the glorious and important objects of your *hope,* to the enjoyment of which God has called or invited you. *The riches of the glory of his inheritance.* That you may understand what is the glorious abundance of the spiritual things to which you are entitled, in consequence of being made children of God; for if children, then heirs, heirs of that glorious inheritance which God has provided for the saints—for all genuine Christians, whether formerly Jews or Gentiles.

19. *The exceeding greatness of his power.* As the apostle is here speaking of the glorious state of believers after death, *the exceeding greatness of his power,* or that power which surpasses all difficulties, being itself omnipotent, is to be understood of that might which is to be exerted in raising the body at the last day; as it will require the same power or energy which He wrought in Christ, when He raised His body from the grave, to raise up the bodies of all mankind, the resurrection of the human nature of Christ being a proof of the resurrection of mankind in general. *According to the working of his mighty power.* "According to the energy of the power of His might." We may understand these words thus: "might" is the

state or simple efficiency of this attribute in God; "power" is this might or efficiency in action; "energy" is the quantum of force, momentum, or velocity with which the power is applied. Though they appear to be synonymous terms they may be thus understood. Passive power is widely different from power in action; and power in action will be in its results according to the energy or momentum with which it is applied.

20. *Set him at his own right hand in the heavenly places.* Gave Him, as Mediator between God and man, the highest honors and dignities, Phil. ii. 9; in which state of exaltation He transacts all the affairs of His Church and rules the universe. The *right hand* is the place of friendship, honor, confidence, and authority.

21. *Far above all principality.* Some think he has reference here to the different orders among good and evil angels; He is superior to all the former, and rules all the latter. Others think he refers to earthly governments; and as *principality*, the first word, signifies the most sovereign and extensive kind of dominion; and "lordship," the last word, signifies the lowest degree of authority; hence we are to understand that to our Lord, in His human nature, are subjected the highest, the intermediate, and the lowest orders of beings in the universe. It is certain that the apostle means that all created power, glory, and influence are under Christ; and hence it is added:

22. *And hath put all things under his feet.* All beings and things are subject to Him, whether they be thrones, dominions, principalities, or powers, Col. i. 16-18 and ii. 10; for He, God the Father, has given *him to be head*—chief, and supreme over all, *to the church*, the Church having no ruler but Jesus Christ. Others may be officers in His Church, but He alone is Head and supreme.

23. *Which is his body.* As he is "head over all things," he is Head to the Church; and this Church is considered as the body of which He is especially the Head; and from Him, as the Head, the Church receives light, life, and intelligence. And is *the fulness of him.* That in which He especially manifests His power, goodness, and truth; for though He fills all the world with His presence, yet He fills all the members of His mystical body with wisdom, goodness, truth, and holiness in an especial manner. Some understand the *fulness* here as signifying the "thing to be filled"; so the Christian Church is to be filled by Him, whose fullness fills all His members, with all spiritual gifts and graces. And this corresponds with what John says, chap. i. 16: "And of his fulness have all we received, and grace for grace." And with what is said in Col. ii. 9-10: "Ye are complete in him"; "And ye are in Him filled full"; i.e., with gifts and grace. How, in any other sense, the Church can be said to be the fullness of Him who fills all in all is difficult to say. However, as Jesus Christ is represented to be the Head, and the Church the body under that Head, the individuals being so many members in that body, and as it requires a body and members to make a head complete, so it requires a Church, or general assembly of believers, to make up the body of Christ. When therefore the Jews and Gentiles are brought into this Church, the body may be said to be complete; and thus Christ

has His visible fullness upon earth, and the Church may be said to be the fullness of Him.

CHAPTER 2

The character of the Ephesians previously to their conversion to Christianity, 1-3. By what virtue they were changed, and for what purpose, 4-7. They were saved by faith, 8-9. And created unto good works, 10. The apostle enters into the particulars of their former miserable state, 11-12. And those of their present happy state, 13. Christ has broken down the middle wall of partition between the Jews and Gentiles, and proclaims reconciliation to both, 14-17. The glorious privileges of genuine believers, 18-22.

1. *And you hath he quickened.* This chapter should not have been separated from the preceding, with which it is most intimately connected. As Christ fills the whole body of Christian believers with His fullness (chap. i. 23), so had He dealt with the converted Ephesians, who before *were dead in trespasses and dead in sins.* Death is often used by all writers, and in all nations, to express a state of extreme misery. *Trespasses* may signify the slightest deviation from the line and rule of moral equity, as well as any flagrant offense; for these are equally transgressions, as long as the sacred line that separates between vice and virtue is passed over. *Sins* may probably mean here habitual transgression, sinning knowingly and daringly.

2. *Wherein in time past ye walked.* There is much force in these expressions. The Ephesians had not sinned casually, or now and then, but continually; they *walked* in trespasses and sins. And this was not a solitary case; all the nations of the earth acted in the same way. It was the *course of this world*, "according to the life," mode of living, or successive ages of this world. The word *aion*, the literal meaning of which is "constant duration," is often applied to things which have a complete course, as the Jewish dispensation, a particular government, and the "term of human life"; so, here, the whole of life is a tissue of sin, from the cradle to the grave; every human soul, unsaved by Jesus Christ, continues to transgress. *The prince of the power of the air.* As the former clause may have particular respect to the Jewish people, who are frequently denominated "this world," this latter clause may especially refer to the Gentiles, who were most manifestly under the power of the devil, as almost every object of their worship was a demon, to whom the worst of passions and practices were attributed, and whose conduct his votaries took care to copy. Satan is termed *prince of the power of the air*, because the air is supposed to be a region in which malicious spirits dwell, all of whom are under the direction and influence of Satan, their chief. *Children of disobedience.* Perhaps a Hebraism for "disobedient children"; but, taken as it stands here, it is a strong expression in which *disobedience* appears to be personified, and wicked men exhibited as her children; the *prince of the power of the air* being their father, while disobedience is their mother.

3. *Among whom also we all had our conversation.* We Jews, as well as you Gentiles, have lived in transgressions and sins; this was the "course of our life." The *lusts*—the evil, irregular, and corrupt affections of the heart, showed themselves in the perversion of the *mind* as well as in our general conduct. The *mind* was

darkened by the lusts of the flesh, and both conjoined to produce acts of unrighteousness.

4. *But God, who is rich in mercy.* As they were corrupt in their nature, and sinful in their practice, they could possess no merit, nor have any claim upon God; and it required much mercy to remove so much misery and to pardon such transgressions. *His great love.* God's infinite love is the groundwork of our salvation; in reference to us that love assumes the form of mercy, and that mercy provides the Saviour, the Lord Jesus Christ. And therefore the apostle adds, v. 5: "By grace ye are saved"—it is by God's free mercy in Christ that you are brought into this state of salvation.

5. *Even when we were dead in sins.* Dead in our souls; dead towards God; dead in law; and exposed to death eternal. *Hath quickened us together with Christ.* God has given us as complete a resurrection from the death of sin to a life of righteousness as the body of Christ has had from the grave. And as this quickening, or making alive, was most gratuitous on God's part, the apostle, with great propriety, says: *By grace ye are saved.*

6. *And hath raised us up together . . . in Christ.* Or rather, "by Christ"; His resurrection being the proof that He had made the full atonement, and that we might be justified by His blood. Believing therefore the record which God gave of His Son, we received this atonement, and were raised from a death of sin to a life of righteousness; and now we sit in heavenly places—we have a right to the kingdom of God, anticipate this glory, and are indescribably happy in the possession of this salvation, and in our fellowship with Christ Jesus.

8. *For by grace are ye saved through faith.* As you are now brought into a state of salvation, your sins being all blotted out, and you made partakers of the Holy Spirit; and, having a hope full of immortality, you must not attribute this to any works or merit of yours; for when this gospel reached you, you were all found "dead in trespasses and sins." Therefore it was God's free mercy to you, manifested through Christ, in whom you were commanded to believe; and having believed by the power of the Holy Spirit, you received, and were sealed by, the Holy Spirit of promise; so that this salvation is in no sense *of yourselves,* but is the "free gift" of God and not of any kind of *works;* so that no man can *boast* as having wrought out his own salvation, or even contributed anything towards it. *By grace are ye saved through faith* in Christ. This is a true doctrine, and continues to be essential to the salvation of man to the end of the world. But whether are we to understand, faith or salvation, as being the *gift of God?* This question is answered by the Greek text: "By this grace ye are saved through faith; and this [*touto,* this salvation] not of you; it is the gift of God, not of works: so that no one can boast." "The relative *touto,* 'this,' which is in the neuter gender, cannot stand for *faith,* which is the feminine; but it has the whole sentence that goes before for its antecedent." But it may be asked: Is not faith the gift of God? Yes, as to the grace by which it is produced; but the grace or power to believe, and the act of believing, are two different things. Without the grace or power to

believe no man ever did or can believe; but with that power the act of faith is a man's own. God never believes for any man any more than He repents for him; the penitent, through this grace enabling him, believes for himself. Nor does he believe necessarily or impulsively when he has that power; the power to believe may be present long before it is exercised, else why the solemn warnings with which we meet everywhere in the Word of God, and threatenings against those who do not believe? Is not this a proof that such persons have the power but do not use it?

10. *For we are his workmanship.* So far is this salvation from being our own work, or granted for our own works' sake, that we are ourselves not only the creatures of God, but our new creation was produced by His power; for we are *created in Christ Jesus unto good works.* He has saved us that we may show forth the virtues of Him who called us from darkness into His marvellous light. For though we are not saved for our good works, yet we are saved that we may perform good works, to the glory of God and the benefit of man. *Which God hath before ordained.* "For which God before prepared us, that we might walk in them." For being saved from sin, we are made partakers of the Spirit of holiness; and it is natural to that Spirit to lead to the practice of holiness; and he who is not holy in his life is not saved by the grace of Christ. The before ordaining, or rather before preparing, must refer to the time when God began the new creation in their hearts; for from the first inspiration of God upon the soul it begins to love holiness, and obedience to the will of God is the very element in which a holy or regenerated soul lives.

11. *Wherefore remember.* That you may ever see and feel your obligations to live a pure and holy life, and be unfeignedly thankful to God for your salvation, remember that you were once heathens, in the flesh—without the pure doctrine, and under the influence of your corrupt nature; such as by the Jews (who gloried, in consequence of their *circumcision,* to be in covenant with God) were *called Uncircumcision;* i.e., persons out of the divine covenant, and having no right or title to any blessing of God.

12. *That at that time ye were without Christ.* Not only were not Christians, but had no knowledge of the Christ or Messiah, and no title to the blessings which were to proceed from Him. *Aliens from the commonwealth of Israel.* You were by your birth, idolatry, etc., alienated from the commonwealth of Israel—from the civil and religious privileges of the Jewish people. *Strangers from the covenants of promise.* Having no part in the promise of the covenant made with Abraham, whether considered as relating to his natural or spiritual seed. *Having no hope.* Either of the pardon of sin or of the resurrection of the body, nor indeed of the immortality of the soul. Of all these things the Gentiles had no rational or well-grounded hope. *Without God in the world.* They had gods many and lords many, but in no Gentile nation was the true God known: nor indeed had they any correct notion of the divine nature. He who has neither *God* nor *Christ* is in a most deplorable state; he has neither a God to worship nor a Christ to justify him. And this is the state of every man who is living without the grace and

Spirit of Christ. All such, whatever they may profess, are no better than practical atheists.

13. *Ye who sometimes were far off.* To be *far off* and to be near are sayings much in use among the Jews. (1) Among them, to be near signifies to be in the approbation or favor of God, and to be *far off* signifies to be under His displeasure. A holy man, or a genuine penitent, might be said to be nigh to God, because such persons are in His favor. (2) Every person who offered a sacrifice to God was considered as having access to Him by the blood of that sacrifice. Hence the priests, whose office it was to offer sacrifices, were considered as being nigh to God; and all who brought gifts to the altar were considered as approaching the Almighty. (3) Being *far off* signified the state of the Gentiles as contradistinguished from the Jews, who were nigh. You Gentiles, who were unacquainted with God, and were even without God in the world, are brought to an acquaintance with Him; and are now, through Christ Jesus, brought into the favor and fellowship of God.

14. *For he is our peace.* Jesus Christ has died for both Jews and Gentiles, and has become a "Peace Offering," to reconcile both to God and to each other. *Who hath made both one.* Formed one Church out of the believers of both people. *The middle wall of partition.* By abolishing the law of Jewish ordinances, He has removed that which kept the two parties not only in a state of separation but also at variance. This expression, *the middle wall,* can refer only to that most marked distinction which the Jewish laws and customs made between them and all other nations whatsoever.

15. *Having abolished in his flesh.* By His incarnation and death He not only made an atonement for sin, but He appointed the doctrine of reconciliation to God and of love to each other, to be preached in all nations. The *enmity* of which the apostle speaks was reciprocal among the Jews and Gentiles. The former detested the Gentiles and could hardly allow them the denomination of men; the latter had the Jews in contempt because of the peculiarity of their religious rites and ceremonies, which were different from those of all the other nations of the earth. *The law of commandments.* Contained in, or rather "concerning," *ordinances;* which law was made merely for the purpose of keeping the Jews a distinct people, and pointing out the Son of God till He should come. *To make in himself.* To make one Church out of both people, which should be considered the body of which Jesus Christ is the Head. Thus He makes *one new man*—one new Church; and thus He makes and establishes *peace.* I think the apostle still alludes to the "peace offering" among the Jews. They have a saying, *Sephra,* fol. 121: "Whosoever offers a peace offering sacrifice, brings peace to the world." Such a peace offering was the death of Christ, and by it peace is restored to the earth.

16. *That he might reconcile both unto God in one body.* That the Jews and Gentiles, believing on the Lord Jesus, might lay aside all their causes of contention and become one spiritual body, or society of men, influenced by the Spirit, and acting according to the precept of the gospel. *Having slain the enmity thereby.* Having by His death upon the Cross made reconciliation between God and man, and by His Spirit in their hearts removed the enmity of their fallen, sinful nature.

17. *And came and preached peace.* Proclaimed the readiness of God to forgive and save both Jews and Gentiles.

18. *For through him,* Christ Jesus, *we both* —Jews and Gentiles—*have access by one Spirit,* through the influence of the Holy Ghost, *unto the Father*—God Almighty. This text is a plain proof of the Holy Trinity. No soul can have access to God but by Jesus Christ, and He introduces none but such as receive His Holy Spirit.

19. *Ye are no more strangers.* In this chapter the Church of God is compared to a city which has a variety of privileges, rights, etc., founded on regular charters and grants. The Gentiles, having believed in Christ, are all incorporated with the believing Jews in this holy city. Formerly, when any of them came to Jerusalem, being *strangers,* they had no rights whatever; nor could they, as mere heathens, settle among them. Again, if any of them, convinced of the errors of the Gentiles, acknowledged the God of Israel but did not receive circumcision, he might dwell in the land, but he had no right to the blessings of the covenant. Such might be called "sojourners"—persons who have no property in the land, and may only rent a house for the time being. *Fellowcitizens with the saints.* Called to the enjoyment of equal privileges with the Jews themselves, who, by profession, were a holy people; who were bound to be holy, and therefore are often called *saints,* or "holy persons," when both their hearts and conduct were far from being right in the sight of God. But the *saints* spoken of here are the converted or Christianized Jews. *Of the household of God.* The house of God is the "temple"; the Temple was a type of the Christian Church. This is now become God's house; all genuine believers are considered as being domestics of this house, the children and servants of God Almighty, having all equal rights, privileges, and advantages.

20. *And are built upon the foundation.* Following the same metaphor, comparing the Church of Christ to a city, and to the Temple, the believing Ephesians are represented as parts of that building; the living stones out of which it is principally formed, 1 Pet. ii. 4-5, having for *foundation*—the ground plan, specification, and principle on which it was builded—the doctrine taught by the *prophets* in the Old Testament and the *apostles* in the New; Jesus Christ being that *corner stone,* the chief angle or foundation Cornerstone, the connecting Medium by which both Jews and Gentiles were united in the same building.

21. *In whom.* By which foundation Cornerstone, Christ Jesus, *all the building,* composed of converted Jews and Gentiles, *fitly framed together,* "properly jointed and connected together," *groweth unto an holy temple*—is continually increasing as new converts from Judaism or heathenism flock into it. It is not a finished building, but will continue to increase and be more and more perfect till the day of judgment.

22. *In whom ye also are builded.* The apostle now applies the metaphor to the purpose for which he produced it, retaining however some

of the figurative expressions. As the stones in a temple are all properly placed so as to form a complete house and be a habitation for the deity that is worshipped there, so you are all, both believing Jews and Gentiles, prepared by the doctrine of the prophets and apostles, under the influence of the Spirit of Christ, to become a habitation of God, a Church in which God shall be worthily worshipped, and in which He can continually dwell.

CHAPTER 3

Paul, a prisoner for the testimony of Jesus, declares his knowledge of what had been a mystery from all ages, that the Gentiles should be fellow heirs and of the same body with the Jews, 1-6. Of which doctrine he was made a minister, that he might declare the unsearchable riches of Christ, and make known to principalities and powers this eternal purpose of God, 7-12. He desires them not to be discouraged on account of his tribulations, 13. His prayer that they might be filled with all the fullness of God, 14-19. His doxology, 20-21.

1. *For this cause.* Because he maintained that the Gentiles were admitted to all the privileges of the Jews and all the blessings of the new covenant, without being obliged to submit to circumcision, the Jews persecuted him and caused him to be imprisoned, first at Caesarea, where he was obliged to appeal to the Roman emperor, in consequence of which he was sent prisoner to Rome. *The prisoner of Jesus Christ for you Gentiles.* For preaching the gospel to the Gentiles, and showing that they were not bound by the law of Moses, and yet were called to be fellow citizens with the saints; for this very cause the Jews persecuted him unto bonds, and conspired his death.

2. *If ye have heard of the dispensation.* The compound particle which is commonly translated "if indeed," in several places means "since indeed, seeing that," and should be translated so in this verse, and in several other places of the New Testament. "Seeing ye have heard of the dispensation of God, *which is given me to you-ward.*" By the *dispensation of the grace of God* we may understand either the apostolic office and gifts granted to Paul for the purpose of preaching the gospel among the Gentiles (see Rom. i. 5) or the knowledge which God gave him of that gracious and divine plan which He had formed for the conversion of the Gentiles.

3. *By revelation he made known unto me.* Instead of *he made known,* "was made known" is the reading of many MSS. It is doubtless the true reading. The apostle wishes the Ephesians to understand that it was not an opinion of his own, or a doctrine which he was taught by others, or which he had gathered from the ancient prophets; but one that came to him by immediate revelation from God, as he had informed them before *in few words,* referring to what he had said in chap. i. 9-12.

4. *Whereby, when ye read.* When you refer back to them. *Ye may understand my knowledge.* You may see what God has given me to know concerning what has been hitherto a *mystery*—the calling of the Gentiles and the breaking down of the middle wall between them and the Jews, so as to make both one spiritual body, and on the same conditions.

5. *Which in other ages was not made known.* That the calling of the Gentiles was made known by the prophets in different ages of the Jewish church is exceedingly clear; but it certainly was not made known in that clear and precise manner in which it was now revealed by the Spirit unto the ministers of the New Testament. Nor was it made known unto them at all that the Gentiles should find salvation without coming under the yoke of the Mosaic law, and that the Jews themselves should be freed from that yoke of bondage; these were discoveries totally new, and now revealed for the first time by the Spirit of God.

6. *That the Gentiles should be fellowheirs.* This is the substance of that mystery which had been hidden from all ages, and which was now made known to the New Testament apostles and prophets, and more particularly to Paul. *His promise in Christ.* That the promise made to Abraham extended to the Gentiles, the apostle has largely proved in his Epistle to the Romans; and that it was to be fulfilled to them by and through Christ, he proves there also; and particularly in his Epistle to the Galatians—see Gal. iii. 14. And that these blessings were to be announced in the preaching of the gospel, and received on believing it, he everywhere declares, but more especially in this Epistle.

7. *Whereof I was made a minister.* A "deacon," a "servant" acting under and by the direction of the great Master, Jesus Christ; from whom, by an especial call and revelation, I received the apostolic gifts and office, and by the "energy," the "in-working of His power," this gospel which I preached was made effectual to the salvation of vast multitudes of Jews and Gentiles.

8. *Less than the least of all saints.* As the design of the apostle was to magnify the grace of Christ in the salvation of the world, he uses every precaution to prevent the eyes of the people from being turned to anything but Christ crucified. And although he was obliged to speak of himself as the particular instrument which God had chosen to bring the Gentile world to the knowledge of the truth, yet he does it in such a manner as to show that the excellency of the power was of God and not of him. To lay himself as low as possible, consistently with his being in the number of divinely commissioned men, he calls himself *less than the least;* and is obliged to make a new word, by strangely forming a comparative degree, not from the positive, which would have been a regular grammatical procedure, but from the superlative. The adjective signifies "little," or *less,* and *least.* On the superlative of "little," Paul forms his comparative, *less than the least,* a word of which it would be vain to attempt a better translation than that given in our own version. It most strongly marks the unparalleled humility of the apostle; and the amazing condescension of God, in favoring him, who had been before a persecutor and blasphemer, with the knowledge of this glorious scheme of human redemption, and the power to preach it so successfully among the Gentiles. *The unsearchable riches of Christ.* The word from *a,* privative, and "to trace out," from *ichnos,* a "step," is exceedingly well-chosen here. It refers to the footsteps of God, the plans He had formed, the dispensations which He had published, and the innumerable providences which He had combined to prepare, mature, and bring to full effect and view His gracious designs in the salvation of a ruined world, by the incarna-

tion, passion, death, and resurrection of His Son. There were in these schemes and providences such *riches*—such an abundance, such a variety, as could not be comprehended even by the naturally vast and, through the divine inspiration, unparalleledly capacious mind of the apostle.

9. *And to make all men see.* "And to illuminate all"; to give information to both Jews and Gentiles; to afford them a sufficiency of light, so that they might be able distinctly to discern the great objects exhibited in this gospel. *What is the fellowship of the mystery.* The word *koinonia,* which we properly translate *fellowship,* was used among the Greeks to signify their religious communities. Here it may intimate the association of Jews and Gentiles in one Church or body, and their agreement in that glorious mystery which was now so fully opened relative to the salvation of both. But instead of *koinonia,* "fellowship," *oikonomia,* "dispensation" or "economy," is the reading of most MSS. Some of the best printed editions of the Greek text have the same reading, and that in our common text has very little authority to support it. "Dispensation" or "economy" is far more congenial to the scope of the apostle's declaration in this place; he wished to show them the economy of that mystery of bringing Jews and Gentiles to salvation by faith in Christ Jesus which God from the beginning of the world had kept hidden in His own infinite mind, and did not think proper to reveal even when He projected the creation of the world, which had respect to the economy of human redemption. *Who created all things by Jesus Christ.* Some very judicious critics are of opinion that this does not refer to the material creation; and that we should understand the whole as referring to the formation of all God's dispensations of grace, mercy, and truth, which have been planned, managed, and executed by Christ, from the foundation of the world to the present time. But the words *by Jesus Christ* are wanting in several MSS. The text therefore should be read: "which from the beginning of the world had been hidden in God who created all things."

10. *That now unto the principalities and powers in heavenly places.* Who are these *principalities and powers?* Some think evil angels are intended, because they are thus denominated, chap. vi. 12. Others think good angels are meant; for as these heavenly beings are curious to investigate the wondrous economy of the gospel, though they are not its immediate objects (see 1 Pet. i. 12), it is quite consistent with the goodness of God to give them that satisfaction which they require. And in this discovery of the gospel plan of salvation, which reconciles things in heaven and things on earth, both men and angels, these pure spirits are greatly interested, and their praises to the Divine Being rendered much more abundant. Others imagine the Jewish rulers and rabbins are intended, particularly those of them who were converted to Christianity, and who had now learned from the preaching of the gospel what, as Jews, they could never have known. *By the church.* That is, by the Christians, and by the wonderful things done in the Church; and by the apostles, who were its pastors. *The manifold wisdom of God.* "That multifarious and greatly diversified wisdom of God"; laying great and infinite plans,

and accomplishing them by endless means, through the whole lapse of ages; making every occurrence subservient to the purposes of His infinite mercy and goodness. God's gracious design to save a lost world by Jesus Christ could not be defeated by any cunning skill or malice of man or devils. Whatever hindrances are thrown in the way, His wisdom and power can remove; and His infinite wisdom can never want ways or means to effect its gracious designs.

11. *According to the eternal purpose.* "According to the purpose concerning the periods." This seems to refer to the complete round of the Jewish system, and to that of the gospel. I have often observed that, though the proper grammatical meaning of the word is "everduring," or "endless duration," yet it is often applied to those systems, periods, and governments which have a complete duration, taking in the whole of them, from their commencement to their termination, leaving nothing of their duration unembraced. So, here, God purposed that the Jewish dispensation should commence at such a time and terminate at such a time; that the gospel dispensation should commence when the Jewish ended, and terminate only with life itself; and that the results of both should be endless. This is probably what is meant by the above phrase. *Which he purposed in Christ Jesus.* "Which He made or constituted in or for Christ Jesus." The manifestation of Christ and the glory which should follow were the grand objects which God kept in view in all His dispensations.

12. *In whom we have boldness.* "By whom we Gentiles have this liberty of speech," so that we may say anything by prayer and supplication, and this "introduction" into the divine presence by faith in Christ. It is only in His name we can pray to God, and it is only by Him that we can come to God; none can give us an "introduction" but Christ Jesus, and it is only for His sake that God will either hear or save us. It is on the ground of such scriptures as these that we conclude all our prayers in the name, and for the sake, of Jesus Christ, our Lord.

13. *I desire that ye faint not.* In those primitive times, when there was much persecution, people were in continual danger of falling away from the faith who were not well-grounded in it. This the apostle deprecates, and advances a strong reason why they should be firm.

14. *For this cause I bow my knees.* That you may not faint, but persevere, I frequently pray to God, who is our God and the Father of our Lord Jesus. Some very ancient and excellent MSS. and versions omit the words *of our Lord Jesus Christ.* And in them the passage reads: "I bow my knees unto the Father." Many parts of this prayer bear a strict resemblance to that offered up by Solomon when dedicating the Temple: "He . . . kneeled down upon his knees before all the congregation of Israel, and spread forth his hands towards heaven," 2 Chron. vi. 13. The apostle was now dedicating the Christian Church, that then was and that ever should be to God; and praying for those blessings which should ever rest on and distinguish it; and he kneels down after the example of Solomon, and invokes Him to whom the first Temple was

dedicated, and who had made it a type of the gospel Church.

15. *Of whom the whole family.* Believers in the Lord Jesus Christ on earth, the spirits of just men made perfect in a separate state, and all the holy angels in heaven make but one family, of which God is the Father and Head. Paul does not say, Of whom the "families," as if each order formed a distinct household; but he says *family,* because they are all one, and of One. And all this family *is named,* derives its origin and being, from God, as children derive their name from him who is the father of the family; holy persons in heaven and earth derive their being and their holiness from God, and therefore His name is called upon them.

16. *That he would grant you.* This prayer of the apostle is one of the most grand and sublime in the whole oracles of God. The riches of the grace of the gospel and the extent to which the soul of man may be saved here below are most emphatically pointed out here. Every word seems to have come immediately from heaven, laboring to convey ideas of infinite importance to mankind. No paraphrase can do it justice, and few commentators seem to have entered into its spirit, perhaps deterred by its unparalleled sublimity. *That he would grant you.* You can expect nothing from Him but as a free gift through Christ Jesus; let this be a ruling sentiment of your hearts when you pray to God. *According to the riches of his glory.* According to the measure of His own eternal fullness, God's infinite mercy and goodness being the measure according to which we are to be saved. In giving alms it is a maxim that everyone should act according to his ability. It would be a disgrace to a king or a nobleman to give no more than a tradesman or a peasant. God acts up to the dignity of His infinite perfections; He gives *according to the riches of his glory.* *To be strengthened with might.* You have many enemies, cunning and strong; many trials, too great for your natural strength; many temptations, which no human power is able successfully to resist; many duties to perform, which cannot be accomplished by the strength of man. Therefore you need divine strength; you must have might; and you must be strengthened everywhere, and every way fortified by that might, mightily and most effectually strengthened. *By his Spirit.* By the sovereign energy of the Holy Ghost. This Fountain of spiritual energy can alone supply the spiritual strength which is necessary for this spiritual work and conflict. *In the inner man.* In the soul. Every man is a compound being; he has a body and a soul. The outward man is that alone which is seen and considered by men; the inward man is that which stands particularly in reference to God and eternity. The outward man is strengthened by earthly food; the inward man, by spiritual and heavenly influences. The soul must be as truly fed and nourished by divine food as the body by natural food.

17. *That Christ may dwell in your hearts by faith.* In this as well as in many other passages, and particularly that in chap. ii. 21, the apostle compares the body or Church of true believers to a temple, which, like that of Solomon, is built to be a habitation of God through the Spirit. And as there could be no indwelling of God but by *Christ,* and no indwelling of Christ

but by *faith,* he prays that they may have such faith in Christ as shall keep them in constant possession of His love and presence. This is what the apostle points out to the believing Ephesians, in praying that Christ might "intensely and constantly dwell in their hearts by faith." *That ye, being rooted and grounded in love.* Here is a double metaphor; one taken from agriculture, the other from architecture. As trees, they are to be *rooted . . . in love*— this is the soil in which their souls are to grow; into the infinite love of God their souls by faith are to strike their roots, and from this love derive all that nourishment which is essential for their full growth, till they have the mind in them that was in Jesus, or, as it is afterwards said, till they are "filled with all the fulness of God." As a building, their foundation is to be laid in this love. "God so loved the world, that he gave his only begotten Son." Here is the ground on which alone the soul, and all its hopes and expectations, can be safely founded. This is a foundation that cannot be shaken; and it is from this alone that the doctrine of redemption flows to man, and from this alone has the soul its form and comeliness. *In* this, as its proper soil, it grows. *On* this, as its only foundation, it rests.

18. *May be able to comprehend with all saints.* These words are so exceedingly full of meaning that it is almost impossible to translate them. The first word, from *ex,* intensive, and *ischyo,* "to be strong," signifies that they might be "thoroughly able," by having been "strengthened with might," by God's power. The second word, from *kata,* intensive, and *lambano,* to "take, catch, or seize on," may be translated, "that you may fully catch, take in, and comprehend" this wonderful mystery of God. The mind must be rendered apt, and the soul invigorated, to take in and *comprehend* these mysteries. *What is the breadth, and length, and depth, and height.* Here the apostle still keeps up the metaphor, comparing the Church of God to a building; and as, in order to rear a proper building, a ground plan and specification must be previously made, according to which the building is to be constructed, the apostle refers to this. They were to be builded up a heavenly house, "an habitation of God through the Spirit"; and this must have its *breadth,* its *length,* its *height,* and its *depth.* But what can the apostle mean by the *breadth, length, depth,* and *height,* of the love of God? Imagination can scarcely frame any satisfactory answer to this question. It takes in the eternity of God. "God is *love";* and in that, an infinity of *breadth, length, depth,* and *height* is included; or rather all *breadth, length, depth,* and *height* are lost in this immensity. It comprehends all that is above, all that is below, all that is past, and all that is to come. In reference to human beings, the love of God, in its *breadth,* is a girdle that encompasses the globe; its *length* reaches from the eternal purpose of the mission of Christ to the eternity of blessedness which is to be spent in His ineffable glories; its *depth* reaches to the lowest fallen of the sons of Adam, and to the deepest depravity of the human heart; and its *height,* to the infinite dignities of the throne of Christ. "He that overcometh will I give to sit down with Me upon My throne, as I have overcome and sat down with the Father upon His throne." Thus we see that the Father, the

Son, and all true believers in Him are to be seated on the same throne! This is the *height* of the love of God, and the height to which that love raises the souls that believe in Christ Jesus!

19. *To know the love of Christ, which passeth knowledge.* It is only by the *love of Christ* that we can know the love of God. The love of God to man induced Him to give Christ for his redemption; Christ's love to man induced Him to give His life's blood for his salvation. The gift of Christ to man is the measure of God's love; the death of Christ for man is the measure of Christ's love. "God so loved the world." "Christ loved us, and gave himself for us." But how can *the love of Christ, which passeth knowledge,* be known? Many have labored to reconcile this seeming contradiction. If we take the verb in a sense in which it is frequently used in the New Testament, "to approve, acknowledge, or acknowledge with approbation," and *gnosis* to signify "comprehension," then the difficulty will be partly removed: "That you may acknowledge, approve, and publicly acknowledge that love of God which surpasseth knowledge." We can acknowledge and approve of that which surpasses our comprehension. We cannot comprehend God; yet we can know that He is; approve of, love, adore, and serve Him. In like manner, though we cannot comprehend the immensity of the love of Christ, yet we know that He has loved us, and washed us from our sins in His own blood; and we approve of, and acknowledge, Him as our only Lord and Saviour. In this sense we may be said to *know* the love of Christ that *passeth knowledge.* But it is more likely that the word *gnosis,* which we translate *knowledge,* signifies here science in general, and particularly that science of which the rabbins boasted, and that in which the Greeks greatly exulted. The former professed to have the key of knowledge, the secret of all divine mysteries; the latter considered their philosophers and their systems of philosophy superior to everything that had ever been known among men, and on this account reputed all other nations as barbarians. When the apostle prays that they may *know the love of Christ, which passeth knowledge,* he may refer to all the boasted knowledge of the Jewish doctors, and to all the greatly extolled science of the Greek philosophers. To know the love of Christ infinitely surpasses all other science. This gives a clear and satisfactory sense. *That ye might be filled with all the fulness of God.* Among all the great sayings in this prayer, this is the greatest. To be filled with God is a great thing; to be filled with the fullness of God is still greater; but to be *filled with all the fulness of God* utterly bewilders the sense and confounds the understanding. By the *fulness of God* we are to understand all those gifts and graces which He has promised to bestow on man, and which He dispenses to the Church. To be *filled with all the fulness of God* is to have the whole soul filled with meekness, gentleness, goodness, love, justice, holiness, mercy, and truth. And as what God fills neither sin nor Satan can fill, consequently it implies that the soul shall be emptied of sin, that sin shall neither have dominion over it nor a being in it.

20. *Now unto him.* Having finished his short but most wonderfully comprehensive and ener-getic prayer, the apostle brings in his doxology, giving praise to Him from whom all blessings come, and to whom all thanks are due. *That is able to do exceeding abundantly.* It is impossible to express the full meaning of these words. God is omnipotent; therefore He is able to do all things, and able to do "superabundantly above the greatest abundance." And who can doubt this who has any rational or scriptural views of His power or His love? *According to the power that worketh in us.* All that He can do and all that He has promised to do will be done *according* to what He has done, by that *power* of the Holy Ghost "which worketh strongly in us"—acts with "energy" in our hearts, expelling evil, purifying and refining the affections and desires, and implanting good.

21. *Unto him,* thus possessed of power and goodness, *be glory in the church*—be unceasing praises ascribed in all the assemblies of the people of God, wherever these glad tidings are preached, and wherever this glorious doctrine shall be credited. *By Christ Jesus.* Through whom, and for whom, all these miracles of mercy and power are wrought. *Throughout all ages.* "Through all succeeding generations"— while the race of human beings continues to exist on the face of the earth. *World without end.* "Throughout eternity"—in the coming world as well as in this. The song of praise, begun upon earth and protracted through all the generations of men, shall be continued in heaven by all that are redeemed from the earth, where eras, limits, and periods are no more forever. *Amen.* So be it! So let it be! And so it will be, for all the counsels of God are faithfulness and truth; and not one jot or tittle of His promise has failed, from the foundation of the world to the present day; nor can fail, till mortality is swallowed up of life. Therefore to the Father, Son, and Holy Ghost be glory, dominion, power, and thanksgiving, now, henceforth, and forever. Amen and Amen.

CHAPTER 4

The apostle exhorts them to walk worthy of their vocation, and to live in peace and unity, 1-6. Shows that God has distributed a variety of gifts, and instituted a variety of offices in His Church, for the building up and perfecting of the body of Christ, 7-13. Teaches them the necessity of being well-instructed and steady in divine things, 14. Teaches how the body or Church of Christ is constituted, 15-16. Warns them against acting like the Gentiles, of whose conduct he gives a lamentable description, 17-19. Points out how they had been changed, in consequence of their conversion to Christianity, 20-21. Gives various exhortations relative to the purification of their minds, their conduct to each other, and to the poor, 22-28. Shows them that their conversation should be chaste and holy, that they might not grieve the Spirit of God; that they should avoid all bad tempers, be kindly affectioned one to another, and be of a forgiving spirit, 29-32.

1. *I therefore.* Therefore, because God has provided for you such an abundant salvation, and you have His testimonies among you, and have full liberty to use all the means of grace. *The prisoner of the Lord.* Who am deprived of my liberty for the Lord's sake. *Beseech you that ye walk.* You have your liberty, and may *walk;* I am deprived of mine, and cannot. This is a fine stroke, and wrought up into a strong argument. You who are at large can show forth the virtues of Him who called you into His marvellous light; I am in bondage, and can only exhort others by my writing, and show

my submission to God by my patient suffering. *The vocation wherewith ye are called.* The "calling" is the free invitation they have had from God to receive the privileges of the gospel, and become His sons and daughters, without being obliged to observe Jewish rites and ceremonies. Their vocation, or calling, took in their Christian profession, with all the doctrines, precepts, privileges, duties, etc., of the Christian religion.

2. *With all lowliness.* It is by acting as the apostle here directs that a man walks worthy of this high vocation; *tapeinophrosyne* signifies "subjection" or "humility of mind." *Meekness.* The opposite to anger and irritability of disposition. *Longsuffering.* "Long-mindedness"— never permitting a trial or provocation to get to the end of your patience. *Forbearing one another.* "Sustaining one another"—helping to "support each" other in all the miseries and trials of life; or if the word be taken in the sense of "bearing with each other," it may mean that, through the love of God working in our hearts, we should bear with each other's infirmities, ignorance, etc., knowing how much others have been or are still obliged to bear with us.

3. *Endeavouring to keep the unity of the Spirit in the bond of peace.* There can be no doubt that the church at Ephesus was composed partly of converted Jews, as well as Gentiles. Now from the different manner in which they had been brought up, there might be frequent causes of altercation. Indeed the Jews, though converted, might be envious that the Gentiles were admitted to the same glorious privileges with themselves without being initiated into them by bearing the yoke and burden of the Mosaic law. The apostle guards them against this, and shows them that they should "intensely labor" (for so the word implies) to promote and preserve *peace* and *unity.* By the *unity of the Spirit* we are to understand, not only a spiritual unity, but also a unity of sentiments, desires, and affections, such as is worthy of and springs from the Spirit of God. By *the bond of peace* we are to understand a peace or union where the interests of all parties are concentrated, cemented, and sealed, the Spirit of God being the Seal upon this knot.

4. *There is one body.* Viz., of Christ, which is His Church. *One Spirit.* The Holy Ghost, who animates this body. *One hope.* Of everlasting glory, to which glory you have been called by the preaching of the gospel; through which you have become the body of Christ, instinct with the energy of the Holy Ghost.

5. *One Lord.* Jesus Christ, who is the Governor of this Church. *One faith.* One system of religion, proposing the same objects to the faith of all. *One baptism.* Administered in the name of the Holy Trinity; indicative of the influences, privileges, and effects of the Christian religion.

6. *One God.* The Fountain of all being, self-existent and eternal; *and Father of all,* both Jews and Gentiles, because He is the Father of the spirits of all flesh. *Who is above all.* "Who is over all"; as the King of Kings, and Lord of Lords. *And through all.* Pervading everything, being present with everything, providing for all creatures, and by His energy supporting all things. *And in you all.* By the energy of His Spirit enlightening, quickening, purifying, and comforting; in a word, making your hearts

the temples of the Holy Ghost. Some think the mystery of the blessed Trinity is contained in this verse: God is "over all," as Father; *through all,* by the Logos or Word; and *in . . . all,* by the Holy Spirit.

7. *Unto every one of us is given grace. Grace* may here signify a particular office; as if the apostle had said: Though we are all equal in the respects already mentioned, yet we have all different offices and situations to fill up in the Church and in the world; and we receive a free gift from Christ, according to the nature of the office, that we may be able to discharge it according to His own mind.

8. *Wherefore he saith.* The reference seems to be to Ps. lxviii. 18, which, however it may speak of the removal of the Tabernacle, appears to have been intended to point out the glorious ascension of Christ after His resurrection from the dead. *When he ascended up on high.* The whole of this verse, as it stands in the psalm, seems to refer to a military triumph. Take the following paraphrase: "Thou hast ascended on high"; the conqueror was placed in a very elevated chariot. "Thou hast led captivity captive"; the conquered kings and generals were usually bound behind the chariot of the conqueror, to grace the triumph. "Thou hast received gifts for [Paul, given gifts unto] men"; at such times the conqueror was wont to throw money among the crowd. Even to "the rebellious"; those who had fought against him now submit unto him, and share his munificence, for it is the property of a hero to be generous. "That the Lord God might dwell among them"; the conqueror being now come to fix his abode in the conquered provinces, and subdue the people to his laws.

9. *But that he also descended.* The meaning of the apostle appears to be this: The Person who *ascended* is the Messiah, and His ascension plainly intimates His descension; that is, His incarnation, humiliation, death, and resurrection.

10. *He that descended.* And He who descended so low is the same who has ascended so high. He came to "the lower parts of the earth" —the very deepest abasement; having emptied himself, taken upon Him the form of a servant, and humbled himself unto death, even the death of the Cross, now He is ascended *far above all heavens*—higher than all height; He has a name above every name. Here His descending into "the lower parts of the earth" is put in opposition to His ascending *far above all heavens.* His abasement was unparalleled; so also is His exaltation. *That he might fill all things.* That He might be the Fountain whence all blessings might flow, dispensing all good things to all His creatures, according to their several capacities and necessities; and, particularly, fill both converted Jews and Gentiles with all the gifts and graces of His Holy Spirit. Hence it follows:

11. *He gave some, apostles.* He established several offices in His Church; furnished these with the proper officers; and, to qualify them for their work, gave them the proper gifts. For a full illustration of this verse, the reader is requested to refer to the notes on 1 Cor. xii. 6-10 and 28-30.

12. *For the perfecting of the saints.* For the complete instruction, purification, and union of

all who have believed in Christ Jesus, both Jews and Gentiles. For the meaning of *perfecting,* see the note on 2 Cor. xiii. 9. *For the work of the ministry.* All these various officers, and the gifts and graces conferred upon them, were judged necessary, by the great Head of the Church, for its full instruction in the important doctrines of Christianity. *Edifying of the body.* The *body of Christ* is His Church, see chap. ii. 20, etc.; and its edification consists in its thorough instruction in divine things, and its being filled with faith and holiness.

13. *In the unity of the faith.* Jews and Gentiles being all converted according to the doctrines laid down in the faith—the Christian system. *The knowledge of the Son of God.* A true understanding of the mystery of the Incarnation: why God was manifest in the flesh, and why this was necessary in order to have human salvation. *Unto a perfect man.* One thoroughly instructed; the whole body of the Church being fully taught, justified, sanctified, and sealed. *Measure of the stature.* The full measure of knowledge, love, and holiness which the gospel of Christ requires.

14. *Be no more children. Children,* here, are opposed to the "perfect man" in the preceding verse; and the state of both is well explained by the apostle's allusions. The man is grown up strong and healthy, and has attained such a measure or height as qualifies him for the most respectable place in the ranks of his country. The child is ignorant, weak, and unsteady, tossed about in the nurse's arms, or whirled round in the giddy sports or mazes of youth; this seems to be the apostle's allusion. *By the sleight of men.* The words refer to the arts used by gamesters, who employ false dice that will always throw up one kind of number, which is that by which those who play with them cannot win. *Cunning craftiness.* It is difficult to give a literal translation of the original words: "By cunning, for the purpose of using the various means of deception." *Panourgia* signifies "craft" and "subtlety" in general, "cheating" and "imposition." *Methodia,* from which we have our term "method," signifies a "wile, a particular sleight, mode of tricking and deceiving." It is applied to the arts which the devil uses to deceive and destroy souls; see chap. vi. 11, called there the "wiles of the devil." From this it seems that various arts were used, by both the Greek sophists and the Judaizing teachers, to render the gospel of none effect or to adulterate and corrupt it.

15. *But speaking the truth in love.* The *truth* recommended by the apostle is the whole system of gospel doctrine; this they are to teach and preach, and this is opposed to the deceit mentioned above. This truth, as it is the doctrine of God's eternal love to mankind, must be preached in *love.* Scolding and abuse from the pulpit or press, in matters of religion, are truly monstrous. *Grow up into him.* This is a continuance of the metaphor taken from the members of a human body receiving nourishment equally and growing up, each in its due proportion to other parts and to the body in general. The truth of God should be so preached to all the members of the Church of God that they may all receive an increase of grace and life; so that each, in whatever state he may be, may get forward in the way of truth and holiness.

16. *From whom the whole body.* This verse is another proof of the wisdom and learning of the apostle. Not only the general ideas here are anatomical, but the whole phraseology is the same: the articulation of the bones, the composition and action of the muscles, the circulation of the fluids, carrying nourishment to every part and depositing some in every place, the energy of the system in keeping up all the functions, being particularly introduced, and the whole terminating in the general process of nutrition, increasing the body, and supplying all the waste that had taken place in consequence of labor.

17. *Walk not as other Gentiles walk.* You are called to holiness by the gospel, The other Gentiles have no such calling; walk not as they walk. In this and the following two verses the apostle gives a most awful account of the conduct of the heathens who were without the knowledge of the true God. (1) They walked *in the vanity of their mind.* "In the foolishness of their mind"; want of genuine wisdom is that to which the apostle refers, and it was through this that the Gentiles became addicted to every species of idolatry; and they fondly imagined that they could obtain help from gods which were the work of their own hands!

18. (2) *Having the understanding darkened.* This is the second instance alleged by the apostle of the degradation of the Gentiles. Having no means of knowledge, the heart, naturally dark, became more and more so by means of habitual transgression, everything in the Gentile system having an immediate tendency to blind the eyes and darken the whole soul. (3) *Being alienated from the life of God.* The original design of God was to live in man; and the life of God in the soul of man was that by which God intended to make man happy, and without which true happiness was never found by any human spirit: from this *through the ignorance that is in them,* through the "substantial" or continually existing ignorance, their moral state became so wretched that they are represented as "abhorring" everything spiritual and pure, for this is the import of the word which we translate *alienated* in some of the best Greek writers. They abhorred everything that had a tendency to lay any restraint on their vicious passions and inclinations. (4) *Blindness of their heart.* Because of the "callousness" of their hearts. "Callous" signifies a thickening of the outward skin of any particular part, especially on the hands and feet, by repeated exercise or use, through which such parts are rendered insensible. This may be metaphorically applied to the conscience of a sinner, which is rendered stupid and insensible by repeated acts of iniquity.

19. (5) *Who being past feeling.* The verb signifies: (*a*) To throw off all sense of shame, and to be utterly devoid of pain, for committing unrighteous acts; (*b*) To be desperate, having neither hope nor desire to reformation; in a word, to be without remorse, and to be utterly regardless of conduct, character, or final blessedness. Several excellent MSS. and versions have "being without hope"; that is, persons who, from their manner of life in this world, could not possibly hope for blessedness in the world to come. (6) *Have given themselves over unto lasciviousness. Lasciviousness* is here personified; and the Gentiles in question are

represented as having delivered themselves over to her jurisdiction. This is a true picture of the Gentile world. (7) *To work all uncleanness with greediness.* This is a complete finish of the most abandoned character. To do an unclean act is bad; to labor in it is worse; to labor in "all uncleanness" is worse still. But to do all this in every case to the utmost extent, "with a desire exceeding" time, place, opportunity, and strength, is worst of all, and leaves nothing more profligate or more abandoned to be described or imagined.

20. *But ye have not so learned Christ.* You have received the doctrines of Christianity, and therefore are taught differently; you have received the Spirit of Christ, and therefore are saved from such dispositions. Some would point and translate the original thus: "But you are not thus; you have learned Christ."

21. *If so be that ye have heard him.* "Seeing that, since indeed," you have heard us proclaim His eternal truth; we have delivered it to you as we received it from Jesus.

22. *That ye put off.* And this has been one especial part of our teaching, that you should abandon all these, and live a life totally opposite to what it was before. *Which is corrupt.* The whole of your former life was corrupt and abominable; you lived in the pursuit of pleasure and happiness; you sought this in the gratification of the lusts of the flesh; and were ever deceived by these lusts, and disappointed in your expectations.

23. *And be renewed in the spirit of your mind.* Their old mode of living was to be abandoned; a new one to be assumed. The mind is to be renovated, and not only its general complexion, but the very spirit of it; all its faculties and powers must be thoroughly, completely, and universally renewed.

24. *Put on the new man.* Get a new nature; for in Christ Jesus, under the Christian dispensation, neither circumcision avails anything, nor uncircumcision, but a new creation. Therefore you must be renewed in the spirit of your mind. *Which after God is created in righteousness.* Here is certainly an allusion to the creation of man. Moses tells us, Gen. i. 27, that "God created man in his own image"; that is, God was the Model according to which he was formed in the spirit of his mind. Paul says here that they should *put on the new man, which after God is created in righteousness and true holiness,* or "in the holiness of truth." Both certainly refer to the same thing, and the one illustrates the other. From the apostle we learn what Moses meant by the "image of God"; it was "righteousness and the truth of holiness."

25. *Wherefore putting away lying.* All falsity, all prevarication, because this is opposite to the truth as it is in Jesus, v. 21, and to the holiness of truth, v. 24. *Speak every man truth with his neighbour.* Truth was but of small account among many of even the best heathens, for they taught that on many occasions a lie was to be preferred to the truth itself. *We are members one of another.* Consider yourselves as one body, of which Jesus Christ is the Head; and as a man's right hand would not deceive or wrong his left hand, so deal honestly with each other.

26. *Be ye angry, and sin not.* Here is the same as "If ye be angry, do not sin." We can never

suppose that the apostle delivers this as a precept, if we take the words as they stand in our version. Perhaps the sense is, "Take heed that you be not angry, lest you sin"; for it would be very difficult, even for an apostle himself, to be angry and not sin. If we consider anger as simply implying displeasure, then there are a multitude of cases in which a man may be innocently—yea, laudably—angry; for he should be displeased with everything which is not for the glory of God and the good of mankind. But, in any other sense, I do not see how the words can be safely taken. *Let not the sun go down upon your wrath.* That is: If you do get angry with anyone, see that the fire be cast with the utmost speed out of your bosom. Do not go to sleep with any unkind or unbrotherly feeling; anger, continued in, may produce malice and revenge.

27. *Neither give place to the devil.* Your adversary will strive to influence your mind and irritate your spirit; watch and pray that he may not get any place in you, or ascendancy over you. As the word *diabolos* is sometimes used to signify a "calumniator, talebearer, whisperer, or backbiter," here it may have the same signification: Do not open your ear to the talebearer, to the slanderer, who comes to you with accusations against your brethren, or with surmisings and evil speakings.

28. *Let him that stole steal no more.* Stealing, overreaching, defrauding, purloining, etc., are consistent with no kind of religion that acknowledges the true God. If Christianity does not make men honest, it does nothing for them.

29. *Let no corrupt communication.* "A "useless, putrid, unsavory, and obscene word or conversation." *But that which is good to the use of edifying.* To be good for a thing is a Graecism, as well as an Anglicism, for to be "fit, proper, suitable." *That it may minister grace.* This may be understood thus: (1) Let your conversation be pure, wise, and holy, that it may be the means of conveying grace, or divine influences, to them that hear. (2) Let it be such as to be grateful or acceptable to the hearers. This is the meaning in some of the most correct Greek writers. Never wound modesty, truth, or religion with your discourse; endeavor to edify those with whom you converse; and, if possible, speak so as to please them.

30. *Grieve not the holy Spirit of God* by giving way to any wrong temper, unholy word, or unrighteous action. Even those who have already a measure of the light and life of God, both of which are not only brought in by the Holy Spirit, but maintained by His constant indwelling, may give way to sin, and so grieve this Holy Spirit that He shall withdraw both His light and presence; and in proportion as He withdraws, then hardness and darkness take place. What is still worse, a state of insensibility is the consequence; for the darkness prevents the fallen state from being seen, and the hardness prevents it from being felt. *Whereby ye are sealed.* The Holy Spirit in the soul of a believer is God's Seal, set on his heart to testify that he is God's property, and that he should be wholly employed in God's service.

31. *Let all bitterness.* It is astonishing that any who profess the Christian name should indulge *bitterness* of spirit. Those who are

censorious, who are unmerciful to the failings of others, who have fixed a certain standard by which they measure all persons in all circumstances, and unchristianize everyone that does not come up to this standard, these have the *bitterness* against which the apostle speaks. *And wrath.* More properly "anger," which may be considered the commencement of the passion. *Anger.* More properly "wrath"—the passion carried to its highest pitch, accompanied with injurious words and outrageous acts, some of which are immediately specified. *And clamour.* Loud and obstreperous speaking, brawling, railing, boisterous talk, often the offspring of wrath; all of which are highly unbecoming the meek, loving, quiet, sedate mind of Christ and His followers. *And evil speaking.* "Blasphemy"; that is, "injurious speaking"—words which tend to hurt those of whom or against whom they are spoken. *With all malice.* "All malignity"; as anger produces wrath, and wrath clamor, so all together produce malice; that is, settled, sullen, fell wrath, which is always looking out for opportunities to revenge itself by the destruction of the object of its indignation.

32. *Be ye kind one to another.* Be kind and obliging to each other; study good breeding and gentleness of manners. A Christian cannot be a savage, and he need not be a boor. Never put any person to needless pain. *Tenderhearted.* "Compassionate." *Forgiving one a n o t h e r.* Should you receive any injury from a brother, or from any man, be as ready to forgive him, on his repentance and acknowledgment, as God was, for Christ's sake, to forgive you when you repented of your sins, and took refuge in His mercy.

CHAPTER 5

Christians should imitate their Heavenly Father, and walk in love, after the example of Christ, 1-2. They should avoid all uncleanness, impurity, covetousness, foolish jesting, and idolatry, because these things exclude from the kingdom of God, 3-7. The Ephesians were once in darkness, but being now light in the Lord, they are exhorted to walk in that light, and bring forth the fruits of the Spirit; and to have no fellowship with the workers of iniquity, whose evil deeds are manifested by the light, 8-13. All are exhorted to awake; to walk circumspectly; to redeem the time; and to learn what the will of the Lord is, 14-17. The apostle gives particular directions relative to avoiding excess of wine, 18. To singing and giving thanks, 19-20. Submission to each other, 21. To husbands that they should love their wives, as Christ loved the Church; for by the marriage union, the union between Christ and the Church is pointed out; and wives are exhorted to reverence their husbands, 22-23.

1. *Be ye therefore followers of God.* The beginning of this chapter is properly a continuation of the preceding, which should have ended with the second verse of this. The word which we translate *followers* signifies such as personate others, assuming it is from this Greek word that we have the word "mimic." Though this term is often used in a ludicrous sense, yet here it is to be understood in a very solemn and proper sense. Let your whole conduct be like that of your Lord; "imitate" Him in all your actions, words, spirit, and inclinations; imitate Him as children do their beloved parents, and remember that you stand in the relation of beloved children to Him.

2. *And walk in love.* Let every act of life be dictated by love to God and man. *As Christ also hath loved us.* Laying down your lives for your brethren if necessary; counting nothing too difficult to be done in order to promote their eternal salvation. *Hath given himself for us.* Christ has died in our stead, and become thereby a Sacrifice for our sins. *An offering.* An oblation, a eucharistic offering. It means any offering by which gratitude was expressed for temporal blessings received from the bounty of God. *A sacrifice.* A "sin offering, a victim for sin." These terms may be justly considered as including every kind of sacrifice, offering, and oblation made to God on any account; and both these terms are with propriety used here, because the apostle's design was to represent the sufficiency of the offering made by Christ for the sin of the world. *For a sweetsmelling savour.* The same as is expressed in Gen. viii. 21; Lev. i. 9; iii. 16: "a sweet savour unto the Lord"; i.e., an offering of His own prescription, and one with which He was well-pleased, and by accepting of which He showed that He accepted the person who offered it. The *sweetsmelling savour* refers to the burnt offerings, the fumes of which ascended from the fire in the act of burning; and as such odors are grateful to man, God represents himself as pleased with them when offered by an upright worshipper according to His own appointment.

3. *But fornication.* It is probable that the three terms used here by the apostle refer to different species of the same thing. The word *fornication* may imply not only fornication but adultery also, as it frequently does; *uncleanness* may refer to all abominable and unnatural lusts —sodomy, bestiality, etc.; and *covetousness,* to "excessive indulgence" in that which, moderately used, is lawful. As the covetous man never has enough of wealth, so the pleasure-taker and the libertine never have enough of the gratifications of sense, the appetite increasing in proportion to its indulgence. If, however, simple *covetousness,* i.e., the "love of gain," be here intended, it shows from the connection in which it stands (for it is linked with fornication and all uncleanness) how degrading it is to the soul of man and how abominable it is in the eye of God. In other places it is ranked with idolatry, for the man who has an inordinate love of gain makes money his god. *Let it not be once named.* Let no such things ever exist among you, for you are called to be saints.

4. *Neither filthiness.* Anything base or vile in words or acts. *Foolish talking.* Scurrility, buffoonery, ridicule, or what tends to expose another to contempt. *Nor jesting.* Artfully turned discourses or words; words that can be easily turned to other meanings; chaste words which, from their connection and the manner in which they are used, convey an obscene or offensive meaning. *Which are not convenient.* "They do not come up" to the proper standard; they are utterly improper in themselves, and highly unbecoming in those who profess Christianity. *But rather giving of thanks.* Prayer or praise is the most suitable language for man; and he who is of a trifling, light disposition is ill fitted for either.

5. *For this ye know.* You must be convinced of the dangerous and ruinous tendency of such a spirit and conduct, when you know that persons of this character can never inherit the kingdom of God.

6. *Let no man deceive you.* Suffer no man to persuade you that any of these things are innocent, or that they are unavoidable frailties of human nature. They are all sins and abom-

inations in the sight of God; those who practice them are *children of disobedience;* and on account of such practices the *wrath of God,* divine punishment, must come upon them.

7. *Be not ye therefore partakers with them.* Do not act as your fellow citizens do; nor suffer their philosophy, *with vain words,* with "empty doctrines," to lead you astray from the path of truth.

8. *For ye were sometimes* ("formerly") *darkness.* While you lived in darkness, you lived in these crimes. *But now are ye light in the Lord.* When you were in heathenish *darkness* you served divers lusts and pleasures, but now you have the *light*—the wisdom and teaching which come from God; therefore *walk as children of the light*—let the world see that you are not slaves to the flesh, but free, willing, rational servants of the Most High.

9. *For the fruit of the Spirit.* Instead of *Spirit,* some MSS., together with several of the fathers, read "light," which is supposed by most critics to be the true reading, because there is no mention made of the Spirit in any part of the context. As light, v. 8, not only means the divine influence upon the soul, but also the gospel, with great propriety it may be said: The fruit of the light, i.e., of the gospel, *is in all goodness and righteousness and truth. Goodness,* in the principle and disposition; *righteousness,* the exercise of that goodness in the whole conduct of life; *truth,* the director of that principle, and its exercise, to the glorification of God and the good of mankind.

10. *Proving what is acceptable.* By walking in the light—under the influence of the divine Spirit, according to the dictates of the gospel—you shall be able to try and bring to full proof that by which God is best pleased. You shall be able to please Him well in all things.

11. *Have no fellowship.* Have no religious connection whatever with heathens or their worship. *Unfruitful works of darkness.* Probably alluding to the mysteries among the heathens, and the different lustrations and rites through which the initiated went in the caves and dark recesses where these mysteries were celebrated; all which he denominates *works of darkness,* because they were destitute of true wisdom; and *unfruitful works,* because they were of no use to mankind, the initiated being obliged, on pain of death, to keep secret what they had seen, heard, and done. *Rather reprove them.* Bear a "testimony" against them; "convince" them that they are wrong; "confute" them in their vain reasons; *reprove* them for their vices, which are flagrant, while pretending to superior illumination. All these meanings has the Greek word which we generally render "to convince" or "reprove."

12. *For it is a shame even to speak.* This no doubt refers to the Eleusinian and Bacchanalian mysteries, which were performed in the night and darkness, and were known to be so impure and abominable, especially the latter, that the Roman senate banished them both from Rome and Italy.

14. *Wherefore he saith.* It is a matter of doubt and controversy whence this saying is derived. Some think it taken from Isa. xxvi. 19: "Thy dead men shall live, together with my dead body shall they arise. Awake and sing, ye that dwell in the dust." Others think that it is taken

from Isa. lx. 1-3: "Arise, shine; for thy light is come." But it seems more natural to understand the words *he saith* as referring to the light, i.e., the gospel, mentioned in v. 13; and should be translated, "Wherefore it saith, Awake thou." That is, This is the general, the strong, commanding voice of the gospel in every part—Receive instruction; leave your sins, which are leading you to perdition; believe on the Lord Jesus Christ, and He will enlighten and save you.

15. *Walk circumspectly.* Our word "circumspect," from the Latin *circumspicio,* signifies to look round about on all hands; to be every way watchful, wary, and cautious, in order to avoid danger, discern enemies before they come too nigh, and secure a man's interest by every possible and lawful means. But the original word signifies "correctly, accurately, consistently, or perfectly." You who have received the truth, be careful of your conduct; walk by the rule which God has given you. Do this as well in little as in great matters. Exemplify your principles, which are holy and good, by a corresponding conduct; do not only profess, but live, the gospel. *Not as fools, but as wise.* The heathens affected to be called "wise men." The apostle here takes the term *sophos,* and applies it to the Christian; and, instead of it, gives the empty Gentile philosopher the title of *fool.*

16. *Redeeming the time.* Buying up those moments which others seem to throw away; steadily improving every present moment, that you may in some measure regain the time you have lost. Let time be your chief commodity; deal in that alone; buy it all up, and use every portion of it yourselves. Time is that on which eternity depends; in time you are to get a preparation for the kingdom of God. If you get not this in time, your ruin is inevitable; therefore buy up the time. *Because the days are evil.* The present times are dangerous; they are full of trouble and temptations, and only the watchful and diligent have any reason to expect that they shall keep their garments unspotted.

17. *Wherefore be ye not unwise.* "Do not become madmen." Here is a most evident allusion to the orgies of Bacchus, in which his votaries acted like madmen: running about, tossing their heads from shoulder to shoulder, appearing to be in every sense completely frantic. *But understanding what the will of the Lord is.* It is the will of God that you should be sober, chaste, holy, and pure. Get a thorough understanding of this; acquaint yourselves with God's will, that you may know how to glorify Him.

18. *Be not drunk with wine, wherein is excess.* This is a further allusion to the Bacchanalian mysteries; in them his votaries got drunk, and ran into all manner of excesses. Plato, though he forbade drunkenness in general, yet allowed that the people should get drunk in the solemnities of that god who invented wine. The word which we translate *excess* means profligacy and debauchery of every kind; such as are the general concomitants of drunkenness, and especially among the votaries of Bacchus in Greece and Italy. *But be filled with the Spirit.* The heathen priests pretended to be filled with the influence of the god they worshipped, and it was in these circumstances that they gave out their oracles. The apostle exhorts the Ephesians not to resemble these, but, instead of being filled with wine, to be filled with the Spirit of

God; in consequence of which, instead of those discoveries of the divine will to which in their drunken worship the votaries of Bacchus pretended, they should be wise indeed, and should understand what the will of the Lord is.

19. *Speaking to yourselves in psalms.* We can scarcely say what is the exact difference between these three expressions. *Psalms* may probably mean those of David. *Hymns.* Extemporaneous effusions in praise of God, uttered under the influence of the divine Spirit, or a sense of His especial goodness. *Songs.* "Odes"; premeditated and regular poetic compositions. But in whatever form they were composed, we learn that they were all *spiritual*, tending to magnify God and edify men. *Singing and making melody in your heart.* The heart always going with the lips. It is a shocking profanation of divine worship to draw nigh to God with the lips while the heart is far from Him. It is too often the case that in public worship men are carried off from the sense of the words by the sounds that are put to them. And how few choirs of singers are there in the universe whose hearts ever accompany them in what they call singing the praises of God!

20. *Giving thanks always.* God is continually loading you with His benefits. You deserve nothing of His kindness; therefore give Him thanks for His unmerited bounties. *God and the Father.* That is, God, who is your Father, and the Father of mercies. *In the name of our Lord Jesus.* He is the only Mediator, and through Him alone can you approach to God.

21. *Submitting yourselves one to another.* Let no man be so tenacious of his own will or his opinion in matters indifferent as to disturb the peace of the church; in all such matters give way to each other, and let love rule. *In the fear of God.* Instead of *in the fear of God,* "in the fear of Christ" is the reading of the best MSS.

22. *Wives, submit yourselves unto your own husbands.* As the *Lord,* viz., Christ, is the Head or Governor of the Church, and the Head of the man, so is the man the head or governor of the woman. The husband should not be a tyrant, and the wife should not be the governor. *As unto the Lord.* The word "Church" seems to be necessarily understood here; that is, Act under the authority of your husbands, as the Church acts under the authority of Christ.

23. *For the husband is the head of the wife.* This is the reason which the apostle gives for his injunctions. *He is the saviour of the body.* As Christ exercises authority over the Church so as to save and protect it, so let the husband exercise authority over his wife by protecting, comforting, and providing her with every necessary and comfort of life, according to his power.

24. *In every thing.* That is, every lawful thing; for it is not intimated that they should obey their husbands in anything criminal, or in anything detrimental to the interests of their souls. The husband may be profligate, and may wish his wife to become such also; he may be an enemy to true religion, and use his authority to prevent his wife from those means of grace which she finds salutary to her soul. In none of these things should she obey him.

25. *Husbands, love your wives.* Here is a grand rule according to which every husband is called to act: "Love your wife as Christ loved

the Church." But how did Christ love the Church? He *gave himself for it*—He laid down His life for it. So then husbands should, if necessary, lay down their lives for their wives. And there is more implied in the words than mere protection and support; for, as Christ gave himself for the Church to save it, so husbands should by all means in their power labor to promote the salvation of their wives and their constant edification in righteousness. Thus we find that the authority of the man over the woman is founded on his love to her, and this love must be such as to lead him to risk his life for her. As the care of the family devolves on the wife, and the children must owe the chief direction of their minds and formation of their manners to the mother, she has need of all the assistance and support which her husband can give her; and if she performs her duty well, she deserves the utmost of his love and affection.

26. *That he might sanctify and cleanse it.* The Church is represented as the spouse of Christ, as the woman is the spouse of the man; and to prepare this Church for himself He washes, cleanses, and sanctifies it. There is certainly an allusion here to the ancient method of purifying women, who were appointed to be consorts to kings. Twelve months, it appears, were in some instances spent in this purification: "Six months with oil of myrrh, and six months with sweet odours, and with other things for the purifying of the women." See the case of Esther, chap. ii. 12; see also Ps. xlv. 13-14; Ezek. xvi. 7-14. *With the washing of water.* Baptism, accompanied by the purifying influences of the Holy Spirit. *By the word.* The "doctrine" of Christ crucified, through which baptism is administered, sin cancelled, and the soul purified from all unrighteousness, the death of Christ giving efficacy to all.

27. *That he might present it to himself.* It was usual to bring the royal bride to the king in the most sumptuous apparel; and is there not here an allusion to Ps. xlv. 13-14: "The king's daughter is all glorious within: her clothing is of wrought gold. She shall be brought unto the king in raiment of needlework"? This presentation here spoken of by the apostle will take place on the last day. *A glorious church.* Every way splendid and honorable, because pure and holy. *Not having spot.* No "blemish" on the face, no spots upon the garment, the heart and life both holy. *Wrinkle.* No mark of decay. The word is commonly applied to wrinkles on the face, indicative of sickness or decrepitude. *Holy and without blemish.* In every sense holy, pure, and perfect. Now it was for this purpose that Christ gave himself for the Church; and for this purpose He continues the different ordinances which He has appointed; and particularly the preaching of the Word—the doctrine of reconciliation through faith in His blood. And it is in this life that all this purification is to take place; for none shall be presented at the day of judgment to Him who has not here been sanctified, cleansed, washed, made glorious, having neither spot, wrinkle, blemish, nor any such thing.

28. *As their own bodies.* For the woman is, properly speaking, a part of the man; for God made man "male and female," and the woman was taken out of his side. Therefore is she flesh of his flesh and bone of his bone; and therefore he that loves his wife loves himself, for they

two are one flesh. The apostle in all these verses refers to the creation and original state of the first human pair.

29. *No man ever yet hated his own flesh.* And this is a natural reason why he should love his wife, and nourish and cherish her.

30. *We are members of his body.* He has partaken of our nature as we have partaken of the nature of Adam. And as He is the Head of the Church and the Saviour of this body, so we, being members of the Church, are members of His mystical body. That is, we are united to Him by one Spirit in the closest intimacy, even similar to that which the members have with the body.

31. *Shall be joined unto his wife.* He shall be "glued" or "cemented" to her; and as a well-glued board will sooner break in the whole wood than in the glued joint, so death alone can part the husband and wife; and nothing but death should dissolve their affection.

32. *This is a great mystery.* "This mystery is great." By *mystery* we may understand a natural thing by which some spiritual matter is signified, which signification the Spirit of God alone can give. So the creation and union of Adam and Eve were intended, in the design of God, to point out the union of Christ and the Church, a union the most important that can be conceived; and therefore the apostle calls it *a great mystery.*

33. *Nevertheless.* "Moreover," or "therefore," on the consideration of God's design in the institution of marriage, *let every one of you . . . love his wife as himself,* because she is both naturally and by a divine ordinance a part of himself. *That she reverence her husband.* Let the wife ever consider the husband as her head; and this he is, not only by nature, but also by the ordinance of God. These are very important matters, and on them the apostle lays great stress.

CHAPTER 6

Children should obey their parents, that they may live long and be happy, 1-3. Parents should be tender towards their children, 4. Servants should show all obedience and fidelity to their masters, 5-8. And masters should treat their servants with humanity, 9. All should be strong in the Lord, and be armed with His armor, because of their wily, powerful, and numerous foes, 10-13. The different parts of the Christian armor enumerated, 14-17. The necessity of all kinds of prayer and watchfulness, 18-20. Tychicus is commissioned to inform the Ephesians of the apostle's affairs, 21-22. The apostolic benediction and farewell, 23-24.

1. *Children, obey your parents.* This is a duty with which God will never dispense; He commands it, and one might think that gratitude, from a sense of the highest obligations, would most strongly enforce the command. *In the Lord.* This clause is wanting in several reputable MSS. and in some versions. *In the Lord* may mean on account of the commandment of the Lord, or as far as the parents' commands are according to the will and word of God. For surely no child is called to obey any parent if he give unreasonable or unscriptural commands.

4. *Fathers, provoke not your children to wrath.* Avoid all severity; this will hurt your own souls, and do them no good; on the contrary, if punished with severity or cruelty, they will be only hardened and made desperate in their sins. Cruel parents generally have bad children. He who corrects his children according to God and reason will feel every blow on his own heart more sensibly than his child feels it on his body. Parents are called to correct, not to punish, their children. Those who punish them do it from a principle of revenge; those who correct them do it from a principle of affectionate concern. *Bring them up.* Literally, "Nourish them in the discipline and instruction of the Lord." The mind is to be nourished with wholesome discipline and instruction, as the body is with proper food. "Discipline" may refer to all that knowledge which is proper for children, including elementary principles and rules for behavior. "Instruction" may imply whatever is necessary to form the mind; to touch, regulate, and purify the passions; and necessarily includes the whole of religion. Both these should be administered in the Lord—according to His will and Word, and in reference to His eternal glory.

5. *Servants, be obedient.* Though *doulos* frequently signifies a "slave" or "bondman," yet it often implies a servant in general, or anyone bound to another, either for a limited time or for life. Even a slave, if a Christian, was bound to serve him faithfully by whose money he was bought, howsoever illegal that traffic may be considered. *According to the flesh.* Your masters in secular things; for they have no authority over your religion nor over your souls. *With fear and trembling.* Because the law gives them a power to punish you for every act of disobedience. *In singleness of your heart.* Not merely through fear of punishment, but from a principle of uprightness, serving them as you would serve Christ.

6. *Not with eyeservice.* Not merely in their presence, when their eye is upon you, as unfaithful and hypocritical servants do, without consulting conscience in any part of their work. *Doing the will of God.* Seeing that you are in the state of servitude, it is the will of God that you should act conscientiously in it.

7. *With good will.* With "cheerfulness"; do not take up your service as a cross or bear it as a burden; but take it as coming in the order of God's providence and a thing that is pleasing to Him.

8. *Whatsoever good thing any man doeth.* Though your masters should fail to give you the due reward of your fidelity and labor, yet, as you have done your work as unto the Lord, He will take care to give you the proper recompense. *Whether he be bond.* A "slave," bought with money. *Or free.* A person who has hired himself of his own free accord.

9. *Ye masters, do the same things unto them.* Act in the same affectionate, conscientious manner towards your slaves and servants as they do towards you. *Forbearing threatening.* If they should transgress at any time, lean more to the side of mercy than justice; and when you are obliged to punish, let it be as light and as moderate as possible; and let revenge have no part in the chastisement, for that is of the devil, and not of God. The words *forbearing threatening* signify to mitigate, relax, or not exact threatening; that is, the threatened punishment. *Knowing that your Master also is in heaven.* You are their masters; God is yours. As you deal with them, so God will deal with you; for

do not suppose, because their condition on earth is inferior to yours, that God considers them to be less worthy of His regard than you are. This is not so, for there is no *respect of persons with Him*.

10. *Finally*. Having laid before you your great and high calling and all the doctrines and precepts of the gospel, it is necessary that I should show you the enemies that will oppose you, and the strength which is requisite to enable you to repel them. *Be strong in the Lord*. You must have strength, and strength of a spiritual kind, and such strength too as the Lord himself can furnish; and you must have this strength through an indwelling God, the power of His might working in you.

11. *Put on the whole armour of God*. The apostle considers every Christian as having a warfare to maintain against numerous, powerful, and subtle foes; and that therefore they would need much strength, much courage, complete armor, and skill to use it. The "panoply" which is mentioned here refers to the armor of the heavy troops among the Greeks; those who were to sustain the rudest attacks, who were to sap the foundations of walls, storm cities. Their ordinary armor was the shield, the helmet, the sword, and the greaves or brazen boots. To all these the apostle refers below. *The wiles of the devil*. "The methods of the devil"; the different means, plans, schemes, and machinations which he uses to deceive, entrap, enslave, and ruin the souls of men.

12. *For we wrestle not against flesh and blood*. Our wrestling or contention is not with men like ourselves. *Flesh and blood* is a Hebraism for "men," or human beings. *Against principalities*. "Chief rulers"; beings of the first rank and order in their own kingdom. *Powers*. "Authorities," derived from and constituted by the above. *Spiritual wickedness*. "The spiritual things of wickedness" or "the spiritualities of wickedness"; highly refined and sublimed evil; disguised falsehood in the garb of truth; antinomianism in the guise of religion. The *spiritual wickedness* is supposed to be the angels which kept not their first estate; who fell from the heavenly places but are ever longing after and striving to regain them; and which have their station in the regions of the air.

13. *Wherefore*. Because you have such enemies to contend with, *take unto you*, assume, as provided and prepared for you, *the whole armour of God;* which armor if you put on and use, you shall be both invulnerable and immortal. The ancient heroes are fabled to have had armor sent to them by the gods. *That ye may be able to withstand*. That you may not only stand fast in the liberty wherewith Christ has made you free, but also discomfit all your spiritual foes; and continuing in your ranks, maintain your ground against them, never putting off your armor, but standing always ready, prepared to repel any new attack. *And having done all, to stand*. Rather, "And having conquered all, stand." This is a military phrase, and is repeatedly uesd in this sense by the best Greek writers. By *evil day* we may understand any time of trouble, affliction, and sore temptation.

14. *Stand therefore*. Prepare yourselves for combat, *having your loins girt about with truth*.

He had told them before to take the whole armor of God, v. 13, and to put on this whole armor. Having got all the pieces of it together, and the defensive parts put on, they were then to gird them close to their bodies with the girdle; and instead of a fine ornamented belt, such as the ancient warriors used, they were to have *truth*. The gospel of Jesus Christ is the truth of God. *Truth* may be taken here for "sincerity"; for if a man be not conscious to himself that his heart is right before God, and that he makes no false pretenses to religion, in vain does he enter the spiritual lists. This alone can give him confidence. *The breastplate of righteousness*. The word *righteousness*, we have often had occasion to note, is a word of very extensive import. It signifies the principle of righteousness; it signifies the practice of righteousness, or living a holy life; it signifies God's method of justifying sinners; and it signifies justification itself. Here it may imply a consciousness of justification through the blood of the Cross; the principle of righteousness or true holiness implanted in the heart; and a holy life, a life regulated according to the testimonies of God. As the *breastplate* defends the heart and lungs, and all those vital functionaries that are contained in what is called the region of the thorax, so this righteousness, this life of God in the soul of man, defends everything on which the man's spiritual existence depends. While he possesses this principle and acts from it, his spiritual and eternal life is secure.

15. *Your feet shod*. The "greaves" were deemed of essential importance in the ancient armor; if the feet or legs are materially wounded, a man can neither stand to resist his foe, pursue him if vanquished, nor flee from him should he have the worst of the fight. That the apostle has obedience to the gospel in general in view, there can be no doubt. But he appears to have more than this, a readiness to publish the gospel; for "how beautiful upon the mountains are the feet of him that bringeth good tidings, that publisheth peace; that bringeth good tidings of good, that publisheth salvation; that saith unto Zion, Thy God reigneth!" (Isa. lii. 7; Rom. x. 15) *The preparation of the gospel*. The word which we translate *preparation* is variously understood. Some think it means a habitual readiness in walking in the way prescribed by the gospel; others, that firmness and solidity which the gospel gives to them who conscientiously believe its doctrines; others, those virtues and graces which in the first planting of Christianity were indispensably necessary to those who published it. Should we take the word *preparation* in its common acceptation, it may imply that, by a conscientious belief of the gospel, receiving the salvation provided by its Author, and walking in the way of obedience which is pointed out by it, the soul is prepared for the kingdom of Heaven. The gospel is termed the *gospel of peace* because it establishes peace between God and man, and proclaims peace and goodwill to the universe. Contentions, strife, quarrels, and all wars being as alien from its nature and design as they are opposed to the nature of Him who is love and compassion to man.

16. *Above all*, "over all" the rest of the armor, *taking the shield of faith*. In the word *thureos* the apostle alludes to the great oblong shield, or

scutum, which covers the whole body. And as *faith* is the grace by which all others are preserved and rendered active, so it is properly represented here under the notion of a *shield,* by which the whole body is covered and protected. Faith, in this place, must mean that evidence of things unseen which every genuine believer has, that God, for Christ's sake, has blotted out his sins, and by which he is enabled to call God his Father, and feel Him to be his Portion. It is such an appropriating faith as this which can quench any dart of the devil. *The fiery darts of the wicked. Belos,* "a dart," signifies any kind of missile weapon; everything that is projected to a distance by the hand, as a javelin or short spear; or by a bow, as an arrow; or a stone by a sling. *The fiery darts of the wicked,* or devil, are evil thoughts and strong injections, as they are termed, which in the unregenerate inflame the passions and excite the soul to acts of transgression. While the truth is strong in Christ it acts as a shield to quench these. He who walks so as to feel the witness of God's Spirit that he is His child has all evil thoughts in abhorrence; and though they pass through his mind, they never fix in his passions. They are caught on this shield, blunted, and extinguished.

17. *Take the helmet of salvation.* Or, as it is expressed, 1 Thess. v. 8, "And for an helmet, the hope of salvation." So the hope of conquering every adversary and surmounting every difficulty, through the blood of the Lamb, is as a helmet that protects the head; an impenetrable one, that the blow of the battle-axe cannot cleave. *The sword of the Spirit.* The *sword* of which Paul speaks is, as he explains it, *the word of God;* that is, the revelation which God has given of himself, or what we call the Holy Scriptures. This is called *the sword of the Spirit* because it comes from the Holy Spirit and receives its fulfilment in the soul through the operation of the Holy Spirit. An ability to quote this on proper occasions, and especially in times of temptation and trial, has a wonderful tendency to cut in pieces the snares of the adversary. In God's Word a genuine Christian may have unlimited confidence, and to every purpose to which it is applicable it may be brought with the greatest effect. The shield, faith, and the *sword . . . the word of God*—or faith in God's unchangeable Word—are the principal armor of the soul.

18. *Praying always.* The apostle does not put praying among the armor; had he done so he would have referred it, as he has done all the rest, to some of the Grecian armor; but as he does not do this, therefore we conclude that his account of the armor is ended, and that now, having equipped his spiritual soldier, he shows him the necessity of praying, that he may successfully resist those principalities, powers, the rulers of the darkness of this world, and the spiritual wickednesses in heavenly places, with whom he has to contend. The "panoply," or whole armor of God, consists in (1) the girdle, (2) the breastplate, (3) the greaves, (4) the shield, (5) the helmet, and (6) the sword. He who had these was completely armed. And as it was the custom of the Grecian armies, before they engaged, to offer prayers to the gods for their success, the apostle shows that these spiritual warriors must depend on the Captain of

their salvation, and pray with all prayer, i.e., incessantly, being always in the spirit of prayer, so that they should be ever ready for public, private, mental, or ejaculatory prayer; always depending on Him who can alone save and who alone can destroy. When the apostle exhorts Christians to pray with all prayer, we may at once see that he neither means spiritual nor formal prayer, in exclusion of the other. *Praying* refers to the state of the spirit as well as to the act. *With all prayer* refers to the different kinds of prayer that are performed in public, in the family, in the closet, in business, on the way, in the heart without a voice, and with the voice from the heart. All these are necessary to the genuine Christian, and he whose heart is right with God will be frequent in the whole. *And supplication.* There is a difference between *prayer* and *supplication.* Some think the former means prayer for the attainment of good; the latter, prayer for averting evil. Supplication however seems to mean prayer continued in, strong and incessant pleadings, till the evil is averted or the good communicated. There are two things that must be attended to in prayer: (1) That it be "in every time, season, or opportunity"; (2) That it should be "in or through the Spirit"—that the heart should be engaged in it, and that its infirmities should be helped by the Holy Ghost. *Watching thereunto.* Being always on your guard lest your enemies should surprise you. Watch, not only against evil, but also for opportunities to do good, and for opportunities to receive good. Without watchfulness, prayer and all the spiritual armor will be ineffectual. *With all perseverance.* Being always intent on your object, and never losing sight of your danger, or of your interest. The word implies "stretching out the neck" and "looking about" in order to discern an enemy at a distance. *For all saints.* For all Christians; for this was the character by which they were generally distinguished.

19. *And for me, that utterance may be given unto me.* Kypke has proved by many examples that *logon didonai* signifies permission and power to defend oneself in a court of justice; and this sense of the phrase is perfectly applicable to the case of Paul, who was "an ambassador in bonds" (v. 20), and expected to be called to a public hearing, in which he was not only to defend himself, but to prove the truth and excellency of the Christian religion. And we learn, from Phil. i. 12-14, that he had his desire in this respect; for the things which happened to him fell out to the furtherance of the gospel, so that his bonds in Christ were manifest in all the palace, and in all other places. Thus God had enabled him to make a most noble defense, by which the gospel acquired great credit.

20. *An ambassador in bonds.* An ambassador being the representative of his king, his person was in all civilized countries held sacred. Contrary to the rights of nations, this ambassador of the King of heaven was put in chains! He had, however, the opportunity of defending himself and of vindicating the honor of his Master.

21. *That ye also.* As well as other churches to whom I have communicated the dealings of both God and man to me. *May know my affairs.* May be acquainted with my situation and circumstances. *And how I do.* How I em-

ploy my time, and what fruit there is of my apostolical labors. *Tychicus, a beloved brother.* We learn, from Acts xx. 4, that Tychicus was of Asia, and that he was a useful companion of Paul. This same person, and with the same character and commendation, is mentioned in the Epistle to the Colossians, chap. iv. 7. He is mentioned also in Titus iii. 12 and in 2 Tim. iv. 12; from all these places it is evident that he was a person in whom the apostle had the highest confidence, and that he was a very eminent minister of Christ.

22. *Whom I have sent unto you for the same purpose.* Namely, that the Ephesians might know his affairs and those of the church at Rome; messengers of this kind frequently passed between the churches in those ancient times. *Comfort your hearts.* By showing you how powerfully he was upheld in all his tribulations, and how God turned his bonds to the furtherance of the gospel. This must have been great consolation to all the followers of God.

23. *Peace.* All prosperity, and continual union with God and among yourselves; *and love* to God and man, the principle of all obedience and union; *with faith,* continually increasing, and growing stronger and stronger, *from God the Father,* as the Fountain of all our mercies, *and the Lord Jesus Christ,* through whose sacrifice and mediation they all come.

24. *Grace be with all them.* May the divine "favor" and all the benedictions flowing from it be with all them who love our Lord Jesus Christ, who has so loved us as to give His life to redeem ours and to save us unto life eternal. *In sincerity.* In "incorruptibility." Those who show the genuineness of their love by walking before Him in holiness of life.

The Epistle to the
PHILIPPIANS

We have already seen, Acts xvi. 12, that Philippi was a town of Macedonia. Philip, king of Macedonia and father of Alexander, having taken possession of it and fortified it, called it Philippi, after his own name. Julius Caesar planted a colony here, which was afterwards enlarged by Augustus; and hence the inhabitants were considered as freemen of Rome.

The gospel was preached first here by Paul. Paul had a vision in the night; a man of Macedonia appeared to him and said, "Come over into Macedonia, and help us." He was then at Troas in Mysia; from thence he immediately sailed to Samothracia, came the next day to Neapolis, and thence to Philippi. There he continued for some time, and converted Lydia, a seller of purple, from Thyatira; and afterwards cast a demon out of a Pythoness, for which he and Silas were persecuted, cast into prison, scourged, and put into the stocks; but the magistrates afterwards finding that they were Romans, took them out of prison and treated them civilly. See the account, Acts xvi. 9.

The Philippians were greatly attached to their apostle, and testified their affection by sending him supplies, even when he was laboring for other churches; and they appear to have been the only church that did so. See chap. iv. 15-16.

There is not much controversy concerning the date of this Epistle; it was probably written in A.D. 62, and about a year after that to the Ephesians.

CHAPTER 1

Paul, in conjunction with Timothy, addresses himself to the saints at Philippi, and gives them his apostolical benediction, 1-2. Thanks God for their conversion and union, and expresses his persuasion that God will continue His work among them, 3-6. Tells them of his strong affection for them, and prays that they may be filled with the salvation of God, 7-11. Shows them how much his persecution had contributed to the success of the gospel, 12-14. Informs that there were some at Rome who preached the gospel from unworthy motives; yet he was convinced that this, which was designed to injure him, should turn to his advantage, 15-19. Mentions his uncertainty whether he should be liberated or martyred, and his perfect readiness to meet either; yet, on the whole, expresses a hope that he should again visit them, 20-26. Exhorts them to a holy life, and comforts them under their tribulations, 27-30.

1. *Paul and Timotheus.* That Timothy was at this time with the apostle in Rome we learn from chap. ii. 19, and also that he was very high in the apostle's estimation. He had also accompanied the apostle on his two voyages to Philippi (see Acts xvi and xx), and was therefore deservedly dear to the church in that city.

It was on these accounts that Paul joined his name to his own, not because he was in any part the author of this Epistle, but he might have been the apostle's amanuensis, though the subscription to the Epistle gives this office to Epaphroditus. Neither in this Epistle nor in those to the Thessalonians and to Philemon does Paul call himself an apostle; the reason of which appears to be that in none of these places was his apostolical authority called in question. *Bishops and deacons.* The "overseers" of the Church of God, and those who ministered to the poor, and preached occasionally. There has been a great deal of paper wasted on the inquiry, "Who is meant by bishops here, as no place could have more than one bishop?" To which it has been answered: "Philippi was a metropolitan see, and might have several bishops." This is the extravagance of trifling. I believe no such officer is meant as we now term "bishop."

3. *Upon every remembrance.* As often as

you recur to my mind, so often do I thank God for the great work wrought among you. Some think that the words should be translated, "for all your kind remembrance," referring to their kind attention to the apostle in supplying his wants.

4. *Always in every prayer.* I pray often for you, and have great pleasure in doing it, seeing what God has already wrought among you.

5. *For your fellowship in the gospel.* If we consider *koinonia* as implying spiritual *fellowship* or "communion," then it signifies, not only their attention to the gospel, their readiness to continue it, and perseverance in it, but also their unity and affection among themselves. Some understand the word as expressing their liberality to the apostle, and to the gospel in general; for the term may not only be applied to communion among themselves, but to communications to others. This sense, though followed by Chrysostom and Theophylact, does not appear to be the best; though we know it to be a fact that they were liberal in supplying the apostle's necessities, and, no doubt, in ministering to the support of others.

6. *Being confident.* There shall be nothing lacking on God's part to support you; and to make you wise, holy, and happy; and bring you at last to His kingdom and glory.

7. *It is meet for me to think this.* It is "just" that I should think so, because *I have you in my heart*—you live in my warmest love and most affectionate remembrance. *Inasmuch as both in my bonds.* Because you have set your hearts upon me in my bonds, sending Epaphroditus to minister to me in my necessities, chap. ii. 25, and contributing of your own substance to me, chap. iv. 14, sending once and again to me while I was in bonds for the defense of the faith, vv. 15-16; those things which, being "a sweet savour, a sacrifice well pleasing and acceptable to God," v. 18, confirm my hope concerning you; especially when I find you yet standing firm under the like afflictions, "having the same conflict which ye saw in me" (when I was among you, Acts xvi. 12, etc.), "and now hear to be in me," chap. i. 30.

8. *For God is my record.* I call God to witness that I have the strongest affection for you, and that I love you with that same kind of tender concern with which Christ loved the world when He gave himself for it; for I am even ready to "be offered upon the sacrifice and service of your faith," chap. ii. 17.

9. *This I pray.* This is the substance of all my prayers for you, *that your love* to God, to one another, and to all mankind, *may abound yet more and more;* that it may be like a river, perpetually fed with rain and fresh streams, so that it continues to swell and increase till it fills all its banks and floods the adjacent plains. *In knowledge.* Of God's nature, perfections, your own duty and interest, His work upon your souls, and His great designs in the gospel. *And in all judgment.* In all "spiritual or moral feeling"; that you may at once have the clearest perception and the fullest enjoyment of those things which concern your salvation.

10. *That ye may approve things that are excellent.* "To the end that you may put to proof the things that differ," or the things that are "more profitable." By the pure and abundant love which they received from God they would be able to try whatever differed from the teaching they had received, and from the experience they had in spiritual things. *That ye may be sincere.* The word which we translate "sincerity" is compounded of *eile,* the "splendor of the sun," and *krino,* "I judge"; a thing which may be examined in the clearest and strongest light without the possibility of detecting a single flaw or imperfection. Be so purified and refined in your souls, by the indwelling Spirit, that even the light of God shining into your hearts shall not be able to discover a fault that the love of God has not purged away. Our word sincerity is from the Latin *sinceritas,* which is compounded of *sine,* "without," and *cera,* "wax," and is a metaphor taken from clarified honey; for the pure or clarified honey is that which is *sine cera,* without wax, no part of the comb being left in it. Sincerity, taken in its full meaning, is a word of the most extensive import; and, when applied in reference to the state of the soul, is as strong as the word "perfection" itself. The soul that is sincere is the soul that is without sin. *Without offence.* Neither offending God nor your neighbor; being neither stumbled yourselves nor the cause of stumbling to others. *Till the day of Christ.* Till He comes to judge the world, or till the day in which you are called into the eternal world. According to this prayer a man, under the power and influence of the grace of God, may so love as never to offend his Maker, to the latest period of his life. Those who deny this must believe that the Spirit of God either cannot or will not do it, or that the blood of Christ cannot cleanse from all unrighteousness.

11. *Being filled with the fruits of righteousness.* By *righteousness* we may understand here the whole work of the Spirit of God in the soul of a believer; and by the *fruits* of righteousness, all holy tempers, holy words, and right actions. And with these they are to be *filled,* "filled up, filled full"; the whole soul and life occupied with them, ever doing something by which glory is brought to God, or good done to man. *By Jesus Christ.* That is, according to His doctrine, through the power of His grace, and by the agency of His Spirit. *Unto the glory and praise of God.* God being honored when the work of His grace thus appears to men in the fruits of righteousness; and God is praised by all the faithful when His work thus appears.

12. *That the things which happened unto me.* Paul was at this time a prisoner at Rome, and it appears probable that he had already been called to make a defense for himself, and to vindicate the doctrines of the gospel; and this he had been enabled to do in such a manner that the honor of the gospel had been greatly promoted by it.

13. *My bonds in Christ are manifest in all the palace.* In consequence of the public defense which he was obliged to make, his doctrines must be fully known in the court and throughout the whole city, as on his trial he would necessarily explain the whole. The *praetorium,* which we here translate *palace,* signifies the court where causes were heard and judged by the *praetor* or civil magistrate; it sometimes signifies the "general's tent," and at others the "emperor's palace." It is supposed that it is used in this latter sense here. There were, no doubt, persons belonging to the emperor's household who would bring the news of so re-

markable a case to the palace; for we find that there were Christians even in Caesar's household; chap. iv. 22.

14. *Waxing confident.* Finding the effect produced by the public defense which the apostle made, they were greatly encouraged, and the more boldly and openly proclaimed the doctrine of Christ crucified.

15. *Some indeed preach Christ even of envy and strife.* These must have been the Judaizing teachers, who insisted on the necessity of connecting the Mosaic rites with the Christian institutions; and probably denounced Paul to the Jews dwelling at Rome as not only an enemy to the law and the prophets, but also as a very imperfect Christian, because he declared strongly against the doctrine of circumcision; and no doubt endeavored to prejudice him with the heathen Romans. *Some also of good will.* Some, through mere benevolence to the apostle, both espoused his doctrine and vindicated his cause.

16. *Preach Christ of contention.* The Judaizing teachers, they also preach Christ; they acknowledge that Jesus is the Christ or promised Messiah, and preach Him as such. *Not sincerely.* "Not chastely," garbling the gospel; not speaking the whole truth, but just what served their purpose; and at the same time they denounced the apostle as an enemy to the divine institutions, because he spoke against circumcision.

17. *The other of love.* Through a sincere desire, not only to make known the way of salvation to the people, but also to vindicate and help the apostle, because they considered him as appointed by God to preach and defend the gospel. The sixteenth and seventeenth verses are transposed by several MSS.

18. *What then?* It is a matter of little importance to me how Christ is preached, provided He be preached. I rejoice that anything is known of Him; and am truly glad that the gospel is even made partially known, for this will lead to further inquiries and in the end be of service to the truth.

19. *This shall turn to my salvation.* That is: It will be the means of my temporal "safety"; of my "deliverance"; for so the word *soteria* is here to be understood. The Jews had denounced the apostle as an enemy to Caesar; but he knew that, when the nature of the gospel should be fully known, the Romans would see that he could be no enemy to Caesar who proclaimed a prince whose kingdom was not of this world. *Through your prayer.* Knowing them to be genuine followers of Christ, he was satisfied that their prayers would be very available in his behalf; and under God he places much dependence upon them. *The supply of the Spirit of Jesus Christ.* The word which we translate *supply* signifies also "furnishing whatever is necessary." The Spirit of God he expected to help all his infirmities and to furnish him with all the wisdom, prudence, strength of reason, and argument which might be necessary for him in the different trials he had to pass through with his persecutors, and the civil powers, at whose judgment seat he stood.

20. *Earnest expectation.* He had the most confident expectation that God would stand by him, so that he should be enabled, with the "utmost liberty of speech," to testify the gospel of the grace of God; and, should he have the liberty of doing so, he was utterly regardless what the issue might be relative to himself.

21. *For to me to live is Christ.* "Whether I live or die, Christ is gain to me." While I live I am Christ's property and servant, and Christ is my Portion. If I die, if I be called to witness the truth at the expense of my life, this will be gain; I shall be saved from the remaining troubles and difficulties in life, and be put immediately in possession of my heavenly inheritance.

22. *But if I live in the flesh.* Should I be spared longer, I shall labor for Christ as I have done; and *this is the fruit of my labour,* that Christ shall be magnified by my longer life, v. 20. *Yet what I shall choose I wot not.* Had I the two conditions left to my own choice, whether to die now and go to glory or whether to live longer in persecutions and affliction (glorifying Christ by spreading the gospel), I could not tell which to prefer.

23. *For I am in a strait betwixt two.* Viz., the dying now and being immediately with God or living longer to preach and spread the gospel and thus glorify Christ among men. *Having a desire to depart, and to be with Christ.* It appears to be a metaphor taken from the commander of a vessel, in a foreign port, who feels a strong desire "to set sail," and get to his own country and family; but this desire is counterbalanced by a conviction that the general interests of the voyage may be best answered by his longer stay in the port where his vessel now rides.

24. *To abide in the flesh.* It would certainly be gain to myself to die, but it will be a gain to you if I live.

25. *Having this confidence, I know that I shall abide.* Convinced that it is necessary that I should live longer, for the spreading and defense of the gospel, I am persuaded that I shall now be liberated. This was in fact the case, for, after having been two years in bonds at Rome, he was released. *For your furtherance.* In the way of righteousness. *And joy of faith.* And happiness in that way.

26. *That your rejoicing may be more abundant.* Men rejoice more in recovering a thing that was lost than they do in a continual possession of what is of much greater value.

27. *Let your conversation be as it becometh the gospel.* The apostle considers the church at Philippi as a free or imperial city, which possesses great honors, dignities, and privileges; and he exhorts them to act "worthy of or suitably to" those honors and privileges. This is the idea that is expressed by the word, "act according to the nature of your political situation," the citizenship and privileges which you possess in consequence of your being free inhabitants of Christ's imperial city, the Church. The apostle resumes the same metaphor, chap. iii. 20: "For our citizenship is in heaven." *Whether I come and see you.* Leaving the matter still in doubt as to them, whether he should again visit them. *In one spirit.* Being all of one mind under the influence of the Holy Ghost. *Striving together.* "Wrestling together," not in contention with each other, but in union against the enemies of the gospel faith.

28. *In nothing terrified by your adversaries.* So it appears that the church at Philippi was then under persecution.

29. *Unto you it is given in the behalf of Christ.* "To you it is graciously given"; it is no small privilege that God has so far honored you as to permit you to suffer on Christ's account. It is only His most faithful servants that He thus honors. Be not therefore terrified by your enemies; they can do nothing to you which God will not turn to your eternal advantage.

30. *Having the same conflict.* When Paul preached the gospel at Philippi he was grievously persecuted, as we learn from Acts xvi. 19-40, being stripped, scourged, thrown into prison, even into the dungeon, and his feet made fast in the stocks. This was the *conflict* they had seen in him; and now they heard that he had been sent prisoner to Rome as an evildoer, and that he was at present in bonds, and shortly to be tried for his life before the Roman emperor, to whom he had been obliged to appeal.

CHAPTER 2

The apostle beseeches them, by various considerations, to live in unity and in the spirit of the gospel, loving each other; and each to prefer his brother to himself, 1-4. He exhorts them to be like-minded with Christ, who, though in the form of God and equal with God, made himself of no reputation, and humbled himself to the death of the Cross for the salvation of man; in consequence of which He was highly exalted, and had a name above every name; to whose authority every knee should bow, and whose glory every tongue should acknowledge, 5-11. They are exhorted to work out their own salvation through His power who works in them, that they may be blameless, and that the apostle's labor may not be in vain, 12-16. He expresses his readiness to offer his life for the gospel, 17-18. Intends to send Timothy to them, of whom he gives a very high character; yet hopes to see them himself shortly, 19-24. In the meantime sends Epaphroditus, who had been near death, and whom he begs them to receive with especial tenderness, 25-30.

1. *If there be therefore any consolation.* The *if* does not express any doubt here, but on the contrary is to be considered as a strong affirmation; "as there is" consolation in Christ, as there is comfort of love. The word translated here *consolation* is in other places rendered "exhortation," and is by several critics understood so here; as if he had said: If exhorting you in the name of Christ has any influence with you. It is extremely difficult to give the force of these expressions; they contain a torrent of most affecting eloquence, the apostle pouring out his whole heart to a people whom with all his heart he loved, and who were worthy of the love even of an apostle. *If any comfort of love.* If the followers of Christ, by giving proofs of their ardent love to each other in cases of distress, alleviate the sufferings of the persecuted. *If any fellowship of the Spirit.* If there be an intimate relation established among all Christians, by their being made mutual partakers of the Holy Ghost. *If any bowels and mercies.* If you, as persons whom I have brought to God at the hazard of my life, feel sympathetic tenderness for me now in a further state of suffering.

2. *Fulfil ye my joy.* You ought to complete my joy, who have suffered so much to bring you into the possession of these blessings, by being *likeminded* with myself, *having the same love* to God, His cause, and me as I have to Him, His cause, and you.

3. *Let nothing be done through strife.* Never be opposed to each other; never act from separate interests. You are all brethren, and of one body; therefore let every member feel and

labor for the welfare of the whole. *But in lowliness of mind.* Have always a humbling view of yourselves, and this will lead you to prefer others to yourselves; for, as you know your own secret defects, charity will lead you to suppose that your brethren are more holy and more devoted to God than you are; and they will think the same of you, their secret defects also being known only to themselves.

4. *Look not every man on his own things.* Do nothing through self-interest in the things of God nor arrogate to yourselves gifts, graces, and fruits which belong to others; you are all called to promote God's glory and the salvation of men.

5. *Let this mind be in you, which was also in Christ Jesus.* Christ labored to promote no separate interest; as man He studied to promote the glory of God and the welfare and salvation of the human race. See then that you have the same "disposition" that was in Jesus.

6. *Thought it not robbery to be equal with God.* The word which we translate *robbery* has been supposed to imply "a thing eagerly to be seized, coveted, or desired," and on this interpretation the passage has been translated: "Who, being in the form of God, did not think it a matter to be earnestly desired to appear equal to God; but made himself of no reputation." Though He was from eternity in the form of God—possessed of the same glory—yet He thought it right to veil this glory and not to appear with it among the children of men; and therefore He was made in the *likeness of men* and took upon Him the *form* or "appearance" of a *servant*. On this account I prefer this sense of the word before that given in our text, which does not agree so well with the other expressions in the context.

7. *But made himself of no reputation.* "He emptied himself"—did not appear in His glory, for He assumed the form of a servant, being made in the likeness of man.

8. *And being found in fashion as a man.* This clause should be joined to the preceding, and thus translated: "Being made in the likeness of man, and was found in fashion as a man." *He humbled himself.* Laid himself as low as possible: (1) In emptying himself—laying aside the effulgence of His glory. (2) In being incarnate—taking upon Him the human form. (3) In becoming a Servant—assuming the lowest innocent character, that of being the Servant of all. (4) In condescending to die, to which He was not naturally liable, as having never sinned, and therefore had a right in His human nature to immortality, without passing under the empire of death. (5) In condescending, not only to death, but to the lowest and most ignominious kind of death, *the death of the cross*, the punishment of the meanest of slaves and worst of felons. What must sin have been in the sight of God when it required such abasement in Jesus Christ to make an atonement for it, and undo its influence and malignity!

9. *Wherefore God also hath highly exalted him.* He has given him a name, "the name," *which is above every name.* This makes it much more emphatic. According to Eph. i. 20-21, the Man Christ Jesus is exalted to the right hand of God, "far above all principality, and power, and might, and dominion, and every name that is named, not only in this world, but also in that which is to come." But if we

refer to any particular epithet, then the name Jesus or "Saviour" must be that which is intended; as no being either in heaven or earth can possess this name as He who is the Redeemer of the world does.

10. *That at the name of Jesus every knee should bow.* That all human beings should consider themselves redeemed unto God by His blood. In a word, that all the spirits of just men made perfect, now in a state of blessedness; all human beings still in their state of probation on earth; and all that are in the shades below, who have, through their own fault, died without having received His salvation; should acknowledge Him.

11. *And that every tongue should confess.* That all those before mentioned should acknowledge that Jesus Christ is Lord, or "absolute Governor," and thus glorify God the Father, who has exalted this human nature to this state of ineffable glory, in virtue of its passion, death, resurrection, and the atonement which it has made, by which so many attributes of the divine nature have become illustrated, the divine law magnified and made honorable, and an eternal glory provided for man. Others by "things in heaven" understand the holy angels; by "things on earth," human beings generally; and by "things under the earth," fallen spirits of every description. Perhaps the three expressions are designed to comprehend all beings of all kinds, all creatures.

12. *As ye have always obeyed.* Continue to act on the same principles and from the same motives; having the same disposition which was in Christ; laboring so as to promote His glory. *Work out your own salvation.* Go on, walking by the same rule and minding the same thing, till your salvation be completed. *With fear and trembling.* Considering the difficulty of the work and the danger of miscarriage.

13. *To will and to do.* The power to will and the power to act must necessarily come from God, who is the Author of both soul and body, and of all their powers and energies; but the act of volition and the act of working come from the man. Because God works in them the power to will and the power to do, therefore the apostle exhorts them to work out their own salvation, most manifestly showing that the use of the powers of volition and action belongs to themselves. They cannot do God's work; they cannot produce in themselves a power to will and to do. And God will not do their work; He will not work out their salvation with fear and trembling.

14. *Do all things without murmurings.* "Without grumblings and altercations."

15. *That ye may be blameless.* In yourselves, and harmless to others. *The sons of God.* Showing by your holy conduct that you are partakers of the divine nature. *Without rebuke.* Persons against whom no charge of transgression can justly be laid. *Among whom ye shine.* Be like the sun and moon; bless even the perverse and disobedient by your light and splendor.

16. *Holding forth the word of life.* An allusion, some think, to those towers which were built at the entrance of harbors, on which fires were kept during the night to direct ships into the port.

17. *Yea, and if I be offered upon the sacrifice and service.* The metaphor appears to be car-

ried on. As it was customary for the weather-beaten mariner, when he had gained his port, to offer a sacrifice to God of some particular animal which he had vowed while in his state of danger, and this was considered to be a "religious service," the apostle, pursuing the idea, states himself to be willing to become the "libation" that was to be "poured upon the sacrifice."

18. *For the same cause also do ye joy.* Should I be thus offered, as I shall rejoice in it, do you also rejoice that I am counted worthy of this high honor.

19. *But I trust in the Lord Jesus.* He is Governor and Disposer of all events, being above all principality and power; and I humbly confide in His power and goodness that I shall be a little longer spared to visit you again, v. 24, and to be able to send Timothy shortly to you. *When I know your state.* By the correct information which I shall receive from Timothy.

20. *For I have no man likeminded.* He is "of the same soul"; a man after my own heart.

21. *For all seek their own.* This must relate to the persons who preached Christ "even of envy and strife," chap. i. 15.

22. *Ye know the proof of him, that, as a son with the father, he hath served with me.* The Philippians had full proof of the affectionate attachment of Timothy to Paul, for he had labored with him there, as we learn from Acts xvi. 1-3 and xvii. 14; and we find from what is said here that Timothy was not a servant to the apostle, but that he had served with him.

23. *How it will go with me.* The apostle was now in captivity; his trial appears to have been approaching, and of its issue he was doubtful, though he seems to have had a general persuasion that he should be spared (see v. 19 and v. 24).

27. *Lest I should have sorrow upon sorrow.* The sorrows of his death, added to the sorrow he endured on account of his sickness; or he may refer to his own state of affliction, being imprisoned and maltreated.

28. *The more carefully.* With the "more haste or dispatch"; because, having suffered so much on account of his apprehended death, they could not be too soon comforted by seeing him alive and restored.

29. *Receive him therefore in the Lord.* For the Lord's sake receive him, and as the Lord's servant.

30. *For the work of Christ.* Preaching the gospel, and ministering to the distressed. *He was nigh unto death.* Having labored far beyond his strength. *Not regarding his life.* Instead of *not regarding his life*, "risking his life" is the reading of some MSS.

CHAPTER 3

The apostle exhorts the Philippians to rejoice in the Lord, 1. And to beware of false teachers, 2. Shows that Christians are the true circumcision, who worship God in the Spirit, 3. And that himself had more reason to trust in the flesh than any of the Jews, 4-6. But that he counted all things loss for Christ, 7-11. He longs after a conformity to Christ in His death, and presses onward to the attainment of His high calling, 12-14. Exhorts them to be like-minded, 15-17. Warns them against certain persons who were enemies to the cross of Christ, 18-19. Shows the nature of their heavenly privileges, and the resurrection and glorification of the human body, 20-21.

1. *Rejoice in the Lord.* Be always happy, but let that happiness be such as you derive from the Lord. *For you it is safe.* It is much better to have these divine things committed to writing than confided to memory.

2. *Beware of dogs.* The Jews, who have here the same appellative which they formerly gave to the Gentiles. *Evil workers.* Judaizing teachers, who endeavored to pervert the gospel. *The concision.* The "cutting" or "excision"; not the "circumcision." The word is used by the apostle to degrade the pretensions which the Jews made to sanctity by the cutting in their flesh. Circumcision was an honorable thing, for it was a sign of the covenant; but as they now had rejected the new covenant, their circumcision was rendered uncircumcision, and is termed a "cutting," by way of degradation.

3. *We are the circumcision.* We who have embraced the faith of Christ crucified are now entered into the new covenant, and according to that new covenant, *worship God in the Spirit,* "exulting," "making our boast of Christ Jesus," as our only Saviour, having *no confidence in the flesh*—in any outward rite or ceremony prescribed by the Jewish institutions.

4. *Though I might also have confidence.* If any of them have any cause to boast in outward rites and privileges, I have as much; yea, *more.*

5. *Circumcised the eighth day.* This was the time that the law required the males to be circumcised. *Of the stock of Israel.* Regularly descended from the patriarch Jacob. *Of the tribe of Benjamin.* The most favorite son of that patriarch; and a tribe that did not revolt with Jeroboam, 1 Kings xii. 21, nor pollute the worship of God by idolatry. *An Hebrew of the Hebrews.* Though born in a heathen country, Tarsus, yet both my parents were Hebrews; nor has there ever been any strange blood mixed with that of our family. *Touching the law, a Pharisee.* One that not only received the law and the prophets as coming from God, but belonged to that sect which, of all others, was most scrupulously attached to it.

6. *Concerning zeal.* As to my zeal for Pharisaism, I gave the fullest proof of it by persecuting the Church of Christ; and this is known to all my countrymen. *Touching the righteousness.* And as to that plan of "justification," which justification the Jews say is to be obtained by an observance of the law, I have done everything so conscientiously from my youth up that in this respect I am *blameless;* and may, with more confidence than most of them, expect that justification which the law appears to promise.

7. *But what things were gain.* The credit and respect which I had, as being zealously attached to the law and to the traditions of the elders, *I counted loss for Christ*—I saw that this could stand me in no stead, that all my acts of righteousness were nothing on which I could depend for salvation, and that Christ crucified could alone profit me.

8. *I count all things but loss.* Not only my Jewish privileges, but all others of every kind. *The excellency of the knowledge of Christ.* That superior light, information, and blessedness which come through the gospel of Jesus Christ. *I have suffered the loss of all things.* Some translate, "for whom I have thrown away all things"—I have made a voluntary choice of Christ, His cross, His poverty, and His reproach;

and for these I have freely sacrificed all I had from the world, and all I could expect from it. *And do count them but dung.* The word means the vilest dross or "refuse" of anything, the worst excrement.

9. *And be found in him.* Be found a believer in Christ, *not having mine own righteousness*—not trusting in anything I have done or could do, in order to my salvation; relying on no scheme of justification, set up formerly either by myself or by others. *But that which is through the faith of Christ.* That justification which is received by faith through the atonement made by Christ. *The righteousness which is of God.* God's method of justifying sinners through faith in His Son.

10. *That I may know him.* To be the true and promised Messiah, and experience all that salvation which He has bought by His blood. *And the fellowship of his sufferings.* Christ died, not only as a Victim for sin, but as a Martyr to the truth. No creature can have *fellowship* with Him in His vicarious sufferings; as a martyr to the truth, Paul wished to imitate Him.

11. *The resurrection of the dead.* That is, the resurrection of those who, having died in the Lord, rise to glory and honor; and hence Paul uses a peculiar word which occurs nowhere else in the New Testament. The words, as they stand in the best MSS., are as follows: "to that resurrection which is of the dead."

12. *Not as though I had already attained.* For I have not yet received the prize; I am not glorified, for I have not finished my course; and I have a conflict still to maintain, and the issue will prove whether I should be crowned. From the beginning of the eleventh to the end of the seventeenth verse there is one continued allusion to the contests at the Olympic games; exercises with which, and their laws, the Philippians were well acquainted. *Either were already perfect.* "Nor am I yet perfect"; I am not yet crowned, in consequence of having suffered martyrdom. I am quite satisfied that the apostle here alludes to the Olympic games, and the word *teteleiomai* is the proof; spoken of those who have completed their race, reached the goal, and are honored with the prize. Paul therefore is not speaking here of any deficiency in his own grace or spiritual state; he does not mean by not being yet *perfect* that he had a body of sin and death cleaving to him, and was still polluted with indwelling *sin*, as some have imagined. He speaks of his not having terminated his course by martyrdom, which he knew would sooner or later be the case. *But I follow after.* "But I pursue." Several are gone before me in this glorious way, and have obtained the crown of martyrdom; I am hurrying after them. *That I may apprehend.* That I may receive those blessings to which I am called by Christ Jesus. There is still an allusion here to the stadium, and exercises there. The apostle considers Christ as the *brabeus,* or Judge in the games, who proclaimed the victor and distributed the prizes; and he represents himself as being introduced by this very *brabeus,* or Judge, into the contest; and this *brabeus* brought him in with the design to crown him, if he contended faithfully. To complete this faithful contention is what he has in view; that he may *apprehend,* or "lay hold" on, *that for which* he had been *apprehended,* or "taken by the hand," *by Christ,*

who had converted, strengthened, and endowed him with apostolical powers, that he might fight the good fight of faith, and "lay hold" on eternal life.

13. *I count not myself to have apprehended.* Whatever gifts, graces, or honors I may have received from Jesus Christ, I consider everything as incomplete till I have finished my course, got this crown, and have my body raised and fashioned after His glorious body. *This one thing I do.* This is the concern, as it is the sole business, of my life. *Reaching forth.* The Greek word points out the strong exertions made in the race; every muscle and nerve is exerted, and he puts forth every particle of his strength in running. He was running for life, and running for his life.

14. *I press toward the mark.* "I pursue along the line"; this is a reference to the white lines that marked the ground in the stadium, from the starting place to the goal, on which the runners were obliged to keep their eyes fixed; for they who transgressed or went beyond this line did not run lawfully, and were not crowned, even though they got first to the goal. What is called *scopos*, "mark" or "scope," here is called *canon*, the "line," i.e., the marked line, v. 16. When it was said to Diogenes, the cynic, "Thou art now an old man, rest from thy labors"; to this he answered: "If I have run long in the race, will it become me to slacken my pace when I come near the end; should I not rather stretch forward?" *For the prize of the high calling of God.* The reward which God from above calls me, by Christ Jesus, to receive. The apostle still keeps in view his crown of martyrdom and his glorious resurrection.

15. *As many as be perfect.* As many as are "thoroughly instructed" in divine things, who have cast off all dependence on the law and on every other system for salvation, and who discern God calling them from above by Christ Jesus. *Be thus minded;* be intensely in earnest for eternal life, nor ever halt till the race is finished. The word *teleioi, perfect,* is taken here in the same sense in which it is taken in 1 Cor. xiv. 20: "Be not *children* in understanding . . . but in understanding be ye *men,*" *teleioi*—"thoroughly instructed, deeply experienced." 1 Cor. ii. 6: "We speak wisdom among them that are perfect," among those who are fully instructed, adults in Christian knowledge. Eph. iv. 13: "Till we all come . . . unto a perfect man"; *teleion,* to the state of adults in Christianity. Heb. v. 14: "But strong meat belongeth to them that are of full age"; *teleion,* "the perfect"—those who are thoroughly instructed and experienced in divine things. *Let us therefore,* says the apostle, *as many as be perfect,* as have entered fully into the spirit and design of the gospel, *be thus minded,* viz., Forget the things which are behind, and stretch forward along the mark for the prize. *If in any thing ye be otherwise minded.* If you have not yet entered into the full spirit and design of this gospel, if any of you have yet remaining any doubts relative to Jewish ordinances or their expediency in Christianity, *God shall reveal even this unto you;* for while you are sincere and upright, God will take care that you shall have full instruction in these divine things.

16. *Whereto we have already attained.* Let us not lose that part of the race which we have already run. *Let us walk by the same rule*—

let us keep the white line continually in view. *Let us mind the same thing,* always considering the glorious prize which is held out by God through Christ Jesus to animate and encourage us.

17. *Brethren, be followers together of me.* In the things of Christ let me be your "line"; and my writing, preaching, and conduct, your "rule." *And mark them.* Still alluding to the "line" in the stadium; keep your eye steadily fixed on those *which walk,* "live," *as ye have us* —myself, Timothy, and Epaphroditus—*for an ensample.*

18. *For many walk.* The Judaizing teachers continue to preach, who wish to incorporate circumcision and other ordinances of the law with the gospel. *They are the enemies of the cross of Christ.* They rather attribute justification to the Levitical sacrifices than to the sacrificial death of Christ; and thus they are enemies to that Cross, and will not suffer persecution for its sake.

19. *Whose end is destruction.* This is the issue of their doctrine and of their conduct. They are here described by three characters: (1) Their *god is their belly*—they live not in any reference to eternity. (2) Their *glory is in their shame*—they lay it down as a proof of their address that they can fare sumptuously every day in consequence of preaching a doctrine which flatters the passions of their hearers. (3) They *mind earthly things*—their whole study and attention are taken up with earthly matters.

20. *Our conversation is in heaven.* "Our citizenship" or "civil rights."

21. *Who shall change our vile body.* Who will "refashion" or "alter the fashion and condition of," the body of our humiliation; this body that is dead—adjudged to death because of sin, and must be putrefied, dissolved, and decomposed. *That it may be fashioned like unto his glorious body.* "That it may bear a similar form to the body of His glory." That is: The bodies of true believers shall be raised up at the great day in the same likeness, immortality, and glory of the glorified humanity of Jesus Christ; and be so thoroughly changed as to be not only capable through their immortality of eternally existing, but also of the infinite spiritual enjoyments at the right hand of God. *According to the working.* "According to that energy, by which He can bring all things under subjection to himself."

CHAPTER 4

The apostle exhorts them to stand fast in the Lord, 1. And beseeches Euodias and Syntyche to be of one mind in divine things, 2. And requests his true yokefellow to help them to a good understanding, 3. Gives them directions concerning their temper and frame of mind, 4-7. And how to act in all respects as becomes the purity and excellence of the gospel, as they had heard from and seen in him, 8-9. Thanks them for their attention to him in his captivity, in sending him what was necessary for his support, though he had learned to be contented in all situations in life, 10-14. Mentions particular cases in which they had ministered to him; promises them, through the riches of glory in Christ, a supply of all their spiritual wants; and renders thanks to God, 15-20. Salutes all the saints, and those particularly of the emperor's household, 21-22. And concludes with his usual apostolical benediction, 23.

1. *Therefore, my . . . beloved.* Because you have this armor, and those enemies, and God for your support, see that you stand fast in Him. This verse most unquestionably belongs to the preceding chapter.

2. *I beseech Euodias, and beseech Syntyche.* These were two pious women, as it is generally supposed, who were deaconesses in the church at Philippi, and who in some points of doctrine and discipline had disagreed. He exhorts them to be of the same mind, that is, to compose their differences; and if they could not perfectly agree, to think and let think, and to avoid all public opposition, as their dissension would strengthen the hands of the common enemy and stumble those who were weak.

3. *Help those women which laboured with me.* Both in the Grecian and Asiatic countries women were kept much secluded, and it was not likely that even the apostles had much opportunity of conversing with them. It was therefore necessary that they should have some experienced Christian women with them who could have access to families and preach Jesus to the female part of them. The apostle tells us that certain women labored with him in the gospel, and were assistants to others also who had assisted him. *With Clement also.* Supposed to be the same who was afterwards bishop of Rome, and who wrote an Epistle to the Corinthians, which is still extant. *Whose names are in the book of life.* Who are genuine Christians; who are enlisted or enrolled in the armies of the Lord, and have received a title to eternal glory.

4. *Rejoice in the Lord alway.* Be continually happy; but this happiness you can find only *in the Lord.* Genuine happiness is spiritual; as it can come only from God, so it infallibly tends to Him.

5. *Let your moderation be known.* The word is of very extensive signification; it means the same as mildness, patience, yieldingness, gentleness, clemency, unwillingness to litigate or contend; but *moderation* is expressive enough as a general term. *The Lord is at hand.* A phrase something similar to the Maranatha of 1 Cor. xvi. 22. The Lord is Judge, and is at hand to punish.

6. *Be careful for nothing.* Be not anxiously solicitous. Do not give place to carking care, let what will occur; for anxiety cannot change the state or condition of anything from bad to good, but will infallibly injure your own souls. *By prayer and supplication.* God alone can help you; He is disposed to do it, but you must ask by prayer and supplication; without this He has not promised to help you. *By prayer*—solemn application to God from a sense of want. *Supplication*—continuance in earnest prayer. *With thanksgiving,* for innumerable favors already received; and for dangers, evils, and deaths turned aside.

7. *And the peace of God.* That harmonizing of all passions and appetites which is produced by the Holy Spirit, and arises from a sense of pardon and the favor of God. *Shall keep your hearts.* Shall keep them as in a strong place or castle. *Your hearts*—the seat of all your affections and passions, *and minds*—your understanding, judgment, and conscience. *Through Christ Jesus;* by whom you were brought into this state of favor, through whom you are preserved in it, and in whom you possess it, for Christ keeps that heart in peace in which He dwells and rules.

8. *Finally, brethren.* The object of the apostle is to recommend holiness and righteousness to them in every point of view; and to show that the gospel of Christ requires all its professors to have the mind that was in Christ, and to walk as He himself also walked. *Whatsoever things are true.* All that is agreeable to unchangeable and eternal truth. *Whatsoever things are honest.* Whatever is "grave, decent, and venerable." Whatever becomes you as men, as citizens, and as Christians. *Whatsoever things are just.* Whatsoever is agreeable to justice and righteousness. All that you owe to God, to your neighbor, and to yourselves. *Whatsoever things are pure.* Whatsoever is "chaste." In reference to the state of the mind and to the acts of the body. *Whatsoever things are lovely.* Whatsoever is "amiable" on its own account and on account of its usefulness to others, whether in your conduct or conversation. *Whatsoever things are of good report.* Whatsoever things the public agree to acknowledge as useful and profitable to men; such as charitable institutions of every kind, in which genuine Christians should ever take the lead. *If there be any virtue.* If they be calculated to promote the general good of mankind, and are thus praiseworthy. *Think on these things.* Esteem them highly, recommend them heartily, and practice them fervently.

9. *Those things, which ye have . . . learned.* From my preaching and writing. *And received.* By faith, as a revelation from God. *And heard.* From my preaching, and that of those who labored with me; and heard from me in my private communications with you; and heard of me from other churches. *And seen in me.* While living and laboring among you. *Do.* Take them for the rule of your faith and practice. *And the God of peace.* He who is the Author of peace, the Lover of peace, and the Maintainer of peace; He who has made peace between heaven and earth, by the mission and sacrifice of His Son, shall be ever with you while you believe and act as here recommended.

10. *But I rejoiced in the Lord.* Every good comes from God, either immediately from His providence or from His grace; therefore the apostle thanks God for the kindness of the Philippians towards him; for it was God who gave them the power, and directed their hearts to use it. *Hath flourished again.* They had helped him before, chap. ii. 25; they had ceased for a time, and now they began again. This is evidently designed by the apostle, as the word implies, which is a metaphor taken from the reviviscence of flowers in spring which seemed dead in winter. For the time in which they were apparently remiss he makes a delicate apology: *Ye were . . . careful, but ye lacked opportunity;* or rather, "You had not ability; you wanted the means."

11. *Not that I speak in respect of want.* I am quite unconcerned in this respect, leaving the whole of my support, while bound for the testimony of Jesus, to the providence of God. *For I have learned.* How true is the proverb, "A contented mind is a continual feast"! What do we get by murmuring and complaining?

12. *I know . . . how to be abased.* I have passed through all these states; I know how to conduct myself in each, and how to extract good from all. And he had passed through these things, especially the hardships, so that he had learned the lesson "perfectly," as the word im-

plies; he was thoroughly instructed, fully initiated into all the mysteries of poverty and want, and of the supporting hand of God in the whole.

13. *I can do all things.* It was not a habit which he had acquired by frequent exercise; it was a disposition which he had by grace; and he was enabled to do all by the power of an indwelling Christ. "Through Him who strengtheneth me" is the reading of some of the best MSS., versions, and fathers, the word *Christ* being omitted.

14. *Ye have well done.* Though I have learned all these important lessons, and am never miserable in want, yet you have done well in sending me relief in the time of affliction.

15. *In the beginning of the gospel.* When, having preached to you, I went forth into Macedonia, I received help from none of the churches which I had founded but from you alone.

16. *For even in Thessalonica.* While laboring to plant the church there, he was supported partly by working with his hands, 1 Thess. ii. 9; 2 Thess. iii. 7-9, and partly by the contributions sent him from Philippi.

17. *Not because I desire a gift.* I do not speak thus to incite you to send me a further gift; I speak this on the general subject because I wish you to bear such fruit as shall abound to your account in the day of the Lord.

18. *I have all.* You have now sent me so much by Epaphroditus that I abound in all the necessaries of life. *Having received . . . the things.* Probably a supply of clothes and such like necessaries, as well as of money. *An odour of a sweet smell.* Alluding to the sacrifices offered up under the law. With what you have done to me, His servant, God is well pleased.

19. *My God shall supply all your need.* As you have given to me in my distress, God will never suffer you to want without raising up help to you, as He raised you up for help to me.

21. *Salute every saint.* Remember to present my affectionate wishes to every Christian at Philippi. *The brethren which are with me.* Those who were fellow laborers with him, generally supposed to be Aristarchus, Mark, Justus, Epaphras, Luke, and Demas.

22. *All the saints.* All the Christians now at Rome. *They that are of Caesar's household.* Nero was at this time emperor of Rome. A more worthless, cruel, and diabolic wretch never disgraced the name or form of man; yet in "his family" there were Christians. But whether this relates to the members of the imperial family, or to guards, or courtiers, or to servants, we cannot tell. If even some of his slaves were converted to Christianity, it would be sufficiently marvellous.

23. *The grace of our Lord.* The word *our* is omitted by many MSS. and several versions, which simply read, "The grace of the Lord Jesus Christ."

The Epistle to the
COLOSSIANS

Colossae was a city of Phrygia in Asia Minor, seated on an eminence on the south side of the river Maeander. It was situated between Laodicea and Hierapolis, and at an equal distance from either; and to this place Xerxes came in his expedition against Greece.

The ancient city of Colossae has been extinct for eighteen hundred years; for about the tenth year of the Emperor Nero, about a year after the writing of this Epistle, not only Colossae, but Laodicea and Hierapolis, were destroyed by an earthquake, according to Eusebius; and the city which was raised in the place of the former was called Chonos or Konos, which name it now bears.

Whether the Colossians to whom the apostle addresses this Epistle were Jews or Gentiles cannot be absolutely determined. It is most probable that they were a mixture of both; but that the principal part were converted Jews is most likely.

CHAPTER 1

The salutation of Paul and Timothy to the church at Colossae, 1-2. They give thanks to God for the good estate of that church, and the wonderful progress of the gospel in every place, 3-6; having received particulars of their state from Epaphroditus, which not only excited their gratitude, but led them to pray to God that they might walk worthy of the gospel; and they give thanks to Him who had made them meet for an inheritance among the saints in light, 7-12. This state is described as a deliverance from the power of darkness, and being brought into the kingdom of God's dear Son, 13-14. The glorious character of Jesus Christ, and what He has done for mankind, 15-20. The salvation which the Colossians had received, and of which the apostle had been the minister and dispenser, 21-26. The sum and substance of the apostle's preaching, and the manner in which he executed his ministry, 27-29.

1. *Paul, an apostle of Jesus Christ by the will of God.* The word *apostle* signifies "one sent," an envoy or messenger. *And Timotheus.* Though Timothy is here joined in the salutation, yet he has never been understood as having any part in composing this Epistle. He has been considered as the amanuensis or scribe of the apostle.

4. *Since we heard of your faith.* This is very similar to Eph. i. 15. And it is certain that the apostle seems to have considered the church at Ephesus and that at Colossae to have been in nearly the same state, as the two Epistles are very similar in their doctrine and phraseology.

5. *For the hope which is laid up for you in heaven.* That eternal life, of both body and soul, which the apostle mentions, Titus i. 2: "In hope of eternal life, which God, that cannot lie, promised before the world began." The *hope* is here used for the object of hope; as every person that is born of God hopes for the resurrection of his body, and the glorification of both it and his soul in the realms of eternal blessedness. *In the word of the truth of the gospel.* In the "doctrine" of that gospel of your salvation which is the *truth* of God. Of this hope, by this doctrine, they had *heard before,* probably by persons who had heard and received the gospel either at Ephesus or some other place, in either Asia Minor or Greece, where the apostles had preached.

6. *And bringeth forth fruit.* Wherever the pure gospel of Christ is preached it is the *seed of the kingdom,* and must be fruitful in all those who receive it by faith, in simplicity of heart. After *bringeth forth fruit,* many MSS., together with many of the fathers, add "and increaseth." It had not only brought forth fruit, but was multiplying its own kind. This reading is very important, and is undoubtedly genuine.

7. *As ye also learned of Epaphras . . . who is for you.* That he was a Colossian is evident from chap. iv. 12: "Epaphras, who is one of you," and some think that he was the first who preached the gospel among this people, and hence called an apostle.

8. *Your love in the Spirit.* The heavenly flame in the heart of this minister communicated itself to those who heard him; it was "like priest, like people." They enjoyed a spiritual, energetic ministry, and they were a spiritual people; they had a loving spirit, and love through the Spirit of God, who dwelt in them.

12. *Giving thanks unto the Father.* Knowing that you have nothing but what you have received from His mere mercy, and that in point of merit you can never claim anything from Him. *Which hath made us meet.* Who has "qualified" us to be partakers. *Of the inheritance.* A plain allusion to the division of the Promised Land by lot among the different families of the twelve Israelitish tribes. *Of the saints in light. Light,* in the sacred writings, is used to express knowledge, felicity, purity, comfort, and joy of the most substantial kind; here it is put to point out the state of glory at the right hand of God.

13. *Delivered us from the power of darkness. Darkness* is here personified and is represented as having *power,* "authority, and sway," all Jews and Gentiles who had not embraced the gospel being under this authority and power. *Translated us into the kingdom.* He has thoroughly changed our state, brought us out of the dark region of vice and impiety, and placed us in the Kingdom under the government of *his dear Son,* "the Son of His love"; the Person whom, in His infinite love, He has given to make an atonement for the sin of the world.

14. *In whom we have redemption.* Who has paid down the redemption price, even His own blood, that our sins might be cancelled, and we made fit to be partakers of the inheritance among the saints in light. The clause *through his blood* is omitted by most MSS. and versions of weight and importance, and by most of the Greek fathers. It is likely that the reading here is not genuine. The same phrase is used Eph. i. 7, where there is no various reading in any of the MSS., versions, or fathers. *The forgiveness of sins.* "The taking away of sins"; all the power, guilt, and infection of sin.

15. *Who is the image of the invisible God.* The Counterpart of God Almighty; and if *the image of the invisible God,* consequently nothing that appeared in Him could be that image. *The firstborn of every creature.* I suppose this phrase to mean the same as that in Phil. ii. 9: "God . . . hath . . . given him a name which is above every name." He is a Man at the head of all the creation of God; nor can He with any propriety be considered as a creature, having himself created all things, and existed before anything was made. If it be said that God created Him first, and that He by a delegated power from God created all things, this is most flatly contradicted by the apostle's reasoning in the sixteenth and seventeenth verses. As the Jews term Jehovah "the firstborn of all the world" or "of all the creation," to signify His having created or produced all things, so Christ is here termed, and the words which follow in the sixteenth and seventeenth verses are the proof of this. The phraseology is Jewish; and as they apply it to the Supreme Being merely to denote His eternal preexistence, and to point Him out as the Cause of all things, it is most evident that Paul uses it in the same way, and illustrates his meaning in the following words, which would be absolutely absurd if we could suppose that by the former he intended to convey any idea of the inferiority of Jesus Christ.

16-17. *For by him were all things created.* Four things are here asserted: (1) That Jesus Christ is the Creator of the universe, of all things visible and invisible. (2) That whatsoever was created was created for himself. (3) That He was prior to all creation, to all beings, whether in the visible or invisible world. (4) That He is the Preserver and Governor of all things; for *by him all things consist.*

18. *He is the head of the body.* What the apostle has said in the preceding two verses refers to the divine nature of Jesus Christ. He now proceeds to speak of His human nature, and to show how highly that is exalted beyond all created things, and how, in that, He is Head of *the church*—the Author and Dispenser of light, life, and salvation, to the Christian world; or in other words, that from Him, as the Man in whom the fulness of the Godhead bodily dwelt, all the mercy and salvation of the gospel system is to be received. *The beginning, the firstborn from the dead.* In 1 Cor. xv. 20, Christ is called "the firstfruits of them that slept"; and here, the chief and *firstborn from the dead;* He being the first that ever resumed the natural life, with the employment of all its functions, nevermore to enter the empire of death, after having died a natural death, and in such circumstances as precluded the possibility of deception. The *arche,* "chief, head, or first," answers in this verse to the *aparche,* or "firstfruits," 1 Cor. xv. 20. Jesus Christ is not only the first who rose from the dead to die no more, but He is the firstfruits of human beings, for as surely as the firstfruits were an indication and pledge of the harvest, so surely was the resurrection of Christ the proof that all mankind should have a resurrection from the dead. *That in all things he might have the preeminence.* That He might be considered, in consequence of His mediatorial office, as possessing the first place in and being chief over all the creation of God. For is it to be wondered at that the human nature, with which the great Creator condescended to unite himself, should be set over all the works of His hands?

19. *For it pleased the Father that in him should all fulness dwell.* As the words *the Father* are not in the original text, some have translated the verse thus: "For in him it seemed right that all fulness should dwell"; that is, that the majesty, power, and goodness of God should be manifested in and by Christ Jesus, and thus by Him the Father reconciles all things to himself. The *fulness* must refer here to the divine nature dwelling in the Man Christ Jesus.

20. *And, having made peace through the blood of his cross.* Peace between God and man. *To reconcile all things unto himself.* The enmity was on the part of the creature; though God is angry with the wicked every day, yet He is never unwilling to be reconciled. But man, whose carnal mind is enmity to God, is naturally averse from this reconciliation; it requires, therefore, the *blood of his cross* to atone for the sin, and the influence of the Spirit to reconcile the transgressor to Him against whom he has offended! *Things in earth, or things in heaven.* If the phrase be not a kind of collective phrase to signify "all the world" or "all mankind," the *things in heaven* may refer, according to some, to those persons who died under the Old Testament dispensation, and who could not have a title to glory but through the sacrificial death of Christ.

21. *And you, that were sometime alienated.* All men are *alienated* from God, and all are *enemies* in their *mind* to Him, and show it by their *wicked works;* but this is spoken particularly of the Gentiles. The word which we render to alienate, "to give to another, to estrange," expresses the state of the Gentiles. While the Jews were, at least by profession, dedicated to God, the Gentiles were *alienated,* that is, "given up to others"; they worshipped not the true God, but had gods many and lords many, to whom they dedicated themselves, their religious service, and their property. *Enemies in your mind.* They had the carnal mind, which is enmity against God; and this was expressed in their outward conduct by *wicked works.* The *mind* is taken here for all the soul, heart, affections, passions.

22. *In the body of his flesh.* By Christ's assumption of a human body, and dying for man, He has made an atonement for sin, through which men become reconciled to God and to each other. *To present you holy.* Having saved you from your sins. *Unblameable.* Having filled you with His Spirit, and written His law in your hearts, so that His love, shed abroad in your hearts, becomes the principle and motive to every action. *And unreproveable.* For, being filled with love, joy, peace, meekness, gentleness, and goodness, against these there is no law. *In his sight.* At the day of judgment. None can enjoy heaven who have not been reconciled to God here, and shown forth the fruits of that reconciliation in being made *holy and*

unblameable, that, when they come to be judged, they may be found *unreproveable.*

23. *If ye continue in the faith.* This will be the case if you, who have already believed in Christ Jesus, continue in that faith, *grounded* in the knowledge and love of God, and *settled,* made firm and perseveringly steadfast, in that state of salvation. *And be not moved away.* Not permitting yourselves to be seduced by false teachers. *The hope of the gospel.* The resurrection of the body, and the glorification of it and the soul together, in the realms of blessedness. This is properly the gospel hope. *To every creature which is under heaven.* A Hebraism for the whole human race.

24. *Rejoice in my sufferings for you.* Paul always considers his persecutions, as far as the Jews were concerned in them, as arising from this simple circumstance—his asserting that God had chosen the Gentiles, and called them to enjoy the very same privileges with the Jews, and to constitute one Church with them. *That which is behind of the afflictions of Christ.* I have still some afflictions to pass through before my race of glory be finished, afflictions which fall on me on account of the gospel, such as Christ bore from the same persecuting people. It is worthy of remark that the apostle does not say the "passion" of Christ, but simply the "afflictions," such as are common to all good men who bear a testimony against the ways and fashions of a wicked world. In these the apostle had his share; in the passion of Christ he could have none. *His body's sake.* Believers, of both Jews and Gentiles, who form that one *body,* of which Christ is the Head.

25. *Whereof I am made a minister.* Having received especial commission from God to preach salvation to the Gentiles. *According to the dispensation.* According to the gospel "economy" of "institution," the scheme or plan of salvation by Christ crucified. *To fulfil the word of God.* The Greek may be translated, "fully to preach the doctrine of God."

26. *The mystery which hath been hid.* The mystery is this: that God had designed to grant the Gentiles the same privileges with the Jews, and make them His people who were not His people. *Made manifest to his saints.* It is fully known to all who have embraced the doctrine of Christ crucified, to all Christians.

27. *The riches of the glory.* God manifests to these how abundantly glorious this gospel is among the Gentiles, and how effectual to the salvation of multitudes is this doctrine of Christ crucified.

29. *Whereunto I also labour.* In order to accomplish this end, I labor with the utmost zeal and earnestness, and with all that strength with which God has most powerfully furnished me. Whoever considers the original words will find that no verbal translation can convey their sense. God worked "energetically" in Paul, and he "wrought energetically" with God; and all this was in reference to the salvation of mankind.

CHAPTER 2

The apostle shows his great concern for the church at Colossae and at Laodicea; and exhorts them to steadfastness in the faith, and to beware of being seduced by specious and enticing words, 1-5. And to walk in Christ, as they had been taught, and to abound in faith and holiness, 6-7. To beware of false teachers, who strove to pervert the gospel, and to lead their minds from Him in whom the fulness of the Godhead dwells; with whom they were filled; by whom they had received spiritual circumcision; and into whom they were baptized and were quickened, and raised from a death of sin to a life of righteousness, 8-12. He points out their former state, and the great things which Christ had done for them, 13-15. Warns them against particular tenets of the Judaizing teachers relative to meats, drinks, holy days, festivals, and the specious pretenses of deceivers, 16-19. And shows that all the things taught by these, though they had a show of wisdom, yet perished in the using, and were the commandments and doctrines of men, 20-23.

1. *What great conflict.* The word *agon*, which we here render *conflict*, is to be understood as implying earnest care and solicitude, accompanied, undoubtedly, with the most fervent application to the throne of grace in their behalf. The *agonizomenos* of the preceding verse gave the apostle occasion to use the word *agon* here. He "agonized" with God, and his "agony" was for them.

2. *That their hearts might be comforted.* That they might have continual happiness in God, having constant affiance in Him. *Being knit together in love.* The word signifies being united, as the beams or the timbers of a building, by mortices and pins. The visible Church of Christ cannot be in union with God unless it have unity in itself, and without love this unity is impossible. *Unto all riches of the full assurance of understanding.* That is, that they might have the most indubitable certainty of the truth of Christianity, of their own salvation, and of the general design of God to admit the Gentiles into His Church. This is the grand mystery of God, which was now laid open by the preaching of the gospel. *And of the Father, and of Christ.* These words are variously written in different MSS., versions, and fathers. This great variety of versions leaves the strongest presumption that the words in question are glosses which have crept into the text and are of no authority.

3. *In whom are hid.* Or rather "in which," referring to the "mystery" mentioned above. In this glorious scheme of Christianity *all the treasures*—the abundance and excellency—*of wisdom and knowledge* are contained.

4. *Lest any man should beguile you.* The word means to deceive by sophistry or subtle reasoning, in which all the conclusions appear to be fairly drawn from the premises, but the premises are either assumed without evidence or false in themselves; but this not being easily discovered, the unthinking or unwary are carried away by the conclusions which are drawn from these premises. And this result is clearly intimated by the term *enticing words*, "plausible conclusions or deductions" from this mode of reasoning. The apostle seems to allude to the Gentile philosophers, who were notorious for this kind of argumentation.

6. *As ye have therefore received Christ Jesus.* Many persons lay a certain stress on the words *as* and *so*, and make various fine heads of discourses from them; viz., *As* you received Christ in a spirit of humility, *so* walk in Him. This may be all proper in itself, but nothing of the kind was intended by the apostle. His meaning is simply this: Seeing you have embraced the doctrine of Christ, continue to hold it fast, and not permit yourselves to be turned aside by sophistical or Judaizing teachers.

7. *Rooted and built up in him.* It is not usual with the apostle to employ this double metaphor, taken partly from the growth of a tree and the increase of a building. They are to be *rooted;* as the good seed had been already sown, it is to take root, and the roots are to spread far, wide, and deep. They are to be "grounded"; as the foundation has already been laid, they are to build thereon. In the one case, they are to bear much fruit; in the other, they are to grow up to be "an habitation of God through the Spirit." See the notes on Eph. ii. 21-22 and iii. 17. *Abounding therein with thanksgiving.* No limitation is ever set to the operations of God on the soul or to the growth of the soul in the knowledge, love, and image of God. Those who are brought into such a state of salvation should abound in gratitude and loving obedience as they grow in grace.

8. *Beware lest any man spoil you.* The word signifies to "rob," or "spoil" of their goods, as if by violence or rapine. Their goods were the salvation they had received from Christ; and both the Gentile and Jewish teachers endeavored to deprive them of these, by perverting their minds and leading them off from the truths of Christianity. *Philosophy and vain deceit.* Or "the vain or empty deceit of philosophy"; such philosophizing as the Jewish and Gentile teachers used. As the term *philosophy* stood in high repute among the Gentiles, the Jews of this time affected it; and both Philo and Josephus use the word to express the whole of the Mosaic institutions. *After the rudiments of the world.* According to the doctrine of the Jewish teachers; or according to the Mosaic institutions, as explained and glossed by the scribes, Pharisees, and rabbins in general. *Not after Christ.* Not according to the simple doctrine of Christ, viz., He died for our offenses; believe on the Lord Jesus, and you shall be saved.

9. *For in him dwelleth all the fulness.* This is opposed to the vain or "empty" doctrine of the Gentile and Jewish philosophers: there is a *fulness* in Christ suited to the empty, destitute state of the human soul; but in the philosophy of the Jews and Gentiles nothing like this was found, nor indeed in the more refined and correct philosophy of the present day. No substitute has ever been found for the grace of the Lord Jesus. By the *Godhead* or "Deity" we are to understand the "state or being of the divine nature"; and by the *fulness* of that Deity, the infinite attributes essential to such a nature. *Bodily.* Signifies "truly, really"; in opposition to "typically, figuratively." There was a symbol of the Divine Presence in the Hebrew Tabernacle, and in the Jewish Temple. But in the body of Christ, the Deity, with all its plenitude of attributes, dwelt "really" and "substantially"; for so the word means.

10. *And ye are complete in him.* "And you are filled with Him." Our word *complete* quite destroys the connection subsisting in the apostle's ideas. The philosophy of the world was "empty," but there was a "fulness" in Christ. The Colossians were empty, spoiled and deprived of every good, while following the empty philosophy and groundless traditions of Jewish and Gentile teachers; but since they had received Christ Jesus they were "filled" with Him. This is the true meaning of the word, and by this the connection and assemblage of ideas in the apostle's mind are preserved. No fanciful "completeness in Christ" of a believer, while

incomplete in himself, is either expressed or intended by Paul. It is too bad a doctrine to exist in the oracles of God.

11. *In whom also ye are circumcised.* All that was designed by circumcision, literally performed, is accomplished in them that believe through the Spirit and power of Christ. It is not a cutting off of a part of the flesh, but a *putting off the body of the sins of the flesh,* through the circumcision of Christ, He having undergone and performed this and all other rites necessary to qualify Him to be a Mediator between God and man. But by the circumcision of Christ, the operation of His grace and Spirit may be intended. The law required the circumcision of the flesh; the gospel of Christ required the circumcision of the heart. The words *of the sins* are omitted by several MSS.

12. *Buried with him in baptism.* Alluding to the immersions practiced in the case of adults, wherein the person appeared to be buried under the water, as Christ was buried in the heart of the earth. His rising again the third day, and their emerging from the water, was an emblem of the resurrection of the body; and, in them, of a total change of life. *The faith of the operation of God.* They were quickened, changed, and saved by means of faith in Christ Jesus, which faith was produced by the operation or energy of God. Believing is the act of the soul; but the grace or power to believe comes from God himself.

14. *Blotting out the handwriting of ordinances.* By the handwriting of ordinances the apostle most evidently means the ceremonial law. This was *against* them, for they were bound to fulfil it; and it was *contrary* to them, as condemning them for their neglect and transgression of it. *Blotting out the handwriting* is probably an allusion to Num. v. 23, where the curses written in the book, in the case of the woman suspected of adultery, are directed to be blotted out with the bitter waters. *Nailing it to his cross.* When Christ was nailed to the Cross, our obligation to fulfill these ordinances was done away.

15. *And having spoiled principalities and powers.* Here is an allusion to the treatment of enemies when conquered. They are "spoiled of their armor"; and they are "exhibited" with contumely and reproach to the populace, especially when the victor has the honor of a "triumph"; to the former of which there is an allusion in the words "making a public exhibition of them"; and to the latter in the words *triumphing over them.* And the *principalities and powers* refer to the emperors, kings, and generals taken in battle, and reserved to grace the victor's triumph. It is very likely that by the *principalities and powers* over whom Christ triumphed the apostle means the *nesioth* and *roshoth,* who were the rulers and chiefs in the Sanhedrin and synagogues, and who had great authority among the people, both in making constitutions and in explaining traditions. The propagation of Christianity in Judea quite destroyed their spiritual power and domination. *In it.* The words refer rather to Christ than to the Cross, if indeed they be genuine; of which there is much reason to doubt, as the versions and fathers differ so greatly in quoting them.

16. *Let no man therefore judge you in meat, or in drink.* The apostle speaks here in refer-

ence to some particulars of the "handwriting of ordinances," which had been taken away, viz., the distinction of meats and drinks, what was clean and what unclean, according to the law; and the necessity of observing certain holy days or festivals, such as the new moons and particular sabbaths, or those which should be observed with more than ordinary solemnity. All these had been taken *out of the way* and nailed to the Cross, and were no longer of moral obligation.

17. *Which are a shadow.* All these things were types, and must continue in force till the Christ, whom they represented, came; the apostle therefore says that the *body*—the substance or design of them, was *of Christ*—pointed Him out, and the excellent blessings which He has procured. The word *shadow* is often used to express anything "imperfect" or "unsubstantial"; while the term *body* was used in the opposite sense, and expressed anything "substantial, solid, and firm." The law was but the shadow or representation of good things to come; none should rest in it. All that it pointed out is to be sought and obtained in Christ.

18. *Let no man beguile you.* Let no man take the "prize" from you which the *brabeus,* or judge in the contests, has assigned you in consequence of your having obtained the victory. *In a voluntary humility and worshipping of angels.* The whole passage has been paraphrased thus: "Let no man spoil you of the prize adjudged to you, who delights in mortifying his body, and walking with the apparent modesty of an angel, affecting superior sanctity in order to gain disciples; intruding into things which he has not seen; and, notwithstanding his apparent humility, his mind is carnal, and he is puffed up with a sense of his superior knowledge and piety." It is very likely that the apostle here alludes to the Essenes, who were remarkably strict and devout, spent a principal part of their time in the contemplation of the Divine Being, abstained from all sensual gratifications, and affected to live the life of angels upon earth.

19. *And not holding the Head.* Not acknowledging Jesus Christ as the only Saviour of mankind, and the only *Head* or "chief" of the Christian Church, on whom every member of it depends, and from whom each derives both light and life. For a further explanation of these words see the notes on Eph. iv. 16, where the figures and phraseology are the same.

20. *If ye be dead with Christ.* See the notes on Rom. vi. 3, 5. *From the rudiments of the world.* You have renounced all hope of salvation from the observance of Jewish rites and ceremonies, which were only *rudiments,* "first elements" or the "alphabet," out of which the whole science of Christianity was composed. We have often seen that *the world* and "this world" signify the Jewish dispensation, or the rites, ceremonies, and services performed under it. *Why, as though living in the world.* Why, as if you were still under the same dispensation from which you have been already freed, are you subject to its ordinances, performing them as if expecting salvation from this performance?

21. *Touch not; taste not; handle not.* These are forms of expression very frequent among the Jews.

22. *Which all are to perish with the using.* These are not matters of eternal moment; the

different kinds of meats were made for the body, and go with it into corruption. In like manner, all the rites and ceremonies of the Jewish religion now perish, having accomplished the end of their institution; namely, to lead us to Christ, that we might be justified by faith. *After the commandments and doctrines of men.* These words should follow the twentieth verse, of which they form a part; and it appears from them that the apostle is here speaking of the traditions of the elders, and the load of cumbrous ceremonies which they added to the significant rites prescribed by Moses.

23. *Which things have indeed a shew of wisdom.* All these prescriptions and rites have indeed the appearance of wisdom, and are recommended by plausible reasons; but they form a worship which God has not commanded, and enjoin macerations of the body, accompanied with a humiliation of spirit, that are neither profitable to the soul nor of any advantage to the body; so that the whole of their religion is worth nothing. What is here termed *will worship* signifies simply a mode of worship which a man chooses for himself, independently of the revelation which God has given.

CHAPTER 3

The apostle exhorts the Colossians to heavenly-mindedness after the example of Christ, that they may be prepared to appear with him in glory, 1-4. Exhorts them also to mortify their members, and calls in their remembrance their former state, 5-7. Shows how completely they were changed from that state, and gives them various directions relative to truth, compassion, meekness, long-suffering, forgiveness, charity, 8-14. Shows that they are called to unity and holiness; and commands them to have the doctrine of Christ dwelling richly in them; and how they should teach and admonish each other, and do everything in the name of the Lord Jesus, 15-17. The relative duties of wives, 18. Of husbands, 19. Of children, 20. Of fathers, 21. Of servants, 22. He concludes by showing that he that does wrong shall be treated accordingly, for God is no respecter of persons, 23-25.

1. *If ye then.* "Seeing then that you are risen with Christ"; this refers to what he had said, chap. ii. 12: "Buried with him in baptism, wherein also ye are risen with him." As therefore you have most cordially received the doctrine of Christ, and profess to be partakers of a spiritual religion that promises spiritual and eternal things, *seek those things,* and look to be prepared for the enjoyment of them.

2. *Set your affection on things above.* This is a very good general rule: "Be as much in earnest for heavenly and eternal things as you formerly were for those that are earthly and perishing."

5. *Mortify therefore your members.* "Put them to death." The verb is used metaphorically to signify "to deprive a thing of its power, to destroy its strength." Use no member of your body to sin against God; keep all under dominion, and never permit the beast to run away with the man. *Inordinate affection.* "Unnatural and degrading passion"; bestial lusts. *Covetousness, which is idolatry.* For the covetous man makes his money his god.

7. *In the which ye also walked sometime.* When you were in your unconverted state, you served divers lusts and pleasures.

8. *But now ye also put off all these.* See on Eph. iv. 22. Being now converted, sin had no more dominion over them. *Anger, wrath.* They had not only lived in the evils mentioned in v. 5, but also in those enumerated here; and

they had not only laid aside the former, but they had laid aside the latter also. *Blasphemy.* The word seems here to mean "injurious and calumnious speaking."

9. *Lie not one to another.* Do not deceive each other; speak the truth in all your dealings. *Ye have put off the old man.* See the notes on Rom. vi. 6, and particularly on Rom. xiii. 11-14. You have received a religion widely different from that you had before; act according to its principles.

10. *And have put on the new man.* See on Rom. xii. 1-2. *Is renewed in knowledge.* Ignorance was the grand characteristic of the heathen state; knowledge, of the Christian. *After the image of him that created him.* The image in which man was made, and in which he must be "remade," "made anew," consists in knowledge, righteousness, and true holiness.

11. *Where there is neither Greek nor Jew.* In which new creation no inquiry is made what nation the persons belonged to or from what ancestry they had sprung, whether in Judea or Greece. *Circumcision nor uncircumcision.* Nor is their peculiar form of religion of any consideration, whether circumcised like the *Jews* or uncircumcised like the heathens. *Bond nor free.* Nor does the particular state or circumstances in which a man may be found either help him to or exclude him from the benefit of this religion, the slave having as good a title to salvation by grace as the freeman. *But Christ is all, and in all.* All mankind are His creatures, all conditions are disposed and regulated by His providence, and all human beings are equally purchased by His blood. He alone is the Source whence all have proceeded, and to Him alone all must return. He is the Maker, Preserver, Saviour, and Judge of all men.

12. *Bowels of mercies.* Be merciful, not in act merely, but in spirit and affection. In all cases of this kind let your heart dictate to your hand; be clothed with bowels of mercy—let your tenderest feelings come in contact with the miseries of the distressed as soon as ever they present themselves.

13. *Forbearing one another.* Avoid all occasions of irritating or provoking each other. *Forgiving one another.* If ye receive offense, be instantly ready to forgive on the first acknowledgment of the fault. *Even as Christ forgave you.* Who required no satisfaction and sought for nothing in you but the broken, contrite heart, and freely forgave you as soon as you returned to Him.

14. *And above all these things.* "Upon all, over all"; as the outer garment envelopes all the clothing, so let *charity* or "love" invest and encompass all the rest. *Which is the bond of perfectness.* Love to God and man is not only to cover all, but also to unite and consolidate the whole. It is therefore represented here under the notion of a girdle, by which all the rest of the clothing is bound close about the body. To love God with all the heart, soul, mind, and strength, and one's neighbor as oneself, is the perfection which the new covenant requires, and which the grace and Spirit of Christ work in every sincerely obedient, humble believer.

15. *And let the peace of God.* Instead of God, "Christ" is the reading of several MSS., with several of the fathers. *Rule in your hearts.*

Let the peace of Christ "judge, decide, and govern" in your hearts, as the *brabeus,* or judge, does in the Olympic contests. No heart is right with God where the peace of Christ does not rule, and the continual prevalence of the peace of Christ is the decisive proof that the heart is right with God. *In one body.* You cannot have peace with God, in yourselves nor among each other, unless you continue in unity; and, as *one body,* continue in connection and dependence on Him who is your only Head; to this *ye are called.* It is a glorious state of salvation, and you should be forever *thankful* that you are thus privileged.

16. *Let the word of Christ dwell in you richly.* I believe the apostle means that the Colossians should be "well instructed in the doctrine of Christ"; that it should be their constant study; that it should be frequently preached, explained, and enforced among them; and that *all* the *wisdom* comprised in it should be well understood. Through bad pointing this verse is not very intelligible; the several members of it should be distinguished thus: "Let the doctrine of Christ dwell richly among you; teaching and admonishing each other in all wisdom; singing with grace in your hearts unto the Lord, in psalms, hymns, and spiritual songs." This arrangement the original will not only bear, but it absolutely requires it, and is not sense without it.

17. *Whatsoever ye do in word or deed.* Let your words be right and your actions upright. *Do all in the name of the Lord Jesus.* Begin with Him and end with Him; invoke His name and pray for His direction and support in all that you do; and thus every work will be crowned with all requisite success. *Giving thanks to God.* Even praises, as well as prayers, must ascend to God through this Mediator.

18. *Wives, submit yourselves.* Having done with general directions, the apostle comes to particular duties, which are commonly called relative, because they belong only to persons in certain situations and are not incumbent on all. The directions here to wives, husbands, children, parents, servants, and masters are so exactly the same in substance with those in Eph. v. 22-33 and vi. 1-9 that there is no need to repeat what has been said on those passages; and to the notes there the reader is requested to refer. *As it is fit in the Lord.* God commands it, and it is both proper and decent.

19. *Be not bitter against them.* Wherever bitterness is, there love is wanting. And where love is wanting in the married life, there is hell upon earth.

20. *Children, obey your parents in all things.* That is, in the Lord, in everything that your parents command you which is not contrary to the will or word of God.

24. *The reward of the inheritance.* Here you have neither lands nor property; you are servants or slaves. Be not discouraged; you have an inheritance in store. Be faithful unto God and to your employers, and Christ will give you a heavenly inheritance.

CHAPTER 4

The duty of masters to their servants, 1. Continuance in prayer recommended, to which watchfulness and thanksgiving should be joined, 2. And to pray particularly for the success of the gospel, 3-4. Directions concerning walking wisely, redeeming of time, and godly conversation, 5-6. He refers them to Tychicus and Onesimus, whom he sends to them, for particulars relative to his present circumstances, 7-9. Mentions the salutations of several then at Rome, of whom he gives some interesting particulars, 10-14. Sends his own salutations to the brethren in Laodicea, and to Nymphas and the church at his house, 15. Directs this Epistle to be read in the church of the Laodiceans, and that to them to be read at Colossae, 16. Directions to Archipus relative to his ministry, 17. Concludes with salutations to the people at Colossae, to whom he sends his apostolical benediction, 18.

1. *Masters, give unto your servants.* This verse should have been added to the preceding, to which it properly belongs; and this chapter should have begun with v. 2. *That which is just and equal.* As they are "bondmen" or "slaves" of whom the apostle speaks, we may at once see with what propriety this exhortation is given. The condition of slaves among the Greeks and Romans was wretched in the extreme; they could appeal to no law, and they could neither expect justice nor equity. The apostle therefore informs the proprietors of these slaves that they should act towards them both according to justice and equity; for God, their Master, required this of them, and would at last call them to account for their conduct in this respect.

2. *Continue in prayer.* This was the apostle's general advice to all; without this neither wives, husbands, children, parents, servants, nor masters could fulfil the duties which God, in their respective stations, required of them. *Watch in the same.* Be always on your guard; and when you have got the requisite grace by praying, take care of it, and bring it into its proper action by watchfulness; by which you will know when, and where, and how to apply it. *With thanksgiving.* Being always grateful to God, who has called you into such a state of salvation, and affords you such abundant means and opportunities to glorify Him.

3. *Praying also for us.* Let the success and spread of the gospel be ever dear to you; and neglect not to pray fervently to God that it may have free course, run, and be glorified. *A door of utterance.* The word *thyra,* which commonly signifies a *door,* or suchlike entrance into a house or passage through a wall, is often used metaphorically for an "entrance" to any business, "occasion" or "opportunity" to commence or perform any particular work. *The mystery of Christ.* The gospel, which had been hidden from all former times, and which revealed that purpose long hidden in the divine councils, that the Gentiles should be called to enjoy the same privileges with the Jews. *For which I am also in bonds.* He was suffering under Jewish malice, and for preaching this very mystery; for they could not bear to hear announced, as from heaven, that the Gentiles, whom they considered eternally shut out from any participation of the divine favor, should be made fellow heirs with them of the grace of life; much less could they bear to hear that they were about to be reprobated and the Gentiles elected in their place. It was for asserting these things that they persecuted Paul at Jerusalem, so that to save his life he was obliged to appeal to Caesar; and being taken to Rome, he was detained a prisoner till his case was fully heard; and he was a prisoner at Rome on this very account when he wrote this Epistle to the Colossians.

4. *That I may make it manifest.* It was a

mystery, and he wished to make it *manifest*—to lay it open, and make all men see it.

5. *Walk in wisdom.* Act wisely and prudently in reference to them who are *without*—who yet continue unbelieving Gentiles or persecuting Jews.

6. *Let your speech be alway with grace, seasoned with salt.* Let all your conversation be such as may tend to exemplify and recommend Christianity; let it not only be holy, but wise, gracious, and intelligent. A harsh method of proposing or defending the doctrines of Christianity only serves to repel men from those doctrines, and from the way of salvation. *Salt,* from its use in preserving good from corruption, and rendering it both savory and wholesome, has always been made the emblem of wisdom. *How ye ought to answer every man.* That your discourse may be so judiciously managed that you may discern how to treat the prejudices and meet the objections of both Jews and Gentiles.

7. *All my state shall Tychicus.* See the note on Eph. vi. 21. Tychicus well knew the apostle's zeal and perseverance in preaching the gospel, his sufferings on that account, his success in converting both Jews and Gentiles, and the converts which were made in Caesar's household.

8. *That he might know your estate.* Instead of "that he may know your affairs," read "that you may know our affairs," which is probably the true reading. Tychicus was sent to them, not to know their affairs, but with Onesimus, to carry this Epistle and make the apostle's state known to them, and comfort their hearts by the good news which he brought. The next verse confirms this meaning.

9. *With Onesimus . . . who is one of you.* Onesimus was a native of some part of Phrygia, if not of Colossae itself; and being lately converted to the Christian faith by the instrumentality of the apostle, he would be able, on this account, to give them satisfactory information concerning the apostle's state, which would be doubly acceptable to them as he was their countryman. See the Epistle to Philemon.

10. *Aristarchus my fellow prisoner.* Concerning Aristarchus, see Acts xix. 29; xx. 4; and xxvii. 2 Aristarchus and Epaphras are mentioned as saluters in this Epistle, and in that to Philemon written at the same time. *Marcus.* See the account of this person, Acts xv. 39. Though there had been some difference between the apostle and this Mark, yet from this, and 2 Tim. iv. 11, we find that they were fully reconciled, and that Mark was very useful to Paul in the work of the ministry.

11. *Jesus, which is called Justus.* Jesus, Joshua or Jehoshua, was his name among his countrymen the Jews; *Justus* was the name which he bore among the Greeks and Romans. *These only.* That is, only Aristarchus, Marcus, and Jesus Justus, who were formerly Jews or proselytes; for they were *of the circumcision,* and assisted the apostle in preaching the gospel.

12. *Epaphras, who is one of you.* A native of some part of Phrygia, and probably of Colossae itself. *A servant of Christ.* A minister of the gospel. *Labouring fervently for you.* "Agonizing"; very properly expressed by our translators, *labouring fervently. That ye may stand perfect and complete.* That you may stand firm, perfectly instructed, and fully persuaded of the truth of those doctrines which have been taught you as the revealed will of God: this I believe to be the meaning of the apostle. Instead of complete or "filled up," almost all the MSS. of the Alexandrian rescension, which are considered the most authentic and correct, have "that ye may be fully persuaded."

13. *He hath a great zeal for you.* Instead of "much zeal," some MSS., versions, and fathers, read "much labor"; they are here nearly of the same meaning, though the latter appears to be the better and genuine reading. *Them that are in Laodicea, and them in Hierapolis.* These were both cities of Phrygia, between which Colossae was situated. The latter was called *Hierapolis,* or the "holy city," from the multitude of its temples. Apollo, Diana, Aesculapius, and Hygeia were all worshipped here, as appears by the coins of this city still extant.

14. *Luke, the beloved physician.* This is generally supposed to be the same with Luke the Evangelist.

15. *Salute . . . Nymphas, and the church which is in his house.* This person, and his whole family, which probably was very numerous, appear to have received the gospel; and it seems that, for their benefit and that of his neighbors, he had opened his house for the worship of God. In those primitive times there were no consecrated places, for it was supposed that the simple setting apart of any place for the worship of God was a sufficient consecration.

16. *Cause that it be read also in the church of the Laodiceans.* That is: Let a copy be taken and sent to them, that it may be read there also. This appears to have been a regular custom in the apostolic Church. *That ye likewise read the epistle from Laodicea.* Some suppose that this was an epistle sent from Laodicea to the apostle, which he now sent by Aristarchus to the Colossians, that they might peruse it. Others think that the Epistle to the Ephesians is the epistle in question, and that it was originally directed to them, and not to the Ephesians. But others, equally learned, think that there was an epistle, different from that to the Ephesians, sent by Paul to the Laodiceans, which is now lost.

17. *Say to Archippus.* Who this person was we cannot tell; there have been various conjectures concerning him. Some think he was bishop, or overseer of the church at Colossae, in the absence of Epaphras.

18. *The salutation by the hand of me Paul.* The preceding part of the Epistle was written by a scribe, from the mouth of the apostle; this, and what follows, was written by the hand of Paul himself. A similar distinction we find in 1 Cor. xvi. 21 and in 2 Thess. iii. 17; and this, it seems, was the means by which the apostle authenticated every Epistle which he sent to the different churches. *Remember my bonds.* See what proof you have of the truth of the gospel; I am in bonds on this account. I suffer patiently, yea, exult in the Lord Jesus, so perfectly am I upheld by the grace of the gospel. *Remember my bonds,* and take courage. How eloquent were these concluding words! *Amen.* This is omitted by the most ancient and correct MSS.

The First Epistle to the
THESSALONIANS

Thessalonica is a seaport town situated on what was called the Thermaic Gulf, and was anciently the capital of Macedonia. According to Stephanus Byzantinus, it was embellished and enlarged by Philip, king of Macedon, father of Alexander the Great, who called it Thessalonica, or the Victory of Thessalia, on account of the victory he obtained there over the Thessalians, prior to which it was called Thermae. Strabo, Tzetzes, and Zonaras say that it obtained the name of Thessalonica from Thessalonica, wife of Cassander, and daughter of Philip.

Paul, in company with Silas, first preached the gospel in this city and the adjacent country. Though the Jews, who were sojourners in this city, rejected the gospel in general, yet a great multitude of the devout Greeks, i.e., such as were proselytes to Judaism, or the descendants of Jewish parents, born and naturalized in Greece, believed and associated with Paul and Silas, and not a few of the chief women of the city embraced the Christian faith, Acts xvii. 4.

As the Jews found that, according to the doctrine of the gospel, the Gentiles were called to enjoy the same privileges with themselves, without being obliged to submit to circumcision and other ordinances of the law, they persecuted that gospel and those who proclaimed it; for, moved with indignation, they employed "certain lewd fellows of the baser sort"—the beasts of the people, "set all the city on an uproar, and assaulted the house of Jason," where the apostles lodged, dragged him and certain brethren before the rulers, and charged them with seditious designs and treason against the Roman emperor! The apostles escaped and got to Berea, where they began anew their important evangelical labors. Thither the Jews of Thessalonica, pursuing them, raised a fresh tumult; so that the apostle, being counselled by the brethren, made his escape to Athens, Acts xvii. 5-15. Thus he followed the command of his Master: Being persecuted in one city, he fled to another; not to hide himself, but to proclaim in every place the saving truths of the gospel of Christ.

It does not appear that Paul stayed long at Athens; he soon went to Corinth, where Timothy and Silas were, but probably not before Timothy met him, for whom he had sent, Acts xvii. 15, to come to him speedily; and whom, it appears, he sent immediately back to Thessalonica, to establish the believers there and comfort them concerning the faith, 1 Thess. iii. 2. While Paul abode at Corinth, Timothy and Silas came to him from Thessalonica, and hearing by them of the steadfastness of the Thessalonian converts in the faith of Christ, he wrote this Epistle, and shortly after the second, to comfort and encourage them; to give them further instructions in the doctrines of Christianity, and to rectify some mistaken views, relative to the day of judgment, which had been propagated among them.

Who the persons were who formed the apostolic church at Thessalonica is not easy to determine. They were not Jews, for these in general persecuted the apostle and the gospel in this place. We are therefore left to infer that the church was formed, (1) of Jewish proselytes, called, Acts xvii. 4, "devout Greeks"; and (2) of converts from heathenism; for, on the preaching of the gospel to them it is said, chap. i. 9, that they "turned to God from idols to serve the living and true God." Though some of the Jews believed on the preaching of Paul and Silas, Acts xvii. 3-4, yet it is evident that the great bulk of the church was composed of Grecian proselytes and converts from heathenism.

CHAPTER 1

The inscription by Paul, Silvanus, and Timotheus to the church of the Thessalonians, 1. Paul gives thanks to God for their good estate, and prays for their continuance in the faith, 2-4. Shows how the gospel came to them, and the blessed effects it produced in their life and conversation, 5-7. How it became published from them through Macedonia and Achaia, and how their faith was everywhere celebrated, 8. He shows, further, that the Thessalonians had turned from idolatry, become worshippers of the true God, and were waiting for the revelation of Christ, 9-10.

1. *Paul, and Silvanus, and Timotheus.* Though Paul himself dictated this letter, yet he joins the names of Silas and Timothy, because they had been with him at Thessalonica, and were well-known there. *And Silvanus.* This was certainly the same as Silas, who was Paul's companion in all his journeys through Asia Minor and Greece; see Acts xv. 22; xvi. 19; xvii. 4, 10. The apostle took him and Timothy with him into Macedonia, and they continued at Berea when the apostle went from thence to Athens; from this place Paul sent for them to come to him speedily, and though it is not said that they came while he was at Athens, yet it is most probable that they did; after which, having sent them to Thessalonica, he proceeded to Corinth, where they afterwards rejoined him, and from whence he wrote this Epistle.

3. *Your work of faith.* This verse contains a very high character of the believers at Thessalonica. They had *faith*, not speculative and indolent, but true, sound, and operative; their faith worked. They had *love*, not that gazed at and became enamored of the perfections of God,

but such a love as labored with faith to fulfill the whole will of God. Faith worked; but love, because it can do more, did more, and therefore labored—worked energetically, to promote the glory of God and the salvation of men. They had *hope*; not an idle, cold, heartless expectation of future good, from which they felt no excitement, and for which they could give no reason, but such a hope as produced a satisfying expectation of a future life and state of blessedness, the reality of which faith had descried, and love anticipated.

4. *Knowing . . . your election of God*. Being assured, from the doctrine which I have delivered to you, and which God has confirmed by various miracles, and gifts of the Holy Spirit, that He has chosen and called the Gentiles to the same privileges to which He chose and called the Jews; and that, as they have rejected the offers of the gospel, God has now elected the Gentiles in their stead. This is the election which the Thessalonians knew; and of which the apostle treats at large in his Epistle to the Romans, and also in his Epistles to the Galatians and Ephesians. No irrespective, unconditional, eternal, and personal election to everlasting glory is meant by the apostle.

5. *For our gospel*. That is, the glad tidings of salvation by Jesus Christ and of your being elected to enjoy all the privileges to which the Jews were called, without being obliged to submit to circumcision or to fulfill the rites and ceremonies of the Mosaic law. *Came not unto you in word only*. It was not by simple teaching or mere reasoning that the doctrines which we preached recommended themselves to you. We did not insist on your using this or the other religious institution; we insisted on a change of heart and life, and we held out the energy which was able to effect it. *And in the Holy Ghost*. By His influence upon your hearts, in changing and renewing them; and by the testimony which you received from Him, that you were accepted through the Beloved, and become the adopted children of God. *And in much assurance*. The Holy Spirit who was given you left no doubt on your mind, with respect to either the general truth of the doctrine or the safety of your own state. *What manner of men we were*. How we preached, and how we lived, our doctrines and our practices ever corresponding. And *for your sake* we sustained difficulties, endured hardships, and were incessant in our labors.

6. *Ye became followers of us*. You became "imitators." *Having received the word in much affliction*. That they received the doctrine of the gospel in the midst of much persecution we may learn from the history in general, and from Acts xvii. 5-6. *With joy of the Holy Ghost*. The consolations which they received in consequence of believing in Christ more than counterbalanced all the afflictions which they suffered from their persecutors.

7. *Ye were ensamples*. "Types," models, or patterns; according to which all the churches in Macedonia and Achaia formed both their creed and their conduct.

8. *From you sounded out*. As Thessalonica was very conveniently situated for traffic, many merchants from thence traded through Macedonia, Achaia, and different parts of Greece. By these, the fame of the Thessalonians having

received the doctrine of the gospel was doubtless carried far and wide.

9. *How ye turned to God from idols*. This could not be spoken either of the Jews or of the devout persons, but of the heathen Greeks; and of such it appears that the majority of the church was formed. The *true God*—in opposition to the whole system of idolatry, which was false in the objects of its adoration, false in its pretensions, false in its promises, and false in all its prospects.

10. *And to wait for his Son from heaven*. To expect a future state of glory, and resurrection of the body, according to the gospel doctrine, after the example of Jesus Christ, who was raised from the dead and ascended unto heaven, ever to appear in the presence of God for us. *Delivered us from the wrath to come*. From all the punishment due to us for our sins, and from the destruction which is about to come on the unbelieving and impenitent Jews.

CHAPTER 2

The apostle sets forth how the gospel was brought and preached to the Thessalonians, in consequence of his being persecuted at Philippi, 1-2. The manner in which the apostles preached, the matter of their doctrine, and the tenor of their lives, 3-11. He exhorts them to walk worthy of God, 12. And commends them for the manner in which they received the gospel, 13. How they suffered from their own countrymen, as the first believers did from the Jews, who endeavored to prevent the apostles from preaching the gospel to the Gentiles, 14-16. Paul's apology for his absence from them; and his earnest desire to see them, founded on his great affection for them, 17-20.

1. *Our entrance in unto you*. His first coming to preach the gospel was particularly owned of the Lord, many of them having been converted under his ministry.

2. *Shamefully entreated . . . at Philippi*. There Paul and Silas had been beaten with many stripes, shut up in the inner prison, and their feet made fast in the stocks. See Acts xvi. 23 ff. *With much contention*. The words not only signify "with intense labor and earnestness," but may here mean "exposed to the greatest danger," "at the peril of our lives."

3. *Our exhortation*. The word has a very extensive meaning; it signifies not only "exhortation" but also "encouragement, consolation," and the like. *Not of deceit*. We did not endeavor to allure you with false pretenses; we did not deceive you, nor were we deceived ourselves. *Nor of uncleanness*. Such as the teachings of the Gentile philosophers were; their supreme gods were celebrated for their adulteries, fornication, uncleannesses, thefts, barbarities, and profligacies of the most odious kind. Our gospel was pure; came from the pure and holy God; was accompanied with the influences of the Holy Spirit, and produced purity both in the hearts and in the lives of all that received it. *Nor in guile*. We had no false pretenses, and were influenced by no sinister motives.

4. *But as we were allowed of God*. "As we were accounted worthy" to be put in trust, as God put confidence in us and sent us on His most especial message to mankind, *even so we speak*, keeping the dignity of our high calling continually in view; and acting as in the sight of God, we speak not to please or flatter men, but to please that God who searches the heart.

5. *Flattering words.* Though we proclaimed the gospel or glad tidings, yet we showed that without holiness none should see the Lord. *Ye know.* That while we preached the whole gospel we never gave any countenance to sin. *Nor a cloke of covetousness.* We did not seek temporal emolument; nor did we preach the gospel for a cloak to our covetousness. *God is witness* that we did not; we sought you, not yours.

6. *Nor of men sought we glory.* As we preached not for worldly gain, so we preached not for popular applause; we had what we sought for—the approbation of God and the testimony of a good conscience. *When we might have been burdensome.* They had a right to their maintenance while they devoted themselves wholly to the work of the gospel for the sake of the people's souls.

7. *But we were gentle among you.* Far from assuming the authority which we had, we acted towards you as a tender nurse or parent does to a delicate child. We fed, counselled, cherished, and bore with you; we taught you to walk, preserved you from stumbling, and led you in a right path.

8. *Being affectionately desirous of you.* We had such intense love for you that we were not only willing and forward to preach the unsearchable riches of Christ to you, but also to give our "own lives" for your sake, *because ye were dear,* "because you were beloved by us." The words used here by the apostle are expressive of the strongest affection and attachment.

9. *Ye remember, brethren, our labour and travail.* From this it appears that Paul spent much more time at Thessalonica than is generally supposed; for the expressions in this verse denote a long continuance of a constantly exercised ministry, interrupted only by manual labor for their own support; *labouring night and day, because we would not be chargeable unto . . . you.* Probably Paul and his companions worked with their hands by day, and spent a considerable part of the night, or evenings, in preaching Christ to the people.

10. *Ye are witnesses, and God also, how holily.* I.e., in reference to God; how *justly* in reference to men; and *unblameably* in reference to our spirit and conduct, as ministers of Christ, *we behaved ourselves among you.* What a consciousness of his own integrity must Paul have had to use the expressions that are here!

11. *How we exhorted.* What pastoral care is marked here! They *exhorted*—were continually teaching and instructing the objects of their charge. *And comforted.* They found many under trials and temptations, and those they encouraged. *And charged.* Continued to "witness" to the people that all the threatenings and promises of God were true; that He required faith, love, and obedience; that He could not behold sin with allowance; that Jesus died to save them from their sins; and that, without holiness, none should see God. And all these things they did, not in a general way only, but they spoke to *every* man; none was left unnoticed, unadmonished, uncomforted. The spirit in which they performed all these branches of the pastoral care was that which was most likely to insure success; as a *father* treats *his children,* so they treated every member of the church.

12. *That ye would walk worthy of God.* That they should, in every respect, act up to their high calling, that it would not be a reproach to the God of holiness to acknowledge them as His sons and daughters. *His kingdom and glory.* His Church here, for that is the kingdom of God among men; and His *glory* hereafter, for that is the state to which the dispensations of grace in His Church lead. The words, however, may signify His "glorious kingdom."

13. *Ye received the word of God.* You received the "doctrine" of God, not as anything fabricated by man, but as coming immediately from God himself, we being only His messengers to declare what He had previously revealed to us. And you have had the fullest proof that you have not believed in vain; for that doctrine, under the power and influence of the Holy Ghost, has "worked most powerfully" in you, filling you with light, life, and holiness.

17. *Being taken from you for a short time.* Through the persecution raised by the Jews, see Acts xvii, he was obliged to leave Thessalonica, and yield to a storm that it would have been useless for him to withstand. *Being taken from you . . . in presence, not in heart.* The apostle had compared himself to a parent or nurse, vv. 7 and 11; and the people he considered as his most beloved children. Here he represents himself as feeling what an affectionate father must feel when "torn from his children"; for this is the import of the word "bereft of children," which we tamely translate *being taken from you. Endeavoured the more abundantly.* His separation from them did not destroy his parental feelings, and the manner in which he was obliged to leave them increased his desire to visit them as soon as possible.

18. *Even I Paul.* He had already sent Timothy and Silas to them; but he himself was anxious to see them, and had purposed this *once and again; but Satan hindered;* i.e., some "adversary," as the word means, whether the devil himself or some of his children.

19. *For what is our hope?* I can have no prospects from earth; I have forsaken all for the gospel. Why then should I continually labor at the risk of my life, preaching the gospel? Is it not to get your souls saved that you may be *my crown of rejoicing* in the day of Christ?

20. *For ye are our glory and joy.* You are the seal of our apostleship; your conversion and steadiness are a full proof that God has sent us.

CHAPTER 3

Paul informs them how, being hindered himself from visiting them, he had sent Timothy to comfort them, of whom he gives a high character, 1-2. Shows that trials and difficulties are unavoidable in the present state, 3-4. Mentions the joy he had on hearing by Timothy of their steadiness in the faith, for which he returns thanks to God; and prays earnestly for their increase, 5-10. Prays also that God may afford him an opportunity of seeing them, 11. And that they may abound in love to God and one another, and be unblamable in holiness at the coming of Christ, 12-13.

1. *Wherefore when we could no longer.* The apostle was anxious to hear of their state, and as he could obatin no information without sending a messenger express, he therefore sent Timothy from Athens, choosing rather to be left alone than to continue any longer in uncertainty relative to their state.

2. *Timotheus, our brother.* It appears that Timothy was but a youth when converted to God; he had now however been some years in the work of God. Paul therefore calls him his *brother;* elsewhere he calls him his "own son," 1 Tim. i. 2; and his "dearly beloved son," 2 Tim. i. 2; because he was brought to the knowledge of the true God and to salvation by Christ through the apostle's instrumentality. *Minister of God.* Employed by God to preach the gospel; this was God's work, and He had appointed Timothy to do it, and to do it at this time in conjunction with Paul; and therefore he calls him his *fellowlabourer.*

3. *That no man should be moved.* That is, caused to apostatize from Christianity. *We are appointed thereunto.* "We are exposed to this; we lie open to such." They are unavoidable in the present state of things.

4. *That we should suffer tribulation.* I prepared you for it, because I knew that it was according to their nature for wicked men to persecute the followers of God.

5. *For this cause.* Knowing that you would be persecuted, and knowing that your apostasy was possible, *I sent to know your faith*—whether you continued steadfast in the truth.

6. *When Timotheus came.* We have already seen that he and Silas stayed behind at Thessalonica, when Paul was obliged to leave it, for the persecution seems to have been principally directed against him. When Paul came to Athens, he sent pressingly to Timothy and Silas to come to him with all speed to that city. We are not informed that they did come, but it is most likely that they did, and that Paul sent Timothy back to Thessalonica to comfort and build up these new converts. After Paul had sent away Timothy, it is likely he went himself straight to Corinth, and there Timothy soon after met him with the good news of the steadiness of the Thessalonian church. *Your faith and charity.* The good tidings which Timothy brought from Thessalonica consisted of three particulars: (1) Their *faith;* they continued steadfast in their belief of the gospel. (2) Their *charity;* they loved one another, and lived in unity and harmony. (3) They were affectionately attached to the apostle; they had *good remembrance* of him, and desired earnestly to see him.

8. *For now we live.* Your steadfastness in the faith gives me new life and comfort; I now feel that I live to some purpose, as my labor in the Lord is not in vain.

10. *Night and day praying exceedingly.* Supplicating God at all times; mingling this with all my prayers; "abounding and superabounding in my entreaties to God" to permit me to revisit you. How strong was his affection for this church! *Might perfect that which is lacking.* That I might have the opportunity of giving you the fullest instructions in the doctrine of Christ, so that the great outlines of truth which you already know may be filled up, that you may be perfectly fitted to every good word and work.

11. *Now God himself and our Father.* That is, God, who is our Father, who has adopted us into the heavenly family, and called us His sons and daughters. *Direct our way.* As he was employed in God's work he dared not consult his own inclinations; he looked for continual directions from God, where, when, and how to do his Master's work.

12. *Make you to increase and abound in love.* They had already love to each other, so as to unite them in one Christian body; and he prays that they may have an increase and an abundance of it, that they might feel the same love to each other which he felt for them all.

13. *To the end he may establish your hearts.* Without love to God and man there can be no establishment in the religion of Christ. It is love that produces both solidity and continuance. *At the coming of our Lord.* God is coming to judge the world. But who in that great day shall give up his accounts with joy? That person only whose heart is established in holiness *before God;* i.e., so as to bear the eye and strict scrutiny of his Judge.

CHAPTER 4

The apostle exhorts them to attend to the directions which he had already given them, that they might know how to walk and please God, 1-2. Gives them exhortations concerning continence, chastity, and matrimonial fidelity, 3-8. Speaks concerning their love to each other, and love to the churches of Christ, and exhorts them to continue and increase in it, 9-10. Counsels them to observe an inoffensive conduct, to mind their own affairs, to do their own business, and to live honestly, 11-12. Not to sorrow for the dead as persons who have no hope of a resurrection, because to Christians the resurrection of Christ is proof of the resurrection of His followers, 13-14. Gives a short but awful description of the appearing of Christ to judge the world, 15-18.

1. *We beseech you, brethren, and exhort.* We give you proper instructions in heavenly things, and request you to attend to our advice. The apostle used the most pressing entreaties; for he had a strong and affectionate desire that this church should excel in all righteousness and true holiness. *Please God . . . more and more.* God sets no bounds to the communications of His grace and Spirit to them that are faithful. And as there are no bounds to the graces, so there should be none to the exercise of those graces.

2. *Ye know what commandments we gave you.* This refers to his instructions while he was among them.

3. *This is the will of God, even your sanctification.* God has called you to holiness; He requires that you should be holy, for without holiness none can see the Lord. *That ye should abstain from fornication.* The word includes all sorts of uncleanness.

4. *How to possess his vessel.* Let every man use his wife for the purpose alone for which God created her and instituted marriage. The word answers to the Hebrew *keli,* which, though it signifies *vessel* in general, has several other meanings. The rabbins frequently express "wife" by it; and to me it appears very probable that the apostle uses it in that sense here. Peter calls the wife the "weaker vessel," 1 Pet. iii. 7. Others think that the body is meant, which is the vessel in which the soul dwells. In this sense Paul uses it in 2 Cor. iv. 7: "We have this treasure in earthen vessels"; and in this sense it is used by both Greek and Roman authors.

6. *That no man go beyond and defraud his brother.* That no man should by any means endeavor to corrupt the wife of another, or to alienate her affections or fidelity from her husband.

7. *God hath not called us unto uncleanness.* He is the Creator of male and female, and the Institutor of marriage, and He has called men and women to this state; but the end of this and all the other callings of God to man is *holiness,* not *uncleanness.* And they who use the marriage state as he directs will find it conducive to their holiness and perfection.

8. *He therefore that despiseth.* He who will not receive these teachings, and is led either to undervalue or despise them, despises not us but God, from whom we have received our commission and by whose Spirit we give these directions. *Hath also given unto us his holy Spirit.* Instead of *unto us,* "unto you" is the reading of a great many MSS. This seems to be the better reading.

9. *Touching brotherly love.* They were remarkable for this; and though the apostle appears to have had this as a topic on which he intended to write to them, yet from the account which he received of their prosperous state by Timothy, he finds that it is unnecessary to spend any time in inculcating a doctrine which they fully understood and practiced.

10. *Ye do it toward all the brethren.* You not only love one another at Thessalonica, but you love all the brethren in Macedonia; you consider them all as children of the same Father.

11. *That ye study to be quiet.* Though in general the church at Thessalonica was pure and exemplary, yet there seem to have been some idle, tattling people among them, who disturbed the peace of others. To these the apostle gives those directions which the whole Church of God should enforce wherever such troublesome and dangerous people are found; viz., that they should *study to be quiet,* "to hold their peace," as their religious cant will never promote true religion; that they should *do their own business,* and let that of others alone; and that they should *work with* their *own hands,* and not be a burden to the Church of God. An idle person, though able to discourse like an angel or pray like an apostle, cannot be a Christian; all such are hypocrites and deceivers. The true members of the Church of Christ walk, work, and labor.

12. *That ye may walk honestly.* "Becomingly, decently, respectably"; as is consistent with the purity, holiness, gravity, and usefulness of your Christian calling. *Them that are without.* The unconverted Gentiles and Jews. *That ye may have lack of nothing.* That you may be able to get your bread by honest labor, which God will ever bless, and be chargeable to no man. He that is dependent on another is necessarily in bondage; and he who is able to get his own bread by the sweat of his brow should not be under obligation even to a king.

13. *I would not have you to be ignorant.* Instead of *have,* "wish," is the reading of many MSS. and many of the Greek fathers. This is undoubtedly the true reading: "Brethren, I would not wish you to be ignorant." This was probably one of the points which were lacking in their faith, that he wished to go to Thessalonica to instruct them in. *Them which are asleep.* That is, those who are dead. It is supposed that the apostle had heard that the Thessalonians continued to lament over their dead, as the heathens did in general who had no

hope of the resurrection of the body, and that they had been puzzled concerning the doctrine of the resurrection.

14. *For if we believe that Jesus died and rose again.* "Seeing that we believe"; knowing that the resurrection of Christ is as fully authenticated as His detah. *Even so them.* It necessarily follows that they who *sleep*—die, in Him—in the faith of the gospel, *will God bring with him*—He will raise them up as Jesus was raised from the dead, in the same manner, i.e., by His own eternal power and energy; and He will bring them *with him*—with Christ, for He is the Head of the Church, which is His body.

15. *This we say unto you by the word of the Lord.* This I have, by express revelation, from the Lord. What he now delivers he gives as coming immediately from the Spirit of God. *We which are alive and remain.* By the pronoun *we* the apostle does not intend himself and the Thessalonians to whom he was then writing; he is speaking of the genuine Christians which shall be found on earth when Christ comes to judgment. From not considering the manner in which the apostle uses this word, some have been led to suppose that he imagined that the day of judgment would take place in that generation, and while he and the then believers at Thessalonica were in life. *Shall not prevent them which are asleep.* Those who shall be found living in that day, though they shall not pass through death, but be suddenly changed, shall not go to glory before them that are dead, for "the dead in Christ shall rise first"— they shall be raised, their bodies made glorious, and be caught up to meet the Lord, before the others shall be changed. And this appears to be the meaning of the apostle's words which we translate *shall not prevent;* for although this word *prevent,* from *prae* and *venio,* literally signifies to "go before," yet we use it now in the sense of "to hinder or obstruct."

16. *The Lord himself.* That is, Jesus Christ. *Shall descend from heaven.* Shall descend in like manner as He was seen by His disciples to ascend; i.e., in His human form, but now infinitely more glorious. *With a shout.* Or "order," and probably in these words: "Arise, ye dead, and come to judgment"; which order shall be repeated by the archangel, who shall accompany it with the sound of the trump of God, whose great and terrible blasts, like those on Mount Sinai, sounding louder and louder, shall shake both the heavens and the earth!

CHAPTER 5

The apostle continues to speak of Christ's coming to judgment, and the uncertainty of the time in which it shall take place, and the careless state of sinners, 1-3. Shows the Thessalonians that they are children of the light; that they should watch and pray, and put on the armor of God, being called to obtain salvation by Christ, who died for them; that whether dead or alive, when the day of judgment comes, they may live forever with Him; and that they should comfort and edify each other with these considerations, 4-11. He exhorts them to remember those who labor among them and are over them in the Lord, and to esteem such highly for their work's sake, 12-13. He charges them to warn, comfort, and support those who stood in need of such assistance, and to be patient and beneficent towards all, 14-15. He points out their high spiritual privileges; warns them against neglecting or misimproving the gifts of the Spirit, and the means of grace, 16-20. They are also exhorted to prove all things; to abstain from all evil; and to expect to be sanctified, through spirit, soul, and body, by Him who has promised this, and who is faithful to His promises, 21-24. Recommends himself and brethren to their prayers; shows them how they are to greet each other; charges them to read this Epistle to all the brethren; and concludes with the usual apostolical benediction, 25-28.

1-2. *But of the times and the seasons.* It is natural to suppose, after what he had said in the conclusion of the preceding chapter concerning the coming of Christ, the raising of the dead, and rendering those immortal who should then be found alive without obliging them to pass through the empire of death, that the Thessalonians would feel an innocent curiosity to know, as the disciples did concerning the destruction of Jerusalem, when those things should take place, and what should be the signs of those times, and of the coming of the Son of Man. And it is remarkable that the apostle answers here to these anticipated questions as our Lord did, in the above case, to the direct question of His disciples; and he seems to refer in these words, *Of the times and the seasons . . . ye have no need that I write unto you. For yourselves know . . . that the day of the Lord . . . cometh as a thief in the night,* to what our Lord said, Matt. xxiv. 44; xxv. 13; and the apostle takes it for granted that they were acquainted with our Lord's prediction on the subject. It is very likely therefore that the apostle, like our Lord, couples these two grand events—the destruction of Jerusalem and the final judgment. And it appears most probable that it is of the former event chiefly that he speaks here, as it was certainly of the latter that he treated in the conclusion of the preceding chapter. In the notes on Acts i. 6-7, it has already been shown that the *times* or *seasons* refer to the destruction of the Jewish commonwealth, and we may fairly presume that they have the same meaning in this place.

3. *For when they shall say, Peace and safety.* This points out, very particularly, the state of the Jewish people when the Romans came against them; and so fully persuaded were they that God would not deliver the city and Temple to their enemies that they refused every overture that was made to them. *Sudden destruction.* In the storming of their city, the burning of their Temple, and the massacre of several hundreds of thousands of themselves; the rest being sold for slaves, and the whole of them dispersed over the face of the earth. *As travail upon a woman.* This figure is perfectly consistent with what the apostle had said before, viz., that the times and seasons were not known, though the thing itself was expected, our Lord having predicted it in the most positive manner. So a woman with child knows that, if she is spared, she will have a bearing time; but the week, the day, the hour, she cannot tell.

4. *But ye, brethren, are not in darkness.* Probably Paul refers to a notion that was very prevalent among the Jews. The words in Midrash Tehillim, on Ps. ix. 8, are the following: "When the holy blessed God shall judge the Gentiles, it shall be in the night season, in which they shall be asleep in their transgressions; but when he shall judge the Israelites, it shall be in the day time, when they are occupied in the study of the law." This maxim the apostle appears to have in view in vv. 4-8.

5. *Ye are all the children of light.* You are children of God, and enjoy both His light and life.

6. *Let us not sleep, as do others.* Let us who are of the day—who believe the gospel and belong to Christ—not give way to a careless, unconcerned state of mind, like to the Gentiles and sinners in general, who are stupefied and blinded by sin. *Let us watch.* Be always on the alert; *and be sober,* making a moderate use of all things.

7. *For they that sleep.* Sleepers and drunkards seek the night season; so the careless and the profligate persons indulge their evil propensities and avoid all means of instruction; they prefer their ignorance to the word of God's grace and to the light of life.

8. *Putting on the breastplate.* We are not only called to work, but we are called also to fight; and that we may not be surprised, we must watch; and that we may be in a condition to defend ourselves, we must be sober; and that we may be enabled to conquer, we must be armed: and what the *breastplate* and *helmet* are to a soldier's heart and head, such are faith, love, and hope to us. *Faith* enables us to endure, "as seeing him who is invisible"; *love* excites us to diligence and activity, and makes us bear our troubles and difficulties pleasantly; *hope* helps us to anticipate the great end, the glory that shall be revealed, and which we know we shall in due time obtain if we faint not.

9. *For God hath not appointed us to wrath.* So then it appears that some were *appointed . . . to wrath,* "to punishment"; on this subject there can be no dispute. But who are they? When did this appointment take place? And for what cause? It is very obvious that in the preceding verses the apostle refers simply to the destruction of the Jewish polity and to the terrible judgments which were about to fall on the Jews as a nation; therefore they are the people who were appointed to wrath; and they were thus appointed, not from eternity, nor from any indefinite or remote time, but from that time in which they utterly rejected the offers of salvation made to them by Jesus Christ and His apostles. The privileges of their election were still continued to them even after they had crucified the Lord of glory; for when He gave commandment to His disciples to go into all the world and preach the gospel to every creature, He bade them begin at Jerusalem. When the Jews were rejected and appointed to wrath, then the Gentiles were elected and appointed to *obtain salvation* by our Lord Jesus Christ, whose gospel they gladly received and continue to prize.

10. *Who died for us.* His death was an atoning sacrifice for the Gentiles as well as for the Jews. *Whether we wake or sleep.* Whether we "live" or "die," whether we are in this state or in the other world, we shall live together with Him—shall enjoy His life and the consolations of His Spirit while here, and shall be glorified together with Him in the eternal world.

11. *Comfort . . . one another.* Rest assured that in all times and circumstances it shall be well with the righteous; let every man lay this to heart; and with this consideration *comfort* and *edify* each other in all trials and difficulties.

12. *Know them.* Act kindly toward them; "acknowledge" them as the messengers of Christ, and treat them with tenderness and respect. This is a frequent meaning of the word. *Them* *which labour among you.* The words have appeared to some as expressing those who had labored among them; but as it is the participle of the present tense, there is no need to consider it in this light. Both it and the word "superintendents" refer to persons then actually employed in the work of God.

13. *Esteem them very highly in love.* Christian ministers who preach the whole truth and labor in the word and doctrine are entitled to more than respect; the apostle commands them to be esteemed, "abundantly, and super-abundantly." And this is to be done *in love;* and as men delight to serve those whom they love, it necessarily follows that they should provide for them, and see that they want neither the necessaries nor conveniences of life.

14. *Warn them that are unruly.* The whole phraseology of this verse is military; I shall consider the import of each term. Those who are "out of their ranks," and are neither in a disposition nor situation to perform the work and duty of a soldier; those who will not do the work prescribed, and who will meddle with what is not commanded. *Comfort the feebleminded.* Those of "little souls"; the "fainthearted"; those who, on the eve of a battle, are dispirited, because of the number of the enemy and their own feeble and unprovided state. *Support the weak.* "Shore up, prop" them that are weak; strengthen those wings and companies that are likely to be most exposed, that they be not overpowered and broken in the day of battle. *Be patient toward all.* The disorderly, *the feebleminded,* and *the weak* will exercise your patience and try your temper. If the troops be irregular, and cannot in every respect be reduced to proper order and discipline, let not the officers lose their temper nor courage; let them do the best they can. God will be with them, and a victory will give confidence to their troops.

15. *See that none render evil for evil.* Every temper contrary to love is contrary to Christianity. A peevish, fretful, vindictive man may be a child of Satan; he certainly is not a child of God. *Follow that which is good.* That by which you may profit your brethren and your neighbors of every description, whether Jews or Gentiles.

16. *Rejoice evermore.* Be always happy; the religion of Christ was intended to remove misery. He that has God for his Portion may constantly exult.

17. *Pray without ceasing.* You are dependent on God for every good; without Him you can do nothing. Feel that dependence at all times, and you will always be in the spirit of prayer; and those who feel this spirit will, as frequently as possible, be found in the exercise of prayer.

18. *In every thing give thanks.* For this reason, that all things work together for good to them that love God; therefore every occurrence may be a subject of gratitude and thankfulness. While you live to God, prosperity and adversity will be equally helpful to you. *For this is the will of God.* That you should be always happy; that you should ever be in the spirit of prayer; and that you should profit by every occurrence in life, and be continually grateful and obedient —for gratitude and obedience are inseparably connected.

19. *Quench not the Spirit.* The Holy Spirit is represented as a fire, because it is His province to enlighten and quicken the soul; and to purge, purify, and refine it. This Spirit is represented as being quenched when any act is done, word spoken, or temper indulged contrary to its dictates. It is the Spirit of love, and therefore anger, malice, revenge, or any unkind or unholy temper will quench it so that it will withdraw its influences; and then the heart is left in a state of hardness and darkness. It has been observed that fire may be quenched as well by heaping earth on it as by throwing water on it; and so the love of the world will as effectually grieve and quench the Spirit as any ordinary act of transgression.

20. *Despise not prophesyings.* Do not suppose that you have no need of continual instruction; without it you cannot preserve the Christian life nor go on to perfection.

21. *Prove all things.* Whatever you hear in these "prophesyings" or preachings, examine by the words of Christ, and by the doctrines which, from time to time, we have delivered unto you in our preaching and writings. Try the spirits, the different teachers, by the Word of God. *Hold fast that which is good.* Whatever in these prophesyings has a tendency to increase your faith, love, holiness, and usefulness, that receive and hold fast.

22. *Abstain from all appearance of evil.* Sin not, and avoid even the *appearance* of it. Do not drive your morality so near the bounds of evil as to lead even weak persons to believe that you actually touch, taste, or handle it. Let not the "form" of it appear with or among you, much less the substance.

23. *And the very God of peace.* That same God who is the Author of peace, the Giver of peace, and who has sent for the redemption of the world the Prince of Peace—may that very God *sanctify you wholly;* leave no more evil in your hearts than His precepts tolerate evil in your conduct. The word *wholly* means precisely the same as our phrase "to all intents and purposes." May He sanctify you to the end and to the uttermost. *Your whole spirit and soul and body.* Some think that the apostle alludes to the Pythagorean and Platonic doctrine, which was acknowledged among the Thessalonians. I should rather believe that he refers simply to the fact that the creature called man is a compound being, consisting: (1) Of a *body,* an organized system, formed by the creative energy of God out of the dust of the earth; (2) Of a *soul,* which is the seat of the different affections and passions, such as love, hatred, anger, with sensations, appetites, and propensities of different kinds; (3) Of *spirit,* the immortal principle, the source of life to the body and soul; and which alone possesses the faculty of intelligence, understanding, thinking, and reasoning, and produces the faculty of speech wherever it resides, if accident have not impaired the organs of speech. The apostle prays that this compound being, in all its parts, powers, and faculties, which he terms their *whole,* comprehending all parts, everything that constitutes man and manhood, may be sanctified and preserved *blameless* till the coming of Christ. Thus we learn that the sanctification is not to take place in, at, or after death.

24. *Faithful is he that calleth you.* In a great

variety of places in His Word, God has promised to sanctify His followers, and His faithfulness binds Him to fulfill His promises; therefore He will do it. He who can believe will find this thing also possible to him.

25. *Pray for us.* Even apostles, while acting under an extraordinary mission, and enjoying the inspiration of the Holy Ghost, felt the necessity of the prayers of the faithful.

27. *I charge you by the Lord that this epistle be read.* There must have been some particular reason for this solemn charge. He certainly had some cause to suspect that the Epistle would be suppressed in some way or other, and that the whole church would not be permitted to hear it; or he may refer to the smaller churches contiguous to Thessalonica, or the churches in Macedonia in general, whom he wished to hear it, as well as those to whom it was more immediately directed. There is no doubt that the apostles designed that their epistles should be copied and sent to all the churches in the vicinity of that to which they were directed. Had this not been the case, a great number of churches would have known scarcely anything of the New Testament. As every Jewish synagogue had a copy of the law and the prophets, so every Christian church had a copy of the Gospels and the Epistles, which were daily, or at least every Sabbath, read for the instruction of the people. This the apostle deemed so necessary that he adjured them by the Lord to read this Epistle to all the brethren; i.e., to all the Christians in that district.

28. *The grace of our Lord Jesus.* As the Epistle began, so it ends; for the grace of Christ must be at the beginning and end of every work, in order to complete it and bring it to good effect. *Amen.* This is wanting in some MSS. It was probably not written by Paul.

The Second Epistle to the
THESSALONIANS

That this Second Epistle was written shortly after the first and from the same place is very probable from this circumstance, that the same persons, Paul, Silvanus, and Timotheus, who addressed the church at Thessalonica in the former Epistle address the same church in this; and as three apostolic men were rarely long together in the same place, it is very likely that the two Epistles were written not only in the same year, but also within a very short time of each other. It appears that the person who carried the First Epistle returned speedily to Corinth, and gave the apostle a particular account of the state of the Thessalonian church; and, among other things, informed him that many were in expectation of the speedy arrival of the day of judgment; and that they inferred from his Epistle already sent, chap. iv. 15, 17 and vv. 4, 6, that it was to take place while the apostle and themselves should be yet alive. And it appears probable, from some parts of this Epistle, that he was informed also that some, expecting this sudden appearance of the Lord Jesus, had given up all their secular concerns as inconsistent with a due preparation for such an important and awful event; see chap. iii. 6-13. To correct such a misapprehension and redeem them from an error which, if appearing to rest on the authority of an apostle, must in its issue be ruinous to the cause of Christianity, Paul would feel himself constrained to write immediately; and this is a sufficient reason why these Epistles should appear to have been written at so short a distance from each other. What rendered this speedy intervention of the apostle's authority and direction the more necessary was that there appear to have been some in that church who professed to have a revelation concerning this thing, and to have endeavored to confirm it by a pretended report from the apostle himself, and from the words already referred to in the former Epistle; see here on chap. ii. 1-2: "We beseech you, brethren . . . be not soon shaken in mind, or be troubled, neither by spirit, nor by word, nor by letter as from us, as that the day of Christ is at hand."

CHAPTER 1

The salutation of Paul and his companions, 1-2. The apostle gives thanks to God for their faith, love, and union; and for their patience under persecutions, 3-4. Speaks of the coming of our Lord Jesus Christ, the punishment of the ungodly, and the glorification of the righteous, 5-10. Prays that God may count them worthy of their calling, that the name of Jesus may be glorified in them, 11-12.

1. *Paul, and Silvanus.* See the notes on 1 Thess. i. 1. This Epistle was written a short time after the former; and as Silas and Timothy were still at Corinth, the apostle joins their names with his own, as in the former case.

3. *Your faith groweth exceedingly.* The word signifies "to grow luxuriantly," as a good and healthy tree planted in a good soil; and if a fruit tree bearing an abundance of fruit to compensate the labor of the husbandman.

4. *We ourselves glory in you in the churches of God.* We hold you up as an example of what the grace of God can produce when communicated to honest and faithful hearts. *For your patience and faith.* From Acts xvii. 5, 13 and from 1 Thess. ii. 14, we learn that the people of Thessalonica had suffered much persecution from both the Jews and their own countrymen; but being thoroughly convinced of the truth of the gospel, and feeling it to be the power of God unto salvation, no persecution could turn them aside from it. And having suffered for

the truth, it was precious to them. Persecution never essentially injured the genuine Church of God.

5. *A manifest token of the righteous judgment of God.* The persecutions and tribulations which you endure are a manifest proof that God has judged righteously in calling you Gentiles into His Church. The words, however, may be understood in another sense, and will form this maxim: "The sufferings of the just, and the triumphs of the wicked, in this life, are a sure proof that there will be a future judgment, in which the wicked shall be punished and the righteous rewarded." This maxim is not only true in itself, but it is most likely that this is the apostle's meaning.

6. *Seeing it is a righteous thing.* Though God neither rewards nor punishes in this life in a general way, yet He often gives proofs of His displeasure, especially against those who persecute His followers. They therefore who have given you tribulation shall have tribulation in recompense.

7. *And to you who are troubled rest with us.* And while they have *tribulation*, you shall have that eternal *rest* which remains for the people of God. *When the Lord Jesus shall be revealed.* But this fullness of *tribulation* to them and *rest* to you shall not take place till the Lord Jesus comes to judge the world. *With his mighty angels.* The coming of God to judge the world is scarcely ever spoken of in the sacred writings without mentioning the holy angels, who are to accompany Him and to form His court or retinue. See Deut. xxxiii. 2; Matt. xxv. 31; xvi. 27; xxvi. 64; Mark viii. 38.

8. *In flaming fire,* in thunder and lightning, *taking vengeance,* inflicting just punishment, *on them that know not God*—the heathen who do not worship the true God, and will not acknowledge Him, but worship idols; and on them *that obey not the gospel*—the Jews, particularly who have rejected the gospel and persecuted Christ and His messengers; and all nominal Christians who, though they believe the gospel as a revelation from God, yet do not obey it as a rule of life.

9. *Who shall be punished.* What this *everlasting destruction* consists in we cannot tell. It is not annihilation, for their being continues; and as the destruction is *everlasting,* it is an eternal continuance and presence of substantial evil and absence of all good; for a part of this punishment consists in being banished *from the presence of the Lord,* excluded from His approbation forever. *The glory of his power.* Never to see the face of God throughout eternity is a heart-rending, soul-appalling thought; and to be banished from the *glory of his power,* that power the glory of which is peculiarly manifested in saving the lost and glorifying the faithful, is what cannot be reflected on without confusion and dismay.

10. *When he shall come to be glorified in his saints.* As the grace of God is peculiarly glorified in saving sinners and making them into saints, this gracious power will be particularly manifested in the great day when countless millions will appear before that throne who have come out of great tribulation, and have washed their robes and made them white in the blood of the Lamb. *And to be admired.*

"To be wondered at among" and on the account of *all them that believe.* Instead of *them that believe,* "them that have believed" is the reading of many MSS. and most of the Greek fathers. This reading is undoubtedly genuine. *Because our testimony among you was believed in that day.* The members of this sentence seem to have been strangely transposed. I believe it should be read thus: "In that day, when He shall come to be glorified in His saints, and admired among all them that have believed; for our testimony was believed among you." The Thessalonians had credited what the apostles had said and written, not only concerning Jesus Christ in general, but concerning the day of judgment in particular.

11. *We pray . . . that our God would count you worthy.* It is our earnest prayer that God would "make you worthy," afford those continual supplies of grace by His Holy Spirit without which you cannot adorn your holy vocation.

12. *That the name of our Lord.* This is the great end of your Christian calling, that Jesus, who has died for you, may have His passion and death magnified in your life and happiness; that you may show forth the virtues of Him who called you from darkness into His marvellous light. *And ye in him.* That His glorious excellence may be seen upon you; that you may be adorned with the graces of His Spirit, as He is glorified by your salvation from all sin. *According to the grace.* That your salvation may be such as God requires, and such as is worthy of His grace to communicate. God saves as becomes God to save, and thus the dignity of His nature is seen in the excellence and glory of His work.

CHAPTER 2

He exhorts the Thessalonians to stand fast in the faith, and not to be alarmed at the rumors they heard concerning the sudden coming of Christ, 1-2. Because, previously to this coming, there would be a great apostasy from the true faith, and a manifestation of a son of perdition, of whose unparalleled presumption he gives an awful description; as well as of his pernicious success among men, and the means which he would use to deceive and pervert the world; and particularly those who do not receive the love of the truth, but have pleasure in unrighteousness, 3-12. He thanks God for their steadfastness, shows the great privileges to which they were called, and prays that they may be comforted and established in every good word and work, 13-17.

1. *We beseech you, brethren, by the coming of our Lord.* It is evident that the Thessalonians, incited by deceived or false teachers, had taken a wrong meaning out of the words of the First Epistle, chap. iv. 15 ff., concerning the day of judgment, and were led then to conclude that that day was at hand; and this had produced great confusion in the church. To correct this mistake the apostle sent them this second letter, in which he shows that this day must be necessarily distant, because a great work is to be done previously to its appearing. Of the day of general judgment he had spoken before, and said that it should "come as a thief in the night," i.e., when not expected; but he did not attempt to fix the time, nor did he insinuate that it was either near at hand or far off. Now, however, he shows that it must necessarily be far off, because of the great transactions which must take place before it can come.

2. *Be not soon shaken in mind.* "From the

mind"; i.e., that they should retain the persuasion they had of the truths which he had before delivered to them; that they should still hold the same opinions, and hold fast the doctrines which they had been taught. *Neither by spirit.* Any pretended revelation. *Nor by word.* Anything which any person may profess to have heard the apostle speak. *Nor by letter.* Either the former one which he had sent, some passages of which have been misconceived and misconstrued, or by any other letter, *as from us* —pretending to have been written by us, the apostles, containing predictions of this kind. There is a diversity of opinion among critics concerning this last clause, some supposing that it refers simply to the First Epistle, others supposing that a forged epistle is intended. I have joined the two senses. The word "to be shaken" signifies to be agitated as a ship at sea in a storm, and strongly marks the confusion and distress which the Thessalonians had felt in their false apprehension of this coming of Christ.

3. *Except there come a falling away first.* We have the original word in our word "apostasy"; and by this term we understand a dereliction of the essential principles of religious truth—either a total abandonment of Christianity itself or such a corruption of its doctrines as renders the whole system completely inefficient to salvation. *That man of sin.* The same as the Hebrew expresses by *ish aven* and *ish beliyaal;* the perverse, obstinate, and iniquitous man. *The son of perdition.* "The son of destruction"; the same epithet that is given to Judas Iscariot, John xvii. 12. The *son of perdition* and the *man of sin* or, as some excellent MSS. and versions, with several of the fathers, read, "the lawless man," must mean the same person or thing. It is also remarkable that the wicked Jews are styled by Isaiah, chap. i. 4, "children of perdition," persons who destroy themselves and destroy others.

4. *Who opposeth and exalteth.* He "stands against" and exalts himself above all divine authority and above every object of adoration and every institution relative to divine worship, himself being the source whence must originate all the doctrines of religion and all its rites and ceremonies; so that sitting in the temple of God—having the highest place and authority in the Christian Church, he acts as God—taking upon himself God's titles and attributes, and arrogating to himself the authority that belongs to the Most High. The words *as God* are wanting in many MSS. and the chief of the Greek fathers. There is indeed no evidence of their being authentic, and the text reads much better without them.

5. *I told you these things.* In several parts of this description of the man of sin, the apostle alludes to a conversation which had taken place between him and the members of this church when he was at Thessalonica; and this one circumstance will account for much of the obscurity that is in these verses. Besides, the apostle appears to speak with great caution, and does not at all wish to publish what he had communicated to them; the hints which he drops were sufficient to call the whole to their remembrance.

6. *And now ye know what withholdeth.* I told you this among other things; I informed you what it was that prevented this man of sin, this son of perdition, from revealing himself fully.

7. *For the mystery of iniquity doth already work.* There is a system of corrupt doctrine which will lead to the general apostasy, already in existence, but it is a *mystery.* It is as yet hidden; it dare not show itself, because of that which "hindereth" or "withholdeth." But when that which now "restraineth" shall be taken out of the way, then shall that wicked one be revealed—it will then be manifest who he is and what he is.

8. *Whom the Lord shall consume.* He shall "blast" him so that he shall "wither" and "die away"; and this shall be done by *the spirit of his mouth*—the words of eternal life, the true doctrine of the gospel of Jesus; this shall be the instrument used to destroy this man of sin. Therefore it is evident his death will not be a sudden but a gradual one; because it is by the preaching of the truth that he is to be exposed, overthrown, and finally destroyed. *The brightness of his coming.* This may refer to that full manifestation of the truth which had been obscured and kept under by the exaltation of this man of sin.

9. *Whose coming is after the working of Satan.* The operation of God's Spirit sends His messengers; the operation of Satan's spirit sends his emissaries. The one comes *after* or "according to the energy" or inward powerful *working of* God; the other comes according to the energy or inward working of Satan. *With all power.* All kinds of miracles, like the Egyptian magicians. *And signs and lying wonders.* The word *lying* may be applied to the whole of these; they were *lying* miracles, *lying* signs, and *lying* wonders; only appearances of what was real, and done to give credit to his presumption and imposture. Whereas God sent His messengers with real miracles, real signs, and real wonders; such Satan cannot produce.

10. *And with all deceivableness of unrighteousness.* With every art that cunning can invent and unrighteousness suggest, in order to delude and deceive. *In them that perish.* "Among them that are destroyed"; and they are destroyed and perish because they would not receive *the love of the truth, that they might be saved.* So they perish because they obstinately refuse to be saved, and receive a lie in preference to the truth.

11. *God shall send them strong delusion. For this* very *cause,* that they would not receive the love of the truth, "but had pleasure in unrighteousness," therefore God permits *strong delusion* to occupy their minds; so that they *believe a lie* rather than the truth, prefer false apostles and their erroneous doctrines to the pure truths of the gospel, brought to them by the well-accredited messengers of God; being ever ready to receive any false Messiah, while they systematically and virulently reject the true One.

12. *That they all might be damned.* "So that they may all be condemned who believed not the truth" when it was proclaimed to them; but took *pleasure in unrighteousness,* preferring that to the way of holiness. Their condemnation was the effect of their refusal to believe the truth, and they refused to believe it because they loved their sins.

13-14. *God hath from the beginning chosen you to salvation.* In your calling God has shown the purpose that He had formed from the beginning, to call the Gentiles to the same privileges with the Jews, not through circumcision and the observance of the Mosaic law, but by faith in Christ Jesus; but this simple way of salvation referred to the same end—holiness, without which no man, whether Jew or Gentile, can see the Lord.

15. *Therefore, brethren, stand fast.* Their obtaining eternal glory depended on their faithfulness to the grace of God; for this calling did not necessarily and irresistibly lead to faith; nor their faith to the sanctification of the spirit; nor their sanctification of the spirit to the glory of our Lord Jesus. Had they not attended to the calling, they could not have believed; had they not believed, they could not have been sanctified; had they not been sanctified they could not have been glorified. All these things depended on each other; they were stages of the great journey; and at any of these stages they might have halted, and never finished their Christian race. *Hold the traditions which ye have been taught.* The word which we render "tradition" signifies anything "delivered" in the way of teaching; and here most obviously means the doctrines delivered by the apostle to the Thessalonians, whether in his preaching, private conversation, or by these Epistles; and particularly the First Epistle, as the apostle here states.

16. *Now our Lord Jesus.* As all your grace came from God through Christ, so the power that is necessary to strengthen and confirm you unto the end must come in the same way. *Everlasting consolation.* The glad tidings of the gospel and the comfort which you have received through believing, a gift which God had in His original purpose in reference to the Gentiles, a purpose which has respected all times and places and which shall continue to the conclusion of time; for the gospel is everlasting, and shall not be superseded by any other dispensation. *And good hope through grace.* The hope of the gospel was the resurrection of the body, and the final glorification of it and the soul throughout eternity. This was the good hope which the Thessalonians had, not a hope that they should be pardoned or sanctified. Pardon and holiness they enjoyed; therefore they were no objects of hope. But the resurrection of the body and eternal glory were necessarily future; these they had in expectation; these they hoped for; and through the *grace* which they had already received they had a *good hope,* a well-grounded expectation, of the glorious state.

17. *Comfort your hearts.* Keep your souls ever under the influence of His Holy Spirit; *and stablish you*—confirm and strengthen you in your belief in every *good word* or doctrine which we have delivered unto you, and in the practice of every *good work* recommended and enjoined by the doctrines of the gospel.

CHAPTER 3

The apostle recommends himself and his brethren to the prayers of the church, that their preaching might be successful, and that they might be delivered from wicked men, 1-2. Expresses his confidence in God and them, and prays that they may patiently wait for the coming of Christ, 3-5. Gives them directions concerning strict discipline in the church; and shows how he and his fellow laborers had behaved among them, not availing themselves of their own power and authority, 6-9. Shows them how to treat disorderly and idle people, and not to get weary in well doing, 10-13. Directs them not to associate with those who obey not the orders contained in this Epistle, 14-15. Prays that they may have increasing peace, 16. And conclude with his salutation and benediction, 17-18.

1. *Finally, brethren.* The words do not mean *finally,* but "furthermore," "to come to a conclusion," "what remains is this," "I shall only add"—any of these phrases expresses the sense of the original. *Pray for us.* God, in the order of His grace and providence, has made even the success of His gospel dependent in a certain measure on the prayers of His followers. Why He should do so we cannot tell, but that He has done so we know; and they are not a little criminal who neglect to make fervent supplications for the prosperity of the cause of God. *May have free course.* They were to pray that "the doctrine of the Lord" "might run," an allusion to the races in the Olympic games; that, as it had already got into the stadium or racecourse, and had started fairly, so it might "run on," get to the goal, and *be glorified;* i.e., gain the crown appointed for him that should get first to the end of the course.

2. *Unreasonable and wicked men.* The word which we translate *unreasonable* signifies rather "disorderly, unmanageable"; persons "out of their place"—under no discipline, regardless of law and restraint, and ever acting agreeably to the disorderly and unreasonable impulse of their own minds. *For all men have not faith.* The word is, without doubt, to be taken here for "fidelity" or "trustworthiness," and not for *faith;* and this is agreeable to the meaning given to it in the very next verse: "But the Lord is faithful."

3. *From evil.* May be translated, "from the evil one." They had disorderly men, wicked men, and the evil one or the devil to contend with; God alone could support and give them the victory. He had promised to do it, and He might ever be confided in as being invariably *faithful.*

4. *And we have confidence.* We have no doubt of God's kindness towards you; He loves you, and will support you; and we can confide in you that you are now acting as we have desired you, and will continue so to do.

5. *The Lord direct your hearts into the love of God.* "Give a proper direction" to all its passions, and keep them in order, regularity, and purity. *The patience of Christ.* Such patience, under all your sufferings and persecutions, as Christ manifested under His. He bore meekly the contradiction of sinners against himself; and when He was reviled, He reviled not again.

6. *That ye withdraw yourselves.* Have no fellowship with those who will not submit to proper discipline; who do not keep their place; such as are "out of their rank," and act according to their own wills and caprices; and particularly such as are idle and busybodies. These he had ordered, 1 Thess. iv. 11-12, that they should study to be quiet, mind their own business, and work with their hands; but it appears that they had paid no attention to this order, and now he desires the church to exclude such from their communion. *And not after the tradition.* This evidently refers to the orders contained in the First Epistle; and that First Epistle was the *tradition* which they had received from him.

7. *We behaved not ourselves disorderly.* "We did not go out of our rank"—we kept our place, and discharged all its duties.

8. *Neither did we eat any man's bread for nought.* We paid for what we bought, and worked with our hands that we might have money to buy what was necessary. *Labour and travail night and day.* We were incessantly employed, either in preaching the gospel, visiting from house to house, or working at our calling. As it is very evident that the church at Thessalonica was very pious, and most affectionately attached to the apostle, they must have been very poor, seeing he was obliged to work hard to gain himself the necessaries of life.

9. *Not because we have not power.* We have the power, the "right," to be maintained by those in whose behalf we labor. "The labourer is worthy of his hire" is a maxim universally acknowledged and respected; and "they which preach the gospel should live of the gospel." The apostle did not claim his privilege, but labored for his own support, that he might be an example to those whom he found otherwise disposed, and that he might spare the poor.

10. *If any would not work, neither should he eat.* This is a just maxim, and universal nature inculcates it to man. If man will work, he may eat; if he do not work, he neither can eat nor should he eat. The maxim is founded on these words of the Lord: "In the sweat of thy face shalt thou eat bread." Industry is crowned with God's blessing; idleness is loaded with His curse.

11. *For we hear that there are some.* It is very likely that Paul kept up some sort of correspondence with the Thessalonian church; for he had heard everything that concerned their state, and it was from this information that he wrote his Second Epistle. *Disorderly.* "Out of their rank"—not keeping their own place. *Working not at all.* Either lounging at home or becoming religious gossips; "doing nothing." *Busybodies.* Doing everything they should not do—impertinent meddlers with other people's business; prying into other people's circumstances and domestic affairs; magnifying or minifying, mistaking or underrating everything; newsmongers and telltales; an abominable race, the curse of every neighborhood where they live, and a pest to religious society.

12. *With quietness they work.* "With silence"; leaving their talebearing and officious inter-

meddling. Less noise and more work! *Eat their own bread.* Their *own* bread because earned by their own honest industry. What a degrading thing to live on the bounty or mercy of another while a man is able to acquire his own livelihood!

13. *Be not weary in well doing.* While you stretch out no hand of relief to the indolent and lazy, do not forget the real poor—the genuine representatives of an impoverished Christ; and rather relieve a hundred undeserving objects than pass by one who is a real object of charity.

14. *If any man obey not.* They had disobeyed his word in the First Epistle, and the church still continued to bear with them; now he tells the church, if they still continue to disregard what is said to them, and particularly his word by this Second Epistle, they are to mark them as being totally incorrigible and have no fellowship with them. Some construe the words, "Give me information of that man by a letter"—let me hear of his continued obstinacy, and send me his name. The words of the original will bear either construction, that in the text or that given above.

15. *Count him not as an enemy.* Consider him still more an enemy to himself than to you; and *admonish him as a brother,* though you have ceased to hold religious communion with him. His soul is still of infinite value; labor to get it saved.

16. *The Lord of peace.* Jesus Christ, who is called "our peace," Eph. ii. 14; and "The Prince of Peace," Isa. ix. 6. May He *give you peace,* for He is the Fountain and Dispenser of it. *The Lord be with you all.* This is agreeable to the promise of our Lord: "Lo, I am with you alway, even unto the end of the world," Matt. xxviii. 20. May the Lord, who has promised to be always with His true disciples, be with you!

17. *The salutation of Paul with mine own hand.* It is very likely that Paul employed an amanuensis generally, either to write what he dictated or to make a fair copy of what he wrote. In either case the apostle always subscribed it, and wrote the salutation and benediction with his own hand; and this was what authenticated all his Epistles. A measure of this kind would be very necessary is forged epistles were carried about in those times.

18. *The grace.* The favor, blessing, and influence of our Lord Jesus Christ. *Be with you all*—be your constant companion. May you ever feel His presence, and enjoy His benediction!

The First Epistle to
TIMOTHY

Paul and Barnabas, in the course of their first apostolic journey among the Gentiles, came to Lystra, a city of Lycaonia, where they preached the gospel for some time, and, though persecuted, with considerable successs. See Acts xiv. 5-6. It is very likely that here they converted to the Christian faith a Jewess named Lois, with her daughter Eunice, who had married a Gentile, by whom she had Timothy, and whose father was probably at this time dead; the grandmother, daughter, and son living together. Compare Acts xvi. 1-3 with 2 Tim. i. 5. It is likely that Timothy was the only child; and it appears that he had been brought up in the fear of God, and carefully instructed in the Jewish religion by means of the Holy Scriptures. Compare 2 Tim. i. 5 with 2 Tim. iii. 15. It appears also that this young man drank into the apostle's spirit, became a thorough convert to the Christian faith, and that a very tender intimacy subsisted between Paul and him.

When the apostle came from Antioch, in Syria, the second time to Lystra, he found Timothy a member of the church, and so highly reputed and warmly recommended by the church in that place that Paul took him to be his companion in his travels, Acts xvi. 1-3. From this place we learn that, although Timothy had been educated in the Jewish faith, he had not been circumcised, because his father, who was a Gentile, would not permit it. When the apostle had determined to take him with him, he found it necessary to have him circumcised, not from any supposition that circumcision was necessary to salvation, but because of the Jews, who would have heard neither him nor the apostle had not this been done. The gospel testimony they would not have received from Timothy, because a heathen; and they would have considered the apostle in the same light, because he associated with such.

It is pretty evident that Timothy had a special call of God to the work of an evangelist, which the elders of the church at Lystra knowing, set him solemnly apart to the work by the imposition of hands, 1 Tim. iv. 14. And they were particularly led to this by several prophetic declarations relative to him, by which his divine call was most clearly ascertained. See 1 Tim. i. 18 and iii. 14.

Timothy, thous prepared to be the apostle's fellow laborer in the gospel, accompanied him and Silas when they visited the churches of Phrygia and delivered to them the decrees of the apostles and elders at Jerusalem, freeing the Gentiles from the law of Moses as a term of salvation. Having gone through these countries, they at length came to Troas, where Luke joined them, as appears from the phraseology of his history, Acts xvi. 10-11. In Troas a vision appeared to Paul, directing them to go into Macedonia. Loosing therefore from Troas, they all passed over to Neapolis; and from thence went to Philippi, where they converted many and planted a Christian church. From Philippi they went to Thessalonica, leaving Luke at Philippi, as appears from his changing the phraseology of his history at verse 40. We may therefore suppose that at their departing they committed the converted at Philippi to Luke's care. In Thessalonica they were opposed by the unbelieving Jews, and obliged to flee to Berea, whither the Jews from Thessalonica followed them. To elude their rage, Paul, who was most obnoxious to them, departed from Berea by night to go to Athens, leaving Silas and Timothy at Berea. At Athens, Timothy came to the apostle and gave him such an account of the afflicted state of the Thessalonian brethren as induced him to send Timothy back to comfort them. After that Paul preached at Athens, but with so little success that he judged it proper to leave Athens and go forward to Corinth, where Silas and Timothy came to him and assisted in converting the Corinthians. And when he left Corinth they accompanied him, first to Ephesus, then to Jerusalem, and after that to Antioch in Syria. Having spent some time in Antioch, Paul set out with Timothy on his third apostolical journey; in which, after visiting all the churches of Galatia and Phrygia, in the order in which they had been planted, they came to Ephesus the second time and there abode for a considerable time. In short, from the time Timothy first joined the apostle as his assistant, he never left him except when sent by him on some special errand. And by his affection, fidelity, and zeal he so recommended himself to all the disciples, and acquired such authority over them, that Paul inserted his name in the inscription of several of the letters which he wrote to the churches, to show that their doctrine was one and the same. His esteem and affection for Timothy the apostle expressed still more conspicuously by writing to him those excellent letters in the canon which bear his name; and which have been of the greatest use to the ministers of the gospel ever since their publication, by directing them to discharge all the duties of their function in a proper manner.

In the third verse of the first chapter of this Epistle the apostle says: "As I entreated thee to abide in Ephesus, when going into Macedonia, so do; that thou mayest charge some not to teach differently." From this it is plain: (1) That Timothy was in Ephesus when the apostle wrote his first letter to him; (2) That he had been left there by the apostle, who at parting with him entreated him to abide at Ephesus; (3) That this happened when Paul was going from Ephesus to Macedonia; and (4) That he had entreated Timothy to abide in Ephesus for the purpose of charging some teachers in that church not to teach differently from the apostles. In the history of the Acts of the Apostles there is no mention of Paul's going from Ephesus to Macedonia but once; viz., after the riot of Demetrius, Acts xx. 1.

The Epistles to the Philippians and to Philemon were written while the apostle was a prisoner at Rome; to the former he says: "I trust in the Lord that I also myself shall come shortly." And to the latter, who was a Colossian, he gives this direction: "But withal prepare me also a lodging: for I trust that through your prayers I shall be given unto you." Colossae was a city of Asia Minor, lying eastward, and at no great distance from Ephesus. Philippi was on the other, i.e., the western, side of the Aegean Sea. Now if the apostle executed his purpose and came to Philemon at Colossae soon after his liberation, it cannot be supposed that he would omit to visit Ephesus, which lay so near it, and where he had spent three years of his ministry. As he was also under a promise to visit the church at Philippi shortly, if he passed from Colossae to Philippi he could hardly avoid taking Ephesus in his way. This, taken in connection with the preceding arguments, can leave little doubt that the date of this Epistle must be referred to a time subsequent to Paul's liberation from Rome.

CHAPTER 1

Paul's salutation to Timothy, 1-2. For what purpose he had left him at Ephesus, 3. What the false apostles taught in opposition to the truth, 4-7. The true use of the law, 8-11. He thanks God for his own conversion, and describes his former state, 12-17. Exhorts Timothy to hold fast faith and a good conscience, and speaks of Hymeneus and Alexander who had made shipwreck of their faith, 18-20.

1. *Paul an apostle . . . by the commandment of God.* We have already seen that the term *apostle* literally signifies a person sent from one to another, without implying any particular dignity in the person or importance in the message. But it is differently used in the New Testament, being applied to those who were sent expressly from God Almighty with the message of salvation to mankind. It is therefore the highest character any human being can have; and the message is the most important which even God himself can send to His intelligent creatures. It was by the express command of God that Paul went to the Gentiles preaching the doctrine of salvation by faith in Christ Jesus. *Jesus Christ . . . our hope.* Without Jesus, the world was hopeless; the expectation of being saved can come to mankind only by His gospel. He is called *our hope*, as He is called our Life, our Peace, our Righteousness, because from Him hope, life, peace, righteousness, and all other blessings proceed.

2. *My own son in the faith.* Brought to salvation through Christ by my ministry alone. Probably the apostle speaks here according to this Jewish maxim: "He who teaches the law to his nighbor's son is considered by the Scripture as if he had begotten him." *In the faith.* The word *faith* is taken here for the whole of the Christian religion, faith in Christ being its essential characteristic. *Grace, mercy, and peace. Grace*, the favor and approbation of God. *Mercy*, springing from that grace, pardoning, purifying, and supporting. *Peace*, the consequence of this manifested mercy, peace of conscience, and peace with God; producing internal happiness, quietness, and assurance.

3. *I besought thee.* The apostle had seen that a bad seed had been sown in the church; and, as he was obliged to go then into Macedonia, he wished Timothy, on whose prudence, piety, and soundness in the faith he could depend, to stay behind and prevent the spreading of a doctrine that would have been pernicious to the people's souls. I have already

supposed that this Epistle was written after Paul had been delivered from his first imprisonment at Rome. When therefore the apostle came from Rome into Asia, he no doubt visited Ephesus, where ten years before he had planted a Christian church; and as he had not time to tarry then, he left Timothy to correct abuses. *That thou mightest charge some.* He does not name any person. The Judaizing teachers are generally supposed to be those intended; and the term *some*, "certain persons," which he uses, is expressive of high disapprobation, and at the same time of delicacy. They were not apostles nor apostolic men; but they were undoubtedly members of the church at Ephesus, and might yet be reclaimed.

4. *Neither give heed to fables.* Idle fancies; things of no moment; doctrines and opinions unauthenticated; silly legends, of which no people ever possessed a greater stock than the Jews. *Endless genealogies.* I suppose the apostle to mean those genealogies which were "uncertain" —that never could be made out, in either the ascending or the descending line; and, principally, such as referred to the great promise of the Messiah, and to the priesthood. The Jews had scrupulously preserved their genealogical tables till the advent of Christ; and the Evangelists had recourse to them and appealed to them in reference to our Lord's descent from the house of David; Matthew taking this genealogy in the descending, Luke in the ascending, line. All was then certain; but we are told that Herod destroyed the public registers. He, being an Idumean, was jealous of the noble origin of the Jews; and that none might be able to reproach him with his descent, he ordered the genealogical tables, which were kept among the archives in the Temple, to be burnt. From this time the Jews could refer to their genealogies only from memory, or from those imperfect tables which had been preserved in private hands; and to make out any regular line from these must have been endless and uncertain. It is probably to this that the apostle refers; I mean the endless and useless labor which the attempts to make out these genealogies must produce, the authentic tables being destroyed. Some learned men suppose that the apostle alludes here to the Aeons among the Gnostics and Valentinians, of whom there were endless numbers to make up what was called their *pleroma*. But it is certain that these heresies had not arrived to any formidable head

in the apostle's time; and it has long been a doubt with me whether they even existed at that time. I think it the most simple way, and most likely to be the intention of the apostle, to refer all to the Jewish genealogies, which he calls "Jewish fables," Titus i. 14. *Which minister questions.* They are the foundation of endless altercations and disputes; for, being uncertain and not consecutive, every person had a right to call them in question; as we may naturally suppose, from the state in which the genealogical tables of the Jews then were, that many chasms must be supplied in different lines and consequently much must be done by conjecture. *Rather than godly edifying.* Such discussions as these had no tendency to promote piety. Many, no doubt, employed much of that time in inquiring who were their ancestors, which they should have spent in obtaining that grace by which, being born from above, they might have become the sons and daughters of God Almighty. Instead of *godly edifying,* "the economy or dispensation of God" is the reading of almost every MS. in which this part of the Epistle is extant, and of almost all the versions, and the chief of the Greek fathers. Of the genuineness of this reading scarcely a doubt can be formed. What had Jewish geneaologies to do with the gospel? Men were not to be saved by virtue of the privileges or piety of their ancestors. The Jews depended much on this. In the "dispensation of God," faith in Christ Jesus was the only means and way of salvation. These endless and uncertain geneaologies produced no faith; indeed they were intended as a substitute for it; for those who were intent on making out their genealogical descent paid little attention to faith in Christ. They ministered questions rather than that economy of God which is by faith.

5. *Now the end of the commandment is charity.* These genealogical questions lead to strife and debate; and the dispensation of God leads to "love" to both God and man, through faith in Christ. These genealogical questions leave the heart under the influence of all its vile tempers and evil propensities; *faith* in Jesus purifies the heart. The *end,* aim, and design of God in giving this dispensation to the world is that men may have an *unfeigned faith,* such as lays hold on Christ crucified, and produces a *good conscience* from a sense of the pardon received, and leads on to purity of heart; love to God and man being the grand issue of the grace of Christ here below, and this fully preparing the soul for eternal glory. He whose soul is filled with love to God and man has a *pure heart,* a *good conscience,* and *faith unfeigned.* "A faith not hypocritical." The apostle appears to allude to the Judaizing teachers, who pretended faith in the gospel merely that they might have the greater opportunity to bring back to the Mosaic system those who had embraced the doctrine of Christ crucified. This is evident from the following verse.

6. *From which some having swerved. From which some,* though they have pretended to aim at the "scope," or "mark," have missed that mark. This is the import of the original word. *Turned aside unto vain jangling.* The original term signifies "empty or vain talking"; discourses that turn to no profit; a great many words and little sense.

7. *Teachers of the law.* To be esteemed or

celebrated as rabbins; to be reputed cunning in solving knotty questions and enigmas, which answered no end to true religion. *Understanding neither what they say.* This is evident from almost all the Jewish comments which yet remain. Things are asserted which are either false or dubious; words, the import of which they did not understand, were brought to illustrate them.

8. *But we know that the law is good.* The law as given by God is both *good* in itself and has a good tendency. This is similar to what the apostle had asserted, Rom. vii. 12-16: "The law is holy, and the commandment holy, and just, and good." *If a man use it lawfully.* That is, interpret it according to its own spirit and design, and use it for the purpose for which God has given it.

9. *The law is not made for a righteous man.* There is a moral law as well as a ceremonial law. As the object of the latter is to lead us to Christ, the object of the former is to restrain crimes, and inflict punishment on those that commit them. It was, therefore, not made for the *righteous* as a restrainer of crimes and an inflicter of punishments; for the righteous avoid sin, and by living to the glory of God expose not themselves to its censures. This seems to be the mind of the apostle; he does not say that the law was not *made for a righteous man,* but it does not "lie against a righteous man," because he does not transgress it: but it "lies against" the wicked. The word "lies" refers to the custom of writing laws on boards and hanging them up in public places within reach of every man, that they might be read by all; thus all would see against whom the law lay. *The lawless.* Those who will not be bound by a law, and acknowledge none, therefore have no rule of moral conduct. *Disobedient.* Those who acknowledge no authority; from *a,* negative, and *hypotasso,* "to subject." *For the ungodly.* The "irreligious"—those who do not worship God or have no true worship; from *a,* negative, and *sebo,* "to worship." *For unholy.* Persons "totally polluted"—unclean within and unclean without; from *a,* negative, and *hosios,* "holy." *And profane.* Such who are so unholy and abominable as not to be fit to attend any public worship. *Murderers of fathers.* The murderer of a father or a mother, notwithstanding the deep fall of man and the general profligacy of the world, has been so rare and is a crime so totally opposite to nature that few civilized nations have found it necessary to make laws against it. Yet such monsters, like the most awful and infrequent *portents,* have sometimes terrified the world with their appearance. But I think the original may mean simply "beating or striking a father or mother." *Manslayers.* "Murderers" simply, all who take away the life of a human being contrary to law.

10. *For whoremongers.* Adulterers, fornicators, and prostitutes of all sorts. *Menstealers.* "Slave dealers"; whether those who carry on the traffic in human flesh and blood or those who steal a person in order to sell him into bondage; or those who buy such stolen men or women, no matter of what color or what country. *For liars.* They who speak for truth what they know to be false; and even they who tell the truth in such a way as to lead others to draw a contrary meaning from it. *For perjured*

persons. Such as do or leave undone anything contrary to an oath or moral engagement, whether that engagement be made by what is called swearing or by an affirmation or promise of any kind. *And if there be any other thing.* Every species of vice and immorality, all must be necessarily included that is contrary to *sound doctrine*—to the immutable moral law of God, as well as to the pure precepts of Christianity where that law is incorporated, explained, and rendered, if possible, more and more binding.

11. *According to the glorious gospel.* The "sound doctrine" mentioned above, which is here called "the gospel of the glory of the blessed or happy God"—a dispensation which exhibits the glory of all His attributes; and by saving man in such a way as is consistent with the glory of all the divine perfections, while it brings peace and goodwill among men, brings glory to God in the highest.

12. *I thank Christ.* I feel myself under infinite obligation to Christ, who hath "strengthened me," and put *me into the ministry,* the "deaconship," the "service" of mankind, by preaching the gospel, for that he *counted me*— He knew that I would be—*faithful* to the charge that was delivered to me.

13. *A blasphemer.* Speaking impiously and unjustly of Jesus, His doctrine, His ways, and His followers. *And a persecutor.* Endeavoring to the uttermost of his power to exterminate all who called on the name of the Lord Jesus. *And injurious.* As full of insolence as I was of malevolence; and yet all the while thinking I did God service, while sacrificing men and women to my own prejudices and intolerance.

14. *The grace of our Lord was exceeding abundant.* The original is very emphatic, "that grace of our Lord hath superabounded"— it manifested itself in a way of extraordinary mercy. *With faith and love.* Not only pardoning such offenses, but leading me to the full experimental knowledge of Christianity, of that *faith* and *love* which are essential to it, and giving me authority to proclaim it to mankind.

15-16. *Christ Jesus came into the world to save sinners.* This is one of the most glorious truths in the Book of God, the most important that ever reached the human ear or can be entertained by the heart of man. This *saying* or "doctrine" he calls, first, a *faithful* or "true" saying. It is a doctrine that may be "credited" without the slightest doubt or hesitation. God himself has spoken it; and the death of Christ and the mission of the Holy Ghost, sealing pardon on the souls of all who believe, have confirmed and established the truth. Secondly, it is *worthy of all acceptation;* as all need it, it is worthy of being received by all. *Of whom I am chief.* Confounding Paul the apostle, in the fullness of his faith and love, with Saul of Tarsus, in his ignorance, unbelief, and persecuting rage, we are in the habit of saying: "This is a hyperbolical expression, arguing the height of the apostle's modesty and humility; and must not be taken according to the letter." I take it not in this light; I take it not with abatement; it is strictly and literally true. Take into consideration the whole of the apostle's conduct previously to his conversion, and was there a greater sinner converted to God from the Incarnation to his own time? Not one; he was the *chief;* and keeping his blasphemy, persecution, and contumely in view, he asserts: Of all that the Lord Jesus came into the world to save, and of all that He had saved to that time, *I am chief.* He could with propriety say, "I am the first"; the "first" who, from a blasphemer, persecutor (and might we not add "murderer"? see the part he took in the martyrdom of Stephen), became a preacher of that gospel which I had persecuted. And hence, keeping this idea strictly in view, he immediately adds (v. 16): *Howbeit for this cause I obtained mercy, that in me first Jesus Christ might shew forth all longsuffering, for a pattern to them which should hereafter believe on him to life everlasting.*

17. *Now unto the King eternal.* This burst of thanksgiving and gratitude to God naturally arose from the subject then under his pen and eye. God has most wondrously manifested His mercy, in this beginning of the gospel, by saving me, and making me a pattern to all them that shall hereafter believe on Christ. He is "the king of eternities": the eternity that was before time was, and the eternity that shall be when time is no more. *Immortal.* "Incorruptible"—not liable to decay or corruption; a simple, uncompounded essence, incapable therefore of decomposition, and consequently permanent and eternal. *Invisible.* One who fills all things, works everywhere, and yet is *invisible* to angels and men; the perfect reverse of false gods and idols, who are confined to one spot, work nowhere, and, being stocks and stones, are seen by everybody. *The only wise God.* The word *wise* is omitted by some MSS. Some of the Greek fathers quote it sometimes and omit it at others; which shows that it was an unsettled reading, probably borrowed from Rom. xvi. 27. Without it the reading is very strong and appropriate: "To the only God," nothing visible or invisible being worthy of adoration but himself. *Be honour,* all the respect and reverence that can be paid by intelligent beings, ascribing to Him at the same time all the *glory*—excellences, and perfections, which can be possessed by an intelligent, unoriginated, independent, and eternal Being; and this *for ever and ever*— through eternity.

18. *This charge.* It was a *charge* that the Judaizing teachers should not teach differently from that doctrine which the apostle had delivered to him. *According to the prophecies.* This may refer to some predictions by inspired men relative to what Timothy should be, and he wishes him to act in all things conformably to those predictions. It was predicted that he should have this high and noble calling; but his behavior in that calling was a matter of contingency, as it respected the use he might make of the grace of his calling. The apostle therefore exhorts him to *war a good warfare.* Some think that "the foregoing prophecies" refer to revelations which the apostle himself had received concerning Timothy; while others think that the word is to be understood of advices, directions, and exhortations which the apostle had previously delivered to him. This is a very sober and good sense of the passage. *War a good warfare.* The trials and afflictions of the followers of God are often represented as a *warfare* or "campaign."

19. *Holding faith.* All the truths of the Christian religion, firmly believing them, and fervent-

ly proclaiming them to others. *And a good conscience.* So holding the truth as to live according to its dictates, that a *good conscience* may be ever preserved. *Which some having put away.* Having "thrust away"; as a foolhardy soldier might his shield and his breastplate or a mad sailor his pilot, helm, and compass. *Concerning faith.* The great truths of the Christian religion. *Have made shipwreck.* Being without the faith, that only infallible system of truth; and a good conscience, that skillful pilot, that steady and commanding helm, that faithful and invariable loadstone; having been driven to and fro by every wind of doctrine, and getting among shoals, quicksands, and rocks, have been shipwrecked and engulfed.

20. *Of whom is Hymenaeus and Alexander.* Who had the faith but thrust it away; who had a good conscience through believing, but made shipwreck of it. Hence we find that all this was not only possible, but did actually take place, though some have endeavored to maintain the contrary; who, confounding eternity with a state of probation, have supposed that if a man once enter into the grace of God in this life he must necessarily continue in it to all eternity. Thousands of texts and thousands of facts refute this doctrine. *Delivered unto Satan.* For the destruction of the flesh, that the spirit might be saved in the day of the Lord Jesus. See what is noted on 1 Cor. v. 5; what this sort of punishment was no man now living knows. There is nothing of the kind referred to in the Jewish writings. It seems to have been something done by mere apostolical authority, under the direction of the Spirit of God. *Hymenaeus,* it appears, denied the resurrection, see 2 Tim. ii. 17-18; but whether this *Alexander* be the same with "Alexander the coppersmith," 2 Tim. iv. 14, or the Alexander in Acts xix. 33, cannot be determined. Probably he was the same with the "coppersmith." Whether they were brought back to the acknowledgment of the truth does not appear. From what is said in the Second Epistle the case seems extremely doubtful. Let him who most assuredly standeth take heed lest he fall.

CHAPTER 2

Prayer, supplication, and thanksgiving, must be made for all men, because God wills that all should be saved, 1-4. There is but one God and one Mediator, 5-7. How men should pray, 8. How women should adorn themselves, 9-10. They are not suffered to teach, nor to usurp authority over men, 11-14. How they may expect to be saved in childbearing, 15.

1. *I exhort therefore, that, first of all.* Prayer for the pardon of sin and for obtaining necessary supplies of grace and continual protection from God, with gratitude and thanksgiving for mercies already received, are duties which our sinful and dependent state renders absolutely necessary; and which should be chief in our view, and *first of all* performed. It is difficult to know the precise difference between the four words used here by the apostle. They are sometimes distinguished thus: *Supplications.* Prayers for averting evils of every kind. *Prayers.* Prayers for obtaining the good things, spiritual and temporal, which ourselves need. *Intercessions.* Prayers in behalf of others. *Giving of thanks.* Praises to God, as the Parent of all good, for all the blessings which we and others have received. It is probable that the

apostle gives directions here for public worship, and that the words may be thus paraphrased: "Now I exhort first of all that in the public assemblies deprecations of evils, and supplications for such good things as are necessary, and intercessions for their conversion, and thanksgiving for mercies be offered in behalf of all men—for heathens as well as for Christians, and for enemies as well as for friends."

2. *For kings.* As it is a positive maxim of Christianity to pray for all secular governors, so it has ever been the practice of Christians. *That we may lead a quiet and peaceable life.* We thus pray for the government that the public peace may be preserved. Good rulers have power to do much good; we pray that their authority may be ever preserved and well-directed. Bad rulers have power to do much evil; we pray that they may be prevented from thus using their power.

4. *Who will have all men to be saved.* Because He wills the salvation of all men, therefore He wills that all men should be prayed for. In the face of such a declaration, how can any Christian soul suppose that God ever unconditionally and eternally reprobated any man?

5. *One mediator.* The word *mediator* signifies literally a "middle person," one whose office it is to reconcile two parties at enmity; and hence Suidas explains it by "a peacemaker."

6. *Who gave himself a ransom.* The word *lytron* signifies a ransom paid for the redemption of a captive; and *antilytron,* the word used here, and applied to the death of Christ, signifies that ransom which consists in the exchange of one person for another, or the redemption of life by life. *To be testified in due time.* The original words are not very clear and have been understood variously. The most authentic copies of the printed Vulgate have simply, "Thus rendering testimony at the appointed time." And this was rendered literally by our first translator: "Whos witnessinge is confermyd in his timis." This appears to be the apostle's meaning: Christ gave himself a Ransom for all. This, in the times which seemed best to the divine wisdom, was to be testified to every nation, and people, and tongue.

7. *I am ordained a preacher.* "I am set apart, appointed." The word does not imply any imposition of hands by either bishop or presbytery. *A teacher of the Gentiles.* Being specially commissioned to preach the gospel, not to the Jews, but to the "nations" of the world. *In faith and verity.* "Faithfully" and "truly"; preaching the truth, the whole truth, and nothing but the truth; and this fervently, affectionately, and perseveringly.

8. *I will therefore.* Seeing the apostle had his authority from Christ, and spoke nothing but what he received from Him, his *I will* is equal to "I command." *That men pray.* That is, for the blessings promised in this testimony of God. For although God has provided them, yet He will not give them to such as will not pray. *Every where.* "In every place." This may refer to a Jewish superstition. They thought at first that no prayer could be acceptable that was not offered at the Temple at Jerusalem; afterward this was extended to the Holy Land. But when they became dispersed among the nations, they built oratories or places

of prayer, principally by rivers and by the seaside; and in these they were obliged to allow that public prayer might be legally offered, but nowhere else. In opposition to this the apostle, by the authority of Christ, commands men to pray *every where;* that all places belong to God's dominions; and, as He fills every place, in every place He may be worshipped and glorified. *Lifting up holy hands.* It was a common custom, not only among the Jews, but also among the heathens, to "lift up" or spread out their arms and hands in prayer. It is properly the action of entreaty and request, and seems to be an effort to embrace the assistance requested. But the apostle probably alludes to the Jewish custom of laying their hands on the head of the animal which they brought for a sin offering, confessing their sins, and then giving up the life of the animal as an expiation for the sins thus confessed. And this very notion is conveyed in the original term. This shows us how Christians should pray. They should come to the altar; set God before their eyes; humble themselves for their sins; bring as a sacrifice the Lamb of God; lay their hands on this Sacrifice; and by faith offer it to God in their souls' behalf, expecting salvation through His meritorious death alone. *Without wrath.* Having no vindictive feeling against any person, harboring no unforgiving spirit, while they are imploring pardon for their own offenses. The *holy hands* refer to the Jewish custom of washing their hands before prayer; this was done to signify that they had put away all sin, and purposed to live a holy life. *And doubting.* "Reasonings, dialogues."

9. *In like manner also.* That is, he wills or commands what follows, as he had commanded what went before. *With shamefacedness* or "modesty." This would lead them to avoid everything unbecoming in the mode or fashion of their dress. With *sobriety.* Moderation would lead them to avoid all unnecessary expense. They might follow the custom or costume of the country as to the dress itself, for nothing was ever more becoming than the Grecian; but they must not imitate the extravagance of those who through impurity or littleness of mind decked themselves merely to attract the eye of admiration or set in lying action the tongue of flattery.

10. *But (which becometh).* That is, good works are the only ornaments with which women professing Christianity should seek to be adorned.

11. *Let the woman learn in silence.* That is generally supposed to be a prohibition of women's preaching. I have already said what I judge necessary on this subject in the notes on 1 Cor. xi. 5, etc., and xiv. 34-35, to which places I beg leave to refer the reader.

12. *Nor to usurp authority.* A woman should attempt nothing, either in public or in private, that belongs to man as his peculiar function. This was prohibited by the Roman laws.

13. *For Adam was first formed, then Eve.* And by this very act God designed that he should have the preeminence. God fitted man by the robust construction of his body to live a public life, to contend with difficulties, and to be capable of great exertions. The structure of woman's body plainly proves that she was never designed for those exertions required in public life.

14. *Adam was not deceived.* It does not appear that Satan attempted the man; the woman said: "The serpent beguiled me, and I did eat." Adam received the fruit from the hand of his wife; he knew he was transgressing; he was not deceived. However, she led the way, and in consequence of this she was subjected to the domination of her husband: "Thy desire shall be to thy husband, and he shall rule over thee," Gen. iii. 16.

15. *She shall be saved in childbearing.* "She shall be saved through childbearing"—she shall be saved by means, or through the instrumentality, of childbearing or of bringing forth a child. There are innumerable instances of women dying in childbed who have lived in faith and charity and holiness, with sobriety; and equally numerous instances of worthless women, slaves to different kinds of vices, who have not only been saved in childbearing, but have passed through their travail with comparatively little pain. Hence that is not the sense in which we should understand the apostle. Yet it must be a matter of great consolation and support to all pious women laboring of child to consider that by the holy Virgin's childbearing salvation is provided for them and the whole human race; and that, whether they die or live, though their own childbearing can contribute nothing to their salvation, yet He who was born of a woman has purchased them and the whole human race by His blood. *If they continue.* "If they live"; for so it signifies in other passages, particularly Phil. i. 25.

CHAPTER 3

Concerning bishops, their qualifications and work, 1-7. Of deacons, and how they should be proved, 8-10. Of their wives and children, and how they should be governed, 11-13. How Timothy should behave himself in the church, 14-15. The great mystery of godliness, 16.

1. *This is a true saying.* "This is a true doctrine." These words are joined to the last verse of the preceding chapter by several of the Greek fathers, and by them referred to the doctrine there stated. *The office of a bishop.* The "episcopacy, overseership, or superintendency." The word *oregetai,* which we translate *desire,* signifies "earnest, eager, passionate desire," and *epithymei,* which we translate *desire,* also signifies "earnestly to desire or covet." *A good work.* A work it then was—heavy, incessant, and painful. There were no unpreaching prelates in those days, and should be none now.

2. *A bishop then must be blameless.* Our term *bishop* comes from the Anglo-Saxon, which is mere corruption of the Greek *episcopos,* and the Latin *episcopus.* The former, being compounded of *epi,* "over," and *skeptomai,* to "look or inspect," signifies one who has the inspection or oversight of a place, persons, or business; what we commonly term a "superintendent." Let us consider the qualifications of a Christian bishop. *First:* This Christian bishop must be blameless; a person against whom no evil can be proved. The word is a metaphor, taken from the case of an expert and skillful pugilist, who so defends every part of his body that it is impossible for his antagonist to give one hit. So this Christian bishop is one that has so conducted himself as to put it out of the

reach of any person to prove that he is either unsound in a single article of the Christian faith or deficient in the fulfillment of any duty incumbent on a Christian. *Second*: He must be *the husband of one wife*. He should be a married man, but he should be no polygamist; and have only *one wife*, i.e., one at a time. It does not mean that, if he has been married and his wife die, he should never marry another. *Third*: He must be *vigilant;* "watchful." *Fourth*: He must be *sober;* "prudent," or, according to the etymology of the word, "a man of a sound mind." *Fifth*: He must be *of good behaviour;* "orderly, decent, grave, and correct" in the whole of his appearance, carriage, and conduct. The preceding term refers to the mind; this latter, to the external manners. *Sixth*: He must be *given to hospitality;* literally, a "lover of strangers"; one who is ready to receive into his house and relieve every necessitous stranger. *Hospitality* in those primitive times was a great and necessary virtue; then there were few inns or places of public entertainment; to those who were noted for benevolence the necessitous stranger had recourse. A Christian bishop, professing love to God and all mankind, preaching a religion one-half of the morality of which was included in "Thou shalt love thy neighbour as thyself," would naturally be sought to by those who were in distress and destitute of friends. *Seventh*: He should be *apt to teach;* one "capable of teaching"; not only wise himself, but ready to communicate his wisdom to others. One whose delight is to instruct the ignorant and those who are out of the way. He must be a preacher; an able, zealous, fervent, and assiduous preacher.

3. An *eighth* article in his character is, he must *not* be *given to wine*. This word not only signifies one who is inordinately attached to wine, a winebibber or tippler, but also one who is imperious, abusive, insolent, whether through wine or otherwise. *Ninth*: He must be *no striker;* not "quarrelsome"; not ready to strike a person who may displease him; no persecutor of those who may differ from him; not prone, as one wittily said,

> To prove his doctrine orthodox
> By apostolic blows and knocks.

Tenth: He must *not* be *greedy of filthy lucre*, "not desirous of base gain," not using base and unjustifiable methods to raise and increase his revenues, not trading or trafficking; for what would be honorable in a secular character would be base and dishonorable in a bishop. Though such a trait should never appear in the character of a Christian prelate, yet there is much reason to suspect that the words above are not authentic. They are omitted in many MSS. and by most of the Greek fathers. Griesbach has left it out of the text, in which it does not appear that it ever had a legitimate place. The word *covetous*, which we have below, expresses all the meaning of this. *Eleventh*: He must be *patient;* "meek, gentle"; the opposite to "a quarrelsome person," which it immediately follows when the spurious word is removed. *Twelfth*: He must *not* be *a brawler;* not "contentious or litigious," but quiet and peaceable. *Thirteenth*: He must *not* be *covetous;* "not a lover of money"; not desiring the office for the sake of its emoluments.

4. The *fourteenth* qualification of a Christian bishop is that he *ruleth well his own house,* one who "properly presides over and governs his own family." One who has the command of his own house, not by sternness, severity, and tyranny, but with all *gravity*.

5. *For if a man know not.* Method is a matter of great importance in all the affairs of life. It is a true saying, "He that does little with his head must do much with his hands"; and even then the business is not half done for want of method. He who has a disorderly family has no government of that family; he probably has none because he has no method, no plan, of presiding.

6. *Fifteenth*: It is required that he be *not a novice*. Not a "young plant," not "recently ingrafted," that is, one not newly converted to the faith. One who has been of considerable standing in the Christian church, if he have the preceding qualifications, may be safely trusted with the government of that church. It is impossible that one who is not long and deeply experienced in the ways of God can guide others in the way of life. Hence presbyters or elders were generally appointed to have the oversight of the rest, and hence presbyter and bishop seem to have been two names for the same office; yet all presbyters or elders certainly were not bishops, because all presbyters had not the qualifications marked above. But the apostle gives another reason: *Lest being lifted up with pride he fall into the condemnation of the devil.* It is natural for man to think himself of more importance than his fellows when they are entrusted to his government. The apostle's term "puffed up, inflated," is a metaphor taken from a bladder when filled with air or wind. From these words of the apostle we are led to infer that *pride* or "self-conceit" was the cause of the devil's downfall.

7. The *sixteenth* requisite is that he should *have a good report of them which are without;* that he should be one who had not been previously a profligate, or scandalous in his life. Such a person, when converted, may be a worthy private member of religious society; but I believe God rarely calls such to the work of the ministry, and never to the episcopate. *Them which are without* are the Jews, Gentiles, and the unconverted of all kinds. *Lest he fall into reproach.* For his former scandalous life. *And the snare of the devil.* Snares and temptations such as he fell in and fell by before. This is called *the snare of the devil;* for as he well knows the constitution of such persons and what is most likely to prevail, he infers that what was effectual before to their transgressing may be so still; therefore on all suitable occasions he tempts them to their old sins.

8. *Likewise must the deacons.* The term deacon simply signifies a "regular or stated servant." As nearly the same qualifications were required in the *deacons* as in the bishops, the reader may consult what is said on the preceding verses. *Grave.* Of a sedate and dignified carriage and conduct. *Not doubletongued.* Speaking one thing to one person and another thing to another on the same subject. This is hypocrisy and deceit. This word might also be translated "liars." *Not given to much wine.* Neither a drunkard, tippler, nor what is called a "jovial companion." All this would be inconsistent with gravity.

10. *Let these also first be proved.* Let them not be young converts or persons lately brought to the knowledge of the truth. This is the same in spirit with what is required of the bishops, v. 6. *Being found blameless.* Being irreproachable; persons against whom no evil can be proved. The same as in v. 2, though a different word is used.

11. *Even so must their wives be grave.* I believe the apostle does not mean here the *wives* of either the bishops or the deacons in particular, but the Christian "women" in general. The original is simply: "Let the women likewise be grave." Whatever is spoken here becomes women in general; but if the apostle had those termed "deaconesses" in his eye, which is quite possible, the words are peculiarly suitable to them. *Not slanderers.* Literally "not devils." See on v. 7. This may be properly enough translated *slanderers,* for all these are of their father, the devil, and his lusts they will do. *Faithful in all things.* The deaconesses had much to do among the poor, and especially among poor women, in dispensing the bounty of the church. They were not only faithfully to expend all they had got, and for the purpose for which they got it, but they must do this with impartiality, showing no respect of persons.

12. *Let the deacons be the husbands of one wife.* This is the same that is required of the bishops. See on vv. 2, 4-5.

13. *That have used the office of a deacon well.* They who, having been tried or proved, v. 10, have shown by their steadiness, activity, and zeal that they might be raised to a higher office are here said to have purchased *to themselves a good degree,* for instead of having to administer to the bodily wants of the poor, the faithful deacons were raised to minister in holy things; and instead of ministering the bread that perisheth, they were raised to the presbyterate or episcopate, to minister the bread of life to immortal souls. And hence the apostle adds: *And great boldness in the faith;* "great liberty of speech"; i.e., in teaching the doctrines of Christianity, and in expounding the Scriptures, and preaching.

14. *These things write I.* That is, I write only these things, because I hope *to come unto thee shortly.*

15. *But if I tarry long.* That is, notwithstanding I hope to come to you shortly, and therefore do not feel the necessity of writing at large; yet, lest I should be delayed, I write what I judge necessary to direct your conduct in the Church of God. *The house of God.* This is spoken in allusion to the ancient Tabernacle, which was God's house, and in which the symbol of the Divine Majesty dwelt. So the Christian Church is God's house, and every believer is a habitation of God through the Spirit. *The church of the living God.* The assembly in which God lives and works; each member of which is a living stone, all of whom, properly united among themselves, grow up unto a holy temple in the Lord. *The pillar and ground of the truth.* To what, or to whom, does *the pillar and ground of the truth* refer? (1) Some say to Timothy, who is called the pillar, because left there to support and defend the truth of God against false doctrines and false teachers; and is so called for the same reason that Peter, James, and John are said to be

"pillars," i.e., supporters of the truth of God, Gal. ii. 9. (2) Others suppose that *the pillar and ground of the truth* is spoken of God, and that "who is" should be supplied as referring immediately to God, just before. (3) Others think that the words should be understood of *the church of the living God.* That is: The full revelation of God's truth is in the Christian Church.

16. *And without controversy.* "And confessedly, by general consent," it is a thing which no man can or ought to dispute; any phrase of this kind expresses the meaning of the original. *God was manifest in the flesh.* Instead of *God,* several MSS., versions, and fathers have "who" or "which." And this is generally referred to the word *mystery;* "Great is the mystery of godliness, which was *manifest in the flesh.*" *Justified in the Spirit.* By the miracles which were wrought by the apostle in and through the name of Jesus, as well as by His resurrection from the dead, through the energy of the Holy Ghost, by which He was proved to be the Son of God with power. Christ was justified from all the calumnies of the Jews, who crucified Him as an impostor. *Seen of angels.* By *angeloi* here, some understand not those celestial or infernal beings commonly called *angels,* but apostles and other persons who became "messengers," to carry far and wide and attest the truth of His resurrection from the dead. If, however, we take the word *seen,* in its Jewish acceptation, for "made known," we may here retain the term *angels* in its common acceptation. For it is certain that previously to our Lord's ascension to heaven these holy beings could have little knowledge of the necessity, reasons, and economy of human salvation; nor of the nature of Christ as God and man. Peter informs us that the "angels desire to look into" these things, 1 Pet. i. 12. And Paul says the same thing, Eph. iii. 9-10. *Preached unto the Gentiles.* This was one grand part of the mystery which had been hidden in God, that the Gentiles should be made fellow heirs with the Jews and be admitted into the kingdom of God. *Believed on in the world.* Was received by mankind as the promised Messiah, the Anointed of God, and the only Saviour of fallen man. *Received up into glory.* Even that human nature which He took of the Virgin Mary was not only raised from the grave but taken up into glory. His reception into glory is of the utmost consequence to the Christian faith; as, in consequence, Jesus Christ in His human nature ever appears before the throne as our Sacrifice and as our Mediator.

CHAPTER 4

Apostasy from the true faith predicted, and in what that apostasy should consist, 1-5. Exhortations to Timothy to teach the truth, 6. To avoid old wives' fables; to exercise himself to godliness, 7-8. To labor, command, and teach, 9-11. To act so that none might despise his youth, 12. To give attendance to reading and preaching, 13-14. To give up himself wholly to the divine work, 15. And so doing he should both save himself and them that heard him, 16.

1. *Now the Spirit speaketh expressly.* "Manifestly, openly." It is very likely that the apostle refers here to a prophecy then furnished by the Holy Ghost, and probably immediately after he had written the words in the preceding verses; and as this prophecy contains things nowhere else spoken of in the sacred writings and of

the utmost moment to the Christian Church, we cannot hear or read them with too much reverence or respect.

In the latter times. This does not necessarily imply the last ages of the world, but any times consequent to those in which the Church then lived. *Depart from the faith.* They will "apostatize" from the faith, i.e., from Christianity; renouncing the whole system in effect, by bringing in doctrines which render its essential truths null and void, or denying and renouncing such doctrines as are essential to Christianity as a system of salvation. A man may hold all the truths of Christianity, and yet render them of none effect by holding other doctrines which counteract their influence; or he may apostatize by denying some essential doctrine, though he bring in nothing heterodox. *Giving heed to seducing spirits.* Pretenders to inspiration and false teachers of every kind belong to this class. *And doctrines of devils.* "Demons."

2. *Speaking lies in hypocrisy.* Persons pretending, not only to divine inspiration, but also to extraordinary degrees of holiness, self-denial, mortification, in order to accredit the *lies* and false doctrines which they taught. *Having their conscience seared with a hot iron.* They bear the marks of their hypocrisy as evidently and as indelibly in their conscience in the sight of God as those who have been cauterized for their crimes do in their bodies in the sight of men. It was customary in ancient times to mark those with a *hot iron* who had been guilty of great crimes, such as sacrilege.

3. *Forbidding to marry.* These hypocritical priests pretending that a single life was much more favorable to devotion and to the perfection of the Christian life. This sentiment was held by the Essenes, a religious sect among the Jews; and we know that it is a favorite opinion among the Romanists, who oblige all their clergy to live a single life by a vow of continency. *To abstain from meats.* Both among the heathens, Jews, and Romanists, certain *meats* were prohibited; some always, others at particular times. This the apostle informs us was directly contrary to the original design of God, and says that those who *know the truth* know this.

4. *For every creature of God is good.* That is, every creature which God has made for man's nourishment is good for that purpose, and to be thankfully received whenever necessary for the support of human life; and *nothing* of that sort is at any time *to be refused,* "rejected or despised."

5. *For it is sanctified by the word of God.* "By the command of God"; probably referring to Gen. i. 29: "And God said . . . I have given you every herb . . . and every tree . . . to you it shall be for meat"; and to chap. ix. 3: "Every moving thing that liveth shall be meat for you; even as the green herb have I given you all things"; i.e., I have given you every animal that is proper for food, as I have given you every herb and fruit proper for nourishment. Therefore all this was sanctified, "set apart," and appropriated to this use by this command. And when man is about to use it, he is to sanctify or set it apart to that use by *prayer* to God.

6. *If thou put the brethren in remembrance of these things.* Show the church that even now there is danger of this apostasy; put them

on their guard against it, for the forewarned are half armed. *Nourished up in the words of faith.* By acting as I command you, you will show that you are a good minister of Jesus Christ, and that you have been nourished from your youth up in the doctrines of faith. The apostle seems to allude here to Timothy's Christian education. *Whereunto thou hast attained.* Which you have "thoroughly understood."

7. *But refuse profane and old wives' fables.* This seems to refer particularly to the Jews, whose Talmudical writings are stuffed with the most ridiculous and profane fables that ever disgraced the human intellect. It may with equal propriety be applied to the legends of the Romish church. *Exercise thyself rather unto godliness.* To understand this expression it is necessary to know that the apostle alludes here to the gymnastic exercises among the Greeks, which were intended as a preparation for their contests at the public games.

8. *For bodily exercise profiteth little.* Those gymnastic exercises, so highly esteemed among the Greeks, are but little worth; they are but of short duration; they refer only to this life, and to the applause of men. But godliness has the promise of this life and the life to come; it is profitable for all things, and for both time and eternity. *But godliness is profitable unto all things.* By *godliness* we are to understand everything that the Christian religion either promises or prescribes: the life of God in the soul of man and the glory of God as the object and end of that life. *Having promise of the life that now is.* The man that fears, loves, and serves God has God's blessing all through life. His religion saves him from all those excesses in both action and passion which sap the foundations of life and render existence itself often a burden. The peace and love of God in the heart produce a serenity and calm which cause the lamp of life to burn clear, strong, and permanent.

10. *For therefore we both labour.* This verse was necessary to explain what he had before said; and here he shows that his meaning was not that the followers of God should enjoy worldly prosperity and exemption from natural evils; for it is because we exercise ourselves to godliness that we have both labor and reproach, and we have these because we trust in the living God. But still we have mental happiness, and all that is necessary for our passage through life; for in the midst of persecutions and afflictions we have the peace of God that passeth knowledge, and have all our crosses and sufferings so sanctified to us that we consider them in the number of our blessings. *Who is the Saviour of all men.* Who has provided salvation for the whole human race, and has freely offered it to them in His Word and by His Spirit. *Specially of those that believe.* What God intends for all He actually gives to them that believe in Christ.

11. *These things command and teach.* Let it be the sum and substance of your preaching that true religion is profitable for both worlds, that vice destroys both body and soul, that Christ tasted death for every man, and that He saves to the uttermost all them that believe in His name.

12. *Let no man despise thy youth.* Act with all the gravity and decorum which become

your situation in the Church. As you are in the place of an elder, act as an elder. *Be thou an example of the believers.* It is natural for the flock to follow the shepherd; if he go wrong, they will go wrong also. *In word.* "In doctrine"; teach nothing but the truth of God, because nothing but that will save souls. *In conversation.* In the whole of your "conduct" in every department which you fill in all your domestic as well as public relations. *In charity.* "In love" to God and man; show that this is the principle and motive of all your conduct. *In spirit.* In the "manner" and "disposition" in which you do all things. These words are wanting in some MSS. They have in all probability been added by a later hand. *In faith.* This word is probably taken here for "fidelity," a sense which it often bears in the New Testament. It cannot mean doctrine, for that has been referred to before. Be faithful to your trust, to your flock, to your domestics, to the public, to your God. "Fidelity" consists in honestly keeping, preserving, and delivering up when required, whatever is intrusted to our care; as also in improving whatever is delivered in trust for that purpose. Lose nothing that God gives, and improve every gift that He bestows. *In purity.* "Chastity" of body and mind; a direction peculiarly necessary for a young minister, who has more temptations to break its rules than perhaps any other person. "Converse sparingly with women, and especially with young women," was the advice of a very holy and experienced minister of Christ.

13. *Give attendance to reading.* Timothy could easily comprehend the apostle's meaning, but at present this is not so easy. What books does the apostle mean? The books of the Old Testament were probably what he intended; these testified of Jesus, and by these he could either convince or confound the Jews. But was the reading of these to be public or private? Probably both. It was customary to read the law and the prophets in the synagogue, and doubtless in the assemblies of the Christians, after which there was generally an exhortation founded upon the subject of the prophecy. Hence the apostle says: *Give attendance to reading, to exhortation, to doctrine.* Timothy was therefore to be diligent in reading the sacred writings at home, that he might be the better qualified to read and expound them in the public assemblies to the Christians and to others who came to these public meetings.

14. *Neglect not the gift that is in thee.* The word here must refer to the "gifts" and "graces" of the divine Spirit, which Timothy received when set apart to the work of an evangelist by the imposition of Paul's hands, 2 Tim. i. 6, and by that of the presbytery or eldership. For it most evidently appears from this verse and that above quoted that he received this double imposition, not probably at different times, but on one and the same occasion. These very gifts and graces might be improved; and we have reason to believe if not improved would be withdrawn by the great Head of the Church. *Given thee by prophecy.* It has already been conjectured that there had been some remarkable prediction relative to the future destiny and usefulness of Timothy. And probably it was in consequence of this that he was set apart to the office of evangelist and bishop in the church at Ephesus.

15. *Meditate upon these things.* Revolve them frequently in your mind; consider deeply their nature and importance; get them deeply fastened in your heart, and let all your conduct flow from this inward feeling and conviction. *Give thyself wholly to them.* "Be thou in these things." Occupy yourself wholly with them; make them not only your chief but your sole concern. You are called to save your own soul and the souls of them that hear you, and God has given you the divine gifts for this and no other purpose. To this let all your reading and study be directed; this is your great business, and you must perform it as the servant and steward of the Lord. *That thy profiting may appear to all.* By being made a universal blessing, convincing and converting sinners, and building up the Church of God on its most holy faith.

16. *Take heed unto thyself.* See that the life of God remains and the work of God prospers in your own soul. *Take heed . . . unto the doctrine,* that the matter be pure and orthodox; that you teach nothing for truth but what God has revealed. *Continue in them.* I.e., in taking heed to yourself and to your doctrine, for this must be your continual study.

CHAPTER 5

Rules to be observed in giving reproofs to the old and to the young, 1-2. Directions concerning widows, 3-16. Of elders that rule well, 17-18. How to proceed against elders when accused, and against notorious offenders, 19-21. Directions concerning imposition of hands, 22. Concerning Timothy's health, 23. Reasons why no person should be hastily appointed to sacred offices, 24-25.

1. *Rebuke not an elder.* That is, an elderly person; for the word is here taken in its natural sense, and signifies one advanced in years. At v. 17 it is taken in what may be termed its ecclesiastical meaning and signifies an officer in the church, what we commonly call a "presbyter" or "bishop"; for sometimes these terms were confounded. There are but few cases in which it at all becomes a young man to reprove an old man, and especially one who is a father in the church. If such a one does wrong or gets out of the way, he should be entreated as a father, with great caution and respect. *The younger men as brethren.* Showing humility, and arrogating nothing to yourself on account of your office. Feel for them as you ought to feel for your own brethren.

2. *The elder women as mothers.* Treating them with the respect due to their age. *With all purity.* With all chastity.

3. *Honour widows that are widows indeed.* One meaning of the word to *honour* is to "support, sustain," Matt. xv. 4-5; and here it is most obviously to be taken in this sense. Provide for those widows especially which are *widows indeed*—persons truly destitute, being aged and helpless, and having neither children nor friends to take care of them, and who behave as becomes their destitute state.

4. *But if any widow have children or nephews.* This shows that "widows indeed" are those that have neither children nor nephews, i.e., no relatives that either will or can help them, or no near relative alive. *Let them learn first to shew piety at home.* Let these children and nephews provide for their aged or helpless parents or relatives, and not burden the church

with them while they are able to support them. *And to requite their parents.* Let them learn to give benefit for benefit. Your parents supported and nourished you when you were young and helpless; you ought therefore to support them when they are old and destitute. This is called showing piety; and there is doubtless allusion to the fifth commandment; "Honour thy father and thy mother"—provide for them in their old age and afflictions; God commands this.

5. *And desolate.* "Left entirely alone"—having neither children nor relatives to take care of her. *Trusteth in God.* Finding she has no other helper, she continues in prayer and supplication, that she may derive that from God which, in the course of His providence, He has deprived her of among men.

6. *But she that liveth in pleasure.* "She that liveth delicately"—voluptuously indulging herself with dainties; it does not indicate grossly criminal pleasures, but simply means one who indulges herself in good eating and drinking, pampering her body at the expense of her mind. The word is used in reference to what we term petted and spoiled children. *Is dead while she liveth.* No purpose of life is answered by the existence of such a person. Seneca, in Epist. 60, says of pleasure-takers and those who live a voluptuous life: "We rank such persons with brutes, not with men; and some of them not even with brutes, but with dead carcasses. They anticipate their own death."

8. *But if any provide not for his own.* His own people or relatives. *Those of his own house.* That is, his own family, or a poor widow or relative that lives under his roof. *Hath denied the faith.* The Christian religion, which strongly inculcates love and benevolence to all mankind. *Is worse than an infidel.* For what are called the dictates of nature lead men to feel for and provide for their own families. Heathen writers are full of maxims of this kind, Tacitus says: "Nature dictates that to every one his own children and relatives should be most dear." And Cicero, in *Epist. ad Caption.*: "Every man should take care of his own family."

9. *Taken into the number.* Let her not be taken into the list of those for which the church must provide. But some think that the apostle means the list of those who were deaconesses in the church, and that no widow was to be admitted into that rank who did not answer to the following character. *Under threescore years.* As it might be supposed that, previously to this age, they might be able to do something towards their own support. *Having been the wife of one man.* Having lived in conjugal fidelity with her husband, or having had but one husband at a time; or, according to others, having never been but once married. But the former is the opinion of some of the most eminent of the Greek fathers, and appears to be that most consistent with the scope of the place and with truth.

10. *Well reported of for good works.* Numbers being able to "bear testimony," as the word implies, that she has not only avoided all sin but that she has walked according to the testimony of God. *Brought up children.* It was customary among the Gentiles to expose their children, when so poor that they were not able to provide for them. Pious and humane people took these up and fed, clothed, and educated them. The words *brought up* may refer to the children of others, who were educated in the Christian faith by pious Christian women. *Lodged strangers.* If she have been given to hospitality, freely contributing to the necessitous, when she had it in her power. *Washed the saints' feet.* This was an office of humanity shown to all strangers and travellers in the Eastern countries, who, either walking barefoot, or having only a sort of sole to defend the foot, needed washing when they came to their journey's end. Pious women generally did this act of kindness. *Relieved the afflicted.* Visited and ministered to the sick. *Diligently followed every good work.* In a word, if she have been altogether a Christian, living according to the precepts of the gospel, and doing the Lord's work with all her heart, soul, and strength. From the character given here of the "widow indeed," it may be doubted whether "widow" was not in some cases the name of an office, which name it might have from being ordinarily filled by widows. It can hardly be supposed that any widow, unless she had considerable property, could have done the things enumerated in this verse, some of which would occasion no small expense. The "widow indeed" may mean a person who was to be employed in some office in the church; and Timothy is enjoined not to take any into that office unless she had been before remarkable for piety and humanity. Some think that the widows of whom the apostle speaks had been deaconesses, and wished now to be taken on what might be termed the superannuated list; and the apostle lays down rules for the admission of such, the sum of which is: Let none come on this superannuated list unless she be at least sixty years of age, and can bring proof of her having conscientiously discharged the office and duty of a deaconess.

11. *But the younger widows refuse.* Do not admit those into this office who are under sixty years of age. Probably those who were received into such a list promised to abide in their widowhood. But as young or comparatively young women might have both occasion and temptations to remarry and so break their engagement to Christ, they should not be admitted. Not that the apostle condemns their remarrying as a crime in itself, but because it was contrary to their engagement. *Wax wanton.* A metaphor taken from a pampered horse, from whose mouth the rein has been removed, so that there is nothing to check or confine him.

12. *Having damnation.* In the sense in which we use this word I am satisfied the apostle never intended it. It is likely that he refers here to some promise or engagement which they made when taken on the list already mentioned, and now they have the guilt of having violated that promise; this is the "condemnation" of which the apostle speaks. *They have cast off their first faith.* By pledging their fidelity to a husband they have cast off their fidelity to Christ, as a married life and their previous engagement are incompatible.

13. *And withal they learn to be idle.* They do not love work, and they will not work. *Wandering about from house to house.* Gadding, gossiping; never contented with home; always visiting. *And not only idle.* If it went no further, this would be intolerable; but they are *tattlers*—talebearers; whisperers; light, tri-

fling persons; all noise and no work. *Busybodies.* Persons who meddle with the concerns of others, who mind everyone's business but their own. *Speaking things which they ought not.* Lies, slanders, calumnies; backbiting their neighbors, and everywhere sowing the seed of dissension.

14. *I will therefore that the younger women marry.* As the preceding discourse has been about the younger widows, and this is an inference from it, it is most evident that by the *younger women* the apostle means the young widows. These he considers unfit for the office of the female diaconate, and therefore wills them to marry, educate children, and give themselves wholly up to domestic affairs. Here the apostle, so far from forbidding second marriages, positively enjoins or at least recommends them. *The adversary.* Any person, whether Jew or Gentile, who might be watching for an occasion to reproach, through the misconduct of its professors, the cause of Christianity.

15. *For some are already turned aside.* Some of these young widows, for he appears to be still treating of them, are turned aside to idolatry, to follow Satan instead of Christ. Slight deviations from a right line may lead at last to an infinite distance from Christ.

16. *If any man or woman that believeth.* If any Christian man or woman have poor *widows,* which are their relatives, let them relieve them —provide them with the necessaries of life, and not burden the church with their maintenance, that the funds may be spared for the support of those widows who were employed in its service, teaching children, visiting the sick.

17. *Let the elders that rule well.* Elder is probably here the name of an ecclesiastical officer, similar to what we now term "presbyter." *Double honour.* Almost every critic of note allows that *time* (Greek) here signifies "reward, stipend, wages." Let him have a double or a larger salary who rules well. And why? Because in the discharge of his office he must be at expense, in proportion to his diligence, in visiting and relieving the sick, in lodging and providing for strangers; in a word, in his being given to hospitality, which was required of every bishop or presbyter. *Especially they who labour in the word and doctrine.* Those who not only preach publicly, but instruct privately, catechize. Some think this refers to distinct ecclesiastical orders; but these technical distinctions were, in my opinion, a work of later times.

18. *The scripture saith, Thou shalt not muzzle the ox.* This is a manifest proof that by "honour" in the preceding verse the apostle means "salary" or "wages": "Let the elders that rule well be accounted worthy of double honour," a larger salary than any of the official widows mentioned before, for "the labourer is worthy of his hire." The maintenance of every man in the church should be in proportion to his own labor, and the necessities of his family.

19. *Against an elder.* Be very cautious of receiving reports against those whose business it is to preach to others and correct their vices. Do not consider an elder as guilty of any alleged crime unless it be proved by two or three witnesses. This the law of Moses required in respect to all.

20. *Them that sin rebuke before all.* That is, before the members of the church; which was the custom of the Jews in their synagogues. *That others also may fear.* This is the grand object of church censures, to reclaim the transgressors and to give warning to others.

21. *I charge thee before God.* The apostle would have Timothy to consider that all he did should be done as in the sight of God, the Father of the spirits of all flesh; in the sight of Christ, the Saviour of sinners, who purchased the Church with His own blood; and in the sight of the most holy, approved, and eminent angels, whose office it was to minister to the heirs of salvation. The word *elect,* applied to the angels here, is supposed to distinguish those who stood when others fell from their first estate. *Without preferring one before another.* "Without prejudice." Promote no man's cause; make not up your mind on any case till you have weighed both sides and heard both parties, with their respective witnesses, and then act impartially, as the matter may appear to be proved. Do not treat any man, in religious matters, according to the rank he holds in life, or according to any personal attachment you may have for him. Every man should be dealt with in the church as he will be dealt with at the judgment seat of Christ.

22. *Lay hands suddenly on no man.* Do not hastily appoint any person to the sacred ministry; let the person be well proved before he receives the imposition of hands. *Neither be partaker of other men's sins.* It is a sin for any improper person to thrust himself into the sacred office; and he partakes of that sin who introduces, helps him forward, or sanctions him in it. *Keep thyself pure.* From this and every other evil.

23. *Drink no longer water, but use a little wine.* The priests under the Mosaic law, while performing sacred rites, were forbidden to drink wine: "Do not drink wine nor strong drink, thou, nor thy sons with thee, when ye go into the tabernacle of the congregation, lest ye die: it shall be a statute for ever throughout your generations," Lev. x. 9; Ezek. xliv. 21. From Athenaeus we learn that the Greeks often mingled their wine with water; sometimes one part of wine to two of water, three parts of water to one of wine, and at other times three parts of water to two of wine. "And among the Romans, no servant, nor free woman, nor youths of quality, drank any wine till they were thirty years of age." And it was a maxim among all that continued water-drinking injured the stomach.

24. *Some men's sins are open beforehand.* In appointing men to sacred offices in the church, among the candidates Timothy would find: (1) Some of whom he knew nothing, but only that they professed Christianity; let such be tried before they are appointed. (2) Some of whose faith and piety he had the fullest knowledge, and whose usefulness in the church was well-known. (3) Some whose lives were not at all or but partially reformed, who were still unchanged in their hearts and unholy in their lives. The sins of these latter were known to all; they go *before to judgment,* "to condemnation." The sins of others might be found out *after,* or in consequence of, this investigation; and those that were otherwise could not

be long hid from his knowledge or the knowledge of the church. On all these accounts the exhortation is necessary: "Lay hands suddenly on no man."

25. *Likewise also the good works of some.* Though those who are very holy and very useful in the church cannot be unknown, yet there are others not less holy who need to be brought forward, who do much good in private and their character and good works are not fully known till after diligent inquiry.

CHAPTER 6

Of the duty of servants, 1-2. Of false teachers, who suppose gain to be godliness, 3-5. Of true godliness and contentment, 6-8. Of those, and their dangerous state, who determine to be rich; and of the love of money, 9-10. Timothy is exhorted to fight the good fight of faith, and to keep the charge delivered to him, 11-14. A sublime description of the majesty of God, 15-16. How the rich should behave themselves, and the use they should make of their property, 17-19. Timothy is once more exhorted to keep what was committed to his trust; and to avoid profane babblings, through which some have erred from the faith, 20-21.

1. *Let as many servants as are under the yoke.* The word here means slaves converted to the Christian faith; and the *yoke* is the state to understand the heathen masters of those Christianized slaves. Even these, in such circumstances and under such domination, are commanded to treat their masters with *all honour* and respect, *that the name of God,* by which they were called, and the *doctrine* of God, Christianity, which they had professed, might *not be blasphemed*—might not be evilly spoken of in consequence of their improper conduct. Civil rights are never abolished by any communications from God's Spirit. The civil state in which a man was before his conversion is not altered by that conversion, nor does the grace of God absolve him from any claims which either the state or his neighbor may have on him.

2. *And they that have believing masters.* Who have been lately converted as well as themselves. *Let them not despise them.* Supposing themselves to be their equals because they are their brethren in Christ. *But rather do them service.* Obey them the more cheerfully *because they are faithful and beloved; faithful* to God's grace, *beloved* by Him and His true followers. *Partakers of the benefit.* "Joint partakers of the benefit." This is generally understood as referring to the master's participation in the services of his slaves. "Because those who are partakers of the benefit of your services are faithful and beloved"; or it may apply to the servants who are partakers of many benefits from their Christian masters. Others think that *benefit* here refers to the grace of the gospel, the common salvation of believing masters and slaves.

3. *If any man teach otherwise.* It appears that there were teachers of a different kind in the church, a sort of religious levellers, who preached that the converted servant had as much right to the master's service as the master had to his. *And consent not to wholesome words.* "Healing doctrines"—doctrines which give nourishment and health to the soul, which is the true character of all the doctrines taught by our Lord Jesus Christ; doctrines which are *according to godliness*—securing as amply the honor and glory of God as they do the peace,

happiness, and final salvation of man. All this may refer to the general tenor of the gospel; and not to anything said, or supposed to have been said, by our Lord relative to the condition of slaves. With political questions or questions relative to private rights, our Lord scarcely ever meddled. He taught all men to love one another; to respect each other's rights; to submit to each other; to show all fidelity; to be obedient, humble, and meek; and to know that His kingdom was not of this world.

4. *He is proud.* He is "blown up" or "inflated" with a vain opinion of his own knowledge; whereas his knowledge is foolishness, for he knows nothing. *Doting about questions.* He is "sick, distempered," about these questions relative to the Mosaic law and the traditions of the elders; for it is most evident that the apostle has the Judaizing teachers in view, who were ever, in questions of theology, straining out a gnat and swallowing a camel. *Strifes of words. Logomachies;* verbal contentions; splitting hairs. *Whereof cometh envy, strife.* How little good have religious disputes ever done to mankind or to the cause of truth! Most controversialists have succeeded in getting their own tempers soured and in irritating their opponents.

5. *Perverse disputings of men of corrupt minds.* Disputations that cannot be settled because their partisans will not listen to the truth; and they will not listen to the truth because their minds are corrupt. Both under the law and under the gospel the true religion was: Thou shalt love the Lord thy God with all thy heart, soul, mind, and strength; and thy neighbor as thyself. Where therefore the love of God and man does not prevail, there there is no religion. *Supposing that gain is godliness.* Professing religion only for the sake of secular profit, defending their own cause for the emoluments it produced, and having no respect to another world. *From such withdraw thyself.* Have no religious fellowship with such people. But this clause is wanting in some MSS. It is probably spurious.

6. *But godliness with contentment is great gain.* The word *godliness* here and in several other places of this Epistle signifies the true religion, Christianity; and the word *contentment* signifies a "competency," a "sufficiency"; that measure or portion of secular things which is necessary for the support of life, while the great work of regeneration is carrying on in the soul. So if a man have the life of God in his soul, and just a sufficiency of food and raiment to preserve and not burden life, he has what God calls *great gain,* an abundant portion.

7. *We brought nothing into this world.* There are some sayings in Seneca which are almost verbatim with this of Paul: "No man is born rich; everyone that comes into the world is commanded to be content with food and raiment."

8. *Having food and raiment let us be therewith content.* Let us consider this a "competency." The word which we translate *raiment* signifies "covering" in general; and here means house or lodging, as well as clothing.

9. *But they that will be rich.* The words are emphatic, and refer to persons who are "determined" to get riches. *And into many foolish and hurtful lusts.* The whole conduct of such a

person is a tissue of folly; scraping, gathering, and heaping up riches, and scarcely affording to take the necessaries of life out of them for himself. These lusts or desires are not only *foolish,* but they are *hurtful.* The mind is debased and narrowed by them; benevolent and generous feelings become extinct; charity perishes; and selfishness, the last and lowest principle in mental degradation, absorbs the soul. For these *foolish and hurtful lusts . . . drown men in destruction and perdition*—the soul is destroyed by them here and brought through them into a state of perdition hereafter.

10. *The love of money is the root of all evil.* Perhaps it would be better to translate "of all these evils"; i.e., the evils enumerated above; for it cannot be true that the love of money is the root of *all evil.* It certainly was not the root whence the transgression of Adam sprang, but it is the root whence all the evils mentioned in the preceding verse spring. This text has been often very incautiously quoted; for how often do we hear, "The Scripture says, Money is the root of all evil"! No, the Scripture says no such thing. Money is the root of no evil, nor is it an evil of any kind; but the love of it is the root of all the evils mentioned here. *While some coveted after.* "Insatiably desiring." *Have erred from the faith.* Have "totally erred"—have made a most fatal and ruinous departure from the religion of Christ. *And pierced themselves through with many sorrows.* The word signifies to be "transfixed in every part"; and is an allusion to one of those "snares" mentioned in v. 9, where a hole is dug in the earth and filled full of sharp stakes, and being slightly covered over with turf, is not perceived; and whatever steps on it falls in and is pierced through and through with these sharp stakes, the "many torments" mentioned by the apostle.

11. *But thou, O man of God.* You who have taken God for your Portion, and are seeking a city that has foundations, *flee these things.* Escape for your life. Even you are not out of the reach of the love of money. *Follow after righteousness*—justice and uprightness in all your dealings with men. *Godliness*—a thorough conformity to the image of God and the mind of Christ. *Faith* in Jesus, and in all that He has spoken; and "fidelity" to the talents you have received and the office with which you are entrusted. *Love* to God and all mankind. *Patience* in all trials and afflictions. *Meekness.* Bearing up with an even mind under all adversities and contradictions.

12. *Fight the good fight of faith.* "Agonize the good agony." You have a contest to sustain in which your honor, your life, your soul, are at stake. *Lay hold on eternal life.* All this is in allusion to the exercises in the public Grecian games. Fight, conquer, and seize upon the prize; carry off the crown of eternal life! *Whereunto thou art also called.* The allusion to the public games is still carried on. You have been called into this palaestra; you have been accepted as one proper to enter the lists with any antagonists that may offer; "in the presence of many witnesses" you have taken the necessary engagements upon yourself, and submitted to be governed by the laws of the stadium; many eyes are upon you, to see whether you will fight manfully and be faithful.

13. *I give thee charge.* This is similar to that in v. 21 of the preceding chapter. *A good confession.* The confession made by Christ before Pontius Pilate is that He was Messiah, the King, but that His kingdom was not of this world; and that hereafter He should be seen coming in the clouds of heaven to judge the quick and dead. See John xviii. 36-37 and Mark xiv. 61-62.

14. *That thou keep this commandment without spot.* Two things are mentioned here: (1) That the *commandment* itself, the whole doctrine of Christ, should be kept entire. (2) That his life should be agreeable to that doctrine. Keep it *without spot*—let there be no blot on the sacred Book; add nothing to it; take nothing from it; change nothing in it. Deliver down to your successors the truth as you have had it from God himself. *Unrebukeable.* Let there be nothing in your conduct or spirit contrary to this truth. Keep the truth, and the truth will keep you. *Until the appearing of our Lord.* Hand it down pure and let your conduct be a comment on it, that it may continue in the world and in the Church till the coming of Christ.

15. *Which in his times he shall shew.* Jesus will appear in the most proper time, the time which the infinite God in His wisdom has appointed for the second coming of His Son. *The blessed and only Potentate. Potentate* is applied to secular governors; but none of these can be styled "the happy and only One"; *the King of kings,* or "the King over all kings"; and "the Lord over all lords or rulers." These are titles which could not be given to any mortals. This is made more specific by the verse following.

16. *Who only hath immortality.* All beings that are not eternal must be mutable; but there can be only one eternal Being, that is, God; and He only can have *immortality. Dwelling in the light which no man can approach unto.* All this is said by the apostle in three words: "inhabiting unapproachable light." Such is the excessive glory of God that neither angel nor man can approach it. *Whom no man hath seen, nor can see.* Moses himself could only see the symbol of the Divine Presence, but the face of God no man could ever see. Because He is infinite and eternal, therefore He is incomprehensible; and if incomprehensible to the mind, consequently invisible to the eye. *To whom,* as the Author of being and the Dispenser of all good, be ascribed *honour and power*—the sole authority of all-pervading, all-superintending, all-preserving, and everlasting might.

17. *Charge them that are rich.* He had before, in vv. 9-10, given them a very awful lesson concerning their obtaining riches; and now he gives them one equally so concerning their use of them. *That they be not highminded.* That they do not value themselves on account of their wealth, for this adds nothing to mind or moral worth. *Nor trust in uncertain riches.* The uncertainty of riches; things which are never at a stay, are ever changing, and seldom continue long with one proprietor. Therefore, as well as on many other accounts, they are not to be trusted in; they cannot give happiness, because they are not fixed and permanent; neither can they meet the wishes of an immortal spirit. *But in the living God,* who is the unchangeable Fountain of perfection. *Who giveth*

us richly all things to enjoy. Who not only has all good, but dispenses it liberally for the supply of the wants of all His creatures; and He does not give merely what is necessary, but He gives what tends to render life comfortable. The comforts of life come from God, as well as the necessaries. He not only gives us a bare subsistence, but He gives us enjoyments.

18. *That they do good.* That they relieve the wants of their fellow creatures, according to the abundance which God has given them—the highest luxury a human being can enjoy on this side of the grave. *Rich in good works.* That their good works may be as abundant as their riches. *Ready to distribute.* That they give nothing through partiality or favor, but be guided in their distribution by the necessities of the objects presented to them; and that they confine not their charity at home, but scatter it abroad. *Willing to communicate.* Bringing every poor person into a state of fellowship with themselves.

19. *Laying up in store for themselves a good foundation.* Paul seems to have borrowed this form of speech from Tobit. See chap. iv. 8-9: "If thou hast abundance, give alms accordingly:

if thou hast but a little, be not afraid to give according to that little: for thou treasurest up a good reward for thyself against the day of necessity."

20. *O Timothy, keep that which is committed to thy trust.* This is another repetition of the apostolic charge. (See chap. i. 5, 18-19; iv. 6-7, 14-16; v. 21; vi. 13.) Carefully preserve that doctrine which I have delivered to you. Nothing can be more solemn and affectionate than this charge. *Avoiding profane and vain babblings.* See on chap. i. 4 and iv. 7.

21. *Which some professing.* Which inspired knowledge some pretending to, have set up Levitical rites in opposition to the great Christian Sacrifice, and consequently *have erred concerning the faith*—have completely mistaken the whole design of the gospel. *Grace be with thee.* May the favor and influence of God be with you, and preserve you from these and all other errors! *Amen.* This word, as in former cases, is wanting in the most ancient MSS. In a majority of cases it appears to have been added by different transcribers nearly in the same way in which we add the word *Finis,* simply to indicate the end of the work.

The Second Epistle to

TIMOTHY

From the whole there seems the fullest evidence: (1) That this Epistle was not written during Paul's first imprisonment at Rome. (2) That he was at Rome when he wrote this Epistle. (3) That he was there a prisoner, and in such confinement as we know, from the Acts of the Apostles, he was not in during the time of his first imprisonment there. (4) That this must have been some subsequent imprisonment. (5) That as the general consent of all Christian antiquity states that Paul was twice imprisoned at Rome, and that from his second imprisonment he was never liberated, but was at its conclusion martyred; therefore this Epistle must have been written while Paul was in his second imprisonment at Rome, and but a short time before his martyrdom. And as the Christian Church has generally agreed that this apostle's martyrdom took place on the twenty-ninth of June, A.D. 66, the Second Epistle to Timothy might have been written sometime towards the end of the spring or beginning of summer of that year. It is supposed that Paul went from Crete to Rome, about the end of the year 65, on hearing of the persecution which Nero was then carrying on against the Christians, on pretense that they had set Rome on fire. For as he knew that the Church must be then in great tribulation, he judged that his presence would be necessary to comfort, support, and build it up. Like a true soldier of Jesus Christ, he was ever at the post of danger; and in this case he led on the forlorn hope.

CHAPTER 1

Paul's address to Timothy, and declaration of his affection for him, 1-4. His account of the piety of Timothy's mother and grandmother, and the religious education they had given their son, 5. He exhorts him to stir up the gift of God that is in him, and not to be ashamed of the testimony of the Lord, 6-8. How God has saved them that believe, and how Christ has brought life and immortality to light by the gospel, 9-10. The apostle's call to preach it, and the persecutions which he had been obliged in consequence to endure, 11-12. Timothy is exhorted to hold fast the form of sound words, 13-14. And is informed of the apostasy of several in Asia; and particularly of Phygellus and Hermogenes, 15. And of the great kindness of Onesiphorus to the apostle in his imprisonment, 16-18.

1. *Paul an apostle.* Paul at once shows his office, the authority on which he held it, and

the end for which it was given him. He was an *apostle*—an extraordinary ambassador from heaven. He had his apostleship by the *will of God*—according to the counsel and design of God's infinite wisdom and goodness. And he was appointed that he might proclaim that eternal *life* which God had in view for mankind by the incarnation of His Son, Jesus Christ, and which was the end of all the promises He had made to men and the commandments He had delivered to all His prophets since the world began.

3. *Whom I serve from my forefathers.* Being born a Jew, I was carefully educated in the knowledge of the true God and the proper

manner of worshipping Him. *With pure conscience.* Ever aiming to please Him, even in the time when through ignorance I persecuted the Church. *Without ceasing I have remembrance of thee.* The apostle thanks God that he has constant remembrance of Timothy in his prayers. It is a very rare thing now in the Christian Church that a man particularly thanks God that he is enabled to pray for others.

4. *Being mindful of thy tears.* Whether the apostle refers to the affecting parting with the Ephesian church, mentioned in Acts xx. 37, or to the deep impressions made on Timothy's heart when he instructed him in the doctrine of Christ crucified, or to some interview between themselves, it is not certainly known. The mention of this by the apostle is no small proof of his most affectionate regard for Timothy, whom he appears to have loved as a father loves his only son.

5. *The unfeigned faith that is in thee.* Timothy had given the fullest proof of the sincerity of his conversion and of the purity of his faith. *Which dwelt first in thy grandmother Lois.* In Acts xvi. 1, we are informed that Paul "came . . . to Derbe and Lystra: and, behold, a certain disciple was there, named Timotheus, the son of a certain woman, which was a Jewess, and believed; but his father was a Greek." Paul, in mentioning the grandmother, mother, and son, passes by the father in silence; which intimates that either the father remained in his unconverted state or was now dead. Lois, the grandmother, appears to have been the first convert to Christianity; she instructed her daughter, Eunice, and both brought up Timothy in the Christian faith.

6. *Stir up the gift of God, which is in thee.* The *gift* which Timothy had received was the Holy Spirit; and through Him, a particular power to preach and defend the truth. This *gift* is represented here under the notion of a fire, which if it be not frequently stirred up and fresh fuel added to it will go out. This is the precise idea which the apostle had in his mind; hence the term which signifies to "stir up the fire; to add fresh fuel to it." *By the putting on of my hands.* See on 1 Tim. iv. 14.

7. *God hath not given us the spirit of fear.* Here is an allusion to the giving of the law on Mount Sinai. This was communicated with such terrible majesty as to engender fear in all the Israelites; even Moses, on the occasion, "did exceedingly fear and tremble." The gospel was ushered in, in a much milder manner; everything was placed on a level with the human intellect and within reach of every human spirit. Nothing was terrific, nothing forbidding; but all was inviting. The very spirit and genius of it was a spirit of power, of love, and of a sound mind. *But of power,* to work miracles, to confound enemies, to support us in trials, and enable us to do that which is lawful and right in His sight. *And of love,* which enables us to hear, believe, hope, and endure all things; and is the incentive to all obedience. *Of a sound mind,* of "self-possession," according to some. But a sound mind implies much more; it means a clear understanding, a sound judgment, a rectified will, holy passions, heavenly tempers; in a word, the whole soul harmonized in all its powers and faculties, and completely regulated and influenced so as to think, speak, and act aright in all things.

8. *Be not . . . ashamed of the testimony.* The testimony of Christ is the gospel in general, which proclaims Christ crucified and redemption through His blood. *Nor of me his prisoner.* When our friends are in power and credit, we can readily acknowledge them, and take opportunities to show that we have such and such connections; but when the person falls into disgrace or discredit, though we cannot pretend not to know him, yet we take care not to acknowledge him. This induced Cicero, in relation to friendships, to give for a maxim, "A true friend is known in adverse circumstances"; and from this we have borrowed our proverb, "A friend in need is a friend indeed." *Be thou partaker of the afflictions of the gospel.* No parent could love a child better than Paul loved Timothy; and, behold! he who could wish him nothing but what was great, honorable, and good wishes him to be a *partaker of the afflictions of the gospel!* Because to suffer for Christ was the highest glory to which any human being in this state could arrive. The royal way to the crown of glory is by the cross of Christ. *According to the power of God.* While you have no more affliction than you have grace to sustain you, you can have no cause to complain. And God will take care that, if a faithful discharge of your duty shall expose you to afflictions, His power manifested in you shall be in proportion to your necessities. His load cannot be oppressive who is strengthened to bear it by the power of God.

9. *Who hath saved us.* From sin; the spirit of bondage, and all tormenting fear. This is the design of the gospel. *And called us with an holy calling.* Invited us to holiness and comfort here and to eternal glory hereafter. *Not according to our works.* We have not deserved any part of the good we have received, and can never merit one moment of the exceeding great and eternal weight of glory which is promised. *Before the world began.* Before the Mosaic dispensation took place, God purposed the salvation of the Gentiles by Christ Jesus; and the Mosaic dispensation was intended only as the introducer of the gospel.

10. *But is now made manifest.* This purpose of God to save the Gentiles as well as the Jews, and call them to the same state of salvation by Jesus Christ, was, previously to the manifestation of Christ, generally hidden; and what was revealed of it was only through the means of types and ceremonies. *Who hath abolished death.* Who has "counterworked death." By death here we are not to understand merely natural death, but that corruption and decomposition which take place in consequence of it, and which would be naturally endless but for the work and energy of Christ. *Brought life and immortality to light.* The literal translation of the original is, "He hath illustrated life and incorruption by the gospel." Jesus Christ died and lay under the empire of death. He arose again from the dead and thus "illustrated" the doctrine of the resurrection. He took the same human body up into heaven, in the sight of His disciples, and ever appears in the presence of God for us; and thus has "illustrated" the doctrine of "incorruption."

11. *Whereunto I am appointed a preacher.*

"A herald." *And an apostle.* Sent immediately from God to man. *A teacher.* One whose business it is to instruct men, and particularly the Gentiles, to whom he was especially sent; to proclaim the doctrines of eternal life, the resurrection and final incorruptibility of the human body; and, in a word, the salvation of both the body and soul of man by Christ Jesus.

12. *I am not ashamed.* Though I suffer for the gospel, I am not ashamed of the gospel; nor am I confounded in my expectation, His grace being at all times sufficient for me. *For I know whom I have believed.* I am well-acquainted with the goodness, mercy, and power of Christ, and know that I cannot confide in Him in vain. *That which I have committed unto him.* This is variously understood. Some think he means his life, which he had put, as it were, into the hands of Christ in order that he might receive it again in the resurrection, at the great day. Others think he means his faithful Creator, knowing that, although wicked men might be permitted to take away his life, yet they could not destroy his soul nor disturb its peace. Others think that he is speaking of the gospel, which he knows will be carefully preserved by the great Head of the Church. For though he shall be soon called to seal the truth with his blood, yet he knows that God will take care that the same truth shall be proclaimed to the world by others whom God shall raise up for that very purpose.

13. *Hold fast the form.* The word signifies the "sketch, plan, or outline" of a building, picture, etc.; and here refers to the plan of salvation which the apostle had taught Timothy. *In faith and love.* Faith credits the divine doctrines. *Love* reduces them all to practice. *Faith* lays hold on Jesus Christ, and obtains that *love* by which every precept is cheerfully and effectually obeyed.

14. *That good thing.* The everlasting gospel. *Keep by the Holy Ghost,* for without a continual spiritual energy man can do nothing.

15. *All they which are in Asia.* It seems as if the apostle must refer to the Asiatic Christians which were then at Rome or had been lately there. Finding the apostle in disgrace and thinking it dangerous to own him or his cause, they neither visited him nor confessed Christianity. He cannot be speaking of any general defection of the Asiatic churches, but of those Asiatics who had professed a particular friendship for him. *Phygellus and Hermogenes.* These were two of the persons of whom he complains; but who they were or what office they held or whether they were anything but private Christians who had for a time ministered to Paul in prison and, when they found the state determined to destroy him, ceased to acknowledge him, we cannot tell.

16. *The Lord give mercy. Onesiphorus* had acknowledged him, and continued to do so; he and his *house,* or "family," ministered to him in prison, and were not ashamed of their imprisoned pastor nor of the cause for which he was in disgrace and suffering. As he showed mercy to the apostle, the apostle prays the Lord to show mercy to him.

17. *When he was in Rome.* Onesiphorus was no doubt an Asiatic who had frequent business at Rome; and when he came sought out the

apostle, who, it is supposed, had been confined in some close and private prison, so that it was with great difficulty he could find him out. This man had entertained the apostle when he was at Ephesus, and now he sought him out at Rome. Pure love feels no loads. Here was a true friend, one "that sticketh closer than a brother."

18. *The Lord grant . . . that he may find mercy of the Lord.* Some think that this is a prayer to God the Father to communicate grace to him, that he might find mercy in the great day at the hand of Jesus Christ, the Judge. It is probably only a Hebraism for "God grant that he may here be so saved by divine grace that in the great day he may receive the mercy of the Lord Jesus Christ unto eternal life." See a similar form of expression, Gen. ix. 16; xix. 24; Exod. xxiv. 1-2.

CHAPTER 2

He exhorts Timothy to constancy, fidelity, and courage; and to acquit himself as a true soldier of Jesus Christ; and patiently to expect the fruit of his labors, 1-7. What the apostle's doctrine was relative to Christ, 8. He mentions his own sufferings and consolations, 9-13. What Timothy is to preach, how he is to acquit himself, and what he is to shun, 14-16. Of Hymenaeus and Philetus, and their errors, 17-18. Of the foundation of God, and its security, 19. The simile of a great house and its utensils, 20-21. Timothy is to avoid youthful lusts, and foolish and unlearned questions, 22-23. How he is to act in reference to false teachers, 24-26.

1. *Be strong in the grace.* Though the genuine import of the word *grace* is "favor," yet it often implies an active principle communicated from God; light directing how to act, and power enabling to act according to the light.

2. *The things that thou hast heard of me.* Those doctrines which I have preached the most publicly and which many persons can attest. But he seems to refer here to the doctrines delivered to him when, in the presence of many witnesses, he laid his hands upon him; see 1 Tim. vi. 12. Then the apostle gave him the proper form of sound words which he was to teach; and now he tells him to commit those truths to faithful men in the same way that they were committed to him, that the truth might be preserved in the Church, and holy men appointed successively to preach it.

3. *Endure hardness.* He considers a Christian minister under the notion of a soldier, not so much for his continual conflicts with the world, the devil, and the flesh, for these are in a certain sense common to all Christians, but for the hardships and difficulties to which he must be exposed who faithfully preaches the gospel of Christ.

4. *No man that warreth entangleth.* It is well remarked by Grotius, on this passage, that the legionary soldiers among the Romans were not permitted to engage in husbandry, merchandise, mechanical employments, or anything that might be inconsistent with their calling. He who will preach the gospel thoroughly, and wishes to give full proof of his ministry, had need to have no other work. He should be wholly in this thing, that his profiting may appear unto all.

5. *If a man also strive for masteries.* "If a man contend in the public games"—the Olympic or Isthmian games among the Greeks. *Is he not crowned,* though he may have conquered, *except he strive lawfully,* unless he enter according

to the rules of the athletae, and act as these direct.

6. *The husbandman that laboureth.* That is: The *husbandman* must *first* till his ground before he can expect a crop; and he must till it according to the proper rules of agriculture, else he cannot have a crop.

7. *Consider what I say.* Apply my metaphors and similitudes in a proper manner. *And the Lord give thee understanding.* But instead of "may He give," several MSS., besides versions and fathers, have "He will give." Consider properly, and God will give you a proper understanding of all things that concern your own peace and the peace and prosperity of His Church. Think as well as read.

8. *Remember that Jesus Christ.* The apostle seems to say: Whatever tribulations or deaths may befall us, let us remember that Jesus Christ, who was slain by the Jews, rose again from the dead, and His resurrection is the proof and pledge of ours. *According to my gospel.* The false teaching of Hymenaeus and Philetus stated that the resurrection was past already. Paul preached the resurrection from the dead, and founded his doctrine on the resurrection and promise of Christ. This was his gospel; the other was of a different nature.

10. *For the elect's sakes.* For the sake of the Gentiles, elected by God's goodness to enjoy every privilege formerly possessed by the Jews, and, in addition to these, all the blessings of the gospel: the salvation of Christ here, and eternal glory hereafter.

11. *If we be dead with him.* That is: As surely as Christ rose again from the dead, so surely shall we rise again, and if we die for Him, we shall surely live again with Him. This, says the apostle, is "a true doctrine."

13. *If we believe not.* Should we deny the faith and apostatize, He is the same, as true to His threatenings as to His promises; *he cannot deny,* act contrary to, *himself.*

14. *That they strive not about words.* Words, not things, have been a most fruitful source of contention in the Christian world; and among religious people, the principal cause of animosity has arisen from the different manner of apprehending the same term, while in essence both meant the same thing. All preachers and divines should be very careful, in both speaking and writing, to explain the terms they use, and never employ them in any sense but that in which they have explained them. *The subverting of the hearers.* This is the general tendency of all polemical divinity and controversial preaching, when angry passions are called in to support the doctrines of the gospel.

15. *Study to shew thyself approved unto God.* Endeavor so to cultivate and improve your heart and mind that you may not be a reproach to Him from whom you profess to receive your commission. *Rightly dividing the word of truth.* The word signifies (1) simply to "cut straight," (2) to "walk in the right way." Therefore, by *rightly dividing the word of truth* we are to understand his continuing in the true doctrine and teaching that to every person.

16. *Shun profane and vain babblings.* This is the character he gives of the preaching of the false teachers. Whatever was not agreeable to the doctrine of truth was, in the sight of God,

"empty and profane babbling"; engendering nothing but *ungodliness,* and daily increasing in that.

17. *Their word will eat as doth a canker.* "As a gangrene"; i.e., as a mortification in the flesh, where the circulation is entirely stopped and putrefaction takes place, which continues to corrupt all the circumjacent flesh, spreading more and more till death takes place, unless stopped by a timely and judicious application of medicine. Such is the influence of false doctrine; it fixes its mortal seed in the soul, which continues to corrupt and assimilate everything to itself till, if not prevented by a timely application of the word of life, under the direction of the heavenly Physician, it terminates in the bitter pains of an eternal death. To such a gangrene the apostle compares the corrupt doctrines of Hymenaeus and Philetus.

18. *Who concerning the truth have erred.* They had the truth, but *erred* or "wandered from it," saying *the resurrection* was already *past,* and thus denying the resurrection of the body and, by consequence, future rewards and punishments.

19. *The foundation of God standeth sure.* The word signifies literally a *foundation,* and especially the foundation of a building; and metaphorically, the building itself, and often a noble mansion or palace. In this place the apostle compares the religion of Christ to a great or noble mansion. See v. 20. And as this religion is founded on the authority and power of the Almighty, it necessarily must stand sure and be permanent. This house has an "inscription" on it, for so *seal* is frequently understood; and this is evidently an allusion to the ancient temples. Above the door of the temple of Delphi there was the Greek word, "Thou art," on which Plutarch has written an express treatise. And we know that there was an inscription on the mitre of the high priest among the Jews, viz., "Holiness to the Lord"; Exod. xxviii. 36; xxxix. 30.

But some suppose here a "contract" or "covenant" by which two parties are bound to fulfill certain conditions and duties, the obligation to which each takes on him by sealing the instrument with his seal. The twofold inscription, i.e., one on the seal of each party, may be here alluded to; that on God's seal is, "*The Lord approveth of them that are his.*" That on the seal of His followers is, "*Let every one that nameth the name of* the Lord (every Christian) *depart from iniquity.*" "Lord," instead of *Christ,* is the reading of almost all the MSS. of importance, and the principal versions. *The Lord knoweth.* I.e., Approves, watches over, and provides for, them that are His true followers. To this His followers most cheerfully subscribe, and say: "Let every one that nameth this Lord avoid every appearance of evil."

20. *But in a great house.* Here the apostle carries on the allusion introduced in the preceding verse. As the "foundation of God" refers to God's building, i.e., the whole system of Christianity, so here the *great house* is to be understood of the same; and the different kinds of vessels mean the different teachers, as well as the different kinds of members. In this sacred house at Ephesus there were *vessels of gold and of silver*—eminent, holy, sincere, and useful teachers and members; and also *vessels*

of wood and of earth—false and heretical teachers, such as Hymenaeus and Philetus, and their followers.

21. *If a man therefore purge himself from these.* He that takes heed to his ways and to his doctrines, and walks with God, will separate himself, not only from all false doctrine, but from all wicked men, and thus be sanctified and proper to be employed by the Master in every good word and work. The apostle has not made the application of these different similes, and it is very difficult to tell what he means.

22. *Flee also youthful lusts.* Not only all irregular and sensual desires, but pride, ambition, and, above all, the lust of power, to which most men will sacrifice all other propensities, their ease, pleasure, health, etc. This is the most bewitching passion in the human heart. Both in church and state it is ruinous, but particularly so in the former. Timothy was now between thirty and forty years of age, the very age in which ambition and the love of power most generally prevail. Carnal pleasures are the sins of youth; ambition and the love of power, the sins of middle age; covetousness and carking cares, the crimes of old age. *Follow righteousness.* Flee from sin, pursue goodness. *Righteousness*—whatever is just, holy, and innocent. *Faith*—fidelity to both God and man, improving that grace by which your soul may be saved, and faithfully discharging the duties of your office. *Charity*—love to God and man. *Peace* among all the members of the church, and as far as possible with all men.

23. *Foolish and unlearned questions.* See the notes on 1 Tim. i. 4; iv. 7; and Titus iii. 9.

24. *The servant of the Lord must not strive.* See on 1 Tim. iii. 2-3.

25. *Those that oppose.* This seems to refer to those who opposed the apostle's authority, and hence the propriety of the allusion to the rebellion of Korah and his company. *If God peradventure.* He was to use every means which he had reason to believe God might bless; and the apostle intimates that, bad as they were, they were not out of the reach of God's mercy.

CHAPTER 3

Dangerous times in the latter days, from the apostasy and wickedness of men, of whom an affecting description is given, 1-7. It shall happen to them as to Jannes and Jambres, who withstood Moses. 8-9. The apostle speaks of his persecutions and sufferings, and shows that all those who will live a godly life must suffer persecution, 10-12, because evil men and seducers will wax worse and worse, 13. Timothy is exhorted to continue in the truths he had received, having known the Scriptures from a child, 14-15. All scripture is given by divine inspiration, 16-17.

1. *In the last days.* This often means the days of the Messiah, and is sometimes extended in its signification to the destruction of Jerusalem, as this was properly the last days of the Jewish state. But the phrase may mean any future time, whether near or distant.

2. *Lovers of their own selves.* "Selfish," studious of their own interest, and regardless of the welfare of all mankind. *Covetous.* "Lovers of money," because of the influence which riches can procure. *Boasters.* Vainglorious: self-assuming; valuing themselves beyond all others. *Proud.* Airy, light, trifling persons; those who love to make a show—who are all outside.

Blasphemers. Those who speak impiously of God and sacred things, and injuriously of men. *Disobedient to parents.* Headstrong children, whom their parents cannot persuade. *Unthankful.* Persons without grace, or gracefulness; who think they have a right to the services of all men, yet feel no obligation, and consequently no gratitude. *Unholy.* Without piety; having no heart reverence for God.

3. *Without natural affection.* Without that affection which parents bear to their young, and which the young bear to their parents. *Trucebreakers.* The word means those who are bound by no promise, held by no engagement, obliged by no oath; persons who readily promise anything because they never intend to perform. *False accusers.* "Devils"; but properly enough rendered *false accusers,* for this is a principal work of the devil. Slanderers; striving ever to ruin the characters of others. *Incontinent.* Those who are slaves to uncleanness. *Fierce.* Wild, impetuous, whatever is contrary to pliability and gentleness. *Despisers of those that are good.* "Not lovers of good men." Here is a remarkable advantage of the Greek over the English tongue, one word of the former expressing five or six of the latter. Those who do not love the good must be radically bad themselves.

4. *Traitors.* Those who deliver up to an enemy the person who has put his life in their hands. *Heady.* Headstrong, precipitate, rash, inconsiderate. *Highminded.* The frivolously aspiring; those who are full of themselves and empty of all good. *Lovers of pleasures more than lovers of God.* Pleasure, sensual gratification, is their god, and this they love and serve; God they do not.

5. *Having a form of godliness.* The original word signifies a "draught, sketch, or summary," and will apply well to those who have all their religion in their creed, confession of faith, catechism, bodies of divinity, while destitute of the life of God in their souls; and are not only destitute of this life, but deny that such life or power is here to be experienced or known. They have religion in their creed, but none in their hearts. *From such turn away*—not only do not imitate them, but have no kind of fellowship with them; they are a dangerous people, and but seldom suspected, because their outside is fair.

6. *For of this sort are they.* He here refers to false teachers and their insinuating manners, practicing upon weak women, who, seeing in them such a semblance of piety, entertain them with great eagerness, and at last become partakers with them in their impurities.

7. *Ever learning,* from their false teachers, *and never able to come to the knowledge of the truth,* because that teaching never leads to the truth.

8. *Now as Jannes and Jambres withstood Moses.* This refers to the history of the Egyptian magicians, given in Exodus vii. *Men of corrupt minds.* It appears as if the apostle were referring still to some Judaizing teachers who were perverting the church with their doctrines, and loudly calling in question the authority and doctrine of the apostle. *Reprobate concerning the faith.* "Undiscerning" or "untried"; they are base metal, unstamped; and should not

pass current, because not standard. This metaphor is frequent in the sacred writings.

9. *But they shall proceed no further.* Such teaching and teachers shall never be able ultimately to prevail against the truth; for "the foundation of God standeth sure." *Their folly shall be manifest.* As the Scriptures, which are the only rule of morals and doctrine, shall ever be preserved; so, sooner or later, all false doctrines shall be tried by them, and the folly of men setting up their wisdom against the wisdom of God must become manifest to all.

10. *Thou hast fully known my doctrine.* And having long had the opportunity of knowing me, the *doctrine* I preached, my "conduct" founded on these doctrines, the "object" I have in view by my preaching, my "fidelity" to God and to my trust, my *longsuffering* with those who walked disorderly, my "love" to them and to the world in general, and my *patience* in all my adversities, you are capable of judging between me and the false teachers, and can easily discern the difference between their doctrines, conduct, motives, temper, spirit, and mine.

11. *Persecutions, afflictions, which came unto me at Antioch.* The *Antioch* mentioned here was Antioch in Pisidia, to which place Paul and Barnabas came in their first apostolic progress, and where Paul delivered that memorable discourse which is preserved in the thirteenth chapter of Acts, vv. 16-43. In this city, it is said, "the Jews stirred up the devout and honourable women, and the chief men of the city, and raised persecution against Paul and Barnabas, and expelled them out of their coasts. But they shook off the dust of their feet against them, and came to Iconium," Acts xiii. 50-51. Here "there was an assault made both of the Gentiles, and also of the Jews with their rulers, to treat them despitefully, and to stone them . . . and [they] fled unto Lystra and Derbe . . . And there came thither certain Jews . . . who persuaded the people, and, having stoned Paul, drew him out of the city, supposing he had been dead." The historian informs us that his life was miraculously restored, and that he departed thence and came to Derbe, and afterwards returned to Lystra, Iconium, and Antioch, where they had lately been so grievously persecuted. See Acts xiv. 5-6, 19-21. These are the persecutions to which the apostle alludes; and we find that he mentions them here precisely in the same order in which, according to the relation of Luke, they occurred.

12. *All that will live godly.* So opposite to the spirit and practice of the world is the whole of Christianity that he who gives himself entirely up to God, making the Holy Scriptures the rule of his words and actions, will be more or less reviled and persecuted.

13. *Evil men and seducers shall wax worse.* They will yet get on for a season, deceiving themselves and deceiving others; but by and by "their folly shall be manifest unto all," v. 9. The word which we render *seducers* signifies "jugglers, pretenders to magical arts"; probably persons dealing in false miracles, with whom the Church in all ages has been not a little disgraced.

14. *But continue thou.* No man, however well-instructed in the things of God or ground-ed in divine grace, is out of the reach of temptation, apostasy, and final ruin; hence the necessity of watching unto prayer, depending upon God, continuing in the faith, and persevering unto the end.

15. *From a child thou hast known the holy scriptures.* The early religious education of Timothy already has been sufficiently noticed; see chap. i. 5. Paul introduces this circumstance again here for the confirmation of Timothy's faith. *Able to make thee wise unto salvation.* The apostle is here evidently speaking of the Jewish Scriptures and he tells us that they are able to make us *wise unto salvation* provided we have faith in Jesus Christ. This is the simple use of the Old Testament. No soul of man can be made wise unto salvation by it but as he refers all to Christ Jesus.

16. *All scripture is given by inspiration of God.* This sentence is not well-translated; the original should be rendered: "Every writing divinely inspired is profitable for doctrine." The apostle is here, beyond all controversy, speaking of the writings of the Old Testament, which, because they came by divine inspiration, he terms "the holy scriptures," v. 15; and it is of them alone that this passage is to be understood; and although all the New Testament came by as direct an inspiration as the Old, yet, as it was not collected at that time, nor indeed complete, the apostle could have no reference to it.

The doctrine of the inspiration of the sacred writings has been a subject of much discussion, and even controversy, among Christians. There are two principal opinions on the subject: (1) That every thought and word were inspired by God, and that the writer did nothing but merely write as the Spirit dictated. (2) That God gave the whole matter, leaving the inspired writers to their own language, and hence the great variety of style and different modes of expression. Is *profitable for doctrine.* To teach the will of God, and to point out Jesus Christ till He should come. *For reproof.* To "convince" men of the truth; and to confound those who should deny it. *For correction.* For "restoring things" to their proper uses and places, correcting false notions and mistaken views. *Instruction in righteousness.* For communicating all initiatory religious knowledge; for schooling mankind. All this is perfectly true of the Jewish Scriptures; and let faith in Christ Jesus be added, see v. 15, and then all that is spoken in the following verse will be literally accomplished.

17. *That the man of God.* The preacher of righteousness, the minister of the gospel, the person who derives his commission from God, and always appears as His herald and servant. *May be perfect.* It properly signifies an "integer" or "whole number" in arithmetic, to which nothing needs to be added to make it complete. *Throughly furnished.* Not only "complete" in himself as to his integrity, religious knowledge, faith in Jesus, and love to God and man, but that he should have all those qualifications which are necessary to complete the character and insure the success of a preacher of the gospel. Timothy was to teach, reprove, correct, and instruct others; and was to be to them a pattern of good works.

CHAPTER 4

The apostle charges Timothy to be diligent, incessant, and faithful in his preaching; to watch, suffer patiently, and give full proof of his ministry, 1-5. He predicts his own approaching death, and expresses the strongest confidence of being eternally happy, 6-8. Desires Timothy to come and see him; shows that several had forsaken him, that others were gone to different districts, and that he had only Luke with him, 9-12. Desires him to bring the cloak, book, and parchments, which he had left at Troas, 13. Of Alexander the coppersmith's opposition, 14-15. Tells Timothy how he was deserted by all when obliged to make his first defense before Nero; but God supported him, and the confidence with which he was inspired, 16-18. Salutations to different persons at Ephesus, and from different persons at Rome, 19-21. The apostolical benediction, 22.

1. *I charge thee therefore before God.* Whose herald you are; and before *the Lord Jesus Christ*, whose salvation you are to proclaim, and who is coming to *judge* the world—all that shall be found then "alive," and all that have died from the foundation of the world.

2. *Preach the word.* "Proclaim the doctrine," the doctrine of Christ crucified for the sins of the whole world; the doctrine that the Gentiles are invited to be fellow heirs with the Jews, and that for Jews and Gentiles there is no salvation but by faith in Christ. *Be instant in season, out of season.* Be urgent whether the times be prosperous or adverse, whenever there is an opportunity; and when there is none, strive to make one. *Reprove.* "Confute" the false teacher. *Rebuke.* Reprove "cuttingly and severely" those who will not abandon their sins. *Exhort.* "Comfort the feebleminded," the diffident and the tempted. *With all longsuffering.* In reference to each and all of these cases. *And doctrine.* The different modes of teaching suited to each.

3. *For the time will come.* There is a time coming to the Church when men will not hear the practical truths of the gospel, when they will prefer speculative opinions, which either do no good to the soul or corrupt and destroy it, to that wholesome doctrine of "Deny thyself, take up thy cross, and follow Me," which Jesus Christ has left in His Church. *But after their own lusts.* For these they will follow, and hate those preachers and that doctrine by which they are opposed. *Shall they heap to themselves teachers.* They will add one teacher to another, run and gad about after all, to find out those who insist not on the necessity of bearing the cross, of being crucified to the world, and of having the mind that was in Jesus. *Having itching ears.* Endless curiosity, an insatiable desire of variety; and they get their ears tickled with the language and accent of the person, abandoning the good and faithful preacher for the fine speaker.

4. *And they shall turn away their ears from the truth.* The truth strips them of their vices, sacrifices their idols, darts its lightnings against their easily besetting sins, and absolutely requires a conformity to a crucified Christ; therefore they turn their ears away from it. *And shall be turned unto fables.* Believe any kind of stuff and nonsense; for as one has justly observed, "Those who reject the truth are abandoned by the just judgment of God to credit the most degrading nonsense."

5. *But watch thou in all things.* It is possible to be overtaken in a fault, to neglect one's duty, and to lose one's soul. Watching unto prayer prevents all these evils. *Endure afflic-*

tions. Let no sufferings affright you; nor let the dread of them either cause you to abandon the truth or relax in your zeal for the salvation of men. *Do the work of an evangelist.* That is: Preach Christ crucified for the sins of the whole world; for this, and this alone, is doing the work of an evangelist, or preacher of the glad tidings of peace and salvation by Christ.

6. *For I am now ready to be offered.* "I am already poured out as a libation." See the note on Phil. ii. 17. He considers himself as on the eve of being sacrificed, and looks upon his blood as the libation which was poured on the sacrificial offering. He could not have spoken thus positively had not the sentence of death already been passed upon him.

7. *I have fought a good fight.* Every reader will perceive that the apostle, as was his very frequent custom, alludes to the contests at the Grecian games: "I have wrestled that good wrestling"—I have struggled hard, and have overcome, in a most honorable cause. *I have finished my course.* I have started for the prize, and have come up to the goal, outstripping all my competitors, and have gained this prize also. *I have kept the faith.* As the laws of these games must be most diligently observed and kept (for though a man overcome, yet is he not crowned except he strive lawfully), so I have kept the rules of the spiritual combat and race; and thus, having contended lawfully and conquered in each exercise, I have a right to expect the prize.

8. *Henceforth there is laid up for me a crown.* This I can claim as my due; but the crown I expect is not one of fading leaves, but *a crown of righteousness;* the reward which God, in His kindness, has promised to them who are faithful to the grace He has bestowed upon them. *The Lord, the righteous judge.* He alludes here to the *brabeus,* or umpire in the Grecian games, whose office it was to declare the victor and to give the crown. *At that day.* The day of judgment; the morning of the resurrection from the dead. *Unto all them also that love his appearing.* All who live in expectation of the coming of Christ, who anticipate it with joyfulness.

9. *Do thy diligence to come shortly unto me.* He appears to have wished Timothy to be present at his death, that he might have his faith confirmed by seeing how a Christian could die; and as he had but a short time to live, he begs Timothy to hasten his visit, and particularly so as he had scarcely now any companions.

10. *Demas hath forsaken me.* This is another proof of the posteriority of this Epistle; for Demas was with the apostle in his first imprisonment, and joins in the salutations, see Col. iv. 14, which were written when Paul was a prisoner at Rome for the first time. *Crescens to Galatia.* Whether the departure of Crescens was similar to that of Demas, as intimated above, or whether he went on an evangelical embassy, we know not. Charity would hope the latter; for we can hardly suppose that Titus, who is here said to have departed to Dalmatia, had abandoned his Cretan churches, his apostolical office, and especially his aged father and friend, now about to seal the truth with his blood! It is probable that both these persons had gone on sacred missions, and perhaps had

been gone some time before the apostle was brought into such imminent danger.

11. *Only Luke is with me.* This was Luke the Evangelist, and writer of the Acts of the Apostles, who was always much attached to Paul, and it is supposed continued with him even to his martyrdom. *Take Mark, and bring him with thee.* This was John Mark, who, after having wavered a little at first, became a steady, zealous, and useful man. *For he is profitable to me for the ministry.* "For service"; that is, he would be very useful to the apostle, to minister to him in his present close confinement.

12. *Tychicus have I sent to Ephesus.* For this person see Acts xx. 4; Eph. vi. 21; Col. iv. 7. It is rather strange that the apostle should say, I have sent Tychicus to Ephesus, if Timothy was at Ephesus at this time; but it is probable that Tychicus had been sent to Ephesus some time before this, and therefore the apostle might say, though writing now to Ephesus, *Tychicus have I sent.*

13. *The cloke that I left at Troas.* By several translated "bag"; and it is most likely that it was something of this kind, in which he might carry his clothes, books, and traveling necessaries. What the *books* were we cannot tell; it is most likely they were his own writings. And as to the *parchments,* they were probably the Jewish Scriptures and a copy of the Septuagint. These he must have had at hand at all times.

14. *Alexander the coppersmith.* We are not to understand this of any tradesman, but of some rabbin; for it was not unusual for the Jews to apply the name of some trade as an epithet to their rabbins and literary men. He is in all probability the very same mentioned in Acts xix. 33, where see the note; and it is not unlikely that he may have been the same whom the apostle was obliged to excommunicate, 1 Tim. i. 20. *The Lord reward him.* But instead of *apodoe,* which has here the power of a solemn imprecation, *apodosei,* "He will reward," is the reading of the very best MSS., several of the versions, and some of the chief Greek fathers. This makes the sentence declaratory: "The Lord will reward him according to his works." This reading is most like the spirit and temper of this heavenly man.

15. *Of whom be thou ware also.* It seems that this rabbin travelled about from place to place for the purpose of opposing the gospel, the Jews putting him forward, as it is said, Acts xix. 33. *He hath greatly withstood our words.* Has been a constant opposer of the Christian doctrines.

16. *At my first answer.* "At my first apology"; this word properly signifies a "defense" or "vindication." This is the meaning of what we call the "apologies" of the primitive fathers; they were vindications or defenses of Christianity. It is generally allowed that when Paul had been taken this second time by the Romans he was examined immediately and required to account for his conduct; and that, so odious was Christianity through the tyranny of Nero, he could procure no person to plead for him. Nero, who had himself set fire to Rome, charged it on the Christians, and they were in consequence persecuted in the most cruel manner. He caused them to be wrapped up in pitched clothes, and then, chaining them to a stake, he ordered them to be set on fire to give light in the streets after night. *I pray God that it may not be laid to their charge.* How much more simple, elegant, and expressive are the apostle's own words: "Let it not be placed to their account!" Let them not have to reckon for it with the supreme Judge at the great day!

17. *The Lord stood with me.* When all human help failed, God, in a more remarkable manner, interposed; and thus the excellency plainly appeared to be of God, and not of man. *That by me the preaching might be fully known.* When called on to make his defense, he took occasion to preach the gospel, and to show that the great God of heaven and earth had designed to illuminate the Gentile world with the rays of His light and glory. This must have endeared him to some, while others might consider him an opposer of their gods and be the more incensed against him. *I was delivered out of the mouth of the lion.* I escaped the imminent danger at that time. Probably he was seized in a tumultuous manner and expected to be torn to pieces. The words "to be rescued from *the mouth* or jaws *of the lion*" are a proverbial form of speech for deliverance from the most imminent danger.

18. *And the Lord shall deliver me from every evil work.* None of the evil designs formed against me to make me unfaithful or unsteady, to cause me to save my life at the expense of faith and a good conscience, shall succeed; my life may go, but He will preserve me *unto his heavenly kingdom.*

19. *Salute Prisca and Aquila.* Several MSS., versions, and fathers have Priscilla instead of Prisca: they are probably the same as those mentioned in Acts xviii. 18, 26. *The household of Onesiphorus.* See chap. i. 16. Onesiphorus was probably dead at this time; his "family" still remained at Ephesus.

20. *Erastus abode at Corinth.* He was treasurer of that city, as we learn from Rom. xvi. 23. The apostle had sent him and Timothy on a mission to Macedonia, Acts xix. 22, whence it is probable he returned to Corinth and there became finally settled. *Trophimus have I left at Miletum sick.* Even the apostles could not work miracles when they pleased; that power was but rarely given, and that for very special purposes. Trophimus was an Ephesian. See Acts xx. 4. Miletus was a maritime town of Ionia, not far from Ephesus; but there was another Miletus, in Crete, which some learned men think to be intended here. It appears that Paul went from Macedonia to Corinth, where he left Erastus; from Corinth he proceeded to Troas, where he lodged with Carpus; from Troas he went to Ephesus, where he visited Timothy; from Ephesus he went to Miletus, where he left Trophimus sick; and having embarked at Miletus, he went by sea to Rome. It is most likely, therefore, that the Miletus of Ionia is the place intended.

21. *Come before winter.* (1) Because the apostle's time was short and uncertain. (2) Because sailing in those seas was very dangerous in winter. Whether Timothy saw the apostle before he was martyred is not known. *Eubulus.* This person is nowhere else mentioned in the New Testament. *Pudens.* Of this person we have traditions and legends, but nothing cer-

tain. The Catholics make him bishop of Rome. *Linus.* He also is made, by the same persons, bishop of Rome; but there is no sufficient ground for these pretensions. *Claudia.* Supposed to be the wife of Pudens. Some think she was a British lady converted by Paul, and that she was the first that brought the gospel to Britain. *All the brethren.* All the Christians, of whom there were many at Rome; though of Paul's companions in travel only Luke remained there.

22. *The Lord Jesus Christ be with thy spirit.* This is a prayer addressed to Christ by one of the most eminent of His apostles; another proof of the untruth of the assertion that prayer is never offered to Christ in the New Testament. He prays that Christ may be with his spirit, enlightening, strengthening, and confirming it to the end. *Grace be with you.* These words show that the Epistle was addressed to the whole church, and that it is not to be considered of a private nature.

The Epistle to
TITUS

It is strange that of a person who must have attained considerable eminence in the Christian Church, and one to whom a canonical Epistle has been written by the great apostle of the Gentiles, we should know so very little. That Titus was a frequent companion of Paul in his journeys we have evidence from his Epistles; and although this was the case, he is not once mentioned in the Book of the Acts of the Apostles!

That he was a Greek, and brought up in heathenism, we learn from Gal. ii. 3: "But neither Titus, who was with me, being a Greek, was compelled to be circumcised." As he was uncircumcised, he was neither a Jew nor a proselyte and probably was a mere heathen till he heard the gospel preached by Paul, by whose ministry he was converted to the Christian faith; chap. i. 4: "To Titus, mine own son ['my genuine son'], after the common faith"; which words sufficiently indicate that Paul alone had the honor of his conversion. That he was very highly and consequently deservedly esteemed by Paul is evident from the manner in which he mentions him in different places: "I had no rest in my spirit till I found Titus, my brother," 2 Cor. ii. 13. "Nevertheless God, that comforteth those who are cast down, comforted us by the coming of Titus; and not by his coming only, but by the consolation wherewith . . . joyed we for the joy of Titus, because his spirit was refreshed by you all. And his inward affection is more abundant toward you, whilst he remembereth . . . how with fear and trembling ye received him," 2 Cor. vii. 6-7, 13, 15. "But thanks be to God, which put the same earnest care into the heart of Titus for you. Whether any do inquire of Titus, he is my partner and fellowhelper concerning you," 2 Cor. viii. 16, 23. "Did Titus make a gain of you? walked we not in the same spirit? walked we not in the same steps?" 2 Cor. xii. 18.

Though Paul's preaching the gospel in Crete is not expressly mentioned anywhere, yet it may be plainly inferred from chap. i. 5: "For this cause left I thee in Crete, that thou shouldest set in order the things that are wanting, and ordain elders in every city." It is supposed that this was sometime in the year 62, after the apostle was released from his first imprisonment in Rome. But not being able to spend much time in that island, he left the care of the churches to Titus, and sailed into Judea in the beginning of 63, taking Timothy with him. Having spent some time in Jerusalem, he proceeded to Antioch, comforting and establishing the churches whithersoever they went. From Antioch he set out on his fifth and last apostolical journey, in which he and Timothy travelled through Syria and Cilicia, and came to Colossae in Phrygia early in the year 64. On this occasion it is supposed he wrote his Epistle to Titus, in which he desires him to meet him in Nicopolis, as he had intended to spend the winter there, Titus iii. 12. From Colossae he went with Timothy to Ephesus, where he left him to regulate and govern the church. From thence he passed into Macedonia, and probably visited Philippi and different churches in that province, according to his intention, Phil. ii. 24; and hence to Nicopolis, where he intended to spend the winter, and where he had desired Titus to meet him.

Whether Titus ever left Crete we know not; nor how, nor where, he died. Some traditions, on which little dependence can be placed, say he lived till he was ninety-four years of age, and died and was buried in Crete. He appears to have been a young man when entrusted with the care of the churches in this island. In such an extensive district an aged or infirm man would have been of little service.

Crete, where Titus was resident, to whom this Epistle was sent, is the largest island in the Mediterranean Sea. According to Strabo, it is 287 miles in length. Pliny states that its greatest breadth is 55 miles.

Many have observed the affinity that subsists between the First Epistle to Timothy and this to Titus. Both Epistles are directed to persons left by the writer to preside in their respective churches during his absence. Both Epistles are principally occupied in describing the qualifications of those who should be appointed to ecclesiastical offices, and the ingredients in this description are nearly the same in both Epistles. Timothy and Titus are both cautioned against the same prevailing corruptions; the phrases and expressions in both letters are nearly the same; and the writer accosts his two disciples with the same salutations, and passes on to the business of his Epistle with the same transition.

The phrase "It is a faithful saying" occurs thrice in the First Epistle to Timothy, once in the second, and once in that to Titus; and in no other part of Paul's writings. These three Epistles were probably written towards the close of his life, and are the only Epistles written after his first imprisonment at Rome.

The same observation belongs to another singularity of expression, viz., the epithet "sound," as applied to words or doctrine. It is thus used twice in the First Epistle to Timothy, twice in the second, and thrice in the Epistle to Titus; besides two cognate expressions, "sound in the faith" and "sound speech." And the word is not found in the same sense in any other part of the New Testament.

The phrase "God our Saviour" stands in the same predicament. It is repeated three times in the First Epistle to Timothy, and thrice in the Epistle to Titus; but does not occur in any other book of the New Testament, except once in the Epistle of Jude.

The most natural accounts which can be given of these resemblances is to suppose that the two Epistles were written nearly at the same time, and whilst the same ideas and phrases dwelt in the writer's mind.

CHAPTER 1

The apostle's statement of his character, his hope, and his function, 1-3. His address to Titus, and the end for which he left him in Crete, 4-5. The qualifications requisite in those who should be appointed elders and bishops in the Church of God, 6-9. Of false teachers, 10-11. The character of the Cretans, and how they were to be dealt with, 12-14. Of the pure, the impure, and false professors of religion, 15-16.

1. *Paul, a servant of God.* In several places of his other Epistles, Paul styles himself the "servant of Jesus Christ," but this is the only place where he calls himself the *servant of God. The faith of God's elect.* The Christians. *The acknowledging of the truth.* For the propagation of that truth, or system of doctrines, which is calculated to promote godliness, or a holy and useful life.

2. *In hope of eternal life.* In expectation of a state of being and well-being which should last through eternity, when time should be no more. *Which God, that cannot lie, promised.* We have often seen that the phrase "the foundation of the world" means the Jewish economy; and "before the foundation of the world," the times antecedent to the giving of the law. This is evidently the meaning here. See 2 Tim. i. 9-11.

3. *But hath in due times.* "In its own times." See 1 Tim. ii. 6; Gal. iv. 4; Eph. i. 10; ii. 7. God caused the gospel to be published in that time in which it could be published with the greatest effect. It is impossible that God should prematurely hasten or causelessly delay the accomplishment of any of His works. Jesus was manifested precisely at the time in which that manifestation could best promote the glory of God and the salvation of man. *Manifested his word.* "His doctrine"—the doctrine of eternal life, by the incarnation, passion, death, and resurrection of Jesus Christ. *Which is committed unto me.* That is, to preach it among the Gentiles. *According to the commandment of God our Saviour.* This evidently refers to the commission which he had received from Christ. See Acts ix. 15; xxvi. 16, etc. This is the commandment, and according to it he became the apostle of the Gentiles. *God our*

Saviour. As the commission was given by Jesus Christ alone, the person whom he terms here *God our Saviour* must be Jesus Christ only; and this is another proof that Paul believed Jesus Christ to be God. This "eternal life" God had "promised" in a comparatively obscure way before the foundation of the world, the Jewish dispensation; but now under the gospel He had "made it manifest"—produced it with all its brightness, illustrations, and proofs.

4. *To Titus, mine own son.* Him whom I have been the instrument of converting to the Christian faith and in whom, in this respect, I have the same right as any man can have in his own begotten son.

5. *For this cause left I thee in Crete.* That Paul had been in Crete, though nowhere else intimated, is clear from this passage. That he could not have made such an important visit and evangelized an island of the first consequence without its being mentioned by his historian Luke, had it happened during the period embraced in the Acts of the Apostles, must be evident. That the journey therefore must have been performed after the time in which Luke ends his history, that is, after Paul's first imprisonment at Rome, seems almost certain. *Set in order the things that are wanting.* It appears from this that the apostle did not spend much time in Crete, and that he was obliged to leave it before he had got the church properly organized. The supplying of this defect, he tells Titus, he had confided to him as one whose spiritual views coincided entirely with his own. *Ordain elders in every city.* That thou mightest "appoint" elders—persons well-instructed in divine things, who should be able to instruct others, and observe and enforce the discipline of the church. It appears that those who are called *elders* in this place are the same as those termed "bishops" in v. 7. We have many proofs that bishops and elders were of the same order in the apostolic Church, though afterwards they became distinct. *In every city.* This seems to intimate that the

apostle had gone over the whole of the "hundred cities" for which this island was celebrated. Indeed it is not likely that he would leave one in which he had not preached Christ crucified.

6. *If any be blameless.* See the notes on 1 Tim. iii. 2. *Having faithful children.* Whose family is converted to God. It would have been absurd to employ a man to govern the church whose children were not in subjection to himself; for it is an apostolic maxim that he who cannot rule his own house cannot rule the church of God, 1 Tim. iii. 5.

7. *Not selfwilled.* Not one who is determined to have his own way in everything, setting up his own judgment to that of all others. *Not soon angry.* Not a choleric man; one who is irritable, who is apt to be inflamed on every opposition; one who has not proper command over his own temper.

8. *A lover of hospitality.* "A lover of strangers." See the note on 1 Tim. iii. 2. *A lover of good men.* "A lover of goodness" or of good things in general. *Sober.* Prudent in all his conduct. Just in all his dealings. Holy in his heart. *Temperate*—self-denying and abstemious in his food and raiment; not too nice on points of honor, nor magisterially rigid in the exercise of his ecclesiastical functions.

9. *Holding fast the faithful word.* Conscientiously retaining, and zealously maintaining, the true Christian doctrine, "according to the instructions," or according to the institutions, form of sound doctrine, or confession of faith, which I have delivered to you. *That he may be able by sound doctrine.* If the doctrine be not sound, vain is the profession of it, and vain its influence. *To exhort* them to hold the faith, that they may persevere. *And to convince.* Refute the objections, confound the sophistry, and convert the gainsayers; and thus defend the truth.

10. *There are many unruly.* Persons who will not receive the sound doctrine nor come under wholesome discipline. *Vain talkers.* Empty boasters of knowledge, rights, and particular privileges; all noise, empty parade, and no work. *Deceivers* of the souls of men by their specious pretensions. *They of the circumcision.* The Judaizing teachers, who maintained the necessity of circumcision and of observing the rites and ceremonies of the Mosaic law in order to the perfecting of the gospel.

11. *Whose mouths must be stopped.* Unmask them at once; exhibit them to the people; make manifest their ignorance and hypocrisy, and let them be confounded before the people whom they are endeavoring to seduce. *Subvert whole houses.* Turn whole Christian families from the faith.

12. *One of themselves, even a prophet of their own.* This was Epimenides, who was born at Gnossus, in Crete. He died about 538 years before the Christian era. When Paul calls him a *prophet of their own,* he only intimates that he was, by the Cretans, reputed a prophet. And according to Plutarch, the Cretans paid him divine honors after his death. *The Cretians are alway liars.* The words quoted here by the apostle are, according to Jerome, Socrates, Nicephorus, and others, taken from a work of Epimenides, now no longer extant, entitled *Concerning Oracles.* The words form a hex-

ameter verse: "The Cretans are always liars; destructive wild beasts; sluggish gluttons." That the Cretans were reputed to be egregious liars several of the ancients declare, insomuch that "to act like a Cretan" signifies "to lie." The other Greeks reputed them liars because they said that among them was the sepulchre of Jupiter, who was the highest object of the Greek and Roman worship. *Evil beasts.* Ferocious and destructive in their manners. *Slow bellies.* Addicted to voluptuousness, idleness, and gluttony; sluggish or hoggish men.

13. *This witness is true.* What Epimenides said of them nearly six hundred years before continued still to be true. *Rebuke them sharply.* "Cuttingly, severely"; show no indulgence to persons guilty of such crimes. *That they may be sound in the faith.* That they may receive the incorrupt doctrine, and illustrate it by a holy and useful life.

14. *Not giving heed to Jewish fables.* See on 1 Tim. i. 4 and iv. 7. *Commandments of men.* The injunctions of the scribes and Pharisees which they added to the law of God. *That turn from the truth.* For such persons made the Word of God of none effect by their traditions. Sometimes the verb signifies to be "averse from, slight, or despise." So here the persons in question despised the truth and taught others to do the same.

15. *Unto the pure all things are pure.* This appears to have been spoken in reference to the Jewish distinctions of clean and unclean meats. To the genuine Christian every kind of meat proper for human nourishment is pure, is lawful and may be used without scruple. This our Lord had long before decided. See on Luke xi. 39-41. *But unto them that are defiled,* in their consciences, and *unbelieving, "unfaithful," is nothing pure.* Their *mind* is contaminated with impure and unholy images and ideas, and their *conscience is defiled* with the guilt of sins already committed against God.

16. *They profess that they know God.* He still speaks concerning the unbelieving Jews, the seducing teachers, and those who had been seduced by their bad doctrine. None were so full of pretensions to the knowledge of the true God as the Jews. *But in works they deny him.* Their profession and practice were at continual variance. Full of a pretended faith, while utterly destitute of those *works* by which a genuine faith is accredited and proved. *Being abominable.* This word sometimes refers to unnatural lusts. *And disobedient.* "Unpersuadable, unbelieving." *Unto every good work reprobate.* "Adulterate"; like a bad coin, deficient in both the weight and the goodness of the metal, and without the proper sterling stamp.

CHAPTER 2

Sundry directions to aged men, 1-2. To aged women, 3. To young women, 4-5. To young men, 6. Directions to Titus relative to his own conduct, 7-8. Directions to servants, 9-10. What the gospel of the grace of God teaches all men, 11-12. The glorious prospect held out by it: salvation from all sin, and final glory, 13-15.

1. *But speak thou the things.* This is a conclusion drawn from the preceding chapter. The Judaizing teachers not only taught a false doctrine, but they led an unholy life. Titus was to act directly opposite; he must teach a sacred doctrine and the things which become it; he

must proclaim the truth and illustrate that truth. The people must not only be well-instructed, but they must be holy in their lives. Principle and practice must go hand in hand.

2. *That the aged men be sober.* It is very likely that the word *aged* is to be taken here in its literal sense; that it refers to advanced years and not to any office in the Church; the whole context seems to require this sense.

3. *The aged women likewise.* I believe elderly women are meant and not deaconesses. *That they be in behaviour.* That they be in their dress, gait, and general deportment such as their holy calling requires; that they be not like the world but like the Church, decent throughout, and adorned with holiness within. *Not false accusers.* "Not devils"; we have had the same expression applied in the same way, 1 Tim. iii. 11. *Not given to much wine.* Not enslaved by much wine, not habitual drunkards or tipplers; habit is a species of slavery. Both among the Greeks and Romans old women were generally reputed to be fond of much wine.

4. *That they may teach the young women to be sober.* That it was natural for the young to imitate the old will be readily allowed; it was therefore necessary that the old should be an example of godly living to the young. Jerome, taking it for granted that drunkenness and impurity are closely connected, asks this serious question: "How can an elderly woman teach young women chastity when, if the young woman should imitate the drunkenness of the matron, it would be impossible for her to be chaste?" *To love their husbands.* The duties recommended in this and the following verses are so plain as to need no comment, and so absolutely necessary to the character of a wife that no one deserves the same who does not live in the practice of them.

5. *Keepers at home.* A woman who spends much time in visiting must neglect her family. Instead of "keepers of the house," or *keepers at home,* some MSS. have "workers at home"; not only staying in the house and keeping the house, but working in the house. *That the word of God be not blasphemed.* The enemies of the gospel are quick-eyed to spy out imperfections in its professors; and if they find women professing Christianity living an irregular life, they will not fail to decry the Christian doctrine on this account.

6. *Young men likewise exhort to be sober minded.* Reformation should begin with the old; they have the authority, and they should give the example. The young of both sexes must also give an account of themselves to God; sober-mindedness in young men is a rare qualification.

7. *In all things shewing thyself a pattern.* As the apostle had given directions relative to the conduct of old men, v. 2; of old women, v. 3; of young women, v. 4; and of young men, v. 6, the words which we translate *in all things* should be rather considered in reference to the above persons and the behavior required in them: "showing thyself a pattern of good works to all these persons"—being in sobriety, gravity, temperance what thou requirest others to be. *In doctrine shewing uncorruptness.* Mixing nothing with the truth; taking nothing from it;

adding nothing to it; and exhibiting it in all its connection, energy, and fullness.

8. *Sound speech. Sound* or "healing doctrine." Human nature is in a state of disease, and the doctrine of the gospel is calculated to remove the disease and restore all to perfect health and soundness. *He that is of the contrary part.* Whether this may refer to the Judaizing teachers in general or to someone who might, by his false doctrine, have been disturbing the peace of the churches in Crete, we cannot tell. *Having no evil thing to say of you.* Against a person who is sound in his doctrine and holy in his life, no evil can be justly alleged. He who reports evil of such a person must be confounded when brought to the test. Instead of *of you,* "of us" is the reading of numerous MSS. and several of the primitive fathers. This reading makes a better sense and is undoubtedly genuine.

9. *Exhort servants to be obedient.* The apostle refers to those who were "slaves" and the property of their masters; even these are exhorted to be obedient "to their own despots." *Please them well in all things.* They were to endeavor to do this in all things, though they could not hope to succeed in everything. *Not answering again.* "Not contradicting or gainsaying." This is no part of a servant's duty; a servant is hired to do his master's work, and this his master has a right to appoint.

10. *Not purloining.* Neither "giving away, privately selling," nor in any way wasting the master's goods. The word signifies not only stealing but embezzling another's property, keeping back a part of the price of any commodity sold on the master's account. In Acts v. 2 we translate it "to keep back part of the price," the crime of which Ananias and Sapphira were guilty. It has been remarked that among the heathens this species of fraud was very frequent.

11. *The grace of God that bringeth salvation hath appeared to all men.* Literally translated, the words stand thus: "For the grace of God, that which saves, hath shone forth upon all men." Or, as it is expressed in the margin of our Authorized Version: "The grace of God, that bringeth salvation to all men, hath appeared." As God's *grace* signifies "God's favor," any benefit received from Him may be termed God's *grace.* Now it cannot be said, except in a very refined and spiritual sense, that this gospel had then *appeared to all men;* but it may be well said that "it bringeth salvation to all men"; this is its design. There is a beauty and energy in the word "hath shined out" that is rarely noted; it seems to be a metaphor taken from the sun. As by his rising in the east and "shining out" he enlightens successively the whole world, so the Lord Jesus, who is called "the Sun of righteousness," Mal. iv. 2, arises on the whole human race "with healing in his wings." And as the light and heat of the sun are denied to no nation nor individual, so the grace of the Lord Jesus also shines out upon all; and God designs that all mankind shall be as equally benefited by it in reference to their souls as they are in respect to their bodies by the sun that shines in the firmament of heaven.

12. *Teaching us that, denying.* Instructing us as children are instructed. *Denying ungodliness.* All things contrary to God. *Worldly lusts.* Such

desires, affections, and appetites as men are governed by who have their portion in this life and live without God in the world. *We should live soberly.* Having every temper, appetite, and desire under the government of reason, and reason itself under the government of the Spirit of God. *Righteously.* Rendering to every man his due; injuring no person in his body, mind, reputation, or property; doing unto all as we would they should do to us. *And godly.* Just the reverse of what is implied in "ungodliness." *In this present world.* Not supposing that anything will be purified in the world to come that is not cleansed in this. The three words above evidently include our duty to God, to our neighbor, and to ourselves. (1) We are to live *soberly* in respect to ourselves, (2) *righteously* in respect to our neighbor, and (3) *godly,* or piously, in respect to our Maker.

13. *Looking for that blessed hope.* Expecting the grand object of our hope, eternal life. This is what the gospel teaches us to expect, and what the grace of God prepares the human heart for. This is called a *blessed* hope; those who have it are "happy" in the sure prospect of that glory which shall be revealed. *The glorious appearing.* This clause, literally translated, is as follows: "And the appearing of the glory of the great God, even our Saviour Jesus Christ." Some think that the *blessed hope* and *glorious appearing* mean the same thing, but I do not think so. The *blessed hope* refers simply to eternal glorification in general; *the glorious appearing,* to the resurrection of the body. For when Christ appears He will change this vile body, and make it "like unto his glorious body, according to the working whereby he is able even to subdue all things unto himself." See Phil. iii. 20-21.

14. *Who gave himself for us.* Who gave His own life as a "ransom price" to redeem ours. This is evidently what is meant, as the (Greek) words imply. Jesus gave His life for the world, and thus has purchased men unto himself; and having purchased the slaves from their thraldom, He is represented as stripping them of their sordid vestments, cleansing and purifying them unto himself, that they may become His own servants. Thus redeemed, they now become His willing servants and are *zealous of good works*—affectionately attached to that noble employment which is assigned to them by that Master whom it is an inexpressible honor to serve.

15. *These things speak.* That is, "teach." *And exhort.* Repeat them again and again, and urge them on their attention and consciences. *And rebuke.* Demonstrate the importance, utility, and necessity of them; and show them that God requires their obedience. *With all authority.* With all that authority with which your office invests you, and which you have received from God. *Let no man despise thee.* That is, act so that no person shall have any cause to despise you, either for your work or the manner and spirit in which you perform it.

CHAPTER 3

The necessity of obedience to the civil powers, and of meek and gentle deportment towards all men, is to be diligently enforced, 1-2. The wretched state of man previously to the advent of Christ, 3. The wonderful change which the grace of God makes, and the means

which it uses to bring men to glory, 4-7. The necessity of a holy life, and of avoiding things which produce strifes and contentions and are unprofitable and vain, 8-9. How to deal with those who are heretics, 10-11. Paul directs Titus to meet him at Nicopolis, and to bring Zenas and Apollos with him, 12-13. Concluding directions and salutations, 14-15.

1. *Put them in mind to be subject to principalities.* By *principalities* we are to understand the Roman emperors, or the supreme civil powers in any place. By *powers* we are to understand the deputies of the emperors, such as proconsuls and all such as are in authority under the supreme civil powers in any place. This doctrine of obedience to the civil powers was highly necessary for the Cretans, who were reputed a people exceedingly jealous of their civil privileges, and ready to run into a state of insurrection when they suspected any attempt on the part of their rulers to infringe their liberties.

2. *To speak evil of no man.* To "blaspheme" no person, to reproach none, to speak nothing to any man's injury.

3. *For we ourselves.* All of us, whether Jews or Gentiles, were before our conversion to Christ foolish, disobedient, and deceived. There is no doubt that the apostle felt he could include himself in the above list previously to his conversion. The manner in which he persecuted the Christians, to whose charge he could not lay one moral evil, is sufficient proof that, though he walked according to the letter of the law, as to its ordinances and ceremonies, blameless, yet his heart was in a state of great estrangement from God, from justice, holiness, mercy, and compassion. *Foolish.* "Without understanding" —ignorant of God, His nature, His providence, and His grace. *Disobedient.* "Unpersuaded, unbelieving, obstinate, and disobedient." *Deceived.* "Erring"—wandering from the right way in consequence of our ignorance, not knowing the right way; and in consequence of our unbelief and obstinacy, not choosing to know it. It is a true saying, "There are none so blind as those who will not see." Such persons are proof against conviction; they will not be convinced by either God or man. *Serving divers lusts and pleasures.* Not served or gratified by our lusts and pleasures, but living, as their "slaves"; a life of misery and wretchedness. *Divers lusts.* Strong and irregular appetites of every kind. *Pleasures*—"Sensual pleasures." Persons intent only on the gratification of sense, living like the brutes, having no rational or spiritual object worthy the pursuit of an immortal being. *Living in malice and envy.* "Spending our lives in wickedness and envy"—not bearing to see the prosperity of others because we feel ourselves continually wretched. *Hateful.* "Abominable"; "hateful as hell." The word comes from Styx, the infernal river by which the gods were wont to swear; and he who (according to the mythology of the heathens) violated this oath was expelled from the assembly of the gods and was deprived of his nectar and ambrosia for a year; hence the river was hateful to them beyond all things.

4. *But after that the kindness.* The "essential goodness" of the divine nature; that which is the spring whence all kindness, mercy, and beneficence proceed. *Love . . . toward man*— "Philanthropy." Philanthropy is a character which God gives here to himself; while human nature exists, this must be a character of the

divine nature. Where love is it will be active and will show itself. So the philanthropy of God *appeared;* it "shone out" in the incarnation of Jesus Christ and in His giving His life for the life of the world.

5. *Not by works of righteousness.* Those who were foolish, disobedient, and deceived, serving divers lusts and pleasures, could not possibly have *works of righteousness* to plead; therefore, if saved at all, they must be saved by *mercy. By the washing of regeneration.* Undoubtedly the apostle here means baptism, the rite by which persons were admitted into the Church, and the visible sign of the cleansing, purifying influences of the Holy Spirit, which the apostle immediately subjoins. Baptism is only a sign, and therefore should never be separated from the thing signified; but it is a rite commanded by God himself, and therefore the thing signified should never be expected without it. By the *renewing of the Holy Ghost* we are to understand, not only the profession of being bound to live a new life, but the grace that renews the heart and enables us thus to live; so the renewing influences are here intended. Baptism changes nothing; the grace signified by it cleanses and purifies.

6. *Which he shed on us abundantly.* "Which He poured out on us," as the water was poured out on them in baptism, to which there is here a manifest allusion. But as this was sometimes only sprinkled on the person, the heavenly gift was "poured out," not in drops, but "richly," in "great abundance." *Through Jesus Christ.* Baptism is nothing in itself, and there had been no outpouring of the Holy Spirit had there been no saving and atoning Christ. Through Him alone all good comes to the souls of men.

7. *That being justified by his grace.* Being freed from sin; for the term "justification" is to be taken here as implying the whole work of the grace of Christ on the heart in order to its preparation for eternal glory. *Should be made heirs.* The gospel not only gave them the hope of an endless state of glory for their souls, but also of the resurrection and final glorification of their bodies, and they who were children of God were to be made *heirs* of His glory.

8. *This is a faithful saying.* "This is the true doctrine," the doctrine that cannot fail. *And these things I will.* "And I will, or desire, you to maintain earnestly what concerns these points." The things to which the apostle refers are those of which he had just been writing. *These things are good and profitable.* They are good in themselves, and calculated to promote the well-being of men.

9. *Avoid foolish questions, and genealogies.* In these the Jews particularly delighted; they abounded in the most frivolous questions; and, as they had little piety themselves, they were solicitous to show that they had descended from godly ancestors. *Contentions, and strivings about the law.* Of legal contentions and different and conflicting decisions about the meaning of particular rites and ceremonies, the Talmud is full.

10. *A man that is an heretick.* Generally defined, one that is obstinately attached to an opinion contrary to the peace and comfort of society, and will submit to neither Scripture nor reason. Here it means a person who maintains Judaism in opposition to Christianity, or who insists on the necessity of circumcision in order to be saved. This is obviously the meaning of the word *heretick* in the only place in which it occurs in the sacred writings. *After the first and second admonition reject.* Labor to convince him of his error; but if he will not receive instruction, if he have shut his heart against conviction, then—"shun him."

11. *Is subverted.* "Is turned out of the way" in which he may be saved, and consequently *sinneth*—enters into that way that leads to destruction. *Being condemned of himself.* This refers to the Judaizing teacher who maintained his party and opinions for filthy lucre's sake. He was conscious of his own insincerity; and that he proclaimed not his system from a conscientious love of truth, but from a desire to get his livelihood.

12. *When I shall send Artemas unto thee, or Tychicus.* These were either deacons or presbyters which the apostle intended to send to Crete to supply the place of Titus. Who Artemas was we know not; he is not mentioned in any other place in the New Testament. Tychicus was a native of Asia, as we learn from Acts xx. 4. *For I have determined there to winter.* Hence the apostle was at liberty, seeing his spending the winter at this or at any other practicable place depended on his own determination. It was probably now pretty late in the autumn, and the apostle was now drawing near to Nicopolis; for he certainly was not yet arrived, else he would not have said, *I have determined there to winter.*

13. *Bring Zenas the lawyer.* This person is mentioned only in this place; whether he was a Jewish, Roman, or Greek lawyer we cannot tell. *And Apollos.* Of this person we have some valuable particulars in Acts xviii. 24; 1 Cor. i. 12; iii. 5-6; and iv. 6. Either Paul had left these at Crete when he visited that island or he had heard that in their evangelical itinerancy they were about to pass through it. *On their journey diligently.* Afford them the means to defray their expenses. The churches through which these evangelists passed bore their expenses from one to the other. See 3 John, v. 6.

14. *And let ours also learn to maintain good works.* There is something very remarkable in this expression. The words which we translate *to maintain good works* occur also in v. 8: and some think they mean "to provide for our own, and the necessities of others, by working at some honest occupation"; and that this was necessary to be taught to the Cretans, *let ours also learn,* who were naturally and practically "idle gluttons." *For necessary uses.* That they may be able at all times to help the Church of God, and those that are in want. *That they be not unfruitful.* As they must be if they indulge themselves in their idle, slothful disposition.

15. *All that are with me.* He means his companions in the ministry. *Salute thee.* Wish thee well, and desire to be affectionately remembered to thee. *Greet them that love us in the faith.* All that love us for Christ's sake, and all that are genuine Christians.

The Epistle to
PHILEMON

It may be thought strange that a short letter, written entirely on a private subject, without reference to the proof or defense of any doctrine of the gospel, should by the general consent of the Church of God from the highest Christian antiquity have been received into the sacred canon, not only as a genuine production of Paul, but as a piece designed by the Holy Spirit for the edification of the Church. However, such is the fact; and we may add that this very piece was held so sacred that even the ancient heretics did not attempt to impugn its authenticity or corrupt its matter, while making dangerously free with the four Gospels and all the other Epistles!

Philemon, the person to whom it is addressed, was undoubtedly, at the time in which this Epistle was sent, an inhabitant of Colossae, and was probably a Colossian by birth, though some suppose that he was of Ephesus. It is evident, from v. 19 of this Epistle, that he was converted to the Christian faith by Paul; this is agreed on all hands. But as some suppose that the apostle had not visited Colossae previously to the writing of this Epistle, they think it probable that he might have met with him at Ephesus or in some other part of Asia Minor, where he formed an acquaintance with him and became the means of his conversion.

That Philemon was a person of some consideration in his own city and in the church in that place is very evident from this Epistle. He had a church in his house, v. 2, and was so opulent as to be extensive in works of charity, and in entertaining those Christians who from different quarters had occasion to visit Colossae. See vv. 5-7.

The occasion of writing this letter was the following: Onesimus, a slave, had on some pretense or other run away from his master, Philemon, and had come to Rome, where Paul was at that time in prison, though not in close confinement; for he dwelt in his own hired house, in which he assiduously preached the gospel, being guarded by only one soldier. See Acts xxviii. 16, 23.

It appears that Onesimus sought out Paul, whose public preaching to both Jews and Gentiles had rendered him famous in the city. Being thus brought back to God, he became affectionately attached to his spiritual father, and served him zealously as his son in the gospel. Onesimus, being thus brought to the acknowledgment of the truth which is according to godliness, gave the apostle a full account of his elopement from his master, and no doubt intimated his wish to return and repair the breach which he had made. Though he was now both dear and necessary to Paul, yet as justice required that reparation should be made, he resolved to send him back; and to remove all suspicion from the mind of Philemon, and to reconcile him to his once unfaithful servant, he wrote the following letter.

It is generally thought that Onesimus had robbed his master; but there is certainly nothing in the Epistle from which this can be legitimately inferred. The words, "If he hath wronged thee, or oweth thee ought, put that on mine account," v. 18, certainly do not prove it. They only state a possible case, that he might have wronged his master or have been under some pecuniary obligation to him; and the apostle, by appearing to assume this, greatly strengthened his own argument, and met the last objection which Philemon could be supposed capable of making. There is neither justice nor piety in making things worse than they appear to be, or in drawing the most unfavorable conclusions from premises which, without constraint, will afford others more consonant to the spirit of charity.

That this Epistle was written about the same time as those to the Philippians and Colossians is proved by several coincidences. It will not be forgotten that Onesimus, the bearer of this Epistle, was one of the bearers of that sent to the Colossians, Col. iv. 9; that when the apostle wrote that, he was in bonds, Col. iv. 3, 18, which was his case also when he wrote this (see vv. 1, 10, 13, 23); from which, and various other circumstances, we may conclude that they were written about the same time.

Paul's salutation to Philemon, and the church at his house, 1-3. He extols his faith, love, and Christian charity, 4-7. Entreats forgiveness for his servant Onesimus, 8-14. Urges motives to induce Philemon to forgive him, 15-17. Promises to repair any wrong he had done to his master, 18-19. Expresses his confidence that Philemon will comply with his request, 20-21. Directs Philemon to prepare him a lodging, 22. Salutations and apostolical benediction, 23-25.

1. *Paul, a prisoner of Jesus Christ.* It has already been noted, in the preface, that Paul was a prisoner at Rome when he wrote this Epistle and those to the Colossians and Philippians. But some think that the term *prisoner* does not sufficiently point out the apostle's state, and that the original word should be translated "bound with a chain." This is certainly its meaning; and it shows us in some measure his circumstances—one arm was bound with a chain to the arm of the soldier to whose custody he had been delivered. *Unto Philemon our dearly beloved.* There is a peculiarity in

the use of proper names in this Epistle which is not found in any other part of Paul's writings. The names to which we refer are Philemon, Apphia, Archippus, and Onesimus. "Affectionate" or "beloved"; this led the apostle to say: *Unto Philemon our dearly beloved.*

2. *Apphia.* Appha is the affectionate address of a brother or sister; or the diminutive of a brother and sister, used to express kindness and affection. *Archippus.* The "ruler" or "master of the horse." Heroes of old were, among both the Greeks and the Trojans, celebrated for their skill in managing and taming the horse and employing him in war; this frequently occurs in Homer. The import of the name of Archippus might suggest this idea to the apostle's mind, and lead him to say: *Archippus our fellowsoldier. Onesimus.* "Useful" or "profitable." The import of this name led the apostle to play upon the word thus: "I beseech thee for my son Onesimus . . . which in time past was to thee unprofitable, but now profitable to thee and to me." *To the church in thy house.* The congregation of Christians frequently assembling in Philemon's house; for at this time the Christians had neither temples, churches, nor chapels. It is very probable that Apphia was the wife of Philemon; and Archippus, their son, the pastor of the church at Philemon's house.

4. *I thank my God.* For all the good He has bestowed upon you, *making mention of thee always in my prayers,* that you may hold fast all that you have, and get all that you need further.

6. *That the communication of thy faith.* The words the "fellowship" or *communication of thy faith* may be understood as referring to the work of love towards the saints—the poor Christians—which his faith in Christ enabled him to perform, faith being taken here for its effects. Indeed the word *koinonia* itself is not unfrequently used to denote "liberality, almsgiving"; and this is very properly remarked by Theophylact here: "He terms almsgiving the communication of faith, because it is the fruit of much faith." Instead of *in you,* "in us" is the reading of all the best MSS., as well as of several versions and fathers.

7. *For we have great joy.* This verse does not read harmoniously. The Greek authorizes the following arrangement: "For we have great joy and consolation in your love, O brother, because the bowels of the saints are refreshed by you." The apostle speaks here of the works of charity in which Philemon abounded towards poor Christians.

8. *Wherefore, though I might be much bold.* It would be better to read: "Wherefore, although I have much authority through Christ to command you to do what is proper, yet, on account of my love to you, I entreat you." There is certainly something very melting and persuasive in this and every part of the Epistle. Yet in my opinion the character of Paul prevails in it throughout. The warm, affectionate, authoritative teacher is interceding with an absent friend for a beloved convert. He urges his suit with an earnestness befitting, perhaps, not so much the occasion as the ardor and sensibility of his own mind. Here also, as everywhere, he shows himself conscious of the weight and dignity of his mission. Nor does he

suffer Philemon, for a moment, to forget it: *I might be much bold in Christ to enjoin thee that which is convenient.* He is careful also to recall, though obliquely, to Philemon's memory the sacred obligation under which he had laid him by bringing him to the knowledge of Christ: "I do not say to thee how thou owest unto me even thine own self besides." Without laying aside, therefore, the apostolic character, our author softens the imperative style of his address by mixing with it every sentiment and consideration that could move the heart of the correspondent. Aged, and in prison, he is content to supplicate and entreat. Onesimus was rendered dear to him by his conversation and his services; the child of his affliction, and ministering unto him "in the bonds of the gospel." This ought to recommend him, whatever had been his fault, to Philemon's forgiveness: "Receive him as myself," as my own bowels. Everything, however, should be voluntary. Paul was determined that Philemon's compliance should flow from his own bounty: "Without thy mind would I do nothing; that thy benefit should not be as it were of necessity, but willingly"; trusting, nevertheless, to his gratitude and attachment for the performance of all that he requested, and for more: "Having confidence in thy obedience I wrote unto thee, knowing that thou wilt also do more than I say."

9. *Paul the aged.* If we allow Paul to have been about twenty-five years of age at the utmost, in the year 31, when he was assisting at the martyrdom of Stephen, Acts vii. 58; as this Epistle was written about A.D. 62, he could not have been at this time more than about fifty-six years old. This could not constitute him an aged man in our sense of the term; yet when the whole length of his life is taken in, being martyred about four years after this, he may not improperly be considered an aged or elderly man, though it is generally allowed that his martyrdom took place in A.D. 66. But the word signifies not only an "old man," but also an "ambassador," because old or elderly men were chosen to fulfill such an office because of their experience and solidity; hence some have thought that we should translate here, "Paul the ambassador." This would agree very well with the scope and even the design of the place.

10. *I beseech thee for my son Onesimus.* It is evident from this that Onesimus was converted by Paul while he was a prisoner at Rome, and perhaps not long before he wrote this Epistle.

11. *Was to thee unprofitable.* Alluding to the meaning of Onesimus' name, as has been already noted, though the apostle uses a different Greek word to express the same idea.

12. *Whom I have sent again.* The Christian religion never cancels any civil relations; a slave, on being converted and becoming a free man of Christ, has no right to claim on that ground emancipation from the service of his master. Justice therefore required Paul to send Onesimus back to his master, and conscience obliged Onesimus to agree in the propriety of the measure; but love to the servant induced the apostle to write this conciliating letter to the master.

13. *That in thy stead he might have ministered unto me.* As Philemon was one of

Paul's converts, he thereby became his spiritual father and had a right to his services when in need. This was a strong argument, to induce Philemon not only to forgive his servant, but to send him back to the apostle, that he might minister to him in his master's stead.

14. *That thy benefit should not be as it were of necessity.* If the apostle had kept Onesimus in his service and written to Philemon to forgive him and permit him to stay, to this it is probable he would have agreed. But the benefit thus conceded might have lost much of its real worth by the consideration that, had he been at Colossae, Philemon would not have sent him to Rome; but, being there and in the apostle's service, he could not with propriety order him home. Thus the benefit to the apostle would have appeared to have been of necessity. The apostle therefore, by sending him back again, gave Philemon the opportunity to do all as if self-moved to it. This is a very delicate touch.

15. *He therefore departed for a season.* This is another most delicate stroke. He departed your slave, your unfaithful slave; he departed "for a short time." But so has the mercy of God operated in his behalf, and the providence of God in thine, that he now returns, not an unfaithful slave, in whom you could repose no confidence, but as a *brother,* a beloved brother in the Lord, to be in the same heavenly family with you forever.

16. *Not now as a servant.* Do not receive him merely as your slave, nor treat him according to that condition; but as *a brother*—as a genuine Christian, and particularly dear to me. *Both in the flesh and in the Lord.* There is no reason to believe that Onesimus was of the kindred of Philemon; and we must take the term *flesh* here as referring to the right which Philemon had in him. He was a part of his property and of his family; as a slave, this was his condition. But he now stood in a twofold relation to Philemon: (1) According to the *flesh,* as above explained, he was one of his family. (2) *In the Lord,* he was now also a member of the heavenly family, and of the church at Philemon's house.

17. *If thou count me therefore a partner.* If you do consider me as a friend, if I still have the place of a friend in your affection, *receive him as myself;* for, as I love him as my own soul, in receiving him you receive me.

18. *If he hath wronged thee, or oweth thee ought.* Had the apostle been assured that Onesimus had robbed his master, he certainly would not have spoken in this hypothetical way. He only puts a possible case: If he have wronged you, or owes you anything, place all to my account; I will discharge all he owes you.

19. *I Paul have written it with mine own hand.* It is likely that the whole of the letter was written by Paul himself, which was not his usual custom. See on 2 Thess. iii. 17. But by thus speaking he bound Phileomon to do what he requested, as an act of common civility, if

he could not feel a higher motive from what he had already urged. *Albeit I do not say to thee how thou owest unto me.* I ask you to do this thing to oblige me, though I will not say how much you owe me; *even thine own self,* as having been the means of your conversion.

20. *Yea, brother.* It is even so that you are thus indebted to me. *Let me have joy of thee,* in forgiving Onesimus and receiving him into your favor. In the words which we should translate, "Let me have profit of thee," there is an evident play on the name of Onesimus. See on vv. 2 and 11. *Refresh my bowels.* Gratify the earnest longing of my soul in this. I ask neither your money nor goods; I ask what will enrich, not impoverish, you to give.

21. *Having confidence in thy obedience.* I know that it will please you thus to oblige your friend; and I know that you will do more than I request, because you feel the affection of a son to your spiritual father. Some think that the apostle hints to Philemon that he should manumit Onesimus.

22. *But withal prepare me also a lodging.* Does not the apostle mention this as conferring an obligation on Philemon? I will begin to repay you by taking up my abode at your house as soon as I shall be freed from prison. But some think he wished Philemon to hire him a house, that he might have a lodging of his own when he returned to Colossae. *For I trust that through your prayers.* It is very likely that this Epistle was written a short time before the liberation of the apostle from his first imprisonment at Rome (see Acts xxviii. 30 and Phil. ii. 24), and that he had that liberation now in full prospect.

23. *Epaphras, my fellowprisoner.* Epaphras was a Colossian, as we learn from Col. iv. 12: "Epaphras, who is one of you." But there is no account there of his being in prison, though the not mentioning of it does not necessarily imply that he was not. Some time or other he had suffered imprisonment for the truth of the gospel, and on that account Paul might, in a general way, call him his fellow prisoner.

24. *Marcus, Aristarchus.* These were all acquaintances of Philemon, and probably Colossians, and may be all considered as joining here with Paul in his request for Onesimus. *Aristarchus* was probably the same with him mentioned in Acts xix. 29; xx. 4; xxvii. 2. See Col. iv. 10. *Demas.* Is supposed to be the same who continued in his attachment to Paul till his last imprisonment at Rome; after which he left him for what is supposed to have been the love of the world, 2 Tim. iv. 10. *Lucas.* Is supposed to be Luke the Evangelist, and author of the Acts of the Apostles.

25. *The grace of our Lord Jesus Christ be with your spirit.* By using the plural *your* the apostle in effect directs or addresses the Epistle, not only to Philemon, but to all the church at his house. *Amen.* Is wanting as usual in the best MSS.

The Epistle to the

HEBREWS

JESUS OF NAZARETH IS THE TRUE GOD

In order to convince the Jews of the truth of this proposition, the apostle uses but three arguments: (1) Christ is superior to the *angels*. (2) He is superior to *Moses*. (3) He is superior to *Aaron*.

These arguments would appear more distinctly were it not for the improper division of the chapters; as he who divided them in the middle ages (a division to which we are still unreasonably attached) had but a superficial knowledge of the Word of God. In consequence of this it is that one peculiar excellency of the apostle is not noticed, viz., his application of every argument, and the strong exhortation founded on it.

That the apostle had a plan on which he drew up this Epistle is very clear, from the close connection of every part. The grand divisions seem to be three:

1. The *proposition*, which is very short, and is contained in chap. i. 1-3. The majesty and preminence of Christ.

2. The *proof* or *arguments* which support the proposition:

CHRIST IS GREATER THAN THE ANGELS

a. Because He has a more excellent name than they, chap. i. 4-5.
b. Because the angels of God adore Him, v. 6.
c. Because the angels were created by Him, v. 7.
d. Because, in His human nature, He was endowed with greater gifts than they, vv. 8-9.
e. Because He is eternal, vv. 10-12.
f. Because He is more highly exalted, v. 13.
g. Because the angels are only the servants of God; He, the Son, v. 14.

In the *application* of this argument he exhorts the Hebrews not to neglect Christ, chap. ii. 1, by arguments drawn:

a. From the minor to the major, vv. 2-3.
b. Because the preaching of Christ was confirmed by miracles, v. 4.
c. Because, in the economy of the New Testament, angels are not the administrators; but the Messiah himself, to whom all things are subject, v. 5.

Here the apostle inserts a twofold *objection*, professedly drawn from divine revelation: Christ is man, and is less than the angels. "What is man . . . Thou madest him a little lower than the angels," vv. 6-7. Therefore He cannot be superior to them.

To this it is answered: (1) Christ as a mortal man, by His death and resurrection, overcame all enemies, and subdued all things to himself; therefore He must be greater than the angels, v. 9. (2) Though Christ died, and was in this respect inferior to the angels, yet it was necessary that He should take on Him this mortal state, that He might be of the same nature with those whom He was to redeem; and this He did without any prejudice to His divinity, vv. 10-18.

CHRIST IS GREATER THAN MOSES

Because Moses was only a servant; Christ, the Lord, chap. iii. 2-6. The *application* of this argument he makes from Ps. xcv. 7-11, which he draws out at length, chap. iii. 7—iv. 13.

CHRIST IS GREATER THAN AARON, AND ALL THE OTHER HIGH PRIESTS

a. Because He has not gone through the veil of the Tabernacle to make an atonement for sin, but has entered for this purpose into heaven itself, chap. iv. 14.
b. Because He is the Son of God, v. 14.
c. Because it is from Him we are to implore grace and mercy, chap. iv. 15-16 and vv. 1-3.
d. Because He was consecrated High Priest by God himself, chap. v. 4-10.
e. Because He is not a priest according to the order of Aaron, but according to the order of Melchisedec, which was much more ancient and much more noble, chap. vii.
f. Because He is not a typical priest, prefiguring good things to come, but the real Priest, of whom the others were but types and shadows, chap. viii. 1—ix. 11.

The *application* of this part contains the following exhortations:
a. That they should carefully retain their faith in Christ as the true Messiah, chap. x. 19-23.
b. That they should be careful to live godly lives, vv. 24-25.
c. That they should take care not to incur the punishment of disobedience, vv. 32-37 and chap. xii. 3-12.

d. That they should place their whole confidence in God, live by faith, and not turn back to perdition, chap. x. 38; xii. 2.

e. That they should consider and imitate the faith and obedience of their eminent ancestors, chap. xi.

f. That they should take courage, and not be remiss in the practice of the true religion, chap. xii. 12-24.

g. That they should take heed not to despise the Messiah, now speaking to them from heaven, chap. xii. 25-29.

3. *Practical and miscellaneous exhortations* relative to sundry duties, chap. xiii.

CHAPTER 1

Different discoveries made of the divine will to the ancient Israelites by the prophets, 1. The discovery now perfected by the revelation of Jesus Christ, of whose excellences and glories a large description is given, 2-13. Angels are ministering spirits to the heirs of salvation, 14.

1. *God, who at sundry times and in divers manners.* We can scarcely conceive anything more dignified than the opening of this Epistle. The sentiments are exceedingly elevated; and the language, harmony itself. The infinite God is at once produced to view, not in any of those attributes which are essential to the divine nature, but in the manifestations of His love to the world, by giving a revelation of His will relative to the salvation of mankind, and thus preparing the way, through a long train of years, for the introduction of that most glorious Being, His own Son. This Son, in the fullness of time, was manifested in the flesh that He might complete all vision and prophecy, supply all that was wanting to perfect the great scheme of revelation for the instruction of the world, and then die to put away sin by the sacrifice of himself. The description which he gives of this glorious personage is elevated beyond all comparison. In short, this first chapter, which may be considered the introduction to the whole Epistle, is, for importance of subject, dignity of expression, harmony and energy of language, compression and yet distinctness of ideas, equal, if not superior, to any other part of the New Testament. *Sundry times. Polymeros,* from *polys,* "many," and *meros,* "a part"; giving portions of revelation at different times. *Divers manners. Polytropos,* from *polys,* "many," and *tropos,* "a manner, turn, or form of speech." The words are rather intended to point out the imperfect state of divine revelation under the Old Testament; it was not complete, nor can it without the New be considered a sufficiently ample discovery of the divine will. Under the Old Testament, revelations were made at various times, by various persons, in various laws and forms of teaching, with various degrees of clearness, under various shadows, types, and figures, and with various modes of revelation, such as by angels, visions, dreams, mental impressions. See Num. xii. 6, 8. But under the New Testament all is done simply by one Person, i.e., Jesus, who has fulfilled the prophets and completed prophecy. One great object of the apostle is to put the simplicity of the Christian system in opposition to the complex nature of the Mosaic economy; and also to show that what the law could not do because it was weak through the flesh, Jesus has accomplished by the merit of His death and the energy of His Spirit.

2. *Last days.* The gospel dispensation, called the *last days* and the "last time" because not to be followed by any other dispensation or the conclusion of the Jewish church and state now at their termination. *By his Son.* It is very remarkable that the pronoun *his* is not found in the text; nor is it found in any MS. or version. We should not therefore supply the pronoun as our translators have done; but simply read "by a son" or "in a son." The apostle begins with the lowest state in which Christ has appeared: (1) His being a Son, born of a woman, and made under the law. He then ascends (2) to His being an *heir,* and an *heir of all things.* (3) He then describes Him as the Creator of all *worlds.* (4) As the "brightness" of the divine glory. (5) As "the express image of his person," or "character of the divine substance." (6) As sustaining the immense fabric of the universe, and this "by the word of his power." (7) As having made an atonement for the sin of the world, which was the most stupendous of all His works. (8) As being on the right hand of God, infinitely exalted above all created beings, and the Object of adoration to all the angelic host. (9) As having an eternal throne, neither His person nor His dignity ever changing or decaying. (10) As continuing to exercise dominion when the earth and the heavens are no more!

3. *The brightness of his glory.* The resplendent outbeaming of the essential glory of God. *The express image of his person.* "The character or impression of His hypostasis or substance." It is supposed that these words expound the former, *image* expounding *brightness,* and *person* "substance," *glory.* The hypostasis of God is that which is essential to Him as God; and the "character" or *image* is that by which all the likeness of the original becomes manifest, and is a perfect facsimile of the whole. It is a metaphor taken from sealing, the die or seal leaving the full impression of its every part on the wax to which it is applied. *Upholding all things by the word of his power.* This is an astonishing description of the infinitely energetic and all-pervading power of God. He spoke, and all things were created; He speaks, and all things are sustained. The Jewish writers frequently express the perfection of the divine nature by the phrases, "He bears all things, both above and below"; "He carries all His creatures"; "He bears his world"; "He bears all worlds by His power." The Hebrews, to whom this Epistle was written, would, from this and other circumstances, fully understand that the apostle believed Jesus Christ to be truly and properly God. *The right hand of the Majesty on high.* As it were associated with the supreme Majesty, in glory everlasting, and in the government of all things in time and in eternity; for the *right hand* is the place of the greatest eminence, I Kings ii. 19.

4. *So much better than the angels.* Another argument in favor of the divinity of our Lord.

The Jews had the highest opinion of the transcendent excellence of angels; they even associate them with God in the creation of the world, and suppose them to be of the privy council of the Most High; and thus they understand Gen. i. 26: "Let us make man in our image, after our likeness"; "And the Lord said to the ministering angels that stood before Him, and who were created the second day, Let us make man." *By inheritance obtained.* The verb signifies generally to "participate, possess, obtain, or acquire." It is not by *inheritance* that Christ possesses a more excellent name than angels, but as God. He has it naturally and essentially; and, as God manifested in the flesh, He has it in consequence of His humiliation, sufferings, and meritorious death. See Phil. ii. 9.

5. *Thou art my Son, this day have I begotten thee.* These words are quoted from Ps. ii. 7, a psalm that seems to refer only to the Messiah; and they are quoted by Paul, Acts xiii. 33, as referring to the resurrection of Christ. And this application of them is confirmed by the same apostle, Rom. i. 4, as by His resurrection from the dead he was "declared," manifestly proved, "to be the Son of God with power." By His resurrection His innocence was demonstrated, as God could not work a miracle to raise a wicked man from the dead. The words *This day have I begotten thee* must refer either to His incarnation, when He was miraculously conceived in the womb of the Virgin by the power of the Holy Spirit, or to His resurrection from the dead, when God by this sovereign display of His almighty energy declared Him to be His Son. This most important use of this saying has passed unnoticed by almost every Christian writer which I have seen, and yet it lies here at the foundation of all the apostle's proofs. If Jesus was not thus the Son of God, the whole Christian system is vain and baseless; but His *resurrection* demonstrates Him to have been the Son of God. *He shall be to me a Son.* This place, which is quoted from 2 Sam. vii. 14, shows us that the Seed which God promised to David, and who was to sit upon his throne, and whose throne should be established forever, was not Solomon, but Jesus Christ; and indeed He quotes the words so as to intimate that they were so understood by the Jews.

6. *And again, when he bringeth in the first-begotten.* This is not a correct translation of the Greek. "But when He bringeth again, or the second time, the Firstborn into the habitable world." This most manifestly refers to His resurrection, which might be properly considered a second incarnation; for as the human soul, as well as the fullness of the Godhead bodily, dwelt in the man Christ Jesus on and during His incarnation, so when He expired upon the Cross both the Godhead and the human spirit left His dead body; and as on His resurrection these were reunited to His revivified manhood, therefore with the strictest propriety does the apostle say that the Resurrection was a second bringing of Him into the world.

I have translated *oikoumene* the "habitable world," and this is its proper meaning; and thus it is distinguished from *cosmos*, which signifies the "globe," independently of its inhabitants, though it often expresses both the inhabited and uninhabited parts. Our Lord's first coming into the world is expressed by this latter word, chap. x. 5: "Wherefore when he cometh into the world" (*cosmos*), and this simply refers to His being incarnated, that He might be capable of suffering and dying for man. But the word is changed on this second coming, I mean His resurrection, and then *oikoumene* is used. And why? Because He was now to dwell with man; to send His gospel everywhere to all the inhabitants of the earth. *Let all the angels of God worship him.* The apostle recurs here to his former assertion, that Jesus is higher than the angels, v. 4. To worship any creature is idolatry. Jesus Christ can be no creature, else the angels who worship Him must be guilty of idolatry, and God the Author of that idolatry, who commanded those angels to worship Christ. There has been some difficulty in ascertaining the place from which the apostle quotes these words; some suppose Ps. xcvii. 7: "Worship him, all ye gods"; which the Septuagint translates thus: "Worship him, all ye his angels." But it is not clear that the Messiah is intended in this psalm, nor are the words precisely those used here by the apostle. Our marginal references send us with great propriety to the Septuagint version of Deut. xxxii. 43, where the passage is found verbatim; but there is nothing answering to the words in the present Hebrew text. In Romans iii there is a large quotation from Psalms xiv, where there are six whole verses in the apostle's quotation which are not found in the present Hebrew text, but are preserved in the Septuagint! How strange it is that this venerable and important version, so often quoted by our Lord and all His apostles, should be so generally neglected, and so little known!

7. *Who maketh his angels spirits.* They are so far from being superior to Christ that they are not called God's sons in any peculiar sense, but His "servants," as tempests and lightenings are. It is very likely that the apostle refers here to the opinions of the Jews relative to the angels. In *Pirkey R. Elieser*, c. 4, it is said: "The angels which were created the second day, when they minister before God, become fire."

8. *Thy throne, O God, is for ever and ever.* If this be said of the Son of God, i.e., Jesus Christ, then Jesus Christ must be God; and indeed the design of the apostle is to prove this. The words here quoted are taken from Ps. xlv. 6-7, which the most intelligent rabbins refer to the Messiah. *A sceptre of righteousness.* The sceptre, which was a sort of staff or instrument of various forms, was the ensign of government, and is here used for government itself. This the ancient Jewish writers understand also of the Messiah.

9. *Thou hast loved righteousness.* This is the characteristic of a just governor: he abhors and suppresses iniquity; he countenances and supports righteousness and truth. *Therefore God, even thy God.* The original may be thus translated: "Therefore, O God, Thy God hath anointed Thee." The form of speech is nearly the same with that in the preceding verse. *With the oil of gladness.* We have often had occasion to remark that, anciently, kings, priests, and prophets were consecrated to their several offices by anointing; and that this signified the gifts and influences of the divine Spirit. Christ signifies "The Anointed One," the same as the Hebrew Messias, and He is here said to be

anointed with the oil of gladness above His fellows. None was ever constituted prophet, priest, and king but himself. Thus He is infinitely exalted "beyond His fellows"—all that had ever borne the regal, prophetic, or sacerdotal offices. *Gladness* is used to express the festivities which took place on the inauguration of kings.

10. *And, Thou, Lord.* This is an address to the Son as the Creator, see v. 2; for this is implied in laying the foundation of the earth. The heavens, which are the work of His hands, point out His infinite wisdom and skill.

11. *They shall perish.* Permanently fixed as they seem to be, a time shall come when they shall be dissolved, and afterward new heavens and a new earth be formed, in which righteousness alone shall dwell. See 2 Pet. iii. 10-13. *Shall wax old as doth a garment.* As a garment by long using becomes unfit to be longer used, so shall all visible things; they shall wear old, and wear out, and hence the necessity of their being renewed. It is remarkable that our word "world" is a contraction of "wear old," a term by which our ancestors expressed the sentiment contained in this verse. That the word was thus compounded and that it had this sense in our language may be proved from the most competent and indisputable witnesses. It was formerly written "weorold."

12. *And they shall be changed.* Not destroyed ultimately or annihilated. They shall be changed and renewed. *But thou art the same.* These words can be said of no being but God; all others are changeable or perishable, because temporal; only that which is eternal can continue essentially and, speaking after the manner of men, formally the same. *Thy years shall not fail.* There is in the divine duration no circle to be run, no space to be measured, no time to be reckoned. All is eternity—infinite—and onward.

13. *But to which of the angels?* We have already seen, from the opinions and concessions of the Jews, that if Jesus Christ could be proved to be greater than the angels, it would necessarily follow that He was God: and this the apostle does most amply prove by these various quotations from their own Scriptures; for he shows that while He is the supreme and absolute Sovereign, they are no more than His messengers and servants.

14. *Are they not all ministering spirits?* That is, "They are *all ministering spirits*"; for the Hebrews often express the strongest affirmative by an interrogation.

CHAPTER 2

The use we should make of the preceding doctrine, and the danger of neglecting this great salvation, 1-4. The future world is not put in subjection to the angels, but all is under the authority of Christ, 5-8. Jesus has tasted death for every man, 9. Nor could He accomplish man's redemption without being incarnated and without dying; by which He destroys the devil, and delivers all that believe on Him from the fear of death and spiritual bondage, 10-15. Christ took not upon Him the nature of angels, but the nature of Abraham, that He might die, and make reconciliation for the sins of the people, 16-18.

1. *Therefore.* Because God has spoken to us by His Son, and because that Son is so great and glorious a Personage, and because the subject which is addressed to us is of such infinite importance to our welfare. *We ought to give*

the more earnest heed. We should hear the doctrine of Christ with care, candor, and deep concern. *Lest at any time we should let them slip.* "Lest at any time we should leak out." Superficial hearers lose the benefit of the word preached as the unseasoned vessel does its fluid; nor can anyone hear to the saving of his soul unless he give "most earnest heed."

2. *If the word spoken by angels.* The law (according to some), which was delivered by the mediation of angels, God frequently employing these to communicate His will to men. See Acts vii. 53 and Gal. iii. 19. But the apostle probably means those particular messages which God sent by angels, as in the case of Lot, Gen. xix, and suchlike. *Was stedfast.* Was so confirmed by the divine authority and so strict that it would not tolerate any offense, but inflicted punishment on *every* act of *transgression*, every case in which the bounds laid down by the law were "passed over," and every act of *disobedience* in respect to the duties enjoined. *Received a just recompence.* That kind and degree of punishment which the law prescribed for those who broke it.

3. *How shall we escape?* If they who had fewer privileges than we have, to whom God spoke in divers manners by angels and prophets, fell under the displeasure of their Maker and were often punished with a sore destruction, *how shall we escape* wrath to the uttermost if we neglect the salvation provided for us and proclaimed to us by the Son of God? Those who *neglect* it are not only they who oppose or persecute it, but they who pay no regard to it. *Which at the first began to be spoken.* Though John the Baptist went before our Lord to prepare His way, yet he could not be properly said to preach the gospel; and even Christ's preaching was only a beginning of the great proclamation. It was His own Spirit in the apostles and evangelists, the men who heard Him preach, that opened the whole mystery of the kingdom of Heaven.

4. *God also bearing them witness.* He did not leave the confirmation of these great truths to the testimony of men; He bore His own testimony to them by *signs, wonders,* various *miracles,* and "distributions of the Holy Ghost." And all these were proved to come from himself; for no man could do those miracles at his own pleasure, but the power to work them was given according to God's *own will;* or rather, God himself wrought them, in order to accredit the ministry of His servants.

5. *The world to come.* That *the world to come* meant the "days of the Messiah" among the Jews is most evident, and has been often pointed out in the course of these notes.

6. *But one in a certain place.* This *one* is David; and the *certain place,* Ps. viii. 4-6. But why does the apostle use this indeterminate mode of quotation? Because it was common thus to express the testimony of any of the inspired writers. So Philo. Thus even the heathens were accustomed to quote high authorities; so Plato. The mode of quotation therefore implies, not ignorance, but reverence. *What is man?* This quotation is verbatim from the Septuagint; the Greek is not so emphatic as the Hebrew: "What is miserable man, that thou rememberest him? and the son of Adam, that thou visitest him?"

7. Thou madest him a little lower than the angels. If this be spoken of man as he came out of the hands of his Maker, it places him at the head of all God's works; for literally translated it is: "Thou hast made him less than God." And this is proved by his being made in the image and likeness of God, which is spoken of no other creature either in heaven or on earth. If we take the words as referring to Jesus Christ, then they must be understood as pointing out the time of His humiliation, as in v. 9; and the *little lower* in both verses must mean "for a short time" or "a little while." And indeed the whole of the passage suits Him better than it does any of the children of men; for it is only under the feet of Jesus that all things are put in subjection, and it was in consequence of His humiliation that He had "a name . . . above every name: that at the name of Jesus every knee should bow, of things in heaven, and things in earth, and things under the earth," Phil. ii. 9-11. *Thou crownedst him with glory and honour.* This was strictly true of Adam in his state of innocence, for he was set over all things in this lower world; "all sheep and oxen . . . the beasts of the field; the fowl of the air, and the fish of the sea, and whatsoever passeth through the paths of the seas," Ps. viii. 7-8. So far all this perfectly applies to Adam; but it is evident the apostle takes *all* in a much higher sense, that of universal dominion; and hence he says, He "left nothing that is not put under him." These verses, collated with the above passage from the Epistle to the Philippians, mutually illustrate each other. And the crowning Christ with glory and honor must refer to His exaltation after His resurrection, in which, as the victorious Messiah, He had all power given to Him in heaven and earth. And although we do not yet see all things put under Him, for evil men and evil spirits are only under the subjection of control, yet we look forward to that time when the whole world shall be bowed to His sway, and when the stone cut out of the mountain without hands shall become great and fill the whole earth.

9. Should taste death for every man. It was a custom in ancient times to take off criminals by making them drink a cup of poison. Socrates was adjudged to drink a cup of the juice of hemlock by order of the Athenian magistrates. The reference in the text seems to point out the whole human race as being accused, tried, found guilty, and condemned, each having his own poisoned cup to drink; and Jesus, the wonderful Jesus, takes the cup out of the hand of each, and cheerfully and with alacrity drinks off the dregs! Thus having drunk every man's poisoned cup, He tasted that death which they must have endured had not their cup been drunk by Another. Is not this the cup to which He refers, Matt. xxvi. 39: "O my Father, if it be possible, let this cup pass from me"? But without His drinking it, the salvation of the world would have been impossible; and therefore He cheerfully drank it in the place of every human soul and thus made atonement for the sin of the whole world; and this He did by the grace, mercy, or infinite goodness of God.

10. For it became him. It was suitable to the divine wisdom, the requisitions of justice, and the economy of grace to offer Jesus as a Sacrifice, in order to bring *many sons* and daughters to *glory. For whom . . . and by whom.* God is the Cause of all things, and He is the Object or End of them. *Perfect through sufferings.* Without suffering He could not have died, and without dying He could not have made an atonement for sin. The sacrifice must be "consummated," in order that He might be qualified to be the *captain* or Author of the salvation of men, and lead all those who become children of God, through faith in Him, into eternal glory. I believe this to be the sense of the passage; and it appears to be an answer to the grand objection of the Jews: "The Messiah is never to be conquered, or die; but shall be victorious, and endure forever."

11. For both he that sanctifieth. The word does not merely signify one who sanctifies or makes holy, but one who makes atonement or reconciliation to God; and answers to the Hebrew *caphar*, "to expiate." See Exod. xxix. 33-36. He that sanctifies is He that makes atonement and they who are sanctified are they who receive that atonement and, being reconciled unto God, become His children by adoption, through grace. In this sense our Lord uses the word, John xvii. 19: "For their sakes I sanctify myself"; on their account I consecrate myself to be a sacrifice. This is the sense in which this word is used generally through this Epistle. *Are all of one.* What this *one* means has given rise to various conjectures. Father, family, blood, seed, race, nature have all been substituted. Nature seems to be that intended (see v. 14), and the conclusion of this verse confirms it. Both the Sanctifier and the sanctified, both Christ and His followers, are all of the same nature; for as the children were partakers of flesh and blood, i.e., of human nature, He partook of the same, and thus He was qualified to become a Sacrifice for man. *He is not ashamed to call them brethren.* Though, as to His Godhead, He is infinitely raised above men and angels, yet as He has become incarnate, notwithstanding His dignity, He blushes not to acknowledge all His true followers as His brethren.

12. I will declare thy name. See Ps. xxii. 22. The apostle certainly quotes this psalm as referring to Jesus Christ, and these words as spoken by Christ unto the Father, in reference to His incarnation; as if He had said: "When I shall be incarnated, I will declare Thy perfections to mankind; and among My disciples I will give glory to Thee for Thy mercy to the children of men." See the fulfillment of this, John i. 18: "No man hath seen God at any time; the only begotten Son, which is in the bosom of the Father, he hath declared him." Nor were the perfections of God ever properly known or declared till the manifestation of Christ.

13. I will put my trust in him. It is not clear to what express place of Scripture the apostle refers. Words to this effect frequently occur; but the place most probably is Ps. xviii. 2, several parts of which psalm seem to belong to the Messiah. *Behold I and the children which God hath given me.* This is taken from Isa. viii. 18. The apostle does not intend to say that the portions which he has quoted have any particular reference, taken by themselves, to the subject in question. They are only catchwords of whole paragraphs, which, taken together, are full to the point; because they are prophecies of the Messiah, and are fulfilled in Him. This is evident from the last quotation: "Behold, I and the children whom the Lord hath given me are for signs and for wonders in Israel." Jesus and His disciples wrought a multitude of the most stupendous signs and wonders in Israel. The expression also may include all genuine Christians; they are for signs and wonders throughout the earth. And as to the eighteenth psalm, the principal part of it seems to refer to Christ's sufferings; but the miracles which were wrought at His crucifixion, the destruction of the Jewish state and polity, the calling of the Gentiles, and the establishment of the Christian Church appear also to be intended.

14. *The children are partakers of flesh and blood.* Since those children of God who have fallen and are to be redeemed are human beings, in order to be qualified to redeem them by suffering and dying in their stead, *He also himself likewise took part of the same*—He became incarnate. By *the children* here we are to understand, not only the disciples and all genuine Christians, as in v. 13, but also the whole human race, all Jews and all Gentiles. *That through death.* That by the merit of His own death, making atonement for sin, and procuring the almighty energy of the Holy Spirit, He might "counterwork" or "render useless and ineffectual" all the operations of him who had the *power* or "influence" to bring death into the world; so that *death,* which was intended by him who was a murderer from the beginning to be the final ruin of mankind, becomes the instrument of their exaltation and endless glory; and thus the death brought in by Satan is counterworked and rendered ineffectual by the death of Christ. *Him that had the power of death.* This is spoken in conformity to an opinion prevalent among the Jews that there was a certain fallen angel who was called the "angel of death."

15. *And deliver them who through fear of death.* It is very likely that the apostle has the Gentiles here principally in view. As they had no revelation and no certainty of immortality, they were continually in bondage to the fear of death.

16. *For verily he took not on him the nature of angels.* "Moreover, He doth not at all take hold of angels; but of the seed of Abraham He taketh hold." This is the marginal reading and is greatly to be preferred to that in the text. Jesus Christ, intending not to redeem angels but to redeem man, did not assume the angelic nature but was made man, coming directly by *the seed* or "posterity" *of Abraham,* with whom the original covenant was made, that in his seed all the nations of the earth should be blessed; and it is on this account that the apostle mentioned *the seed of Abraham,* and not the seed of Adam. The word itself signifies not only to "take hold of" but to "help, succor, save from sinking." The rebel angels, who sinned and fell from God, were permitted to "fall downe, alle downe," as one of our old writers expresses it, till they fell into perdition. Man sinned and fell, and was falling "downe, alle downe," but Jesus laid hold on him and prevented him from falling into endless perdition.

17. *Wherefore in all things.* Because He thus laid hold on man in order to redeem him, it was necessary that He should in all things become like to man, that He might suffer in his stead, and make an atonement in His nature. *That he might be a merciful and faithful high priest.* "That He might be merciful"—that He might be affected with a feeling of our infirmities, that, partaking of our nature with all its innocent infirmities and afflictions, He might know how to compassionate poor, afflicted, suffering man. And that He might be a "faithful high priest in those things which relate to God," whose justice requires the punishment of the transgressors, or a suitable expiation to be made for the sins of the people—"to make propitiation or atonement for sins by sacrifice."

18. *For in that he himself hath suffered.* The maxim on which this verse is founded is the following: A state of suffering disposes persons to be compassionate, and those who endure most afflictions are they who feel most for others. The apostle argues that, among other causes, it was necessary that Jesus Christ should partake of human nature, exposed to trials, persecutions, and various sufferings, that He might the better feel for and be led to succor those who are afflicted and sorely tried. Were the rest of the Scripture silent on this subject, this verse might be an ample support for every tempted soul.

CHAPTER 3

Jesus is the High Priest of our profession, 1. And is counted worthy of more honor than Moses, as the son is more worthy than the servant, 2-6. We should not harden our hearts against the voice of God, as the Israelites did, and were excluded from the earthly rest in Canaan, 7-11. We should be on our guard against unbelief, 12. And exhort each other, lest we be hardened through the deceitfulness of sin; and we should hold fast the beginning of our confidence to the end, and not provoke God as the Israelites did, who were destroyed in the wilderness, 13-17. They were promised the earthly rest, but did not enter because of unbelief, 18-19.

1. *Holy brethren.* Persons "consecrated to God," as the word literally implies, and called, in consequence, to be holy in heart, holy in life, and useful in the world. The Israelites are often called a "holy people, saints," because consecrated to God, and because they were bound by their profession to be holy; and yet these appellations are given to them in numberless instances where they were very unholy. The not attending to this circumstance, and the not discerning between actual positive holiness and the call to it as the consecration of the persons, has led many commentators and preachers into destructive mistakes. A man may be a Christian in profession and not such in heart; and those who pretend that, although they are unholy in themselves, they are reputed holy in Christ, because His righteousness is imputed to them, most awfully deceive their own souls. *Heavenly calling.* The Israelites had an earthly calling; they were called out of Egypt to go into the Promised Land. Christians have a heavenly calling; they are invited to leave the bondage of sin and go to the kingdom of God. *Apostle and High Priest of our profession.* Among the Jews the high priest was considered to be also the apostle of God, and it is in conformity to this notion that the apostle speaks. And he exhorts the Hebrews to *consider* Jesus Christ to be both their *High Priest* and *Apostle,* and to expect these offices to be henceforth fulfilled by Him, and by Him alone. This was the fullest intimation that the Mosaic economy was at an end and

the priesthood changed. By *our profession,* or "that confession of ours," the apostle undoubtedly means the Christian religion. Moses was the apostle under the old testament, and Aaron the priest. When Moses was removed, the prophets succeeded him; and the sons of Aaron were the priests after the death of their father. This system is now annulled; and Jesus is the Prophet who declares the Father's will, and He is the Priest who ministers in the things pertaining to God.

2. *Who was faithful to him.* In Num. xii. 7, God gives this testimony to Moses: "My servant Moses . . . is faithful in all mine house"; and to this testimony the apostle alludes. *House* means not only the place where a family dwells, but also the family itself. The whole congregation of Israel was the house or family of God; and Moses was His steward, and was faithful in the discharge of his office. Jesus Christ has His house—the whole great family of mankind, for all of whom He offered His sacrificial blood to God; and the Christian Church, which is especially His own household, is composed of His own children and servants, among and in whom He lives and constantly resides. He has been *faithful* to the trust reposed in Him as the Apostle of God; He has faithfully proclaimed the will of the Most High.

3. *For this man was counted.* The pronoun should have been translated "this person," and this would have referred immediately to Jesus Christ, v. 1. *More glory than Moses.* We have already seen that the apostle's design is to prove that Jesus Christ is higher than the angels, higher than Moses, and higher than Aaron. That He is higher than the angels has been already proved; that He is higher than Moses he is now proving. *He who hath builded the house.* There can be no doubt that a man who builds a house for his own accommodation is more honorable than the house itself; but the *house* here intended is the Church of God. This Church, here called a *house* or "family," is built by Christ; He must therefore be greater than Moses, who was only a member and officer in that Church.

4. *For every house is builded by some man.* The literal sense is plain enough: "Every structure plainly implies an architect, and an end for which it was formed. The architect may be employed by him for whose use the house is intended; but the efficient cause of the erection is that which is here to be regarded." The word *house* here is still taken in a metaphorical sense as above; it signifies "family" or Church. Now the general meaning of the words, taken in this sense, is: "Every family has an author, and a head or governor. Man may found families, civil and religious communities, and be the head of these; but God alone is the Head, Author, and Governor of all the families of the earth; He is the Governor of the universe."

5. *As a servant.* The fidelity of Moses was the fidelity of a *servant;* he was not the framer of that Church or house; He was employed, under God, to arrange and order it; he was steward to the Builder and Owner. *For a testimony of those things.* Every ordinance under the law was typical; everything bore a *testimony* to the things which were to be spoken after; i.e., to Jesus Christ, His suffering, death, and the glory which should follow; and to His gospel in all

its parts. The faithfulness of Moses consisted in his scrupulous attention to every ordinance of God, his framing everything according to the pattern showed him by the Lord, and his referring all to that Christ of whom he spoke as the Prophet who should come after him.

6. *But Christ as a son over his own house.* Moses was faithful as a servant *in* the house; Jesus was faithful as the firstborn Son *over* the house of which He is the Heir and Governor. Here then is the conclusion of the argument in reference to Christ's superiority over Moses. Moses did not found the house or family; Christ did. Moses was but in the house, or one of the family; Christ was over the house as its Ruler. Moses was but servant in the house; Christ was the Son and Heir. Moses was in the house of another; Christ, in His own house. *Whose house are we.* We Christians are His Church and "family"; He is our Father, Governor, and Head. *If we hold fast the confidence.* We are now His Church, and shall continue to be such and be acknowledged by Him *if* we maintain our Christian profession, "that liberty of access to God," which we now have, and the *rejoicing of the hope,* i.e., of eternal life, which we shall receive at the resurrection of the dead. The word which is here translated *confidence,* and which signifies "freedom of speech, liberty of access," seems to be used here to distinguish an important Christian privilege. Under the old testament no man was permitted to approach to God; even the very mountain on which God published His laws must not be touched by man nor beast; and only the high priest was permitted to enter the holy of holies, and that only once a year, on the great Day of Atonement; and even then he must have the blood of the victim to propitiate the divine justice. Under the Christian dispensation the way to the holiest is now laid open; and we have "liberty of access," even to the holiest, by the blood of Jesus. Having such access unto God, by such a Mediator, we may obtain all that grace which is necessary to fit us for eternal glory; and having the witness of His Spirit in our heart, we have a well-grounded hope of endless felicity and exult in the enjoyment of that hope. But *if* we retain not the grace, we shall not inherit the glory.

7. *Wherefore (as the Holy Ghost saith, To day.* These words are quoted from Ps. xcv. 7; and as they were written by David, and attributed here to the Holy Ghost, it proves that David wrote by the inspiration of God's Holy Spirit. As these words were originally a warning to the Israelites not to provoke God, lest they should be excluded from that rest which He had promised them, the apostle uses them here to persuade the Christians in Palestine to hold fast their religious privileges and the grace they had received, lest they should come short of that state of future glory which Christ had prepared for them. The words strongly imply, as indeed does the whole Epistle, the possibility of falling from the grace of God and perishing everlastingly; and without this supposition these words and all suchlike, which make more than two-thirds of the whole of divine revelation, would have neither sense nor meaning. Why should God entreat man to receive His mercy if He have rendered this impossible? Why should He exhort a believer to persevere if it be impossible for him to fall away?

8. *Harden not your hearts.* Which you will infallibly do if you will not hear His voice. *Provocation.* The "exasperation" or "bitter provocation."

9. *When your fathers tempted me.* It would be better to translate "where" than *when,* as the Vulgate has done in its *ubi;* and this translation has been followed by Wycliffe, Coverdale, Tyndale, and our first translators in general.

10. *Wherefore I was grieved.* God represents himself as the Father of this great Jewish family, for whose comfort and support He had made every necessary provision, and to whom He had given every proof of tenderness and fatherly affection; and because they disobeyed Him, and walked in that way in which they could not but be miserable, therefore He represents himself as grieved and exceedingly displeased with them.

11. *So I sware in my wrath.* God's grief at their continued disobedience became *wrath* at their final impenitence, and therefore He excluded them from the promised rest.

12. *Take heed, brethren, lest there be in any of you.* Take warning by those disobedient Israelites; they were brought out of the house of bondage, and had the fullest promise of a land of prosperity and rest. By their disobedience they came short of it, and fell in the wilderness. You have been brought from the bondage of sin, and have a most gracious promise of an everlasting inheritance among the saints in light. Through unbelief and disobedience they lost their rest; through the same you may lose yours. *An evil heart of unbelief* will lead away *from the living God.*

13. *But exhort one another daily.* This supposes a state of close church fellowship, without which they could not have had access to each other. *While it is called To day.* Use time while you have it, for by and by there will be no more present time. All will be future; all will be eternity. *Daily* signifies time continued; *to day,* all present time.

14. *For we are made partakers of Christ.* Having believed in Christ as the promised Messiah and embraced the whole Christian system, they were consequently made partakers of all its benefits in this life, and entitled to the fulfillment of all its exceeding great and precious promises relative to the glories of the eternal world. The former they actually possessed; the latter they could have only in case of their perseverance. Therefore the apostle says, *If we hold the beginning of our confidence stedfast unto the end,* i.e., of life. For our participation of glory depends on our continuing steadfast in the faith, to the end of our Christian race. The word *hypostasis,* which we here translate *confidence,* signifies properly a "basis" or "foundation"; that on which something else is builded, and by which it is supported. Their faith in Christ Jesus was this *hypostasis* or "foundation"; on that all their peace, comfort, and salvation was builded. If this were not held fast to the end, Christ in His saving influences could not be held fast; and no Christ, no heaven.

16. *For some, when they had heard, did provoke.* There is a various reading here, which consists merely in the different placing of an accent, and yet gives the whole passage a different turn—*tines;* if read with the accent on the

epsilon. *Tines* is the plural indefinite, and signifies *some,* as in our translation; if read with the accent on the iota, it has an interrogative meaning; and, according to this, the whole clause, "But who were those hearers who did bitterly provoke? Were they not all they who came out of the land of Egypt by Moses?" Or the whole clause may be read with one interrogation: "But who were those hearers that did bitterly provoke, but all those who came out of Egypt by Moses?" It is more likely that this is the true reading, as all that follows to the end of the eighteenth verse is a series of interrogations.

17. *Whose carcasses fell.* "Whose members fell," the members of the body.

18. *To whom sware he.* God never acts by any kind of caprice; whenever He pours out His judgments, there are the most positive reasons to vindicate His conduct.

19. *So we see that they could not enter in.* It was no decree of God that prevented them; it was no want of necessary strength to enable them; it was through no deficiency of divine counsel to instruct them. All these they had in abundance; but they chose to sin, and *would* not believe. Unbelief produced disobedience, and disobedience produced hardness of heart and blindness of mind; and all these drew down the judgments of God, and wrath came upon them to the uttermost.

CHAPTER 4

As the Christian rest is to be obtained by faith, we should beware of unbelief, lest we lose it as the Hebrews did theirs, 1. The reason why they were not brought into the rest promised to them, 2. The rest promised to the Hebrews was a type of that promised to Christians, 3-10. Into this rest we should earnestly labor to enter, 11. A description of the Word of God, 12-13. Jesus is our sympathetic High Priest, 15. Through Him we have confidence to come to God, 16.

1. *Let us therefore fear.* Seeing the Israelites lost the rest of Canaan through obstinacy and unbelief, let us be afraid lest we come short of the heavenly rest through the same cause. *Should seem to come short of it.* "Lest any of us should actually come short of it"; i.e., miss it. *Come short.* The verb is applied here metaphorically; it is an allusion, of which there are many in this Epistle, to the races in the Grecian games.

2. *For unto us was the gospel preached.* "For we also have received good tidings as well as they." They had a gracious promise of entering into an earthly rest; we have a gracious promise of entering into a heavenly rest. God gave them every requisite advantage; He has done the same to us. Moses and the elders spoke the word of God plainly and forcibly to them; Christ and His apostles have done the same to us. They might have persevered; so may we. They disbelieved, disobeyed and fell; and so may we. *But the word preached did not profit them.* "But the word of hearing did not profit them." The word and promise to which the apostle most probably refers is that in Deut. i. 20-21. "Ye are come unto the mountain of the Amorites, which the Lord our God doth give unto us. Behold, the Lord thy God hath set the land before thee: go up and possess it, as the Lord God of thy fathers hath said unto thee; fear not." But instead of attending to the word of the Lord by Moses, the whole congregation murmured against him and Aaron, and "said one to another, Let us make a captain, and let us return into

Egypt," Num. xiv. 2, 4. *Not being mixed with faith in them that heard.* The word *mixed* is peculiarly expressive; it is a metaphor taken from the nutrition of the human body by mixing the aliment taken into the stomach with the saliva and gastric juice, in consequence of which it is concocted, digested, reduced into chyle, which, absorbed by the lacteal vessels and thrown into the blood, becomes the means of increasing and supporting the body, all the solids and fluids being thus generated; so that on this process, properly performed, depend (under God) strength, health, and life itself. Should the most nutritive aliment be received into the stomach, if not *mixed* with the above juices, it would be rather the means of death than of life; or, in the word of the apostle, it would *not profit* because not thus *mixed. Faith* in the word preached, in reference to that God who sent it, is the grand means of its becoming the power of God to the salvation of the soul.

3. *For we which have believed do enter into rest.* The great spiritual blessings, the fore-runners of eternal glory, which were all typified by that earthly rest or felicity promised to the ancient Israelites, we Christians do, by believing in Christ Jesus, actually possess. We have peace of conscience and joy in the Holy Ghost, are saved from the guilt and power of sin, and thus enjoy an inward rest. But this is a rest differing from the seventh day's rest, or Sabbath, which was the original type of Canaan, the blessings of the gospel, and eternal glory; seeing God said, concerning the unbelieving Israelites in the wilderness, *I have sworn in my wrath* that they shall not *enter into my rest*, notwithstanding *the works* of creation *were finished*, and the seventh day's rest was instituted *from the foundation of the world*; consequently the Israelites had entered into that rest before the oath was sworn. *From the foundation of the world.* The foundation of the world means the completion of the work of creation in six days.

4. *For he spake in a certain place.* This *certain place* or "somewhere" is probably Gen. ii. 2; and refers to the completion of the work of creation, and the setting apart the seventh day as a day of rest for man, and a type of ever-lasting felicity.

5. *And in this place again.* In the ninety-fifth psalm, already quoted, v. 3. This was a second rest which the Lord promised to the believing, obedient seed of Abraham; and as it was spoken of in the days of David, when the Jews actually possessed this long promised Canaan, therefore it is evident that that was not the rest which God intended, as the next verse shows.

6. *It remaineth that some must enter therein.* Why our translators put in the word *must* here I cannot even conjecture. I hope it was not to serve a system, as some have since used it: "Some *must* go to heaven, for so is the doctrine of the decree; and there *must* be certain persons infallibly brought thither as a reward to Christ for His sufferings; and in this the will of man and free agency can have no part." Now supposing that even all this was true, yet it does not exist either positively or by implication in the text. The words literally translated are as follows: "Seeing then it remaineth for some to enter into it"; or, "Whereas therefore it remaineth that some enter into it, and they to whom it was first preached (they to whom the promise

was given; they who first received the good tidings; i.e., the Israelites, to whom was given the promise of entering into the rest of Canaan) did not enter in because of their unbelief"; and the promise still continued to be repeated even in the days of David; therefore some other rest must be intended.

7. *He limiteth a certain day.* The term *day* signifies not only time in general, but also present time, and a particular space. *Day* here seems to have the same meaning as "rest" in some other parts of this verse. The day or time of rest relative to the ancient Jews being over and past, and a long time having elapsed between God's displeasure shown to the disobedient Jews in the wilderness and the days of David, and the true rest not having been enjoyed, God in His mercy has instituted another day—has given another dispensation of mercy and goodness by Christ Jesus; and now it may be said, as formerly, *To day, if ye will hear his voice, harden not your hearts.* God speaks now as He spoke before; His voice is in the gospel as it was in the law. Believe, love, obey, and you shall enter into this rest.

8. *For if Jesus had given them rest.* It is truly surprising that our translators should have rendered the text *Jesus*, and not "Joshua," who is most clearly intended. They must have known that the *Yehoshua* of the Hebrew, which we write "Joshua," is everywhere rendered *Jesus* by the Septuagint; and it is their reading which the apostle follows. It is "Joshua" in Coverdale's Testament, 1535; in Tindal's 1548; several modern translators, Wesley, Macknight, Wakefield, etc., read "Joshua," as does our own in the margin. What a pity it had not been in the text, as all the smaller Bibles have no marginal readings and many simple people are bewildered with the expression! The apostle shows that, although Joshua did bring the children of Israel into the Promised Land, yet this could not be the intended rest, because long after this time the Holy Spirit, by David, speaks of this rest. The apostle therefore concludes,

9. *There remaineth therefore a rest to the people of God.* It was not (1) the rest of the Sabbath; it was not (2) the rest in the Promised Land, for the Psalmist wrote long after the days of Joshua. Therefore there is another rest, a state of blessedness, for the people of God; and this is the gospel, the blessings it procures and communicates, and the eternal glory which it prepares for, and has promised to, genuine believers.

There are two words in this chapter which we indifferently translate *rest, katapausis* and *sabbatismos*, the first signifying a "cessation from labour," so that the weary body is rested and refreshed; the second meaning, not only a rest from labor, but a "religious rest"—a rest of a sacred kind, of which both soul and body partake. This is true whether we understand the rest as referring to gospel blessings, or to eternal felicity, or to both.

10. *For he that is entered into his rest.* The man who has believed in Christ Jesus has entered into His rest, the state of happiness which He has provided and which is the forerunner of eternal glory. *Hath ceased from his own works.* No longer depends on the observance of Mosaic rites and ceremonies for his justification and

final happiness. He rests from all these works of the law as fully as God has rested from His works of creation. Those who restrain the word *rest* to the signification of eternal glory say that ceasing from our own works relates to the sufferings, tribulations, afflictions of this life, as in Rev. xiv. 13. I understand it as including both.

11. *Let us labour therefore.* The word implies every exertion of body and mind which can be made in reference to the subject. *Lest any man fall.* Lest he fall off from the grace of God, from the gospel and its blessings, and perish everlastingly. This is the meaning of the apostle, who never supposed that a man might not make final shipwreck of faith and of a good conscience as long as he was in a state of probation.

12. *For the word of God is quick, and powerful.* Commentators are greatly divided concerning the meaning of the phrase *the word of God;* some supposing the whole of divine revelation to be intended; others, the doctrine of the gospel faithfully preached; others, the mind of God or the divine intellect; and others, the Lord Jesus Christ, who is thus denominated in John i and Rev. xix. 13, the only places in which He is thus incontestably characterized in the New Testament. Mr. Wesley's note on this verse is expressed with his usual precision and accuracy: "*For the word of God*—preached, v. 2, and armed with threatenings, v. 3, *is living and powerful*—attended with the power of the living God, and conveying either life or death to the hearers; *sharper than any twoedged sword*—penetrating the heart more than this does the body; *piercing* quite through, and laying open, *the soul and spirit, joints and marrow*—the inmost recesses of the mind, which the apostle beautifully and strongly expresses by this heap of figurative words; *and is a discerner, not only of the thoughts,* but also of the *intentions.*" The law, the Word of God in general, is repeatedly compared to *a twoedged sword* among the Jewish writers. *Is a discerner of the thoughts.* "Is a critic of the propensities and suggestions of the heart." How many have felt this property of God's Word where it has been faithfully preached! How often has it happened that a man has seen the whole of his own character and some of the most private transactions of his life held up as it were to public view by the preacher, and yet the parties absolutely unknown to each other! Some, thus exhibited, have even supposed that their neighbors must have privately informed the preacher of their character and conduct; but it was the Word of God which, by the direction and energy of the divine Spirit, thus searched them out, was a critical Examiner of the propensities and suggestions of their hearts, and had pursued them through all their public haunts and private ways. Every genuine minister of the gospel has witnessed such effects as these under his ministry in repeated instances.

13. *Neither is there any creature that is not manifest.* God, from this word comes and by whom it has all its efficacy, is infinitely wise. And so infinite is He in His knowledge, and so omnipresent is He, that the whole creation is constantly exposed to His view; nor is there a creature of the affections, mind, or imagination that is not constantly under His eye. *But all things are naked and opened.* The verb *opened* signifies to have the "neck bent back" so as to expose the face to full view, that every feature might be seen; and this was often done with criminals, in order that they might be the better recognized and ascertained. *With whom we have to do.* "To whom we must give an account." He is our Judge, and is well-qualified to be so, as all our hearts and actions are *naked* and *opened* to him.

14. *Seeing then that we have a great high priest.* It is contended, and very properly, that the particle which we translate *seeing,* as if what followed was an immediate inference from what the apostle had been speaking, should be translated "now"; for the apostle, though he had before mentioned Christ as the "High Priest of our profession," chap. iii. 1, and as the High Priest who made "reconciliation for the sins of the people," chap. ii. 17, does not attempt to prove this in any of the preceding chapters, but now enters upon that point, and discusses it at great length to the end of chap. x.

After all, it is possible that this may be a resumption of the discourse from chap. iii. 6, the rest of that chapter and the preceding thirteen verses of this being considered as a parenthesis. These parts left out, the discourse runs on with perfect connection. It is very likely that the words here are spoken to meet an objection of those Jews who wished the Christians of Palestine to apostatize: "You have no Tabernacle—no Temple—no high priest—no sacrifice for sin. Without these there can be no religion; return therefore to us, who have the perfect Temple service appointed by God." To these he answers: "*We have a . . . high priest, that is passed into the heavens, Jesus the Son of God;* therefore *let us hold fast our profession.*" Three things the apostle professes to prove in this Epistle: (1) That Christ is greater than the *angels.* (2) That He is greater than *Moses.* (3) That He is greater than *Aaron* and all *high priests.* The former two arguments, with their applications and illustrations, he has already dispatched; and now he enters on the third. See the preface to this Epistle.

15. *For we have not an high priest.* To the objection, "Your High Priest, if entered into the heavens, can have no participation with you, and no sympathy for you, because out of the reach of human feelings and infirmities," he answers: "We have not a high priest who cannot sympathize with our weakness." Though He be the Son of God and equal in His divine nature with God, yet, having partaken of human nature, and having submitted to all its trials and distresses, and being *in all points tempted like as we are . . . without* feeling or consenting to *sin,* He is able to succor them that are tempted. See chap. ii. 18. The words might be translated "in all points according to the likeness," i.e., as far as His human nature could bear affinity to ours. For though He had a perfect human body and human soul, yet that body was perfectly tempered; it was free from all morbid action, and consequently from all irregular movements. His mind, or human soul, being free from all sin, being every way perfect, could feel no irregular temper, nothing that was inconsistent with infinite purity.

16. *Let us therefore come boldly unto the throne of grace.* The allusion to the high priest and his office on the Day of Atonement is

here kept up. The approach mentioned here is to the propitiatory or mercy seat. This was the covering of the ark of the testimony or covenant, at each end of which was a cherub, and between them the *shechinah,* or symbol of the divine majesty, which appeared to, and conversed with, the high priest. The throne of grace in heaven answers to this propitiatory, but to this *all* may approach who feel their need of salvation; and they may approach with freedom, confidence, liberty of speech, in opposition to the fear and trembling of the Jewish high priest. Here nothing is to be feared, provided the heart be right with God, truly sincere, and trusing alone in the sacrificial Blood. *That we may obtain mercy.* "That we may take mercy"—that we may receive the pardon of all our sins; there is mercy for the taking. *And find grace.* Mercy refers to the pardon of sin, and being brought into the favor of God. *Grace* is that by which the soul is supported after it has received this mercy, and by which it is purified from all unrighteousness, and upheld in all trials and difficulties, and enabled to prove faithful unto death. *To help in time of need.* "For a seasonable support"; that is, support when necessary, and as necessary, and in due proportion to the necessity. The word is properly rendered "assistance, help, or support"; but it is an assistance in consequence of the earnest cry of the person in distress, for the word signifies "to run at the cry."

CHAPTER 5

The nature of the high priesthood of Christ; His preeminence, qualifications, and order, 1-10. Imperfect state of the believing Hebrews, and the necessity of spiritual improvement, 11-14.

1. *For every high priest taken from among men.* This seems to refer to Lev. xxi. 10, where it is intimated that the high priest shall be taken from his brethren; i.e., he shall be of the tribe of Levi, and of the family of Aaron. *Is ordained for men.* Is appointed to preside over the divine worship in those things which relate to man's salvation. *That he may offer both gifts and sacrifices for sins.* God ever appeared to all His followers in two points of view: (1) as the Author and Dispenser of all temporal good; (2) as their Lawgiver and Judge. In reference to this twofold view of the Divine Being, His worship was composed of two different parts: (1) "offerings" or *gifts;* (2) *sacrifices.* As the Creator and Dispenser of all good, He had "offerings" by which His bounty and providence were acknowledged. As the Lawgiver and Judge, against whose injunctions offences had been committed, He had *sacrifices* offered to Him to make atonement for sin. The *gifts* mentioned here by the apostle included every kind of eucharistical offering. The *sacrifices* included victims of every sort, or animals whose lives were to be offered in sacrifice and their blood poured out before God as an atonement for sins.

2. *Who can have compassion on the ignorant.* The word signifies not merely to *have compassion* but to "acts with moderation" and to "bear with each in proportion" to his ignorance, weakness, and untoward circumstances, all taken into consideration with the offenses he has committed; in a word, to pity, feel for, and excuse as far as possible; and when the provoca-

tion is at the highest, to moderate one's passion towards the culprit, and be ready to pardon; and when punishment must be administered, to do it in the gentlest manner. The reason given why the high priest should be slow to punish and prone to forgive is that he himself is also "compassed with weakness"; "weakness lies all around him."

3. *And by reason hereof.* As he is also a transgressor of the commands of God, and unable to observe the law in its spirituality, he must offer sacrifices for sin, not only for the people, but for himself also; this must teach him to have a fellow feeling for others.

4. *This honour.* "The office," which is one meaning of the word in the best Greek writers. It is here an honorable office, because the man is the high priest of God, and is appointed by God himself to that office. *But he that is called of God, as was Aaron.* God himself appointed the tribe and family out of which the high priest was to be taken, and Aaron and his sons were expressly chosen by God to fill the office of the high priesthood.

5. *Christ glorified not himself.* The man Jesus Christ was also appointed by God to this most awful yet glorious office of being the High Priest of the whole human race. *Thou art my Son.* See on chap. i. 5.

6. *He saith also in another place.* That is, in Ps. cx. 4, a psalm of extraordinary importance, containing a very striking prediction of the birth, preaching, suffering, death, and conquests of the Messiah. For the mode of quotation here, see the note on chap. ii. 6. *Thou art a priest for ever.* As long as the sun and moon endure, Jesus will continue to be High Priest to all the successive generations of men, as He was the Lamb slain from the foundation of the world. If He be *a priest for ever,* there can be no succession of priests. *After the order of Melchisedec.* Who this person was must still remain a secret. We know nothing more of him than is written in Gen. xiv. 18, etc.

7. *Who in the days of his flesh.* The time of His incarnation, during which He took all the infirmities of human nature upon Him, and was afflicted in His body and human soul just as other men are, irregular and sinful passions excepted. The Redeemer of the world appears here as simply man; but He is the Representative of the whole human race. He must make expiation for sin by suffering, and He can suffer only as men. Suffering was as necessary as death; for man, because he has sinned, must suffer, and because he has broken the law, should die. Jesus took upon himself the nature of man, subject to all the trials and distresses of human nature. Though He was the Son of God, conceived and born without sin, or anything that could render Him liable to suffering or death, yet to constitute Him a complete Saviour, He must submit to whatever the law required; and therefore He is stated to have "learned . . . obedience by the things which he suffered," v. 8, that is, subjection to all the requisitions of the law; "and being made perfect," that is, having finished the whole by dying, He by these means became the "author of eternal salvation unto all them that obey him," v. 9; to them who, according to His own command, repent and believe the gospel, and

under the influence of His Spirit walk in holiness of life. *Prayers and supplications.* There may be an allusion here to the manner in which the Jews speak of prayer. "There are three degrees of prayer, each surpassing the other in silence; crying, with a loud voice; but tears surpass all" (*Synops. Sohar,* p. 33). The apostle shows that Christ made every species of prayer, and those especially by which they allowed a man must be successful with his Maker.

The word *hiketerias,* which we translate *supplications,* exists in no other part of the New Testament. *Hiketes* signifies a supplicant: "He who, in the most humble and servile manner, entreats and begs anything from another." *To save him from death.* I have already observed that Jesus Christ was the Representative of the human race; and have made some observations on the peculiarity of His sufferings, following the common acceptation of the words in the text, which things are true, howsoever the text may be interpreted. But here we may consider the pronoun *him* as implying the collective body of mankind. So he made *supplications with strong crying and tears unto him that was able to save them from death;* for I consider "them," of chap. ii. 15, the same or implying the same thing as *him* in this verse; and, thus understood, all the difficulty vanishes away. On this interpretation I shall give a paraphrase of the whole verse: "Jesus Christ, in the days of His flesh (for He was incarnated that He might redeem the seed of Abraham, the fallen race of man), and in His expiatory sufferings, when representing the whole human race, offered up prayers and supplications with strong crying and tears to Him who was able to save them from death. The intercession was prevalent, the passion and sacrifice were accepted, the sting of death was extracted, and Satan was dethroned."

9. *And being made perfect.* "And having finished all"—having died and risen again. Signifies to have "obtained the goal"; to have ended one's labor, and enjoyed the fruits of it. So when Christ had finished His course of tremendous sufferings and consummated the whole by His death and resurrection, He became the Cause of *eternal salvation unto all them that obey him.* He was consecrated both High Priest and Sacrifice by His offering upon the Cross. He "tasted death for every man"; but He is the *author* and "cause of eternal salvation only to them who *obey him.* It is not merely believers, but obedient believers, who shall be finally saved. Therefore this text is an absolute, unimpeachable evidence that it is not the imputed obedience of Christ that saves any man.

10. *Called of God an high priest.* Being "constituted, hailed, and acknowledged" to be a High Priest.

11. *Of whom we have many things to say.* The words which we translate *of whom* are variously applied: (1) To Melchisedec; (2) To Christ, (3) To the endless priesthood. It is likely that the words are to be understood as meaning Jesus, or that endless priesthood of which he was a little before speaking, and which is a subject that carnal Christians cannot easily comprehend. *Hard to be uttered.* "Difficult to be interpreted," because Melchisedec was a typical person. Or if it refer to the priesthood of Christ, that is still more difficult to be explained, as it implies not only His being constituted a Priest

after this typical order, but His paying down the ransom for the sins of the whole world. *Dull of hearing.* Your souls do not keep pace with the doctrines and exhortations delivered to you. Signifies a person who walks heavily and makes little speed.

12. *For when for the time.* They had heard the gospel for many years, and had professed to be Christians for a long time; on these accounts they might reasonably have been expected to be well-instructed in divine things, so as to be able to instruct others. *Which be the first principles.* "Certain first principles or elements." The literal translation of the passage is this: "You have need that one teach you a second time certain elements of the doctrines of Christ, or oracles of God"; i.e., the notices which the prophets gave concerning the priesthood of Jesus Christ, such as are found in Psalms cx and in Isaiah liii. By the *oracles of God* the writings of the Old Testament are undoubtedly meant. *And are become such.* The words seem to intimate that they had once been better instructed, and had now forgotten that teaching; and this was occasioned by their being "dull of hearing." Either they had not continued to hear or they had heard so carelessly that they were not profited by what they heard. They had probably totally omitted the preaching of the gospel and consequently forgotten all they had learned. Indeed it was to reclaim those Hebrews from backsliding and preserve them from total apostasy that this Epistle was written. *Such as have need of milk. Milk* is a metaphor by which many authors, both sacred and profane, express the first principles of religion and science. On the contrary, those who had well learned all the first principles of religion and science and knew how to apply them were considered as adults who were capable of receiving "solid food"; i.e., the more difficult and sublime doctrines. The rabbins abound with this figure; it occurs frequently in Philo, and in the Greek ethic writers also. But all these are to derive their nourishment or spiritual instruction from *the oracles of God.* The word oracle is used by the best Greek writers to signify a "divine speech, or answer of a deity to a question proposed." It always implied a speech or declaration purely celestial, in which man had no part; and it is thus used wherever it occurs in the New Testament. (1) It signifies the law received from God by Moses, Acts vii. 38. (2) The Old Testament in general, the holy men of old having spoken by the inspiration of the divine Spirit, Rom. iii. 2. (3) It signifies divine revelation in general, because all delivered immediately from God, I Thess. ii. 13; I Pet. iv. 11. When we consider what respect was paid by the heathens to their oracles, which were supposed to be delivered by those gods who were the objects of their adoration, but which were only impostures, we may then learn what respect is due to the true *oracles of God.*

13. *For every one that useth milk.* It is very likely that the apostle, by using this term, refers to the doctrines of the law, which were only the rudiments of religion and were intended to lead us to Christ, that we might be justified by faith. *The word of righteousness.* "The doctrine of justification." I believe this to be the apostle's meaning. He that uses *milk,* rests in the ceremonies and observances of the

law, *is unskilful in* "the doctrine of justification"; for this requires faith in the sacrificial death of the promised Messiah.

14. *But strong meat.* The high and sublime doctrines of Christianity: the atonement, justification by faith, the gift of the Holy Ghost, the fullness of Christ dwelling in the souls of men, the resurrection of the body, the glorification of both body and soul in the realms of blessedness, and an endless union with Christ in the throne of His glory. This is the "strong food" which the genuine Christian understands, receives, digests, and by which he grows. *By reason of use.* Who, by constant hearing, believing, praying, and obedience, *use* all the graces of God's Spirit; and in the faithful use of them find every one improved, so that they daily grow in grace and in the knowledge of Jesus Christ, our Lord. *Have their senses exercised.* The word signifies the different organs of sense through which we gain the sensations called seeing, hearing, tasting, smelling, and feeling. There is something in the soul that answers to all these senses in the body. In the adult Christian these senses are said to be *exercised,* a metaphor taken from the athletes or contenders in the Grecian games, who were wont to employ all their powers, skill, and agility in mock fights, running, wrestling, that they might be the better prepared for the actual contests when they took place.

CHAPTER 6

We must proceed from the first principles of the doctrine of Christ unto perfection, and not lay the foundation a second time, 1-3. Those who were once enlightened, and have been made partakers of the Holy Ghost and the various blessings of the gospel, if they apostatize from Christ, and finally reject Him as their Saviour, cannot be renewed again to repentance, 4-6. The double similitude of the ground blessed of God and bearing fruit and of that ground which is cursed of God and bears briers and thorns, 7-8. The apostle's confidence in them, and his exhortation to diligence and perseverance, 9-12. God's promise and oath to Abraham, by which the immutability of His counsel is shown, in order to excite our hope, 13-18. Hope is the anchor of the soul, and enters within the veil, 19-20.

1. *Therefore.* Because you have been so indolent, slow of heart, and still have so many advantages *Leaving the principles of the doctrine of Christ.* Ceasing to continue in the state of babes, who must be fed with milk—with the lowest doctrines of the gospel, when you should be capable of understanding the highest. The words might be translated "the discourse of the beginning of Christ," as in the margin; that is, the account of His incarnation, and the different types and ceremonies in the law by which His advent, nature, office, and miracles were pointed out. *Let us go on unto perfection.* Let us never rest till we are adult Christians— till we are saved from all sin, and are filled with the Spirit and power of Christ. The original is very emphatic: "Let us be carried on to this perfection." God is ever ready by the power of His Spirit to carry us forward to every degree of light, life, and love necessary to prepare us for an eternal weight of glory. Many make a violent outcry against the doctrine of *perfection,* i.e., against the heart being cleansed from all sin in this life and filled with love to God and man, because they judge it to be impossible! Is it too much to say of these that they know neither the Scripture nor the power of God? Surely the Scripture promises

the thing, and the power of God can carry us on to the possession of it. *Laying again the foundation of repentance.* The phrase *dead works* occurs but once more in the sacred writings, and that is in chap. ix. 14 of this Epistle; and in both places it seems to signify "such works as deserve death"—works of those who were dead in sins, and dead by sentence of the law, because they had by these works broken the law. Repentance may be properly called the *foundation* of the work of God in the soul of man, because by it we forsake sin and turn to God to find mercy. *Faith toward God* is also a *foundation,* or fundamental principle, without which it is impossible to please God, and without which we cannot be saved. By repentance we feel the need of God's mercy; by faith we find that mercy.

2. *Of the doctrine of baptisms.* I am inclined to think that all the terms in this verse, as well as those in the former, belong to the Levitical law and are to be explained on that ground. *Baptisms,* or immersions of the body in water, sprinklings, and washings, were frequent as religious rites among the Hebrews, and were all emblematical of that purity which a holy God requires in His worshippers, and without which they cannot be happy here nor glorified in heaven. *Laying on of hands* was also frequent, especially in sacrifices. The person bringing the victim laid his hands on its head, confessed his sins over it, and then gave it to the priest to be offered to God, that it might make atonement for his transgressions. This also had respect to Jesus Christ, that Lamb of God who takes away the sins of the world. The doctrines also of the *resurrection of the dead* and of *eternal judgment* were both Jewish, but were only partially revealed and then referred to the gospel. Daniel has taught both, chap. xii. 2: "And many of them that sleep in the dust of the earth shall awake, some to everlasting life, and some to shame and everlasting contempt."

3. *And this will we do.* God being my Helper, I will teach you all the sublime truths of the gospel, and show you how all its excellences were typified by the law, and particularly by its sacrificial system.

4. *For it is impossible for those who were once enlightened.* Before I proceed to explain the different terms in these verses, it is necessary to give my opinion of their design and meaning: (1) I do not consider them as having any reference to any person professing Christianity. (2) They do not belong, nor are they applicable, to backsliders of any kind. (3) They belong to apostates from Christianity; to such as reject the whole Christian system, and its Author, the Lord Jesus. (4) And to those of them only who join with the blaspheming Jews, call Christ an impostor, and vindicate His murderers in having crucified Him as a malefactor; and thus they render their salvation impossible, by willfully and maliciously rejecting the Lord that bought them. No man believing in the Lord Jesus as the great Sacrifice for sin, and acknowledging Christianity as a divine revelation, is here intended, though he may have unfortunately backslidden from any degree of the salvation of God. *Once enlightened.* Thoroughly instructed in the nature and design of the Christian religion, having received the knowledge of the truth, chap. x. 32; and being con-

vinced of sin, righteousness, and judgment; and led to Jesus, the Saviour of sinners. *Tasted of the heavenly gift.* Having received the knowledge of salvation by the remission of sins, through the Dayspring which from on high had visited them; such having received Christ, the *heavenly gift* of God's infinite love, John iii. 16. *Partakers of the Holy Ghost.* The Spirit himself witnessing with their spirits that they were the children of God, and thus assuring them of God's mercy towards them, and of the efficacy of the atonement through which they had received such blessings.

5. *And have tasted the good word of God.* Have had this proof of the excellence of the promise of God in sending the gospel, the gospel being itself the good word of a good God, the reading and preaching of which they find sweet to the taste of their souls. Genuine believers have an appetite for the Word of God; they taste it, and then their relish for it is the more abundantly increased. *The powers of the world to come.* These words are understood two ways: (1) They may refer to the stupendous miracles wrought in confirmation of the gospel, the gospel dispensation being "the world to come" in the Jewish phraseology, as we have often seen; and that *dynamis* is often taken for a "mighty work" or "miracle" is plain from various parts of the Gospels. The prophets had declared that the Messiah, when He came, should work many miracles, and should be as mighty in word and deed as was Moses; see Deut. xviii. 15-19. And they particularly specify the giving sight to the blind, hearing to the deaf, strength to the lame, and speech to the dumb, Isa. xxxv. 5-6. All these miracles Jesus Christ did in the sight of this very people; and thus they had the highest evidence they could have that Jesus was this promised Messiah, and could have no pretense to doubt His mission or apostatize from the Christian faith which they had received. (2) The words have been supposed to apply to those communications and foretastes of eternal blessedness, or of the joys of the world to come, which they who are justified through the Blood of the covenant, and walk faithfully with their God, experience; and to this sense the word *have tasted* is thought more properly to apply. But "to taste," signifies "to experience or have full proof" of a thing. Thus, to "taste of death," Matt. xvi. 28, is "to die." It seems, therefore, that the first opinion is the best founded.

6. *If they shall fall away.* "And having fallen away." I can express my own mind on this translation nearly in the words of Dr. Macknight: "The participles *who were enlightened, have tasted,* and *were made partakers,* being aorists, are properly rendered by our translators in the past time; wherefore *parapesontas,* being an aorist, ought likewise to have been translated in the past time, 'HAVE *fallen away.*' Nevertheless, our translators, following Beza, who without any authority from ancient MSS. has inserted in his version the word '*if,*' have rendered this clause, IF *they fall away,* that this text might not appear to contradict the doctrine of the perseverance of the saints. But as no translator should take upon him to add to or alter the Scriptures, for the sake of any favourite doctrine, I have translated *parapesontas* in the past time, '*have fallen away,*' according to the true import of the word, as standing in connection with the other aorists in the preceding verses." *To renew them again unto repentance.* As *repentance* is the first step that a sinner must take in order to return to God, and as sorrow for sin must be useless in itself unless there be a proper sacrificial offering, these having rejected the only available sacrifice, their repentance for sin, had they any, would be nugatory, and their salvation impossible on this simple account; and this is the very reason which the apostle immediately subjoins. *Seeing they crucify to themselves the Son of God.* They reject Him on the ground that He was an impostor, and justly put to death. And thus they are said to crucify Him to themselves—to do that in their present apostasy which the Jews did; and they show thereby that, had they been present when He was crucified, they would have joined with His murderers. *And put him to an open shame.* "And have made Him a public example"; or, "crucifying unto themselves and making the Son of God a public example." That is, they show openly that they judge Jesus Christ to have been worthy of the death which He suffered, and was justly made a public example by being crucified. This shows that it is final apostasy, by the total rejection of the gospel and blasphemy of the Saviour of men, that the apostle has in view. See the note on v. 4.

7. *For the earth which drinketh in the rain.* As much as if he had said: In giving up such apostates as utterly incurable, we act as men do in cultivating their fields; for as the ground, which drinketh in the rain by which the providence of God waters it, brings forth fruit to compensate the toil of the tiller, and continues to be cultivated, God granting His blessing to the labors of the husbandman; so,

8. *That which beareth thorns and briers is rejected.* That is: The land which, notwithstanding the most careful cultivation, receiving also in due times the early and latter rain, produces nothing but thorns and briers, or noxious weeds of different kinds, is rejected, is given up as unimprovable; its briers, thorns, and brushwood burnt down; and then left to be pastured on by the beasts of the field. This seems to be the custom in husbandry to which the apostle alludes. *Is nigh unto cursing.* It is acknowledged, on almost all hands, that this Epistle was written before the destruction of Jerusalem by the Romans. This verse is in my opinion a proof of it, and here I suppose the apostle refers to that approaching destruction; and perhaps he has this all along in view, but speaks of it covertly, that he might not give offense.

There is a good sense in which all these things may be applied to the Jews at large, who were favored by our Lord's ministry and miracles. They were "enlightened" by His preaching; "tasted" of the benefits of the "heavenly gift"—the Christian religion established among them; saw many of their children and relatives "made partakers of the Holy Ghost"; "tasted the good word of God," by the fulfillment of the promise made to Abraham; and saw the almighty power of God exerted, in working a great variety of miracles. Yet after being convinced that never man spake as this Man, and that none could do those miracles which He did except God were with him; after having followed Him in thousands for three years while He preached to them the gospel of the kingdom of God; they "fell away" from all this, crucified Him who, even in His sufferings as well as His resurrection, was demonstrated by miracles to be the Son of God; and then to vindicate their unparalleled wickedness, endeavored to make Him a public example by reproaches and blasphemies. Therefore their state, which had received much moral cultivation from Moses, the prophets, Christ and His apostles; and now bore nothing but the most vicious fruits—pride, unbelief, hardness of heart, contempt of God's Word and ordinances, blasphemy, and rebellion —was *rejected*, reprobated, of God; was *nigh unto cursing*—about to be cast off from the divine protection; and their city and Temple were shortly to be burnt up by the Roman armies. Thus the apostle, under the case of individuals, points out the destruction that was to come upon this people in general, and which actually took place about seven years after the writing of this Epistle! And this appears to be the very subject which the apostle has in view in the parallel solemn passages, chap. x. 26-31; and, viewed in this light, much of their obscurity and difficulty vanishes away.

9. *But, beloved.* Here he softens what he had before said. Having given them the most solemn warning against apostasy, he now encourages them to persevere, commends the good that is in them, and excites them to watchfulness and activity. *Better things of you.* Than that you shall resemble that unfruitful ground that can be improved by no tillage, and is thrown into waste, and is fit only for the beasts of the forests to roam in. *Things that accompany salvation.* "Things that are suitable to a state of salvation"; you give proofs still that you have not, whatever others have done, departed from the living God. Several of your brethren have already apostatized, and the whole nation is in a state of rebellion against God; and in consequence of their final rejection of Christ and His gospel are about to be finally rejected by God. They must meet with destruction; they have the things that are suitable to, and indicative of, a state of reprobation; the wrath of God will come upon them to the uttermost; but while they meet with destruction, you shall meet with salvation. It is worthy of remark that no genuine Christians perished in the destruction of Jerusalem; they all, previously to the siege of Titus, escaped to Pella.

10. *God is not unrighteous.* God is bound to men only by His own promise. This promise He is not obliged to make; but, when once made, His righteousness or justice requires Him to keep it. Therefore whatever He has promised He will certainly perform. The word *labour*, prefixed to *love*, is wanting in almost every MS. and version of importance. *Ministered to the saints.* Have contributed to the support and comfort of the poor Christians who were suffering persecution in Judea. As they had thus ministered, and were still ministering, they gave full proof that they had a common cause with the others; and this was one of the things that proved them to be in a state of salvation.

11. *We desire.* We "earnestly wish" that each person among you may continue to "manifest, exhibit to full view," the same diligence. There might be reason to suspect that some, through fear of man, might not wish the good they did

to be seen, lest they also should suffer persecution. *To the full assurance of hope.* The person who has this *full assurance of hope* is he who not only knows and feels that his sins are forgiven through Christ Jesus, but also that his heart is purified from all unrighteousness, that the whole body of sin and death is destroyed, and that he is fully made a partaker of the divine nature. As without holiness—complete, entire holiness—no man can see God, so without this none can scripturally or rationally hope for eternal glory, it being a contradiction to profess to have the full assurance of hope to enjoy a state and place for which the soul is conscious it is not prepared.

12. *That ye be not slothful.* This shows how the full assurance of hope is to be regulated and maintained. They must be diligent; slothfulness will deprive them of both hope and faith. That "faith which worketh by love" will maintain hope in its full and due exercise. *Followers of them.* "That you be imitators of them who are inheriting the promises." And they inherited these promises by faith in Him who is invisible, and who, they knew, could not lie; and they patiently endured, through difficulties and adversities of every kind, and persevered unto death.

13. *When God made promise to Abraham.* The promise referred to is that made to Abraham when he had offered his son Isaac on the altar, Gen. xxii. 16-18: "By myself have I sworn, saith the Lord, for because thou hast done this thing, and hast not withheld thy son, thine only son: that in blessing I will bless thee, and in multiplying I will multiply thy seed as the stars of the heaven, and as the sand which is upon the sea shore; and thy seed shall possess the gate of his enemies; and in thy seed shall all the nations of the earth be blessed." *He sware by himself.* He pledged His eternal power and Godhead for the fulfillment of the promise; there was no being superior to himself to whom He could make appeal, or by whom He could be bound.

14. *Saying, Surely blessing I will bless thee.* I will continue to bless you. *Multiplying I will multiply thee.* I will continue to increase your posterity. In the most literal manner God continues to fulfill this promise; genuine Christians are Abraham's seed, and God is increasing their number daily.

15. *He obtained the promise.* Isaac was supernaturally born; and in his birth God began to fulfill the promise. While he lived, he saw a provision made for the multiplication of his seed; and, having continued steadfast in the faith, he received the end of all the promises in the enjoyment of an eternal glory. And the inference from this is: If we believe and prove faithful unto death, we shall also inherit the promises.

16. *Men verily swear by the greater.* One who has greater authority.

17. *The heirs of promise.* All the believing posterity of Abraham, and the nations of the earth or Gentiles in general. *The immutability of his counsel.* His unchangeable purpose, to call the Gentiles to salvation by Jesus Christ; to justify every penitent by faith; to accept faith in Christ for justification in place of personal righteousness; and finally to bring every

persevering believer, whether Jew or Gentile, to eternal glory.

18. *That by two immutable things.* The promise and oath of God: the promise pledged His faithfulness and justice; the oath, all the infinite perfections of His Godhead, for He sware by himself. *We might have a strong consolation.* There appears to be an allusion here to the cities of refuge and to the persons who fled to them for safety. As the person who killed his neighbor unawares was sure if he gained the city of refuge he should be safe, and had strong consolation in the hope that he should reach it, this hope animated him in his race to the city. He ran, he fled, knowing that, though in danger the most imminent of losing his life, yet as he was now acting according to an ordinance of God, he was certain of safety provided he got to the place.

19. *Which hope we have as an anchor.* The apostle here changes the allusion; he represents the state of the followers of God in this lower world as resembling that of a vessel striving to perform her voyage through a troublesome, tempestuous, dangerous sea. At last she gets near the port; but the tempest continues; the water is shallow, broken, and dangerous, and she cannot get in. In order to prevent her being driven to sea again, she heaves out her sheet anchor, which she has been able to get within the pierhead by means of her boat, though she could not herself get in. Then, swinging at the length of her cable, she rides out the storm in confidence, knowing that her anchor is sound, the ground good in which it is fastened, and the cable strong. The comparison of *hope* to an *anchor* is frequent among the ancient heathen writers, who supposed it to be as necessary to the support of a man in adversity as the anchor is to the safety of the ship when about to be driven on a lee shore by a storm.

20. *Whither the forerunner.* The word *prodromos* does not merely signify one that goes or runs before another, but also one who shows the way, he who first does a particular thing. So in the Septuagint, Isa. xxviii. 4, *prodromos sykou* signifies the "first fruits of the fig tree." To this meaning of the word Pliny refers, *Hist. Nat.,* xvi, c. 26: "The fig tree produces some figs which are ripe before the rest, and these are called by the Athenians *prodromos,* forerunner." The word is interpreted in the same way by Hesychius; it occurs in no other part of the New Testament, but may be found in Ecclus. xii. 8 and in Isa. xxviii. 4, quoted above from the Septuagint. From this we may at once perceive the meaning of the phrase: Jesus is the "Firstfruits" of human nature that has entered into the heavenly Kingdom. And He is entered *for us,* as the Firstfruits of all who have found redemption in His blood. *After the order of Melchisedec.* After a long digression the apostle resumes his explanation of Ps. cx. 4, which he had produced, chap. v. 6, 10, in order to prove the permanency of the high priesthood of Christ.

CHAPTER 7

Concerning the greatness of Melchisedec, after whose order Christ is a High Priest, 1-4. The Levites had authority to take tithes of the people; yet Abraham, their representative, paid tithes to Melchisedec, 5-10. Perfection cannot come by the Mosaic law, else there could be no need for another priest after the order of Melchisedec, according to the prediction of David in Psalms cx, which priest is sprung from a tribe to which the priesthood, according to the law, did not appertain; but Christ is a Priest forever, not according to the law, "but after the power of an endless life," 11-17. The law therefore is disannulled because of its unprofitableness and imperfection; and Christ has an unchangeable priesthood, 18-24. He is therefore able always to save them that come unto Him, being in every respect a suitable Saviour; and He has offered up himself for the sins of the people, 25-27. The law makes those priests who have infirmity; but He who is consecrated by the oath is perfect, and endures forever, 28.

1. *For this Melchisedec, king of Salem.* The name Melchisedec is thus expounded in *Bereshith Rabba,* "The Justifier of those who dwell in him." *Salem* is generally understood to be Jerusalem; but some think that it was that city of Shechem mentioned in Josh. xx. 7. Jerome was of this opinion.

2. *Gave a tenth part of all.* It was an ancient custom among all the nations of the earth to consecrate a part or tenth of the spoils taken in war to the objects of their worship.

3. *Without father, without mother.* The object of the apostle in thus producing the example of Melchisedec was to show: (1) That Jesus was the Person prophesied of in the 110th psalm, which psalm the Jews uniformly understood as predicting the Messiah. (2) To answer the objections of the Jews against the legitimacy of the priesthood of Christ, taken from the stock from which He proceeded. The objection is this: If the Messiah is to be a true Priest, He must come from a legitimate stock, as all the priests under the law have regularly done; otherwise we cannot acknowledge Him to be a Priest. But Jesus of Nazareth has not proceeded from such a stock; therefore we cannot acknowledge Him for a Priest, the Antitype of Aaron. To this objection the apostle answers that it was not necessary for the priest to come from a particular stock, for Melchisedec was a priest of the most high God, and yet was not of the stock of either Abraham or Aaron, but a Canaanite. He who could not support his pretensions by just genealogical evidences was said by the Jews to be *without father.* In this way both Christ and Melchisedec were *without father* and *without mother;* i.e., were not descended from the original Jewish sacerdotal stock. Yet Melchisedec, who was a Canaanite, was a priest of the most high God. The old Syriac has given the true meaning by translating thus: "Whose father and mother are not inscribed among the genealogies." The Arabic is nearly the same: "He had neither father nor mother; the genealogy not being reckoned." The Aethiopic: "He had neither father nor mother upon earth, nor is his genealogy known." *Made like unto the Son of God.* Melchisedec was without father and mother, *having neither beginning of days, nor end of life.* His genealogy is not recorded; when he was born and when he died are unknown. His priesthood, therefore, may be considered as perpetual. In these respects he was like to Jesus Christ, who, as to His Godhead, had neither father nor mother, beginning of time, nor end of days; and has an everlasting priesthood.

4. *Consider how great this man was.* There is something exceedingly mysterious in the person and character of this king of Salem, and to find out the whole is impossible. He seems to have been a sort of universal priest, having none superior to him in all that region; and

confessedly superior even to Abraham himself, the father of the faithful and the source of the Jewish race.

5. *They that are of the sons of Levi.* The priests who are of the posterity of the Levites, and receive the priesthood in virtue of their descent from Aaron, have authority from the law of God to receive tithes from the people. *According to the law.* That is, the Levites received a tenth from the people. The priests received a tenth of this tenth from the Levites, who are here called their brethren, because they were of the same tribe and employed in the same sacred work. The apostle is proceeding to show that Melchisedec was greater even than Abraham, the head of the fathers, for to him Abraham gave tithes; and as the Levites were the posterity of Abraham, they are represented here as paying tithes to Melchisedec through him. Yet Melchisedec was not of this family, and therefore must be considered as having a more honorable priesthood than even Aaron himself; for he took the tenth from Abraham, not for his maintenance, for he was a king, but in virtue of his office as universal high priest of all that region.

6. *Blessed him that had the promises.* This is a continuation of the same argument, namely, to show the superiority of Melchisedec, and in consequence to prove the superiority of the priesthood of Christ beyond that of Aaron. As in the seed of Abraham all the nations of the earth were to be blessed, Abraham received a sacerdotal blessing from Melchisedec, who was the representative of the Messiah, the promised Seed, to show that it was through Him, as the High Priest of the human race, that this blessing was to be derived on all mankind.

7. *The less is blessed of the better.* That the superior blesses the inferior is a general proposition. But Abraham was blessed of Melchisedec; therefore Melchisedec was greater than Abraham.

8. *Here men that die receive tithes.* The apostle is speaking of the ecclesiastical constitution of the Jews, which was standing at the time this Epistle was written. Under the Jewish dispensation, though the priests were successively removed by death, yet they were as duly replaced by others appointed from the same family, and the payment of tithes was never interrupted. But as there is no account of Melchisedec ceasing to be a priest or of his dying, he is represented as still living, the better to point him out as a type of Christ, and to show his priesthood to be more excellent than that which was according to the law, as an unchanging priesthood must be more excellent than that which was continually changing. *But there he receiveth them.* The *here* in the first clause of this verse refers to Mosaical institutions, as then existing; the *there* in this clause refers to the place in Genesis (chap. xiv. 20) where it is related that Abraham gave tithes to Melchisedec, who is still considered as being alive or without a successor, because there is no account of his death nor of any termination of his priesthood.

9. *And as I may so say.* "And so to speak a word." This form of speech, which is very frequent among the purest Greek writers, is generally used to soften some harsh expression, or to limit the meaning when the proposition might otherwise appear to be too general. It answers fully to our "so to speak—as one would say—I had almost said—in a certain sense." *Payed tithes in Abraham.* The Levites, who were descendants of Abraham, paid tithes to Melchisedec "through" Abraham, their progenitor and representative.

10. *For he was yet in the loins of his father.* That is, Levi was seminally included in Abraham, his forefather.

11. *If therefore perfection were by the Levitical priesthood.* The word *teleiosis* signifies the "completing" or "finishing" of anything, so as to leave nothing imperfect and nothing wanting. Applied here to the Levitical priesthood, it signifies the accomplishment of that for which a priesthood is established, viz., giving the Deity an acceptable service, enlightening and instructing the people, pardoning all offenses, purging the conscience from guilt, purifying the soul and preparing it for heaven, and regulating the conduct of the people according to the precepts of the moral law. This perfection never came, and never could come, by the Levitical law; it was the shadow of good things to come, but was not the substance. It represented a perfect system, but was imperfect in itself. *For under it the people received the law.* That is, as most interpret this place, under the priesthood, because on the priesthood the whole Mosaical law and the Jewish economy depended. But it is much better to understand "on account of it," instead of *under it*; for it is a positive fact that the law was given before any priesthood was established, for Aaron and his sons were not called nor separated to this office till Moses came down the second time from the mount with the tables renewed, after that he had broken them, Exod. xl. 12-14. But it was in reference to the great sacrificial system that the law was given, and on that law the priesthood was established; for why was a priesthood necessary but because that law was broken and must be fulfilled? *That another priest should rise.* The law was given that the offense might abound and sin appear exceeding sinful, and to show the absolute necessity of the sacrifice and mediation of the great Messiah. But it was neither perfect in itself, nor could it confer perfection, nor did it contain the original priesthood. Melchisedec had a priesthood more than four hundred years before the law was given; and David prophesied, Ps. cx. 4, that another priest should arise after the order of Melchisedec, nearly five hundred years after the law was given. The law therefore did not contain the original priesthood; this existed typically in Melchisedec, and really in Jesus Christ.

12. *The priesthood being changed.* That is, the order of Aaron being now abrogated to make way for that which had preceded it, the order of Melchisedec. *There is made of necessity a change also of the law.* The very essence of the Levitical law consisting in its sacrificial offerings; and as these could not confer perfection, could not reconcile God to man, purify the unholy heart, nor open the kingdom of Heaven to the souls of men, consequently it must be abolished, according to the order of God himself.

13. *For he of whom these things are spoken.* That is, Jesus, the Messiah, spoken of in Ps. cx. 4, who came, not from the tribe of Levi, but from the tribe of Judah, of which tribe **no priest**

ever ministered at a Jewish altar, nor could minister according to the law.

14. *For it is evident.* As the apostle speaks here with so much confidence, it follows that our Lord's descent from the tribe of Judah was incontrovertible. The genealogical tables, in both Matthew and Luke, establish this point.

15. *And it is yet far more evident.* "And besides, it is more abundantly, strikingly manifest." It is very difficult to translate these words, but the apostle's meaning is plain, viz., that God designed the Levitical priesthood to be changed, because of the oath in Ps. cx, where, addressing the Messiah, he says: "Thou art a priest for ever after the order [or similitude] of Melchisedek," who was not only a priest, but also a king. None of the Levitical priests sustained this double office; but they both, with that of prophet, appear and were exercised in the person of our Lord, who is the Priest to which the apostle alludes.

16. *Who is made.* Appointed to this high office by God himself, not succeeding one that was disabled or dead. This is probably all that the apostle intends by the words *carnal commandment,* for *carnal* does not always mean sinful or corrupt, but feeble, frail, or what may be said of or concerning man in his present dying condition. *But after the power of an endless life.* Not dying, or ceasing through weakness to be a priest, but properly immortal himself, and having the power to confer life and immortality on others.

17. *For he testifieth.* That is, either the Scripture, in the place so often quoted, or God by that Scripture. *Thou art a priest for ever.* This is the proof that He was not appointed according to the carnal commandment, but according to the power of an endless life, because He is a Priest *for ever;* i.e., One that never dies and is never disabled from performing the important functions of His office.

18. *For there is verily a disannulling.* There is a total abrogation "of the former law" relative to the Levitical priesthood. See v. 19. *For the weakness.* It had no energy; it communicated none; it had no Spirit to minister; it required perfect obedience, but furnished no assistance to those who were under it. *And unprofitableness.* No man was benefited by the mere observance of its precepts. It pardoned no sin, changed no heart, reformed no life; it found men dead in trespasses and sins, and it consigned them to eternal death. It was therefore weak in itself and unprofitable to men.

19. *For the law made nothing perfect.* It completed nothing; it was only the outline of a great plan, the shadow of a glorious substance; see on v. 11. It neither pardoned sin or purified the heart, nor gave strength to obey the moral precepts. *Nothing* is put here for "no person." *But the bringing in of a better hope.* The original is very emphatic, the "superintroduction" or the "after introduction"; and this seems to be put in opposition to the "the preceding commandment," or former Levitical law, of v. 18. This went before to prepare the way of the Lord, to show the exceeding sinfulness of sin and the strict justice of God. The *better hope,* which referred not to earthly but to spiritual good, not to temporal but eternal felicity, founded on the priesthood and atonement of Christ, was after-

wards introduced for the purpose of doing what the law could not do, and giving privileges and advantages which the law would not afford. One of these privileges immediately follows: *By the which we draw nigh unto God.* This is a sacerdotal phrase. The high priest alone could approach to the Divine Presence in the holy of holies; but not without the blood of the sacrifice, and that only once in the year. But through Christ, as our High Priest, all believers in Him have an entrance to the holiest by His blood, and through Him perform acceptable service to God. The *better hope* means, in this place, Jesus Christ, who is the Author and Object of the hope of eternal life, which all His genuine followers possess.

21. *Those priests,* the Levitical, *were made without an oath,* to show that the whole system was changeable and might be abolished. *But this,* the everlasting priesthood of Christ, *with an oath,* to show that the gospel dispensation should never change and never be abolished. *By him,* God the Father, *that said unto him,* the promised Messiah, Ps. cx. 4, *The Lord sware,* to show the immutability of His counsel, *and will not repent,* can never change His mind nor purpose, *Thou art a priest for ever*—as long as time shall run and the generations of men be continued on earth. Till the necessity of the mediatorial Kingdom be superseded by the fixed state of eternity, till this Kingdom be delivered up unto the Father, and God shall be All in All, shall this priesthood of Christ endure.

22. *By so much,* this solemn, unchangeable oath of God, *was Jesus made a surety,* a "Mediator," One who brings the two parties together, witnesses the contract, and offers the covenant sacrifice on the occasion. *A better testament.* "A better covenant"; thus contradistinguished from the Mosaic, which was the old covenant; and this is called the new and better covenant, because God has in it promised other blessings, to other people, on other conditions, than the old covenant did. The new covenant is better than the old in the following particulars: (1) God promised to the Jewish nation certain secular blessings, peculiar to that nation, on condition of their keeping the law of Moses; but under the new covenant He promises pardon of sin, and final salvation to all mankind, on condition of believing on Jesus Christ and walking in His testimonies. (2) The Jewish priests, fallible, dying men, were mediators of the old covenant by means of their sacrifices, which could not take away sin, nor render the comers thereunto perfect. But Jesus Christ, who liveth forever, who is infinite in wisdom and power, by the sacrifice of himself has established this new covenant, and by the shedding of His blood has opened the kingdom of Heaven to all believers.

23. *And they truly were many priests.* Under the Mosaic law it was necessary there should be a succession of priests because, being mortal, they were not suffered to continue always by reason of death.

24. *But this.* "But He," that is, Christ, *because he continueth ever,* is eternal, *hath an unchangeable priesthood,* "a priesthood that passeth not away" from Him. He lives forever, and He lives a Priest forever.

25. *Wherefore.* Because He is an everlasting Priest and has offered the only available sacrifice, *he is able . . . to save* from the power, guilt, nature, and punishment of sin. *To the uttermost,* to all intents, degrees, purposes; and always, and in and through all times, places, and circumstances; for all this is implied in the original word. But "in and through all times" seems to be the particular meaning here, because of what follows, *he ever liveth to make intercession for them;* this depends on the perpetuity of His priesthood and the continuance of His mediatorial office. But none can be saved by His grace that do not *come unto God by [through] him;* i.e., imploring mercy through Him as their Sacrifice and Atonement. The phrase "to make intercession" for a person has a considerable latitude of meaning. It signifies: (1) To come to or meet a person on any cause whatever. (2) To intercede, pray for, or entreat in the behalf of, another. (3) To defend or vindicate a person. (4) To commend. (5) To furnish any kind of assistance or help.

26. *Such an high priest became us.* Such a High Priest was in every respect suitable to us, every way qualified to accomplish the end for which He came into the world. There is probably here an allusion to the qualifications of the Jewish high priest: (1) He was required to be *holy,* answering to the Hebrew *chasid,* "merciful." Holiness was his calling; and, as he was the representative of his brethren, he was required to be merciful and compassionate. (2) He was to be *harmless,* "without evil"—holy without and holy within; injuring none, but rather living for the benefit of others. (3) He was *undefiled,* answering to the Hebrew "without blemish"—having no bodily imperfection. Nothing low, mean, base, or unbecoming in his conduct. (4) He was *separate from sinners.* By his office he was separated from all men and worldly occupations, and entirely devoted to the service of God. (5) Higher than the heavens. There may be some reference here to the exceeding dignity of the high priesthood; it was the highest office that could be sustained by man, the high priest himself being the immediate representative of God. But these things suit our Lord in a sense in which they cannot be applied to the high priest of the Jews. (1) He was *holy,* infinitely so; and "merciful." Witness His shedding His blood for the sins of mankind. (2) *Harmless*—perfectly without sin in His humanity as well as His divinity. (3) *Undefiled*—contracted no sinful infirmity in consequence of His dwelling among men. (4) *Separate from sinners*—absolutely unblameable in the whole of His conduct, so that He could challenge the most inveterate of His enemies with, "Which of you convicteth me of sin?" (5) *Higher than the heavens*—more exalted than all the angels of God, than all created beings, whether thrones, dominions, principalities, or powers, because all these were created by Him and for Him, and derive their continued subsistence from His infinite energy.

27. *Who needeth not daily.* Though the high priest offered the great atonement only once in the year, yet in the Jewish services there was a daily acknowledgement of sin, and a daily sacrifice offered by the priests, at whose head was the high priest, for their own sins and the sins of the people. The Jews held that a priest who neglected his own expiatory sacrifice would be smitten with death. *For this he did once.* For himself He offered no sacrifice; and the apostle gives the reason—he needed none, because he was "holy, harmless, undefiled, separate from sinners"; and for the people He offered himself once for all, when He expired upon the Cross.

28. *For the law maketh men high priests.* The Jewish priests have need of these repeated offerings and sacrifices because they are fallible, sinful men. *But the word of the oath* (still referring to Ps. cx. 4), *which was since the law.* For David, who mentions this, lived nearly five hundred years after the giving of the law; and consequently that oath, constituting another priesthood, abrogates the law. And by this the *Son . . . is consecrated,* "is perfected," *for evermore.* Being a High Priest without blemish, immaculately holy, every way perfect, immortal, and eternal, He is a Priest "to eternity."

CHAPTER 8

The sum, or chief articles, of what the apostle has spoken concerning the eternal priesthood of Christ, 1-5. The excellency of the new covenant beyond that of the old, 6-9. The nature and perfection of the new covenant stated from the predictions of the prophets, 10-12. By this new covenant the old is abolished, 13.

1. *Of the things which we have spoken this is the sum.* The word which we translate *sum* signifies the "chief," the "principal," or "head." *Who is set on the right hand of the throne.* This is what the apostle states to be the chief or most important point of all that he had yet discussed. His sitting down at the right hand of the throne of God, proves: (1) That He is higher than all the high priests that ever existed. (2) That the sacrifice which He offered for the sins of the world was sufficient and effectual, and as such accepted by God. (3) That He has all power in the heavens and in the earth, and is able to save and defend to the uttermost all that come to God through Him. (4) That He did not, like the Jewish high priest, depart out of the holy of holies after having offered the atonement; but abides there at the throne of God as a continual Priest, in the permanent act of offering His crucified body unto God in behalf of all the succeeding generations of mankind.

2. *A minister of the sanctuary.* "A public minister of the holy things" or places. The word means a person who officiated for the public, a public officer, in whom, and his work, all the people had a common right; hence our word "liturgy," the public work of prayer and praise, designed for the people at large. Properly speaking, the Jewish priest was the servant of the public; he transacted the business of the people with God. Jesus Christ is also the same kind of public officer; both as Priest and Mediator, He transacts the business of the whole human race with God. He performs the "holy things" or acts in the *true tabernacle,* heaven, of which the Jewish Tabernacle was the type. The Tabernacle was the place among the Jews where God, by the symbol of His presence, dwelt. This could only typify heaven, where God in His essential glory dwells; and hence heaven is called here the *true tabernacle* to distinguish it from the type. *Which the Lord pitched.* The Jewish Tabernacle was man's work, though made by God's direction; the heavens, this *true tabernacle,* the work of God alone. The

Tabernacle was also a type of the human nature of Christ, John i. 14: "And the Word was made flesh, and dwelt among us" (and "tabernacled" among us). For, as the Divine Presence dwelt in the Tabernacle, so the fullness of the Godhead, bodily, dwelt in the Man Christ Jesus. And this human body was the peculiar work of God, as it came not in the way of natural generation.

3. *Every high priest is ordained.* "Is set apart," for this especial work. *Gifts and sacrifices.* Eucharistic "offerings," and *sacrifices* for sin. By the former, God's government of the universe and His benevolence to His creatures in providing for their support were acknowledged. By the latter, the destructive and ruinous nature of sin and the necessity of an atonement were confessed. *Wherefore it is of necessity.* If Christ be a High Priest, and it be essential to the office of a high priest to offer atoning sacrifices to God, Jesus must offer such. Now it is manifest that, as he is the Public Minister, officiating in the true tabernacle as High Priest, He must make an atonement; and His being at the right hand of the throne shows that He has offered and continues to offer such an atonement.

4. *For if he were on earth.* As the Jewish Temple was standing when this Epistle was written, the whole Temple service continued to be performed by the legal priests, descendants of Aaron, of the tribe of Levi. Therefore if Christ had been then on earth, He could not have performed the office of a priest, being of the tribe of Judah, to which tribe the office of the priesthood did not appertain. *There are priests that offer gifts.* This is an additional proof that this Epistle was written before the destruction of Jerusalem.

5. *Who serve.* Who perform divine worship. *Unto the example and shadow.* "With the representation and shadow." The whole Levitical service was a representation and shadow of heavenly things; it appears, therefore, absurd to say that the priests served *unto* an *example* or "representation" *of heavenly things;* they served rather unto the substance of those things, with appropriate representations and shadows. *As Moses was admonished.* As Moses was divinely warned or admonished of God. *According to the pattern.* According to the "type," plan, or form. It is very likely that God gave a regular plan and specification of the Tabernacle and all its parts to Moses, and that from this divine plan the whole was constructed. See on Exod. xxv. 40.

6. *Now hath he obtained a more excellent ministry.* His office of priesthood is more excellent than the Levitical because the covenant is better, and established on better promises. The old covenant referred to earthly things; the new covenant, to heavenly. The old covenant had promises of secular good; the new covenant, of spiritual and eternal blessings. As far as Christianity is preferable to Judaism, as far as Christ is preferable to Moses, as far as spiritual blessings are preferable to earthly blessings, and as far as the enjoyment of God throughout eternity is preferable to the communication of earthly good during time, so far does the new covenant exceed the old.

7. *If that first . . . had been faultless.* This is nearly the same argument with that in chap. vii. 11. The simple meaning is: If the first covenant had made a provision for and actually conferred pardon and purity, and given a title to eternal life, then there could have been no need for a second. But the first covenant did not give these things; therefore a second was necessary.

8. *For finding fault with them.* The meaning is evidently this: God, in order to show that the first covenant was inefficient, saith to *them,* the Israelites, *Behold, the days come . . . when I will make a new covenant."* He found fault with the covenant, and addressed the people concerning His purpose of giving another covenant, that should be such as the necessities of mankind required. As this place refers to Jer. xxxi. 31-34, the words *finding fault with them* may refer to the Jewish people, of whom the Lord complains that they had broken His covenant though He was a Husband to them. *With the house of Israel and with the house of Judah.* That is, with all the descendants of the twelve sons of Jacob. This is thought to be a promise of the conversion of all the Jews to Christianity, both of the lost tribes and of those who are known to exist in Asiatic and European countries.

9. *Not according to the covenant.* The new covenant is of a widely different nature to that of the old; it was only temporal and earthly in itself, though it pointed out spiritual and eternal things. The new covenant is totally different from this, as we have already seen; and such a covenant, or system of religion, the Jews should have been prepared to expect, as the Prophet Jeremiah had in the above place so clearly foretold it. *And I regarded them not.* "And I neglected them or despised them"; but the words in the Hebrew text of the prophet we translate, "although I was an husband unto them." Let it be observed: (1) That the apostle quotes from the Septuagint. (2) The Hebrew words will bear a translation much nearer to the Septuagint and the apostle than our translation intimates. The words might be literally rendered, "And I was Lord over them," or, "I lorded or ruled over them"; i.e., I chastised them for their transgressions and punished them for their iniquities; "I took no further care of them," and gave them up into the hands of their enemies, and so they were carried away into captivity. This pretty nearly reconciles the Hebrew and the Greek, as it shows the act of God in reference to them is nearly the same when the proper meaning of the Hebrew and Greek words is considered.

10. *This is the covenant.* This is the nature of that glorious system of religion which I shall publish among them *after those days,* i.e., in the times of the gospel. *I will put my laws into their mind.* I will influence them with the principles of law, truth, holiness; and their understandings shall be fully enlightened to comprehend them. *And write them in their hearts.* All their affections, passions, and appetites shall be purified and filled with holiness and love to God and man; so that they shall willingly obey, and feel that love is the fulfilling of the law. Instead of being written on tables of stone, they shall be written on the fleshly tables of their hearts. *I will be to them a God.* These are the two grand conditions by which the parties in this covenant or agreement are bound: (1) "I will be your God." (2) "Ye shall be my people." To be God's people implies that they should

give God their whole hearts, serve Him with all their might and strength, and have no other object of worship or dependence but himself. Any of these conditions broken, the covenant is rendered null and void, and the other party absolved from his engagement.

11. *They shall not teach every man his neighbour.* The prophecy here indicates that there should be, under the gospel dispensation, a should be, under the gospel dispensation, a profusion of divine light; and this we find to be the case by the plentiful diffusion of the sacred writings, and by an abundant gospel ministry. And these blessings are not confined to temples or palaces, but are found in every corner of the land; so that, literally, all the people, *from the least to the greatest,* know and acknowledge the only true God, and Jesus Christ, whom He has sent. Almost every man, at least in this land, has a Bible, and can read it; and there is not a family that has not the opportunity of hearing the gospel preached, explained, and enforced. Some have thought that *from the least to the greatest* is intended to signify the order in which God proceeds with a work of grace; He generally begins with the poor, and through these the great and the high often hear the gospel of Christ.

12. *I will be merciful to their unrighteousness.* In order to be their God, as mentioned under the preceding verse, it is requisite that their iniquity should be pardoned; this is provided for by the immolation of Jesus Christ as the covenant Sacrifice. All spiritual evil against the nature and law of God is represented here under the following terms: (1) *Unrighteousness,* "injustice" or "wrong." This is against God, his neighbor, and himself. (2) Sin, deviation from the divine law; "missing the mark." (3) Iniquity, "lawlessness"; not having, knowing, or acknowledging a law; having no law written in their hearts, and restrained by none in the conduct of their lives.

13. *He hath made the first old.* That is, He has considered it as "antiquated," and as being no longer of any force. *That which decayeth and waxeth old.* Here is an allusion to the ancient laws which either had perished from the tables on which they were written through old age, or were fallen into disuse, or were abrogated. *Is ready to vanish away.* "Is about to be abolished." The word is used to express the abolition of the law. The apostle therefore intimates that the old covenant was just about to be abolished; but he expresses himself cautiously and tenderly, that he might not give unnecessary offense.

CHAPTER 9

Of the first covenant and its ordinances, 1. The Tabernacle, candlestick, table, shewbread, veil, holy of holies, censer, ark, pot of manna, Aaron's rod, tables of the covenant, cherubim of glory, and mercy seat, 2-5. How the priests served, 6-7. What was signified by the service, 8-10. The superior excellency of Christ's ministry and sacrifice, and the efficacy of His blood, 11-26. As men must once die and be judged, so Christ was once offered to bear the sins of many, and shall come without a sin offering, a second time, to them that expect Him, 27-28.

1. *The first covenant had also ordinances.* Our translators have introduced the word *covenant,* the whole context showing that *covenant* is that to which the apostle refers, as that was

the subject in the preceding chapter and this is a continuation of the same discourse. *Ordinances.* Rites and ceremonies. *A worldly sanctuary.* It is supposed that the term worldly here is opposed to the term "heavenly," chap. viii. 5, and that the whole should be referred to the secular nature of the Tabernacle service. But I think there is nothing plainer than that the apostle is speaking here in praise of this sublimely emblematic service, and hence he proceeds to enumerate the various things contained in the first Tabernacle, which added vastly to its splendor and importance; such as the table of the shewbread, the golden candlestick, the golden censer, the ark of the covenant overlaid round about with gold, in which was the golden pot that had the manna, Aaron's rod that budded, and the two tables which God had written with His own finger. Hence I am led to believe that *cosmicos* is here taken in its proper, natural meaning and signifies "adorned, embellished, splendid"; hence *cosmos,* "the world." So Pliny, *Hist. Nat.,* l. ii, c. 5: "That which the Greeks call *cosmos,* 'ornament,' we, (the Latins,) from its perfect and absolute elegance call *mundum,* world."

2. *For there was a tabernacle made; the first, wherein.* The sense is here very obscure and the construction involved: leaving out all punctuation, which is the case with all the very ancient MSS., the verse I suppose an indifferent person, who understood the language, would without hesitation render, "For there was the first Tabernacle constructed, in which were the candlestick," etc. And this Tabernacle or dwelling may be called the first dwelling place which God had among men, to distinguish it from the second dwelling place, the Temple built by Solomon; for *tabernacle* here is to be considered in its general sense, as implying a dwelling. To have a proper understanding of what the apostle relates here, we should endeavor to take a concise view of the Tabernacle erected by Moses in the wilderness. It comprised: (1) The court where the people might enter. (2) In this was contained the altar of burnt offerings, on which were offered the sacrifices in general, besides offerings of bread, wine, and other things. (3) At the bottom or lower end of this court was the tent of the covenant. The two principal parts of the Tabernacle were the holy place and the holy of holies. In the holy place, as the apostle observes, there were: (1) The golden *candlestick* of seven branches, (2) the golden altar, or altar of incense, (3) the altar or *table* of the *shewbread;* where the twelve loaves, representing the twelve tribes, were laid before the Lord. *Which is called the sanctuary.* "This is called holy." This clause may apply to any of the nouns in this verse, in the nominative case, which are all of the feminine gender; and the adjective "holy" may be considered here as the nominative singular feminine. The word *tabernacle* may be the proper antecedent.

3. *And after the second veil.* The first veil, of which the apostle has not yet spoken, was at the entrance of the holy place, and separated the temple from the court, and prevented the people, and even the Levites, from seeing what was in the holy place. The second veil, of which the apostle speaks here, separated the holy place from the holy of holies. *The tabernacle which is called the Holiest of all.* That is, that

part of the Tabernacle which is called the holy of holies.

4. *Which had the golden censer.* The apostle says that the *golden censer* was in the holy of holies, but this is nowhere mentioned by Moses. But he tells us that the high priest went in, once every year, with the golden censer to burn incense; and Calmet thinks this censer was left there all the year, and that its place was supplied by a new one, brought in by the priest the year following. Others think it was left just within the veil, so that the priest by putting his hand under the curtain could take it out and prepare it for his next entrance into the holiest. *The ark of the covenant.* This was a sort of chest overlaid with plates of gold, in which the two tables of the law, Aaron's rod, the pot of manna, etc., were deposited. Its top, or lid, was the propitiatory or mercy seat.

5. *And over it the cherubims of glory.* Cherubim is the plural of cherub, and it is absurd to add our plural termination (*s*) to the plural termination of the Hebrew. The *glory* here signifies the Shechinah or symbol of the Divine Presence. *Shadowing the mercyseat.* One at each end of the ark, with their faces turned toward each other, but looking down on the cover or proptiatory, here called the *mercyseat. Of which we cannot now speak particularly.* What these point out or signify is thus explained by Cyril: "Although Christ be but one, yet he is understood by us under a variety of forms. He is the *Tabernacle,* on account of the human body in which he dwelt. He is the *Table,* because he is our Bread of life. He is the *Ark* which has the law of God enclosed within, because he is the Word of the Father. He is the *Candlestick,* because he is our spiritual light. He is the *Altar of Incense,* because he is the sweet-smelling odour of sanctification. He is the *Altar of Burnt Offering,* because he is the victim, by death on the Cross, for the sins of the whole world."

6. *When these things were thus ordained.* When the Tabernacle was made, and its furniture placed in it, according to the divine direction. *The priests went always into the first tabernacle.* That is, into the first part of the Tabernacle, or holy place, into which he went every day twice, *accomplishing the service,* which included his burning the incense at the morning and evening sacrifice, dressing the lamps, and sprinkling the blood of the sin offerings before the veil, Lev. iv. 6.

7. *But into the second.* That is, the holy of holies, or second part of the Tabernacle, *The high priest alone once every year;* that is, on one day in the year only, which was the day on which the general atonement was made. The high priest could enter into this place only on one day in the year, but on that day he might enter several times. See Leviticus xvi. *Not without blood.* The day prescribed by the law for this great solemnity was the tenth of the month Tisri, in which the high priest brought in the incense or perfumes, which he placed on the golden censer. He brought also the blood of the bullock, and sprinkled some portion of it seven times before the ark and the veil which separated the holy place from the holy of holies. See Lev. xvi. 14. He then came out, and taking some of the blood of the goat which had been sacrificed, he sprinkled it between the veil and

the ark of the covenant, v. 15. *Which he offered for himself, and for the errors of the people.* For transgressions of which they were not conscious.

8. *The Holy Ghost this signifying.* These services were divinely appointed, and by each of them the Holy Spirit of God is supposed to speak. *The way into the holiest.* That full access to God was not the common privilege of the people while the Mosaic economy subsisted. That the apostle means that it is only by Christ that any man and every man can approach God is evident from chap. x. 19-22. I have already observed that the apostle appears to use the word *tabernacle* in the general sense of a dwelling place and therefore applies it to the Temple, which was reputed the house or dwelling place of God, as well as the ancient Tabernacle. Therefore what he speaks here concerning the *first tabernacle* may be understood as applying with propriety to the then Jewish Temple, as well as to the ancient Tabernacle, which, even with all their sacrifices and ceremonies, could not make the way of holiness plain nor the way to God's favor possible.

9. *Which,* Tabernacle and its services, *was a figure,* a dark enigmatical representation, *for the time then present—*for that age and dispensation, and for all those who lived under it. *In which,* "during which," time or dispensation *were offered both gifts and sacrifices,* eucharistic offerings and victims for sin, *that could not make him that did the service,* whether the priest who made the offering or the person who brought it in the behalf of his soul, *perfect, as pertaining to the conscience—*could not take away guilt from the mind nor purify the conscience from dead works. The whole was a *figure,* or dark representation, of a spiritual and more glorious system; and although a sinner who made these offerings and sacrifices according to the law might be considered as having done his duty, and thus he would be exempted from many ecclesiastical and legal disabilities and punishments, yet his *conscience* would ever tell him that the guilt of sin was still remaining. The words *in which,* referred in the above paraphrase to *the time,* are read by several versions as referring to the Tabernacle, and this is the reading which our translators appear to have followed.

10. *In meats and drinks, and divers washings.* He had already mentioned eucharistic and sacrificial offerings, and nothing properly remained but the different kinds of clean and unclean animals which were used, or forbidden to be used, as articles of food; together with the different kinds of drinks, *washings,* "baptisms," immersions, sprinklings, and washings of the body and the clothes, and *carnal ordinances,* or things which had respect merely to the body and could have no moral influence upon the soul, unless considered in reference to that of which they were the similitudes or figures. *Carnal ordinances.* Rites and ceremonies pertaining merely to the body. *Imposed on them until the time of reformation.* These rites and ceremonies were enacted, by divine authority, as proper representations of the gospel system, which should reform and rectify all things. *The time of reformation,* "the time of rectifying," signifies the gospel dispensation, under which everything is set straight; everything referred to

its proper purpose and end; the ceremonial law fulfilled and abrogated; the moral law exhibited and more strictly enjoined (see our Lord's sermon upon the mount); and the spiritual nature of God's worship taught, and grace promised to purify the heart. So that, through the power of the eternal Spirit, all that was wrong in the soul is "rectified"; the affections, passions, and appetites purified; the understanding enlightened; the judgment corrected; the will refined; in a word, all things made new.

11. *But Christ being come an high priest of good things.* I think this and the succeeding verses not happily translated; indeed, the division of them has led to a wrong translation. Therefore they must be taken together thus: "But the Christ, the High Priest of those good things (or services) which were to come, through a greater and more perfect tabernacle, not made with hands, that is, not of the same workmanship, entered once for all into the sanctuary; having obtained eternal redemption for us, not by the blood of goats and calves, but by His own blood. For if the blood of goats, and bulls, and calves, and a heifer's ashes, sprinkled on the unclean, sanctifieth to the cleansing of the flesh, how much more shall the blood of Christ, who, through the eternal Spirit, offered himself without spot to God, cleanse your consciences from dead works, in order to worship (or that you may worship) the living God?"

In the above translation I have added, in v. 13, "of goats," on the authority of several MSS. *High priest of good things.* Or "services," *to come.* He is the High Priest of Christianity. *A greater and more perfect tabernacle.* This appears to mean our Lord's human nature. That, in which dwelt all the fullness of the Godhead bodily, was fitly typified by the Tabernacle and Temple, in both of which the majesty of God dwelt. *Not made with hands.* Though our Lord's body was a perfect human body, yet it did not come in the way of natural generation; His miraculous conception will sufficiently justify the expressions used here by the apostle.

12. *But by his own blood.* Here the redemption of man is attributed to the blood of Christ; and this Blood is stated to be shed in a sacrificial way, precisely as the blood of bulls, goats, and calves was shed under the law. *Once.* "Once for all," in opposition to the annual entering of the high priest into the holiest with the blood of the annual victim. *The holy place,* or "sanctuary," signifies heaven, into which Jesus entered with His own blood, as the high priest entered into the holy of holies with the blood of the victims which he had sacrificed. *Eternal redemption.* A redemption price which should stand good forever, when once offered; and an endless redemption from sin, in reference to the pardon of which, and reconciliation to God, there needs no other sacrifice. It is eternal in its merit and efficacy.

13. *Sanctifieth to the purifying of the flesh.* Answers the end proposed by the law; namely, to remove legal disabilities and punishments, having the body and its interests particularly in view, though adumbrating or typifying the soul and its concerns.

14. *Who through the eternal Spirit.* This expression is understood two ways: (1) Of the Holy Ghost himself. As Christ's miraculous conception was by the Holy Spirit, and He

wrought all His miracles by the Spirit of God, so His death or final offering was made through or by the eternal Spirit; and by that Spirit He was raised from the dead, I Pet. iii. 18. (2) Of the eternal Logos or Deity which dwelt in the Man Christ Jesus, through the energy of which the offering of His humanity became an infinitely meritorious victim; therefore the deity of Christ is here intended. But we cannot well consider one of these distinct from the other. It is probable that the Holy Ghost, not the Logos, is what the apostle had more immediately in view. But still we must say that the Holy Spirit, with the eternal Logos and the almighty Father, equally concurred in offering up the sacrifice of the human nature of Christ in order to make atonement for the sin of the world. *Purge your conscience.* "Purify your conscience." The term "purify" should be everywhere, both in the translation of the Scriptures and in preaching the gospel, preferred to the word *purge,* which at present is scarcely ever used in the sense in which our translators have employed it. *Dead works.* Sin in general, or acts to which the penalty of death is annexed by the law.

15. *And for this cause.* Some translate "on account of this" (Blood). Perhaps it means no more than a mere inference, such as "therefore" or "wherefore." *He is the mediator of the new testament.* There was no proper reason why our translators should render *diatheke* by *testament* here, when in almost every other case they render it "covenant," which is its proper ecclesiastical meaning, as answering to the Hebrew *berith.* Very few persons are satisfied with the translation of the following verses to the twentieth, particularly the sixteenth and seventeenth; at all events the word "covenant" must be retained. *He,* Jesus Christ, *is the mediator;* the *mediator* was the person who witnessed the contract made between the two contracting parties, slew the victim, and sprinkled each with its blood. *Of the new testament.* The "new contract" betwixt God and the whole human race, by Christ Jesus, the Mediator, distinguished here from the old covenant between God and the Israelites, in which Moses was the mediator. *That by means of death.* His own death upon the Cross. *For the redemption of the transgressions.* To make atonement for the transgressions which were committed under the old covenant, which the blood of bulls and calves could not do; so the death of Jesus had respect to all the time antecedent to it, as well as to all the time afterward till the conclusion of the world. *They which are called,* the Gentiles, *might receive the promise*—might, by being brought into a covenant with God, have an equal right with the Jews, not merely to an inheritance such as the Promised Land, but to an *eternal inheritance,* and consequently infinitely superior to that of the Jews.

16. *For where a testament is.* A learned and judicious friend furnishes me with the following translation of this and the seventeenth verse: "For where there is a covenant, it is necessary that the death of the appointed victim should be exhibited, because a covenant is confirmed over dead victims, since it is not at all valid while the appointed victim is alive. Mr. Wakefield has translated the passage in nearly the same way: "For where a covenant is, there

must be necessarily introduced the death of that which establisheth the covenant; because a covenant is confirmed over dead things, and is of no force at all whilst that which establisheth the covenant is alive." This is undoubtedly the meaning of this passage; and we should endeavor to forget that *testament* and *testator* were ever introduced, as they totally change the apostle's meaning.

18. *Whereupon.* "Wherefore," as a victim was required for the ratification of every covenant, the first covenant made between God and the Hebrews, by the mediation of Moses, *was* not *dedicated,* "renewed" or solemnized, *without blood*—without the death of a victim and the aspersion of its blood.

19. *When Moses had spoken every precept.* The place to which the apostle alludes is Exod. xxiv. 4-8. *And sprinkled both the book.* The sprinkling of the *book* is not mentioned in the place to which the apostle refers, nor did it in fact take place. The words "and the book itself" should be referred to "having taken," and not to "he sprinkled." The verse should therefore be read thus: "For after every commandment of the law had been recited by Moses to all the people, he took the blood of the calves, and of the goats, with water and scarlet wool, and the book itself, and sprinkled all the people." The rite was performed thus: Having received the blood of the calves and goats into basins, and mingled it with water to prevent it from coagulating, he then took a bunch of *hyssop,* and having bound it together with thread made of *scarlet wool,* he dipped this in the basin, and sprinkled the blood and water upon the people who were nearest to him, and who might be considered on this occasion the representatives of all the rest.

20. *This is the blood of the testament* (covenant). Our Lord refers to the conduct of Moses here, and partly quotes his words in the institution of the Eucharist: "This is my blood of the new testament [covenant], which is shed for many for the remission of sins," Matt. xxvi. 28. And by thus using the words and applying them, He shows that His sacrificial blood was intended by the blood shed and sprinkled on this occasion, and that by it alone the remission of sins is obtained.

21. *He sprinkled with blood . . . all the vessels of the ministry.* To intimate that everything used by sinful man is polluted, and that nothing can be acceptable in the sight of a holy God that has not in effect the sprinkling of the atoning Blood.

22. *And almost all things are by the law purged with blood.* The apostle says *almost,* because in some cases certain vessels were purified by water, some by fire, Num. xxxi. 23, and some with the ashes of the red heifer, Num. xix. 2-10, but it was always understood that everything was at first consecrated by the blood of the victim. *And without shedding of blood is no remission.* The apostle shows fully here what is one of his great objects in the whole of this Epistle, viz., that there is no salvation but through the sacrificial death of Christ, and to prefigure this the law itself would not grant any remission of sin without the blood of a victim. This is a maxim even among the Jews themselves, "There is no expiation but by blood." Every sinner has forfeited his life by

his transgressions, and the law of God requires his death; the blood of the victim, which is its life, is shed as a substitute for the life of the sinner. By these victims the sacrifice of Christ was typified. He gave His life for the life of the world; human life for human life, but a life infinitely dignified by its union with God.

23. *The patterns of things in the heavens.* That is, the Tabernacle and all its utensils, services, etc., must be purified by *these,* viz., the blood of calves and goats, and the sprinkling of the blood and water with the bunch of hysop bound about with scarlet wool. These are called *patterns,* "exemplars," earthly things, which were the representatives of *heavenly things.* Purification implies, not only cleansing from defilement, but also dedication or consecration. All the utensils employed in the Tabernacle service were thus *purified* though incapable of any moral pollution. *But the heavenly things themselves.* Some think this means heaven itself, which, by receiving the sacrificed body of Christ, which appears in the presence of God for us, may be said to be *purified,* i.e., "set apart," for the reception of the souls of those who have found redemption in His blood. Others think the body of Christ is intended, which is the tabernacle in which His divinity dwelt; and that this might be said to be purified by its own sacrifice, as He is said, John xvii. 19, to sanctify himself; that is, to "consecrate" himself unto God as a Sin Offering for the redemption of man. Others suppose the Church is intended, which He is to present to the Father without entrance to the holy of holies must be made by the sprinkling of the blood of the sacrifice, and as that holy of holies represented heaven, the apostle's meaning seems to be that there was and could be no entrance to the holiest but through His blood. And therefore, when by "a more perfect tabernacle," vv. 11-12, He passed into the heavens, not with the blood of bulls and goats, but by His own blood, He thus purified or laid open the entrance to the holiest, by a more valuable sacrifice than those required to open the entrance of the holy of holies. *It was . . . necessary,* therefore, for God had appointed it so, that the Tabernacle and its parts, which were *patterns of things in the heavens,* should be "consecrated" and entered with such sacrifices as have already been mentioned. But the heaven of heavens into which Jesus entered, and whither He will bring all His faithful followers, must be propitiated, consecrated, and entered by the infinitely better sacrifice of His own body and blood. That this is the meaning appears from the following verse.

24. *Christ is not entered into the holy places made with hands.* He is not gone into the holy of holies of the Tabernacle or Temple, as the Jewish high priest does once in the year with the blood of the victim, to sprinkle it before the mercy seat there; but *into heaven itself,* which He has thus opened to all believers, having made the propitiatory offering by which both He and those whom He represents are entitled to enter and enjoy eternal blessedness.

25. *Nor yet that he should offer himself often.* The sacrifice of Christ is not like that of the Jewish high priest. His must be offered every year; Christ has offered himself once for all.

26. *For then must he often have suffered.* In the counsel of God, Christ was considered the

"Lamb slain from the foundation of the world," Rev. xiii. 8, so that all believers before His advent were equally interested in His sacrificial death with those who have lived since His coming. *The end of the world.* The conclusion of the Jewish dispensation, the Christian dispensation being that which shall continue till the end of time. *To put away sin.* "To abolish the sin offerings"; i.e., to put an end to the Mosaic economy by His one offering of himself. Some think that the expression should be applied to the putting away the guilt, power, and being of sin from the souls of believers.

27. *As it is appointed.* It is "laid before" them by the divine decree: "Dust thou art, and unto dust shalt thou return." *Unto men* generally, during the course of the present world.

28. *So Christ was once offered.* He shall die no more; He has borne away the sins of many, and what He has done once shall stand good forever. Yet He will appear a second time *without sin,* "without a sin offering"; that He has already made. *Unto salvation.* To deliver the bodies of believers from the empire of death, to reunite them to their purified souls, and bring both into His eternal glory. This is salvation, and the very highest of which the human being is capable.

CHAPTER 10

The insufficiency of the legal sacrifices to take away sin, 1-4. The purpose and will of God, as declared by the Psalmist, relative to the salvation of the world by the incarnation of Christ; and our sanctification through that will, 5-10. Comparison between the priesthood of Christ and that of the Jews, 11-14. The new covenant which God promised to make and the blessings of it, 15-17. The access which genuine believers have to the holiest by the blood of Jesus, 18-20. Having a High Priest over the Church of God, we should have faith, walk uprightly, hold fast our profession, exhort and help each other, and maintain Christian communion, 21-25. The danger and awful consequences of final apostasy, 26-31. In order to our perseverance, we should often reflect on past mercies, and the support afforded us in temptations and afflictions; and not cast away our confidence, for we shall receive the promise if we patiently fulfill the will of God, 32-37. The just by faith shall live, but the soul that draws back shall die, 38. The apostle's confidence in the believing Hebrews, 39.

1. *The law having a shadow of good things to come.* (1) *A shadow* signifies, literally the shade cast from a body of any kind. (2) It signifies, technically, a sketch, rude plan, or imperfect draught of a building, landscape, man, beast, etc. (3) It signifies, metaphorically, any faint adumbration, symbolical expression, imperfect or obscure image of a thing; and is opposed to "body," or the thing intended to be thereby defined. *And not the very image.* Image signifies: (1) a simple representation, (2) the form or particular fashion of a thing, (3) the model according to which anything is formed, (4) the perfect image of a thing as opposed to a faint representation. The law, with all its ceremonies and sacrifices, was only a *shadow* of spiritual and eternal good. The gospel is the *image* or thing itself, as including every spiritual and eternal good. *Can never . . . make the comers thereunto perfect.* Cannot remove guilt from the conscience or impurity from the heart.

2. *Would they not have ceased to be offered?* Had they made an effectual reconciliation for the sins of the world, and contained in their once offering a plenitude of permanent merit, they would have ceased to be offered.

4. *For it is not possible.* Common sense must have taught them that shedding the blood of bulls and goats could never satisfy divine justice nor take away guilt from the conscience; and God intended that they should understand the matter so; and this the following quotation from the Psalmist sufficiently proves.

5. *When he* (the Messiah) *cometh into the world,* was about to be incarnated, *he saith* to God the Father, *Sacrifice and offering thou wouldest not*—It was never Thy will and design that the sacrifices under Thy own law should be considered as making atonement for sin; they were only designed to point out My incarnation and consequent sacrificial death. And therefore *a body hast thou prepared me,* by a miraculous conception in the womb of a virgin, according to Thy word, "The seed of the woman shall bruise the head of the serpent." *A body hast thou prepared me.* The quotation in this and the following two verses is taken from Ps. xl. 6-8, as they stand now in the Septuagint, with scarcely any variety of reading; but although the general meaning is the same, they are widely different in verbal expression in the Hebrew. David's words we translate, "Mine ears hast thou opened"; but they might be more properly rendered, "My ears hast Thou bored"; that is, Thou hast made me Thy servant forever, to dwell in Thine own house; for the allusion is evidently to the custom mentioned in Exod. xxi. 2, etc.: "If thou buy an Hebrew servant, six years he shall serve: and in the seventh he shall go out free . . . but if the servant shall plainly [positively] say, I love my master . . . I will not go out free: then his master shall bring him to . . . the door post; and . . . shall bore his ear through with an aul; and he shall serve him for ever." But how is it possible that the Septuagint and the apostle should take a meaning so totally different from the sense of the Hebrew? Dr. Kennicott supposes that the Septuagint and apostle express the meaning of the words as they stood in the copy from which the Greek translation was made, and that the present Hebrew text is corrupted. It is remarkable that all the offerings and sacrifices which were considered to be of an atoning or cleansing nature, offered under the law, are here enumerated by the Psalmist and the apostle, to show that none of them nor all of them could take away sin, and that the grand sacrifice of Christ was that alone which could do it. Four kinds are here specified, by both the Psalmist and the apostle, viz., sacrifice, offering, burnt offering, sin offering. Of all these we may say, with the apostle, it was impossible that the blood of bulls and goats should take away sin.

6. *Thou hast had no pleasure.* Thou couldst never be pleased with the victims under the law; Thou couldst never consider them as atonements for sin, as they could never satisfy Thy justice nor make Thy law honorable.

7. *In the volume of the book.* "In the roll of the book." Anciently, books were written on skins and rolled up. Among the Romans these were called *volumina,* from *volvo,* "I roll"; and Pentateuch, in the Jewish synagogues, is still written in this way. There are two wooden rollers; on one they roll on, on the other they roll off, as they proceed in reading. The *book* mentioned here must be the Pentateuch, or five books of Moses, for in David's time no other

part of divine revelation had been committed to writing. This whole *book* speaks about Christ and His accomplishing the *will* of God. *To do thy will.* God willed not the sacrifices under the law, but He willed that a human victim of infinite merit should be offered for the redemption of mankind. That there might be such a victim, a "body" was prepared for the eternal Logos and in that body He came to do the will of God, that is, to suffer and die for the sins of the world.

9. *He taketh away the first.* The offerings, sacrifices, burnt offerings, and sacrifices for sin which were prescribed by the *law. That he may establish the second.* The offering of the body of Jesus once for all.

10. *By the which will we are sanctified.* Closing in with this so solemnly declared will of God that there is no name given under heaven among men by which we can be saved but Jesus the Christ, we believe in Him, find redemption in His blood, and are sanctified unto God through the sacrificial offering of His body.

11. *Every priest standeth.* The office of the Jewish priest is here compared with the office of our High Priest. The Jewish priest stands daily at the altar, like a servant ministering, repeating the same sacrifices; our High Priest offered himself once for all, and sat down at the right hand of God, as the only begotten Son and Heir of all things, v. 12. This continual offering argued the imperfection of the sacrifices. Our Lord's once offering proves His was complete.

13. *Till his enemies be made his footstool.* Till all that oppose His high priesthood and sacrificial offering shall be defeated, routed, and confounded; and acknowledge in their punishment the supremacy of His power as universal and eternal King, who refused to receive Him as their atoning and sanctifying Priest.

14. *For by one offering.* His death upon the Cross. *He hath perfected for ever.* He has procured remission of sins and holiness; for it is well observed here, and in several parts of this Epistle, that "to make perfect" is the same as "to procure remission of sins." *Them that are sanctified.* Them that have received the sprinkling of the Blood of this offering. These, therefore, receiving redemption through that blood, have no need of any other offering; as this was a complete atonement, purification, and title to eternal glory.

15. *The Holy Ghost also is a witness to us.* The words are quoted from Jer. xxxi. 33-34, and here we are assured that Jeremiah spoke by the inspiration of the Spirit of God. *Had . . . said before.* See chap. viii. 10, 12.

18. *Now where remission of these is.* In any case, where sin is once pardoned, there is no further need of a sin offering; but every believer on Christ has his sin blotted out, and therefore needs no other offering for that sin.

19. *Having therefore, brethren, boldness.* The apostle, having now finished the doctrinal part of his Epistle and fully shown the superiority of Christ to all men and angels, and the superiority of His priesthood to that of Aaron and his successors, the absolute inefficacy of the Jewish sacrifices to make atonement for sin, and the absolute efficacy of that of Christ to make reconciliation of man to God, proceeds now to show what influence these doctrines should have on the hearts and lives of those who believe in His merits and death. *Boldness to enter.* "Liberty, full access to the entrance of the holy place." This is an allusion to the case of the high priest going into the holy of holies. He went with fear and trembling, because, if he had neglected the smallest item prescribed by the law, he could expect nothing but death. Genuine believers can come even to the throne of God with confidence, as they carry into the divine presence the infinitely meritorious Blood of the great atonement.

20. *By a new and living way.* It is a *new* way; no human being had ever before entered into the heaven of heavens. Jesus in human nature was the first, and thus He has opened the way to heaven to mankind, His own resurrection and ascension to glory being the proof and pledge of ours. *Through the veil.* As the high priest lifted up or drew aside the veil that separated the holy from the most holy place, in order that he might have access to the Divine Majesty; and as the veil of the Temple was rent from the top to the bottom at the crucifixion of Christ, to show that the way to the holiest was then laid open; so we must approach the throne through the mediation of Christ, and through His sacrificial death. Here the veil—His humanity—is rent, and the kingdom of Heaven opened to all believers.

21. *An high priest over the house of God.* The *house* or family *of God* is the Christian Church, or all true believers in the Lord Jesus. Over this Church, house, or family Christ is the High Priest—in their behalf He offers His own blood, and their prayers and praises.

22. *Let us draw near.* Let us come with the blood of our Sacrifice to the throne of God; the expression is sacrificial. *With a true heart.* Deeply convinced of our need of help, and truly in earnest to obtain it. *In full assurance of faith.* Being fully persuaded that God will accept us for the sake of His Son, and that the sacrificial death of Christ gives us full authority to expect every blessing we need. *Having our hearts sprinkled.* Not our bodies, as was the case among the Hebrews, when they had contracted any pollution, for they were to be sprinkled with the water of separation (see Num. xix 2-10); but our *hearts,* sprinkled by the cleansing efficacy of the blood of Christ, without which we cannot draw nigh to God. *From an evil conscience.* Having that deep sense of guilt which our conscience felt taken all away, and the peace and love of God shed abroad in our hearts by the Holy Ghost given unto us. *Our bodies washed with pure water.* The high priest, before he entered into the inner tabernacle or put on his holy garments, was to wash his flesh in water, Lev. xvi. 4, and the Levites were to be cleansed the same way, Num. viii. 7. The apostle probably alludes to this in what he says here, though it appears that he refers principally to baptisms, the washing by which was an emblem of the purification of the soul by the grace and Spirit of Christ. But it is most likely that it is to the Jewish baptisms, and not the Christian, that the apostle alludes.

23. *Let us hold fast the profession.* The word implies that general consent that was among Christians on all the important articles of their faith and practice; particularly their acknowl-

edgment of the truth of the gospel, and of Jesus Christ as the only Victim for sin and the only Saviour from it. If the word "washed" above refer to Christian baptism in the case of adults, then the profession is that which the baptized then made of their faith in the gospel, and of their determination to live and die in that faith. The various readings on this clause are many in the MSS. But among all these, the confession or "profession of hope" is undoubtedly the genuine reading. Now among the primitive Christians the hope which they professed was the resurrection of the body and everlasting life. The apostle exhorts them to *hold fast* this "confession" *without wavering*—never to doubt the declarations made to them by their Redeemer, but having the "full assurance of faith" that their hearts were sprinkled from an evil conscience, that they had found redemption in the blood of the Lamb, they might expect to be glorified with their living Head in the kingdom of their Father. *He is faithful that promised.* The eternal life, which is the object of your hope, is promised to you by Him who cannot lie. As He then is *faithful* who has given you this promise, hold fast the profession of your hope.

24. *And let us consider one another.* Let us "diligently and attentively consider" each other's trials, difficulties, and weaknesses; feel for each other, and "excite" each other to an increase of *love* to God and man; and, as the proof of it, to be fruitful in *good works.* The words "to the provocation" are often taken in a good sense, and signify "excitement, stirring up" to do anything laudable, useful, honorable, or necessary.

25. *Not forsaking the assembling of ourselves.* Whether this means public or private worship is hard to say; but as the word is but once more used in the New Testament, (2 Thess. ii. 1) and there means the "gathering together" of redeemed of the Lord at the day of judgment, it is as likely that it means here private religious meetings for the purpose of mutual exhortation; and this sense appears the more natural here because it is evident that the Church was now in a state of persecution, and therefore their meetings were most probably held in private. For fear of persecution it seems as if some had deserted these meetings, "as the custom of certain persons is." They had given up these strengthening and instructive means, and the others were in danger of following their example. *The day.* "That day"—the time in which God would come and pour out His judgments on the Jewish nation. We may also apply it to the day of death and the day of judgment. Both of these are approaching to every human being. He who wishes to be found ready will carefully use every means of grace, and particularly the communion of saints, if there be even but two or three in the place where he lives, who statedly meet together in the name of Christ. Those who relinquish Christian communion are in a backsliding state; those who backslide are in danger of apostasy. To prevent this latter, the apostle speaks the awful words following.

26. *For if we sin wilfully.* If we deliberately, for fear of persecution or from any other motive, renounce the profession of the gospel and the Author of that gospel, after having *received the knowledge of the truth* so as to be convinced that Jesus is the promised Messiah, and that He

had sprinkled our hearts from an evil conscience—for such *there remaineth no . . . sacrifice for sins.* For as the Jewish sacrifices are abolished, as appears by the declaration of God himself in the fortieth psalm, and Jesus being now the only Sacrifice which God will accept, those who reject Him have none other; therefore their case must be utterly without remedy. This is the meaning of the apostle, and the case is that of a deliberate apostate—one who has utterly rejected Jesus Christ and His atonement, and renounced the whole gospel system. It has nothing to do with backsliders in our common use of that term. A man may be overtaken in a fault, or he may deliberately go into sin, and yet neither renounce the gospel nor deny the Lord that bought him. His case is dreary and dangerous, but it is not hopeless; no case is hopeless but that of the deliberate apostate, who rejects the whole gospel system, after having been saved by grace or convinced of the truth of the gospel. To him there remaineth no more sacrifice for sin; for there was but the one, Jesus, and this he has utterly rejected.

27. *A certain fearful looking for of judgment.* From this it is evident that God will pardon no man without a sacrifice for sin. *And fiery indignation.* A "zeal," or fervor of fire"; something similar to the fire that came down from heaven and destroyed Korah and his company, Num. xvi. 35.

28. *He that despised Moses' law.* He that rejected it, "threw it aside," and denied its divine authority by presumptuous sinning, *died without mercy*—without any extenuation or mitigation of punishment, Num. xv. 30. *Under two or three witnesses.* That is, when convicted by the testimony of two or three respectable witnesses. See Deut. xvii. 6.

29. *Of how much sorer punishment?* Such offenses were trifling in comparison of this, and in justice the punishment should be proportioned to the offense. *Trodden under foot the Son of God.* Treated Him with the utmost contempt and blasphemy. *The blood of the covenant . . . an unholy thing.* The blood of the covenant means here the sacrificial death of Christ, by which the new covenant between God and man was ratified, sealed, and confirmed. And counting this *unholy,* or "common," intimates that they expected nothing from it in a sacrificial or atoning way. How near to those persons, and how near to their destruction do they come in the present day who reject the atoning Blood and say "that they expect no more benefit from the blood of Christ than they do from that of a cow or a sheep"! Is not this precisely the crime of which the apostle speaks here, and to which he tells us God would show no mercy? *Despite unto the Spirit of grace.* Hath "insulted" the Spirit of grace. The apostle means the Holy Spirit, whose gifts were bestowed in the first age on believers for the confirmation of the gospel. See chap. vi. 4-6. Wherefore if one apostatized in the first age, after having been witness to these miraculous gifts, much more after having possessed them himself, he must, like the scribes and Pharisees, have ascribed them to evil spirits, than which a greater indignity could not be done to the Spirit of God.

30. *Vengeance belongeth unto me.* This is the

saying of God, Deut. xxxii. 35, in reference to the idolatrous Gentiles, who were the enemies of His people; and is here with propriety applied to the above apostates, who, being enemies to God's ordinances and Christ's ministry and merits, must also be enemies to Christ's people. *The Lord shall judge his people.* That is, He shall execute judgment *for* them; for this is evidently the sense in which the word is used in the place from which the apostle quotes, Deut. xxxii. 36: "For the Lord shall judge his people, and repent himself for his servants, when he seeth that their power is gone." So God will avenge and vindicate the cause of Christianity by destroying its enemies, as He did in the case of the Jewish people, whom He destroyed from being a nation.

31. *It is a fearful thing to fall into the hands of the living God.* To fall into the hands of God is to fall under His displeasure. How dreadful to have the displeasure of an eternal, almighty Being to rest on the soul forever!

32. *But call to remembrance.* It appears from this, and indeed from some parts of the gospel history, that the first believers in Judea were greatly persecuted. Our Lord's crucifixion, Stephen's martyrdom, the persecution that arose after the death of Stephen, Acts viii. 1, Herod's persecution, Acts xii. 1, in which James was killed, and the various persecutions of Paul, sufficiently show that this disposition was predominant among that bad people. *A great fight of afflictions.* "A great combat or contention of sufferings." Here we have an allusion to the combats at the Grecian games or to exhibitions of gladiators at the public spectacles.

33. *Ye were made a gazingstock.* You were exhibited as wild beasts and other shows at the theaters. *Companions of them that were so used.* It appears, from I Thess. ii. 14-15, that the churches of God in Judea were greatly persecuted, and that they behaved with courage and constancy in their persecutions. When any victim of persecuting rage was marked out, the rest were prompt to take his part and acknowledge themselves believers in the same doctrine for which he suffered.

34. *Ye had compassion of me in my bonds.* "You suffered with me; you sympathized with me," when bound for the testimony of Jesus. This probably refers to the sympathy they showed towards him and the help they afforded him during his long imprisonment in Caesarea and Jerusalem. But instead of *my bonds,* "the prisoners" is the reading of several MSS. This reading appears to be so well-supported that Griesbach has admitted it into the text. If it be genuine, it shows that there had been, and perhaps were then, several bound for the testimony of Jesus, and that the church in Judea had shown its attachment to Christ by openly acknowledging these prisoners and ministering to them. *Took joyfully the spoiling of your goods.* They were deprived of their inheritances, turned out of their houses, and plundered of their goods; "they wandered about in sheepskins and goatskins; being destitute, afflicted, tormented." To suffer such persecution patiently was great; to endure it without a murmur was greater; to rejoice in it was greatest of all. But how could they do all this? The next clause informs us. *Knowing in yourselves.* They had the fullest evidence that they were the children of God, the Spirit itself bearing this witness to their spirits; "and if children then heirs; heirs of God, and joint-heirs with Christ." They knew that heaven was their portion, and that to it they had a sure right and indefeasible title by Christ Jesus. This accounts, and this alone can account, for their taking joyfully the spoiling of their goods.

35. *Cast not away therefore your confidence.* "Your liberty of access" to God; your title and right to approach His throne; your birthright as His sons and daughters; and the clear evidence you have of His favor, which, if you be not steady and faithful, you must lose. "Do not throw it away." There is a reference here to cowardly soldiers who throw away their shields and run away from the battle. The Lacedemonian women, when they presented the shields to their sons going to battle, were accustomed to say: "Either bring this back, or be brought back upon it"; alluding to the custom of bringing back a slain soldier on his own shield, a proof that he had preserved it to the last, and had been faithful to his country. They were accustomed also to excite their courage by delivering to them their fathers' shields with the following short address: "This shield thy father always preserved; do thou preserve it also, or perish." Thus spake the Lacedemonian mothers to their sons; and what say the oracles of God to us? "Cast not away your confession of faith." This is your shield; keep it, and it will ever be your sure defense; for by it you will quench every fiery dart of the wicked one. The Church of Christ speaks this to all her sons, and especially to those employed in the work of the ministry. *Great recompence of reward.* No less than God's continual approbation, the peace that passeth all understanding ruling the heart here, and the glories of heaven as an eternal portion. Conscientiously keep the shield, and all these shall be yours. This will be your *reward.*

36. *Ye have need of patience.* Having so great a fight of sufferings to pass through, and they of so long continuance. God furnishes the grace; you must exercise it. *Patience* and "perseverance" are nearly the same. *Have done the will of God.* By keeping the faith and patiently suffering for it.

37. *For yet a little while.* "For yet a very little time." In a very short space of time the Messiah will come, and execute judgment upon your rebellious country. This is determined, because they have filled up the measure of their iniquity, and their destruction slumbereth not. The apostle seems to refer to Hab. ii. 3-4, and accommodates the words to his own purpose.

38. *Now the just shall live by faith.* "But the just by faith," i.e., he who is justified by faith, *shall live*—shall be preserved when this overflowing scourge shall come. *But if any man draw back.* "But if he draw back"; he, the man who is justified by faith; for it is of him, and none other, that the text speaks. The insertion of the words *any man,* if done to serve the purpose of a particular creed, is a wicked perversion of the words of God. They were evidently intended to turn away the relative from the antecedent, in order to save the doctrine of final and unconditional perseverance, which doctrine this text destroys. *My soul shall have no pleasure in him.* My very heart shall be

opposed to him who makes shipwreck of faith and a good conscience. The word *hypostellein* signifies not only to *draw back*, but to "slink away and hide through fear." In this sense it is used by the very best Greek writers, as well as by Josephus and Philo.

39. *But we are not of them who draw back.* "We are not the cowards, but the courageous." I have no doubt of this being the meaning of the apostle, and the form of speech requires such a translation; it occurs more than once in the New Testament. We are not cowards who slink away, and notwithstanding meet destruction; but we are faithful, and have our souls saved alive. The words signify the "preservation of the life." He intimates that, notwithstanding the persecution was hot, yet they should escape with their lives. It is very remarkable, and I have more than once called the reader's attention to it, that not one Christian life was lost in the siege and destruction of Jerusalem. Every Jew perished, or was taken captive; all those who had apostatized and slunk away from Christianity perished with them; all the genuine Christians escaped with their lives. This very important information, which casts light on many passages in the New Testament, and manifests the grace and providence of God in a very conspicuous way, is given by Eusebius: "When the whole congregation of the Church in Jerusalem, according to an oracle given by revelation to the approved persons among them before the war, were commanded to depart from the city, and inhabit a certain city which they call Pella, beyond Jordan, to which, when all those who believed in Christ had removed from Jerusalem, and when the saints had totally abandoned the royal city which is the metropolis of the Jews; then the Divine vengeance seized them who had dealt so wickedly with Christ and his apostles, and utterly destroyed that wicked and abominable generation."

CHAPTER 11

A definition of faith, 1-2. What are its immediate objects, 3. What are its effects, instanced in Abel, 4. In Enoch. 5-6. In Noah. 7. In Abraham, 8-10. In Sara, 11. In their righteous posterity, 12-16. In Abraham's offering of his son Isaac, 17-19. In Isaac. 20. In Jacob, 21. In Joseph, 22. In Moses, 23-28. In the Israelites in the wilderness, 29. In the fall of Jericho, 30. In Rahab, 31. In several of the judges, and in David, Samuel, and the prophets, 32-34. The glorious effects produced by it in the primitive martyrs, 35-40.

1. *Faith is the substance of things hoped for.* "Faith is the subsistence of things hoped for," "the demonstration of things not seen." The word *hypostasis*, which we translate *substance* signifies "subsistence," that which becomes a foundation for another thing to stand on. And *elenchos* (*evidence*) signifies such a "conviction" as it produced in the mind by the "demonstration" of a problem, after which demonstration no doubt can remain, because we see from it that the thing is, that it cannot but be, and that it cannot be otherwise than as it is and is proved to be. Such is the faith by which the soul is justified; or rather, such are the effects of justifying faith. *Elenchos* is defined by logicians, "A demonstration of the certainty of a thing by sure arguments and indubitable reasons." Aristotle uses it for a mathematical demonstration, and properly defines it thus: "Elenchos, or Demonstration, is that which cannot be otherwise, but is so as we assert."

Things hoped for are the peace and approbation of God, and those blessings by which the soul is prepared for the kingdom of Heaven. A penitent hopes for the pardon of his sins and the favor of his God; faith in Christ puts him in possession of this pardon, and thus the thing that was hoped for is enjoyed by faith. In an extended sense the *things hoped for* are the resurrection of the body, the new heavens and the new earth, the introduction of believers into the heavenly country, and the possession of eternal glory. The things unseen, as distinguished from the things hoped for, are, in an extended sense, the creation of the world from nothing, the destruction of the world by the deluge, the miraculous conception of Christ, His resurrection from the dead, His ascension to glory, His mediation at the right hand of God, His government of the universe, etc., all which we as firmly believe on the testimony of God's Word as if we had seen them. But this faith has particular respect to the being, goodness, providence, grace, and mercy of God, as the subsequent verses sufficiently show.

2. *For by it the elders obtained a good report.* By the *elders* are meant "ancestors, forefathers," such as the patriarchs and prophets, several of whom he afterwards particularly names and produces some fact from the history of their lives. It is very remarkable that among the whole there is not one word concerning poor Adam and his wife, though both Abraham and Sarah are mentioned. There was no good report concerning them; not a word of their repentance, faith, or holiness. The word which we translate *obtained a good report* literally signifies "were witnessed of"; and thus leads us naturally to God, who by His Word, as the succeeding parts of the chapter show, bore testimony to the faith and holiness of His servants. The apostle does not mention one of whom an account is not given in the Old Testament. This therefore is God's witness or testimony concerning them.

3. *Through faith we understand.* By *worlds* we are to understand the material fabric of the universe: and as the word is used in the plural number, it may comprehend, not only the earth and visible heavens, but the whole planetary system; the different worlds which, in our system at least, revolve round the sun. The apostle states that these things were not made out of a preexistent matter.

4. *By faith Abel offered unto God a more excellent sacrifice.* "More sacrifice"; as if he had said: Abel, by faith, made more than one offering; and hence it is said, God testified of his gifts. The plain state of the case seems to have been this: Cain and Abel both brought offerings to the altar of God, probably the altar erected for the family worship. As Cain was a husbandman, he brought a eucharistic offering, of the fruits of the ground, by which he acknowledged the being and providence of God. Abel, being a shepherd or a feeder of cattle, brought, not only the eucharistic offering, but also of the produce of his flock as a sin offering to God, by which he acknowledged his own sinfulnsss, God's justice and mercy, as well as His being and providence. Cain, not at all apprehensive of the demerit of sin or God's holiness, contented himself with the thank offering. This God could not, consistently with His

holiness and justice, receive with complacency; the other, as referring to Him who was the Lamb slain from the foundation of the world, God could receive, and did particularly testify His approbation. Now by this faith, thus exercised, in reference to an atonement, he, Abel, though "dead, yet speaketh"; i.e., preacheth to mankind the necessity of an atonement, and that God will accept no sacrifice unless connected with this.

5. *By faith Enoch was translated.* It is said, in Gen. v. 24, that Enoch walked with God, and "he was not; for God took him." Here the apostle explains what God's taking him means, by saying that he *was translated that he should not see death;* from which we learn that he did not die, and that God took him to a state of blessedness without obliging him to pass through death. See his history explained at large in the above place, in Gen. v. 22-24.

6. *He that cometh to God.* The man who professes that it is his duty to worship God must, if he act rationally, do it on the conviction that there is such a Being, infinite, eternal, unoriginated, and self-existent; the Cause of all other being; on whom all being depends; and by whose energy, bounty, and providence all other beings exist, live, and are supplied with the means of continued existence and life. He must believe also that He rewards *them that diligently seek him;* that He is not indifferent about His own worship; that He requires adoration and religious service from men; and that He blesses and especially protects and saves those who in simplicity and uprightness of heart seek and serve Him. This requires faith, such a faith as is mentioned above; a faith by which we can *please* God; and now that we have an abundant revelation, a faith according to that revelation; a faith in God through Christ, the great Sin Offering, without which a man can no more please Him or be accepted of Him than Cain was.

7. *By faith Noah.* See the whole of this history, Gen. vi. 13. *Warned of God.* As we know from the history in Genesis that God did "warn" Noah, we see from this the real import of the verb as used in various parts of the New Testament; it signifies "to utter oracles, to give divine warning." *Moved with fear.* "Influenced by religious fear or reverence towards God." This is mentioned to show that he acted not from a fear of losing his life, but from the fear of God, and hence that fear is here properly attributed to faith. *He condemned the world.* He credited God; they did not. He walked in the way God had commanded; they did not. He repeatedly admonished them, I Pet. iii. 20; they regarded it not. This aggravated their crimes, while it exalted his faith and righteousness. *Became heir of the righteousness.* He became entitled to that justification which is by faith, and his temporal deliverance was a pledge of the salvation of his soul.

8. *Abraham, when he was called.* See on Gen. xii. 1-4. *Not knowing whither he went.* Therefore his obedience was the fullest proof of his faith in God, and his faith was an implicit faith. He obeyed, and went out from his own country, having no prospect of any good or success but what his implicit faith led him to expect from God, as the "rewarder of them that diligently seek him." In all the preceding cases, and in all that follow, the apostle keeps this maxim fully in view.

9. *By faith he sojourned in the land of promise.* It is remarkable that Abraham did not acquire any right in Canaan except that of a burying place; nor did he build any house in it. His faith showed him that it was only a type and pledge of a better country, and he kept that better country continually in view. He, *with Isaac and Jacob,* who were *heirs . . . of the same promise,* were contented to dwell in tents, without any fixed habitation.

10. *For he looked for a city which hath foundations.* He knew that earth could afford no permanent residence for an immortal mind, and he looked for that heavenly building of which God is the Architect and Owner. *Whose builder and maker is God.* The word *technites* signifies an "architect," one who plans, calculates, and constructs a building. The word *demiourgos* signifies the "governor of a people," one who forms them by institutions and laws, the framer of a political constitution. God is here represented the Maker or Father of all the heavenly inhabitants, and the Planner of their citizenship in that heavenly country.

11. *Through faith also Sara.* Her history, as far as the event here is concerned, may be seen in Gen. xvii. 19 and xxi. 2. Sarah at first treated the divine message with ridicule, judging it to be absolutely impossible, not knowing then that it was from God; and this her age and circumstances justified, for, humanly speaking, such an event was impossible. But when she knew that it was God who said this, it does not appear that she doubted anymore, but implicitly believed that what God had promised He was able to perform.

12. *Him as good as dead.* According to nature, long past the time of the procreation of children. The birth of Isaac, the circumstances of the father and mother considered, was entirely supernatural; and the people who proceeded from this birth were a supernatural people, and were and are most strikingly singular through every period of their history to the present day.

13. *These all died in faith.* That is, Abraham, Sarah, Isaac, and Jacob continued to believe, to the end of their lives, that God would fulfill this promise; but they neither saw the numerous seed nor did they get the promised rest in Canaan. *Strangers and pilgrims. Strangers,* persons who are out of their own country, who are in a foreign land. *Pilgrims,* sojourners only for a time, not intending to take up their abode in that place nor to get naturalized in that country. How many use these expressions, professing to be *strangers and pilgrims* here below, and yet the whole of their conduct, spirit, and attachments show that they are perfectly at home!

14. *Declare plainly that they seek a country.* A man's *country* is that in which he has constitutional rights and privileges; no stranger or sojourner has any such rights in the country where he sojourns. These, by declaring that they felt themselves strangers and sojourners, professed their faith in a heavenly country and state, and looked beyond the grave for a place of happiness.

15. *If they had been mindful of that country.* They considered their right to the promises of

God as dependent on their utter renunciation of Chaldea, and it was this that induced Abraham to cause his steward Eliezer to swear that he would not carry his son Isaac to Chaldea; see Gen. xxiv. 5-8. There idolatry reigned; and God had called them to be the patriarchs and progenitors of a people among whom the knowledge of the true God, and the worship required by Him, should be established and preserved.

16. *But now they desire a better.* They all expected spiritual blessings and a heavenly inheritance. They sought God as their Portion, and in such a way and on such principles that He is not *ashamed to be called their God;* and He shows His affection for them by preparing *for them a city,* to wit, heaven, as themselves would seek no city on earth, which is certainly what the apostle has here in view. And from this it is evident that the patriarchs had a proper notion of the immortality of the soul and expected a place of residence widely different from Canaan.

17. *Abraham, when he was tried.* See the history of this whole transaction explained at large in the notes on Gen. xxii. 1-9. *Offered up his only begotten.* Abraham did, in effect, offer up Isaac; he built an altar, bound his son, laid him upon the altar, had ready the incense, took the knife, and would immediately have slain him had he not been prevented by the same authority by which the sacrifice was enjoined. Isaac is here called *his only begotten,* as he was the only son he had by his legitimate wife, who was heir to his property, and heir of the promises of God. The man who proved faithful in such a trial deserved to have his faith and obedience recorded throughout the world.

19. *To raise him up, even from the dead.* Abraham "staggered not at the promise . . . through unbelief; but was strong in faith, giving glory to God." The resurrection of the dead must have been a doctrine of the patriarchs; they expected a heavenly inheritance. They saw they died as did other men, and they must have known that they could not enjoy it but in consequence of a resurrection from the dead. *He received him in a figure. Parabole* sometimes means a "daring exploit, a jeoparding of the life." I think it should be so understood here, as pointing out the very imminent danger he was in of losing his life. The clause may therefore be thus translated: "Accounting that God was able to raise him up from the dead, from whence he had received him, he being in the most imminent danger of losing his life." It is not therefore the natural deadness of Abraham and Sarah to which the apostle alludes, but the death to which Isaac on this occasion was exposed, and which he escaped by the immediate interference of God.

20. *By faith Isaac blessed Jacob and Esau.* He believed that God would fulfill His promise to his posterity, and God gave him to see what would befall them in their future generations. The apostle does not seem to intimate that one should be an object of the divine hatred and the other of divine love in reference to their eternal states.

21. *Blessed both the sons of Joseph.* That is, Ephraim and Manasseh. See the account in Gen. xlviii. 5, etc. *Worshipped, leaning upon the top of his staff.* This subject is particularly considered in the note on Gen. xlvii. 31. It appears that at the time Joseph visited his father he was very weak and generally confined to his couch, having at hand his staff; either that with which he usually supported his feeble body or that which was the ensign of his office as patriarch or chief of a very numerous family. The ancient chiefs in all countries had this staff or sceptre continually at hand. It is said, Gen. xlviii. 2, that when Joseph came to see his father, Jacob, who was then in his last sickness, "Israel strengthened himself, and sat upon the bed, with his feet on the floor, he supported himself with his staff. When Joseph sware to him that he should be carried up from Egypt, he "bowed himself upon the bed's head," still supporting himself with his staff, which probably with this last act he laid aside, "gathered up his feet," and reclined wholly on his couch. It was therefore indifferent to say that he worshipped or bowed himself on his staff or on his bed's head. But as *shachah* signifies not only to "bow," but also to "worship," because acts of adoration were performed by bowing and prostration; and as *mittah,* a "bed," by the change of the vowel points becomes *matteh,* a "staff," hence the Septuagint have translated the passage, "And Israel bowed or worshipped on the head of his staff." This reading the apostle follows here.

22. *Joseph, when he died.* "When he was dying."

23. *By faith Moses.* See the notes on Exod. ii. 2 and Acts vii. 20. We know that Moses was brought up at the Egyptian court, and there was considered to be the son of Pharaoh's daughter, and probably might have succeeded to the throne of Egypt. But finding that God had visited His people and given them a promise of spiritual and eternal blessings, he chose rather to take the lot of this people, i.e., God as his Portion forever, than to "enjoy the pleasures of sin," which, however gratifying to the animal senses, could only be "temporary."

26. *The reproach of Christ.* The *Christ* or Messiah had been revealed to Moses; of Him he prophesied, Deut. xviii. 15; and the *reproach* which God's people had, in consequence of their decided opposition to idolatry, may be termed *the reproach of Christ,* for they refused to become one people with the Egyptians, because the promise of the rest was made to them, and in this rest Christ and His salvation were included. But, although it does not appear these things were known to the Hebrews at large, yet it is evident that there were sufficient intimations given to Moses concerning the great Deliverer (of whom himself was a type) that determined his conduct in the above respect, as he fully understood that he must renounce his interest in the promises and in the life eternal to which they led, if he did not obey the divine call in the present instance. Many have been stumbled by the word *Christ* here, because they cannot see how Moses should have any knowledge of Him. It may be said that it was just as easy for God Almighty to reveal Christ to Moses as it was for Him to reveal Him to Isaiah, or to the shepherds, or to John Baptist; or to manifest Him in the flesh. After all, there is much reason to believe that by *Christ* the apostle means the whole body of the Israelitish or Hebrew people; for as the word signifies "the anointed," and anointing was a consecration to

God, all the Hebrew people were considered thus anointed or consecrated; and it is worthy of remark that *Christos* is used in this very sense by the Septuagint, I Sam. ii. 35; Ps. cv. 15; and Hab. iii. 13, where the word is necessarily restrained to this meaning. *He had respect unto the recompence.* He "looked attentively" to it; his eyes were "constantly directed" to it. This is the import of the original word, and the whole conduct of Moses was an illustration of it.

27. *He forsook Egypt.* He believed that God would fulfill the promise He had made, and he cheerfully changed an earthly for a heavenly portion. *Not fearing the wrath of the king.* The apostle speaks here of the departure of Moses with the Israelites, not of his flight to Midian, Exod. ii. 14-15; for he was then in great fear. But when he went to Pharaoh with God's authority, to demand the dismission of the Hebrews, he was without fear, and acted in the most noble and dignified manner; he then feared nothing but God. *As seeing him who is invisible.* He continued to act as one who had the Judge of his heart and conduct always before his eyes. By calling the Divine Being the *invisible*, the apostle distinguishes Him from the gods of Egypt, who were visible, corporeal, gross, and worthless. The Israelites were worshippers of the true God, and this worship was not tolerated in Egypt.

28. *He kept the passover.* God told him that He would destroy the firstborn of the Egyptians, but would spare all those whose doors were sprinkled with the blood of the paschal lamb. Moses believed this, kept the Passover, and sprinkled the blood. See the notes on Exodus xii.

29. *By faith they passed through the Red sea.* See the notes on Exod. xiv. 22. The Egyptians thought they could walk through the sea as well as the Israelites; they tried, and were drowned, while the former passed in perfect safety. The one walked by faith, the other by sight; one perished, the other was saved.

30. *The walls of Jericho fell down.* This is particularly explained Josh. vi. 1, etc. God had promised that the walls of Jericho should fall down if they compassed them about seven days. They believed, did as they were commanded, and the promise was fulfilled.

31. *The harlot Rahab perished not.* See this account in Josh. ii. 1, 9, 11 and vi. 23, where it is rendered exceedingly probable that the word *zonah* in Hebrew and *porne* in Greek, which we translate *harlot*, should be rendered "innkeeper," as there is no proper evidence that the person in question was such a woman as our translation represents her. As to her having been a harlot before and converted afterwards, it is a figment of an idle fancy. She was afterwards married to Salmon, a Jewish prince; see Matt. i. 5. *Received the spies with peace.* "Giving them a kind welcome, good fare, and protection."

32. *Time would fail me.* A very usual mode of expression with the best Greek writers, when they wish to intimate that much important intelligence remains to be communicated on the subject already in hand, which must be omitted because of other points which have not yet been handled. *Gedeon.* Who by faith in God, with 300 men, destroyed a countless multitude of Midianites and Amalekites, and delivered Israel from oppression and slavery, Judges vi–viii. *Barak.* Who overthrew Jabin, king of Canaan, and delivered Israel from servitude, Judges iv. *Samson.* Who was appointed by God to deliver Israel from the oppressive yoke of the Philistines; and by extraordinary assistance discomfited them on various occasions, Judges xiii–xvi. *Jephthae.* Who, under the same guidance, defeated the Ammonites, and delivered Israel, Judges xi–xii. *David.* King of Israel, whose whole life was a life of faith and dependence on God. *Samuel.* The last of the Israelitish judges, to whom succeeded a race of kings, of whom Saul and David were the first two, and were both anointed by this most eminent man.

33. *Who through faith subdued kingdoms.* As *Joshua*, who subdued the seven Canaanitish nations; and *David*, who subdued the Moabites, Syrians, Ammonites, and Edomites, 2 Samuel viii; etc. *Wrought righteousness.* Did a great variety of works indicative of that faith in God without which it is impossible to do anything that is good. *Obtained promises.* This is supposed to refer to Joshua and Caleb, who through their faith in God obtained the Promised Land, while all the rest of the Israelites were excluded; to Phineas also, who for his act of zealous faith in slaying Zimri and Cosbi got the promise of an everlasting priesthood; and to David, who for his faith and obedience obtained the kingdom of Israel, and had the promise that from his seed the Messiah should spring. *Stopped the mouths of lions.* Daniel, who, though cast into a den of lions for his fidelity to God, was preserved among them unhurt and finally came to great honor.

34. *Quenched the violence of fire.* As in the case of the three faithful Hebrews—Shadrach, Meshach, and Abed-nego—who for their steady attachment to God's worship were cast into a fiery furnace, in which they were preserved and from which they escaped unhurt, Daniel iii. *Escaped the edge of the sword.* Moses, who escaped the sword of Pharaoh, Exod. xviii. 4; Elijah, that of Jezebel; and David, that of Saul; and many others. *Out of weakness were made strong.* Were miraculously restored from sickness, which seemed to threaten their life; as Hezekiah, Isa. xxxviii. 21. *Waxed valiant in fight.* Like Gideon, who overthrew the camp of the Midianites, and Jonathan, that of the Philistines, in such a way as must have proved that God was with them.

35. *Women received their dead.* As did the widow of Zarephath, I Kings xvii. 21, and the Shunammite, 2 Kings iv. 34. *Others were tortured.* This word signifies to "beat violently."

36. *Had trial of cruel mockings and scourgings.* We do not know the cases to which the apostle refers. The *mockings* here can never mean such as those of Ishmael against Isaac or the youths of Bethel against Elisha. It is more probable that it refers to public exhibitions of the people of God at idol feasts and the like; and Samson's case before Dagon, when the Philistines had put out his eyes, is quite in point. As to *scourgings*, this was a common way of punishing minor culprits; and even those who were to be punished capitally were first scourged. See the case of our Lord. *Bonds and imprisonment.* Joseph was cast into prison; Jeremiah was cast into a dungeon full of mire,

chap. xxxvii. 16 and xxxviii. 6; and the Prophet Micaiah was imprisoned by Ahab, I Kings xxii. 27.

37. *They were stoned.* As Zechariah, the son of Barachiah or Jehoida, was, between the altar and the Temple; see the account in 2 Chron. xxiv. 21. And as Naboth the Jezreelite, who, on refusing to give up his father's inheritance to a covetous king, because it had respect to the promise of God, was falsely accused and stoned to death, 1 Kings xxi. 1-14. *They were sawn asunder.* There is a tradition that the Prophet Isaiah was thus martyred. In *Yevomoth*, fol. 49, 2, it is thus written: "Manasseh slew Isaiah; for he commanded that he should be slain with a wooden saw. They then brought the saw, and cut him in two; and when the saw reached his mouth, his soul fled forth." *Were tempted. Epeirasthesan.* I believe this word has vexed the critics more than any other in the New Testament. How being *tempted* can be ranked among the heavy sufferings of the primitive martyrs and confessors is not easy to discern, because to be tempted is the common lot of every godly man. This difficulty has induced learned men to mend the text by conjecture. Alberti thinks the original reading was *espeir- asthesan,* "they were strangled." Many more differences have been proposed by learned men, all bearing a very near resemblance to the words now found in the Greek text. *Were slain with the sword.* As in the case of the eighty-five priests slain by Doeg, see 1 Sam. xxii. 18; and the prophets, of whose slaughter by the sword Elijah complains, 1 Kings xix. 10. Probably the word means being "beheaded," which was formerly done with a *sword* and not with an axe, and in the East is done by the sword to the present day. *They wandered about in sheep- skins.* "Sheepskins dressed with the wool on." This was probably the sort of mantle that Elijah wore, and which was afterwards used by Elisha; for the Septuagint, in 2 Kings ii. 8, 13, expressly say: "And Elijah took his sheepskin" (mantle); "And he [Elisha] took the sheepskin of Elijah which had fallen from off him." It is likely that the prophets themselves wore such garments, and that the false prophets imitated them in this, in order that they might gain the greater credit. "And it shall come to pass in that day, that the prophets shall be ashamed every one of his vision . . . neither shall they wear a rough garment to deceive," Zech. xiii. 4; "a hairy skin," Septuagint, probably the *goatskins* mentioned above. In general, this was an upper garment; but in the cases to which the apostle alludes, the *sheepskins and goatskins* seem to have been the only covering. *Being destitute.* "In want" of all the comforts and conveniences of life, and often of its necessaries. *Afflicted.* In consequence of enduring such privations. *Tor- mented.* "Maltreated, harassed," variously perse- cuted by those to whom they brought the message of salvation.

38. *Of whom the world was not worthy.* Yet they were obliged to wander by day in *deserts* and *mountains,* driven from the society of men, and often obliged to hide by night *in dens and caves of the earth* to conceal themselves from the brutal rage of men. Perhaps he refers here principally to the case of Elijah and the hundred prophets hidden in caves by Obadiah and fed with bread and water. See 1 Kings xviii. 4.

David was often obliged thus to hide himself from Saul, 1 Sam. xxiv. 3, etc.

39. *Having obtained a good report* (having been witnessed to; see v. 2) *through faith.* It was faith in God which supported all those eminent men who, in different parts of the world and in different ages, were persecuted for righ- teousness' sake. *Received not the promise.* They all heard of the promises made to Abraham of a Messiah, for this was a constant tradition; but they died without having seen this Anointed of the Lord. This must be the promise without receiving of which the apostle says they died.

40. *God having provided some better thing for us.* This is the dispensation of the gospel, with all the privileges and advantages it confers. *That they without us should not be made per- fect.* Believers before the Flood, after the Flood, under the law, and since the law, make but one Church. The gospel dispensation is the last, and the Church cannot be considered as "complete," *perfect,* till the believers under all dispensations are gathered together. As the gospel is the last dispensation, the preceding believers cannot be consummated even in glory till the gospel Church arrive in the heaven of heavens.

CHAPTER 12

Having so many incitements to holiness, patience, and perseverance, we should lay aside every hindrance, and run with patience the race that is set before us, taking our blessed Lord for our Example, 1-4. These sufferings are to be considered as fatherly chastisements from God, and to be patiently submitted to on account of the benefits to be derived from them, 5-11. They should take courage and go forward, 12-13. Directions to follow peace with all men, and to take heed that they fall not from the grace of God, 14-15. References to the case of Esau, 16-17. The privileges of Christians, compared with those of the Jews, by which the superior excellence of Christianity is shown, 18-24. They must take care not to reject Jesus, who now addressed them from heaven, and who was shortly to be their Judge, 25-27. As they were called to receive a Kingdom, they should have grace, whereby they might serve God acceptably, 28-29.

1. *Wherefore.* This is an inference drawn from the examples produced in the preceding chapter, and on this account both should be read in connection. *Compassed about.* Here is another allusion to the Olympic games. The agonistae, or contenders, were often greatly animated by the consideration that the eyes of the principal men of their country were fixed upon them; and by this they were induced to make the most extraordinary exertions. *Cloud of witnesses.* Both the Greeks and Latins fre- quently use the term *cloud* to express a great number of persons or things. *Let us lay aside every weight.* As those who ran in the Olympic races would throw aside everything that might impede them in their course, so Christians, pro- fessing to go to heaven, must throw aside every- thing that might hinder them in their Christian race. Whatever weighs down our hearts or affections to earth and sense is to be carefully avoided; for no man with the love of the world in his heart can ever reach the kingdom of Heaven. *The sin which doth so easily beset.* "The well-circumstanced sin"; that which has everything in its favor, time, and place, and opportunity; the heart and the object; and a sin in which all these things frequently occur, and consequently the transgression is frequently committed; the sin that stands well, or is favor- ably situated, ever surrounding the person and soliciting his acquiscence. What we term the

"easily besetting sin" is the sin of our constitution, the sin of our trade, that in which our worldly honor, secular profit, and sensual gratification are most frequently felt and consulted. Some understand it of original sin, as that by which we are inveloped in body, soul, and spirit. Whatever it may be, the word gives us to understand that it is what meets us at every turn; that it is always presenting itself to us; that as a pair of compasses describe a circle by the revolution of one leg while the other is at rest in the center, so this, springing from that point of corruption within, called the "carnal mind," surrounds us in every place; we are bounded by it, and often hemmed in on every side. In laying aside the weight there is an allusion to the long garments worn in the Eastern countries, which, if not laid aside or tucked up in the girdle, would greatly incommode the traveller, and utterly prevent a man from running a race. *Let us run with patience the race.* "Let us start, run on, and continue running" till we get to the goal. This figure is a favorite among the Greek writers.

2. *Looking unto Jesus.* "Looking *off* and *on*, or *from* and *to*"; looking off or from the world and all secular concerns to Jesus and all the spiritual and heavenly things connected with Him. This is still an allusion to the Grecian games. Those who ran were to keep their eyes fixed on the mark of the prize; they must keep the goal in view. The exhortation implies (1) That they should place all their hope and confidence in Christ, as their sole Helper in this race of faith; (2) That they should consider Him their Leader in this contest and imitate His example. *The author and finisher of our faith.* *Archegos,* translated here *author,* signifies in general captain or leader, or the first inventor of a thing; see chap. ii. 10. But the reference here seems to be to the *brabeus,* or judge in the games, whose business it was to admit the contenders and to give the prize to the conqueror. Jesus is here represented as this Officer; every Christian is a contender in this race of life, and for eternal life. The heavenly course is begun under Jesus, and under Him it is completed. He is the *finisher* by awarding the prize to them that are faithful unto death. Thus He is the *author* or the Judge under whom and by whose permission and direction, according to the rules of the heavenly race, they are permitted to enter the lists and commence the race; and He is the *finisher,* the "Perfecter," by awarding and giving the prize which consummates the combatants at the end of the race. *Who for the joy that was set before him.* The joy of fulfilling the will of the Father, Ps. xl. 6, etc., in tasting death for every man; and having endured the Cross and despised the shame of this ignominious death, He is set down at the right hand of God, ever appearing in the presence of God for us, and continuing His exhibition of himself as our Sacrifice, and His intercession as our Mediator.

3. *For consider him.* "Attentively observe" and "analyze" every part of His conduct, enter into His spirit, examine His motives and object, and remember that, as He acted, you are called to act; He will furnish you with the same Spirit, and will support you with the same strength. He bore a continual opposition of sinners against himself, but He conquered by meekness, patience, and perseverance; He has left you an example that you should follow His steps. If you trust in Him, you shall receive strength. Therefore, howsoever great your opposition may be, you shall not be weary; if you confide in and attentively look to Him, you shall have continual courage to go on, and never *faint* in your minds. Here is a continued allusion to the contenders in the Grecian games, who, when exhausted in bodily strength and courage, yielded the palm to their opponents, and were said "to be weary or exhausted"; "to be dissolved, disheartened, or to have lost all bravery and courage."

4. *Ye have not yet resisted unto blood.* Many of those already mentioned were martyrs for the truth; they persevered unto death, and lost their lives in bearing testimony to the truth. Though you have had opposition and persecution, yet you have not been called, in bearing your testimony against sin and sinners, to seal the truth with your blood. *Striving against sin.* An allusion to boxing at the Grecian games. In the former passages the apostle principally refers to the footraces.

5. *And ye have forgotten.* Or "Have you forgotten the exhortation?" This quotation is made from Prov. iii. 11-12, and shows that the address there, which at first sight appears to be from Solomon to his son or from some fatherly man to a person in affliction, is properly from God himself to any person in persecution, affliction, or distress. *Despise not thou the chastening.* "Do not neglect the correction of the Lord." That man neglects correction and profits not by it who does not see the hand of God in it or, in other words, does not fear the rod and Him who hath appointed it, and consequently does not humble himself under the mighty hand of God, deplore his sin, deprecate divine judgment, and pray for mercy. *Nor faint.* Do not be discouraged nor despair, for the reasons immediately alleged.

6. *For whom the Lord loveth he chasteneth.* Here is the reason why we should neither neglect correction nor faint under it. It is a proof of the fatherly love of God Almighty, and shows His most gracious designs towards us, from which we may be fully convinced that the affliction will prove the means of good to our souls if we make a proper use of it. *And scourgeth every son whom he receiveth.* This is a quotation from the Septuagint of Prov. iii. 12, of which place our version is: "Even as a father the son in whom he delighteth." But howsoever near this may appear to be the Hebrew, it bears scarcely any affinity to the apostle's words. The translation therefore of the Septuagint and apostle is perfectly consonant to the Hebrew text, and our version of Prov. iii. 12 is wrong.

7. *If ye endure chastening.* If you submit to His authority, humble yourselves under His hand, and pray for His blessing, you will find that He deals with you as beloved children, correcting you that He may make you partakers of His holiness. *God dealeth with you as with sons.* He acknowledges by this that you belong to the family, and that He, as your Father, has you under proper discipline. It is a maxim among the Jewish rabbins that "the love which is not conjoined with reproof is not genuine."

8. *Then are ye bastards.* This proceeds on the general fact that bastards are neglected in their manners and education; the fathers of such, feeling little affection for, or obligation to regard,

their spurious issue. But *all* that are legitimate children *are partakers* of *chastisement* or "discipline"; for the original word does not imply stripes and punishments, but the whole "discipline" of a child, both at home and at school.

9. *We have had fathers of our flesh.* The fathers of our flesh, i.e., our natural parents, were correctors; and we reverenced them, notwithstanding their corrections often arose from whim or caprice. But *shall we not rather be in subjection to the Father of spirits;* to Him from whom we have received both body and soul; who is our Creator, Preserver, and Supporter; to whom both we and our parents owe our life and our blessings; and who corrects us only for our profit, that we may *live* and be "partakers of his holiness"? The apostle in asking, *Shall we not much rather be in subjection unto the Father of spirits, and live?* alludes to the punishment of the stubborn and rebellious son, Deut. xxi. 18-21: "If a man have a stubborn and rebellious son, which will not obey the voice of his father, or the voice of his mother, and that, when they have chastened him, will not hearken unto them: then shall his father and his mother lay hold on him, and bring him out unto the elders of his city . . . and they shall say . . . This our son is stubborn and rebellious, he will not obey our voice . . . And all the man of his city shall stone him with stones, that he die."

10. *For . . . a few days.* The chastisement of our earthly parents lasted only a short time; that of our Heavenly Father also will be but a short time, if we submit. And as our parents ceased to correct when we learned obedience, so will our Heavenly Father when the end for which He sent the chastisement is accomplished. God delights not in the rod; judgment is His strange work.

11. *No chastening for the present seemeth to be joyous.* Neither correction, wholesome restraint, domestic regulations, nor gymnastic discipline are pleasant to them that are thus exercised; but it is by these means that obedient children, scholars, and great men are made. And it is by God's discipline that Christians are made. He who does not bear the yoke of Christ is good for nothing to others, and never gains rest to his own soul. *The peaceable fruit of righteousness.* I.e., the joyous, prosperous fruits; those fruits by which we gain much, and through which we are made happy. *Exercised thereby.* "To the trained." There is still an allusion to the Grecian games, and in the word before us to those "gymnastic exercises" by which the candidates for the prizes were trained to the different kinds of exercises in which they were to contend when the games were publicly opened.

12. *Wherefore lift up the hands.* The apostle refers to Isa. xxxv. 3. The words are an address to persons almost worn out with sickness and fatigue, whose *hands* hang down, whose *knees* shake, and who are totally discouraged. These are exhorted to exert themselves, and take courage, with the assurance that they shall infallibly conquer if they persevere.

13. *Make straight paths for your feet.* That is, Take the straight path that is before you; do not go in crooked or rough ways, where are stones, briers, and thorns, by which you will be inevitably lamed, and so totally prevented from proceeding in the way; whereas if you go in

the even, proper path, though you have been wounded by getting into a wrong way, that which was wounded will *be healed* by moderate, equal exercise, all impediments being removed. The application of all this to a correct, holy deportment in religious life is both natural and easy.

14. *Follow peace with all men.* Cultivate, as far as you possibly can, a good understanding, with both Jews and Gentiles. "Pursue peace" with the same care, attention, and diligence as beasts do their game; follow it through all places; trace it through all winding circumstances; and have it with all men, if you can with a safe conscience. *And holiness.* That state of continual "sanctification," that life of purity and detachment from the world and all its lusts, without which detachment and sanctity *no man shall see the Lord*—shall never enjoy His presence in the world of blessedness. "To see God," in the Hebrew phrase, is to "enjoy Him"; and without holiness of heart and life this is impossible. No soul can be fit for heaven that has not suitable dispositions for the place.

15. *Looking diligently.* "Looking about, over, and upon"; being constantly on your guard. *Lest any man fail of the grace of God.* "Lest any person should come behind, or fall off from, this grace or gift of God"; this state of salvation, viz., the gospel system or Christianity, for this is most evidently the meaning of the apostle. It is not the falling from a work of grace in their own souls, but from the gospel, to apostatize from which they had now many temptations; and to guard them against this, the whole Epistle was written. *Lest any root of bitterness springing up.* A root of bitterness signifies a "poisonous plant." The Hebrews call every species of poison a "bitter," and with considerable propriety, as most plants are poisonous in proportion to the quantum of the bitter principle they possess. The *root of bitterness* is here used metaphorically for a bad man, or a man holding unsound doctrines, and endeavoring to spread them in the church. *Trouble you.* This alludes to the effects of poison taken into the body. The blood itself (the principle, under God, of life) becomes putrescent; and probably to this the intelligent apostle alludes when he says, *and thereby many be defiled,* "corrupted or contaminated."

16. *Lest there be any fornicator.* Any licentious person who would turn the gospel of the grace of God into lasciviousness. *Or profane person, as Esau.* It is not intimated that Esau was a *fornicator;* and the disjunctive *or* separates the *profane person* from the *fornicator.* And Esau is here termed *profane* because he so far disregarded the spiritual advantages connected with his rights of primogeniture that he alienated the whole for a single mess of pottage. See the note on Gen. xxv. 34. The word which we translate *profane* was applied to those who were not initiated into the sacred mysteries or who were despisers of sacred things, and consequently were to be denied admittance to the Temple and were not permitted to assist at holy rites. Indeed, among the Greeks it signified any thing or person which was "not consecrated to the gods." The Latin *profanus,* from which we have our word, is compounded of *procul a fano,* "far from the temple," properly an "irreligious man." *Sold his birthright.* The firstborn,

in patriarchal times: (1) Had a right to the priesthood, Exod. xxii. 29; (2) And a double portion of all the father's possessions, Deut. xxi. 17; (3) And was lord over his brethren, Gen. xxvii. 29, 37; xlix. 3; (4) And in the family of Abraham the firstborn was the very source whence the Messiah, as the Redeemer of the world, and the Church of God were to spring. In short, the rights of primogeniture were among the most noble, honorable, and spiritual in the ancient world.

17. *When he would have inherited the blessing.* When he wished to have the lordship over the whole family conveyed to him, and sought it earnestly with tears, he found no place for a "change" in his father's mind and counsel, who now perceived that it was the will of God that Jacob should be made lord of all. *Repentance.* Here *metanoia* is not to be taken in a theological sense, as implying contrition for sin, but merely "change of mind or purpose"; nor does the word refer here to Esau at all, but to his father, whom Esau could not, with all his tears and entreaties, persuade to reverse what he had done. "I have blessed him," said he, "yea, and he must be blessed"; I cannot reverse it now. Nothing spoken here by the apostle, nor in the history in Genesis to which he refers, concerns the eternal state of either of the two brothers. The use made of the transaction by the apostle is of great importance: Take heed lest, by apostatizing from the gospel, you forfeit all right and title to the heavenly birthright, and never again be able to retrieve it; because they who reject the gospel reject the only means of salvation.

18-21. *For ye are not come unto the mount that might be touched.* I believe the words should be translated "to a palpable or material mountain"; for that it was not a mountain that on this occasion *might be touched,* the history, Exod. xix. 12-13, shows; and the apostle himself, in v. 20, confirms. It is called here a palpable or material mount to distinguish it from that spiritual "mount Sion," of which the apostle is speaking. The apostle's design is to show that the dispensation of the law engendered terror; that it was most awful and exclusive; that it belonged only to the Jewish people; and that, even to them, it was so terrible that they *could not endure that which was commanded,* and entreated that God would not communicate with them in His own person, but by the ministry of Moses. And even to Moses, who held the highest intimacy with Jehovah, the revealed glories, the burning fire, the blackness, the darkness, the tempest, the loud-sounding trumpet, and the voice of words were so terrible that he said, "I exceedingly fear and tremble." These were the things which were exhibited on that material mountain; but the gospel dispensation is one grand, copious, and interesting display of the infinite love of God. It is all encouragement; breathes nothing but mercy; is not an exclusive system; embraces the whole human race; has Jesus, the sinner's Friend, for its Mediator; is ratified by His blood; and is suited, most gloriously suited, to all the wants and wishes of every soul of man.

22. *But ye are come unto mount Sion.* In order to enter fully into the apostle's meaning we must observe: (1) That the Church, which is called here *the city of the living God, the heavenly Jerusalem,* and *mount Sion,* is represented under the notion of a city. (2) That the great assembly of believers in Christ is here opposed to the congregation of the Israelites assembled at Mount Sinai. (3) That the *innumerable company of angels* is here opposed to those angels by whom the law was ushered in, Acts vii. 53; Gal. iii. 19. (4) That the gospel "firstborn," whose names are "written in heaven," are here opposed to the enrolled firstborn among the Israelites, Exod. xxiv. 5; xix. 22. (5) That the "mediator of the new covenant," the Lord Jesus, is here opposed to Moses, the mediator of the old. (6) And that "the blood of sprinkling," of Christ, our High Priest, refers to the act of Moses, Exod. xxiv. 8: "And Moses took the blood, and sprinkled it on the people, and said, Behold the blood of the covenant, which the Lord hath made with you concerning all these words." *The heavenly Jerusalem.* This phrase means the Church of the New Testament. *To an innumerable company of angels.* "To myriads, tens of thousands, of angels." These are represented as the attendants upon God when He manifests himself in any external manner to mankind. When He gave the law at Mount Sinai, it is intimated that myriads of these holy beings attended Him. "The chariots of God are twenty thousand, even thousands of angels: the Lord is among them, as in Sinai, in the holy place," Ps. lxviii. 17. And when He shall come to judge the world, He will be attended with a similar company. "Thousand thousands ministered unto him, and ten thousand times ten thousand stood before him," Dan. vii. 10. In both these cases, as in several others, these seem to be, speaking after the manner of men, the bodyguard of the Almighty.

23. *To the general assembly.* This word is joined to the preceding by some of the best MSS., and is quoted in connection by several of the fathers: "Ye are come . . . to the general assembly of innumerable angels"; and this is probably the true connection. *The firstborn.* Those who first received the gospel of Christ, and who are elsewhere termed the "firstfruits." This is spoken in allusion to the firstborn among the Israelites, who were all considered as the Lord's property, and were dedicated to Him. The Jews gave the title "firstborn" to those who were very eminent or excellent, what we would term the head or top of his kin. The *church of the firstborn* is the assembly of the most excellent. *Which are written in heaven.* Who are enrolled as citizens of the New Jerusalem, and are entitled to all the rights, privileges, and immunities of the Church here and of heaven above. This is spoken in allusion to the custom of enrolling or writing on tables, etc., the names of all the citizens of a particular city; and all those thus registered were considered as having a right to live there, and to enjoy all its privileges. *God the Judge of all.* The supreme God is ever present in this general assembly. To Him they are all gathered; by Him they are admitted to all those rights, etc.; under His inspection they continue to act; and it is He alone who erases from the register those who act unworthily of their citizenship. *Judge* here is to be taken in the Jewish use of the term, i.e., one who exercises sovereign rule and authority. *The spirits of just men made perfect.* We cannot understand these terms without the assistance of Jewish phraseology. The Jews divide mankind into three classes: (1) the just perfect,

(2) the wicked perfect, (3) those between. The "just perfect" are those (1) who have conquered all brutal appetites and gross passions, (2) who have stood in the time of strong temptation, (3) who give alms with a sincere heart, (4) who worship the true God only, (5) who are not invidious, (6) from whom God has taken evil concupiscence, and given the good principle. In several parts of this Epistle *teleios*, "the just man," signifies one who has a full knowledge of the Christian system, who is justified and saved by Christ Jesus; and the *teteleiomenoi* used here are the adult Christians, who are opposed to the babes in knowledge and grace. See chap. v. 12-14; viii. 11; and Gal. iv. 1-3. *The spirits of just men made perfect,* or the "righteous perfect," are the full-grown Christians; those who are justified by the blood and sanctified by the Spirit of Christ. Being come to such implies that spiritual union which the disciples of Christ have with each other, and which they possess how far soever separate. For they are all joined in one Spirit, Eph. ii. 18; they are "in the unity of the Spirit," Eph. iv. 3-4; "and of one soul," Acts iv. 32. This is a unity which was never possessed even by the Jews themselves in their best state; it is peculiar to real Christianity.

24. *And to Jesus the mediator of the new covenant.* The old covenant and its mediator, Moses, are passed away. See chap. viii. 13. The new covenant, i.e., the gospel, is now in force, and will be to the end of the world; and Jesus, the Son of God, the brightness of the Father's glory, the Maker and Preserver of all things, the Saviour and the Judge of all men, is its Mediator. *To the blood of sprinkling.* This is an allusion, as was before observed, to the sprinkling of the blood of the covenant sacrifice upon the people when that covenant was made upon Mount Sinai; to the sprinkling of the blood of the sin offerings before the mercy seat; and probably to the sprinkling of the blood of the paschal lamb on their houses, to prevent their destruction by the destroying angel. But all these sprinklings were partial and inefficacious, and had no meaning but as they referred to the Blood of sprinkling under the new covenant. *Better things than that of Abel.* God accepted Abel's sacrifice, and was well-pleased with it; for Abel was a righteous man, and offered his sacrifice by faith in the great promise. But the blood of Christ's sacrifice was infinitely more precious than the blood of Abel's sacrifice, as Jesus is infinitely greater than Abel; and the blood of Christ avails for the sins of the whole world, whereas the blood of Abel's sacrifice could avail only for himself.

25. *See,* "take heed," *that ye refuse not him,* the Lord Jesus, the Mediator of the new covenant, who now *speaketh from heaven,* by His gospel, to the Jews and to the Gentiles, having in His incarnation come down from God. *Him that spake on earth.* Moses, who spoke on the part of God to the Hebrews, every transgression of whose word "received a just recompence of reward," none being permitted to escape punishment. Consequently, if you turn away from Christ, who speaks to you from heaven, you may expect a much sorer punishment, the offense against God being so much the more heinous as the privileges slighted are more important and glorious.

26. *Whose voice then shook the earth.* Namely, at the giving of the law on Mount Sinai; and from this it seems that it was the voice of Jesus that then shook the earth, and that it was He who came down on the mount. *Not the earth only, but also heaven.* Probably referring to the approaching destruction of Jerusalem and the total abolition of the political and ecclesiastical constitution of the Jews, the one being signified by the *earth,* the other by *heaven;* for the Jewish state and worship are frequently thus termed in the prophetic writings. And this seems to be the apostle's meaning, as he evidently refers to Hag. ii. 6, where this event is predicted. It may also remotely refer to the final dissolution of all things.

27. *The removing of those things that are shaken.* The whole of the Jewish polity, which had been in a shaken state from the time that Judea had fallen under the power of the Romans. *As of things that are made.* That is, subjects intended to last only for a time. God never designed that the Jewish religion should become general, nor be permanent. *Those things which cannot be shaken.* The whole gospel system, which cannot be moved by the power of man. *May remain.* Be permanent, God designing that this shall be the last dispensation of His grace and mercy, and that it shall continue till the earth and the heavens are no more.

28. *We receiving a kingdom.* The gospel dispensation, frequently termed the "kingdom of God" and the "kingdom of heaven," because in it God reigns among men, and He reigns in the hearts of them that believe; and His kingdom is righteousness, peace, and joy in the Holy Ghost. *Which cannot be moved.* Which never can fail, because it is the last dispensation. *Let us have grace.* "Let us have, keep, or hold fast, the benefit or gift," that is, the heavenly Kingdom which God has given us. This is the meaning of the word, 2 Cor. viii. 4, and is so rendered by our translators; and it is only by this heavenly gift of the gospel that we can serve God acceptably, for He can be pleased with no service that is not performed according to the gospel of His Son. If we prefer the common meaning of the word *grace,* it comes to the same thing. Without the *grace,* the especial succor and influence of Christ, we cannot *serve,* "pay religious worship to," *God;* for He receives no burnt offering that is not kindled by fire from His own altar. *Acceptably.* In such a way as to "please" Him well. And the offering with which He is well pleased, He will graciously accept; and if He accept our service, His Spirit will testify in our conscience that our ways please Him. When Abel sacrifices, God is well-pleased; where Cain offers, there is no approbation. *Reverence.* With "modesty." *Godly fear.* "Religious fear." We have "boldness to enter into the holiest by the blood of Jesus," but let that boldness be ever tempered with "modesty" and "religious fear"; for we should never forget that we have sinned, and that God "is a consuming fire."

29. *For our God is a consuming fire.* The apostle quotes Deut. iv. 24, and by doing so he teaches us this great truth, that sin under the gospel is as abominable in God's sight as it was under the law; and that the man who does not labor to serve God with the principle and in the way already prescribed will find that

fire to consume him which would otherwise have consumed his sin.

CHAPTER 13

Exhortations to hospitality to strangers, 1-2. Kindness to those in bonds, 3. Concerning marriage, 4. Against covetousness, 5-6. How they should imitate their teachers, 7-8. To avoid strange doctrines, 9. Of the Jewish sin offerings, 10-11. Jesus suffered without the gate, and we should openly confess Him and bear His reproach, 12-13. Here we have no permanent residence, and while we live should devote ourselves to God and live to do good, 14-16. We should obey them that have the rule over us, 17. The apostle exhorts them to pray for him, that he might be restored to them the sooner, 18-19. Commends them to God in a very solemn prayer, 20-21. Entreats them to bear the word of exhortation, mentions Timothy, and concludes with the apostolical benediction, 22-25.

1. *Let brotherly love continue.* Feel for, comfort, and support each other; and remember that he who professes to love God should love his brother also. They had this brotherly love among them; they should take care to retain it. As God is remarkable for His "philanthropy," or love to man, so should they be for *philadelphia,* or love to each other. See the note on Titus iii. 4.

2. *To entertain strangers.* In those early times, when there were scarcely any public inns or houses of entertainment, it was an office of charity and mercy to receive, lodge, and entertain travellers; and this is what the apostle particularly recommends. *Entertained angels.* Abraham and Lot are the persons particularly referred to. Their history, the angels whom they entertained, not knowing them to be such, and the good they derived from exercising their hospitality on these occasions, are well-known; and have been particularly referred to in the notes on Gen. xviii. 3; xix. 2.

3. *Remember them that are in bonds.* He appears to refer to those Christians who were suffering imprisonment for the testimony of Jesus. *As bound with them.* Feel for them as you would wish others to feel for you were you in their circumstances, knowing that, being in the body, you are liable to the same evils, and may be called to suffer in the same way for the same cause.

4. *Marriage is honourable in all.* Let this state be highly esteemed as one of God's own instituting, and as highly calculated to produce the best interests of mankind. This may have been said against the opinions of the Essenes, who held marriage in little repute, and abstained from it themselves as a state of comparative imperfection. At the same time it shows the absurdity of the popish tenet that marriage in the clergy is both dishonorable and sinful; which is, in fact, in opposition to the apostle, who says *marriage is honourable in all;* and to the institution of God, which evidently designed that every male and female should be united in this holy bond; and to nature, which in every part of the habitable world has produced men and women in due proportion to each other. *The bed undefiled.* Every man cleaving to his own wife, and every wife cleaving to her own husband, because *God will judge,* i.e., punish, all "fornicators and adulterers."

5. *Let your conversation.* That is, the whole tenor of your conduct, the "manner of your life," or rather the disposition of your hearts in reference to all your secular transactions; for in this sense the original is used by the best Greek writers. *Be without covetousness.* Desire nothing more than what God has given you; and especially covet nothing which the Divine Providence has given to another man, for this is the very spirit of robbery. *Content with such things as ye have.* "Being satisfied with present things." The covetous man is ever running out into futurity with insatiable desires after secular good; and, if this disposition be not checked, it increases as the subject of it increases in years. Covetousness is the vice of old age. *I will never leave thee, nor forsake thee.* These words were, in sum, spoken to Joshua, chap. i. 5: "As I was with Moses, so will I be with thee: I will not fail thee, nor forsake thee." They were spoken also by David to Solomon, 1 Chron. xxviii. 20: "David said to Solomon his son, Be strong and of good courage, and do it: fear not, nor be dismayed: for the Lord God, even my God, will be with thee; he will not fail thee, nor forsake thee." The apostle, in referring to the same promises, feels authorized to strengthen the expressions, as the Christian dispensation affords more consolation and confidence in matters of this kind than the old covenant did. The words are peculiarly emphatic. There are no less than five negatives in this short sentence, and these connected with two verbs and one pronoun twice repeated. To give a literal translation is scarcely possible; it would run in this way: "No, I will not leave thee; no, neither will I not utterly forsake thee." Those who understand the genius of the Greek language and look at the manner in which these negatives are placed in the sentence will perceive at once how much the meaning is strengthened by them, and to what an emphatic and energetic affirmative they amount. This promise is made to those who are patiently bearing affliction or persecution for Christ's sake; and may be applied to any faithful soul in affliction, temptation, or adversity of any kind. Trust in the Lord with your whole heart, and never lean to your own understanding; for He hath said, "No, I will never leave thee; not I: I will never, never cast thee off."

6. *So that we may boldly say.* We, in such circumstances, while cleaving to the Lord, may confidently apply to ourselves what God spoke to Joshua and to Solomon; and what He spoke to David, *The Lord is my helper, and I will not fear what man shall do.* God is omnipotent; man's power is limited; howsoever strong he may be, he can do nothing against the Almighty.

7. *Remember them which have the rule over you.* This clause should be translated, "Remember your guides who have spoken unto you the doctrine of God." Theodoret's note on this verse is very judicious: "He intends the saints who were dead, Stephen the first martyr, James the brother of John, and James called the Just. And there were many others who were taken off by the Jewish rage. 'Consider these (said he), and, observing their example, imitate their faith.'" *Considering the end of their conversation.* "The issue of whose course of life most carefully consider." They lived to get good and do good; they were faithful to their God and His cause; they suffered persecution, and for the testimony of Jesus died a violent death. God never left them; no, He never forsook them; so that they were happy in their afflictions and glorious in their death.

8. *Jesus Christ the same yesterday.* In all past times there was no way to the holiest but through the blood of Jesus, either actually shed or significantly typified. *To day*—He is the Lamb newly slain, and continues to appear in the presence of God for us. *For ever*—to the conclusion of time, He will be "the way, the truth, and the life," none coming to the Father but through Him; and throughout eternity it will appear that all glorified human spirits owe their salvation to His infinite merit.

9. *Be not carried about.* "Be not whirled about." But almost every MS. of importance has "be not carried away," which is undoubtedly the true reading, and signifies here, "Do not apostatize," permit not yourselves to be carried off from Christ and His doctrine. *Divers and strange doctrines.* "Variegated doctrines"; those that blended the law and the gospel, and brought in the Levitical sacrifices and institutions in order to perfect the Christian system. Remember the old covenant is abolished; the new alone is in force. *Strange doctrines*, "foreign" doctrines, such as have no apostolical authority to recommend them. *That the heart be established with grace.* It is well to have the heart, the mind, and conscience fully satisfied with the truth and efficacy of the "gospel"; for so the word *charis* should be understood here, which is put in opposition to *bromasin, meats,* signifying here the Levitical institutions, and especially its sacrifices, these being emphatically termed *meats* because the offerers were permitted to feast upon them after the blood had been poured out before the Lord. See Lev. vii. 15; Deut. xii. 6-7. *Which have not profited them.* Because they neither took away guilt, cleansed the heart, nor gave power over sin.

10. *We have an altar.* The altar is here put for the sacrifice on the altar; the Christian *altar* is the Christian Sacrifice, which is Christ Jesus, with all the benefits of His passion and death. To these privileges they had no right who continued to offer the Levitical sacrifices and to trust in them for remission of sins.

11. *For the bodies of those beasts.* Though in making covenants, and in some victims offered according to the law, the flesh of the sacrifice was eaten by the offerers, yet the flesh of the sin offering might no man eat. When the blood was sprinkled before the holy place to make an atonement for their souls, the skins, flesh, entrails, etc., were carried without the camp, and there entirely consumed by fire; and this entire consumption, according to the opinion of some, was intended to show that sin was not pardoned by such offerings. For as eating the other sacrifices intimated they were made partakers of the benefits procured by those sacrifices, so not being permitted to eat of the sin offering proved that they had no benefit from it, and that they must look to the Christ, whose sacrifice is pointed out, that they might receive that real pardon of sin which the shedding of His blood could alone procure. While therefore they continued offering those sacrifices and refused to acknowledge the Christ, they had no right to any of the blessings procured by Him, and it is evident they could have no benefit from their own.

12. *That he might sanctify the people.* That He might consecrate them to God and make an atonement for their sins, He *suffered without the gate* at Jerusalem, as the sin offering was consumed "without the camp" when the Tabernacle abode in the wilderness. Perhaps all this was typical of the abolition of the Jewish sacrifices and the termination of the whole Levitical system of worship. He left the city, denounced its final destruction, and abandoned it to its fate; and *suffered without the gate* to bring the Gentiles to God.

13. *Let us go forth therefore unto him.* Let us leave this city and system, devoted to destruction, and take refuge in Jesus alone, *bearing his reproach*—being willing to be accounted the refuse of all things, and the worst of men, for His sake who bore the contradiction of sinners against himself and was put to death as a malefactor.

14. *For here have we no continuing city.* Here is an elegant and forcible allusion to the approaching destruction of Jerusalem. The Jerusalem that was below was about to be burned with fire and erased to the ground; the Jerusalem that was from above was that alone which could be considered to be "permanent."

15. *By him therefore let us offer the sacrifice of praise.* He has now fulfilled all vision and prophecy, has offered the last bloody sacrifice which God will ever accept; and as He is the Gift of God's love to the world, let us through Him offer the sacrifice of praise to God continually, this being the substitute for all the Levitical sacrifices. The Jews allowed that in the time of the Messiah all sacrifices, except the sacrifice of praise, should cease. To this maxim the apostle appears to allude; and understood in this way, his words are much more forcible. "Rabbi Phineas, Rabbi Levi, and Rabbi Jochanan, from the authority of Rabbi Menachem of Galilee, said, 'In the time of the Messiah all sacrifice shall cease except the sacrifice of praise.'" This was in effect quoting the authority of one of their own maxims, that now was the time of the Messiah, that Jesus was that Messiah, that the Jewish sacrificial system was now abolished, and that no sacrifice would now be accepted of God except the sacrifice of praise for the gift of His Son. *That is, the fruit of our lips.* This expression is probably borrowed from Hos. xiv. 2, in the version of the Septuagint, which in the Hebrew text is "the heifers of our lips." This may refer primarily to the sacrifices, heifers, calves, etc., which they had vowed to God; so that the "calves of their lips" were the sacrifices which they had promised. But how could the Septuagint translate "calves" by *fruit*? Very easily, if they had in their copy *peri*, the *mem* being omitted; and thus the word would be literally *fruit*, and not "calves."

16. *But to do good and to communicate.* These are continual sacrifices which God requires, and which will spring from a sense of God's love in Christ Jesus. Praise to God "for his unspeakable gift," and acts of kindness to men for God's sake. No reliance, even on the infinitely meritorious sacrifice of Christ, can be acceptable in the sight of God if a man have not love and charity towards his neighbor. Praise, prayer, and thanksgiving to God, with works of charity and mercy to man, are the sacrifices which every genuine follower of Christ must offer: and they are the proofs that a man belongs to Christ; and he who does not bear these fruits gives full

evidence, whatever his creed may be, that he is no Christian.

17. *Obey them that have the rule over you.* "Obey your leaders." He is not fit to rule who is not capable of guiding. See on v. 7 in the former verse the apostle exhorts them to remember those who had been their leaders and to imitate their faith; in this he exhorts them to obey the leaders they now had, and to submit to their authority in all matters of doctrine and discipline, on the ground that they watched for their souls, and should have to give an account of their conduct to God. If this conduct were improper, they must give in their report before the great tribunal with *grief*, but it must be given; if holy and pure, they would give it in with *joy*.

18. *Pray for us.* Even the success of apostles depended, in a certain way, on the prayers of the Church. Few Christian congregations feel, as they ought, that it is their bounden duty to pray for the success of the gospel, both among themselves and in the world. The Church is weak, dark, poor, and imperfect because it prays little. *We trust we have a good conscience.* We are persuaded that we have a conscience that not only acquits us of all fraud and sinister design, but assures us that in simplicity and godly sincerity we have labored to promote the welfare of you and of all mankind. *To live honestly.* "Willing in all things to conduct ourselves well" —to behave with decency and propriety.

19. *The rather to do this.* That is, pray for us, that, being enabled to complete the work which God has given us here to do, we may be the sooner enabled to visit you. It is evident from this that the people to whom this Epistle was written knew well who was the author of it, nor does there appear in any place any design in the writer to conceal his name; how the Epistle came to lack a name it is impossible to say.

20. *Now the God of peace.* We have often seen that *peace* among the Hebrews signifies "prosperity" of every kind. *The God of peace* is the same as the God of all blessedness, who has at His disposal all temporal and eternal good; who loves mankind, and has provided them a complete salvation. *Brought again from the dead our Lord.* As our Lord's sacrificial death is considered as an atonement offered to the divine justice, God's acceptance of it as an atonement is signified by His raising the human nature of Christ from the dead; and hence this raising of Christ is, with the utmost propriety, attributed to God the Father, as this proves His acceptance of the sacrificial offering. *That great shepherd of the sheep.* This is a title of our blessed Lord, given to Him by the prophets; so Isa. xl. 11; "He shall feed his flock like a shepherd: he shall gather the lambs with his arm, and carry them in his bosom, and shall gently lead those that are with young"; and Ezek. xxxiv. 23; "I will set up one shepherd over them, and he shall feed them, even my servant David [i.e., the beloved, viz., Jesus]; he shall feed them, and he shall be their shepherd"; and Zech. xiii. 7; "Awake, O sword, against my shepherd . . . smite the shepherd, and the sheep shall be scattered." In all these places the term *shepherd* is allowed to belong to our blessed Lord; and He appropriates it to himself, John x. 11, by calling himself "the good shepherd"

who lays down "his life for the sheep." *Through the blood of the everlasing covenant.* Some understand this in the following way, that "God brought back our Lord from the dead on account of His having shed His blood to procure the everlasting covenant." Others, that "the Lord Jesus became the great Shepherd and Saviour of the sheep by shedding His blood to procure and ratify the everlasting covenant." The sense, however, will appear much plainer if we connect this with the following verse: "Now the God of peace, that brought again from the dead our Lord Jesus, that great shepherd of the sheep, make you, through the blood of the everlasting coveant, perfect in every good work to do his will." The Christian system is termed the *everlasting covenant*, to distinguish it from the temporary covenant made with the Israelites at Mount Sinai, and to show that it is the last dispensation of grace to the world and shall endure to the end of time.

21. *Make you perfect.* "Put you completely in joint." See the note on 2 Cor. xiii. 9. From the following terms we see what the apostle meant by the perfection for which he prays. They were to do the will of God in every good work, from God *working* in them *that which is wellpleasing in his sight.* (1) This necessarily implies a complete change in the whole soul, that God may be well-pleased with whatsoever He sees in it; and this supposes its being cleansed from all sin, for God's sight cannot be pleased with anything that is unholy. (2) This complete inward purity is to produce an outward conformity to God's will, so they were to be made *perfect in every good work.* (3) The perfection within and the perfection without were to be produced by "the blood of the everlasting covenant"; for although "God is love," yet it is not consistent with His justice or holiness to communicate any good to mankind but through His Son, and through Him as having died for the offenses of the human race. *To whom be glory for ever.* As God does all in, by, and through Christ Jesus, to Him be the honor of His own work ascribed through time and eternity.

22. *Suffer the word of exhortation.* Bear the word or doctrine of this exhortation. This seems to be an epithet of this whole Epistle; and as the apostle had in it shown the insufficiency of the Levitical system to atone for sin and save the soul, and had proved that it was the design of God that it should be abolished, and had proved also that it was now abolished by the coming of Christ, whom he had shown to be a greater Priest than Aaron, higher than all the angels, the only Son of God as to His human nature, and the Creator, Governor, and Judge of all, and that their city was shortly to be destroyed, he might suppose that they would feel prejudiced against him, and thus lose the benefit of his kind intentions toward them. Therefore he entreats them to bear the exhortation which, notwithstanding the great extent of the subject, he had included in a short compass. *I have written a letter unto you in few words.* Perhaps it would be better to translate, "I have written to you briefly."

23. *Know ye that our brother Timothy.* The word *our*, which is supplied by our translators, is very probably genuine, as it is found in several MSS. and in the Syriac, the Coptic, Armenian, Slavonic, and Vulgate. *Is set at liberty.*

"Is sent away," for there is no evidence that Timothy had been imprisoned. It is probable that the apostle refers here to his being sent into Macedonia, Phil. ii. 19-24, in order that he might bring the apostle an account of the affairs of the church in that country. In none of Paul's Epistles, written during his confinement in Rome, does he give any intimation of Timothy's imprisonment, although it appears from Phil. i. 1; Col. i. 1; and Philemon 1 that he was with Paul during the greatest part of the time. *With whom, if he come shortly, I will see you.* Therefore Paul himself, or the writer of this Epistle, was now at liberty, as he had the disposal of his person and time in his own power. Some suppose that Timothy did actually visit Paul about this time, and that both together visited the churches in Judea.

24. *Salute all them that have the rule over you.* "Salute all your leaders" or "guides." See on vv. 7 and 17. *And all the saints.* All the Christians, for this is the general meaning of the term in most parts of Paul's writings. But a Christian was then a saint, i.e., by profession a holy person; and most of the primitive Christians were actually such. But in process of time the term was applied to all that bore the Christian name, as "elect, holy people, sanctified" were to the nation of the Jews when both their piety and morality were at a very low ebb. *They of Italy salute you.* Therefore it is most likely that the writer of this Epistle was then in some part of Italy, from which he had not as yet removed after his being released from prison. By *they of Italy* probably the apostle means the Jews there who had embraced the Christian faith. These salutations show what a brotherly feeling existed in every part of the Christian Church; even those who had not seen each other yet loved one another, and felt deeply interested for each other's welfare.

25. *Grace be with you all.* May the divine favor ever rest upon you and among you; and may you receive, from that source of all good, whatsoever is calculated to make you wise, holy, useful, and happy! And may you be enabled to persevere in the truth to the end of your lives!

The Epistle of
JAMES

This Epistle, with those of Peter, John, and Jude, is termed *catholic*. Oecumenius gives the following reason: "These epistles are called catholic, universal, or circular, because they were not written to one nation or city, but to believers everywhere."

Yet as these Epistles had some difficulty at first to get into general circulation, but at last were everywhere received, it is more likely that they obtained the term "catholic" from the circumstance of their being at last universally acknowledged as canonical; so that the word "catholic" is to be understood here in the same sense as "canonical."

Who the writer of the Epistle in question was is difficult to say; all that we know certainly is, from his own words, that his name was James, and that he was a servant of God and of the Lord Jesus. Two persons of this name are mentioned in the New Testament: James the son of Zebedee, called also James the elder; and James "the less" or the "little one," called the son of Alphaeus, and brother of our Lord. Michaelis leans to the opinion that James the son of Zebedee was the author. Other great authorities ascribe it to James, called the brother of our Lord, who was president, or bishop, of the church in Jerusalem. Even allowing this opinion to be correct, it is not agreed in what sense James is called our Lord's brother, there being *four* or *five* different opinions concerning the meaning of this term. From Matt. xiii. 55-56 we learn that there were four persons called brethren of our Lord: "Is not this the carpenter's son? is not his mother called Mary? and his brethren, James, and Joses, and Simon, and Judas? And his sisters, are they not all with us?" Now it is generally allowed that the James here is the author of this Epistle, and the Jude or Judas mentioned with him the author of that which stands last in this collection. But with respect to the meaning of the term "brother," as here used, it will be necessary to state the opinions of learned men:

1. It is supposed that these were children of Joseph, by a former marriage; this is a very ancient opinion, as there is nothing improbable in the supposition that Joseph was a widower when he married the blessed Virgin.

2. They are supposed to have been children of Joseph and his wife Mary, all born after the birth of our Lord. This is an opinion extremely probable.

3. That they were called our Lord's brethren because children of Joseph by the wife of one of his brothers, who had died childless and whose widow Joseph took, according to the Mosaic law, to raise up seed to his deceased brother. This is very unlikely because, in this case, it would have been only requisite for Joseph to have had one male by his brother's wife; but here we find four, besides several sisters.

4. That Cleophas, called also Alphaeus, married a sister of the blessed Virgin, called also Mary, by whom he had the above issue; and that these were called brethren of our Lord, from

the common custom among the Hebrews to term cousins "brethren." The first and second of these opinions appear to me the most probable.

The Epistle itself is entirely different in its complexion from all those in the sacred canon; the style and manner are more that of a Jewish prophet than a Christian apostle. It scarcely touches on any subject purely Christian. Our blessed Lord is mentioned only twice in it, chap. i. 1; ii. 1; but it has nothing of His miracles or teaching, of His death or resurrection, nor of any redemption by Him. It begins without any apostolical salutation and ends without any apostolical benediction. In short, had it not been for the two slight notices of our blessed Lord, we had not known it was the work of any Christian writer. It may be considered a sort of connecting link between Judaism and Christianity, as the ministry of John Baptist was between the old covenant and the new. There is neither plan nor arrangement in it; but it contains many invaluable lessons which no serious person can read without profit.

CHAPTER 1

He addresses the dispersed of the twelve tribes, 1. Shows that they should rejoice under the cross, because of the spiritual good which they may derive from it, especially in the increase and perfecting of their patience, 2-4. They are exhorted to ask wisdom of God, who gives liberally to all, 5. But they must ask in faith, and not with a doubting mind, 6-8. Directions to the rich and the poor, 9-11. The blessedness of the man that endures trials, 12. How men are tempted and drawn away from God, 13-15. God is the Father of lights, and all good proceeds from Him, 16-18. Cautions against hasty words and wrong tempers, 19-21. We should be doers of the Word, and not hearers merely, lest we resemble those who, beholding their natural faces in a glass, when it is removed forget what manner of persons they were, 22-24. We should look into the perfect law of liberty and continue therein, 25. The nature and properties of pure religion, 26-27.

1. *James, a servant of God.* He neither calls himself an apostle nor does he say that he was the brother of Christ or bishop of Jerusalem. *To the twelve tribes which are scattered abroad.* To the Jews, whether converted to Christianity or not, who lived out of Judea and sojourned among the Gentiles for the purpose of trade or commerce. *Greeting.* "Health"; a mere expression of benevolence, a wish for their prosperity; a common form of salutation; see Acts xv. 23; xxiii. 26.

2. *Count it all joy.* The word which we translate *temptations* signifies affliction, persecution, or trial of any kind; and in this sense it is used here, not intending diabolic suggestion, or what is generally understood by the word *temptations.*

3. *The trying of your faith.* Trials put religion, and all the graces of which it is composed, to proof. The man that stands in such trials gives proof that his religion is sound, and the evidence afforded to his own mind induces him to take courage, bear patiently, and persevere.

4. *Let patience have her perfect work.* That is, continue faithful, and your patience will be crowned with its full reward; for in this sense is *ergon,* which we translate *work,* to be understood. The *perfect work* is the "full reward." *That ye may be perfect and entire.* "Fully instructed" in every part of the doctrine of God and in His whole will concerning you. Having all your parts, members, and portions; that you may have every grace which constitutes the mind that was in Christ, so that your knowledge and holiness may be complete, and bear a proper proportion to each other. These expressions in their present application are by some thought to be borrowed from the Grecian games. The man was *perfect* who in any of the athletic exercises had got the victory; he was *entire,* having everything complete, who had the victory in each of the five exercises. Of this use in the last term I do not recollect

an example, and therefore think the expressions are borrowed from the sacrifices under the law. A victim was *perfect* that was perfectly sound, having no disease; it was *entire* if it had all its members, having nothing deficient.

5. *If any of you lack wisdom.* Wisdom signifies, in general, knowledge of the best end and the best means of attaining it; but in Scripture it signifies the same as true religion, the thorough practical knowledge of God, of oneself, and of a Saviour. *Let him ask of God.* Because God is the only Teacher of this wisdom. *That giveth to all men liberally.* Who has all good, and gives all necessary good to everyone that asks fervently. He who does not ask thus does not feel his need of divine teaching. The ancient Greek maxim appears at first view strange, but it is literally true: "The knowledge of ignorance is the beginning of knowledge."

6. *Let him ask in faith.* Believing that God is, that He has all good, and that He is ever ready to impart to His creatures whatever they need. *Nothing wavering.* "Not judging otherwise"; having no doubt concerning the truth of these grand and fundamental principles, never supposing that God will permit him to ask in vain, when he asks sincerely and fervently. *Is like a wave of the sea.* The man who is not thoroughly persuaded that if he ask of God he shall receive resembles *a wave of the sea;* he is in a state of continual agitation; *driven with the wind and tossed;* now rising by hope, then sinking by despair.

7. *Let not that man think.* The man whose mind is divided, who is not properly persuaded either of his own wants or God's sufficiency. Such persons may pray, but having no faith, they can get no answer.

8. *A double minded man.* The "man of two souls," who has one for earth and another for heaven; who wishes to secure both worlds; he will not give up earth, and he is loath to let heaven go. This was a usual term among the Jews to express the man who attempted to worship God and yet retained the love of the creature. Perhaps James refers to those Jews who were endeavoring to incorporate the law with the gospel, who were divided in their minds and affections, not willing to give up the Levitical rites and yet unwilling to renounce the gospel. Such persons could make no progress in divine things.

9. *Let the brother of low degree.* The poor, destitute Christian may "glory" in the cross of Christ, and the blessed hope laid up for him in heaven; for, being a child of God and an heir of God and a joint heir with Christ,

10. *But the rich, in that he is made low.* "In his humiliation"—in his being brought to the foot of the Cross to receive, as a poor and miserable sinner, redemption through the Blood of the Cross; and especially let him rejoice in this, because all outward glory is only as the flower of the field and, like that, will wither and perish.

11. *For the sun is no sooner risen.* All human things are transitory; rise and fall, or increase and decay, belong to all the productions of the earth, and to all its inhabitants.

12. *Blessed is the man that endureth temptation.* Every man is in this life in a state of temptation or trial, and in this state he is a candidate for another and a better world; he that stands in his trial *shall receive the crown of life, which the Lord hath promised to them that love him.* There may be an allusion here to the contests in the Grecian games. He is crowned who conquers, and none else.

13. *Let no man say.* Lest the former sentiment should be misapplied, as the word temptation has two grand meanings—solicitation to sin, and trial from providential situation or circumstances—James, taking up the word in the former sense, after having used it in the latter, says: *Let no man say, when he is tempted* [solicited to sin], *I am tempted of God; for God cannot be tempted with evil, neither tempteth he* [thus] *any man."*

14. *But every man is tempted,* successfully solicited to sin, *when he is drawn away of his own lust*—when, giving way to the evil propensity of his own heart, he does that to which he is solicited by the enemy of his soul. Among the rabbins we find some fine sayings on this subject. "Evil concupiscence is, at the beginning, like the thread of a spider's web: afterwards it is like a cart rope" (*Sanhedrim,* fol. 99). In the words *drawn away of his own lust, and enticed,* there is a double metaphor: the first referring to the dragging a fish out of the water by a hook which it had swallowed, because concealed by a bait; the second, to the enticements of impure women, who draw away the unwary into their snares and involve them in their ruin.

15. *When lust hath conceived.* When the evil propensity works unchecked, *it bringeth forth sin*—the evil act between the parties is perpetrated. *And sin, when it is finished.* When this breach of the law of God and of innocence has been a sufficient time completed, it *bringeth forth death*—the spurious offspring is the fruit of the criminal connection, and the evidence of that *death* or "punishment" due to the transgressors. Sin is a small matter in its commencement; but by indulgence it grows great, and multiplies itself beyond all calculation. To use the rabbinical metaphor lately adduced, it is, in the commencement, "like the thread of a spider's web"—almost imperceptible through its extreme fineness, and as easily broken; afterwards it becomes like a cart rope. It has, by being indulged, produced strong desire and delight; next, consent. Then time, place, and opportunity serving, that which was conceived in the mind and finished in the purpose is consummated by act.

16. *Do not err.* By supposing that God is the author of sin or that He impels any man to commit it.

17. *Every good gift and every perfect gift is from above.* Whatever is good is from God; whatever is evil is from man himself. As from the sun all light comes, so from God all good comes. *With whom is no variableness.* The sun, the fountain of light to the whole of our system, may be obscured by clouds; or the different bodies which revolve round him, and particularly the earth, may from time to time suffer a diminution of his light by the intervention of other bodies eclipsing his splendor, and his apparent *shadow of turning;* when for instance, in our winter, he has declined to the southern tropic, so that our days are greatly shortened, and we suffer in consequence a great diminution of both light and heat. But there is nothing of this kind with God; He is never affected by the changes and chances to which mortal things are exposed.

18. *Of his own will begat he us.* God's will here is opposed to the lust of man, v. 15; His truth, the means of human salvation, to the sinful means referred to in the above verse; and the new creatures, to the sin conceived and brought forth, as above. As the will of God is essentially good, all its productions must be good also; as it is infinitely pure, all its productions must be holy. The *word* or doctrine of *truth,* what Paul calls "the word of the truth of the gospel," Col. i. 5, is the means which God uses to convert souls. *A kind of firstfruits.* By *creatures* we are here to understand the Gentiles, and by *firstfruits* the Jews, to whom the gospel was first sent; and those of them that believed were the firstfruits of that astonishing harvest which God has since reaped over the whole Gentile world.

19. *Swift to hear.* "Talk little and work much," is a rabbinical adage (*Pirkey Aboth,* cap. i. 15). "The righteous speak little, and do much; the wicked speak much, and do nothing" (*Bava Metzia,* fol. 87). *Slow to wrath.* Those who are hasty in speech are generally of a peevish or angry disposition. A person who is careful to consider what he says is not likely to be soon angry.

21. *All filthiness.* This word signifies any impurity that cleaves to the body; but applied to the mind, it implies all impure and unholy affections, such as those spoken of in v. 15, which pollute the soul. In this sense it is used by the best Greek writers. *Superfluity of naughtiness.* The "overflowing of wickedness." *The engrafted word.* That doctrine which has already been planted among you, which has brought forth fruit in all them that have meekly and humbly received it, and is as powerful to save your souls as the souls of those who have already believed. When those who were Jews, and who had been originally planted by God as altogether a right vine, received the faith of the gospel, it is represented as being engrafted on that right stock, the pure knowledge of the true God and His holy moral law. This indeed was a good stock on which to implant Christianity.

22. *But be ye doers of the word.* They had heard this doctrine; they had believed it; but they had put it to no practical use. *Deceiving your own selves.* Imposing on your own selves by sophistical arguments; this is the meaning of the words. They had reasoned themselves

into a state of carnal security, and the object of James is to awake them out of their sleep.

23. *Beholding his natural face in a glass.* This metaphor is very simple, but very expressive. A man wishes to see his own face, and how, in its natural state, it appears; for this purpose he looks into a mirror, by which his real face, with all its blemishes and imperfections, is exhibited. He is affected with his own appearance; he sees deformities that might be remedied; spots, superfluities, and impurities that might be removed. While he continues to look into the mirror he is affected, and wishes himself different to what he appears, and forms purposes of doing what he can to render his countenance agreeable. On going away he soon forgets "what manner of person he was." The doctrines of God, faithfully preached, are such a mirror; he who hears cannot help discovering his own character and being affected with his own deformity. He sorrows and purposes amendment; but when the preaching is over, the mirror is removed, and not being careful to examine the records of his salvation, the "perfect law of liberty," v. 25, or not continuing to look therein, he soon forgets "what manner of man he was."

25. *But whoso looketh into the perfect law.* The word which we translate *looketh into* is very emphatic and signifies that deep and attentive consideration given to a thing or subject which a man cannot bring up to his eyes, and therefore must "bend his back and neck, stooping down," that he may see it to the greater advantage. The *law of liberty* must mean the gospel. It is a *law,* for it imposes obligations from God and prescribes a rule of life; and it punishes transgressors and rewards the obedient. It is, nevertheless, a law that gives *liberty* from the guilt, power, dominion, and influence of sin; and it is *perfect,* providing a fullness of salvation for the soul: and it may be called *perfect* here in opposition to the law, which was a system of types and representations of which the gospel is the sum and substance. *And continueth.* Takes time to see and examine the state of his soul, the grace of his God, the extent of his duty, and the height of the promised glory. The metaphor here is taken from those females who spend much time at their glass, in order that they may decorate themselves to the greatest advantage, and not leave one hair, or the smallest ornament, out of its place. *He being not a forgetful hearer.* This seems to be a reference to Deut. iv. 9: "Only take heed to thyself, and keep thy soul diligently, lest thou forget the things which thine eyes have seen, and lest they depart from thy heart all the days of thy life." "He who studies and forgets is like to a woman who brings forth children, and immediately buries them" (*Aboth R. Nathan,* cap. 23). *Shall be blessed in his deed.* In *Pirkey Aboth,* cap. v. 14, it is said: "There are four kinds of men who visit the synagogues: (1) He who enters but does not work; (2) He who works but does not enter; (3) He who enters and works; (4) He who neither enters nor works. The first two are indifferent characters; the third is the righteous man; the fourth is wholly evil." As the path of duty is the way of safety, so it is the way of happiness; he who obeys God from a loving heart and pure conscience will infallibly find continual blessedness.

27. *Pure religion and undefiled.* James's definition rather refers to the effects of *pure religion* than to its nature. The "life of God in the soul of man," producing love to God and man, will show itself in the acts which James mentions here. It is *pure* in the principle, for it is divine truth and divine love. It is *undefiled* in all its operations. It can produce nothing unholy, because it ever acts in the sight of God; and it can produce no ungentle word nor unkind act, because it comes from the *Father.* The words *pure* and *undefiled* are supposed to have reference to a diamond or precious stone, whose perfection consists in its being free from flaws. True religion is the ornament of the soul; and its effects, the ornament of the life. *To visit the fatherless and widows in their affliction.* Works of charity and mercy are the proper fruits of religion, and none are more especially the objects of charity and mercy than the orphans and widows. False religion may perform acts of mercy and charity: but its motives not being pure, and its principle being defiled, the flesh, self, and hypocrisy spot the man, and spot his acts. True religion does not merely give something for the relief of the distressed, but it visits them, it takes the oversight of them, it takes them under its care.

CHAPTER 2

We should not prefer the rich to the poor, nor show any partiality inconsistent with the gospel of Christ, 1-4. God has chosen the poor, rich in faith, to be heirs of His kingdom, even those whom some among their brethren despised and oppressed, 5-6. They should love their neighbor as themselves, and have no respect of persons, 7-9. He who breaks one command of God is guilty of the whole, 10-11. They should act as those who shall be judged by the law of liberty; and he shall have judgment without mercy who shows no mercy, 12-13. Faith without works of charity and mercy is dead; nor can it exist where there are no good works, 14-20. Abraham proved his faith by his works, 21-24. And so did Rahab, 25. As the body without the soul is dead, so is faith without good works, 26.

1. *My brethren, have not.* This verse should be read interrogatively: "My brethren, do you not make profession of the faith or religion of our glorious Lord Jesus Christ with acceptance of persons?" That is, preferring the rich to the poor merely because of their riches, and not on account of any moral excellence, personal piety, or public usefulness. *Faith* is put here for religion; and *of glory* should, according to some critics, be construed with it as the Syriac and Coptic have done. Some connect it with *our Lord Jesus Christ*—"the religion of our glorious Lord Jesus Christ." Others translate thus, "the faith of the glory of our Lord Jesus." There are many various readings in the MSS. and versions on this verse; the meaning is clear enough, though the connection be rather obscure.

2. *If there come unto your assembly.* "Into the synagogue." It appears from this that the apostle is addressing Jews who frequented their synagogues. Our word *assembly* does not express the original; and we cannot suppose that these synagogues were at this time occupied with Christian worship, but that the Christian Jews continued to frequent them for the purpose of hearing the law and the prophets read, as they had formerly done, previously to their conversion to the Christian faith. *With a gold ring, in goodly apparel.* The ring on the finger and the splendid garb were proofs of the man's

opulence; and his ring and his coat, not his worth, moral good qualities, or the righteousness of his cause, procured him the respect of which James speaks. *There come in also a poor man.* In ancient times petty courts of judicature were held in the synagogues; and it is probable that the case here adduced was one of a judicial kind, where, of the two parties, one was rich and the other poor; and the master or ruler of the synagogue, or he who presided in this court, paid particular deference to the rich man and neglected the poor man; though, as plaintiff and defendant, they were equal in the eye of justice, and should have been considered so by an impartial judge.

3. *Sit here under my footstool.* Thus evidently prejudging the cause, and giving the poor man to see that he was to expect no impartial administration of justice in his cause.

4. *Are ye not then partial?* "Do you not make a distinction," though the case has not been heard and the law has not decided? *Judges of evil thoughts.* "Judges of evil reasonings"; that is, "judges who reason wickedly"; who in effect say in your hearts, We will espouse the cause of the rich, because they can befriend us; we will neglect that of the poor, because they cannot help us, nor have they power to hurt us.

5. *Hath not God chosen the poor of this world?* This seems to refer to Matt. xi. 5: "And the poor have the gospel preached to them." These believed on the Lord Jesus and found His salvation; while the rich despised, neglected, and persecuted Him.

6. *Do not rich men oppress you?* The administration of justice was at this time in a miserable state of corruption among the Jews; but a Christian was one who was to expect no justice anywhere but from his God. The words "exceedingly oppress" and "drag you to courts of justice" show how grievously oppressed and maltreated the Christians were by their countrymen the Jews, who made law a pretext to afflict their bodies and spoil them of their property.

7. *Blaspheme that worthy name.* They took every occasion to asperse the Christian name and the Christian faith.

8. *The royal law.* This epithet, of all the New Testament writers, is peculiar to James; but it is frequent among the Greek writers in the sense in which it appears James uses it. *Royal* is used to signify anything that is of general concern, is suitable to all, and necessary for all, as brotherly love is. This commandment, *Thou shalt love thy neighbour as thyself,* is a *royal law,* not only because it is ordained of God, and proceeds from His kingly authority over men, but because it is so useful, suitable, and necessary to the present state of man.

9. *But if ye have respect to persons,* in judgment or in any other way; *ye commit sin* against God and against your brethren, *and are convinced,* "convicted," by *the law;* by this royal law, "Thou shalt love thy neighbour as thyself"; *as transgressors,* having shown this sinful acceptance of persons which has led you to refuse justice to the poor man and uphold the rich in his oppressive conduct.

10. *For whosoever shall keep the whole law.*

This is a rabbinical form of speech. In the tract *Shabbath,* fol. 70, where they dispute concerning the thirty-nine works commanded by Moses, Rabbi Yochanan says: "But if a man do the whole, with the omission of one, he is guilty of the whole, and of every one."

11. *For he that said.* That is, the Authority that gave one commandment gave also the rest; and he who breaks one resists this Authority; so that the breach of any one commandment may be justly considered a breach of the whole law.

12. *So speak ye, and so do.* Have respect to every commandment of God, for this the *law of liberty,* the gospel of Jesus Christ, particularly requires; and this is the law by which all mankind who have had the opportunity of knowing it shall be judged. But all along James particularly refers to the precept, "Thou shalt love thy neighbour as thyself."

13. *For he shall have judgment.* He who shows no mercy to man, or in other words, he who does not exercise himself in works of charity and mercy to his needy fellow creatures, shall receive no mercy at the hand of God; for He has said, "Blessed are the merciful: for they shall obtain mercy." *Mercy rejoiceth against judgment.* These words are variously understood. (1) *Mercy,* the merciful man, the abstract for the concrete, exults over judgment; that is, he is not afraid of it, having acted according to the law of liberty, "Thou shalt love thy neighbour as thyself." (2) You shall be exalted by mercy above judgment. (3) For He (God) exalts mercy above judgment. (4) A merciful man rejoices rather in opportunities of showing mercy than in acting according to strict justice. (5) In the great day, though justice might condemn every man according to the rigor of the law, yet God will cause mercy to triumph over justice in bringing those into His glory who, for His sake, had fed the hungry, clothed the naked, ministered to the sick, and visited the prisoners. See what our Lord says, Matt. xxv. 31-46. In the MSS. and versions there is a considerable variety of readings on this verse, and some of the senses given above are derived from those readings. The spirit of the saying may be found in another scripture, "I will have mercy, and not sacrifice"—I prefer works of charity and mercy to everything else, and especially to all acts of worship.

14. *What doth it profit . . . though a man say he hath faith?* We now come to a part of this Epistle which has appeared to some eminent men to contradict other portions of the divine records. In short, it has been thought that James teaches the doctrine of justification by the merit of good works, while Paul asserts this to be insufficient, and that man is justified by faith. Luther, supposing that James did actually teach the doctrine of justification by works, which his good sense showed him to be absolutely insufficient for salvation, was led to condemn the Epistle in toto, as a production unauthenticated by the Holy Spirit, and consequently worthy of no regard; he therefore termed it "a chaffy epistle," an "epistle of straw," fit only to be burned. Learned men have spent much time in striving to reconcile these two writers, and to show that Paul and James perfectly accord: one teaching the pure doctrine, the other guarding men against the abuse

of it. Mr. Wesley sums the whole up in the following words, with his usual accuracy and precision: "From chap. i. 22 the apostle has been enforcing Christian practice. He now applies to those who neglect this under the pretense of faith. Paul had taught that a man is justified by faith without the works of the law. This some already began to wrest to their own destruction. Wherefore James, purposely repeating, vv. 21, 23, 25, the same phrases, testimonies, and examples which Paul had used, Rom. iv. 3; Heb. xi. 17, 31, refutes, not the doctrine of Paul, but the error of those who abused it. There is therefore no contradiction between the apostles; they both delivered the truth of God, but in a different manner, as having to do with different kinds of men. This verse is a summary of what follows: 'What profiteth it?' is enlarged on, vv. 15-17; *though a man say*, vv. 18-19; *can that faith save him?* v. 20. It is not *though he have faith*, but *though he say, I have faith*. Here therefore true, living faith is meant. But in other parts of the argument the apostle speaks of a dead, imaginary faith. He does not therefore teach that true faith *can*, but that it *cannot*, subsist without works. Nor does he oppose *faith* to *works*, but that empty name of faith to real faith working by love. *Can that faith which is without works save him?* No more than it can profit his neighbor."

15. *If a brother or sister be naked.* That is, ill-clothed; for *naked* has this meaning in several parts of the New Testament, signifying bad clothing, or the want of some particular article of dress. See Matt. xxv. 36, 38, 43-44 and John xxi. 7.

16. *Be ye warmed and filled.* Your saying so to them while you give them nothing will profit them just as much as your professed faith, without those works which are the genuine fruits of true faith, will profit you in the day when God comes to sit in judgment upon your soul.

17. *If it hath not works, is dead.* The faith that does not produce works of charity and mercy is without the living principle which animates all true faith; that is, love to God and love to man.

18. *Shew me thy faith without thy works.* Your pretending to have faith while you have no works of charity or mercy is utterly vain. For as *faith*, which is a principle in the mind, cannot be discerned but by the effects—that is, good works—he who has no good works has, presumptively, no faith. *I will shew thee my faith by my works.* My works of charity and mercy will show that I have faith; and that it is the living tree, whose root is love to God and man, and whose fruit is the good works here contended for.

19. *Thou believest that there is one God.* This is the faith in which these persons put their hope of pleasing God and of obtaining eternal life. Believing in the being and unity of God distinguished them from all the nations of the world; and having been circumcised, and thus brought into the covenant, they thought themselves secure of salvation. The insufficiency of this James immediately shows. *The devils also believe, and tremble.* It is well to believe there is one only true God; this truth universal nature proclaims. Even the devils believe it; but far from justifying or saving them, it leaves

them in their damned state, and every act of it only increases their torment. "They shudder with horror"; they *believe, and tremble*, are increasingly tormented; but they can neither love nor obey.

20. *But wilt thou know?* Are you willing to be instructed in the nature of true saving faith? Then attend to the following examples.

21. *Was not Abraham our father?* Did not the conduct of Abraham, in offering up his son Isaac on the altar, sufficiently prove that he believed in God, and that it was his faith in Him that led him to this extraordinary act of obedience?

22. *Seest thou how faith wrought?* Here is a proof that faith cannot exist without being active in works of righteousness. His faith in God would have been of no avail to him had it not been manifested by works. For *by works*, by his obedience to the commands of God, his *faith was made perfect.* It dictated obedience; he obeyed; and thus faith "had its consummation." Even true faith will soon die if its possessor does not live in the spirit of obedience.

23. *The scripture was fulfilled.* He *believed God.* This faith was never inactive; it was accounted to *him for righteousness;* and, being justified by thus believing, his life of obedience showed that he had not received the grace of God in vain. *The Friend of God.* The highest character ever given to man.

24. *Ye see then how.* It is evident from this example that Abraham's faith was not merely believing that there is a God, but a principle that led him to credit God's promises relative to the future Redeemer and to implore God's mercy; this he received and was justified by faith. His faith now began to work by love, and therefore he was found ever obedient to the will of his Maker. He brought forth the fruits of righteousness; and his works *justified*—proved the genuineness of his faith. Obedience to God is essentially requisite to maintain faith. Faith lives, under God, by works; and works have their being and excellence from faith. Neither can subsist without the other, and this is the point which James labors to prove, in order to convince the antinomians of his time that their faith was a delusion, and that the hopes built on it must needs perish.

25. *Rahab the harlot.* See the notes on Josh. ii. 1 ff. and Heb. xi. 31 ff. Rahab had the approbation due to genuine faith, which she actually possessed, and gave the fullest proof that she did so by her conduct. As justification signifies, not only the pardon of sin, but receiving the divine approbation, James seems to use the word in this latter sense. God approved of them because of their obedience to His will, and He approves of no man who is not obedient.

26. *For as the body without the spirit is dead.* There can be no more a genuine faith without good works than there can be a living human body without a soul.

CHAPTER 3

They are exhorted not to be many masters, 1. And to bridle the tongue, which is often an instrument of much evil, 2-12. The character and fruits of true and false wisdom, 13-18.

1. *Be not many masters.* Do not affect the "teacher's" office, for many wish to be teachers

who have more need to learn. There were many teachers or rabbins among the Jews, each affecting to have the truth and to draw disciples after him. We find a caution against such persons, and of the same nature with that of James, in *Pirkey Aboth.* c. i. 10: "Love labour, and hate the rabbin's office." This caution is still necessary; there are multitudes whom God has never called and never can call, because He has never qualified them for the work, who earnestly wish to get into the priest's office. Their case is awful; they *shall receive the greater condemnation* than common sinners. They have not only sinned in thrusting themselves into that office to which God has never called them, but through their insufficiency the flocks over whom they have assumed the mastery perish for lack of knowledge, and their blood will God require at the watchman's hand.

2. *In many things we offend all.* "We all stumble or trip." Some have produced these words as a proof that "no man can live without sinning against God; for James himself, a holy apostle, speaking of himself, all the apostles, and the whole Church of Christ, says, *In many things we offend all.*" This is a very bad and dangerous doctrine; and pushed to its consequences, would greatly affect the credibility of the whole gospel system. *Offend not in word, the same is a perfect man.* To understand this properly we must refer to the caution James gives in the preceding verse: "Be not many masters" (or teachers)—do not affect that for which you are not qualified. But, says he, *if any man offend not,* "trip not in doctrine," teaching the truth, the whole truth, and nothing but the truth, *the same is* "a man fully instructed" in divine things. How often the term *logos,* which we render *word,* is used to express "doctrine," and the doctrine of the gospel, we have seen in many parts of the preceding comment. And how often the word *teleios,* which we translate *perfect,* is used to signify an "adult Christian," one "thoroughly instructed" in the doctrines of the gospel, may be seen in various parts of Paul's writings. See, among others, 1 Cor. ii. 6; xiv. 20; Eph. iv. 13; Phil. iii. 15; Col. iv. 12; Heb. v. 14. The man, therefore, who advanced no false doctrine and gave no imperfect view of any of the great truths of Christianity, that man proved himself thereby to be "thoroughly instructed" in divine things; to be no novice, and consequently, among the many teachers, to be a perfect master and worthy of the sacred vocation. *Able also to bridle the whole body.* Grotius, by *body,* believed that the Church of Christ was intended; and this the view we have taken of the preceding clauses renders very probable. But some think the passions and appetites are intended; yet these persons understand "not offending in word" as referring simply to well-guarded speech. Now how a man's cautiousness in what he says can be a proof that he has every passion and appetite under control, I cannot see. Indeed, I have seen so many examples of a contrary kind that I can have no doubt of the impropriety of this exposition.

3. *Behold, we put bits in the horses' mouths.* In order to show the necessity of regulating the tongue, to which James was led by his exhortation to them who wished to thrust themselves into the teacher's office, supposing, be-

cause they had the gift of a ready flow of speech, that therefore they might commence teachers of divine things, he proceeds to show that the tongue must be bridled as the horse and governed as the ships; because, though it is small, it is capable of ruling the whole man, and of irritating and offending others.

5. *Boasteth great things.* That is, can do great things, whether of a good or evil kind. He seems to refer here to the powerful and all-commanding eloquence of the Greek orators. They could carry the great mob whithersoever they wished; calm them to peaceableness and submission, or excite them to furious sedition. *Behold, how great a matter!* See what a flame of discord and insubordination one man, merely by his persuasive tongue, may kindle among the common people.

6. *The tongue is a fire.* It is often the instrument of producing the most desperate contentions and insurrections. *A world of iniquity.* This is an unusual form of speech, but the meaning is plain enough; *world* signifies here a mass, a great collection, an abundance. We use the term in the same sense—a "world of troubles," a "world of toil." *Setteth on fire the course of nature.* "And setteth on fire the wheel of life." I question much whether this verse be in general well understood. There are three different interpretations of it: (1) James does not intend to express the whole circle of human affairs, so much affected by the tongue of man; but rather the penal wheel of the Greeks, and not unknown to the Jews, on which they were accustomed to extend criminals to induce them to confess or to punish them for crimes; under which wheels, fire was often placed to add to their torments. (2) But is it not possible that by the "wheel of life" James may have the circulation of the blood in view? Angry or irritating language has an astonishing influence on the circulation of the blood: the heart beats high and frequently; the blood is hurried through the arteries to the veins, through the veins to the heart, and through the heart to the arteries again, and so on; an extraordinary degree of heat is at the same time engendered; the eyes become more prominent in their sockets; the capillary vessels suffused with blood; the face flushed; and, in short, the whole wheel of nature is set on fire of hell. (3) It is true, however, that the rabbins use the term "the wheel of generations" to mark the successive generations of men, and it is possible that James might refer to this; as if he had said: "The tongue has been the instrument of confusion and misery through all the ages of the world." But the other interpretations are more likely.

7. *Every kind of beasts.* That is, every "species" of wild beasts *is tamed,* i.e., brought under man's power and dominion.

8. *But the tongue can no man tame.* No cunning, persuasion, or influence has ever been able to silence it. *It is an unruly evil.* "An evil that cannot be restrained"; it cannot be brought under any kind of government; it breaks all bounds. *Full of deadly poison.* He refers here to the tongues of serpents, supposed to be the means of conveying their poison into wounds made by their teeth. Throughout the whole of this poetic and highly declamatory description James must have the tongue of the slanderer, calumniator, backbiter, whisperer, and talebear-

er particularly in view. Vipers and rattlesnakes are not more dangerous to life than these are to the peace and reputation of men.

9. *Therewith bless we God.* The tongue is capable of rehearsing the praises and setting forth the glories of the eternal King; what a pity that it should ever be employed in a contrary work! It can proclaim and vindicate the truth of God, and publish the gospel of peace and goodwill among men; what a pity that it should ever be employed in falsehoods, calumny, or in the cause of infidelity! *And therewith curse we men.* In the true Satanic spirit, many pray to God the Father to destroy those who are objects of their displeasure! These are the common swearers, whose mouths are generally full of direful imprecations against those with whom they are offended.

10. *Out of the same mouth.* This saying is something like that of Prov. xviii. 21: "Death and life are in the power of the tongue."

11. *Doth a fountain send forth . . . sweet water and bitter?* In many things nature is a sure guide to man; but no such inconsistency is found in the natural world as this blessing and cursing in man. No fountain, at the same opening, sends forth sweet water and bitter; no fig tree can bear olive berries; no vine can bear figs; nor can the sea produce salt water and fresh from the same place. These are all contradictions, and indeed impossibilities, in nature. And it is depraved man alone that can act the monstrous part already referred to.

12. *So can no fountain both yield salt water and fresh.* For the reading of the common text, which is, "So no fountain can produce salt water and sweet," there are various other readings in the MSS. and versions. The true reading appears to be, "Neither can salt water produce sweet," or, "Neither can the sea produce fresh water"; and this is a new comparison, and not an inference from that in v. 11. There are therefore four distinct comparisons here: (1) A fountain cannot produce sweet water and bitter. (2) A fig tree cannot produce olive berries. (3) A vine cannot produce figs. (4) Salt water cannot be made sweet. That is, according to the ordinary operations of nature, these things are impossible.

13. *Who is a wise man?* One truly religious; who, although he can neither bridle nor tame other men's tongues, can restrain his own. *And endued with knowledge.* And qualified to teach others. *Let him shew.* Let him by a holy life and chaste conversation show, through meekness and gentleness, joined to his divine information, that he is a Christian indeed; his works and his spirit proving that God is in him of a truth; and that, from the fullness of a holy heart, his feet walk, his hands work, and his tongue speaks. We may learn from this that genuine wisdom is ever accompanied with meekness and gentleness. Those proud, overbearing, and disdainful men who pass for great scholars and eminent critics may have learning, but they have not wisdom.

14. *If ye have bitter envying and strive.* If you are under the influence of an unkind, fierce, and contemptuous spirit, even while attempting or pretending to defend true religion, "do not boast" of either your exertions or success in silencing an adversary. You have no religion, and no true wisdom; and to profess either is to *lie . . . against the truth.*

15. *This wisdom descendeth not from above.* God is not the author of it, because it is bitter—not meek. *Is earthly.* Having this life only in view. *Sensual.* "Animal"—having for its object the gratification of the passions and animal propensities. *Devilish.* "Demoniacal"—inspired by demons.

16. *For where envying and strife is.* "Zeal," fiery, inflammatory passion, and "contention," altercations about the different points of the law, of no use for edification; such as those mentioned in Titus iii. 9.

17. *The wisdom that is from above.* The pure religion of the Lord Jesus, bought by His blood and infused by His Spirit. See the rabbinical meaning of this phrase at the end of this chapter. *Is first pure.* "Chaste, holy, and clean." *Peaceable.* Living in peace with others, and promoting peace among men. *Gentle.* "Meek, modest, of an equal mind," taking everything in good part, and putting the best construction upon all the actions of others. *Easy to be intreated.* Not stubborn nor obstinate; of a yielding disposition in all indifferent things. *Full of mercy.* Ready to pass by a transgression, and to grant forgiveness to those who offend, and performing every possible act of kindness. *Good fruits.* Each temper and disposition producing fruits suited to and descriptive of its nature. *Without partiality.* "Without making a difference"—rendering to every man his due; and being never swayed by self-interest, worldly honor, or the fear of man. *Without hypocrisy.* Without pretending to be what it is not; acting always in its own character; never working under a mask.

18. *And the fruit of righteousness is sown.* The whole is the principle of righteousness in the soul, and all the above virtues are the fruits of that righteousness. *Is sown in peace.* When the peace of God rules the heart, all these virtues and graces grow and flourish abundantly. *Of them that make peace.* The peacemakers are continually recommending this wisdom to others, and their own conduct is represented as a sowing of heavenly seed, which brings forth divine fruit. Some render this verse, which is confessedly obscure, thus: "And the peaceable fruits of righteousness are sown for the practicers of peace. He who labors to live peaceably shall have peace for his reward."

Almost the whole of the preceding chapter is founded on maxims highly accredited in the rabbinical writings, and without a reference to those writings it would have been impossible, in some cases, to have understood James's meaning. There is one phrase, the rabbinical meaning and use of which I have reserved for this place, viz. "The wisdom that is from above." This they seem to understand to be a peculiar inspiration of the Almighty, or a teaching communicated immediately by the angels of God. In *Sohar Yalcut Rubeni,* fol. 19, Rabbi Chiya said: "The wisdom from above was in Adam more than in the supreme angels, and he knew all things." In *Sohar Chadash,* fol. 35, it is said concerning Enoch, "That the angels were sent from heaven, and taught him the *wisdom that is from above.*" It is another word for the life of God in the soul of man, or true religion; it is the teaching of God in the human heart.

CHAPTER 4

The origin of wars and contentions, and the wretched lot of those who are engaged in them, 1-2. Why so little heavenly good is obtained, 3. The friendship of the world is enmity with God, 4-5. God resists the proud, 6. Men should submit to God, and pray, 7-8. Should humble themselves, 9-10. And not speak evil of each other, 11-12. The impiety of those who consult not the will of God, and depend not on His providence, 13-15. The sin of him who knows the will of God and does not do it, 16-17.

1. *From whence come wars and fightings?* About the time in which James wrote we find, according to the accounts given by Josephus, that the Jews, under pretense of defending their religion, and procuring that liberty to which they believed themselves entitled, made various insurrections in Judea against the Romans, which occasioned much bloodshed and misery to their nation. The factions also into which the Jews were split had violent contentions among themselves, in which they massacred and plundered each other. In the provinces, likewise, the Jews became very turbulent; particularly in Alexandria and different other parts of Egypt, of Syria, and other places, where they made war against the heathens, killing many, and being massacred in their turn. These are probably the *wars* and *fightings* to which James alludes. *Come they not hence, even of your lusts?* This was the principle from which these Jewish contentions and predatory wars proceeded, and the principle from which all the wars that have afflicted and desolated the world have proceeded.

2. *Ye lust, and have not.* You are ever covetous, and ever poor. *Ye kill, and desire to have.* You are constantly engaged in insurrections and predatory wars, and never gain any advantage. *Ye have not, because ye ask not.* You get no especial blessing from God, as your fathers did, because you do not pray. Worldly good is your god; you leave no stone unturned in order to get it; and as you ask nothing from God but to consume it upon your evil desires and propensities, your prayers are not heard.

3. *Ye ask, and receive not.* Some think that this refers to their prayers for the conversion of the heathen; and on the pretense that they were not converted thus, they thought it lawful to extirpate them and possess their goods. *Ye ask amiss.* "Ye ask evilly, wickedly." You have not the proper dispositions of prayer, and you have an improper object. You ask for worldly prosperity, that you may employ it in riotous living. This is properly the meaning of the original, "That ye may expend it upon your pleasures." The rabbins have many good observations on asking amiss or asking improperly, and give examples of different kinds of this sort of prayer; the phrase is Jewish, and would naturally occur to James in writing on this subject.

4. *Ye adulterers and adulteresses.* The Jews, because of their covenant with God, are represented as being espoused to Him; and hence their idolatry and their iniquity in general are represented under the notion of adultery. And although they had not since the Babylonish captivity been guilty of idolatry, according to the letter, yet what is intended by idolatry—having their hearts estranged from God, and seeking their portion in this life and out of God—is that of which the Jews were then notoriously guilty. *Whosoever therefore will be a friend of the world.* How strange it is that people professing Christianity can suppose that with a worldly spirit, worldly companions, and their lives governed by worldly maxims, they can be in the favor of God, or ever get to the kingdom of Heaven! When the world gets into the Church, the Church becomes a painted sepulchre, its spiritual vitality being extinct.

5. *Do ye think that the scripture saith in vain?* This verse is exceedingly obscure. We cannot tell what scripture James refers to; many have been produced by learned men as that which he had particularly in view. Some think Gen. vi. 5: "Every imagination of the thoughts of his heart was only evil continually." Gen. viii. 21: "The imagination of man's heart is evil from his youth." Num. xi. 29: "Moses said unto him, Enviest thou for my sake?" and Prov. xxi. 10: "The soul of the wicked desireth evil." None of these scriptures, nor any others, contain the precise words in this verse; and therefore James may probably refer, not to any particular portion, but to the spirit and design of the Scripture in those various places where it speaks against envying, covetousness, worldly associations. Perhaps the word in this and the two succeeding verses may be well paraphrased thus: "Do you think that concerning these things the Scripture speaks falsely, or that the Holy Spirit, who dwells in us, can excite us to envy others instead of being contented with the state in which the providence of God has placed us? Nay, far otherwise; for He gives us more grace to enable us to bear the ills of life, and to lie in deep humility at His feet, knowing that His Holy Spirit has said, Prov. iii. 34: 'God resisteth the proud, but giveth grace to the humble.' Seeing these things are so, submit yourselves to God; resist the devil, who would tempt you to envy, and he will flee from you; draw nigh to God, and He will draw nigh to you." I must leave this sense as the best I can give, without asserting that I have hit the true meaning. There is not a critic in Europe who has considered the passage that has not been puzzled with it. I think the fifth verse should be understood as giving a contrary sense to that in our translation. Every genuine Christian is a habitation of the Holy Ghost, and that Spirit "excites strong desires against envy"; a man must not suppose that he is a Christian if he have an envious or covetous heart.

6. *But he giveth more grace.* "A greater benefit" than all the goods that the world can bestow; for He gives genuine happiness, and this the world cannot confer. May this be James's meaning? *God resisteth the proud.* "Sets himself in battle array" against him. *Giveth grace unto the humble.* The sure way to please God is to submit to the dispensations of His grace and providence; and when a man acknowledges Him in all his ways, He will direct all his steps. The covetous man grasps at the shadow and loses the substance.

7. *Submit . . . to God.* Continue to bow to all His decisions and to all His dispensations. *Resist the devil.* He cannot conquer you if you continue to resist. Strong as he is, God never permits him to conquer the man who continues to resist; he cannot force the human will.

8. *Draw nigh to God.* Approach Him, in the name of Jesus, by faith and prayer, and *he will draw nigh to you*—He will meet you at your coming. When a soul sets out to seek God, God sets out to meet that soul; so that while we are

drawing near to Him, He is drawing near to us. *Cleanse your hands, ye sinners.* This I think to be the beginning of a new address, and to different persons, and should have formed the commencement of a new verse. Let your whole conduct be changed. "Cease to do evil; learn to do well." Washing or cleansing the hands was a token of innocence and purity. *Purify your hearts.* Separate yourselves from the world, and consecrate yourselves to God; this is the true notion of sanctification. We have often seen that to sanctify signifies to separate a thing or person from profane or common use, and consecrate it or him to God. The person or thing thus consecrated or separated is considered to be "holy" and to be God's property. There are therefore two things implied in a man's sanctification: (1) That he separates himself from evil ways and evil companions, and devotes himself to God; (2) That God separates guilt from his conscience and sin from his soul, and thus makes him internally and externally "holy." This double sanctification is well expressed in *Sohar,* Levit., fol. 33, col. 132, on the words, "Be ye holy, for I the Lord am holy": "A man sanctifies himself on the earth, and then he is sanctified from heaven." As a man is a sinner, he must have his hands cleansed from wicked works; as he is *double minded,* he must have his heart sanctified.

9. *Be afflicted, and mourn.* Without true and deep repentance you cannot expect the mercy of God. *Let your laughter be turned to mourning.* It appears most evidently that many of those to whom James addressed this Epistle had lived very irregular and dissolute lives. He had already spoken of their lust and pleasures, and he had called them adulterers and adulteresses; and perhaps they were so in the grossest sense of the words. He speaks here of their *laughter* and their *joy;* and all the terms taken together show that a dissolute life is intended.

10. *Humble yourselves in the sight of the Lord.* In v. 7 they were exhorted to submit to God; here they are exhorted to humble themselves in His sight. Submission to God's authority will precede humiliation of soul, and genuine repentance is performed as in the sight of God; for when a sinner is truly awakened to a sense of his guilt and danger, he seems to see, whithersoever he turns, the face of a justly incensed God turned against him. *He shall lift you up.* Mourners and penitents lay on the ground and rolled themselves in the dust. When comforted and pardoned, they arose from the earth, shook themselves from the dust, and clothed themselves in their better garments. God promises to raise these from the dust, when sufficiently humbled.

11. *Speak not evil one of another.* Perhaps this exhortation refers to evil speaking, slander, and backbiting in general, the writer having no particular persons in view. It may, however, refer to the contentions among the different factions then prevailing among this wretched people, or to their calumnies against those of their brethren who had embraced the Christian faith. *He that speaketh evil of his brother.* It was an avowed and very general maxim among the rabbins that "no one could speak evil of his brother without denying God, and becoming an atheist." *Speaketh evil of the law.* The law

condemns all evil speaking and detraction. He who is guilty of these, and allows himself in these vices, in effect judges and condemns the law; i.e., he considers it unworthy to be kept, and that it is no sin to break it. *Thou art not a doer of the law, but a judge.* You reject the law of God, and set up your own mischievous conduct as a rule of life; or, by allowing this evil speaking and detraction, intimate that the law that condemns them is improper, imperfect, or unjust.

12. *There is one lawgiver.* "And judge" is added here by about thirty MSS. On this evidence Griesbach has received it into the text. The man who breaks the law, and teaches others so to do, thus in effect sets himself up as a *lawgiver* and judge. But there is only one such "lawgiver and judge"—God Almighty, who is *able to save* all those who obey Him, and *able . . . to destroy* all those who trample underfoot His testimonies. *Who art thou that judgest another?* Who are you who dare to usurp the office and prerogative of the supreme Judge? But what is that law of which James speaks? and who is this *lawgiver* and "judge"? Most critics think that the law mentioned here is the same as that which he elsewhere calls "the royal law" and "the law of liberty," thereby meaning the gospel; and that Christ is the Person who is called the Lawgiver and Judge. This, however, is not clear to me. I believe James means the Jewish law; and by the *lawgiver* and "judge," God Almighty, as acknowledged by the Jewish people. I find, or think I find, from the closest examination of this Epistle, but few references to Jesus Christ or His gospel. His Jewish creed, forms, and maxims, this writer keeps constantly in view; and it is proper he should, considering the persons to whom he wrote. Some of them were doubtless Christians; some of them, certainly no Christians; and some of them, half Christians and half Jews. The two latter descriptions are those most frequently addressed.

13. *Go to now.* "Come now," the same in meaning as the Hebrew "come," Gen. xi. 3-4, 7. "Come, and hear what I have to say, *ye that say,*" To day or to morrow we will go. This presumption on a precarious life is here well reproved. *And continue there a year, and buy and sell.* This was the custom of those ancient times; they traded from city to city, carrying their goods on the backs of camels.

14. *Whereas ye know not.* This verse should be read in a parenthesis. It is not only impious, but grossly absurd, to speak thus concerning futurity when you know not what a day may bring forth. *It is even a vapour.* "It is a smoke," always fleeting, uncertain, evanescent. This is a frequent metaphor with the Hebrews. See Ps. cii. 11; "My days are like a shadow"; Job viii. 9; "Our days upon earth are a shadow"; 1 Chron. xxix. 15; "Our days on the earth are as a shadow, and there is none abiding."

16. *But now ye rejoice in your boastings.* You glory in your proud and self-sufficient conduct, exulting that you are free from the trammels of superstition, and that you can live independently of God Almighty. "All such boasting is wicked."

17. *To him that knoweth to do good.* As if he had said: After this warning none of you can plead ignorance; if therefore any of you shall be found to act their ungodly part, not ac-

knowledging the divine providence, the uncertainty of life, and the necessity of standing every moment prepared to meet God—as you will have the greater sin, you will infallibly get the greater punishment. This may be applied to all who know better than they act. He who does not the Master's will because he does not know it will be beaten with few stripes; but he who knows it and does not do it shall be beaten with many; Luke xii. 47-48. James may have the Christians in view who were converted from Judaism to Christianity. They had much more light and religious knowledge than the Jews had, and God would require a proportionable improvement from them.

CHAPTER 5

The profligate rich are in danger of God's judgments because of their pride, fraudulent dealings, riotous living, and cruelty, 1-6. The oppressed followers of God should be patient, for the Lord's coming is nigh; and should not grudge against each other, 7-9. They should take encouragement from the example of the prophets and of Job, 10-11. Swearing forbidden, 12. Directions to the afflicted, 13-15. They should confess their faults to each other, 16. The great prevalence of prayer instanced in Elijah, 17-18. The blessedness of converting a sinner from the error of his way, 19-20.

1. *Go to now.* See on chap. iv. 13. *Weep and howl for your miseries.* James seems to refer here, in the spirit of prophecy, to the destruction that was coming upon the Jews, not only in Judea, but in all the provinces where they sojourned.

2. *Your riches are corrupted.* Are "putrefied." The term *riches* is to be taken here, not for gold, silver, or precious stones (for these could not putrefy), but for the produce of the fields and flocks, the different stores of grain, wine, and oil, which they had laid up in their granaries, and the various changes of raiment which they had amassed in their wardrobes.

3. *Your gold and silver is cankered.* Instead of helping the poor, and thus honoring God with your substance, you have, through the principle of covetousness, kept all to yourselves. *The rust of them shall be a witness against you.* Your putrefied stores, your moth-eaten garments, and your tarnished coin are so many proofs that it was not for want of property that you assisted not the poor, but through a principle of avarice; loving money, not for the sake of what it could procure, but for its own sake, which is the genuine principle of the miser. This was the very character given to this people by our Lord himself; He called them "lovers of money." *Shall eat your flesh as it were fire.* This is a very bold and sublime figure. He represents the rust of their coin as becoming a canker that should produce gangrenes in their flesh, till it should be eaten away from their bones. By the *last days* we are not to understand the day of judgment, but the last days of the Jewish commonwealth, which were not long distant from the date of this Epistle.

4. *The hire of the labourers.* The law, Lev. xix. 13, had ordered: "The wages of him that is hired shall not abide with thee all night until the morning," every day's labor being paid for as soon as ended. This is more clearly stated in another law, Deut. xxiv. 15: "At his day thou shalt give him his hire, neither shall the sun go down upon it . . . lest he cry against thee unto the Lord, and it be sin unto thee." And

that God particularly resented this defrauding of the hireling we see from Mal. iii. 5: "I will come near to you in judgment; and I will be a swift witness against . . . those who oppress the hireling in his wages." And on these laws and threatenings is built what we read in *Synopsis Sohar*, p. 100, n. 45: "When a poor man does any work in a house, the vapour proceeding from him, through the severity of his work, ascends toward heaven. Woe to his employer if he delay to pay him his wages." To this James seems particularly to allude when he says: *"The cries of them which have reaped are entered into the ears of the Lord of hosts."* *The Lord of sabaoth.* James often conceives in Hebrew though he writes in Greek. It is well-known that *Yehovah tsebaoth,* "Lord of hosts," or "Lord of armies," is a frequent appellation of God in the Old Testament; and signifies His uncontrollable power and the infinitely numerous means He has for governing the world, and defending His followers, and punishing the wicked.

5. *Ye have lived in pleasure.* "You have lived luxuriously"; feeding yourselves without fear, pampering the flesh. *And been wanton.* "You have lived lasciviously." You have indulged all your sinful and sensual appetites to the uttermost. *Ye have nourished your hearts.* "You have fattened your hearts," and have rendered them incapable of feeling, *as in a day of slaughter,* "a day of sacrifice," where many victims are offered at once and where the people feast upon the sacrifices: many no doubt turning, on that occasion, a holy ordinance into a riotous festival.

6. *Ye have condemned and killed the just; and he doth not resist you.* Several by "the just one" understand Jesus Christ, who is so called, Acts iii. 14; vii. 52; xxii. 14. But the structure of the sentence and the connection in which it stands seem to require that we should consider this as applying to the just or righteous in general, who were persecuted and murdered by those oppressive rich men; and their death was the consequence of their dragging them before the judgment seats, chap. ii. 6, where, having no influence, and none to plead their cause, they were unjustly condemned and executed. *And he doth not resist you.* In the word *he doth not resist* the idea is included of defense in a court of justice. These poor righteous people had none to plead their cause; and if they had it would have been useless, as their oppressors had all power and all influence, and those who sat on these judgment seats were lost to all sense of justice and right. Some think that *he doth not resist you* should be referred to God; as if he had said, God permits you to go on in this way at present, but He will shortly awake to judgment, and destroy you as enemies of truth and righteousness.

7. *Be patient therefore.* Because God is coming to execute judgment on this wicked people, therefore be patient till He comes. He seems here to refer to the coming of the Lord to execute judgment on the Jewish nation, which shortly afterwards took place. *The husbandman waiteth.* The seed of your deliverance is already sown, and by and by the harvest of your salvation will take place. God's counsels will ripen in due time. *The early and latter rain.* The rain

of seedtime and the rain of ripening before harvest. The first fell in Judea about the beginning of November, after the seed was sown; and the second, toward the end of April, when the ears were filling, and this prepared for a full harvest. Without these two rains the earth would have been unfruitful. These God had promised: "I will give you the rain of your land in his due season, the first rain and the latter rain, that thou mayest gather in thy corn, and thy wine, and thine oil," Deut. xi. 14.

8. *Be ye also patient.* Wait for God's deliverance, as you wait for His bounty in providence. *Stablish your hearts.* Take courage; do not sink under your trials. *The coming of the Lord draweth nigh.* "Is at hand." He is already on His way to destroy this wicked people, to raze their city and Temple, and to destroy their polity forever; and this judgment will soon take place.

9. *Grudge not.* "Groan not"; grumble not; do not murmur through impatience; and let not any ill treatment which you receive induce you to vent your feelings in imprecations against your oppressors. Leave all this in the hands of God. *Lest ye be condemned.* By giving way to a spirit of this kind you will get under the condemnation of the wicked. *The judge standeth before the door.* His eye is upon everything that is wrong in you and every wrong that is done to you, and He is now entering into judgment with your oppressors.

10. *Take . . . the prophets.* The prophets who had spoken to their forefathers by the authority of God were persecuted by the very people to whom they delivered the divine message; but they suffered affliction and persecution with patience, commending their cause to Him who judgeth righteously; therefore, imitate their example.

11. *We count them happy which endure.* According to that saying of our blessed Lord, "Blessed are ye, when men shall revile you, and persecute you . . . for so persecuted they the prophets which were before you," Matt. v. 11, etc. *Ye have heard of the patience of Job.* Stripped of all his worldly possessions, deprived at a stroke of all his children, tortured in body with sore disease, tempted by the devil, harassed by his wife, and calumniated by his friends, he nevertheless held fast his integrity, resigned himself to the divine dispensations, and charged not God foolishly. *And have seen the end of the Lord.* The issue to which God brought all his afflictions and trials, giving him children, increasing his property, lengthening out his life, and multiplying to him every kind of spiritual and secular good. This was God's end with respect to him; but the devil's end was to drive him to despair, and to cause him to blaspheme his Maker. This mention of Job shows him to have been a real person, for a fictitious person would not have been produced as an example of any virtue so highly important as that of patience and perseverance. *The end of the Lord* is a Hebraism for the "issue" to which God brings any thing or business. *The Lord is very pitiful, and of tender mercy. Very pitiful* might be rendered "of much sympathy."

12. *Above all things . . . swear not.* What relation this exhortation can have to the subject in question, I confess I cannot see. It may not have been designed to stand in any connection, but to be a separate piece of advice, as in the several cases which immediately follow. That the Jews were notoriously guilty of common swearing is allowed on all hands; and that swearing by heaven, earth, Jerusalem, the Temple, the altar, different parts of the body, was not considered by them as binding oaths has been sufficiently proved. Rabbi Akiba taught that "a man might swear with his lips, and annul it in his heart; and then the oath was not binding." See the notes on Matt. v. 33. *Let your yea be yea.* Do not pretend to say *yea* with your lips, and annul it in your heart; let the *yea* or the *nay* which you express be bona fide such. Do not imagine that any mental reservation can cancel any such expressions of obligation in the sight of God. *Lest ye fall into condemnation.* "Lest you fall under judgment."

13. *Is any among you afflicted? let him pray.* The Jews taught that the meaning of the ordinance, Lev. xiii. 45, which required the leper to cry, "Unclean! unclean!" was "that thus making known his calamity, the people might be led to offer up prayers to God in his behalf." They taught also that when any sickness or affliction entered a family they should go to the wise men and implore their prayers.

14. *Is any sick among you? let him call for the elders.* This was also a Jewish maxim. Rabbi Simeon, in *Sepher Hachaiyim,* said: "What should a man do who goes to visit the sick? *Ans.* He who studies to restore the health of the body should first lay the foundation in the health of the soul. The wise men have said, No healing is equal to that which comes from the word of God and prayer. Rabbi Phineas, the son of Chamma, hath said, 'When sickness or disease enters into a man's family, let him apply to a wise man, who will implore mercy in his behalf.'"

15. *And the prayer of faith shall save the sick.* That is, God will often make these the means of a sick man's recovery; but there often are cases where faith and prayer are both ineffectual, because God sees it will be prejudicial to the patient's salvation to be restored; and therefore all faith and prayer on such occasions should be exerted on this ground: "If it be most for Thy glory, and the eternal good of this man's soul, let him be restored; if otherwise, Lord, pardon, purify him, and take him to Thy glory." *And if he have committed sins.* So as to have occasioned his present malady, *they shall be forgiven him;* for being the cause of the affliction, it is natural to conclude that, if the effect be to cease, the cause must be removed. We find that in the miraculous restoration to health under the powerful hand of Christ, the sin of the party is generally said to be forgiven, and this also before the miracle was wrought on the body. Hence there was a maxim among the Jews, and it seems to be founded in common sense and reason, that God never restores a man miraculously to health till He has pardoned his sins; because it would be incongruous for God to exert His miraculous power in saving a body the soul of which was in a state of condemnation to eternal death because of the crimes it had committed against its Maker and Judge.

16. *Confess your faults one to another.* This is a good general direction to Christians who endeavor to maintain among themselves the communion of saints. This social confession

tends much to humble the soul and to make it watchful. *The effectual fervent prayer.* The words signify "energetic supplication," or such a prayer as is suggested to the soul and wrought in it by a divine energy. When God designs to do some particular work in His Church, He pours out on His followers the spirit of grace and supplication; and this He does sometimes when He is about to do some especial work for an individual. When such a power of prayer is granted, faith should be immediately called into exercise, that the blessing may be given; the spirit of prayer is the proof that the power of God is present to heal. Long prayers give no particular evidence of divine inspiration. The following was a maxim among the ancient Jews, "The prayers of the righteous are short." This is exemplified in almost every instance in the Old Testament.

17. *Elias was a man subject to like passions.* This was Elijah, and a consistency between the names of the same persons as expressed in the Old and the New Testaments should be kept up. The word *homoiopathes* signifies of "the same constitution," a human being just as ourselves are. *And he prayed earnestly.* "He prayed with prayer"; a Hebraism for "He prayed fervently." *That it might not rain.* See this history, 1 Kings xvii. 1 ff. *And it rained not on the earth.* "On that land," viz., the land of Judea; for this drought did not extend elsewhere. *Three years and six months.* This is the term mentioned by our Lord, Luke iv. 25; but this is not specified in the original history. In 1 Kings xviii. 1 it is said, "In the third year" "the word of the Lord came to Elijah," that is, concerning the rain; but this third year is to be computed from the time of his going to live at Zarephath, which happened many days after the drought began, as is plain from this, that he remained at the brook Cherith till it was dried up, and then went to Zarephath, in the country of Zidon; 1 Kings xvii. 7-9. Therefore the *three years and six months* must be computed from his announcing the drought, at which time that judgment commenced.

18. *And he prayed again.* This second prayer is not mentioned in the history in express words. But as in 1 Kings xviii. 42, it is said, "He cast himself down upon the earth, and put his face between his knees," that was probably the time of the second praying, namely, that rain might come, as this was the proper posture of prayer.

19. *Err from the truth*—stray away from the gospel of Christ; *and one convert him*—reclaim him from his error and bring him back to the fold of Christ.

20. *Let him know.* Let him duly consider, for his encouragement, that he who is the instrument of converting a sinner shall save a soul from eternal death, and a body from ruin, *and shall hide a multitude of sins;* for in being the means of his conversion we bring him back to God, who, in His infinite mercy, hides or blots out the numerous sins which he had committed during the time of his backsliding. It is not the man's sins who is the means of his conversion, but the sins of the backslider, which are here said to be hidden.

The First Epistle of
PETER

CHAPTER 1

Of the persons to whom this Epistle was directed, and their spiritual state, 1-2. He describes their privileges, and thanks God for the grace by which they were preserved faithful in trials and difficulties, 3-5. The spiritual benefit they were to receive out of their afflictions, 6-7. Their love to Christ, 8. And the salvation they received through believing, 9. This salvation was predicted by the prophets, who only saw it afar off, and had only a foretaste of it, 10-12. They should take encouragement, and be obedient and holy, 13-16. They should pray, and deeply consider the price at which they were purchased, that their faith and hope might be in God, 17-21. As their souls had been purified by obeying the truth through the Spirit, they should love each other with a pure and fervent love, 22-23. The frailty of man and the unchangeableness of God, 24-25.

1. *Peter, an apostle.* Simon Peter, called also Cephas. He was a fisherman, son of Jonah, brother of Andrew, and born at Bethsaida; and one of the first disciples of our Lord. *The strangers scattered throughout.* Jews first, who had believed the gospel in the different countries here specified; and converted Gentiles also. Though the word *strangers* may refer to all truly religious people, yet the inscription may have a special reference to those who were driven by persecution to seek refuge in those heathen provinces to which the influence of their persecuting brethren did not extend. *Pontus.* An ancient kingdom of Asia Minor, originally a part of Cappadocia. *Galatia.* The ancient name of a province of Asia Minor. *Cappadocia.* An ancient kingdom of Asia, comprehending all the country lying between Mount Taurus and the Euxine Sea. *Asia.* That province of Asia Minor of which Ephesus was the capital. It appears that it is in this sense that it is used here by Peter, because Pontus, Galatia, and Bithynia, are comprised in the provinces of Asia Minor. *Bithynia.* An ancient kingdom of Asia, formerly called Mysia.

2. *Elect according to the foreknowledge of God.* If the apostle had directed his letter to persons elected to eternal life, no one, as Drs. Lardner and Macknight properly argue, could have received such a letter, because no one could have been sure of his election in this way till he had arrived in heaven. But the persons to whom the apostle wrote were all, with propriety, said to be *elect according to the foreknowledge of God;* because, agreeably to

the original purpose of God, discovered in the prophetical writings, Jews and Gentiles, indiscriminately, were called to be the visible Church, and entitled to all the privileges of the people of God, on their believing the gospel. *Through sanctification of the Spirit*—through the renewing and purifying influences of His Spirit on their souls, *unto obedience*—to engage and enable them to yield themselves up to all holy obedience, the foundation of all which is the *sprinkling of the blood of Jesus Christ*—the atoning blood of Jesus Christ which was typified by the sprinkling of the blood of sacrifices under the law, in allusion to which it is called the "blood of sprinkling."

3. *Blessed be the God and Father.* "Blessed be God even the Father" or "Blessed be God, the Father of our Lord Jesus Christ." *Begotten us again unto a lively hope.* I think the apostle has a reference here to his own case, and that of his fellow apostles, at the time that Christ was taken by the Jews and put to death. Previously to this time they had strong confidence that He was the Messiah, and that it was He who should redeem Israel; but when they found that He actually expired upon the Cross, and was buried, they appear to have lost all hope of the great things which before they had in prospect. This is feelingly expressed by the two disciples whom our Lord, after His resurrection, overtook on the road going to Emmaus; see Luke xxiv. 13-24. And the hope that with them died with their Master, and seemed to be buried in His grave, was restored by the certainty of His resurrection. The expressions, however, may include more particulars than what are above specified; as none can inherit eternal life except those who are children in the heavenly family, and none are children but those who are born again, then Peter may be considered as laying here the foundation of the hope of eternal life in the regeneration of the soul.

4. *To an inheritance.* Called an *inheritance* because it belongs to the children of God. *Incorruptible.* It has no principles of dissolution or decay in it. *Undefiled.* Nothing impure can enter it. *Fadeth not away.* "It cannot wither"; it is always in bloom—a metaphor taken from those flowers that never lose their hue nor their fragrance. *Reserved in heaven.* Such a place as that described above is not to be expected on earth.

5. *Who are kept.* Who are "defended as in a fortress or castle." There is a remarkable correspondence between the two verbs used in this sentence. The verb *tereo* signifies to "keep, watch, guard"; and *phroureo* signifies to "keep as under a military guard." The true disciples of Christ are under the continual watchful care of God, and the inheritance is "guarded" for them. *By the power of God.* By the mighty and miracle-working power of God. But this *power of God* is interested in the behalf of the soul by *faith.* To believe is our work; the exertion of the almighty power is of God. *Ready to be revealed.* Or rather, "prepared to be revealed." The inheritance is prepared for you; but its glories will not be revealed till the *last time*— till you have done with life and passed through your probation, having held fast faith and a good conscience. Some by *salvation* understand the deliverance of the Christians from the sackage of Jerusalem, the end of the Jewish polity

being called the *last time;* others suppose it to refer to the day of judgment, and the glorification of the body and soul in heaven.

6. *Wherein ye greatly rejoice.* Some refer *wherein* to the "salvation" mentioned above; others, to the "last time" in v. 5; others think that it applies to the being kept by the power of God through faith; and others, that it refers to all the preceding advantages and privileges. It was in the present salvation of God that they rejoiced or gloried, though not without having an eye to the great recompense of reward. *Though now for a season.* "A little while yet"— during your pilgrimage here below, which is but a point when compared with eternity. *If need be.* "If it be necessary"—if your situation and circumstances be such that you are exposed to trials and persecutions which you cannot avoid, unless God were to work a miracle for your deliverance, which would not be for your ultimate good, as He purposes to turn all your trials and difficulties to your advantage. Those to whom Peter wrote rejoiced greatly, "danced for joy," while they were "grieved" with "various trials."

7. *That the trial of your faith, being much more precious than of gold.* As by the action of fire gold is separated from all alloy and heterogeneous mixtures, and is proved to be gold by its enduring the action of the fire without losing anything of its nature, weight, color, or any other property, so genuine faith is proved by adversities, especially such as the primitive Christians were obliged to pass through.

8. *Whom having not seen, ye love.* Those to whom the apostle wrote had never seen Christ in the flesh; and yet, such is the realizing nature of faith, they loved Him as strongly as any of His disciples could to whom He was personally known. *Ye rejoice with joy unspeakable.* You have unutterable happiness through believing; and you have the fullest, clearest, strongest evidence of eternal glory.

9. *Receiving the end of your faith.* You are put in possession of the salvation of your souls, which was the thing presented to your faith when you were called by the gospel of Christ. The word *end* is often used so as to imply the "issue" or "reward" of any labor or action. *Salvation of your souls.* The object of the Jewish expectations in their Messiah was the salvation or deliverance of their bodies from a foreign yoke; but the true Messiah came to save the soul from the yoke of the devil and sin. This glorious salvation these believers had already received.

10. *Of which salvation the prophets have enquired.* The incarnation and suffering of Jesus Christ and the redemption procured by Him for mankind were made known, in a general way, by the prophets; but they themselves did not know the time when these things were to take place, nor the people among and by whom He was to suffer. They therefore "inquired accurately or earnestly," and *searched diligently.*

11. *The glory that should follow.* Not only the glory of His resurrection, ascension, exaltation, and the effusion of His Spirit; but that grand manifestation of God's infinite love to the world in causing the gospel of His Son to be everywhere preached, and the glorious moral

changes which should take place in the world under that preaching, and the final glorification of all them who had here received the report and continued faithful unto death.

12. *Unto whom it was revealed.* We may presume that in a great variety of cases the prophets did not understand the meaning of their own predictions. They had a general view of God's designs; but of particular circumstances connected with those great events they seem to have known nothing, God reserving the explanation of all particulars to the time of the issue of such prophecies. If all succeeding interpreters of the prophecies had been contented with the same information relative to the predictions still unaccomplished, we should have had fewer books and more wisdom. *Angels desire to look into.* "To stoop down to"; the posture of those who are earnestly intent on finding out a thing, especially a writing difficult to be read. They bring it to the light, place it so that the rays may fall on it as collectively as possible, and then stoop down in order to examine all the parts, that they may be able to make out the whole. We learn from the above that it was "the Spirit of Christ" in the Jewish prophets that prophesied of Christ; it was that Spirit which revealed Him; and it is the same Spirit which takes of the things of Christ and shows them unto us.

13. *Gird up the loins of your mind.* The allusion here is to the long robes of the Asiatics, which, when they were about to perform any active service, they tucked in their girdles. *Hope to the end for the grace.* Continue to expect all that God has promised, and particularly that utmost salvation, that glorification of body and soul, which you shall obtain at the revelation of Christ, when He shall come to judge the world.

14. *Not fashioning yourselves.* As the offices of certain persons are known by the garb they wear, so are transgressors.

15. *But as he which hath called you.* Here Christianity has an infinite advantage over heathenism. God is holy, and He calls upon all who believe in Him to imitate His holiness; and the reason why they should be holy is that God, who has called them, *is holy,* v. 15.

17. *Who without respect of persons.* God is said to be "no respecter of persons" for this reason among many others, that, being infinitely righteous, He must be infinitely impartial. He cannot prefer one to another, because He has nothing to hope or fear from any of His creatures. God's judgment will be according to *every man's work,* and a man's work or "conduct" will be according to the moral state of his mind. No favoritism can prevail in the day of judgment; nothing will pass there but holiness of heart and life.

18. *Ye were not redeemed with corruptible things.* To "redeem" signifies to procure life for a captive or liberty for a slave by paying a price, and the precious blood of Christ is here stated to be the price at which the souls of both Jews and Gentiles were redeemed. *Vain conversation.* Empty, foolish, and unprofitable conduct.

19. *The precious blood of Christ.* "The valuable Blood"; how valuable neither is nor could be stated. *As of a lamb.* Such as was

required for a sin offering to God; the Lamb of God that takes away the sin of the world. *Without blemish* in himself *and without spot* from the world, being perfectly pure in His soul and righteous in His life.

20. *Who verily was foreordained.* "Foreknown"; appointed in the divine purpose to be sent into the world, because infinitely approved by the divine justice. *Before the foundation of the world.* Before the law was given, or any sacrifice prescribed by it. Its whole sacrificial system was appointed in reference to this fore-appointed Lamb, and consequently from Him derived all its significance and virtue. The phrase *foundation of the world* occurs often in the New Testament, and is supposed by some learned men and good critics to signify the commencement of the Jewish state. Perhaps it may have this meaning in Matt. xiii. 35; Luke xi. 50; Eph. i. 4; Heb. iv. 3; and ix. 26. But if we take it here in its common signification, the creation of universal nature, then it shows that God, foreseeing the fall and ruin of man, appointed the remedy that was to cure the disease. *Last times.* The gospel dispensation, called the *last times,* as we have often seen, because never to be succeeded by any other.

21. *Who by him do believe in God.* This is supposed to refer to the Gentiles, who never knew the true God till they heard the preaching of the gospel. *Gave him glory.* Raised Him to His right hand. *That your faith* in the fulfillment of all His promises, and *hope* of eternal glory, *might be in God,* who is unchangeable in His counsels and infinite in His mercies.

22. *Seeing ye have purified your souls*—having purified your souls, *in obeying the truth* —by believing in Christ Jesus, *through* the influence and teaching of *the Spirit,* and giving full proof of it by *unfeigned love* to the *brethren,* you *love one another,* or "you will love each other," *with a pure heart fervently,* "intensely or continually"; the full proof that their brotherly love was *unfeigned*—"without hypocrisy."

23. *Being born again.* For being born of Abraham's seed will not avail to the entering of the kingdom of Heaven. *Not of corruptible seed.* By no human generation or earthly means; *but of incorruptible*—a divine and heavenly principle which is not liable to decay, nor to be affected by the changes and chances to which all sublunary things are exposed. *By the word of God.* "By the doctrine of the living God, which remaineth forever."

25. *But the word of the Lord.* The doctrine delivered by God concerning Christ endureth forever. *And this is the word.* "What is spoken," by the gospel preached unto you.

CHAPTER 2

We should lay aside all evil dispositions, and "desire the sincere milk of the word," that we may grow thereby, 1-3. And come to God to be made living stones, and be built up into a spiritual temple, 4-5. The prophecy of Christ as chief Cornerstone, precious to believers, but a Stumbling Stone to the disobedient, 6-8. True believers are a chosen generation, a royal priesthood, etc., 9-10. They should abstain from fleshly lusts, 11. Walk uprightly among the Gentiles, 12. Be obedient to civil authority, according to the will of God, 13-15. Make a prudent use of their Christian liberty, 16. Fear God and honor the king, 17. Servants should be subject to their masters, serve them faithfully, and suffer indignities patiently, after the example of Christ, 18-23. Who bore the punishment due to our sins in His own body upon the tree, 24. They were formerly like sheep going astray, but are now returned unto the Shepherd and Bishop of their souls, 25.

1. *Wherefore laying aside.* This is in close connection with the preceding chapter, from which it should not have been separated; and the subject is continued to the end of the tenth verse. *Laying aside all malice.* See the notes on Eph. iv. 22-31. These tempers and dispositions must have been common among the Jews, as they are frequently spoken against. Christianity can never admit of such; they show the mind, not of Christ, but of the old murderer.

2. *As newborn babes.* In the preceding chapter, v. 23, the apostle states that they had been "born again"; and as the newborn infant desires that aliment which nature has provided for it, so they, being born again, born from above, should as earnestly require that heavenly nourishment which is suited to their new nature. And this the apostle calls the *sincere milk of the word*, or, as some translate, "the rational unadulterated milk"; i.e., the pure doctrines of the gospel, as delivered in the Epistles and Gospels, and as preached by the apostles and their successors. *That ye may grow thereby.* "Unto salvation" is added here by about forty MSS. The reading is undoubtedly genuine, and is very important. It shows why they were regenerated, and why they were to desire the unadulterated doctrines of the gospel, viz., that they might "grow up unto salvation."

3. *If so be ye have tasted.* "Seeing ye have tasted." *That the Lord is gracious.* This seems to refer to Ps. xxxiv. 8: "O taste and see that the Lord is good."

4. *To whom coming, as unto a living stone.* This is a reference to Isa. xxviii. 16: "Behold, I lay in Zion for a foundation a stone, a tried stone, a precious corner stone, a sure foundation." Jesus Christ is, in both the prophet and apostle, represented as the Foundation on which the Christian Church is built, and on which it must continue to rest; and the stone or foundation is called here *living*, to intimate that He is the Source of life to all His followers, and that it is in union with Him that they live. *Disallowed indeed of men.* That is, rejected by the Jews. This is a plain reference to the prophecy, Ps. cxviii. 22: "The stone which the builders refused is become the head stone of the corner." *Chosen of God.* To be the Saviour of the world and the Founder of the Church, and the Foundation on which it rests. *Precious.* "Honorable." Howsoever despised and rejected by men, Jesus, as the Sacrifice for a lost world, is infinitely honorable in the sight of God.

5. *Ye also, as lively stones.* "Living stones"; each being instinct with the principle of life, which proceeds from Him who is the Foundation, called above "a living stone." The metaphor in this and the following verse is as bold as it is singular; and commentators and critics have found it difficult to hit on any principle of explanation. The Church of Christ is represented under the figure of a *house*, or rather "household"; and as a household must have a place of residence, hence, by a metonymy, the house itself, or material building, is put for the household or family which occupies it. This point will receive the fullest illustration if we have recourse to the Hebrew. *Beith* signifies both a "house" and a "family"; *ben*, a

son; *bath*, a daughter; and *eben*, a stone. Of all these nouns, *banah*, "he built," is, I believe, the common root. Now as *beith*, "a house," is built of *abanim*, "stones," hence *banah*, "he built," is a proper radix for both "stones" and "building"; and as *beith*, "a family or household" (Ps. lxviii. 6), is constituted or made up of *banim*, "sons," and *banoth*, "daughters," hence the same root, *banah*, "he built," is common to all; for sons and daughters build up or constitute a family, as stones do a building. Here then is the ground of the metaphor: The spiritual house is the holy or Christian family or household; this family or household is composed of the sons and daughters of God Almighty; and hence the propriety of "living stones," because this is the living house or spiritual family. And as all the stones, sons and daughters, that constitute the spiritual building are made partakers of the life of Christ, consequently they may with great propriety be called "living stones," that is, sons and daughters of God, who live by Christ Jesus, because He lives in them. Now, following the metaphor, these various living stones become one grand temple, in which God is worshipped, and in which He manifests himself as He did in the Temple of old. Every stone, son and daughter, being a spiritual sacrificer or priest, they all offer up praise and thanksgiving to God through Christ; and such sacrifices, being offered up in the name and through the merit of His Son, are all acceptable in His sight.

6. *Behold, I lay in Sion.* This intimates that the foundation of the Christian Church should be laid at Jerusalem; and there it was laid, for there Christ suffered, and there the preaching of the gospel commenced. *A chief corner stone.* This is the same as the foundation stone; and it is called here the *chief corner stone* because it is laid in the foundation, at an angle of the building where its two sides form the groundwork of a side and end wall. And this might probably be designed to show that, in Jesus, both Jews and Gentiles were to be united. *Elect, precious.* "Chosen" and "honorable." *Shall not be confounded.* These words are quoted from Isa. xxviii. 16; but rather more from the Septuagint than from the Hebrew text. The latter we translate, "He that believeth shall not make haste"—he who comes to God, through Christ, for salvation, shall never be confounded; he need not "haste" to flee away, for no enemy shall ever be able to annoy him.

7. *Unto you therefore which believe.* You, both Jews and Gentiles. *He is precious.* "The honor is to you who believe"; i.e., the honor of being in this building, and of having your souls saved through the blood of the Lamb, and becoming sons and daughters of God Almighty. *Them which be disobedient.* The Jews who continue to reject the gospel; that very Person whom they reject is *head of the corner*—is Lord over all, and has all power in the heavens and the earth.

8. *A stone of stumbling.* Because in Him all Jews and Gentiles who believe are united, and because the latter were admitted into the Church and called by the gospel to enjoy the same privileges which the Jews, as the peculiar people of God, had enjoyed for two thousand years before, therefore they rejected the Christian religion; they would have no partakers with themselves in the salvation of God. This was the true cause why the Jews rejected the gospel; and they rejected Christ because He did not come as a secular prince. In the one case He was a *stone of stumbling*—He was poor, and affected no worldly pomp; in the other He was a *rock of offence,* for His gospel called the Gentiles to be a peculiar people whom the Jews believed to be everlastingly reprobated and utterly incapable of any spiritual good. *Whereunto also they were appointed.* Some good critics read the verse thus, carrying on the sense from the preceding: "Also a stone of stumbling, and a rock of offense: The disobedient stumble against the word, to which verily they were appointed." Peter refers to Isa. viii. 14-15: "And he shall be for a sanctuary; but for a stone of stumbling and for a rock of offence to both the houses of Israel, for a gin and for a snare to the inhabitants of Jerusalem. And many among them shall stumble, and fall, and be broken." The *disobedient,* therefore, being appointed to stumble against the Word, or being prophesied of as persons that should stumble, necessarily means, from the connection in which it stands and from the passage in the prophet, that their stumbling, falling, and being broken is the consequence of their disobedience or unbelief; but there is no intimation that they were *appointed* or "decreed" to disobey, that they might stumble and fall and be broken. They stumbled and fell through their obstinate unbelief; and thus their stumbling and falling, as well as their unbelief, were of themselves. In consequence of this they were *appointed* to be broken; this was God's work of judgment.

9. *Ye are a chosen generation.* The titles formerly given to the whole Jewish church. The Israelites were a *chosen* or "elected race," to be a special people unto the Lord their God, "above all people that are upon the face of the earth," Deut. vii. 6. They were also *a royal priesthood,* or what Moses calls "a kingdom of priests," Exod. xix. 6. They were *an holy nation,* Exod. xix. 6; for they were separated from all the people of the earth, that they might worship the one only true God, and abstain from the abominations that were in the heathen world. They were also a *peculiar people,* a "purchased people"; a "private property," belonging to God Almighty, Deut. vii. 6. But they were called to this state of salvation *out of darkness,* idolatry, superstition, and ungodliness, *into his marvellous light,* the gospel dispensation, which, in reference to the discoveries it had made of God, His nature, will, and gracious promises towards mankind, differed as much from the preceding dispensation of the Jews as the light of the meridian sun from the faint twinkling of a star. And they had these privileges that they might *shew forth the praises of him who* had thus *called* them; "the virtues," those perfections of the wisdom, justice, truth, and goodness of God, that shone most illustriously in the Christian dispensation. These they were to exhibit in a holy and useful life, being transformed into the image of God, and walking as Christ himself walked.

10. *Which in time past were not a people.* This is a quotation from Hos. i. 9-10 and ii. 23, where the calling of the Gentiles by the preaching of the gospel is foretold. From this it is

evident that the people to whom the apostle now addresses himself had been Gentiles.

11. *Which war against the soul.* Which are "marshalled and drawn up in battle array," to fight against the soul; either to slay it or to bring it into captivity. This is the object and operation of every earthly and sensual desire. How little do those who indulge them think of the ruin which they produce!

12. *Having your conversation honest.* Living in such a manner among the Gentiles, in whose country you sojourn, as becomes the gospel which you profess. *In the day of visitation.* I believe this refers to the time when God should come to execute judgment on the disobedient Jews in the destruction of their civil polity and the subversion of their Temple and city. That *the day of visitation* means a time in which punishment should be inflicted is plain from Isa. x. 3: "And what will ye do in the day of visitation, and in the desolation which shall come from far?"

13. *Submit yourselves to every ordinance of man.* In every settled state, and under every form of political government, where the laws are not in opposition to the laws of God, it may be very soundly and rationally said: "Genuine Christians have nothing to do with the laws but to obey them." The words literally signify, not *every ordinance of man,* but "every human creature"; it is better to understand the words thus, "All the constituted authorities." The meaning of Peter appears to be this: The Jews thought it unlawful to obey any ruler that was not of their own stock; the apostle tells them they should obey the civil magistrate, let him be of what stock he may, whether a Jew or a Gentile, and let him exercise the government in whatsoever form. This is the general proposition: and then he instances "emperors" and their "deputies"; and, far from its being unlawful for them to obey a heathen magistrate, they were to do it *for the Lord's sake,* "on account of the Lord," whose will it was and who commanded it.

14. *Or unto governors.* By "king, as supreme" the Roman emperor is meant; and by *governors* are meant leaders, governors, presidents, proconsuls, and other chief magistrates, sent by him into the provinces dependent on the Roman Empire. *For the punishment of evildoers.* This was the object of their mission; they were to punish delinquents, and encourage and protect the virtuous.

15. *For so is the will of God.* God, as their supreme Governor, shows them that it is His will that they should act uprightly and obediently at all times, and thus confound *the ignorance of foolish men,* who were ready enough to assert that their religion made them bad subjects. The word which we translate *put to silence* signifies to "muzzle," i.e., stop their mouths, leave them nothing to say.

16. *As free.* The Jews pretended that they were a free people, and owed allegiance to God alone; hence they were continually rebelling against the Roman government, to which God had subjected them because of their rebellion against Him. Thus they used their liberty *for a cloke of maliciousness*—for a pretext of rebellion, and by it endeavored to vindicate their seditious and rebellious conduct. *But as the*

servants of God. These were free from sin and Satan, but they were the *servants of God*— "bound" to obey Him; and as He had made it their duty to obey the civil magistrate, they served God by submitting "to every ordinance of man for the Lord's sake."

17. *Honour all men.* That is, give honor to whom honor is due, Rom. xiii. 7. *Love the brotherhood.* All true Christians, who form one great family of which God is the Head. *Fear God,* who gives you these commandments, lest He punish you for disobedience. *Honour the king.* Pay that respect to the "emperor" which his high authority requires, knowing that civil power is of God.

18. *Servants, be subject.* See the notes on Eph. vi. 5; Col. iii. 22; and Titus ii. 9. *With all fear.* With all submission and reverence. *The froward.* The crooked, perverse, unreasonable, morose, and austere.

19. *For this is thankworthy.* If, in a conscientious discharge of your duty, you suffer evil, this is in the sight of God thankworthy, pleasing, and proper.

20. *For what glory is it?* It appears from this that the poor Christians, and especially those who had been converted to Christianity while in a state of slavery, were often grievously abused; they were *buffeted* because they were Christians, and because they would not join with their masters in idolatrous worship.

21. *Hereunto were ye called.* You were called to a state of suffering when you were called to be Christians; for the world cannot endure the yoke of Christ, and they that will live godly in Christ must suffer persecution; they will meet with it in one form or other. *Christ also suffered for us.* And left us the example of His meekness and gentleness; for when He was reviled, He reviled not again. You cannot expect to fare better than your Master; imitate His example, and His Spirit shall comfort and sustain you. Many MSS. and most of the versions, instead of *Christ also suffered for us, leaving us,* read, "suffered for you, leaving you." This reading, which I think is genuine, is noticed in the margin.

22. *Who did no sin.* He suffered, but not on account of any evil He had either done or said. It is very likely that the apostle mentions *guile,* because those who do wrong generally strive to screen themselves by prevarication and lies. These words appear to be a quotation from Isa. liii. 9.

23. *But committed himself.* Though He could have inflicted any kind of punishment on His persecutors, yet to give us, in this respect also, an example that we should follow His steps, He committed His cause to Him who is the righteous Judge. To avoid evil tempers and the uneasiness and danger of avenging ourselves, it is a great advantage in all such cases to be able to refer our cause to God, and to be assured that the Judge of all the earth will do right.

24. *Bare our sins in his own body.* Bore the punishment due to our sins. In no other sense could Christ bear them. To say that they were so imputed to Him as if they had been His own, and that the Father beheld Him as blackened with imputed sin, is monstrous, if not blasphemous. *That we, being dead to sins.* "That

we, being freed from sin"—delivered out of its power, and from under its tyranny. *Should live unto righteousness.* That *righteousness* should be our master now, as sin was before. *By whose stripes ye were healed.* The apostle refers here to Isa. liii. 4-6; and he still keeps the case of these persecuted servants in view, and encourages them to suffer patiently by the example of Christ, who was buffeted and scourged, and who bore all this that the deep and inveterate wounds, inflicted on their souls by sin, *might be healed.*

25. *For ye were as sheep going astray.* Formerly you were not in a better moral condition than your oppressors; you were like stray sheep, in the wilderness of ignorance and sin, till Christ, the true and merciful Shepherd, called you back from your wanderings by sending you the gospel of His grace. *Bishop of your souls.* Unless we consider the word *Bishop* as a corruption of the word *episcopos,* and that this literally signifies an "overseer," an "inspector," or "one that has the oversight," it can convey to us no meaning of the original. Jesus Christ is the "Overseer of souls"; He has them continually under His eye; He knows their wants, wishes, dangers, and provides for them. As their *Shepherd,* He leads them to the best pastures, defends them from their enemies, and guides them by His eye. Jesus is the good Shepherd that laid down His life for His sheep. All human souls are inexpressibly dear to Him, as they are the purchase of His blood. He is still supreme *Bishop* or "Overseer" in His Church.

CHAPTER 3

The duty of wives to their husbands, how they are to be adorned, and be in subjection as Sarah was to Abraham, 1-6. The duty of husbands to their wives, 7. How to obtain happiness, and live a long and useful life, 8-11. God loves and succors them that do good; but His face is against the wicked, 12-13. They should suffer persecution patiently, and be always ready to give a reason of the hope that is in them, and preserve a good conscience, though they suffer for righteousness, 14-17. Christ suffered for us and was put to death in the flesh, but quickened by the Spirit, 18. How He preached to the old world while Noah was preparing the ark, 19-20. The salvation of Noah and his family a type of baptism, 21. Christ is ascended to heaven, all creatures being subject to Him, 22.

1. *Ye wives, be in subjection.* Consider that your husband is, by God's appointment, the head and ruler of the house. Do not, therefore, attempt to usurp his government; for even though he *obey not the word,* is "not a believer in the Christian doctrine," his rule is not thereby impaired. For Christianity never alters civil relations; and your affectionate, obedient conduct will be the most likely means of convincing him of the truth of the doctrine which you have received. *Without the word.* That your holy conduct may be the means of begetting in them a reverence for Christianity, the preaching of which they will not hear. See the notes on 1 Cor. xiv. 34.

2. *Chaste conversation coupled with fear.* While they see that you join modesty, chastity, and the purest manners, to the fear of God. Or perhaps *fear* is taken, as in Eph. v. 33, for the "reverence" due to the husband.

3. *Whose adorning.* See the note on Heb. ix. 1, where the word *cosmos,* "world" or "ornament," is defined. *Plaiting the hair, and of wearing of gold.* Plaiting the hair, and variously

folding it about the head, was the most ancient and most simple mode of disposing of this chief ornament of the female head. Thin plates of gold were often mixed with the hair, to make it appear more ornamental by the reflection of light. Small golden buckles were also used in different parts; and among the Roman ladies, pearls and precious stones of different colors. But it is evident, from many remaining monuments, that in numerous cases the *hair* differently plaited and curled was the only ornament of the head. Often a simple pin, sometimes of ivory, pointed with gold, seemed to connect the plaits. In monuments of antiquity the heads of the married and single women may be known, the former by the hair being parted from the forehead over the middle of the top of the head, the latter by being quite close, or being plaited and curled all in a general mass. There is a remarkable passage in Plutarch very like that in the text: "An ornament, as Crates said, is that which becomes her best. This is neither gold, nor pearls, nor scarlet; but those things which are an evident proof of gravity, regularity, and modesty." The wife of Phocion, a celebrated Athenian general, receiving a visit from a lady who was elegantly adorned with gold and jewels, and her hair with pearls, took occasion to call the attention of her guest to the elegance and costliness of her dress, remarking at the same time, "My ornament is my husband, now for the twentieth year general of the Athenians."

4. *The hidden man of the heart.* This phrase is of the same import with that of Paul, Rom. vii. 22, the "inner man"; that is, the soul, with the whole system of affections and passions. Every part of the Scripture treats man as a compound being: the "body" is the outward or visible man; the "soul," the inward, hidden, or invisible man. *A meek and quiet spirit.* That is, a mind that will not give provocation to others, nor receive irritation by the provocation of others. Meekness will prevent the first; "quietness" will guard against the last. *Great price.* All the ornaments placed on the head and body of the most illustrious female are, in the sight of God, of no worth; but a "meek and silent spirit" are, in His sight, invaluable.

5. *For after this manner.* Simplicity reigned in primitive times; natural ornaments alone were then in use. Trade and commerce brought in luxuries; and luxury brought pride, and all the excessive nonsense of dress. *Being in subjection unto their own husbands.* It will rarely be found that women who are fond of dress and extravagant in it have any subjection to their husbands but what comes from mere necessity. Indeed, their dress, which they intend as an attractive to the eyes of others, is a sufficient proof that they have neither love nor respect for their own husbands.

6. *Even as Sara obeyed.* Almost the same words are in *Rab. Tanchum,* fol. 9, 3: "The wife of Abraham reverenced him, and called him lord, as it is written, Gen. xviii. 12: 'And my lord is old.'" The words of the apostle imply that she acknowledged his superiority, and her own subjection to him, in the order of God. *Whose daughters ye are.* As Abraham is represented the father of all his male believing descendants, so Sara is represented as the mother of all her believing female posterity. *As long as ye do well.* For you cannot maintain

your relationship to her longer than you believe, and you cannot believe longer than you continue to obey. *And are not afraid with any amazement.* It is difficult to extract any sense out of this clause. The original is not very easy: "And not fearing with any terror." If you do well, and act conscientiously your part as faithful wives, you will at no time live under the distressing apprehension of being found out, or terrified at every appearance of the discovery of infidelities or improper conduct.

7. *Dwell with them according to knowledge.* Give your wives, by no species of unkind carriage, any excuse for delinquency. How can a man expect his wife to be faithful to him if he be unfaithful to her? *Giving honour unto the wife.* Using your superior strength and experience in her behalf, and thus honoring her by becoming her protector and support. But the word *honour* signifies "maintenance" as well as "respect"—maintain, provide for the wife. *As unto the weaker vessel.* Being more delicately, and consequently more slenderly, constructed. Roughness and strength go hand in hand; so likewise do beauty and frailty. The female has what the man wants—beauty and delicacy. The male has what the female wants—courage and strength. The one is as good in its place as the other; and by these things God has made an equality between the man and the woman, so that there is properly very little superiority on either side. *Being heirs together.* Both the man and woman being equally called to eternal glory; and as prayer is one great means of obtaining a meetness for it, it is necessary that they should live together in such a manner as to prevent all family contentions, that they may not be prevented, by disputes or misunderstandings, from uniting daily in this most important duty—family and social prayer.

8. *Be ye all of one mind.* Unity, both in the family and in the Church, being essentially necessary to peace and salvation. See on Rom. xii. 16 and xv. 5. *Having compassion.* "Being sympathetic"; feeling for each other; bearing each other's burdens. *Love as brethren.* "Be lovers of the brethren." *Pitiful.* "Tenderhearted." *Courteous.* Be "friendly-minded," is the reading of more than twenty MSS. and some of the fathers. This is probably the true reading.

9. *Not rendering evil for evil.* Purposing, saying, doing nothing but good; and invariably returning good for evil. *Ye are thereunto called.* This is your calling, your business in life—to do good, and to do good for evil, and to implore God's blessing even on your worst enemies.

10-11. *For he that will love life.* This is a quotation from Ps. xxxiv. 12-16, as it stands in the Septuagint; only the aorist of the imperative is changed from the second into the third person. He who wishes to live long and prosperously must act as he is here directed. (1) He must refrain from evil speaking, lying, and slandering. (2) He must avoid flattery and fair speeches, which cover hypocritical or wicked intentions. (3) He must "avoid" *evil,* keep "going away" from evil. (4) He must *do good;* he must walk in the way of righteousness. (5) He must live peaceably with all men; *seek peace* where it has been lost; and "pursue it" where it seems to be flying away. He who lives thus must live happy in himself.

12. *The eyes of the Lord are over the righteous.* That is, he is continually under God's notice and His care; God continually watches for him and watches over him, and he is under His constant protection. *And his ears are open unto their prayers.* The original is very emphatic: "The eyes of the Lord are upon the righteous, and His ears to their prayers." The righteous man ever attracts the divine notice, and wherever he is, there is the ear of God; for, as every righteous man is a man of prayer, wherever he prays, there is the ear of God, into which the prayer, as soon as formed, enters. *But the face of the Lord.* Far from His eye being upon them, or His ear open to their requests (for prayer they have none), His *face,* His "approbation," His providence and blessing, are turned away from them.

13. *Who is he that will harm you?* Is it possible that a man can be wretched who has God for his Friend? *If ye be followers.* "If you are imitators of the good One," i.e., of God. "The good One" is one of God's prime epithets, see Matt. xix. 17; and Satan is distinguished by the reverse, "the evil one," Matt. xxiii. 19. Instead of *followers,* or rather "imitators," "zealous" of what is good is the reading of numerous MSS., with some of the fathers. This is a very probable reading.

14. *But and if ye suffer.* God may permit you to be tried and persecuted for righteousness' sake, but this cannot essentially harm you; He will press even this into your service and make it work for your good. *Happy are ye.* This seems to refer to Matt. v. 10, "Blessed or happy are you when men persecute you." *Be not afraid of their terror.* "Fear not their fear"; see Isa. viii. 12. Sometimes fear is put for the object of a man's religious worship; see Gen. xxxi. 42; Prov. i. 26; and the place in Isaiah just quoted. The exhortation may mean, "Fear not their gods," they can do you no hurt; and supposing that they curse you by them, yet be not troubled. "He who fears God need have no other fear."

15. *But sanctify the Lord God in your hearts.* To sanctify God may signify to offer Him the praises due to His grace; but as to *sanctify* literally signifies to "make holy," it is impossible that God should be thus sanctified. We have often already seen that *hagiazo* signifies to separate from earth, that is, from any common use or purpose, that the thing or person thus separated may be devoted to a sacred use. Perhaps we should understand Peter's words thus: Entertain just notions of God; of His nature, power, will, justice, goodness, and truth. Thus *sanctify the Lord God in your hearts,* and you will ever be ready . . . to give . . . a *reason of the hope that is in you* to every serious and candid inquirer after truth. Most religious systems and creeds are incapable of rational explanation, because founded on some misconception of the divine nature. Instead of *God,* some MSS. have "Christ." "Sanctify Christ in your hearts" as Lord. The word *apologia,* which we translate *answer,* signifies a "defense"; from this we have our word "apology," which did not originally signify an excuse for an act but a defense of that act. The defenses of Christianity by the primitive fathers are called "apologies." *With meekness and fear.* Several excellent MSS. add the word "but" here, and it improves the sense considerably: "Be ready always to give an answer to every man that asketh you a reason of the hope that is in you, but with meekness and fear." Do not permit your readiness to answer, nor the confidence you have in the goodness of your cause, lead you to answer pertly or superciliously to any person. Defend the truth with all possible gentleness and fear, lest while you are doing it you should forget His presence whose cause you support, or say anything unbecoming the dignity and holiness of the religion which you have espoused, or inconsistent with that heavenly temper which the Spirit of your indwelling Lord must infallibly produce.

16. *Having a good conscience.* The testimony of God in your own soul "that in simplicity and godly sincerity" you have your "conversation in the world." *Whereas they speak evil of you.* See the same sentiment in chap. ii. 11, and the note there.

17. *For it is better.* See on chap. ii. 19-20.

18. *Christ also hath once suffered.* See the notes on Rom. v. 6; Heb. ix. 28. *Put to death in the flesh.* In His human nature. *But quickened by the Spirit.* That very dead body revived by the power of His divinity.

19. *By which.* Spirit, His own divine energy and authority. *He went and preached.* By the ministry of Noah, 120 years. *Unto the spirits in prison.* The inhabitants of the antediluvian world, who, having been "disobedient" and convicted of the most flagrant transgressions against God, were sentenced by His just law to destruction. But their punishment was delayed to see if they would repent; and "the longsuffering of God waited" 120 years, which were granted to them for this purpose; during which time, as criminals tried and convicted, they are represented as being *in prison*—detained under the arrest of divine justice, which waited either for their repentance or the expiration of the respite, that the punishment pronounced might be inflicted. This I have long believed to be the sense of this difficult passage, and no other that I have seen is so consistent with the whole scope of the place. That the Spirit of God did strive with, convict, and reprove the antediluvians, is evident from Gen. vi. 3: "My spirit shall not always strive with man, for that he also is flesh: yet his days shall be an hundred and twenty years." And it was by this Spirit that Noah became a "preacher of righteousness," and condemned that ungodly world, Heb. xi. 7, who would not believe till wrath, divine punishment, came upon them to the uttermost. The word *spirits* is supposed to render this view of the subject improbable, because this must mean disembodied spirits; but this certainly does not follow, for "the spirits of just men made perfect," Heb. xii. 23, certainly means righteous men, and men still in the Church militant; and the "Father of spirits," Heb. xii. 9, means men still in the body; and "the God of the spirits of all flesh," Num. xvi. 22 and xxvii. 16, means men not in a disembodied state. There is no ground to believe that the text speaks of Christ's going to hell to preach the gospel to the damned, or of His going to some feigned place where the souls of the patriarchs were detained, to whom He preached, and whom He delivered from that place and took with Him to paradise.

20. *When once the longsuffering of God waited.* In *Pirkey Aboth,* cap. v. 2, we have these words: "There were ten generations from Adam to Noah, that the long-suffering of God might appear; for each of these generations provoked him to anger, and went on in their iniquity, till at last the deluge came." *Were saved by water.* *While the ark was a preparing,* only Noah's family believed; these amounted to *eight persons.* And only these were saved from the deluge on the water; all the rest perished in the water.

21. *The like figure whereunto.* There are many difficulties in this verse, but the simple meaning of the place may be easily apprehended. Noah believed in God, walked uprightly before Him, and found grace in His sight; he obeyed Him in building the ark, and God made it the means of his salvation from the waters of the deluge. *Baptism* implies a consecration and dedication of the soul and body to God, the Father, Son, and Holy Spirit. He who is faithful to his baptismal covenant, taking God through Christ, by the eternal Spirit, for his Portion, is saved here from his sins; and through the resurrection of Christ from the dead has the well-grounded hope of eternal glory. This is all plain; but was it the deluge itself, or the ark, or the being saved by that ark from the deluge, that was the antetype of which Peter speaks? Noah and his family were "saved by water"; i.e., it was the instrument of their being saved through the good providence of God. So the water of *baptism,* typifying the regenerating influence of the Holy Spirit, is the means of salvation to all those who receive this Holy Spirit in His quickening, cleansing efficacy. Now as the waters of the Flood could not have saved Noah and his family had they not made use of the ark, so the water of baptism saves no man but as it is the means of his getting his heart purified by the Holy Spirit, and typifying to him that purification.

22. *Who is gone into heaven.* Having given the fullest proof of His resurrection from the dead, and of His having accomplished the end for which He came into the world. *On the right hand of God.* In the place of the highest dignity, honor, and influence. *Angels and authorities and powers.* That is, all creatures and beings, both in the heavens and in the earth, are put under subjection to Jesus Christ.

CHAPTER 4

We should suffer patiently, after the example of Christ, 1. And no longer live according to our former custom, but disregard the scoffs of those who are incensed against us because we have forsaken their evil ways, who are shortly to give account to God for their conduct, 2-5. How the gospel was preached to Jews and Gentiles, 6. As the end of all things was at hand, they should be sober, watchful, charitable, benevolent, good stewards of the bounty of Providence; and when called to instruct others, speak as the oracles of God, 7-11. Of the persecutions and trials which were coming upon them, and how they were to suffer so as not to disgrace their Christian character, 12-16. Judgment was about to begin at the house of God, and even the righteous would escape with difficulty from the calamities coming upon the Jews; but they must continue in well-doing, and thus commit the keeping of their souls to their faithful Creator, 17-19.

1. *As Christ hath suffered.* He is your proper Pattern; have the same disposition He had; the same forgiving spirit, with meekness, gentleness, and complete self-possession. *He that hath suffered in the flesh hath ceased from sin.* The man who suffers generally reflects on his ways, is humbled, fears approaching death, loathes himself because of his past iniquities, and ceases from them.

2. *That he no longer should live . . . in the flesh*—Governed by the base principle of giving up his faith to save his life; *to the lusts of men*—according to the will of his idolatrous persecutors; *but to the will of God*—which will of God is that he should retain the truth and live according to its dictates, though he should suffer for it.

3. *The time past of our life.* This is a complete epitome of the Gentile or heathen state, and a proof that those had been Gentiles to whom the apostle wrote. They *walked in lasciviousness,* every species of lewdness and impurity; *lusts,* strong irregular appetites and desires of all kinds; *excess of wine,* "inflamed with wine"; *revellings,* lascivious feastings, with drunken songs; *banquetings,* "wine feasts, drinking matches"; *abominable idolatries,* that is, the abominations practiced at their idol feasts, where they not only worshipped the idol, but did it with the most impure, obscene, and abominable rites. This was the general state of the Gentile world, and with this monstrous wickedness Christianity had everywhere to struggle.

4. *They think it strange.* They wonder and are astonished at you, that you can renounce these gratifications of the flesh for a spiritual something, the good of which they cannot see. *Excess of riot.* "Flood of profligacy"; bearing down all rule, order, and restraints before it. *Speaking evil of.* Literally, "blaspheming"; i.e., speaking impiously against God, and calumniously of *you.*

5. *To judge the quick and the dead.* They shall give account of these irregularities to Him who is prepared to judge both the Jews and the Gentiles. The Gentiles, previously to the preaching of the gospel among them, were reckoned to be "dead in trespasses and sins," Eph. ii. 1-5; under the sentence of death, because they had sinned. The Jews had at least, by their religious profession, a name to live; and by that profession were bound to live to God.

6. *Was the gospel preached also to them that are dead.* But if the apostle had the same fact in view which he mentions in chap. iii. 19-20, then the antediluvians are the persons intended. *For this cause*—that Christ is prepared "to judge the quick and the dead," and to dispense righteous judgment in consequence of having afforded them every necessary advantage; *was the gospel preached* by Noah *also to them that are dead*—the antediluvian world, then dead in trespasses and sins, and condemned to death by the righteous judgment of God. But in His great compassion He afforded them a respite, that though they were condemned as *men in the flesh* (Gen. vi. 3), yet, hearing this gospel by Noah, they might believe, *and live according to God in the spirit*—live a blessed life in eternity according to the mercy of God, who sent His Spirit to strive with them.

7. *But the end of all things is at hand.* I think that here also Peter keeps the history of the deluge before his eyes, finding a parallel to the state of the Jews in his own time in that of the antediluvians in the days of Noah. In Gen. vi. 13, God said unto Noah, "The end of all flesh is come before me." This was spoken at a time when God had decreed the destruction

of the world by a flood. Peter says, *The end of all things is at hand;* and this he spoke when God had determined to destroy the Jewish people and their polity by one of the most signal judgments that ever fell upon any nation or people. The end of the Temple, the end of the Levitical priesthood, the end of the whole Jewish economy, was then at hand. *Be . . . sober, and watch unto prayer. Be . . . sober*—make a prudent and moderate use of all you possess; and *watch* against all occasions of sin; and pray for the supporting hand of God to be upon you for good, that you may escape the destruction that is coming upon the Jews, and that you may be saved from among them when the scourge comes.

8. *Have fervent charity.* "Intense love; for love shall cover a multitude of sins." A loving disposition leads us to pass by the faults of others, to forgive offenses against ourselves, and to excuse and lessen, as far as is consistent with truth, the transgressions of men. It does not mean that our love to others will induce God to pardon our offenses.

9. *Use hospitality.* Be ever ready to divide your bread with the hungry, and to succor the stranger. *Without grudging.* "Without grumblings." Do nothing merely because it is commanded, but do it from love to God and man; then it will be without grumbling.

10. *Hath received the gift.* "A gift"; any blessing of providence or grace. I cannot think that the word means here the Holy Ghost, or any of His supernatural gifts or influences; it may include those, but it signifies anything given by the mere mercy and bounty of God. But perhaps in this place it may signify some or any office in the Church; and this sense, indeed, the connection seems to require. *Stewards of the manifold grace.* Whatever gifts or endowments any man may possess, they are, properly speaking, not his own; they are the Lord's property, and to be employed in His work, and to promote His glory.

11. *If any man speak.* In order to explain or enforce God's Word, and edify his neighbor, let him do it as those did to whom the living oracles were committed; they spoke as they were inspired by the Holy Ghost. *Of the ability which God giveth.* Perhaps the ministering here may refer to the care of the poor, and the *ability* is the means which God may have placed in their hands; and they are to minister this as coming immediately from God, and lead the minds of the poor to consider Him as their Benefactor, that He in all things may be glorified through Christ Jesus.

12. *Think it not strange concerning the fiery trial.* "The burning." The metaphor is old, but noble; it represents the Christians at Pontus as having fire cast upon them for the trying of their faith, as gold is tried by fire, chap. i. 7, to which the apostle alludes.

14. *If ye be reproached for the name of Christ.* To be reproached for the *name of Christ* is to be reproached for being a Christian. This is the highest honor to which any man can arrive in this world, and therefore the apostle says to such, *Happy are ye. On their part he is evil spoken of.* "By them He is blasphemed, by you He is honored."

15. *But let none of you suffer . . . as a busybody in other men's matters.* "The inspector of another"; meddling with other people's concerns, and forgetting their own.

16. *Yet if any man suffer as a Christian.* If he be persecuted because he has embraced the Christian faith, *let him not be ashamed; but let him* rather *glorify God* on this very account. Christ suffered by the Jews because He was holy; Christians suffer because they resemble Him. The word *Christian* is used only here and in Acts xi. 26; xxvi. 28.

17. *Judgment must begin at the house of God.* Our Lord had predicted that, previously to the destruction of Jerusalem, His own followers would have to endure various calamities; see Matt. xxiv. 9, 21-22; Mark xiii. 12-13; John xvi. 2 ff. Here His true disciples are called *the house* or "family" *of God.* That the converted Jews suffered much from their own brethren needs little proof. But probably the word which we here translate *judgment* may mean no more than affliction and distress; for it was a Jewish maxim that, when God was about to pour down some general judgment, He began with afflicting His own people in order to correct and amend them, that they might be prepared for the overflowing scourge. *And if it first begin at us*—Jews who have repented and believed on the Son of God; *what shall the end be of them*—the Jews who continue impenitent, and obey not the gospel of God?

18. *And if the righteous scarcely be saved?* If it shall be with extreme difficulty that the Christians shall escape from Jerusalem when the Roman armies shall come against it with the full commission to destroy it, *where shall the ungodly and the sinner appear?* Where shall the proud, Pharisaic boaster in his own outside holiness, and the profligate transgressor of the laws of God, "show themselves," as having escaped the divine vengeance? It is rather strange, but it is a fact, that this verse is the Septuagint translation of Prov. xi. 31: "Behold, the righteous shall be recompensed in the earth: much more the wicked and the sinner." For this the Septuagint and Peter have, *If the righteous scarcely be saved, where shall the ungodly and the sinner appear?*

19. *Suffer according to the will of God.* A man suffers according to the will of God who suffers for righteousness' sake; and who, being reviled, reviles not again. *Commit the keeping of their souls.* Place their lives confidently in His hand who, being their *Creator,* will also be their Preserver, and keep that safely which is committed to His trust. God is here represented as *faithful,* because He will always fulfill His promises, and withhold no good thing from them that walk uprightly.

CHAPTER 5

Directions to the elders to feed the flock of God, and not to be lords over God's heritage, that when the chief Shepherd does appear, they may receive a crown of glory, 1-4. The young are to submit themselves to the elder, and to humble themselves under the mighty hand of God, and cast all their care upon Him, 5-7. They should be sober and watchful, because their adversary the devil is continually seeking their destruction, whom they are to resist, steadfast in the faith, 8-9. They are informed that the God of all grace had called them to His eternal glory, 10-11. Of Silvanus, by whom this Epistle was sent, 12. Salutations from the church at Babylon, 13. The apostolic benediction, 14.

1. *The elders which are among you.* In this place the term *elders* or presbyters is the name of an office. They were as pastors or shepherds of the flock of God, the Christian people among whom they lived. They were the same as bishops, 1 Tim. v. 17. *Who am also an elder.* "A fellow elder"; one on a level with yourselves. *A witness of the sufferings of Christ.* He was with Christ in the garden; he was with Him when He was apprehended; and he was with Him in the high priest's hall. *A partaker of the glory.* He had the promise from his Lord and Master that he should be with Him in heaven, to behold His glory, John xvii. 21, 24.

2. *Feed the flock.* Do not fleece the flock. *Taking the oversight.* Discharging the office of bishops or superintendents. This is another proof that bishop and presbyter were the same order in the apostolic times, though afterwards they were made distinct. *Not by constraint.* The office was laborious and dangerous, especially in these times of persecution; it is no wonder then that even those who were best qualified for the office should strive to excuse themselves. *Not for filthy lucre.* Could the office of a bishop, in those early days and in the time of persecution, be a lucrative office? Does not the Spirit of God lead the apostle to speak these things rather for posterity than for that time? But of a ready mind. Doing all for Christ's sake, and through love to immortal souls.

3. *Neither as being lords over God's heritage.* This is the voice of Peter in his catholic Epistle to the catholic Church! According to him there are to be no *lords over God's heritage.* The bishops and presbyters who are appointed by the Head of the Church to feed the flock, to guide and to defend it, not to fleece and waste it; and they are to look for their reward in another world, and in the approbation of God in their consciences. And in humility, self-abasement, self-renunciation, and heavenly-mindedness they are to be *ensamples*, "types," to the flock.

4. *When the chief Shepherd.* That is, the Lord Jesus Christ, whose is the flock, and who provides the pasture, and from whom, if you are legally called to the most awful work of preaching the gospel, you have received your commission. When he *shall appear* to judge the world in righteousness, you who have fed His flock, who have taken the superintendency of it, "not by constraint," nor for filthy lucre's sake, not as lords over the heritage, but with a ready mind, employing body, soul, spirit, time, and talents in endeavoring to pluck sinners as brands from eternal burnings, and build up the Church of Christ on its most holy faith—*ye shall receive a crown of glory that fadeth not away*, an eternal nearness and intimacy with the ineffably glorious God.

5. *Likewise, ye younger.* Probably means here "inferiors," or those not in sacred offices; and may be understood as referring to the people at large who are called to obey them that have the rule over them in the Lord. *Be subject one to another.* Strive all to serve each other; let the pastors strive to serve the people, and the people the pastors; and let there be no contention, but who shall do most to oblige and profit all the rest. *Be clothed with humility.* To be *clothed* with a thing or person is a Greek mode of speech for being that thing or person with which a man is said to be clothed. Be truly humble, and let your outward garb and conduct be a proof of the humility of your hearts.

6. *Humble yourselves.* Those who submit patiently to the dispensations of God's providence, He lifts up; those who lift themselves up, God thrusts down.

7. *Casting all your care.* Your "anxiety," your "distracting care." *Upon him; for he careth for you.* "For He concerns himself with the things that interest you." This is a plain reference to Ps. lv. 22: "Cast thy burden upon the Lord, and he shall sustain thee." He will bear both you and your burden.

8. *Be sober.* Avoid drunkenness of your senses, and drunkenness in your souls; be not overcharged with the concerns of the world. *Be vigilant.* Awake, and keep awake; be always "watchful"; never be off your guard. Your enemies are alert; they are never off theirs. *Your adversary the devil.* This is the reason why you should be sober and vigilant; you have an ever active, implacable, subtle enemy to contend with. He *walketh about*—he has access to you everywhere; he knows your feelings and your propensities, and informs himself of all your circumstances. Only God can know more and do more than he; therefore your care must be cast upon God. *As a roaring lion.* Satan tempts under three forms: (1) The subtle serpent; to beguile our senses, pervert our judgment, and enchant our imagination. (2) As an angel of light; to deceive us with false views of spiritual things. (3) As a roaring lion; to bear us down, and destroy us by violent opposition, persecution, and death. Thus he was acting towards the followers of God at Pontus, etc., who were now suffering a grievous persecution. *Walketh about.* Traversing the earth; a plain reference to Job ii. 2. *Seeking whom he may devour.* "Whom he may gulp down." There is a beauty in this verse, and a striking apposition between the first and last words, which I think have not been noticed: Be *sober*, from *ne*, "not," and *piein*, "to drink"—"do not drink, do not swallow down"; and the word from *kata*, "down," and *piein*, "to drink." If you swallow strong drink down, the devil will swallow you down.

9. *Whom resist.* Stand against him. *The same afflictions are accomplished in your brethren.* It is the lot of all the disciples of Christ to suffer persecution. The "brotherhood," the Christian Church, everywhere is exposed to the assaults of men and devils. You are persecuted by the heathen among whom you live, and from among whom you are gathered into the fold of Christ; but even those who profess the same faith with you, and who are resident among the Jews (for so I think *in the world* is here to be understood), are also persecuted, both heathens and Jews being equally opposed to the pure and holy doctrines of the gospel. Any man who has read the Greek Testament with any attention must have observed a vast number of places in which the word *cosmos*, which we translate *world*, means the Jewish people and the Jewish state, and nothing else.

10. *But the God of all grace.* The Fountain of infinite compassion, mercy, and goodness. *Who hath called us.* By the preaching of the

gospel. *After that ye have suffered a while.* "Having suffered a little time"; that is, while you are enduring these persecutions, God will cause all to work together for your good. *Make you perfect.* All these words are read in the future tense by the best MSS. and versions. "He will make you perfect"—put you in "complete joint" as the timbers of a building. *Stablish.* Make you "firm" in every part. *Strengthen.* Cramp and bind every part so that there shall be no danger of warping, splitting, or falling. *Settle.* Cause all to rest so evenly and firmly upon the best and surest foundation that you may grow together to a holy temple in the Lord. In a word, that you may be "complete" in all the mind that was in Christ; "supported" in all your trials and difficulties; "strengthened" to resist and overcome all your enemies; and after all abide, firmly "founded," in the truth of grace. All these phrases are architectural; and the apostle has again in view the fine image which he produced in chap. ii. 5.

11. *To him*—the God of all grace; *be glory*—all honor and praise be ascribed; and *dominion*—the government of heaven, earth, and hell; *for ever*—through time; and *ever*—through eternity. *Amen*—so be it, so let it be, and so it shall be.

12. *By Silvanus, a faithful brother unto you, as I suppose.* To say the least of this translation, it is extremely obscure, and not put together with that elegance which is usual to our translators. I see no reason why the clause may not be thus translated: "I have written to you, as I consider, briefly, by Silvanus, the faithful brother." On all hands it is allowed that this

Silvanus was the same as Silas, Paul's faithful companion in travel, mentioned in Acts xv. 40; xvi. 19; and if he were the same, Peter could never say *as I suppose* to his faith and piety: but he might well say this to the shortness of his Epistle, notwithstanding the many and important subjects which it embraced. *Exhorting.* Calling upon you to be faithful, humble, and steady. *And testifying.* "Earnestly witnessing" that it *is the true grace*—the genuine gospel of Jesus Christ, "in which ye stand," and in which you should persevere to the end.

13. *Elected together with you.* "Fellow elect," or "elected jointly" with you. *And so doth Marcus my son.* This is supposed to be the same person who is mentioned in Acts xii. 12, and who is known by the name of John Mark; he is the same who wrote the Gospel that goes under his name. He is called here Peter's son, i.e., according to the faith, Peter probably having been the means of his conversion. This is very likely, as Peter seems to have been intimate at his mother's house. See the account in Acts xii. 6-17.

14. *Greet ye one another with a kiss of charity.* See the notes on Rom. xvi. 16 and on 1 Cor. xvi. 20. In the above places the kiss is called "a holy kiss"; here, "a kiss of love"; i.e., as a mark of their love to each other, in order that misunderstandings might be prevented. *Peace be with you all.* May all "prosperity," spiritual and temporal, be with all *that are in Christ Jesus*—that are truly converted to Him, and live in His Spirit obedient to His will. *Amen.* Is wanting, as usual, in some of the principal MSS. and versions.

The Second Epistle of
PETER

CHAPTER 1

The apostolical address, and the persons to whom the Epistle was sent described by the state into which God had called, and in which He had placed, them, 1-4. What graces they should possess in order to be fruitful in the knowledge of God, 5-8. The miserable state of those who either have not these graces or have fallen from them, 9. Believers should give diligence to make their calling and election sure, 10-11. The apostle's intimations of his speedy dissolution, and his wish to confirm and establish those churches in the true faith, 12-15. The certainty of the gospel, and the convincing evidence which the apostle had of its truth from being present at the Transfiguration, by which the word of prophecy was made more sure, 16-19. How the prophecies came, and their nature, 20-21.

1. *Simon Peter.* "Symeon" is the reading of almost all the versions, and of all the most important MSS. And this is the more remarkable, as the surname of Peter occurs upwards of seventy times in the New Testament, and is invariably read *Simon*, except here, and in Acts xv. 14, where James gives him the name of "Symeon." *A servant.* Employed in his Master's work. *And an apostle.* Commissioned immediately by Jesus Christ himself to preach to the Gentiles, and to write these Epistles for the edification of the Church. *Precious faith.* "Valuable faith"; faith worth a great price, and

faith which cost a great price. *With us.* God having given to you, believing Gentiles, the same faith and salvation which He had given to us, believing Jews. *Through the righteousness of God.* Through His method of bringing a lost world, both Jews and Gentiles, to salvation by Jesus Christ; through His gracious impartiality, providing for Gentiles as well as Jews. *Of God and our Saviour Jesus Christ.* This is not a proper translation of the original, which is literally, "Of our God and Saviour Jesus Christ"; and this reading, which is indicated in the margin, should have been received into the text; and it is an absolute proof that Peter calls Jesus Christ "God," even in the properest sense of the word, with the article prefixed.

2. *Grace*—God's favor; *peace*—the effects of that favor in the communication of spiritual and temporal blessings. *Through the knowledge of God.* "By the acknowledging of God, and of Jesus our Lord."

3. *As his divine power.* His power, which no power can resist, because it is *divine*—that which properly belongs to the infinite Godhead. *Hath given unto us.* "Hath endowed us with

the gifts," or hath "gifted us." By *life and godliness* we may understand: (1) a godly life; or (2) eternal life as the end, and godliness the way to it; or (3) what was essentially necessary for the present life, and what was requisite for the life to come. *That hath called us to glory and virtue.* To *virtue* or "courage" as the means; and *glory*—the kingdom of Heaven, as the end. This is the way in which these words are commonly understood, and this sense is plain enough, but the construction is harsh. Others have translated "by His glorious benignity," and read the whole verse thus: "God by His own power hath bestowed on us everything necessary for a happy life and godliness, having called us to the knowledge of himself, by His own infinite goodness." It is certain that the word which we translate *virtue* or "courage," is used, 1 Pet. ii. 9, to express the perfection of the divine nature. But there is a various reading here which is of considerable importance, and which, from the authorities by which it is supported, appears to be genuine: Through the knowledge of Him who hath called us "by His own glory and power," or "by His own glorious power."

4. *Whereby are given unto us.* By His own glorious power He hath "freely given unto us exceeding great and invaluable promises." Peter intimates to these Gentiles that God had given unto them exceeding great promises; indeed all that He had given to the Jews, the mere settlement in the Promised Land excepted; and this also He had given in all its spiritual meaning and force. And besides these "superlatively great" promises, which distinguished the Mosaic dispensation, He had given them the "valuable" promises, those which came through the great price: enrollment with the Church of God, redemption in and through the Blood of the Cross, the continual indwelling influence of the Holy Ghost, the resurrection of the body, and eternal rest at the right hand of God. *That by these ye might be partakers.* The object of all God's promises and dispensations was to bring fallen man back to the image of God, which he had lost. This, indeed, is the sum and substance of the religion of Christ. We have partaken of an earthly, sensual, and devilish nature; the design of God by Christ is to remove this, and to make us *partakers of the divine nature;* and save us from all the *corruption* in principle and fact which *is in the world;* the source of which is *lust*—irregular, unreasonable, inordinate, and impure desire. *Lust* is the source whence springs all the corruption which is in the world. Lust conceives and brings forth sin; sin is finished or brought into act, and then brings forth death. This destructive principle is to be rooted out, and love to God and man is to be implanted in its place. This is every Christian's privilege. God has promised to purify our hearts by faith; and that as sin hath reigned unto death, even so shall grace reign through righteousness unto eternal life; that here we are to be delivered out of the hands of all our enemies, and have even "the thoughts of our hearts so cleansed by the inspiration of God's Holy Spirit that we shall perfectly love Him, and worthily magnify His holy name."

5. *And beside this.* Notwithstanding what God hath done for you, in order that you may not receive the grace of God in vain. *Giving all diligence.* "Furnishing all earnestness" and activity. The original is very emphatic. *Add to your faith.* "Lead up hand in hand." *Virtue.* "Courage" or "fortitude," to enable you to profess the faith before men in these times of persecution. *Knowledge.* True wisdom, by which your faith will be increased, and your courage directed.

6. *Temperance.* A proper and limited use of all earthly enjoyments, keeping every sense under proper restraints, and never permitting the animal part to subjugate the rational. *Patience.* Bearing all trials and difficulties with an even mind, enduring in all, and persevering through all. *Godliness.* Piety towards God; a deep, reverential, religious fear.

7. *Brotherly kindness.* "Love of the brotherhood"—the strongest attachment to Christ's flock. *Charity.* "Love" to the whole human race, even to your persecutors. True religion is neither selfish nor insulated; where the love of God is, bigotry cannot exist. Narrow, selfish people, and people of a party, who scarcely have any hope of the salvation of those who do not believe as they believe and who do not follow with them, have scarcely any religion, though in their own apprehension none is so truly orthodox or religious as themselves.

8. *For if these things be in you, and abound.* If you possess all these graces, and they increase and abound in your souls, *they* will *make,* show, you to be neither "idle" nor unfruitful, "in the acknowledgment" of our Lord Jesus Christ." The common translation is here very unhappy. *Barren* and *unfruitful* certainly convey the same ideas; but "idle" or "inactive," which is the proper sense, takes away this tautology and restores the sense. The graces already mentioned by the apostle are in themselves active principles; he who was possessed of them, and had them abounding in him, could not be "inactive"; and he who is not inactive in the way of life must be fruitful.

9. *But he that lacketh these things.* He, whether Jew or Gentile, who professes to have faith in God, and has not added to that faith "fortitude, knowledge, temperance, patience, godliness, bortherly kindness, and universal love," is *blind*—his understanding is darkened; *and cannot see afar off,* "shutting his eyes against the light, winking," not able to look truth in the face, nor to behold that God whom he once knew was reconciled to him: and thus it appears he is willfully blind; *and hath forgotten that he was purged from his old sins*—has at last, through his non-improvement of the grace which he received from God, lost the evidence of things not seen.

10. *Wherefore.* Seeing the danger of apostasy and the fearful end of them who obey not the gospel, *give all diligence,* "hasten," be deeply careful, labor with the most intense purpose of soul. *To make your calling.* From deep Gentile darkness into the marvellous light of the gospel. *And election.* Your being chosen, in consequence of obeying the heavenly calling, to be the people and Church of God. *Sure.* "Firm, solid." For your calling to believe the gospel, and your election to be members of the Church of Christ, will be ultimately unprofitable to you unless you hold fast what you have received by adding to your faith virtue, knowledge, temperance. *For if ye do these things*—if

you are careful and diligent to work out your own salvation, through the grace which you have already received from God. *Ye shall never fall*—"You shall at no time stumble or fall"; as the Jews have done, and lost their election, Rom. xi. 11, where the same word is used. We find, therefore, that they who do not these things shall fall; and thus we see that there is nothing absolute and unconditional in their election.

11. *For so an entrance shall be ministered.* If you give diligence, and do not fall, an abundant, free, honorable, and triumphant *entrance shall be ministered unto you . . . into the everlasting kingdom.* There seems to be here an allusion to the triumphs granted by the Romans to their generals who had distinguished themselves by putting an end to a war or doing some signal military service to the state. "You shall have a triumph, in consequence of having conquered your foes, and led captivity captive."

12. *Wherefore I will not be negligent.* He had already written one Epistle; this is the second.

13. *As long as I am in this tabernacle.* By *tabernacle* we are to understand his body.

14. *Knowing that shortly I must put off.* Peter plainly refers to the conversation between our Lord and himself related in John xxi. 18-19. And it is likely that he had now a particular intimation that he was *shortly* to seal the truth with his blood. But as our Lord told him that his death would take place when he should be old, being aged now he might on this ground fairly suppose that his departure was at hand.

15. *Moreover, I will endeavour.* And is not this endeavor seen in these two Epistles? By leaving these among them, even after his decease they had *these things always in remembrance. After my decease.* "After my going out," i.e., of his tabernacle.

16. *Cunningly devised fables.* I think from the apostle's using *eyewitnesses,* or rather "beholders," in the end of the verse, it is probable that he means those *cunningly devised fables* among the heathens, concerning the appearance of their gods on earth in human form. And to gain the greater credit to these fables, the priests and statesmen instituted what they called the "mysteries" of the gods, in which the fabulous appearance of the gods was represented in mystic shows. But one particular show none but the fully initiated were permitted to behold; hence they were entitled "beholders." This show was probably some resplendent image of the god, imitating life, which, by its glory, dazzled the eyes of the beholders, while their ears were ravished by hymns sung in its praise; to this it was natural enough for Peter to allude when speaking about the transfiguration of Christ. Here the indescribably resplendent majesty of the great God was manifested, as far as it could be, in conjunction with that human body in which the fullness of the Divinity dwelt. "And we," says the apostle, "were beholders of His own majesty." Here was no trick, no feigned show; we saw Him in His glory whom thousands saw before and afterwards; and we have made known to you the *power and coming,* the appearance and presence, of our Lord Jesus; and we call you to feel the exceeding greatness of this power in your conversion, and the glory of this appearance in His revelation by the power of His Spirit to your souls. These things we have witnessed, and these things you have experienced; and therefore we can confidently say that neither you nor we have followed cunningly devised fables, but that blessed gospel which is the power of God to the salvation of everyone that believes.

17. *For he received . . . honour and glory.* In His transfiguration our Lord received from the Father *honour* in the voice or declaration which said, "This is My Son, the beloved One, in whom I have delighted." And He received *glory* when, penetrated with and involved in that excellent glory, "the fashion of his countenance was altered," for His face did shine as the sun, "and his raiment was white and glistering," exceeding white like snow.

18. *And this voice . . . we heard.* That is, himself, James, and John heard it, and saw this glory; for these only were the "beholders" on the holy mount. It is worthy of remark that our blessed Lord, who came to give a new law to mankind, appeared on this *holy mount* with splendor and great glory, as God did when He came on the *holy mount,* Sinai, to give the old law to Moses. And when the voice came from the excellent glory, "This is My Son, the beloved One, in whom I have delighted; hear Him," the authority of the old law was taken away.

19. *We have also a more sure word of prophecy.* "We have the prophetic doctrine more firm or more confirmed"; for in this sense the word is used in several places in the New Testament. See 1 Cor. i. 6: "Even as the testimony of Christ was confirmed in [among] you"; 2 Cor. i. 21; Col. ii. 7; Heb. ii. 3; vi. 16. This is the literal sense of the passage in question, and this sense removes that ambiguity from the text which has given rise to so many different interpretations. Taken according to the common translation, it seems to say that *prophecy* is a surer evidence of divine revelation than miracles; and so it has been understood. The meaning of the apostle appears to be this: The voice from heaven and the miraculous transfiguration of His person have confirmed the prophetic doctrine concerning Him. And to this doctrine, thus confirmed, you do well to take heed; for it is that light that shines in the dark place, in the Gentile world, as well as among the Jews; and this you must continue to do till the day of His second, last, and most glorious appearing to judge the world comes; and the *day star—phosphoros,* "this light-bringer"—*arise in your hearts*—manifest himself to your eternal consolation. The word *phosphoros* generally signified the planet Venus, when she is the morning star; and thus she is called in most European nations.

20. *Knowing this first.* Considering this as a first principle, *that no prophecy of the scripture,* whether it referred to above or any other, *is of any private interpretation*—proceeds from the prophet's own knowledge or invention. The word signifies also "impetus, impulse"; and probably this is the best sense here: not by the mere private impulse of his own mind.

21. *For the prophecy came not in old time.* That is, in any former time, *by the will of man,* by a man's own searching, conjecture, or calculation; *but holy men of God,* persons separat-

ed from the world and devoted to God's service, *spake . . . moved by the Holy Ghost.* So far were they from inventing these prophetic declarations concerning Christ or any future event that they were "carried away," out of themselves and out of the whole region, as it were, of human knowledge and conjecture, by the Holy Ghost, who, without their knowing anything of the matter, dictated to them what to speak and what to write.

CHAPTER 2

False teachers foretold, who shall bring in destructive doctrines and shall pervert many, but at last be destroyed by the judgments of God, 1-3. Instances of God's judgments in the rebellious angels, 4. In the antediluvians, 5. In the cities of Sodom and Gomorrah, 6-8. The Lord knows how to deliver the godly, as well as to punish the ungodly, 9. The character of those seducing teachers and their disciples; they are unclean, presumptuous, speak evil of dignities, adulterous, covetous, and cursed, 10-14. Have forsaken the right way, copy the conduct of Balaam, speak great swelling words, and pervert those who had escaped from error, 15-19. The miserable state of those who, having escaped the corruption that is in the world, have turned back like the dog to his vomit, and the washed swine to her wallowing in the mire, 20-22.

1. *But there were false prophets.* There were not only holy men of God among the Jews, who prophesied by divine inspiration, but there were also false prophets, whose prophecies were from their own imagination, and perverted many. *As there shall be false teachers among you.* At a very early period of the Christian Church many heresies sprang up. *Damnable heresies.* "Heresies of destruction"; such as, if followed, would lead a man to perdition. And these they will "bring in privately"—cunningly, without making much noise, and as covertly as possible. It would be better to translate "destructive heresies" than *damnable.*

2. *Many shall follow.* "Will follow," because determined to gratify their sinful propensities. *Pernicious ways.* "Their destructions"; i.e., the "heresies of destruction," or "destructive opinions," mentioned above. But instead of "destructions," "lasciviousnesses or uncleannesses" is the reading of upwards of sixty MSS., most of which are among the most ancient, correct, and authentic. The word "lasciviousnesses" is undoubtedly the true reading, and this points out what the nature of the heresies was. It was a sort of antinomianism; they pampered and indulged the lusts of the flesh. *By reason of whom.* These were persons who professed Christianity; and because they were called Christians, and followed such abominable practices, *the way of truth,* the Christian religion, was "blasphemed." Had they called themselves by any name but that of Christ, His religion would not have suffered.

3. *And through covetousness,* that they might get money to spend upon their lusts, *with feigned words,* with "counterfeit tales, false narrations" of pretended facts, "lying miracles, fabulous legends." *Whose judgment now of a long time.* From the beginning God has condemned sin and inflicted suitable punishments on transgressors; and has promised in His Word, from the earliest ages, to pour out His indignation on the wicked. The punishment, therefore, so long ago predicted shall fall on these impure and incorrigible sinners; and the "condemnation" which is denounced against them *slumbereth not*—it is alert; it is on its way; it is hurrying on, and must soon overtake them.

4. *For if God spared not the angels.* The angels were originally placed in a state of probation, some having fallen and some having stood proves this. How long that probation was to last to them, and what was the particular test of their fidelity, we know not; nor indeed do we know what was their sin, nor when nor how they fell. Jude says, They "kept not their first estate, but left their own habitation"; which seems to indicate that they got discontented with their lot and aspired to higher honors, or perhaps to celestial domination. *But cast them down to hell, and delivered them into chains of darkness.* "But with chains of darkness confining them in Tartarus, delivered them over to be kept to judgment"; or, "Sinking them into Tartarus, delivered them over into custody for punishment, to chains of darkness." *Chains of darkness* is a highly poetic expression. Darkness binds them on all hands; and so dense and strong is this darkness that it cannot be broken through; they cannot deliver themselves nor be delivered by others. As the word "Tartarus" is found nowhere else in the New Testament, nor does it appear in the Septuagint, we must have recourse to the Greek writers for its meaning. The ancient Greeks appear to have received, by tradition, an account of the punishment of the "fallen angels," and of bad men after death; and their poets did, in conformity I presume with that account, make Tartarus the place where the giants who rebelled against Jupiter, and the souls of the wicked, were confined.

5. *Spared not the old world.* The apostle's argument is this: If God spared not the rebellious angels, nor the sinful antediluvians, nor the cities of Sodom and Gomorrah, He will not spare those wicked teachers who corrupt the pure doctrines of Christianity. *Saved Noah, the eighth.* Some think that the words should be translated, "Noah, the eighth preacher of righteousness"; but it seems most evident, from 1 Pet. iii. 20, that eight persons are here meant, which were the whole that were saved in the ark, viz., Shem, Ham, Japheth, and their three wives, six; Noah's wife, seven; and Noah himself, the eighth. The form of expression, *Noah, the eighth,* i.e., Noah and seven more, is most common in the Greek language. *World of the ungodly.* A whole race without God—without any pure worship or rational religion.

7. *Vexed with the filthy conversation.* "Being exceedingly pained with the unclean conduct of those lawless persons." What this was, see in the history, Genesis xix.

8. *That righteous man dwelling among them.* Lot, after his departure from Abraham, lived at Sodom a space of about twenty years. The word "tormented" is not less emphatic than the word "grievously pained" in the preceding verse, and shows what this man must have felt in dwelling so long among a people so abandoned.

9. *The Lord knoweth how to deliver the godly.* The preservation and deliverance of Lot gave the apostle occasion to remark that God knew as well to save as to destroy; and that His goodness led Him as forcibly to save righteous Lot as His justice did to destroy the rebellious in the instances already adduced.

10. *But chiefly them that walk.* That is, God will in the most signal manner punish them that walk after the flesh--addict themselves to

sodomitical practices, and the "lust of pollution," probably alluding to those most abominable practices where men abuse themselves and abuse one another. *Despise government.* They brave the power and authority of the civil magistrate, practicing their abominations so as to keep out of the reach of the letter of the law. And they *speak evil of dignities*—they blaspheme civil government; they abhor the restraints laid upon men by the laws, and would wish all governments destroyed that they might live as they list. *Presumptuous are they.* They are bold and daring, headstrong, regardless of fear. *Selfwilled.* Self-sufficient; presuming on themselves; following their own opinions, which no authority can induce them to relinquish. *Are not afraid to speak evil of dignities.* They are lawless and disobedient, spurn all human authority, and speak contemptuously of all legal and civil jurisdiction.

11. *Whereas angels.* This is a difficult verse, but the meaning seems to be this: The holy angels, who are represented as bringing an account of the actions of the fallen angels before the Lord in judgment, simply state the facts without exaggeration, and without permitting anything of a bitter, reviling, or railing spirit to enter into their accusations. See Zech. iii. 1 and Jude 9, to the former of which Peter evidently alludes.

12. *But these, as natural brute beasts.* "As those natural animals void of reason," following only the gross instinct of nature, being governed by neither reason nor religion. *Made to be taken and destroyed.* Intended to be taken with nets and gins and then destroyed, because of their fierce and destructive nature. So these false teachers and insurgents must be treated; first incarcerated, and then brought to judgment, that they may have the reward of their doings. And thus, by "blaspheming what they do not understand," they at last perish in their own corruption; i.e., their corrupt doctrines and vicious practices.

13. *They that count it pleasure to riot in the day time.* Most sinners, in order to practice their abominable pleasures, seek the secrecy of the night; but these, bidding defiance to all decorum, decency, and shame, take the open day, and thus proclaim their impurities to the sun. *Spots . . . and blemishes.* They are a disgrace to the Christian name. *Sporting themselves.* Forming opinions which give license to sin and then acting on those opinions, and thus rioting in their own deceits. *While they feast with you.* It appears they held a kind of communion with the Church, and attended sacred festivals, which they desecrated with their own unhallowed opinions and conduct.

14. *Having eyes full of adultery.* "Of an adulteress"; being ever bent on the gratification of their sensual desires, so that they are represented as having an adulteress constantly before their eyes, and that their eyes can take in no other object but her. *Cannot cease from sin.* "Which cease not from sin"; they might cease from sin, but they do not; they love and practice it. *Beguiling unstable souls.* The metaphor is taken from adulterers seducing unwary, inexperienced, and light, trifling women; so do those false teachers seduce those who are not established in righteousness. *Exercised with covetous practices.* The metaphor is taken from the

agonistae in the Grecian games, who exercised themselves in those feats, such as wrestling, boxing, running, in which they proposed to contend in the public games. These persons had their hearts schooled in nefarious practices; they had exercised themselves till they were perfectly expert in all the arts of seduction, overreaching, and every kind of fraud. *Cursed children.* Such not only live under God's curse here, but they are heirs to it hereafter.

15. *Which have forsaken the right way.* As Balaam did, who, although God showed him the right way, took one contrary to it, preferring the reward offered him by Balak to the approbation and blessing of God. *The way of Balaam* is the counsel of Balaam. He counselled the Moabites to give their most beautiful young women to the Israelitish youth, that they might be enticed by them to commit idolatry. See the notes on Num. xxii. 5 ff. and xxiii. 1 ff.

16. *The dumb ass speaking with man's voice.* See the note on Num. xxii. 28.

17. *These are wells without water.* Persons who by their profession should furnish the water of life to souls athirst for salvation, but they have not this water. *Clouds that are carried with a tempest.* In a time of great drought, to see clouds beginning to cover the face of the heavens raises the expectation of rain; but to see these "carried off" by a sudden *tempest* is a dreary disappointment. These false teachers were equally as unprofitable as the empty well, or the light, dissipated cloud. *To whom the mist of darkness is reserved.* That is, an eternal separation from the presence of God and the glory of His power. They shall be thrust into "outer darkness," Matt. viii. 12. Instead of *clouds*, "and mists" is the reading in a number of MSS. and in several of the fathers.

18. *They speak great swelling words of vanity.* The word signifies things of great magnitude, grand, superb, sublime; it sometimes signifies "inflated, bombastic." *Those that were clean escaped.* Those who, through hearing the doctrines of the gospel, had been converted were perverted by those false teachers.

19. *While they promise them liberty.* Either to live in the highest degrees of spiritual good or a freedom from the Roman yoke; or from the yoke of the law, or what they might term needless restraints. Their own conduct showed the falsity of their system, for they were slaves to every disgraceful lust. *For of whom a man is overcome.* This is an allusion to the ancient custom of selling for slaves those whom they had conquered and captivated in war.

20. *The pollutions of the world.* Sin in general, and particularly superstition, idolatry, and lasciviousness. These are called *miasmata*, things that "infect, pollute, and defile." The word was anciently used, and is in use at the present day, to express those noxious particles of effluvia proceeding from persons infected with contagious and dangerous diseases; or from dead and corrupt bodies, stagnant and putrid waters, marshes, etc., by which the sound and healthy may be infected and destroyed. The world is here represented as one large, putrid marsh, or corrupt body, sending off its destructive *miasmata* everywhere and in every direction, so that none can escape its contagion, and none can be healed of the great epidemic disease of

sin, but by the mighty power and skill of God. Now it is by *the knowledge of the Lord and Saviour Jesus Christ,* as says Peter, that we escape the destructive influence of these contagious *miasmata.* But if, after having been healed, and *escaped* the death to which we were exposed, we get *again entangled,* "enfolded, enveloped" with them, then *the latter end* will be *worse . . . than the beginning,* forasmuch as we shall have sinned against more light.

21. *For it had been better for them not to have known.* For the reasons assigned above; because they have sinned against more mercy, are capable of more sin, and are liable to greater punishment. *The holy commandment.* The whole religion of Christ is contained in this one commandment, "Thou shalt love the Lord thy God with all thy heart, with all thy soul, with all thy mind, and with all thy strength; and thy neighbor as thyself."

22. *According to the true proverb.* This seems to be a reference to Prov. xxvi. 11: "As a dog returneth to his vomit, so a fool returneth to [repeateth] his folly."

CHAPTER 3

The apostle shows his design in writing this and the preceding Epistle, 1-2. Describes the nature of the heresies which should take place in the last times, 3-8. A thousand years with the Lord are but as a day, 9. He will come and judge the world as He has promised, and the heavens and the earth shall be burned up, 10. How those should live who expect these things, 11-12. Of the new heavens and the new earth, and the necessity of being prepared for this great change, 13-14. Concerning some difficult things in Paul's Epistles, 15-16. We must watch against the error of the wicked, grow in grace, and give all glory to God, 17-18.

1. *This second epistle.* In order to guard them against the seductions of false teachers, he calls to their remembrance the doctrine of the ancient prophets, and the commands or instructions of the apostles, all founded on the same basis.

3. *There shall come . . . scoffers.* Persons who shall endeavor to turn all religion into ridicule, as this is the most likely way to depreciate truth in the sight of the giddy multitude. The scoffers, having no solid argument to produce against revelation, affect to laugh at it, and get superficial thinkers to laugh with them. *Walking after their own lusts.* Here is the true source of all infidelity. The gospel of Jesus is pure and holy, and requires a holy heart and holy life. They wish to follow their own *lusts,* and consequently cannot brook the restraints of the gospel; therefore they labor to prove that it is not true. There is a remarkable addition here in almost every MS. and version of note: "There shall come in the last days, in mockery, scoffers walking after their own lusts." This is the reading of a number of MSS. and several of the fathers. They come "in mockery"; this is their spirit and temper. They have no desire to find out truth; they take up the Bible merely with the design of turning it into ridicule. *The last days* probably refer to the conclusion of the Jewish polity, which was then at hand.

5. *For this they willingly are ignorant of.* They shut their eyes against the light and refuse all evidence; what does not answer their purpose they will not know. *By the word of God the heavens were of old.* Moses: "In the beginning God created the heaven and the earth. And the earth was without form, and void; and

darkness was upon the face of the deep." Now these heavens and earth which God made in the beginning, and which He says were at first formless and empty, and which He calls "the deep," are in the very next verse called "waters"; from which it is evident that Moses teaches that the earth was made out of some fluid substance, to which the name of "water" is properly given. The *earth,* which was originally formed *out of the water,* "subsists by water."

7. *But the heavens and the earth, which are now.* The present earth and its atmosphere, which are liable to the same destruction, because the same means still exist (for there is still water enough to drown the earth, and there is iniquity enough to induce God to destroy it and its inhabitants), are nevertheless *kept in store,* "treasured up," kept in God's storehouse, to be destroyed, not by water, but by *fire* at *the day of judgment.*

8. *Be not ignorant.* Though they are willfully ignorant, neglect not the means of instruction. *One day is with the Lord as a thousand years.* That is: All time is as nothing before Him, because in the presence as in the nature of God all is eternity; therefore nothing is long, nothing short, before Him. The words of the apostle seem to be a quotation from Ps. xc. 4.

9. *But is longsuffering.* It is not slackness that induced God to prolong the respite of ungodly men, but His long-suffering, His unwillingness that any should perish; and therefore He spared them, that they might have additional offers of grace and be led to repentance. As God is *not willing that any should perish,* and as He is willing *that all should come to repentance,* consequently He has never devised nor decreed the damnation of any man, nor has He rendered it impossible for any soul to be saved.

10. *The day of the Lord will come.* See Matt. xxiv. 43, to which the apostle seems to allude.

11. *All these things shall be dissolved.* They will all be "separated," all "decomposed," but none of them destroyed. And as they are the original matter out of which God formed the terraqueous globe, consequently they may enter again into the composition of a new system; and therefore the apostle says, v. 13: "We . . . look for new heavens and a new earth"—the others being decomposed, a new system is to be formed out of their materials. *What manner of persons ought ye to be?* Some put the note of interrogation at the end of this clause, and join the remaining part with the twelfth verse, thus: "Seeing then that all these things shall be dissolved, what manner of persons ought ye to be? By holy conversation and godliness, expecting and earnestly desiring the coming of the day of God," etc.

12. The word which we translate *hasting unto* should be rendered "earnestly desiring" or "wishing for," which is a frequent meaning of the word in the best Greek writers.

13. *We, according to his promise, look for new heavens.* The promise to which it is supposed the apostle alludes is found Isa. lxv. 17: "Behold, I create new heavens and a new earth: and the former shall not be remembered, nor come into mind"; and chap. lxvi. 22: "For as the new heavens and the new earth, which I

will make, shall remain before me, saith the Lord, so shall your seed." Now although these may be interpreted of the glory of the gospel dispensation, yet, if Peter refer to them, they must have a more extended meaning.

14. *Seeing that ye look for such things.* As you profess that such a state of things shall take place and have the expectation of enjoying the blessedness of it, *be diligent* in the use of every means and influence of grace, *that ye may be found of him*—the Lord Jesus, the Judge of quick and dead; *without spot*—any contagion of sin in your souls; *and blameless*—being not only holy and innocent, but useful in your lives.

15. *And account that the longsuffering of our Lord.* Conclude that God's long-suffering with the world is a proof that He designs men to be saved. *According to the wisdom given unto him.* That is, according to the measure of the divine inspiration by which he was qualified for the divine work and by which he was so capable of entering into the deep things of God. It is worthy of remark that Paul's Epistles are ranked among the "scriptures"; a term applied to those writings which are divinely inspired, and to those only.

16. *As also in all his epistles, speaking in them of these things.* For example, he has spoken of Christ's coming to judgment, 1 Thess. iii. 13; iv. 14-18; 2 Thess. i. 7-10; Titus ii. 13. And of the resurrection of the dead, 1 Cor. xv. 22; Phil. iii. 20-21. And of the burning of the earth, 2 Thess. i. 8. And of the heavenly country, 2 Cor. v. 1-10. And of the introduction of the righteous into that country, 1 Thess. iv. 17; Heb. iv. 9; xii. 14, 18, 24. And of the judgment of all mankind by Christ, Rom. xiv. 10.

17. *Seeing ye know these things before.* Seeing that by prophets and apostles you have been thus forewarned, *beware,* "keep watch, be on your guard"; cleave to God and the word of His grace, lest you be *led away* from the truth delivered by the prophets and apostles, *by the error of the wicked,* "of the lawless"—those who wrest the Scriptures to make them countenance their lusts and lawless practices. *Fall from your own stedfastness.* From that faith in Christ which has put you in possession of that grace which establishes the heart.

18. *But grow in grace.* Increase in the image and favor of God. *To him,* the Lord Jesus, *be glory*—all honor and excellency attributed *both now,* in this present state, *and for ever,* "to the day of eternity"—that in which death, and misery, and trial, and darkness, and change, and time itself are to the righteous forever at an end. It is eternity; and this eternity is one unalterable, interminable, unclouded, and unchangeable day!

The First Epistle of

JOHN

On the term *epistle,* as applied to this work of John, it may be necessary to make a few remarks. There is properly nothing of the epistolary style in this work; it is addressed neither to any particular person nor to any church.

The writer does not mention himself in either the beginning or the ending; and, although this can be no objection against its authenticity, yet it is some proof that the work was never intended to be considered in the light of an epistle.

(1) Is it a tract or dissertation upon the more sublime parts of Christianity? (2) Is it a polemical discourse against heretics, particularly the Gnostics, or some of their teachers, who were disturbing the churches where John dwelt? (3) Is it a sermon, the subject of which is God's love to man in the mission of Jesus Christ, from which our obligations to love and serve Him are particularly inferred? (4) Or is it a collection of Christian aphorisms, made by John himself; and put together as they occurred to his mind, without any intended order or method? Much might be said on all these heads of inquiry, and the issue would be that the idea of its being an epistle of any kind must be relinquished; and yet *epistle* is its general denomination through all antiquity.

It is a matter, however, of little importance what its title may be or to what species of literary composition it belongs, while we know that it is the genuine work of John; of the holiest man who ever breathed; of one who was most intimately acquainted with the doctrine and mind of his Lord; of one who was admitted to the closest fellowship with his Saviour; and who has treated of the deepest things that can be experienced or comprehended in the Christian life.

As to distinct heads of discourse, it does not appear to me that any were intended by the apostle; he wrote just as the subjects occurred to his mind, or rather as the Holy Spirit gave him utterance; and although technical order is not here to be expected, yet nothing like disorder or confusion can be found in the whole work.

CHAPTER 1

The testimony of the apostle concerning the reality of the person and doctrine of Christ; and the end for which he bears this testimony, 1-4. God is Light, and none can have fellowship with Him who do not walk in the light; those who walk in the light are cleansed from all unrighteousness by the blood of Christ, 5-7. No man can say that he has not sinned; but God is faithful and just to cleanse from all unrighteousness them who confess their sins, 8-10.

1. *That which was from the beginning.* That glorious Personage, Jesus Christ the Lord, who was from eternity; Him, being manifested in the flesh, we have heard proclaim the doctrine of eternal life; with our own eyes have we seen Him, not transiently, for we have looked upon Him frequently; *and our hands have handled*—frequently touched—His person; and we have had every proof of the identity and reality of this glorious Being that our senses of hearing, seeing, and feeling could possibly require.

2. *For the life was manifested.* The Lord Jesus, who is the Creator of all things and the Fountain of life, was manifested in the flesh, *and we have seen* Him, and in consequence bear witness to Him as the Fountain and Author of eternal life. For He who was from eternity with the Father *was manifested unto us,* His apostles, and to the whole of the Jewish nation, and preached that doctrine of *eternal life* which I have before delivered to the world in my gospel, and which I now further confirm by this Epistle.

3. *That which we have seen and heard.* We deliver nothing by hearsay, nothing by tradition, nothing from conjecture; we have had the fullest certainty of all that we write and preach. *That ye also may have fellowship with us.* That you may be preserved from all false doctrine, and have a real "participation" with us, apostles of the grace, peace, love, and life of God.

4. *That your joy may be full.* You have already tasted that the Lord is good; but I am now going to show you the height of your Christian calling, that your happiness may be complete, being thoroughly cleansed from all sin, and filled with the fullness of God.

5. *This then is the message.* This is the grand principle on which all depends, *which we have heard* from *him. God is light*—the Source of wisdom, knowledge, holiness, and happiness; and *in him is no darkness at all*—no ignorance, no imperfection, no sinfulness, no misery.

6. *If we say that we have fellowship.* Having *fellowship,* "communion," with God necessarily implies a partaking of the divine nature. Now if a man profess to have such communion, and *walk in darkness*—live an irreligious and sinful life—he lies in the profession which he makes, and does *not the truth*—does not walk according to the directions of the gospel.

7. *But if we walk in the light.* If, having received the principle of holiness from Him, we live a holy and righteous life, deriving continual light, power, and life from Him, then we *have fellowship one with another;* that is, *we* have communion with God, and God condescends to hold communion with us. *The blood of Jesus Christ.* The meritorious efficacy of His passion and death has purged our consciences from dead works, and *cleanseth us,* "continues to cleanse us," i.e., to keep clean what it has made clean. And being cleansed from all sin is what every believer should look for, what he has a right to expect, and what he must have in this life in order to be prepared to meet his God. Christ is not a partial Saviour; He saves to the uttermost, and He cleanses from all sin.

8. *If we say that we have no sin.* This is tantamount to v. 10: "If we say that we have not sinned." "All have sinned, and come short of the glory of God"; and therefore every man needs a Saviour, such as Christ is. It is very likely that the heretics, against whose evil doctrines the apostle writes, denied that they had any sin or needed any Saviour. Indeed the Gnostics even denied that Christ suffered; the Aeon, or Divine Being that dwelt in the man Christ Jesus, according to them, left Him when He was taken by the Jews; and He being but a common man, His sufferings and death had neither merit nor efficacy. *We deceive ourselves.* By supposing that we have no guilt, no sinfulness, and consequently have no need of the blood of Christ as an atoning sacrifice. *The truth is not in us.* We have no knowledge of the gospel of Jesus, the whole of which is founded on this most awful truth—all have sinned, all are guilty, all are unholy; and none can redeem himself. Hence it was necessary that Jesus Christ should become incarnated and suffer and die to bring men to God.

9. *If we confess our sins.* If, from a deep sense of our guilt, impurity, and helplessness, we humble ourselves before God, acknowledging our iniquity, His holiness, and our own utter helplessness, and implore mercy for His sake who has died for us. *He is faithful,* because to such He has promised mercy, Ps. xxxii. 5; Prov. xxviii. 13; *and just,* for Christ has died for us, and thus made an atonement to the divine justice; so that God can now be just, and yet the Justifier of him who believes in Jesus. *And to cleanse us from all unrighteousness.* Not only to forgive the sin, but to purify the heart. Observe, (1) Sin exists in the soul after two modes or forms: (*a*) In *guilt,* which requires forgiveness or pardon; (*b*) In *pollution,* which requires cleansing. (2) *Guilt,* to be forgiven, must be confessed; and *pollution,* to be cleansed, must be also confessed. In order to find mercy, a man must know and feel himself to be a sinner, that he may fervently apply to God for pardon; in order to get a clean heart, a man must know and feel its depravity, acknowledge and deplore it before God, in order to be fully sanctified. (3) Few are pardoned, because they do not feel and confess their sins; and few are sanctified or cleansed from all sin, because they do not feel and confess their own sore, and the plague of their hearts. (4) As the blood of Jesus Christ, the merit of His passion and death, applied by faith, purges the conscience from all dead works, so the same cleanses the heart from all unrighteousness. (5) As all unrighteousness is sin, so he that is cleansed from all unrighteousness is cleansed from all sin. To attempt to evade this, and plead for the continuance of sin in the heart through life, is ungrateful, wicked, and even blasphemous; for as he who says he has not sinned, v. 10, makes God a liar, who has declared the contrary through every part of His revelation; so he that says the blood of Christ either cannot or will not cleanse us from all sin in this life gives also the lie to his Maker, who has declared the contrary, and thus shows that the word, the doctrine of God, is not in him. Reader, it is the birthright of every child of God to be cleansed from all sin, to keep himself unspotted from the world, and so to live as nevermore to offend his Maker. All things are possible to him that believes, because all things are possible to the infinitely meritorious blood and energetic Spirit of the Lord Jesus.

CHAPTER 2

He exhorts them not to sin; yet encourages those who may have fallen, by the hope of mercy through Christ, who is a Propitiation for the sins of the whole world, 1-2. He who knows God keeps His commandments; and he who professes to abide in Christ ought to walk as Christ walked, 3-6. The old and new commandment, that we should walk in the light and love the brethren, 7-11. The apostle's description of the different states in the family of God: little children, young men, and fathers; and directions to each, 12-15. A statement of what prevails in the world, 16-17. Cautions against antichrists, 18-23. Exhortations to persevere in what they had received, and to continue to follow that anointing of the Divine Spirit by which they could discern all men, and know all things necessary to their salvation, and proper to prepare them for eternal glory, 24-29.

1. *My little children.* "My beloved children"; the address of an affectionate father to children whom he tenderly loves. The term also refers to the apostle's authority as their spiritual father, and their obligation to obey as his spiritual children. *That ye sin not.* This is the language of the whole Scripture; of every dispensation, ordinance, institution, doctrine, and word of God. *And if any man sin.* If, through ignorance, inexperience, the violence of temptation, unwatchfulness, you have fallen into sin and grieve the Spirit of God, do not continue in the sin nor under the guilt; do not despair of being again restored to the favor of God. Your case, it is true, is deeply deplorable, but not desperate; there is still hope, for—*we have an advocate with the Father.* We still have Him before the throne who died for our offenses and rose again for our justification; and there He makes intercession for us. He is the *righteous;* He who suffered, "the just for the unjust, that he might bring us to God." Do not therefore despair, but have immediate recourse to God through Him.

2. *And he is the propitiation,* the "atoning sacrifice," *for our sins.* This is the proper sense of the word as used in the Septuagint, where it often occurs; and is the translation of *asham,* an "oblation for sin," Amos viii. 14; *chattath,* a "sacrifice for sin," Ezek. xliv. 27; *kippur,* an "atonement," Nom. v. 8. The word is used only here and in chap. iv. 10. *And not for ours only.* It is not for us apostles that He has died, nor exclusively for the Jewish people, but for *the whole world,* Gentiles as well as Jews, all the descendants of Adam. The apostle does not say that He died for any select part of the inhabitants of the earth, but for all mankind, and the attempt to limit this is a violent outrage against God and His Word. For the meaning of the word which we here translate "advocate" see the note on John xiv. 16.

3. *And hereby we do know that we know him.* If we keep the commandments of God, loving Him with all our hearts, and our neighbors as ourselves, we have the fullest proof that we have the true saving knowledge of God and His Christ. The Gnostics pretended to much knowledge, but their knowledge left them in possession of all their bad passions and unholy habits; they therefore gave no proof that they had known either God or His Son, Jesus; nor is any man properly acquainted with God who is still under the power of his sins.

4. *He that saith, I know him.* This is a severe blow against those false teachers, and against all pretenders to religious knowledge, who live under the power of their sins; and against all antinomians, and false boasters in the righteous-

ness of Christ as a covering for their personal unholiness. They are all liars, and no *truth* of God is in them.

5. *But whoso keepeth his word.* Conscientiously observes His doctrine, the spirit and letter of the religion of Christ. *Is the love of God perfected.* The design of God's love in sending Jesus Christ into the world to die for the sin of man "is accomplished" in that man who receives the doctrine and applies for the salvation provided for him. *That we are in him.* That we have entered into His spirit and views, received His salvation, have been enabled to walk in the light, and have communion with Him by the Holy Spirit.

6. *Abideth in him.* He who not only professes to have known Christ, but also that he has communion with Him and abides in His favor, should prove the truth of his profession by walking as Christ walked; living a life of devotion and obedience to God, and of benevolence and beneficence to his neighbor. Thus Christ walked; and He has left us an example that we should follow His steps. To "be in Christ," v. 5, is to be converted to the Christian faith, and to have received the remission of sins. To "abide in Christ," v. 6, is to continue in that state of salvation, growing in grace, and in the knowledge of our Lord Jesus Christ.

7. *Brethren, I write no new commandment.* There seems a contradiction between this and the next verse. But the apostle appears to speak, not so much of any difference in the essence of the precept itself, as in reference to the degrees of light and grace belonging to the Mosaic and Christian dispensations. It was ever the command of God that man should receive His light, walk by that light, and love Him and one another. But this commandment was renewed by Christ with much latitude and spirituality of meaning; and also with much additional light to see its extent, and grace to observe it. It may therefore be called the "old commandment," which was "from the beginning"; and also a "new commandment" revealed afresh and illustrated by Christ. Instead of *brethren,* a number of MSS., along with several of the fathers, have "beloved." This is without doubt the true reading.

8. *Which thing is true in him and in you.* It is true that Christ loved the world so well as to lay down His life for it; and it was true in them, in all His faithful followers at that time, who were ready to lay down their lives for the testimony of Jesus. *The darkness is past.* The total thick darkness of the heathen world and the comparative darkness of the Mosaic dispensation are now passing away, and the pure and superior light of Christianity is now diffusing its beams everywhere. He does not say that the darkness was all gone by, but "is passing away"; he does not say that the fullness of the light had appeared, but it "is now shining," and will shine more and more to the perfect day; for the darkness passes away in proportion as the light shines and increases.

9. *He that saith he is in the light.* He that professes to be a convert to Christianity, even in the lowest degree. *And hateth his brother*—not only does not love him, but wills and does him evil, as the Jews did the Gentiles. *Is in darkness*—has received no saving knowledge of the truth.

10. *He that loveth his brother.* That is, his neighbor, his fellow creature, whether Jew or Gentile, so as to bear him continual goodwill, and to be ready to do him every kind office. *Abideth in the light*—not only gives proof that he has received Christ Jesus the Lord, but that he walks in Him, that he retains the grace of his justification, and grows therein. *And there is none occasion of stumbling in him.* "And there is no stumbling block in him"; he neither gives nor receives offense. Love prevents him from giving any to his neighbor; and love prevents him from receiving any from his neighbor, because it leads him to put the best construction on everything.

11. *But he that hateth his brother is in darkness.* He is still in his heathen or unconverted state. *And walketh in darkness,* his conduct being a proof of that state. *And knoweth not whither he goeth*—having no proper knowledge of God or eternal things; and cannot tell whether he is going to heaven or hell, *because that darkness hath blinded his eyes*—darkened his whole soul, mind, and heart.

12. *I write unto you, little children.* "Beloved children" (see on v. 1), those who were probably the apostle's own converts, and members of the church over which he presided. But it may be applied to young converts in general; therefore he says of them that their sins were forgiven them for His name's sake; i.e., on account of Jesus, the Saviour.

13. *I write unto you, fathers.* By *fathers* it is very likely that the apostle means persons who had embraced Christianity on its first promulgation in Judea and in the Lesser Asia, some of whom had probably seen Christ in the flesh; for this appears to be what is meant by *Ye have known him . . . from the beginning.* But *him that is from the beginning* may mean Jesus Christ in the eternity of His nature; see John i. 1-2. *I write unto you, young man.* These were confirmed disciples of Christ; persons who were well-grounded in the truth, had been thoroughly exercised in the Christian warfare, were no longer agitated by doubts and fears, but had arrived at the abiding testimony of the Spirit of God in their consciences; hence they are said to have *overcome the wicked one,* v. 14. They were persons in the prime of life, and in the zenith of their faith and love. *I write unto you, little children.* A very different term from that used in the twelfth verse, which means "beloved children," as we have already seen. This is another class, and their state is differently described: *Ye have known the Father.*

14. *The word of God abideth in you.* You have not only thoroughly known and digested the divine doctrine, but your hearts are molded into it.

15. *Love not the world.* The Holy Spirit saw it necessary to caution these against the love of the world, the inordinate desire of earthly things. Covetousness is the predominant vice of old age: Ye "fathers," *love not the world.* The things which are in the world, its profits, pleasures, and honors, have the strongest allurements for youth; therefore, you "young men, little children, and babes," love not *the things* of this world. *The love of the Father is not in him.* The love of God and the love of earthly things are incompatible.

16. *For all that is in the world.* All that it can boast of, all that it can promise, is only sensual, transient gratification, and even this promise it cannot fulfill; so that its warmest votaries can complain loudest of their disappointment. *Is not of the Father.* Nothing of these inordinate attachments either comes from or leads to God. They are of this world; here they begin, flourish, and end. They deprave the mind, divert it from divine pursuits, and render it utterly incapable of spiritual enjoyments.

17. *The world passeth away.* All these things are continually fading and perishing, and the very state in which they are possessed is changing perpetually. *And the lust thereof.* The men of this world, their vain pursuits, and delusive pleasures are passing away in their successive generations, and their very memory perishes. *But he that doeth the will of God*—that seeks the pleasure, profit, and honor that comes from above—shall abide *for ever,* always happy through time and eternity, because God, the unchangeable Source of felicity, is his Portion.

18. *Little children, it is the last time.* This is the last dispensation of grace and mercy to mankind. *Antichrist shall come.* Who is this antichrist? Any person, thing, doctrine, system of religion, polity, which is opposed to Christ, and to the spirit and spread of His gospel, is antichrist. *Many antichrists.* Many false prophets, false Messiahs, heretics, and corrupters of the truth. *Whereby we know that it is the last time.* That time which our Lord has predicted, and of which He has warned us.

19. *They went out from us.* These heretics had belonged to our Christian assemblies; they professed Christianity, and do so still. They are not Christians; we abhor their conduct and their creed. We never sent them to teach. *They were not of us.* For a considerable time before they left our assemblies they gave proofs that they had departed from the faith; *for if they had been of us,* if they had been apostles, and continued in the firm belief of the Christian doctrines, they would not have departed from us to form a sect of themselves. *That they were not all of us.* These false teachers probably drew many sincere souls away with them; and to this it is probable the apostle alludes when he says, *They were not all of us.* Some were; others were not.

20. *But ye have an unction.* The word *chrisma* signifies, not an *unction,* but an "ointment," the very thing itself by which anointing is effected; and so it was properly rendered in our former translations. Probably this is an allusion to the holy anointing oil of the law, and to Ps. xlv. 7: "God . . . hath anointed thee with the oil of gladness"; He hath given Thee the plenitude of the Spirit, which none of "thy fellows," none of the prophets, ever received in such abundance. By this it is evident that not only the gifts of the Spirit, but the Holy Spirit himself, is intended. As oil was used among the Asiatics for the inauguration of persons into important offices, and this oil was acknowledged to be an emblem of the gifts and graces of the Holy Spirit, without which the duties of those offices could not be discharged; so it is put here for the Spirit himself, who presided in the Church, and from whom all gifts and graces flowed. The *chrism* or

"ointment" here mentioned is also an allusion to the holy anointing ointment prescribed by God himself, Exod. xxx. 23-25, which was composed of fine myrrh, sweet cinnamon, sweet calamus, cassia lignea, and olive oil. This was an emblem of the gifts and graces of the divine Spirit. *Ye know all things.* Every truth of God necessary to your salvation and the salvation of man in general, and have no need of that knowledge of which the Gnostics boast.

But although the above is the sense in which this verse is generally understood, yet there is reason to doubt its accuracy. The adjective *panta*, which we translate *all things*, is most probably in the accusative case singular, having "man," or some such substantive, understood. The verse therefore should be translated: "You have an ointment from the Holy One, and you know or discern every man." This interpretation appears to be confirmed by v. 26, "those who are deceiving or misleading you"; and in the same sense should v. 27 be understood: "But as the same anointing teacheth you," not "of all things," but "of all men." It is plain from the whole tenor of the Epistle that John is guarding the Christians against seducers and deceivers, who were even then disturbing and striving to corrupt the Church.

21. *I have not written.* It is not because you are ignorant of these things that I write to you, *but because* you *know* them, and can by these judge of the doctrines of those false teachers, and clearly perceive that they are liars; for they contradict the truth which you have already received.

22. *Who is a liar but he that denieth that Jesus is the Christ?* Here we see some of the false doctrines which were then propagated in the world. There were certain persons who, while they acknowledged Jesus to be a divine teacher, denied Him to be the *Christ*, i.e., the Messiah. *He is antichrist, that denieth the Father and the Son.* He is antichrist who denies the supernatural and miraculous birth of Jesus Christ, who denies Jesus to be the Son of God, and who denies God to be the Father of the Lord Jesus; thus he denies the Father and the Son. The Jews in general, and the Gnostics in particular, denied the miraculous conception of Jesus; with both He was accounted no more than a common man, the son of Joseph and Mary. But the Gnostics held that a divine person, aeon, or angelic being, dwelt in him; but all things else relative to His miraculous generation and divinity they rejected. These were antichrists, who denied Jesus to be the Christ.

23. *Whosoever denieth the Son.* He who denies Jesus to be the Son of God, and consequently the Christ or Messiah, *he hath not the Father*—he can have no birth from above; he cannot be enrolled among the children of God, because none can be a child of God but by faith in Christ Jesus. *He that acknowledgeth the Son hath the Father also.* This clause is printed by our translators in Italics to show it to be of doubtful authority, as it was probably wanting in the chief of those MSS. which they consulted, as it was in Coverdale's Bible, printed 1535; and in all the early printed editions (which I have seen) previously to 1566. But that the clause is genuine, and should be restored to the text without any mark of spurious-

ness, is evident from the authorities by which it is supported. It is found in many MSS. of the best authority.

24. *Let that therefore abide in you.* Continue in the doctrines concerning the incarnation, passion, death, resurrection, ascension, and intercession of the Lord Jesus, which you have heard preached from the beginning by us, His apostles. *Ye also shall continue in the Son, and in the Father.* You who are preachers shall not only be acknowledged as ministers of the Church of Christ, but be genuine children of God, by faith in the Son of His love; and you all, thus continuing, shall have fellowship with the Father and with the Son.

25. *This is the promise.* God has promised eternal life to all who believe on Christ Jesus. So they who receive His doctrine, and continue in communion with the Father and the Son, shall have this *eternal life.*

26. *These things have I written.* Either meaning the whole Epistle or what is contained in the preceding verses, from the beginning of the eighteenth to the end of the twenty-fifth. *Them that seduce you.* That is, the "deceivers" that were among them, and who were laboring to pervert the followers of Christ.

27. *But the anointing which ye have received.* That "ointment," the gifts of the Holy Spirit, mentioned in v. 20. *Ye need not that any man teach you.* John does not say that those who had once received the teaching of the divine Spirit had no further need of the ministry of the gospel. No, but he says they had no need of such teaching as their false teachers proposed to them; nor of any other teaching that was different from that anointing, i.e., the teaching of the Spirit of God. No man, howsoever holy, wise, or pure, can ever be in such a state as to have no need of the gospel ministry; they who think so give the highest proof that they have never yet learned of Christ or His Spirit. *And is truth.* Because it is the Spirit of truth, John xvi. 13.

28. *And now, little children,* "beloved children," *abide in him*—in Christ Jesus. Let His word and Spirit continually abide in you, and have communion with the Father and the Son. *That, when he shall appear,* to judge the world, *we may have confidence,* "freedom of speech, liberty of access, boldness," from a conviction that our cause is good, and that we have had proper ground for exultation; *and not be ashamed,* confounded, when it appears that those who were brought to Christ Jesus have apostatized.

29. *If ye know that he is righteous,* that God is a holy God, *ye know* also, *that every one who doeth righteousness,* who lives a holy life, following the commandments of God, *is born of him,* "begotten of Him"—is made a partaker of the divine nature, without which he could neither have a holy heart nor live a holy life. This verse properly belongs to the following chapter and should not be separated from it. The subject is the same, and does not stand in any strict relation to that with which the twenty-eighth verse concludes.

CHAPTER 3

The extraordinary love of God towards mankind, and the effects of it, 1-3. Sin is the transgression of the law, and Christ was manifested to take away our sins,

4-6. The children of God are known by the holiness of their lives, the children of the devil by the sinfulness of theirs, 7-10. We should love one another, for he that hates his brother is a murderer; as Christ laid down His life for us, so we should lay down our lives for the brethren, 11-16. Charity is a fruit of brotherly love; our love should be active, not professional merely, 17-18. How we may know that we are of the truth, 19-21. They whose ways please God have an answer to all their prayers, 22. The necessity of keeping the commandment of Christ, that He may dwell in us and we in Him by His Spirit, 23-24.

1. *Behold, what manner of love.* Whole volumes might be written upon this and the following two verses without exhausting the extraordinary subject contained in them, viz., the love of God to man. *What manner of love.* "What great love," as to both quantity and quality, for these ideas are included in the original term. The length, the breadth, the depth, the height, he does not attempt to describe. *The Father hath bestowed.* For we had neither claim nor merit that we should be called, that is, "constituted" or "made," *the sons of God,* who were before children of the wicked one. After "that we might be called," "and we are" is added by several MSS. *Therefore the world*—the Jews, and all who know not God, and are seeking their portion in this life. *Knoweth us not*—do not "acknowledge, respect, love, or approve" of us. In this sense the word is here to be understood. We have often seen that this is a frequent use of the term "know," in both Hebrew and Greek, in the Old Testament and also in the New. *Because it knew him not.* The Jews did not "acknowledge" Jesus; they "approved" neither of Him, His doctrine, nor His manner of life.

2. *Now are we the sons of God.* He speaks of those who are begotten of God and who work righteousness. *And it doth not yet appear what we shall be.* "It is not yet manifest"; though we know that we are the children of God, we do not know that state of glorious excellence to which, as such, we shall be raised. *When he shall appear.* "When He shall be manifested"; i.e., when He comes the second time, and shall be manifested in His glorified human nature to judge the world. *We shall be like him,* for our vile bodies shall be made like unto His glorious body; *we shall see him as he is,* in all the glory and majesty of both the divine and human nature. See Phil. iii. 21; and John xvii. 24: "Father, I will that they also, whom thou hast given me, be with me where I am; that they may behold my glory."

3. *And every man that hath this hope in him.* All who have the hope of seeing Christ as He is; that is, of enjoying Him in His own glory. *Purifieth himself*—abstains from all evil, and keeps himself from all that is in the world, viz., the lusts of the flesh, of the eye, and the pride of life. God having purified his heart, it is his business to keep himself "in the love of God, looking for the mercy of our Lord Jesus Christ unto eternal life." The apostle does not here speak of any man purifying his own heart, because this is impossible; but of his persevering in the state of purity into which the Lord has brought him. The words, however, may be understood of a man's anxiously using all the means that lead to purity; and imploring God for the sanctifying Spirit, to "cleanse the thoughts of his heart by its inspiration, that he may perfectly love Him, and worthily magnify His name." *As he is pure.*

Till he is as completely saved from his sins as Christ was free from sin. Many tell us that "this never can be done, for no man can be saved from sin in this life." Will these persons permit us to ask, How much sin may we be saved from in this life? Something must be ascertained on this subject: (1) That the soul may have some determinate object in view; (2) That it may not lose its time, or employ its faith and energy, in praying for what is impossible to be attained. Now, as "he was manifested to take away our sins," v. 5, to "destroy the works of the devil," v. 8; and as his blood cleanseth from all sin and unrighteousness, chap. i. 7, 9; is it not evident that God means that believers in Christ shall be saved from all sin? For if His blood cleanses from all sin, if He destroys the works of the devil (and sin is the work of the devil), and if he who "is born of God doth not commit sin," v. 9, then he must be cleansed from all sin; and while he continues in that state he lives without sinning against God; for the "seed [of God] remaineth in him: and he cannot sin, because he is born [or begotten] of God," v. 9. How strangely warped and blinded by prejudice and system must men be who, in the face of such evidence as this, will still dare to maintain that no man can be saved from his sin in this life; but must daily commit sin, in thought, word, and deed, as the Westminster divines have asserted! That is, every man is laid under the fatal necessity of sinning as many ways against God as the devil does through his natural wickedness and malice; for even the devil himself can have no other way of sinning against God except by thought, word, and deed. And yet, according to these, and others of the same creed, "even the most regenerate sin thus against God as long as they live." Could not the grace that saved them partially save them perfectly? Could not that power of God that saved them from habitual sin save them from occasional or accidental sin? Shall we suppose that sin, how potent soever it may be, is as potent as the Spirit and grace of Christ?

4. *Sin is the transgression of the law.* The spirit of the law as well as of the gospel is that "we should love God with all our powers, and our neighbor as ourselves." All disobedience is contrary to love; therefore *sin is the transgression of the law,* whether the act refers immediately to God or to our neighbor.

5. *And ye know that he was manifested to take away our sins.* He came into the world to destroy the power, pardon and guilt, and cleanse from the pollution of sin. *In him is no sin.* And therefore He is properly qualified to be the atoning Sacrifice for the sins of men.

6. *Whosoever abideth in him.* By faith, love, and obedience. *Sinneth not.* Because his heart if purified by faith. *Hath not seen him.* It is no unusual thing with this apostle, both in his Gospel and in his Epistles, to put occasionally the past for the present, and the present for the past tense. It is very likely that here he puts, after the manner of the Hebrew, the preterite for the present: He who sins against God "doth not see Him, neither doth he know Him."

7. *Let no man deceive you.* By asserting either that "you cannot be saved from sin in this life" or "that sin will do you no harm and cannot alter your state, if you are adopted into

the family of God; for sin cannot annul this adoption." Hear God, you deceivers! *He that doeth righteousness is righteous,* according to his state, nature, and the extent of his moral powers, *Even as he is righteous.* Allowing for the disparity that must necessarily exist between that which is bounded and that which is without limits. As God, in the infinitude of His nature, is righteous, so they, being filled with Him, are in their limited nature righteous.

8. *He that committeth sin is of the devil.* Hear this, you who cannot bear the thought of that doctrine that states believers are to be saved from all sin in this life! *He that committeth sin is a child of the devil,* and shows that he has still the nature of the devil in him; *for the devil sinneth from the beginning*—he was the father of sin, brought sin into the world, and maintains sin in the world by living in the hearts of his own children, and thus leading them to transgression; and persuading others that they cannot be saved from their sins in this life, that he may secure a continual residence in their hearts. He knows that if he has a place there throughout life, he will probably have it at death; and, if so, throughout eternity. *For this purpose.* For "this very end," with this very design, was Jesus manifested in the flesh, *that he might destroy,* "that He might loose," the bonds of sin, and dissolve the power, influence, and connection of sin.

9. *Whosoever is born of God,* "begotten" of God, *doth not commit sin.* "That is," say some, "as he used to do; he does not sin habitually as he formerly did." This is bringing the influence and privileges of the heavenly birth very low indeed. We have the most indubitable evidence that many of the heathen philosophers had acquired, by mental discipline and cultivation, an entire ascendency over all their wonted vicious habits.

10. *In this the children of God are manifest.* Here is a fearful text. Who is a child of the devil? He that commits sin. Who is a child of God? He that works righteousness. By this text we shall stand or fall before God, whatever our particular creed may say to the contrary. *Neither he that loveth not his brother.* No man is of God who is not ready on all emergencies to do any act of kindness for the comfort, relief, and support of any human being. For, as God made of one blood all the nations of men to dwell upon the face of the whole earth, so all are of one family; and consequently all are brethren, and should love as brethren.

11. *For this is the message.* See chap. i. 5. *From the beginning* God has taught men that they should *love one another.*

12. *Not as Cain.* Men should not act to each other as Cain did to his brother, Abel. He murdered him because he was better than himself. But who was Cain? "He was of the devil."

13. *Marvel not . . . if the world hate you.* Expect no better treatment from unconverted Jews and Gentiles than Abel received from his wicked and cruel brother.

14. *We know that we have passed from death unto life. Death* and *life* are represented here as two distinct territories, states, or kingdoms, to either of which the inhabitants of either may be removed. This is implied in the term denoting "change of place," and "I go." It is the same figure which Paul uses, Col. i. 13: "Who hath delivered us from the power of darkness, and hath translated us into the kingdom" of the Son of His love. *We know,* says the apostle, *that* "we are passed over from the territory of death to the kingdom of life," *because we love the brethren,* which those who continue in the old kingdom—under the old covenant—can never do; for *he that loveth not his brother abideth in death.* He has never changed his original residence. He is still an unconverted, unrenewed sinner.

15. *Whosoever hateth his brother is a murderer.* He has the same principle in him which was in Cain, and it may lead to the same consequences. *No murderer hath eternal life.* Eternal life springs from an indwelling God, and God cannot dwell in the heart where hatred and malice dwell. This text has been quoted to prove that no murderer can be saved. This is not said in the text; and there have been many instances of persons who have been guilty of murder having had deep and genuine repentance, and who doubtless found mercy from His hands who prayed for His murderers, "Father, forgive them; for they know not what they do."

16. *Hereby perceive we the love of God.* This sixteenth verse of this third chapter of John's First Epistle is, in the main, an exact counterpart of the sixteenth verse of the third chapter of John's Gospel: "God so loved the world, that he gave his only begotten Son." Here the apostle says, We *perceive,* "we have known," *the love of God, because he laid down his life for us. Of God* is not in the text, but it is preserved in one MS. and in two or three of the versions; but though this does not establish its authenticity, yet *of God* is necessarily understood or "of Christ."

17. *But whoso hath this world's good.* Here is a test of this love; if we do not divide our bread with the hungry, we certainly would not lay down our lives for Him. Whatever love we may pretend to mankind, if we are not charitable and benevolent, we give the lie to our profession. *This world's good.* "The life of this world," i.e., the means of life. *How dwelleth the love of God in him?* That is, it cannot possibly dwell in such a person. Hardheartedness and God's love never meet together; much less can they be associated.

18. *My little children,* "my beloved children," *let us not love in word*—in merely allowing the general doctrine of love to God and man to be just and right. *Neither in tongue*—in making professions of love, and of a charitable and humane disposition, and resting there. *But in deed*—by humane and merciful acts. *And in truth*—feeling the disposition of which we speak.

19. *Hereby we know that we are of the truth,* that we have the true religion of the Lord Jesus, *and shall assure our hearts,* be persuaded in our consciences that we have the truth as it is in Jesus, as no man can impose upon himself by imagining he loves when he does not. He may make empty professions to others, but if he loves either God or man, he knows it because he feels it. And love unfelt is not love; it is "word" or "tongue." This the apostle lays down as a test of a man's Christianity, and it is the strongest and most infallible test that can be given.

20. *If our heart condemn us.* If we be conscious that our love is feigned, we shall feel inwardly condemned in professing to have what we have not. And *if our heart condemn us, God is greater than our heart,* for He knows every hypocritical winding and turning of the soul. He searches the heart, and tries the reins, and sees all the deceitfulness and desperate wickedness of the heart which we cannot see.

21. *If our heart condemn us not*—if we be conscious to ourselves of our own sincerity, that we practice not deceit, and use no mask; then *have we confidence toward God*—we can appeal to Him for our sincerity, and we can come with boldness to the throne of grace, to "obtain mercy, and find grace to help in time of need." And therefore says the apostle,

22. *Whatsoever we ask,* in such a spirit, *we receive of him;* for He delights to bless the humble, upright, and sincere soul. *Because we keep his commandments.* Viz., by loving Him and loving our neighbor. These are the great commandments of both the old covenant and the new. And whoever is filled with this love to God and man will *do those things that are pleasing* to Him, for love is the very soul and principle of obedience. The word "heart" is used in the preceding verses for conscience, and so the Greek fathers interpret it; but this is not an unfrequent meaning of the word in the sacred writings.

23. *That we should believe on the name of his Son.* We are commanded to believe on Christ; and being through Him redeemed from the guilt of sin, restored to the divine favor, and made partakers of the Holy Ghost, we are enabled to *love one another, as he gave us commandment;* for without a renewal of the heart, love to God and man is impossible, and this renewal comes by Christ Jesus.

24. *Dwelleth in him,* i.e., in God; *and he, God, in him,* the believer. *And hereby we know.* We know *by the Spirit which he hath given us* that we dwell in God, and God in us.

CHAPTER 4

We must not believe every teacher who professes to have a divine commission to preach, but try such, whether they be of God; and the more so because many false prophets are gone out into the world, 1. Those who deny that Jesus Christ is come in the flesh have the spirit of antichrist, 2-3. The followers of God have been enabled to discern and overcome them, 4-6. The necessity of love to God and one another shown from God's love to us, 7-11. Though no man hath seen God, yet every genuine Christian knows Him by the Spirit which God has given him, 12-13. The apostles testified that God sent His Son to be the Saviour of the world, and God dwelt in those who confessed this truth, 14-15. "God is love," 16. The nature and properties of perfect love, 17-18. We love Him because He first loved us, 19. The wickedness of pretending to love God while we hate one another, 20-21.

1. *Beloved, believe not every spirit.* Do not be forward to believe every teacher to be a man sent of God. As in those early times every teacher professed to be inspired by the Spirit of God, because all the prophets had come thus accredited, the term *spirit* was used to express the man who pretended to be and teach under the Spirit's influence. See 1 Cor. xii. 1-12; 1 Tim. iv. 1. *Try the spirits.* Put these teachers to the proof. Try them by that testimony which is known to have come from the Spirit of God, the word of revelation already given. *Many false prophets.* Teachers not inspired by the Spirit of God.

2. *Hereby know ye the Spirit of God.* We know that the man who teaches that Jesus Christ is the promised Messiah, and that he *is come in the flesh, is of God*—is inspired by the divine Spirit; for no man can call Jesus Lord but by the Holy Ghost.

3. *Every spirit,* every teacher, *that confesseth not* Jesus *is not of God*—has not been inspired by God. The words *is come in the flesh* are wanting in several MSS. Griesbach has left them out of the text. *Ye have heard that it should come.* See 2 Thess. ii. 7. *Even now already is it in the world.* Is working powerfully among both Jews and Gentiles.

4. *Ye are of God.* You are under the influence of the divine Spirit. *And have overcome them*—your testimony, proceeding from the Spirit of Christ, has invalidated theirs, which has proceeded from the influence of Satan; for *greater* is the Holy Spirit which *is in you, than* the spirit which *is in the world.*

5. *They are of the world.* They have no spiritual views; they have no spirituality of mind; they seek the present world and its enjoyments. Their conversation is worldly, and worldly men hear them in preference to all others.

6. *We are of God.* We apostles have the Spirit of God, and speak and teach by that Spirit. *He that knoweth God,* who has a truly spiritual discernment, *heareth us,* acknowledges that our doctrine is from God; that it is spiritual, and leads from earth to heaven.

7. *Beloved, let us love one another.* And ever be ready to promote each other's welfare, both spiritual and temporal. *For love is of God.* And ever acts like Him; He loves man, and daily loads him with His benefits. He that loveth most has most of God in him; and he that loveth God and his neighbor, as before described and commanded, *is born of God,* "is begotten of God"—is a true child of his Heavenly Father.

8. *He that loveth not,* as already described, *knoweth not God,* has no experimental knowledge of Him. *God is love.* How can a decree of absolute, unconditional reprobation of the greater part or any part of the human race stand in the presence of such a text as this? It has been well observed that, although God is holy, just, righteous, He is never called "holiness, justice," in the abstract, as He is here called *love.* This seems to be the essence of the divine nature, and all other attributes to be only modifications of this.

9. *In this was manifested the love of God.* The mission of Jesus Christ was the fullest proof that God could give, or that man could receive, of His infinite love to the world. *That we might live through him.* The whole world was sentenced to death because of sin, and every individual was dead in trespasses and sins; and Jesus came to die in the stead of the world, and to quicken every believer, that all might live to Him who died for them and rose again. This is another strong allusion to John iii. 16.

10. *Not that we loved God,* and that He was thereby induced to give His Son *to be a propitiation for our sins.*

11. *If God so loved us*—without any reason or consideration on our part, and without any

desert in us. *We ought also, in like manner, to love one another.*

12. *No man hath seen God at any time.* We may feel Him, though we cannot see Him; and if we love one another, He *dwelleth in us, and his love is perfected in us*—it has then its full accomplishment, having molded us according to its own nature.

14. *And we have seen* Jesus Christ manifested in the flesh; see chap. i. 1. *And do testify*—bear witness, in consequence of having the fullest conviction—*that the Father sent the Son to be the Saviour of the world.* We have had the fullest proof of this from His doctrine and miracles, which we heard and saw during the whole time that He sojourned among men.

15. *Whosoever shall confess.* Much stress is laid on this confession, because the false teachers denied the reality of the Incarnation; but this confession implied also such a belief in Christ as put them in possession of His pardoning mercy and indwelling Spirit.

16. *God is love.* See on v. 8. *He that dwelleth in love*—he who is full of love to God and man is full of God, for *God is love.*

17. *Herein is our love made perfect.* By God dwelling in us and we in Him, having cast out all the carnal mind that was "enmity" against himself, and filled the whole heart with the spirit of love and purity. *May have boldness in the day of judgment.* "Freedom of speech," and "liberty of access," seeing in the person of our Judge Him who has died for us, regenerated our hearts, and who himself fills them. *As he is*—pure, holy, and loving. *So are we in this world,* being saved from our sins, and made like to himself in righteousness and true holiness. No man can contemplate the day of judgment with any comfort or satisfaction but on this ground, that the blood of Christ hath cleansed him from all sin; and that he is kept by the power of God, through faith, unto salvation. This will give him boldness in the day of judgment.

18. *There is no fear in love.* The man who feels that he loves God with all his heart can never dread Him as his Judge. As he is now made a partaker of His Spirit, and carries a sense of the divine approbation in his conscience, he has nothing of that *fear* that produces "terror" or brings *torment.* The *perfect love,* that fullness of love which he has received, *casteth out fear,* removes all terror relative to this day of judgment, for it is of this that the apostle particularly speaks. *He that feareth*—he who is still uncertain concerning his interest in Christ. *Is not made perfect in love*—has not yet received the abiding witness of the Spirit that he is begotten of God; nor that fullness of love to God and man which excludes the "enmity" of the "carnal mind," and which it is his privilege to receive. We are not to suppose that the love of God casts out every kind of fear from the soul; it casts out only that which has *torment.*

20. *If a man say, I love God, and hateth his brother.* This, as well as many other parts of this Epistle, seems levelled against the Jews who pretended much love to God while they hated the Gentiles.

21. *This commandment have we.* The love of God and the love of man can never be separated.

He who loves God will love his brother; he who loves his brother gives this proof that he loves God.

CHAPTER 5

He that believeth is born of God; loves God and His children; and keeps His commandments, which are not grievous, 1-3. Faith in Christ overcomes the world, 4-5. The three earthly and heavenly witnesses, 6-9. He that believeth hath the witness in himself, 10. God has given unto us eternal life in His Son, 11-12. The end for which John writes these things, 13-15. The sin unto death, and the sin not unto death, 16-17. He that is born of God sinneth not, 18. The whole world lieth in the wicked one, 19. Jesus is come to give us an understanding, that we may know the true God, 20. All idolatry to be avoided, 21.

1. *Whosoever believeth.* "He that believeth that Jesus is the Messiah," and confides in Him for the remission of sins, "is begotten of God"; and they who are pardoned and begotten of God love Him in return for His love, and love all those who are His children.

2. *By this we know that we love the children of God.* Our love of God's followers is a proof that we love God. Our love to God is the cause why we love His children, and our keeping the *commandments* of God is the proof that we love Him.

3. *For this is the love of God.* This the love of God necessarily produces. It is vain to pretend love to God while we live in opposition to His will. *His commandments,* to love Him with all our hearts, and our neighbor as ourselves, *are not grievous,* are not burdensome; for no man is burdened with the duties which his own love imposes. The old proverb explains the meaning of the apostle's words, "Love feels no loads."

4. *Whatsoever is born of God.* "Whatsoever [the neuter for the masculine] is begotten of God overcometh the world."

6. *This is he that came by water and blood.* Jesus was attested to be the Son of God and promised Messiah by *water,* i.e., His baptism, when the Spirit of God came down from heaven upon Him, and the voice from heaven said, "This is my beloved Son, in whom I am well pleased." Jesus Christ came also by *blood.* He shed His blood for the sins of the world, and this was in accordance with all that the Jewish prophets had written concerning Him. Here the apostle says that the Spirit witnesses this; that He came *not by water only*—being baptized, and baptizing men in His own name that they might be His followers and disciples; but by *blood* also—by His sacrificial death, without which the world could not have been saved, and He could have had no disciples.

7. *There are three that bear record in heaven.* It is likely that this verse is not genuine. It is wanting in every MS., one excepted.

8. *The spirit, and the water, and the blood.* This verse is supposed to mean "the Spirit—in the word confirmed by miracles; the *water*—in baptism, wherein we are dedicated to the Son (with the Father and the Holy Spirit), typifying His spotless purity, and the inward purifying of our nature; *and the blood*—represented in the Lord's Supper, and applied to the consciences of believers: and all these harmoniously agree in the same testimony, that Jesus Christ is the divine, the complete, the only Saviour of the world" (Mr. Wesley's notes).

9. *If we receive the witness of men.* Which all are obliged to do, and which is deemed a sufficient testimony to truth in numberless cases. *The witness of God is greater*—He can neither be deceived nor deceive.

10. *He that believeth on the Son of God.* This is God's witness to a truth, the most important and interesting to mankind. God has witnessed that whosoever believeth on His Son shall be saved and have everlasting life; and shall have the witness of it in himself, the Spirit bearing witness with his spirit that he is a child of God. To know his sin forgiven, to have the testimony of this in the heart from the Holy Spirit himself, is the privilege of every true believer in Christ.

11. *This is the record.* The great truth to which the Spirit, the water, and the Blood bear testimony. *God hath given to us eternal life*— a right to endless glory, and a meetness for it. *And this life is in his Son;* it comes by and through Him.

12. *He that hath the Son hath life.* As the eternal life is given "in" the Son of God, it follows that it cannot be enjoyed without Him. No man can have it without having Christ; therefore *he that hath the Son hath life, and he that hath not the Son of God hath not life.*

13. *That ye may know that ye have eternal life.* It is not a blind reliance for, but an actual enjoyment of, salvation; Christ living, working, and reigning in the heart. *And that ye may believe.* That is, "continue to believe"; for Christ dwells in the heart only by faith, and faith lives only by love, and love continues only by obedience; he who believes loves, and he who loves obeys.

14. *This is the confidence,* the "liberty of access and speech," *that, if we ask any thing according to his will,* that is, which He has promised in His Word. All that God has promised we are justified in expecting; and what He has promised and we expect, we should pray for. Prayer is the language of the children of God.

15. *And if we know that he hear us.* Seeing we are satisfied that He hears the prayer of faith, requesting the things which himself has promised, *we know,* consequently, *that we have the petitions*—the answer to the *petitions*—*that we desired of him.* For He cannot deny himself; and we may consider them as sure as if we had them; and we shall have them as soon as we plead for and need them.

16. *A sin which is not unto death.* This is an extremely difficult passage, and has been variously interpreted. What is the *sin not unto death,* for which we should ask, and life shall be given to him that commits it? And what is the *sin unto death,* for which we should not pray? *The sin unto death* means a case of transgression, particularly of grievous backsliding from the life and power of godliness, which God determines to punish with temporal death, while at the same time He extends mercy to the penitent soul. The disobedient prophet, 1 Kings xiii. 1-32, is, on this interpretation, a case in point. Many others occur in the history of the Church, and of every religious community. The *sin not unto death* is any sin which God does not choose thus to punish. This view of the subject is that taken by the late Rev. J. Wesley, in a sermon entitled "A Call to Backsliders." I do not think the passage has anything to do with what is termed "the sin against the Holy Ghost." See the note on Matt. xii. 31-32.

17. *All unrighteousness is sin.* Every act contrary to justice is sin—is a transgression of the law which condemns all injustice.

18. *Whosoever is born of God sinneth not.* This is spoken of adult Christians; they are cleansed from all unrighteousness, consequently from all sin, chap. i. 7-9. *Keepeth himself.* That is, in the love of God, Jude 21, by building up himself on his most holy faith, and praying in the Holy Ghost; *and that wicked one,* the devil, *toucheth him not,* finds nothing of his own nature in him on which he can work.

19. *The whole world lieth in wickedness.* "Lieth in the wicked one."

20. *We know that the Son of God is come.* in the flesh, and has made His soul an offering for sin; *and hath given us an understanding,* a more eminent degree of light than we ever enjoyed before.

21. *Little children.* "Beloved children"; he concludes with the same affectionate feeling with which he commenced. *Keep yourselves from idols.* That is a man's *idol* or god from which he seeks his happiness. That is a man's idol which prevents him from seeking and finding his all in God.

The Second Epistle of

JOHN

The apostle's address to a Christian matron and her children, 1-3. He rejoices to find that certain of her family had received, and continued to adorn, the truth; and he exhorts them to continue to love one another according to the commandment of Christ, 4-6. And particularly cautions them against deceivers, and to be watchful that they might not lose the benefit of what they had received, 7-8. The necessity of abiding in the doctrine of Christ, 9. He cautions them against receiving, or in any way forwarding, those who did not bring the true doctrine of Christ, 10-11. Excuses himself from writing more largely, and purposes to pay her and family a visit shortly, 12-13.

1. *The elder.* John the apostle, who was now a very old man, generally supposed to be about ninety, and therefore he uses the term presbyter or *elder,* not as the name of an office, but as designating his advanced age. He is allowed to have been the oldest of all the apostles, and to have been the only one who died a natural death. *The elect lady.* As *kuria* may be the feminine of *kurios,* "lord," therefore it may signify *lady;* and so several, both ancients and moderns, have understood it. But others have considered it the proper name of a woman, Kyria; and that this is a very ancient opinion is evident from the Peshito Syriac, which uses it as a proper name, as does also the Arabic. Some have thought that Eclecta was the name of this matron, from the word which we translate *elect,* and which here signifies the same as "excellent, eminent, honorable," or the like. Others think that a particular church is intended, which some suppose to be the church at Jerusalem, and that the "elect sister," v. 13, means the church at Ephesus; but these are conjectures which appear to me to have no good ground. I am satisfied that no metaphor is here intended; that the Epistle was sent to some eminent Christian matron, not far from Ephesus, who was probably deaconess of the church, who, it is likely, had a church at her house, or at whose house the apostles and travelling evangelists frequently preached, and were entertained. *Whom I love in the truth.* Whom I love as the Christian religion requires us to love one another. *And not I only.* She was well-known in the churches; many had witnessed or heard of her fidelity, and partook of her hospitality.

2. *For the truth's sake.* On account of the gospel. *And shall be with us.* For God will preserve not only the Christian religion but its truth, all its essential doctrines, *for ever.*

3. *Grace be with you.* This is addressed to her, her household, and probably that part of the church which was more immediately under her care. *The Son of the Father.* The apostle still keeps in view the miraculous conception of Christ, a thing which the Gnostics absolutely denied, a doctrine which is at the groundwork of our salvation.

4. *That I found of thy children walking in truth.* I have already supposed this Christian matron to be mother of a family, probably a widow, for no mention is made of her husband; and that she was also a deaconess in the church, and one in whose house the travelling evangelists preached, and where they were entertained. The *children* mentioned here may either be her own children or those members of the church which were under her care, or some of both. The apostle was glad to find, probably by an epistle sent from herself to him or from the information of some of the itinerant evangelists, that the work of God was prospering in the place where she lived, and also in her own household. He does not say that all were walking in the truth, but "some" of her children.

5. *That which we had from the beginning.* The commandment to *love one another* was what they had heard from the first publication of Christianity, and what he wishes this excellent woman to inculcate on all those under her care. The mode of address here shows that it was a person, not a church, to which the apostle wrote.

6. *And this is love.* That is, our love is shown and proved by our walking according to the commandments of God; for love is the principle of obedience.

7. *For many deceivers.* Of these he had spoken before, see 1 John iv. 1 ff. And these appear to have been Gnostics, for they denied that Jesus was *come in the flesh.* And this doctrine, so essential to salvation, none could deny but a deceiver and an antichrist. Instead of *are entered into,* many excellent MSS. and versions have "are gone out." The sense is nearly the same.

8. *Look to yourselves.* Be on your guard against these seducers; watch, pray, love God and each other, and walk in newness of life. *That we lose not those things which we have wrought.* That we apostles, who have been the means of your conversion, may not be deprived of you as our crown of rejoicing in the day of the Lord Jesus. Instead of the first person plural, *we lose,* many MSS., versions, and fathers read the whole clause in the second person plural, "ye lose": "Take heed to yourselves, that ye lose not the things which ye have wrought, but that ye receive a full reward." This reading is more consistent and likely, and is supported by at least as good evidence as the other.

9. *Whosoever transgresseth*—he who "passes over" the sacred enclosure, or "goes beyond" the prescribed limits. *And abideth not in the doctrine*—does not remain within these holy limits, but indulges himself either in excesses of action or passion. *Hath not God* for his Father, nor the love of God in his heart. *Hath both the Father and the Son.* He who abideth in the doctrine of Christ, his body is a temple of the

Holy Trinity, and he has communion with the Father as his Father, and with the Son as his Saviour and Redeemer.

10. *If there come any unto you,* under the character of an apostle or evangelist, to preach in your house. *And bring not this doctrine,* that Jesus is come in the flesh, and has died for the redemption of the world; *Receive him not into your house.* Give him no entertainment as an evangelical teacher. Let him not preach under your roof. *Neither bid him God speed.* "And do not say, Health to him"—do not salute him with "Peace be to you!" The words mean, according to the Eastern use of them, "Have no religious connection with him, nor act towards him so as to induce others to believe you acknowledge him as a brother."

11. *Is partaker of his evil deeds.* He that acts towards him as if he considered him a Christian brother, and sound in the faith, puts it in his power to deceive others, by thus apparently accrediting his ministry.

12. *Having many things to write.* That is, I have many things that I might write to you, but I think it best not to commit them to paper, because I hope to visit you shortly, and speak fully of those matters, which will be a means of increasing the comfort of both you and your family, as well as my own. There is more comfort in mutual interviews among friends than in epistolary correspondence.

13. *The children of thy elect sister.* Probably her own sister, who lived at Ephesus and, being acquainted with the apostle's writing, desired to be thus remembered to her. *Elect,* in both this and the first verse, signifies "excellent, eminent, or honorable." *Amen* is wanting in the most ancient MSS. and in most of the versions.

The Third Epistle of
JOHN

The apostle's address to Gaius, and his good wishes for his prosperity in body and soul, 1-2. He commends him for his steadiness in the truth, and his general hospitality, especially to the itinerant evangelists, 3-8. Speaks of the bad conduct of Diotrephes, his abuse of his power in the church, and his slander of the apostles, 9-10. Exhorts Gaius to avoid his example, and to follow what is good, 11. Commends Demetrius, 12. Excuses himself from writing more fully, and proposes to pay him a visit shortly, 13-14.

1. *The elder.* See on the first verse of the preceding Epistle. *The wellbeloved Gaius. Gaius* is the Greek mode of writing the Roman name Caius, and thus it should be rendered in European languages. Several persons of the name of Gaius occur in the New Testament. In the Epistle to the Romans, chap. xvi. 23, Paul mentions a Gaius who lived at Corinth, whom he calls his "host," and the host "of the whole church." In 1 Cor. i. 14, Paul mentions a Gaius who lived at Corinth, whom he had baptized; but this is probably the same with the above. In Acts xix. 29, mention is made of a Gaius who was a native of Macedonia, who accompanied Paul, and spent some time with him at Ephesus. In Acts xx. 4 we meet a Gaius of Derbe, who was likewise a fellow traveller of Paul. Now whether this Gaius was one of the persons just mentioned or whether he was different from them all is difficult to determine, because Gaius was a very common name. Yet if we may judge from the similarity of character it is not improbable that he was the Gaius who lived at Corinth, and who is styled by Paul the "host . . . of the whole church"; for hospitality to his Christian brethren was the leading feature in the character of this Gaius to whom John wrote, and it is on this very account that he is commended by the apostle.

2. *I wish above all things.* Above all things I pray *that thou mayest prosper and be in health.*

3. *When the brethren came.* Probably the same of whom he speaks in the fifth and following verses, and who appear to have been itinerant evangelists. *The truth that is in thee.* The soundness of your faith and the depth of your religion.

4. *To hear that my children.* From this it has been inferred that Gaius was one of John's converts, and consequently not the Corinthian Gaius, who was converted, most probably, by Paul. But the apostle might use the term *children* here as implying those who were immediately under his pastoral care, and being an old man, he had a right to use such terms in addressing his juniors in both age and grace.

6. *Which have borne witness of thy charity.* Of your love and benevolence. *Before the church.* The believers at Ephesus, for to this church the apostle seems to refer. *Whom if thou bring forward.* If you continue to assist such, as you have done, *thou shalt do well. After a godly sort.* "Worthy of God"; and in such a way as He can approve.

7. *For his name's sake they went forth.* For the sake of preaching the gospel of the grace of God, and making known Jesus to the heathen. *Taking nothing of the Gentiles.* Receiving no emolument for their labor, but in every respect showing themselves to be truly disinterested. Sometimes, and on some special occasions, this may be necessary; but "The labourer is worthy of his hire" is the maxim of the Author of Christianity. And those congregations of Christians are ever found to prize the gospel most, and profit most by it, who bear all expenses incident to it.

9. *I wrote unto the church,* the church where Gaius was. *But Diotrephes, who loveth to have the preeminence,* "who loves the presidency, or

chief place" in the church. He was doubtless an officer in the church, at least a deacon, probably a bishop; and being one, he magnified himself in his office; he loved such eminence, and behaved himself haughtily in it. *Receiveth us not.* Does not acknowledge the apostolical authority.

10. *If I come, I will remember.* I will show him the authority which, as an apostle of Jesus Christ, I possess. *Prating against us.* Diotrephes might have been a converted Jew who was unwilling that the Gentiles should be received into the church; or a Judaizing Christian who wished to incorporate the law with the gospel, and calumniated the apostles who taught otherwise. This haughty and unfeeling man would give no countenance to the converted Gentiles; so far from it that he would not receive any of them himself, forbade others to do it, and excommunicated those who had been received into the church by the apostles.

11. *Follow not that which is evil.* "Do not imitate that wicked man," i.e., the conduct of Diotrephes; be merciful, loving, and kind.

12. *Demetrius hath good report.* Perhaps another member of the church where Gaius was; or he might have been one of those whom the apostle recommends to Gaius; or possibly the bearer of this letter from John to Gaius.

13. *I had many things to write.* That is, I have many things that I might write; but having the hope of seeing you shortly, I will not commit them to paper. *Ink* and *pen* are here mentioned, paper and ink in the preceding Epistle.

14. *Peace be to thee.* May you possess every requisite good, of both a spiritual and a temporal kind. *Our friends salute thee.* Desire to be affectionately remembered to you. *Greet the friends by name*—remember me to all those with whom I am acquainted, as if I had specified them by name.

The Epistle of

JUDE

The address and apostolical benediction, 1-2. The reasons which induced Jude to write this Epistle, to excite the Christians to contend for the true faith, and to beware of false teachers, lest, falling from their steadfastness, they should be destroyed after the example of backsliding Israel, the apostate angels, and the inhabitants of Sodom and Gomorrah, 3-7. Of the false teachers, 8. Of Michael disputing about the body of Moses, 9. The false teachers particularly described; they are like brute beasts, going the way of Cain, running after the error of Balaam, and shall perish, as did Korah in his gainsaying, 10-11. Are impure, unsteady, fierce, shameless, etc., 12-13. How Enoch prophesied of such, 14-15. They are further described as murmurers and complainers, 16. We should remember the cautions given unto us by the apostles, who foretold of these men, 17-19. We should build up ourselves on our most holy faith, 20-21. How the Church of Christ should treat such, 22-23. The apostle's farewell, and his doxology to God, 24-25.

1. *Jude, the servant of Jesus Christ.* Probably Jude the apostle, who was surnamed Thaddaeus and Lebbaeus, was son to Alphaeus, and brother to James the less, Joses, and Simon. *Brother of James.* Supposed to be James the less, bishop of Jerusalem, mentioned here because he was an eminent person in the Church. *To them that are sanctified by God.* Instead of "to the sanctified," several MSS., with several of the fathers, have "to them that are beloved." Jude writes to all believers everywhere, and not to any particular church; hence this Epistle has been called a general Epistle.

2. *Mercy unto you.* For even the best have no merit, and must receive every blessing and grace in the way of *mercy. Peace* with God and your consciences, *love* to both God and man, *be multiplied,* be unboundedly increased.

3. *When I gave all diligence.* This phrase is a Grecism for being "exceedingly intent" upon a subject, taking it up seriously with determination to bring it to good effect. The meaning of the apostle seems to be this: "Beloved brethren, when I saw it necessary to write to

you concerning the common salvation, my mind being deeply affected with the dangers to which the Church is exposed from the false teachers that are gone out into the world, I found it extremely necessary to write and exhort you to hold fast the truth which you had received, and strenuously to contend for that only faith which, by our Lord and His apostles, has been delivered to the Christians." *The common salvation.* The Christian religion and the salvation which it brings. This is called *common* because it belongs equally to Jews and Gentiles.

4. *For there are certain men crept in unawares.* They had got into the Church under specious pretenses; and, when in, began to sow their bad seed. *Before of old ordained.* Such as were long ago "proscribed, and condemned in the most public manner"; this is the import of the word in this place, and there are many examples of this use of it in the Greek writers. *To this condemnation.* To a similar punishment to that immediately about to be mentioned. In the sacred writings all such persons, false doctrines, and impure practices have been most openly proscribed and condemned; and the apostle immediately produces several examples, viz., the disobedient Israelites, the unfaithful angels, and the impure inhabitants of Sodom and Gomorrah. *Turning the grace of our God into lasciviousness.* Making the grace and mercy of God a covering for crimes, intimating that men might sin safely who believe the gospel, because in that gospel grace abounds. *The only Lord God, and our Lord Jesus Christ.* God is omitted by more than sixteen MSS., and by many of the fathers. It is very likely that it was originally inserted as a gloss, to ascertain to whom the title of "the only Sovereign," belonged; and thus make two persons where only

one seems to be intended. The passage I believe belongs solely to Jesus Christ, and may be read thus: "Denying the only sovereign Ruler, even our Lord Jesus Christ."

5. *I will therefore put you in remembrance.* That is, how such persons were proscribed, and condemned to bear the punishment due to such crimes. *Though ye once knew this.* The word here translated *once* has greatly puzzled many interpreters. It has two meanings in the sacred writings, and indeed in the Greek writers also. It signifies (1) "once, one time"; (2) "altogether, entirely, perfectly." This appears to be the sense of the word in Heb. vi. 4: "those who were fully enlightened." Heb. x. 2: "thoroughly cleansed." Jude is to be understood as saying, "I will therefore put you in remembrance, though you are thoroughly instructed in this." *Saved the people.* Delivered them from the Egyptian bondage. *Afterward destroyed them.* Because they neither believed His word nor were obedient to His commands. This is the first example of what was mentioned in v. 4.

6. *The angels which kept not their first estate.* "Their own principality." The words may be understood of their having invaded the office or dignity of some others, or of their having by some means forfeited their own. This is spoken of those generally termed the "fallen angels"; but from what they fell, or from what cause or for what crime, we know not. They are produced as the second example. *But left their own habitation.* This seems to intimate that they had invaded the office and prerogatives of others, and attempted to seize on their place of residence and felicity. *He hath reserved in everlasting chains.* That is, in a state of confinement from which they cannot escape. *Under darkness.* Alluding probably to those dungeons or dark cells in prisons where the most flagitious culprits were confined. *The judgment of the great day.* The final judgment, when both angels and men shall receive their eternal doom.

7. *Even as Sodom and Gomorrha.* What their sin and punishment were may be seen in Genesis xix, and the notes there. This is the third example to illustrate what is laid down in v. 4. *Are set forth for an example.* Both of what God will do to such transgressors and of the position laid down in v. 4, viz., that God has in the most open and positive manner declared that such and such sinners shall meet with the punishment due to their crimes. *Suffering the vengeance of eternal fire.* Subjected to such a punishment as an endless fire can inflict.

8. *Likewise also these filthy dreamers.* He means to say that these false teachers and their followers were as unbelieving and disobedient as the Israelites in the wilderness, as rebellious against the authority of God as the fallen angels, and as impure and unholy as the Sodomites; and that consequently they must expect similar punishment. *Despise dominion.* They "set all government at nought"—they will come under no restraints; they despise all law, and wish to live as they list. *Speak evil of dignities.* "They blaspheme or speak injuriously of supreme authority."

9. *Yet Michael the archangel.* Let it be observed that the word *archangel* is never found in the plural number in the sacred writings There can be properly only one archangel, one chief or head of all the angelic host. Nor is the word "devil," as applied to the great enemy of mankind, ever found in the plural; there can be but one monarch of all fallen spirits. Michael is this archangel, and head of all the angelic orders; the devil, great dragon, or Satan, is head of all the diabolic orders. When these two hosts are opposed to each other they are said to act under these two chiefs, as leaders. Hence in Rev. xii. 7, it is said: "Michael and his angels fought against the dragon . . . and his angels." *Disputed about the body of Moses.* What this means I cannot tell, or from what source Jude drew it, unless from some tradition among his countrymen. *Durst not bring against him a railing accusation.* It was a Jewish maxim, as may be seen in *Synopsis Sohar*, page 92, note 6: "It is not lawful for man to prefer ignominious reproaches, even against wicked spirits."

10. *Speak evil of those things which they know not.* They do not understand the origin and utility of civil government; they revile that which ever protects their own persons and their property. *But what they know naturally.* They are destitute of reflection; their minds are uncultivated; they follow mere natural instinct, and are slaves to their animal propensities. *As brute beasts.* Like the irrational animals; but, in the indulgence of their animal propensities, *they corrupt themselves,* beyond the example of the brute beasts.

11. *They have gone in the way of Cain.* They are haters of their brethren, and they that are such are murderers; and by their false doctrine they corrupt and destroy the souls of the people. *The error of Balaam.* For the sake of gain they corrupt the Word of God and refine away its meaning and let it down so as to suit the passions of the profligate. *Gainsaying of Core.* See the account of the rebellion of Korah, Dathan, and Abiram, and their company, in Numbers xxii. It appears that these persons opposed the authority of the apostles of our Lord, as Korah and his associates did that of Moses and Aaron; and Jude predicts them a similar punishment.

12. *Spots in your feasts of charity.* It appears that these persons, unholy and impure as they were, still continued to have outward fellowship with the Church! The *feasts of charity,* the "love feasts," of which the apostle speaks, were in use in the primitive Church till the middle of the fourth century, when, by the Council of Laodicea, they were prohibited to be held in the churches; and, having been abused, fell into disuse. In later days they have been revived, in all the purity and simplicity of the primitive institution, among the Moravians and the people called Methodists. *Feeding themselves without fear.* Eating, not to suffice nature, but to pamper appetite. It seems the provision was abundant, and they ate to gluttony and riot. It was this which brought the love feasts into disrepute in the Church, and was the means of their being at last wholly laid aside. *Clouds . . . without water.* The doctrine of God is compared to the rain, Deut. xxxii. 2, and *clouds* are the instruments by which the rain is distilled upon the earth. In arid or parched countries the very appearance of a cloud is delightful, because it is a token of refreshing showers; but when sudden winds arise and disperse these clouds, the hope of the husband-

man and shepherd is cut off. These false teachers are represented as *clouds;* they have the form and office of the teachers of righteousness, and from such appearances pure doctrine may be naturally expected. But these are *clouds . . . without water*—they distill no refreshing showers, because they have none; they are *carried* away and *about* by their passions, as those light, fleecy clouds are carried by the winds. *Trees whose fruit withereth.* "Galled or diseased trees." They have the appearance of ministers of the gospel, but they have no fruit. *Twice dead.* First, naturally and practically dead in sin, from which they had been revived by the preaching and grace of the gospel. Secondly, dead by backsliding or apostasy from the true faith, by which they lost the grace they had before received; and now likely to continue in that death because *plucked up* from *the roots,* their roots of faith and love being no longer fixed in Christ Jesus.

13. *Raging waves of the sea, foaming out their own shame.* The same metaphor as in Isa. lvii. 20: "The wicked are like the troubled sea, when it cannot rest, whose waters cast up mire and dirt." *Wandering stars.* These are uncertain, anomalous meteors, wills-o'-the-wisp. *The blackness of darkness.* They are such as are going headlong into that outer darkness where there are wailing, and weeping, and gnashing of teeth.

14. *Enoch also, the seventh from Adam.* He was the *seventh* patriarch, and is distinguished thus from Enoch, son of Cain, who was but the third from Adam; this appears plainly from the genealogy, 1 Chron. i. 1. Of the *Book of Enoch,* from which this prophecy is thought to have been taken, much has been said; but as the work is apocryphal, and of no authority, I shall not burden my page with extracts. Perhaps the word *prophesied* means no more than "preached, spoke, made declarations," concerning these things and persons; for doubtless he reproved the ungodliness of his own times. *Ten thousands of his saints.* This seems to be taken from Dan. vii. 10.

15. *To execute judgment.* This was originally spoken to the antediluvians, and the coming of the Lord to destroy that world was the thing spoken of in this prophecy or declaration.

16. *Having men's persons in admiration.* Timeservers and flatterers. *Because of advantage.* "For the sake of lucre." All the flatterers of the rich are of this kind; and especially those who profess to be ministers of the gospel and who, for the sake of a more advantageous living, will soothe the rich even in their sins.

17. *Remember ye the words.* Instead of following those teachers and their corrupt doctine, remember what Christ and His apostles have said, for they foretold the coming of such false teachers and impostors.

19. *Who separate themselves.* From the true Church, which they leave from an affectation of superior wisdom. *Sensual.* "Animal"—living as brute beasts, guided simply by their own lusts and passions. For they have *not the Spirit* —they are not spiritually minded, and have no Holy Ghost, no inspiration from God.

20. *Building up yourselves.* Having the *most holy faith*—the gospel of our Lord Jesus, and the writings of His apostles—for your foundation. *Praying in the Holy Ghost.* Holding fast the divine influence which you have received, and under that influence making prayer and supplication to God. The prayer that is not sent up through the influence of the Holy Ghost is never likely to reach heaven.

21. *Keep yourselves in the love of God.* By "building up yourselves on your most holy faith," and "praying in the Holy Ghost"; for without this we shall soon lose the love of God.

22. *And of some have compassion, making a difference.* The general meaning of this exhortation is supposed to be, "You are not to deal alike with all those who have been seduced by false teachers; you are to make a difference between those who have been led away by weakness and imprudence and those who, in the pride and arrogance of their hearts and their unwillingness to submit to wholesome discipline, have separated themselves from the Church and become its inveterate enemies."

24. *Now unto him that is able to keep you from falling.* Who alone can preserve you from the contagion of sin, and preserve you from falling into any kind of error that might be prejudicial to the interests of your souls; and thus to *present you faultless. Before the presence of his glory,* where nothing can stand that does not resemble himself; *with exceeding* great *joy* in finding youselves eternally out of the reach of the possibility of falling, and for having now arrived at an eternity of happiness.

25. *To the only wise God.* Who alone can teach, who alone has declared the truth; that truth in which you now stand. *Our Saviour.* Who has by His blood washed us from our sins, and made us kings and priests unto God the Father. *Be glory.* Be ascribed all light, excellence, and splendor. *Majesty.* All power, authority, and preeminence. *Dominion.* All rule and government in the world and in the Church, in earth and in heaven. *And power.* All energy and operation to everything that is wise, great, good, holy, and excellent. *Both now.* In the present state of life and things. *And ever.* To the end of all states, places, dispensations, and worlds; and to a state which knows no termination, being that eternity in which this glory, majesty, dominion, and power ineffably and incomprehensibly dwell.

After *to the only wise God our Saviour,* many excellent MSS., etc., add "by Jesus Christ our Lord"; and after *dominion and power* they add "before all time"; and both these readings Griesbach has received into the text. The text therefore may be read thus: "To the only wise God our Saviour, by Christ Jesus our Lord, be glory and majesty, dominion and power, before all time; and now, and through all futurity. Amen."

The Book of
THE REVELATION

Among the interpreters of the Apocalypse, in both ancient and modern times, we find a vast diversity of opinions, but they may be all reduced to four principal hypotheses or modes of interpretation: (1) The Apocalypse contains a prophetical description of the destruction of Jerusalem, of the Jewish war, and the civil wars of the Romans. (2) It contains predictions of the persecutions of the Christians under the heathen emperors of Rome, and of the happy days of the Church under the Christian emperors, from Constantine downwards. (3) It contains prophecies concerning the tyrannical and oppressive conduct of the Roman pontiffs, the true antichrist; and foretells the final destruction of popery. (4) It is a prophetic declaration of the schism and heresies of Martin Luther, those called Reformers, and their successors; and the final destruction of the Protestant religion.

The first opinion has been defended by Professor Wetstein and other learned men on the continent. The second is the opinion of the primitive fathers in general, both Greek and Latin. The third was first broached by the Abbe Joachim, who flourished in the thirteenth century, was espoused by most of the Franciscans, and has been and still is the general opinion of the Protestants. The fourth seems to have been invented by popish writers, merely by way of retaliation.

Who the writer of the Apocalypse was, learned men are not agreed. This was a question, as well in ancient as in modern times. Many have attributed it to the Apostle John; others, to a person called John the presbyter, who they say was an Ephesian, and totally different from John the apostle. Whether it was written by John the apostle, John the presbyter, or some other person is of little importance if the question of its inspiration be fully established.

My readers will naturally expect that I should either give a decided preference to some one of the opinions stated above or produce one of my own; I can do neither, nor can I pretend to explain the book. I do not understand it; and in the things which concern so sublime and awful a subject I dare not, as my predecessors, indulge in conjectures. I have read elaborate works on the subject, and each seemed right till another was examined. I am satisfied that no certain mode of interpreting the prophecies of this book has yet been found out, and I will not add another monument to the littleness or folly of the human mind by endeavoring to strike out a new course. I repeat it, I do not understand the book; and I am satisfied that not one who has written on the subject knows anything more of it than myself.

A conjecture concerning the design of the book may be safely indulged; thus then it has struck me that the book of the Apocalypse may be considered as a prophet continued in the Church of God, uttering predictions relative to all times, which have their successive fulfilment as ages roll on; and thus it stands in the Christian Church in the place of the succession of prophets in the Jewish church; and by this especial economy prophecy is still continued, is always speaking; and yet a succession of prophets is rendered unnecessary.

I had resolved for a considerable time not to meddle with this book, because I foresaw that I could produce nothing satisfactory on it; but when I reflected that the literal sense and phraseology might be made much plainer by the addition of philological and critical notes; and that, as the diction appeared in many places to be purely rabbinical (a circumstance to which few of its expositors have attended), it might be rendered plainer by examples from the ancient Jewish writers; and that several parts of it spoke directly of the work of God in the soul of man, and of the conflicts and consolations of the followers of Christ, particularly in the beginning of the book, I changed my resolution, and have added short notes, principally philological, where I thought I understood the meaning.

CHAPTER 1

The preface to this book, and the promise to them who read it, 1-3. John's address to the seven churches of Asia, whose high calling he particularly mentions; and shows the speedy coming of Christ, 4-8. Mentions his exile to Patmos, and the appearance of the Lord Jesus to him, 9-11. Of whom he gives a most glorious description, 12-18. The command to write what he saw, and the explanation of the seven stars and seven golden candlesticks, 19-20.

1. *The Revelation of Jesus Christ.* The word from which we have our word Apocalypse signifies literally a "revelation, or discovery of what was concealed or hidden." It is here said that this revelation, or discovery of hidden things, was given by God to Jesus Christ, that Christ gave it to His angel, that this angel showed it to *John,* and that John sent it to the churches. *Things which must shortly come to pass.* On the mode of interpretation devised by Wetstein, this is plain; for if the book were written before the destruction of Jerusalem, and the prophecies in it relate to that destruction, and the civil wars among the Romans, which lasted but three or four years, then it might be said the Revelation is of things which *must shortly come to pass*. But if we consider the book as referring to the state of the Church in all ages, the words here and those in v. 3 must be understood of the commencement of the events predicted; as if he had said: In a short time the train of these visions will be put in motion.

2. *Who bare record of the word of God.* Is there a reference here to the first chapter of John's Gospel, "In the beginning was the Word, and the Word was with God"? Of this *Word*, John did bear record. Or does the writer mean the fidelity with which he noted and related the word—doctrines or prophecies—which he received at this time by revelation from God? This seems more consistent with the latter part of the verse.

3. *Blessed is he that readeth.* This is to be understood of the happiness or security of the persons who, reading and hearing the prophecies of those things which were to come to pass shortly, took proper measures to escape from the impending evils. *The time is at hand.* Either in which they shall be all fulfilled or begin to be fulfilled. See the note on v. 1. These three verses contain the introduction; now the dedication to the seven churches commences.

4. *John to the seven churches.* The apostle begins this much in the manner of the Jewish prophets. They often name themselves in the messages which they receive from God to deliver to the people. The *Asia* here mentioned was what is called Proconsular Asia; the *seven churches* were those of Ephesus, Smyrna, Pergamos, Thyatira, Sardis, Philadelphia, and Laodicea. These seven were those which lay nearest to the apostle, and were more particularly under his care; though the message was sent to the churches in general, and perhaps it concerns the whole Christian world. But the number *seven* may be used here as the number of perfection. *Grace be unto you.* This form of apostolical benediction we have often seen in the preceding Epistles. *From him which is, and which was, and which is to come.* This phraseology is purely Jewish, and probably taken from the Tetragrammaton, *Yehovah;* which is supposed to include in itself all time, past, present, and future. In *Chasad Shimuel,* Rab. Samuel ben David asks: "Why are we commanded to use three hours of prayer? Answer: These hours point out the holy blessed God; he who was, who is, and who shall be. The morning prayer points out him who was before the foundation of the world; the noonday prayer points out him who is; and the evening prayer points out him who is to come." This phraseology is exceedingly appropriate, and strongly expresses the eternity of God; for we have no other idea of time than as past, or now existing, or yet to exist. That which was is the eternity before time; that which is, is time itself; and that which is to come is the eternity which shall be when time is no more. *The seven Spirits which are before his throne.* The ancient Jews, who represented the throne of God as the throne of an Eastern monarch, supposed that there were seven ministering angels before this throne, as there were seven ministers attendant on the

throne of a Persian monarch. We have an ample proof of this, *Tobit* xii. 15: "I am Raphael, one of the seven holy angels which present the prayers of the saints, and which go in and out before the glory of the Holy One." And in *Jonathan ben Uzziel's* Targum, on Gen. xi. 7: "God said to the seven angels which stand before him." That seven angels are here meant, and not the Holy Spirit, is most evident from the place, the number, and the tradition. Those who imagine the Holy Ghost to be intended suppose the number seven is used to denote His manifold gifts and graces. That these seven spirits are angels, see chap. iii. 1; iv. 5; and particularly v. 6, where they are called "the seven Spirits of God sent forth into all the earth."

5. *The faithful witness.* The true Teacher, whose testimony is infallible, and whose sayings must all come to pass. *The first begotten of the dead.* See the note on Col. i. 18. *The prince of the kings.* The "Chief" or "Head" of all earthly potentates. *Unto him that loved us.* This should begin a new verse, as it is the commencement of a new subject. Our salvation is attributed to the love of God, who gave His Son; and to the love of Christ, who died for us. See John iii. 16. *Washed us from our sins.* The redemption of the soul, with the remission of sins and purification from unrighteousness, is here, as in all the New Testament, attributed to the blood of Christ shed on the Cross for man.

6. *Kings and priests.* See on 1 Pet. ii. 5, 9. But instead of *kings and priests* the most reputable MSS., versions, and fathers have "a kingdom and priests"; i.e., a Kingdom of priests, or a royal priesthood. The regal and sacerdotal dignities are the two highest that can possibly exist among men; and these two are here mentioned to show the glorious prerogatives and state of the children of God. *To him be glory.* That is, to Christ; for it is of Him that the prophet speaks, and of none other. *For ever and ever.* "To ages of ages"; or rather, through all indefinite periods; through all times, and through all eternity. *Amen.* A word of affirmation and approbation; so it shall be, and so it ought to be.

7. *Behold, he cometh with clouds.* This relates to His coming to execute judgment on the enemies of His religion. *And all kindreds of the earth.* "All the tribes of the land." By this the Jewish people are most evidently intended, and therefore the whole verse may be understood as predicting the destruction of the Jews, and is a presumptive proof that the Apocalypse was written before the final overthrow of the Jewish state. *Even so, Amen.* "Yea, Amen." It is true, so be it.

8. *I am Alpha and Omega.* I am from eternity to eternity. This mode of speech is borrowed from the Jews, who express the whole compass of things by *aleph* and *tau,* the first and last letters of the Hebrew alphabet; but as John was writing in Greek, he accommodates the whole to the Greek alphabet, of which *alpha* and *omega* are the first and last letters. With the rabbins "from aleph to tau" expressed the whole of matter, "from the beginning to the end." *The beginning and the ending.* This clause is wanting in almost every MS. and version of importance. It appears to have been added first as an explanatory note, and in process of time crept into the text.

9. *Your brother.* A Christian, begotten of God, and incorporated in the heavenly family. *Companion in tribulation.* Suffering under the persecution in which you also suffer. *In the kingdom.* For we are a Kingdom of priests unto God. *And patience of Jesus.* Meekly bearing all indignities, privations, and sufferings for the sake and after the example of our Lord and Master. *The isle that is called Patmos.* This island lies in the Aegean Sea. It has derived all its celebrity from being the place to which John was banished by one of the Roman emperors; whether Domitian, Claudius, or Nero is not agreed on, but it was most probably the latter. The whole island is about thirty miles in circumference. *For the testimony of Jesus Christ.* For preaching Christianity and converting heathens to the Lord Jesus.

10. *I was in the Spirit.* That is, I received the Spirit of prophecy, and was under its influence when the first vision was exhibited. *The Lord's day.* The first day of the week, observed as the Christian Sabbath, because on it Jesus Christ rose from the dead; therefore it was called *the Lord's day,* and has taken place of the Jewish Sabbath throughout the Christian world. *And heard behind me a great voice.* This voice came unexpectedly and suddenly. He felt himself under the divine afflatus, but did not know what scenes were to be represented. *As of a trumpet.* This was calculated to call in every wandering thought, to fix his attention, and solemnize his whole frame. Thus God prepared Moses to receive the law. See Exod. xix. 16, 19.

11. *I am Alpha and Omega, the first and the last: and.* This whole clause is wanting in many MSS. Griesbach has left it out of the text. *Saying . . . What thou seest, write in a book.* Carefully note down everything that is represented to you. John had the visions from heaven, but he described them in his own language and manner. *Send it unto the seven churches.* The names of which immediately follow. *In Asia.* This is wanting in the principal MSS. and versions. *Ephesus.* This was a city of Ionia, in Asia Minor, situated at the mouth of the river Cayster, on the shore of the Aegean Sea, about fifty miles south of Smyrna. *Smyrna,* now called also Ismir, is the largest and richest city of Asia Minor. It is situated about one hundred and eighty-three miles west by south of Constantinople, on the shore of the Aegean Sea. *Pergamos.* A town of Mysia, situated on the river Caicus. It was anciently famous for its library, which contained, according to Plutarch, two hundred thousand volumes. It was here that the *membranae Pergameniae,* Pergamenian skins, were invented; from which we derive our word "parchment." *Thyatira.* A city of Natolia, in Asia Minor, seated on the river Hermus, in a plain eighteen miles broad, and is about fifty miles from Pergamos. *Sardis.* Now called Sardo and Sart, a town of Asia, in Natolia, about forty miles east from Smyrna. *Philadelphia.* A city of Natolia, seated at the foot of mount Tmolus, by the river Cogamus. It is about forty miles east-southeast of Smyrna. *Laodicea.* A town of Phrygia, on the river Lycus. It was built by Antiochus Theos, and named after his consort Laodice.

12. *And I turned.* For he had heard the voice behind him. *To see the voice;* i.e., the person from whom the voice came. *Seven golden candlesticks.* "Seven golden lamps." These seven lamps represented the seven churches, in which the light of God was continually shining and the love of God continually burning. And they are here represented as *golden,* to show how precious they were in the sight of God. This is a reference to the Temple at Jerusalem, where there was a candlestick or chandelier of seven branches; or rather six branches—three springing out on either side, and one in the centre. See Exod. xxxvii. 17-23. This reference to the Temple seems to intimate that the Temple of Jerusalem was a type of the whole Christian Church.

13. *Like unto the Son of man.* This seems a reference to Dan. vii. 13. This was our blessed Lord himself, v. 18. *Clothed with a garment down to the foot.* This is a description of the high priest, in his sacerdotal robes. Jesus is our High Priest, even in heaven. He is still discharging the sacerdotal functions before the throne of God. *Golden girdle.* The emblem of both regal and sacerdotal dignity.

14. *His head and his hairs were white like wool.* This was not only an emblem of His antiquity, but it was the evidence of His glory; for the whiteness or splendor of His head and hair doubtless proceeded from the rays of light and glory which encircled His head, and darted from it in all directions. *His eyes were as a flame of fire.* To denote His omniscience, and the all-penetrating nature of the divine knowledge.

15. *His feet like unto fine brass.* An emblem of His stability and permanence, brass being considered the most durable of all metallic substances or compounds. The original word means the famous metal which, according to Suidas, was "a kind of amber, more precious than gold." It seems to have been a composition of gold, silver, and brass, and the same with the Corinthian brass, so highly famed and valued. It may however mean no more than copper melted with *lapis calaminaris,* which converts it into brass; and the flame that proceeds from the metal during this operation is one of the most intensely and unsufferably vivid that can be imagined. I have often seen several furnaces employed in this operation, and the flames bursting up through the earth (for these furnaces are underground) always called to remembrance this description given by John: *His feet of fine brass, as if they burned in a furnace. His voice as the sound of many waters.* The same description we find in Ezek. xliii. 2: "The glory of the God of Israel came from the way of the east: and his voice was like a noise of many waters; and the earth shined with his glory."

16. *In his right hand seven stars.* The *stars* are afterwards interpreted as representing the seven angels, messengers, or bishops of the seven churches. Their being in the right hand of Christ shows that they are under His special care and most powerful protection. *Out of his mouth went a sharp twoedged sword.* The *sharp twoedged sword* may represent the Word of God in general, according to that saying of the apostle, Heb. iv. 12: "The word of God is quick, and powerful, and sharper than any twoedged sword, piercing even to the dividing asunder of soul and spirit." And "the word of God" is termed "the sword of the Spirit," Eph. vi. 17. *And his countenance was as the sun shineth in his*

strength. His face was like the disk of the sun in the brightest summer's day, when there were no clouds to abate the splendor of his rays. A similar form of expression is found in Judges v. 31: "Let them that love him be as the sun when he goeth forth in his might."

17. *I fell at his feet as dead.* The appearance of the glory of the Lord had the same effect upon Ezekiel, chap. i. 28; and the appearance of Gabriel had the same effect on Daniel, chap. vii. 17. The terrible splendor of such majesty was more than the apostle could bear, and he fell down deprived of his senses, but was soon enabled to behold the vision by a communication of strength from our Lord's *right hand.*

18. *I am he that liveth, and was dead.* I am Jesus, the Saviour, who, though the Fountain of life, have died for mankind; and being raised from the dead I shall die no more, the great sacrifice being consummated. *And have the keys of death and the grave,* so that I can destroy the living and raise the dead. The key here signifies the power and authority over life, *death,* and the grave. This is also a rabbinical form of speech. We should understand *hades* here, not as *hell,* nor the place of separate spirits, but merely as the "grave"; and the key we find to be merely the emblem of power and authority. Christ can both save and destroy, can kill and make alive. Death is still under His dominion, and He can recall the dead whensoever He pleases. He is "the resurrection, and the life."

20. *The mystery.* That is, the allegorical explanation of the *seven stars* is the seven *angels* or ministers of the churches; and the allegorical meaning of the "seven golden lamps" is the *seven churches* themselves.

CHAPTER 2

The epistle to the church of Ephesus, commending their labor and patience, 1-3. And reprehending their having left their first love, exhorting them to repent, with the promise of the tree of life, 4-7. The epistle to the church of Smyrna, commending their piety, and promising them support in their tribulation, 8-11. The epistle to the church of Pergamos, commending their steadfastness in the heavenly doctrine, 12-13. And reprehending their laxity in ecclesiastical discipline, in tolerating heretical teachers in the church, 14-15. The apostle exhorts them to repent, with the promise of the white stone and a new name, 16-17. The epistle to the church of Thyatira, with a commendation of their charity, faith, and patience, 18-19. Reprehending their toleration of Jezebel, the false prophetess, who is threatened with grievous punishment, 20-24. Particular exhortations and promises to this church, 24-29.

I must here advise my readers: (1) That I do not perceive any metaphorical or allegorical meaning in the epistles to these churches. (2) I consider the churches as real; and that their spiritual state is here really and literally pointed out; and that they have no reference to the state of the Church of Christ in all ages of the world, as has been imagined; and that the notion of what has been termed the Ephesian state, the Smyrnian state, the Pergamenian state, the Thyatirian state, etc., is unfounded, absurd, and dangerous; and such expositions should not be entertained by any who wish to arrive at a sober and rational knowledge of the Holy Scriptures. (3) I consider the angel of the church as signifying the messenger, the pastor, sent by Christ and His apostles to teach and edify that church. (4) I consider what is spoken to this angel as spoken to the whole church; and that it is not his particular state that is described,

but the state of the people in general under his care.

THE EPISTLE TO THE CHURCH AT EPHESUS

1. *Unto the angel of the church of Ephesus.* By *angel* we are to understand the "messenger" or person sent by God to preside over this church; and to him the epistle is directed, not as pointing out his state, but the state of the church under his care. *Angel of the church* here answers exactly to that officer of the synagogue among the Jews called the messenger of the church, whose business it was to read, pray, and teach in the synagogue. The church at Ephesus is first addressed, as being the place where John chiefly resided; and the city itself was the metropolis of that part of Asia. *Holdeth the seven stars.* Who particularly preserves and guides and upholds, not only the ministers of those seven churches, but all the genuine ministers of His gospel, in all ages and places. *Walketh in the midst of the seven golden candlesticks.* Is the supreme Bishop and Head, not only of those churches, but of all the churches or congregations of His people throughout the world.

2. *I know thy works.* For the eyes of the Lord are throughout the earth, beholding the evil and the good; and, being omnipresent, all things are continually open and naked before Him. It is worthy of remark that whatsoever is praiseworthy in any of these churches is first mentioned, thereby intimating that God is more intent on finding out the good than the evil in any person or church, and that those who wish to reform such as have fallen or are not making sufficient advances in the divine life should take occasion, from the good which yet remains, to encourage them to set out afresh for the kingdom of Heaven. Exhortations and encouragements of this kind are sure to produce the most blessed effects; and under such the work of God infallibly revives.

3. *And hast borne.* The same things mentioned in the preceding verse, but in an inverted order, the particular reason of which does not appear. Perhaps it was intended to show more forcibly to this church that there was no good which they had done, nor evil which they had suffered, that was forgotten before God. *And hast not fainted.* They must therefore have had a considerable portion of this love remaining, else they could not have thus acted.

4. *Nevertheless I have somewhat against thee.* The clause should be read, according to the Greek, thus: "But I have against you that you have left your first love." They did not retain that strong and ardent affection for God and sacred things which they had when first brought to the knowledge of the truth, and justified by faith in Christ.

5. *Remember.* Consider the state of grace in which you once stood; the happiness, love, and joy which you felt when you received remission of sins; the zeal you had for God's glory and the salvation of mankind; your willing, obedient spirit, your cheerful self-denial, your fervor in private prayer, your detachment from the world, and your heavenly-mindedness. *Whence thou art fallen.* Or "Remember what a loss you have sustained." *Repent.* Be deeply humbled before God for having so carelessly

guarded the divine treasure. *Do the first works.* Resume your former zeal and diligence; watch, fast, pray, reprove sin, carefully attend all the ordinances of God, walk as in His sight, and rest not till you have recovered all your lost ground, and got back the evidence of your acceptance with your Maker. *I will come unto thee quickly.* In the way of judgment. *And will remove thy candlestick.* Take away My ordinances, remove your ministers, and send you a famine of the word.

6. *The deeds of the Nicolaitanes.* These were, as is commonly supposed, a sect of the Gnostics, who taught the most impure doctrines and followed the most impure practices.

7. *He that hath an ear.* Let every intelligent person, and every Christian man, attend carefully to what the Holy Spirit, in this and the following epistles, says to the churches. See the note on Matt. xi. 15, where the same form of speech occurs. *To him that overcometh.* To him who continues steadfast in the faith and uncorrupt in his life, who faithfully confesses Jesus and neither imbibes the doctrines nor is led away by the error of the wicked, *will I give to eat of the tree of life.* As he who conquered his enemies had, generally, not only great honor but also a reward, so here a great reward is promised "to the conqueror." And as in the Grecian games, to which there may be an allusion, the conqueror was crowned with the leaves of some tree, here it is promised that they should *eat of the fruit of the tree of life, which is in the midst of the paradise of God;* that is, that they should have a happy and glorious immortality. *The tree of life* is frequently spoken of by the rabbins; and by it they generally mean the immortality of the soul and a final state of blessedness.

THE EPISTLE TO THE CHURCH AT SMYRNA

8. *These things saith the first and the last.* He who is eternal; from whom all things come, and to whom all things must return. *Which was dead,* for the redemption of the world; *and is alive* to die no more forever, His glorified humanity being enthroned at the Father's right hand.

9. *I know thy works.* As He had spoken to the preceding church, so He speaks to this: I know all that you have done, and all that you have suffered. The *tribulation* here mentioned must mean persecution, either from the Jews, the heathens, or from the heretics, who, because of their flesh-pampering doctrine, might have had many partisans at Smyrna. *And poverty.* Stripped probably of all their temporal possessions because of their attachment to the gospel. *But thou art rich.* Rich in faith, and heir of the kingdom of Christ. *The blasphemy of them which say they are Jews.* There were persons there who professed Judaism, and had a synagogue in the place, and professed to worship the true God; but they had no genuine religion, and they served the devil rather than God. They applied a sacred name to an unholy thing; and this is one meaning of the word *blasphemy* in this book.

10. *Ten days.* As the *days* in this book are what is commonly called "prophetic days," each answering to a year, the *ten days* of tribulation may denote "ten years of persecution"; and this was precisely the duration of the persecution under Diocletian, during which all the Asiatic churches were grievously afflicted. Others understand the expression as implying frequency and abundance, as it does in other parts of Scripture. Gen. xxxi. 7, 41: Thou hast "changed my wages ten times"; i.e., you have frequently changed my wages. Num. xiv. 22: "Those men . . . have tempted me now these ten times"; i.e., They have frequently and grievously tempted and sinned against Me. Neh. iv. 12: "The Jews which dwelt by them came . . . [and] said unto us ten times," i.e., They were frequently coming and informing us that our adversaries intended to attack us. Job xix. 3; "These ten times have ye reproached me"; i.e., you have loaded me with continual reproaches. *Be thou faithful unto death.* Be firm, hold fast the faith, confess Christ to the last and at all hazards, and you shall have *a crown of life*—you shall be crowned with life, have an eternal happy existence, though you suffer a temporal death. It is said of Polycarp that when brought before the judge, and commanded to abjure and blaspheme Christ, he firmly answered, "Eighty and six years have I served Him, and He never did me wrong. How then can I blaspheme my King, who hath saved me?" He was then adjudged to the flames, and suffered cheerfully for Christ, the Lord and Master.

11. *He that overcometh.* The "conqueror" who has stood firm in every trial and vanquished all his adversaries. *Shall not be hurt of the second death.* That is, an eternal separation from God and the glory of His power, as what we commonly mean by final perdition. This is another rabbinical mode of speech in very frequent use, and by it they understand the punishment of hell in a future life.

THE EPISTLE TO THE CHURCH AT PERGAMOS

12. *Which hath the sharp sword.* See on chap. i. 16. The "sword of the Spirit, which is the word of God," cuts every way; it convinces of sin, righteousness, and judgment; pierces between the joints and the marrow, divides between the soul and spirit, dissects the whole mind, and exhibits a regular anatomy of the soul. It not only reproves and exposes sin, but it slays the ungodly, pointing out the punishment they shall endure. Jesus has the *sword with two edges,* because He is the Saviour of sinners and the Judge of quick and dead.

13. *Where Satan's seat is.* "Where Satan has his throne"—where he reigns as king and is universally obeyed. It was a maxim among the Jews that, where the law of God was not studied, there Satan dwelt; but he was obliged to leave the place where a synagogue or academy was established. *Thou holdest fast my name.* Notwithstanding that the profession of Christianity exposed this church to the bitterest persecution, they held fast the name of Christian, which they had received from Jesus Christ, and did not deny His faith; for when brought to the trial they openly professed themselves disciples and followers of their Lord and Master. *Antipas was my faithful martyr.* Who this *Antipas* was we cannot tell. We only know that he was a Christian, and probably bore some office in the church, and became illustrious by his martyrdom in the cause of Christ.

14. *I have a few things against thee.* Their good deeds are first carefully sought out and

commended; what was wrong in them is touched with a gentle but effectual hand. The followers of Balaam, the Nicolaitans, and the Gnostics were probably all the same kind of persons, but see on v. 6. What the doctrine of Balaam was, see the notes on Num. xxiv; xxv; and xxxi. It appears that there were some then in the church at Pergamos who held eating things offered to idols in honor of those idols, and fornication, indifferent things. They associated with idolaters in the heathen temples and partook with them in their religious festivals.

15. *The doctrine of the Nicolaitanes.* See on v. 6.

16. *Will fight against them with the sword of my mouth.* See on v. 12. He now speaks for their edification and salvation; but if they do not repent, He will shortly declare those judgments which shall unavoidably fall upon them.

17. *The hidden manna.* It was a constant tradition of the Jews that the ark of the covenant, the tables of stone, Aaron's rod, the holy anointing oil, and the pot of manna were hidden by King Josiah when Jerusalem was taken by the Chaldeans; and that these should all be restored in the days of the Messiah. This *manna* was *hidden,* but Christ promises to give it to him that is conqueror. Jesus is the Ark, the Oil, the Rod, the Testimony, and the Manna. He who is partaker of His grace has all those things in their spiritual meaning and perfection. *And will give him a white stone.* It is supposed that by the white stone is meant pardon or acquittance, and the evidence of it; and that there is an allusion here to the custom observed by judges in ancient times, who were accustomed to give their suffrages by *white* and black pebbles. Those who gave the former were for absolving the culprit; those who gave the latter were for his condemnation. Others suppose there is an allusion here to conquerors in the public games, who were not only conducted with great pomp into the city to which they belonged, but had a *white stone* given to them, with their name inscribed on it; which badge entitled them, during their whole life, to be maintained at the public expense. The most remarkable of these instruments were the *tesserae hospitales,* which were given as badges of friendship and alliance, and on which some device was engraved, as a testimony that a contract of friendship had been made between the parties. A small, oblong, square piece of wood, bone, stone, or ivory was taken and divided into two equal parts, on which each of the parties wrote his own name, and then interchanged it with the other. This was carefully preserved; and by producing this when they travelled, it gave a mutual claim to the bearers of kind reception and hospitable entertainment at each other's houses. The *tessera* taken in this sense seems to have been a kind of tally, and the two parts were compared together to ascertain the truth. Now it is very probable that John may allude to this, for on this mode of interpretation every part of the verse is consistent. The word does not necessarily signify a *stone* of any kind, but a suffrage, sentence, decisive vote; and in this place seems answerable to the *tessera.* The names of the contracting persons, or some device, were written on the *tessera,* which commemorated the friendly contract; and as the parts were interchanged, none could know that name or device,

or the reason of the contract, but he who received it. This, when produced, gave the bearer a right to the offices of hospitality; he was accommodated with food, lodging, as far as these were necessary; and to this the eating *of the hidden manna* may refer.

THE EPISTLE TO THE CHURCH AT THYATIRA

19. *I know thy works.* And of these he first sets forth their *charity,* their "love" to God and each other, and particularly to the poor and distressed; and hence followed their *faith,* their "fidelity," to the grace they had received; and *service,* "ministration"; properly pious and benevolent service to widows, orphans, and the poor in general. *And thy patience.* Your "perseverance" under afflictions and persecutions, and your continuance in well-doing. I put *faith* before *service* according to the general consent of the best MSS. and versions. *Thy works.* The continued labor of love and thorough obedience. *The last to be more than the first.* They not only retained what they had received at first, but grew in grace, and in the knowledge and love of Jesus Christ. This is a rare thing in most Christian churches; they generally lose the power of religion and rest in the forms of worship, and it requires a powerful revival to bring them to such a state that their last works shall be more than their first.

20. *That woman Jezebel.* There is an allusion here to the history of Ahab and Jezebel, as given in 2 Kings ix—x; and although we do not know who this Jezebel was, yet from the allusion we may take it for granted she was a woman of power and influence in Thyatira, who corrupted the true religion and harassed the followers of God in that city, as Jezebel did in Israel. Instead of *that woman Jezebel,* many excellent MSS., and almost all the ancient versions, read "thy wife Jezebel"; which intimates, indeed asserts, that this bad woman was the wife of the bishop of the church, and his criminality in suffering her was therefore the greater. This reading Griesbach has received into the text.

21. *I gave her space to repent.* It is worthy of remark that the Gnostics called their doctrine "the depths of God" and "the depths of Bythos," intimating that they contained the most profound secrets of divine wisdom. Christ here calls them the "depths of Satan," being masterpieces of his subtlety. Perhaps they thought them to be of God, while all the time they were deceived by the devil.

25. *That which ye have*—that is, the pure doctrine of the gospel; *hold fast till I come*—till I come to execute the judgments which I have threatened.

26. *Power over the nations.* Every witness of Christ has power to confute and confound all the false doctrines and maxims of the nations of the world, for Christianity shall at last rule over all; the kingdom of Christ will come, and the kingdom of this world become the kingdoms of our God and of His Christ.

27. *He shall rule them with a rod of iron.* He shall restrain vice by the strictest administration of justice; and those who finally despise the word and rebel shall be *broken* and destroyed, so as never more to be able to make head against the truth.

CHAPTER 3

The epistle to the church of Sardis, 1-6. The epistle to the church of Philadelphia, 7-13. The epistle to the church of Laodicea, 14-22.

EPISTLE TO THE CHURCH AT SARDIS

1. *The seven Spirits of God.* See the note on chap. i. 4. *Thou hast a name that thou livest.* You have the reputation of Christians, and consequently of being alive to God, through the quickening influence of the divine Spirit; but *art dead*—you have not the life of God in your souls; you have not walked consistently and steadily before God, and His Spirit has been grieved with you, and He has withdrawn much of His light and power.

2. *Be watchful.* You have lost ground by carelessness and inattention. Awake, and keep awake! *Strengthen the things which remain.* The convictions and good desires, with any measure of the fear of God and of a tender conscience, which, although still subsisting, are about to perish, because the Holy Spirit, who is the Author of them, being repeatedly grieved, is about finally to depart. *Thy works perfect.* "Filled up." They performed duties of all kinds, but no duty completely. They were constantly beginning, but never brought anything to a proper end. Their resolutions were languid, their strength feeble, and their light dim. They probably maintained their reputation before men, but their works were not perfect before God.

3. *Remember.* Enter into a serious consideration of your state. *How thou hast received.* With what joy, zeal, and gladness you heard the gospel of Christ when first preached to you. *Hold fast.* Those good desires and heavenly influences which still remain. *And repent.* Be humbled before God. *I will come on thee as a thief.* As the thief comes when he is not expected.

4. *Thou hast a few names even in Sardis.* A few "persons," *names* being put for those who bore them. And as the members of the church were all enrolled, or their names entered in a book, when admitted into the church or when baptized, *names* are here put for the people themselves. *Have not defiled their garments.* Their souls. The Hebrews considered holiness as the garb of the soul, and evil actions as stains or spots on this garb. *They shall walk with me in white.* They shall be raised to a state of eternal glory, and shall be forever with their Lord.

5. *I will not blot out his name.* This may be an allusion to the custom of registering the names of those who were admitted into the church in a book kept for that purpose. These are properly *book[s] of life*, as there those who were born unto God were registered. Or there may be allusions to the *white raiment* worn by the priests, and the erasing of the name of any priest out of the sacerdotal list who had either sinned or was found not to be of the seed of Aaron. "The great council of Israel sat and judged the priests. If in a priest any vice was found they stripped off his white garments and clothed him in *black*, in which he wrapped himself, went out, and departed. Him in whom no vice was found they clothed in *white*, and he went and took his part in the ministry among his brother priests." *I will confess his name.*

I will acknowledge that this person is My true disciple and a member of My mystical body.

EPISTLE TO THE CHURCH AT PHILADELPHIA

7. *He that is holy.* In whom holiness essentially dwells, and from whom all holiness is derived. *He that is true.* He who is the Fountain of truth. *He that hath the key of David.* See this metaphor explained, Matt. xvi. 19. *Key* is the emblem of authority and knowledge; *the key of David* is the regal right or authority of David. David could shut or open the kingdom of Israel to whom he pleased. The Kingdom of the gospel and the kingdom of Heaven are at the disposal of Christ. He can shut against whom He will; He can open to whom He pleases. If He shuts, no man can open; if He opens, no man can shut.

8. *I have set before thee an open door.* I have opened to you a door to proclaim and diffuse My word; and notwithstanding there are many adversaries to the spread of My gospel, yet none of them shall be able to prevent it. *Thou hast a little strength.* May refer either to the smallness of the numbers or to the littleness of their grace.

9. *I will make them*, show them to be, *of the synagogue of Satan, who say they are Jews,* pretending thereby to be of the synagogue of God, and consequently His true and peculiar children. *I will make them to come and worship.* I will so dispose of matters in the course of My providence that the Jews shall be obliged to seek unto the Christians for toleration, support, and protection, which they shall be obliged to sue for in the most humble and abject manner. *To know that I have loved thee.* That the love which was formerly fixed on the Jews is now removed and transferred to the Gentiles.

10. *The word of my patience.* The doctrine which has exposed you to so much trouble and persecution, and required so much patience and magnanimity to bear up under its attendant trials. *The hour of temptation.* A "time" of sore and peculiar trial which might have proved too much for their strength. He who is faithful to the grace of God is often hidden from trials and difficulties which fall without mitigation on those who have been unfaithful in His covenant. Many understand by the *hour of temptation* the persecution under Trajan, which was greater and more extensive than the preceding ones under Nero and Domitian. *To try them.* That is, such persecutions will be the means of trying and proving those who profess Christianity and showing who were sound and thorough Christians and who were not.

12. *A pillar in the temple.* There is probably an allusion here to the two pillars in the Temple of Jerusalem, called Jachin and Boaz, "stability and strength." The Church is the *temple;* Christ is the Foundation on which it is built; and His ministers are the pillars by which, under Him, it is adorned and supported. *I will write upon him the name of my God.* As the high priest had on his breastplate the names of the twelve tribes engraved, and these constituted the city or church of God, Christ here promises that in place of them the twelve apostles, representing the Christian Church, shall be written, which is called the New Jerusalem, and which God has adopted in place of the twelve Jewish tribes. *My new name.* The Saviour of all, the Light that

lightens the Gentiles, the Christ, the Anointed One, the only Governor of His Church, and the Redeemer of all mankind. There is here an intimation that the Christian Church is to endure forever, and the Christian ministry to last as long as time endures: *He shall go no more out* forever.

EPISTLE TO THE CHURCH OF THE LAODICEANS

14. *These things saith the Amen.* That is, He who is true or faithful; from *aman,* "he was true"; immediately interpreted, *the faithful and true witness. The beginning of the creation of God.* That is, the Head and Governor of all creatures, the King of the creation. See on Col. i. 15. By His titles here He prepares them for the humiliating and awful truths which He was about to declare, and the authority on which the declaration was founded.

15. *Thou art neither cold nor hot.* You are neither heathens nor Christians—neither good nor evil—neither led away by false doctrine nor thoroughly addicted to that which is true. In a word, they were listless and indifferent, and seemed to care little whether heathenism or Christianity prevailed. Though they felt little zeal either for the salvation of their own souls or that of others, yet they had such a general conviction of the truth and importance of Christianity that they could not readily give it up. *I would thou wert cold or hot.* That, is, you should be decided; adopt some part or other, and be in earnest in your attachment to it. Epictetus, Ench., chap. 36: "Thou oughtest to be one kind of man, either a good man or a bad man."

16. *Because thou art lukewarm.* Irresolute and undecided. *I will spue thee out of my mouth.* He alludes here to the known effect of tepid water upon the stomach; it generally produces a nausea. I will cast you off.

17. *I am rich.* You suppose yourself to be in a safe state, perfectly sure of final salvation, because you have begun well and laid the right foundation. It was this most deceitful conviction that cut the nerves of their spiritual diligence; they rested in what they had already received, and seemed to think that once in grace must be still in grace. *Thou art wretched.* "Most wretched." Instead of being children of God, as they supposed, and infallible heirs of the Kingdom, they were, in the sight of God, in the condition of the most abject slaves. *And miserable.* Most deplorable, to be pitied by all men. *And poor.* Having no spiritual riches, no holiness of heart. *Rich* and *poor* are sometimes used by the rabbins to express the righteous and the wicked. *And blind.* The eyes of your understanding being darkened, so that you do not see your state. *And naked.* Without the image of God, not clothed with holiness and purity. A more deplorable state in spiritual things can scarcely be imagined than that of this church. And it is the true picture of many churches and of innumerable individuals.

18. *White raiment.* Holiness of heart and life. *Anoint thine eyes.* Pray for, that you may receive, the enlightening influences of My Spirit, that you may be convinced of your true state, and see where your help lies.

19. *As many as I love.* So it was the love He still had to them that induced Him thus to reprehend and thus to counsel them. *Be zealous.*

Be in earnest to get your souls saved. They had no zeal; this was their bane. He now stirs them up to diligence in the use of the means of grace, and repentance for their past sins and remissness.

20. *Behold, I stand at the door, and knock.* There are many sayings of this kind among the ancient rabbins; thus in *Shir Hashirim Rabba,* fol. 25, 1: "God said to the Israelites, My children, open to me one door of repentance, even so wide as the eye of a needle, and I will open to you doors through which calves and horned cattle may pass." In *Sohar Levit.* fol. 8, col. 32, it is said: "If a man conceal his sin, and do not open it before the holy King, although he ask mercy, yet the door of repentance shall not be opened to him. But if he open it before the holy blessed God, God spares him, and mercy prevails over wrath; and when he laments, although all the doors were shut, yet they shall be opened to him, and his prayer shall be heard." Christ stands, waits long, at the *door* of the sinner's heart; He knocks—uses judgments, mercies, reproofs, exhortations, to induce sinners to repent and turn to Him; He lifts up His *voice*— calls loudly by His Word, ministers, and Spirit. *If any man hear.* If the sinner will seriously consider his state and attend to the voice of his Lord. *And open the door.* This must be his own act, receiving power for this purpose from his offended Lord, who will not break open the door; He will make no forcible entry. *I will come in to him.* I will manifest myself to him, heal all his backslidings, pardon all his iniquities, and love him freely. *Will sup with him.* Hold communion with him, feed him with the bread of life.

21. *To sit with me in my throne.* In every case it is *to him that overcometh,* to the "conqueror," that the final promise is made. He that conquers not is not crowned; therefore every promise is here made to him that is faithful unto death. Here is a most remarkable expression: Jesus has conquered and is set down with the Father upon the Father's throne; he who conquers through Christ sits down with Christ upon His throne; but Christ's throne and the throne of the Father are the same; and it is on this same throne that those who are faithful unto death are finally to sit!

This is the worst of the seven churches, and yet the most eminent of all the promises are made to it, showing that the worst may repent, finally conquer, and attain even to the highest state of glory.

CHAPTER 4

John sees the throne of God in heaven surrounded by twenty-four elders; and four living creatures, full of eyes; which all join in giving glory to the Almighty, 1-11.

1. *A door was opened in heaven.* This appears to have been a visible aperture in the sky over his head.

2. *I was in the Spirit.* Rapt up in an ecstasy.

3. *And he that sat.* There is here no description of the Divine Being, so as to point out any similitude, shape, or dimensions. The description rather aims to point out the surrounding glory and effulgence than the person of the almighty King.

4. *Four and twenty elders.* Perhaps this is in reference to the smaller Sanhedrin at Jerusalem,

which was composed of twenty-three elders; or to the princes of the twenty-four courses of the Jewish priests which ministered at the Tabernacle and the Temple, at first appointed by David. *Clothed in white raiment.* The garments of the priests. *On their heads crowns of gold.* An emblem of their dignity.

5. *Seven lamps of fire.* Seven angels, the attendants and ministers of the supreme King. See chap. i. 4.

6. *Four beasts.* "Four living creatures." The word beast is very improperly used here and elsewhere in this description. Wycliffe first used it, and translators in general have followed him in this uncouth rendering.

7. *The first beast was like a lion.* It is supposed that there is a reference here to the four standards or ensigns of the four divisions of the tribes in the Israelitish camp, as they are described by Jewish writers. The first living creature was like a *lion;* this was, say the rabbins, the standard of Judah on the east, with the two tribes of Issachar and Zabulon. The second, like a *calf* or "ox," which was the emblem of Ephraim, who pitched on the west, with the two tribes of Manasseh and Benjamin. The third, with the *face* of a *man,* which, according to the rabbins, was the standard of Reuben, who pitched on the south, with the two tribes of Simeon and Gad. The fourth, which was like a *flying* (spread) *eagle,* was, according to the same writers, the emblem on the ensign of Dan, who pitched on the north, with the two tribes of Asher and Naphtali. This traditionary description agrees with the four faces of the cherub in Ezekiel's vision.

8. *The four beasts had each of them six wings.* I have already observed, in the preface to this book, that the phraseology is rabbinical; I might have added, and the imagery also. We have almost a counterpart of this description in *Pirkey Elieser,* chap. 4. In *Shemoth Rabba,* sec. 23, fol. 122, 4, Rabbi Abin says: "There are four which have principality in this world: among intellectual creatures, *man;* among birds, the *eagle;* among cattle, the *ox;* and among wild beasts, the *lion:* each of these has a kingdom and a certain magnificence, and they are placed under the throne of glory, Ezek. i. 10, to show that no creature is to exalt itself in this world, and that the kingdom of God is over all." These creatures may be considered the representatives of the whole creation.

10. *Cast their crowns before the throne.* Acknowledge the infinite supremacy of God, and that they have derived their being and their blessings from Him alone. This is an allusion to the custom of prostrations in the East, and to the homage of petty kings acknowledging the supremacy of the emperor.

11. *Thou art worthy, O Lord, to receive.* Thus all creation acknowledges the supremacy of God; and we learn from this song that He made all things for His pleasure; and through the same motive He preserves.

CHAPTER 5

acknowledge that they were redeemed to God by His blood, 11-12. And then, of the whole creation, who ascribe blessing, honor, glory, and power to God and the Lamb forever, 13-14.

1. *A book written within and on the backside.* That is, the book was full of solemn contents *within,* but it was sealed; and on the *backside* was a superscription indicating its contents. It was a labelled book, or one written on each side of the skin, which was not usual. *Sealed with seven seals.* As seven is a number of perfection, it may mean that the book was so sealed that the seals could neither be counterfeited nor broken; i.e., the matter of the book was so obscure and enigmatical, and the work it enjoined and the facts it predicted so difficult and stupendous, that they could neither be known nor performed by human wisdom or power.

2. *A strong angel.* One of the chief of the angelic host. *Proclaiming.* As the "herald" of God. *To open the book, and to loose the seals.* To loose the seals that he may open the book. Who can tell what this book contains? Who can open its mysteries? The book may mean the purposes and designs of God relative to His government of the world and the Church.

3. *And no man.* No "person" or "being." *In heaven.* Among all the angels of God. *Nor in the earth.* No human being. *Neither under the earth.* No disembodied spirit, nor any demon. Neither angels, men, nor devils can fathom the decrees of God. *Neither to look thereon.* None can look into it unless it be opened, and none can open it unless the seals be unloosed.

4. *I wept much.* Because the world and the Church were likely to be deprived of the knowledge of the contents of the book.

5. *The Lion of the tribe of Juda.* Jesus Christ, who sprang from this tribe, as His genealogy proves; see on Matthew i and Luke iii. There is an allusion here to Gen. xlix. 9, "Judah is a lion's whelp"; the lion was the emblem of this tribe, and was supposed to have been embroidered on its ensigns. *The Root of David.* See Isa. xi. 1. Christ was *the Root of David* as to His divine nature; He was a "Branch" "out of the stem of Jesse" as to His human nature. *Hath prevailed.* By the merit of His incarnation, passion, and death. *To open the book.* To explain and execute all the purposes and decrees of God, in relation to the government of the world and the Church.

6. *Stood a Lamb.* Christ, so called because He was a sacrificial Offering; "a little or delicate Lamb." *As it had been slain.* As if now in the act of being offered. This is very remarkable; so important is the sacrificial offering of Christ in the sight of God that He is still represented as being in the very act of pouring out His blood for the offenses of man. Thus all succeeding generations find they have the continual sacrifice ready, and the newly shed Blood to offer. *Seven horns.* As horn is the emblem of power, and *seven* the number of perfection, the *seven horns* may denote the all-prevailing and infinite might of Jesus Christ. He can support all His friends; He can destroy all His enemies; and He can save to the uttermost all that come unto God through Him. *Seven eyes.* To denote His infinite knowledge and wisdom; but as these *seven eyes* are said to be *the seven Spirits of God,* they seem to denote rather His providence,

in which He often employs the ministry of angels. Therefore these are said to be *sent forth into all the earth.* See on chap. i. 4.

7. *He came and took the book.* This verse may be properly explained by John, chap. i. 18. "No man hath seen God at any time; the only begotten Son, which is in the bosom of the Father, he hath declared him." With Jesus alone are all the counsels and mysteries of God.

8. *The four beasts . . . fell down before the Lamb.* The whole Church of God, and all His children in heaven and earth, acknowledge that Jesus Christ is alone worthy and able to unfold and execute all the mysteries and counsels of God. *Having every one of them harps.* There were *harps* and *vials;* and each of the *elders* and living creatures had one. *Odours, which are the prayers of saints.* The frankincense and odors offered at the Tabernacle were emblems of the prayers and praises of the Lord. That prayers are compared to incense, see Ps. cxli. 2: "Let my prayer be set forth before thee as incense."

9. *A new song.* Composed on the matters and blessings of the gospel, which was just now opened on earth. But *new song* may signify a "most excellent song"; and by this the gospel and its blessings are probably signified. The gospel is called a *new song,* Ps. xcvi. 1. And perhaps there is an allusion in the "harps" here to Ps. cxliv. 9: "I will sing a new song unto thee, O God: upon a psaltery and an instrument of ten strings." The same form of speech is found, Isa. xlii. 10: "Sing unto the Lord a new song"; and there the prophet seems to have the gospel dispensation particularly in view. *Thou . . . hast redeemed us to God by thy blood out of every . . . nation.* It appears, therefore, that the living creatures and the elders represent the aggregate of the followers of God; or the Christian Church in all nations, and among all kinds of people, and perhaps through the whole compass of time; and all these are said to be redeemed by Christ's *blood,* plainly showing that His life was a sacrificial offering for the sins of mankind.

10. *Kings and priests.* See Exod. xix. 6; 1 Pet. ii. 5, 9, and the notes there.

11. *The voice of many angels.* These also are represented as joining in the chorus with redeemed mortals. *Ten thousand times ten thousand.* "Myriads of myriads and chiliads of chiliads"; that is, an infinite or innumerable multitude. This is in reference to Dan. vii. 10.

12. *To receive power.* That is, Jesus Christ is worthy "to take," to have ascribed to Him, *power*—omnipotence; *riches*—beneficence; *wisdom*—omniscience; *strength*—power in prevalent exercise; *honour*—the highest reputation for what He has done; *glory*—the praise due to such actions; *and blessing*—the thankful acknowledgments of the whole creation. Here are seven different species of praise; and this is exactly agreeable to the rabbinical forms, which the author of this book keeps constantly in view. See *Sepher Rasiel,* fol. 39, 2: "To thee belongs glory; magnitude; might; the kingdom; the honour; the victory; and the praise."

13. *Every creature.* All parts of the creation, animate and inanimate, are represented here, by that figure of speech called "personification," as giving praise to the Lord Jesus, because by

Him all things were created. We find the whole creation gives precisely the same praise, and in the same terms, to Jesus Christ, who is undoubtedly meant here by the Lamb just slain, as they give to God who sits upon the throne. Now if Jesus Christ were not properly God, this would be idolatry, as it would be giving to the creature what belongs to the Creator.

14. *The four beasts said, Amen.* Acknowledged that what was attributed to Christ was His due. *The four and twenty elders.* The word twenty-four is wanting in the most eminent MSS. and versions. *Fell down and worshipped.* Fell down on their knees, and then "prostrated themselves" before the throne. This is the Eastern method of adoration: first, the person worshipping fell down on his knees; and then, bowing down, touched the earth with his forehead. This latter act was "prostration." *Him that liveth for ever.* This clause is wanting in many MSS. and is undoubtedly spurious.

CHAPTER 6

What followed on the opening of the seven seals. The opening of the first seal; the white horse, 1-2. The opening of the second seal; the red horse, 3-4. The opening of the third seal; the black horse and the famine, 5-6. The opening of the fourth seal; the pale horse, 7-8. The opening of the fifth seal; the souls of men under the altar, 9-11. The opening of the sixth seal; the earthquake, the darkening of the sun and moon, and falling of the stars, 12-14. The terrible consternation of the kings and great men of the earth, 15-17.

1. *When the Lamb opened one of the seals.* It is worthy of remark that the opening of the seals is not merely a declaration of what God will do, but is the exhibition of a purpose then accomplished; for whenever the seal is opened, the sentence appears to be executed. It is supposed that, from chaps. vi to xi inclusive, the calamities which should fall on the enemies of Christianity, and particularly the Jews, are pointed out under various images, as well as the calamities. *One of the four beasts.* Probably that with the face of a lion. See chap. iv. 7. *Come and see.* Attend to what is about to be exhibited. It is very likely that all was exhibited before his eyes as in a scene; and he saw every act represented which was to take place, and all the persons and things which were to be the chief actors.

2. *A white horse.* Supposed to represent the gospel system, and pointing out its excellence, swiftness, and purity. *He that sat on him.* Supposed to represent Jesus Christ. *A bow.* The preaching of the gospel, darting conviction into the hearts of sinners. *A crown.* The emblem of the Kingdom which Christ was to establish on earth. *Conquering, and to conquer.* Overcoming and confounding the Jews first, and then the Gentiles, spreading more and more the doctrine and influence of the Cross over the face of the earth.

3. *The second beast.* That which had the face of an ox.

4. *Another horse that was red.* The emblem of war; perhaps also of severe persecution, and the martyrdom of the saints. *Him that sat thereon.* Some say, Christ; others, Vespasian; others, the Roman armies. *Take peace from the earth.* To deprive Judea of all tranquillity. *They should kill one another.* This was literally the case with the Jews, while besieged by the

Romans. *A great sword.* Great influence and success, producing terrible carnage.

5. *The third beast.* That which had the face of a man. *A black horse.* The emblem of famine. Some think that which took place under Claudius. See Matt. xxiv. 7; the same which was predicted by Agabus, Acts xi. 28. *A pair of balances.* To show that the scarcity would be such that every person must be put under an allowance.

6. *A measure of wheat for a penny.* It contained as much as one man could consume in a day; and a *penny*, the Roman *denarius*, was the ordinary pay of a laborer. So it appears that in this scarcity each might be able to obtain a bare subsistence by his daily labor; but a man could not, in such cases, provide for a family. *Three measures of barley.* This seems to have been the proportion of value between the wheat and the barley. Barley was allowed to afford a poor aliment, and was given to the Roman soldiers instead of wheat, by way of punishment. *Hurt not the oil and the wine.* Be sparing of these; use them not as delicacies, but for necessity, because neither the vines nor the olives will be productive.

7. *The fourth beast.* That which had the face of an eagle.

8. *A pale horse.* The symbol of death. Of this symbol there can be no doubt, because it is immediately said, *His name that sat on him was Death. And Hell followed with him.* The "grave," or "state of the dead," received the slain. *Over the fourth part of the earth.* One-fourth of mankind was to feel the desolating effects of this seal. *To kill with sword* (war), *and with hunger* (famine), *and with death* (pestilence), *and with the beasts of the earth* (lions, tigers, hyaenas, which would multiply in consequence of the devastations occasioned by war, famine, and pestilence).

9. *The fifth seal.* There is no animal nor any other being to introduce this seal, nor does there appear to be any new event predicted; but the whole is intended to comfort the followers of God under their persecutions, and to encourage them to bear up under their distresses. *I saw under the altar.* A symbolical vision was exhibited, in which he saw an *altar;* and under it *the souls of them that were slain for the word of God*—martyred for their attachment to Christianity—are represented as being newly slain as victims to idolatry and superstition.

10. *And they cried with a loud voice.* That is, their blood, like that of Abel, cried for vengeance; for we are not to suppose that there was anything like a vindictive spirit in those happy and holy souls who had shed their blood for the testimony of Jesus. We sometimes say, "Blood cries for blood"; that is, in the order of divine justice every murderer, and every murdering persecutor, shall be punished. *O Lord.* Sovereign Lord. *Holy.* In Thy own nature, hating threatenings. *Dost thou not judge the persecutors, and avenge our blood, inflict signal punishment, on them that dwell on the earth?* Probably meaning the persecuting Jews; they dwelt "upon that land," a form of speech by which Judea is often signified in the New Testament.

11. *White robes.* The emblems of purity, innocence, and triumph. *They should rest yet for*

a little season. This is a declaration that, when the cup of the iniquity of the Jews should be full, they should then be punished in a mass. If this book was written before the destruction of Jerusalem, as is most likely, then this destruction is that which was to fall upon the Jews and the "little time" or *season* was that which elapsed between their martyrdom, or the date of this book, and the final destruction of Jerusalem by the Romans, under Vespasian and his son Titus, about A.D. 70. What follows may refer to the destruction of the heathen Roman Empire.

12. *The sixth seal.* This seal also is opened and introduced by Jesus Christ alone. *A great earthquake.* A most stupendous change in the civil and religious constitution of the world. If it refer to Constantine the Great, the change that was made by his conversion to Christianity might be very properly represented under the emblem of an *earthquake,* and the other symbols mentioned in this and the following verses. The *sun*—the ancient pagan government of the Roman Empire—was totally darkened; and, like a black hair *sackcloth,* was degraded and humbled to the dust. The *moon*—the ecclesiastical state of the same empire—became as *blood*—was totally ruined, their sacred rites abrogated, their priests and religious institutions desecrated, their altars cast down, their temples destroyed, or turned into places for Christian worship.

13. *The stars of heaven.* The gods and goddesses, demigods, and deified heroes of their poetical and mythological heaven were prostrated indiscriminately, and lay as useless as the figs or fruit of a tree shaken down before ripe by a "tempestuous wind."

14. *And the heaven departed as a scroll.* The whole system of pagan and idolatrous worship, with all its spiritual, secular, and superstitious influence, was blasted, shrivelled up, and rendered null and void, as a parchment scroll when exposed to the action of a strong fire. *And every mountain.* All the props, supports, and dependencies of the empire, whether regal allies, tributary kings, dependent colonies, or mercenary troops, were all *moved out of their places,* so as to stand no longer in the same relation to that empire, and its worship, support, and maintenance, as they formerly did. *And island.* The heathen temples, with their precincts and enclosures, cut off from the common people, and into which none could come but the privileged, may be here represented by islands, for the same reasons.

15. *The kings of the earth.* All the secular powers who had endeavored to support the pagan worship by authority, influence, riches, political wisdom, and military skill; with *every bondman*—all "slaves," who were in life and limb addicted to their masters or owners. *And every free man.* Those who had been manumitted, commonly called "freedmen," and who were attached, through gratitude, to the families of their liberators. All *hid themselves*—were astonished at the total overthrow of the heathen empire and the revolution which had then taken place.

16. *Said to the mountains and rocks.* Expressions which denote the strongest perturbation and alarm. They preferred any kind of death to that which they apprehended from this most

awful revolution. *From the face of him that sitteth on the throne.* They now saw that all these terrible judgments came from the Almighty; and that Christ, the Author of Christianity, was now judging, condemning, and destroying them for their cruel persecutions of is followers.

17. *For the great day of his wrath.* The decisive and manifest time in which He will execute judgment on the oppressors of His people. *Who shall be able to stand?* No might can prevail against the might of God. All these things may literally apply to the final destruction of Jerusalem, and to the revolution which took place in the Roman Empire under Constantine the Great. Some apply them to the "day of judgment"; but they do not seem to have that awful event in view.

CHAPTER 7

The four angels holding the four winds of heaven, 1. The angel with the seal of the living God, and sealing the servants of God out of the twelve tribes, whose number amounted to 144,000, 2-8. Besides these, there was an innumerable multitude from all nations, who gave glory to God and the Lamb, 9-12. One of the elders shows who these are, and describes their most happy state, 13-17.

1. *And after these things.* Immediately after the preceding vision. *I saw four angels.* Instruments which God employs in the dispensation of His providence; we know not what. *On the four corners of the earth.* On the extreme parts of the land of Judea, called "the land," or *earth,* by way of eminence. *Holding the four winds.* Preventing evil from every quarter. *Earth . . . sea, nor on any tree;* keeping the whole of the land free from evil, till the Church of Christ should wax strong, and each of His followers have time to prepare for his flight from Jerusalem, previously to its total destruction by the Romans.

2. *The seal of the living God.* This angel is represented as the chancellor of the supreme King, and as *ascending from the east,* "from the rising of the sun." Some understand this of Christ, who is called "the east," Luke i. 78. *Four angels, to whom it was given to hurt.* Particular agents employed by divine providence in the management of the affairs of the earth, but whether spiritual or material we know not.

3. *Till we have sealed the servants of our God.* There is manifestly an allusion to Ezek. ix. 4 here. By sealing we are to understand consecrating the persons in a more especial manner to God, and showing, by this mark of God upon them, that they were under His more immediate protection, and that nothing should hurt them. It was a custom in the East, and indeed in the West too, to stamp with a hot iron the name of the owner upon the forehead or shoulder of his slave. It is worthy of remark that not one Christian perished in the siege of Jerusalem; all had left the city and escaped to Pella.

4. *I heard the number of them which were sealed.* In the number of 144,000 are included all the Jews converted to Christianity; 12,000 out of each of the 12 tribes. But this must be only a certain for an uncertain number; for it is not to be supposed that just 12,000 were converted out of each of the 12 tribes.

5-8. *Of the tribe of Juda.* First, we are to observe that the tribe of Levi is here mentioned, though that tribe had no inheritance in Israel; but they now belonged to the spiritual priesthood. Secondly, that the tribe of Dan, which had an inheritance, is here omitted, as also the tribe of Ephraim. Thirdly, that the tribe of *Joseph* is here added in the place of Ephraim. Ephraim and Dan, being the principal promoters of idolatry, are left out in this enumeration.

9. *A great multitude.* This appears to mean the Church of Christ among the Gentiles, for it was different from that collected from the twelve tribes; and it is here said to be *of all nations, and kindreds, and people, and tongues. Clothed with white robes,* as emblems of innocence and purity. *With palms in their hands,* in token of victory gained over the world, the devil, and the flesh.

10. *Salvation to our God.* That is, God alone is the Author of the salvation of man; and this salvation is procured for and given to them through the *Lamb,* as their propitiatory Sacrifice.

11. *All the angels.* As there is joy in the presence of God among these holy spirits when one sinner repents, no wonder that they take such an interest in the gathering together of such innumerable multitudes who are fully saved from their sins.

12. *Saying, Amen.* Giving their most cordial and grateful assent to the praises attributed to God and the Lamb. *Blessing, and glory.* There are here seven different species of praise attributed to God, as in chap. v. 12, where see the note.

13. *One of the elders answered.* A Hebraism for "spoke." The question is here asked, that the proposer may have the opportunity of answering it.

14. *Sir, thou knowest.* That is, I do not know, but you can inform me. *Came out of great tribulation.* Persecutions of every kind. *And have washed their robes.* Have obtained their pardon and purity through the *blood of the Lamb.* Their white robes cannot mean the righteousness of Christ, for this cannot be washed and made white in His own blood. This white linen is said to be "the righteousness of saints," chap. xix. 8, and this is the righteousness in which they stand before the throne. Therefore it is not Christ's righteousness, but it is a righteousness wrought in them by the merit of His blood and the power of His Spirit.

15. *Therefore.* Because they are washed in the blood of the Lamb, *are they before the throne*—admitted to the immediate presence, *of God. And serve him day and night.* Without ceasing; being filled with the spirit of prayer, faith, love, and obedience. *Shall dwell among them.* He lives in is own Church, and in the heart of every true believer.

16. *They shall hunger no more.* They shall no longer be deprived of their religious ordinances and the blessings attendant on them, as they were when in a state of persecution. *Neither shall the sun light on them.* Their secular rulers, being converted to God, became nursing fathers to the Church. *Nor any heat.* Neither persecution nor affliction of any kind. These the Hebrews express by the term "heat, scorching."

17. *The Lamb.* The Lord Jesus, enthroned with His Father in ineffable glory. *Shall feed*

them. Shall communicate to them everything calculated to secure, continue, and increase their happiness. *Living fountains of waters.* A "spring" in the Hebrew phraseology is termed "living water," because constantly boiling up and running on. By these perpetual fountains we are to understand endless sources of comfort and happiness, which Jesus Christ will open out of His own infinite plenitude to all glorified souls. These eternal living fountains will make an infinite variety in the enjoyments of the blessed. *God shall wipe away,* in the most affectionate and fatherly manner, *all tears from their eyes,* all causes of distress and grief. They shall have pure, unmixed happiness.

CHAPTER 8

The opening of the seventh seal, 1. The seven angels with the seven trumpets, 2-6. The first sounds, and there is a shower of hail, fire, and blood, 7. The second sounds, and the burning mountain is cast into the sea, 8-9. The third sounds, and the great star Wormwood falls from heaven, 10-11. The fourth sounds, and the sun, moon, and stars are smitten; and a threefold woe is denounced against the inhabitants of the earth, because of the three angels who are yet to sound, 12-13.

1. *The seventh seal.* This is ushered in and opened only by the Lamb. *Silence in heaven.* This must be a mere metaphor, *silence* being put here for the deep and solemn expectation of the stupendous things about to take place, which the opening of this seal had produced. When anything prodigious or surprising is expected, all is silence, and even the breath is scarcely heard to be drawn. *Half an hour.* As *heaven* may signify the place in which all these representations were made to John, the *half an hour* may be considered as the time during which no representation was made to him, the time in which God was preparing the august exhibition which follows. There is here, and in the following verses, a strong allusion to different parts of the Temple worship; a presumption that the Temple was still standing, and the regular service of God carried on. The *silence* here refers to this fact—while the priest went in to burn incense in the holy place, all the people continued in silent mental prayer without till the priest returned. See Luke i. 10. The angel mentioned here appears to execute the office of priest, as we shall by and by see.

2. *The seven angels which stood before God.* Probably the same as those called "the seven Spirits which are before his throne," chap. i. 4. There is still an allusion here to the seven ministers of the Persian monarchs. See Tobit, chap. xii. 15.

3. *Another angel.* About to perform the office of priest. *Having a golden censer.* This was a preparation peculiar to the day of expiation. "On other days it was the custom of the priest to take fire from the great altar in a silver censer, but on the day of expiation the high priest took the fire from the great altar in a golden censer; and when he was come down from the great altar, he took incense from one of the priests, who brought it to him, and went with it to the golden altar; and while he offered the incense the people prayed without in silence, which is the silence in heaven for half an hour." See Sir Isaac Newton. *Much incense, that he should offer it.* Judgments of God are now about to be executed. The *saints,* the genuine Christians, pray much to God for protection. The angelic

priest comes with *much incense,* standing between the living and those consigned to death, and offers his incense to God *with the prayers of all saints.*

4. *The smoke of the incense, which came with the prayers.* Though incense itself be an emblem of the prayers of the saints, Ps. cxli. 2, yet here they are said to ascend *before God,* as well as the incense. It is not said that the angel presents these prayers. He presents the incense, and the prayers ascend with it. The ascending of the incense shows that the prayers and offering were accepted.

5. *Cast it into the earth.* That is, upon the land of Judea; intimating the judgments and desolations which were now coming upon it, and which appear to be further opened in the sounding of the seven trumpets. *There were voices.* All these seem to point out the confusion, commotions, distresses, and miseries which were coming upon these people in the wars which were at hand.

6. *Prepared themselves to sound.* Each took up his trumpet, and stood prepared to blow his blast. Wars are here indicated; the trumpet was the emblem of war.

7. *Hail and fire mingled with blood.* This was something like the ninth plague of Egypt. See Exod. ix. 18-24: "The Lord sent thunder and hail . . . and fire mingled with the hail"—"and the fire ran along upon the ground. *They were cast upon the earth.* "Into that land"; viz., Judea, thus often designated. *And the third part of trees.* Before this clause the Codex Alexandrinus and some thirty-five others have, "And the third part of the land was burnt up." This reading, which is undoubtedly genuine, is found also in the Complutensian Polyglot. Griesbach has received it into the text. The land was wasted; the *trees*—the chiefs of the nation—were destroyed; and the *grass*—the common people—slain or carried into captivity. High and low, rich and poor were overwhelmed with one general destruction. This seems to be the meaning of these figures.

8. *A great mountain burning with fire.* Mountain, in prophetic language, signifies a "kingdom," Jer. li. 25, 27, 30, 58. Great disorders, especially when kingdoms are moved by hostile invasions, are represented by "mountains" being cast "into the midst of the sea," Ps. xlvi. 2. Seas mean peoples, as is shown in this book, chap. xvii. 15. Therefore great commotions in kingdoms and among their inhabitants may be here intended; but to whom, where, and when these happened, or are to happen, we know not. *The third part of the sea became blood.* Another allusion to the Egyptian plagues, Exod. vii. 20-21. *Third part* is a rabbinism expressing a considerable number. "When Rabbi Akiba prayed, wept, rent his garments, put off his shoes, and sat in the dust, the world was struck with a curse; and then the third part of the olives, the third part of the wheat, and the third part of the barley, was smitten."

9. *The third part of the ships were destroyed.* These judgments seem to be poured out upon some maritime nation, destroying much of its population, and much of its traffic.

10. *There fell a great star from heaven.* This has given rise to various conjectures. Some say the star means Attila and his Huns; others,

Genseric with his Vandals falling on the city of Rome; others, Eleazer, the son of Annus, spurning the emperor's victims, and exciting the fury of the Zealots; others, Arius, infecting the pure Christian doctrine with his heresy. It certainly cannot mean all these, and probably none of them. Let the reader judge.

11. *The star is called Wormwood.* So called from the bitter or distressing effects produced by its influence.

12. *The third part of the sun . . . moon . . . stars . . . was darkened.* Supposed to mean Rome, with her senates, consuls, eclipsed by Odoacer, king of the Heruli, and Theodoric, king of the Ostrogoths, in the fifth century. But all this is uncertain.

13. *I . . . heard an angel flying.* Instead of *an angel flying,* almost every MS. and version of note has "an eagle flying." The eagle was the symbol of the Romans, and was always on their ensigns. The three woes which are here expressed were probably to be executed by this people, and upon the Jews and their common-wealth. Taken in this sense the symbols appear consistent and appropriate; and the reading "eagle" instead of *angel* is undoubtedly genuine, and Griesbach has received it into the text.

CHAPTER 9

The fifth angel sounds, and a star falls from heaven to earth, 1. The bottomless pit is opened, and locusts come out upon the earth, 2-3. Their commission, 4-6. Their form, 7-10. Their government, 11-12. The sixth angel sounds, and the four angels bound in the Euphrates are loosed, 13-15. The army of horsemen, and their description, 16-19. Though much evil is inflicted upon men for their idolatry, etc., they do not repent, 20-21.

1. *A star fall from heaven.* An angel en-compassed with light suddenly descended, and seemed like a *star* falling from heaven. *The key of the bottomless pit.* Power to inundate the earth with a flood of temporal calamities and moral evils.

2. *He opened the bottomless pit.* "The pit of the bottomless deep." Some think the angel means Satan, and the bottomless pit hell. Some suppose Mohammed is meant. *There arose a smoke.* False doctrine, obscuring the true light of heaven.

3. *Locusts.* Vast hordes of military troops; the description which follows certainly agrees better with the Saracens than with any other people or nation, but may also apply to the Romans. *As the scorpions of the earth have power.* Namely, to hurt men by stinging them.

4. *They should not hurt the grass.* Neither the common people, the men of middling con-dition, nor the nobles. However, this appears rather to refer to the prudent counsels of a military chief, not to destroy the crops and herbage, of which they might have need in their campaigns. *Which have not the seal of God.* All false, hypocritical, and heterodox Christians.

5. *To them it was given.* That is, they were *permitted. That they should be tormented five months.* Some take these months literally, and apply them to the conduct of the Zealots who, from May to September, in the year of the siege, produced dreadful contests among the people; or to the afflictions brought upon the Jews by Cestius Gallus when he came against Jerusalem, before which he lay one whole sum-

mer, or nearly five months. Others consider the *months* as being prophetical months, each day being reckoned for a year; therefore this period must amount to 150 years, counting 30 days to each month, as was the general custom of the Asiatics. *Their torment was as the tor-ment of a scorpion.* The phraseology here is peculiar, and probably refers to the warlike weapon called a *scorpion,* several of which, or men armed with them, Cestius Gallus brought with him in his army. Isidore describes this *scorpion* thus: "The scorpion is a poisoned arrow shot from a bow or other instrument, which, when it wounds a man, deposits the poison with which it is covered in the wound; whence it has the name of scorpion."

6. *In those days shall men seek death.* So distressing shall be their sufferings and torment that they shall long for death in any form, to be rescued from the evils of life.

7. *The locusts were like unto horses.* This description of the locusts appears to be taken from Joel ii. 4. The whole of this symbolical description of an overwhelming military force agrees very well with the troops of Mohammed. The Arabs are the most expert horsemen in the world; they live so much on horseback that the horse and his rider seem to make but one animal. The Romans also were eminent for their cavalry. *Crowns like gold.* Not only al-luding to their costly turbans, but to the extent of their conquests and the multitude of powers which they subdued. *Their faces were as the faces of men.* That is, though locusts symboli-cally, they are really men.

8. *Hair as the hair of women.* No razor passes upon their flesh; their hair long, and their beards unshaven. *Their teeth were as the teeth of lions.* They are ferocious and cruel.

9. *They had breastplates . . . of iron.* They seemed to be invulnerable, for no force availed against them. *The sound of their wings.* Their hanging weapons and military trappings, with the clang of their shields and swords when they make their fierce onsets. This simile is borrowed from Joel ii. 5-7.

10. *They had tails like unto scorpions.* This may refer to the consequences of their victories. They infected the conquered with their perni-cious doctrines. *Their power was to hurt men five months.* The locusts make their principal ravages during the five summer months. But probably these may be prophetic months, as above, in v. 5—150 years.

11. *A king over them.* A supreme head; some think Mohammed, some think Vespasian. *The angel of the bottomless pit.* The chief envoy of Satan. *Abaddon.* From *abad,* "he destroyed." *Apollyon.* From *apo,* intensive, and *ollyo,* "to destroy." The meaning is the same in both Hebrew and Greek.

12. *One woe is past.* That is, the woe or deso-lation by the symbolical scorpions. *There come two woes more.* In the trumpets of the sixth and seventh angels.

13. *The four horns of the golden altar.* This is another not very obscure indication that the Jewish Temple was yet standing.

14. *Loose the four angels.* These four angels *bound,* hitherto restrained, in the *Euphrates,* are by some supposed to be the Arabs, the Saracens, the Tartars, or the Turks; by others,

Vespasian's four generals, one in Arabia, one in Africa, one in Alexandria, and one in Palestine.

15. *For an hour, and a day, and a month, and a year.* We have in this place a year resolved into its component parts. Twenty-four hours constitute a day; seven days make a week; four weeks make a month; and twelve months make a year. Probably no more is meant than that these four angels were "at all times" prepared and permitted to inflict evil on the people against whom they had received their commission. There are some who understand these divisions of time as prophetical periods, and to these I must refer, not professing to discuss such uncertainties.

16. *Two hundred thousand thousand.* "Two myriads of myriads"; that is, 200,000,000; an army that was never yet got together from the foundation of the world, and could not find forage in any part of the earth. Perhaps it only means vast numbers, multitudes without number. Such a number might be literally true of the locusts. Those who will have their particular system supported by the images in this most obscure book tell us that the number here means all the soldiers that were employed in this war, from its commencement to its end! Those who can receive this saying let them receive it.

17. *Breastplates of fire, and of jacinth, and brimstone.* That is, red, blue, and yellow; the first is the color of fire, the second of jacinth, and the third of sulphur. *And the heads of the horses.* Is this an allegorical description of great ordnance? Fire, smoke, and brimstone is a good allegorical representation of gunpowder. The Ottomans made great use of heavy artillery in their wars with the Greeks of the lower empire.

18. *By these three was the third part of men killed.* That is, By these was great carnage made.

19. *Their power is in their mouth.* From these the destructive balls are projected. *And in their tails,* the breech where the charge of gunpowder is lodged. *Their tails were like unto serpents, and had heads.* If cannons are intended, the description, though allegorical, is plain enough; for brass ordnance especially are frequently thus ornamented, both at their muzzles and at their breech.

20. *Yet repented not.* The commission which these horsemen had was against idolaters; and though multitudes of them were destroyed, yet the residue continued their senseless attachment to dumb idols, and therefore heavier judgments might be expected. These things are supposed to refer to the desolation brought upon the Greek church by the Ottomans, who entirely ruined that church and the Greek empire. The church which was then remaining was the Latin or Western church, which was not at all corrected by the judgments which fell upon the Eastern church, but continued its senseless adoration of angels, saints, relics, and does so to the present day. If therefore God's wrath be kindled against such, this church has much to fear.

21. *Neither repented they of their murders.* Their cruelties towards the genuine followers of God the Albigenses, and Waldenses, and others, against whom they published crusades, and hunted them down, and butchered them in the most shocking manner. The innumerable murders by the horrible Inquisition need not be mentioned. *Their sorceries.* Those who apply this also to the Romish church understand by it the various tricks, sleights of hand, or legerdemain by which they impose on the common people in causing images of Christ to bleed, and the various pretended miracles wrought at the tombs of pretended saints, holy wells, and suchlike. *Fornication.* Giving that honor to various creatures which is due only to the Creator. *Their thefts.* Their exactions and impositions on men for indulgences, pardons. These things may be intended, but it is going too far to say that this is the true interpretation. And yet to express any doubt on this subject is with some little else than heresy. If such men can see these things so clearly in such obscure prophecies, let them be thankful for their sight, and indulgent to those who still sit in darkness.

CHAPTER 10

The description of a mighty angel with a little book in his hand, 1-2. The seven thunders, 3-4. The angel swears that there shall be time no longer, 5-7. John is commanded to take the little book and eat it; he does so, and receives a commission to prophesy to many peoples, 8-11.

1. *Another mighty angel,* either Christ or His representative; *clothed with a cloud,* a symbol of the divine majesty. *A rainbow was upon his head.* The token of God's merciful covenant with mankind. *His face was as it were the sun.* So intensely glorious that it could not be looked on. *His feet as pillars of fire.* To denote the rapidity and energy of his motions and the stability of his counsels.

2. *A little book open.* Meaning probably some design of God long concealed, but now about to be made manifest. But who knows what it means? *His right foot upon the sea, and his left foot on the earth.* To show that he had the command of each, and that his power was universal, all things being under his feet.

3. *Seven thunders.* Seven being a number of perfection, it may here mean many, great, loud, and strong peals of thunder, accompanied with distinct voices; but what was said John was not permitted to reveal, v. 4.

5. *Lifted up his hand to heaven.* As one making an appeal to the Supreme Being.

6. *By him that liveth for ever and ever.* The eternal, self-existent Jehovah, the Maker of all things. *That there should be time no longer.* That the gerat counsels relative to the events already predicted should be immediately fulfilled, and that there should be no longer "delay." This has no reference to the day of judgment.

7. *The mystery of God should be finished.* What this mystery refers to, who knows? Nor have we more knowledge concerning the sounding of the seventh angel. On these points there is little agreement among learned men. Whether it mean the destruction of Jerusalem, or the destruction of the papal power, or something else, we know not. And yet with what confidence do men speak of the meaning of these hidden things! *Declared to his servants the prophets.* It is most likely, therefore, that this trumpet belongs to the Jewish state.

8. *Take the little book which is open.* Learn from this angel what should be published to the world.

9. *Take it, and eat it up.* Fully comprehend its meaning; study it thoroughly.

10. *It was in my mouth sweet as honey.* There was in it some pleasing, some unpleasing, intelligence. I read of the consolations and protection of the true worshippers of God, and did rejoice; I read of the persecutions of the Church, and was distressed.

11. *Thou must prophesy again.* You must write, not only for the instruction of the Jews in Palestine, but of those in the different provinces, as well as the heathens and heathen emperors and potentates in general.

CHAPTER 11

The command to measure the Temple, 1-2. The two witnesses which should prophesy 1,260 days, 3. The description, power, and influence of these witnesses, 4-6. They shall be slain by the beast which shall arise out of the bottomless pit; and shall arise again after 3½ days, and ascend to heaven, 7-12. After which shall be a great earthquake, 13. The introduction to the third woe, 14. The sounding of the seventh angel, and "the four and twenty elders" give glory to God, 15-19.

1. *And there was given me a reed.* See Ezek. xl. 3, etc. *Measure the temple of God.* This must refer to the Temple of Jerusalem; and this is another presumptive evidence that it was yet standing.

2. *But the court . . . is given unto the Gentiles.* The measuring of the Temple probably refers to its approaching destruction, and the termination of the whole Levitical service; and this we find was to be done by the Gentiles (Romans), who were to tread it down 42 months; i.e., just 3½ years, or 1,260 days. This must be a symbolical period.

3. *My two witnesses.* This is extremely obscure; the conjectures of interpreters are as unsatisfactory as they are endless on this point. Those who wish to be amused or bewildered may have recourse both to ancients and moderns on this subject.

4. *These are the two olive trees.* Mentioned in Zech. iv. 14, which there represent Zerubbabel and Joshua, the high priest. The whole account seems taken from Zech. iv. 1-14. Whether the prophet and the apostle mean the same things by these emblems, we know not.

5. *Fire proceedeth out of their mouth.* That is, they are commissioned to denounce the judgments of God against all who would attempt to prevent them from proceeding in their ministry.

6. *These have power to shut heaven.* As Elijah did, 1 Kings xvii and xviii. *To turn them to blood.* As Moses did, Exodus vii. They shall have power to afflict the land with plagues, similar to those which were inflicted on the Egyptians.

7. *The beast that ascendeth out of the bottomless pit.* This may be what is called "antichrist," some power that is opposed to genuine Christianity. But what or whence, except from the bottomless pit, i.e., under the influence and appointment of the devil, we cannot tell; nor do we know by what name this power or being should be called. The conjectures concerning the "two witnesses" and the "beast" have been sufficiently multiplied. If the whole passage,

as some think, refers to the persecution raised by the Jews against the Christians, then some Jewish power or person is the beast from the bottomless pit. If it refer to the early ages of Christianity, then the beast may be one of the persecuting heathen emperors. If it refer to a later age of Christianity, then the beast may be the papal power, and the Albigenses and Waldenses the two witnesses, which were nearly extinguished by the horrible persecutions raised up against them by the church of Rome. Whatever may be here intended, the earth has not yet covered their blood.

8. *The great city.* Some say Rome, which may be spiritually called *Sodom* for its abominations, *Egypt* for its tyrannous cruelty, and the place *where also our Lord was crucified* because of its persecution of the members of Christ; but Jerusalem itself may be intended. All these things I must leave to others.

9. *Shall not suffer their dead bodies to be put in graves.* They shall be treated with the greatest barbarity. Refusal of burial to the dead was allowed to be the sum of brutality and cruelty.

10. *Shall send gifts.* This was a custom in days of public rejoicing. They sent gifts to each other, and gave portions to the poor. See Esther ix. 19, 22.

11. *They stood upon their feet.* Were restored to their primitive state.

12. *They ascended up to heaven.* Enjoyed a state of great peace and happiness.

13. *A great earthquake.* Violent commotions among the persecutors, and revolutions of states. *Slain of men seven thousand.* Many perished in these popular commotions. *The remnant were affrighted.* Seeing the hand of God's judgments so remarkably stretched out. *Gave glory.* Received the pure doctrines of the gospel, and glorified God for His judgments and their conversion.

14. *The second woe is past.* That which took place under the sixth trumpet, and has been already described. *The third woe cometh.* Is about to be described under the seventh trumpet, which the angel was now prepared to sound. Of the three woes which were denounced, chap. viii. 13, the first is described in chap. ix. 1-12, the second in chap. ix. 13-21. These woes are supposed by many learned men to refer to the destruction of Jerusalem: the first woe—the seditions among the Jews themselves; the second woe—the besieging of the city by the Romans; the third woe—the taking and sacking of the city, and burning the Temple. This was the greatest of all the woes, as in it the city and Temple were destroyed, and nearly a million men lost their lives.

15. *There were great voices in heaven.* All the heavenly host—angels and redeemed human spirits—joined together to magnify God, that He had utterly discomfited His enemies and rendered His friends glorious. This will be truly the case when the kingdoms of this world become the kingdoms of God and of His Christ. But when shall this be? Some say what is meant by these words has already taken place in the destruction of the Jewish state and sending the gospel throughout the Gentile world. Others say that it refers to the millennium and to the consummation of all things.

16. *The four and twenty elders.* The representatives of the universal Church of Christ. See on chap. v. 8-10.

17. *O Lord God Almighty, which art.* This gives a proper view of God in His eternity; all times are here comprehended, the present, the past, and the future. This is the infinitude of God. *Hast taken to thee.* Thou hast exercised that power which Thou ever hast; and Thou hast broken the power of Thy enemies, and exalted Thy Church.

18. *The nations were angry.* Were enraged against Thy gospel and determined to destroy it. *Thy wrath is come.* The time to avenge Thy servants and to destroy all Thy enemies. *The time of the dead, that they should be judged.* The word "to judge" is often used in the sense of "to avenge." The dead, here, may mean those who were slain for the testimony of Jesus, and the judging is the avenging of their blood. *Give reward unto thy servants.* Who have been faithful unto death. *The prophets*—the faithful teachers in the Church; *the saints*—the Christians. *And them that fear thy name.* All Thy sincere followers. *Destroy them which destroy the earth.* All the authors, fomenters, and encouragers of bloody wars.

19. *The temple of God was opened in heaven.* The true worship of God was established and performed in the Christian Church; this is the true temple, that at Jerusalem being destroyed. *And there were lightnings, and voices, and thunderings, and an earthquake, and great hail.* These great commotions were intended to introduce the following vision; for the twelfth chapter is properly a continuation of the eleventh, and should be read in strict connection with it.

CHAPTER 12

The woman clothed with the sun, and in travail, 1-2. The great red dragon waiting to devour the child as soon as born, 3-4. The woman is delivered of a son, who is caught up unto God; and she flees to the wilderness, 5-6. The war in heaven between Michael and the dragon, 7-8. The dragon and his angels are overcome and cast down to the earth, whereupon the whole heavenly host give glory to God, 9-11. The dragon, full of wrath at his defeat, persecutes the woman, 12-13. She flees to the wilderness, whither he attempts to pursue her; and he makes war with her seed, 14-17.

CHAPTER 13

The beast rising out of the sea with seven heads, ten horns, and ten crowns, 1. His description, power, blasphemy, cruelty, etc., 2-10. The beast coming out of the earth with two horns, deceiving the world by his false miracles, and causing everyone to receive his mark in the right hand, 11-17. His number, 666, 18.

CHAPTER 14

The Lamb on Mount Sion, and His company and their character, 1-5. The angel flying in the midst of heaven with the everlasting gospel, 6-7. Another angel proclaims the fall of Babylon, 8. A third angel denounces God's judgments against those who worship the beast or his image, 9-11. The patience of the saints, and the blessedness of them who die in the Lord, 12-13. The man on the white cloud, with a sickle, reaping the earth, 14-16. The angel with the sickle commanded by another angel, who had power over fire, to gather the clusters of the vines of the earth, 17-18. They are gathered and thrown into the great winepress of God's wrath, which is trodden without the city, and the blood comes out 1,600 furlongs, 19-20.

1. *A Lamb stood on the mount Sion.* This represents Jesus Christ in His sacrificial office;

mount Sion was a type of the Christian Church. *And with him an hundred forty and four thousand.* Representing those who were converted to Christianity from among the *Jews.* See chap. vii. 4. *His Father's name written in their foreheads.* They were professedly, openly, and practically the children of God by faith in Christ Jesus. Different sects of idolaters have the peculiar mark of their god on their foreheads. Almost every MS. of importance, as well as most of the versions and many of the fathers, read this clause thus: "Having His name and His Father's name written upon their foreheads." This is undoubtedly the true reading, and is properly received by Griesbach into the text.

2. *The voice of many waters.* That is, of multitudes of various nations. *The voice of harpers.* Though the sounds were many and apparently confused, yet both harmony and melody were preserved.

3. *They sung . . . a new song.* See on chap. v. 9. *No man could learn that song.* As none but genuine Christians can worship God acceptably, because they approach Him through the only Mediator, so none can understand the deep things of God but such; nor can others know the cause why true believers exult so much in God through Christ, because they know not the communion which such hold with the Father and the Son through the Holy Ghost.

4. *These are they which were not defiled with women.* They are pure from idolatry, and are presented as unspotted virgins to their Lord and Saviour, Christ. There may be an allusion here to the Israelites committing idolatry, through the means of their criminal connection with the Midianitish women. See Num. xxv. 1-4 and xxxi. 16. *The firstfruits unto God.* The reference appears to be to those Jews who were the first converts to Christianity.

5. *In their mouth was found no guile.* When brought before kings and rulers they did not dissemble, but boldly confessed the Lord Jesus.

6. *Another angel fly in the midst of heaven, having the everlasting gospel.* Whether this angel means any more than a particular dispensation of providence and grace, by which the gospel shall be rapidly sent throughout the whole world; or whether it means any especial messenger, order of preachers, people, or society of Christians, whose professed object it is to send the gospel of the Kingdom throughout the earth, we know not. But the vision seems truly descriptive of a late institution entitled "The British and Foreign Bible Society," whose object it is to print and circulate the Scriptures of the Old and New Testaments through all the habitable world, and in all the languages spoken on the face of the earth.

7. *Fear God, and give glory to him.* This is the general language of the sacred writings. Worship the true God, the Creator and Governor of all things; and give Him glory; for to Him alone, not to idols or men, all glory and honor belong.

8. *Babylon is fallen, is fallen.* This is generally understood to be a prediction concerning Rome; and it is certain that Rome, in the rabbinical writings, is termed Babylon. *That great city.* Among the same writers this city is styled "the great city" and "the great Rome." But which Rome is meant? Pagan or papal

Rome? Some parts of the description apply best to the former. *The wine of the wrath of her fornication.* There is an allusion here to a custom of impure women, who give love potions to those whom they wish to seduce and bind to their will; and these potions are generally of an intoxicating nature, greatly inflaming the blood, and disturbing the intellect. Fornication and adultery are frequently used in Scripture as emblems of idolatry and false worship. No nation of the earth spread their idolatries so far as the ancient Romans; they were as extensive as their conquests. And papal Rome has been not less active in disseminating her superstitions. She has given her rituals, but not the everlasting gospel, to most nations of the earth.

10. *The wine of the wrath of God.* As they have drunk the intoxicating wine of idolatry or spiritual fornication, they shall now drink the wine of God's wrath, which is poured out into the cup of His indignation. This is an allusion to the poisoned cup which certain criminals were obliged to drink, on which ensued speedy death. *Shall be tormented with fire and brimstone.* An allusion to the punishment of Sodom and Gomorrah for their unnatural crimes. *Presence of the holy angels, and . . . of the Lamb,* these being the instruments employed in their destruction; the *Lamb*—the Lord Jesus Christ—acting as Judge.

11. *The smoke of their torment.* Still an allusion to the destruction of Sodom and Gomorrah.

12. *Here is the patience of the saints.* Here the faith of the true Christians shall be proved; they will "follow the Lamb whithersoever he goeth"; they keep the commandments of God, and are steadfast in the faith of our Lord Jesus Christ. Sometimes *patience* or "perseverance" is taken for the reward of these virtues. The text therefore may be thus understood: Here is the reward of the perseverance of the true Christians; for although they die for the testimony of Jesus, yet they shall be unutterably blessed. See the next verse.

13. *I heard a voice from heaven.* As the information now to be given was of the utmost importance, it is solemnly communicated by a voice from heaven, and the apostle is commanded to write or record what is said. *Blessed are the dead.* Happy are they. They do not see the evil that shall come upon the world, and are exempted from any further sufferings. "Happy are the dead" is a proverb frequently to be met in the Greek and Roman poets. *From henceforth.* "From this time; now; immediately." This word is joined to the following by many MSS. and some versions. It was a maxim among the Jews that as soon as the souls of the just departed from this life they ascended immediately to heaven. *Yea, saith the Spirit.* The Holy Spirit confirms the declaration from heaven and assigns the reasons of it. *That they may rest from their labours.* Have no more tribulation and distress. *And their works do follow them.* "And their works follow with them." Here is an elegant personification; their good works, sufferings, etc., are represented as so many companions escorting them on their way to the kingdom of God.

14. *A white cloud.* It is supposed that, from this verse to the end of the chapter, the destruction of Rome is represented under the symbols

of harvest and vintage; images very frequent among the ancient prophets, by which they represented the destruction and excision of nations. See Joel iii. 12-14; Isa. xvii. 5; lxiii. 1; and Matt. xiii. 37 *A golden crown* In token of victory and regal power.

15. *Thrust in thy sickle.* Execute the judgments which God has decreed. *For the harvest of the earth is ripe.* The cup of the people's iniquity is full.

16. *The earth was reaped.* The judgments were executed.

18. *Power over fire.* Probably meaning the same angel which is mentioned in chap. viii. 3; ix. 13, who stood by the altar of burnt offering, having authority over its fire to offer that incense to God which represents the prayers of the saints.

19. *The great winepress of the wrath of God.* The place or kingdom where God executes His judgments on the workers of iniquity, whether pagans or persecuting Christians—Rome pagan or Rome papal.

20. *Even unto the horse bridles.* A hyperbolical expression, to denote a great effusion of blood. The Jews said, "When Hadrian besieged the city called Bitter, he slew so many that the horses waded in blood up to their mouths."

CHAPTER 15

The seven angels with the seven last plagues, 1. The sea of glass, and those who had a victory over the beast, 2. The song of Moses and the Lamb, 3-4. The temple in heaven opened, 5. Seven angels come out of the temple, who receive from one of the four living creatures seven golden vials full of the wrath of God, 6-8.

1. *Seven angels having the seven last plagues.* Under the emblems of harvest and vintage God's judgments on the enemies of His Church have already been pointed out; but these are further signified by the seven vials, which are called *the seven last plagues* of God. *The seven last plagues* appear to fall under the seventh and last trumpet. As the seventh seal contained the seven trumpets, so the seventh trumpet contains the seven vials. And as seven angels sounded the seven trumpets, so seven angels are appointed to pour out the seven vials, angels being always the ministers of Providence. This chapter contains the opening vision which is preparatory to the pouring out of the vials.

2. *A sea of glass.* A spacious, lucid plain around the throne, from which fiery coruscations were continually emitted; or the reflection of the light upon this lucid plain produced the prismatic colors of the most vivid rainbow.

3. *They sing the song of Moses.* That which Moses sang, Exod. xv. 1, when he and the Israelites, by the miraculous power of God, had got safely through the Red Sea, and saw their enemies all destroyed. *And the song of the Lamb.* The same song adapted to the state of the suffering, but now delivered, Christians. *Great and marvellous are thy works.* God's works are descriptive of His infinite power and wisdom. *Lord God Almighty.* Nearly the same as "Jehovah God of hosts." *Just and true are thy ways.* Every step God takes in grace or providence is according to justice, and He carefully accomplishes all His threatenings and all His promises; to this He is bound by His truth.

4. *Who shall not fear thee?* That is, "All should fear" and worship this true God, because He is just and true and *holy;* and His saints should love and obey Him, because He is their King; and they and all men should acknowledge His *judgments,* because they are *made manifest.*

5. *The temple of the tabernacle of the testimony.* The *temple* which succeeded the *tabernacle,* in which was the *testimony,* viz., the two tables, Aaron's rod, pot of manna, holy anointing oil, etc. All bearing testimony to the truth of God and His miraculous interposition in their behalf.

6. *The seven angels came out of the temple.* To show that they were sent from God himself. *Clothed in pure and white linen.* Habited as priests. For these habits see Exod. xxviii. 6, 8; and see the note on chap. i. 13.

8. *The temple was filled with smoke.* So was the Tabernacle when consecrated by Moses, Exod. xl. 34-35, and the Temple when consecrated by Solomon, 1 Kings viii. 10-11; 2 Chron. v. 14. See Isa. vi. 4. This account seems at least partly copied from those above.

CHAPTER 16

The angels are commanded to pour out their vials upon the earth, 1. The first pours out his vial on the earth, by which a grievous sore is produced, 2. The second angel pours out his vial on the sea, and it is turned into blood, 3. The third angel pours out his vial on the rivers and fountains, and they are turned also into blood, 4-7. The fourth angel pours out his vial on the sun, and men are scorched with fire, 8-9. The fifth angel pours out his vial on the throne of the beast, 10-11. The sixth angel pours out his vial on the river Euphrates, 12. Three unclean spirits come out of the mouth of the beast, dragon, and false prophet: and go forth to gather all the kings of the world to battle, in the place called Armageddon, 13-16. The seventh angel pours out his vial on the air, on which followed thunders, lightnings, earthquakes, and extraordinary hail, 17-21.

1. *Go your ways, and pour out.* These ministers of the divine justice were ready to execute vengeance upon transgressors, having full power, but could do nothing in this way till they received especial commission. Nothing can be done without the permission of God, and in the manifestation of justice or mercy by divine agency there must be positive command.

2. *A noisome and grievous sore.* This is a reference to the sixth Egyptian plague, boils and blains, Exod. ix. 8, etc.

3. *As the blood of a dead man.* Either meaning blood in a state of putrescency or an effusion of blood in naval conflicts; even the sea was tinged with the blood of those who were slain in these wars. This is most probably the meaning of this vial. These engagements were so sanguinary that both the conquerors and the conquered were nearly destroyed; *every living soul died in the sea.*

4. *Upon the rivers and fountains of waters.* This is an allusion to the first Egyptian plague. Exod. vii. 20; and to those plagues in general there are allusions throughout this chapter. It is a sentiment of the rabbins that "whatever plagues God inflicted on the Egyptians in former times, he will inflict on the enemies of his people in all later times."

5. *The angel of the waters.* The rabbins attribute angels, not only to the four elements so called, but to almost everything besides. We have already seen the "angel of the bottomless

pit," chap. ix. 11, and "the angel of the fire," chap. xiv. 18.

6. *Thou hast given them blood to drink.* They thirsted after blood and massacred the saints of God, and now they have got blood to drink!

10. *The seat of the beast.* "Upon the throne of the wild beast." The regal family was smitten by the fourth vial; they did not repent; then the fifth angel pours out his vial on the throne of the wild beast, or anti-Christian idolatrous power. *Was full of darkness.* Confusion, dismay, and distress.

11. *Blasphemed the God of heaven.* Neither did they repent; therefore other judgments must follow.

12. *Upon the great river Euphrates.* Probably meaning the people in the vicinity of this river, though some think that the Tiber is intended. *The water thereof was dried up.* The people discomfited and all impediments removed. *The kings of the east.* There seems to be an allusion here to the ruin of Babylon by Cyrus, predicted by the Prophet Jeremiah, chaps. l and li.

13. *Three unclean spirits.* Perhaps false teachers, called afterwards "spirits of devils," which persuade the kings of the earth by lying miracles to come forth to the place of general slaughter, vv. 14, 16.

15. *Behold, I come as a thief.* Here is a sudden but timely warning to put every man on his guard, when this sudden and generally unexpected tribulation should take place. *Keepeth his garments, lest he walk naked.* Here is a plain allusion to the office of him who was called the prefect or overseer of the mountain of the Temple. His custom was to go his rounds during the watches of the night; and if he found any of the Levites sleeping on his watch, he had authority to beat him with a stick and burn his vestments. Such a person being found on his return home *naked,* it was at once known that he had been found asleep at his post, had been beaten, and his clothes burned; thus his *shame* was seen—he was reproached for his infidelity and irreligion.

16. *Armageddon.* The original of this word has been variously formed and variously translated. It is "the mount of the assembly"; or "the destruction of their army"; or it is "Mount Megiddo," the valley of which was remarkable for two great slaughters: one of the Israelites, 2 Kings xxiii. 29, the other of the Canaanites, Judg. iv. 16; v. 19. But what is the battle of Armageddon? How ridiculous have been the conjectures of men relative to this point! Within the last twenty years this battle has been fought at various places, according to our purblind seers and self-inspired prophets! At one time it was Austerlitz, at another Moscow, at another Leipsic, and now Waterloo! And thus they have gone on, and will go on, confounding and being confounded.

17. *Poured out his vial into the air.* To signify that this plague was to be widely diffused, and perhaps to intimate that pestilences and various deaths would be the effect of this vial. *It is done.* It is said, chap. x. 7, that in the days of the seventh trumpet "the mystery of God should be finished"; so here we find it completed. "All's over!"

18. *A great earthquake.* Most terrible com-

motions, both civil and religious. Or a convulsion, shaking, or revolution.

19. *The great city.* Some say Jerusalem, others Rome pagan, others Rome papal. *The cup of the wine of the fierceness of his wrath.* Alluding to the mode of putting certain criminals to death, by making them drink a cup of poison.

20. *Every island fled away.* Probably meaning the capture of seaport towns, and fortified places.

21. *A great hail . . . every stone about the weight of a talent.* Has this any reference to cannon balls and bombs? It is very doubtful; we are all in the dark in these matters. The words "as a talent" are used to express something "great, excessively oppressive."

CHAPTER 17

The judgment of the great whore, which sits on many waters, 1-2. Her description, name, and conduct, 3-6. The angel explains the mystery of the woman, of the beast, etc., 7-18.

CHAPTER 18

A luminous angel proclaims the fall of Babylon, and the cause of it, 1-3. The followers of God are exhorted to come out of it, in order to escape her approaching punishment, 4-8. The kings of the earth lament her fate, 9-10. The merchants also bewail her, 11. The articles in which she trafficked enumerated, 12-16. She is bewailed also by shipmasters, sailors, etc., 17-19. All heaven rejoices over her fall, and her final desolation is foretold, 20-24.

1. *The earth was lightened with his glory.* This may refer to some extraordinary messenger of the everlasting gospel, who, by his preaching and writings, should be the means of diffusing the light of truth and true religion over the earth.

2. *Babylon the great is fallen, is fallen.* This is a quotation from Isa. xxi. 9: "And he . . . said, Babylon is fallen, is fallen; and all the graven images of her gods he hath broken unto the ground." This is applied by some to Rome pagan, by others to Rome papal, and by others to Jerusalem. *Is become . . . the hold of every foul spirit.* See the parallel passages in the margin. The figures here point out the most complete destruction. A city utterly sacked and ruined, never to be rebuilt.

3. *The wine of the wrath.* The punishment due to her transgressions, because they have partaken with her in her sins. See the note on chap. xiv. 8.

4. *Come out of her, my people.* These words appear to be taken from Isa. xlviii. 20; Jer. i. 8; li. 6, 45.

5. *Her sins have reached unto heaven.* They are become so great and enormous that the long-suffering of God must give place to His justice.

6. *Reward her even as she rewarded you.* These words are a prophetic declaration of what shall take place: God will deal with her as she dealt with others.

8. *Therefore shall her plagues come.* Death, by the sword of her adversaries; *mourning,* on account of the slaughter; and *famine,* the fruits of the field being destroyed by the hostile bands.

9. *The kings of the earth.* Those who copied her superstitions and adopted her idolatries.

10. *Standing afar off.* Beholding her desolations with wonder and astonishment, utterly unable to afford her any kind of assistance.

11. *The merchants of the earth.* These are represented as mourning over her, because their traffic with her was at an end.

13. *Slaves.* The "bodies of men"; probably distinguished here from *souls of men,* to express bondmen and freemen.

14. *Dainty and goodly.* "Delicacies for the table"; what is "splendid and costly in apparel."

16. *Clothed in fine linen, and purple.* The verb which we here translate *clothed* signifies often "to abound, be enriched, laden with," and is so used by the best Greek writers. These articles are not to be considered here as personal ornaments, but as articles of trade or merchandise, in which this city trafficked.

17. *Every shipmaster.* Captains of vessels; some think pilots are meant, and this is most likely to be the meaning of the original word. This description appears to be at least partly taken from Ezek. xxvii. 26-28. *And all the company in ships.* The crowd or passengers aboard. But the best MSS. and versions have "those who sail from place to place."

18. *What city is like unto this great city!* Viz., in magnitude, power, and luxury.

19. *They cast dust on their heads.* They showed every sign of the sincerest grief. The lamentation over this great ruined city, from vv. 9 to 19, is exceedingly strong and well-drawn. Here is no dissembled sorrow; all is real to the mourners, and affecting to the spectators.

20. *Rejoice over her, thou heaven.* This is grand and sublime; the fall of this bad city was cause of grief to bad men. But as this city was a persecutor of the godly and an enemy to the works of God, angels, apostles, and prophets are called to rejoice over her fall.

21. *Thus with violence shall that great city Babylon be thrown down.* This action is finely and forcibly expressed by the original words. The millstone will in falling have not only an accelerated force from the law of gravitation, but that force will be greatly increased by the projectile force impressed upon it by the power of the destroying angel. *Shall be found no more at all.* In her government, consequence, or influence. This is true of ancient Babylon. It is also true of Jerusalem; her government, consequence, and influence are gone. It is not true of Rome pagan; nor, as yet, of Rome papal. The latter still exists, and the former is most intimately blended with it; for in her religious service Rome papal has retained her language and many of her heathen temples she dedicated to saints real or reputed, and incorporated many of her superstitions and absurdities in a professedly Christian service. It is true also that many idols are now restored under the names of Christian saints!

22. *The voice of harpers.* This seems to indicate not only a total destruction of influence, etc., but also of being. It seems as if this city was to be swallowed up by an earthquake, or burnt up by fire from heaven.

23. *By thy sorceries.* Political arts, state tricks, counterfeit miracles, and deceptive maneuvers of every kind. This may be spoken of many great cities of the world, which still continue to flourish.

24. *In her was found the blood of prophets.* She was the persecutor and murderer of prophets and of righteous men. *And of all that were slain upon the earth.* This refers to her counsels and influence, exciting other nations and people to persecute and destroy the real followers of God.

CHAPTER 19

The whole heavenly host give glory to God, because He has judged the great whore, and avenged the blood of His saints, 1-6. The marriage of the Lamb and His bride, 7-9. John offers to worship the angel, but is prevented, 10. Heaven is opened, and Jesus, the Word of God, appears on a white horse; He and His armies described, 11-16. An angel in the sun invites all the fowls of heaven to come to the supper of the great God, 17-18. The beast, the false prophet, and the kings of the earth gather together to make war with Him who sits on the white horse; but they are all discomfited, and utterly destroyed, 19-21.

1. *I heard a great voice of much people in heaven.* The idolatrous city being destroyed, and the blood of the martyred saints being avenged, there is a universal joy among the redeemed of the Lord, which they commence with the word Hallelu-Yah, "Praise ye Jah or Jehovah"; which the Septuagint, and John from them, put into Greek letters thus: *Allelou-ia. Salvation.* He is the sole Author of deliverance from sin; the *glory* of this belongs to Him, the *honour* should be ascribed to Him, and His *power* is that alone by which it is effected.

2. *For true and righteous.* His judgments displayed in supporting His followers and punishing His enemies are *true*—according to His predictions; and *righteous*, being all according to infinite justice and equity.

3. *Her smoke rose up.* There was, and shall be, a continual evidence of God's judgments executed on this great whore or idolatrous city; nor shall it ever be restored.

4. *The four and twenty elders.* The true Church of the Lord Jesus converted from among the Jews. See chap. iv. 10; v. 14.

5. *Praise our God.* Let all, whether redeemed from among Jews or Gentiles, give glory to God.

6. *The voice of a great multitude.* This is the catholic or universal Church of God gathered from among the Gentiles. *The Lord God omnipotent reigneth.* Many excellent MSS., most of the versions, add "our," and according to this the text reads emphatically thus: "Our Lord God, the Almighty, reigneth." What consolation to every genuine Christian that his Lord and God is the Almighty, and that this Almighty never trusts the reins of the government of the universe out of His hands!

7. *The marriage of the Lamb is come.* The meaning of these figurative expressions appears to be this: After this overthrow of idolatry and superstition, and the discomfiture of Antichrist, there will be a more glorious state of Christianity than ever was before.

8. *Arrayed in fine linen.* A prediction that the Church should become more pure in her doctrines, more pious in her experience, and more righteous in her conduct than she had ever been from her formation. *The fine linen*

here spoken of is not the righteousness of Christ imputed to believers, for it is here called *the righteousness of the saints*—that which the grace and Spirit of Christ have wrought in them.

9. *Blessed are they which are called unto the marriage supper.* This is an evident allusion to the marriage of the king's son, Matt. xxii. 2, etc., where the incarnation of our Lord and the calling of Jews and Gentiles are particularly pointed out. *Blessed* are all they who hear the gospel, and are thus invited to lay hold on everlasting life.

10. *I fell at his feet to worship him.* Great as this angel was, John could not mistake him either for Jesus Christ or for God the Father; nor was his prostration intended as an act of religious worship. This was merely an act of that sort of reverence which any Asiatic would pay to a superior. His mistake was the considering that he was under obligation to the angel for the information which he had now received. This mistake the angel very properly corrects, showing him that it was from God alone this intelligence came, and that to Him alone the praise was due. *I am thy fellowservant.* No higher in dignity than yourself; employed by the same God, on the same errand, and with the same testimony; and therefore not entitled to your prostration. *Worship God*—prostrate yourself to Him, and to Him give thanks. *The testimony of Jesus is the spirit of prophecy.* As this is a reason given by the angel why he should not worship him, the meaning must be this: I, who have received this *spirit of prophecy,* am not superior to you, who have received the *testimony* of Christ, to preach Him among the Gentiles. Or the spirit of prophecy is a general testimony concerning Jesus, for He is the Scope and Design of the whole Scriptures.

11. *A white horse.* This is an exhibition of the triumph of Christ after the destruction of His enemies. The white horse is the emblem of this, and *Faithful and True* are characters of Christ. See chap. iii. 14. *In righteousness he doth judge and make war.* The wars which He wages are from no principle of ambition, lust of power, or extension of conquest and dominion; they are righteous in their principle and in their object.

12. *His eyes were as a flame of fire.* To denote the piercing and all-penetrating nature of His wisdom. *On his head were many crowns.* To denote the multitude of His conquests and the extent of His dominion. *A name written, that no man knew.* This is a reference to what the rabbins call the tetragrammaton, YHVH; or what we call "Jehovah." This name the Jews never attempt to pronounce; when they meet with it in the Bible, they read *Adonai* for it. But, to a man, they all declare that no man can pronounce it; and that the true pronunciation has been lost, at least since the Babylonish captivity; and that God alone knows its true interpretation and pronunciation. This, therefore, is the *name* . . . *that no man knew, but he himself.*

13. *He was clothed with a vesture dipped in blood.* To show that He was just come from recent slaughter. The description is taken from Isa. lxiii. 2-3. *The Word of God.* Written in the Targum, and in other Jewish writings, "The

word of Jehovah;" by which they always mean a Person, and not a word spoken.

14. *The armies which were in heaven.* Angels and saints, over whom Jesus Christ is Captain. *Clothed in fine linen.* All holy, pure, and righteous.

15. *Out of his mouth goeth a sharp sword.* See on chap. i. 16. This appears to mean the word of the gospel, by which His enemies are confounded and His friends supported and comforted. *With a rod of iron.* He shall execute the severest judgment on the opposers of His truth. *He treadeth the winepress.* As the grapes are trodden to express the juice, so His enemies shall be bruised and beaten, so that their life's blood shall be poured out.

17. *An angel standing in the sun.* Exceedingly luminous, every part of Him emitting rays of light.

18. *That ye may eat the flesh of kings.* There shall be a universal destruction; the kings, generals, captains, and all their host shall be slain.

20. *That worshipped his image.* The *beast* has been represented as the Latin empire; the *image of the beast,* the popes of Rome; and *the false prophet,* the papal clergy. *Were cast alive into a lake of fire.* Were discomfited when alive, in the zenith of their power, and destroyed with an utter destruction.

21. *With the sword of him that sat upon the horse.* He who sat on the white horse is Christ; and His sword is His word—the unadulterated gospel.

CHAPTER 20

An angel binds Satan a thousand years, and shuts him up in the bottomless pit, 1-3. They who were beheaded for the testimony of Jesus, who have part in the first resurrection, and shall reign with Christ a thousand years, 4-6. When the thousand years are expired, Satan shall be loosed out of his prison, shall go forth and deceive the nations, and shall gather Gog and Magog from the four corners of the earth, 7-8. These shall besiege the holy city; but fire shall come down from heaven and consume them, and they and the devil be cast into a lake of fire, 9-10. The great white throne, and the dead, small and great, standing before God, and all judged according to their works, 11-12. The sea, death, and hades give up their dead, and are destroyed; and all not found in the book of life are cast into the lake of fire, 13-15.

1. *An angel came down from heaven.* One of the executors of the divine justice, who receives criminals, and keeps them in prison, and delivers them up only to be tried and executed. The *key* of the prison and the *chain* show who He is; and as the *chain* was *great,* it shows that the culprit was impeached of no ordinary crimes.

2. *That old serpent, which is the Devil, and Satan.* He who is called the *old serpent* is the *Devil*—the "calumniator," and *Satan*—the "opposer." *A thousand years.* In what this binding of Satan consists, who can tell? How many visions have been seen on this subject both in ancient and modern times! This and what is said in vv. 3-5 no doubt refer to a time in which the influence of Satan will be greatly restrained, and the true Church of God enjoy great prosperity, which shall endure for a long time. But it is not likely that the number, *a thousand years,* is to be taken literally here, and "year" symbolically and figuratively in all the book beside. The doctrine of the "millennium," or of the saints reigning on earth a thousand years, with Christ for their Head, has

been illustrated and defended by many Christian writers, among both the ancients and the moderns. Were I to give a collection of the conceits of the primitive fathers on this subject, my readers would have little reason to applaud my pains. It has long been the idle expectation of many persons that the millennium, in their sense, was at hand; and its commencement has been expected in every century since the Christian era. It has been fixed for several different years, during the short period of my own life! I believed those predictions to be vain, and I have lived to see them such. Yet there is no doubt that the earth is in a state of progressive moral improvement; and that the light of true religion is shining more copiously everywhere, and will shine more and more to the perfect day. But when the religion of Christ will be at its meridian of light and heat, we know not. In each believer this may speedily take place; but probably no such time shall ever appear, in which evil shall be wholly banished from the earth, till after the day of judgment, when the earth having been burned up, a new heaven and a new earth shall be produced out of the ruins of the old, by the mighty power of God; righteousness alone shall dwell in them. The phraseology of the apostle here seems partly taken from the ancient prophets and partly rabbinical; and it is from the Jewish use of those terms that we are to look for their interpretation.

3. *He should deceive the nations no more.* Be unable to blind men with superstition and idolatry as he had formerly done.

4. *I saw thrones.* Christianity established in the earth, the kings and governors being all Christians. *Reigned with Christ a thousand years.* I am satisfied that this period should not be taken literally. It may signify that there shall be a long and undisturbed state of Christianity; and so universally shall the gospel spirit prevail that it will appear as if Christ reigned upon earth; which will in effect be the case, because His Spirit shall rule in the hearts of men; and in this time the martyrs are represented as living again; their testimony being revived, and the truth for which they died, and which was confirmed by their blood, being now everywhere prevalent. As to the term *thousand years,* it is a mystic number among the Jews. It appears therefore that this phraseology is purely rabbinical.

5. *The rest of the dead lived not again.* It is generally supposed from these passages that all who have been martyred for the truth of God shall be raised a thousand years before the other dead, and reign on earth with Christ during that time, after which the dead in general shall be raised; but this also is very doubtful.

6. *Blessed* ("happy") *and holy.* He was holy and therefore he suffered for the testimony of Jesus in the time when nothing but holiness was called to such a trial. *The first resurrection.* Supposed to be that of the martyrs, mentioned above. *The second death.* Punishment in the eternal world; such is the acceptation of the phrase among the ancient Jews. *Hath no power.* "Hath no authority"—no dominion over him. This is also a rabbinical mode of speech.

7. *Satan shall be loosed.* How can this bear any kind of literal interpretation? Satan is bound a thousand years, and the earth is in peace; righteousness flourishes, and Jesus Christ

alone reigns. This state of things may continue forever if the imprisonment of Satan be continued. Satan, however, is loosed at the end of the thousand years, and goes out and deceives the nations, and peace is banished from the face of the earth, and a most dreadful war takes place. These can be only symbolical representations, utterly incapable of the sense generally put upon them.

8. *Gog and Magog.* This seems to be almost literally taken from the Jerusalem Targum, and that of *Jonathan ben Uzziel,* on Num. xi. 26. I shall give the words at length: "And there were two men left in the camp, the name of the one was Eldad, the name of the other was Medad, and on them the spirit of prophecy rested. Then they both prophesied together, and said, 'In the very end of time Gog and Magog and their army shall come up against Jerusalem, and they shall fall by the hand of the King Messiah; and for seven whole years shall the children of Israel light their fires with the wood of their warlike engines, and they shall not go to the wood nor cut down any tree.'" This account seems most evidently to have been copied by John, but how he intended it to be applied is a question too difficult to be solved by the skill of man; yet both the account in the rabbins and in John is founded on Ezekiel xxxviii—xxxix. The rabbinical writings are full of accounts concerning *Gog and Magog.* Under these names the enemies of God's truth are generally intended.

9. *The beloved city.* Primarily, Jerusalem; typically, the Christian Church.

10. *And the devil . . . was cast into the lake.* Before Satan was "bound," that is, his power was curtailed and restrained; now he is *cast into the lake of fire,* his power being totally taken away.

11. *A great white throne.* Refulgent with glorious majesty. *Him that sat on it.* The indescribable Jehovah. *From whose face the earth and the heaven fled away.* Even the brightness of His countenance dissolved the universe, and annihilated the laws by which it was governed. This is a very majestic figure, and finely expressed. *There was found no place for them.* The glorious majesty of God filling all things, and being all in all.

12. *The dead, small and great.* All ranks, degrees, and conditions of men. This description seems to refer to Dan. vii. 9-10. *And the books were opened.* See Dan. xii. 1. "Rab Jehuda said: All the actions of men, whether good or bad, are written in a book, and of all they shall give account" (*Sohar* Gen., fol. 79, col. 298). "In the first day of the new year the holy blessed God sits that he may judge the world; and all men, without exception, give an account of themselves; and the books of the living and the dead are opened" (*Sohar Chadash,* fol. 19, 1). The books mentioned here were the books of the living and the dead, or the "book of life" and the "book of death"; that is, the account of the good and evil actions of men; the former leading to life, the latter to death. John evidently alludes here to Dan. vii. 10, on which the rabbinical account of the books appears to be founded. The expressions are figurative in both.

13. *The sea gave up the dead.* Those who had been drowned in it. *And death.* All who died by

any kind of disease. Death is here personified, and represented as a keeper of defunct human beings; probably no more than earth or the grave is meant, as properly belonging to the empire of death. *And hell.* Hades, the place of separate spirits. The sea and death have the bodies of all human beings; *hades* has their spirits. That they may be judged, and punished or rewarded according to their works, their bodies and souls must be reunited; *hades,* therefore, gives up the spirits; and the sea and the earth give up the bodies.

14. *And death and hell were cast into the lake.* Death himself is now abolished, and the place for separate spirits is no longer needful. All dead bodies and separated souls being rejoined, and no more separation of bodies and souls by death to take place, consequently the existence of these things is no further necessary. *This is the second death.* The first death consisted in the separation of the soul from the body for a season; the second death in the separation of body and soul from God forever. The first death is that from which there may be a resurrection; the second death is that from which there can be no recovery.

CHAPTER 21

The new heaven and the new earth, 1. The new Jerusalem, 2. God dwells with men; the happy state of His followers, 3-7. The wretched state of the ungodly, 8. An angel shows John the holy city, the New Jerusalem, 9-10. Her light, wall, gates, and foundations described, 11-21. God and the Lamb are the Temple and Light of it, 22-23. The nations and kings of the earth bring their glory and honor to it; the gates shall never be shut, nor shall any defilement enter into it, 24-27.

1. *A new heaven and a new earth.* See the notes on 2 Pet. iii. 13. The ancient Jews believed that God would renew the heavens and the earth at the end of seven thousand years. The general supposition they founded on Isa. lxv. 17. *There was no more sea.* The sea no more appeared than did the first heaven and earth. All was made new; and probably the new sea occupied a different position and was differently distributed from that of the old sea.

2. *And I John.* The writer of this book. *New Jerusalem.* See the notes on Gal. iv. 24-27. This doubtless means the Christian Church in a state of great prosperity and purity, but some think eternal blessedness is intended.

3. *The tabernacle of God is with men.* God, in the most especial manner, dwells among His followers, diffusing His light and life everywhere.

4. *There shall be no more death.* Because there shall be a general resurrection. And this is the inference which Paul makes from his doctrine of a general resurrection, 1 Cor. xv. 26, where he says, "The last enemy that shall be destroyed is death."

5. *Behold, I make all things new.* As the creation of the world at the beginning was the work of God alone, so this new creation. *These words are true and faithful.* Truth refers to the promise of these changes; faithfulness, to the fulfillment of these promises.

6. *It is done.* All is determined, and shall be fulfilled in due time. The great drama is finished, and what was intended is now completed, referring to the period alluded to by the

angel. *I am Alpha and Omega.* See on chap. i. 8. *The fountain of the water of life.* See on John iv. 10, 14; vii. 37, etc. The rabbins consider "the fountain of the world to come" as one of the particular blessings of a future state.

7. *Inherit all things.* Here he had no inheritance; there he shall inherit the kingdom of Heaven, and be with God and Christ, and have every possible degree of blessedness.

8. *But the fearful.* Those who, for fear of losing life or their property, either refused to receive the Christian religion, though convinced of its truth and importance, or having received it, in times of persecution fell away, not being willing to risk their lives. *And unbelieving.* Those who resist against full evidence. *The abominable.* Those who are polluted with unnatural lust. *And murderers.* Those who take away the life of man for any cause but the murder of another, and those who hate a brother in their heart. *And whoremongers.* Adulterers, fornicators, whores, prostitutes, and rakes of every description. *Idolaters.* Those who offer any kind of worship or religious reverence to anything but God. *And all liars.* Everyone who speaks contrary to the truth when he knows the truth, and even he who speaks the truth with the intention to deceive; i.e., to persuade a person that a thing is different from what it really is, by telling only a part of the truth, or suppressing some circumstance which would have led the hearer to a different and to the true conclusion. All these shall have their portion, their "share," what belongs to them, their right, *in the lake which burneth with fire and brimstone: which is the second death,* from which there is no recovery.

9. *The bride, the Lamb's wife.* The pure and holy Christian Church.

10. *To a great and high mountain.* That, being above this city, he might see every street and lane of it.

11. *Having the glory of God.* Instead of the sun and moon, it has the splendor of God to enlighten it. *Unto a stone most precious, even like a jasper stone, clear as crystal.* Among precious stones there are some even of the same species more valuable than others; for their value is in proportion to their being free from flaws, and of a uniform and brilliant transparency. A *crystal* is perfectly clear; the Oriental *jasper* is a beautiful sea-green.

12. *Had a wall great and high.* An almighty defense. *Twelve gates.* A gate for every tribe of Israel, in the vicinity of which gate that tribe dwelt, so that in coming in and going out they did not mix with each other. This description of the city is partly taken from Ezek. xlviii. 30-35.

13. *On the east three gates.* The city is here represented as standing to the four cardinal points of heaven, and presenting one side to each of these points.

14. *The wall of the city had twelve foundations.* Probably twelve stones, one of which served for a foundation or "threshold" to each gate; and on these were inscribed the names of the twelve apostles, to intimate that it was by the doctrine of the apostles that souls enter into the Church, and thence into the New Jerusalem.

15. *Had a golden reed.* Several excellent MSS. add "a measure"; he had "a measuring rod made of gold." This account of measuring the city seems to be copied, with variations, from Ezek. xl. 3, etc.

16. *The city lieth foursquare.* The quadrangular form intimates its perfection and stability, for the square figure was a figure of perfection among the Greeks; the "square" or "cubical man" was, with them, a man of unsullied integrity, perfect in all things.

17. *The wall . . . an hundred and forty and four cubits.* This is twelve, the number of the apostles, multiplied by itself. *The measure of a man, that is, of the angel.* The cubit, so called from *cubitus,* the "elbow," is the measure from the tip of the elbow to the tip of the middle finger, and is generally reckoned at one foot and a half, or eighteen inches. By the cubit of a man we may here understand the ordinary cubit, and that this was the angel's cubit who appeared in the form of a man.

18. *The building of the wall of it was of jasper.* The Oriental jasper is exceedingly hard and almost indestructible. Pillars made of this stone have lasted some thousands of years, and appear to have suffered scarcely anything from the tooth of time. *Pure gold, like unto clear glass.* Does not this imply that the walls were made of some beautifully bright yellow stone, very highly polished? This description has been most injudiciously applied to heaven; and in some public discourses, for the comfort and edification of the pious, we hear of heaven with its golden walls, golden pavements, gates of pearl, not considering that nothing of this description was ever intended to be literally understood, and that gold and jewels can have no place in the spiritual and eternal world.

19. *The foundations of the wall.* Does not this mean the foundations or "thresholds" of the gates? The gates represented the twelve tribes, v. 12; and these foundations or thresholds, the twelve apostles, v. 14. There was no entrance into the city but through those gates, and none through the gates but over these thresholds. *The first foundation was jasper.* A stone very hard, some species of which are of a sea-green color; but it is generally a bright reddish brown. *The second, sapphire.* This is a stone of a fine blue color, next in hardness to the diamond. *The third, a chalcedony.* A genus of the semipellucid gems. *The fourth, an emerald.* This is of a bright green color without any mixture, and is one of the most beautiful of all the gems.

20. *The fifth, sardonyx.* The onyx is an accidental variety of the agate kind; it is of a dark horny color, in which is a plate of a bluish white, and sometimes of red. *The sixth, sardius.* The sardius is a precious stone of a blood-red color. *The seventh, chrysolite.* The gold stone. It is of a dusky green with a cast of yellow. It is a species of the topaz. *The eighth, beryl.* This is a pellucid gem of a bluish green color. *The ninth, a topaz.* A pale, dead green, with a mixture of yellow. It is considered by the mineralogists as a variety of the sapphire. *The tenth, a chrysoprasus.* A variety of the chrysolite, called by some a yellowish green and cloudy topaz. *The eleventh, a jacinth.* A precious stone of a dead red color, with a mixture of yellow. *The twelfth, an amethyst.* A gem

generally of a purple or violet color, composed of a strong blue and deep red. These stones are nearly the same with those on the breastplate of the high priest, Exod. xxviii. 17 ff., and probably were intended to express the meaning of the Hebrew words there used.

21. *The twelve gates were twelve pearls.* This must be merely figurative, for it is out of all the order of nature to produce a pearl large enough to make a gate to such an immense city.

22. *I saw no temple.* There was no need of a temple where God and the Lamb were manifestly present.

23. *No need of the sun.* This is also one of the traditions of the ancient Jews, that "in the world to come the Israelites shall have no need of the sun by day, nor the moon by night" (*Yalcut Rubeni,* fol. 7, 3). God's light shines in this city, and in the Lamb that light is concentrated, and from Him everywhere diffused.

24. *The nations of them which are saved.* This is an allusion to the promise that the Gentiles should bring their riches, glory, and excellence to the Temple at Jerusalem, after it should be rebuilt.

25. *The gates of it shall not be shut at all.* The Christian Church shall ever stand open to receive sinners of all sorts, degrees, and nations. *There shall be no night there.* No more idolatry, no intellectual darkness; the Scriptures shall be everywhere read, the pure Word everywhere preached, and the Spirit of God shall shine and work in every heart.

26. *The glory and honour of the nations into it.* Still alluding to the declarations of the prophets that the Gentiles would be led to contribute to the riches and glory of the Temple by their gifts.

27. *There shall in no wise enter into it any thing that defileth.* See Isa. xxxv. 8; lii. 1. Neither an impure person—he who turns the grace of God into lasciviousness, nor a liar—he that holds and propagates false doctrines.

CHAPTER 22

The river of the water of life, 1. The tree of life, 2. There is no curse nor darkness in the city of God, 3-5. The angel assures John of the truth of what he has heard, and states that the time of the fulfillment is at hand, 6-7. He forbids John to worship him, 8-9. Again he states that the time of the fulfillment of the prophecies of this book is at hand, 10-12. Christ is Alpha and Omega, 13. The blessedness of those who keep His commandments; they enter through the gates into the city, 14. All the unholy are excluded, 15. Christ sent His angel to testify of those things in the churches, 16. The invitation of the Spirit and the bride, 17. A curse denounced against those who shall either add to or take away from the prophecies of this book, 18-19. Christ cometh quickly, 20. The apostolical benediction, 21.

1. *Pure river of water of life.* This is evidently a reference to the garden of paradise, and the river by which it was watered; and there is also a reference to the account, Ezek. xlvii. 7-12. *Water of life,* as we have seen before, generally signifies spring or running water; here it may signify incessant communications of happiness proceeding from God.

2. *In the midst of the street of it.* That is, of the city which was described in the preceding chapter. *The tree of life.* An allusion to Gen. ii. 9. The account in Ezekiel is this: "And by the river upon the bank thereof, on this side and on that side, shall grow all trees for meat,

whose leaf shall not fade . . . it shall bring forth new fruit according to his months . . . and the fruit thereof shall be for meat, and the leaf thereof shall be for medicine," chap. xlvii. 12. *Twelve manner of fruits.* "Twelve fruits"; that is, fruit twelve times in the year, as is immediately explained, *yielded her fruit every month.* As this was a great and spacious city, one fountain was not sufficient to provide water for it; therefore a river is mentioned, a great river, by which it was sufficiently watered. Some think that by this *tree of life* the gospel is indicated; the *twelve . . . fruits* are the twelve apostles; and the *leaves* are gospel doctrines by which nations—the Gentiles—are healed of the disease of sin. But this seems to be a fanciful interpretation.

3. *No more curse.* Instead of *curse* the best MSS., versions, etc., read "cursed person." As there shall be no more sinning against God, so there shall be no more curse of God upon the people; for they shall all be His *servants,* and *serve him.* Our first parents came under the curse by sinning against their Maker in paradise. These shall never apostatize; therefore neither they nor the earth shall be cursed.

4. *See his face.* Enjoy what is called the beatific vision; and they shall exhibit the fullest evidence that they belong entirely to Him, for *his name* shall be written *on their foreheads.*

5. *There shall be no night there.* See the twenty-third and twenty-fifth verses of the preceding chapter.

6. *These sayings are faithful and true.* See the preceding chapter, v. 5. From this verse to the end of the chapter is reckoned the epilogue of this book. (1) The angel affirms the truth of all that had been spoken, vv. 6-11. (2) Jesus Christ confirms what has been affirmed, and pledges himself for the fulfilment of all the prophecies contained in it, vv. 12-17. (3) John cautions his readers against adding or diminishing, and concludes with the apostolical blessing, vv. 18-21.

8. *I fell down to worship.* I prostrated myself before him as before a superior being, to express my gratitude, and give him thanks for the communications he had made. See on chap. xix. 10.

10. *Seal not the sayings.* Do not lay them up for future generations; they concern the present times; "They must shortly come to pass," *for the time is at hand.* See above, v. 6. What concerned the Jews was certainly *at hand.*

11. *He that is unjust, let him be unjust still.* The time of fulfilment will come so suddenly that there will be but little space for repentance and amendment. What is done must be done instantly; and let him that is holy persevere, and hold fast what he has received.

12. *Behold, I come quickly.* I come to establish My cause, comfort and support My followers, and punish the wicked.

13. *I am Alpha and Omega.* See on chap. i. 8, 18.

14. *Blessed are they that do his commandments.* They are happy who are obedient. *That they may have right to the tree of life.* The original is much more expressive, "That they may have authority over the tree of life"; an authority founded on right, this right founded

on obedience to the commandments of God, and that obedience produced by the grace of God working in them.

15. *Without are dogs.* All those who are uncircumcised in heart. The Jews call all the uncircumcised *dogs.* "Who is a dog? Ans. He who is not circumcised" (*Pirkey Elieser,* chap. 29).

16. *I Jesus.* The Maker, the Redeemer, and Judge of all men. *Have sent mine angel.* An especial messenger from heaven. *I am the root and the offspring of David.* Christ is the *root* of David as to His divine nature, for from that all the human race sprang. And He is the *offspring* of David as to His human nature, for that He took of the stock of David. *The bright and morning star.* I am splendor and glory to My kingdom; as the *morning star* ushers in the sun, so shall I usher in the unclouded and eternal glories of the everlasting Kingdom.

17. *The Spirit and the bride.* All the prophets and all the apostles; the Church of God under the Old Testament, and the Church of Christ under the New. *Say, Come.* Invite men to Jesus, that by Him they may be saved and prepared for this Kingdom. *Let him that heareth.* Let all who are privileged with reading and hearing the Word of God join in the general invitation to sinners. *Him that is athirst.* He who feels his need of salvation and is longing to drink of the living fountain. *And whosoever will.* No soul is excluded: Jesus died for every man; every man may be saved; therefore let him who wills, who wishes for salvation, come and *take the water of life freely*—without money or price!

18. *If any man shall add.* Shall give any other meaning to these prophecies, or any other application of them, than God intends, he, though not originally intended, shall have the plagues threatened in this book for his portion.

19. *If any man shall take away.* If any man shall lessen this meaning, curtail the sense, explain away the spirit and design, of these prophecies, *God shall take away his part out of the book of life,* etc. Thus Jesus Christ warns all those who consider this book to beware of indulging their own conjectures concerning it. I confess that this warning has its own powerful influence upon my mind, and has prevented me from indulging my own conjectures concerning its meaning, or of adopting the conjectures of others. These visions and threatenings are too delicate and awful a subject to trifle with, or even to treat in the most solemn manner, where the meaning is obscure. I must leave these things to time and event, the surest interpreters. This is termed a revelation, but it is a revelation of symbols; an exhibition of enigmas, to which no particular solution is given, and to which God alone can give the solution.

20. *Surely I come quickly.* This may be truly said to every person in every age; Jesus, the Judge, is at the door! *Even so, come, Lord Jesus.* The wish and desire of the suffering Church, and of all the followers of God, who are longing for the coming of His kingdom.

21. *The grace of our Lord Jesus Christ.* May the favor and powerful influence of Jesus Christ *be with you all;* you of the seven churches, and the whole Church of Christ in every part of the earth, and through all the periods of time.